CHILTON'S IMPORT CAR REPAIR MANUAL 1972-1977

Import Cars and Light Trucks

President	William A. Barbour
Executive Vice President	James Miades
Vice President & General Manager	John P. Kushnerick
Editorial Director	Alan F. Turner
Managing Editor	Kerry A. Freeman, S.A.E.
Senior Editor	Richard J. Rivele, S.A.E.
Service Editors	Carl Canfield
	Lance Ealey
	Martin J. Gunther
	Dean Morgantini
	Ron Webb
Editorial Production	Dru Brown
Production Manager	Warren Owens
Assistant Production Manager	Timothy Frelick
Production Assistant	Nancy Hassler

 CHILTON BOOK COMPANY
Chilton Way, Radnor, Pa. 19089

Manufactured in USA
© 1977 by Chilton Book Company
ISBN 0-8019-7125-X
234567890 987654

CONTENTS

SPECIFICATIONS

INTRODUCTION

The Audi, produced by Auto Union of Germany and distributed in the United States by Porsche Audi, a division of Volkswagen of America, has been available in the United States since 1970. Three models, the Super 90, Super 90 station wagon (Variant), and the 100 LS, were initially imported using one basic engine. A 1,760 cc. slanted four-cylinder, OHV engine was used. Displacement has since been increased to 1,871 cc. The Super 90 was dropped in 1972, after an estimated 4,-500 sales. The 100 was introduced in

1972, to replace the Super 90 as a lower cost alternative to the 100 LS. The top of the line 100 GL, with automatic transmission as standard equipment, was added in 1973. The only 100 series car available beginning 1974 was the 100 LS. In mid-1973, a new smaller car, the Fox, was introduced. It had a 1,471 cc overhead camshaft engine and shares many of the familiar Audi features such as McPherson strut suspension and front-wheel drive. The Fox engine was enlarged to 1,588 cc in 1975.

The Audi uses a transaxle behind the forward mounted engine to transmit power to the front drive axle, while a dead axle is used in the rear. Also standard are inboard mounted front disc brakes (outboard on the Fox and the 100 Series beginning 1975), rear drum brakes, and rack and pinion steering. A four-speed transmission is standard but can be replaced with an optional three-speed automatic.

MODEL IDENTIFICATION

Super 90

100 LS, all 100 series models are quite similar

1973-76 Fox

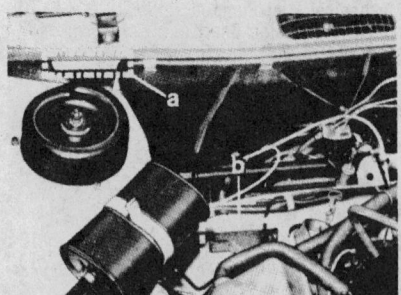

1977 Fox

SERIAL NUMBER IDENTIFICATION

Vehicle

Super 90

The chassis number is on a plate on top of the instrument panel. It is also stamped into the crossmember behind the battery, in the engine compartment. The vehicle identification plate is mounted on the right side of the engine compartment. The chassis number follows the words "Fahrgest.-Nr." on the plate.

100, 100 LS, 100 GL

The chassis number is on a plate on top of the instrument panel. It is also stamped into the upper right corner of the firewall. The vehicle identification plate is mounted on the support directly behind the engine, except on 1973 and later models. On these it is on the right

1972 100, 100 LS, 100 GL vehicle identification, (a) is the chassis number, (b) is the vehicle identification plate.

wheel housing. The chassis number follows the words "Fahrgest.-Nr." on this plate.

Fox

The chassis number is on a plate on the

left windshield pillar. It is also stamped into the top center of the firewall. The vehicle identification plate is on the right wheel housing. The chassis number follows the words "Fahrgest.-Nr." on this plate.

Engine

Super 90

Up to chassis numbers 6842 025 559, 6843 018 078 and 6834 000 156 the engine number is stamped on the engine block above the fuel pump. After the above chassis numbers, the engine number is located on the left side of the engine block.

An engine code number indicating the exact cylinder bore of the particular engine is stamped on the starter end of the

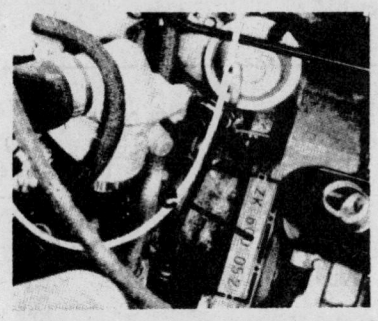

Engine number location for 100, 100 LS, and 100 GL.

cylinder block, just below the cylinder head.

100, 100 LS, 100 GL

The engine number is stamped on the left side of the engine block (clutch housing).

In addition to the engine number, an engine code number is also stamped on the starter end of the cylinder block, just below the cylinder head. This number indicates the exact cylinder bore of the particular engine.

Fox

The engine number is stamped on the left side of the engine block, just above the fuel pump.

In addition to the engine number, an engine code number is also stamped into the left front side of the cylinder block, just above the water pump. This number indicates the exact cylinder bore of the particular engine.

GENERAL ENGINE SPECIFICATIONS

Year and Model	Engine Cu in. Displacement	Carburetor Type	SAE Horsepower @ rpm	SAE Torque @ rpm (ft lbs)	Bore x Stroke (in.)	Compression Ratio	Normal Oil Pressure (psi)*
1972 Super 90	107.5 (1,760 cc)	2 bbl	N.A.	105 @ 3,000	3.21 x 3.32	8.2:1	14-85
1972-75 100, 100 LS, 100 GL	114.2 (1,871 cc)	2 bbl	91 @ 5,200	110 @ 3,500	3.31 x 3.32	8.2:1	14-85
1976-77 100	114.2 (1,871 cc)	F.I.	92 @ 5,500	106 @ 3,300	3.31 x 3.32	8.0:1	14-85
1973-74 Fox	89.7 (1,471 cc)	2 bbl	75 @ 6,000	82 @ 4,000	3.01 x 3.15	8.2:1	14-100
1975 Fox	97 (1,588 cc)	CIS	81 @ 5,800, 79 Calif.	99 @ 3,300	3.13 x 3.15	8.0:1	9-100
1976-77 Fox	97 (1,588 cc)	F.I.	79 @ 5,500	89 @ 3,300	3.13 x 3.15	8.0:1	64-74

* Idle—5000 rpm
F.I. Fuel Injection
CIS Continuous Injection System

TUNE-UP SPECIFICATIONS

Year and Model	Engine Cu in. Displacement	SPARK PLUGS Type	SPARK PLUGS Gap (in.)	DISTRIBUTOR Point Dwell (deg)	DISTRIBUTOR Point Gap (in.)	IGNITION TIMING (deg) MT	IGNITION TIMING (deg) AT	Intake Valve Opens (deg)	Pressure Fuel Pump (psi)	IDLE SPEED (rpm) MT	IDLE SPEED (rpm) AT	VALVE CLEAR. (in.) ① In	VALVE CLEAR. (in.) ① Ex	% CO @ idle
1972 Super 90	107.5 (1,760 cc)	N8Y ④	0.024- 0.028	47-53	0.016	9A @ 950 rpm②	—	5B	3	950	—	0.008	0.016	1.0
1972 100 100 LS	114.2 (1,871 cc)	N7Y	0.024- 0.030	47-53	0.016	8A @ idle ③	8A @ idle ③	5B	3.6	850- 1000	850- 1000	0.006- 0.008	0.014- 0.016	1.0
1973 100 100 LS 100 GL	114.2 (1,871 cc)	N7Y	0.024- 0.030	47-53	0.016	8A @ idle ⑤	8A @ idle ⑤	58	3.6	850- 1000	850- 1000	0.006- 0.008	0.014- 0.016	1.0
1974-75 100 LS	114.2 (1,871 cc)	N7Y	0.024- 0.030	47- 53	0.016	6A @ idle ⑤	6A @ idle ⑤	5B	3.6	850- 1000	850- 1000	0.006- 0.008	0.014- 0.016	1.0 ⑦

TUNE-UP SPECIFICATIONS

Year and Model	Engine Cu in. Displacement	SPARK PLUGS Type	SPARK PLUGS Gap (in.)	DISTRIBUTOR Point Dwell (deg)	DISTRIBUTOR Point Gap (in.)	IGNITION TIMING (deg) MT	IGNITION TIMING (deg) AT	Intake Valve Opens (deg)	Pressure Fuel Pump (psi)	IDLE SPEED (rpm) MT	IDLE SPEED (rpm) AT	VALVE CLEAR. (in.) ① In	VALVE CLEAR. (in.) ① Ex	% CO @ idle
1976-77 100	114.2 (1,871 cc)	N7Y	.027-.035	44-50	0.016	6A	6A	5B	4.8-5.4	850-1000	850-1000	0.008-0.010	0.016-0.018	0.9 Fed. 0.5 Cal.
1975 100 LS	114.2 (1,871 cc)	N7Y	0.035	47-53	0.016	6A @ idle	6A @ idle	5B	66.8-75.3⑧	850-1000	850-1000	0.004-0.006	0.014-0.016	1.5/1.0 Calif.
1973 Fox	89.7 (1,471 cc)	N8Y	0.028	47-53	0.016	0 @ idle ⑥	0 @ idle ⑥	4B	2.5-3.5	850-1000	850-1000	0.008-0.012	0.016-0.020	0.6-2.0
1974 Fox	89.7 (1,471 cc)	N8Y	0.028	47-53 ⑨	0.016	3A @ idle	3A @ idle	4B	2.5-3.5	950	950	0.008-0.012	0.016-0.020	1.3 ⑩
1975 Fox	97 (1,588 cc)	N8Y	0.028	47-53	0.016	3A @ idle 1000	3A @ idle 1000	4B	66.8-75.3	900-950	900-950	0.008-0.012	0.016-0.020	1.0
1976 Fox	97 (1,588 cc)	N7Y	.028	44-50	.016	3A @ idle	3A @ idle	4B	4.8-5.4	850-1000	850-1000	0.008-0.012	0.016-0.020	1.0AT (Fed.) 1.5MT (Fed.) 0.5 Cal.

① Set hot, warm for Fox
② 18B @ 3,000 with vacuum hose disconnected
③ 27B @ 2,500 with vacuum hose disconnected
④ N4 for continuous highway speeds
⑤ 30B @ 2,750 with vacuum hose disconnected
⑥ 30B @ 3,000 with vacuum hose disconnected

⑦ 1.5 with air pump, hose off
⑧ Fuel injection
⑨ 47-53 in Calif., 44-50 otherwise.
⑩ 1.0 with air pump, without—0.6-2.0 to engine No. XW001013, 0.4-1.6 from No. XW001014
AT   Automatic transmission
MT   Manual transmission

NOTE: The underhood specifications sticker often reflects tune-up specification changes made in production. Sticker figures must be used if they disagree with those in this chart.

FIRING ORDER

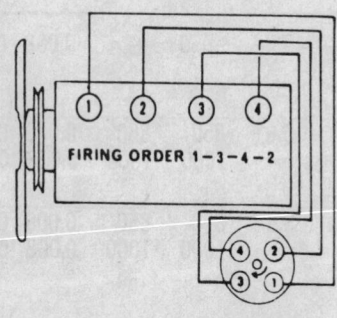

FIRING ORDER 1—3—4—2

Super 90 and 100 series

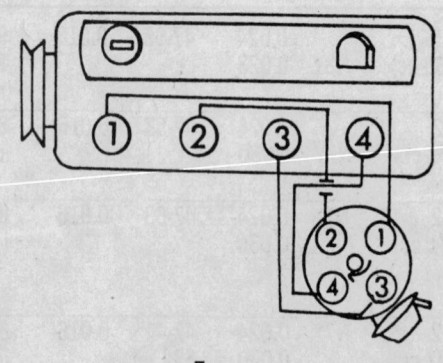

Fox

CAPACITIES

Model	ENGINE CRANKCASE (qts) With Filter	Transmission (pts) Manual	Transmission (pts) Automatic	Drive Axle (pts) ①	Gasoline Tank (gals)	Cooling System (qts)
Super 90, 100, 100 LS, 100 GL	4.3	4.2	12.5 6.0 change	3	15.3	8
Fox	3.2	3.4	12.5 fill 6.0 change	2.1	12	6.5

① Only with automatic transmission.

CRANKSHAFT AND CONNECTING ROD SPECIFICATIONS

All measurements are given in inches.

Engine	CRANKSHAFT Main Brg. Journal Dia.*	CRANKSHAFT Main Brg. Oil Clearance	CRANKSHAFT Shaft End-Play	CRANKSHAFT Thrust on No.	CONNECTING ROD Journal Diameter*	CONNECTING ROD Oil Clearance	CONNECTING ROD Side Clearance
Super 90, 100, 100 LS, 100 GL	2.3622	0.002-0.004	0.003-0.007	3	1.8898	0.001-0.003	0.004-0.009
Fox	2.1260	0.001-0.003	0.003-0.007	3	1.8110	0.0011-0.0034	0.010

*Standard size

VALVE SPECIFICATIONS

Engine	Seat Angle (deg)	Face Angle (deg)	STEM TO GUIDE CLEARANCE (in.) Intake	STEM TO GUIDE CLEARANCE (in.) Exhaust	STEM DIAMETER (in.) Intake	STEM DIAMETER (in.) Exhaust
Super 90	45	45°15′	0.001	0.002	0.3507	0.3890
100, 100 LS, 100 GL	45	45°15′	0.001	0.002	0.3507	0.3499
Fox	45	45	0.001-0.002	0.001-0.002	0.314	0.313

NOTE: Valve guides are removable.

PISTON AND RING SPECIFICATIONS

All measurements in inches

Engine	Piston Clearance	RING GAP Top Compression	RING GAP Bottom Compression	RING GAP Oil Control	RING SIDE CLEARANCE Top Compression	RING SIDE CLEARANCE Bottom Compression	RING SIDE CLEARANCE Oil Control
Super 90	0.001	0.012-0.018	0.010-0.020	0.010-0.016	0.003-0.005	0.002-0.003	0.001-0.002
100, 100 LS, 100 GL	0.001	0.039	0.039	0.039	0.006	0.006	0.006
Fox	0.001	0.039	0.039	0.039	0.006	0.006	0.006

NOTE: Three oversizes of pistons are available to accommodate overbores up to 0.040 in.

TORQUE SPECIFICATIONS

All readings in ft lbs

Engine	Cylinder Head Bolts	*Rod Bearing Bolts	Main Bearing Bolts	Crankshaft Pulley Bolt	Flywheel To Crankshaft Bolts	MANIFOLD	
						Intake	Exhaust
Super 90	65	25-31	29①	130-180	65	17	17
100, 100 LS, 100 GL	65	25-31	58②	130-180	65	18	18
Fox	48-60 cold③ 56-67 warm	25 33	47	58	36	18	17

① 23 on bearing cap no. 5
② 24 on bearing cap no. 5
③ 1976-77 54 cold
      61 warm

* Use new bolts

TORQUE SEQUENCES

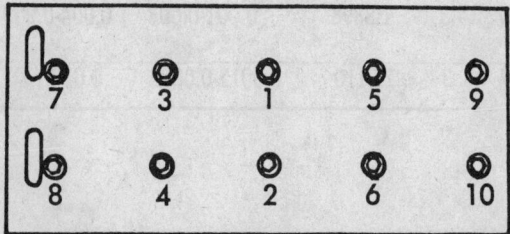
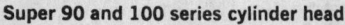

Super 90 and 100 series cylinder head

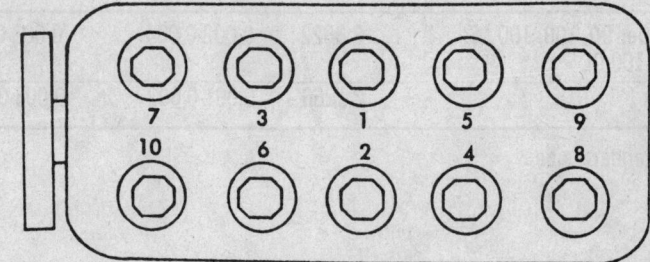

Fox cylinder head

ALTERNATOR AND REGULATOR SPECIFICATIONS

Year	ALTERNATOR Part No. or Manufacturer	Output (amps.)	REGULATOR Part No. or Manufacturer	Volts
Super 90, 100, 100 LS, 100 GL Early models	Bosch K1 14V 35A 20	35	Bosch AD 1/14V	13.9-14.8
Super 90, 100, 100 LS, 100 GL Late models	Bosch K1 14V 55A 20	55	Bosch AD 1/14V or EE 14V (integral)	13.9-14.8
Fox	Bosch K1 14V 55A	55	Bosch EF 14V (integral)	13.5-14.5

BATTERY AND STARTER SPECIFICATIONS

All cars use 12 volt, negative ground electrical systems

Year	Model	Battery Amp Hour Capacity	Starter							Brush Spring Tension (oz)	Min. Brush Length (in.)
			Lock Test			No Load Test					
			Amps	Volts	Torque (ft/lbs)	Amps	Volts	RPM			
All	Super 90, 100 100 LS, 100 GL	45/55	250-300	7	N.A.	30-55	11.5	6000-9000		N.A.	0.47
All	Fox	45/54	250-300	7	N.A.	30-55	11.5	6000 9000		N.A.	0.5

BRAKE SPECIFICATIONS

All measurements given are (in.) unless noted

Year	Model	Lug Nut Torque (ft/lb)	Master Cylinder Bore	Brake Minimum Thickness	Disc Maximum Run-Out	Diameter	Brake Drum Max. Machine O/S	Max. Wear Limit	Minimum Lining Thickness	
									Front	Rear
1972	Super 90	85	0.743	0.36	0.005	7.87	7.89	7.91	0.078	0.098
1972-77	100, 100 LS	85	0.813①	0.36	0.002	7.87	7.89	7.91	0.078	0.098
1973-77	Fox	65	0.825	0.413	0.002	7.87	7.89	7.91	0.078	0.098

① 0.874—1973-77
NOTE: Minimum lining thickness is as recommended by the manufacturer. Due to variations in state inspection regulations, the minimum allowable thickness may be different than recommended by the manufacturer.

WHEEL ALIGNMENT

Model	CASTER		CAMBER		Toe-in (in.)	WHEEL PIVOT RATIO	
	Range (deg)	Pref Setting (deg)	Range (deg)	Pref Setting (deg)		Inner Wheel	Outer Wheel
1972 Super 90	0°10′N to 0°30′P	0°10′P	0°5′N to 0°35′P	0°15′P	0.00-0.08①	20	18°50′ to 19°30′
1972-74 100, 100 LS, 100 GL	0°14′N to 0°26′P	0°6′P	0°9′N to 0°31′P	0°11′P	0.00-0.08①	20	18°30′ to 19°30′
1975-77 100 LS	0°11′N to 0°29′P	0°9′	0°20′N to 0°20′P	0°	0.00	20	19°40′ to 20°20′
1975-77 100 LS, Power Steering	0°19′P to 0°59′P	0°39′	0°20′N to 0°20′P	0°	0.00	20	19°40′ to 20°20′
1973-77 Fox	0 to 1P	0°30′P	0°5′P to 0°55′P③	0°30′P②	0.00-0.08	20	18°36′ to 19°36′

N Negative
P Positive

① Toe-out
② 0°30′N (Rear wheel) not adjustable
③ In-0° (Rear wheel) not adjustable

TUNE-UP PROCEDURES

All the tune-up steps should be followed, as each adjustment complements the effects of the other adjustments. If the tune-up specifications sticker in the engine compartment disagrees with the Tune-Up Specifications Chart, the sticker figures must be followed.

Spark Plugs

1. Disconnect each spark plug wire by pulling on the rubber cap, not on the wire.

2. Wipe the wires clean with a cloth dampened in kerosene and wipe them dry. If the wires appear to be cracked, they should be replaced.

3. Blow or brush the dirt away from each of the spark plugs. Sometimes this is done by loosening the plugs and cranking the engine with the starter.

4. Remove each spark plug with a spark plug socket. Be careful that the socket is all the way down on the plug to prevent it from slipping and cracking the porcelain insulator.

5. Evaluate the condition of the plugs. In general, a tan or medium gray color on the business end of the plug indicates normal combustion conditions. Refer to the Tune-Up Specifications Chart for the proper spark plug type.

6. If the plugs are to be reused, file the center and side electrodes with a small, fine file. It is often suggested that plugs be tested and cleaned on a service station sandblasting machine; however, this piece of equipment is becoming rare. Check the gap between the two electrodes with a spark plug gap gauge. The round wire type is the most accurate. If the gap is not as specified, use the adjusting device on the gap gauge to bend the outside electrode to correct. Be careful not to bend the electrode too far, because excessive bending may cause it to weaken and possibly fall off into the engine. This would require cylinder head removal to reach the broken piece, and could result in cylinder wall and ring damage.

7. Clean the plug threads with a wire brush. Crank the engine with the starter to blow out any dirt particles from the cylinder head threads.

8. Put a drop of oil on the threads and screw the plugs in finger tight. Tighten them with the plug socket. If a torque wrench is available, tighten them to 22 ft lbs.

9. Reinstall the wires. If there is any doubt as to their proper locations, refer to "Firing Order".

Breaker Points and Condenser

The condenser need not be replaced each time the points are replaced, since this item is not cheap and does not often give trouble. It should be replaced, however, if the points are severely burned. After every breaker point adjustment or replacement, the ignition timing must be checked and, if necessary, adjusted. No special equipment other than a feeler gauge is required for point replacement or adjustment, although a dwell meter should be used to ensure the accuracy of the adjustment.

1. Detach the two spring clips securing the distributor cap. Remove the cap.

2. Clean the cap inside and out. Check for cracks and carbon paths. A carbon path shows up as a dark line, usually from one of the cap sockets or inside terminals to a ground. Check the condition of the button inside the center of the cap and the four inside terminals. Replace the cap if necessary.

3. Pull the rotor up and off the shaft. Clean off the metal end if it is burned or corroded. Replace the rotor if necessary. Remove the dust cap, if there is one.

4. The manufacturer states that the points must be replaced, not reconditioned. Experience also shows that it is more economical and reliable in the long run to replace the point set while the distributor is open, than to have to do this at a later (and possibly more inconvenient) time.

Breaker point installation

(c)—Lead to coil	(n)—Raised lugs
(g)—Vacuum line connection	(o)—Screwdriver slot
(m)—Flat plug wire terminal	(p)—Holddown screw

5. Pull off the flat plug terminal on the wire from the point set. Remove the point set hold-down screw, being very careful not to drop it into the inside of the distributor. If this happens, the distributor will probably have to be removed to get at the screw. If the screw is lost elsewhere, it must be replaced with one that is no longer than the original to avoid interference with distributor workings. Remove the point set.

6. Remove the condenser by removing the screw and pulling the assembly out. Detach the lead from the coil. The condenser, wire, flat plug connection, and plastic sealing boot are a single assembly.

7. Install the new condenser, attaching the lead to the coil.

8. Apply a small amount of high melting point grease to the pivot side of the point set rubbing block.

9. Replace the point set and tighten the screw tightly. Replace the flat plug terminals.

10. Check that the contacts meet squarely. If they do not, bend the tab supporting the fixed contact.

11. Turn the engine until a high point on the cam that opens the points contacts the rubbing block on the point arm. This is easier if the spark plugs have been removed.

12. There is a screwdriver slot and two raised lugs near the contacts. Insert a screwdriver and lever the points open or closed until they appear to be open about the correct gap.

13. Insert the correct size feeler gauge and adjust the gap with the screwdriver until you can push the gauge in and out between the contacts with a slight drag but without moving the point arm. Another check is to try the gauges 0.001–0.002 larger and smaller than the setting size. The larger one should disturb the point arm, whereas the smaller one should not drag at all. Tighten the point set hold-down screw snugly. Recheck the

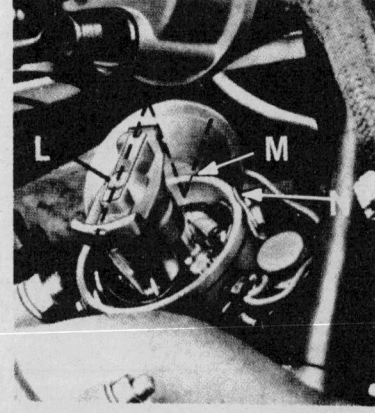

The distributor rotor (L) aligned with the No. 1 cylinder mark (M) on the rim of the distributor body. The dust cap is removed here.

gap, because it often changes when the screw is tightened.

14. After all the point adjustments are complete, pull a white business card through (between) the contacts to remove any traces of oil. Oil will cause rapid point burning.

15. Replace the dust cap.

16. Push the rotor firmly down into place. It will only go on one way. If it is not installed properly, it will probably break when the starter is operated.

17. Replace the distributor cap and install the spring clips.

18. Check the dwell with a meter. Dwell can be checked with the engine running or cranking. Decrease dwell by increasing the point gap; increase by decreasing the gap. Dwell angle is simply the number of degrees of distributor shaft rotation during which the points stay closed. Theoretically, if the point gap is correct, the dwell should also be correct or nearly so. However, dwell is a more accurate setting. If dwell varies more than 3 degrees from idle speed to 2,500 engine rpm, the distributor is worn.

NOTE: *Some tachometers, dwell-meters, and oscilloscopes will not work with the capacitive discharge ignition system used on all 1973 and later 100 series cars. Some may be damaged. Check with the manufacturer of your test equipment if there is any doubt.*

19. Start the engine. If it won't start, check:

a. That all the spark plug wires are in place.

b. That the rotor has been installed.

c. That the wire inside the distributor is connected.

d. That the points open and close when the engine turns.

e. That the gap is correct and the hold-down screw is tight.

f. That the condenser lead to the coil is attached.

20. After the first 200 miles on a new set of points, the point gap often closes up due to initial rubbing block wear. For best performance, recheck the gap or dwell at this time.

21. Since changing the point gap affects the ignition timing setting, the timing should be checked and adjusted if necessary after each point replacement or adjustment.

Ignition Timing

Static

A basic timing adjustment can be made in the following manner. Turn the engine until the basic ignition timing mark is aligned with the ignition timing pointer and the distributor rotor points toward the No. 1 cylinder mark on the rim of the distributor body. Timing marks are on the flywheel on the Fox, and on the crankshaft pulley on the other models. This will put No. 1 cylinder at TDC (0° T). Connect a 12 volt test lamp between the ignition coil terminal, No. 1 connected to the distributor, and a ground. Rotate the distributor clockwise until the lamp goes out. Turn the distributor counterclockwise until the lamp just lights, and tighten the clamp on the distributor at that point. The ignition timing is now approximately set. As soon as possible, check the adjustment with a timing light.

Dynamic

To check with a timing light, connect a timing light to No. 1 cylinder and connect a tachometer.

NOTE: *Some tachometers, dwell-meters, and oscilloscopes will not work with the capacitive discharge ignition system used on all 1973 and later 100 series cars. Some may be damaged. Check with the manufacturer of your test equipment if there is any doubt.*

Loosen the distributor clamp screw until it is just possible to turn the distributor by hand. Run the engine at idle speed

Timing marks for 100, 100 LS, and 100 GL. The Super 90 has a similar arrangement with different numbers. (M) is the timing cover pointer and (K) is the ignition timing mark used at 2,500 rpm.

Fox flywheel ignition timing marks and pointer, the 30° setting shown is for 3,000 rpm

and point the timing light at the pulley (flywheel on the Fox). Turn the distributor until the specified notch (on the flywheel or pulley) aligns with the pointer. Disconnect the vacuum hoses and check the timing at 2,500, 2,750, or 3,000 rpm if specified. Adjust as necessary.

NOTE: *Timing should always be checked both at idle and at 2,500, 2,-750, or 3,000 rpm if specified.*

Valve Lash

Super 90, 100 Series

The valve clearance should be adjusted in firing order, with the engine at operating temperature. See the specifications for the proper clearances. Remove the air filter and rocker cover. Set the engine at TDC on No. 1 cylinder by aligning the 0°T mark on the crankshaft pulley with the timing cover pointer and aligning the distributor rotor with the No. 1 cylinder mark on the rim of the distributor body. Turn the engine in the normal direction of rotation. The valve clearance of cylinder No. 1 should be adjusted when the valves of No. 4 cylinder overlap, i.e. when both arms move in opposite directions simultaneously. When this occurs, the exhaust valve is closing and the intake opening.

Thus adjust:

A. Valve clearance of cylinder No. 3 at overlap of cylinder No. 2

B. Valve clearance of cylinder No. 4 at overlap of cylinder No. 1

C. Valve clearance of cylinder No. 2 at overlap of cylinder No. 3

When making adjustments, tighten the self-locking adjustment nut until it is just possible to remove the feeler gauge.

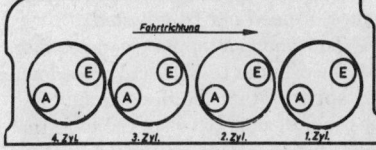

Super 90 and 100 series exhaust valve location is indicated by (A) and intake valve by (E). The arrow points to the front.

Fox

The valve clearances should be checked in firing order, with the engine at normal operating temperature.

1. Remove the camshaft cover and the distributor cap.

2. Set the engine at TDC on No. 1 cylinder by aligning the 0°T mark on the flywheel with the pointer and aligning the distributor rotor with the No. 1 cylinder mark on the rim of the distributor body.

NOTE: *Always turn the crankshaft in the normal direction of rotation. There is a hole in the body behind the front* license plate through which a wrench can be used on the crankshaft.

3. The valve clearances of cylinder No. 1 should be checked when the valves of No. 4 cylinder overlap, i.e. when both No. 4 cylinder valves move in opposite directions simultaneously. You may have to move the crankshaft slightly to find this position. When this happens, the exhaust valve is closing and the intake opening. Check and note the clearance of both the intake and exhaust valves for No. 1 cylinder. Use a feeler gauge between each valve tappet and camshaft lobe.

4. Turn the crankshaft 180° (90° at the distributor rotor) in the normal direction of rotation. Check and note the valve clearances of cylinder No. 3 at the overlap position of cylinder No. 2.

5. Turn the crankshaft 180°. Check and note the valve clearances of cylinder No. 4 at the overlap position of cylinder No. 1.

6. Turn the crankshaft 180°. Check and note the valve clearances of cylinder No. 2 at the overlap position of cylinder No. 3.

7. Now the crankshaft has been turned two complete revolutions (one for the distributor rotor) and all the valve tappet to camshaft lobe clearances have been noted. Compare the noted clearances with those listed in the Tune-Up Specifications Chart. Normal wear usually results in the clearances becoming too small. Adjustment is made by replacing the tappet clearance disc in the top of each tappet. These are available in 26 sizes ranging from 3.0 mm (0.119 in) to 4.25 mm (0.166 in) in increments of 0.05 mm (0.002 in). The thickness of each disc is marked on the bottom.

NOTE: *If a valve clearance deviates 0.002 in or less from the specified clearance, it need not be adjusted.*

8. To remove a tappet clearance disc, turn the cylinder to TDC and press down the tappet so that the disc can be lifted out. Audi dealers have special tools that make this operation much easier. Once the disc is removed, check its size and determine what size will be needed to produce the required adjustment.

NOTE: *Before depressing the tappets, turn them so their openings are at right angles to the camshaft.*

9. Install the required disc and turn the tappet back to its normal direction.

When all the clearances have been corrected, check them again to catch any possible error caused by worn discs.

Carburetor

Idle Speed and Mixture

The idle speed and mixture should be adjusted only after the engine has reached normal operating temperature. The air cleaner must be in place and the preheater hose from the exhaust manifold disconnected. The high beam headlights must be on. The ignition system must be properly adjusted before any carburetor adjustments are attempted. The only accurate way to set the idle mixture is with a CO meter. The allowable percentage of CO in the exhaust gases is shown on the engine compartment emission control sticker.

Standard carburetor adjustments. (E) is the idle speed adjusting screw and (R) is the idle mixture adjusting screw.

Standard Carburetors

The carburetor has only two adjusting screws: one on the throttle linkage for idle speed, and one in the carburetor body for idle mixture. These carburetors are found mainly on early Super 90 and 100 series and non-US models.

1. Set the idle speed with the idle speed adjusting screw.

2. Turn the mixture screw in until the engine just begins to slow down and to run roughly. If turning this screw has no effect, the carburetor idle passages are probably clogged.

3. Back the mixture adjusting screw out ⅛–¼ turn. The engine should resume smooth operation.

4. Reset the idle speed if necessary.

5. Check the CO content of the exhaust gases. Reset the mixture screw if the allowable percentage is exceeded.

6. Complete the job by making a final adjustment of idle speed.

Idle Air Bypass Carburetors

The carburetor has three adjusting screws. The one on the throttle linkage controls the position of the throttle plate. This screw is sealed and is not to be adjusted. The fuel-air mixture bypasses around the throttle plate at idle. There is an idle mixture adjusting screw and an air control screw in the carburetor body. On some models, the air control screw is called an auxiliary fuel control screw. These carburetors are the current emission control type.

1. Use the mixture adjusting screw to set the idle speed to specifications.

2. Tighten the air control screw (auxiliary fuel control screw) all the way in gently. Back it out slightly less than a full turn.

3. Adjust the mixture adjusting screw to obtain the specified percentage of CO in the exhaust gases at idle.

4. If the idle speed is now too high, tighten the mixture adjusting screw to correct. Then tighten the air control screw to get the proper CO content.

NOTE: *It is normal for idle speed to be low on new engines. This need not be adjusted unless the condition persists after break-in.*

On this Fox carburetor, 13 is the idle mixture screw and 14 is the auxiliary fuel control screw (air control screw) which is used to adjust CO readings. On other models, the air control screw is level with and to the right of the mixture screw.

Fuel Injection

Idle Speed Adjustment

1. Operate engine at normal operating temperature.

2. With high beams on and A/C on, ignition timing set to 3A with vacuum hose connected, adjust idle to 850-1000 rpm.

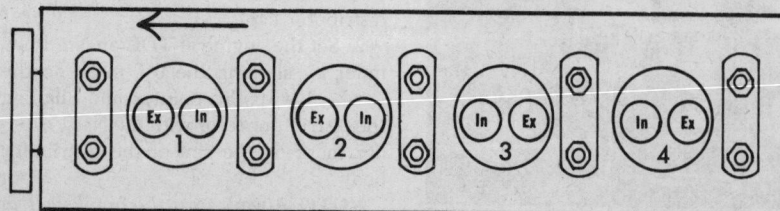

Fox exhaust valve location is indicated by (EX) and intake valve by (IN). The arrow points to the front.

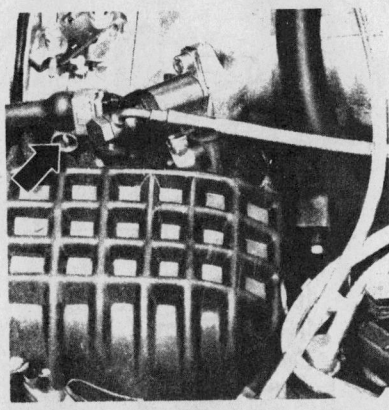

Idle speed adjustment point—Fox with fuel injection

CO adjusting tool and locations—fuel injected Fox

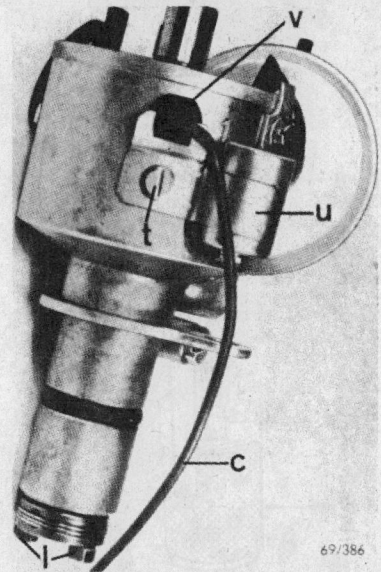

Super 90 and 100 series distributor body removed from the engine. The projections (1) engage the slots in the oil pump driveshaft.

    (c)—Green condenser lead
    (t)—Condenser clamp screw
    (u)—Condenser
    (v)—Plastic boot

ENGINE ELECTRICAL

Distributor

Removal and Installation

Remove the air cleaner. Pry back the retaining clips and remove the distributor cap. Mark the relationship between the distributor body and the engine block. Disconnect the green condenser lead at the ignition coil. Detach the vacuum line, being careful not to damage the plastic tube. Remove the bolt at the retaining clamp and pull the distributor from the housing. If the distributor is difficult to remove, the rubber seal is probably sticking. Carefully pry the distributor loose with a screwdriver.

Distributor installation is the reverse of removal. When installing the distributor, the projections on the shaft, at the bottom of the distributor, must engage the slots in the oil pump driveshaft. Turn the rotor slightly until the two engage. The projections and grooves have been milled off center, making it impossible to install the distributor incorrectly. The gear-driven fox distributor has a slot at the bottom which mates with a dog on top of the oil pump driveshaft. Lubricate the seal with a small amount of oil before

installation. Align the marks made on removal, then tighten the clamp bolt.

NOTE: *If the engine has been turned while the distributor was out, or if a new distributor is being installed, refer to the Static Ignition Timing procedure.*

Alternator

Alternator Precautions

All Audi models are equipped with alternators. When performing any service to the alternator or alternator system the following precautions should be observed.

    A. Leads or cables to any part of the charging circuit should be disconnected only after the engine has been switched off and has stopped running.

    B. When working on the electrical system, always disconnect the lead from the negative battery terminal.

    C. When performing tests with the engine running, the battery must always be connected.

    D. Temporary connections should never be made to the alternator. Always make firm connections.

The alternator warning light on the instrument panel should go out when the engine reaches idle speed, or shortly after.

Removal and Installation

1. Disconnect the battery ground strap.

2. Disconnect all the leads to the alternator, tagging them first. Various ar-

rangements of plug-in or bolt-on connections have been used. On some models the wiring may be unplugged from the back of the alternator; on others, it must be unplugged at the voltage regulator on the right front wheelhousing.

NOTE: *Current models have a voltage regulator built into the alternator.*

3. Remove the belt tensioning bolt from the slotted adjusting bracket.

4. Remove the drive belt.

5. Unbolt and remove the alternator.

To install the unit:

6. Install the hinge bolts. On super 90 and 100 series models, make sure that the head of the rear bolt is to the rear of the car.

7. Install the drive belt and the belt tensioning bolt.

8. Adjust the belt tension.

9. Replace all the electrical connections, making sure that they are installed in their original locations.

10. Connect the battery ground strap.

Belt Tension Adjustment

The alternator drive belt is correctly tensioned when the longest span of belt between pulleys can be depressed about ½ in., by moderate thumb pressure. To adjust, loosen the slotted adjusting bracket bolt on the alternator. If the alternator hinge bolts are very tight, it may be necessary to loosen them slightly to move the alternator. Move the alternator in or out by hand to get the correct tension, then tighten the adjusting bolt.

NOTE: *Be careful not to overtighten the belt, as this may damage the alternator bearings.*

Regulator

The earlier models have a voltage regulator on the right front wheelhousing in the engine compartment. If there is none there, as on current models, it is built into the alternator.

Removal and Installation

To remove the regulator, disconnect the battery ground cable, disconnect the three-pronged plug, and unscrew the unit from the wheelhousing. Be careful to make a good ground connection on reinstallation. The manufacturer does not recommend any adjustments to the regulator.

Starter

Removal and Installation

Super 90, 100 Series

Disconnect the battery ground lead. Remove the oil filter.

NOTE: *When the oil filter is removed, a certain amount of oil will escape.*

Disconnect both leads from the upper terminal of the solenoid. Remove the open cable shoe lead from the lower solenoid terminal. The screw need only be slightly opened to permit removal. On the Super 90, the crossbrace under the starter must be unbolted and removed. Unbolt the starter from the mounting flanges and remove it forward.

Installation is the reverse of removal. Be sure that all leads are positioned correctly and are not pinched. If necessary, replace the lower mounting bolt with the head to the front of the car. Thoroughly clean the seal and oil filter sealing surface. Lightly lubricate both surfaces and tighten the oil filter to approximately 14–18 ft lbs or about one turn by hand. Replace the oil that escaped and run the engine, checking the filter for leaks. **CAUTION:** *Some starters are equipped with an additional terminal (16) which is under full battery voltage, with a direct connection to the ignition coil. This connection bridges the ignition coil series resistor to create higher ignition voltage.*

Fox

1. Disconnect the battery ground lead.
2. Remove the mounting bolt at the engine block.
3. Disconnect the three starter wires.
4. Remove the mounting bolts and nuts and the starter.
5. Reverse the procedure for installation.

Starter Drive Replacement

1. Remove starter.
2. Remove snap ring from armature shaft.
3. Remove stop ring.
4. Slide starter drive from shaft.
5. Reverse the above to install. Use a new snap ring.

Battery

Location

The battery in the 100 series and Fox is located under the rear seat and is accessible by lifting the front edge of the rear seat. The battery in the Super 90 is located in the engine compartment. Be sure that the terminals are clean and provide an adequate connection. The terminals should be coated (lightly) periodically with grease to prevent corrosion.

Water should be added only to bring the solution level up to the bottom of the cell filler well, but not above.

ENGINE MECHANICAL

The Audi engine is a four-cylinder, four-stroke, carbureted, in-line unit. The Fox has an overhead camshaft driven by

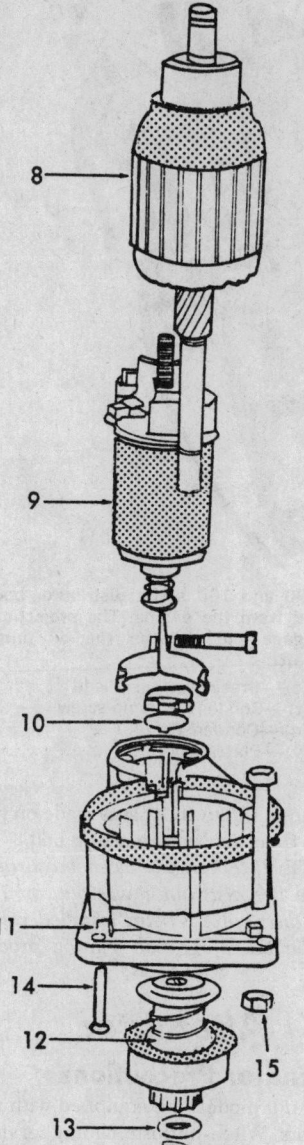

1. Mounting bracket	9. Solenoid
2. End cap screws	10. Disc
3. Housing screws	11. Mounting housing
4. Cupped washer	12. Drive pinion
5. End plate bushing	13. Stop ring
6. Brushes	14. Solenoid bolt
7. Field coil housing	15. Starter bolt and nut
8. Armature	16. Circlip

Exploded view of typical starter

a toothed rubber belt. 1975 and later models have the Continuous Injection System (CIS). The engine is canted at an angle of 40 degrees to the right in the Super 90 and 100 series; 20 degrees in the Fox. The engine/transmission unit is mounted in the integral body and frame by engine carriers bolted to the engine block and supports on the transmission.

Engine Removal and Installation

Super 90, 100 Series

The transmission and engine must be lowered from the car as a unit. The following procedure is for manual transmission cars; see Automatic Transmission Removal and Installation for details on items that must be disconnected on the automatic transmission.

1. Remove the hood (only if using a hoist to remove the engine).
2. Unbolt and remove the apron just below the front bumper.
3. Remove the negative connection from the battery. Remove the air cleaner and carburetor breather hose at the air filter. Drain the coolant. Disconnect all hoses between the radiator and engine and the heater and engine. Disconnect the fuel hose at the fuel pump and plug the end of the line. Remove the power brake unit vacuum hose at the intake manifold.
4. Disconnect the speedometer cable at the transmission, the clutch cable at the mount and the gearshift linkage at the transmission.
5. Disconnect the accelerator linkage at the carburetor, mounting point, and connecting rod, and remove the throttle shaft.
6. Separate the brake line at the body

mount and plug the line to prevent loss of fluid.

7. Remove the guard plate from the right engine mount.

8. Disconnect the following electrical wiring from the engine and transmission: ignition leads, idle cut-off valve (if installed), temperature switch, four pole plug of regulator, oil pressure switch, starter connections, backup light switch and ground leads.

9. Remove the Super 90 oil filter.

10. Remove the radiator and the fan support together with the fan and stop pad.

NOTE: *This operation is only necessary if working with a frame contact hoist or in a pit where the opening in the pit is not large enough to permit lowering the engine with the fan attached. If the opening is large enough, unscrew the stop only.*

11. Remove the front exhaust pipe at the exhaust manifold and at the primary muffler.

12. Unbolt the driveshaft flange at the brake disc. Do not lose the thin insulator from between the brake disc and the flange. Turn the driveshaft flange slightly in the direction of the wheel and wire it to the upper wishbone.

13. Detach the stabilizer from the lower wishbone, left and right.

14. Position the jack or lifting apparatus and lift the weight from the engine mounts. Remove the bolts retaining the rear crossmember to the body. Remove the retaining nut at the right engine/transmission mount. Note the position of the washers and sleeve on the right engine/transmission mount.

15. Remove the retaining nut from the left engine/transmission mount, but do not move the locknut. Lower the engine/transmission unit from the car.

16. Installation procedures are the reverse of removal. The engine and transmission unit must be aligned in such a way that the same distance between brake disc and wishbone exists on each side. The distance between the pulley and front end of the side-member must also be the same on each side. After installation, bleed the brakes.

Fox, Manual Transmission, Without A/C

This procedure explains how to lift the engine out of the chassis. If the car has air-conditioning, it will be necessary to lower the engine, transmission, and front suspension from the car as a unit.

1. Remove the hood and disconnect the battery ground cable. Detach the starter wires.

2. Remove the air cleaner.

3. Disconnect the accelerator linkage and the fuel cutoff solenoid wire.

4. Disconnect the ignition coil primary

(g) is the fan support, (h) is the stop pad, and (i) is the stop on the super 90 and 100 series.

When installing the super 90 and 100 series engine, the same distance (y) must be maintained between the pulley and the front of the side member on both sides. The maximum allowable deviation is 0.08 in.

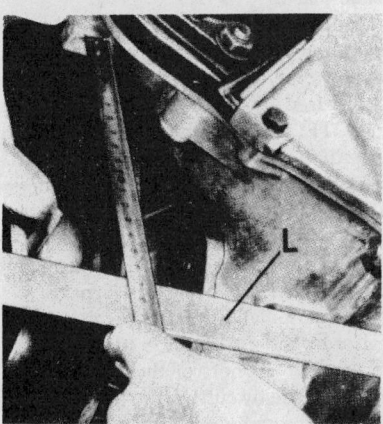

When installing the Super 90 and 100 series engine, the distance between the transmission casting at the point shown and a straightedge (L) must not vary more than 0.16 in. from side to side.

and secondary wires, the oil pressure sending unit, and the coolant temperature sending unit.

5. Loosen the clutch cable adjusting nuts and disconnect the cable. Disconnect the fuel line at the pump. Unplug the alternator.

6. Remove the grille.

7. Remove the bolts holding the panel

When installing the super 90 and 100 series engine, the same distance (X) must be maintained on both sides between the brake discs and the suspension wishbones. The maximum allowable deviation is 0.08 in.

at the side of the radiator through the grille opening.

8. Drain the coolant. Disconnect the lower radiator hose and the radiator fan switch at the bottom of the radiator. Remove the lower radiator panel and the lower radiator mounting nuts.

9. Loosen the mounting bar and slide the upper radiator panel toward the center of the car to remove it. Unbolt the upper radiator mounts and detach the upper radiator hose.

10. Disconnect the heater and intake manifold coolant hoses. Remove the radiator side mounting bolt and remove the radiator and electric fan together.

11. Disconnect the exhaust pipe at the manifold.

12. Attach an engine hoist to the cast lifting eye at the left rear of the cylinder head and to the alternator bracket. Take up the slack.

13. Remove the front engine mount and unbolt the engine mounts on both sides.

14. Unbolt and pull the engine and transmission apart and turn the front of the engine to the left to remove.

15. On installation, stick the transmission-to-engine connecting plate to the back of the engine block with grease. The

front engine mount must be installed so that there is no strain on it with the engine in place. Torque the engine to transmission bolts to 40 ft lbs.

Fox, Automatic Transmission, Without A/C

This procedure is to LIFT the engine out of the chassis. If the car has air-conditioning, it will be necessary to LOWER the engine, transmission, and front suspension from the car as a unit.

1. Steps 1–4 are the same as for manual transmission models.

5. Disconnect the fuel line at the pump. Unplug the alternator.

6. Drain the coolant. Disconnect the upper and lower radiator hoses and the heater and intake manifold coolant hoses. You don't need to remove the radiator.

7. Disconnect the exhaust pipe at the manifold.

8. Attach an engine hoist to the cast lifting eye at the left rear of the cylinder head and to the alternator bracket. Take up the slack.

9. Loosen the engine mounts on both sides and remove the front engine mount.

10. Remove the starter wires and unscrew the mounting bolt at the engine block. Remove the starter.

11. Unbolt the engine from the transmission. Support the transmission. Remove the torque converter guard and detach the vacuum hose.

12. Working through the starter opening, remove the three torque converter/drive shell connecting bolts.

13. Separate the engine from the transmission and lift it out straight.

14. Use a strap to prevent the torque converter from falling out of the transmission.

15. On installation, stick the transmission-to-engine connecting plate to the back of the engine block with grease. The front engine mount must be installed so that there is no strain on it with the engine in place. New torque converter/drive shell connecting bolts must be installed and torqued to 25 ft lbs. Torque the engine to transmission bolts to 40 ft lbs.

Fox, With A/C

On air-conditioned models, it is necessary to lower the engine, transmission, and front suspension from the car as a unit.

1. Raise the car, allowing the front wheels to hang down. Disconnect the battery ground cable.

2. Drain the coolant.

3. Disconnect all connections between engine, transmission, and body as explained for models without A/C.

4. Remove the radiator.

5. Disconnect the gearshift rod coupling at the transmission.

6. Detach the front engine mount at the engine block.

7. Use a removal tool to separate the tie rod ends from the steering levers.

8. Push the brake pedal down about 1½ in and fasten it in place to keep the system from draining. Disconnect and plug the brake lines at the brackets on the wheel housing.

9. Attach a framework to keep the assembly steady to a sturdy floor jack and clamp it to the crossmember. Lift slightly and disconnect both coil spring units from the wheel housings. Unbolt the crossmember.

10. Disconnect the backup light switch wire and lower the engine, transmission, and front suspension assembly.

11. On installation, tighten the coil spring units to the body to 16 ft lbs, and the crossmember to the body to 33 ft lbs.

Cylinder Head

Removal and Installation

Super 90, 100 Series

1. Drain the coolant from the radiator. Disconnect the spark plug wires.

2. Remove the sheet metal cover from the exhaust manifold. Remove the intake and exhaust manifolds.

3. Disconnect the hoses from the thermostat housing.

4. Remove the valve cover. Loosen the valve rocker arm adjusting nuts and remove the pushrods. Note their original locations; they must all go back in the same place.

5. Loosen the cylinder head bolts in the same order as shown for tightening. Remove the bolts. A metric allen wrench is required for the head bolts.

NOTE: *Do not loosen the head bolts until the engine has thoroughly cooled.*

6. Remove the head. If it sticks, operate the starter to loosen it by compression or rap it upward with a soft hammer. Do not force anything between the head and block. Check the head for warpage.

7. Reinstallation of the head is made easier by the use of guide studs installed in opposite corners of the block. These can be made by cutting the heads off two bolts of the same size as the head bolts.

8. Put the gasket in place on the block.

9. Guide the cylinder head into place.

10. Coat the head bolt threads with a graphite lubricant. Install them finger tight.

11. Tighten the bolts in the sequence shown in four stages until the proper torque is reached. The bolts should be torqued again after the first 500–1000 miles.

12. Install the pushrods in their original locations. Make a preliminary valve lash adjustment.

13. Replace the valve cover, using a new gasket. Replace the manifolds. Connect the coolant hoses and the spark plug wires.

14. Refill the cooling system.

15. Run the engine until it reaches normal operating temperature, watching for leaks. Make a final valve adjustment with the engine warm.

16. On overhaul, if the rocker studs and pushrod guide plates have been removed, the guides must be aligned so that the pushrods will not contact them. The cylinder head must be heated to 248°F in an oven in order to install or remove the valve guides.

Fox

1. Disconnect the battery ground cable.

2. Drain the coolant. Disconnect the hoses.

3. Unbolt the exhaust pipe from the manifold.

4. Disconnect the electrical wires. Detach the accelerator linkage.

5. Remove the alternator belt and the timing belt.

6. Loosen the cylinder head bolts in the reverse of the order shown for tightening. Remove the bolts. A metric allen wrench is required for the head bolts.

CAUTION: *Don't loosen the head bolts until the engine is thoroughly cool. Don't loosen the camshaft bearing cap nuts.*

7. Remove the head. If it sticks, loosen it by compression or rap it upward with a soft hammer. Do not force anything between the head and block. Check the head for warpage.

CAUTION: *Do not attempt to remove the camshaft from the head without checking the Camshaft Removal and Installation procedure. Special tools are required.*

8. On installation, make sure that the head gasket is installed with the word OBEN up and to the left side of the engine. Put the head in place and install the right front and left rear head bolts first.

9. Tighten the bolts in the sequence shown in four stages until the proper torque is reached. The bolts should be torqued again after the first 300 miles.

10. On overhaul, valve guides must be pressed out or in from above. The cylinder head must be heated to 176–212°F in an oil bath or an oven to install new valve guides.

NOTE: *New cylinder head bolts and a new, soft head gasket are available to correct coolant leakage problems. The new bolts are marked 12.9 and should be torqued to normal specifications. Anytime there is a leakage problem, both the head and block should be checked for warpage.*

11. Make sure to align the timing belt and sprockets as explained under Timing Belt Removal and Installation.

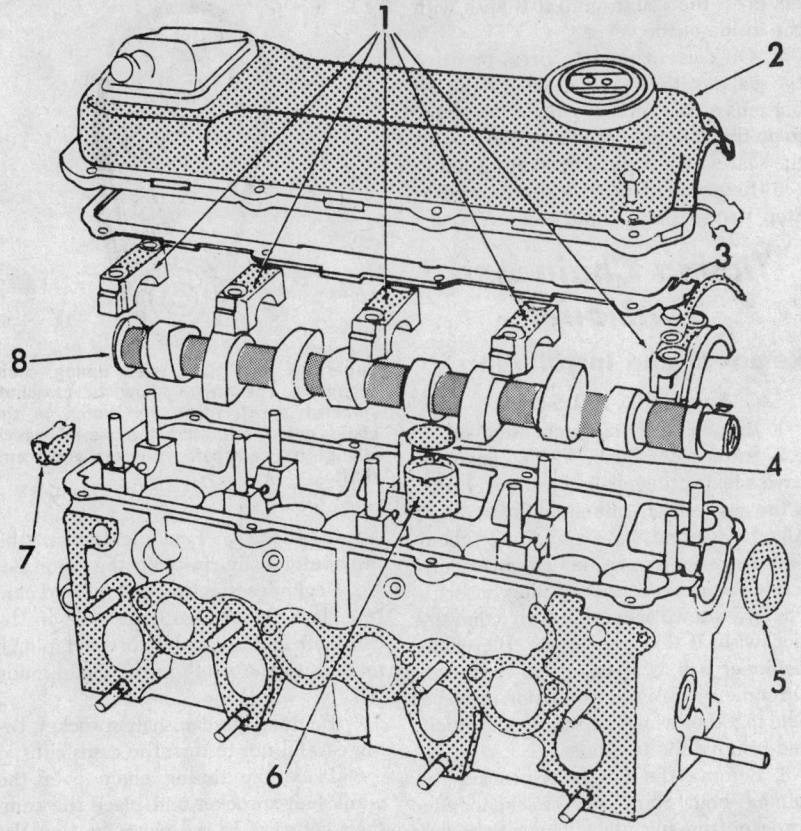

Fox cylinder head and camshaft

1. Camshaft bearing caps
2. Camshaft cover
3. Gasket
4. Valve adjusting disc
5. Oil seal
6. Cam follower
7. End plug
8. Camshaft

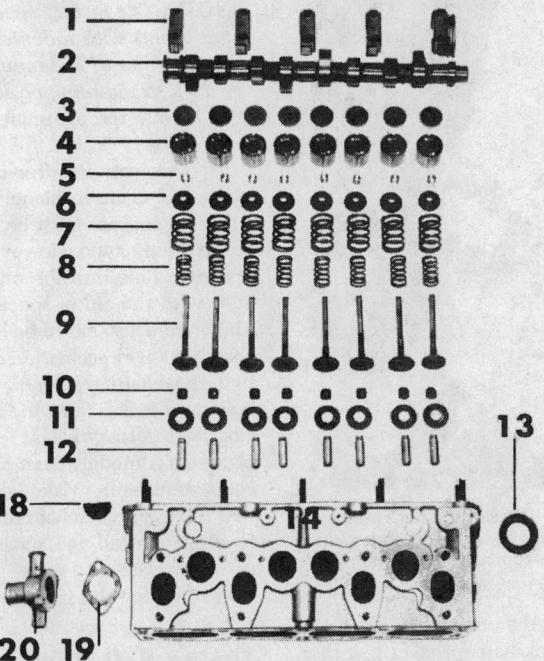

Details of the Fox cylinder head and valve train

1. Bearing cap
2. Camshaft
3. Tappet clearance disc
4. Tappet
5. Lock
6. Spring retainer
7. Outer spring
8. Inner spring
9. Valve
10. Valve seal
11. Spring retainer
12. Valve guide
13. Shaft seal
14. Cylinder head
18. Plug
19. Gasket, water adapter
20. Water adapter

CAUTION: *Do not attempt to start the engine until you are sure of this alignment.*

For cylinder head overhaul, see the Engine Rebuilding section of this manual.

Intake Manifold
Removal and Installation

1. Drain the coolant.
2. Remove the air cleaner.
3. Disconnect the coolant hoses from the manifold and the automatic choke. Remove the wire from the electric choke.
4. Disconnect the vacuum hose and the lead to the idle cutoff valve. Detach the fuel line and the accelerator linkage.
5. Remove the manifold nuts and the manifold support.
6. Pull the manifold off the studs. If it sticks, rap it with a soft hammer. Do not force anything between the manifold and the cylinder head. Discard the gaskets.
7. Installation is the reverse of the removal procedure. New gaskets must be used. Tighten the nuts to 18 ft. lb. After refilling the cooling system, start the engine and check for leaks.

Exhaust Manifold
Removal and Installation

1. Disconnect the heated air intake hose from the manifold.
2. Unbolt the exhaust pipe from the manifold.
3. Remove the sheet metal cover.
4. Remove the manifold nuts. Pull the manifold off the studs. If it sticks, rap it with a soft hammer. Do not force anything between the manifold and the cylinder head. Discard the gaskets.
5. Installation is the reverse of the removal procedure. New gaskets must be used. If the gaskets are the type with round openings, they must be installed with the beaded side outward from the head and the notched edge down. Gaskets with oval openings must be installed with the beaded edge outward from the head. Tighten the manifold nuts to the specified torque. Torque the front exhaust pipe flange nuts to 18–22 ft lbs, in steps. A new gasket should also be used between the exhaust pipe and the manifold.

Timing Chain Cover
Removal and Installation

1. Place the car on a lift or pit.
2. Remove the apron under the front bumper.
3. Have an assistant place the car in first gear and hold the brake on. Remove the crankshaft pulley nut. On cars with automatic transmission the nut can be

Audi

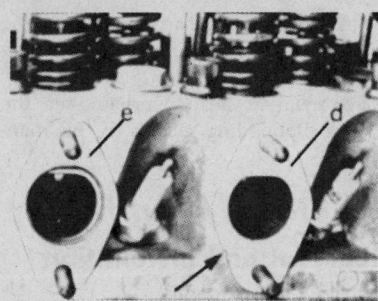

Super 90 and 100 series exhaust manifold gaskets. (d) is the type with the oval opening which must be installed with the notched (arrow) side down, (e) is the type with the round opening. Both types must have the beaded edge around the opening outward.

removed by affixing a heavy wrench and rapping the wrench with a hammer. The nut must be unscrewed in the opposite direction of normal engine rotation.

4. Loosen the fan and alternator adjustments and remove the belts.

5. Remove the pulley, rapping it with a soft hammer if necessary. Be careful not to lose the shaft key.

6. Drain the oil.

7. Remove first the oil pan, then the timing chain cover.

8. Reverse the procedure to install, using new gaskets. Timing chain cover bolt torque is 7 ft lbs.

Timing Chain Cover Oil Seal Replacement

Current models have the lip retaining the oil seal in the cover to the inside. Thus the oil seal is pressed in from the front of the cover. Older models have the retaining lip toward the outside of the cover; the seal is pressed in from the inside of the cover. The result of this is that the oil seal may be replaced with the cover in place on the current models, while on older models the cover must be removed to replace the seal. The only way to determine which cover is installed is by inspection, after removing the crankshaft pulley. Virtually all US models use the current type. The seal can be replaced without removing the engine.

To replace either type:

1. Remove the timing chain cover on older models. Follow Steps 1–6 of the "Timing Chain Cover Removal and Installation" procedure for current models.

2. Carefully pry out the old seal with a screwdriver, being careful not to damage the housing.

3. Apply grease between the lips of the seal and apply a little oil to the outside edge.

4. On older models press in the seal from the inside of the cover. Press or drive it in with a seal installer or a suitable improvised tool, until it bottoms on the retaining lip. If there is no retaining

lip, press the seal in until it is flush with the inside of the cover.

5. On current models, press or drive the seal in with the metal side out until it bottoms on the retaining lip. A good way to do this is to tighten a flat plate against the seal with the pulley retaining nut.

6. Reverse the procedure followed in Step 1 to reassemble the engine.

Timing Chain and Tensioner

Removal and Installation

Super 90, 100 Series

1. Remove the timing chain cover.

2. Some older Super 90 engines may have a leaf spring chain tensioner. If this is the case, simply unbolt and remove it. All other engines have a hydraulic chain tensioner. Bend open the lock plate, unscrew the chain tensioner plug, insert a Phillips screwdriver and turn counterclockwise. If this is not done, the chain tensioner will fly apart as it is removed. On some models, the tensioner must be held together while it is removed. Unbolt and remove the tensioner.

3. Remove the camshaft sprocket retaining bolt. Some way to keep the sprocket from turning will have to be devised.

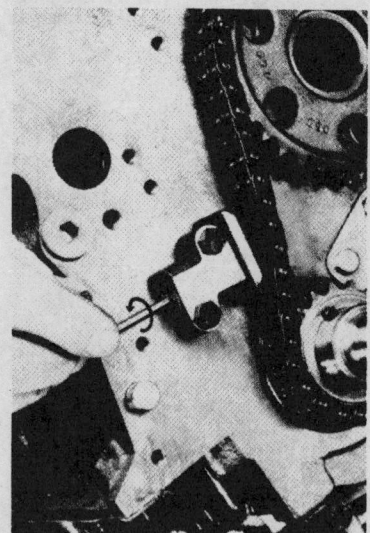

Use a Phillips screwdriver as shown to prevent the Super 90 and 100 series chain tensioner from coming apart when it is removed.

4. Remove the camshaft sprocket, chain, and crankshaft sprocket together, using a puller on the crankshaft sprocket. Be careful not to lose the key for the crankshaft sprocket.

5. On reinstallation, heat the crankshaft sprocket to 140°F in an oven. Do not heat it with a flame, as it will be warped. Install the shaft key and slide the sprocket into place until it rests against the stop.

Super 90 and 100 series timing chain alignment. The arrows show the camshaft sprocket punch mark, the notch in the chain guide rail, and the dowel which aligns the camshaft sprocket and camshaft.

6. Align the No. 1 cylinder mark on the distributor body rim with the rotor. Set No. 1 cylinder precisely at top dead center. Place the camshaft sprocket on the camshaft and align the sprocket punch mark with the notch in the chain guide rail.

7. Remove the camshaft sprocket, being careful not to turn the camshaft.

8. Place the timing chain over the crankshaft sprocket and place the camshaft sprocket in the chain, so that the camshaft sprocket can be installed without moving either the camshaft or the crankshaft.

NOTE: *The factory specifies that timing chains with indented links should not be reused. They must be replaced with a straight-link chain.*

9. Torque the camshaft sprocket bolt to 58 ft lbs.

10. The manufacturer states that the leaf spring chain tensioner used on older Super 90 engines must be replaced with the hydraulic type. However, this entails drilling a hole into the engine block oil bore with the aid of special equipment. The engine also has to be lowered in the chassis to gain access. Assemble and install the chain tensioner, torquing the bolts to 9 ft lbs. Turn the chain plunger clockwise to release it. Current production models have a self-releasing chain tensioner. Make absolutely sure that the hydraulic chain tensioner is free to move. Install the tensioner plunger and lock plate.

11. Replace the timing cover.

Timing Belt Removal and Installation

Fox

1. Remove the grille.

2. Remove the alternator belt and the timing belt cover.

3. Loosen the belt tensioner locknut and turn the tensioner counterclockwise (facing it) to release the belt tension.

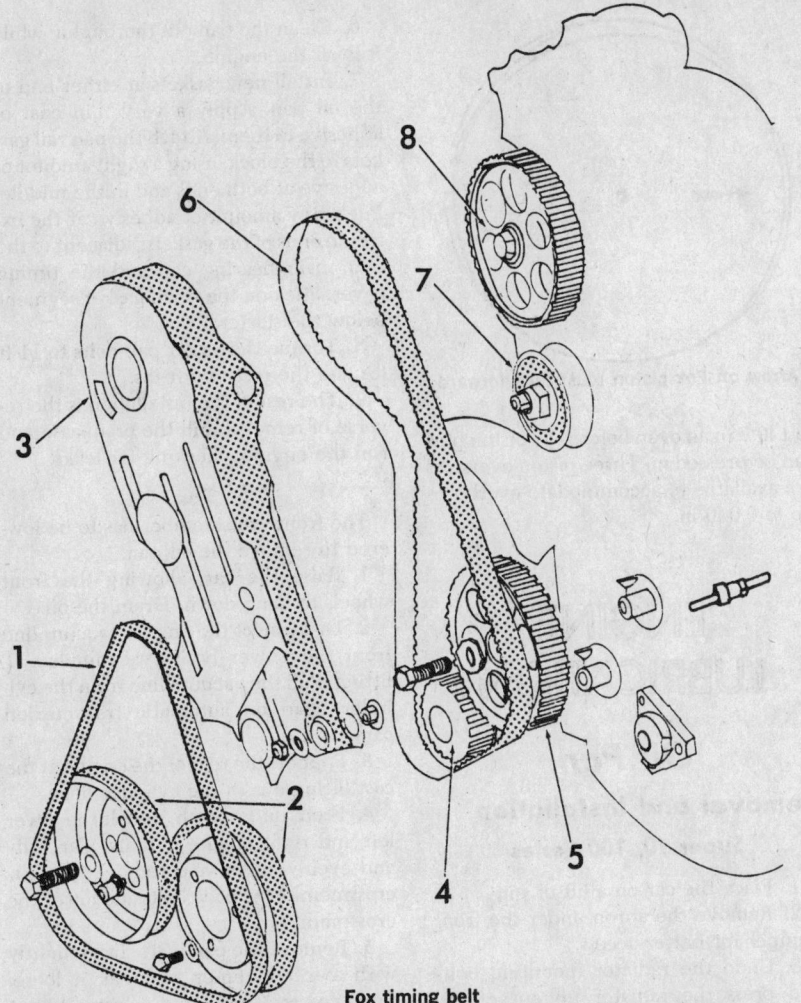

Fox timing belt

1. Alternator belt
2. Belt pulleys
3. Timing gear cover
4. Crankshaft sprocket
5. Intermediate sprocket
6. Drive belt
7. Tensioner
8. Camshaft sprocket

Fox crankshaft pulley and intermediate sprocket alignment for timing belt installation. With the pulley and sprocket as shown, No. 1 cylinder should be at TDC and the distributor rotor aligned with the No. 1 cylinder notch.

4. Slide the belt off the camshaft sprocket.

5. Belt installation is easier if the water pump pulley is removed.

6. Set the flywheel timing mark at TDC (0°T).

7. Make sure that the camshaft is positioned so that the No. 4 cylinder valves

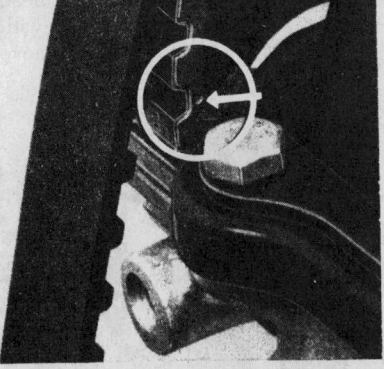

Fox camshaft sprocket aligned for timing belt installation. With the sprocket as shown, No. 4 cylinder valves should be in the overlap position.

are overlapping; i.e. the exhaust valve is opening and the intake closing. If there is a punch mark on the back of the camshaft sprocket, align it with the camshaft cover gasket (left side).

8. Turn the intermediate shaft so that the distributor rotor points to the No. 1 cylinder mark on the rim of the distributor body. If there is a notch on the crankshaft pulley, it should now align with the punch mark on the front of the intermediate shaft sprocket.

9. Taking care not to disturb any of the three sprockets, install the timing belt.

NOTE: *Audi dealers have a special tool which can be used to hold the sprockets in alignment. It can also be used to check alignment on early engines which do not have the punch mark on the back of the camshaft sprocket and the notch on the crankshaft sprocket.*

10. Recheck that the No. 1 (and 4) cylinder is at TDC, that the camshaft is in the No. 4 cylinder overlap position, and that the distributor rotor is in the No. 1 cylinder firing position.

11. Turn the belt tensioner clockwise (facing it) until it is just possible to turn the longest span of belt about 90° with your thumb and forefinger. Lock the tensioner in place.

NOTE: *It is not necessary to recheck the belt tension during the normal life span of the belt (about 60,000 miles).*

12. Again recheck the alignment as in Step 10 and replace the belt cover, water pump pulley, alternator belt, and grille. Check the ignition timing when the job is complete.

Camshaft
Removal and Installation
Super 90, 100 Series

This operation requires that the engine be removed from the car and rather extensively disassembled.

1. Remove the timing chain and tensioner.

2. Remove the cylinder head.

3. Remove the tappets (valve lifters). A special tool is used by dealers to lift them out. Keep them in order so they can be replaced in their original locations.

4. Remove the distributor.

5. Remove the oil pump.

6. Unbolt and remove the camshaft locating plate.

7. Carefully guide the camshaft out of the block, being cautious not to bang the lobes into the bearings. This is a lot easier if a bolt is threaded into the front of the camshaft for use as a handle.

8. On reinstallation, oil the camshaft bearing surfaces. Insert the camshaft carefully.

9. Install the locating plate, torquing the bolts to 18 ft lbs.

10. Check the camshaft end-play in and out of the block, using a dial indicator. If it exceeds 0.004 in., install a new locating plate.

11. The rest of the reassembly procedure is the reverse of disassembly. Make sure to align the chain and sprockets as explained under Timing Chain and Tensioner Removal and Installation. Check the ignition timing when the job is complete.

Fox

NOTE: *The manufacturer says that the camshaft must not be removed unless a special removal tool is used. This device bolts to the cylinder head and presses down on the camshaft at two places: between the lobes for cylinder 3 and between the lobes for cylinder 2. The following alternate procedure may be used, but great caution must be exercised. The alternate procedure is not recommended by the manufacturer.*

1. Remove the timing belt.
2. Remove the camshaft sprocket.
3. Remove the air cleaner.
4. Remove the camshaft cover.
5. Unscrew and remove the No. 1, 3, and 5 bearing caps (No. 1 is at the front).
6. Unscrew the No. 2 and 4 bearing caps, diagonally and in increments.
7. Lift the camshaft out of the cylinder head.
8. Lubricate the camshaft journals and lobes with assembly lube or gear oil before installing it in the cylinder head.
9. Replace the camshaft oil seal with a new one whenever the cam is removed.
10. Install the No. 1, 3, and 5 bearing caps and tighten the nuts to 14 ft. lbs. The caps should be installed so they read right side up from the driver's seat.
11. Install the No. 2 and 4 bearing caps and diagonally tighten the nuts to 14 ft. lbs.

NOTE: *If checking end play, install a dial indicator so that the feeler touches the camshaft snout. Endplay should be no more than 0.006 in.*

12. Replace the seal in the No. 1 bearing cap. If necessary, replace the end plug in the cylinder head.
13. Install the camshaft cover.
14. Install the camshaft pulley and the timing belt.
15. Check the valve clearance.

Pistons and Connecting Rods

Super 90, 100 Series

The connecting rods must be installed in the engine with the grooved side toward the camshaft. New connecting rod bolts must always be used. Both the pistons and the piston pins must be heated to 140°F in an oven in order to install the pins. Three oversizes of pistons are available to accommodate overbores up to 0.040 in.

Fox

The pistons must be installed in the block with the arrow at the edge of the crown facing to the front of the car. The connecting rod and cap alignment casting grooves must face the intermediate shaft. New connecting rod bolts must always be used. The pistons must be heated

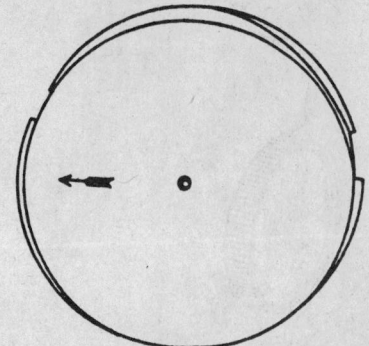

Arrow on Fox piston must face forward

to 140°F in an oven before the piston pins can be pressed in. Three piston oversizes are available to accommodate overbores up to 0.040 in.

ENGINE LUBRICATION

Oil Pan

Removal and Installation

Super 90, 100 Series

1. Place the car on a lift or pit.
2. Remove the apron under the front bumper for better access.
3. Undo the radiator mounting bolts and press the radiator up out of the brackets.
4. Drain the oil.
5. Loosen and remove the Allen head bolts holding the pan. Tap it lightly with a soft hammer to break it loose. Remove the pan.

6. Clean the pan out thoroughly while it is off the engine.
7. Install new gaskets at either end of the oil pan. Apply a very thin coat of adhesive to them. Attach the pan rail gaskets to the block, using a slight amount of adhesive at both ends and in the middle. Put a tiny amount of adhesive at the extreme ends of the gaskets, adjacent to the rear main bearing cap and the timing cover. Stick on the small gasket segment below the starter.
8. Torque the larger pan bolts to 11 ft lbs and the rest to 6 ft lbs.
9. The rest of the installation is the reverse of removal. Fill the crankcase and run the engine, checking for leaks.

Fox

The front crossmember has to be lowered to remove the oil pan.

1. Raise the car, allowing the front wheels to hang down. Drain the oil.
2. Disconnect the engine vacuum line from the power brake vacuum line T fitting. Pull the vacuum line from the cylinder head on automatic transmission cars.
3. Support the rear of the engine at the cast lifting eye in the cylinder head.
4. From underneath, unbolt the lower left and right engine mounts. Carefully and evenly loosen and remove the four crossmember to body bolts and lower the crossmember.
5. Remove the pan bolts. Tap it lightly with a soft hammer to break it loose. Remove the pan and clean it out thoroughly while it is off the engine.
6. On installation, use a new gasket with no sealer. Torque the pan bolts in a criss-cross pattern, in steps, to 6 ft lbs. Torque the crossmember bolts to 33 ft lbs.

(1) is the Super 90 and 100 series oil pan rail gaskets, stuck to the block at (x). (n) is a small separate gasket segment. Arrows show adhesive application locations.

Rear Main Bearing Oil Seal Replacement

When this seal fails, the usual result is oil leakage onto the clutch. This, of course, causes clutch slippage or failure to disengage.

Super 90, 100 Series

This repair requires that the engine be removed from the car and extensively disassembled.

1. Remove the engine.
2. Remove the transmission (and clutch) from the engine.
3. Remove the flywheel. Some method of preventing the flywheel from turning will have to be devised.

NOTE: *Mark the relationship between the flywheel and crankshaft to preserve balance.*

4. Remove the oil pan.
5. Unbolt and remove the rear main bearing cap.
6. The circular seal may now be removed.
7. Press the new seal evenly into place with the sealing lip toward the front of the engine. This is rather difficult without special seal installing tools.
8. Torque the bearing cap to specifications.
9. The remainder of the procedure is the reverse of disassembly. Make sure to align the flywheel marks made in Step 3.

Fox

1. Remove the engine. Refer to the Engine Removal and Installation procedures.
2. Remove the transmission (and clutch) from the engine.
3. Remove the flywheel. Some method of preventing the flywheel from turning will have to be devised.

NOTE: *Mark the relationship between the flywheel and crankshaft to preserve balance.*

4. The circular seal may now be removed by placing a screwdriver under the sealing lip or behind the support ring

When intalling the Super 90 and 100 series distributor, the rotor (r) must be aligned with the No. 1 cylinder notch (s). The vacuum unit (t) should parallel the engine block. (us) is the distributor mounting bolt.

carefully. Be very cautious not to damage the seal bearing surface.

5. Press the new seal evenly in place. This is rather difficult without special seal installing tools.
6. The remainder of the procedure is the reverse of removal. Make sure to align the flywheel marks made in Step 3.

Oil Pump

Removal and Installation

Super 90, 100 Series

1. Remove the distributor. Remove the oil pan.
2. Disconnect the oil line from the block and the pump.
3. Unbolt the pump and pull it out of the block, being careful not to lose the bolt spacer.
4. Place No. 1 cylinder on top dead center. This can be done by turning the engine with a finger held over the No. 1 spark plug hole. When compression is felt, turn the engine to align the 0°T mark on the crankshaft pulley with the timing pointer.
5. On replacement, turn the pump un-

til the wide segment of the pump driveshaft faces forward. Turn the shaft 15 degrees counterclockwise and slide the oil pump shaft into the gear teeth of the camshaft.

6. Install the spacer under the pump and mounting bolt and tighten the bolt finger tight.
7. Put the oil line in place. Turn the pump or add extra gaskets at either end of the oil line to prevent any strain on the line.
8. Torque the pump mounting bolt to 18 ft lbs and the oil line bolts to 7 ft lbs. Use the lock plates to hold the oil line bolts.
9. Align the distributor rotor with the No. 1 cylinder notch in the rim of the housing. Insert the distributor with the vacuum unit parallel to the engine block and pointing to the rear of the engine. When installing the distributor, wiggle the rotor back and forth to allow the shaft projections to engage the oil pump driveshaft slots. Tighten the distributor mounting bolt.
10. Replace and fill the oil pan.
11. Start the engine and watch for oil leaks. If it won't start, check the basic ignition timing as described in Chapter 2. If it does start, check the final ignition timing with a timing light.

Fox

To remove the pump, remove the oil pan and the pump mounting bolts. Pull the pump straight down. Pump bolt torque is 13–16 ft lbs.

ENGINE COOLING

The radiator drain plug is at the bottom, adjacent to the lower hose on all models. The engine drain plug is at the front, adjacent to the alternator except on the Fox. The Super 90 also has a drain plug at the bottom of the heater, inside the car. There is a breather plug in the

The wide segment (c) on the Super 90 and 100 series oil pump driveshaft must face forward when installing the pump.

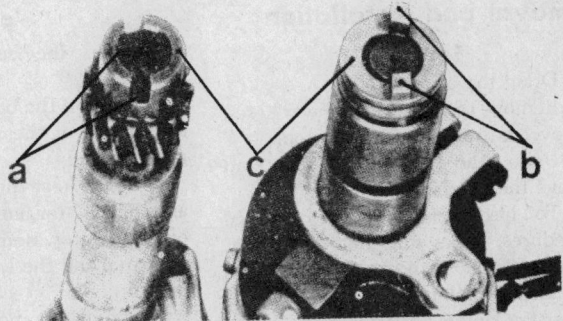

The slots (a) in the Super 90 and 100 series oil pump driveshaft and the projections (b) on the distributor driveshaft are offset. (c) indicates the wide segment of each shaft. Because of this construction, the shafts can mate in only one way.

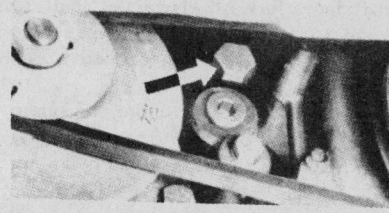

Super 90 and 100 series engine block coolant drain plug.

Radiator drain plug; 100, 100 LS, and 100 GL shown.

Cooling system breather plug; 100, 100 LS, and 100 GL shown.

upper heater hose, near the firewall on Super 90 and 100 series cars. The breather plug must be used to remove air from the system, when the engine is first started after refilling.

Radiator

Removal and Installation

Super 90

1. Drain the coolant.
2. Remove the upper and lower hoses. Remove the small hose at the top.
3. Undo the mounting nuts and remove the radiator downward.
4. To install, reverse the removal procedures. Make sure that the gasket between the cowl and the radiator seals the crack completely. Be sure that the rubber fan ring is flat around the cowl.

100, 100 LS, 100 GL

1. Drain the coolant.
2. Remove the upper radiator hose.

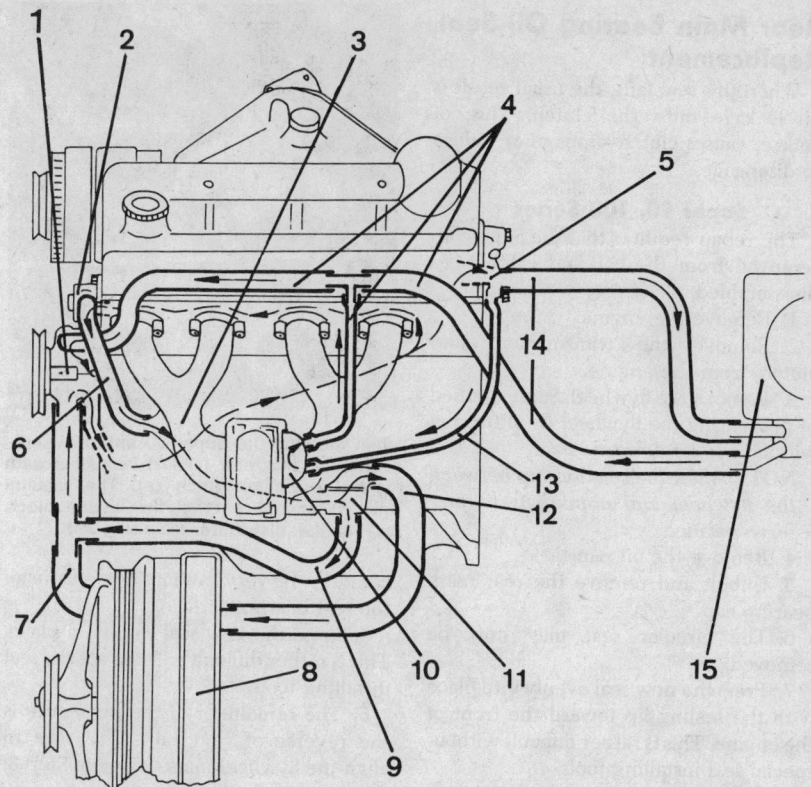

Coolant flow; 1972 100 series shown, later models have the thermostat at the front of the engine block.

1. Water pump
2. Flange, front of cylinder head
3. Intake manifold
4. Return line, heater and automatic choke
5. Flange, rear of cylinder head
6. Connecting line to intake manifold
7. Radiator circuit from radiator to water pump
8. Radiator and fan (or electric fan)
9. Bypass line from intake manifold to water pump
10. Preheating, automatic choke
11. Thermostat, intake manifold
12. Radiator circuit
13. Automatic choke circuit
14. Heater circuit
15. Heat exchanger, heater

3. Detach the mounting strut at the top of the radiator, and swing it forward.
4. Detach the lower radiator hose. Detach the fan thermostatic switch.
5. Unbolt the radiator mountings.
6. Lift the radiator out.
7. To install, reverse the removal procedures. Make sure that the rubber sealing strips between the radiator and radiator cowl are in place.

Fox

1. Drain the coolant. Remove the grille.
2. Remove the bolts holding the panel at the side of the radiator through the grille opening.
3. Disconnect the lower radiator hose and the radiator fan switch at the bottom of the radiator. Remove the lower radiator panel and the lower radiator mounting nuts.
4. Loosen the mounting bar and slide the upper radiator panel toward the center of the car to remove it. Unbolt the upper radiator mounts and detach the upper radiator hose.

5. Disconnect the heater and intake manifold coolant hoses at the fan shroud. Remove the radiator side mounting bolt and remove the radiator and electric fan together.

Water Pump

Removal and Installation

Super 90

1. Loosen the adjustment and remove the water pump drive belt.
2. Drain the coolant.
3. Remove the bolt that holds the small diameter hose to the front of the pump.
4. Detach the inlet and outlet hoses from the pump.
5. Remove the three Allen head bolts and remove the pump.
6. Reverse the procedure for installation, using new gaskets and adjusting the water pump drive belt tension. Tighten the pump mounting bolts to 18 ft lbs.

100, 100 LS, 100 GL

1. Loosen the adjustment and remove the water pump drive belt.

2. Drain the coolant.

3. Remove the alternator pivot bolt at the front.

4. Loosen the clamp and pull the lower hose off the pump.

5. Remove the thermostat housing.

6. Unbolt the fan pulley. The pulley may be prevented from turning by wedging a screwdriver between the pulley hub and one of the bolts.

7. The pulley may be carefully pried off the hub with two large screwdrivers.

8. Loosen the clamp and pull the upper hose off the pump.

9. Remove the five bolts and remove the pump.

10. Reverse the procedure for installation, using new gaskets and adjusting the alternator drive belt tension. Pump mounting bolt torque is 15 ft lbs for the large bolts, and 9 ft lbs for the small ones. Thermostat housing bolt torque is 15 ft lbs. Pulley bolt torque is 7 ft lbs.

Fox

1. Drain the coolant.

2. Remove the alternator.

3. Remove the timing belt cover.

4. Loosen the clamps and detach the hoses from the pump.

5. Unbolt the pump, turn it slightly, and lift it out.

6. On installation, use a new pump to block seal and torque the pump bolts to 14 ft lbs.

Thermostat

The thermostat normally installed in the super 90 and 100 series is rated at 181°F (83°C). There is also available a winter thermostat rated at 189°F (87°C).

Removal and Installation

1. Drain the coolant from the radiator.

2. Remove the air cleaner on the Super 90.

3. The thermostat is inside a cast housing on the engine or the water pump, connected to the upper radiator hose. On most 100 series models through 1972, it is on the rear end of the intake manifold. Some early models may have it on the front of the engine. Unbolt the cover and remove the gasket and the thermostat.

4. When replacing the thermostat on the 100 series with the front mounted thermostat, the bar on the thermostat should be facing up and running from front to rear. On the Super 90, the bar should be facing up and pointing at the projection on the housing. Some thermostats have an arrow on the bar which should also point at the projection. In any case, the bar should be up. The housing bolts should be torqued to 7 ft lbs. Always use a new gasket.

5. Replace the Super 90 air cleaner and refill the radiator.

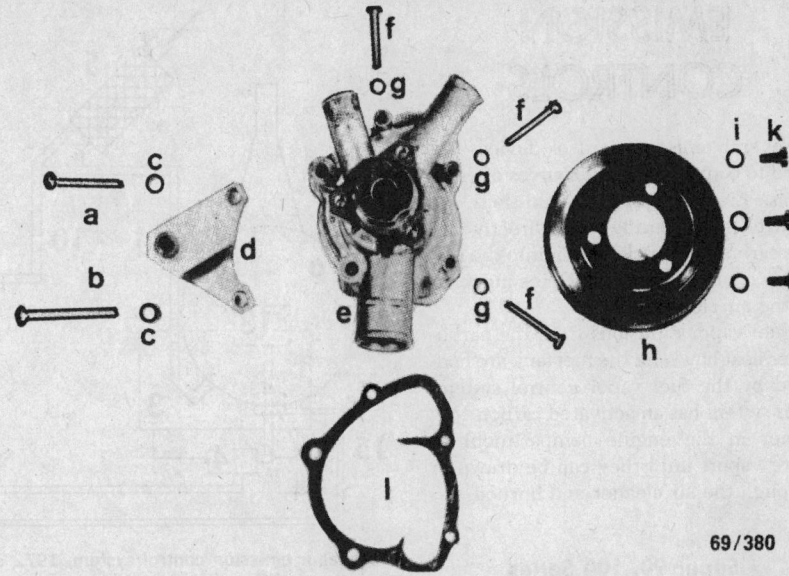

69/380

Exploded view of 100, 100 LS, and 100 GL water pump

(a)—Bolt	(e)—Water pump	(k)—Bolt
(b)—Bolt	(f)—Bolt	(l)—Water pump gasket
(c)—Lockwasher	(g)—Lockwasher	
(d)—Mounting plate, alternator	(h)—Pulley	
	(i)—Lockwasher	

When installing the Super 90 thermostat, the bar (or arrow) should point at the projection (a). (b) points to the front.

Correct installation of the front mounted 100 series thermostat

Radiator Fan

On the Super 90, the radiator fan is driven by the same belt that drives the water pump. On the early 100, 100 LS, and 100 GL, the radiator fan is driven by a separate belt, the water pump being driven by the same belt that drives the alternator. Late 100 series models and the Fox have an electric fan which requires no belt or adjustment. On models through 1972 and the Fox, the fan thermostatic switch is in the bottom of the radiator. Beginning 1973, it is in the lower radiator hose.

Belt Tension Adjustment

1. Loosen the two bolts holding the fan housing to the fan support arm.

2. Move the fan and housing out to tighten the belt. The belt is correctly tensioned when the longest span of belt between pulleys can be depressed about ½ in. by moderate thumb pressure.

3. Tighten the bolts.

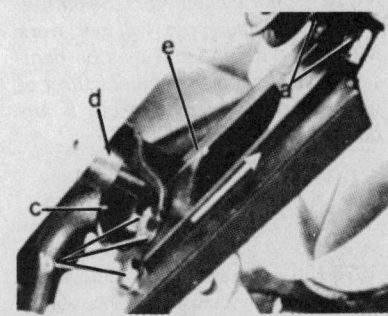

Radiator fan belt tension is adjusted with the bolts (a).

(b)—Mounting bolts	(d)—Stop
(c)—Pad	(e)—Fan support

Audi

EMISSION CONTROLS

Several emission control devices are used to control different sources of emissions. Engine crankcase emissions are controlled by routing them directly into the carburetor air cleaner or into the fuel vapor control system, which is connected to the air cleaner.

Fuel vapor emissions from the carburetor float bowl and the fuel tank are handled by the fuel vapor control system. This system has an activated carbon container in the engine compartment to store vapors until they can be drawn in through the air cleaner and burned.

Super 90, 100 Series

The 100, 100 LS, and 100 GL use certain basic equipment to control exhaust emissions. The Super 90 uses some of this equipment. The parts of the system are: a triple port intake manifold, an air cleaner with a temperature controlled inlet beginning in 1972, and a heating circuit to preheat the intake manifold.

The triple port intake manifold has a separate intake for water, used to preheat the manifold. The preheating and the conduction of the fuel/air mixture from each stage separately leads to more complete combustion and a lower level of exhaust emissions.

The distributor uses both centrifugal and vacuum advance mechanisms.

All 1973 and later 100 series models are equipped with a capacitive discharge ignition system. This system reduces the normal decline in ignition system performance between tune-ups, keeping exhaust emissions at a minimum. It does this primarily by reducing the electrical load on the breaker points and supplying very high voltage to the spark plugs.

NOTE: *Some tachometers, dwell meters, and oscilloscopes will not work with this system. Some may be damaged. Check with the manufacturer of your test equipment if there is any doubt.*

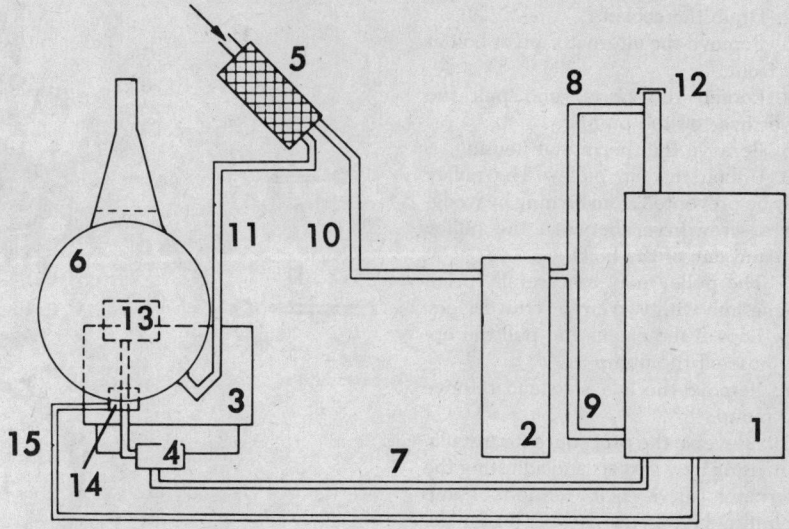

Fuel vapor emission control system, 1972 and later. Earlier versions and the Fox do not have items (14) and (15).

1. Fuel tank
2. Vapor expansion container
3. Engine
4. Fuel pump
5. Activated carbon container
6. Air cleaner
7. Fuel line from tank to pump
8. Breather line from neck to expansion container
9. Breather line from tank to expansion container
10. Breather line to carbon container
11. Line from carbon
11. Line from carbon container to air cleaner
12. Non-vented tank filler cap
13. Carburetor
14. Fuel return valve
15. Line from return valve to tank

Emission control schematic for 100LS

— Exhaust and air lines
- - - Vacuum control lines
······ Electrical wiring

1. Air cleaner
2. Carburetor venturi
3. Throttle valve
4. Intake manifold
5. Cylinder head intake port
6. Cylinder head exhaust port
7. Belt drive for air pump
8. Air pump
9. Air filter for air pump
10. Pressure regulating valve
11. Check valve
12. Diverter valve
13. Distributor
14. EGR filter
15. EGR valve
16. Vacuum booster
17. Vacuum reserve
18. Solenoid vacuum valve
19. Temperature switch for cooling circuit
20. Crankcase ventilation

1973 100 series automatic transmission models have an exhaust gas recirculation system, while manual transmission models have a transmission controlled spark advance system which permits distributor vacuum advance only in fourth gear.

The exhaust gases to be recirculated are picked up from the exhaust pipe ahead of the muffler and directed through a filter into the intake manifold. A valve operated by carburetor vacuum allows recirculation only at light throttle cruising conditions. Exhaust gas recirculation reduces the high combustion chamber temperatures caused by lean mixtures, retarded timing, and other emission-reducing measures, thereby reducing the emission of oxides of nitrogen. The manual transmission spark advance control system has a solenoid valve in the vacuum line to the distributor. When the transmission is in fourth gear, a switch on the case operates the solenoid valve to connect the distributor vacuum advance unit to its vacuum source. This reduces (in fourth gear) the hesitation and surging at light throttle caused by lean mixtures and retarded timing.

In 1974, the exhaust gas recirculation system was slightly modified and used on all models. The exhaust gas was taken from the exhaust port of No. 4 cylinder. Carburetor vacuum still controlled the EGR valve, but intake manifold vacuum was used to operate the valve through a vacuum booster and a vacuum reservoir. The manual transmission spark advance control system was replaced, on all 1974 models, by the dual vacuum unit distributor, The retard unit is activated by intake manifold vacuum. The advance unit is activated by carburetor vacuum, but only when the engine is warmed up and above idle speed. The carburetor to vacuum unit line is blocked by a solenoid valve regulated by a temperature switch in the coolant bypass circuit when coolant temperature is below 40°F. An air injection system was used on all 1974 California models. The belt driven air pump takes in air through a filter and forces it into the exhaust ports through a pressure regulating valve, a check valve, and the intake manifold. To prevent backfiring on deceleration, a diverter valve injects air into the intake manifold under these conditions. The diverter valve is regulated by intake manifold vacuum.

1975 and later models have the Audi continuous fuel injection system and the air injection system. California models only have a catalytic converter in the exhaust system.

Fox

The Fox uses emission control systems very similar to those on the 100 series. The fuel evaporation control system differs only in that it does not require a fuel recirculation line. The dual vacuum unit distributor spark advance system is the same as on the 1974 100 series except that there is no temperature switch or solenoid valve. The air injection system, used on some 1974 models, differs only in minor details from the 100 series arrangement. The exhaust gas recirculation system picks up the exhaust gases to be recirculated from the exhaust manifold and directs them through a filter to the vacuum controlled EGR valve and then into the intake manifold. The EGR valve is operated by carburetor vacuum from two different points; the valve regulates the amount of exhaust gas to be recirculated and the operating conditions under which it will be recirculated.

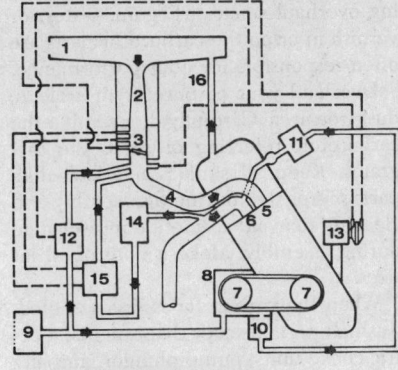

——— Exhaust and air lines
--- Vacuum control lines

Emission control schematic for Fox

1. Air cleaner
2. Carburetor venturi
3. Throttle valve
4. Intake manifold
5. Cylinder head intake port
6. Cylinder head exhaust port
7. Belt drive for air pump
8. Air pump
9. Air pump filter
10. Pressure relief valve
11. Check valve
12. Diverter valve
13. Distributor
14. EGR filter
15. EGR valve
16. Crankcase ventilation

1975 and later models have the Audi continuous fuel injection system. California models only have a catalytic converter in the exhaust system.

FUEL SYSTEM

Fuel Pump

Removal and Installation

Super 90

The Super 90 fuel pump is on the side of the block, beneath the intake manifold.

1. Detach the hose at the carburetor, since the other end is hard to reach.
2. Remove and plug the pump intake hose.
3. Remove the mounting bolts.
4. Remove the crankcase dipstick and reach around the radiator to pull the pump out to the rear. Be careful not to spill any fuel into the crankcase.
5. When replacing the pump, use new gaskets, one on each side of the insulator, and rock the pump back and forth to make sure that the lever rests on the camshaft.

100, 100 LS, 100 GL

The fuel pump is on the left side of the engine block.

1. Disconnect the hoses from the pump. Plug the inlet hose.
2. Remove the mounting bolts and pull out the pump.
3. When replacing the pump, use a new insulator. No other gaskets are required.

Fox

The fuel pump is on the left side of the engine, in front of the distributor.

1. Disconnect the hoses from the pump. Plug the inlet hose.
2. Remove the mounting bolts and remove the pump with the plastic insulator.
3. Reverse the procedure on installation.

Measuring Output Pressure

A fuel pump pressure testing gauge can be connected between the fuel pump and the carburetor. With the engine running at about 2,000 rpm, the pressure should be approximately as specified in the "Tune-Up Specifications Chart".

Fuel Recirculation Valve

100 Series models, beginning 1972, have a fuel recirculation line to relieve

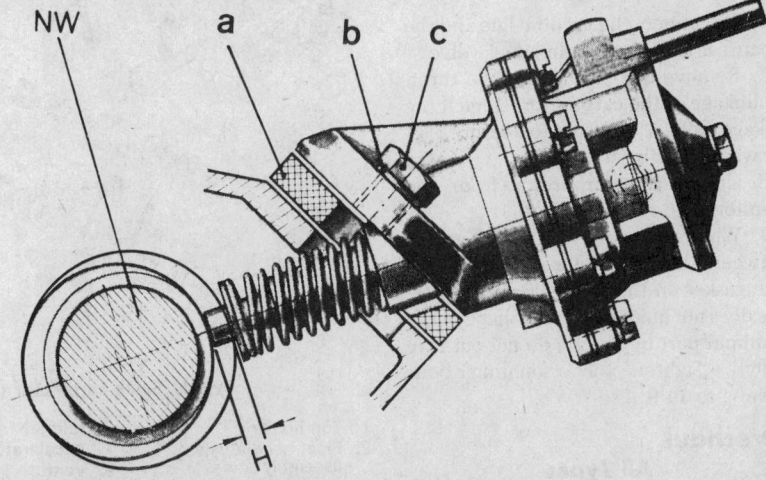

100, 100 LS, 100 GL fuel pump. (NW) is the camshaft, (a) is the insulator, (b) is the lockwasher, and (c) is the mounting bolt.

excess pressure in the line between the fuel pump and the carburetor. The line returns fuel to the tank. 1972 models have a vacuum operated recirculation valve. Beginning 1973, the recirculation valve was replaced by a calibrated orifice inserted in the recirculation line. The calibrated orifice can be installed on 1972 models to replace the recirculation valve.

Carburetors

The carburetors used are:

Carburetor Usage

Model	Year	Carburetor
Super 90	1972	Solex 32/32 TDID
100, 100 LS, 100 GL, Fox	1972-1975	Solex 32/35 TDID
Fox	1973-1975	Solex 32/35 DIDTA

Carburetor Usage

NOTE: *Solex carburetors are marked with the model number on the float bowl and on the outside of the throttle bore.*

These are all progressive two-barrel units; that is, the secondary throttle opens only on wide throttle opening. This results in good high rpm performance, as well as smooth and economical low-speed operation.

Removal and Installation

1. Remove the air cleaner.
2. Disconnect the fuel hose, being careful not to spill any fuel on hot engine parts.
3. If a choke with coolant connections is used, remove the radiator cap. Disconnect the coolant lines and fasten them up in some way to avoid losing any coolant. Disconnect the lead from the electric choke.
4. Disconnect the vacuum line and the electrical lead to the idle cutoff valve.
5. Remove the clip holding the throttle linkage at the carburetor. Detach the linkage, being careful not to lose any plastic washers or bushings.
6. Unbolt the carburetor from the manifold and remove.
7. When replacing, use a new gasket between the carburetor and manifold. The gasket on the Super 90 and 100 series does not quite match the shape of the manifold port by design; do not cut it to match. Tighten the mounting bolts evenly, to 14 ft lbs.

Overhaul

All Types

Efficient carburetion depends greatly on careful cleaning and inspection dur-

ing overhaul since dirt, gum, water, or varnish in or on the carburetor parts are often responsible for poor performance.

Overhaul your carburetor in a clean, dust-free area. Carefully disassemble the carburetor, referring often to the diagrams. Keep all similar and look-alike parts segregated during disassembly and cleaning to avoid accidental interchange during assembly. Make a note of all jet sizes.

When the carburetor is disassembled, wash all parts (except diaphragms, electric choke units, pump plunger, and any other plastic, leather, fiber, or rubber parts) in clean carburetor solvent. Do not leave parts in the solvent any longer than is necessary to sufficiently loosen the deposits. Excessive cleaning may remove the special finish from the float bowl and choke valve bodies, leaving these parts unfit for service. Rinse all parts in clean solvent and blow them dry with compressed air or allow them to air dry. Wipe clean all cork, plastic, leather, and fiber parts with a clean, lint-free cloth.

Blow out all passages and jets with compressed air and be sure that there are no restrictions or blockages. Never use wire or similar tools to clean jets, fuel passages, or air bleeds. Clean all jets and valves separately to avoid accidental interchange.

Check all parts for wear or damage. If wear or damage is found, replace the defective parts. Especially check the following:

1. Check the float needle and seat for wear. If wear is found, replace the complete assembly.
2. Check the float hinge pin for wear and the float(s) for dents or distortion. Replace the float if fuel has leaked into it.
3. Check the throttle and choke shaft bores for wear or an out-of-round condition. Damage or wear to the throttle arm, shaft, or shaft bore will often require replacement of the throttle body. These parts require a close tolerance of fit; wear may allow air leakage, which could affect starting and idling.

NOTE: *Throttle shafts and bushings are not included in overhaul kits. They can be purchased separately.*

4. Inspect the idle mixture adjusting needles for burrs or grooves. Any such condition requires replacement of the needle, since you will not be able to obtain a satisfactory idle.
5. Test the accelerator pump check valves. They should pass air one way but not the other. Test for proper seating by blowing and sucking on the valve. Replace the valve if necessary. If the valve is satisfactory, wash the valve again to remove breath moisture.

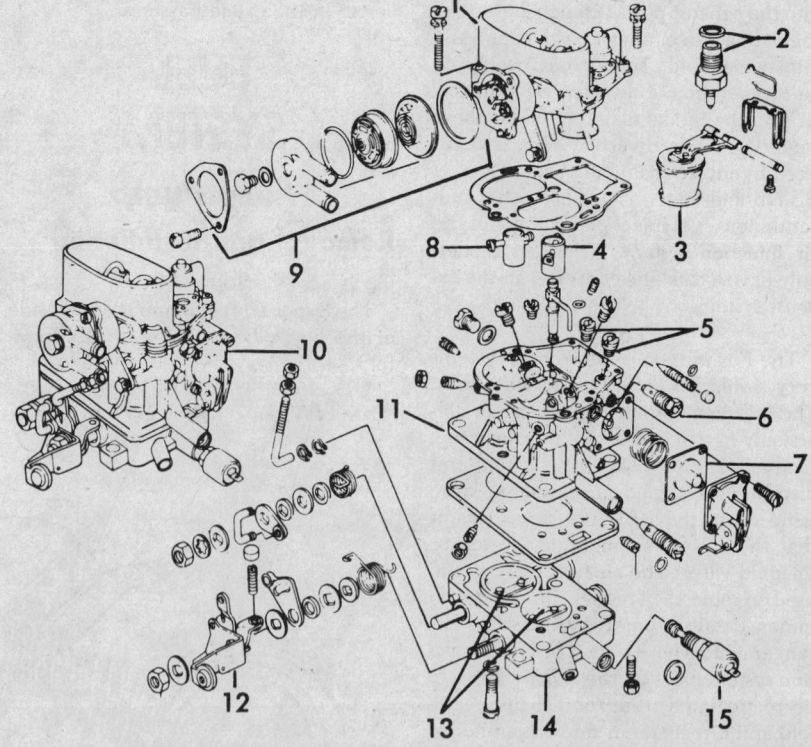

Typical Solex carburetor used on Audi. Solex 32/35 shown

1. Top housing
2. Float needle valve assembly
3. Float
4. Venturi
5. Main jets
6. Idle jet
7. Accelerator pump assembly
8. Venturi
9. Automatic choke assembly
10. Assembled view of carburetor
11. Carburetor bowl assembly
12. Throttle lever assembly
13. Throttle valves
14. Throttle plate
15. By-pass cutoff valve

6. Check the bowl cover for warped surfaces with a straightedge.

7. Closely inspect the valves and seats for wear and damage, replacing as necessary.

8. After the carburetor is assembled, check the choke valve for freedom of operation.

Carburetor overhaul kits are recommended for each overhaul. These kits contain all gaskets and new parts to replace those that deteriorate most rapidly. Failure to replace all parts supplied with the kit (especially gaskets) can result in poor performance later.

Some carburetor manufacturers supply overhaul kits of three basic types: minor repair; major repair; and gasket kits. Basically, they contain the following:

Minor Repair Kits:

All gaskets
Float needle valve
Volume control screw
All diaphragms
Spring for the pump diaphragm

Major Repair Kits:

All jets and gaskets
All diaphragms
Float needle valve
Volume control screw
Pump ball valve
Main jet carrier
Float
Complete intermediate rod
Intermediate pump lever
Complete injector tube
Some cover hold-down screws and washers

Gasket Kits:

All gaskets

After cleaning and checking all components, reassemble the carburetor, using new parts and referring to the exploded view. When reassembling, make sure that all screws and jets are tight in their seats, but do not overtighten. Tighten all screws gradually, in rotation. Do not tighten needle valves into their seats; uneven jetting will result. Always use new gaskets. Be sure to adjust the float level when reassembling.

Throttle Linkage Adjustment

Throttle linkage adjustments are not normally required. However, it is a good idea to check that the throttle valve(s) in the carburetor open all the way when the accelerator pedal is held in the wide-open throttle position. Only the primary throttle valve will open on the 32/32 or 32/35 DIDTA carburetor; the secondary throttle is vacuum operated. On the Super 90, there is an adjustment point on the linkage inside the car. To adjust, simply loosen the clamp bolt and vary the position of the two levers. There is also an adjustable accelerator pedal stop on the floor to prevent overtravel of the linkage.

Fuel Level Adjustment— 32/32 DIDTA

This adjustment is made with the carburetor installed on the engine.

1. Idle the engine for one minute.

2. Stop the engine. Remove the air cleaner.

3. Detach the fuel line.

4. Remove the five carburetor cover mounting screws.

5. Plug the fuel inlet with a finger and lift off the carburetor cover and gasket. Set them to the side, leaving the linkages attached.

6. Using a sliding T-scale, measure the distance from the top of the fuel surface to the edge of the housing. It should be 0.67–0.74 in. on carburetors with finned floats (after No. 7279), and 0.63–0.71 in. on earlier models.

7. The measurement may be corrected by varying the thickness of the fiber sealing ring under the float needle valve.

Float Level Adjustment— 32/32 and 32/35 TDID

This adjustment can be made with the carburetor either installed or removed.

1. If the carburetor is on the car, perform Steps 1–5 of "Fuel Level Adjustment—32/32 DIDTA."

2. Disconnect the linkage between the upper and lower parts of the carburetor.

3. Turn the carburetor cover upside down.

4. Measure the distance between the upper edge of the bead around the float and the carburetor cover flange surface. It should be as follows:

Carburetor Float Level

Carburetor	Float Level (in.)
32/32 TDID	0.51–0.59
32/35 TDID	0.61–0.69

5. The metal tab of the float lever can be bent to correct the height.

6. If necessary, the fuel level can also be checked as described for the 32/32 DIDTA. It should be 0.53–0.55 in. for both models.

Accelerator Pump Injection Rate Adjustment

This adjustment applies to all carburetors. It must be done with the carburetor removed from the car.

1. Place the carburetor over a clean container. Make sure that the float bowl is full.

2. Pump the throttle linkage full stroke 10–20 times. Injection should start as soon as the linkage is moved.

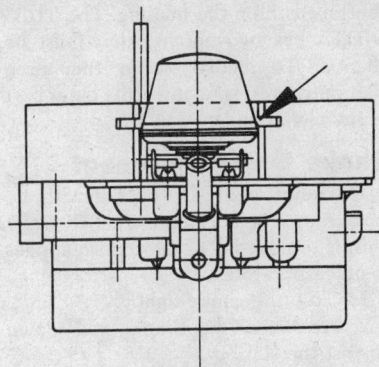

Float level adjustment—the arrow points to the upper edge of the float bead

3. Measure the amount of fuel pumped, with a chemist's graduated cylinder. Divide the amount in cc (ml) by the number of strokes to get the average volume per stroke. The figure should be:

Carburetor Injection Rate

Carburetor	Injection Rate (cc)
32/32 TDID, Super 90	1.1–1.4
32/35 TDID, 100, 100 LS, 100 GL	1.4–1.9
1973–74 Fox	0.8–1.1

4. To increase the injection rate, place more washers between the cotter pin and the pump lever. To decrease the rate, remove washers or move the cotter pin further out. It is not adjustable on Fox carburetors.

5. If the specified rate cannot be obtained, check the diaphragm and the injection tube.

Automatic Choke Adjustment

The standard adjustment on all versions of the automatic choke is with the movable notch aligned with the large

Accelerator pump output is adjusted with washers between the cotter pin and the pump lever (b).

central tooth on the housing. The 32/35 DIDTA has two notches that must be aligned. To adjust, loosen the three clamping screws and move the outer part of the choke unit.

Choke Gap Adjustment

This adjustment can be made with the carburetor in place, but it is much easier with it removed. The procedure applies to all carburetors.

1. Close the choke tightly.
2. Press the diaphragm rod down against the stop.
3. Hold the follower against the stop.
4. Check the gap between the upper edge of the choke valve and the housing wall with a drill. The gap should be:

Carburetor Choke Gap

Carburetor	Choke gap (in.)
32/32 TDID, Super 90	0.094-0.106
32/35 TDID, 100,100 LS, 100 GL	0.132-0.144
1973 Fox	0.145
1974 Fox to engine No. XW001013	0.137
1974 Fox from engine No. XW001014	0.145

5. To correct the gap, bend the pin up or down slightly.

Throttle Gap Adjustment

This adjustment could possibly be made with the carburetor in place, but it is much easier with it removed.

1. Close the choke tightly. The stop lever should rest on the highest step of the stepped washer, holding the throttle open slightly.
2. Check the gap between the lower edge of the throttle valve and the housing wall with a drill. The measurement should be:

Carburetor Throttle Gap

Carburetor	Throttle Gap (in.)
32/32 TDID	0.051-0.059
32/35 TDID, 100, 100 LS, 100 GL	0.055-0.059
1973 Fox	0.025 Std 0.031 Auto
1974 Fox to engine No. XW001013, all Canadian manual	0.025
1974 Fox from engine No. XW001014, all Canadian automatic	0.031

Bend pin (k) to adjust the choke gap

Automatic choke is correctly adjusted when (a), (b), and (f) are aligned. (h) is an insulator.

When checking choke gap, press the diaphragm rod (h) down against the stop and hold the follower (e) against the stop.

Accelerator pump diaphragm assembly, (c) is the cover screws, (d) is the cover, (e) is the diaphragm, and (f) is the spring.

3. Adjust the gap by means of the two nuts on the connecting rod.

Idle Speed and Mixture Adjustments

See "Tune-Up Procedures" for these

When checking the throttle gap, the stop lever (1) should rest on the highest step of the stepped washer (m) and hold the throttle open by means of the connecting rod, (p) indicates the adjusting nuts.

adjustments. The procedure to be used depends on the type of carburetor. There are two types: standard and idle air bypass. The standard has only one adjusting screw, the idle mixture screw, on the body of the carburetor. These units are found mainly on early Super 90 and 100 Series and non-US models. The idle air bypass carburetor is the current emission control type. It can be identified by the two adjusting screws on the body of the carburetor. These are the idle mixture and idle air control screws.

Carburetor Jet Sizes

Carburetor	Main Jet Primary	Secondary	Air Correction Jet Primary	Secondary
32/32 TDID, Super 90	102.5	145	120	100
32/35 TDID, 100, 100 LS, 100 GL	127.5	135	150	100
32/35 TDID, automatic, 100, 100 LS, 100 GL	125	135	150	100
32/35 TDID, Fox	120	140	140	140
32/35 TDID, automatic, Fox	115	140	140	140

FUEL INJECTION

Sensor Plate Position Adjustment

1. Loosen fuel line-to-control pressure regulator connection at fuel distributor.
2. Upper edge of sensor plate must be flush with edge of air cone. Adjust if too high. Plate may be lower, but not by

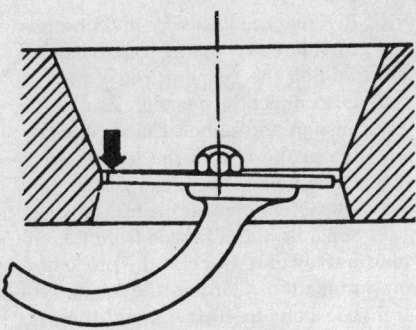

Sensor plate rest position

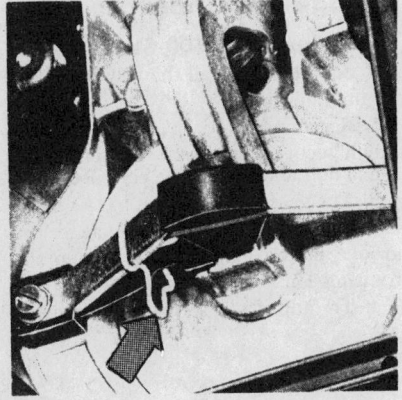

Adjustment point on wire bracket—bend here

more than .019".

3. To adjust, remove air flow sensor with upper part of air cleaner.

4. Remove air filter.

5. Adjust spring stop by bending wire bracket.

6. Check and adjust idle, if necessary.

Control Pressure Test-Engine Cold

1. Connect a pressure gauge in-line from fuel distributor to control pressure regulator.

2. Remove electrical connector from regulator.

3. Run engine at idle for no more than one minute.

4. Note control pressure. At room temperature, pressure should be 18-24 psi.

Fuel Pump Delivery Check

1. Connect ground wire to #1 coil terminal.

2. Remove fuel return line and hold it in a measuring flask.

3. Crank engine for 30 seconds. Delivery reading must be 24 ounces. If less, replace the pump.

Thermo-time Switch Check

1. With engine cold, remove harness plug from cold start valve and connect test light across harness plug connectors.

2. Connect jumper wire from coil terminal #1 to ground.

3. Operate starter. If test light does not

light for about 8 seconds, replace the switch.

Cold Start Valve Check

1. Remove electrical connector from valve.

2. Remove valve and hold in a measuring flask.

3. Connect jumper wire from cold start valve to coil terminal #15. Connect another wire from cold start valve to ground.

4. Run pump by removing relay and connecting terminals L13 and L14 on plate. (8 amp fuse should be connected in jumper wire.)

5. Turn on ignition switch and observe spray pattern. Pattern should be cone-shaped and steady.

6. Turn ignition off and wipe nozzle dry with a clean cloth. No drops should form within one minute.

7. If spray pattern is incorrect or leakage is observed, replace the valve.

Auxiliary Air Regulator Check

1. With engine cold, remove and plug auxiliary air regulator hose.

2. Run engine at idle; after 5 minutes the gate valve must be closed.

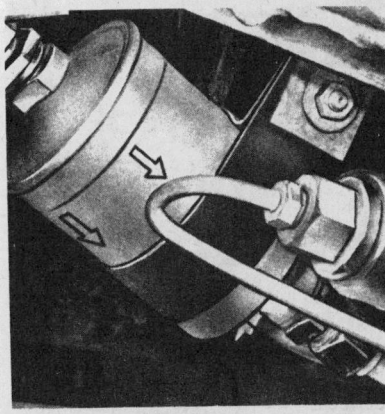

Auxiliary air regulator—arrow shows gate valve

Injector Removal, Testing, and Installation

1. Remove injector from engine, but leave it connected to the fuel line.

2. Point injector into measuring flask and operate starter for 15 seconds. Spray should be even and conical.

3. Turn off ignition. Injector should not drip.

4. Moisten rubber seal on injector with fuel.

5. Press injectors fully into seat.

Fuel Filter Removal and Installation

The fuel filter is bolted in-line and must be uncoupled for replacement. Filter is installed with arrows pointing in direction of flow.

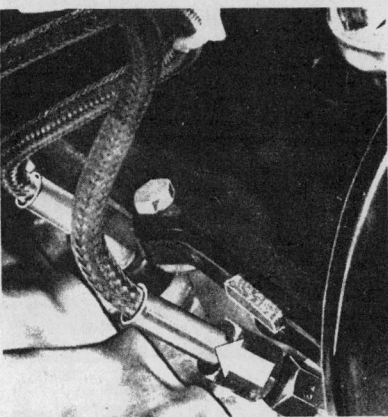

Checking fuel injector

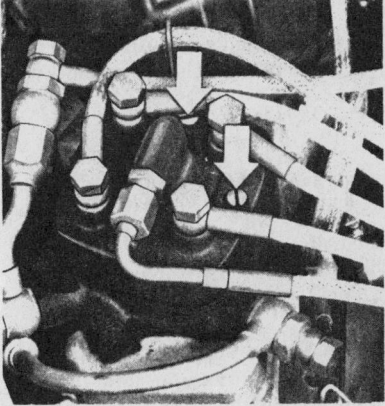

Installing fuel filter

Fuel distributor attaching screws

Fuel Distributor Removal and Installation

1. Clean and remove fuel lines at distributor.

2. Remove retaining bolts and carefully lift out distributor. Take care not to drop control piston.

3. If control plunger has been removed, moisten with fuel before installing and insert small shoulder first.

4. Reinstall distributor using new O-rings.

Fuel Pump Check Valve Replacement

1. Remove right rear wheel.

Fuel pump connections

Fuel pump check valve location

2. Remove gas tank filler cap.

3. Clean and disconnect fuel line connections.

4. Remove screw connector, which contains check valve, and replace using a new seal.

5. Torque connector to 14-18 in. lb.

6. Reconnect fuel line using new seals.

MANUAL TRANSMISSION

The transmission is combined with the differential in a transaxle.

Removal and Installation

Super 90, 100 Series

The engine/transaxle unit must be removed from the car as explained under "Engine Removal and Installation". Then the transmission can simply be unbolted from the engine and slid back. On replacement, tighten the bolts to 54, 33, and 18 ft lbs, respectively, for the three sizes of bolts.

It is possible to remove the transaxle only from the Super 90, but this procedure is fully as difficult as removing the whole unit. It requires moving the engine and transaxle about in the chassis while supporting them with some rather elaborate lifting and supporting brackets. The front crossmember must also be removed.

Fox

The transaxle can be lowered from the car, leaving the engine in place.

1. Disconnect the battery ground cable. Raise the car on a chassis lift.

2. Detach and wire up the entire exhaust system.

3. Release the lockplates and remove the axle shaft bolts. Wire the shafts up.

4. Use pliers to unscrew the speedometer cable nut.

5. Support the transaxle. Remove the engine to transaxle bolts and the clutch guard plate.

When adjusting the Super 90 and 100 series manual transmission floorshift linkage, the spring loaded ball should engage the slot (N) in the shift rod (33) with the transmission in Neutral. If it does not, loosen bolts (8) and move the bracket.

6. Remove the lock wire and unscrew the gearshift rod coupling square headed bolt. Pull off the gearshift rod.

7. Disconnect the gearshift strut at the transmission and unbolt the small crossmember at the rear of the transmission.

8. Disconnect the backup light and seat belt system wires at the transmission.

9. Separate the transaxle from the engine and lower it. Reverse the procedure on installation. Torque the engine to transaxle bolts to 40 ft lbs. and the axle shaft bolts to 28 ft lbs.

Linkage Adjustment

Super 90, 100 Series

1. Slide the seats all the way back and set the handbrake.

2. Remove the six sheetmetal screws which secure the console. Unscrew the shift knob and lift off the console.

3. The shift lever bracket has a spring-loaded ball which should engage the groove in the long shift rod when the transmission is in Neutral.

4. To adjust, loosen the four bolts

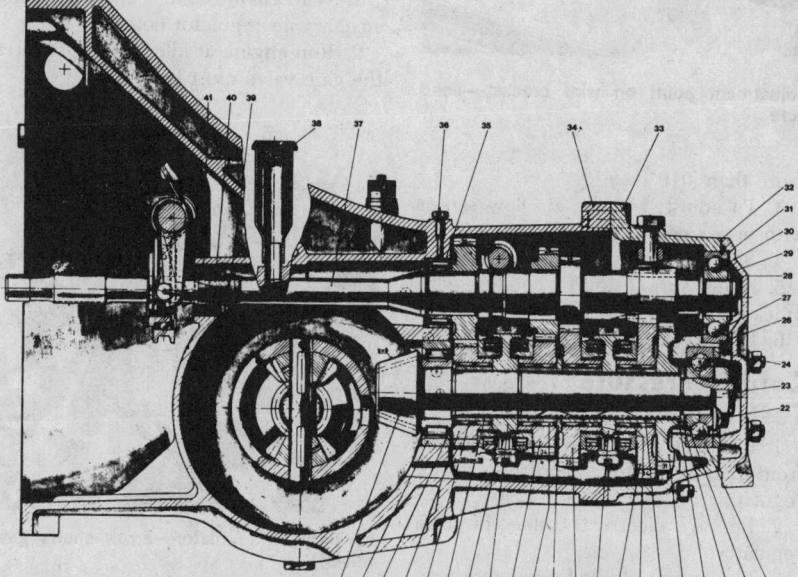

Cross-section of the Super 90 and 100 series manual transmission (transaxle).

1. Drive pinion
2. Roller bearing
3. Spacer
4. Sliding gear, 4th gear
5. Needle bearing
6. Needle bearing inner race
7. Operating sleeve
8. Guide sleeve
9. Sliding gear, 3rd gear
10. Needle bearing
11. Thrust washer
12. Sliding gear, 2nd gear
13. Guide sleeve
14. Sliding gear, 1st gear
15. Needle bearing
16. Needle bearing, inner race
17. Reverse gear
18. Shim
19. Shim
20. Shim
21. Four point bearing

22. Lock plate
23. Hex nut
24. Shim
25. Reverse gear ass. (not illustrated)
26. Snap-ring
27. Grooved ball bearing
28. Circlip
29. Support disc
30. End cover
31. Shim
32. Gasket, end cover
33. Transmission cover
34. Transmission case
35. Needle bearing
36. Hex head screw
37. Main shaft
38. Breather valve
39. Oil slinger
40. Shaft
41. Bushing

which hold the shift lever bracket to the floor and move the bracket to the front or rear. Tighten the bolts and recheck the adjustment. Beginning 1974, there is an adjustable linkage rod above the rear of the transmission for easier adjustment.

5. If the long shift rod has a rubber damper apparatus in the middle, make sure that it is in good condition and not causing any unnecessary play.

6. Grease the moving parts lightly.

7. Replace the console and the shift knob.

Fox

1. Remove the rubber boot at the base of the shift lever.

2. Loosen the two bolts at the base of the lever and move the lever to the far right of the neutral slot against the stop. Tighten the bolts.

3. If there is a problem with the lever sticking or jamming, loosen the two shift gate bolts from under the car and adjust the gate backward or forward. Tighten the bolts.

CLUTCH

Removal and Installation

Super 90, 100 Series

1. Remove the engine and transaxle as a unit.

2. Separate the engine and transaxle.

3. Mark the relationship of the pressure plate to the flywheel.

4. Unbolt the pressure plate from the flywheel, loosening the bolts alternately a little bit at a time to prevent warpage.

5. To install the clutch, place the driven plate on the pressure plate, making sure that it is facing the right way.

6. Hold the clutch assembly against the flywheel, aligning the marks in Step 3, and insert a dummy shaft through the pressure plate and the driven plate into the crankshaft pilot bearing.

7. Install the pressure plate bolts finger tight. Then tighten the bolts evenly, in rotation, to avoid distortion. Torque the

bolts to 24–27 ft lbs. Remove the dummy shaft.

8. The clutch release bearing in the front of the transmission housing should be checked before reassembly. It is retained by two springs.

9. Bolt the transaxle back to the engine. Bolt torque is 54, 33, and 18 ft lbs, respectively, for the three sizes of bolts.

10. Replace the engine/transaxle unit in the car. Check the clutch adjustment.

Fox

1. Remove the transaxle.

2. Mark the relationship of the pressure plate to the flywheel.

3. Unbolt the pressure plate from the flywheel, loosening the bolts alternately, a little at a time, to prevent warpage.

4. To install the clutch, place the driven plate on the pressure plate, making sure that it is facing the right way.

5. Hold the clutch assembly against the flywheel, aligning the marks made in Step 2 and the three dowel pins on the flywheel with the pressure plate, and insert a dummy shaft through the pressure plate and the driven plate into the crankshaft pilot bearing.

6. Install the pressure plate bolts finger tight. Then tighten the bolts evenly, in rotation, to avoid distortion. Torque the bolts to 24 ft lbs. Remove the dummy shaft.

7. The clutch release bearing in the front of the transaxle should be checked before reassembly. It is retained by two springs.

8. Replace the transaxle. Torque the engine to transaxle bolts to 40 ft lbs and the axle shaft to 28 ft lbs.

Pedal Free-Play Adjustment

The pedal free-play is adjusted at the clutch end of the cable. Free-play is the distance that the pedal travels from the released position to the point at which clutch spring pressure can be felt. This can be measured by placing a yardstick alongside the clutch pedal. Play should be 0.6–0.8 in. (0.6 on the Fox).

1. On the 100, 100 LS, and 100 GL, loosen the upper cable nut. Turn both

nuts clockwise to reduce play, and counterclockwise to increase. After the adjustment is made, tighten the upper nut to lock the cable in place.

2. On the Super 90, turn the adjusting nut at the end of the inner cable clockwise to increase play, and counterclockwise to reduce play. Make sure that the toggle is seated in the notch on the clutch arm.

3. The total pedal travel on the super 90 and 100 series should be at least 6.1 in. If it is not adequate, the pedal pivot can be loosened and moved up.

Clutch Cable

Removal and Installation

1. Loosen the adjustment.

2. Disengage the cable from the clutch arm.

3. Unhook the cable from the pedal. Remove the threaded eye from the end of the cable. Remove the adjustment nut(s).

4. Remove the C-clip which holds the outer cable at the adjustment point. Remove all the washers and bushings, first noting their locations.

5. Pull the cable out of the firewall toward the engine compartment side.

6. Install and connect the new cable. Adjust the pedal free-play.

AUTOMATIC TRANSMISSION

The Audi automatic transmission is a hydraulically operated three-speed unit, with a torque converter.

Removal and Installation

100 Series

The automatic transmission can be disconnected from the engine and removed with the engine in the car.

1. Drain the transmission. Remove the grille and front apron. The engine must be mounted to the frame in some manner or suspended on a lift or jack to prevent it from falling from the mounts when the mounts are disconnected.

2. Loosen the brake pipe lines from the brake hoses and plug the ends of the brake hoses.

3. Disconnect the accelerator linkage.

4. Remove the front exhaust pipe.

5. Remove the oil filter and starter.

6. Disconnect both driveshafts and suspend them from the upper wishbones. Disconnect the stabilizer bar at both lower wishbones.

7. Unbolt the holder for the selector cable at the transmission. Remove the selector cable from the lever at the transmission. Remove the selector cable holder.

Before removing the pressure plate bolts (a) mark the pressure plate (b) and the flywheel as shown at the arrow. The dummy shaft (d) is used to center the driven plate (clutch disc) on reinstallation.

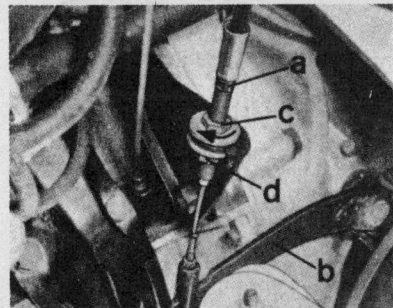

Clutch adjustment point on the 100 series and Fox. (a) is the clutch cable, (b) is the clutch lever, (c) and (d) are the adjusting nuts.

8. Disconnect the crossmember at the engine mounting and at the support. Place a jack or support under the transmission.

9. Remove the guard and disconnect the left and right engine mounts. Be careful not to alter the position of the left mount, which is fixed by means of locknuts.

10. Insert bolts (⅜ in. x 8 in.) through each side in place of the engine mounts. Lower the complete power plant until the unit rests on the bolts.

11. Disconnect the transmission vacuum hose at the vacuum unit or at the T adaptor.

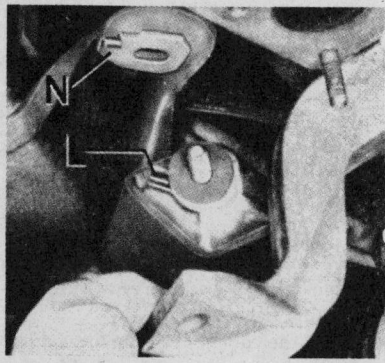

Be sure that the projection (N) engages the groove (L) of the 100 series mount.

12. Unbolt the torque converter Allen bolts by working through the hole for the starter.

13. Unbolt the engine-to-transmission connections and remove the transmission. Secure the torque converter in the transmission with a strap.

14. To install the transmission, reverse the removal procedure, noting the following: Lift the transmission and bolt it to the engine. Lift both the engine and transmission and install the selector lever holder. When installing the engine mounts, be sure that the projection engages the groove of the mount. After installing the engine and transmission assembly, check the alignment of the unit. Refer to "Engine Installation." Torque converter bolt torque is 22 ft lbs. Transmission-to-engine bolt torque is 54, 33, and 18 ft lbs, respectively, for the three bolt sizes. Refill the transmission.

Fox

The transaxle can be lowered from the car, leaving the engine in place.

1. Disconnect the battery ground cable.

2. Raise the car on a chassis hoist.

3. Remove the lockplates and remove the axle shaft bolts. Wire the shafts up.

4. Disconnect the vacuum hose. Remove the torque converter guard plate. Disconnect the kickdown switch wire.

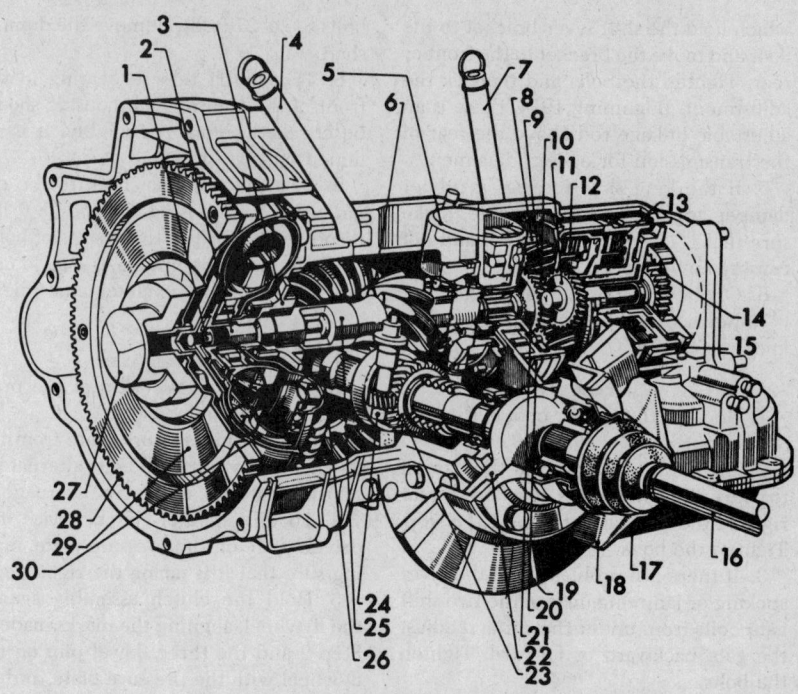

Cross-section of the 100 series automatic transmission (transaxle)

1. Pump shaft	12. Forward clutch	23. Impeller, governor and speedometer
2. Turbine shaft	13. Direct and reverse clutch	24. Speedometer pinion shaft
3. Stator support	14. Oil pump	25. Drive pinion shaft
4. Oil filler tube, differential	15. 2nd gear brake band	26. Differential
5. Governor	16. Driveshaft	27. Crankshaft, engine
6. Drive pinion	17. Oil pan	28. Gear ring
7. Filler tube, planetary gear	18. Brake caliper	29. Drive plate
8. Annulus	19. Brake disc	30. Torque converter
9. Small planetary gear	20. Ist gear and reverse brake band	(P)—Impeller
10. Large sun gear	21. Planetary gear carrier	(L)—Stator
11. Large planetary pinion	22. Stub axle	(T)—Turbine

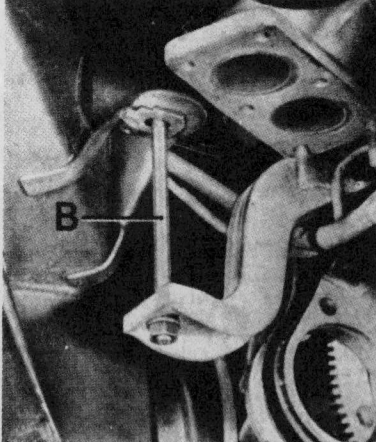

Insert bolts (B) through each engine mount to support the 100 series engine.
Note that the starter has been removed for access to the torque converter bolts.

5. Use pliers to unscrew the speedometer cable nut.

6. Support the transaxle.

7. Remove the upper engine to transaxle bolts.

8. Remove the starter and remove the three torque converter bolts through the starter opening.

9. Unbolt the small crossmember at the rear of the transmission.

10. Lower the transaxle slightly.

11. Detach the shift linkage cable at the transmission.

12. Remove the lower engine to transaxle bolts.

13. Separate the transaxle from the engine and lower it. Secure the torque converter in the transmission with a strap. Reverse the procedure on installation. Torque the engine to transaxle bolts to 40 ft lbs and the torque converter bolts to 20–23 ft lbs. New torque converter bolts and washers must be used. Torque the axle shaft bolts to 28 ft lbs.

14. Check the shift linkage adjustment.

Pan Removal and Installation

The automatic transmission fluid should be changed and the pan cleaned out every 18,000 miles (20,000 miles beginning 1973). The interval should be shortened to 12,000 miles under severe use such as city driving or trailer towing.

To change the fluid:

1. Run the engine in Neutral for a minute or two.

2. Make sure that the vehicle is parked on level ground. Stop the engine.

3. Place a pan of at least four quarts capacity under the transmission.

4. Remove the plug from the transmission bottom pan, after wiping the area clean.

5. Remove the starter.

6. Remove and clean out the pan.

7. Replace the pan, using a new gasket. Torque the bolts to 7 ft lbs. Wait ten minutes and retorque the bolts.

8. Clean off the plug, particularly the threads, and replace it.

9. Replace the starter on the 100 series.

10. Pour in five pints of fluid through the dipstick filler tube. The proper transmission fluid is Dexron with the prefix letter B.

11. Start the engine and shift through all the lever positions.

12. The level should reach the tip of the dipstick. Add fluid until the level reaches this point.

13. Take a short test drive. Fill the transmission until the level is between the marks on the dipstick. Retorque the bolts.

NOTE: *If the transmission is overfilled, the excess must be drained.*

Kickdown Switch

100 Series

The kickdown switch is mounted behind the accelerator pedal. With the ignition switch on, the switch should make an audible click when the pedal is pressed all the way down.

The transmission should downshift when the accelerator is depressed to the wide open throttle position at speeds between 39 and 65 mph for second gear, and 16 and 36 mph for first gear.

Neutral Safety Switch Adjustment

The neutral safety switch prevents the engine from being started with the transmission in any position other than Park or Neutral. It also activates the backup lights. The switch is at the base of the shift lever, inside the floorshift console.

To replace or adjust the switch:

1. Remove the four screws which hold the console to the floor.

2. Shift into Neutral. Remove the two screws which hold the shift position indicator plate to the console. Remove the shift knob and the console.

3. Disconnect the switch electrical leads. These are: red/black—neutral safety; black—backup lights; blue/red—backup lights. The backup light wires are at the front.

4. Remove the two switch retaining screws. Remove the switch.

5. Install the new switch so that the

neutral safety switch contacts are together.

6. Install the electrical connectors. Hold the footbrake while making sure that the engine will start only in Neutral and Park. Make sure that the backup lights operate only in Reverse. If the switch does not operate properly, it may have to be moved on its slotted mounting bracket.

7. Replace the console cover.

Shift Linkage Adjustment

The function of this adjustment is to make sure that the transmission is fully engaged in each shift position. If this is not done, the transmission may be only partially engaged in a range position. This would result in severe damage due to slippage.

1. Place the selector lever in Park.

2. Loosen the cable clamp nut at the transmission end. On the Fox, remove the rubber cover from the bottom of the shifter (underneath the car) and loosen the cable clamp screw.

3. Press the selector lever on the transmission back to the stop.

4. Tighten the clamp nut or screw.

Vacuum Modulator Adjustment

100 Series

The vacuum modulator, on the rear of the transmission, regulates the firmness and timing of shifts in relation to speed and throttle opening. A leaking modulator will result in transmission fluid being sucked into the engine through the vacuum modulator and burned. This will produce a smoky exhaust and a continually low transmission fluid level. The modulator must be adjusted any time it, or its seal, has been replaced. This adjustment is also necessary if the gearshift timing is incorrect.

1. Disconnect and plug the vacuum hose at the modulator.

2. Remove the test plug from the right side of the transmission. Connect a pressure gauge with a scale up to 150 psi.

3. Place the selector lever in Neutral and idle the engine at 1,000 rpm. Adjust the modulator until the gauge shows 48.4 psi. Stop the engine.

The two (Bs) show where the automatic transmission test gauge is to be connected.

Automatic transmission second gear brake band adjusting screw and locknut (66) and (67). First gear brake band adjusting screw and locknut (60 and 67).

4. Remove the gauge and replace the plug and vacuum line.

5. The transmission should upshift with wide open throttle from First to Second gear at 19—21 mph, and from Second to Third at 54—58 mph.

Band Adjustments

100 Series

Second Gear Band

1. Loosen the locknut.

2. Tighten the adjusting screw to 87 in. lbs.

3. Loosen the adjusting screw and retighten to 44 in. lbs.

4. Turn the adjusting screw out 1¾–2 turns.

5. Tighten the locknut.

First Gear Band

1. Loosen the locknut.

2. Tighten the adjusting screw to 87 in. lbs.

3. Loosen the adjusting screw and retighten to 44 in. lbs.

4. Turn the adjusting screw out 3¼–3¾ turns.

5. Tighten the locknut.

Fox

First Gear Band

1. Loosen locknut.

2. Tighten first gear band adjusting screw to 7 ftlb.

3. Loosen adjusting screw and retighten to 3.5 ftlb.

4. Back off screw 3.25 to 3.5 turns and tighten locknut.

Second Gear Band

1. Loosen locknut.

2. Tighten adjusting screw to 7 ftlb.

3. Loosen screw and retighten to 3.5 ftlb.

4. Back off screw exactly 2.5 turns and tighten locknut.

NOTE: *Transmission must be horizontal when adjusting bands or bands may jam.*

TRANSAXLE

The transmission and differential are combined in a transaxle. On models with manual transmission, the transmission and differential share a common lubricant supply. No transaxle overhaul procedures are given here due to the extensive specialized tools, knowledge, and procedures required.

Removal and Installation

Super 90 and 100 Series

The transaxle is removed from the car in unit with the engine. See "Engine Removal and Installation" for details. On the automatic, it is possible to remove the transaxle only, leaving the engine in place. See "Automatic Transmission Removal and Installation" for details.

Fox

The transaxle can be removed from the car alone, leaving the engine in place. See Transmission Removal and Installation for details.

DRIVE AXLES

Each front wheel drive axle shaft has two Rzeppa constant velocity joints. These joints can handle lateral movement caused by suspension travel, as well as steering movements.

Driveshafts

Removal and Installation

Super 90, 100 Series

The steering knuckles must be removed along with the shafts.

1. Support the vehicle and remove the wheels. Let the front suspension hang free.

2. Have an assistant hold the brakes. Unbolt the driveshaft from the transmission stub axle and brake disc. There should be an insulator between the driveshaft and brake disc.

3. Remove the cotter pin and the castellated nut from the steering tie-rod end. Press out the tie-rod end from the steering knuckle arm. A small puller or press is required to free the tie-rod end.

4. Remove the two steering knuckle mounting bolts.

5. Remove the steering knuckle and driveshaft assembly.

6. Reverse the procedure for installation.

7. Check the wheel alignment.

Fox

1. With the wheels on the ground, remove the front wheel spindle nut.

2. Unbolt the inner driveshaft coupling. If you are removing the right shaft,

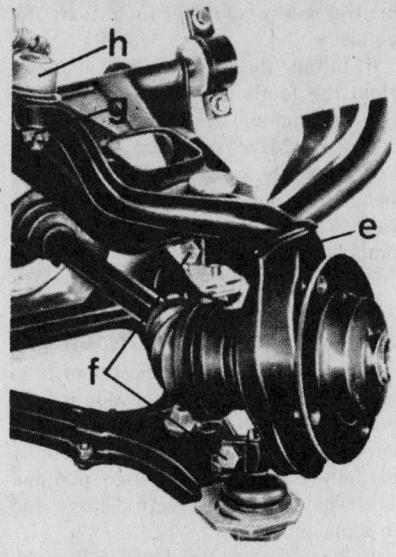

The castellated nut (g) and the cotter pin (h) must be removed before pulling out the tie-rod end (h) from the Super 90 and 100 series steering knuckle (e). (f) indicates the steering knuckle mounting bolts.

disconnect the front exhaust pipe at the manifold and the support on the transaxle. Push the inner end of the shaft up and let it rest on the transaxle.

3. Turn the steering wheel all the way in the direction of the side you are working on. Pull the driveshaft out of the steering knuckle.

4. Only the outer joint is available for replacement. If the inner joint is damaged, a new driveshaft must be installed. The outer joint can be removed by removing the snap-ring (inboard side) and hitting the axle end with a soft hammer.

5. On installation, torque the driveshaft coupling bolts to 25 ft lbs.

Disassembly

Super 90, 100 Series

This operation requires the use of a press or puller setup. It is necessary in order to replace the rubber boots.

1. Clamp the steering knuckle in a vise.

2. Remove the cotter pin. Unscrew the castellated nut and reverse it on the threads to protect them from damage.

3. Press the driveshaft from the steering knuckle. Steps 4–8 cover steering knuckle service.

4. Press out the wheel hub from the steering knuckle.

5. Remove the spacer, Nilos ring, and ball bearing inner race.

6. Drive the outer ball bearing race from the knuckle. Remove the internal snap-rings, using snap-ring pliers, and press out the second ball bearing outer race.

7. Replace the snap-rings. Press in the outer races. Fill the space between the races with high melting point wheel bearing grease.

8. Place the spacer and Nilos ring in the wheel hub. Press on the ball bearing inner race and install a new spacer bushing. Place the hub in the steering knuckle and press in the second ball bearing inner race.

9. Remove both rubber boot clamps and slide the boots off the joints.

10. Clamp the inner driveshaft in a vise. Spread the snap-ring in the joint and have an assistant hit the outer end of the shaft with a soft hammer. A "powerful" blow is required.

11. Drive the joint housing off the inner shaft, using the soft hammer.

12. Pull off the rubber boots.

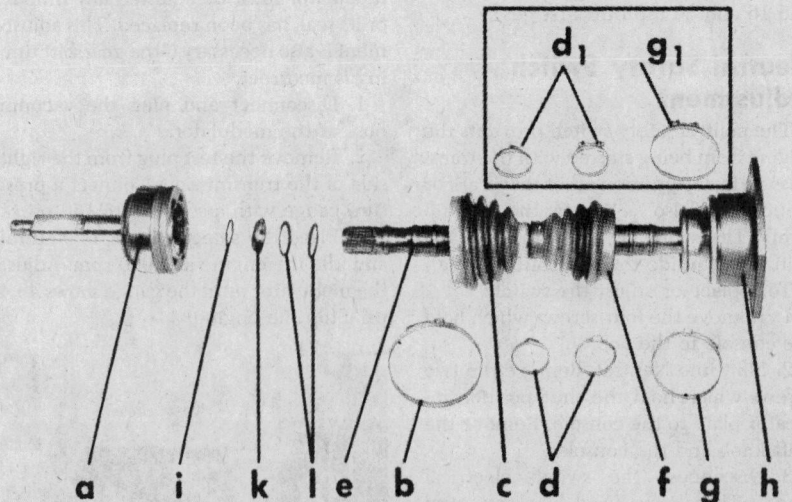

Super 90 and 100 series driveshaft assembly

(a)—Outer driveshaft with Rzeppa joint
(b)—Clamp
(c)—Rubber boot
(d)—Clamps
(dl)—Clamps
(e)—Inner driveshaft
(f)—Rubber boat
(g)—Clamp
(Gl)—Clamp
(h)—Rzeppa joint with flange
(i)—Snap-ring
(k)—Pressure ring
(l)—Disc springs

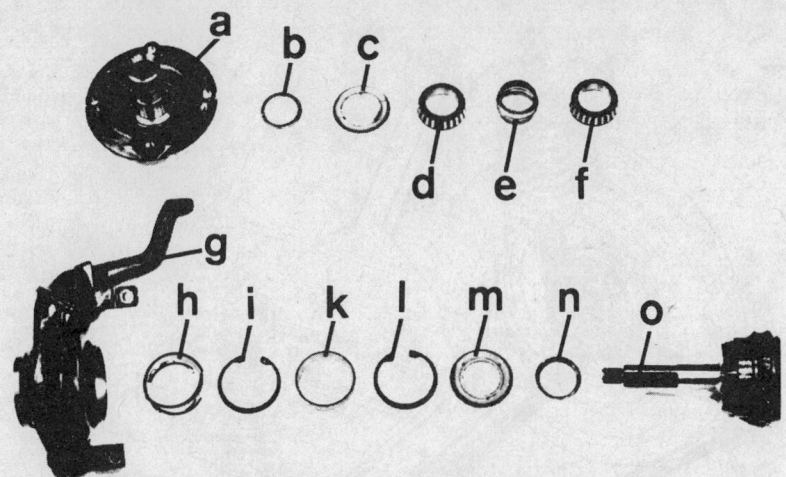

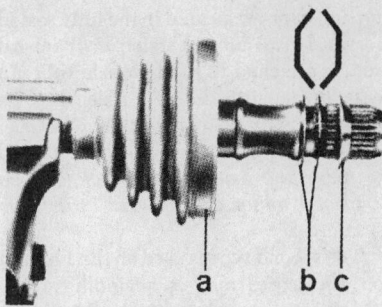

Installation of disc springs and pressure ring on Super 90 and 100 series inner drive shaft. The Fox has only the inner disc spring.

(a)—Outer rubber boot
(b)—Disc springs
(c)—Pressure ring

Super 90 and 100 series steering knuckle and wheel hub assembly

(a)—Wheel hub
(b)—Spacer
(c)—Nilos ring
(d)—Ball bearing inner race
(e)—Spacer bushing
(f)—Ball bearing inner race
(g)—Right steering knuckle
(h)—Ball bearing outer race
(i)—Snap-ring
(k)—Outer ball bearing race
(l)—Snap-ring
(m)—Nilos ring
(n)—Spacer
(o)—Driveshaft

13. Clean the joint with alcohol and air dry.

14. Install new rubber boots.

15. Place two new disc springs on the inner shaft with their concave side out. Install a pressure ring with the convex side out.

16. Place a new snap-ring in the joint. Place the ends in the machined groove.

17. Slide the joint onto the inner shaft, so that the snap-ring begins to go into place. Drive the joint into place, hitting the outer end of the driveshaft with a soft hammer. The snap-ring should snap into place. The outer end of the shaft may also be pounded on with a wooden block.

18. Fill each joint with 60 cc of Moly-kote® grease or its equivalent.

19. Put the rubber boots in place. Install the boot clamps, making sure that the free ends trail in the normal direction of rotation.

20. Grease and install the spacer and Nilos ring. Press the driveshaft into the wheel hub. Adjust the hub nut so that there is 0.002–0.003 in. wheel bearing play, measured with a dial indicator at the outer edge of the wheel hub.

REAR SUSPENSION

There are two basic types of rear suspension used on Audi cars. The first is used on the Super 90 and the 100 series through 1973. The rear axle assembly is bolted to the body as a unit. The rear axle is attached to two suspension arms. The

Rear suspension components for Super 90 and 100 series through 1973

(a)—Brake drum and wheel hub
(b)—Brake assembly
(c)—Stop pad
(d)—Shock absorber
(e)—Suspension arm
(f)—Handbrake cable
(g)—Brake line
(h)—Transverse (panhard) rod
(i)—Axle tube
(k)—Stabilizer
(l)—Cross tube
(m)—Torsion bar
(n)—Mounting tube
(o)—Torsion bar
(p)—Handbrake adjustment
(r)—Stop pad
(s)—Shock absorber
(t)—Rubber bearing
(u)—Wheel cylinder
(v)—Rear axle, outer
(w)—Brake drum and wheel hub
(x)—Grease cap
(y)—Mounting bolt
(z)—Mounting bolt

torsion bars are located in the fully sealed forward cross tube. A stabilizer (Panhard rod) is attached to the rear axle tube. In case of repairs, the rear axle may be removed with or without the cross tube.

NOTE: *A jack must never be placed under the axle tube. A jack can be placed under the forward cross tube safely.*

The second type is used on the Fox and on 100 series models beginning 1974. This system is very much like the earlier arrangement, but the forward cross tube and torsion bars are not used. The shock absorbers are replaced by coil/shock struts.

NOTE: *This suspension system is less susceptible to damage than the early type, but the car should still be raised only at the frame members directly behind the front wheel openings and in front of the rear wheel openings.*

Rear Axle
Removal and Installation
Super 90 and 100 Series Through 1973, Without Cross Tube

1. Depress the brake pedal approximately 1.2 in. and hold the pedal in this position to close the compensating bore in the brake master cylinder.
2. Remove both shock absorbers.
3. Raise and support the vehicle and remove the rear wheels. Support the axle tube.
4. Disconnect the handbrake cable. Push out the protective sleeve on either side of the cable. Remove the rubber boot and pull the handbrake cable out. Pull the cable down through the slot in the bracket.
5. Disconnect the brake lines.
6. Remove the handbrake cable from the suspension arms by bending open the retaining clamps.
7. Remove the transverse stabilizer bar.
8. Unbolt the right and left suspension arms.
9. Lift the rear axle from the suspension arms.
10. Installation is the reverse of removal.

Super 90 and 100 Series Through 1973, With Cross Tube

It is not advisable to remove the cross tube or complete rear axle, since a special centering gauge is required for proper installation of the cross tube.

Fox, 1974 And Later 100 Series

1. Remove the rear wheels. Support the axle, but don't put any load on the springs.
2. Remove the rear muffler and tailpipe.
3. Disconnect the parking brake cable at the yoke where the two cables merge

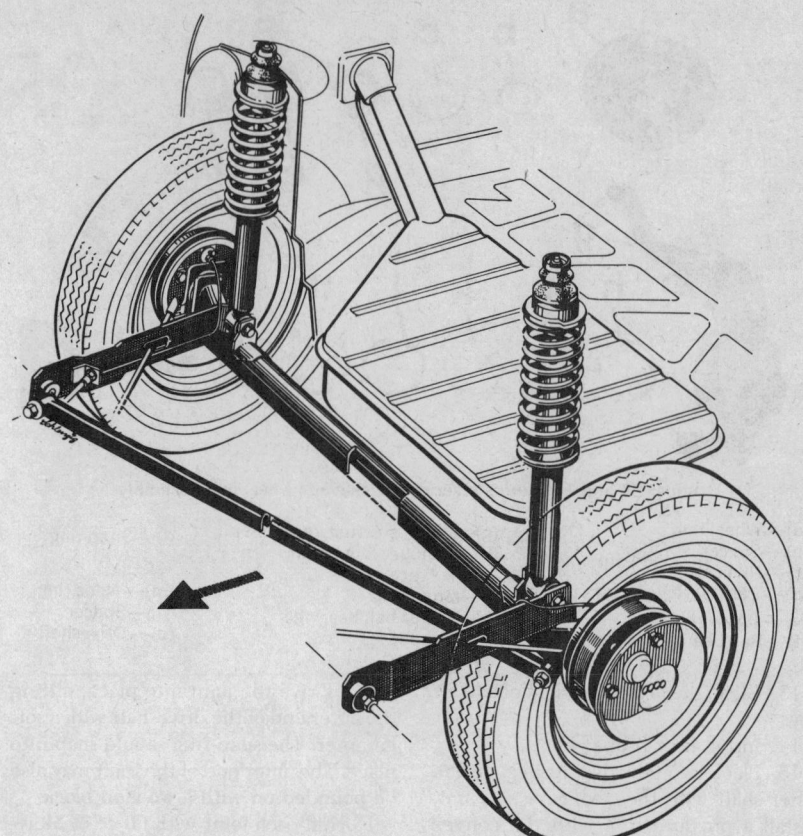

Rear suspension, Fox and 1974 and later 100 series

into one. Detach the cable holders from the underbody.
4. Detach both rear brake lines.
5. Unbolt the control arms and the diagonal arm from the body.
6. Unbolt the bottom of the shock absorber struts from the axle.
7. Remove the axle.
8. On installation, torque the control arm to body bolts to 32 ft lbs and the diagonal arm to body bolts to 61 ft lbs. Torque the lower shock absorber strut to axle bolts to 43 ft lbs. Bleed the brakes.

Wheel Bearings and Stub Axles
Removal and Installation

1. Depress the brake pedal approximately 1.2 in. and hold it in that position to close the master cylinder compensating bore.
2. Detach the brake lines on both sides and plug the lines.
3. Pry off the grease cap and remove the cotter pin, castellated nut, and washer. Remove the wheel and brake drum.
4. Remove the bearing inner race from the brake drum.
5. Carefully (the spring can fly out) pry out the brake shoe retaining spring. Remove the brake shoes complete with pressure rod and spring, bottom bracket first. Disconnect the handbrake cable.

6. Unbolt the rear stub axle and brake backing plate.
7. Pry out the shaft seal (which should be replaced) and remove the inner race of the roller bearing.
8. Drive the roller bearing outer race from the brake drum. Remove the snapring and drive the outer roller bearing race from the drum.
9. Replace the snap-ring and drive in the outer race of the outer roller bearing.
10. Press in the outer race of the inner roller bearing.
11. Lightly coat the inner race of the inner roller bearing with wheel bearing grease and push it into the outer race.
12. Drive a new shaft seal into position (the open side of the seal should face the roller bearing). Fill the space between the two roller bearings with approximately 10 oz of wheel bearing grease.
13. Coat the inner race of the outer roller bearing with grease and install the inner race.
14. Replace the stub axle and brake backing plate with the groove in the stub axle facing upward. Bolt torque is 14–15 ft lbs for 8G bolts and 22 ft lbs for 10K bolts.
15. Assemble the brake shoes, connect the handbrake cable, and insert the brake shoes on the bottom bracket first, then at the wheel cylinder. Replace the retaining spring.
16. Replace the brake drum and

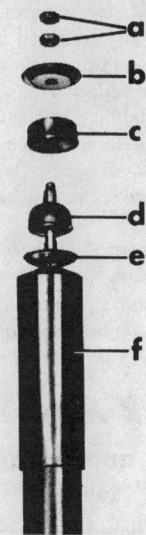

Details of the upper end of the Super 90 and 100 series through 1973 rear shock absorbers, parts (a-c) are installed inside the trunk.

(a)—Nuts
(b)—Disc, edge up
(c)—Rubber pad, curved side up
(d)—Rubber pad, curved side up
(e)—Disc, part of shock absorber
(f)—Shock absorber

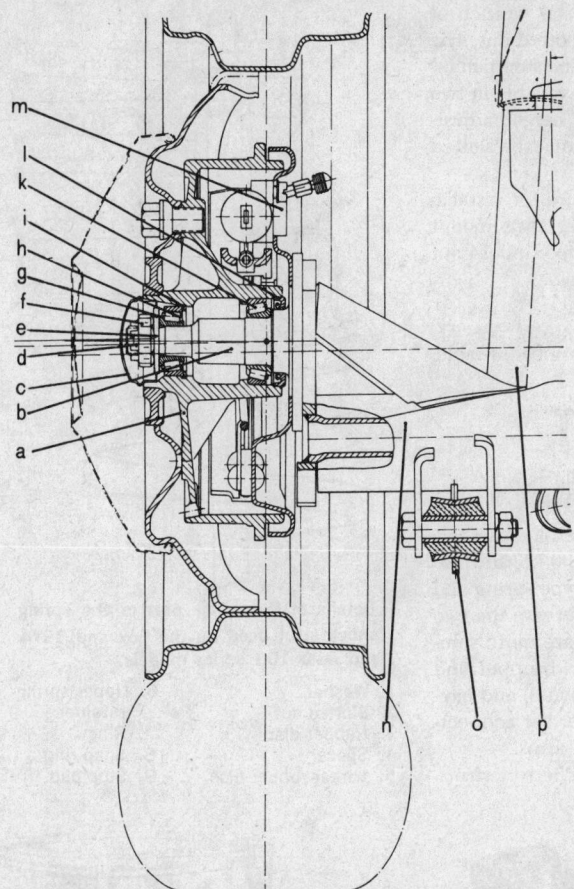

(a)—Brake drum
(b)—Rear stub axle
(c)—Cap
(d)—Cotter pin
(e)—Nut

(f)—Castellated nut
(g)—Washer
(h)—Roller bearing
(i)—Snap-ring
(k)—Roller bearing

(l)—Shaft seal
(m)—Brake assembly
(n)—Rear axle
(o)—Suspension arm
(p)—Shock absorber

Rear wheel bearing and stub axle assembly

wheel, special washer, nut, castellated nut, and a new cotter pin. Wheel bearing play should be 0.001–0.002 in. It can be measured with a dial indicator. Fill the dust cap with approximately 10 oz of wheel bearing grease and replace it.

Shock Absorbers

Removal and Installation
Super 90 and 100 Series Through 1973

1. Raise and support the car. Support the weight of the axle tube.
2. Remove the Panhard rod.
3. Unbolt the bottom of the shock absorber.
4. Hold the flats on the top of the shock absorber rod in the trunk with a wrench and remove the nuts, disc, and rubber pad.
5. Remove the shock absorber.
6. Install the rubber bumper, rounded side up, on top of the new shock absorber rod.
7. Install the shock absorber through the floor pan.
8. Inside the trunk, install a rubber pad with the curved side up, a disc with the edge up, and the nuts. Use the second nut to lock the first.
9. Bolt the bottom of the shock absorber in place. Replace the Panhard rod.

Struts

Removal and Installation
Fox And 1974–75 100 Series

1. On the Fox, remove the bottom

Rear brake drum and wheel bearing components

(a)—Cap
(b)—Cotter pin
(c)—Castellated nut
(d)—Nut
(e)—Washer
(f)—Inner race roller bearing

(g)—Outer race roller bearing
(h)—Brake drum
(i)—Snap-ring
(k)—Outer race roller bearing
(l)—Inner race roller bearing
(m)—Shaft seal

cushion of the rear seat. Release the mounting tabs at the bottom of the seat-back and pull it forward to detach its upper clips.

2. Support the rear of the chassis. Support the axle too, but don't put any load on the springs. Remove the rubber guard from the top of the strut, from inside the trunk.

3. On the Fox, peel back the insulation on the bulkhead to expose the access hole.

4. Remove the mounting nut, washer, and rubber disc.

5. Unbolt the strut from the axle and remove it.

6. You can disassemble these struts carefully without a spring compressor,

but you will need a special wrench of some sort to remove the slotted nut. The springs are color coded. The stop pad inside the top of the coil is available in two sizes for slight rear end height adjustment. On reassembly, torque the slotted nut to 11 ft lbs.

7. Reverse the procedure for installation and torque the lower strut mount bolt to 43 ft lbs and the upper mount nut to 23 ft lbs.

Adjustments

Rear wheel alignment is not adjustable.

FRONT SUSPENSION

The Super 90 front suspension uses torsion bars, while the 100, 100 LS, and 100 GL use McPherson strut type spring and shock absorber units. Otherwise the two front suspension systems are quite similar, being independent with upper and lower control arms (wishbones) and having a cross-chassis stabilizer bar connecting the two lower control arms.

The Fox also uses McPherson struts.

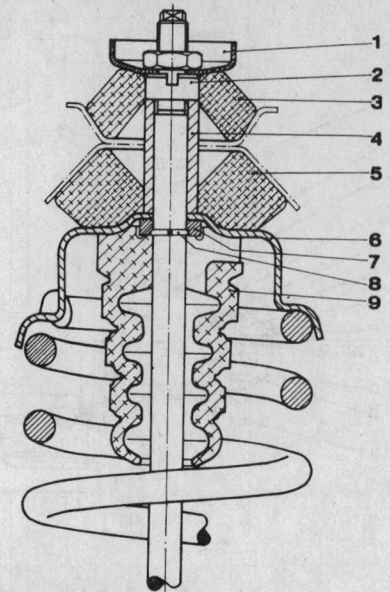

Details of the upper part of the spring /shock strut used on the Fox and 1974 and later 100 series models.

1. Washer
2. Slotted nut
3. Rubber disc
4. Spacer
5. Larger rubber disc
6. Upper spring retainer
7. Ring
8. Snap ring
9. Stop pad

The strut unit, steering arm, and steering knuckle are all combined in one assembly; there is no upper control arm. The system is designed with negative roll-radius; this stabilizes the car when different retarding forces are applied to the front wheels, as would happen if one front tire were on wet pavement and the other on dry.

NOTE: *Exercise extreme caution when working with the front suspension. Coil springs and torsion bars are under great tension and can cause severe injury if released suddenly.*

Shock Absorbers

Removal and Installation
Super 90

This operation is best performed with the vehicle resting on its wheels.

1. Unbolt the shock absorber from the lower control arm.

2. Inside the engine compartment, hold the flats on top of the shock absorber rod with a wrench. Remove the locknut and nut. Remove the disc and upper mounting pad.

3. Remove the shock absorber.

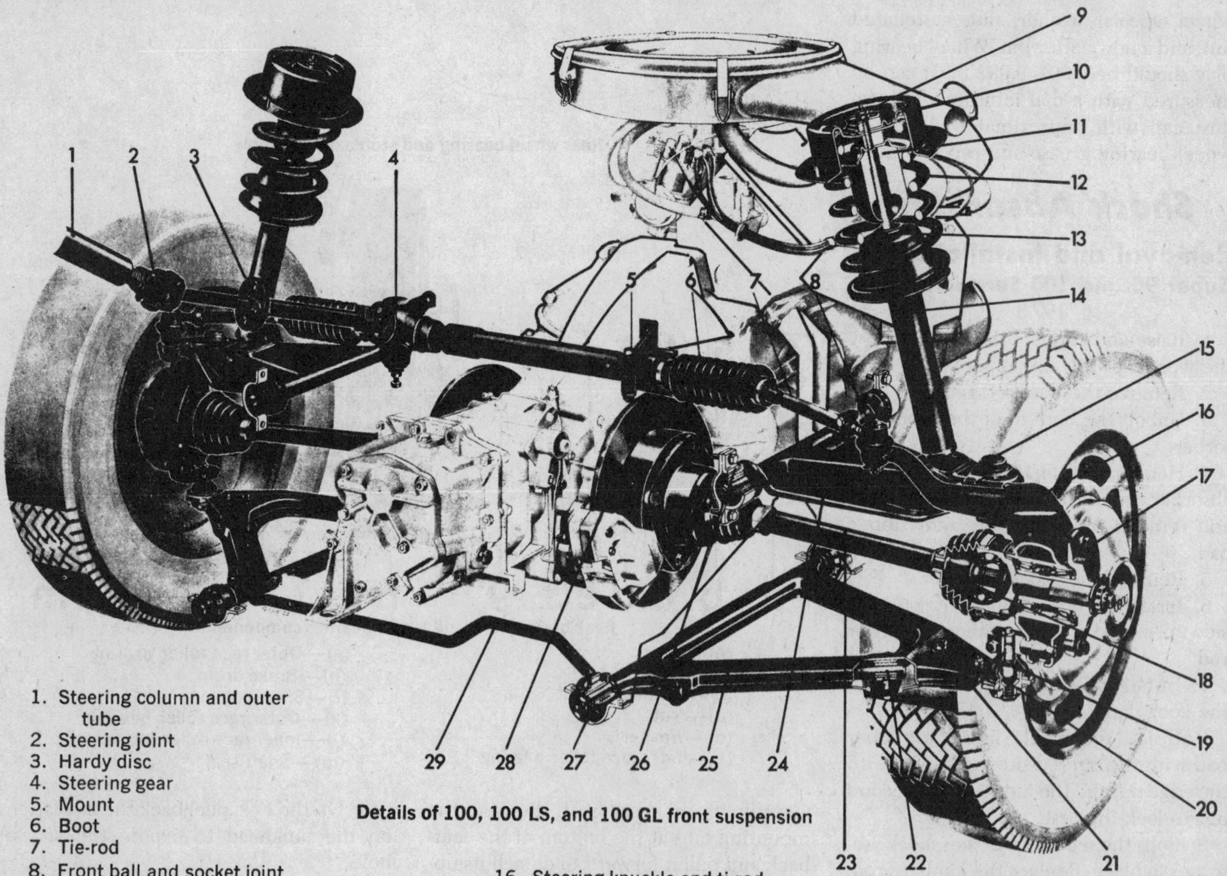

1. Steering column and outer tube
2. Steering joint
3. Hardy disc
4. Steering gear
5. Mount
6. Boot
7. Tie-rod
8. Front ball and socket joint
9. Spring retainer, upper
10. Rubber ring
11. Stop pad
12. Spring
13. Spring retainer, lower
14. Shock absorber
15. Support joint

16. Steering knuckle and ti-rod arm
17. Wheel hub
18. Rzeppa joint
19. Wishbone joint
20. Caster adjustment
21. Camber adjustment
22. Stabilizer bearing

23. Driveshaft
24. Wishbone, upper
25. Wishbone, lower
26. Wishbone bearing, upper
27. Wishbone bearing, lower
28. Brake disc
29. Stabilizer

Details of 100, 100 LS, and 100 GL front suspension

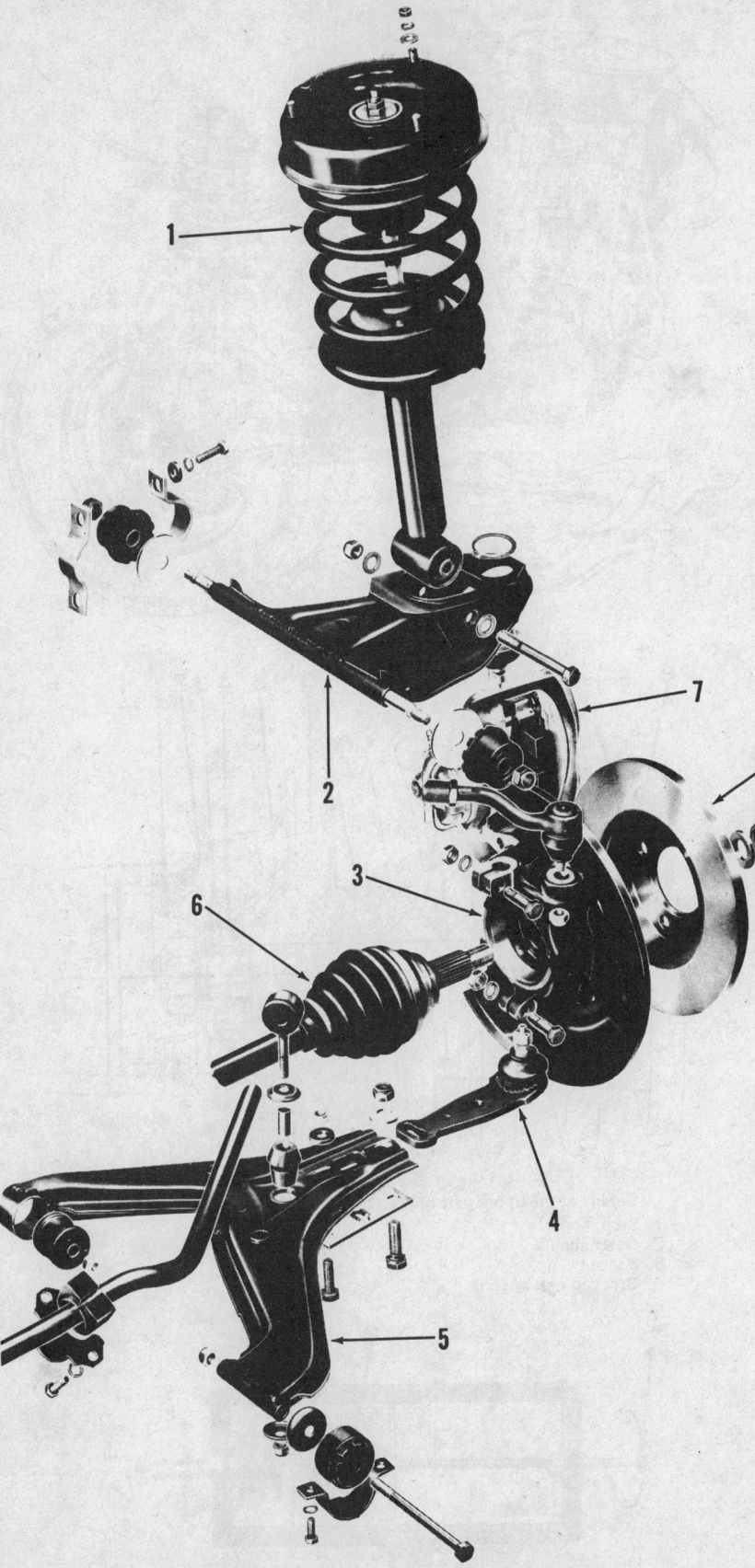

The 100 Series front suspension introduced in 1975

1. Coil spring
2. Upper control arm
3. Steering knuckle
4. Lower ball joint
5. Lower control arm
6. Driveshaft
7. Caliper
8. Disc

4. Install the lower mounting pad (it has deep cavities on both sides) and disc on the new shock absorber rod.

5. Install the shock absorber from underneath.

6. Inside the engine compartment, install the upper mounting pad and disc. Install the nuts, torquing the first to 30 ft lbs, and using the second to lock the first.

7. Bolt the bottom of the shock absorber in place. Torque the bolt to 34 ft lbs.

McPherson Strut

Removal and Installation

100, 100 LS, 100 GL

1. Support the vehicle and remove the wheels. Let the front suspension hang free.

2. Unbolt the strut unit from the upper control arm.

3. Inside the engine compartment, remove the three nuts which hold the top of the strut unit. Do not remove the nut and locknut in the center.

4. Pull the unit down and pull the top out through the wheel opening. It may be necessary to pull the steering knuckle down a bit for clearance.

5. It is not recommended that the strut unit be disassembled unless the necessary special tools to do this safely are available. The units should be serviced in pairs to maintain equal shock absorbing qualities and ride height. Spacers are available to correct ride height. The strut unit must be disassembled to install these. The proper ride height with standard size tires is 8.2–8.7 in., measured from the floor to the 0.32 in. diameter hole in the front bearing shell of the lower control arm inner pivot.

6. When replacing the strut unit, torque the three bolts and nuts, which hold the upper end of the strut to the body, to 13–15 ft lbs, and the lower end to 62–69 ft lbs. The torque for the shock absorber to spring retaining nut is 18–26 ft lbs.

7. Check the wheel alignment.

Fox

1. With the car resting on its wheels, remove the axle nut.

2. Raise the car and remove the wheel.

3. Unbolt the brake caliper, remove the brake line clip, and rest the caliper on the lower control arm.

4. Remove the bolt holding the steering knuckle to the lower control arm.

5. Detach the steering arm from the tie-rod end.

6. Unbolt the stabilizer bar pivots from the lower control arm. Disconnect the lower control arm from the steering knuckle by removing the bolt at the ball joint.

7. Remove the strut mounting nuts in

the engine compartment and remove the strut.

8. It is not recommended that the strut unit be disassembled unless the necessary special tools to do this safely are available. The units should be serviced in pairs to maintain equal shock absorbing qualities and ride height.

9. When replacing the strut unit, use a new nut and bolt to attach the lower control arm to the steering knuckle. Torque the strut to body bolts to 16 ft lbs, the control arm to steering knuckle bolt to 16 ft lbs, the brake caliper mounting bolts to 43 ft lbs, and the stabilizer bar pivots to 7 ft lbs.

10. Torque the axle nut to 180 ft lbs and check the wheel alignment.

Upper Control Arm And Ball Joint

Removal and Installation

Super 90

1. Raise the vehicle and let the front suspension hang free. Remove the wheels.

2. Remove the upper control arm-to-steering knuckle bolt.

3. Pull the control arm up so that the control arm upper joint comes loose from the steering knuckle.

4. Remove the two nuts and bolts which hold the outer end of the control arm together.

5. Hold the long control arm inner pivot bolt in place and loosen the nut about three turns. Remove the control arm joint from the end of the control arm.

6. Remove the front crossmember. Remove the nuts from the pivot bracket bolts from inside the engine compartment.

7. Pull the pivot bracket away from the body. It is located by two pins.

8. Remove the bolts and take the control arm off around the shock absorber.

NOTE: *Upper ball joint may be replaced at this time. It is a simple press fit.*

9. Reverse the procedure for installation. Make sure that the pivot bracket mounting bolts are in position.

10. Check the wheel alignment.

100, 100 LS, 100 GL

1. Remove the McPherson strut unit.

2. Remove the upper control arm to steering knuckle bolt.

3. Pull the control arm up so that the control arm upper joint comes loose from the steering knuckle.

4. Remove the four mounting bolts and the control arm.

NOTE: *Upper ball joint is a press fit and may be replaced at this time.*

5. Reverse the procedure for installation.

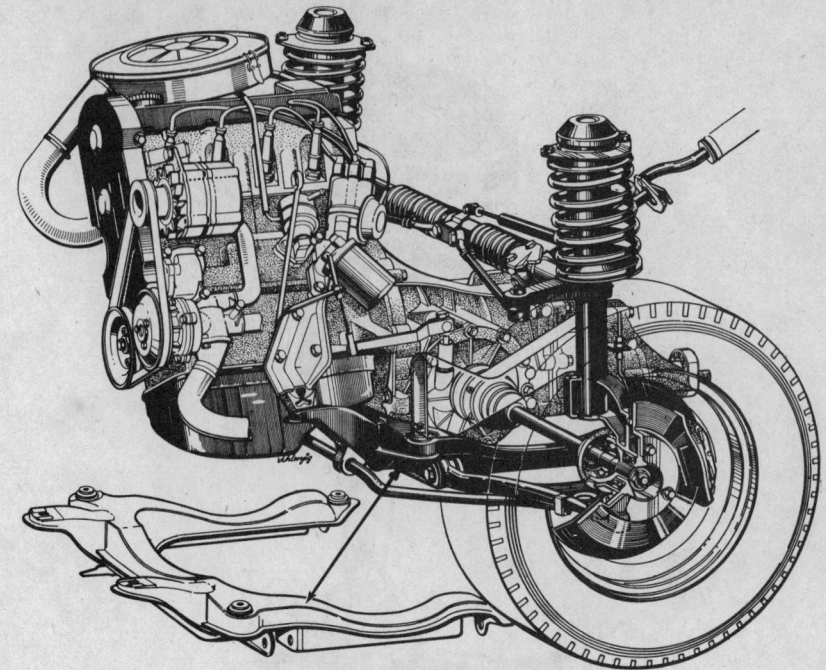

Fox front suspension

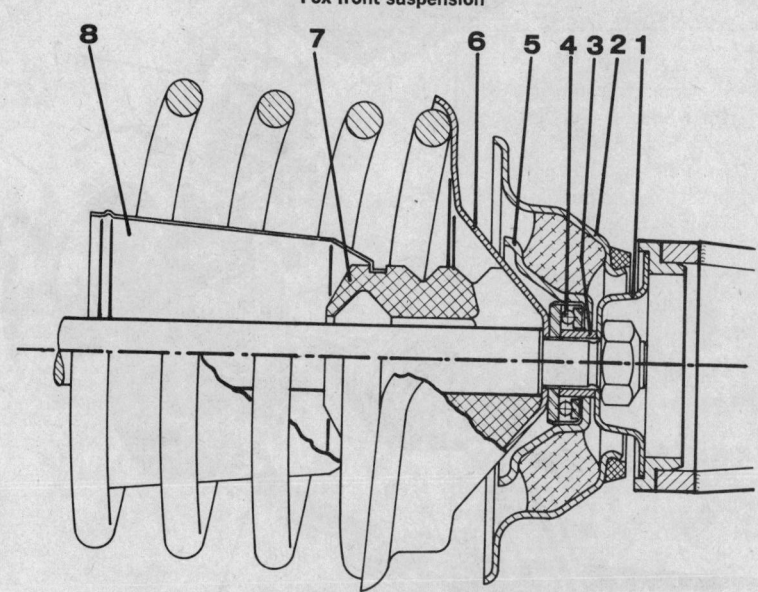

Details of the upper part of the Fox front spring/shock strut

1. Stop
2. Outer shell
3. Spacer
4. Grooved ball bearing
5. Inner shell
6. Upper spring retainer
7. Stop pad
8. Guard

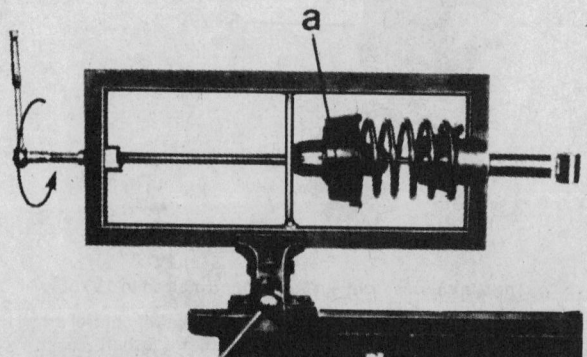

A coil spring compressor is necessary to overhaul the front suspension strut.

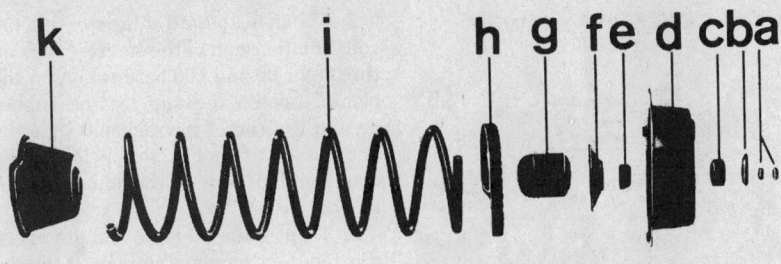

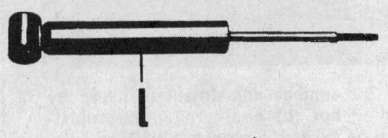

Exploded view of 100 series front suspension strut unit

(a)—Nut
(b)—Plate
(c)—Mounting pad, upper
(d)—Spring retainer, upper
(e)—Mounting pad, lower
(f)—Plate
(g)—Stop pad
(h)—Ring
(i)—Spring
(k)—Spring retainer, lower
(l)—Shock absorber

6. Check the wheel alignment.

Lower Control Arm And Ball Joint

Removal and Installation

Super 90

1. Disconnect the steering knuckle as described in Steps 1–5 of "Driveshaft Removal and Installation."

2. Remove the stabilizer bar.

3. Detach the bottom of the shock absorber. This is easier if the spring load is temporarily taken off the lower control arm by prying upward. Let the suspension hang free after this is done.

4. Loosen the bolt at the front of the torsion bar until only 4–5 threads are still engaged. This can be seen by lifting the floor covering above the crossmember.

5. Remove the bolt which holds the two parts of the control arm together.

6. Remove the bolt at the front of the torsion bar.

7. Pull the front of the control arm off the front of the torsion bar after unbolting the bearing.

8. Unbolt the rear bearing and pull the rear of the control arm off to the front.

1. Cotter pin
2. Tie-rod
3. Axle driveshaft
4. Circlip
5. Retainer nut
6. Brake caliper
7. Wheel bearing
8. Hub
9. Brake disc
10. Axle nut

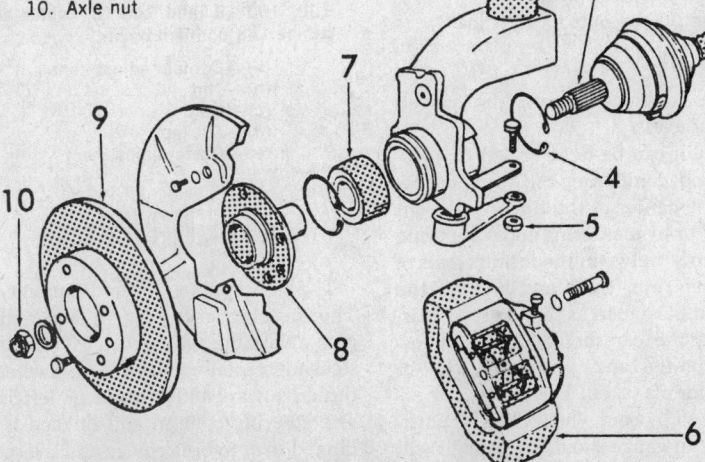

Fox front suspension

9. Reverse the procedure for installation.

10. Check the wheel alignment.

100, 100 LS, 100 GL

1. Raise the vehicle and let the suspension hang free. Remove the wheels.

2. Remove the stabilizer bar. It may be necessary to move the exhaust pipe.

3. Support the lower control arm. Remove the lower control arm to steering knuckle bolt. Let the arm down to pull the joint loose from the steering knuckle.

4. Unbolt the bearing bolts and remove the control arm.

NOTE: *To remove lower ball joint, remove retaining ring & nut and pull ball joint from joint plate.*

5. Reverse the procedure for installation.

6. Check the wheel alignment.

Track Control Arm and Ball Joint

Fox

1. Remove bolts securing control arm to subframe. Before removing ball joint, mark its position on the subframe.

2. Pull ball joint retaining clamp and pull ball joint from knuckle.

3. Remove bolts securing ball joint flange to control arm.

4. To install, position new ball joint on control arm and tighten bolts to 47 ftlb.

5. Install control arm in reverse of above. Torque control arm-to-subframe bolts to 32 ftlb.

Adjustments

Ride Height

Super 90

Rear ride height is not readily adjustable. Front ride height is measured from the floor to the underside of the lower control arm inner bearing. With standard size tires it should be 6.9–8.3 in. for the sedan and 6.2–7.6 in. for the station wagon. The car should be bounced and settled before making the measurement. To adjust the ride height turn the rear torsion bar adjusting bolt. The measurements on both sides should be alike, or different by no more than 0.4 in.

100, 100 LS, 100 GL

The suspension strut units must be removed and be disassembled and new springs or spacers installed to adjust ride height on these models. It is not recommended that the strut unit be disassembled unless the necessary special tools to do this safely are available. The proper front ride height with standard size tires is 8.2–8.7 in., measured from the floor to the 0.32 in. diameter hole in the front bearing shell of the lower control arm

100, 100 LS, and 100 GL ride height is adjusted by inserting spacers (D) on the strut unit (A). (S) is the special strut compressor.

inner pivot. The measurements on both sides should be alike, or different by no more than 0.3 in. The car should be bounced and settled before making the measurement. Rear ride height is not readily adjustable, except on 1974 and later models. See "Rear Suspension Strut Removal and Installation."

Wheel Alignment

Before checking wheel alignment, tire pressures should be brought up to specifications and the front ride height checked. The car should be bounced and settled before each alignment check or adjustment. The adjustments should be made in this order: caster, camber, toe-in. There is no caster adjustment on the Fox.

Caster

Super 90
1. Loosen the front nut on the upper control arm inner pivot bolt.
2. Using a thin wrench in front of the upper control arm mounting bracket, adjust the caster angle.
3. Leave the nut loose for the camber adjustment. Otherwise, tighten it to 54 ft lbs while holding the bolt head.

100, 100 LS, 100 GL
1. Loosen the large locknut at the bottom of the outer end of the lower control arm.

Super 90 caster adjustment is made by loosening nut (b) and turning eccentric (a) with a thin wrench, SW32.

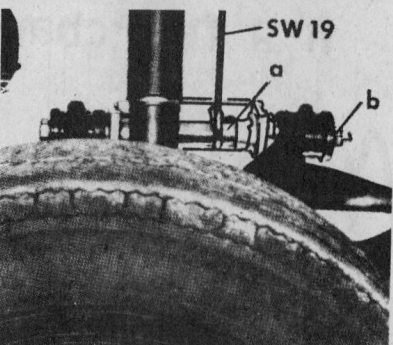

Super 90 camber adjustment is made by loosening nut (b) and turning the adjustment tube (a) with a wrench, SW19.

2. Turn the eccentric bolt, which passes through the locknut, to adjust caster.

Camber

Camber is checked with the wheels straight ahead.

Super 90
1. Loosen the front nut on the upper control arm inner pivot bolt.
2. Turn the adjustment tube in the center of the upper control arm mounting bracket to adjust camber.
3. Hold the bolt head and tighten the nut to 54 ft lbs.

100, 100 LS, 100 GL
1. Loosen the nut (on the top) on the bolt that passes through the outer end of the lower control arm.
2. Loosen the bolt (on the bottom) inboard of the nut loosened in Step 1.
3. Adjust camber by turning the large nut on top of the bolt loosened in Step 2.
4. Tighten the bolt and nut to 32 ft lbs.

Fox
1. Loosen the two nuts holding the ball joint to the lower control arm.
2. Push the ball joint in or out to adjust the camber. Dealers have a special tool to lever the ball joint in or out, using the holes in the control arm.
3. Tighten the nuts to 47 ft lbs.

Toe-In

Toe-in is checked with the wheels straight ahead.
1. Toe-in can be determined by measuring and comparing the distance between the center of the tire tread, front and rear, or by measuring and comparing the distance between the inside edges of the wheel rims, front and rear. If the wheel rims are used as the basis of measurement, the car should be rolled forward slightly and a second set of measurements taken. This avoids any error induced by bent wheels. If at all possible, a toe-in gauge should be used; it will give a much more accurate measurement.

2. Toe-in is adjusted at the steering tie-rods at either end of the steering rack on the Super 90 and 100 Series. Loosen the clamp. Loosen the clip for the rubber boot at the end of the rack and slide the boot back. On the Fox, simply loosen the clamp and locknut on the adjustable left tie-rod.
3. Turn both rods to lengthen or shorten them an equal amount. If the tie-rods are not adjusted equally, the steering wheel will be crooked and the turning arcs of the front wheels will be changed. On the Fox, only the left tie-rod is adjustable. If the steering wheel is crooked, it must be removed and repositioned.
4. Tighten the clamps and replace the boots.

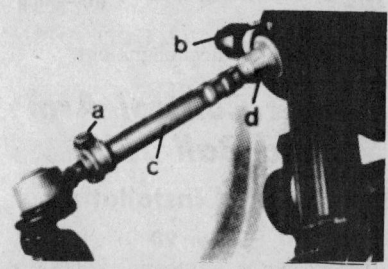

Toe-in on Super 90 and 100 series is adjusted by loosening nut (a) on each steering tie-rod (c) and pushing back the rubber boot and clamp (b) in order to use a wrench on the flats (d).

100, 100 LS, and 100 GL caster and camber adjustment points.

(a)—Camber adjustment
(b)—Nut
(c)—Bolt
(d)—Locknut
(e)—Caster adjustment

STEERING

The steering is a rack and pinion type. The steering geometry is designed to give a variable ratio effect, giving faster steering response as the steering wheel is turned toward either right or left lock. The steering column and linkage is arranged so as to break away and telescope safely in an accident, rather than penetrating into the passenger compartment.

Steering Wheel
Removal and Installation

1. Center the wheel. Disconnect the battery ground cable.
2. Pry off the wheel pad (horn button). The Super 90 has two small holes in the back of the wheel. A small screwdriver may be inserted to push the pad off.
3. Unbolt and remove the wheel. A steering wheel puller should not be necessary.
4. On installation, torque the bolt to 36 ft lbs. Do not pound on the wheel, as the collapsible column may be damaged.

Turn Signal and Headlight Dimmer Switch Replacement
Super 90, 100 Series

1. Remove the steering wheel.
2. Disconnect the battery ground cable.
3. Remove the wire from the horn contact ring. Remove the two screws and the horn contact ring.
4. Remove the screws which hold the column casing at the top and just below the instrument panel. The Super 90 has an additional screw in the top edge of the casing. It may be necessary, for access, to remove the padding from the underside of the instrument panel.
5. Remove the casing. Be careful to note the arrangement of any springs and washers removed from the top of the column.
6. The switch may now be disconnected, unscrewed, and removed. The wires are color coded for ease of replacement.

Fox

1. Disconnect the battery ground cable.
2. Remove the steering wheel.
3. Remove the screws in the top of the switch housing, lift off the housing and unplug the connectors, and remove the switch housing along with the wiper and turn signal levers.

Ignition and Steering Lock Switch
Removal and Installation
Super 90, 100 Series

To perform this operation, proceed with Steps 1–5 of "Turn Signal and Headlight Dimmer Switch Replacement". The lock switch is clamped to the steering column with special bolts whose heads shear off on installation. These must be drilled out in order to remove the switch. When replacing the unit, make sure that the lock tang is aligned with the slot in the steering column.

Fox

1. Remove the column shroud for access to the screws.

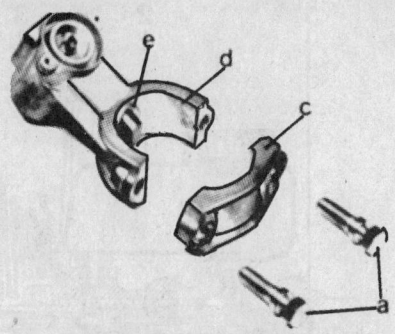

The ignition and steering lock switch is held in place by two bolts (a) whose heads shear on installation to deter theft.

(c)—Lower housing
(d)—Upper housing
(e)—Steering lock tang

2. Drill off the special shear bolt heads. CAUTION: *These bolts also support the steering column. Support the column while removing the bolts.*
3. On installation, make sure the two projections on the lock clamp assembly engage the two depressions in the column. Tighten the new bolts until their heads shear off.

Steering Gear
Removal and Installation
Super 90

1. Point the front wheels straight ahead. Loosen the bolt and open the clamp at the bottom of the steering column, inside the car.
2. Remove the four bolts and slide up the plate at the base of the steering column.
3. Bend open the lockplate and remove the coupling bolts.
4. Disconnect the ends of the steering tie-rods from the steering knuckles by removing the cotter pins and nuts and pressing out the tie-rod ends. A small puller or press is required to free the tie-rod ends.
5. Unbolt the support brackets from below.
6. Pry the brackets loose inside the engine compartment.
7. Pull the steering gear out to the left, after turning the coupling down.
8. On installation, center the steering gear and the steering wheel.

100 Series, Manual Steering

1. Point the front wheels straight ahead. Disconnect the steering column from the firewall.
2. Disconnect the steering shaft from the steering gear.
3. Disconnect the ends of the steering tie-rods from the steering knuckles by removing the cotter pins and nuts and pressing out the tie-rod ends. A small puller or press is required to free the tie-rod ends.

4. Unbolt the steering gear from the firewall. Slide the unit toward the right and pull it up and out through the engine compartment.
5. On installation, center the steering gear and the steering wheel.

Fox

1. Pry off the lock plate and remove both tie-rod mounting bolts from the steering rack, inside the engine compartment. Pry the tie rods out of the mounting pivot.
2. Remove the lower instrument panel trim.
3. Remove the shaft clamp bolt, pry off the clip, and drive the shaft toward the inside of the car with a brass drift.
4. Remove the steering gear mounting bolts at both ends. There is a single bolt at the right end.
5. Turn the wheels all the way to the right and remove the steering gear through the opening in the right wheel-housing.
6. For installation, temporarily install the tie-rod mounting pivot to the rack with both mounting bolts. Remove one bolt, install the tie-rod, and replace the bolt. Do the same on the other tie-rod. Make sure to install the lock plate. Torque the tie-rod bolts to 39 ft lbs, the mounting pivot bolt to 15 ft lbs, and the steering gear to body mounting bolts to 15 ft lbs.

Power Steering Pump
Removal and Installation

1. Remove hoses from pump. Plug openings.
2. Remove belt adjusting bolt, push pump to one side and remove belt.
3. Support pump, remove mounting bolts and lift out pump.

Steering Linkage
Tie-Rod Removal and Installation
Super 90, 100 Series

1. Jack up the car and remove the wheels.
2. Disconnect the end of the steering tie-rod from the steering knuckle by removing the cotter pin and nut and

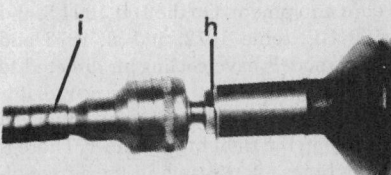

Nut (h) is loosened to remove the tie-rod (i) from the Super 90 and 100 series steering gear.

pressing out the tie-rod end. A small puller or press is required to free the tie-rod end.

3. The steering gear boots can be replaced with no further disassembly at this point.

4. Loosen the clamp and slide the rubber boot as far back as possible.

5. Turn the steering all the way to the side being worked on. Do not force it against the stops.

6. Bend open the lockplate behind the knurled cylinder on the tie-rod. Unscrew the tie rod.

7. Reverse the procedure for installation. Adjust the new tie-rod to the same length as the old one. Torque the tie-rod to 51 ft lb, then set the lockplate. Tie-rod outer end torque is 26 ft lbs.

8. Check the toe-in.

Fox

1. Raise the car and remove the front wheels.

2. Disconnect the outer end of the steering tie-rod from the steering knuckle by removing the cotter pin and nut and pressing out the tie-rod end. A small puller or press is required to free the tie-rod end.

3. Under the hood, pry off the lock plate and remove the mounting bolts from both tie-rod inner ends. Pry the tie-rod out of the mounting pivot.

4. First install the mounting pivot to the rack with both mounting bolts. Remove one bolt, install the tie-rod, and replace the bolt. Do the same on the other tie-rod. Make sure to install the lock plate. The inner tie-rod end bolts should be torqued to 40 ft lbs.

5. If you are replacing the adjustable left tie-rod, adjust it to the same length as the old one. Check the toe-in when the job is done.

6. Use new cotter pins when installing the outer tie-rod ends. Torque the nut to 28 ft lbs.

BRAKE SYSTEMS

All models have dual circuit hydraulic brakes with front disc brakes and rear drum brakes. Inboard front disc brakes are used on the super 90 and 100 series. A vacuum operated power assist is standard equipment. On the 100, 100 LS, and 100 GL, some 1972, and all 1973 and later models have cooling air directed to the brake discs from the electric radiator fan. The fan is switched on by a thermal switch in the right brake caliper. There is sometimes a fan switch in the air conditioner circuit also. 1973 and later 100 series, and all Fox models have a brake pad lining thickness warning light.

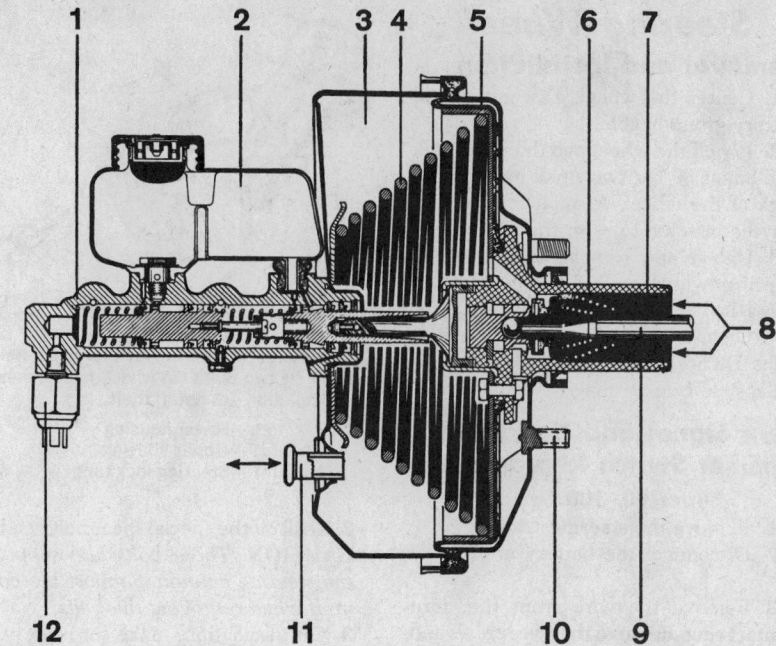

Cross-section of brake master cylinder and vacuum brake booster

1. Master cylinder	5. Diaphragm	9. Pressure rod
2. Brake fluid container	6. Timing housing	10. Mounting bolts
3. Vacuum cylinder	7. Filter	11. Vacuum connection
4. Spring	8. Air intake	12. Brake light switch

Adjustment

The front disc brakes are self-adjusting. The rear drum brakes must be adjusted periodically, or whenever free travel is one third or more of the total pedal travel.

1. Raise the rear of the car. Do not place a jack under the rear axle tube on 1973 and earlier super 90 and 100 series models.

2. Block the front wheels and release the parking brake. Step on the brake pedal hard to center the linings.

3. Turn the front adjusting nut on the brake backing plate until the wheel can't be rotated forward by hand.

4. Loosen the adjusting nut until the wheel can be turned freely without drag.

5. Repeat Steps 3 and 4 for the rear adjusting nut.

6. Repeat Steps 3, 4, and 5 for the other rear wheel.

When adjusting the rear brakes, turn adjusting nuts (A) toward (a) to tighten and (b) to loosen.

7. Step on the brake pedal hard and make sure the wheels still rotate without drag.

Master Cylinder

Removal and Installation

1. Have an assistant hold the brake pedal down about 1½ in. Disconnect the brake line nearest the firewall.

2. Hold a container under the fitting disconnected in Step 1 and have the assistant release the pedal. The contents of the reservoir will drain into the container. Discard the used fluid.

3. Disconnect the other brake line.

4. Disconnect the stoplight switch from the master cylinder.

5. Unbolt and remove the master cylinder from the power brake unit. Be careful not to lose the sealing ring between the two units.

6. Installation is the reverse of removal. Master cylinder bolt torque is 17 ft lbs. Fill and bleed the system. There should be a pedal free-play of 0.2 in. It can be adjusted on the linkage, inside the car.

Overhaul

1. Clean the outside of the master cylinder.

2. Remove the brake fluid reservoir, unscrew the brake light switch, remove the snap-ring and dismantle the unit. It will be necessary to partially unscrew the stop screw to remove the secondary piston.

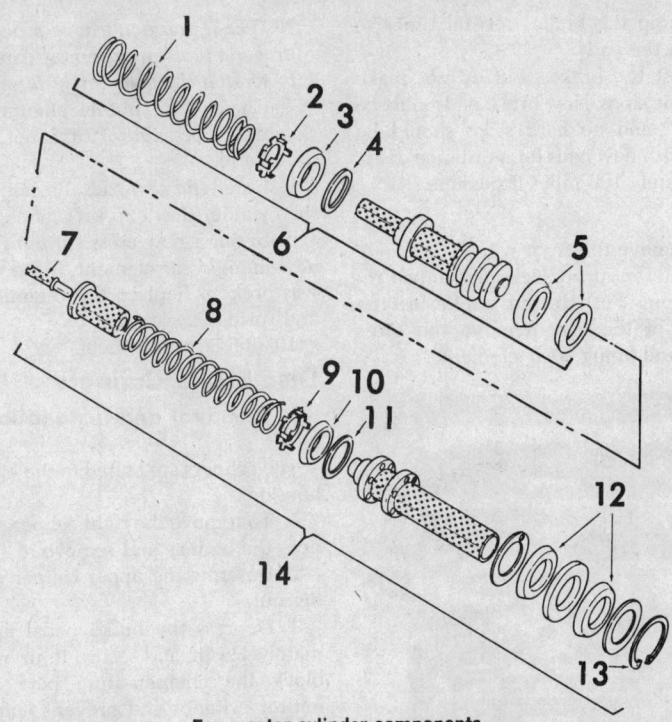

Fox master cylinder components

1. Conical spring
2. Spring seat
3. Primary cup
4. Washer
5. Secondary cups
6. Primary piston assembly
7. Stroke limiting screw
8. Cylindrical spring
9. Spring seat
10. Primary cup
11. Washer
12. Secondary cups
13. Circlip
14. Secondary piston assembly

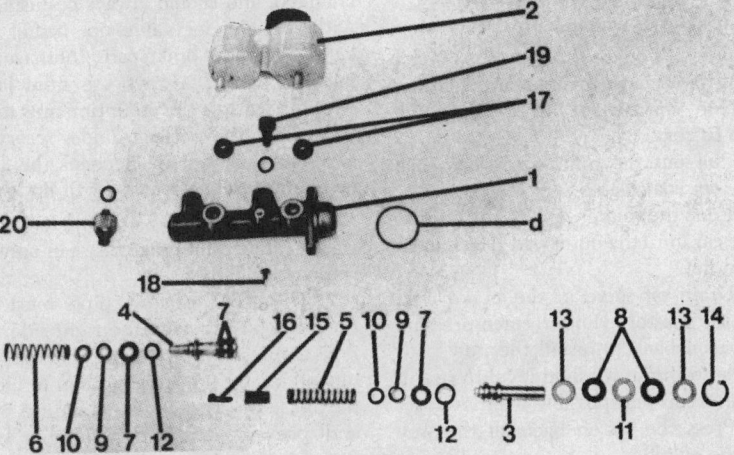

Exploded view of brake master cylinder

1. Master cylinder
2. Brake fluid container
3. Primary piston
4. Secondary piston
5. Primary spring
6. Secondary spring
7. Primary boot
8. Secondary boot
9. Support ring
10. Spring retainer
11. Intermediate ring
12. Filler disc
13. Stop disc
14. Snap-ring
15. Stop sleeve
16. Inner stop screw
17. Container plug
18. Outer stop screw
19. Pressure valve
20. Brake light switch

3. All parts must be thoroughly cleaned in alcohol or clean brake fluid only. Dry the parts with compressed air and be sure that the compensating port is not plugged.

4. Visually inspect all components. Replace any that are suspect. Rubber boots and container plugs should always be replaced.

5. On assembly, lubricate all metal parts with clean brake fluid.

6. Preassemble and install the piston.

7. Be sure that the boots are installed correctly and are not damaged.

8. Check the pistons for ease of operation. If the pistons do not return quickly to the stop screw or disc, dismantle the master cylinder and lightly polish the cyl-

inder surface.

9. Further assembly is the reverse of disassembly. Grease should not be applied to the pushrod, as it will swell the rubber boots.

Bleeding

The hydraulic system must be bled whenever the pedal feels spongy, indicating that compressible air has entered the system. The system must also be bled whenever any component has been disconnected or there has been a leak.

1. Clean off the top of the master cylinder. Check that the fluid level in each reservoir is between the marks.

2. Attach a hose to the bleeder valve at the first wheel to be bled. Mechanics customarily start at the wheel farthest from the master cylinder and work closer. Some 100 Series cars with automatic transmission and inboard brakes have three bleeder screws on each front brake caliper. On these cars, the bleeding sequence should be: upper right front, upper left front, lower outer right front, lower inner right front, lower outer left front, lower inner left front, left rear, and right rear. Pour a few inches of brake fluid into a clear container and stick the end of the tube below the surface.

NOTE: *The tube and container of brake fluid are not absolutely necessary, but this is a very sloppy job without them.*

3. Open the bleed valve about ½ turn. Have a helper slowly depress the pedal. Close the valve just before the pedal reaches the end of its travel. Have the helper let the pedal back up.

4. Check the fluid level. If the reservoir runs dry, the procedure will have to be restarted from the beginning.

5. Repeat Step 3 until no more bubbles come out the hose.

6. Repeat the bleeding operation, Steps 3 to 5, at the other three wheels.

7. Check the master cylinder level again.

8. If repeated bleeding has no effect, there is an air leak, probably internally in the master cylinder or in one of the wheel cylinders.

Front Disc Brakes

All super 90 and 100 series models use the same type of two-piston front disc brakes, except for some automatic transmission models, primarily 1972, which use four-piston brakes. These four-piston units can be readily identified by the presence of three bleeder screws instead of the usual one. Procedures for the two-piston brakes may be adapted to the four-piston units. The Fox uses single piston disc brakes.

Audi

Disc Brake Pads

Removal and Installation

Super 90, 100 Series

Although the four front brake pads may wear unevenly, they must not be switched around to equalize wear. They must always be replaced in sets of four. Minimum permissible friction pad thickness is 0.08 in.

NOTE: *This is the factory recommendation. State inspection laws may not allow this much wear.*

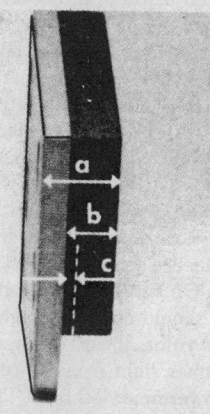

(a) is the thickness of the new pad and the backplate (b) is the thickness of the new pad, and (c) is the minimum safe pad thickness, 0.08 in.

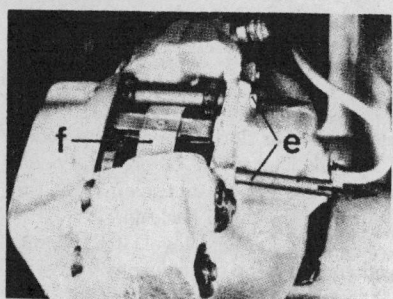

(e) is the pad retaining pins and (f) is the cross spring.

1. Pull out the lock clips and remove the retaining pins. While doing this, hold the cross springs in place.

2. Remove the cross springs and pull the brake pads from the calipers. On 1972 and later models, disconnect the electrical leads.

3. To install new pads, drain off some of the brake fluid from the master cylinder, since pressing the pistons back to install pads will cause the brake fluid level to rise.

4. Press the pistons completely into the cylinder and check their alignment. They should be at an angle of 20°; if not they must be rotated. A gauge may be made up to check this.

5. Slide the pads into the caliper recess.

6. Replace the retaining spring and install the cross springs, retaining pins, and new lock clips.

7. Pump the brakes several times to position the pads.

8. Test the brakes, but do not make any panic stops. New brake pads must be "run-in" and no hard stops should be made with new pads for a distance of approximately 100 miles if possible.

Fox

1. Remove the front wheel.

2. Pull the spring locks off the pad retaining pins. Push the pins out toward the outside of the car. Remove the cross spring and lining wear elements.

If the Fox brake lining wear elements (arrows) have broken off, they must be replaced when new pads are installed.

NOTE: *If the pads have worn excessively causing the lining wear elements to break, they must be replaced along with their wiring up to the firewall connector. The right connector is behind the battery.*

3. Pull out the inner pad. A special hook tool is available to do this.

4. Press the caliper toward the outside of the car until the outer pad is free to be pulled out.

5. Drain off some of the brake fluid from the master cylinder, since pressing the piston back to install the new pads will cause the brake fluid level to rise in the reservoir and possibly overflow.

6. Press the piston back all the way into the cylinder.

NOTE: *If you don't have a piston depressing tool, be extremely careful not to scratch the cylinder wall.*

7. Check the piston alignment. It should be at an angle of 20°. If not, it must be rotated.

8. Install the new pads. Be careful that the cylinder dust cup isn't damaged.

9. Install a new cross spring. Install a new lining wear element, if the old one was broken. Replace the retaining pins and spring locks.

10. Replace the wheel.

Disc Brake Calipers

Removal and Installation

Super 90

The calipers are bolted to the transaxle housing.

1. To remove the right caliper, disconnect the battery and remove it.

2. Unscrew the upper caliper mounting nut.

3. Depress the brake pedal approximately 1½ in. and secure it, in order to block the compensating port in the master cylinder and prevent fluid from running out.

4. Disconnect the brake line.

5. Remove the lower caliper mounting nut.

6. Installation is the reverse of removal. Note the following points: The left and right calipers must not be interchanged, and should always be installed with the bleeder valve up. Install the calipers without brake pads (these can be installed later). Always use new lockwashers. Torque the mounting nuts to 69 ft lbs. Refill the master cylinder reservoir and bleed the system. Recheck the fluid level and test the brakes (with no load).

100, 100 LS, 100 GL

The caliper and brake disc can only be removed together.

1. The front exhaust pipe must be removed for access to the right side.

2. Depress the brake pedal about 1½ in. and secure it in this position to block the master cylinder compensating port and prevent fluid from running out. Remove the brake pads.

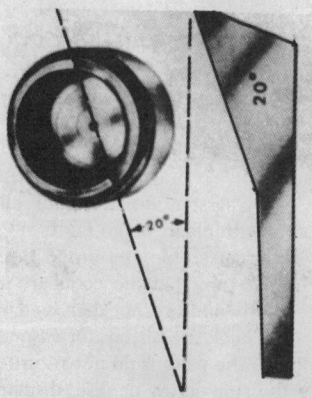

The pistons must be aligned at 20° in the caliper

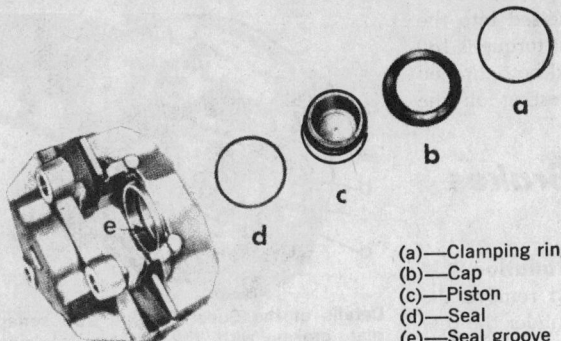

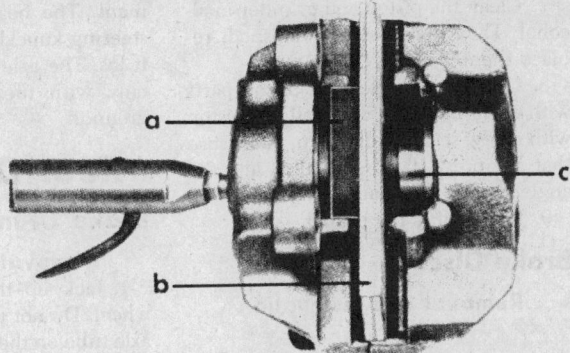

(a)—Clamping ring
(b)—Cap
(c)—Piston
(d)—Seal
(e)—Seal groove

The Super 90 and 100 series caliper with one piston and cylinder assembly disassembled.

Air pressure is used to remove the piston (c) from the caliper. An old pad (a) and a piece of wood (b) are installed in the caliper.

3. Disconnect the brake line at the caliper and plug the opening. On 1972 and later models, disconnect the electrical lead to the right caliper.

4. Remove the caliper nuts.

5. Unbolt the driveshaft flange and slide it back and upward.

6. Remove the brake disc and caliper, noting the insulating washer between the flange and brake disc.

7. Installation is the reverse of removal. Make sure that the calipers are not interchanged. On calipers with single bleeder screws, the screw must be at the top. Torque the caliper mounting nuts to 69–76 ft lbs, and the driveshaft flange bolts to 70–78 ft lbs. Refill the master cylinder reservoir and bleed the system. Recheck the fluid level and test the brakes.

Fox

1. Remove the wheel.

2. Disconnect the brake line from the caliper.

3. Unbolt the caliper from the steering knuckle.

4. On installation, torque the caliper

mounting bolts to 43 ft lbs. Bleed the brakes.

Overhaul

Super 90, 100 Series

NOTE: *The two halves of the caliper must not be separated, nor should the connecting screws be loosened.*

1. Remove the pads.

2. Plug the brake line connection.

The caliper mounting nuts (a) on the 100, 100 LS, and 100 GL.

Clean off the outside of the caliper unit, using hot water and a non-alkaline detergent.

3. Pry off the clamping ring from one cylinder, using a screwdriver.

4. Remove the cap from the same cylinder by hand.

5. Clamp an old pad in place on the cylinder opposite to the one being removed. Do not use a good pad; it will be ruined. Place a piece of wood across the center of the caliper to catch the piston. Apply air pressure to the brake line connection to force out the piston. Be careful, as the piston may be blown out of the caliper.

6. The seal can be removed from the cylinder groove with a plastic instrument. Be extremely careful not to damage the cylinder finish.

7. The cylinder and the piston may not be resurfaced; they must be replaced if damaged. The piston and cylinder parts should be cleaned in alcohol.

8. Coat the cylinder and piston parts with clean brake fluid. Install the piston with a new seal, cap, and clamping ring. Make sure that the piston face is installed at a 20° angle, as discussed under "Brake Pad Replacement."

9. Steps 3–8 may now be repeated for the second piston.

Fox

1. Remove the caliper.

2. Pry the mounting frame off the floating frame.

3. Pry the brake cylinder and guide spring off the floating frame.

4. Remove the clamp and dust cup from the cylinder.

5. Pull the piston out of the cylinder. If it won't come out, you can apply air pressure through the brake line connection.

CAUTION: *When forcing the piston out with air pressure, make sure to hold it face down on the bench so that the piston doesn't fly out.*

6. Pull the seal out of the cylinder. Be extremely careful not to damage the cylinder wall.

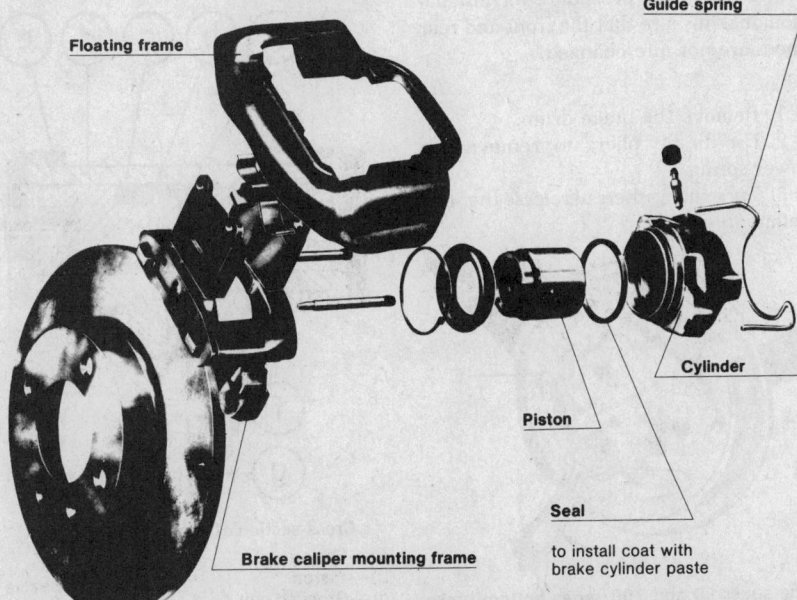

Guide spring

Floating frame

Cylinder

Piston

Seal

Brake caliper mounting frame

to install coat with brake cylinder paste

Fox single piston floating front disc brake components

7. Clean the piston and cylinder in alcohol. They may not be refinished; replace them if damaged.

8. Coat the cylinder and piston parts with clean brake fluid. Install the piston with a new seal and dust cup. Make sure that the piston face is installed at a 20° angle. See "Brake Pad Replacement".

9. Reassemble the caliper.

Brake Disc

Removal and Installation

Super 90

1. Jack up the vehicle and remove the wheel.

2. Disconnect the steering knuckle from the upper wishbone. See "Upper Control Arm Removal and Installation" for details.

3. Unbolt the driveshaft flange and move it toward the outside.

4. Remove the brake disc downward, being careful not to drop it.

5. Installation is the reverse of removal. Torque the driveshaft flange bolts to 77 ft lbs.

100, 100 LS, 100 GL

Follow the procedure for "Caliper Removal and Installation." The caliper and disc must be removed together.

Fox

1. Jack up the car and remove the wheel.

2. Unbolt and set aside the caliper. Don't disconnect the brake line. Don't let the caliper hang on the brake line.

3. Remove the screw and take off the disc. Be very careful not to touch the disc surface with greasy fingers.

4. On installation, torque the caliper bolts to 43 ft lbs.

Inspection

Super 90, 100 Series

Maximum permissible disc runout is 0.005 in. The disc may be reground but no more than 0.026 in. thickness may be removed from each side. Original disc thickness is 0.410 in. Maximum permissible thickness variation is 0.001 in.

Fox

Maximum permissible disc runout is 0.002 in. The disc may be machined but minimum safe thickness is 0.43 in. The original thickness is 0.47 in. Maximum permissible thickness variation is 0.001 in.

Front Wheel Bearings

Removal and Installation, Adjustment

Super 90, 100 Series

Refer to "Transaxle—Driveshaft Disassembly" for these procedures.

Fox

There is no front wheel bearing adjust-

ment. The bearing is pressed into the steering knuckle. Axle nut torque is 180 ft lbs. The axle nut should be tightened only with the wheels resting on the ground.

Rear Drum Brakes

Brake Drums

Removal and Installation

1. Jack up the car and remove the wheel. Do not use a jack under the rear axle tube on the Super 90 and 100 Series models through 1973. Release the parking brake.

2. Pry off the grease cap.

3. Remove the cotter pin and the nuts.

4. Pull off the brake drum by hand, making sure that the washer and roller bearing don't fall out. If the drum is held by the brakes, back off on the brake adjustment.

5. On reinstallation, tighten the nut to force the brake drum into place, then loosen it until there is 0.001–0.002 in. bearing play measured with a dial indicator.

6. Replace the castellated nut and install a new cotter pin.

7. Fill the grease cap with about 10 oz of wheel bearing grease.

8. Adjust the brakes if necessary.

Brake Shoes

Removal and Installation

Super 90, 100 Series

1. Remove the brake drum.

2. Remove the big retaining spring at the bottom. Be careful it doesn't fly out.

3. Disconnect the parking brake cable and pull the shoes from the wheel cylinder.

4. Remove the shoes.

5. Reverse the procedure for installation, making sure that the front and rear shoes are not interchanged.

Fox

1. Remove the brake drum.

2. Use brake pliers to remove the lower spring.

3. Turn the washers to release the shoe retaining springs.

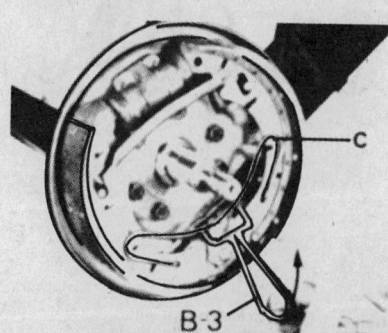

The super 90 and 100 series bottom brake shoe retaining spring (c) is being replaced. Tool B-3 can be fabricated.

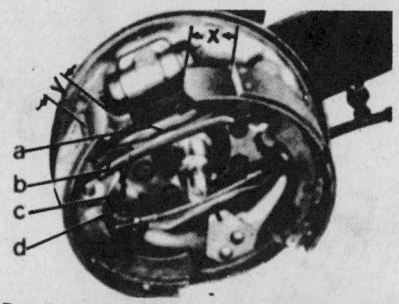

Details of the Super 90 and 100 series rear brakes with the bottom retaining spring removed. The measurement (x) for the front shoe is greater than (y) for the rear shoe.

(a)—Retaining clip
(b)—Spring (long end at the rear)
(c)—Handbrake lever
(d)—Pressure rod

4. Disconnect the parking brake cable by pressing the spring toward the front of the car and unhooking the cable from the lever.

5. Reverse the procedure for installation.

Wheel Cylinders

Removal and Installation

1. Remove the brake shoes.

2. Depress the brake pedal about 1½ in. to block the master cylinder compensating port and prevent leakage. Secure the pedal in this position.

3. Disconnect the brake line and plug the opening.

4. Remove the two mounting screws from the backing plate.

5. Remove the cylinder.

6. Reverse the procedure for installation.

Overhaul

1. Clean the outside of the cylinder, using alcohol or clean brake fluid.

Cross-section of a rear wheel cylinder

(a)—Spring
(b)—Piston
(c)—Grooved cup
(d)—Cylinder
(e)—Cap
(f)—Bleeder valve
(g)—Dust cap
(h)—Brake line connection

2. Remove the rubber boots and disassemble the cylinder.

3. Clean all parts in alcohol.

4. Air dry all parts.

5. If there are any pits or roughness inside the cylinder, it must be replaced.

6. Replace the piston if it is scratched or damaged in any way.

7. Lubricate all internal parts with clean brake fluid and reassemble the cylinder. Replace all rubber parts.

8. Make sure that the cylinder slides freely. If it does not, disassemble the cylinder and polish the inside of the cylinder lightly by revolving the cylinder around a piece of crocus cloth held by a finger. Do not polish the cylinder in a lengthwise direction. Clean the cylinder again after polishing. Air dry.

9. Replace the boots.

10. Replace the cylinder and tighten the bolts evenly. Bleed the system after it is reassembled.

Rear Wheel Bearings

Removal and Installation, Adjustment

Refer to "Rear Suspension—Wheel Bearings and Stub Axle Removal and Installation" for these procedures.

Parking Brake

Adjustment

The handbrake (parking brake) must be adjusted periodically to compensate for lining wear and cable stretching. The adjuster is at the cable junction, under the center of the car.

1. Block the front wheels. Raise and support the rear of the vehicle. Do not use a jack under the rear axle tube.

2. Pull the brake up to the first or second notch.

3. If the wheels will not rotate freely, loosen the adjusting nut. Some early Super 90 models may have two wing nuts for adjustment; adjust them individually for equal tension.

4. Tighten the adjusting nut until there is a slight drag on the rear wheels.

5. Pull the handle up to the third or fourth notch; the wheels should lock.

6. Check that there is no drag when the brake handle is fully released.

Cable

Removal and Installation

1. Jack up the rear of the car. Do not place a jack under the axle tube on the Super 90 and 100 Series models through 1973.

2. Block the front wheels and release the handbrake.

3. Remove the rear brake shoes.

4. Remove the cable adjusting nut(s) and detach the cable guides from the floorpan.

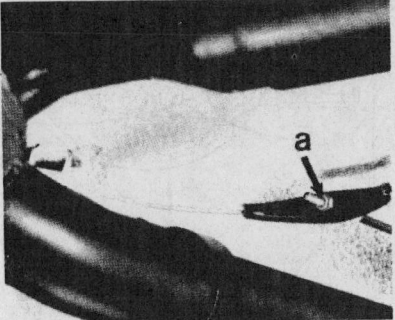

(a) indicates the adjusting point for one piece rear handbrake cables used on most models.

5. Replace the cable and brake shoes. Check the parking brake adjustment.

CHASSIS ELECTRICAL

Heater

Removal and Installation

Super 90

To remove either the heater blower or the core, it is necessary to remove the heater unit from the car and disassemble it.

1. Drain the radiator coolant, disconnect the battery and remove the instrument panel lower trim.

2. Drain the remaining coolant from the plug in the bottom of the heater.

3. If necessary, unscrew the blower duct at the bottom of the heater and remove.

4. Unbolt and remove the hood latch cable.

5. Disconnect the brown and red wires.

6. Remove the right and left defroster hoses and push them toward the engine compartment.

7. Disconnect the heater control cable from the lever, to the right of the steering column. Disconnect the cables from the lower and center heater control levers.

8. Remove the left and right water drain hoses.

9. Unbolt and remove the heater.

10. Installation is the reverse of removal. Adjust the control cables so that they allow the control levers full movement.

100, 100 LS, 100 GL

To remove either the heater blower or the core, it is necessary to remove the heater unit from the car and disassemble it.

1. Drain the coolant, disconnect the battery, and remove the lower instrument panel trim and center shelf.

2. Remove the breather screw from

the hose inside the engine compartment, being careful not to damage the firewall seal.

3. Detach both heater hoses.

4. Disconnect the cables that control the foot area heater flaps, the windshield flap and the heater valve.

5. Remove the plug connector from the heater controls and the lead from terminal 15 of the emergency warning light switch.

6. From the passenger compartment unbolt the heater and pull it down.

7. Installation is the reverse of removal.

8. When installing the cables, place the heater levers in the Off position. Place the leg of the spring clip in the mount and install the spring clip. The cable sleeve must protrude at least 0.2 in. beyond the spring clip.

Radio

The radio is usually a dealer installed or aftermarket unit. Thus no specific removal and installation procedures can be given. The following information applies generally to all car radios.

Care should be taken during installation to avoid reversing the ground and power leads. Reversal of these leads will cause serious damage to the radio. The power lead usually has an in-line fuse.

If the speaker needs replacement, it should be replaced with one of the same impedance, measured in ohms. Mismatched impedance can cause rapid transistor failure as well as poor radio performance. This should also be taken into consideration when adding a second speaker.

The radio should never be operated without a speaker connected or with the speaker leads shorted. This will result in transistor failure.

Wiper Motor and Linkage

Removal and Installation

Super 90

The wiper motor and the linkage can be removed from inside the engine compartment after removing the heater.

1. Disconnect the battery ground cable. Remove the wiper arm. It is mounted either with a cap nut and domed washer, or, by a spring which engages a groove.

2. Pull the windshield washer pump from the instrument panel and remove the hoses (long connection to the jets and short connection to the water supply).

3. Remove the ring nut from the instrument panel, remove the switch, and pull off the cables.

4. Remove the brown cable from the instruments.

5. Drain the coolant and remove the heater.

6. Remove the nuts from the wiper arm mounts.

7. Disconnect the hoses from the washer jets.

8. Tilt the wiper motor and linkage assembly to remove it.

9. Installation is the reverse of removal. Seal the cable hole in the firewall with a plastic sealant if necessary. Operate the wiper motor to be sure that the wipers park properly. Remove the motor crank arm and mount it properly if this does not occur.

Wiper Motor
Removal and Installation
100, 100 LS, 100 GL

The motor can be removed from inside the engine compartment.

1. Disconnect the battery negative terminal.

2. Remove the right and left knee padding.

3. From the engine compartment, pull out the rubber grommet to give the wiring harness more play. Pull out the wiper switch and remove the leads.

4. Bend open the metal tabs holding the wiring harness and remove the harness which runs below the spray jets, together with the spray jet line.

5. Loosen the nut and pry off the lever for the linkage.

6. Remove the motor and harness.

7. Reverse the procedure for installation.

Wiper Linkage
Removal and Installation
100, 100 LS, 100 GL

The linkage can be removed from inside the engine compartment.

1. Remove the windshield wiper arms from the studs by prying off the cap and removing the retaining nut. Remove the lower nut, washer and seal from the recess in the body.

2. Remove the mounting screws in the engine compartment and tilt the wiper base to remove.

3. Installation of the wiper linkage and the motor is done by reversing the removal procedures. The lever connected to the wiper motor should be installed at approximately 90° to the front and rear centerline of the vehicle. The wiper arm blades have different angles. The arm with the blade at the greater angle is installed on the driver's side.

Windshield Wiper Motor and Linkage
Fox

1. Pry off wiper arms and remove nuts

Fox heater system (models with A/C)

1. Fresh air inlet with control flap (opens with heater on)
2. Dry air flap (opens with A/C on)
3. Heater—A/C blower
4. Air outlets for ends of instrument panel
5. Heater core
6. Center air outlet
7. Floor air outlet
8. Evaporator

from studs in cowl.

2. Remove brace-to-body screws.

3. Disconnect multiple connector at wiper motor.

4. Remove motor mounting screw, and pry off connecting rod.

5. Remove linkage followed by motor.

Instruments

The instruments can be removed separately in the Super 90, but the entire instrument cluster must be removed in the 100 Series and Fox.

Fuel and Water Temperature Gauge
Removal and Installation
Super 90

1. Disconnect the battery ground cable.

2. Unscrew and remove the blower duct from the bottom of the heater.

3. Remove the instrument panel bottom trim. If it is held in place by round plastic clips, use a punch to drive the plastic pins through. The pins will be needed for installation.

4. Pull the three bulbs from the back of the housing.

5. Unscrew the knurled nuts and remove the retaining bracket.

6. Pull the instrument through the panel and detach all the connections.

7. Reverse the procedure for installation.

Speedometer
Removal and Installation
Super 90

1. Follow Steps 1–3 of "Fuel and Wa-

ter Temperature Gauge Removal and Installation—Super 90."

2. Unscrew the cable from the back of the case.

3. Remove the nut and the retaining bracket.

4. Remove the speedometer and detach the wires.

5. Reverse the procedure for installation.

Instrument Cluster
Removal and Installation
100 Series

1. Disconnect the battery ground cable.

2. Remove the screws which hold the padding on top of the instrument panel. Remove the padding.

3. Remove the nuts at the rear of the instrument cluster and remove the cover.

4. Pull the cluster out toward the driver's seat.

5. Pull off the electrical connections and unscrew the speedometer cable.

6. Remove the instrument cluster. It may be further disassembled as necessary.

Fox

1. Disconnect the battery ground cable.

2. Remove the lower instrument panel trim.

3. Disconnect the speedometer cable from the back of the speedometer. Detach the electrical plug at the back of the fuel and temperature gauge.

4. Detach the spring at either end and pull the cluster forward.

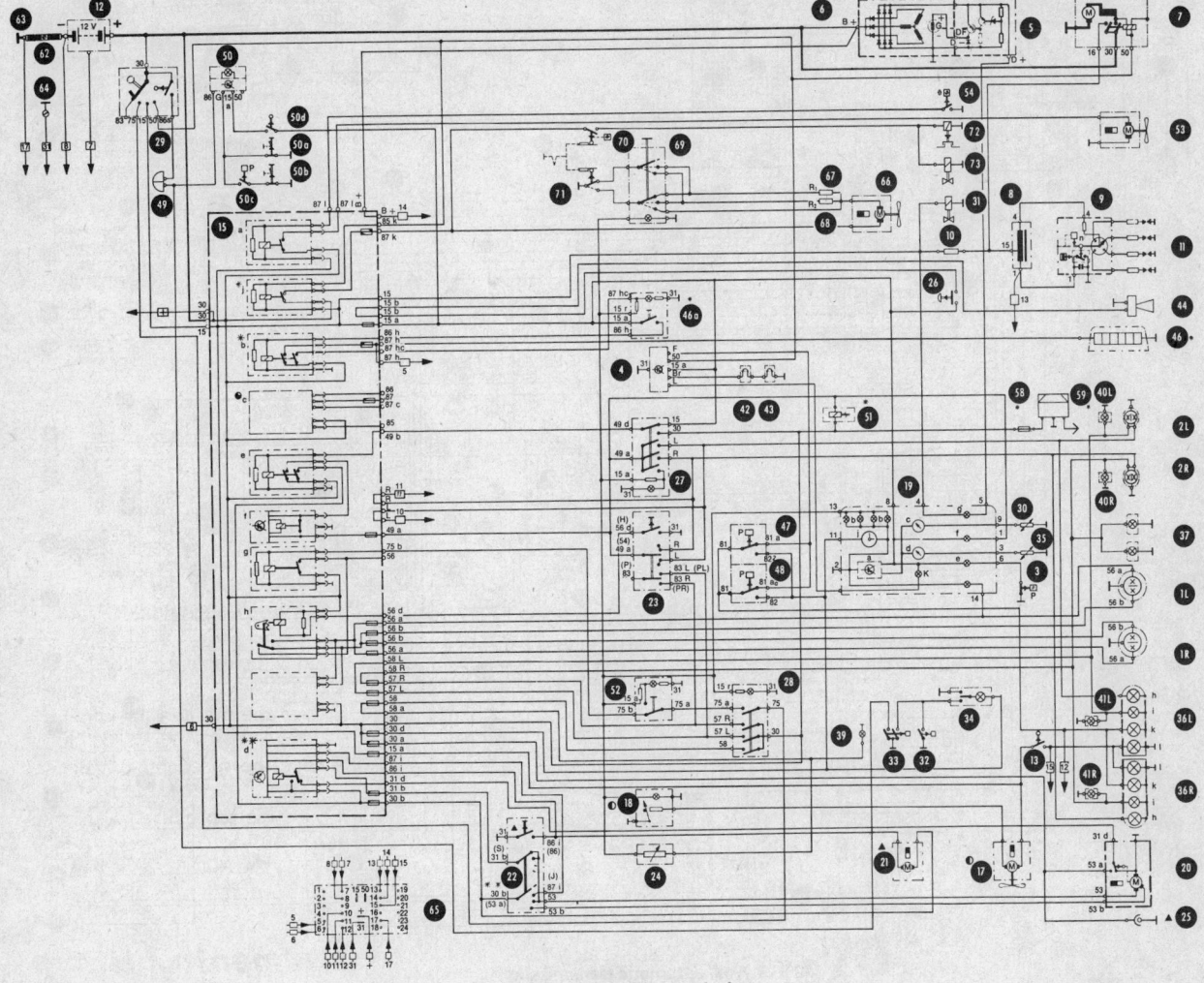

1973 Fox manual transmission

1R.	Headlight, right	
1L.	Headlight, left	
2R.	Turn signal, right	
2L.	Turn signal, left	
3.	Oil pressure switch	
4.	Electronic switch, position 19k	
5.	Governor	
6.	Alternator	
7.	Starter	
8.	Ignition coil	
9.	Distributor with contact breaker	
10.	Resistor, ignition coil	
11.	Spark plugs	
12.	Battery	
13.	Backup light switch	
15.	Relay, central electric control	
15a.	Relay, fan motor (coolant)	
*15b.	Relay, rear window defogger	
15d.	Relay, intermittent wiper/washer	
15e.	Relay, wiper motor, turn signal/hazard warning lights	
15f.	Relay, turn signal	
15g.	Relay, main light	
15h.	Relay, high and low beam	
15j.	Relay, air conditioner	
17.	Blower motor, heater and ventilation	
18.	Resistor, blower motor	
19.	Combination instrument	
19a.	Electronic voltage stabilizer	
19b.	Instrument light	
19c.	Temperature gauge	
19d.	Fuel gauge	
19e.	Oil indicator	
19f.	Turn signal indicator	

19g.	Charge indicator	
19i.	High beam indicator	
19j.	Clock	
19k.	Brake indicator, items 47, 48, 42 and 43	
20.	Wiper motor	
21.	Washer motor	
22.	Wiper/washer switch	
23.	Turn signal/low beam switch	
24.	Resistor, switch and instrument light	
25.	Cigar lighter	
26.	Horn button	
27.	Hazard light (four-way flasher) switch	
28.	Light switch	
29.	Steering/ignition lock	
30.	Temperature transmitter	
31.	Idle cutoff valve	
32.	Door contact switch, right	
33.	Door contact switch, left	
34.	Interior light and switch	
35.	Fuel level transmitter	
36R.	Taillight, right	
36L.	Taillight, left	
36h.	Turn signal	
36i.	Taillight	
36k.	Brake light	
36l.	Backup light	
37.	License plate light	
39.	Glove compartment light	
40R.	Side marker light, front, right	
40L.	Side marker light, front, left	
41R.	Side marker light, rear, right	
41L.	Side marker light, rear, left	
42.	Brake wear control 1	

43.	Brake wear control 2
44.	Horn
*46.	Rear window defogger
*46a.	Switch, rear window defogger
47.	Brake pressure control 1
48.	Brake pressure control 2
49.	Buzzer
50.	Fasten seat belt switch
50a.	Seat belt switch (driver's side)
50b.	Seat belt switch (passenger's side)
50c.	Seat contact switch (passenger's side)
50d.	Transmission switch
*51.	Acoustic turn signal indicator
52.	Parking light switch
53.	Fan motor, coolant
54.	Thermo switch, fan motor
*58.	Fuse, radio
*59.	Radio
60.	Parking brake indicator switch
61.	Parking brake indicator switch
62.	Ground strap, battery/engine block
63.	Ground, engine block
64.	Ground, body
65.	Diagnosis socket
66.	Blower motor, air conditioning
67.	Resistor 1, blower motor
68.	Resistor 2, blower motor
69.	Push button switch, blower motor
70.	Thermo switch, blower motor
71.	Control switch, blower motor
72.	Solenoid, air conditioning
73.	Electric valve, engine speed booster

*optional extra

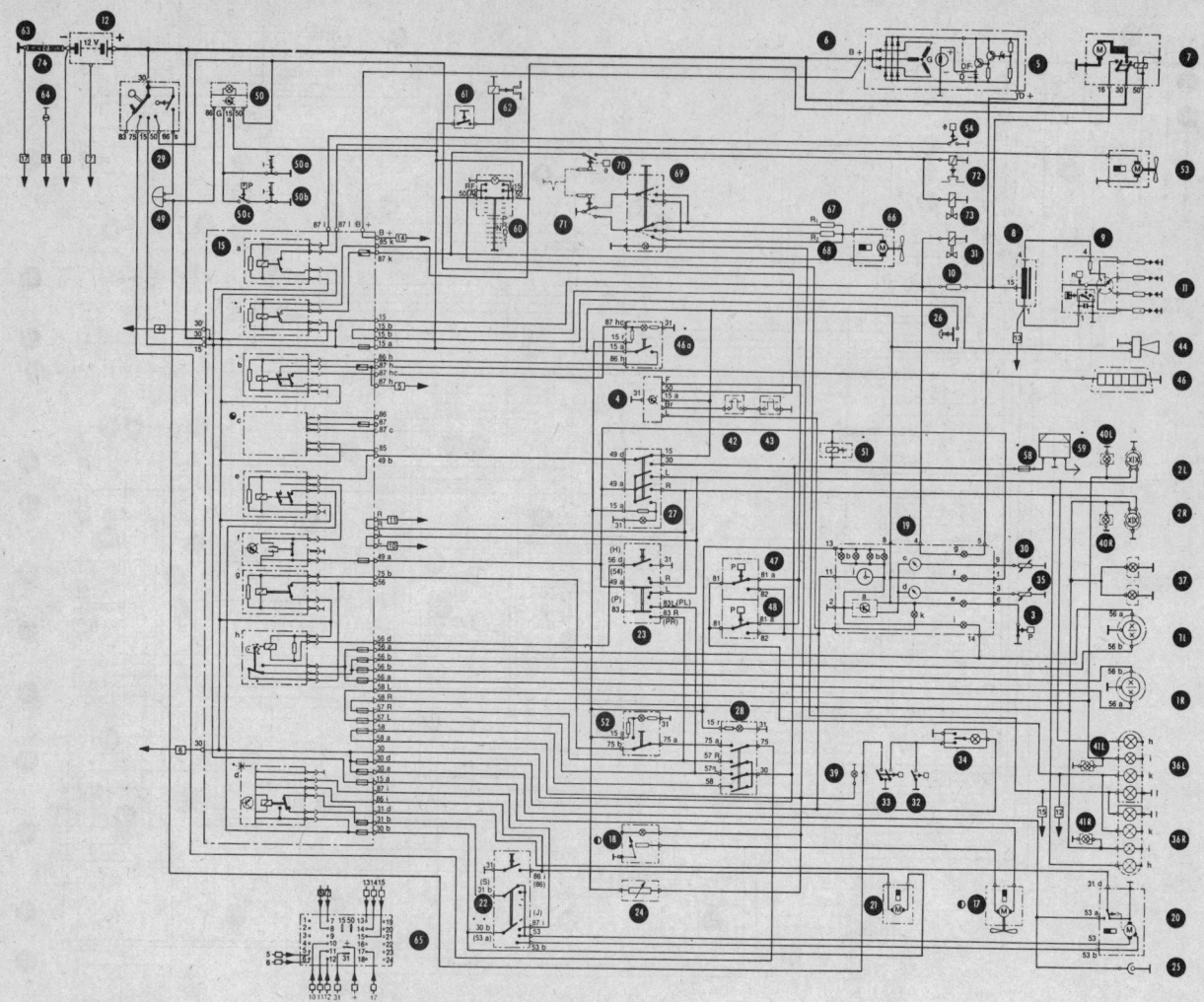

1973 Fox, automatic transmission

1R. Headlight, right	19i. High beam indicator	44. Horn
1L. Headlight, left	19j. Clock	*46. Rear window defogger
2R. Turn signal, right	19k. Brake indicator, item 47, 48, 42	46a. Switch, rear window defogger
2L. Turn signal, left	and 43	47. Brake pressure control 1
3. Oil pressure switch	20. Wiper motor	48. Brake pressure control 2
4. Electronic switch, item 19k	21. Washer motor	49. Buzzer
5. Governor	22. Wiper/washer switch	50. Fasten seat belt switch
6. Alternator	23. Turn signal/low beam switch	50a. Seat belt switch (driver's side)
7. Starter	24. Resistor, switch and instrument light	50b. Seat belt switch (passenger's side)
8. Ignition coil	25. Cigar lighter	50c. Seat contact switch (passenger's side)
9. Distributor with contact breaker	26. Horn button	*51. Acoustic turn signal indicator
10. Resistor, ignition coil	27. Hazard light (four-way flasher) switch	52. Parking light switch
11. Spark plugs	28. Light switch	53. Fan motor, coolant
12. Battery	29. Steering/ignition lock	54. Thermo switch, fan motor
15. Relay, central electric control	30. Temperature transmitter	*58. Fuse, radio
15a. Relay, fan motor (coolant)	31. Solenoid valve	*59. Radio
*15b. Relay, rear window defogger	32. Door contact switch, right	60. Selector lever, automatic transmission
15d. Relay, intermittent wiper/washer	33. Door contact switch, left	61. Kickdown switch, automatic
15e. Relay, wiper motor, turn signal/hazard	34. Interior light and switch	transmission
warning lights	35. Fuel level transmitter	62. Solenoid, automatic tranmission
15f. Relay, turn signal	36R. Taillight, right	63. Ground, engine block
15g. Relay, main light	36L. Taillight, left	64. Ground, body
15h. Relay, high and low beam	36h. Turn signai	65. Diagnosis socket
15j. Relay, air conditioner	36i. Taillight	66. Blower motor, air conditioning
17. Blower motor, heater and ventilation	36k. Brake light	67. Resistor 1, blower motor
18. Resistor, blower motor	36l. Backup light	68. Resistor 2, blower motor
19. Combination instrument	37. License plate light	69. Push button switch, blower motor
19a. Electronic voltage stabilizer	39. Glove compartment light	70. Thermo switch, blower motor
19b. Instrument light	40R. Side marker light, front, right	71. Control switch, blower motor
19c. Temperature gauge	40L. Side marker light, front, left	72. Solenoid, air conditioning
19d. Fuel gauge	41R. Side marker light, rear, right	73. Electric valve, engine speed booster
19e. Oil indicator	41L. Side marker light, rear, left	74. Ground strap, battery/engine Block
19f. Turn signal indicator	42. Brake wear control 1	
19g. Charge indicator	43. Brake wear control 2	*optional extra

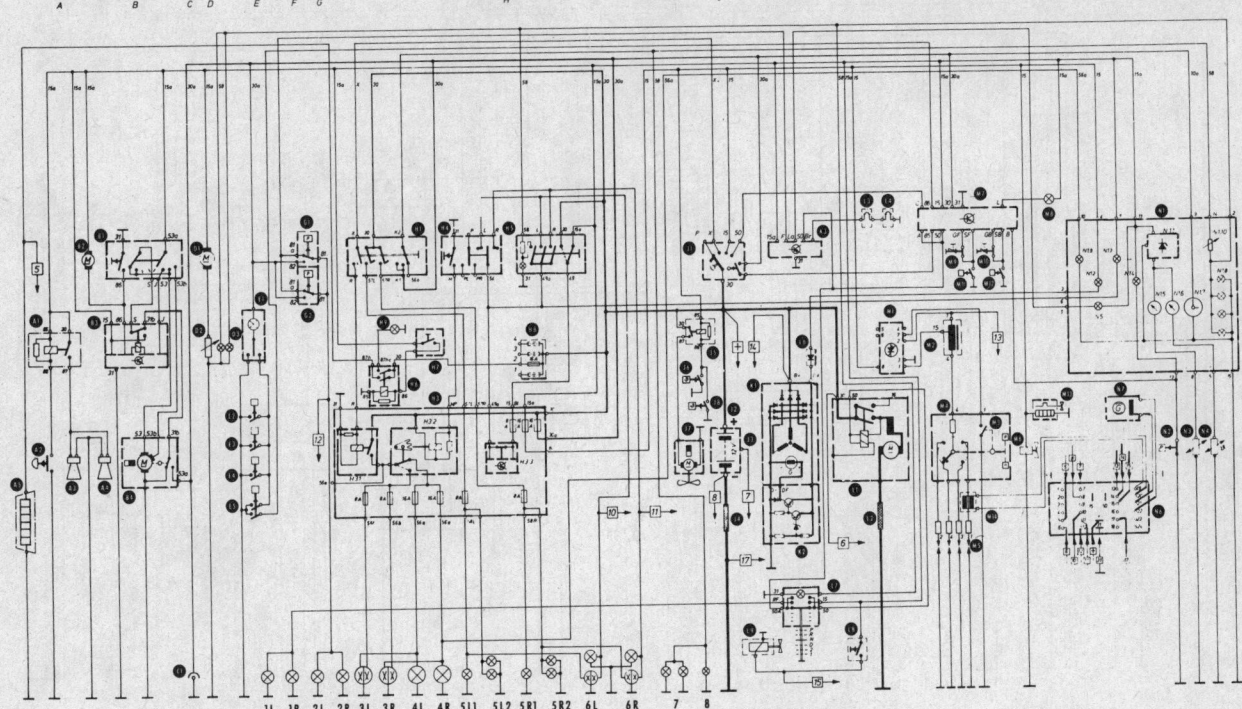

100 LS, automatic transmission, 1974

A1.	Horn relay (strut 1)	J5.	Relay for J7
A2.	Horn button (steering wheel)	J6.	Thermo switch for J7
A3.	Horn, deep tone (engine compartment)	J7.	Fan motor, coolant
A4.	Horn, high tone (engine compartment)	J8.	Thermo switch, brake temperature control
A5.	Rear window defogger	K1.	Alternator (engine)
B1.	Wiper/washer switch	K2.	Regulator (built in alternator)
B2.	Washer motor (engine compartment)	K3.	Electric control unit for G1, G2, L3, L4
B3.	Intermittent wiper/washer relay	L1.	Starter (engine)
B4.	Wiper motor	L2.	Ground (engine/body)
C1.	Socket (cigarette lighter/instrument panel)	L3.	Brake indicator 1 (breakoff element)
D1.	Blower motor (heater + fresh air)	L4.	Brake indicator 2 (breakoff element)
D2.	Brightness control (instrument panel)	L6.	Locking diode (capacitive discharge ignition)
D3.	Light (heater controls)		
E1.	Interior light (roof frame)	L7.	Selector lever (automatic transmission)
E2-5.	Door contact switches	L8.	Kickdown switch (accelerator pedal)
G1.	Brake light switch 1	L9.	Solenoid (automatic transmission)
G2.	Brake light switch 2	M1.	Capacitive discharge ignition control unit
H1.	Main light switch (instrument panel)	M2.	Ignition coil (wheelhouse in engine compartment)
H3.	Combination relay (left of clutch pedal)		
H3.1.	Headlight relay	M3.	Contact breaker points (engine)
H3.2.	Dimmer relay	M4.	Distributor (engine)
H3.3.	Flasher relay	M5.	Spark plugs 1–4 (engine)
H4.	Turn signal switch (steering column)	M6.	Fuel valve (carburetor)
H5.	Hazard warning light switch (instrument panel)	M7.	Seat belt indicator control unit
		M8.	Fasten seat belt light
H6.	Relay, rear window defogger	M9.	Seat belt switch (driver side)
H7.	Switch, relay (H6)	M10.	Seat belt switch (passenger side)
H8.	Auxiliary fusebox	M11.	Seat contact (driver side)
H9.	Rear window defogger indicator light	M12.	Seat contact (passenger side)
1L.	Backup light, left	M13.	Enrichment valve
1R.	Backup light, right	M14.	Trigger impulse transmitter
2L.	Brake light, left	N1.	Combination instrument (instrument panel)
2R.	Brake light, right	N1.1.	Voltage stabilizer control
3L.	Low and high beam, left	N1.2.	Battery charge indicator
3R.	Low and high beam, right	N1.3.	Turn signal indicator
4L.	High beam, left	N1.4.	Oil pressure indicator
4R.	High beam, right	N1.5.	Fuel gauge
5L1.	Side marker light, front, left	N1.6.	Temperature gauge
5L2.	Side marker light, rear, left	N1.7.	Clock
5R1.	Side marker light, front right	N1.8.	Instrument light
5R2.	Overnight and side marker light, rear, right	N1.9.	High beam indicator
6L.	Turn signal and parking light, front, left	N1.10.	Potentiometer
6R.	Turn signal and parking light, front, right	N2.	Oil pressure switch (engine)
7.	License plate light	N3.	Fuel level transmitter (tank)
8.	Glove compartment light	N4.	Temperature transmitter (engine)
J1.	Ignition lock (steering column)	N5.	Brake indicator light for G1, G2, L3 and L4
J2.	Battery (underneath rear seat)	N6.	Diagnosis socket
J3.	Acid indicator (battery)	N7.	Tdc transmitter
J4.	Ground (battery/body)		

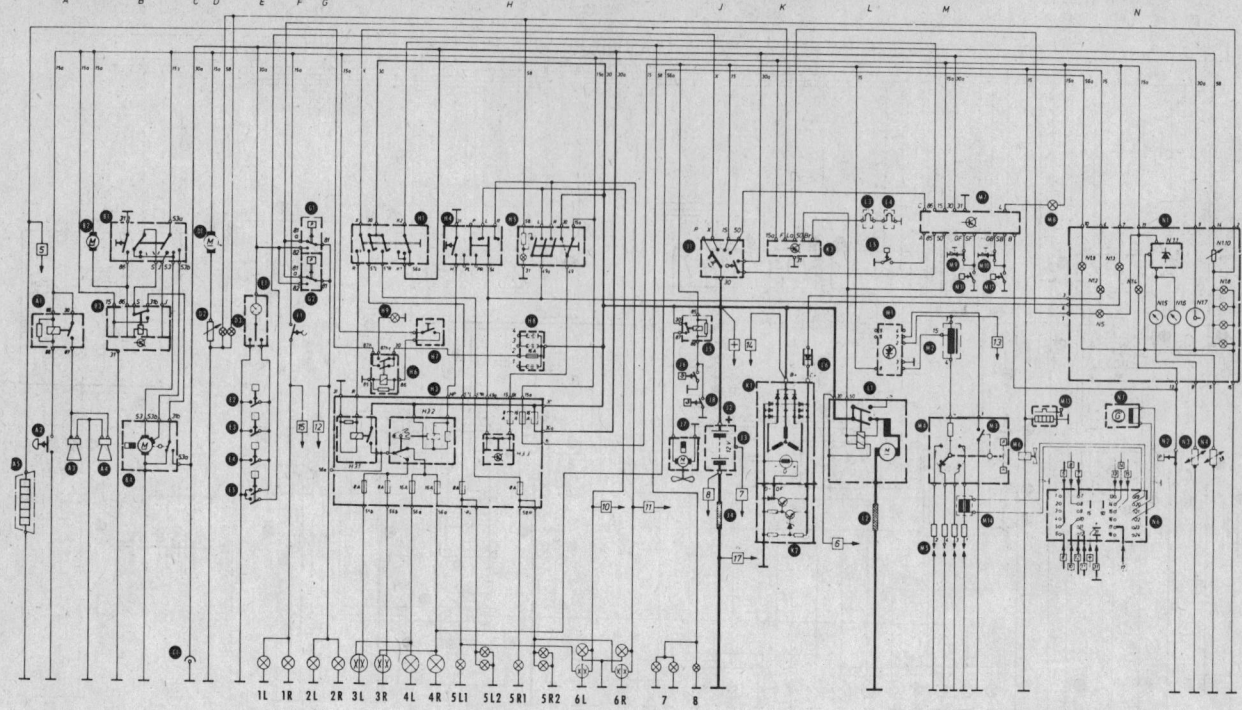

100 LS, manual transmission, 1974

A1. Horn relay (strut 1)	J7. Fan motor, coolant	N6. Diagnosis socket
A2. Horn button (steering wheel)	J8. Thermo switch, brake temperature control	N7. Tdc transmitter
A3. Horn, deep tone (engine compartment)	K1. Alternator (engine)	
A4. Horn, high tone (engine compartment)	K2. Regulator (alternator)	
A5. Rear window defogger	K3. Electric control unit for G1, G2, L3, L4	
B1. Wiper/washer switch	L1. Starter (engine)	
B2. Washer motor (engine compartment)	L2. Ground (engine/body)	
B3. Intermittent wiper/washer relay	L3. Brake indicator 1 (breakoff element)	
B4. Wiper motor	L4. Brake indicator 2 (breakoff element)	
C1. Socket (cigarette lighter/instrument panel)	L5. Parking brake switch	
D1. Blower motor (heater + fresh air)	L6. Locking diode (capacitive discharge ignition)	
D2. Brightness control (instrument panel)	M1. Capacitive discharge ignition control unit	
D3. Light (heater controls)	M2. Ignition coil (wheelhouse/engine compartment)	
E1. Interior light (roof frame)	M3. Contact breaker points (engine)	
E2-5. Door contact switches	M4. Distributor (engine)	
F1. Backup light switch (transmission)	M5. Spark plugs 1–4 (engine)	
G1. Brake light switch 1	M6. Fuel valve (carburetor)	
G2. Brake light switch 2	M7. Seat belt indicator control unit	
H1. Main light switch (instrument panel)	M8. Fasten seat belt light	
H3. Combination relay (left of clutch pedal)	M9. Seat belt switch (driver side)	
H3.1. Headlight relay	M10. Seat belt switch (passenger side)	
H3.2. Dimmer relay	M11. Seat contact (driver side)	
H3.3. Flasher relay	M12. Seat contact (passenger side)	
H4. Turn signal switch (steering column)	M13. Enrichment valve	
H5. Hazard warning light switch (instrument panel)	M14. Trigger impulse transmitter	
H6. Relay, rear window defogger	N1. Combination instrument (instrument panel)	
H7. Switch, relay (H6)	N1.1. Voltage stabilizer control	
H8. Auxiliary fusebox	N1.2. Battery charge indicator	
H9. Rear window defogger indicator light	N1.3. Turn signal indicator	
1L. Backup light, left	N1.4. Oil pressure indicator	
1R. Backup light, right	N1.5. Fuel gauge	
2L. Brake light, left	N1.6. Temperature gauge	
2R. Brake light, right	N1.7. Clock	
3L. Low and high beam, left	N1.8. Instrument light	
3R. Low and high beam, right	N1.9. High beam indicator	
4L. High beam, left	N1.10 Potentiometer	
4R. High beam, right	N2. Oil pressure switch (engine)	
5L1. Side marker light, front, left	N3. Fuel level transmitter (tank)	
5L2. Side marker light, rear, right	N4. Temperature transmitter (engine)	
6L. Turn signal and parking light, front, left	N5. Brake indicator light for G1, G2, L3 and L4	
6R. Turn signal and parking light, front, right		
7. License plate light		
8. Glove compartment light	**NOTE:** From chassis No. 8462042542 the fuel pump wiring has been changed as follows:	
J1. Ignition lock (steering column)		
J2. Battery (underneath rear seat)	1. Fuel pump relay with 5 terminals	
J3. Acid indicator (battery)	2. Air flow sensor has no terminals or terminal is vacant	
J4. Ground (battery/body)	3. No wiring between terminal 50 on starter and terminal 50 on fuel pump relay	
J5. Relay for J7	4. A blue wire runs from terminal 1 on ignition coil to fuse box terminal A3	
J6. Thermo switch for J7		

SPECIFICATIONS

INTRODUCTION

Capri, imported by Lincoln-Mercury, is a product of Ford of Europe; it has been imported to the United States since 1970. In 1970 the car was offered with a 1600 cc engine and manual transmission. As popularity grew, the option list was extended to include a 2000 cc engine and automatic transmission. In 1972, in addition to the 1600 and 2000 cc engines, a 2600 cc V6 engine was made available.

The 1600 cc engine was dropped for 1973, and the V6 enlarged to 2800 cc in 1974. In 1975, a 2300 cc OHC engine was introduced, replacing the 2000 cc.

MODEL IDENTIFICATION

1972

1973

1974

Capri II

SERIAL NUMBER IDENTIFICATION

Engine

NOTE: *Engine type can be determined by using the Vehicle Identification Plate.*

Engine Identification

No. of Cyl.	Displace. (cc)	Type	Engine Model Code
4	1600	OHV	L1/L4
4	2000	OHC	NB, NA, N
4	2300	OHC	YA
6	2600	OHV	UX
6	2800	OHV	PX

Vehicle Identification Plate

The vehicle identification plate is located on the right-side front fender apron in the engine compartment. This plate gives details of the engine, axle, body, and transmission. The vehicle identification number is also visible through the driver's side of the windshield.

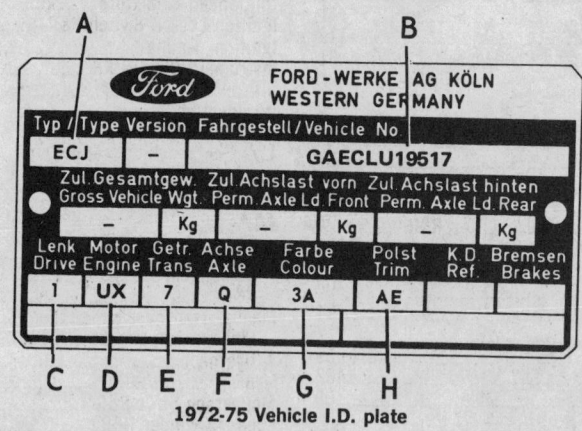

1972-75 Vehicle I.D. plate

A) Body Type
  ECJ—Tudor Coupe
B) Vehicle Number
  consists of eleven symbols
  G A E C K U 78175

  1) G—assembled in Germany
  2) A—denotes Cologne Plant
    B—denotes Genk Plant
  3) model type (EC-Capri)
  4) year and month of manufacture, first letter—year, second—month: L-1971, M-1972, K-1973, P-1974
  5) serial number
C) Drive code
  1—left hand drive
D) Engine code
  L1. L4—1600 cc
  NB, NA, N—2000 cc
  UX—2600 cc
  P—2800 cc

E) Transmission code
  5, B—manual shift
  7, C—automatic
F) Rear Axle Code
  V, C—3.89:1
  Q, S—3.44:1
  R—3.22:1
G) Paint code
  1—Sapphire Metallic
  3—Silver Fox Metallic
  6—Evergreen Metallic
  7—Tawny Metallic
  J—Sunset
  T—Yellow
  B—Ermine White
  A—Vinyl Roof Black
H) Trim code
  AE—Black
  FE—Marquis Blue
  JE—Tan
  KE—Parchment

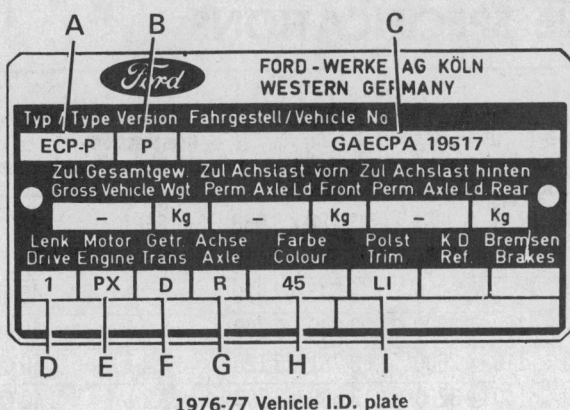

1976-77 Vehicle I.D. plate

A. Body Type
ECP—three door hatchback

B. Version
P—decor option
D—standard
T—Ghia

C. Vehicle number
GAECPA19517
G—built in Germany
A—Cologne assembly plant
EC—model type
PA—assembly code
    first letter—year; second letter—month
Sequence number—a five digit code ranging from 00001-99999

D. Drive code
l—left hand drive

E. Engine code
YA-2300
PX-2800

F. Transmission code
B—4sp.
D—automatic

G. Rear axle code
S—3.44:1
R—3.22:1
L—3.09:1

H. Paint code
B5—White 691
T5—Yellow 779
J5—Orange 913
05—Dk. red 979
35—Silver met. 888
45—Bronze met. 884B
15—Med. blue met. 859
55—Lt. green met. 924

I. Trim code
AA—black vinyl
LA—saddle vinyl
KA—lt. tan vinyl
AI—black cloth
LI—saddle cloth
KI—lt. tan cloth

TUNE-UP SPECIFICATIONS

Year	Engine Displacement (cc)	SPARK PLUGS Type	Gap (in.)	DISTRIBUTOR Point Dwell (deg)	Point Gap (in.)	IGNITION TIMING (deg)▲ MT	AT	Intake Valve Opens (deg)	Fuel Pump Pressure (psi)	Compression Press. (psi)	IDLE SPEED (rpm) MT	AT	Valve Clearance (in.) In	Ex
1972	1600	AGR-22	0.030	36-40	0.025	12B	—	17B	3½-4½	④	900/500⑤	—	0.010	0.017
1972	2000	BF-32D	0.034	36-40	0.025	6B	10B⑪	24B	3½-4½	④	750/500⑦	650/500⑦	0.008③	0.010③
1973	2000	BF-42	0.030	37-41	0.025	⑫	⑫	24B	3½-4½	④	⑫	⑫	⑫	⑫
1974-75	2000	AGR-32	0.034	37-41	0.025	6B	10B	24B	3½-4½	④	750	650	⑫	⑫
1972	2600	AGR-32	0.035	37-40	0.025	12B	12B	20B	3½-4½	④	750	650	0.014⑥	0.016⑥
1973	2600	AGR-32	0.025	37-41	0.025	⑫	⑫	20B	3½-4½	④	⑫	⑫	0.014⑥	0.016⑥
1974-75	2800	AGR-42	0.034	37-41	0.025	⑫	⑫	20B	3½-4½	④	⑫	⑫	0.014⑥	0.016⑥
Capri II	2300	⑫	⑫	Electronic		⑫	⑫	22	3½-4½	④	⑫	⑫	—	—
Capri II	2800	⑫	⑫	Electronic		⑫	⑫	20	3½-4½	④	⑫	⑫	0.014⑥	0.016⑥

▲ With the vacuum lines disconnected and plugged
B Before top dead center
① At 650 rpm in Drive (AT); 750 rpm in Neutral (MT)
② At 900 rpm
③ Between the cam and follower, cold
④ Lowest 75 per cent of the highest
⑤ Higher speed with solenoid energized
⑥ Cold
⑦ Air conditioner on, if so equipped

⑧ California Automatic, 9°
⑨ 12 Degrees Before With 28mm Carburetor
⑩ 6 Degrees Before With 25 mm Carburetor
⑪ 9B in California
⑫ See engine compartment sticker
MT Manual Transmission
AT Automatic Transmission
— Not Applicable

NOTE: The underhood specifications sticker often reflects tune-up specification changes made in production. Sticker figures must be used if they disagree with those in this chart.

GENERAL ENGINE SPECIFICATIONS

Year	Engine Displacement Cu. In. (cc)	Carburetor Type	Horsepower (@ rpm)	Torque @ rpm (ft lbs)	Bore x Stroke (in.)	Compression Ratio	Oil Pressure @ rpm (psi)
1972	97.6 (1600)	Motorcraft 1V	71 @ 5000	91 @ 3000	3.188 x 3.056	8.0:1	35 @ 1000
1972-75	122 (1600)	Motorcraft 2V	100 @ 5600	120 @ 3600	3.575 x 3.029	8.2:1	35 @ 1500
1972-73	158.6 (2600)	Motorcraft 2V	107 @ 5700	N.A.	3.545 x 2.630	8.2:1	40 @ 1500
1974-75	170 (2800)	Motorcraft 2V	105 @ 4600	140 @ 3200	3.660 x 2.700	8.2:1	40 @ 1500
Capri II	140 (2300)	Motorcraft 2V	88 @ 5000	116 @ 2600	3.781 x 3.126	8.4:1	50 @ 2000
Capri II	170 (2800)	Motorcraft 2V	105 @ 4600	140 @ 3200	3.660 x 2.700	8.2:1	40 @ 1500

N.A. Not Available

FIRING ORDER

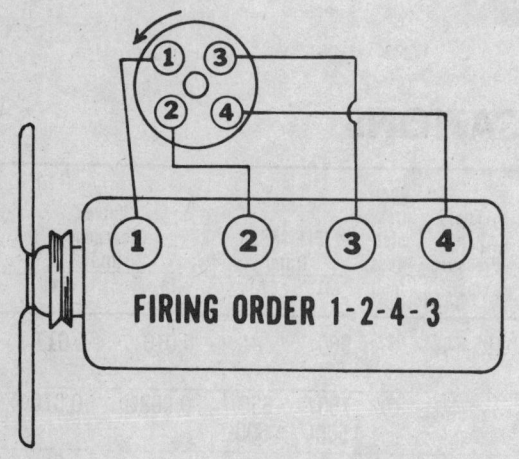

1600 cc engine

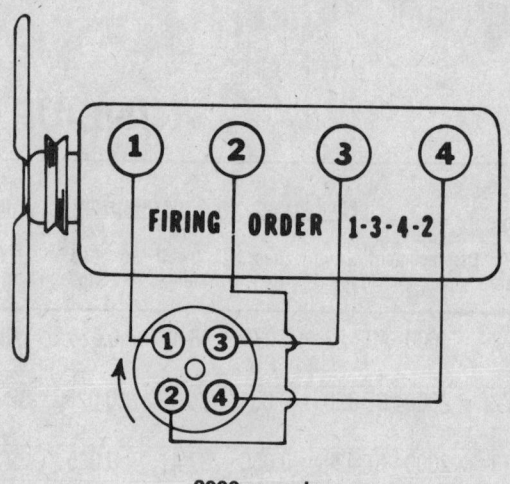

2000 cc engine

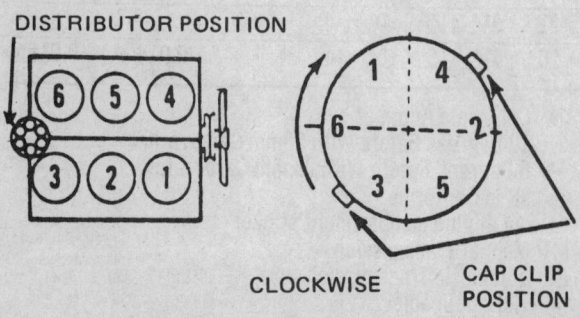

FIRING ORDER-1-4-2-5-3-6

V6 engine

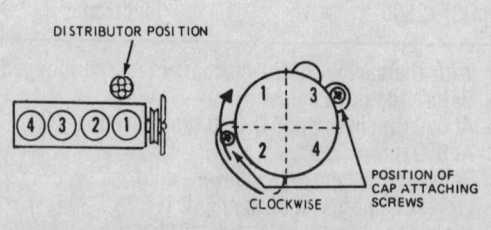

2300 cc engine

CAPACITIES

Model		ENGINE CRANKCASE REFILL after draining (qt)		TRANSMISSION REFILL after draining (pt)			Differential (pt)	Fuel Tank (gal)	Cooling System (qt)
		With filter	Without filter	Manual 4 speed	Automatic (total cap.)				
					C3, C4	Borg Warner			
1972	1600	3.5	3.2	2.8	—	—	5.8	12	6.8
1972	2000	4	3.5	2.8	14.3	13.5	5.8	12	8.1
1973-75	2000	4	3.5	2.8	12.5	13.5	2.3	12	8.1
1972	2600	4.7	4.2	2.8	14.4	13.5	5.8	12	8.2
1973	2600	4.7	4.2	2.8	14.4	13.5	2.3	12	10.8
1974-75	2800	4.5	4	2.8	14.4	13.5	2.3	12	10.8
Capri II	2300	5	4	2.8	16	—	2.3	12	7.6
Capri II	2800	5	4.5	2.8	16	—	2.3	12	8.5

— Not Applicable

CRANKSHAFT AND CONNECTING ROD SPECIFICATIONS

All measurements are given in inches

Year	Engine Displacement (cu in.)	CRANKSHAFT				CONNECTING ROD		
		Main Brg Journal Dia	Main Brg Oil Clearance	Shaft End-Play	Thrust on No.	Journal Diameter	Oil Clearance	Side Clearance
1972	97.6 (1600)	2.1253-2.1257① 2.1257-2.1261②	0.0005-0.0016	0.003-0.011	3	1.9368-1.9376	0.0004-0.0024	0.004-0.010
1972-75	122 (2000)	2.2432-2.2440	0.0006-0.0016	0.003-0.011	3	2.0464-2.0472	0.0006-0.0026	0.004-0.011
1972-73	158.6 (2600)	2.244① 2.243②	0.0005-0.002	0.004-0.008	3	2.126① 2.125②	0.0005-0.002	0.004-0.011
1974-75	170 (2800)	2.2437-2.2441① 2.2433-2.2437②	0.0006-0.0019	0.004-0.008	3	2.1256-2.1260 ① 2.1252-2.1256 ②	0.0006-.0021	0.004-0.011
Capri II	140 (2300)	2.3982-2.3990	0.0008-0.0026	0.004-0.008	3	2.0465-2.0472	0.0008-0.0015	0.004-0.011
Capri II	170 (2800)	2.433-2.441	0.0006-0.0019	0.004-0.008	3	2.1252-2.1260 ②	0.0006-0.0021	0.004-0.011

① Red   ② Blue   — Not Specified

VALVE SPECIFICATIONS

Year	Engine Displacement Cu. In. (cc)	Seat Angle (deg)	Face Angle (deg)	Spring Test Pressure (lbs @ in.)	Spring Installed Height (in.)	STEM TO GUIDE CLEARANCE (in.)		STEM DIAMETER (in.)	
						Intake	Exhaust	Intake	Exhaust
1972	97.6 (1600)	44	45	48-53 @ 1.263	1.263	0.0008-0.0027	0.0017-0.0036	0.3098-0.3105	0.3098-0.3096
1972-75	122 (2000)	44	45	64-73 @ 1.417	1.417	0.0008-0.0025	0.0018-0.0035	0.3159-0.3167	0.3149-0.3156
1972-73	158.6 (2600)	45	N.A.	N.A.	N.A.	0.002	0.003	0.316	0.315
1974-75	170 (2800)	44.5	45.5	N.A.	N.A.	0.0015-0.0018	0.0025-0.0027	0.3159-0.3166	0.3149-0.3157
Capri II	140 (2300)	45	44	75 @ 1.56	1.563	0.0010-0.0027	0.0015-0.0032	0.3420	0.3415
Capri II	170 (2800)	45	44	66.5 @ 1.59	1.594	0.0008-0.0025	0.0018-0.0035	0.3159-0.3166	0.3149-0.3157

① Cold   N.A. Not Available

PISTON AND RING SPECIFICATIONS
All measurements in inches

Year	Engine Displacement Cu In. (cc)	Piston Clearance	RING GAP			RING SIDE CLEARANCE		
			Top Compression	Bottom Compression	Oil Control	Top Compression	Bottom Compression	Oil Control
1972	97.6 (1600)	0.0016-0.0022	0.009-0.014	0.009-0.014	0.009-0.014	0.0016-0.0036	0.0016-0.0036	0.0018-0.0038
1972-75	122 (2000)	0.001-0.002	0.015-0.023	0.015-0.023	0.016-0.055	0.0019-0.0038	0.0019-0.0038	SNUG
1972-73	158.6 (2600)	0.001-0.003	0.015-0.023	0.015-0.023	0.015-0.055	0.0020-0.0033	0.0020-0.0033	SNUG
1974-75	170 (2800)	0.001-0.003	0.015-0.023	0.015-0.023	0.015-0.055	0.0020-0.0033	0.0020-0.0033	SNUG
Capri II	140 (2300)	0.001-0.002	0.010-0.020	0.010-0.020	0.015-0.055	0.0020-0.0040	0.0020-0.0040	SNUG
Capri II	170 (2800)	0.0011-0.0019	0.015-0.023	0.015-0.023	0.015-0.055	0.0020-0.0033	0.0020-0.0033	SNUG

TORQUE SPECIFICATIONS
All readings in ft lbs

Year	Engine Displacement Cu In.	Cylinder Head Bolts	Rod Bearing Bolts	Main Bearing Bolts	Crankshaft Bolt	Flywheel-to-Crankshaft Bolts	MANIFOLDS	
							Intake	Exhaust
1972	97.6 (1600)	65-70	30-35	65-70	24-28	50-55	12-15	15-18
1970-75	122 (2000)	65-80	29-34	65-75	39-43	47-51	12-15	12-15
1972-73	158.6 (2600)	65-80	22-26	65-75	32-36	45-50	15-18	15-18
1974-75	170 (2800)	65-80	21-25	65-75	31-36	47-52	15-18	15-18
Capri II	140 (2300)	80-90	30-36	80-90	80-114	54-64	14-21	16-23
Capri II	170 (2800)	65-80	21-25	65-75	92-103	47-52	15-18①	16-23

① Stud: 10-12

Torque Sequences

Cylinder Head

1600 cc engine

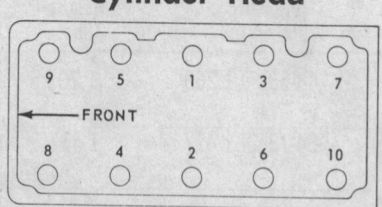

2000 and 2300 cc engines

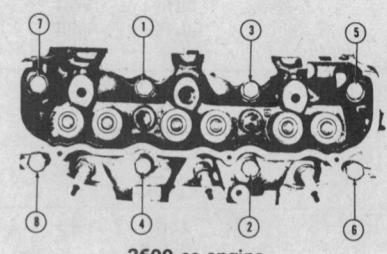

2600 cc engine

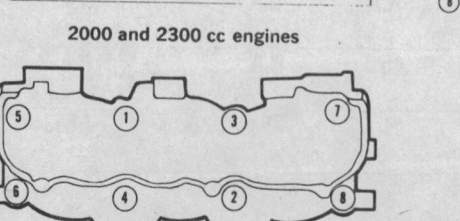

2800 cc engine

Intake Manifold

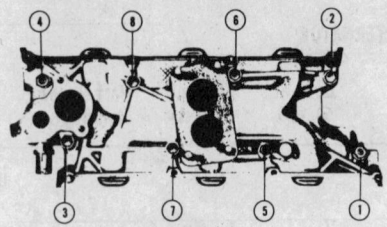

2000 cc engine

2600 cc engine

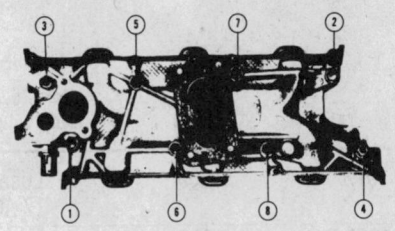

2800 cc engine

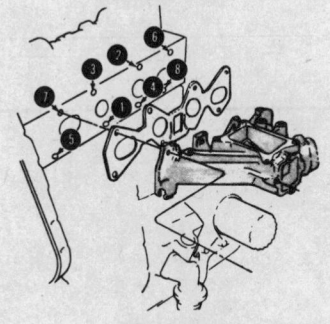

2300 cc engine

Exhaust Manifold

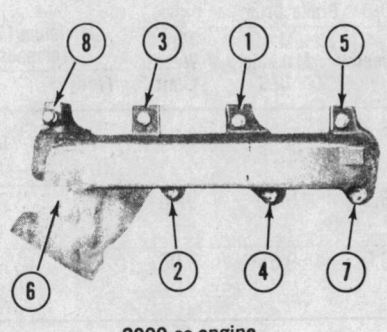

2000 cc engine

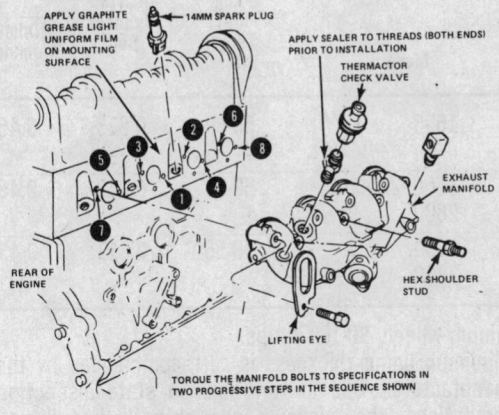

APPLY GRAPHITE GREASE LIGHT UNIFORM FILM ON MOUNTING SURFACE

14MM SPARK PLUG

APPLY SEALER TO THREADS (BOTH ENDS) PRIOR TO INSTALLATION

THERMACTOR CHECK VALVE

EXHAUST MANIFOLD

HEX SHOULDER STUD

LIFTING EYE

REAR OF ENGINE

TORQUE THE MANIFOLD BOLTS TO SPECIFICATIONS IN TWO PROGRESSIVE STEPS IN THE SEQUENCE SHOWN

2300 cc engine

BATTERY AND STARTER SPECIFICATIONS

All cars use 12 volt, negative ground electrical systems

Year	Model	Battery Amp Hour Capacity	Starter						Brush Spring Tension (oz)	Min. Brush Length (in.)
			Lock Test			No Load Test				
			Amps	Volts	Torque (ft/lbs)	Amps	Volts	RPM		
1972	97.6 (1600)	55	— Not Recommended —			N.A.	N.A.	N.A.	28 (Lucas) 42 (Bosch)	0.375
1972-77	4 cyl.	55① 66②	— Not Recommended —			54	N.A.	N.A.	42	0.375
1972-73	158.6 (2600)	66	— Not Recommended —			54	N.A.	N.A.	42	0.375
1974-77	170 (2800)	66	— Not Recommended —			54	N.A.	N.A.	42	0.375

① Manual transmission   ② Automatic transmission

ALTERNATOR AND REGULATOR SPECIFICATIONS

| | | ALTERNATOR | | | REGULATOR | | | | | | |
| | | | | | | Field Relay | | | Regulator | | |
Year	Model	Part No. or Manufacturer	Field Current @ 12 v	Output (amps)	Part No. or Manufacturer	Air Gap (in.)	Point Gap (in.)	Volts to Close	Air Gap (in.)	Point Gap (in.)	Volts @ 75°
1972	1600	Lucas 17 ACR	—	35	—	Integral with alternator					14.1-14.5
1972-73	1600, 2000, 2600	Bosch K-1	—	35	—	Not adjustable					14.1-14.4
1974-77	2000, 2300 2800	Bosch K-1	—	35①	—	Not adjustable					13.7-14.4

① 55 Amps w/AC

BRAKE SPECIFICATIONS
All measurements given are (in.) unless noted

| Year | Model | Lug Nut Torque (ft/lb) | Master Cylinder Bore | Brake Disc | | Brake Drum | | | Minimum Lining Thickness | |
				Minimum Thickness	Maximum Run-Out	Diameter	Max. Machine O/S	Max. Wear Limit	Front	Rear
1972	1600	50-55	0.813	0.45	0.0035	9.0	9.05	9.06	⅛	1/32 above rivets
1972-73	1600, 2000, 2600	50-55	0.813	0.45	0.0035	9.0	9.05	9.06	⅛	1/32 above rivets
1974-77	2000, 2800	50-55①	0.813	0.45	0.0035	9.0	9.05	9.06	⅛	1/32 above rivets

① Aluminum wheels 90-100 ft. lbs.
NOTE: Minimum lining thickness is as recommended by the manufacturer. Due to variations in state inspection regulations, the minimum allowable thickness may be different than recommended by the manufacturer.

WHEEL ALIGNMENT

Year	Caster (deg)	Camber (deg)	Toe-In (in)	King Pin Inclination (deg)
1972	½N to 1½P	¼N to ¾N	¼ to ⅜	7½ to 8½
1973	¾P to 1¾P	½N to ½P	¼ to ⅜	7½ to 8½
1974-75	½P to 1½P	½N to ½P	¼ to ⅜	7½ to 8½
1976-77	1P to 2¼ P	¾P to 2¼P	¼ to ⅜	7½ to 8½

N Negative
P Positive

TUNE-UP PROCEDURES

Spark Plugs

Before removing the spark plugs, clean the surrounding area. Grasp the plug wire by the rubber boot at the end of the wire and pull the wire from the plug. When removing wires, be careful not to confuse which wire goes on which plug. A piece of tape should be placed on the wire to identify the cylinder number. Loosen and remove each spark plug with a spark plug socket. Be especially careful not to crack the porcelain insulator. If a plug is tight, use a breaker bar on the socket to remove the spark plug. Once the spark plugs are removed, be careful not to let any dirt fall into the cylinders. Examine the plugs. If you decide to reuse the spark plugs, clean them in the following manner.

1. File the center electrode flat.
2. Inspect the porcelain insulator for cracks.
3. Clean all deposits on the base of the plug with a wire brush.

Before installing the spark plugs, adjust the plug gap according to the "Tune-Up Specifications Chart" with a wire feeler gauge. When installing new spark plugs, the gap must also be checked and set. Hand-tighten each of the plugs and then torque them to 15 ft lbs.

Breaker Points and Condenser

The point set and condenser should be replaced as a unit. Whenever the points are adjusted, the ignition timing should be checked since adjusting the points will change the timing.

Release the clips which secure the distributor cap. Remove the cap and the rotor. Inspect the inside of the distributor cap for cracks or excessive wear and also check the rotor for burning or excessive wear.

If the breaker points are not pitted or burned, they may be cleaned rather than replaced. If you decide to clean them, proceed in the following manner.

1. Pry open the points with a screwdriver.
2. Place a point file between the contacts.
3. Release the points (Let the points exert their own pressure; don't apply any external pressure.)
4. File the contacts.
5. Adjust the points. (See "Breaker Point Adjustment.")

Removal and Installation

When replacing the points and condenser, special care should be taken to

Electronic ignition distributor

prevent dropping any of the attaching screws into the distributor or on the ground. To remove the points and condenser follow this procedure:

1. Remove the screws which retain the points and condenser.
2. Remove the condenser and distributor wires.
3. Remove the points and condenser.
4. Apply a small amount of heat-resistant white grease to the distributor cam.
5. Replace the points and condenser.
6. Replace the screws, being careful not to strip the threads.
7. Replace the condenser and distributor wires.
8. Adjust the points.

Breaker Point Adjustment

Using a socket and breaker bar, turn the bolt on the crankshaft pulley to rotate the engine until the rubbing block of the points is on a high point of the distributor cam.

CAUTION: *The 2000 cc engine must only be rotated clockwise.* Insert the correct size feeler gauge between the contacts and adjust them to the proper gap. (See "Tune-Up Specifications Chart.")

Slightly loosen the attaching screws, insert a screwdriver in the notch on the breaker plate, and twist the screwdriver to open or close the points to the proper gap. The feeler gauge should have a slight drag on it at the proper gap. Retighten the attaching screws. Replace the rotor, aligning the tab inside the rotor with the notch on the distributor shaft. Replace the distributor cap and snap the retaining clips into place.

Dwell Angle

The dwell angle is the angle that the distributor cam rotates while the breaker points are closed. This is a more precise adjustment than point gap. To adjust the dwell angle, remove the distributor cap and connect a dwell meter between the primary lead (the distributor wire terminal on the coil) and ground. Crank the engine with the key and observe the dwell angle on the meter. You can also

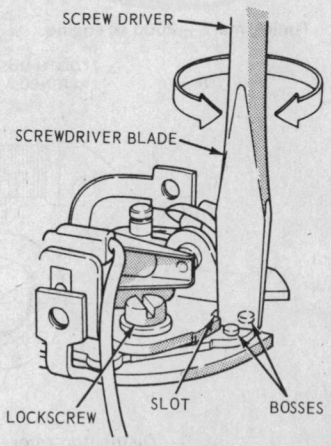

Adjusting breaker points

check the dwell with the engine running. Refer to the "Tune-up Specifications Chart" for the proper dwell angle. If it is necessary to adjust the angle, adjust it by opening or closing the point gap as previously described. Remove the dwell meter and replace the distributor cap.

Spark Plug Wires

Wipe the spark plug wires clean and inspect them for cracks, breaks, or frayed insulation. Replace any damaged wires. If you replace any wires, make sure you replace them with the same type (resistor or non-resistor type).

Ignition Timing

Set the dwell angle before setting the timing. Disconnect and plug the vacuum lines. Locate the timing mark on the pulley and the pointer on the engine block. Clean the pointer and the timing mark. Mark the correct timing position on the pulley with a piece of chalk or paint. (See the "Tune-up Specifications Chart.") Install a timing light and set the idle at 600 rpm. Loosen the distributor locknut at the base of the distributor. Adjust the ignition timing to the proper specifications by turning the distributor. (Align the pointer and the mark.) On the 1600 cc engine, turn the distributor counterclockwise to advance the spark. On the

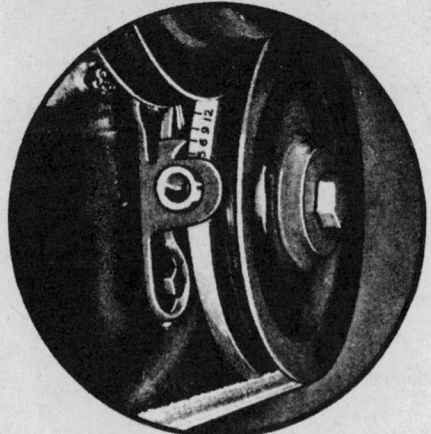

Timing mark—2000 cc engine

Timing mark—1600 cc engine

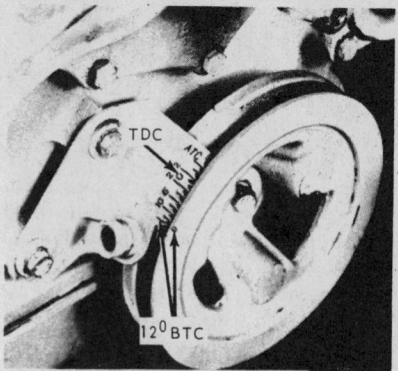

Timing mark—V6 engine

Adjusting valve clearance—2000 cc engine

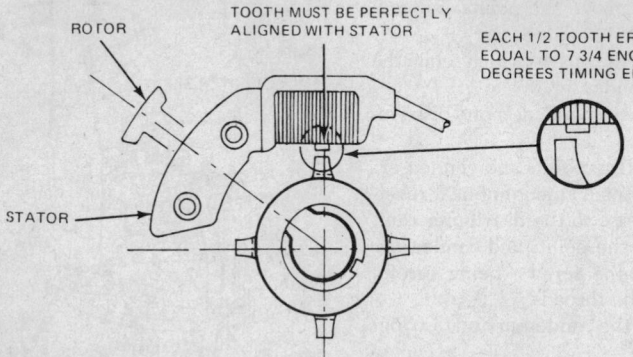

Distributor rotor position for static timing

2000, 2300 and V6 engines, turn the distributor clockwise to advance timing. Make sure that the locknut is retightened and the vacuum lines are reconnected.

Breakerless Ignition Systems

In relation to tune-ups, breakerless systems require very little maintenance. There are no points or condenser to replace, and no adjustments to be made other than timing. An occasional check of the rotor and cap contacts for excessive burning and pitting should be performed.

Ignition timing can be performed in the same manner as with older point type systems.

Valve Lash Adjustment

1600 Engine

Allow the engine to run until operating temperature is reached. Stop the engine and remove the rocker arm cover. Using a socket and a breaker bar, rotate the engine to open the valves by turning the nut on the crankshaft pulley. Turn the engine until the valves listed in the first column are fully open, then adjust the valves in the second column.

1600 Valve Adjustment

Using a feeler gauge and a 7/16 in. box

1600 Valve Adjustment

Valve Open	Valves to adjust (intake)	Valves to adjust (exhaust)
1	3	8
2	7	5
3	6	1
5	2	4

wrench, insert the feeler gauge between the valve stem and rocker arm, and turn the adjustment screw in or out to adjust the clearance. There should be a slight drag on the feeler gauge at the proper clearance. Refer to the "Tune-up Specifications Chart" for the proper valve lash adjustment of all engines. Clean all material from the cylinder head and rocker arm cover. Install a new gasket and install the rocker arm cover. Run the engine and check for oil leaks.

2000 cc Engine

The valves should be set when the engine is cold. If the engine has been running, allow it to cool. Remove the valve cover. Using a socket and a breaker bar, rotate the engine by turning the bolt on the crankshaft pulley clockwise. **CAUTION:** *Do not turn the pulley counterclockwise; the timing belt may slip and alter the valve timing.* Rotate the engine

until the high point of the number cam lobe is pointing straight down. Remove the number 6 and 7 rocker arm retaining springs by inserting a screwdriver under the spring at the rocker arm and snapping the spring up and off. Loosen the locknut with a ¾ in. wrench. Adjust the clearance between the cam lobe and the rocker arm by inserting the feeler gauge. Turn the adjustment screw in or out, with a 15 mm wrench, to obtain the proper clearance. Retighten the locknuts when the adjustment is complete. Repeat the procedure for the rest of the valves, adjusting each with its cam lobe pointing straight down. Adjust the valves in the following order:

2000 Valve Adjustment

Snap the retaining spring back into place. Install a new valve cover gasket and install the valve cover. Run the engine and check for oil leaks.

2000 and 2300 Valve Adjustment

Valve Open	Valves to Adjust to 0.008 (intake)	Valve to Adjust to 0.010 (exhaust)
1	6	7
2	8	3
3	2	5
6	4	1

2300 cc Engine

This engine employs hydraulic valve lifters. To check valve lash: use the special tool available from Ford, or its equivalent and depress the cam follower

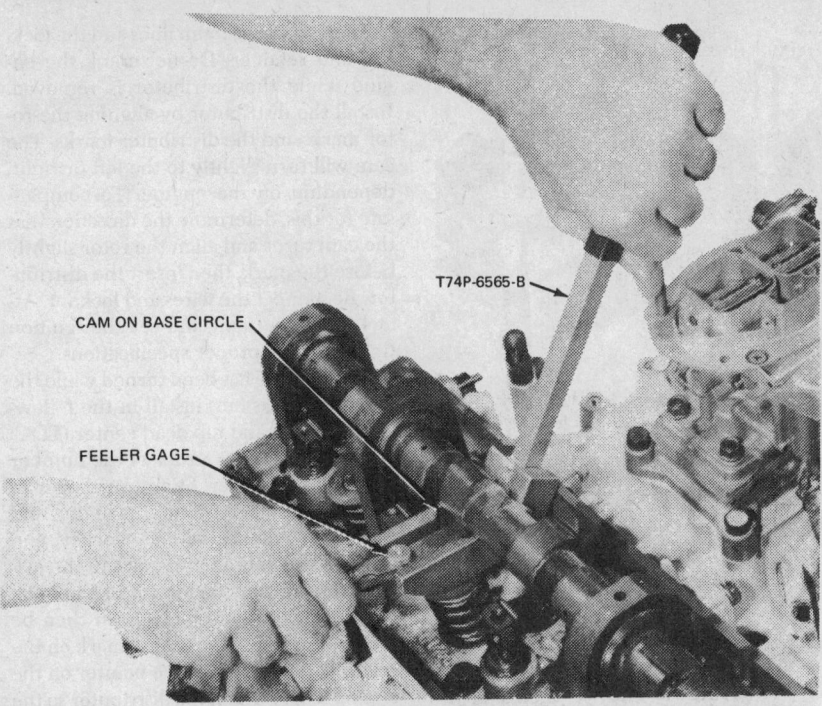

CAM ON BASE CIRCLE

T74P-6565-B

FEELER GAGE

Checking hydraulic valve lash

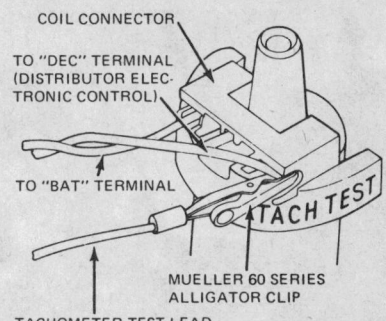

COIL CONNECTOR

TO "DEC" TERMINAL
(DISTRIBUTER ELEC-
TRONIC CONTROL)

TO "BAT" TERMINAL

TACH TEST

MUELLER 60 SERIES
ALLIGATOR CLIP

TACHOMETER TEST LEAD

Electronic ignition tachometer connections

until the lash adjuster is completely collapsed. Insert the proper feeler gauge (.008int.; .010 exh) between the base circle of the cam and the follower. The should be done when the camshaft is in a position with the base circle of the lobe facing the follower. If the clearance is excessive, remove the follower and check for damage. If the follower is okay, check the spring assembled height to make sure the valve is not sticking. If the spring height is okay, check the camshaft lobe for excessive wear.

Replace damaged or worn parts as necessary.

V6 Engine

If some component of the valve system is replaced, the valves must be set cold before starting the engine. If the valves are set for a tune-up, adjust them hot and running. When setting the valves of the cold engine, rotate No. 1 cylinder so that the piston is at top dead center (TDC). Remove the valve covers. Place a socket and breaker bar on the nut of the crankshaft pulley. Remove the spark plug from the cylinder where you are adjusting the valves and have an assistant place their finger in the hole. Rotate the engine (clockwise as viewed from the front) until the pressure pops the finger out. Now that cylinder is at TDC; both valves should be closed and the timing pointer and pulley mark aligned. Adjust the valves as explained in the 1600 cc engine section. Adjust the valves in the rest of the cylinders in firing order (1–4–2–5–3–6). This can be done by turning the crankshaft 120 degrees clockwise each time. After two full revolutions, each cylinder will have been at TDC once. To adjust

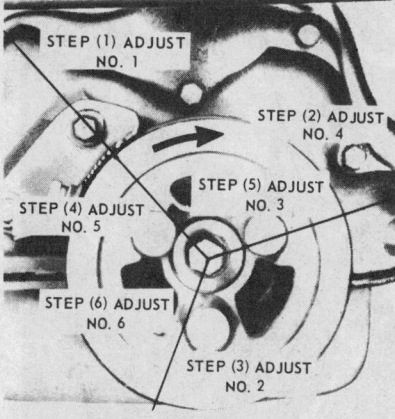

STEP (1) ADJUST NO. 1

STEP (2) ADJUST NO. 4

STEP (5) ADJUST NO. 3

STEP (4) ADJUST NO. 5

STEP (6) ADJUST NO. 6

STEP (3) ADJUST NO. 2

Step-by-step procedure for V6 engine cold valve adjustment. The procedure is started by placing No. 1 cylinder on TDC.

the valves when the engine is hot, run the engine until it reaches operating temperature. With the engine running at idle speed, insert a feeler gauge between the valve stem and rocker arm and adjust the valve. After adjusting each valve recheck the valve clearance.

Carburetor

Idle Speed and Mixture

The 1600 cc engine uses a single-barrel downdraft carburetor with an automatic choke. Other engines use two-barrel carburetors. The carburetor number is stamped on the fuel bowl opposite the accelerator pump. Idle speed and ignition settings are located on the emission decal in the engine compartment. Single-barrel carburetors should be adjusted in the following manner:

1. Remove the air cleaner.

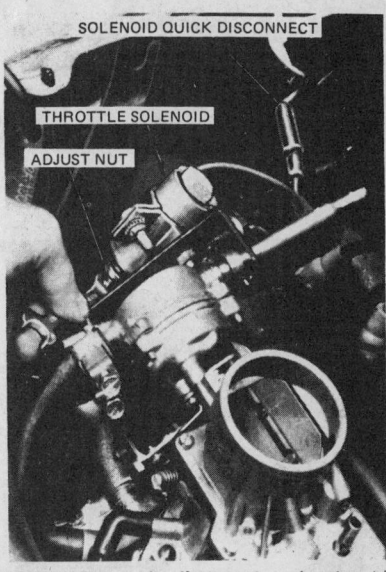

SOLENOID QUICK DISCONNECT

THROTTLE SOLENOID

ADJUST NUT

Throttle solenoid adjustment and solenoid lead disconnect.

2. Connect a tachometer to the engine.

3. Allow the engine to run until it reaches operating temperature.

4. Disconnect the throttle solenoid lead from the wiring harness. Make sure the idle limiter cap is against the maximum rich stop.

5. Disconnect the hose which runs from the carburetor to the decel valve and plug the decal valve fitting.

6. Turn the curb idle adjusting screw to set the engine at the lower specified idle speed (See the "Tune-up Specifications Chart.") It may be necessary to use the adjusting screw on the throttle solenoid as well as the curb idle screw to achieve the proper idle.

7. Reconnect the throttle solenoid. Set the higher specified idle speed using the solenoid plunger.

8. Move the throttle lever to allow the solenoid plunger to extend.

9. Turn the idle mixture screw to the right or left to obtain the smoothest idle.

10. Reconnect the decel valve hose and the air cleaner.

Use the following procedure for two-barrel carburetors:

1. Remove the air cleaner.

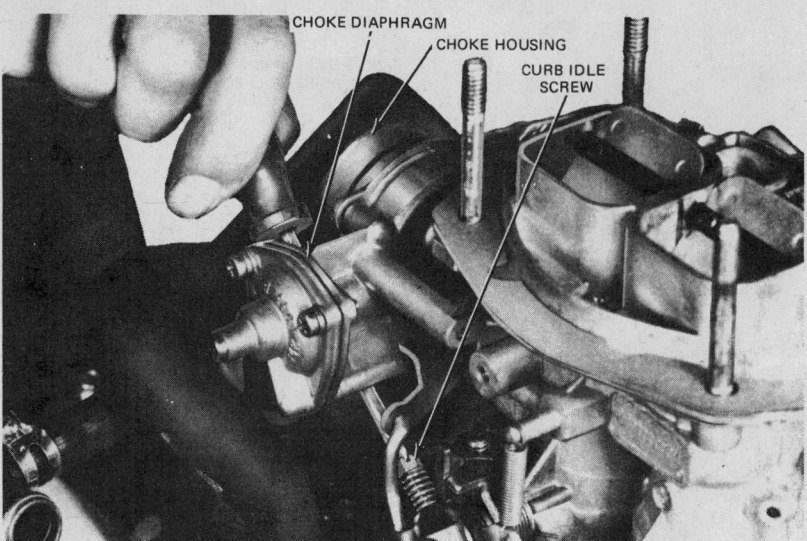

Setting curb idle—2000 cc and V6 engines.

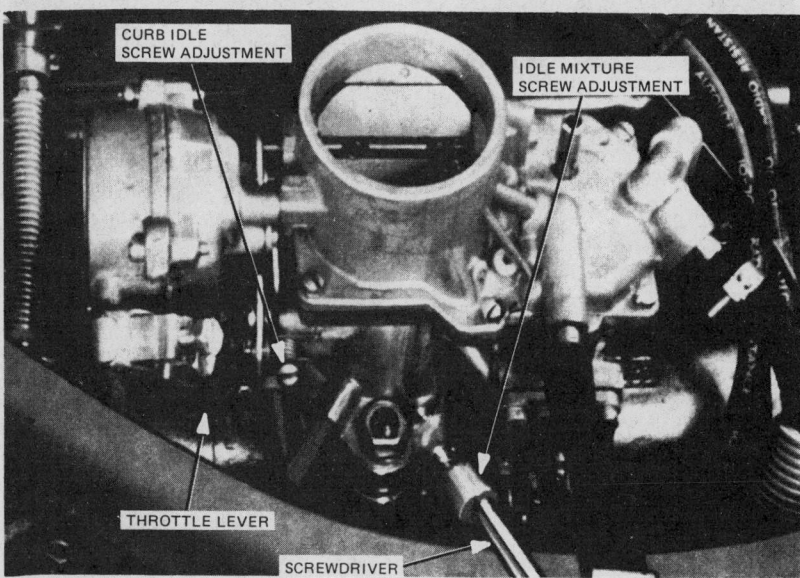

Curb idle and idle mixture adjustment screw—1600.

2. Connect a tachometer.

3. Allow the engine to run until it reaches operating temperature.

4. Check the ignition timing as in the previous section, and make sure it is set to proper specifications.

5. Disconnect the hose which runs from the carburetor to the decel valve (if equipped) and plug the decel valve fitting.

6. Place the car in Drive, if the car is equipped with an automatic transmission, and in neutral if it has a manual transmission.

7. Set the idle speed to the speed listed in the "Tune-Up Specifications Chart" by using the curb idle screw. This reading must be taken with the air cleaner connected.

8. Turn the idle mixture screw to the right or left to obtain the smoothest idle.

ENGINE ELECTRICAL

Distributor

Removal and Installation

The distributor is located on the right side of the 1600 cc engine, on the left side of the 2000 cc and 2300 cc engines, and at the rear of the V6 engine.

Before removing the distributor, match mark the distributor body and engine block with chalk or paint, and mark the engine block so the two marks align. Remove the distributor cap and mark the distributor body to show the direction in which the rotor is pointing. This will ensure correct distributor installation and timing.

Remove the vacuum lines and the locknut and retainer. Do not crank the engine while the distributor is removed. Install the distributor by aligning the rotor marks and the distributor marks. The cam will turn slightly to the left or right, depending on the engine. To compensate for this, determine the direction that the cam turns and align the rotor slightly before the mark, then insert the distributor. Reconnect the wires and locknut. Attach a timing light and set the ignition timing to the proper specifications.

If the engine has been turned while the distributor was out, install in the following manner. Find top dead center (TDC) of the compression stroke of the number one (no. 1) cylinder. Stick your finger in the spark plug hole of no. 1 cylinder, and turn the engine with a socket and breaker bar until the pressure in the cylinder forces your finger out of the hole. The exact location of TDC can then be found by aligning the timing mark on the crankshaft pulley with the pointer on the engine block. Install the distributor so the rotor is pointing to the no. 1 spark plug wire on the distributor cap and the points are just opening. Again, use a timing light to set the timing to the proper specifications.

Alternator

The alternator used on 1600 cc models is either a Lucas or Bosch. Other models use only Bosch. Types can be determined by the codes stamped on the alternator, 17 ACR for Lucas and K–1 for Bosch.

Alternator Precautions

When servicing an alternator or a circuit incorporating one, the following precautions should be observed:

1. The alternator is used on a negative ground system only.

2. When installing a battery, connect the positive cable first, then connect the negative (ground) cable.

3. Never disconnect the battery while the engine is running.

4. Remove the molded connections from the alternator when you are welding.

5. Never attempt to polarize the alternator.

Removal and Installation

Lucas

1. Disconnect the negative (ground) cable from the battery.

2. Disconnect the wires from the rear of the alternator.

3. Remove the alternator mounting bolts and the alternator.

4. Position the alternator and install the mounting bolts.

5. Install the fan belt and adjust it so it has ½ in. free-play.

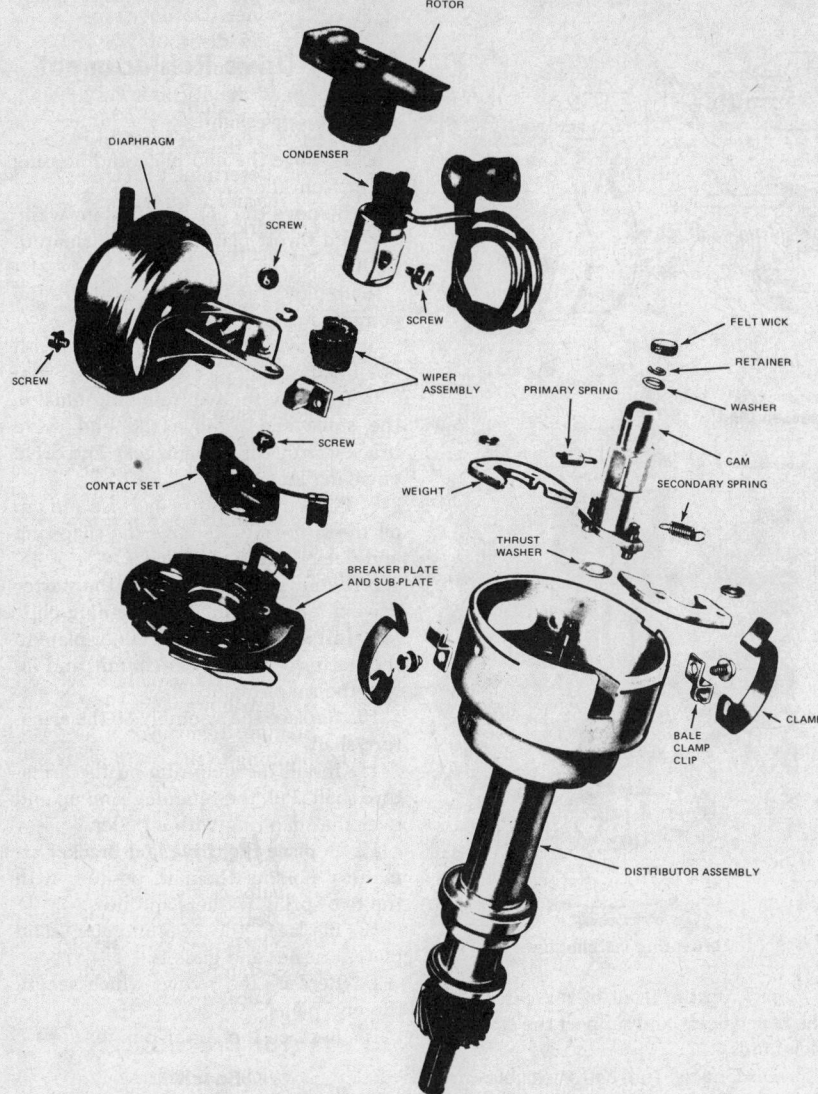

V6 distributor components; 2000 is similar

9. Install the heat duct and the air cleaner.

10. Connect the battery.

Fan Belt Tension Adjustment

The fan belt free-movement should be ½ in. measured midway between the water pump pulley and the alternator. To adjust the fan belt, loosen the front and rear lower alternator mounting bolts and the front adjusting bolt. Move the alternator to give the belt the correct tension. Retighten the adjusting bolt, then the mounting bolts.

Voltage Regulator

The voltage regulator used on the Lucas charging systems is integral with the alternator and is not adjustable. If it does not function properly, it should be replaced. There are three types of regulator used with this system. The Lucas regulators are located at the rear of the alternator. The regulator on the Bosch charging system is located on the right fender apron. It is not adjustable and if it does not function properly it should be replaced.

Removal and Replacement

Lucas

1. Remove the screws which hold the plastic cover to the rear of the alternator and remove the cover.

2. Disconnect the wires from the regulator to the brush gear.

3. Remove the screws which attach the regulator and remove the regulator.

4. Install the new regulator.

5. Reconnect the wires to the brush gear.

6. Install the plastic cover and screws.

Bosch

1. Unplug the wiring from the alternator to the regulator.

2. Remove the regulator attaching screws and remove the regulator.

3. Position the new regulator on the fender apron and install the mounting bolts.

4. Reconnect the wiring plug to the regulator.

Starter

Removal and Installation

A Bosch starter is used on most Capris. A Lucas unit was used on some 1600s. They can be identified by the different exterior housing appearance. The Bosch unit has a round solenoid.

Lucas

1. Disconnect the wires from the battery.

2. Remove the wires from the starter.

3. Remove the solenoid attaching nuts,

6. Connect the wires on the back of the alternator.

7. Connect the battery.

Bosch (4 cylinder)

1. Disconnect the negative (ground) battery cable.

2. Remove the clip which holds the wire plug connector to the rear of the alternator, and disconnect the wiring plug.

3. Disconnect the regulator-to-alternator wiring at the alternator.

4. Disconnect the heater hose bracket from the alternator.

5. Loosen the mounting bolts and remove the alternator.

6. Remove the mounting bolts and the alternator.

7. Position the alternator and install the mounting bolts.

8. Install the fan belt and adjust it to ½ in. free-play.

9. Connect the heater hose bracket to the alternator.

10. Connect the plug and the clip at the rear of the alternator.

11. Connect the battery.

Bosch (6 cylinder)

1. Disconnect the negative (ground) cable from the battery.

2. Remove the connectors at the rear of the alternator.

3. Remove the air cleaner and exhaust manifold heat duct.

4. Remove the adjusting bolt from the rear of the alternator.

5. Remove the mounting bolts. Slide the alternator back and away from the mounting bracket and lift it out between the battery and the exhaust manifold.

6. Position the alternator to the mounting bracket and install the mounting bolts.

7. Install the fan belt and adjust it to ½ in. free-play.

8. Connect the multiple connectors to the rear of the alternator.

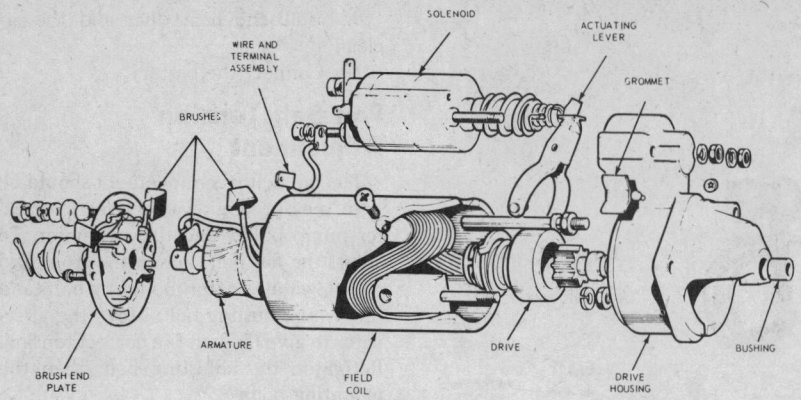

Lucas starter—disassembled

washers, and connecting strap, and then remove the solenoid.

4. Apply the parking brake and block the rear wheels. Jack the front of the car and place jackstands under it.

5. Remove the lower mounting bolts.

6. Loosen the upper mounting bolt.

7. Support the starter, remove the upper mounting bolt, and remove the starter.

8. Reverse the procedure to install the starter. (When installing the solenoid, be sure to have the correct location of the plunger extension on the fork mechanism.)

Bosch, 4 cylinder

1. Disconnect the battery ground cable.

2. Disconnect the wires at the solenoid.

3. Remove the attaching screws and then the starter.

4. Reverse the procedure to install the starter.

Bosch, 6 cylinder

1. Disconnect the battery ground cable.

Thrust-ring installation

2. Jack up the front of the car, block the rear wheels, and support the car with jackstands.

3. Disconnect the battery cable and the two push-on wire connectors from the solenoid.

4. Remove the mounting bolts and the starter.

5. Reverse the procedures to install the starter.

Starter Drive Replacement

Lucas

1. Remove the starter from the car.

2. Remove the end plate and housing cover from the starter.

3. Remove the cotter pin, shim washers, and thrust plate from the armature shaft.

4. Remove the bolts which secure the commutator end plate.

5. Remove the end plate with brush box molding and gasket.

6. Unscrew the two retaining nuts on the studs and remove the end drive bracket, armature, pinion gear, and drive engaging lever.

7. Place the armature in a vise and tap off the snap-ring. Remove the snap-ring and detach the starter drive.

8. Remove the spring from the starter drive after removing the retaining clip.

9. Install the ring and retainer plate to the starter drive and clutch unit, and install the snap-ring.

10. Replace the assembly on the armature shaft.

11. Install the snap-ring on the armature shaft. Pull the retaining ring up and over the snap-ring with a puller.

12. Replace the drive and bracket armature, holding them in position with the two spring washers and nuts.

13. Replace the commutator end plate, brushes and gaskets.

14. Replace the screws which secure the end plate.

15. Replace the cotter pin.

Bosch

1. Remove the starter from the engine.

2. Detach the field winding cable and remove the solenoid.

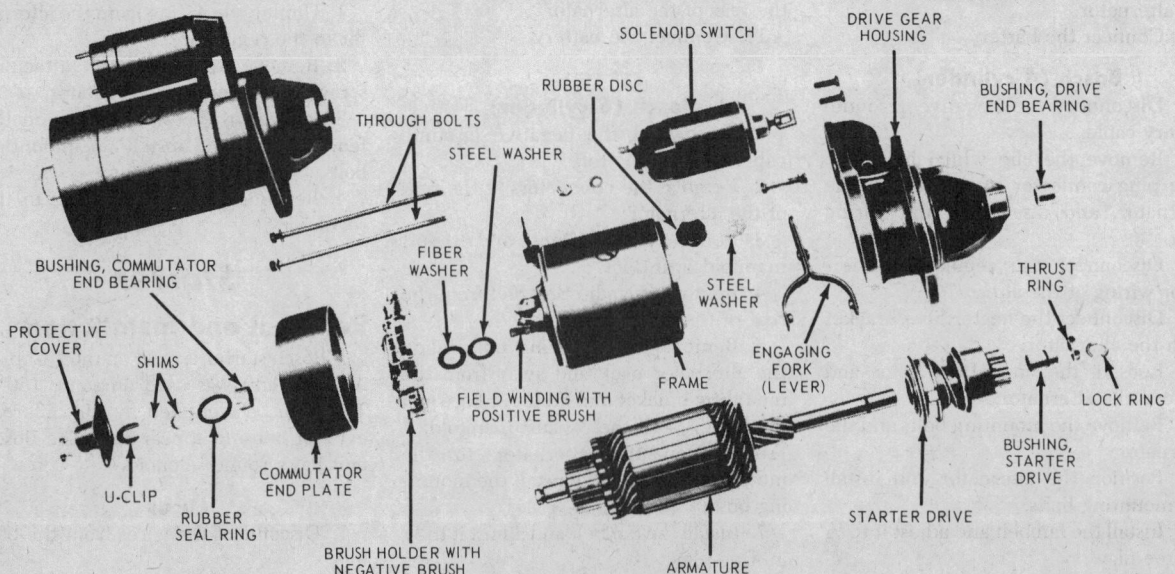

Bosch starter—disassembled

3. Remove the engaging lever guide screw.

4. Remove the end plate through bolts.

5. Remove the drive end plate.

6. Press the stop-ring toward the pinion.

7. Remove the snap-ring.

8. Remove the stop-ring and the starter drive gear.

9. Put silicone grease on the armature shaft thread and the starter drive gear engaging ring. Install the stop-ring and snap-ring on the armature shaft.

10. Press the snap-ring in the groove of the shaft.

11. Press on the stop-ring.

12. Install the engaging lever on the engaging ring and install the drive end plate.

13. Attach the engaging fork to the guide screw.

14. Install the steel washer, and then the rubber washer, with the tab pointing toward the armature.

15. Install the housing and rubber washer.

16. Insert the end plate bolts.

17. Hook the solenoid to the engaging fork and attach the screws.

18. Connect the field winding cable.

Starter Solenoid Replacement

Lucas

1. Disconnect the battery.

2. Disconnect the wires from the solenoid.

3. Remove the solenoid retaining nuts, washers, and connecting strap.

4. Remove the solenoid.

5. Replace the solenoid.

6. Reconnect the wires to the solenoid.

7. Reconnect the battery.

Bosch

1. Remove the starter.

2. Disconnect the field winding cable from the solenoid.

3. Unscrew the mounting bolts and remove the solenoid.

4. Link the new solenoid to the engaging lever and install the two screws.

5. Connect the field winding cable to the solenoid.

6. Seal the joints and screw heads with lacquer.

ENGINE MECHANICAL

Design

Five different engines have been available in the Capri; a 1600 cc four, a 2000 cc four, a 2300 cc four, a 2600 cc V6, and a 2800 cc V6.

1600 cc Engine

The 1600 cc engine is a four-cylinder, inline, overhead valve type. The cylinder head and the engine block are made of cast iron. The pistons are made of an aluminum alloy and are fitted to the steel connecting rods by full-floating piston pins. The cast-iron crankshaft is supported by five main bearings.

The camshaft is driven by a chain at one-half engine speed, by the crankshaft. A helical gear on the camshaft drives the distributor and oil pump, while the fuel pump is actuated by an eccentric on the camshaft.

NOTE: *The intake valves on the 1600 cc engine are aluminum-coated and cannot be refaced.*

2000 cc Engine

The 2000 cc engine is a four-cylinder inline engine with an overhead camshaft. The camshaft is mounted on the top of the cylinder head in three bearings and opens the valves by means of rocker arms. The overhead cam eliminates the need for valve lifters and pushrods. The cylinder head and engine block are made of cast-iron, while the intake manifold is aluminum.

The pistons are made from an aluminum alloy with steel struts. The cast iron crankshaft is supported by five main bearings. The camshaft is driven at one-half engine speed by a rubber belt. Since the camshaft is mounted on the top of the engine, the oil pump, fuel pump, and distributor must be driven by an auxiliary shaft off the camshaft belt.

2300cc Engine

The 4 cylinder 2300cc overhead cam engine is of lightweight iron construction. The crankshaft is supported on five main bearings and the camshaft by four. Main, connecting rod, camshaft and auxiliary shaft bearings are all replaceable.

The camshaft is driven from the crankshaft by a cogged belt, which also operates the auxiliary shaft, and thusly the oil pump, fuel pump and distributor. Belt tension is maintained by a pre-loaded and locked idler pulley bearing on the outside of the belt.

Water pump and fan are separately driven from the crankshaft by a conventional V-belt which also drives the alternator.

Hydraulic adjusters are used on the valve train. These units are placed at the fulcrum point of the cam followers. Their action is similar to lifters in an OHV engine. The head is drilled to supply oil to these units.

Although similar in design to the 2000cc the 2300cc is different in detail and few parts will interchange. A set of metric tools is needed for service.

V6 Engine

The 2600 and 2800 cc engines are a V6 overhead valve design. The cylinder heads and engine block are made of cast iron. Four main bearings support the crankshaft. The distributor and the oil pump are driven by an eccentric at the front of the camshaft. The connecting rods are forged steel with replaceable copper-lead alloy insert bearings. The intake manifold is made from aluminum and has individual passages to the openings in the cylinder heads. The V6 has a full pressure lubrication system fed by a rotor type oil pump mounted at the rear of the crankcase.

Engine Cautions

Metric and standard thread bolts are mixed throughout the engine and transmission. Since some of the metric threads are very similar to the standard threads, caution should be used when installing or removing bolts.

Metric bolts and screws will have the letters "M" or "ISOM" embossed on the head. Metric nuts will have the letter "M" on the sides.

If any repair operation requires the removal of any component of the air conditioning system, do not disconnect any of the lines of the system. If it is impossible to move the component out of the way with the lines attached, have the air conditioning system evacuated by a trained serviceman.

When installing nuts or bolts (refer to the torque specification chart), oil the threads with light-weight engine oil. Do not oil threads that require oil-resistant or water-resistant sealers.

Engine Removal and Installation

1600 cc

1. Remove the hood.

2. Disconnect the battery cables.

3. Drain the cooling system, from the radiator and engine block.

4. Remove the air cleaner assembly.

5. Disconnect the radiator hoses and remove the radiator.

6. Disconnect the heater hoses from the water pump and the intake manifold.

7. Disconnect the accelerator linkage from the carburetor.

8. Disconnect the temperature gauge, oil pressure sending unit, and the alternator wires.

9. Remove the exhaust pipes from the manifold and the hot air pipes from the manifold, where applicable.

10. Disconnect the fuel line from the fuel pump.

11. Disconnect the distributor wires from the coil and the high-tension leads from the spark plugs. Remove the distributor cap.

12. Jack up the front of the car and support it with jackstands.

13. Remove the starter motor.

14. Remove the lower bolts and cover of the clutch housing.

15. Drain the crankcase oil.

16. Put the car back on the ground.

17. Support the transmission.

18. Remove the bolts which attach the clutch housing to the engine.

19. Install a lifting device.

20. Remove the front motor mounts while supporting the engine with the chain hoist or other lifting apparatus.

21. Pull the engine slightly forward to separate the transmission imput shaft from the clutch, and then lift the engine out of the car.

To install:

22. Attach a chain hoist to the engine.

23. Position the engine assembly in the engine compartment and engage the unit on the transmission shaft. Make sure that the engine flywheel cover is located on the dowel pins. If the drive gear does not mesh, turn the crankshaft pulley slowly until the gear meshes.

24. Reconnect the motor mounts.

25. Position the engine to the clutch housing bolts. Make sure that the engine ground wire is held in place by the top left bolt.

26. Remove the chain hoist.

27. Remove the transmission support.

28. Connect the fuel line to the fuel pump.

29. Install the distributor cap. Connect the wires from the coil to the distributor. Connect the high-tension leads to the spark plugs.

30. Connect the alternator wires, the temperature gauge, and the oil pressure sending unit.

31. Connect the exhaust pipe and tighten the clamp bolts.

32. Connect the accelerator linkage to the carburetor.

33. Connect the heater hoses and the automatic choke hose.

34. Install the radiator and connect the hoses.

35. After you have made sure that the drain plugs are closed, open the cooling system. Refill the cooling system.

36. Install the air cleaner assembly.

37. Jack up the front of the car and support it with jackstands.

38. Install the starter motor and wires.

39. Install the clutch housing, lower cover, and bolts.

40. Put the front of the car back on the ground.

41. Connect the battery.

42. Refill the engine with oil.

43. Install the hood.

44. Run the engine, check it for leaks, and adjust the applicable components.

2000 cc, 2300 cc

NOTE: *If the engine has the thermactor air pump system, any interfering components will have to be removed.*

1. Remove the hood.

2. Remove the lower splash shield from the radiator and drain the coolant.

3. Remove the air cleaner assembly.

4. Disconnect the battery.

5. Remove the upper radiator shield, disconnect the upper and lower radiator hoses, and remove the radiator.

6. Disconnect the heater hoses from the water pump and the carburetor choke fitting.

7. Disconnect the alternator wiring.

8. Disconnect the accelerator cable from the carburetor. Disconnect the automatic transmission kickdown cable.

9. Disconnect the flexible fuel line at the fuel tank line and plug the fuel tank line.

10. Disconnect the coil wires.

11. Disconnect the oil pressure and the water temperature sending unit wires at the sending units.

12. Jack up the front of the car and support it with jackstands.

13. Remove the starter motor.

14. Disconnect the muffler pipe at the exhaust manifold.

15. Remove the flywheel or converter housing lower front cover. On vehicles with automatic transmissions, disconnect the converter from the flexplate. Remove the converter housing-to-cylinder block lower attaching screws.

16. Mark the flywheel and torque converter so they can be correctly mated during installation.

17. Support the transmission.

18. Disconnect the motor mounts at the underbody bracket.

19. Lower the car to the ground.

20. Attach a chain hoist and remove the engine.

To install:

21. Place a new gasket over the exhaust inlet pipe.

22. Lower the engine into the engine compartment.

23. Line up the dowel pins on the rear face of the cylinder block with the corresponding holes in the flywheel or converter housing. Make sure that the studs in the exhaust manifold are aligned with the holes in the muffler inlet pipe. Line up the engine mount studs.

24. On a vehicle with a manual transmission, start the transmission shaft into the clutch disc. If the engine hangs up after the shaft enters, turn the crankshaft slowly until the shaft spline meshes with the clutch disc splines.

25. Install the flywheel or converter housing upper attaching screws.

26. Remove the chain hoist.

27. Remove the transmission support.

28. Jack up the front of the car and support it with jackstands.

29. Install the flywheel or converter lower attaching capscrews.

30. On a vehicle with an automatic transmission, install the converter-to-flexplate capscrews and torque them to the proper specifications.

31. Install the flywheel converter housing front cover.

32. Install the engine mounts.

33. Install the starter and wires.

34. Install the exhaust manifold-to-muffler inlet pipe retaining nuts.

35. Lower the car to the ground.

36. Connect the flexible fuel line to the fuel tank line.

37. Connect the oil pressure and temperature sending unit wires.

38. Connect the coil wires and the battery.

39. Install the bellcrank assembly to the intake manifold and connect the accelerator cable to the bellcrank assembly.

40. Connect the heater hose to the water pump and choke housing.

41. Connect the alternator wires.

42. Install the radiator and connect the hoses.

43. Fill the crankcase with oil.

44. Refill the cooling system.

45. Run the engine, check for leaks, and adjust any applicable components.

46. Install the upper and lower radiator shields.

47. Install the air cleaner assembly and hood.

V6 Engine

NOTE: *If the engine has the thermactor air pump system, any interfering components will have to be removed.*

1. Remove the hood.

2. Disconnect the battery and drain the cooling system.

3. Remove the air cleaner assembly and remove the radiator hoses.

4. Remove the fan shroud attaching bolts and position the shroud over the fan. Remove the radiator and shroud.

5. Remove the alternator and bracket and remove the alternator ground wire.

6. Disconnect the fuel line from the fuel pump and plug the fuel tank line.

7. Disconnect the accelerator linkage at the carburetor and intake manifold. Disconnect the transmission downshift linkage if so equipped.

8. Disconnect the coil wires and the brake booster lines.

9. Jack up the front of the car and support it with jackstands.

10. Disconnect the muffler inlet pipes at the exhaust manifold.

11. Remove the starter.

12. Disconnect the engine from the motor mounts.

13. If equipped with an automatic transmission, remove the converter inspection cover and disconnect the

flywheel from the converter. Remove the downshift rod.

14. Remove the converter housing-to-engine block bolts and the adaptor plate-to-converter housing bolt.

On vehicles equipped with manual transmissions, remove the clutch linkage and remove the bell housing-to-engine block bolts.

15. Support the transmission.

16. Install a chain hoist and remove the engine.

To install:

17. Lower the engine into the compartment.

18. Start the transmission shaft into the clutch disc. If the engine hangs up, turn the crankshaft until the gear meshes. On a vehicle with an automatic transmission, start the converter pilot into the crankshaft.

19. Install the bell housing or converter housing upper bolts, making sure that the dowel pins in the cylinder block engage the flywheel housing. Remove the transmission support.

20. Remove the hoist.

21. On vehicles with an automatic transmission, position the downshift cable on the transmission and engine.

22. Jack up the car and support it with stands.

23. On a vehicle with an automatic transmission, position the transmission linkage bracket and install the remaining converter housing bolts. Install the adaptor plate-to-converter housing bolt. Install the converter-to-flywheel nuts and install the inspection cover.

On a vehicle with a manual transmission, remove the pilot studs, and then install the lower bell housing bolts and connect the clutch linkage to the engine block.

24. Install the starter and connect the wires.

25. Connect the muffler inlet pipes at the exhaust manifold.

26. Install the front motor mounts.

27. Lower the car to the ground.

28. Install the wires to the coil, and connect the wires to the temperature sending unit and the oil pressure sending unit. Connect the brake booster line.

29. Install the accelerator linkage and connect the downshift rod if so equipped. Connect the vacuum lines. Connect the fuel tank line at the fuel pump.

30. Connect the ground wire at the cylinder block. Install the heater hoses at the water pump and cylinder block.

31. Install the alternator and bracket. Connect the alternator ground wire to the cylinder block. Install the fan belts and adjust them to the proper specifications.

32. Position the fan shroud over the fan. Install the radiator and connect the hoses. Install the fan shroud attaching bolts.

33. Refill the cooling system. Fill the crankcase with oil. Adjust the transmission downshift linkage if so equipped.

34. Run the engine and check for leaks.

35. Install the air cleaner assembly and adjust any applicable components.

36. Install the hood.

Cylinder Head

NOTE: *To prevent distortion or warping of the cylinder head, allow the engine to cool completely before removing the head bolts.*

Removal and Installation
1600 cc Engine

1. Remove the air cleaner assembly.

2. Drain the cooling system.

3. Disconnect the fuel line at the fuel pump and carburetor.

4. Disconnect the spark plug leads and position them out of the way.

5. Disconnect the heater and vacuum hoses at the intake manifold and the hoses at the choke housing.

6. Disconnect the wire from the temperature sending unit.

7. Disconnect the exhaust pipe from the exhaust manifold.

8. Disconnect the throttle from the carburetor and disconnect the carburetor vacuum line from the distributor.

9. Remove the thermostat housing and the thermostat.

10. Remove the rocker arm cover and the gasket.

11. Remove the rocker arm shaft bolts evenly, and lift off the rocker arm assembly.

12. Lift out the pushrods and keep them in the order in which they were removed.

13. Remove the cylinder head bolts and lift off the cylinder head and gasket.

CAUTION: *Do not lay the cylinder head flat on its face or damage may result to the spark plugs or gasket surface.*

14. Clean the bottom of the head and the top of the cylinder block of all gasket material.

15. Position a new head gasket on the engine block.

16. Install the cylinder head on the engine and install the bolts hand tight.

17. Follow the proper order to tighten the bolts, in stages, to 65–70 ft lbs. with a torque wrench.

18. Install the pushrods in their original locations.

19. Install the rocker arm assembly and tighten the bolts evenly to 25–30 ft lbs.

20. Adjust the valve clearances.

21. Connect the exhaust pipe.

22. Connect the distributor vacuum advance line and the throttle linkage to the carburetor. Connect the vacuum line at the intake manifold.

23. Connect the wire to the temperature sending unit.

24. Connect the heater and vacuum hoses to the intake manifold. Connect the hoses to the choke housing.

25. Replace the thermostat and housing and use a new gasket.

26. Refill the cooling system.

27. Connect the fuel lines.

28. Connect the spark plug wires.

29. Install the rocker arm cover and the air cleaner assembly.

30. Adjust the idle speed and mixture settings.

2000 cc, 2300 cc Engines

1. Drain the cooling system.

2. Remove the air cleaner assembly.

3. Remove the valve cover.

4. Remove the exhaust manifold. (See the Exhaust Manifold Removal procedures.)

5. Remove the intake manifold, carburetor, and the decel valve as an assembly. (See the Intake Manifold Removal procedures.)

6. Remove the camshaft drive belt cover. Note the location of the belt cover attaching bolts that have rubber grommets.

7. Loosen the drive belt tensioner and remove the drive belt.

8. Remove the water outlet elbow from the cylinder head with the hose attached.

9. Using an Allen socket, remove the cylinder head bolts. (This tool is available at automotive stores and parts houses.)

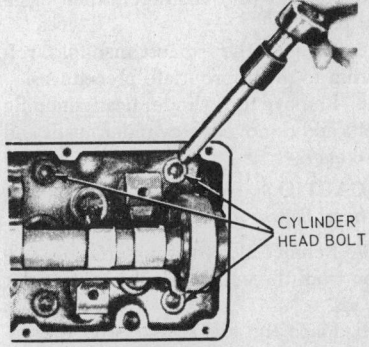

Removing or installing cylinder head bolts —2000 cc engine.

10. Lift the cylinder head and camshaft assembly from the engine.

11. Remove all the gasket material and carbon from the top of the engine block and pistons and from the bottom of the cylinder head.

12. Place a new cylinder head gasket on the engine block and position the cylinder head on the engine.

NOTE: *If you encounter difficulty in positioning the cylinder head on the engine block, it may be necessary to install guide studs in the engine block* to correctly align the head on the block.

13. Tighten the head bolts in sequence, and in steps, to 65–80 ft lbs. for the 2000 cc, and 80–90 ft lbs. for the 2300 cc with a torque wrench.

14. Install the camshaft drive belt. (See the Camshaft Drive Belt Installation procedures in the following sections.)

15. Install the camshaft drive belt cover with its attaching bolts. Make sure that the rubber grommets are installed on the bolts. Tighten them to 6–13 ft lbs.

16. Install the water outlet elbow and a new gasket.

17. Install the intake and exhaust manifolds. (See the Intake and Exhaust Manifold installation sections.)

18. Adjust the valve clearance.

19. Install the valve cover and air cleaner assembly.

20. Fill the cooling system.

V6 Engine

1. Remove the air cleaner assembly and disconnect the battery and accelerator linkage. Drain the cooling system.

2. Remove the distributor cap with the spark plug wires attached. Remove the distributor vacuum line and the distributor. Remove the hose from the water pump to the water outlet which is on the carburetor.

3. Remove the valve covers, fuel line and filter, carburetor, and the intake manifold.

4. Remove the rocker arm shaft (by loosening two bolts at a time, in sequence) and oil baffles. Remove the pushrods, keeping them in the proper sequence for reinstallation in their original positions.

5. Remove the exhaust manifold, referring to the appropriate procedures.

6. Remove the cylinder head retaining bolts and remove the cylinder heads and gaskets.

CAUTION: *Do not lay the cylinder head flat on its surface.*

7. Remove all gasket material and carbon from the engine block and cylinder heads.

8. Place the head gaskets on the engine block.

NOTE: *The left and right gaskets are not interchangeable. They are marked "front" and "top".*

9. Install guide studs in the engine block. Install the cylinder head assemblies on the engine block one at a time. Tighten the cylinder head bolts in sequence, and in steps, to 65–80 ft lbs.

10. Install the intake and exhaust manifolds.

11. Install the pushrods in the proper sequence. Install the oil baffles and the rocker arm shaft assemblies. Adjust the valve clearances.

12. Install the valve covers with new gaskets.

13. Install the distributor and set the ignition timing.

14. Install the carburetor and the distributor cap with the spark plug wires.

15. Connect the accelerator linkage, fuel line, with fuel filter installed, and distributor vacuum line to the carburetor. Fill the cooling system.

Cylinder Head Overhaul

The procedure for the 2000 cc and 2300 cc engines is the same as for OHV engines with this exception; if the camshaft is removed from the cylinder head, it must be installed along with the camshaft thrust plate and the camshaft drive gear and attaching bolt. The cylinder head must be removed to remove the camshaft.

For cylinder head overhaul, see the Engine Rebuilding Section of this Manual.

Rocker Shaft

Disassembly and Assembly

These procedures do not apply to the 2000 cc or 2300 cc engines because they are equipped with an overhead camshaft and do not employ a rocker arm assembly.

1. Remove the air cleaner assembly and any interfering emission control equipment.

2. Disconnect the spark plug wires and move them aside. Disconnect the throttle rod if necessary.

3. Remove the rocker arm cover and its gasket.

4. Remove the rocker arm attaching bolts (by loosening two bolts at a time, in sequence) and lift off the rocker arm assembly.

5. Remove the pin from one end of the shaft and slip off the spring washer from the shaft. The 1600 has a cotter pin, flat washer, crimped washer, and another flat washer. The supports, springs, and rocker arms may now be removed.

6. Check the shaft and its component parts for excessive wear or damage. Replace any parts that show these conditions.

7. Clean the component parts of the shaft assembly in a suitable degreasing solvent.

NOTE: *Ordinarily, the rocker shaft itself is not cleaned. If there is an insufficient amount of engine oil being circulated through the rocker arm assembly, however, the inside of the shaft should be cleaned in this manner:* Remove the plugs in the rocker shaft ends by drilling a hole in one plug. Insert a long rod through the drilled hole and knock out the opposite plug. Remove the drilled plug in the same manner. Clean the shaft in a degreasing solvent and replace the plugs.

8. Assemble the rocker arm shaft. On the 1600, the bolt holes in the rocker shaft supports must be on the same side as the rocker adjusting screws. Note that the 1600 rocker arms are right and left handed, each being inclined toward the support. The cotter pins should be installed with their heads up.

9. Replace the rocker arm assembly on the cylinder head. Make sure that the notch on the end of the V6 rocker shaft is down. Install the attaching bolts hand tight and then torque them down evenly to 25–30 ft lbs. for the 1600, 32–36 ft lbs. for the 2600, and 43–49 ft lbs. for the 2800.

10. Adjust the valve clearances. (Be sure to set the valves on the V6 engine when it is cold and then again, when it is hot.)

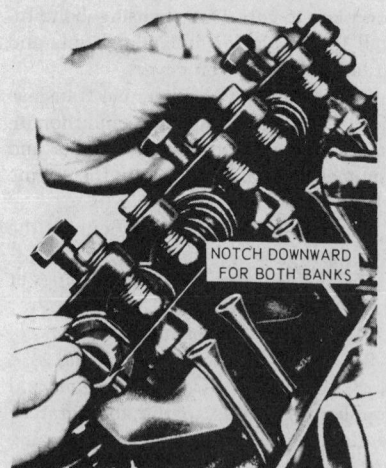

NOTCH DOWNWARD FOR BOTH BANKS

Removing rocker arm shaft assembly— V6 engine.

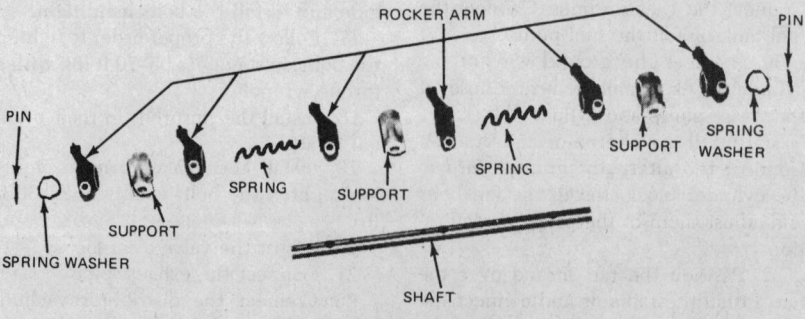

V6 rocker shaft assembly

11. Clean the cylinder head and valve cover of any dirt or gasket material and replace the valve cover.

12. Replace the spark plug wires.

Intake Manifold
Removal and Installation
1600 cc Engine

1. Remove the air cleaner assembly.
2. Partially drain the cooling system.
3. Disconnect the throttle shaft from the carburetor throttle lever.
4. Disconnect the fuel and vacuum lines from the carburetor.
5. Remove the choke thermostatic spring and water housing.
6. Disconnect the water outlet hose and the crankcase ventilation hose from the intake manifold.
7. Disconnect the decel valve to carburetor pipe at the carburetor.
8. Remove the attaching nut and bolts and remove the intake manifold and gasket.
9. If a new manifold is being installed, transfer all the necessary components to the new manifold.
10. Use a large allen wrench to remove the decel valve adaptor from the old manifold.
11. Position the decel valve against the adaptor face, engage and tighten the securing nut, and torque to 1–2 ft lb with the valve held in a vertical position.
12. Apply a sealing compound on both sides of the gasket around the water port and fit it to the cylinder head.
13. Install the intake manifold and tighten the nuts and bolts evenly to 15–18 ft lbs.
14. Connect the water hose and the crankcase ventilation hose to the intake manifold.
15. Connect the distributor vacuum line and fuel line to the carburetor.
16. Connect the decel valve to the carburetor.
17. Connect the throttle lever.
18. Install the thermostatic spring and water housing, locate the spring in the center slot, and align the housing marks before tightening the screws.
19. Install the air cleaner assembly and refill the cooling system.

OHC Engines

1. Remove the air cleaner assembly.
2. Disconnect the fuel line from the carburetor. Remove the carburetor.
3. Disconnect the vacuum lines at the intake manifold. On 2300 cc, disconnect the water lines at the manifold.
4. Disconnect the crankcase ventilation hose at the intake manifold.
5. Remove the intake manifold attaching bolts and remove the manifold, car- buretor, and decel valve from the studs, as an assembly.
6. Clean all dirt and gasket material from the surfaces on the cylinder head and intake manifold.
7. Position a new gasket and the mani- fold on the studs. Torque the bolts and nuts to 12–15 ft lbs. for the 2000 cc and 14–21 for the 2300 cc.
8. Connect the crankcase ventilation hose to the manifold.
9. Connect the distributor vacuum lines to the manifold.
10. Connect the fuel line to the carbu- retor.
11. Install the air cleaner assembly.

V6 Engine

1. Remove the air cleaner assembly and disconnect the battery.
2. Disconnect the throttle cables.
3. Drain the cooling system. Discon- nect and remove the hose from the water outlet to the radiator and the hoses and the line from the water outlet to the wa- ter pump.
4. Remove the distributor cap and spark plug wires as an assembly. Discon- nect the distributor wire and the vacuum line.
5. Mark the position of the distributor and remove it.
6. Remove the fuel line and filter be- tween the fuel pump and the carburetor and then remove the rocker arm covers.
7. Remove the intake manifold bolts and nuts. Tap the manifold lightly with a plastic hammer to break the gasket seal; and then lift off the manifold.
8. Remove all the gasket material and dirt from the manifold and cylinder heads.
9. Apply sealing compound to the join- ing surfaces. Place the manifold gasket in place. (Make sure that the tab on the right bank of the cylinder head gasket fits into the cutout of the manifold gasket.) Apply sealant to the manifold retaining bolt bosses.
10. Install the intake manifold. Tighten the attaching bolts until they are hand tight, and then torque them, in se- quence, to 15–18 ft lbs.

NOTE: *Tightening one of the bolts with a torque wrench will require a "crow's foot." This tool can be obtained from an automotive supply house or parts store.*

11. Install the distributor so the rotor is pointing to the mark made previously.
12. Connect the distributor wire and vacuum line.
13. Install the carburetor, fuel line, fuel filter, and the rocker arm covers.
14. Install the distributor cap and wires.
15. Install and adjust the carburetor linkage.
16. Install the air cleaner assembly and air cleaner tube to the carburetor. Con- nect the battery.
17. Fill the cooling system. Adjust the ignition timing.

Exhaust Manifold
Removal and Installation
1600 cc Engine

1. Support the front muffler pipe and remove the two nuts which hold the manifold to the muffler pipe flange. Sepa- rate the joint.
2. Disconnect the hot air pipe from the air cleaner to the manifold.
3. Remove the nuts and bolts which hold the manifold to the cylinder head and remove the manifold.
4. Discard the old gaskets and clean all mating surfaces of any gasket material.
5. If the manifold is to be replaced, remove the heat baffle and transfer it to the new manifold.
6. Position the center gasket on the studs, then locate the manifold on the studs.
7. Position the other gaskets between the manifold flanges and the cylinder head.
8. Install the nuts and bolts hand tight and then torque them evenly to 15–18 ft lbs.
9. Position the manifold and muffler pipe flanges together and secure them with the two nuts.
10. Connect the hot air pipe at the manifold.
11. Start the engine and check for leaks.

OHC Engines

1. Remove the air cleaner.
2. Remove the two attaching nuts from the top of the exhaust manifold shroud.
3. Disconnect the two attaching nuts from the muffler inlet pipe. If engine is equipped with thermactor, disconnect the line at the check valve.
4. Remove the manifold attaching nuts and remove the manifold from the cylinder head.
5. This manifold does not use a gasket. When installing the manifold, smear a light coat of graphite grease on the mat- ing surfaces of the exhaust manifold.
6. Position the manifold on the guide studs and install the attaching bolts hand tight, then torque them in sequence to 12–15 ft lbs. for the 2000 cc and 16–23 ft. lb. for the 2300 cc.
7. Install a new exhaust pipe gasket and install the two nuts.
8. Position the exhaust manifold shroud on the manifold and install the two nuts.
9. Install the air cleaner.

V6 Engine

1. Remove the air cleaner.

2. Remove the four attaching nuts from the exhaust manifold shroud (right side only).

3. Disconnect the attaching nuts from the muffler inlet pipe.

4. Remove the exhaust manifold attaching nuts and remove the manifold.

5. These manifolds do not use gaskets. When installing the manifold, smear a light coat of graphite grease on the mating surfaces.

6. Position the manifold on the studs and install the bolts hand-tight then torque them evenly to 15–18 ft lbs.

7. Install a new inlet pipe gasket and the attaching nuts.

8. Position the exhaust manifold shroud on the manifold and install the attaching nuts (right side).

Timing Gear Cover

NOTE: *These procedures apply to the 1600 and V6 engines only.*

Removal and Installation

1600 cc Engine

1. Drain the cooling system and remove the radiator hoses.

2. Remove the radiator assembly.

3. Remove the fan belt and then the fan and the water pump pulley.

4. Remove the water pump. (See the Cooling System Section in this chapter.)

5. Remove the crankshaft pulley using a two-jawed puller. Remove the four front oil pan bolts and the oil dipstick. Remove the attaching bolts of the front cover and remove the front cover.

Reverse the procedure to install the cover. Torque the attaching bolts to 7–9 ft lbs. and the oil pan bolts to 7–9 ft lbs. Be sure to clean all gasket material from the cover and joining places on the block. Use a new gasket on the cover and, if necessary, replace the cork packing strip on the front cover.

V6 Engine

1. Remove the oil pan as described in a following section.

2. Remove the radiator and any other necessary parts to allow clearance.

3. Remove the alternator and drive belts. Remove the water pump and water lines.

Removing or installing guide sleeves—V6 engine.

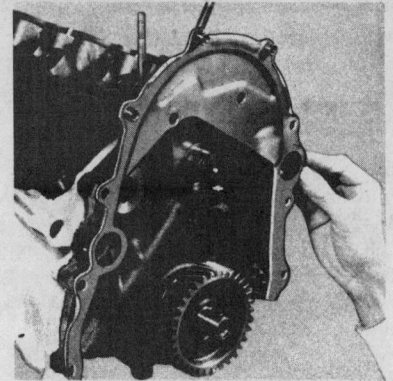

Removing or installing front cover plate—V6 engine.

4. Remove the fan.

5. Remove the crankshaft pulley with a puller and, if necessary, remove the guide sleeves from the cylinder block.

6. Remove the front cover retaining bolts and remove the front cover. If the front cover plate gasket needs replacement, remove the two screws and the plate to replace the gasket.

7. To install, reverse the procedures, cleaning all surfaces of gasket material and installing new gaskets and sealing compound.

NOTE: *If the guide sleeves were removed, install them with new seal rings but do not use sealing compound.*

Oil Seal Replacement

1600 cc Engine

The oil seal can be removed after the timing chain cover has been removed. Support the front cover and drive out the seal using a suitably sized socket.

Drive the new seal into the housing from the rear while supporting the housing around the seal. When fitting the cover to the engine, be sure that the seal is lined up with the crankshaft and pulley boss.

V6 Engine

Remove the front cover as previously described. Support the front cover and drive out the seal with a socket of a suitable size. To install the new seal, support the cover and drive the new seal in with a socket.

Timing Chain, Gears, and Tensioner

Removal and Installation

1600 cc Engine

Remove the timing gear cover as previously explained. Also remove the camshaft oil slinger and camshaft sprocket retainer and bolts. Remove the camshaft sprocket and disconnect the timing chain. Remove the timing chain tensioner and bolts.

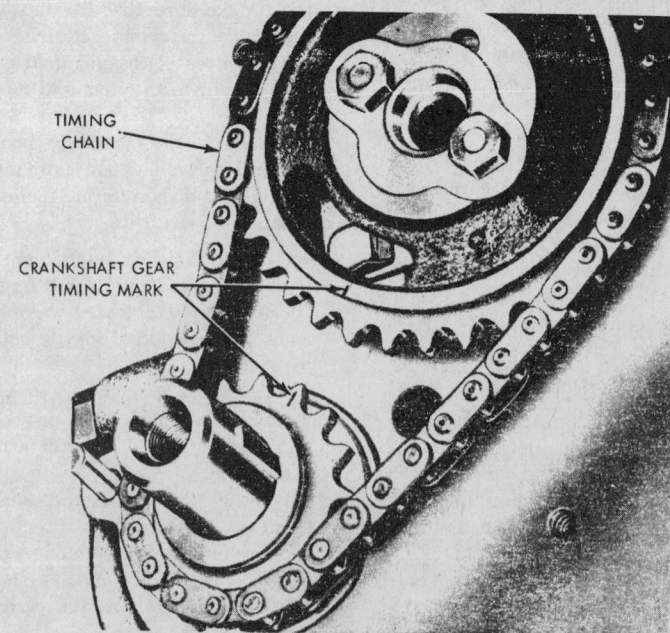

Timing chain tensioner—1600 cc engine

Timing marks—1600 cc engine

1. Position the timing chain over the camshaft and crankshaft sprockets so that the timing marks are aligned when the sprocket is fitted. Tighten the bolts to 12–15 ft lbs. and bend up the locking pads.

2. Install the oil slinger on the crankshaft. Install the camshaft sprocket retainer and bolts. Torque the bolts to 12–15 ft lbs. Install the timing chain tensioner.

3. Clean all surfaces of old gasket material. Install new gaskets with sealer.

4. Tighten the cover attaching bolts to 7–9 ft lbs. and the oil pan bolts to 7–9 ft lbs.

5. Position the crankshaft pulley, aligning the pulley slot with the crankshaft key. Tighten the bolts to 24–28 ft lbs.

6. Install the water pump, pulley, water pump, fan belt, fan, radiator, and hoses. Fill the cooling system.

7. Set the ignition timing as previously outlined.

V6 Engine

1. Drain the cooling system.

2. Remove the timing chain cover as previously described.

3. Remove the crankshaft gear with a puller. Remove the key from the crankshaft.

4. Remove the bolt and washer which hold the camshaft gear, then pry the camshaft gear from the camshaft. Pry off the gear carefully. Do not push the camshaft toward the rear of the engine or you might knock out the oil plug at the rear of the engine. Remove the thrust plate, spacer, and key.

5. Place the spacer and thrust plate on the camshaft. Install the key in the camshaft. Align the keyway in the gear with the key and press the gear onto the shaft, making sure that it seats tight against the spacer.

6. Camshaft end-play should be 0.001–0.004 in; it can be corrected by replacing the thrust plate. Position the crankshaft key, align the keyway and press on the gear, making sure the timing marks are aligned.

7. Install the timing chain cover and fill the cooling system.

8. Set the ignition timing.

Timing Belt Cover, Belt, and Tensioner

These procedures apply only to the 2000 cc and 2300 cc engines which have a camshaft belt and an overhead camshaft, rather than timing gears or chains.

Removal and Installation; Tensioner Adjustment

1. Remove the camshaft drive belt cover.

2. Remove the distributor cap and po-

Aligning timing marks—V6 engine

sition it out of the way.

3. Using a large socket and a breaker bar, turn the bolt on the crankshaft pulley in a clockwise direction until the following conditions exist.

A. The timing pointer on the front of the engine is aligned with the O or V mark on the pulley.

B. The pointer on the camshaft sprocket is aligned with the ball in the belt guide plate.

C. The distributor rotor is aligned with the timing mark on the upper lip of the distributor housing.

NOTE: *If the drive belt has slipped and is out of timing, disregard the preceding operations.*

4. Loosen the drive belt tensioner bolt and move the tensioner as far to the left as possible. Tighten the tensioner adjustment bolt. This will remove the preload of the tensioner from the belt.

5. Remove the belt from the pulleys.

6. If the timing marks on the camshaft, crankshaft, and distributor were not aligned before the belt was removed, align them at this time. Turn the crankshaft (A), camshaft (B), or the auxiliary shaft (C) until the components are in the positions described in Step 3.

7. Install the belt on the three sprockets, making sure the cogs on the belt fully engage the slots in the sprockets.

8. Loosen the tensioner adjustment bolt and allow the full spring pressure of the tensioner to force the tensioner against the belt.

Timing marks—2000 cc engine

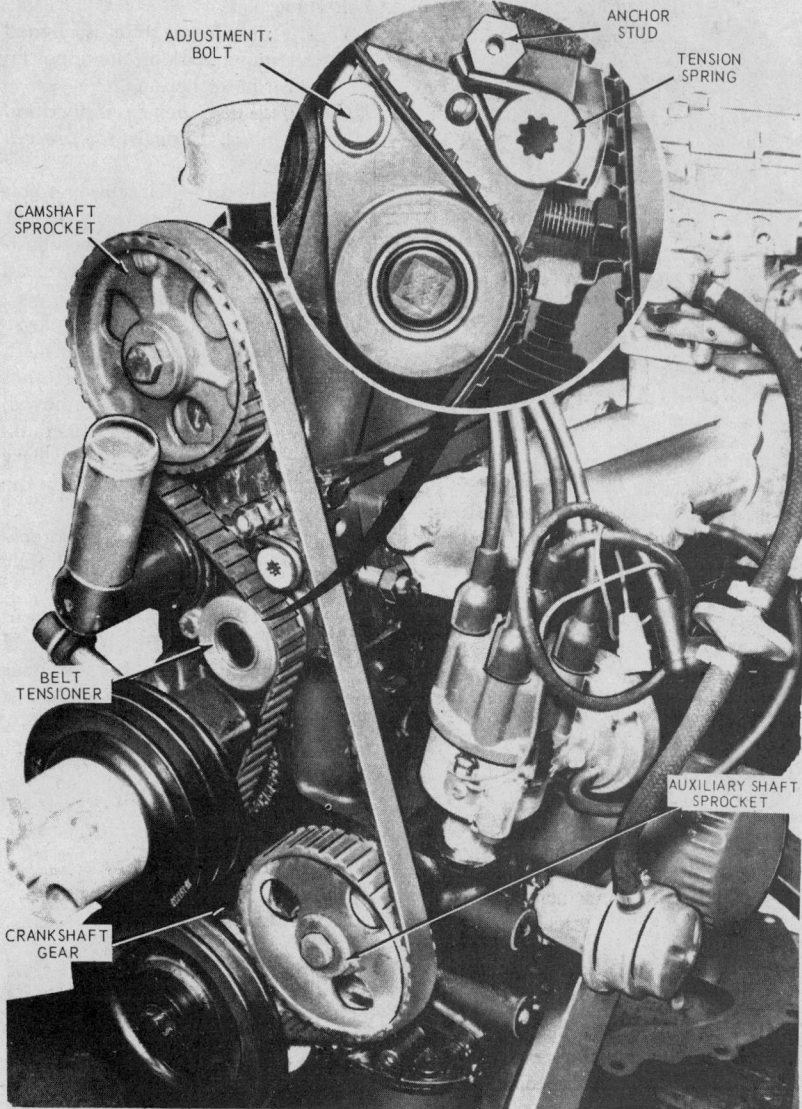

ADJUSTMENT BOLT

ANCHOR STUD

TENSION SPRING

CAMSHAFT SPROCKET

BELT TENSIONER

AUXILIARY SHAFT SPROCKET

CRANKSHAFT GEAR

Camshaft drive train—2000 cc engine

9. Using a socket and breaker bar on the crankshaft pulley bolt, turn the crankshaft two complete turns in a clockwise direction to remove all slack from the belt. Tighten the tensioner adjustment pivot bolt to 32–26 ft lbs.

10. Continue to turn the crankshaft until the three marks described in step 3 of the belt removal procedure are aligned. If the belt has slipped, remove the belt and repeat the installation procedure.

11. Install the distributor cap and the drive belt cover.

On vehicles where the timing belt has jumped engine timing without a known cause e.g., foreign material, snow or ice, behind the belt, or a loose tensioner, remove the camshaft sprocket from the engine. Wrap the drive belt around the sprocket for at least 300 degrees (300°). Visually check to make sure that each cog of the belt is properly seated in the valley between the teeth on the camshaft sprocket.

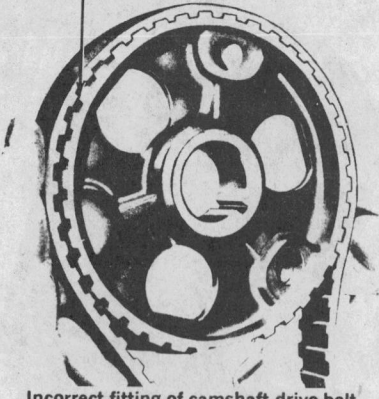

DRIVE BELT COG NOT SEATING PROPERLY BETWEEN THE TEETH

Incorrect fitting of camshaft drive belt sprocket —2000 cc engine

Auxiliary Shaft

Removal and Installation (OHC Engine only)

1. Remove the camshaft drive belt cover.

2. Remove the drive belt and auxiliary shaft sprocket.

3. Remove the distributor and fuel pump.

4. Remove the auxiliary shaft cover and thrust plate.

5. Withdraw the auxiliary shaft from the engine block.

6. Slide the auxiliary shaft into the housing and insert the thrust plate to hold the shaft.

7. Install a new gasket and auxiliary shaft cover.

8. Fit a new gasket to the fuel pump and install the fuel pump.

9. Insert the distributor and install the auxiliary shaft sprocket.

10. Align the timing marks and install the drive belt.

11. Install the drive belt cover.

12. Set the ignition timing.

Camshaft and/or Valve Lifters

Removal and Installation

1600 cc Engine

The mechanical lifters have an inverted, "mushroom" design. This means that the portion of the valve lifter that contacts the camshaft has a larger diameter than the top of the lifter. Because of this it is necessary to remove the engine from the car, remove most of the external components from the engine, and invert the engine, to remove the lifters and/or the camshaft.

Engine removal procedures have been described earlier; therefore, the following operations will only cover details not previously mentioned.

1. Remove the engine from the car and place it on a work stand.

2. Remove the fuel and oil pumps.

3. Remove the distributor.

4. Remove the valve cover, rocker arm shaft, and pushrods.

5. Remove the front cover and timing chain.

6. Place a drain pan under the engine and invert the engine on the stand.

7. Remove the oil pan.

8. Remove the camshaft thrust plate and the camshaft and lifters.

Installation is generally the reverse of the removal procedure. Several things should be kept in mind when replacing certain parts of the engine.

1. Make sure the timing marks on the timing sprockets are aligned.

2. The distributor should be installed with the rotor pointing in the same direction as it did when removed.

3. Replace the pushrods in the same bores from which they were removed.

4. Set the ignition timing.

5. Run the engine and check for leaks.

OHC Engine

The camshaft is mounted on the cylinder head. The bearings are mounted in carriers that are an integral part of the cylinder head. On 2000 cc engines the bearings and their journals have a progressively larger diameter from front to rear; therefore, the cylinder head must be removed and the camshaft must be removed from the rear. The opposite is true on 2300 cc engines.

1. Remove the cylinder head.
2. Remove the rocker arms.
3. Remove the camshaft drive gear attaching bolt and washer, and remove the gear and belt guide plate.
4. Remove the camshaft thrust plate from the rear of the cylinder head.
5. Carefully slide the camshaft out of the rear of the cylinder head.

To install, reverse the procedures.

V6 Engine

1. Drain the cooling system.
2. Remove the radiator, fan, spacer, water pump pulley, and belt.
3. Remove the distributor cap, with the spark plug wires attached. Remove the distributor vacuum line, distributor, alternator, rocker arm covers, fuel line and filter, carburetor, and intake manifold.
4. Remove the rocker arm and shaft assemblies. Lift out the pushrods and mark them so they can be replaced in the same location.
5. Remove the oil pan.
6. Remove the timing chain cover and water pump as an assembly.
7. Remove the camshaft gear retaining bolt and slide the gear off the camshaft. Remove the camshaft thrust plate.
8. Remove the valve lifters from the engine block with a magnet. Lifters should be identified to permit installation in the same location.
9. Carefully pull the camshaft from the engine block, avoiding damage to the camshaft bearings. Remove the key and spacer ring.
10. Coat the camshaft with a cam lubricant or heavy engine oil.
11. Install the camshaft, carefully avoiding damage to the bearings.

NOTE: *When installing the camshaft, do not push it hard into the engine. There is an oil plug at the rear of the engine block called the "bore plug". If the camshaft is forced into the engine, it could push this plug out, resulting in oil leaking on the clutch and pressure plate.*

12. Install the spacer ring with the chamfered side toward the camshaft. Insert the camshaft key. Install the thrust plate. Camshaft end-play should be 0.-001–0.004 in. The spacer ring and thrust plate are available in two sizes for adjustment.

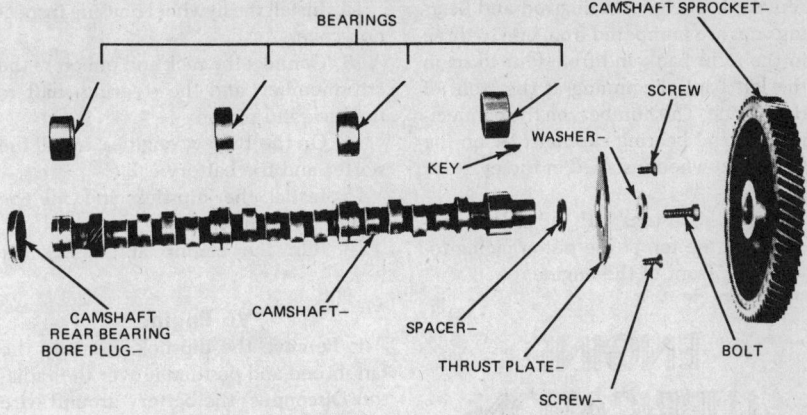

Camshaft and related parts—V6 engine

13. Align the timing marks and install the camshaft timing gear. Install the retaining washer and bolt.
14. Install the valve lifters.
15. Install the timing cover and water pump.
16. Install the belt drive pulley and secure it with the washer and retaining bolt.
17. Install the oil pan.
18. Install the pushrods in the same locations from which they were removed. Install the intake manifold.
19. Install the oil baffles and rocker arm shaft assemblies. Adjust the valves to the cold setting.
20. Install the water pump pulley, fan spacer, fan and belt, carburetor, fuel line and filter, alternator, distributor cap, and wires.
21. Fill the cooling system.
22. Install the rocker arm covers but not permanently. Run the engine, check for leaks, and set the ignition timing.
23. Set the valves at their hot setting. Install the valve covers permanently.

Pistons and Connecting Rods

Identification and Positioning

1600 cc Engine

When assembling a connecting rod to the piston, make sure it is positioned correctly. The marking "front" is stamped on the web to facilitate this.

Connecting rods and caps are numbered. The number is stamped on the camshaft side of the big end so that the cap installed with its numbers together must be in its original position. *Never assemble a bearing cap to another connecting rod.*

The wrist pins are selected to give the correct fit in the piston bore and bushing in the connecting rod. Pistons are only supplied complete with the piston pin to ensure the correct fit. The piston pins should not be interchanged.

Three piston rings are used: one for oil and two for compression. The two compression rings have a top marking and must be installed with the mark pointing up.

Always make sure that the arrow on the piston is pointing toward the front of the engine.

OHC Engine

Install the pistons in the same cylinders from which they were removed. The connecting rod and bearing caps are numbered on the left side from one to four, beginning at the front of the engine. The numbers on the connecting rods and bearing cap must be on the same side when installed in the cylinder bore.

Install the pistons with the arrow or notch on the top facing toward the front of the engine.

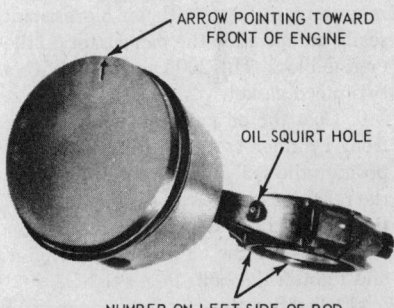

Piston and rod assembly—2000 cc engine

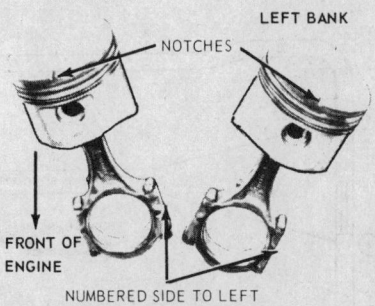

Piston and rod assemblies—V6 engine

V6 Engine

Pistons must be installed in the same cylinders from which they were removed. The connecting rod and bearing caps are numbered from one to three in the right bank and from four to six in the left bank, beginning at the front of the engine. The numbers on the connecting rod and bearing cap must be on the same side when installed in the cylinder bore.

Install the pistons with the indentation notch on the top of the piston facing toward the front of the engine.

ENGINE LUBRICATION
Oil Pan
Removal and Installation
4 cyl Engines

1. Remove the dipstick and drain the crankcase oil.

2. On 1600 cc engines, disconnect the ground cable of the battery and remove the starter motor from the engine.

3. Disconnect the steering shaft connection from the rack and pinion.

4. Disconnect the rack and pinion from the crossmember and move it forward to provide clearance.

5. Remove the flywheel housing inspection cover.

6. Remove the oil pan attaching bolts and also remove the pan.

7. Clean the gasket mounting surfaces on the pan and block.

8. Coat the block surfaces and oil pan mounting surfaces with an oil-resistant sealer and position the pan gasket on the engine block. The 2000 and 2300 have a two piece gasket.

9. Coat the oil pan front seal and the front cylinder cover with a sealer, and position the seal on the front cover. Coat the rear oil pan seal with sealer and install the seal in the rear main bearing cap.

10. Position the oil pan on the engine and tighten the bolts finger-tight.

11. Tighten the bolts in sequence to 7–9 ft lbs for M6 bolts and 11–13 ft lb. for M8 bolts.

12. Install the flywheel housing inspection cover.

13. Connect the rack and pinion to the crossmember, and the steering shaft to the rack and pinion.

14. On the 1600 cc engines, install the starter and the battery cable.

15. Install the dipstick and fill the crankcase with oil.

16. Run the engine and check for leaks.

V6 Engine

1. Remove the dipstick. Remove the fan shroud and position it over the radiator. Disconnect the battery ground wire and loosen the alternator bracket and adjusting bolts.

2. Raise the vehicle and drain the oil.

3. Remove the splash pan and starter.

4. Remove the engine front support nuts. Raise the engine and place wood blocks between the engine supports and the chassis.

5. Remove the clutch or converter housing cover.

6. Remove the oil pan retaining bolts and the pan.

7. Clean the surfaces of the oil pan and the engine block. Coat the block surface and the oil pan gasket with sealer. Position the pan gasket on the engine block.

8. Position the oil pan front seal on the cylinder front cover. Position the oil pan rear seal on the rear main bearing cap.

9. Position the oil pan on the engine block and install two front and two rear bolts. Install the rest of the bolts. Torque the bolts in steps (2–4 ft lbs, then 5–7 ft lbs).

10. Replace the converter housing or clutch cover.

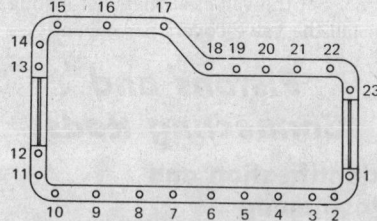

2000 cc engine oil pan bolts are to be torqued to 7-9 ft lbs in numerical sequence

11. Remove the wood blocks and install the support nuts.

12. Replace the starter and splash shield.

13. Lower the car. Position the alternator and tighten the bolts. Adjust the belt tension and connect the battery cable.

14. Install the fan shroud.

15. Install the dipstick. Fill the crankcase with oil. Run the engine and check for leaks.

Crankshaft Rear Oil Seal
Removal and Installation
1600 cc

1. Remove the right and left engine mountings from the cylinder block.

2. Position and mount the engine on a stand.

3. Remove the pressure plate bolts evenly and remove the pressure plate and clutch disc.

4. Remove the flywheel.

5. Remove the oil pan and gaskets.

6. Remove the rear oil seal carrier.

7. Install a new crankshaft rear oil seal using remover/replacer.

8. Locate a new gasket on the rear oil seal carrier, using a suitable joining compound at the ends, and fit the carrier to the block rear face using an aligner. Tighten the bolts evenly to a torque of 12 to 15 ft-lb and remove the aligner.

9. Position new gaskets on the block flange using a suitable joining compound at each end. Position the cork packing strips with the chamfered ends into the grooves, again using a suitable joining compound and refit the oil pan. Tighten the bolts to the correct torque and in sequence.

10. Locate the flywheel squarely upon the crankshaft flange. Tighten the bolts evenly to a torque of 50 to 55 ft-lb.

11. Check the flywheel run-out using the gauge at the rim. The flywheel run-out should not exceed 0.005 inch total indicator reading. Centralize the clutch disc with the hub assembly away from the flywheel. Tighten the bolts evenly to a torque of 12 to 15 ft-lb then remove the disc locator.

INSTALL THESE BOLTS FIRST

FRONT OF ENGINE

V6 engine oil pan bolts are to be torqued to 5-7 ft lbs in the circular, numerical, sequence shown

1600 cc engine oil pan bolts are to be torqued to 7-9 ft lbs, first in alphabetical, then in numerical sequence.

12. Remove the engine from the stand using lifting brackets.

13. Install the right and left engine mountings to the cylinder block and bend over locking tabs.

2000, 2300

1. Remove the transmission assembly. Remove clutch pressure plate and clutch disc, if so equipped.

2. Remove flywheel, flywheel housing and rear plate.

3. Use an awl to punch two holes in the crankshaft rear oil seal. Punch the holes on opposite sides of the crankshaft and just above the bearing cap to cylinder block split line. Install a sheet metal screw in each hole. Use two large screwdrivers or small pry bars and pry against both screws at the same time to remove the crankshaft rear oil seal. It may be necessary to place small blocks of wood against the cylinder block to provide a fulcrum point for the pry bars. Use caution throughout this procedure to avoid scratching or otherwise damaging the crankshaft oil seal surface.

4. Clean the oil seal recess in the cylinder block and main bearing cap. Inspect and clean the oil seal contact surface on the crankshaft.

5. Coat the oil seal to cylinder block surface of the oil seal with oil. Coat the seal contact surface of the oil seal and crankshaft with Lubriplate. Start the seal in the recess and install it. Drive the seal into position until it is firmly seated.

6. Install rear plate, flywheel housing, and flywheel. Tighten flywheel bolts to specifications.

7. Install clutch disc and clutch pressure plate, if so equipped. Align clutch disc before tightening pressure plate retaining screws.

V6

1. Remove the transmission, clutch and flywheel or the automatic transmission, converter and flywheel.

2. Remove the crankshaft rear seal with a sheet metal screw.

3. Install the new crankshaft rear seal.

4. Install the flywheel, clutch and transmission on the flywheel, converter and the automatic transmission.

5. Start the engine and check for oil leaks.

Oil Pump

Removal and Installation

1600 cc Engine

The oil pump is mounted on the left side of the engine and is attached to the engine by three bolts. To remove the pump, remove the three bolts and the pump and oil filter as an assembly. Use a new gasket and fill the pump with oil when reinstalling.

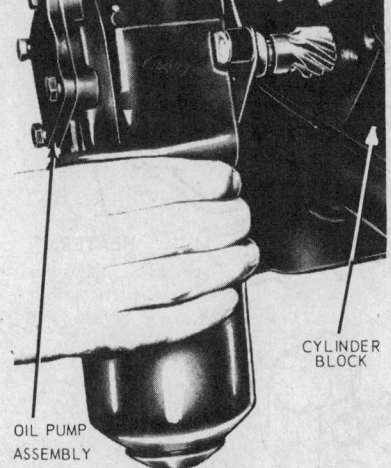

Removing oil pump—1600 cc engine

OHC Engine

The oil pump is mounted on the bottom of the engine block and is enclosed by the oil pan. To remove the pump, remove the oil pan, the attaching bolts, and the pump. When installing, use a new gasket and fill the pump with oil to prime it.

V6 Engine

Remove the oil pan and remove the bolt that retains the oil pick-up screen to the main bearing cap. Remove the oil pump retaining bolts. Lift off the oil pump and pull out the oil pump driveshaft. When installing the pump, insert the drive shaft into the engine block with the pointed end facing inward. Use a new gasket and fill the pump with oil to prime it.

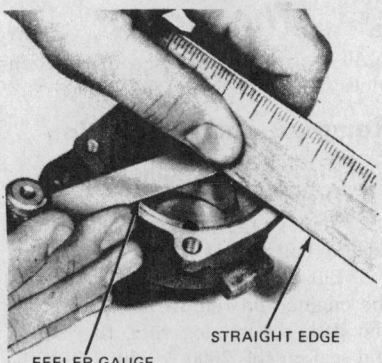

Checking oil pump rotor end clearance

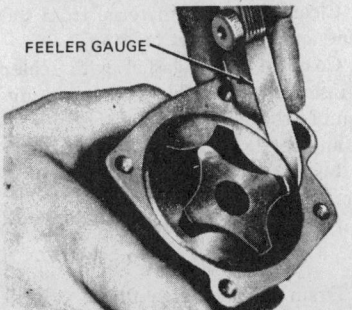

Checking oil pump outer race to housing clearance.

Checking Clearances

Inspect the inside of the oil pump housing, the outer race, and the rotor, for wear or damage. Measure the outer race-to-housing clearance.

With the rotor assembly installed in the housing, place a ruler over the rotor assembly and the housing. Check the clearance between the ruler and the rotor outer race.

Oil Pump Clearance Specifications

Model	Outer Race-to-Housing	Rotor Assembly End Clearance
1600	0.005	0.005
2000, V6	0.005-0.011	0.001-0.004

ENGINE COOLING

The four-cylinder engines employ a pressurized cooling system with the pump fan assembly bolted to the front face of the cylinder block. Coolant is circulated from the base of the radiator up through the water pump and into the cylinder block. The coolant circulates through the engine block and cylinder head to the thermostat, located at the front of the cylinder head. It then returns to the top radiator tank, flows down the radiator tubes, and is cooled by passing air.

The V6 system has a three-stage system which uses a centrifugal type water pump with the thermostat located in the water inlet housing at the lower left corner of the engine front cover. In the first stage, coolant flow to the radiator is blocked off to allow a quick warmup. In the second, normal temperature stage, some coolant is returned from the engine directly through a bypass hose to the water pump. In the third, overheat stage, the bypass hose is blocked off by the thermostat so that all coolant must circulate through the radiator.

NOTE: *On the V6, it may be necessary to disconnect the heater hose from the water outlet on top of the engine while filling the radiator. When water comes from both the hose and the outlet, the system is free of air.*

Radiator

Removal and Installation

1. Except on the 1600 engine remove the radiator upper splash shield. Unbolt the shroud and place it over the fan.

2000 cc engine cooling system

2. Place a drain pan under the radiator, remove the cap, open the drain plug, and drain the radiator.

3. Disconnect the upper and lower radiator hoses.

4. Disconnect the automatic transmission cooling lines from the radiator, if so equipped.

5. Remove the retaining screws and lift out the radiator.

6. Reverse the procedures to install.

7. Refill the cooling system with antifreeze solution.

8. Run the engine, with the cap off and heater on, to relieve any air pockets, then install the radiator cap, run the engine, and check for leaks.

Water Pump

Removal and Installation

1. Drain the cooling system.

2. Disconnect the lower radiator hose and heater hose from the water pump.

3. Remove the alternator belt. Remove the fan shroud.

4. Remove the fan attaching bolts and remove the fan, spacer, and water pump pulley. Remove the camshaft drive belt cover from OHC engines.

5. Remove the water pump attaching bolts and the water pump. Note that there are different lengths of bolts on the V6.

6. Clean all gasket material from all mounting surfaces.

7. Transfer the heater hose fitting to the new water pump.

8. Coat the new gasket with sealer and position the pump and gasket on the engine.

9. Install the pump mounting bolts. Install the camshaft drive belt cover on OHC engines.

10. Install the fan, spacer, and water pump pulley.

11. Install the alternator belt. Install the fan shroud.

12. Connect the heater and radiator hoses.

13. Fill the cooling system, run the engine, and check for leaks.

Thermostat

All thermostats installed in these engines start to open at 185–192° F.

Removal and Installation

4 cyl. Engines

1. Drain the cooling system.

2. Remove the thermostat housing attaching bolts.

3. Lift the thermostat housing from the engine and remove the thermostat and gasket (retaining ring, thermostat, and seal on the 2000 & 2300) from the engine.

4. Clean all gasket material from the engine and thermostat housing.

5. Coat the 1600 gasket with sealer and install it to the thermostat housing. Assemble the 2000 & 2300 thermostat, seal, and retaining ring to the housing.

6. Install the housing bolts and tighten them.

7. Fill the cooling system.

V6 Engine

1. Drain the cooling system.

2. Disconnect the radiator and heater hose from the thermostat housing cover.

3. Remove the three screws which hold the thermostat housing to the water pump. Pull the housing cover away from the water pump and remove the thermostat.

4. Clean the thermostat housing cover and water pump surfaces of all gasket material.

5. Position the thermostat in the water pump and install a new gasket and thermostat housing cover.

6. Connect the radiator and heater hoses. Fill the cooling system, run the engine, and check for leaks.

EMISSION CONTROLS

PCV Valve

(Positive Crankcase Ventilation Valve)

The PCV valve is located in the oil separator on 4 cylinder engines. On the V6 engine the PCV valve is located at the left front of the intake manifold and screws out.

Removal and Replacement

1. Pull or screw out the PCV valve.

2. Remove the PCV valve from the hose. Inspect the inside of the hose and if it is dirty, disconnect it from the intake manifold and clean it.

3. If the PCV valve hose was removed, connect it to the intake manifold.

4. Install the new PCV valve.

NOTE: *Do not attempt to clean the PCV valve; it should be replaced at the proper interval.*

Testing

With the engine running, remove the PCV valve from its mounting. Block off the end of the valve with your finger. You should feel a vacuum when the valve is blocked. Another test is to remove the valve (engine stopped) and shake it. There will be a clicking sound if the valve is free.

Decel Valve

The decel valve is mounted on the intake manifold, adjacent to the carburetor. The purpose of this valve is to meter an additional amount of fuel and air to the engine during deceleration. Additional fuel and air permits a more complete combustion, resulting in lower levels of exhaust emissions. During deceleration, the manifold vacuum forces the diaphragm assembly in the decel valve against the spring which in turn raises the decel valve. With the valve now open, existing manifold vacuum pulls a metered amount of fuel and air from the carburetor and travels through the valve body assembly into the intake manifold. The decel valve remains open and continues to feed additional fuel and air for a specified time.

Testing

To prevent unnecessary replacement of the decel valve, the following test should be performed. If the decel valve is found to be out of adjustment, the complete adjustment procedure should be performed before the valve is replaced.

Idle speed and initial ignition timing settings are detailed for all engines on the emission sticker located in the engine compartment.

1. Run the engine until it reaches operating temperature and then turn it off.

2. Connect a tachometer and timing light to the engine.

3. Disconnect both distributor vacuum lines and plug the intake manifold line.

4. With the engine running at the idle speed specified on the emission decal, check to see that timing is to specifications.

5. Adjust the timing as required.

6. Set the idle limiter cap to the maximum rich position.

7. Connect a vacuum gauge between the carburetor and the decel valve. The ID (inside diameter) of the connections and pipes must not be less than the ID of the decel valve inlet tube. The length of the tube between the decel valve and the vacuum gauge should not exceed 60 in.

8. Increase the engine speed to 3000 rpm and hold this speed for about two (five for 1974) seconds.

9. Release the throttle and observe the time interval between the throttle re-

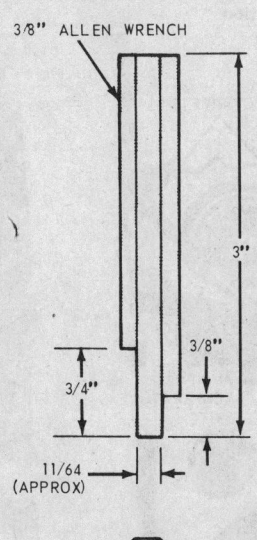

Decel valve adjusting tool

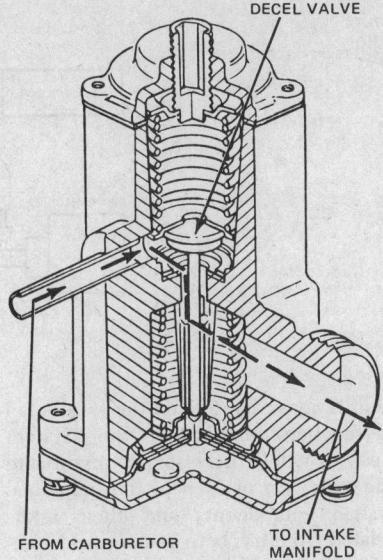

SECTIONAL VIEW
(VALVE SHOWN IN OPEN POSITION)

Decel valve

lease and a zero (0) reading on the vacuum gauge. Refer to the following chart for proper timing.

Decel Valve Timing Chart

Engine	Valve Timing
1600	2.5-3.5 sec
2000 (manual trans)	2.5-3.5 sec
2000 (auto. trans)	1.5-3.5 sec
2600 (manual trans)	1.5-3.5 sec
2600 (auto. trans)	1.5-3.5 sec
All 1974 models	2-5 sec

10. If the decel valve needs adjustment, remove and discard the colored cap (if so equipped) for access to the nylon adjuster. Use the tool shown in the illustration to adjust the decel valve. This tool can be made by grinding down a ⅜ in. allen wrench to the dimensions shown.

11. Insert the tool into the decel valve nylon adjusting screw. To increase the valve timing, back out the screw (counterclockwise). To decrease the valve timing, turn the adjusting screw inward (clockwise). One turn of the adjuster in either direction will increase or decrease the valve timing approximately ½ second.

12. Snap in a new colored cap in the top of the decel valve, if so equipped.

13. Remove the vacuum gauge and connect the tube between the carburetor and the decel valve. Remove the tachometer and the timing light. Connect the vacuum lines.

Removal and Installation

1. Disconnect the air-fuel hose from the decel valve.

2. Loosen the union nut that attaches the decel valve to the intake manifold and remove the decel valve.

3. Position the decel valve on the intake manifold and tighten the union nut.

4. Connect the air-fuel hose to the valve.

5. Test and adjust the valve as required. (See the previous section.)

Dual Diaphragm Distributor

The dual diaphragm is a two-chambered housing which is mounted on the side of the distributor. The outer side of the housing is a distributor vacuum advance mechanism. The vacuum advance is connected to the carburetor by a vacuum hose. The purpose of the vacuum advance is to advance the ignition timing according to the conditions under which the engine is operating.

The second side of the dual diaphragm has been added to the older type of distributor to help control engine exhaust emissions at idle and on deceleration. This inner side of the diaphragm is connected by a vacuum hose to the intake manifold. When the engine is idling, intake manifold vacuum is high and the carburetor vacuum is low. Under these conditions, intake manifold vacuum, applied to the inner side of the dual diaphragm, retards the ignition timing to promote more complete combustion of the air-fuel mixture in the engine combustion chambers.

Testing and adjustments of these distributors requires the use of an off-the-car distributor machine.

NOTE: *1974 non-California V6 engines have the dual diaphragm installed, but with the retard diaphragm open to the atmosphere.*

TRS (Transmission Regulated Spark Control System)

This system is used on all 1600 cc engines sold in California for 1972, and all 1973 models. The complete system consists of a distributor modulator valve, ambient temperature switch, transmission switch, the necessary vacuum hose, and the electrical wiring to connect the three components.

The TRS system reduces the exhaust emissions of an engine by retarding the distributor vacuum advance while the car is in First and Second gears. A transmission-operated switch activates the distributor modulator (solenoid) valve and advances the spark when the car is in high gear.

The vacuum is retarded through the

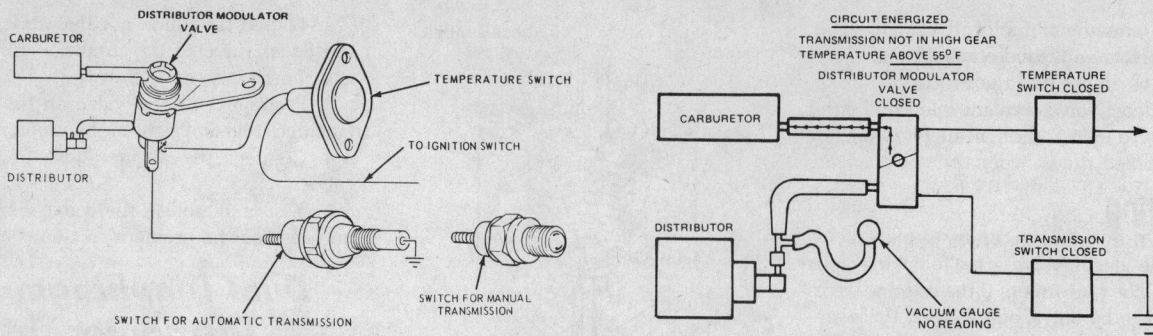

TRS system

TRS circuit energized

use of a distributor modulator valve inserted in the vacuum line between the carburetor port and the distributor primary (outer diaphragm) vacuum advance connection. The modulator valve is located in the engine compartment and is normally open. When energized electrically, it closes off to cut the vacuum supply from the carburetor to the primary vacuum advance unit on the distributor (outer diaphragm) and prevents vacuum advance.

A temperature switch and connector is located under the right-side kick panel within the front passenger compartment, with the sensor of the switch assembly protruding outward to the outside atmosphere, at the right front door hinge. The function of the temperature switch is to close the electrical circuit at approximately 65° F or higher, and to open the circuit at approximately 49° F or lower. Remember; the spark can be retarded only with warm outside air available.

With a vacuum gauge connected to the TRS system between the modulator valve and the distributor and the temperature switch above 65° F (use a hot sponge on the switch to raise the temperature if necessary), proceed as follows:

System Test

1. Start the engine in neutral or park. No vacuum should be indicated on the gauge (circuit energized).

2. Increase the engine speed to 1000–1500 rpm. The vacuum indication should read zero.

3. Disengage the clutch, then place the transmission in high gear. With the engine running at 1000–1500 rpm and the clutch disengaged, at least 6 in. Hg should appear on the vacuum gauge. Make sure that the engine is stopped before engaging the clutch.

Malfunction of the electrical circuit affects the vacuum, but the vacuum portion has no effect on the electrical circuit. Therefore, if the distributor modulator valve does not function as outlined above, neither will the vacuum. In this event, there is either an absence of electrical feed or poor ground is indicated and a functional check of each compo-

nent is necessary. Should the system fail to function according to the "System Test," it will be necessary to investigate the operation of each of the individual system components and their interrelated circuitry, both vacuum and electrical.

Testing

Transmission Switch Test

Disconnect the transmission switch lead from the modulator valve blade terminal and connect it in series with a test

light to the positive terminal of the battery. With the engine and ignition off, move the gears through all positions. The light should stay on until high gear is entered (when the switch is open). If the light stays on, the circuit is grounded or the switch is inoperative. If it does not go on at all, the circuit is open or the switch is inoperative. Replace the switch as necessary.

Temperature Switch Test

To test the temperature switch, disconnect the temperature switch lead from

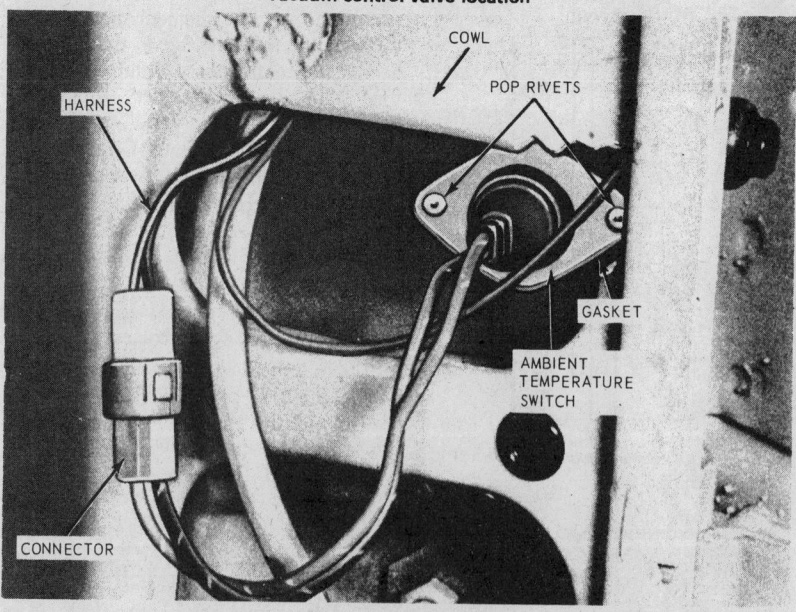

Vacuum control valve location

Temperature control switch

the blade terminal of the distributor modulator valve and connect it in series with a test light to a good ground. Turn on the ignition switch and warm the temperature switch with a hot sponge. The light should go on when the temperature of the switch reaches 65° F. (Anything approaching body temperature is sufficient.) Cool the switch until its temperature reaches below 49° F and then the light should go out. (An aerosol spray, such as starting fluid, should provide sufficient cooling.) If the light does not go *on* when *the switch is warmed,* the circuit is either open or grounded or else the switch is inoperative. If it does not go *out* when *cooled,* either it is not cold enough or the switch is inoperative. Reconnect the blade terminal to the modulator valve when the tests are completed.

Distributor Modulator Valve Test

With two of the three variables known to be good (the transmission and temperature switches) the distributor modulator valve can be tested by conducting the "System Test" again. If vacuum is not present when it should be, or vice versa, either the valve is inoperative, the hoses are pinched, plugged, or improperly connected, or there is no venturi vacuum from the carburetor.

Removal and Installation

Distributor Modulator Valve

1. Remove the two wires from the distributor modulator valve.
2. Disconnect each vacuum line from the valve. Tag the vacuum lines so they can be installed in their original position.

TRS Troubleshooting Chart

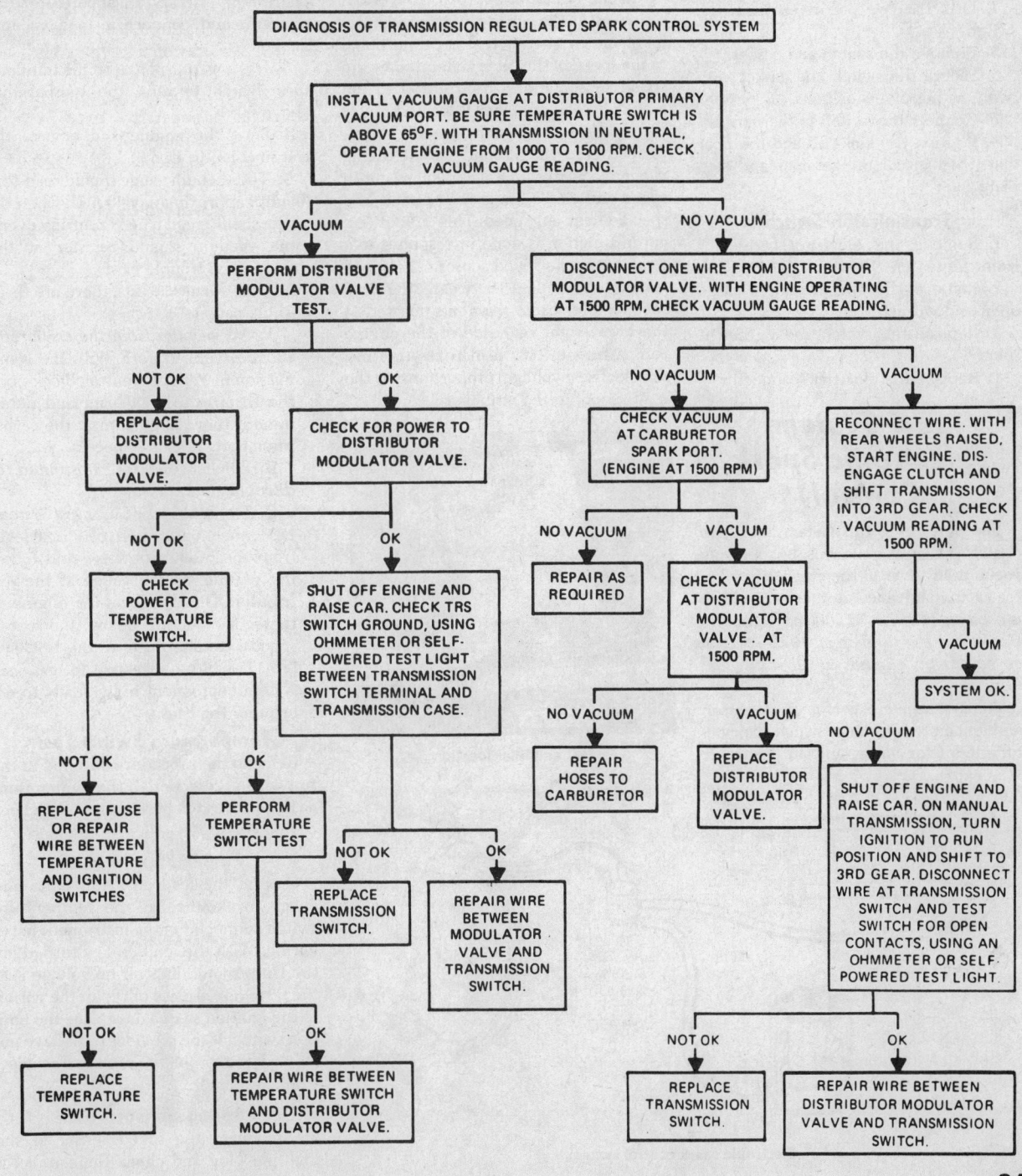

3. Remove the attaching screw, valve, and bracket.

4. Position the new modulator valve and install the attaching screw.

5. Connect the two vacuum lines to their respective ports.

6. Connect the two wires to their respective terminals.

Temperature Switch

1. Open the right door.

2. Remove the two step plate screws and remove the kick-pad retainer and weatherstrip.

3. Lift the floor mat and support the kick-pad in the raised position. Disconnect the switch at the connector.

4. Drill the two pop rivets from the switch.

5. Remove the switch and gasket.

6. Secure the switch and gasket with two new pop-rivets or bolts.

7. Connect the switch to the harness.

8. Position the kick-pad and the floor mat, then install the retainer and step plate.

Transmission Switch

1. Remove the electrical connector from the switch.

2. Remove the switch with a large open-end wrench.

3. Replace the switch and tighten it snugly.

4. Replace the electrical connector.

ESC System (Electronic Spark Control)

The purpose of this system is to help control exhaust emissions by delaying vacuum advance to the engine distributor vacuum advance unit, as required. *It is used on all 1972–73 2000 cc engines in California. It is used on all 1972–73 2600 cc automatic engines in all states and Canada.*

The system consists of a speed sensor, ambient air temperature switch, distributor modulator valve, and an electronic amplifier. The vacuum is retarded by the use of a distributor modulator valve inserted in the vacuum line between the carburetor and the distributor primary vacuum advance (outer diaphragm). The valve is normally open and, when it is energized electrically, closes to cut off the vacuum supply from the carburetor to the primary vacuum advance unit on the distributor, preventing vacuum advance.

The temperature switch is located under the right-side kick panel within the front passenger compartment. This switch closes the circuit to the amplifier at approximately 65° F or higher, and opens the circuit at approximately 49° F or lower. As the car begins to accelerate, a voltage frequency that is proportional to the speed of the car is generated by the speed sensor and is transmitted to the amplifier. The amplifier is located under the right-side instrument panel. The amplifier opens the ground circuit to the vacuum control valve at a specified cut-in speed and closes the ground circuit at a specified cut-out speed. This cut-out and cut-in function is done in response to a signal from the speed sensor. The speed sensor is installed between the two speedometer cable segments, located at the lower right rear side of the engine compartment. Two lead wires transmit the electrical voltage, proportional to the road speed, to the amplifier.

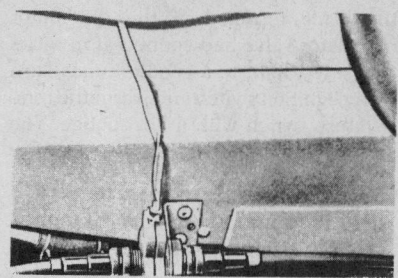

Speed sensor location

Testing

1. Raise the rear wheels.

2. Disconnect the vacuum hose at the distributor primary advance (outer diaphragm) and connect it to a vacuum gauge.

3. Use a warm sponge on the temperature switch to raise the temperature above 65° F.

4. Start the engine and engage the transmission in Drive.

5. The vacuum gauge should read zero (0) until approximately 40 mph when the gauge should read 6 in. Hg. In any event, some vacuum should register at this speed unless trouble exists.

6. If no vacuum exists, there are three possible causes:

A. *No vacuum from the carburetor vacuum venturi port.* With the transmission in Park or Neutral, block open the throttle to 1500 rpm and determine if there is vacuum at the carburetor port. Repair as necessary.

B. *Pinched, blocked, misrouted, or disconnected hoses.*

C. *Inoperative ESC Control System.* Disconnect one or both electrical leads from the modulator valve and follow the vacuum to the gauge at the distributor. Throttle down the engine. If there is vacuum below the cut-in speeds, trouble exists in the ESC system. It will be necessary to test each system component individually to determine the cause.

Temperature Switch Test

Refer to the procedure outlined in the previous TRS section. If the temperature switch proves to operate properly, check the power supply.

Power Supply Test

Ground the lead on a test lamp and check for voltage at the temperature switch connector of the instrument panel wiring. With the ignition key turned on, the lamp should light. If no voltage is at the terminal, replace or repair the wiring to the ignition switch or replace the ignition switch. If the previous steps have not located the problem, replace the electronic amplifier.

Speed Sensor Test

Disconnect the speed sensor at the multiple plug and check the sensor for

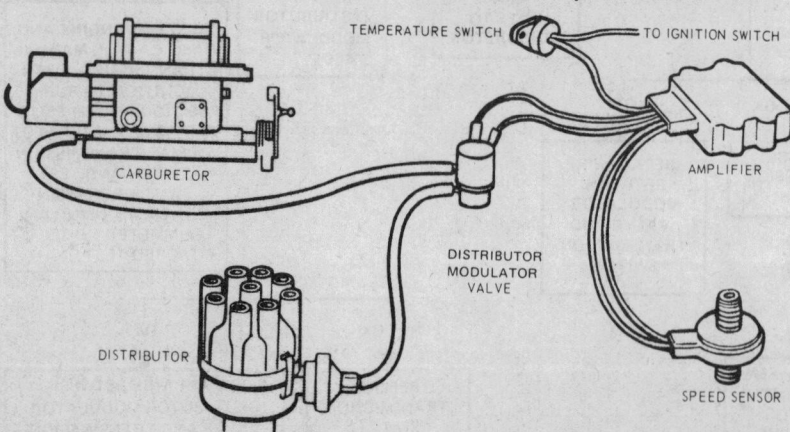

ESC amplifier location

Electronic spark control system

continuity with an ohmmeter. Resistance of the speed sensor at room temperature is 40–60 ohms.

Check the resistance of the speed sensor to ground. The resistance should be an open circuit because no continuity is permitted between the black wire and the case. Replace the black wire if the resistance readings are incorrect.

Removal and Replacement

Speed Sensor

1. Disconnect the speed sensor lead wires at the connector.
2. Disconnect the speedometer cable nut from each side of the sensor.
3. Remove the two attaching screws, then remove the sensor and the bracket.
4. Place an O-ring on each end of the speed sensor.
5. Connect the speedometer cable to each end of the sensor.
6. Connect the sensor leads to the harness.

Electronic Amplifier

1. Remove the access cover from the instrument panel.
2. Disconnect the harness plug from the amplifier.
3. Remove the attaching screw and then remove the amplifier from the mounting bracket.
4. Hold the new amplifier in position and install the attaching screw.
5. Plug the harness into the amplifier.
6. Install the instrument panel access cover.

Temperature switch and Distributor Valve

To remove these components refer to the removal and replacement procedures outlined in the TRS system.

Thermactor (Air Pump) System

The Thermactor system is used on 1974 and later models to reduce carbon monoxide and hydrocarbon content of exhaust gases. It does this by injecting air into the hot exhaust gases as they leave the combustion chamber. A belt-driven air pump with a centrifugal filter fan on the intake forces the air through external air passages on the 4 cyl., and internal passages on the V6. A vacuum-operated bypass valve dumps excess air during deceleration to prevent backfiring in the exhaust manifold. A check valve in the system prevents reverse flow of exhaust gases in case of pump failure.

Testing

Pump Supply Test

1. The engine should be at normal operating temperature.
2. Disconnect the air supply hose at

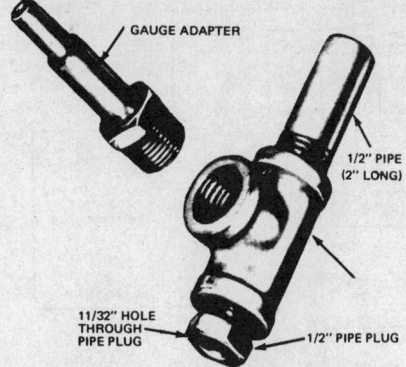

Thermactor system test gauge adapter

the check valve. If there are two check valves, clamp a plug in the end of one hose.

3. Clamp an adapter and pressure gauge into the air supply hose.
4. Start the engine and slowly increase its speed to 1500 rpm.
5. Air pressure should be 1 psi or more. If not, the pump must be replaced.

Check Valve Test

1. The engine should be at normal operating temperature.
2. Disconnect the air supply hose at the check valve. If there are two, disconnect them both.
3. The valve plate inside the valve body should be lightly against the seat, and away from the air or exhaust manifold.
4. Depress the valve plate with a screwdriver. It should return freely to the seat when released.
5. Leave the hose or hoses off and start the engine. Increase speed slowly to 1500 rpm.
6. Feel for exhaust gas leakage at the valve or valves. Replace any leakers.

NOTE: *It is normal for the valve to flutter or vibrate at idle speed.*

Bypass Valve Test

1. Disconnect the bypass to check valve hose at the bypass valve.
2. Start the engine and let it idle.
3. Air should be coming from the hose.
4. Pinch the vacuum line to the bypass valve shut for 5–8 seconds.
5. Air flow through the bypass valve should stop for a while when you release the vacuum hose. No time length is specified.
6. Check the bypass valve for leaks:
   a. Tee a vacuum gauge into the bypass valve vacuum hose.
   b. Plug the end of the hose.
   c. Note the gauge reading with the engine running.
   d. Remove the plug and connect the vacuum hose to the bypass valve. Check the vacuum reading after 60 seconds.
   e. If readings c. and d. differ, replace the bypass valve.

EGR (Exhaust Gas Recirculation) System

The EGR system is used on all 1974 and later models to reduce combustion temperatures and production of oxides of nitrogen by introducing a small volume of exhaust gas into the combustion chamber. The vacuum operated EGR valve is mounted on a spacer plate under the carburetor. The amount of exhaust gas recirculated and when it is recirculated are controlled by engine vacuum and temperature. A venturi vacuum amplifier is used to operate the EGR valve with manifold vacuum, under the control of carburetor vacuum.

System Test

1. With the engine running at normal operating temperature, about 8 in. Hg

Vacuum gauge hookup for Thermactor system bypass valve test

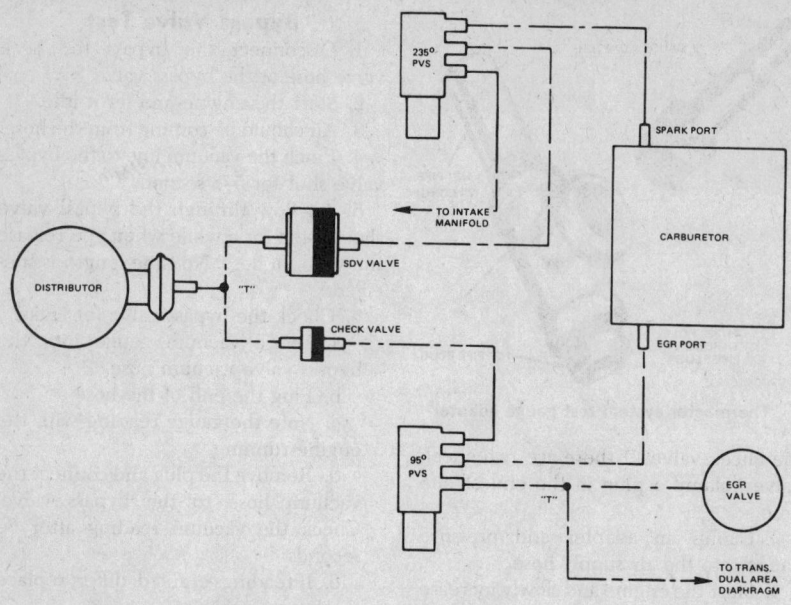

1974 combined EGR and distributor vacuum advance control system

vacuum should be sufficient to open the EGR valve.

2. If the valve is operating properly, the engine should slow and idle roughly when the valve is opened at idle.

3. A rough idle may be caused by an EGR valve or gasket that isn't sealing properly.

Evaporative Emission System

This emission system is designed to limit the emission of fuel vapors into the atmosphere and prevent raw gas from escaping from the fuel tank. The system consists of four components: the fuel tank; a pressure-sensitive and vacuum-sensitive fuel tank cap; a restrictor in the vapor line; and a vapor-absorbing charcoal canister.

This system allows fuel vapors to escape but prevents liquid gasoline from

escaping. The fuel vapors enter the vapor separator outlet hose to the charcoal canister which is mounted in the engine compartment. The vapors enter the canister, pass through a charcoal filter, and then exit through a hole in the bottom. As the vapors pass through the charcoal they are cleansed of hydrocarbons so the air that passes from the canister is free of pollutants.

When the engine is running, vacuum from the carburetor draws fresh air into the charcoal canister. As the entering air passes through the charcoal in the canister, it picks up the hydrocarbons that were deposited by the gasoline vapors. This gas mixture is then carried to the carburetor where it combines with incoming air and enters the combustion chambers of the engine to be burned.

Removal and Installation
Charcoal Canister

1. Slacken the clip retaining the large

hose at the charcoal canister and remove the hose.

2. Release the spring clip retaining the vapor line hose and disconnect the hose from the canister.

3. Remove the center holding bolt and remove the canister.

4. Position the canister and install the center bolt.

5. Reconnect the two hoses to the canister and secure them with their retaining clips.

Heated Air Intake Duct

The heated air intake portion of the air cleaner consists of a thermostat and a spring-loaded temperature control door in the snorkel of the air cleaner. The temperature control door is located between the end of the air cleaner snorkel, which draws in air from the engine compartment, and the duct that carries heated air up from the exhaust manifold. When the temperature under the hood is below 85° F (100° on the V6), the temperature control door blocks off under-hood air from entering the air cleaner and allows only heated air from the exhaust manifold to be drawn into the air cleaner. When the temperature under the hood rises above 110° F (135° F on the V6), the temperature control door blocks off heated air from the exhaust manifold and allows only under-hood air to be drawn into the air cleaner. Between 90 and 110° (135°) F, a mixture of heated and under-hood air is provided. By controlling the temperature of the engine intake air this way, exhaust emissions are lowered and fuel economy increased.

Testing
4 cyl. engines

1. With the engine cold and the temperature under the hood below 85° F, check the position of the temperature door in the air cleaner. It should be in the up (open) position, blocking off under-hood air.

2. Remove the air cleaner from the car. Immerse the air cleaner duct assembly in water, raise the water temperature to 85° F, and allow the temperature to stabilize for five minutes. The flap should be open to hot air. Now raise the temperature to 110° F stabilize. The temperature control door should be in the down position, blocking off the heated air from the exhaust manifold.

If the temperature door does not react in this manner, and the door is not binding, replace the valve and duct assembly.

V6 engine

1. With the engine cold and the underhood temperature less than 100° F, the valve plate should be in the heat on position.

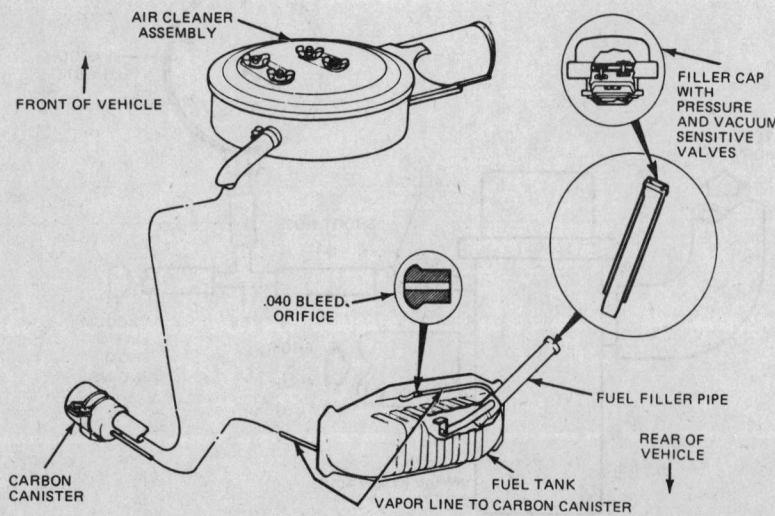

Fuel evaporative system—V6 engine

2. Immerse the duct assembly in water, raise the temperature to 100° F, and allow the temperature to stabilize for five minutes. The valve should still be in the heat on position.

3. Now raise the temperature to 135° F and stabilize. The valve plate should be in the heat off position. Replace the duct and valve assembly if large variations from the specified temperatures were found.

FUEL SYSTEM

Fuel Filter Replacement

1. Remove air cleaner.
2. Loosen the clamps securing the fuel filter to the fuel line hoses.
3. Remove the fuel filter and discard the clamps.
4. Install a new filter using new clamps.
5. Crimp clamps securely, start engine and check for leaks.
6. Install air cleaner.

Fuel Pump

A single-action fuel pump is used on all models. On the 1600 cc engine, the fuel pump is on the right side of the engine and is operated by the camshaft. On 2000 engines through 1973, the pump is actuated by a pushrod driven by the auxiliary shaft. On the 2000, 2300 and V6 engines, the fuel pump is on the left side of the engine and is actuated by an eccentric on the auxiliary shaft on OHC engines or a rod driven by the camshaft (V6).

Testing

Pressure Test

Disconnect the fuel line from the carburetor and attach a pressure tester to the line. Idle the engine and note the reading on the tester. The readings should be 3.5–5.0 psi for the 1600 cc engine, and 3.5–5.5 for the others.

Capacity Test

Disconnect the fuel line from the carburetor and insert it into a one quart container. Crank the 1600 cc engine for 38 seconds, the 2000 cc and 2300 cc engines for 35–43 seconds, and the V6 engine for 15 seconds (25 starting 1976). The bottle should be half-full (one pint).

Removal and Installation

1. Disconnect the inlet line and outlet fuel lines at the fuel pump.
2. Remove the fuel pump retaining bolts and remove the pump and gasket. Discard the gasket.
3. Remove all the gasket material from

the engine block and pump mounting surface. Apply oil-resistant sealer to both sides of the new gasket. Position the gasket on the fuel pump flange and hold the pump in position against the engine block.

NOTE: *Make sure the rocker arm or rod is riding on the camshaft eccentric.*

4. Press the pump tightly against the engine block, install the retaining bolts and tighten them securely.
5. Connect the fuel lines. Start the engine and check for leaks.

Carburetors

The 1600 cc engine is equipped with a model 1250 one barrel. The 2000, 2300 and 2600 cc engines are equipped with a model 5200 two barrel carburetor. The 2800 cc engines are equipped with a model 2150 carburetor. On the 2bbl carburetor, the primary venturi is smaller than the secondary venturi. The two are connected by mechanical linkage and, when the primary throttle plate opens approximately 45° the secondary plate begins to open.

Removal and Installation

1. Remove the air cleaner.
2. On the 2000, 2300 and V6 engines, remove the bolt that attaches the choke water housing to the carburetor and remove the water cover with its hoses attached. On 1974 and later models, detach the electrically assisted choke wire. On the 1600 cc engine, remove the three screws that attach the water housing to the carburetor. Remove the housing.

3. Note the location of all fuel lines and vacuum hoses that attach to the carburetor, then disconnect them from the carburetor.
4. Disconnect the throttle linkage from the carburetor.
5. Disconnect the throttle solenoid wire at the push-on connection.
6. On all 1600 cc engines, remove the two nuts that attach the carburetor to the intake manifold. On the 2000, 2300 and the V6 engines, remove the four nuts that attach the carburetor to the intake manifold.
7. Inspect the carburetor base gasket. If it is damaged in any way, replace it. Clean any foreign matter from the base of the carburetor.
8. Position the carburetor on the intake manifold and tighten the nuts.
9. Connect the vacuum lines and the fuel lines to the carburetor.
10. Connect the throttle linkage to the carburetor.
11. Connect the water housing to the carburetor.
12. On those models equipped with a throttle solenoid, connect the lead wire at the push-on connector.
13. Replace any coolant that was lost in the removal of the water hoses.

Overhaul

All Types

Efficient carburetion depends greatly on careful cleaning and inspection during overhaul since dirt, gum, water, or varnish in or on the carburetor parts are

Fuel pump pressure and capacity test

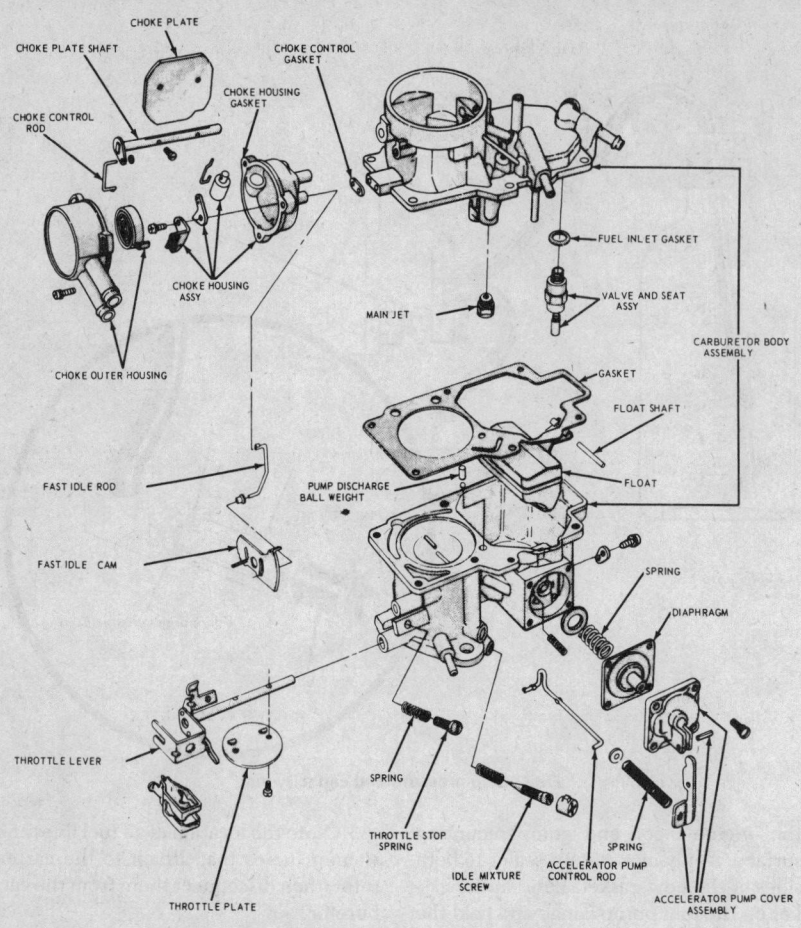

Exploded view of 1250 carburetor used on 1600 cc engine

wear or damage is found, replace the defective parts. Especially check the following:

1. Check the float needle and seat for wear. If wear is found, replace the complete assembly.

2. Check the float hinge pin for wear and the float(s) for dents or distortion. Replace the float if fuel has leaked into it.

3. Check the throttle and choke shaft bores for wear or an out-of-round condition. Damage or wear to the throttle arm, shaft, or shaft bore will often require replacement of the throttle body. These parts require a close tolerance of fit; wear may allow air leakage, which could affect starting and idling.

NOTE: *Throttle shafts and bushings are not included in overhaul kits. They can be purchased separately.*

4. Inspect the idle mixture adjusting needles for burrs or grooves. Any such condition requires replacement of the needle, since you will not be able to obtain a satisfactory idle.

5. Test the accelerator pump check valves. They should pass air one way but not the other. Test for proper seating by blowing and sucking on the valve. Replace the valve if necessary. If the valve is satisfactory, wash the valve again to remove breath moisture.

6. Check the bowl cover for warped surfaces with a straightedge.

often responsible for poor performance.

Overhaul your carburetor in a clean, dust-free area. Carefully disassemble the carburetor, referring often to the exploded views. Keep all similar and looka-like parts segregated during disassembly and cleaning to avoid accidental interchange during assembly. Make a note of all jet sizes.

When the carburetor is disassembled, wash all parts (except diaphragms, electric choke units, pump plunger, and any other plastic, leather, fiber, or rubber parts) in clean carburetor solvent. Do not leave parts in the solvent any longer than is necessary to sufficiently loosen the deposits. Excessive cleaning may remove the special finish from the float bowl and choke valve bodies, leaving these parts unfit for service. Rinse all parts in clean solvent and blow them dry with compressed air or allow them to air dry. Wipe clean all cork, plastic, leather, and fiber parts with a clean, lint-free cloth.

Blow out all passages and jets with compressed air and be sure that there are no restrictions or blockages. Never use wire or similar tools to clean jets, fuel passages, or air bleeds. Clean all jets and valves separately to avoid accidental interchange.

Check all parts for wear or damage. If

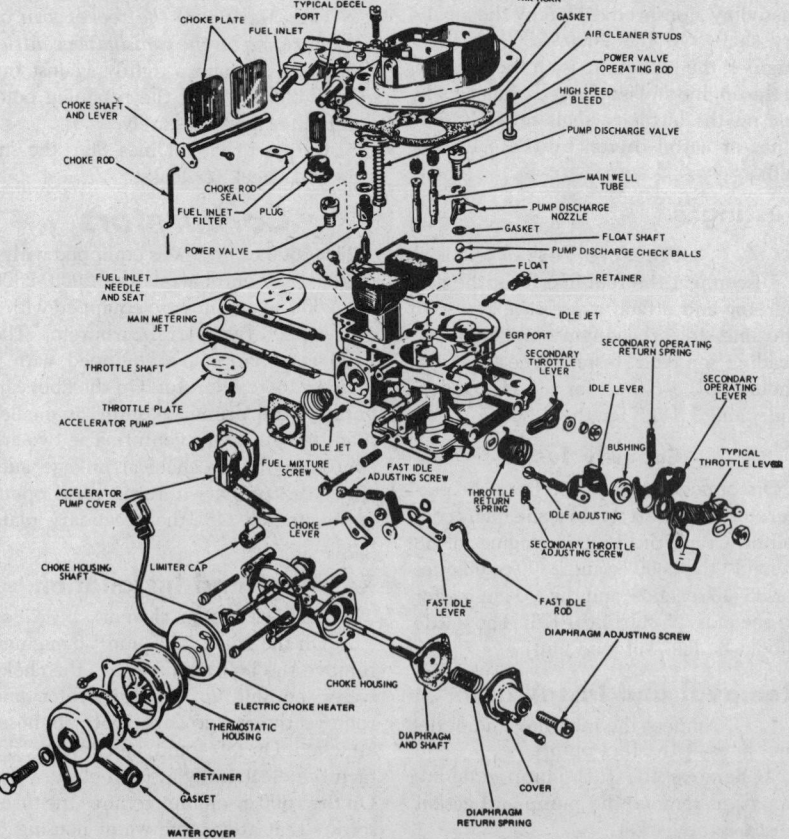

Exploded view of 5200 carburetor used on 2000 cc and V6 engines

7. Closely inspect the valves and seats for wear and damage, replacing as necessary.

8. After the carburetor is assembled, check the choke valve for freedom of operation.

Carburetor overhaul kits are recommended for each overhaul. These kits contain all gaskets and new parts to replace those that deteriorate most rapidly. Failure to replace all parts supplied with the kit (especially gaskets) can result in poor performance later.

After cleaning and checking all components, reassemble the carburetor, using new parts and referring to the exploded view. When reassembling, make sure that all screws and jets are tight in their seats, but do not overtighten, as the tips will be distorted. Tighten all screws gradually, in rotation. Do not tighten needle valves into their seats; uneven jetting will result. Always use new gaskets. Be sure to adjust the float level when reassembling.

Choke Unloader Adjustment

1250 Carburetor

1. Remove the air cleaner and fully depress the throttle control lever.

2. Measure the clearance between the bottom of the choke plate and the carburetor wall. The clearance should be 0.210 in. (no. 4 drill bit).

3. If the clearance is not within specifications, bend the fast idle cam to adjust it.

2150 and 5200 Carburetor

1. Hold the carburetor throttle lever in the wide-open position.

2. Insert a 0.256 in. drill bit into the air horn of the carburetor.

3. Apply light pressure to the choke plate to remove all slack.

4. With the drill bit against the carburetor wall, the bottom of the choke plate should just contact the drill. If it does not, bend the tab on the fast idle lever where it contacts the fast idle cam to correct it.

Automatic Choke Adjustment

1250 Carburetor

1. Remove the air cleaner.

2. Loosen the three screws that attach the choke water housing to the choke housing.

3. Turn the choke water housing to align the index mark on the water housing with the large index mark on the choke housing and tighten the water cover attaching screws.

5200 Carburetor

1. Loosen the three screws that attach the choke water housing to the choke housing.

2. Turn the choke water housing as required to align the index mark on the

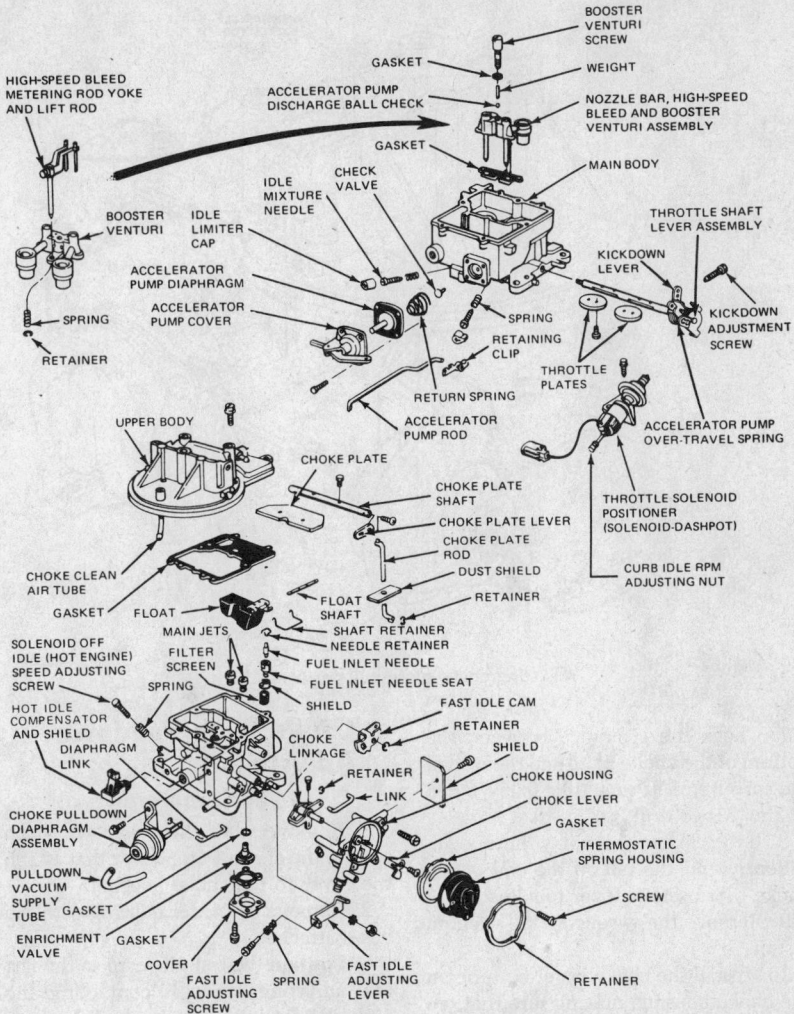

Exploded view of 2150 carburetor used on Capri II V6

water housing with the specified mark on the choke housing. If the choke cap setting is index, align the notch on the water cover with the large index mark in the center of the top of the choke housing. If the choke setting is one lean, align the notch on the water cover with the first notch to the left of the large index mark on the choke housing.

Choke Specifications

Model	Carburetor	Setting
1600	All	Index
2000, 2600	Manual	1 Lean
2000, 2600	Automatic	Index
All 1974 and later models	See engine compartment sticker	

Choke Linkage Adjustment

1250 Carburetor

1. Remove the air cleaner.

2. Remove the three screws that attach the choke water housing to the choke housing.

3. Depress the choke piston assembly in the choke housing until the vacuum

bleed slot in the wall of the piston housing is exposed.

4. Insert the bent tip of a piece of 0.040 in. (thick) wire into this slot, then raise the piston to trap the wire.

5. Close the choke plate in the top of the carburetor until it stops.

6. Partially open the throttle plates in the carburetor to disengage the fast idle screw from the fast idle cam.

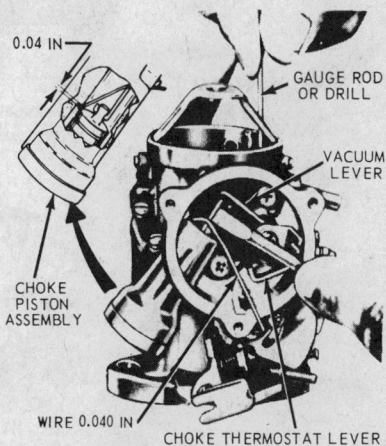

1250 carburetor choke linkage adjustment

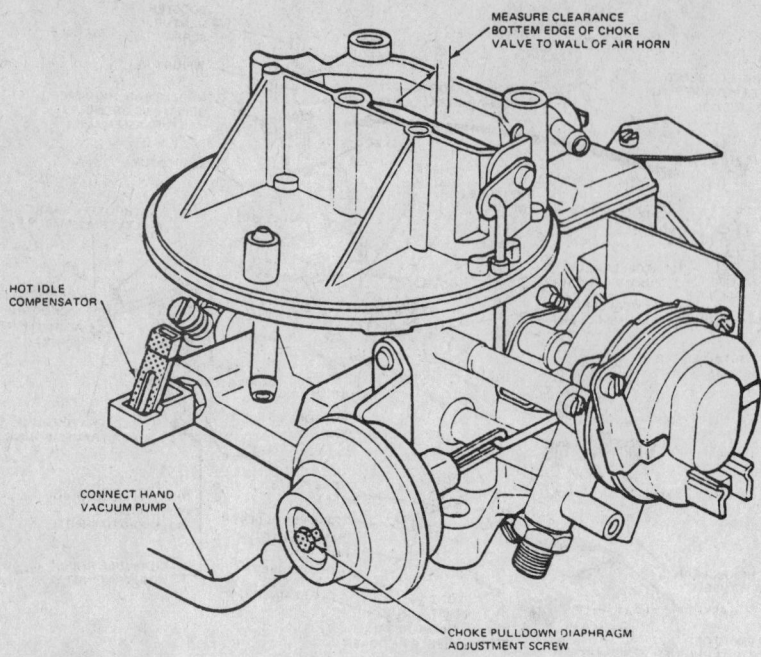

MEASURE CLEARANCE
BOTTOM EDGE OF CHOKE
VALVE TO WALL OF AIR HORN

HOT IDLE
COMPENSATOR

CONNECT HAND
VACUUM PUMP

CHOKE PULLDOWN DIAPHRAGM
ADJUSTMENT SCREW

Adjusting choke plate pull-down—2150

7. Check the clearance between the bottom of the choke plate and the wall of the carburetor. It should be 0.064–0.085 in. (no. 51–46 drill bit).

8. If the clearance is not within specifications, bend the tab on the end of the choke thermostatic lever to adjust it.

9. Remove the wire from the vacuum piston.

10. Install the choke water housing on the choke housing, making sure that tab on the end of the choke coil spring engages the slot in the choke control lever. Align the index mark on the water cover with the large index mark on the choke housing before tightening the water cover.

Choke Plate Pulldown Adjustment

1250 Carburetor

1. Remove the three screws from around the choke water cover that attach the cover to the choke housing.

2. Remove the water housing with the hoses attached.

3. Position the fast idle cam so the fast idle adjusting screw is contacting the highest step on the cam.

4. Using a screwdriver, push the vacuum diaphragm stem back into the diaphragm housing until it stops. Hold the stem in this position.

5. Insert a ¼ in. (13/64 in. for 1976–77 5200; 9/64 in. for 1976–77 2150 drill bit

into the air horn of the carburetor and apply light pressure to the choke plate to remove all slack. With the drill bit against the air horn wall, the bottom of the choke plate should just contact the drill bit.

6. If the clearance is incorrect, remove the vacuum diaphragm adjusting screw plug and insert a screwdriver into the exposed hole, then adjust the screw inward or outward as required.

7. Install the choke water housing on the choke housing, making sure the tab on the end of the coil spring engages the slot in the choke housing shaft.

8. Install the three choke water housing attaching screws and tighten them finger-tight. Adjust the automatic choke as previously described.

2150 and 5200 Carburetor

1. Set the throttle on the fast idle cam top step.

2. Loosen the screws and rotate the choke cap 90° in the rich direction.

3. Force the pulldown control diaphragm link in the direction of applied vacuum.

4. Measure the clearance between the bottom edge of the choke plate and the center of the carburetor air horn wall nearest the fuel bowl.

5. Pulldown should be 0.178–0.218. Reset if necessary by adjusting diaphragm stop on the end of the choke pulldown diaphragm.

6. Reset choke cap to original position.

Float Level Adjustments

1250 Carburetor

1. Remove the air cleaner.

2. Disconnect the fuel inlet hose and the decel valve hose at the carburetor.

3. Remove the choke fast idle cam pivot screw.

4. Remove the screws retaining the thermostatic spring housing and spring and then remove the spring.

5. Remove the screws and spring washers retaining the carburetor upper

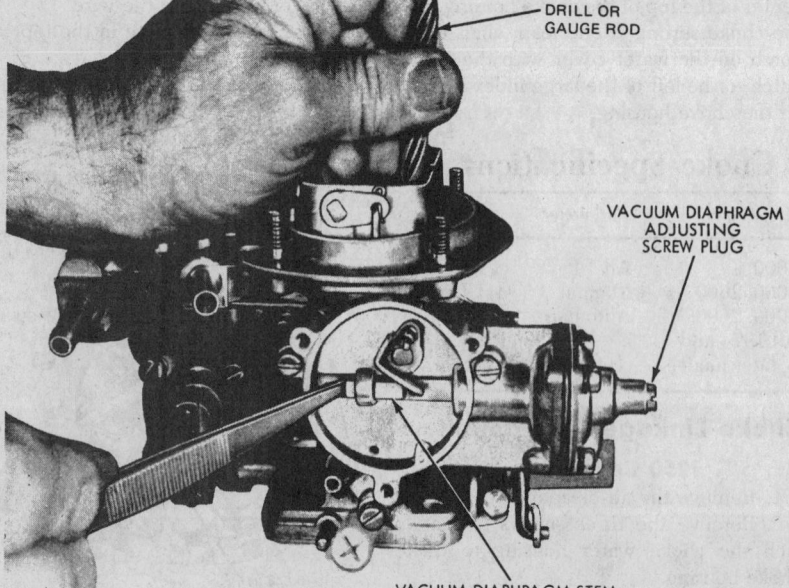

DRILL OR
GAUGE ROD

VACUUM DIAPHRAGM
ADJUSTING
SCREW PLUG

VACUUM DIAPHRAGM STEM

5200 carburetor choke linkage adjustment

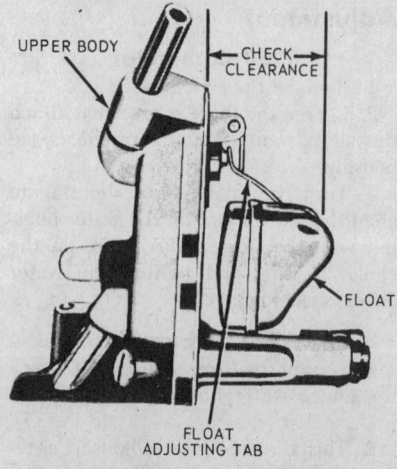

UPPER BODY

CHECK
CLEARANCE

FLOAT

FLOAT
ADJUSTING TAB

1250 carburetor float level adjustment

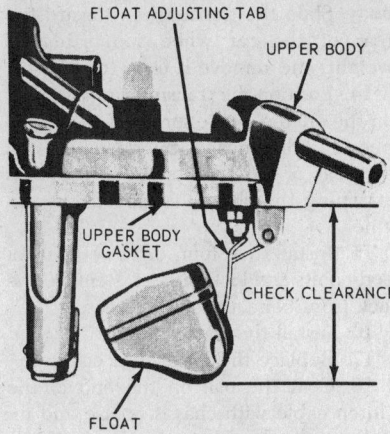

FLOAT ADJUSTING TAB
UPPER BODY
UPPER BODY GASKET
CHECK CLEARANCE
FLOAT

1250 carburetor float drop adjustment

body to the lower body. Carefully lift off the body.

6. Hold the carburetor upper body in a vertical position with the float hanging down.

7. Measure the distance from the bottom of the float to the upper body gasket. Adjust the distance to 1.20 in. by bending the tab which rests against the needle valve.

8. Turn the upper body to the upright position and again measure the distance from the bottom of the float to the gasket. Adjust the distance to 1.40 in. by bending the tab which rests on the needle valve housing.

9. Position the air horn gasket to the upper body.

10. Carefully position the upper body to the lower body and install the retaining screws.

11. Install the fuel inlet hose and decel valve hose to the carburetor.

12. Install the choke thermostatic housing with the bimetallic spring in the center slot of the lever. The index mark on the housing should be aligned with the specified mark on the body. Secure the housing with the retaining screws.

13. Replace the air cleaner assembly.

2150 Carburetor

A two stage adjustment procedure is necessary.

1. Remove and invert the air horn. With the inlet needle seated, check the distance between the top surface of the main body gasket and the top of the float. Setting should be ⅜″.

2. Bend float tab, if necessary, to adjust.

3. Replace air horn and operate engine to normal operating temperature. Place vehicle on as flat a surface as possible.

4. Stop engine and remove the air horn attaching screws.

5. Start engine and remove air horn.

6. While the engine is idling, use a standard depth scale to measure the vertical distance from the top of the ma-

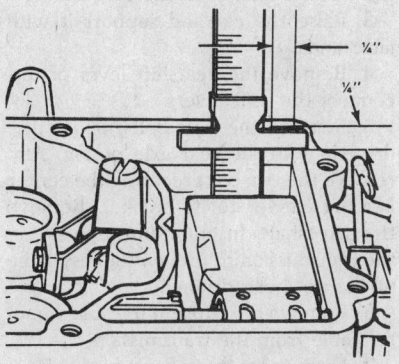

FLOAT LEVEL GAUGE
FoMoCo
FLOAT SHOULD JUST TOUCH AT THIS POINT

Dry float level adjustment—2150

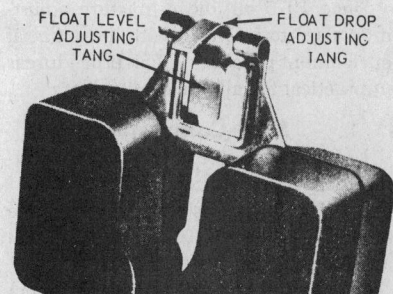

¼″
¼″

Wet float level adjustment—2150

chined surface of the carburetor main body to the level of the fuel in the bowl. The measurement must be made at least ¼″ away from any vertical surface. Setting should be ¾″.

7. If adjustment is necessary, stop engine and bend tab on float to adjust.

5200 Carburetor

1. Remove the air cleaner.

2. Disconnect the fuel and decel valve hoses from the carburetor.

3. Remove the small clip that attaches the choke rod to the choke plate shaft

and disconnect the rod from the shaft.

4. Remove the screws that attach the upper body of the carburetor to the main body of the carburetor and carefully lift the upper body off the main body. Be careful not to tear the upper body gasket.

5. Turn the carburetor upper body upside down and measure the clearance between the bottom of each float and the bottom of the carburetor upper body. The clearance should be 0.420 in. (0.460 for the 1974 2000 cc and 1976–77 2300 cc).

6. If the clearance is incorrect, bend the float level adjusting tang to correct it. **NOTE:** *Both floats must be adjusted to the same clearance.*

7. With the upper body still in the inverted position, measure the clearance between the tang on the rear of the float mounting bracket and the bumper spring on the float pivot pin. The clearance should be 0.020–0.050 in. If the clearance is incorrect, bend the float drop tang to adjust it.

8. Position the upper body and gasket of the main body of the carburetor and connect the choke rod to the choke plate lever. Install the choke rod attaching clip in the hole in the rod.

9. Install the upper body attaching screws.

10. Connect the fuel and decel valve hoses to the carburetor.

11. Install the air cleaner.

FLOAT LEVEL ADJUSTING TANG
FLOAT DROP ADJUSTING TANG

5200 carburetor float drop adjustment

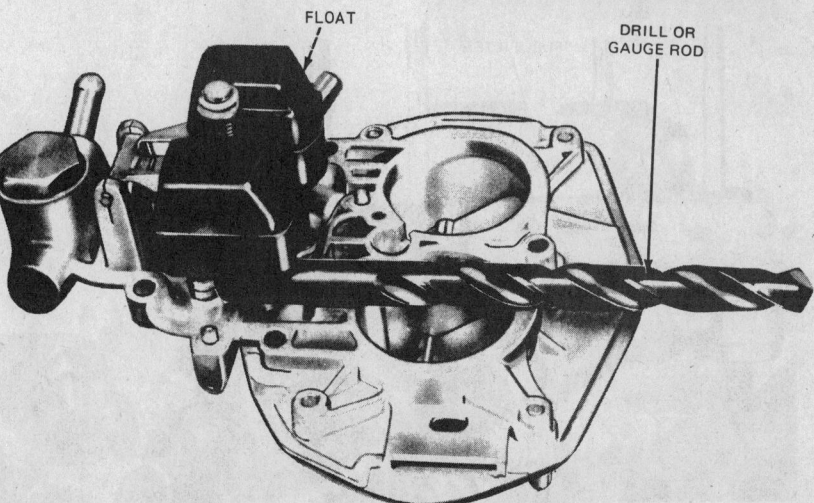

FLOAT
DRILL OR GAUGE ROD

5200 carburetor float level adjustment

Fast Idle Cam Clearance

2150 & 5200 Carburetor

1. Place a 5/32 (3/32 for 1976 and later) drill bit between the lower edge of the choke plate and the air horn wall.

2. Set the fast idle screw on the second step of the fast idle cam and measure the clearance between the choke lever tang and the arm on the fast idle cam.

3. The clearance should be about ⅛ in.

4. If the clearance is excessively large or small, bend the choke lever tang up or down. Don't bend it any more than necessary; it can break off.

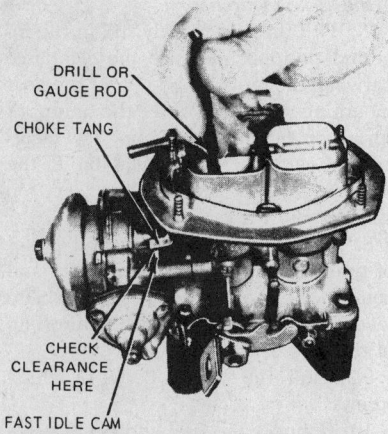

DRILL OR GAUGE ROD
CHOKE TANG
CHECK CLEARANCE HERE
FAST IDLE CAM

5200 carburetor fast idle cam clearance

Fast Idle Adjustment

Since 1975 all idle & mixture adjustments are to be made with the artificial enrichment procedure. This procedure is impractical for all but Ford dealers.

5200 Carburetor

1. Run the engine until normal operating temperature is reached.

2. Position the fast idle screw on the second step of the fast idle cam and against the shoulder of the first step.

3. Adjust the speed to 1600–1800 rpm by turning the adjusting screw.

FUEL FILTER
FAST IDLE ADJUSTING SCREW
CHOKE HOUSING

5200 carburetor fast idle adjustment

MANUAL TRANSMISSION

There are two types of transmissions used on the Capri. On Capris with the 1600 cc engine shift linkage is located inside the tailshaft. Manual transmissions used on the 2000, 2300 and V6 engines have their shift linkage located externally. Before removing these transmissions it is necessary to remove the shifter and/or linkage.

Removal and Installation

1. Disconnect the ground cable from the battery.

2. On the 1600 cc engine, disconnect the throttle linkage at the carburetor.

3. Raise the car and support it with jackstands.

4. Remove the gearshift lever or disconnect the shift levers.

5. Remove the four bolts joining the driveshaft to the rear axle pinion. Also remove the two bolts securing the center bearing carrier to its bracket. Remove the driveshaft. Install a dummy yoke in the transmission to prevent oil loss if the oil has not been drained.

6. Remove the clip and the speedometer cable from the transmission.

7. Disconnect the exhaust pipe(s) from the exhaust manifold.

8. Move the clutch release lever boot and free the clutch operating cable from the lever.

9. Remove the starter motor attaching bolts and move the starter to one side.

10. Remove the bolts holding the clutch housing to the engine.

11. Remove the bolts holding the lower dust cover from the clutch housing and detach the cover.

12. Support the rear of the engine with a jack.

13. Remove the four bolts attaching the transmission crossmember to the

body. Slide the transmission toward the rear of the car while supporting its weight, and remove it from the car.

14. Position the transmission assembly on the engine. Make sure that the clutch housing fully engages the dowel pins on the rear of the engine. Install the bolts attaching the clutch housing to the engine.

15. Install the four crossmember-to-body bolts and lockwashers. Remove the jack from beneath the engine.

16. Install the starter motor.

17. Replace the lower dust cover.

18. Coat the ball on the end of the clutch cable with chassis grease and install the clutch cable to the clutch release lever. Adjust the cable. (See the clutch section.) Locate the boot in the release lever opening.

19. Install the shift rods to the shifter, if so equipped (See the following section.)

20. Connect the exhaust pipe(s) to the exhaust manifold.

21. Install the speedometer cable and secure it with the retaining clip.

22. Install the driveshaft, aligning the mating marks. Replace the four nuts and bolts at the rear axle pinion. Locate the center bearing carrier in position and attach it to its bracket with the two bolts.

23. On the 1600 cc engine, install the gearshift lever.

24. Refill the transmission if the oil was drained.

25. Remove the jackstands and lower the car to the ground. Check the transmission and the clutch for proper operation.

Overhaul

NOTE: *Two types of manual transmission are used on the Capri. The 2000, 2300, and V6 engines use transmissions that have the shift linkage located on the outside. The 1600 cc engine uses a transmission that has the linkage located inside the top. Follow the procedure that applies to your transmission.*

Transmission Disassembly

1600 cc. Engine

1. Remove four bolts and top cover plate.

2. Pry the plug from the rear of the extension housing.

3. Remove the plunger screw from the right side of the case.

4. Working through the top cover opening, use a punch to remove the pin which secures the shift selector arm to the shift shaft.

5. Pull the shift shaft rearward, being careful not to drop the shift selector arm and the interlock plate.

6. Move the First-Second and Third-Fourth gear synchronizer hubs toward the input shaft bearing.

7. If necessary, remove the shift shaft plunger spring from the case. The plunger screw was removed in Step 3.

8. Remove the pin from the Third-Fourth shift fork. Remove the fork.

9. Unbolt the extension housing from the case. With a plastic hammer, tap the extension housing slightly rearward. Rotate the housing until the countershaft lines up with the notch in the housing flange.

10. Tap the countershaft rearward with a brass drift until it is just clear of the front of the case. Push the countershaft out with a dummy shaft. Lower the cluster gear to the bottom of the case.

11. Remove the extension housing and output shaft assembly. The third-fourth synchronizer sleeve must be pushed forward for clearance.

12. Unbolt the front bearing retainer from the case. Remove the retainer and the gasket.

13. Remove the input shaft oil seal.

14. Remove the snap-ring from around the input shaft bearing. Tap the input shaft gear and bearing assembly out of the transmission with a brass drift. Remove the needle roller bearing from the recess in the end of the input shaft gear.

15. Remove the cluster gear, two thrust washers, and the dummy shaft, from the case. Remove 20 needle rollers and a retaining washer from each end of the cluster gear.

16. Assemble a nut, a flat washer, and a sleeve on a 5/16 in. × 24 UNF threaded bolt. Screw the bolt into the reverse idler shaft and tighten to pull out the shaft.

17. Remove the low-reverse shift fork from the lever pin inside the case. Do not remove the pin.

Component Disassembly

Third-Fourth Synchronizer

1. Remove fourth gear blocking ring from the input shaft gear side of the assembly.

2. Remove the synchronizer hub snap-ring from the forward end of the output shaft and discard.

3. Support third gear. Press the output shaft out of the third-fourth gear synchronizer and third gear. Be careful not to drop the output shaft.

4. Pull the sleeve from the hub. Remove the inserts and springs.

5. Check all parts for wear. The synchronizer hub and sleeve should be replaced if worn or damaged.

First-Second Synchronizer

1. Remove the plug in the extension housing. Remove the speedometer driven gear.

2. Remove the snap-ring which holds the output shaft bearing to the extension housing. With a plastic hammer, tap the output shaft assembly out of housing.

3. Remove the snap-ring which holds the speedometer drive gear. Pull off the gear. Remove the snap-ring which holds the output shaft bearing.

4. Support low and reverse sliding gear. Press low and reverse sliding gear, spacer, and output shaft bearing from the output shaft.

5. Remove the snap-ring which holds the first-second synchronizer assembly to the output shaft.

6. Support second gear. Press the Second gear and First-Second synchronizer assembly from the output shaft.

7. Dismantle the synchronizer assembly. Replace the synchronizer hub or sleeve if worn or damaged. The output shaft bearing must be replaced.

Input Shaft and Gear

1. Remove and discard the input shaft snap-ring.

2. Press off the input shaft bearing.

Component Assembly

Third-Fourth Synchronizer

1. Slide the gear over the hub. Place an insert in each slot.

2. Install a synchronizer spring inside the sleeve beneath the inserts; the spring tang should fit into an insert. Install the other spring on the opposite side, fitting the tang into the same insert. When viewed from the edge, the springs should run in opposite directions.

3. Place the third gear on the output shaft with the dog teeth forward. Assemble the blocking ring on the third gear cone.

4. Place the synchronizer assembly on the output shaft with the boss forward.

5. Support the hub. Press the hub on the output shaft and install a new snap-ring.

First-Second Synchronizer

1. Install the second gear on the output shaft with the cone and dog teeth to the rear.

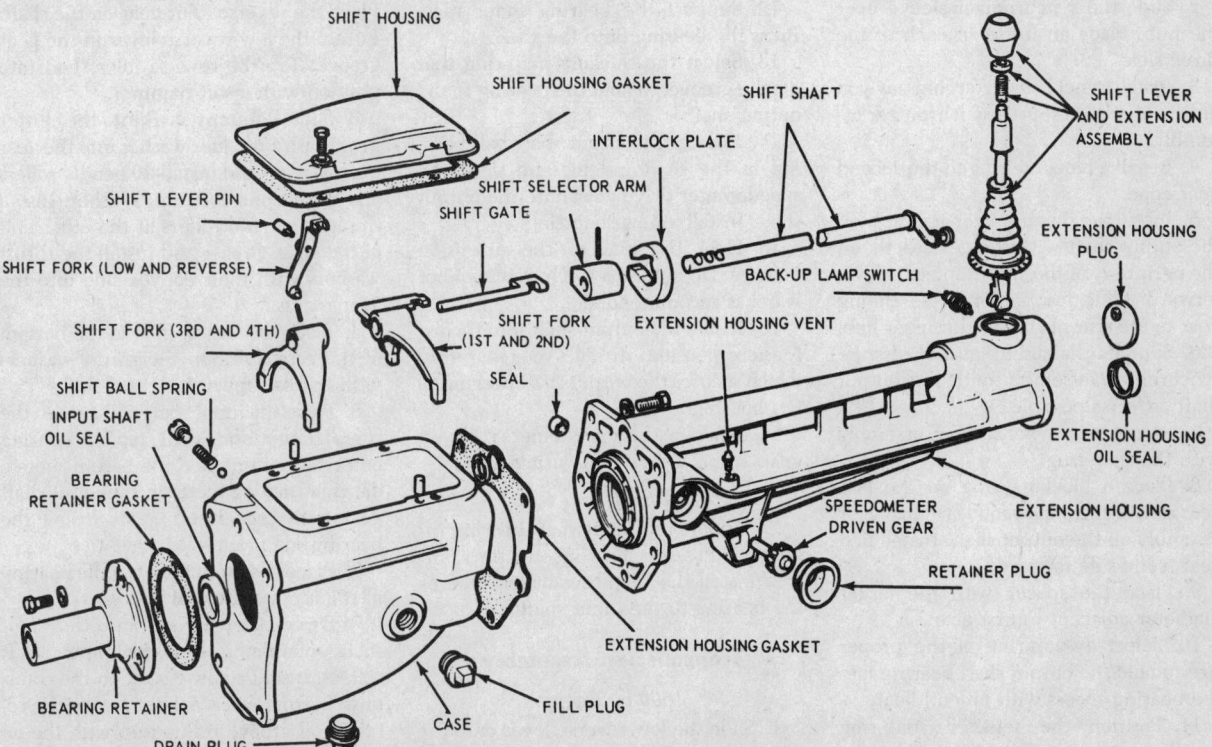

Case exploded view of the transmission used with the 1600 cc engine

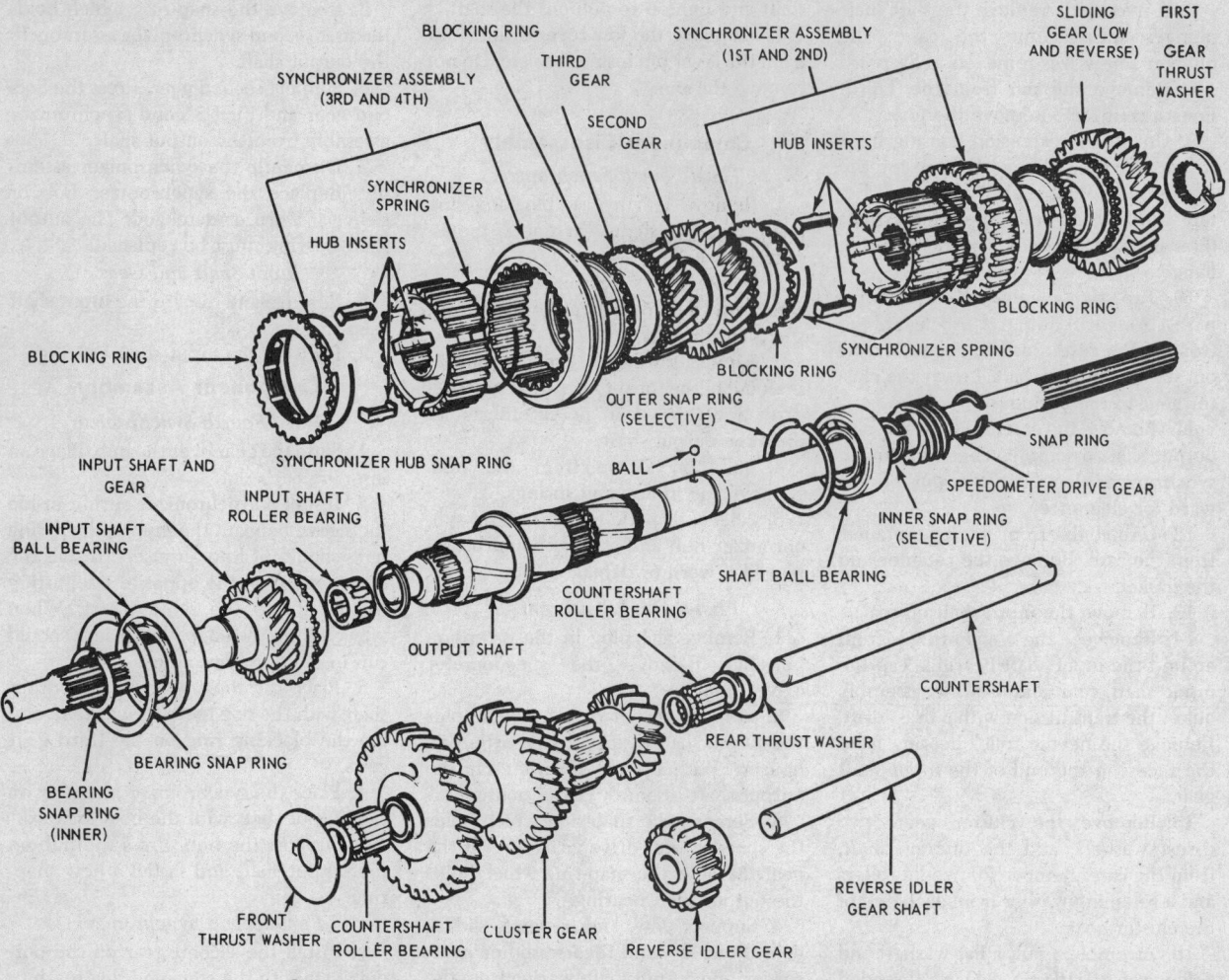

Gear train exploded view of the transmission used with the 1600 cc engine

2. Slide the synchronizer sleeve over the hub. Place an insert in each of the three slots.

3. Install synchronizer springs as you did for the third-fourth synchronizer assembly.

4. Install a blocking ring to the second gear cone.

5. Install the synchronizer assembly on the output shaft with the gear teeth, on the periphery of the synchronizer sleeve, forward. Slide low and reverse sliding gear to the rear of the synchronizer hub.

6. Support the sliding gear. Press the synchronizer assembly onto the output shaft as far as possible.

7. Secure the synchronizer assembly with the snap-ring.

8. Place a blocking ring on the first gear side of the first-second synchronizer assembly on the output shaft. Install first gear, cone side forward.

9. Place the spacer with the larger diameter adjacent to first gear.

10. Select a snap-ring of the proper size to hold the output shaft bearing into the bearing recess with no end float.

11. Position the selected snap-ring loosely on the output shaft next to the spacer.

12. Support the bearing inner race. Press the bearing onto the shaft.

13. Select the thickest snap-ring that fits the groove, to hold the bearing to the output shaft.

14. Locate the output shaft ball bearing in the shaft indent, and push the speedometer drive gear onto the output shaft. Install a new snap-ring.

15. Heat the end of the extension housing. Do not use a torch. A pan of hot water is recommended.

16. Install the output shaft into the extension housing. Install the snap-ring which secures the output shaft bearing to the housing.

17. Replace the speedometer driven gear. Install a new plug, using sealer.

Input Shaft and Gear

1. Support the input shaft bearing inner race. Press the bearing onto the shaft.

2. Install the snap-ring which secures the bearing to the input shaft.

Transmission Assembly

1600 cc Engine

1. Slide the low-reverse lever onto the lever pin inside the case.

2. Push the idler shaft into the case.

Place the reverse idler gear on the shaft. Locate the low-reverse lever in the gear groove. Tap the reverse idler shaft into position with a soft hammer.

3. Slide a dummy shaft into the cluster gear. Push a retainer washer into the gear bore. Grease and install 20 needle rollers and the second retaining washer. Install the washers and rollers at the other end of the gear. Grease and install the thrust washers with their convex side into the gear recess.

4. Place the cluster gear in the bottom of the case. Position the thrust washers with the flat upward.

5. Place the input shaft and gear in the case. Using a brass drift, tap the bearing outer race into place. Be careful not to damage the dog teeth on the input shaft gear with the cluster gear. Install the bearing snap-ring.

6. Place the input shaft needle bearing in the input shaft gear recess.

7. Drive a new oil seal into the input shaft retainer. Cover the input shaft splines. Install a new gasket on the transmission front face. Make sure that the retainer oil groove is lined up with the oil passage in the case. Coat the bolts with sealer and install them with lock-washers.

8. Locate the fourth gear blocking ring on the input shaft gear cone.

9. Install a new oil seal in the shift shaft aperture. Drive the seal in with a socket.

10. Install a new sealer coated gasket to the extension housing.

11. Pull the third-fourth synchronizer sleeve forward. Slide the extension housing and output shaft into position. Align the cutaway on the extension housing with the countershaft aperture in the rear face of the case.

12. Using loops of cord, lift the cluster gear into mesh with the output and input shaft gears. Take care not to drop the countershaft thrust washers.

13. Tap the countershaft into place, driving out the dummy shaft, and make sure that the lug on the rear of the countershaft fits into the recess on the extension housing flange.

14. Push the extension housing onto the transmission case. Apply sealer to bolts. Torque to 30–35 ft lbs.

15. Replace both shift forks. Secure the third-fourth fork with a new pin.

16. Position the shift forks to the synchronizer sleeves. Move synchronizer hubs into neutral positions.

17. Grease the shift shaft oil seal in the rear of the case. Slide the shift shaft through the extension housing. Position the shift selector arm and interlock plate so that the interlock plate locates in the cutouts in the shift forks. Pass the shift shaft through the shift selector arm and forks until the pin holes are aligned.

18. Replace the plunger ball and spring. Replace the retaining screw, using sealer.

19. Install the pin through the shift selector arm and shift shaft.

20. Apply sealer to plug. Tap plug into rear of extension housing.

21. Install top cover and gasket.

22. Refill transmission.

Transmission Disassembly

2000 cc, 2300 cc and V6 Engines

1. Remove the retaining clips and the flat washers from the shift rods at the shift levers. Remove the rods.

2. Remove the bolts which secure the shift linkage cover and remove the cover from the side of the transmission. Remove the shifter forks from the gear box.

3. Remove the bolts which hold the tailshaft to the gear box and twist the tailshaft until the countershaft becomes fully visible.

4. Remove the countershaft by driving it from the front of the gear box toward the rear using a brass drift. The countershaft should just clear the front of the case. Push the countershaft out the rest of the way with a dummy shaft. Lower the cluster gear to the bottom of the gear box.

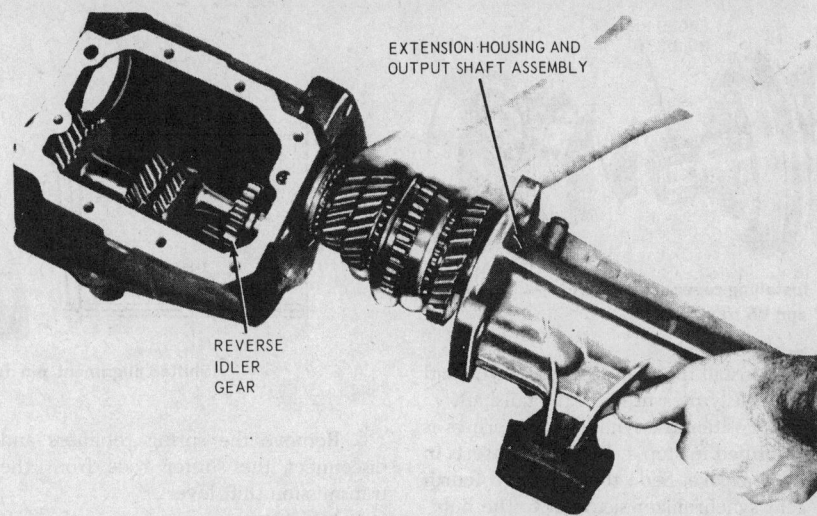

Removing tailshaft—2000, 2300, and V6 transmissions

EXTENSION HOUSING AND
OUTPUT SHAFT ASSEMBLY

REVERSE
IDLER
GEAR

5. Remove the snap ring which secures the input shaft bearing and press off the bearing.

6. Remove the tailshaft and the output shaft assembly from the gearbox.

7. Disassemble the cluster gear by allowing the dummy countershaft to fall out. Remove the needle bearings and the spacers from the cluster gear.

8. Drive out the reverse idler gear shaft toward the rear of the gear box.

9. Remove the snap-ring, in front of the third and fourth gear synchronizer, from the output shaft assembly. Remove the synchronizer assembly including third gear.

10. Remove the snap-ring and the thrust washer in front of the second gear. Remove second gear and the blocking ring.

11. Remove the first and second gear synchronizer sleeve and remove the synchronizer inserts.

12. Remove the speedometer drive gear.

13. Remove the snap-ring which retains the output bearing in the tailshaft.

14. Using a soft faced mallet, remove the output shaft from the tail shaft.

15. Remove the snap-ring from the output shaft and press off the bearing using an arbor press. Remove the spacer and first gear with the blocking ring and insert spring.

3rd/4th SYNCRONIZER

Removing third gear snap-ring—2000, 2300, and V6 transmissions

Transmission Assembly

2000 cc, 2300 cc and V6 Engines

NOTE: *Before assembling the transmission, clean all parts in a suitable solvent and check them for wear and damage. Use sealer on bolts which extend into the transmission case.*

1. Slide the insert spring, blocking ring, first gear, and the spacer onto the rear of the output shaft. Make sure that the broad side of the spacer is pointing toward the shaft bearing.

2. Install a new snap-ring on the tailshaft output shaft.

When installing a new bearing on the tail shaft, a new snap-ring should be selected as follows: Place a dummy bearing into the tailshaft and determine the distance between the top face of the bearing and the outer edge of the retaining groove, using a feeler gauge.

The thickness of the dummy bearing (0.688 in.) plus the feeler gauge blades is the total width between the stop for the bearing, and the outer edge of the snap-ring retaining groove. Measure the width of the new bearing and subtract that number from the total width just obtained. This figure is the thickness that the new snap-ring should be.

3. Install the speedometer gear along the output shaft by pressing it into place.

4. Position the first and second gear synchronizer springs in the synchronizer hub by placing one end of each spring into the same groove.

5. Position the inserts in their grooves and then slide the first and second gear synchronizer sleeve onto the synchronizer hub.

6. Slide the blocking ring, second gear and the thrust washer onto the output shaft. Install the snap-ring.

7. Heat the tailshaft. Do not use a torch. A pan of hot water is recommended. Install the output shaft and bearing into the tailshaft. Do not use a press.

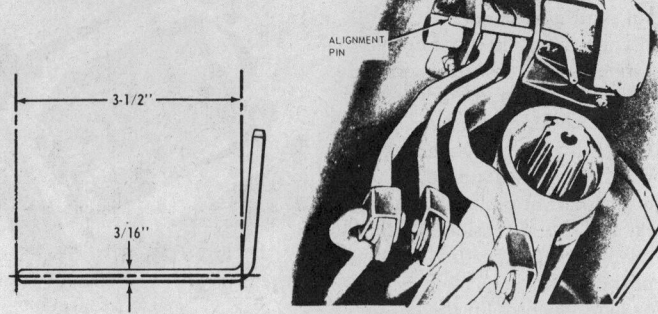

Installing caged roller bearing—2000, 2300, and V6 transmissions

Shifter alignment pin for 2000, 2300, and V6

8. Install the snap-ring which you had previously measured, in the tailshaft.

9. Position the synchronizer springs as described in step 4. Install the inserts in their groove. Slide the third and fourth gear synchronizer sleeve onto the hub.

10. Install the third and fourth gear synchronizer assembly by sliding it onto the output shaft and install the snap-ring.

11. Press the input shaft bearing onto the input shaft and install a snap-ring that gives the least possible end-play.

12. Install the input shaft and gear to the gear box using a brass drift. Install the snap-ring.

13. Install the front bearing retainer to the gear box with the gasket in place. The oil groove in the retainer should be in line with the oil passage in the gear box.

14. Install the reverse idler gear, with the collar for the selector fork facing rearward, then drive the idler gear shaft into position until it is flush against the case.

15. With a dummy pinion installed in the bottom of the gear box, install the countershaft. Position the thrust washers in the gear box.

16. Install the tailshaft using sealer on both ends. Slide the tailshaft and the output shaft into position.

17. Using cords, raise the cluster gear into mesh with the main gear train and install the countershaft. The offset lug on the rear of the countershaft must be positioned to allow final installation of the tailshaft.

18. Use a sealer and install the tailshaft bolts, torquing them to 30–35 ft lbs. Install the speedometer driven gear.

19. Install the shifter forks for first-second, and third-fourth gears so that the numbers stamped on the forks face the front of the transmission. Install the reverse fork with the number facing the *rear*.

20. Install the retaining clips and the flat washers on the shift levers and install the shift rods to the shift levers.

Linkage Adjustment

NOTE: *This procedure applies only to the 2000 cc, 2300 cc and V6 engines.*

1. Make an alignment pin out of 3/16 in. rod stock.

2. Place the gearshift lever in neutral and raise the car off the ground.

3. Remove the spring retainers and disconnect the shifter rods from the transmission shift levers.

4. Insert the alignment pin in the shift levers.

5. Place all the transmission shift levers in the neutral position.

6. Adjust the length of the shifter rods so they fit into the holes in the transmission shift levers. Install the shifter rods and the spring retainers.

7. Remove the alignment pin and lower the car to the ground. Check the transmission for proper operation.

CLUTCH

Removal and Installation

1. Remove the transmission from the car.

2. Loosen each of the pressure plate-to-flywheel attaching bolts gradually to relieve the spring pressure.

3. If the same pressure plate is being used again, match-mark it with the flywheel so it may be installed in its original position.

4. Remove the clutch disc and the pressure plate from the car.

5. Position the pressure plate and the clutch disc on the flywheel and install the attaching bolts by hand, but do not tighten them with a wrench.

6. Install a clutch (dummy or pilot) shaft to the center of the clutch disc.

7. Tighten the pressure plate attaching bolts evenly to 12–15 ft lbs.

8. Remove the dummy shaft.

9. Install the transmission.

Clutch Adjustment
1600, 2000, 2600

Loosen the locknut (1600 and 2000 cc only) and position the clutch pedal back against the stop on the pedal bracket. Pull the outer cable forward. Turn the adjusting nut as necessary to obtain a clearance of 0.125–0.145 in. between the nut and the clutch housing on the 1600 and 2000 cc. On the V6, the rear of the adjuster nut should be even with the front of the recess. With this setting, clutch pedal free-play should be ¾– 15/16 in. for the 1600 (29/32–1 7/32 for 1976 and later) 2000, and 2300 and 15/16–1 1/16 in. for the V6 clutch pedal free-play.

2. Lock the locknut but do not overtighten it.

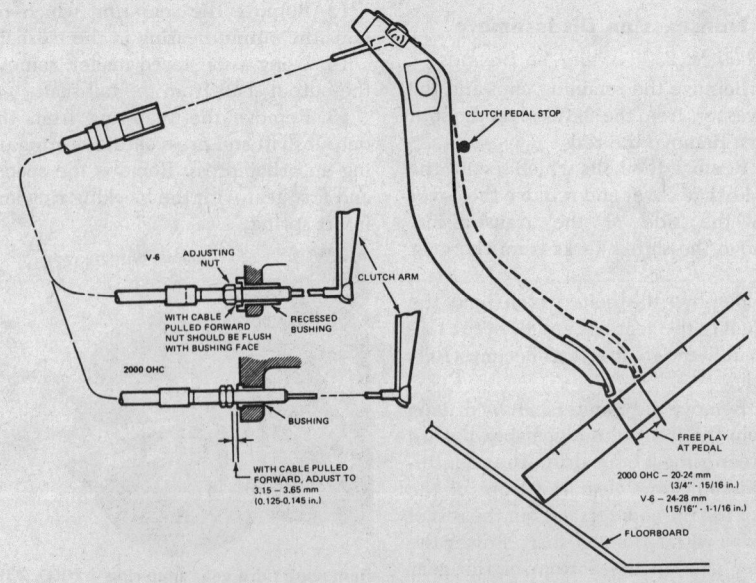

Clutch adjustment, 1600 cc engine adjustment is similar to that for 2000 OHC

3. Lubricate the pedal end of the clutch cable.

2300 cc

Pull the pedal back hard against its backstop and secure with a block of wood.

1. Raise the vehicle on a hoist and loosen the adjusting locknut. Pull the conduit forward to take up slack. While holding the cable forward, turn the adjusting nut to obtain a clearance of 3.-15–3.65 mm between the adjusting nut and the clutch housing cable bushing.

2800 cc

Block the clutch as above.

1. Raise the vehicle on a hoist and pull the conduit forward until the adjusting nut is pulled from its recess in the clutch housing cable bushing. Pull the cable forward just enough to take up slack in the release lever.

2. Turn the adjusting nut until it just comes in contact with the hexagonal recess. Release the forward pull on the cable allowing the nut to enter the recess.

AUTOMATIC TRANSMISSION

The transmission in the car can readily be identified by the vehicle identification plate. The Borg Warner Model 35 has the number 7 in the "Trans." space; the C4 has a C; the C3 has a D.

Removal and Installation

C3 Transmission

1. Raise the vehicle on a hoist.

2. Place a drain pan under the transmission fluid pan. Starting at the rear of the pan and working toward the front, loosen the attaching bolts and allow the fluid to drain. Then remove all of the pan attaching bolts except two at the front, to allow the fluid to further drain. After all the fluid has drained, install two bolts on the rear side of the pan to temporarily hold it in place.

3. Remove the converter drain plug access cover and adapter plate bolts from the lower end of the converter housing.

4. Remove the three converter-to-flywheel attaching bolts. Crank the engine to turn the converter to gain access to the bolts, using a wrench on the crankshaft pulley attaching bolt. On belt driven overhead camshaft engines, never turn the engine backwards.

5. Crank the engine until the converter drain plug is accessible and remove the plug. Place a drain pan under the converter to catch the fluid. After all the fluid has been drained from the converter, reinstall the plug and torque to specification.

6. Remove the drive shaft and install the extension housing seal replacer tool in the extension housing.

7. Remove the speedometer cable from the extension housing.

8. Disconnect the shift rod at the transmission manual lever. Disconnect the downshift rod at the transmission downshift lever.

9. Remove the starter-to-converter housing attaching bolts and position the starter out of the way.

10. Disconnect the neutral start switch wires from the switch.

11. Remove the vacuum lines from the transmission vacuum unit.

12. Position a transmission jack under the transmission and raise it slightly.

13. Remove the engine rear support-to-crossmember nut.

14. Remove the crossmember-to-frame side support attaching bolts and remove the crossmember.

15. Remove the inlet pipe steady rest from the inlet pipe and rear engine support; then disconnect the muffler inlet pipe at the exhaust manifold and secure it.

16. Lower the jack under the transmission and allow the transmission to hang.

17. Position a jack to the front of the engine and raise the engine to gain access to the two upper converter housing-to-engine attaching bolts.

18. Disconnect the oil cooler lines at the transmission. Plug all openings to keep out dirt.

19. Remove the lower converter housing-to-engine attaching bolts.

20. Remove the transmission filler tube.

21. Secure the transmission to the jack with a safety chain.

22. Remove the two upper converter housing-to-engine attaching bolts. Move the transmission to the rear and down to remove it from under the vehicle.

23. Torque the converter drain plug to specification if not previously done.

24. Position the converter to the transmission making sure the converter hub is fully engaged in the pump gear.

25. With the converter properly installed, place the transmission on the jack and secure with safety chain.

26. Rotate the converter so the bolt drive lugs and drain plug are in alignment with their holes in the flywheel.

27. With the transmission mounted on a transmission jack, move the converter and transmission assembly forward into position being careful not to damage the flywheel and the converter pilot.

During this move, to avoid damage, do not allow the transmission to get into a nosed down position as this will cause the converter to move forward and disengage from the pump gear. The converter must rest squarely against the flywheel. This indicates that the converter pilot is not binding in the engine crankshaft.

28. Install the two upper converter housing-to-engine attaching bolts and torque them to 28–38 ft lb.

29. Remove the safety chain from the transmission.

30. Insert the filler tube in the stub tube and secure it to the cylinder block with the attaching bolt. Torque the bolt to 7–10 ft. lb. If the stub tube is loosened or dislodged, it should be replaced.

31. Install the oil cooler lines in the retaining clip at the cylinder block. Connect the lines to the transmission case.

32. Remove the jack supporting the front of the engine.

33. Position the muffler inlet pipe support bracket to the converter housing and install the four lower converter housing-to-engine attaching bolts. Torque the bolts to 28–38 ft. lb.

34. Raise the transmission. Position the crossmember to the frame side supports and install the attaching bolts. Torque the bolts to 48–52 ft. lb.

35. Lower the transmission and install the rear engine support-to-crossmember nut. Torque the nut to 30–35 ft. lb.

36. Remove the transmission jack.

37. Install the vacuum hose on the transmission vacuum unit. Install the vacuum line into the retaining clip.

38. Connect the neutral start switch plug to the switch.

39. Install the starter and torque the attaching bolts to 20–25 ft. lb.

40. Install the three flywheel-to-converter attaching bolts.

Flywheel assemblies used with C3 Automatic Transmissions are designed with a pilot hole to be sure of proper flywheel-to-converter alignment. Prior to installing the transmission to the engine, the flywheel must be indexed with the pilot hole, in the six o'clock position.

When assembling the flywheel to the converter, first install the attaching bolt through the pilot hole and torque to specification (27–37 ft-lb). Install the remaining two bolts and torque to 30–35 ft. lb.

If the first bolt is not installed in the pilot hole, a misalignment of the flywheel holes and the mating converter weld nuts may occur. This misalignment will cause difficulty in installing the remaining bolts, crossthreaded bolts, or interference between flywheel and bolt threads. Any of these conditions will result in improperly torqued flywheel-to-converter attaching bolts, which may contribute to transmission or flywheel failures.

41. Install the converter drain plug access cover and adapter plate bolts. Torque the bolts to 5–7 ft lb.

42. Connect the muffler inlet pipe to the exhaust manifold.

43. Connect the transmission shift rod to the manual lever.

44. Connect the downshift rod to the downshift lever.

45. Connect the speedometer cable to the extension housing.

46. Install the drive shaft. Torque the companion flange U-bolt attaching nuts to 17–23 ft. lb.

47. Adjust the manual and downshift linkage as required.

48. Lower the vehicle. Fill the transmission to the proper level with the specified fluid.

Pour in five quarts of fluid; then run the engine and add fluid as required.

49. Check the transmission, converter assembly and oil cooler lines for leaks.

C4 Transmission

1. Raise the car on a lift.

2. Drain the fluid from the transmission. Place a pan under the transmission. Loosen the transmission pan attaching bolts and allow the fluid to drain. After some fluid has drained remove all the bolts and remove the pan.

3. Remove the ground cable from the battery at the engine block. Disconnect the starter cable from the starter. Remove the starter attaching bolts and remove the starter.

4. Remove the access cover from the lower part of the converter housing.

5. Remove the nuts which hold the converter to the flywheel. You must rotate the flywheel in order to gain access to the bolts. To rotate the flywheel, place a socket on the crankshaft pulley bolt and turn it.

6. Cars equipped with a V6 engine have a drain plug on the converter. Rotate the flywheel as previously described to gain access to the converter plug. Remove the plug and drain the fluid. Replace the plug after draining the fluid.

6. Mark the driveshaft for correct alignment when installing.

7. Remove the bolts which hold the driveshaft center bearing to the body.

8. Lower the driveshaft assembly and remove it from the car.

9. Remove the speedometer cable from the tailshaft.

10. Disconnect the shift cable from the lever on the transmission.

11. Remove the shift cable bracket from the converter housing.

12. Disconnect the downshift cable from the transmission downshift lever bracket.

13. Disconnect the neutral safety switch wires and the connectors from the switch.

14. Remove the vacuum line from the modulator on the transmission.

15. Support the transmission with a transmission jack and then remove the crossmember bolts and the crossmember.

16. Disconnect the transmission fluid cooler lines at the transmission.

17. Remove the transmission filler tube.

18. Secure the transmission to the jack with a chain.

19. Remove the converter housing attaching bolts. Move the transmission to the rear and down in order to remove it.

20. To install, move the transmission into position. The converter must rest squarely against the flywheel.

21. Install the converter housing to engine attaching bolts and tighten them to 23–33 ft lbs. Remove the chain from the transmission.

22. Install the transmission filler tube.

23. Install the transmission fluid cooler lines to the transmission.

24. Position the crossmember to the frame and install the bolts.

25. Install the flywheel-to-converter nuts and tighten them to 23–28 ft lbs.

26. Remove the transmission jack. Install the vacuum hose to the modulator.

27. Connect the neutral safety switch.

28. Connect the downshift cable to the downshift bracket. Connect the shift cable bracket to the converter housing.

29. Connect the down shift cable to the lever on the transmission.

30. Connect the speedometer cable to the tailshaft.

31. Install the driveshaft and align the marks. Install the center driveshaft bearing.

32. Install the converter housing access cover. Install the starter and the starter cable. Install the battery ground cable.

33. Lower the car to the ground and fill the transmission to the correct level with the proper fluid.

Borg Warner Transmission

1. Remove the transmission dipstick and disconnect the downshift valve cable.

2. Raise the car on a hoist and remove the transmission pan drain plug and drain the fluid.

3. Mark the driveshaft with paint, for correct alignment when installing. Remove the bolts from the flange.

4. Remove the bolts which hold the driveshaft center bearing to the body.

5. Lower the driveshaft assembly and remove it from the car.

6. Disconnect the exhaust pipe bracket from the transmission. Loosen the exhaust pipe and move it to one side.

7. Remove the speedometer cable from the transmission.

8. Disconnect the starter wires and remove the starter.

9. Remove the torque converter front cover. Remove the cap screws which hold the flex plate to the converter.

10. Disconnect the linkage control cable at the transmission. Disconnect the neutral safety switch wires.

11. Place a transmission jack under the transmission transmission, and secure the transmission to the jack with a chain.

12. Remove the four engine mount to body bolts.

13. Remove the converter housing bolts. Remove the transmission filler tube. Using a bar, apply pressure to the converter to prevent the converter from coming off the transmission when the assembly is removed.

14. Lower the transmission and converter assembly and remove it from the car.

15. To install, raise the transmission into position and install five of the six housing attaching bolts. Position the rear engine support to the body and install the bolts.

16. Remove the chain from the transmission.

17. Install the bolts which hold the flex plate to the converter. Install the converter front cover.

18. Install the starter and connect the wires.

19. Install the exhaust pipe bracket to the transmission.

20. Install the speedometer cable. Install the manual linkage control cable.

21. Connect the wires to the neutral safety switch. Install the driveshaft, aligning the marks then install the retaining bolts. Position the center bearing to the body and install the holding bolts.

22. Lower the car to the ground and install the downshift cable.

23. Fill the transmission to the proper level with specified transmission fluid.

24. Adjust the downshift cable.

Pan Removal & Installation
C4 Transmission

1. Raise the car on a hoist.

2. Place a drain pan under the transmission.

3. Starting at the rear of the pan and working toward the front, loosen the attaching bolts and allow the transmission fluid to drain.

4. Remove the bolts and the pan.

5. Remove all gasket material from the pan and the transmission mounting surface.

6. Apply gasket sealer to the oil pan and position the gasket on the pan.

7. Position the pan on the transmission and install the bolts hand-tight.

8. Torque the bolts evenly to 12–16 ft lbs. Fill the transmission to the proper level with the specified fluid.

Borg Warner Transmission

Follow the previous procedures for removal and installation. The fluid can be removed through the drainplug. The torque for the pan bolts is 8–13 ft lbs.

Pan Removal and Filter Service

C3 Transmission

1. Loosen the pan attaching bolts to drain the fluid from the transmission.

2. When the fluid has stopped draining from the transmission, remove and thoroughly clean the pan and the screen. Discard the pan gasket. Remove & clean filter screen in solvent and blow it dry.

3. Place a new gasket on the pan, and install the pan on the transmission.

4. Add three quarts of fluid to the transmission through the filler tube.

5. Run the engine at idle speed for about two minutes, and then run it at fast idle speed (about 1200 rpm) until it reaches its normal operating temperature. Do not race the engine.

6. Shift the selector lever through all the positions, place it at P, and check the fluid level. The fluid level should be above the ADD mark. If necessary, add enough fluid to the transmission to bring the level between the ADD and FULL marks on the dipstick. Do not overfill the transmission.

Filter Service

C4 and Borg Warner Transmissions

Remove the transmission pan. Remove the screws attaching the filter screen to the transmission. Wash the filter in a solvent and blow it clean of solvent with an air gun. Install the filter screen and replace the oil pan.

NOTE: *Cleaning the filter screen is not a regular maintenance procedure. It should be cleaned when the oil pan has been removed for other service procedures.*

Front Band Adjustment

C3 Transmission

1. Remove the downshift rod from the transmission downshift lever.

2. Clean all dirt from the band adjusting screw area. Remove and discard the locknut.

3. Install a new locknut on the adjusting screw and torque to 18–23 ft lb.

4. Back off the adjusting screw exactly one and a half turns.

5. Hold the adjusting screw from turning and torque the locknut to 23 ft. lb.

6. Install the downshift rod on the transmission downshift lever.

Intermediate Band Adjustment

C4 Transmission

1. Wipe the area clean around the adjusting screw on the side of the transmission.

2. Remove the adjusting screw locknut and discard it.

3. Install a new locknut on the adjusting screw but do not tighten it.

4. Tighten the adjusting screw to exactly 10 ft lbs.

5. Back off the adjusting screw exactly 1 ¾ turns.

6. Hold the adjusting screw so that it does not turn and tighten the locknut to 35–45 ft lbs.

NOTE: *The tools used in the illustration of band adjustment are: a torque wrench, an extension, and an allen socket.*

Borg Warner Transmission

1. Drain the transmission fluid. Remove the pan.

2. Remove the servo rear mounting bolt, the two fluid transfer tubes, and the cam plate.

3. Pull out on the servo actuating lever and insert a ¼ in. spacer between the adjusting screw and the servo piston stem.

4. Tighten the adjusting screw to 10 in lbs.

5. Hold the adjusting screw stationary and position the one-way clutch spring two threads away from the actuating lever with the long leg of the spring to the rear. Now install the cam plate, being careful to engage the leg of the spring in the ramp.

6. Install the two fluid transfer tubes. Install the pan with a new gasket.

7. Refill the transmission.

Low-Reverse Band Adjustment

C4 Transmission

1. Wipe the area clean around the adjustment screw on the side of the transmission.

2. Remove the adjusting screw locknut and discard it.

3. Install a new locknut but do not tighten it.

4. Tighten the adjusting screw to exactly 10 ft lbs.

5. Back off the adjusting screw exactly three full turns.

6. Hold the adjusting screw so that it does not turn and tighten the locknut to 35–45 ft lbs.

Borg Warner Transmission

1. Snap out the woodgrain panel at the rear of the console. Remove the two screws and slide the plastic cross panel forward to remove.

2. Lift up the rear corners of the handbrake boot and remove the two screws. Pry up the rear edge of the front woodgrain panel and remove the center retaining screw. Remove the two screws, one on each side of the lower forward console edge, and remove the console. Pull the carpet back on the right.

3. If there isn't an access hole, cut one.

4. Loosen the locknut and tighten the adjusting screw to 10 ft lbs. Back off the adjusting screw one complete turn.

5. Tighten the locknut to 25–30 ft lbs without disturbing the adjusting screw.

6. Plug the hole in the transmission tunnel and replace the carpet and console.

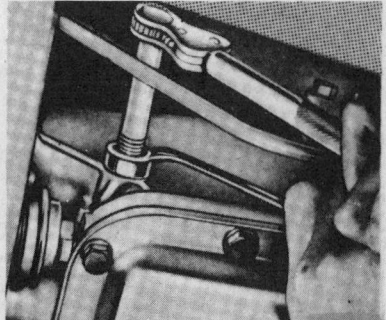

Adjusting low-reverse band—C4 automatic transmission.

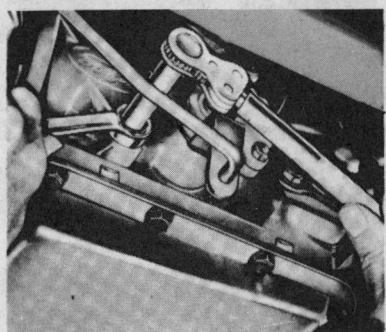

Adjusting intermediate band—C4 automatic transmission.

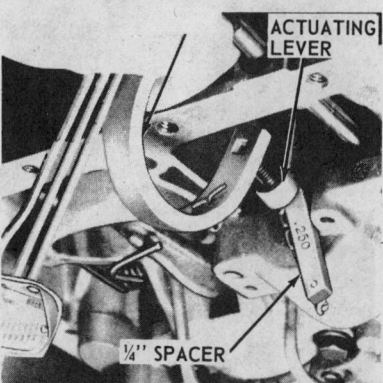

Borg Warner automatic intermediate band adjustment. The U-shaped device is a special wrench.

C-3 front band adjustment

Shift Linkage Adjustment

1. Position the transmission selector lever in the Drive position.

2. Raise the car and remove the clevis pin and disconnect the cable and the bushing from the transmission.

3. Move the transmission lever to the Drive position, which is the third detent from the back of the transmission on the Borg Warner and C4. It is the third detent from the front on the C3.

4. With the transmission selector lever and the transmission lever in the Drive positions, adjust the cable length until the clevis pin holes in the transmission lever and the end of the cable are aligned.

5. Connect the cable, lower the car, and check the operation of the transmission in each selector lever position.

Downshift Linkage Adjustment

C3 Transmission

The transmission kick-down cable is

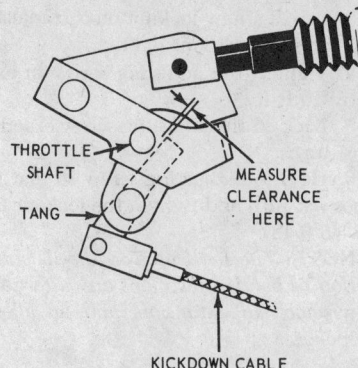

C4 automatic transmission kickdown linkage adjustment.

adjusted by varying the position of the cable housing in its mounting bracket. To adjust:

1. Hold the accelerator pedal in full throttle position with a suitable wedge.

2. Place the transmission lever in full kick-down position.

3. Loosen the top nut and adjust bottom nut to give a 0.020 to 0.080 inch clearance between the carburetor linkage kick-down lever and the throttle operating shaft. Tighten the top nut.

4. Remove the weight from the accelerator and operate the linkage several times to be sure that wide open throttle and full transmission kick-down can be achieved.

C4 Transmission

1. Press the gas pedal to the floor to completely open the throttle.

2. Position the kick-down cable so that the tang just contacts the throttle shaft.

3. If an adjustment is required, loosen the two kick-down cable adjusting nuts at the bracket and move the cable as required. Tighten the adjusting nuts.

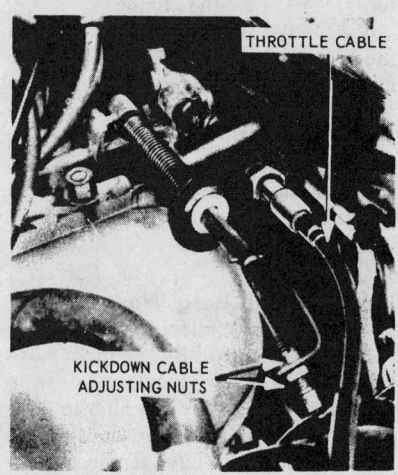

C4 automatic transmission kickdown linkage adjustment nuts.

Borg Warner Transmission

The downshift valve control cable governs the transmission control pressure which, in turn, determines the shift points. It also manually downshifts the transmission at full throttle.

NOTE: *This procedure is recommended only for service personnel skilled in automatic transmission adjustment. The instructions must be followed exactly.*

1. Connect a tachometer to the engine.

2. Attach a pressure gauge to the control pressure take-off at the rear of the transmission.

3. Allow the engine to warm up (in Neutral) to normal operating temperature.

4. Apply the parking brake and block the wheels securely. Do not stand in front of the car.

5. Adjust the idle speed to 630–680 rpm in Drive. The pressure should be 50–65 psi.

6. Apply the footbrakes and increase the engine speed 500 rpm above idle, in Drive. The pressure should increase 15–20 psi over idle.

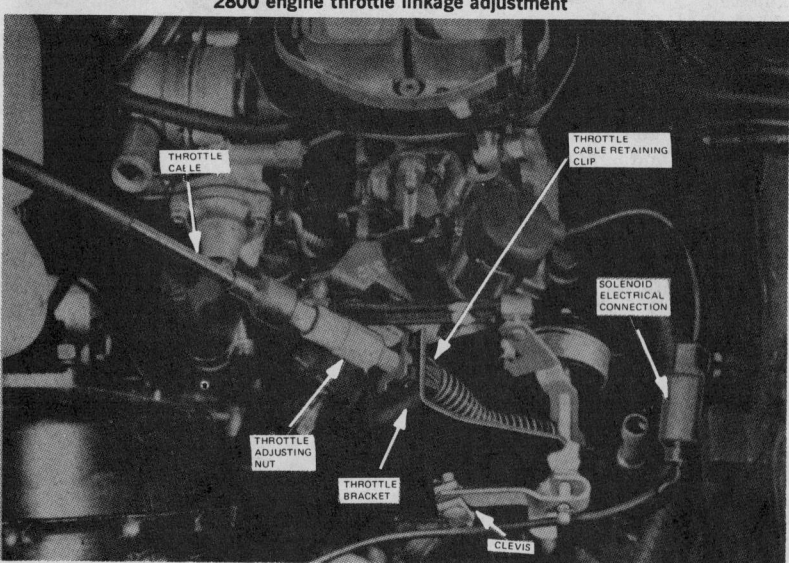

2800 engine throttle linkage adjustment

2300 engine throttle linkage adjustment

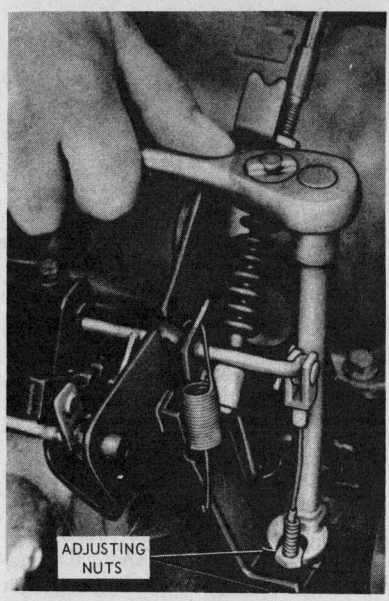

Borg Warner automatic transmission down-shift cable adjustment

CAUTION: *Do not operate the engine at this speed, in Drive, for more than 20 seconds. If the engine speed exceeds 500 rpm over idle speed, release the accelerator and let the engine idle before restarting the test. Do not perform the test repeatedly.*

7. Adjust the downshift valve control cable to get the pressures specified in Steps 5 and 6.

Neutral Safety Switch

Removal and Installation, Adjustment

C3 Transmission

1. Raise car on hoist.
2. Disconnect cable connector from switch.
3. Use a thin wall socket to remove the neutral start switch and O-ring.
4. Install new O-ring and neutral start switch. Tighten switch to specified torque.
5. Install cable connector.
6. Check the operation of the switch in each detent position. Check to see the back-up light operates in reverse only. The engine should start only with the transmission selector lever in N (neutral) and P (park).

C4 Transmission

1. Remove the downshift cable from the transmission downshift lever.
2. Remove the transmission downshift outer lever retaining nut and lever. It may be necessary to apply penetrating oil to the lever shaft and nut in order to remove the nut and lever.
3. Remove the neutral safety switch attaching bolts.
4. Disconnect the multiple wire connector. Remove the switch.

5. Install the new switch on the transmission. Install the attaching bolts.
6. With the transmission lever in neutral, rotate the switch and insert a gauge pin (no. 43 drill) into the gauge pin hole.
7. Tighten the switch attaching bolts to 4–8 ft lbs and remove the gauge pin.
8. Install the outer downshift lever and attaching nut, and install the downshift cable to the downshift lever.
9. Install the switch wires. Connect the multiple wire connector. Check the operation of the switch in each lever position. The engine should start only with the transmission lever in the Neutral or Park position.

Borg-Warner Transmission

1. Place the transmission lever in Drive.
2. Raise the car and disconnect the four leads from the neutral safety switch.
3. Loosen the locknut using a 11/16 in. "crow's foot" and unscrew the switch from the transmission. Remember the number of turns required to remove it.
4. Screw the new switch in about the same number of turns as required to remove the old one. Back out a couple of turns.
5. Connect a battery powered test light across the backup light terminals (the two big ones).
6. Screw the switch in until the test light goes out. Make a mark on the switch and transmission case at this point.
7. Connect the test light to the two small terminals, the starter terminals.
8. Screw in the switch until the test light lights. Mark this position.
9. Unscrew the switch to a point halfway between the marks made in Steps 6 and 8. Tighten the locknut and connect the leads.
10. Check that the engine will start only with a transmission in Neutral or Park. Have an assistant check the backup lights.

DRIVE AXLES

Driveshaft and Universal Joints

Through 1974

A two-piece, tubular driveshaft is splined to the transmission output shaft and transmits power through three universal joints and a center bearing, situated in front of the middle universal joint, to the rear axle pinion flange. A constant velocity type center universal joint is used. When this joint requires service, the manufacturer recommends that the entire driveshaft assembly be replaced.

Capri II

The Capri II uses a one-piece drive-shaft with two serviceable universal joints. There is no center bearing.

Driveshaft

Removal and Installation

1. Mark the driveshaft and the rear axle pinion flange for correct realignment when installing and then remove the four attaching bolts and lockwashers.
2. Remove the two bolts and the lockwashers securing the center bearing to the body.
3. Lower the driveshaft assembly and withdraw it from the transmission. A slight amount of oil may leak from the transmission.
4. Slide the front yoke into the transmission, engaging the output shaft splines, taking care not to damage the oil seal or bearing in the tail shaft.
5. Lift the rear of the driveshaft assembly, and align the marks on the driveshaft and the rear axle pinion flange. Fit the four bolts and the lockwashers, and tighten them.
6. Secure the center bearing carrier to its bracket and tighten the attaching bolts to 13–17 ft lbs.
7. Check the level of the transmission lubricant.

Universal Joint Overhaul

NOTE: *This procedure is for service replacement and 1972–73 original equipment U-joints with snap-ring bearing cap retainers. 1974 and later original equipment retainers are pressed in with a preload and staked in place.*

1. Remove the driveshaft.
2. Position the driveshaft assembly in a vise.
3. Remove the snap-rings which retain the bearing caps.
4. Using a suitably sized socket or an arbor press, drive one of the bearing caps in toward the center of the universal joint. This will force the opposite bearing cap out.
5. As each bearing cap is pressed or punched far enough out of the universal joint assembly so that it is accessible, grip it with a pair of pliers and pull it from the driveshaft yoke. Drive or press the spider in the opposite direction in order to make the opposite bearing cap accessible and pull it free with a pair of pliers. Use this procedure to remove all bearings from the universal joints.
6. After removing the bearings, lift the spider from the yoke.
7. Thoroughly clean the yoke areas on the driveshaft.

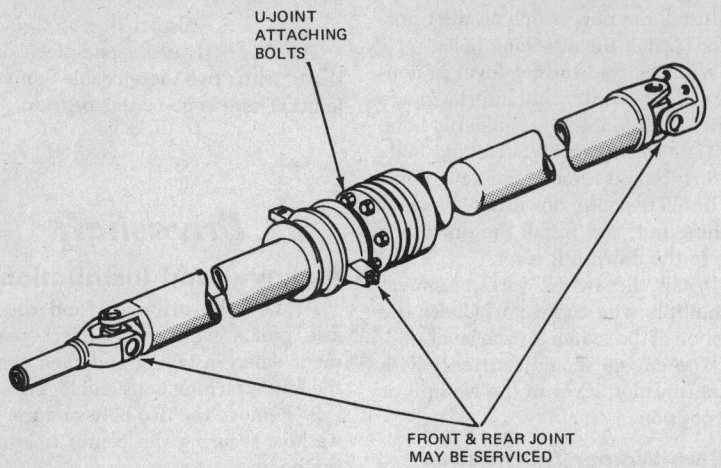

The constant velocity center universal joint is to be serviced by replacement of the complete assembly.

CAUTION: *Use extreme care when installing a new bearing into position. A heavy jolt can cause one or more of the needle bearings to fall out of place which will stop the cap from sitting properly on the spider.*

8. Start a new bearing into the yoke.

9. Position the spider in the yoke and press or drive the new bearing cap ¼ in. below the surface of the yoke.

10. With the bearing cap in position, install a new snap-ring.

11. Start a new bearing cap into the opposite side of the yoke.

12. Press or drive the bearing cap until the opposite bearing—which you have just installed—contacts the inner surface of the snap-ring.

13. Install a new snap-ring on the second bearing cap.

14. Position the slip yoke on the spider and install new bearings and snap-rings.

15. Check the reassembled joints for freedom of movement. Never install a driveshaft in a car if there is any binding in the universal joints.

Center Bearing

Removal and Installation

1. Remove the driveshaft.

2. Mark the center universal yoke and the front universal yoke for correct realignment when installing. On the constant velocity center universal joint,

mark the two halves of the joint housing before removing the six bolts to separate the halves. Bend back the locktab in the center of the universal yoke and loosen the retaining bolt. Remove the U-shaped plate and separate the two halves of the driveshaft.

3. Remove the driveshaft and the bearing assembly from the rubber insulator.

4. Bend back the tabs securing the rubber insulator into its carrier and then remove the insulator.

5. Remove the bearing and the protective caps from the driveshaft with a puller.

6. Drive the ball bearing and the protective caps onto the driveshaft.

7. Insert the rubber insulator into its carrier with the boss upward. Bend the tabs on the carrier back over the beaded edge of the rubber insulator.

8. Slide the carrier and the rubber insulator over the bearing assembly.

9. Screw the retaining bolt with a new locktab onto the end of the front driveshaft, leaving enough space to allow for the U-shaped plate.

10. Align the mating marks on the two universal joint yokes and assemble the driveshaft. Insert the U-shaped plate, with the smooth surface toward the bolt under the retaining bolt head and tighten the bolt to 25–30 ft lbs. Bend the locktab up.

11. Install the driveshaft.

Axle Shaft and/or Bearing Replacement

Removal and Installation

1. Jack up the rear of the car and support it with jackstands.

2. Remove the wheel, brake drum securing screw, and the brake drum. Be sure that the parking brake is released.

3. Remove the bolts that secure the bearing retaining plate to the backing plate. These bolts are accessible through holes in the axle shaft flange.

4. Pull the axle and bearing assembly out of the axle housing with a slide hammer.

5. Loosen the inner retaining ring by nicking it deeply with a chisel in several places. It will then slide off easily.

6. Press off the bearing and seal assembly and install the new one by pressing it into position.

7. Press on the new retainer.

8. Assemble the shaft and the bearing in the housing.

9. Install the retaining nuts, drum, wheel, and tire.

Differential

Removal

1. Jack up the car and pull the axle shafts.

2. Mark the driveshaft and pinion flanges for realignment. Remove the four bolts and washers, the ten retaining bolts, the cover, the gasket, and drain the axle.

3. Match mark and remove the differential bearing caps. Using two pry bars, remove the differential.

Overhaul

1. Pull off the bearings from each side of the differential assembly. Remove the shims.

2. Unscrew the ring gear retaining bolts and remove the ring gear from the differential assembly.

3. Drive out the locking pin which secures the differential pinion shaft in the differential case. Remove the pinion shaft, differential pinions, differential side gears and adjusting shims.

4. Hold the drive pinion flange and remove the nut. Pull off the pinion flange using a puller. Remove the pinion and bearing spacer from the pinion.

5. Press off the large roller bearing from the pinion shaft, remove the spacer shim from the pinion shaft.

6. Remove the small tapered roller bearing together with the oil seal from the axle housing.

7. Drive the bearing races out from the axle housing.

8. Install the pinion bearing races, pulling them squarely into position.

9. To determine total side play of the differential case in the housing, press the

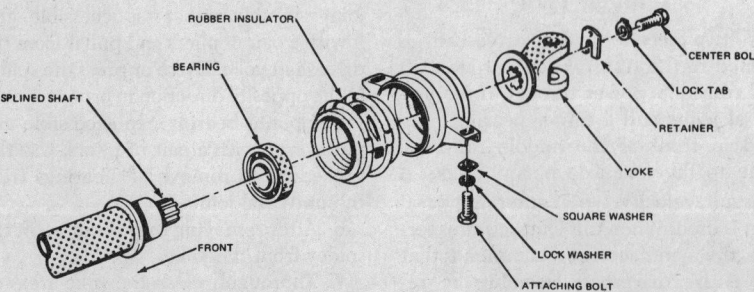

Details of the center driveshaft bearing

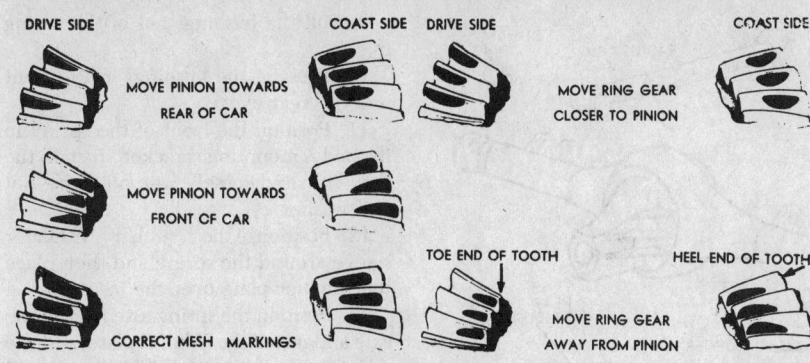

DRIVE SIDE   COAST SIDE   DRIVE SIDE   COAST SIDE

MOVE PINION TOWARDS REAR OF CAR

MOVE RING GEAR CLOSER TO PINION

MOVE PINION TOWARDS FRONT OF CAR

TOE END OF TOOTH   HEEL END OF TOOTH

CORRECT MESH MARKINGS

MOVE RING GEAR AWAY FROM PINION

Pinion mesh markings

taper roller bearings on the differential case without shims. Install pressure blocks into the axle tubes and install the differential into the housing. Install the bearing caps, tighten, loosen, then retighten finger tight. Mount a dial indicator gauge on the axle housing so the feeler contacts the side of the ring gear and the dial reads zero. By moving the differential, the total side play can be measured. Record this measurement. Remove the differential and pressure blocks.

10. To determine the thickness of the pinion bearing spacer, use the trial and error method. Install the pinion with a selected spacer, small taper bearing, drive pinion flange, and the old self-locking nut. Tighten the nut to 72–87 ft lbs. and rotate the pinion several times using an in. lbs. torque wrench. If the rotating torque required is too high, the spacer is too thin, and should be replaced with a thicker one. If the torque is too low, a thinner spacer should be used. Correct torque is 13–19 in. lbs. Remove the old nut. To check the spacer thickness, use the method described in "Pinion Mesh Markings."

11. Make sure that the new oil seal has grease between the two sealing lips and is coated with sealing compound on the other side. Install it with a new self locking nut and torque to 72–87 ft lbs.

12. Remove the differential case bearings. Position the shims as indicated by the total side play figure, one half of the required amount on each side, on the differential case. Press the taper roller bearings on the differential case. Insert the case in the axle housing and center it. Position the bearing caps as marked. Insert the screws and torque to 43–49 ft lbs.

13. Position the dial indicator feeler in a vertical position on one ring gear tooth and check the tooth flank backlash. If the backlash is not within 0.005–0.009 in. (0.-12–0.22 mm.) the differential must be removed again. If the backlash is too large, remove the shims from the ring gear face side and transfer to ring gear back side. Reverse procedure if backlash is too small. Do not increase or decrease

Measuring ring gear backlash

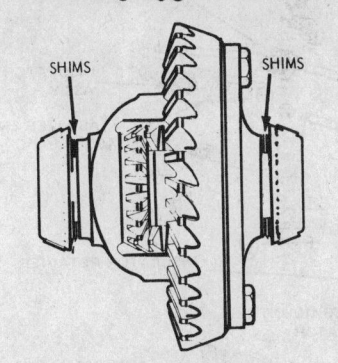

SHIMS   SHIMS

Location of differential case side shims

number of shims, but only interchange between one side and the other.

14. For proper tooth contact pattern check, see "Pinion Mesh Markings."

15. Position a new gasket and the axle case cover on the axle case, secure with bolts and torque to 22–29 ft lbs.

16. Install the driveshaft, axles and wheels.

Pinion Mesh Markings

The following method of determining the relative position of the ring gear and pinion, and whether or not they are in proper mesh, will prove satisfactory for all pinion and ring gears. This should be followed by a final check, even when the pinion depth has been determined by special tools. Assemble the pinion in the housing, without preload, and tighten the pinion nut until a preload of about 10 in. lbs. is developed on the bearings to insure that they are completely free of end play.

This, of course, is not the final bearing

preload setting, but is a good one for checking the pinion mesh markings.

Install the differential assembly and adjust it to provide from 0.004–0.008 in. backlash of the ring gear, measured at the rim of the gear.

Paint five or six of the ring gear teeth with red lead and, while a helper brakes the ring gear with a piece of wood, slowly turn the pinion until the ring gear makes at least one full revolution. The mesh of the pinion with the ring gear will be indicated as a mark in the red lead on the ring gear teeth. Compare this mark with the accompanying illustrations. The caption on each photograph explains whether the mark indicates the pinion is too deep or too shallow, the ring gear too close or too far away.

When the marking is found to be improper, it is customary to make trial changes in increments of 0.005 or 0.007 in. If changing the shim 0.005–0.007 throws the marking from too deep to too shallow, the proper distance is about halfway between.

If, after changing this increment of shims, the mark still indicates that more must be changed, it is advisable to continue changing in the same increments.

While considerable time is generally required to disassemble the unit, press off the bearings, change the shims, press the bearing back on and reassemble the unit, this is still the only positive method of determining that the differential will operate quietly after it is finally installed in the car.

Differential Specifications

	1600	2000	2600	2300 & 2800
Axle Ratio	3.89:1*	3.44:1	3.22:1	3.08:1
No. teeth in pinion	9	9	9	11
No. teeth in ring gear	35	31	29	34
Oil capacity	2.3	2.3	2.3	2.3
Side gear play	0.004-0.006			
Bearing pre-load	0.0012-0.0031			
Backlash	0.047-0.086			

* 1600 cc only

REAR SUSPENSION

The rear axle is suspended by two three leaf springs. Two radius arms, which are attached to the body at one end and the rear axle at the other, assist the springs in controlling lateral movement of the rear axle on models through

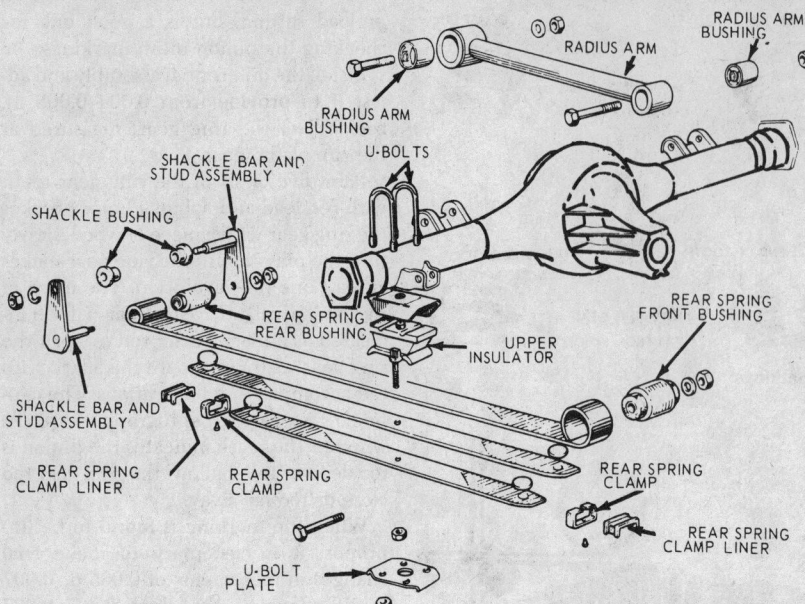

Rear suspension through 1972—exploded view.

Capri rear suspension beginning 1973—exploded view

1972. This function is handled by a stabilizer bar on 1973 and later models. Sealed, hydraulic shock absorbers are positioned between the rear axle and the reinforced mountings on the floor pan. The shock absorbers are staggered on the axle. The right-hand shock absorber axle mounting is located in front of the rear axle and the left-hand shock is mounted to the rear of the axle.

Springs

Removal and Installation

1. Block each front wheel.
2. Jack up the rear of the car and support it with jackstands.

3. Position a jack under the rear axle and extend it sufficiently to support the axle.

4. Remove the rear shackle nuts and the washers and then detach the combined shackle bolt and the plate assemblies. Remove the two rubber bushings.

NOTE: *Skip steps 5–10 if you are not replacing the bushings.*

5. Unscrew the nut from the front mounting bracket and then withdraw the thru-bolt.

6. Remove the U-bolts and then the attaching plate.

7. Remove the spring assembly.

8. Remove the insulator sleeve and the retaining plate from the spring.

9. Pull the bushings out of the spring eyes.

10. Press in the bushings in the front and the rear eyes.

11. Position the front of the spring in its body mounting bracket. Install the thru-bolt and loosely assemble the nut and washer.

12. Position the rubber insulator sleeve around the spring and then place the retainer plate over the insulator.

13. Position the spring assembly to the axle and install the U-bolts, plate, and the nuts. Tighten the nuts initially to about 5 ft lbs to compress the rubber insulators.

14. Place the spring into position and assemble the rear shackle bolt and plate assemblies. Install the nuts and washers but do not tighten them.

15. Remove the jack supporting the rear axle.

16. Lower the car to the ground.

17. Tighten the U-bolts, front hanger nuts, and the axle shackle nuts. Refer to the following chart for torque specifications.

Shock Absorbers

Removal and Installation

Through 1974

1. Block each front wheel.
2. Jack up the rear of the car and support it with jackstands.
3. From inside the trunk, remove the two nuts from the top of the shock absorbers.
4. Lift off the top steel washer and the rubber bushing.
5. Detach the lower end of the shock absorber from the bracket on the axle by removing the nut, lockwasher, and bolt. Remove the shock absorber from the car.
6. Remove the rubber bushing and the steel washer from the top of the shock absorber.
7. Assemble the large steel washer and the rubber bushing on the top of the shock absorber.
8. Extend the upper end of the shock absorber through the mounting hole in the body. Position the rubber bushing

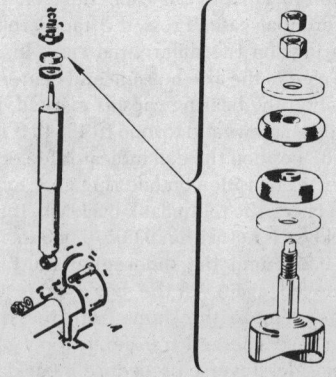

Rear shock absorber assembly

and the washer over the piston rod and hold it in place by installing the nut, but do not tighten it.

9. Install the lower end of the shock absorber into the bracket on the axle and line up the holes in the bracket with the hole in the shock absorber. Install the bolt, lockwasher, and nut. Tighten the bolt to 40–45 ft lbs.

10. Remove the jackstands and lower the car to the ground.

11. Tighten the shock absorber retaining nut, from inside the trunk, to 15–20 ft lbs. Install the locknut and tighten it securely.

1975–77

1. Remove the two rear seat attaching bolts and remove the rear seat.

2. Unscrew the seat belt retaining bolt from the upper end of the B post. Remove belt.

3. Remove the B post trim.

4. Remove the upper quarter window trim.

5. Remove two screws at the rear end of the rocker panel and pull off the door weatherstrip in the side trim area.

6. Remove the side trim panel and remove the luggage compartment carpet.

7. Tilt the rear seat back rest forward and remove the rear panel trim and the side panel.

8. Remove the two nuts from the top of the shock absorber and lift off the top steel washer and the rubber bushing.

9. Raise the car on a hoist.

10. Remove the lower end of the shock absorber from the bracket on the axle by removing the nut, lock washer and bolt. Remove the shock absorber from the car.

11. Remove the rubber bushing and steel washer from the top of the shock absorber.

12. Assemble the large steel washer and the rubber bushing to the top of the shock absorber.

13. Extend the shock absorber upward and pass it through the mounting hole in the body. Position the rubber bushing to the mounting hole in the body. Position washer and nut on the piston rod but do not tighten.

14. Position the lower end of the shock absorber in the bracket on the axle. Install the bolt, lock washer and nut. Tighten to 40–45 ft-lbs (5.54–6.22 m-kg).

15. Lower the car to the ground.

16. Tighten the shock absorber upper attaching nut to 15–20 ft-lbs (2.07-2.76 m-kg). Install the lock nut and tighten securely.

17. Replace the rear panel, and side trim panel. Replace the luggage compartment carpet.

18. Replace the side trim panel, fit the door weatherstrip in place and attach the rocker panel.

19. Replace the upper quarter window and B post trim.

20. Replace the seat belt attachment at the B post and fit the rear seat.

Radius Arm

Removal and Installation

1. Block each front wheel. Jack up the rear of the car and support it with jackstands.

2. Remove the rear end of the radius arm from the rear axle by removing the nut, washer, and bolt. Use a C-clamp and a screwdriver (if required) to remove the load from the arm.

3. Remove the front end of the radius arm.

4. Position the front end of the radius arm to the body mounting.

5. Pull the radius arm back, using a C-clamp (if required) to align the radius arm bushing with the mounting arm bracket on the rear axle. Slide the thru-bolt into position and loosely assemble the nut and washer.

6. Remove the jackstands and lower the car to the ground.

7. Tighten the securing nuts to 25–30 ft lbs.

262 ± 2,5 mm (10·24 ± 01 in)

Stabilizer bar lever arm length should be adjusted to the dimension shown

Stabilizer Bar

Removal and Installation

1. Raise and safely support the rear of the car.

2. Disconnect the parking brake primary cable from the relay lever on the rear axle.

3. Push the stabilizer bar back for access and unbolt the clamps from the axle.

4. Remove the bar.

5. On installation, if the bushing fittings at the end of the bar have been disturbed, check, that the lever arm length of the bar is correct on both sides. Adjust by screwing the bushing fittings in or out. Tighten the locknuts.

6. Locate the bar on the axle and position the bushing fittings in the frame channels. Install the bolt heads inside the frame. Replace the plain washers and self-locking nuts loosely.

7. Hold the bar in place and start the retaining clamp bolts. Lower the car to rest on its wheels. Torque the clamp bolts to 29–37 ft lbs. Tighten the bushing fitting pivot bolts to 33–37 ft lbs.

FRONT SUSPENSION

This independent front suspension uses McPherson struts. These units combine vertically mounted shock absorbers surrounded by coil springs. Side-to-side movement of each front wheel is controlled by a track control arm, and fore and aft movement is controlled by the stabilizer bar.

Downward movement of the wheel is limited by a rebound stop inside the shock absorber, and the upward movement by the spring reaching its limit of compression and by a rubber bumper around the suspension unit Piston rod.

Front suspension geometry figures (i.e. camber, caster, and the kingpin inclination angles) are set when the car is manufactured and are not adjustable. Toe-in, however, is adjustable.

Strut Assembly

Removal and Installation

1. Jack up the front of the car and support it with jackstands.

2. Remove the wheel.

3. Remove and plug the brake line.

4. Position a jack under the track control arm and jack up the suspension unit.

5. Remove the cotter pin and unscrew the castle nut holding the connecting rod end to the steering arm. Using a ball joint separator, separate the joint. Remove the jack from under the control arm.

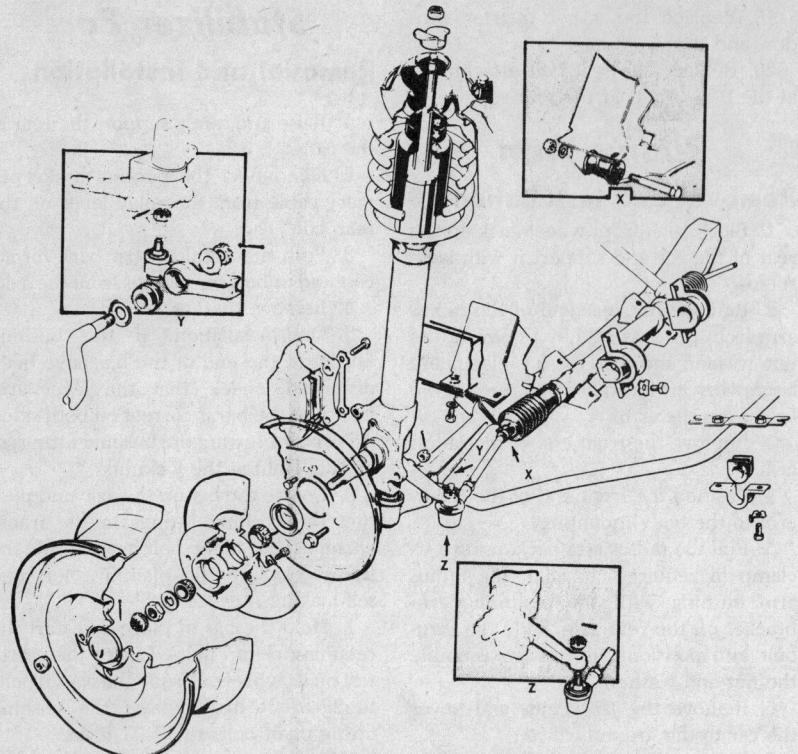

Front suspension—exploded view

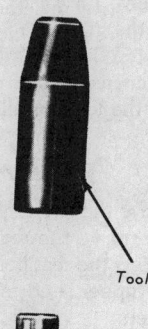

Tool

Replacing the gland and bushing assembly on the piston rod with the bushing guide tool

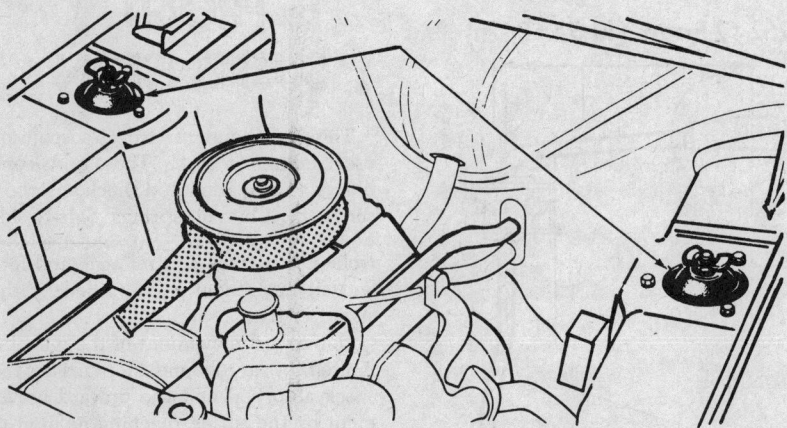

Cranked retainers

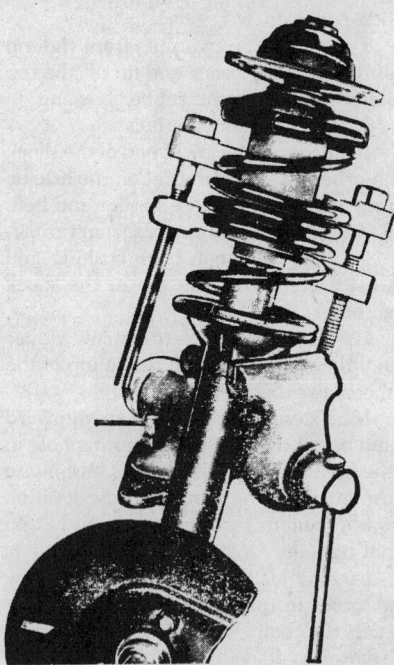

Coil spring compressor installation

6. Remove the cotter pin and unscrew the castle nut holding the track control arm to the base of the suspension unit and disconnect the track control arm.

7. Remove the three bolts holding the top mount assembly to the side apron panel and remove the suspension assembly from the car, complete with the disc brake caliper.

8. Lift the suspension assembly into position and secure it with the three bolts through the side apron panel, to the top mount assembly. Tighten the bolts to 15–18 ft lbs.

9. Assemble the track control arm ball stud to the base of the suspension unit and tighten the securing nut to 30–35 ft lbs. Install a new cotter pin.

10. Install the connecting rod end to the steering arm and tighten the castle nut to 18–22 ft lbs. Install a new cotter pin.

11. Remove the brake line plug and install the brake line.

12. Bleed the brakes.

13. Replace the wheel and lower the car

Disassembly and Assembly
Through 1974

1. Remove the strut assembly.

2. Install a coil spring compressor on the spring.

3. Unscrew the piston rod nut and then remove the cranked retainers at the top.

4. Detach the top mount and lift off the spring upper seat, the coil spring, and the rubber bumper.

5. Using a suitable size pipe wrench, carefully unscrew the bumper stop platform and then lift it off.

6. Remove the O-ring from the upper guide and gland assembly. Remove any burrs from the top edge of the machined area of the piston rod with a stone. If this isn't done, removing and replacing the gland and bushing assembly will damage the coated surface of the bushing.

7. Lift the piston rod upward until the gland and the bushing assembly are clear of the outer casing. Slide the gland assembly off the rod.

8. Empty the fluid.

9. Pull the piston rod, complete with the piston, cylinder, and the compression valve, out of the casing.

10. Remove the piston rod from the cylinder by pushing the compression valve out of the base and then pushing the rod inward and withdrawing it from the cylinder.

11. Wash all components in a suitable solvent and examine them for wear or damage. Replace any worn or damaged parts. Do not remove the piston from the piston rod; these parts are available only as an assembly.

12. Insert the piston rod into the cylinder and push the compression valve into the base of the cylinder.

13. Carefully pass the cylinder and the piston rod assembly into the outer casing. Fill the unit with shock absorber fluid.

14. Install the gland and the bushing guide (a special tool) onto the end of the piston rod and slide the gland and bushing over the guide. Push it down until it fits into the end of the cylinder and the complete internal assembly is below the top of the outer casing.

15. Place the O-ring on the top of the gland and the bushing assembly, and then place it correctly around the bore of the outer casing.

16. Screw the bumper stop platform into the top of the outer casing and tighten it to 55–60 ft lbs.

17. Install the other parts of the unit and pull the piston rod fully upward, then install the rubber bumper, suspension spring, spring upper seat, and dished washer.

18. Assemble the top mount and the cranked retainer. Install the piston rod nut with locking compound on the threads and tighten it to 5–10 ft lbs.

19. Remove the spring compressor.

20. Loosen the piston rod and retighten the nut to 28–32 ft. lbs. after the unit is installed in the car. When tightening the piston rod nut with the car on the ground, the wheels must be facing straight-ahead and the cranked retainer must face inward.

1975–77

1. Install adjustable spring retainers, to the front spring.

2. Remove the piston rod nut by forcing the nut collar out of the piston rod keyway with a small punch. Remove and discard the nut.

3. Remove the cranked retainer.

4. Remove the top mount and lift off the spring upper seat, suspension spring and the rubber bumper.

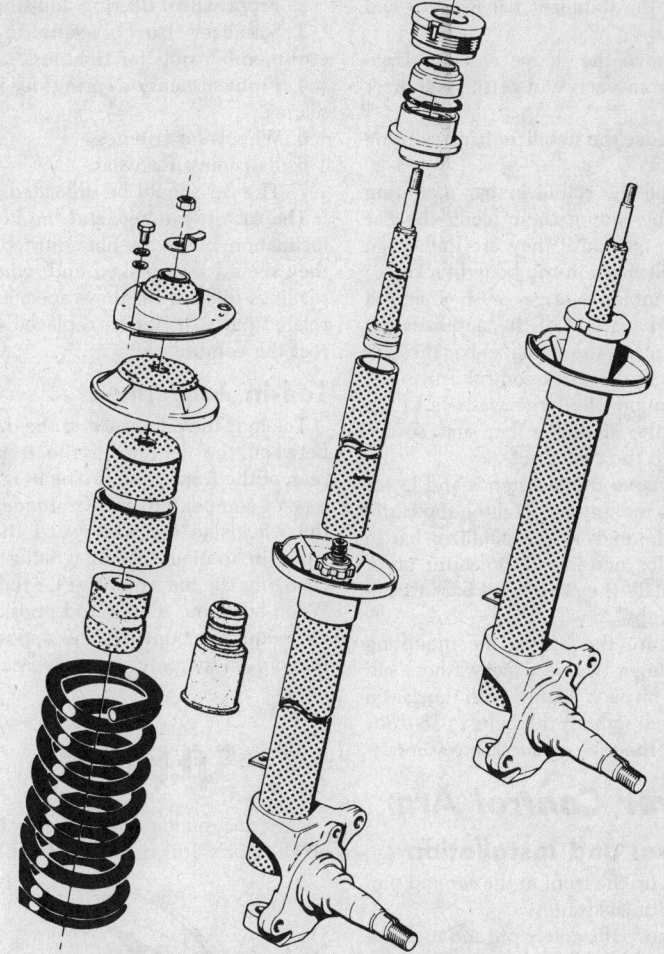

Strut assembly—exploded view

5. Using a suitable wrench, remove shock cartridge.

6. Screw the shock cartridge into the top of the outer casing. Using a suitable wrench, tighten it securely to 55–60 ft-lbs (7.60–8.29 m-kg).

7. Install the suspension spring, rubber bumper, plug, and the spring upper seat.

8. Assemble the top mount and the cranked retainer. Install a new collared piston rod nut and tighten to 5–10 ft-lbs (0.7–1.4 m-kg). Do not bend the nut collar into the piston rod keyway at this time.

9. Remove adjustable spring retainers from the front spring.

10. Loosen the piston rod nut and retighten to 28–32 ft-lbs (3.9–4.4 m-kg) when the suspension unit is assembled into the car and the car is on the ground. When tightening the piston rod nut, the wheels must be in the straight-ahead position and the cranked retainer must face inwards, i.e. towards the engine.

11. After retightening the piston rod nut, force its collar into the piston rod keyway with a small punch.

Coil Springs
Removal and Installation

1. Remove the strut assembly and install a spring compressor.

2. Unscrew the piston rod nut and remove the cranked retainer.

3. Detach the top mount and lift off the spring upper seat, and the spring.

4. Mount the spring in a vise and remove the compressor.

5. Install the new spring in a vise and install the spring compressor. Replace the spring on the strut.

6. Install the rubber bumper and the upper seat.

7. Replace the cranked retainer and the piston rod nut. See the section on strut assembly for the proper torque and procedures when installing the piston rod nut.

Stabilizer Bar
Removal and Installation

1. Jack up the front of the car and support it with jackstands.

2. Remove the two attachment clamps from the front of the stabilizer bar after bending back the locktabs and removing the four bolts.

3. Remove the cotter pins and unscrew the stabilizer bar nuts which hold the ends of the stabilizer bar to the track control arm. Remove the nuts and pull off the large washers.

4. Pull the stabilizer bar forward and remove it.

5. Remove the sleeve and the large washer from each end of the stabilizer bar.

6. Remove the stabilizer bar mounting bushings.

7. Install the stabilizer bar mounting bushing by sliding them along the bar from one end until they are under the clamp bolt holes in the body bracket.

8. Assemble a large washer and a sleeve to each end of the stabilizer bar and then insert the stabilizer bar through the holes in the track control arms.

9. Assemble the large washers to the ends of the stabilizer bar and secure them with the castle nuts.

10. Remove the jackstands and lower the car to the ground. Tighten the castle nuts on the ends of the stabilizer bar to 15–45 ft lbs. and install the cotter pins.

11. Install the stabilizer bar attachment clamps.

12. Secure the bar to the mounting points using a two new lockwashers and two bolts on each clamp. With the car on the ground, tighten the bolts to 15–18 ft lbs. Turn the tabs on the lockwashers.

Lower Control Arm

Removal and Installation

1. Jack up the front of the car and support it with jackstands.

2. Remove the cotter pin and unscrew the castle nut holding the control arm to the stabilizer bar. Pull off the large dish washer.

3. Remove the self-locking nut and the flat washer from the rear of the lower control arm pivot and release the inner end of the control arm.

4. Remove the cotter pin and unscrew the nut securing the control arm ball joint to the base of the strut unit and then separate the joint.

5. Assemble the control arm ball stud to the base of the strut unit, and tighten it to 30–35 ft lbs. Install a new cotter pin.

6. Position the control arm so that it is in place over the stabilizer bar and then secure the inner end. Slide the pivot bolt into position from the front and install the flat washer and the self-locking nut from the rear. Tighten the nut to 22–27 ft lbs. with the car resting on its wheels.

7. Assemble the dished washer to the end of the stabilizer bar. Install the castle nut, lower the car to the ground, and tighten the nut to 15–45 ft lbs. Install a new cotter pin.

Front-End Alignment

Before any alignment checks are made, the following points should be checked and, if necessary, corrected.

1. Correct tire inflation.

2. Front wheel bearing adjustment.

3. Stabilizer bar brackets to body crossmember nuts for tightness.

4. Front suspension springs for proper seating.

5. Wheels for trueness.

6. Ball joints for wear.

7. The car should be unloaded.

The caster, camber, and the king pin inclination angles are not adjustable, but they should be checked and, when the readings differ from those specified, the related parts should be replaced to correct the condition.

Toe-in Adjustment

Toe-in is the difference of the distance between the centers of the front and rear, of the front wheels. Toe-in is necessary to compensate for the tendency of the wheels to deflect toward the rear while in motion. Toe-in is adjusted by changing the length of the tie rod ends. When adjusting the tie rod ends, adjust each equal amounts (in the opposite direction) to increase or to decrease the toe-in.

STEERING

Rack and pinion steering gear is used on all Capris. It is mounted in rubber insulators on brackets attached to the front crossmember.

The steering wheel is mounted on a collapsible can, so that it will collapse under a heavy impact. Movement of the steering wheel is transmitted by the steering shaft through a universal joint and a flexible coupling to the pinion. Rotation of the pinion causes the rack to move from side-to-side and the connecting rods, attached to the ends of the rack, transmit this movement to the spindle arms and cause the wheels to turn.

The steering gear holds three tenths (0.3) of a pint of SAE 90 hypoid oil. Never fill the gear completely with oil. This would result in a buildup of pressure which could burst or blow off the bellows in the gear.

Steering Wheel

Removal and Installation

1. Make sure that the front wheels are facing straight ahead. On 1973 and later models, remove the two screws holding the steering column shroud and remove the lower half. Pull off the upper shroud.

2. Pry out the steering wheel center emblem. Matchmark the steering shaft and wheel so they can be correctly realigned.

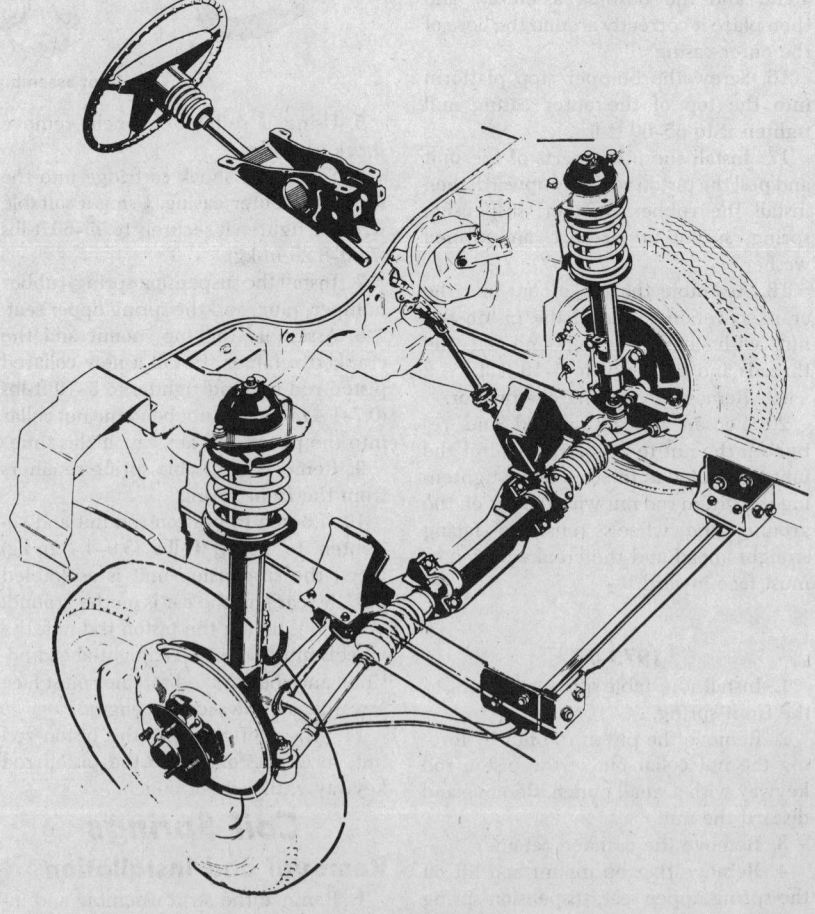

Steering gear and linkage

Steering column details

3. Remove the steering wheel retaining nut and then pull the steering wheel off the steering shaft by hand.

4. Align the steering wheel in the correct position and push it onto the shaft. Be sure that the turn signal cancelling cam is in the groove on the underside of the wheel.

5. Install the steering wheel retaining nut and tighten it to 20–25 ft lbs. (25–30 on Capri II).

6. Install the steering wheel center Replace the shrouds, if removed.

Turn Signal Switch

Removal and Installation

1972

1. Disconnect the battery ground cable.

2. Remove the bolts securing the column to the underside of the instrument panel and the lower column.

3. Remove the two screws securing the steering column shrouds and remove the shrouds.

4. Remove the two screws holding the switch to the steering column.

5. Disconnect the multipin plug and remove the switch.

6. Connect the multipin plug to the harness.

7. Position the switch on the steering column and secure it with the two screws.

8. Locate the steering column shrouds and secure them with the two screws.

9. Secure the steering column to the underside of the instrument panel with the two bolts.

10. Connect the battery ground cable and check the operation of the switch.

1973–77

1. Disconnect the battery ground cable.

2. Remove the steering column shroud screws and remove the lower shroud half. Pull sharply up to release the upper shroud half.

3. Remove the switch retaining screws, disconnect the electrical plug, and remove the switch.

4. On reinstallation, connect the electrical plug and screw the switch in place.

5. Replace the shroud halves.

6. Connect the battery.

Ignition Switch

Switch Removal and Installation

1972

1. Disconnect the battery ground cable.

2. Unscrew the steering column shroud retaining screw and remove the steering column shroud.

3. Make sure that the ignition key is in the "O" position.

4. Disconnect the leads at the ignition switch, noting their positions.

5. Remove the two screws which secure the ignition switch to the lock and withdraw the switch.

6. Assemble the switch and lock, make sure the key remains in the "O" position, and is installed in the correct direction.

7. Engage and tighten the two switch retaining screws.

8. Reconnect the wires to their respective terminals on the ignition switch.

9. Replace the steering column shroud.

10. Connect the battery ground cable.

11. Test the switch for proper operation.

1973–74

1. Disconnect the negative battery cable.

2. Remove the steering column shroud screws. Remove the lower shroud half and pull the upper half sharply upward to remove.

3. Make sure that the key is in the O position.

4. Remove the ashtray. Remove the hazard warning (four-way flasher) switch and disconnect the wiring at the connector.

5. Unscrew the turn signal switch and leave it hanging on the wiring harness.

6. Unscrew the lower dash trim panel. Pull the panel forward and down to get at the lighter and clock connectors. Discon-

nect the connectors and remove the trim panel.

7. Pull off the instrument panel illumination control knob. Remove the lower instrument cluster bezel screws, pull the bezel down, and disconnect the seat belt warning light connector.

8. Disconnect the oil pressure line at the fitting.

9. Unscrew the instrument cluster, disconnect the speedometer cable and electrical plug at the back of the cluster, and remove the cluster.

10. Pull the plug from the ignition switch. Remove the screws holding the switch to the lock and remove the switch.

11. Remove the shear bolts holding the two lock halves together by tapping the heads lightly with a hammer and center punch to unscrew them. If this doesn't work, drill the bolts out.

12. On installation, put the key in the lock and make sure that it is in the 0 position.

13. Install the switch retaining screws. Make sure that the lock pawl is projecting; engage it in the column cutout. Assemble the two lock halves and install new shear bolts. Tighten them until their heads shear off.

14. Connect the ignition switch plug.

15. Connect the speedometer cable and instrument wiring plug and replace the instrument cluster. Connect the oil pressure gauge line.

16. Connect the seat belt wiring. Replace the instrument cluster bezel and the instrument panel illumination control knob.

17. Connect the lighter and clock connectors, replace the lower dash trim panel.

18. Install the turn signal switch. Replace and connect the hazard warning switch.

19. Install the ashtray.

20. Install the steering column shroud, replace the battery cable, and check operation of the switch.

1976–77

1. Disconnect the negative cable from the battery.

2. Remove the screws securing the steering column shroud. Remove the lower half of the shroud and release the shroud upper half retaining lug from its spring clip on the steering column by pulling sharply upward.

3. Be sure that the ignition key is in the O position.

4. Remove the screws holding the lower left dash trim panel. Pull the trim panel forward and down and remove the connector from the hazard warning flasher switch. Remove the trim panel from the dash.

5. Disconnect ignition wires at the connector.

6. Remove the screws securing the ignition switch to the lock and withdraw the switch.

7. Position the switch to the lock, being sure that the key remains in the O position and is correctly inserted.

8. Engage and tighten the switch retaining screws.

9. Connect ignition wires at the connection.

10. Position the lower left dash trim panel under the dash panel and connect the hazard warning flasher switch. Press the trim panel into its location and install and tighten the screws.

11. Mount the upper and lower halves of the steering column shroud and secure with screws.

12. Connect the battery negative cable and check the operation of the switch.

Lock Removal and Installation

Through 1974

1. Disconnect the battery ground cable.

2. Remove the steering column shroud screws and the upper bolts holding the steering column.

3. Remove the shroud and turn the column for access to the headless bolts.

4. Disconnect the electrical leads from the switch and lock body.

5. Remove the shear bolts by tapping the heads lightly with a center punch and hammer to unscrew them. If this doesn't work, drill the bolts out. Remove the lock assembly.

6. On installation, position the new lock assembly, with the key in place, to the column.

7. Make sure that the lock pawl is projecting; engage it in the column cutout. The lock should be in the O Position.

8. Assemble the two lock halves and install new shear bolts. Tighten them until their heads shear off. While tightening, make sure that the lock pawl works freely.

9. Connect the electrical leads.

10. Turn the column to the correct position. Replace the column mounting bolts and the column shroud.

11. Reconnect the battery ground cable.

1976–77

1. Disconnect the negative cable from the battery.

2. Remove the screws holding the steering column shroud. Remove the lower half of the shroud and release the shroud upper half retaining lug from its spring clip on the steering column by pulling sharply upward.

3. Remove the screws holding the left and right lower dash trim panels and lower the panels.

4. Remove the screws holding the turn signal switch. Move the switch out of the way.

5. Disconnect the ignition wires at the connector.

6. Remove the screws holding the steering column to the dash.

7. Turn the steering column to gain access to the headless bolts.

8. Remove lock from steering column by drilling out headless bolts or removing bolts with a screw extractor.

9. Position the new lock assembly, with the key in the lock, to the steering column.

10. Withdraw the lock to allow the pawl to enter the steering shaft.

11. Locate the loose half of the clamp to the lock, engage the shear head bolts and tighten evenly until the bolt heads shear off. While tightening the bolts, check the pawl for free operation.

12. Reconnect the ignition wires at the connector.

13. Turn the steering column in the correct position. Install the screws holding the steering column.

14. Install the turn signal switch.

15. Install the lower dash trim panels.

16. Install the upper and lower halves of the steering column shroud.

17. Connect the battery ground cable.

Steering Gear

Removal and Installation

Manual Steering

1. Set the steering wheel so the front wheels are facing straight ahead.

2. Jack up the front of the car and support it with jackstands.

3. Remove the nut and the bolt retaining the flexible coupling to the pinion splines.

4. Bend back the locktabs and remove the screws holding the steering gear to the mounting brackets on the crossmember. Remove the screws, locking plates, and the U-clamps.

5. Remove the cotter pins and slacken the castle nuts securing the connecting rod ends to the spindle arms.

6. Using a ball joint separator tool, separate the connecting rod ends from the spindle arms. Remove the castle nuts and withdraw the steering gear from the car. It may be necessary to turn one wheel to the stop to permit the steering gear assembly to be moved sideways enough to allow the other end to clear the stabilizer bar.

7. Remove the connecting rods and the locknuts. Note the number of turns required to unscrew them.

8. Replace the locknuts and the connecting rod ends; screw them in the same

number of turns required to take them out.

9. Make sure the steering wheel is aligned straight ahead.

10. Set the steering gear in the straight ahead position.

11. Position the steering gear and align the mating splines on the flexible coupling and the pinion shaft.

12. Secure the steering gear assembly to its mounting brackets on the crossmember. Tighten the screws to 15–18 ft lbs.

13. Assemble the connecting rod ends to the spindle arms. Install the castle nuts and tighten them to 18–22 ft lbs. Install new cotter pins.

14. Tighten the flexible coupling-to-pinion shaft securing bolt to 12–15 ft lbs.

15. Remove the jackstands and lower the car to the ground.

16. Check the front end wheel alignment. Check the position of the steering wheel.

Power Steering

1. Disconnect negative battery cable.

2. Raise car on hoist and remove engine splash shield if equipped.

3. Disconnect fluid pipes from rack and drain power steering fluid.

4. Remove steering coupling lower clamp bolt.

5. Disconnect tie rod ends from steering arm.

6. Remove the two steering rack mounting bolts and remove rack from vehicle.

7. Remove tie rod ends from track rods. Count number of turns required to disengage threads and note the number for assembly purposes.

8. Install tie rod ends on tie rods. Screw on each tie rod end the same number of turns as required to remove it.

9. Position steering rack into vehicle and locate pinion in steering coupling. Ensure bolt hole in steering coupling aligns with flat on steering pinion shaft.

10. Secure steering rack to cross-member with the two bolts.

11. Install steering coupling lower clamp bolt. Be sure coupling segments are all in same plane. Align as necessary by sliding coupling up or down on pinion shaft.

12. Connect tie rod ends to steering arms, and connect fluid lines to rack. Torque pressure lines 19 to 23 ft-lbs and return lines 12 to 15 ft-lbs.

13. Install engine splash shield, if equipped.

14. Check and adjust front wheel toe-in.

15. Connect negative cable battery, fill power steering reservoir, and bleed system.

16. Lower car from hoist.

Power Steering Pump

Removal and Installation

1. Open hood and disconnect negative cable from battery.
2. Raise car on hoist.
3. Remove engine splash shield, if so equipped.
4. Loosen alternator mounting bolts (2300 cc) or idler pulley bolts (2800 cc) and remove drive belt.
5. Disconnect fluid lines and drain fluid.
6. On 2300 cc engines disconnect fuel pump from engine. Do not disconnect fuel pump lines, but move pump away from power steering pump mounting bolts.
7. Remove power steering pump (2300 cc). On 2800 cc equipped cars remove the pump and bracket assembly.
8. Remove pulley from pump and pump from adaptor bracket, if so equipped.
9. Secure pump properly to bracket.
10. Install pulley on pump.
11. Install pump (2300 cc) and bracket assembly.
12. Reinstall fuel pump on 2300 cc engines.
13. Connect power steering fluid lines. Torque pressure lines to 19 to 23 ft-lbs and return lines to 12 to 15 ft-lbs.
14. Install drive belts and adjust tension. Cooling.
15. Install engine splash shield, if so equipped.
16. Lower hoist and fill reservoir with Power Steering Fluid. Bleed system.
17. Connect negative battery cable and close hood.

Air Bleeding

1. Open hood and check the fluid level. If the fluid is low, add Power Steering to maximum level.
2. After adding fluid, allow fluid to stand for two minutes. Start car and run engine to 1500 rpm.
3. Slowly turn steering wheel from lock to lock. At the same time check fluid level, add fluid until lever is steady and air bubbles no longer appear.
4. Check pipe connections, bellows, valve body and pump for leaks and repair.
5. Close hood.

Manual Steering Gear Adjustments

Support Yoke and Pinion Bearing Pre-Load

1. Carefully mount the steering gear in a vise (with protected jaws), so that the pinion is horizontal and the rack pre-load cover plate is on top.
2. Remove the two screws attaching the rack pre-load cover plate to the housing.

3. Lift off the cover plate, shim pack and gasket. Withdraw the spring and support yoke.
4. Remove the two screws attaching the pinion bearing pre-load cover plate to the housing.
5. Lift off the cover plate, shim pack and gasket.
6. Position shim pack and pinion cover plate on bearing and install the retaining screws. The shim pack must be made up of at least three shims. One shim must be 0.093 inch thick and positioned immediately next to plate.
7. Tighten the cover retaining screws then loosen until the plate just touches shim pack.
8. Using feeler gages, measure the gap between the cover plate and the steering gear housing. The gap should measure 0.011 to 0.013 inches. (To confirm that the cover plate has been pulled down evenly by the retaining screws, take feeler gage measurements adjacent to each screw.)
9. If the gap measured exceeds 0.011 to 0.013 inches the shim pack must be made smaller. If the gap is smaller than specification, the shim pack must be made larger. The shim pack must still use a 0.093 inch thick shim, positioned next to plate.
10. Remove the cover plate, assemble the shim pack and reinstall the cover plate. Install the attaching screws, using sealer on the threads, and tighten to 6–8 ft-lbs (0.85–1.1 m-kg).
11. Set the support yoke adjustment. For the spring to exert the correct pressure on the support yoke, it is necessary for the distance between the underside of the cover plate and the top of the support yoke to be accurately set to 0.0005–0.0035 inch (0.0127–0.089 mm).
12. Assemble the support yoke to the rear of the rack and push it fully into position. Using a straight edge and feeler gages, measure the distance between the top of the support yoke and the surface of the steering gear housing at the cover plate. Note this dimension.
13. Assemble a shim pack (including two gaskets which must sandwich the shim pack), the thickness of which is 0.-0005–0.0035 inch (0.0127–0.089 mm) greater than the dimension obtained in the previous paragraph.
It is most important that the dimension is correctly set. If it is not, it may result in a knocking noise from the steering gear or heavy steering effort.
14. Install the spring into the recess in the support yoke.
15. Position the shim pack and gaskets and replace the cover plate.
16. Assemble the attaching screws to the cover plate, using sealer on the threads. Tighten the screws to 6–8 ft-lbs (0.85–1.1 m-kg).

17. Install an in-lbs torque wrench to the splined end of the pinion shaft.
18. Determine the torque required to start the pinion rotating. This should be 10–18 in-lbs (11.53–20.74 cm-kg). If the actual torque is not within the prescribed limits, the adjustment is incorrect (check the shimming) or there is some malfunction within the gear assembly (tight bearings, damaged gear teeth, lack of lubricant, etc.) which is increasing the friction level.

BRAKE SYSTEMS

All Capris are equipped with floating caliper type disc brakes on the front wheels and conventional drum brakes on the rear. A twin-reservoir hydraulic system is used to operate the brakes. This provides separate hydraulic circuits for the front and rear brakes. If one circuit fails, the driver is still able to stop the car by using the other system.

All models use a floor-mounted handbrake which is located between the front seats. This parking brake operates through a two-cable linkage and its operation causes the self-adjusting mechanism in the rear brakes to operate.

A power brake vacuum booster is installed in the engine compartment. The booster operates through a rod and clevis assembly which is attached to the brake pedal at one end and the brake master cylinder at the other end.

Adjustment

The front disc brakes are not adjustable. The rear drum brakes normally are self adjusting, but can be adjusted by the use of the parking brake lever on models through 1974. Operate the parking brake lever at the rear wheel backing plate. Pull and then release the lever until the clicking of the adjuster stops. The brakes should then be sufficiently adjusted. Make sure that the parking brake lever returns to the fully off position.

Hydraulic System

Master Cylinder

Removal and Installation

1. Siphon the fluid from the reservoir.
2. Disconnect the brake lines from the master cylinder.
3. Remove the master cylinder-to-brake booster retaining nuts.
4. Lift the master cylinder away from the brake booster, being careful not to damage the vacuum seal.
5. Position the master cylinder, including the fluid seal, correctly onto the push-rod and hold it in position. With the

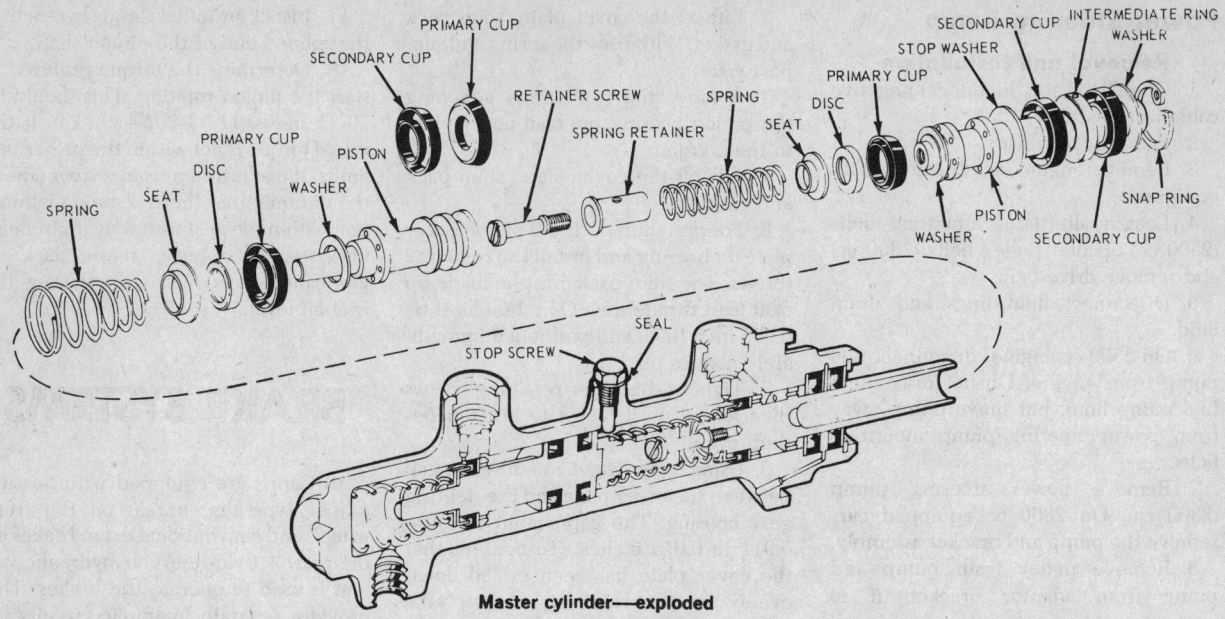

Master cylinder—exploded

cylinder in this position, screw in all union nuts of the brake lines a few turns.

6. Connect the master cylinder to the brake booster and tighten the nuts.

7. Connect the brake lines.

8. Fill the reservoir with heavy-duty brake fluid designated for disc brake systems. Bleed the entire brake system.

9. Check the operation of the brakes.

Overhaul

1. Remove the master cylinder.

2. Remove the reservoir from the cylinder assembly. Remove the rubber plugs.

3. Loosen the stopscrew at the center of the cylinder.

4. Push the piston inward and, using snap-ring pliers, remove the cylinder retaining snap-ring.

5. Remove the stopwasher and the primary piston assembly from the first chamber.

6. Press the secondary piston assembly out of the second chamber of the cylinder with compressed air.

7. Clean the master cylinder and the pistons with commercial alcohol or methylated spirit. Blow the parts dry with moisture-free air. Master cylinders with scored or otherwise damaged surfaces must not be reused.

8. Lightly coat the inner surfaces, pistons, and cups with brake fluid.

9. Assemble the piston of the second chamber with the filler washer, cups, pressure disc, pressure spring, and spring seat, and carefully insert the piston into the cylinder. Press the piston inward slightly and screw in the stopscrew, with the seal. Release the piston and let it contact the stopscrew.

10. Assemble the piston of the first chamber. Do not overtighten the retainer screw.

11. Insert the piston and press it in slightly. Don't move the piston against the stopscrew until the chambers have been filled with fluid. Install the rubber plug and the reservoir.

Pressure Differential Valve and Switch
Removal and Installation

1. Disconnect the five brake lines from the ports on the valve and the switch assembly. Plug the end of the lines from the master cylinder.

2. Disconnect the wire from the switch.

3. Unscrew the bolt securing the assembly to the rear of the engine compartment. Remove the assembly.

4. Position the assembly in place on the firewall and loosely install the attaching bolt.

5. Connect the hydraulic lines. Tighten the attaching bolt.

6. Connect the wiring to the switch.

Power Brake Booster
Removal and Installation

1. Remove the brake pushrod clevis pin from the brake pedal and remove the pin.

2. Remove the master cylinder retaining nuts and position the master cylinder assembly away from the brake booster.

3. Remove the vacuum hose from the brake booster.

4. Remove the brake booster-to-dash panel retaining screws and remove the brake booster assembly and seal.

5. Remove the retaining bracket and the gasket from the brake booster.

6. Assemble the brake booster retaining bracket with a new gasket to the brake booster.

7. Position the booster assembly and the bracket onto the bolts protruding

through the dash panel. Use a new gasket. Connect the pushrod with the clevis pin to the brake pedal.

8. Install and tighten the bracket retaining screws. Connect the vacuum hose to the booster.

9. Position the master cylinder assembly with a new seal ring on the booster and tighten the master cylinder-to-booster retaining nuts.

Bleeding

To make sure that the brake warning light will go out after bleeding the brakes, the piston in the pressure valve must be centralized. Fabricate the tool shown in the illustration from a screwdriver. Insert the tool in the base of the pressure valve during the bleeding operation.

NOTE: *This isn't necessary on the Capri II; the piston is self-centering*

1. Make sure that the master cylinder is full with brake fluid.

2. Remove the rubber dust cap from the right front bleed valve on the rear of the backing plate.

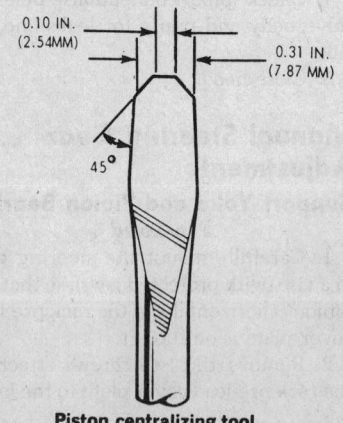

Piston centralizing tool

3. Install a box wrench on the bleed valve. Push a piece of rubber tubing over the bleeder until it is flush with the wrench. Place the other end of the tube in a glass jar that contains a small amount of brake fluid. During the bleeding operation the end of the tube must always be kept in the brake fluid.

Start with the right-front wheel then bleed the left-front, left-rear, and the right-rear, in that order.

NOTE: *The Capri II doesn't have a right rear bleeder valve.*

4. Unscrew the bleed valve about half a turn, then depress the brake pedal fully, release it, and allow it to return to its normal position. Brake fluid and/or air bubbles should have been pumped into the jar; if not, unscrew the valve further.

5. Pause for about five seconds to allow the master cylinder to be refilled with fluid.

6. Continue to depress the brake pedal, pausing after each return stroke of the brake pedal, until the fluid entering the jar is free of air bubbles.

NOTE: *Check the master cylinder periodically during bleeding, making sure not to let it run out of fluid.*

7. Press the pedal to the floor and tighten the bleed valve. Remove the tool from the pressure valve.

Front Brakes

Disc Brake Pad Inspection

An inspection of the pad contact surface should be routinely made. Check for scoring or cracking, glazing or signs of abnormal or uneven wear. Also check for signs of oil or grease contamination.

If any of the above are found, discard the shoes and replace with a new set on both sides.

Disc Brake Pads

Removal and Installation

1. Jack up the front of the car and support it with jackstands.
2. Remove the front wheels.
3. Pull out the retaining clips and retaining pins, and remove the brake pads from the caliper. Remove the brake pad tension springs and shims. (It may be necessary to use a pair of thin-nosed pliers.) Remove the master cylinder reservoir cap and siphon off a third of the fluid in the reservoir.
4. Push the pistons into their bores with a screwdriver.
5. Place the brake pad tension springs on the brake pads and shims. Install new brake pads and shims. The shims must be installed with the arrows up.
6. Install the retaining pins and clips. Refill the reservoir to the proper level.
7. Operate the brake pedal several times to bring the pads into correct adjustment.
8. Install the wheel and lower the car to the ground.

Disc Brake Calipers

Removal and Installation

1. Jack up the front of the car and support it with jackstands. Remove the wheels.
2. Remove the retaining pins and lift out the brake pads. If you plan to overhaul the calipers, press on the brake pedal to force the pistons out.
3. Remove the brake line from the rear of the caliper and install a plug into each open end.
4. Bend back the locktabs and remove the two caliper retaining bolts and the caliper assembly.
5. Replace the caliper assembly, using a new locking plate, and tighten the retaining bolts to 45–50 ft lbs. Bend up the locktabs.
6. Install the brake lines. Install the brake pads and bleed the brakes.

Overhaul

The caliper is made in two paired halves, which are bolted together. Under no circumstances should the halves be separated.

1. Remove the caliper assembly.
2. Partially remove the piston from one cylinder bore. Remove the securing circlip and also the sealing bellows from its location in the lower part of the piston skirt. Remove the piston.
3. Pull the sealing bellows from its location in the annular ring machined in the cylinder bore. Remove the piston sealing ring.
4. Repeat these operations for the other cylinders.
5. Wash the pistons and the piston bores in commercial alcohol, methylated spirits, or brake fluid.

6. Check the pistons and their bores for score marks or other imperfections.
7. Assemble a piston seal in the groove of the piston bore.
8. Install the rubber bellows to the cylinder, with the lip that is turned outward installed in the groove provided in the cylinder.
9. Lubricate the piston with clean brake fluid. Place the piston—crown first —through the rubber sealing bellows and into the cylinder.
10. When the piston is located in the cylinder, install the inner edge of the bellows in the groove in the piston skirt.
11. Push the piston as far down in the cylinder as possible.
12. Secure the sealing bellows to the caliper with the circlip.
13. Install the caliper assembly.
14. Bleed the brakes.

Rotor (disc) Inspection

Routinely check the surface of the rotors for signs of heat checking (bluish tints), uneven wear, waviness or grooving and scoring. See the brake specifications chart at the beginning of this section for wear limits. In most instances rotors can be resurfaced rather than replaced.

Brake Disc

Removal and Installation

1. Jack up the front of the car and support it with jackstands.
2. Remove the front wheels.
NOTE: *In order to remove the disc, the caliper must be removed.*
3. Loosen, but do not remove, the upper caliper attaching bolt.
4. Remove the lower attaching bolt.

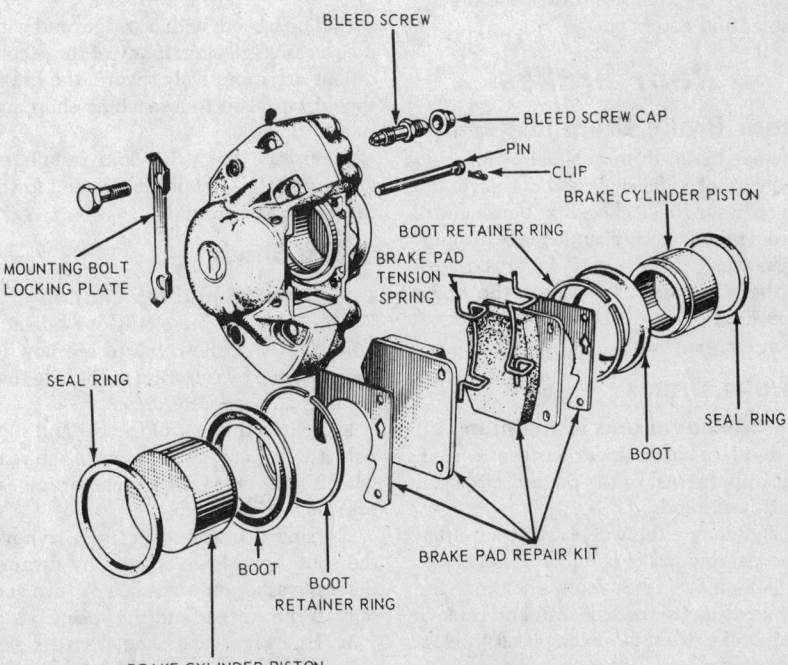

Caliper assembly—exploded view

When the caliper is removed from the disc, it must be wired out of the way of the disc. Also, the brake pads will fall out if they are not held in place when the caliper is removed. Insert a small piece of wood or fold a piece of heavy cardboard to fit between the shoes to hold them in place.

5. Hold the caliper in place and remove the upper attaching bolt.

6. Slide the caliper off the brake disc, inserting a piece of wood between the brake pads.

7. When the caliper is clear of the disc, wire it out of the way.

8. Remove the dust cap from the wheel hub. Remove the cotter pin, nut retainer, nut, thrust washer, and outer wheel bearing.

9. Remove the disc from the spindle. Reverse the procedures to install. Adjust the bearings.

Wheel Bearings

1. Remove the wheel cover and dust cap.

2. Jack up the car.

3. Remove the cotter pin, nut retainer, adjusting nut, washer, and bearing.

4. Wash all parts in a solvent.

5. Hand-pack the wheel bearing with wheel bearing grease.

6. Reassemble, reversing the removal procedure.

NOTE: *When installing the cotter pin it may be necessary to move the nut retainer in various positions on the nut to allow the cotter pin to go through the hole in the axle.*

7. Torque the adjusting nut to 17–20 ft lbs. while turning the disc. Back the nut off one-half turn then tighten it hand-tight or 10–15 in. lbs. Install the nut retainer and cotter pin.

Rear Brakes

Rear Brake Drum Inspection

Rear brake drums should be periodically checked for signs of abnormal or uneven wear, heat checking (bluish tints), grooving or scoring, and cracks. In most instances, drums can be resurfaced rather than replaced. Check the brake specifications at the beginning of this section for wear limits.

Brake Drums

Removal and Installation

1. Place blocks under the front wheels. Jack up the rear of the car and support it with jackstands.

2. Remove the wheel. Make sure that the parking brake is fully released.

3. Remove the screw holding the brake drum to the half-shaft and remove the brake drum by pulling it off the lug-nut studs.

4. Inspect the inside of the drum. It

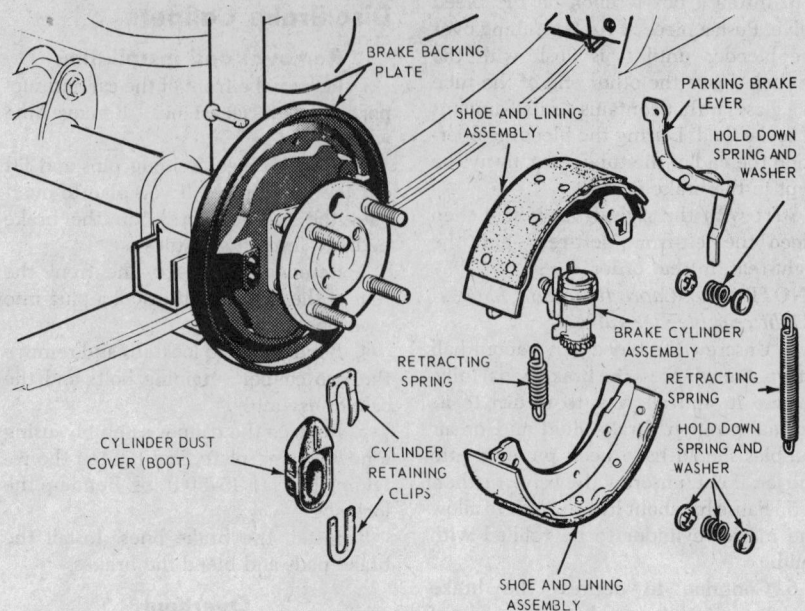

Rear brake—exploded view

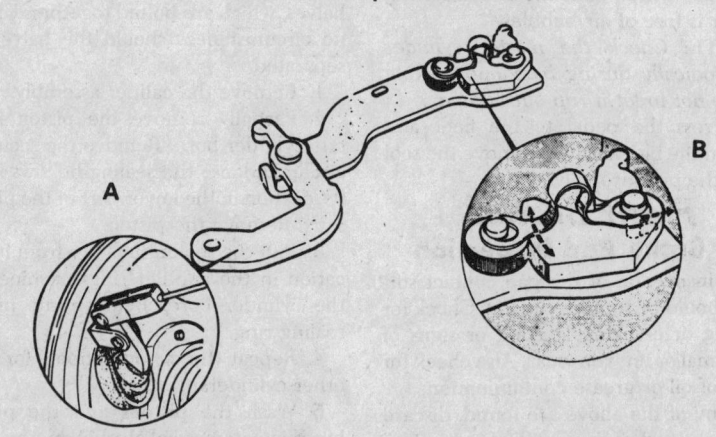

Details of Capri II rear brake self adjusters (shown inverted)

should be smooth with no ridges and with no excessive glazing. If any of these conditions are excessively severe, the brake should be taken to a machine shop and turned down.

5. Replace the drum and install the holding screw. Install the tire and lower the car to the ground.

Brake Shoes

Removal and Installation

Remove and replace only one side at a time. This will allow you to see how to replace parts by referring to the side that is still intact as a reference.

1. Jack up the rear of the car and support it with jackstands. Remove the rear wheels and remove the brake drums (as previously described).

2. Using a brake spring tool remove the shoe hold down springs by turning the top washer on each shoe ¼ turn and pull off the washer and the spring.

3. Disengage each shoe from its slot and remove it from the wheel cylinder. Remove the shoes. To prevent the piston

from falling out of the wheel cylinder, it should be held in place with a clip or a rubber band around the cylinder.

4. Remove the retracting spring from the brake shoes.

5. On models through 1974, remove and turn the adjustment wheel on the wheel cylinder until it is against the slot head bolt shoulder. This moves the brake shoes (when installing) to the fully off adjustment. If this is not done, difficulty may be encountered when installing the brake drum.

6. Assemble the retracting springs between the two shoes on the drum side of the shoes. Apply white grease on the brake shoe support pads, brake shoe pivots, and to the adjustment wheel threads of the wheel cylinder.

7. Fit the shoe assembly to the backplate with the hold-down springs and washers.

8. Check to see that the shoes are seated firmly and that the springs are not binding. On the Capri II, reset the self adjusting unit by prying the adjusting

arm away from the serrated wheel with a screwdriver and gently pushing the arm toward the backing plate. Make sure the lever returns to the fully off position. Install the brake drum and the holding screw.

9. Operate the parking brake lever at the backplate for as long as necessary to adjust the brakes, until the clicking stops. Make sure that the lever returns to the fully off position.

10. Install the wheel. Remove the jackstands and lower the car to the ground. Check the operation of the brakes on a road test.

Wheel Cylinders

Removal and Installation through 1974

1. Remove the brake line (two on the right side) from the rear of the backplate and install plugs.

2. Remove the spring pin and the clevis pin from the handbrake link on the inside of the brake plate.

3. Pry the rubber boot on the rear of the wheel cylinder away from the brake plate and remove it. Pull off the two U-shaped retainers that hold the cylinder to the brake plate.

4. Remove the wheel cylinder and the parking brake link.

5. Install the parking brake link and the wheel cylinder in the hole in the brake plate. Make sure that the pivot on the parking brake link is correctly located in the slot in the wheel cylinder body.

6. Secure the wheel cylinder to the brake plate using the U-shaped retainers.

7. Install the rubber boot over the wheel cylinder and the parking brake link. Make sure that the wheel cylinder can slide in the carrier plate. Lubricate with waterproof grease. Check the parking brake link and see that it operates properly.

8. Connect the parking brake linkage to the parking brake link using a clevis pin, and retain it in position with the spring clip.

9. Remove the plug and connect the brake line to the wheel cylinder. Bleed the brake system.

Removal and Installation, 1976–77

1. Remove the wheel and drum.
2. Remove the brake shoes.
3. Disconnect, but don't pull away the brake line.
4. Remove the wheel cylinder bolts and lockwashers and remove it.
5. Position the cylinder and start the tubing connection.
6. Fasten the cylinder down.
7. Tighten the tubing connection.
8. Replace and adjust the shoes.

9. Replace the drums and bleed the brakes.

Overhaul through 1974

1. Remove the wheel cylinder.
2. Remove the boot retainer, pry off the boot, and withdraw the piston—complete with seal—from the wheel cylinder bore.
3. Detach the seal from the piston.
4. Remove the return spring from the cylinder bore.
5. Remove the adjustment wheel and the screw assembly from the other end of the wheel cylinder.
6. Wash all parts in commercial alcohol or brake fluid, inspect them for wear or damage, and replace any necessary parts.
7. Dip the piston and seal in brake fluid and then reassemble them. Install the seal to the piston with the flat face of the seal adjacent to the piston rear shoulder.
8. Install the return spring in the wheel cylinder.
9. Dip the piston and the seal assembly in brake fluid and insert them into the cylinder bore, seal end first.
10. Install the dust cover on the wheel cylinder and then install the retainer.
11. Replace the adjustment wheel and screw the assembly into the wheel cylinder. Turn the rachet wheel until it is flush with the shoulder of the slot head bolt. Replace the cylinder.

Overhaul, 1976–77

1. Remove the two rubber dust covers.
2. Slide out the piston assemblies from each end.
3. Remove the spring.
4. Wash all parts in alcohol or brake fluid, inspect them for wear or damage, and replace any necessary parts.

NOTE: *Rebuilding kits are usually available for wheel cylinders.*

5. Install new seals on the pistons. Slide one piston into place. Insert the spring

and the second piston from the other end.

6. Replace the dust covers.

Parking Brake

Cable Removal and Installation through 1974

1. Place blocks in front and back of the front wheels. Jack up the rear of the car and support it with jackstands. Release the parking brake.

2. Unscrew the nuts holding the end of the primary brake cable to the relay lever on the rear of the axle housing. On 1975–77 models the cable is attached by a spring clip to the transverse rod.

3. Remove the primary cable from the end of the parking brake lever by removing the spring and the clevis pin.

4. Free the cable from its guides on the underbody and then remove it from under the car.

5. Attach the cable to the end of the parking brake lever by installing the clevis pin and securing it with the spring clip.

6. Apply grease to the cable guides and thread the cable through the guides.

7. Connect the cable to the relay lever by threading it through the pivot pin, installing the spacer, and securing it with the two nuts. Adjust the cable.

8. Remove the jackstands and lower the car to the ground. Remove the blocks from the front wheels.

1976–77

1. Release the parking brake.
2. Remove the spring clip and clevis pin holding the cable to the handle.
3. Remove the spring clip and clevis pin holding the cable to the right rear brake lever.
4. Remove the clip holding the cable to transverse rod. Slide the cable clear of the rod bracket.
5. Slide the cable, adjusting nut, and

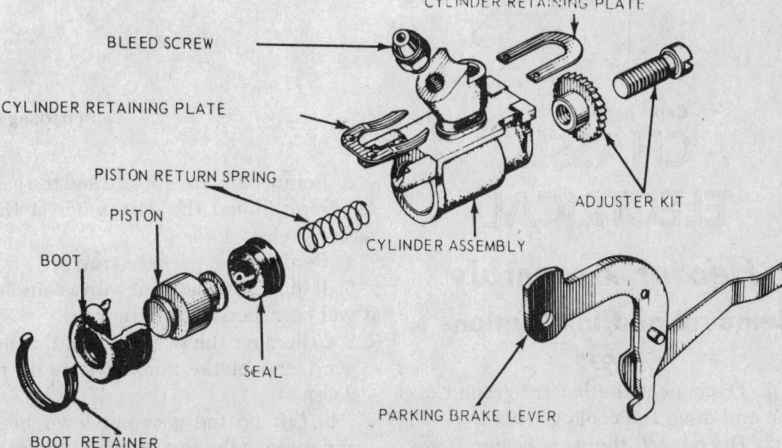

Wheel cylinder—exploded view

guide clear of the abutment bracket and remove.

6. Reverse the procedure for installation. Grease the pivot points. Adjust the parking brake.

Adjustment through 1974

1. Block the front wheels of the car. Jack up the rear of the car and support it with jackstands.

2. Adjust the length of the primary cable by tightening or loosening the adjusting nut on the relay lever so the cable has no slack.

3. Adjust the length of the transverse cable so that the cable has no slack in it. Do this by adjusting the nut on the end of the cable adjacent to the right-hand rear brake.

Remove the jackstands and lower the car to the ground. Remove the blocks from the front wheels. Check the operation of the parking brake.

1976–77

1. Raise and support the rear axle. Block the front wheels.

2. Check the clearance between each brake lever abutment (stop) and the backing plate. It should be 0.039–0.059 in.

3. To adjust, engage the keyed cable sleeve into the abutment slot and turn the adjuster nut to remove cable slack.

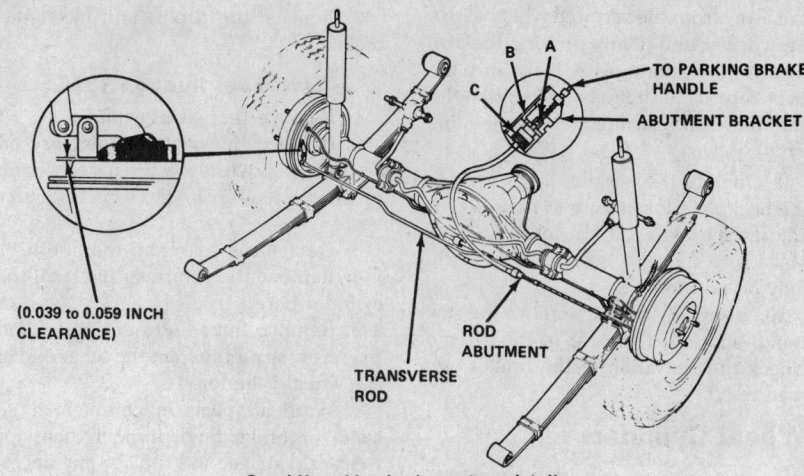

(0.039 to 0.059 INCH CLEARANCE)

Capri II parking brake system details

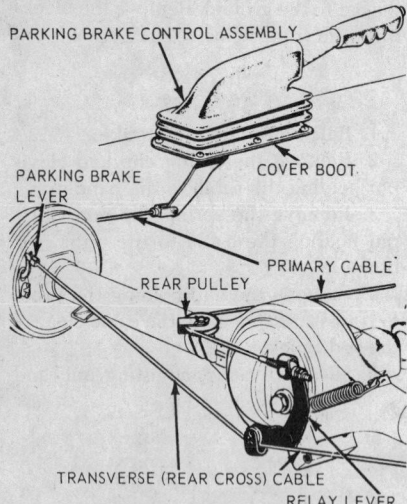

Capri parking brake

CHASSIS ELECTRICAL

Heater Assembly

Removal and Installation

1972

1. Disconnect the battery ground cable and drain the cooling system.

2. Disconnect the two heater hoses from the heater core.

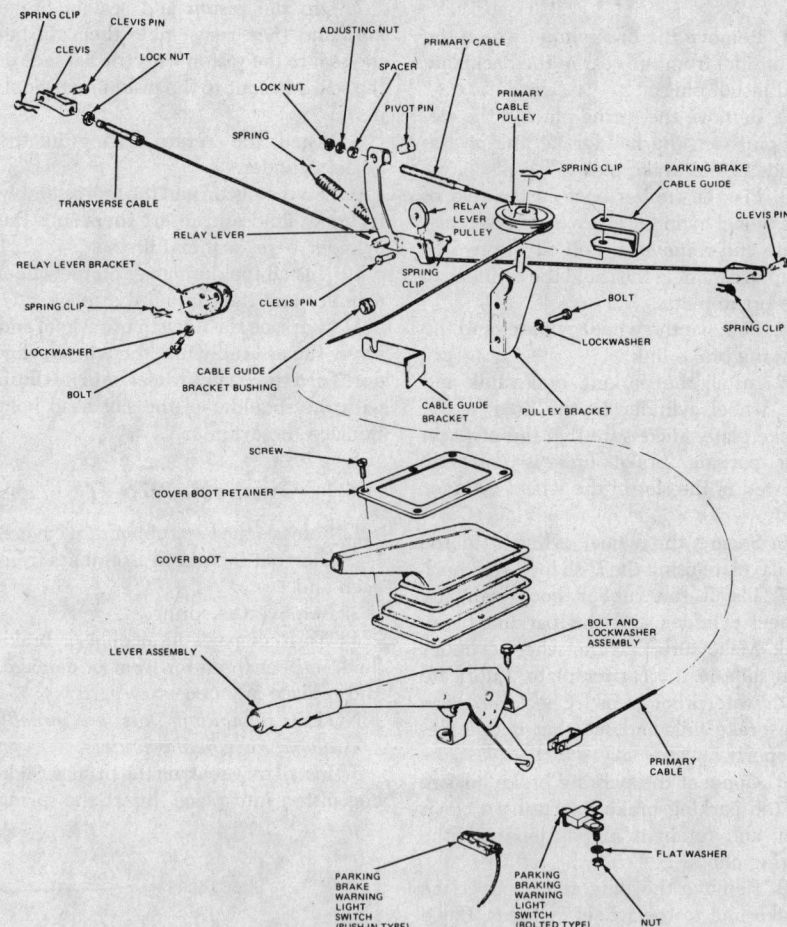

Capri parking brake system details

3. Remove the cover plate and the gasket from around the core tubes at the dash panel.

4. Remove the package tray.

5. If the car is equipped with a console, it will be necessary to remove it.

a. Remove the two screws at the forward end of the console (console to floor).

b. Lift up the gearshift lever boot and remove the two screws at the rear end of the console.

c. Pry up the rear panel and remove the two attaching screws.

d. Gently pry up the clock panel and disconnect the two electrical connectors and the light bulb.

e. Remove the main screw at the rear end of the area under the clock panel.

f. Slide the plastic brace below the handbrake lever forward and remove it. Then lift the console out of the car.

6. Remove the control cable retaining

clips and disconnect the cables from the control levers.

7. Disconnect the three wire connectors from the terminals on the heater and disconnect the bullet connector from the other wire.

8. Disconnect the left and right vent ducts and the left and right defroster ducts from the heater.

9. Remove the windshield wiper motor for better access to one of the mounting screws at the left side of the heater. (See the following section.)

10. Remove the four heater-to-dash panel mounting screws and then remove the heater assembly from the car.

11. Position the heater assembly to the dash panel and install the four mounting screws.

12. Install the windshield wiper motor.

13. Connect the left and right vent ducts and the left and right defroster ducts to the assembly.

14. Connect the three wire connectors to the terminals on the heater and connect the wire with the bullet connectors.

15. Connect the control cables to the levers and adjust them. (See the section on adjustment.)

16. Install the gasket and the cover plate around the heater core tubes at the engine side of the dash panel.

17. Connect the heater hoses to the heater core tubes and secure them with wire clips.

18. On those models that are equipped with a console, make the proper electrical connections and replace the console.

19. Install the package tray.

20. Fill the cooling system and connect the battery cable. Run the engine and check the operation of the cooling system. Check for leaks and once removed, the two halves must be separated.

1973–77 except w/Factory A/C

1. Remove the lower dash trim panel and the glove box. To do this, the steering column shroud, ashtray, hazard flasher switch, and turn signal switch must be removed.

2. Remove the four-speed shift knob. Remove the screws for the center console. Pry the rear console panel up and remove the two screws. Pry up the clock panel and disconnect the electrical connections. Remove the main screw at the rear end of the area under the clock panel. Slide the plastic brace forward below the parking brake lever and remove it. Lift the console out.

3. Drain the coolant, with the heater controls on.

4. Disconnect the hoses from the heater core and detach the gasket.

5. Disconnect the right and left vent and defroster ducts from the heater assembly.

6. Disconnect the control cables from the heater and water valve.

7. Unscrew the seat belt buzzer and let it hang.

8. Disconnect the wiring harness connector from the heater blower.

9. Remove the wiper motor bracket.

10. Remove the heater assembly bolts and remove the unit.

11. On installation, replace the heater assembly and the wiper motor bracket.

12. Install the left vent and defroster ducts.

13. Connect the blower wiring.

14. Connect the control cables. Adjust the upper lever in the WARM position and the lower in the OFF position.

15. Install the right vent and defroster ducts.

16. Replace the gasket and heater hoses.

17. Fill the cooling system.

18. Replace the console, shift knob, glove box, and lower dash trim panel.

With Factory-Installed A/C

CAUTION: *This operation requires discharging the A/C system. This should not be attempted by untrained personnel.*

The assembly to be removed in this procedure is the evaporator case assembly.

1. Discharge the system.

2. Disconnect the refrigerant lines from the evaporator core and the heater hoses from the heater core in the engine compartment.

3. Remove the glove box and the lower right trim panel. Remove the control head assembly and lower instrument panel.

4. Disconnect the vacuum hoses from the evaporator case.

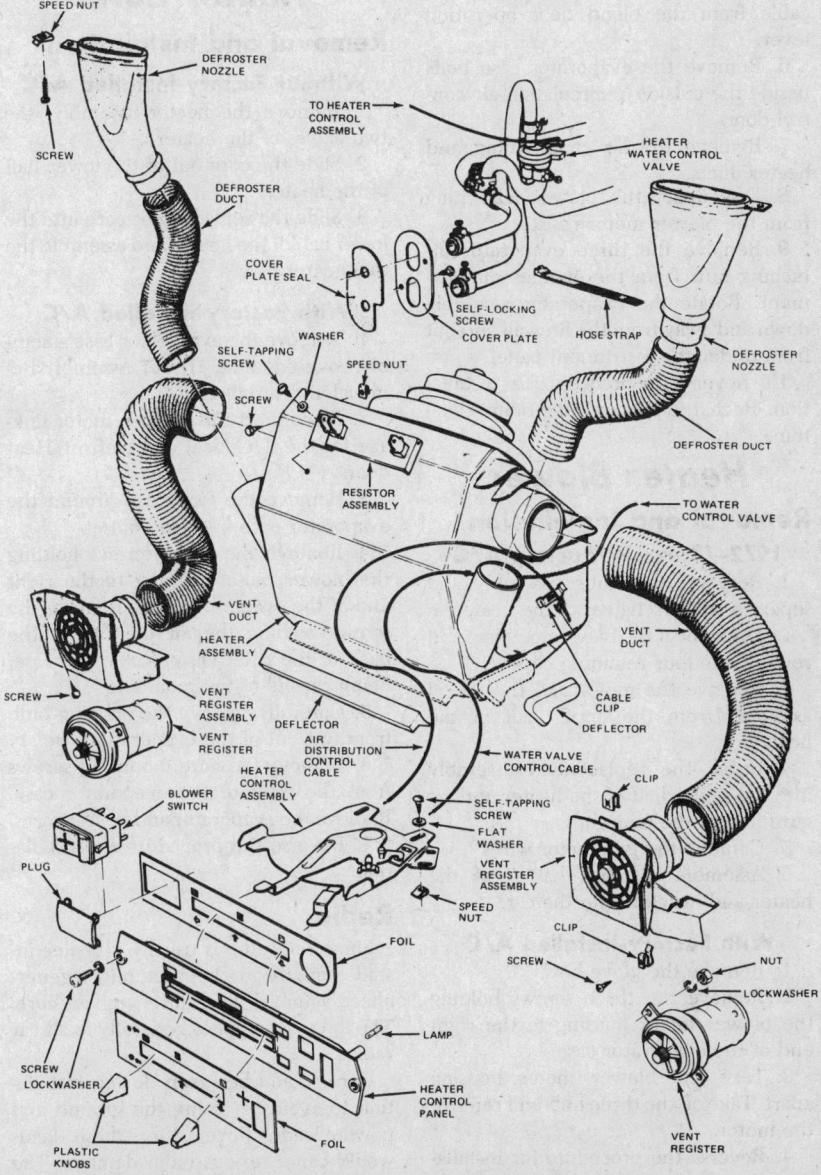

1973-75 Capri heating and ventilating system, without factory-installed A/C

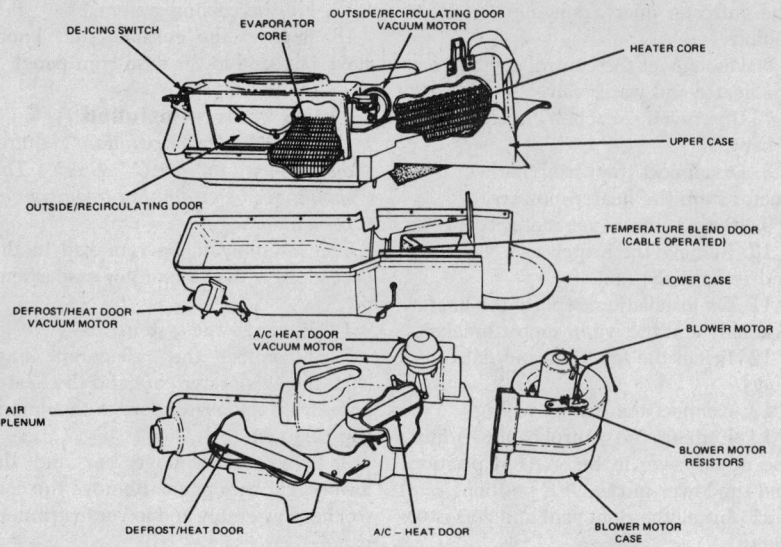

1974-75 Capri evaporator case assembly—factory-installed A/C

5. Disconnect the temperature control cable from the blend door operating lever.

6. Remove the evaporator case bolts beside the outside/recirculation air control door.

7. Remove the air conditioning and heater ducts.

8. Disconnect the blower lead plug from the blower motor resistor.

9. Remove the three evaporator attaching nuts from the engine compartment. Rotate the evaporator assembly down and away from the firewall and out from under the instrument panel.

10. Reverse the procedure for installation. Recharge the air conditioning system.

Heater Blower

Removal and Installation

1972–77 exc W/Factory A/C

1. Remove the heater assembly and separate the two halves of the heater.

2. Disconnect the two motor wires and remove the four retaining clips.

3. Remove the motor and the wheel assembly from the upper half of the heater.

4. Install the replacement assembly into the upper half of the heater and secure it with the four clips.

5. Connect the two motor wires.

6. Assemble the two halves of the heater and install it into the car.

With Factory-Installed A/C

1. Remove the glove box.

2. Remove the three screws holding the blower motor housing to the right end of the evaporator case.

3. Take the blower motor housing apart. Take off the three nuts and remove the motor.

4. Reverse the procedure for installation.

Heater Core

Removal and Installation

Without Factory-Installed A/C

1. Remove the heater assembly, the two halves of the heater.

2. Slide the core out of the lower half of the heater.

3. Slide the replacement core into the lower half of the heater and assemble the two heater halves.

With Factory-Installed A/C

1. Remove the evaporator case assembly, covered under Heater Assembly Removal and Installation.

2. Disconnect the vacuum motor linkage for the A/C-Heat and Defrost/Heat doors.

3. Remove the foam pad around the evaporator core inlet and outlet.

4. Remove the three screws holding the blower motor housing to the right end of the evaporator case. Remove the screws holding the air plenum to the back of the case. Disassemble the case, being careful of the moulding.

5. Carefully remove the de-icing bulb from in front of the evaporator core.

6. Remove the core mounting screws from the front of the evaporator case. Remove the evaporator and heater cores.

7. Reverse the procedure for installation.

Radio

Since the radio is usually a dealer installed or aftermarket unit, only a generalized removal procedure is given here. The following applies generally to all car radios.

Care should be taken during installation to avoid reversing the ground and power leads. Reversal of these leads would cause serious radio damage. The power lead usually has an inline fuse.

If the speaker needs replacement, it should be replaced with one of the same impedance, measured in ohms (Ω). Mismatched impedance can cause rapid transistor failure as well as low volume output. This should also be considered when adding a second speaker; it must be of the same impedance and wired in parallel with the original.

The radio should never be operated without a speaker connected or with the speaker leads shorted. This will result in transistor failure.

Removal and Installation

NOTE: *This is a general procedure; it is not specific to any car.*

1. Remove the package tray, if any.

2. Remove the radio knobs and unscrew the retaining nuts.

3. Remove the wire connectors from the radio and remove the brackets from the rear of the radio.

4. Remove the radio.

5. Place the radio in position and install the brackets and the wiring connectors.

6. Install the package tray.

Windshield Wiper Motor

Removal and Installation

1972

1. Disconnect the battery ground cable.

2. Remove the package tray.

3. Remove the wiper arms and the two nuts securing the wiper pivots to the body.

4. Detach the heater-to-defroster vent hose.

5. Disconnect the two control cables from the heater.

6. Remove the attaching screws holding the wiper motor to the mounting bracket.

7. Disconnect the wiper motor wires, making note of their position.

8. Remove the wiper motor assembly.

9. Position the wiper motor behind the instrument panel.

10. Secure the motor to the body with the two wiper pivot nuts.

11. Connect the wiper motor wiring.

12. Position the wiper motor and install the attaching bolt.

13. Connect the two heater control cables.

14. Install the package tray.

15. Replace the wiper arm and blades.

16. Connect the battery ground cable.

1973–74

NOTE: *This procedure is for cars without factory A/C but can be adapted for those with it.*

1. Remove the heater assembly.

2. Unscrew the left defroster.

3. Detach the wiper motor wiring.

4. Remove the wiper arm and blade assemblies from the spindles, remove the spindles from the cowl top panel. Remove the sleeves and sealing washers.

5. Remove the wiper motor, linkage, and left defroster simultaneously.

6. Remove the linkage from the motor shaft.

7. On installation, attach the motor to the bracket.

8. Put the linkage on the motor shaft, making sure that the tab fits into the driveshaft slot.

9. Install the motor, linkage, and left defroster together. Put the sealing washers and sleeves over the wiper spindles and mount the spindles loosely to the cowl panel.

10. Connect the motor wiring.

11. Replace the heater assembly.

12. Fasten down the wiper motor mounting bracket.

13. Tighten the wiper spindle nuts. Fasten the left defroster in place. Install the wipers and arms.

1976–77 Front Motor

1. Disconnect the negative cable from the battery.

2. Remove wiper arms and blades.

3. Remove the screws securing the steering column shroud. Remove the lower half of the shroud and release the shroud upper half retaining lug from its spring clip on the steering column by pulling sharply upward.

4. Remove retaining screws and pull lower dash panel assembly clear of dash panel.

5. Disconnect cigar lighter wiring and remove panel assembly from vehicle.

6. Remove instrument cluster bezel.

7. Remove instrument cluster.

8. Remove glovebox catch striker and glovebox assembly. Disconnect glovebox light wiring.

9. Disconnect heater control cables from heater controls.

10. Disconnect left-side defroster tube connector from heater and remove connector and tube.

11. Disconnect and remove left-side face-level vent tube.

12. Disconnect wiring at heater and wiper motor.

13. Remove left defroster vent retaining screw and remove vent.

14. Remove wiper spindle retaining nuts and motor bracket retaining screw and remove motor and linkage assembly from vehicle.

15. Separate motor from linkage.

16. Attach motor to linkage.

17. Install wiper motor and linkage assembly. Secure with spindle retaining nuts and motor bracket retaining screw.

18. Install left side defroster vent.

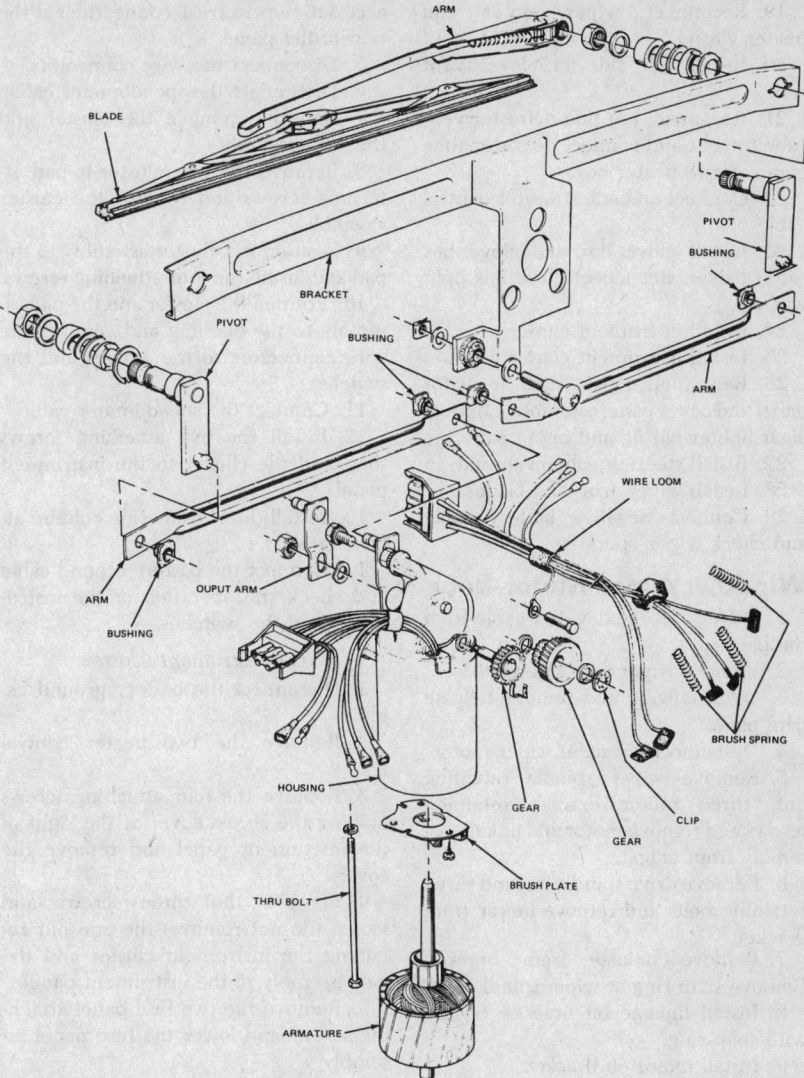

Windshield wiper system components

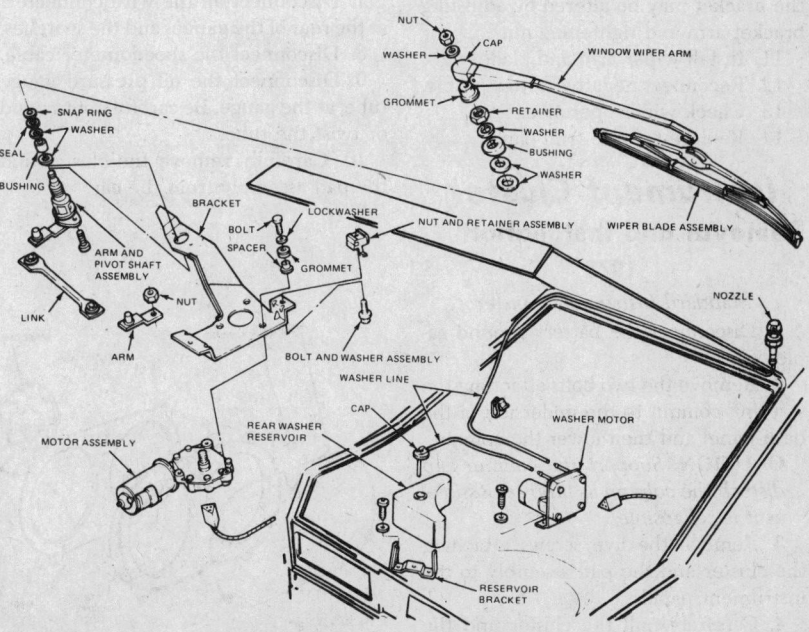

Rear window wiper assembly—Capri II

19. Reconnect wiper motor and heater wiring.

20. Install left side face-level vent tube.

21. Reconnect left side defroster vent tube to vent and connect defroster tube connector to heater box.

22. Connect and adjust heater control cables.

23. Install glove box and glove box catch striker. Reconnect glove box light wiring.

24. Install instrument cluster.

25. Install instrument cluster bezel.

26. Reposition lower dash insulator panel and cover panel assembly. Connect cigar lighter wiring and install panel.

27. Install steering column shroud.

28. Install wiper arms and blades.

29. Connect negative battery cable and check wiper operation.

Window Wiper Motor-Rear

1. Disconnect the negative cable from the battery.

2. Remove wiper arm and blade.

3. Open tailgate and remove tailgate trim panel.

4. Disconnect wiring at wiper motor.

5. Remove wiper spindle retaining nut, three motor bracket retaining screws and remove motor and linkage assembly from tailgate.

6. Remove drive spindle nut and three retaining bolts and remove motor from bracket.

7. Remove linkage from bracket. Remove snap ring at wiper spindle end.

8. Install linkage on bracket. Secure with snap ring.

9. Install motor on bracket.

10. Install wiper motor and bracket on tailgate and reconnect wiper motor wiring. To avoid water leaks the position of the bracket may be altered by adjusting bracket arm and tightening nut.

11. Install wiper arm and blade.

12. Reconnect negative battery cable.

13. Check wiper operation.

14. Replace tailgate trim panel.

Instrument Cluster
Removal and Installation
1972

Standard Instrument Cluster

1. Disconnect the battery ground cable.

2. Remove the two bolts attaching the steering column to the underside of the dash panel and then lower the column.

CAUTION: *Support the column and disturb the column as little as possible, as it is collapsible.*

3. Remove the five screws attaching the cluster and the pad assembly to the instrument panel.

4. Carefully pull the cluster and the pad assembly slightly toward you to gain

access to the electrical connections at the rear of the panel.

5. Disconnect the wire connectors.

6. Disconnect the speedometer cable.

7. Carefully remove the cluster and the pad assembly.

8. Remove the four cluster-to-pad attaching screws and remove the cluster assembly.

9. Position the cluster assembly to the pad and install the four attaching screws.

10. Position the cluster and the pad assembly to the opening and connect the wire connectors to the gauges and the switches.

11. Connect the speedometer cable.

12. Install the five attaching screws that hold the cluster to the instrument panel.

13. Install the two steering column attaching bolts.

14. Connect the battery ground cable and check the operation of the instruments and the switches.

GT Instrument Cluster

1. Disconnect the battery ground cable.

2. Remove the two heater control knobs.

3. Remove the four attaching screws holding the access cover at the right of the instrument panel and remove the cover.

4. Remove the three screws and loosen (do not remove) the one nut retaining the instrument cluster and the pad assembly to the instrument panel.

5. Remove the two fuse panel attaching screws and lower the fuse panel assembly.

6. Carefully pull the cluster and the pad assembly toward you to gain access to the connections at the back of the panel.

7. Disconnect all the wire connectors at the rear of the gauges and the switches.

8. Disconnect the speedometer cable.

9. Disconnect the oil pressure gauge tube, at the gauge. Be careful not to bend or twist the tube.

10. Carefully remove the cluster and the pad assembly from the car.

11. Remove the four cluster-to-pad attaching screws and remove the cluster assembly.

12. Position the cluster assembly to the pad and install the four attaching screws.

13. Position the cluster and the pad assembly to the opening and connect the wire connectors to the gauges and the switches.

14. Connect the speedometer cable.

15. Install the three cluster and pad retaining screws, and tighten the one retaining nut.

16. Position the fuse panel and install the two retaining screws.

17. Position the access cover at the right of the instrument panel and install the four attaching screws.

18. Install the two heater knobs.

19. Connect the battery ground cable and check the operation of the gauges and the switches.

1973–77 W/O Factory A/C

1. Disconnect the battery ground cable.

2. Remove the steering column shroud and the ashtray.

3. Unfasten the hazard warning switch and disconnect its connector.

4. Unfasten the turn signal switch and let it hang.

5. Remove the lower trim panel screws. Pull the panel forward and down to disconnect the lighter and clock. Remove the trim panel.

6. Pull off the panel illumination control knob.

7. Remove the lower cluster bezel screws, pull the bezel down, and disconnect the seat belt warning light connector.

8. Disconnect the oil pressure line fitting.

9. Remove the cluster screws, pull cluster forward and disconnect the speedometer cable and wiring plug. Remove the cluster.

10. On installation, connect the speedometer cable and wiring plug, and replace the cluster screws.

11. Connect the oil pressure line.

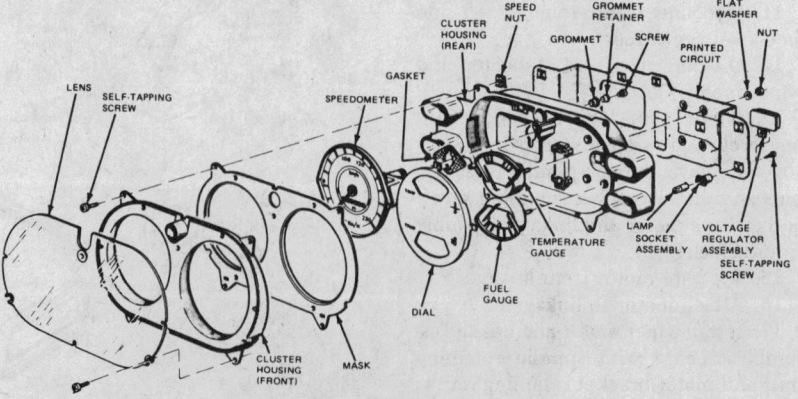

Capri 2000 cc instrument cluster

12. Connect the seat belt warning wire.

13. Hook the upper bezel retaining clips behind the tongues on the instru- ment panel. Push the bezel in and install the screws.

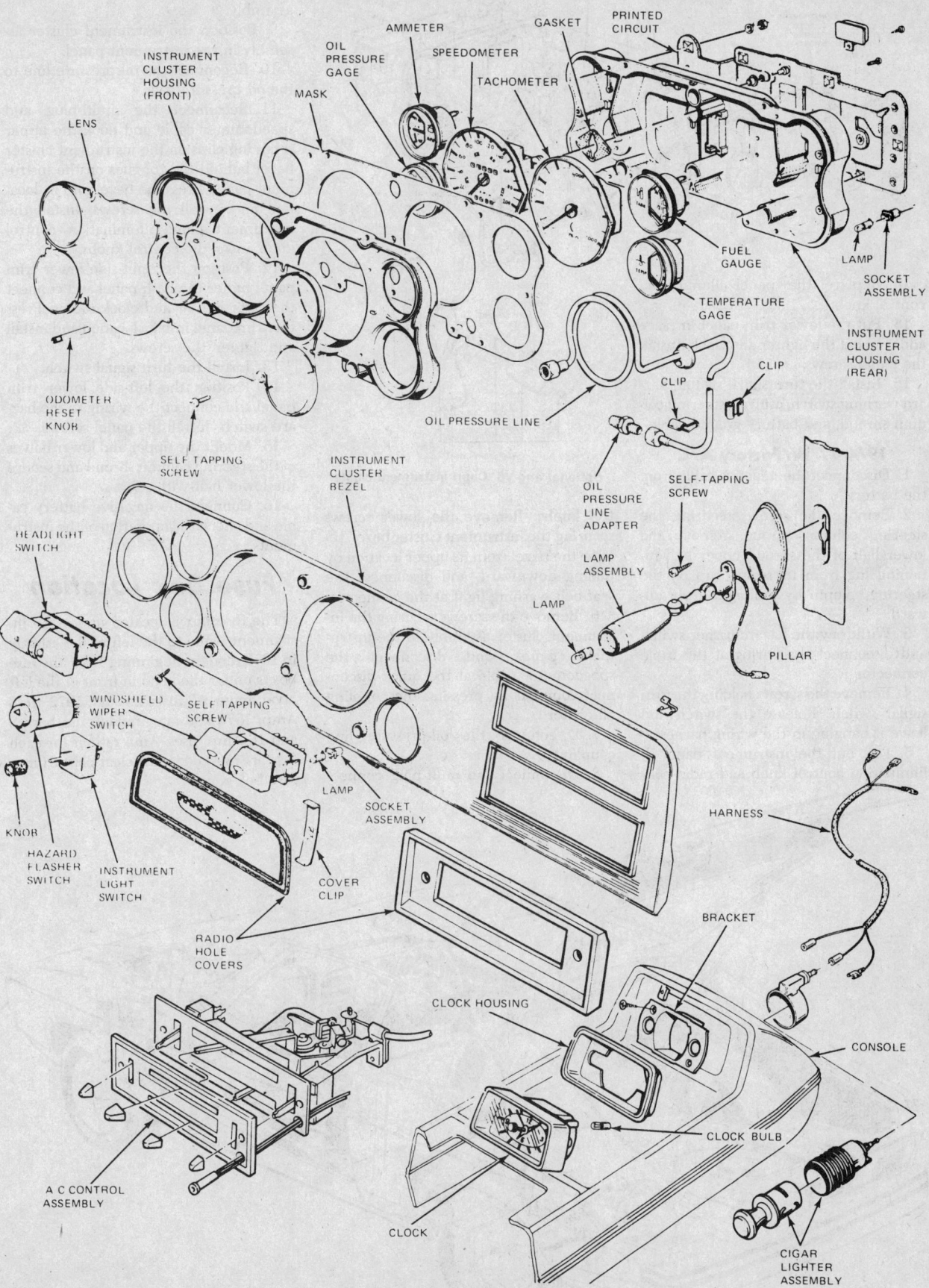

Capri II instrument cluster—with A/C

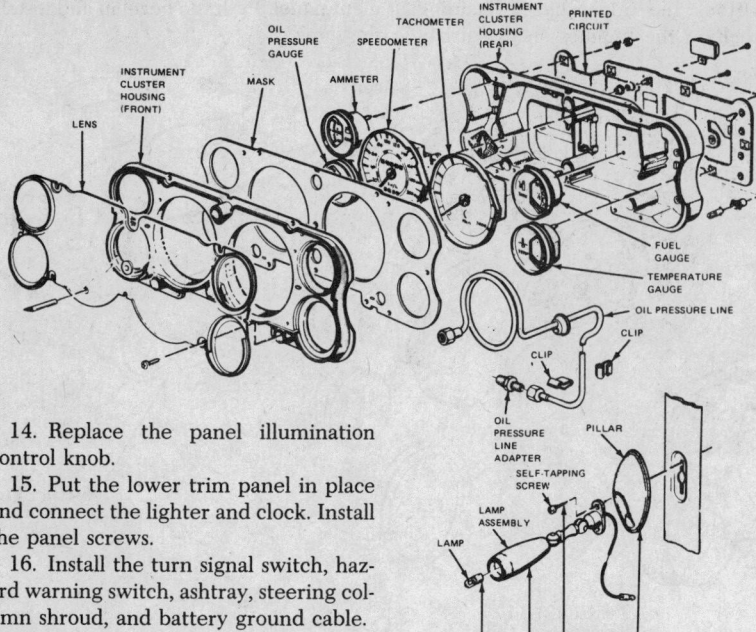

14. Replace the panel illumination control knob.

15. Put the lower trim panel in place and connect the lighter and clock. Install the panel screws.

16. Install the turn signal switch, hazard warning switch, ashtray, steering column shroud, and battery ground cable.

1974–77 W/Factory A/C

1. Disconnect the negative cable from the battery.

2. Remove the screws securing the steering column shroud; remove the lower half of the shroud upper half retaining lug from its spring clip on the steering column by pulling sharply upward.

3. Withdraw the hazard flasher switch and disconnect the wiring at the cable connector.

4. Remove the screws holding the turn signal switch. Release the switch and leave it hanging in the wiring harness.

5. Pull out the instrument panel illumination control knob and radio con-

Optional and V6 Capri instrument cluster

trol knobs. Remove the lower screws securing the instrument cluster bezel, release the bezel from its upper location by pulling downward, and disconnect the seat belt warning light at the connector.

6. Remove the screws securing the instrument cluster assembly to the instrument panel, and disconnect the speedometer cable at the quick disconnect coupling by pressing the coupling off-center.

7. Disconnect the oil-pressure line coupling.

8. Disconnect the mult-plug connec-

tor from the rear of the instrument cluster. Remove the instrument cluster assembly.

9. Position the instrument cluster assembly in the instrument panel.

10. Reconnect the oil pressure line to the oil pressure gage.

11. Reconnect the multi-plug and speedometer cable and hook the upper retaining clips on the instrument cluster bezel behind the tongues on the instrument panel. Press the bezel into its location and install the screws. Install the instrument panel illumination control knob and radio control knobs.

12. Position the right-side lower trim panel under the dash panel and connect the cigar lighter and clock cables. Press the trim panel into its location and install and tighten the screws.

13. Install the turn signal switch.

14. Position the left-side lower trim panel and connect the wiring to the hazard switch. Install the panel screws.

15. Mount the upper and lower halves of the steering column shroud and secure the lower half with screws.

16. Connect the negative battery cable and check the operation of the instruments.

Fuse Box Location

The fuse box is located under the instrument panel to the left of the ashtray in 1972 models. Beginning 1973, the fuse box is under the hood in front of the left hood hinge. All fuses through 1972 are 8 Amp; 1973 and later models use both 8 and 16 Amp fuses. Amp ratings for each fuse are marked on the clear plastic inner fuse box cover.

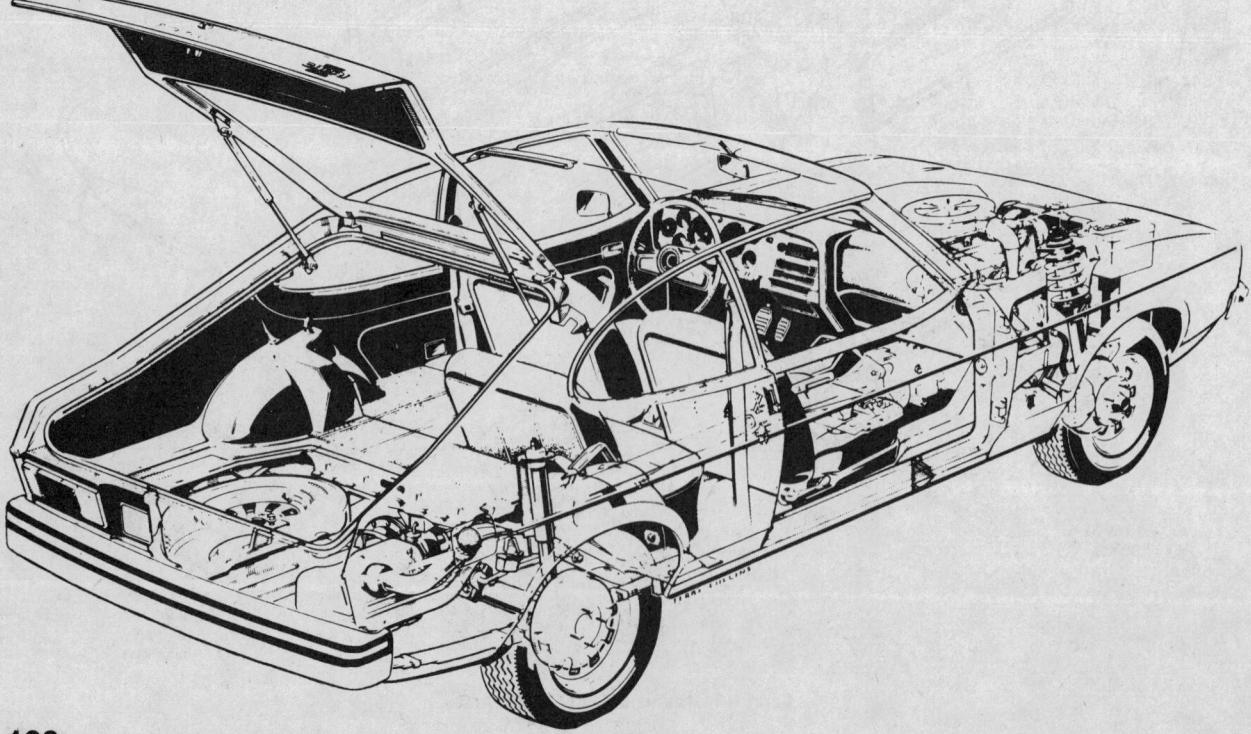

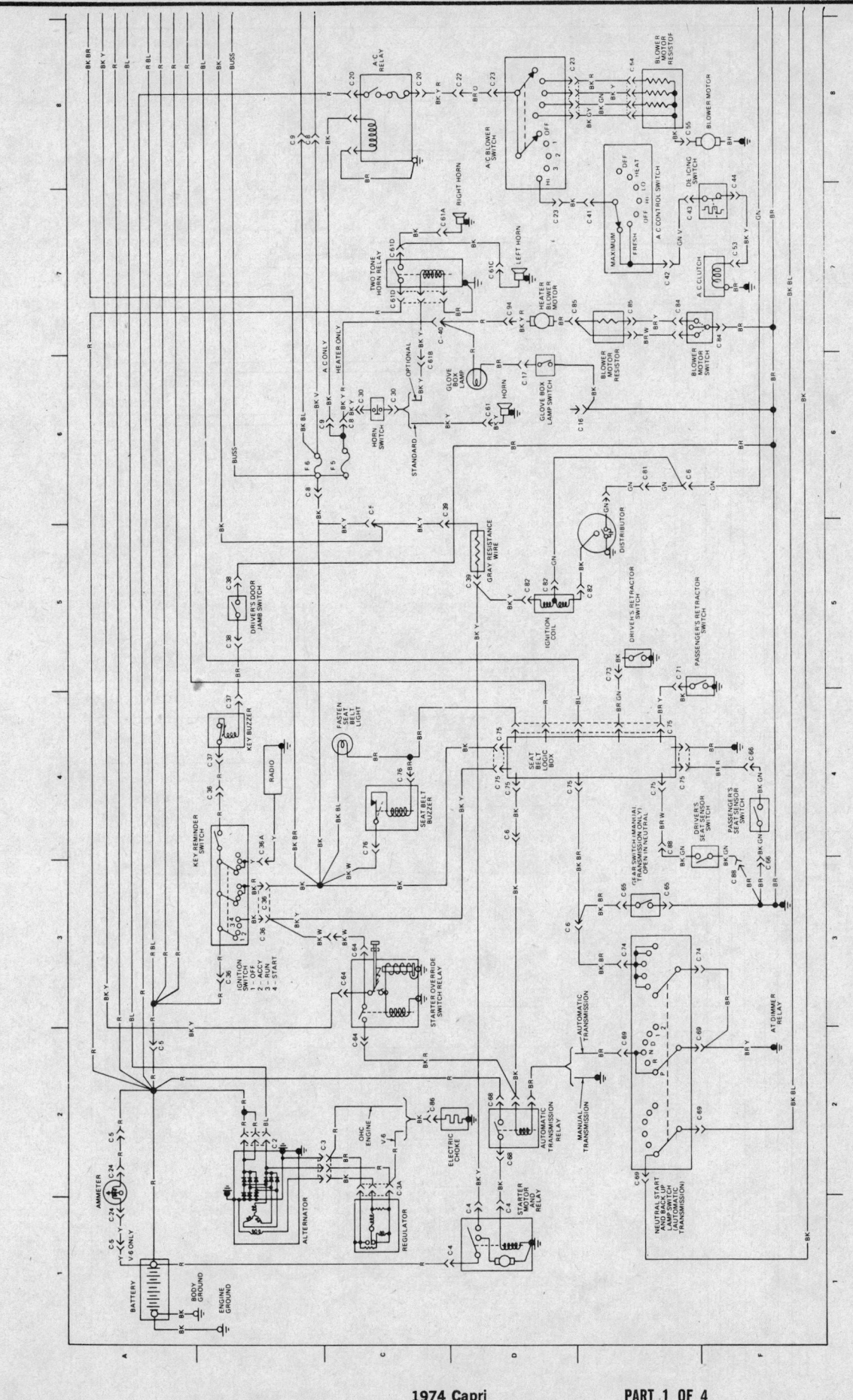

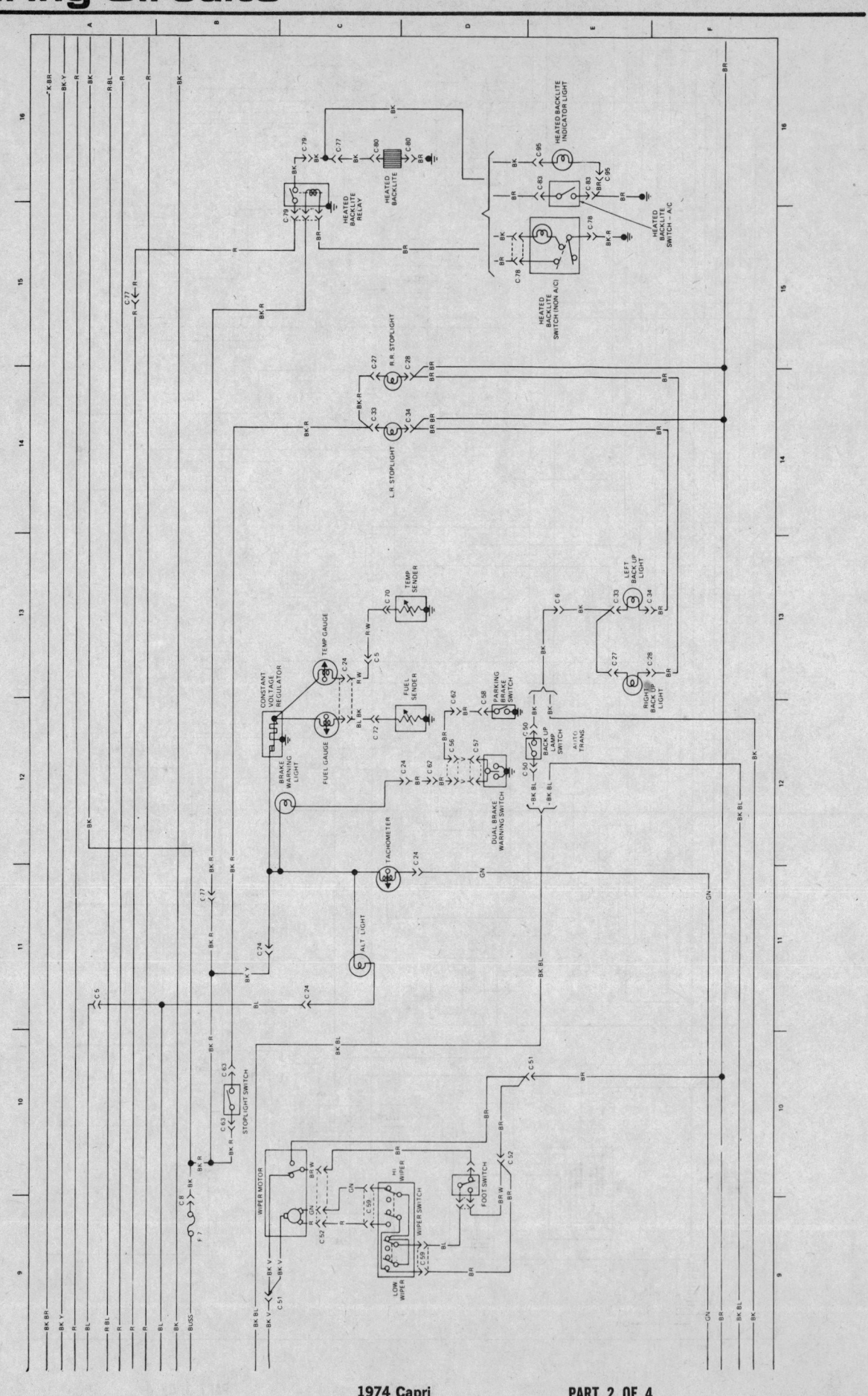

1974 Capri   PART 2 OF 4

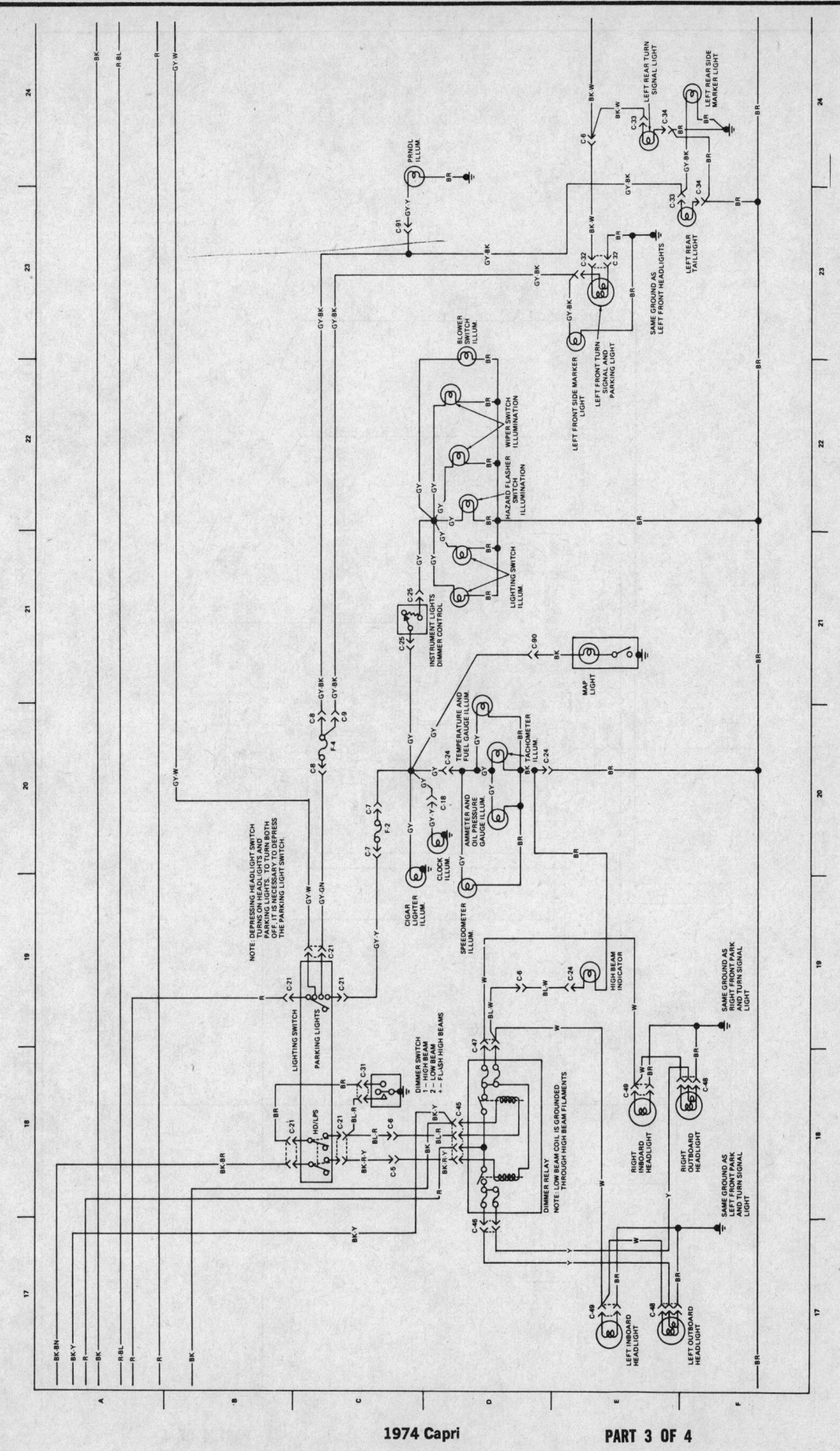

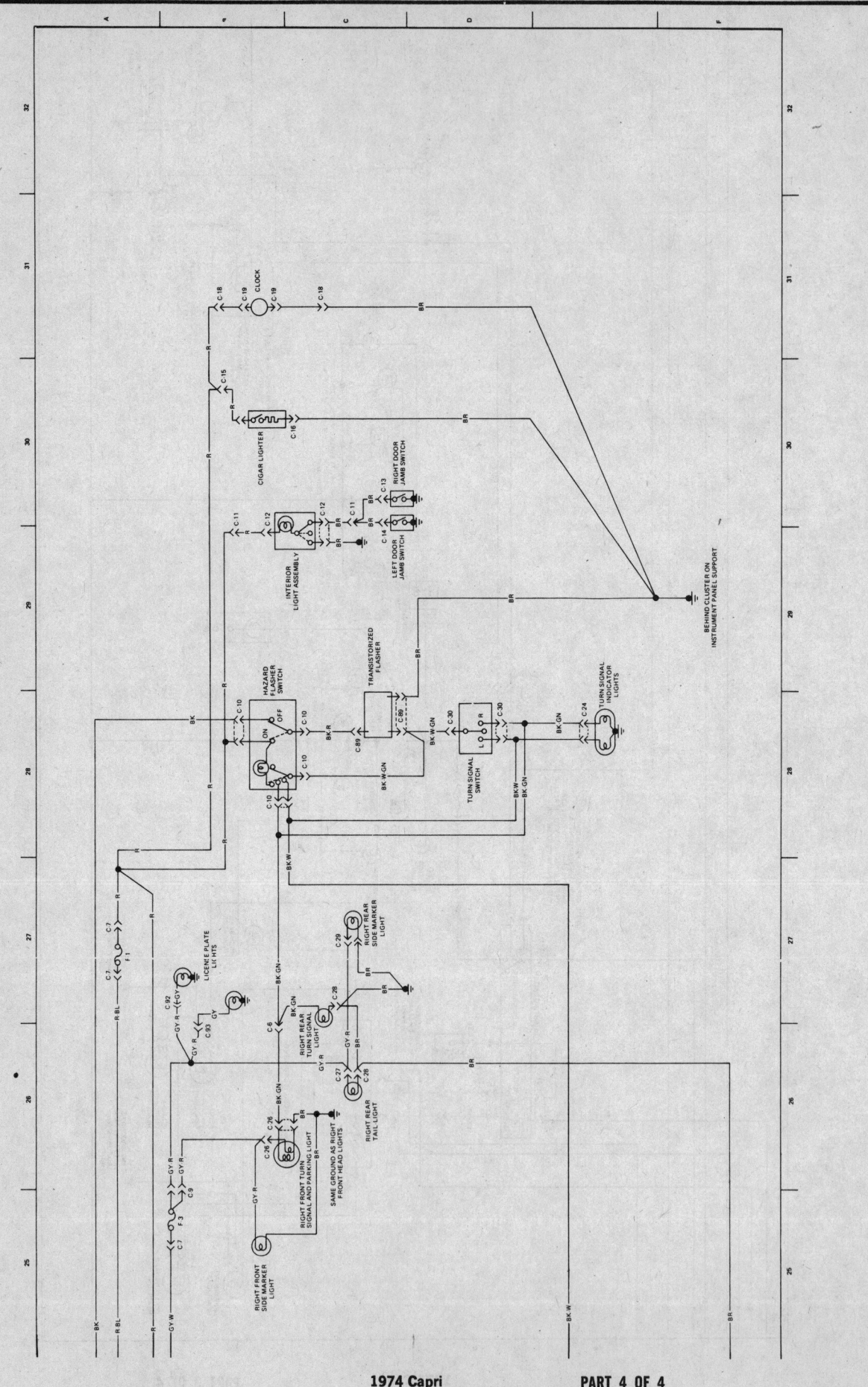

1974 Capri   PART 4 OF 4

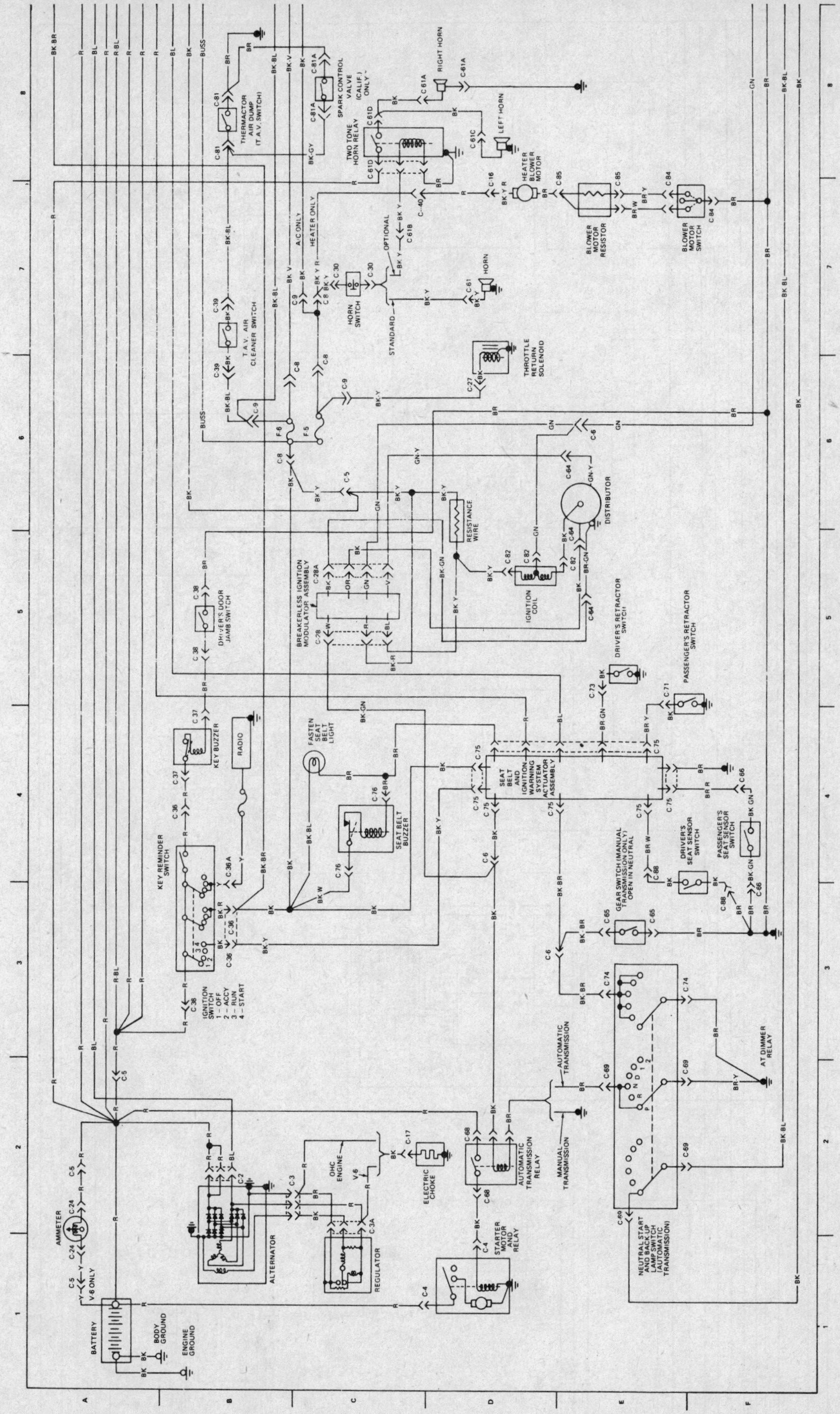
BATTERY
BODY GROUND
ENGINE GROUND
AMMETER
V-6 ONLY
ALTERNATOR
REGULATOR
OHC ENGINE
ELECTRIC CHOKE
STARTER MOTOR AND RELAY
AUTOMATIC TRANSMISSION RELAY
AUTOMATIC TRANSMISSION
MANUAL TRANSMISSION
NEUTRAL START AND BACK-UP LAMP SWITCH (AUTOMATIC TRANSMISSION)
AT DIMMER RELAY
IGNITION SWITCH
1 – OFF
2 – ACCY
3 – RUN
4 – START
KEY REMINDER SWITCH
KEY BUZZER
RADIO
DRIVER'S DOOR JAMB SWITCH
FASTEN SEAT BELT LIGHT
SEAT BELT BUZZER
SEAT BELT AND IGNITION WARNING SYSTEM ACTUATOR ASSEMBLY
GEAR SWITCH (MANUAL TRANSMISSION ONLY) OPEN IN NEUTRAL
DRIVER'S SEAT SENSOR SWITCH
PASSENGER'S SEAT SENSOR SWITCH
DRIVER'S RETRACTOR SWITCH
PASSENGER'S RETRACTOR SWITCH
BREAKERLESS IGNITION MODULATOR ASSEMBLY
RESISTANCE WIRE
IGNITION COIL
DISTRIBUTOR
THROTTLE RETURN SOLENOID
T.A.V. AIR CLEANER SWITCH
THERMACTOR AIR DUMP (T.A.V. SWITCH)
SPARK CONTROL VALVE (CALIF. ONLY)
TWO TONE HORN RELAY
RIGHT HORN
LEFT HORN
HORN
HORN SWITCH
OPTIONAL
STANDARD
A/C ONLY
HEATER ONLY
HEATER BLOWER MOTOR
BLOWER MOTOR RESISTOR
BLOWER MOTOR SWITCH
BUSS

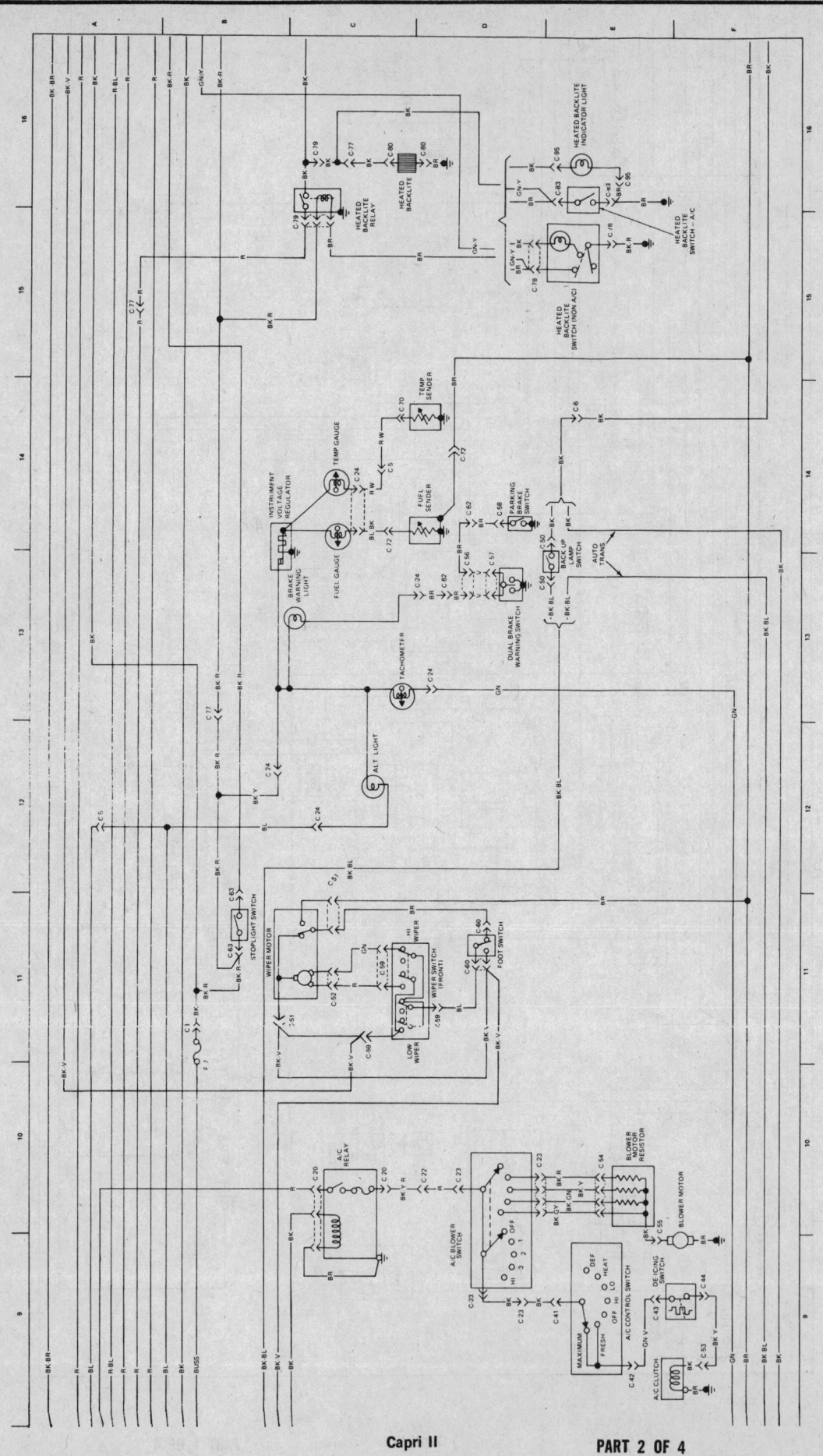

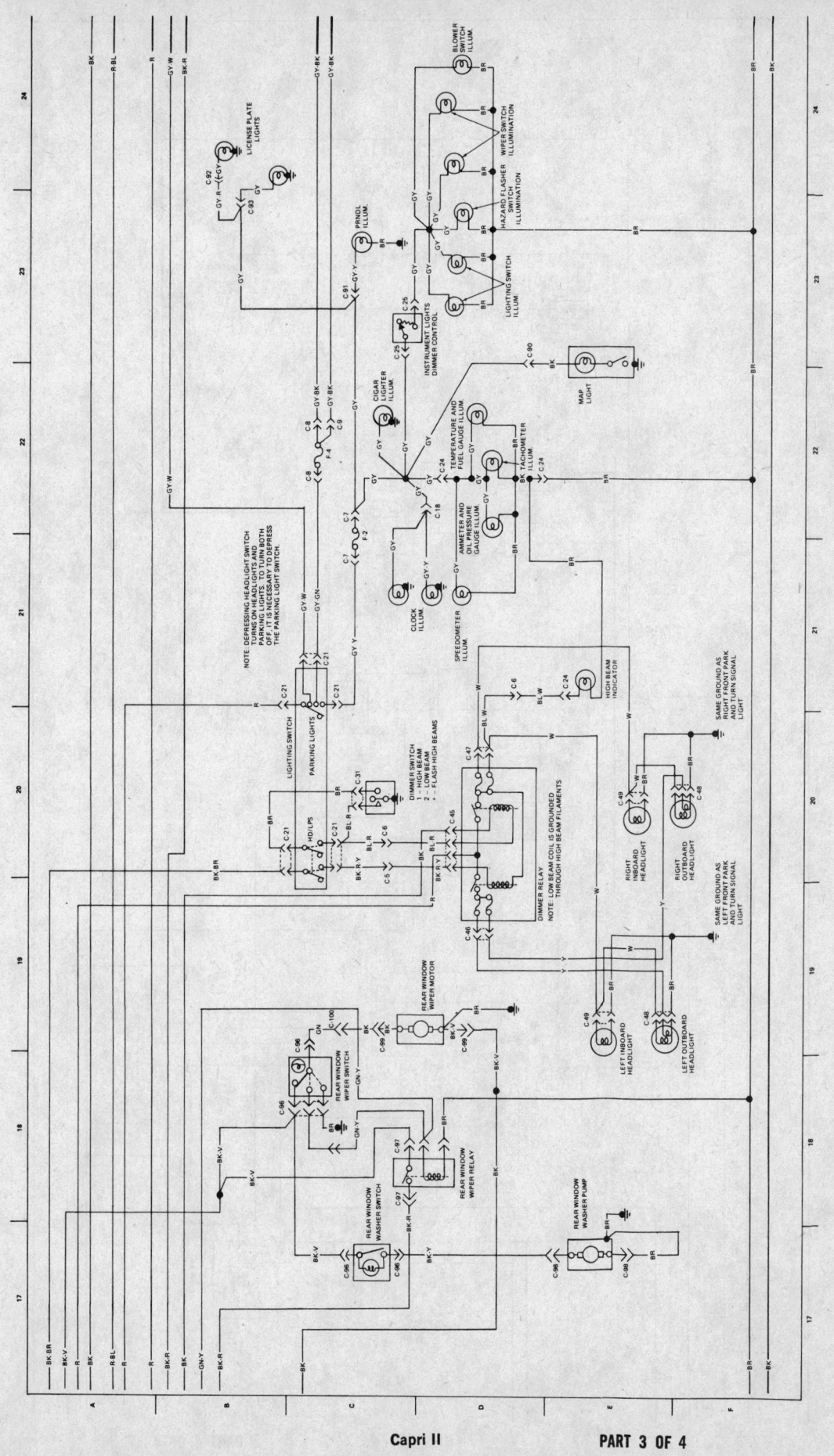

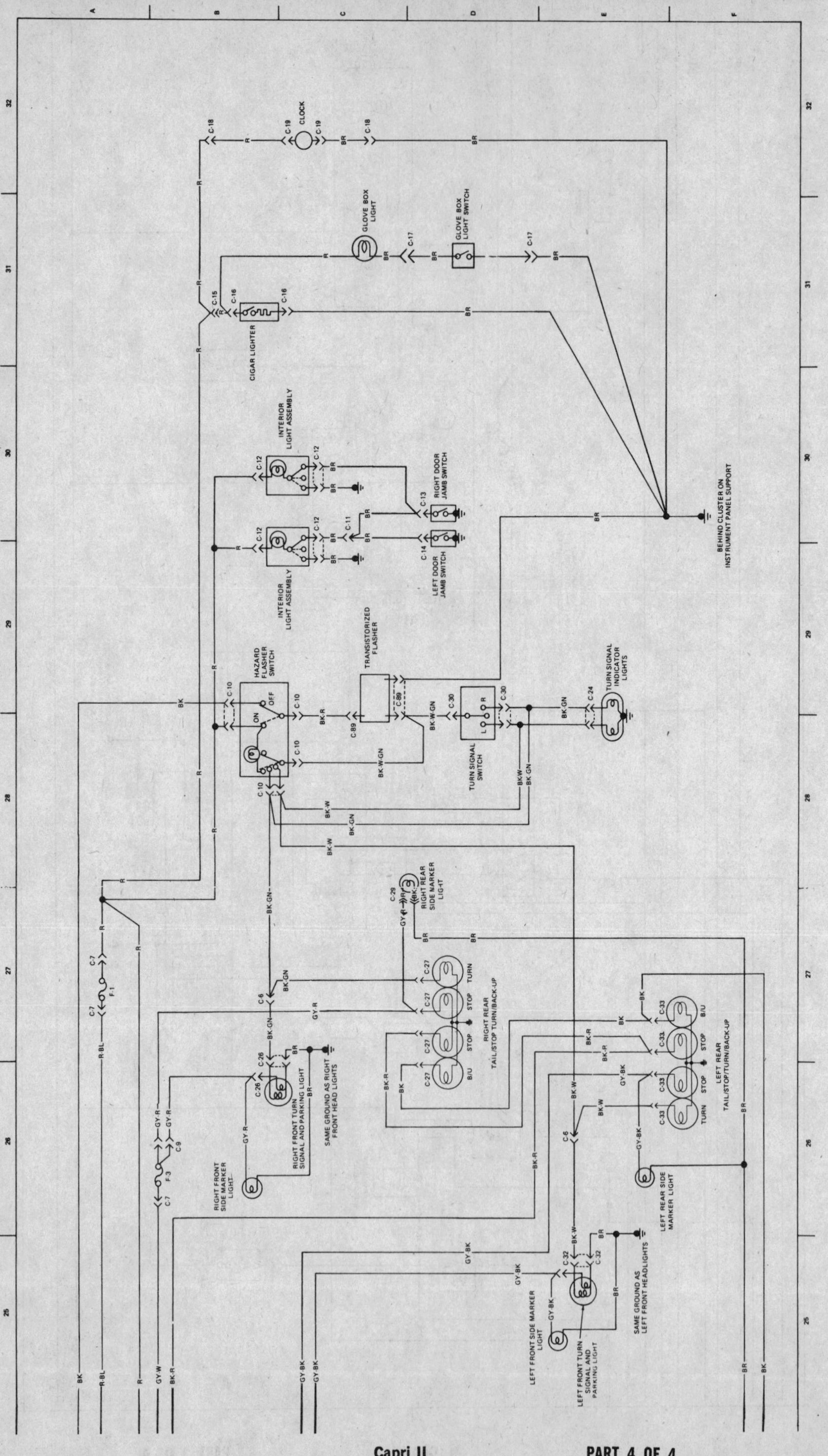
CLOCK
GLOVE BOX LIGHT
GLOVE BOX LIGHT SWITCH
CIGAR LIGHTER
INTERIOR LIGHT ASSEMBLY
RIGHT DOOR JAMB SWITCH
LEFT DOOR JAMB SWITCH
BEHIND CLUSTER ON INSTRUMENT PANEL SUPPORT
HAZARD FLASHER SWITCH
TRANSISTORIZED FLASHER
TURN SIGNAL SWITCH
TURN SIGNAL INDICATOR LIGHTS
RIGHT REAR SIDE MARKER LIGHT
RIGHT REAR TAIL/STOP TURN/BACK-UP
LEFT REAR TAIL/STOP/TURN/BACK-UP
LEFT REAR SIDE MARKER LIGHT
RIGHT FRONT SIDE MARKER LIGHT
RIGHT FRONT TURN SIGNAL AND PARKING LIGHT
SAME GROUND AS RIGHT FRONT HEAD LIGHTS
LEFT FRONT SIDE MARKER LIGHT
LEFT FRONT TURN SIGNAL AND PARKING LIGHT
SAME GROUND AS LEFT FRONT HEADLIGHTS

SPECIFICATIONS

Dodge Colt / Plymouth Arrow

INTRODUCTION

The Dodge Colt is the first combined effort of Dodge and Mitsubishi Heavy Industries, Ltd. It is a descendant of the Mitsubishi Colt, which has been sold in Japan for several years. The Colt joins a growing field of small, low priced, but well equipped economy cars which are becoming popular in the United States. The Colt is sold and serviced as part of the Dodge dealer network, rather than having its own, and is considered a Dodge product.

The Plymouth Arrow is also a Mitsubishi built car which is smaller and less expensive than the Colt. The Arrow is sold and serviced as a part of the Plymouth dealer network.

MODEL IDENTIFICATION

1972-73 Dodge Colt sedan

1972-73 Dodge Colt station wagon

1972-73 Dodge Colt hardtop

1975-76 Dodge Colt station wagon

1975-76 Dodge Colt sedan

1977 Dodge Colt sedan

1977 Plymouth Arrow sedan

SERIAL NUMBER IDENTIFICATION

Vehicle Number

The vehicle identification plate is mounted on the instrument panel, adjacent to the lower corner of the windshield on the driver's side, and is visible through the windshield. The thirteen digit vehicle number is composed of a seven digit identification code, and a six digit sequential number.

Engine model number

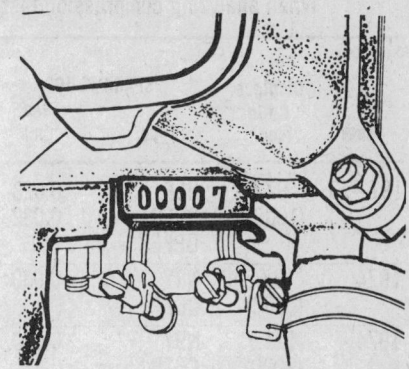

Engine number location

Serial number location

Engine Number

The engine model number is embossed on the lower left side of the block. The sequential engine number is stamped on a pad at the upper right front of the engine, adjacent to the exhaust manifold.

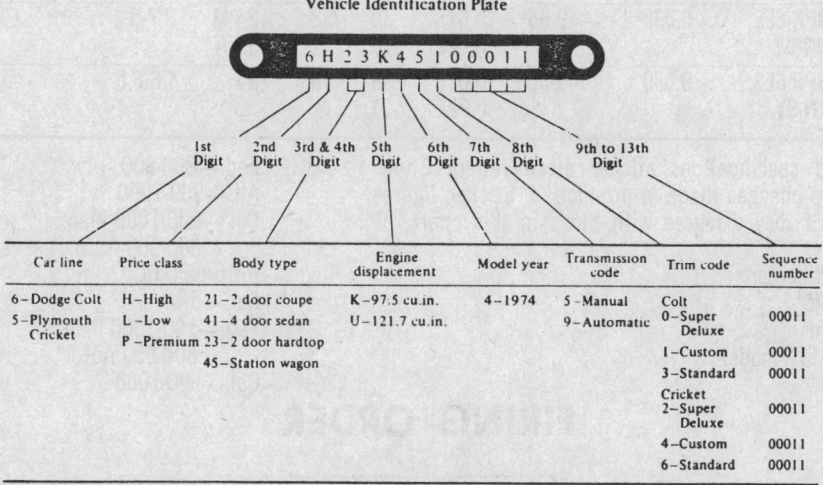

Vehicle I.D. Plate (Typical)

Vehicle Identification Plate

	1st Digit	2nd Digit	3rd & 4th Digit	5th Digit	6th Digit	7th Digit	8th Digit	9th to 13th Digit
	Car line	Price class	Body type	Engine displacement	Model year	Transmission code	Trim code	Sequence number
	6–Dodge Colt	H–High	21–2 door coupe	K–97.5 cu.in.	4–1974	5–Manual	Colt	
	5–Plymouth Cricket	L–Low	41–4 door sedan	U–121.7 cu.in.		9–Automatic	0–Super Deluxe	00011
		P–Premium	23–2 door hardtop				1–Custom	00011
			45–Station wagon				3–Standard	00011
							Cricket	
							2–Super Deluxe	00011
							4–Custom	00011
							6–Standard	00011

GENERAL ENGINE SPECIFICATIONS

Year	Engine Displacement Cu In. (cc)	Carburetor Type	Horsepower @ rpm	Torque @ rpm (ft lbs)	Bore x Stroke (in.)	Compression Ratio	Oil Pressure (psi)
1972-73	97.5 (1600)	1 x 2 bbl	100 @ 6300	101 @ 4000	3.03 x 3.39	8.5:1	28-57
1974	97.5 (1600)	1 x 2 bbl	83 @ 5600MT 81 @ 5600AT	83 @ 5600MT 81 @ 5600AT	3.03 x 3.39	8.5:1	28-57
	121.7 (2000)	1 x 2 bbl	94 @ 5500	108 @ 3600	3.31 x 3.54	8.5:1	57-71①
1975	97.5 (1600)	1 x 2 bbl	79 @ 5300	86 @ 3000	3.03 x 3.39	8.5:1	57-71①
	121.7 (2000)	1 x 2 bbl	89 @ 5200	105 @ 3000	3.31 x 3.54	8.5:1	57-71①
1976-77	97.5 (1600)	1 x 2 bbl	83 @ 5500	89 @ 3500	3.03 x 3.39	8.5:1	②
	121.7 (2000)	1 x 2 bbl	96 @ 5500	109 @ 3500	3.31 x 3.54	8.5:1	②

MT Manual Transmission
AT Automatic Transmission
① At 2000 RPM

② 97.5—58-73 @ 4000
57-71 w/Silent Shaft @ 2000
121.7—50-64 @ 2000

TUNE-UP SPECIFICATIONS

When analyzing compression test results, look for uniformity among cylinders, rather than specific pressures.

Year	Engine Displace. Cu In. (cc.)	SPARK PLUGS Type	Gap (in.)	DISTRIBUTOR Point Dwell (deg)	Point Gap (in.)	IGNITION TIMING (deg) MT	AT	Intake Valve Opens (deg)	Fuel Pump Pressure (psi)	Idle Speed (rpm)	VALVE CLEAR (in) In	Ex
1972-73	97.5 (1600)	B6E, B6ES, BP6ES	0.028-0.032	49-55	0.018 0.022	TDC	TDC①	32	3.7-5.1	700-750① 1350-1450② 800-850③	0.003 cold	0.007 cold
1974	97.5 (1600)	N9Y C62P	0.030	49-55	0.018-0.022	TDC	3B	32 M 22 A	3.7-5.1	800-900	0.006 hot	0.010 hot
1974	121.7 (2000)	N9Y C62P	0.030	49-55	0.018-0.022	3B	3B 850 rpm	25	3.7-5.1	800-900	0.006	0.010
1975	97.5 (1600)	BP6ES or N9Y	0.030	49-55	0.018-0.022	5A	5A	32 M 22 A	3.7-5.1	800-900	0.006 hot	0.010 hot
	121.7 (2000)	BP6ES or N9Y	0.030	49-55	0.018-0.022	5A	5A	20	3.7-5.1	800-900	0.006 hot	0.010 hot
1976	97.5 (1600)	BPR-6ES RN-9Y	0.030	49-55	0.018 0.022	TDC	TDC	32 M 22 A	3.7-5.1	900-1000 M 800-900 A	0.006 hot	0.010 hot
	121.7 (2000)	BPR-6ES RN-9Y	0.030	49-55	0.018 0.022	3B	3B	20	3.7-5.1	900-1000 M 800-900 A	0.006 hot	0.010 hot
1977	97.5 (1600)	BPR-6ES RN-9Y	0.030	49-55	0.018 0.022	5B ⑤	5B ⑤	24 M 19 A	3.7-5.1	④	0.006 hot	0.010 hot
	121.7 (2000)	BPR-6ES RN-9Y	0.030	49-55	0.018 0.022	5B ⑤	5B ⑤	24	4.6-6.0	⑥	0.006 hot	0.010 hot

NOTE: The underhood specifications sticker often reflects tune-up specification changes made in production. Sticker figures must be used if they disagree with those in this chart.

TDC Top dead center
B Before top dead center
① With solenoid off
② With solenoid on
③ Idle speed for 1972 model

④ Fed.—800-900
   Alt.—900-1000
   Cal.—900-1000 Man.
       800-900 Auto.
⑤ Altitude (TDC)
   Cal.—5A
⑥ Fed.—900-1000 Man.
       800-900 Auto.
   Cal.—900-1000

FIRING ORDER

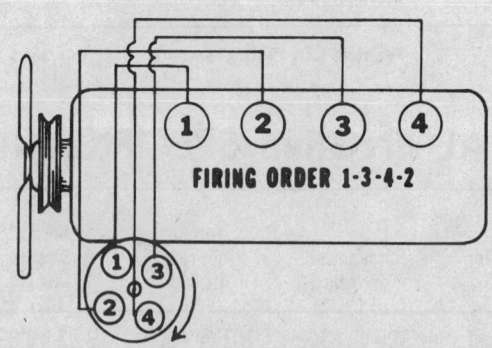

FIRING ORDER 1-3-4-2

CAPACITIES

Year	Model	Engine Displacement Cu In. (cc)	ENGINE CRANKCASE (qts) With Filter	Without Filter	TRANSMISSION (pts) Manual 4-spd	5-spd	Automatic	Drive Axle (pts)	Gasoline Tank (gals)	Cooling System (qts) W/ AC	W/O AC
1972-73	All	1600	4.2	3.7	3.6	—	6.2	2.0	13①	7.2	7.2

CAPACITIES

Year	Model	Engine Displacement Cu In. (cc)	ENGINE CRANKCASE (qts)		TRANSMISSION (pts)			Drive Axle (pts)	Gasoline Tank (gals)	Cooling System (qts)	
			With Filter	Without Filter	Manual		Automatic			W/ AC	W/O AC
					4-spd	5-spd					
1972-73	All	1600	4.2	3.7	3.6	—	6.2	2.0	13①	7.2	7.2
1974-75	All	1600	4.2	3.7	3.6	—	5.8	1.9	13①	6.6	6.6
		2000	5.0	4.0	3.6	—	5.8	1.9	13①	8.3	8.3
1976-77	All	1600	4.2	3.7	3.6	4.3	6.8	2.4②	13①	6.4③	6.4③
		2000	4.5	4.0	3.6	4.9	6.8	2.4②	13①	8.0④	8.0④

① Station Wagon—11   ② 1977—1.92   ③ 1977—7.7   ④ 1977—9.5
— Not Applicable

CRANKSHAFT AND CONNECTING ROD SPECIFICATIONS

All measurements are given in inches

Year	Engine Displace. (Cu In.)	CRANKSHAFT				CONNECTING ROD		
		Main Brg. Journal Dia.	Main Brg. Oil Clearance	Shaft End-Play	Thrust on No.	Journal Diameter	Oil Clearance	Side Clearance
1972-73	97.5	2.2433-2.2441	0.0006-0.0030	0.002-0.007	3	1.7709-1.7717	0.0003-0.0028	0.0039-0.0098
1974-76	97.5	2.2441	0.0006-0.0031	0.002-0.007	3	1.7717	0.0004-0.0028	0.004-0.010
	121.7	2.5984	0.008-0.0028	0.002-0.007	3	2.0866	0.0006-0.0025	0.004-0.010
1977	97.5	2.441	0.0008-0.0022	0.002-0.007	3	1.772	0.0006-0.0020	0.004-0.010
	121.7	2.5984	0.008-0.0017	0.002-0.007	3	2.087	0.0007-0.0022	0.004-0.010

VALVE SPECIFICATIONS

Year	Engine Displacement Cu In. (cc)	Seat Angle (deg)	Face Angle (deg)	Spring Test Pressure (lbs @ in.)	Spring Installed Height (in.)	STEM TO GUIDE CLEARANCE (in.)		STEM DIAMETER (in.)	
						Intake	Exhaust	Intake	Exhaust
1972-75	97.5 (1600)	45	44	59-65 @ 1.47	1.47	0.0010-0.0022	0.002-0.003	0.3133-0.3139	0.3121-0.0033
1974-75	121.7 (2000)	43.5 44	45- 45.5	55-62 @ 1.6	1.47	0.001-0.00	0.002-0.003	0.313-0.314	0.313-0.314
1976-77	97.5 (1600)	44	45	61 @ 1.47	1.47	0.001-0.0022	0.002-0.0033	0.313-0.314	0.312-0.313
	121.7 (2000)	44	45	61 @ 1.59	1.59	0.001-0.0022	0.002-0.0033	0.313-0.314	0.312-0.313

PISTON AND RING SPECIFICATIONS

All measurements in inches

Year	Engine Displace. Cu In. (cc)	Piston Clearance	RING GAP			RING SIDE CLEARANCE		
			Top Compression	Bottom Compression	Oil Control	Top Compression	Bottom Compression	Oil Control
1972-73	97.5 (1600)	0.0008- 0.0016	0.006-0.014	0.006-0.014	0.006-0.014	0.0012-0.0028	0.0008-0.0024	0.0010-0.0030
1974-75	97.5 (1600)	0.0008- 0.0016	0.0008-0.0169	0.0008-0.0169	0.006-0.014	0.0012-0.0028	0.0008-0.0024	0.0010-0.0030
	121.7 (2000)	0.0008- 0.0016	0.0118-0.0197	0.0098-0.0177	0.010-0.018	0.0012-0.0028	0.0008-0.0024	0.0008-0.0026

PISTON AND RING SPECIFICATIONS
All measurements in inches

| Year | Engine Displace. Cu In. (cc) | Piston Clearance | RING GAP | | | RING SIDE CLEARANCE | | |
			Top Compression	Bottom Compression	Oil Control	Top Compression	Bottom Compression	Oil Control
1976-77	97.5 (1600)	0.0008-0.0016	0.008-0.016	0.008-0.016	0.008-0.020	0.0012-0.0028	0.0008-0.0024	0.0008-0.0024
	121.7 (2000)	0.0008-0.0016	0.010-0.016	0.010-0.016	0.010-0.018	0.0024-0.0039	0.0008-0.0024	0.0008-0.0024

TORQUE SPECIFICATIONS
All readings in ft lbs

| Year | Engine Displace. (Cu In.) | Cylinder Head Bolts | Rod Bearing Bolts | Main Bearing Bolts | Crankshaft Pulley Bolt | Flywheel To Crankshaft Bolts | MANIFOLD | |
							Intake	Exhaust
1971-73	97.5	51-55① (cold) 7-9②	23-25	36-40	43-51	69-76	11-14	11-14
1974-77	97.5	51-54 (cold) 58-61 (hot)	23-25	36-39	43-50	83-90	11-14	11-14
	121.7	65-72 (cold) 72-77 (hot)	33-35	54-61	80-93	83-90③	11-14	11-14

① bolts   ② nuts   ③ 1976-77—95-100

TORQUE SEQUENCES

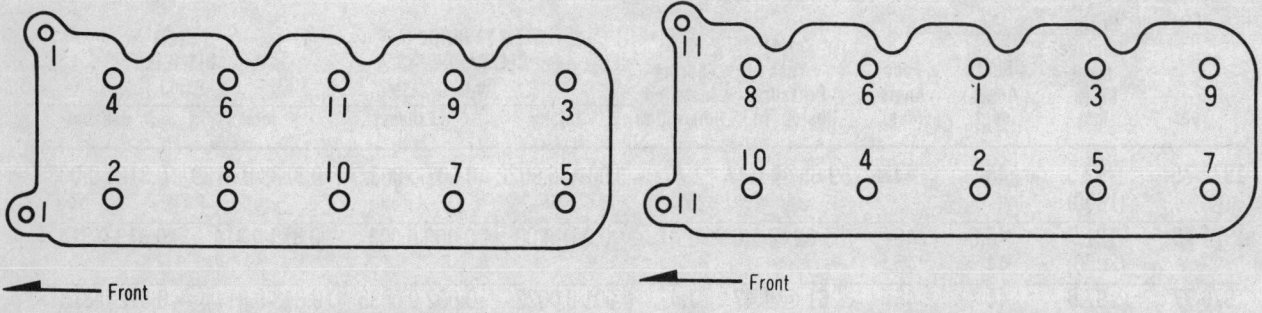

Head bolt removal sequence   Head bolt tightening sequence

BATTERY AND STARTER SPECIFICATIONS

| Year | Model | Battery Amp Hour Capacity | Starter | | | | | | | Brush Spring Tension (oz) | Min. Brush Length (in.) |
| | | | Lock Test | | | No Load Test | | | | |
			Amps	Volts	Torque (ft/lbs)	Amps	Volts	RPM		
1972-75	1600	60	500	6.0	11.2	55	11	5500	56	0.453
1974-75	2000	60	Less than 730	6.0	18.0	62	11	4500	53	0.453
1976-77	1600	60	150	8.6④	2.53①	53	10.5	5000	38	.669
	2000	60	200③	9.6⑤	3.83②	62	11	6500	38	.669

① Auto. Trans.—2.24   ③ Man. Trans.—150   ⑤ Auto. Trans.—9.2
② Man. Trans.—2.24   ④ Auto. Trans.—9.6

ALTERNATOR AND REGULATOR SPECIFICATIONS

Year	Model	Part No. or Manufacturer	Field Current @ 12 v	Output (amps)	Part No. or Manufacturer	Air Gap (in.)	Point Gap (in.)	Volts to Close	Air Gap (in.)	Point Gap (in.)	Volts @ 75°
		ALTERNATOR				Field Relay			Regulator		
1972-73	All	AC2040K	—	16.5-32.0	RQB2220D	0.035-0.047	0.030-0.043	14.3-15.3	0.032-0.047	0.012-0.016	
1974-75	All	AH2040K₁	—	40	RQB2220D	—See Note—		14.3-15.8	—See Note—		
1976-77	All	AH2045K₁③	—	45	RQB2220D	————See Note————					

NOTE: 1974-77 models are equipped with sealed voltage regulators which cannot be adjusted if the readings vary from the specifications
① No Load
② Load
③ 2000 cc eng.—AH2045G₁
— Not available

BRAKE SPECIFICATIONS

All measurements given are (in.) unless noted

Year	Model Cu In. (cc)	Lug Nut Torque (ft/lb)	Master Cylinder Bore	Minimum Thickness	Run-Out Maximum	Diameter	Max. Machine O/S	Max. Wear Limit	Front	Rear
				Brake Disc		Brake Drum			Minimum Lining Thickness	
1972-73	97.5 (1600)	51-58	¹¹/₁₆	0.331	0.006	9.0	9.079	9.079	0.08	0.04
1974-77	97.5 (1600)	51-58	①	0.450	0.006	9.0	9.079	9.079	0.08	0.04
	121.7 (2000)	51-58	¹³/₁₆	0.450	0.006	9.0	9.079	9.079	0.08	0.04

NOTE: Minimum lining thickness is as recommended by the manufacturer. Due to variations in state inspection regulations, the minimum allowable thickness may be different than recommended by the manufacturer.

① ¹¹/₁₆ Non Power
¹³/₁₆ Power

WHEEL ALIGNMENT

Year	Model Cu In. (cc)	Range (deg)	Pref Setting (deg)	Range (deg)	Pref. Setting (deg)	Toe-in (in.)	Steering Axis Inclination
		CASTER		CAMBER			
1972-76	97.5 (1600)	1¼P-1½P	1⅜P	½P-1½P	1P	0.08-0.23	8°50'
1977	97.5 (1600)	½P-1¼P	¾P	⅓P-1⅓P	⅚P	0.08-0.24	9.01°
1974-76	121.7 (2000)	¾P-1¾P	1¼P	⅓P-1⅓P	⅚P	0.08-0.23	9°
1977	121.7 (2000)	½P-1¼P	¾P	⅓P-1⅓P	⅚P	0.08-0.24	9.01°

TUNE-UP PROCEDURES

Spark Plugs

The plugs should be checked every 12,-000 miles. If defective they should be replaced. Check for cracked insulators, burned or worn electrodes, or accumulated carbon. If plugs are reused, clean them thoroughly with a wire brush and file, and regap them to 0.028–0.030″.

To remove plugs:

1. Clean the area around the plugs to remove particles which could enter combustion chambers.

2. Remove plugs carefully to avoid breaking porcelain insulator.

When installing plugs:

3. Take care not to cross thread plugs.

4. A little oil on the plug threads makes the job easier.

5. Tighten the plugs firmly. If a torque wrench is available, tighten them to 18–22 ft lb.

Breaker Points and Condenser

Snap off the two retaining clips on the distributor cap. Remove the cap and examine it for cracks, deterioration, or carbon tracking. Replace the cap, if necessary, by transferring one wire at a time from the old cap to the new one. Examine the rotor for corrosion or wear and replace it if it's at all questionable. Check the points for pitting and burning. Slight imperfections on the contact surface may be filed off with a point file (fine emery paper will also do), but it is usually wise to replace the breaker point set when tuning. Always replace the condenser when you replace the point set, unless you have access to a condenser tester.

To replace the breaker points:

1. Remove the rotor.

2. Observe which screws retain the ground and primary wires. Remove the two retaining screws and lift out the lubricator wick plate and the point set.

3. Install the new point set, making sure that the pin on the bottom engages the hole in the breaker plate.

4. Install the lubricator wick plate, primary and ground wires, and then the two retaining screws (hand-tight).

5. Turn the fan belt or crankshaft pulley until the breaker arm rubbing block is on the high point of one of the cam lobes.

6. A 0.20 in. feeler gauge should just slip through the points. If the gap is incorrect, turn the eccentric screw in or out as necessary to bring it within specifications.

On 1975–77 models, adjustment is made by inserting a screwdriver in the slot and pivoting it to correct the gap.

7. When the gap is correct, tighten the two retaining screws.

8. Lubricate the distributor cam wick with engine oil or silicone grease.

9. Install the rotor and distributor cap.

10. Check the dwell angle and the ignition timing as outlined in the following sections.

11. The condenser is mounted on the outside of the distributor. Undo the mounting screw and the terminal screw to replace the condenser.

Dwell Angle

The dwell angle or cam angle is the number of degrees that the distributor cam rotates while the points are closed. There is an inverse relationship between dwell angle and point gap. Increasing the point gap will decrease the dwell angle and vice versa. Checking the dwell angle with a meter is a far more accurate method of measuring point opening than the feeler gauge method.

After setting the point gap to specification with a feeler gauge as described above, check the dwell angle with a meter. Attach the dwell meter according to the manufacturer's instruction sheet. The negative lead is grounded and the positive lead is connected to the primary wire that runs from the coil to the distributor. Start the engine, let it idle and reach operating temperature, and observe the dwell on the meter. The reading should fall within the allowable range. If it does not, the gap will have to be reset or the breaker points will have to be replaced.

Ignition Timing

CAUTION: *When performing this or any other adjustment with the engine running, be very careful of the fan belt and pulley.*

Ignition timing should always be checked as a part of any tune-up. Timing is checked after the points have been adjusted or replaced. An accurate stroboscopic timing light is a necessity for timing the engine.

1971–74

1. Attach the timing light according to the manufacturer's instructions.

2. Locate the timing tab on the front of the engine near the crankshaft pulley. Mark the "T" or appropriate line (according to the tune-up specifications), and the notch in the crankshaft pulley with chalk so that they will be more visible.

3. Disconnect and plug the hose to the vacuum advance unit on the distributor.

4. Start the engine and allow it to reach the normal operating temperature.

5. Shine the timing light at the crankshaft pulley marks. The marked line should align with pulley notch.

6. If the marks do not align, loosen the distributor mounting nut and rotate it slowly to align the timing marks.

7. Tighten the mounting nut when the ignition timing is correct.

The vacuum advance can be adjusted by means of the phillips screw located near the diaphragm. This adjustment is rarely needed. The checking procedure is performed in the same manner as out-

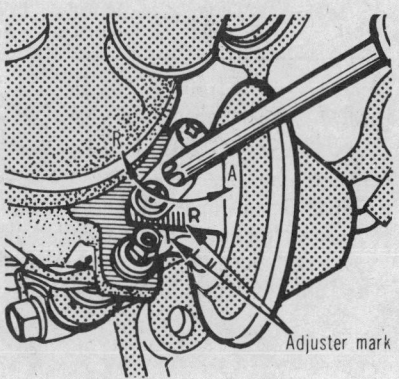

1600 cc timing adjustment

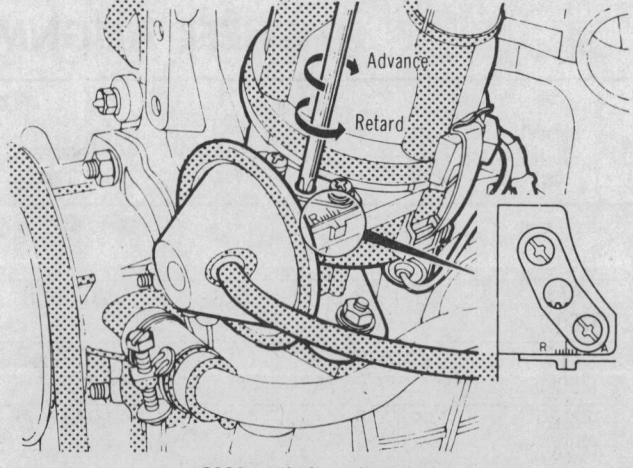

2000 cc timing adjustment

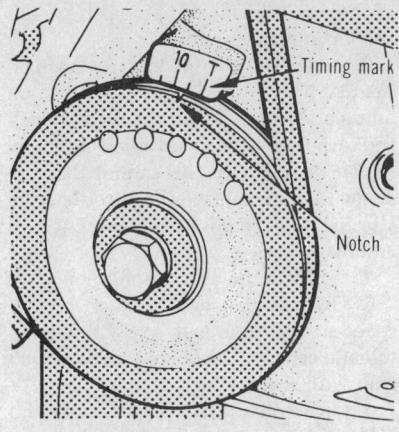

1600 cc timing mark

2000 cc timing mark

lined above, except that the vacuum hose is left in place. Loosen the two retaining screws and turn the adjusting screw as necessary.

1975–77

These models are equipped with vacuum advance/retard distributors. Vacuum retard functions at idle to retard the spark to 5° ATDC. Basic timing is checked by removing the rubber plug from the vacuum advance/retard unit on the distributor.

Check and adjust basic timing (with the exception of plugging the vacuum line), as outlined in the preceding Steps 1 through 7. Replace the rubber plug and check the retarded timing. Adjustment, if necessary, is made in the manner outlined in the last paragraph above.

Valve Lash

Valve clearance is adjusted with the engine stopped. When adjusting the valves cold, for example after an engine rebuild, proceed as follows:

1. Adjust the valves in the firing order 1–3–4–2.
2. Turn the crankshaft pulley to bring the piston to TDC of the compression stroke on the cylinder being adjusted.

3. Loosen the two rocker adjusting screw locknuts.
4. Using a 0.003 in. feeler gauge for the intake and a 0.007 in. gauge for the exhaust, turn the adjusting screw until the clearance is correct.
5. Tighten the lock nuts to 7–9 ft lbs.

The normal valve clearance adjustment, or final adjustment after the above initial cold adjustment, is performed as follows:

1. Run the engine until it reaches normal operating temperature and then turn it off.
2. Undo the wing nut and remove the air cleaner. Pull the large crankcase ventilation hose off of the front of the air cleaner. Disconnect the two smaller hoses, one goes to the rear of the rocker arm cover and one to the intake manifold.
3. Loosen and remove the nuts and one bracket which attach the air cleaner to the rocker arm cover.
4. Lift the bottom housing of the air cleaner off of the carburetor and, with it, the hose coming up from the exhaust manifold heat stove.
5. Unsnap the spark plug wires from their clips on the rocker arm cover.
6. Loosen and remove the two rocker arm cover bolts. The rear bolt is a crankcase ventilation fitting, so you will have to use a deep socket or a box wrench.
7. Carefully lift the rocker arm cover off of the cylinder head. Using a 5/16 in. allen socket (1600 cc) or regular socket (2000 cc) and torque wrench, make sure that the cylinder head bolts are all tightened to 58–62 ft lbs on 1600 cc engines, 72–79 ft lbs on 2000 cc engines.
8. Hot valve clearance is 0.006 in. (intake) and 0.010 in. (exhaust). Valves for each cylinder are adjusted in the firing order: 1–3–4–2.
9. Turn the crankshaft pulley to bring the piston to TDC of the compression stroke. Both valves will be closed at this point and the rocker arms will be resting on the "heel" of the camshaft lobe (the round side, not the egg-shaped side).

10. Loosen the two rocker arm adjusting screw locknuts.
11. Using the correct thickness feeler gauge, turn the adjusting screw until the gauge just snaps through the valve stem and the rocker arm.
12. Proceed to adjust the valves of each cylinder in the firing order. Remember to bring each piston to TDC of its compression stroke.

CAUTION: *The importance of correctly setting the valve clearance cannot be overemphasized. The clearance must be right or peak performance and efficiency will never be realized. Loose valve clearances will result in excessive wear and valve train clatter; tight valve clearances will result in valve seat burning.*

13. Apply non-hardening sealer to the rocker arm cover gasket. Replace the gasket if its condition is at all questionable.
14. Install the cover, hoses, spark plug wires, and air cleaner in the reverse order of removal. Tighten the rocker arm cover bolts to 4–5 ft lbs.
15. Start the engine and check for leaks.

Carburetor

1971–72 Idle Speed and Throttle Positioner Adjustment

The Colt carburetor is equipped with five adjustment screws, but don't become immediately alarmed and confused. For tune-up purposes, we will only be using two of these screws: the curb idle screw and the throttle positioner screw.

To set the idle speed:
1. Start the engine and run it until the normal operating temperature is reached.
2. Attach a dwell/tachometer to the engine and observe the idle speed.
3. If your idle speed differs from those specified in the "Tune-Up Specifications" chart, turn the curb idle screw to correct it.

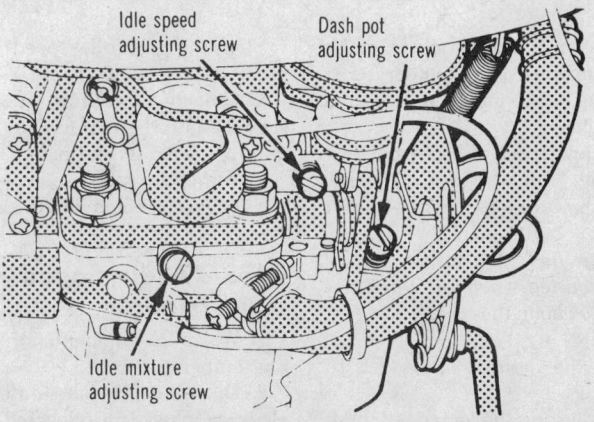

Idle speed adjusting screw

NOTE: *Make sure that you are turning the correct screw as shown in the illustration. Do not mistake the throttle positioner screw for the curb idle screw.*
CAUTION: *Do not adjust the air/fuel mixture screw, readily identified by its plastic limiter cap. A CO meter is required to check any adjustment, so refer this service to your dealer or garage. If a CO meter is available, the specified CO values are 3.5%–5% for 1971, 3.5% ± 1% for 1972.*

To adjust the throttle positioner:

1. Bring the engine to operating temperature.

2. Attach a dwell/tachometer to the engine.

3. Disconnect and plug the hose which connects the air cleaner and the intake manifold at the manifold end.

4. Remove the air cleaner.

5. Disconnect the negative (green) solenoid lead from the terminal.

6. Accelerate the engine to 2500 rpm a few times.

7. Maintain the engine speed and ground the green negative wire on the carburetor to switch the solenoid ON.

8. Release the throttle and check the engine rpm, which should be 1350–1450 rpm.

9. If the engine speed is incorrect, adjust the throttle positioner screw.
NOTE: *Some 1971 models are equipped with an adjusting nut rather than a screw, but the adjustment procedure is the same.*

10. Install the solenoid wire and vacuum hose. Install the air cleaner.

1973–74 Idle Speed and Dashpot Adjustment

This carburetor is similar to the one used on previous models except that the decel throttle positioner has been eliminated. 1974 1600 cc models equipped with a manual transmission and sold in California are additionally equipped with a decel dashpot.

Idle speed and mixture screws are in the same locations as 1971–72 models. Don't confuse them with the fast idle or dashpot screws.

1. Run the engine at idle speed until it reaches normal operating temperature.

2. Hook-up a tachometer and observe the idle speed.

3. If the idle speed differs from that given in the "Tune-Up Specifications" chart, turn the curb idle screw to correct it.
NOTE: *Air/fuel idle mixture should only be adjusted when a CO meter is available to obtain the correct CO level of 3–4.5%.*

To adjust the dashpot on models so equipped:

1. After adjusting the idle speed, push up on the lower end of the dashpot until

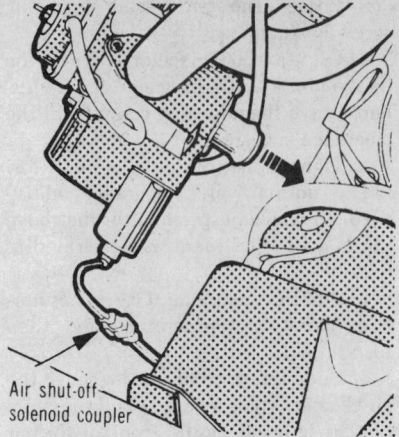

Air shut-off solenoid coupler

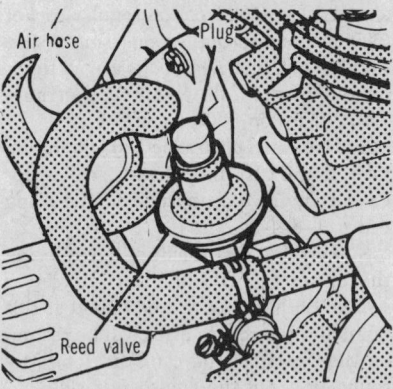

Removing air hose—1976-77 1600 cc

Air hose removal—1976-77 2000 cc

it stops. Engine idle speed should increase to 1500–2000 rpm.

2. Quickly releasing the pushrod should cause the idle to drop to normal after a 1.5–3.5 second pause.

3. If the idle speed returns to normal too slowly, correct it with the adjustment screw.

1975–77 Idle Speed Adjustment

1. Warm the engine to normal operating temperature.

2. Disconnect the air shut-off solenoid electrical plug. This is located under the air control valve which is on the left-side

of the engine. This equipment is part of the air injection system.

3. Adjust the idle speed to 900 rpm on manual transmission cars or 800 rpm on automatic transmission cars. Do this with the carburetor idle speed adjusting screw (B) on manual cars. Be careful that the screw doesn't contact the throttle arm. Use the throttle positioner screw (C) on automatic cars.

4. Connect the air shut-off solenoid.

5. On manual cars, adjust engine speed to 1000 rpm with screw B. On automatic cars, set the engine speed to 900 rpm with screw C.

6. On automatic cars only, remove the rubber plug from the vacuum unit on the distributor. Adjust the idle speed to 800 rpm with screw band, reinstall the rubber plug.

7. Race the engine to about 2500 rpm a few times and observe that it returns to normal idle speed.

ENGINE ELECTRICAL

Distributor

Removal and Installation

1972–74

1. Remove the distributor cap.

2. Mark the position of the distributor.

3. Remove the distributor.

4. If the engine has not been disturbed while the distributor was out i.e., the crankshaft was not turned, reinstall the distributor in the reverse order of removal.

If the engine has been rotated while the distributor was out, then proceed as follows:

5. Turn the crankshaft so that No. 1 piston is on its compression stroke and the timing marks are aligned as described in "Ignition Tuning".

6. Turn the distributor so that the rotor points approximately 15° before the No. 1 cylinder position in the cap.

7. If the oil pump drive doesn't engage, remove the distributor and turn the pump shaft so that it is perpendicular to the centerline of the crankshaft on 1600 cc engines; parallel on 2000 cc engines.

1975

1. Remove the distributor cap and the vacuum hoses and remove the distributor.

2. To install adjust the alignment mark of the timing adjuster to the center position. One division of the timing adjuster equals 4° of the crankshaft angle.

3. Set No. 1 cylinder at TDC and align the timing marks.

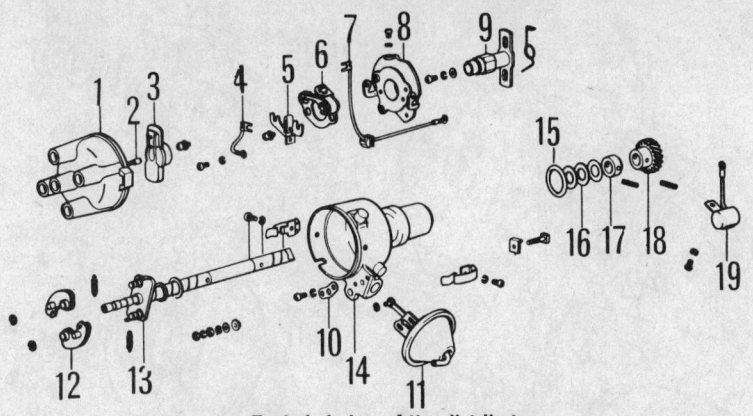

Exploded view of the distributor

1. Cap
2. Carbon
3. Rotor
4. Ground wire
5. Cam felt
6. Arm support
7. Lead wire
8. Breaker base
9. Cam
10. Locking plate
11. Vacuum control
12. Governor weight
13. Shaft
14. Housing
15. O-ring
16. Washer
17. Thrust collar
18. Gear
19. Condenser

Positioning the oil pump driveshaft groove —1975-77 1600 cc

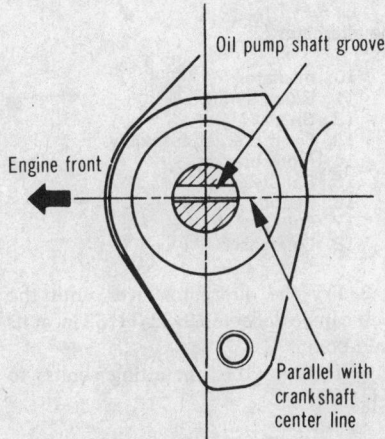

Positioning the oil pump driveshaft groove —1975-77 2000 cc

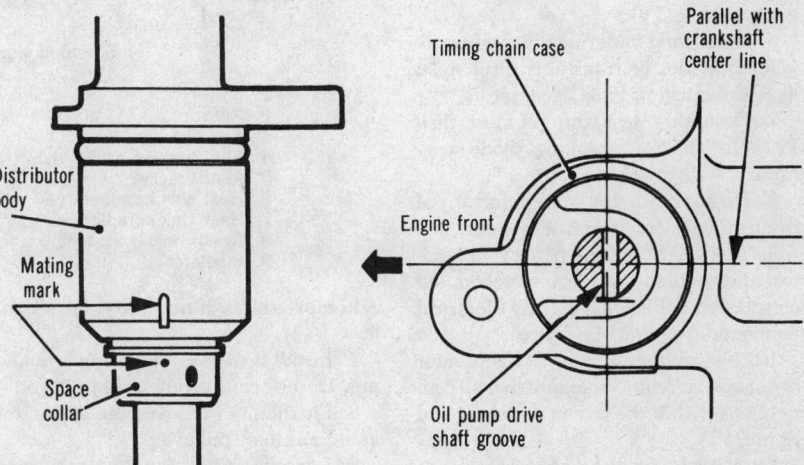

(The top end of oil pump shaft viewed from the distributor fitting area.)

Distributor installation—1976-77 1600 cc

4. On the 1600 cc engine, the lug at the lower end of the distributor shaft fits the groove in the upper end of the oil pump driveshaft. The groove should be parallel with the crankshaft center line.

5. Adjust the distributor position so the stud will be at the center of the oblong hole in the distributor flange.

1976–77

Remove the distributor cap and vacuum hoses and distributor.

2. Installation is the reverse of removal.

3. If the engine was disturbed, set No. 1 cylinder at TDC and align the timing marks.

4. On the 1600 cc engine turn the oil pump drive shaft until the groove is parallel with the crankshaft. Align the mating mark on the lower end of the distributor body with that on the spacer.

5. On the 2000 cc engine align the mating mark line of the distributor housing with the punch mark on the distributor driven gear.

Distributor installation—1975-77 2000 cc

Alternator

Alternator Precautions

All Colts and Arrows are equipped with alternating current (AC) generators (alternators). Unlike the direct current (DC) generators used in many older cars, there are several precautions which must be strictly observed in order to avoid damaging the unit. They are:

1. Reversing the battery connections will result in damage to the diodes.

2. Booster batteries should be connected from negative to negative, and positive to positive.

3. Never use a fast charger as a booster to start cars with AC circuits.

4. When servicing the battery with a fast charger, always disconnect the car battery cables.

5. Never attempt to polarize an AC generator.

6. Avoid long soldering times when replacing diodes or transistors. Prolonged heat is damaging to AC generators.

7. Do not use test lamps of more than 12 volts (V) for checking diode continuity.

8. Do not short across or ground any of the terminals on the AC generator.

9. The polarity of the battery, generator, and regulator must be matched and considered before making any electrical connections within the system.

10. Never operate the AC generator on an open circuit. Make sure that all connections within the circuit are clean and tight.

11. Disconnect the battery terminals when performing any service on the electrical system. This will eliminate the possibility of accidental reversal of polarity.

12. Disconnect the battery ground cable if arc welding is to be done on any part of the car.

Removal and Installation

1. Disconnect the battery cables and the alternator wires. Note or tag the wires so that you can reinstall them correctly.

2. Loosen and remove the top mounting bolt.

3. Loosen the elongated lower mounting nut. Slide the alternator over in its attaching bracket and remove the fan belt.

4. Remove the lower mounting nut and bolt, being sure not to lose any of the mounting shims.

5. Remove the alternator.

NOTE: *Remember when installing the alternator that it is not necessary to polarize an AC generating system.*

6. Trial fit the alternator on the engine. The shims are installed on the inside of both alternator mounting legs.

Exploded view of the alternator

1. Stator
2. Rotor
3. Ball bearing
4. Rear bracket assembly
5. Rear bracket
6. Heat sink complete (+)
7. Heat sink complete (−)
8. Brush holder assembly
9. Insulator
10. Insulator
11. Brush spring
12. Brush
13. Front bracket assembly
14. Front bracket
15. Ball bearing
16. Bearing retainer
17. Pulley
18. Condenser

Add more shims, if necessary, for a tight fit.

7. Install the lower mounting bolt and nut. Do not completely tighten it yet.

8. Fit the fan belt over the alternator and crankshaft pulleys.

9. Loosely install the top mounting bolt and pivot the alternator over until the fan belt is correctly tensioned as outlined in the next procedure.

10. Finally tighten the top and bottom bolts to 14–18 ft lbs.

11. Connect the alternator wires and the battery cables.

Belt Replacement and Tensioning

1. Check the fan belt(s) for cracking, fraying, and any other deterioration. Replace it if it is at all suspect.

2. To replace the belt, loosen the mounting bolts and pivot the alternator in its bracket. Remove the old belt and slip the replacement belt over the pulleys.

Fan belt adjustment

3. Pry the alternator over until the belt can be deflected 9/32–11/32 in. at its mid-point.

4. Tighten the mounting bolts to 14–18 ft lbs.

Regulator

Removal and Installation

1. Disconnect the ground cable from the battery.

2. Disconnect the electrical connector plug.

3. Loosen and remove the two mounting screws. Remove the regulator.

4. Clean the attaching area for proper grounding of the regulator.

5. Install the regulator. Do not over-tighten the mounting screws or you will distort the case.

6. Connect the electrical plug and the battery cable.

CAUTION: *Never operate the engine with the regulator disconnected.*

Voltage Check and Adjustment

1. Connect a voltmeter to the A and E terminals of the regulator connector plug.

NOTE: *Do not disconnect the plug.*

2. Disconnect one of the battery terminals while the engine is idling to unload the alternator.

3. Increase the engine speed to 2000 rpm. The voltmeter should show a value

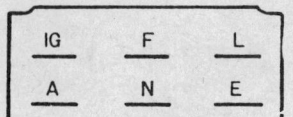

Regulator terminals

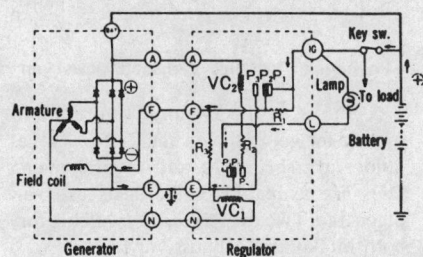

Schematic diagram of the regulator

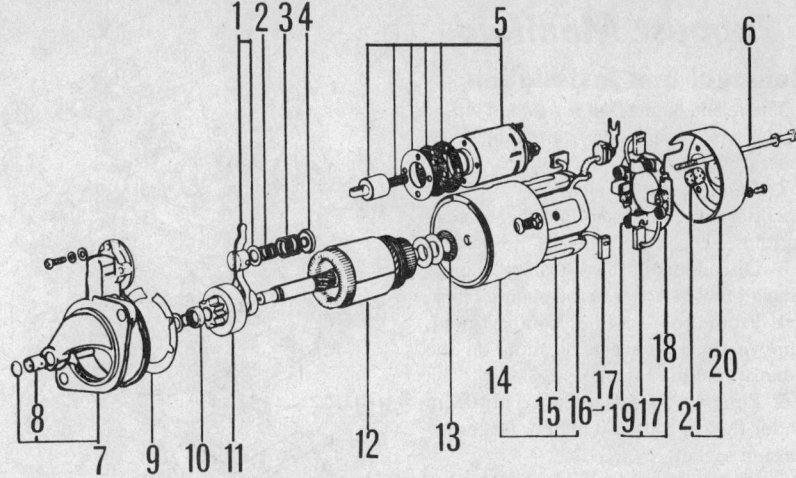

Exploded view of starter

1. Lever assembly	8. Front bracket bearing
2. Lever spring (A)	9. Plate
3. Lever spring (B)	10. Stop ring
4. Spring retainer	11. Overrunning clutch
5. Electromagnetic switch	12. Armature
6. Through bolt	13. Insulating washer
7. Front bracket	

14. Yoke assembly	
15. Pole piece	
16. Field coil	
17. Brush	
18. Brush holder	
19. Brush spring	
20. Rear bracket	
21. Rear bracket bearing	

of 14.3–15.8 V at room temperature.

If the reading is not within specifications:

4. Remove the regulator cover.

5. Adjust the constant voltage relay (located on the left) by bending the end of the coil side plate up or down.

Bending the plate down reduces the voltage, bending it up increases the voltage.

6. The field relay is adjusted in the same manner as the voltage relay.

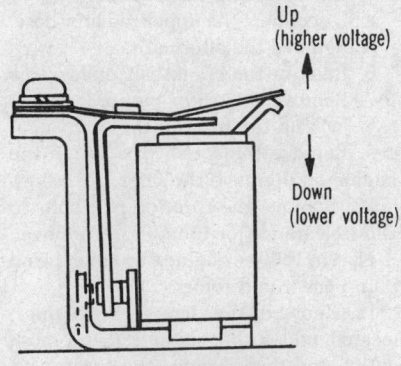

Adjusting the voltage

Starter

Removal and Installation

1. Disconnect the battery ground cable, starter wires and remove the starter.

2. Installation is the reverse of removal.

Starter Overhaul

1. Remove the starter.

2. Remove the solenoid.

3. Remove the through-bolts and separate the armature and the housing.

4. Carefully remove the armature and lever from the pinion housing.

5. Remove the rear housing.

6. Remove the brushes and brush retainer. Replace them if they are worn past the Mitsubishi (three diamond) symbol.

7. Remove the snap-ring. Slide the starter drive off of the shaft.

8. Installation is the reverse of removal. Starter drive gear-to-stop ring clearance should be 0.02–0.08 in. Adjust with gaskets.

ENGINE MECHANICAL

Engine/Transmission Removal

The engine and transmission must be removed as a unit.

1. Remove the hood. Remove the bridge panel and front grill. Drain and remove the radiator. Remove the battery.

2. Disconnect the ground strap, ignition coil wiring and vacuum and fuel solenoid valves.

3. Disconnect the following: alternator, starter, transmission switch, back-up light switch, temperature gauge and oil pressure gauge.

4. Disconnect all hoses and remove the air cleaner.

5. Disconnect all carburetor linkage. Remove the heater hose.

6. Unbolt the exhaust pipe at the manifold flange and disconnect the muffler pipe bracket at the transmission.

7. Remove the hose between the fuel filter and the fuel pump return line.

8. Remove the vacuum hose from the purge control valve.

9. Disconnect the speedometer cable backup light and distributor switches.

10. Disconnect the clutch cable and shift lever.

11. Remove the cross shaft and control rod from the bracket under the transmission. On automatic transmission, remove the tie-rod.

12. Remove the leatherette cover inside the car and remove the shifter assembly.

13. Attach a hoist and remove weight from the engine mounts. Remove the attaching bolts from the engine mounts and lift the engine upward and forward.

14. Installation is the reverse of removal.

Intake Manifold

Removal and Installation

CAUTION: *The intake manifold is cast aluminum.*

1. Remove the air cleaner.

2. Disconnect the fuel line and EGR lines on models so equipped.

3. Disconnect the throttle positioner solenoid and fuel cut-off solenoid wires.

4. Disconnect the accelerator and, if equipped with automatic transmission, the shift cables at the carburetor.

5. Drain the coolant.

6. Remove the water hose from carburetor and cylinder head.

7. Remove the heater and water outlet hoses.

8. Disconnect the water temperature sending unit.

9. Remove the manifold and carburetor.

10. Installation is the reverse of removal.

Exhaust Manifold

Removal and Installation

The inside flange bolt is reached with a 6 inch socket extension from underneath the car.

1. Remove the air cleaner.
2. Remove the manifold heat stove and hose. Disconnect the EGR lines.
3. Disconnect the exhaust pipe bracket that attaches to the engine block.
4. From the engine compartment, remove the two accessible nuts on the exhaust manifold flange.
5. Remove the inside flange nut from under the car with a 6 inch or larger extension socket.
6. Remove the manifold.
7. Installation is the reverse of removal.

Cylinder Head

Removal and Installation

The timing chain and gear must be removed and hung on wire. 1600 cc engines require a 5/16 in. Allen socket; 2000 engines are hex head.

CAUTION: *Never remove the cylinder head unless the engine is absolutely cold; the cylinder head could warp.*

1. Remove the intake and exhaust manifolds. Put No. 1 piston at TDC.
2. Remove the crankcase ventilation hoses, fuel lines and fuel pumps.
3. Remove the rocker arm cover.
4. Remove the camshaft sprocket and chain.

NOTE: *Unless you are also removing the timing gear cover, attach a wire around the sprocket and chain. On the 1600 cc engine, align the sprocket mark and the plated link; on the 2000 cc engine, paint alignment marks on the sprocket and chain.*

5. Remove the cylinder head. A 5/16 in. allen socket is required to remove the ten head bolts on the 1600 cc engine; the 2000 cc bolts are hex head type.
6. Installation is the reverse of removal. Be sure timing marks are aligned. If it is difficult to install the gear and chain, loosen the chain tensioner.

Camshaft and Rocker Arm

Removal and Installation

It is easier to remove the cylinder head and disassemble the head on the bench, then to remove the camshaft or rocker arms with the head installed.

1. Remove the rocker arms.

NOTE: *The first and the fourth pair of bearing cap nuts also retain the rocker cover brackets. Don't lose the dowel pins which locate the bearing caps.*

2. Drive out the retaining pins and slide off the washer, rocker arms, and

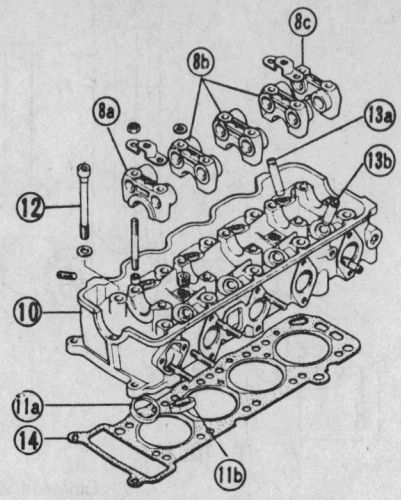

Exploded view of the cylinder head

- 8a. Camshaft bearing cap
- 8b. No. 2, 3 and 4 caps
- 8c. Camshaft bearing cap (rear)
- 10. Cylinder head
- 11a. Intake valve seat ring
- 11b. Exhaust valve seat ring
- 12. Cylinder head bolt
- 13a. Exhaust valve guide
- 13b. Intake valve guide
- 14. Cylinder head gasket

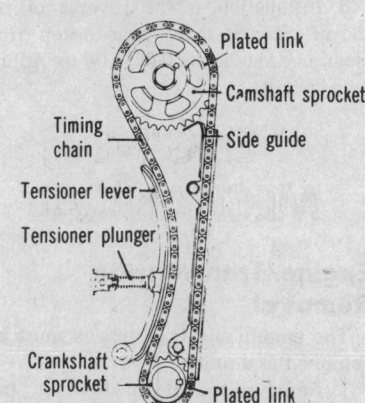

1600 cc timing chain and tensioner

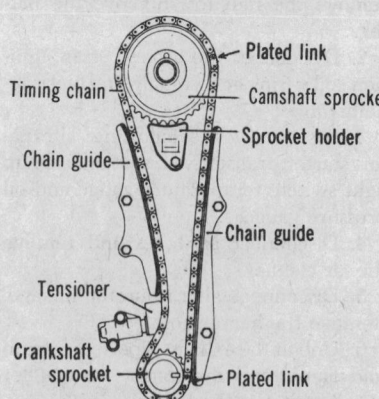

2000 cc timing chain and tensioner

springs.

3. Remove the camshaft.
4. Disassemble the keys, retainer, spring, and valves.
5. Pry off the valve stem seals.
6. Refer to the cylinder head overhaul

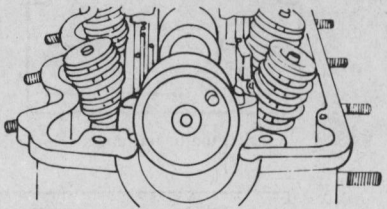

Position of installed camshaft dowel pin

procedures in the General Information section for general overhaul notes. Valve guides are shrunk fit and several oversizes are available. Valve seats are replaceable. Two oversizes are available for both intake and exhaust valves.

7. Installation is the reverse of removal.

Timing Gear Cover, Chain, and Tensioner

Removal and Installation

NOTE: *The timing chain case is cast aluminum, so exercise caution when handling this part.*

1. Remove the distributor.
2. Remove the fan.
3. Remove the cylinder head.
4. Disconnect the upper radiator hose.
5. Remove the alternator.
6. Remove the crankshaft pulley.
7. Remove the water pump.
8. Jack up the front of the car.
9. Remove the splash pan. Drain the engine oil. Remove the filter.
10. Remove the front oil pan bolts to allow clearance for timing case removal.
11. On 1600 cc engines, remove the oil pump cover and rotors.
12. Remove the tensioner retainer, located under the upper radiator hose outlet, and then remove the spring and plunger.
13. Pry off the cover, being careful not to destroy the oil pan gasket. If the gasket is damaged, remove the oil pan and replace the gasket.
14. Remove the timing chain.
15. Pry the crankshaft opening seal out of the timing gear cover. Install a new

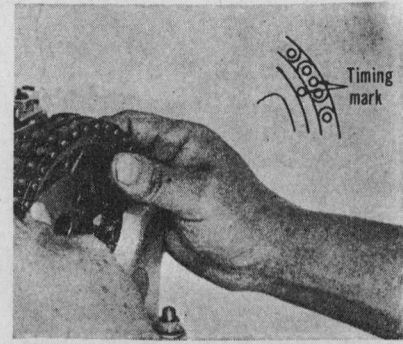

Camshaft sprocket installation

seal, using a pipe of similar diameter and a rubber or plastic mallet.

16. Remove the chain tensioner lever and the chain guide (also sprocket holder on 2000 cc engine).

17. Install the pivot in the rear of the tensioner lever hole. Mount the lever on the block.

18. Install timing chain guide. The openings face in toward the chain.

19. Rotate the crankshaft so that No. 1 piston is at TDC.

20. With the punch mark on the crankshaft gear aligned with the chrome plated link on the chain, install the gear onto its key on the crankshaft.

21. Install the second key, if it was removed. Install the distributor drive gear with the stamped "F" (on 1600 cc engines), or "C" or "A" (on 2000 cc engines) facing forward. The oil slinger should be installed with its cupped side out.

22. With the crankshaft timing marks aligned, suspend the camshaft sprocket with its "O" chrome plated link on the chain aligned.

23. Using a non-hardening sealer, glue the two timing gear cover gaskets to the engine block. Apply sealer to the exposed oil pan surface.

24. Still holding the camshaft sprocket and chain, install the timing gear cover.

25. On the 1600, insert the chain tensioner lever plunger and the spring into the timing cover opening.

NOTE: *The camshaft sprocket and the chain are supported and stretched respectively by the tensioner lever. Double check that the timing marks are aligned.*

26. Further installation is the reverse of removal.

Counterbalance Shafts

Removal

2000 cc Engine

1. Remove the crankshaft pulley.
2. Remove the timing chain case.
3. Remove the chain guides.
4. Remove the crankshaft sprocket, counterbalance shaft sprocket and chain.
5. Remove the crankshaft sprocket, camshaft sprocket and timing chain.

NOTE: *Since the timing chain tensioner stands in the way of the chain removal, depress the tensioner as the chain is removed.*

6. Remove the camshaft sprocket holder and the right and left timing chain guides.
7. Remove the bolt locking the oil pump driven gear and right counterbalance shaft remove the oil pump mounting bolts. Remove the oil pump assembly

and the right counterbalance shaft from the cylinder block.

NOTE: *If the bolt locking the oil pump driven gear and counterbalance shaft is hard to loosen, remove the oil pump and counterbalance shaft as an assembly, and then remove the lock bolt to disassemble.*

8. Remove the thrust plate by threading two bolts into the threaded holes of the flange and turn down the bolts at the same time.
9. Withdraw the left counterbalance shaft.
10. Installation is the reverse of removal. No. 1 cylinder should be at TDC. The thrust plate is easier to install if guide bolts are used.

Install the camshaft sprocket and crankshaft sprocket on the timing chain (for driving the camshaft). Make sure that the punched mating marks on the sprocket teeth correspond with the two plated links on the chain.

Install the two counterbalance shaft sprockets on the chain (for driving the counterbalance shaft), while aligning the punched mating marks on the sprockets with the three plated links on the chain.

While holding the chain and sprockets, first install the chain in alignment with the mating mark of the crankshaft sprocket, and then install the sprocket on the counterbalance shaft and oil pump driven gear at the same time and tighten the sprocket lock bolts.

Temporarily install chain guides A, B and C.

Adjust the tension of the chain in the following sequence.

(a) Tighten the chain guide A mounting bolt firmly.

(b) Tighten the chain guide C mounting bolt firmly.

(c) Shake the right and left sprockets to collect chain slackness at point P. Adjust the position of chain guide C so that when the chain is pulled in the

direction of arrow Y with finger tips, the clearance between the chain guide B and the links of the chain will be .04 to .14 in. and then tighten the bolts.

Piston Identification

On 1972–75 models the pistons are designated by a letter into three weight groups, A, B, and C. Always replace a piston with another from the same weight group. On 1976–77 models the pistons are stamped with a size mark.

1976-77 Piston Size Markings

Size	Size mark
S.T.D.	None
.010 in. O.S.	25
.020 in. O.S.	50
.030 in. O.S.	75
.039 in. O.S.	100

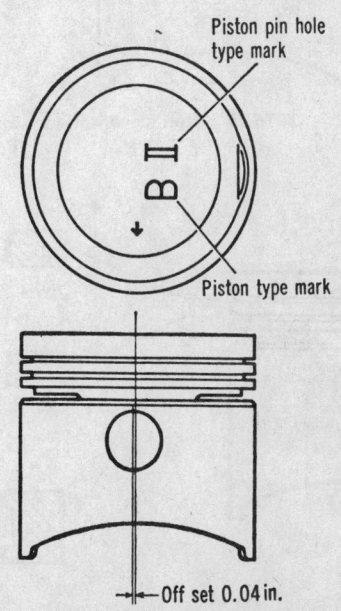

1972-75 piston weight designation

2000 cc balancer system (1976-77)

When replacing the piston and connecting rod assembly always direct the front mark on the piston head toward the front of the engine.

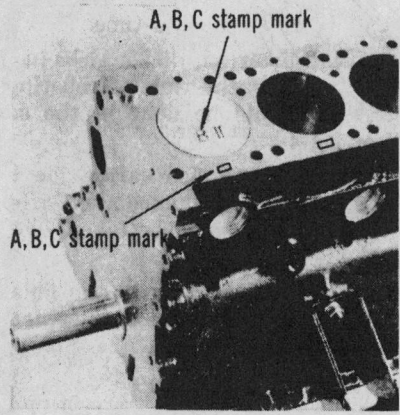

1972-75 cylinder block and piston designation

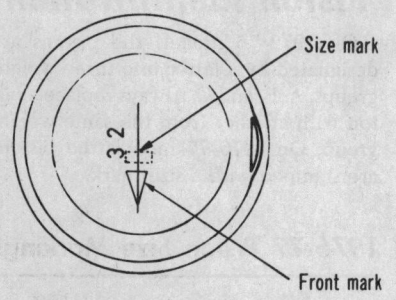

1976-77 piston identification

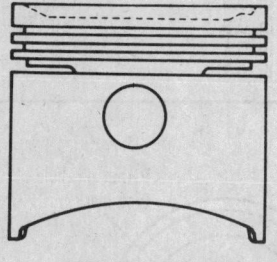

Piston ring installation

Ring end-gap positioning

ENGINE LUBRICATION

Oil Pan

Removal and Installation

The engine must be raised off its mounts for the pan to clear the suspension crossmember.

1. Remove the underbody splash shield.
2. Unbolt the left and right engine mounts.
3. Jack the engine under the bell housing.
4. Remove the oil pan.
5. Installation is the reverse of removal.

Rear Main Oil Seal

Replacement

The rear main oil seal is located in a housing on the rear of the block. To replace the seal, remove the transmission and do the work from underneath the car or remove the engine and do the work on the bench.

1. Remove the housing from the block.
2. Remove the separator from the housing.
3. Pry out the old seal.
4. Lightly oil the replacement seal. The oil seal should be installed so that the seal plate fits into the inner contact surface of the seal case. Install the separator with the oil holes facing down.

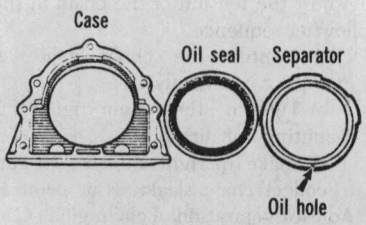

Rear main oil seal

Oil Pump—1600 CC

The oil pump is a trochoid gear-type which is built into the bottom of the timing gear cover.

Removal and Installation

1. Drain the oil.
2. Remove the splash shield.
3. Remove the oil filter.
4. Remove the oil pump cover and rotor assembly.
5. Installation is the reverse of removal. Use only the special 3-piece gasket.

Oil Pump—2000 CC

The oil pump is located inside the oil pan under the timing chain cover. The pump is driven directly by a gear on the crankshaft and in turn drives the distributor.

Removal and Installation

1974–75

The engine must be raised to remove the oil pan.

1. Put No. 1 cylinder at TDC
2. Remove the oil pan.
3. Remove the oil pump.
4. To install the pump, make sure that the distributor shaft pawl is exactly parallel with the crankshaft. Align the punch mark on the gear with the mark on the oil pump body.

1976–77

Refer to Counterbalance Shaft Removal And Installation procedures given in the Engine Mechanical section.

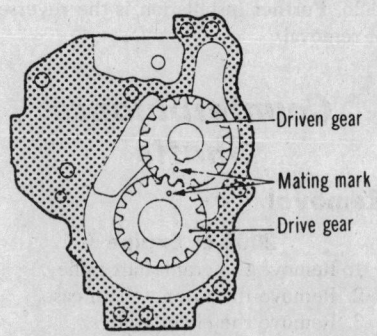

2000 cc oil pump alignment marks

Oil Pump Clearances

1972–77

Check the oil pump clearances against those specified.

Chain case-to-shaft clearance: 0.005 in. or less

Inner-to-outer rotor clearance: 0.010 in. or less

Rotor-to-cover end-play: 0.008 in. or less

Outer rotor-to-chain case clearance: 0.012 in. or less

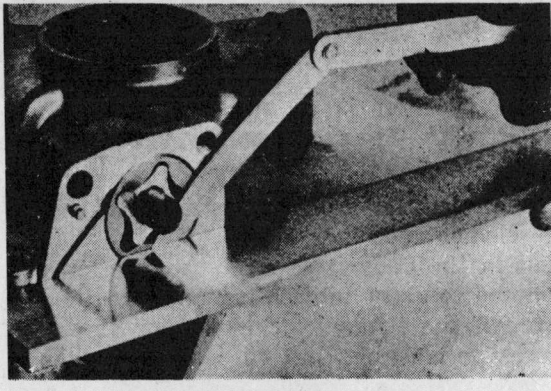

Oil pump gear end play

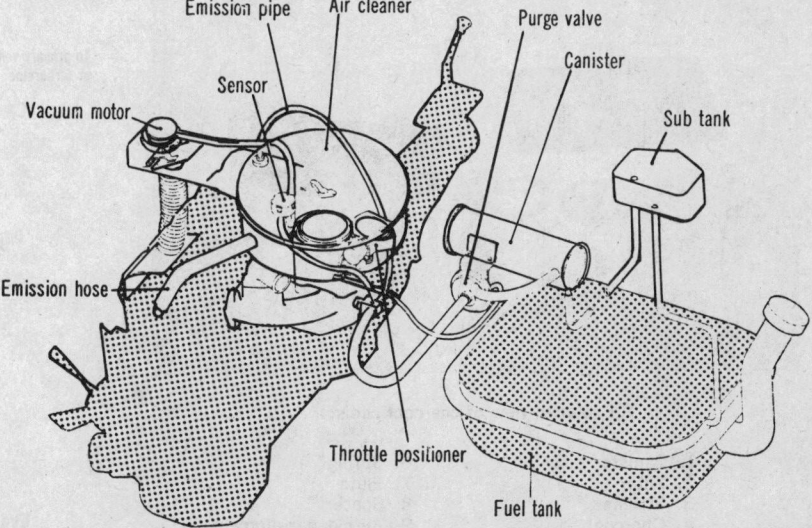

Exploded view of oil pump

ENGINE COOLING

Radiator

Removal and Installation

1. Remove the splash panel from the bottom of the car. Drain the radiator by opening the petcock. Remove the shroud on models so equipped.

2. Disconnect the radiator hoses at the engine. On automatic transmission cars, disconnect and plug the transmission lines to the bottom of the radiator.

3. Remove the two retaining bolts from either side of the radiator. Lift out the radiator.

4. Install the radiator in the reverse order of removal. Tighten the retaining bolts gradually in a criss-cross pattern.

Water Pump

Removal

1. Drain cooling system.

2. Remove fan belt, fan and alternator brace.

3. Remove water pump.

4. Installation is the reverse of removal.

Thermostat

Removal and Installation

The thermostat is located in the intake manifold under the upper radiator hose.

1. Drain the coolant below the level of the thermostat.

2. Remove the two retaining bolts and lift the thermostat housing off the intake manifold with the hose still attached.

NOTE: *If you are careful, it is not necessary to remove the upper radiator hose.*

3. Lift the thermostat out of the manifold.

4. Install the thermostat in the reverse order of removal. Use a new gasket and coat the mating surfaces with sealer.

EMISSION CONTROLS

Crankcase Ventilation

The Colt and Arrow are equipped with a closed crankcase ventilation system which doesn't use a PCV valve. The only maintenance necessary is a periodic check of the ventilation hoses. A thin hose runs from a fitting on the top rear of the valve cover to the intake manifold. A larger diameter hose runs from the front of the valve cover to the air cleaner. Replace any brittle hoses.

Evaporative Emission System

Component Removal and Installation

Expansion Tank
NOTE: *The expansion tank is located*

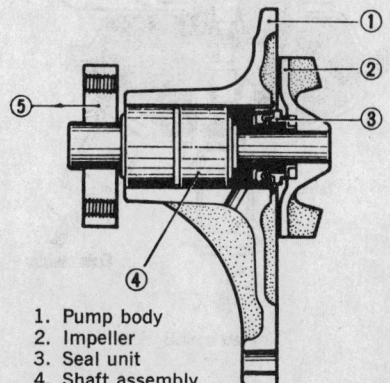

1. Pump body
2. Impeller
3. Seal unit
4. Shaft assembly
5. Bracket

Cross-section of the water pump

1972-73 emission controls

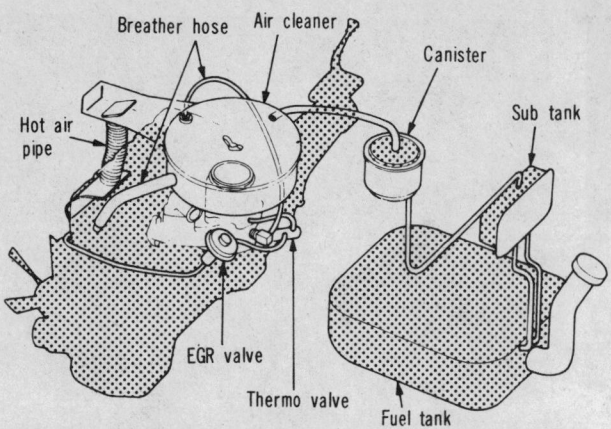

1974-77 emission controls

in the trunk of all models except the station wagon. Remove the left rear trim panel on station wagons for access to the tank.

1. Remove the hoses, unbolt and remove the tank.

2. Installation is the reverse of removal.

Charcoal Canister

1971–72

1. Remove the two purge valve retaining bolts. Leave the hoses attached to the valve.

2. Remove the purge valve-to-canister hose.

3. Remove the two canister bracket bolts and remove the canister.

4. Install the replacement canister in the reverse order of the removal.

1973–77

1. Remove the two connecting hoses.

2. Loosen and remove the canister retaining band bolt.

3. Remove the canister.

4. Installation is the reverse of removal. Replace any brittle hoses.

Thermostatically Controlled Air Cleaner

1972–73

The Colt and Arrow is equipped with a thermostatically controlled air cleaner which maintains the intake air admitted to the carburetor between 95° F and 105° F.

Testing

Air Door

1. Start the engine. With the engine cold and the outside temperature less than 90° F, the door should be in the "heat on" position (closed to outside air).

2. Operate the throttle lever rapidly to ½–¾ of its opening and release it. The air door should open to allow outside air to enter and then it should close again.

3. Warm the engine to normal operating temperature. Watch the door. When it opens to the outside air, remove the top from the air cleaner. The temperature should be over 90° F and no more than

130° F; 115° F is about normal. If the door does not work within these temperature ranges or fails to work at all, check for linkage or door binding.

If binding is not present and the air door is not working, proceed with the vacuum tests given below. If these indicate no faults in the vacuum motor and the door is not working, the temperature sensor is defective and must be replaced.

Vacuum Motor

1. Check all of the vacuum lines and fittings for leaks.

2. Remove the hose which runs from the sensor to the vacuum motor. Run a hose directly from the manifold vacuum source to the vacuum motor.

3. If the motor closes the air door, it is functioning property and the temperature sensor is defective.

4. If the motor does not close the door and no binding is present in its operation, the vacuum motor is defective and must be replaced.

NOTE: *If an alternate vacuum source is applied to the motor, insert a vacuum gauge in the line by using a T-fitting. Apply at least 9 in. Hg. of vacuum in order to operate the motor.*

1974–77

This heated air system is operated directly by a bimetal coil located in the snorkel which responds to underhood air temperature. Below 41° F, the hot air control valve is in the position, to allow heated air to flow through the cowl and into the air cleaner. Above 108° F, the valve allows air to flow directly into the air cleaner.

Inspection

1. When the air cleaner has cooled down, crank the engine and check to see if the hot air control valve operates properly.

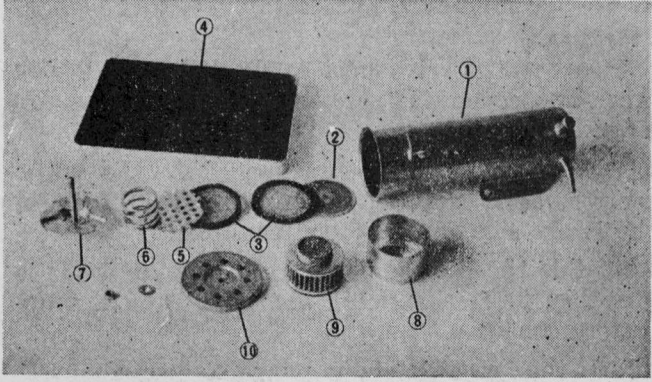

Exploded view of charcoal canister

1. Canister body	6. Spring
2. Filter	7. Plate
3. Strainer	8. Spacer
4. Charcoal	9. Air cleaner element
5. Plate	10. Cup

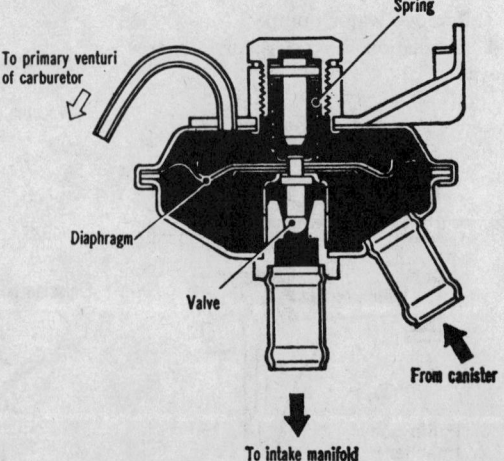

Evaporative emission system schematic diagram.

To ignition coil
To ignition switch
Throttle positioner
Leak jet
Governor switch
1 2
3 4
A Transmission switch
B Clutch switch
Solenoid valve
Fast idle adjust nut
Lock nut
Primary throttle lever

A Transmission switch

B Clutch switch
Clutch pedal

Operation of throttle positioner

2. Make sure the heated air intake port is closed fully at an underhood air temperature of 108° F. If the bimetal valve is found defective replace the air cleaner base.

Carburetor Controls

The two-barrel carburetor is equipped with several emission reducing features. The throttle body is connected to the cooling system which prevents carburetor icing and provides a more uniform fuel mixture when the engine is cold. The choke housing also receives coolant to provide more responsive choke operation. A fuel cut-off solenoid stops the fuel flow in the primary idle system when the ignition switch is turned off. This permits the use of a relatively high idle speed without the problem of dieseling. On 1972 models, a throttle positioner is used to reduce emissions during deceleration. It consists of a vacuum activator linked to a lever which contacts the primary throttle lever. A solenoid valve controls the positioner vacuum unit. The solenoid is operated by a speed-sensitive electronic governor. The governor switch is located under the passenger seat and counts ignition pulses. On deceleration the solenoid activates the positioner which prevents the primary throttle valve from closing until the engine drops below 1600 rpm.

Exhaust Gas Recirculation

Some 1974 and all 1975–77 models are equipped with EGR. An EGR valve mounted on the intake manifold meters the amount of exhaust gas to be recirculated. The EGR valve is controlled by intake manifold vacuum. The vacuum applied to the EGR valve is controlled by a thermo valve, located in the vacuum passage, which prevents EGR until the coolant temperature reaches 104° for better warm-up and initial driveability. On

1975–77 models, the thermovalve is also used to control the dual diaphragm distributor.

Component Removal and Installation

EGR Valve

1. Remove the vacuum hose.
2. Disconnect the exhaust line from the EGR valve.
3. Remove the EGR valve.
4. Installation is the reverse of removal.

Thermo Valve

The thermo valve is threaded into the left side of the intake manifold.
1. Disconnect the vacuum lines.
2. Turn the thermo valve out of the intake manifold.
3. Apply a good sealer to the valve threads before installation.
4. Connect the vacuum lines. The "A" nipple should be connected to the vacuum hose from the carburetor and the "B" nipple to the EGR valve.

Decel Dashpot

1974 1600 cc California models with manual transmission are equipped with a decel dashpot to hold the throttle plates slightly open during deceleration.

Dual Diaphragm Distributor

The 1975–77 Colt and the 1976–77 Arrow are equipped with a dual diaphragm distributor. This provides vacuum advance or retard. Timing is retarded under most conditions, except when the engine coolant temperature rises above 203° F. On automatic transmission cars, a carburetor throttle adjuster prevents higher engine speeds and creeping in gear.

Air Injection System

Used on all 1975s, the AIR system con-

sists of a belt-driven air pump, an air shut-off solenoid and diverter valve, and check valve.

Component Removal and Installation

Air Pump

1. Disconnect the air hose.
2. Remove the drive belt.
3. Remove the air pump.
4. Installation is the reverse of removal.
Adjust the belt tension.

Testing

Air Control Valve

Check the air discharge, by running the engine at idle and disconnecting the hose from the check valve. The check valve is satisfactory if air is being discharged. No air should leak from the relief side.
Check the air shut-off valve operation.
1. The air shut-off solenoid should be energized when the ignition is ON.
2. Remove the air hose from the discharge side.
3. At 3000 rpm, disconnect the shut-off solenoid coupler. Air should be discharged from the relief side only.
4. Gradually run the engine to 3500 rpm. If air is discharged from the relief port, system is functioning normally.

Thermal Reactor

1975–77 California models use a thermal reactor in place of a conventional exhaust manifold.

Removal and Installation

1. Remove the air cleaner and disconnect the hose from the check valve.
2. Disconnect the check valve support.
3. Disconnect the air injection pipe and remove the heat cowl.
4. Disconnect the EGR line.
5. Remove the thermal reactor.
6. Installation is the reverse of removal.

FUEL SYSTEM
Fuel Filter

Replacement

All models use an in-line filter which should be replaced every 12,000 miles.

Mechanical Fuel Pump

Removal and Installation

1. Remove the fuel lines.
2. Unbolt the pump mounting bolts,

and remove the pump, insulator, and gasket.

3. Coat both sides of a new insulator and gasket with sealer, and install the pump in the reverse order of removal.

Testing

Disconnect the fuel line from the carburetor and attach a pressure tester to the end of the line. Crank the engine. The tester should show 3.7–5.1 psi.

Electric Fuel Pump

1975 models are equipped with an electric fuel pump mounted in the trunk on sedans and hardtops and in the left rear wheel housing on station wagons.

Removal and Installation

1. Disconnect the battery ground cable.
2. Disconnect the fuel lines.
3. Disconnect all electrical connections.
4. Remove the pump.
5. Installation is the reverse of removal.

Troubleshooting

If the fuel pump doesn't work:
1. Check the fuse.
2. Check all wiring connections.
3. Check the control relay which is located in the engine compartment, next to the ignition coil. If the engine starts when the ignition switch is turned to "START" but stops when it is turned to "ON," the relay is defective.

Carburetors

Removal and Installation

1. Remove the solenoid valve wiring.
2. Disconnect the air cleaner breather hose, air duct and vacuum tube.
3. Remove the air cleaner.
4. Remove the air cleaner case.
5. Disconnect the accelerator and shift cables (automatic transmission) at the carburetor.
6. Disconnect the purge valve hose; remove the vacuum compensator, and fuel lines.
7. Drain the coolant.
8. Remove the water hose between the carburetor and the cylinder head.
9. Remove the carburetor.
10. Installation is the reverse of removal.

Overhaul

Efficient carburetion depends greatly on careful cleaning and inspection during overhaul, since dirt, gum, water, or varnish in or on the carburetor parts are often responsible for poor performance.

Exploded view of the carburetor

1. Throttle positioner solenoid	18. Float	34. By-pass screw
2. Compensator	19. Secondary pilot jet	35. Fuel cut solenoid
3. Stud	20. Secondary main jet	36. Intermediate lever
4. Throttle positioner	21. Primary main jet	37. Idle limiter
5. Adjusting nut	22. Pump weight	38. Pilot screw
6. Locknut	23. Steel ball	39. Accelerator pump
7. Auto-choke	24. Inner secondary venturi	40. Enrichment body assembly
8. Choke shaft	25. Inner primary venturi	41. Enrichment jet
9. Water hose	26. Primary pilot jet	42. Main body
10. Return spring	27. Choke valve	43. Insulator
11. Depression chamber	28. Throttle stop screw	44. Throttle chamber packing
12. Piston chamber	29. Abatement plate	45. Carburetor gasket
13. Float chamber cover	30. Lever	46. Throttle body
14. Float chamber packing	31. Lever spring	47. Throttle stop screw
15. Fuel joint	32. Throttle lever	
16. Filter	33. Throttle return spring	
17. Needle valve		

Overhaul your carburetor in a clean, dust-free area. Carefully disassemble the carburetor, referring often to the exploded views. Keep all similar and looka-like parts segregated during disassembly and cleaning to avoid accidental interchange during assembly. Make a note of all jet sizes.

When the carburetor is disassembled, wash all parts (except diaphragms, electric choke units, pump plunger, and any other plastic, leather, fiber, or rubber parts) in clean carburetor solvent. Do not leave parts in the solvent any longer than is necessary to sufficiently loosen the deposits. Excessive cleaning may remove the special finish from the float bowl and choke valve bodies, leaving these parts unfit for service. Rinse all parts in clean solvent and blow them dry with compressed air or allow them to air dry. Wipe clean all cork, plastic, leather, and fiber parts with a clean, lint-free cloth.

Blow out all passages and jets with compressed air and be sure that there are no restrictions or blockages. Never use wire or similar tools to clean jets, fuel passages, or air bleeds. Clean all jets and valves separately to avoid accidental interchange.

Check all parts for wear or damage. If wear or damage is found, replace the defective parts. Especially check the following:

1. Check the float needle and seat for wear. If wear is found, replace the complete assembly.

2. Check the float hinge pin for wear and the float(s) for dents or distortion. Replace the float if fuel has leaked into it.

3. Check the throttle and choke shaft bores for wear or an out-of-round condition. Damage or wear to the throttle arm, shaft, or shaft bore will often require replacement of the throttle body. These parts require a close tolerance of fit; wear may allow air leakage, which could affect starting and idling.

NOTE: *Throttle shafts and bushings are not included in overhaul kits. They can be purchased separately.*

4. Inspect the idle mixture adjusting needles for burrs or grooves. Any such condition requires replacement of the needle, since you will not be able to obtain a satisfactory idle.

5. Test the accelerator pump check valves. They should pass air one way but not the other. Test for proper seating by blowing and sucking on the valve. Replace the valve if necessary. If the valve is satisfactory, wash the valve again to remove breath moisture.

6. Check the bowl cover for warped surfaces with a straight edge.

7. Closely inspect the valves and seats for wear and damage, replacing as necessary.

8. After the carburetor is assembled, check the choke valve for freedom of operation.

Carburetor overhaul kits are recommended for each overhaul. These kits contain all gaskets and new parts to replace those that deteriorate most rapidly. Failure to replace all parts supplied with the kit (especially gaskets) can result in poor performance later.

After cleaning and checking all components, reassemble the carburetor, using new parts and referring to the exploded view. When reassembling, make sure that all screws and jets are tight in their seats, but do not overtighten as the tips will be distorted. Tighten all screws gradually, in rotation. Do not tighten needle valves into their seats; uneven jet-

ting will result. Always use new gaskets. Be sure to adjust the float level when reassembling.

Throttle Linkage Adjustment

Throttle linkage is adjusted at the clamp which joins the accelerator pedal rod to the carburetor rod. With the carburetor throttle valve closed and the accelerator pedal not depressed, the distance between the clamp and the floor should be 1.2 inches. Make sure that the accelerator rod moves smoothly.

Float and Fuel Level Adjustment

The Colt and Arrow carburetor is equipped with a see through float bowl window which allows you to check the fuel level without disassembling the carburetor. With the engine at idle, the fuel level should be within the white dots on the window. If not, remove the float chamber cover and bend the float support plate to correct the fuel level.

Fast Idle Adjustment

The fast idle should be set at 1700–1750 rpm with a cold engine. On earlier models, bend the cam operating link rod to alter the fast idle. Later models are equipped with a fast idle screw which allows easier adjustment.

Automatic Choke Adjustment

The choke case has three small projections. Align the center projection with the yellow punch mark of the bimetal case.

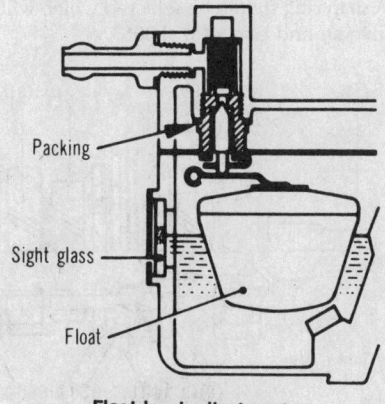

Packing

Sight glass

Float

Float level adjustment

MANUAL TRANSMISSION
Four and Five Speed
Removal and Installation

1. Remove the battery. Remove the starter. Withdraw the two large transmis-

sion top bolts (located in the engine compartment).

2. Remove the gearshift assembly from inside the vehicle.

3. Drain the transmission. Disconnect the speedometer and back-up light switch.

4. Remove the driveshaft. Disconnect the muffler pipe from its bracket and disconnect the clutch cables.

5. Support the transmission and unbolt the rear support.

6. Unbolt the bellhousing.

7. Remove the transmission.

8. To install the transmission, reverse the removal procedure. When replacing the gearshift assembly, place the shifter in the second-speed position in case of the four-speed transmission, or in the first-speed position in the five-speed transmission, so that the nylon bushing hole is vertical.

Overhaul

NOTE: *Proper transmission overhaul requires the use of certain special tools. If these are not available, the job should not be undertaken.*

4 Speed (KM110)

1. Remove clutch control lever shaft and shift arm.

2. Remove the speedometer driven gear.

3. Remove the backup light switch.

4. Remove the extension housing. It may be necessary to tap it off with a soft mallet.

5. Lay the transmission upside down and remove the bottom cover.

6. Remove the snap ring and take out the speedometer drive gear.

7. Tap off the main drive gear bearing retainer.

8. Remove the countershaft retainer.

9. Remove the countershaft from the rear of the case and remove the countergear. Forty needle bearings, both front and rear spacers and the front and rear thrust washers may also be removed.

10. Remove the reverse idler gear, needle bearing, spacer and front thrust washer from the reverse idler gear shaft.

11. Remove the reverse idler gear shaft locking bolt and pull the shaft out the rear of the case.

12. Remove the three plugs on the right side of the case and remove the poppet springs and balls.

13. Remove the reverse gear, reverse shift rail and fork.

14. Drive the shift rail and fork spring pins off with a 3/16″ punch.

15. Remove each shift rail and selector out the rear of the case and then remove the shift fork.

16. Pull the mainshaft assembly rearward and off the bearing retainer.

17. Remove the main drive gear syn-

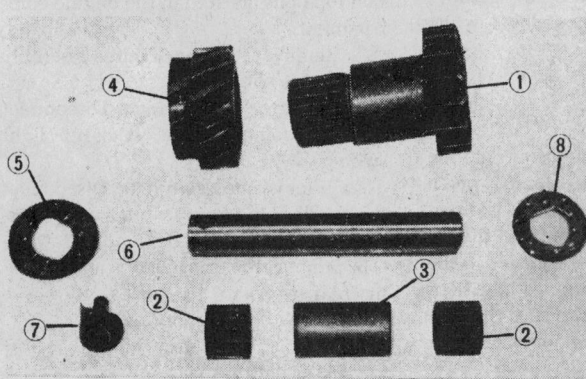

Exploded view of the reverse idler gear

1. Reverse idler gear
2. Needle bearing
3. Spacer
4. Front idler gear
5. Thrust washer
6. Gear shaft
7. Bolt
8. Selective rear thrust washer

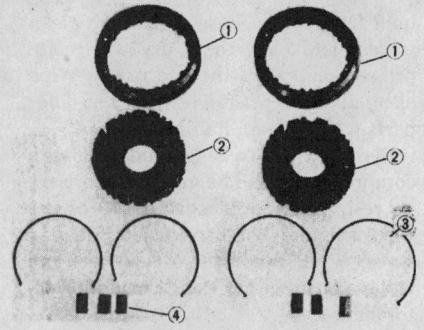

Exploded view of synchronizers
1. Synchronizer sleeve
2. Synchronizer hub
3. Springs
4. Synchronizer pieces

chronizer ring and the pilot needle bearing.

18. Remove the snap ring and pull the mainshaft rear bearing retainer off the bearing.

19. Remove the locknut.

20. Hold the mainshaft with the forward end down and strike it against the work bench to make the bearing fall off.

21. Remove the spacer, first gear needle bearing, spacer bushing, synchronizer ring, first-second speed synchronizer assembly, synchronizer ring, second speed gear and needle bearing.

22. Remove the snap ring from the front end of the mainshaft and then remove the third-fourth speed synchronizer assembly, synchronizer ring, third speed gear and needle bearing.

23. Remove the main drive gear assembly out the front of the case.

24. Remove each snap ring, and, using a puller, remove the bearing.

25. Remove the shifter and control shaft lock pin with a 3/16″ punch.

26. Remove the return spring and pull off the control shaft.

To assemble:

27. Press the main drive gear bearing into place and install a select-fit snap ring to bring play down to 0–.002″.

28. Assemble the synchronizers in reverse order of disassembly. After installing the needle bearings and third speed gear onto the mainshaft from the front, install the synchronizer ring and the third-fourth synchronizer assembly.

29. Install the first-second speed synchronizer.

30. Install a snap ring to bring the synchronizer end play down to 0–0.003″. Third gear end play should be 0.001–0.007″.

31. Install needle bearing, second speed gear, synchronizer ring and first-second speed synchronizer assembly onto the mainshaft.

32. Force the synchronizer assembly forward and check the second speed gear end play. Play should be 0.001–0.007″.

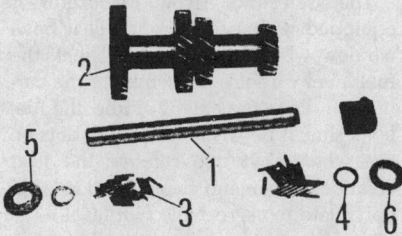

Exploded view of the counter gear
1. Countershaft
2. Counter gear
3. Needle rollers
4. Spacer
5. Thrust washer
6. Thrust washer

33. Install the first gear spacer ring, needle bearing, synchronizer ring, first speed gear and spacer. Force these parts forward and check the end play. Play should be 0.001–0.007″.

34. Using a bearing installer guide, a hammer or press, install the mainshaft bearing. Tighten the locknut to 72 ft lb. and install the locking key.

35. Install the snap ring on the rear bearing retainer and install the retainer. A snap ring should be selected which will give an end play of 0–0.006″.

36. Temporarily install the countergear, front and rear thrust washers and shaft, and measure the end play of the countergear. If the end play does not agree with the specified value of 0.002–0.007″, correct it by selecting a suitable rear thrust washer. Make certain that the thrust washer tongue fits properly in the slot made in the case.

37. Install the needle rollers and the bearing spacers in the front and rear bores of the counter gear. Applying grease to the rollers will keep them from dropping. The spacers should be installed on the outside of the needle rollers.

38. Attach the front thrust washer and the rear thrust washer selected for counter gear end play, to the counter gear. Hold them in place with grease. Install the countergear in the case.

39. Secure the rear of the countergear by tightening the stopper plate.

40. Fill the front bearing oil seal lip with grease. Apply sealant to the packing. Install the seal, using a special oil seal installer.

41. When installing the front bearing

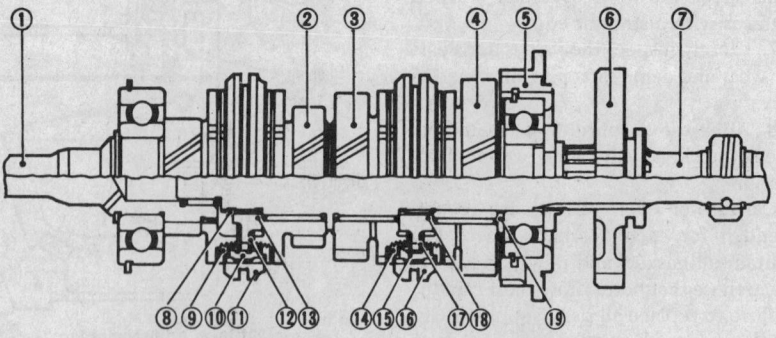

Assembled view of the mainshaft
1. Main drive gear
2. Third speed gear
3. Second speed gear
4. First speed gear
5. Rear bearing retainer
6. Reverse gear
7. Mainshaft
8. Snap-ring
9. Synchronizer ring
10. Synchronizer piece
11. Synchronizer sleeve
12. Synchronizer spring
13. Synchronizer hub (third-fourth)
14. Synchronizer ring
15. Synchronizer piece
16. Synchronizer sleeve
17. Synchronizer spring
18. Synchronizer hub (first-second)
19. Spacer

Synchronizer inspection—Dimension A = 0.059 in.

retainer, check the thickness of the packing. Thickness, top and bottom, should be 0.012″. Adjust bearing-to-shim clearance to 0–0.004″ with a shim.

42. Install the speedometer driven gear onto the mainshaft.

43. Apply sealant to the packing and locking bolts and install the extension housing to the transmission case.

44. Install the backup light switch and ball.

45. Install the speedometer driven gear and lockplate.

46. Install the bottom cover. Tighten the bolts, in a criss-cross manner, to 6–7 ft lb.

47. Install the control lever assembly to the case.

NOTE: *the shifter should be placed in the second speed position and the nylon bushing in the vertical position.*

5-Speed (1976–77 1600 cc.)

1. Drain the oil and remove the inspection cover.

2. Remove the backup light switch and ball.

3. Loosen the extension housing bolts, but do not remove them.

4. Loosen the return plunger plug, place the shift lever in reverse, remove the bolts and pull off the extension housing.

5. Remove the snap ring, speedometer drive gear and ball.

6. Remove the snap ring, mainshaft rear bearing, and bearing front snap ring.

7. Remove the reverse idler gear and related parts.

8. Loosen and remove the mainshaft intermediate locknut and the countershaft gear rear end lock nut.

9. Remove the three poppet spring covers, springs and balls from the right side of the case.

10. Using a 3/16″ punch, remove the split pin retaining the 1–2 and 3–4 shift forks to their rails.

11. Pull the 1–2 shift rail toward the rear of the case. Remove the counter 5th gear and ball bearing with the rail.

12. Pull the 3–4 shift rail toward the rear of the case.

13. Remove the mainshaft nut.

14. Remove the 5th-reverse synchronizer assembly, the 5th gear and the 5th-reverse shift rail and fork.

15. Remove the two interlock plungers.

16. Remove the spacer and reverse counter gear.

17. Remove the rear retainer.

18. Remove the front bearing retainer and spacer.

19. At this point, special tools, Rear Stopper Plate MD998244 and Front Stopper Plate MD998243, are needed. These are Mitsubishi tool numbers, but the equivalent, in function, of these tools will be satisfactory.

20. Insert the rear stopper plate tool between the clutch gear and synchronizer ring of the 3rd speed gear, and the front stopper plate tool between the

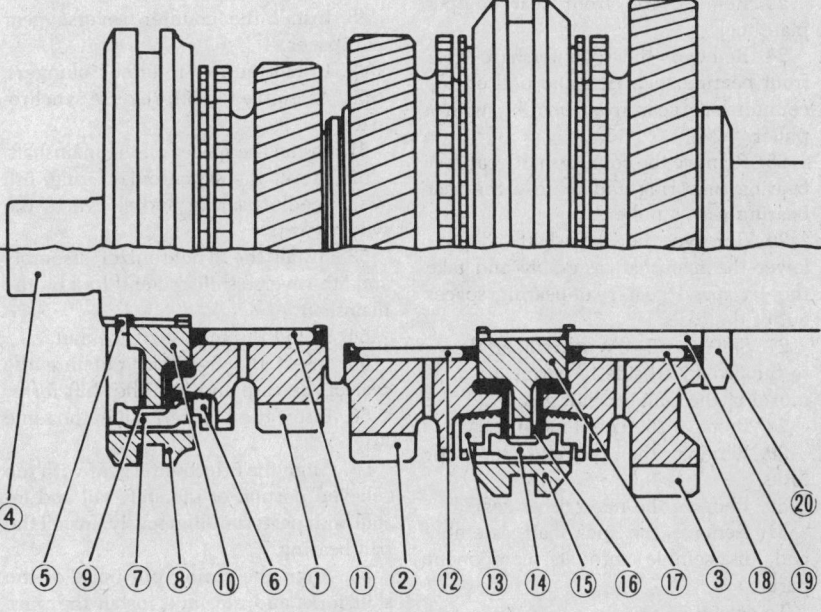

Assembled view of mainshaft

1. 3rd speed gear
2. 2nd speed gear
3. 1st speed gear
4. Mainshaft
5. Snap ring
6. Synchronizer ring (3-4 speed)
7. Synchronizer piece
8. Synchronizer sleeve (3-4 speed)
9. Synchronizer spring (3-4 speed)
10. Synchronizer hub (3-4 speed)
11. Needle bearing (3rd speed gear)
12. Needle bearing (2nd speed gear)
13. Synchronizer ring (1-2 speed)
14. Synchronizer piece
15. Synchronizer sleeve (1-2 speed)
16. Synchronizer spring (1-2 speed)
17. Synchronizer hub (1-2 speed)
18. Needle bearing (1st speed gear)
19. 1st gear bearing sleeve
20. Bearing spacer

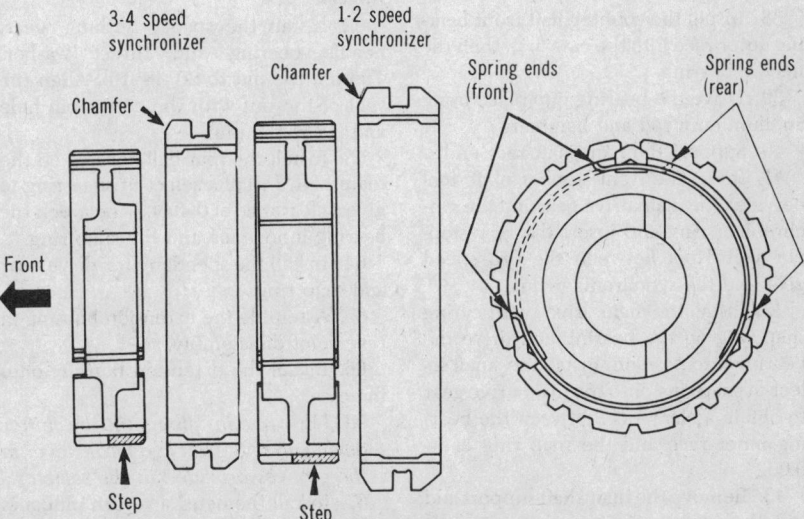

Assembled view of synchronizers

clutch gear and the synchronizer ring of the main drive gear.

21. Remove the mainshaft bearing snap ring and ball bearing. Slide the mainshaft support tool, MD998241, in place of the bearing over the mainshaft to support it.

22. Remove the main drive gear bearing snap rings. Using a puller, remove the bearing.

23. Remove the front rear stopper plate tools.

24. Remove the countershaft gear front bearing snap ring and pull off the countershaft gear front bearing with a puller.

25. Remove the countershaft gear rear bearing snap ring and remove the rear bearing with a puller.

26. Remove the mainshaft adapter, lower the mainshaft assembly and take the 1st speed gear rear bearing spacer out of the case.

27. Shift the 3–4 synchronizer sleeve to the 3rd speed side to permit easy removal of the countershaft gear.

28. Remove the countershaft gear.

29. Remove the 1–2 and 3–4 shift forks.

30. Remove the main drive gear.

31. Remove the mainshaft assembly and disassemble into its component parts.

To assemble:

32. Assemble the mainshaft in reverse of disassembly.

33. Insert the mainshaft into the case.

34. Install the synchronizer ring and needle bearing on the main drive gear and insert it into the case from the front.

35. Install the 1–2 and 3–4 shift forks, the 3–4 synchronizer sleeve and the countershaft.

36. Install the countershaft gear.

37. Support the countershaft gear, install the snap ring and press on the bearing.

38. Install the countershaft front bearing outer race into the case first, then the needle bearing.

39. Drive the bearing into place using an aluminum rod and hammer.

40. Support the mainshaft rear end.

41. Insert the front stopper plate tool between the main drive gear and the synchronizer ring and insert the rear stopper plate tool between the 3rd speed gear and the synchronizer ring.

42. Install the main drive gear bearing snap ring on the bearing and drive the bearing into position. Install the small select-fit snap ring onto the main drive gear to obtain a clearance between the bearing inner race and the snap ring of 0–0.002″.

43. Remove the mainshaft support and install the snap ring on the mainshaft bearing. Drive the bearing into position

and remove the front and rear stopper plate tools.

44. Apply grease to the front bearing oil seal lip and drive the oil seal into place in the front bearing retainer.

45. Check the clearance between the front bearing retainer and the main drive gear. Select and install a spacer to provide a clearance of 0–0.004″.

46. Install the front bearing retainer.

47. Install the rear retainer.

48. Install the counter reverse gear and spacer.

49. Install the two interlock plungers.

50. Assemble the 5th-reverse synchronizer.

51. Install the spacer on the mainshaft.

52. Install the synchronizer ring, 5th gear, needle bearing and sleeve to the synchronizer.

53. Install the synchronizer assembly and 5th-reverse shift rod and fork on the mainshaft.

54. Install the mainshaft locknut.

55. Insert the 3–4 shift rail into the rear of the case and into the shift forks.

56. Insert the 1–2 shift rail in the same way.

57. Align the 5th countergear with the relieved portion of the shift rail and install both parts simultaneously. Install the ball bearing.

58. Align the spring pin holes of the shift forks and rails and install the pins. The pins must not project out of the forks and the slit of the pin must be parallel with the rail.

59. Install the poppet balls and springs. Install the plugs until the heads are flush with the case surface. The springs must be installed with the tapered ends inside on the balls. The 1–2 spring is longest.

60. Torque the mainshaft locknut to 70–90 ftlb. and the countershaft locknut to 50–70 ftlb.

61. Insert the reverse idler shaft into the case.

62. Install the spacer bushing, gear, needle bearing and thrust washer. Tighten the nut to 20–40 ftlb. Align the split of the nut with the cotter pin hole and insert the pin.

63. Install the rear ball bearing on the mainshaft. Install a select-fit snap ring to give a clearance of 0–0.007″ between the bearing inner race and the snap ring.

64. Install the speedometer drive gear and snap ring.

65. Assemble the extension housing in reverse of disassembly.

66. Install the extension housing onto the case.

NOTE: *when installing, tilt the shifter down and to the left and fit the lever in the grooves provided in the selector.*

67. Install the neutral return plungers and ball; screw in the plugs until they are flush with the case.

68. Install the backup light switch and ball.

69. Install the bottom cover and torque the bolts to 6–7 ftlb.

70. Install the control lever assembly.

5-Speed (1975 All, 1976–77 2000 cc.)

1. Drain the oil and remove the case cover.

2. Remove the backup light switch and ball.

3. Remove the extension housing attaching bolts, back off the plug of the neutral return plunger, turn the shift lever down to the left and pull off the extension housing.

4. Remove the snap ring and speedometer drive gear.

5. Remove the snap ring and mainshaft rear bearing.

6. Remove the three plugs and remove the poppet springs and balls.

7. Remove the 1–2 and 3–4 shift fork pins with a 3/16″ punch. Pull each rail toward the rear of the case and remove the forks and interlock plunger.

8. In the same manner, remove the 5th-reverse forks.

9. Engage the reverse and 2nd gears and mainshaft and countershaft rear locknuts.

10. Remove the 5th counter gear and bearing with a puller. Remove the spacer and reverse counter gear.

11. Remove the 5th gear and sleeve from the mainshaft. Remove the 5th synchronizer and spacer.

12. Remove the cotter pin, nut and reverse idler gear.

13. Remove the rear bearing retainer.

14. Drive the reverse idler gear shaft from the case.

15. Remove the front bearing retainer.

16. Press the counter gear to the rear and remove the rear bearing snap ring.

17. Using a puller, remove the counter rear bearing.

18. Remove the snap ring and pull the counter front bearing. Remove the counter gear from the case.

19. Remove the main drive pinion from the case.

20. Remove the two snap rings and pull the bearing.

21. Remove the snap ring and pull the mainshaft bearing.

22. Remove the mainshaft from the case.

23. Disassemble the mainshaft.

24. Disassemble the extension housing.

To assemble:

25. Install the bearing on the main drive pinion and select a snap ring which will give a clearance of 0–0.0024″ between the snap ring and the bearing.

26. Assemble the mainshaft. Use a spacer which will give a 3–4 synchronizer

1. Clutch control shaft
2. Transmission case
3. Main drive gear
4. Synchronizer (3-4 speed)
5. 3rd speed gear
6. 2nd speed gear
7. Synchronizer (1-2 speed)
8. 1st speed gear
9. Rear bearing retainer
10. Synchronizer (reverse and overtop)
11. Overtop gear
12. Control shaft
13. Control lever
14. Front bearing retainer
15. Countershaft gear
16. Under cover
17. Mainshaft
18. Counter reverse gear
19. Reverse idler gear
20. Reverse idler gear shaft
21. Counter overtop gear
22. Extension housing
23. Speedometer drive gear

Sectional view of transmission (5-speed w/1600 cc)

end play of 0–0.003″. Use a snap ring which will give a 1–2 gear end play of 0.002–0.008″.

27. Insert the mainshaft into the case and drive in the center bearing.

28. Install the needle bearing and synchronizer ring, then insert the main drive pinion into the case from the front.

29. Insert the countershaft gear into the case.

30. Install the snap ring on the countershaft front needle bearing and drive the bearing into the case by hammering the outer race.

31. Install the snap ring on the countershaft rear bearing and install it in place.

32. Install the front bearing retainer using a spacer which will give a clearance of 0–0.004″ between the bearing and retainer.

33. Install the front retainer oil seal.

34. Install the rear retainer.

35. Install the reverse idler gear shaft.

36. Install the needle bearing, reverse idler gear and thrust washer. Tighten the locknut and install the cotter pin. Idler gear end play should be 0.0047–0.0110″. If not, replace the thrust washer.

37. Assemble the 5th synchronizer.

38. Install the spacer, stop plate and 5th synchronizer assembly, the 5th gear bearing sleeve and needle bearing, the synchronizer ring and 5th gear, in that order, to the mainshaft from the rear. 5th gear end play should be 0.004–0.010″.

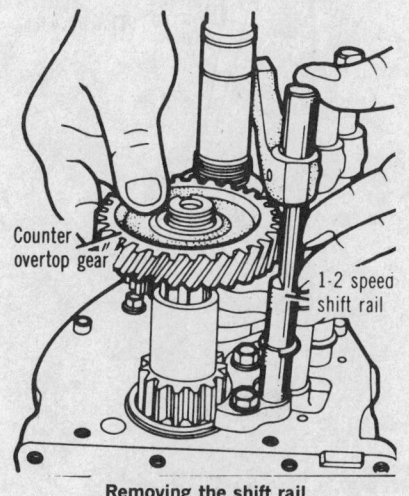

Counter overtop gear

1-2 speed shift rail

Removing the shift rail

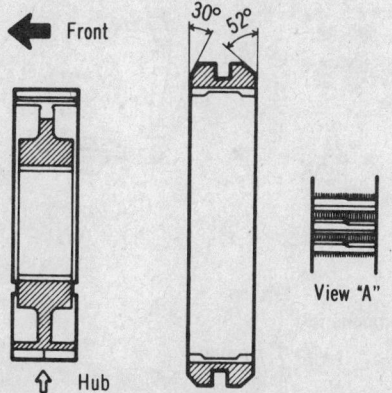

Front

Hub
A

Sleeve

View "A"

1-2 speed synchronizer

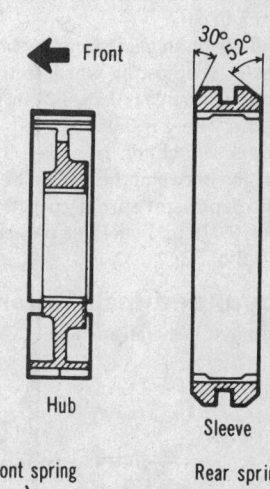

Front

Hub

Sleeve

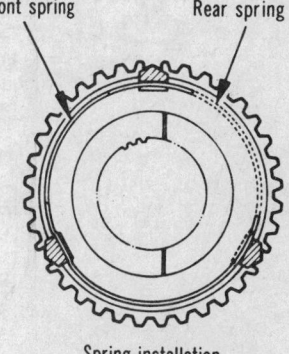

Front spring

Rear spring

Spring installation

3-4 speed synchronizer

39. Install the spacer, counter reverse gear, spacer, counter 5th gear and the ball bearing onto the countershaft gear from the rear. Tighten and lock the nut.

153

40. Insert the 3–4 and 1–2 forks into their synchronizer sleeves. Insert each shift rail from the rear of the case. Install the spring pins and interlock plunger.

NOTE: *the slit in the pins should be parallel with the rail.*

41. Insert the ball and poppet spring into each shift rail. Tighten the plugs flush with the case.

42. Install the ball bearing on the rear of the mainshaft.

43. Install the speedometer drive gear.

44. Turn the shifter down and to the left and install the extension housing.

45. Install the neutral return plungers, spring, and resistance spring and ball. Tighten the plugs flush with the case.

46. Install the speedometer driven gear sleeve and lock plate.

47. Install the backup light switch and ball.

48. Install the bottom cover and torque the bolts to 6–7 ftlb.

49. Install the control lever assembly.

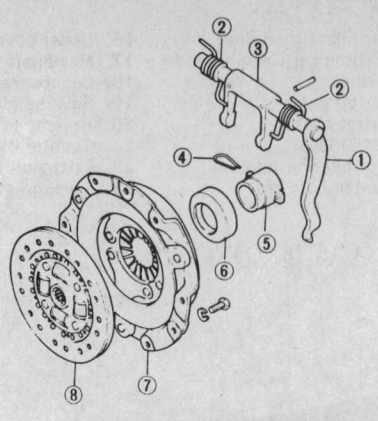

Exploded view of the clutch

1. Clutch control shaft
2. Return spring
3. Clutch shift arm
4. Return clip
5. Release bearing carrier
6. Release bearing
7. Pressure plate assembly
8. Clutch disc

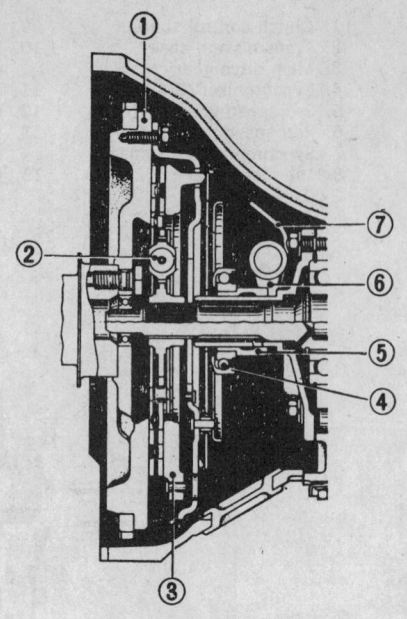

Cross-section of the clutch

1. Flywheel
2. Clutch disc
3. Pressure plate
4. Release bearing
5. Release bearing carrier
6. Clutch shift arm
7. Return spring

CLUTCH

Adjustment

Adjust the clutch switch so that the distance between the toe board and pedal face is 6.7 in.

1. Pull the outer cable from the holder.

2. Turn the adjusting wheel so the cable holder clearance is 0.20–0.24 in. (each turn of the wheel is 0.06 in.).

3. Check the clutch free play. This is the distance between the release bearing and the diaphragm spring operation. It should be 0.079 in. Pedal free play should be 0.8–1.2 in.

Removal and Installation

1. Remove the transmission.

Clutch switch adjustments

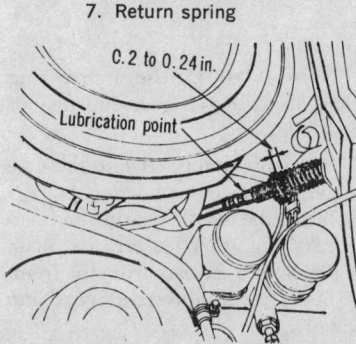

Clutch lubrication and adjustment

2. Remove the pressure plate.

3. Lift off the return clip on the transmission side and remove the release bearing and carrier.

4. Remove the control lever and the spring pin with a 3/16 in. punch.

5. Installation is the reverse of removal.

AUTOMATIC TRANSMISSION

The automatic transmission used in all Colt models from 1971–73 is a Borg-Warner with an aluminum case. In 1974 Chrysler introduced a Torqueflite model for use with the optional 121.7 CID engine, while still using the Borg Warner unit for the 97.5 CID engine through 1976. In 1977 the Torqueflite became standard on both engines.

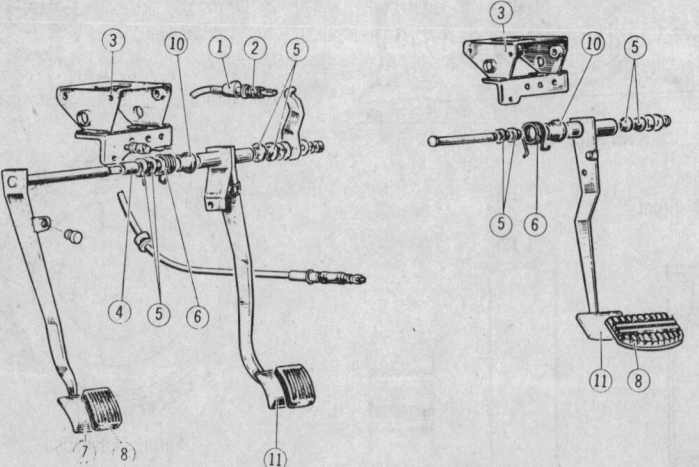

Clutch pedal components

1. Clutch cable
2. Spring
3. Pedal support
4. Spacer
5. Bushing
6. Spring
7. Clutch pedal
8. Pedal pad
10. Silencer
11. Brake pedal

Removal and Installation

Borg-Warner

The exhaust system must be removed from the connecting pipe to the muffler.

1. Remove the air cleaner, battery with cables, starter, and the upper bolts which attach the engine to the transmission.

2. Drain the transmission. Remove the speedometer cable and driveshaft.

3. Remove the exhaust system from the connecting pipe rearward to the muffler.

4. Remove the transmission oil lines.

5. Remove the control rod.

6. Remove the bellhousing. Rotate the torque converter, and remove the four exposed bolts.

7. Place a jack under the transmission.

8. Remove the insulator attaching bolts, ground cable, and spacer. Remove the insulator.

9. Remove the torque converter and pull out the transmission.

10. To install the transmission, reverse the removal procedure.

Torqueflite

The transmission and converter must be removed as an assembly; otherwise, the converter drive plate, pump bushing, or oil seal may be damaged. The drive plate will not support a load; therefore, none of the weight of the transmission should be allowed to rest on the plate during removal.

1. Drain the transmission and remove cooler lines at transmission.

2. Remove starter and cooler line bracket.

3. Rotate engine clockwise and remove bolts attaching torque converter to drive plate.

4. Remove the driveshaft.

5. Disconnect gearshift rod and torque shaft.

6. Disconnect throttle rod from lever at the left side of transmission. Remove linkage bellcrank from transmission if so equipped.

7. Remove the oil filler tube and speedometer cable.

8. Support the rear of the engine with jack.

9. Raise transmission slightly.

10. Remove crossmember.

11. Remove all bell housing bolts.

12. Carefully work transmission converter assembly rearward off engine block dowels and disengage converter hub from end of crankshaft. Attach a small C-clamp to edge of bell housing to hold converter in place during transmission removal.

13. Remove transmission.

14. Installation is the reverse of removal.

Oil pan removal sequence Borg-Warner

Oil Pan and Filter Removal and Installation

Borg-Warner

1. Raise and support vehicle.

2. Remove pan bolts in a criss-cross fashion allowing fluid to drain at the same time.

3. Remove gasket and magnet. The magnet is used to pickup metallic foreign objects.

4. Install magnet and new gasket and attach pan, tightening bolts in a criss-cross pattern to 6–9 ftlb. Refill with Dexron type fluid.

Torqueflite

1. Raise and support vehicle.

2. Loosen the pan bolts from one end to the other allowing the fluid to drain out.

3. Unbolt the old filter from the pan.

4. Clean the pan and install a new filter. Tighten filter bolts to 35 inlb.

5. Install the pan and new gasket. Torque pan bolts to 6–9 ftlb.

6. Add four quarts of Dexron fluid, start the engine and move the lever through all positions, pausing momentarily in each. Add enough fluid to bring the level to the full mark on the dipstick.

Downshift Cable Adjustment

All Models

Run the engine to operating temperature. Adjust the cable by turning the outer adjusting screw until the bottom just contacts the caulked stopper. Adjust to 0.002–0.004 in. clearance. If further adjustment is necessary, perform the following: Remove the transmission pipe plug. Connect the transmission pressure gauge. Set both the parking and the foot brake. With the engine at idle, place the car in gear. Check the line pressure. Normal is 49.7–65.3 psi. Increase the engine speed to 1,000 rpm. Line pressure should be 65.3–85.2 psi. The difference in pressure readings should be 15.6–19.6 psi. If

it is not, tighten the outer cable with the adjusting screw to increase the pressure or loosen the outer cable to decrease the pressure.

Front Band Adjustment— Borg-Warner

1. Remove the transmission pan.

2. Loosen the locknut and move the servo lever out of the way.

3. Insert a 0.35 in. feeler gauge between the servo piston pin and the adjusting screw.

4. Torque the servo screw to 10 in. lbs.

5. Tighten the locknut and remove the feeler gauge.

Rear Band Adjustment— Borg-Warner

This screw is located on the right-hand outer wall of the transmission case.

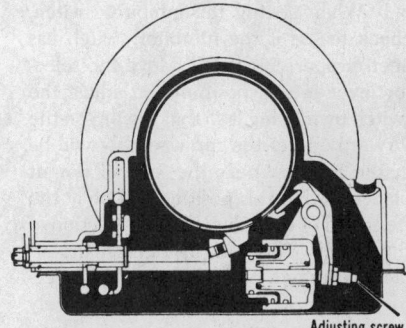

Front band adjusting screw location Borg-Warner.

Rear band adjusting screw location Borg-Warner.

Loosen the locknut. Tighten the nut to 10 ft lbs. Loosen the nut ¾ turn. Tighten down the locknut.

Kickdown Band— Torqueflite

The kickdown band adjusting screw is located on the left side of the transmission case.

1. Loosen locknut and back off approximately 5 turns. Test adjusting screw for free turning in the transmission case.

2. Using wrench, Tool C–3380A or commercial substitute with adapter C–3705 tighten band adjusting screw 47–50 in. lbs. If adapter C–3705 is not used, tighten adjusting screws to 72 in. lbs. which is the true torque.

NOTE: *Tool C–3380A is basically an adaptation of an in. lbs. torque wrench with an extension (C–3705) a commercial substitute may accomplish the same service.*

3. Back off adjusting screw 3 turns from Step 2. Tighten locknut to 35 ft lbs.

Low & Reverse Band— Torqueflite

1. Raise vehicle, drain transmission fluid and remove the pan.

2. This transmission has an allen socket adjustment screw at the servo end of lever. After removing locknut this screw is tightened to 41 in. lbs. true torque then backed off the 7½ turns from 41 in. lbs. Tighten locknut to 30 ft lbs.

3. Reinstall the pan.

Neutral Safety Switch— Torqueflite

1. When testing the inhibitor switch, check to see if the inhibitor switch has been properly installed. Move the selector lever into N position and adjust the switch by moving it so that the pin on the forward end of the rod assembly will be in the position near the lobe of detent plate and that this position will be at the front end of the range of N connection of the switch. Temporarily tighten the attaching screws. After adjusting the selector lever clearance to 0.059 in. securely tighten the screws.

2. Test the continuity of the switch circuit by using a test light with switch connector disconnected.

Shift Linkage Adjustment— Torqueflite

For exploded view of transmission control, refer to illustration. To adjust the shift linkage, the control cover must be removed.

Removal and Installation

1. Remove the shift handle assembly from the lever.

2. Take the position indicator assembly out upward.

Exploded view of Torqueflite automatic transmission control

1. Push button
2. Shift handle
3. Rod adjusting nut
4. Rod return spring
5. Selector lever assembly
6. Position indicator assembly
7. Indicator lamp socket assembly
8. Inhibitor switch
9. Shift lever rod
10. Shift lever bracket assembly
11. Lever bracket cover
12. Transmission control arm
13. Transmission control rod

Remove the position indicator lamp.

3. Disconnect the control rod from the arm.

Remove the lever bracket assembly.

4. Installation is the reverse of removal.

If the turning effort (13–29 in. lbs) is not obtained, adjust it by using a selective wave washer of proper size.

CAUTION: *When the turning effort at the pivot A is checked, the pin at the forward end of the rod assembly must not slide with the detent plate. If the arm is loose, the bushing should be replaced.*

Adjust the rod adjusting nut at the top end of the selector lever assembly so that when the selector lever is in N position, the nut may be flush with the bottom of the lever notch.

To connect the control rod to the selector lever assembly, first make certain that the selector lever is held in N position, and then move the control rod 3 detent stops from L position to place transmission in N neutral.

Throttle Rod Adjustment— Torqueflite

Warm the engine until it reaches the normal operating temperature. With the

Throttle rod adjustment—Torqueflite

carburetor automatic choke off the fast idle cam, adjust the engine idle speed by using a tachometer. Then make the throttle rod adjustment.

1. Install each linkage. Loosen its bolts so that the rods B and C can slide properly.

2. Lightly push the rod A or the transmission throttle lever and the rod C toward the idle stopper and set the rods to idle position. In this case the carburetor automatic choke must be fully released. Tighten the bolt securely to connect the rods B and C.

3. Make sure that when the carburetor throttle valve is wide-open, the transmission throttle lever smoothly moves from idle to wide-open position (operating angle; 45°–54°) and that there is some room in the lever stroke.

DRIVE AXLES

Driveshafts and U-Joints

The driveshaft and U-joints are of conventional design and construction. Driveshaft length differs between the manual and automatic transmission equipped vehicles.

Driveshaft

Removal and Installation

1. Drain the transmission fluid.

2. Remove the driveshaft from the transmission end by withdrawing it rearward.

3. Installation is the reverse of removal.

U-Joint Overhaul

1. Remove the snap rings at each cap.

2. Using a drift, drive out one cap by hammering on the other, until the opposite cap is almost all the way out of the yoke. Remove the driven cap with a pliers.

3. Drive out the remaining caps in a similar fashion.

4. To install, place the spider in the yoke.

1. Sleeve yoke
2. Snap-ring
3. Needle bearing
4. Dust seal
5. Universal joint journal
6. Driveshaft
7. Balance weight
8. Driveshaft flange yoke

Driveshaft components

5. Force grease into the passages in the spider and apply grease to the needles in the caps.

6. Place a cap in one end of the yoke from the outside, place the assembly in a vise.

7. Press the cap into the yoke with the vise. When the cap is flush with the yoke and starting over the spider, use a suitable socket to press it in the remaining distance. Repeat with the other caps. Take great care that the needles don't fall over during the operation.

8. Install proper size snap rings.

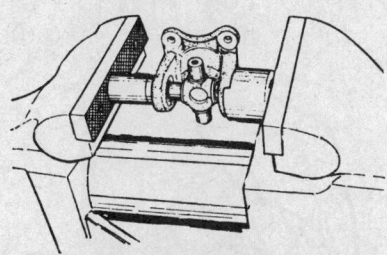

U-Joint bearing removal

Snap-Ring Code (in.)

Yellow–0.0516   Blue–0.0528
None–0.0504   Purple–0.0539

Bearing-to-snap-ring clearance is 0.00–0.001 in. When the snap-rings are installed, press each bearing toward the opposite shaft ends to measure the maximum clearance.

Measure the snap-ring clearance

Drive Axle

Removal and Installation

1. Remove the rear wheels.
2. Remove the driveshaft.
3. Disconnect all foot and parking rear brake lines.
4. Remove the rear U-bolts and the shock absorbers.
5. Remove the spring shackle pin nuts and the shackle plate. With the axle housing resting on the jack, remove the rear springs.
6. To replace the axle assembly, reverse the removal procedure. Bleed the brakes.

Rear Axle Shaft

Removal and Installation

1. Remove the rear wheels and the brake backing plate.
2. The axle shaft may be pulled out manually or with a slide hammer.
3. Installation is the reverse of removal.

Axle Shaft Bearing/Oil Seal

Removal and Installation

1. Remove the axle shaft.
2. Grind a small notch on the inner

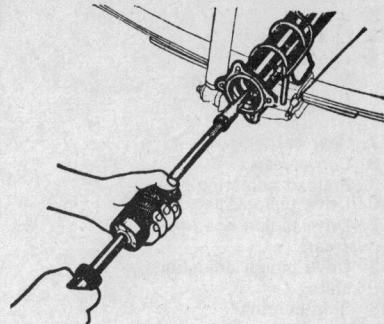

Oil seal removal

bearing retainer and split the retainer at that point with a chisel.

3. Remove the bearing.
4. The oil seal can be removed after the axle shaft is removed.
5. Install the outer bearing retainer (raised surface facing the wheel hub), axle shaft bearing and retainer. Using packing, set the clearance between the outer bearing retainer and the bearing to 0.-00–0.01 in.

Differential

Removal and Installation

1. Drain the oil.
2. Remove the driveshaft.
3. Pull out both axle shafts to disengage the axle shafts from the differential gears. They need only be pulled out about 2 in.
4. Unbolt and remove the differential carrier.
5. Installation is the reverse of removal.

Overhaul

1. Remove the bearing caps and pry the differential from the carrier.
2. Remove the differential side bearings. Be sure to keep the right and left bearing shims separated.
3. Remove the ring gear.
4. Drive out the pinion shaft lockpin from the rear of the ring gear, and remove the pinion shaft.
5. Remove the pinions and side gears

Exploded view of axle shaft

1. Wheel hub bolt
2. Rear axle shaft oil seal
3. Packing
4. Bearing retainer (inner)
5. Bearing
6. Bearing retainer (outer)
7. Bearing retainer bolt
8. Rear axle shaft

1. Locknut
2. Washer
3. End yoke
4. Slinger
5. Oil seal
6. Drive pinion bearing (front)
7. Gear carrier
8. Carrier cap
9. Preload adjusting shim
10. Drive pinion spacer
11. Drive pinion bearing (rear)
12. Drive pinion adjusting shim
13. Side bearing
14. Side bearing adjusting shim
15. Differential pinion
16. Differential pinion washer
17. Air breather
18. Final drive gear set
19. Differential pinion shaft
20. Differential case
21. Lockwasher
22. Differential side gear
23. Side gear spacer
24. Packing
25. Rear axle housing

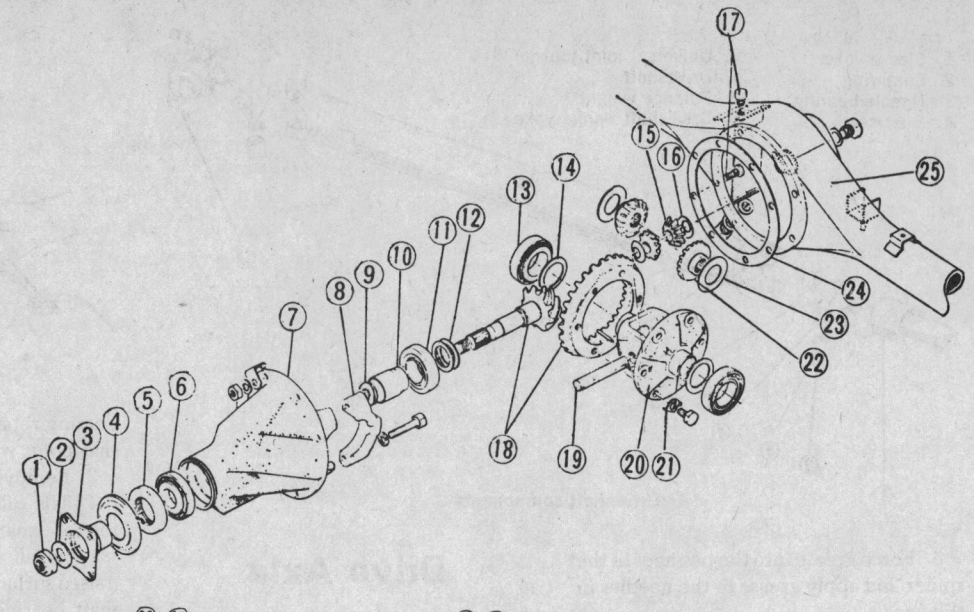

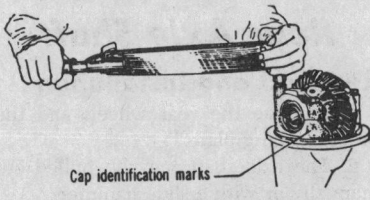

Exploded view of differential

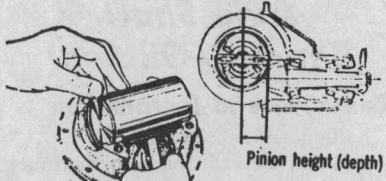

Bearing cap identification marks

Cap identification marks

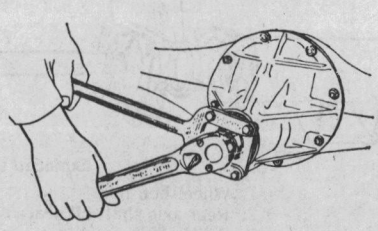

Measuring pinion height

Pinion height (depth)

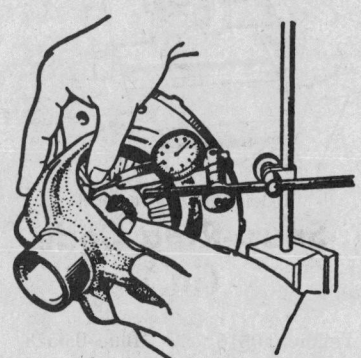

Checking pinion gear and side gear backlash

with spacers. Note the position of the side gear spacers.

6. Hold the end yoke and remove the pinion nut.

7. Remove the end yoke.

8. Tap the drive pinion shaft with a plastic faced mallet and remove the drive pinion with the adjusting shim, rear inner race, spacer and preload adjusting shim.

9. Remove the front pinion bearing outer race and oil seal.

10. Remove the pinion bearing rear outer race.

NOTE: *If the unit is to be assembled using no replacement parts, the same spacers and shims can generally be used. If either pinion bearing or ring gear and drive pinion are being replaced, new shims should be used. Only replace the drive pinion and ring gear in matched sets.*

11. Assemble the side gears in the differential case. Install the thrust washers in the same place as they were installed.

12. With washers, insert both differential gears at the same time to mesh with the side gears. Insert the pinion shaft.

13. Measure the backlash of the differential gears and side gears. The backlash should be (1972–73) 0.003–0.005 in. (1974–77) 0–.003 in. and can be adjusted with the use of spacers listed below.

Removing the end yoke

Side Gear Spacers

14. Align the pinion shaft hole with the case and drive the lockpin in.

15. Install the ring gear.

16. To assemble the drive pinion, press the front and rear outer races into the gear carrier.

17. Insert a shim between the drive pinion and rear bearing. If the original gear set is being replaced, the original shims may be used. If a new gear set is being installed, calculate the shim di-

Side Gear Spacers

Part No.	Thickness of spacer (in.)
MA180860	0.0394 0 −0.0028
MA180861	0.0394 −0.0031 −0.0067
MA180862	0.0394 −0.0071 −0.0098
MA180876	0.0394 +0.0063 −0.0035
MA180875	0.0394 +0.0031 −0.0004

mension in the following manner. Assuming the pinion height before disassembly is correct, subtract the new pinion variation marking (on the pinion head) from the old pinion variation marking. If the answer is positive, add shims in the corresponding amount. If the answer is negative, subtract shims in the corresponding amount. This will produce a reasonable starting point for assembly. If the shim choice is proved incorrect, the entire pinion must be disassembled, and the shim changed accordingly. The etched marking on the face of the pinion represents a positive or negative variation from the standard in millimeters.

18. Assemble the front bearing, end yoke, pinion spacer and washer and torque the pinion nut gradually. Torque the pinion nut constantly checking the preload, until a preload of 6–9 in. lbs is reached (without the oil seal).

Shims are available in the following sizes:

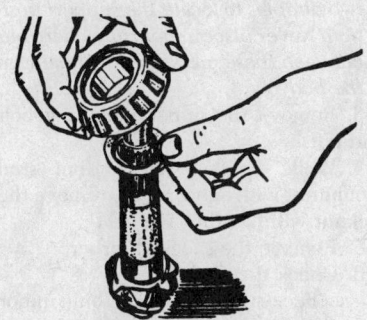

Pinion height shim installation

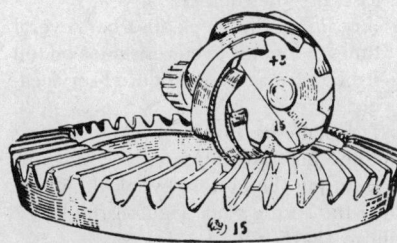

Pinion and ring gear markings

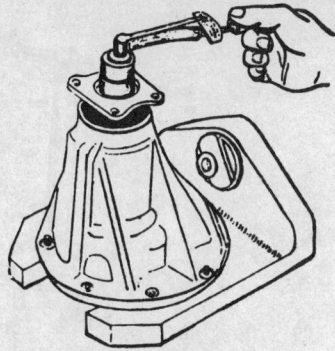

Measuring pinion preload

Pinion Bearing Preload Shims

19. Remove the end yoke and insert the bearing preload adjusting shim between the pinion spacer and the bearing and torque the pinion nut to 8–11 in. lbs of preload with oil seal).

The pinion nut torque should be 100–145 ft lbs.

20. Install each side bearing into the differential case without the adjusting shim.

Pinion Bearing Preload Shims

Part No.	Thickness of shim (in.)
MA180842	0.0543 ± 0.0004
MA180843	0.0555 ± 0.0004
MA180844	0.0567 ± 0.0004
MA180845	0.0579 ± 0.0004
MA180846	0.0591 ± 0.0004
MA180847	0.0603 ± 0.0004
MA180848	0.0614 ± 0.0004
MA180849	0.0626 ± 0.0004
MA180850	0.0638 ± 0.0004
MA180851	0.0650 ± 0.0004
MA180852	0.0118 ± 0.0005

21. Install the differential case assembly on the gear carrier and measure the clearance between the side bearing outer race and the gear carrier.

22. The thickness of the shim on each side is determined by the following formula:

The 0.004 in dimension is added as the side bearing preload (0.002 in. on each side). Side bearing preload shims are available in the following sizes:

Measuring side bearing-to-carrier clearance

Side Bearing Preload Shims

23. Align the gear carrier and bearing cap positioning marks and torque the cap bolts to 25–29 ft lbs.

24. Install a dial indicator and measure ring gear run-out. If the run-out exceeds 0.002 in., change the position of the ring gear on the differential carrier by 90°. If the run-out still exceeds 0.002 in., replace the ring gear or differential carrier.

Side Bearing Preload Shims

Part No.	Shim thickness (in.)
MA180828	0.0787 ± 0.0004
MA180829	0.0799 ± 0.0004
MA180830	0.0811 ± 0.0004
MA180831	0.0823 ± 0.0004
MA180832	0.0835 ± 0.0004
MA180833	0.0846 ± 0.0004
MA180834	0.0858 ± 0.0004
MA180835	0.0870 ± 0.0004
MA180836	0.0882 ± 0.0004
MA180837	0.0894 ± 0.0004
MA180838	0.0906 ± 0.0004
MA180839	0.0917 ± 0.0004

25. Measure the backlash of the ring gear at four points, 90° apart. Ring gear backlash should not exceed 0.005–0.007 in. (1972–73) or 0.000–0.002 in. (1974–77). if the measured backlash is greater than the specification, shift shims in a corresponding thickness from the ring gear tooth side to the rear of the ring gear. If backlash is less than specified, shift shims from the rear side of the ring gear to the tooth side. Side gear adjusting shims are available in the following sizes:

Side Bearing Adjusting Shims

26. Make a ring gear tooth pattern check. See General Information.

Side Bearing Adjusting Shims

Part No.	Thickness (in.)
MA180822	0.0028 ± 0.0004
MA180823	0.0051 ± 0.0006
MA180824	0.0098 ± 0.0010
MA180825	0.0020 ± 0.0002
MA180826	0.0062 ± 0.0008
MA180827	0.0157 ± 0.0012

Proper tooth contact

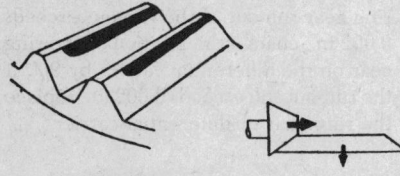

Face contact

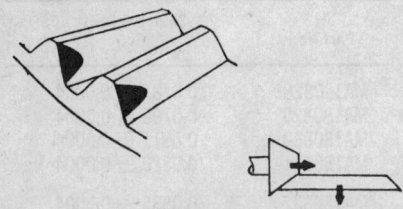

Heel contact

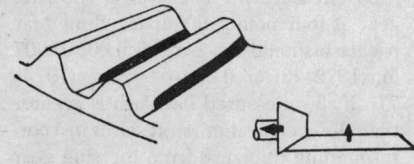

Toe contact

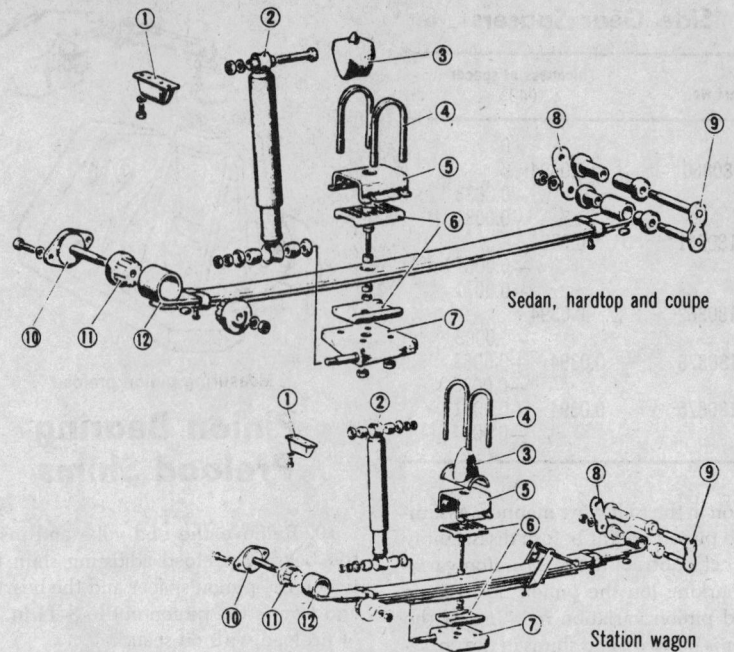

Flank contact

Sedan, hardtop and coupe

Station wagon

Colt rear suspension (Arrow similar)

1. Carrier bumper
2. Shock absorber
3. Rubber cushion
4. Spring U-bolt
5. Pad bracket
6. Pad
7. U-bolt seat
8. Shackle plate
9. Spring shackle assembly
10. Spring pin assembly
11. Front eye bushing
12. Leaf spring assembly

REAR SUSPENSION

Springs

Removal and Installation

1. Remove the hub cap or wheel cover. Loosen the lug nuts.

2. Raise the rear of the car. Install a stand at the exact point of the sill shown in the drawing. Two dimples locate the support point on the sill flange.

CAUTION: *Damage to the unit body can result from installing a stand at any other location.*

3. Disconnect the lower mounting nut of the shock absorber.

4. Remove the four U-bolt fastening nuts from the spring seat.

NOTE: *It's not necessary to remove the shock absorber, leave the top connected.*

5. Place a floor jack under the rear axle and raise it just enough to remove the load from the springs. Remove the spring pad and seat.

6. Remove the two rear shackle attaching nuts and remove the rear shackle.

7. Remove the front pin retaining nut. Remove the two pin retaining bolts and take off the pin.

8. Remove the spring.

NOTE: *It is a good safety practice to replace used suspension fasteners with new parts.*

9. Install the front spring eye bushings from both sides of the eye with the bushing flanges facing out.

10. Insert the spring pin assembly from the body side and fasten it with the bolts. Temporarily tighten the spring pin nut.

11. Install the rear eye bushings in the same manner as the front, insert the shackle pins from the outside of the car, and temporarily tighten the nut after installing the shackle plate.

12. Install the pads on both sides of the spring, aligning the pad center holes with the spring center bolt collar, and then install the spring seat with its center hole through the spring center collar.

13. Attach the assembled spring and spring seat to the axle housing with the axle housing spring center hole meeting the spring center bolt and install the U-bolt nuts. Tighten the nuts to 33–36 ft lbs.

14. Tighten the lower shock absorber nut to 12–15 ft lbs on all models.

15. Lower the car to the floor, jounce it a few times, and then tighten the spring pin and shackle pin nuts to 36–43 ft lbs.

Shock Absorbers

Removal and Installation

1. Remove the hub cap or wheel cover. Loosen the lug nuts.

2. Raise the rear of the car. Support the car with jackstands.

NOTE: *The body sill is marked with two dimples to locate the support position. Never place a stand anywhere but between these marks or you'll damage the body.*

3. Remove the upper mounting bolt and nut.

4. While holding the bottom stud mount nut with one wrench, remove the locknut with another wrench.

5. Remove the shock absorber.

6. Check the shock for:
   a. Excessive oil leakage, some minor weeping is permissible;
   b. Bent center rod, damaged outer case, or other defects;
   c. Pump the shock absorber several times, if it offers even resistance on full strokes it may be considered serviceable.

7. Install the upper shock mounting nut and bolt. Hand-tighten the nut.

8. Install the bottom eye of the shock over the spring stud. Tighten the lower nut to 12–15 ft lbs.

9. Finally, tighten the upper nut to

47–58 ft lbs on all models except station wagons, which are tightened to 12–15 ft lbs.

Shock Absorbers

Removal and Installation

1. Support the car with jackstands. **NOTE:** *The body sill is marked with two dimples to locate the support position. Never place a stand anywhere but between these marks or you'll damage the body.*
2. Remove the upper mounting bolt and nut.
3. Remove the lower locknut.
4. Remove the shock absorber.
5. Installation is the reverse of removal.

FRONT SUSPENSION

Strut

Removal and Installation

1. Remove the front and caliper. Remove the front hub with disc and dust cover.
2. Disconnect the stabilizer linkage and the lower arm. Remove the strut assembly, knuckle arm and strut insulator retaining bolts and remove the strut assembly from the wheelhouse.
3. Installation is the reverse of removal.

Spring

Removal and Installation

The strut assembly must be removed to the bench.
1. Clamp the strut assembly in a vise.
2. Install a coil spring compressor.
3. Remove the dust cover.
4. Remove the insulator.
5. Remove the spring.
6. Installation is the reverse of re-

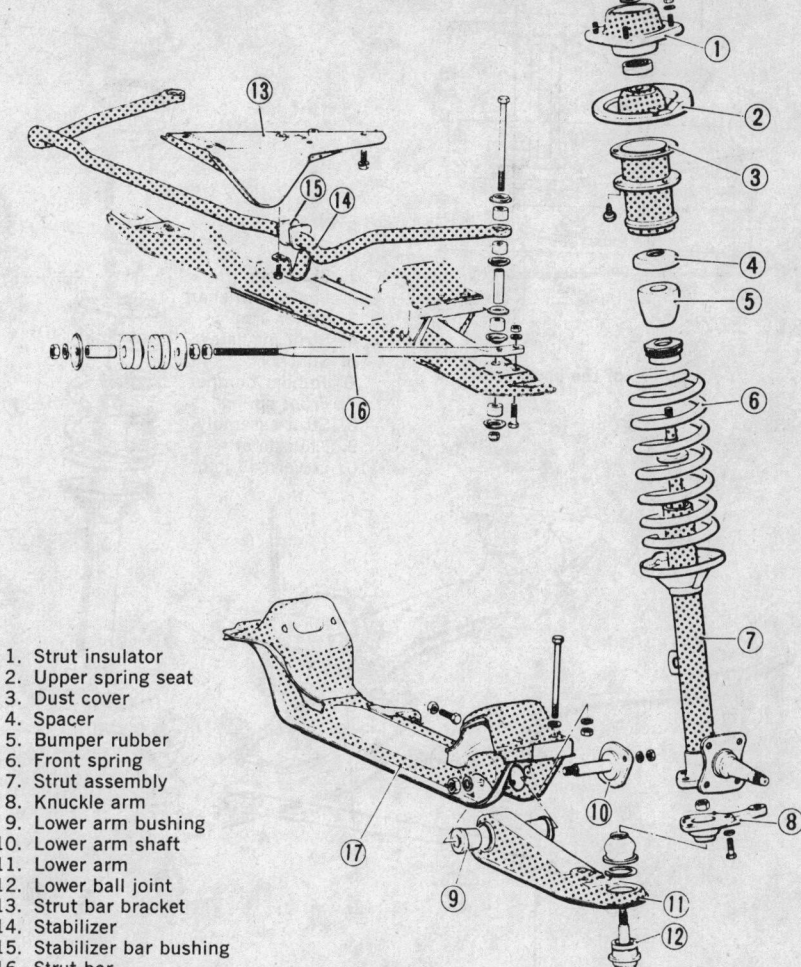

1. Strut insulator
2. Upper spring seat
3. Dust cover
4. Spacer
5. Bumper rubber
6. Front spring
7. Strut assembly
8. Knuckle arm
9. Lower arm bushing
10. Lower arm shaft
11. Lower arm
12. Lower ball joint
13. Strut bar bracket
14. Stabilizer
15. Stabilizer bar bushing
16. Strut bar
17. Crossmember

Arrow front suspension

moval. Align the spring seat upper assembly with the indentation on the piston rod and the D-shaped hole.

Ball Joint

Removal and Installation

1. Remove strut assembly and tie rod.
2. Remove the lower arm ball joint

dust seal by prying up the dust seal ring evenly with a screwdriver.
3. Next remove the snap-ring using snap-ring pliers.
4. Using ball joint remover and installer tool, press off ball joint.
5. To install the ball joint, press the ball joint properly into the burred hole, with the ball joint and lower arm mating marks aligned.
6. Replace the lower arm on the ball joint if the standard ball joint installation pressure is obtained.

Lower Control Arm

Removal and Installation

1. After disconnecting the stabilizer ring from the lower arm, remove strut assembly.
2. Disconnect the steering knuckle arm and the tie rod ball joint.
3. Using the knuckle arm puller, disconnect the knuckle arm and the lower arm ball joint.
4. Remove the bolts holding the lower arm to the sub frame, and remove the

Exploded view of the front suspension strut.

1. Knuckle arm
2. Knuckle
3. Strut sub-assembly (shock absorber)
4. Front suspension spring
5. Rubber bumper
6. Dust cover plate
7. Dust cover
8. Upper spring seat
9. Ball bearing
10. Insulator
11. Dust cover

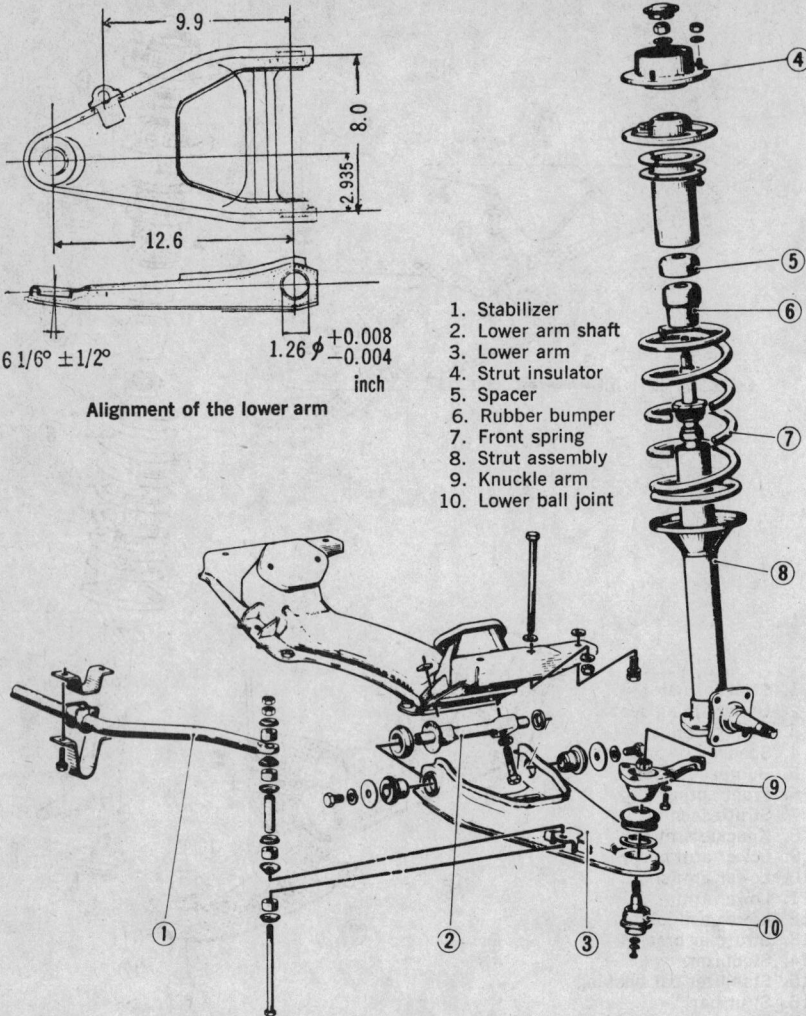

Alignment of the lower arm

1. Stabilizer
2. Lower arm shaft
3. Lower arm
4. Strut insulator
5. Spacer
6. Rubber bumper
7. Front spring
8. Strut assembly
9. Knuckle arm
10. Lower ball joint

Colt front suspension

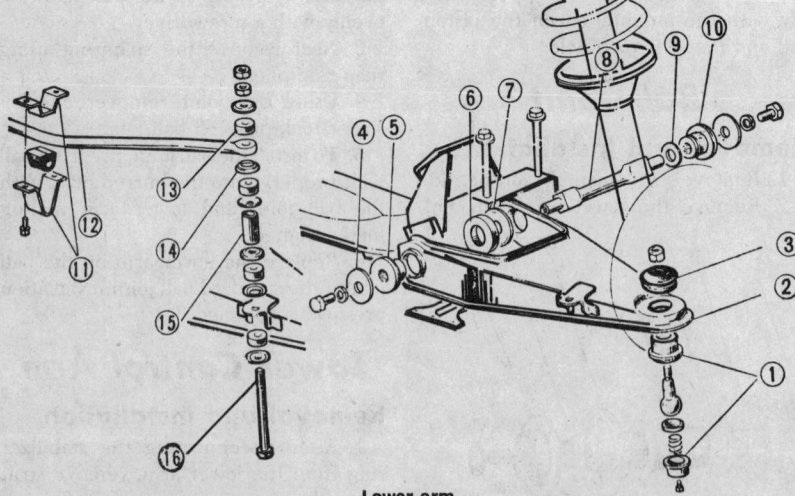

Lower arm

1. Joint assembly
2. Lower arm
3. Joint cover
4. Washer
5. Bushing (front)
6. Stopper rubber
7. Stopper washer
8. Lower arm shaft
9. Spacer
10. Bushing (rear)
11. Stabilizer fixture
12. Stabilizer
13. Rubber bushing
14. Seat
15. Collar
16. Stabilizer bolt

lower arm assembly.

Installation is the reverse of removal.

Front End Alignment

Caster and Camber

Caster and camber are preset at the factory. They require adjustment only if the suspension and steering linkage components are damaged, in which case, repair is accomplished by replacing the damaged part.

Toe-In

Toe-in is the difference in the distance between the front wheels, as measured at both the front and the rear of the front tires.

Toe-In is equal to the difference between the front and rear measurements. This difference should be between 5/64 in. and 15/64 in.

Toe-In is adjusted by turning the tie rod turnbuckle in or out as necessary. Left side toe-in may be reduced by turning the tie-rod turnbuckle toward the front of the car, and right side toe-in by turning the turnbuckles toward the rear of the car. The turnbuckles should always be tightened or loosened the same amount for both tie rods; the difference in length between the two tie-rods should not exceed 0.2 in.

STEERING

Steering Wheel

Removal and Installation

1. Pry off the steering wheel center foam pad.

2. Remove the steering wheel retaining nut.

3. Using a steering wheel puller, remove the wheel.

4. Be sure the front wheels are in a straight ahead position. Reverse the removal procedure.

Steering Gear

Removal and Installation

1. Remove the upper and lower control rods.

2. Disconnect the gear box main shaft. Pull out the steering shaft.

3. Disconnect, but do not remove, the pitman arm and relay rod.

4. Installation is the reverse of removal. Adjust the end clearance of the upper control rod.

Adjustments

Steering gear adjustments are not required during normal vehicle operation. Adjustments are made only as a part of gear box overhaul.

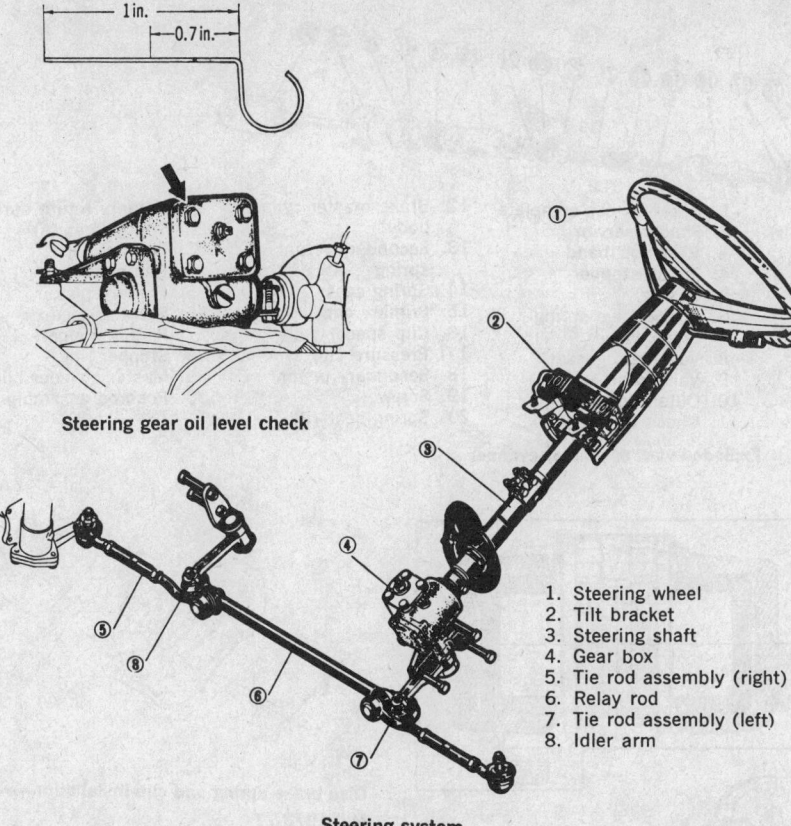

Steering gear oil level check

1. Steering wheel
2. Tilt bracket
3. Steering shaft
4. Gear box
5. Tie rod assembly (right)
6. Relay rod
7. Tie rod assembly (left)
8. Idler arm

Steering system

Turn Signal Switch

Removal and Installation

1. Remove the steering wheel.
2. Remove the instrument cluster.
3. Remove the top and bottom steering column covers.
4. Disconnect each column switch connector and then remove the column switch.
5. Remove the turn signal and flasher switch contact points.
6. Switch installation is the reverse of the removal procedure. Be sure that the switch is centered in the column or the self-cancelling will be affected.

Ignition Lock and Switch

Removal and Installation

1. Cut a notch in the lock bracket bolt head with a hacksaw.
2. Remove the bolt and lock.
3. Remove the column cover and unbolt and remove the ignition switch.
4. Install both lock and switch in reverse of removal.
NOTE: *when installing lock, the bolt should be tightened until the head is crushed. When installing switch, install the switch bolt loosely and insert and work the key a few times to make sure everything checks out before tightening the bolt.*

BRAKE SYSTEMS

Adjustment

The front disc brakes require no periodic adjustment. Rear drum brakes are adjusted as follows.
1. Make sure that the hand brakes are fully released.
2. The square-lugged adjuster is located on the rear of the backing plate. Turn the adjuster as far as it will go clockwise.
3. Back the adjuster off slightly until, while turning the wheel, you feel no drag. Maximum brake shoe-to-drum clearance should be less than 0.012 in. Each 90° turn of the adjuster decreases clearance by 0.006 in.

Master Cylinder

Removal and Installation

1. Remove all lines connected to the master cylinder. Slowly depress the brake pedal to remove the fluid.
2. Remove the clevis pin from between the master cylinder push rod and the pedal.
3. Remove the master cylinder from the firewall and thoroughly clean it.
4. Installation is the reverse of removal. Bleed the brakes.

Overhaul

Refer to the exploded view. Do not disassemble the primary piston.

Combination Valve

The combination valve has three functions:
    a. rear brake pressure control
    b. warning light control
    c. differential failure control

Removal and Installation

NOTE: *the valve should not be disassembled. If it is faulty, replace it.*
1. Disconnect and plug brake lines at the valve.
2. Remove the valve.
3. Install the valve and tighten the attaching bolts to 6–9 ftlb. Tighten the brake tube nuts to 9–12 ftlb.

System Bleeding

1. Check the mater cylinder fluid level.
2. Remove the cap from the bleeder screw of the wheel farthest from the master cylinder.
3. Connect a length of rubber tubing to the screw and place the other end in a jar half full of clean brake fluid.
4. Pump the brake pedal until no bubble are visible in the container.
5. Hold the pedal in the depressed position and tighten the screw. Replace the cap and proceed to each wheel in turn.
NOTE: *periodically check the master cylinder during the bleeding operation to check the fluid level does not go too low. If it does, air will enter the master cylinder and it will have to be bled as well.*

Front Disc Brakes

Brake Pad

Removal and Installation— 1972–Mid–1973

1. Pry the cross-spring from the pads. Pull out the retaining clips and remove the pins.
2. Using a pair of locking pliers, pull the one pad out of the caliper.
3. Siphon off about ½ of the brake fluid in the reservoir.
4. Push the caliper piston back.
5. Insert the new pad along with its shim (arrow on shim pointing forward).
NOTE: *On early 1972 Colt's, replace the shims with the newer square type to cure brake squeaking.*
6. Remove the opposite pad and repeat Steps 4 and 5.
7. Install the retaining pins and clips.
8. Install cross-spring.

Removal and Installation— Mid–1973–77

1. Remove the wheel.

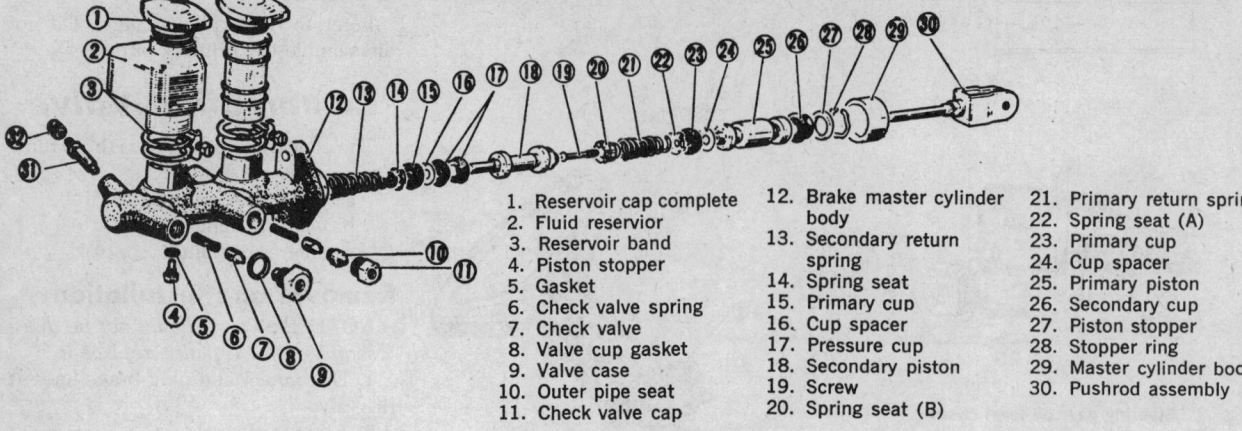

1. Reservoir cap complete
2. Fluid reservoir
3. Reservoir band
4. Piston stopper
5. Gasket
6. Check valve spring
7. Check valve
8. Valve cup gasket
9. Valve case
10. Outer pipe seat
11. Check valve cap
12. Brake master cylinder body
13. Secondary return spring
14. Spring seat
15. Primary cup
16. Cup spacer
17. Pressure cup
18. Secondary piston
19. Screw
20. Spring seat (B)
21. Primary return spring
22. Spring seat (A)
23. Primary cup
24. Cup spacer
25. Primary piston
26. Secondary cup
27. Piston stopper
28. Stopper ring
29. Master cylinder boots
30. Pushrod assembly

Exploded view of master cylinder

1. Pin retaining clip
2. Pad retaining pin
3. Connector bolt
4. Gasket
5. Connector
6. Gasket
7. Caliper seal
8. Bleeder cap
9. Bleeder screw
10. Cross-spring
11. Pad shim
12. Retaining ring
13. Dust seal
14. Front brake piston
15. Piston seal
16. Caliper (outer)
17. Caliper (inner)
18. Pad assembly

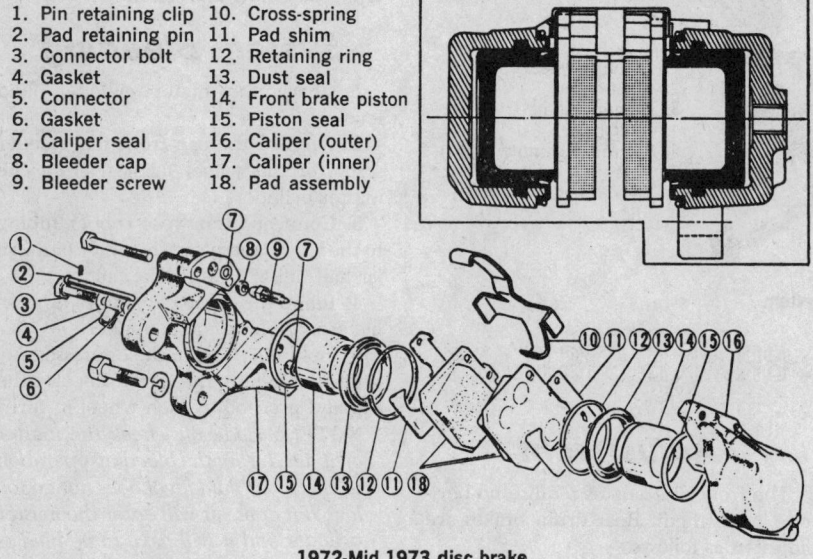

1972-Mid 1973 disc brake

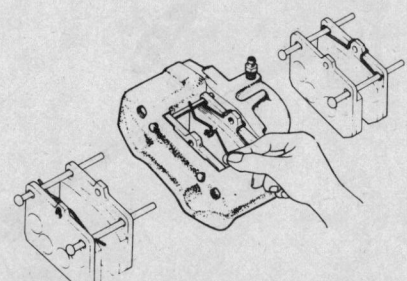

Disc brake spring and clip installation— Mid 1973-77

8. Install the pad protector in proper direction, as shown.

9. Check brake dragging torque. Drive the car for about 330 ft. Apply the parking brakes and then check the dragging torque with a force of less than 13 lbs at a wheel bolt. If the standard value (39 in. lbs or less) is exceeded, disassemble the piston sliding part and check for dirtiness and rust and the piston seal for elasticity.

2. Remove the protector.

3. Holding the center of the clip detach it from the pad and its ends from the retaining pins. Remove the clip.

4. Pull the retaining pins from the caliper assembly. Remove the spring.

5. Remove the pad by holding the backing plate area of the pad with pliers.

6. To replace the brake pad, spread the piston and insert the pad through the shim.

7. Install the spring and clip. In this case, do not confuse their positions.

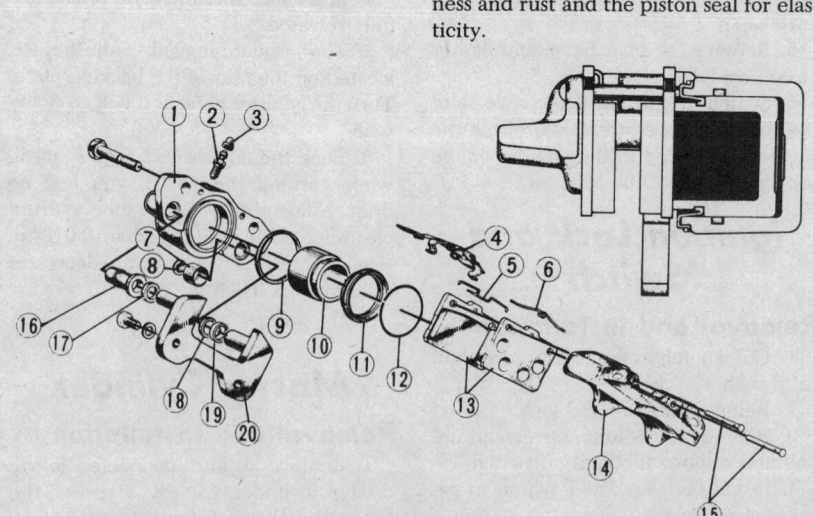

Mid 1973-77 disc brake

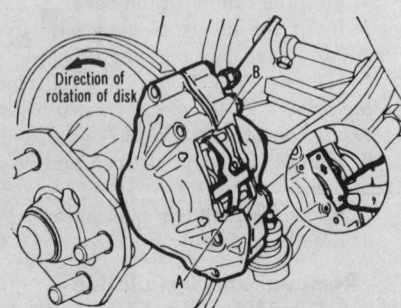

Cross-spring and shim installation

1. Inner caliper
2. Bleeder screw
3. Bleeder screw cap
4. Pad protector
5. Spring
6. Clip
7. Torque plate pin cap
8. Cap plug
9. Piston seal
10. Piston
11. Dust seal
12. Retaining ring
13. Pad assembly
14. Outer caliper
15. Pad retaining pin
16. Torque plate pin bushing
17. Spacer
18. Wiper seal retainer
19. Wiper seal
20. Torque plate

CAUTION: *When the pad has been replaced, the brake is likely to drag before the initial run-in is made, but they may be considered servicable if the dragging torque is within the specified limit.*

Brake Caliper

Removal and Installation— 1972–Mid–1973

1. Remove the wheel.
2. Disconnect the brake line. Remove the union bolt of the flexible hose.
3. Remove the cross-spring. Remove the clips and the retaining pins.
4. Remove both brake pads and shims. Mark them left and right, if they are being reused.
5. Unscrew the two retaining bolts from the bracket behind the disc and remove the caliper.
6. Installation is the reverse of removal. Bleed the brakes.

Removal and Installation— Mid–1973–77

1. Remove the disc brake pad.
2. Remove the brake hose clip from the strut area, then disconnect the brake hose from the caliper.
3. Remove the caliper assembly by loosening torque plate and adapter mounting bolts.
4. Installation is the reverse of removal. If the brake pedal stroke is excessively long, remove the brake pad and replace it with a piece of metal about the same size. Press the piston into the caliper about ⅛ in. Reinstall the brake pad and pump the pedal several times. Repeat until the pedal stroke is normal.

Overhaul—1972–Mid–1973

1. Remove the caliper. Remove the retaining ring and seal the outer piston.
2. While holding the piston with a piece of hardwood, apply air pressure through the brake line fitting and force the outer piston from the caliper.
3. Remove the inner piston by inserting a drift through the union bolt opening and tapping it out.
4. Remove the piston seals.
5. Assembly is the reverse of disassembly.

Overhaul—Mid–1973–1977

1. Remove the caliper.
2. Separate the two caliper halves.
3. Remove the dust seal, and piston by applying compressed air to the hose fitting.
4. Carefully remove the piston seal.
5. Reassemble the caliper.

Apply brake fluid to the piston before assembly. Insert the piston seal into the piston so that the seal isn't twisted.

Whenever the torque plate has been removed from the inner caliper half, it is necessary to clean the torque plate shaft and the shaft bore of the caliper and apply brake assembly grease to the rubber bushing, wiper seal inner surface, and torque plate shaft before assembly.

Brake Disc and Wheel Bearing

Removal and Installation

1. Remove the caliper.
2. Pry off the dust cap. Tap out and discard the cotter pin. Remove the locknut.
3. Remove the brake disc and wheel hub.
4. Using a brass drift, carefully drive the outer bearing race out of the hub.
5. Remove the inner bearing seal and bearing.
6. Check the bearings for wear or damage and replace them if necessary. Drift the bearing race into place in the hub.
7. Pack the inner and outer wheel bearings with grease.
8. Install the inner bearing in the hub. Drive the seal on until its outer edge is even with the edge of the hub.
9. Install the hub/disc assembly on the spindle, being careful not to damage the oil seal.
10. Install the outer bearing, washer, and spindle nut. Adjust the bearing as follows.

Adjustment

1. Tighten the spindle nut to 15 ft lbs and then loosen it.
2. Tighten the nut to 4 ft lbs.
3. Install the cap on the nut. Do not back off the nut more than 15° for cotter pin hole-to-slot alignment.

Rear Drum Brakes

Brake Shoe and Wheel Cylinder

Removal and Installation

1. Remove the wheel, brake drum, and hold-down spring.

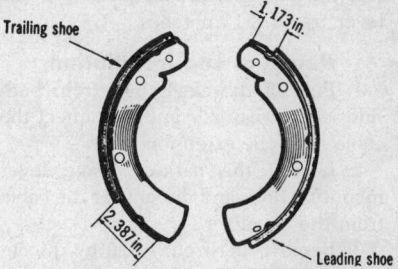

Brake lining installed position

2. Disassemble the shoe return spring.
3. Remove the clevis pin from between the extension lever and the parking brake cable. Remove the adjusting assembly.
4. Remove the brake lines from the wheel.
5. Remove the wheel cylinder from the backing plate.
6. Installation is the reverse of removal. Adjust the brakes.

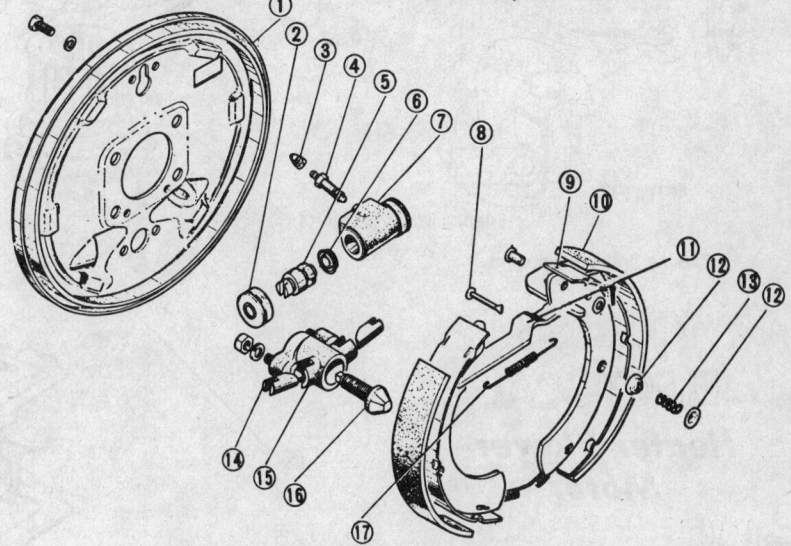

Exploded view of the rear brakes

1. Backing plate	11. Parking brake extension lever
2. Wheel cylinder boot	12. Shoe hold-down spring seat
3. Bleeder screw cap	13. Shoe hold-down spring
4. Bleeder screw	14. Slack adjuster anchor
5. Wheel cylinder piston	15. Slack adjuster body
6. Piston cup	16. Slack adjuster
7. Wheel cylinder body	17. Shoe return spring
8. Shoe hold-down spring pin	
9. Brake shoe assembly	
10. Brake lining	

Parking Brake

Cable

Adjustment

1. Release the brake cable.
2. Loosen the adjusting nuts on either side of the cable.
3. Move the cable lever to each side and tighten the nuts to the tension.
4. Cable tightening should provide back plate and extension lever clearance of *less* than 0.04 in.
5. Be certain the drum does not contact the lining. Standard parking brake lever travel is 10 notches.

Removal and Installation

1. Pull off the clevis pins from both sides of the rear axle and disconnect the cable from the extension lever.
2. Loosen the parking brake lever mounting bolts and disconnect the cable from the equalizer.
3. Remove the front cable by disconnecting it from the lever.
4. Install in reverse of the above. Apply multipurpose grease to all sliding parts. After installation, release the brake and adjust the extension lever-to-backing plate clearance to 0–0.04" by turning the nut on the cable. Parking brake lever should be in the fully applied position at the 4th to 6th notch. If not, replace the cable.

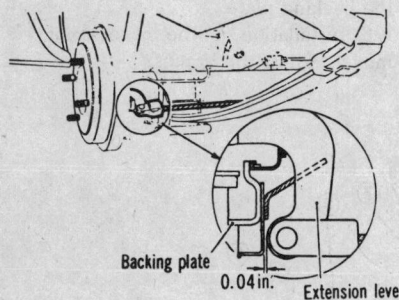

Parking brake adjustment

Backing plate 0.04 in. Extension lever

CHASSIS ELECTRICAL

Heater Blower Motor

Colt

Removal and Installation

The heater is located directly under the center of the dashboard.

1. Unplug the two electrical leads from the motor.
2. Remove the three retaining screws and remove the motor.
3. Install the motor in the reverse order of removal.

Exploded view of parking brake linkage

1. Parking brake lever cover
2. Parking brake lever assembly
3. Parking brake cable
4. Clip
5. Bolt
6. Clip
7. Bushing
8. Clevis pin

Heater Unit

NOTE: *This procedure doesn't apply to air conditioned cars. The heater core is contained within the heater unit and is not serviced separately.*

Removal and Installation

1971–73

1. Drain the coolant.
2. Loosen the retaining screws at the bottom of the radio which are tightened together with the center cover.
3. Remove the top center padding.
4. Remove the heater control knobs.
5. Remove the retaining screws at the bottom of the console cover which are

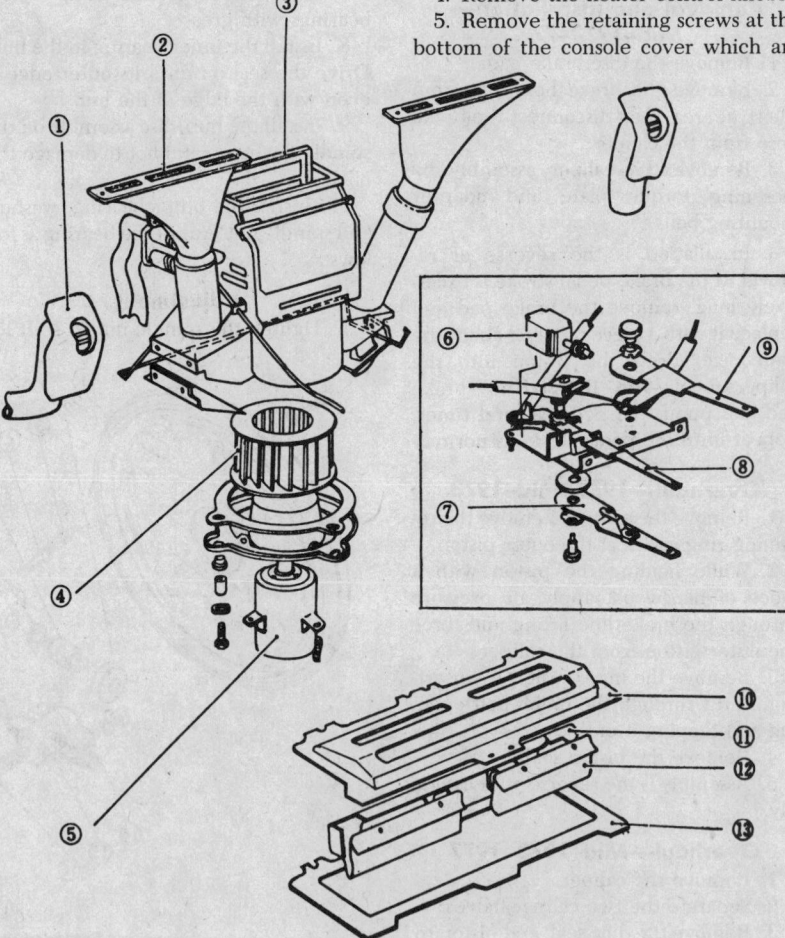

Exploded view of the heater

1. Ventilator duct assembly
2. Defroster nozzle
3. Heater assembly
4. Turbo fan
5. Motor
6. Fan motor switch
7. Air control level
8. Heater-defroster changeover and fan motor switch lever
9. Temperature control lever
10. Upper panel
11. Plate
12. Non-return valve
13. Lower panel

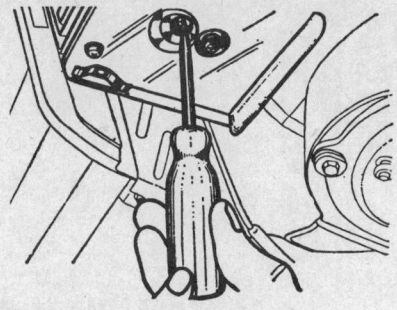

Adjusting heater control position

tightened together with the ashtray.

6. Slide the console and radio out.

7. Disconnect the radio wiring and remove the console.

8. Remove the two heater control wires at the heater.

9. Remove the heater control assembly.

10. Disconnect the two water hoses. Disconnect the two ducts at the heater.

11. Remove the heater unit.

12. Install the heater in the reverse order of removal.

1974–77

1. Drain the radiator.

2. Remove the glovebox, instrument cluster, and console compartment (if so equipped).

3. Disconnect each heater control wire at the heater unit.

4. Remove the heater control assembly.

5. Disconnect the heater hoses and ducts.

Arrow

Removal and Installation

1. Remove the air intake control knob, the ash tray and heater control knobs and the radio knobs and retaining nuts.

2. Remove the three upper screws and a lower screw, a screw located behind the blind cover above the air intake control panel, and the three screws behind and in the upper inside part of the ash tray.

3. Pull the ash tray out a little and disconnect the heater, meter and speedometer connectors.

4. Remove the ground cable which is attached to the body by a screw and remove the cluster.

5. To install reverse the removal procedure.

Windshield Wipers

Motor and Linkage

Removal and Installation

1. Remove wiper arm. Remove arm shaft locknut and push in the shaft.

NOTE: On 1974–77 models, before proceeding with removal work, uncover the wiper removing hole located on the left side of the front deck.

2. Remove the bolts that hold the motor bracket to the body, and pull out the wiper motor assembly.

3. Remove the nut at the top of the wiper arm on the drivers seat side and take off the wiper arm together with the blade. Loosen the wiper arm shaft locknut and pull out the wiper motor assembly.

4. Disconnect the motor crank arm and linkage. The bushing can be easily removed by pushing by hand with the arm and linkage held parallely.

NOTE: The crank arm and motor have been installed so that the wiper blades will stop at a prescribed automatic angle, and shouldn't be removed unless specially required.

5. Installation is the reverse of removal.

Radio

Colt

Removal and Installation—1972–73

1. Remove the fastenings and extract the padding from on top of the radio.

2. Remove all radio switches. In addition, remove all heater control levers and knobs. Remove the wing nut on the radio right-hand side.

3. Remove the screws at the bottom of the ash tray and console cover.

4. Pull the radio slightly forward. Disconnect all wiring and lift out.

5. To replace the radio, reverse the removal procedure.

Removal and Installation—1974–77

1. Remove glove box then loosen the knobs and attaching nuts on the front of the radio.

2. Remove speaker, antenna, and power wires from the back of the radio. Remove the radio attaching bracket and take out the radio.

3. Installation is the reverse of removal.

Arrow

Removal and Installation

1. Remove the instrument cluster.

2. Remove the radio knobs from the radio panel.

3. Remove the nuts from behind the knobs, the screw from the bracket and remove the radio (AM radio). Remove the bolts from under the brackets and remove the radio (AM/FM radio).

NOTE: The AM radio circuit fuse block is located on the right rear side of the radio, the AM/FM circuit fuse block is installed in the line with the power cable.

Instrument Cluster

Colt

Removal and Installation

1. Loosen screws at the upper and lower part of the instrument cluster. Loosen the screws holding the heater control knobs, ash tray, and cigarette lighter (1974–77 only) from their respective brackets. Remove blind cover (1974–77) on the right side of the glove box and remove the attaching screws on the right side of the cluster.

2. Remove the harness cover at the bottom of the instrument panel and disconnect lighting switch and the instrument panel harness.

3. Pull the instrument panel cluster a little toward you, disconnect multiple connector, antenna feeder, speaker connector, heater fan connector (1974–77) and meter cables and then remove instrument cluster assembly.

4. Installation is the reverse of removal.

After the instrument cluster has been installed, draw out the meter cables as long as the marking tape can be seen from the engine compartment.

Arrow

Removal and Installation

1. Remove the air intake control knob, the ash tray and heater control knobs and the radio knobs and retaining nuts.

2. Remove the three upper screws and a lower screw, a screw located behind the blind cover above the air intake control panel, and the three screws behind and in the upper inside part of the ash tray.

3. Pull the ash tray out a little and disconnect the heater, meter and speedometer connectors.

4. Remove the ground cable which is attached to the body by a screw and remove the cluster.

5. To install reverse the removal procedure.

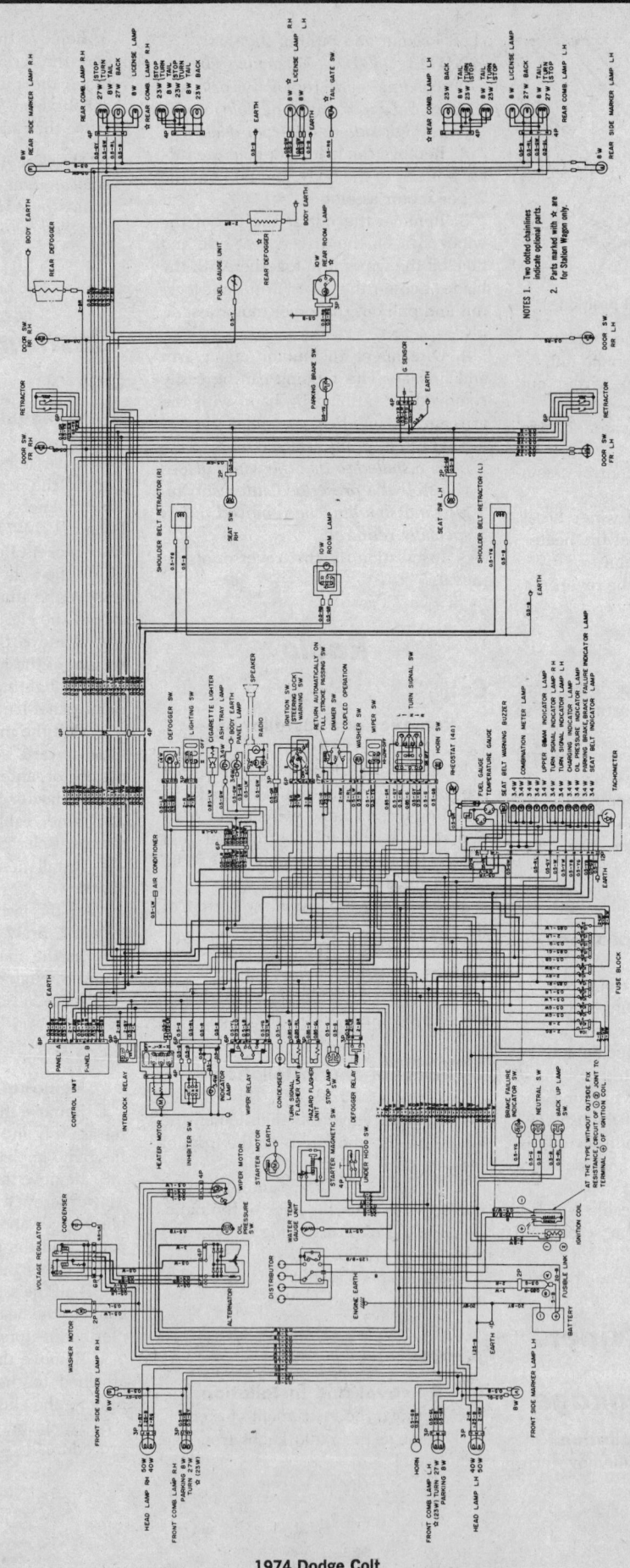

1974 Dodge Colt

1975 Dodge Colt

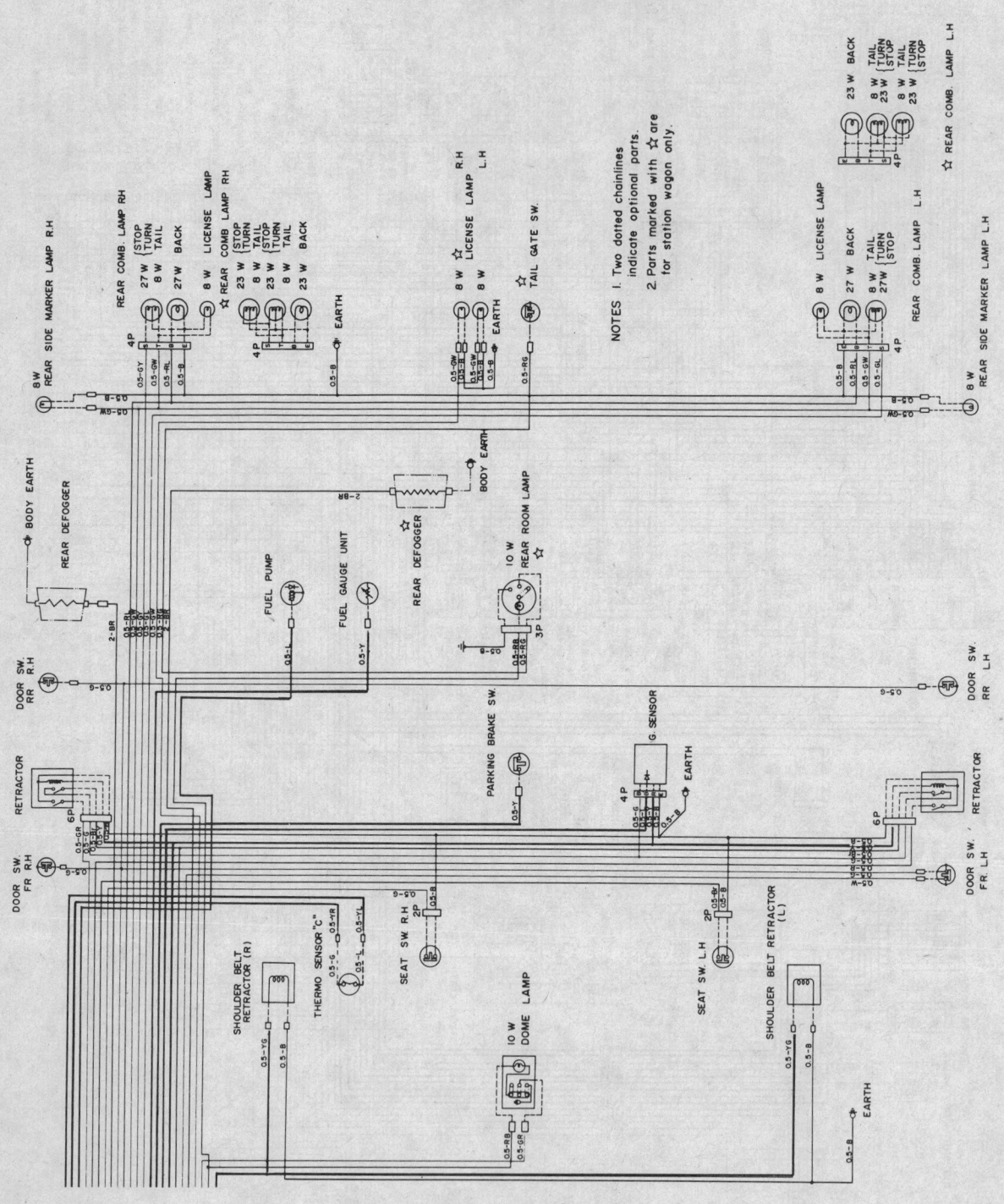

1975 Dodge Colt

1976 Dodge Colt

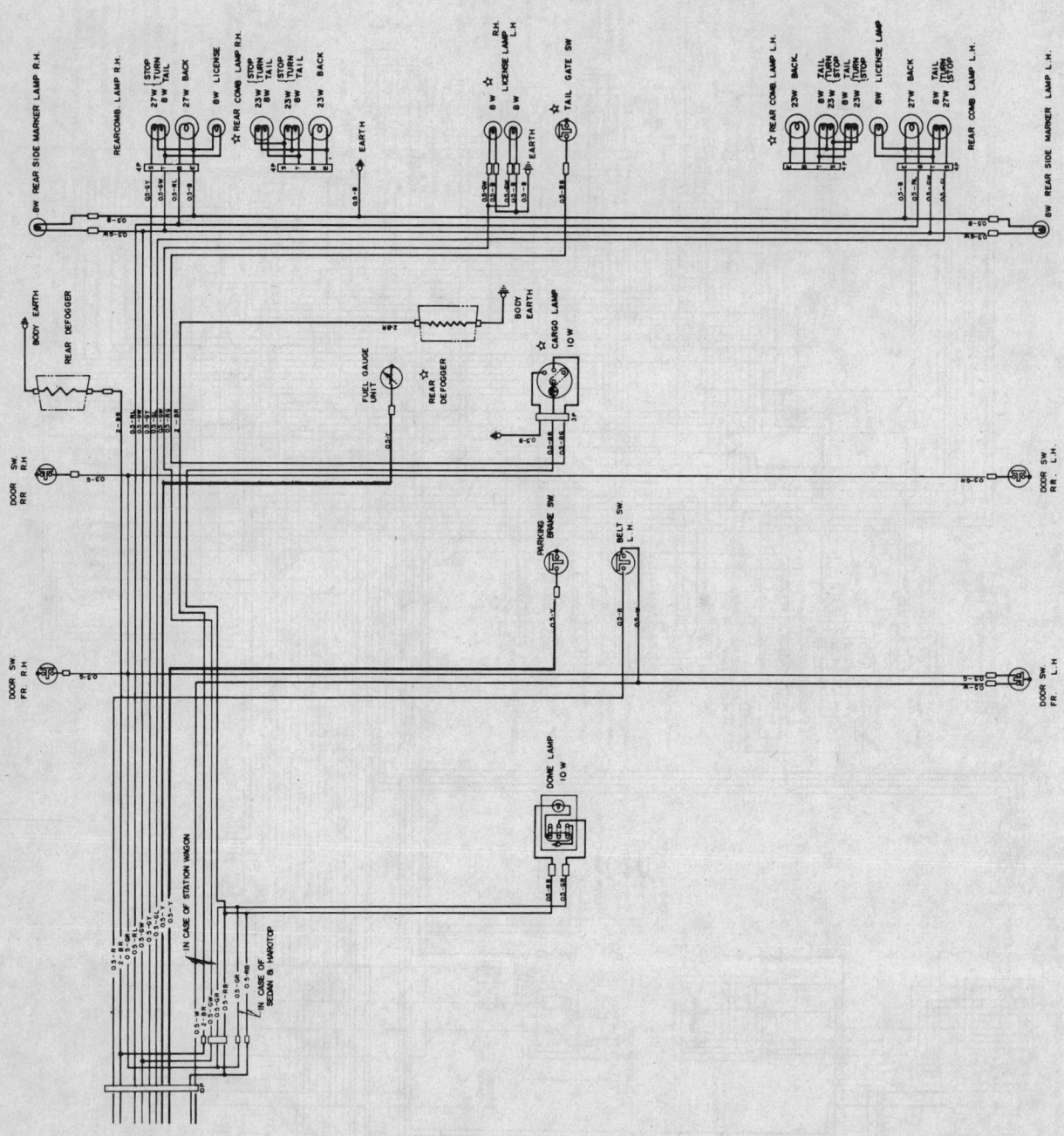

1976 Dodge Colt

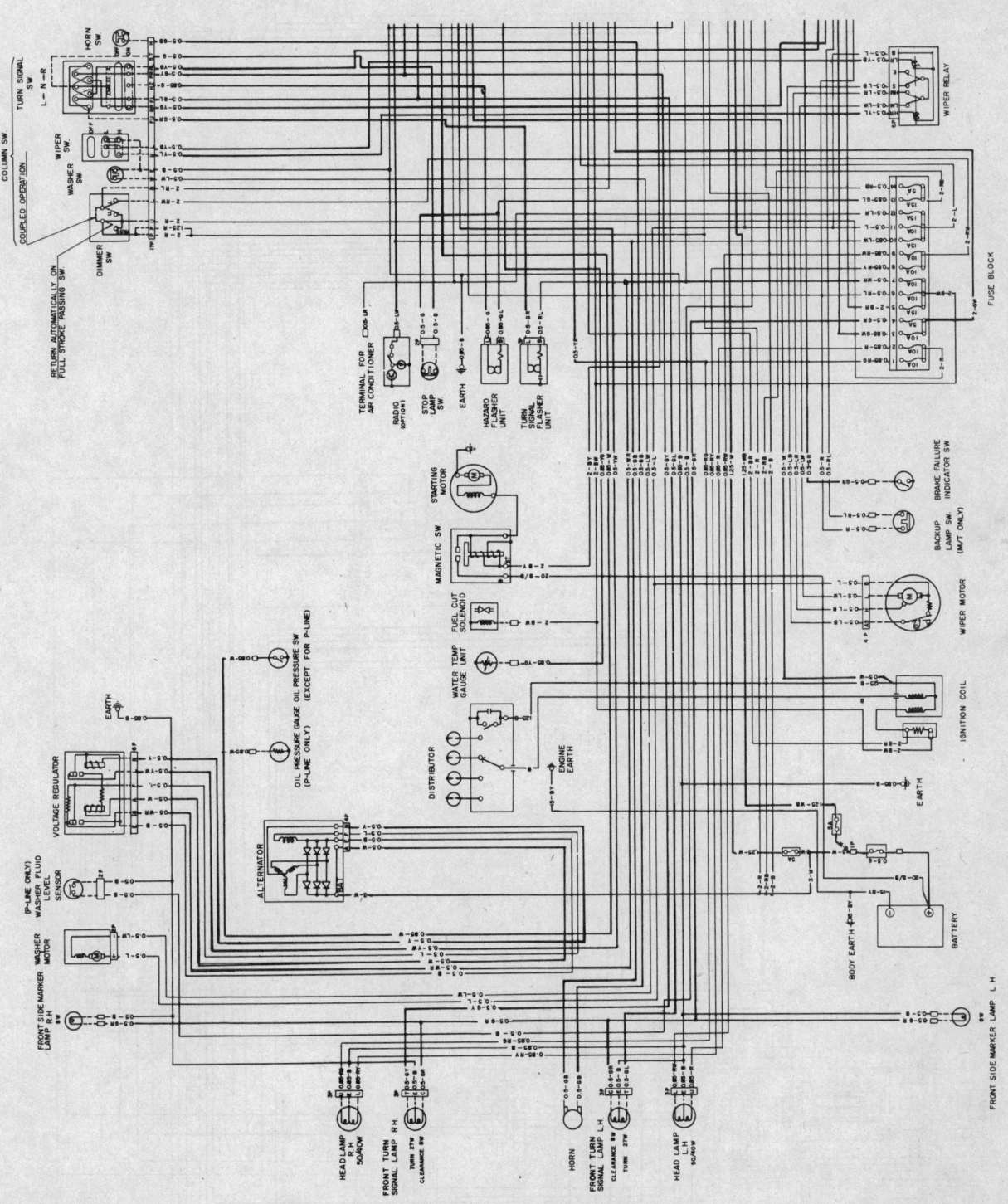

1976 Plymouth Arrow

1976 Plymouth Arrow

SPECIFICATIONS

INTRODUCTION

The Courier was introduced by Ford in 1972 to compete with the already well established Toyotas and Datsuns. The Courier along with others of its ilk, fills the need for a vehicle between the family car and an all-out truck. The small wheelbase and stiff suspension to accomodate the substantial payload capacity all blend together to form a pleasant compromise.

Very similar, both in appearance and performance to its four counterparts, the Courier sports one of the few automatic transmissions in trucks of this type and also has one of the higher GVWs, rated at 3,935 lbs. It also comes equipped with a skid plate under the oil pan, a worthwhile feature for off-roaders.

Power for the Courier is supplied by a SOHC engine of 1796 cc providing sufficient on or off-road performance with excellent gas mileage. A 4-speed manual, fully synchronized transmission is standard with the 3-speed automatic and 5-speed manual optional. Drum brakes front and rear provide stopping power.

SERIAL NUMBER IDENTIFICATION

Vehicle

The vehicle identification information is stamped on the model plate riveted to the body at the right rear corner of the engine compartment. This plate contains the truck model code and year, the engine model codes, the cylinder displacement of the engine, the chassis number (which is the same as the vehicle and warranty identification number) and the name of the manufacturer.

Vehicle Safety Certification Label

The Vehicle Safety Certification Label is attached to the left door lock pillar and contains the following information:

GVWR—Gross Vehicle Weight Rating, which is the maximum loaded weight at which the vehicle can be operated;

GAWR—Gross Axle Weight Rating, which is the maximum loaded weight of each axle measured at the ground. However, if one axle is loaded to its maximum, the weight on both axles cannot exceed the vehicle's weight at the ground;

This label also contains the name of the manufacturer, the month and year of manufacture and the statement of certification;

The VIN (Vehicle Identification Number) is also located on the certification label and is used for warranty identification.

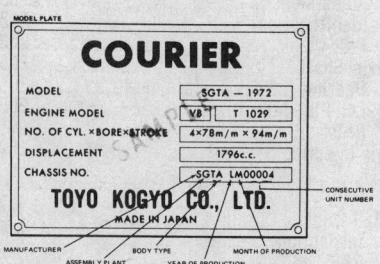

Vehicle certification label and model plate

TUNE-UP SPECIFICATIONS

When analyzing compression results, look for uniformity among cylinders, rather than specific pressures.

Year	Engine Cu in. Displacement (cc)	Spark Plugs Type	Spark Plugs Gap (in.)	Distributor Point Dwell (deg)	Distributor Point Gap (in)	Ignition Timing (deg) MT	Ignition Timing (deg) AT	Intake Valve Opens (deg)	Fuel Pump Pressure (psi)	Idle Speed (rpm) MT	Idle Speed (rpm) AT	Valve Clearance (in.) In ▲	Valve Clearance (in.) Ex ▲
1972	109.6 (1796) Federal	AG32A	0.029-0.033	49-55	0.018-0.022	5B	—	13B	2.8-3.6	①	—	0.012	0.012
1972	109.6 (1796) California	AG32A	0.029-0.033	49-55	0.018-0.022	5B	—	26B	2.8-3.6	①	—	0.014	0.016
1973	109.6 (1796) All	AG32A	0.029-0.033	49-55	0.018-0.022	5B	—	26B	2.8-3.6	①	—	0.012	0.013
1974	109.6 (1796) All	AG32A	0.029-0.033	49-55	0.018-0.022	3B	3B	13B	2.8-3.6	①	—	0.012	0.012
1975-76	109.6 (1796) All	①	①	①	①	①	①	13B	2.8-3.6			0.012	0.012

Federal—49 states (except California)
California—California only
— Not applicable
① See emission control decal under the engine hood.
▲ Measured at the valve (hot)

NOTE: The underhood specifications sticker often reflects tune-up specification changes made in production. Sticker figures must be used if they disagree with those in this chart.

GENERAL ENGINE SPECIFICATIONS

Year	Engine Displacement cu in. (cc)	Carb Type	Advertised Horsepower (@ rpm)	Advertised Torque @ rpm (ft lbs)	Bore and Stroke (in.)	Advertised Compression Ratio	Oil Pressure (@ rpm)
1972-1976	109.6 (1796)	One Zenith Stromberg 2-bbl	74 @ 5000 ①	92 @ 3500 ②	3.07 x 3.70	8.6:1	50-64 @ 3000

① 1976-77: 67 @ 5000
② 1976-77: 88 @ 3000

FIRING ORDER

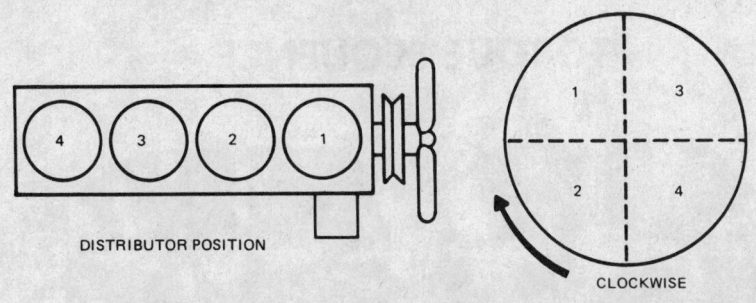

DISTRIBUTOR POSITION

CLOCKWISE

FIRING — 1-3-4-2

All Models

CAPACITIES

Year	Model	Engine Displacement Cu in. (cc)	Engine Crankcase (qts) With Filter	Engine Crankcase (qts) Without Filter	Transmission (pts) Manual 4-spd	Transmission (pts) Manual 5-spd	Transmission (pts) Automatic	Drive Axle (pts)	Gasoline Tank (gals)	Cooling System (qts) w/heater
1972	All	109.6 (1796)	4	3	3	—	—	3.2	11.7	7.5
1973-76	All	109.6 (1796)	5	4	3	4.5	6.6	3.2	11.7	7.5

① Available on 1974-75 models only

PISTON AND RING SPECIFICATIONS
All measurements in inches

Year	Engine Displacement cu. in. (cc)	Piston Clearance	RING GAP Top Compression	RING GAP Bottom Compression	RING GAP Oil Control	RING SIDE CLEARANCE Top Compression	RING SIDE CLEARANCE Bottom Compression	RING SIDE CLEARANCE Oil Control
1972-76	109.6 (1800)	0.0022-0.0028	0.008-0.016	0.008-0.016	0.008-0.016	0.0014-0.0028	0.0012-0.0026	0.0012-0.0025

TORQUE SPECIFICATIONS
(All readings in ft lbs unless noted)

Year	Engine Displacement cu in. (cc)	Cylinder Head Bolts	Rod Bearing Bolts	Main Bearing Bolts	Camshaft sprocket -to-Cam	Flywheel-to-crankshaft Bolts	Manifolds Intake	Manifolds Exhaust
1972	109.6 (1796)	①	30	60	55	115	20	20
1973	109.6 (1796)	①	30	60-65	50-58	115	20	20
1974	109.6 (1796)	①	29-33	60-65	50-64	115	20	20
1975	109.6 (1796)	①	29-33	60-65	50-64	115	20	20
1976-77	109.6 (1796)	①	29-33	60-65	50-64	115	16	18

① 60-65 ft lbs (cold); 70 ft lbs (normal operating temperature)

NOTE: The following chart gives torque limits for various size bolts; if the torques listed above conflict with those listed below, use the torques above.

6 mm—6 ft lbs
8 mm—15 ft lbs
10 mm—30 ft lbs

12 mm—50 ft lbs
14 mm—65 ft lbs

TORQUE SEQUENCE

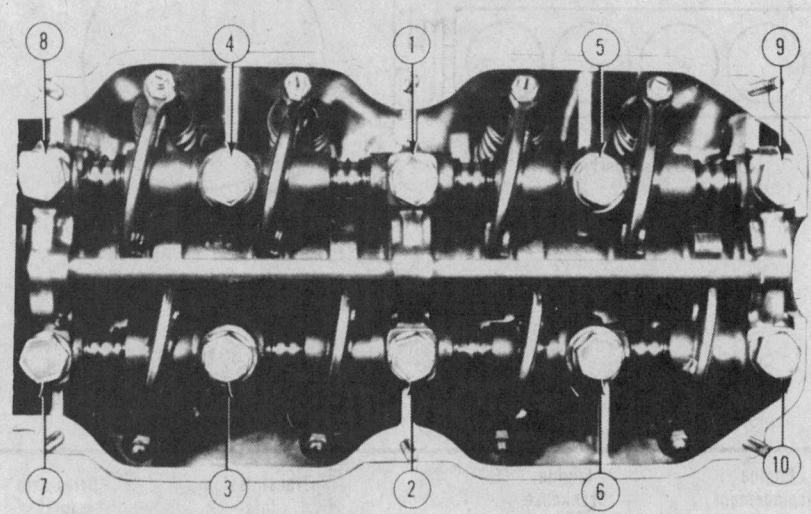

Cylinder head-all models

CRANKSHAFT AND CONNECTING ROD SPECIFICATIONS
(All measurements given in in.)

Year	Engine Displacement cu in. (cc)	Crankshaft Main Brg Journal Dia	Crankshaft Main Brg Oil Clearance	Crankshaft Shaft End Play	Crankshaft Thrust on No.	Connecting Rod Journal Dia	Connecting Rod Oil Clearance	Connecting Rod Side Clearance
1972	109.6 (1796)	2.4784-2.4804	0.0005-0.0015 ①	0.003-0.012	4	2.0842-2.0866	0.001-0.011 ②	0.004-0.008 ③
1973	109.6 (1796)	2.4746-2.4780	0.0005-0.0015 ①	0.003-0.012	4	2.0842-2.0866	0.001-0.011 ②	0.004-0.008 ③
1974	109.6 (1796)	2.4779-2.4785	0.0005-0.0015 ①	0.003-0.012	4	2.0842-2.0848	0.001-0.011 ②	0.004-0.008 ③
1975-76	109.6 (1796)	2.4779-2.4785	0.0005-0.0015 ①	0.003-0.012	4	2.0842-2.0848	0.001-0.011 ②	0.004-0.008 ③

① Wear limit: 0.0012-0.0024 in.   ② Wear limit: 0.0008-0.003 in.   ③ Wear limit: 0.014 in.

VALVE SPECIFICATIONS

Year	Engine Displacement cu in. (cc)	Seat Angle (deg)	Face Angle (deg)	Spring Test Pressure (lbs @ in.)	Stem to Guide Clearance (in.)		Stem Diameter (in.)	
					Intake	Exhaust	Intake	Exhaust
1972	109.6 (1796)	45	45	31½ @ 1-¹¹⁄₃₂ ③	0.0007-0.0023 ①	0.0007-0.0023 ①	0.3150-0.3168	0.3150-0.3168
1973	109.6 (1796)	45	45	31½ @ 1-¹¹⁄₃₂ ③	0.0007-0.0021 ①	0.0007-0.0021 ①	0.3161-0.3167	0.3159-0.3161
1974	109.6 (1796)	45	45	26.8 @ 1.36 ②	0.0007-0.0021 ①	0.0007-0.0023 ①	0.3161-0.3167	0.3159-0.3167
1975-76	109.6 (1796)	45	45	26.8 @ 1.36 ②	0.0007-0.0021 ①	0.0007-0.0023 ①	0.3161-0.3167	0.3159-0.3167

N.A. Not Available
① Wear limit: 0.008 in.
② Inner: 16.3 @ 1.25
③ Inner: 20.9 @ 1.25

BATTERY AND STARTER SPECIFICATIONS

All cars use 12 volt, negative ground electrical systems

Year	Model	Battery Amp Hour Capacity	Starter Lock Test Amps	Volts	Torque (ft/lbs)	No Load Test Amps	Volts	RPM	Brush Spring Tension (oz.)	Min. Brush Length (in.)
1972-76	All	60①	—Not Recommended—			50 (or less)	11	5000 (or more)	38	0.16②

① 70 amp/hr battery optional
② New length—0.55 in.

BRAKE SPECIFICATIONS

All measurements given are (in.) unless noted

Year	Model	Lug Nut Torque (ft/lb)	Master Cylinder Bore	Brake Disc Minimum Thickness	Maximum Run-Out	Brake Drum Diameter	Max. Machine O/S	Max. Wear Limit	Minimum Lining Thickness Front	Rear
1972-76	All	55-65	0.750	—	—	10.236	10.296	10.30	0.039①	0.039①

① or within ¹⁄₃₂ in. of the shoe. New lining thickness is 0.217 in.
— Not Applicable
NOTE: Minimum lining thickness is as recommended by the manufacturer. Due to variations in state inspection regulations, the minimum allowable thickness may be different than recommended by the manufacturer.

WHEEL ALIGNMENT SPECIFICATIONS

Year	Model	Caster Range (deg)	Pref. Setting (deg)	Camber Range (deg)	Pref. Setting (deg)	Toe-in (in.)	Front Wheel Turning Angle (deg) Inward	Outward
1972	All	¾P-1-¼P	1P	1P-1-¾P	⅜P	⁵⁄₆₄-⅛	37	32
1973-76	All	¾P-1-¼P	1P	1P-1-¾P	⅜P	0-¼	34-38	32-33

P Positive

TUNE-UP PROCEDURES

Spark Plugs

Removal and Installation

1. Disconnect the wire from the plug by twisting and pulling the molded cap from the plug. Don't yank the wire from the plug, as the connection inside the cap can be damaged.

2. Loosen the plug a few turns and blow the dirt away from the base of the plug with compressed air.

3. Remove the plug the rest of the way.

4. To gap the spark plugs, remove each one in turn and measure the gap with a round feeler gauge of the appropriate thickness. The round feeler gauge is inserted between the center and side electrode, To adjust the gap, bend the side electrode with the tool on the end of the feeler gauge until the specified gap is obtained.

5. Insert the plugs into the engine and tighten them finger-tight.

6. Be sure that the plugs are not cross-threaded. If the plugs use metal gaskets, new gaskets should be installed each time the plugs are removed and installed.

7. Tighten the spark plugs.

8. Install the spark plug wires on their respective plugs. Be sure that each wire is firmly connected.

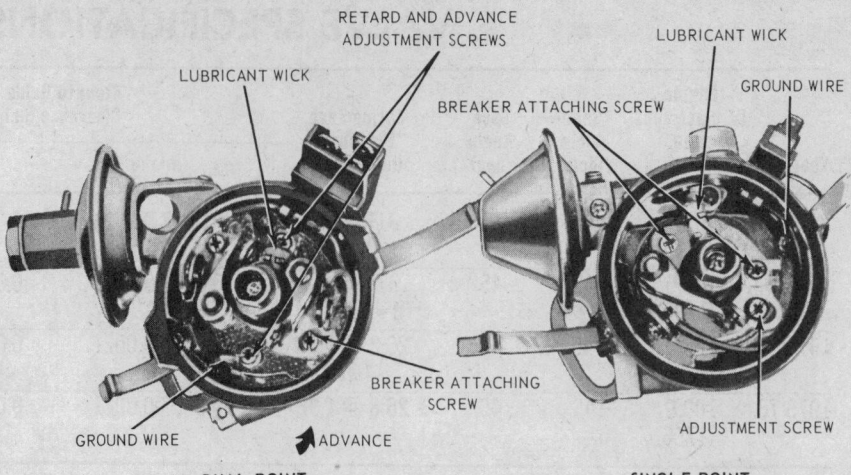

DUAL POINT   SINGLE POINT

Distributor with cap removed

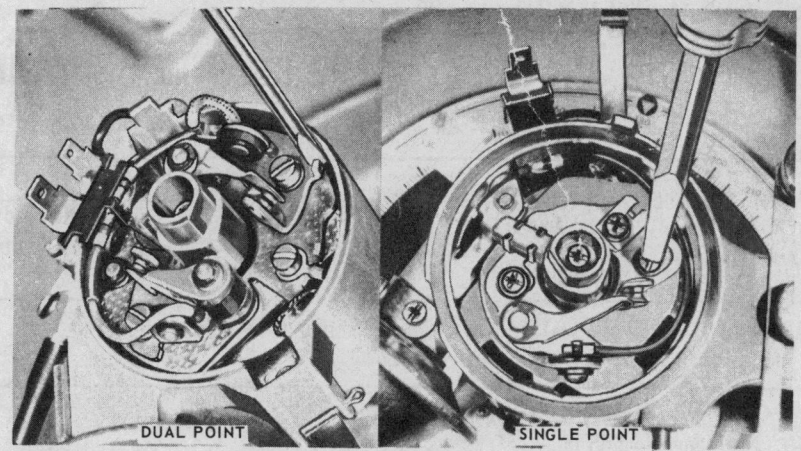

DUAL POINT   SINGLE POINT

Adjusting point gap

Breaker Points and Condenser

Removal and Installation

NOTE: *In 1972, 2 types of distributors were used; a dual point distributor was used in 49 states and Canada. A single point distributor was used for 1972 California models. In 1973–76, the single point distributor was used on all models.*

1. Remove the distributor cap and rotor.

2. Disconnect the primary and condenser wires.

3. Remove the breaker points from the base plate.

4. Place the breaker point(s) assemblies on the base plate. Install the attaching screws, again using a magnetic screwdriver.

5. Install the condenser. It is always best to install a new condenser each time you replace the points.

6. Connect the primary and condenser wires to the point(s) terminal and tighten the connection.

7. Be sure that the points are aligned.

8. Set the point gap or dwell angle and install the rotor and distributor cap. Use the alignment marks made previously to get the cap on correctly.

Dwell Angle

When setting ignition contact points, it is advisable to observe the following general rules:

1. If the points are used, they should not be adjusted using a feeler gauge. The gauge will not give an accurate reading on a pitted surface.

2. Never file the points—this removes their protective coating and results in rapid pitting.

3. When using a feeler gauge to set new points, be certain that the points are fully open. The fiber rubbing block must rest on the highest point of the cam lobe.

4. Always make sure that a feeler gauge is free of oil or grease before setting the points.

5. Make sure that the points are properly aligned and that the feeler gauge is not tilted. If points are misaligned, bend the fixed contact support only, never the movable breaker arm.

A dwell meter virtually eliminates errors in point gap caused by the distributor cam lobes being unequally worn, or human error. In any case, point dwell should be checked as soon as possible after setting with a feeler gauge because it is a far more accurate check of point operation under normal operating conditions. The dwell meter is also capable of detecting high point resistance (oxidation) or poor connections within the distributor.

To connect the dwell meter, switch the meter to the six-, four- or eight-cylinder range, as the case may be, and connect one lead to ground. The other lead should be connected to the coil distributor terminal (the one having the wire going to contact points). Follow the manufacturer's instructions if they differ from those listed. Zero the meter, start the engine and gradually allow it to assume normal idle speed. (See "Tune-Up Specifications.") The meter should agree with the specifications. Any excessive variation in dwell indicates a worn distributor shaft or bushings, or perhaps a worn distributor cam or breaker plate.

Adjustment—Single Point Distributors

There are two methods to adjust the breaker point gap. By far the more accurate is the method of measuring dwell angle electronically.

Feeler Blade Method

1. Check and adjust the breaker point alignment. Bend the fixed contact support only.

2. Crank the engine in short bursts until the rubbing block rests on a peak of a cam lobe.

3. Insert a feeler blade of the specified thickness between the breaker points. Adjust the gap until the feeler blade will slide through the gap with a slight drag, by loosening the adjustment screw and moving the point base. When the correct gap is obtained, tighten the adjustment screw.

4. Clean the breaker cam and apply a thin coating of distributor cam lubricant to the cam. Do not use engine oil.

5. After setting the breaker point gap, set the ignition timing.

6. Install the distributor rotor and cap.

Dwell Meter Method—Single Point Distributors

1. Connect a dwell/tach to the engine.

2. Remove the distributor cap and rotor.

3. If the dwell angle is not as specified, adjust the point gap. Crank the engine again and note the dwell reading. Repeat this process until the dwell is within specifications.

Adjustment—Dual Point Distributors

Dual point distributors are adjusted in much the same manner as single point distributors. Adjust the dwell of each set of points separately to get the specified dwell. A piece of insulated material can be inserted between the contacts of one set of points to take it out of the circuit, while adjusting the other set.

Ignition Timing

1. Clean and mark the timing marks.

2. Disconnect and plug the vacuum line to the distributor.

3. Connect a timing light and tachometer.

4. Start the engine and reduce the idle to 700–750 rpm to be sure that the centrifugal advance mechanism is not working.

5. With the engine running, shine the timing light at the timing pointer and observe the position of the pointer in relation to the timing mark on the crankshaft pulley.

6. If the timing is not as specified, adjust the timing by loosening the distributor hold down bolt and rotating the distributor in the proper direction. When the proper ignition timing is obtained,

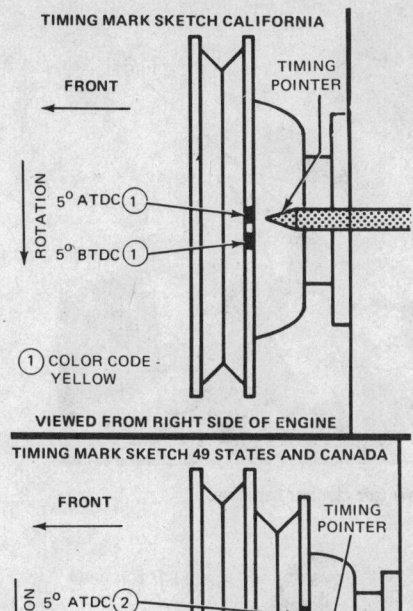

TIMING MARK SKETCH CALIFORNIA

FRONT

ROTATION

TIMING POINTER

5° ATDC ①
5° BTDC ①

① COLOR CODE - YELLOW

VIEWED FROM RIGHT SIDE OF ENGINE

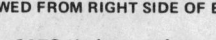

TIMING MARK SKETCH 49 STATES AND CANADA

FRONT

ROTATION

TIMING POINTER

5° ATDC ②
TDC ①
5° BTDC ②

① COLOR CODE - WHITE
② COLOR CODE - YELLOW

VIEWED FROM RIGHT SIDE OF ENGINE

1972 timing marks

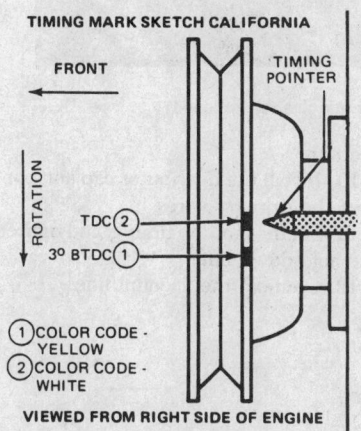

TIMING MARK SKETCH CALIFORNIA

FRONT

ROTATION

TIMING POINTER

TDC ②
3° BTDC ①

① COLOR CODE - YELLOW
② COLOR CODE - WHITE

VIEWED FROM RIGHT SIDE OF ENGINE

1973-76 timing marks

tighten the hold down bolt on the distributor.

7. Check the centrifugal advance mechanism by accelerating the engine to about 2,000 rpm. If the ignition timing advances, the mechanism is working properly.

8. Stop the engine and remove the timing light.

9. Reset the idle to specifications.

10. Remove the tachometer.

Valve Lash

1. Run the engine until normal operating temperature is reached.

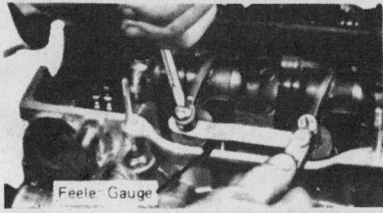

Checking valve clearance at the valve

Checking valve clearance at the camshaft

2. Remove the rocker cover.

3. Torque the cylinder head bolts to specifications.

4. Rotate the crankshaft so that No. 1 cylinder (front) is in the firing position. This can be determined by removing the spark plug from No. 1 cylinder and putting your thumb over the spark plug port. When compression is felt, No. 1 cylinder is on the compression stroke. Rotate the engine with a wrench on the crankshaft pulley and stop it at TDC of the compression stroke on No. 1 cylinder.

5. Check the valve clearance. The clearance can be checked at the camshaft or at the valve.

6. Loosen the adjusting screw locknut and adjust the clearance by turning the adjusting screw with the feeler blade inserted. Tighten the locknut.

7. Rotate the crankshaft, adjusting the valves for each cylinder at TDC of the compression stroke for each cylinder in the firing order—1–3–4–2.

8. Install the rocker arm cover.

Carburetor

Idle Speed and Mixture

1. Put the transmission in Neutral.

2. Connect a tachometer.

3. Set the curb idle speed to specifications, using the curb idle speed adjusting screw.

4. Check the idle mixture with a HC/CO analyzer, to prevent disturbing the emissions level by over-richening it.

ENGINE ELECTRICAL
Distributor

Removal and Installation

1. Remove the distributor cap.

2. Disconnect the vacuum hose.

3. Scribe matchmarks on the distribu-

Idle mixture adjusting screw (air cleaner removed)

Curb idle speed adjusting screw (air cleaner removed)

tor body and the cylinder block to indicate the relative positions.

4. Scribe another mark on the distributor body indicating the position of the rotor.

5. Disconnect the primary wires.

6. Remove the distributor from the engine.

NOTE: *Do not crank the engine while the distributor is removed.*

To install the distributor:

7. If the engine was cranked while the distributor was removed, turn the crankshaft until No. 1 cylinder is at the top of the compression stroke. This can be determined by feeling compression with your thumb through the spark plug port. The TDC mark on the crankshaft pulley should also be aligned with the timing pointer. Slide the distributor into the engine with the rotor pointing to No. 1 firing position (see "Firing Order").

8. If the engine has not been cranked while the distributor was removed, slide the distributor (with the O-ring) into the engine, aligning the matchmarks made during removal.

9. Install the flat washer, lockwasher and hold-down nut, but do not tighten

the nut.

10. Install the distributor cap and connect the primary wires.

11. Set the ignition timing, and tighten the hold-down nut.

12. Connect the vacuum line.

Alternator

The alternator is protected by a 40 amp fuse on the right fender splash shield.

Alternator Precautions

Some precautions should be taken when working on this, or any other, AC charging system.

1. Never switch battery polarity.

2. When installing a battery, always connect the grounded terminal first.

3. Never disconnect the battery while the engine is running.

4. If the molded connector is disconnected from the alternator, never ground the hot wire.

5. Never run the alternator with the main output cable disconnected.

6. Never electric weld around the truck without disconnecting the alternator.

7. Never apply any voltage in excess of battery voltage while testing.

8. Never "jump" a battery for starting purposes with more than 12 volts.

Removal and Installation

1. Disconnect the wire at the terminal at the rear of the alternator.

2. Pull the multiple connector from the rear of the alternator.

3. Remove the fan belt.

4. Remove the distributor cap and rotor from the distributor.

5. Remove the alternator.

6. Installation is the reverse of removal. Be sure to adjust the drive belt tension and to connect the battery properly.

Regulator

An external regulator is located on the fender splash shield.

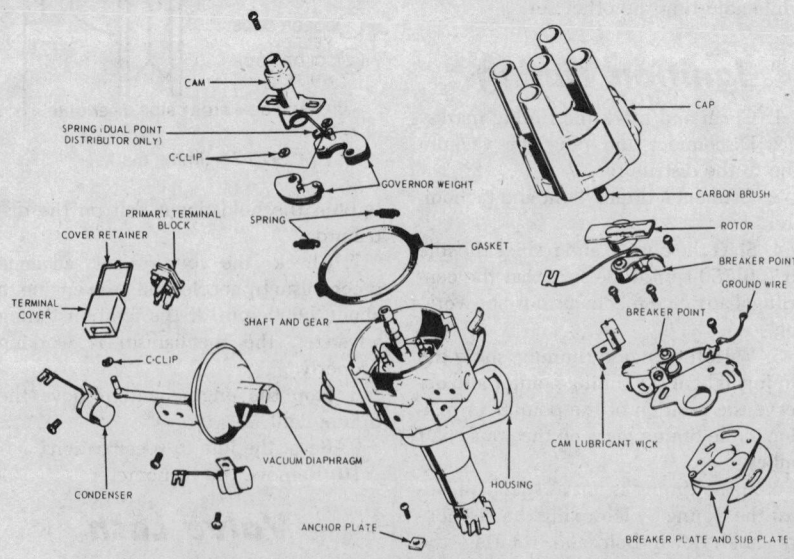

Exploded view of the dual point distributor

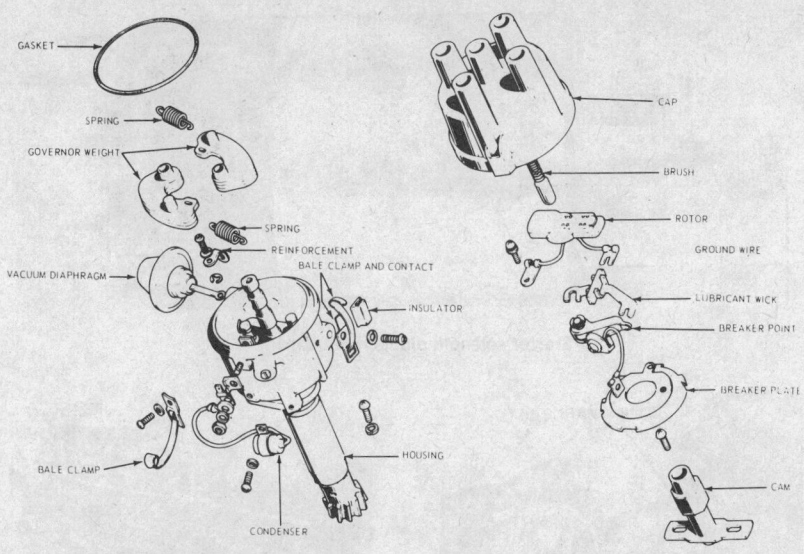

Exploded view of the single point distributor

Removal and Installation

1. Disconnect the regulator wires at the multiple connector.

2. Remove the regulator from the splash shield.

3. Installation is the reverse of removal.

Regulator Test

The alternator regulator is not adjustable, but if it is suspected to be malfunctioning, the following test can be performed.

1. Connect a tachometer.

2. Connect the positive lead of a voltmeter to the alternator B terminal, and the negative lead to ground.

3. Set the voltmeter of the 20 volt scale.

4. Put the transmission in Neutral and set the parking brake.

5. Start the engine and run it at 1,800 rpm. The voltmeter should read 14–15 volts. If not replace it.

Starter

Removal and Installation

1. Raise the hood and disconnect the battery ground cable.

2. Remove the carburetor air cleaner and air intake tube.

3. Disconnect the battery cable from the starter solenoid battery terminal.

4. Pull the ignition switch wire from the solenoid 50 terminal.

5. Raise and support the truck on jackstands.

6. Working under the truck, remove the two starter attaching bolts, washers and nuts.

7. Tilt the drive end of the starter and remove the starter by working it out below the emission system hoses.

To install the starter:

8. Install the starter and 2 bolts, washers and nuts.

9. Connect the ignition switch wire to the solenoid 50 terminal.

10. Connect the battery cable to the solenoid battery terminal.

11. Install the carburetor air cleaner and air intake tube.

12. Connect the ground cable to the battery.

13. Lower the truck and check the operation of the starter.

Starter Drive Replacement

1. Remove the field strap.

2. Disengage the solenoid plunger hook from the shift fork and remove the solenoid.

3. Remove the shift fork pivot bolt, nut and lock washer.

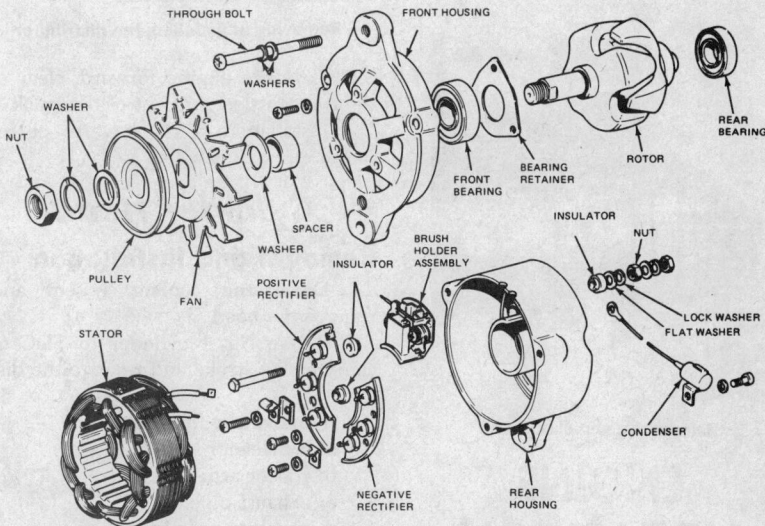

Exploded view of the alternator

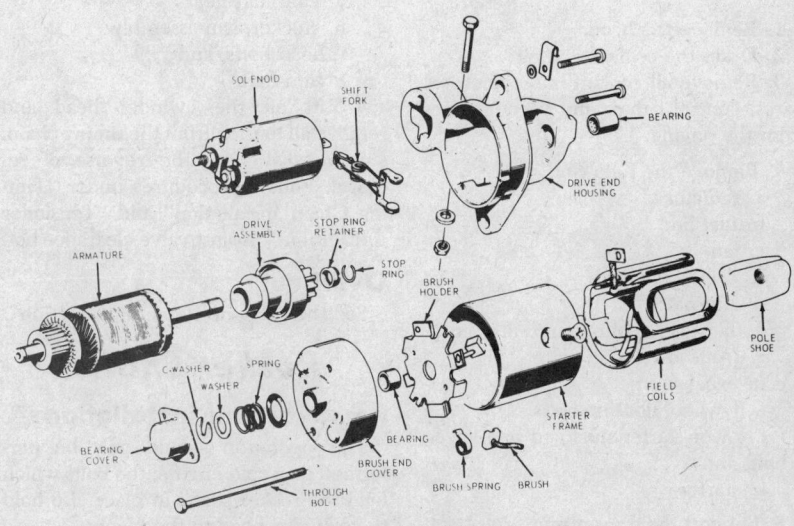

Exploded view of the starter

4. Remove the drive end housing while disengaging the shift fork.

5. Slide the drive stop-ring retainer toward the armature and remove the stop-ring.

6. Slide the retainer and drive assembly from the shaft.

7. Installation is the reverse of removal.

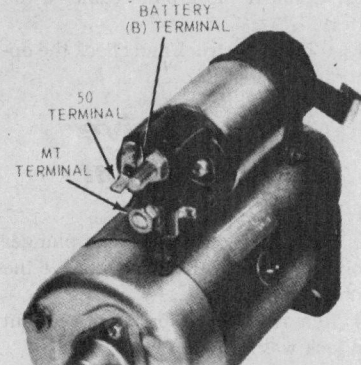

Starter solenoid terminals

Starter drive end-clearance

ENGINE MECHANICAL

Removal and Installation

1. Remove the hood.
2. Drain the coolant and oil.
3. Remove all coolant lines, electrical wires, control cables and vacuum lines from the engine.
4. Remove the following:
   a. radiator
   b. fuel line
   c. fan
   d. drive belts
   e. alternator
   f. thermactor pump and filter hose
   g. front lower skid plate
   h. exhaust pipe
   i. flywheel housing bolts
   j. lower starter nuts and one lower bolt, and
   k. starter.
5. Support the transmission and attach an engine hoist.

Starter solenoid plunger adjustment

Removing or installing the distributor

6. Slide the engine forward, clear of the transmission, and out of the truck.

7. Installation is the reverse of removal.

Cylinder Head

Removal and Installation

1. Drain the cooling system and remove the hood.
2. Rotate No. 1 cylinder to TDC of compression stroke and remove the distributor.
3. Remove the following:
   a. air cleaner
   b. rocker arm cover
   c. exhaust pipe
   d. accelerator linkage
   e. exhaust pipe
   f. distributor gear from camshaft
   g. camshaft gear
   h. Rocker arm assembly
   i. head bolts, and
   j. camshaft.
4. Lift off the cylinder head and remove all tension from the timing chain.
5. Installation is the reverse of removal. Follow procedures under "Timing Chain Installation" and "Tensioner Adjustment". Adjust valve clearance hot.

Overhaul

See the "Engine Rebuilding Section".

Rocker Shafts

Removal and Installation

This operation should only be performed on a cold engine; the bolts which hold the rocker shafts in place also hold the cylinder head to the block.

1. Disconnect the choke cable.

Removing or installing the camshaft

Cylinder head-to-front cover bolt

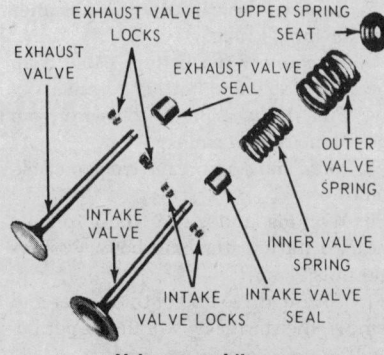

Valve assemblies

ROCKER ARMS — EXHAUST

ROCKER ARMS — EXHAUST

ROCKER ARM SHAFT SUPPORTS

CAMSHAFT BEARING CAPS (PART OF CYLINDER HEAD ASSEMBLY)

SPRINGS

SPRINGS

CAMSHAFT THRUST PLATE

ROCKER ARM SHAFT — EXHAUST

O-RING 6594

OIL DISTRIBUTION PIPE

ROCKER ARM SHAFTS — INTAKE

SPRINGS

SPRINGS

ROCKER ARM SHAFT SUPPORTS

ROCKER ARMS — INTAKE

ROCKER ARMS — INTAKE

Exploded view of rocker arm and shafts

2. If equipped, disconnect the air by-pass valve cable.

3. Disconnect the spark plug wires.

4. Remove the rocker cover.

5. Remove the rocker arm shaft attaching bolts evenly and remove the rocker arm shafts.

6. Installation is the reverse of removal. Torque the rocker arm bolts and adjust the valves cold. Later perform a hot adjustment.

Intake Manifold

Removal and Installation

1. Drain the cooling system.
2. Remove the air cleaner.
3. Remove the accelerator linkage.
4. Disconnect the choke cable and fuel line. Plug the fuel line.
5. Disconnect the Thermactor hoses, if equipped.
6. Disconnect the PCV valve hose.
7. Disconnect the heater return hose and by-pass hose.

8. Remove the manifold and carburetor as an assembly.

9. Installation is the reverse of removal.

Exhaust Manifold

Removal and Installation

1. Raise and support the truck.
2. Unbolt the exhaust pipe at the manifold.
3. Remove the manifold.
4. Installation is the reverse of removal.

Cylinder Front Cover

Removal and Installation

1. Scribe alignment marks on the hood hinges and remove the hood.
2. Drain the cooling system.
3. Remove the radiator.
4. Remove the drive belts.
5. Remove the crankshaft pulley and the water pump.

6. Remove the cylinder head-to-front cover bolt.

7. Raise and support the truck.

8. Remove the engine skid plate.

9. Disconnect the emission line from the oil pan. Drain the oil.

10. Remove the oil pan.

11. Remove the alternator and bracket and lay the alternator aside.

12. Remove the Thermactor pump (if equipped) and lay the pump aside.

13. Remove the steel tube from the front of the engine.

14. Unbolt and remove the front cover.

15. Installation is the reverse of removal.

Front Cover Oil Seal

Removal and Installation

The front cover oil seal can be removed and a new one installed without removing the front cover.

1. Drain the cooling system.
2. Remove the radiator.
3. Remove the drive belt(s).
4. Remove the crankshaft pulley.
5. Pry the front oil seal from the front cover.
6. Press a new front seal into position (flush).
7. Install the crankshaft pulley.
8. Install the drive belt(s) and adjust the tension.
9. Install the radiator. Fill the cooling system.

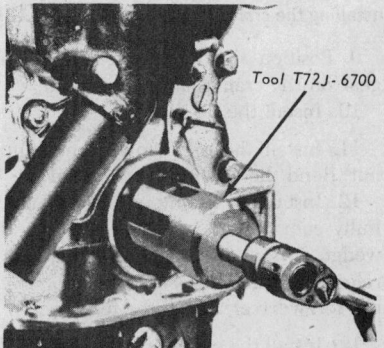

Tool T72J-6700

Removing the front cover oil seal

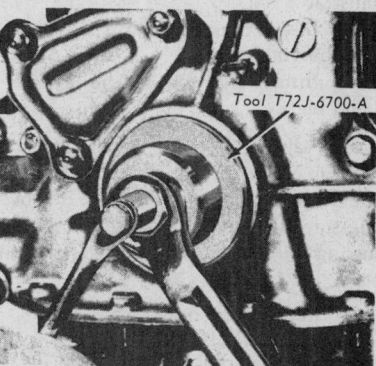

Tool T72J-6700-A

Installing the front cover oil seal

Timing Chain and Tensioner

Removal and Installation

1. Remove the cylinder head and front cover. It is not necessary that the intake and exhaust manifolds be removed.

2. Remove the oil pump and chain.

3. Remove the timing chain tensioner.

4. Loosen the timing chain guide strip screws.

5. Remove the oil slinger.

6. Remove the oil pump gear and chain as an assembly.

7. Remove the timing chain, crankshaft gear and camshaft gears from the engine.

To install the timing chain, timing gears and tensioner:

8. Position the crankshaft gear in the timing chain.

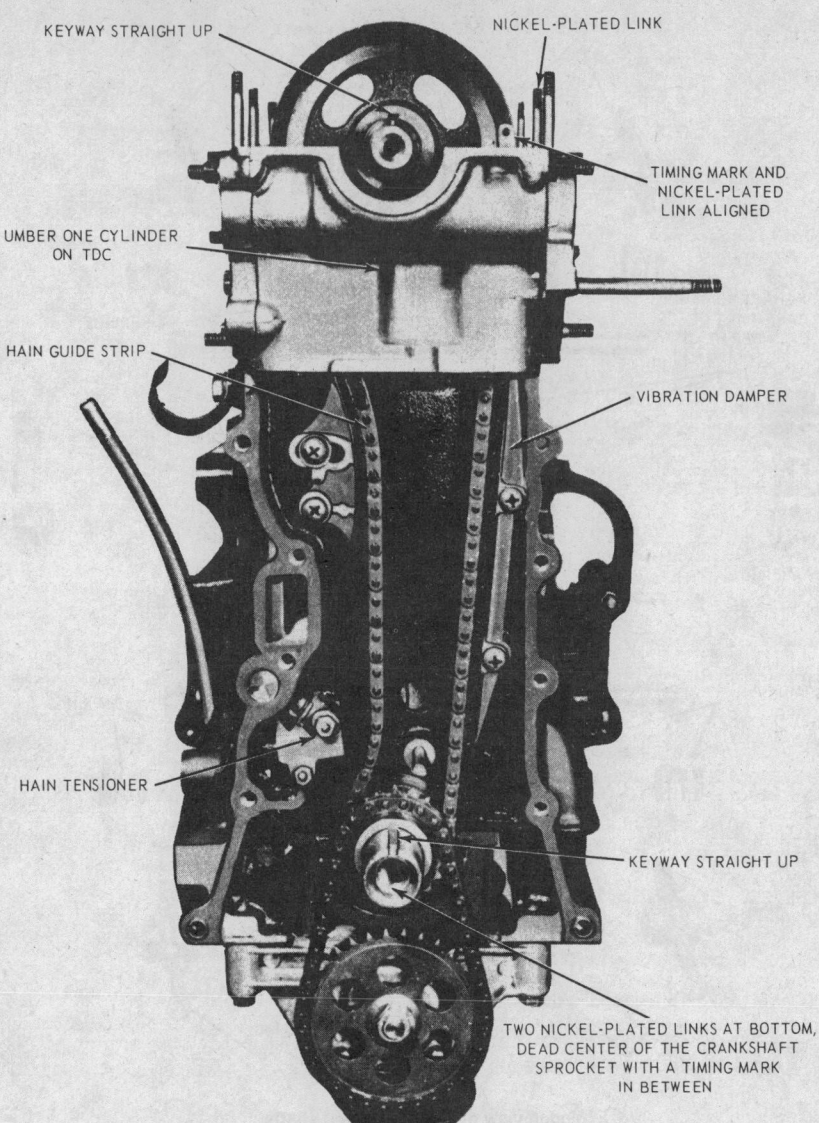

Correct valve timing

Installing the crankshaft gear and timing chain

9. Position the oil pump chain and gear on the crankshaft and oil pump.

10. Install the oil slinger.

11. Install the oil pump washer and nut. Bend the washer over the nut.

12. Install the timing chain tensioner. Fully compress the snubber spring and wedge a screwdriver into the tensioner release mechanism. Without removing the screwdriver, install the tensioner.

13. Install the cylinder head and camshaft. Be sure that the valve timing is as illustrated.

14. Install the rocker arm shafts and cam bearing caps.

15. Install and torque the cylinder head bolts.

16. Adjust the timing chain tension. Press in on the chain guide strip. Tighten the guide strip attaching screws. Remove the screwdriver from the tensioner, allowing the snubber to take up the chain slack.

17. Replace the front cover.

18. Adjust the valve clearance cold. Torque the cylinder head bolts and adjust the valve clearance hot.

Timing Chain Tensioner

Removal and Installation

This operation can be performed with front cover installed.

1. Remove the water pump.

2. Remove the tensioner cover.

Removing the timing chain tensioner

3. Remove the attaching bolts from the tensioner. Remove the tensioner.

To install the tensioner:

4. Fully compress the snubber spring. Insert a screwdriver into the tensioner release mechanism.

5. Without removing the screwdriver, insert the tensioner and align the bolt holes. Install and torque the bolts.

6. Adjust the chain tension as follows:

Timing Chain Tensioner Adjustment

1. Remove the two blind plugs and aluminum washers from the front cover.

2. Loosen the guide strip attaching screws.

3. Press the top of the chain guide strip through the adjusting hole in the cylinder head.

4. Tighten the guide strip attaching screws.

5. Remove the screwdriver from the

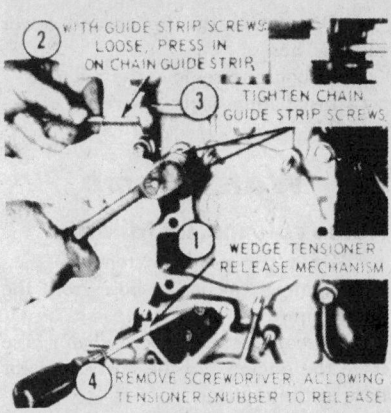

Adjusting the timing chain tensioner-front cover installed

tensioner and let the snubber take up the slack in the chain.

6. Install the blind plugs and aluminum washers.

7. Install the tensioner cover and gasket.

8. Install a new gasket and water pump. Install the crankshaft pulley and drive belt and adjust the tension. Check the coolant level.

Camshaft

Removal and Installation

Perform this operation on a cold engine.

1. Scribe alignment marks on the hood hinges and remove the hood (if necessary).

2. Remove the water pump.

3. Disconnect the coil wire and vacuum line from the distributor.

4. Rotate the crankshaft to place No. 1 cylinder on TDC of the compression stroke. This can be determined by removing the spark plug and feeling compression with your thumb. When compression is felt, rotate the crankshaft until the pointer aligns with the TDC mark on the pulley.

5. Remove the plug wires and distribu-tor cap. Remove the distributor.

6. Remove the valve cover.

7. Release the tension on the timing chain.

8. Remove the cylinder head bolts.

9. Remove the rocker arm assembly.

10. Remove the nut, washer and distributor gear from the camshaft.

11. Remove the nut and washer holding the camshaft gear.

12. Remove the camshaft. Do not remove the camshaft gear from the timing chain. Be sure that the gear teeth and chain relationship is not disturbed. Wire the chain and cam gear in place so that they will not fall behind the front cover.

To install the camshaft:

13. Clean all the gasket surfaces.

14. Clean the cylinder head bolt holes.

15. Install the camshaft on the head and install the camshaft gear.

16. Check the valve timing.

17. Install the rocker arm assembly.

18. Install and torque the head bolts.

19. Install the cam gear washer and nut.

20. Install the distributor gear, washer, and nut.

21. Adjust the timing chain tension.

22. Check the camshaft end-play. It should be 0.001–0.007 in. If it exceeds 0.008 in., replace the thrust plate with a new one.

23. Install the distributor, distributor cap and plug wires.

24. Connect the vacuum line and coil wire.

25. Adjust the valve clearance cold. Install the valve cover and fill the cooling system.

26. Run the engine and check for leaks. When normal operating temperature is reached, adjust the hot valve clearance.

27. Adjust the carburetor and ignition timing.

28. Install the air cleaner and hood.

Pistons and Connecting Rods

Removal and Installation

Refer to the "Engine Rebuilding" section for general engine service.

Piston and Connecting Rod Positioning

Correct installation of piston and rod

ENGINE LUBRICATION

Oil Pan

Removal and Installation

1. Raise and support the truck.

2. Remove the engine skid plate.

3. Drain the engine oil.

4. Remove and support the clutch release cylinder.

5. Remove the engine rear brace and loosen the bolts on the left-side.

6. Disconnect the emission line from the oil pan.

7. Remove the oil pan and rest it on the crossmember.

8. Remove the oil pump pickup tube from the pump.

9. Remove the oil pan.

To install the oil pan:

10. Clean all the gasket surfaces.

11. Clean the oil pan, oil pump pickup tube and oil pump screen.

12. Install a new oil pan gasket with oil-resistant sealer.

13. Install the oil pump pickup tube and screen.

14. Install the oil pan on the block. Torque the nuts and bolts to specifications.

15. Connect the emission line to the oil pan.

16. Attach the rear engine bracket. Torque the bolts to specification.

17. Reinstall the clutch release cylinder. Torque the nuts to specification.

18. Replace the engine skid plate.

19. Lower the truck. Fill the crank-

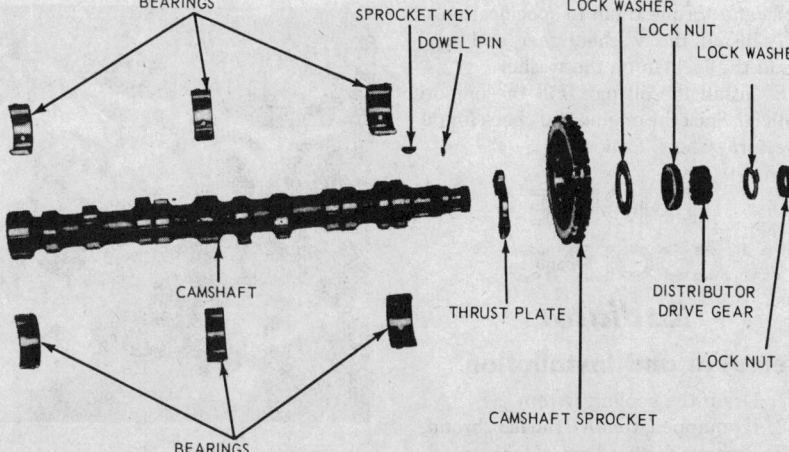

Camshaft and related parts

case, and run the engine. Check for leaks and oil pressure.

Rear Main Oil Seal

Replacement

If the rear main oil seal in being replaced independently of any other parts, it can be done with the engine in place. If the rear main oil seal and the rear main bearing are being replaced, together, the engine must be removed.

1. Remove the transmission.
2. Remove the clutch disc, pressure plate and flywheel.
3. Using an awl, punch two holes in the crankshaft rear oil seal. They should be punched on opposite sides of the crankshaft, just above the bearing cap-to-cylinder block split line.
4. Install a sheet metal screw in each hole. Pry against both screws at the same time to remove the oil seal. Do not scratch the oil seal surface on the crankshaft.

Removing the crankshaft rear main oil seal

5. Clean the oil recess in the cylinder block and bearing cap. Clean the oil seal surface on the crankshaft.
6. Coat the oil seal surfaces with oil. Coat the oil seal surface and the seal surface on the crankshaft with Lubriplate. Install the oil seal and be sure that it is not cocked. Be sure that the seal surface was not damaged.
7. Install the flywheel. Coat the threads of the flywheel attaching bolts with oil-resistant sealer.
8. Install the clutch, pressure plate, and transmission.

Oil Pump

Removal and Installation

1. Remove the oil pan.
2. Remove the oil pump gear attaching nut.
3. Remove the bolts attaching the oil pump to the block. Loosen the gear on the pump.
4. Remove the oil pump and gear.
To install the oil pump:
5. Install the oil pump gear in the chain.
6. Prime the oil pump and install it on the gear and cylinder block. Install the

Installing the oil pump

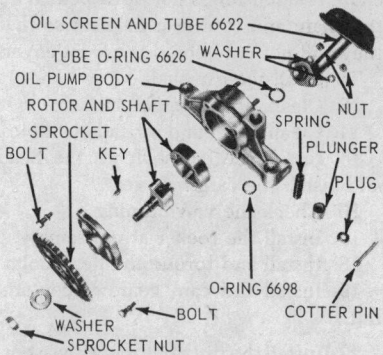

Exploded view of the oil pump and related parts

Installing the oil pump drive gear and chain

bolts and torque them to specification.
7. Install the washer, gear and nut. Bend the locktab on the washer.
8. Install the oil pan. Fill the engine with oil. Start the engine and check for oil pressure. Check for leaks.

ENGINE COOLING

Radiator

Removal and Installation

1. Drain the cooling system.
2. If equipped, remove the fan shroud.
3. Remove the fan. On California models remove the fan clutch.

4. Disconnect the upper and lower radiator hoses.
5. Unbolt and remove the radiator.
6. Installation is the reverse of removal.

Water Pump

Removal and Installation

1. Drain the cooling system.
2. Remove the lower hose from the water pump.
3. Disconnect the upper-radiator hose from the engine and the lower radiator hose at the radiator.
4. Remove the radiator.
5. Remove the drive belts.
6. Remove the fan and pulley. Remove the crankshaft pulley.
7. Unbolt and remove the water pump.
To install the water pump:
8. Clean the gasket surfaces of the water pump and cylinder block.
9. Install the water pump and new gasket on the block. Torque the bolts to specification.
10. Install the lower hose on the water pump.
11. Install the fan and pulley. Install the crankshaft pulley.
12. Install the drive belts and adjust the tension.
13. Install the radiator.
14. Refill the cooling system with the specified amount and type of coolant. Install the radiator cap and start the engine. Check for leaks.

Thermostat

Removal and Installation

1. Drain enough coolant to bring the coolant level down below the thermostat housing. The thermostat housing is located on the left front side of the cylinder block. Disconnect the temperature sending unit wire.

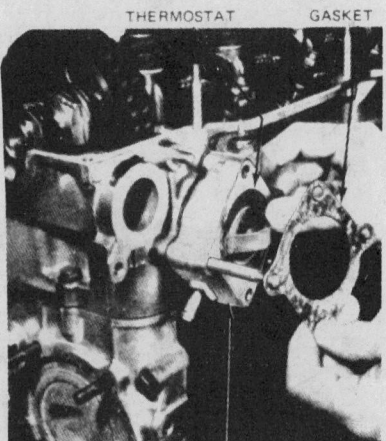

Thermostat installation

2. Remove the coolant outlet elbow. If so equipped, position the vacuum control valve out of the way. The vacuum control valve is not used on California models.

3. Disconnect the coolant by-pass hose from the thermostat housing.

4. Remove the thermostat and housing from the engine.

5. Remove the thermostat from the housing and note the position of the jiggle pin.

To install the thermostat:

6. Remove all gasket material from the parts.

7. Install the thermostat housing using a new gasket with water-resistant sealer.

8. Position the thermostat in the housing with the jiggle pin up. Coat a new gasket with sealer and install it on the thermostat housing.

9. Install the coolant outlet elbow and vacuum control valve (if equipped).

10. Connect the by-pass and radiator hoses.

11. Connect the temperature sending unit wire.

12. Fill the cooling system with the proper coolant. Operate the engine and check the coolant level. Check for leaks.

EMISSION CONTROLS

Hydrocarbons, carbon monoxide (CO), oxides of nitrogen (NO) and fuel vapors are controlled by four basic systems. A Thermactor air injection system is used on California trucks only. A positive crankcase ventilation (PCV) system is used on all trucks. All Couriers use an evaporative emission control system to absorb fuel vapors and a deceleration control system to augment the Thermactor air pump.

Thermactor Air Injection System

The Thermactor system consists of an air pump, check valve, one air injection nozzle for each cylinder, an air injection manifold, air by-pass valve and the associated hoses and connection.

Testing the System

Air Pump Drive Belt

Be sure that the air pump drive belt is adjusted to the proper tension.

Air Pump

1. Disconnect the air pump outlet hose from the air by-pass valve.

2. Connect a "T" fitting and pressure gauge into the outlet line.

3. Start the engine and run it briefly at 1,500 rpm.

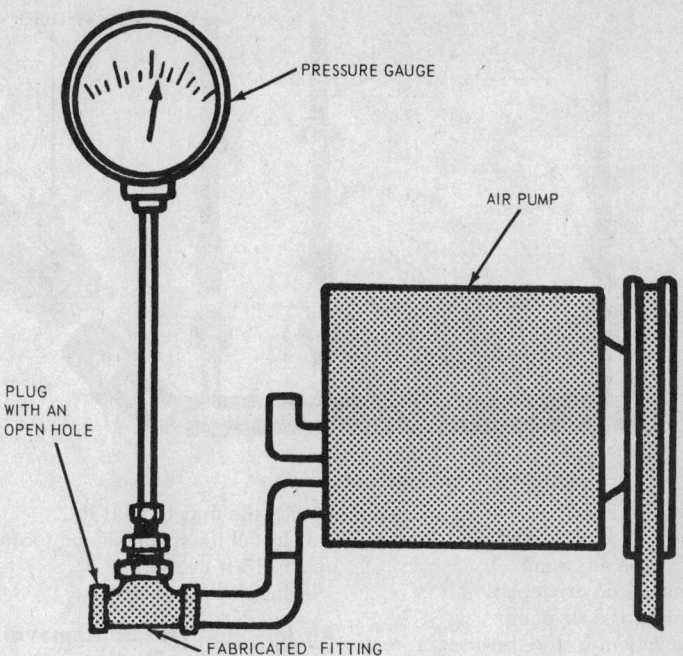

Checking air pump pressure

4. If the pressure reading is below 1 psi, replace the pump.

Air Pump Relief Valve

1. Operate the engine at idle.

2. Check the relief valve for airflow. No flow should be evident. If airflow out is noted, replace the relief valve and air pump.

3. Increase the engine speed to 3,000 rpm. If air flows out of the relief valve, the valve is in good condition. If air does not flow from the relief valve, or if the valve is excessively noisy, the relief valve and air pump assembly should be replaced.

Air Manifold Check Valve

1. Remove the check valve from the air injection manifold. Blow through the valve from the intake side and the outlet side. Air should pass through the valve from the intake side only. If air passes through the valve from the outlet side, replace the valve.

Air By-pass Valve

1. Disconnect the air line at the check valve.

2. Push the choke knob all the way in.

3. Run the engine at 1,500 rpm.

4. Hold your hand over the end of the air pump air line. Air should flow from the hose.

5. Pull the choke knob all the way out. No air should flow from the air line.

6. If the valve is not operating properly, replace the valve.

Adjustments

Air Pump Drive Belt

1. Be sure the drive belt is adjusted properly.

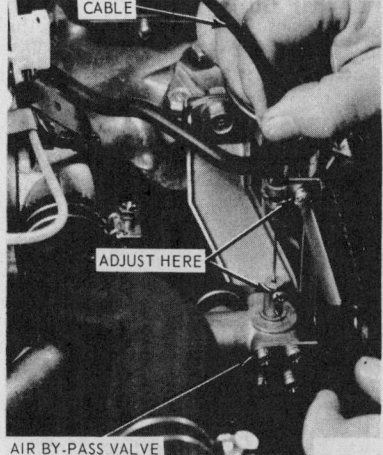

Adjusting the air by-pass valve

Air By-pass Valve

1. Push the choke handle all the way in. Be sure that the choke plate is fully open.

2. Loosen the cable retaining screw in the valve plunger and the screw in the cable retaining bracket.

3. Be sure that the plunger is fully bottomed.

4. Insert the cable in the plunger and tighten the retaining screw.

5. Push down on the cable as much as possible without bending the control wire, then tighten the bracket screw.

6. Pull the choke knob all the way out. The valve plunger should be pulled to the top of the bracket.

Service

Air Pump Removal and Installation

1. Remove the battery, alternator and

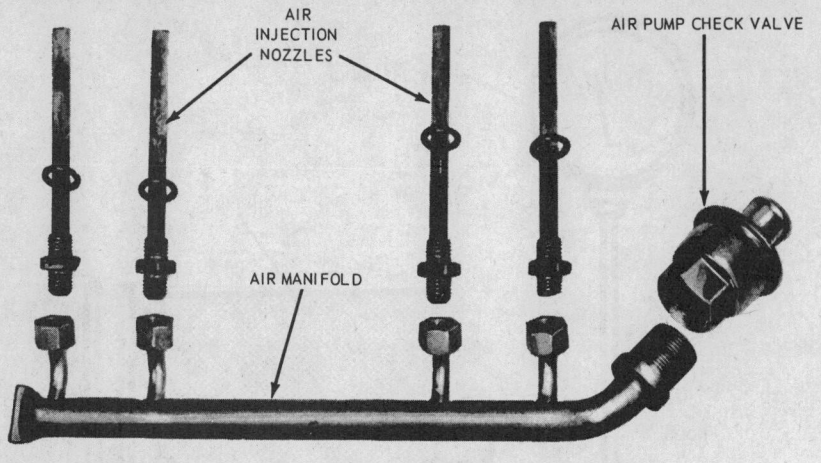

Air manifold assembly

alternator drive belt.

2. Disconnect the inlet and outlet hoses from the air pump.

3. Remove the drive belt.

4. Remove the air pump.

5. Installation is the reverse of removal. Adjust drive belt tension.

Air Pump Check Valve Removal and Installation

1. Disconnect the air hose from the check valve and unscrew it from the air manifold.

2. Installation is the reverse of removal.

Air Manifold Removal and Installation

1. Remove the check valve.

2. Remove the nozzles from the manifold by removing the attaching nuts from the nozzles.

3. Unbolt and remove the manifold.
To install the manifold:

4. Install the nozzles in the manifold.

Torque the nuts to 20 ft lbs.

5. Install the manifold and torque the nuts to 15 ft lbs.

6. Install the check valve.

Air Injection Nozzle Removal and Installation

1. Disconnect the air line from the check valve.

2. Remove the nozzles from the manifold.

3. Remove the heat stove from the exhaust manifold.

4. Remove the nozzles.
To install the nozzles:

5. Install the nozzles. Torque the nuts to 20 ft lbs.

6. Install the heat stove on the exhaust manifold.

7. Connect the air line to the manifold check valve.

Air By-Pass Valve Removal and Installation

1. Loosen the cable attaching screws

at the valve plunger and the cable retaining bracket.

2. Pull the cable out of the valve.

3. Unscrew and remove the valve from the mounting bracket.

4. Install the valve on the mounting bracket.

5. Push the choke knob all the way in.

6. Insert the end of the cable in the valve plunger and tighten the retaining screw.

7. Pull the cable to remove all slack between the plunger and cable bracket. Tighten the cable retaining screw at the bracket.

Deceleration Control System

The system uses an anti-afterburn valve to prevent fuel detonation in the exhaust system and a coasting richer valve to prevent overly lean fuel mixtures. The coasting richer valve is controlled by three switches; the speedometer switch, the accelerator switch and the clutch switch. In order for the coasting richer valve to operate, all three switches must be closed. The accelerator switch closes when the accelerator pedal is in the released position. The speedometer switch closes at speeds above approximately 17–23 mph. The clutch switch is closed when the clutch pedal is released.

Testing the System

Anti-Afterburn Valve

1. Remove the outlet hose from the anti-afterburn valve.

2. Hold a hand over the outlet fitting and raise the engine rpm. Quickly re-

Deceleration Control System—all except 1972 California only

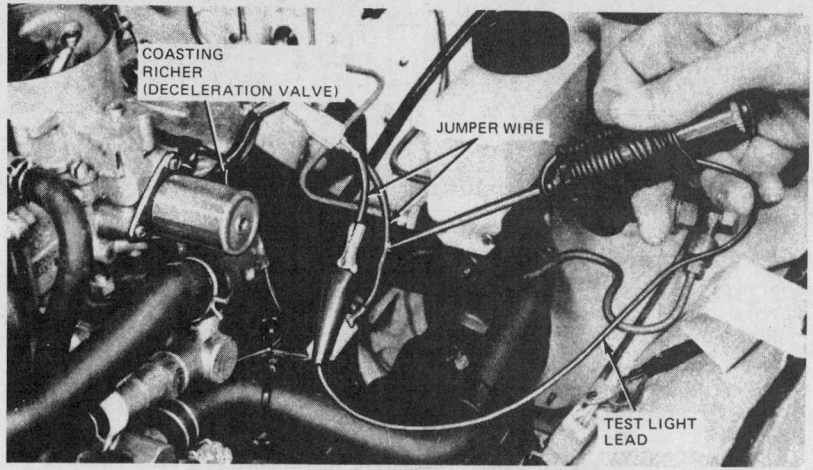

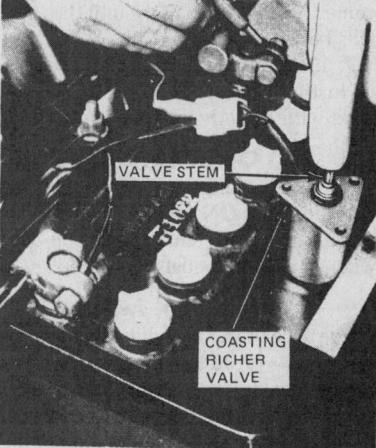

Testing the Coasting Richer Valve with a test light

Testing the Coasting Richer Valve with the battery

lease the accelerator. Air should flow for approximately three seconds. If the valve passes air for more than three seconds, or does not pass air at all, it should be replaced.

Coasting Richer Valve (Deceleration Valve)

1. Remove the coasting richer valve from the carburetor.

2. Connect the coasting richer valve to the battery.

3. As power is applied to the valve, the solenoid plunger should be pulled into the valve body.

4. Reinstall the coasting richer valve. Connect a test light.

5. Raise the rear wheels and support the truck on stands.

6. Start the engine and raise the engine speed above 30 mph. Release the accelerator pedal. The test light should

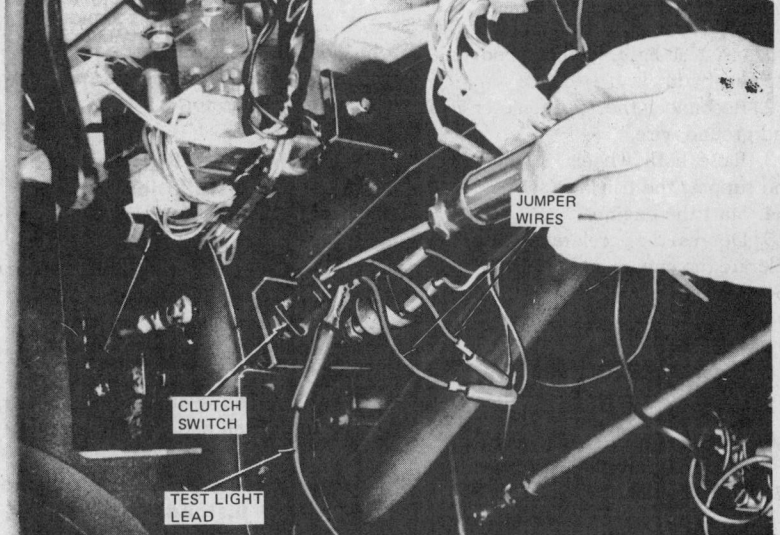

Checking the clutch switch

Deceleration Control System—1972 except California

come ON and remain ON until the speed falls below 17–23 mph.

7. If the system is operating properly, no further tests are required. If not, proceed with the other tests.

Clutch Switch

When checking the circuit the test light should be ON when the clutch pedal is fully released, and should be OFF when the clutch pedal is fully depressed.

Accelerator Switch

The accelerator switch is actuated by a throttle lever link on the carburetor. When checking the switch with a circuit tester, the test light should be ON when the accelerator pedal is fully released and should be OFF when the pedal is depressed.

Speed Switch

1. Remove the instrument cluster and attach a test light to the speedometer switch.
2. Reconnect the speedometer cable and ground wire.
3. Raise both wheels off the ground and support the truck on stands.
4. Start the engine.
5. Depress the accelerator pedal to accelerate the engine and confirm that the speed switch is ON at speeds of 17–23 mph and OFF at speeds below 17–23 mph.
6. If not, replace the switch.

Speed Switch Relay

Check the speed switch relay with a test light to be sure that it is operating at 17–23 mph.

Service

Anti-Afterburn Valve Removal and Installation

1. Remove the two air hoses from the valve.
2. Remove the vacuum line to the intake manifold.
3. Unbolt and remove the valve.

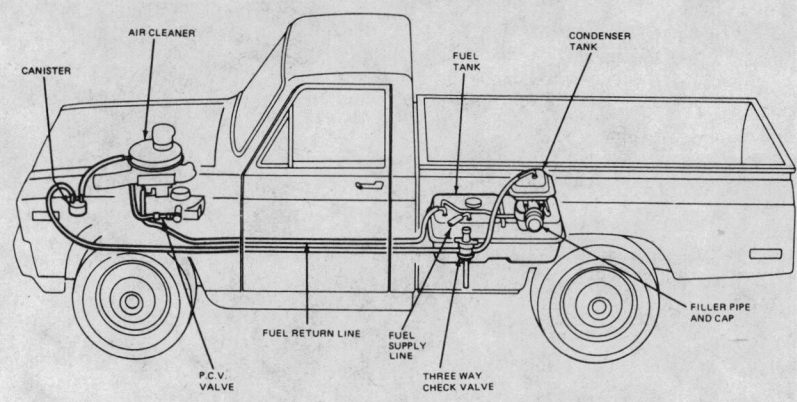

Evaporative Emission Control System

Coasting Richer (Deceleration Valve) Removal and Installation

1. Disconnect the valve electrical lead at the quick-disconnect.
2. Unscrew and remove the valve from the carburetor.

Clutch Switch Removal and Installation

1. Remove the nut on the back side of the switch mounting bracket.
2. Disconnect the switch electrical lead at the quick-disconnect.
3. Remove the switch
4. Installation is the reverse of removal.
5. Adjust the switch until it clicks when the clutch pedal is depressed.

Accelerator Switch Removal and Installation

1. Disconnect the switch electrical lead at the quick-disconnect.
2. Remove the screws attaching the switch to the throttle return spring bracket and remove the switch.

Accelerator Switch Adjustment

1. Be sure that the throttle valve is fully closed.

2. Loosen the switch adjusting screw and turn the switch off.
3. Gradually tighten the adjusting screw until the switch produces a clicking sound and is turned on.
4. Tighten the adjusting screw another 1½ turns.

Speed Switch Removal and Installation

The speed switch is integral with the speedometer head located in the instrument panel.

Positive Crankcase Ventilation (PCV) System

The function of the PCV valve is to divert blow-by gases from the crankcase to the intake manifold to be burned in the cylinders. The system consists of a PCV valve, an oil separator and the hoses necessary to connect the components.

Testing the System

PCV Valve

1. Remove the hose from the PCV valve.
2. Start the engine and run it at approximately 700–1,000 rpm.
3. Cover the end of the PCV valve with a finger. A distinct vacuum should be felt. If no vacuum is felt, replace the valve.

Service

PCV Valve Removal and Installation

Remove the valve from the fitting on the intake manifold.

Evaporative Emission Control System

The system consists of a fuel tank, a condenser tank and a check valve.

Checking the speedometer relay

Service

Condenser Tank Removal and Installation

1. Raise and support the rear of the truck.
2. Disconnect the hoses from the condenser tank.
3. Unbolt and remove the condenser tank.

Check Valve Removal and Installation

1. Disconnect the hoses from the check valve.
2. Unscrew and remove the valve.

FUEL SYSTEM

Couriers use an electric fuel pump and a Zenith-Stromberg 2-barrel downdraft carburetor with a manual choke.

Fuel Filter

Replacement

An in-line disposable filter is used. Unclip the lines from the filter to replace.

Electric Fuel Pump

An external electric fuel pump is mounted on the left frame rail adjacent to the fuel tank.

Testing the Fuel Pump

To determine that the fuel pump is in good operating condition, tests for both volume and pressure should be performed. The tests are performed with the fuel pump installed, and the engine at normal operating temperature and idle speed.

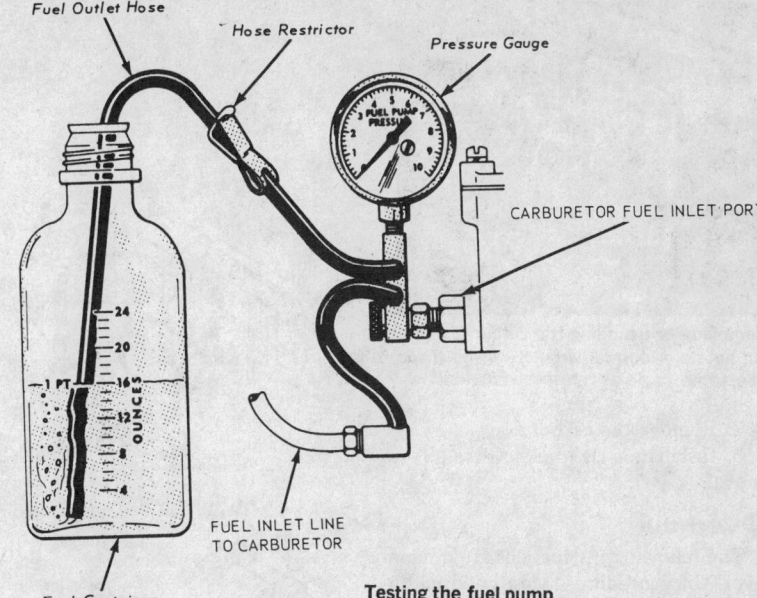

Testing the fuel pump

Be sure that the fuel filter is in good condition.

Pressure Test

1. Remove the air cleaner.
2. Disconnect the fuel inlet line at the carburetor.
3. Connect a pressure gauge, a restrictor and a flexible hose between the fuel filter and the carburetor. Position the flexible hose and restrictor so that the fuel can be discharged into a suitable graduated container.
4. Operate the engine at idle speed and vent the system into the container by momentarily opening the hose restrictor.
5. Close the hose restrictor and allow the pressure to stabilize and note the reading. It should be 2.8–3.6 psi.

6. If the pump pressure is not within specifications, and the fuel filter and fuel lines are not blocked, the pump is malfunctioning and should be replaced.
7. If the pressure is within specifications, perform the volume test.

Volume Test

1. Open the hose restrictor and expel the fuel into the container, while observing the time required to discharge 1 pint. Close the restrictor. Fuel pump volume should be approximately 2 pints/minute.
2. If the pump volume is below specifications, repeat the test using an auxiliary fuel supply and a new filter. If the pump volume meets specifications while using the auxiliary fuel supply, check for a restriction in the fuel lines.

Removal and Installation

1. Remove the fuel pump shield from the frame. Disconnect the electrical leads from the pump.
2. Disconnect the inlet and outlet lines from the pump. Plug the lines.
3. Unbolt and remove the pump from its mounting bracket.
4. Installation is the reverse of removal.

Carburetor

Removal and Installation

1. Remove the air cleaner and duct.
2. Disconnect the accelerator shaft from the throttle lever.
3. Disconnect and plug the fuel supply and return lines.
4. Disconnect the throttle solenoid and deceleration valve at the quick-disconnects.
5. Disconnect the carburetor-to-distributor vacuum line.
6. Disconnect the throttle return and choke cable.

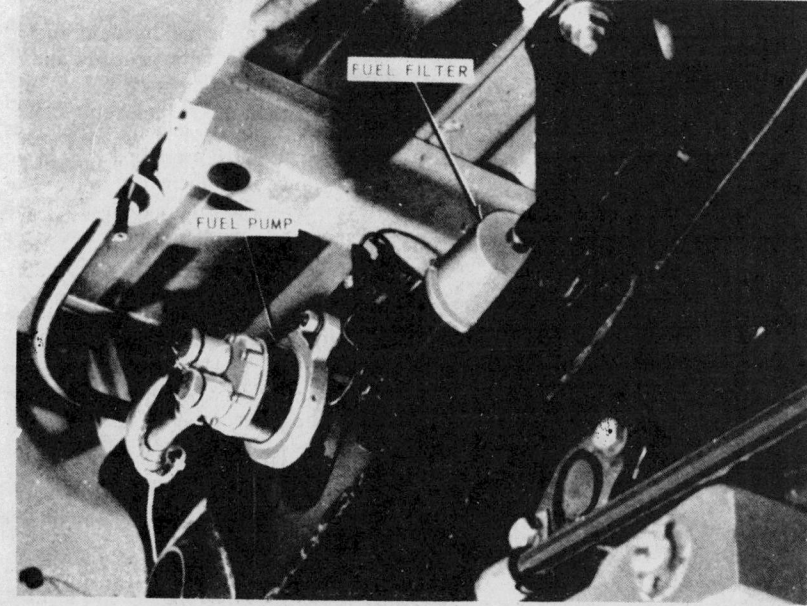

Fuel pump installed

Removing or installing the carburetor attaching nuts. A normal wrench can be made to the same angle as the special tool shown.

7. Remove the carburetor.

8. Installation is the reverse of removal.

Overhaul

The following instructions are general overhaul procedures. Most good carburetor rebuilding kits come replete with exploded views and specific instructions.

Efficient carburetion depends greatly on careful cleaning and inspection during overhaul, since dirt, gum, water, or varnish in or on the carburetor parts are often responsible for poor performance.

Overhaul your carburetor in a clean, dust-free area. Carefully disassemble the carburetor, referring often to the exploded views. Keep all similar and lookalike parts segregated during disassembly and cleaning to avoid accidental interchange during assembly. Make a note of all jet sizes.

When the carburetor is disassembled, wash all parts (except diaphragms, electric choke units, pump plunger, and any other plastic, leather, fiber, or rubber

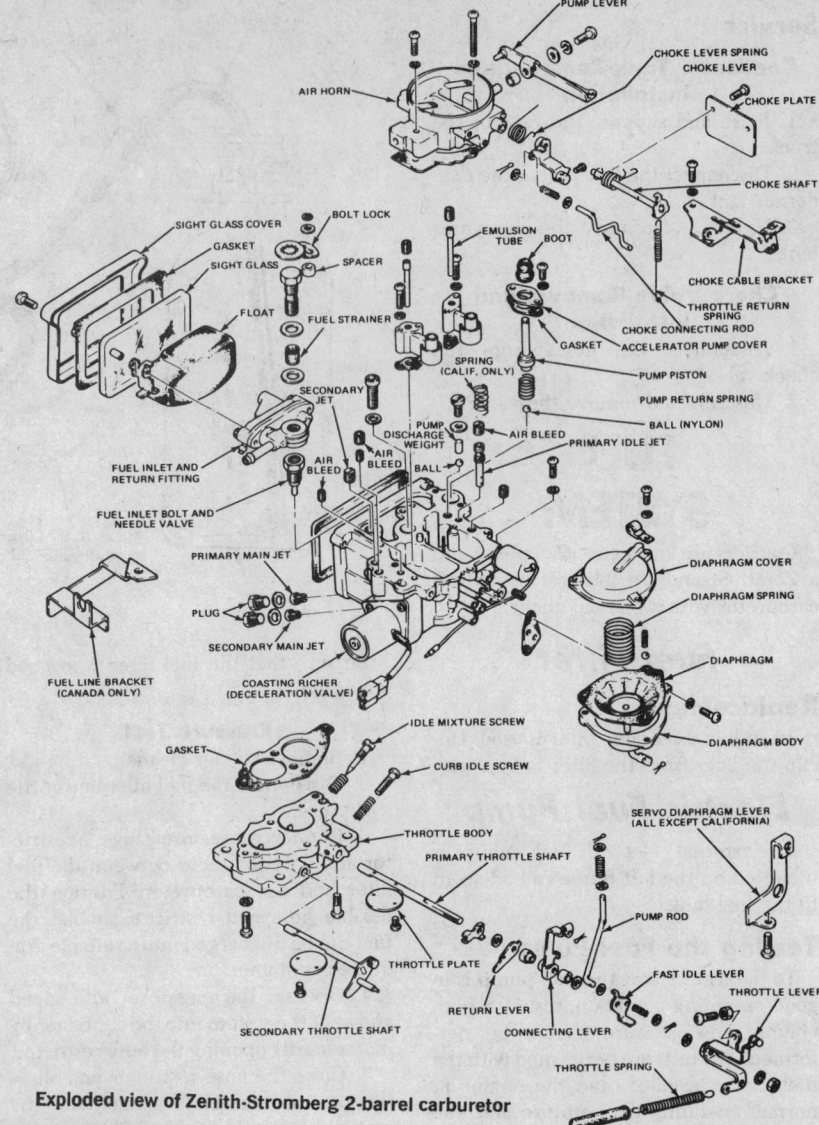

Exploded view of Zenith-Stromberg 2-barrel carburetor

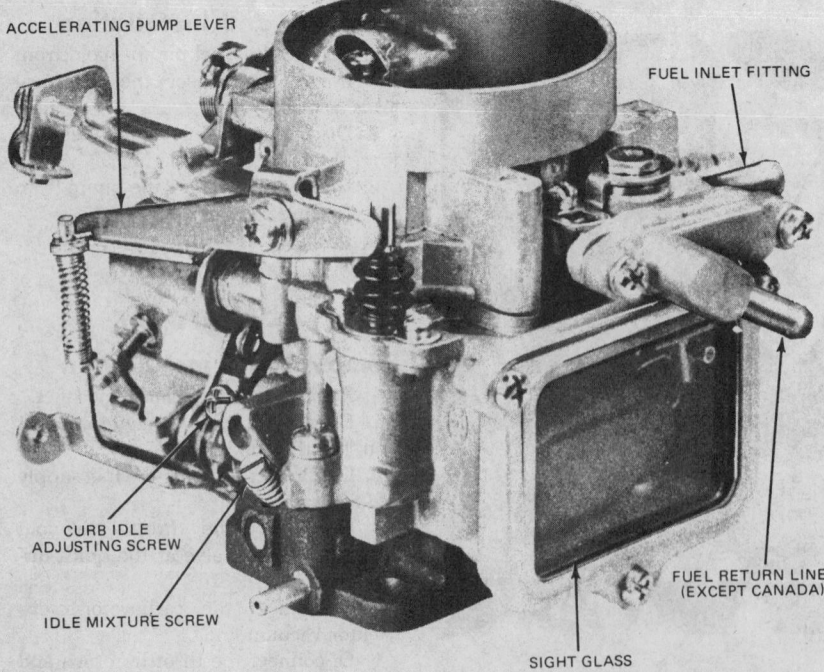

Zenith-Stromberg 2-barrel carburetor

parts) in clean carburetor solvent. Do not leave parts in the solvent any longer than is necessary to sufficiently loosen the deposits. Excessive cleaning may remove the special finish from the float bowl and choke valve bodies, leaving these parts unfit for service. Rinse all parts in clean solvent and blow them dry with compressed air or allow them to air dry. Wipe clean all cork, plastic, leather, and fiber parts with a clean, lint-free cloth.

Blow out all passages and jets with compressed air and be sure that there are no restrictions or blockages. Never use wire or similar tools to clean jets, fuel passages, or air bleeds. Clean all jets and valves separately to avoid accidental interchange.

Check all parts for wear or damage. If wear or damage is found, replace the defective parts. Especially check the following:

1. Check the float needle and seat for wear. If wear is found, replace the complete assembly.

2. Check the float hinge pin for wear and the float(s) for dents or distortion. Replace the float if fuel has leaked into it.

3. Check the throttle and choke shaft bores for wear or an out-of-round condition. Damage or wear to the throttle arm, shaft, or shaft bore will often require replacement of the throttle body. These parts require a close tolerance of fit; wear may allow air leakage, which could affect starting and idling.

NOTE: *Throttle shafts and bushings are not included in overhaul kits. They can be purchased separately.*

4. Inspect the idle mixture adjusting needles for burrs or grooves. Any such condition requires replacement of the needle, since you will not be able to obtain a satisfactory idle.

5. Test the accelerator pump check valves. They should pass air one way but not the other. Test for proper seating by blowing and sucking on the valve. Replace the valve if necessary. If the valve is satisfactory, wash the valve again to remove breath moisture.

6. Check the bowl cover for warped surfaces with a straightedge.

7. Closely inspect the valves and seats for wear and damage, replacing as necessary.

8. After the carburetor is assembled, check the choke valve for freedom of operation.

Carburetor overhaul kits are recommended for each overhaul. These kits contain all gaskets and new parts to replace those which deteriorate most rapidly. Failure to replace all parts supplied with the kit (especially gaskets) can result in poor performance later.

After cleaning and checking all components, reassemble the carburetor, using new parts and referring to the exploded view. When reassembling, make sure that all screws and jets are tight in their seats, but do not overtighten as the tips will be distorted. Tighten all screws gradually, in rotation. Do not tighten needle valves into their seats; uneven jetting will result. Always use new gaskets. Be sure to adjust the float level when reassembling.

Fast Idle Adjustment

1. Remove the air cleaner.
2. With the choke plate fully closed, measure the clearance between the primary throttle plate and the wall of the throttle bore. The clearance can be measured with the shank end of a #55 drill bit.
3. If the clearance is not as specified, (0.0508 in.) bend the fast idle lever where it contacts the throttle lever tang until

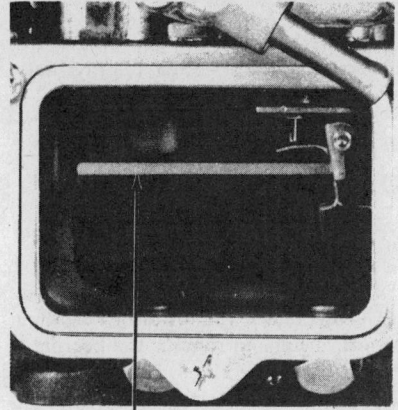

FUEL LEVEL MARK

Fuel level mark on the sight glass

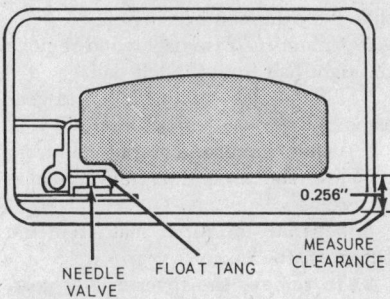

NEEDLE VALVE   FLOAT TANG   MEASURE CLEARANCE 0.256"

Float level adjustment—measure the clearance between the float and the edge of the bowl

the proper clearance is obtained.

Float and Fuel Level Adjustment

1. With the engine running, check the fuel level in the sight glass.
2. If the fuel level is not at the mark on the sight glass, remove the carburetor.
2. Remove the fuel bowl cover.
4. Invert the carburetor and lower the

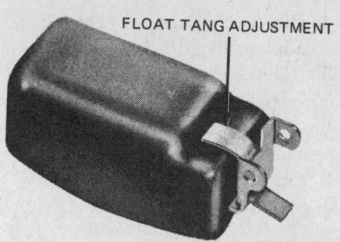

FLOAT TANG ADJUSTMENT

Bend the tang to adjust the float level

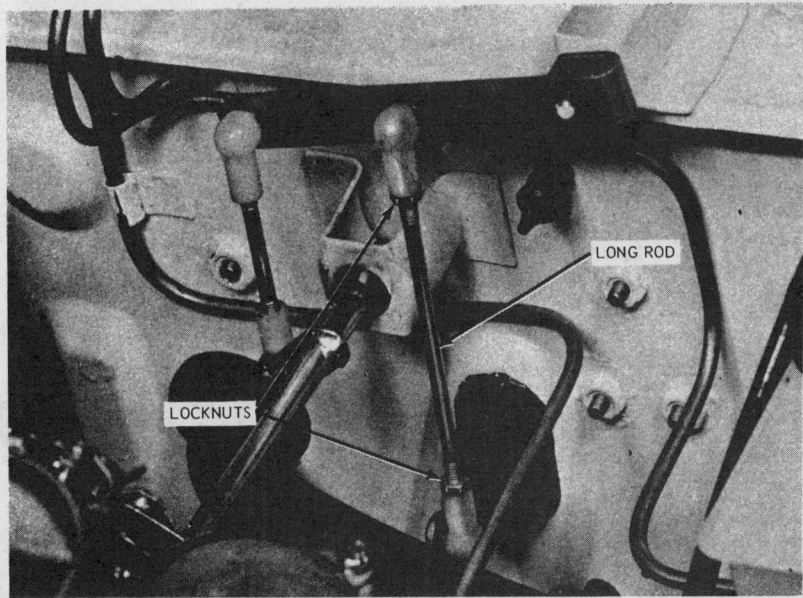

CHOKE CABLE ATTACHING SCREWS

Choke adjustment

float until the tang on the float just contacts the needle valve.

5. Measure the clearance between the float and the edge of the bowl.
6. If the clearance is not 0.256 in. bend the float tang until the proper clearance is obtained.
7. Install the fuel bowl cover.
8. Reinstall the carburetor.
9. Recheck the fuel level at the sight glass.

Choke Adjustment

1. Push the choke knob all the way in.
2. Loosen the choke cable attaching screws at the choke lever and the choke cable bracket.
3. Be sure that the choke plate is fully open.

LONG ROD

LOCKNUTS

Throttle linkage adjustment

4. Insert the choke cable into the choke lever. Tighten the screw.

5. Pull the cable outward to remove all slack between the choke lever and choke cable bracket and tighten the attaching screw at the choke cable bracket.

6. Operate the choke to be sure that there is no binding.

Throttle Linkage Adjustment

1. Loosen the locknut on the longer linkage rod and rotate both ends in the sockets until the proper accelerator travel from idle to wide-open throttle is obtained.

2. Tighten the locknuts to set the adjustment.

MANUAL TRANSMISSION

Couriers are equipped with a fully synchronized 4-speed manual transmission.

The manual transmission is known as a top loader and there are no linkage or shifter adjustments.

Removal and Installation

4-Speed

1. Remove the following:
   a. gearshift boot
   b. shift lever, tower and gasket assembly
   c. driveshaft
   d. exhaust pipe brackets
   e. exhaust pipe
   f. clutch return spring and slave cylinder
   g. speedometer cable from case
   h. starter cables and backup light wires, and
   i. starter.

2. Support the transmission and engine with separate jacks.

3. Unbolt the transmission from the engine.

4. Remove the transmission crossmember.

5. Remove the transmission.

6. Installation is the reverse of removal.

5 Speed

1. Remove the gearshift boot and retainer cover from the lever.

2. Pull the lever, shim and bushing straight up and away from the retainer.

3. Disconnect the driveshaft.

4. Remove the following:
   a. exhaust pipe brackets
   b. exhaust pipe and resonator
   c. slave cylinder
   d. speedometer cable
   e. starter and backup light wires
   f. starter, and
   g. transmission-to-engine rear plate bolts.

5. Support the transmission and unbolt it from the crossmember; remove the crossmember and lower the transmission.

6. Installation is the reverse of removal.

Overhaul

4 Speed

Transmission Disassembly

1. Drain and remove the transmission.

2. Disconnect the throwout bearing return spring and remove the bearing.

3. Remove the clutch housing, gasket and input shaft bearing thrust washer.

4. Unbolt the extension housing. With the control lever in Neutral, press the lever as far downward as possible and slide the extension housing off.

5. Unbolt the case halves and remove the right half from the left half.

6. Lift out the countershaft and gear assembly.

7. Roll the input and output shaft from under the shift forks and remove them as an assembly.

8. Separate the input shaft from the output shaft.

9. To remove the reverse idler gear, push the center (3rd and 4th) shift rail as far forward as possible. This will provide working clearance. Remove the gear.

10. Remove the setscrew on the outside of the case to remove the reverse idler shaft.

Input Shaft Disassembly and Assembly

1. Remove the bearing from the bearing pocket in the shaft.

2. Remove the snap-ring that holds the input bearing on the shaft.

3. Press the input bearing off the shaft.

4. Position the input shaft bearing on the input shaft and press it into position.

5. Install the snap-ring.

6. Install the bearing in the bearing pocket.

Output Shaft Disassembly and Assembly

1. Remove the snap-ring at the front end of the output shaft and remove the 3rd and 4th gear synchronizer, synchro-

nizer ring and 3rd gear. The part number on the 3rd gear should face rearward; if not, mark the gear for reassembly.

2. Remove the rearmost snap-ring and slide the speedometer gear and drive ball off the shaft. Remove the other speedometer gear snap-ring.

3. Remove the selective fit snap-ring and washer holding reverse gear, output shaft bearing, low gear, low gear bushing, 1st and 2nd gear synchronizer and 2nd gear on the shaft. Slide the parts off the shaft. Note that the oil groove on the synchronizer hub should face forward.

4. Assemble 3rd gear and the synchronizer ring on the front end of the output shaft, along with the 3rd and 4th gear synchronizer.

5. Be sure the part number on the synchronizer hub faces rearward.

6. Install the front snap-ring.

7. Slide the 2nd gear and synchronizer ring on the rear end of the shaft.

8. Install the 1st and 2nd gear synchronizer and ring on the shaft with the oil groove in the synchronizer forward.

9. Install the 1st gear synchronizer ring, 1st gear and sleeve, thrust washer, bearing and reverse gear on the shaft.

10. Slide the selective fit thrust washer on the shaft and install the selective fit snap-ring. Check the clearance between the rear face of reverse gear and the selective thrust washer. The clearance should be 0–0.004 in. Adjust the end-play using combinations of thrust washers and snap rings.

Countershaft Disassembly and Assembly

1. Remove the snap-ring from the rear end of the shaft and slide off reverse gear and the bearing.

2. If it is necessary to replace the bearing sleeve, it can be pressed off using sharp edged press plates.

3. Remove the snap-ring on the front end of the shaft and press the bearing off.

4. If the sleeve on the rear end of the shaft was removed, press it into position.

5. Install the bearing and reverse gear. Install the snap-ring.

6. Press the ball bearing onto the front

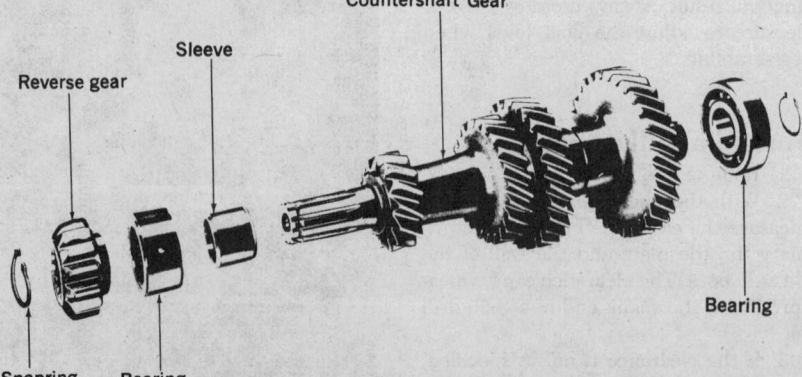

Exploded view of 4-speed countershaft

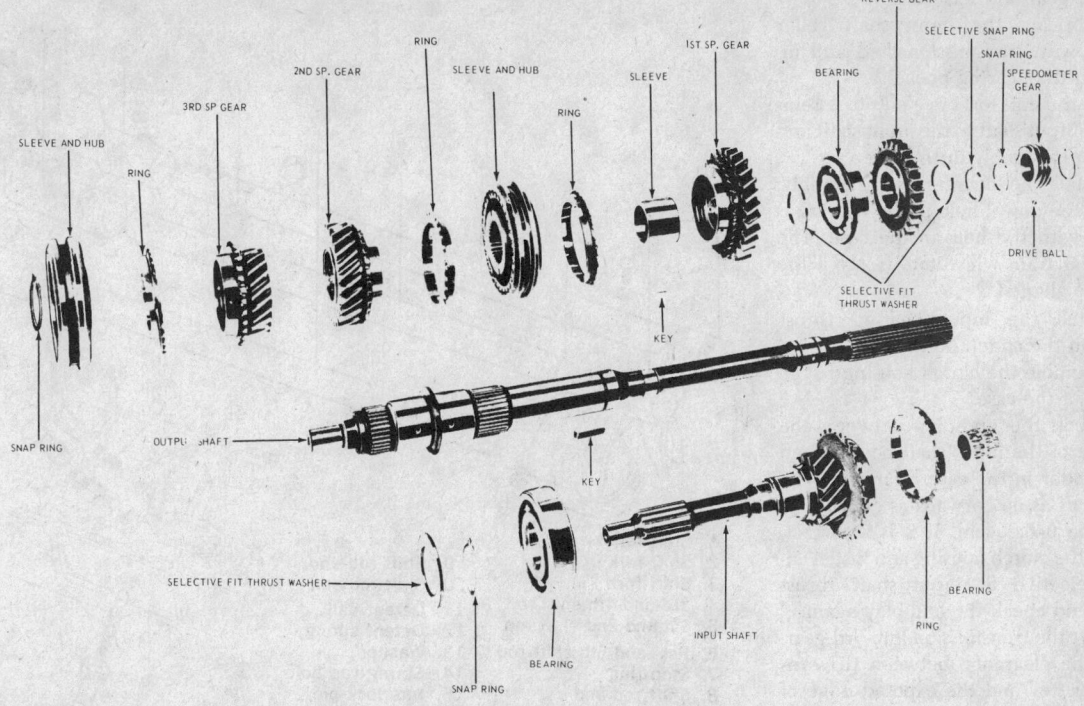

Exploded view of 4-speed input and output shafts

of the shaft and install the snap-ring.

Reverse Idler Shaft and Gear Disassembly and Assembly

See Steps 9–10 of "Transmission Disassembly".

Shift Rails Disassembly and Assembly

Detent assemblies, caps, plates, shims, gaskets, springs and balls should be reinstalled in their original locations.

1. Remove each spring cap, one at a time, and shake out the spring, ball and shim.

2. Remove the interlock bore plug. Shake out the interlock pins.

3. Remove the shift forks from the case.

4. Install the shift fork and slide the 1st and 2nd shift rail into the case and fork.

5. Install 2 dummy shift rails.

6. Align the holes in the dummy shift rails with the holes in the 1st and 2nd gear shift rail.

7. Holding the case on edge, drop a detent pin into position.

8. Remove a dummy shaft.

9. Install the 3rd and 4th gear shift fork rail and slide the 3rd and 4th gear shift rail (and washer, if used) into the case.

10. Align the detent holes in the remaining dummy rail and the 3rd and 4th gear shift rail. Install another interlock pin.

11. Remove the remaining dummy shaft rail and install the reverse shifter rail and fork. Align the interlock hole and install the remaining interlock pin.

12. Install the interlock bore plug.

13. Align the shift forks on the shift

rails and install the lockbolts.

14. Position the case open side down and install each detent into the bore from which it was removed. Lubricate the moving parts.

Extension Housing Disassembly and Assembly

1. Place the housing on its right side and remove the speedometer gear, back-up light switch and spring loaded friction piece.

2. Disconnect the control lever from the control rod and slide the rod from the housing. Remove the key.

3. Assembly is the reverse of disassembly. Lubricate the speedometer gear housing seal before installation.

Transmission Assembly

1. Install the reverse idler gear. Install

Checking 4-speed input shaft end-play

the idler gear and setscrew.

2. Lubricate the input shaft roller bearing with transmission fluid and install it in the bearing pocket.

3. Set the shift forks in Neutral. Assemble the output shaft to the input shaft and install the assembly in the case.

4. Install the countershaft assembly. Be sure the dowel hole in the bearing is aligned with the hole in the case. The main gear train will rotate freely if the holes are aligned.

5. Install the input bearing thrust washer in the clutch housing.

6. Assemble the clutch housing to the left half of the case.

7. Check the end-play between the rear face of the input shaft bearing and the shoulder in the case by moving the input shaft as far forward as possible. It should be 0–0.004 in. If it is incorrect, remove the clutch housing and install another selective fit input shaft thrust washer and check the end-play again.

8. Shift the transmission into 3rd gear. Check the clearance between the synchronizer key and the exposed edge of the synchronizer ring. It should be 0.030–0.080 in. If not, remove the clutch housing, countershaft, and the input shaft and output shaft as an assembly. Disassemble the output shaft and substitute a thicker selective fit washer for the key slotted thrust washer. Assemble the complete output shaft and adjust the overall end-play at the reverse gear using the selective fit thrust washer described under "Output Shaft Disassembly and Assembly".

9. Install the input and output shaft assembly into the case. Install the countershaft. Install the clutch housing.

10. Recheck the synchronizer key clearance as described in Step 8.

11. Recheck the input shaft end-play as described in Step 7.

12. Shift the transmission into 4th gear. Measure the distance between the shift gate end of the shift rail and transmission case boss. The clearance should be 0–0.028 in. If the clearance is excessive, install a selective fit thrust washer (or washers) on the 3rd and 4th gear shift rail between the shift gate fitting and the transmission case boss.

13. Remove the clutch housing.

14. Lubricate all moving parts with transmission fluid. Lubricate the input shaft and output shaft seals in the clutch and extension housings.

15. Coat the mating surfaces of the case halves with a thin coat of sealer and allow them to dry.

16. Shift the transmission into Neutral.

17. Assemble the case halves.

18. Install a new extension housing gasket and install the extension housing.

19. Install the clutch housing using a new gasket.

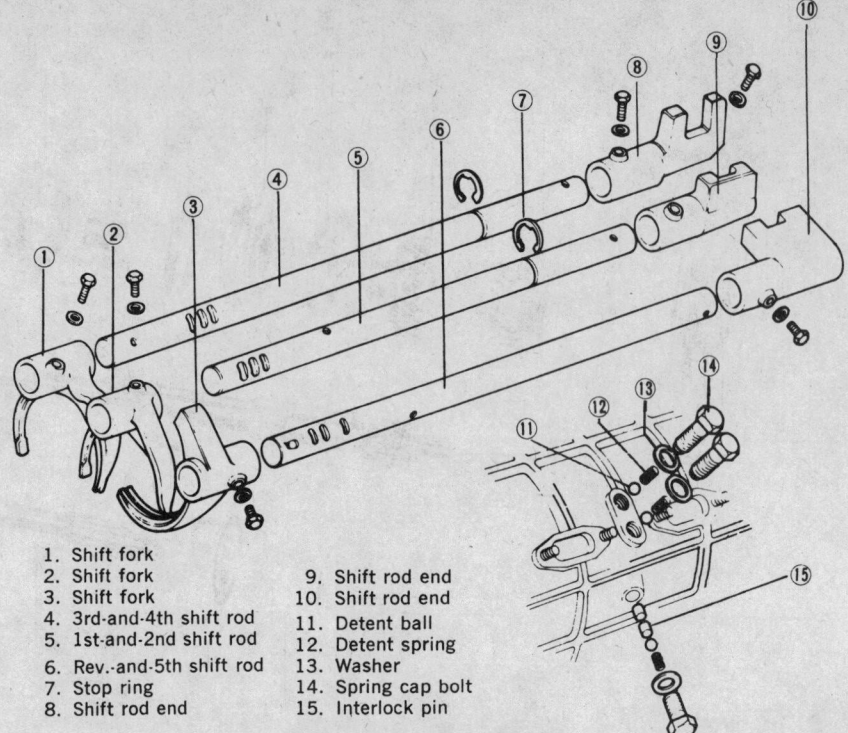

1. Shift fork
2. Shift fork
3. Shift fork
4. 3rd-and-4th shift rod
5. 1st-and-2nd shift rod
6. Rev.-and-5th shift rod
7. Stop ring
8. Shift rod end
9. Shift rod end
10. Shift rod end
11. Detent ball
12. Detent spring
13. Washer
14. Spring cap bolt
15. Interlock pin

5-speed shift rod and forks

20. Install the clutch release lever, bearing and related parts.

21. Install the transmission.

5 Speed

NOTE: *The use of special tools is required for the following procedure.*

1. Pull the release fork outward until the spring clip of the fork releases from the ball pivot.

2. Remove the fork and release bearing from the clutch housing.

3. Remove the nuts attaching the clutch housing and remove the housing, shim and gasket.

4. Remove the bolts attaching the gearshift lever retainer to the extension housing and remove the retainer and gasket.

5. Remove the spring and steel ball, select lock spindle and spring from the gearshift lever retainer.

6. Unbolt and remove the extension housing with the control lever end down to the left as far as it will go.

7. Unbolt and remove the control lever end, key and control rod.

8. Remove the lock plate and speedometer gear assembly from the extension housing.

9. Remove the back-up light switch from the extension housing.

10. Remove the snap ring and slide the speedometer drive gear from the mainshaft.

11. Remove the bottom cover and gasket.

12. Unbolt and remove the shift rod ends.

13. Remove the rear bearing housing from the intermediate housing.

14. Remove the snap ring and remove the main shaft rear bearing, thrust washer and race. A puller may be necessary.

15. Using the puller, remove the washer and countershaft rear bearing.

16. Remove the counter fifth gear.

17. Remove the intermediate housing from the case.

18. Unbolt and remove the springs and shift locking balls.

19. Remove the two blind covers and gaskets from the case.

20. Unbolt and remove the reverse/fifth shift rod, fork and interlock pin.

21. Unbolt and remove the first/second and third/fourth shift forks, rods and interlock pins.

22. Remove the snap ring and slide the washer, fifth gear and synchronizer ring from the main shaft. Also, remove the steel ball and needle bearing.

23. Lock the rotation of the mainshaft with second and reverse.

24. Remove the locknut and slide the reverse/fifth clutch hub and sleeve assembly, synchronizer ring, reverse gear and needle bearing from the mainshaft.

25. Remove the spacer and counter reverse gear from the countershaft.

26. Remove the reverse idler gear, thrust washers and shaft from the transmission case.

27. Remove the bearing rear cover plate.

28. Remove the snap ring from the front end of the countershaft and install

Mazda tool number 49 0839 445 synchronizer ring holder or its equivalent between the fourth synchronizer ring and the synchromesh gear on the main driveshaft.

29. Using a bearing puller, remove the countershaft front bearing.

30. Remove the adjusting shim from the countershaft front bearing bore.

31. With the puller, remove the countershaft center bearing outer race.

32. With a special puller and attachment, remove the mainshaft front bearing, thrust washer and inner race along with the adjusting shim front the mainshaft front bearing bore.

33. Remove the snap ring, and using the puller, remove the main drive shaft bearing.

34. Remove the countershaft center bearing inner race with the puller.

35. Separate the input shaft from the mainshaft and remove the input shaft from the case.

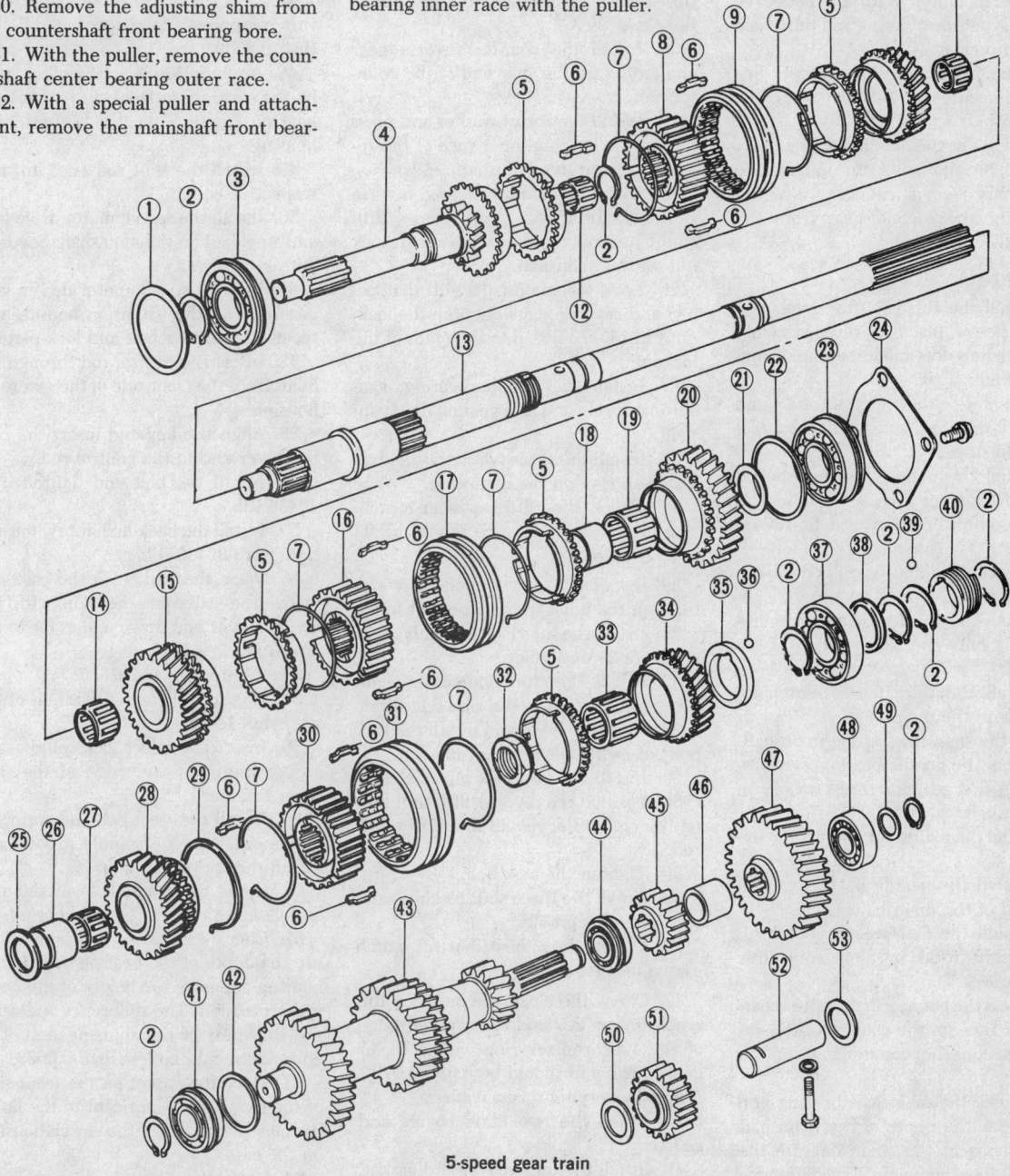

5-speed gear train

1. Shim	28. Reverse gear
2. Snap ring	29. Stop ring
3. Main drive shaft bearing	30. Rev.-and-5th clutch hub
4. Main drive shaft gear	31. Clutch sleeve
5. Synchronizer ring	32. Main shaft lock nut
6. Synchronizer key	33. Needle bearing
7. Synchronizer key spring	34. 5th gear
8. 3rd-and-4th clutch hub	35. Thrust washer
9. Clutch sleeve	36. Lock ball
10. 3rd gear	37. Main shaft rear bearing
11. Needle bearing	38. Thrust washer
12. Needle bearing	39. Lock ball
13. Main shaft	40. Speedometer drive gear
14. Needle bearing	41. Counter shaft front bearing
15. 2nd gear	42. Shim
16. 1st-and-2nd clutch hub	43. Counter shaft
17. Clutch sleeve	44. Counter shaft center bearing
18. Bearing inner race	45. Counter reverse gear
19. Needle bearing	46. Spacer
20. 1st gear	47. Reverse gear
21. Thrust washer	48. Counter shaft rear bearing
22. Shim	49. Thrust washer
23. Main shaft front bearing	50. Thrust washer
24. Bearing cover	51. Reverse idler gear
25. Thrust washer	52. Idler gear shaft
26. Bearing inner race	53. Thrust washer
27. Needle bearing	

36. Remove the synchronizer ring and needle bearing from the input shaft.

37. Remove the mainshaft assembly from the case.

38. Remove the first/second and third-/fourth shift forks from the case.

39. Remove the snap ring and slide the third/fourth clutch hub and sleeve assembly, synchronizer ring and third gear from the mainshaft.

40. Remove the thrust washer, first gear and needle bearing from the rear of the mainshaft.

41. Press out the needle bearing inner race, synchronizer ring, first and second clutch hub, sleeve assembly, synchronizer ring and second gear from the mainshaft.

Assembly

1. Install the third/fourth clutch hub into the sleeve, place the three keys into the clutch hub slots and install the springs onto the hub.

2. Assemble the first/second and reverse/fifth clutch hub and sleeve as described in step 1.

3. Install the needle bearing, second gear, synchronizer ring, and first/second clutch assembly on the rear section of the mainshaft.

4. Press on the first gear needle bearing inner race.

5. Install the third gear and synchronizer ring onto the front section of the mainshaft.

6. Install the third/fourth clutch assembly onto the mainshaft.

7. Fit the snap ring on the mainshaft.

8. Install the needle bearing, synchronizer ring, first gear and thrust washer on the mainshaft.

9. Install the mainshaft assembly in the case.

10. Install the needle bearing on the front end of the mainshaft.

11. Install the first/second and third-/fourth shift forks in their respective clutch sleeves.

12. Press the countershaft center bearing inner race on the countershaft.

13. Position the countershaft in the case.

14. Check the mainshaft bearing end play. Check the depth of the mainshaft bearing bore in the case. Measure the mainshaft bearing height. The difference indicates the required adjusting shim to give a total end play of less than 0.0039".

15. Install the synchronizer ring holder tool between the fourth synchronizer ring and the synchromesh gear on the *input shaft*.

16. Position the shims and mainshaft bearing in the bore and install with a press.

17. Install the input shaft bearing in the same way.

18. Check the countershaft front bearing end play in the same way as the mainshaft bearing end play.

19. Install the front bearing snap ring.

20. Press the countershaft center bearing into position.

21. Install the bearing cover plate.

22. Install the reverse idler gear shaft, thrust washers and reverse idler gear in the case.

23. Install the counter reverse gear and spacer on the rear end of the countershaft.

24. Install the thrust washer and press the needle bearing inner race of the reverse gear on the mainshaft.

25. Install the needle bearing, reverse gear, synchronizer ring, reverse/fifth clutch assembly and new mainshaft lock nut on the mainshaft.

26. Lock the mainshaft with the second and reverse gears. Tighten the locknut to 115–173 ftlb. Bend the tabs of the locknut.

27. Install the needle bearing, synchronizer ring and fifth gear on the mainshaft.

28. Install the thrust washer, steel ball and snap ring on the mainshaft.

29. Check the thrust washer-to-snap ring clearance. Clearance should be 0.-0039–0.0118".

30. Install the first/second shift rod through the holes in the case and fork.

31. Install the interlock pin with a special installer and guide.

32. Install the third/fourth shift rod through the holes in the case and fork.

33. Align the holes and install the lock bolts of each shift fork and rod.

34. Install the interlock pin as above.

35. Position the reverse/fifth shift fork on the clutch sleeve and install the shift rod.

36. Tighten the lock bolt.

37. Install the three shift locking balls, springs and cap bolts.

38. Place the third/fourth clutch sleeve in third gear.

39. Check the clearance between the synchronizer key and the exposed edge of the synchronizer ring with a feeler gauge. The gap should be 0.026–0.079". Adjust by varying thrust washers.

40. Install the two blind covers and gaskets.

41. Install the undercover and gasket. Torque to 4–7 ftlb.

42. Apply a thin coat of sealer to the mating edges and install the intermediate housing on the transmission case. Align the lock bolt holes of the housing and reverse idler gear shaft, install and tighten the lock bolt.

43. Position the counter fifth gear and bearing to the rear end of the countershaft and install with a press.

44. Install the thrust washer and snap ring.

45. Check the clearance between the washer and snap ring. Clearance should be less than 0.0039".

45. Install the mainshaft rear bearing with a press.

46. Install the thrust washer and snap ring.

47. Check the thrust washer-to-snap ring clearance. Clearance should be less than 0.0059".

48. Apply a thin coat of sealing agent to the mating surfaces and install the bearing housing on the intermediate housing.

49. Install the shift rod ends on their respective rods.

50. Install the speedometer drive gear and steel ball on the mainshaft. Secure it with a snap ring.

51. Install a speedometer driven gear assembly on the extension housing and secure it with the bolt and lock plate.

52. Insert the control rod through the holes from the front side of the extension housing.

53. Align the key and insert the control lever end in the control rod.

54. Install the bolt and tighten it to 20–30 ftlb.

55. Install the back-up light switch and tighten to 20–30 ftlb.

56. Place the gasket on the case and install the extension housing with the control lever end down and as far to the left as it will go.

57. Tighten the bolts.

58. Check for proper operation of the gear shift lever.

59. Insert the select lock spindle and spring from the underside of the shift lever retainer.

60. Install the steel ball and spring in alignment with the spindle groove and install the spring cap bolt.

61. Install the gearshift lever retainer and gasket on the extension housing.

62. Check the bearing end play. Measure the depth of the bearing bore in the housing. Measure the height of the bearing protrusion. The difference indicates the thickness of the shim needed. The end play should be less than 0.0039".

63. Place the gasket on the front side of the case. Apply lubricant to the lip of the oil seal and install the clutch housing on the case.

64. Install the release bearing and fork on the clutch housing.

CLUTCH
Pedal Height Adjustment (Free-Play)

Adjust the pushrod length by rotating the rod. The clutch should have a free travel of 13/16–1-3/16 in. measured at the pedal pad.

CLUTCH MASTER CYLINDER   ASSIST SPRING

ADJUSTABLE PEDAL STOP

CLUTCH PEDAL

FREE TRAVEL ADJUSTMENT POINT

FREE TRAVEL DIMENSION

Clutch pedal adjustment

Clutch Release Lever Adjustment

NOTE: *This adjustment must be maintained to prevent release bearing and clutch damage.*

1. Raise and support the truck.
2. Disconnect the release lever return spring at the lever.
3. Loosen the locknut and rotate the adjusting nut until a clearance of 1/8–9/64 in. (0.12–0.14 in.) is obtained between the bullet nosed end of the adjusting nut and the release lever.
4. Tighten the locknut.

Removal and Installation

1. Remove the transmission.

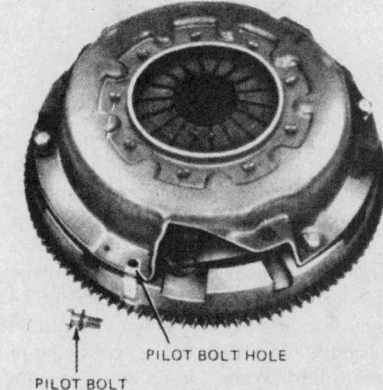

PILOT BOLT HOLE

PILOT BOLT

Clutch pilot bolt holes and alignment marks for pressure plate

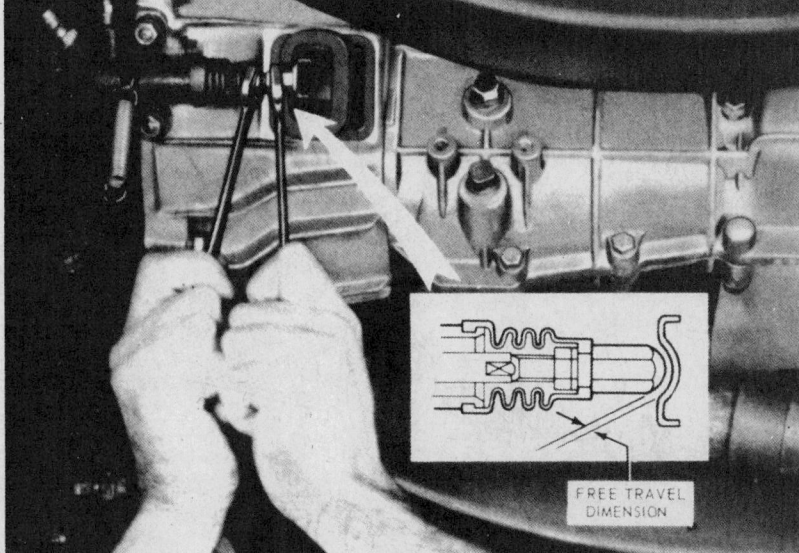

FREE TRAVEL DIMENSION

Clutch release lever adjustment

2. Remove the four attaching and two pilot bolts holding the clutch cover to the flywheel. Loosen the bolts evenly and a turn or two at a time. If the clutch cover is to be reinstalled, mark the flywheel and clutch cover to show the location of the two pilot holes.
3. Remove the clutch disc.

To install the clutch:

4. Install the clutch disc on the flywheel. Do not touch the facing or allow the facing to come in contact with grease or oil. The clutch disc can be aligned using a tool made for that purpose, or with an old mainshaft.
5. Install the clutch cover on the flywheel and install the four standard bolts and the two pilot bolts.
6. To avoid distorting the pressure plate, tighten the bolts evenly a few turns at a time until they are all tight.
7. Torque the bolts to 13–20 ft lbs using a crossing pattern.
8. Remove the aligning tool.
9. Apply a light film of lubricant to the release bearing, release lever contact area on the release bearing hub and to the input shaft bearing retainer.
10. Install the transmission.
11. Check the operation of the clutch and if necessary, adjust the pedal free-play and the release lever.

Clutch Master Cylinder

Removal and Installation

1. Disconnect and plug the hydraulic line.
2. Unbolt and remove the master cylinder.

Overhaul

1. Remove the master cylinder.
2. Clean the outside of the cylinder thoroughly and drain the fluid.
3. Remove the dust cover.
4. Use a screwdriver to remove the piston stop-ring. Remove the stop washer.
5. Remove the piston, piston cup and piston return spring from the cylinder.
6. Carefully remove and disassemble the one-way valve.
7. Wash all parts (except rubber parts) in clean alcohol or brake fluid. Never use mineral spirits of any kind to clean a master cylinder.
8. Check the rubber cups. If they have become worn, softened or swelled, replace them.
9. Check the clearance between the cylinder bore and piston. If it exceeds 0.004 in., replace the cylinder or piston.
10. Be sure that the one-way valve is free to operate.

To assemble the master cylinder:

11. Dip the piston and cups in clean brake fluid.

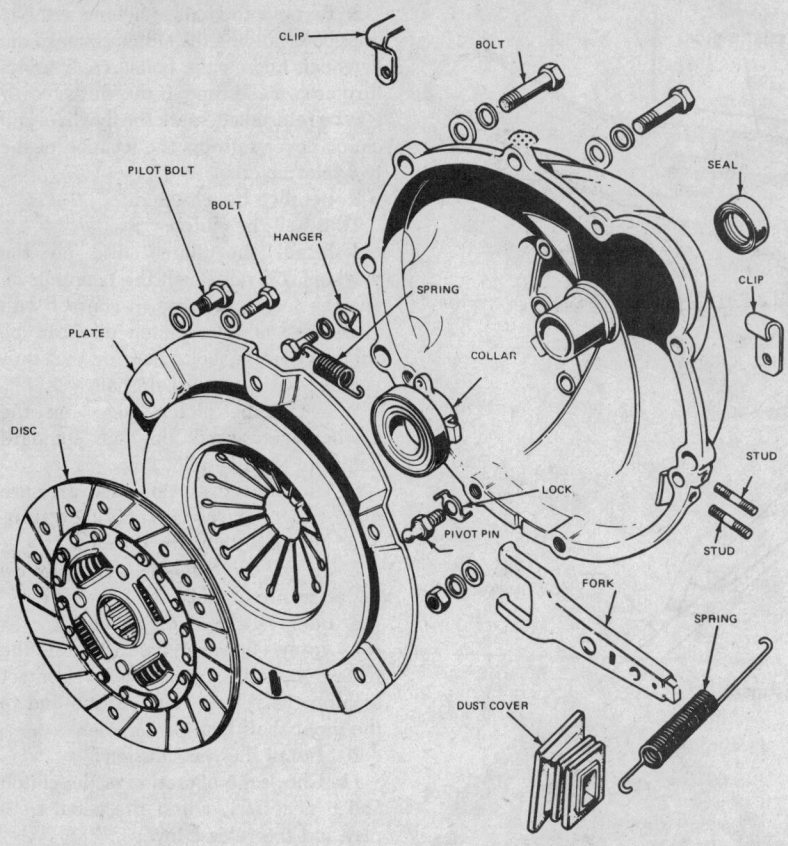

Exploded view of the clutch and housing

pearing, close the bleeder valve and remove the tube.

During the bleeding process, the master cylinder must be kept at least ¾ full. After the bleeding operation is finished, install the cap on the bleeder valve and fill the master cylinder to the proper level. Always use fresh brake fluid, and above all, do not use the fluid that was in the jar for bleeding, since it contains air. Install the master cylinder reservoir cap.

Clutch Slave Cylinder

Removal and Installation

1. Disconnect and plug the slave cylinder hydraulic line.
2. Unhook the release lever return spring.
3. Remove the nuts and washers attaching the slave cylinder to the clutch housing.

To install the slave cylinder:

4. Install the slave cylinder on the clutch housing, torquing the nuts to 12–17 ft lbs.
5. Connect the slave cylinder inlet line to the slave cylinder.
6. Fill the master cylinder and bleed the hydraulic system.
7. Check and adjust the release lever.
8. Connect the return spring.

Overhaul

1. Remove the slave cylinder.
2. Clean the outside thoroughly.
3. Remove the dust cover and release rod.

12. Install the return spring in the cylinder bore.

13. Install the primary cup so that the flat side of the cup is toward the piston.

14. Install the secondary cup on the piston and insert the cup and piston into the cylinder.

15. Install the stop washer and stopring.

16. Assemble and install the one-way valve.

17. Fill the reservoir with clean brake fluid and operate the piston with a screwdriver until fluid is ejected through the outlet fitting.

18. Install the master cylinder.

19. Bleed the hydraulic system.

Bleeding the Hydraulic System

The clutch hydraulic system must be bled whenever the line has been disconnected.

To bleed the system, remove the rubber cap from the bleeder valve and attach a rubber hose to the valve. Submerge the other end of the hose in a large jar of clean brake fluid. Open the bleeder valve. Depress the clutch pedal and allow it to return slowly. Continue this pumping action and watch the jar of brake fluid. When air bubbles stop ap-

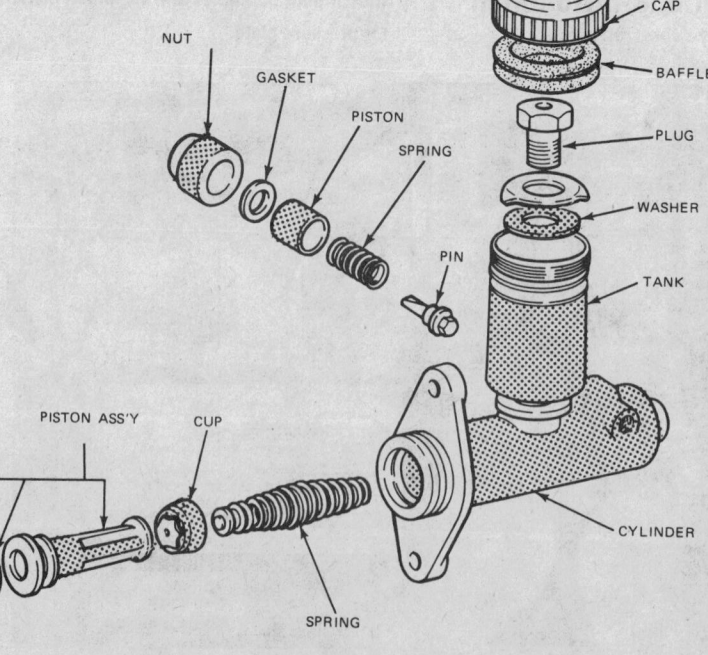

Exploded view of the clutch master cylinder

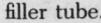

Cross-sectional view of the clutch slave cylinder

4. Remove the piston from the cylinder.

5. Disassemble the bleeder valve.

6. Inspect the cylinder, using Steps 7–9 of the "Master Cylinder Overhaul" procedure.

To assemble the slave cylinder:

7. Dip the pistons and cups in clean brake fluid.

8. Assemble the cups to the piston as shown and install the piston.

9. Install the release rod and release rod boot.

10. Install the steel ball and bleeder into the bleeder orifice. Install the bleeder cap.

11. Install the slave cylinder.

AUTOMATIC TRANSMISSION

Couriers use a JATCO automatic transmission as optional equipment in 1974–76. It is model 3N71B, a 3-speed unit with manual selection of 1st and 2nd gears possible.

NOTE: *The adjustments should be performed in the order given. Be sure the idle speed is set before performing any adjustments.*

Removal and Installation

1. Disconnect the battery.

2. Raise and support the truck.

3. Drain the transmission fluid.

4. Unbolt the exhaust pipe bracket from the right side of the converter housing.

5. Disconnect the driveshaft at the rear axle.

6. Remove the driveshaft center bearing support.

7. Remove the driveshaft.

8. Disconnect the speedometer cable.

9. Disconnect the shift rod from the manual lever at the transmission.

10. Remove the vacuum hose from the vacuum diaphragm, the wires from the downshift solenoid and the inhibitor switch.

11. Disconnect and plug the oil cooler lines.

12. Remove the access cover from the lower end of the converter housing. Matchmark the drive plate and torque converter for reassembly. Remove the 4 bolts attaching the drive plate to the torque converter.

13. Unbolt the rear transmission support from the crossmember.

14. Support the transmission with a jack and unbolt and remove the crossmember.

15. Lower the transmission enough to remove the starter.

16. Remove the converter housing-to-engine bolts.

17. Remove the transmission fluid filler tube.

18. Using a pry bar, exert pressure between the flex plate and the converter to prevent the converter from disengaging from the transmission as the transmission is moved rearward.

19. Remove the transmission and converter as an assembly.

20. Installation is the reverse of removal.

Manual Linkage Adjustment

1. Put the gearshift lever in Neutral.

2. Raise and support the truck.

3. Disconnect the clevis from the lower end of the selector lever operating arm.

4. Move the transmission manual lever to Neutral, the 3rd detent position from the rear of the transmission.

5. Loosen the two clevis retaining nuts and adjust the clevis so that it freely enters the hole of the lever. Tighten the retaining nuts to secure the adjustment.

6. Connect the clevis to the lever and attach it with the spring washer, flat washer and retaining clip.

Throttle Linkage Adjustment

See "Fuel System".

Kick-Down Switch Adjustment

1. Turn the ignition switch to the ON position.

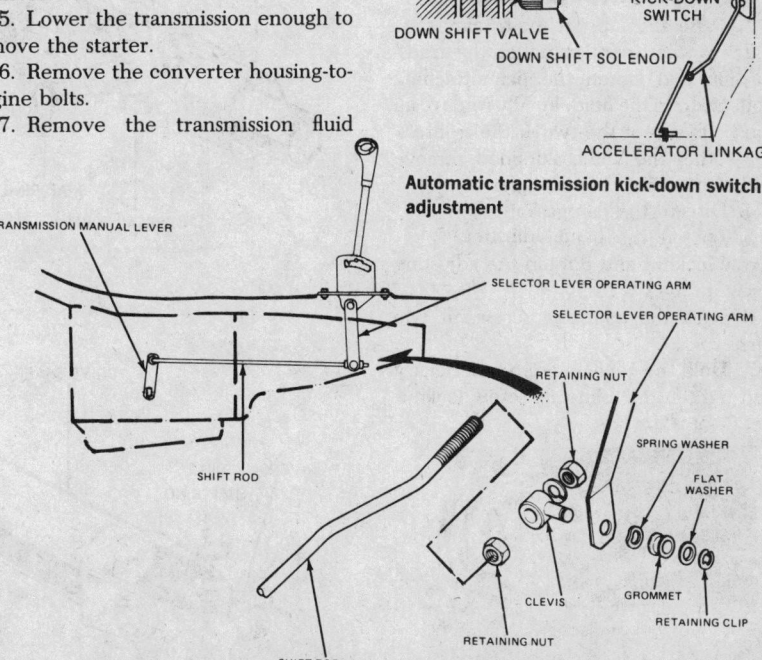

Automatic transmission kick-down switch adjustment

Automatic transmission manual linkage adjustment

2. Loosen the kick-down switch attaching nut and adjust the switch to engage when the accelerator pedal is depressed about ⅞ of the way. The downshift solenoid will click when the switch engages.

Inhibitor Switch Adjustment

1. Adjust the manual linkage.

2. Place the transmission manual lever in Neutral (3rd detent from the rear of the transmission).

3. Remove the transmission manual lever retaining nut and lever.

4. Loosen the inhibitor switch attaching bolts. Remove the screw from the alignment pin hole at the bottom of the switch.

5. Rotate the switch and insert a 0.059 in. (#53 or #54 drill bit) into the alignment pin hole and internal rotor.

6. Tighten the two switch attaching bolts and remove the alignment pin.

7. Reinstall the alignment pin hole screw in the switch body.

8. Install the manual lever. The engine should only start with the transmission selector lever in Neutral or Park.

![Automatic transmission inhibitor switch adjustment]

INHIBITOR SWITCH   0.059" ALIGNMENT PIN

Automatic transmission inhibitor switch adjustment

Band Adjustment

1. Raise and support the truck.

2. Place a drainpan under the transmission and loosen the pan attaching bolts to drain the fluid. Finally remove all the bolts except the two at the front.

3. When the fluid has drained, remove and thoroughly clean the pan.

4. Discard the pan gasket.

5. Loosen the band adjusting screw locknut and tighten the adjusting screw to 9–11 ft lbs.

6. Back the adjusting screw off two turns.

7. Hold the adjusting screw stationary and tighten the adjusting screw locknut to 22–29 ft lbs.

ADJUSTING SCREW   LOCK NUT

Automatic transmission brake band adjustment

8. Install a new pan gasket and install the pan on the transmission. Fill the transmission.

Pan Removal and Installation

See Steps 1, 2, 3, 4, 8 and 9 of the preceding procedure.

DRIVE AXLE
Driveshaft and U-Joints

Removal and Installation

1. Mark the driveshaft and companion flange for correct alignment when it is installed.

2. Remove the center support bearing bracket.

3. Pull the driveshaft rearward and remove it from the transmission.

To install the transmission:

4. Position the driveshaft and slide the front yoke into the extension housing of the transmission.

5. Attach the center support bearing bracket.

6. Install the rear shaft to the companion flange and torque the bolts to 39–47 ft lbs. Be sure that the alignment marks made during removal are aligned.

U-Joint Overhaul

1. Remove the driveshaft from the vehicle and place it in a vise, being careful not to damage it.

2. Remove the snap-rings which retain the bearings in the flange and in the driveshaft.

3. Remove the driveshaft tube from the vise and position the U-joint in the vise with a socket smaller than the bearing cap on one side and a socket larger than the bearing cap on the other side.

4. Slowly tighten the jaws of the vise so that the small socket forces the U-joint spider and the opposite bearing into the larger socket.

5. Remove the other side of the spider in the same manner (if applicable) and remove the spider assembly from the driveshaft. Discard the spider assemblies.

6. Clean all foreign matter from the yoke areas at the end of the driveshaft(s).

7. Start the new spider and one of the bearing cap assemblies into a yoke by positioning the yoke in a vise with the spider positioned in place with one of the bearing cap assemblies positioned over one of the holes in the yoke. Slowly close the vise, pressing the bearing cap assembly in the yoke. Press the cap in far enough so that the retaining snap-ring can be installed. Use the smaller socket to recess the bearing cap.

8. Open the vise and position the opposite bearing cap assembly over the proper hole in the yoke with the socket that is smaller than the diameter of the bearing cap located on the cap. Slowly close the vise, pressing the bearing cap

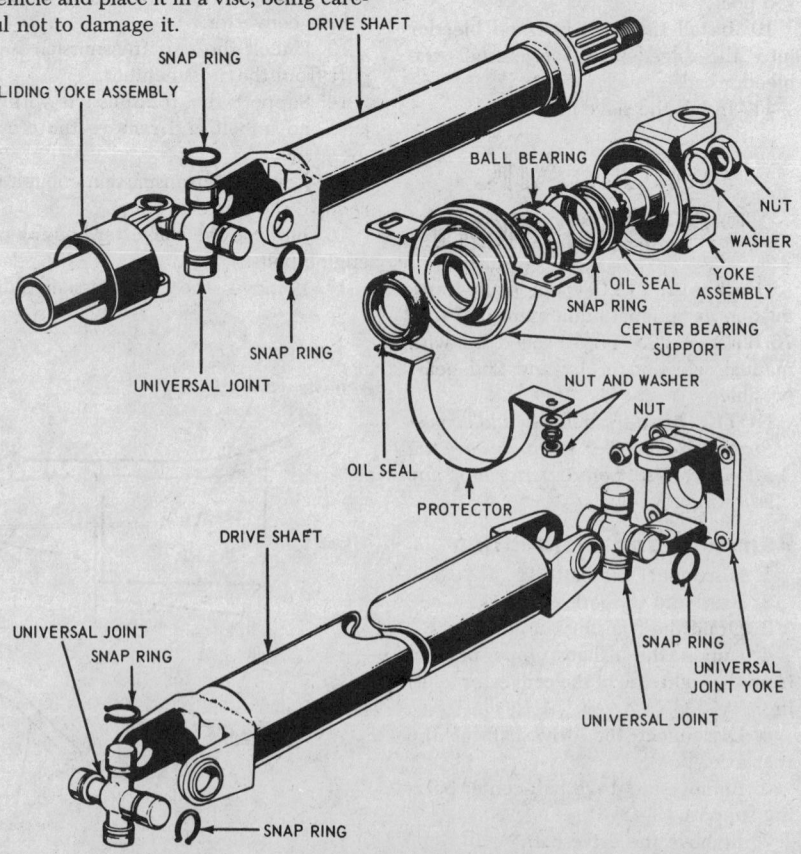

Driveshaft disassembled

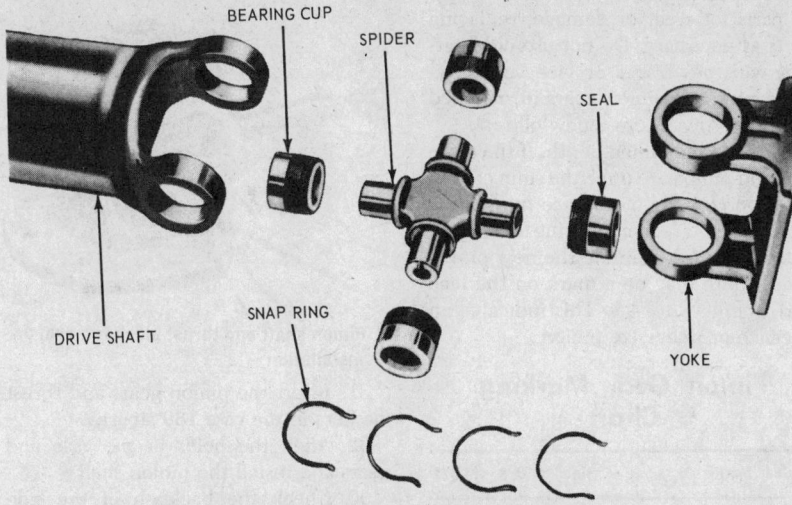

Exploded view of a U-joint

into the hole in the yoke with the socket. Make sure that the spider assembly is in line with the bearing cap as it is pressed in. Press the bearing cap in far enough so that the retaining snap-ring can be installed. Snap-rings are available in 0.057–0.064 in. thicknesses to assure good centering of the yokes and spiders, preventing out-of-balance. When selecting snap-rings, to give a suitable slight drag fit (not binding), use similar snap-rings in any given yoke. For example, do not use a 0.059 in. snap-ring opposite a 0.063 in. snap-ring, as this would create an out-of-balance condition.

9. Install all remaining U-joints in the same manner. The nut attaching the yoke and bearing to the front coupling shaft should be torqued to 115–130 ft lbs.

10. Install the driveshaft and grease the new U-joints.

Axle Shaft

Removal and Installation

1. Raise and support the truck.
2. Remove the rear wheel and brake drum.
3. Remove the brake shoes.
4. Remove the parking brake cable retainer.
5. Disconnect and plug the hydraulic brake lines.
6. Unbolt the backing plate and bearing housing.
7. Slide the complete axle shaft from the housing. If necessary, remove the oil seal from the housing.

To install the axle shaft:
8. Install a new axle oil seal in the housing if the old one was removed.
9. Install the axle shaft assembly.
10. Using two bolts and nuts, temporarily install the bearing housing and backing plate to the housing flange.
11. Check the axle shaft end-play with a dial indicator mounted on the backing plate.

Checking axle shaft end-play

12. If only one axle shaft has been removed, the end-play should be 0.002–0.006 in. If both axle shafts have been removed, check the end-play after the first shaft is installed. It should be 0.026–0.033 in. The end-play of the second shaft should then be 0.002–0.006 in. Shims are available to adjust the end-play.

13. After adjusting the end play, install all bolts and torque them to 12–16 ft lbs.
14. Install the brake shoes.
15. Install the brake drum and wheel.
16. Connect the brake lines.
17. Bleed the brakes.

Differential

Removal and Installation

1. Raise and support the truck.
2. Drain the fluid.
3. Remove the axle shafts.
4. Matchmark the driveshaft and companion flange for reassembly. Remove the driveshaft.
5. Unbolt and remove the carrier.
6. Installation is the reverse of removal. Clean the magnetic drain plug.

Overhaul

Before disassembling the carrier, perform a few tests for future reference.

1. Wipe the lubricant from the gear teeth and perform a tooth contact pattern test.

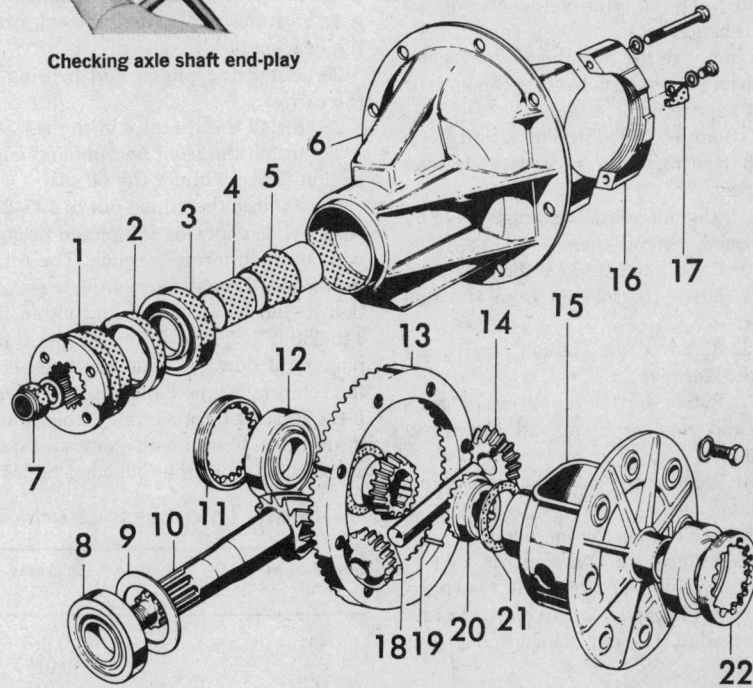

Exploded view of differential

1. Pinion flange
2. Pinion oil seal
3. Pinion front bearing
4. Pinion bearing collar
5. Collapsible pinion bearing spacer
6. Carrier
7. Pinion nut
8. Pinion rear bearing
9. Adjusting washer (Adjusting spacer)
10. Drive pinion
11. Pinion side adjusting nut
12. Side bearing
13. Ring gear
14. Pinion gear
15. Differential gear case
16. Bearing cap
17. Adjusting nut lock
18. Pinion shaft
19. Pinion shaft lock pin
20. Side gear
21. Thrust washer
22. Ring gear side adjusting nut

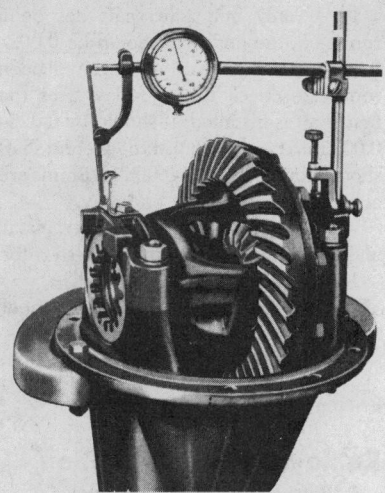

Checking side bearing preload

2. Measure and record the ring gear backlash. The limits are 0.007–0.008 in.

3. Measure and record the ring gear run-out.

4. Matchmark the carrier, differential bearing caps and the adjusters for reassembly.

5. Remove the adjuster lockplates.

6. Set up a dial indicator to read the side bearing preload. Loosen the nuts securing the bearing cap and slowly back off the adjuster to relieve the preload. As this is being done, observe and record the preload. The adjuster on the left side has a left-hand thread.

7. Remove the nuts, bearing caps and adjusters. Keep each bearing cap with its own adjuster.

8. Remove the differential and keep each bearing outer race with its own bearing.

9. If the differential bearings are to be replaced, remove them.

10. Unbolt and remove the ring gear.

11. Drive the lockpin from the ring gear.

12. Remove the pinion shaft and thrust block.

13. Rotate the differential pinion gears 90° and remove them and the thrust washers.

14. Remove the side gears and thrust washers.

15. Remove the pinion nut.

16. Remove the companion flange.

17. Remove the pinion and rear bearing from the carrier with a plastic or rubber mallet. Do not damage the gear teeth.

18. Remove the pinion oil seal and front bearing.

19. The pinion bearing outer races can be removed with a drift.

20. Remove and save the shims from underneath the outer race.

21. Remove the bearing from the pinion.

With the carrier disassembled, check all parts for wear or damage, replacing parts as necessary. Do not use old bearings with new races or vice versa. Replace ring and pinion gears in matched sets only. Always use a new oil seal.

22. Find the pinion depth. If the same ring and pinion are used, the shim combination under the outer race may prove satisfactory. If replacing a ring and pinion with a new set, examine the new pinion gear. There may be a mark on the face end from −1 to +1. This indicates an oversize or undersize pinion.

Pinion Gear Marking Chart

Gear Mark	Inches O/S or U/S
± 1	± 0.0004
± 2	± 0.0008
± 3	± 0.0012

If there is no mark, the shim pack already with the carrier should be satisfactory. For example, if the new pinion is marked +3 and the old pinion is marked +2, the shim pack must be increased by 0.0004 in. In any case, no more than 4 shims should be used.

23. Position the determined shim pack and bearing races.

24. Find the pinion bearing preload. If the bearing was removed from the pinion gear or a new gear is being used, press the bearing on the pinion.

25. Install the pinion and bearing in the carrier.

26. Install the spacer and shims.

27. Install the front bearing and companion flange without the oil seal.

28. Tighten the pinion nut to 145–250 ft lbs, while checking the pinion preload with an in. lb torque wrench. The rotating torque, through one complete revolution should be 1.3–2.5 ft lbs, within the 145-250 ft lbs of nut torque. Tighten the pinion nut slowly in small increments as the rotating torque builds up in a hurry. If the rotating torque is not within limits, it must be adjusted with shims and spacers selected from the following tables.

Shim Thickness Chart

Identification Mark	Thickness (in.)
4	0.013
6	0.014
8	0.015

29. Following this adjustment, install a new oil seal and tighten the pinion nut to 200 ft lbs.

To assemble the differential:

30. Install the thrust washer on each differential side gear and install the side gears.

Pinion shaft and thrust block removal or installation

31. Insert the pinion gears and thrust washers in the case 180° apart.

32. Align the holes in the case and gears and install the pinion shaft.

33. Check the backlash of the side gears which should not exceed 0.008 in. If it does, adjust the backlash with the side gear thrust washers.

Side Gear Thrust Washer Chart

Identification Mark	Thickness (in.)
6	0.063
7	0.067
8	0.071

34. After adjustment, remove the pinion shaft and install the thrust block. The hole should be centered between the side gears. Reinstall the pinion shaft until the lockpin hole in the pinion shaft is aligned with the hole in the case.

35. Install the lockpin in the pinion shaft and stake it in place.

36. Install the ring gear and torque the bolts to 40–45 ft lbs. Bend the locktabs over the bolts.

37. Install each differential bearing in the case. Install the outer races on their respective bearings.

38. Install the differential gear assembly in the carrier so that the marks on the face of the pinion and ring gear are in alignment.

39. Note the identification marks on the adjusters (right and left-hand) and install these.

40. Install the bearing caps and align the matchmarks previously made.

41. Turn the adjusters until the bearings are properly positioned and some amount of backlash exists in the ring gear teeth. End-play in the bearings should be eliminated.

42. Slightly tighten one of the bearing cap nuts on each side and adjust the backlash.

43. Install a dial indicator on the carrier flange and index it at right angles to one of the ring gear teeth. Check the backlash at 4 or 5 different teeth. Turn both adjusters equally, until the backlash

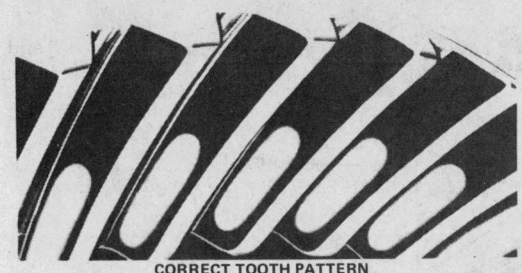

CORRECT TOOTH PATTERN
THIS PATTERN PROVIDES PROPER GEAR MESH AND AXLE PERFORMANCE.
ALL ADJUSTMENTS MUST BE MADE TO SECURE THIS TYPE OF PATTERN.

LOW CONTACT
THE PINION IS IN TOO FAR.
REMOVE SHIMS, AND READJUST BACKLASH.

HIGH CONTACT
THE PINION IS OUT TOO FAR.
ADD SHIMS, AND READJUST BACKLASH.

CONTACT ON THE HEAL
TOO MUCH BACKLASH.
MOVE RING GEAR TOWARD PINION.

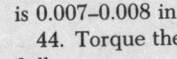

Gear tooth patterns

CONTACT ON THE TOE
NOT ENOUGH BACKLASH.
MOVE RING GEAR AWAY FROM PINION.

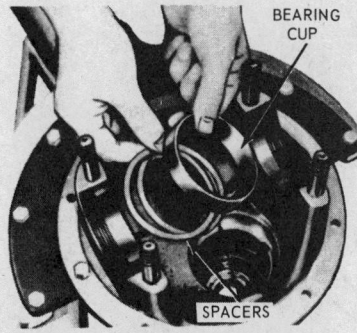

Positioning shims and bearing races

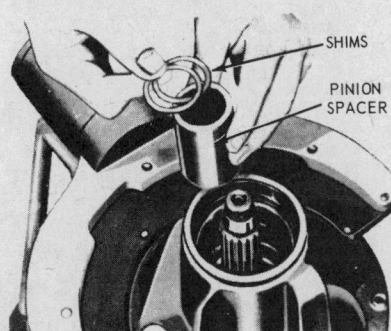

Installing pinion spacer and shims

is 0.007–0.008 in.

44. Torque the bearing cap nuts to 45 ft lbs.

45. Install the adjuster lockplates.

REAR SUSPENSION

Springs

Removal and Installation

1. Raise and support the truck.

2. Support the rear axle.

3. Disconnect the shock absorber at the lower mount.

4. Remove the spring clip nuts and the spring plate.

5. Remove the spring pin nut and remove the two bolts and nuts attaching the spring pin to the frame bracket.

6. Remove the spring pin and remove the front end of the spring from the truck.

7. Remove the shackle plate nuts and the shackle plate.

8. Remove the spring from the truck.

To install the spring:

9. Install the rubber bushings in the front eye of the spring and position it in the frame bracket. Align the holes of the bushings with the hole of the frame bracket.

10. Insert the spring pin from the outside through the rubber bushing.

11. Install the spring pin plate to the frame bracket and torque the nuts to 15–18 ft lbs.

12. Install the rubber bushings in the rear spring eye and shackle plate. Install the spring and shackle plate to the frame bracket. Do not tighten the nuts.

13. Lower the rear axle and place the center hole of the axle spring clip plate over the head of the spring center bolt.

14. Install the spring plate under the spring and install the spring clips. Torque the nuts to 46–58 ft lbs.

15. Connect the shock absorber at the lower mount and torque the mount to 18–26 ft lbs.

16. Lower the vehicle and bounce it several times to seat the springs.

17. Tighten the spring pin nuts to 62–76 ft lbs. and the shackle plate nuts to 44–58 ft lbs.

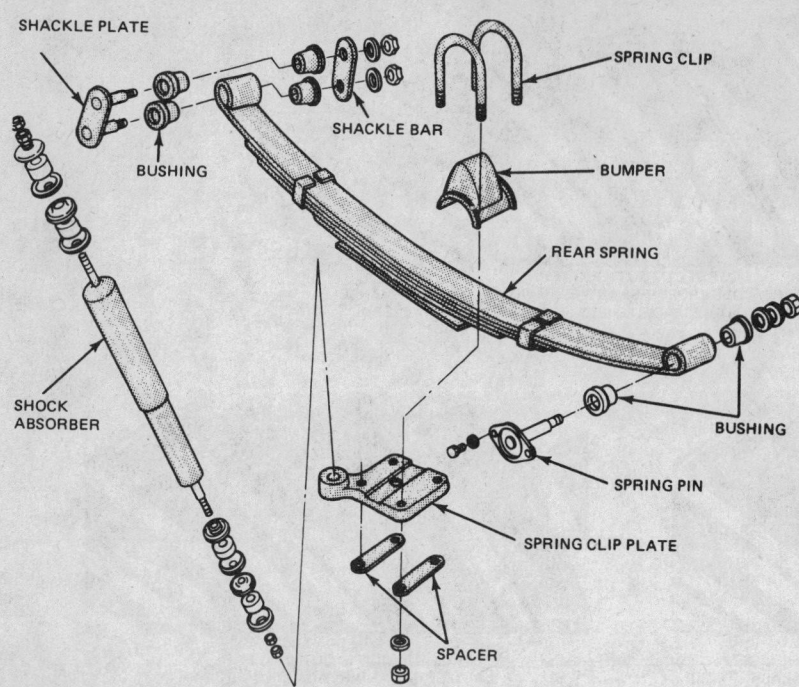

SHACKLE PLATE

BUSHING

SHACKLE BAR

SPRING CLIP

BUMPER

REAR SPRING

SHOCK ABSORBER

BUSHING

SPRING PIN

SPRING CLIP PLATE

SPACER

Exploded view of the rear suspension

Shock Absorber

Removal and Installation

1. Raise and support the truck.
2. Remove the nuts, washers and bushings from the upper and lower shock mounts.
3. Compress the shock absorber and remove it.

To install the shock absorber:

4. If the rubber bushings are worn or damaged, use new ones.
5. Compress the shock absorber and install it in the truck.

6. Install the rubber bushings, washers and nuts on both the upper and lower mounts. Torque all mounts to 18–26 ft lbs.
7. Lower the truck.

FRONT SUSPENSION
Shock Absorber

Removal and Installation

1. Raise and support the truck.
2. Unbolt the upper mount from the crossmember.
3. Remove the rubber bushings and washers.
4. Unbolt the lower end from the control arm.
5. Remove the shock from under the lower control arm.

To install the shock absorber:

6. Replace any worn or damaged bushings.
7. From under the lower control arm, install the shock with bushings and attach the shock to the lower control arm. Torque the lower mount to 12–17 ft lbs.
8. Attach the upper end of the shock to the crossmember and torque the upper mount bolt to 18–26 ft lbs.
9. Lower the truck.

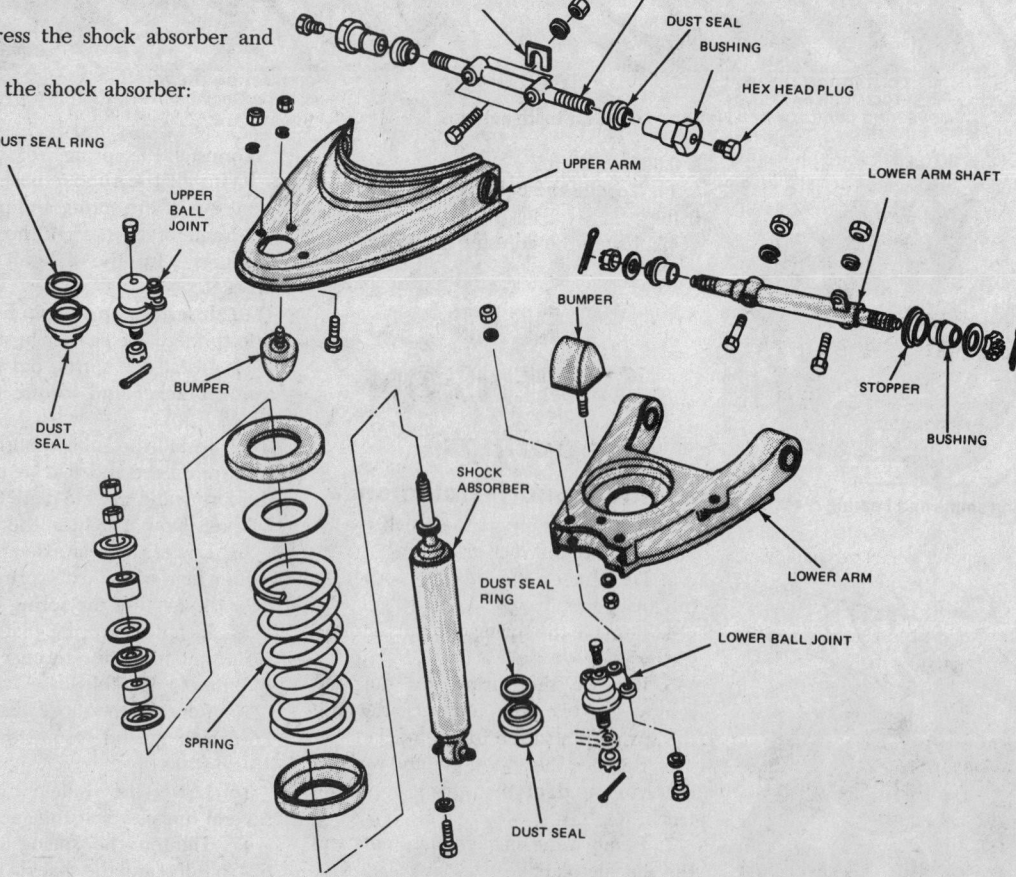

SHIM

UPPER ARM SHAFT

DUST SEAL

BUSHING

HEX HEAD PLUG

DUST SEAL RING

UPPER ARM

LOWER ARM SHAFT

UPPER BALL JOINT

BUMPER

BUMPER

STOPPER

BUSHING

DUST SEAL

SHOCK ABSORBER

LOWER ARM

DUST SEAL RING

LOWER BALL JOINT

SPRING

DUST SEAL

Exploded view of the front suspension

Spring Removal and Installation

Follow procedures under "Upper Control Arm".

Upper Control Arm

Removal and Installation

1. Raise and support the truck.
2. Support the lower control arm.
3. Lower the truck until the upper control arm is off the bumper stop.
4. Remove the wheel. Install a spring compressor.
5. Remove the cotter pin and nut retaining the upper ball joint.
6. Separate the ball joint from the spindle.
7. From under the hood, remove the two upper arm retaining bolts and remove the arm from the vehicle.
8. Remove the ball joint from the upper arm.
9. Install the ball joint in the upper control arm.
10. Position the upper control arm in the truck and install the alignment shims from where they were removed.
11. Install the spindle on the ball joint.
12. Remove the spring compressor.

Lower Control Arm

Removal and Installation

1. Raise and support the front of the truck.
2. Remove the wheel.
3. Disconnect the shock absorber and push the shock up into the spring.
4. Remove the front stabilizer bar.
5. Position a floor jack under the lower control arm and raise the arm to take the spring pressure off. Install a spring compressor.
6. Unbolt the ball joint from the lower control arm.
7. Pull the spindle and ball joint away from the lower arm.
8. If necessary, the lower ball joint can be removed by removing the cotter pin and nut and loosening the ball joint with a hammer.
9. Remove the lower control arm.
10. Install the lower control arm. Do not tighten. If removed, install the ball joint.
11. Install the spring.
12. Use a C-clamp to clamp the spring to the lower control arm.
13. Raise the lower control arm with a floor jack and position the ball joint and spindle in the lower arm.
14. Loosely install the three lower arm-to-ball joint bolts. Remove the spring compressor, and remove the floor jack and C-clamp.
15. Torque the three ball joint retaining nuts to 60–70 ft lbs.

16. Pull the shock absorber down and install the bolts and nuts.
17. Install the stabilizer bar on the lower control arm.
18. Check front wheel alignment.

Ball Joints

Checking

1. Check the ball joint dust seals and replace them if they are defective.
2. Check the end-play of the upper and lower ball joints. If the end-play exceeds 0.031 in., replace the ball joint.

Replacement

Use the applicable procedures under "Upper Control Arm Removal and Installation", or "Lower Control Arm Removal and Installation".

Front End Alignment

Caster

Caster is adjusted by changing the shim(s) between the upper arm shaft and the frame, or, by turning the eccentric shaft until the correct angle is obtained.

Camber

Camber is adjusted by adding or subtracting the shim(s) between the upper arm shaft and the frame. The shims are available in thicknesses of 0.040 in., 0.064 in., 0.080 in., and 0.128 in.

Toe-In

Toe-in can be increased or decreased by changing the length of the tie-rods.

Front Wheel Turning Angle

The turning stop screws are located at the steering knuckle. If necessary, the screws can be adjusted to adjust the turning angle.

STEERING
Steering Wheel

Removal and Installation

1. Disconnect the negative battery cable.
2. Remove the horn button by turning it counterclockwise. Remove the horn contact spring.
3. Matchmark the steering wheel and

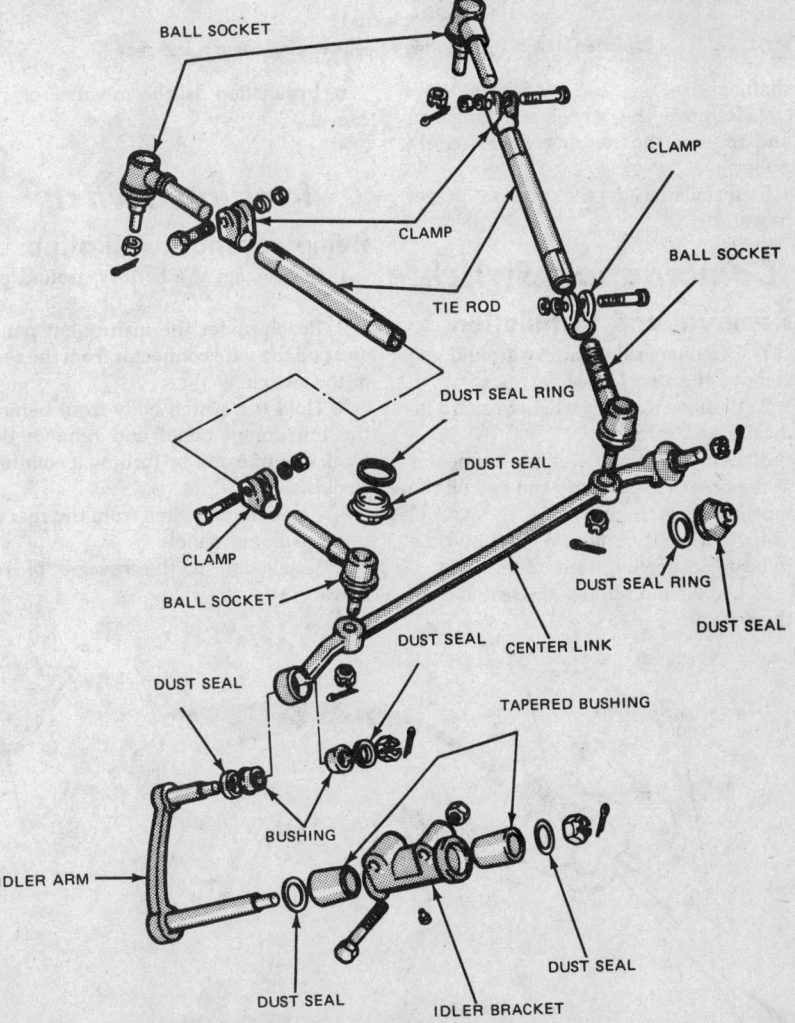

Exploded view of the steering linkage

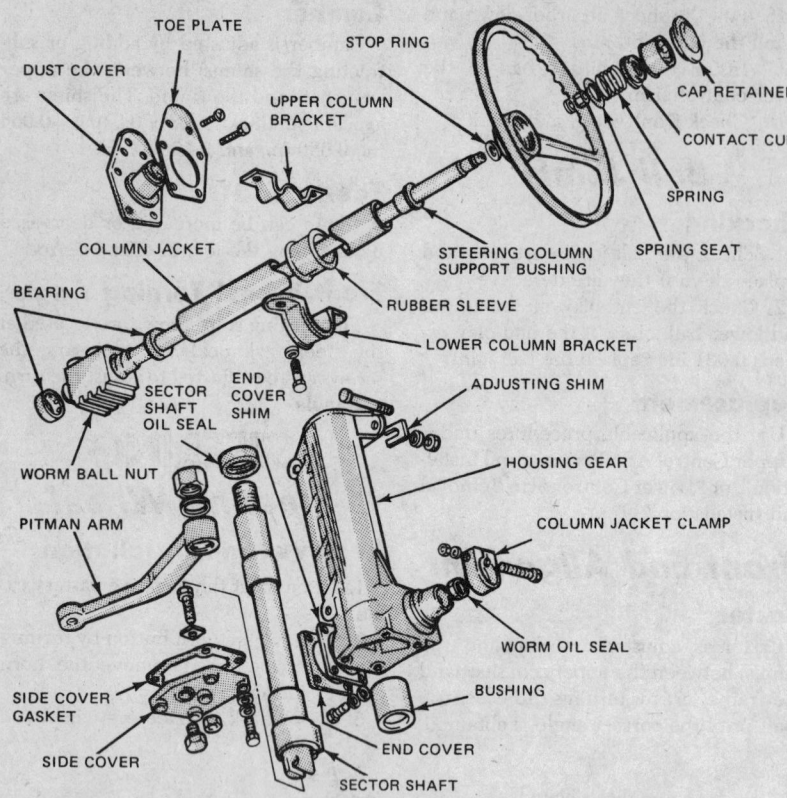

TOE PLATE
STOP RING
DUST COVER
CAP RETAINER
UPPER COLUMN
BRACKET
CONTACT CUP
SPRING
COLUMN JACKET
STEERING COLUMN
SUPPORT BUSHING
SPRING SEAT
BEARING
RUBBER SLEEVE
LOWER COLUMN BRACKET
SECTOR
SHAFT
OIL SEAL
END
COVER
SHIM
ADJUSTING SHIM
WORM BALL NUT
HOUSING GEAR
PITMAN ARM
COLUMN JACKET CLAMP
WORM OIL SEAL
SIDE COVER
GASKET
BUSHING
SIDE COVER
END COVER
SECTOR SHAFT

Exploded view of the steering wheel, steering column and gear

shaft.

4. Remove the wheel attaching nut and remove the steering wheel with a puller.

5. Installation is the reverse of removal.

Combination Switch

Removal and Installation

1. Disconnect the battery ground and remove the steering wheel.

2. Remove the plastic lights, hazard indicator and shroud.

3. Disconnect the multiple connector at the base of the column and pull off the headlight switch knob.

4. Remove the snap-ring and pull the indicator cancelling cam off the shaft.

5. Unbolt and remove the switch from the column.

6. Installation is the reverse of removal.

Ignition Switch

Removal and Installation

1. Disconnect the battery ground cable.

2. Reach under the instrument panel and pull the wire connector from the rear of the switch.

3. Hold the switch body from behind the instrument panel and remove the black retaining nut by turning it counterclockwise.

4. Remove the switch from the rear of the instrument panel.

5. Installation is the reverse of removal.

Steering Column and Gear

Removal and Installation

1. Disconnect the negative battery cable.

2. Remove the steering wheel.

3. Remove the canceling cam snapring and cam from the top of the steering shaft.

4. Remove the dimmer and turn signal wires from the switch.

5. Remove the steering column support bracket.

6. Remove the floor covering and insulator pad from the bottom end of the steering column.

7. Unbolt the toe plate and boot from the dash.

8. Remove the column jacket from the shaft.

9. Remove the air cleaner.

10. Disconnect the heater hoses and brackets and position them aside.

11. Remove and plug the hydraulic lines from the clutch and master cylinders.

12. Remove the brake and clutch master cylinders.

13. Raise and support the truck. Disconnect the pitman arm.

14. Unbolt the steering gear from the frame. Check for the presence of an aligning shim between the gear and the frame.

15. Lower the truck and remove the gear and shaft.

16. Installation is the reverse of removal. Reinstall the aligning shim in its original location, if equipped. Bleed the clutch and master cylinders. Bleed the brakes.

Worm Bearing Preload Adjustment

1. It is necessary to drain the steering gear to make this adjustment. Refill the steering gear after adjustment.

2. Disconnect the pitman arm from the gear.

3. Loosen the sector adjusting screw locknut and turn the adjusting screw counterclockwise.

4. Rotate the worm shaft with a torque wrench. The preload should be 1–3.5 in. lb. If it is not, unscrew the end cover bolts and remove the end cover with the shim pack. If the preload is less than specified, reduce the shim size. If it is more than specified, increase the shim size. Shims are available in 0.002, 0.003, 0.004 and 0.008 in.

5. Reconnect the Pitman arm.

Sector Gear and Ball Nut Mesh Load

This adjustment must be done after the worm bearing preload is adjusted.

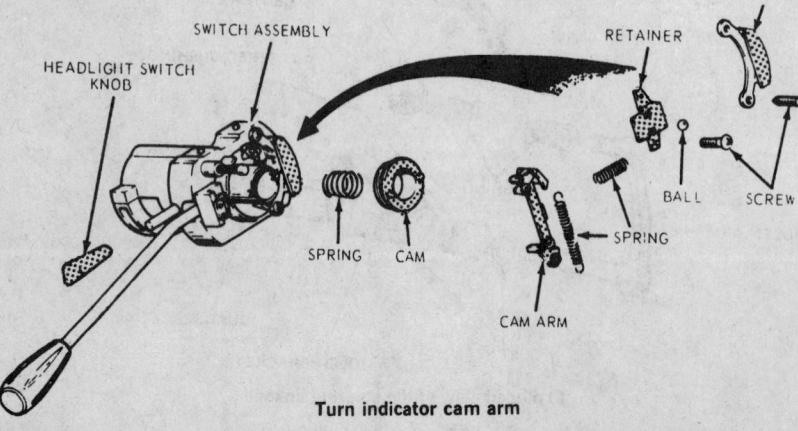

SWITCH ASSEMBLY
PLATE
RETAINER
HEADLIGHT SWITCH
KNOB
SPRING
CAM
BALL
SCREW
SPRING
CAM ARM

Turn indicator cam arm

1. Disconnect the pitman arm from the center link.

2. Loosen the locknut on the sector adjusting screw.

3. Turn the steering wheel slowly to either stop. Turn it to the other stop, counting the number of turns. Position the steering wheel in the center, by dividing the number of turns in half.

4. Turn the sector adjusting screw clockwise until a torque of 5–7 in. lbs is obtained while rotating the worm past the center (high spot).

5. Tighten the locknut while holding the adjusting screw. Recheck the mesh load.

6. Reconnect the pitman arm to the center link.

BRAKE SYSTEMS
Adjustment

Front Brakes

1. Raise and support the truck.

2. Remove the adjusting slot covers from the brake backing plate.

3. Insert a brake adjusting spoon and rotate the starwheel of one wheel cylinder toward the inside of the brake drum until the wheel is locked. Then back off the starwheel 6–8 notches.

4. Repeat Step 3 for each wheel cylinder of each wheel.

5. Install the adjusting slot covers.

6. Check the brake adjustment by spinning the wheel by hand. There should be no drag.

Rear Brakes

1. Be sure that the parking brake is fully released. Disconnect the equalizer clevis pin.

2. Raise and support the truck.

3. Remove the adjusting slot covers from the brake backing plate.

4. Insert a brake spoon into the lower adjusting slot to contact the starwheel of the lower wheel cylinder.

5. Turn the lower wheel cylinder starwheel to expand the brake shoe until it locks against the drum. Back the starwheel off 6–8 notches. Check the wheel, by rotating it, to be sure that there is no drag.

6. Repeat Step 5 for each wheel cylin-

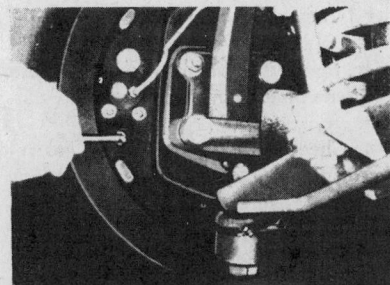

Adjusting the front brake shoes

Adjusting the rear brake shoes

der of each wheel.

7. Connect the parking brake equalizer clevis pin and check the parking brake adjustment.

8. Install the adjusting hole covers.

9. Lower the truck and road-test the brakes. Readjust if necessary.

Brake Pedal Free-Travel Adjustment

1. Loosen the locknut on the master cylinder pushrod at the clevis, which attaches the pushrod to the pedal.

2. Turn the master cylinder pushrod either in or out to obtain ⅝–1 in. free travel.

3. Tighten the locknut.

HYDRAULIC SYSTEMS
Master Cylinder

Removal and Installation

1. Disconnect and plug the brake lines.

2. Unbolt the master cylinder and lift it and the boot outward and upward

away from the firewall and brake pushrod.

To install the master cylinder:

3. Install the master cylinder and boot on the firewall, while carefully guiding the brake pushrod into contact with the master cylinder piston.

4. Install the two nuts and lockwashers and tighten the nuts to 11–17 ft lbs.

5. Connect the brake lines to the master cylinder outlet ports.

6. Bleed the brake system.

7. Check the brake pedal free-travel adjustment.

Overhaul

1. Remove the master cylinder.

2. Remove the master cylinder reservoir and drain the master cylinder.

3. Remove the two grommets from the master cylinder body.

4. Remove the dust boot.

5. Use a small screwdriver to remove the piston stopring.

6. Remove the piston stopwasher, primary piston and primary piston return spring.

7. Remove the secondary piston stopscrew and O-ring.

8. Remove the secondary piston and secondary return spring.

9. Remove the outlet port fittings, gaskets, check valves and check valve springs.

10. Clean all the parts (except rubber) in isopropyl alcohol. Do not use mineral base fluids. Allow all parts to air dry.

To assemble the master cylinder:

11. Dip all parts (except rubber) in clean brake fluid before assembly.

12. Install the check valve spring and check valves into the cylinder outlets and install the outlet port fittings and gaskets.

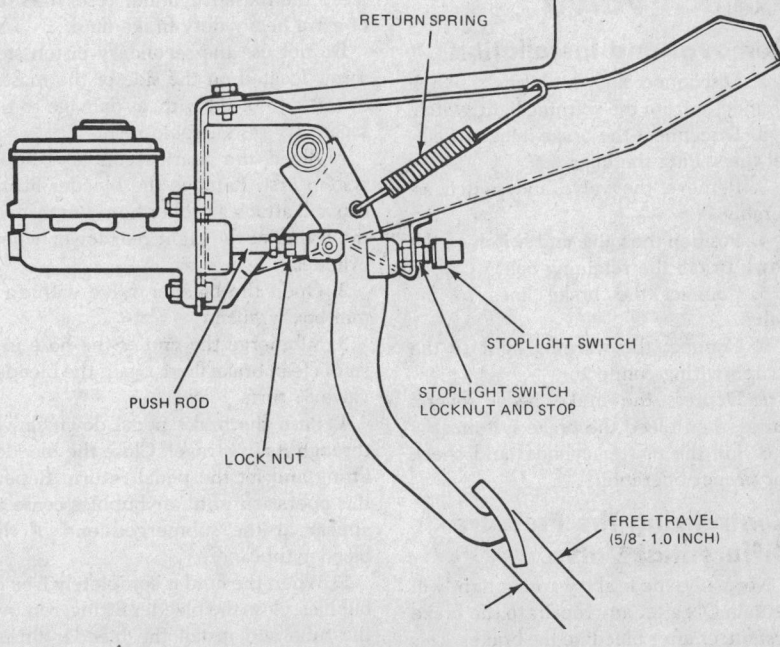

RETURN SPRING

STOPLIGHT SWITCH

STOPLIGHT SWITCH LOCKNUT AND STOP

PUSH ROD

LOCK NUT

FREE TRAVEL (5/8 - 1.0 INCH)

Brake pedal free-travel adjustment

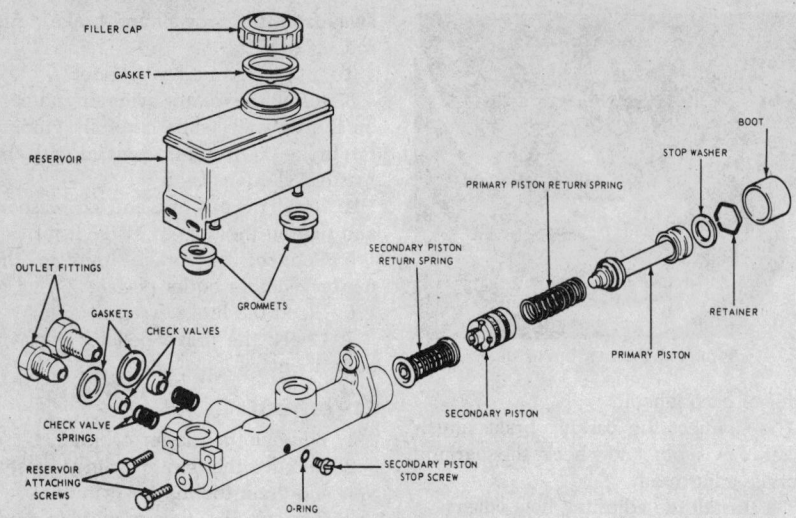

Exploded view of the master cylinder

13. Position the secondary piston return spring on the secondary piston and install the assembly spring first.

14. Position the primary piston spring on the primary piston and install the assembly, spring first into the cylinder.

15. Install the piston stopwasher and piston stopring.

16. Install the secondary piston stopbolt.

17. Install the two grommets in the cylinder body.

18. Install the reservoir so that the outlet tubes are seated in the grommets.

19. Fill the master cylinder and pump the piston with a screwdriver until fluid flows from the outlet ports.

20. Install the master cylinder and bleed the brakes.

Pressure Differential Valve

Removal and Installation

1. Disconnect the warning light switch connector from the warning light switch.

2. Disconnect the brake inlet and outlet lines. Plug the lines.

3. Remove the valve and switch assembly.

4. Position the valve and switch on the cowl. Install the retaining bolt.

5. Connect the brake lines to the valve.

6. Connect the warning light to the switch wiring connector.

7. Depress the brake pedal several times, then bleed the brake system.

8. Fill the master cylinder and check for proper operation.

Centralizing the Pressure Differential Valve

Normally, the brake warning light will remain ON after any repairs to the brake system, or after bleeding the brakes. This is caused by the pressure differential valve remaining in the off center position.

1. Turn the ignition switch to ON.

2. Check the fluid levels in the master cylinder reservoirs and fill them to within ¼ in. of the top, if necessary.

3. Depress the brake pedal and the piston will center itself, causing the warning light to go out.

4. Turn the ignition switch OFF. The light should go out.

Bleeding

The primary and secondary (front and rear) systems are independent systems and are bled separately. Bleed the longest line first on an individual system. In the case of the rear brakes, bleed at the lower right rear wheel cylinder then at the upper right rear wheel cylinder. Keep the master cylinder reservoirs full of extra heavy duty brake fluid.

Do not use the secondary piston stop screw located on the side of the master cylinder to bleed with, as damage to the secondary piston could result.

1. Bleed the rear (secondary) brake system first. Remove the bleeder fitting cap and attach a rubber hose snugly over the fitting at the right rear lower wheel cylinder.

2. Open the bleeder valve with an 8 mm box wrench.

3. Submerge the end of the hose in a jar of clean brake fluid. Open the bleeder valve ¾ turn.

4. Push the brake pedal down slowly through its full travel. Close the bleeder fitting and let the pedal return. Repeat this operation until air bubbles cease to appear at the submerged end of the bleeder tube.

5. When the fluid is completely free of bubbles, close the bleeder fitting, remove the tube and install the bleeder fitting cap.

6. Repeat this procedure at the upper right wheel cylinder.

7. Repeat the procedure at the left rear wheel cylinders. Refill the master cylinder reservoir after each wheel cylinder is bled.

8. Bleed the primary (front) brake system in the same manner, ending by bleeding each left front wheel cylinder.

9. When the bleeding operation is complete, the master cylinder should be filled to within ¼ in. of the top. Install the master cylinder cover.

10. Centralize the pressure differential valve.

Front Drum Brakes

Brake Drum

Removal and Installation

1. Raise and support the truck.

2. Remove the wheel.

3. Remove the brake drum attaching screws and install them in the tapped holes in the brake drum.

4. Turn these screws in evenly to force the brake drum away from the wheel hub.

5. Remove and inspect the brake drum.

To install the brake drum:

6. Install the brake drum with the attaching screw holes aligned with the holes in the hub.

7. Transfer the attaching screws from the tapped holes in the brake drum to the attaching holes in the hub.

8. Tighten the screws evenly to secure the hub.

9. Install the wheel.

10. Lower the truck check the brake adjustment.

Inspection

1. Check the brake drum diameter with a brake drum gauge. Replace any drums which have a diameter greater than 10.2962 in.

2. Inspect the brake drums for cracks.

Brake Shoes

Inspection

1. If compressed air is available, blow out the accumulated dust and grit.

2. If the lining is worn to within 1/32 in. of the shoe or if the shoes are damaged, they must be replaced.

3. Replace any linings (in axle sets only) that are contaminated with grease or brake fluid from leaking wheel cylinders.

4. Check the condition of the shoes, retracting springs and hold-down springs for signs of overheating. If the shoes have a slight blue color, this indicates overheating and replacement of the springs as well as the linings is recommended.

5. If signs of overheating are present,

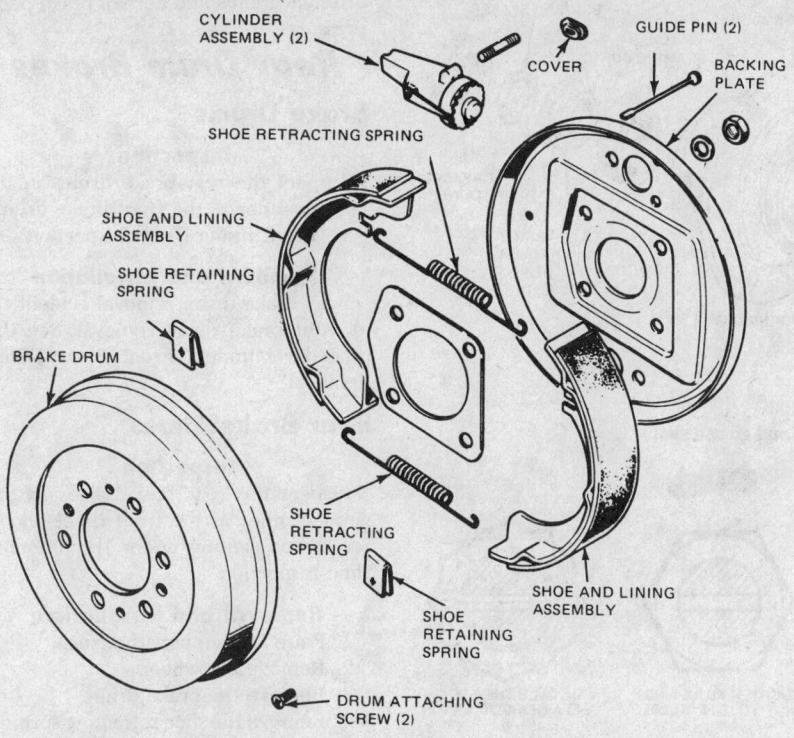

Front brakes

11. Adjust the brakes.

12. Bleed the brakes and centralize the pressure differential valve.

13. Lower the truck.

Overhaul

1. Remove the wheel cylinder.

2. Remove the piston and adjusting screw with the boot attached to the cylinder. Separate the adjuster and boot from the adjuster.

3. Using compressed air (if possible), blow the piston cup, cup expander and spring. Lay the cylinder face down and apply air pressure to the brake line port.

4. Wash all parts in isopropyl alcohol, except the rubber boot.

5. Examine the cylinder bore, piston and adjuster for wear, roughness or damage. Check the clearance between the piston and cylinder bore. If the clearance is greater than 0.006 in., replace with new parts. Discard the piston cups.

To assemble the wheel cylinder:

6. Lubricate the cylinder bore, adjuster and new piston cup with clean brake fluid.

7. Position the piston return spring in the piston cup expander. Install the return spring, piston cup expander and piston cup in the cylinder. The flat side of the piston cup goes out.

8. Install the piston boot to the piston adjuster (smaller lip of the boot in the groove of the piston adjuster.)

9. Insert the piston adjuster into the cylinder and install the larger lip of the boot in the groove on the cylinder body.

10. Install the adjusting screw in the piston adjuster.

11. Install the wheel cylinder.

Front Wheel Bearings

Adjustment

The front wheel bearings should be adjusted if the wheel is loose on the spindle or if the wheel does not rotate freely.

1. Raise and support the truck.

2. Remove the wheel cover and pry

the wheel cylinders should be rebuilt as a precaution against future problems.

Removal and Installation

1. Raise and support the truck.

2. Remove the wheel.

3. Remove the brake drum.

4. Remove the brake shoe retracting springs.

5. Remove the shoe retaining spring guide pin and the retaining spring.

6. Remove the brake shoes.

To install new brake shoes:

7. Lubricate the threads of the adjusting screw with brake paste and one or two spots on the adjuster wheel inside threads. Lubricate the backing plate shoe pads.

8. Position each brake shoe on the brake backing plate so that the slot in the shoe web is toward the starwheel in the wheel cylinder.

9. Install the shoe retaining spring guide pin. Install the retaining spring over the guide pin, hold the guide pin in place and depress the retaining spring. Turn it 90° to lock the spring in place.

10. Install the brake shoe retracting spring. Be careful not to bend the springs or stretch the hooks.

11. Install the brake drum.

12. Install the wheel.

13. Adjust the brakes.

14. Bleed the brakes.

15. Lower the truck and check for proper operation.

Wheel Cylinder

Removal and Installation

1. Raise and support the truck.

2. Remove the wheel.

3. Remove the brake drum and brake shoes.

4. Disconnect and plug the brake line at the wheel cylinder.

5. Remove the stud nuts and bolt attaching the wheel cylinder to the backing plate and remove the wheel cylinder.

To install the wheel cylinder:

6. Install the wheel cylinder on the backing plate.

7. Clean the end of the brake line and attach it to the wheel cylinder. Tighten the tube fitting nut.

8. Install the links in the end of the wheel cylinder.

9. Install the shoes and adjuster assemblies.

10. Install the brake drum and wheel.

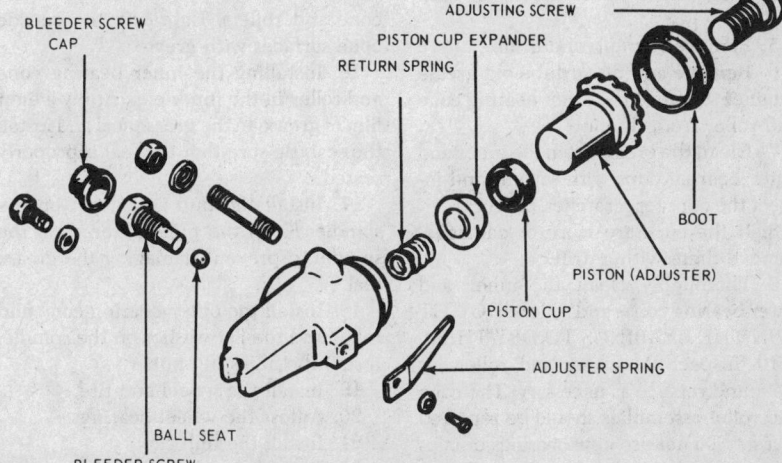

Exploded view of the front wheel cylinder

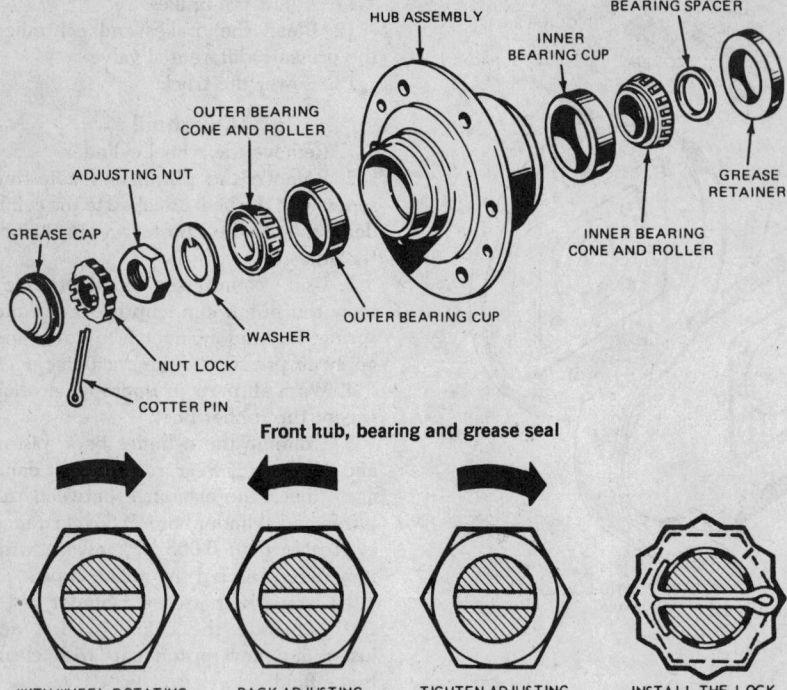

OUTER BEARING
CONE AND ROLLER

HUB ASSEMBLY

INNER
BEARING CUP

BEARING SPACER

INNER
BEARING CUP

GREASE
RETAINER

ADJUSTING NUT

GREASE CAP

INNER BEARING
CONE AND ROLLER

WASHER

OUTER BEARING CUP

NUT LOCK

COTTER PIN

Front hub, bearing and grease seal

WITH WHEEL ROTATING,
TORQUE ADJUSTING NUT,
TO 17-25 FT. LBS.

BACK ADJUSTING
NUT OFF 1/2 TURN

TIGHTEN ADJUSTING
NUT TO 10-15 IN.-LBS.

INSTALL THE LOCK
AND A NEW COTTER PIN

Front wheel bearing adjustment

the grease cap from the hub.

3. Remove the cotter pin and locknut.

4. While rotating the wheel, drum and hub, tighten the adjusting nut to 17–25 ft lbs.

5. Back the adjusting nut off ½ turn. Retighten the adjusting nut to 6–8 ft lbs.

6. Install the nut lock on the adjusting nut so that the castellations are aligned with the cotter pin hole in the spindle.

7. Install a new cotter pin.

Removal, Installation and Packing

1. Raise and support the truck.

2. Remove the wheel cover.

3. Remove the wheel and tire.

4. Remove the grease cap from the hub. Remove the cotter pin, nut lock, adjusting nut and flat washer from the spindle.

5. Remove the hub and drum.

6. Remove and discard the old grease retainer. Remove the inner bearing cone and roller from the hub.

7. Clean the grease from the inner and outer bearing cups with solvent and inspect the cups for scratches, pits, or wear.

8. If the cups are worn or damaged, remove them with a drift.

9. Thoroughly clean the inner and outer bearing cones and rollers. DO NOT SPIN THE BEARINGS TO DRY THEM.

10. Inspect the cones and roller for wear and replace as necessary. The cone and roller assemblies should be replaced as a set. Do not use new bearings or cups with old bearings or cups.

11. Clean the spindle and the inside of

the hub with solvent to remove all of the old grease.

12. Cover the spindle with a cloth and clean the dirt from the dustshield. Remove the cloth carefully. Do not get dirt on the spindle.

13. If the inner or outer bearing cups were removed, install the new replacement cups in the hub. Be sure that they are seated squarely and properly.

14. Pack the inside of the hub with wheel bearing grease.

NOTE: *It is important that all the old grease is removed, because lithium base grease is not compatible with the sodium base grease that was originally installed.*

15. Pack the bearing cone and roller with wheel bearing grease. Work as much grease as possible between the cone and rollers. Lubricate the outside cone surfaces with grease.

16. Installing the inner bearing cone and roller in the inner cup. Apply a light film of grease to the grease seal and install the seal. Be sure that the seal is properly seated.

17. Install the hub and drum on the spindle. Keep the hub centered on the spindle to prevent damaging the grease seal.

18. Install the outer bearing cone and roller and the flat washer on the spindle. Install the adjusting nut.

19. Install the wheel and tire.

20. Adjust the wheel bearings.

21. Install the hub cap.

22. Pump the brake pedal several times to restore normal brake lining-to-

drum clearance and normal brake pedal pressure.

Rear Drum Brakes

Brake Drums

Inspection

Inspect the rear brake drums in the same manner as the front brake drums. See "Front Brake Drum Inspection".

Removal and Installation

Rear brake drum removal is identical to front brake drum removal. See the procedures under "Front Brake Drum Removal".

Rear Brake Shoes

Inspection

Inspect the rear brake shoes in the same manner as the front brake shoes. See the procedures under "Front Brake Shoe Inspection".

Removal and Installation

1. Raise and support the truck.

2. Remove the wheel.

3. Remove the brake drum.

4. Remove the shoe retracting springs.

5. Remove the shoe retaining spring guide pins and retaining spring by holding the guide pin to the backing plate, and compressing and turning the retaining spring 90°.

6. Remove the parking brake link.

7. Disconnect the parking brake cable from the parking brake lever.

To install the brake shoes.

8. Lubricate the threads of the adjusting screws, mating surfaces of the shoe webs and brake backing plate with a small amount of brake paste or Lubriplate.

9. Install the parking brake lever on the rear shoe and install the retaining clip. Hold the rear brake shoe near the brake backing plate and connect the eye of the parking brake cable to the parking brake operating lever.

10. Position both brake shoes on the backing plate and connect the parking brake link between both shoes. Engage the brake shoes with the slots in the wheel cylinder pistons and adjusting screws.

11. Install the shoe retaining guide pins. Depress the retaining springs and turn them 90° to lock them in place.

12. Install the brake shoe retracting springs. Be careful not to bend the hooks or stretch the springs too far.

13. Install the brake drum.

14. Install the wheel.

15. Adjust the brakes.

16. Lower the truck and check the operation of the brakes.

Wheel Cylinder

Removal and Installation

1. Raise and support the truck.

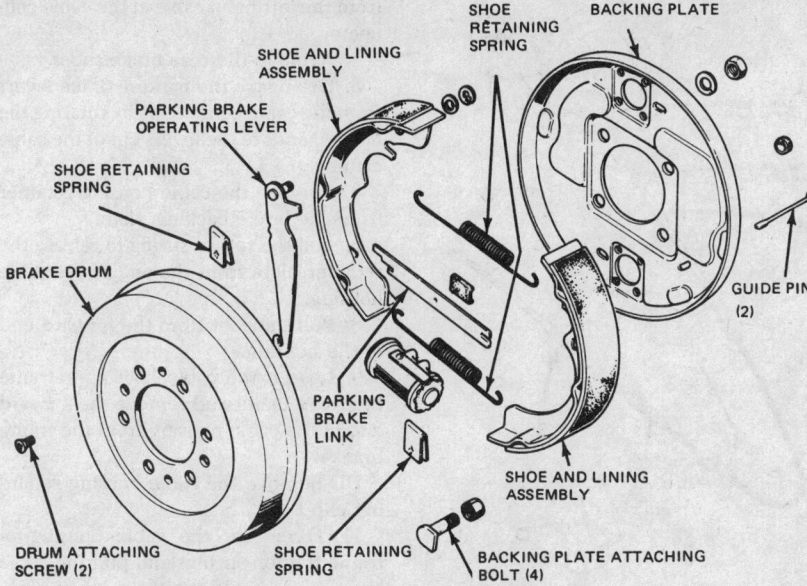

Rear brake assembly

Installing the parking brake operating lever (rear brakes)

2. Remove the wheel, brake drum and brake shoes.

3. Disconnect the brake line at the wheel cylinder and plug the line.

4. Remove the four nuts attaching the wheel cylinder to the backing plate and remove the wheel cylinder.

To install the wheel cylinder:

5. Wipe the end of the hydraulic line to clean it of any foreign material.

6. Install the wheel cylinder on the backing plate.

7. Connect the brake line to the wheel cylinder and tighten the tube fitting.

8. Install the links in the end of the wheel cylinder. Install the brake shoes and adjusters.

9. Install the brake drum and wheel.

10. Adjust the brakes.

11. Bleed the brakes.

12. Centralize the pressure differential valve.

13. Lower the truck and test the operation of the brakes.

Overhaul

1. Perform Steps 1, 2, and 3 of the "Wheel Cylinder Removal" procedure.

2. Remove the piston and adjusting screw with the boot attached to the adjuster.

3. Separate the adjuster screw and boot from the adjuster.

4. Remove the other piston and boot and separate the boot from the piston.

5. Press in on either piston cup and force the piston cups, cup expanders, and return spring from the cylinder.

6. Wash all parts (except the boots) in clean isopropyl alcohol. Examine the cylinder bore for roughness or scoring.

7. Check the piston-to-cylinder bore clearance. If it exceeds 0.006 in., replace with new parts.

To assemble the wheel cylinder:

8. Lubricate the cylinder bore, adjuster and new piston cups with clean brake fluid, before assembly. Always use new piston cups.

9. Install the piston return spring in a piston cup expander. Place the other piston cup expander and new piston cup on the return spring. Install the return spring, piston cup expanders and piston cups into the cylinder (flat side of the piston cups out).

10. Install the piston boot to the piston adjuster with the smaller lip of the boot on the groove of the piston adjuster.

11. Insert the piston adjuster into the cylinder assembly and install the larger lip of the boot in the groove of the cylinder.

12. Install the adjusting screw in the piston adjuster.

13. Perform Steps 5 and 6–13 of the "Wheel Cylinder Removal and Installation" procedure.

PARKING BRAKE

Adjustment

1. Adjust the service brakes before attempting to adjust the parking brake.

2. Use the adjusting nut to adjust the length of the front cable so that the rear brakes are locked when the parking brake lever is pulled out 5–10 notches.

3. After adjustment, apply the parking brake several times. Release the parking brake and make sure that the rear wheels rotate without dragging. If they drag, repeat the adjustment.

Front Parking Brake Cable

Removal and Installation

1. Raise and support the truck.

2. Remove the serrated adjusting nut.

3. Separate the front brake cable from the equalizer and remove the jam nut.

4. Remove the cable return spring and pull the protective boot from the lower end of the front cable housing.

5. Pull the lower cable housing forward out of the slotted frame bracket and slip the cable shaft sideways through the slot until the cable and housing is free of the bracket.

6. Disengage the upper cable connector from the brake lever by removing the clevis pin and retainer.

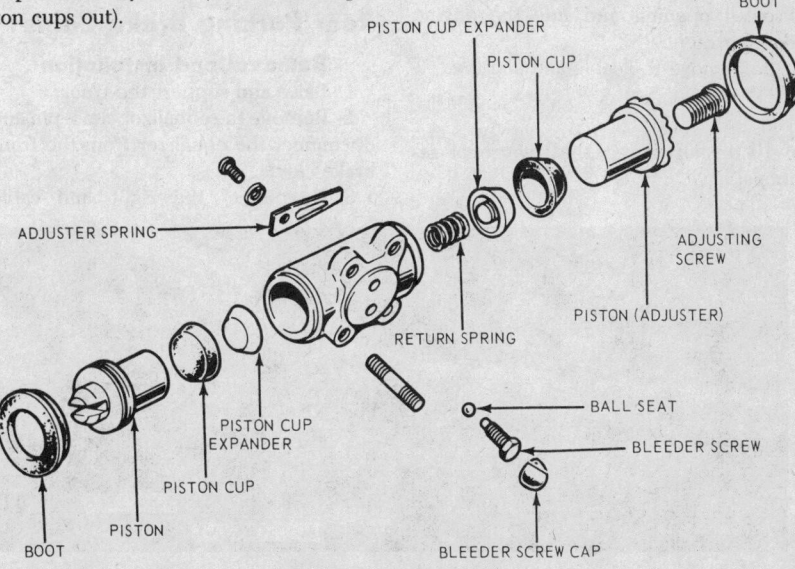

Exploded view of a rear wheel cylinder

7. Remove the upper cable housing retaining clip and pull the upper cable and housing from out of the slotted bracket on the firewall.

8. Push the upper cable, cable housing, and dust shield grommet through the

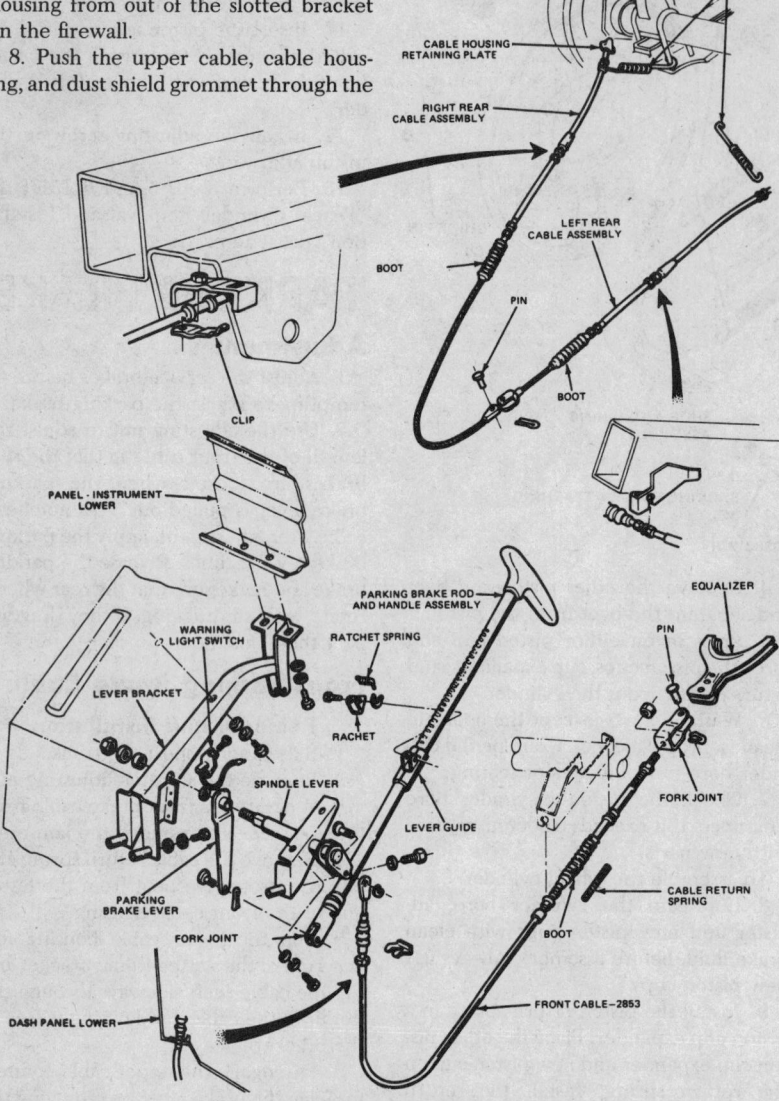

Parking brake linkage

firewall opening and into the engine compartment.

9. Remove the cable and housing.

10. Installation is the reverse of removal.

Rear Parking Brake Cable

Removal and Installation

1. Raise and support the truck.

2. Remove the equalizer clevis pin and disconnect the equalizer from the front brake clevis.

3. Disconnect the right-hand cable

from the left-hand cable at the cable connector.

4. Remove the rear brake shoes.

5. Disengage the parking brake levers from the cable connectors by rotating the hooked ends of the levers out of the cable connector.

6. Remove the cable housing retainer from the brake backing plate.

7. Pull the return spring to release the retainer plate from the end of the cable housing.

8. Pull the boot from the forward end of the housing.

9. Loosen the cable housing-to-frame bracket locknut and remove the forward end of the cable housing from the frame bracket.

10. Remove the cable housing retaining clip bolts.

11. Disengage the cable housing-to-frame tension springs and pull the cable housing and cable out of the brake backing plate.

12. Installation is the reverse of removal.

Chassis Electrical

Heater Assembly

Removal and Installation

1. Disconnect the battery.

2. Drain the cooling system.

3. Remove the water valve shield at the left-side of the heater.

4. Disconnect the two hoses from the left-side of the heater.

5. At the heat-defrost door, at the water valve and at the outside recirculation door, disengage the control cable housing from the mounting clip on the heater. Disconnect each of the three cable wires from the crank arms.

6. Disconnect the fan motor electrical lead.

7. Remove the glove compartment for clearance.

8. At the engine side of the dash, remove the retaining nut and bolt.

9. Disconnect the two defroster ducts from the heater and remove the heater.

10. Installation is the reverse of removal. Note the following:

a. Connect the heat-defrost door control cable to the door crank arm. Set the control lever (upper) in the HEAT position and turn the crank arm toward the mounting clip as far as it will go. Engage the cable housing in the clip and install the screw in the clip.

b. Connect the water valve control cable wire to the crank arm on the water valve lever. Locate the cable housing in the mounting clip. Set the control lever in the HOT position and

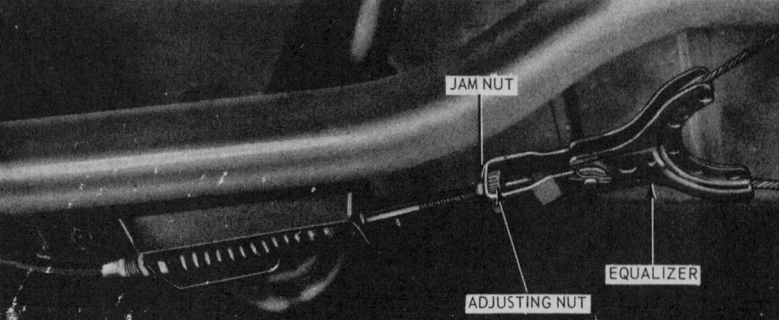

Adjusting the parking brake

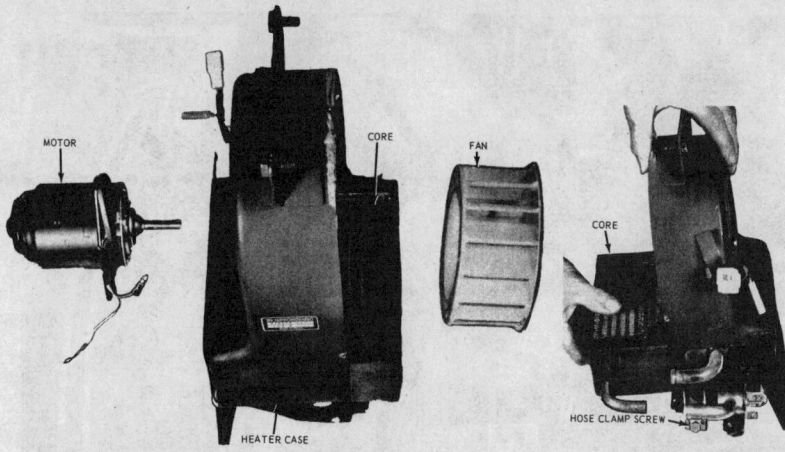

Heater motor and fan

Disassembled view of heater

pull the valve plunger and lever to the full outward position. This will move the lever crank arm toward the cable mounting clip as far as it will go. Tighten the clip and screw.

c. Insert the outside-recirculation door control cable into the hole in the door crank arm. Bend the wire over and tighten the screw. Set the center control lever in the REC position and turn the door crank arm toward the mounting clip as far as it will go. Engage the cable housing in the clip and install the screw in the clip.

Heater Motor and Fan

Removal and Installation

1. Remove the heater.
2. Remove the five screws and separate the halves of the heater assembly.
3. Loosen the fan retaining nut. Lightly tap on the nut to loosen the fan. Remove the fan and nut from the motor shaft.
4. Remove the three motor-to-case retaining screws and disconnect the bullet connector to the resistor and ground screw.

5. Rotate the motor and remove it from the case.

Heater Core

Removal and Installation

1. Remove the heater.
2. Separate the halves of the case.
3. Loosen the hose clamps and slide the heater core from the case.
4. Slide the replacement core into the case. At the same time, connect the core tube to the water valve tube with the short hose and clamps.
5. Assemble the halves of the heater and install the five screws.
6. Install the heater.

Radio

Removal and Installation

1. Remove the ash tray, ash tray retainer and rear retainer support. Remove the heater control knobs, heater control bezel and right-hand defroster hose.
2. Remove the heater control and position it to the left.
3. Remove the radio chassis rear support bracket.
4. Bend the bracket down 90°.

5. Remove the radio knobs, attaching nuts and bezel.
6. Pull the chassis forward until the control shafts clear the holes in the instrument panel. Disconnect the speaker wires, power lead and antenna lead. Rotate the chassis so that the control shafts point upward and lower the radio.
7. Installation is the reverse of removal.

Wiper Motor, Linkage and Bracket

Removal and Installation

1. Disconnect the battery.
2. Remove the wiper arms and blades by removing the retaining nuts.
3. Remove the rubber cap, nut, tapered spacer and rubber grommet from each pivot shaft.
4. Remove the two motor and bracket retaining bolts and washers.
5. Disconnect the wiper motor leads at the multiple connector.
6. Remove the motor and bracket assembly. Note the position of the ground washer and the rubber washer at the bracket mounting holes. Remove the plastic water shield.
7. To disconnect the motor from the bracket, remove the retaining clip that holds the linkage to the motor output arm. Note the position of the washers before removing the motor from the bracket.
8. Remove the four motor-to-bracket retaining bolts and remove the motor.
9. Installation is the reverse of removal.

Instrument Cluster

Removal and Installation

1. Disconnect the battery.
2. Remove the screws holding the instrument cluster to the dash.
3. Pull the cluster rearward enough to gain access to the cluster assembly.
4. Reach behind the cluster and disconnect the speedometer cable.
5. Pull the multiple connector from the printed circuit.
6. Note the position of the two ammeter leads and disconnect them.
7. Remove the screw attaching the ground wire to the rear of the cluster. On trucks equipped with a Thermactor air pump, remove the two connectors at the speedometer sensor switch.
8. Remove the instrument cluster.
9. Installation is the reverse of removal.

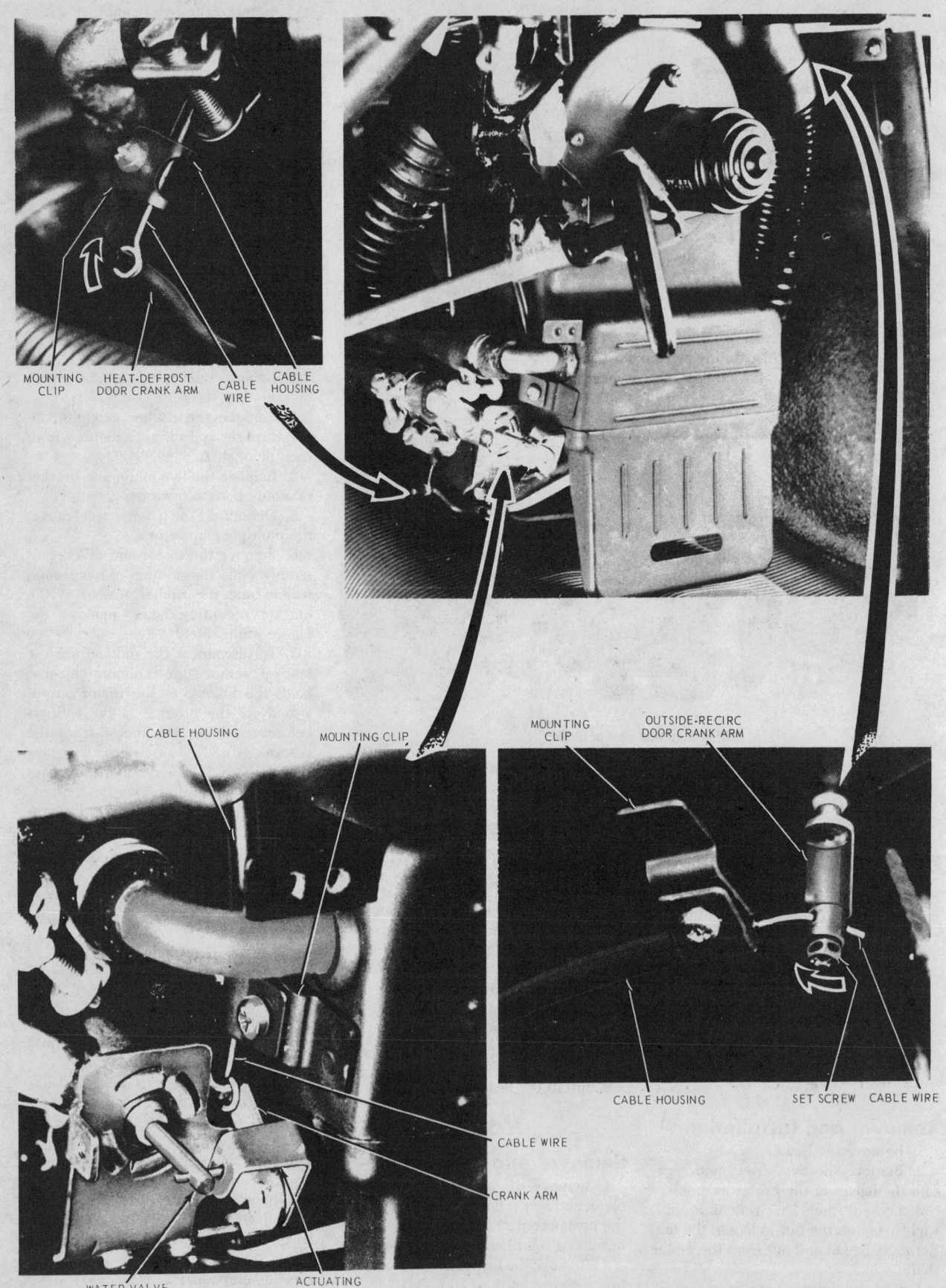

MOUNTING
CLIP

HEAT-DEFROST
DOOR CRANK ARM

CABLE
WIRE

CABLE
HOUSING

CABLE HOUSING

MOUNTING CLIP

MOUNTING
CLIP

OUTSIDE-RECIRC
DOOR CRANK ARM

CABLE HOUSING

SET SCREW

CABLE WIRE

CABLE WIRE

CRANK ARM

WATER VALVE

ACTUATING
LEVER

Heater control cable connections

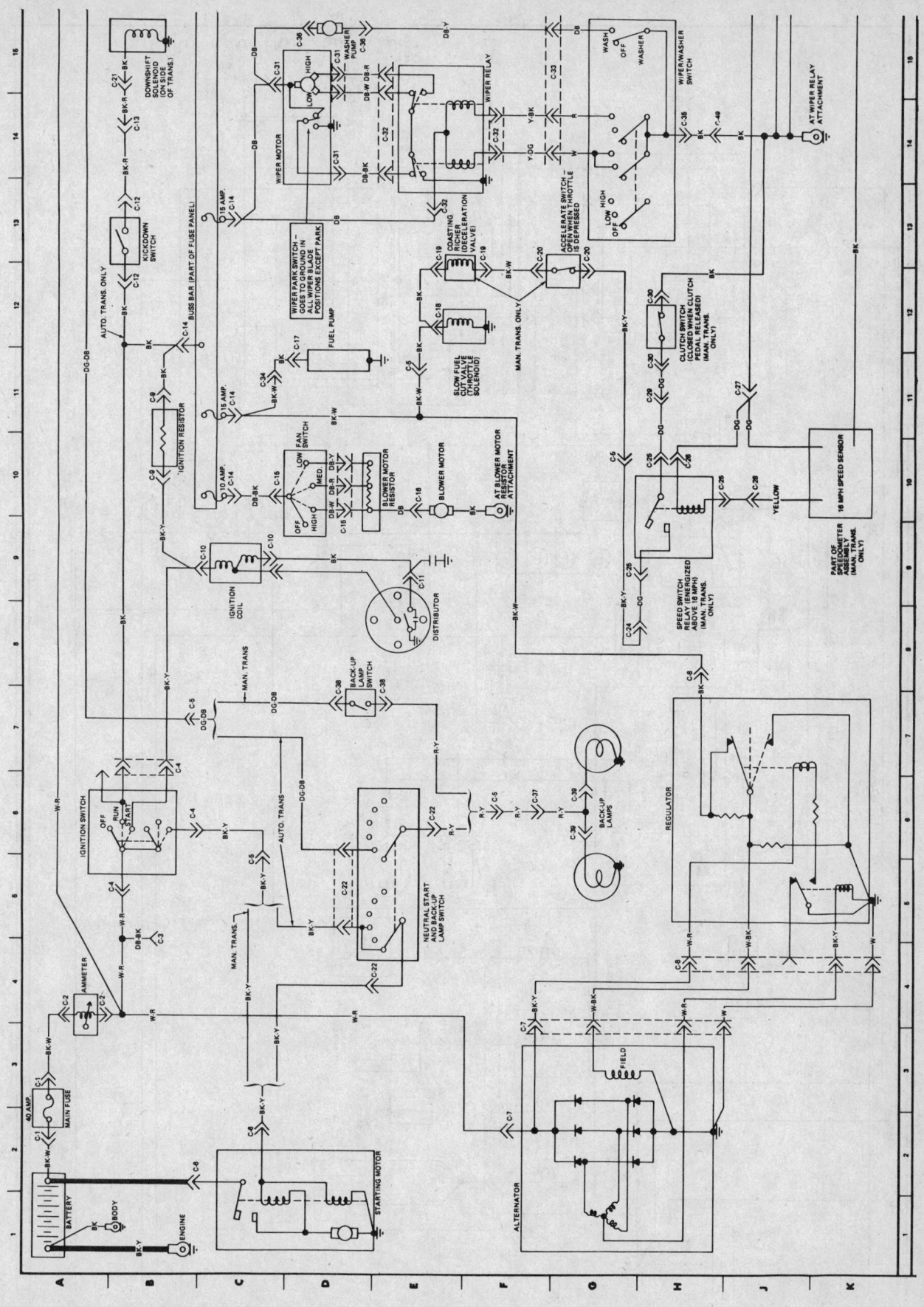

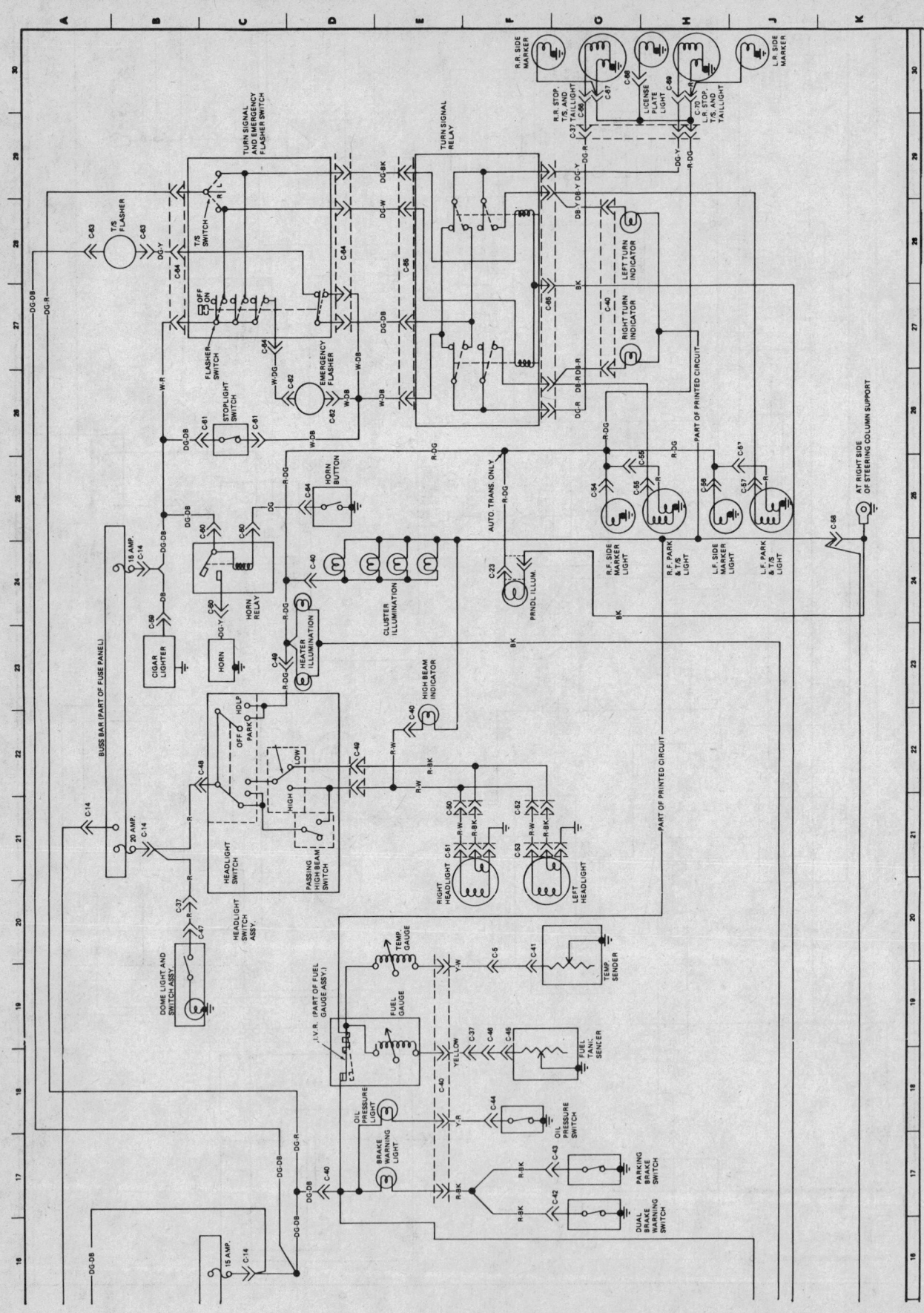

1974-76

SPECIFICATIONS

Datsun

INTRODUCTION

Nissan Motor Company Limited, the producer of Datsun vehicles, was established in 1933. Nissan was Japan's first mass producer and exporter of cars and trucks. The 5,000,000th Nissan-built vehicle was produced in 1969. Small economy sedans, pickup trucks, and sportscars are included in the Datsun line imported to the United States. They gained international recognition in 1969 by winning the team championship in the East African Safari Rally. The team took the first six places in its class. Datsun is also a frequent entrant in the grueling Mexican 1000 mile off-road race and also won the 1970 SCCA C-production championship.

MODEL IDENTIFICATION

PL521 1,600 cc pickup, PL520 is similar

PL510 sedan, two-door and wagon are similar

KLB110 coupe, sedan is similar

240-260-280 Z

KPL610 fastback coupe, sedan and wagon are similar with vertical grille bars added

B210 Coupe

PL710 Sedan

PL620

F-10 Wagon- Hatchback and Sedan are similar

SERIAL NUMBER IDENTIFICATION

Engine Number

The engine number is stamped on the right side top edge of the cylinder block. The engine serial number is preceded by the engine model code.

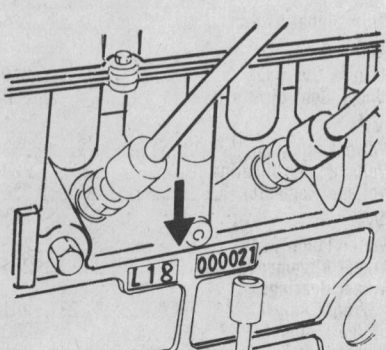
Engine serial and code number

Chassis Number

The car chassis number is on the firewall under the hood. On pickups, it is on top of the right frame member, in the engine compartment. The chassis number is also on a plate attached to the top of the instrument panel on the driver's side. The chassis serial number is preceded by the model designation.

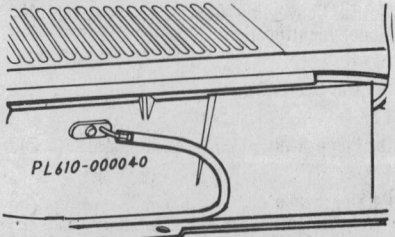
Chassis number location for all models except pickup

Vehicle Identification Plate

The vehicle identification plate is attached to the hood ledge or the firewall. This plate is mounted on the right front suspension strut housing on the 240 Z, 260 Z and 280 Z. The identification plate gives the vehicle model, engine displacement in cc., SAE horsepower rating, wheelbase, engine number, and chassis number.

DATSUN	TYPE	HLS30
ENGINE CAPACITY		2,393 cc
MAX. HP at RPM		151 HP at 5,600 rpm
WHEEL BASE		2,305 mm
ENGINE NO.		L24- ☐☐☐☐☐
CAR NO.		HLS30- ☐☐☐☐☐

NISSAN MOTOR CO., LTD.
YOKOHAMA JAPAN

Vehicle identification plate

FIRING ORDER

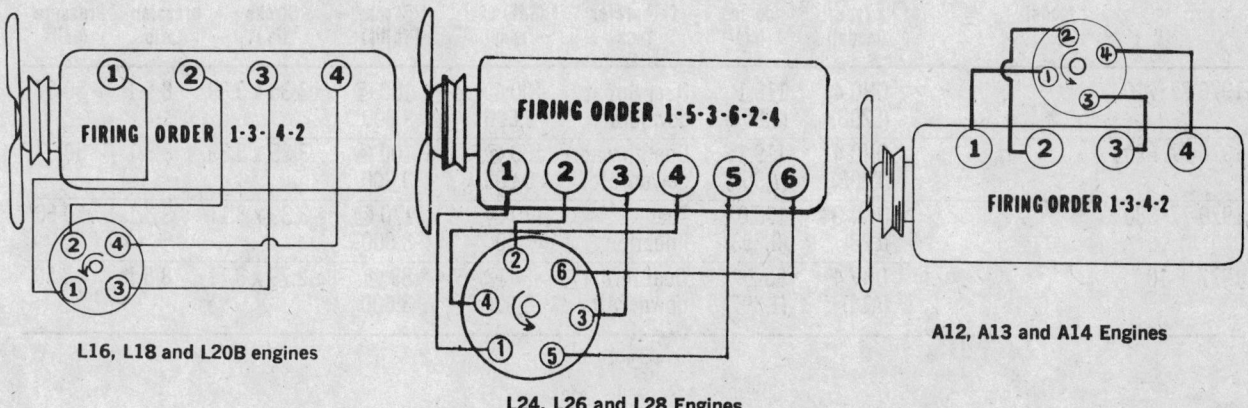

FIRING ORDER 1-3-4-2

L16, L18 and L20B engines

FIRING ORDER 1-5-3-6-2-4

L24, L26 and L28 Engines

FIRING ORDER 1-3-4-2

A12, A13 and A14 Engines

GENERAL ENGINE SPECIFICATIONS

Year and Model	Type (model)	Engine Displacement cu. in. (cc)	Carburetor Type	Horse-power (SAE) @ rpm	Torque @ rpm (ft lbs)	Bore x Stroke (in.)	Com-pression Ratio	Normal Oil Pressure (psi)
1972-1973 510/521	OHC 4 (L16)	97.3 (1,595)	Dual throat downdraft	96 @ 5,600	100 @ 3,600	3.27 x 2.90	8.5:1	54-57
1972-1973 240 Z Coupe	OHC 6 (L24)	146.0 (2,393)	Two CU type sidedraft	151 @ 5,600	146 @ 4,400	3.27 x 2.90	8.8:1	50-57
1972-1973 1200	OHV 4 (A12)	71.5 (1,171)	Dual throat downdraft	69 @ 6,000	70 @ 4,000	2.87 x 2.76	8.5:1	54-60
1973 610	OHC 4 (L18)	108.0 (1,770)	Dual throat downdraft	100 @ 5,600	100 @ 3,600	3.35 x 3.307	8.5:1	50-57
1973-1974 PL620 1800 Pickup	OHC 4 (L18)	108.0 (1,770)	Dual throat downdraft	93 @ 6,000	99 @ 3,200	3.35 x 3.07	8.5:1	50-57
1974 610	OHC 4 (L20B)	119.1 (1,952)	Dual throat downdraft	112 @ 5,600	108 @ 3,600	3.35 x 3.39	8.5:1	50-57
1974 710	OHC 4 (L18)	108 (1,770)	Dual throat downdraft	100 @ 5,600	100 @ 3,600	3.35 x 3.07	8.5:1	50-57
1974 B210 Sedan, Coupe	OHV 4 (A13)	78.59 (1,288)	Dual throat downdraft	78 @ 6,000	75 @ 4,000	2.87 x 3.03	8.5:1	43-50
1974 260Z Coupe	OHC 6 (L26)	156.52 (2,565)	Two SU type sidedraft	162 @ 5,600	154 @ 4,400	3.27 x 3.11	8.8:1	50-57
1975 710	OHC 4 (L20B)	119.1 (1,952)	Dual throat downdraft	100 @ 5,600	100 @ 3,600	3.35 x 3.39	8.5:1	50-57
1975 B210 Sedan, Coupe	OHV 4 (A14)	85.24 (1,397)	Dual throat downdraft	78 @ 6,000	75 @ 4,000	2.99 x 3.03	8.5:1	43-50
1975 PL620 Pick-up	OHC 4 (L20B)	119.1 (1,952)	Dual throat downdraft	100 @ 5,600	100 @ 3,600	3.35 x 3.39	8.5:1	50-57
1975 280 Z	OHC 6 (L28)	168.0 (2,753)	Fuel injection	170 @ 5,600	170 @ 5,600	3.39 x 3.11	8.3:1	50-57
1976-77 B-210	OHV 4 (A14)	85.2 (1,397)	Dual throat downdraft	80 @ 6,000	83 @ 3,600	2.79 x 3.03	8.5:1	43-50
1976-77 610	OHC 4 (L20B)	119.1 (1,952)	Dual throat downdraft	112 @ 5,600	108 @ 3,600	3.35 x 3.39	8.5:1	50-57

GENERAL ENGINE SPECIFICATIONS

Year and Model	Type (model)	Engine Displacement cu. in. (cc)	Carburetor Type	Horse-power (SAE) @ rpm	Torque @ rpm (ft lbs)	Bore x Stroke (in.)	Compression Ratio	Normal Oil Pressure (psi)
1976-77 710	OHC 4 (L20B)	119.1 (1,952)	Dual throat downdraft	100 @ 5,600	100 @ 3,600	3.35 x 3.39	8.5:1	50-57
1976-77 620	OHC 4 (L20B)	119.1 (1,952)	Dual throat downdraft	100 @ 5,800	100 @ 3,600	3.35 x 3.39	8.5:1	50-57
1976-77 280 Z	OHC 6 (L28)	168.0 (2,753)	Fuel injection	170 @ 5,600	170 @ 3,600	3.39 x 3.11	8.3:1	50-60
1977 F-10	OHV 4 (A14)	85.2 (1,397)	Dual throat downdraft	80 @ 6,000	83 @ 3,600	2.79 x 3.11	8.5:1	43-50

TUNE-UP SPECIFICATIONS

When analyzing compression test results, look for uniformity among cylinders, rather than specific pressures.

Year	Model	SPARK PLUGS Type	SPARK PLUGS Gap (in.)	DISTRIBUTOR Point Dwell (deg)	DISTRIBUTOR Point Gap (in.)	IGNITION TIMING (deg) MT	IGNITION TIMING (deg) AT	Fuel Pump Pressure (psi)	IDLE SPEED (rpm) MT	IDLE SPEED (rpm) AT①	VALVE CLEARANCE (in.) In	VALVE CLEARANCE (in.) Ex	Percentage of CO at idle
1972	PL521	BP-5ES	0.032-0.036	49-55	0.018-0.022	7B @ 700	7B @ 600	2.6 3.4	700	600	0.008 cold, 0.010 hot	0.010 cold, 0.012 hot	2
1973-1974	PL620	BP-6ES	0.028-0.031	49-55	0.018-0.022	5B @ 800	5B @ 650	2.6 3.4	800	650	0.008 cold, 0.010 hot	0.010 cold, 0.012 hot	1.5
1972	PL510, WPL510	BP-5ES	0.032-0.036	49-55	0.018-0.022	7B @ 700	7B @ 600	2.6 3.4	700	600	0.008 cold, 0.010 hot	0.010 cold, 0.012 hot	2
1973	PL510	BP-6ES	0.028-0.031	49-55	0.018 0.022	5B @ 800	5B @ 650	2.6-3.4	800	650	0.008 cold, 0.010 hot	0.010 cold, 0.012 hot	1.5
1972	240 Z	BP-6ES	0.032-0.036	35-41 man., 33-39 auto.	0.018-0.022	5B @ 750	TDC @ 600 ③	3.4-4.3	750	600	0.008 cold, 0.010 hot	0.010 cold, 0.012 hot	6②
1973	240 Z	BP-6ES	0.032-0.036	35-41 man., 33-39 auto.	0.018-0.022	7B @ 750	5B @ 600 ④	3.4-4.3	750	600	0.008 cold, 0.010 hot	0.010 cold, 0.012 hot	3②
1972	LB110, KLB110	BP-5ES	0.032-0.036	49-55	0.020	5B @ 700	5B @ 600	N.A.	700	600	0.010 cold, 0.014 hot	0.012 cold, 0.014 hot	2
1973	LB110, KLB110	BP-5ES	0.032-0.036	49-55	0.020	5B @ 700	5B @ 600	N.A.	700	600	0.010 cold, 0.014 hot	0.010 cold, 0.014 hot	1.5

TUNE-UP SPECIFICATIONS—(Continued)

Year	Model	SPARK PLUGS		DISTRIBUTOR		IGNITION TIMING (deg)		Fuel Pump Pressure (psi)	IDLE SPEED (rpm)		VALVE CLEARANCE (in.)		Percentage of CO at idle
		Type	Gap (in.)	Point Dwell (deg)	Point Gap (in.)	MT	AT		MT	AT①	In	Ex	
1973	PL610, KPL610, WPL610	BP-6ES	0.028-0.031	49-55	0.018-0.022	5B @ 800	5B @ 650	2.6 3.4	800	650	0.008 cold, 0.010 hot	0.010 cold, 0.012 hot	1.5
1974	PL610 KPL610, WPL610	B6ES	0.028-0.031	49-55	0.017-0.022	12B @ 750	12B @ 650	3-3.8	750	650	0.010 hot	0.012 hot	3
1974	PL710, PL620 KPL710	B6ES	0.028-0.031	49-55	0.017-0.022	12B @ 800	12B @ 650	2.6-3.4	800	650	0.010 hot	0.012 hot	1.5
1974	B210	BP5ES	0.031-0.035	49-55	0.017-0.022	5B @ 800	5B @ 650	3.4	800	650	0.014 hot	0.014 hot	1.5
1974	260 Z	B6ES	0.031-0.035	⑤	⑤	8B @ 750	8B @ 600	3.4-4.3	750	600	0.010 hot	0.012 hot	1.3
1975	B210 (Federal)	BP-5ES	0.031-0.035	49-55	0.017-0.022	10B	10B	3.8	700	650	0.014 hot	0.014 hot	2.0
1975	PL620	BP-6ES	0.031-0.035	49-55	0.017-0.022	12B ⑥	12B	3.8	750	650	0.010 hot	0.012 hot	2.0
1975	280 Z Federal	BP-6ES	0.028-0.031	Electronic	⑦	7B⑧	7B⑧	36.3	800	800	0.010 hot	0.012 hot	2.0
1975	280 Z (California)	BP-6ES	0.028-0.031	Electronic	⑦	10B	10B	36.3	800	800	0.010 hot	0.012 hot	2.0
1975	610	BP-6ES	0.031-0.035	49-55	0.017-0.022	12B	12B	3.8	750	650	0.010 hot	0.012 hot	2.0
1975	710	BP-6ES	0.031-0.035	49-55	0.017-0.022	12B	12B	3.8	750	650	0.010 hot	0.012 hot	2.0
1975	B210 (California)	BP-6ES	0.031-0.035	Electronic	⑦	10B	10B	3.8	750	650	0.014 hot	0.014 hot	2.0
1975	710, 610 (California)	BP-6ES	0.031-0.035	Electronic	⑦	12B	12B	3.8	750	650	0.010 cold	0.012 cold	2.0
1976	B-210 (Federal)	BP-5ES	0.031-0.035	49-55	0.017-0.022	10B	10B	3.8	700	650	0.014 hot	0.014 hot	2.0
1976	B-210 (California)	BP-5ES	0.031-0.035	Electronic	⑦	10B	10B	3.8	700	650	0.014 hot	0.014 hot	2.0
1976	610, 710 (Federal)	BP-6ES	0.031-0.035	Electronic	0.018-0.022	12B	12B	3.8	750	650	0.010 hot	0.012 hot	2.0
1976	610, 710 (California)	BP-6ES	0.031-0.035	Electronic	⑦	12B	12B	3.8	750	650	0.010 hot	0.012 hot	2.0
1976	620 (Federal)	BP-6ES	0.031-0.035	49-55	0.018-0.022	12B	12B	3.8	750	650	0.010 hot	0.012 hot	2.0
1976	620 (California)	BP-6ES	0.039-0.043	Electronic	⑦	10B	12B	3.8	750	650	0.010 hot	0.012 hot	2.0
1976	280 Z (Federal)	BP-6ES	0.028-0.031	Electronic	⑦	7B⑧	7B⑧	36.3	800	700	0.010 hot	0.012 hot	2.0
1976	280 Z (California)	BP-6ES	0.028-0.031	Electronic	⑦	10B	10B	36.3	800	700	0.010 hot	0.012 hot	2.0
1977	B-210 (Federal)	BP-5ES	0.039-0.043	49-55	0.018-0.022	10B	8B	3.8	700	650	0.014 hot	0.014 hot	2.0
1977	B-210 (California)	BP-5ES	0.039-0.043	Electronic	⑦	10B	10B	3.8	700	650	0.014 hot	0.014 hot	2.0
1977	610, 710 (Federal)	BP-6ES	0.031-0.035	49-55	0.018-0.022	12B	12B	3.8	750	650	0.010 hot	0.012 hot	2.0

TUNE-UP SPECIFICATIONS—(Continued)

Year	Model	SPARK PLUGS Type	SPARK PLUGS Gap (in.)	DISTRIBUTOR Point Dwell (deg)	DISTRIBUTOR Point Gap (in.)	IGNITION TIMING (deg) MT	IGNITION TIMING (deg) AT	Fuel Pump Pressure (psi)	IDLE SPEED (rpm) MT	IDLE SPEED (rpm) AT①	VALVE CLEARANCE (in.) In	VALVE CLEARANCE (in.) Ex	Percentage of CO at idle
1977	610, 710 (California)	BP-6ES	0.039-0.043	Electronic	⑦	12B	12B	3.8	750	650	0.010 hot	0.012 hot	2.0
1977	620 (Federal)	BP-6ES	0.031-0.035	49-55	0.018-0.022	12B	12B	3.8	750	650	0.010 hot	0.012 hot	2.0
1977	620 (California)	BPR-6ES	0.031-0.035	Electronic	⑦	10B	12B	3.8	750	650	0.010 hot	0.012 hot	2.0
1977	280 Z	BP-6ES	0.039-0.043	Electronic	⑦	10B	10B	36.3	800	700	0.010 hot	0.012 hot	2.0
1977	F-10 (Federal)	BP-5ES	0.039-0.043	49-55	0.018-0.022	10B	10B	3.8	700	700	0.014 hot	0.014 hot	2.0
1977	F-10 (California)	BP-5ES	0.039-0.043	Electronic	⑦	10B	10B	3.8	700	700	0.014 hot	0.014 hot	2.0

NOTE: The underhood specifications sticker sometimes reflects tune-up specification changes made in production. Sticker figures must be used if they disagree with this chart.

① In Drive
② Air pump disconnected
③ Automatic—10B @ 600 below 30°F
④ Automatic—15B @ 600 below 30°F
⑤ Reluctor Gap 0.012-0.016
⑥ 10B—California
⑦ Reluctor Gap 0.008-0.016 in.
⑧ 13 BTDC—Advanced

CAPACITIES

Model	ENGINE CRANKCASE With Filter	ENGINE CRANKCASE Without Filter	TRANSMISSION (pts) MANUAL 4-Sp	TRANSMISSION (pts) Automatic (total capacity)	Drive Axle (pts)	Gas Tank (gals)	Cool. Syst. (qts)
PL510	5.2	4.4	6.4	11.4 ①	1.7	11.9	6.8, 7.2 ②
WPL510	5.2	4.4	6.4	11.4 ①	2.1	11.9	6.8, 7.2 ②
PL521	4.4	3.6	4.2	—	1.7	10.8	6.8, 7.4 ②
240 Z	4.7	4.3	3.2	12.8	2.1	15.9	8.5
LB110, KLB110	N.A.	2.9	4.3	11.8	1.8	9.3	5.7
PL610 KPL610	5.0	4.5	4.0	11.8	1.8	13.8	9.0
WPL610	5.0	4.5	4.0	11.8	2.8	13.8	9.0
PL620	5.0	4.5	4.0	11.8	2.0	11.8	6.5
1974 B210 Sedan Coupe	3.45	—	2.5	10.9	1.88	11.6 11.45	5.45

Model	ENGINE CRANKCASE With Filter	ENGINE CRANKCASE Without Filter	TRANSMISSION (pts) MANUAL 4-Sp	TRANSMISSION (pts) Automatic (total capacity)	Drive Axle (pts)	Gas Tank (gals)	Cool. Syst. (qts)
1974 PL610 KPL610 WPL610	4.5	—	4.0	10.9	1.75 ③	14.5 14.5 13.75	6.88
1974 PL710 KPL710	4.45	—	4.5	10.9	2.75	13.25	6.88
260 Z	5.0	—	3.12	10.9	2.2	15.9	10.0②
1975 PL620	5.0	4.5	3.5	11.8	2.0	11.8	10.5②
1975 B210	4.2	3.7	2.7	12.0	2.0	11.5	12.5④
1975 PL610 KPL610 WPL610	4.5	4.0	4.25	11.8	1.4⑤	14.5⑥	7.25
1975 PL710 KPL710	4.5	4.0	4.25	11.8	2.75	13.2⑦	7.25
1976-77 B-210	4.0	3.5	2.75	11.8	2.0	11.5	5.25⑧

CAPACITIES

Model	ENGINE CRANKCASE With Filter	ENGINE CRANKCASE Without Filter	TRANSMISSION (pts) MANUAL 4-Sp	TRANSMISSION (pts) Automatic (total capacity)	Drive Axle (pts)	Gas Tank (gals)	Cool. Syst. (qts)
1976-77 610	4.5	4.0	4.25	11.8	1.37⑨ ⑩		7.25
1976-77 710	4.5	4.0	4.25	11.8	2.75	⑪	7.25
1976 620	4.5	4.0	2.5	11.8	2.12	11.8	7.0
1977 620	4.5	4.0	⑫	11.8	2.12	11.8	7.0

Model	ENGINE CRANKCASE With Filter	ENGINE CRANKCASE Without Filter	TRANSMISSION (pts) MANUAL 4-Sp	TRANSMISSION (pts) Automatic (total capacity)	Drive Axle (pts)	Gas Tank (gals)	Cool. Syst. (qts)
1976 280 Z	5.0	4.25	3.12	11.8	2.75	17.2	9.0
1977 280 Z	5.0	4.25	⑮	11.8	⑯	17.2	9.0
1977 F-10	4.0	3.5	⑬	—	⑬	10.5	6.0⑭

① 1.5 pts—oil cooler
② With heater
③ With manual trans.—2.12
　 With auto trans.—2.75
④ Auto trans.—12.0 pts.
⑤ Wagon—1.75 pts.
⑥ Wagon—13.7; Calif.—13.0
⑦ Wagon—11.8; Calif.—13.2
⑧ 5.0 with automatic
⑨ 1.75 on station wagon
⑩ 14.5—sedan, hardtop
　 13.75—station wagon

　 13.0—California
⑪ 13.25—Sedan, hardtop
　 11.8—station wagon
　 13.25—California
⑫ 4-spd—3.7
　 5-spd—4.25
⑬ Transaxle case—5.0 pts
⑭ W/o heater—5.0 qts.
⑮ 4-spd—3.6 pts.
　 5-spd—4.25 pts.
⑯ R-180 differential—2.12 pts.
　 R-200 differential—2.75 pts.

CRANKSHAFT AND CONNECTING ROD SPECIFICATIONS

All measurements are given in inches.

Engine Model	CRANKSHAFT Main Brg. Journal Dia.	CRANKSHAFT Main Brg. Oil Clearance	CRANKSHAFT Shaft End-Play	CRANKSHAFT Thrust on No.	CONNECTING ROD BEARINGS Journal Dia.	CONNECTING ROD BEARINGS Oil Clearance	CONNECTING ROD BEARINGS Side Clearance
L16	2.1631-2.1636	0.001-0.003	0.002-0.006	3	1.9670-1.9675	0.001-0.003	0.008-0.012
L24	2.1631-2.1636	0.001-0.003	0.002-0.007	Center	1.9670-1.9675	0.001-0.002	0.008-0.012
A12	1.9671-1.9668	0.001-0.002	0.002-0.006	3	1.7701-1.7706	0.001-0.002	0.008-0.012
L18	2.1631-2.1636	0.001-0.002	0.002-0.007	3	1.9670-1.9675	0.001-0.002	0.008-0.012
L20B	2.333-2.360	0.0008-0.002	0.002-0.007	3	1.9660-1.9670	0.001-0.002	0.008-0.012
L18 (710)	2.3599-2.360	0.0008-0.002	0.002-0.007	3	1.967-1.9675	0.001-0.002	0.008-0.012
A13	1.966-1.967	0.0008-0.002	0.002-0.006	3	1.7701-1.7706	0.0008-0.002	0.008-0.012
L26	2.1631-2.1636	0.0008-0.003	0.002-0.007	Center	1.9670-1.9675	0.001-0.002	0.008-0.012
A14	1.966-1.967	0.0008-0.002	0.002-0.006	3	1.7701-1.7706	0.0008-0.002	0.008-0.012
L28	2.1631-2.1636	0.0008-0.0028	0.002-0.007	Center	1.9670-1.9675	0.001-0.002	0.008-0.012

VALVE SPECIFICATIONS

Engine Model	Seat Angle (deg)	VALVE SPRING PRESSURE (lb. @ in.) Outer	VALVE SPRING PRESSURE (lb. @ in.) Inner	VALVE SPRING FREE LENGTH (in.) Outer	VALVE SPRING FREE LENGTH (in.) Inner	STEM TO GUIDE CLEARANCE (in.) Intake	STEM TO GUIDE CLEARANCE (in.) Exhaust	Valve Guide Removable
L16	45	105 @ 1.21 64 @ 1.53	56 @ .96 27 @ 1.38	2.05	1.77	0.001-0.002	0.002-0.003	Yes

VALVE SPECIFICATIONS

Engine Model	Seat Angle (deg)	VALVE SPRING PRESSURE (lb. @ in.)		VALVE SPRING FREE LENGTH (in.)		STEM TO GUIDE CLEARANCE (in.)		Valve Guide Removable
		Outer	Inner	Outer	Inner	Intake	Exhaust	
L24	45	47 @ 1.57 108 @ 1.16	56 @ .96	1.97	1.76	0.001-0.002	0.002-0.003	Yes
A12	45	66 @ 1.52 135 @ 1.23	—	1.80	—	0.001-0.002	0.002-0.003	Yes
L18	45	108 @ 1.16	56 @ .97	1.97	1.77	0.001-0.002	0.002-0.003	Yes
A13	45	129 @ 1.19	—	1.831	—	0.0006-0.0018	0.0016-0.0028	Yes
L20B	45	108 @ 1.16	56 @ 0.965	1.968	1.766	0.0008-0.0021	0.0016-0.0029	Yes
L26	45	108 @ 1.16	56 @ 0.965	1.968	1.766	0.0008-0.0021	0.0016-0.0029	Yes
A14	45	129 @ 1.19	—	1.831	—	0.0008-0.002	0.0016-0.002	Yes
L28	45	108 @ 1.16	56 @ 0.965	1.968	1.766	0.0008-0.0021	0.0016-0.0029	Yes

— Not Applicable

PISTON AND RING SPECIFICATIONS

All measurements in inches

Engine Model	Piston Clearance	RING GAP			RING SIDE CLEARANCE		
		Top Compression	Bottom Compression	Oil Control	Top Compression	Bottom Compression	Oil Control
L16	0.001-0.002	0.009-0.015	0.006-0.012	0.006-0.012	0.002-0.003	0.001-0.003	0.001-0.003
L24	0.001-0.002	0.009-0.015	0.006-0.012	0.006-0.012	0.002-0.003	0.001-0.003	0.001-0.003
A12	0.001-0.002	0.008-0.014	0.008-0.014	0.010-0.014	0.002-0.003	0.002-0.003	0.002-0.003
L18	0.001-0.002	0.014-0.022	0.012-0.020	0.012-0.035	0.002-0.003	0.002-0.003	0.002-0.003
A13	0.001-0.002	0.008-0.010	0.008-0.010	0.010-0.030	0.002-0.003	0.002-0.003	N.A.
A14	0.001-0.002	0.008-0.012	0.006-0.012	0.012-0.035	0.002-0.003	0.001-0.002	Combined ring
L20B	0.001-0.002	0.010-0.020	0.010-0.020	0.010-0.020	0.002-0.003	0.002-0.003	N.A.
L26	0.001-0.002	0.009-0.020	0.006-0.010	0.006-0.010	0.002-0.003	0.002-0.003	N.A.
L20B (1975)	0.001-0.002	0.010-0.016	0.012-0.020	0.012-0.022	0.002-0.003	0.001-0.003	N.A.
A14 (1975)	0.0009-0.002	0.008-0.014	0.006-0.012	0.012-0.035	0.002-0.003	0.001-0.002	Combined ring
L28	0.001-0.002	0.009-0.015	0.006-0.012	0.006-0.012	0.002-0.003	0.001-0.003	N.A.

N.A. Not Applicable

TORQUE SPECIFICATIONS

All readings in ft lbs

Engine Model	Cylinder Head Bolts	Main Bearing Bolts	Rod Bearing Bolts	Crankshaft Pulley Bolt	Flywheel to Crankshaft Bolts
L16	40	33-40	20-24	116-130	69-76
L24	47	33-40	20-24	116-130	101
A12	33-35	36-38	25-26	108-116	47-54
L18	47-62	33-40	33-40	87-116	101-116
A13	54-58	36-43	23-27	108-145	54-61
L20B	47-61	33-40	33-40	87-116	101-116
L26	54-61	33-40	27-31	94-108	94-108
A14	51-54	36-43	23-27	108-145	54-61
L28	54-61	33-40	33-40	94-108	94-108

TORQUE SEQUENCES

Cylinder Head

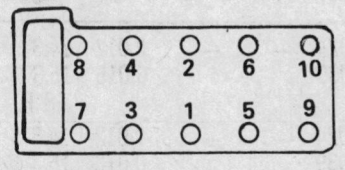

L16, L18, and L20B engines

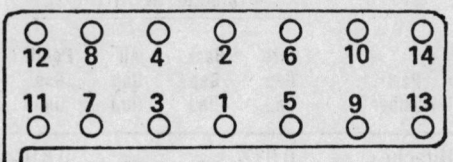

L24, L26 and L28 Engines

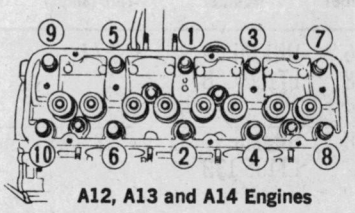

A12, A13 and A14 Engines

BATTERY AND STARTER SPECIFICATIONS

All cars use 12 volt, negative ground electrical systems

Year	Model	Battery Amp Hour Capacity	Lock Test Amps	Lock Test Volts	Lock Test Torque (ft/lbs)	No Load Test Amps	No Load Test Volts	No Load Test RPM	Brush Spring Tension (oz)	Min. Brush Length (in.)
All	110	N.A.	420	6.3	6.5	60	12	7,000	3.9	0.37
All	510	50,60	480	6.0	7.9	60	12	7,000	62	0.28
All	520	40,50	480	6.0	7.9	60	12	7,000	62	0.28
All	521	40,50,60	480	6.0	7.9	60	12	7,000	62	0.28
All	240 Z 260 Z	60	460	6.0	10.1	60	12	5,000	62	0.49
All	610 620 710	N.A.	430 MT / 540 AT	6.0 / 5.0	6.3 / 6.0	60	12	7,000 / 6,000	49-64	0.7283
All	280 Z	65	——Not Recommended——			60	12	5,000 MT 6,000 AT	49-64	0.47
All	F10	N.A.	——Not Recommended——			60	12	7,000	49-64	0.47

MT Manual Transmission
AT Automatic Transmission
N.A. Not Available

ALTERNATOR AND REGULATOR SPECIFICATIONS

Engine Model	Part Number	Output @ 2,500 Alternator rpm (amps)	Part Number	CHARGE RELAY① Core Gap (in.)	Back Gap (in.)	Air Gap (in.)	Point Gap (in.)	VOLTAGE REGULATOR② Core Gap (in.)	Back Gap (in.)	Air Gap (in.)	Point Gap (in.)	Regulated Voltage
L16	Hitachi LT130-41	22	Hitachi TL1Z-17	—	0.007	0.020-0.024	0.016-0.020	—	0.035-0.039	0.032-0.047	0.012-0.016	14-15
L24	Hitachi LT145-35	34	Hitachi TL1Z-37	0.032-0.039	—	—	0.016-0.024	0.024-0.039	—	—	0.012-0.016	14.3 15.3 @ 50°F.
A12	Hitachi LT135-05	24	Hitachi TL1Z-37	0.032-0.039	—	—	0.016-0.024	0.024-0.039	—	—	0.012-0.016	14.3-15.3 @ 50°F.

Datsun

ALTERNATOR AND REGULATOR SPECIFICATIONS

Engine Model	Part Number (Alternator)	Output @ 2,500 Alternator rpm (amps)	Part Number (Regulator)	CHARGE RELAY① Core Gap (in.)	Back Gap (in.)	Air Gap (in.)	Point Gap (in.)	VOLTAGE REGULATOR② Core Gap (in.)	Back Gap (in.)	Air Gap (in.)	Point Gap (in.)	Regulated Voltage
L16, L18	Hitachi LT150-05B	37.5	Hitachi TL1Z-58	0.032-0.039	—	—	0.016-0.024	0.024-0.039	—	—	0.012-0.016	14.3-15.3 @ 68°F.
L18	Hitachi LT135-13B	28	Hitachi TL1Z-57	0.032-0.039	—	—	0.016-0.024	0.024-0.039	—	—	0.012-0.016	14.3-15.3 @ 68°F.
A13	Hitachi LT135-13B LT150-05	28.0 37.5	Hitachi TL1Z-79	0.031-0.035	—	—	0.016-0.024	0.024-0.039	—	—	0.012-0.016	14.3-15.3 @ 68°F.
A14	Hitachi LT150-26	37.5	TL1Z-85C	0.031-0.039	—	—	0.012-0.016	0.024-0.039	—	—	0.014-0.018	14.3-15.3 @ 68°F.
L20B	Hitachi LT150-05B	37.5	Hitachi TL1Z-58	0.031-0.039	—	—	0.016-0.024	0.024-0.039	—	—	0.012-0.016	14.3-15.3 @ 68°F.
L26	Hitachi LT150-10	50.0	Hitachi TL1Z-79	0.031-0.039	—	—	0.016-0.024	0.024-0.039	—	—	0.012-0.016	14.3-15.3 @ 68°F.
L28	Hitachi LT160-23C	45	TL1Z-85C	0.031-0.039	—	—	0.016-0.024	0.024-0.039	—	—	0.014-0.018	14.3-15.3 @ 68°F.
A14	Hitachi LT150-19	37.5	Hitachi TL1Z-82	0.031-0.039	—	—	0.016-0.024	0.024-0.039	—	—	0.012-0.016	14.3-15.3 @ 68°F.
L20B	Hitachi LT150-13	37.5	Hitachi TL1Z-82	0.031-0.039	—	—	0.016-0.024	0.024-0.039	—	—	0.012-0.016	14.3-15.3 @ 68°F.
L20B (1975 PL620 only)	Hitachi LT135-13B w/o air LT135-19B w/air	35	Hitachi TL1Z-85	0.031-0.039	—	—	0.016-0.024	0.024-0.039	—	—	0.012-0.016	14.3-15.3 @ 68°F.

① Right unit in regulator case (left unit in TL1Z-17, upper unit in TL1Z-57/58)
② Left unit in regulator case (right unit in TL1Z-17, lower unit in TL1Z-57/58)
NOTE: Right and left are determined with the regulator terminals or harness plug downward.

— Not Applicable

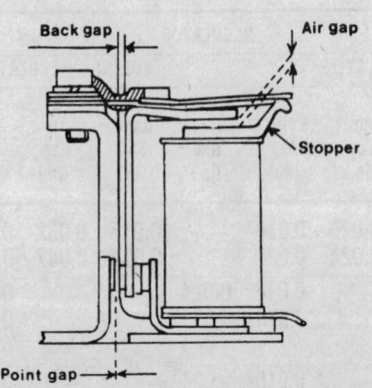

Regulator and charge indicator relay—all except Hitachi TL1Z 57/58

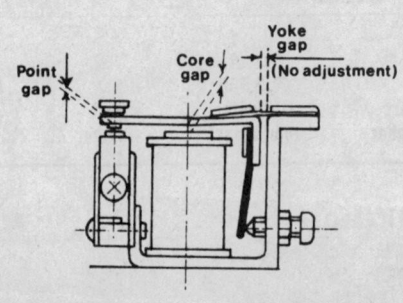

Regulator and charge indicator relay—Hitachi TL1Z 57/58

BRAKE SPECIFICATIONS
All measurements given are (in.) unless noted

Model	Lug Nut Torque (ft/lb)	Brake Disc			Brake Drum			Minimum Lining Thickness	
		Master Cylinder Bore	Minimum Thickness	Maximum Run-Out	Diameter	Max. Machine O/S	Max. Wear Limit	Front	Rear
510	58-65	0.750	0.331	0.0047	9.0	9.04	9.093	0.059 (drum) 0.04 (disc)	0.059 0.059
521	58-65	0.750	—	—	10.0	10.04	10.032	0.059	0.059
240 Z	58-65	0.875	0.413	0.006	9.0	9.04	9.055	0.079	0.059
610	58-65	0.750	0.331	0.0047	9.0	9.04	9.055	0.079	0.059
620	58-65	0.750	0.331	0.0047	8.0	8.04	8.051	0.063	0.059
210	58-65	0.750	0.331	0.0039	8.0	8.04	8.051	0.063	0.059
710	58-65	0.750	0.331	0.0047	9.0	9.04	9.055	0.079	0.059
260 Z	58-65	0.875	0.413	0.006	9.0	9.04	9.055	0.079	0.059
280 Z	58-65	0.875	0.413	0.006	9.0	9.04	9.06	0.079	0.059
F-10	58-65	0.750	0.339	0.0047	8.0	8.04	8.051	0.063	0.039

— Not Applicable

NOTE: Minimum lining thickness is as recommended by the manufacturer. Due to variation in state inspection regulations, the minimum allowable thickness may be different than recommended.

WHEEL ALIGNMENT SPECIFICATIONS

Model	Year	CASTER		CAMBER		Toe-In (in.)	Steering Axis Inclination (deg)	WHEEL PIVOT RATIO (deg)	
		Range (deg)	Preferred Setting (deg)	Range (deg)	Preferred Setting (deg)			Inner Wheel	Outer Wheel
PL510	All	—	1°40'	—	1	0.35-0.47	8	38°-39°	22°30'-33°30'
WPL510	All	—	2	—	1°10'	0.12-0.24	7°50'	38°-39°	22°30'-33°30'
PL521	All	—	3°50'	50'-1°50'	1°20'	0.08-0.12	6	34°	29°30'
240 Z		2°25'-3°25'	2°55'	20'-1°20'	50'	0.08-0.20	11°40'-12°40'	32°-33°	31°24'-32°24'
LB110, KLB110	All	40'-1°40'	1°10'	35'-1°35'	1°05'	0.16-0.24	7°55'	42°-44°	35°-37°
PL610, KPL610	1974	0°45'-2°15'	—	1°-2°30'	—	0.24-0.35	7°05'	37°-38°	30°40'-32°40'
WPL610	1974	0°55'-2°25'	—	1°10'-2°40'	—	0.32-0.43	6°55'	37°-38°	30°40'-32°40'
PL620	1974	—	1°50'	—	1°15'	0.08-0.12	6°15'	36°	31°
B210	1974	1°15'2°15'	—	40'-1°40'	—	0.079-0.157	7°47'-8°47'	37°-39°	31°-33°
PL610 KPL610 WPL610	1974	1°15'2°45'	—	1°15'-2°45' 1°30'-3°	—	0.430-0.550	5°55'-7°25' 5°45'-7°15'	37°	30°42'-32°42'
PL710 KPL710	1974	1°10'2°40'	—	1°25'-2°55'	—	0.550-0.670	6°25'	37°-38°	30°42'-32°42'
260 Z	All	2°09'-3°39'	—	01'-1°31'	—	0.080-0.197	12°10'	33°	31°07'
PL620	1975-77	1°15'2°15'	1°50'	0°15'-2°15-	1°15'	0.04-0.20	6°15'	35°-37°	30°-32°
PL610 KPL610	1975	1°15'2°15'	1°50'	1°15'-2°45-	2°	0.43-0.55	5°55'-7°25'	32°-33°	29°-30' 31°30'

WHEEL ALIGNMENT SPECIFICATIONS

Model	Year	CASTER		CAMBER		Toe-In (in.)	Steering Axis Inclination (deg)	WHEEL PIVOT RATIO (deg)	
		Range (deg)	Preferred Setting (deg)	Range (deg)	Preferred Setting (deg)			Inner Wheel	Outer Wheel
WPL610	1975	1°15'2°15'	1°50'	1°30'-3°00'	2°15'	0.43-0.55	5°45'-7°15'	32°-33°	29°-30' 31°30'
PL710 KPL710	1975	1°10'-2°40'	1°55'	1°25'2°55'	2°10'	0.32-0.43	6°25'	32°-33°	29°-30' 31°30'
B210	1975	1°00'-2°30'	1°45'	0°25'1°55'	1°10'	0.08-0.16	7°32'-9°02'	37°-39°	31°-33°
710	1976-77	1°-2°35'	1°45'	1°15'2°45'	2°	①	6°15'-7°45'	32°-33°	29°30'-31°30'
610	1976-77	1°-2°35'	1°45'	1°15'2°45'	2°	①	6°15'-7°45'	32°-33°	29°30'-31°30'
280Z Coupe	1976-77	2°-3°30'	2°45'	0°20'-1°50'	1°05'	0-0.12	11°15'-12°45'	34°-35°	32°-34°
280Z 2+2	1976-77	2°-3°30'	2°45'	0°20'-1°50'	1°05'	0-0.12	11°15'-12°45'	36°-37°	34°-36°
F-10	1977	0°20'-1°50'	0°55'	0°50'-2°10'	1°30'	②	9°15'-10°45'	36°30'-39°30'	31°-34°

① 0.16-0.24 Radial tires   ② 0-0.08 Radial tires   — Not specified
   0.24-0.31 Bias tires   0.20-0.28 Bias tires

OIL PUMP SPECIFICATIONS

Engine	Pump type	Clearance between inner and outer rotor (in.)	Tip clearance—gear or rotor to cover or outer rotor (in.) (max.)	Clearance between outer rotor and body (in.)	Maximum oil pressure (psi)	Minimum oil pressure (psi) at idle	Relief valve spring free length (in.)	Relief valve opening pressure (psi)
L16, L18, L24	Rotor	0.002-0.005	0.005	0.006-0.008	54-60	14-17	2.24	54.0-59.7
A12	Rotor	0.002-0.005	0.005	0.006-0.008	54-60	13-17	1.71	54.0-59.7
L26	Rotor	0.001-0.003	0.005	0.006-0.008	71	11	2.067	51
L20B	Rotor	0.001-0.003	0.005	0.006-0.008	71	11	2.067	50
A13	Rotor	0.002-0.005	0.005	0.006-0.008	60	11	1.712	54
A14	Rotor	0.002-0.0047	0.0047	0.0059-0.0083	54-74	11	1.7122	54-60
L28	Rotor	N.A.	0.0047	0.0059-0.0083	80	N.A.	2.067	N.A.

TUNE-UP PROCEDURES

Spark Plugs

Clean any foreign material from around the spark plugs prior to removing them. Use a spark plug socket with a rubber insert to remove the plugs. This will prevent cracking the porcelain insulator. Each spark plug should be individually inspected and, if necessary, replaced. Refer to the Troubleshooting Section for an analysis of plug tip conditions. Clean reusable spark plugs and file the center electrode flat. Adjust the spark plug gap, according to the Tune-Up Specifications chart, with a wire type feeler gauge. Lightly oil the threads and torque the spark plugs to 11–15 ft lbs.

Breaker Points and Condenser

Release the distributor cap latches and remove the cap and rotor. Check the points for pitting or burning. Use a point file to clean them. Turn the engine by hand until the distributor cam opens the points. Loosen the setscrew. Adjust the points to the specified gap using a feeler gauge. Tighten the setscrew and recheck the gap. Apply a trace of bearing lubricant to the breaker cam. Replace the cap and rotor. Point dwell should be checked at this time. The figures are given in the Tune-Up Specifications Chart. Ignition timing should be checked each time the breaker points are adjusted.

NOTE: *Some distributors are equipped with dual points.*

Dwell Angle

A dwell meter hookup is shown in the Troubleshooting section. If the distributor has two sets of points, proceed as follows:

1. Unplug the distributor from the engine wiring harness.
2. Connect the two black wires with a jumper wire. This activates the advanced set of points.
3. Check and adjust the dwell of the advanced set of points.
4. Take one end of the jumper wire from the distributor side of the plug. Connect the black wire in the engine harness to the yellow wire from the distributor. This activates the retarded set of points.
5. Check and adjust the dwell of the retarded set of points.
6. Reconnect the plug. Adjust both point sets to the specified gap.

Solid State Breakerless Ignition

Air Gap

Reluctor air gap should be checked periodically. Standard air gap is 0.012–0.016 in. for both single and dual gap distributors. If the gap is incorrect, adjustment may be made by loosening the pick-up coil screws and inserting a feeler gauge.

NOTE: *The use of a non-magnetic feeler gauge such as plastic or brass, is recommended for accurate gapping.*

Remove the rubber cap from the tip of the rotor shaft. Add grease if necessary. The reluctor cannot be removed. To remove the pick-up coil, take out the two pick-up coil assembly and core screws clamping the primary wire. Reverse the sequence to install.

Ignition Timing

Ignition timing should be adjusted with the distributor vacuum line disconnected and plugged. The engine should be running at idle speed. A timing light must be used to obtain an accurate setting. The setting is indicated by the pointer on the engine front cover and the markings on the crankshaft pulley. The top dead center, or 0°, mark is located at the extreme left. The next mark may be either 5° or 10° before top dead center, depending on the engine model. The succeeding marks are 5° apart.

To set the timing, disconnect the vacuum line and loosen the distributor clamp. Connect the timing light, start the engine, and allow it to idle. Point the timing light at the pulley markings and turn the distributor head until the timing pointer and the correct pulley mark are aligned. Some early distributors have a knurled knob for fine adjustments. Tighten the clamp and replace the vacuum line.

Timing settings for each model are given in the Tune-Up Specifications Chart. Engines with emission controls must be set exactly to the manufacturer's recommendations.

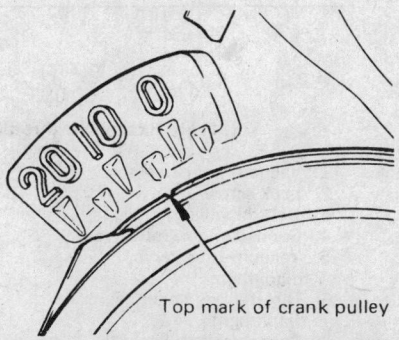

Timing Marks—A12, A13 and A14 Engines

NOTE: *There are two different timing settings for the 240 Z and 260 Z with automatic transmission: an advanced setting for temperatures below 30°F, and a retarded setting for temperatures above 50°F.*

Valve Lash

Remove the valve or camshaft cover. Both valves for each cylinder may be adjusted while they are fully closed, on the compression stroke. After the valves have closed, turn the engine another quarter turn to insure the cam lobes are not putting pressure on the valves. This can readily be seen on overhead camshaft engines. Loosen the locknuts and insert the proper feeler gauge between the valve stem and rocker arm on overhead valve engines, or between the cam lobe and cam follower on overhead cam engines. Valve clearance figures are given in the Tune-Up Specifications Chart. Tighten the adjusting screw until you feel a slight drag on the feeler gauge. Tighten the locknut and recheck the clearance.

After adjusting the valves for the first cylinder, turn the engine in the normal direction of rotation until the valves for the next cylinder in the firing order close. Repeat the adjusting procedure until all valves have been adjusted. Install a new gasket and replace the cover.

NOTE: *Do not run the engine with the rocker arm or camshaft cover removed. Do not adjust the valves with the engine running.*

Carburetor

See the Fuel System Section for further adjustments. Two Hitachi sidedraft carburetors are used on L24 and L26 engines. All other carbureted engines use one down-draft carburetor of various makes and types.

Synchronization and Idle Mixture

Hitachi Type, L24, L26 Engines

Two types of dual carburetor linkages have been used. The early type utilizes a flexible cable from the accelerator pedal. The cable turns a cable drum attached to a throttle shaft, mounted on the intake manifold. The throttle shaft is connected to each throttle by a threaded turnbuckle. Each carburetor has an individual throttle adjusting (idle speed) screw. Some models have another idle adjusting screw on the throttle shaft. Synchronization adjustments are made at the turnbuckles.

The late type uses rod linkage from the accelerator pedal to turn an auxiliary throttle shaft. This shaft is connected by a nonadjustable rod to a throttle shaft linking the carburetor throttles. Each carburetor has an individual throttle adjusting (idle speed) screw. There is also an idle speed adjusting screw on the auxiliary throttle shaft. Synchronizing adjustments are made at a balance screw on the throttle shaft. 1972–1973 models have a fast idle setting screw which is not to be disturbed.

The engine must be at normal operating temperature to perform carburetor adjustments. Make sure the piston damper oil level is correct. If the plunger has one mark, the oil level should be within 0.2 in. of the mark. If the rod has two marks, the oil level should be between the marks. SAE 20 oil should be used in the dampers, except in extremely cold areas where a lighter viscosity may be necessary. To adjust the carburetors:

1. Remove the air cleaner.

2. Back out the individual carburetor throttle adjusting screws.

3. On early linkage, disconnect the front turnbuckle. On late linkage, back out the balance screw.

4. On early linkage, adjust the rear turnbuckle to the standard measurement.

5. Tighten both carburetor mixture adjusting nuts fully. Back them off an equal number of turns (2–3) until they reach their stops. Tighten both nuts about ½ turn.

6. Turn in the individual carburetor throttle adjusting screws a few turns and start the engine. Adjust both screws equally to obtain a reasonable idle speed.

7. Using an air flow meter (Unisyn), measure air flow through each carburetor. Equalize the readings at each carburetor by adjusting the individual throttle adjusting screws. An alternate, and more difficult method is to equalize flow by listening to the hiss of each carburetor air intake through a length of rubber hose. The carburetors are now synchronized. This can be checked visually by stopping the engine, raising both carburetor pistons, and observing whether the throttle plates are parallel.

8. Tighten both mixture adjusting nuts simultaneously ⅛ turn at a time. Tightening the nut leans the mixture. Stop at the point which gives the fastest, smooth idle. If the nuts are tightened all the way and idle is still unsatisfactory, return the nuts to their initial positions as in Step 5. Loosen the nuts simultaneously ⅛ turn at a time. Loosening the nuts richens the mixture. Stop at the point which gives the fastest, smooth idle.

NOTE: *On engines with emission control, the mixture adjusting nuts are held by locknuts and are not to be adjusted, except after carburetor overhaul. Adjust the mixture to obtain the percentage of CO at idle speed spe-*

Early Hitachi/SU Throttle Linkage

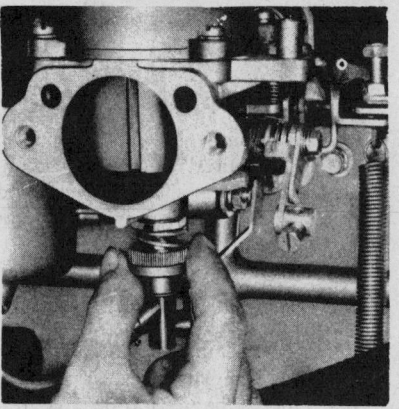

Hitachi/SU carburetor mixture adjusting nut

cified in the Tune-Up Specifications Chart.

9. Lift the piston of the rear carburetor ½ in. This makes the carburetor inoperative. If the engine stalls, richen the front carburetor until it will keep the engine running. Now lift the piston of the front carburetor, and adjust the mixture of the back carburetor. The mixture adjustment is now completed.

10. On early linkage, adjust and connect the front turnbuckle. On late linkage, turn in the balance screw to interlock the front and rear throttle shafts.

11. Open the throttle suddenly. The engine should accelerate immediately with no hesitation. Both pistons should

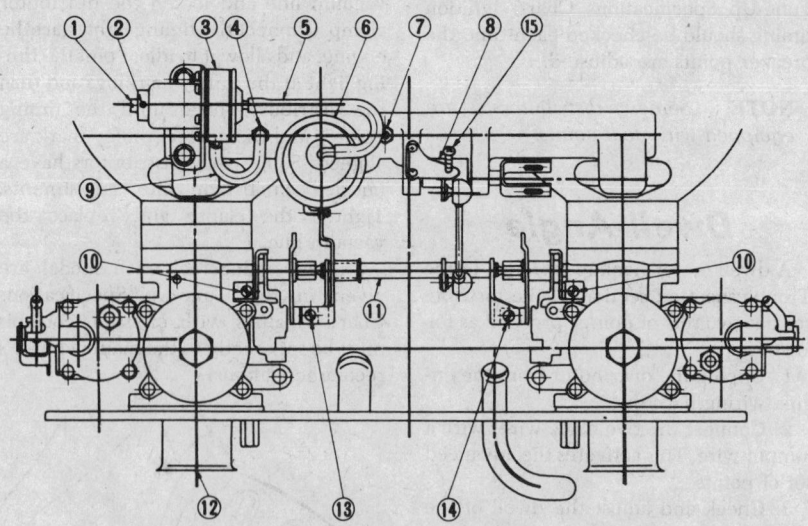

Late Hitachi/SU throttle linkage—1972 and later

1. Vacuum adjusting screw
2. Lock screw
3. Control valve
4. Connector-control valve
5. Vacuum tube-servo diaphragm
6. Throttle positioner servo diaphragm
7. Connector-anti-backfire valve
8. Auxiliary throttle shaft
9. Vacuum tube-control weights
10. Throttle adjusting screw
11. Throttle shaft
12. Air cleaner air horn
13. Positioner adjusting screw
14. Balance screw
15. Fast idle setting screw

rise an equal amount. If this is not the case, recheck the synchronization and mixture adjustments.

12. Adjust the idle speed to that specified in the Tune-Up Specifications Chart. If there is a manufacturer's sticker in the engine compartment, it takes precedence.

Downdraft Carburetors

These carburetors have only one idle mixture adjusting screw. Tighten the screw to lean the mixture and loosen to richen it.

1. For a starting point, gently turn the idle mixture adjusting screw all the way in and back out 2–3 turns.

2. Start the engine and adjust the mixture screw for the fastest smooth idle.

3. Adjust the idle speed screw to obtain the idle speed given in the Tune-Up Specifications Chart.

4. Open the throttle suddenly. The engine should accelerate immediately, without hesitation. If it stumbles or stalls, richen the mixture slightly.

5. On engines with emission control, adjust the idle mixture to obtain the percentage of CO at idle speed given in the Tune-Up Specifications Chart. Some carburetors have idle mixture limiter caps to prevent excessive idle mixture adjustments.

NOTE: *If turning the idle mixture screw has no effect, the idling passages are probably clogged.*

280Z Fuel Injection

Idle RPM and Mixture Ratio

CAUTIONS: *On models equipped with an automatic transmission, all checks should be performed with the shift lever in the "D" position. Be sure to engage the parking brake and chock all four wheels.*

Depress the brake pedal while accelerating the engine to prevent movement of the car. After the idle adjustment has been made, shift the lever to "P" or "N" and remove the wheel chocks.

NOTE: *Idle mixture adjustment requires a CO-meter. Before attempting adjustment, warm-up meter and calibrate.*

1. Warm engine to the operating temperature.

2. Race engine (1,500 to 2,000 rpm) two or three times under no load, then idle the engine for one minute. Check the idle speed. If necessary, adjust to specifications. Manual Transmission - 800 RPM Automatic Transmission - 700 RPM in "D."

3. Check the ignition timing, if necessary, adjust to specifications. Manual - 10°

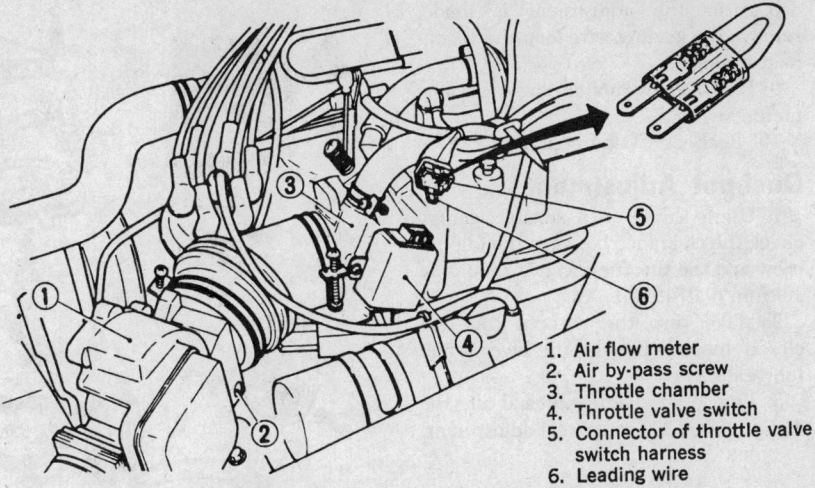

Idle mixture adjustment—Fuel injection models

1. Air flow meter
2. Air by-pass screw
3. Throttle chamber
4. Throttle valve switch
5. Connector of throttle valve switch harness
6. Leading wire

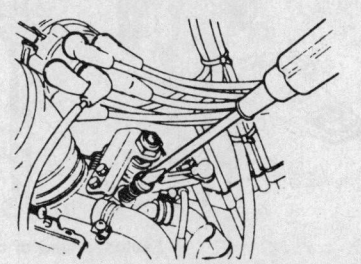

Adjusting idle speed—Fuel injection models

BTDC@800, Automatic - 10° BTDC@700.

4. Check the CO percentage. It should be as follows:

California models - 0.5% max.
Non-California models - 1.0% max.

NOTE: *When checking the idle mixture ratio (CO percentage) make sure the following are in good order.*

Battery
Ignition system
Engine oil and coolant levels
Fuses
E.F.I Unit and connectors
Hoses
Oil filler cap and level gauge
Valve clearance and engine compression

5. Remove throttle valve switch connector.

6. Construct a wire loop as indicated by the arrow in the illustration and insert in place of the connector. This maintains continuity in the system.

7. Adjust idle CO to altitude specifications by turning air by-pass screw.

NOTE: *Remove the plastic plug from the air by-pass screw and turn screw clockwise for richer mixture and counter-clockwise for leaner.*

The following are the idle CO percentages for altitudes.

0 to 2,000 ft. - 3.3%
2,000 to 4,000 ft. - 4.7%
4,000 to 6,000 ft. - 5.7%
Above 6,000 ft. - 6.7%

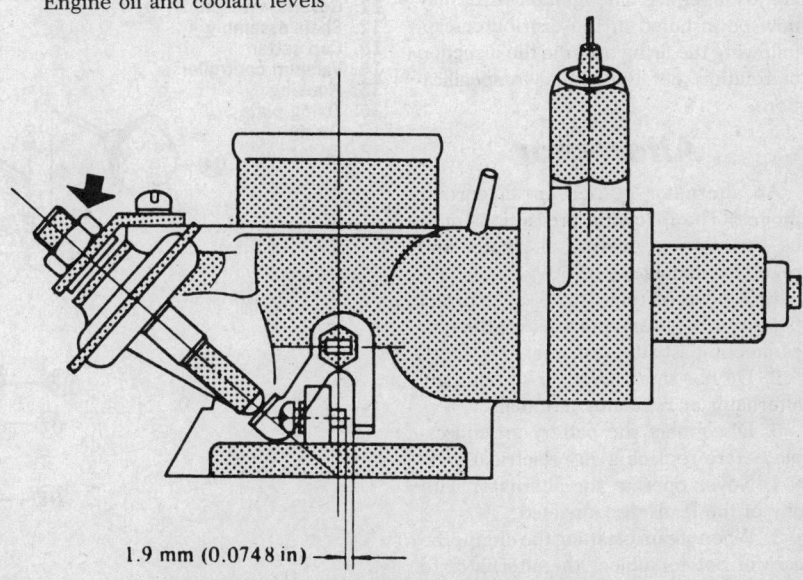

1.9 mm (0.0748 in)

Dashpot adjustment—Fuel injection models

8. After the adjustment is made, remove the leading wire loop and reconnect harness.

9. Install a new rubber plug on air flow meter.

10. Recheck CO percentage.

Dashpot Adjustment

1. Using shims or a suitable gauge, check the clearance between the idle set crew and the throttle lever. It should be 1.9 mm (0.0748 in.).

2. Make sure the dashpot rod end closely touches the throttle lever when fully extended.

3. If necessary, loosen nut and turn the dashpot assembly to correct adjustment.

ENGINE ELECTRICAL
Distributor
Removal and Installation

When removing the distributor for any reason, note the location of the rotor and mark the relationship of the distributor body to the engine. The distributor can then be replaced precisely in its original location, if the engine has not been turned. If the engine has been turned while the distributor was removed, or the distributor location was not marked, proceed as follows: Find top dead center of the compression stroke of No. 1 cylinder by holding a finger in the spark plug hole and rotating the engine. Compression pressure will force the finger from the hole. The exact location of top dead center can then be found by use of the crankshaft pulley timing marks. Install the distributor so that the rotor is pointing at the No. 1 spark plug wire and the points are just opening. The ignition wires may now be installed in the distributor cap, following the firing order in the direction of rotation. Set the timing to specifications.

Alternator

An alternator is used on all current models. The following precautions must be observed to prevent alternator and regulator damage:

1. Be absolutely sure of correct polarity when installing a new battery, or connecting a battery charger.

2. Do not short across or ground any alternator or regulator terminals.

3. Disconnect the battery ground cable before replacing any electrical unit.

4. Never operate the alternator with any of the leads disconnected.

5. When steam cleaning the engine, be careful not to subject the alternator to excessive heat.

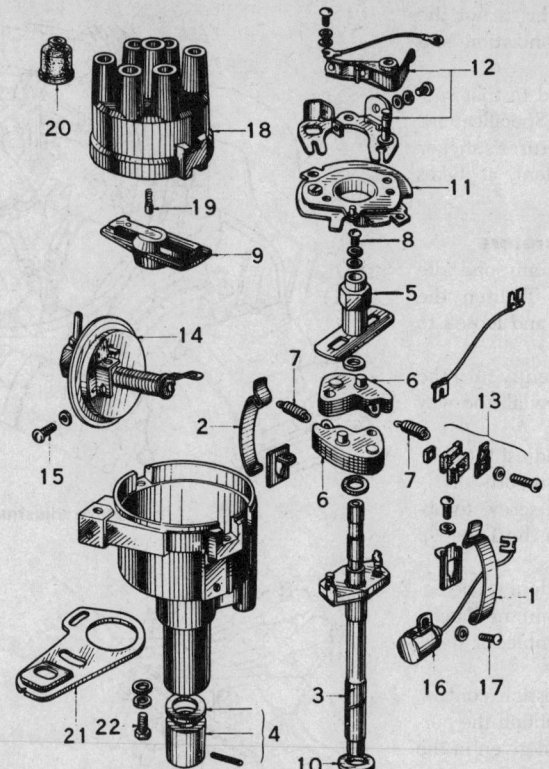

1. Cap holddown spring
2. Cap holddown spring
3. Shaft
4. Drive pinion
5. Cam
6. Centrifugal advance weights
7. Centrifugal advance springs
8. Screw
9. Rotor
10. Thrust washer
11. Breaker plate
12. Contact set
13. Terminal assembly
14. Vacuum control unit
15. Screw
16. Condenser
17. Screw
18. Cap
19. Carbon brush
20. Rubber boot
21. Holddown plate
22. Bolt

Exploded view of distributor, L16 engine

6. When charging the battery, remove it from the car or disconnect the alternator output terminal.

1. Cap
2. Rotor head
3. Rollpin
4. Reluctor
5. Pick-up coil
6. Contactor
7. Breaker plate assembly
8. Packing
9. Rotor shaft
10. Governor spring
11. Governor weight
12. Shaft assembly
13. Cap setter
14. Vacuum controller
15. Housing
16. Fixing plate
17. O-ring
18. Collar

Removal and Installation

1. Disconnect the battery ground.
2. Disconnect lead wires from alternator.

Exploded view of L28 and A-14 distributor

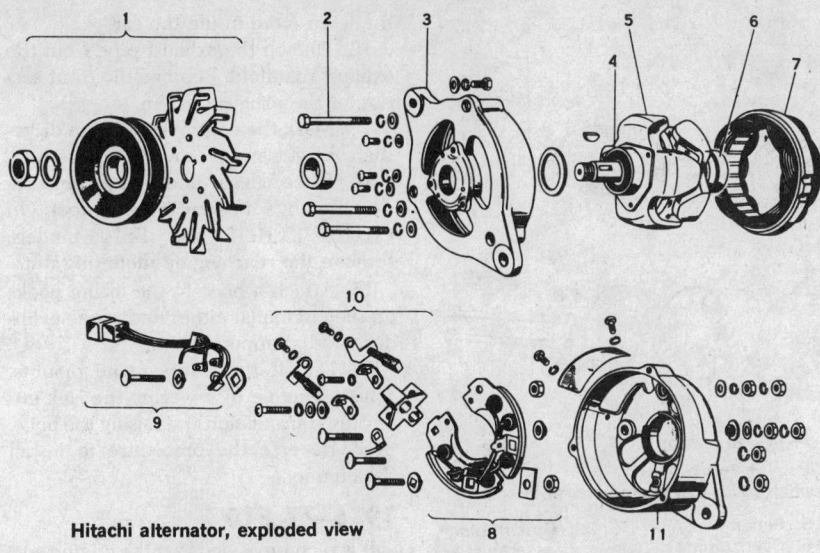

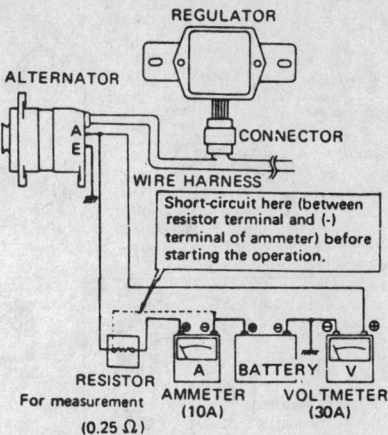

Test setup for Hitachi TL1Z 57/58 regulator

Hitachi alternator, exploded view

1. Pulley assembly
2. Through bolt
3. Front cover
4. Front bearing
5. Rotor
6. Rear bearing
7. Stator
8. Diode plate assembly
9. Lead wire assembly
10. Brush assembly
11. Rear cover

3. Remove adjusting bolt and slip off belt.

4. Support unit and remove mounting bolts.

5. Reverse the above to install.

Belt Tension Adjustment

The correct belt tension for all alternators gives about ½ in. play on the longest span of the belt. The adjustment is usually made by pivoting the alternator. Overtightening the belt will cause rapid wear to the alternator and water pump bearings.

Regulator

Adjustment

All Regulators Except Hitachi TL1Z–57/58

1. Perform this test with the regulator cool. If voltage is not measured within one minute after starting the engine, stop the engine and allow the regulator to cool. It is imperative that the battery be fully charged.

2. Connect an ammeter and voltmeter as shown.

3. Run the engine at 2,500 rpm. Make sure that the charging current is less than 5 amps, and that the regulated voltage is as specified in the Alternator and Regulator Specifications Chart. If the charging current is too high, replace the battery with a fully charged one.

4. If the voltage is incorrect, set the regulator unit gaps to the specified clearances.

5. Recheck the voltage. If it is still incorrect, readjust the air gap. Bend the stopper up to raise the voltage and down to lower.

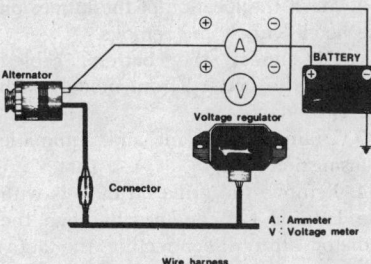

Test setup for all regulators except Hitachi TL1Z-37/57/58

Voltage Specifications

Ambient temperature (°F)	Regulated voltage
14	14.6-15.6
32	14.5-15.5
50	14.3-15.3
68	14.2-15.2
86	14.0-15.0
104	13.9-14.9

Hitachi TL1Z–57/58 Regulator

1. Connect an ammeter, voltmeter, fully charged battery, and resistor as shown.

2. Since this regulator is temperature compensated, the temperature of the regulator cover must be noted. Regulated voltage varies with ambient temperature.

3. Before starting the check, bypass the ammeter as shown to prevent ammeter damage.

4. Start the engine, increase engine speed to 2,500 rpm gradually, and continue for several minutes.

5. If ammeter reading is not below 5 amps, the battery is not fully charged. Replace it with a good one.

6. Return the engine to idle speed.

7. Increase engine speed to 2,500 rpm and check the voltage.

Temperature Voltage Chart

8. If the voltage is incorrect, set the regulator unit gaps to the specified figures.

9. Recheck the voltage. If it is still incorrect, turn in the adjusting screw on the voltage regulator unit to increase voltage, and turn it out to decrease voltage.

Starter

The starter is mounted at the right rear of the engine. The solenoid is mounted on top of the starter and engages the drive pinion through a pivot yoke shift lever.

Removal and Installation

1. Disconnect the battery ground cable.

2. Disconnect the switch lead from the solenoid switch terminal. This terminal is usually labeled S.

3. Disconnect the battery cable from the solenoid battery terminal. This terminal is usually labeled B. There is a third solenoid terminal, labeled M, connected to the starter motor.

4. Remove both starter mounting bolts. Pull the starter assembly forward and out.

5. Reverse the procedure to install.

Starter Drive Replacement

1. Remove the solenoid.

2. Remove the dust cover, E-ring and thrust washer.

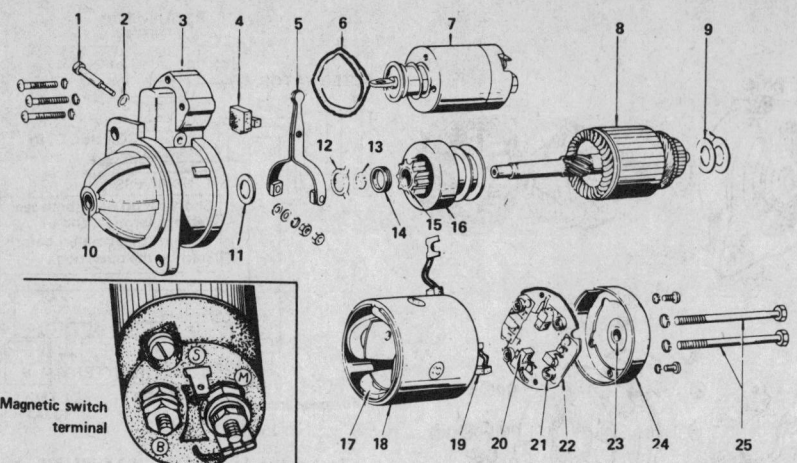

Magnetic switch terminal

Starter with top-mounted solenoid (magnetic switch). The L16 engine starter is shown.

1. Shift lever pin
2. Packing
3. Gear case
4. Dust cover
5. Shift lever
6. Dust cover
7. Solenoid assembly
8. Armature
9. Thrust washer
10. Bushing
11. Thrust washer
12. Stopper washer
13. Stopper clip
14. Pinion stopper
15. Pinion
16. Overrunning clutch
17. Field coil
18. Housing
19. Positive brush
20. Negative brush
21. Brush spring
22. Brush holder assembly
23. Brushing
24. Rear cover
25. Through bolt

3. Remove the brush holder assembly screws.

4. Remove the two through-bolts and the rear cover.

5. Remove the brushes and brush holder.

6. Disengage the yoke and remove the armature assembly.

7. Remove the retaining clip, collar and drive gear.

8. Reverse the above for installation.

Battery

All Datsun models are equipped with a 12-volt battery. The battery is located under the hood in all models. To gain access to the battery in the 240 Z and 260 Z coupe, first open the hood, then the inspection flap in the fender. The inspection flap must be closed before the hood.

ENGINE MECHANICAL

Datsun engines are all inline, with either four or six cylinders. Some have overhead valves with a rocker arm arrangement and others have a single overhead camshaft. Engine displacements range from 1,171 to 2,753 cc. Refer to the Engine Identification Chart for identification of engines by model, number of cylinders, displacement, and camshaft location. Engines are referred to by model designation codes throughout this section.

PL510, PL610, KPL610, WPL510, WPL610, PL521, PL620, LB110, KLB110, 240 Z, B210, PL710, KPL710, 260 Z, 280 Z

It is best to remove the engine and transmission as a unit.

1. Mark the location of the hinges on the hood. Unbolt and remove.

2. Disconnect the battery cables. Remove the battery from models with the L16 engine.

3. Drain the coolant and automatic transmission fluid.

4. Remove the grille on models with the L16 or L18 engine. Remove the radiator after disconnecting the automatic transmission coolant tubes.

5. Remove the air cleaner.

6. Remove the fan and pulley from the L16 engine.

7. Disconnect:
  a. water temperature gauge wire
  b. oil pressure sending unit wire
  c. ignition distributor primary wire
  d. starter motor connections
  e. fuel hose
  f. alternator leads
  g. heater hoses
  h. throttle and choke connections
  i. engine ground cable
  j. thermal transmitter wire—B210, 260 Z, 280 Z
  k. fuel cut-off switch wire—B210
  l. vacuum cut solenoid wire—B210

8. Disconnect the power brake booster hose from the engine.

9. Remove the clutch operating cylinder and return spring.

10. Disconnect the speedometer cable from the transmission. Disconnect the backup light switch and any other wiring or attachments to the transmission. On cars with the L18 engine, disconnect the parking brake cable at the rear adjuster.

11. Disconnect the column shift linkage. Remove the floorshift lever. On LB110 and KLB110 models, remove the boot, withdraw the lock pin, and remove

the lever from inside the car.

12. Detach the exhaust pipe from the exhaust manifold. Remove the front section of the exhaust system.

13. Mark the relationship of the driveshaft flanges and remove the driveshaft.

14. Place a jack under the transmission. Remove the rear crossmember. On LB110, KLB110 and B210 models, remove the rear engine mounting nuts.

15. Attach a hoist to the lifting hooks on the engine (at either end of the cylinder head). Support the engine.

16. Unbolt the front engine mounts. Tilt the engine by lowering the jack under the transmission and raising the hoist.

17. Reverse the procedure to install the engine.

1976–77 F10

It is recommended that the engine and transmission be removed as a unit. If need be, the units may be separated after removal.

1. Remove the hood by holding at both sides and unscrewing bolts. This requires two people.

2. Remove the battery and drain radiator coolant.

3. Remove the air cleaner and disconnect the accelerator wire from the carburetor.

4. Disconnect the following wires and hoses:
  Ignition wire from the coil to the distributor
  Ignition coil ground wire and the engine ground cable
  Disconnect the block connector from the distributor
  Remove fusible links
  Unplug all engine harness connectors
  Remove the fuel and fuel return hoses
  Disconnect the upper and lower radiator hoses
  Detach the heater inlet and outlet
  Remove the Master-Vac vacuum hose
  Disconnect the carbon canister hoses and the air pump air cleaner hose

5. Remove the airpump air cleaner.

6. Remove the carbon canister.

7. Remove the auxiliary fan and the washer tank.

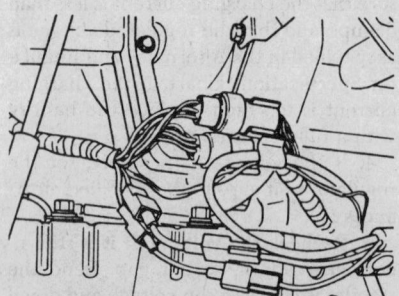

Engine harness connector—F-10

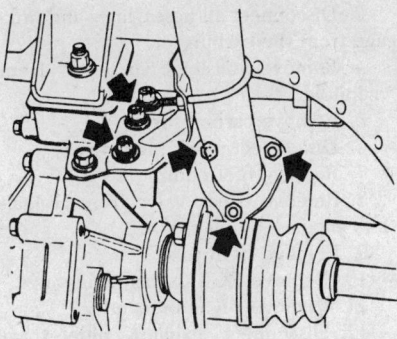

Disconnecting the front exhaust pipe—F-10

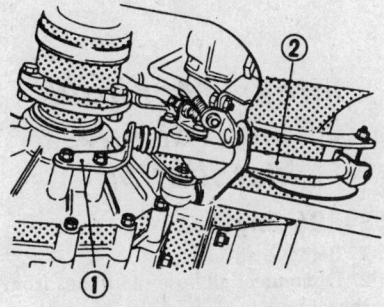

Removing radius link support—F-10

1. Link support
2. Radius link

8. Remove the grille and radiator with the fan assembly.

9. Remove the clutch cylinder from the clutch housing.

10. Remove both buffer rods and disconnect the speedometer cable.

11. Remove the spring pins from the transmission gear selection rods.

12. Attach suitable engine slingers to the block and attach chain or cable. Keep the lifting source slack at this point.

13. Disconnect the exhaust pipe at both the manifold connection and the clamp holding the pipe to the engine.

14. Disconnect the right and left side drive shafts from their side flanges and remove the bolt holding the radius link support.

15. Lower the shifter and selector rods and remove the securing bolts from the motor mounts.

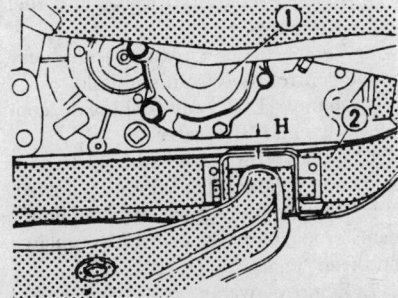

Clearance between frame and clutch housing

1. Clutch housing
2. Sub-frame

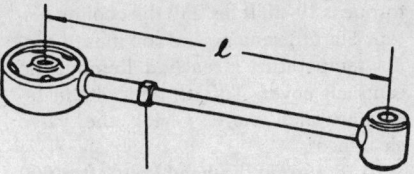

Tightening torque
0.8 to 1.2 kg-m (5.8 to 8.7 ft-lb)

Adjusting buffer rod length

a. Remove the nuts holding the front and rear motor mounts to the frame.

16. Lift the engine up and away from the car.

Installation is the reverse of removal with the following cautions and observations.

1. When lowering the engine into the car and onto the frame, make sure to keep it as level as possible.

2. Check the clearance between the frame and clutch housing and make sure that the engine mount bolts are seated in the groove of the mounting bracket.

a. Distance "H" should be 0.394–0.472 in.

3. After installing the motor mounts, adjust and install the buffer rods. The right side should be 8.23–8.31 in. and the left 5.39–5.47 in.

Cylinder Head
Removal and Installation

NOTE: *To prevent distortion or warping of the cylinder head, allow the engine to cool completely before removing the head bolts.*

For overhaul see the Engine Rebuilding Section

A12, A13 and A14 Overhead Valve Engines

To remove the cylinder head on OHV engines:
1. Drain the coolant.
2. Disconnect the battery ground cable.
3. Remove the upper radiator hose. Remove the water outlet elbow and the thermostat.
4. Remove the air cleaner, carburetor, rocker arm cover, and both manifolds.
5. Remove the spark plugs.
6. Disconnect the temperature gauge connection.
7. Remove the head bolts and remove the head and rocker arm assembly together. Rap the head with a mallet to loosen it from the block. Remove it and discard the gasket.
8. Remove the pushrods, keeping them in order.

To replace the cylinder head on OHV engines:

1. Make sure that head and block surfaces are clean. Check the cylinder head surface with a straightedge and a feeler gauge for flatness. If the head is warped more than 0.003 in., it must be trued. If this is not done, there will probably be a leak. The block surface should also be checked in the same way. If the block is warped more than 0.003 in., it must be trued.

2. Install a new head gasket. Most gaskets have a TOP marking. Make sure that the proper head gasket is used so that no water passages are blocked off.

3. Install the head. Install the pushrods in their original locations. Install the rocker arm assembly. Loosen the rocker arm adjusting screws to prevent bending pushrods when tightening the head bolts. Tighten the head bolts finger tight. The single bolt marked T must go in the No. 1 position on the center right side of the engine.

4. Refer to the Torque Specifications Chart for the correct head bolt torque. Tighten the bolts to one third of the specified torque in the order shown in the head bolt tightening sequence illustration. Torque the rocker arm mounting bolts to 15–18 ft lbs.

5. Tighten the bolts to two thirds of the specified torque in sequence.

6. Tighten the bolts to the full specified torque in sequence.

7. Adjust the valves. If no cold setting is given, adjust the valves to the normal hot setting.

8. Reassemble the engine. Intake and exhaust manifold bolt torque is 7–10 ft lbs. Fill the cooling system. Start the engine and run it until normal temperature is reached. Remove the rocker arm cover. Torque the bolts in sequence once more. Check the valve clearances.

9. Retorque the head bolts after 600 miles of driving. Check the valve clearances after torquing, as this may disturb the settings.

L16, L18, L24, L20B, L26, L28 Overhead Cam Engines

To remove the cylinder head on OHC engines:
1. Drain the coolant.

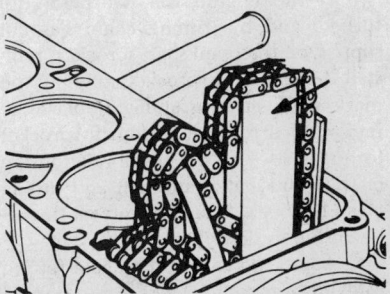

On overhead cam engines, the wedge shown by the arrow can be used to prevent the timing chain from slipping off the crankshaft sprocket.

2. Disconnect the battery ground cable.

3. Remove the upper radiator hose. Remove the water outlet elbow and thermostat.

4. Remove the air cleaner, carburetor, camshaft cover, and both manifolds.

5. Disconnect the temperature gauge at the head.

6. Remove the spark plugs.

7. Mark the relationship between the camshaft, camshaft sprocket, and timing chain. Remove the camshaft sprocket. A wooden wedge may be used to prevent the timing chain from slipping off the crankshaft sprocket. If this tool is not available, support the timing chain in some way so that the relationship of the crankshaft sprocket and the timing chain will be unchanged.

8. Remove the cylinder head front plate and chain tensioner.

9. Unbolt the cylinder head from the block and from the front timing cover. These engines use three different size head bolts. Note the original locations of these bolts.

To replace the cylinder head on OHC engines:

1. Make sure that the head and block surfaces are clean. Check the cylinder head surface for flatness. If the head is warped more than 0.003 in., it must be trued. If this is not done, there will probably be a leak. The block surface should also be checked. If the block is warped more than 0.003 in., it must be trued.

2. Install the new gasket. On L16 engines, apply sealant to both sides of the gasket.

3. Install the head. Install the bolts in their proper locations. Tighten the bolts finger tight.

4. Refer to the Torque Specifications Chart for the correct bolt torque. Tighten the bolts to one third of the specified torque in the order shown in the head bolt tightening sequence illustration.

5. Tighten the bolts to two thirds of the specified torque in sequence.

6. Tighten the bolts to the full specified torque in sequence.

7. If the engine has not been disturbed, and the timing chain has not slipped off the crankshaft sprocket, reinstall the camshaft sprocket, aligning the marks made on disassembly. Replace the fuel pump drive cam. Camshaft sprocket torque is 36–43 ft lbs. If the relationship of the crankshaft, camshaft, and timing chain has been disturbed, correct this relationship as described.

8. Adjust the valves. If no cold setting is given, adjust the valves to the normal hot setting.

9. Reassemble the engine. On U20 engines, intake and exhaust manifold bolt torque is 10–20 ft lbs. Fill the cooling system. Start the engine and run it until normal temperature is reached. Remove the camshaft cover. Torque the bolts in sequence once more. Check the valve clearances.

10. Retorque the head bolts after 600 miles of driving.

Valve Guide Replacement

When replacing cylinder head valve guides, be sure that the guide height above the top of the cylinder head surface is as follows.

Valve Guide Height Specifications

Engine	Guide height (in.)
L16, L18, L24	0.409–0.417
A12	0.709
L20B	0.417
L26, L28	0.409–0.417
A13, A14	0.728

Rocker Shaft Removal and Installation

A12, 13, 14 Engines

1. Remove rocker cover.

2. Loosen rocker adjusting bolts and push adjusting screws away from pushrods.

3. Unbolt and remove rocker shaft assembly.

4. To install, reverse the above. Tighten rocker shaft bolts to 14–18 ft lbs. in a circular sequence.

Intake Manifold Removal and Installation

A12, 13, 14 Engines

1. Disconnect all hoses from air cleaner and remove air cleaner.

2. Disconnect linkage and fuel line and remove carburetor.

3. Remove the EGR control valve.

4. Unbolt and remove the manifold.

5. Install by reversing the above. Torque bolts to 11–15 ft lbs.

Intake and Exhaust Manifold Assembly

L16, 18, 20B Engines

1. Disconnect all hoses and remove the air cleaner.

2. Disconnect all hoses from intake manifold.

3. Disconnect all hoses, lines and linkage from the carburetor.

4. Remove dashpot bracket from manifold.

5. Remove carburetor.

6. Disconnect spark plug wires.

7. Remove fuel pump.

8. Remove check valve from air gallery pipe.

9. Remove EGR tube.

10. Remove EGR passage and valve.

11. Remove FICD bracket.

12. Disconnect exhaust pipe from manifold.

13. Unbolt and remove manifold assembly.

Intake Manifold Removal and Installation

L24, 26 Engines

1. Remove air cleaners.

2. Disconnect all hoses and lines from carburetors.

3. Remove both carburetors.

4. Remove EGR control tube and control valve.

5. Disconnect rear coolant piping and exhaust gas inlet tube from intake manifold.

6. Remove FICD and bracket.

7. Remove fuel inlet and outlet tube assemblies.

8. Remove coolant tube and balance tube.

9. Remove exhaust heat shield plate.

10. Remove fuel evaporative hose bracket from water elbow bracket.

11. Remove intake manifold.

Intake Manifold Removal and Installation

L28 Engine

1. Remove air regulator and hose assembly.

2. Remove cold start valve and fuel pipe assembly.

3. Remove back pressure transducer valve control tube from manifold.

4. Remove EGR heat shield plate, control valve and BPT valve.

5. Remove throttle chamber, dashpot and boost controlled deceleration device.

6. Remove fuel return and feed hoses, canister purge hose, pressure regulator and front engine slinger.

7. Remove water hose, thermostat housing, PVC valve hose, heat shield plate and EGR tube.

8. Remove manifold.

Exhaust Manifold Removal and Installation

All exc. L16, 18 20B

For exhaust manifold removal, see procedures under Intake Manifold Removal.

Timing Chain Cover

Removal and Installation, Oil Seal Replacement

A12, A13 and A14 Overhead Valve Engines

1. Remove the radiator. Loosen the alternator adjustment and remove the belt. Loosen the air pump adjustment and remove the belt on engines with the air pump system.
2. Remove the fan and unbolt and remove water pump.
3. Bend back the lock tab from the crankshaft pulley nut. Remove the nut with a heavy wrench. Rap the wrench with a hammer. The nut must be unscrewed opposite normal engine rotation. Pull off the pulley.
4. It is recommended that the oil pan be removed or loosened before the front cover is removed.
5. Unbolt and remove the timing chain cover.
6. Replace the crankshaft oil seal in the cover. Most models use a felt seal.
7. Reverse the procedure to install, using new gaskets. Apply sealant to both sides of the timing cover gasket. Front cover bolt torque is 4 ft lbs, water pump bolt torque is 7–10 ft lbs, and oil pan bolt torque is 4 ft lbs.

L16, L18, L24, L20B, L26 and L28 Overhead Cam Engines

While it may be possible to perform this operation with the engine in place, Datsun recommends that the engine be removed from the vehicle.

1. Loosen and remove the alternator and air pump belts. Remove the alternator and air pump.
2. Remove the distributor. Remove the cylinder head. This may not be necessary on some engines.
3. Remove the fan and pulley.
4. Bend back the lock tab from the crankshaft pulley nut. Remove the nut with a heavy wrench. Rap the wrench with a hammer. The nut must be unscrewed opposite normal engine rotation.
5. Remove the water pump.
6. Remove the oil pan.
7. Remove the timing chain cover.
8. Remove the old crankshaft oil seal from the cover. Press in a new seal.

9. Reverse the procedure to install, applying sealant to both sides of the cover gasket. On L16 and L18 engines, check that the height difference between the cylinder block upper surface and the front cover upper surface is less than 0.-006 in. Oil pan bolt torque is 4–5 ft lbs for all three engines.

Timing Chain and Camshaft

Removal and Installation

A12, A13 and A14 Overhead Valve Engines

It is recommended that this operation be done with the engine removed from the vehicle.

1. Remove the timing chain cover.
2. Unbolt and remove the chain tensioner.
3. Remove the camshaft sprocket retaining bolt.
4. Pull off the camshaft sprocket, easing off the crankshaft sprocket at the same time. Remove both sprockets and chain as an assembly. Be careful not to lose the shims and oil slinger from behind the crankshaft sprocket.
5. Remove the distributor, distributor drive spindle, pushrods, and valve lifters. **NOTE:** *The lifters cannot be removed until the camshaft has been removed.* Remove the oil pump and pump driveshaft.
6. Unbolt and remove the camshaft locating plate.
7. Remove the camshaft carefully. This will be easier if the block is inverted to prevent the lifters from falling down.
8. The camshaft bearings can be pressed out and replaced. They are available in undersizes, should it be necessary to regrind the camshaft journals.
9. Reinstall the camshaft. If the locating plate has an oil hole, it should be to the right of the engine. The locating plate is marked with the word LOWER and an arrow. A12 engine locating plate bolt torque is 3–4 ft lbs. Be careful to engage the drive pin in the rear end of the camshaft with the slot in the oil pump driveshaft.

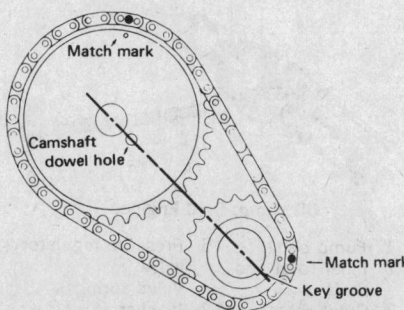

Assembly of sprockets and timing chain— A12, A13 and A14 Engines

10. Camshaft end-play can be measured after temporarily replacing the camshaft sprocket and securing bolt.

Camshaft End-Play Specifications

Engine	Camshaft end-play (in.)
A12	0.001-0.003
A13, A14	0.0004-0.002
L20B	0.0031-0.0150
L26, L28	0.0031-0.0150

If end-play is excessive, replace the locating plate. They are available in several sizes.

11. If the crankshaft or camshaft has been replaced, install the sprockets temporarily and make sure that they are parallel. Adjust by shimming under the crankshaft sprocket.
12. Assemble the sprockets and chain, aligning them.
13. Turn the crankshaft until the keyway and No. 1 piston is at top dead center. Install the sprockets and chain. The oil slinger behind the crankshaft sprocket must be replaced with the concave surface to the front. If the chain and sprocket installation is correct, the sprocket marks must be aligned between the shaft centers when No. 1 piston is at top dead center. Engine camshaft sprocket retaining bolt torque is 33–36 ft lbs.
14. The rest of the reassembly procedure is the reverse of disassembly. Engine chain tensioner bolt torque is 4–6 ft lbs.

L16, L18, L24, L20B, L26, L28 Overhead Cam Engines

These engines are of true overhead camshaft design, using only a single timing chain. To remove the timing chain:

1. Remove the timing chain cover. Remove the camshaft sprocket if the head has not been removed.
2. Remove the chain and tensioner.
3. Remove the oil slinger and distributor drive gear from the crankshaft. Pull off the sprocket.

To replace the chain:
4. Install the cylinder head (removed during timing chain cover removal).
5. Install the crankshaft sprocket, distributor drive gear, and oil slinger with the concave side out.
6. Set the crankshaft and camshaft keys upward. When turning the shafts, be careful not to force the valves against the pistons.
7. Install the sprockets to the chain, aligning the marks on the chain with the marks on the sprockets at the left side of the engine. There are 42 links between

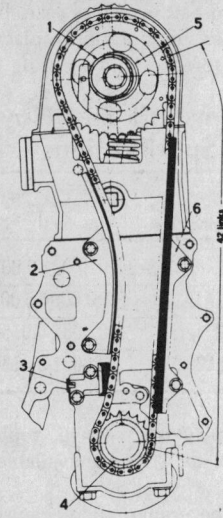

Camshaft chain installation—OHC Engines

1. Fuel pump drive cam
2. Chain guide
3. Chain tensioner
4. Crankshaft sprocket
5. Camshaft sprocket
6. Chain guide

the two chain marks.

8. Install the chain and sprockets to the engine. Install the fuel pump drive cam. Torque the camshaft sprocket bolt to 36–43 ft lbs.

9. Install the chain tensioner.

10. Replace the timing chain cover.

The camshaft can be removed from the cylinder head with the head either in place on the engine or removed. To remove the camshaft:

1. Remove the camshaft cover or cylinder head. Remove the fuel pump drive cam and camshaft sprocket. Remove the rocker arm springs.

2. Loosen the rocker pivot lock nuts and remove the rocker arms by pressing down the valve springs.

3. Remove the camshaft locating plate.

4. Withdraw the camshaft carefully. Do not remove the camshaft bearings. If these bearings are removed, an alignment boring procedure will be required to properly realign them.

To replace the camshaft:

5. Replace the camshaft. Install the locating plate.

6. Check camshaft end-play. It should be 0.003–0.015 in. Adjust by replacing the locating plate.

7. Replace the sprocket, torquing the bolt to 36–43 ft lbs.

8. Install the rocker arms, pressing down the valve springs with a screwdriver. Install the rocker arm springs.

9. Adjust the valves.

Pistons and Connecting Rods

On all engines, it is advisable to mark the connecting rods on removal so that they will be reinstalled in the same cylinder, facing in the same direction. On early engines with a clamp bolt at the top of the connecting rod, the clamp bolt must face toward the camshaft side of the engine. The oil hole at the bottom of the connecting rod must face to the right side. These engines have F marks on the tops of their pistons.

ENGINE LUBRICATION

Oil Pump

Removal and Installation

A12, A13, A14

The oil pump is mounted on the right side of the engine.

1. Drain the oil.
2. Remove the front stabilizer.
3. Remove the splash shield.
4. Unbolt and withdraw the pump from the side of the engine.
5. Prime the pump. Reverse the procedure to install. Torque the pump mounting bolts to 9–11 ft lbs.

L16, L18, L24, L20B, L26, L28

These oil pumps are mounted at the bottom of the engine front cover.

1. Remove the distributor.
2. Drain the oil.
3. Remove the front stabilizer on L16 engine models.
4. Remove the splash shield.
5. Unbolt and remove the oil pump.
6. Before replacing the pump, prime the pump and position No. 1 cylinder at top dead center. Install the oil pump with the spindle punch mark toward the front. Torque the mounting bolts to 11–15 ft lbs.
7. Install the distributor with the rotor pointing to the No. 1 spark plug lead in the cap.
8. Reverse the rest of the removal procedure.

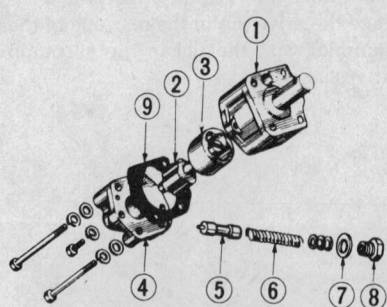

Oil pump, OHC Engines

1. Pump body
2. Inner rotor and shaft
3. Outer rotor
4. Pump cover
5. Pressure regulator valve
6. Valve spring
7. Washer
8. Cap
9. Gasket

Inspection

The pump can readily be disassembled and checked for wear. Refer to the Oil Pump Specifications Chart for clearances. The rotor pump used on J engines has a chamfered edge on the outer rotor. On reassembly, the chamfer must be toward the base of the pump body.

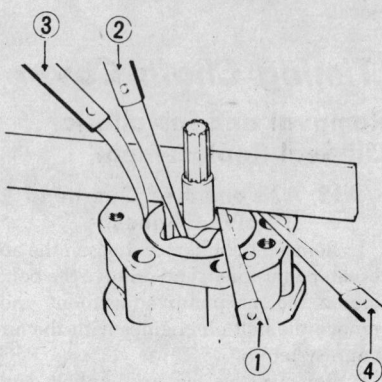

Clearance to be checked in rotor oil pumps

1. Side clearance
2. Tip clearance
3. Outer rotor to pump body clearance
4. Rotor to cover clearance

ENGINE COOLING

Water Pump

Removal and Installation

1. Drain the coolant.
2. Loosen the adjusting bolt at the alternator and remove the fan belt.
3. Remove the fan and pulley and unbolt the pump. This job will be easier if you remove the radiator beforehand.
4. Reverse the procedure for installation.

Thermostat

Removal and Installation

The engine thermostat is housed in the water outlet casting on the cylinder head.

1. Drain the coolant.
2. Remove the upper radiator hose and unbolt the water outlet elbow.
3. The thermostat may now be removed.
4. Refer to the accompanying chart for data on original equipment thermostats.
5. Reverse the removal procedure to replace the thermostat. When installing be sure that the side with the spring faces into the engine. Use a new gasket.

Radiator

Removal and Installation

To remove the radiator:
1. Drain the coolant.

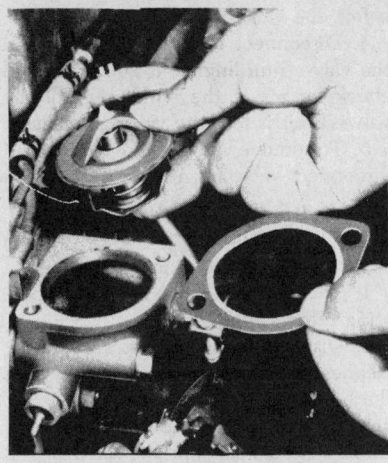

Correct thermostat installation

Thermostat Specifications

Engine	Opening Temperature of Thermostat (°F)	Full Opening of Thermostat (in.)
L16, L18, L24, A12, A13, L20B, L26, A14, L28	183	0.315 @ 203°F

2. Disconnect the upper hose, lower hose, and expansion tank hose.

3. Disconnect the automatic transmission oil cooler lines after draining the transmission. Cap the lines to exclude dirt.

4. Remove the radiator mounting bolts and radiator.

5. Reverse the procedure to replace the radiator. Fill the automatic transmission to the proper level. Fill the cooling system.

6. If the valve is plugged, replace it. Do not clean it.

EMISSION CONTROLS

Various systems are used to control crankcase vapors, exhaust emissions, and fuel vapors. The accompanying chart shows the systems used with various models and engines.

Crankcase Ventilation System

The sealed system consists simply of a tube connecting the valve cover to the carburetor air cleaner. The oil filler cap and the dipstick are sealed. No provision is made for admitting ventilation air into the crankcase. Crankcase vapors are drawn through the carburetor and burned along with the air/fuel mixture.

Emission Control Equipment Applications Table

Year	Model	Engine	Emission Control Systems
1972-1973	PL510 WPL510 PL521	L16	1,4,5
1973	PL610 KPL610 WPL610	L18	1,4,5
1973-1975	PL620	L18	1,4,5
1972-1973	240Z	L24	1,3,4,5
1972-1973	LB110 KLB110	A12	1,4,5
1974	260Z	L26	1,3,5,6
1974	PL610 KPL610 WPL610	L20B	1,3,5,6
1974	PL710 KPL710	L18	1,3,5,6
1974	B210	A13	1,3,4,5,6
1975	B210	A14	1,3,4,5,6,7
1975	PL710 KPL710	L20B	1,3,4,5,6,7
1975	PL610 KPL610 WPL610	L20B	1,3,4,5,6,7
1976-1977	610	L20B	1,3,4,6,7,8,9,10,11
1976-1977	710	L20B	1,3,4,6,7,8,9,10,11
1976-1977	B210	A14	1,3,4,6,7,8,10,11
	280Z	L28	1,6,7,9,11,12
1976-1977	620	L20B	1,3,4,6,7,8,9,10
1977	280Z	L28	1,6,7,9,12
1977	F-10	A14	1,3,4,6,7,8,10,11

1. Closed Crankcase Ventilation System
2. Sealed Crankcase Ventilation System
3. Air Pump System
4. Engine Modification System
5. Fuel Vapor Control System
6. Exhaust Gas Recirculation System
7. Catalytic Converter California Cars Only
8. Early Fuel Evaporation System
9. Boost Controlled Deceleration Device
10. High Altitude Compensator—California Option
11. TCS—Manual Transmission exc. California
12. Floor Temperature Sensing Device

The closed system is identical to the sealed system, with the addition of a tube containing a variable orifice valve between the crankcase and the intake manifold. Under high vacuum conditions (idle), vapors are drawn into the intake manifold through the valve. The tube connected to the air cleaner admits ventilation air through the crankcase. Under

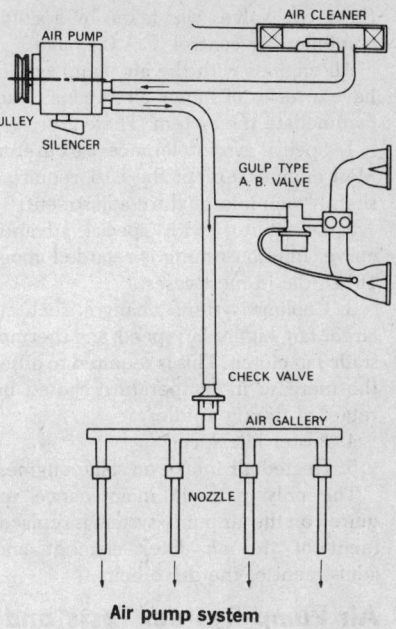

Air pump system

low vacuum conditions (full-throttle), vapors are drawn through the carburetor as in the sealed system.

The crankcase ventilation system requires no periodic maintenance other than replacement of the variable orifice valve, should it become clogged.

Variable Orifice Valve Test

1. With the engine idling, remove the hose from the valve on the intake manifold.

2. A hissing sound should be heard and a vacuum felt at the valve inlet.

Air Pump System

In this system, an air injection pump, driven by the engine, compresses, distributes, and injects filtered air into the exhaust port of each cylinder. The air combines with unburned hydrocarbons and carbon monoxide to produce harmless compounds. The system includes an air cleaner, the belt driven air pump, a check valve, and an anti-backfire valve.

The air pump draws air through a hose connected to the carburetor air cleaner or to a separate air cleaner. The pump is a rotary vane unit with an integral pressure regulating valve. The pump outlet pressure passes through a check valve which prevents exhaust gas from entering the pump in case of insufficient pump outlet pressure. An anti-backfire valve admits air from the air pump into the intake manifold on deceleration to prevent backfiring in the exhaust manifold.

In 1976 California models utilized a secondary system consisting of an air control valve which limits injection of secondary air and an emergency relief valve which controls the supply of secondary air. This system protects the converter from overheating. In 1977 the function of these two valves was taken by a single combined air control (C.A.C.) valve.

All engines with the air pump system have a series of minor alterations to accommodate the system. These are:

1. Special close-tolerance carburetor. Most engines, except the L16, require a slightly rich idle mixture adjustment.

2. Distributor with special advance curve. Ignition timing is retarded about 10° at idle in most cases.

3. Cooling system changes such as larger fan, higher fan speed, and thermostatic fan clutch. This is required to offset the increase in temperature caused by retarded timing at idle.

4. Faster idle speed.

5. Heated air intake on some engines.

The only periodic maintenance required on the air pump system is replacement of the air filter element and adjustment of the drive belt.

Air Pump System Tests and Repairs

Air Pump Test. Removal and Installation

To test air pump output pressure:

1. The engine must be at normal operating temperature.

2. Stop the engine. Disconnect the air supply hose from the check valve at the exhaust manifold. Disconnect the vacuum hose from the air control valve (Calif. cars only).

3. Start the engine. Check the pump pressure output at 1,500 rpm. With the L16 engine, the pressure should be 0.47 in. (12 mm.) Hg or more. With an L24, L26 or L28 engine, the pressure should be 0.063 in. (16 mm.) Hg or more. 1975 and later L20B and A14 engines should have at least 3.94 in./Hg. pressure.

4. If air pressure is not as specified, disconnect the air hose at the anti-backfire valve. Plug the hose opening and repeat the pressure test.

5. At 1500 rpm, close the hole of the gauge with a finger. If leaking air is felt at the relief valve, replace the relief valve.

6. Replace the pump if it does not show proper pressure.

To remove and replace the air pump:

1. Disconnect the hoses from the pump.

2. Remove the bolt holding the pump to the belt adjustment arm or adjusting bracket.

3. Unbolt the pump from the mounting bracket. Remove the belt.

4. Remove the pump from the car.

5. Reverse the procedure to install, adjusting the belt to have about ½ in. play under thumb pressure at the longest span between pulleys.

Check Valve Test, Removal and Installation

To test the check valve action:

1. The engine must be at normal operating temperature.

2. Stop the engine. Disconnect the air supply hose from the check valve at the exhaust manifold.

3. The valve plate inside the valve body should be lightly positioned against the valve seat away from the air distributor manifold.

4. Insert a small screwdriver into the valve and depress the valve plate. The plate should reset freely when released.

5. Start the engine. Increase the idle speed to 1,500 rpm and check for exhaust leakage. Valve pulsation or vibration at idle is a normal condition.

To remove and replace the check valve:

1. Remove the check valve from the air gallery pipe, holding the air gallery flange with a wrench.

2. On reinstallation, the proper torque is 65–76 ft lbs.

Air Control Valve Test, Removal and Installation

1. Warm engine to normal operating temperature.

2. Check all hoses for leaks.

3. Disconnect the outlet side hose of the valve and check for air flow. If no air is felt, replace the valve.

4. Disconnect the vacuum hose from the valve. If air flow from the air hose stops, the valve is working correctly, if air flow continues, replace the valve.

5. To replace valve, disconnect hoses and remove from bracket.

Emergency Air Relief Valve Test, Removal and Installation

1. Warm engine to normal operating temperature.

2. Check all vacuum hoses for leaks.

3. Run engine at 2000 rpm and check for air flow at outlet port of valve. If no air is felt, the valve is normal.

4. Disconnect the vacuum hose from the valve. Run engine at 2000 rpm and check for air at the outlet port of the valve. If air is felt, the valve is normal.

5. To remove valve, remove hoses and disconnect valve from mounts.

Anti-Backfire Valve Test, Removal and Installation

To test the anti-backfire valve:

1. The engine must be at normal operating temperature.

2. Disconnect the air hose from the air cleaner at the anti-backfire valve. Plug the hose.

3. Open and close the throttle rapidly. Air flow should be felt at the valve for 1–2 seconds on deceleration. If no air flow is felt or flow is felt continuously for more than 2 seconds, replace the valve.

To remove the anti-backfire valve, simply disconnect the hoses.

Engine Modification System

Engine modifications used on vehicles with the L16 or L18 prior to 1975, and 1974–77 L18 and L20B, are:

1. A distributor with a secondary set of contact points which are retarded 5° (7° in 1972–1973. For 1974–77 models, a single set of points is used. These secondary points are operational only when cruising or accelerating with a partially open throttle in third gear with manual transmission, or over 13 mph with automatic transmission. For 1973, the timing is advanced only at idle, full throttle, and in fourth gear. A speed sensor is located at the speedometer on automatic transmission models. On 1972–1977 models, a temperature sensor in the engine compartment allows retarded timing only

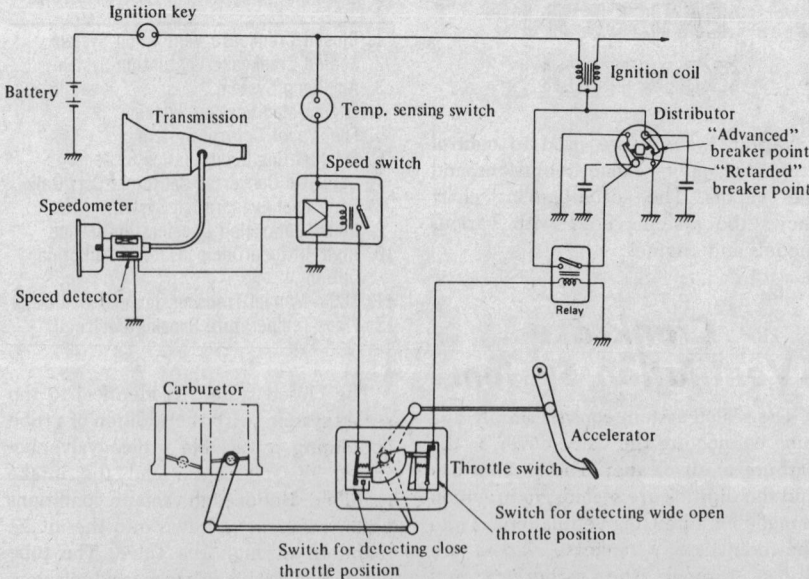

Engine modification system, 1972 PL510 and WPL510, automatic transmission

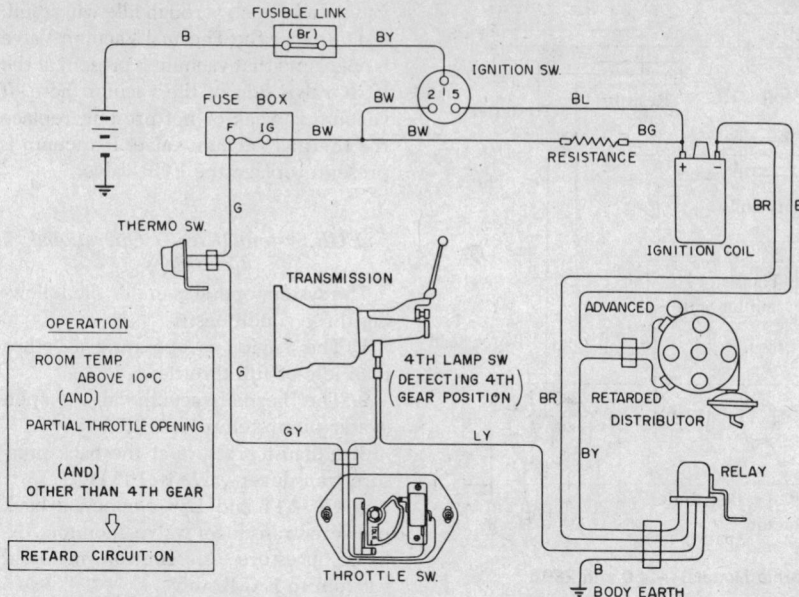

OPERATION

ROOM TEMP
ABOVE 10°C
(AND)
PARTIAL THROTTLE OPENING
(AND)
OTHER THAN 4TH GEAR

⇩

RETARD CIRCUIT ON

Engine modification system, 1973 L16 and L18 engine models, and 1974 L18 and L20B engines. Automatic transmission vehicles don't have the transmission switch shown

when the temperature inside the car is 50°F or above.

2. A solenoid valve in the carburetor opens to supply a lean fuel and air mixture, bypassing the throttle valve, in third gear or over 13 mph as above. The solenoid valve will not open if overridden by a closed throttle switch, a wide open throttle switch, a neutral switch, or a clutch disengaged switch. This arrangement is operational primarily during deceleration, when high intake manifold vacuum is present. For 1972–1977, this system is replaced with a vacuum controlled device in the carburetor to perform the same function.

The engine modification system used on the 1200 series with the A12 and the B210 series with the A13 and A14 engine is relatively simple. It requires only a throttle positioner which holds the throttle slightly open on deceleration. A vacuum control valve connected to the intake manifold causes a vacuum servo to hold the throttle open slightly during the high vacuum condition of deceleration. The control valve is compensated for the effects of altitude and atmospheric pressure. The carburetor and distributor are specially calibrated for this engine. A transmission-controlled vacuum advance system is used on 1972–1975 manual transmission models.

The engine modification system for the 240 Z sports coupe with the L24 engine and the 260 Z with the L26 engine is quite similar to that for the A12, A13 engine, using a vacuum control valve, vacuum servo, and throttle positioner. 1973–74 models have a solenoid to prevent running on, mounted on the vacuum control valve. The 240 Z with automatic transmission has a dual point distributor. One set of points has a timing

setting of 0°TDC and the other a setting of 10°BTDC. A thermo-switch under the instrument panel activates the advanced timing set of points for easier starting and warmup when the temperature inside the car drops below 30°F. 1974–77 260 Z and 280 Z models have breakerless distributors. A dual gap type is used with automatic transmissions. Timing is the same as the 240 Z.

For 1973 L24 engines and all 1974–77 engines, an exhaust gas recirculation (E.G.R.) system is used. This system uses vacuum from the rear carburetor to actuate a valve which allows a small amount of exhaust gases to be drawn into the intake manifold. This results in a decrease in oxides of nitrogen in the exhaust gases. The vacuum required to operate the system is not available at idle or wide throttle openings. A thermostatic switch inside the car shuts off the vacuum to the system when the temperature is below 30°F, thus allowing good cold starting and driveability.

Engine Modification System Tests, Adjustments

Throttle Positioner Adjustment—A12, A13, L24, L26 Engines

1. The engine must be at normal operating temperature. A tachometer must be connected. If there is a dashpot, back off its adjustment to prevent interference.

2. Increase engine speed to 3,000 rpm for the A12, A13 or 2,000 rpm for the L24, L26.

3. Release the throttle. The time required to slow to 1,000 rpm should be:

Engine		Transmission	Time in seconds
A12	A13	Manual	3.5-4.5
A12	A13	Automatic	2.5-3.5
L24	L26	Manual	3.0

4. To adjust the time lag, first loosen the lockscrew on the vacuum control valve. Turn the adjusting screw clockwise to increase time lag, and counterclockwise to decrease.

5. Tighten the lockscrew.

6. Repeat Steps 2–5 to check the adjustment. If the adjustment is correct, the engine will settle down to the correct idle speed.

EGR System—1973 L24 and all 1974–75 Engines

1. Make sure that the temperature inside the engine compartment is at least 55°F.

2. Increase the engine speed from idle to about 3,500 rpm. The EGR valve shaft should move up.

3. If the valve does not move, check the solenoid valve by applying direct battery current. Check the EGR valve. If the

Transmission controlled vacuum advance introduced in 1972 on A12 engine and continued on the A13 and A14.

Datsun

----- A/T model only

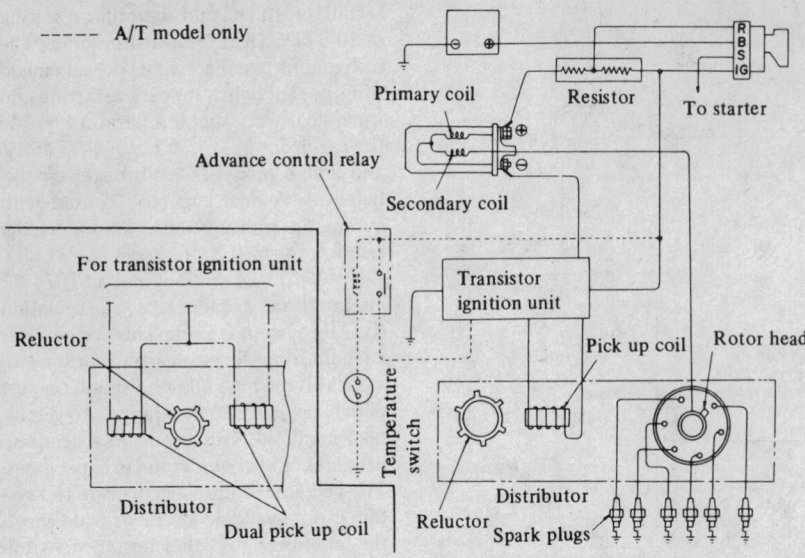

Breakerless Distributor System (California Models)—260 and 280Z

For transistor ignition unit

Reluctor

Distributor

Dual pick up coil

Primary coil

Advance control relay

Secondary coil

Resistor

To starter

Transistor ignition unit

Temperature switch

Reluctor

Distributor

Spark plugs

Pick up coil

Rotor head

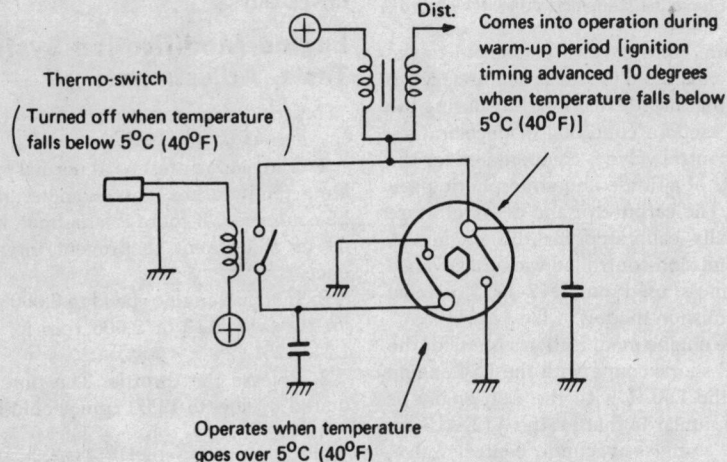

Thermo-switch
(Turned off when temperature falls below 5°C (40°F))

Dist.

Comes into operation during warm-up period [ignition timing advanced 10 degrees when temperature falls below 5°C (40°F)]

Operates when temperature goes over 5°C (40°F)

Dual point distributor system, 240 Z automatic

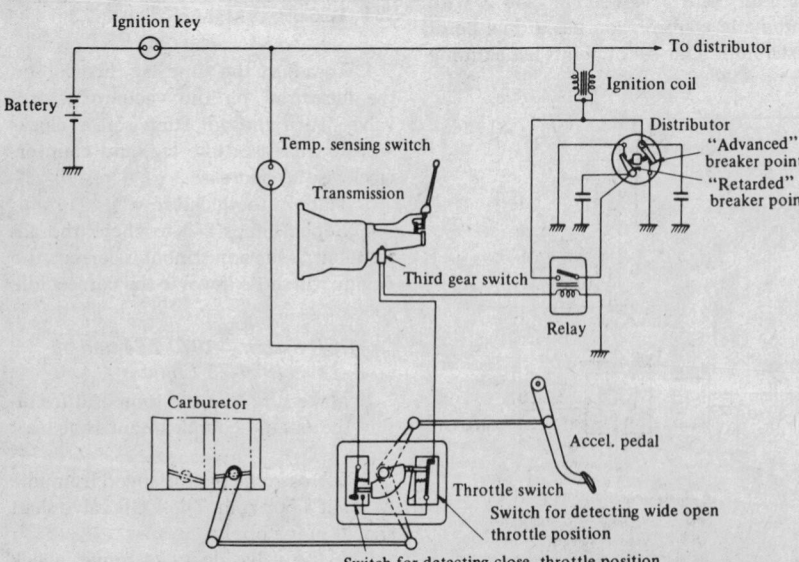

Ignition key

Battery

Temp. sensing switch

Transmission

Carburetor

Third gear switch

Relay

Accel. pedal

Throttle switch
Switch for detecting wide open throttle position
Switch for detecting close throttle position

To distributor

Ignition coil

Distributor

"Advanced" breaker point
"Retarded" breaker point

Engine modification system, 1972 PL510 and WPL510, manual transmission

valve sticks open, a rough idle will result.

4. Be sure the Thermal Vacuum Valve is open, and that vacuum is present at the EGR valve side of the vacuum hose. If vacuum is weak or not present, replace the thermal vacuum valve. If vacuum is present, replace the EGR valve.

EGR System 1976–77 Operational Conditions

The system operates under the following three conditions:

1. The engine is operating at other than idle or full throttle.

2. The thermal vacuum valve is open (water pump temp 117°–127°F).

3. Exhaust pressure at the back pressure transducer valve is .10" HG.

4. On A14 and L28 engines, a back pressure transducer valve monitors exhaust pressure to control manifold vacuum to E.G.R. valve.

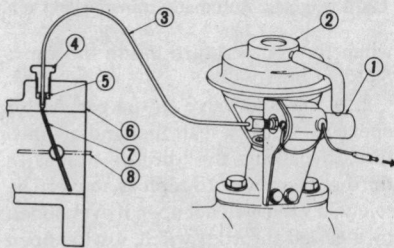

L24, L26 engine EGR system

1. Solenoid valve
2. EGR valve
3. EGR vacuum tube
4. Attaching nut
5. Sealing nut
6. Rear carburetor
7. Throttle valve
8. Throttle valve fully open

Transmission Controlled Vacuum Advance—1972–1977 A12, A13, A14, 1975–77 L26, L28, 1975–77 L20B Engines With Manual Transmission

1. Place the car on a lift with the rear wheels free.

2. Pull off the distributor vacuum hose.

3. Place the transmission in high gear.

4. Run the engine to about 3,000 rpm.

5. Vacuum should be available at the hose. It should be available only in high gear, unless the temperature inside the car is above 50°F. If this is the case, vacuum should be available regardless of the gear selected.

6. If the system does not function properly, check:

a. the fuse. If it is blown, the electric choke won't work either.

b. the high gear switch on the right side of the transmission.

c. the temperature sensing switch inside the passenger compartment.

d. the solenoid valve between the engine vacuum source and the distributor. Vacuum advance is allowed when no current goes to the solenoid.

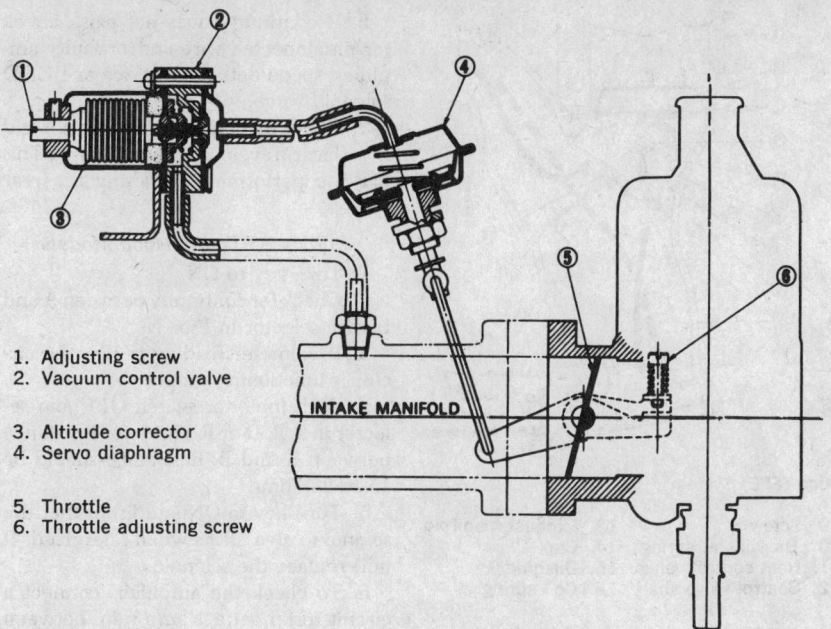

1. Adjusting screw
2. Vacuum control valve

3. Altitude corrector
4. Servo diaphragm

5. Throttle
6. Throttle adjusting screw

INTAKE MANIFOLD

Engine modification system, 240Z, 260Z, the 1973-74 models have a solenoid on the vacuum control valve

Spark Delay Valve—A14, L20B engines with Automatic Transmission

1. Remove the valve.

2. Blow air through the port on the carburetor side, then through the distributor side port. The valve is in good condition if air flow resistance is greater on one side than the other.

Solenoid Bypass Valve—L16 Engine With Manual Transmission

The solenoid valve is opened by electric current and spring-loaded to the closed position. To test system operation:

1. Disconnect the solenoid valve ground lead (black wire). Connect an ammeter between the lead terminal and ground. A test light can also be used, but this only indicates whether current is present or not, while an ammeter measures the amount of current.

2. Switch the ignition on.

3. With the throttle closed, the transmission in gear, and the clutch pedal released, the ammeter should read about 0.4 amps. In any other condition, the ammeter should read 0 amps.

4. If the ammeter reading is not as specified, check each switch and adjust or replace it as necessary. On the throttle valve switch, clearance between the cam and microswitch body should be 0.032 in.

5. Remove the ammeter and replace the solenoid valve ground lead. Start the engine. Connect a jumper wire between the battery output terminal and the solenoid input terminal. The engine speed should rise to about 1,100 rpm.

6. If engine speed does not rise, check the solenoid operation.

7. Reconnect the leads in their normal locations.

Solenoid Bypass Valve—L16 Engine With Automatic Transmission

1. Disconnect the solenoid valve ground lead (black wire). Connect an ammeter between the lead terminal and ground. A test light can also be used, but this only indicates whether current is present or not, while an ammeter measures the amount of current.

2. When speed is over 13 mph with a closed throttle, the ammeter should read about 0.4 amps. Below 13 mph or with the throttle open, the ammeter should read 0 amps.

3. If the ammeter reading is not as specified, check each switch and adjust or replace it as necessary.

4. Remove the ammeter and replace the solenoid valve ground lead. Start the engine. Connect a jumper wire between the battery output terminal and the solenoid input terminal. The engine speed should rise to about 1,100 rpm.

5. If engine speed does not rise, check the solenoid operation.

6. Reconnect the leads in their normal locations.

Vacuum Bypass Valve—1972–74 L16, L18, L20B Engine

If this device is not adjusted correctly, the engine will take a long time to settle down to idle speed after the throttle is released.

1. With the engine warmed up, it should take 4–5 seconds for the engine speed to fall from 3,000 rpm to 1,000 rpm after the throttle is released. If it does not, proceed with the following.

2. Loosen the lock screw at the bottom of the vacuum bypass valve on the carburetor.

3. Remove the vacuum bypass valve cover.

4. Turn the adjusting screw clockwise to increase the time lag, and counterclockwise to decrease. Do not fit the screwdriver tightly into the slot.

5. Replace the cover and tighten the lock screw.

Dual Point Distributor—L16 Engine With Manual Transmission through 1972

1. Disconnect the lead wires from the retarded and advanced terminals on the distributor. Connect an ammeter between the lead wire for the retarded points and ground.

2. Switch the ignition on.

3. With the throttle partially open, the shift lever in third gear, and the clutch pedal released, the ammeter should indicate about 3 amps. The temperature must be above 50°F in the passenger compartment on 1972–1973 models.

4. With the throttle valve wide open or nearly closed, or the shift lever in some position other than third, or the clutch pedal depressed, the ammeter should indicate 0 amps.

5. If the ammeter reads 0 amps in Step 3, disconnect the terminals of the relay (E1 on 521) and measure the voltage between the terminal with the No. 1 punch mark and ground. If voltage is about 12 volts, replace the relay. If voltage is 0 volts, check each switch and wiring.

6. If the ammeter reads 3 amps in Step 4, check the clutch switch, neutral switch, and third gear switch. On the PL510 and WPL510, check the throttle switch. On the PL521, check the throttle switch and accelerator switch.

Dual Point Distributor—L16 Engine With Automatic Transmission through 1972

1. Disconnect the lead wire of the retarded side of the distributor. Connect an ammeter between the lead wire and the retarded side terminal.

2. Start the engine and drive the vehicle.

3. The ammeter should not read 0 amps when speed is over 13 mph with a partially open throttle. Otherwise, the ammeter should read 0 amps.

4. If the ammeter reading is not as specified, check the speed switch, throttle switch, speed detector, and relay.

Early Fuel Evaporation System (E.F.E.)

1976–77 Cars Exc. 280 Z

In this system, a control valve is welded to the valve shaft and installed on the exhaust manifold through bushing. This heat control valve and is actuated by a coil spring, thermostatic spring and counterweight which are assembled on the valve shaft projecting at the rear outside

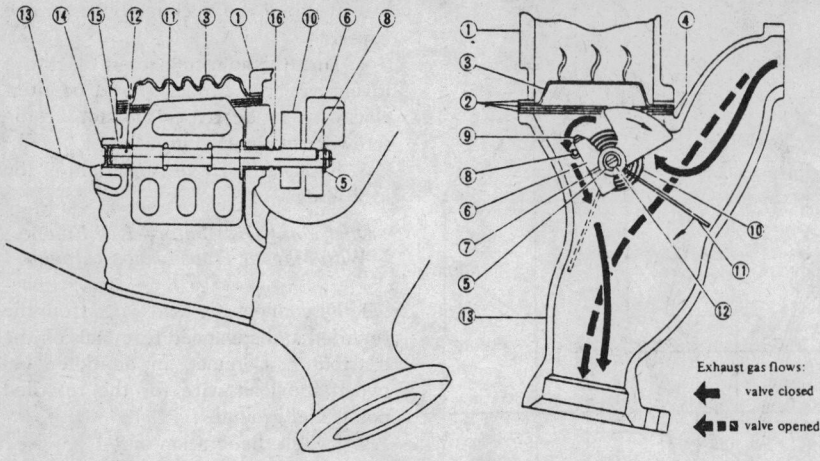

Early Fuel Evaporation (EFE) System

1. Intake manifold
2. Stove gasket
3. Manifold stove
4. Heat shield plate
5. Snap ring
6. Counterweight
7. Key
8. Stopper pin
9. Screw
10. Thermostat spring
11. Heat control valve
12. Control valve shaft
13. Exhaust manifold
14. Cap
15. Bushing
16. Coil spring

of the manifold. The counterweight is secured to the shaft with a key, bolt and snap-ring. A chamber between the intake and exhaust manifolds above the manifold stove heats the air-fuel mixture by means of exhaust gases. This results in better atomization and lower HC content.

Testing

1. Run engine and visually check for movement.

2. In cold weather, the counterweight will move counterclockwise until it reaches the stop pin. As the engine warms up the counterweight gradually moves down.

3. As engine speed increases, the flow of exhaust gases causes the counterweight to move clockwise. When the heat control valve is full open the counterweight should again be in contact with the stop pin.

Check for bent stop pin, broken heat valve key, axial clearance between heat control valve and manifold of 0.028–0.059", and cracks or flaking at the heat control valve weld.

Boost Controlled Deceleration Device (B.C.D.D.)

All 1976–77 Cars exc. B210, F-10 and 1976 280 Z

The B.C.D.D. is installed under the throttle chamber as a part of it. It supplies additional air to the intake manifold during coasting to maintain manifold vacuum at the proper operating pressure.

There are two diaphragms in the device. Diaphragm I detects the manifold vacuum and opens the vacuum control valve when vacuum exceeds operating pressure. Diaphragm II operates the air

control valve by way of the vacuum transmitted through the vacuum control valve. The air control valve regulates the amount of additional air so that the manifold vacuum can be kept at operating pressure.

On manual transmission models, in addition to the B.C.D.D., the system consists of a vacuum control solenoid valve, speed detecting switch and amplifier.

On automatic transmission models, in addition to the B.C.D.D., the system consists of vacuum control solenoid and inhibitor switch.

Testing

Manual Transmission Models

1. Check for continuity between terminals A and B with engine off.

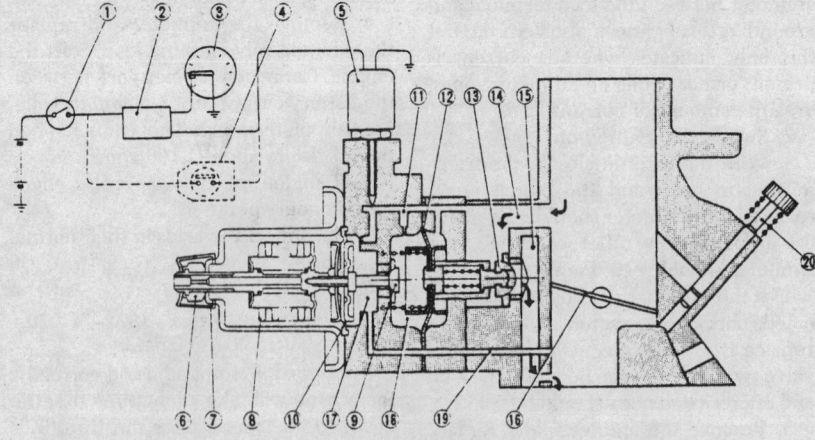

BCDD sectional view

1. Ignition switch
2. Amplifier
3. Speed detecting switch Blow 10 M.P.H.: ON (For M/T)
4. Inhibitor switch "N" or "P" position: ON (For A/T)
5. Vacuum control solenoid valve
6. Adjusting nut
7. Lock spling
8. Altitude corrector
9. Vacuum control valve
10. Diaphragm I
11. Air passage
12. Diaphragm II
13. Air control valve
14. Air passage
15. Air passage
16. Throttle valve
17. Vacuum chamber I
18. Vacuum chamber II
19. Vacuum passage
20. Idle speed adjusting screw

2. If continuity does not exist, check for disconnected wire and/or faulty amplifier, speed detecting device or BCDD solenoid valve.

3. Check for continuity between A and B with car traveling at least 10 mph. This may be performed by raising the rear wheels.

Automatic Transmission Models

1. Turn key to ON.

2. Check for continuity between A and B with selector in P or N.

3. If volmeter reading is 12v, the circuit is functioning properly.

4. With inhibitor switch OFF and selector in 1, 2, D or R, check for resistance between A and B. Resistance should be 15 to 28 ohms.

5. Turn key to ON and listen that the solenoid valve clicks when energized. If not, replace the solenoid.

6. To check the amplifier, connect a circuit tester set a 1 amp min. between the amplifier and the solenoid valve. Turn the key to ON. The tester pointer should deflect if the system is working properly. If not, replace the amplifier.

Setting BCDD Pressure

A tachometer and a vacuum gauge are needed for this job.

1. Remove the harness from the solenoid vacuum valve.

2. Connect the vacuum gauge to the intake manifold.

3. Run the engine to normal operating temperature.

4. Adjust the engine to proper idle speed: 800 manual, 700 auto in D.

5. Increase the speed to 3000–3500 rpm and suddenly close the throttle.

6. Vacuum should increase abruptly to

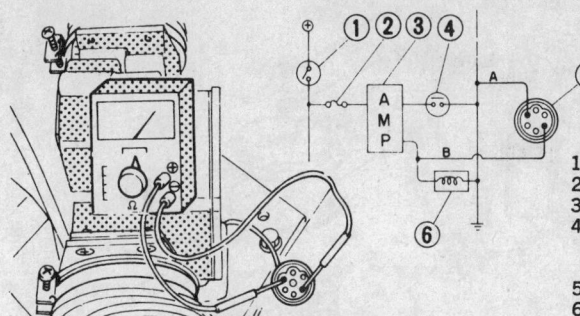

1. Ignition key
2. Fuse
3. Amplifier
4. Speed detecting switch
   Above 10 mph: OFF
   Below 10 mph: ON
5. Function test connector
6. Vacuum control solenoid valve

BCDD functional test—manual transmission

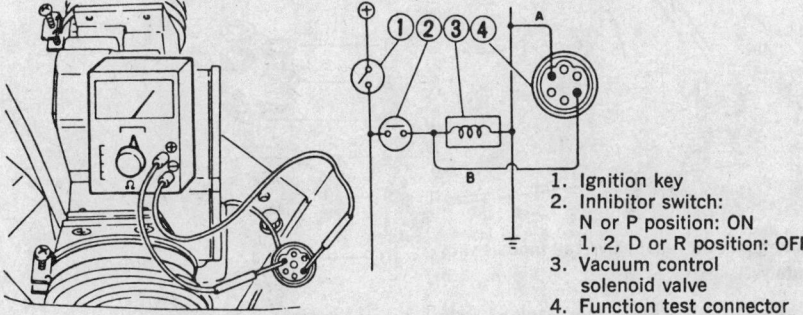

1. Ignition key
2. Inhibitor switch:
   N or P position: ON
   1, 2, D or R position: OFF
3. Vacuum control solenoid valve
4. Function test connector

BCDD functional test—automatic transmission

23–24 in. Hg., and gradually decrease at idle.

7. BCDD set pressure should be 18–19 in. Hg. at idle.

8. Pressure is adjusted by means of a bolt in the end of the BCDD.

Fuel Vapor Control System

The fuel vapor control system is used on all vehicles sold in the U.S., starting 1970. It has four major components:

1. A sealed gas tank filler cap to prevent vapors from escaping at this point.

2. A vapor separator which returns liquid fuel to the fuel tank, but allows vapors to pass into the system.

3. A vapor vent line connecting the vapor separator to a flow guide valve.

4. A flow guide valve which allows air into the fuel tank and prevents vapors from the crankcase ventilation system from passing into the vapor vent line and fuel tank.

When the engine is not running, fuel vapors accumulate in the fuel tank, vapor separator, and vapor vent line. When the vapor pressure exceeds 0.4 in. (10 mm) Hg, the flow guide valve opens to allow the vapors to pass into the crankcase ventilation system. Fuel vapors are thus accumulated in the crankcase. When the engine starts, the vapors are disposed of by the crankcase ventilation system. When enough fuel has been used to create a slight vacuum in the fuel tank and fuel vapor control system, the flow guide

valve opens to let fresh air from the carburetor air cleaner into the tank.

On engines with sidedraft carburetors, float bowl vapors are routed through the float bowl overflow tubes to the carburetor air cleaner.

Flow Guide Valve Test

The flow guide valve is mounted in the engine compartment. The valve fittings are usually marked A, from air cleaner; F, from fuel tank; and C, to crankcase.

1. Blow into the F fitting. Air should come out the C fitting.

2. Blow into the C fitting. Air should not escape.

3. Blow into the A fitting. Air should come out either the F or C fitting, or both.

4. Replace the valve if defective.

Catalytic Converter

All California Cars except Pick-Up

In addition to the air injection system, EGR and the engine modifications, the catalyst further reduces pollutants. Through catalytic action, it changes residual hydrocarbons and carbon monoxide in the exhaust gas into carbon dioxide and water before the exhaust gas is discharged into the atmosphere.

NOTE: *Only unleaded fuel must be used with catalytic converters; lead in fuel will quickly pollute the catalyst and render it useless.*

The emergency air relief valve is used as a catalyst protection device. When the temperature of the catalyst goes above maximum operating temperature, the temperature sensor signals the switching module to activate the emergency air re-

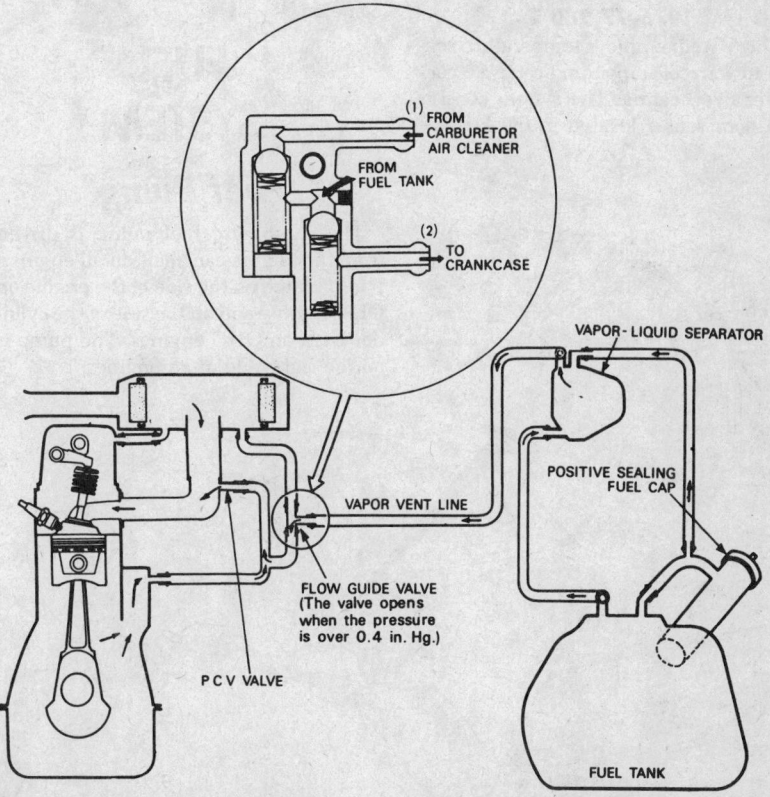

Fuel vapor control system for engines with downdraft carburetors

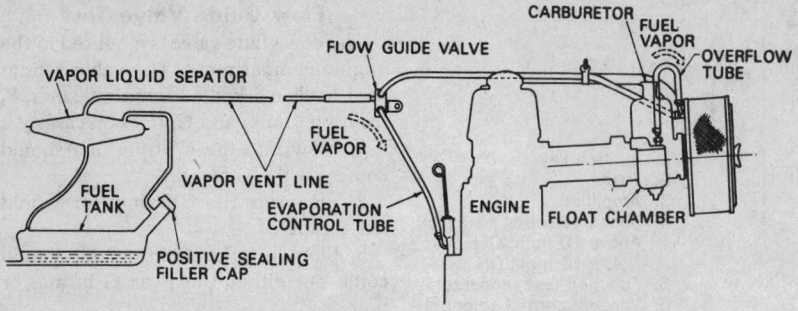

Fuel vapor control system for engines with sidedraft carburetors

lief valve. This stops air injection into the exhaust manifold and lowers the temperature of the catalyst.

Removal and Installation

1. Apply the parking brake.
2. Disconnect the temperature sensor connectors and pull the connectors outside of the floor.
3. Block the wheels.
4. Jack and support the car.
5. Remove the temperature sensor protector.
6. Remove the catalytic converter shield.
7. Unbolt and remove the catalytic converter. Handle the converter gently; it is very delicate.
8. Installation is the reverse of removal.

Floor Temperature Warning System

1976–77 280 Z

This system employs temperature sensors to warn of impending catalytic converter overheating. The system consists of a floor sensor located in the luggage

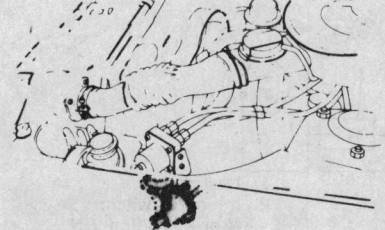

Emergency air relief valve (all models with catalyst)

compartment, a floor sensor relay located under the front passenger seat and a warning lamp located on the left side of the instrument panel.

Testing

Lamp should light when ignition is turned to ON.

To test sensor, wait until floor temperature is below 80°F. Then heat floor area around sensor to 239°F. Light should come on.

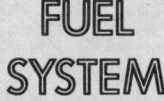

FUEL SYSTEM

Fuel Pump

The diaphragm fuel pump is driven from the engine camshaft on all engines. It is mounted on the side of the engine on OHV engines and on the side of the cylinder head on OHC engines. The pump is on the right side of all engines.

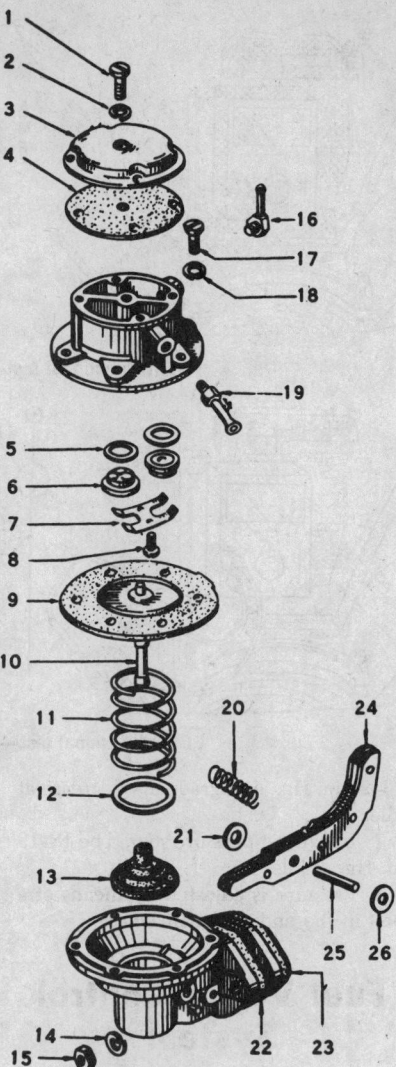

Fuel pump

1. Screw
2. Lockwasher
3. Cover
4. Cover gasket
5. Packing
6. Valve
7. Valve retainer
8. Valve retainer screw
9. Diaphragm
10. Pull rod
11. Spring
12. Seal washer
13. Seal
14. Lockwasher
15. Nut
16. Elbow
17. Screw
18. Lockwasher
19. Connector
20. Spring
21. Rocker arm slide spacer
22. Spacer
23. Gasket
24. Rocker arm
25. Pin
26. Rocker arm slide spacer

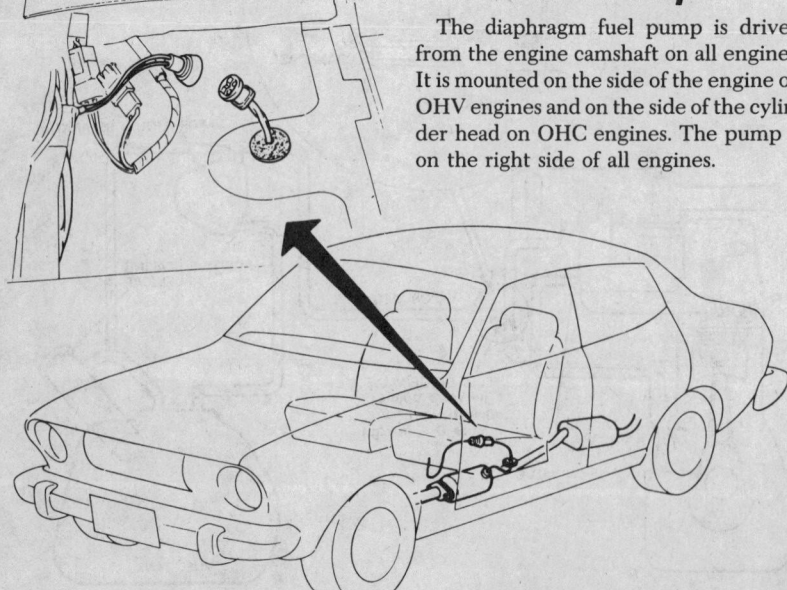

Catalyst temperature sensor location (all models with catalyst)

Removal and Installation

1. Disconnect the inlet and outlet lines from the pump.

2. Remove the mounting bolts.

3. Remove the pump and discard the gasket.

4. Lubricate the pump rocker arm, rocker arm pin, and lever pin before reinstallation.

5. Bolt the pump into position, using a new gasket.

6. Connect the fuel lines.

Fuel Pump Tests

Static Pressure Test

1. Disconnect fuel line at carburetor.

2. Attach adapter and tee to fuel line and connect a pressure gauge.

3. Run engine at varying speeds. Pressure should remain constant, 3–4 psi.

Capacity Test

1. With static pressure within specifications, disconnect fuel line at carburetor.

2. Fuel in bowl should be sufficient to start and run engine at 1000 rpm for one minute. Fuel delivery should be 600cc in one minute.

Carburetors

Three Hitachi sidedraft carburetors are used on L24 and L26 engines. These carburetors are virtually identical to the British SU carburetors. All other engines use one downdraft carburetor of various makes and types.

Hitachi/SU Type—1972

Fuel Level Adjustment

Float bowl fuel level should be 0.87–0.95 in. from the top edge of the bowl

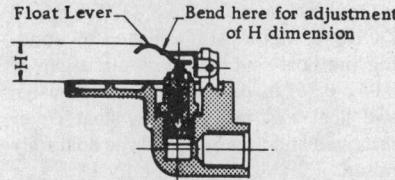

Float bowl fuel level adjustment for Hitachi/SU type carburetor with free float

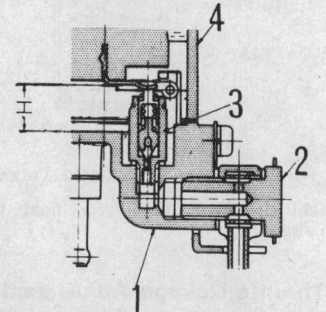

Float bowl fuel level adjustment for Hitachi/SU type carburetor with float in unit with float lever

    1. Float chamber cover
       (unit shown inverted)
    2. Filter bolt
    3. Needle valve
    4. Float chamber

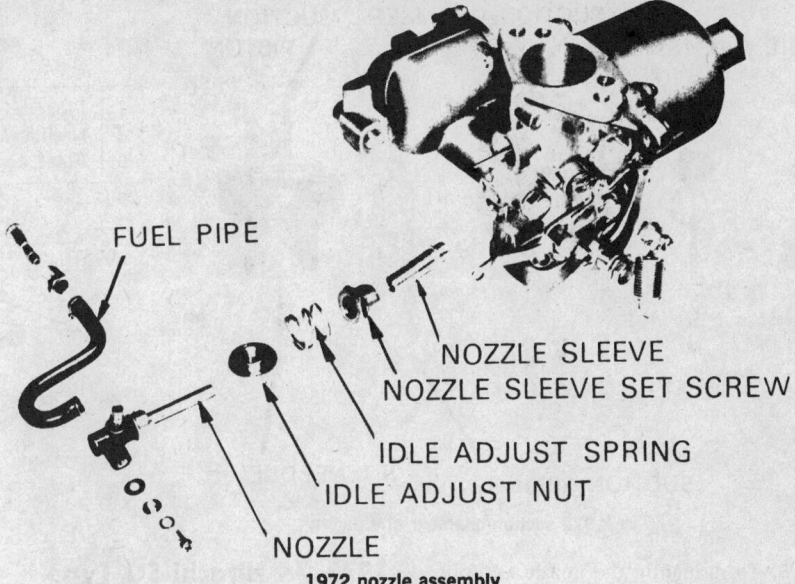

1972 nozzle assembly

with the float in place.

To adjust the level:

1. Remove the float chamber covers.

2. Place the covers upside down.

3. Lift the float lever and slowly lower it until the float lever seat just contacts the valve stem.

4. Check dimension H. It should be 0.55–0.59 in. Note that some carburetors have free floats and others have the float in unit with the float lever.

Overhaul—1972

These carburetors, being precision devices, are capable of being very finely adjusted. For the same reason, they require periodic attention. The factory recommends that they be disassembled and cleaned every six months. The suction piston and chamber often accumulate deposits of grit and varnish. To check for this condition, remove the air cleaner and raise the suction piston about ½ in. with a finger. Release the piston. It should come down smoothly and evenly. If not, the carburetor must be disassembled and cleaned. If turning the mixture nuts seems to have no effect, the difficulty is probably an air leak. The remedy is to replace all packings and gaskets. The same applies to fuel leaks. A common cause of air leaks is wear of the throttle shafts and the throttle shaft bore. The remedy is to install new throttle shafts and bushings. If the carburetor has no throttle shaft bushings, it may be necessary to drill out the throttle shaft bore to install them. The float chambers of these carburetors are very similar to those in conventional carburetors. However, the venturi and fuel system are precision made and require careful handling.

To disassemble the carburetors:

1. Remove the screws and the suction chamber.

2. Remove the suction spring, nylon packing, and suction piston from the chamber. Be extremely careful not to bend the jet needle.

3. Do not remove the jet needle from the suction piston unless it must be replaced. To remove it, loosen the jet needle setscrew. Hold the needle with pliers at a point no more than 0.1 in. from the piston. Remove the needle by pulling and turning slowly. Replace the needle with the shoulder portion flush with the piston surface. Check this with a straightedge. Tighten the setscrew.

4. Clean all parts of the suction chamber assembly with a safe solvent. Reassemble, using all the new parts supplied in the overhaul kit. Do not lubricate the piston.

1972 Float chamber disassembly

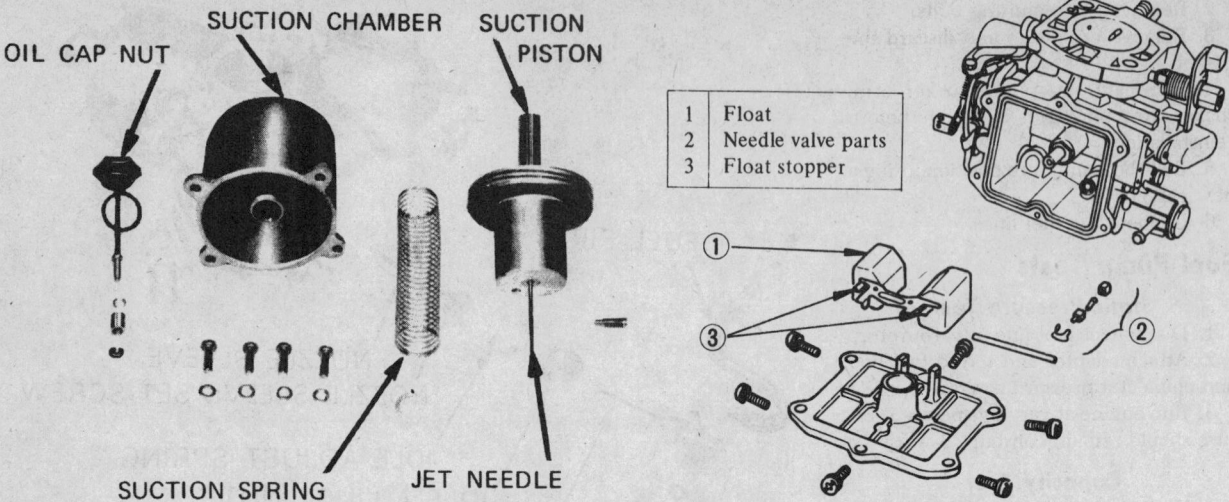

OIL CAP NUT   SUCTION CHAMBER   SUCTION PISTON

1	Float
2	Needle valve parts
3	Float stopper

SUCTION SPRING   JET NEEDLE

1972 suction chamber and piston

1973 and later float chamber

5. To dismantle the nozzle assembly, remove the 4 mm. screw and remove the connecting plate from the nozzle head by pulling lightly on the starter (choke) lever. Remove the fuel line and nozzle. Be careful not to bend the jet needle if the suction chamber assembly is mounted on the carburetor. Remove the idle (mixture) adjusting nut and spring. Do not remove the nozzle sleeve unless absolutely necessary. Special care is required to replace this part. Remove the nozzle sleeve setscrew and nozzle sleeve.

6. Clean all parts of the nozzle assembly with a safe solvent. Be very careful of the nozzle. Do not pass anything through the nozzle for cleaning purposes.

7. The jet needle must now be carefully centered in the nozzle, unless the nozzle sleeve and setscrew were not disturbed. Even so, it is a good idea to check this. To center the jet needle, insert the nozzle sleeve into the carburetor body with the setscrew loose. Carefully install the suction piston assembly without the plunger rod. Insert the nozzle without the spring and mixture adjusting nut until the nozzle contacts the nozzle sleeve. Position the nozzle sleeve so that the jet needle is centered inside the sleeve and does not contact the sleeve. Test centering by raising and releasing the suction piston. It should drop smoothly, making a metallic sound when it hits the stop. Tighten the nozzle sleeve setscrew when the needle is centered.

8. Reassemble the nozzle assembly. Replace the fuel line. Replace the damper plunger rod.

9. Pull the starter lever slightly, replace the connecting plate and 4 mm. screw.

10. Carburetor synchronization and mixture adjustments must be performed after reinstalling the carburetors.

1973–74 Hitachi SU Type HMB46W

Due to stringent air pollution control requirements, these carburetors have been altered to provide cleaner burn of the fuel-air mixture. As a result, the adjustment of the metering system, especially the jet needle, is almost impossible without using the proper metering equipment. Errors will adversely effect the emission control system.

Disassembly of the carburetor is strongly advised against by the manufacturer. Only the following should be disassembled and adjusted. Otherwise, the manufacturer recommends that the entire unit be replaced.

Float

1. Loosen six screws and take off the float.
2. Take off the clip and remove needle valve parts.
3. Do not touch jet needle setting nut or bend the float stopper.
4. For installation, reverse the disassembly procedure.

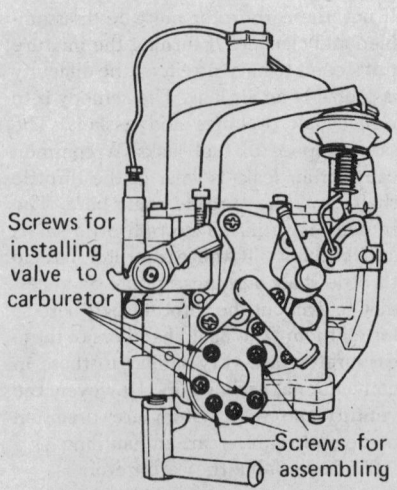

Screws for installing valve to carburetor

Screws for assembling

1973 and later power valve

Power Valve

1. Remove the three mounting screws and the power valve from carburetor body.
2. Unscrew three screws and disassemble the valve.
3. If the diaphragm is defective, replace the valve by reversing the removal procedure.

Downdraft Carburetors

Fuel Level Adjustment

All Nihonkikaki (Nikki) carburetors have a glass float chamber side cover marked with a fuel level line. Fuel level is adjusted by varying the thickness of the washer under the float valve.

On the Hitachi DAF328, DCG306, and DCH340, fuel level is adjusted by bending the float seat tab to obtain a gap of 0.051–0.067 in. between the needle valve and float seat tab with the float cover removed and inverted, and the float fully raised.

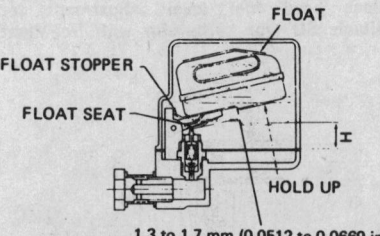

FLOAT

FLOAT STOPPER

FLOAT SEAT

HOLD UP

1.3 to 1.7 mm (0.0512 to 0.0669 in)

Hitachi downdraft carburetor float level adjustment

Throttle Linkage Adjustment

On all models, make sure the throttle is wide open when the accelerator pedal is floored. Some models have an adjustable accelerator pedal stop to prevent strain on the linkage.

Dashpot Adjustment

A dashpot is used on carburetors of cars

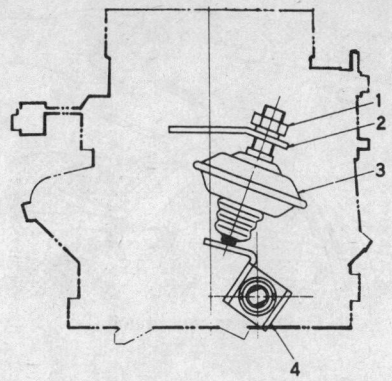

Dashpot installation on Hitachi downdraft carburetor

1. Locknut
2. Mounting arm
3. Dashpot
4. Throttle lever

with automatic transmissions. It slows the closing of the throttle valve to prevent stalling. The dashpot should be adjusted so it contacts the throttle lever at about 2,000–2,500 rpm on deceleration.

Secondary Throttle Adjustment

On most two-throat carburetors the secondary throttle should begin to open when the primary throttle is open 48°. On the Hitachi DCG306, 48° corresponds to a measurement of 0.23 in. between the lower edge of the primary throttle valve and the inside edge of the primary bore. On the Hitachi DAF328, the secondary throttle begins to open when the primary throttle is open 59° or 0.35 in. On the Hitachi DCH340, the secondary begins to open when the primary is open 50° or 0.29 in. Adjust the point of secondary throttle opening by bending the linkage between the two throttles.

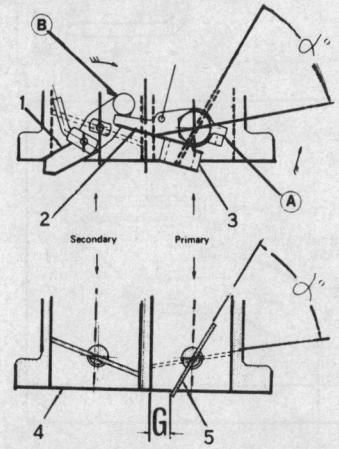

Measurement of point at which secondary throttle starts to open, Hitachi downdraft carburetor

1. Connecting lever
2. Return plate
3. Adjusting plate
4. Secondary throttle chamber
5. Primary throttle valve
a. Primary throttle opening in degrees
G. Primary throttle opening in inches

Vacuum Break Adjustment

A12, 13, 14 Engines

1. Close choke valve completely.
2. Hold choke valve by stretching a rubber band between choke shaft lever and carburetor.
3. Pull vacuum break arm fully straight with pliers.
4. Adjust the gap between the top edge of the choke plate and the air horn to:

    Auto Trans.   1.44–1.56mm
    Manual Trans.   1.36–1.48mm

Vacuum Break Adjustment

L16, 18, 20B Engines

Proceed as above. Adjust gap to:
Non-California Models   1.42mm
California Models   1.5mm

Automatic Choke Index Adjustment

1. Start engine and close choke valve completely.
2. Check for choke valve binding.
3. Loosen choke cover screws and set cover index mark at center notch only.
4. Tighten screws.

Choke Unloader Adjustment

1. Close choke valve completely.
2. Hold choke valve by stretching a rubber band between choke shaft lever and carburetor.
3. Pull throttle lever until it completely opens.
4. Adjust gap between the choke plate and the carburetor body to:

    A12, 13, 14 engines - 2.01mm
    L16, 18, 20B engines - 2.45mm

Overhaul

Carburetor overhaul involves separating the major components, removing and blowing out all jets, blowing out all passages, washing the parts in a safe solvent, and reassembling with new gaskets. After overhaul, the idle mixture and speed must be adjusted. Carburetor overhaul kits are available and generally contain complete instructions, a full set of gaskets, a new float needle valve and accelerator pump parts.

Overhaul your carburetor in a clean, dust-free area. Carefully disassemble referring often to the exploded views. Keep all similar and lookalike parts apart during disassembly and cleaning to avoid accidental interchange during assembly. Make a note of all jet sizes.

When the carburetor is disassembled, wash all parts (except diaphragms, electric choke units, pump plunger, and any other plastic, leather, fiber, or rubber parts) in clean carburetor solvent. Do not leave parts in the solvent any longer than is necessary to sufficiently loosen the deposits. Excessive cleaning may remove

the special finish from the float bowl and choke valve bodies, leaving these parts unfit for service. Rinse all parts in clean solvent and blow them dry with compressed air or allow them to air dry. Wipe clean all cork, plastic, leather, and fiber parts with a clean, lint-free cloth.

Blow-out all passages and jets with compressed air and be sure there are no restrictions or blockages. Never use wire or needles to clean jets, fuel passages, or air bleeds. Clean all jets and valves separately to avoid accidental mixing.

Check all parts for wear or damage. If any is found, replace the defective parts. Especially check the following:

1. Check the float needle and seat for wear. If wear is found, replace the complete assembly.
2. Check the float hinge pin for wear and the float(s) for dents or distortion. Replace the float if fuel has leaked into it.
3. Check the throttle and choke shaft bores for wear or an out-of-round condition. Damage or wear to the throttle arm, shaft, or shaft bore will often require replacement of the throttle body. These parts require a close tolerance; wear may allow air leakage, which could affect starting and idling.

NOTE: *Throttle shafts and bushings are not included in overhaul kits. They can be purchased separately.*

4. Inspect the idle mixture adjusting needles for burrs or grooves. This type of wear requires replacement to obtain a satisfactory idle.
5. Test the accelerator pump check valves. They should pass air one way but not the other. Test for proper seating by applying a vacuum to the valve. Replace if necessary. If the valve is satisfactory, wash the valve again to remove breath moisture.
6. Check the bowl cover with a straight edge for warped surfaces.
7. Closely inspect the valves and seats for wear and damage, replacing as necessary.
8. After the carburetor is assembled, check the choke valve for free movement.

Carburetor overhaul kits are recommended for each overhaul. These kits contain all gaskets and new parts to replace those that deteriorate most rapidly. Failure to replace all parts supplied with the kit (especially gaskets) may result in poor performance later.

Some carburetor manufacturers supply overhaul kits of three basic types: minor repair; major repair; and gasket kits. Basically, they contain the following:

Minor Repair Kits:

All gaskets
Float needle valve
Volume control screw

All diaphragms
Spring for the pump diaphragm

Major Repair Kits:

All jets and gaskets
All diaphragms
Float needle valve
Volume control screw
Pump ball valve
Main jet carrier
Float
Complete intermediate rod
Intermediate pump lever
Complete injector tube
Some cover hold-down screws and washers

Gasket Kits:

All gaskets

After cleaning and checking all components, reassemble the carburetor, using new parts and referring to the exploded view. When reassembling, make sure all screws and jets are tight. Do not overtighten or you may distort the tips. Tighten all screws gradually, in rotation. Do not tighten needle valves into their seats; uneven jetting will result. Always use new gaskets. Be sure to adjust the float level when reassembling.

Fuel Injection—L28

The Fuel Injection system used in the 1975–77 280Z is an electronic type, using various types of sensors to convert engine operating conditions into electrical signals. The information generated is fed to a control unit, giving it the right figures to set the injector open-valve period.

Checking Functional Parts

For the processes described you will need a small testing light and an ohmmeter.

Control Unit

1. Connect the testing lamp to the harness-side connector of the injector.
2. Crank the engine. If the light flashes due to the pulse voltage applied to the injector, the control unit is operating.

Because two different transistors are used in the system, you will have to test both the No. 1 and 4 cylinders.

To confirm your findings, remove the connector on the coolant sensor. The installed testing lamp should flash more brightly. It is only necessary to run this test on the No. 1 or No. 4 cylinders.

Checking Potentiometer

CAUTION: *Before checking the air*

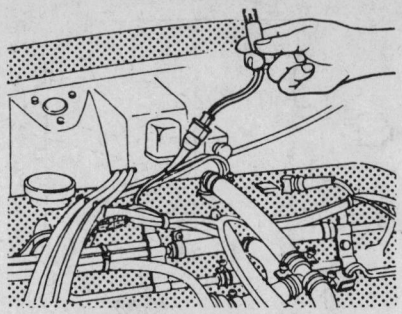

Checking control unit

flow meter, remove the battery ground cable.

1. Remove the air flow meter.
2. Measure the resistance between terminals 8 and 6 as indicated in the illustration. The standard resistance should be 180 ohms.
3. Measure the resistance between terminals 8 and 9. The resistance here should be 100 ohms.
4. Connect a 12-volt battery to terminal 9 (positive) and terminal 6 (negative).
5. Connect the positive lead of a volt meter to terminal 8 and the negative lead to terminal 7.
6. Reaching into the air flow meter, slowly open the flap so that the volt flow

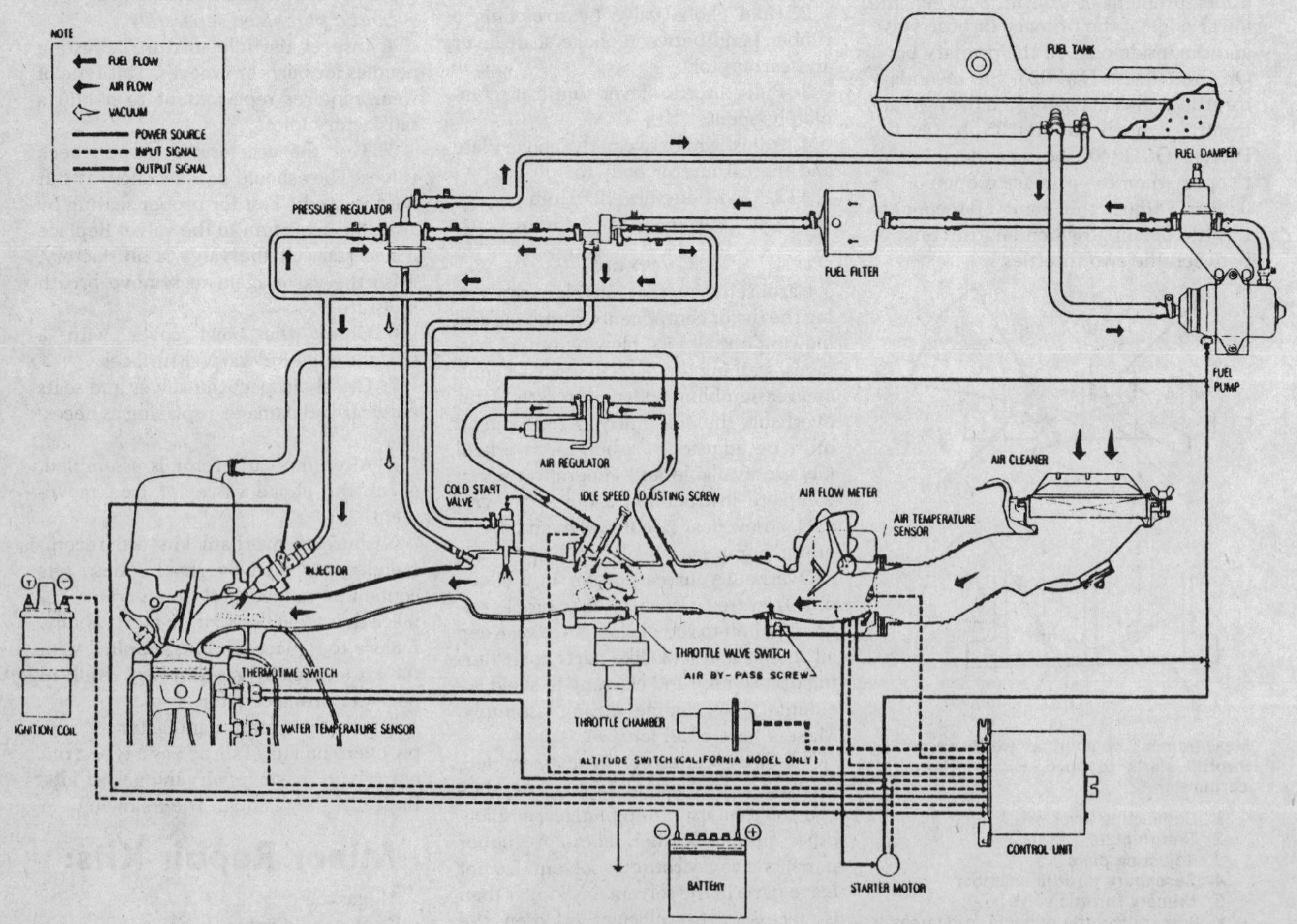

NOTE

- ← FUEL FLOW
- ← AIR FLOW
- ← VACUUM
- —— POWER SOURCE
- ---- INPUT SIGNAL
- --- OUTPUT SIGNAL

FUEL TANK

FUEL DAMPER

PRESSURE REGULATOR

FUEL FILTER

FUEL PUMP

AIR REGULATOR

AIR CLEANER

COLD START VALVE

IDLE SPEED ADJUSTING SCREW

AIR FLOW METER

AIR TEMPERATURE SENSOR

INJECTOR

THROTTLE VALVE SWITCH

AIR BY-PASS SCREW

THERMOTIME SWITCH

THROTTLE CHAMBER

IGNITION COIL

WATER TEMPERATURE SENSOR

ALTITUDE SWITCH (CALIFORNIA MODEL ONLY)

CONTROL UNIT

BATTERY

STARTER MOTOR

Fuel injection system

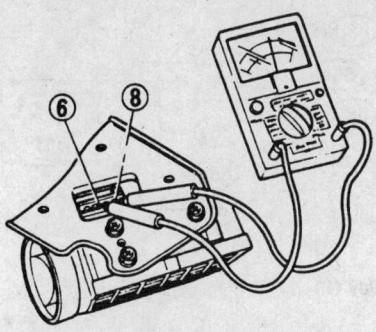

Measuring terminal resistance

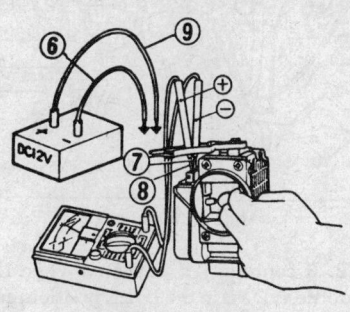

Checking terminal voltage variation

slowly decreases. If the indicator varies suddenly, the problem may be in the potentiometer.

Air Flow Meter Insulation Check

Connect an ohmmeter to any one terminal on the flow meter. Touch the flow meter body with the other connector. If any continuity is indicated, the unit is out of order.

Checking Flap

Reach into the air flow meter with your fingers. If the flap opens and closes smoothly, without binding, the mechanical portion of the unit is working.

Fuel Pump Contact Points

Connect an ohmmeter to terminals 36 and 39 of the fuel pump, on the side of the air flow meter.

Reach into the meter and move the flap. A current flow should be indicated when you have opened the flap about 8 degrees. There should be no continuity with the flap closed. If there is a deviation, replace the entire air flow meter.

Air Temperature

Checking Continuity

1. Disconnect the battery ground cable.
2. Remove the air flow meter.
3. Check the temperature of your surroundings and make note of it.
4. Connect an ohmmeter to terminals 27 and 8 on the air flow meter connector and check the resistance indicated. Make note of it.

Air Flow Meter Resistance Specifications

Air temperature °C (°F)	Resistance (kΩ)
—30 (—22)	20.3 to 33.0
—10 (—14)	7.6 to 10.8
10 (50)	3.25 to 4.15
20 (68)	2.25 to 2.75
50 (122)	0.74 to 0.94
80 (176)	0.29 to 0.36

The resistance values should be as indicated in the chart. Should the test results vary far from the ranges provided, replace the air temperature sensor and air flow meter as a unit.

Insulation Resistance

Connect an ohmmeter to terminal 27 of the air flow meter and touch the body with the other connector. Should continuity be indicated, replace the unit.

Water Temperature Sensor

This test may be done either on or off the vehicle. The test should be done with the coolant both hot and cold.

1. Disconnect the battery ground cable.
2. Disconnect the water temperature sensor harness.

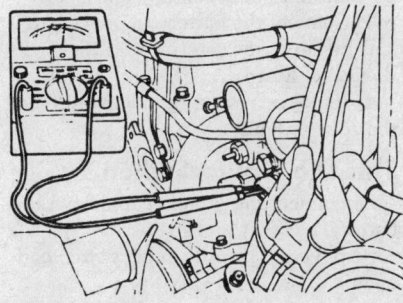

Resistance test of the water temperature sensor

3. Place a thermometer in the coolant when the engine is cold. Make note of the indication.
4. Read the resistance indicated on the meter and compare it with the chart for temperature/resistance values.

To measure the coolant temperature and resistance values when hot:
1. Connect the water temperature sensor harness.
2. Connect the battery ground cable.
3. Warm the engine and disconnect the harness and battery cable.
4. Read the sensor resistance as described in the cold process.

Sensor Check Off The Engine

1. Remove the sensor and dip the unit into water maintained at 68°F. Read resistance.

Water Temperature Sensor Resistance Specifications

Cooling water temperature °C (°F)	Resistance (kΩ)
—30 (—22)	20.3 to 33.0
—10 (—14)	7.6 to 10.8
10 (50)	3.25 to 4.15
20 (68)	2.25 to 2.75
50 (122)	0.74 to 0.94
80 (176)	0.29 to 0.36

2. Heat the water to 176°F and check the resistance.

In either type of check, should the resistance be far outside the ranges provided, replace the sensor unit.

Sensor Insulation Check

This check is done on the engine.
1. Disconnect the battery ground cable.
2. Disconnect the sensor harness connector.
3. Connect an ohmmeter to one of the terminals on the sensor and touch the engine block with the other. Any indication of continuity indicates need to replace the unit.

Thermotime Switch

1. Disconnect the ground cable from the battery.
2. Disconnect the electric connector of the thermotine switch and measure the resistance between terminal No. 46 and the switch body.

The resistance should be zero with water temperatures less than 57°F.

The resistance should be zero or infinite with temperatures of 57° to 72°F.

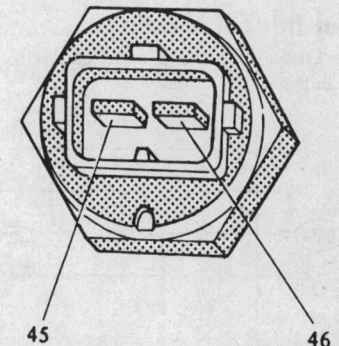

Terminals—thermotime switch

The resistance should be infinite with a temperature of 72°F.

3. Measure the resistance between terminal No. 45 and the switch body.

70 to 86 ohms .... OK

Any different reading than shown indicates replacement.

Datsun

Cold Start Valve

1. Disconnect the lead wire from the "S" terminal of the starter motor.

2. Turn the ignition switch to START and make sure the fuel pump is working. You should be able to hear it.

3. Disconnect the ground cable from the battery.

4. Remove the screws holding the cold start valve to the intake manifold and remove the valve.

5. Disconnect the start valve electrical connector.

6. Put the start valve into a large glass container and plug the neck of the jar.

7. Connect the ground cable of the battery and turn the ignition switch to START. The valve should not inject fuel.

8. Turn the switch to OFF and connect a jumper wire between the valve and the battery terminals. Leave the valve in the jar.

At this point, the valve should inject fuel. If not, proceed to the next step.

9. With the ignition switch in the START position, and the jumper wire installed as described, check for fuel flow. If the fuel is injected to the jar, the unit is operating. If not, replace.

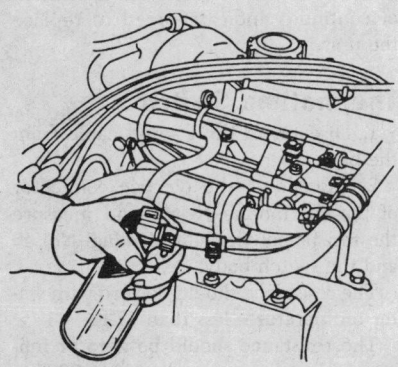

Checking fuel flow from start valve—280Z

Fuel Injection Relay

1. Disconnect the ground cable from the battery.

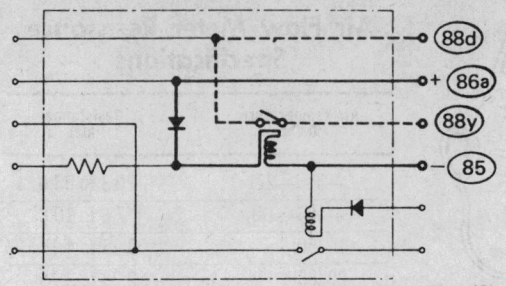
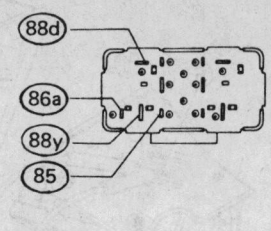

Fuel pump relay (2)

2. Remove the relay from the automobile.

Main Relay Check

Connect a battery (12-volt) between the positive (86c) terminal and the negative (85). Clicks should be heard and continuity indicated between terminals 88z and 88a, and between 88z and 88b.

Connect the battery (12-volt) between positive (85) and negative (86c) terminals. No clicks should be heard.

If the results are not as described in the two tests, the unit is faulty.

Fuel Pump Relay

1. Make sure there is continuity between terminals 88d and 88c and between 86a and 86.

2. Connect a 12-volt battery to positive (86a) and negative (85) terminals. Clicks should be heard and there should be continuity between 88y and 88d.

3. Connect the battery to positive (85) and negative (86a) terminals. No clicks should be heard.

4. If the test results are not as outlined, the relay is faulty.

Throttle Valve Switch

Disconnect the ground cable from the battery.

Remove the throttle valve switch connector.

Idle Switch

Connect an ohmmeter between terminals 2 and 18.

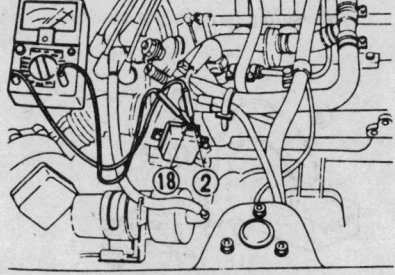

Idle switch check

2. If continuity is indicated when the throttle valve is in the IDLE position, and does not exist when the valve opens about 4° the switch is normal.

Full Switch Check

1. Connect an ohmmeter between terminals 3 and 18.

2. Gradually open the throttle valve and read the indication when the valve is open about 34°. If the indication is higher at all settings other than 34°, the full switch is operating properly.

Throttle Valve Switch Insulation

Connect an ohmmeter between body metal and terminals 2, 3 and 18. Meter reading should be infinite.

Dropping Resistor

Disconnect the ground cable from the battery.

Disconnect the 4-pin and 6-pin connectors from the injection system harness and conduct resistance checks between

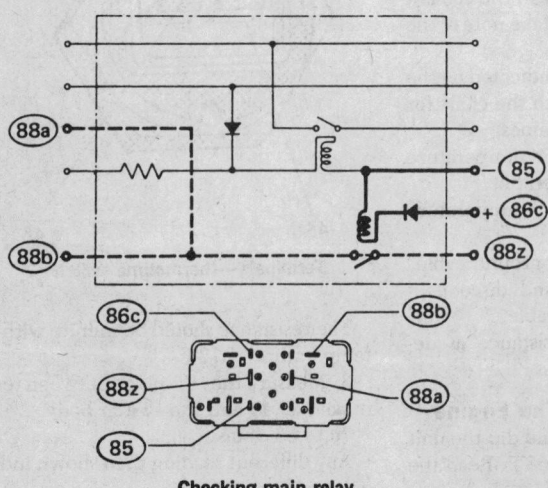

Checking main relay

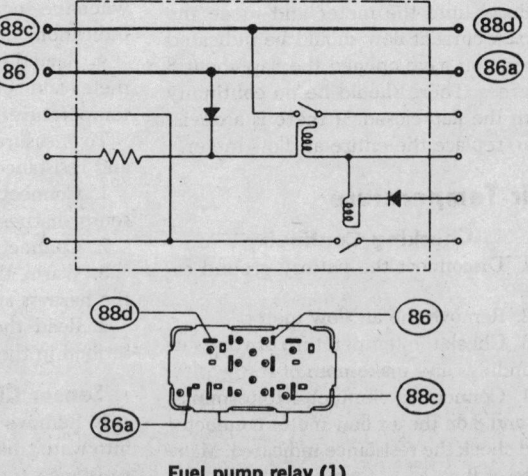

Fuel pump relay (1)

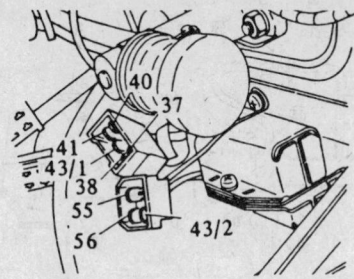

Dropping resistor terminal numbers

the following points.

43/1 and No. 41 - #4 cylinder
43/1 and No. 40 - #3 cylinder
43/1 and No. 38 - #2 cylinder
43/1 and No. 37 - #1 cylinder

The resistance readings should be approximately 6 ohms.

Also conduct checks between:

43/2 and No. 56 - #6 cylinder
43/2 and No. 55 - #5 cylinder

The resistance should again be 6 ohms.

Altitude Switch (California Models Only)

Disconnect the ground cable from the battery and remove the switch from the automobile.

Attach an ohmmeter to the connector and blow or suck through the discharge port. If a click is heard and continuity exists, the switch is in good order.

There is no adjustment possible on the switch. Should it be found to be defective, replace the unit.

Fuel Pump

Functional Test

Disconnect the lead wire from the "S" terminal of the starter motor.

Move the ignition switch to the START position and the fuel pump should sound, indicating normal operation. If you do not hear the sound, check all pump circuits. If they check, replace the unit.

Discharge Pressure

1. Disconnect the ground cable from the battery.

2. Disconnect the cold start valve harness.

3. Using two jumper wires, connect each terminal to the battery terminals. You may release pressure by connecting jumper wires to the cold start valve connector for a few seconds.

4. Install a pressure gauge in the fuel line before the fuel filter.

5. Disconnect the lead wire from the "S" terminal of the starter motor.

6. Disconnect cold start valve connector.

7. Connect ground cable to battery.

8. Turn the ignition switch to the START position to run fuel pump. A pressure of 36.3 psi should be indicated. If the pressure is not as noted, replace pressure regulator and repeat.

Should the pressure still not equal 36.3 psi, check for blocked lines and, if clear, replace the fuel pump.

Fuel Discharge

Install a pressure gauge as indicated and, with an observer, operate the automobile to speeds between 13 and 38 mph in second gear.

If the pressure is not equal to 36.3 psi, check for clogged lines or replace pump.

Fuel Damper

Install a pressure gauge in the fuel line and check for fluctuating readings. If found, replace damper.

Injector

For continuity, remove the ground cable from the battery and disconnect the electrical connectors from the injectors.

Check for continuity readings between the two terminals. If there is no indication, the injector is faulty.

Check the injectors for sound as follows:

If the engine is running, run it at idle

and place a screwdriver tip against each injector and your ear to the handle to check for operating sounds. If there is low sound from any injector, it is faulty.

If the engine is not running, disconnect the connector of the cold start valve and crank the engine. Check for sounds as described.

If there are low sounds from any injector, that injector is faulty.

If there is no sound from all the injectors, check the harness. If the harness is normal, check the operation of the control unit.

If sounds are heard from numbers 1, 2 and 3 injectors or numbers 4, 5 or 6, replace the control unit.

Air Regulator

Hold the rubber tubing between the throttle chamber and the air regulator with your fingers and squeeze. The engine speed should be reduced.

If it does not, remove the hoses from both ends of the regulator and check to see if the valve opens. The opening should be as indicated by the gray area in the illustration.

Direction of bimetal movement with increasing temperature

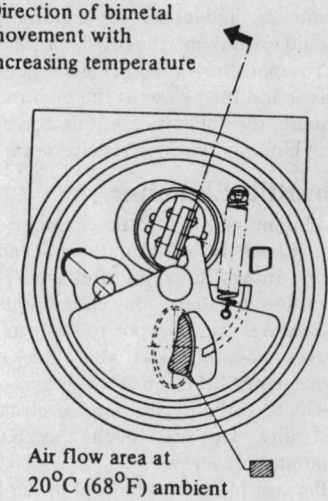

Air flow area at 20°C (68°F) ambient

Valve opening at 68° F.

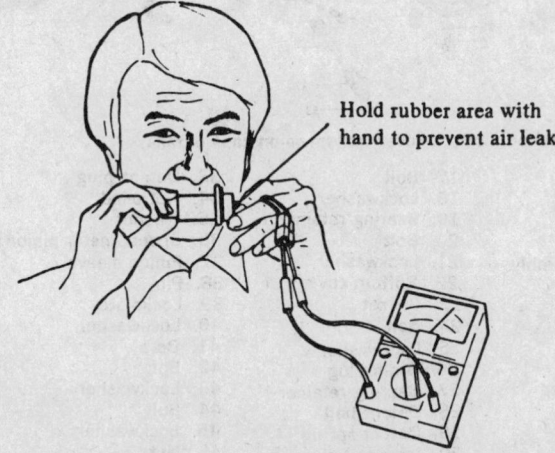

Hold rubber area with hand to prevent air leak.

Checking the altitude switch

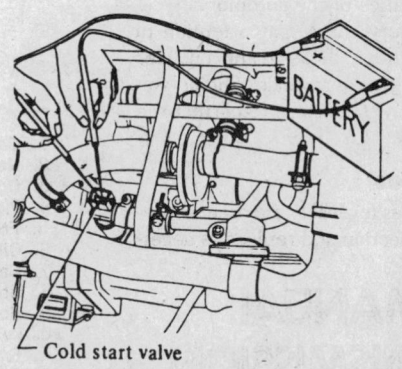

Cold start valve

Releasing fuel pressure

1. Air cleaner element
2. Air duct (air cleaner to AFM)
3. Air duct (AFM to throttle chamber)
4. Flange (throttle chamber to intake manifold)
5. Cold start valve mounting surface
6. Blind plug (E.G.R.),
7. Injector mounting surface in intake manifold
8. Cylinder head mounting surface in intake manifold
9. Hose (throttle chamber to 3-way connector), both sides
10. Hose (3-way connector to rocker cover), both sides
11. Hose (3-way connector to air regulator), both sides
12. Hose (air regulator to throttle chamber connector), both sides
13. Throttle chamber connector mounting surface
14. Hose (pipe connector to P.C.V. valve), both sides
15. Distributor vacuum line
16. E.G.R. vacuum line
17. Canister vacuum and purge line
18. Automatic transmission vacuum line
19. Cooler vacuum line

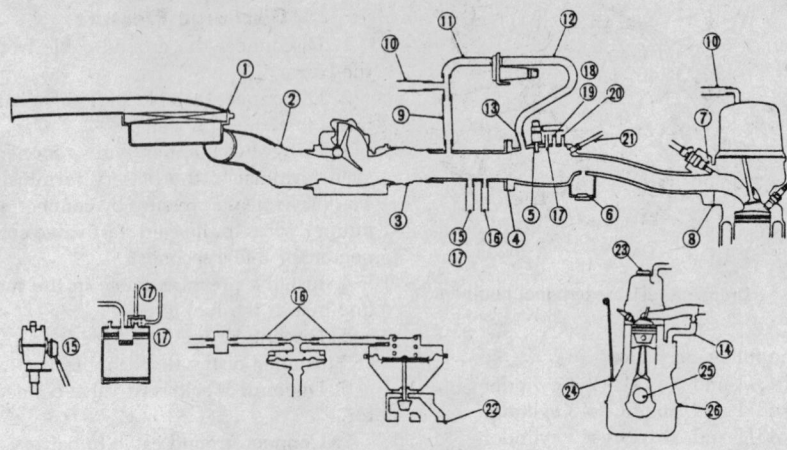

20. Master-Vac line
21. Pressure regulator vacuum line
22. E.G.R. valve mounting surface
23. Oil filler cap
24. Oil level gauge
25. Oil seal (on front and rear of crankshaft)
26. Oil pan gasket mounting surface.

Air leak check points in the intake system

Disconnect the regulator electrical connector and check for continuity, it should exist. It not, the regulator is faulty.

To open the valve, pry with a screwdriver and then close. If the operation is smooth, the valve is operating correctly. Any binding indicates replacement.

Throttle Chamber

1. Remove the throttle chamber.

2. Check to see that the idle adjust screw moves smoothly and adjust the throttle valve to the fully closed position.

3. Move the dash pot rod to see if it moves smoothly and also check the movement of the throttle valve.

4. Check the bypass port for obstacles and dirt. Do not touch the E.G.R. vacuum port screw.

Because of the sensitivity of the air flow meter, there cannot be any air leaks in the fuel system. Even the smallest leak could unbalance the system and affect the performance of the automobile.

During every check, pay attention to hose connections, dipstick and oil filler cap for evidence of air leaks. Should you encounter any, take steps to correct the problem.

Fuel Hoses

Check hoses for leaks or looseness. Retighten connection and replace as necessary.

MANUAL TRANSMISSION

Removal and Installation

The transmission may be removed separately from under the vehicle. Trans-

mission removal and replacement procedure for early models is generally similar.

1972–1974 All Models

1. Raise and support the vehicle. Disconnect the battery. On the 510 disconnect the handbrake cable at the equalizer pivot. Disconnect the backup light switch on all models.

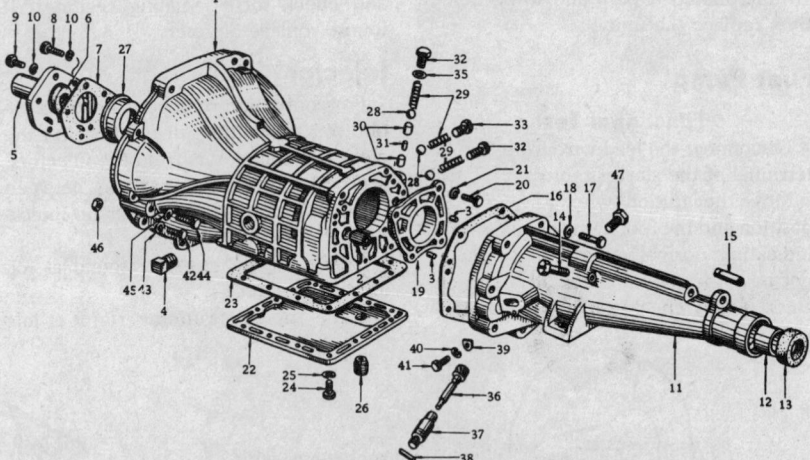

2. On the 510 loosen the muffler clamps and turn the muffler to one side to allow room for driveshaft removal. On the 240 Z, remove the exhaust system. On models with the A12, A13, A14, L18, L20B, L26 or L28 engine, disconnect the exhaust pipe from the manifold. On the 260 and 280 Z, disconnect the accelerator linkage.

Four speed, bottom cover transmission case details

1. Case	17. Bolt	33. Detent plug
2. Needle bearing	18. Lockwasher	34. Not used
3. Dowel pin	19. Bearing retainer	35. Washer
4. Plug	20. Bolt	36. Speedometer pinion
5. Front cover assembly	21. Lockwasher	37. Pinion sleeve
6. Oil seal	22. Bottom cover	38. Pin
7. Gasket	23. Gasket	39. Lockplate
8. Bolt	24. Bolt	40. Lockwasher
9. Bolt	25. Lockwasher	41. Bolt
10. Lockwasher	26. Drain plug	42. Bolt
11. Extension housing	27. Bearing retainer	43. Lockwasher
12. Bushing	28. Detent ball	44. Bolt
13. Oil seal	29. Detent spring	45. Lockwasher
14. Breather	30. Interlock plunger	46. Nut
15. Striker bushing	31. Interlock pin	47. Plug for backup light
16. Gasket	32. Detent plug	switch

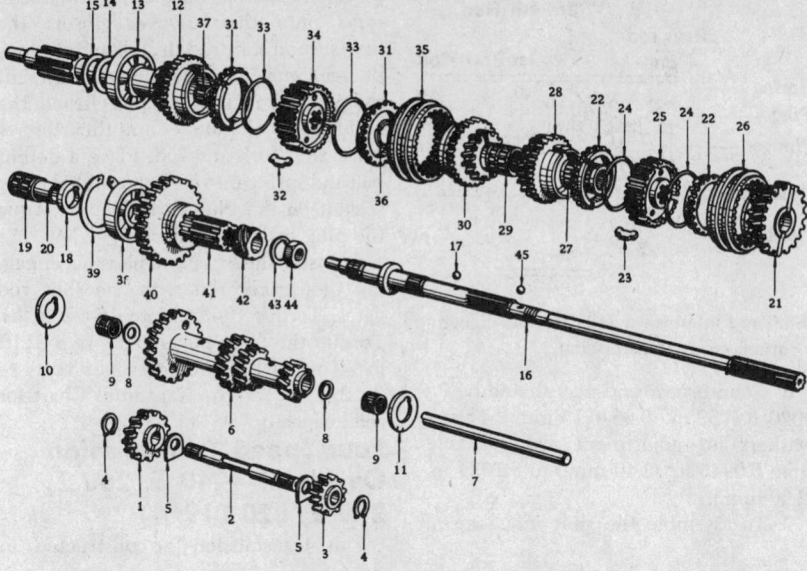

Four speed, bottom cover transmission

1. Reverse idler gear
2. Reverse idler shaft
3. Main reverse idler gear
4. Snap-ring
5. Thrust washer
6. Countergear
7. Countershaft
8. Spacer
9. Needle bearing
10. Front countershaft thrust washer
11. Rear countershaft thrust washer
12. Main drive gear
13. Main drive gear bearing
14. Washer
15. Snap-ring
16. Mainshaft
17. 5/32″ steel ball
18. Thrust washer
19. Needle bearing
20. First gear bushing
21. First gear
22. Baulk ring
23. Shifting insert
24. Spreader ring
25. First/second synchro hub
26. Coupling sleeve
27. Needle bearing
28. Second gear
29. Needle bearing
30. Third gear
31. Baulk ring
32. Shifting insert
33. Spreader ring
34. Third/fourth synchro hub
35. Coupling sleeve
36. Snap-ring
37. Pilot bearing
38. Bearing
39. Snap-ring
40. Reverse gear
41. Reverse gear hub
42. Speedometer drive gear
43. Lockwasher
44. Nut
45. Steel ball

3. Unbolt the driveshaft at the rear and remove. If there is a center bearing, unbolt it from the crossmember. Seal the end of the transmission extension housing to prevent leakage.

4. Disconnect the speedometer drive cable from the transmission.

5. Remove the shift lever.

6. Remove the clutch operating cylinder from the clutch housing.

7. Support the engine with a large wood block and a jack under the oil pan.

8. Unbolt the transmission from the crossmember. Support the transmission with a jack and remove the crossmember.

9. Lower the rear of the engine to allow clearance.

10. Remove the starter.

11. Unbolt the transmission. Lower and remove it to the rear.

12. Reverse the procedure for reinstallation. Check the clutch linkage adjustment.

1976–77 F10

You must remove the engine/transmission unit as a whole. Refer to "Engine Mechanical" for instructions.

After removal, remove the bolts holding the transmission to the engine and separate by pulling the transmission to-wards the clutch housing.

NOTE: *The clutch assembly will remain attached to the engine.*

Installation is the reverse of removal. The bolts holding the transmission should be torqued to 10 to 13 ft lbs.

CAUTION: *If the clutch has been removed, it will have to be re-aligned and when connecting drive shafts, insert O-rings between differential side flanges and drive shafts.*

Four Speed, Bottom Cover Transmission Overhaul— 521, 620 (1973), 510, 610, 710

The reverse and reverse idler drive gears are contained in the extension housing of this transmission. On late units, the cast, ribbed bottom cover is replaced by a stamped steel cover. Virtually all of these transmissions imported to the US have a modified extension housing incorporating a floorshift mechanism. The transmission model number is F4W63.

Disassembly

1. Drain the transmission.

2. Remove the clutch withdrawal lever and release bearing.

3. Remove the clevis pin which connects the striker rod to the shift lever.

4. Remove the speedometer drive pinion assembly.

5. Unbolt and remove the extension housing, disengaging the striker rod from the shift rod gates.

6. Remove the bottom and front covers.

7. Remove the three detent plugs, springs, and balls.

8. Drive out the shift fork retaining pins. Remove the rods and forks.

9. Move the first/second and third-/fourth coupling sleeves into gear at the same time to lock the mainshaft.

10. Pull out the countershaft and countergear with the two needle roller bearings and spacers.

11. Remove the snap-ring, reverse idler gears, and shaft.

12. Unbolt the mainshaft rear bearing retainer.

13. Pull out the mainshaft assembly to the rear. Pull out the clutch shaft to the front.

14. To disassemble the mainshaft, remove the snap-ring, third/fourth synchronizer hub and coupling sleeve. Remove third gear, with the roller bearing. Remove the mainshaft nut, lockplate, speedometer drive gear, and steel ball. Take off reverse gear and the hub. Press off the bearing and retainer. Remove the thrust washer and first gear with the needle roller bearing and bushing. Be careful not to lose the steel ball which locates the thrust washer. Take off the first/second synchronizer and hub. Remove second gear with the needle roller bearing.

Inspection

1. Clean all parts with a safe solvent. Lubricate the bearings with gear oil.

2. Check the mainshaft for straightness. Runout at the rear of the shaft should not exceed 0.0059 in. (0.15 mm.). Make sure the synchronizer hubs slide freely without excessive clearance.

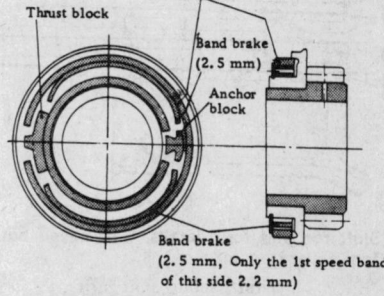

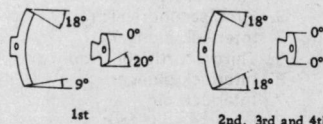

Servo type synchronizer assembly details

3. Place the synchronizer baulk ring in position on the cone of its gear. Check the gap between the baulk ring end face and the front face of the clutch teeth. The gap should be 0.0472–0.0360 in. (1.2–1.6 mm.). If it is less than 0.0315 in. (0.8 mm.), replace the ring.

4. The clearance between the shift forks and their grooves should be 0.0059–0.0118 in. (0.15–0.30 mm.).

5. Replace all O-rings and oil seals.

Assembly

Assembly procedures are generally the reverse of disassembly, however the following special instructions are required.

1. On the clutch shaft, there should be no end-play between the bearing and the snap-ring. Snap-rings are available in sizes from 0.0598 in. (1.52 mm.) to 0.0697 in. (1.77 mm.).

2. Some of these transmissions use a servo type synchronizer which utilizes brake bands. To assemble these synchronizers, place each gear on a flat surface. Install the synchronizer ring into the clutch gear. Place the thrust block and anchor block and install the circlip into the groove.

3. Third gear should be adjusted to give an end-play of 0.0020–0.0059 in. (0.05–0.15 mm.). Snap-rings for adjustment are available in sizes from 0.0551 in. (1.40 mm.) to 0.0630 in. (1.60 mm.).

4. Tighten the mainshaft nut to 65–80 ft lbs.

5. Install the reverse idler driving gear on the reverse shaft and fasten with a snap-ring. Install the shaft and gear into the case, placing a thrust washer between the gear and case. Place a thrust washer, idler gear, and snap-ring on the inside end of the shaft. Idler gear end-play should be 0.0039–0.0118 in. (0.1–0.3 mm.). Snap-rings are available in sizes from 0.0433 in. (1.1 mm.) to 0.0591 in. (1.5 mm.).

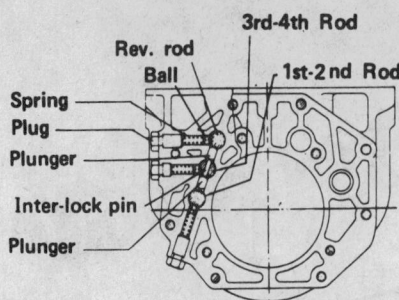

Shift rod interlock details for four speed bottom cover transmission

6. Countergear end-play should be 0.0020–0.0059 in. (0.05–0.15 mm.). Thrust washers for adjustment are available from 0.0945 in. (2.40 mm.) to 0.1024 in. (2.60 mm.).

7. To assemble the shift mechanism, place the first/second and third/fourth forks onto their sleeves. Insert the first/second shift rod. Install an interlock plunger and then the third/fourth shift rod with the interlock pin. Install the other interlock plunger and then the reverse shift fork and rod. Place a detent ball and spring into each detent hole. Use sealant on the plug threads and torque the plug to 12–15 ft lbs.

8. Install the extension housing, engaging the striker rod with the shift rod gates. Torque the bolts to 16–22 ft lbs. Torque the front cover bolts to 8–12 ft lbs. Torque the bottom cover bolts to 8–12 ft lbs. See the Capacities Chart for refill capacity.

Four Speed Transmission Overhaul—240 Z, 260 Z, 280 Z, 620 (1974)

This transmission is constructed in

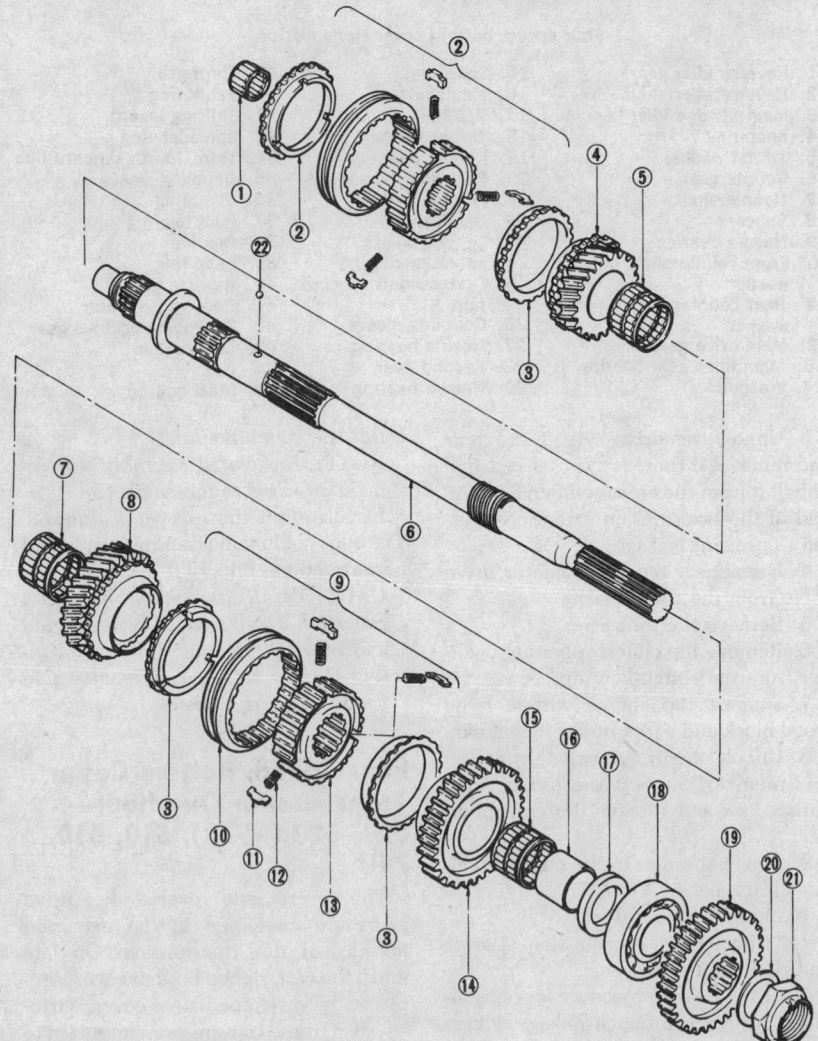

240Z, 260Z, 280Z and 1974 620 mainshaft

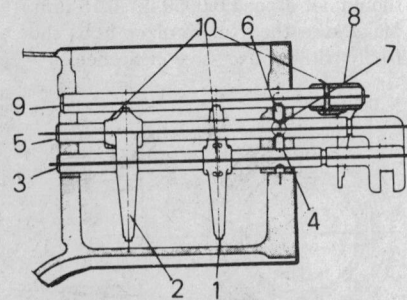

Shift rod and fork details, four speed bottom cover transmission

1. First/second shift fork
2. Third/fourth shift fork
3. First/second shift rod
4. Interlock plunger
5. Third/fourth shift rod
6. Interlock plunger
7. Interlock pin
8. Reverse shift fork
9. Reverse shift rod
10. Fork retaining pin

1. Pilot bearing
2. 3rd & 4th synchromesh assembly
3. Baulk ring
4. 3rd gear, mainshaft
5. Needle bearing
6. Mainshaft
7. Needle bearing
8. 2nd gear, mainshaft
9. 1st & 2nd synchromesh assembly
10. Coupling sleeve
11. Shifting insert
12. Spread spring
13. Synchronizer hub
14. 1st gear, mainshaft
15. Needle bearing
16. Bushing, 1st gear
17. Thrust washer, mainshaft
18. Mainshaft bearing
19. Reverse gear, mainshaft
10. Thrust washer
21. Nut
22. Steel ball

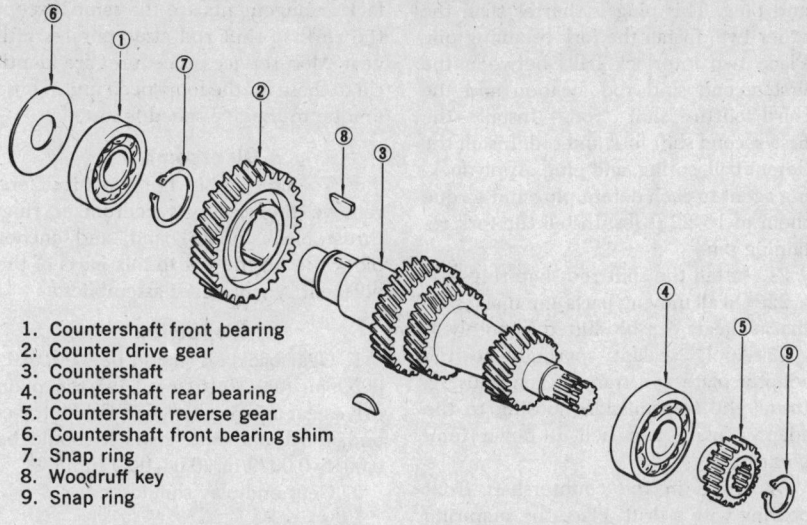

1. Countershaft front bearing
2. Counter drive gear
3. Countershaft
4. Countershaft rear bearing
5. Countershaft reverse gear
6. Countershaft front bearing shim
7. Snap ring
8. Woodruff key
9. Snap ring

240Z, 260Z, 280Z and 1974 620 countershaft

three sections: clutch housing, transmission housing, and extension housing. There are no case cover plates. There is a cast iron adapter plate between the transmission and extension housings. The transmission model number is F4W71.

Disassembly

1. Remove the clutch housing dust cover. Remove the retaining spring, release bearing sleeve, and withdrawal lever.

2. Remove the backup light/neutral safety switch.

3. Unbolt and remove the clutch housing, rapping with a soft hammer if necessary. Remove the gasket, mainshaft bearing shim, and countershaft bearing shim.

4. Remove the speedometer pinion sleeve.

5. Remove the striker rod pin from the rod. Separate the striker rod from the shift lever bracket.

6. Unbolt and remove the rear extension. It may be necessary to rap the housing with a soft hammer.

7. Remove the mainshaft bearing snap-ring.

8. Remove the adapter plate and gear assembly from the transmission case by rapping with a soft hammer. Hold the adapter plate in a vise.

9. Punch out the shift fork retaining pins. Remove the shift rod snap-rings.

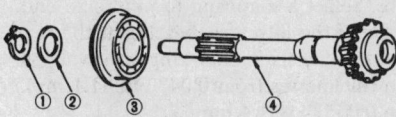

240Z 4-speed clutch shaft

1. Snap ring
2. Spacer
3. Main drive bearing with snap ring
4. Main drive shaft

Remove the detent plugs, springs, and balls from the adapter plate. Remove the shift rods, being careful not to lose the interlock balls.

10. Remove the snap-ring, speedometer drive gear, and locating ball.

11. Bend back the mainshaft lock tab. Remove the nut, lockwasher, thrust washer, reverse hub, and reverse gear.

12. Remove the snap-ring and countershaft reverse gear. Remove the snap-ring, reverse idler gear, thrust washer, and needle bearing.

13. Support the gear assembly while rapping on the rear of the mainshaft with a soft hammer. An assistant would be helpful to avoid dropping any of the parts. The mainshaft will separate into the forward clutch shaft and the rear mainshaft.

14. Remove the setscrew from the adapter plate. Remove the shaft nut, spring washer, plain washer, and reverse idler shaft.

15. Remove the machine screws holding the bearing retainer with an impact tool. Remove the bearing retainer and the mainshaft rear bushing.

16. To disassemble the mainshaft (rear section), remove the front snap-ring, third/fourth synchronizer assembly, third gear, and needle bearing. From the rear, remove the thrust washer, locating ball, first gear, needle bearing, first gear bushing, first/second synchronizer assembly, second gear, and needle bearing.

17. To disassemble the clutch shaft, remove the snap-ring and bearing spacer and press off the bearing.

18. To disassemble the countershaft, press off the front bearing . . . Press off the rear bearing, press off the gears and remove the keys.

19. Remove the retaining pin, control arm pin, and shift control arm from the rear of the extension housing.

Inspection

1. Wash all parts in a safe solvent. Oil bearings immediately. Check all parts for wear or damage. Replace all seals, O-rings, and gaskets.

2. When reassembling, gear backlash between mating gears should be 0.0020–0.0059 in. (0.05–0.15 mm.). If excessive, replace both driving and driven gears.

3. Gear end-play should be 0.0047–0.0075 in. (0.12–0.19 mm.) for all gears except the reverse idler. Reverse idler gear end-play should be 0.0020–0.0138 in. (0.05–0.35 mm.). End-play is adjusted by installing snap-rings of different thicknesses.

4. Check the synchronizer baulk ring inside serration for wear. The slot should be 0.0472–0.0550 in. (1.2–1.4 mm.) wide.

Assembly

1. Place the O-ring in the front cover. Install the front cover to the clutch housing with a press. Put in the front cover oil seal.

2. Install the rear extension oil seal with a drift.

3. Assemble the first/second and third/fourth synchronizer assemblies. Make sure that the ring gaps are not both on the same side of the unit.

4. On the rear end of the mainshaft, install the needle bearing, second gear, baulk ring, first/second synchronizer assembly, baulk ring, first gear bushing, needle bearing, first gear, locating ball, and thrust washer.

5. Drive or press on the mainshaft rear bearing.

6. Install the countershaft rear bearing to the adapter plate. Drive or press the mainshaft rear bearing into the adapter plate until the bearing snap-ring groove comes through the rear side of the plate. Install the snap-ring. If it is not tight against the plate, press the bearing back in slightly.

7. Insert the countershaft bearing ring between the countershaft rear bearing and bearing retainer. Install the bearing retainer to the adapter plate, torquing

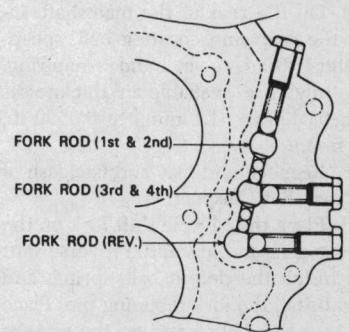

FORK ROD (1st & 2nd)

FORK ROD (3rd & 4th)

FORK ROD (REV.)

240Z, 260Z, 280Z and 1974 620 interlock and detent

the screws to 9–13 ft lbs. Stake both ends of the screws with a punch.

8. Insert the reverse idler shaft from the rear of the adapter plate. Torque the setscrew to 9–13 ft lbs. Install the spring washer and plain washer to the idler shaft. Torque the shaft nut to 43–58 ft lbs.

9. Place the two keys on the countershaft and oil the shaft lightly. Press on third gear and install a snap-ring.

10. Install the countershaft into its rear bearing.

11. From the front of the mainshaft, install the needle bearing, third gear, baulk ring, third/fourth synchronizer assembly, and snap-ring. Snap-rings are available in thicknesses from 0.0561 in. (1.425 mm.) to 0.0640 in. (1.625 mm.) to adjust gear end-play to the figure specified under "Inspection."

12. Press the main drive bearing onto the clutch shaft. Install the main drive gear spacer and a snap-ring. Snap-rings are available in thicknesses from 0.0710 in. (1.80 mm.) to 0.0820 in. (2.08 mm.) to adjust gear end-play to the figure specified under "Inspection."

13. Insert a key into the countershaft. Insert the pilot bearing in the clutch shaft assembly. Engage the countershaft drive gear with fourth gear and drive on the countershaft fourth gear with a drift. The rear end of the countershaft should be held steady while driving on the gear, to prevent rear bearing damage.

14. Install the reverse hub, reverse gear, thrust washer, and lock tab on the rear of the mainshaft. Install the shaft nut temporarily.

15. Oil the reverse idler shaft lightly. Install the needle bearing, reverse idler gear, thrust washer, and snap-ring.

16. Place the countershaft reverse gear and snap-ring on the rear of the countershaft. Snap-rings are available in thicknesses from 0.0433 in. (1.1 mm.) to 0.0590 in. (1.5 mm.) to adjust gear end-play to the figure specified under "Inspection."

17. Engage both first and second gears to lock the shaft. Torque the mainshaft nut to 130–152 ft lbs. and bend up the lock tab.

18. On the rear of the mainshaft, install the snap-ring, locating ball, speedometer drive gear, and snap-ring. Snap-rings are available in thicknesses from 0.0433 in. (1.1 mm.) to 0.0590 in. (1.5 mm.).

19. Recheck end-play and backlash of all gears. See "Inspection."

20. Place the reverse shift fork on the reverse gear and install the reverse shift rod. Install the detent ball, spring, and plug. Install the fork retaining pin. Place two interlock balls between the reverse shift rod and the third/fourth shift rod location. Install the third/fourth shift fork and rod. Install the detent ball, spring,

and plug. This plug is shorter than the other two. Install the fork retaining pin. Place two interlock balls between the first/second shift rod location and the third/fourth shift rod. Install the first/second shift fork and rod. Install the detent ball, spring, and plug. Apply locking agent to each detent plug and torque them to 16–22 ft lbs. Install the fork retaining pin.

21. Install the shift rod snap-rings.

22. Oil all moving parts and make sure that all gears can be shifted smoothly.

23. Apply sealant sparingly to the adapter plate and transmission housing. Install the transmission housing to the adapter plate and bolt it down temporarily.

24. Drive in the countershaft front bearing with a drift. Place the snap-ring in the mainshaft front bearing.

25. Apply sealant sparingly to the adapter plate and extension housing. Align the shift rods in the neutral positions. Position the striker rod to the shift rods and bolt down the extension housing. Torque to 11–16 ft lbs. Be careful not to damage the extension housing oil seal in installation.

26. Insert the striker rod pin, connect the rod to the shift lever bracket, and install the striker rod pin retaining ring. Replace the shift control arm.

27. To select the proper mainshaft bearing shim, first measure the amount the bearing protrudes from the front of the transmission case. This is measurement (B). Then measure the depth of the bearing recess in the rear of the clutch housing. This is measurement (A). Required shim thickness is found by subtracting (B) from (A). Shims are available in thicknesses of 0.0551 in. (1.4 mm.) and 0.0630 in. (1.6 mm.).

28. To select the proper countershaft front bearing shim, measure the amount that the bearing is recessed into the transmission case. Shim thickness should equal this measurement. Shims are available in thicknesses from 0.0157 in. (.4 mm.) to 0.0394 in. (1.0 mm.).

29. Apply sealant sparingly to the clutch and transmission housing mating surfaces and torque the bolts to 11–16 ft lbs.

30. Replace the clutch operating mechanism.

31. Install the shift lever temporarily and check shifting action.

32. Refill the transmission. See the Capacities Chart.

Five Speed Transmission Overhaul, 240 Z, 260 Z, 280Z

This transmission is quite similar to the four speed 240 Z unit. The model number is FS5C71A. Servo type synchromesh is used, instead of the Borg Warner type in the four speed. Shift linkage and inter-

lock arrangements are the same, except the reverse shift rod also operates fifth gear. Most service procedures are identical to those for the four speed unit. Those unique to the five-speed follow.

Disassembly

1. To disassemble the synchronizers, remove the circlip, synchronizer ring, thrust block, brake band, and anchor block. Be careful not to mix parts of the different synchronizer assemblies.

Inspection

1. Gear backlash should be 0.0016–0.0059 in. (0.04–0.15 mm.) for the main drive gear and reverse gear. For first, second, third, and fifth gears it should be 0.0016–0.0079 in. (0.04–0.20 mm.).

2. Gear end-play should be:

5-Speed Transmission End-Play Specifications

Gear	End-Play in. (mm.)
First, Second, Fifth	0.0039–0.0075 (0.12–0.19)
Third	0.0039–0.0094 (0.12–0.24)
Reverse Idler	0.0019–0.0137 (0.05–0.35)

Assembly

1. The synchronizer assemblies for second, third, and fourth are identical. When assembling the first gear synchronizer, be sure to install the 0.0866 in. (2.2 mm.) thick brake band at the bottom.

2. When assembling the mainshaft, select a third gear synchronizer hub snap-ring to minimize hub end-play. Snap-rings are available in thicknesses of 0.0610–0.0630 in. (1.55–1.60 mm.), 0.0591–0.0610 in. (1.50–1.55 mm.), and 0.0571–0.0591 in. (1.45–1.50 mm.). The synchronizer hub must be installed with the longer boss to the rear.

3. When reassembling the gear train, install the mainshaft, countershaft, and gears to the adapter plate. To tighten the mainshaft locknuts, tighten the front nut to 15–22 ft lbs. and the rear nut to 7–15 ft lbs. Hold the rear nut and force the front nut against it to a torque of 217 ft lbs. Select a snap-ring to minimize end-play of the fifth gear bearing at the rear of the mainshaft. Snap-rings are available in thicknesses from 0.0433 in. (1.1 mm.) to 0.0551 in. (1.4 mm.).

Four Speed Transmission Overhaul—B110, B210

This F4W56 transmission is constructed in two sections: a combined clutch and transmission housing, and an extension housing. There is a cast iron adapter plate between the housings. There are no case cover plates.

Disassembly

1. Drain the oil.

1. Remove the dust cover, spring, clutch withdrawal lever, and release bearing.

3. Remove the front cover from inside the clutch housing.

4. Remove the speedometer drive pinion from the extension housing. Remove the striker rod return spring plug, spring, plunger, and bushing. Remove the striker rod pin and separate the striker rod from the shift lever bracket.

5. Remove the extension housing. Tap it with a soft hammer, if necessary.

6. Separate the adapter plate from the transmission case, being careful not to lose the countershaft bearing washer.

7. Clamp the adapter plate in a vise with the reverse idler gear up.

8. Drive out the retaining pin and remove the reverse shift fork and reverse idler gear.

9. Remove the mainshaft rear snap-ring, washer, and reverse gear.

10. Drive out the remaining shift fork retaining pins. Remove all three detent plugs, springs, and balls. Remove the forks and shift rods. Be careful not to lose the interlock plungers.

11. Tap the rear of the mainshaft with a soft hammer to separate the mainshaft and countershaft from the adapter plate. Be careful not to drop the shafts. Separate the clutch shaft from the mainshaft.

12. From the front of the mainshaft, remove the needle bearing, synchronizer hub thrust washer, steel locating ball, third/fourth synchronizer, baulk ring, third gear, and needle bearing.

13. Press off the mainshaft bearing to the rear. Remove the thrust washer, first gear, needle bearing, baulk ring, first/second synchronizer, baulk ring, second gear, and needle bearing.

14. Remove the countergear bearing and the clutch shaft snap-ring and bearing.

Inspection

1. Clean all parts in a safe solvent. Oil the bearings immediately. Check all parts for wear or damage.

2. Backlash for each pair of gears should be 0.0031–0.0059 in. (0.08–0.15 mm.). If it is excessive, replace both drive and driven gears.

3. Gear end-play is adjusted by using snap-rings of different thicknesses.

4. Place each baulk ring on the cone of its gear. Check the gap between the baulk ring end face and the clutch teeth front face. The gap should be 0.0413–0.0551 in. (1.05–1.40 mm.). If it is less than 0.0197 in. (0.5 mm.), replace the baulk ring.

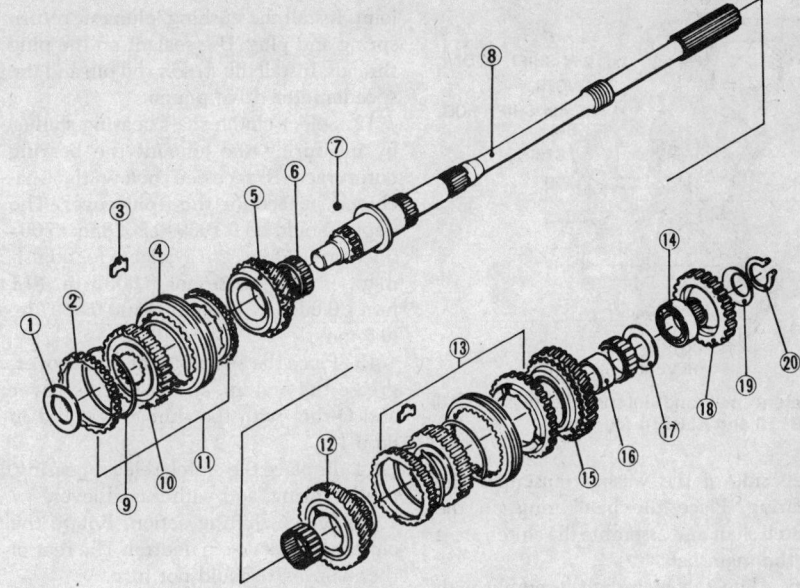

Mainshaft Assembly—LB110, KLB110, B210

1. Thrust washer
2. Baulk ring
3. Shifting insert
4. Coupling sleeve
5. 3rd gear, mainshaft
6. Needle bearing
7. Steel ball
8. Mainshaft
9. Spread ring
10. Synchronizer hub
11. 3rd & 4th synchronizer assembly
12. 2nd gear, mainshaft
13. 1st & 2nd synchronizer assembly
14. Mainshaft bearing
15. 1st gear, mainshaft
16. Bushing, 1st speed gear
17. Thrust washer, mainshaft
18. Reverse gear, mainshaft
19. Thrust washer
20. Snap-ring

Assembly

1. Press on the countershaft bearings. Install the countershaft assembly to the transmission case and replace the adapter plate temporarily. Countershaft end-play should be 0–0.0079 in. (0–0.2 mm.). Front bearing shims are available for adjustment in thicknesses from 0.0315 in. (0.8 mm.) to 0.0512 in. (1.3 mm.). Remove the countershaft assembly from the case.

2. Oil all moving parts when installing.

3. Install the coupling sleeve, shifting inserts, and spring on the synchronizer hub. Be careful not to hook the front and rear ends of the spring to the same insert. Make sure that the hub and sleeve operate smoothly.

4. Install the needle bearing from the rear of the mainshaft. Install second gear, the baulk ring, and synchronizer hub assembly. Align the shifting insert to the baulk ring groove. Install the first gear side needle bearing, baulk ring, and first gear. Install the mainshaft thrust washer and press on the rear bearing.

On the mainshaft front end, replace the needle bearing, third gear, baulk ring, synchronizer hub assembly, steel locating ball, thrust washer, and pilot bearing. Be sure to grease the sliding surface of the steel ball and thrust washer. The dimpled side of the thrust washer must face to the front and the oil grooved side to the rear.

5. Replace the main bearing, washer, and snap-ring onto the clutch shaft. The

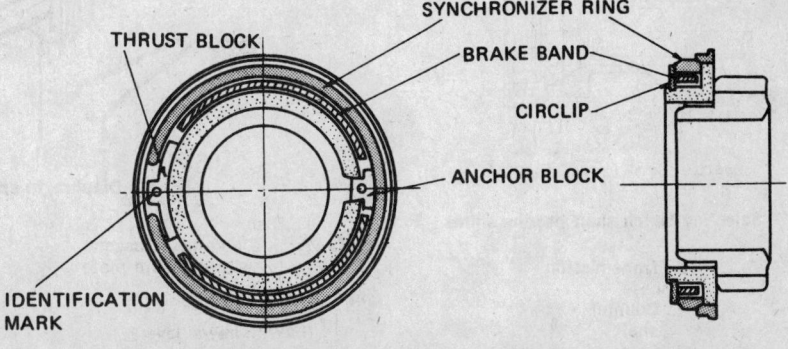

Servo type synchronizer assembled

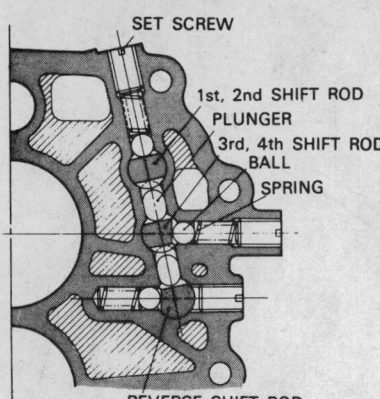

Detent ball and interlock details, B210, LB110 and KLB110 four speed

SET SCREW
1st, 2nd SHIFT ROD
PLUNGER
3rd, 4th SHIFT ROD
BALL
SPRING
REVERSE SHIFT ROD

web side of the washer must face the bearing. Place the baulk ring on the clutch shaft and assemble the clutch shaft to the mainshaft.

6. Align the mainshaft assembly with the countershaft assembly and install them to the adapter plate by lightly tapping on the clutch shaft with a soft hammer.

7. Place the first/second and third-/fourth shift forks on the shift rods, being careful that the forks are not reversed. Install all three shift rods and the detent and interlock parts. Apply locking agent to the detent plug threads and screw the plugs in flush. Make sure the shift forks are in their grooves and drive in the retaining pins.

8. Install the mainshaft reverse gear, thrust washer, and snap-ring. Face the web side of the thrust washer to the gear.

9. Replace the reverse idler gear and pin on the reverse shift fork. Check interlock action by attempting to shift two shift rods at once.

10. Install the adapter plate to the transmission case. Make sure to install the countergear front shim selected in Step 1. Use sealant on the joint and seat the plate by tapping with a soft hammer.

11. Align the striker lever and install

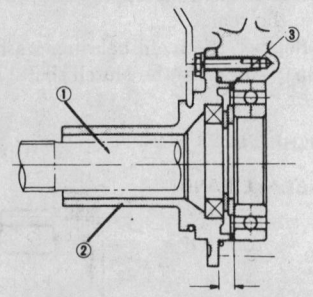

5.00 to 5.15 mm (0.1969 to 0.202 8 in.)

Selecting clutch shaft bearing shims

1. Transmission case
2. Counter-shaft
3. Shim

the extension housing. Use sealant on the joint. Install the bushing, plunger, return spring and plug. Use sealant on the plug threads. Install the striker rod pin and the speedometer drive pinion.

12. Select clutch shaft bearing shim(s) by measuring the amount the bearing outer race is recessed below the machined surface for the front cover. The depth should be 0.1969–0.2028 in. (5.00–5.15 mm.). Shims are available for adjustment in thicknesses of 0.0039 in. (0.1 mm.), 0.0079 in. (0.2 mm.), and 0.0197 in. (0.5 mm.).

13. Place the oil seal in the front cover, grease the seal lip, and install the cover and O-ring with the shim(s) selected in Step 12.

14. Replace the clutch release bearing, return spring, and withdrawal lever.

15. Check shifting action. Rotate the clutch shaft slowly in neutral. The rear of the mainshaft should not turn.

16. Refer to the Capacities Chart for refill capacity.

CLUTCH

Removal and Installation

Models With Coil Spring Clutch

1. Remove the transmission from the engine.

2. On the L16 engine, temporarily lock the release lever.

3. Loosen the retaining bolts in sequence, a turn at a time. Remove the bolts.

4. Remove the pressure plate and disc.

5. Replace the disc with the longer chamfered splined end of the hub toward the transmission.

6. Align the disc to the flywheel with a splined dummy shaft.

7. Install the pressure plate. Most models have two pressure plate locating dowels in the flywheel. Tighten the pressure plate bolts in sequence, a turn at a time.

Clutch release mechanism, A12, A13, L24 and L26 engines. (1) is withdrawal lever, (2) is return spring, and (3) is the release bearing.

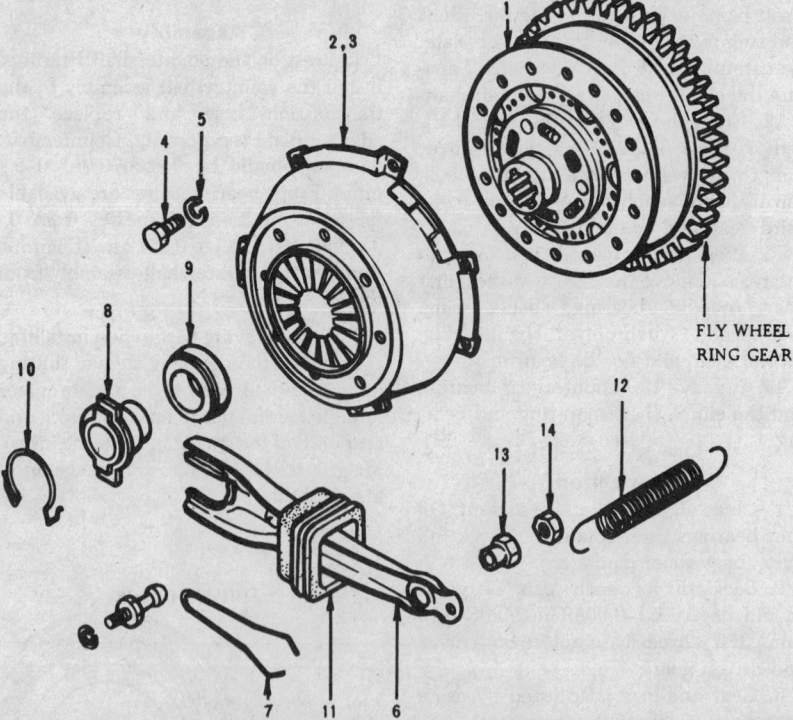

FLY WHEEL RING GEAR

Diaphragm spring clutch—510

1. Disc
2, 3. Clutch cover assembly with pressure plate
4. Bolt
5. Lockwasher
6. Withdrawal lever
7. Retainer spring
8. Bearing sleeve
9. Release bearing
10. Bearing sleeve holder spring
11. Dust cover
12. Return spring
13. Withdrawal lever push nut
14. Locknut

Torque to 35 ft lbs., except on the L16 engine. L16 torque is 17–19 ft lbs.

8. Remove the dummy shaft. Unlock the release lever on the L16.

9. Replace the release bearing and transmission.

Models With Diaphragm Spring Clutch

1. Remove the transmission from the engine.

2. Loosen the bolts in sequence, a turn at a time. Remove the bolts.

3. Remove the pressure plate and clutch disc.

4. On A12, A13, A14, L24, L26 and L28 engines, remove the release mechanism. Apply multi-purpose grease to the bearing sleeve inside groove, the contact point of the withdrawal lever and bearing sleeve, the contact surface of the lever ball pin and lever. Replace the release mechanism.

5. Install the disc, aligning it with a splined dummy shaft.

6. Install the pressure plate and torque the bolts to 17–18 ft lbs. on L16, L24, L26 and L28 engines, and 11–16 ft lbs. on A12, A13, A14, L18 and L20B engines.

7. Remove the dummy shaft.

8. Replace the transmission.

F10 Transaxle Clutch

Because of the unique configuration of the F10 transmission/drive shaft system (transaxle), the transmission is impossible to remove from the car without removing the engine.

Due to this problem, Datsun has made provisions for clutch service through an access plate (cover) on the top of the housing. The engine and transmission need not be removed to permit repair or replacement.

NOTE: *The clutch cover and pressure plate are balanced as a unit. If replacement is necessary, replace both parts.*

1. Disconnect the following cables, wires and hoses:

    Battery ground cable

    Fresh air duct

    Engine harness connectors on the clutch housing

    Ignition wire between the coil and the distributor

    Carbon canister hoses

2. Remove the inspection plate from the top of the clutch housing and remove the six bolts holding the clutch cover.

NOTE: *In order to reach all six bolts, you are going to have to jack up the car and, as you loosen the bolts, rotate the right front wheel with the car in top gear. This will rotate the clutch cover.*

CAUTION: *Be sure to loosen the bolts evenly in order.*

3. Rotate the steering wheel all the way to the right and remove the inspection plate inside the right wheel well.

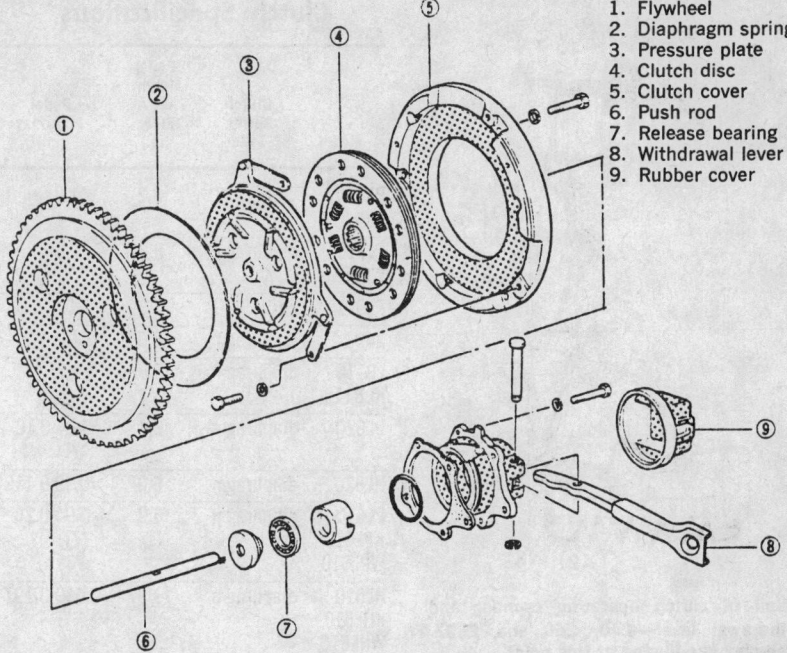

1. Flywheel
2. Diaphragm spring
3. Pressure plate
4. Clutch disc
5. Clutch cover
6. Push rod
7. Release bearing
8. Withdrawal lever
9. Rubber cover

F-10 clutch components

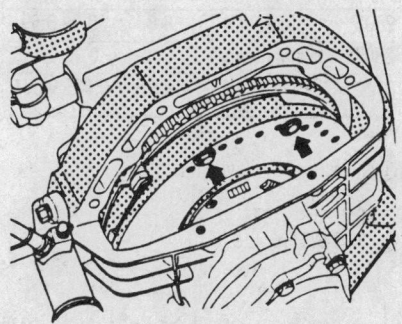

Removing clutch cover bolts—F-10

4. Disconnect the withdrawal lever and remove the six bolts on the bearing house. Reaching through the wheel well inspection hole, pull out the primary drive gear assembly.

5. After removing the drive gear, go back to the engine compartment and lift the clutch cover and disc assembly out through the open section of the clutch housing. You may also remove the diaphragm at the same time.

6. Remove the strap holding the pressure plate to the clutch cover and remove the clutch from the center.

NOTE: *This strap must be replaced in the same position it had before removal. Mark the relative position before removal. Installing it out of position will cause an imbalance.*

Installation

Installation is the reverse of removal. But, you must observe the following:

1. Paying particular attention to the alignment marks, reassemble the disc and cover to the pressure plate. Tighten the strap bolts to 5–6 ft. lbs.

2. Put the diaphragm spring and cover assembly onto the flywheel and screw the bolts in with your fingers.

NOTE: *These bolts should remain loose enough to shift the assembly when installing the drive gear. There are a pair of aligning pins on the flywheel.*

3. Install the drive gear assembly by aligning the disc hub with the gear spline. After alignment, tighten the cover bolts to 5–7.2 ft lbs.

Clutch Linkage

Adjustment

Refer to the Clutch Specifications Chart for clutch pedal height above floor and pedal free play.

All models have a hydraulically operated clutch. Pedal height is usually adjusted with a stopper limiting the upward travel of the pedal. Pedal free-play is adjusted at the master cylinder pushrod. If the pushrod is nonadjustable, free-play is adjusted by placing shims between the master cylinder and the firewall. On a few models, pedal free play can also be adjusted at the operating (slave) cylinder pushrod.

Hydraulic System Bleeding

Bleeding is required to remove air trapped in the hydraulic system. This operation is necessary whenever the system has been leaking or dismantled. The bleed screw is usually located on the clutch operating (slave) cylinder.

1. Remove the bleed screw dust cap.

2. Open the bleed screw about ¾ turn.

3. Attach a tube to the bleed screw, immersing the free end in a clean con-

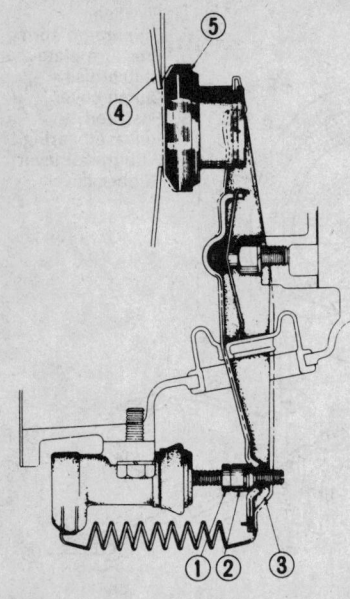

Detail of clutch operating cylinder and withdrawal level—240, 260 and 280Z. Free-play is adjusted at this point.

1. Locknut
2. Adjusting nut
3. Withdrawal lever
4. Diaphragm spring
5. Release bearing

tainer of brake fluid.

4. Fill the master cylinder with fluid.

5. Depress the clutch pedal quickly. Hold it down. Have an assistant tighten the bleed screw. Allow the pedal to return slowly. Bleeder screw torque: 5–65 ft lbs.

Clutch Specifications

Model	Clutch Spring Type	Pedal Height Above Floor (in.)	Pedal Free-Play (in.)
PL510 WPL510	coil	8.2	1.0
PL510 WPL510	diaphragm	8.2	1.0
PL521	coil	5.3	1.0
240Z	diaphragm	8.0	1.0
LB110 KLB110	diaphragm	5.6	1.2
PL620	diaphragm	6.4 ③	0.04-0.12 ①
HL620	diaphragm	6.02	0.39-0.118
PL610 KPL610 WPL610	diaphragm	6.9 ②	0.04-0.20 ①
HL610 KHL610 WHL610	diaphragm	7.087	0.039-0.197
710	diaphragm	7.1	0.04-0.20
B210	diaphragm	6.3	0.39-0.59
260Z	diaphragm	8.8	0.39-0.59
280Z	diaphragm	8.8	0.39-0.118
F10	diaphragm	6.75	0.236-0.551

① Measured at clevis pin
② 7.08 in.—1975
③ 6.02 in.—1975
④ 6.02-6.3 in.—1975

Clutch master cylinder—1200 and B210

1. Snap-ring
2. Dust cover
3. Pushrod
4. Piston
5. Spring
6. Inlet valve spring
7. Inlet valve
8. Spring retainer
9. Shims
10. Inlet valve release pin
11. Housing
12. Fluid reservoir
13. Reservoir cap

6. Repeat Steps 2 and 5 until no more air bubbles are seen in the fluid container.

7. Remove the bleed tube. Replace the dust cap. Refill the master cylinder.

Hydraulic System Repairs

Clutch master and slave cylinders are repaired in much the same way as are brake master and wheel cylinders. Bleeding is required whenever the clutch hydraulic system has been dismantled.

AUTOMATIC TRANSMISSION

Only external transmission adjustments and repairs, and transmission removal and replacement, are covered in this book.

The 510 up to serial number PL510-117464, and up to serial number WPL510-853595 use a British built Borg Warner automatic transmission with a cable operated downshift. The 240 Z (1972 and later models) use a Japanese unit. There is a model and serial number tag on the left side of the Borg Warner units and on the right side of the Japanese transmission.

Automatic Transmission I.D.

Model no.	Nissan Part no.	Transmission
AS14-35EC	31010-24500	British built BW
AS2-41	31010A8500	American built BW
3N71B	X0120, 2710, 2402	JATCO
3N71	—	JATCO

Shift Linkage Adjustment

Floorshift

1. Loosen the trunnion locknuts at the lower end of the control lever. Remove the selector lever knob and console.

2. Place the selector lever in Neutral.

3. Place the transmission shift lever in neutral position by pushing it all the way back, then pulling it forward two stops.

4. Check the vertical clearance between the top of the shift lever pin and transmission control bracket. The clearance, should be 0.020–0.059 in. Adjust by turning the nut at the lower end of the selector lever compression rod.

5. Check the horizontal clearance, of the shift lever pin and transmission control bracket. This should be 0.020 in. Adjust with the trunnion locknuts.

6. Replace the console, making sure that the shift pointer is correctly aligned. Install the knob.

1. Converter housing
2. Housing to case bolt
3. Lockwasher
4. Screen
5. Captive nut
6. Screw
7. Converter assembly
8. Not used
9. Case assembly
10. Rear band adjusting screw
11. Locknut
12. Seal
13. Adapter
14. Neutral safety switch
15. Park pawl
16. Toggle link
17. Toggle link pin
18. Washer
19. Spring
20. Toggle lever
21. Toggle pin
22. Washer
23. Retaining clip
24. Toggle pin
25. O-ring
26. Cotter pin
27. Pin
28. Toggle lift lever
29. Spring
30. Torsion lever
31. Washer
32. Retaining clip
33. Park linkage
34. Retaining clip
35. Downshift cable assembly
36. Manual valve shaft
37. Spring
38. Roll pin
39. Collar
40. Roll pin
41. Detent spring
42. Detent ball
43. Pan
44. Pan gasket
45. Drain plug
46. Bolt
47. Extension housing
48. Oil seal
52-57 Not used
49. Gasket
50. Bolt
51. Lockwasher
58. Filler, dipstick and
breather tube
59. Dipstick
60. Drive plate to
converter bolt
61. Lockwasher

British built Borg Warner automatic transmission

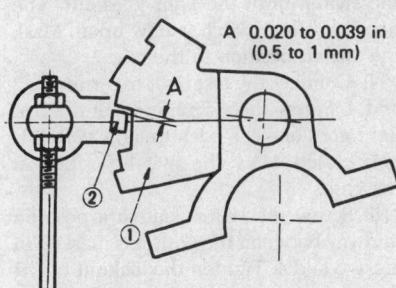

Column shift automatic transmission linkage adjustment. (1) is the selector position plate, (2) is the stop pin

Column Shift

1. Loosen the trunnion locknuts on the upper selector rod. (On the steering column inside the engine compartment).

2. Place the selector lever in Neutral. Place the transmission shift lever in neutral position, the central of its five positions.

3. Adjust the locknuts to make the clearance between the stop pin on the lower selector lever and the position plate 0.020–0.039 in.

Downshift Cable Adjustment

This adjustment is necessary only on early models with the British-built Borg Warner transmission. The adjustment is made at the carburetor end of the cable.

1. Check the transmission fluid level. Connect a tachometer to the engine.

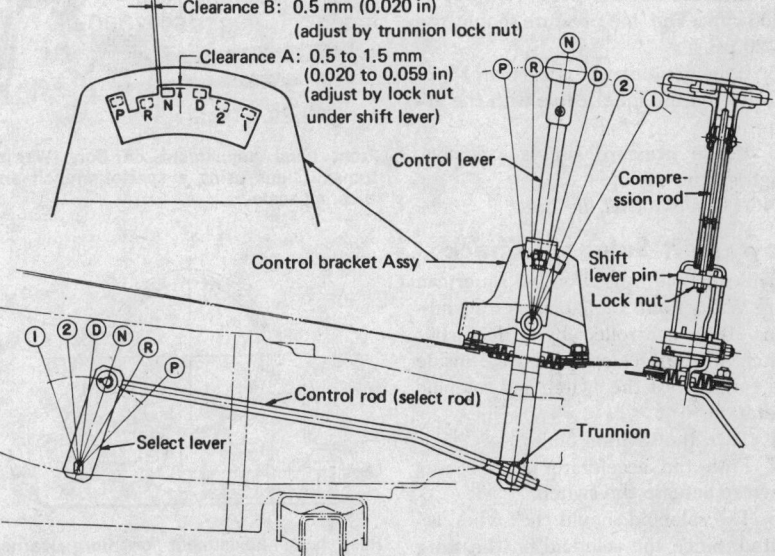

Floorshift automatic transmission linkage adjustment

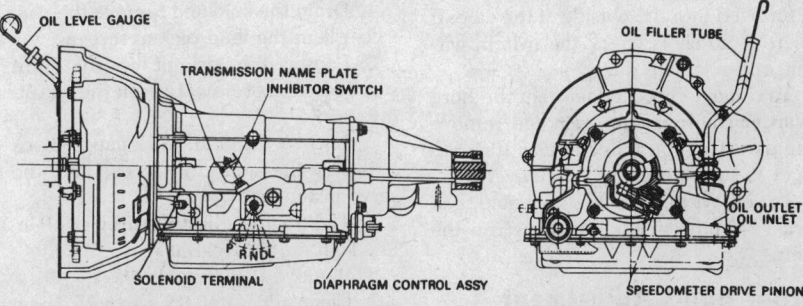

American built Borg Warner automatic transmission

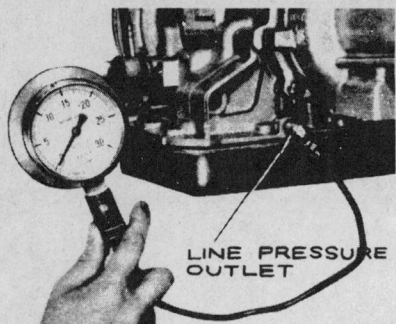

Pressure gauge connected to the British built Borg Warner automatic transmission

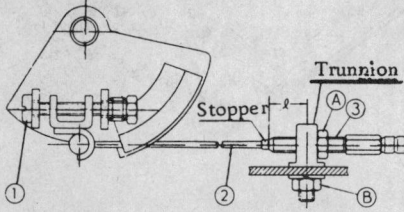

Downshift cable adjuster. (1) is adjuster, (2) is inner cable, (3) is outer cable.

2. Connect a pressure gauge to the transmission line pressure outlet.

3. Start the engine and shift into Drive. The car should be safely blocked and the hand and footbrakes set.

4. Increase engine speed from 500 to 1,000 rpm. The line pressure should rise 15–20 psi.

5. If the pressure rise is less than 15–20 psi, shorten the inner cable with the adjuster.

6. If the pressure rise is excessive, lengthen the cable.

NOTE: *Do not oil the cable.*

Downshift Solenoid Check

This solenoid is used on the American Borg Warner and the Japanese transmissions. It is controlled by a downshift switch on the accelerator linkage inside the car. To test the switch and solenoid operation:

1. Turn the ignition on.

2. Push the accelerator all the way down to actuate the switch.

3. The solenoid should click when actuated. Since the solenoid on the Borg Warner transmission is mounted inside the pan, it may be difficult to hear the click. The Japanese transmission solenoid is screwed into the outside of the case. If there is no click, check the switch, wiring, and solenoid.

To remove the solenoid from the Borg Warner transmission, drain and remove the pan. Then push in and turn the solenoid ½ turn clockwise to remove.

To remove the Japanese solenoid, first drain 2–3 pints of fluid, then unscrew the unit.

Front Band Adjustment

This adjustment procedure is for the

Removal of Borg Warner transmission downshift solenoid

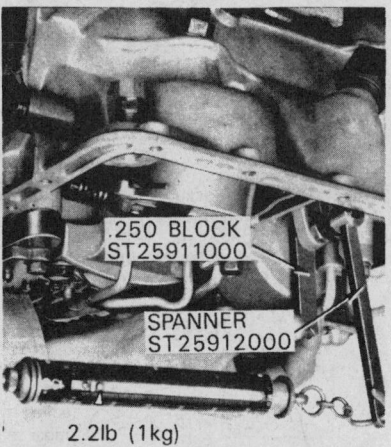

Front band adjustment on Borg Warner transmissions using a special wrench and a spring scale

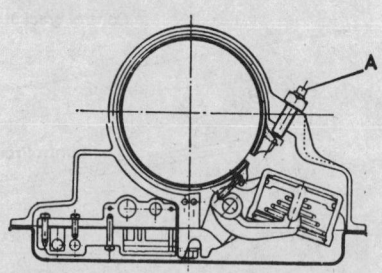

Rear band adjustment on Borg Warner transmissions. (A) is the adjusting screw.

Borg Warner transmissions only.

1. Drain the fluid and remove the pan.

2. Clean the fluid pickup screen.

3. Loosen the locknut on the front servo adjusting screw. Loosen the adjusting screw.

4. Insert a 0.250 in. thick gauge block between the adjusting screw and the servo piston rod.

5. Tighten the adjusting screw to 10 in. lbs. Tighten the locknut to 18 ft lbs.

6. Remove the gauge block.

7. Clean and install the pan with a new gasket.

Rear Band Adjustment

This adjustment procedure is for the Borg Warner transmissions only. It may be necessary to unbolt the crossmember and lower the rear of the transmission to get at the adjusting screw on the right side of the case.

1. Loosen the locknut. Tighten the adjusting screw to 10 ft lbs.

2. Back off the adjusting screw ¾ turn on the American unit and one turn on the British unit.

3. Tighten the locknut to 28 ft lbs.

Neutral Safety and Backup Light Switch Adjustment

Borg Warner Transmission

The switch unit is screwed into the left side of the transmission case. The switch terminals marked 1 and 3 are for the neutral safety switch which prevents the engine from being started except in Park or Neutral. The terminals 2 and 4 are for the backup light switch.

1. Shift into Drive or Low with the engine off. Disconnect the switch leads.

2. Connect a test light in series with terminals 1 and 3 and battery current.

3. Loosen the switch locknut. Screw in the switch until the light goes out. The neutral safety switch is now open. Mark the switch position in the case.

4. Connect the test light to terminals 2 and 4. Screw the switch in until the test light goes on. The backup light switch is now closed. Mark the switch position in the case.

5. Screw the switch out to a position midway between the positions marked in Steps 3 and 4. Tighten the locknut to 5 ft lbs.

6. Make sure while holding the brakes on, that the engine will start only in Park or Neutral transmission positions. Check that the backup lights go on only in reverse.

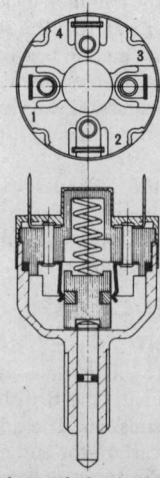

Neutral safety and backup light switch, Borg Warner transmission

Japanese Transmission

The switch unit is bolted to the left side of the transmission case, behind the transmission shift lever. The switch prevents the engine from being started in any transmission position except Park or Neutral. It also controls the backup lights.

1. Remove the transmission shift lever retaining nut and the lever.

2. Remove the switch.

3. Remove the machine screw in the case under the switch.

4. Align the switch to the case by inserting a 0.059 in. (1.5 mm.) diameter pin through the hole in the switch into the screw hole. Mark the switch location.

5. Remove the pin, replace the machine screw, install the switch as marked, and replace the transmission shift lever and retaining nut.

6. Make sure while holding the brakes on, that the engine will start only in Park or Neutral. Check that the backup lights go on only in reverse.

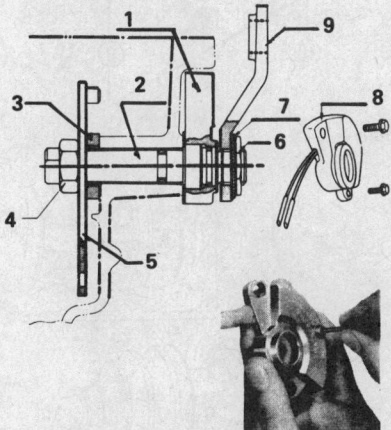

Neutral safety and back-up light switch—JATCO transmission

1. Neutral safety switch
2. Manual shaft
3. Washer
4. Nut
5. Manual plate
6. Nut
7. Washer
8. Neutral safety switch
9. Transmission shift lever

Removal and Installation

510 With British BW Unit

1. Disconnect the downshift cable from the carburetor.

2. Drain the transmission oil pan.

3. Remove the driveshaft.

4. Disconnect the handbrake mechanism if necessary.

5. Disconnect the speedometer cable from the transmission. Disconnect the neutral safety switch.

6. Disconnect the transmission shift linkage. Disconnect the oil cooler tubes.

7. Remove the filler tube.

8. Unbolt the transmission from the rear crossmember.

9. Support the engine with a jack under the torque converter housing.

10. Remove the crossmember. Lower the rear of the engine slightly.

11. Support the transmission with a jack. Place a pan under the torque converter.

12. Remove the starter.

13. Remove the four bolts holding the torque converter to the drive plate. Access is from the front through the engine mounting plate.

14. Remove the converter and transmission assembly towards the rear. Be careful not to let the converter fall when separating the assembly from the engine.

15. Reverse the procedure to install. Make sure the drive plate is not warped more than 0.020 in. Plate-to-crankshaft bolt torque is 40–50 ft lbs. To insure correct engagement of the front oil pump drive, rotate the converter so that the drive fingers on the hub will be in 9 and 3 o'clock positions. Rotate the slots of the front oil pump driving gear to the same positions. Torque the drive plate-to-torque converter bolts to 25–30 ft lbs. Torque the ⅜ in. converter housing-to-engine bolts to 30–34 ft lbs. and the 5/16 in. bolts to 7–10 ft lbs. There are two dowels for aligning the converter housing to the engine.

16. Refill the transmission and check the fluid level.

510 with American BW Unit

1. Disconnect the battery.

2. Remove the carburetor torsion shaft and starter.

3. Remove the two torque converter housing-to-engine capscrews at the top.

4. Raise and support the car.

5. Disconnect the handbrake front cable from the center lever.

6. Loosen the oil pan bolts and drain the transmission.

7. Loosen the muffler clamps and turn the muffler for clearance. Remove the driveshaft.

8. Disconnect the speedometer cable, vacuum hose, and neutral safety switch wiring. Disconnect the solenoid wire at the transmission.

9. Detach the oil cooler tubes. Remove the filler tube and plug opening.

10. Disconnect the lower selector rod and remove the cross shaft assembly.

11. Support the transmission with a suitable jack.

12. Remove the rear crossmember. Lower the transmission and the rear of the engine for access to the converter-to-drive plate bolts. Place a pan under the converter.

13. Remove the engine rear plate. Mark the relationship of the converter and drive plate. Remove the torque converter-to-drive plate bolts, screwing the bolts out completely one at a time. Remove the remaining converter housing-to-engine capscrews. Pull the trans-

mission away from the engine.

To replace the American built Borg Warner transmission:

14. Make sure the drive plate is not warped more than 0.020 in. Plate-to-crankshaft bolt torque is 50 ft lbs. Place the transmission and converter assembly on a jack. Pull the transmission forward to start the converter hub into the crankshaft. Align the engine block dowel pin with the converter housing aligning hole. Install the two lower converter housing attaching bolts and tighten to pull the transmission assembly into place. Torque the converter housing bolts to 32 ft lbs. Tighten the drive plate-to-converter bolts to 28 ft lbs.

15. Install the starter motor, shift linkage, speedometer cable, filler tube, and oil cooler tubes.

16. Connect the vacuum hose and kickdown solenoid wire.

17. Raise the transmission until it contacts the floor pan, attach the rear crossmember to the side rails, lower the transmission, and bolt the transmission to the crossmember.

18. Replace the driveshaft, exhaust pipe, and handbrake cable.

19. Lower the vehicle, replace the battery cable, and carburetor torsion shaft.

20. Pour in 3 quarts of transmission fluid. Set the handbrake and start the engine. Add 3 more quarts. Move the selector lever through all ranges. Add enough fluid to bring the level up to the F mark.

All Models with Japanese Transmission

1. Disconnect the battery cable.

2. Remove the accelerator linkage.

3. Detach the shift linkage.

4. Disconnect the neutral safety switch and downshift solenoid wiring.

5. Remove the drain plug and drain the torque converter. If there is no converter drain plug, drain the transmission. If there is no transmission drain plug, remove the pan to drain. Replace the pan to keep out dirt.

6. Remove the front exhaust pipe.

7. Remove the vacuum tube and speedometer cable.

8. Disconnect the fluid cooler tubes.

9. Remove the driveshaft and starter.

10. Support the transmission with a jack under the oil pan. Support the engine also.

11. Remove the rear crossmember.

12. Mark the relationship between the torque converter and the drive plate. Remove the four bolts holding the converter to the drive plate through the hole at the front, under the engine. Unbolt the transmission from the engine.

13. Reverse the procedure for installation. Make sure the drive plate is warped no more than 0.020 in. Torque the drive plate-to-torque converter and converter

housing-to-engine bolts to 29–36 ft lbs.
Drive plate-to-crankshaft bolt torque is
101–116 ft lbs.

14. Refill the transmission and check
the fluid level.

TRANSAXLE

Due to the complexity of the job, and
the special tools required, no transaxle
overhaul is given.

Shift Linkage Adjustment

F-10 4 speed

1. Loosen control lever adjusting nuts.
2. Measure the initial clearance between the case cover and the shift lever
when the shift lever is pushed completely
into the case cover.
3. Relocate the shift lever to increase
the clearance by 8mm. Move shift lever
fully downward (hand lever in 4th gear).
4. Push select lever fully upward so
that hand lever guide plate touches detent pin.
5. Turn upper adjusting nut until it
contacts trunnion plate then back off one
full turn.
6. Tighten lower adjusting nut.

F-10 5 speed

1. Loosen all 4 locknuts and move shift
lever completely into transmission case,
then back out 8mm.
2. Move shift lever down so that gears
are in 3rd position.
3. Push select lever fully down so that
hand lever guide plate touches detent
pin.
4. Turn selector shaft upper adjusting
nut until it touches the trunnion plate.
Then turn it one complete turn more and
tighten lower nut.
5. Place hand lever in neutral and adjust hand lever to detent gap to one to
two millimeters. Tighten lock nuts.

DRIVE AXLES

Driveshaft and U-Joints

F10 Front Wheel Drive

Because of the front wheel drive installation in the F10, driveshafts (as commonly thought of) do not exist. However,
there are definitely driveshafts.

Leading from the transmission/differential to the front wheels, particular care
should be taken when removing or installing.

Removal

1. Raise the car and support it.
Remove the front wheels and tires.
2. Remove the cotterpin and take off
the lock nut from the drive shaft while

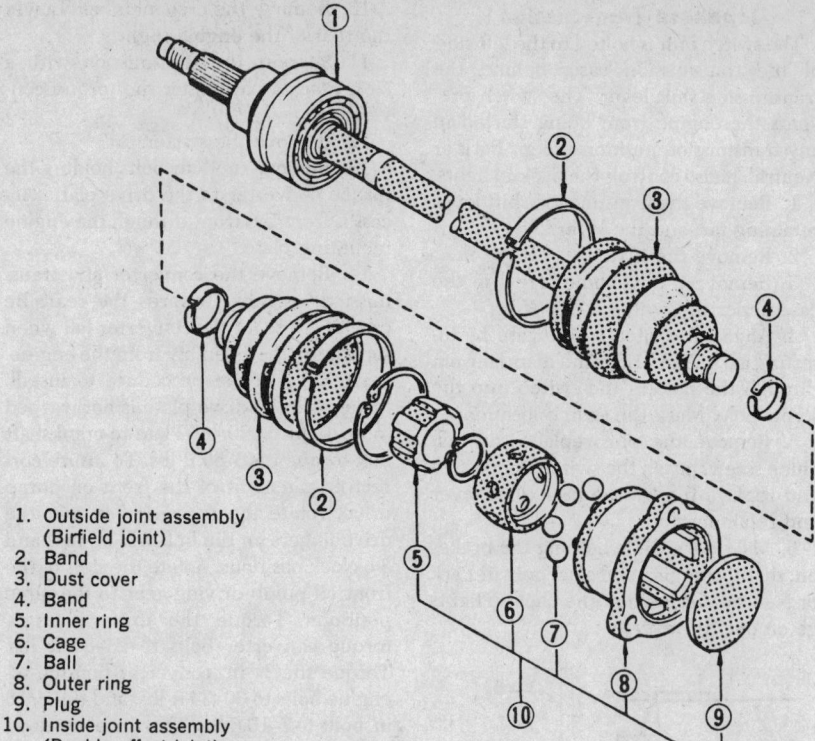

1. Outside joint assembly (Birfield joint)
2. Band
3. Dust cover
4. Band
5. Inner ring
6. Cage
7. Ball
8. Outer ring
9. Plug
10. Inside joint assembly (Double offset joint)

Driveshaft assembly—F-10

Special Datsun tool ST35100000 for removing driveshaft

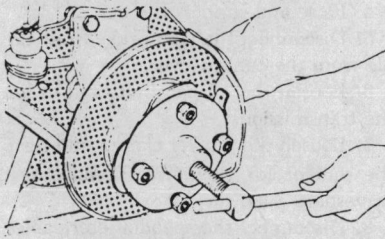

Removing driveshaft

holding the wheel hub.
3. Install a drive shaft remover (screw
type), remove the bolts holding the drive
shaft and pull the shaft. The shaft may be
removed from under the engine compartment.
NOTE: *When removing, do not damage the seal on the knuckle.*

Disassembly

1. Place the drive shaft in a "soft" vise
and straighten and remove boot band,
then remove the dust cover from the
joint outer ring and slide back.
2. Pry off the clip with a screwdriver
and pull out the outer ring (with flange).
3. Wipe the grease from the ball cage
and drive out the ball bearings. Turn the
cage half a turn and remove from the
inner ring.

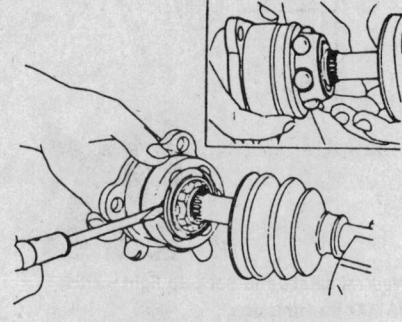

Removing the clip and outer ring

4. Pry off the retaining ring and
remove the inner ring. It is easily
removed by tapping with a mallet. Then
remove the dust cover.

Inspection

Clean all parts with a safe solvent and
dry with compressed air. Check all the
parts for wear, deformation, rust, burn or
excessive play. Replace any part that
seems damaged.

Assembly

Assembly is the reverse procedure,
with the following steps added:

To securely fasten the dust cover, wrap
a band around it and tighten with pliers
and a screwdriver. Lock the band with a
punch, leaving about the same length as
its width protruding. Bend that portion
back over itself.

NOTE: *Renew grease and take care
not to allow any dirt inside the dust
cover.*

Installation

Installation is the reverse of removal. Add the following steps to your procedure:

Do not damage the grease seal.

Lubricate the grease seal lip with grease.

Install an O-ring on the flange surface of the Double offset joint.

Be sure that the drive shaft thread is clear of the hub before tightening.

If the fit seems to be tight, lightly hammer the flange surface until threads are exposed. Torque hub nut to 87–145 ft lbs. and shaft bolts to 28–36 ft lbs.

Removal and Installation

PL521, LB110, KLB110, B210, PL610, KPL610, PL710, KPL710

These driveshafts are all one piece units with a U-joint and flange at the rear, and a U-joint and a splined sleeve yoke which fits into the rear of the transmission, at the front. Early models and trucks generally have U-joints with grease fittings. U-joints without grease fittings must be disassembled for lubrication, usually at 24,000 mile intervals. The splines are lubricated by transmission oil.

1. Be ready to catch oil coming from the rear of the transmission and to plug the extension housing.
2. Unbolt the rear flange.
3. Pull the driveshaft down and back.
4. Plug the transmission extension housing.
5. Reverse the procedure to install, oiling the splines. Flange bolt torque is 15–20 ft lbs.

PL510, PL610, KPL610, WPL510

These driveshafts are the one piece type with a U-joint and flange at the rear, and a U-joint and a splined sleeve yoke which fits into the rear of the transmis-

1. Sleeve yoke
2. Spider with four bearing journals
3. Bearing race snap-ring
4. Bearing race with needle rollers
5. Spider with four bearing journals
6. Flange yoke
7. Bearing race snap-ring

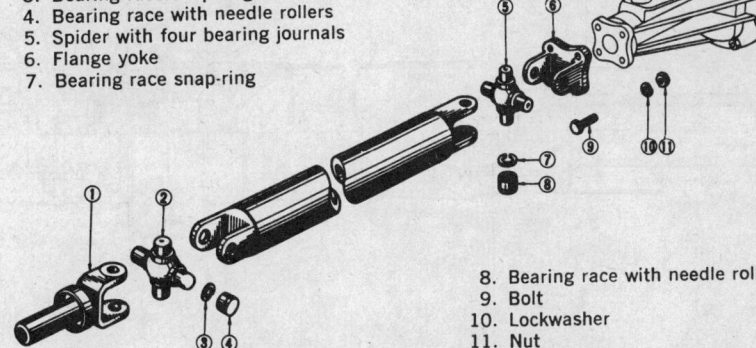

8. Bearing race with needle rollers
9. Bolt
10. Lockwasher
11. Nut

LB110, KLB110 driveshaft with late type U-joints

sion, at the front. The U-joints must be disassembled for lubrication at 24,000 mile intervals. The splines are lubricated by transmission oil.

1. Release the handbrake.
2. Loosen the PL510 muffler and rotate it out of the way.
3. On the PL510, remove the handbrake rear cable adjusting nut and disconnect the left handbrake cable from the adjuster.
4. Unbolt the rear flange.
5. Pull the driveshaft down and back.
6. Plug the transmission extension housing.
7. Reverse the procedure to install, oiling the splines. Flange bolt torque is 29–62 ft lbs. on the PL510 and WPL510, and 15–20 ft lbs. on the PL610 and KPL610.

240, 260 and 280 Z Four Speed

This driveshaft is the same type used on the PL510 and WPL510. It is balanced as an assembly.

1. Make sure that there are spline/-

flange yoke match marks in two places. If not, make some with chalk.

2. Remove the submuffler and, on the 260 and 280 Z, the main muffler.
3. Unbolt the rear flange.
4. Pull the driveshaft down and back.
5. Plug the transmission extension housing.
6. Reverse the procedure to install, aligning the match marks and oiling the splines. Flange bolt torque is 18 ft lbs.

240, 280 Z Five Speed

This driveshaft has a flange at either end and a splined coupling in the center.

1. Carry out Steps 1–3 for 240 Z—Four Speed.
2. Unbolt the front flange.
3. Remove the driveshaft.
4. Reverse the procedure to install, aligning the match marks. Flange bolt torque is 18 ft lbs.

WPL610, PL620

These models use a driveshaft with three U-joints and a center support bearing. The driveshaft is balanced as an assembly. It is not recommended that it be disassembled.

1. Mark the relationship of the driveshaft flange to the differential flange.
2. Unbolt the center bearing bracket.
3. Unbolt the driveshaft flange from the differential flange.
4. Pull the driveshaft back under the rear axle. Plug the rear of the transmission to prevent oil or fluid loss.
5. On installation, align the marks made in Step 1. Torque the flange bolts to 15–20 ft lbs. Center bearing bracket bolt torque is 12–16 ft lbs. on the PL620 and 26–35 ft lbs. on the WPL610.

U-Joint Overhaul

Disassembly

1. Mark the relationship of all components for reassembly.
2. Remove the snap-rings. The snap-rings seat in the needle bearing races.
3. Tap the yoke with a soft hammer to release one bearing cap. Be careful not to

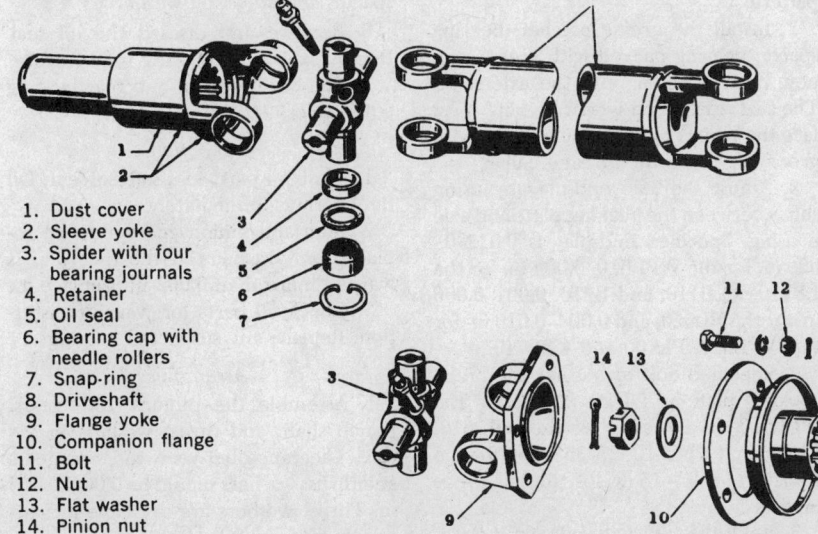

1. Dust cover
2. Sleeve yoke
3. Spider with four bearing journals
4. Retainer
5. Oil seal
6. Bearing cap with needle rollers
7. Snap-ring
8. Driveshaft
9. Flange yoke
10. Companion flange
11. Bolt
12. Nut
13. Flat washer
14. Pinion nut

Driveshaft with early type U-joints

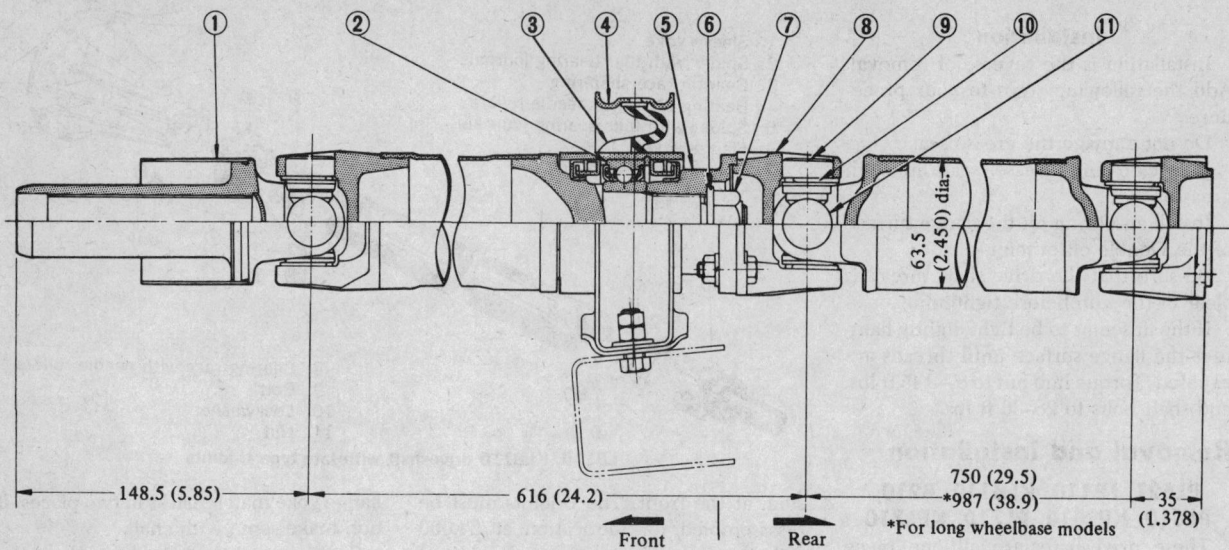

63.5
(2.450) dia.

148.5 (5.85)   616 (24.2)

750 (29.5)
*987 (38.9)   35 (1.378)

*For long wheelbase models

Front   Rear

WPL610 and PL620 driveshaft

1. Sleeve yoke assembly
2. Center bearing
3. Center bearing insulator
4. Center bearing bracket
5. Companion flange
6. Plain washer
7. Self locking nut
8. Flange yoke
9. Bearing race assembly
10. Snap ring
11. Journal assembly

lose the needle rollers.

4. Remove the other bearing caps. Remove the spiders from the yokes.

Inspection

1. Spline backlash should not exceed 0.0197 in. (.5 mm.).

2. Driveshaft runout should not exceed 0.015 in. (.4 mm.).

3. On units with snap-rings seated in the needle bearing races, different thicknesses of snap-rings are available for U-joint adjustment. Play should not exceed 0.0008 in. (0.02 mm.).

4. U-joint spiders must be replaced if their bearing journals are worn more than 0.0059 in. (0.15 mm.) from their original diameter.

Assembly

1. Place the needle rollers in the races and hold them in place with grease.

2. Put the spider into place in its yokes.

3. Replace all seals.

4. Tap the races into position and secure with the snap-rings.

Differential

All models have solid rear drive axles except the PL510, PL610, KPL610, 240, 260 and 280 Z, which have independent rear suspension with the differential carrier solidly mounted.

Solid Rear Axle—PL521, PL620, WPL510, WPL610, LB110, KLB110, PL710, KPL710, B210

Axle Unit Disassembly

1. Remove the rear axle assembly from the vehicle. Disconnect the brake lines at the wheel cylinders.

2. Remove the handbrake linkage.

3. Drain the oil.

4. Unbolt the backing plate from the axle housing. Pull the axle shaft and backing plate out with a slide hammer.

5. From the rear of the backing plate, press off the bearing collar or cut it off with a cold chisel. The collar should not be reused. Pull out the bearing.

NOTE: *Some units use a locknut instead of a bearing collar.*

6. Unbolt and pull out the differential carrier from the axle housing.

Axle Unit Assembly

1. Use a new gasket between the axle housing and differential carrier. Torque the bolts to 14–18 ft lbs. in a diagonal pattern.

2. Install the grease catcher, bearing spacer, bearing packed with grease, and new bearing collar onto the axle shaft. The seal side of the wheel bearing must face the wheel. Coat the oil seal lips with grease. Press on the bearing collar.

3. Adjust the axle end-play by using shims between the backing plate and axle housing. Specified end-play is 0.012–0.020 in. for the WPL510, 0.004 in. for the LB110, KLB110, and B210, 0.001–0.006 in. for the PL620, and 0.004–0.018 in. for the WPL610, PL700 and KPL710.

4. Specified bolt torque for the brake backing plate is 20–28 ft lbs. for the WPL510, 16–20 ft lbs. for the WPL610, PL710 and KPL710, 27–35 ft lbs. for the PL620, and 11–15 ft lbs. for all other models.

5. Refill the unit with oil. See the Capacities Chart.

Differential Overhaul

Disassembly

1. Remove the side bearing caps, marking their locations for reassembly. Remove the differential assembly from the carrier.

2. Pull off the side bearings. Do not mix left and right side parts.

3. Flatten the lock tabs and unbolt the ring gear, loosening the bolts diagonally.

4. Drive out the pinion shaft lock pin from left to right. Remove the pinion shaft and pinions, side gears, and thrust washers. Separate these parts by original location.

5. Remove the drive pinion nut and pull off the flange. Tap the drive pinion back with a soft hammer and remove it with the rear bearing inner race, bearing spacer, and adjusting washer.

6. Remove and discard the oil seal. Remove the front bearing inner race.

7. Pull out the front and rear bearing outer races.

Inspection

1. Wash all parts in a safe solvent. Oil the bearings immediately.

2. Ring and pinion gears must be replaced only in pairs. If the ring gear is warped more than 0.002 in., replace it.

3. Check all parts for wear or distortion. Replace any suspected bearings.

Assembly

1. Assemble the pinions, side gears, pinion shaft, and thrust washers in the case. Clearance between the side gears and thrust washers should be 0.004–0.008 in. Thrust washers are available in various thicknesses for adjustment.

2. Drive in and peen over the lock pin.

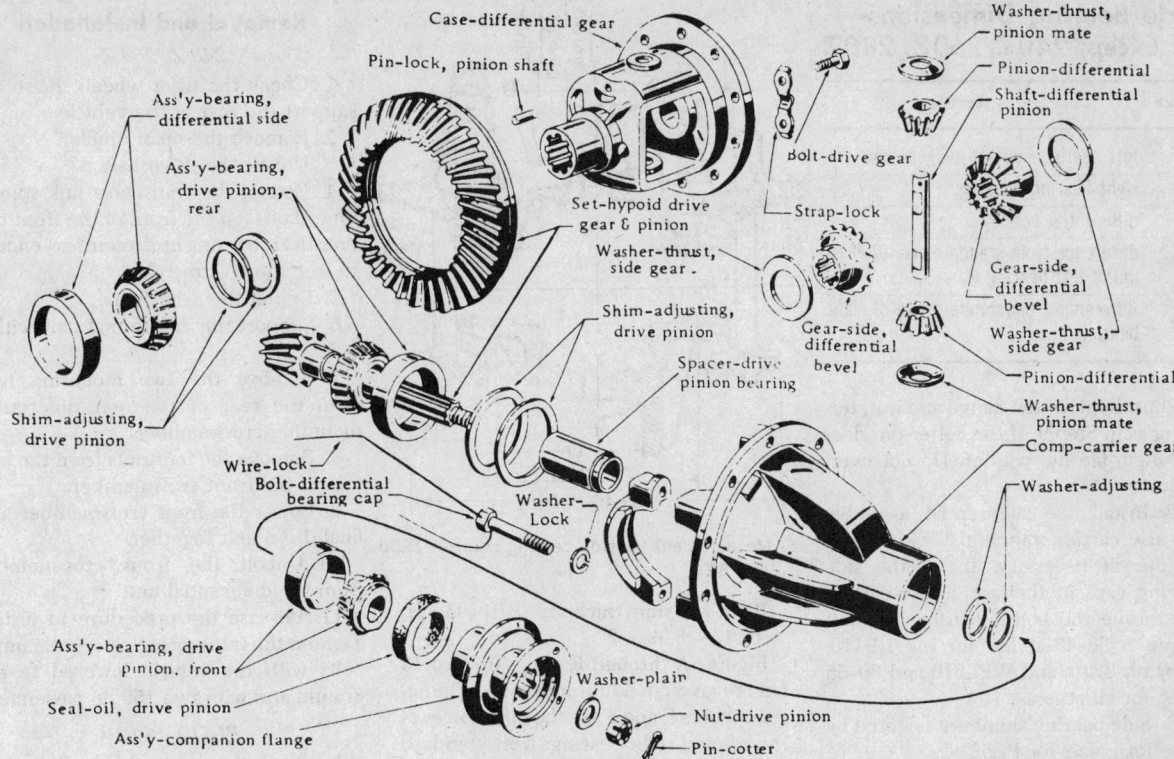

Differential details, WPL510

3. Bolt on the ring gear using new lock tabs. Tighten the bolts diagonally. Specified bolt torques are:

4. Press the side bearing inner races onto the differential case without shims.

5. The drive pinion height is adjusted with shims behind the rear bearing race. Dealers have special tools for making this measurement. Specified standard pinion heights are:

Standard pinion height is measured from the axle centerline to the pinion face. The deviation of the drive pinion from standard size is marked on the pinion face with + for larger and − for smaller. All PL521 are marked in thousandths of an inch. The pinion on all other models is marked in hundredths of a millimeter. There is usually an M mark on pinions graded in hundredths of a millimeter. If no standard pinion height is specified, the adjustment must be made

by use of special tools or by comparing the marks on the old and new drive pinion and adjusting the original shim pack to suit.

6. Press in the drive pinion rear bearing outer race and shims. Press in the front bearing outer race. Press the rear bearing inner race onto the drive pinion.

7. Install the drive pinion and collapsible spacer into the differential carrier without the oil seal. Install the oil seal on the PL620. The front bearing inner race and the flange should be installed. Tighten the flange nut until the torque required to turn the shift (bearing preload) is:

On the WPL610, PL710 and KPL710, preload is adjusted by selecting the proper size washer and spacer. This is done because this model does not use a collapsible spacer. Preload should be 6–9 in. lbs. without an oil seal.

8. Check the drive pinion height again.

9. Torque the flange nut to the specified torque.

10. Make sure that pinion bearing preload is as in Step 7. If it is excessive, a new spacer must be installed.

11. Remove the nut and flange. Press in a new oil seal. Pack grease between the

Pinion face marking, 1200 and B210 is shown

Pinion Bearing Preload (with Oil Seal)

Model	New Bearing (in. lbs.)	Used Bearing (in. lbs.)
LB110, KLB110	5.2-6.9	2.6-3.5
WPL510	8.7-11.3	3.5-4.3
PL620	6-13①	—
HL620	8.7-11.0	—
260Z	7.0-9.1	—
280Z	8.7-11.4	—
B210	5.2-6.9	—
PL610	6.9-9.5	—
HL610	6.1-8.7	—
WPL610	9.5-12.2	—
710	6.1-8.7	—

Drive Axle Flange Nut Torque Specifications

Model		Torque (ft lbs)
WPL510, WPL610		101-130
LB110, KLB110		87-123
L520, SPL311		100-120
PL620		94-145
HL620		101-123
610		123-145
WPL610	W/MT	101-123
	W/AT	101
710		101-123
B210		87-123
HLB210		101-217
260Z 280Z		123-145

Side Bearing Dimensions—All Except 240 Z, 260 Z, 280 Z

Figure	Location
A	left bearing housing of gear carrier
B	right bearing housing
C,D	differential case
E	difference from standard size (0.7874 in.) of left bearing
F	difference from standard size of right bearing

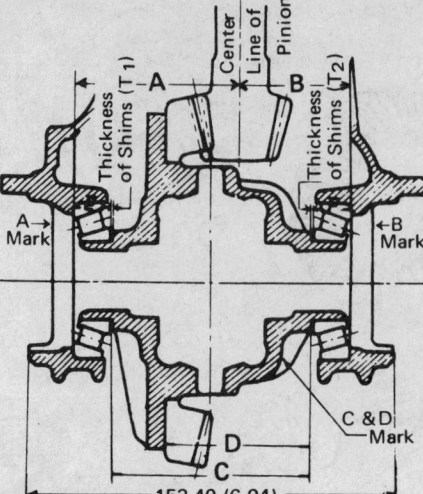

Measurement for side bearing shims—1200 and B210

seal lips. Replace the flange and nut, torquing as in Step 9. If the cotter pin does not align, file the washer. Do not over-torque.

12. Install the differential assembly into the carrier, tapping it with a soft hammer if necessary. Install the side bearing caps in their original locations and torque the bolts. Bearing cap bolt torque is 36–43 ft lbs. for the LB110, KLB110, B210, and WPL610 and 30–35 ft lbs. for all others.

13. Side bearing shims are selected by these formulae, for PL521:

Left side shim thickness=A−C+D+E+0.007 in.

Right side shim thickness=B−D+F+0.006 in.

All figures are read in thousandths of an inch. If old bearings are being reused, the required shim thickness on each side should be reduced by 0.001–0.003 in. to prevent excessive bearing preload.

14. LB110, KLB110 and B210 side bearing shims are selected by these formulae:

Left side shim thickness=A−C+D+E+0.2 mm.

Right side shim thickness=B−D+F+0.2 mm.

Figures A, B, C, and D are as in Step 13, but are read in hundredths of a millimeter. Figures E and F are the differences of the left and right bearings from standard size (17.5 mm.), read in hundredths of a millimeter.

15. WPL610, PL710 and KPL710 side bearing shims are selected by these formulae:

Left side shim thickness = $(A-C+D-H) \times 0.01 + 0.20 + E$

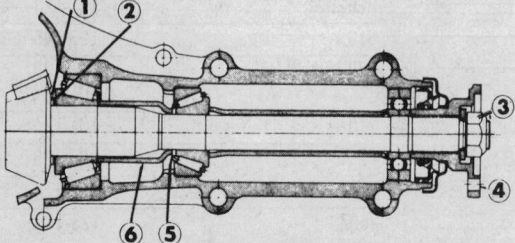

Details of installed drive pinion

Right side shim thickness = $(B-D+H) \times 0.01 + 0.09 + F$

Figures A through F are as in Step 13 but are given in hundredths of a millimeter. Figures E and F are the differences of the left and right bearings from standard size. Figure H is marked on the ring gear.

16. PL620 side bearing shims are selected by these formulae:

Left side shim thickness = $(A-C+D-H) \times 0.01 + 0.175 + E$

Right side shim thickness = $(B-D+H) \times 0.01 + 0.150 + F$

Figures A through H are as in Step 15.

17. Ring and pinion gear backlash should be .006–.008 in., measured with a dial indicator. It should be 0.005–0.007 on the WPL610. If it is excessive, remove some right side shims and place them on the left. If it is too small, change shims from left to right.

18. Make a tooth contact pattern check with red lead. Adjust the drive pinion height and side bearing shims as required.

Final Drive Unit—240, 260, 280 Z, PL510, PL610, KPL610

These vehicles have independent rear suspension with the final drive unit mounted solidly. Although the suspension arrangements differ, the final drive units are virtually identical.

1. Pinion bearing adjusting washer
2. Pinion height adjusting shims
3. Pinion nut
4. Pinion flange
5. Pinion bearing adjusting washer
6. Pinion bearing adjusting spacer

Removal and Installation
240 Z, 260 Z

1. Chock the front wheels. Raise and support the rear of the vehicle.
2. Remove the main muffler.
3. Unbolt the driveshaft.
4. Loosen the transverse link spindle inner bolts (on the front of the front differential mounting crossmember) enough to free the crossmember.
5. Unbolt the axle shafts.
6. Support the differential unit with a jack.
7. Remove the two mounting nuts from the rear of the rear differential mounting crossmember.
8. Remove the four nuts from the bottom of the front crossmember.
9. Lower the front crossmember and final drive unit together.
10. Unbolt the front crossmember from the differential unit.
11. Reverse the procedure to install. Tighten the transverse link spindle inner bolts with the vehicle lowered to the ground and with two 150 lb. passengers.

PL510, PL610

1. Chock the front wheels. Raise and support the rear of the vehicle.
2. Disconnect the handbrake rear cable driveshaft, and axle shafts.
3. Support the differential unit with a jack.
4. Unbolt the differential rear mounting crossmember from body.
5. Remove the four bolts holding the differential to the rear suspension crossmember.
6. Remove the differential to the rear.
7. Support the rear suspension crossmember with stands to prevent damage to the insulators.
8. Unbolt the differential rear mounting crossmember from the differential.
9. Reverse the procedure to install. Pry the differential unit into position.

Disassembly

1. Drain the oil and remove the rear cover.
2. Clamp the housing down securely.
3. Check the tooth contact pattern with red lead.
4. Check the backlash between the ring and pinion with a dial indicator. It should be 0.004–0.008 in.
5. If the tooth contact pattern or gear backlash is incorrect, make sure that runout at the rear of the ring gear does not exceed 0.002 in.
6. Remove the side flange bolts and pull off the side flanges with a slide hammer.
7. Unbolt and pull off the side retainers. Note the original locations of retainers and shims.
8. Remove the differential assembly from the carrier.

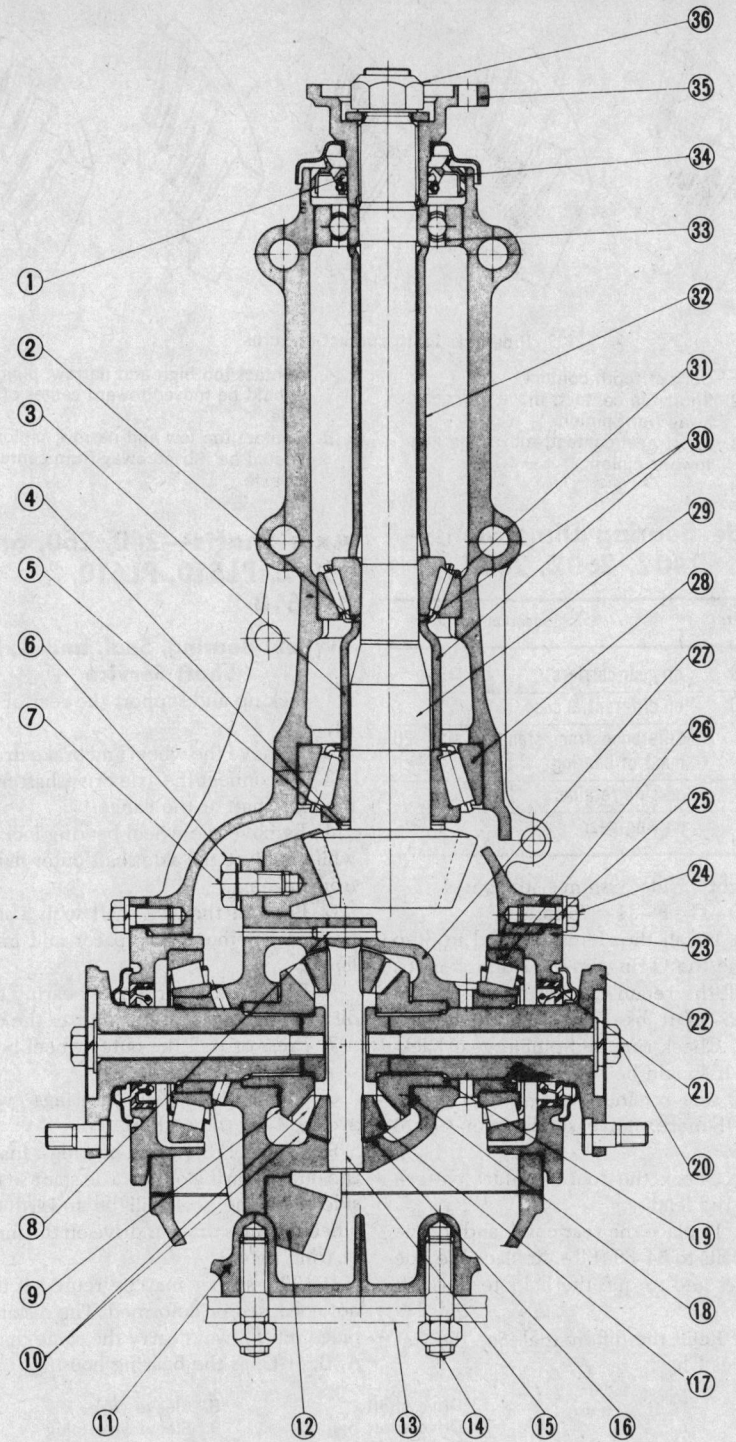

Details of independent rear suspension differential assembly

1. Oil seal
2. Pinion bearing adjusting washer
3. Pinion bearing adjusting spacer
4. Pinion height adjusting shims
5. Pinion height adjusting washer
6. Lock strap
7. Ring gear retaining bolt
8. Pinion shaft lock pin
9. Side gear thrust washer
10. Side gear
11. Rear cover
12. Ring gear
13. Differential mount
14. Nut
15. Pinion shaft
16. Thrust washer
17. Pinion gear
18. Thrust washer
19. Side gear
20. Side flange bolt
21. Oil seal
22. Side flange
23. Side retainer
24. Bolt
25. O-ring
26. Side bearing
27. Differential gear case
28. Drive pinion rear bearing
29. Drive pinion
30. Drive pinion preload adjusting spacer and washer
31. Pinion front bearing
32. Front pilot bearing spacer
33. Front pilot bearing
34. Oil seal
35. Drive pinion flange
36. Drive pinion nut

9. Remove the bearing outer races from the side retainers with an oil seal puller.

10. Hold the drive pinion flange and loosen the nut. Tighten the nut to 123–145 ft lbs. and check the torque required to turn the drive pinion. It should be 2.-6–13 in lbs. Remove the nut and pull off the flange.

11. Press the drive pinion from the gear carrier with the front and rear bearing inner races, bearing spacers, and adjusting washers. Press out the front pilot bearing.

12. Press the drive pinion from the rear bearing.

NOTE: *If the tooth contact pattern and backlash was correct in Steps 3 and 4 and the original ring gear, carrier, drive pinion, rear bearing, and washers are to be reused, it is not necessary to remove the rear bearing.*

13. Press the front and rear bearing outer races from the carrier.

14. Pull off the right differential side gear. Spread the lock straps, loosen and remove the ring gear bolts in a diagonal pattern. Remove the ring gear and pull off the left differential side gear. Do not mix right and left side parts.

15. Punch out the pinion shaft lock pin from the ring gear side. Remove the shaft, differential gears, and thrust washers. Note the original location of all parts.

16. To replace the front oil seal, pull off the seal retainer and pull out the seal. Apply grease between the lips of the new oil seal and drive it into place. Replace the retainer.

NOTE: *The front oil seal can be replaced with the differential mounted on the vehicle, after the driveshaft and flange are removed.*

17. To replace the side oil seals, pull out the seal and drive in the new one, applying grease between the seal lips.

NOTE: *The side oil seals can be replaced with the differential mounted on the vehicle, after the axle shafts, flanges, and retainers are removed.*

Assembly

1. Wash all parts in a safe solvent and oil the bearings immediately.

2. Install the side and pinion gears into the differential case. Replace the pinion shaft. Check the clearance between the side gears and thrust washers. It should be 0.004–0.008 in. Various thicknesses of thrust washers are available for adjustment.

3. Drive in the pinion shaft lock pin. Stake the end of the pin with a punch.

4. Install the ring gear to the differential assembly. Use new lock straps under the bolts. Torque the bolts to 51–58 ft lbs. in a diagonal pattern, tapping the bolt heads lightly before final torquing.

5. Before pressing on new differential

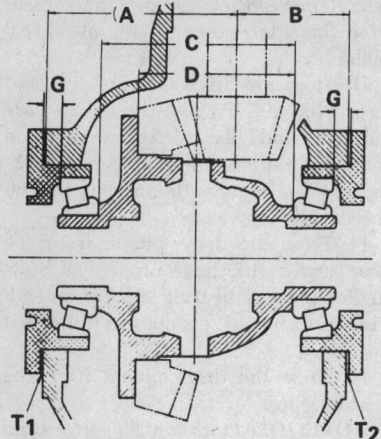

T1   T2

Measurements used in selecting side bearing shims

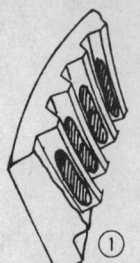 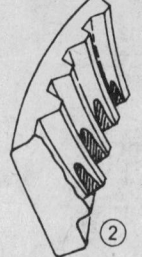 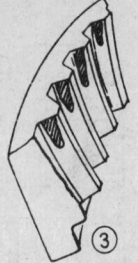 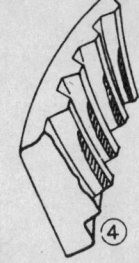 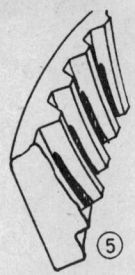

Ring gear tooth contact patterns

1. Correct tooth contact
2. Short toe contact; move ring gear away from pinion.
3. Short heel contact; move ring gear toward pinion.
4. Contact too high and narrow; pinion should be moved toward center of axle.
5. Contact too low and narrow; pinion should be moved away from center of axle.

side bearings, check bearing width. Standard width is 0.787 in (20 mm.).

6. Press the front and rear drive pinion bearing outer races into the gear carrier.

7. Drive pinion bearing preload turning torque should be 6–9 in. lbs, with the pinion flange nut torqued to 123–145 ft lbs. and without the oil seal. This is normally checked and adjusted with special tools.

8. Normal PL510 drive pinion height is 1.909 in. (48.5 mm.) from the axle centerline to the pinion face. Special tools are required to make this adjustment. The height is adjusted by a washer and shims between the rear bearing and the drive pinion gear. The deviation of the drive pinion from standard size, in hundredths of a millimeter, is marked on the pinion face with + for larger and − for smaller. If the drive pinion is replaced, compare the old and new marks and adjust the shim pack to suit.

9. Install the drive pinion, front pilot bearing, and oil seal. Replace the flange and torque the bolt to 123–145 ft lbs.

10. Side bearing shims are selected by these formulae:
Left side shim thickness = $A + C + G - D - E + H + .76$ mm.

Side Bearing Dimensions—240Z, 260Z, 280Z

Figure	Location
A,B	on gear carriers
C,D	on differential case
E,F	difference from standard size (20 mm.) of bearing
G	on side retainers
H	on ring gear

Right side shim thickness = $B + D + G - F - H + .76$ mm.

11. Install the shims selected in Step 10 and the O-rings in the side retainers. Install the retainers. Bolt torque should be 6.5–8.7 ft lbs.

12. Check ring and pinion gear backlash. It should be 0.004–0.008 in. If less, move side retainer shims from right to left. If more, move shims from left to right.

13. Check the tooth contact pattern with red lead.

14. Replace the rear cover and torque the bolts to 54–69 ft lbs. Replace the side flanges and torque the bolts to 14–19 ft lbs.

15. Refill the differential. See the Capacities Chart.

Axle Shafts—240, 260, and 280 Z, PL510, PL610, KPL610

Wheel Bearing, Seal, and Axle Shaft Service

1. Jack up and support the rear of the car.

2. Remove the wheel and brake drum.

3. Disconnect the axle driveshaft from the axle shaft at the flange.

4. Remove the wheel bearing locknut while holding the axle shaft outer flange from turning.

5. Pull out the axle shaft with a slide hammer. Remove the spacer and inner flange.

6. Drive the inner wheel bearing and oil seal out toward the center of the car.

7. Press or pull the outer wheel bearing from the axle shaft.

8. Pack the wheel bearings with grease. Coat the seal lip.

9. Reinstall the wheel bearings. Install the outer bearing on the axle shaft so the side with the seal will be toward the wheel. Always press or drive on the inner bearing race.

10. The spacer may be reused if it is not collapsed or deformed. The distance piece must always carry the same mark, A, B, or C, as the bearing housing.

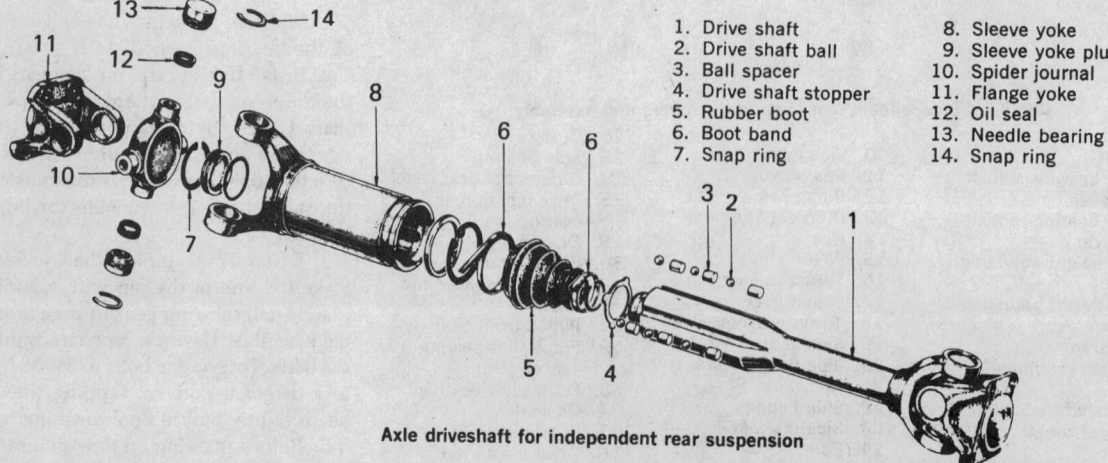

1. Drive shaft
2. Drive shaft ball
3. Ball spacer
4. Drive shaft stopper
5. Rubber boot
6. Boot band
7. Snap ring
8. Sleeve yoke
9. Sleeve yoke plug
10. Spider journal
11. Flange yoke
12. Oil seal
13. Needle bearing
14. Snap ring

Axle driveshaft for independent rear suspension

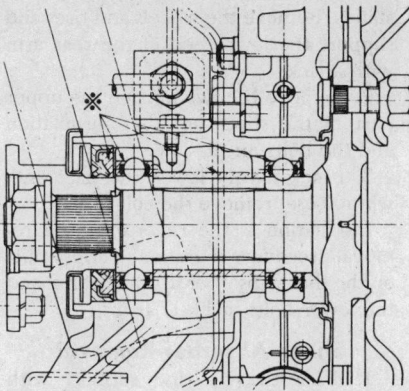

* indicates areas to receive grease

11. Fill the area illustrated with grease.

12. Replace the axle shaft and flange. Tighten the bearing locknut to the specified torque.

13. The torque required to start the axle shaft turning should be 3.9 in. lbs. or less. This is a 28.7 oz or less pull at the hub bolt. Axle shaft end-play, checked with a dial indicator, should be 0–0.006 in.

14. If the turning torque or axle shaft play is incorrect, disassemble the unit and install a new distance piece.

Driveshaft

The axle driveshafts must be removed and disassembled to lubricate the ball splines every 30,000 miles. Handle the driveshaft carefully; it is easily damaged. No repair parts for the driveshafts are available. If a driveshaft is defective in any way, it must be replaced as an assembly.

To disassemble:

1. Remove the U-joint spider from the differential end of the shaft.

2. Remove the snap-ring and sleeve yoke plug.

3. Compress the driveshaft and remove the snap-ring and stopper.

4. Disconnect the boot and separate the driveshaft carefully so as not to lose the balls and spacer.

5. Pack about 10 grams (0.35 oz) of grease into the ball grooves. Also pack about 35 grams (1.23 oz) of grease into the area illustrated.

6. Twisting play between the two shaft halves should not exceed 0.004 in. Check play with the driveshaft completely compressed.

7. While reassembling, adjust the U-joint side play to 0.001 in. or less by selecting suitable snap-rings. Four different thicknesses are available for adjustment. Axle driveshaft flange nut torque is 36–43 ft lbs.

REAR SUSPENSION
Leaf Spring Type B210

Spring Removal and Installation

1. Raise the rear axle until the wheels hang free. Support the car on stands. Support the rear axle with a jack.

2. Unbolt the bottom end of shock absorber.

3. Unbolt the axle from the spring leaves. Unbolt and remove the front spring bracket. Lower the front of the spring to the floor.

4. Unbolt and remove the spring rear shackle.

5. Before reinstallation, coat the front bracket pin, bushing, shackle pin, and shackle bushing with a soap solution.

6. Reverse the procedure to install. The front pin nut and the shock absorber mounting should be tightened before the vehicle is lowered to the floor.

Shock Absorber Removal and Installation

To remove the rear shock absorbers, simply unbolt the lower and upper ends. The upper nuts are under the rear seat back. The shock absorbers are not serviceable and should be replaced if defective. Mounting bolt torques are given under "Spring Removal and Installation".

WPL510, WPL610, PL710, KPL710

Spring Removal and Installation

1. Raise the rear axle until the wheels hang free. Support the car on stands. Support the rear axle with a floor jack.

2. Remove the spare tire.

3. Unbolt the bottom end of the shock absorber.

4. Unbolt the axle from the spring leaves.

5. Unbolt the front spring bracket from the body. Lower the spring end and bracket to the floor.

6. Unbolt and remove the rear shackle.

7. Unbolt the bracket from the spring.

8. Before reinstallation, coat the front bracket pin and bushing, and the shackle pin and bushing with a soap solution.

9. Reverse the procedure to install. The front pin nut and the shock absorber mounting should be tightened after the vehicle is lowered to the floor. Make sure that the elongated flange of the rubber bumper is to the rear.

Shock Absorber Removal and Installation

When removing the WPL510 shock absorber, unbolt the upper bracket from the body and remove the shock absorber and bracket as a unit. The WPL610 shock absorbers have a conventional strap mounting at the top. The shock absorbers are not serviceable and should be replaced if defective. Mounting bolt torques are given under "Spring Removal and Installation".

Independent Rear Suspension—PL510, PL610, KPL610, 240, 260, and 280Z

Coil Spring Removal and Installation—PL510, PL610, KPL610

1. Raise the rear of the vehicle and support it on stands.

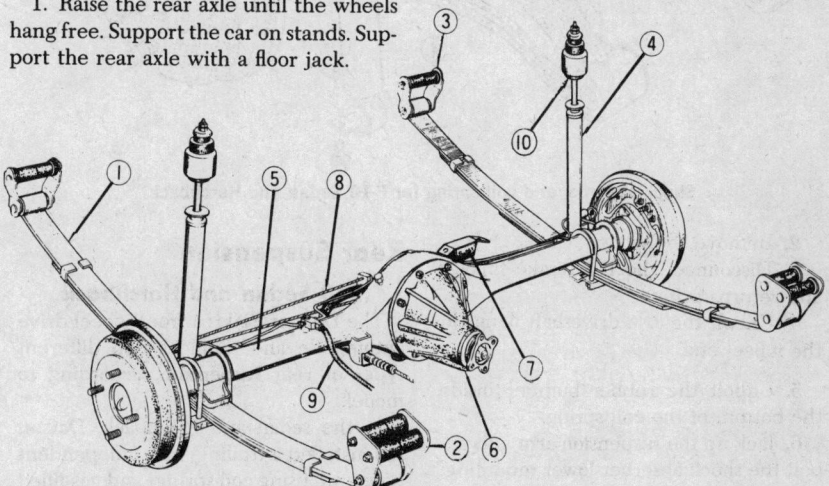

Leaf spring rear suspension, LB110, KLB110, B210 shown

1. Leaf spring
2. Front mounting
3. Shackle
4. Shock absorber
5. Axle housing
6. Differential carrier
7. Torque arrester
8. Handbrake cable
9. Brake hose
10. Bound bumper

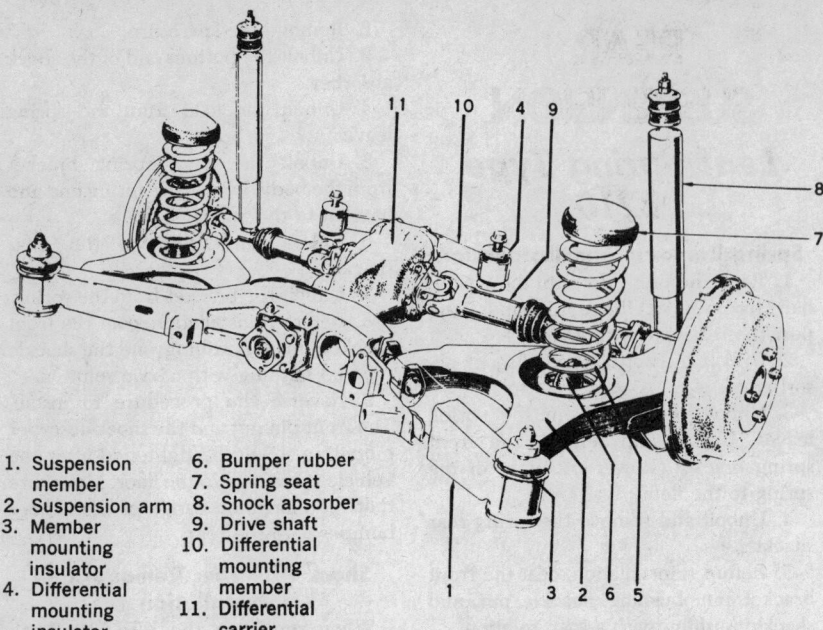

1. Suspension member
2. Suspension arm
3. Member mounting insulator
4. Differential mounting insulator
5. Coil spring
6. Bumper rubber
7. Spring seat
8. Shock absorber
9. Drive shaft
10. Differential mounting member
11. Differential carrier

Sedan independent rear suspension

1. Rubber seat
2. Coil spring
3. Rear arm
4. Shock absorber

Shock absorber and coil spring for F-10 Sedan and Hatchback

2. Remove the wheels.

3. Disconnect the handbrake linkage and return spring.

4. Unbolt the axle driveshaft flange at the wheel end.

5. Unbolt the rubber bumper inside the bottom of the coil spring.

6. Jack up the suspension arm and unbolt the shock absorber lower mounting.

7. Lower the jack slowly and cautiously. Remove the coil spring, spring seat, and rubber bumper.

8. Reverse the procedure to install, making sure that the flat face of the spring is at the top.

Rear Suspension

F10 Sedan and Hatchback

The Datsun F10 is a front wheel drive automobile and employs two different types of rear suspension, according to model.

In the sedan and hatchback, Datsun has installed a trailing arm, independent type unit, using coil springs and gas-filled shock absorbers.

In the Sport Wagon, Datsun uses a semi-elliptic leaf spring unit on a rigid axle tube equipped with the same shocks as the sedan and hatchback.

Coil Spring Removal

1. Raise the car and support with jack

stands. Remove the wheels and tires and support the lower end of the rear arm with a jack.

2. Remove the two nuts on the upper part of the shock absorber installation and the bolts on the lower.

3. Progressively lower the jack and, when loose, remove the coil spring.

Installation is the reverse of the removal procedure. Torque the upper nuts on the shock absorber to 12–16 ft lbs. and the lower bolts to 11–17 ft lbs.

Shock Absorber Removal

1. Raise the car and support with safety stands.

2. Remove the wheel and tire and securely support the lower end of the rear arm with a jack. Remove nuts (upper side) and bolts (lower) from the shock absorber.

3. Slowly lower the jack and remove the shock absorber.

Installation is the reverse of removal. Torque the upper nuts to 12–16 ft lbs. and the lower bolts to 11–17 ft lbs.

Sport Wagon Leaf Spring Removal

1. Raise the car and support it with safety stands. Remove the wheels and tires.

2. Remove the nuts from the lower shock absorber bracket.

3. Remove the nuts from the U-bolts and remove the bumper rubber and spring seat.

4. Using a jack, raise the axle until it clears the spring and remove the hand brake clamp.

5. Remove the front pin and shackle and remove the spring from the automobile.

Installation is the reverse of removal.
U-bolt nut torque - 26–29 ft lbs.
Shackle nut torque - 12–14 ft lbs.
Front Pin nut torque - 12–16 ft lbs.
Front Pin bolt torque - 6.5–10 ft lbs.
NOTE: *When putting shackle and front pin in place, the leaf spring should be under a normal load.*

Shock Absorber Removal

1. Raise the car and support with safety stands. Remove the wheels and tires.

2. Remove the nuts from the lower shock bracket and, after removing the cover from the upper bracket, remove the nuts. Take out the shock absorber.

Installation is the reverse of removal. The nuts (upper and lower) should be torqued to 12–16 ft lbs.

Sedan and Hatchback Rear Arm Removal

1. Raise the car and support it with safety stands. Remove the wheels and tires.

2. Loosen the flare nut on the brake

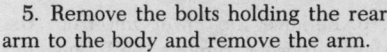

NOTE: *Replace any bushings that are cracked or damaged before installation.*

Installation is the reverse of removal. The torques are:

Rear Arm bolt - 40–48 ft lbs.
Lower Shock bolt - 11–17 ft lbs.
Upper Shock nut - 12–16 ft lbs.
Disc bolt - 18–25 ft lbs.
Brake Tube Flare nut - 11–13 ft lbs.
Brake Hose Connector - 10–13 ft lbs.
Lug Nut - 58–65 ft lbs.

Sport Wagon Axle Tube Removal

1. Raise the car and support with safety stands. Remove the wheels and tires.

2. Remove the brake tube flare nut, clevis pin and remove the hand brake rear cable.

3. Remove the brake hose and cable bracket and detach the hand brake cable from the tube.

4. Remove the bearing cap, cotterpin and lock nut and pull the drum and bearing.

5. Remove the brake assembly and support the lower end of the tube with a jack.

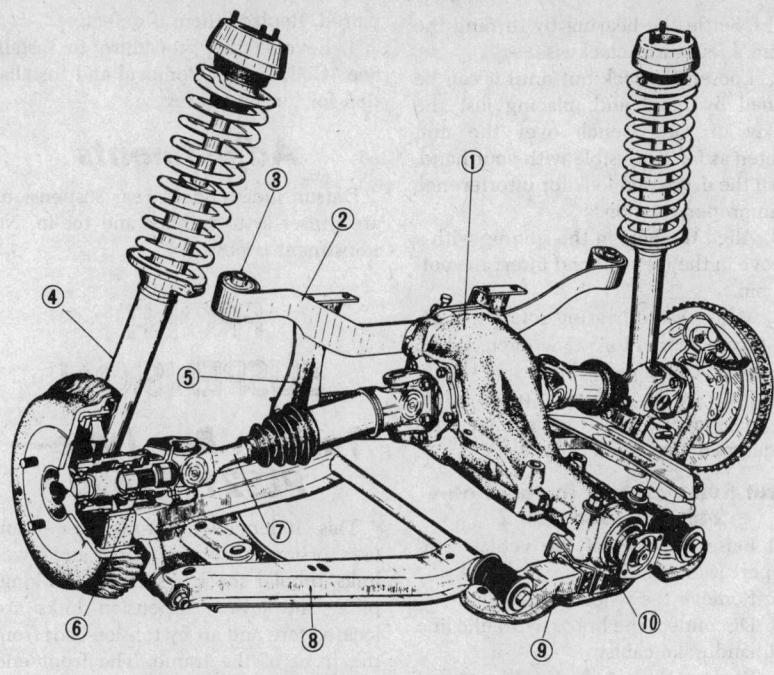

240 Z, 260 Z independent rear suspension

1. Differential carrier
2. Differential case mount rear member
3. Differential case mount rear insulator
4. Strut assembly
5. Link mount brace

6. Rear axle shaft
7. Drive shaft
8. Transverse link
9. Differential case mount front member
10. Differential case mount front insulator

tube and remove it. Install a plug to prevent leakage.

3. Remove the hand brake wire, bearing cap, cotter pin and lock nut. Remove the drum and roller bearing.

4. Remove the rear brake assembly and securely support the rear arm with a jack.

Remove the nuts from the upper shock bracket and the bolts from the lower. As the jack is slowly lowered, remove the shock absorber and coil spring.

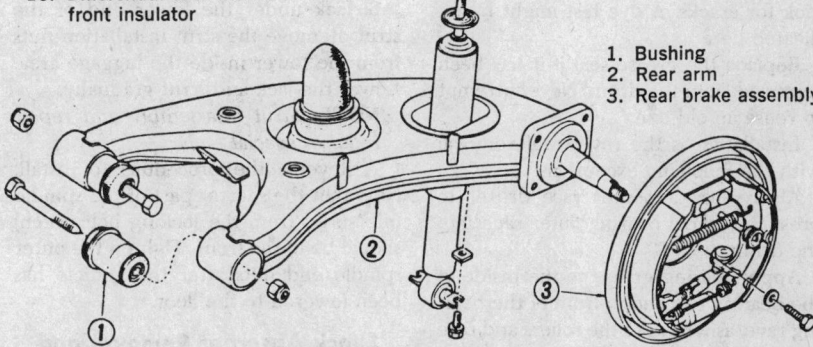

1. Bushing
2. Rear arm
3. Rear brake assembly

Rear arm—F-10 sedan and hatchback

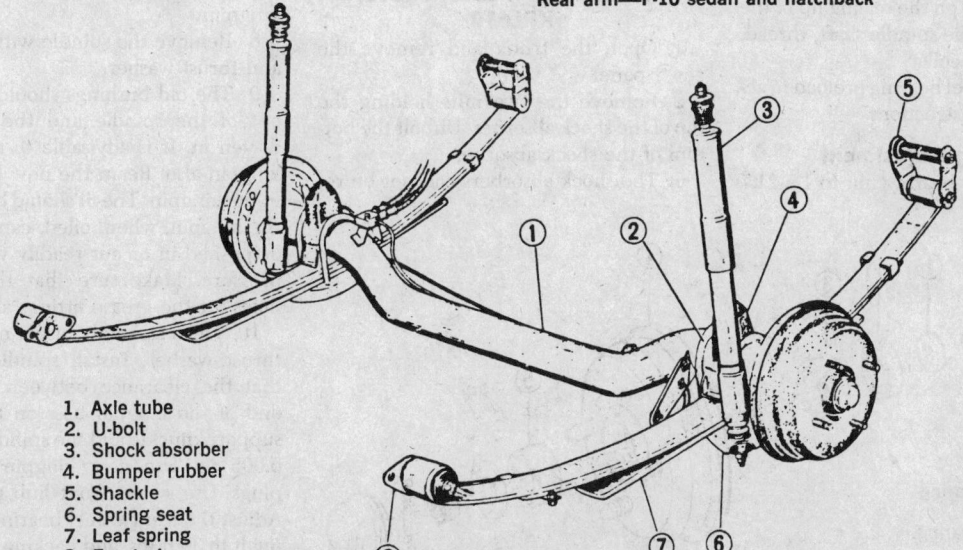

1. Axle tube
2. U-bolt
3. Shock absorber
4. Bumper rubber
5. Shackle
6. Spring seat
7. Leaf spring
8. Front pin

Rear suspension—F-10 Sports Wagon

6. Remove the lower nut from the shock absorber, remove the U-bolts and take off the axle tube.

Installation is the reverse of removal, with the following torque values:
Brake flare nut - 11–13 ft lbs.
Brake hose connector - 2.2–2.9 ft lbs.
Disc attaching bolt - 18–25 ft lbs.
Shock absorber nut - 12–16 ft lbs.
U-bolt nut - 25–29 ft lbs.
Lug Nut - 54–61 ft lbs.

F10 Rear Wheel Bearing and Drum Service

1. Raise the car and support with safety stands. Remove the wheel and tire.
2. Remove the bearing cap, cotter pin and lock nut and pull the drum and bearing.
3. Pry out the seal from the rear of the drum with a screwdriver and drive out the bearing outer race, using a drift and mallet. Apply even blows through the two grooves inside the drum.

Check the drum for cracks or distortion and clean the bearing with solvent, blowing dry with compressed air.

Check the bearing for free movement, noise and cracks and check the condition of the outer race.

Look over the spindle for evidence of bearing creep or damaged threads and look for cracks. A dye test might be indicated here.

Replace the grease seal if it has been removed from the drum. Never attempt to reuse an old one.

Installation is the reverse of removal with the following exceptions:

Always use an outer race drifter to press the wheel bearing outer race into the drum.

Apply bearing grease to the inside of the bearing cap and in front of the bearing race, as well as to the rollers and race surface of the bearing. Put a small amount of grease on the sealing lip of the grease seal and the spindle shaft, thread, lock washer and collar.

Adjust the wheel bearing preload in accordance with instructions.

Bearing Adjustment

1. Tighten the bearing nut to 18–21.7

ft lbs. Settle the bearing by turning the drum a few turns clockwise.
2. Loosen the lock nut until it can be turned by hand and, placing just the socket of the wrench over the nut, tighten as far as possible with your hand. Turn the drum and look for interference or improper rotation.
3. Align the hole in the spindle with a groove in the lock nut and insert the cotter pin.
4. Measure the bearing rotation starting torque with a torque wrench. When the grease seal is new, the torque should be 2.6–6.1 in. lbs. and when used, 3.5 in. lbs. maximum. Repeat adjustment until torque matches specifications.

Strut Removal and Installation— 240, 260, and 280 Z

1. Raise the rear of the vehicle and support it on stands.
2. Remove the wheels.
3. Disconnect the brake hydraulic line and handbrake cable.
4. Remove the nuts from either end of the transverse link outer spindle. Remove the spindle center locking bolt. Pull out the spindle. Separate the bottom of the strut from the transverse link.
5. Unbolt the axle driveshaft flange at the wheel end.
6. Jack under the lower end of the strut. Remove the strut installation nuts from the tower inside the luggage area. Lower the jack and strut gradually.

NOTE: Strut disassembly and repair requires special tools.

7. Reverse the procedure to install. Note that the shorter part of the spindle (measured from the locking bolt notch) should be to the front. Tighten the outer spindle end nuts after the vehicle has been lowered to the floor.

Shock Absorber Removal and Installation—PL510, PL610, KPL610

1. Open the trunk and remove the cover panel.
2. Remove the two nuts holding the top of the shock absorber. Unbolt the bottom of the shock absorber.
3. The shock absorbers can not be re-

paired. Replace them if defective.
4. Reverse the procedure to install. See "Coil Spring" Removal and Installation for torque figures.

Adjustments

Datsun independent rear suspensions are preset as to camber and toe-in. No adjustment is possible.

FRONT SUSPENSION

Torsion Bar Type— PL521, PL620

This independent front suspension uses torsion bar springs, upper and lower links, tubular shock absorbers, and kingpins. The lower suspension links are located fore and aft by tension rods from the front of the frame. The front end height can be adjusted to compensate for normal spring sagging.

Kingpin and Bushing Replacement

1. Block the front of the truck.
2. Remove the wheels.
3. Unscrew the front wheel brake hose connections.
4. Remove the hubcap and spindle nut. Remove the hub and drum with the wheel bearing.
5. Remove the brake backing plate from the spindle.
6. Disconnect the tie rod from each spindle.
7. Take out the kingpin lock bolt and remove the upper spindle plug. It may be necessary to drill and tap a hole to pull the plug out. Drive the kingpin down to remove the bottom plug. Tap out the kingpins.
8. Remove the spindle with the shims and thrust washer.
9. The old bushings should be driven out of the spindle and the new ones driven in. It is advisable to replace the kingpin also. Ream the new bushings to fit the kingpin. The fit should be such that the kingpin, when oiled, can be turned or pushed in or out readily with thumb pressure. Make sure that the bushing holes for the grease fittings are open.
10. On reassembly, use a new spindle thrust washer. Install spindle shims so that the clearance between the upper end of the kingpin boss on the spindle support knuckle and the spindle is 0.003– 0.005 in. Use new kingpin expansion plugs. Use a new front hub grease seal. Adjust the front wheel bearing by torquing it to 30 ft lbs. and backing off ⅛ turn. On the PL620, the torque should be 22–25 ft lbs.

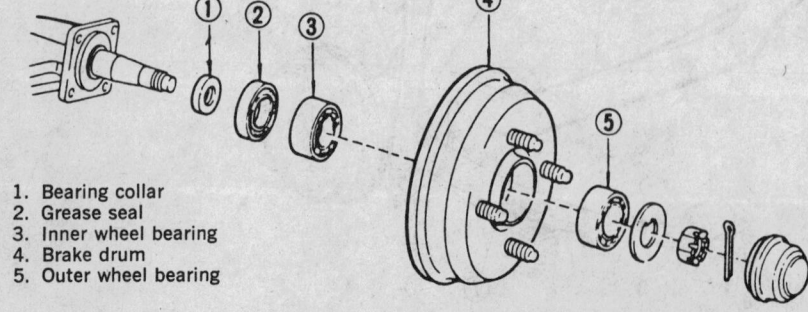

1. Bearing collar
2. Grease seal
3. Inner wheel bearing
4. Brake drum
5. Outer wheel bearing

F-10 rear brake drum and bearing assembly

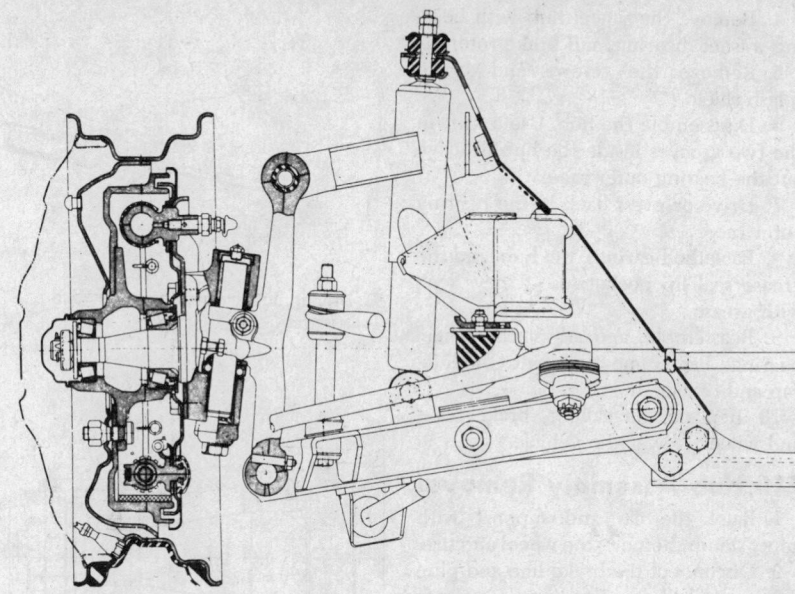

Front Suspension—Sectional View, PL620

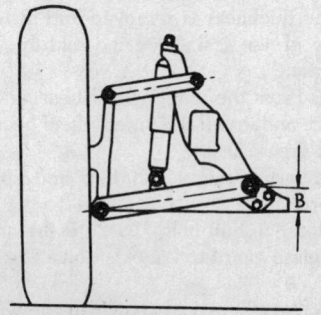

Check measurement (B) after adjusting front suspension height

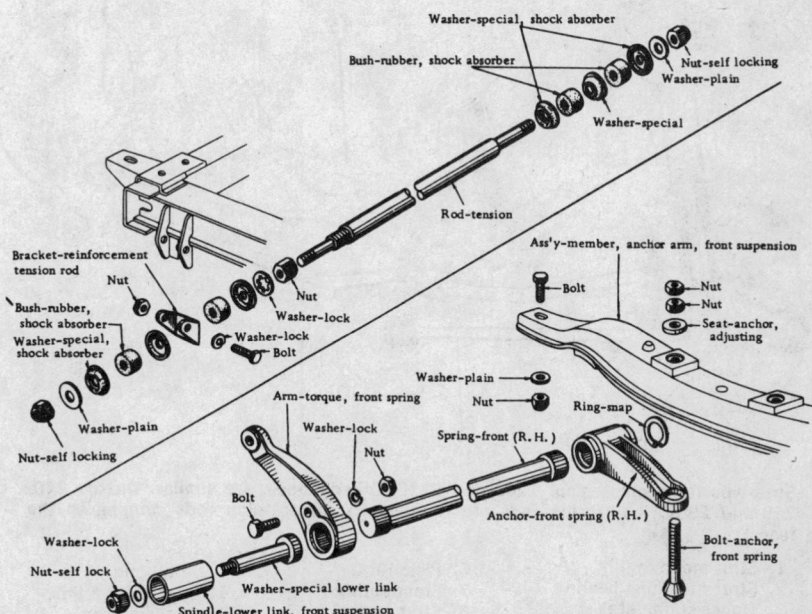

Tension rod assembly, top, and torsion bar assembly, bottom

bines the function of coil spring and shock absorber. The spindle is mounted to the lower part of the strut which has a single ball joint. No upper suspension arm is required in this design. The spindle and lower suspension transverse link (control arm) are located fore and aft by tension rods to the front part of the chassis on most models. Compression rods, which run rearward, are used on the 240, 260 and 280 Z. A cross-chassis sway bar is used on all models.

Wheel Bearing Adjustment

1. Jack up the car and remove the wheel.
2. Remove the hubcap and cotter pin.
3. Torque the spindle nut to:

Spindle Nut Torque Specifications

Model	Torque (ft lbs)
240Z, 260Z, 710, 280Z	18-22
510, 610, B210	22-25
110	16-17
F-10	87-145

4. Turn the hub a few turns in each direction and retorque the nut.
5. Loosen the nut 60–75° on the "Z" series, 90° on the PL510, PL610, KPL610, WPL510, WPL610, PL710 and KPL710, and 40–70° on the LB110, KLB110 and B210. Insert the cotter pin.
6. Turn the hub a few more turns.
7. Hub turning torque, with the disc brake pads removed, should be:

11. Grease the suspension and bleed the brake system.

Tension Rod Adjustment

There are three adjusting nuts on each tension rod. There is one at the lower suspension link end and two at the frame end. Adjust these nuts until both rubber bushings at the frame end are compressed to 0.43 in.

Suspension Height Adjustment

1. Jack up the vehicle under the front suspension crossmember to unload the torsion bars.
2. Turn the rear torsion bar anchor bolt right to lower the vehicle and left to raise it.
3. Dimension B in the illustration should be 3.07–3.23 in. on the PL620, with the vehicle empty and resting on its wheels.

Wheel Alignment

Caster and camber are adjusted by shims placed between the upper suspension link spindle and the crossmember.

Toe-in is adjusted at the center tie-rod. See the Wheel Alignment Specifications Chart for alignment specifications.

Strut Type—PL510, PL610, KPL610, PL710, KPL710, WPL510, WPL610, LB110, KLB110, B210, F-10, 240, 260, and 280 Z

This independent front suspension uses McPherson struts. Each strut com-

Front Wheel Bearing Adjustment Specifications

Model	Torque (ft lbs)	Pull at hub bolt lbs
240Z	3.5-7.4	1.5-3.3
260Z, 280Z	—	3.5-7.4
B210	—	2.6
110	15.6-20.0	7.1-8.8
510 (w/new bearing and Seal)	6.1	—
510 (w/used bearing and Seal)	3.5	—
610	—	1.5
710	—	3.3
F-10	—	3-11

If torque is excessive, check the wheel bearing condition. There should be no hub end-play.

8. Replace the hubcap, brake pads, and wheel. Lower the car.

Hub Assembly Removal and Installation

1. Jack up the vehicle, remove the wheel, and disconnect the brake hose.
2. Unbolt and remove the brake caliper assembly.
3. Remove the hubcap, cotter pin, and spindle nut.

4. Remove the wheel hub with bearing washer, bearing, and brake rotor.
5. Remove the screws and brake splash shield.
6. Disassemble the hub. Use a drift in the two grooves inside the hub to drive out the bearing outer race.
7. Drive or press back in the bearing outer race.
8. Pack the bearings, the hub, and the grease seal lip pocket (use a new seal) with grease.
9. Reassemble, and adjust the wheel bearings. Pack some grease into the hub-cap and replace it.
10. Replace the caliper, brake hose, and wheel. Lower the vehicle.

F10 Hub Assembly Removal

1. Raise the car and support with safety stands. Remove the wheel and tire.
2. Disconnect the brake line and plug to prevent leakage. Remove the caliper assembly.
3. Pull out the cotter pin and remove the lock nut from the hub and driveshaft. Hold the hub steady to prevent turning.

NOTE: *It is good policy to install lug nuts during this operation to prevent damage to the threads.*

4. Pull the hub from the driveshaft

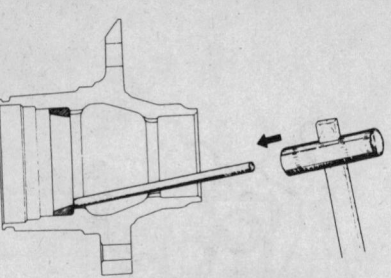

Driving out the bearing outer race

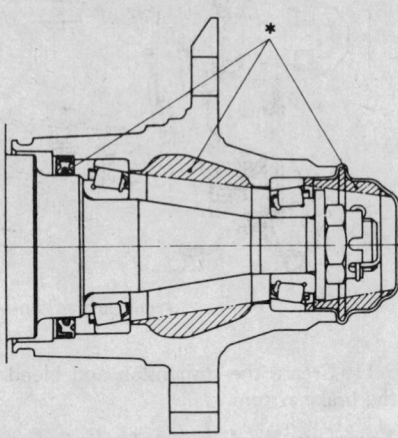

*indicates areas to be filled with grease

with a hub puller. Make sure the wheel are pointed straight ahead to prevent undue forces on the driveshafts.
5. Remove the driveshaft, being careful not to damage the grease seal on the knuckle.
6. Remove the splash guard and disconnect the lower ball joint and side rod ball joint from the knuckle. Be careful not to damage the ball joint dust cover.
7. Remove the bolts holding the knuckle to the strut and remove the knuckle.
8. Using a bearing puller, remove the wheel bearing and grease seal from the hub, should they need replacement, and drive the bearing races and grease seal from the knuckle using a drift.

Installation

1. Lubricate the wheel bearings and, using an outer race drifter, install the outer race in the knuckle and the outside bearing outer race in place.
2. Replace the spacer with one of the same thickness as removed and install a new grease seal. Pack the seal lip with grease.
3. Press the outer wheel bearing into place and install the inner wheel bearing and grease seal.
4. Install the wheel hub and splash guard.

Rotor to hub bolt - 18–25 ft lbs.

Splash guard to knuckle bolt - 18–25 ft lbs.

5. Put the proper spacer in the wheel hub assembly and place the drive shaft into the knuckle and fit to wheel hub.

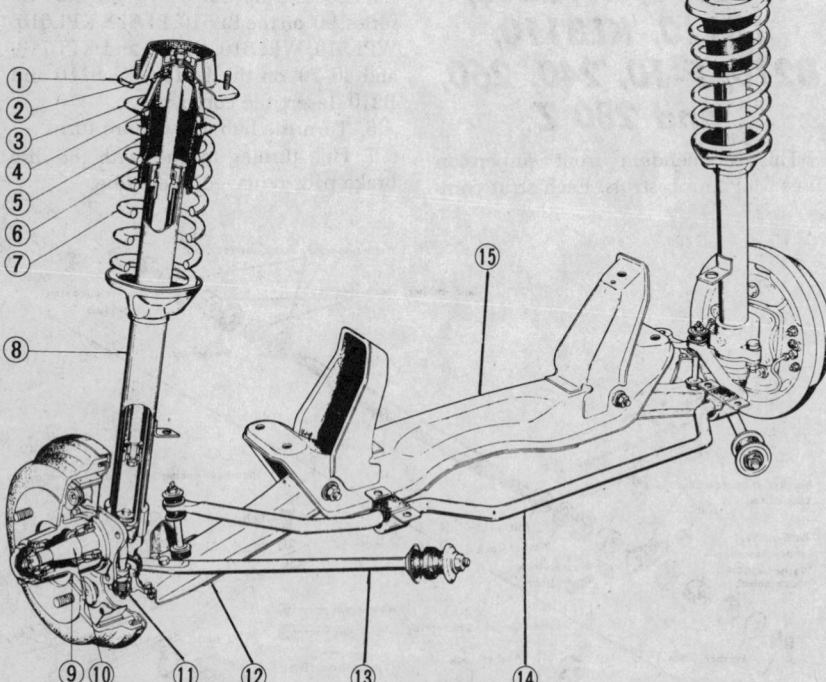

Strut-type front suspension, 1200 and B210. Other models are similar. On the 240, 260 and 280Z, the tension rods are replaced by compression rods running to the rear.

1. Strut mounting
2. Strut mounting bearing
3. Upper spring seat
4. Bumper rubber
5. Dust cover
6. Piston rod
7. Front spring
8. Strut assembly
9. Hub assembly
10. Spindle
11. Ball joint
12. Transverse link
13. Tension rod
14. Stabilizer
15. Suspension member

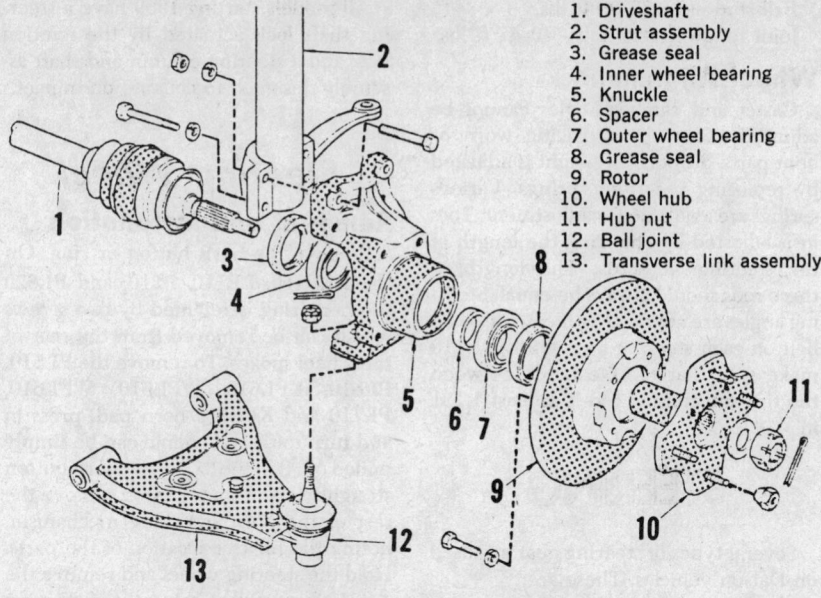

1. Driveshaft
2. Strut assembly
3. Grease seal
4. Inner wheel bearing
5. Knuckle
6. Spacer
7. Outer wheel bearing
8. Grease seal
9. Rotor
10. Wheel hub
11. Hub nut
12. Ball joint
13. Transverse link assembly

F-10 wheel hub and knuckle

izer bar from the transverse link.

4. Unbolt the steering arm.

5. Place a jack under the bottom of the strut.

6. Open the hood and remove the nuts holding the top of the strut.

7. Lower the jack slowly and cautiously until the strut assembly can be removed.

8. Reverse the procedure to install. The self locking nuts holding the top of the strut must be replaced.

Ball Joint Inspection

Ball joints cannot be disassembled. Check ball stud turning torque with ball joint properly lubricated. If torque is excessively higher or lower than specified, replace ball joint.

New parts: 65–109 in lbs.
Used parts: 43 in lbs.

Ball Joint Removal and Installation

The lower ball joint should be replaced when up and down (axial) play exceeds the standard play of 0.012–0.040 in. for the LB110 and KLB110, 0.004–0.012 in.

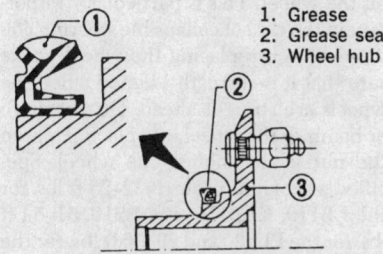

1. Grease
2. Grease seal
3. Wheel hub

Wheel bearing grease seal installation—F-10

6. The inner wheel bearing will install itself to the hub while you tighten the hub nut. Tighten the nut to 87–145 ft lbs.

7. Spin the hub several times in both directions to check for freedom of movement. Then measure bearing preload.

Rotation start at wheel hub bolt is 3–11 lbs.

NOTE: *If the bearing preload does not meet specifications, replace as follows: If preload is lower - install a smaller spacer.*

If preload is greater - install a larger.

8. Bolt the knuckle to the strut and lower Ball joint. Secure the drive shaft to the side flange, the caliper to the splash guard and the side rod ball joint to the knuckle arm.

Knuckle to strut bolt - 24–33 ft lbs.
Lower ball stud nut - 22–29 ft lbs.
Drive shaft bolt - 29–36 ft lbs.
Caliper bolt - 40–47 ft lbs.
Side rod ball stud nut - 40–47 ft lbs.

9. Reconnect the brake line and tighten flare to 11–13 ft lbs.

10. Install the wheel and tire, lower the car and bleed the brake system.

Strut Removal and Installation All Models

1. Jack up the car and support it safely. Remove the wheel.

2. Disconnect and plug the brake hose.

3. Disconnect the tension rod (compression rod on the "Z" series) and stabil-

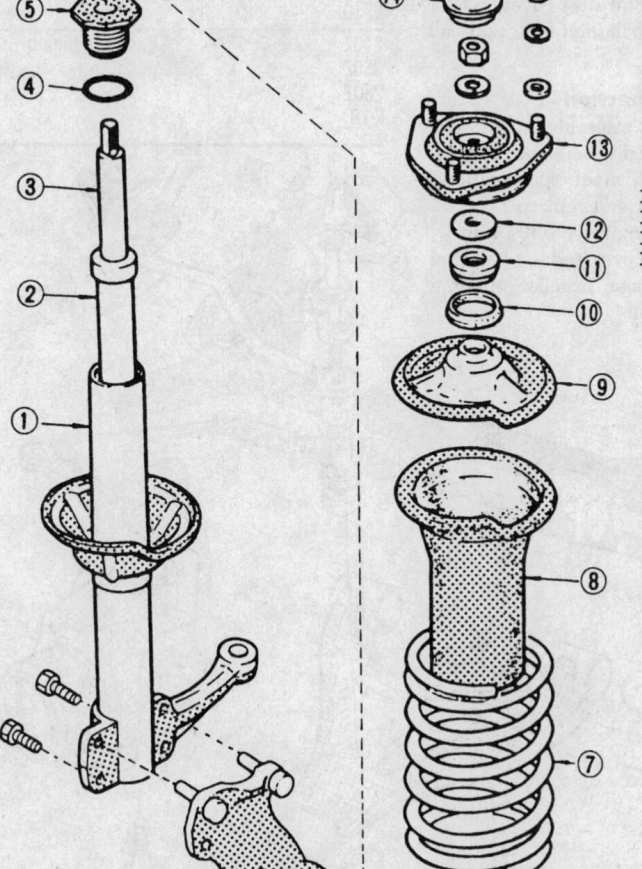

1. Strut
2. Cylinder
3. Piston rod
4. O-ring
5. Gland packing
6. Bumper rubber
7. Coil spring
8. Dust cover
9. Spring seat
10. Dust seal
11. Seat
12. Plate
13. Mounting insulator
14. Cap

F-10 suspension strut

for the B210, 0.040 in. for the PL610, KPL610, WPL610, PL710 and KPL710, or 0.012–0.014 in. for the other models. The ball joint should be greased every 30,000 miles. There is a plugged hole in the bottom of the joint for installation of a grease fitting.

1. Raise and support the car so the wheels hang free. Remove the wheel.

2. Unbolt the tension rod (compression rod on "Z" series) and stabilizer bar from transverse link.

3. Unbolt the strut from the steering arm.

4. Remove the cotter pin and ball joint stud nut. Separate the ball joint and steering arm.

5. Unbolt the ball joint from the transverse link.

6. Reverse the procedure to install a new ball joint. Grease the joint after installation.

F10 Ball Joint Removal

1. Raise the car and support with safety stands. Remove the wheel and tire.

2. Remove the nut holding the ball stud to the knuckle and force out the stud with a suitable tool, being careful not to damage the ball joint dust cover.

3. Remove the ball joint bolts and ball joint.

Inspection

The ball joint is assembled at the factory and cannot be disassembled. If measurements do not meet specifications, discard entire unit and replace.

Ball stud swinging force - 30 in. lbs.

Check the dust cover and the ball stud for cracks or damage. Installation is the reverse of removal.

Ball stud nut - 22–29 ft lbs.
Joint to lower arm bolt - 40–47 ft lbs.

Wheel Alignment

Caster and camber angles cannot be adjusted except by replacing worn or bent parts. Suspension height is adjusted by replacing the front springs. Various springs are available for adjustment. Toe-in is adjusted by changing the length of the steering side-rods. The length of these rods should always be equal. Steering angles are adjusted by means of a stop bolt on each steering arm. On the B110 make sure that the clearance between the tire and tension rod is at least 1.181 in.

STEERING

Several types of steering gear are used on Datsun vehicles. These are:

Steering Applications

Model	Type
110, 510, 610, 521, 620, 710, B210	Recirculating ball
240Z 260Z 280Z F-10	Rack and pinion

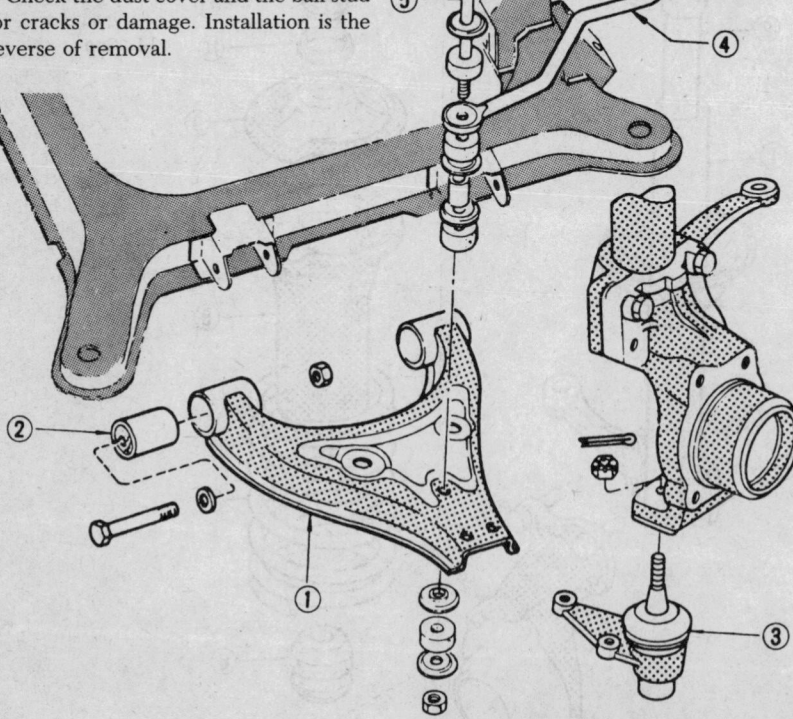

F-10 control arm

All models starting 1969 have a steering shaft lock actuated by the ignition lock and a steering column and shaft assembly designed to collapse on impact.

Steering Wheel

Removal and Installation

Remove the horn button or ring. On the KLB110, LB110, B210, and PL620 the horn ring is retained by two screws which can be removed from the rear of the wheel spokes. To remove the PL510, PL610, KPL610, WPL510, WPL610, PL710 and KPL710 horn pad, press in and turn to the left. Some can be simply pulled off. Pull the "Z" series horn button straight out to remove. Next remove the rest of the horn switching mechanism, noting the relative location of the parts. Hold the steering wheel and remove the nut. Using a puller, remove the steering wheel. Do not attempt to pry or hammer off the wheel. This is particularly important in the case of collapsible steering columns. When replacing the wheel, make sure that it is correctly aligned when the wheels are straight ahead. Do not drive or hammer the wheel into place. Tighten the nut while holding the wheel. Specified wheel nut torque is 22–25 ft lbs. for the LB110, KLB110, and B210, 51–54 ft lbs. for the PL620 and 29–36 ft lbs. for the "Z" series, PL610, KPL610, and WPL610. Reinstall the horn button, pad, or ring.

Turn Signal Switch

Removal and Installation

Follow procedures under Steering Wheel Removal and Installation. Remove shell covers and remove switch.

Steering Gear

Removal and Installation

PL521, PL620

1. Remove the steering wheel.

2. Unbolt the steering column from the instrument panel. On models with column shift, unbolt the shift linkage from the column.

3. Disconnect the horn wire.

4. Disconnect the steering rod from the steering arm.

5. Unbolt the steering gear box from the frame.

6. Pull the box, column, and shaft down and out of the vehicle.

7. Reverse the procedure to install.

510, 610, 710 Collapsible Column

1. Remove the steering shaft U-joint clamp bolt.

2. Remove the stud nut and pull the steering rod ball joint from the steering arm.

3. Unbolt the steering gear box from the frame and remove. If necessary, remove the horn button and pull the steering wheel and shaft up slightly.

4. Reverse the procedure to install. Torque the U-joint clamp bolt to 22 ft lbs. (29–36 ft lbs. for the PL610, KPL610, WPL610, PL710). If the upper and lower shaft sections of the collapsible column have been separated, the slit of the universal joint must align with the punch mark on the upper end of the upper steering shaft.

510—Rigid Column B110, B210— Collapsible Column

1. Remove the steering wheel.

2. Separate and remove the upper steering column shell.

3. Remove the turn signal and light switch assembly. Disconnect the automatic transmission linkage.

4. Unbolt the steering column from the instrument panel.

5. Remove the steering column hole cover from the floorboards.

6. Unbolt the steering box from the body.

7. Pull the assembly out of the car toward the engine compartment. Be extremely cautious with the B110 and B210 collapsible column. Merely dropping or

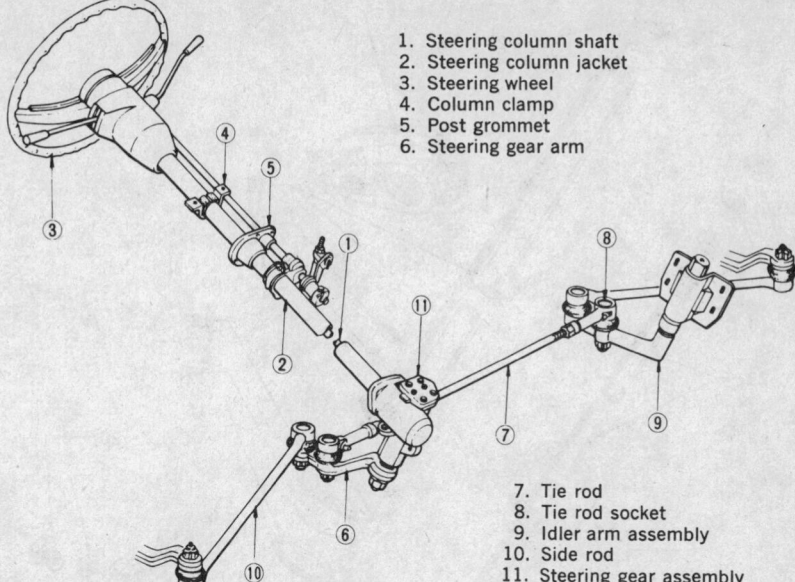

1. Steering column shaft
2. Steering column jacket
3. Steering wheel
4. Column clamp
5. Post grommet
6. Steering gear arm

7. Tie rod
8. Tie rod socket
9. Idler arm assembly
10. Side rod
11. Steering gear assembly

Steering assembly, PL620 shown. Most sedans and pickups are similar.

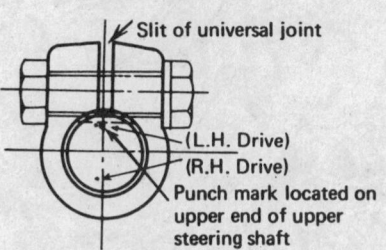

Slit of universal joint
(L.H. Drive)
(R.H. Drive)
Punch mark located on upper end of upper steering shaft

Reassembly details for collapsible column steering shaft

leaning on the assembly could cause enough damage to require replacement.

8. Reverse the procedure to install.

240, 260 and 280 Z

1. Raise and support the front end. Remove the front wheels.

2. Loosen the clamp bolts at both U-joints. Remove the lower joint and shaft assembly from the engine compartment.

3. Remove the splash shields.

4. Remove the steering side rod stud

1. Steering gear housing
2. Bushing
3. Bushing
4. Stud
5. Oil seal
6. Drain plug
7. Cover
8. Gasket
9. Bolt
10. Bolt
11. Lockwasher
12. Filler plug
13. Adjusting screw
14. Locknut
15. Cover
16. O-ring
17-20. Shims
21. Nut
22. Lockwasher
23. Bolt
24. Rear cover
25. Oil seal
26. O-ring
27. Nut
38. Lockwasher
29. Bolt
30. Bearing
31. Worm gear
32. U-joint yoke
33. U-joint spider
34. Oil seal retainer
35. Oil seal
36. Bearing
37. Snap-ring
38. Bolt
39. Nut
40. Rocker shaft (lever)
41. Needle roller race
42. Roller ball pug
43. Needle roller cover

44-46. Roller ball
47-49. Needle rollers
50. Roller spacer
51. Thrust washer
52. Shaft adjusting thrust washer
53. Steering arm
54. Nut
55. Washer
56. Cotter pin

57. Steering column
58. Column bushing
59. Bolt
60. Lockwasher
61. Washer

62. Steering shaft
63. Lockwasher
64. Mounting bolt
65. Nut
66. Lockwasher

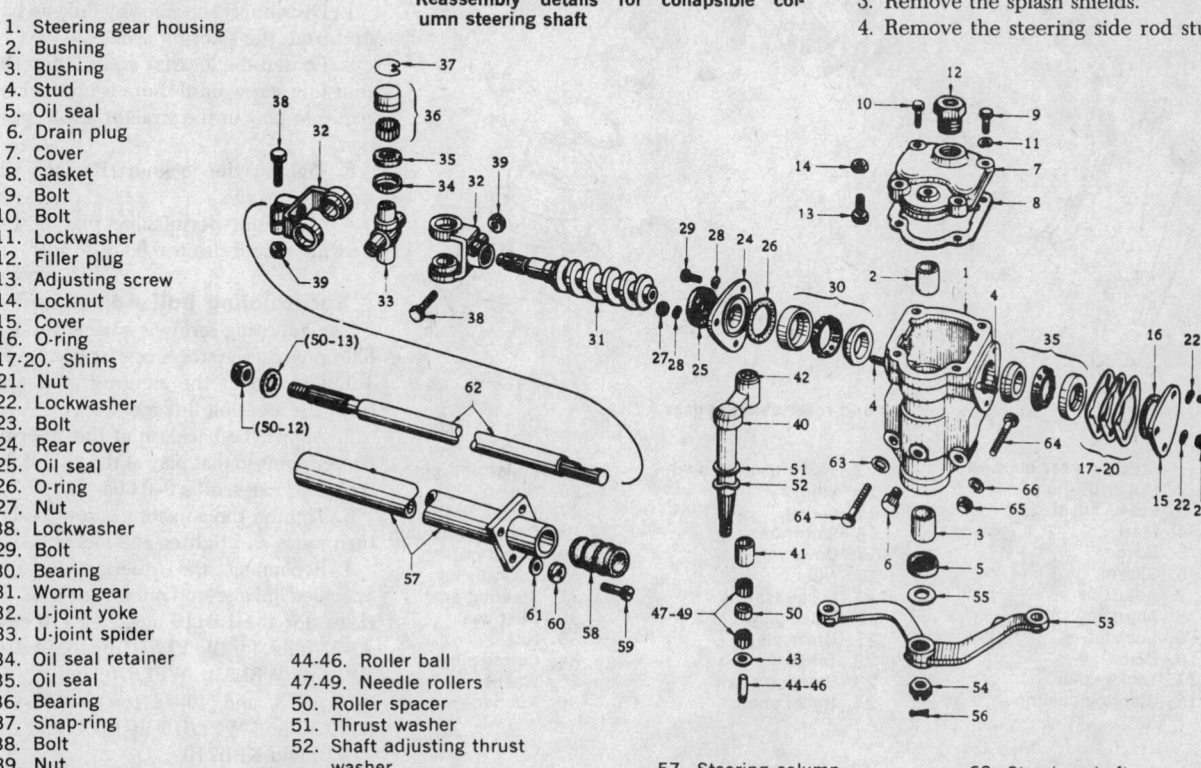

Cam and lever steering gear

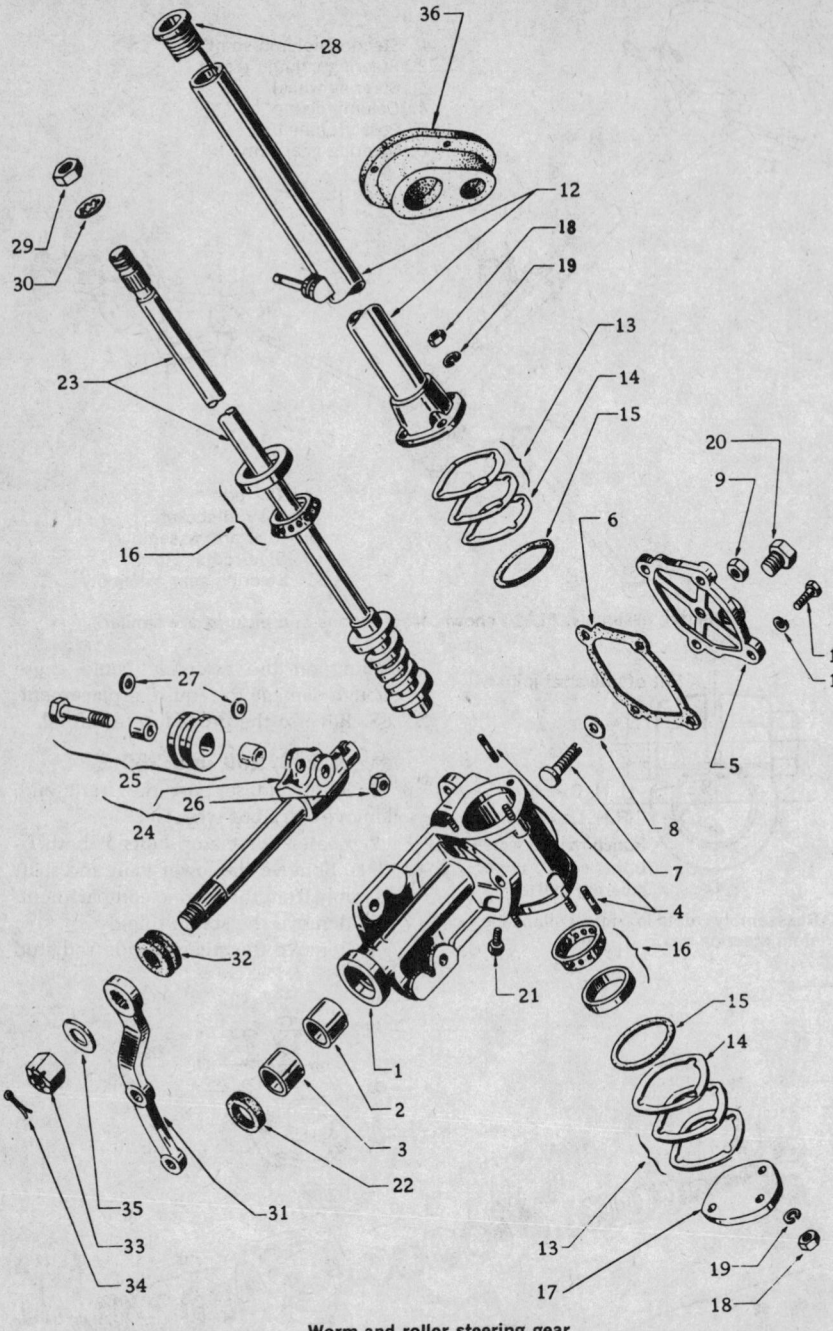

Worm and roller steering gear

1. Steering gear housing
2. Upper bushing
3. Lower bushing
4. Stud
5. Cover
6. Gasket
7. Adjusting screw
8. Adjusting shim
9. Locknut
10. Bolt
11. Lockwasher
12. Steering column

13. Worm bearing shim
14. Shims
15. O-ring
16. Worm bearing
17. Cover
18. Nut
19. Lockwasher
20. Filter plug
21. Drain plug
22. Oil seal
23. Steering shaft
24. Roller shaft

25. Roller and pin
26. Nut
27. Thrust washers
28. Column bushing
29. Wheel nut
30. Lockwasher
31. Steering arm
32. Dust seal
33. Nut
34. Cotter pin
35. Washer
36. Rubber grommet

the upper and lower shaft sections of the collapsible column have been separated, the slit of the universal joint must align with the punch mark on the upper end of the upper steering shaft.

Adjustment

Worm and Roller Adjustment

The backlash adjusting screw is located next to the filler plug on the steering gear box cover.

1. Disconnect the drag link from the steering arm.

2. Loosen the locknut and turn the adjusting screw in clockwise until the mechanism binds.

3. Back off the screw until the unit operates smoothly. Tighten the locknut.

4. Check free play at tne end of the steering arm, with the steering gear in the central (straight ahead) position. Free play should be 0–0.008 in.

5. Check the force required to turn the steering wheel with a spring scale attached to the wheel rim. It should be 1.-1.5 lbs.

6. Replace the drag link.

7. Maximum permissible play at the steering wheel rim is 1–1.4 in.

Cam and Lever Adjustment

The adjusting screw is adjacent to the filler plug on the steering gear box cover.

1. Disconnect the steering linkage ball stud from the steering arm.

2. Loosen the locknut and tighten the adjusting screw until there is no steering arm free play in the straight ahead position.

3. Tighten the locknut. Replace the steering linkage.

4. Maximum permissible play at the steering wheel rim is 0.98–1.38 in.

Recirculating Ball Adjustment

The adjusting screw is adjacent to the filler plug on the steering gear box cover.

1. Disconnect the steering gear arm from the steering linkage.

2. Adjust the backlash at the steering center point so that play at the end of the steering gear arm is 0–0.004 in.

3. Tighten the adjusting screw ⅛–1/6 turn more and tighten the locknut.

4. Reconnect the steering linkage. Specified linkage stud nut torque is 22–36 ft lbs. for the LB110 and KLB110 and 40–55 ft lbs. for the PL510, B210, PL610, KPL610, WPL510, WPL610, and PL620 thru 1973, and 40–72 for the PL610, KPL610 and WPL610 in 1974, and the PL710 and KPL710.

5. Maximum free play at steering wheel rim should be 0.79–0.98 in. for the LB110 and KLB110, 0.98–1.18 in. for the PL510 and WPL510, and 1–1.4 in. for all other models.

nuts and pull the studs from the spindle steering arms.

5. Raise the engine slightly, being careful not to damage the accelerator linkage.

6. Unbolt the steering gear housing from the suspension crossmember.

7. Remove the rack and pinion assembly.

8. Reverse the procedure to install. If

Steering Lock

The steering lock/ignition switch-/warning buzzer switch assembly is attached to the steering column by special screws whose heads shear off on installation. The screws must be drilled out to remove the assembly. The ignition switch or warning switch can be replaced without removing the assembly. The ignition switch is on the back of the assembly, and the warning switch on the side.

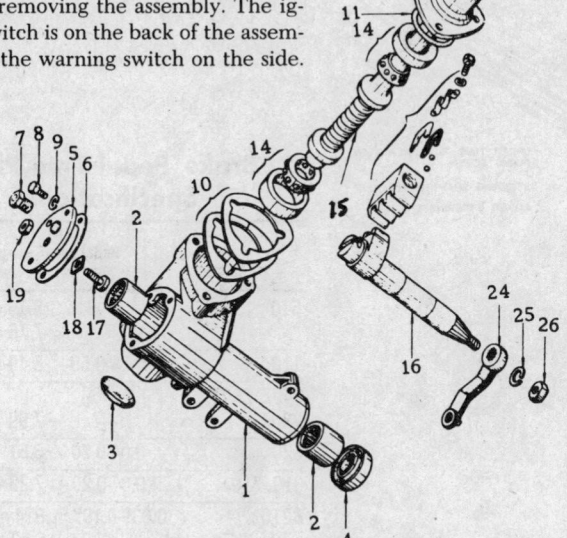

Recirculating ball steering gear

1. Steering gear housing	10. Shims for worm bearing	18. Adjusting shim
2. Needle bearing	11. O-ring	19. Locknut
3. Plug	12. Steering column	20. Bolt
4. Oil seal	13. Bearing	21. Lockwasher
5. Sector shaft cover	14. Bearing	22. Nut
6. Gasket	15. Steering shaft	23. Washer
7. Plug (filler)	16. Sector shaft	24. Steering arm
8. Bolt	17. Adjusting screw	25. Lockwasher
9. Lockwasher		26. Nut

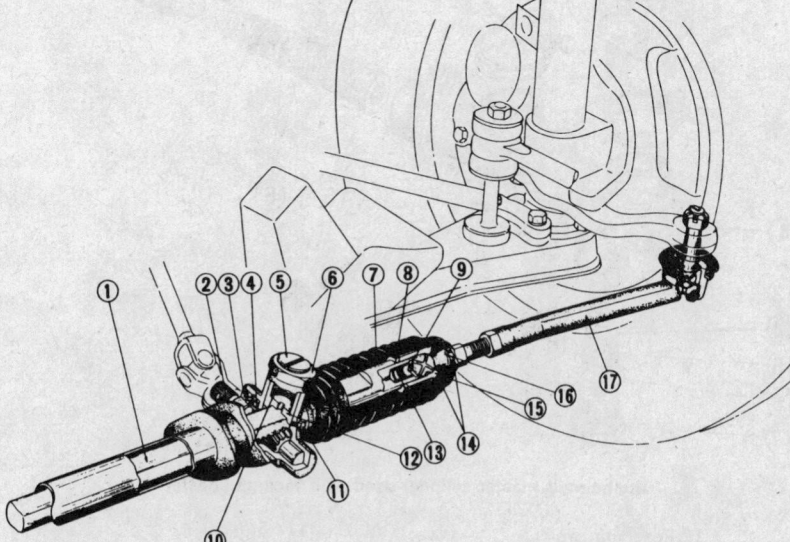

Rack and pinion steering gear, left side shown

1. Rack	6. Locknut	12. Retainer
2. Pinion	7. Boot	13. Side rod inner spring
3. Oil seal	8. Locknut	14. Dust cover clamp
4. Pinion bearing	9. Side rod spring seat	15. Side rod inner socket
5. Retainer adjusting screw	10. Retainer spring	16. Ball stud
	11. Filler plug	17. Side rod

The warning buzzer, which sounds when the driver's door is opened with the steering unlocked, is located behind the instrument panel. It is on the left side of the instrument panel on the B210, LB110 and KLB110, and on the steering support on the "Z" series and behind the center reinforcement behind cover on the F10.

BRAKE SYSTEMS

Front disc brakes are used on all current car models, with drum brakes at the rear. All pickups have a drum brake system front and rear. The "Z" series, B210, 710, 610, 620 and F10 have a vacuum booster system to lessen required pedal pressure. The parking brake operates the rear brakes through a cable system.

Adjustment

There are four basic types of brake adjusting system used.

To adjust the brakes, raise the wheels, disconnect the handbrake linkage from the rear wheels, apply the brakes hard a few times to center the drums, and proceed as follows:

Bolt Adjuster

Turn the adjuster bolt on the backing plate until the wheel can no longer be turned, then back off until the wheel is free of drag. Repeat the procedure on the other adjuster bolt on the same wheel. Some models may have only one adjuster bolt per wheel.

Bolt Adjuster With Click Arrangement

The adjuster is located on the backing plate. The adjustment proceeds in clicks or notches. The wheel will often be locked temporarily as the adjuster passes over center for each click. Thus the adjuster is alternately hard and easy to turn. When the wheel is fully locked, back off 1–3 clicks.

Star Wheel Adjuster

Remove the rubber boot from the backing plate. Insert a screwdriver through the adjusting hole to engage the toothed wheel. Turn the adjuster teeth down until the wheel is locked, then push them up about 12 notches so that the wheel is free of drag.

Self Adjusting

No manual adjustment is required. The self adjusters operate whenever the hand or foot brakes are used.

After Adjustment

After adjusting the brakes, reconnect the handbrake linkage. Make sure that

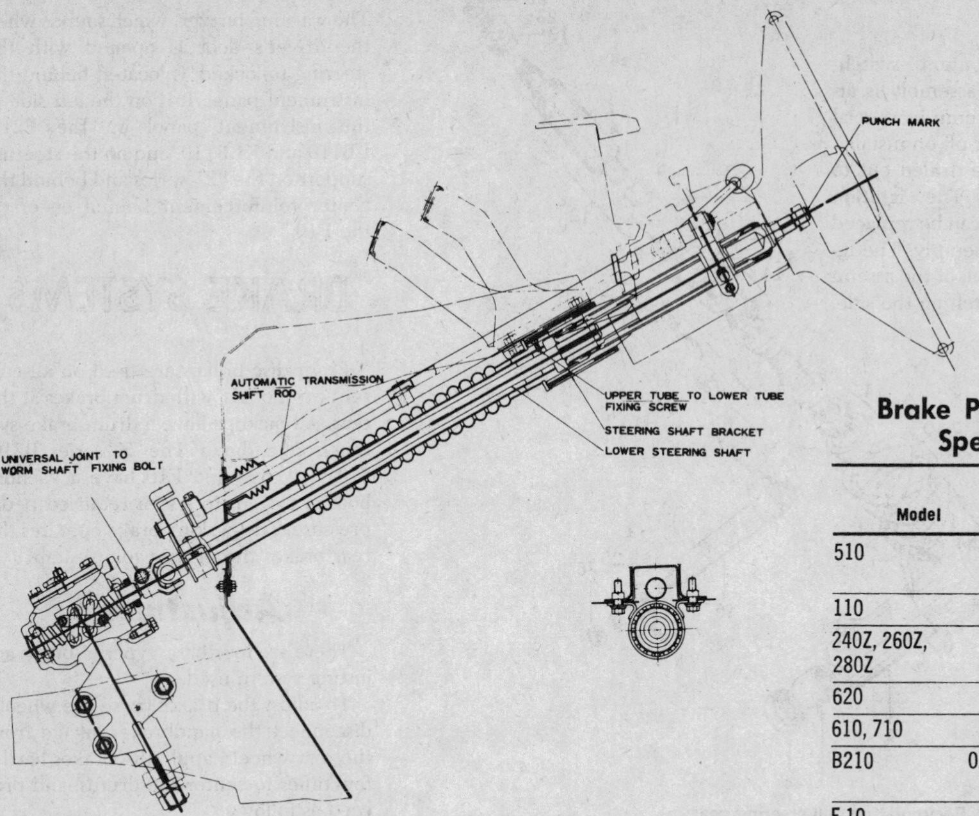

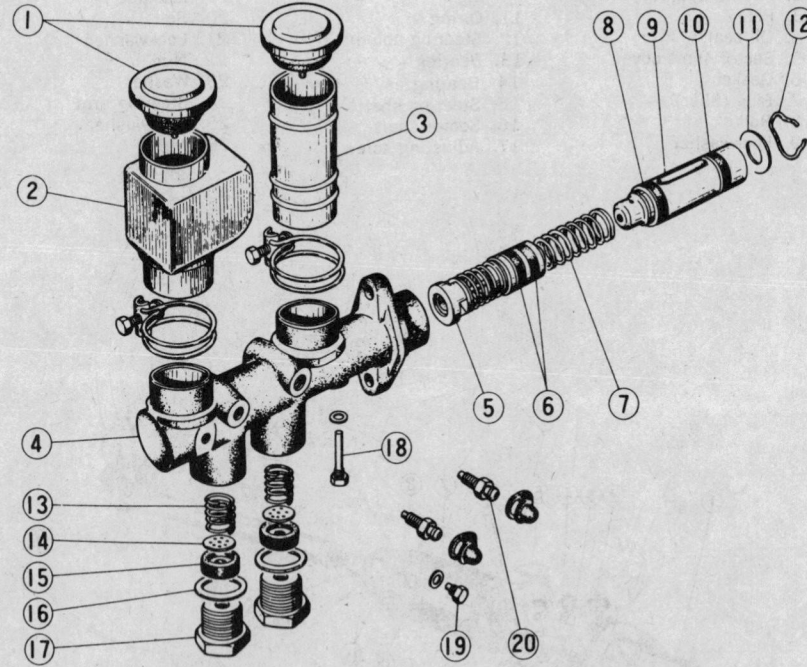

PUNCH MARK

AUTOMATIC TRANSMISSION
SHIFT ROD

UNIVERSAL JOINT TO
WORM SHAFT FIXING BOLT

UPPER TUBE TO LOWER TUBE
FIXING SCREW

STEERING SHAFT BRACKET

LOWER STEERING SHAFT

Collapsible shaft and column assemby

Brake Pedal Free-Play Specifications

Model	Pedal free play (in.)	Pedal pad free height (in.)
510	—	8.15 manual, 7.76 automatic
110	0.24-0.59	5.49-6.65
240Z, 260Z, 280Z	—	7.99
620	0.04-0.20	5.51
610, 710	0.04-0.20	7.28
B210	0.039-0.197	614 manual, 6.22 automatic
F-10	—	6.85-7.09

there is no rear wheel drag with the handbrake released. Loosen the handbrake adjustment if necessary.

Master Cylinder

Removal and Installation

Clean the outside of the cylinder thoroughly, particularly around the cap and fluid lines. Disconnect the fluid lines and cap them to exclude dirt. Remove the clevis pin connecting the pushrod to the brake pedal arm inside the vehicle. This pin need not be removed on models with the vacuum booster. Unbolt the master cylinder from the firewall and remove. If the pushrod is not adjustable, there will be shims between the cylinder and the firewall. These shims, or the adjustable pushrod, are used to adjust brake pedal free play. After installation, bleed the system and check the pedal free play.

NOTE: *Ordinary brake fluid will boil and cause brake failure under the high temperatures developed in disc brake systems. Special fluid for disc brake systems must be used.*

Pedal Adjustment

Before adjusting the pedal, make sure that the wheelbrakes are correctly adjusted.

Dual circuit master cylinder used with vacuum booster

1. Reservoir cap
2. Brake fluid reservoir
3. Brake fluid reservoir
4. Brake master cylinder
5. Piston assembly
6. Piston cup
7. Cylinder spring
8. Primary piston cup
9. Pistom assembly
10. Secondary piston cup
11. Stopper
12. Snap ring
13. Valve spring
14. Check valve assembly
15. Check valve assembly
16. Packing
17. Valve cap screw
18. Stopper bolt
19. Stopper bolt
20. Bleeder

Adjust the pedal free-play by means of an adjustable pushrod or shims between the master cylinder and the firewall. Adjust the pedal height by means of the pedal arm stop pad.

Overhaul

The master cylinder can be disassembled using the illustrations as a guide. Clean all parts in clean brake fluid. Replace the cylinder or piston as necessary if clearance between the two exceeds 0.-006 in. Lubricate all parts with clean brake fluid on assembly. Master cylinder rebuilding kits, containing all the wearing parts, are available to simplify overhaul.

Bleeding

Bleeding is required whenever air in the hydraulic fluid causes a spongy feeling pedal and sluggish response. This is almost always the case after some part of the hydraulic system has been repaired or replaced.

1. Fill the master cylinder reservoir with the proper fluid. Special fluid is required for disc brakes.

2. The usual procedure is to bleed at the points furthest from the master cylinder first.

3. Fit a rubber hose over the bleeder screw. Submerge the other end of the hose in clean brake fluid in a clear glass container. Loosen the bleeder screw.

4. Slowly pump the brake pedal several times until fluid free of bubbles is discharged. An assistant is required to pump the pedal.

5. On the last pumping stroke, hold the pedal down and tighten the bleeder screw. Check the fluid level periodically during the bleeding operation.

6. Bleed the front brakes in the same way as the rear brakes. Note that some front drum brakes have two hydraulic cylinders and two bleeder screws. Both cylinders must be bled.

7. Check that the brake pedal is now firm. If not, repeat the bleeding operation.

FRONT DISC BRAKES

Lockheed type disc brakes are used on the PL610, KPL610, WPL510, WPL610, PL710, KPL710 and F10. Girling type brakes are used on the 240 Z, KLB110, LB110, B210, 260 Z, 280 Z.

Disc Brake Pads

Removal and Installation

All four front brake pads must always be replaced as a set. Several grades of pads are available for most models for

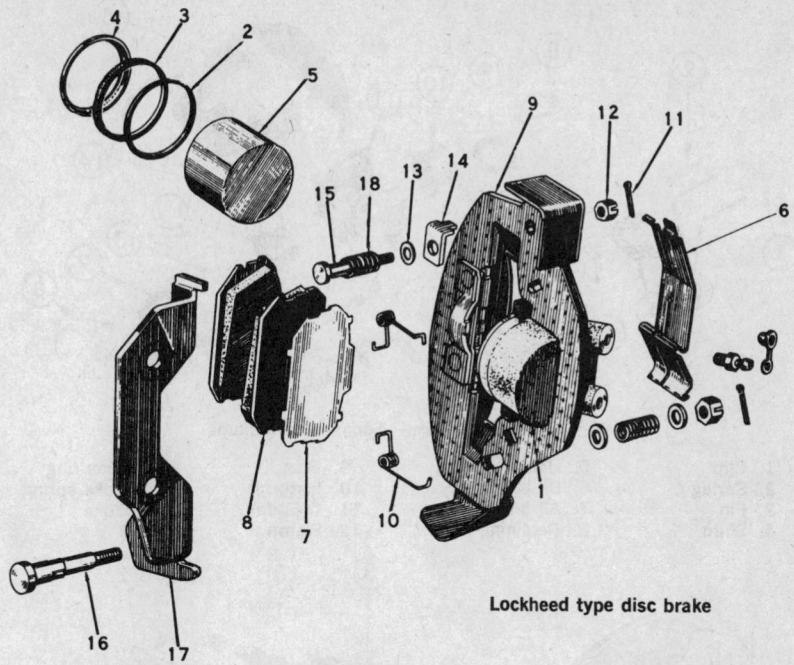

Lockheed type disc brake

1. Cylinder	7. Shim	13. Washer
2. Piston seal	8. Pad	14. Support bracket
3. Wiper seal	9. Caliper plate	15. Hold down pin
4. Retainer	10. Tension spring	16. Pivot pin
5. Piston	11. Cotter pin	17. Mounting bracket
6. Clip	12. Nut	18. Spring

road use, or racing.

Lockheed Type

1. Jack up the car and remove the wheel.

2. Loosen the anti-rattle clip.

3. Loosen the bleed screw. Pull the caliper plate toward the outer end of the spindle and push the piston in 0.12–0.16 in. Be careful not to scratch the pistons or bores.

4. The outer pad can now be pulled out.

5. Pull the caliper plate inward and remove the inner pad.

6. Thoroughly clean the exposed end of each piston and the caliper assembly. Check the rotor (disc) for scoring. If it is badly scored, it must be removed for resurfacing or replacement.

7. If the piston has been pushed in far enough, the new pads can be installed.

8. Install the new pads. Tighten the bleeder screw.

Girling Type

1. Jack up the car and remove the wheel.

2. Remove the clip(s), retaining pins, and anti-squeal clips. Remove the coil spring on the LB110, KLB110, and B210.

3. Using pliers, pull out the pads and anti-squeal shims.

4. Thoroughly clean the exposed end of each piston and the caliper assembly. Check the rotor (disc) for scoring. If it is badly scored, it must be removed for resurfacing or replacement.

5. Before installing the new pads, the pistons must be pushed back into their cylinders. Be careful not to scratch the pistons or bores.

NOTE: *The master cylinder may overflow when the pistons are pushed back. The bleeder screw can be loosened to prevent overflow.*

Be careful not to push the pistons in too far or the seals will be damaged. The pistons need not be pushed in past a position flush with the edge of the cylinder. Install the new pads and tighten the bleeder screw if it was loosened.

6. Install the anti-squeal shims with the arrow marks pointing in the direction of rotor rotation. On the LB110, the coil spring should be installed on the retaining pin furthest from the bleed screw.

7. Replace the wheels and pump the brake pedal a few times to seat the pads. This must be done before the car is driven.

Calipers and Brake Discs

Overhaul

Lockheed Type

1. Jack up and support the car. Remove the wheel.

2. Disconnect and cap the brake hose.

3. Unbolt and remove the caliper assembly.

4. Remove the spindle nut and rotor with the hub.

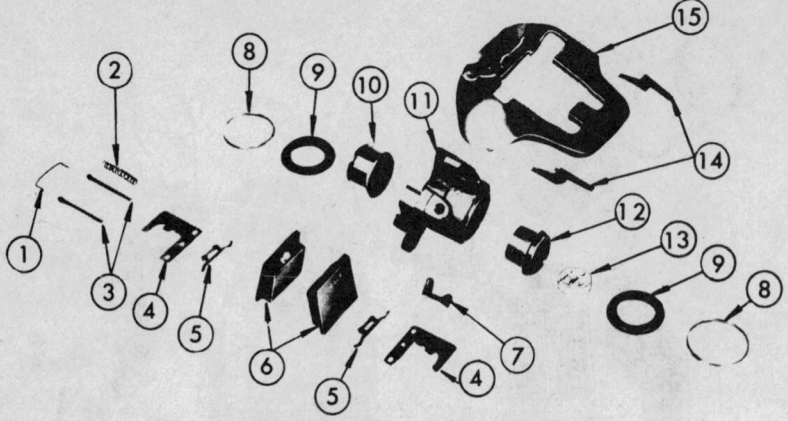

Girling-type disc brake—Sedans and pickups

1. Clip
2. Spring
3. Pin
4. Shim
5. Hanger spring
6. Brake pad
7. Air bleeder
8. Retaining ring
9. Boot
10. Piston B
11. Cylinder
12. Piston A
13. Bias ring
14. Yoke spring
15. Yoke

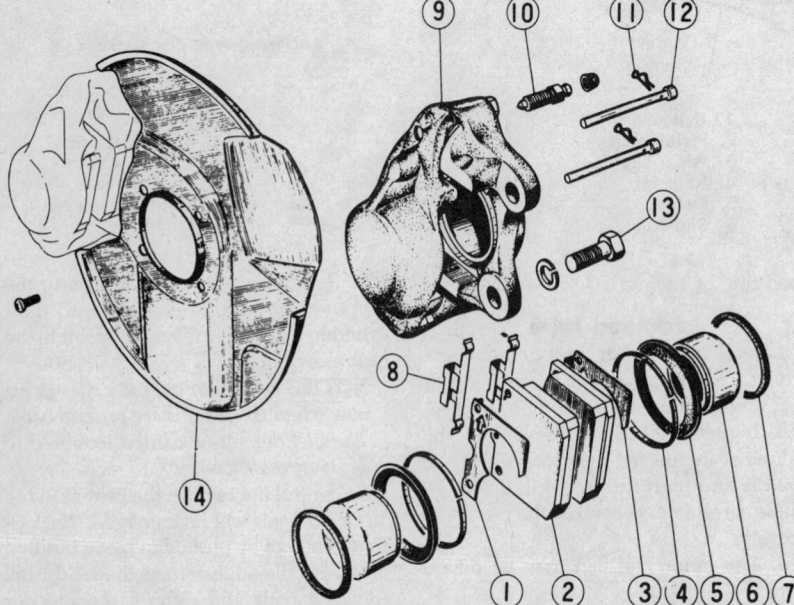

Girling-type disc brake—"Z" series

1. Anti-squeal shim, right
2. Pad
3. Anti-squeal shim, left
4. Retaining ring
5. Dust cover
6. Piston
7. Piston seal
8. Anti-squeal spring
9. Caliper assembly
10. Bleeder
11. Clip
12. Retaining pin
13. Caliper fixing bolt
14. Baffle plate

5. Unbolt and remove the rotor from the hub.

6. Remove the pads. Remove the tension springs and pull out the cylinder. Apply air or hydraulic pressure to the inlet hole to remove the piston from the cylinder. Remove the retainer and seals. The piston seal also serves to retract the piston and should be replaced at every overhaul.

7. If the rotor (disc) is scored, it can be machined. Minimum safe rotor thickness is 0.331 in. Rotor runout must not exceed 0.004.

8. Wash all parts in clean brake fluid.

Replace all seals. If the cylinder or piston is damaged, replace both.

9. Bolt the rotor to the hub, torquing the bolts to 28–38 ft lbs. Pack the bearings, install the hub on the spindle, and adjust the wheel bearing.

10. Insert a new seal in the cylinder groove and attach the wiper seal. Lubricate the cylinder bore with brake fluid. Insert the piston cautiously until the piston head is almost flush with the wiper seal retainer. The relieved part of the piston must face the pivot pin.

11. Install the cylinder into the caliper plate and secure it with the tension springs.

12. Install the hold down pin, washer, and nut on the support bracket. Install a new cotter pin in the nut.

13. Assemble the mounting bracket and caliper plate with the pivot pin. Install the washer, spring, washer, and nut. Tighten the nut completely and lock it with a cotter pin.

14. Install the caliper assembly to the spindle, torquing the mounting bolts to 53–65 ft lbs. Make sure that the caliper plate can slide smoothly.

15. Install the pads and shims, making sure that they are seated correctly. Seat the inner pad first. Make sure the anti-rattle clip is positioned correctly.

16. Reconnect the brake hose and bleed the system.

Girling Type—B110, B210

1. Remove the pads.

2. Disconnect the brake tube.

3. Remove the two bottom strut assembly installation bolts to obtain clearance.

4. Remove the caliper assembly mounting bolts.

5. Loosen the bleeder screw and press the pistons into the cylinder.

6. Clamp the yoke in a vise and tap the yoke head with a hammer to loosen the cylinder. Be careful that primary piston does not fall out.

7. Remove the bias ring from primary piston. Remove the retaining rings and boots from both pistons. Depress and remove the pistons from the cylinder. Remove the piston seal from the cylinder carefully with the fingers so as not to mar the cylinder wall.

8. Remove the yoke springs from the yoke.

9. Wash all parts with clean brake fluid.

10. If the piston or cylinder is badly worn or scored, replace both. The piston surface is plated and must not be polished with emery paper. Replace all seals. The rotor can be removed and machined if scored, but final thickness must be at least 0.331 in. Runout must not exceed 0.001 in.

11. Lubricate the cylinder bore with clean brake fluid and install the piston seal.

12. Insert the bias ring into primary piston so that the rounded ring portion comes to the bottom of the piston. Primary piston has a small depression inside, while secondary does not.

13. Lubricate the pistons with clean brake fluid and insert into the cylinder. Install the boot and retaining ring. The yoke groove of the bias ring of primary piston must align with the yoke groove of the cylinder.

14. Install the yoke springs to the yoke so the projecting portion faces to the disc (rotor).

15. Lubricate the sliding portion of the cylinder and yoke. Assemble the cylinder and yoke by tapping the yoke lightly.

16. Replace the caliper assembly and pads. Torque the mounting bolts to 33–41 ft lbs. Rotor bolt torque is 20–27 ft lbs. Strut bolt torque is 33–44 ft lbs. Bleed the system of air.

Girling Type—"Z" Series

The caliper halves must not to be separated. If brake fluid leaks from the bridge seal, replace the caliper assembly.

1. Remove the pads.
2. Disconnect the brake line and caliper mounting bolts.
3. Hold the piston in one side and force the other one out with air pressure. Remove the other piston.
4. Remove the piston seal from the cylinder carefully with the fingers so as not to mar the cylinder wall.
5. Wash all parts with clean brake fluid.
6. If the piston or cylinder is badly worn or scored, replace both. The piston surface is plated and must not be polished with emery paper. Replace all seals.
7. With the wheel bearing properly adjusted, runout at the center of the rotor surface should be less than 0.006 in. The rotor can be resurfaced if scored, but must be at least 0.413 in. thick after resurfacing.
8. Lubricate the piston seal with clean brake fluid and install it.
9. Install dust seals on the pistons, lubricate the pistons with clean brake fluid, and install the pistons into the cylinders. Clamp the dust seals with retaining rings.
10. Reinstall the caliper assembly. Mounting bolt torque is 53–71 ft lbs. Rotor mounting bolt torque is 28–38 ft lbs.
11. Replace the pads and brake line. Bleed the system of air.

Wheel Bearing Adjustment

All Models with Disc Brakes exc. F-10

1. Jack and support car.
2. Remove wheel, cotter pin and brake pads.
3. Tighten spindle nut to 18–22 ft lbs.
4. Rotate wheel a few times in each direction to seat bearing. Retighten nut.
5. Loosen nut 60°.
6. Install adjusting cap and tighten within 15° until grooves are aligned with hole in spindle.
7. Spin wheel several times to check for free rotation.
8. Measure bearing preload with a spring scale at wheel hub lug as follows:
Rotation starting torque—
    New parts 7.9 in. lb.
    Old parts 63 in. oz.
9. Install new cotter pin.
10. Install pads and wheel.

Models with Drum Brakes

1. Tighten wheel bearing lock nut to 16–18 ft lbs.
2. Turn the wheel a few turns each way to seat the bearing. Retighten the nut.
3. Back-off the nut 40–70° to line it up with the hole in the spindle.
4. Again turn the wheel a few turns in each direction. Measure bearing rotation starting torque with a spring scale attached to a wheel lug. Starting torque should be:
    New bearing - 3.46 lb.
    Used bearing - 1.54 lb.
5. Install a new cotter pin and the dust cap.

Front Wheel Bearing

Removal and Installation

All Models with Disc Brakes exc. F-10

1. Jack and support car.
2. Remove wheel.
3. Remove dust cap from spindle.
4. Remove cotter pin.
5. Remove spindle nut.
6. Remove caliper retaining bolts and suspend caliper out of the way.
7. Remove hub from spindle along with bearings.
8. Remove outer bearing from hub.
9. With a brass drift, remove inner bearing and oil seal.
10. Remove inner and outer races with a drift.
11. Install in reverse of the above. Races may be hammered into position with a drift. Take care not to nick race surface.
12. Install inner bearing and oil seal.

All Models with Front Drum Brakes

1. Jack up and support car.
2. Remove wheel.
3. Remove dust cap, cotter pin and spindle nut.
4. Pull hub from spindle taking care not to drop outside wheel bearing.
5. Drive inside wheel bearing and oil seal out of hub with a brass drift. Likewise drive out bearing races.
6. To install, drive races into position with a brass drift or installing tool. Take care not to nick race surfaces.
7. Assemble other parts in reverse order.
8. Adjust wheel bearing.

NOTE: *New wheel bearings should be thoroughly packed with clean multipurpose grease. Hub and dust cap should also be packed to points indicated by a stamped asterisk.*

Rear Wheel Bearing

Adjustment

F-10

1. Jack up and support car.
2. Remove wheel.
3. Tighten wheel bearing lock nut to 18–22 ft lbs.
4. Turn drum a few turns in both directions to seat bearing.
5. Back off lock nut until it is finger tight.
6. Check drum for free rotation.
7. Align cotter pin hole by turning nut clockwise. Install new cotter pin.
8. Check wheel bearing rotating torque using a spring scale at the hub lug. Starting torque should be:
    New grease seal: 1.1–2.6 lb.
    Used grease seal: 1.5 lb.

Rear Wheel Bearing Removal and Installation

F-10

1. Jack up and support car.
2. Remove wheel.
3. Remove dust cap, cotter pin and lock nut.
4. Remove drum with bearing.
5. Pry off grease seal with screwdriver.
NOTE: *If it is necessary to remove race, take note that it must be replaced using a press.*
6. Drive wheel bearing outer race from drum using a brass drift. Apply hammer evenly around race.
7. Wheel bearing race must be pressed into drum.
8. Pack hub and dust cap with grease to fill indentations. Do not over-pack.
9. Wheel bearing should be thoroughly packed with multi-purpose grease, by hand.
10. Apply thin coating of grease to lip of new grease seal, spindle and lock nut. Old grease seal should never be reused.
11. Install all parts in reverse of removal.
12. Adjust wheel bearing as described above.

DRUM BRAKES

Front drum brakes on all models so equipped have two shoes and two hydraulic cylinders at each wheel. The cylinders are bolted to the front brake backing plate. All models have rear drum brakes. Each rear brake assembly has two brake shoes and a single hydraulic cylinder which is free to slide back and forth in a slot in the brake backing plate. On some models the hydraulic cylinder is bolted and the adjuster slides.

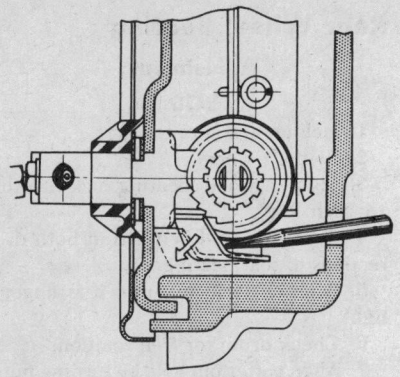

Loosening the "Z" series rear brake adjuster

Drum, Lining and Wheel Cylinder Replacement

510, 610, 710, and F10 Rear

1. Raise the vehicle and remove the wheels.

2. Release the parking brake. Disconnect the cross rod from the lever of the brake cylinder. Remove the brake drum. Place a heavy rubber band around the cylinder to prevent the piston from coming out.

3. Remove the return springs and shoes.

4. Clean the backing plate and check the wheel cylinder for leaks. To remove the wheel cylinder, remove the brake line, dust cover, plates, and adjusting shims. Clearance between the cylinder and the piston should not exceed 0.006 in.

5. The drums must be machined if scored or out of round more than 0.002 in. The drum inside diameter should not

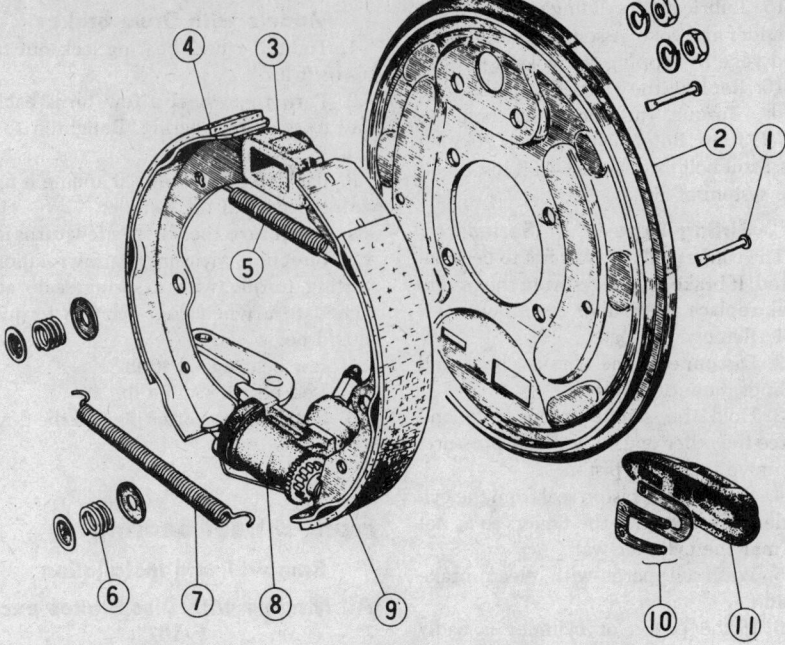

240 Z, 260 Z rear brake

1. Anti-rattle pin
2. Brake backing plate
3. Anchor block
4. After shoe assembly
5. Return spring
6. Anti-rattle spring
7. Return spring
8. Wheel cylinder
9. Fore shoe assembly
10. Retaining shim
11. Dust cover

be machined beyond 9.04 in. Minimum safe lining thickness is 0.059 in. (0.039—F10).

6. Hook the return springs into the new shoes. The springs should be be-

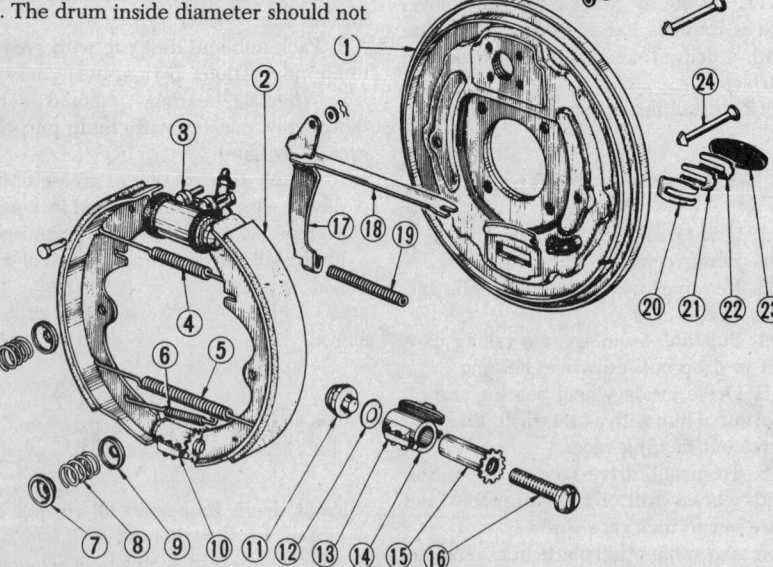

Rear Brake Assembly—PL620

1. Brake disc
2. Brake shoe assembly
3. Wheel cylinder assembly
4. Upper return spring
5. Lower return spring
6. Rear shoe return spring
7. Retainer
8. Anti-rattle spring
9. Spring seat
10. Adjuster assembly
11. Adjuster head
12. Adjuster head shim
13. Lock spring
14. Adjuster housing
15. Adjuster wheel
16. Adjuster screw
17. Toggle lever
18. Extension link
19. Return spring
20. Adjuster spring
21. Lock plate
22. Adjuster shim
23. Rubber boot
24. Anti-rattle pin

tween the shoes and the backing plate. The longer return spring must be adjacent to the wheel cylinder. A very thin film of grease may be applied to the pivot points at the ends of the brake shoes. Grease the shoe locating buttons on the backing plate, also. Be careful not to get grease on the linings or drums.

7. Place one shoe in the adjuster and piston slots, and pry the other shoe into position.

8. Replace the drums and wheels. Adjust the brakes. Bleed the hydraulic system of air if the brake lines were disconnected.

9. Reconnect the handbrake, making sure that it does not cause the shoes to drag when it is released.

B110, B210 Rear

1. Raise the vehicle and remove the wheels.

2. Loosen the handbrake cable, remove the clevis pin from the wheel cylinder lever, disconnect the handbrake cable, and remove the return pull spring.

3. Remove the brake drum, shoe retainers, return springs, and brake shoes. Loosen the brake adjusters if the drums are difficult to remove. Place a heavy rubber band around the cylinder to prevent the piston from coming out.

4. Clean the backing plate and check the wheel cylinder for leaks. To remove the wheel cylinder, remove the brake line, dust cover, plates, and adjusting shims. Clearance between cylinder and

piston should not exceed 0.006 in.

5. The drums must be machined if scored or out of round more than 0.001 in. The drum inside diameter must not be machined beyond 8.04 in. Minimum safe lining thickness is 0.059 in.

6. Follow Steps 6–9 for 510 Rear.

240 Z, 260 Z, 280 Z Rear

1. Raise and support the vehicle. Remove the wheel.

2. Remove the brake drum. If it is difficult to remove, remove the wheel cylinder lever handbrake clevis pin. Remove the brake drum adjusting hole plug and pry the adjusting lever away from the adjusting wheel with a screwdriver inserted through the adjusting hole. Turn the adjusting wheel down with the screwdriver to loosen the brake shoes. Remove the brake drum.

3. Remove the brake shoe retainers and springs. Remove the shoes and return springs. Place a heavy rubber band around the cylinder to prevent the piston from coming out.

4. Clean the backing plate and check for wheel cylinder leaks. To remove the wheel cylinder, detach the brake tube and dust cover, drive the lock plate out toward the front, pull the adjusting plate to the rear, and remove the cylinder. Clearance between the cylinder and piston should not exceed 0.006 in.

5. The drums should be machined if scored or out of round more than 0.002 in. The drum inside diameter should not be machined beyond 9.04 in. Minimum safe lining thickness is 0.060 in.

6. On reassembly, apply a very light film of grease to all sliding surfaces. Be careful not to get any on the linings or drums. The wheel cylinder must be free to slide. The longer black return spring must be adjacent to the wheel cylinder.

All Other Models

Lining replacement procedures for models not specifically covered above are generally quite similar to the above procedures. Brake drums should not be machined more than 0.040 in. beyond their original inside diameter, and should be machined if scored or out of round more than 0.002 in. Minimum safe lining thickness is 0.060 in.

Parking Brake

Adjustment

Handbrake adjustments are generally not needed, unless the cables have stretched.

All Models except the "Z" Series

There is an adjusting nut on the cable under the car, usually at the end of the front cable and near the point at which the two cables from the rear wheels come together (the equalizer). The LB110 and KLB110 have a turnbuckle in the cable. LB110, KLB110 and B210 handbrake lever stroke should be 3.1 in. or 6 notches. PL510 handle travel should be 3.-4–3.7 in.; WPL510 handle travel should be 4.3–4.7 in.; PL620 handle travel should be 3.1–3.9 in.; PL610, KPL610, WPL610, PL710 and KPL710 handle travel should be 3.5–3.9 in.; F10 Hatchback and Sedan should be 3.15–3.74 and the Sports Wagon, 3.74–5.12 in. Some models also have a turnbuckle in the rear cable to compensate for cable stretching.

240 Z, 260 Z, 280 Z

The driveshaft must be removed gain access to the adjusting nut on the front linkage rod.

Removal and Installation

NOTE: *When installing any cable, it is necessary to apply a light coating of multi-purpose grease to the cable.*

510

Front Cable

1. Release brake and disconnect clevis pin from the lever.

2. Screw out the adjusting nut from the rear end of the front cable and disconnect it from the lever.

3. Remove the cable clamp from the floor pan.

4. Remove the lock plate attaching the front cable to the retainer and remove the cable.

5. Remove the cable by unfastening its outer casing from the hand brake control bracket.

6. Installation is the reverse of removal.

Rear Cable—Independent Rear Suspension

1. Remove the adjusting nut from the adjuster and disconnect the left rear cable from the adjuster.

2. Pull out the lock plates and remove the clevis pins which connect the rear cable with the wheel cylinder levers.

3. Installation is the reverse of removal.

Rear Cables—Solid Rear Axle

1. Disconnect clevis pins at each backing plate.

2. Disconnect cable at center connector.

3. Installation is the reverse of removal.

610, 710

Front Cable

1. Remove center console.

2. Disconnect terminal from warning switch.

3. Remove control stem bracket from floor.

4. Remove front cable bracket assembly, pin and front cable.

5. Installation is the reverse of removal.

Rear Cable—Station Wagon

1. Remove clevis pin securing rear cable to balance lever.

2. Remove parking brake return spring.

3. Remove cotter pin from cross-rod and wheel cylinder and remove cable.

4. Installation is the reverse of removal.

Rear Cable—Sedan and Hardtop

1. Remove return spring.

2. Disconnect rear cable from adjuster.

3. Remove cable lock plate from rear suspension.

4. Remove clevis pin from rear wheel cylinders and remove cable.

5. Installation is the reverse of removal.

1200

1. Loosen the turnbuckle adjusting nut and separate the front and rear cables.

2. Remove the lock plate from in front of the turnbuckle, remove the clip in the passenger compartment and disconnect the front cable.

3. Remove the hand brake lever cover. Remove the lever assembly with the front cable connected in the passenger compartment.

4. Remove the hanger strap bolt, remove the lock plate from the axle housing bracket and disconnect the rear cable.

5. Disassemble the hanger strap unit, and remove the cables from the wheel cylinders.

6. Installation is the reverse of removal.

B210

Front Cable

1. Loosen turnbuckle adjusting nut and separate front and rear cables.

2. Remove lock plate from in front of turnbuckle, clip in passenger compartment and detach cable from floor panel.

3. Remove hand brake lever cover.

4. Disconnect handbrake switch wire and remove lever assembly along with cable.

5. Installation is the reverse of removal.

Rear Cable

1. Separate front and rear cables.

2. Remove return spring.

3. Disconnect cable from shank.

4. Remove lock plate from axle housing bracket and detach cable from bracket.

5. Loosen hanger strap bolt and remove cable from hanger.

6. Remove the cotter pin from each wheel cylinder lever and remove the cables.

7. Installation is the reverse of removal.

F-10
Front Cable

1. On hatchback and sedan, loosen parking brake adjusting nut and separate cable from equalizer. On sport wagon, remove clevis pin on counter lever and separate cable from lever.

2. Remove cable supporter.

3. Remove console.

4. Disconnect parking brake warning switch wire.

5. Remove handbrake lever (2 bolts) and cable.

6. Installation is the reverse of removal.

Rear Cable
Hatchback and Sedan

1. Release parking brake.

2. Separate rear cable ends from clevis by pulling out clevis pin.

3. Loosen clamp on trailing arm and remove rear cable.

4. Separate rear cable from front cable and remove return spring.

5. Installation is the reverse of removal.

Sport Wagon

1. Release brake lever.

2. Separate rear cable ends from clevis by pulling pin out.

3. Remove return spring and adjusting nuts at counter lever.

4. Pull front end of rear cable out through bracket and hole in body.

5. Remove brackets on left rear spring and axle tube.

6. Remove snap ring and pull cable assembly out to the left through guide bracket. At the same time, disconnect the left rear cable from the equalizer.

7. Installation is the reverse of removal.

Z Series Cars

1. Remove the lock nut and adjusting nut from the rear end of the front rod; clevis pin from the front end and remove the front rod.

2. Remove the hanger spring and clevis pin.

3. Remove the clevis pin at each wheel cylinder and remove the cable ends.

4. Remove retaining brackets at wheels and remove equalizer side retainers. Remove rear cables.

5. Installation is the reverse of removal.

Pickup
Front Cable

1. Release brake.

2. Loosen adjusting nut at balance lever.

3. Disconnect front cable from control lever.

4. Remove retainer spring at cable guide bushing.

5. Disconnect rear cables from balance lever.

6. Remove balance lever brackets from crossmember.

7. Detach front cable clip and pull cable rearward.

Rear Cable

1. Release brake.

2. Remove both rear brake drums and disconnect cables from toggle levers.

3. Detach spring and retainer.

4. Remove rear cable from brake backing plate.

5. Disconnect rear cable from balance lever.

6. Detach cable clips and remove cable.

7. Installation is the reverse of removal.

CHASSIS ELECTRICAL

Heater Unit

Removal and Installation
510

1. Drain the coolant.

2. Disconnect the water pipes to the engine.

3. Disconnect the blower motor electrical connector.

4. Remove the three heater control wires at the heater unit.

5. Remove the two bolts and ventilator.

6. Remove the four bolts and detach the heater unit.

7. Reverse the procedure for installation.

B110

1. Remove the package tray and ashtray.

2. Disconnect the two hoses between the heater and engine.

3. Disconnect the cables from the heater unit and heater controls. Disconnect the wiring.

4. Disconnect the two control wires from the water cock and interior valve, and the control rod from the shut valve. Set the heater control upper lever to DEF and lower lever to OFF.

5. Pull off the right and left defroster hoses.

6. Remove the four screws holding the heater unit to the firewall. Remove the control knob and remove the screws holding the control unit to the instrument panel. Remove the heater unit.

7. Reverse the procedure for installation.

610

1. Disconnect the battery ground cable.

2. Drain the coolant.

3. Detach the coolant inlet and outlet hoses.

4. Remove the center ventilator grille from the bottom of the instrument panel.

5. Remove the heater duct hose.

6. Detach the defroster hose from each side of the heater unit.

7. Disconnect the control cables.

8. Disconnect the wires at the connectors.

9. Remove the bolt at each side of the unit and the one on the top for models 1972–1973 and two on each side for 1974 models.

10. Remove the unit.

11. Reverse the procedure for installation. Run the engine for a few minutes with the heater on to make sure the system is filled with coolant.

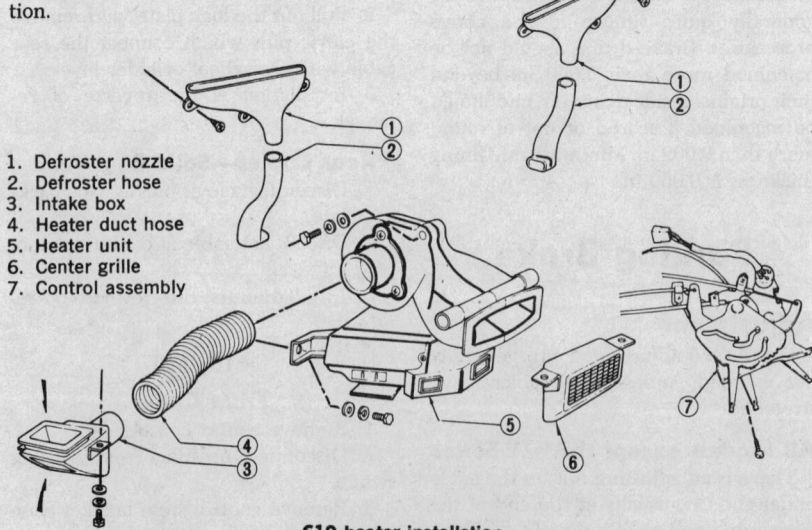

1. Defroster nozzle
2. Defroster hose
3. Intake box
4. Heater duct hose
5. Heater unit
6. Center grille
7. Control assembly

610 heater installation

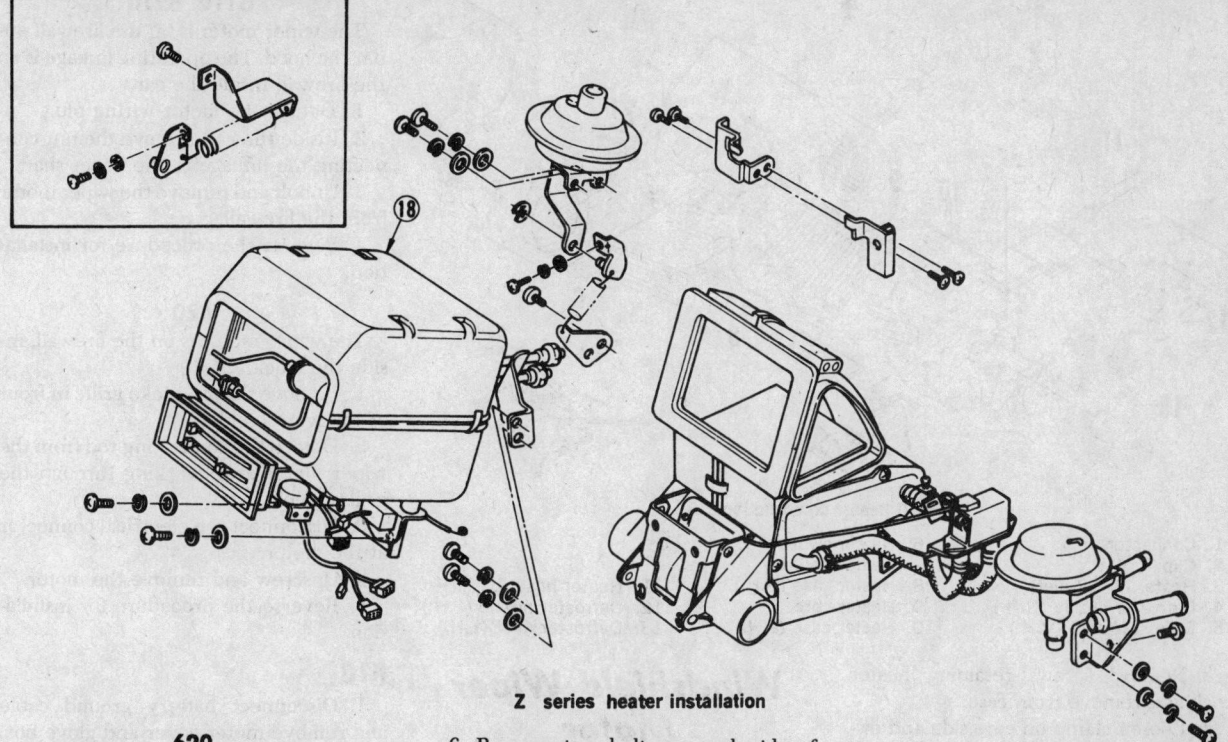

Z series heater installation

620

1. Disconnect the battery ground cable.
2. Drain the coolant.
3. Remove the defroster hoses.
4. Disconnect the control cables.
5. Disconnect the wires at the connectors.
6. Disconnect the coolant inlet and outlet hoses.
7. Remove the three mounting bolts and remove the heater unit.
8. Reverse the procedure for installation. Run the engine for a few minutes with the heater on to make sure the system is filled with coolant.

B210

1. Disconnect battery ground strap.
2. Drain engine coolant.
3. Remove defroster hose from both sides of heater unit.
4. Disconnect electrical wires from heater unit.
5. Remove clamps and disconnect water hose from right side of heater.
6. Remove one attaching bolt from each side of the unit and remove unit by pulling forward and out.
7. Reverse procedure for installation.

710

1. Disconnect battery ground strap.
2. Drain engine coolant.
3. Remove intake duct hose and defroster duct from both sides of heater unit. Remove console box if so equipped.
4. Disconnect electrical wires at connectors.
5. Loosen retaining clamps and remove control cables.

6. Remove two bolts on each side of unit and one on top. Remove unit from vehicle.
7. Install in reverse of the above.

240 Z, 260 Z, 280 Z

1. Disconnect battery ground and drain coolant.
2. Remove console box by removing the five attaching screws.
3. Remove the four attaching screws and lift off finisher. Disconnect wires.
4. Remove attaching screws and lift out three way duct to instrument panel.
5. Remove the control cables at the intake duct, water cock and floor mode doors.
6. Disconnect defroster ducts and two right side heater hoses from the unit.
7. Remove heater control and vent ducts from the unit.
8. Remove two bolts retaining the unit to the dash panel from inside the passenger compartment and two bolts retaining the unit to the firewall from the engine compartment.
9. Move heater unit to the right and out.
10. Reverse the above for installation.

F10

1. Disconnect battery ground cable and drain coolant.
2. Disconnect inlet and outlet hoses and remove defroster hoses from each side of the heater unit.
3. Remove the cable retaining clamps for the heater valve, floor door and intake door.
4. Disconnect electrical connectors and remove the heater unit.

Installation is the reverse of removal.

Heater Core
Removal and Installation

510

1. Remove the four clips and separate the lower cover.
2. Unbolt and remove the heater core.
3. Installation is the reverse of removal.

610, 620, 710

The heater unit need not be removed to remove the heater core. It must be removed to remove the blower motor.

1. Drain the coolant.
2. Detach the coolant hoses.
3. Disconnect the control cables on the sides of the heater unit.
4. Remove the clips and the cover from the front of the heater unit.
5. Pull out the core.
6. Reverse the procedure for installation. Run the engine with the heater on for a few minutes to make sure the system fills with coolant.

B110, B210, F-10

1. Remove heater from car.
2. Remove clip and slide hose from cock.
3. Pry off five clips and separate left and right sides of heater case.
4. Lift out heater core.

240 Z, 260 Z, 280 Z

1. Remove heater from car.
2. Loosen clamp on heater cock side.

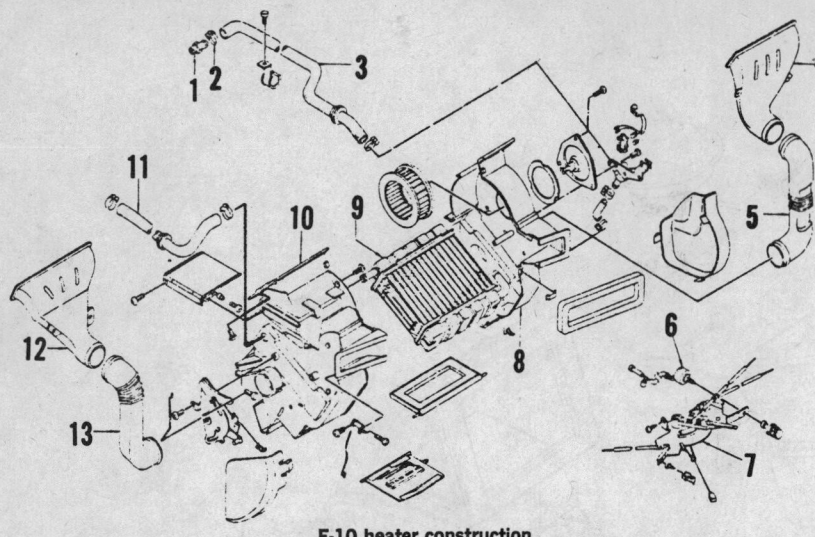

F-10 heater construction

1. Connector
2. Clip
3. Heater hose (inlet)
4. Defroster nozzle (R.H.)
5. Defroster duct (R.H.)
6. Heater switch
7. Heater control
8. Heater case (R.H.)
9. Heater core
10. Heater case (L.H.)
11. Heater hose (outlet)
12. Defroster nozzle (L.H.)
13. Defroster duct (L.H.)

3. Remove screws retaining heater cock and remove from case.

4. Loosen clamp on core side and disconnect hose.

5. Remove E-ring from floor door operating rod.

6. Remove five screws and take off side cover. Pull out heater core.

7. Assemble in reverse of the above.

Radio

Removal and Installation

510, 610, 620, 710, and F10

1. Detach all electrical connections.
2. Remove the radio knobs and retaining nuts.
3. Remove the mounting screws, tip the radio down at the rear, and remove.
4. Reverse the procedure for installation.

B110, B210

1. Remove the instrument cluster.
2. Detach all electrical connections.
3. Remove the radio knobs and retaining nuts.
4. Remove the rear support bracket.
5. Remove the radio.
6. Reverse the procedure for installation.

240 Z, 260 Z, 280 Z

The radio is mounted in the center console panel and the speaker in the left fender inner panel. The front face plate of the console must be removed to remove the radio.

Windshield Wiper Motor

Removal and Installation

510, 610, 710, 240 Z, 260 Z, 280 Z

The wiper motor and operating linkage is on the firewall under the hood.

1. Lift the wiper arms. Remove the securing nuts and detach the arms.

2. Remove the nuts holding the wiper pivots to the body. Remove the air intake grille for access.

3. Open the hood and unscrew the motor from the firewall.

4. Disconnect the wiring connector and remove the wiper motor with the linkage.

5. Reverse the procedure for installation.

NOTE: *If the wipers do not park correctly, adjust the position of the automatic stop cover on the wiper motor.*

B110, B210

The wiper motor is on the firewall under the hood. The operating linkage is on the firewall inside the car.

1. Detach the motor wiring plug.

2. Inside the car, remove the nut connecting the linkage to the wiper shaft.

3. Unbolt and remove the wiper motor from the firewall.

4. Reverse the procedure for installation.

620

The wiper motor is on the firewall, inside the truck.

1. Remove the air intake grille in front of the windshield.

2. Detach the connecting rod from the wiper motor arm, working through the grille opening.

3. Disconnect the electrical connector at the motor.

4. Unscrew and remove the motor.

5. Reverse the procedure for installation.

F10

1. Disconnect battery ground cable and remove meter cover and glove box.

2. Remove the base of the wiper arm from the pivot shaft by raising the wiper blade away from the glass and loosening the attaching nut.

3. Remove the wiper motor by removing the ball joint connecting the motor shaft to the wiper link. Remove the motor from the dash.

4. Remove the pivot bolts and remove the link assembly.

Installation is the reverse of removal. Make sure the angle is correct to obtain the right sweeping zone.

Instrument Cluster

Removal and Installation

510

1. Disconnect the speedometer cable by unscrewing the nut at the back of the speedometer.

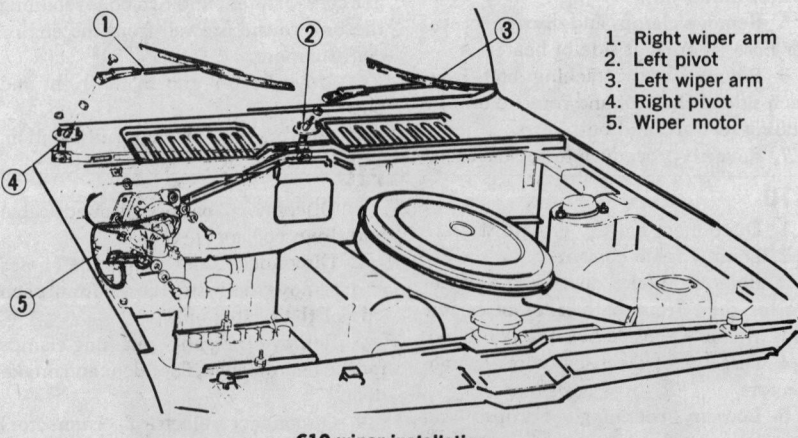

1. Right wiper arm
2. Left pivot
3. Left wiper arm
4. Right pivot
5. Wiper motor

610 wiper installation

2. Remove the screws holding the instrument cluster to the instrument panel.

3. Pull out the instrument cluster enough to detach the wiring.

4. Remove the cluster. Individual instrument units can be removed from the rear of the cluster.

B110, B210

1. Disconnect the battery negative lead.

2. Depress the wiper, light switch, and choke knobs, turning them counterclockwise to remove.

3. From the rear, disconnect the lighter wire. Turn and remove the lighter outer case.

4. Remove the radio and heater knobs.

5. Remove the shell cover from the steering column.

6. Remove the screws which hold the instrument cluster to the instrument panel. Pull out the cluster.

7. Disconnect the wiring connector. Disconnect the speedometer cable by unscrewing the nut at the back of the speedometer.

8. Individual instruments may be removed from the rear of the cluster.

610, 710

1. Disconnect the battery ground cable.

2. Remove the four screws and the steering column cover.

3. Remove the screws which attach the cluster face. Two are just above the steering column, and there is one inside each of the outer instrument recesses.

4. Pull the cluster lid forward.

5. Disconnect the multiple connector.

6. Disconnect the speedometer cable.

7. Disconnect any other wiring.

8. Remove the cluster face.

9. Remove the odometer knob if the vehicle has one.

10. Remove the six screws and the cluster.

11. Instruments may now be readily replaced.

12. Reverse the procedure for installation.

620

1. Disconnect the battery ground cable.

2. Remove the three cluster face retaining screws from inside the instrument recesses.

3. Remove the cluster face retaining screw from underneath the instrument panel.

4. Pull the cluster face outward.

5. Disconnect the speedometer cable and the multiple electrical connector. Disconnect any other wiring. Remove the four screws which hold the cluster to the cluster face. Remove the cluster.

6. Reverse the procedure for installation.

F10

1. Disconnect the battery ground cable and remove all knobs, nuts and exposed screws.

2. Remove the ashtray and the retaining screws. Pull the panel downward and forward. Disconnect the cigarette lighter connector. Remove panel.

Installation is the reverse of removal.

Instruments

Removal and Installation—240 Z, 260 Z, 280 Z

The speedometer and tachometer are both attached at the rear with two wingnuts. Access is from under the instrument panel. After the wingnuts are removed, the instrument can be pulled out through the instrument panel. The other three gauge units are held to brackets by slotted head hex bolts. To gain access, the center console panel must be removed.

FUSE BOX LOCATION CHART

Model	Fuse Box Location	Fusible Link Location
521, 510	Engine compartment right rear	None
110	Under instrument panel, right of steering column	Between battery and alternator
240Z	Under ash tray in console	At alternator, at starter
610	Below hood release knob	Adjacent to battery
620	Below head-light switch	Between battery and alternator
710	Engine compartment Right rear	Relay bracket right front of engine compartment
260Z, 280Z	Under dash at extreme right	Right rear of engine compartment*
B210	Above brake light switch	Engine compartment below voltage regulator
F-10	Under dash at extreme left	Off (+) cable on battery

*A fusing link for the fuel injection is in (+) battery cable

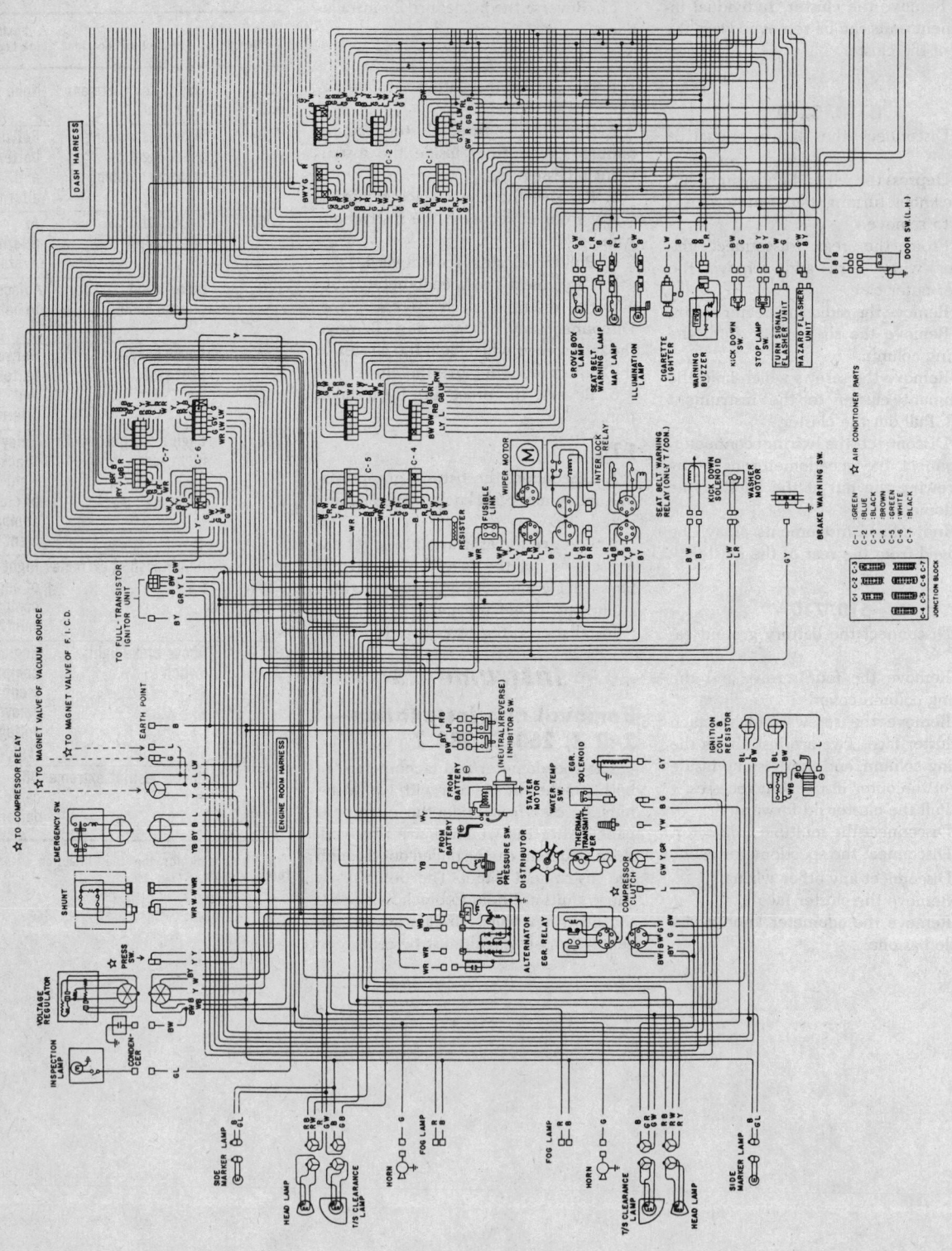

1974-75 260Z automatic transmission

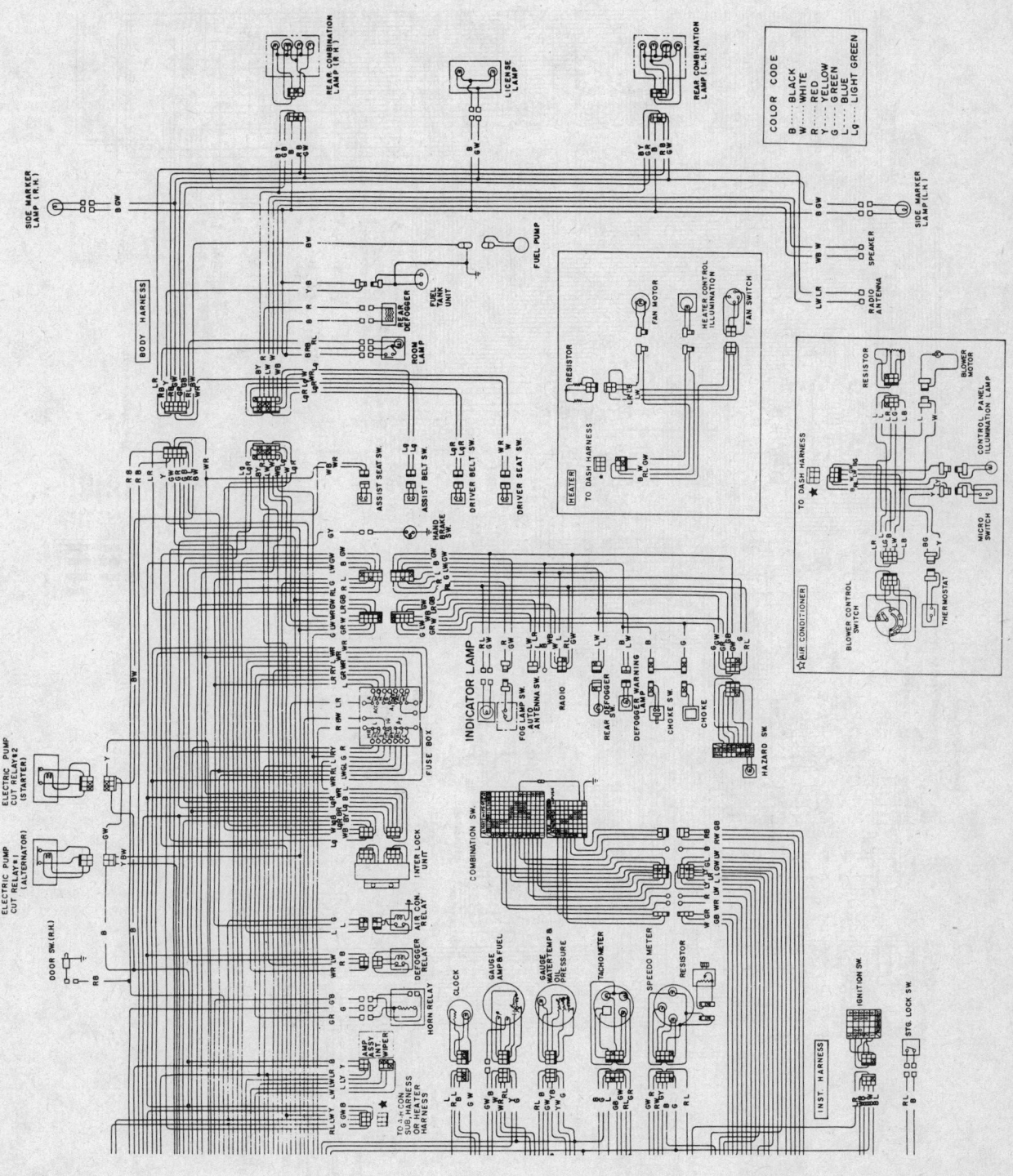

1974-75 260Z automatic transmission

Wiring Circuits

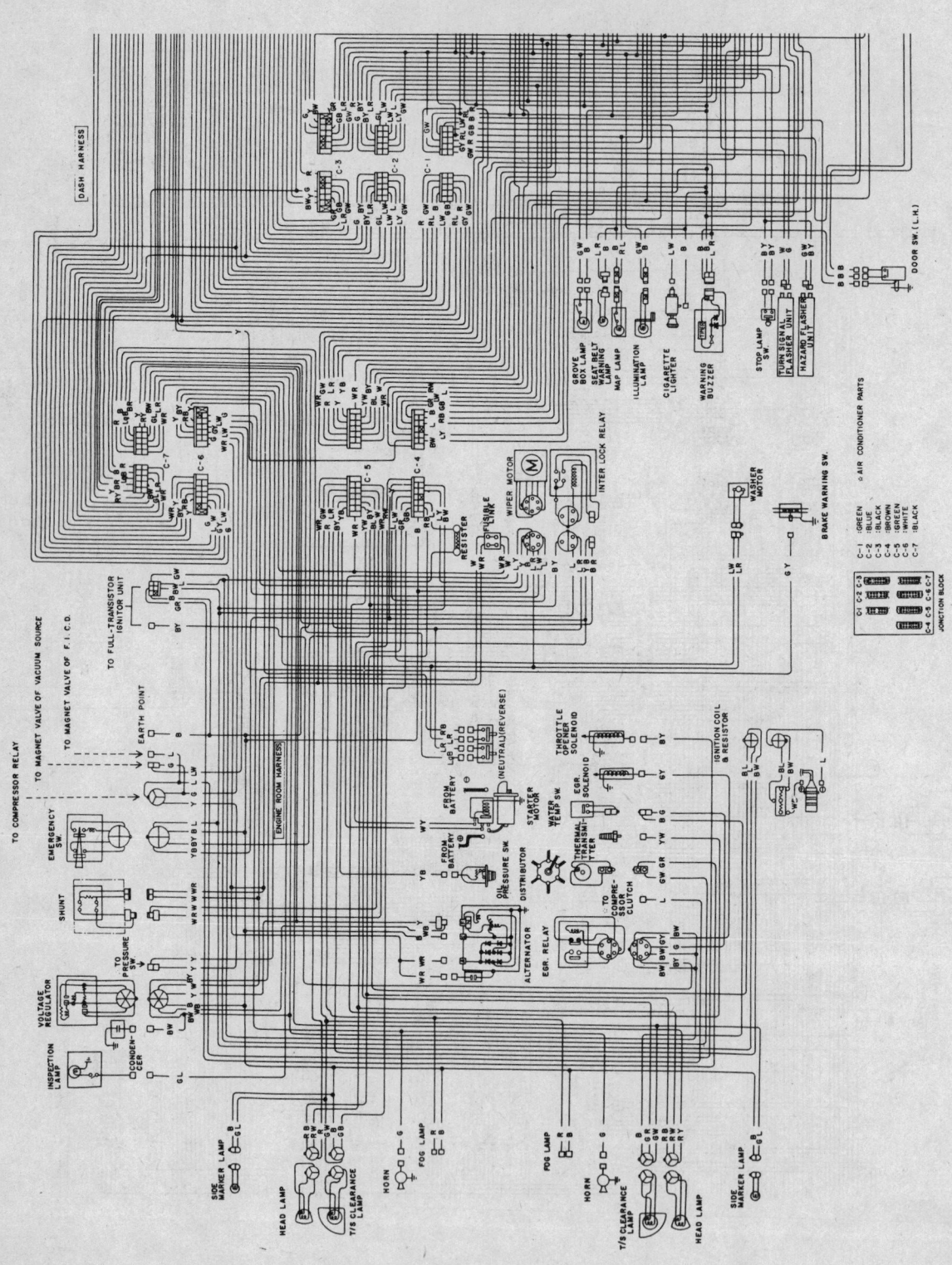

1974-75 260Z manual transmission

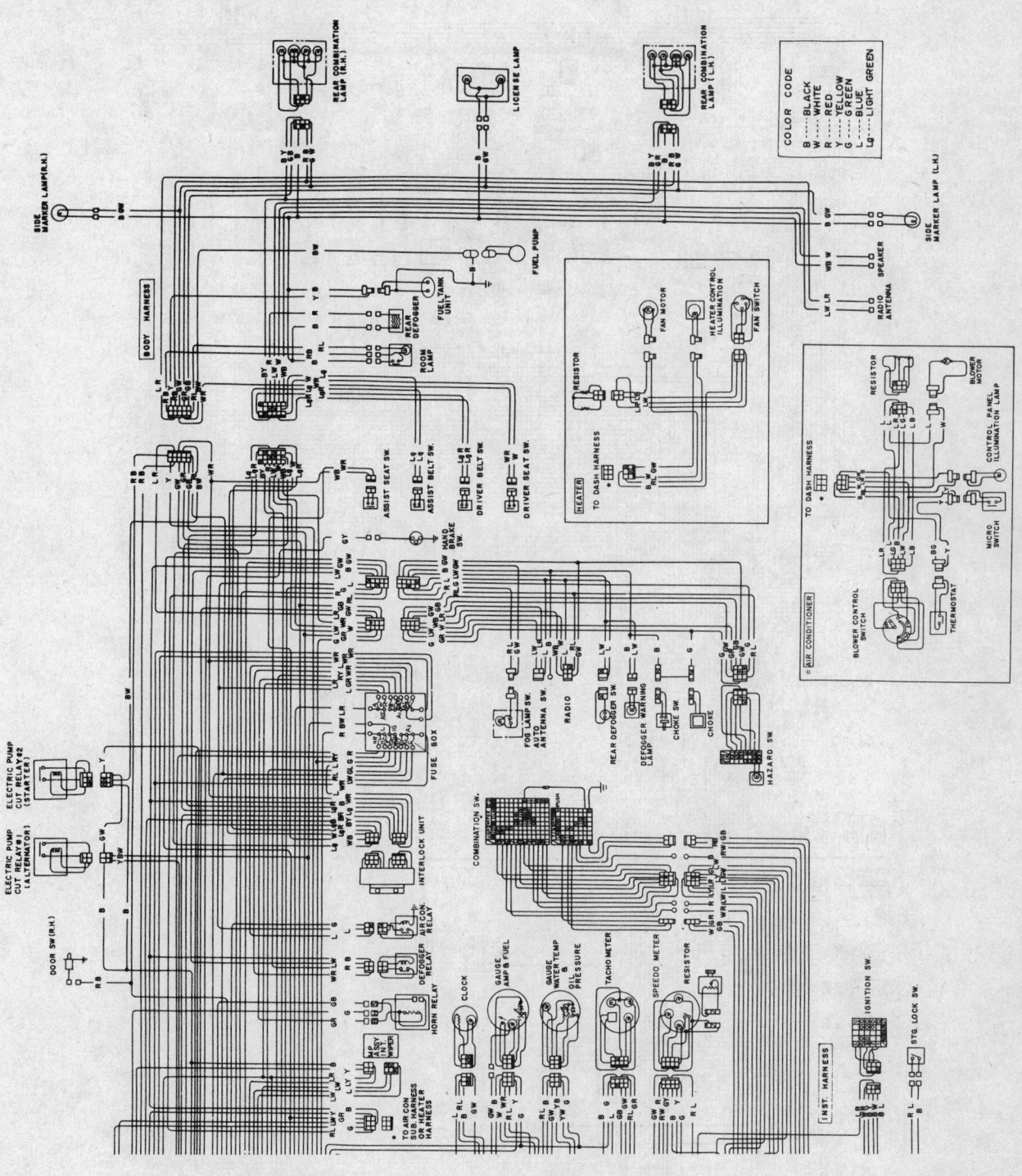

1974-75 260Z manual transmission

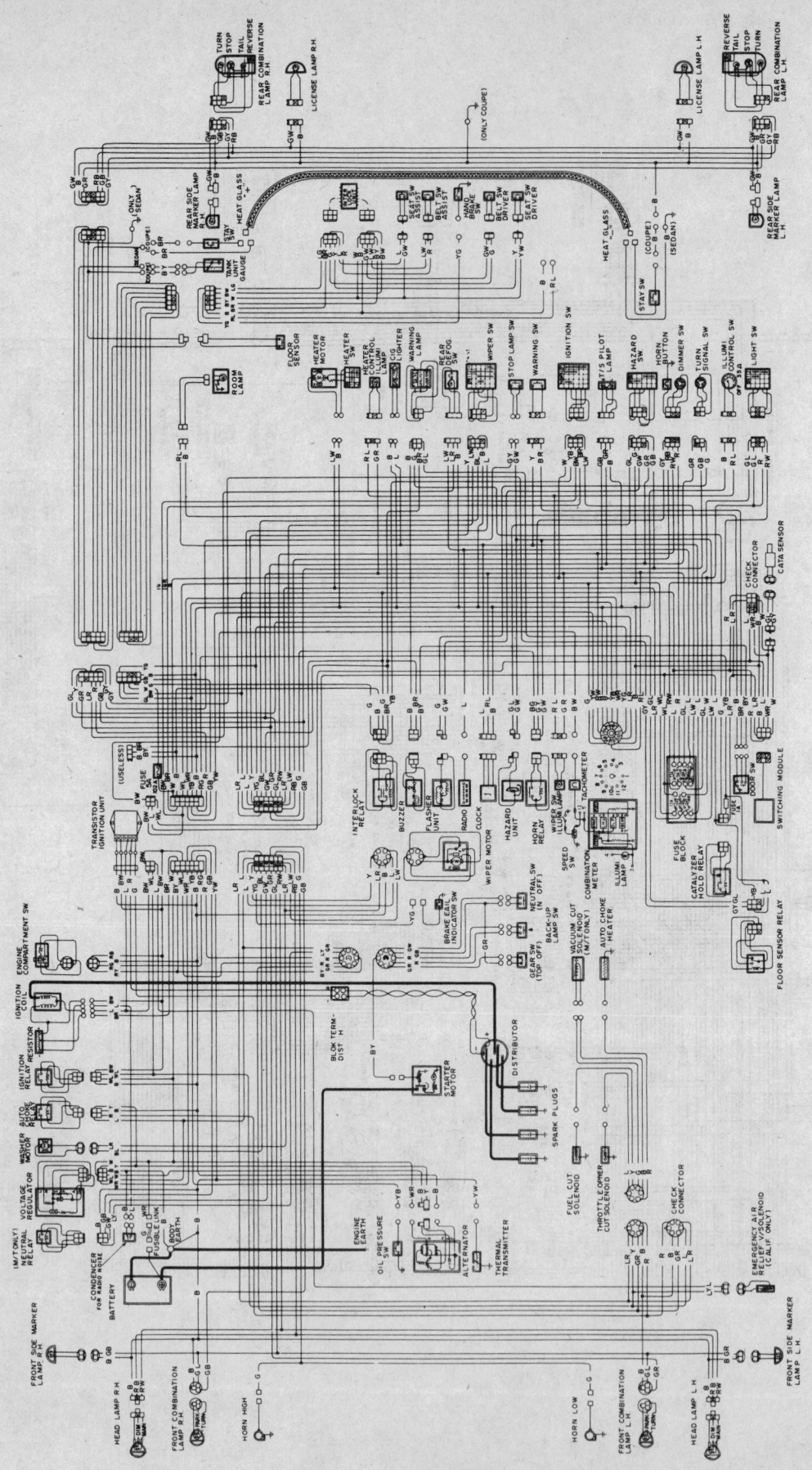

1975 B210 wiring diagram (California w/manual transmission)

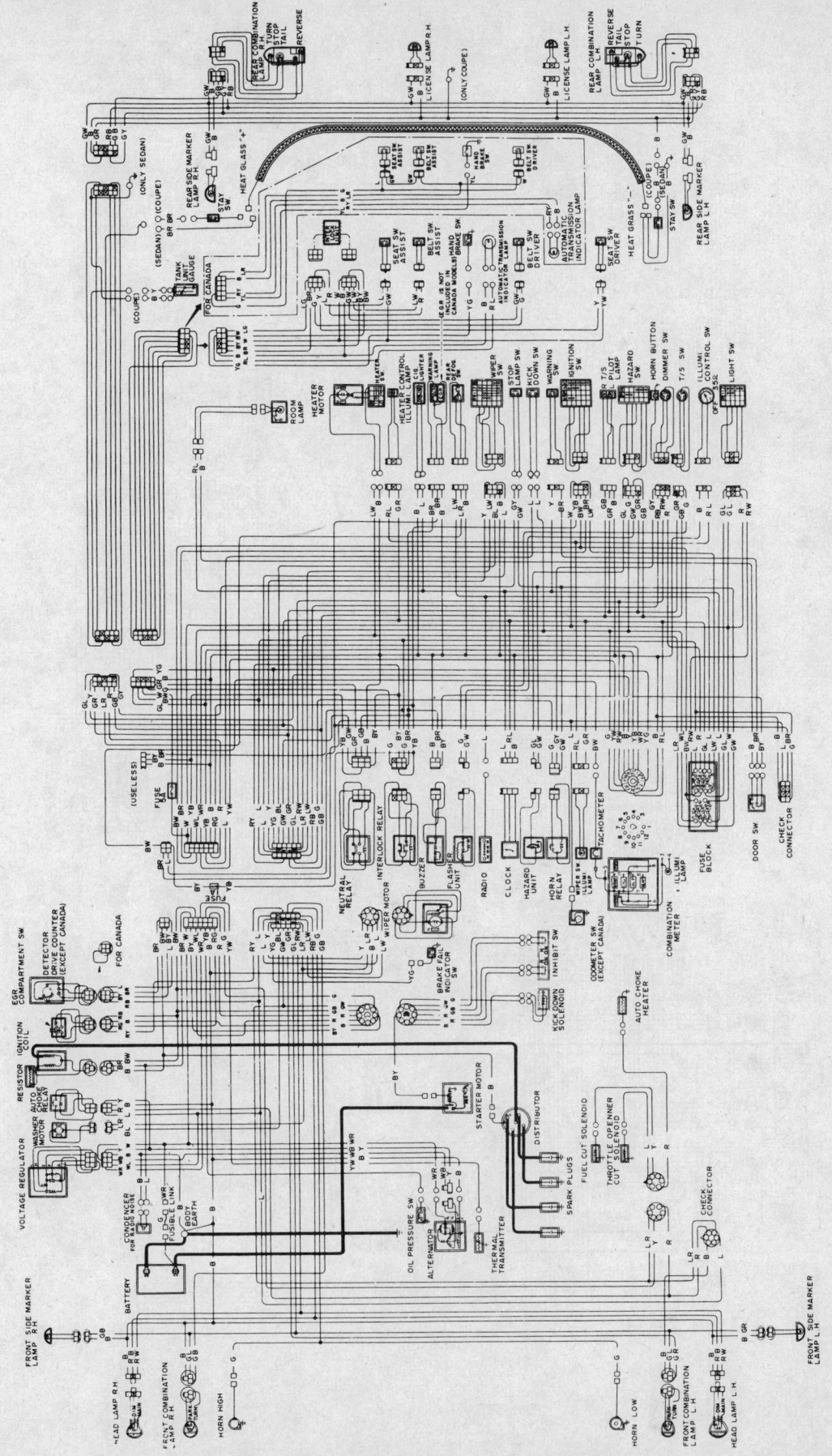

1975 B210 wiring diagram (Federal w/automatic transmission)

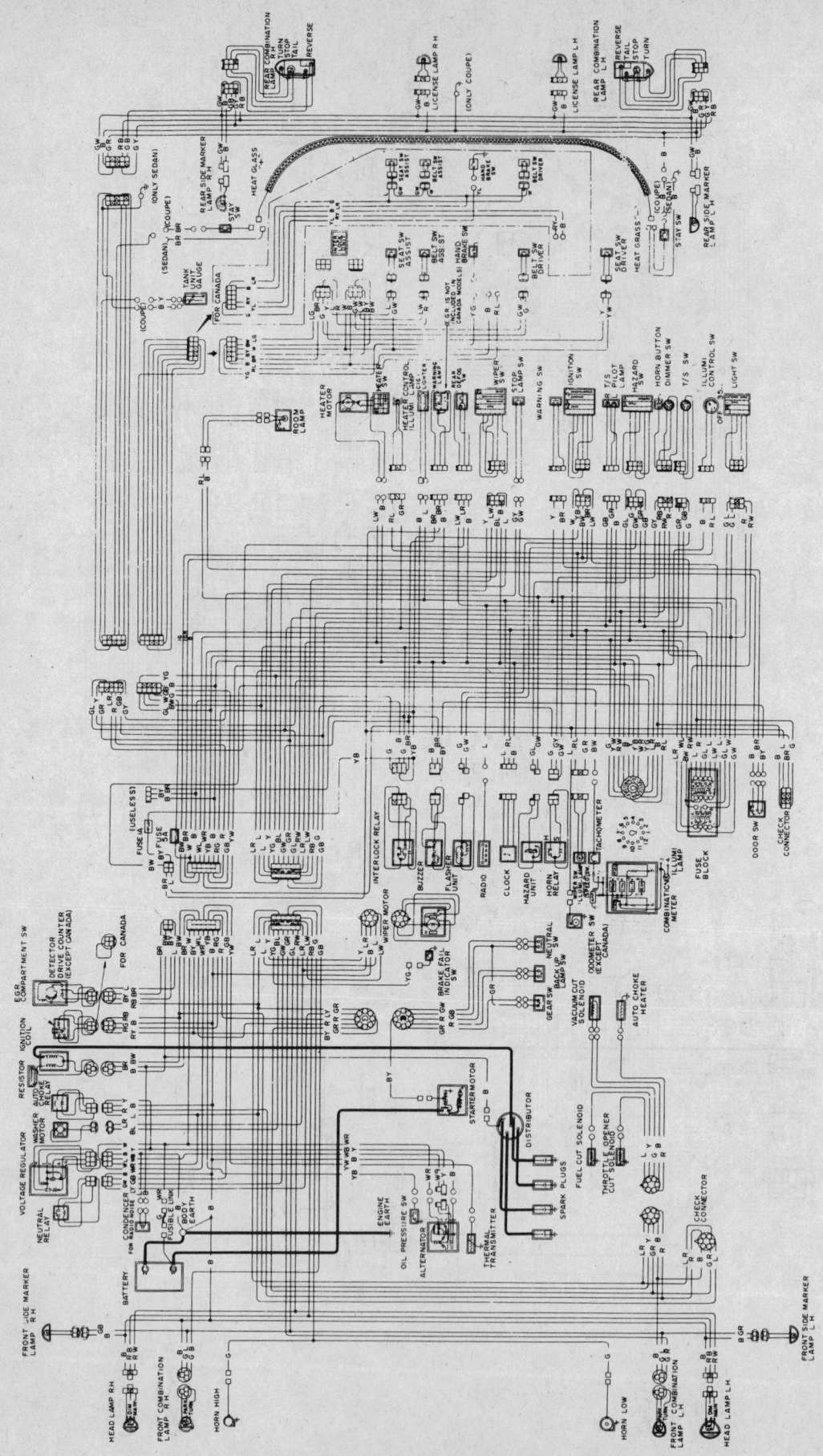

1975 B210 wiring diagram (Federal w/manual transmission)

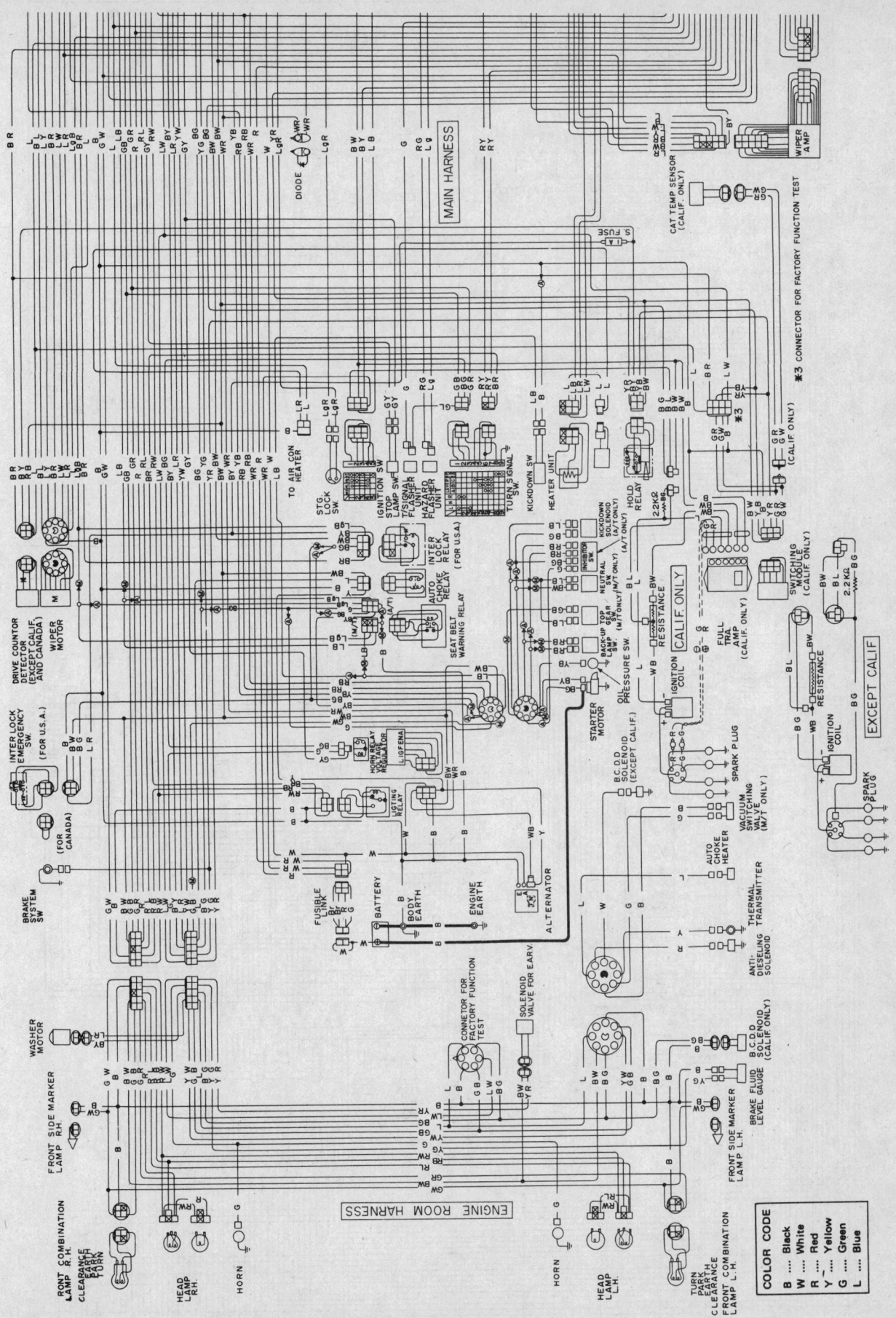

Datsun

1975 610 sedan, fastback, and wagon

305

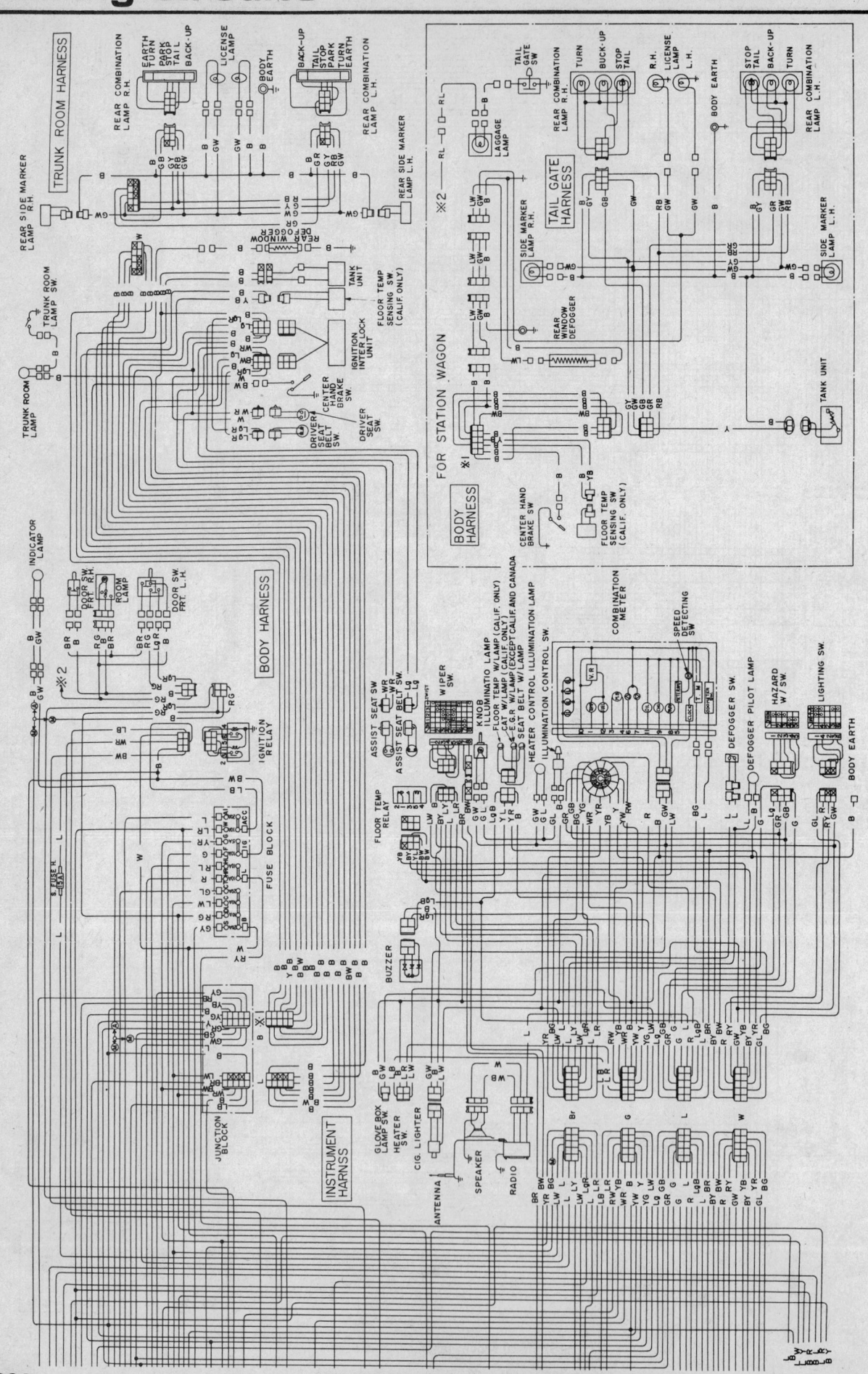

1975 610 sedan, fastback, and wagon

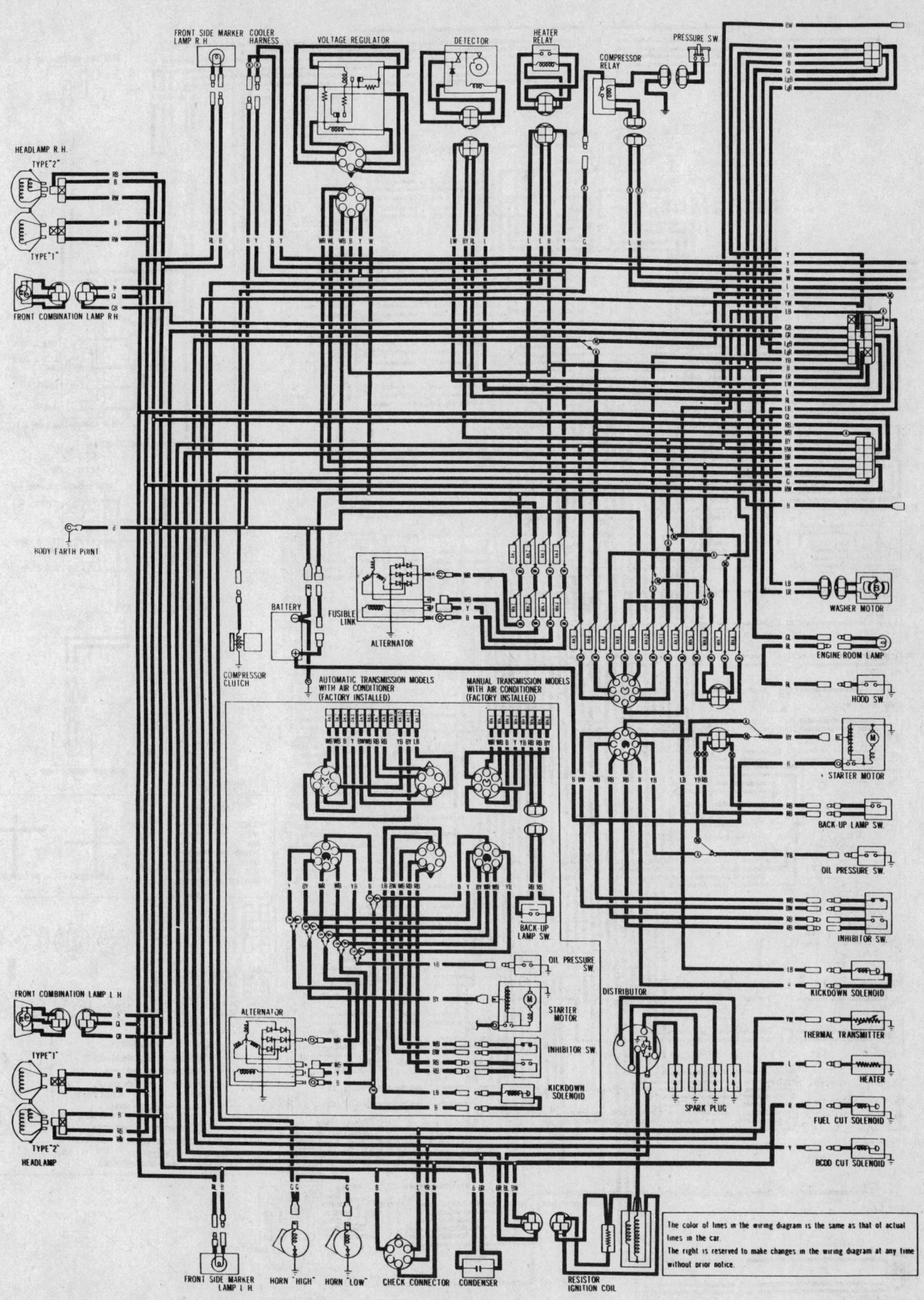

1975 620 pick-up

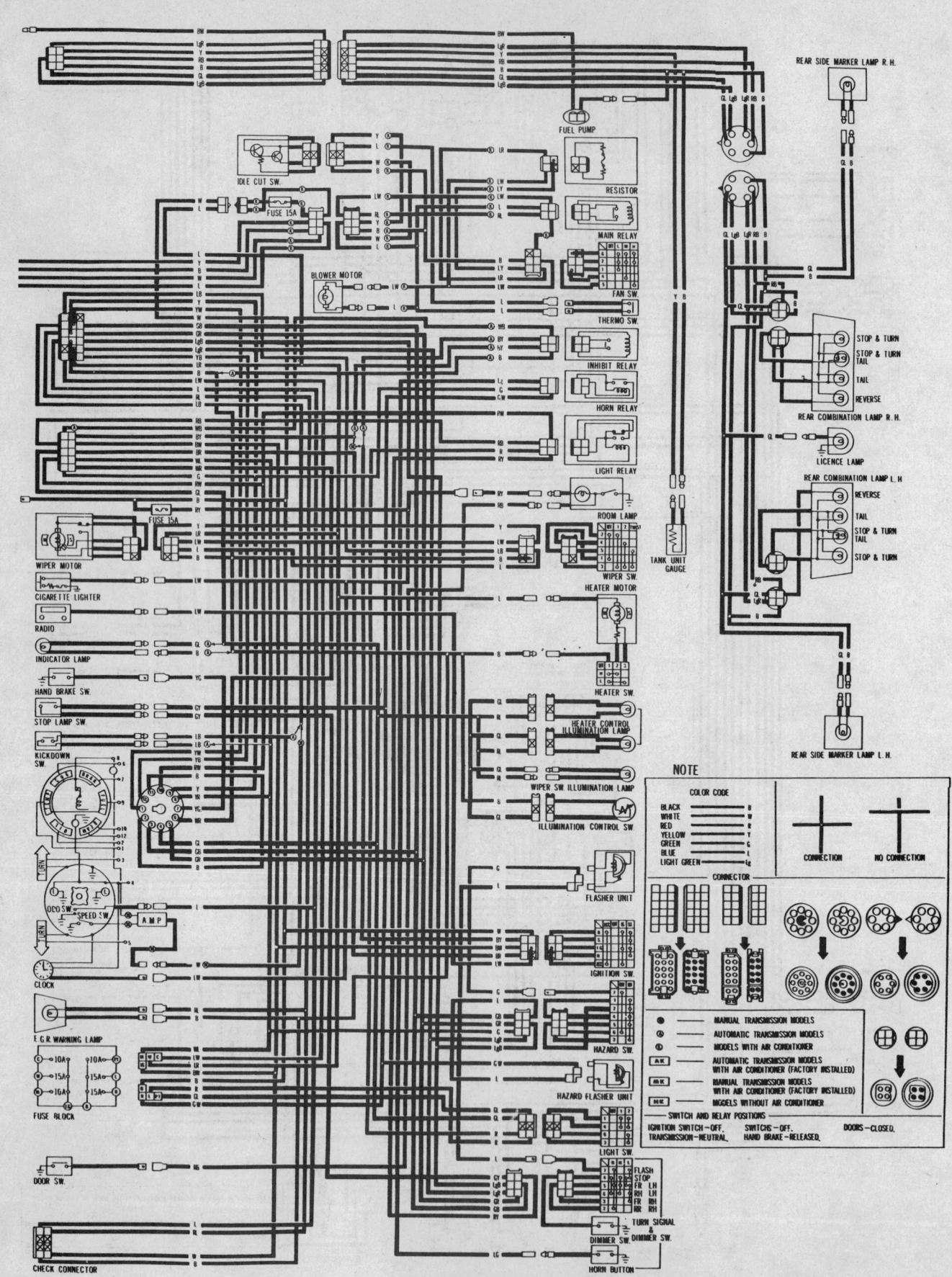

1975 620 pick-up

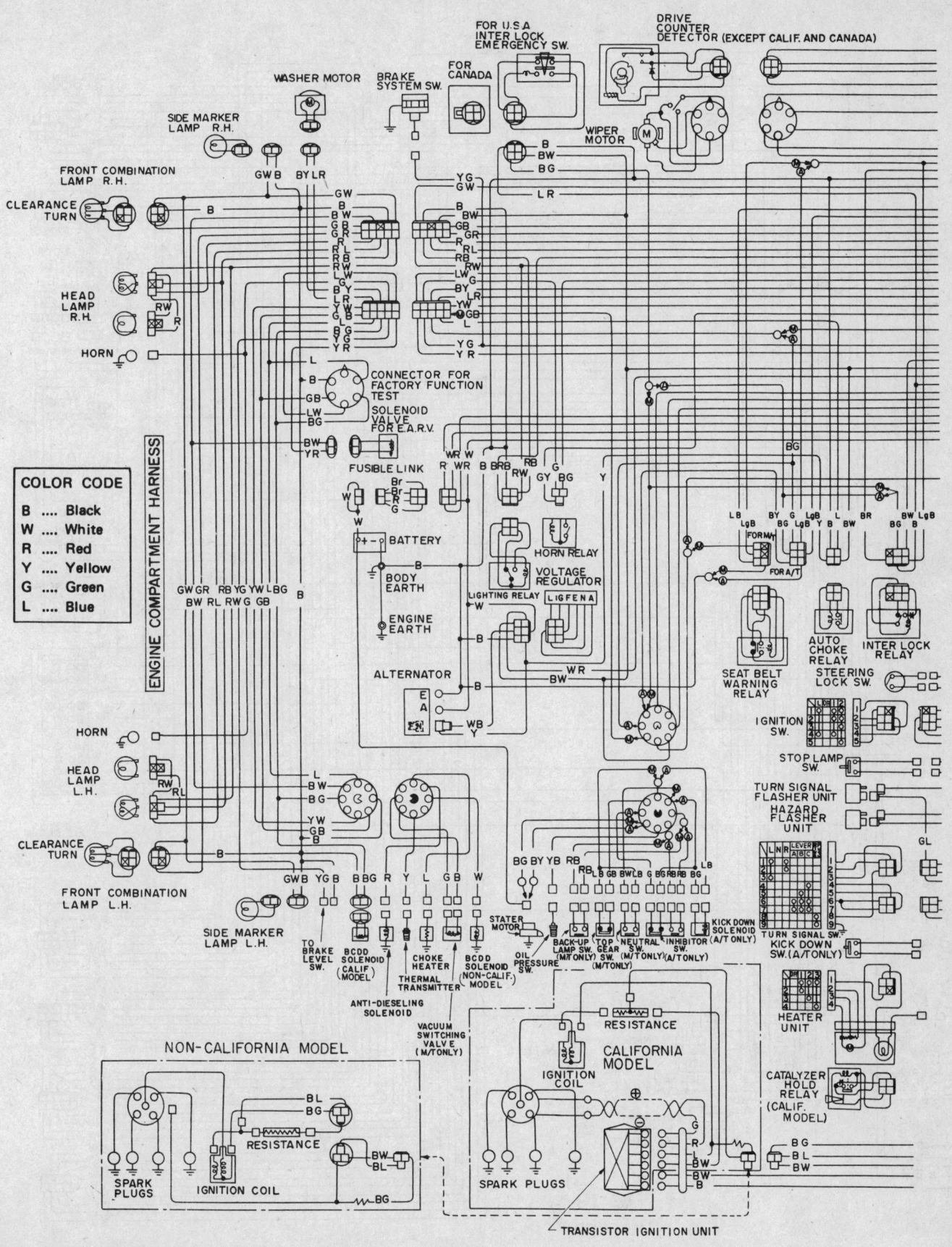

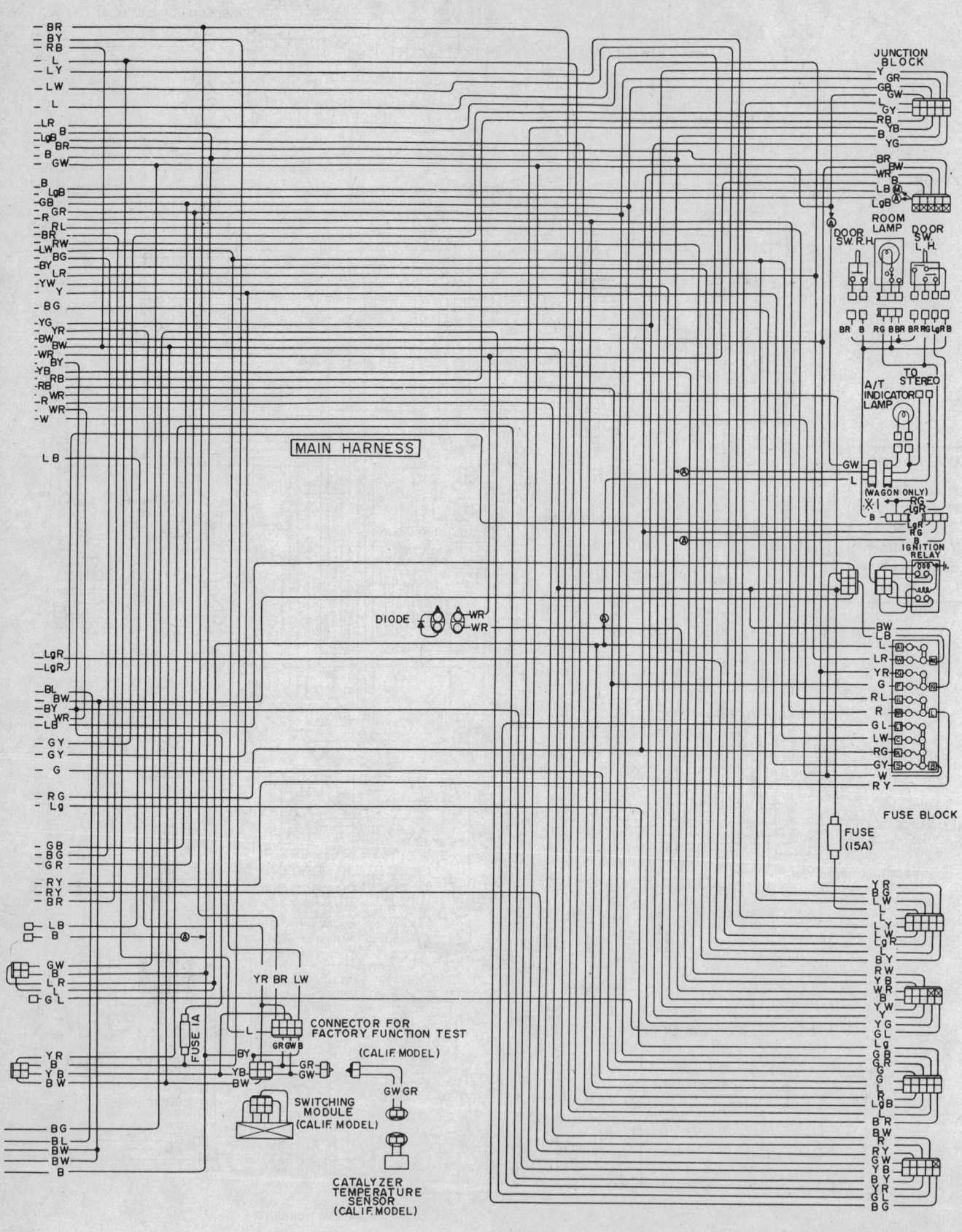

MAIN HARNESS

1975 710   PART 2 OF 3

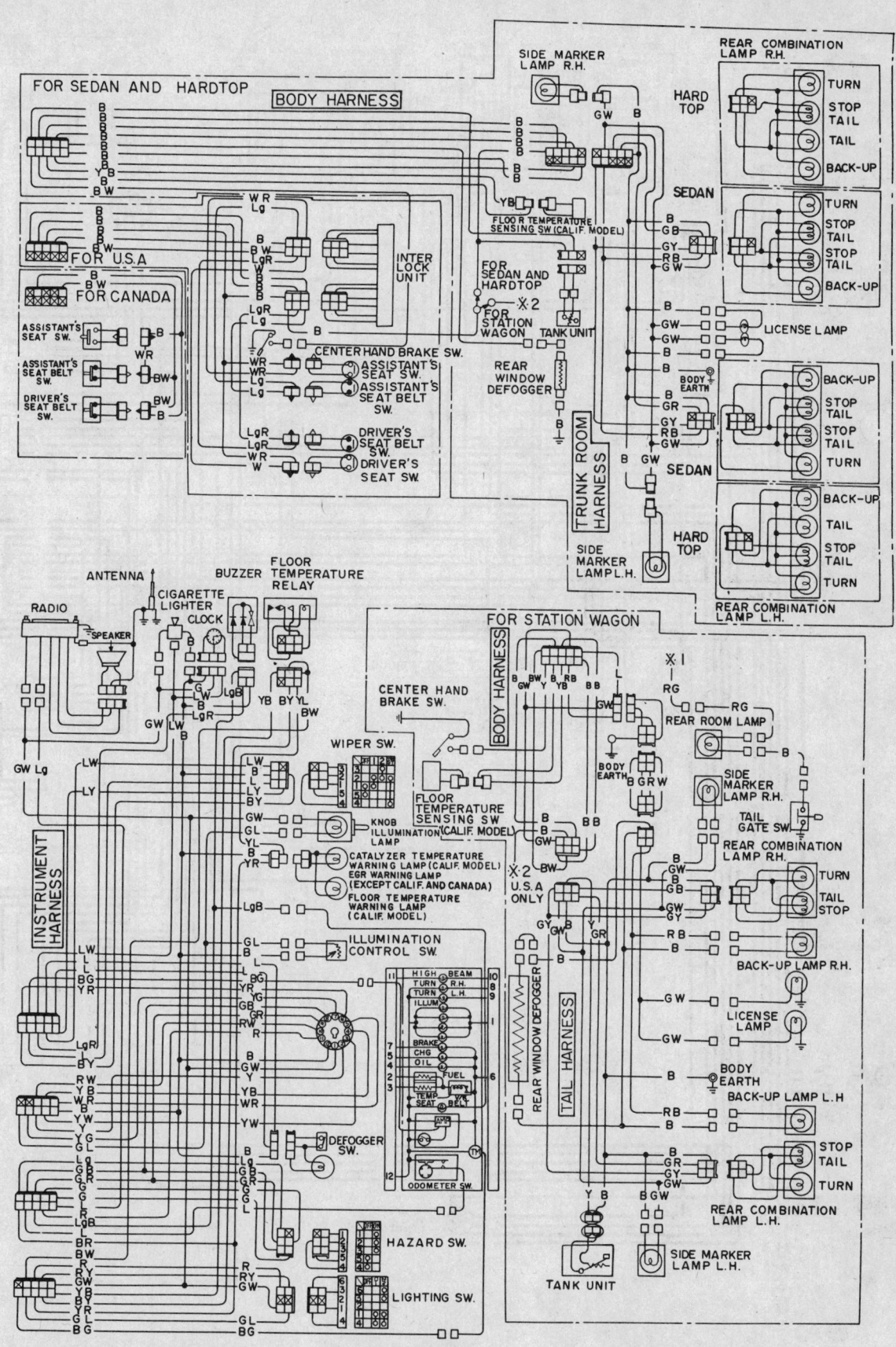

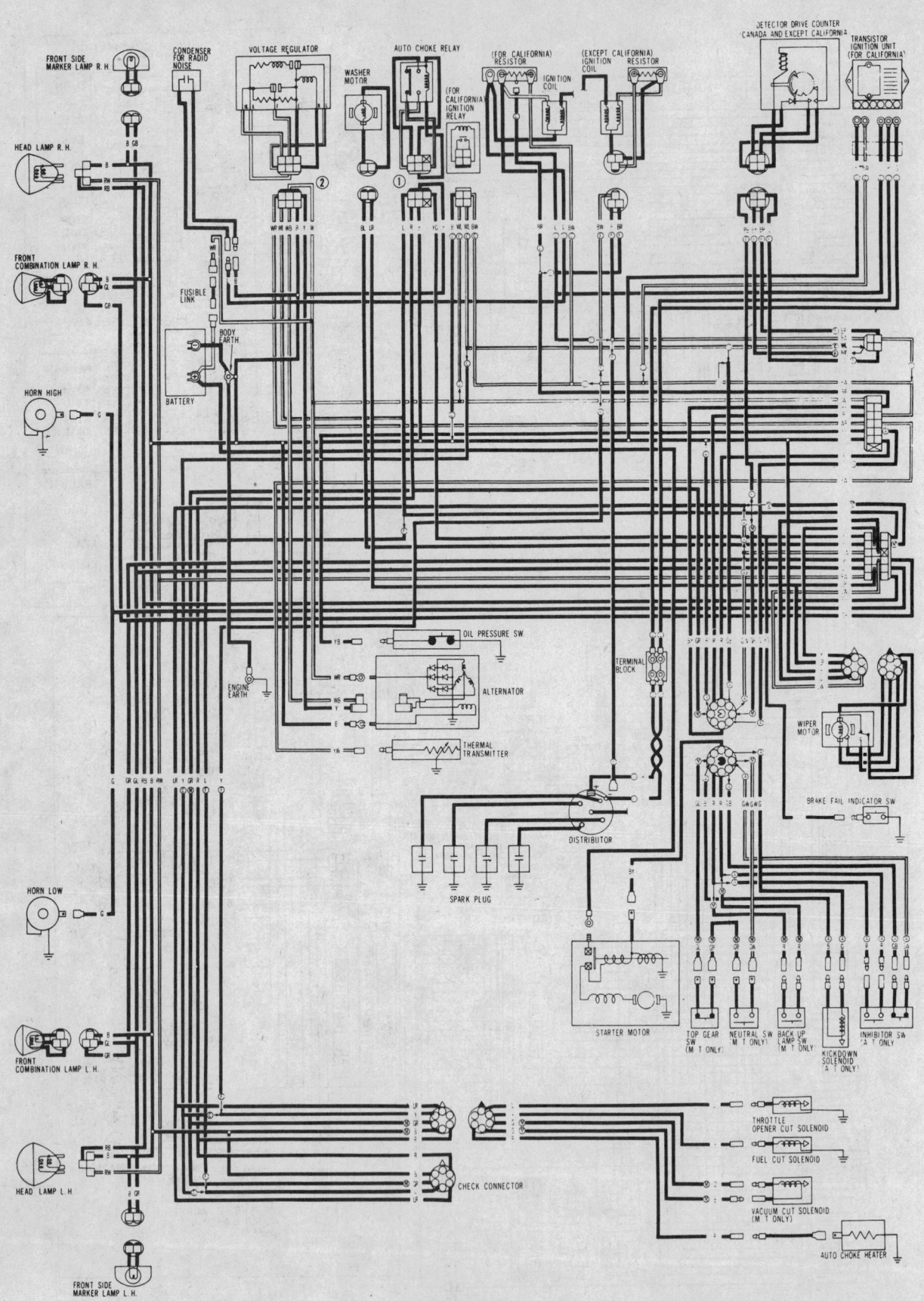

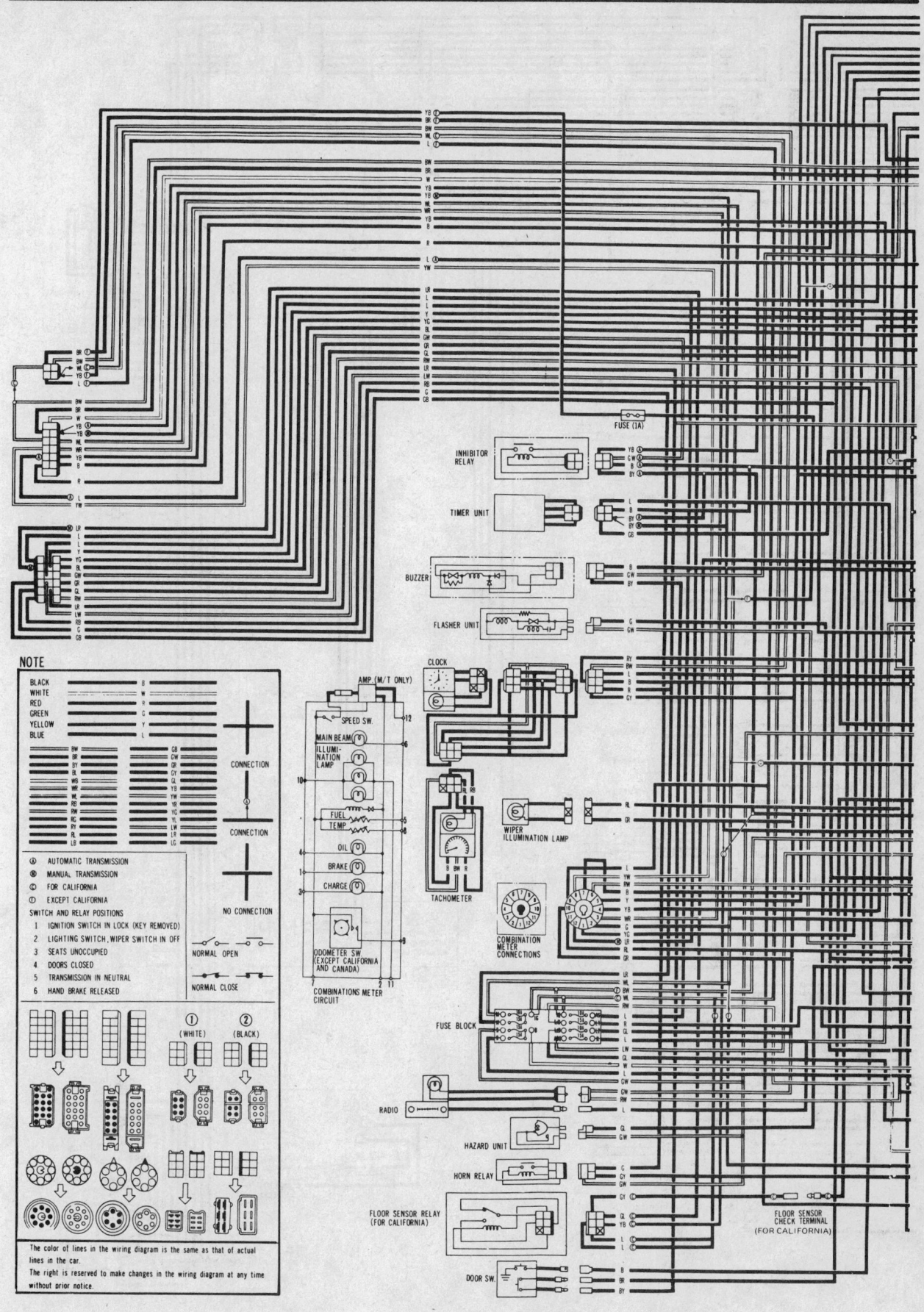

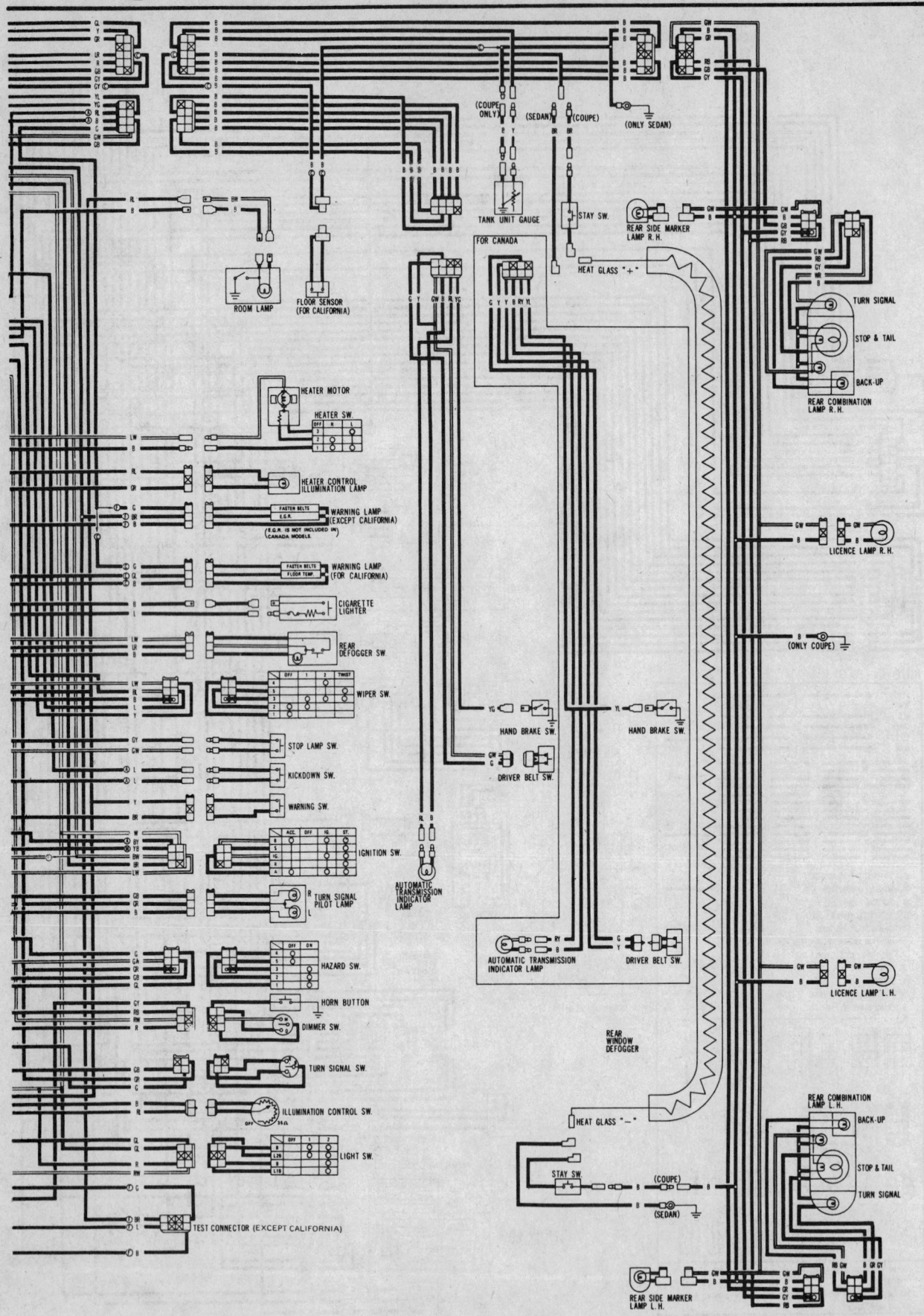

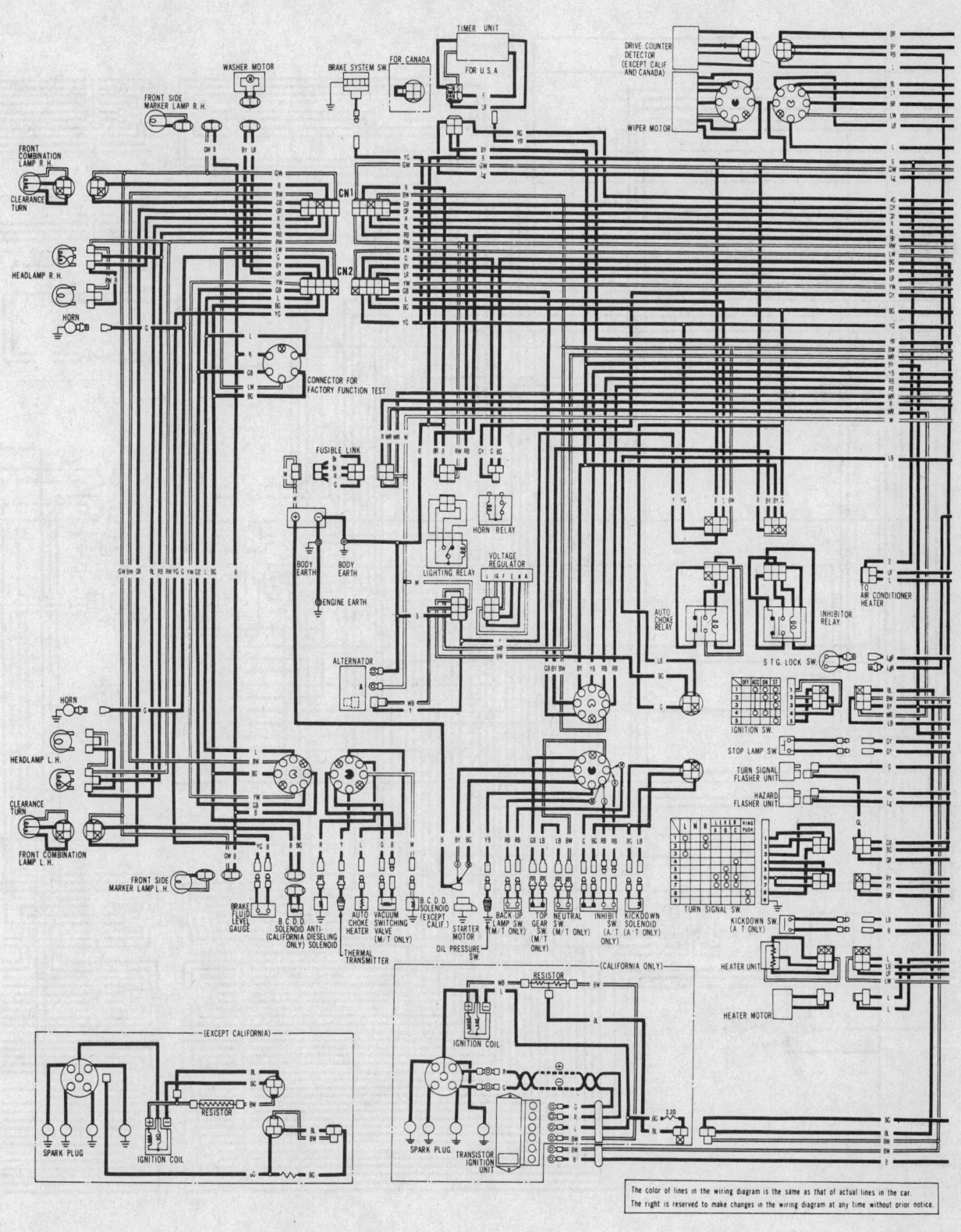

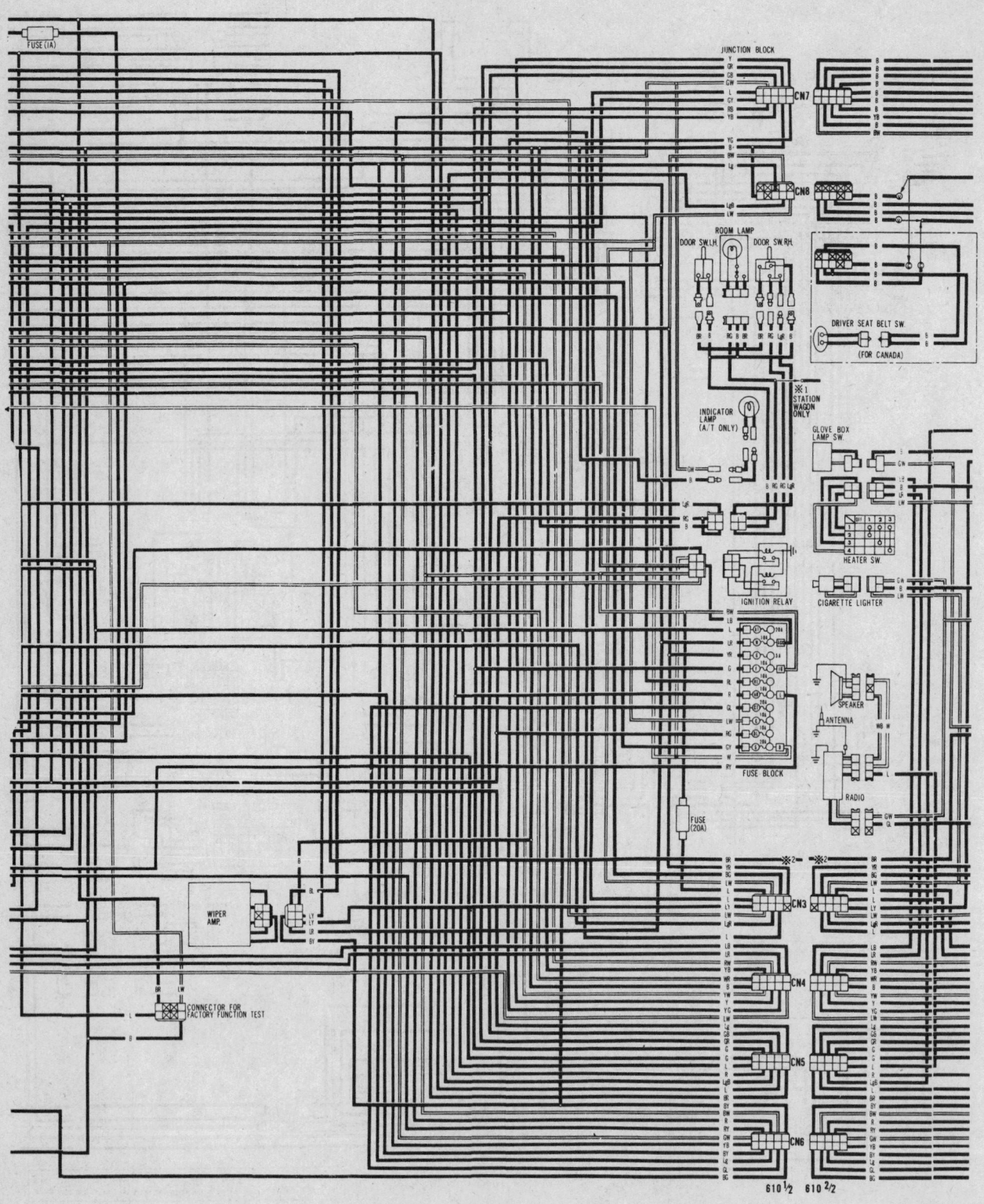

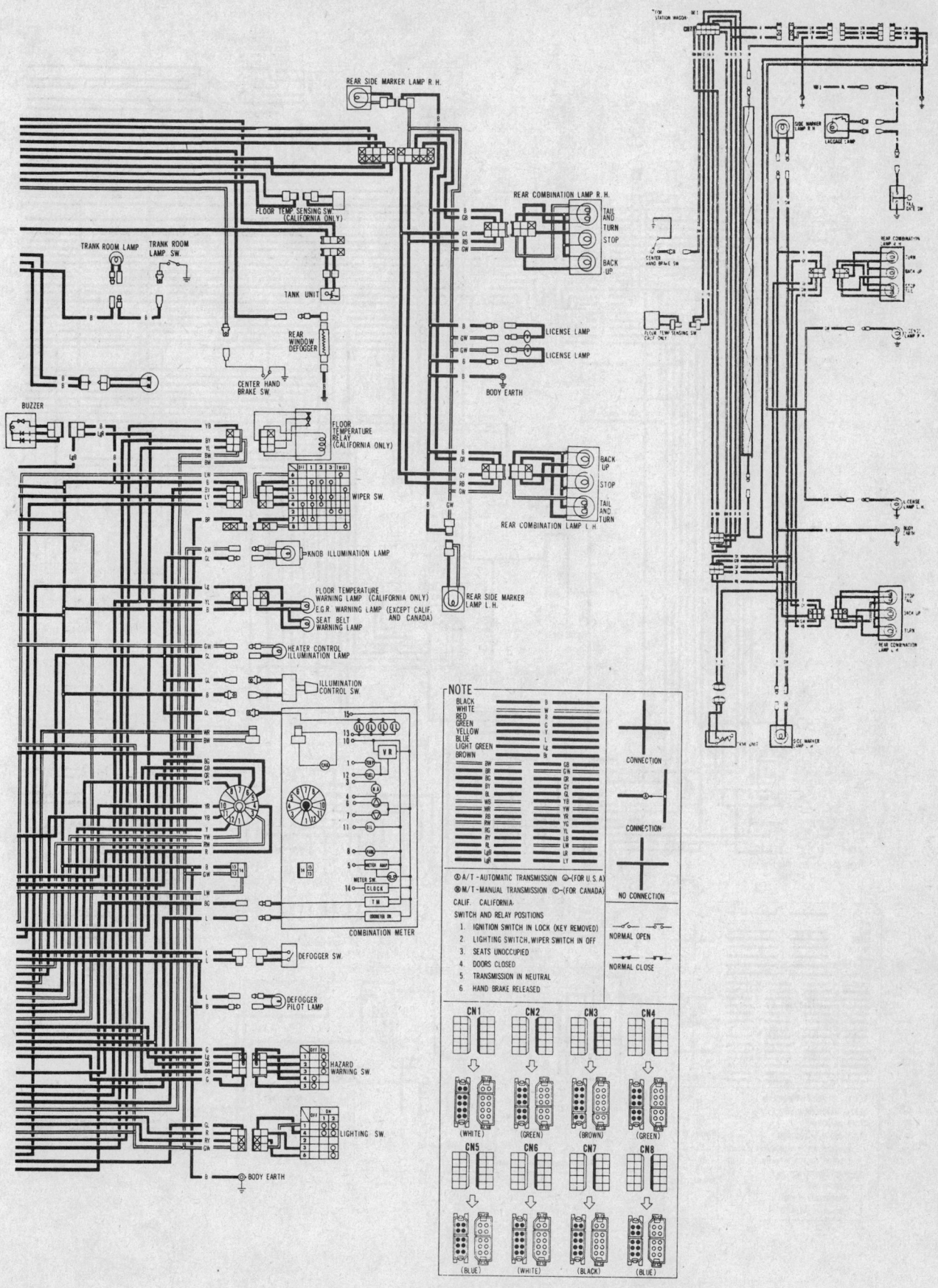

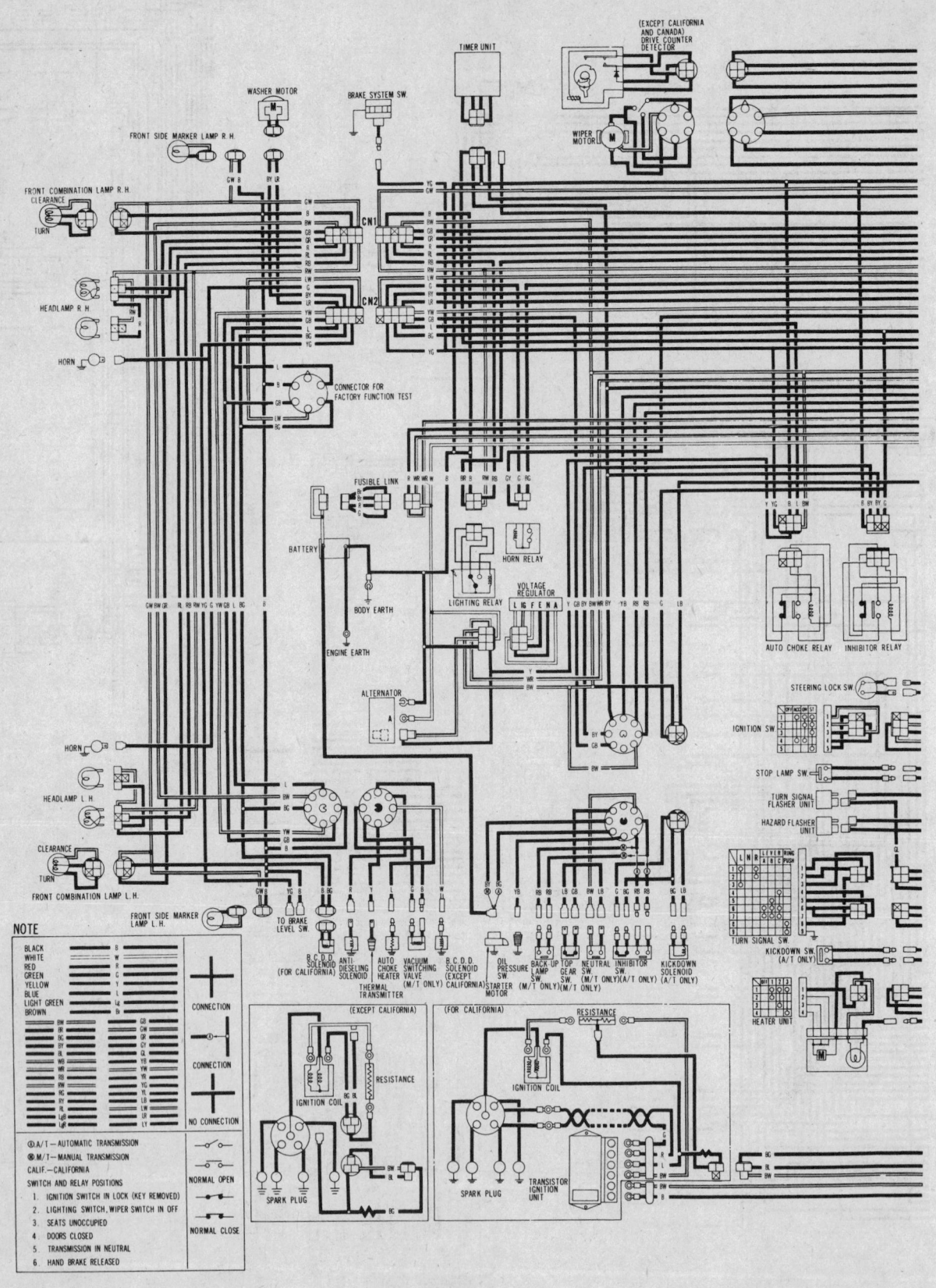

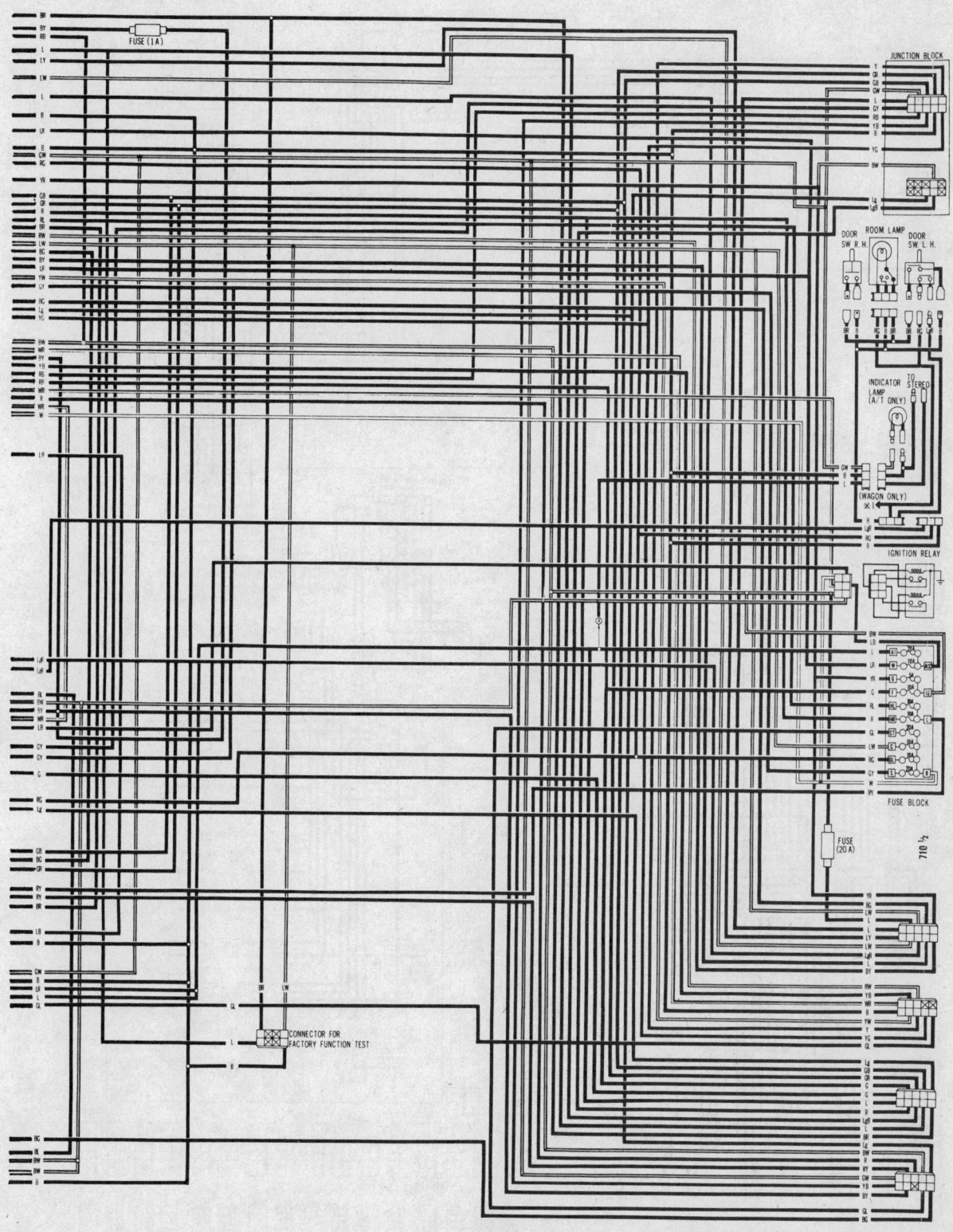

Wiring Circuits

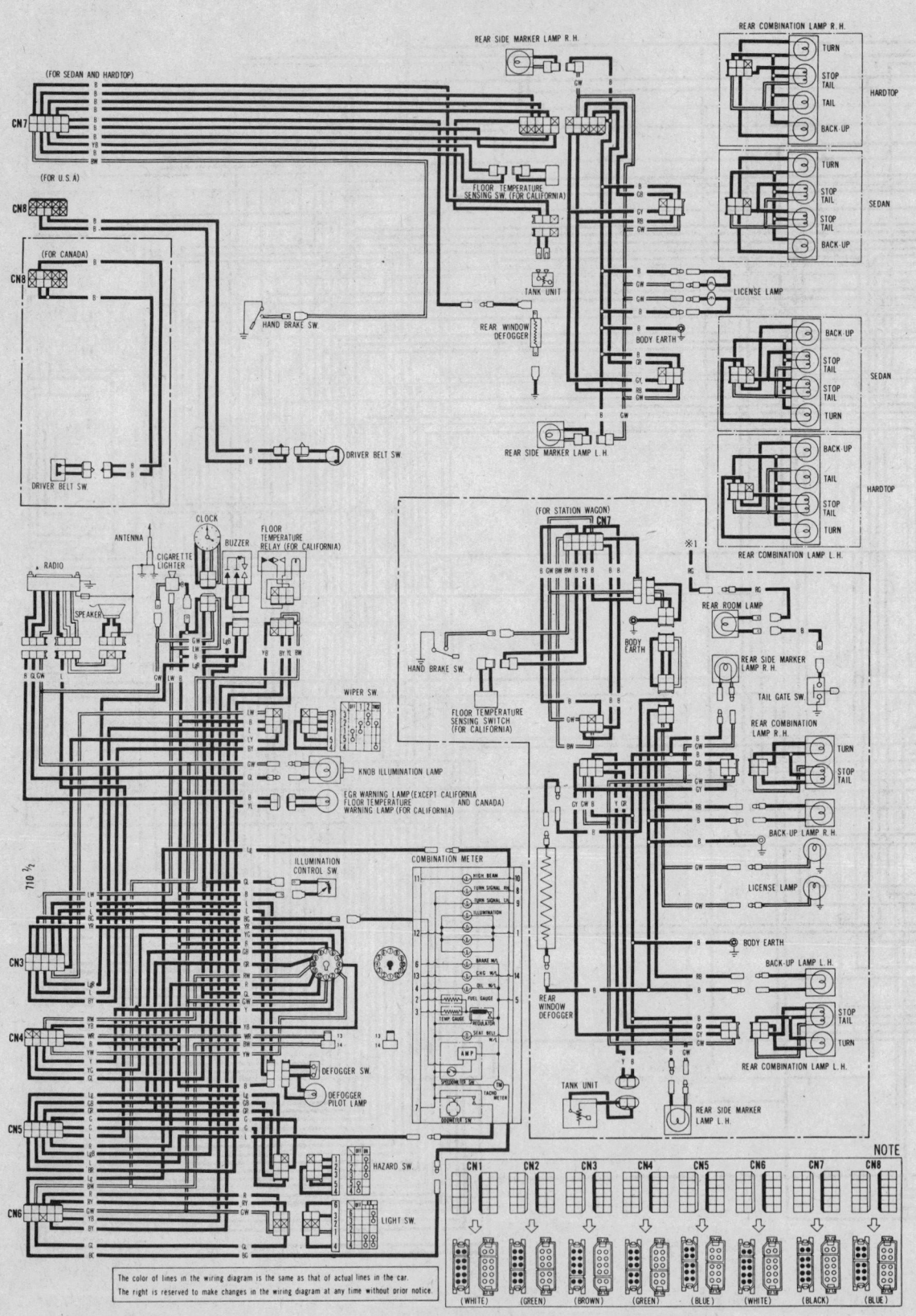

1976-77 710   PART 3 OF 3

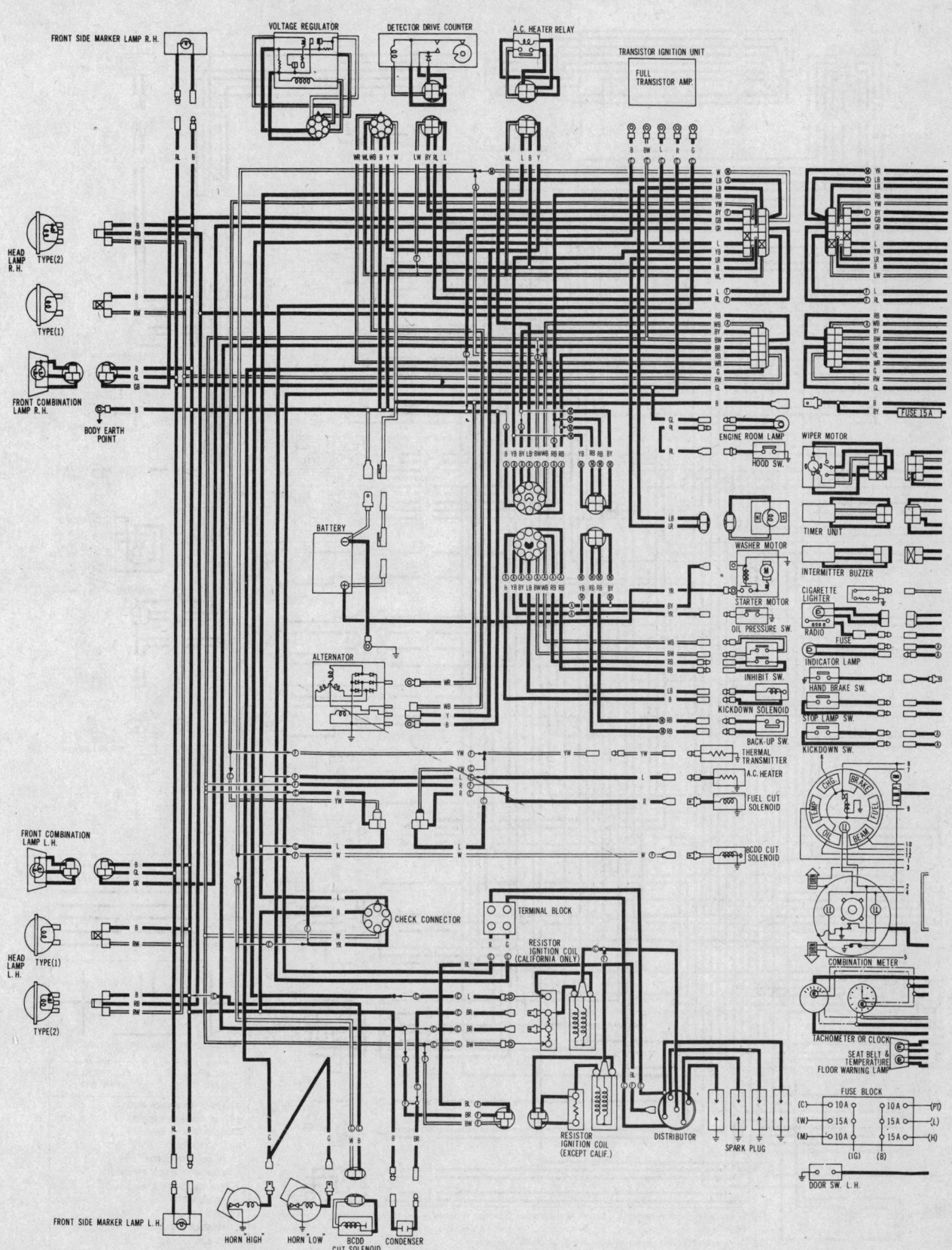

1976 620 pick-up

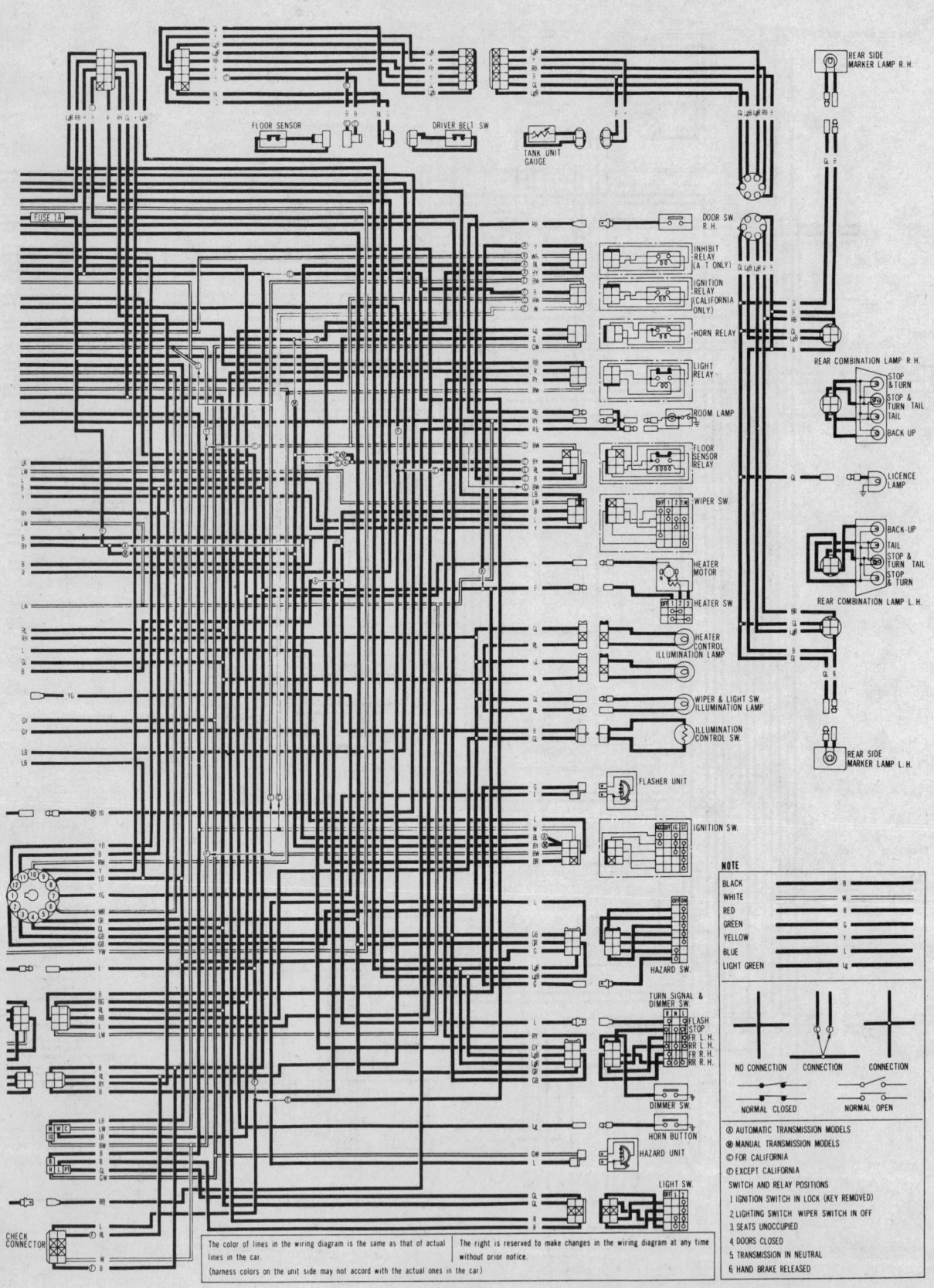

1976 620 pick-up

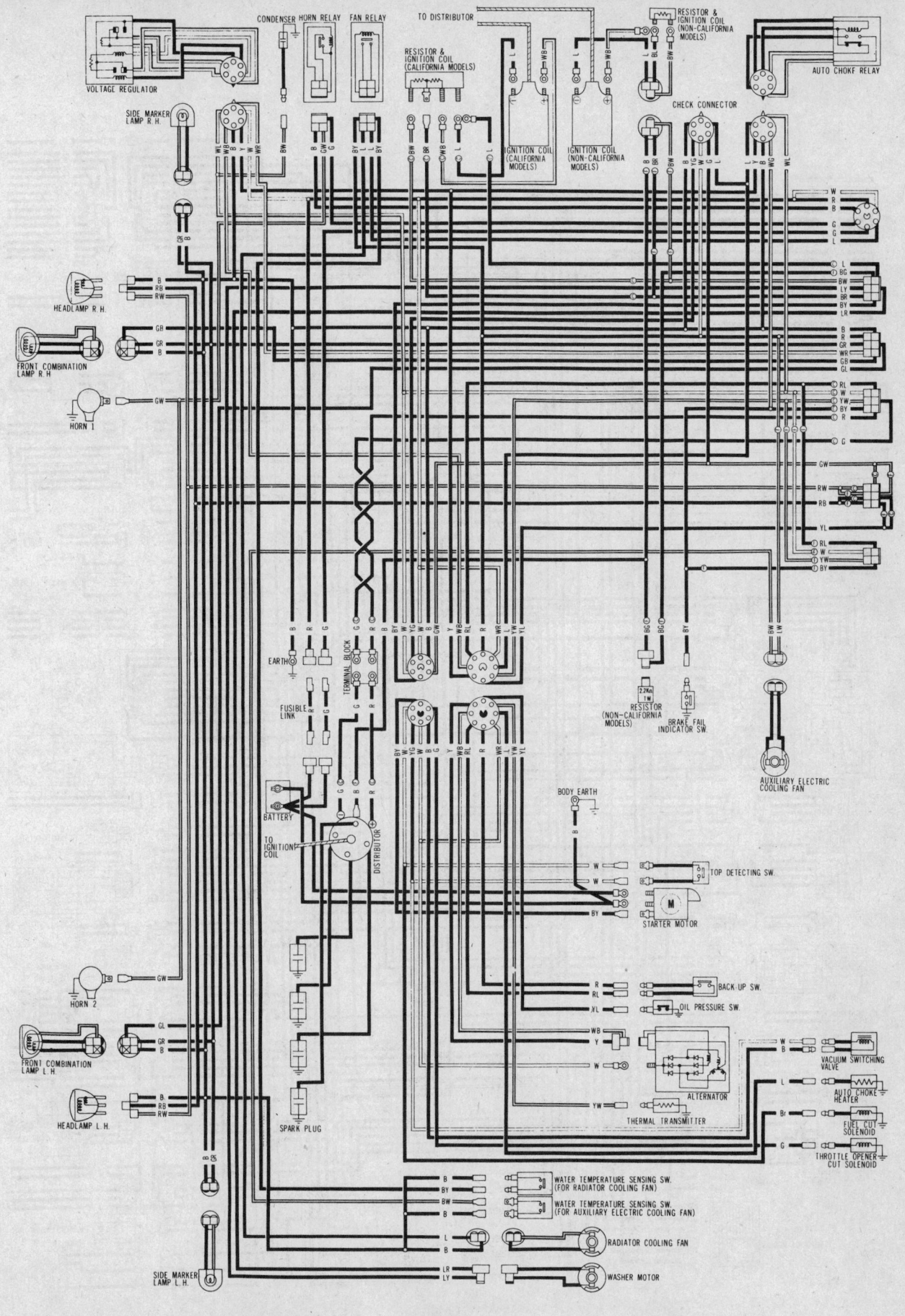

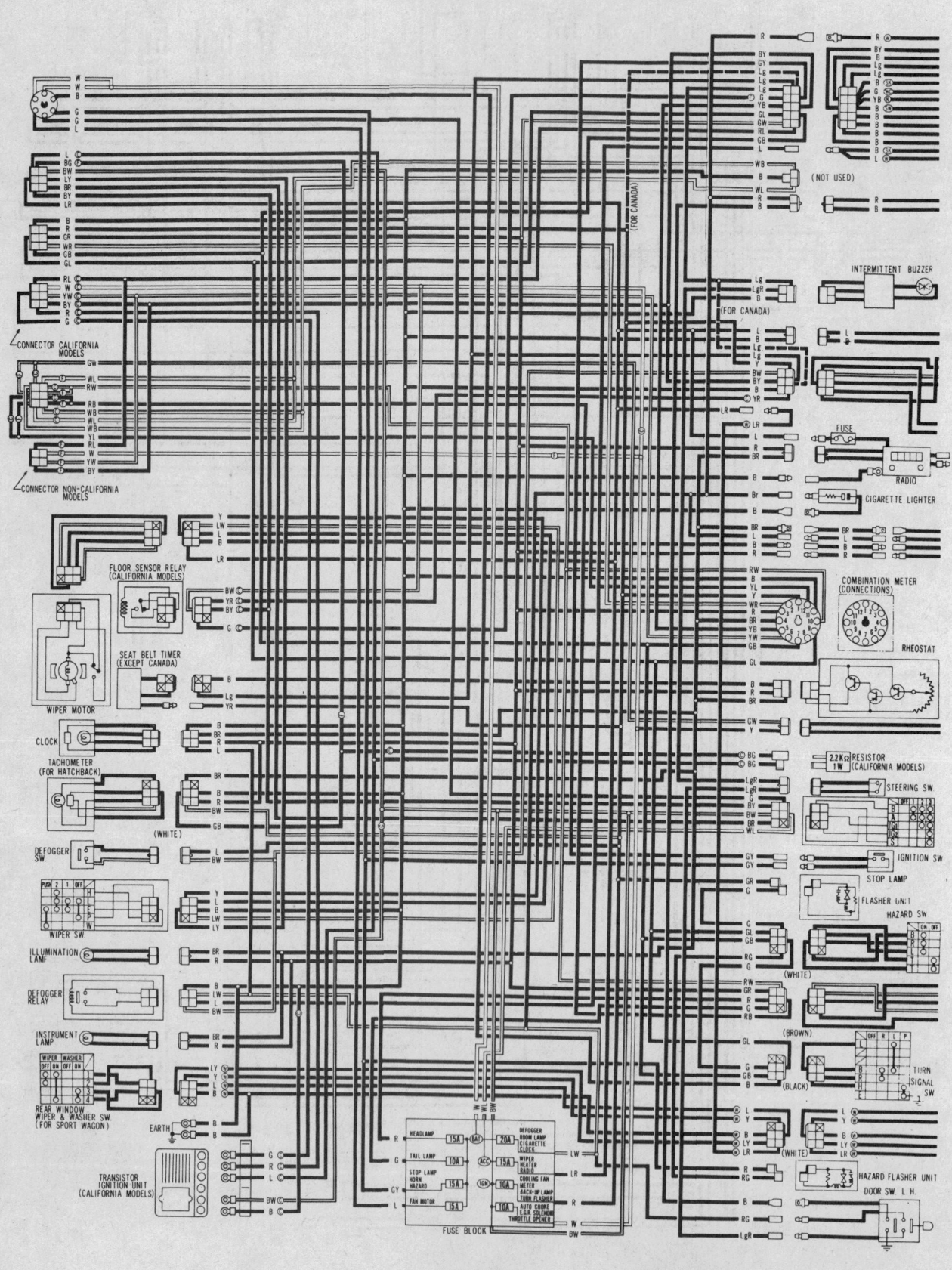

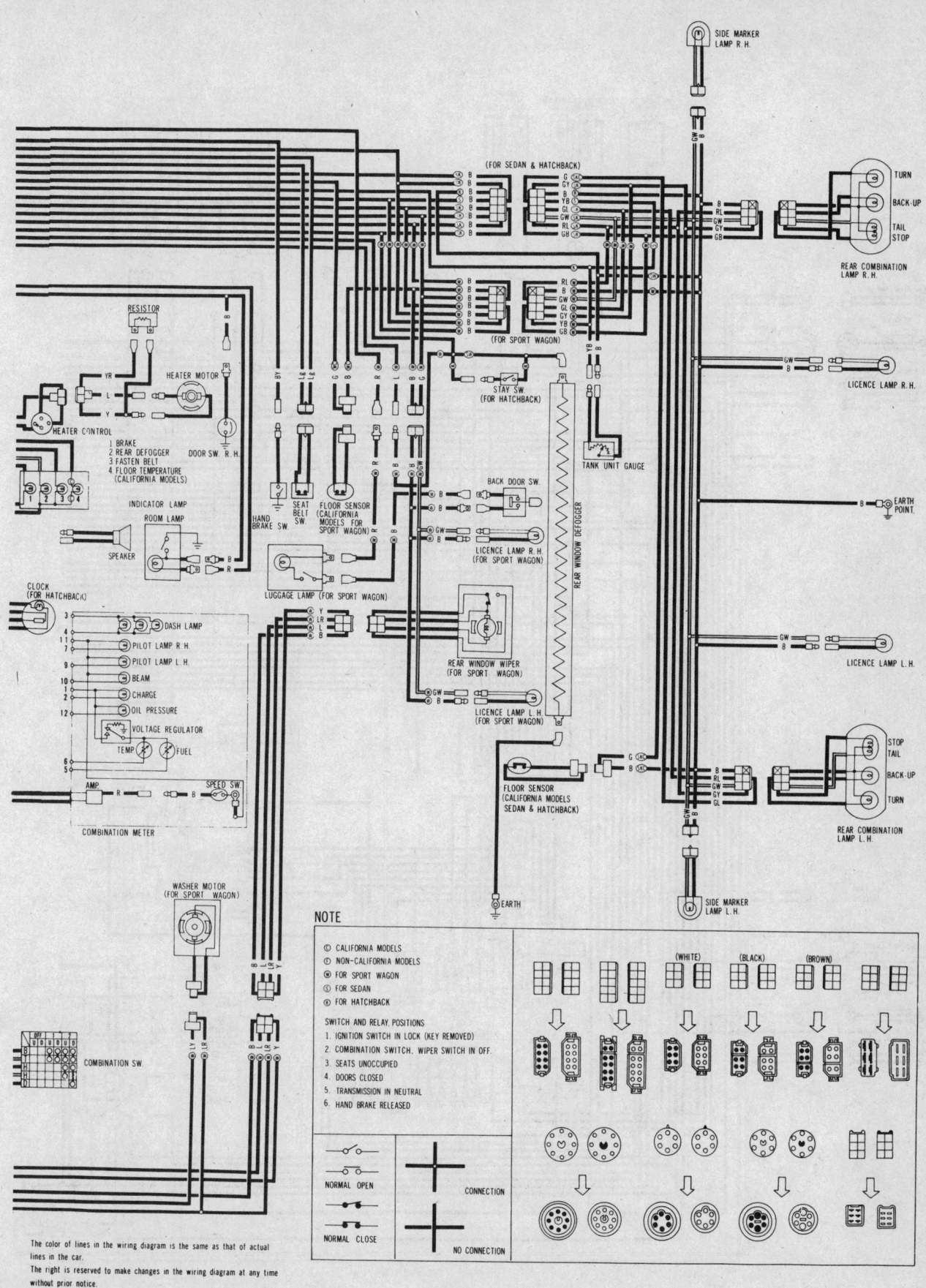

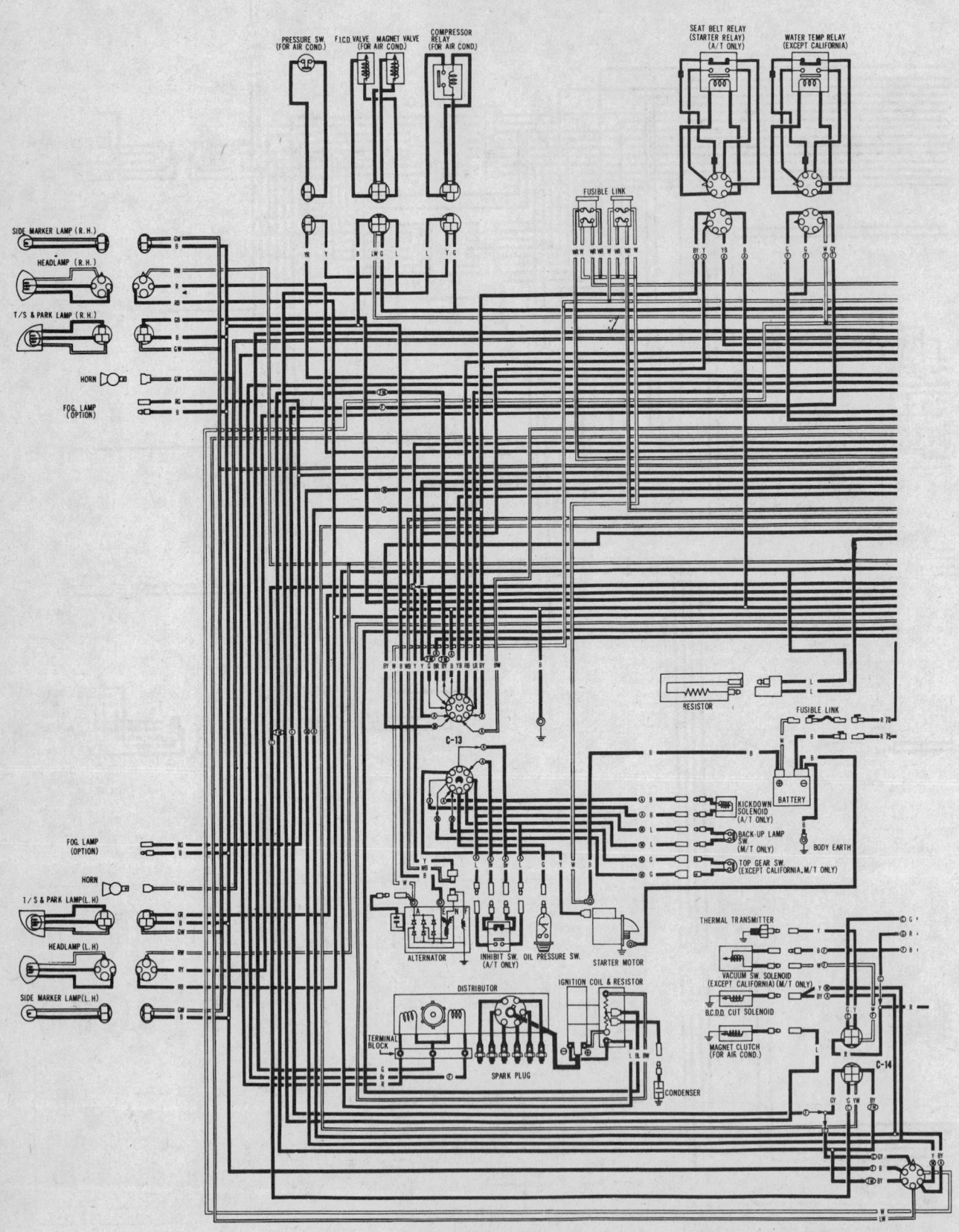

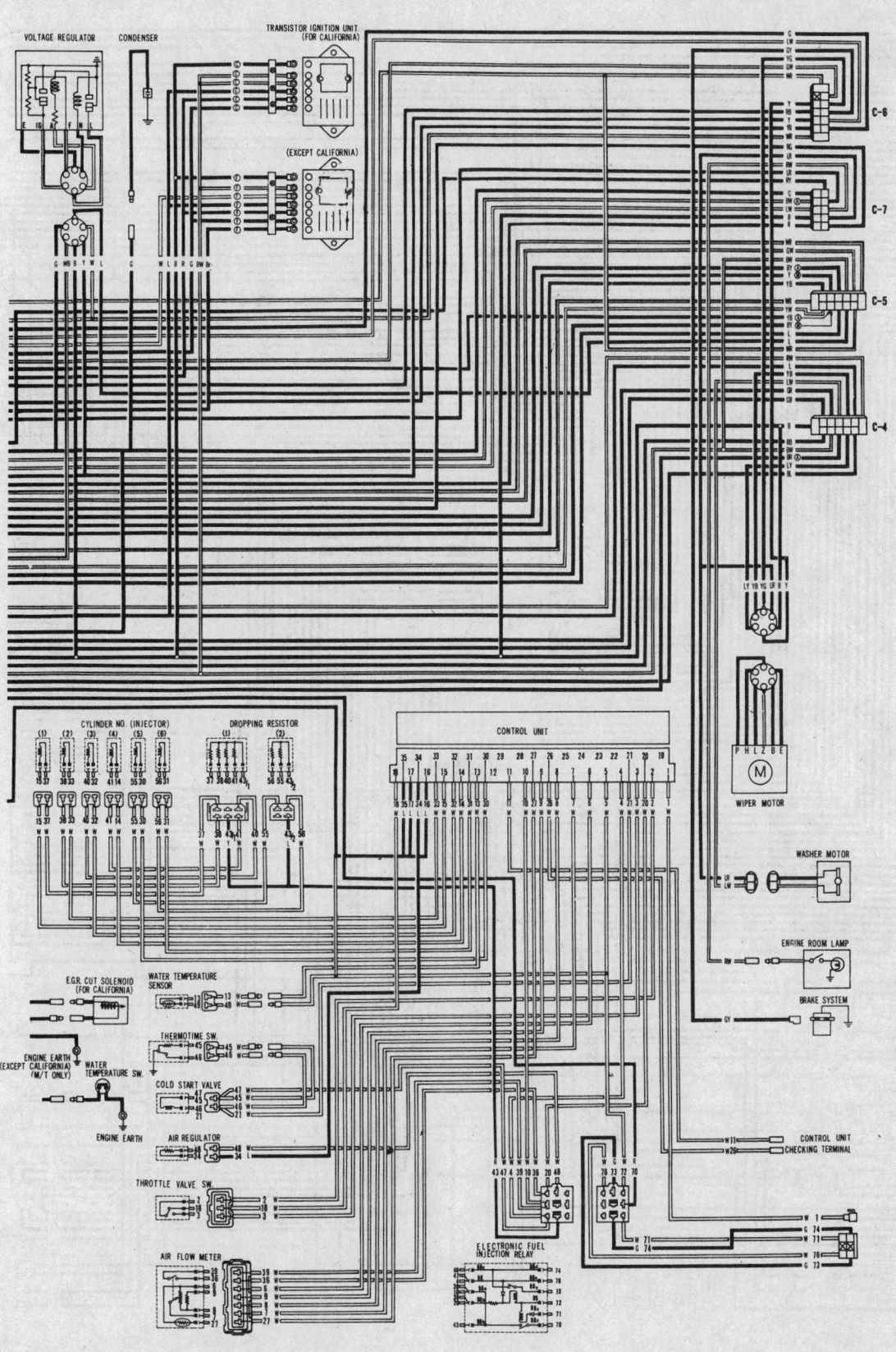

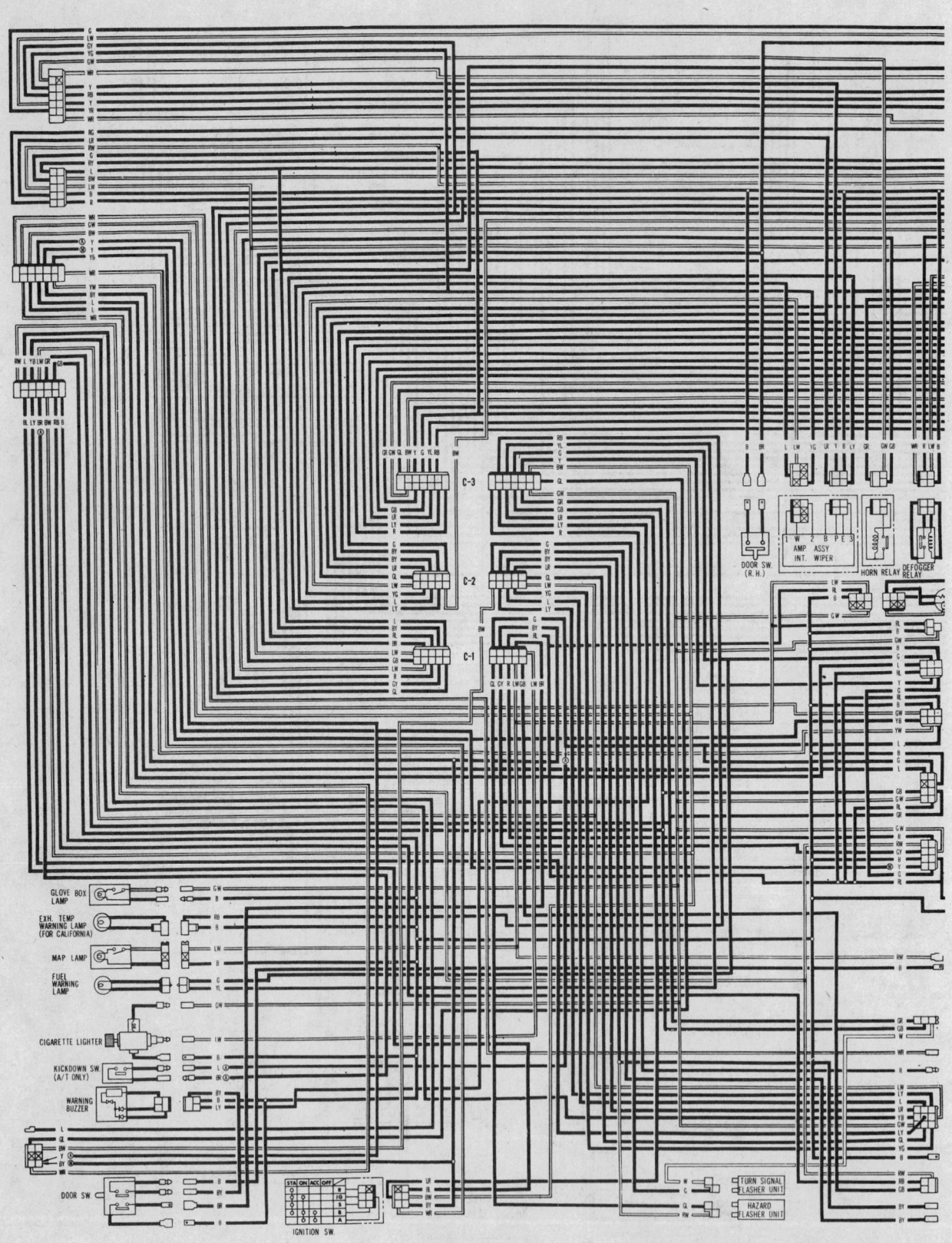

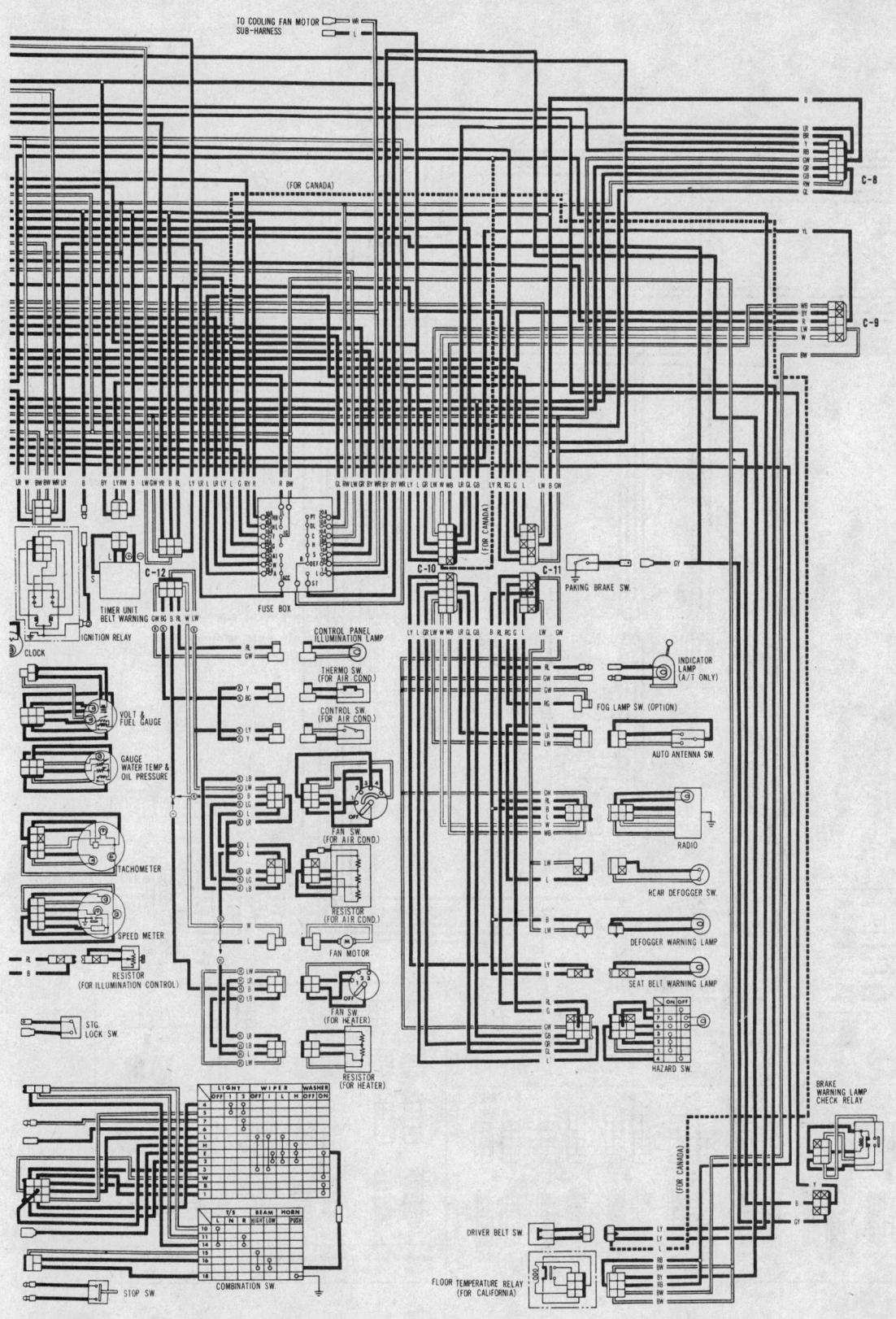

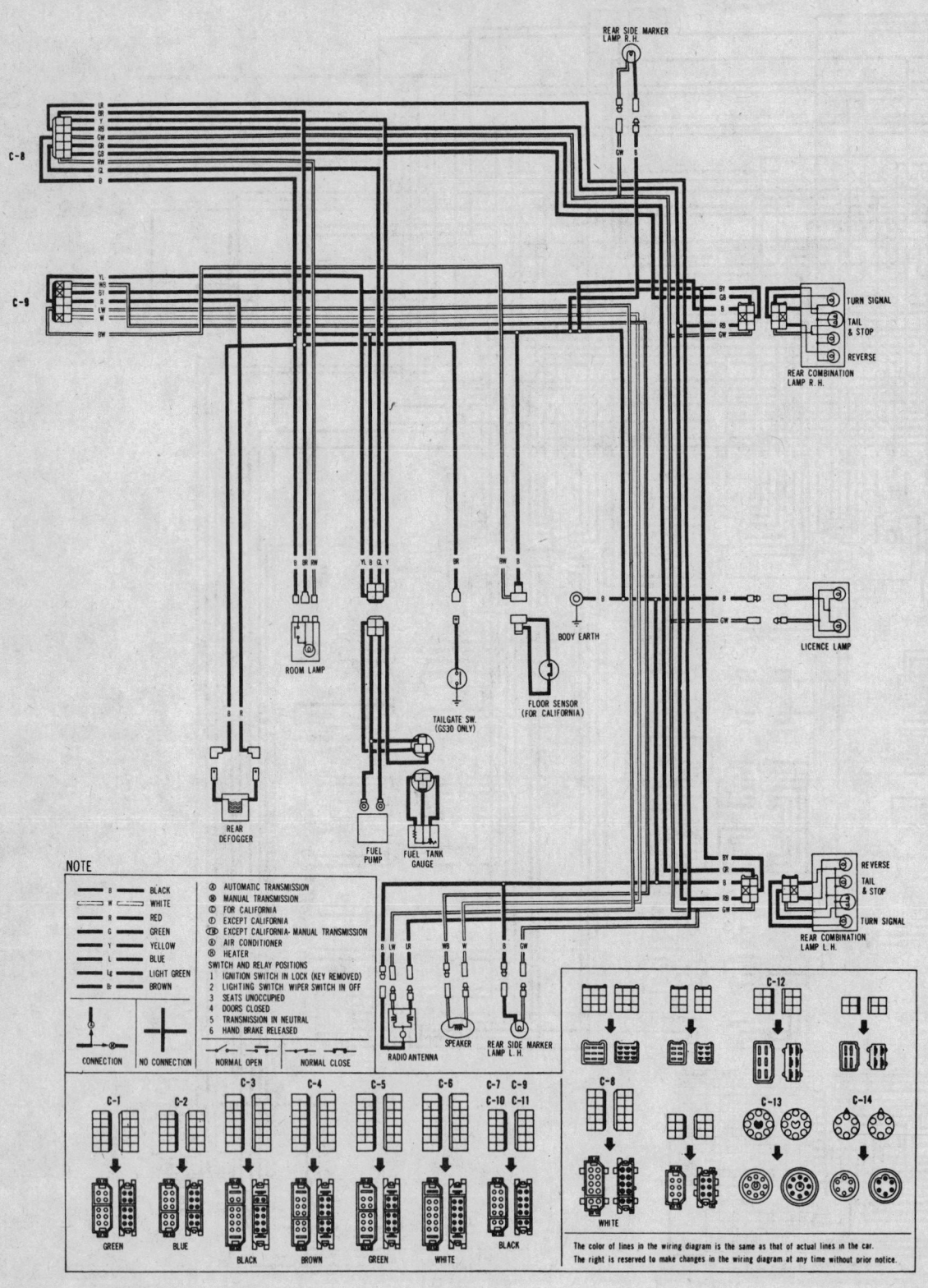

NOTE

B	BLACK	Ⓐ AUTOMATIC TRANSMISSION
W	WHITE	Ⓜ MANUAL TRANSMISSION
R	RED	Ⓒ FOR CALIFORNIA
G	GREEN	Ⓔ EXCEPT CALIFORNIA
Y	YELLOW	Ⓔ Ⓜ EXCEPT CALIFORNIA- MANUAL TRANSMISSION
L	BLUE	Ⓐ AIR CONDITIONER
Lg	LIGHT GREEN	Ⓗ HEATER
Br	BROWN	

SWITCH AND RELAY POSITIONS
1 IGNITION SWITCH IN LOCK (KEY REMOVED)
2 LIGHTING SWITCH WIPER SWITCH IN OFF
3 SEATS UNOCCUPIED
4 DOORS CLOSED
5 TRANSMISSION IN NEUTRAL
6 HAND BRAKE RELEASED

CONNECTION   NO CONNECTION   NORMAL OPEN   NORMAL CLOSE

The color of lines in the wiring diagram is the same as that of actual lines in the car.
The right is reserved to make changes in the wiring diagram at any time without prior notice.

SPECIFICATIONS

MODEL IDENTIFICATION

1972-73 850 Sport Spider

1972-73 128 Sedan, Wagon

1974 128 Sedan, Wagon

1975-77 128 Sedan, Wagon

1972-73 128SL Coupe

1974 128SL Coupe

1975 128SL Coupe

1976-77 128 3P Coupe

1974 X1/9

1975-77 X1/9

**1973 124 Special Sedan
(1972 similar)**

1974 124 TC Special Sedan

**1973 124 Special Wagon
(1972 similar)**

1974 124 TC Special Wagon

1972 124 Sport Coupe

1973 124 Sport Coupe

1974 124 Sport Coupe

1975 124 Sport Coupe

1972 124 Sport Spider

1973 124 Sport Spider

1974 124 Sport Spider

1975-77 124 Sport Spider

1975-77 131 Sedan, Wagon

SERIAL NUMBER IDENTIFICATION

Vehicle and Engine

An identification plate, mounted on the engine compartment wall, (front trunk X1/9), carries the chassis number and the spare parts ordering number. The engine number is stamped on a pad on the engine block.

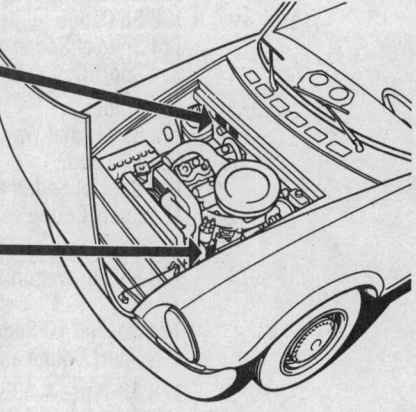

Fiat 124 Identification: (A) Chassis type and number, engine type and spares ordering number; (B) Chassis number; (C) Engine number.

Fiat 850 Identification: (A) Model number: (B) Chassis type and serial number; (C) Engine type and serial number.

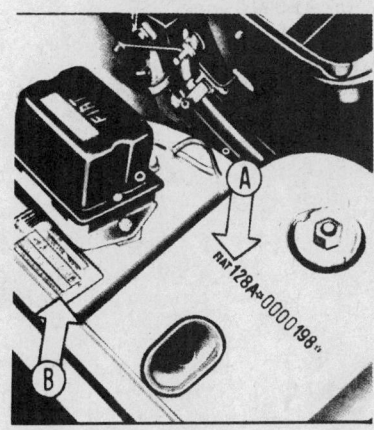

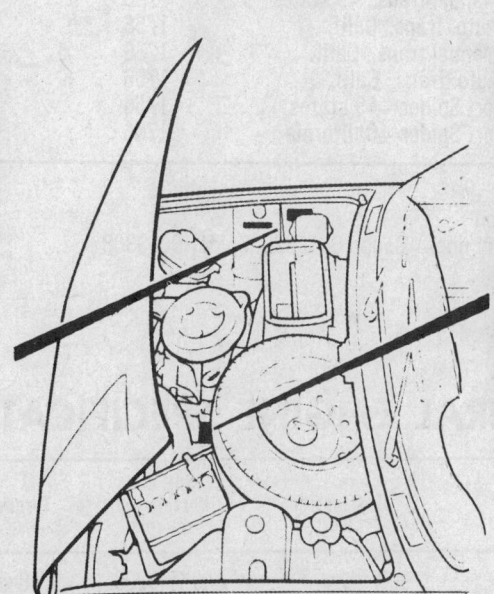

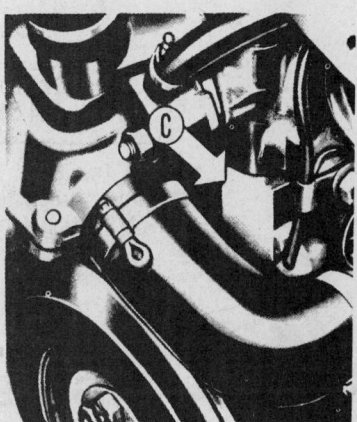

Fiat 128 Identification: (A) Chassis type and serial number; (B) Identification plate; and (C) Engine type and serial number.

ENGINE IDENTIFICATION

Year	Model	Displace-ment (cc)	Engine Serial Prefix
1972	850 Spider	903	100 GBS 040
	128 Sedan and Wagon	1116	128 A 040
	128 SL Coupe	1290	128 A1 040
	124 Special Sedan and Wagon	1438	124 B2 040
	124 Sport Coupe and Spider	1608	125 BC 040
1973	850 Spider	903	100 GBS 040
	128 Sedan and Wagon	1116	128 A 040
	128 SL Coupe	1290	128 A1 040
	124 Special Sedan and Wagon	1438	124 B2 040
	124 Sport Coupe and Spider	1608 (early prod.)	125 BC 040
		1592① (late prod.)	132 AC 040 3
1974	128 Sedan, Wagon and SL Coupe	1290	128 A1 040 4
	X1/9	1290	128 AS 040 4
	124 Special TC Sedan and TC Wagon	1592	132 A 040 4
	124 Sport Coupe and Spider	1756	132 A1 040 4
1975	128 All Types—49 states	1290	128 A1 040 5
	128 All Types—California	1290	128 A1 031 5
	X1/9	1290	128 AS 031 5
	131 All Types—49 states	1756	132 A1 040 5
	131 All Types—California	1756	132 A1 031 5
	124 Sport Coupe, Spider—49 states	1756	132 A1 040 5
	124 Sport Coupe, Spider—California	1756	132 A1 031 5
1976	128 All Types—49 states	1290	128 A1 040 6
	128 All Types—California	1290	128 A1 031 6
	X1/9—49 states	1290	128 AS 031 6
	X1/9—California	1290	128 AS 031 5
	131 All Types—49 states	1756	132 A1 040 5
	131 All Types—California	1756	132 A1 031 5
	124 Sport Spider—49 states	1756	132 A1 040 5
	124 Sport Spider—California	1756	132 A1 031 5
1977	128 All Types—49 states	1290	128 A1 040 6
	128 All Types—California	1290	128 A1 031 6
	X1/9—49 states	1290	128 AS 031 6
	X1/9—California	1290	128 AS 031 5
	131—Manual trans., 49 states	1756	132 A1 040 6
	131—Auto. trans., Calif.	1756	132 A1 040 5
	131—Manual trans., Calif.	1756	132 A1 031 6
	131—Auto. trans., Calif.	1756	132 A1 031 5
	124 Sport Spider—49 states	1756	132 A1 040 6
	124 Sport Spider—California	1756	132 A1 031 6

TC Twin Cam
prod.—production
① Starting serial nos.—Coupe 0213370; Spider 0063308

GENERAL ENGINE SPECIFICATIONS

Year	Model	Displacement (cc)	SAE net Horsepower @ rpm	Torque (ft-lbs) @ rpm	Bore & Stroke (in.)	Compression ratio
1972	850 Spider	903	49 @ 6200	48 @ 4000	2.56 x 2.68	9.5:1
	128 Sedan and Wagon	1116	49 @ 6000	57 @ 3600	3.15 x 2.10	8.5:1
	128 SL Coupe	1290	66 @ 6000	67 @ 3600	3.39 x 2.19	8.5:1
	124 Special Sedan and Wagon	1438	68 @ 5400	81 @ 3300	3.15 x 2.81	9.0:1
	124 Sport Coupe and Spider	1608	94 @ 6600	94 @ 4000	3.15 x 3.15	8.5:1

GENERAL ENGINE SPECIFICATIONS

Year	Model	Displacement (cc)	SAE net Horsepower @ rpm	Torque (ft-lbs) @ rpm	Bore & Stroke (in.)	Compression ratio
1973	850 Spider	903	49 @ 6200	48 @ 4000	2.56 x 2.68	8.5:1
	128 Sedan and Wagon	1116	49 @ 6000	57 @ 3600	3.15 x 2.19	8.5:1
	128 SL Coupe	1290	66 @ 6000	67 @ 3600	3.39 x 2.19	8.5:1
	124 Special Sedan and Wagon	1438	68 @ 5400	81 @ 3300	3.15 x 2.81	8.5:1
	124 Sport Coupe and Spider	1608 (early prod.)	90 @ 6600	88 @ 3600	3.15 x 3.15	8.5:1
		1592① (late prod.)	87 @ 6200	85 @ 4200	3.15 x 3.12	8.0:1
1974	128 Sedan, Wagon, and SL Coupe	1290	66 @ 6000	67 @ 3600	3.39 x 2.19	8.5:1
	X1/9	1290	67 @ 6000	67 @ 4000	3.39 x 2.19	8.5:1
	124 Special TC Sedan & TC Wagon	1592	78 @ 5800	85 @ 3400	3.15 x 3.12	8.0:1
	124 Sport Coupe and Spider	1756	93 @ 6200	92 @ 3000	3.31 x 3.12	8.0:1
1975-77	128 All Types—49 states	1290	62 @ 6000	67 @ 4000	3.39 x 2.19	8.5:1
	128 All Types—California	1290	61 @ 5800	67 @ 4000	3.39 x 2.19	8.5:1
	X1/9	1290	61 @ 5800	67 @ 4000	3.39 x 2.19	8.5:1
	131 All Types—49 states	1756	86 @ 6200	90 @ 2800	3.31 x 3.12	8.0:1
	131 All Types—California	1756	83 @ 5800	89 @ 2800	3.31 x 3.12	8.0:1
	*124 Sport Cpe., Spider—49 States	1756	86 @ 6200	89 @ 2800	3.31 x 3.12	8.0:1
	*124 Sport Cpe., Spider—Calif.	1756	83 @ 5800	90 @ 2800	3.31 x 3.12	8.0:1

TC Twin Cam

① Starting serial numbers: 0213370 Coupe; 0063308 Spider

* 124 Sport Coupe not sold in 1976-77

TUNE-UP SPECIFICATIONS

Year	Model	Displacement (cc)	Spark Plug Type #	Spark Plug Gap (in.)	Points Gap (in.)	Points Dwell (deg.)	Ignition Timing (deg.)	Idle Speed (rpm)	Valve Lash Intake (in.)	Valve Lash Exh. (in.)	Intake Valve Opens (deg)	Idle Mixture (% CO)
1972	850 Spider	903	Champion N7Y	.022	.016	55	TDC	850	.006	.008	25B	2±0.5
	128 Sedan and Wagon	1116	Champion N9Y	.022	.016	55	TDC	850	.012	.016	10B	2±0.5
	124 Special Sedan and Wagon	1438	Champion N9Y	.022	.018	60	TDC	MT-850 AT-750	.008	.008	19B	3±0.5
	124 Sport Coupe and Spider	1608	Champion N6Y	.022	.016	55	TDC	850	.018	.020	22B	2±0.5
1973	850 Spider	903	Champion N7Y	.022	.016	55	TDC	850	.006	.008	25B	2±0.5
	128 Sedan and Wagon	1116	Champion N9Y	.022	.016	55	TDC	850	.012	.016	10B	2±0.5
	128 SL Coupe	1290	Champion N9Y	.022	.016	55	TDC	850	.012	.016	10B	2±0.5
	124 Special Sedan and Wagon	1438	Champion N9Y	.022	.018	60	TDC	MT-850 AT-750	.008	.008	19B	3±0.5
	124 Sport Coupe and Spider	1608	Champion N6Y	.022	.016	55	TDC	850	.018	.020	22B	2±0.5
		1592①	Champion N6Y	.021	.016DP	55	TDC	850	.018	.020	22B	2±0.5
1974	128 Sedan, Wagon, and SL Coupe	1290	Champion N9Y	.022	.016	55	TDC	850	.012	.016	10B	1±0.5
	X1/9	1290	Champion N9Y	.022	.016	55	TDC	850	.012	.016	10B	1±0.5
	124 Special TC Sedan and TC Wagon	1592	Champion N9Y	.022	.016DP	55	TDC	MT-850 AT-750	.018	.020	22B	0.5±0.3
	124 Sport Coupe and Spider	1756	Champion N7Y	.022	.016DP	55	TDC	850	.018	.020	22B	0.7±0.2

TUNE-UP SPECIFICATIONS

Year	Model	Displacement (cc)	Spark Plug Type #	Spark Plug Gap (in.)	Points Gap (in.)	Points Dwell (deg.)	Ignition Timing (deg.)	Idle Speed (rpm)	Valve Lash Intake (in.)	Valve Lash Exh. (in.)	Intake Valve Opens (deg)	Idle Mixture (% CO)
1975-77	128 All Types— 49 states	1290	Champion N9Y	.023	.016	55	TDC	850	.012	.016	10B	1±0.5③
	128 All Types— California	1290	Champion N9Y	.023	.016	55	TDC	825	.012	.016	10B	3±0.5③
	X1/9	1290	Champion N9Y	.023	.016	55	TDC②	825	.012	.016	10B	3±0.5③
	131 All Types— 49 states	1756	Champion N9Y	.023	.016DP	55	TDC	MT-850 AT-725	.018	.020	5B	MT-0.5±0.2 AT-0.7±0.2
	131 All Types— California	1756	Champion N9Y	.023	.016DP	55	TDC	MT-825 AT-725	.018	.020	5B	3±0.5
	*124 Sport Cpe., Spider— 49 states	1756	Champion N7Y ④	.023	.016DP	55	TDC	850	.018	.020	5B	0.5±0.2
	*124 Sport Cpe., Spider— Calif.	1756	Champion N7Y ④	.023	.016DP	55	TDC	825	.018	.020	5B	3±0.5

TC Twin Cam
* Sport Coupe not available in 1976-77
\# Original equipment spark plugs; similar characteristic plugs of different manufacture may be used without damage to the engine
DP Dual point distributor; see text for explanation

MT Manual transmission
AT Automatic transmission
① Starting serial nos.: 0213370 Coupe; 0063308 Spider
② 10 BTDC on 1976-77 California models
③ 1976-77 models 2% CO ± 0.5
④ 1977 models—N9Y plugs or equivalent

NOTE: The underhood specifications sticker often reflects tune-up specification changes made in production. Sticker figures must be used if they disagree with those in this chart.

CAPACITIES

Model	Engine Disp. (cc)	Crankcase (qts) With Filter	Crankcase (qts) Without Filter	Transaxle (pts)	Transmission Manual (pts)	Transmission Automatic (pts)	Rear Axle (pts)	Fuel Tank (gals)	Cooling System (qts)
850	903	4.5	4.0	4.5	—	—	—	7.4	8.0
128 Sedan, Wagon	1116, 1290	5.3	4.5	6.6	—	—	—	9.5	6.8
128 SL, 3P	1290	5.3	4.5	6.6	—	—	—	12.5	7.0
X1/9	1290	5.3	4.5	6.6	—	—	—	12.7①	11.6②
124 Special Sedan and Wagon	1438	4.0	3.5	—	2.8	6.0④	2.8	Sed. 10.3 Wag. 12.5	8.0
124 TC Sedan and TC Wagon	1592	4.5	4.0	—	3.0	6.0④	2.8	Sed. 9.6 Wag. 11.4	8.0
124 Sport Coupe and Spider	1608, 1592, 1756	4.5	4.0	—	3.5	—	2.8	11.4	8.0③
131 Sedan and Wagon	1756	4.5	4.0	—	3.8	6.0④	2.1	12.2	8.0

Sed. Sedan
Wag. Wagon
① 1974 models; 12.5 gal.

② 1974 models; 11.2 qts.
③ 1975-77 models; 8.8 qts.
④ 12 pints to refill after total disassembly and rebuild

FIRING ORDER

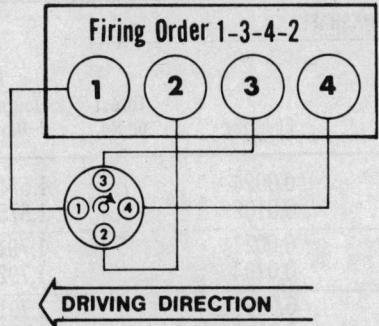

Firing order—1972-73 124 Sedan, Wagon

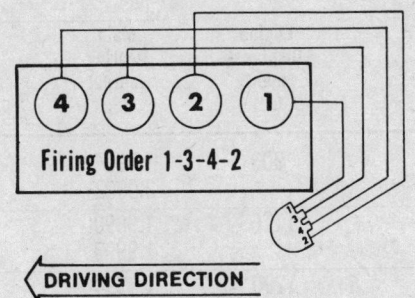

Firing order—1972-73 850 Spider

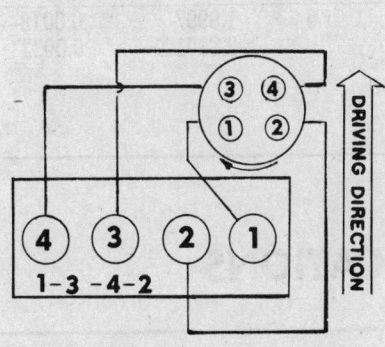

Firing order—1972-77 128

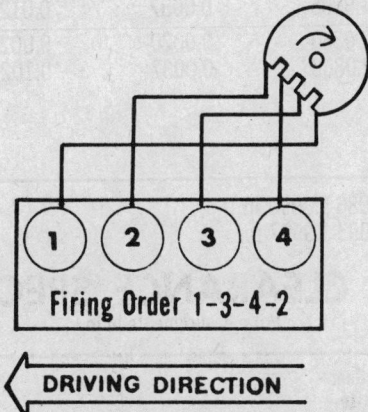

Firing order—1972-77 124 Sport Spider and Coupe, 1974 124 TC Sedan and Wagon, 1975-77 131

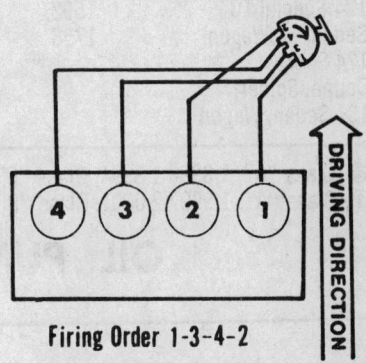

Firing order—1974-77 X1/9

TORQUE SEQUENCE

Cylinder Head

NOTE: *It is a common rule that most torque sequences start at the center and work outward.*

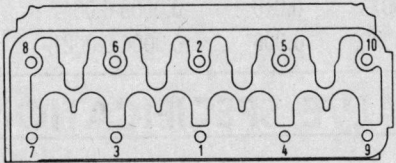

Cylinder head bolt tightening sequence——1972-73, 124 Sedan, Wagon

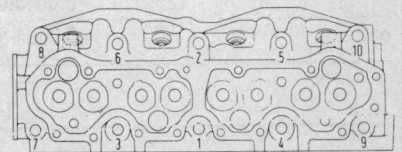

Cylinder head bolt tightening sequence—128, X1/9

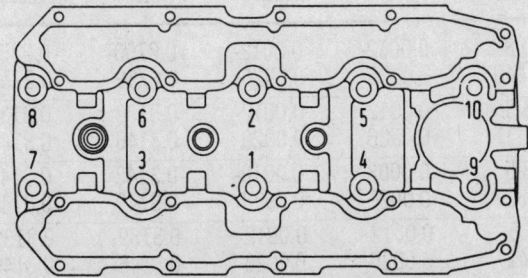

Cylinder head bolt tightening sequence—1972-77 124 Sport Coupe and Spider, 1974 124 TC Sedan and Wagon, 1975-77 131

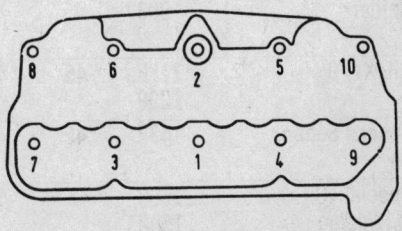

Cylinder head bolt tightening sequence, 850

CRANKSHAFT AND CONNECTING ROD SPECIFICATIONS

(All measurements in inches)

Model	Engine Displacement (cc)	CRANKSHAFT				CONNECTING ROD	
		Main Bearing Journal Dia.	Main Bearing Oil Clearance	End-Play	Thrust on No.	Journal Dia.	Oil Clearance
850 Spider	903	1.9994-2.0002	0.0008-0.0028	0.0024-0.0102	2	1.5742-1.5750	0.0010-0.0028
128 Sedan, Wagon	1116	1.9990-1.9998	0.0019-0.0037	0.0021-0.0104	5	1.7913-1.7920	0.0014-0.0034
128, X1/9 128SL, 128 3P	1290	1.9994-2.0002	0.0016-0.0033	0.0021-0.0104	5	1.7913-1.7920	0.0014-0.0034
124 Special Sedan, Wagon	1438	1.9990-1.9998	0.0019-0.0037	0.0021-0.0104	5	1.7916-1.7924	0.0010-0.0029
124 Sport Coupe, Spider	1608	1.9990-1.9998	0.0020-0.0037	0.0021-0.0120	5	1.8990-1.8994①	0.0018-0.0032
124 Special TC Sedan, TC Wagon; 124 Sport Coupe, Spider; 131 Sedan, Wagon	1592, 1756	2.0860-2.0868	0.0020-0.0037	0.0021-0.1020	5	1.9997-2.0001②	0.0018-0.0032

① Class "A", 1.8990-1.8994; Class "B", 1.8986-1.8990 in.
② Class "A", 1.9997-2.0001; Class "B", 1.9993-1.9997 in.

OIL PUMP CLEARANCE SPECIFICATIONS

(All measurements in in.)

Model	Engine Displacement (cc)	Gear-to-Housing Clearance		Gear End-Play		Gear Backlash	
		New	Replace	New	Replace	New	Replace
128, X1/9	1116 and 1290	0.004-0.007	0.010	0.0008-0.0041	0.0060	0.006	0.010
124	1608	0.0043-0.0071	0.010	0.0012-0.0045	0.0070	0.0059	0.0098
	1438	0.0043-0.0070	0.010	0.0008-0.0041	0.0059	0.0059	0.0098
	1290	0.0043-0.0070	0.010	0.0008-0.0041	0.0059	0.0059	0.0098
850	903	0.0004-0.0040	0.006	0.0004-0.0021	0.0040	0.0031	0.0060

VALVE SPECIFICATIONS

Model	Engine Displacement (cc)	Seat Angle (deg)	Face Angle (deg)	Spring Test Pressure (lbs @ in.)		Stem to Guide Clearance (in.)		Stem Diameter (in.)	
				Inner	Outer	Intake	Exhaust	Intake	Exhaust
850 Spider	903	45	45.5	12.1 1.280	40.8 1.440	0.0012-0.0025	0.0012-0.0025	0.2750-0.2756	0.2750-0.2756
128 All; X1/9	1116, 1290	45	45.5	32.7 1.220	75.5 1.417	0.0012-0.0026	0.0012-0.0026	0.3139-0.3146	0.3139-0.3146
124 Special Sedan, Wagon	1438	45	45.5	30.6 1.173	63.5 1.327	0.0008-0.0021	0.0010-0.0023	0.3143-0.3149	0.3142-0.3148
124 Special TC Sedan, Wagon; 124 Sport Coupe, Spider; 131 Sedan, Wagon	1608, 1592, 1756	45	45.5	32.7 1.220	75.5 1.417	0.0012-0.0026	0.0012-0.0026	0.3139-0.3146	0.3139-0.3146

PISTON AND RING SPECIFICATIONS

Model	Engine Displacement (cc)	Piston Clearance	RING GAP			RING SIDE CLEARANCE		
			Top Compression	Top Oil Control	Bottom Oil Control	Top Compression	Top Oil Control	Bottom Oil Control
850 Spider	903	0.0024-0.0031①	0.0079-0.0138	0.0079-0.0138	0.0079-0.0138	0.0018-0.0028	0.0010-0.0022	0.0008-0.0018
128 Sedan, Wagon	1116	0.0020-0.0028	0.0118-0.0177	0.0079-0.0138	0.0079-0.0138	0.0018-0.0030	0.0006-0.0022	0.0008-0.0020
128, X1/9, 128SL, 128 3P	1290	0.0028-0.0035	0.0118-0.0176	0.0118-0.0176	0.0098-0.0157	0.0018-0.0030	0.0016-0.0028	0.0012-0.0024
124 Special Sedan, Wagon	1438	0.0024-0.0031	0.0118-0.0176	0.0079-0.0138	0.0079-0.0138	0.0018-0.0030	0.0012-0.0028	0.0012-0.0024
124 Special TC Sedan, TC Wagon; 124 Sport Coupe, Spider	1592	0.0025-0.0033	0.0118-0.0176	0.0079-0.0138	0.0079-0.0138	0.0018-0.0030	0.0011-0.0027	0.0011-0.0024
124 Sport Coupe, Spider; 131 Sedan, Wagon	1608, 1756	0.0016-0.0024	0.0118-0.0176	0.0079-0.0138	0.0079-0.0138	0.0018-0.0030	0.0011-0.0027	0.0011-0.0024

① Top of bore: 0.0024-0.0031 in.
Near piston skirt: 0.0020-0.0027 in.

TORQUE SPECIFICATIONS

(All readings in ft lbs)

Model	Engine Displacement (cc)	Cylinder Head Bolts	Rod Bearing Bolts	Main Bearing Bolts	Crankshaft Pulley Bolt	Flywheel to Crankshaft Bolts	MANIFOLDS	
							Intake	Exhaust
850 Spider	903	33-40	29	43	72	33-36	—	18
128 Sedan, Wagon	1116	61	40	61	101	61	22	22
128 Sedan, Wagon; 128SL, 128 3P; X1/9	1290	69	36	58	101	61	22	22
124 Special Sedan, Wagon	1438	58	36	58	87	61	18	18
124 Sport Coupe, Spider	1608	61	36	58	180	61	18	18
124 Special TC Sedan, TC Wagon; 124 Sport Coupe, Spider; 131 Sedan, Wagon	1592, 1756	54	47	83①	180	61	18	18

① Smaller front main bearing cap bolt—58 ft-lbs.

Fiat

ALTERNATOR AND REGULATOR SPECIFICATIONS

Year	Model	ALTERNATOR Part No. or Manufacturer	Field Current @ 14v	Max. Output (amps)	REGULATOR Part No. or Manufacturer	1st Stage Testing Current (amps)	1st Stage Regulating Voltage (volts)	2nd Stage Testing Current (amps)	2nd Stage Regulating Voltage (volts)	Contact Gap (in.)	Armature to Core Gap (in.)
1972-73	850	Fiat A12M 124/12/42B	42	53	Marelli RC1/12B	25-35	13.5-13.8	2-12	14.2	.018	.059
1972-73	128	Bosch G1-14V 33A27	29	38	Bosch AD1/14V	2.0	13.6-14.1	0.6-0.7	14.2	—	—
1974	128, X1/9	Marelli A124-14V Variant 3	44	53	Bosch AD1/14V	2.0-2.2	13.5-14.0	0.8-1.0	14.2	—	—
1975-77	128, X1/9	Marelli A124-14V 60A Variant 1①	60	70	Marelli RC2/12E①	40-45①	13.7-14.2	10-14	14.2	.018	.059
1972-77	124 (All Models)	Fiat A12M 124/12/42M	42	53	Marelli RC2/12B	25-35	13.5-14.0	2-12	14.2	.018	.059
1975-77	131	Marelli A-124-14V-44A②	43	53	Marelli RC2/12D②	25-35②	13.5-14.0	2-12	14.2	.018	.059

① X1/9 not equipped with A/C uses Marelli A124-14V-44A alternator and Marelli RC2/12D regulator with 1st stage testing current of 25-35 amps

② 131 models equipped with A/C use Marelli A124-14V-60A alternator and Marelli RC2/12E regulator with 1st stage testing current of 40-45 amps

BATTERY AND STARTER SPECIFICATIONS

All cars use 12 volt, negative ground electrical systems

Year	Model	Battery Amp Hour Capacity	Lock Test Amps	Lock Test Volts	Lock Test Torque (ft/lbs)	No Load Test Amps	No Load Test Volts	No Load Test RPM	Brush Suring Tension (oz)	Manufacturer or Part No.
1972-73	850	50	258	7.7	5.3	30	12	8500	40	Fiat E76-0.5/12 Variant 9
1972-74	128, X1/9	50①	315	7	6.4	30	11.9	7000	40	Fiat E84-0.8/12 Variant 1
1975-77	128, X1/9	50①	370	8.3	7.9	35	11.7	7000	40	Fiat E84-0.8/12 Variant 1
1972-73	124 Special Sedan, Wagon	60	315	7	6.4	25	11.9	7500	18	Fiat E84-0.8/12
1927-73 and 1974-77	124 Sport Coupe, Spider; 124 TC Sedan, TC Wagon; 124 Sport Coupe, Spider; 131 Sedan, Wagon	60	530	7	12.6	28	12	5200	35	Fiat E100-1.3/12

① X1/9—60 amp hour battery

BRAKE SPECIFICATIONS

All measurements given are (in.) unless noted

Year	Model	Lug Nut Torque (ft/lb)	Master Cylinder Bore	Brake Disc		Brake Drum			Minimum Lining Thickness	
				Minimum Thickness	Maximum Run-Out	Diameter	Max. Machine O/S	Max. Wear Limit	Front	Rear
1972-73	850 Spider	45	0.75	Regrind 0.374 Wear Limit 0.354	0.006	7.2915-7.3032	7.3230-7.3347	7.3540	0.08	0.06
1972-77	128 All Models	50	0.75	Regrind 0.368 Wear Limit 0.354	0.006	7.2929-7.3043	7.3234-7.3358	7.3554	0.08	0.06
1972-77	124 All Models	51	0.75	Regrind front—0.368 rear—0.371 Wear Limit 0.354	0.006	—	—	—	0.08	0.08
1975-77	131	51	0.75	Regrind 0.368 Wear Limit 0.354	0.006	8.9882-9.000	9.0182-9.0300	9.0551	0.06	0.18
1974-77	X1/9	50	0.75	Regrind 0.368 Wear Limit 0.354	0.006	—	—	—	0.08	0.08

WHEEL ALIGNMENT SPECIFICATIONS

(Applies only to unladen vehicle)

Year	Model	CASTER Front (deg)	CAMBER Front (deg)	Rear (deg)	TOE-IN Front (in.)	Rear (in.)
1972-73	850 Spider	8P to 10P	1½P to 2⅙P	0 to 1N	+0.510-+0.590	+0.020-+0.180
1972-73	128 Sedan, Wagon	1⅓P to 1½P	1⅓P to 2P	½N to ⅙P① ⅓P to 1P②	−0.120-+0.040	+0.100-+0.260
1974-77	128 Sedan, Wagon	1⅙P to 2⅙P	1⅙P to 2⅙P	⅔N to ⅓P① ⅙N to 1⅙P②	−0.120-+0.040	+0.059-+0.217
1972-73	128 SL	1⅓P to 1½P	1P to 1⅔P	⅚N to 1½N	−0.060-+0.100	+0.160-+0.320
1974-77	128 SL, 3P	1⅙P to 2⅙P	½P to 1½P③	⅔N to 1⅔N	−0.060-+0.100	+0.079-+0.236
1972-73	124 Sedan, Wagon	2⅔P to 3⅓P	1/12N to ½P	Fixed	+0.200-+0.360	Fixed
1974	124 Sedan, Wagon	2⅙P to 3⅙P	¼N to ½P	Fixed	+0.200-+0.360	Fixed
1972-73	124 Sport Coupe	2⅔P to 3⅓P	1/12N to ½P	Fixed	+0.200-+0.360	Fixed
1974-75	124 Sport Coupe	2½P to 3½P	¼N to ½P	Fixed	+0.200-+0.360	Fixed
1972-73	124 Sport Spider	2⅚P to 3½P	⅙N to ½P	Fixed	+0.160-+0.320	Fixed
1974-77	124 Sport Spider	2⅔P to 3⅔P	⅓N to ⅔P	Fixed	+0.160-+0.320	Fixed
1974-77	X1/9	6½P to 7½P	0 to 1N	1⅙N to 2⅙N	+0.080-+0.240	+0.157-+0.236
1975-77	131 Sedan, Wagon	3¼P to 4¼P	¼P to 1¼P	Fixed	+0.236-+0.393	Fixed

① Sedan
② Wagon
③ 1974 models; ⅚P to 1½P

P Postive
N Negative

TUNE-UP PROCEDURES

Spark Plugs

Spark plugs should be cleaned and re-gapped at 6,000 mile intervals, and replaced every 12,000 miles.

Since all late model Fiat engines use aluminum alloy cylinder heads, care should be exercised to prevent damage to the spark plug threads. When reinstalling used plugs, clean the threads and lightly oil or use graphite grease (such as Never-SeezR) on the threads. Do not over-tighten the spark plugs. Thread the plugs into the head by hand until tight, and then torque to specifications (see chart) using a torque wrench of known accuracy. All that is necessary is to seat the plug snugly against the head, forming a good compression seal.

If cross-threaded or stripped threads are encountered, see the engine rebuilding section at the end of this book.

Breaker Points and Condenser

Breaker points should be inspected and regapped at 6,000 mile intervals, and replaced with the condenser(s) every 12,000 miles.

Removal and Installation

1972-73 124 Special Sedan and Wagon

NOTE: *On these models, it may be easier to remove the distributor to install the points and condenser, as the centrifugal advance mechanism blocks access to the top of the distributor.*

1. Remove the two distributor cap hold-down screws. The screws will stay with the cap. Lift off the cap.

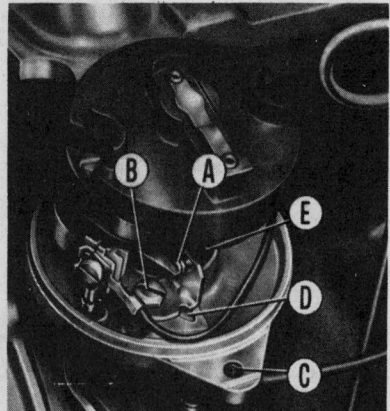

Ignition points—1972-73 124 Special Sedan and Wagon

    A. Contacts
    B. Adjusting screw
    D. Adjusting slot
    E. Lubricating wick

2a. If you are going to remove the distributor, mark the position of the rotor and distributor housing on a stationary object such as the cylinder block. Then disconnect the distributor primary lead and remove the distributor hold-down nut and retainer. Pull out the distributor.

2b. If you are going to service the points and condenser with the distributor installed, remove the two rotor retaining screws and lift off the rotor. (At this time it is a good idea to smear a little white grease on the contact surfaces of the centrifugal weights of the advance mechanism).

3. Disconnect the breaker points lead and condenser lead at the primary connection. Remove the breaker point retaining screw and lift out the points. Remove the condenser bracket retaining screw (outside the distributor below breaker plate level) and remove the condenser. Apply a light film of silicone based grease to the distributor cam lobes.

4. Install new breaker points and condenser. To adjust point gap, rotate the distributor shaft so that the breaker point rubbing block contacts one of the four high points of the distributor cam lobes. If the distributor is still in the car, turn the engine over by hand, push the car in 4th gear, or use a remote starter switch. Slightly loosen the breaker points retaining screw and insert the proper sized feeler gauge between the point contacts. Move the fixed arm in or out to obtain the specified clearance, and tighten the retaining screw in this position. Install the rotor (if removed); it will go on only one way.

5. If the distributor was removed, install it (together with the oil slinger doughnut), taking care to align the marks made prior to removal. Install the distributor hold-down nut and retainer. Connect the primary wire.

6. Install the distributor cap and screws.

7. Check dwell angle and ignition timing.

850, 128, X1/9, and 1972–73 124 Sport (1608cc)

NOTE: *On the X1/9, Fiat recommends servicing the points and condenser with the distributor removed. See "Distributor Removal and Installation" in the Engine Electrical section.*

1. Unsnap the two distributor cap clasps and remove the cap with high tension wires connected. On some models, the cap is retained by two screws that stay with the cap.

2. Pull straight up and remove the rotor. At this time, it is good practice to apply a few drops of light (10W) oil to the lubricating wick at the top of the distributor shaft.

3. Disconnect the breaker points lead

Ignition points—1972-73 850, 128

    A. Adjusting screw
    B. Lubricating wick
    C. Contact gap
    D. Adjusting slot

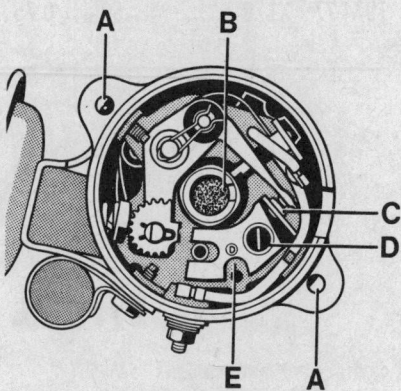

Ignition points—1974-77 128, X1/9

    B. Lubricating wick
    C. Contact gap
    D. Adjusting screw
    E. Adjusting slot

and condenser lead at the primary connection. Remove the condenser bracket retaining screws, and replace the condenser. Remove the breaker point retaining screws (and wire clip on 1974–77 128 and X1/9 models) and remove the points. Apply a light film of silicone based grease to the distributor cam lobes. Wipe off any excess.

4. Install new breaker points and condenser. To adjust point gap, rotate the crankshaft pulley until the breaker point rubbing block rests on the high point of the distributor cam lobe. Slightly loosen the breaker points retaining screw and insert the proper sized feeler gauge between the point contacts. Move the fixed arm in or out to obtain the specified clearance. Tighten the retaining screw.

5. Connect the electrical leads for the breaker points and condenser. Install the cap and rotor.

6. Check dwell angle and ignition timing.

131, 1973–77 124 Sport Coupe and Spider (1592, 1756cc), and 1974 124 Special TC Sedan and Wagon

NOTE: *These models are equipped with a dual point distributor. The dual point sets do not operate simultaneously; one set is used for starting, and the other for running. The starting set provides 10 degrees of additional spark advance during starter cranking. The running set returns the spark timing to Top Dead Center. On 1973–74 models, the starting set is actuated by pulling out the manual choke knob. On 1975–77 models with automatic choke, the starting set is actuated by coolant temperatures of 36-46°F or less. On both systems, the starting set cuts out and the running set takes over when full cold oil pressure is reached.*

1. Remove the two distributor cap retaining screws. The screws will stay with the cap. Remove the cap.

2. Pull straight up and remove the rotor. Apply a few drops of light (10W) oil to the lubricating wick atop the distributor shaft.

3. Crank the engine over, or rotate the crankshaft pulley by hand or push the car in 4th gear, until both point sets open with their rubbing blocks on the high points of the distributor cam lobes. Disconnect both breaker points leads and condensers leads at the primary connections. Remove and replace both point sets and condensers. Apply a light film of silicone based grease to the distributor cam lobes. Wipe off any excess.

4. Adjust the point gap for both breaker point sets by inserting the feeler gauge between the point contacts; 0.012-0.019 in. for the starting set, and 0.014-0.017 in. for the running set.

NOTE: *For longer service, set the gap to the maximum specification, as the rubbing block will wear down in service and slowly close the gap. Adjust gap by moving the fixed arm of each set in or out, then tighten the retaining screws.*

5. Install the rotor. Install the distributor cap.

6. Check dwell angle and ignition timing.

Dwell Angle

Dwell angle should always be checked after adjusting or installing new points. Using a dwell meter of known accuracy, connect the negative lead to a good ground (such as an engine bolt), and the positive lead to the primary connection at the distributor. On dual-point distributors, make sure you connect the dwell meter positive lead to the primary connection for the running breaker contacts —not the starting set.

Dwell angle is the amount of degrees of distributor shaft rotation that the points remain closed (making contact). Increasing the point gap decreases dwell, while decreasing the point gap increases dwell. Dwell angle may be checked with the engine running, or with the engine cranking over at starter speed. With a running engine, the dwell angle reading should be fairly constant. When the engine is being cranked over, the dwell angle reading will fluctuate between zero and the maximum figure for that angle.

Following a dwell angle adjustment, ignition timing should be checked. A one degree increase in dwell results in the ignition timing being retarded two degrees, and vice versa.

Ignition Timing

Fiat recommends that the ignition timing be checked at 6,000 mile intervals, or whenever the breaker points, dwell angle setting, or distributor body is disturbed. All timing checks are made with the engine warmed to operating temperature, and idling in neutral (manual transmission cars) or Drive (automatic equipped cars).

Locate the timing marks on the crankshaft pulley and front timing case.

NOTE: *Because of the difficult access to the timing marks on the crankshaft pulley on 1975 and later 128 models, an additional set of marks are provided on the flywheel, visible through the bell housing. Remove the spare tire to observe these marks.*

Find the TDC timing mark and highlight with chalk or paint. Then, using a stroboscopic timing light, set the timing to specifications. Timing is adjusted by loosening the distributor hold-down nut and rotating the distributor body in the required direction.

Ignition timing marks—124 Sport Coupe and Spider, 131, and 1974 124 TC Sedan and Wagon

A = 10° (Adv.)
B = 5° (Adv.)
C = 10° (TDC)

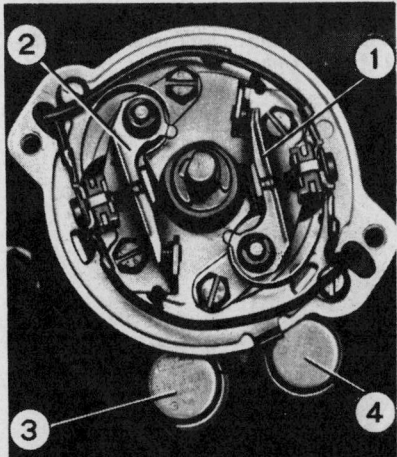

Ignition points—1973-77 124 Sport Spider and Coupe, 1974 124 TC Sedan and Wagon, 1975-77 131

1. Main breaker points
2. Auxiliary breaker points
3. Capacitor, main breaker points
4. Capacitor, auxiliary breaker points

Timing Marks—128, X1/9

1. 10° BTDC
2. 5° BTDC
3. 0° TDC
4. Timing mark on the crankshaft pulley

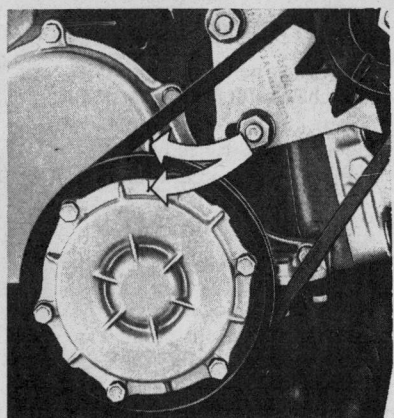

Ignition timing marks—850

Ignition timing marks on flywheel—1975 and later 128 models

A = 0° (Adv.)
B = 5° (Adv.)
C = 10° (T.D.C.)

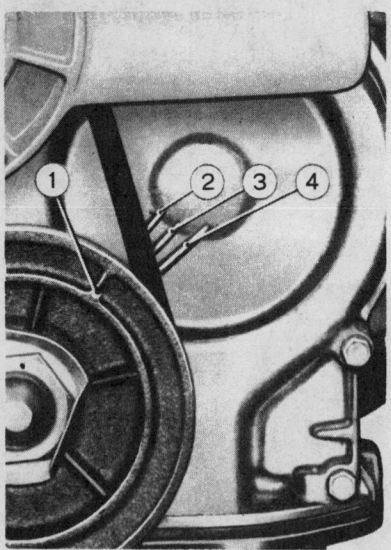

Ignition timing marks—1972-73 124 Sedan and Wagon

1. Index on driving pulley
2. Index showing 10° advance
3. Index showing 5° advance
4. Index showing 0° advance

NOTE: *On 1974 and later 128 and X1/9 models, leave the vacuum line attached to the distributor for the timing check.*

Valve Clearance Adjustment

Valve clearance should be checked every 12,000 miles—sooner if the head is removed or if excessive valve train noise is noticed. On overhead valve engines (850, 1972–73 124 Special Sedan and Wagon), valve clearance adjustment is a simple matter of loosening a locknut and rotating the adjusting screw on the rocker arm in the required direction. However, on both single and double overhead cam engines (128, X1/9, 131, 124 Sport, and 124 Special TC), valve clearance is adjusted by the thickness of the Shim (plate) between the cam lobe and tappet bucket, requiring special service tools.

850, 1972–73 124 Special Sedan and Wagon

NOTE: *Valve clearance is checked with the engine cold.*

There are two ways you can adjust the valves on these engines; a two position method and a four position method. On the two position method, first bring no. 1 cylinder to Top Dead Center (double-check this by rotor position), and adjust the clearance on valves (counting from the front of the engine) 1, 2, 3, and 5. Then, rotate the crankshaft pulley one full turn to bring no. 4 cylinder to TDC (again check rotor position) and adjust valves 4, 6, 7, and 8. This is the quick way. The official Fiat approved method is the following:

1. Remove the valve cover. Also remove the spark plugs to make it easier to rotate the crankshaft pulley by hand.

2. Rotate the crankshaft pulley or push the car in fourth gear until the valves of no. 1 cylinder are in the "rock" or "at balance" position. At this position, the #1 exhaust valve has just closed and the #1 intake valve is slightly open; and

there should be clearance between both valves and rocker arms of no. 4 cylinder. Here is the way it works, following the firing order; with the valves for cylinder #3 "at balance", check the clearances for the valves of #2 cylinder; cylinder #4 "at balance", check cylinder #1; and finally cylinder #2 "at balance", check cylinder #3.

3. If the clearance needs adjusting, loosen the locknut and rotate the adjusting screw in the required direction so that the feeler gauge slides between the valve stem and rocker arm with a slight drag. Then, while holding the adjusting screw from turning, tighten the locknut. Recheck the clearance.

4. Install the spark plugs and valve cover.

128, X1/9, 131, 124 Sport, and 1974 124 Special TC Sedan and Wagon

NOTE: *Special tools required for this job include a tappet depressor tool #A 60421 (128, X1/9) or #A 60422 (124, 131), a pair of curved tip needle nose pliers (such as #A 87001), a lever #A*

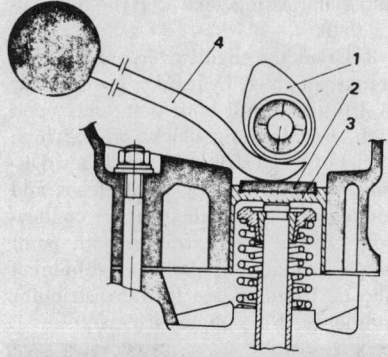

Depressing tappet with lever #A60443— 124, 131 Twin cam

1. Camshaft lobe
2. Tappet plate
3. Tappet

Measuring valve clearance on a 128 or X1/9 engine; 124, 131 Twin cam engine similar

1. Camshaft lobe   3. Tappet
2. Adjustment plate 4. Feeler gauge

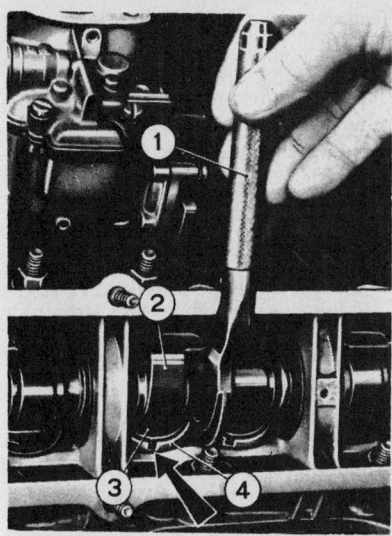

Depressing tappet with tool #A60421— 128, X1/9

1. Tool A. 60421
2. Camshaft lobe
3. Plate
4. Tappet

The arrow shows one of the two notches in the tappet to help plate removal

60443 (Twin cam only), and a compressed air source and air chuck to blow out the old adjusting shim.

NOTE: *The engine must be cold for a valve clearance check.*

1. Remove the retaining screws and remove the camshaft cover.

2. Turn the crankshaft until the lobe controlling the tappet being checked is pointing upward and is at a right angle to the tappet plate.

3. Measure the clearance between the tappet plate and the camshaft lobe with a feeler gauge.

4. If the clearance is not at the proper specification, a tappet plate of the required thickness will have to be installed.

5. To remove the old tappet plate (shim), the tappet must be depressed and held in that position. On the 128 and X1/9, this is accomplished with special tool #A 60421 (see illustration). However, on the 124 and 131 twin cam engines, this is a two step process. First, depress the tappet with special lever #60443 or rotate the camshaft until the lobe depresses the tappet. Then, install the tappet clamping tool # 60422 which will keep the tappet depressed. If you rotated the camshaft to depress the tappet, rotate it again to give clearance for plate removal. Finally, using compressed air through the notch in the tappet or needle nose pliers, or both, remove the old plate.

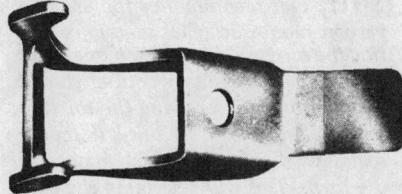

Tappet clamping tool #A60422—124, 131 Twin Cam

6. Install a new tappet plate after determining its thickness by comparing it to the clearance measurement taken in step 3.

Tappet clearance adjustment plates are available in a range of thicknesses from 0.146 in. to 0.185 in. with a difference between each plate of 0.002 in.

The thickness of the plate is shown on one of the plate's flat sides. This side

should be installed facing the tappet. It is recommended that the plate's thickness be checked to make sure that it is actually the thickness specified.

Carburetor

Often mistaken for an improperly adjusted carburetor is an incorrectly adjusted air cleaner climatic setting. This adjustment provides warmed intake air for cold climates and cool intake air for warm climates. See "Emission Controls" for details.

Idle Speed and Mixture Adjustment—All Models

NOTE: *On 1975 and later models equipped with a catalytic converter (california models, and all X1/9 cars), idle speed and mixture is checked with the air injection hose between the diverter valve and check valve pinched shut with locking pliers.*

1. Start the engine and warm to operating temperature (176°F min.). Make sure the choke plate is open.

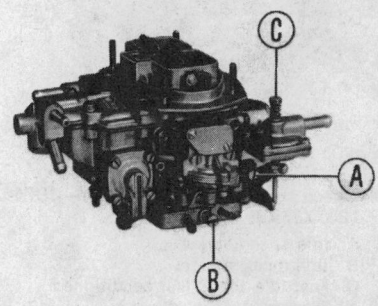

Idle speed and mixture adjustments—1972-74 124 (all)

A. Idle speed screw
B. Idle mixture screw
C. Fast idle screw

Idle speed and mixture adjustments—1972-73 128

A. Fast idle screw
B. Idle mixture screw
C. Idle speed screw

NOTE: *If possible, make all adjustments with the air cleaner on, as removal may artificially lean out the mixture.*

2. Adjust the idle speed to specifications with the idle speed screw. The idle

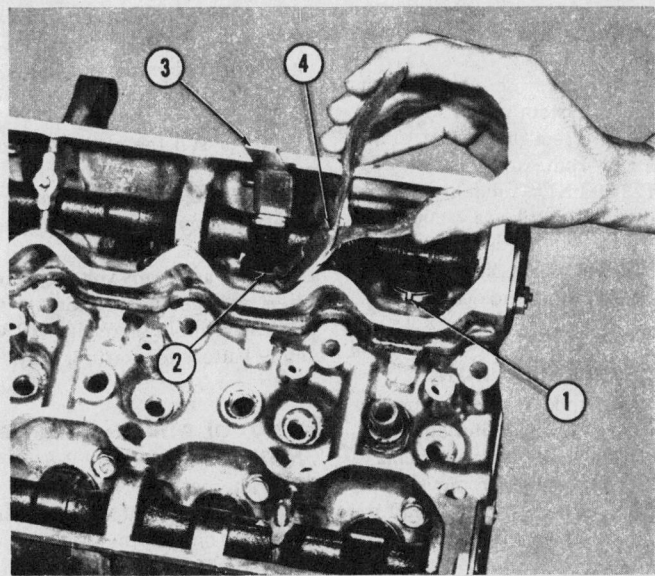

Remove tappet shim—124, 131 Twin Cam

1. Tappet notch
2. Tappet plate (shim)
3. Clamping tool #A60422
4. Needle nose pliers

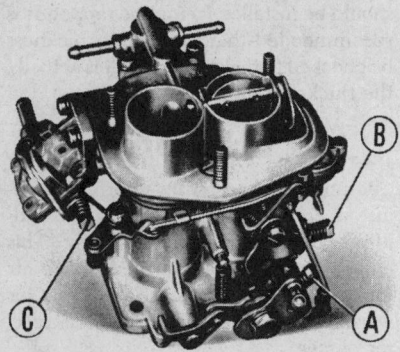

Idle speed and mixture adjustments—1972-73 850

A. Idle speed screw
B. Idle mixture screw
C. Fast idle screw

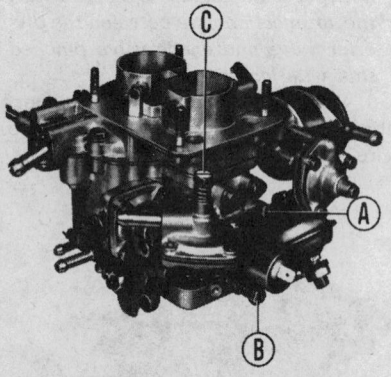

Idle speed and mixture adjustments—1974-77 128, X1/9

A. Idle speed screw
B. Idle mixture screw
C. Fast idle screw (Air conditioned cars only)

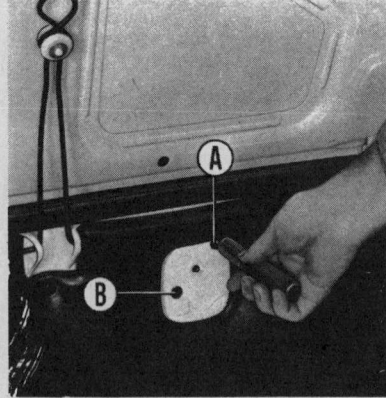

Access holes for carburetor adjustments—X1/9

A. Idle speed
B. Idle mixture

speed is set with the transmission in neutral on manual transmission cars, and is set in Drive with the parking brake firmly applied on automatic cars.

3. Adjust the idle mixture (% CO) to specifications (see "Tune-up" chart) with the idle mixture metering screw.

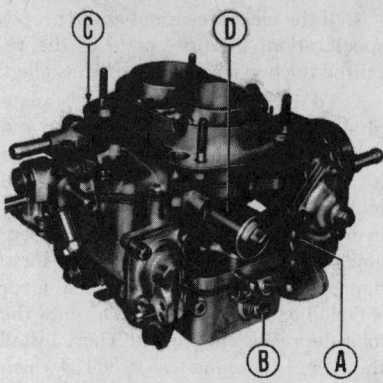

Idle speed and mixture adjustments—1975-77 124, 131

A. Idle speed screw
B. Idle mixture screw
C. Fast idle screw
D. Idle stop solenoid

NOTE: *Fiat recommends the use of a carbon monoxide (CO) meter for setting the mixture. However, if one is not available, a satisfactory setting should be found by first screwing the mixture screw all the way in until it lightly seats, and then backing it out about 2 to 3½ turns. This will get you in the ballpark, and then you can adjust the mixture for the highest possible rpm within that range. Screw clockwise to lean (decrease CO). and counterclockwise to richen (increase CO).*

4. After adjusting mixture, recheck idle speed and adjust if necessary.

ENGINE ELECTRICAL

Distributor

All Fiat distributors use a centrifugal ignition advance system which advances spark timing in direct proportion to increasing engine rpm. In addition, 1974 and later 128 and X1/9 models with the Ducellier distributor utilize a vacuum retard system which retards the ignition timing about 10° under high vacuum situations such as idling and deceleration.

Removal and Installation

The quick method of distributor removal is to mark the distributor body and rotor positions relative to some stationary engine component before removal, and then put it back the way you found it. However, on the 1608, 1592 and 1756cc engines installed in the 124 and 131 (these are the ones with the distributor located at the right rear of the engine above the exhaust manifold), the distributor drive gear is helical (slanted drive).

Therefore, the rotor will rotate about 30–40 degrees during removal or installation. For this reason, mark the position of the rotor before removal and just after removal. When you go to install the distributor, align the rotor with the mark you made just after removal so when the distributor is installed, the rotor will correctly align with the first mark.

The Fiat approved method of distributor removal is the following:

1. Remove the high tension wires from the distributor.
2. Remove the low tension leads and disconnect the vacuum control (if equipped).
3. Rotate the crankshaft to bring No. 1 cylinder to TOP DEAD CENTER (TDC) of compression stroke (both valves closed). Align the timing marks.
4. Position the distributor rotor opposite the No. 1 contact in the cap. At this point the contact breaker points are about to open.
5. Fit the distributor into its housing and tighten the clamp bolt.
6. Replace the distributor cap and connect the spark plug wires in the correct firing order.
7. Check the ignition timing with a timing light and the point dwell with a dwell meter.

Alternator

Alternator Precautions

Certain precautions should be observed when working on this, or any other AC charging system.

1. Never switch battery polarity.
2. When installing a battery, never connect the hot cable first.
3. Never disconnect the battery while the engine is running.
4. If the molded connector is disconnected from the alternator, do not ground the hot wire.
5. Never run the alternator with the main output cable disconnected.
6. Never electric weld around the vehicle, without disconnecting the alternator.
7. Never apply any voltage, other than battery voltage, when testing.
8. Never apply more than 12 volts to jump a battery for starting purposes.

Removal and Installation

NOTE: *Disconnect the battery first.*

The alternator is removed by disconnecting the electrical leads and unscrewing the nut on the upper bracket and the screw which attaches the bracket to the engine. Remove the two nuts of the lower brackets, fan, generator and water pump belt. Installation is the reverse of removal.

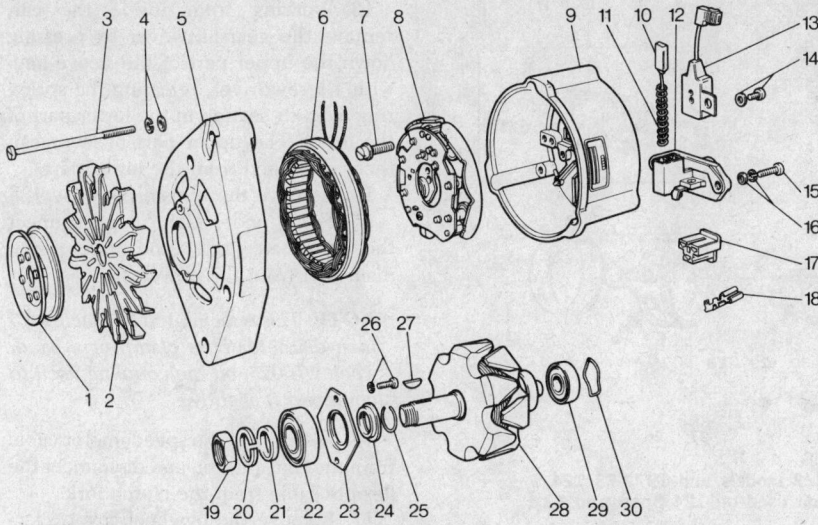

Bosch GI-14V 33A27 alternator—1972-73 128

1. Pulley	11. Spring	21. Thrust ring
2. Blower	12. Brush holder	22. Bearing
3. Through-bolt	13. Condenser	23. Bearing retainer plate
4. Washers	14. Screw and washer	24. Thrust ring
5. Frame	15. Screw	25. Spring washer
6. Stator	16. Washers	26. Screw and washer
7. Screw	17. Power socket	27. Key
8. Diode plate	18. Plug	28. Rotor
9. Frame	19. Nut	29. Bearing
10. Brush	20. Spring washer	30. Backing washer

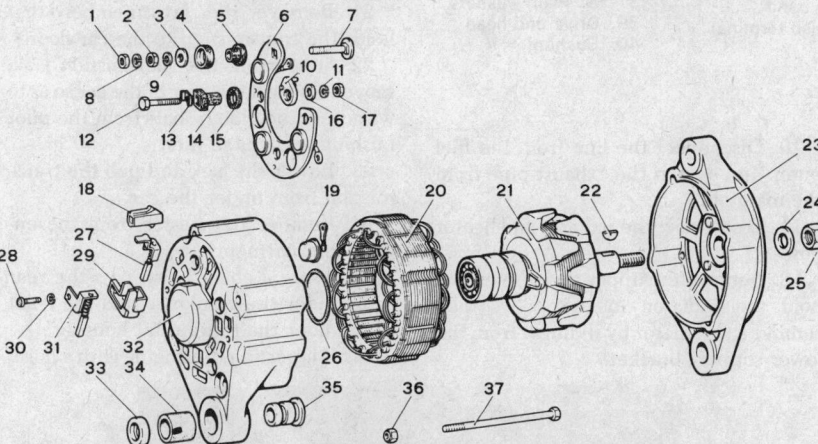

Fiat A 12M 124/12/42M alternator—all 124 models; similar to Marelli A 124-14V 60A unit used on 1975-76 128, X1/9 and 131 models

1-2. Nuts	14-15. Insulators	26. Rubber seal, bearing outer race
3. Flat washer	16. Flat washer	27. Positive brush
4-5. Positive clamp insulators	17. Nut	28. Screw
6. Positive diode plate	18. Insulated connector for charge indicator blade plug	29. Brush holder
7. Screw, positive clamp		30. Spring washer
8-9. Spring washers	19. Negative diode	31. Negative brush
10. Diode terminal connector insulator	20. Stator	32. Diode end frame
	21. Rotor	33-34-35. Rubber bushing components
11. Spring washer	22. Key	
12. Screw, positive diode plate, diode terminals and stator phases ends attachment	23. Drive end frame	36. Nut
	24. Spring washer	37. Through-bolt
13. Plate	25. Pulley nut	

Generator Voltage Regulator

Adjustments

Cut-out

1. Measure the air gap for the cut-out relay between the clapper and the edge of the core nearest the contacts.

2. Make the cut-in adjustment with the unit at 65–95° F.

3. Adjust by bending the spring tension arm until the points close at the proper specification.

4. Check the reverse current by connecting a two-way ammeter in series with the battery lead to the regulator.

5. Run the generator to 4500 rpm and gradually reduce speed, noting the reverse current at the point where the contacts open. (See specifications for the proper amperage.)

6. The range between cut-in and cut-out action can be adjusted by enlarging or reducing the air gap.

Starter

Removal and Installation

Front Engine Models

1. Jack up the car and place jackstands beneath the frame.

2. Disconnect the battery positive terminal to prevent accidental shorting.

3. Remove the exhaust manifold and muffler to provide clearance.

4. Disconnect the wires from the starter, tagging each wire to facilitate later identification.

5. Remove the mounting bolts and pull the starter from the housing.

6. Installation is the reverse of removal.

Rear Engine Models

1. Raise the car at the rear and set it on two stands at the control arms.

2. Disconnect the battery (positive) cable to prevent shorting.

3. Disconnect and remove the lower linings of the compartment.

4. If necessary, remove the exhaust manifold and muffler.

5. Disconnect the wires from the starter motor and tag each wire to facilitate later identification.

6. Remove the mounting bolts and the starter.

7. Installation is the reverse of removal.

Overhaul

The starter can be broken down into the following subassemblies: solenoid, commutator end head, frame, armature, drive and pinion end head.

1. To disassemble, disconnect the starter motor lead from the solenoid and remove the solenoid.

2. Remove the brush cover and disconnect the brush holder.

3. Lift the brushes slightly and retain them in their holders by arranging springs against their sides.

4. Unscrew the two self-locking nuts and take off the brush holder bracket, saving the fiber and steel thrust washers.

5. Slide the frame off the pinion end.

6. Remove the cotter pin from the linkage pivot and remove the pivot. The armature can then be taken out, along with the drive and fork lever.

7. Assembly is the reverse of removal.

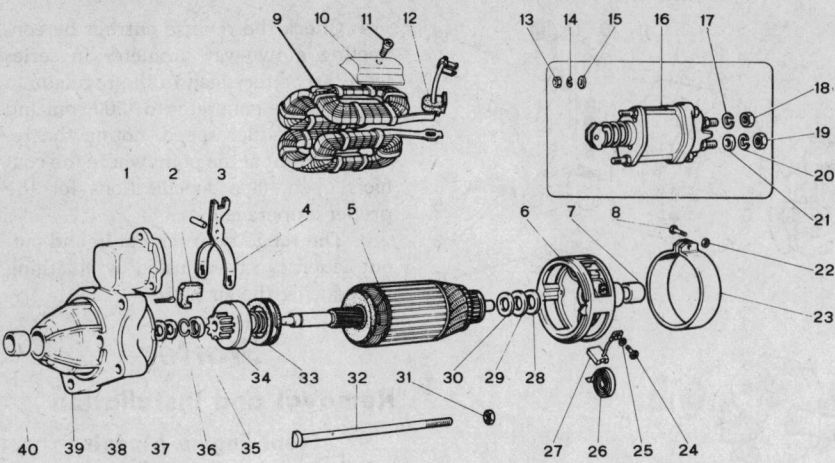

Fiat E84-0.8/12 starter—all 128, X1/9 models and 1972-73 124 S pecial; similar to Fiat E100-1.3/12 unit used on 124 Sport and 131 models

1. Split pin
2. Rubber pad
3. Lever pivot pin
4. Starter drive pinion shifter fork
5. Armature
6. Commutator end head
7. Bushing
8. Protection band screw
9. Field winding
10. Pole shoe
11. Pole shoe attaching screw
12. Grommet
13. Nut, solenoid to drive end head

14. Lock washer
15. Plain washer
16. Solenoid assembly
17. Lock washer
18. Nut, current lead clamping
19. Nut, field winding terminal
20. Lock washer
21. Plain washer
22. Nut, protection band screw
23. Commutator end head protection band
24. Screw, brush terminal clamping

25. Lock washer
26. Brush spring
27. Brush
28-29. Plain washers
30. Fibre thrust washer
31. Thru-bolt nut
32. Starter thru-bolt
33. Starter drive sleeve
34. Drive pinion
35. Stop ring
36. Snap ring
37-38. Plain washers
39. Drive end head
40. Bushing

ENGINE MECHANICAL

Engine Removal and Installation

All 124 Models, 131

1. Removal of 124 sedan and sports car engines is facilitated by removing the radiator and the transmission. Proceed as follows:

2. Jack up the car and place it on jackstands.

3. Drain the radiator, auxiliary tank, block and heater system by first moving the heater lever to far right, then opening the radiator drain cock and removing the plug on the right-hand side of the block.

4. Speed drainage by removing the radiator and auxiliary tank caps.

5. Disconnect the battery leads.

6. Then disconnect the ignition coil, generator, starter, low oil pressure and water temperature indicator wires.

7. Disconnect the accelerator rod, sliding it out of the lever ball joint end toward the dash.

8. Remove the air filter.

9. Detach the choke cable from the carburetor.

10. Disconnect the line from the fuel pump and detach the exhaust pipe from the manifold.

11. Disconnect the radiator and heater hoses.

12. Remove the upper two screws that hold the radiator to the body, then remove the radiator by sliding it from the lower support bracket.

13. Working from inside the car, remove the gearshift lever by pressing down the upper part of the sleeve and, with a screwdriver, releasing the spring ring from its seating in the lower part of the lever. The upper part of lever can then be slipped from the lower part.

14. Remove the transmission cover.

15. From under the car, disconnect the driveshaft spider and transmission mainshaft from the universal.

NOTE: *This is facilitated by placing a 5 inch diameter hose clamp or a band, Tool A.70025, on the coupling itself to compress it slightly.*

16. Disconnect the speedometer cable from the transmission and disconnect the flexible cable from the clutch fork.

17. Remove the flywheel cover, electrical ground cable and exhaust pipe bracket clip.

18. Remove the heat shield from the exhaust manifold and the three bolts that hold the starter to the front of the transmission.

19. Position a hydraulic jack under the transmission for support.

20. Remove the four bolts which mount the transmission to the crankcase.

21. Remove the crossmember that holds the transmission to the car floor.

22. Supporting the transmission jack, move it toward the rear of the car so as to withdraw the clutch shaft from the pilot bushing and clutch hub.

23. Lower the jack and pull the transmission from under the car.

24. Remove the starter from the engine compartment.

25. Using a chain hoist, pass the rear sling under the crankcase and the front sling under the thermostat housing.

26. Supporting the engine with a hoist,

A clamp holds universal (4) together while removing drive shaft screws (1) and transmission spider screws.

remove the front mounts and lift the engine clear.

27. Installation is the reverse of removal.

850

1. Jack up the car from the rear and place it on jackstands.
2. Disconnect the positive terminal of the battery and the fuel line at the tank.
3. Tilt the back of the rear seat forward and remove the screws and floor covering.
4. Remove the starter and the two upper bolts that hold the transmission to the engine.
5. Remove the apron from under the engine.
6. Unbolt the flywheel housing from the transmission.
7. Disconnect the exhaust pipe at the manifold and the muffler at the oil sump.
8. Drain the cooling system and disconnect the water hoses at the radiator.
9. Disconnect the fuel line at the fuel pump.
10. Disconnect the oil pressure and water temperature indicators.
11. Remove the air cleaner and disconnect the carburetor choke and accelerator linkage.
12. Disconnect the ignition coil and generator.
13. Attach a chain hoist to the engine and lightly take up the slack.
14. Remove the two bottom bolts that hold the engine to the transmission.
15. Remove the rear central engine support nut, washer and rubber bushing.
16. Remove the two nuts, one on each side, that hold the bumper to the brackets and the four nuts and two screws that hold the lower body panel.
17. Lift the engine from the car.
18. Installation is the reverse of removal.

128

1. Place the car on jackstands and be sure the car is in a stable position before removal.
2. Raise the hood and unhook the stay rod. Place covers on the fenders.
3. Loosen the wing nut and remove the spare tire.
4. Take off the lower guards.
5. Drain the water from the radiator, supply tank, cylinder block and passenger compartment heating system in the following way:
   a. Completely lower the heater lever inside the car.
   b. Open the cock at the bottom of the radiator and remove the radiator cap.
   c. Open the cock at the inner side of the engine block and take the cap off the supply tank to help water drainage.
6. Disconnect the battery cables.

7. Disconnect the primary and secondary wires from the coil to the distributor.
8. Disconnect the wires from the generator.
9. Disconnect the wires from the starter, the oil pressure sending unit, and the water temperature sending unit.
10. Disconnect the air cleaner.
11. Disconnect the linkage and choke wire from the carburetor.
12. Disconnect the fuel inlet hose from the fuel pump.
13. Disconnect the exhaust pipe from the manifold.
14. Remove the two rubber hoses from the union with the thermostat to the radiator.
15. Disconnect the water inlet and outlet hoses from the engine to the passenger compartment heater.
16. Disconnect the speedometer drive from the transmission housing by unscrewing the retaining ring.
17. Remove the adjustable rod of the flexible cable from the clutch release lever by unscrewing the locknut and nut.
18. Detach the anti-roll bar by removing the screws which clamp the brackets and insulators to the body. Then unscrew the nuts which fasten the ends to the control arms.
19. Remove the exhaust pipe support bracket from the transmission housing.
20. Disconnect the rod from the gearshift control lever.
21. Remove the earth plate from the transmission housing.
22. Take off the left hand wheel. Unscrew the left tie rod-to-steering nut and disconnect the ball joint.
23. Remove the shock absorber from the pillar.
24. Unscrew the constant-speed joint nuts from both front wheels.
25. From above the car, working in the engine compartment, disconnect the reaction strut.
26. Hook up the engine and put the cable under light tension. Then, working from above, unscrew the engine to body clamping bolt and, from below, detach the crossmember from the underbody.
27. Work the shaft of each constant-speed joint out of its seat in the pillars and secure the axle shafts with wire to prevent them from coming away from their seats in the differential.
28. Using a hoist lower the engine group to remove.
29. Install in the reverse order.

X1/9

1. Disconnect the battery and drain the cooling system.
2. Remove the air cleaner assembly.
3. Disconnect the air pump inlet hose and outlet hose from the pump.
4. Disconnect the heater return hose

at the coupling joint and disconnect the heater hose from the pump.
5. Disconnect the wires from the alternator.
6. Remove the two bolts retaining the louvered protection panel below the carbon trap in the rear firewall.
7. Disconnect the choke linkage from the carburetor.
8. Disconnect the vacuum hoses from the base of the carburetor. Disconnect the electrical leads from the solenoid and the carburetor vent hose from the carburetor.
9. Disconnect the coil wires at the distributor. Disconnect the leads from the oil pressure and water temperature sending units. Disconnect the electrical wires from the starter.
10. Remove the clamp securing the fuel lines to the firewall and disconnect the fuel supply and return lines from the firewall.
11. Remove the stopbolt from the accelerator cable, slide the seal off the cable, remove the retainer clip from the cable sheath and remove the cable from the support.
12. Remove the bolts securing the coolant expansion tank, top and bottom, and lift the tank, allowing the water to drain into the engine. Disconnect the hoses from the tank at the thermostat and remove the tank.
13. Remove the hoses from the thermostat.
14. Remove the cotter pin holding the slave cylinder pushrod to the clutch shaft. Loosen the two bolts securing the slave cylinder to the transmission. Open the bleeder screw of the slave cylinder and allow the pushrod to retract. Swing the slave cylinder out of the way.
15. From underneath the vehicle, remove the remaining bolt holding the louvered panel and remove the panel from the firewall. Remove the heat shield located behind the alternator. Remove the three panels from the bottom of the engine compartment and the panel in board of each rear wheel.
16. Drain the transmission/differential lubricant.
17. Disconnect the electrical connectors for the seatbelt interlock system and the back-up lights. Remove any clamps as necessary to allow the wires to be removed with the engine.
18. Disconnect the speedometer cable from the differential and secure the cable out of the way.
19. Remove the bolts retaining the gearshift linkage to the shifting tube. Loosen the bolt at the transmission end of the flexible link and swing the link to one side.
20. Remove the bolts holding the ground strap to the body.
21. Straighten the lock-tabs on the ex-

haust manifold flange. Remove the four nuts and lock-tab plates. Remove the 2 bolts from the upper bracket at the left end of the muffler. Remove the two nuts retaining the center support of the muffler to the crossmember and remove the muffler assembly. Remove the two nuts and bolt retaining the upper bracket to the differential case and remove the bracket.

22. Remove the three bolts securing the axle boots retaining ring on the right and left sides and slide the boots away from the differential, draining excess oil.

23. Remove the handbrake cable bracket at the forward end of each suspension control arm.

24. Take note of and record the number of shims at each suspension control arm mounting point.

25. Remove the four bolts and nuts plus the shims holding the control arms to the body and swing the control arms downward out of their brackets. Move the control arms away from the differential until the axles are free of the differential. Secure the axle assemblies to the control arms.

NOTE: *If necessary, the entire suspension assemblies may be removed at this time by removing the wheels and brake calipers and the three nuts securing the top of the shock absorbers.*

26. Straighten the lock-tabs on the two bolts on each end of the lower crossmember and loosen the bolts. Lower the vehicle until the engine is resting on a support.

CAUTION: *Support the engine in such a manner so as not to do damage to the oil pan or any cast aluminum parts.*

Remove the bolts from the lower crossmember.

27. From the top of the engine compartment, disconnect the engine torque rod from the bracket on the engine.

28. Remove the bolt from the engine mount, raise the car slightly and rock the engine/transmission assembly in order to clear the front engine mount.

29. Carefully raise the vehicle while supporting the engine.

30. Install the engine in the reverse order of removal.

Cylinder Head

Removal and Installation

124, 131 DOHC Engine

1. Drain the cooling system and disconnect the upper radiator hose.

2. Remove the air cleaner.

3. Disconnect all linkage and hoses from the carburetor and cylinder head.

4. Remove the carburetor and intake manifold as an assembly.

5. Disconnect the exhaust manifold from the side of the cylinder head.

Install timing belt (3) with camshaft gears at top (exhaust left, intake right) locked by tool (4) and positioned with reference marks opposite pointers on (1). Idler pulley (8), locked by screws (7 and 9), exerts tension on belt. Auxiliary drive gear is held in place by (6).

6. Remove the timing belt shroud from the front of the engine.

7. Loosen the timing belt tensioner (idler) and remove the timing belt from the camshaft drive pulleys.

8. Remove the spark plug wires from the spark plugs.

9. Unscrew the cylinder head attaching bolts and carefully lift off the cylinder head. Lift the head straight up so as not to damage any of the open valves.

10. Clean the mating surfaces of all gasket material.

11. Before placing the cylinder head on the engine block, position the camshafts so that the reference marks on the intake and exhaust camshaft gears are aligned with the fixed pointers on the front of the cylinder head. While aligning the marks and the pointers, be careful that the valves do not interfere with each other. Once the timing marks are aligned, avoid turning the camshafts until the drive belt has been installed.

12. Turn the crankshaft until no. 1 and 4 pistons are at TDC with no. 1 on the compression stroke.

13. Carefully place the cylinder head on the block. Do not allow any of the open valves to contact the cylinder block to avoid bending them.

14. Install the cylinder head bolts and tighten to specification in the proper sequence.

15. Fit the camshaft drive belt around the camshaft pulleys without turning the crankshaft or the camshafts.

16. Attach a spring scale to the hole in the upper right arm of the drive belt idler pulley. Apply a load of 60 lbs to the belt

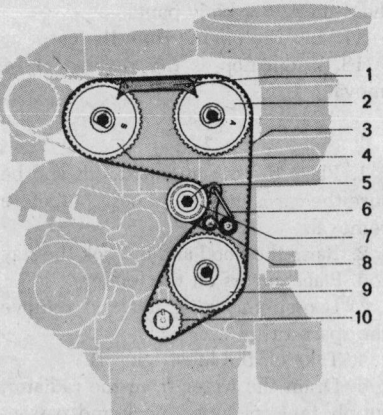

124, 131 Twin cam engine valve gear drive

1. Valve timing pointers
2. Intake camshaft drive pulley
3. Timing belt
4. Exhaust camshaft/distributor drive pulley
5. Roller retaining nut
6. Tensioner spring
7. Tensioner roller
8. Tensioner retaining screw
9. Oil pump drive pulley
10. Crankshaft pulley

by pulling the spring scale on a line bisecting the angle between the two runs of the belt where it passes around the idler pulley. Tighten the idler pulley attaching nut.

17. Check the belt tension after turning the crankshaft two or three times.

18. Check for proper valve timing.

19. Assemble the remaining components in the reverse order of removal.

124 OHV Engine

1. Drain the radiator and cylinder block.

2. Remove the air filter.

3. Disconnect the water temperature sending unit cable.

4. Disconnect the spark plug wires.

5. Disconnect the accelerator rods from the cylinder head cover.

6. Remove the cylinder head cover.

7. Disconnect all water hoses.

8. Disconnect the fuel line.

9. Disconnect the starter relay cable.

10. Disconnect the exhaust pipe from the manifold.

11. Remove the starter motor heat shield.

   NOTE: *It is best to leave the intake and exhaust manifolds and the carburetor assembled to the head; they can be removed easily on the work bench.*

12. Remove the rocker shaft assembly to include the supports and rockers.

13. Withdraw the pushrods.

14. Remove the ten cylinder head hold-down bolts.

15. Remove the head and its gasket.

16. The remaining parts can be removed on the work bench. These include: thermostat and housing, intake and exhaust manifolds, the carburetor and the heater.

17. Installation is the reverse of the above procedure, observing the following points:

   a. Always use a new head gasket.

   b. Tighten the head bolts in sequence.

   c. Tighten the cylinder head bolts to 29 ft lbs the first time and then go to the specified 56 ft lbs.

850 OHV Engine

1. Drain the cooling system.

2. Remove the air cleaner.

3. Remove the carburetor.

4. Remove the distributor.

5. Remove the rocker cover.

6. Disconnect the coolant inlet and outlet pipes.

7. Disconnect the exhaust pipes from the manifold and the exhaust manifold from the head.

8. Disconnect the spark plug wires from the spark plugs and the heat indicator sending unit lead from the sending unit.

9. Unscrew the rocker shaft assembly attaching bolts and lift the rocket shaft

assembly from the cylinder head. Loosen the four attaching bolts 1 to 2 turns at a time in sequence so to avoid bending the rocker shaft.

10. Remove the pushrods.

11. Remove the cylinder head attaching screws and lift the cylinder head from the cylinder block.

12. Remove all gasket material from the mating surfaces of the cylinder head and block.

13. Install the cylinder head in the reverse order of removal. Tighten the cylinder head bolts in the proper sequence in two stages; 22 ft lbs the first time and to final specification the second time.

128 SOHC Engine

1. Drain the cooling system.

2. Remove the spare tire from the engine compartment.

3. Remove the air cleaner.

4. Disconnect the spark plug cables.

5. Disconnect the accelerator control linkage from the carburetor.

6. Disconnect the fuel line and the choke control cable from the carburetor.

7. Disconnect the temperature sending unit electrical lead.

8. Disconnect the heater inlet hose, the upper and lower radiator hoses, and

the coolant pump delivery hose from the thermostat housing.

9. Disconnect the exhaust pipe from the manifold and remove the bracket.

10. Remove the belt guard cover, working from below the vehicle to get at the lower screw after removing a guard.

11. Loosen the belt tensioner pulley retaining nut and remove the belt from the camshaft sprocket.

12. Unscrew the belt guard lower screw.

13. Remove the shroud by unscrewing the set screws.

14. Disconnect the reaction rod from the bracket in the cylinder head.

15. Remove the cylinder head retaining screws and nuts and remove the cylinder head along with the intake and exhaust manifolds, carburetor, and the camshaft housing. Removal of these parts is best performed with the cylinder head out of the vehicle.

16. Install the cylinder head, with the intake and exhaust manifolds, carburetor and camshaft housing assembled to it, in the reverse order of removal. Tighten the cylinder head bolts in the proper sequence in two stages; 29 ft lbs the first time and to specifications the second time.

Removing the belt tensioner pulley nut

1. Camshaft sprocket	5. Tensioner
2. Tensioner pulley	6. Belt guard
3. Drive pulley	7. Bracket
4. Auxiliary shaft sprocket	

X1/9

1. Drain the cooling system and disconnect the battery.

2. Remove the air cleaner assembly.

3. Disconnect the fuel hoses from the carburetor and pull the two hoses out of the bracket on the camshaft cover.

4. Disconnect the accelerator linkage leading from the carburetor at the camshaft cover.

5. Disconnect the spark plug cables from the spark plugs.

6. Disconnect the distributor vacuum hose from the fitting in the cylinder head.

7. Remove the stop-bolt from the accelerator cable.

8. Slide the seal off of the cable and remove the clip retaining the cable to the camshaft cover. Remove the cable.

9. Disconnect the expansion tank hose, water pump inlet and outlet hoses, and the water pump-to-union hose.

10. Remove the bolt retaining the engine torque rod in its bracket and move the rod out of the way.

11. Disconnect the hose from the exhaust shroud.

12. Disconnect the electrical leads of the termostatic switch on the carburetor.

13. Disconnect the evaporative hose from the carburetor.

14. Remove the air pump hoses.

15. Disconnect the muffler from the exhaust manifold flange.

16. Remove the bolts and washers attaching the timing cover.

17. Remove the lower right shield from under the engine.

18. Remove the alternator and the drive belt.

19. Remove the air pump.

20. Loosen the nut on the timing belt tensioner pulley and remove the timing belt.

21. Remove the lower bolt through the belt guard.

22. Remove the cylinder head attaching bolts and nuts and lift the cylinder head straight up and off of the engine. The carburetor and intake and exhaust manifolds are removed with the cylinder head as an assembly and removed from the cylinder head on the work bench.

23. Install the cylinder head in the reverse order of removal. Tighten the cylinder head bolts in the proper sequence. The valve timing is adjusted in the same manner as for the 128.

Cylinder Head Overhaul

See Engine Rebuilding Section

Rocker Shafts

Removal and Installation

The removal and installation of the rocker shaft assemblies of the 124 OHV and 850 OHV engines is covered under the cylinder head removal and installation procedures for each of these engines. The rocker shaft mounting studs are removed from the cylinder head by double-nutting them and unscrewing them out. Screw the new studs into the head and stake them in place with a punch. Tighten the rocker shaft retaining nuts to 15 ft lbs on the 850 and 29 ft lbs on the 124.

Intake and Exhaust Manifolds

Removal and Installation

1. Remove the air cleaner.

2. Remove the fuel line, all vacuum lines, coolant lines (128 and X1/9), and accelerator linkage from the carburetor.

3. The carburetor can be removed at this point or removed after the manifold is removed from the vehicle.

4. Disconnect the exhaust pipe from the manifold. This is not necessary if removing just the intake manifold on DOHC engines.

5. Remove the manifold retaining bolts from the cylinder head and remove the manifold from the engine.

6. Install the manifold(s) in the reverse order of removal, tighten the retaining bolts to specification in an alternating sequence starting at the center and working toward the ends.

Timing Gear Cover

Removal and Installation

850

1. Remove the crankshaft/centrifugal oil filter drive belt.

2. Remove the centrifugal oil filter cover and gasket.

3. Remove the crankshaft pulley nut. It will be necessary to prevent the crankshaft from turning in order to remove the nut.

4. Remove the pulley from the crankshaft.

5. Remove the timing cover retaining nuts and remove the cover.

6. Install the timing gear cover in the reverse order of removal.

124 OHV

1. Remove the alternator and fan drive belt.

2. Remove the crankshaft pulley retaining nut.

3. Remove the crankshaft pulley.

4. Remove the timing gear cover retaining screws and remove the cover.

5. Install the timing gear cover in the reverse order of removal.

128, X1/9, 131 and 124 OHC Engines

The valve mechanism drive belt cover on these engines is removed by simply removing the retaining screws and lifting the cover from the engine. Install in reverse order.

Timing Chain or Belt

Removal and Installation

850

1. Remove the timing gear cover.

2. Remove the nuts retaining the camshaft drive sprocket.

3. Remove the camshaft drive sprocket together with the timing chain.

4. The crankshaft sprocket has to be removed with a puller.

5. Install the crankshaft drive sprocket on the crankshaft aligning the slot in the sprocket with the key and keyway in the crankshaft.

6. Turn the crankshaft until the timing mark on the drive sprocket is at ten o'clock position.

7. Install the camshaft sprocket, with the timing chain positioned around both sprockets, on the camshaft with the timing mark on the camshaft sprocket aligned with the mark on the crankshaft sprocket. Turn the camshaft as necessary. The chain stretchers on the timing chain

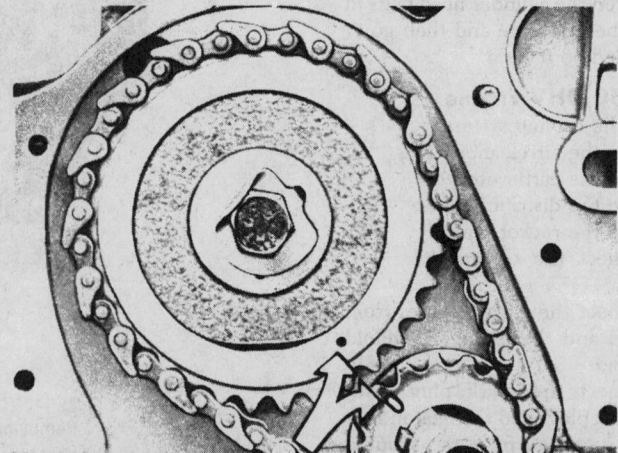

The valve timing marks on the crankshaft and camshaft sprockets of the 850 engine. The chain tensioners should always be turned outward as shown

should be pointing toward the camshaft side of the engine at the top of the camshaft sprocket.

8. Install the lockplate on the camshaft and screw on the camshaft sprocket retaining nut. Prevent the crankshaft from turning and tighten the nut to 36 ft lbs, then bend the lockplate to lock the nut in place.

9. Install the timing gear cover.

124 OHV

1. Remove the timing gear cover.

2. Bend the tab washer to release the camshaft sprocket retaining bolt. Remove the bolt, tab washer and flat washer.

3. Remove the camshaft sprocket together with the timing chain.

4. If necessary, remove the crankshaft sprocket with a gear puller.

5. Install the crankshaft sprocket onto the crankshaft together with the positioning key.

6. Position the camshaft drive sprocket on the camshaft together with the timing chain placed around the crankshaft sprocket. Make sure that the timing marks on both sprockets are aligned with each other.

Timing marks aligned on 124 camshaft drive sprockets.

7. Attach the camshaft driven sprocket to the camshaft with the flat washer, tab washer and the bolt. Tighten the bolt to 35 ft lbs. Turn up the tab against the head of the bolt to lock it in position.

124 DOHC Engines

1. Drain the cooling system.

2. Remove the upper radiator hose and the top section of the air duct.

3. Remove the timing belt cover after placing the timing mark on the crankshaft pulley at TDC.

4. Remove the lower protection plate from the engine.

5. Loosen the alternator mounting bolts and remove the drive belt.

6. Slacken the timing belt idler pulley and remove the timing belt.

7. Install the new belt over the camshaft gears and the idler pulley.

8. Position the spring balance to the hole in the upper right arm of the idler pulley.

9. Adjust the belt tension by applying a load of 60 lbs in the direction of a line bisecting the angle between the two runs of the belt where it passes around the idler pulley. Tighten the idler pulley attaching nuts.

10. Check the valve timing and reassemble the timing gear cover, radiator air duct, and refill the cooling system to the proper level.

128 SOHC Engines

1. Remove the timing gear cover. The lower retaining screw of the cover must be removed from under the car after removing the right side guard.

2. Check the valve timing by aligning the timing mark on the camshaft sprocket with the fixed mark on the engine and making sure that the timing mark on the crankshaft sprocket is simultaneously aligned with its fixed index mark.

3. Remove the water pump and generator drive belt.

4. Loosen the tensioner pulley retaining nut and relieve the spring action to remove the timing belt.

5. Install the new belt, making sure the belt and sprocket teeth engage perfectly.

6. Tighten the tensioner pulley nut to 33 ft lbs.

X1/9

1. Turn the crankshaft until no. 4 piston is at TDC of the compression stroke. The timing mark on the front (right) crankshaft pulley should be at TDC and the camshaft timing pulley mark should be aligned with the cast finger of the support, visible through the hole in the camshaft cover.

NOTE: *Throughout this entire procedure remember that if the camshaft is turned independently of the crankshaft the valves may hit the pistons causing damage.*

2. Remove the bolts attaching the timing cover, remove the right guard from under the engine, remove the lower bolt retaining the timing cover and remove the cover.

3. Loosen the alternator and remove the alternator and water pump drive belt.

4. Remove the drive pulley from the crankshaft.

5. Loosen the air pump and remove the drive belt.

6. Remove the camshaft cover. Check and make sure the cam lobes of no. 4 cylinder are pointing up.

7. Remove the distributor.

8. Loosen the idler pulley locknut, push it on the support and tighten the

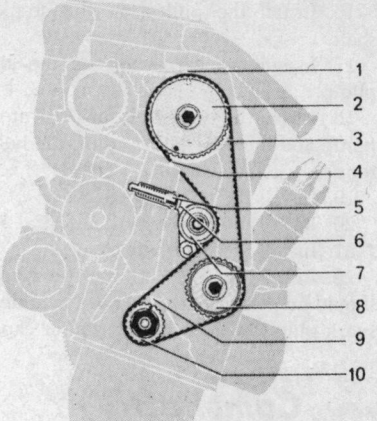

128, X1/9 engine valve gear drive

1. Camshaft timing reference mark (engine on car)
2. Camshaft drive pulley
3. Toothed timing belt, driving the camshaft and pulley 8
4. Camshaft timing reference mark (engine on bench)
5. Idler pulley tensioner
6. Idler pulley support
7. Idler pulley
8. Drive pulley for oil pump and ignition distributor
9. Reference mark for pulley 10 setting
10. Crankshaft sprocket

locknut. Remove the timing belt, starting at the idler pulley.

9. Install the new timing belt, starting at the crankshaft. Twist the belt gently into position around the crankshaft pulley. Do not kink the belt.

10. Slip the belt over the camshaft pulley. The camshaft pulley may have to be turned *slightly* to align the slots with the belt cogs.

11. Install the belt over the idler pulley last.

12. Loosen the idler pulley locknut and retighten after tension is on the belt. Turn the crankshaft of the engine one half of a turn in the direction of normal rotation by either pushing the car with it in fourth gear or bumping the starter.

13. Release the idler pulley locknut to make sure all slack is removed from the belt and then retighten the locknut.

14. Continue to turn the crankshaft of the engine in the direction of normal rotation by either method mentioned in step 12 until no. 4 piston reaches TDC of the compression stroke (one and one-half turns).

NOTE: *Never push the car backward in gear or allow the engine to rock backward while pushing the car. Slack will develop in the belt, allowing the belt to jump timing.*

15. Position the belt cover on the engine and check to make sure the crankshaft timing mark is at TDC and that the camshaft mark is aligned with the pointer. Tighten the tensioner pulley nut to 32 ft lbs.

16. Install the pulley on the crankshaft.

17. Install the drive belt on the air pump.

18. Install the drive belt for the water pump and the alternator. Adjust the belt tension.

19. Install the timing gear cover.

20. Install the lower right guard.

21. Install the camshaft cover.

22. Install the distributor. The rotor should be pointing toward no. 4 cylinder spark plug tower of the distributor cap.

Camshaft(s)

Removal and Installation

128 and X1/9 SOHC Engine

1. Remove the camshaft drive belt.

2. Remove the camshaft carrier attaching bolts and remove the camshaft carrier assembly from the engine.

3. Remove the camshaft drive sprocket.

4. Remove the camshaft thrust plate from the opposite end (opposite the belt end) of the camshaft carrier.

5. Carefully slide the camshaft out of the camshaft carrier.

6. Install the camshaft in the reverse order of removal, making sure the valve timing marks on the camshaft sprocket and the crankshaft sprocket are properly aligned before installing the timing belt. See timing belt removal and installation procedure.

124, 131 DOHC Engine

The camshafts on the 124 DOHC engines are removed in the same manner as

Removing the camshaft retainer attaching bolts on the 124 OHV engine

the camshaft in a 128 SOHC engine; the procedure for which is given above.

124 OHV Engine

NOTE: *If the camshaft is to be removed from the engine while the engine is still in the car, it will be necessary to gain sufficient clearance in front of the engine by removing any obstructing components such as the radiator or body parts.*

1. Remove the distributor and fuel pump.

2. Remove the cylinder head and valve lifters.

3. Remove the timing chain cover.

4. Remove the camshaft timing sprocket together with the timing chain.

5. Remove the two bolts and washers attaching the camshaft retainer plate and remove the plate.

6. Carefully slide the camshaft out of the cylinder block. Be careful not to damage any of the camshaft bearings with the camshaft lobes.

7. Install the camshaft in the reverse order of removal. Coat the camshaft with clean engine oil before inserting into the cylinder block. Make sure the timing marks on the crankshaft and camshaft sprocket are aligned when the timing chain and sprockets are installed.

8. Reassemble the remaining components in the reverse order of disassembly. Install the distributor so that the rotor is pointing toward the no. 1 spark plug tower when the piston in no. 1 cylinder is at TDC of the compression stroke.

850 OHV Engine

1. Remove the engine from the vehicle.

2. Remove the rocker cover and remove the rocker shaft assembly and the pushrods.

3. Remove the timing chain cover, camshaft timing chain sprocket and timing chain.

4. Remove the flywheel.

5. Turn the engine upside down and tap on the cylinder block in order to make sure that the valve tappets move away from the camshaft lobes.

6. Remove the camshaft retaining plate from the rear of the engine block.

7. Carefully slide the camshaft out of the cylinder block, avoiding damage to the camshaft bearings caused by the lobes.

8. Install the camshaft in the reverse order of removal. Coat the camshaft with clean engine oil before sliding it into the cylinder block. Make sure the valve timing marks on the crankshaft and camshaft

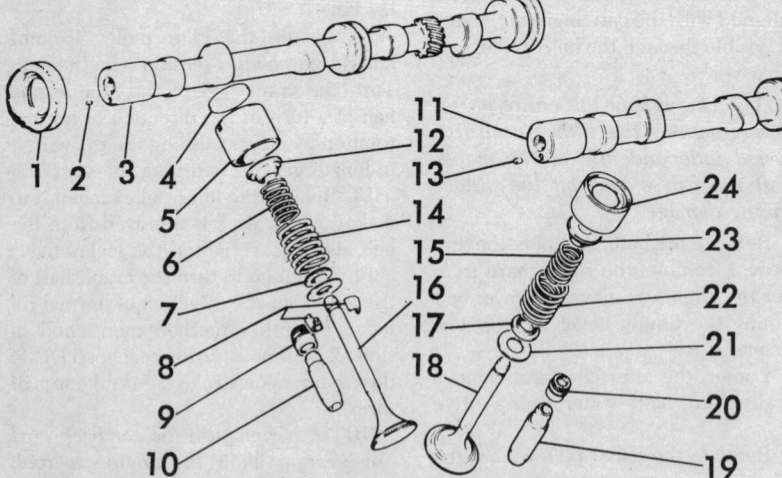

124, 131 Twin cam valve mechanism

1. Camshaft seal	9. Exhaust valve oil seal
2. Exhaust camshaft dowel	10. Exhaust valve guide
3. Exhaust camshaft	11. Intake camshaft
4. Tappet plate	12. Upper cup
5. Exhaust valve tappet	13. Dowel
6. Exhaust valve inner spring	14. Exhaust valve outer spring
7. Lower cup	15. Intake valve inner spring
8. Locks	16. Exhaust valve
17. Lower cup	
18. Intake valve	
19. Intake valve guide	
20. Oil seal	
21. Washer	
22. Intake valve outer spring	
23. Upper cup	
24. Intake valve tappet	

are aligned when the timing chain is installed. Install the distributor with the rotor pointing toward no. 1 tower of the distributor cap when the piston in no. 1 cylinder is at TDC of the compression stroke.

Piston and Connecting Rod Identification and Positioning

If the connecting rod and piston assemblies are going to be reinstalled in the engine, they should be clearly identified during disassembly so they can be reinstalled in their original positions.

850 OHV Engines

Standard size pistons have three different size wrist pin bores; classes 1, 2, and 3. The numbers 1, 2, or 3 are stamped on the bottom of the piston. Wrist pins must be matched to the pistons in accordance with these numbers.

There are three classes of pistons denoting size. They are classes A, C, and E; A being the standard size and E being the largest oversize piston. The piston class letter is also stamped on the bottom of the piston.

The connecting rods and the bearing caps are matched by numbers stamped on the sides of the bearing bosses. The number designates which cylinder the connecting rod assembly is to be installed. The numbers range from 1 to 4, of course.

The piston and connecting rod assembly is installed in the engine with the connecting rod and bearing cap identifications numbers matched on the same side and facing away from the cam-

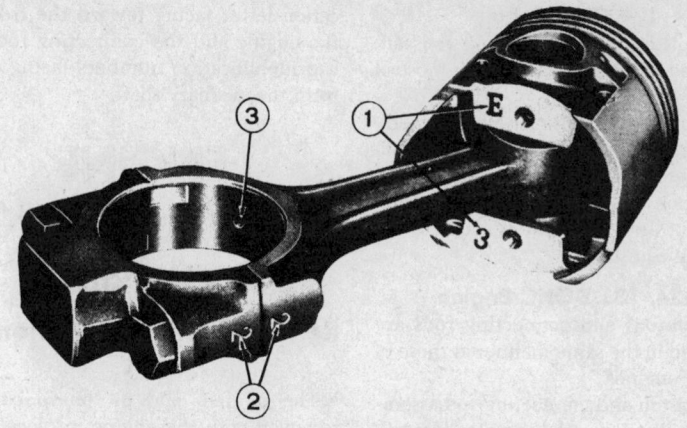

Piston and connecting rod identification for the 850

1. Piston size letter and wrist pin size number
2. Connecting rod and bearing cap cylinder number
3. Oil hole

shaft (oil hole in connecting rod toward the camshaft). The piston is installed on the connecting rod so that piston identification *letter* is facing toward the timing chain end of the engine.

128 and X1/9 SOHC Engine

Piston and piston wrist pin, and connecting rod and connecting rod cap identification is the same as for the 850 OHV engine.

The piston and connecting rod assembly is installed in the cylinder block with piston identification *letter* toward the timing belt end of the engine and the connecting rod and cap identification numbers facing away from the auxiliary shaft.

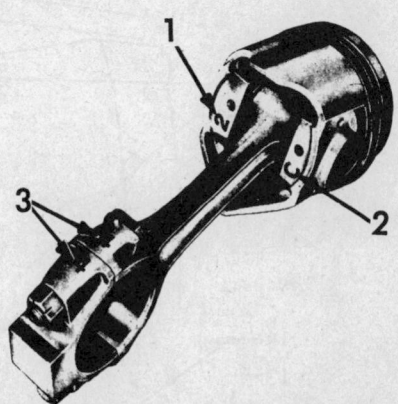

128, X1/9 piston and rod assemblies are marked for (1) size of bore, (2) wrist pin size, and (3) cylinder number. Metal may be removed from areas (1) and (2) to equalize rod weights

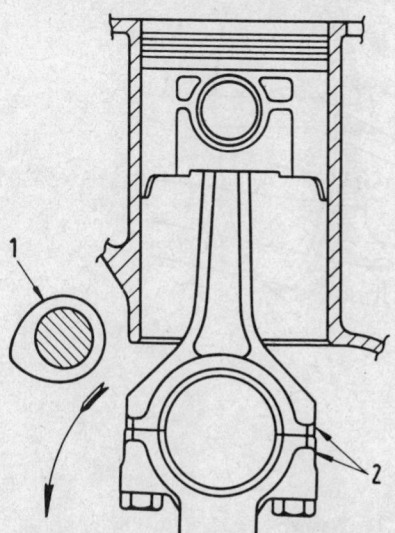

Piston and connecting rod installation for the 850

1. Camshaft
2. Location of the connecting rod and bearing cap identification and cylinder number

NOTE: Arrow shows the direction of crankshaft rotation

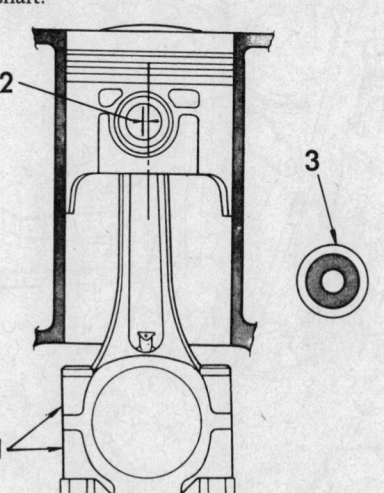

Piston and connecting rod installation for 128, X1/9, 124 Twin cam, and 131

1. Location of the connecting rod and bearing cap identification and cylinder number
2. Piston pin offset 0.08 in.
3. Auxiliary shaft

NOTE: Arrow shows direction of crankshaft rotation

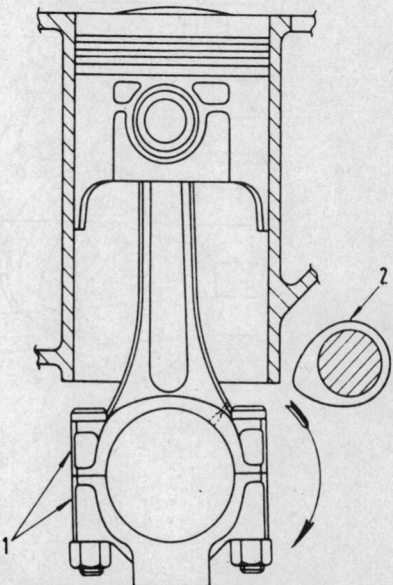

Piston and connecting rod installation for 1972-73 124 OHV. Cylinder number (1) faces away from camshaft (2). Arrow shows crankshaft rotation from front

124 OHV Engine

The pistons and connecting rods are identified in the same manner as those of the 850 engines.

The piston and connecting rod assemblies are installed with the piston identification letter facing toward the front of the engine and the connecting rod and cap identification numbers facing away from the camshaft.

124, 131 DOHC Engine

The pistons and connecting rods are identified in the same manner as those of the 850 engines.

The piston and connecting rod assemblies are installed with the piston identifi- cation letter facing toward the front of the engine and the connecting rod and cap identification numbers facing away from the auxiliary shaft.

ENGINE LUBRICATION
Oil Pan
Removal and Installation
850

The oil pan and oil pump can be removed with the engine in place. Jack up the rear of the car and support it on stands.

124, 131

Oil pan and oil pump removal is not possible with the engine in the car unless the mounts are unbolted and the engine is hoisted high enough to allow the pan to be removed (about 6–8 inches).

128 and X1/9

The oil pan may be removed from the bottom if the engine is supported with a hoist or other lifting device which will allow the engine mounting crossmember and splash shields to be removed.

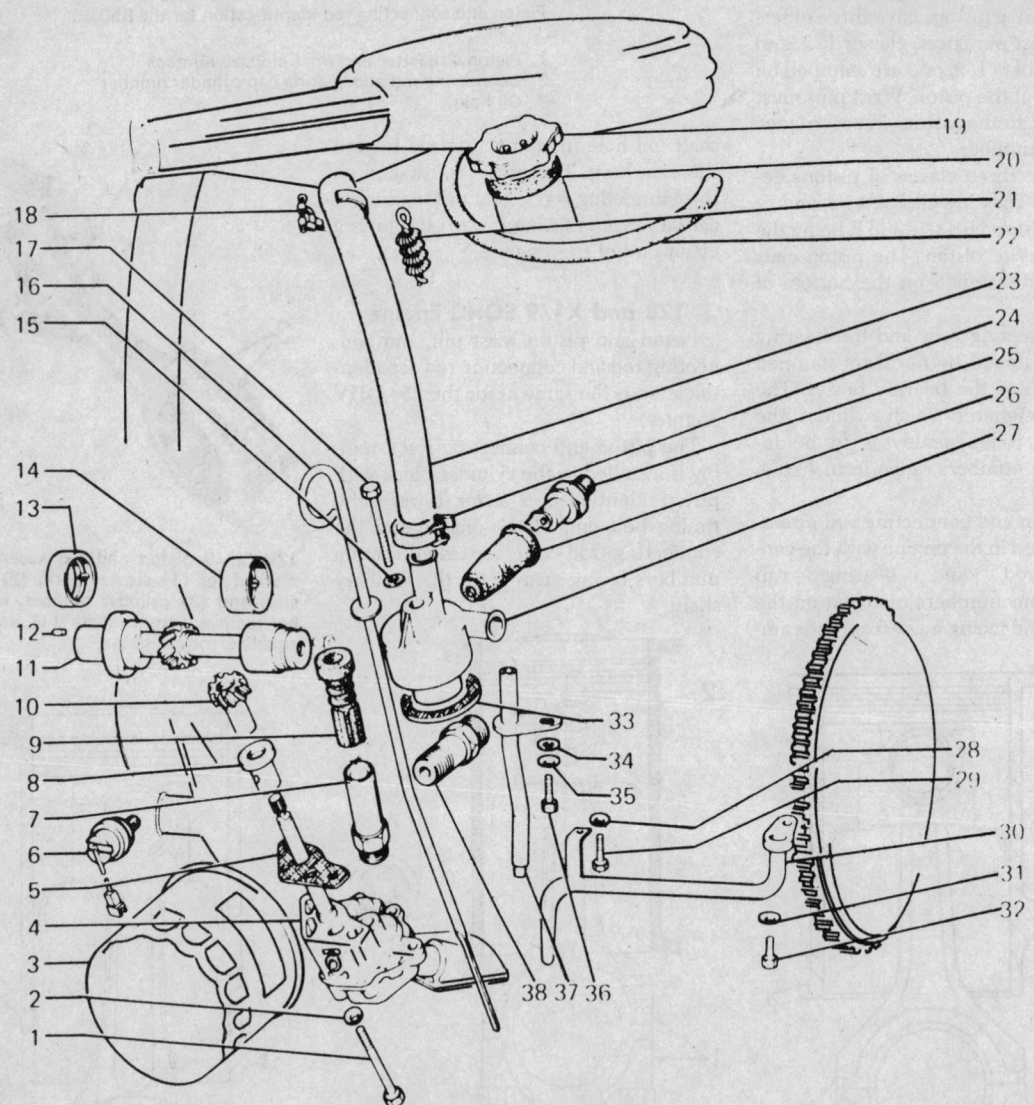

128, X1/9 engine lubrication components

1. Bolt	11. Shaft	21. Flame trap	31. Washer
2. Washer	12. Pin	22. Hose	32. Bolt
3. Filter	13. Bushing	23. Hose	33. Gasket
4. Oil pump	14. Bushing	24. Clamp	34. Washer
5. Gasket	15. Washer	25. Switch	35. Lockwasher
6. Sending unit	16. Dip stick	26. Boot	36. Bolt
7. Pipe	17. Bolt	27. Boot	37. Pipe
8. Bushing	18. Clamp	28. Washer	38. Connector
9. Seal	19. Oil cap	29. Bolt	
10. Gear	20. Gasket	30. Pipe	

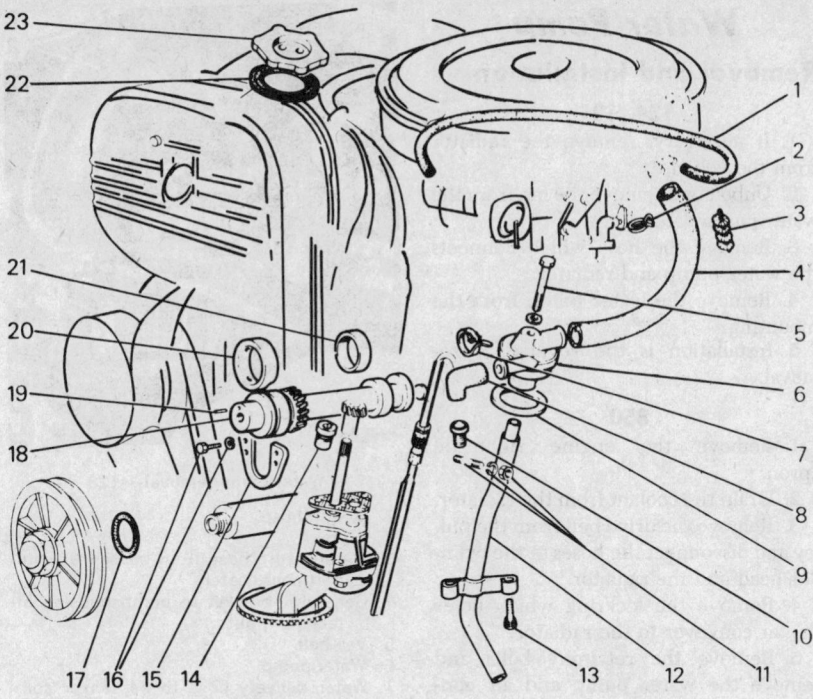

124, 131 Twin cam engine lubrication components

1. Blow-by gas and oil vapor hose
2. Collar
3. Flam trap
4. Breather hose
5. Bolt and washer
6. Breather
7. Collar
8. Hose
9. Seal
10. Vapor return connection
11. Stud, lockwasher, and nut
12. Breather tube
13. Bolt
14. Gear bushing
15. Retaining plate
16. Bolt and lockwasher
17. Spring washer
18. Auxiliary shaft
19. Dowel
20. Front bushing
21. Rear bushing
22. Seal
23. Oil filler cap

Oil Pump

Removal and Installation

1. Remove the oil pan.
2. Remove the oil pump assembly attaching bolts and remove the oil pump.
3. Install the oil pump in the reverse order of removal.

Checking Clearances

1. Remove the oil pump from the engine.
2. Remove the pump cover to expose the oil pump gears.
3. Measure the clearance between the gear teeth and the pump housing with a feeler gauge.
4. Place a straight edge across the pump housing and measure the clearance between the straight edge and the ends of the gears with a feeler gauge.
5. Place the blade of the feeler gauge between the teeth of the two gears and measure the gear backlash.

6. Replace any worn parts and reassemble the oil pump in the reverse order of disassembly.

Rear Main Seal

Rear seal replacement is performed with the crankshaft removed. See the Engine Rebuilding Section.

ENGINE COOLING

Radiator

Removal and Installation

124, 131

1. Open the petcock at the bottom of the radiator and drain the coolant from the radiator and cylinder block.
2. Remove the hose which connects the radiator and thermostat cover.
3. Remove the hose which connects the radiator and water pump.
4. Remove the pipe which connects the radiator to the auxiliary tank.
5. Unbolt and remove the radiator.
6. Installation is the reverse of removal.

850

1. Remove the engine right-side apron and drain the coolant from the radiator.
2. Disconnect the coolant intake and outlet hoses from the radiator.
3. Disconnect the lockring which secures the air conveyor to the radiator.
4. Disconnect the engine ground cable and the pipe from the radiator to the expansion tank.
5. Remove the radiator mounting screws and lift out the radiator.
6. Installation is the reverse of removal.

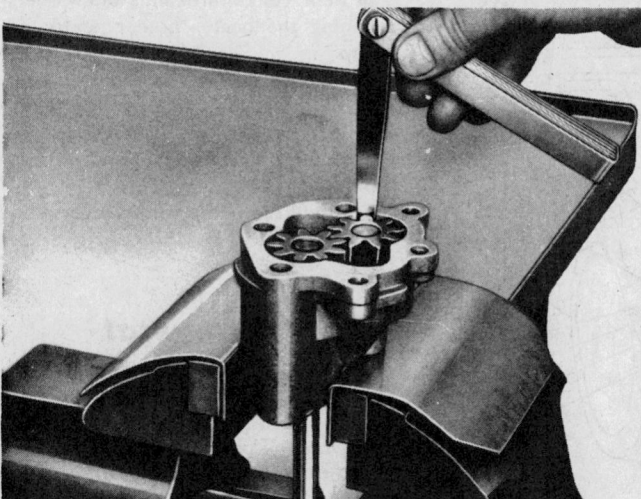

Measuring the clearance between the gear and housing of an oil pump

Measuring clearance between ends of the gears and a straight edge

Fiat

128

1. Drain the radiator and the cylinder block.
2. Disconnect the thermal fan switch and the fan relay switch.
3. Disconnect the hose running from the radiator to the expansion tank.
4. Remove the hoses running from the thermostat union to the radiator.
5. Remove the screws that attach the top part of the radiator to the brackets fitted on the body, together with the rubber pads, washers, and spacers.
6. Slide the radiator, fan, and shroud out of the top of the engine compartment.
7. Installation is the reverse of removal.

X1/9

1. Drain the cooling system.
2. Remove the three lower screws securing the grille to the crossrail.
3. Remove the four nuts retaining the guard plate to the body and remove the plate.
4. Disconnect the hoses at the radiator.
5. Disconnect the electrical connector for the fan motor and the wires from the thermostatic switch.
6. Remove the bolt and nut holding the bottom crossrail at each side and remove the crossrail.
7. Lower the radiator out from under the car, being careful of the fan.
8. Install the radiator in the reverse order of removal.

1. Fan motor	9. Gasket	16. Washer
2. Fan	10. Conveyor	17. Nut
3. Washer	11. Washer	18. Relay
4. Nut	12. Lockwasher	19. Thermostatic switch
5. Plate	13. Nut	20. Gasket
6. Washer	14. Nut	21. Lockring
7. Lockwasher	15. Lockwasher	22. Spacer
8. Nut		

X1/9 Electric cooling fan installation

Water Pump

Removal and Installation

124, 131

1. If necessary, remove the radiator from the vehicle.
2. Unbolt and remove the fan from the water pump flange.
3. Remove the hose which connects the water pump and radiator.
4. Remove the water pump from the mounting.
5. Installation is the reverse of removal.

850

1. Remove the engine right-side apron.
2. Drain the coolant from the radiator.
3. Remove the drive belt from the pulley and disconnect the hoses at the cylinder head and the radiator.
4. Remove the lockring which holds the air conveyor to the radiator.
5. Remove the retaining bolts and remove the water pump and air conveyor assembly.

128

1. Remove the spare wheel.
2. Place protective coverings on the fenders.
3. Drain the water from the cooling system.
4. Disconnect the hot air hose and the accelerator rod from the shroud.
5. Remove the shroud.
6. Disconnect the passenger compart-

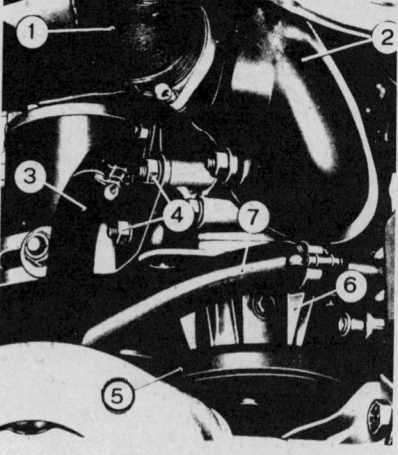

Water pump removal—128

1. Hot air hose
2. Shroud
3. Water return hose from passenger compartment heater
4. Generator bracket to pump housing attachment nuts
5. Vee belt
6. Water pump
7. Water delivery hose to passenger compartment heater

ment heater water delivery and return hoses.
7. Slacken the nuts that hold the generator on the two lower brackets and remove the top bracket.
8. Unscrew the nuts which attach the pump to the crankcase and slide off the pump assembly.
9. Installation is the reverse of removal.

X1/9

1. Drain the cooling system.
2. Remove the protection panels from the bottom right side of the engine.
3. Remove the alternator and drive belt.
4. Disconnect the hoses from the water pump.
5. Remove the three nuts and washers retaining the heater hose pipe to the pump.
6. Remove the bolt holding the support for the air pump to the water pump.
7. Remove the four bolts holding the water pump to the engine and remove the pump.
8. Install the pump in the reverse order of removal.

Thermostat

Removal and Installation

124, 131

1. Drain off part of the coolant in the radiator (to a level below the inline bypass thermostat).
2. Disconnect the 3 hoses to the inline

FAN RELAY 39

THERMAL SWITCH 104

TO FUSE L 10   30/51 86 85 87

TO BATTERY   M FAN 37/1

Water pump on the X1/9 engine

1. Support bracket
2. Water pump
3. Alternator
4. Water pipe attaching screw
5. Water pipe
6. Water pump attaching screws

thermostat and withdraw the thermostat.

Immerse the thermostat in the water and heat the water. When the temperature reaches 185–192° F, the thermostat valve should begin to open. The valve should be completely open when the water temperature reaches 212° F. If the thermostat does not meet specifications, it is defective and must be replaced.

3. Installation is the reverse of removal.

850

1. Drain the coolant below the level of the thermostat.
2. Remove the retaining bolts from the thermostat housing.
3. Without removing the hose, carefully lift the housing off the cylinder head.
4. Remove the thermostat.
5. Clean the mating surfaces and install the replacement thermostat using a new gasket.
6. Replace the housing over the thermostat and tighten the bolts. Refill the cooling system.

128 and X1/9

1. Drain the water from the cooling system.
2. Remove the spare wheel from the engine compartment on the 128.
3. Disconnect the hoses from the thermostat union.
4. Unscrew the attachment screws and remove the union, complete with the thermostat.
5. Unscrew the union cover and slide out the thermostat and its seal.
6. Installation is the reverse of removal.

EMISSION CONTROLS

Application

Crankcase Ventilation System—All 1972–77 models

Evaporative Control System—All 1972–77 models

Engine Modification System—All 1972–77 models

Deceleration Throttle Positioner System–1972–73 850, 128; 1972–77 124, 131

Air Injection System—All 1974–77 models

Exhaust Gas Recirculation System —1974–77 124, 131

Catalytic Converter System—1975–77 California models; All 1975–77 X1/9 models (50 states)

Crankcase Ventilation System

This is a closed system in which all crankcase vapors are drawn into the engine's combustion chambers to be consumed, rather than being vented to the atmosphere.

During idle and part-throttle engine operation, intake vacuum draws the vapors from the crankcase and a connecting hose (with a flame trap) conveys them to the air cleaner and into the carburetor.

During full-throttle engine operation, the crankcase vapors are conveyed directly to the intake manifold downstream of the carburetor by an additional smaller diameter hose; this part of the circuit is

controlled by a valve which is activated by the throttle mechanism of the carburetor.

Maintenance

Every 12,000 miles, this blowby gas and oil vapor recirculation system, including the carburetor, vent valve and flame trap must be cleaned and flushed with solvent.

Evaporative Emission Control

This system is designed to prevent the escape of raw fuel vapors into the atmosphere—that is, in effect, a "sealed" fuel system.

The fuel tank is of the "limited filling" type—that is, it maintains a volume of air space which is normally slightly pressurized. The tank and filler cap are non-vented. Fuel vapors originating in the fuel tank are conveyed to the separator; this component passes vapors but is designed to return liquid fuel to the tank. The vapors are then conveyed to a three-way valve. With the fuel tank slightly pressurized, fuel vapors are passed through this valve to the active carbon trap and become absorbed there.

As the engine is operated, intake manifold vacuum is applied to the trap. This draws warm air from a collector, normally near the exhaust manifold, into the trap and up through the carbon trap; the warm air regenerates the carbon, purifying it and releasing the fuel vapors to be drawn into the intake manifold.

Maintenance

It is recommended that the components of this system be visually inspected periodically in order to determine that all units and hoses are intact and hose connections are secure. On 1974 and later models, replace the charcoal canister every 25,000 miles.

Engine Modification System

This system is a catch-all for all the emission control features and components that do not fall under any of the other headings. Basically, it consists of a leaner, more carefully controlled carburetor; a recalibrated distributor that brings in the ignition advance at a higher rpm; a revised camshaft and valve timing; and a lower compression ratio.

To help the engine burn the leaner air/fuel mixture, a climatic setting is provided on the air cleaner (all models except X1/9). In cold weather, the air cleaner can be adjusted to draw in only exhaust manifold heated intake air, providing for better fuel atomization and overall better driveability when cold. In warm climates, the air cleaner can be adjusted to draw in only cool (ambient) intake air.

On 1975 and later models, an idle stop solenoid is used on the carburetor linkage to prevent dieseling or "running on" after the key is shut off. The solenoid cuts off the fuel supply to the engine, closing the throttle plate completely.

Maintenance

The only maintenance item is the air cleaner climatic setting. In temperate zones, the setting is adjusted in spring and autumn. Adjust the air intake as per the following illustrations:

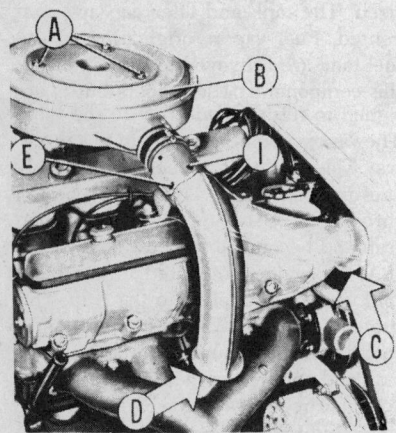

Air cleaner climatic adjustment—1972-73 124 Sport Coupe and Spider

Warm climate—Align snorkel rib with reference "I" ("C" position)
Cold climate—Align snorkel rib with reference "E" ("D" position)

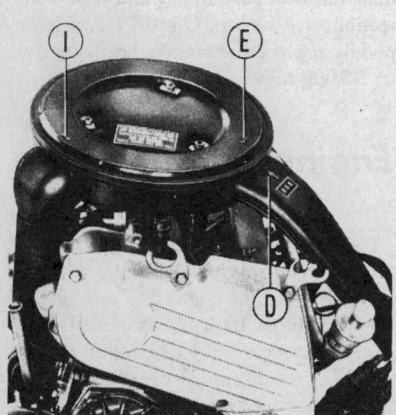

Air cleaner climatic adjustment—1974-77 128, 1972-74 124 Sedan and Wagon, 1974-77 124 Sport and 131

Warm climate—Align arrow "D" with reference "E"
Cold climate—Align arrow "D" with reference "I"

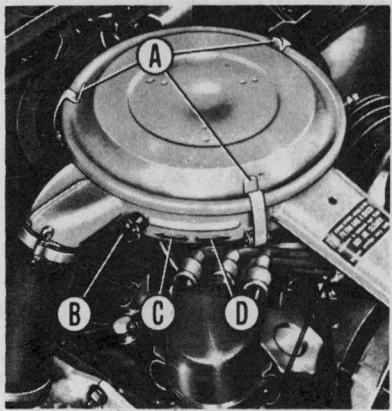

Air cleaner climatic adjustment—1972-73 850, 128

Warm climate—Push and turn knob "B" in direction of arrow "C"
Cold climate—Push and turn knob "B" in direction of arrow "D"

Deceleration Throttle Positioner System

This system, also known as the Fast Idling System, reduces emissions by holding the throttle slightly open when decelerating in third or fourth gears (manual transmission), and when decelerating in second or third gears (automatic

transmission). If uncontrolled, deceleration from speed causes a high vacuum condition when the throttle plate closes with the engine in the middle to upper rpm range. This high vacuum draws in raw fuel which causes an overrich condition. With the throttle positioner holding the throttle open to the fast idle position, extra air is admitted with the fuel, leaning out the mixture and reducing emissions.

The carburetor is provided with a vacuum-sensitive diaphragm which is linked to the primary throttle plate shaft. Vacuum to operate this diaphragm is derived from the intake manifold through an electropneumatic valve. This valve is mounted on the vehicle firewall or side wall of the engine compartment, depending on car model, and is operated by applying an electrical ground to complete the activating circuit.

Switch "A" is fitted to the transmission, and is closed (activating the circuit) when 3rd or 4th gears are engaged.

Switch "B" is fitted at the clutch pedal and is connected in *series* with switch "A". It is closed when the pedal is released and opens as the pedal is depressed. Thus, with 3rd or 4th gear engaged and the clutch pedal released, both switches are closed and the electrovalve is energized. Under such conditions,

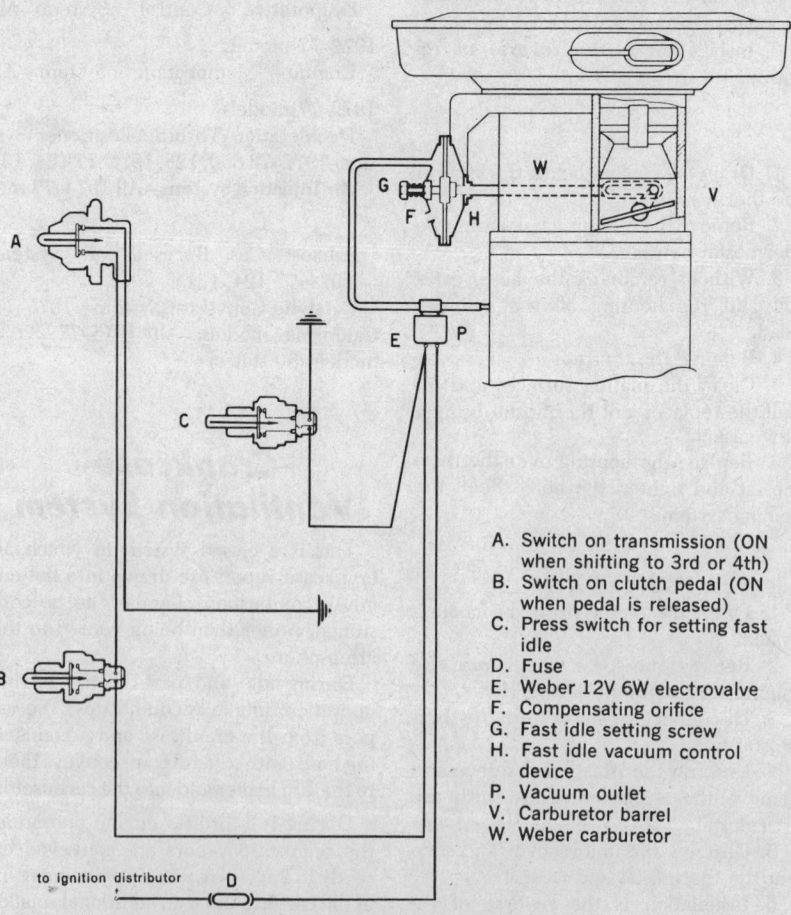

A. Switch on transmission (ON when shifting to 3rd or 4th)
B. Switch on clutch pedal (ON when pedal is released)
C. Press switch for setting fast idle
D. Fuse
E. Weber 12V 6W electrovalve
F. Compensating orifice
G. Fast idle setting screw
H. Fast idle vacuum control device
P. Vacuum outlet
V. Carburetor barrel
W. Weber carburetor

Deceleration throttle positioner system—1972-73

manifold vacuum is applied to the diaphragm keeping the throttle plate from returning completely to the closed or idle position. If the transmission is in a position other than 3rd or 4th gears (opening switch "A") or the clutch pedal is depressed regardless of conditions existing in the transmission (opening switch "B"), the activating circuit is broken and the device is rendered inoperative.

In order to be able to check and/or adjust the fast idle setting, pushbutton switch "C" is provided to manually ground, or activate, the electrovalve. This switch is mounted on the firewall or side of the engine compartment, depending on the car model. Fast idle speed is then adjusted with the screw "G" on the vacuum diaphragm unit on the carburetor.

NOTE: *This circuitry is fused through the windshield wiper system; therefore, if that circuit is inoperative, the device will not function.*

Maintenance

The only adjustment on the system is the fast idle speed, which can be checked after setting normal idle speed and mixture. With the engine warm and idling in neutral, depress and hold down the fast idle electrovalve button (located inside the engine compartment on the firewall, radiator support or fender apron) while accelerating the engine to approximately 2500 rpm. This will activate the system and simulate a deceleration condition. While still depressing the button, allow the engine speed to decrease to the fast idle speed; 1600 rpm on a manual transmission car and 1300 rpm with an automatic. Adjust as necessary with the fast idling adjusting screw on the fast idle diaphragm and recheck. Finally, release the pushbutton switch and check that the engine speed returns to normal idle speed, within 1–3 seconds.

1974-77 Fast idle electrovalve button—1975-77 124 Spider location shown

Air Injection System

All 1974 and later Fiats are equipped with this system (also known as a thermal reactor system) to control emissions. A belt-driven air pump delivers filtered air to the exhaust ports. Here, the additional oxygen supplied by the vane type pump reacts with the uncombusted fuel mixture, promoting an afterburning effect in the hot exhaust manifold. To prevent a damaging reverse flow in the air injection manifold when exhaust gas pressure exceeds air supply pressure, a non-return check valve is used. Also, to prevent backfiring in the exhaust system during deceleration, a diverter valve is used to divert pump air to the atmosphere under these conditions. On 1975 and later models, the diverter valve also serves to cut-out the air pump air during cold temperature starts.

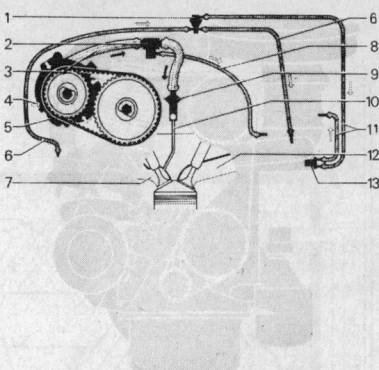

1974 124 Air injection and EGR systems schematic

1. Exhaust gas recirculation (EGR) control valve
2. Diverter valve
3. Air distributor line
4. Air intake
5. Air pump
6. Exhaust gas recirculation line
7. Exhaust manifold
8. Vacuum tapping line, intake manifold, for diverter valve
9. Air injection non-return valve
10. Air injector
11. Vacuum tapping line, carburetor, for EGR valve
12. Intake manifold
13. EGR valve control thermovalve

Maintenance

On 128 and X1/9 models with the Bosch or Nippondenso air pump, replace the air pump filter cartridge at 12,000 mile intervals; sooner if the car is driven in dusty areas. On 124 and 131 models with the Saginaw air pump, the filter is integral with the pump and does not require servicing.

1. Dashpot
2. Air pump intake line with filter
3. Pump air discharge safety valve
4. Air pump
5. Electrovalve 8 thermo switch
6. Intake manifold
7. Exhaust manifold
8. Electrovalve (normally closed) for diverter valve
9. Diverter valve
10. Vacuum tapping line, intake manifold, for diverter valve
11. Air distribution line
12. Air injection non-return valve
13. Vacuum tapping line, carburetor, for diaphragm 17
14. Air injector
15. Vacuum control thermovalve
16. Delay valve
17. Distributor advance diaphragm control unit
18. Catalytic converter thermocouple
19. Catalytic converter
20. Exhaust pipe

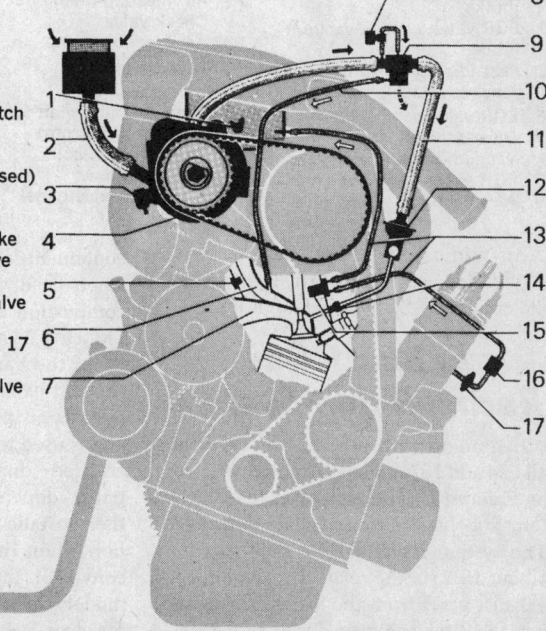

1975-77 128, X1/9 emission control systems schematic

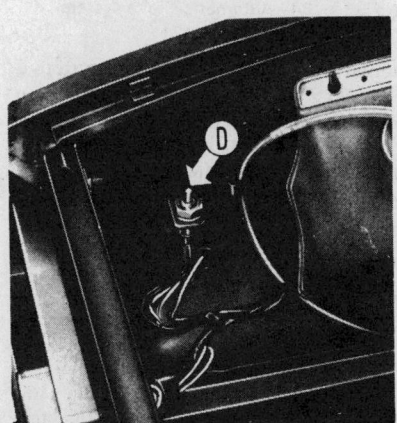

1972-73 Fast idle electrovalve button "D"—850 Spider location shown

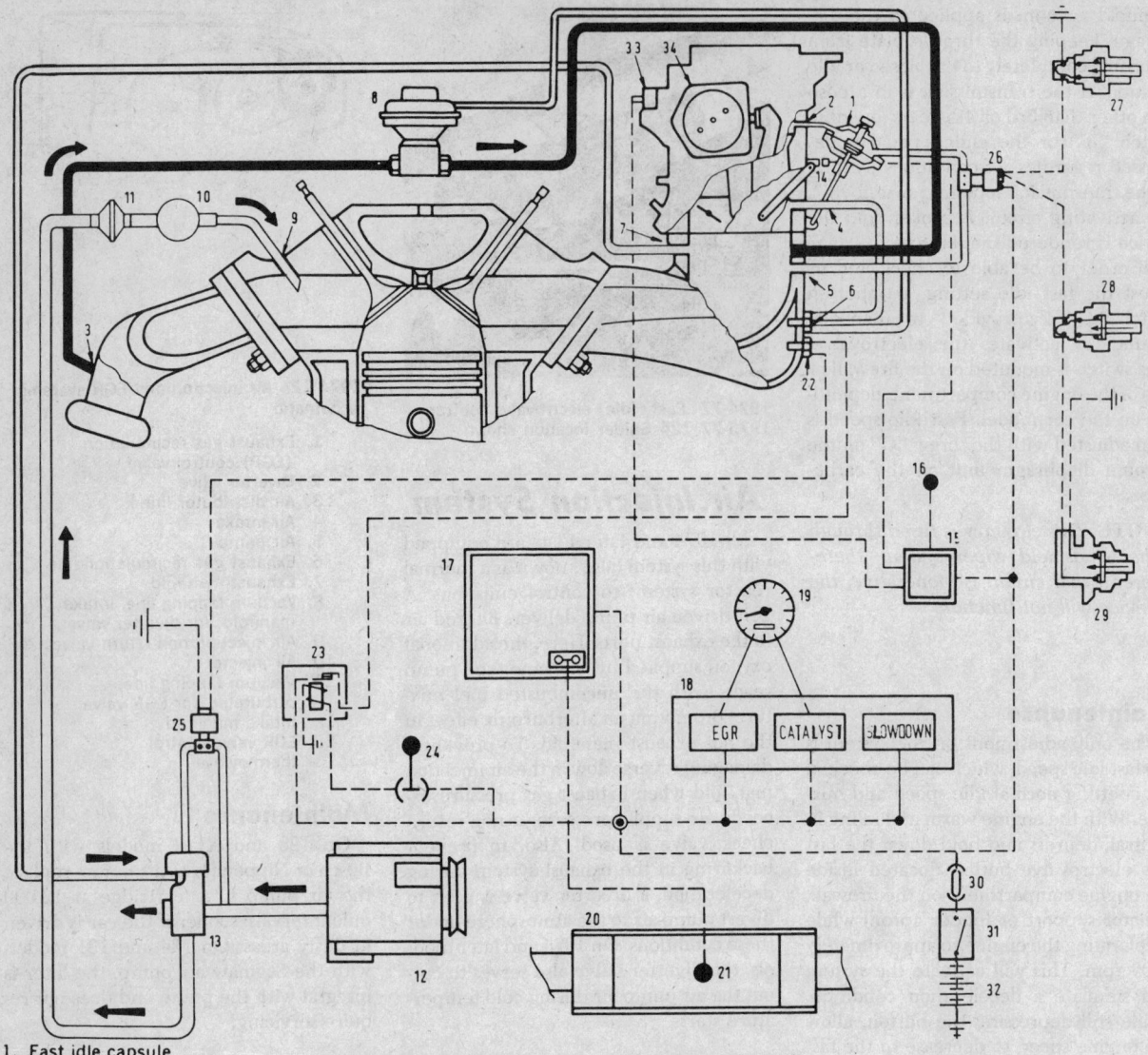

1975-76 124 131 emission control systems schematic

1. Fast idle capsule
2. Continuity hole
3. Exhaust gas recirculation intake
4. EGR valve control vacuum intake
5. Fast idle valve control vacuum intake
6. EGR valve control thermovalve
7. Diverter valve control vacuum intake
8. EGR valve
9. Air injector

10. Air injection manifold
11. Check valve
12. Air injection pump
13. Diverter valve
14. Inhibitor switch
15. Tachymetric switch (operates at 2650 ± 50 rpm)
16. From ignition coil
17. Control unit
18. Warning device panel

19. Odometer
20. Catalytic converter
21. Thermocouple
22. Thermoswitch
23. Magnetic reversing switch
24. Gearshift lever (switch open with transmission in neutral)
25. Electrovalve (normally closed)
26. Electrovalve
27. Fast idle control switch

28. Switch closed when clutch is engaged
29. Switch contacts closed by transmission on 3rd-4th gear
30. Fuse
31. Ignition contact matched switch
32. Battery
33. Idle stop solenoid
34. Automatic choke system

Air pump belt tension cannot be adjusted. Replace belt if worn. Average belt life should be 25,000–35,000 miles.

Exhaust Gas Recirculation System

Beginning with the 1974 model year, all 124 and 131 models are equipped with an Exhaust Gas Recirculation (EGR) System to control nitrogen oxide emissions. The system recirculates a small portion (about 10%) of the relatively oxygen-free exhaust gases from the exhaust manifold into the intake mixture during part-throttle conditions. Since the exhaust gases

contain little oxygen, they cannot burn when fired, thereby lowering the peak combustion chamber temperatures and reducing NOx. To ensure good driveability of the car, an EGR valve is used to prevent exhaust gas recirculation during periods of idling or wide open throttle, and is used to meter the degree of recirculation during part-throttle applications, depending on engine load. A thermostatic switch cuts out recirculation when the engine is cold. (catalytic converter models only). Also, on 1977 models, recirculation is prevented when 5th gear is engaged.

On 1975–76 models only, an odometer

actuated EGR service reminder system is used. At 25,000 mile intervals, the system will light an "EGR" service warning lamp on the dash. Beginning with the 1977 model year, the EGR system has been "re-certified" for 50,000 miles eliminating the need for the 25,000 mile service reminder system.

Maintenance

On 1974–76 models, check the vacuum lines for leaks or cracks every 25,000 miles. Also check the EGR valve and exhaust gas line for deposits, particularly if a steady diet of leaded fuel is used. Clean with a bristle bore brush, or replace as necessary. 1977 models have no regularly scheduled EGR maintenance specified.

On 1975–76 models with the EGR service reminder system, the warning light is extinguished by resetting the odometer counter, located on the firewall of the engine compartment.

To reset the switch:

1. Remove the odometer counter lockwire (5) and unscrew the cap. (6).

2. Rotate the screw switch to "50".

3. Replace the fuse in holder (6). Install the cap and lockwire.

4. At 50,000 mile EGR service, repeat step 1 and rotate screw back to "25". Repeat step 3.

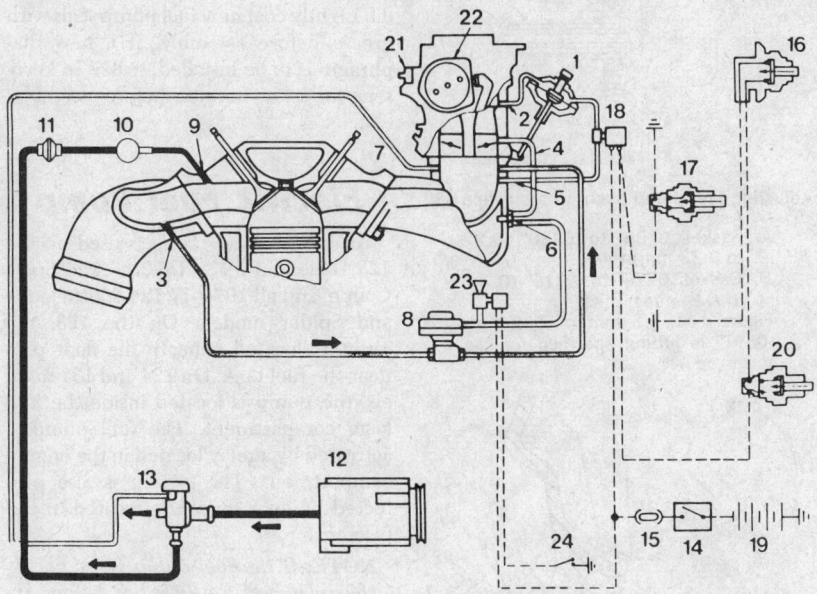

Standard version.

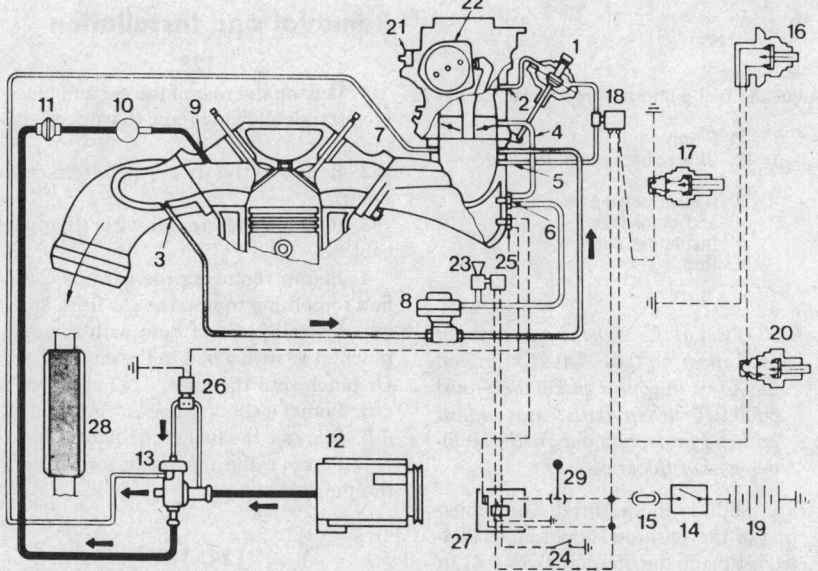

1977 124, 131 emission control systems schematic

1. Fast idle capsule
2. Continuity hole
3. Exhaust gas recirculation intake
4. EGR valve control vacuum intake
5. Fast idle valve control vacuum intake
6. EGR valve control thermovalve
7. Diverter valve control vacuum intake
8. EGR valve
9. Air injector
10. Air injection manifold
11. Check valve
12. Air pump
13. Diverter valve
14. Ignition contact matched switch
15. Fuse
16. Switch contacts closed by transmission on 3rd-4th gear
17. Fast idle control switch
18. Electrovalve
19. Battery
20. Switch closed when clutch is engaged
21. Idle stop solenoid
22. Automatic choke system
23. Electrovalve
24. Transmission switch (closed with 5th gear engaged)
25. Thermoswitch
26. Electrovalve
27. Magnetic reversing switch
28. Catalytic converter
29. Gear shift lever (switch open with transmission in neutral)

Catalytic Converter System

All 1975 and later models manufactured for sale in California, as well as all (50 states) 1975–77 X1/9 models are equipped with a catalytic converter to further reduce emissions. The converter is located in the exhaust system, upstream from the muffler. The converter is filled with a platinum/palladium pellet substrate which rapidly oxidizes emissions of hydrocarbons and carbon monoxide into carbon dioxide and water.

On 1975–76 models, a catalyst protection system is used to prevent overheating of the catalyst. Whenever the throttle is released fully while the engine speed is 2650 rpm or greater (such as deceleration from speed), the carburetor idle stop solenoid will shut off the fuel supply until engine speed drops below 2650 rpm. This prevents raw fuel from being sucked into the intake during deceleration. On 1977 models, this system is not used.

Also on 1975–76 models, a catalyst temperature warning system is used. If a malfunction in the fuel system should occur, leading to an overrich condition and subsequent converter overheating, a thermo sensor in the converter will activate a dash warning light which reads "slow down". The hotter the catalyst, the faster the warning light will blink on and off. 1977 models do not use this system.

Also on 1975–76 models only is an odometer actuated catalytic converter replacement reminder system. Identical to the EGR service reminder, at 25,000 mile intervals, a dash warning light will display "catalyst", indicating that its time to replace the converter. Beginning with the 1977 model year, the converter has been re-certified for 50,000 miles or more, with no regularly scheduled replacement intervals. Maintenance

On 1975–76 models, replace the converter at 25,000 mile intervals, and reset the odometer switch. The switch, and resetting procedure is the same as that listed under EGR Maintenance. 1977 models do not require replacement of the converter in normal service.

FUEL SYSTEM

Mechanical Fuel Pump

A mechanical type fuel pump is used on the 850, X1/9, 124 Special sedan and wagon, 1972–73 124 Sport Coupe and Spider with the 1608 cc engine, and the 1973 1592 cc 124 Sport Spider. The pump is located on the engine block and is driven by the camshaft (pushrod engines) or auxiliary shaft (overhead cammers). A pushrod (850 and X1/9) or pump lever (124) riding on the camshaft or auxiliary shaft eccentric operates the fuel pump diaphragm.

Removal and Installation

850, X1/9, 124

1. Remove and plug the fuel lines leading to the fuel pump.
2. Remove the mounting nuts and carefully remove the fuel pump from the block (or crankcase).
3. If the pump is equipped with a pushrod, remove the pushrod, gasket and insulator from the mounting.
4. Installation is the reverse of removal. Perform the following additional steps on the 850, and X1/9.

  a. Before replacing the fuel pump, adjust the projection of the pump pushrod.

  b. Fit the insulating spacer to its seat with a gasket.

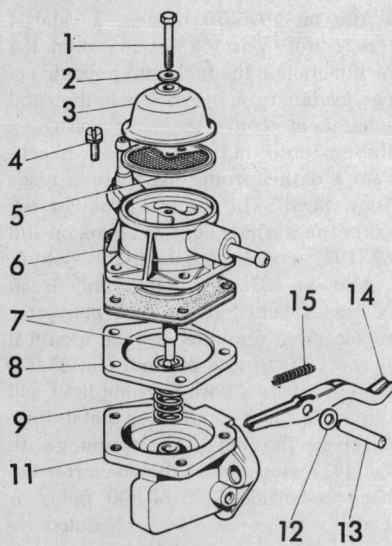

Mechanical fuel pump—124

1. Screw
2. Lockwasher
3. Cover
4. Screw
5. Filter
6. Upper body
7. Diaphragm
8. Spacer
9. Spring
11. Lower body
12. Flat washer
13. Pivot pin
14. Operating lever
15. Spring

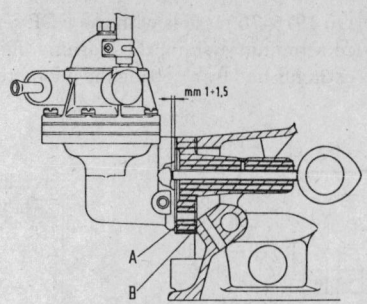

Adjusting fuel pump pushrod projection 850

A. Gasket .0106" to .0130" (0.27 to 0.33 mm) thick
B. Gasket .0276" to .0315" (0.7 to 0.8 mm) thick
Figure 1 ÷ 1,5 mm = .0394" to .0591" is jutting specified for the push rod

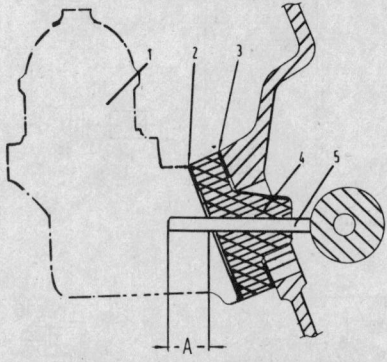

Adjusting fuel pump pushrod projection X1/9

1. Pump
2. Gasket between pump and support
3. Gasket between support and crankcase
4. Insulating support
5. Rod

NOTE: *On the 850, the outer gasket used must be 0.0106–0.0130 in.; on the X1/9, the outer gasket used must be 0.012 in. In both cases, adjust pushrod projection only with the inner gasket thickness.*

  c. Slide in the pushrod. The projection of the pushrod should be 0.0394–0.0591 in. on the 850, and 0.59–0.61 in. on the X1/9. If the projection is not within specified limits, adjust the projection by replacing the inner gasket with another. 850 service gaskets are available in the following thicknesses:
A = .0106"–.0130"
B = .0276"–.0315"
C = .0472"–.0512"
X1/9 service gaskets are available in the following thicknesses: 0.012 in. (0.3 mm), 0.027 in. (0.7 mm), and 0.047 in. (1.2 mm).

Service

Sludge deposited in the fuel chamber or on the filter may be removed with the pump cover off. Intake and outlet valves should be inspected and replaced if damaged. Check springs for good condition.

Control mechanism for the intake chamber diaphragm should be washed in kerosene and lightly lubricated with thin oil. Lightly coat new fuel pump seals with grease before assembly. If a new diaphragm is to be installed, soak it in kerosene for a few minutes before assembly.

Electric Fuel Pump

An electric fuel pump is used on the 128, 131, and 1973 1592 cc 124 Sport Coupe, and all 1974–77 124 Sport Coupe and Spider models. On the 128, the pump is located beneath the floor pan, near the fuel tank. On 124 and 131 models, the pump is located inside the luggage compartment. The fuel pump is activated by a relay located in the engine compartment. The system is also protected by an 8 amp fuse located in the fuse box.

NOTE: *If the fuel pump stops, check the relay and the fuse box before attempting any repairs.*

Removal and Installation

128

1. Jack up the rear of the car and place it on stands allowing room to work on the pump.
2. Remove the hot wire from the pump.
3. Remove the ground wire. (If applicable.)
4. Before removing the gas inlet line, find something to stop the gas from flowing. A small piece of hose with the end pinched or with a bolt in the end will do. Or pinch shut the lines.
5. Remove the gas lines.
6. Remove the fuel recirculating lines.
7. Remove the mounting screws and the pump.

124, 131

It is located in the luggage compartment. Use the steps 2–7 given above for the 128.

Removal and Installation

1. Disconnect the accelerator rod, sliding it out of the lever ball joint end toward the dashboard.
2. Remove the air filter.
3. Detach the choke cable. (1972–74 models only.)
4. Disconnect the fuel line.
5. Disconnect all of the vacuum lines.
6. Remove the mounting bolts or nuts.
7. Remove the carburetor and gasket.
8. Installation is the reverse of the above procedure.

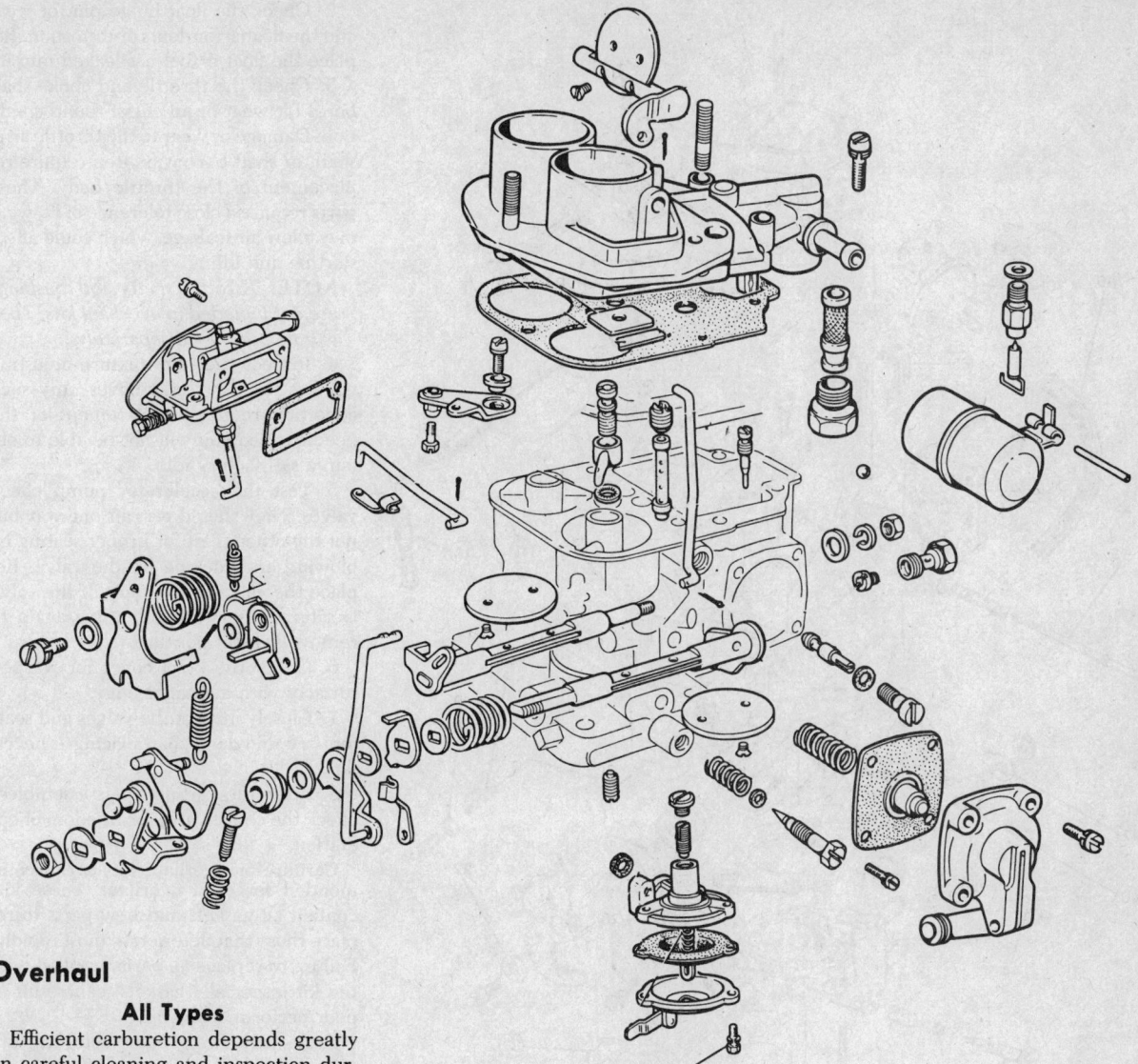

Exploded view of Weber 30 DICA 1—1972-73 850

Overhaul

All Types

Efficient carburetion depends greatly on careful cleaning and inspection during overhaul, since dirt, gum, water, or varnish in or on the carburetor parts are often responsible for poor performance.

Overhaul your carburetor in a clean, dust-free area. Carefully disassemble the carburetor, referring often to the exploded views. Keep all similar and look-alike parts segregated during disassembly and cleaning to avoid accidental interchange during assembly. Make a note of all jet sizes.

When the carburetor is disassembled, wash all parts (except diaphragms, electric choke units, pump plunger, and any other plastic, leather, fiber, or rubber parts) in clean carburetor solvent. Do not leave parts in the solvent any longer than is necessary to sufficiently loosen the deposits. Excessive cleaning may remove the special finish from the float bowl and choke valve bodies, leaving these parts unfit for service. Rinse all parts in clean solvent and blow them dry with compressed air or allow them to air dry. Wipe clean all cork, plastic, leather, and fiber parts with a clean, lint-free cloth.

CARBURETOR APPLICATION

Year	Model	Carburetor
1972-73	850	Weber 30 DICA 1
	128	Weber 32 ICA 1
	124 Special	Weber 32 DHSA 1
	124 Sport	Weber 28/36 DHSA 2
1974	128, X1/9	Weber 32 DMTRA 1/200
	124 Special TC	Weber 32 DMSA
	124 Sport	Weber 34 DMSA 1
1975-76	128; (49 states)	Weber 32 DATRA 1/100
	X1/9; (50 states), 128 (Calif.)	Weber 32 DATRA 4/100
	131; manual trans. (49 states)	Weber 32 ADFA 1/100
	131; auto. trans. (49 states)	Weber 32 ADFA 3/100
	131; manual trans (Calif.)	Weber 32 ADFA 4/100
	131; auto. trans. (Calif.)	Weber 32 ADFA 6/100
	124 Sport (49 states)	Weber 32 ADFA 2/100
	124 Sport (Calif.)	Weber 32 ADFA 5/100

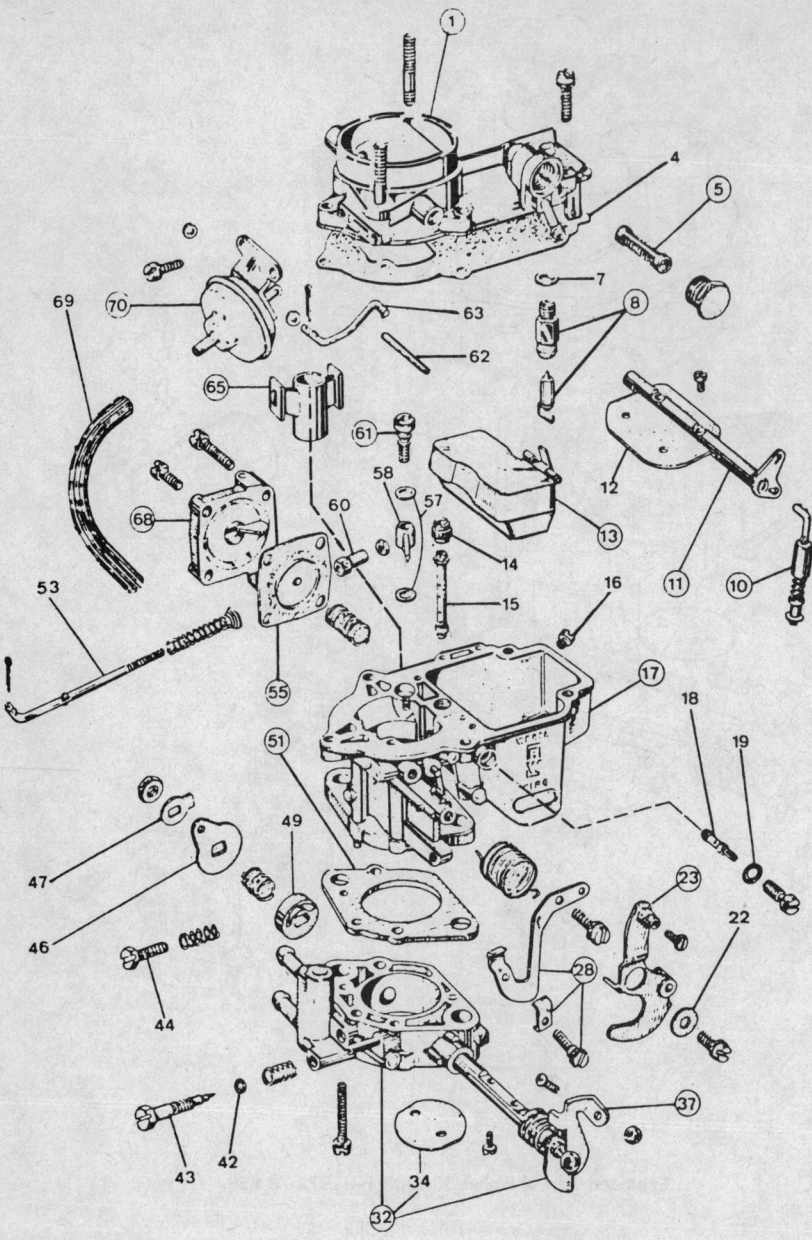

Exploded view of Weber 32 ICA 1—1972-73 128

1. Float chamber cover
4. Gasket
5. Filter
7. Washer
8. Needle valve
10. Choke control link
11. Choke valve spindle
12. Choke valve
13. Float
14. Air correction jet
15. Emulsion tube
16. Main jet
17. Body
18. Idling jet
19. Washer
22. Washer
23. Choke control lever
28. Control cable bracket
32. Throttle body
34. Throttle valve
37. Throttle control and spindle
42. Seal
43. Volume control screw
44. Slow-running screw
46. Accelerator pump lever
47. Tab washer
49. Oil vapor recirculating valve
51. Flange
53. Accelerator pump rod
55. Diaphragm
57. Washers
58. Discharge tube
60. Accelerator pump stroke adjusting nut
61. Check valve
62. Float spindle
63. Vacuum system choke control rod
65. Small venturi
68. Accelerator pump cover
69. Depression system tube
70. Vacuum diaphragm chamber

2. Check the float hinge pin for wear and the float(s) for dents or distortion. Replace the float if fuel has leaked into it.

3. Check the throttle and choke shaft bores for wear or an out-of-round condition. Damage or wear to the throttle arm, shaft, or shaft bore will often require replacement of the throttle body. These parts require a close tolerance of fit; wear may allow air leakage, which could affect starting and idling.

NOTE: *Throttle shafts and bushings are not included in overhaul kits. They can be purchased separately.*

4. Inspect the idle mixture adjusting needles for burrs or grooves. Any such condition requires replacement of the needle, since you will not be able to obtain a satisfactory idle.

5. Test the accelerator pump check valves. They should pass air one way but not the other. Test for proper seating by blowing and sucking on the valve. Replace the valve if necessary. If the valve is satisfactory, wash the valve again to remove breath moisture.

6. Check the bowl cover for warped surfaces with a straight edge.

7. Closely inspect the valves and seats for wear and damage, replacing as necessary.

8. After the carburetor is assembled, check the choke valve for freedom of operation.

Carburetor overhaul kits are recommended for each overhaul. These kits contain all gaskets and new parts to replace those that deteriorate most rapidly. Failure to replace all parts supplied with the kit (especially gaskets) can result in poor performance later.

Some carburetor manufacturers supply overhaul kits of three basic types: minor repair; major repair; and gasket kits. Basically, they contain the following:

Minor Repair Kits:

All gaskets
Float needle valve
Volume control screw
All diaphragms
Spring for the pump diaphragm

Major Repair Kits:

All jets and gaskets
All diaphragms
Float needle valve
Volume control screw
Pump ball valve
Main jet carrier
Float
Complete intermediate rod
Intermediate pump lever
Complete injector tube
Some cover hold-down screws and washers

Blow out all passages and jets with compressed air and be sure that there are no restrictions or blockages. Never use wire or similar tools to clean jets, fuel passages, or air bleeds. Clean all jets and valves separately to avoid accidental interchange.

Check all parts for wear or damage. If wear or damage is found, replace the defective parts. Especially check the following:

1. Check the float needle and seat for wear. If wear is found, replace the complete assembly.

Gasket Kits:

All gaskets

After cleaning and checking all components, reassemble the carburetor, using new parts and referring to the exploded view. When reassembling, make sure that all screws and jets are tight in their seats, but do not overtighten as the tips will be distorted. Tighten all screws gradually, in rotation. Do not tighten needle valves into their seats; uneven jetting will result. Always use new gaskets. Be sure to adjust the float level when reassembling.

Throttle Linkage Adjustment

All Fiat models use cable type throttle linkage. Adjustments can be made at the carburetor by loosening the hold-down screw of the eye in which the cable slides. Proper adjustment will allow the gas pedal to be fully released from the floor boards and at the same time the carburetor will be in the fully-closed position.

NOTE: *If the gas pedal suddenly becomes sloppy, before checking the adjustment be sure that the cable housing is securely mounted.*

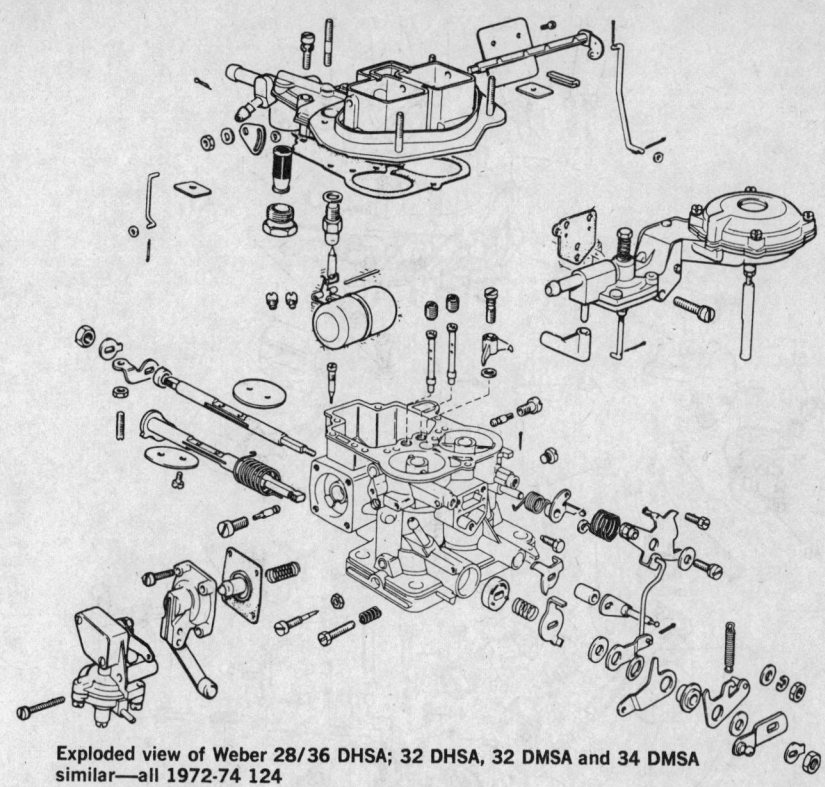

Exploded view of Weber 28/36 DHSA; 32 DHSA, 32 DMSA and 34 DMSA similar—all 1972-74 124

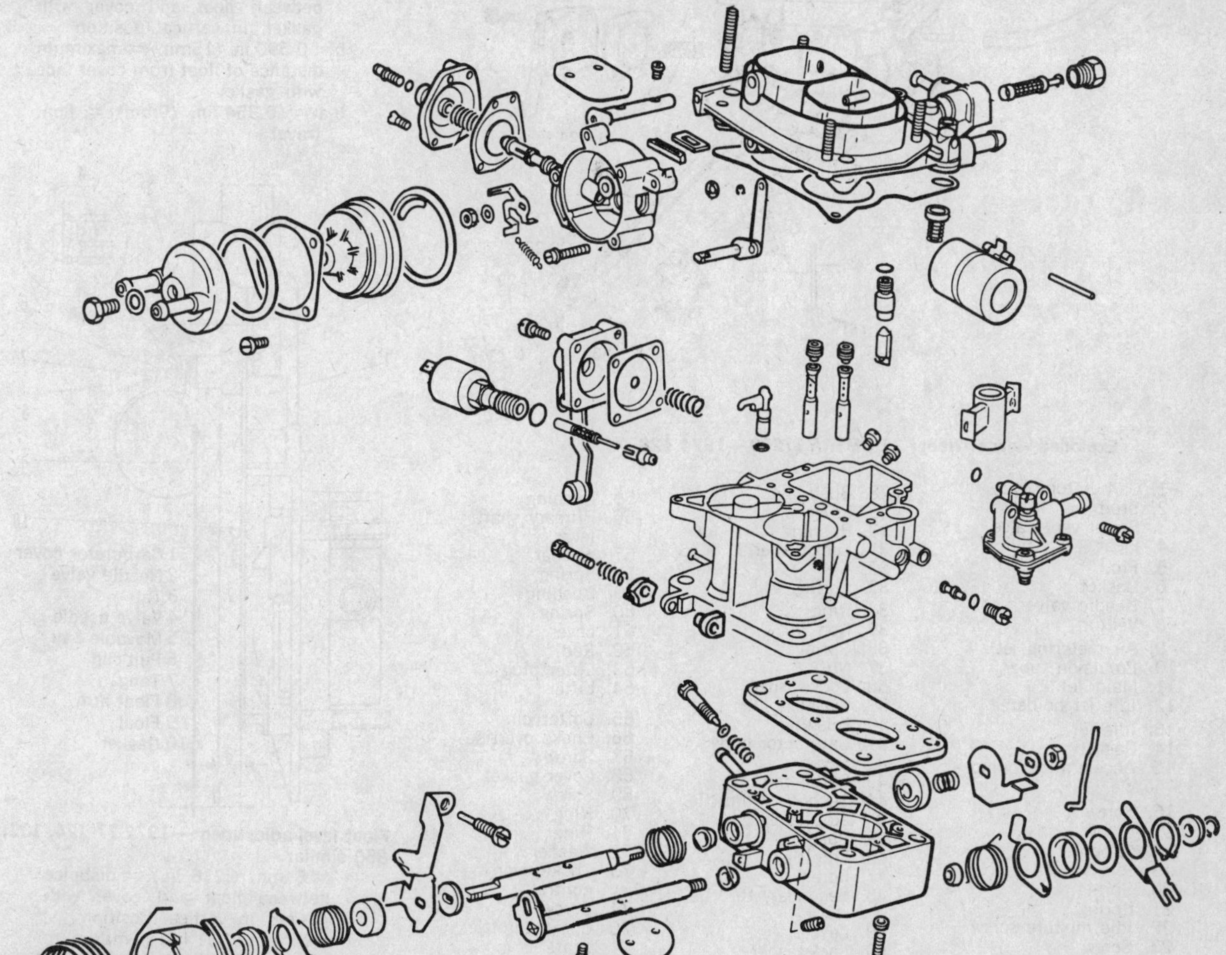

Exploded view of Weber 32 ADFA—1975-77 124, 131

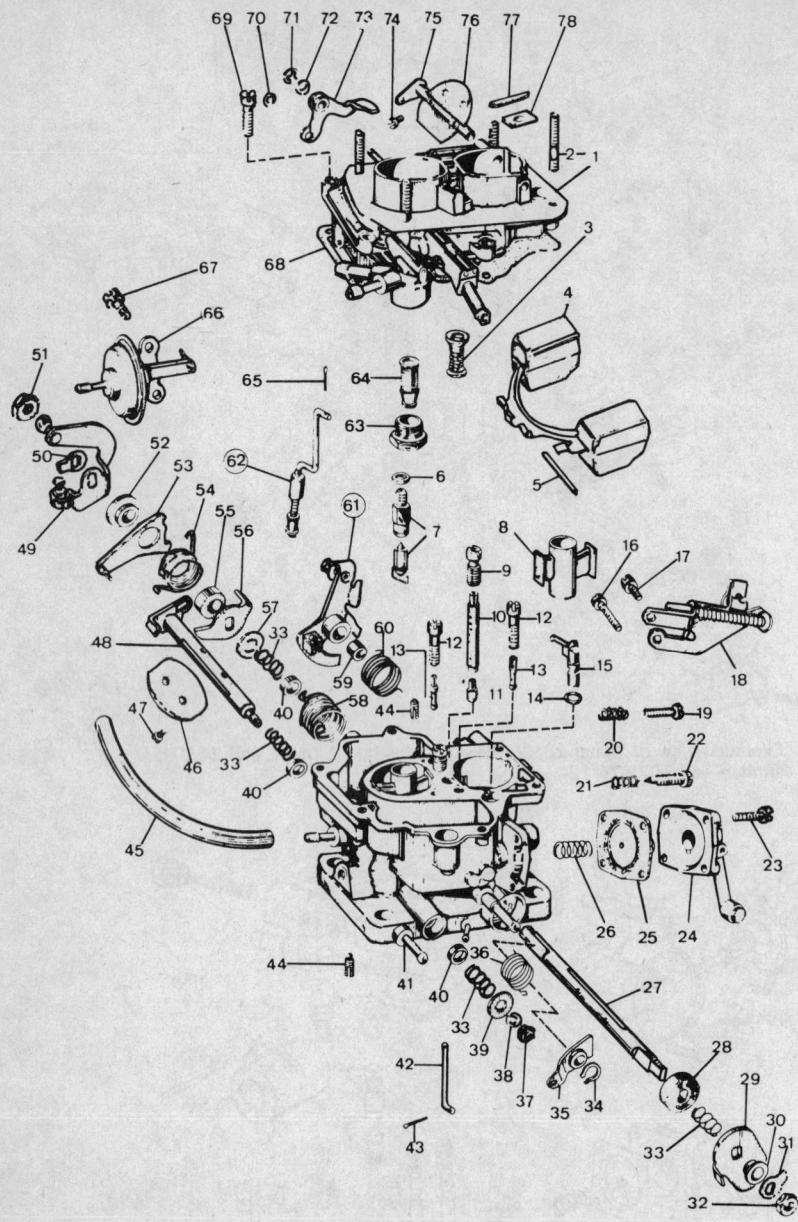

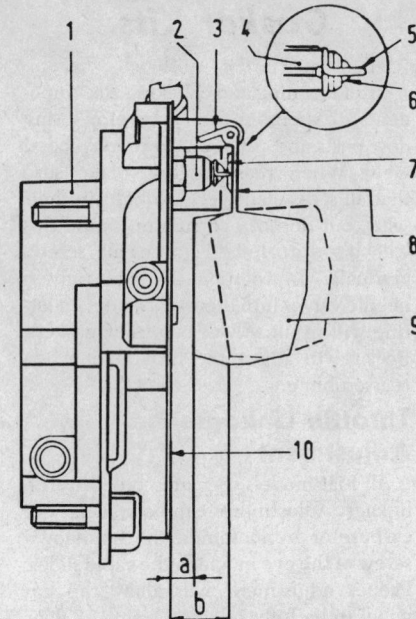

Float level adjustment—1974-77 128, X1/9

1. Carburetor cover	6. Movable ball
2. Needle valve	7. Tang
3. Lug	8. Float arm
4. Valve needle	9. Float
5. Return hook	10. Gasket

a = 0.236 in. (6mm) = distance between float and cover with gasket, in vertical position

b = 0.590 in. (15mm) = maximum distance of float from cover face with gasket

b-a = 0.354 in. (9mm) = float travel

Exploded view of Weber 32 DMTRA 1/200—1974 128, X1/9

1. Carburetor cover	28. Bushing	55. Bushing
2. Stud	29. Lever	56. Primary shaft
3. Bowel vent valve	30. Bushing	lever
4. Float	31. Lockwasher	57. Washer
5. Pin	32. Nut	58. Spring
6. Gasket	33. Spring	59. Bushing
7. Needle valve	34. Ring	60. Spring
8. Venturi	35. Rod	61. Lever
9. Air metering jet	36. Spring	62. Rod
10. Emulsion tube	37. Nut	63. Lifter plug
11. Main Jet	38. Lockwasher	64. Lifter
12. Idle jet holder	39. Washer	65. Cotter pin
13. Idle jet	40. Bushing	66. Choke override
14. Gasket	41. Carburetor body	67. Screw
15. Acceleration pump	42. Lever	68. Cover gasket
nozzle	43. Cotter pin	69. Screw
16. Screw	44. Secondary throttle	70. Ring
17. Screw	stop screw	71. Ring
18. Support	45. Hose	72. Washer
19. Idle screw	46. Throttle	73. Choke override
20. Spring	47. Screw	control
21. Spring	48. Secondary throttle	74. Screw
22. Idle mixture screw	shaft	75. Choke throttle
23. Screw	49. Lever	shaft
24. Accelerator pump cover	50. Lockwasher	76. Choke throttle
25. Diaphragm	51. Nut	77. Plug
26. Spring	52. Bushing	78. Dust cover
27. Throttle shaft, primary	53. Lever	
	54. Spring	

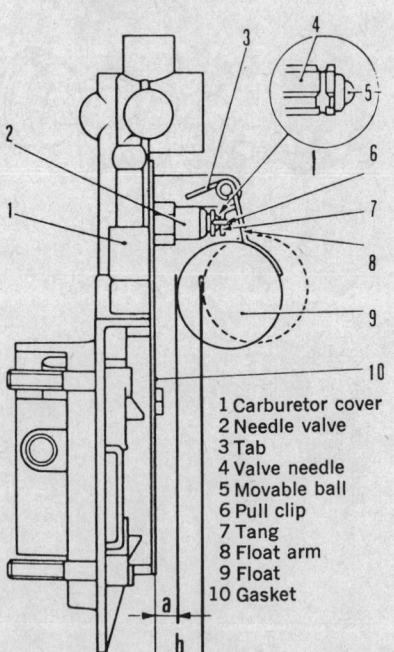

Float level adjustment—1972-77 124, 131; 850 similar

1 Carburetor cover
2 Needle valve
3 Tab
4 Valve needle
5 Movable ball
6 Pull clip
7 Tang
8 Float arm
9 Float
10 Gasket

a = 6 mm (.236 in.) = distance between float and cover with gasket, in vertical position

b = 14 mm (.551 in.) = maximum distance of float from cover face, with gasket

b-a = 8 mm (.315 in.) = float travel

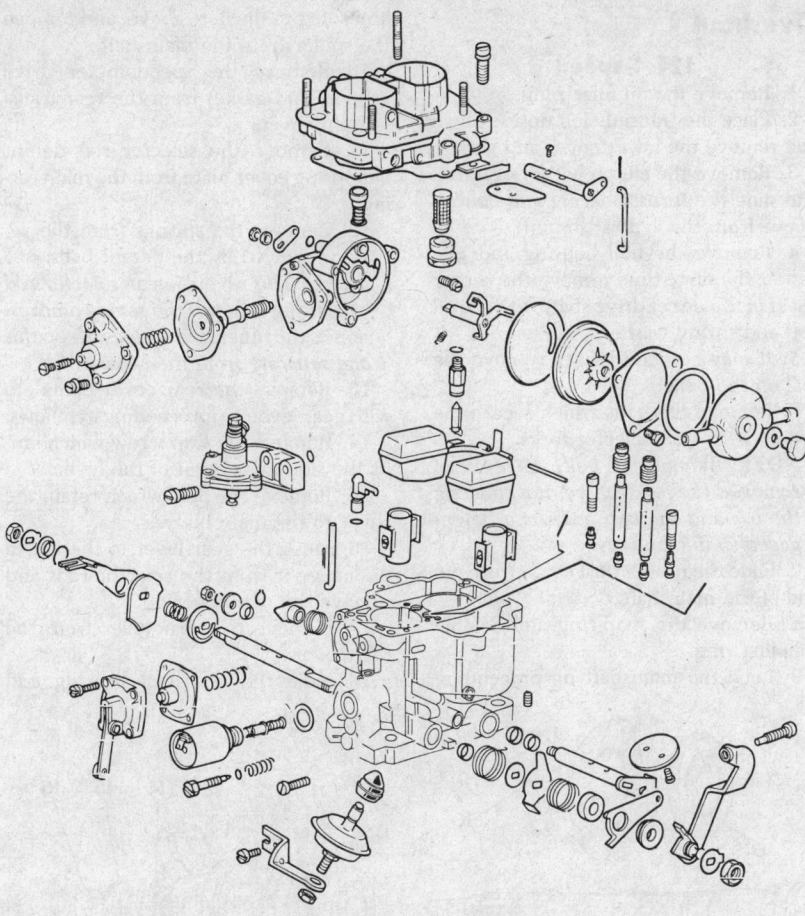

Exploded view of Weber 32 DATRA—1975-77 128, X1/9

Float Level Adjustment

1. Remove the air horn section of the carburetor from the rest of the carburetor assembly.

2. Check to make sure that the needle valve is screwed all the way into its seat. Make sure that the float is not dented or punctured and can turn freely on its hinge.

3. Holding the air horn assembly so that the float hangs vertically, the distance between the top side of the float and the cover with the gasket in place should be 0.236 in. On the 1972–73 128 *only*, check *instead* the distance between the bottom side of the float and the cover, which should be 1.4114 in. This is distance "a".

4. Holding the air horn assembly in the normal horizontal position, the float should drop so that the maximum distance between the end of the float and the cover mating surface with the gasket in place is distance "b" (see illustrations). Total float travel is b-a.

5. To adjust the float level, *carefully* bend the tang of the float that attaches to the needle valve.

Fast Idle Speed Adjustment

See the "Deceleration Throttle Posi-

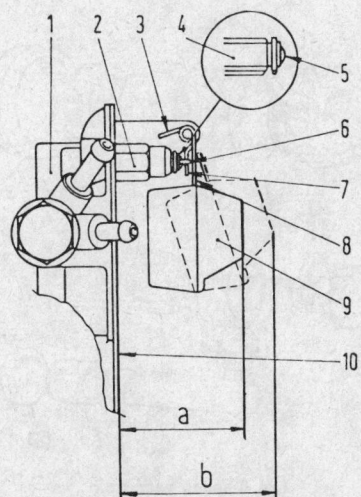

Float level adjustment—1972-73 128

1. Carburetor cover	6. Return hook
2. Needle valve	7. Tang
3. Lug	8. Float arm
4. Valve needle	9. Float
5. Movable ball	10. Gasket

a = 1.4114" (35.85 mm) = distance between float and cover with gasket, in vertical position

b = 1.7520" (44.5 mm) = maximum distance of float from cover face, with gasket

b-a = .3406" (8.65 mm) = float travel

tioner Maintenance" portion of the Emission Control section

Choke Adjustment

1972–74 Fiats use hand-operated manual chokes and can be adjusted at the eye on the butterfly choke valve where the cable is secured by a setscrew.

NOTE: *For proper operation of the choke be sure that the cable housing is mounted properly.*

MANUAL TRANSMISSION

Removal and Installation

124, 131

1. Working from the inside of the car, remove the gear lever and cover plate.

2. Underneath the car, remove the flexible coupling from the spider on the mainshaft. Remove the drain plug and drain the transmission.

3. Remove the speedometer drive from the support on the transmission.

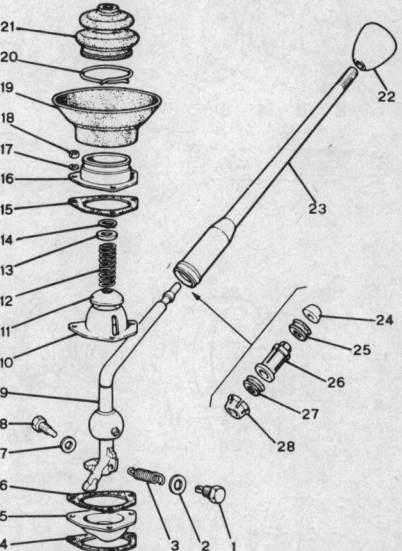

Exploded view of 124 4-speed shifter assembly

1. Gear lever return spring anchor screw	14. Retaining snap-ring
2. Flat washer	15. Gasket
3. Lever return spring	16. Flange
4. Gasket	17. Spring washer
5. Socket plate	18. Nut
6. Gasket	19. Grommet
7. Flat washer	20. Spring clip
8. Gear lever stop screw	21. Rubber boot
9. Lower part of gear lever with ball	22. Knob
10. Upper socket plate	23. Upper part of gear lever
11. Dome washer	24. Shoulder block
12. Spring	25. Rubber bushings
13. Cup washer	26. Spacer
	27. Rubber bushings
	28. Spring-ring

4. Disconnect the clutch withdrawal fork return spring.

5. Remove the locknut and unscrew the adjusting rod from the flexible clutch cable.

6. Remove the flywheel cover from the bellhousing.

7. Remove the bolt which secures the exhaust pipe bracket to the transmission. On the 131, remove the driveshaft protection bracket.

8. Detach the exhaust piping.

9. Remove the starter motor heat shield and the starter motor. Disconnect clutch and transmission emission control switch wires.

10. Support the transmission, and disconnect the transmission mount from the underbody. Remove the 4 bolts which secure the transmission to the engine.

11. Move the transmission carefully away from the engine and lower it to the ground. Do not rest input shaft on clutch disc or release bearing.

12. To install, reverse the removal procedure.

Overhaul

124 4-speed

1. Remove the oil filler plug.

2. Place the transmission upside down and remove the lower cover and gasket.

3. Remove the clutch withdrawal fork and slide the thrust bearing and control sleeve from the central support.

4. Remove the bell housing and gasket. At the same time remove the center cover of the direct drive shaft with the oil seal and spring washer.

5. It may be necessary to remove the seal on the bench.

6. Remove the bolts which secure the 3rd and 4th gear selector forks.

NOTE: *When the bolts have been removed the fork can be moved along the bar and the two gears can be engaged simultaneously.*

7. Slide the rubber dust cover from the end of the mainshaft.

8. Remove the snap-ring and flexible coupling ring.

9. Lock the mainshaft by proceeding

according to the note above, and remove the spider from the mainshaft.

10. Remove the speedometer drive support and gasket from the rear transmission cover.

11. Remove the selector rod detent ball spring cover plate from the main casing.

12. Remove the springs from the recesses, followed by the detent balls.

NOTE: *The reverse gear selector rod ball spring is not of the same compression as the other two springs. Keep this one separate from the other two.*

13. Remove the rear cover complete with gear lever, by proceeding as follows.

14. Remove the stop screw which limits the side movement of the lever.

15. Remove the nuts which retain the cover to the main body.

16. Move the gear lever to the left to disengage it from the selector rods and remove the rear cover.

17. Remove the gear lever from the rear cover.

18. Slide the rear ball bearing and

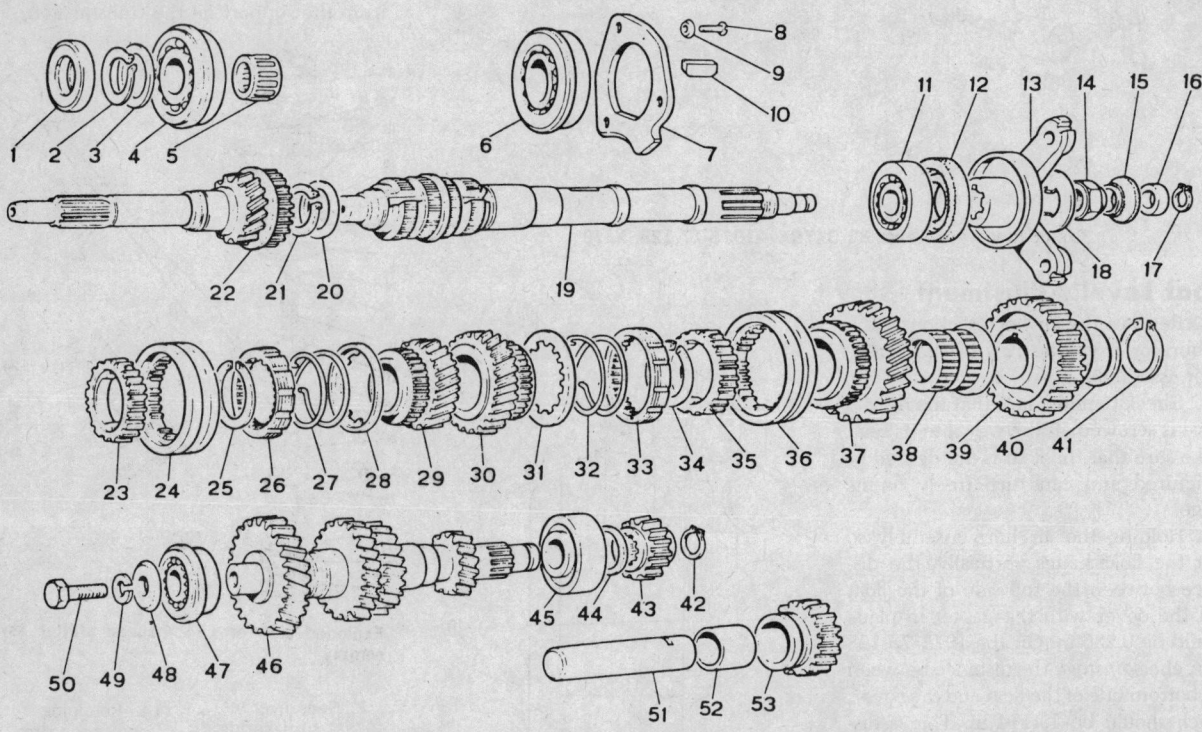

124 4-speed gear train

1. Inner cover seal	12. Rear cover oil seal	24 and 36. Sliding sleeves	43. Reverse driving gear
2. Bearing snap ring	13. Flexible coupling spider	25 and 34. Lock rings	44. Spring washer
3. Spring washer	14. Spider fixing nut	26 and 33. Synchronizing rings	45. Countershaft rear roller bearing
4. Direct drive shaft ball bearing	15. Sealing ring	27 and 32. Synchronizer springs	46. Countershaft with 1st, 2nd and 3rd speed gears
5. Needle roller bearing between direct drive and mainshaft	16. Flexible coupling centering ring	28 and 31. Cups	47. Countershaft front double-row ball bearing
6. Mainshaft intermediate ball bearing	17. Snap ring	29. 3rd speed driven gear	48. Flat washer
7. Mainshaft intermediate ball bearing retaining plate	18. Lockwasher	30. 2nd speed driven gear	49. Spring washer
8. Bearing retaining plate fixing screw	19. Mainshaft	35. 1st-2nd gear sliding sleeve hub	50. Countershaft front ball bearing fixing bolt
9. Bearing retaining plate screw washer	20. Spring washer	37. 1st speed driven gear	51. Reverse idler gear spindle
10. Key	21. Mainshaft assembly retaining snap ring	38. 1st gear bushing	52. Reverse idler gear bushing
11. Mainshaft rear ball bearing	22. Direct drive and 4th gear shaft	39. Reverse driven gear	53. Reverse idler gear
	23. 3rd-4th gear sliding sleeve hub	40. Spring washer	
		41. Reverse driven gear retaining snap ring	
		42. Snap ring	

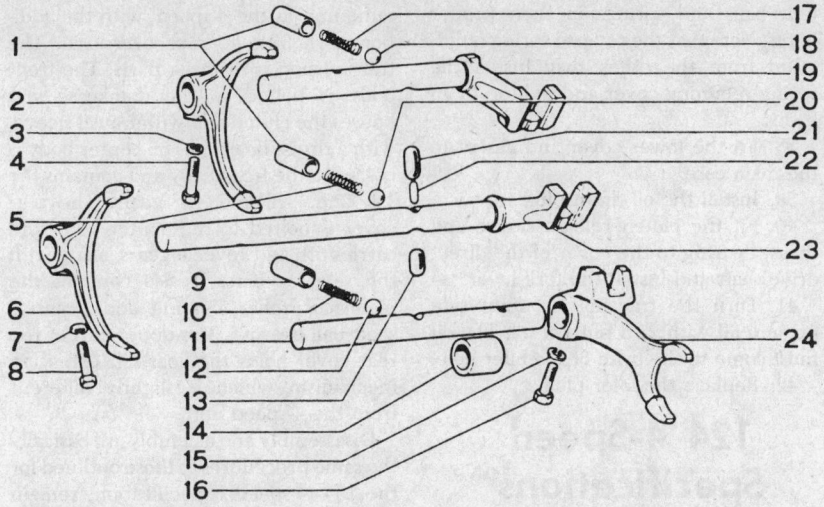

Exploded view of 124 4-speed internal shifting components

1. Bushing
2. 1st and 2nd gear selector fork
3. Lock washer
4. Bolt
5. Spring
6. 3rd and 4th gear selector fork
7. Lock washer
8. Bolt
9. Bushing
10. Spring
11. Reverse selector rod
12. Ball
13. Roller
14. Spacer
15. Lock washer
16. Bolt
17. Spring
18. Ball
19. 1st and 2nd gear selector rod
20. Ball
21. Roller
22. Roller
23. 3rd and 4th gear selector rod
24. Reverse selector fork

speedometer drive gear from the mainshaft.

19. Slide the reverse gear selector rod, complete with fork, from its seat in the main case and, at the same time, remove reverse gear from its spindle.

20. Remove the snap-ring which retains the reverse driving gear and remove the gear from the end of the layshaft.

21. Remove the snap-ring which retains the driven gear from the reverse gear train.

22. Remove the spring washers, driven gear of the reverse gear train, and remove the Woodruff key from its seat.

NOTE: *Before removing the retaining clip of the reverse gear driven train, the spring washer must be compressed.*

23. Engage the two gears to prevent the shafts from turning and remove the retaining bolt and front ball bearing from the layshaft.

24. Tilt the layshaft and remove it from the main case.

25. Remove the 3rd and 4th selector rods from the case and remove the bolt and spring washer holding the 1st and 2nd gear selector forks to the rod.

26. Remove the rod, followed by the 1st-2nd and 3rd-4th gear forks. The three safety rollers will be released as the selector rods are removed.

27. Remove the plate which retains the mainshaft intermediate ball bearing.

28. Withdraw the bearing from its housing.

29. Withdraw the reverse gear spindle from the main case.

30. Remove the direct drive and 4th gear shaft from the mainshaft, complete with ball bearing and 4th gear synchronizing ring.

31. Tilt the mainshaft and remove it from the case, complete with gears, hubs, sliding sleeves and synchronizing rings.

32. Remove the following parts from the mainshaft: 1st gear with synchronizer and bushing 1st and 2nd gear hub and sliding sleeve, 2nd gear, and synchronizer assembly.

33. Remove the snap-ring from its seat in the front end of the mainshaft and remove the following parts: spring washer, 3rd-4th gear hub, 3rd gear, and synchronizer assembly.

34. Remove the snap-ring from the direct drive and 4th gear shaft and remove the spring washer and ball bearing.

To assemble the transmission:

1. Assemble the following parts on the front of the mainshaft, in the order given: 3rd gear and synchronizing ring, 3rd-4th gears and spring washer.

2. Insert the snap-ring in the groove, securing the parts listed above to the front of the mainshaft.

3. Slide the 2nd gear and synchronizing ring, 1st-2nd gear sliding sleeve and hub and 1st speed synchronizing ring and gear with bushing onto the rear end of the shaft.

4. Tilt the mainshaft and insert it into the transmission case.

5. Working from the rear end of the mainshaft, use a driver and insert the intermediate ball bearing.

6. Install the reverse idler gear shaft, then fit the shaft and bearing retaining plate.

7. Secure the plate to the main case and stake the nuts in place.

8. Fit the ball bearing and spring washer to the direct drive shaft and 4th gear shaft, and insert the spring retaining clip of the bearing in the groove.

9. Install the direct drive roller bearing onto the mainshaft.

10. Insert the direct drive shaft in the main case and slide it onto the end of the mainshaft.

11. Fit the 1st and 2nd gear selector fork to the sliding sleeve and slide the corresponding selector rod into the fork from outside.

12. Replace the locating roller of this bar to its seat and secure the fork to the rod.

13. Install the 3rd-4th gear selector fork and rod in the same manner.

NOTE: *Do not lock the fork to the rod at this point, since it will be necessary to use this fork to lock the transmission at a later time.*

14. Insert the layshaft into the main case.

15. Replace the front ball bearing and rear ball bearing of the layshaft.

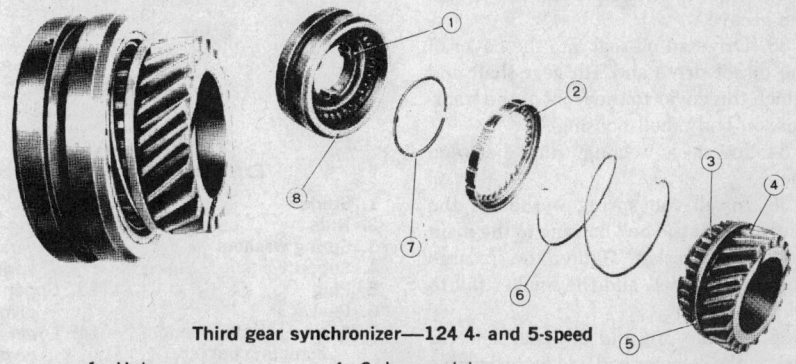

Third gear synchronizer—124 4- and 5-speed

1. Hub
2. Synchronizing ring
3. Blocker ring
4. 3rd gear pinion
5. Cup ring
6. Spring
7. Circlip
8. Sliding sleeve

16. Lock the shafts by engaging two gears at the same time.

17. Use the flat washer, spring washer and bolt to secure the front bearing to the layshaft. Tighten the retaining bolt to 69 ft. lbs.

18. Fit the key to the mainshaft and install the reverse driving gear and spring washer.

19. Retain these with a snap-ring.

NOTE: *When installing the reverse driven gear snap-ring, center the spring washer so that the snap-ring cannot snap into the groove of the shaft.* Fit the spring washer and reverse driving gear to the rear end of the layshaft and secure them with a snap-ring.

20. Insert the reverse selector rod locating roller in its seating, and fit the selector fork to the rod.

21. Retain this with a bolt and spring washer.

22. Install the selector rod in its guide and at the same time, fit the reverse idler gear to its spindle.

23. Install the speedometer drive gear and rear ball bearing on the mainshaft.

24. Fit the gear shifting assembly to the rear transmission cover, as follows.

25. Drive a new oil seal with inner spring into place.

26. Fit the gear shifting lever to the cover.

27. Attach the gear lever return spring to the lever and replace the screw in the cover.

28. Mount the lever assembly on the rear cover and fit the rear cover to the main transmission case. Be sure to fit a gasket between the two cases. Install the back-up light switch and torque to 32.5 ft. lbs.

29. Replace the speedometer drive support with a gasket under it. It is held in place by a nut on a stud in the cover.

30. Install the flexible spider and flat washer on the tail of the mainshaft.

31. Lock the gears and tighten the nut, (to 58 ft. lbs.), bending up the tab washer.

32. Install the dust cover on the mainshaft and drive the coupling centering ring into place and insert the snap-ring in the groove.

33. Drive an oil seal into the cover of the direct drive and 4th gear shaft and attach this cover to the front of the transmission body (bell housing).

34. Insert a sealing ring between them.

35. Install the spring washer of the cover and fit the bell housing to the main case, with a gasket. Tighten the six large nuts to 36 ft. lbs., and the smaller nut to 18 ft. lbs.

36. Fit the 3rd and 4th gear selector fork to the selector rod and secure with a bolt and washer.

37. Replace the three selector rod de-tent balls and springs in their proper bores. Note that the reverse spring is different from the other two. Install the spring retaining cover and tighten to 18 ft. lbs.

38. Fit the lower cover and gasket to the main case.

39. Install the oil drain plug.

40. Fit the clutch release sleeve and thrust bearing to the cover of the direct drive shaft and install the fork lever.

41. Turn the transmission right side up, and fill with 2.75 pints of oil. The oil must come to the brim of the filler hole.

42. Replace the filler plug.

124 4-Speed Specifications

Gear blacklash	0.0039 in.
Clearance between 1st gear and bushing	0.0019-0.0039 in.
2nd and 3rd gears and seats	0.0019-0.0039 in.
Clearance between reverse gear and bushing	0.0019-0.0039 in.
Clearance between flanks of sleeve splines and hub splines	0.0027-0.0063 in
Radial bearing clearance	0.0019 in. (max.)
Axial bearing clearance	0.0196 in. (max.)
Shaft runout	0.00098 in. (max.)

124 (5-Speed)

This transmission is used on 124 Spyder and Coupe models. Basically, it is the same unit as the 4-speed, with the addition of a fifth gear or overdrive. The transmission is in three parts. The front body is bolted to the crankcase and houses the clutch and withdrawal sleeve, with a thrust bearing. The center body is bolted to the front body and contains the 1st, 2nd, 3rd and 4th gears. The rear cover is bolted to the center body and carries 5th and reverse gears, along with the selector bars. It also contains the mainshaft roller bearing and countershaft ball bearing. The upper part of the rear cover holds the gearshift extension mechanism which is slightly different from the 4-speed unit.

Disassembly and assembly are basically the same procedures as those outlined for the 124 (4-speed). Specifications remain identical to those for the 4-speed unit.

When assembling a synchronizer, be sure that the returned ends of the spring are inserted in the slots in the blocker ring, without distorting the normal diameter of the spring. This should be done before the circlip is fitted.

131 5-Speed

1. Pull the output yoke off of the output shaft.

2. Remove the speedometer driven gear retainer and gasket.

3. Remove the gearshift support and gasket from the rear housing.

4. Remove the seven bolts and washers retaining the rear housing to the main

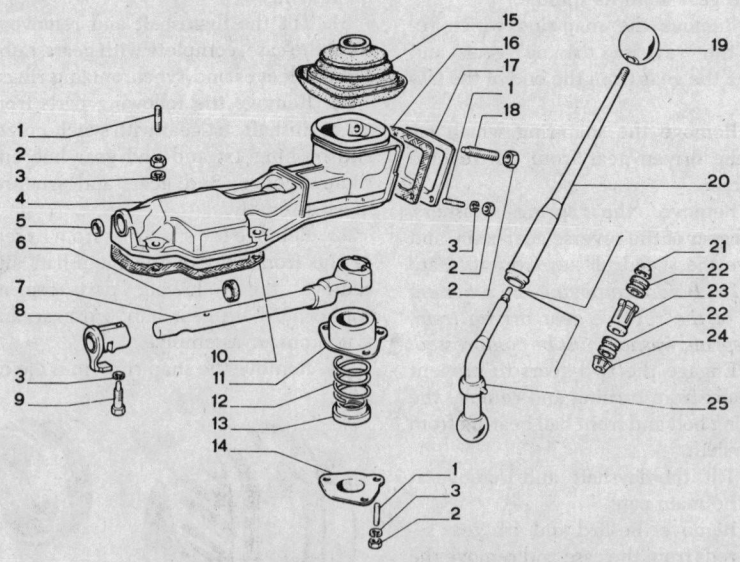

Exploded view of 124 5 speed gearshift mechanism.

1. Studs
2. Nuts
3. Spring washers
4. Support
5. Plug
6. Gasket
7. Gear selector and actuating bar
8. Dog
9. Screw
10. Gasket
11. Cover, spring retaining
12. Reverse stiffening spring
13. Upper ball socket, pivot lever
14. Lower ball socket, pivot lever
15. Boot
16. Gasket
17. Cover
18. Pin
19. Grip
20. Lever jacket
21. Pad
22. Resilient bushings
23. Spacer
24. Snap-ring, lever jacket
25. Pivot lever, gearshift

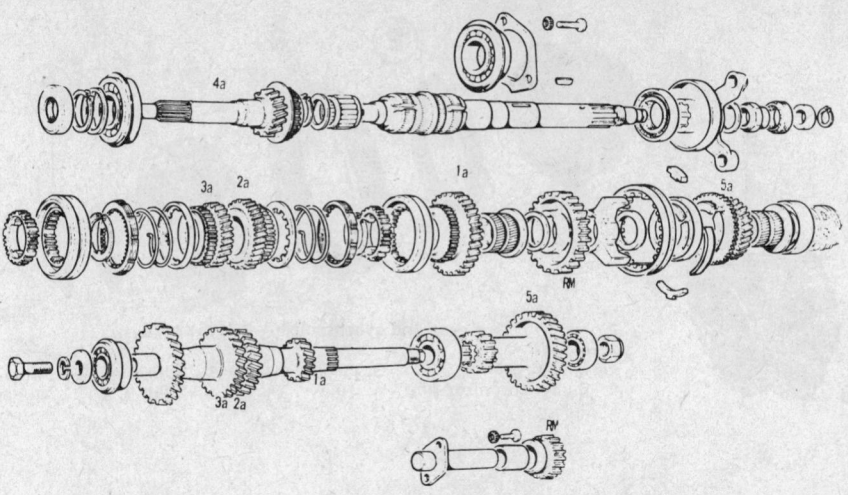

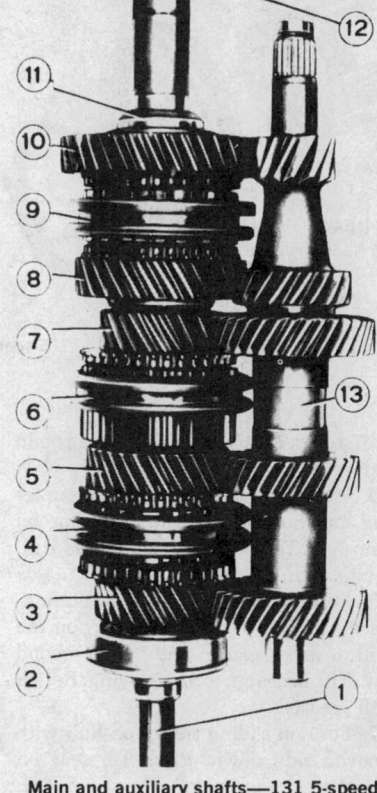

124 5-speed gear train

1A. 1st gear	3A. 3rd gear	5A. 5th gear
2A. 2nd gear	4A. 4th gear	RM. Reverse gear

case. Tap lightly with wooden or plastic hammer and pull off to the rear.

5. Disconnect clutch release lever from ball joint pivot. Remove release bearing support and release lever.

6. Inside bell housing, remove the seven bolts retaining bell housing to main case. Tap lightly and remove bell housing.

7. Remove snap ring for speedometer drive gear and slide gear off output shaft.

8. Remove snap ring in front of input shaft bearing.

9. Apply pressure to spring washer behind snap ring at rear of output shaft and remove snap ring. Remove spring washer.

10. Remove bolt retaining reverse shifting fork to shifting rod, and remove fork and reverse idler gear. Remove shifting rod spacer. Remove reverse gear from the mainshaft.

11. Remove bolt retaining extension for 3rd and 4th gear shifting rod. Remove extension.

12. Remove snap ring retaining reverse drive gear onto auxiliary shaft, and remove the gear.

13. Remove two bolts retaining detent ball cover. Remove cover, springs and balls.

14. Remove woodruff key from output shaft. Slide main case off of shafts. Remove magnet for front housing slot.

15. Remove bolt retaining fork to shifting rod, and remove rod. Assemble fork to rod for reference. Repeat for other shifting rods.

16. Remove mainshaft and auxiliary shaft from housing.

17. Disconnect input shaft from mainshaft. Remove bearing from inside input shaft.

18. Position mainshaft in vice with protective jaws. Using two screwdrivers, pry outer bearing race off of shaft. Then,

slide 1st gear, outer race for thrust bearing, thrust bearing, inner race, and thrust washer off of mainshaft.

19. Remove roller bearing (122 rollers) and separator for bearings.

20. Remove snap ring retaining 1st and 2nd gear synchronizer hub. Place mainshaft in press with block beneath 2nd gear. Press off hub, synchronizer ring, gear, and washers. Remove roller bearing (134 rollers) from shaft.

21. Invert mainshaft. Depress spring washer and remove snap ring and washer from other end. Pull the 3rd and 4th gear synchronizer hub from shaft. Remove 3rd gear.

22. Remove snap ring retaining 5th gear synchronizer hug. Pull off hub. Remove 5th gear.

23. Depress spring washer and remove snap ring. Pull bearing from mainshaft.

To assemble the transmission:

1. Press bearing on input shaft. Position spring washer and snap ring on shaft. Depress spring washer and install snap ring in groove.

2. Place 5th gear and synchronizer ring on mainshaft. Tap hub for 5th gear

Main and auxiliary shafts—131 5-speed

1. Input shaft	7. 5th gear
2. Bearing	8. 2nd gear
3. 4th gear	9. 1st and 2nd gear
4. 3rd and 4th gear	synchronizer
synchronizer	10. 1st gear
5. 3rd gear	11. Bearing outer race
6. 5th gear	12. Main shaft
synchronizer	13. Auxiliary shaft

synchronizer down with brass drift until ring seats correctly in hub. Secure with snap ring. Position sliding sleeve on hub with beveled teeth facing 5th gear.

3. Place 3rd gear and synchronizer on mainshaft. Tap hub down with brass drift. Install sliding sleeve on hub with grooved side down. Position spring washer and snap ring on shaft. Depress spring washer and install snap ring in groove.

4. Invert mainshaft. Position two rows

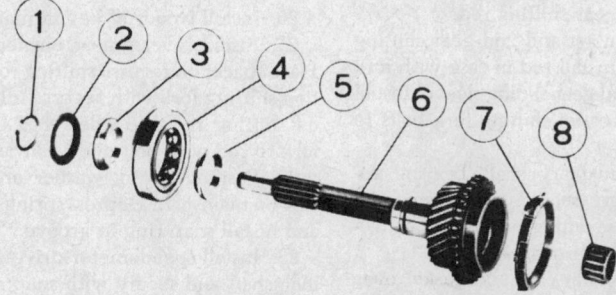

131 5-speed input shaft

1. Snap ring	5. Outer race
2. Spring washer	6. Input shaft
3. Outer race	7. Synchronizer ring
4. Bearing	8. Bearing

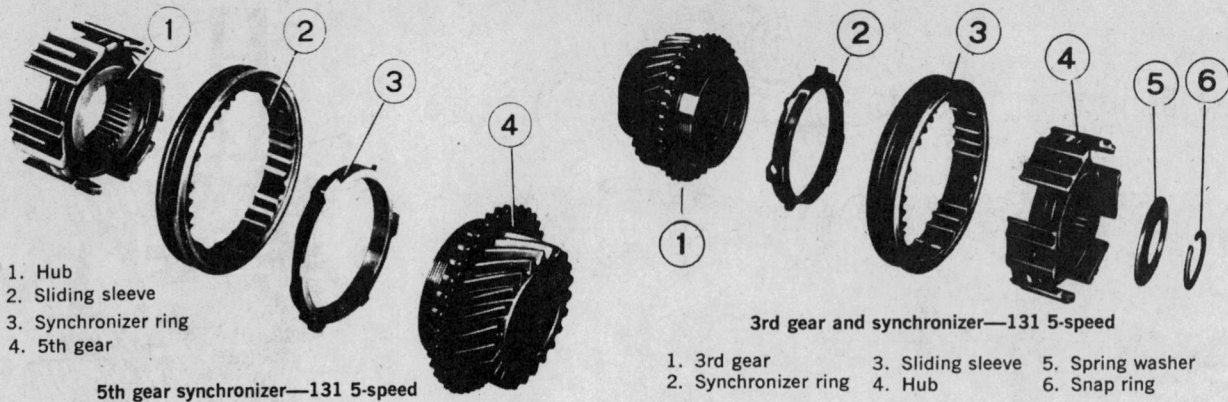

1. Hub
2. Sliding sleeve
3. Synchronizer ring
4. 5th gear

5th gear synchronizer—131 5-speed

3rd gear and synchronizer—131 5-speed

1. 3rd gear
2. Synchronizer ring
3. Sliding sleeve
4. Hub
5. Spring washer
6. Snap ring

of 67 roller bearings on shaft and retain with clean wheel bearing grease.

5. Place 2nd gear and synchronizer ring and hub for 1st and 2nd gear on mainshaft. Tap hub down with brass drift. Retain with snap ring.

6. Position flat washer on mainshaft. Place a row of 61 roller bearings on the shaft, install a spacer, and then a second row of 61 bearings, forming a ring. Retain with grease.

7. Position sliding sleeve on hub with grooved side down. Place 1st gear on mainshaft, then install thrust washer, thrust bearing and washer.

8. Press bearing onto input shaft. Position flat washer and outer bearing race on shaft. Tap outer race down with brass drift.

9. Place lockwasher on bearing in front housing for auxiliary shaft. Position magnet in case with magnetic face toward gears.

10. Install input shaft in mainshaft. Mesh together mainshaft and auxiliary shaft gears and install in front housing.

11. Remove allen bolt from front housing. Position 5th gear shifting fork on rod in case with fork on 5th gear sliding sleeve. Install detent ball in front housing adjacent to 5th gear shifting rod.

12. Position 3rd and 4th gear shifting fork on rod. Install rod in case with fork on 3rd and 4th gear sliding sleeve. Install detent ball in front housing adjacent to 3rd and 4th gear shifting rod.

13. Position 1st and 2nd gear shifting fork on rod. Install rod in case with fork on 1st and 2nd gear sliding sleeve. Install allen bolt. Tighten shifting fork bolts to 14.5 ft. lbs.

14. Coat auxiliary shaft bearing retainer with grease. Position retainer on bearing in case with grooved surface facing away from bearing.

15. Install main case and gasket over shafts and shifting rods. Position outer race for mainshaft bearing on shaft, and tap down with brass drift. Position washer and retainer plate on shaft.

16. Place reverse gear idle shaft in

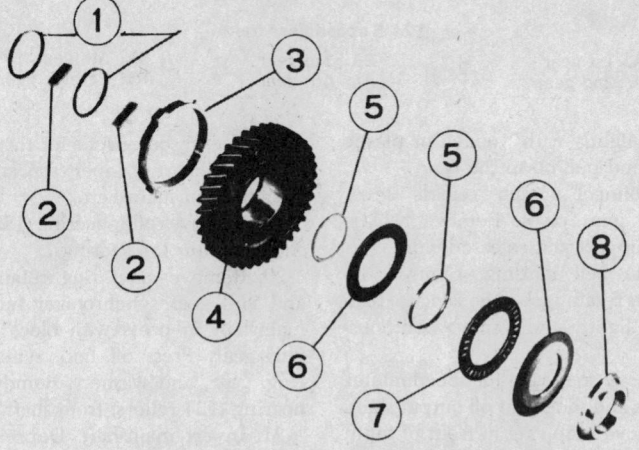

1st gear and synchronizer—131 5-speed

1. Spacer
2. Roller bearings
3. Synchronizer ring
4. 1st gear
5. Flat washer
6. Thrust washer
7. Thrust bearing
8. Outer race

case. Position retainer plate tab in shaft groove. Secure with 4 bolts.

17. Position detent balls and springs in case, and retain plate with 2 bolts. Tighten to 18 ft. lbs.

18. Install reverse drive gear on auxiliary shaft with washer and secure with snap ring.

19. Position 3rd and 4th gear shifting rod extension on rod. Install extension retaining bolt and lockwasher and tighten.

20. Install woodruff key in mainshaft.

21. Install reverse gear on mainshaft. Place spacer on reverse shifting rod. Position shifting fork with reverse idler gear on shifting rod and idler shaft. Secure fork to rod with bolt and lockwasher.

22. Position spring washer and snap ring on mainshaft. Depress spring washer and install snap ring in groove.

23. Install speedometer drive gear on mainshaft and secure with snap ring.

24. Install input shaft outer bearing retaining snap ring.

25. Position bell housing with gasket to main case, and secure with seven bolts and washers. Install clutch release lever

and release bearing on input shaft and connect lever to ball joint pivot.

26. Position rear housing with gasket to main case and secure with seven bolts and washers.

27. Place both ends of shifter spring in rear housing slotted plate. Then, flip

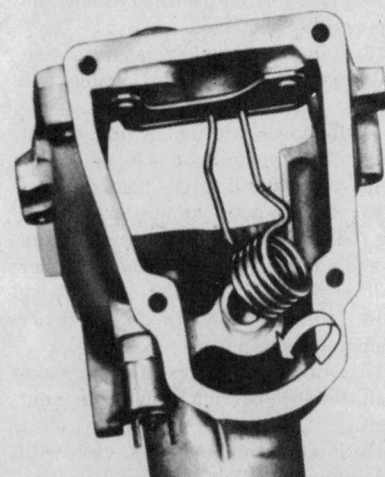

Installing shifter spring—131 5-speed

spring over and install over spring support boss.

28. Install gearshift support with gasket on rear housing. Install retaining bolts and check shifting action.

29. Install speedometer driven gear housing and gasket.

30. Slide output shaft yoke onto shaft.

CLUTCH

A single, dry clutch disc and diaphragm spring pressure plate are utilized on all models. Clutch actuation is by cable, except on the X1/9, which uses a hydraulic master and slave cylinder system.

Removal and Installation

124 and 850

1. Jack up the car and remove the transmission or transaxle (850) as previously outlined.

NOTE: *It is important that the input shaft never be allowed to rest on the withdrawal flange, since the support plates of the flange will be bent.*

2. Mark the position of the clutch in relation to the flywheel to facilitate assembly.

3. Remove the bolts (in stages) which secure the clutch cover to the flywheel. The bolts should be removed evenly to prevent distortion of the clutch.

4. Remove the pressure plate and clutch disc.

5. Check the condition of the pilot bushing which is pressed into the crankshaft. If necessary, replace the bushing. Installation of the clutch is the reverse of removal. Use an old input shaft or wooden dummy shaft to center the clutch disc. Tighten the clutch cover bolts diagonally, in rotation, to 22 ft. lbs.

128, X1/9

1. Raise the car and support it on support stands.

2. Remove the transaxle.

3. Mark the clutch in respect to the flywheel so that correct balance can be maintained.

4. Remove the retaining bolts which secure the clutch cover to the flywheel and then remove the clutch assembly.

5. Installation is the reverse of removal with the following notes:

a. The clutch disc should be positioned with the protruding part of the hub facing the transmission housing.

b. Before tightening the clutch-to-flywheel mounting screws, be sure to center the disc with a discarded transmission mainshaft, or an aligning tool.

c. Tighten the clutch cover bolts diagonally, in rotation, to 11 ft. lbs.

Clutch Pedal Adjustment

NOTE: *On all models check the clutch*

control cable grommet for damage. A damaged grommet will not allow the cable sheath to react correctly, thus causing a clutch malfunction. To correct this problem, replace the grommet. Lubricate to prevent clutch "shudder".

128

1. Open hood, remove the spare tire and locate the cable nut and locknut shown in the illustration.

2. Adjust the nut until the pedal has one in. of free-play. Tighten the locknut.

Clutch free play adjusting location—128

1. Cable
2. Nut and locknut for adjusting the tie-rod
3. Forked lever

X1/9

1. Jack up the rear of the car.

2. Clutch pedal free play (distance before resistance is felt when depressing pedal) should be 1.25 in.

3. If not, adjust as necessary by loosening the locknut and turning the adjusting nut on the slave cylinder pushrod where it contacts the clutch release lever. Tighten locknut.

4. Lower car and recheck adjustment. If slave cylinder does not operate at all, check for air in system and bleed circuit.

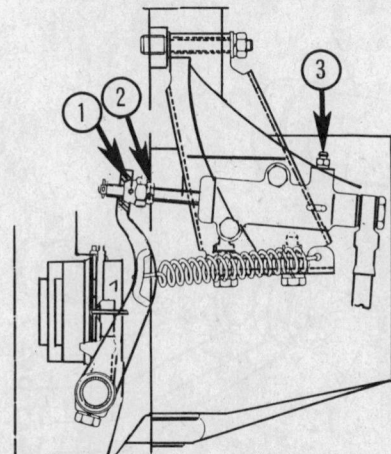

Clutch free play adjusting location—X1/9

1. Adjusting nut
2. Locknut
3. Bleed nipple

131

1. Open the hood.

2. Check that clutch pedal free play is 1 in.

3. If not, adjust as necessary by adjusting the cable at the firewall. Loosen cable locknut, and, while holding the cable housing from turning, rotate adjusting nut in required direction. Tighten locknut.

4. Recheck adjustment.

Clutch free play adjusting location—131

850

1. Jack up the rear of the car.

2. Adjust by loosening the locknut of the adjustable rod of the throwout (release) lever and turning the cable adjusting nut.

3. Adjust travel to one in. Tighten locknut.

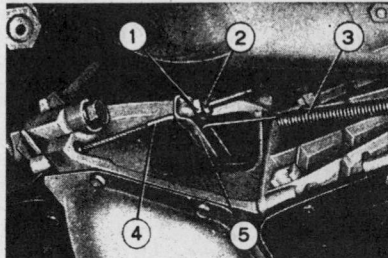

Clutch free play adjusting location —124; 850 similar

1. Pullrod adjusting nut
2. Locknut
3. Clutch fork return spring
4. Flexible cable
5. Fork lever

124

1. Jack up the front of the car.

2. Adjustment is made at the cable nut at the clutch release lever as shown in the illustration.

3. Adjust the pedal travel to 0.98 in.

Clutch Master Cylinder

Removal and Installation

X1/9

NOTE: *The upper steering column assembly must first be removed to gain access to the clutch master cylinder.*

1. Disconnect the battery.

2. Remove the five screws retaining the steering column upper and lower trim halves.

3. Disconnect the column wiring (three connectors and one wire).

4. Remove the two nuts and two bolts retaining the upper column assembly to the underside of the dashboard. Support the column and steering wheel assembly and pull it straight back and out, disconnecting it from the steering box shaft. Remove the complete column and steering wheel assembly from the car.

5. Place absorbant rags over the driver's side floor carpets. Locate the master cylinder up over the clutch pedal. Disconnect and plug the fluid line to the slave cylinder.

6. Remove the two retaining bolts. Pull the cylinder out far enough to disconnect and plug the fluid line to the reservoir. Pull the cylinder off the pushrod. Remove from car.

7. Reverse steps 1–6 to install. Refill the fluid reservoir and bleed the hydraulic system.

Clutch Slave Cylinder

Removal and Installation

X1/9

1. Disconnect and plug the fluid line banjo connector from the rear of the slave cylinder.

2. Remove the cotter pin from the end of the slave cylinder pushrod.

3. Disconnect the release arm return spring.

4. Remove the two slave cylinder retaining bolts and remove the cylinder.

5. Reverse steps 1–4 to install, using

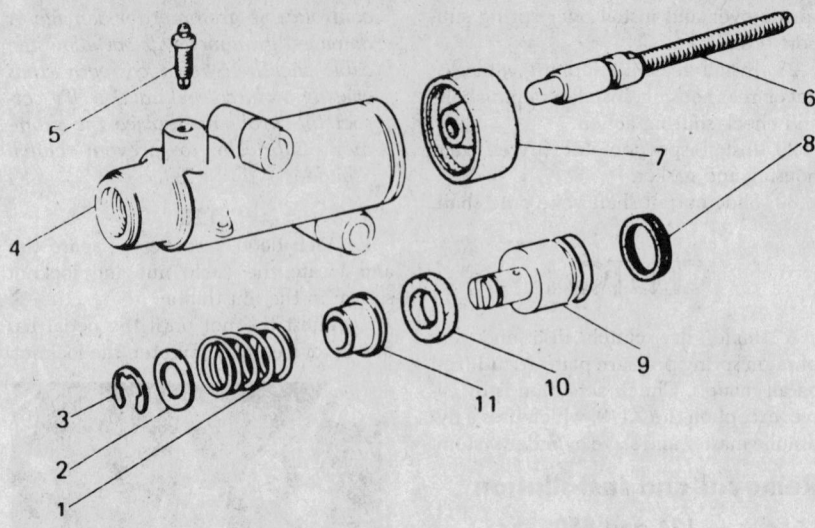

Exploded view of clutch slave cylinder—X1/9

1. Spring
2. Washer
3. Lockring
4. Housing
5. Bleeding screw
6. Rod
7. Boot
8. Seal
9. Piston
10. Seal
11. Bushing

new copper gaskets at the fluid line banjo connector. Bleed the hydraulic system. Adjust clutch pedal free-play, if necessary.

Hydraulic System Bleeding

X1/9

1. Connect a bleeder hose to the slave cylinder bleeder nipple. Place the other end of the hose in a container partially filled with brake fluid. Make sure the hose end is immersed in fluid.

2. Fill up the clutch fluid reservoir with clean brake fluid. Open the bleeder nipple screw.

3. Have an assistant pump the clutch pedal until all air bubbles stop coming

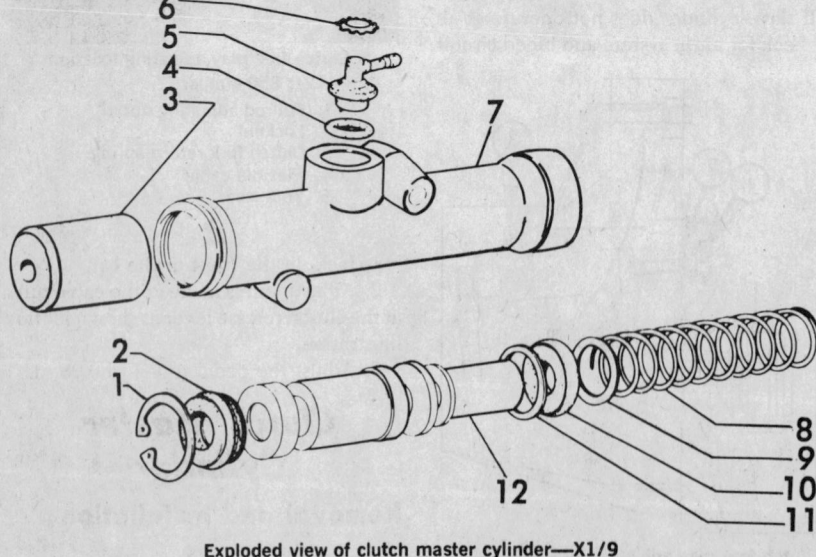

Exploded view of clutch master cylinder—X1/9

1. Lockring
2. Seal
3. Boot
4. Gasket
5. Connector
6. Lockplate
7. Cylindetr
8. Spring
9. Seal
10. Seal
11. Gasket
12. Plunger

out of the hose. Periodically check the reservoir level so that it doesn't run dry.

4. When all air is expelled, close the nipple screw and remove the hose. Discard the old clutch (brake) fluid. Refill the reservoir and check clutch operation.

AUTOMATIC TRANSMISSION

The automatic transmission available in the 124 and 131 series is the GM/Adam Opel Trimatic. It is a three-speed unit with a variable torque multiplication ratio of between 2.4 to 1 and 1 to 1.

Pan Removal and Filter Service

1. Raise the car and support it safely.

2. Drain all fluid from the oil pan.

3. Remove the oil pan and gasket. Discard the old gasket.

4. Remove the strainer assembly and strainer gasket and discard the gasket.

5. Install a new oil strainer gasket. Install a new strainer assembly.

6. Install a new gasket on the oil pan and install the pan. Tighten the attaching bolts to 7–10 ft. lbs.

7. Lower the car and add approximately three (3) pints of transmission fluid (Dexron) through the filler tube.

8. With the manual control lever in the Park position, start the engine. DO NOT RACE THE ENGINE. Move the manual control lever through each range.

9. Immediately check the fluid level with the selector lever in Neutral, engine running, and vehicle on a level surface.

10. Add additional fluid to bring the level to ¼ in. below the ADD mark on the dipstick. Do not overfill.

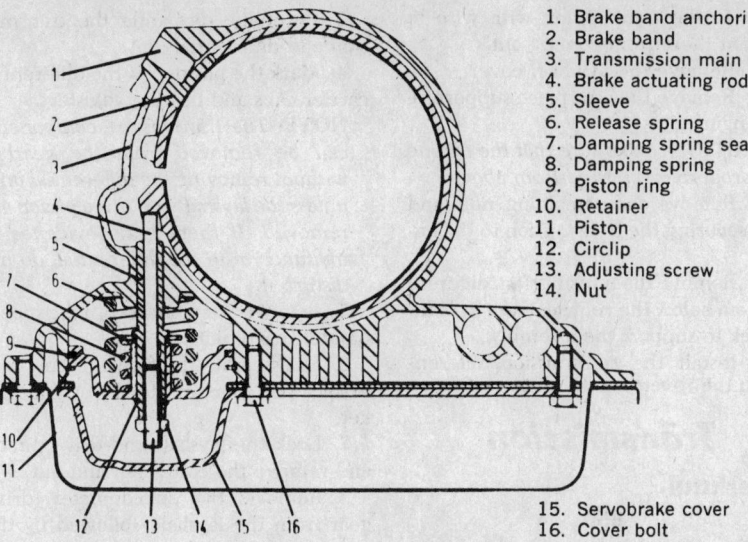

1. Brake band anchoring pin
2. Brake band
3. Transmission main case
4. Brake actuating rod
5. Sleeve
6. Release spring
7. Damping spring seat
8. Damping spring
9. Piston ring
10. Retainer
11. Piston
12. Circlip
13. Adjusting screw
14. Nut
15. Servobrake cover
16. Cover bolt

Band adjustment—124, 131 automatic

Band Adjustment

1. Drain the transmission.
2. Remove the pan and gasket.
3. Remove the servo brake band cover.
4. Loosen the locknut for the servo brake adjusting screw.
5. Tighten the adjusting screw to 40 *inch pounds.* Then, back off the adjusting screw five full turns.
6. Without disturbing the adjustment, tighten the locknut to 12-15 ft-lbs.
7. Install the servo brake band cover, using a new gasket. Tighten to 17–19 ft-lbs.
8. Install the pan and gasket. Tighten to 7–10 ft-lbs.

9. Fill the transmission with Dexron automatic transmission fluid. Follow steps 7–10 under "Pan Removal and Filter Service".

Gear Selector Linkage Adjustment

1. With the engine off, place the shift lever in Drive.
2. Jack up the front of the car and support with jackstands.
3. Disconnect the shifter tie rod at the relay lever (shift lever).
4. Move the cross shaft actuating lever (shift lever on transmission) to the Drive position, which is third detent from the front.

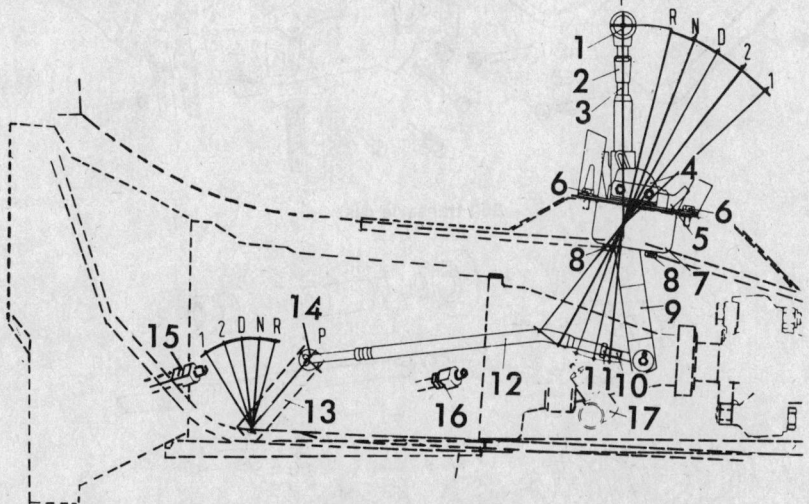

Selector lever linkage adjustment—124, 131 automatic

1. Upper handle
2. Lower handle
3. Selector lever
4. Starter inhibitor switch
5. Gear selector
6. Bolt
7. Support
8. Bracket bolt
9. Relay lever
10. Tie rod adjustable end
11. Adjusting nut
12. Tie rod
13. Cross shaft actuating lever
14. Flat washer
15. Oil union
16. Oil union
17. Speedometer drive support
18. Bracket
19. Flat washer
20. Bushing
21. Cotter pin
22. Cotter pin
23. Gear selector bolt

5. Without disturbing either of the two levers, try to insert the end of the shifter tie rod into the relay lever. If necessary, loosen the adjusting nut and rotate until the tie rod end will just slip into the eye of the relay lever. Then, tighten the adjusting nut. Connect the tie rod to the relay lever using a new circlip.

6. Remove the jackstands and lower the car. Check shifter operation.

TRANSAXLE

Removal and Installation

850

The transmission and differential are incorporated into a single case. The transmission uses four forward gears, all synchronized, the 4th gear being an overdrive. Synchronizing rings are of the sliding type.

1. Disconnect the cable from positive terminal of battery.
2. Remove the engine compartment lid, upper headlining, generator and starter.
3. Jack car up at the rear and place it on stands.
4. Disconnect the shock absorbers from lower mountings.
5. Remove the axle shaft universal joints.
6. Disconnect the clutch and speedometer cables and the gearshift rod.
7. Support the transaxle unit with a jack and remove the unit mounting screws from the engine.
8. Remove the flywheel cover and the screws which hold the transaxle support bracket to the body.
9. Adjust the position of the jack to permit disengagement of the clutch shaft from the plate, then lift out the transaxle.
10. Reverse the removal procedure to install the transaxle.

128

1. Disconnect the battery.
2. Remove the spare tire.
3. Remove the speedometer drive.
4. Disconnect the flexible cable adjusting rod from the clutch release lever and unhook the return spring.
5. Unscrew the guard-to-body nut.
6. Unscrew the transmission-to-crankcase attachment screws and nuts, accessible from above.
7. Attach the engine support crosspiece.
8. Remove the hub caps from the front wheels and unscrew the constant speed joint-to-wheel hub nuts.
9. Remove the left front wheel.
10. Disconnect the left tie-rod from the steering arm.
11. Remove the stabilizer bar.
12. Unscrew the two lower left shock absorber-to-pillar attaching screws and nuts.

13. Remove the two lower guards.

14. Unscrew the nuts which fasten the exhaust clamping bracket to the transmission.

15. Disconnect the gearshift and selection lever control rod.

16. Unscrew the starter motor-to-transmission assembly bolts.

17. Remove the engine support crossmember.

18. Remove the flywheel cover.

19. Unscrew the remaining transmission-to-engine attachment screws.

20. Disconnect the ground cable from the transmission assembly.

21. Using wire, fix the axle shafts complete with constant-speed joints, to the transmission in order to prevent them from coming away from their seats in the differential.

22. Remove the transmission-differential assembly from beneath the car using a hydraulic jack.

23. Installation is the reverse of removal.

X1/9

1. Remove the air cleaner and the carburetor cooling duct.

2. Disconnect the battery cables from the battery.

3. Disconnect the clutch slave cylinder from the clutch linkage, remove the two slave cylinder attaching bolts and move the cylinder out of the way.

4. Support the engine and remove the nuts and bolts holding the transmission to the crankcase that are accessible from above.

5. Raise the vehicle and remove the rear wheels.

6. Remove the three lower guards on the left side.

7. Mark the position of the shift tube where it is connected to the gearshift flexible link.

8. Remove the two bolts holding the flexible link to the shift tube, loosen the bolt at the transmission end of the link and swing the link out of the way.

9. Disconnect the electrical connector for the backup lights and remove the clamp securing the wires to the body.

10. Disconnect the connector for the seat belt system in the transmission. The connector is located inboard and forward of the transmission ear the engine water hoses.

11. Remove the starter from the transmission.

12. Disconnect the ground strap.

13. Remove the exhaust pipe.

14. Remove the hub nuts holding the constant speed joints to the wheel hubs.

15. Remove the two bolts and nuts securing the suspension control arms to their supports. Pull the hub off the constant speed joints and attach the axle

shafts to the transmission with wire to prevent them from coming out.

16. Remove the flywheel cover.

17. Remove the crosspiece supporting the engine.

CAUTION: *Make sure that the engine is properly supported from above.*

18. Remove the remaining nuts and bolts securing the transmission to the engine.

19. Remove the transmission/differential from below the vehicle. Use a hydraulic jack to support the assembly.

20. Install the transmission/differential in the reverse order of removal.

Transmission

Overhaul

850

1. Remove the left side mounting bracket and tie the axle shafts up, to prevent them from falling or being damaged.

2. Place the transaxle on a work stand or large smooth bench and drain the oil.

3. Carefully, dismantle the transmission and differential unit.

4. Mark the position of the differential carrier caps and bearing adjusters.

NOTE: *The transmission components can be removed from the gearbox without removing the differential unit, unless the layshaft and drive pinion are removed. If there is no evidence of malfunction in the differential, do not disturb it.*

5. Remove the support with the speedometer drive pinion.

6. Disassemble the front housing and extract the gear selector lever and gasket.

7. Lock the layshaft and drive pinion and remove the cotter pin and nut.

8. Remove the speedometer drive gear from the layshaft, followed by the retainer cover, springs and detent balls.

9. Remove the second gear sliding sleeve with fork and selector rod and the hub (with springs).

10. Slide out the reverse control upper rod and fork, red locking ball, intermedi-

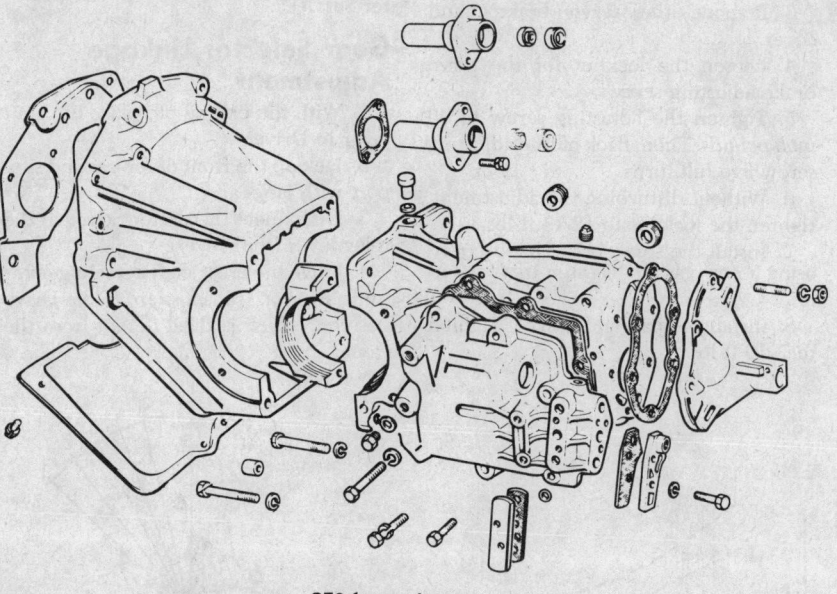

850 transaxle case

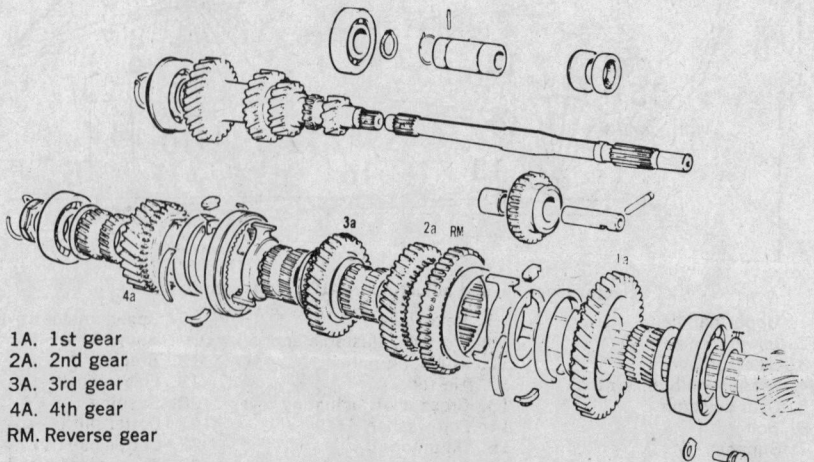

1A. 1st gear
2A. 2nd gear
3A. 3rd gear
4A. 4th gear
RM. Reverse gear

850 transmission gears

ate rod and safety roller and 3rd and 4th gear selector forks.

11. Remove the synchronizer ring, 2nd speed driven gear and bushing.

12. Unscrew the primary shaft nut and remove the washer.

13. Remove the 2nd speed drive gear, ball bearing and reverse shaft retaining plate and slide out the reverse shaft with gear.

14. Remove the front housing-to-center body mounting plate and from the plate, remove the primary shaft front bearing and layshaft front bearing.

15. Remove from the layshaft: 3rd speed driven gear and bushing; synchronizer; 3rd and 4th speed sliding sleeve and hub; first and reverse driven gear; 4th speed synchronizer and driven gear with bushing.

16. Through the front end, remove the primary shaft containing the 1st, 3rd, 4th and reverse drive gears, rear bearing and clutch shaft.

17. Remove the clutch release control assembly from the rear housing. The seal ring and intermediate support bushing will remain in the gearbox rear housing.

Thoroughly clean all parts and inspect them for cracks, burrs, wear and runout. Any parts not meeting specifications should be replaced. Carefully file away all burrs with a dead file.

1. Through the casing front end, install the primary shaft with 1st, 3rd, 4th and reverse speeds drive gear assembly, complete with rear bearing and clutch shaft.

2. Fit the layshaft with the following parts: 4th speed gear and bushing, 3rd and 4th speed gear synchronizer assembly, hub and 3rd and 4th speed sliding sleeve (to which the 1st speed driven gear must be keyed), 3rd speed synchronizer ring and driven gear with bushing.

3. Install the mounting plate for the center housing to front body.

4. Install the primary shaft front bearing and the layshaft front bearing.

5. Fit the reverse shaft with gear and bushing and install the retaining plate.

6. Key the 2nd speed driving gear in position and secure with a nut and washer.

7. Tighten this nut to a torque of 43 ft lbs. (early type) and 73 ft lbs. (later gearboxes).

8. Fit the 2nd speed driven gear, bushing, synchronizing ring and sliding sleeve hub to the layshaft.

9. Install the sliding sleeve with 1st and 2nd speed selector rod and fork.

10. Position the three synchronizer inner springs.

11. Insert the selector rod safety roller.

12. Slide the following parts into position: 3rd and 4th speed intermediate selector rod and fork; safety roller and ball set and reverse speed upper selector rod and fork.

13. Lock the forks on rods.

14. Install the three detent balls and springs and secure with the cover.

15. Install the speedometer driven gear.

16. Screw the nut into place on the layshaft and torque to 40 ft lbs.

17. Fit the speed selector lever and gasket to the front housing.

18. Fit the front housing to the central body and at the same time insert the speed selector lever on the selector lever dogs.

19. Install the speedometer drive pinion support.

20. Install the cotter pin and nut on the shaft.

850 Transmission Rebuilding Specifications

Ball bearing radial clearance	0.002 in. (max.)
Ball bearing axial clearance	0.02 in. (max.)
Shaft runout	0.0008 in. (max.)
Differential cage bearings	
Preload (divarication	
measured at carrier caps	
with dial indicator)	0.008-0.010 in.
Final drive backlash	0.004-0.006 in.
Oil	
Type	Fiat W 90M
Quantity	4.44 pts.

128 and X1/9

1. Remove the drain plug and drain the lubricant from the transmission/differential.

2. Remove the screws securing the oil boots and remove the axle shafts together with the oil boots.

3. Remove the nuts retaining the cover and remove the cover and gasket.

4. Remove the snap-ring from the mainshaft bearing.

5. Compress the spring washer in the countershaft and remove the snap-ring from the countershaft.

6. Remove the detent ball spring cover and gasket for the shift control rods. Remove the three ball spring and balls.

7. Remove the two ball bearings from the mainshaft and countershaft.

8. Remove the nuts attaching the transmission housing to the main case and lift the case off of the studs.

9. Remove the screws retaining the gearshift forks and dogs to the rods. Remove the rods, forks, and dogs from their seats in the housing.

10. Remove the gear selector and engagement lever support.

11. Remove the gasket between the maincase and the housing.

12. Remove the nut securing the reverse gear shaft retaining plate and remove the plate and the reverse gear shaft.

13. Remove the mainshaft and countershaft assemblies together with the differential assembly.

14. Remove the screw retaining the shift lever and remove the gear shift control rod.

15. Clean all of the parts with solvent and check the main case, housing, and cover for cracks and wear or damage to the bearing seats. Check all of the seals for deterioration or wear. Check all shafts for chipping or excessive wear. Check the splines for wear or damage.

Check and make sure that the sliding sleeve hubs for the engagement of first/second and third/fourth gears are not nicked. Check the sleeve sliding surface.

Check the synchronizer rings for signs

Compressing the spring washer on the countershaft in order to remove the snap ring

1. Spring washer compressing tool
2. Countershaft
3. Countershaft bearing
4. Snap-ring
5. Mainshaft bearing

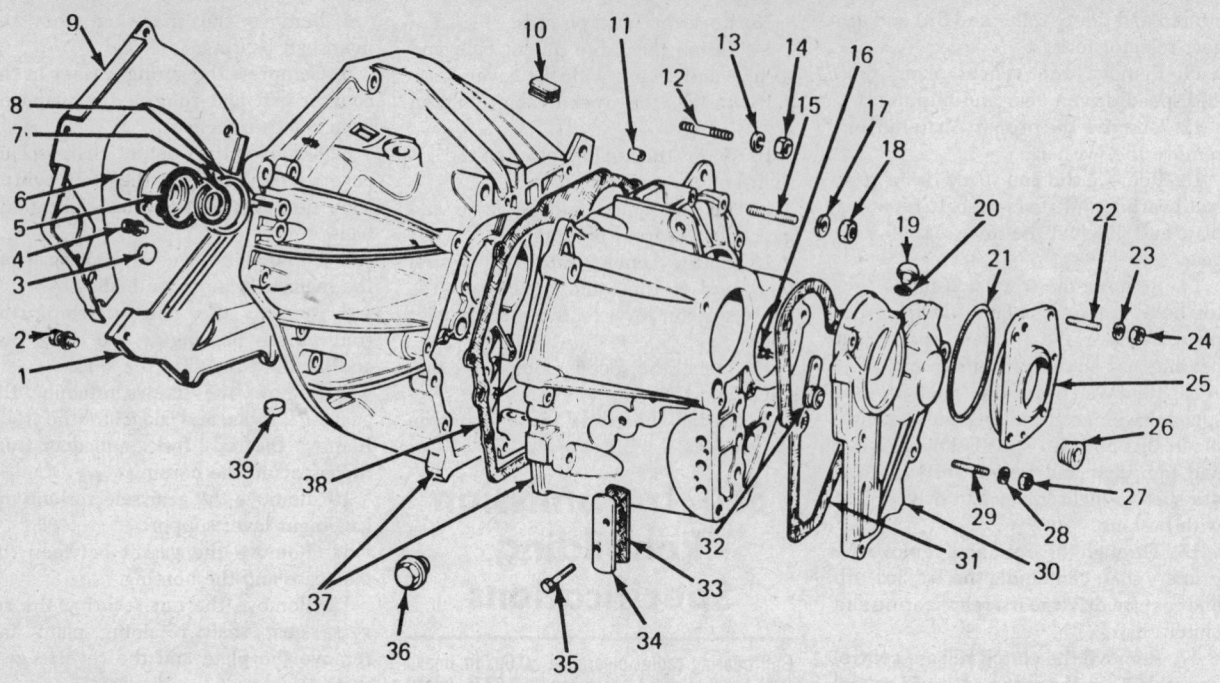

128, X1/9 transmission case

1. Cover	11. Dowel	21. Seal	31. Gasket
2. Bolt and washer	12. Stud	22. Stud	32. Magnet
3. Plug	13. Lockwasher	23. Lockwasher	33. Gasket
4. Bolt and washer	14. Nut	24. Nut	34. Cover
5. Gasket	15. Stud	25. Flange	35. Bolt
6. Cover	16. Bolt and washer	26. Plug	36. Plug
7. Seal	17. Lockwasher	27. Nut	37. Case
8. Plug	18. Nut	28. Lockwasher	38. Gasket
9. Cover	19. Vent	29. Stud	39. Plug
10. Plug	20. Gasket	30. Cover	

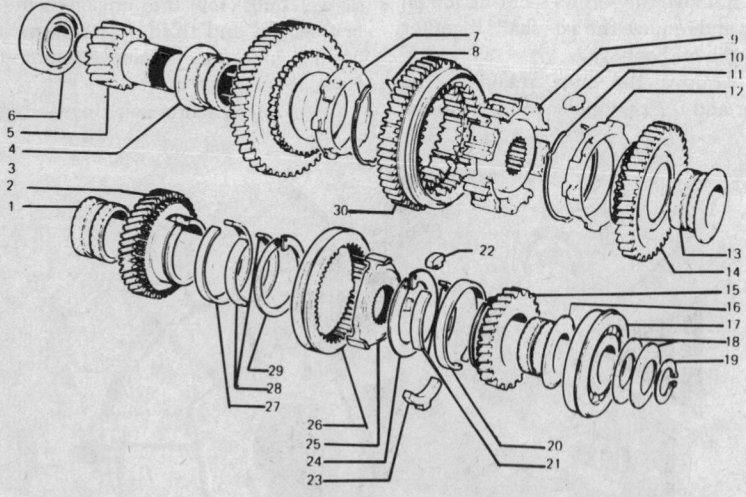

128, X1/9 countershaft

1. Bushing	11. Spring	21. Spring
2. Driven gear	12. Synchronizer	22. Pad
3. Driven gear	13. Bushing	23. Pad
4. Bushing	14. Driven gear	24. Snap ring
5. Countershaft	15. Gear	25. Hub
6. Bearing	16. Bushing	26. Sleeve
7. Synchronizer	17. Bearing	27. Synchronizer
8. Spring	18. Spring washer	28. Spring
9. Hub	19. Snap ring	29. Snap ring
10. Pad	20. Synchronizer	30. Sleeve

of deterioration on the inside surface and on the teeth that mesh with the sliding sleeves. The rings must not be loose in its gear seat.

If splined parts do not slide easily and smoothly, remove the cause with a very fine file or replace the defective parts.

16. Install the bearing for the countershaft into the clutch cover end of the transmission case.

17. Install the outer bearing race for the differential bearing into the case.

18. Install the gear shift control rod in the housing with the spring, gasket, cover, and boot. Next install the control lever.

19. Install the differential assembly in the housing.

20. Install the countershaft assembly in the housing.

21. Install the mainshaft assembly in the housing.

22. Install the reverse gear shaft with its gasket in the housing. Secure the reverse gear shaft assembly with the plate and nut.

23. Install the gasket onto the housing mating surface.

24. Make sure that the gear selector and engagement lever is seated on the control lever attached to the gear control rod. Install the support for the selector

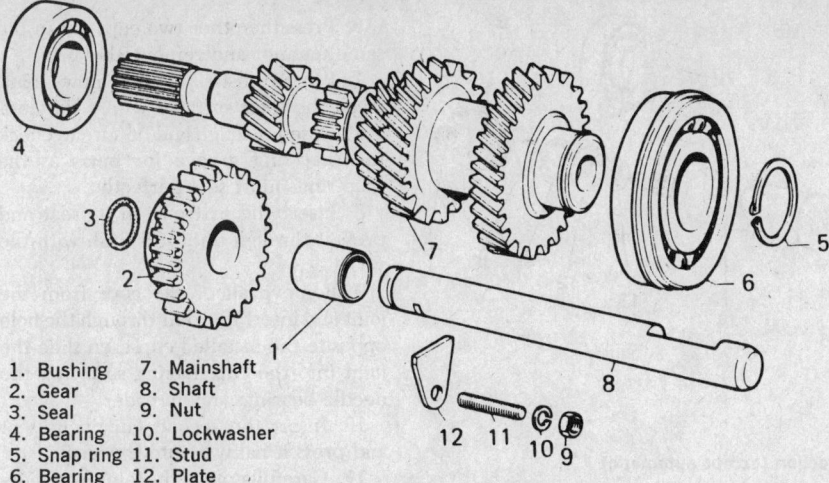

1. Bushing
2. Gear
3. Seal
4. Bearing
5. Snap ring
6. Bearing
7. Mainshaft
8. Shaft
9. Nut
10. Lockwasher
11. Stud
12. Plate

128, X1/9 mainshaft and reverse gear

and engagement lever on the housing. Secure the support with the nut.

25. Install the rod detent rollers in their seats on the support.

26. Install the gear selector rods, forks, and dogs.

27. Install the transmission case on the housing.

28. Secure the two halves of the transmission case together with the washers and nuts.

29. Install the three detent balls and springs in the transmission case.

30. Install the gasket and spring retainer cover. Secure the cover with the two bolts.

31. Install the bearing on the mainshaft and the bearing on the countershaft. Install the two spring washers and snap-ring on the countershaft. Install the snap-ring on the mainshaft.

32. Install the gasket and cover on the transmission.

33. Set the differential bearing. (See differential overhaul.)

34. Install the clutch release forked lever and sliding sleeve.

35. Place the axle shafts in the differential. Place the oil boots covers on the differential and secure the covers with the three bolts. Tie up the shafts to prevent them from falling out.

Shift Linkage Adjustment

128 and X1/9

1. Place the transmission in Neutral.

2. Loosen the two adjustment screws at the transmission end of the shift rod.

3. Place the gear shift lever in the neutral position (centered and straight up and down) and tighten the two adjusting screws at the transmission end of the shift rod. The holes in the flexible shift rod are slotted to allow for adjustment.

850

1. Jack up the rear of the car.

2. Place the transmission in neutral.

3. Loosen the gear selector and actuating lever rod retaining screws at the transmission.

4. Place the gear shift lever in the neutral position and tighten the gear selector and actuating lever rod retaining screws.

5. Lower the rear of the vehicle.

DRIVE AXLES
Driveshaft and U-Joints

124 and 131

Fiat 124 and 131 driveshafts are in two parts; a splined tubular front piece connected to the transmission through a flexible spider coupling and a solid rear piece, connected to the front piece by a

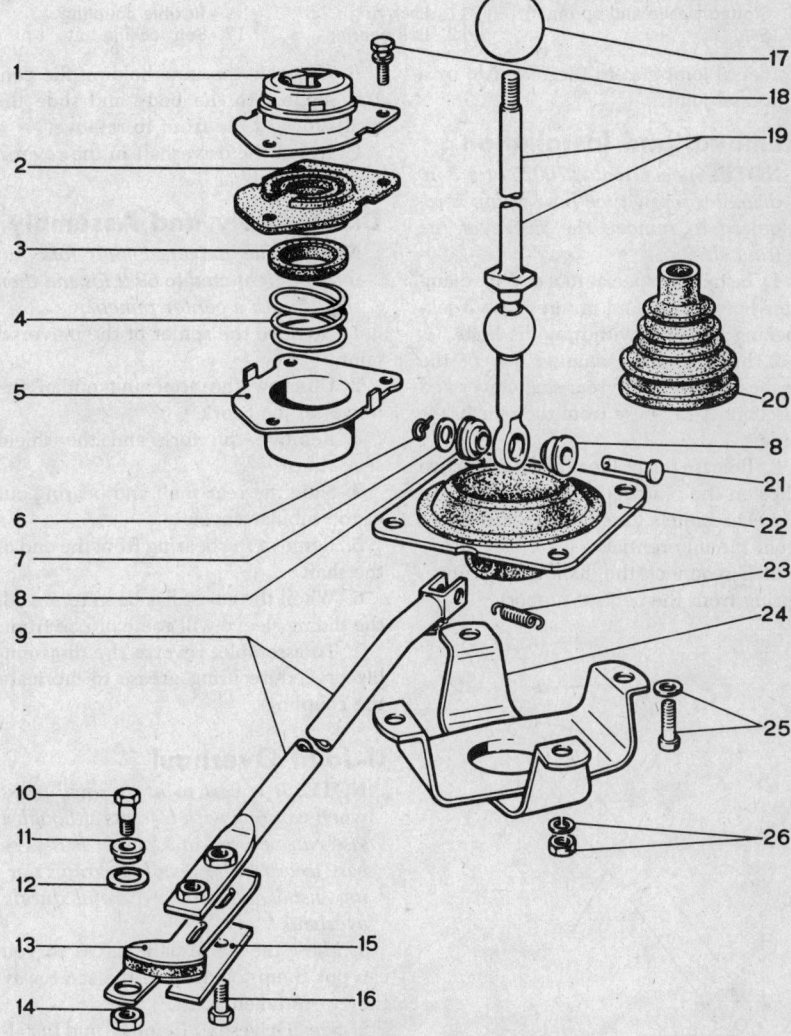

Gear shift mechanism for 128, X1/9 similar

1. Guide plate
2. Upper socket
3. Lower socket
4. Spring
5. Support
6. Cotter pin
7. Flat washer
8. Bushings
9. Rod
10. Screw
11. Bushing
12. Spring washer
13. Flexible rod
14. Nut
15. Plate
16. Screw
17. Knob
18. Screw
19. Lever
20. Dust boot
21. Pin
22. Guard and boot
23. Return spring
24. Guard
25. Screw and washer
26. Nut and spring washer

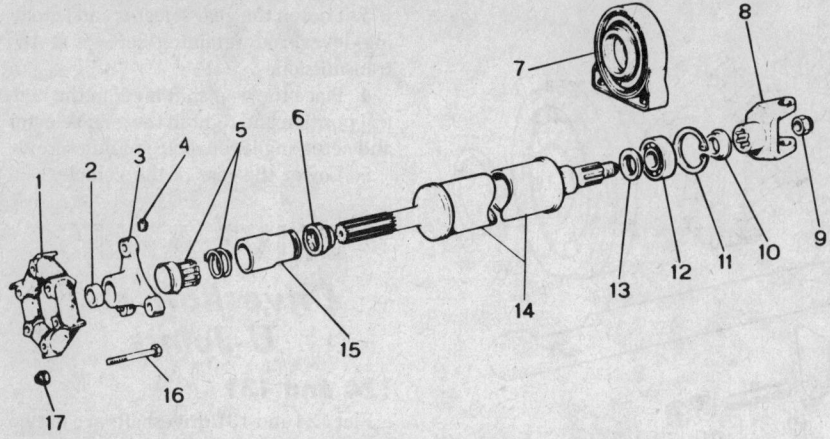

124, 131 driveshaft front section (except automatic)

1. Flexible coupling
2. Bushing
3. Sleeve
4. Lubrication fitting
5. Slotted sleeve and spring
6. Seal
7. Resilient pad
8. Yoke
9. Nut
10. Disc
11. Lock ring
12. Ball bearing
13. Disc
14. Front prop shaft
15. Socket
16. Bolts securing sleeve to flexible coupling
17. Self locking nut

universal joint and to the rear axle by a universal joint.

Removal and Installation

NOTE: *Special tool A.70025 or a 5 in. diameter screw type hose clamp is required to remove the sleeve of the front shaft.*

1. Install the special tool or 5 in. diameter hose clamp and unscrew the 3 self-locking nuts and withdraw the bolts.

2. Remove the retaining clip of the brake hose from the rear shaft cover and disconnect the hose from the rear brake pipe.

3. Release the brake pipe from the two clips on the rear shaft cover.

4. Disconnect the rear shaft cover from the differential.

5. Disconnect the handbrake return spring from the central support.

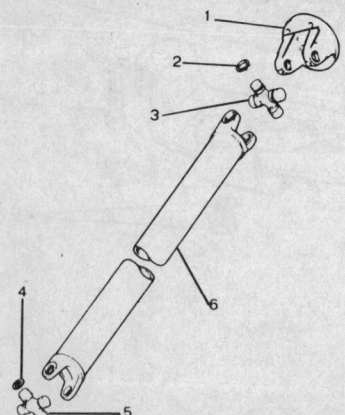

124, 131 driveshaft rear section

1. Fork connecting rear prop shaft to drive pinion sleeve
2. Spider snap ring
3. Spider assy.
4. Snap ring
5. Spider assy.
6. Rear prop shaft

6. Unscrew the nuts holding the central support to the body and slide the shafts toward the front to remove.

7. Install the driveshaft in the reverse order of removal.

Disassembly and Assembly

NOTE: *The universal joint fork nut must be tightened to 69 ft lbs and then staked with a center punch.*

1. Remove the spider of the universal joint.

2. Unscrew the attaching nut of the universal joint fork.

3. Remove the fork and the shield snap-ring.

4. Slide the rear shaft and bearing out of the tubular cover.

5. Remove the bearing from the end of the shaft.

6. When the cover has been removed, the sliding sleeve will come off the front.

7. To assemble, reverse the disassembly procedure using grease to lubricate the couplings.

U-Joint Overhaul

NOTE: *It is best to use a small press when working with U-joints although a vise can be used in a pinch. It is very easy to crush the needle bearings during installation, so be careful during overhaul.*

1. Mark the driveshaft halves so you can put them together in the same way they were taken apart.

2. See "Driveshaft Removal and Installation" and remove the shaft.

3. Remove the snap-rings which retain the cups.

4. Press the joint toward the center. This will make one of the cups accessible with pliers.

5. Remove the cup, turn the shaft over and press out the other side.

6. Press the other two cups out in the same manner and remove the joint.

7. Before installing the new joint, clean the shaft surfaces where the cups are pressed through and be sure to check the snap-ring groove for burrs as the snap-rings must seat perfectly.

8. Insert the first cup in its seat and press it through until it is flush with the shaft.

9. Remove all of the cups from the joint and insert the joint through the hole opposite the installed cup then slide the joint into the cup making sure that the needle bearings stay in order.

10. Insert the second cup in its seat and press it halfway into the shaft.

11. Carefully move the joint from side-to-side until it reaches the point where the joint is making contact with the needle bearings in both cups then press them together driving the second cup in far enough to insert the snap-ring.

12. Insert the ring, turn the shaft over and press the cup in and insert the other ring.

13. Use the same procedure to connect the shaft halves observing the marks made in Step 1.

14. It is best to have someone assist you in connecting the shafts together because of the weight and awkwardness of the assembly.

Axle Shafts

Removal and Installation

124

1. Jack up the rear of the car. Remove the wheels. Remove the caliper support bracket assembly without disconnecting the brake fluid lines.

2. Remove the snap-ring which retains the bearing dust cover.

3. Using a slide hammer, remove the axle shaft, complete with snap-ring, dust cover, bearing and bearing retained collar.

4. Extract the shaft oil seal and O-ring.

NOTE: *Always use a hydraulic press to remove the axle shaft bearing retaining collar.*

5. Fit the oil seal and O-ring to the housing.

6. Insert the complete axle shaft and fit the snap-ring to the housing.

7. Fit the brake disc to the axle shaft hub with two centering screws.

8. Fit the caliper support bracket and caliper assembly to the axle.

9. Fit the wheel and lower the car to the ground.

131

1. Jack up the rear of the car and block the front wheels. Release the parking brake. Remove the rear wheel.

2. Remove the two brake drum retaining bolts and pull off the drum.

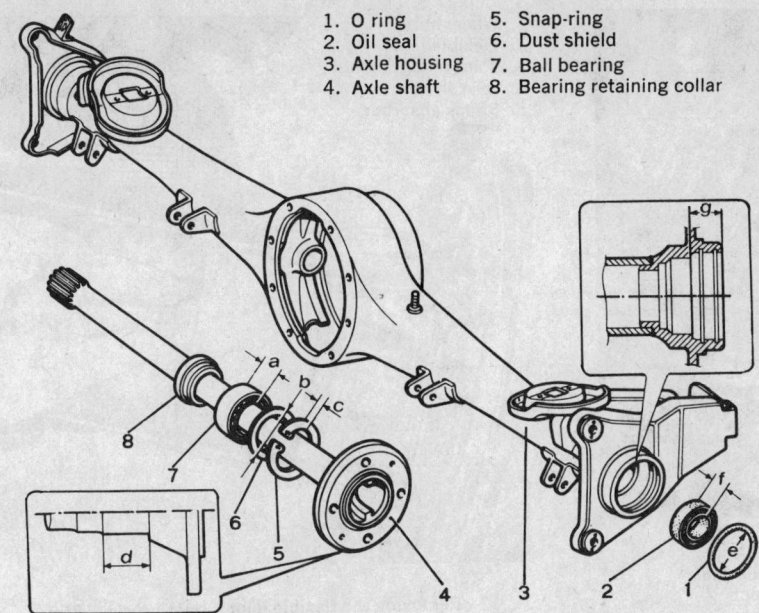

1. O ring
2. Oil seal
3. Axle housing
4. Axle shaft
5. Snap-ring
6. Dust shield
7. Ball bearing
8. Bearing retaining collar

Exploded view of 124 rear axle and axle shaft assembly

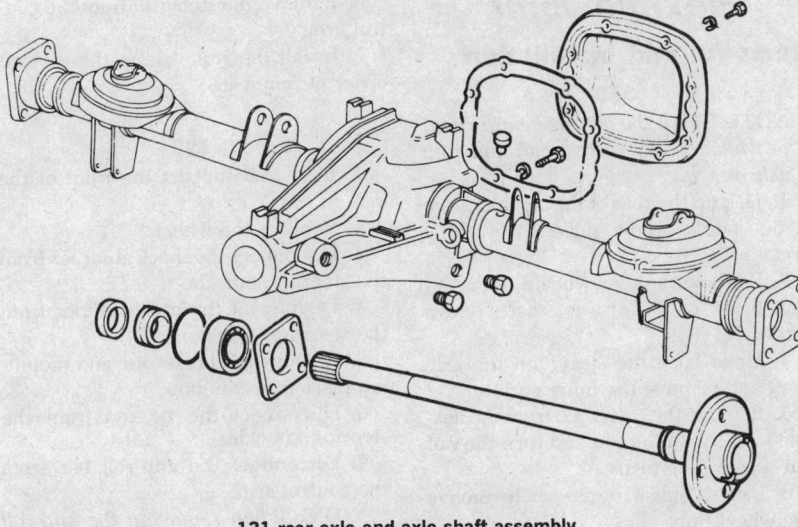

131 rear axle and axle shaft assembly

3. Working through the axle shaft flange, remove the four backing plate bolts.

4. Attach a slide hammer to the axle shaft flange and pull out the axle shaft, bearing and retainer.

NOTE: *Do not stretch or bend brake line.*

5. Remove and replace the oil seal in the axle housing.

6. Check that the axle bearing is tight against its retainer and axle shaft shoulder. If replacement is necessary, press off the retainer with an arbor press. Never reuse the retainer. To install the new retainer, heat to 578°F and press on so that the bearing inner race is locked between the retainer and axle shaft shoulder.

7. Install the axle shaft assembly. Install the backing plate bolts, brake drum, and wheel.

128

1. Drain the transmission oil.

2. Unscrew the oil seal boot at the transmission.

3. Remove the outer clamps on the boot at the constant-speed joint and pull back both boots enough to uncover both joints.

4. Clean the grease off both joints.

5. Open the sealing ring on the constant-speed joints and remove the shaft ends from their seats in the joint.

6. Turn the car wheels to enable the shafts to be fully removed from their seats in the differential.

NOTE: *Some early cars are equipped with twin type axle shafts. If it becomes necessary to replace one of these shafts it can be replaced with the later integral type shaft.*

7. Installation is the reverse of the removal procedure, bearing the following in mind.

8. When each axle shaft end has been inserted into the constant-speed joint, check that the snap-ring is lying in its axle shaft groove.

CAUTION: *Make sure that the axle shaft snap-ring is, in fact, lying in its groove. Move the shaft inward and outward a few times; this operation is necessary as correct ring setting is vital.*

9. Grease the constant-speed joint sockets and the protection boot. No more than 3 oz of grease should be used.

X1/9

1. Remove the wheel/tire assembly.

2. Remove the two bolts and nuts securing the shock absorber to the pillar.

3. Remove the nut holding the ball joint of the control arm in the pillar and remove the ball joint from the pillar.

4. Remove the nut retaining the strut ball joint to the pillar and remove the ball joint from the pillar.

5. Drain some oil from the transmission.

6. Remove the three bolts and washers retaining the oil seal boot to the differential.

7. Pull the axle shaft and wheel hub from the differential.

8. Remove the brake caliper and support bracket from the pillar.

9. Remove the bolts securing the retaining plate and brake rotor to the hub and remove the plate and rotor.

10. Remove the clamp retaining the

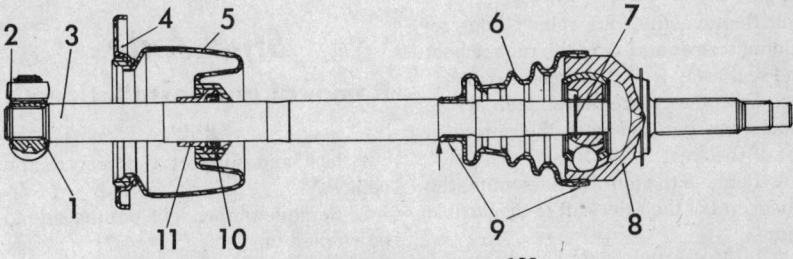

Left axle shaft assembly—128

1. Tripod joint
2. Circlip
3. Axle shaft
4. Flange
5. Oil seal boot
6. Boot
7. Snapring
8. Constant-speed joint
9. Boot clamps
10. Sealing ring
11. Bushing

The arrow indicates the shoulder with which the boot
(6) should be in contact after installation

383

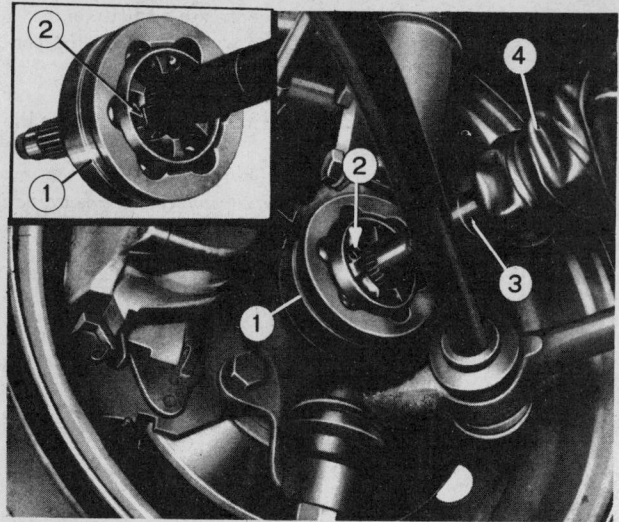

Removing axle shaft for constant-speed joint—128

1. Constant-speed joint
2. Sealing ring
3. Axle shaft
4. Boot

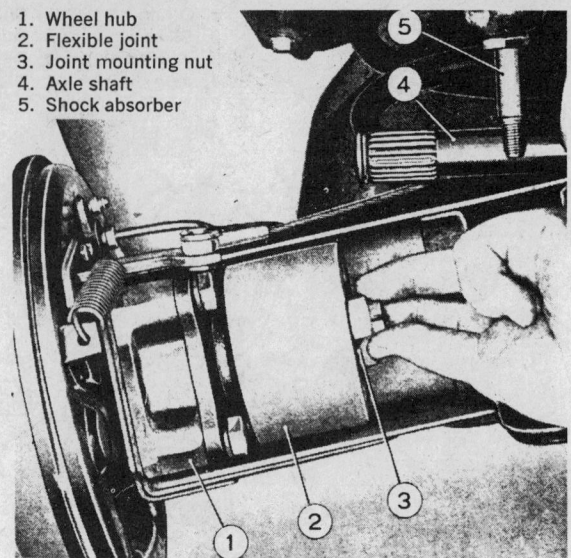

1. Wheel hub
2. Flexible joint
3. Joint mounting nut
4. Axle shaft
5. Shock absorber

Removing the flexible joint mounting nut—850

boot to the constant-speed joint and pull the boot back to uncover the joint. Clean the grease off of the joints.

11. Remove the lock-ring from the constant-speed joints, using a pair of pliers.

12. Remove the axle shaft from the constant-speed joint.

13. Install the axle shaft in the reverse order of removal. After installing the axle shaft in the constant-speed joint and installing the snap-ring in the groove of the axle shaft, make sure the snap-ring is properly seated by moving the shaft in and out. Grease the constant-speed joint with no more than 3 ozs of grease.

850

The axle shafts are coupled to the differential through slip joints which allow the shafts to slide and swing along an internal spline in the side gear.

At the opposite end of the axle shafts are connected to the wheel shafts through a flexible joint splined sleeve.

1. Jack up the rear of the vehicle and support it.

2. Remove the four rubber boot retaining screws and slide the rubber boot and seal away from the transmission.

3. Disconnect the lower end of the shock absorber and push the piston up out of the way.

4. Remove the four bolts retaining the wheel end of the axle shaft to the flexible joint.

5. Push the axle shaft into the transmission slightly so to clear the flexible joint and then withdraw the axle shaft from the transmission and out from under the vehicle.

6. Install the axle shaft in the reverse order of removal.

Flexible Joint
Removal and Installation
850

NOTE: *This is the outside bearing joint to which the axle driveshaft and stub axle attach.*

1. Jack up the rear of the car and place it on stands. Allow sufficient working area.

2. Remove the rear wheels.

3. Back out the axle shaft sleeve screws.

4. Move back the sleeve on the axle shaft and remove the inner spring.

5. Remove the cotter pin from the flexible joint mounting nut and turn the nut out 4 complete turns.

6. Using a slide hammer partly remove the wheel hub.

7. Turn the mounting nut out all of the way and remove the flexible joint.

8. Install the new joint and torque the mounting nut to 101 ft lbs.

9. Insert a new cotter pin. If the slots do not align, tighten the nut until the pin slides freely into its seat.

Stub Axle
Removal and Installation
850

1. Jack and support the rear of the vehicle.

2. Remove the wheel from the side to be worked on.

3. Disconnect the axle shaft flange from the flexible joint.

4. At this point you must decide if the brake drum is to be removed from the stub axle now or after the stub axle and drum are removed from the vehicle.

5. Remove the flexible joint.

6. Remove the stub axle from the control arm.

7. Install the stub axle in the reverse order of removal.

128

1. Raise and support the front of the car.

2. Remove the wheel.

3. Disconnect the shock absorber from the steering knuckle.

4. Disconnect the brake caliper from the steering knuckle.

5. Remove the brake disc and mounting plate from the hub.

6. Disconnect the tie rod from the steering knuckle.

7. Disconnect the anti-roll bar from the control arm.

NOTE: *When removing the anti-roll bar from the control arms, make sure to take note of the number of adjustment shims inserted between the ends of the bar and the control arm bushings so they can be replaced in their original positions.*

8. Disconnect the control arm from the body.

9. If necessary, remove the control arm from the steering knuckle.

10. Remove the stub axle from the steering knuckle with a press.

11. Install the stub axle in the reverse order.

X1/9

1. Remove the axle shaft.

2. Remove the hub and pillar assembly from the car.

3. Remove the hub nut and washer.

4. Pull the constant-speed joint out of the hub.

5. Press the hub from the pillar.

6. Remove the ring nut securing the

bearing in the pillar and remove the bearing from the pillar.

7. Install the new bearing in the pillar.

8. Screw the *new* ring nut into the pillar to hold the bearing. Tighten the nut to 43 ft lbs. Fiat tool A.57123 is the socket used to tighten the nut.

NOTE: *Whenever the bearing in the pillar is replaced, use a new ring nut. It is necessary to replace the bearing every time the hub (stub axle) is removed from the pillar.*

9. Press the hub into the pillar.

10. Install the constant-speed joint into the hub.

11. Install the washer and hub nut and tighten the nut to 100 ft lbs. Stake the nut with a punch.

Differential

Removal

124

To remove only the differential, use the following procedure.

1. Unscrew the drain plug in the lower part of the axle housing and drain the gear oil.

2. Jack the rear of the car and remove the rear wheels. Disconnect the driveshaft.

3. Withdraw the axle shafts far enough to disengage them from the side gears.

4. Unbolt and remove the differential from the housing.

Disassembly

1. Matchmark the bearing caps and bosses. Remove the bolts and lockplates from the bearing caps. The lockplates hold the bearing adjusters in place.

2. Remove the caps, adjuster rings and roller bearing cups.

3. Withdraw the differential case from the carrier, complete with gears, ring gear and bearing cones.

4. Turn the carrier upside down and by locking the pinion, unscrew the pinion nut.

5. Withdraw the pinion, complete with thrust ring, rear roller bearing cone and collapsible spacer.

6. Remove the oil seal, oil slinger and front bearing cone.

7. Remove the cup of the rear roller bearing with a drift. Remove the front roller bearing cone with a driver.

8. Slide the collapsible spacer from the pinion and pull the cone of the rear roller bearing and thrust washer from the pinion.

9. Remove the cones of the bearings in which the differential case runs.

10. Remove the screws retaining the ring gear to the case and drift out the pinion gears shaft from the case.

11. Rotate the side and pinion gears and remove these and their thrust washers from the case.

Inspection

Check all gears for damage or wear. Very slight wear damage can be corrected with very fine abrasive paper. Inspect the side gear thrust washers. If the thrust washers are only slightly defective polish them. Be sure that the case and carrier are not cracked.

Assembly

Assemble the side gears and thrust washers in the case. Insert the pinion gears through the opening in the case and engage them with the side gears. Align the holes in the pinion gears with the holes in the case and insert the pinion gears shaft. Check the axial play in each

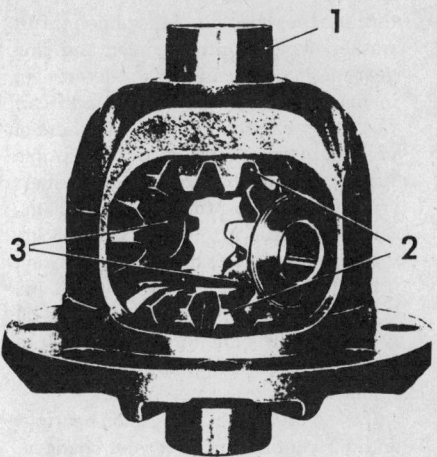

Assembly of side gears in the differential case.

1. Differential case
2. Side gears
3. Pinion gears

Arrange the pinion gears as shown in the figure and push them into place by rolling them on the side gear.

side gear. The play should be from 0.004 in. max. If the side gear play is excessive, replace the thrust washers with thicker ones, to bring the axial play within specifications. Service thrust washers are supplied in the following sizes: 0.070 in., 0.072 in., 0.074 in., 0.076 in., 0.078 in., 0.080 in. and 0.082 in. If the thrust washers were changed, measure the clearance again. If new thrust washers fail to bring the clearance within specifications, the side gears are excessively worn and must be replaced. Fit the ring gear to the case and torque the bolts to 72 ft lbs. Fit the cones of both roller bearings with a driver of proper size.

At this point, assembly of the pinion requires a trial and error method to de-

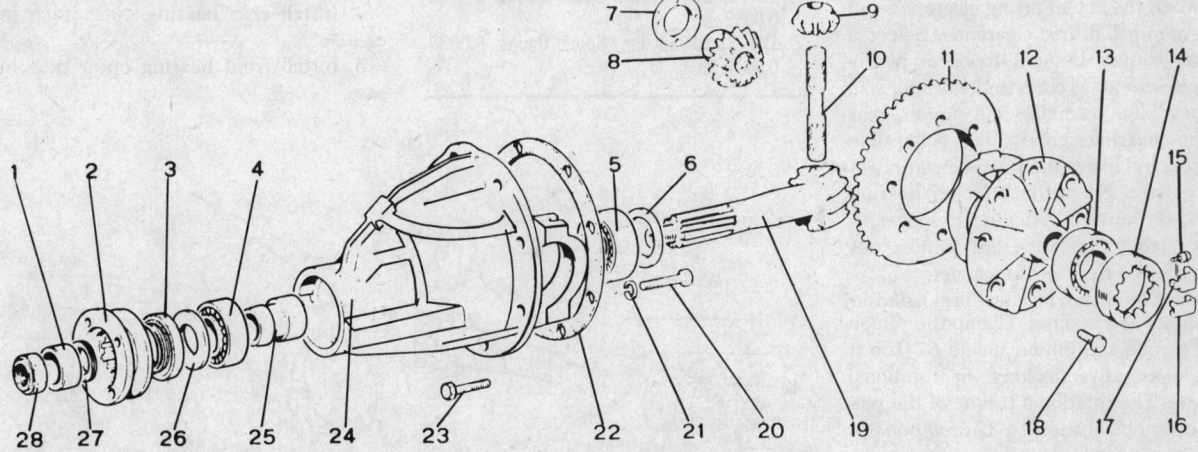

124 differential assembly

1. Spacer
2. "U" joint sleeve
3. Oil seal
4. Front roller bearing
5. Rear roller bearing
6. Pinion shaft rear roller bearing thrust washer
7. Side gear thrust washer
8. Side gear
9. Pinion gear
10. Pinion gear shaft
11. Ring gear
12. Differential case
13. Differential case roller bearing
14. Bearing adjuster ring
15. Locking plate bolt
16-17. Locking plates
18. Bolt fixing ring gear to differential case
19. Bevel pinion
20. Carrier cap bolt
21. Spring washer
22. Gasket
23. Differential carrier to axle housing bolt
24. Differential carrier
25. Collapsible spacer
26. Oil slinger
27. Plain washer
28. Bevel pinion nut

termine the thickness of the pinion thrust washer, which controls pinion and ring gear mesh, compensating for differences in machining between pinion and carrier. Assemble several thrust washers of varying thickness and several collapsible spacers. Pinion bearing thrust washers are in the following thicknesses: 0.100 in., 0.102 in., 0.104 in., 0.106 in., 0.108 in., 0.110 in., 0.112 in., 0.114 in., 0.116 in., 0.118 in., 0.120 in., 0.122 in., 0.124 in., 0.126 in., 0.128 in., 0.130 in. and 0.132 in.

Arrange the pinion gears as shown in the figure and push them into place by rolling them on the side gear.

If the pinion, ring gear, pinion bearings and differential carrier are not changed, the same collapsible spacer and pinion thrust washer may be re-used. However, if any of those parts are installed new, the thrust washer and collapsible spacer will have to be replaced with new parts.

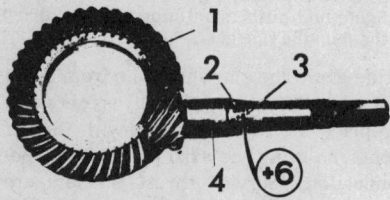

Ring gear and pinion markings

1. Ring gear
2. Serial production and matching number
3. Centesimal value of difference between actual and nominal distance
4. Bevel pinion

By comparing the number stamped on the pinion and ring gear (old or new gear sets), a reasonable determination of thrust washer thickness can be made. The number, stamped on the pinion and preceded by a (+) or (−) sign, is the difference, in hundredths of a millimeter, between the actual fitting clearance and the nominal fitting clearance. Select a thrust washer thought to be of nearly proper size (or as close to the proper size as possible). Assemble the pinion, rear roller bearing cone and collapsible spacer, and insert the pinion assembly in the carrier. Fit the front roller bearing cone, the oil seal, oil slinger, spacer u-joint sleeve, washer, and pinion nut through the front of the carrier.

The pinion bearings are preloaded in the following manner. Clamp the pinion and torque the pinion nut to 87–166 ft lbs., constantly checking the rotational torque. The rotational torque of the pinion must be between 14–17 *inch-pounds.*

NOTE: *If the tightening torque is exceeded, the collapsible spacer will have to be replaced. If the proper rotational torque cannot be obtained, the spacer will have to be removed and replaced with another.*

Fit the differential case into the carrier, complete with bearing outer races. Fit

the two bearing retaining and adjusting rings and bring them into light contact with the bearings. Fit the bearing caps and torque the bolts to 36.0 ft lbs. Temporarily adjust the ring gear and pinion backlash to 0.0031–0.0051 in. Alternately, tighten the two bearing adjusting rings the same number of turns, until the differential case bearing cap divergence measures 0.0055–0.0071 in. The ring gear backlash must remain as set.

Using a dial gauge, adjust the ring gear backlash to 0.0032–0.0051 in. It is important that if one adjuster ring is turned, the other be turned an equal amount in an opposite direction, ensuring that the preload is not altered.

Coat the ring gear with red lead and check the tooth contact pattern. Depending on the results of this test, the pinion thrust washer may have to be replaced with another of different thickness, either thicker or thinner, depending on the direction in which the pinion must be moved. Bear in mind that if this operation is necessary, the entire process will have to be repeated.

124 Differential Specifications

Pinion nut torque	87–166 ft. lbs.
Pinion turning torque	14-17 inch pounds
Bearing preload	
Differential cap spread	0.0055-0.0071 in.①
Side gear axial clearance	0.004 in. max.
Pinion and ring gear	
backlash	0.0031-0.0051②
Oil	
Type	Fiat W 90/M
Quantity	1 pt. 26 oz.

① 124 Sport Spyder, Sport Coupe 0.0063-0.0059 in.

② 124 Sport Spyder, Sport Coupe 0.0039-0.0078 in.

131

Disassembly

NOTE: *A case spreader is required to remove the carrier assembly.*

1. Drain the lubricant.
2. Pull out the axle shafts.
3. Position a case spreader on the axle housing. Matchmark the carrier bearing caps and bosses. Remove carrier bearing bolts, washers and caps. Spread case and remove carrier, bearings and shims, noting position of bearing outer races and shims.
4. Lock pinion flange and remove pinion nut and washer. Remove flange.
5. Remove oil seal and plate from pinion shaft.
6. Push out pinion shaft.
7. Remove front and rear pinion bearing outer rings.
8. Press off rear pinion bearing. Keep shims in order.
9. Pull off carrier bearings. Keep outer race, caps and shims from same side in order.
10. Remove bolts retaining ring gear to carrier.
11. Drift out pinion shaft from carrier. Remove pinion side gears and thrust washers.

Assembly

1. Position thrust washers under side gears. Install side gears in carrier.
2. Mesh pinion gears with side gears and rotate until aligned with hole for pinion shaft. Install pinion shaft in carrier.
3. Check that the rotating torque required to turn one side gear while holding the other is 22–36 ft.-lbs. If not, adjust thrust washer thickness. Washers are available in sizes from 0.0709 in. to 0.0817 in., in increments of 0.002 in.
4. Install rear bearing outer race in case.
5. Install front bearing outer race in case.

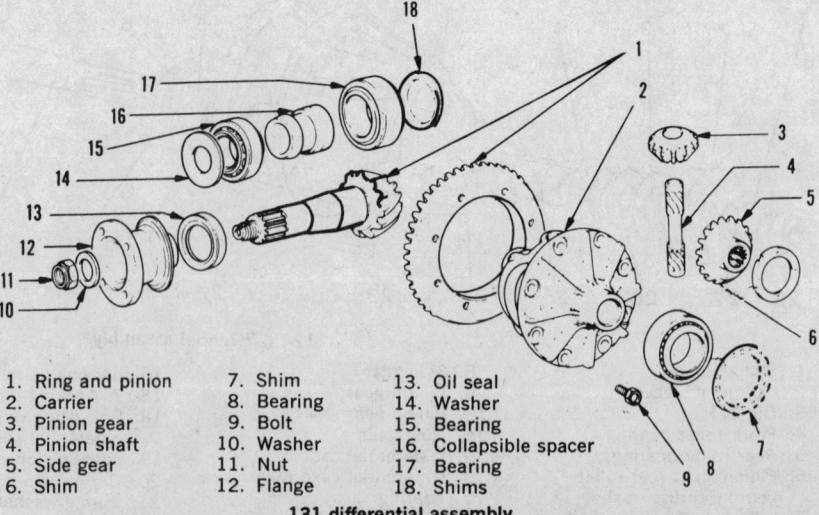

1. Ring and pinion	7. Shim	13. Oil seal
2. Carrier	8. Bearing	14. Washer
3. Pinion gear	9. Bolt	15. Bearing
4. Pinion shaft	10. Washer	16. Collapsible spacer
5. Side gear	11. Nut	17. Bearing
6. Shim	12. Flange	18. Shims

131 differential assembly

6. Install ring gear on carrier. Tighten bolts to 72 ft.-lbs.

7. Press bearings into carrier. If reusing old bearings, install in original position.

8. To determine drive pinion shim thickness, proceed as follows:

Check marking on old pinion and measure shim thickness. Add shim thickness to marking on old pinion (in hundreths of a millimeter) to obtain nominal dimension. If old pinion marking is +10 and old shim thickness is 2.90mm, nominal dimension is 3.00mm. So, if the new pinion marking is +20, then required shim thickness is 2.80mm.

9. Position shim on drive pinion and press bearing onto pinion shaft.

10. Install drive pinion in case. Install collapsible spacer, front pinion bearing and plate on pinion. Install a new oil seal in case.

11. Position U-joint flange, washer and nut on pinion. Oil pinion bearings and tighten flange nut so that rotating torque is 14–18 *inch pounds*.

12. If reusing old bearings, outer races and shims, install spreader on case. Spread case and install carrier with outer races and shims in their original positions. Install caps. Tighten bolts to 36 ft-lbs and check backlash.

13. If using new bearings or carrier, position carrier and outer race assembly in case. Install an equal amount of shims at either side; sufficient to remove any end-play. Install cap bolts and washers and tighten.

14. To measure backlash, a dial indicator is used. Block the drive pinion flange from turning. Move ring gear one way as far as it will go ans zero the indicator. Then, move it the other way as far as it will go and check the reading. If reading is not 0.003–0.005 in., adjust shim size accordingly.

15. If using new bearings or carrier, increase size of each shim by 0.002 in. Install case spreader and spread case. Install carrier bearing outer races and shims. Remove the spreader. Install bearing caps in original positions and tighten bolts to 36 ft-lbs.

16. Install rear cover with new gasket. Tighten bolts to 18 ft-lbs. Install axle shafts. Fill with lubricant.

REAR SUSPENSION
Removal and Installation
128

1. Jack up the rear of vehicle and place safety stands underneath.

2. Remove the rear wheels.

3. Plug the outlet hole of the brake fluid reservoir.

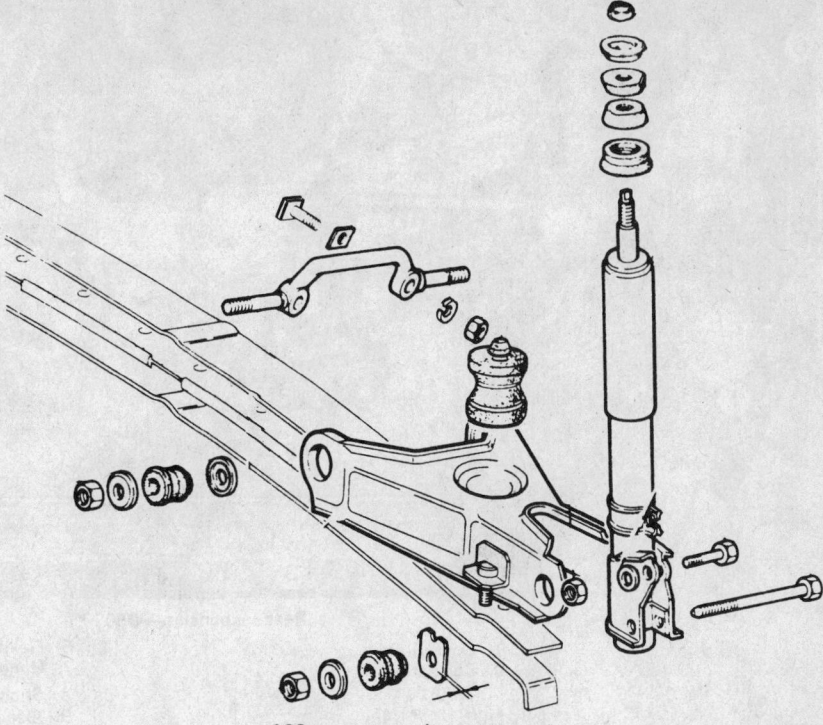

128 rear suspension components

4. Detach the flexible fluid hose from the metal pipe.

5. Release the handbrake relay lever and detach the cable from the shoe control levers on the brake backing plate.

6. Disconnect the braking regulator torsion bar from the left control arm.

7. Place a hydraulic jack under the control arm, raise the suspension, and detach the shock absorbers inside the luggage compartment. Remove the jack.

8. Detach the rubber pads which attach the leaf spring to the control arms.

9. Unscrew the nuts that attach the swivels of the control arms to the screws which pass through the plate that mounts the suspension to the body.

10. Attach the control arm to the body by passing the two screws through the plate. Finger tighten the nuts.

11. Reattach the rubber pads used to anchor the leaf spring.

12. Link the braking regulator torsion bar to the left control arm.

13. Slip the bottom rubber bushing onto the top stud of the shock absorber. Apply a hydraulic jack under the suspension and lift the whole assembly to enable the top stud of the shock absorber to be inserted into the special hole provided in the luggage compartment.

14. Mount the top rubber bushings, the retainer cap, and the self-locking nut to the top stud of the shock absorber.

15. Tighten the shock absorber nuts.

16. Reattach the handbrake control cable to the lever on the brake backing plate and reconnect the brake fluid hose and metal pipe to each other.

17. Restore the brake fluid and bleed the system.

850

1. Jack up the rear of the car and place safety stands underneath.

2. Remove a wheel and disconnect a shock absorber at the rear.

3. Tie the axle shaft off from the wheel shaft joint.

4. Disconnect the handbrake control cable from the brake shoe actuating lever.

5. Plug the brake fluid reservoir outlet and detach the brake hose from the brake line.

6. Disconnect the sway bar at the control arm and the transmission mounting bracket.

7. Back out the screws which mount the control arm to the body, at the front and the rear, noting the number of shims.

8. Using a hydraulic jack, lower the rear suspension.

9. Repeat this procedure to lower the other arm.

10. Reverse the removal procedure to install the rear suspension.

NOTE: *Upon disassembly of the rear hub, once the roller bearing in the hub has been removed it must be replaced with a new one.*

X1/9

1. Remove the wheel.

2. Disconnect the flexible brake tube from the caliper if the caliper is to be removed with the suspension assembly or, in order to save from bleeding the

Rear suspension—850

1. Control arms
2. Coil springs
3. Sway bar
4. Brake lines
5. Transmission mounting brackets
6. Flexible joints
7. Handbrake cable
8. Shocks
9. Axle shafts

brake hydraulic system, remove the caliper from the suspension assembly and support with heavy gauge wire attached to the body.

3. Disconnect the parking brake cable from the caliper, depending on whether or not it is being removed from the vehicle or not.

4. Remove the exhaust pipe.

5. Note the number of shims and their position on the control arm. Remove the nut, washer, and bolt attaching the control arm to the bracket at the front of the suspension. Allow the shims to remain between the arm and bracket.

6. Remove the nut, washer, and bolt securing the arm to the bracket at the rear of the suspension. Take note to the number of shims and their position. Al-

low the shims to remain between the arm and bracket.

7. Remove the hub nut and washer.

8. Remove the three nuts and washers securing the top of the shock absorber.

9. Slide the suspension assembly off of the constant-speed joint shaft. Position the axle shaft so that it will not come out of the differential.

To install the suspension assembly:

10. Install the shims in their original positions and loosely attach the arm to the brackets.

11. Raise the assembly and mount the hub to the constant-speed joint.

12. Insert the upper attachment of the shock absorber in the holes in the body and install the three attaching nuts and spring washers.

13. Place the washer on the axle shaft and thread a new hub nut onto the shaft. Tighten the nut to 101 ft lbs and stake the nut.

NOTE: *Always use a new hub nut.*

14. Install the exhaust pipe.

15. Install the wheel.

16. Lower the car to the ground.

17. With the vehicle laden (two people sitting inside), tighten the control arm attaching nuts to 72 ft lbs. Tighten the three upper shock absorber attaching nuts to 43 ft lbs.

124, 131

1. Jack up the rear of the car. Remove the rear wheels after placing the car on jackstands.

2. Disconnect the driveshaft.

3. Disconnect the brake lines.

4. Disconnect the handbrake cables.

5. Free the cables from their clips on the body.

6. Disconnect the shocks from inside the trunk. On 131 wagons, disconnect the shocks from their upper mounts, beneath the car.

7. Disconnect the two stabilizer bar links.

8. Disconnect the brake regulator link.

9. Support the rear axle with a hydraulic jack.

10. Disconnect the anchor rods and the sway bar.

11. Remove the assembly by lowering the jack.

12. Remove the stabilizer bar brackets and the bar.

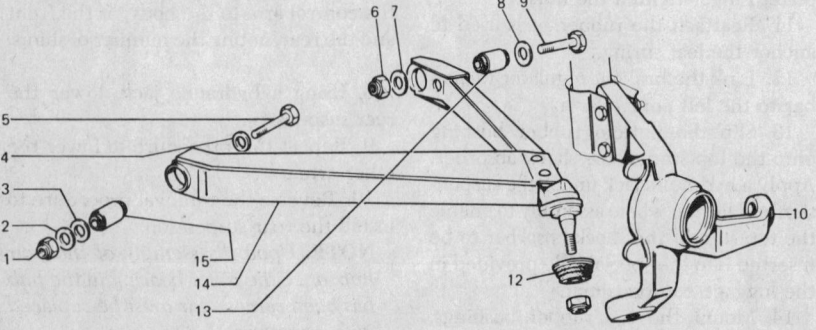

Exploded view of the rear control arm assembly for an X1/9

1. Nut
2. Washer
3. Washer
4. Washer
5. Bolt
6. Nut
7. Washer
8. Washer
9. Bolt
10. Pillar
12. Boot
13. Bushing
14. Control arm
15. Bushing

13. Remove the shocks at the spring mounts, or lower attachment (131 Wagon).

14. Remove the anchor rods and sway bar from the axle.

NOTE: *Do not tighten any bolts during assembly unless otherwise instructed. Bolts should be tightened in sequence with the vehicle on a level surface.*

15. Connect the anchor rods and the sway bar to the housing.

16. Bolt the shocks to the spring seats or lower mount (131 wagon), and tighten them.

17. Bolt up the stabilizer bar with its links, but do not tighten it completely.

18. Seat the springs with pads to the axle plates.

19. Place the jack in position.

20. Connect the axle to the body, but do not fully tighten the anchor rods to their brackets.

21. Connect the stabilizer bar links to the housing, but do not tighten fully.

22. Connect the brake regulator rod to the housing.

23. Tighten the shocks at the luggage compartment, or upper mount (131 wagon).

24. Install the driveshaft and tighten.

25. Install brake lines and handbrake cables.

26. Bleed the brake system.

27. Install the wheels. Lower the vehicle and torque the wheels to 51 ft lbs.

28. Tighten the nuts on the pivot bolts.

NOTE: *The following bolts should be tightened in the order in which they appear. They should be gradually loaded until the specified torque is obtained.*

    a. Anchor rod-to-the housing (124)— 72 ft lbs.

    b. Sway bar-to-the axle (124)—72 ft lbs.

    c. Stabilizer bar links-to-axle—25 ft lbs.

    d. Reaction strut nuts (131)—58 ft lbs.

    e. Transverse strut nuts (131)—58 ft lbs.

NOTE: *The above procedure prevents the rubber bushings from being unduly stressed.*

Adjustments

850

Toe-in is adjusted at the front mounting bracket from the trailing arm. Slotted bolt holes provide the adjustment.

128

Rear wheel camber and toe-in are adjusted at the lower control arm-to-body attaching bolts by means of shims. To increase the negative camber angle, add an equal number of shims. To decrease the negative camber angle, remove an equal number of shims. To increase toe-in, add

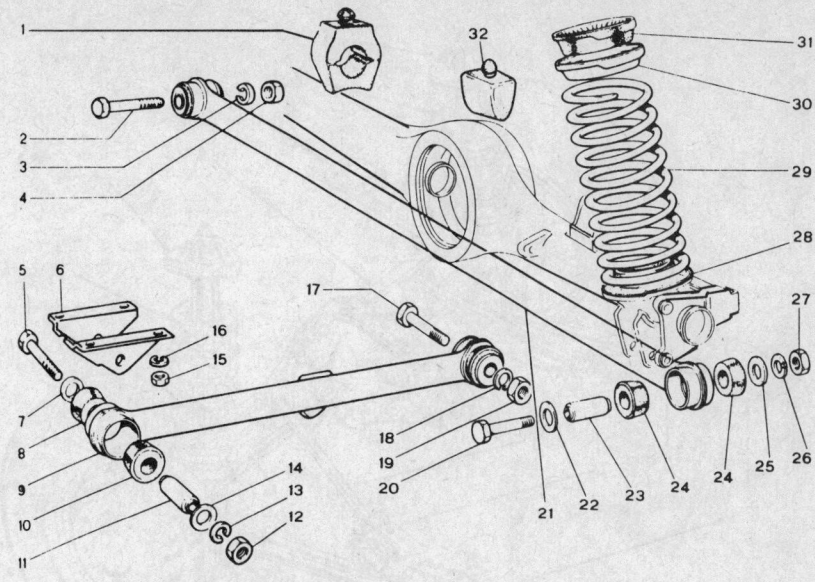

124 rear suspension rods and springs

1. Rubber pad	11. Spacer	21. Cross rod
2. Bolt anchoring cross rod to body	12. Nut	22. Flat washer
3. Lock washer	13. Lock washer	23. Spacer
4. Nut	14. Flat washer	24. Rubber bushings
5. Bolt anchoring lower side rod to bracket 6	15. Nut	25. Flat washer
6. Bracket	16. Lock washer	26. Lock washer
7. Flat washer	17. Bolt anchoring lower side rod to axle housing	27. Nut
8. Rubber bushing	18. Lock washer	28. Lower ring-pad
9. Lower side rod	19. Nut	29. Coil spring
10. Rubber bushing	20. Bolt anchoring cross rod to axle housing	30. Upper seating ring
		31. Upper rubber ring-pad
		32. Rubber buffer

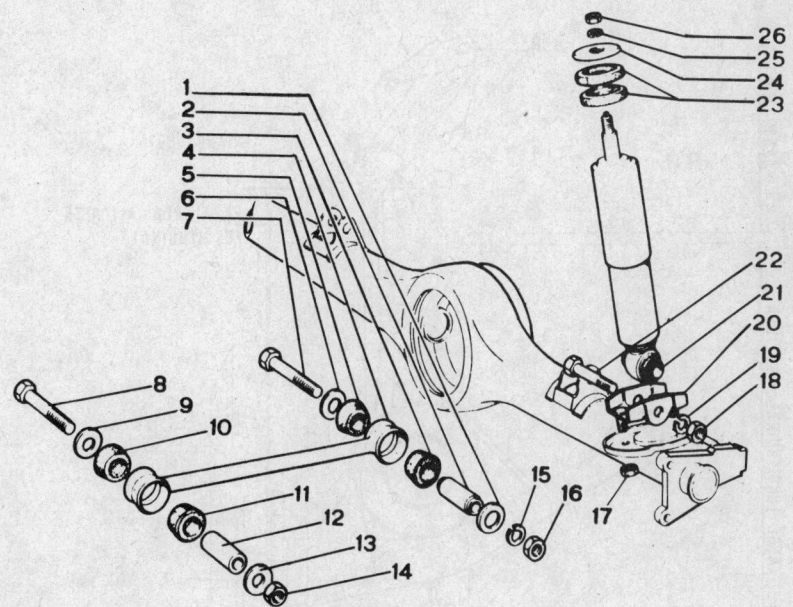

124 rear suspension shock absorbers

1. Flat washer	9. Flat washer	19. Lock washer
2. Spacer	10. Rubber bushing	20. Lower bracket
3. Rubber bushing	11. Rubber bushing	21. Shock absorber, complete
4. Upper side rod	12. Spacer	22. Bolt fixing shock absorber to lower bracket
5. Rubber bushing	13. Flat washer	23. Rubber bushing
6. Flat washer	14. Nut	24. Upper cup
7. Bolt anchoring upper side rod to axle housing	15. Lock washer	25. Lock washer
8. Bolt anchoring upper side rod to body	16. Nut	26. Nut
	17. Nut	
	18. Nut	

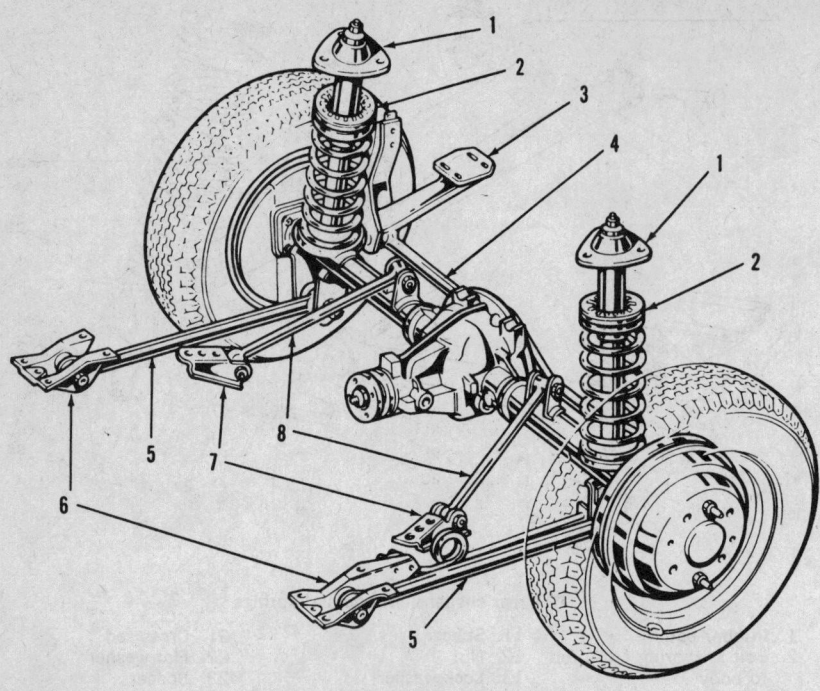

131 rear suspension (typical)

1. Shock absorber
2. Coil spring
3. Transverse strut support

4. Transverse strut
5. Lower reaction strut
6. Lower reaction strut support

7. Upper reaction strut support
8. Upper reaction strut

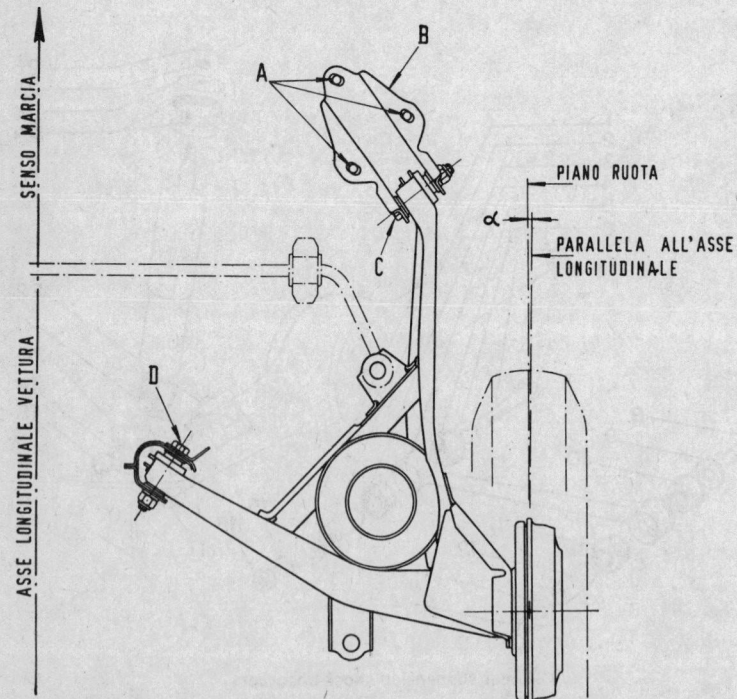

Rear wheel alignment—850

A. Screws, front bracket to underbody (recommended torque 28.9 to 36.2 ft. lbs.—4 to 5 kgm.). Tighten these screws after adjusting toe-in with wheel in vertical position —B. Front bracket of control arm—C-D. Screws and nuts, control arm to underbody. These nuts should be drawn up with 65.1 lbs. (9 kgm) of torque with care under full load—Toe in angle, with wheel in vertical position: 0° 12′ ± 6′.
Senso marcia—Direction drive. Asse longitudinale vettura—car centerline. Piano ruota—Wheel plane. Parallela al'asse longitudinale—Parallel to car centerline.

shims to the rear bolt or remove shims from the front bolt. To decrease toe-in, add shims to the front bolt or remove shims from the rear bolt.

To adjust, proceed as follows:

1. Raise the rear of the vehicle

2. Compress one end of the leaf spring to shift it from the flexible guide which anchors it to the control arm.

3. Remove the guide.

4. Slowly release the spring.

5. Unscrew the nuts which attach the pivot to the body.

6. Partly remove the screw to free the adjustment shims.

7. Carry out the required variation in the number of shims.

8. Reinsert the screw.

9. Carry out this operation on both control arm-to-body screws.

10. Adjust the other wheel as necessary.

11. Reassemble the two flexible guides which anchor the leaf spring to the control arms and tighten the attachment nuts to 22 ft lbs.

X1/9

Toe-in is adjusted by turning the reaction rod, thus lengthening or shortening the rod to the desired toe-in specification. Toe-in with the vehicle unladen should be between + 0.360 and + 0.510 in.

Camber should be −1°10′ to −2°10′.

FRONT SUSPENSION

The 124 model range is equipped with parallel upper and lower control arm front suspension. A coil spring is located between the control arms, along with a shock absorber. The steering knuckles are located in ball joints. A stabilizier bar is used on all models.

The 850 uses a transverse leaf spring front suspension. The leaf spring acts as the lower mounting point for the steering knuckle. A control arm is located on top of the knuckle. A shock absorber attaches to the steering knuckle at the bottom and to the body at the top. A stabilizer bar is used on all models.

The 128, 131, and X1/9 are equipped with MacPherson front suspension. The suspension strut acts as shock absorber, suspension (with a concentric coil spring), and upper locating member. A control arm is located at the bottom of the steering knuckle. A stabilizer bar is used on all models.

Removal and Installation

124

1. Support the front of the car with safety stands.

2. Remove the front wheels.

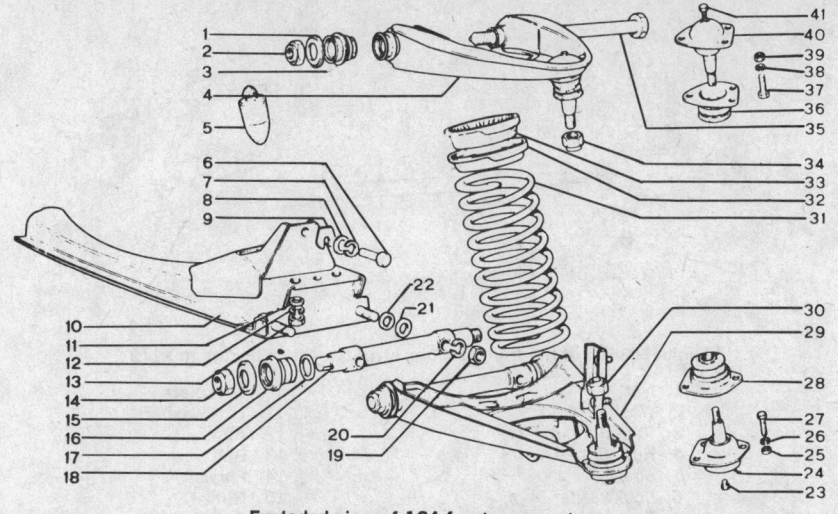

Exploded view of 124 front suspension

1. Cup
2. Nut fixing upper control arm to body
3. Resilient bushing
4. Upper control arm
5. Buffer
6. Bolt
7. Spring washer
8. Flat washer
9. Tab strip
10. Crossmember
11. Flat washer
12. Spring washer
13. Nut
14. Nut fixing pivot bar 18 to lower control arm
15. Cup
16. Resilient bushing
17. Flat washer
18. Pivot bar
19. Nut fixing lower control arm to crossmember 10
20. Spring washer
21. Flat washer
22. Tab strip
23. Plug
24. Lower ball joint
25. Nut
26. Spring washer
27. Bolt
28. Seal
29. Lower control arm
30. Self-locking nut fixing steering knuckle to lower control arm
31. Spring
32. Spring seat
33. Rubber pad
34. Self-locking nut fixing steering knuckle to upper control arm
35. Bolt
36. Seal
37. Bolt
38. Spring washer
39. Nut
40. Upper ball joint
41. Plug

3. Remove the shock.

4. Using a spring compressor, compress the spring until it is free from pressuring the control arm.

5. Disconnect the stabilizer bar at the lower control arm.

6. Disconnect the brake hoses.

7. Disconnect the tie-rod at the steering knuckle arm.

8. Unscrew the fixing nut and remove the pivot bolt to allow the control arm to separate from the body.

9. Remove the nuts which secure the lower control arm to the crossmember. Be sure to mark the number of shims removed and from which stud they were removed.

10. The assembly can now be removed and disassembled.

NOTE: *Shims are located between the body and the pivot bar to which the control arm is mounted.*

11. Install the stabilizer bar to the body.

12. Insert the shims and install the wishbone assembly, bolting the lower control arm to the crossmember.

13. Insert the spring with tool attached into its seat in the control arm.

14. Compress the spring until its height will allow you to connect the upper control arm.

15. Connect the upper control arm, but do not tighten it fully.

16. Connect the stabilizer bar to the control arm.

17. Connect the tie-rod to the steering arm.

18. Connect the brake lines.

19. Bleed the brake system.

20. Seat the spring by unloading the compressor.

21. Remove the compressor and install the shock.

22. Install the tires, lower the car and torque the wheels to 50 ft lbs.

23. With the vehicle on a level surface, gradually tighten the following bolts in the order in which they appear and to the proper specification.

  a. Nut on the pin connecting the upper control arm to the body—72 ft lbs.

  b. Nuts retaining the lower control arm to the crossmember—43 ft lbs.

  c. Nuts fixing the lower control arm to the pin—72 ft lbs.

850

1. Jack up the front of the car and support beneath the subframe on jackstands.

2. Remove the wheels and disconnect the shock absorbers.

3. Disconnect the tie- rod and ball joints.

4. Disconnect the sway bar from the leaf spring.

5. Disconnect and plug the brake lines.

6. Support, in turn, under each out-

board eye of the leaf spring, and remove each outboard spring eye bolt.

7. Remove the spring center support bolts and lower out the spring.

8. Remove the upper control arm-to-body retaining nuts and remove the suspension assembly.

NOTE: *Take note of the number and location of the caster/camber adjusting shims.*

9. Prior to installation, check the condition of the upper control arm and king pin bushings. Drive out and replace as necessary.

10. Slide each upper control arm onto its mounting studs with the correct amount of shims. Do not tighten the retaining nuts yet.

11. Install the spring center support bolts and tighten to 43 ft-lbs.

12. Install the shocks.

13. Place a floor jack, in turn, beneath each spring eye, and very carefully raise the spring end until the eye bolt will go through the spring eye and kingpin housing. Snug up these bolts, but do not tighten until the car is on the ground.

14. Install the sway bar and torque the shackle nuts to 10.8 ft-lbs.

15. Tighten the upper control arm retaining nuts to 32–36 ft-lbs.

16. Connect the tie rod ends.

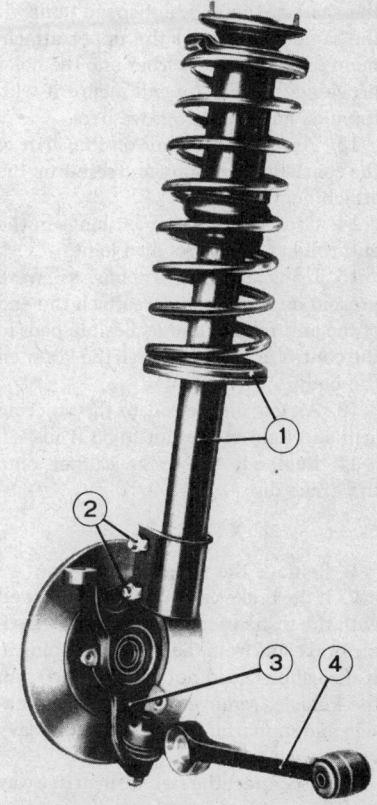

Left front suspension assembly—128; 131 similar

1. Shock absorber and spring
2. Screws and nuts attaching the shock absorber to the pillar
3. Pillar
4. Control arm

17. Connect the brake lines and bleed the brakes. Install the wheels.

18. Lower the car to the ground. Torque the spring eye bolts to 65 ft-lbs.

128

1. Loosen the front wheel stud bolts.
2. Loosen the front wheel hub nuts.
3. Place the vehicle on jackstands.
4. Remove the front wheels.
5. Unscrew the nuts which attach the brake caliper to the pillar and secure the caliper to the body.
6. Unscrew the nut which attaches the tie-rod ball joint to the steering arm and then remove the swivel with a puller.
7. Unscrew the nut which attaches the end of the anti-roll bar to the control arm.
8. Detach the control arm from the body.
9. Remove the hub nut.
10. Release the top attachment of the shock absorber by unscrewing the 3 mounting nuts in the engine compartment and slide the suspension assembly off the constant-speed joint shaft and support the axle shaft in such a way as to prevent it from slipping out of the differential.
11. Attach the anti-roll bar to the body.
12. Take up each completely reassembled control arm and mount the hub on the shaft of the constant-speed joint. At the same time, insert the upper attachment of the shock absorber into the holes provided in the body and secure it with the nuts and the spring washers.
13. Place a flat washer on the shaft of the constant-speed joint and screw up the attachment nut.
14. Grease the rubber bushings in the anti-roll bar-to-control arm joint.
15. Using as many shims as were present on disassembly, reattach the end of the anti-roll bar and its flexible pads to the control arm and reinstall the latter on the body.
16. Attach the tie-rod to the steering arm and tighten the nut to 58 ft lbs.
17. Remount the brake caliper onto the brake disc.

X1/9, 131

1. Remove the wheel and tire.
2. If the brake caliper is to be removed with the suspension, disconnect the flexible brake line from the caliper and plug it. If the caliper need not be removed from the vehicle, remove it from the suspension and support it with a length of heavy gauge wire.
3. Disconnect the stabilizer strut (sway bar) from the suspension.
4. Remove the bolt holding the control arm to the body mount.
5. Remove the nut holding the tie rod ball joint to the steering arm and remove the ball joint.

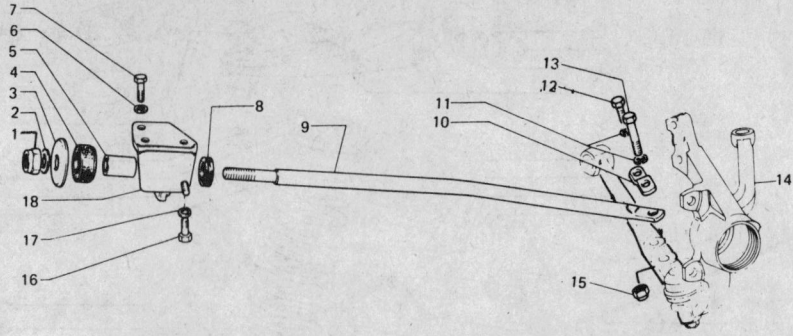

Exploded view of the front reaction strut bar assembly for an X1/9

1. Nut
2. Washer
3. Retainer cup
4. Rubber pad
5. Spacer
6. Lockwasher
7. Bolt
8. Rubber ring
9. Reaction strut bar
10. Lockplate
11. Lockwasher
12. Bolt
13. Bolt
14. Pillar
15. Nut
16. Bolt
17. Washer
18. Body support

6. Support beneath the steering knuckle. Disconnect the top of the shock absorber by removing the three nuts and washers.

7. Lower the suspension strut assembly out of the car.

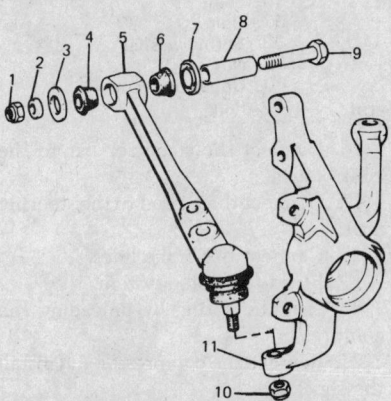

Exploded view of the front control arm assembly for an X1/9

1. Nut
2. Washer
3. Washer
4. Rubber bushing
5. Control arm
6. Rubber bushing
7. Washer
8. Spacer
9. Bolt
10. Nut
11. Pillar

8. Install the suspension assembly in the reverse order. Tighten the attaching nuts and bolts with the vehicle under a load. Tighten the knuckle-to-tie rod attaching nut to 58 ft lbs; the control arm-to-lower pillar attaching nut to 51 ft lbs (X1/9) 58 ft lbs (131); the control arm-to-body attaching bolt to 29 ft lbs (X1/9) 65 ft lbs (131); and the stabilizer strut bar attaching bolt to 29 ft. lbs (X1/9) 43 ft lbs (131).

Shock Absorber

Removal and Installation

124

1. Working from inside the engine compartment, disconnect the upper end of the shock holding the shank from turning with a wrench.
2. Remove the nut and bolt fixing the shock to the lower control arm.
3. Remove the shock through the lower control arm.
4. Installation is the reverse of the removal procedure to include replacing all the worn bushings and washers.

Removing front shock upper attachment—128, X1/9, 131

Removing front shock lower attachment—128, X1/9, 131

1. Screws and nuts attaching the lower end of the shock absorber to the pillar

131, 128 and X1/9

NOTE: *A coil spring compressor is required.*

1. Detach the shock at the top by unscrewing the three nuts that attach it to the body.

2. Jack up the front of the car and support beneath the subframe with jackstands. Remove the wheel.

3. Remove the two bolts retaining the lower end of the strut to the knuckle or pillar.

4. Remove the shock and coil spring (strut assembly).

5. Using a spring compressor, compress the spring making sure that the compressor is installed properly.

CAUTION: *Be sure that the lips of the compressor are gripping the spring firmly. If the spring should escape, great damage or injury could result.*

6. Unscrew the pad mounting nut and release the spring compressor. Remove the spring.

7. Remove the old shock, insert the new one and reverse the removal proce-

Unbolting shock from spring cap—128, X1/9. 131

1. Coil spring check plate clearance screws
2. Upper check plate
3. Shock absorber wrench

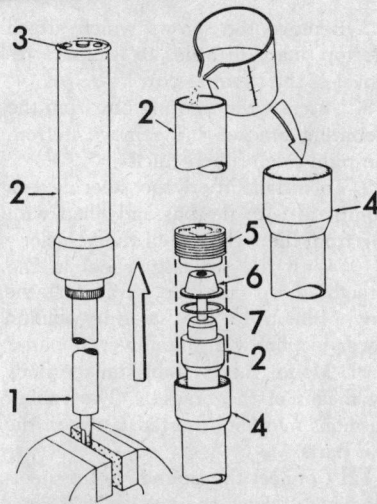

Refilling X1/9, 128 and 131 shock inserts —method "A"

1. Stem
2. Inner cylinder
3. Valve
4. Outer cylinder
5. Threaded plug
6. Cap
7. Ring seal

Place stem (1) of inner cylinder (2) in vise. Extend cylinder. Carefully and gently tape around and under valve (3) to remove it. Pour fluid into cylinder (2) until full. Add remaining fluid to outer cylinder (4). Install valve (3) by carefully tapping it around edge. Insert cylinder (2) into cylinder (4). Assemble absorber using new ring seal (7) and Cap (6). Screw threaded plug (5) on absorber.

dure. With the suspension loaded, torque the lower strut attaching bolts to 36 ft-lbs.

850

1. Jack up the front of the car and place it on stands, be sure to allow sufficient area to work on the shocks.

2. Remove the front tires.

3. Remove the upper mounting bolts.

4. Remove the lower mounting nut.

5. Withdraw the shock through the top control arm.

6. To install, reverse the removal procedure.

Adjustments

Camber

124

Camber angle adjustments are made by changing the number of shims under the two bolts that hold the lower control arm to the frame crossmember. Camber is increased by removing shims and reduced by adding shims. Add or remove the same number for each bolt, otherwise caster will be affected.

X1/9, 131, 128

Camber cannot be adjusted and is built into the suspension.Replace weak, worn, or damaged springs or other suspension components to gain the proper camber measurement.

850

1. To adjust the caster or camber, the spring must be loaded.

2. Install the shims between the control arm pivot bar and the body.

3. To increase the caster, shift the shims from the rear to the front.

4. To decrease the caster, shift the shims from the front to the rear.

5. To increase the camber, add an equal number of shims to both studs. Reverse to decrease camber.

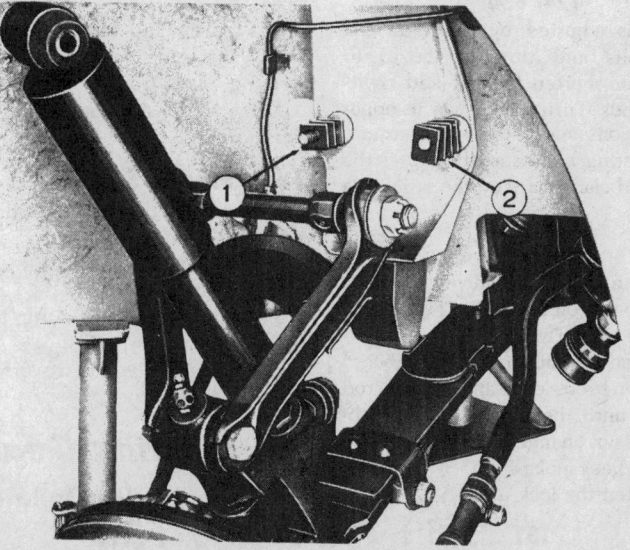

Caster and camber shims on 850 (1 and 2)

Caster

124

Caster angle is increased by moving these shims from the front bolt to the rear and decreased by moving them from the rear bolt to the front.

131

Caster is adjusted by adding or removing shims between the sway bar and lower support (control) arm.

850

See the procedure for adjusting the camber on the 850.

128

If the caster angles are incorrect, the necessary corrections must be made by varying the number of shims inserted between the end of the anti-roll bar and the rubber pad of the control arm. The angle is reduced by about 15 minutes for each extra shim.

1. Raise the front of the vehicle on a pneumatic jack.
2. Remove the nut which anchors the anti-roll bar to the control arm.
3. Disconnect the control arm from the body.
4. Withdraw the end of the anti-roll bar from the control arm.
5. Add or remove as many shims as necessary to correct the caster angle.
6. Reassemble the various components. Lower the vehicle and rock it a few times to settle down the suspension before tightening the two attachment nuts to their correct torque values.

X1/9

Caster is adjusted on the X1/9 by adding or subtracting shims between the front reaction struts and body-end supports.

Toe-In

124, 850

Toe-in is adjusted by loosening the clamp bolts and turning sleeves to lengthen or shorten the left and right-hand tie-rods. Turn the sleeves in opposite directions and to an equal extent. After adjusting, make sure the gaps in the sleeves and clamps are on the same side and flush.

X1/9, 128

1. Set the wheels straight ahead. Make sure the spokes on the steering wheel are positioned properly.
2. Loosen the locknut on the inboard end of the tie rod sleeve and turn the rod in or out until the proper toe-in is obtained. Do not change the position of the steering wheel spokes.
3. Tighten the lock nut.

131

131 toe-in is adjusted in the same man-

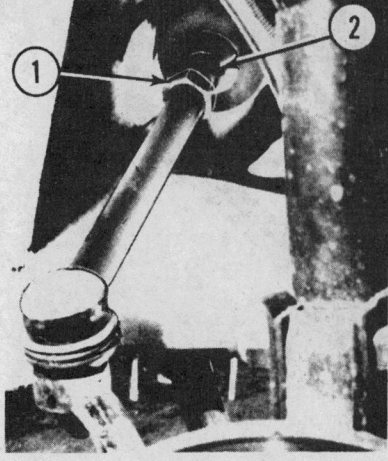

Toe-in adjustment—128, X1/9
1. Nut   2. Ball joint

ner as the 128 and X1/9, except that the outboard locknut is loosened to rotate the tie-rod.

NOTE: *Lubricate the steering rod boot so it doesn't tear.*

STEERING
Steering Wheel
Removal and Installation

128 and X1/9, 131

1. Disconnect the battery. Remove the screws attaching the horn button cover.
2. Remove the screws holding the steering column masking sleeves and remove the sleeves.
3. Unscrew the steering wheel attaching nut and remove the steering wheel.
4. Install in the reverse order.

850, 124

1. Disconnect the battery. Pry off the horn button by inserting a screwdriver between the button and the wheel hub.
2. Disconnect the horn wire at the button.
3. Unscrew and remove the steering wheel attaching nut and remove the steering wheel from the shaft.
4. Install the steering wheel in the reverse order.

Turn Signal Switch

1. Remove horn button and steering wheel.
2. Disconnect switch wiring. Remove shroud, except on 850.
3. Remove attaching clamp and slide off switch.
4. Installation is the reverse of removal.

Steering Gear
Removal and Installation

128

1. Disconnect the battery leads.

2. Rest the front of the car on stands.
3. Unscrew the stud bolts and remove the front wheels.
4. Remove the spare wheel.
5. Disconnect the drive pinion from the lower section of the steering column at the universal joint.
6. Using a puller, remove the tie-rods from the steering arms.

U-joint connecting drive pinion to steering column lower section—128

1. Universal joint of lower steering column section
2. Drive pinion
3. Screw and nut

7. Remove the screws which attach the top guard in order to facilitate removal of the steering box.
8. Unscrew the steering box from the mounting bracket and remove it from the right-side of the vehicle.
9. To install, insert the steering box (complete with tie-rods and filled with oil), from the right-side of the vehicle.
10. With the steering wheel in the straight-ahead position, connect the drive pinion to the steering column lower section, with the universal joints.
11. Mount the assembly on the body by means of the brackets. The rubber cushions must be inserted between the two parts.
12. Connect the tie-rods to the steering arms. Torque the nuts to 58 ft lbs.
13. Attach the top guard to the body.
14. Replace the front wheels and return the spare wheel to the engine compartment.

X1/9, 131

1. Remove the bolt and nuts retaining the universal on the bottom of the steering column to the pinion shaft of the steering box.
2. Remove the three screws securing the gasket cover to the steering box on the floor boards.
3. Jack up the front of the vehicle and remove the two front wheels.

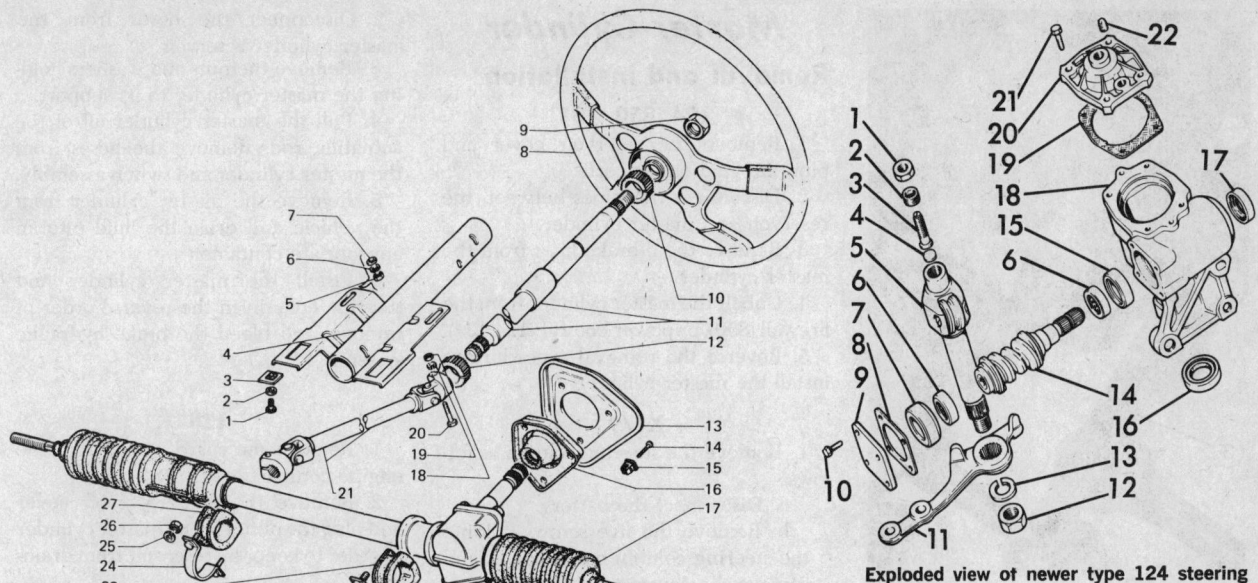

Exploded view of the steering column and steering gear of the X1/9

1. Bolt	10. Bushing	19. Lockwasher
2. Washer	11. Steering column	20. Bolt
3. Retainer	12. Bushing	21. Shaft
4. Support	13. Cover	22. Clamp
5. Nut	14. Screw	23. Pad
6. Lockwasher	15. Pad	24. Clamp
7. Washer	16. Gasket	25. Lockwasher
8. Steering wheel	17. Steering box	26. Nut
9. Nut	18. Nut	27. Pad

Exploded view of newer type 124 steering gear.

1. Adjusting screw nut
2. Screw ring
3. Adjusting screw
4. Plug
5. Roller shaft
6. Ball bearings
7. Bearing retainer
8. Shims
9. Worm screw thrust cover
10. Cover screws
11. Pitman arm
12. Nut, pitman arm to roller shaft
13. Washer
14. Worm screw
15. Bearing retainer
16. Roller shaft seal
17. Steering column seal
18. Steering gear housing
19. Gasket
20. Steering housing upper cover
21. Upper cover screws
22. Oil filter plug

4. Remove the nuts securing the ball joints in both knuckles. Remove the tie rods from the knuckles.

5. Remove the four bolts securing the steering box to the body and remove the steering box from the vehicle.

6. Install the steering box in the reverse order of removal.

124

1. Disconnect the battery.

2. Remove the horn button and emblem cover.

3. Remove the steering wheel retaining nut and pull the steering wheel from the shaft, using a wheel puller.

4. Remove the turn signal switch half covers and unscrew the retaining collar of the turn signal switch. This is located on the bracket which fixes the steering column to the body.

5. Disconnect the steering column bracket from the ignition switch (threaded ring) and remove the retaining collar of the turn signal switch.

6. Remove the screw which clamps the steering column to the worm shaft and remove the steering colum from inside the car.

7. Unscrew the nuts which fix the left-hand steering arm and intermediate arm pins.

8. Remove the pins with an appropriate puller.

9. Remove the steering box from the body by removing the 3 mounting screws.

NOTE: *Shims can be placed on the steering box bolts to ensure proper alignment.*

Note the number and placement of such shims.

10. Drain the oil from the steering box.

11. Using a puller, remove the drop arm from the roller shaft.

12. Remove the roller shaft cover, complete with roller shaft adjusting screw, adjusting disc, lockwasher and locknut.

13. Remove the roller shaft assembly from the steering box.

14. Remove the worm shaft thrust cover and the front bearing adjusting shims.

15. Turn the worm shaft to withdraw the front roller bearing.

16. Use a puller and remove the outer race of the rear roller bearing.

17. Remove the worm and shaft from the steering box along with the inner race of the inner roller bearing.

850

1. Disconnect the battery. Pry off the horn button by inserting a screwdriver between the button and wheel hub.

2. Disconnect the horn and remove the steering wheel, using a wheel puller.

3. Working from the luggage compartment, loosen the steering column-to-worm screw.

4. Jack the front of the car up and support it on stands.

5. Disconnect the steering rods from the pitman arm.

6. Remove the mounting nuts and the steering gear.

7. To install, reverse the removal procedure.

Adjustments

124 and 850

1. Measure the amount of free-play in the steering wheel by moving it back and forth until the wheels will not respond. At this point whatever movement is left in the wheel is free-play.

2. To adjust this condition, loosen the locknut and turn the adjusting screw in.

3. Gradually adjust the free-play out of the steering wheel until it becomes minimal.

4. Tighten the locknut while holding the adjustment screw in place.

Adjusting worm and roller clearance—124, 850

1. Lockwasher
2. Adjusting screw
3. Drop arm

NOTE: *Serious damage may result from turning the adjustment screw in too far. A small amount of free-play should remain to insure against this condition.*

BRAKE SYSTEMS
Adjustment

Rear Drum Brakes

1. Jack up the car and put it on stands.
2. Push the brake pedal to lock the shoes against the drum.
3. Rotate the adjustment nuts outward until locked.
4. Rotate them back about 20° and be sure that the wheels turn freely.

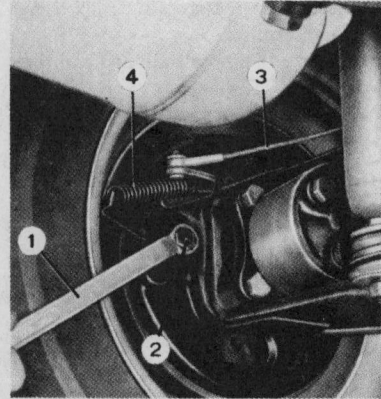

Adjusting the rear drum brakes on an 850; others similar

1. Wrench
2. Brake shoe actuating cam nut
3. Handbrake control cable
4. Brake shoe actuating lever return sprin[g]

Master Cylinder
Removal and Installation
124, 850, 131

1. Remove the reservoir cover and plug the fluid outlet port.
2. Disconnect the pipes between the reservoir and master cylinder.
3. Remove the 3 brake lines from the master cylinder.
4. Unbolt the master cylinder from the firewall (850), or power booster (124,131).
5. Reverse the removal procedure to install the master cylinder.

X1/9

1. Remove the steering column as follows:
   a. Disconnect the battery.
   b. Remove the five screws holding the steering column cover halves and remove the covers.
   c. Disconnect the three electrical connectors and one wire.
   d. Remove the two nuts and washers holding the column to the top of the dashboard.
   e. Remove the two bolts and washers holding the column to the bottom of the dash board.
   f. Slide the shaft off of the steering box shaft and remove the column from the vehicle.

2. Disconnect the hoses from the master cylinder reservoir.
3. Remove the nuts and washers holding the master cylinder to its support.
4. Pull the master cylinder off of the actuating rod. Remove the hoses from the master cylinder and switch assembly.
5. Remove the master cylinder from the vehicle and drain the fluid into an appropriate container.
6. Install the master cylinder and steering column in the reverse order of removal and bleed the brake hydraulic system.

128

1. Remove the spare wheel from the engine compartment.
2. Remove the fluid reservoir cover and plug the outlet to the master cylinder in order to keep the reservoir from draining.
3. Disconnect the reservoir-to-master cylinder tubes.
4. Disconnect the fluid delivery tubing to the front and rear brakes, removing the fastening screws.
5. Remove both nuts and spring washers which secure the master cylinder to the body (1972–73 Sedan and Wagon) or power booster (1974–77 Sedan and Wagon and all Coupe models) and remove the master cylinder.

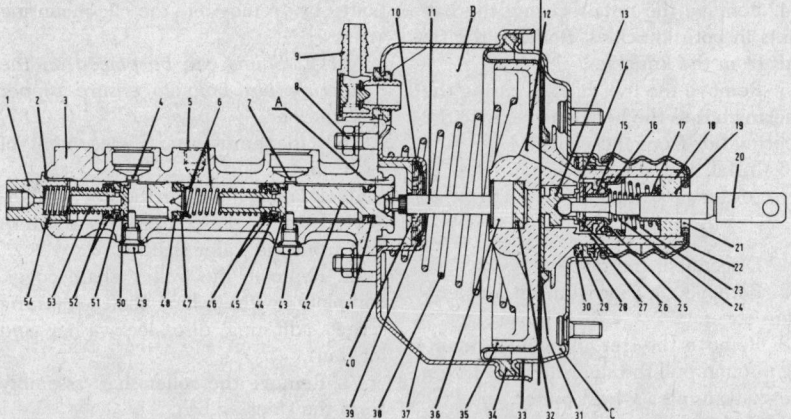

Longitudinal section of power brake booster and master cylinder, Distance "A" (projection of power piston pushrod from master cylinder mounting plate is 0.041-0.051 in. on 1972-74 124 and 128; 0.0408-0.0758 in. on 1975-77 124 Sport; and 0.0325-0.0404 in. on 1975-77 128 and 131

1. Plug	19. Filtering element	37. Front body
2. Seal	20. Valve control rod	38. Piston return spring
3. Cylinder body	21. Air inlet	39. Cup
4. Connector seat	22. Dust boot	40. Guide bushing
5. Front wheel brake connector	23. Piston-valve return spring	41. Seal
6. Spring and cup	24. Valve return spring	42. Rear piston
7. Connector seat	25. Valve (15) cup	43. Plug and seal
8. Nut	26. Atm. press. air passage	44. Spacer
9. Vacuum line fitting	27. Vacuum orifice	45. Seal
10. Front seal	28. Rear seal	46. Spring and cup
11. Piston control rod	29. Shoulder ring	47. Flat washer
12. Vacuum duct	30. Lockwasher	48. Seal
13. Piston-valve	31. Piston retainer	49. Plug and seal
14. Vacuum duct orifice	32. Reaction disc	50. Spacer
15. Valve	33. Rear body	51. Seal
16. Cup	34. Diaphragm	52. Spring and cup
17. Cup	35. Control piston	53. Front piston
18. Control piston guide tube	36. Working piston	54. Spring and cup

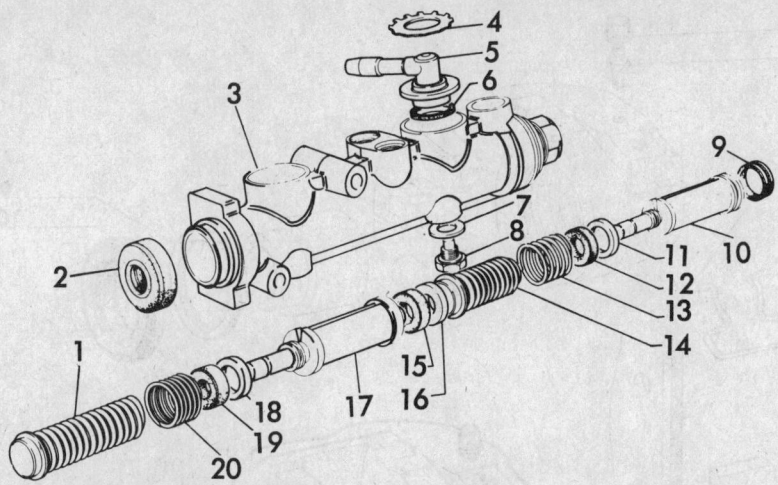

Exploded view of master cylinder—X1/9 shown; others similar

1. Spring	6. Gasket	11. Spacer	16. Spacer
2. Boot	7. Gasket	12. Seal	17. Piston
3. Housing	8. Screw	13. Spring	18. Spacer
4. Lockplate	9. Gasket	14. Spring	19. Seal
5. Connection	10. Piston	15. Seal	20. Spring

6. Installation is the reverse of removal.

Overhaul

All Models

1. Disconnect the fluid inlet connector from the cylinder.

2. Remove the boot from its groove in the cylinder body.

3. Back out the setscrews and the end plug.

4. Remove from the cylinder body the piston return springs, cups, seal rings, and spacers.

5. Check the valve carriers, reaction springs, and rubber seal rings.

6. Inspect the cylinder bore for pits or roughness. If this condition exists, hone the bore to prevent excessive wear of seals or fluid loss.

NOTE: *If the cylinder bore is badly scored or corroded, the cylinder body must be replaced.*

7. Be sure to lubricate all parts with clean brake fluid.

8. Assembly is the reverse of disassembly.

Brake Pressure Regulator

This device, located near the rear axle is used on 124, 128 and 131 models only. It serves to adjust hydraulic line pressure to prevent rear wheel lock-up under hard braking. An important safety factor, the pressure regulator will apply a reduced line pressure to the rear brakes (roughly half that of the front brakes) when the rear suspension is off-loaded. A torsion bar, anchored to the rear axle, senses suspension angle, and transmits this mechanically to the pressure regulator

valve. The result is straight line stopping and more even braking effect.

Adjustment

The pressure regulator need only be adjusted upon initial installation, or if its mounting bolts become loose in service. By loosening the mounting bolts, the regulator may be pivoted to adjust the travel of the torsion bar.

124, 131, 128

1. Raise rear of car and support on stands.

2. Disconnect regulator torsion bar (E) at axle connecting link (G).

3. Pivot axle end of the torsion bar to distance "X" from the rubber buffer resting surface.

4. Lift dust boot (C) and check that regulator piston (D) contacts other end of torsion bar.

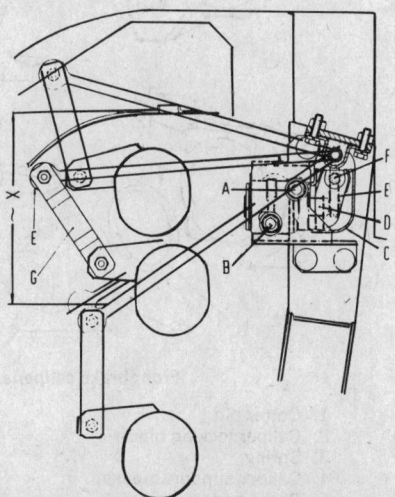

Brake pressure regulator adjustment—124 sedan and coupe shown; others similar

5. If not, loosen regulator mounting screws (A+B) and pivot regulator until piston just grazes torsion bar.

6. Then tighten the mounting screws and connect the torsion bar. On the 128, torque the bolts to 14 ft-lbs. Distance "X" is:

5.78 in.—124 Special Sedan and 124 Sport Coupe

5.0 in.—124 Wagon

3.74 in.—124 Sport Spider

12.0 in.—131 Sedan

12.25 in.—131 Wagon

2.126 in.—128 All

Bleeding

All Models

NOTE: *When bleeding the rear brakes on 124, 128, and 131 models, the line pressure regulator will limit the pressure to the rear wheel brake units when the rear suspension is jacked up. This will make bleeding difficult. To prevent this, temporarily disconnect the regulator torsion bar from the rear axle link and tie it up to simulate normal suspension height. This will allow full pressure to the rear brakes and speed up bleeding.*

1. Fill the reservoir and hydraulic system with brake fluid.

2. Clean all dirt from the bleeder screws and remove the protective caps.

3. Install a bleeder hose over the fitting in the brake caliper or the wheel cylinder and submerge the other end of the bleeder hose in a clean jar half-filled with brake fluid.

4. Loosen the bleeder screw a few turns and have a helper press the brake pedal down quickly, allowing it to return slowly.

5. Do this procedure several times until no more air bubbles escape from the rubber hose.

6. Keeping the brake pedal depressed, remove the bleeder hose and tighten the bleeder screw.

7. Clean the bleeder screw and refit the protective cap.

8. Repeat Steps 2, 3, 4 and 5 on the other wheels. Make sure that the reservoir is full after each wheel cylinder is bled.

Front Disc Brakes

Brake Pads

Removal and Installation

1. Remove the caliper from the mounting brackets.

2. Remove the retaining plates and slide off the pins.

3. Tip the clamps to remove the caliper from the bracket.

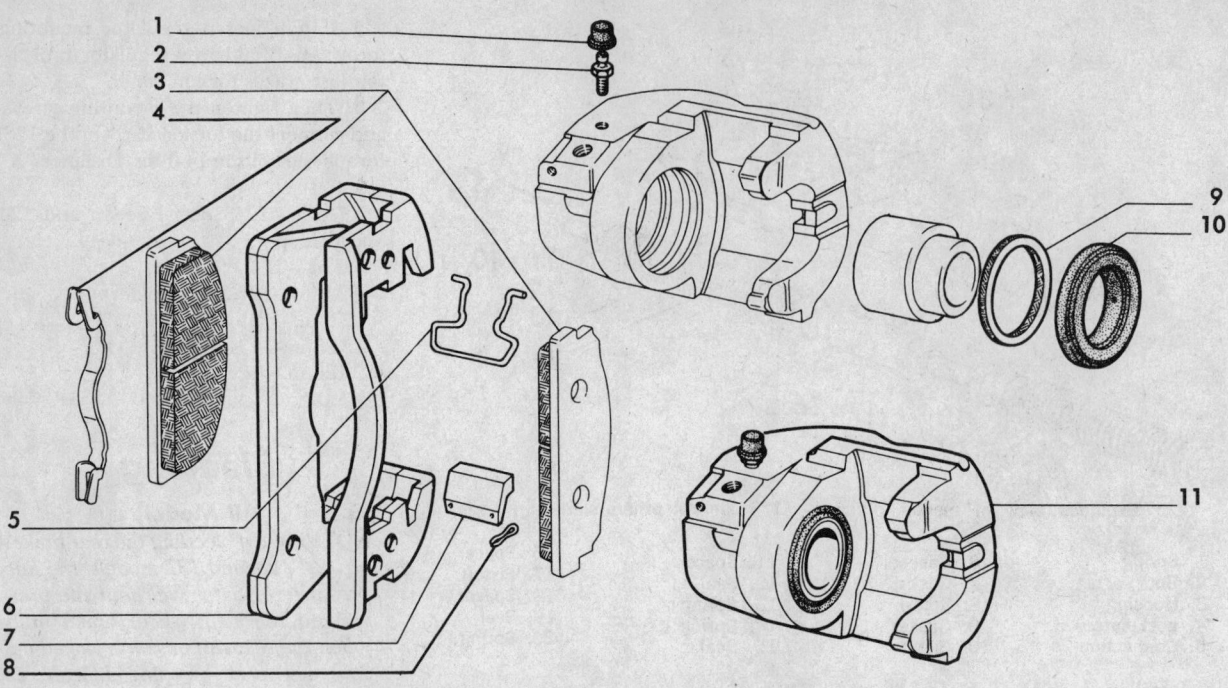

Exploded view of front brake caliper—850, 128, 124, 131

1. Bleeder screw cap
2. Bleeder screw
3. Brake pads
4. Spring
5. Caliper fastener spring
6. Caliper support bracket
7. Caliper locking block
8. Cotter pin
9. Piston seal
10. Piston dust boot
11. Assembled caliper

4. Replace the pads and push the piston (using a flat piece of wood or a putty knife) to the bottom of the cylinder.

5. Make sure that the mark on the piston faces the bleeder screw. Replace the caliper.

Brake Calipers

Removal and Installation

1. Jack up the car, put it on stands, and remove the wheels.

2. Plug the outlet port of the brake fluid reservoir.

3. Disconnect the brake hose from the caliper by unscrewing the junction.

4. Remove the cotter pins, which hold the locking blocks in place, and remove the locking blocks.

5. Remove the caliper flat springs, friction pads and springs.

6. Without removing the brake disc from the car, check the brake disc runout with a dial indicator.

7. If there are any deep score marks on the disc, be sure that they do not exceed 0.019 in. Past this dimension, the discs must be replaced.

8. Fit the spring and friction pads to the caliper bracket.

9. Install the flat spring and caliper to the caliper bracket.

10. Insert the locking blocks to retain the caliper.

11. Replace the cotter pins.

12. Connect the brake hose to the caliper and tighten the connection.

13. Unplug the brake fluid reservoir and fill the reservoir.

14. Bleed the brakes.

Overhaul

850, 124, 128, 131

1. Remove the dust boot.

2. Direct a jet of air into the fluid inlet coupling to remove the piston from the caliper cylinder.

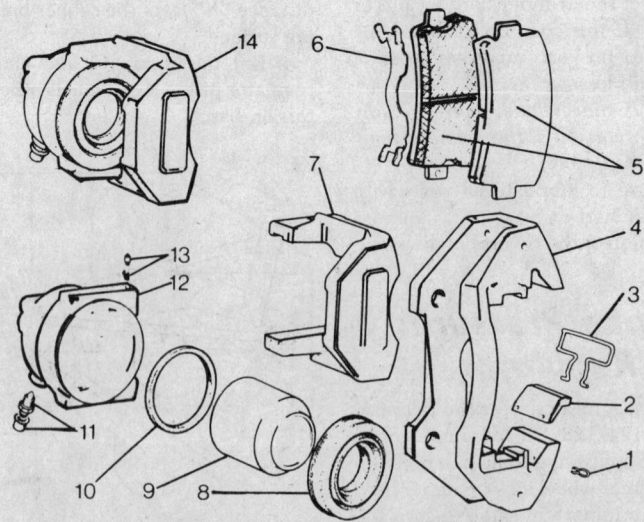

Front brake caliper assembly on the X1/9

1. Cotter pin
2. Caliper locking block
3. Spring
4. Caliper support bracket
5. Brake pads
6. Brake pad retainer spring
7. Cylinder housing
8. Dust boot
9. Piston
10. Piston seal
11. Bleeder screw and dust cap
12. Cylinder
13. Spring and attaching
14. Assembled caliper assembly

3. Remove the seal.

NOTE: *When pistons are removed, piston seals always must be changed.*

4. Wash all parts in hot water and dry them with compressed air.

5. Fit the piston seal to the caliper cylinder.

6. Insert the piston and push it to the far end of the cylinder.

7. Fit the dust boot, making sure that the lip enters the undercut in the caliper body.

X1/9

1. Remove the dust boot.

2. Depress the dowel holding the caliper cylinder to the caliper support bracket with a thin drift or rod.

3. Separate the cylinder from the support bracket.

4. Apply compressed air to the brake hose port and blow the piston out of the cylinder. Remove the piston seal.

5. Check the piston and caliper cylinder for scoring or binding. The cylinder bore can be refinished by honing.

6. Clean and flush the parts with clean brake fluid. Make sure that all metal particles are removed from the cylinder bore.

7. Assemble the caliper in the reverse order of removal, keeping the parts liberally coated with clean brake fluid.

Brake Disc

All exc. 128

Removal and Installation

1. Raise and support the front of the car.

2. Remove the wheel.

3. Unbolt the caliper from its bracket and suspend it out of the way.

4. Remove the wheel bearing nut and slide the hub and disc from the spindle.

5. Installation is the reverse of removal. For wheel bearing adjustment, see the wheel bearing paragraph below.

128

1. Unbolt the caliper bracket from the steering knuckle and support the assembly out of the way.

2. Remove the two bolts securing the disc to the hub.

3. Using a brass drift, remove the disc from the hub.

4. Install in reverse of the above.

Rear Drum Brakes

Brake Drums

Removal and Installation

850, 128, 131

1. Jack up the rear of the vehicle and support it.

2. Remove the wheel and tire assembly. Release the parking brake.

3. Back off the adjustment of the brake

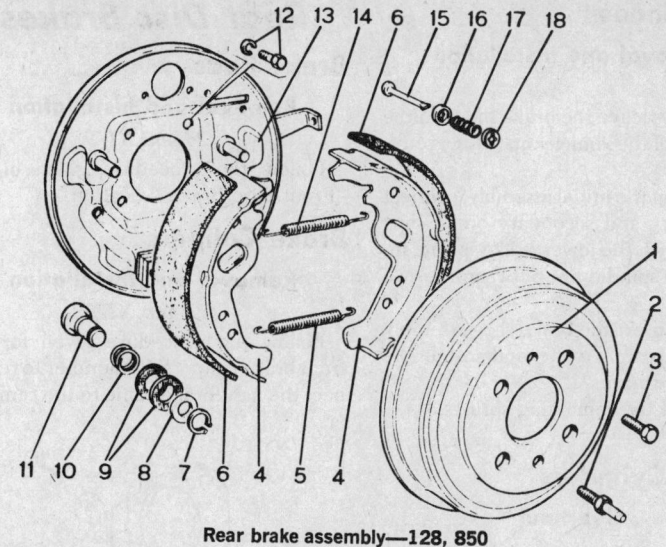

Rear brake assembly—128, 850

1. Brake drum	7. Snap ring	13. Brake backing plate
2. Drum attaching screw wheel location dowel	8. Plain washer	14. Upper shoe return spring
3. Brake drum attaching screw	9. Friction washers	15. Pivot pin
4. Shoe side	10. Spring	16. Inner cup
5. Lower shoe return spring	11. Casing	17. Shoe guide spring
6. Brake linings	12. Screw and washer	18. Outer cup

shoes, if necessary. Remove the two drum retaining bolts.

4. Remove the brake drum from the hub or axle shaft flange by pulling it straight out and off the locating dowels.

5. Install in the reverse order.

Inspection

After the brake drum has been removed from the vehicle, it should be inspected for run-out, severe scoring, cracks, and the proper inside diameter.

Minor scores on a brake drum can be removed with fine emery cloth, provided that all grit is removed from the drum before it is installed on the vehicle.

A badly scored, rough, or out-of-round (run-out) drums can be ground or turned on a brake drum lathe. Do not remove any more material from the drum than is necessary to provide a smooth surface for the brake shoe to contact. The maximum diameter of the braking surface is shown on the inside of each brake drum. Brake drums that exceed the maximum braking surface diameter shown on the brake drum, either through wear or refinishing, must be replaced. This is because after the outside wall of the brake drum reaches a certain thickness (thinner than the original thickness) the drum loses its ability to dissipate the heat created by the friction between the brake drum and the brake shoes, when the brakes are applied. Also, the brake drum will have more tendency to warp and/or crack.

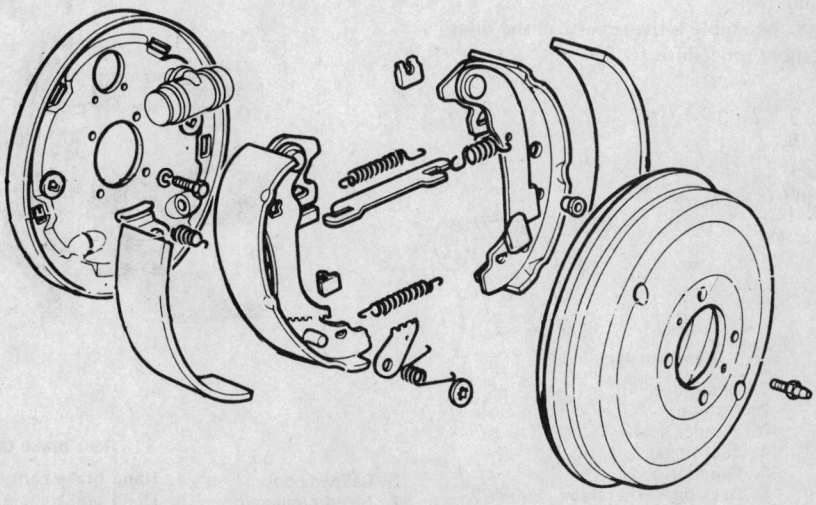

Rear brake assembly—131

Fiat

Brake Shoes

Removal and Installation

1. Always leave the brake shoes on the other side of the vehicle intact for a reference.

2. During the initial assembly, connect the primary and secondary brake shoe together with the lower brake spring, inserting the spindle nut between the two shoes.

3. Now insert the brake shoe assembly onto the backing plate and install the hold-down springs.

4. Install the remaining springs.

Wheel Cylinders

Overhaul

NOTE: *When overhauling a wheel cylinder still on the backing plate, take care not to get brake fluid on the linings.*

1. Jack up the car and place it on stands.

2. Remove the wheels and brake drums. Release the upper shoe springs and tilt the shoes away from the wheel cylinder.

3. Unfasten and remove the rubber boots from the ends of the wheel cylinder.

4. The plunger, valve rings and cups on the end of the reaction spring will be pushed out by the expansion of the spring.

5. Check the condition inside of the cylinder.

6. Slightly hone the cylinder, if needed.

NOTE: *The cleaning process is only to smooth the inside surface of the cylinder. Do not try to remove deep pits or grooves by honing.*

7. Valve rings should be replaced and all parts lubricated, with clean brake fluid.

8. Assembly is the reverse of the disassembly procedure.

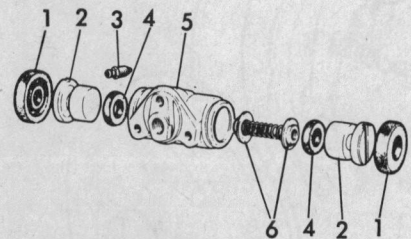

Rear wheel cylinder

1. Dust boot
2. Pistons
3. Bleeder screw
4. Seal rings
5. Cylinder body
6. Backing washers and piston reaction spring

Rear Disc Brakes

Brake Pads

Removal and Installation
124 and X1/9

Follow the procedure given in the "Front Disc Brakes" Section.

Brake Calipers

Removal and Installation
124 and X1/9

Follow the procedure given for the front brake calipers. Remember to reconnect the handbrake cable to the cam levers.

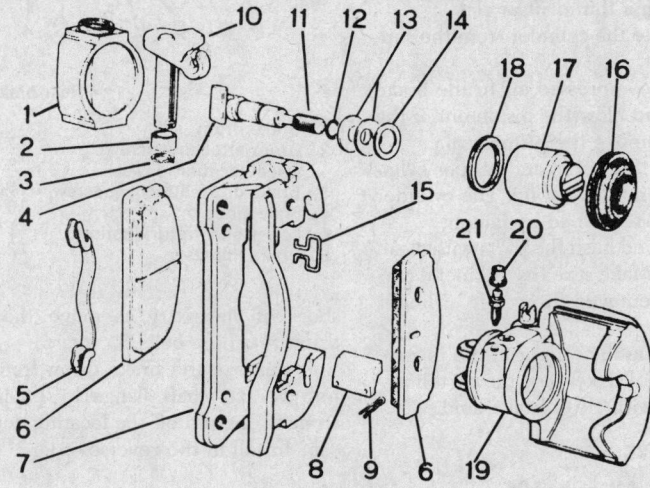

Rear brake assembly—124

1. Boot over hand brake lever end	8. Caliper locking block	15. Flat radial spring cap
2. Bushing	9. Cotter pin	16. Boot
3. Snap ring	10. Hand brake cam lever	17. Piston
4. Pawl	11. Self-adjusting plunger	18. Piston seal
5. Friction pad locking spring	12. Plunger sealing ring	19. Caliper body
6. Friction pad	13. Disc springs	20. Cap for bleed connection
7. Caliper bracket	14. Disc spring thrust washer	21. Bleed connection

Overhaul
124

1. Remove the dust boot and unscrew the piston from the handbrake plunger.

2. To do this, insert a screwdriver into the slot in the head of the piston.

3. Remove the seal and the handbrake gaiter.

4. Remove the pivot pin on which the cam lever turns and remove the lever along with the plunger seal, disc spring and spring thrust washer.

NOTE: *When the pistons are removed from the caliper, the piston seals always must be changed.*

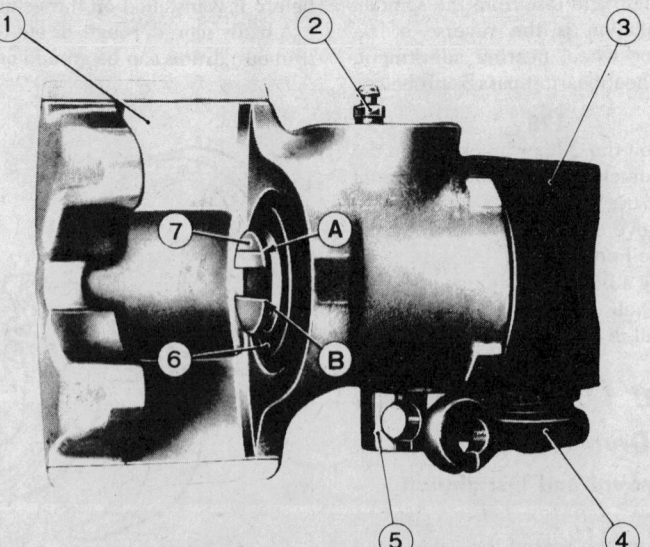

Rear brake caliper—124

1. Caliper body	4. Hand brake cam lever	7. Piston
2. Bleed connection	5. Hand brake cable anchorage	A. Reference mark
3. Gaiter	6. Piston protection boot	B. Slot engaging friction pad rib

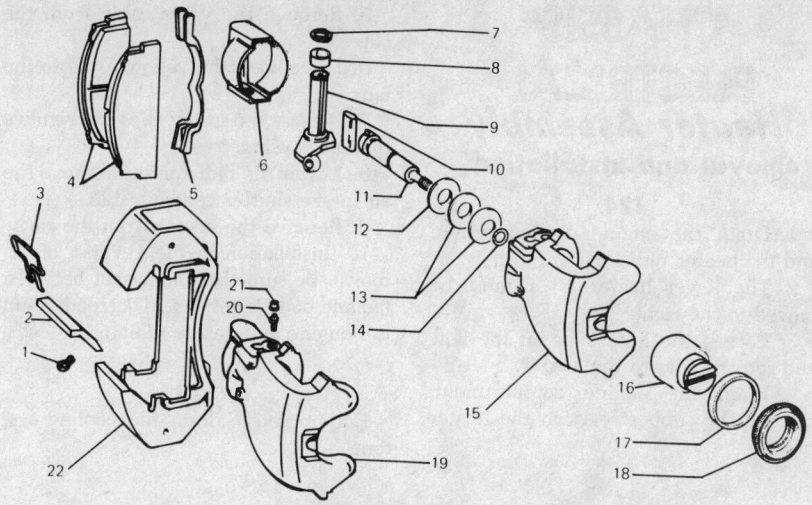

Rear brake caliper assembly on the X1/9

1. Cotter pin	12. Spring washer
2. Caliper locking block	13. Spring washers
3. Caliper locking block locking spring	14. Seal
4. Brake pads	15. Caliper cylinder
5. Brake pad retaining spring	16. Piston
6. Rubber boot	17. Piston seal
7. Snap ring	18. Dust boot
8. Spacer	19. Assembled caliper
9. Handbrake	20. Bleeder screw
10. Pawl	21. Bleeder screw dust boot
11. Plunger	22. Support bracket

5. Fit the self-adjusting plunger with seal, spring and thrust washer.

6. Install the handbrake cam lever and fit the pivot pin in the fork of the caliper body.

7. Fit the handbrake lever gaiter.

8. Replace the rubber piston seal in the caliper body.

9. Screw in the piston until it is properly seated and the mark cut in the piston is opposite the bleed connection.

X1/9

1. Remove the dust boot.

2. Unscrew the piston from the plunger.

3. Use a screwdriver placed in the slot in the plunger and remove the seal.

4. Remove the lockring from the handbrake shaft and remove the shaft.

5. Remove the handbrake plunger together with the plunger pawl, seal and spring washers.

6. The cylinder bore can be refinished by honing. Flush all metal particles out of the cylinder bore with clean brake fluid. Replace all worn or damaged parts.

7. Assemble the caliper in the reverse order of removal, keeping all of the parts liberally coated with clean brake fluid.

Brake Discs

Removal and Installation

1. Raise and support the rear of the vehicle.

2. Remove the wheel.

3. Remove the caliper support bracket

by removing the two screws which secure it to the axle housing.

4. Remove the bolts retaining the brake disc to the wheel hub.

5. Remove the disc, using an ordinary drift.

6. Install the disc in the reverse order of removal.

Parking Brake

Cable

Adjustment

1. Disengage the handbrake cable, using the lever.

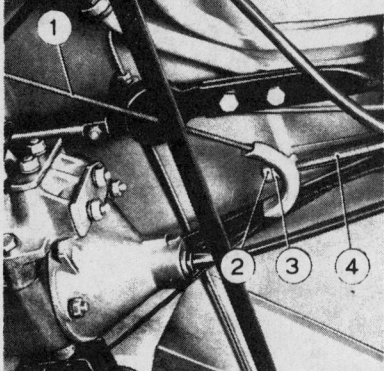

Parking brake adjustment—850, 124

1. Parking brake control cable
2. Locknut
3. Adjusting nut
4. Threaded tensioner

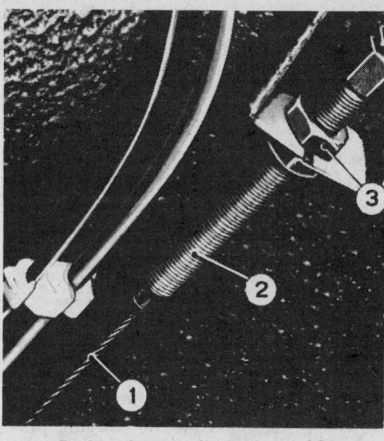

Parking brake adjustment—128

1. Main cable
2. Threaded tensioner
3. Adjusting nut and locknut

Parking brake adjustment access window—X1/9

2. Pull the lever up three or four notches.

3. Loosen the locknut on the tensioner and turn the adjusting nut until the cable is stretched and the wheels are locked.

4. Tighten the locknut.

5. The cable is correctly tensioned when the car is held by a movement of the lever through 3 notches.

6. Release the lever and check that the wheels are free to turn.

Wheel Bearings

Packing

128

The packing of the 128 wheel bearings is performed during assembly and installation of the front suspension assembly. See the "Front Suspension Removal and Installation" Section, Chapter 8. After removing the bearings proceed as follows:

1. Clean the bearings with solvent.

2. If possible, blow them dry with air. **NOTE:** *Do not spin the bearing around on your finger with an air blast; hold the bearing from spinning with your finger.*

3. Insert a finger full of grease into your left palm and with your right hand, dip the bearing into the grease. Allow the grease to seep between the rollers.

4. Continue packing until the grease has tightened the bearing considerably.

NOTE: *The easiest way to insert the grease is between the race and the roller housing from the wide side of the taper until it begins to come out of the thin side.*

X1/9

1. Jack up the front end of the vehicle and remove the wheel.

2. Disconnect the brake calipers and support bracket from the steering pillar.

3. Remove the bolt and centering stud holding the brake rotor and plate and remove the rotor and plate.

4. Remove the nut securing the tie rod to the pillar and remove the ball joint from the pillar.

5. Remove the nut holding the control arm to the pillar and remove the control arm ball joint from the pillar.

6. Remove the two nuts and bolts holding the shock absorbers to the pillar and remove the pillar from the vehicle.

7. Remove the nut and washers holding the hub to the pillar and press the hub out of the pillar.

8. Remove the ring nut holding the bearing in the pillar and pull the bearing out of the pillar.

NOTE: *The removal and installation of the bearing is facilitated by using special Fiat tools A.57123 socket to remove the bearing ring nut and 8015 bearing puller/installer to remove and install the bearing.*

9. Clean the bearing and pack it with grease as oulined above for the 128.

10. Install the new bearing.

11. Screw a *new* ring nut into the pillar. Tighten the nut to 43 ft lbs. Always use a new ring nut.

12. Stake the ring nut with a punch.

13. Install the hub in the pillar and press it into place with a press. Install the two washers and a nut and tighten the nut to 100 ft lbs. Stake the nut with a punch.

14. Install the steering pillar to the car in the reverse order of removal.

124, 131 and 850

1. Jack up the front of the car and place it on stands.

NOTE: *A pulley puller is required to remove the wheel hub.*

2. Remove the front tire.

3. Remove the brake caliper.

4. Remove the brake disc by unbolting the two mounting screws.

5. The bearing can now be removed, after removing the wheel hub with a puller.

6. Follow Steps 1–4 of the 128 procedure, above.

CHASSIS ELECTRICAL
Heater Assembly
Removal and Installation

124

1. Drain the engine cooling system and the heater radiator.

2. The lower heater lever must be moved to the right.

3. Loosen the hose clips on the flow and return pipes to the heater.

4. From the engine compartment, remove the rubber seals on the heater pipes.

5. Remove the valve cable from the clip.

6. Disconnect the yellow cable to the fan.

7. Release the spring clips and remove the fan housing.

8. Lower the radiator and remove the air intake shutter control cable.

9. Remove the heater from the car.

10. Installation is the reverse of removal. Be sure that the gasket between fan and body is positioned correctly. Run the engine and fill the radiator.

128

1. Completely drain the cooling system.

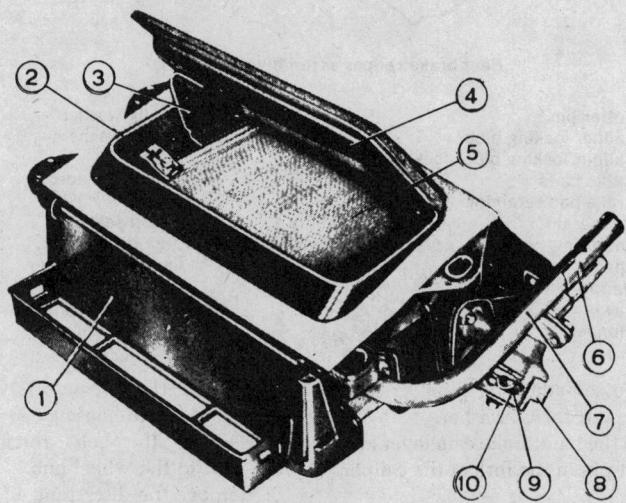

Heater core housing—124

1. Heater core housing	6. Inlet pipe
2. Operating cable clip	7. Outlet pipe
3. Support	8. Water valve lever
4. Air inlet shutter	9. Water valve
5. Heater core	10. Water valve operating cable clamp

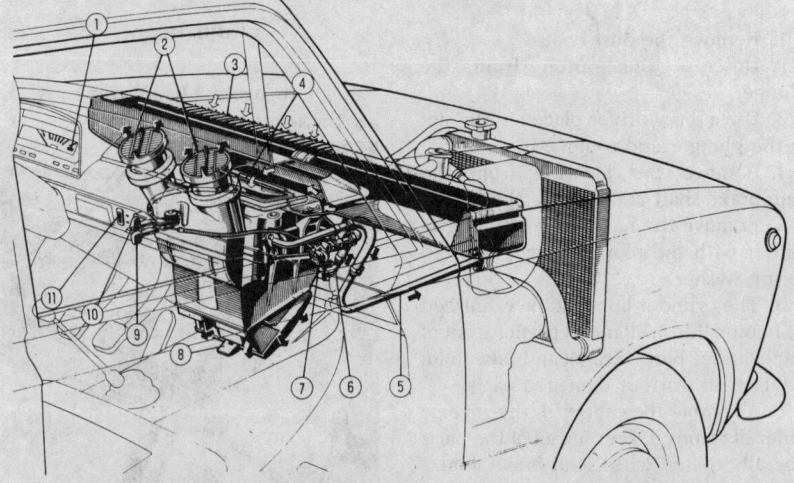

Heater system—124

1. Engine temperature warning light	7. Heater water control valve
2. Air adjuster	8. Shutter
3. Air intake slots	9. Lever operating valve (7)
4. Air intake shutter	10. Lever to control air shutter (4)
5. Heater water return line	11. Heater fan switch
6. Heater water delivery line	

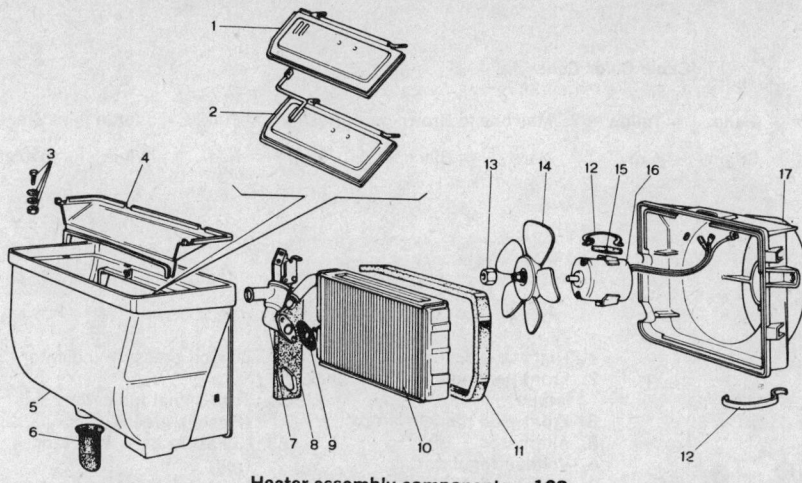

Heater assembly components—128

1. Upper shutter, for fresh air admission to car interior
2. Lower shutter, for air flow onto radiator (10)
3. Attaching screw, washers and nut
4. Water shield
5. Housing
6. Water drain plug
7. Valve
8. Gasket
9. Gasket
10. Radiator
11. Gasket
12. Spring clips
13. Nut, attaching impeller to motor
14. Impeller
15. Rubber pad
16. Motor
17. Fan housing

Starting from car with chassis No. 215963 a grid has been added to the heater housing

2. Loosen the clips which retain the inlet and outlet hoses.

3. Remove the screw and nut from the air shutter actuating rod.

4. Remove the air conveyor.

5. Slide out the radiator housing spring clips.

6. Withdraw the outside shutter actuating rod.

7. Remove the heater valve control cable.

8. Remove the heater core.

9. Remove the fan housing attaching nuts.

10. Disconnect the cables which feed the motor at the fan switch.

11. Installation is the reverse of removal.

850

1. Drain the cooling system.

2. Back out the six retaining screws and remove the utility shelf.

3. Loosen the clamps and remove the inlet and outlet hoses.

4. Disconnect the fan electrical lead.

5. Remove the heater mounting screws.

6. Withdraw the heater assembly.

7. Installation is the reverse of the above order to include bleeding the radiator core.

NOTE: *Be sure to check all hoses and clamps and the drain cock and gaskets before reinstalling the heater core. Heater disassembly is done easily by removing or prying out the case clips. The electric fan is also mounted with clips.*

Windshield Wiper Motor

Removal and Installation

124

The windshield wiper motor is removed from the engine compartment side in the following manner.

1. Unscrew the left-hand spacer nut and remove the left-hand wiper blade and arm.

2. Remove the retaining nuts from the bracket and pull the motor back slightly.

3. Remove the clip connecting the right half-link to the motor and remove the motor.

4. Installation is the reverse of removal.

128

1. Remove the wiper blades and arms.

2. Back out the attaching nuts and remove the wiper blade pivot spacers.

3. Remove the spare wheel.

4. Remove the speedometer cable clip from the body.

5. Remove the screws which attach the wiper assembly to the mounting bracket.

6. Disconnect the connector block and remove the unit completely.

7. Installation is the reverse of removal.

850 Spider

1. Disconnect the negative battery cable.

2. Raise the compartment lid to gain access to the windshield wiper motor.

3. Disconnect the linkage, electrical lead and the motor attaching bolts and remove the wiper motor from the vehicle.

4. Install in the reverse order of removal.

Instrument Cluster

Removal and Installation

124 Spider

1. Unscrew the 4 mounting screws securing the cluster.

2. Disconnect the speedometer cable.

3. Disconnect the 5 cluster connectors.

4. Remove the cluster.

5. Install the cluster in the reverse order of removal.

124 Special

1. Depress spring from the front of the panel.

2. Remove the speedometer cable.

3. Unplug the connectors.

4. Remove the cluster.

5. Install the cluster in the reverse order of removal.

850 Spider

1. Disconnect the steering column mounting bracket.

2. Remove the locknuts which hold the toggle switches and the trip odometer.

3. Disconnect the speedometer.

4. Remove the panel mounting screws.

5. Withdraw the cluster.

6. To install, reverse the removal procedure.

128 Sedan

1. Open the hood and remove the spare wheel.

2. Back out the speedometer cable retainer plate screw.

3. Remove the instrument cluster retainer screw from inside the car.

4. Withdraw the instrument cluster.

5. To install, reverse the removal procedure.

X1/9

1. Remove the five screws retaining the instrument cluster to the instrument panel.

2. Slide the cluster out enough to disconnect the three electrical connectors and the speedometer cable.

3. Remove the instrument cluster from the instrument panel.

4. Install the instrument cluster in the reverse order of removal.

Wiring Circuits

Cable Color Code

Arancio = Amber	Bianco = White	Giallo = Yellow	Marrone = Brown	Rosa = Pink	Verde = Green
Azzurro = Light blue	Blu = Dark Blue	Grigio = Grey	Nero = Black	Rosso = Red	Viola = Violet

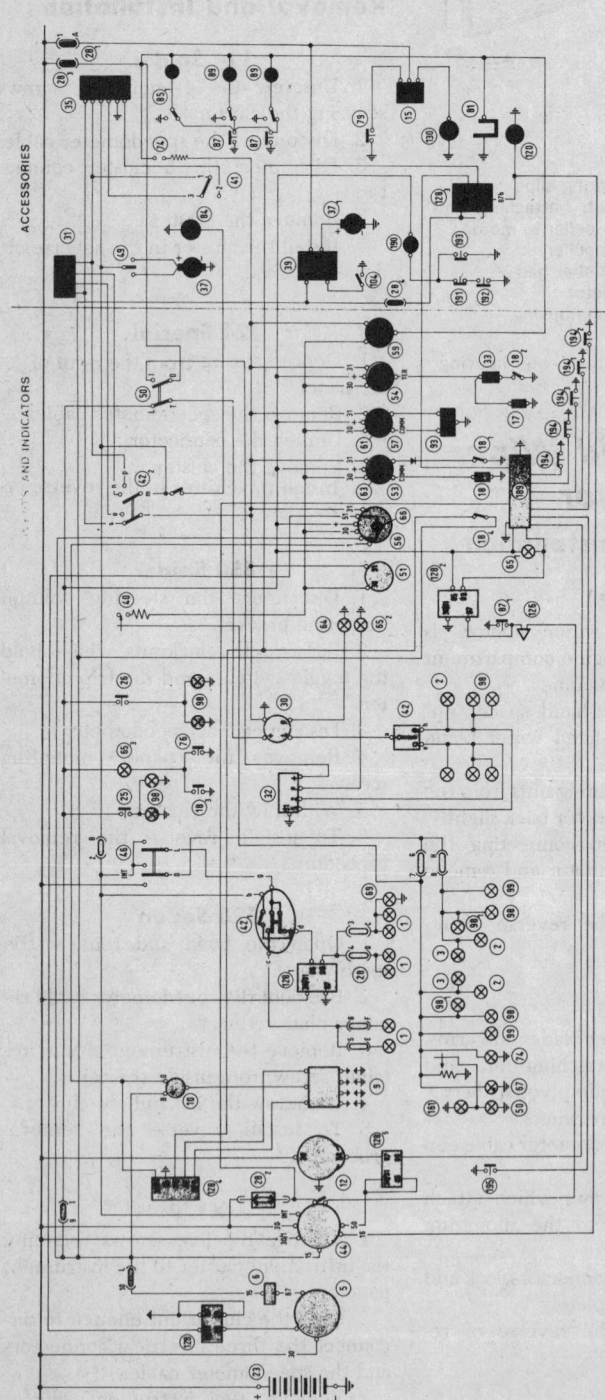

1974 124 Sport Coupe

1. High/Low beam headlights
2. Front parking and turn signal lamps
3. Front side marker lamps
5. Alternator
6. Voltage regulator
9. Ignition distributor
10. Ignition coil
12. Starter motor
15. Horn relay
17. Engine water temperature gauge sending unit
18. Oil pressure gauge sending unit
18/1. Low oil pressure indicator sending unit
18/2. Thermostatic switch to engine water temperature gauge
18/3. Brake system effectiveness indicator switch
18/4. Thermostatic switch for ignition mode selection relay control
23. Battery
25. Back-up lights switch
26. Stop light switch
28. Fuses
28/1. 16-Amp fuse
28/2. 3-Amp inline fuse
28/3. 8-Amp inline fuse
28/4. 8-Amp inline fuse
30. Turn signal flasher
31. Windshield wiper intermittent cycling switch
32. Vehicular hazard warning signal flasher
33. Engine water temperature gauge resistor
35. Two-speed windshield wiper motor
37. Two-speed heater fan motor
37/1. Engine fan motor
39. Relay for motor 37/1
40. Instrument cluster light rheostat-switch unit
41. Windshield wiper motor speed selection relay
42. Turn signal indicator switch
42/1. High/Low beams change-over switch
42/2. Wiper/washer three-position switch
44. Steering lock ignition switch
46. Lighting switch (controls also headlights)
49. Heater fan motor three-position switch
50. Vehicular hazard warning signal switch with incorporated light
51. Speedometer
53. Oil pressure gauge
54. Engine water temperature gauge
56. Tachometer
57. Fuel gauge
59. Clock
61. Fuel reserve indicator (red)

63. Low oil pressure indicator (red)
64. Turn signal indicator (Flashes green)
65/1. Fasten belts indicator (red)
65/2 Vehicular hazard warning indicator (Flashes red)
65/3 Brake system effectiveness indicator (red)
66. Battery charge indicator (red)
67. Parking and tail lights indicator (green)
69. High beams indicator (blue)
74. Cigar lighter with housing indicator
76. Hand brake ON switch
79. Horn button
81. Current receptacle
84. Washer pump motor
85/1. Dash courtesy light with switch
87. Courtesy light jamb switches
87/1. Remove key indicator jamb switch (driver's door)
89. Pillar courtesy lights with switch
93. Fuel gauge sending unit
98. Tail, turn signal, stop and back-up lights unit
98/1. Rear side marker lamps
99. License plate lamps
104. Thermostatic switch (on radiator) for motor 37/1
120. Fuel pump
126. Fasten belts and remove key buzzer
128. Battery charge relay
128/1. High beam relay
128/2. Relay for buzzer 126
128/3. Fuel pump and ignition mode relay control switch
128/4. Ignition mode selection relay
128/5. Starter relay
130. Horn compressor
161. Light source, optical fiber illumination
189. Interlock system electronic control unit
190. Exhaust gas recirculation control valve
191. Button switch on clutch for EGR valve control
192. Button switch on transmission for EGR valve control
193. Exhaust emission control device electrovalve
194. Button switches on seat belts
194/1. Strip switch in passenger's seat cushion
194/2. Gear-engaged signal button switch
194/3. Strip switch in driver's seat cushion
195. Interlock by-pass switch

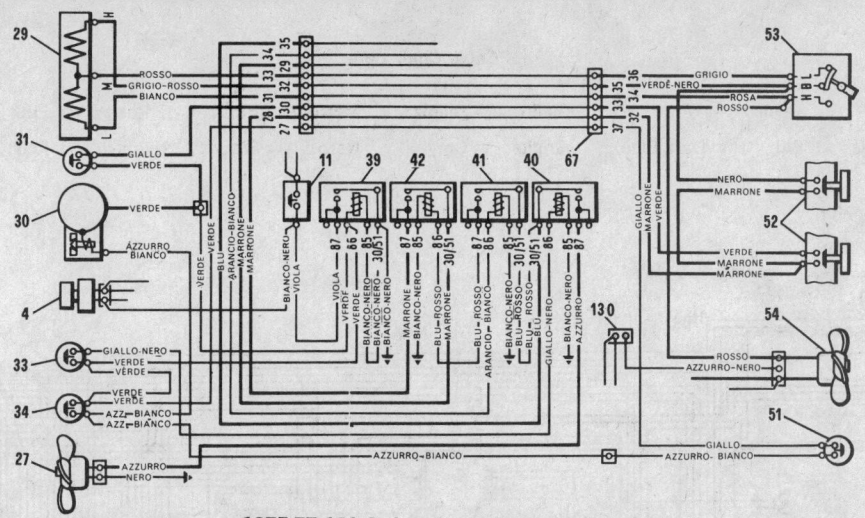

1975-77 131 Sedan air conditioner option

4. Fast idle electrovalve
11. Fast idle switch
27. Condenser cooling fan
29. Conditioner fan speed selector resistor
30. Compressor and defroster valve

31. Low pressure switch
33. Condenser cooling fan temperature switch
34. Safety temperature switch
39. Relay for fast idle electrovalve

40. Condenser cooling fan relay
41. Master relay
42. Conditioner fan relay
51. Defroster valve temperature switch
52. Conditioner control board

53. Conditioner fan motor speed switch
54. Conditioner cooling fan
67. Central control box
130. Terminal

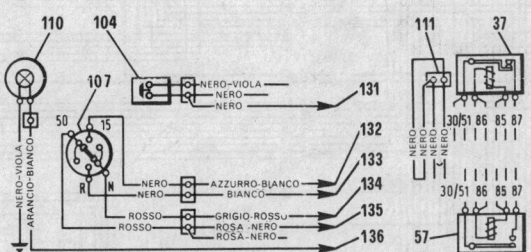

1975-77 131 Sedan automatic transmission option

37. Gear-engaged starter inhibitor relay
57. Starter inhibitor relay
104. Fast idle switch

107. Starter inhibitor switch and back-up light (replaces switch 113)
110. Selected gear indicator light

111. Connector for fast idle switch thru clutch
131. To terminal of switch 101
132. To terminal 5 of rear cable connector of central control box 67

133. To back-up lights 125
134. To terminal 85 of relay 58
135. To switch 107
136. To terminal 12 of rear cable connector of central control box 67

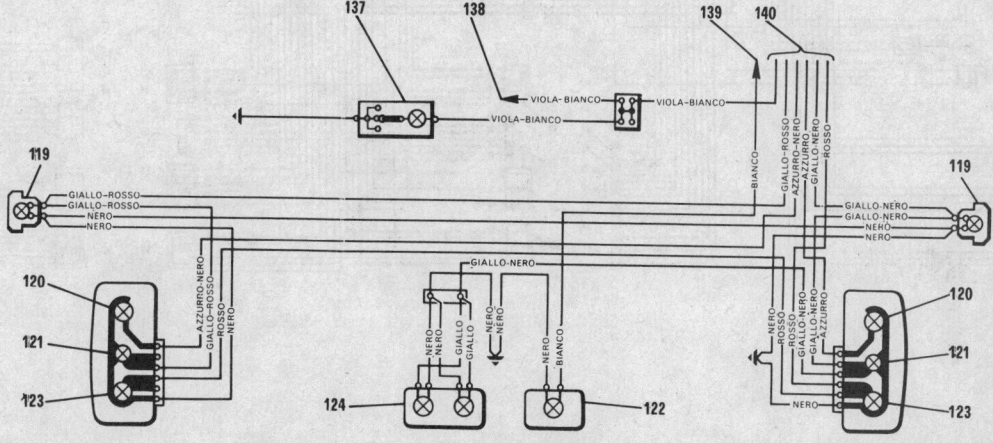

1975-77 131 Sedan Station Wagon supplement

119. Rear side marker lights
120. Rear turn signal lights
121. Rear tail lights

122. Back-up light
123. Stop lights
124. License plate lights

137. Rear interior light and switch
138. To lights 115

139. To switch 112
140. To terminals of rear cable connector of central control box 67

Cable Color Code

| Arancio = Amber | Bianco = White | Giallo = Yellow | Marrone = Brown | Rosa = Pink | Verde = Green |
| Azzurro = Light blue | Blu = Dark Blue | Grigio = Grey | Nero = Black | Rosso = Red | Viola = Violet |

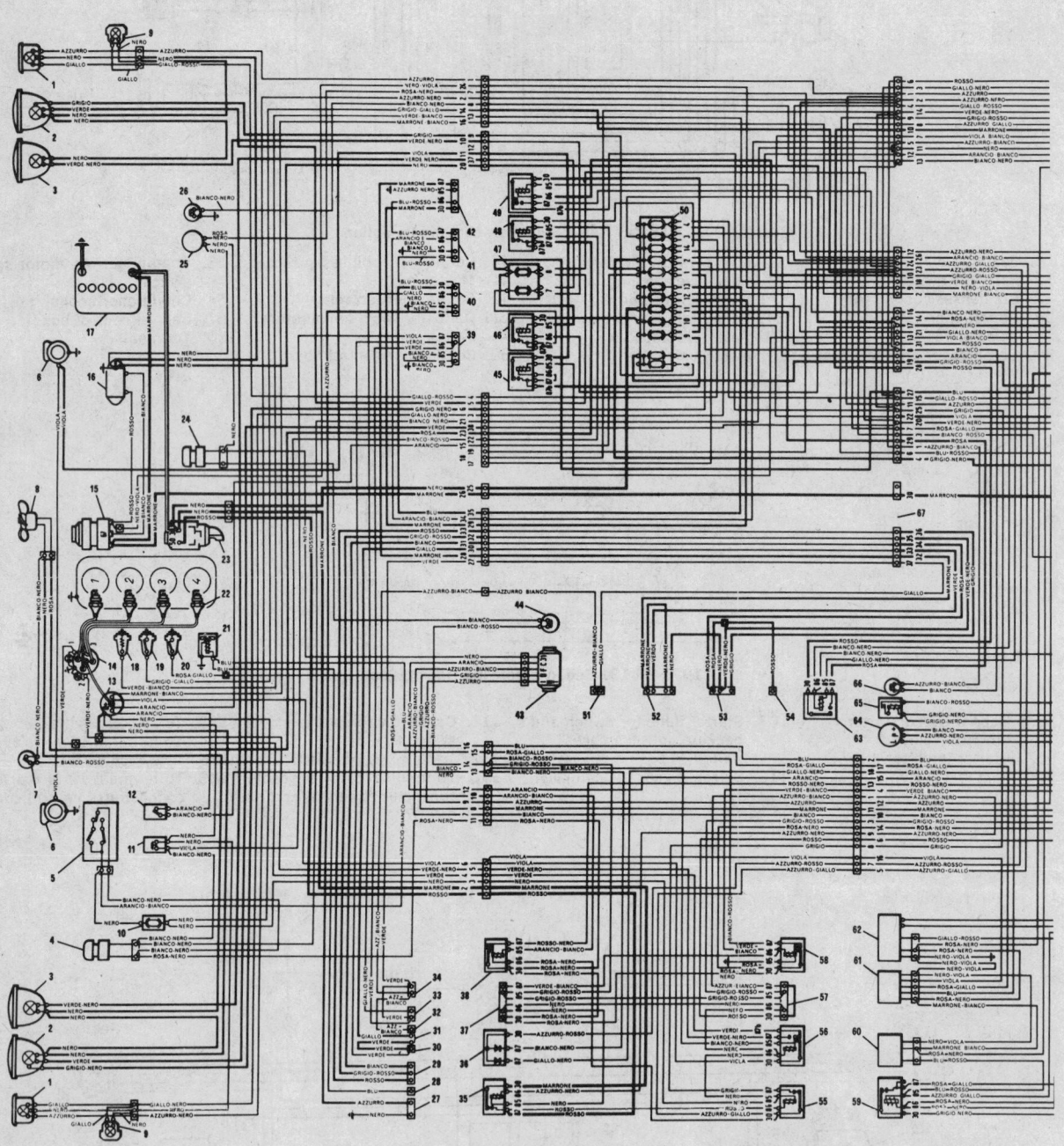

1975-77 131 Sedan

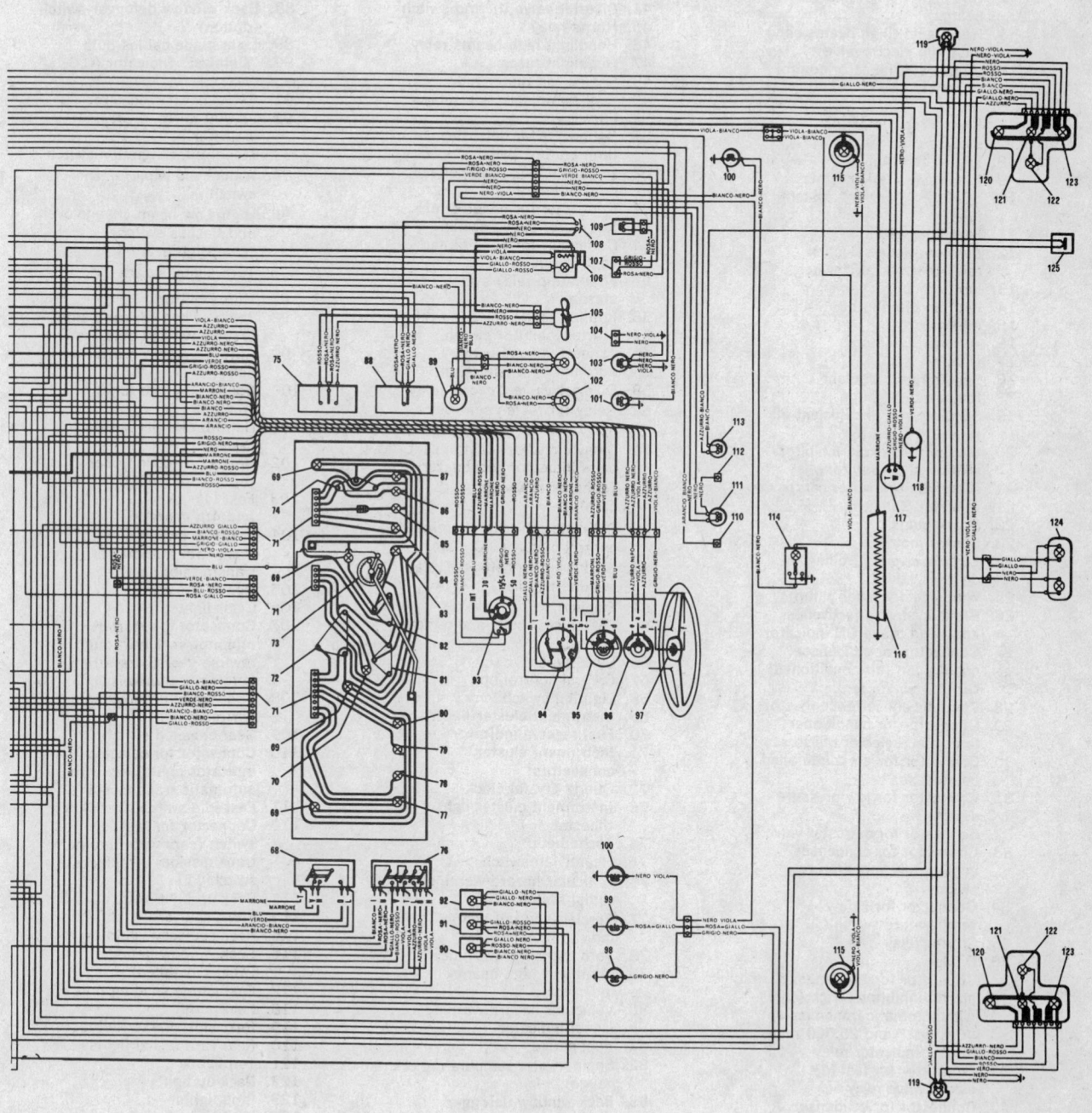

1975-77 131 Sedan

Wiring Circuits

1. Front parking and turn signal lamps
2. Headlights (high and low beams)
3. Headlights (high beams only)
4. Fast idle electrovalve
5. "Catalyst" indicator control switches
6. Horns
7. Engine fan motor thermostatic switch
8. Engine fan motor
9. Front side marker lights
10. "Catalyst" warning system fuse
11. Fast idle switch
12. Ignition mode selection relay thermostatic switch
13. Ignition coil
14. Ignition distributor
15. Alternator
16. Voltage regulator
17. Battery
18. Sending unit, coolant temperature gauge
19. Sending unit, insufficient oil pressure indicator
20. Idle stop solenoid inhibitor switch on carburetor (Catalytic Converter cars)
21. Idle stop solenoid
22. Spark plugs
23. Starter motor
24. Electrovalve controlling diverter valve
25. Windshield washer pump
26. Brake system effectiveness and hand brake ON indicator
27. Connector for condenser cooling fan (air conditioned cars)
28. Catalytic converter connector
29. Connector for conditioner fan speed selector resistor
30. Connector for air conditioned compressor
31. Connector for low pressure switch
32. Connector for defroster valve
33. Connector for condenser cooling fan temperature switch
34. Connector for safety temperature switch
35. Starter relay
36. Diodes
37. Connector for gear-engaged starter inhibitor switch (cars with automatic transmission)
38. "Catalyst" and 25,000 miles "EGR" indicator relay
39. Connector for fast idle electrovalve relay
40. Connector for condenser cooling fan relay
41. Connector for air conditioner master relay

42. Connector for conditioner fan relay
43. Windshield wiper motor
44. Diverter valve thermo switch
45. Horns relay
46. Headlight high beams relay
47. Headlight fuses
48. Engine fan motor relay
49. Fuel pump selection relay
50. Fuses
51. Connector for defroster valve temperature switch
52. Connector for conditioner control board
53. Connector for conditioner fan motor speed switch
54. Connector for conditioner cooling fan
55. Fuel pump relay switch on starting
56. Ignition mode selection relay
57. Starter inhibitor switch connector (cars with automatic transmission)
58. Diverter valve air feed relay
59. Relay for fasten seat belts and remove key circuit
60. Delay circuit for fasten seat belts indicator and buzzer
61. Tachometer switch (C.C. cars)
62. Catalytic converter electronic control circuit (C.C. cars)
63. Back window defogger relay (where installed)
64. Flasher
65. Fasten seat belts and remove key buzzer
66. Stop switch
67. Central control box
68. Lighting switch
69. Instrument cluster lights
70. Fuel reserve indicator
71. Instrument cluster connectors
72. Quartz crystal clock
73. Instrument cluster light rheostat
74. Tachometer
75. Heater fan switch
76. Vehicular hazard warning signal switch
77. Parking and tail lights indicator
78. Turn signal arrow indicator
79. Headlight high beams indicator
80. Vehicular hazard warning signal indicator
81. Fuel gauge
82. Engine water temperature gauge
83. Back window defogger indicator (option)
84. Battery charge indicator
85. Low oil pressure indicator

86. Brake system effectiveness/hand brake ON indicator
87. Fasten seat belts indicator
88. Back window defogger switch (option)
89. Light guide cables bulb
90. "Catalyst" indicator (C.C. cars)
91. "Slow down" indicator
92. 25,000 miles "EGR" indicator
93. Steering lock ignition switch
94. Windshield wiper/washer switch
95. High/Low beam change-over and flashes switch (O = High beam)
96. Turn signal switch
97. Horns button
98. Jamb switch (driver's side) for remove key buzzer
99. Button switch on driver's belt
100. Courtesy lamps jamb switches
101. Hand brake ON button switch
102. Heater/air conditioner controls illumination bulbs
103. Fast idle switch (thru 3rd and 4th gears)
104. Fast idle switch connector (cars with automatic transmission)
105. Heater fan motor
106. Cigar lighter
107. Connector for starter inhibitor switch through reverse gear (cars with automatic transmission)
108. Connector for glove compartment light
109. Gear-engaged switch
110. Connector for selected gear indicator light (cars with automatic transmission)
111. Fast idle switch thru clutch
112. Connector for fast idle switch (cars with automatic transmission)—replaces switch 111
113. Back-up light switch
114. Front courtesy light
115. Rear courtesy lights
116. Back window defogger (where installed)
117. Fuel gauge sending unit
118. Fuel pump
119. Rear side marker lights
120. Rear turn signal lights
121. Tail lights
122. Back-up lights
123. Stop lights
124. License plate lights
125. Catalytic converter thermocouple (where installed)

1975-77 131 Sedan

1. Front parking lamps
2. Front turn signal lamps
3. Headlights
4. Front side marker lamps
5. Engine fan motor thermostatic switch
6. Battery charge selection relay
7. Fuel pump selection relay (at starting)
8. Ignition advance selection relay
9. Selection relay for diverter valve control electrovalve (C.C. cars)
10. Engine fan motor relay
11. Alternator
12. Ignition distributor
13. Thermostatic switch, engine coolant temperature gauge
14. Sending unit, engine coolant temperature gauge
15. Spark plugs
16. Voltage regulator
17. Thermostatic switch, ignition selection relay
18. Starter motor
19. Ballast resistor, engine coolant temperature gauge
20. Sending unit, insufficient oil pressure indicator
21. Sending unit, oil pressure gauge
22. Ignition coil
23. Engine fan motor
24. Fast idle switch
25. Idle stop solenoid
26. Horns compressor
27. EGR cut-out electrovalve on 5th gear
28. Fast idle switch through clutch
29. Fast idle electrovalve
30. Electrovalve controlling diverter valve (C.C. cars)
31. Thermostatic switch, electrovalve controlling diverter valve (C.C. cars)
32. Selection relay, fasten belts/remove key indicator circuit
33. Horns relay.
34. Windshield washer pump
35. Fasten belts/remove key buzzer
36. Delay circuit for fasten belts indicator and buzzer
37. Windshield wiper interrupter
38. Turn signal flasher
39. Hazard warning signal flasher
40. Windshield wiper motor
41. Low brake fluid level indicator (if fitted)
42. Brake system effectiveness indicator
43. Stop lights switch
44. 16-A inline fuse
45. 8-A inline fuse
46. Power point
47. Instrument cluster lamps rheostat

48. Brake system effectiveness/ Hand brake ON indicator
49. Fasten belts indicator
50. Ideogram light potentiometer
51. Vehicular hazard warning signal indicator
52. Windshield wiper sweep rate knob
53. Clock light
54. Quartz crystal clock
55. Engine coolant temperature gauge light
56. Engine coolant temperature gauge
57. Engine tachometer
58. Battery charge indicator
59. Tachometer light
60. Oil pressure gauge light
61. Low oil pressure indicator
62. Oil pressure gauge
63. High beam indicator
64. Speedometer light
65. Turn signal arrow indicator
66. Parking and tail lights indicator
67. Fuel gauge light
68. Fuel reserve indicator
69. Fuel gauge
70. Lighting switch
71. Courtesy lamp/remove key buzzer jamb switch
72. Heater fan motor, two-speed
73. Courtesy lamp with incorporated switch

74. Vehicular hazard warning signal switch with incorporated light
75. Ideogram illumination optical fibers light source
76. Heater fan motor switch, three-position
77. Cigar lighter and housing indicator
78. Fast idle switch thru 3rd/4th gear
79. Hand brake ON switch
80. Back-up light/EGR cut-out on 5th gear switch
81. Gear-engaged switch
82. Steering lock ignition switch
83. Fuses
84. High/low beams change-over switch lever
85. Turn signal switch
86. Windshield wiper/washer switch
87. Horns button
88. Button switch on driver's belt
89. Rear side marker lights
90. Battery
91. Trunk light
92. Fuel gauge sending unit
93. Fuel pump
94. Rear turn signal lamps
95. Stop lamps
96. Tail lamps
97. Back-up lamps
98. License plate lamps

1975-77 124 Sport Spider

Cable Color Code

Arancio	= Amber	Bianco	= White	Giallo	= Yellow	Marrone	= Brown	Rosa	= Pink	Verde	= Green
Azzurro	= Light blue	Blu	= Dark Blue	Grigio	= Grey	Nero	= Black	Rosso	= Red	Viola	= Violet

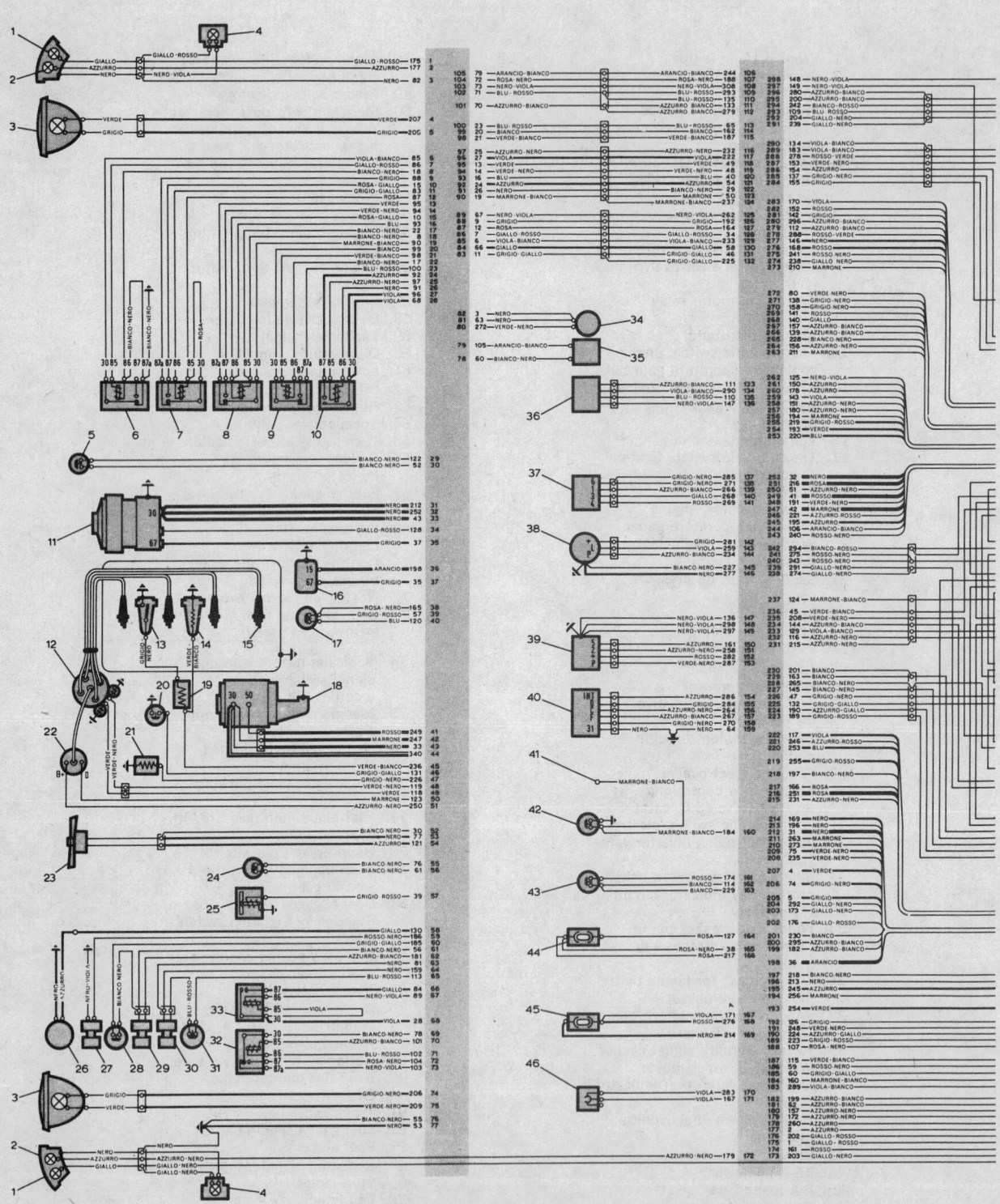

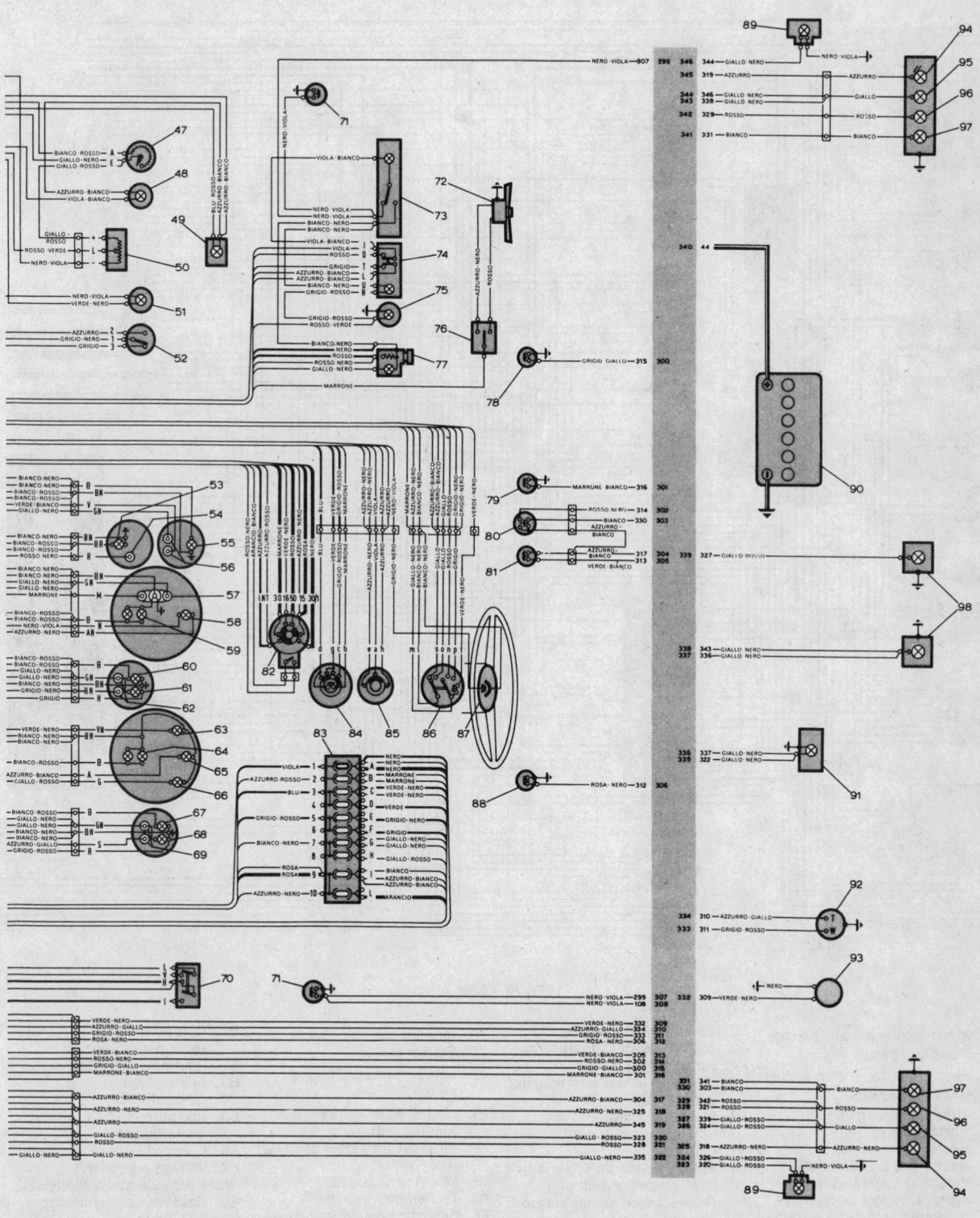

1975-77 124 Sport Spider

Wiring Circuits

Cable Color Code

Arancio = Amber	Bianco = White	Giallo = Yellow	Marrone = Brown	Rosa = Pink	Verde = Green
Azzurro = Light blue	Blu = Dark Blue	Grigio = Grey	Nero = Black	Rosso = Red	Viola = Violet

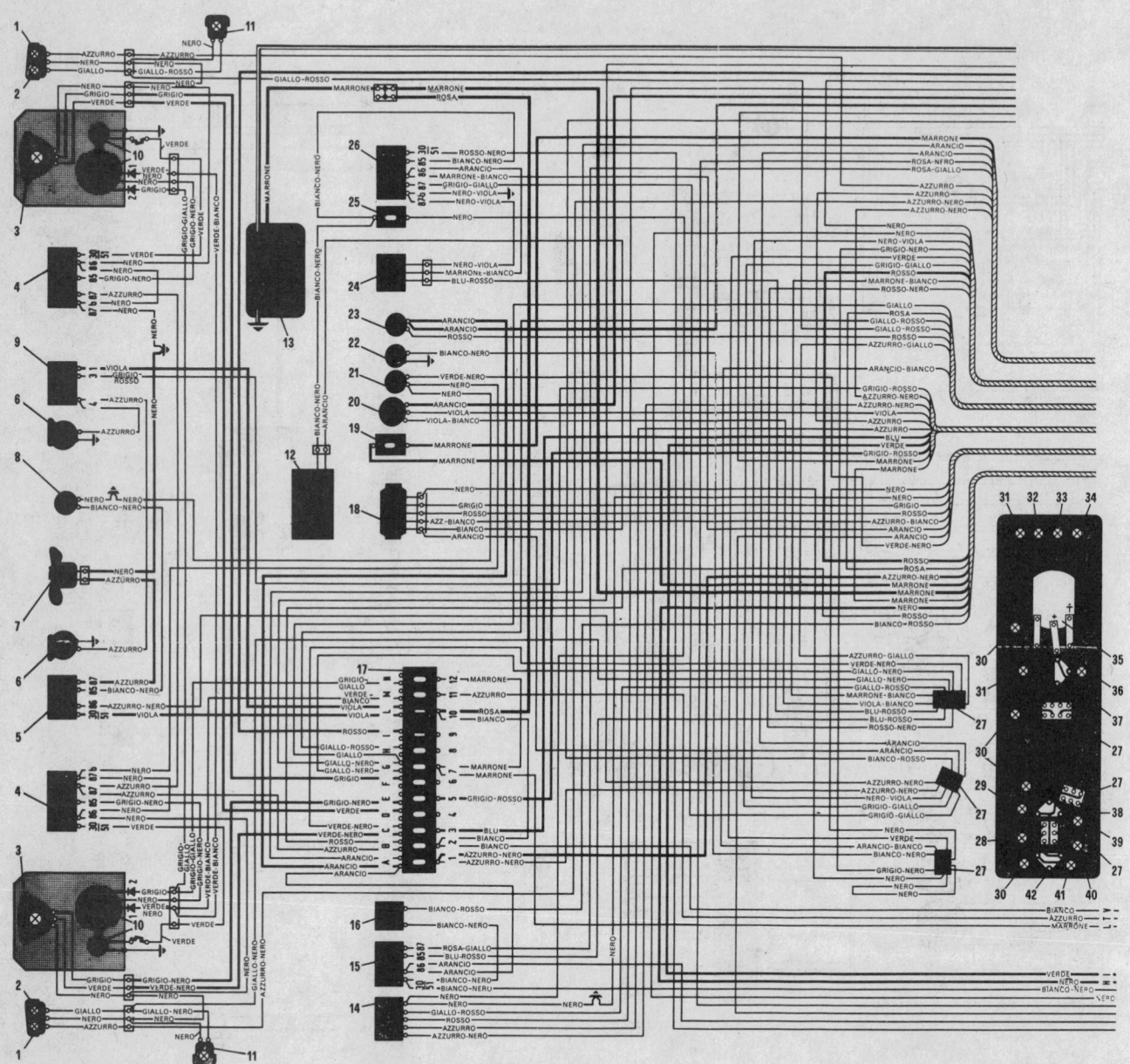

1975-77 X1/9

49. Windshield wiper and washer 3-position switch
50. High/Low beams change-over and flashes switch
51. Turn signal switch
52. Horns control
53. Heater fan 2-speed motor
54. Heater fan 3-position switch
55. Vehicular hazard warning signal switch, 2-position
56. Instrument cluster 3-position switch
57. Ideogram illumination optical fiber light source
58. Ideogram illumination optical fiber light source

59. Courtesy light switch
60. Ballast resistor, instrument cluster lights intensity
61. Cigarette lighter and housing indicator
62. Ideogram lighting potentiometer
63. Courtesy light
64. Button switch on driver's belt
65. Fuel gauge sending unit
66. Gear-engaged signal button switch
67. Back-up lamp switch
68. Switch for hand brake ON signal
69. Carburetor cooling motor relay

70. Ignition coil
71. Starter motor
72. Low oil pressure indicator switch
73. Engine water temperature sending unit
74. Oil pressure gauge sending unit
75. Idle stop solenoid
76. Tachometer switch
77. Catalytic converter electronic control unit
78. Diverter valve relay
79. Diverter valve air discharge electrovalve
80. Carburetor cooling motor

81. Carburetor cooling motor thermostatic switch
82. Ignition distributor
83. Spark plugs
84. Alternator
85. Idle stop inhibitor switch on carburetor
86. Diverter valve thermoswitch
87. Voltage regulator
88. Rear side marker lamps
89. Rear turn signal lights
90. Tail lights
91. Stop lights
92. Back-up lights
93. License plate lights
94. Catalytic converter thermocouple

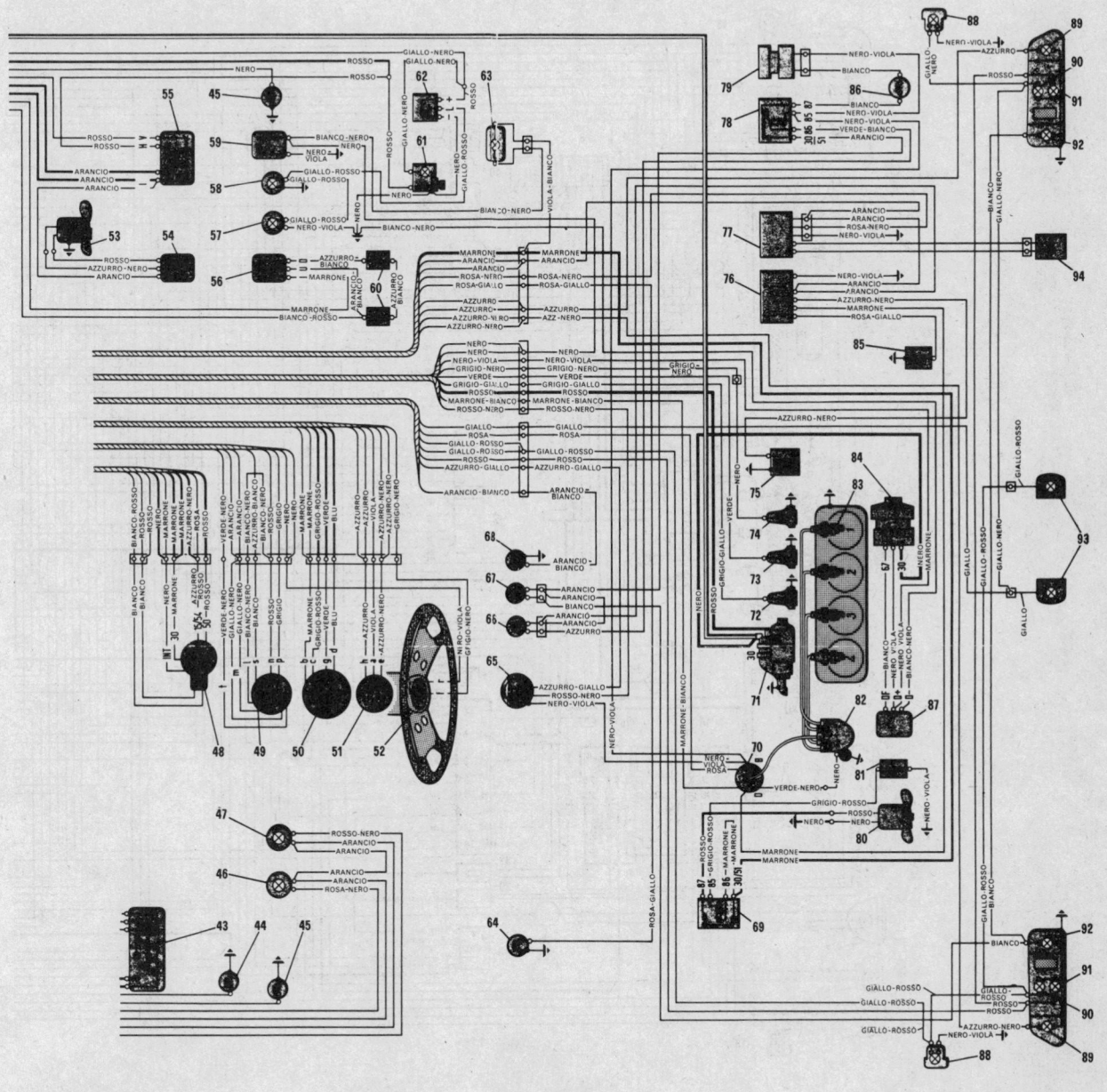

1975-77 X1/9

1. Front turn signal lights
2. Front parking lights
3. Headlights (low and high beams)
4. Headlight motors relay
5. Engine fan motor relay
6. Horns
7. Engine fan motor
8. Engine fan motor thermostatic switch
9. Horns relay
10. Headlight motors
11. Front side marker lights
12. "Catalyst" indicator control switches (25,000 miles)
13. Battery
14. Flasher, vehicular hazard warning signal
15. Fasten belts buzzer relay
16. Fasten belts buzzer
17. Fuses
18. Windshield wiper motor
19. Fuse protecting courtesy light and carburetor cooling motor
20. Flasher, turn signal lights
21. Windshield washer pump
22. Brake system effectiveness indicator
23. Stop lights switch
24. Delay circuit for fasten belts indicator and buzzer
25. "Catalyst" warning system fuse
26. "Catalyst" indicator relay
27. Instrument cluster connectors
28. Brake system effectiveness/ hand brake ON indicator
29. Spare indicator
30. Instrument cluster lights
31. "Fasten belts" indicator (red)
32. Vehicular hazard warning signal indicator (flashing)
33. Parking and tail lights indicator (green)
34. High beams indicator (blue)
35. Engine tachometer (electronic)
36. Fuel reserve indicator (red)
37. Fuel gauge
38. Engine water temperature gauge
39. Battery charge indicator (red)
40. Back window defogger indicator (where installed)
41. Insufficient oil pressure indicator (red)
42. Oil pressure gauge
43. Lighting and headlight motors 3-position switch
44. Jamb switch on driver's door for remove key buzzer
45. Jamb switches for courtesy light
46. "Catalyst" indicator
47. "Slow down" indicator
48. Ignition switch

Wiring Circuits

Cable Color Code

Arancio = Amber	Bianco = White	Giallo = Yellow	Marrone = Brown	Rosa = Pink	Verde = Green
Azzurro = Light blue	Blu = Dark Blue	Grigio = Grey	Nero = Black	Rosso = Red	Viola = Violet

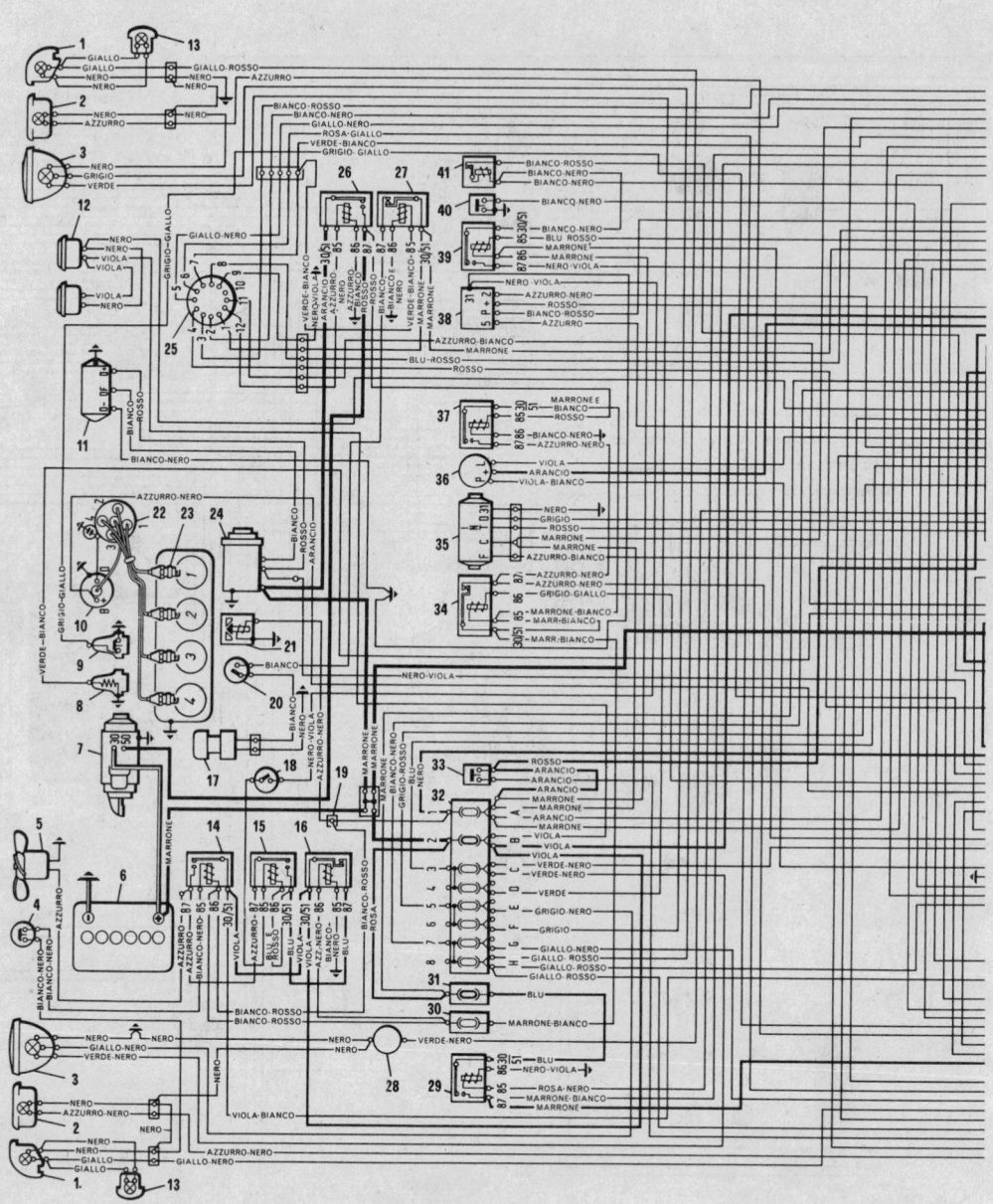

1975-77 128 Sedan

1. Front parking lamps
2. Front turn signal lamps
3. Headlamps
4. Engine fan motor thermostatic switch (on radiator)
5. Engine and carburetor fan motor
6. Battery
7. Starter
8. Sending unit, coolant temperature gauge
9. Sending unit, low oil pressure indicator
10. Ignition coil
11. Voltage regulator
12. Horns

13. Front side marker lamps
14. Relay for motor 5—Engine fan operation
15. Relay for motor 5—Carburetor cooling with engine OFF
16. Relay for motor 5—Carburetor cooling with engine ON
17. Diverter valve air discharge electrovalve
18. Engine fan motor thermostatic switch (intake manifold)
19. Catalytic converter connector
20. Diverter valve thermo switch
21. Idle stop solenoid

22. Ignition distributor
23. Spark plugs
24. Alternator
25. Interlock system electronic control unit
26. Starter relay
27. Catalytic converter air feed relay
28. Windshield washer pump
29. Relay for defogger 81 (where installed)
30. Fuse for fuel pump
31. Fuse for defogger 81 (where installed)
32. fuses
33. Stop lights switch

34. Fuel pump relay
35. Windshield wiper motor
36. Flasher, turn signal lights
37. Fuel pump relay starting switch
38. Flasher, vehicular hazard warning signal
39. Relay for buzzer 41
40. Switch for indicator 66
41. Remove key and fasten belts buzzer
42. Fuse, remove key buzzer
43. Connectors, instrument cluster
44. Turn signal indicator (green)
45. Instrument cluster lights

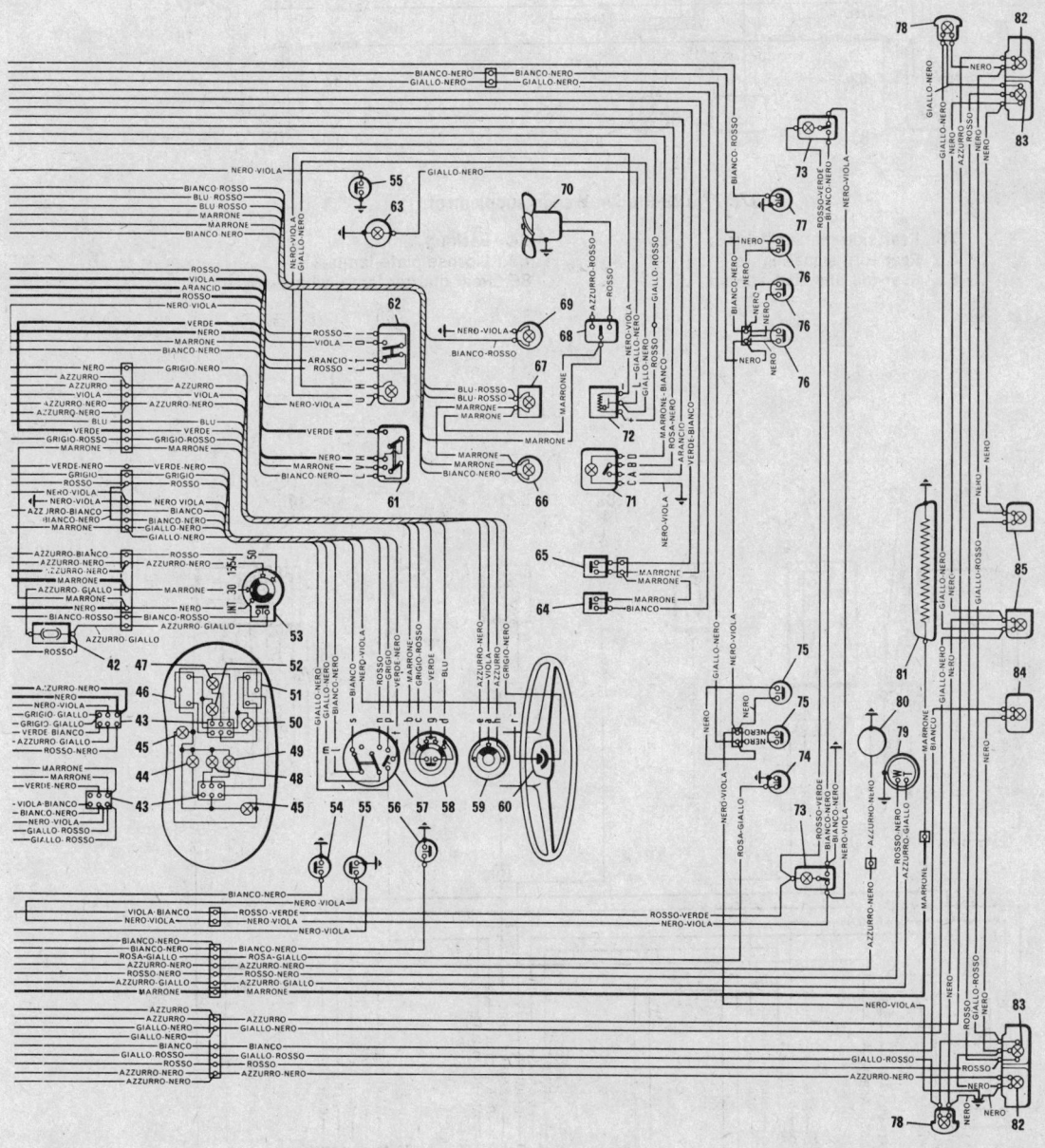

1975-77 128 Sedan

46. Coolant temperature gauge
47. Battery charge indicator (red)
48. Parking and tail lights indicator (green)
49. High beams indicator (blue)
50. Fuel reserve indicator (red)
51. Fuel gauge
52. Low engine oil pressure indicator (red)
53. Ignition switch
54. Jamb switch for remove key buzzer
55. Jamb switches for pillar lamps
56. Switch, hand brake ON and indicator 66 operation check

57. Windshield wiper and washer 3-position switch
58. High/Low beams change-over and flashes switch
59. Turn signal switch
60. Horn button
61. Lighting and instrument cluster 3-position switch
62. Switch, with light, vehicular hazard warning signal
63. Ideogram illumination optical fiber light source
64. Switch, back-up lamp
65. Gear-engaged signal button switch

66. Indicator, hydraulic service brake effectiveness and hand brake ON
67. Fasten belts indicator (red)
68. Heater fan 3-position switch
69. Vehicular hazard warning signal indicator
70. Heater fan 2-speed motor
71. Switch, with indicator, for defogger 81 (where installed)
72. Ideogram lighting potentiometer
73. Pillar lamps, with switch
74. Button switch on driver's belt
75. Strip switches in driver's seat cushion

76. Strip switches in passenger's seat cushion
77. Button switch on passenger's belt
78. Rear side marker lights
79. Fuel gauge sending unit
80. Fuel pump
81. Back window defogger (where installed)
82. Rear turn signal lights
83. Rear tail and stop lights
84. Back-up lamp
85. License plate lamp

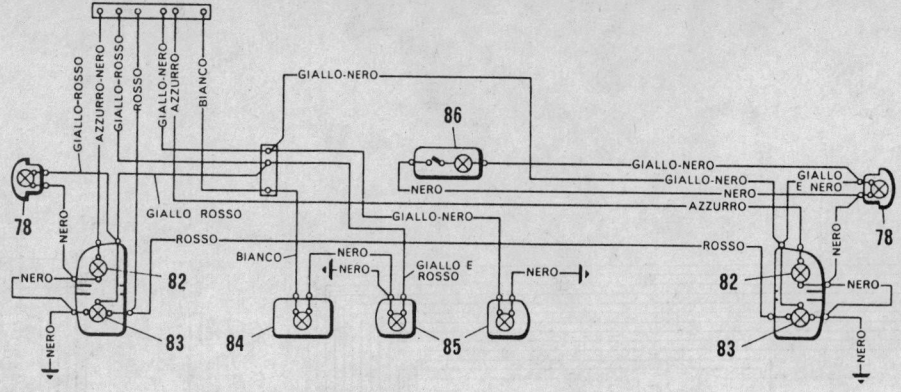

1975-77 128 Station Wagon supplement

78. Rear side marker lights
82. Rear turn signal lights
83. Rear tail and stop lights
84. Back-up lamp
85. License plate lamp
86. Rear quarter lamp, with switch

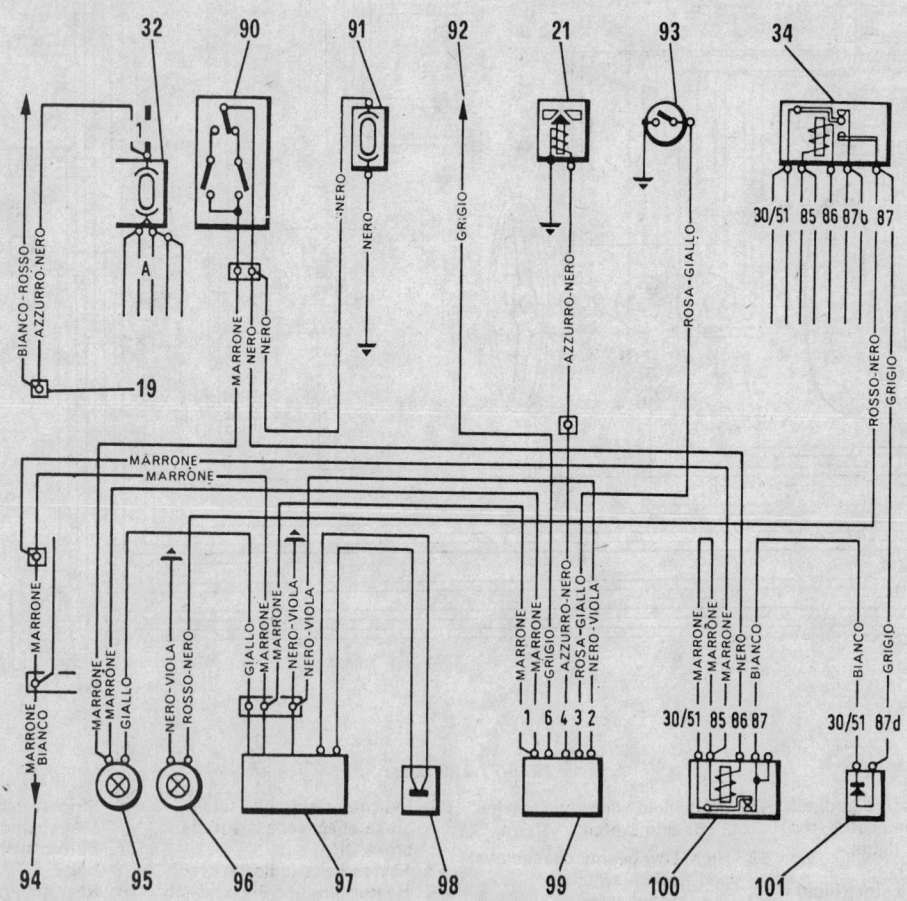

1975-77 128 California supplement

32. Fuses
90. "Catalyst" indicator control switches (25,000 miles)
91. "Catalyst" warning system fuse
92. To terminal D of ignition distributor

21. Idle stop solenoid
93. Idle stop solenoid inhibitor switch on carburetor
34. Fuel pump and "catalyst" indicator selection relay
19. Connector for catalytic conveter version

94. To terminal 1 of interlock system electronic control unit
95. "Slow down" indicator
96. "Catalyst" indicator
97. Catalytic converter electronic control unit

98. Catalytic converter thermocouple
99. Tacho switch
100. "Catalyst" indicator relay
101. Indicator diodes

SPECIFICATIONS

Honda

INTRODUCTION

Honda Motor Company has been selling motorcycles in the United States for over a decade, earning the distinction of number one in sales in the motorcycle world. Until 1971 its automotive sales were limited to Asia. However this was changed with the introduction of the Honda 600. This two-cylinder "mini" was first marketed on the West Coast and Hawaii, and as 1971 drew to a close, Honda placed 19th in import sales. After Honda's decision to sell its models on a nationwide basis, the 600 rose to 12th in import sales by the middle of 1972.

Both models, the 600 sedan and Z600 coupe, share the same front-wheel drive, air-cooled SOHC engine. Only the sheet metal and styling, in the usual American practice, are changed—with everything done in miniature. Excellent examples of clever design and engineering, the 600's are cheap to operate and maintain.

The 600, however, was discontinued after the 1972 model run and replaced by the larger Honda Civic. Although still smaller than sub-compact in size, this "stretched" version of the 600 style sports a water-cooled, transversely mounted four-cylinder engine and much improved performance.

MODEL IDENTIFICATION

1973 1170 cc Civic

1974-76 1237 cc Civic

1975-76 Civic CVCC Sedan

1975-76 Civic CVCC Wagon

1976 Accord CVCC

SERIAL NUMBER IDENTIFICATION

Vehicle Identification (Chassis) Number

Honda vehicle identification numbers are on the top edge of the instrument panel visible from the outside. In addition, there is a Vehicle/Engine Identification plate under the hood on the hood mounting bracket.

Engine Serial Number

The engine serial number is stamped into the clutch casing and appears on the VIN plate. The first three digits indicate engine model identification. The remaining numbers refer to production sequence.

Transmission Serial Number

The transmission serial number is stamped on the top of the transmission/-clutch case.

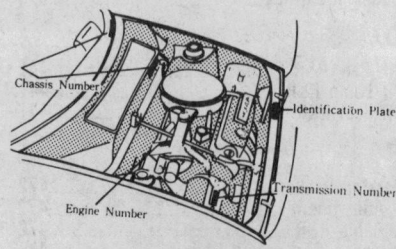
Serial number locations

SERIAL NUMBER IDENTIFICATION CHART

Year	Model	Body Type	Trans.	VIN (Chassis Number)	Engine No.
1973 Civic	SBA	2-Dr	4-Sp	SBA-1007001—1100000	EB1-1000001—1069000
	SBB	2-Dr	Hondamatic	SBB-1007001—1100000	EB1-1000001—1069000
	SBC	3-Dr	4-Sp	SBC-1007001—1100000	EB1-1000001—1069000
	SBD	3-Dr	Hondamatic	SBD-1007001—1100000	EB1-1000001—1069000
1974 Civic	SBA	2-Dr	4-Sp	SBA-2100001—3300000	EB2-1000001—1076643
	SBB	2-Dr	Hondamatic	SBB-2100001—3300000	EB2-1000001—1076643
	SBC	3-Dr	4-Sp	SBC-2100001—3300000	EB2-1000001—1076643
	SBD	3-Dr	Hondamatic	SBD-2100001—3300000	EB2-1000001—1076643
1975 Civic	SBA	2-Dr	4-Sp	SBA-3300001—4000000	EB2-2000001—3000000
	SBB	2-Dr	Hondamatic	SBB-3300001—4000000	EB2-2000001—3000000
	SBC	2-Dr	4-Sp	SBC-3300001—4000000	EB2-2000001—3000000
	SBD	3-Dr	Hondamatic	SBD-3300001—4000000	EB2-2000001—3000000
1975 CVCC Civic	SGA	2-Dr	4-Sp	SGA-1000001—2000000	ED1-1000001—2000000
	SGB	2-Dr	Hondamatic	SGB-1000001—2000000	ED1-1000001—2000000
	SGC	3-Dr	4-Sp	SGC-1000001—2000000	ED1-1000001—2000000
	SGD	3-Dr	Hondamatic	SGD-1000001—2000000	ED1-1000001—2000000
	SGE	3-Dr	5-Sp	SGE-1000001—2000000	ED1-1000001—2000000
	WBA	Wagon	4-Sp	WBA-1000001—2000000	ED2-1000001—2000000
1976 Civic	SBA	2-Dr	4-Sp	SBA-4000001—5000000	EB2-3000001—4000000
	SBB	2-Dr	Hondamatic	SBB-4000001—5000000	EB2-3000001—4000000
	SBC	3-Dr	4-Sp	SBC-4000001—5000000	EB2-3000001—4000000
	SBD	3-Dr	Hondamatic	SBD-4000001—5000000	EB2-3000001—4000000
1976 CVCC Civic	SGA	2-Dr	4-Sp	SGA-2000001—3000000	ED3-2000001—3000000
	SGB	2-Dr	Hondamatic	SGB-2000001—3000000	ED3-2000001—3000000
	SGC	3-Dr	4-Sp	SGC-2000001—3000000	ED3-2000001—3000000
	SGD	3-Dr	Hondamatic	SGD-2000001—3000000	ED3-2000001—3000000
	SGE	3-Dr	5-Sp	SGE-2000001—3000000	ED3-2000001—3000000
	WBA	Wagon	4-Sp	WBA-2000001—3000000	ED4-2000001—3000000
	WBB	Wagon	Hondamatic	WBB-2000001—3000000	ED4-2000001—3000000
1976 CVCC Accord	SJD	3-Dr	Hondamatic	SJD-1000001—2000000	EF1-1000001—2000000
	SJE	3-Dr	5-Sp	SJE-1000001—2000000	EF1-1000001—2000000

GENERAL ENGINE SPECIFICATIONS

Model	Year	Engine Displacement (cc)	Carburetor Type	Horsepower @ rpm	Bore x Stroke (in.)	Compression Ratio	Torque @ rpm (ft lbs)
Civic	1973	1170	Hitachi 2 bbl	50 @ 5000	2.76 x 2.99	8.3:1	59 @ 3000
Civic	1974	1237	Hitachi 2 bbl	N.A.	2.83 x 2.99	8.1:1	N.A.
Civic AIR	1975-76	1237	Hitachi 2 bbl	N.A.	2.83 x 2.99	8.1:1	N.A.
Civic CVCC	1975	1487	Keihin 3 bbl	53 @ 5000	2.91 x 3.41	8.1:1	68 @ 3000
Civic CVCC	1976	1487	Keihin 3 bbl	53 @ 5000	2.91 x 3.41	7.9:1	68 @ 3000
Accord CVCC	1976	1600	Keihin 3 bbl	68 @ 5000	2.91 x 3.66	8.0:1	85 @ 3000

N.A. Not Available

TUNE-UP SPECIFICATIONS

When analyzing compression test results, look for uniformity among cylinders, rather than specific pressures.

Year	Model	Engine Displacement (cc)	Original Equipment Spark Plugs Type	Gap (in.)	Distributor Point Dwell (deg)	Point Gap (in.)	Basic Ignition Timing (deg) MT	AT	Intake Valve Opens (deg)	Fuel Pump Pressure (psi)	Idle Speed (rpm) MT	AT	Valve Clearance (in.) Intake (cold)	Auxiliary (cold)	Exhaust (cold)
1973	Civic	1170	BP-6ES or W-20EP ①	0.028-0.031	49-55	0.018-0.022	TDC ③⑧	TDC ③⑧	32B	2.56	750-850 ④	700-800 ⑤	0.005-0.007	—	0.005-0.007
1974	Civic	1237	BP-6ES or W-20EP ①	0.028-0.031	49-55	0.018-0.022	5B ⑧	5B ⑧	31B	2.56	750-850 ④	700-800 ⑤	0.004-0.006	—	0.004-0.006
1975-76	Civic AIR	1237	BP-6ES or W-20EP ①	0.028-0.032	49-55	0.018-0.022	7B ⑧	7B ⑧	31B	2.56	750-850 ④	700-800 ⑤	0.004-0.006	—	0.004-0.006
1975	Civic CVCC	1487	BP-6ES or W-20ES ②	0.028-0.032	49-55	0.018-0.022	TDC ⑨	3A ⑨	N.A.	1.85-2.56	800-900 ④	700-800 ⑤	0.005-0.007	0.005-0.007	0.005-0.007
1976	Civic CVCC	1487	BP-6ES or W-20ES ②	0.028-0.032	49-55	0.018-0.022	2B ⑥⑨	2B ⑦⑨	N.A.	1.85-2.56	800-900 ④	700-800 ⑤	0.005-0.007	0.005-0.007	0.005-0.007
1976	Accord CVCC	1600	BP-6ES or W-20ES ①②	0.028-0.031	49-55	0.018-0.022	2B ⑨	TDC ⑨	10A	1.85-2.56	750-850 ④	630-730 ⑤	0.005-0.007	0.005-0.007	0.005-0.007

① For continuous highway use over 70 mph, use cooler NGK BP-7ES, Nippon Denso W-22EP or equivalent
② For continuous low-speed use under 30 mph, use hotter NGK BP-5ES, Nippon Denso W-16ES or equivalent
③ Static ignition timing—5B
④ In neutral, with headlights on
⑤ In drive range, with headlights on
⑥ 5-speed sedan (hatchback) from engine number 2500001-up—6B
⑦ Station wagon—TDC
⑧ Aim timing light at red notch on crankshaft pulley with distributor vacuum hose(s) connected at specified idle speed
⑨ Aim timing light at red mark on flywheel or torque converter drive plate with distributor vacuum hose connected at specified idle speed

TDC—Top Dead Center   B—Before Top Dead Center   — Not Applicable
  A—After Top Dead Center   N.A. Not Available

FIRING ORDER

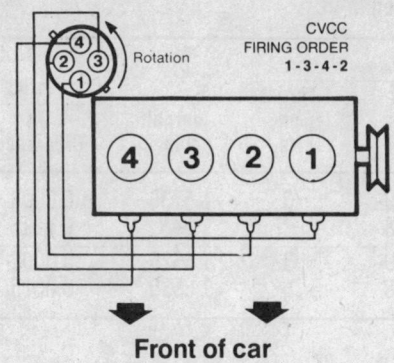

CVCC
FIRING ORDER
1 - 3 - 4 - 2

Rotation

Front of car

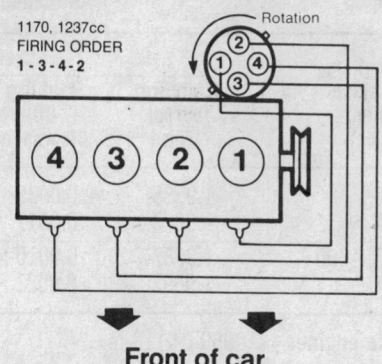

1170, 1237cc
FIRING ORDER
1 - 3 - 4 - 2

Rotation

Front of car

CAPACITIES

Year	Model	Engine Displacement (cc)	Engine Crankcase (qts) w/filter	Transmission (qts)			Gasoline Tank (gals)	Cooling System (qts\)
				Manual		Automatic		
				4-sp	5-sp			
1973	Civic	1170	3.2	2.6	—	2.6	10.0	4.2
1974	Civic	1237	3.2	2.6	—	2.6	10.0	4.2
1975-76	Civic	1237	3.2	2.6	—	2.6	10.6	4.2
1975-76	CVCC Sedan	1487	3.2	2.6	2.6	2.6	10.6	4.2
1975-76	CVCC Wagon	1487	3.2	2.6	—	2.6	11.0	4.2
1976	CVCC Accord	1600	3.8	—	2.6	4.4	13.2	6.0

— Not Applicable

VALVE SPECIFICATIONS

Year	Engine Displacement (cc)	Seat Angle (deg)	Face Angle (deg)	Spring Installed Height (in.)	Stem to Guide Clearance (in.)			Stem Diameter (in.)		
					Intake	Exhaust	Auxiliary	Intake	Exhaust	Auxiliary
1973-76	1170, 1237	45	45	Inner— 1.6535 Outer— 1.5728	0.005- 0.007	0.005- 0.007	—	0.2591- 0.2594	0.2579- 0.2583	—
1975-76	1487 CVCC	45	45	Inner— 1.358 Outer— 1.437 Auxiliary— 0.906	0.0004- 0.0016	0.0020- 0.0031	0.0008- 0.0020	0.2592- 0.2596	0.2580- 0.2584	0.2162- 0.2166
1976	1600 CVCC	45	45	Inner— 1.358 Outer— 1.437 Auxiliary— 0.906	0.0008- 0.0020	0.0008- 0.0020	0.0020- 0.0032	0.2591- 0.2594	0.2579- 0.2583	0.2157- 0.2161

— Not Applicable

CRANKSHAFT AND CONNECTING ROD SPECIFICATIONS

All measurements given in in.

Year	Engine Displacement (cc)	Crankshaft: Main Brg Journal Dia	Crankshaft: Main Brg Oil Clearance	Crankshaft: Shaft End Play	Crankshaft: Thrust on No.	Connecting Rod: Journal Dia	Connecting Rod: Oil Clearance	Connecting Rod: Side Clearance
1973-76	1170, 1237	1.9685-1.9673	0.0009-0.0017	0.0039-0.0138	3	1.5736-1.548	0.0008-0.0015	0.0079-0.0177①
1975-76	1487, 1600 CVCC	1.9687-1.9697	0.0010-0.0021	0.0039-0.0138	3	1.6525-1.6535	0.0008-0.0015	0.0059-0.0118

① 1974-76 1237 cc engines—0.0059-0.0118 in.

PISTON AND RING SPECIFICATIONS

All measurements are given in inches

Year	Engine Displacement (cc)	Piston Clearance	Ring Gap: Top Compression	Ring Gap: Bottom Compression	Ring Gap: Oil Control	Ring Side Clearance: Top Compression	Ring Side Clearance: Bottom Compression	Ring Side Clearance: Oil Control
1973	1170	0.0012-0.0039	0.008-0.016	0.008-0.016	0.008-0.035	0.0008-0.0018	0.0008-0.0018	0.0008-0.0018
1974-76	1237	0.0012-0.0039	0.0098-0.0157	0.0098-0.0577	0.0118-0.0394	0.0008-0.0018	0.0008-0.0018	Snug
1975-76	1487, 1600 CVCC	0.0012-0.0039	0.0079-0.0157	0.0079-0.0157	0.0079-0.0354①	0.0008-0.0018	0.0008-0.0018	Snug

① 1600 engine Oil control ring gap—0.0118-0.0354

ALTERNATOR AND REGULATOR SPECIFICATIONS

Year	Alternator: Engine Displacement (cc)	Alternator: Part No. or Manufacturer	Alternator: Field Current @ 12 V (amps)	Alternator: Output (amps) @ 5,000 rpm	Regulator: Part No. or Manufacturer	Field Relay: Yoke Gap (in.)	Field Relay: Point Gap (in.)	Field Relay: Volts to Close	Regulator: Yoke Gap (in.)	Regulator: Point Gap (in.)	Regulator: Volts @ 5,000 rpm
1973-76	1170, 1237 Civic	Hitachi	2.5	40① 35②	Hitachi	0.008-0.018	0.0016-0.0472	4.5-5.8	0.008-0.024	0.010-0.018	13.5-14.5
1975-76	1487 CVCC Civic	Nippon Denso	2.5	35③ 45④	Nippon Denso	—	—	—	—	0.016-0.020	13.5-14.5
1976	1600 CVCC Accord	Nippon Denso	2.5	50	Nippon Denso	—	—	—	—	—	—

① From No. 1011759
② Up to No. 1011158
③ Without A/C
④ With A/C
— Not Applicable

TORQUE SPECIFICATIONS
All readings are given in ft lbs

Year	Engine Displacement (cc)	Cylinder Head Bolts	Main Bearing Bolts	Rod Bearing Bolts	Crankshaft Pulley Bolts	Flywheel to Crankshaft Bolts	Manifold		Spark Plugs	Oil Pan Drain Bolt
							In	Ex		
1973-76	1170, 1237	30-35① 37-42②	27-31	18-21	34-38	34-38	13-17	13-17③	11-18	29-36
1975-76	1487, 1600 CVCC	40-47	30-35	18-21	34-38	34-38	15-17	15-17	11-18	29-36

① To engine number EB 1-1019949
② From engine number EB 1-1019950
③ 1975-76 models w/AIR—22-33 ft lbs

TORQUE SEQUENCES

CVCC cylinder head torque sequence

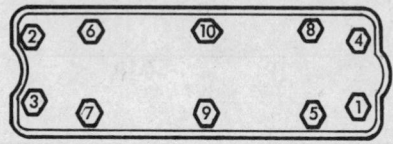

1170, 1237 cc cylinder head torque sequence

BATTERY AND STARTER SPECIFICATIONS
All cars use 12 volt, negative ground electrical systems

Year	Model (cc)	Battery Amp Hour Capacity	Lock Test			Starter No Load Test			Brush Spring Tension (oz)	Min. Brush Length (in.)
			Amps	Volts	Torque (ft/lbs)	Amps	Volts	RPM		
1973-76	Civic (1170,1237)	45	380 or less	4.9	5.4	less than 70	12	7000 or more	56-57	N.A.
1975-76	Civic CVCC (1487)	45	160	9.6	N.A.	less than 80	11.5	N.A.	N.A.	0.39
1976	CVCC Accord (1600)	47	N.A.	N.A.	N.A.	N.A.	N.A.	N.A.	N.A.	0.39

N.A. Not Available

BRAKE SPECIFICATIONS
All measurements given are (in.) unless noted

Year	Model	Lug Nut Torque (ft/lb)	Brake Disc		Brake Drum			Minimum Lining Thickness	
			Minimum Thickness	Maximum Run-Out	Inner Diameter	Max. Machine O/S	Max. Wear Limit	Front	Rear
1973-76	Civic Sedan, Hatchback	51-65	0.354	0.006	7.087	7.126	7.146	0.063	0.079
1975-76	Civic Wagon	51-65	0.449	0.006	7.874	7.913	7.933	0.300	0.118
1976	Accord Hatchback	51-65	0.354	0.006	7.087	7.126	7.146	0.039	0.079

WHEEL ALIGNMENT SPECIFICATIONS

Year	Model	CASTER		CAMBER		Toe-Out (in.)	Steering Axis Inclination (deg)
		Range (deg)	Preferred Setting (deg)	Range (deg)	Preferred Setting (deg)		
1973-76	Civic—all exc. station wagon	1¼P-2¼P	1¾P	0-1P	½P	0.04	8.9
1975	Civic station wagon	1½P-2½P	2P	0-1P	½P	0.04	9.3
1976	Civic station wagon	½P-1½P	1P	0-1P	½P	0.04	9.3
1976	Accord Hatchback	1⅓P-2⅓P	1⅚P	⅙P-1⅙P	⅔P	0.04	12.2

P—Positive

TUNE-UP PROCEDURES
Spark Plugs

Removal

1. Place a piece of masking tape around each spark plug wire and number it according to its corresponding cylinder.

2. Pull the wires from the spark plugs, grasping the wire by the end of the rubber boot and twisting off.

NOTE: *Avoid spark plug removal while the engine is hot. Since the cylinder head spark plug threads are aluminum, the spark plug becomes tight due to the different coefficients of heat expansion. If a plug is too tight to be removed even while the engine is cold, apply a solvent around the plug followed with an application of oil once the solvent has penetrated the threads. Do this only when the engine is cold.*

3. Loosen each spark plug with a 13/16 in. spark plug socket. When the plug has been loosened a few turns, stop to clean any material from around the spark plug holes. Compressed air is preferred; however, if air is not available, simply use a rag to clean the area.

NOTE: *In no case should foreign matter be allowed to enter the cylinders. Severe damage could result.*

4. Finish unscrewing the plugs and remove them from the engine.

Inspection and Cleaning

Before attempting to clean and re-gap plugs, be sure that the electrode ends aren't worn or damaged and that the insulators (the white porcelain covering) are not cracked. Replace the plug if this condition exists.

Clean reusable plugs with a plug cleaner or a wire brush. The plug gap should be checked and readjusted, if necessary, by bending the ground electrode with a spark plug gapping tool.

NOTE: *Do not use a flat gauge to check plug gap; an incorrect reading will result. Use a wire gauge only.*

Installation

1. Lightly oil the spark plug threads and hand tighten them into the engine.

2. Tighten the plugs securely with a spark plug wrench (about 10 ft lbs of torque).

CAUTION: *Do not overtighten because of the aluminum threads.*

3. Reconnect the wires to the plugs, making sure that each is securely fitted.

Breaker Points and Condenser

NOTE: *There are two rules that should*

Distributor—all models except CVCC Hondamatic
1. Hold-down screws
2. Ground wire
3. Adjusting screw
4. Breaker arm pivot
5. Primary lead

always be followed when adjusting or replacing points. The points and condenser are a matched set; never replace one without replacing the other. If you change the point gap or dwell of the engine, you also change the ignition timing. Therefore, if you adjust the points, you must also adjust the timing.

Inspection

1. Disconnect the high-tension wire from the coil.

2. Unfasten the two retaining clips to remove the distributor cap.

3. Remove the rotor from the distributor shaft by pulling it straight up. Examine the condition of the rotor; if it is cracked or the metallic tip is excessively burned, replace it.

4. Pry the breaker points open with a screwdriver and examine the condition of the contact points. If the points are excessively worn, burned, or pitted they should be replaced.

NOTE: *Contact points which have been used for several thousand miles will have a gray, rough surface, but this is not necessarily an indication that they are malfunctioning. The roughness between the points matches so*

that a large contact area is maintained.

5. If the points are in good condition, polish them with a point file.

NOTE: *Do not use emery cloth or sandpaper as they may leave particles on the points which could cause them to arc.*

After polishing the points, refer to the section following the breaker point replacement procedures for proper adjustment. If the points need replacing, refer to the following procedure.

Removal and Installation

1. Remove the small square nut from the terminal screw located in the side of the distributor housing and remove the nut, screw, condenser wire, and primary wire from the terminal. Remove the terminal from the slot in the distributor housing.

2. Remove the screw(s) which attaches the condenser to the outside of the distributor housing (most models), or to the breaker plate inside the distributor (CVCC Hondamatic models), and remove the condenser.

3. Unscrew the phillips head screw which holds the ground wire to the

breaker point assembly and lift the end of the ground wire out of the way.

4. Remove the two phillips head screws which attach the point assembly to the breaker plate and remove the point assembly.

NOTE: *You should use a magnetic or locking screwdriver. Trying to locate one of these tiny screws after you've dropped it can be an excruciating affair.*

5. Wipe all dirt and grease from the distributor plate and cam with a lint-free cloth. Apply a small amount of heat-resistant lubricant to the distributor cam. Although the lube is supplied with most breaker point kits, you can buy it at any auto parts store if necessary.

6. Properly position the new points on the breaker plate of the distributor and secure with the two point screws. Attach the ground wire, with its screw, to the breaker plate assembly. Screw the condenser to its proper position on the distributor housing, or breaker plate.

7. Fit the terminal back into its notch in the distributor housing and attach the condenser and primary wires to the terminal screw and fasten with the nut.

Adjustment

With a Feeler Gauge

1. Rotate the crankshaft pulley until the point gap is at its greatest (where the rubbing block is on the high point of the cam lobe). This can be accomplished by using either a remote starter switch or by rotating the crankshaft pulley by hand.

2. At this position, insert the proper sized feeler gauge between the points. A slight drag should be felt. Point gap should be 0.018–0.022 in.

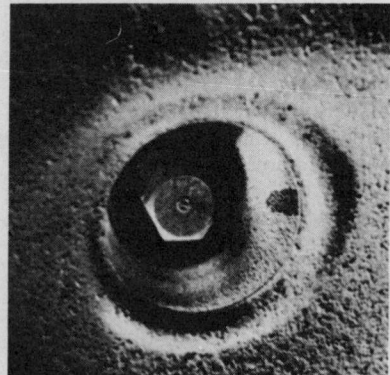

Crankshaft pulley bolt access window inside the left front fender—CVCC models

3. If no drag is felt, or if the feeler gauge cannot be inserted, loosen, but do not remove the two breaker point set screws.

4. Adjust the points as follows:

Insert a screwdriver through the hole in the breaker point assembly and into the notch provided on the breaker plate. Twist the screwdriver to open or close the points. When the correct gap has

been obtained, retighten the point set screws.

5. Recheck the point gap to be sure that it did not change when the breaker point attaching screws were tightened.

6. Align the rotor with the distributor shaft and push the rotor onto the shaft until it is fully seated.

7. Reinstall the distributor cap and the coil high-tension wire.

With a Dwell Meter

Connect a dwell/tachometer, in accordance with its manufacturer's instructions, between the distributor primary lead and a ground.

With the engine warmed up and running at the specified idle speed (see the tune-up chart, above), take a dwell reading.

If the point dwell is not within specifications, shut the engine off and adjust the point gap, as outlined above.

NOTE: *Increasing the point gap decreases the dwell angle and vice versa.*

Install the dust cover, rotor, and cap. Check the dwell reading again and adjust it, as required.

Ignition Timing

Honda recommends that the ignition timing be checked at 12,000 mile intervals (1973–74 models), or 15,000 mile intervals (1975–76 models). Also, the timing should always be adjusted after installing new points or adjusting the dwell angle. On all 1973–76 1170 and 1237 cc engines, the timing marks are located on the crankshaft pulley, with a pointer on the timing belt cover; all visible from the driver's side of the engine compartment. On all CVCC engines, the timing marks are located on the flywheel (manual transmission) or torque converter drive plate (automatic transmission), with a pointer on the rear of the cylinder block; all visible from the front right-side of the engine compartment after removing a special rubber access plug in the timing mark window. In all cases, the timing is checked with the engine warmed to operating temperature (176° F), idling in Neutral (manual trans.) or 2nd gear (Hon-

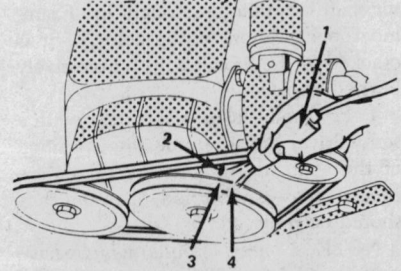

1. Timing light
2. Reference mark
3. 5° Timing mark (red)
4. 0° Timing mark—TDC (white)

1973-74 ignition timing marks

damatic), and with all vacuum hoses *connected.*

1. Stop the engine, and hook up a tachometer. The positive lead connects to the distributor side terminal of the ignition coil, and the negative lead to a good ground, such as an engine bolt.

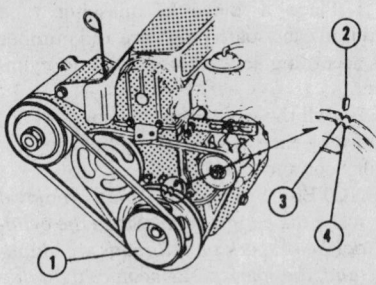

1975-76 1237 cc ignition timing marks

1. Crankshaft pulley   3. 7° BTDC mark
2. Timing pointer   4. TDC mark

NOTE: *On some models, you will have to pull back the rubber ignition coil cover to reveal the terminals.*

2. Hook up a DC stroboscopic timing light to the engine. The positive and negative leads connect to their corresponding battery terminals and the spark plug lead to No. 1 spark plug. The No. 1 spark plug is the one at the driver's side of the engine compartment.

3. Make sure that all wires are clear of the cooling fan and hot exhaust manifolds. Start the engine. Check that the idle speed is set to specifications with the transmission in Neutral (manual transmission) or 2nd gear (Hondamatic).

If not, adjust as outlined later . At any engine speed other than the specified idle speed, the distributor advance or retard mechanisms will actuate, leading to an erroneous timing adjustment.

CAUTION: *Make sure that the parking brake is firmly applied and the front wheels blocked to prevent the car from rolling forward when the automatic transmission is engaged.*

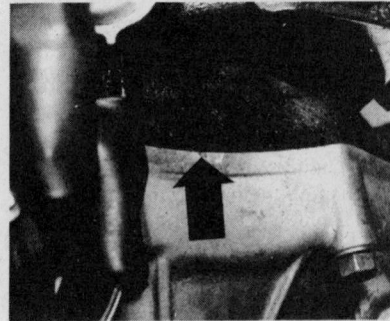

CVCC timing mark window location

4. Point the timing light at the timing marks. On Non-CVCC cars, align the pointer with the "F" or red notch on the crankshaft pulley. On CVCC cars, align the pointer with the red notch on the flywheel or torque converter drive plate

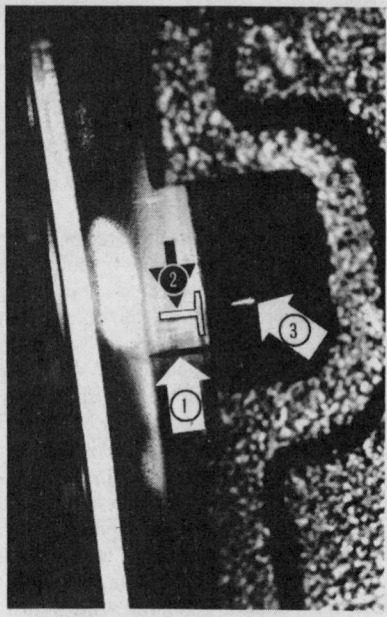

CVCC engine timing marks

1. Ignition timing mark (red notch)
2. Top Dead Center (T) mark
3. Ignition timing pointer

(except on cars where the timing specifications is TDC in which case the "T" or white notch is used).

5. If necessary, adjust the timing by loosening the larger distributor hold-down (clamp) bolt and slowly rotate the distributor in the required direction while observing the timing marks.

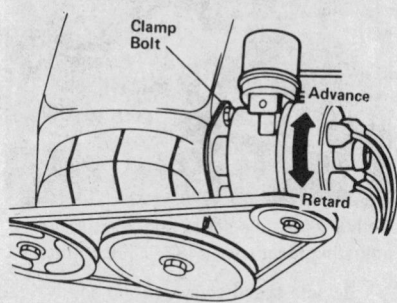

Adjusting ignition timing—1170, 1237 cc shown, CVCC similar

CAUTION: *Do not grasp the top of the distributor cap while the engine is running as you might get a nasty shock. Instead, grab the distributor housing to rotate.*

After making the necessary adjustment, tighten the hold-down bolt, taking care not to disturb the adjustment.

NOTE: *There are actually two bolts which may be loosened to adjust ignition timing. There is a smaller bolt on the underside of the distributor swivel mounting plate. This smaller bolt should not be loosened unless you cannot obtain a satisfactory adjustment using the upper bolt. Its purpose is to provide an extra range of adjustment, such as in cases where the distributor*

was removed and then installed one tooth off.

Valve Lash Adjustment

Honda recommends that the valve clearance be checked at 12,000 mile intervals (1973–74 models), or 15,000 mile intervals (1975–76 models).

NOTE: *While all valve adjustments must be as accurate as possible, it is better to have the valve adjustment slightly loose than slightly tight, as burned valves may result from overly tight adjustments.*

All 1973–74 Models and 1975–76 1237 cc Models

1. Adjust valves when the engine is cold (100°F or less).
2. Remove the valve cover and align the TDC (Top Dead Center) mark on the crankshaft pulley with the index mark on the timing belt cover. The TDC notch is the one immediately following the red 5° BTDC notch used for setting ignition timing.

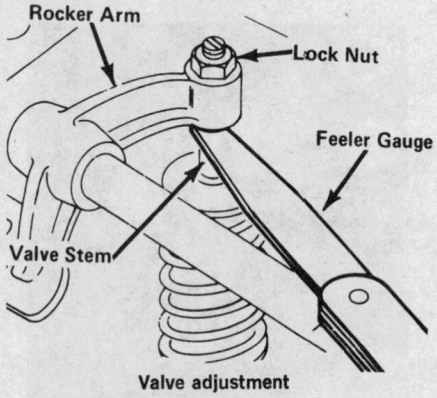

Valve adjustment

3. When No. 1 cylinder is at TDC on the compression stroke, check and adjust the following valves (numbered from the crankshaft pulley end of the engine):

Intake—Nos. 1 and 2 cylinders
Exhaust—Nos. 1 and 3 cylinders
Adjust the valves as follows

a. Check valve clearance with a feeler gauge between the tip of the rocker arm and the top of the valve. There should be a slight drag on the feeler gauge;

b. If there is no drag or if the gauge cannot be inserted, loosen the valve adjusting screw locknut;

c. Turn the adjusting screw with a screwdriver to obtain the proper clearance;

d. Hold the adjusting screw and tighten the locknut;

e. Recheck the clearance before reinstalling the valve cover.

4. Then rotate the crankshaft 360° and adjust:

Intake—Nos. 3 and 4 cylinders
Exhaust—Nos. 2 and 4 cylinders

1975–76 CVCC Models

1. Make sure that the engine is cold (cylinder head temperature below 100° F).

2. Remove the valve cover. From the front of the engine, take a look at the forward face of the camshaft timing belt gear. When No. 1 cylinder as at Top Dead Center (TDC), the keyway for the woodruff key retaining the timing gear to the camshaft will be facing up. On 1976 models, the word "UP" will be at the top of the gear. You can doublecheck this by distributor rotor position. Take some chalk or crayon and mark where the No. 1 spark plug wire goes into the distributor cap on the distributor body. Then, remove the cap and check that the rotor points toward that mark.

3. With the No. 1 cylinder at TDC, you can adjust the following valves (numbered from the crankshaft pulley end of the engine):

Intake—Nos. 1 and 2 cylinders
Auxiliary Intake—Nos. 1 and 2 cylinders
Exhaust—Nos. 1 and 3 cylinders
Adjust the valves as follows:

a. Check valve clearance with a feeler gauge between the tip of the rocker arm and the top of the valve. There should be a slight drag on the feeler gauge;

b. If there is no drag or if the gauge cannot be inserted, loosen the valve adjusting screw locknut;

c. Turn the adjusting screw with a screwdriver to obtain the proper clearance;

d. Hold the adjusting screw and tighten the locknut;

e. Recheck the clearance before reinstalling the valve cover.

4. To adjust the remaining valves, rotate the crankshaft to the No. 4 cylinder TDC position. To get the No. 4 cylinder to the TDC position, rotate the crankshaft 360 degrees. This will correspond to an 180 degree movement of the distributor rotor and camshaft timing gear. The rotor will now be pointing opposite the mark you made for the No. 1 cylinder. The camshaft timing gear keyway or "UP" mark will now be at the bottom (6 o'clock position). At this position, you may adjust the remaining valves:

Intake—Nos. 3 and 4 cylinders
Auxiliary Intake—Nos. 3 and 4 cylinders
Exhaust—Nos. 2 and 4 cylinders

Carburetor
Idle Speed and Mixture Adjustment

NOTE: *All carburetor adjustments must be made with the engine fully warmed up to operating temperature (176° F).*

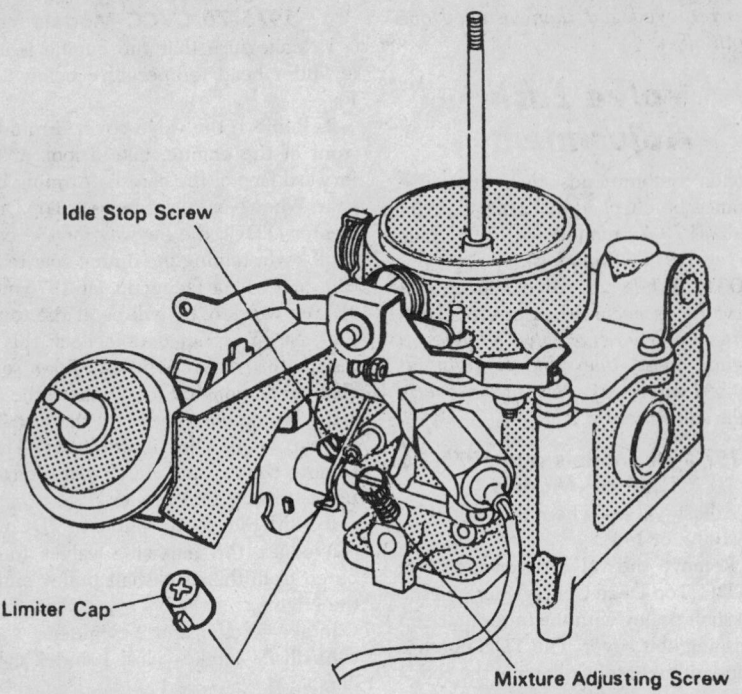

Hitachi 2-bbl idle speed and mixture screw adjusting locations—1170, 1237 cc models

1973 Civic 1170 cc With Hitachi 2-bbl

1. Adjust the idle speed with the headlights on and the cooling fan off. The cooling fan can be disconnected by removing the leads from either the fan motor or the thermoswitch screwed into the base of the radiator, on the engine side (see the illustration).

Manual transmission models should be set in Neutral. Cars equipped with Hondamatic transmissions should be set in gear "1". Set the parking brake and block the front wheels.

2. Remove the limiter cap and turn the idle mixture screw counterclockwise, until engine speed drops. Now turn the idle speed screw in the reverse direction (clockwise) until the engine reaches its highest rpm. (If the idle speed is now above specification, repeat Steps 1 & 2.)

3. Continue to turn the idle mixture screw clockwise to obtain the specified rpm drop:

4-speed—40 rpm
Hondamatic—20 rpm

4. Replace the limiter cap and reconnect the cooling fan lines.

1974 Civic 1237 cc and 1975–76 Civic 1237 cc with Hitachi 2-bbl

1. The idle speed is adjusted with the headlights on and the radiator cooling fan off. To make sure that the cooling fan stays off while you are making your adjustments, disconnect the fan leads.

NOTE: *Do not leave the cooling fan leads disconnected for any longer than necessary, as the engine may overheat.*

Cooling fan quick disconnect

Manual transmission cars are adjusted with the transmission in Neutral. On Hondamatic cars, the idle adjustments are made with the car in gear "1." As a safety precaution, firmly apply the parking brake and block the front wheels.

2. Remove the plastic limiter cap from the idle mixture screw. Hook up a tachometer to the engine with the positive lead connected to the distributor side (terminal) of the coil and the negative lead to a good ground. On 1976 models, disconnect the breather hose from the valve cover.

3. Start the engine and adjust first the mixture screw (turn counterclockwise to richen), and then the idle speed screw for the best quality idle at 870 rpm (manual transmission), or 770 rpm (Hondamatic in gear).

4. Then, lean out the idle mixture (turn mixture screw clockwise), until the idle speed drops to 800 rpm (manual

transmission), or 750 rpm (Hondamatic in gear).

5. Replace the limiter cap, connect the cooling fan, and disconnect the tachometer.

1975–76 Civic CVCC with Keihin 3-bbl

1. The idle speed is adjusted with the headlights on and the radiator cooling fan on. With the engine warmed to operating temperature and idling, the cooling fan should come on. But, if it doesn't, you can load the engine's electrical system (for purposes of adjusting the idle speed), by turning the high-speed heater blower on instead. Do not have both the cooling fan and heater blower operating simultaneously, as this will load the engine too much and lower the idle speed abnormally. Manual transmission cars are adjusted with the transmission in Neutral. On Hondamatic cars, the idle adjustments are made with the car in gear "2" (that's right, Hi gear). As a safety precaution, apply the parking brake and block the front wheels.

Keihin 3-bbl idle speed and mixture screw adjusting locations—1487, 1600 cc models

1. Idle speed screw
2. Mixture screw with limiter cap

2. Remove the plastic cap from the idle mixture screw. Hook up a tachometer to the engine with the positive lead connected to the distributor side (terminal) of the coil and the negative lead to a good ground.

3. Start the engine and rotate the idle mixture screw counterclockwise (rich), until the highest rpm is achieved. Then, adjust the idle speed screw to 910 rpm (manual transmission), or 810 rpm (Hondamatic in Second gear).

4. Finally, lean out the idle mixture (turn mixture screw in clockwise), until the idle speed drops to 850 rpm (manual transmission), or 750 rpm Hondamatic in Second gear).

5. Replace the limiter cap and disconnect the tachometer.

1976 Accord CVCC with Keihin 3-bbl

1. Follow steps 1 and 2 for "1975–76 Civic CVCC"

2. Start the engine and turn the idle mixture screw counterclockwise until the highest rpm is reached. Then, adjust the idle speed screw to 880 rpm (5-speed) or 730 rpm (Hondamatic in second gear).

3. Then, lean out the mixture by turning the idle mixture clockwise until the idle speed drops to 800 rpm (5-speed) or 680 rpm (Hondamatic in second gear).

4. Replace the limiter cap and disconnect the tachometer.

ENGINE ELECTRICAL
Distributor

Removal and Installation

1. Disconnect the high tension and primary lead wires that run from the distributor to the coil.

2. Unsnap the two distributor cap retaining clamps and remove the distributor cap. Position it out of the way.

3. Using chalk or paint, carefully mark the position of the distributor rotor in relation to the distributor housing, and mark the relation of the distributor housing to the engine block. When this is done, you should have a line on the distributor housing directly in line with the tip of the rotor, and another line on the engine block directly in line with the mark on the distributor housing.

NOTE: *This aligning procedure is very important because the distributor must be reinstalled in the exact location from which it was removed, if correct ignition timing is to be maintained.*

4. Note the position of the vacuum line(s) on the vacuum diaphragm with masking tape and then disconnect the lines from the vacuum unit.

5. Remove the bolt which attaches the distributor to the engine block or distributor extension housing (CVCC), and remove the distributor from the engine.

CAUTION: *Do not disturb the engine while the distributor is removed. If you attempt to start the engine with the distributor removed, you will have to retime the engine.*

6. To install, place the rotor on the distributor shaft and align the tip of the rotor with the line that you made on the distributor housing.

7. With the rotor and housing aligned, insert the distributor into the engine while aligning the mark on the housing with the mark on the block, or extension housing (CVCC).

NOTE: *Since the distributor pinion gear has helical teeth, the rotor will*

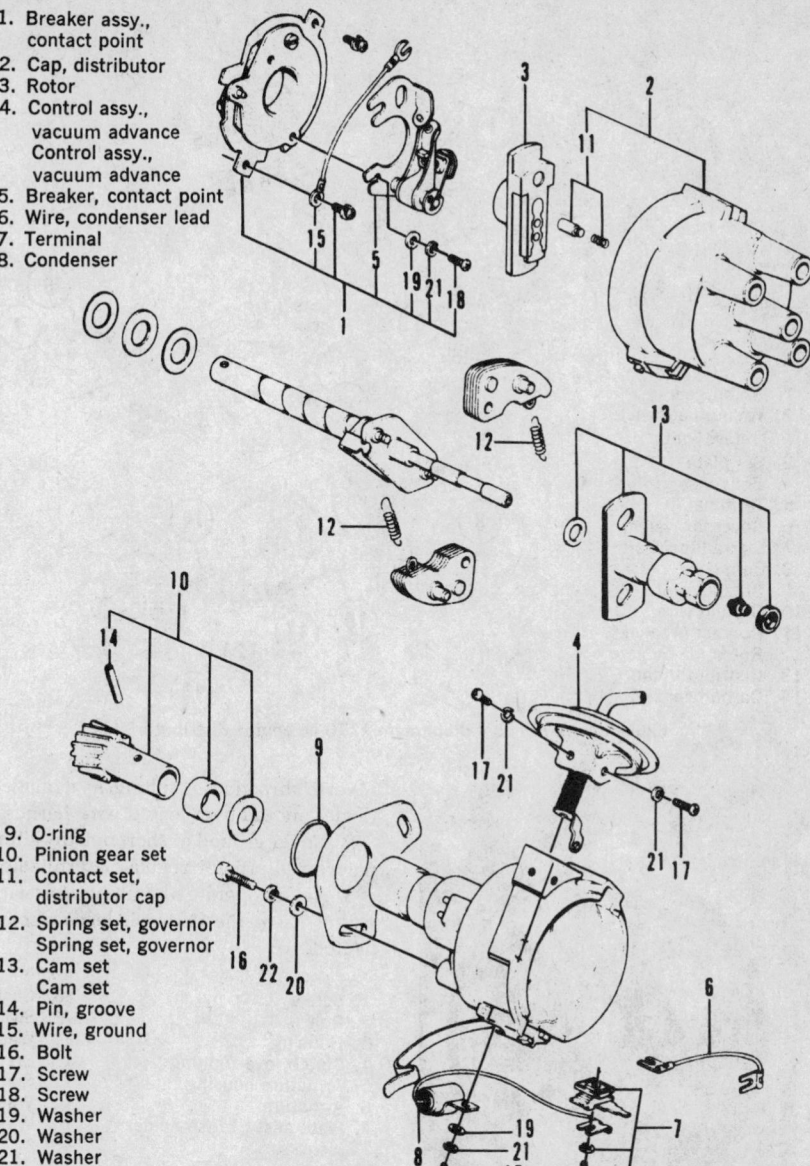

1. Breaker assy., contact point
2. Cap, distributor
3. Rotor
4. Control assy., vacuum advance
   Control assy., vacuum advance
5. Breaker, contact point
6. Wire, condenser lead
7. Terminal
8. Condenser
9. O-ring
10. Pinion gear set
11. Contact set, distributor cap
12. Spring set, governor
    Spring set, governor
13. Cam set
    Cam set
14. Pin, groove
15. Wire, ground
16. Bolt
17. Screw
18. Screw
19. Washer
20. Washer
21. Washer
22. Washer

Exploded view of CVCC manual transmission distributor with vacuum advance

turn slightly as the gear on the distributor meshes with the gear on the camshaft. Allow for this when installing the distributor by aligning the mark on the distributor with the mark on the block, but positioning the tip of the rotor slightly to the side of the mark on the distributor.

8. When the distributor is fully seated in the engine, install and tighten the distributor retaining bolt.

9. Align and install the distributor cap and snap the retaining clamps into place.

10. Install the high-tension and primary wires onto the coil.

11. Check the ignition timing as outlined in

Installation When Engine Has Been Disturbed

If the engine was cranked with the distributor removed, it will be necessary to

retime the engine. If you have installed the distributor incorrectly and the engine will not start, remove the distributor from the engine and start from scratch.

1. Install the distributor with No. 1 cylinder at the top dead center position on the compression stroke (the "TDC" mark on the crankshaft pulley (or flywheel) aligned with the index mark on the timing belt cover or crankcase).

2. Line up the metal end of the rotor head with the protrusion on the distributor housing.

3. Carefully insert the distributor into the cylinder head opening with the attaching plate bolt slot aligned with the distributor mounting hole in the cylinder head. Then secure the plate at the center of the adjusting slot. The rotor head must face No. 1 cylinder.

NOTE: *Since the distributor pinion*

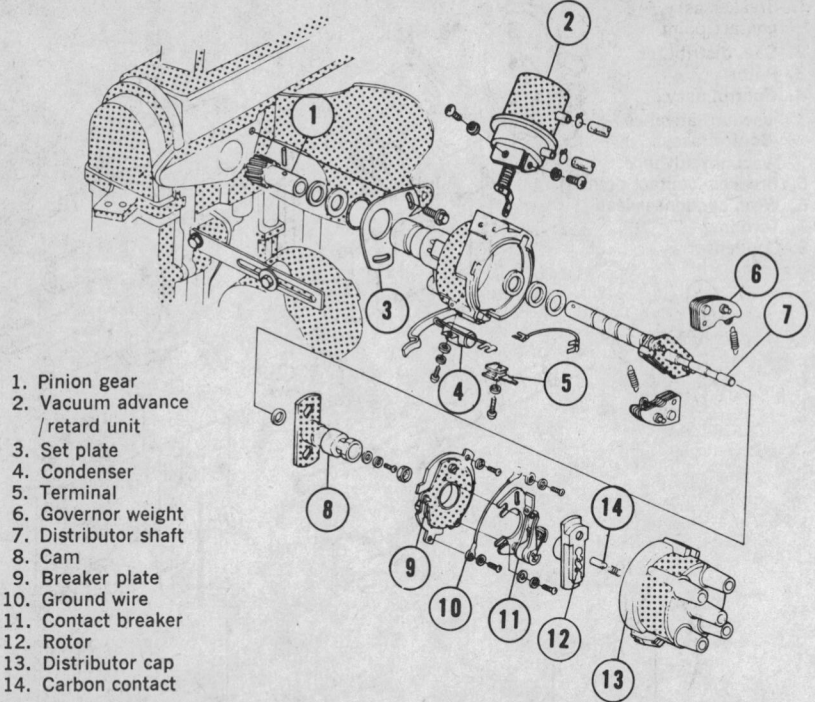

1. Pinion gear
2. Vacuum advance /retard unit
3. Set plate
4. Condenser
5. Terminal
6. Governor weight
7. Distributor shaft
8. Cam
9. Breaker plate
10. Ground wire
11. Contact breaker
12. Rotor
13. Distributor cap
14. Carbon contact

Exploded view of dual diaphragm 1170 cc engine distributor

The rotor will move about 30° during removal or installation

gear has helical teeth, the rotor will turn slightly as the gear on the distributor meshes with the gear on the camshaft. Allow for this when installing the distributor by positioning the tip of the rotor to the side of the protrusion.

4. Inspect and adjust the point gap and ignition timing.

Alternator

Precautions

1. Observe the proper polarity of the battery connections by making sure that the positive (+) and negative (−) terminal connections are not reversed. Misconnection will allow current to flow in the reverse direction, resulting in damaged diodes and an overheated wire harness.

2. Never ground or short out any alternator or alternator regulator terminals.

3. Never operate the alternator with any of its or the battery's leads disconnected.

1. Screw
2. Bolt
3. Housing
4. Clutch, overrunning
5. Armature housing
6. Armature
7. Plate assy., brush holder
8. Gasket
9. Switch assy., magnetic
10. Washer
11. Bracket
12. Screw
13. Washer
14. Washer

4. Always remove the battery or disconnect its output lead while charging it.

5. Always disconnect the ground cable when replacing any electrical components.

6. Never subject the alternator to excessive heat or dampness of the engine is being steam-cleaned.

7. Never use arc-welding equipment with the alternator connected.

Removal and Installation

1. Disconnect the negative (−) battery terminal.

2. Unplug the wires from the "E", "F", and "N" plugs on the rear of the alternator.

3. Loosen and remove the two alternator mounting bolts and remove the V-belt and alternator assembly.

4. To install, reverse the removal procedure. Adjust the alternator belt tension according to the "Belt Tension Adjustment" section below.

Belt Tension Adjustment

The initial inspection and adjustment to the alternator drive belt should be performed after the first 3,000 miles or if the alternator has been moved for any reason. Afterwards, you should inspect the belt tension every 12,000 miles. Before adjusting, inspect the belt to see that it is not cracked or worn. Be sure that its surfaces are free of grease and oil.

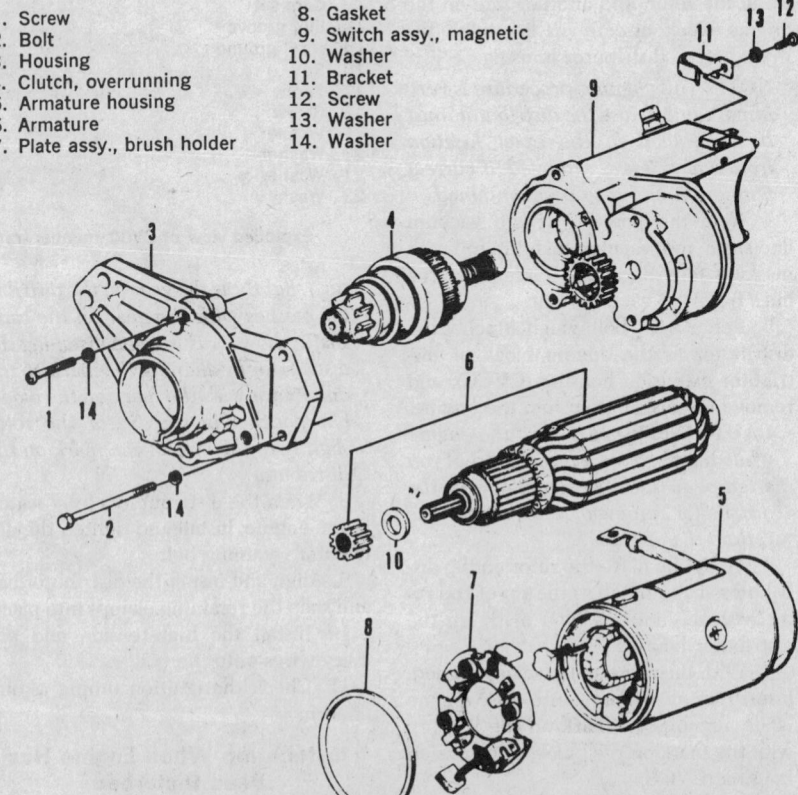

Exploded view of alternator—1170, 1237 cc unit shown; CVCC unit similar

1. Push down on the belt halfway between pulleys with a force of about 24 lbs. The belt should deflect 0.47–0.67 in. (12–17 mm).

2. If the belt tension requires adjustment, loosen the adjusting link bolt and move the alternator with a pry bar positioned against the front of the alternator housing.

CAUTION: *Do not apply pressure to any other part of the alternator.*

3. After obtaining the proper tension, tighten the adjusting link bolt.

CAUTION: *Do not overtighten the belt; damage to the alternator bearings could result.*

Voltage Regulator

Removal and Installation

The regulator is inside the engine compartment, attached to the right fenderwall just above the battery.

1. Disconnect the negative (−) terminal from the battery.

2. Remove the regulator terminal lead wires.

NOTE: *You should label these wires to avoid confusion during installation.*

3. Unscrew the two regulator retaining bolts and remove the regulator from the car.

4. To install, reverse the removal procedure.

Starter

Removal and Installation

1. Disconnect the ground cable at the battery negative (−) terminal, and the starter motor cable at the positive terminal.

2. Disconnect the starter motor cable at the motor.

3. Remove the starter motor by loosening the two attaching bolts. On CVCC models, the bolts attach from opposing ends of the starter.

4. Reverse the removal procedure to install the motor. Be sure to tighten the attaching bolts to 29–36 ft lbs and make sure that all wires are securely connected.

Starter Drive Replacement

1170, 1237 cc Models

1. Remove the solenoid by loosening and removing the attaching bolts.

2. Remove the two brush holder plate retaining screws from the rear cover. On the Civic motor, also pry off the rear dust cover along with the clip and thrust washer(s).

3. Remove the two through bolts from the rear cover and lightly tap the rear

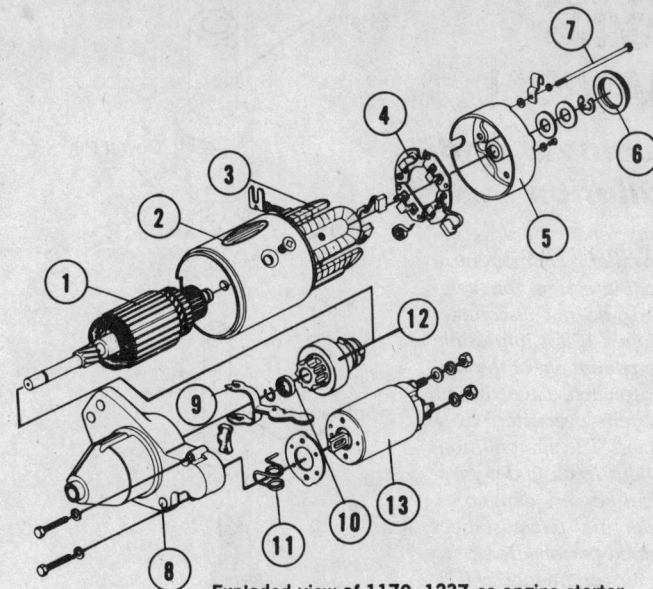

1. Armature
2. Yoke
3. Field coil
4. Brush holder
5. Rear cover
6. Dust cover
7. Through-bolt
8. Gear case
9. Shift lever
10. Stop collar
11. Spring
12. Pinion
13. Solenoid

Exploded view of 1170, 1237 cc engine starter

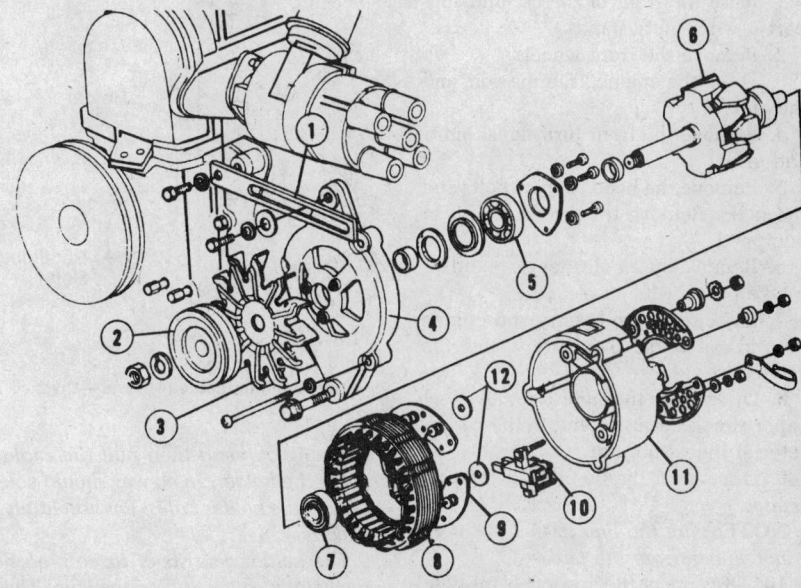

Exploded vew of CVCC engine starter

1. Alternator stay	7. Ball bearing
2. Pulley	8. Stator
3. Fan	9. Rectifier
4. Drive end frame	10. Brush holder
5. Ball bearing	11. Rectifier end frame
6. Rotor	12. Insulation washer

cover with a mallet to remove it.

4. Remove the four carbon brushes from the brush holder and remove the brush holder.

5. Separate the yoke from the case. The yoke is provided with a hole for positioning, into which the gear case lock pin is inserted.

6. On the Civic, simply pull the yoke assembly from the gear case, being sure to carefully detach the shift lever from the pinion.

7. Remove the armature unit from the

yoke casing and the field coil.

8. To remove the pinion gear from the armature, first set the armature on end with the pinion end facing upward and pull the clutch stop collar downward toward the pinion. Then remove the pinion stop clip and pull the pinion stop and gears from the armature shaft as a unit.

9. To assemble and install the starter motor, reverse the disassembly and removal procedures. Be sure to install new clips, and be careful of the installation direction of the shift lever on the Civic.

ENGINE MECHANICAL

Engine Removal and Installation

CAUTION: *If any repair operation requires the removal of a component of the air conditioning system (on vehicles so equipped), do not disconnect the refrigerant lines. If it is impossible to move the component out of the way with the lines attached, have the air conditioning system evacuated by a trained serviceman. The air conditioning system contains freon under pressure. This gas can be very dangerous. Therefore, under no circumstances should an untrained person attempt to disconnect the air-conditioner refrigerant lines.*

1170, 1237 cc Models

1. Raise the front of the car and support it with safety stands.
2. Remove the front wheels.
3. Drain the engine, transmission, and radiator.
4. Remove the front turn signal lights and grille.
5. Remove the hood support bolts and the hood. Remove the fan shroud, if so equipped.
6. Remove the air cleaner case, and air intake pipe at the air cleaner.
7. Disconnect the battery and engine ground cables at the battery and the valve cover.
8. Disconnect the hose from the fuel vapor storage canister and to the carburetor at the carburetor.
9. Disconnect the fuel line at the fuel pump.
   NOTE: *Plug the line so that gas does not siphon from the tank.*
10. Disconnect the lower coolant hose at the water pump connecting tube and the upper hose at the thermostat cover.
11. Disconnect the following control cables and wires from the engine:
    a. Throttle and choke cables at the carburetor;
    b. Clutch cable at the release arm;
    c. Ignition coil wires at the distributor;
    d. Starter motor positive battery cable connection and solenoid wire;
    e. Back-up light switch and T.C.S. (Transmission Controlled Spark) switch wires from the transmission casing;
    f. Speedometer and tachometer cables;
    CAUTION: *When removing the speedometer cable from the transmission, it is not necessary to remove the entire cable holder. Remove the end boot (gear holder seal) and the cable*

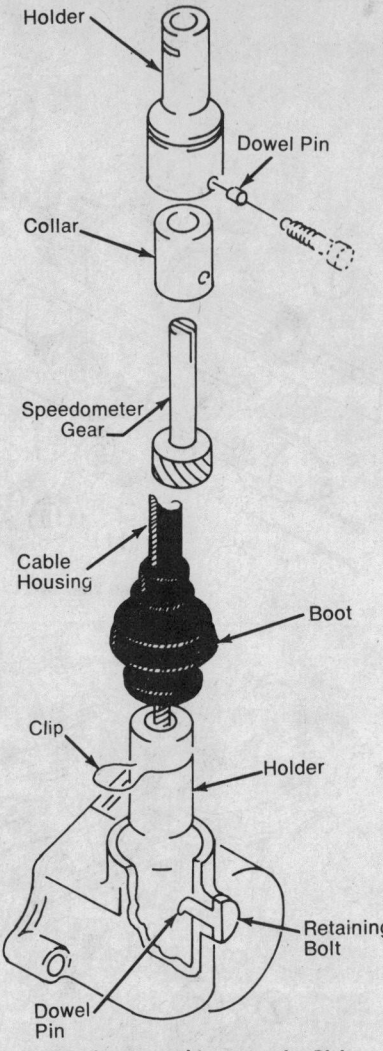

Speedometer cable removal—Civic

retaining clip and then pull the cable out of the holder. In no way should you disturb the holder unless it is absolutely necessary.

The holder consists of three pieces: the holder, collar, and a dowel pin. The dowel pin indexes the holder and collar and is held in place by the bolt that retains the holder. If the bolt is removed and the holder rotated, the dowel pin can fall into the transmission case, necessitating transmission disassembly to remove the pin. To insure that this does not happen when the holder must be removed, do not rotate the holder more than 30° in either direction when removing it. Once removed, make sure that the pin is still in place. Use the same precaution when installing the holder.

    g. Alternator wire and wire harness connector;
    h. The wires from both water temperature thermal switches on the intake manifold;
    i. Cooling fan connector and radiator thermoswitch wires;

    j. Oil pressure sensor;
    k. On 1975–76 models, vacuum hose to throttle opener at opener, and vacuum hose from carburetor insulator to throttle opener;
    l. On 1975–76 models, by-pass valve assembly and bracket.
    NOTE: *It would be a good idea to tag all of these wires to avoid confusion during installation.*
12. Disconnect the heater hose by removing the "H" connector from the two hoses in the firewall.
13. Remove the engine torque rod from the engine and firewall.
14. Remove the starter motor.
15. Remove the radiator from the engine compartment.
16. Remove the exhaust pipe-to-manifold clamp.
17. Remove the exhaust pipe flange nuts and lower the exhaust pipe.
18. Disconnect the left and right lower control arm ball joints at the knuckle, using a ball joint remover (or special tool 07941–6340000).
19. Hold the brake disc and pull the right and left drive shafts out of the differential case.
20a. Manual transmission only: Drive out the gearshift rod pin (8 mm) with a drift and disconnect the rod at the transmission case.
    NOTE: *Do not disconnect the shift lever end of the gearshift rod and extension.*
20b.—Hondamatic only: Disconnect shift cable at console and cooler line at transmission.
21. Disconnect the gearshift extension at the engine (man. trans. only).
22. Screw in two engine hanger bolts in the torque rod bolt hole and the bolt hole just to the left of the distributor. Then, engage the lifting chain hooks to the hanger bolts and lift the engine just enough to take the load off the engine mounts.
23. After being sure that the engine is properly supported, remove the two center mount bracket nuts.
24. Remove the center beam (1973–74 only).
25. Remove the left engine mount.
26. Lift the engine out slowly, taking care not to allow the engine to damage other parts of the car.
27. To install, reverse the removal procedure. Pay special attention to the following points:
    a. Tighten all mounting bolts and nuts to their specified torque;
    b. Lower the engine into position and install the left mount. On 1973–74 models, install the center beam with the front end between the stabilizer bar and frame. Do not attach mounting bolts at this time.
    NOTE: *On 1973–74 models, be sure*

that the lower mount has the mount stop installed between the center beam and the rubber mount.

c. Align the center mount studs with the beam and tighten the nuts and washer several turns (just enough to support the beam). On 1973–74 models, attach the rear end of the center beam to the subframe;

d. On 1973–74 models, attach the front end of the center beam. Torque the center beam bolts to specification but do not tighten the lower mount nuts. Lower the engine so it rests on the lower mount. Torque the lower mount nuts to the proper specifications;

e. Use a new shift rod pin;

f. After installing the driveshafts, attempt to move the inner joint housing in and out of the differential housing. If it moves easily, the driveshaft end clips should be replaced;

g. Make sure that the control cables and wires are connected properly;

h. When connecting the heater hoses, the upper hose goes to the water pump connecting pipe and the lower hose to the intake manifold;

i. Refill the engine, transmission, and radiator with their respective fluids to the proper levels;

j. On Hondamatic cars, check shift cable adjustment.

1487 cc Civic CVCC

1. Raise the front of the car and support it with jackstands. Remove both front wheels.
2. Remove the headlight rim attaching screws and the rims.
3. Open the hood. Disconnect both parking light connectors. Remove the parking light retaining bolts and backing plate and remove the parking lights.
4. Remove the lower grille molding and remove the six grille retaining bolts and the grille.
5. Disconnect the windshield washer hose and remove it from the underside of the hood.
6. Disconnect the negative battery cable and the transmission bracket-to-body ground cable.
7. Remove the upper torque (engine locating) arm.
8. Disconnect the vacuum hose at the power brake booster, thermosensors "A" and "B" at their wiring connectors, and the coolant temperature gauge sending unit wire.
9. Drain the radiator. After all coolant has drained, install the drain bolt finger-tight.
10. Disconnect all four coolant hoses. Disconnect cooling fan motor connector and the temperature sensor. Remove the radiator hose to the overflow tank.

11. On Hondamatic cars only, remove both ATF cooler line bolts.
NOTE: *Save the washers from the cooler line banjo connectors and replace if damaged.*
12. Remove the radiator.
13. Label and disconnect the starter motor wires. Remove the two starter mounting bolts (one from each end of the starter), and remove the starter.
14. Label and disconnect the spark plug wires at the plugs. Remove the distributor cap and scribe the position of the rotor on the side of the distributor housing. Remove the top distributor swivel bolt and remove the distributor (the rotor will rotate 30° as the drive gear is beveled).
15. On manual transmission cars, remove the C-clip retaining the clutch cable at the firewall. Then, remove the end of the clutch cable from the clutch release arm and bracket. First, pull up on the cable, and then push it out to release it from the bracket. Remove the end from the release arm.
16. Disconnect the back-up light switch wires. Disconnect the control valve vacuum hose, the air intake hose, and the preheat air intake hose. Disconnect the air bleed valve hose from the air cleaner. Label and disconnect all remaining vacuum hoses from the underside of the air cleaner. Remove the air cleaner.
17. Label and disconnect all remaining emission control vacuum hoses from the engine. Disconnect the emission box wiring connector and remove the black emission box from the firewall.
18. Remove the engine mount heat shield.
19. Disconnect the engine-to-body ground strap at the valve cover.
20. Disconnect the alternator wiring connector and oil pressure sensor leads.
21. Disconnect the vacuum hose from the start control and electrical leads to both cut-off solenoid valves.
22. Disconnect the vacuum hose from the charcoal canister and both fuel lines to the carburetor. Mark the adjustment and disconnect the choke and throttle cables at the carburetor.
23. On Hondamatic cars only, remove the center console and disconnect the gear selector control cable at the console. This may be accomplished after removing the retaining clip and pin.
24. Drain the transmission oil.
25. Remove the fender well shield under the right fender, exposing the speedometer drive cable. Remove the set screw securing the speedometer drive holder. Then, slowly pull the cable assembly out of the transmission, taking care not to drop the pin or drive gear. Finally, remove the pin, collar, and drive gear from the cable assembly.
26. Disconnect the front suspension

stabilizer bar from its mounts on both sides. Also, remove the bolt retaining the lower control arm to the sub-frame on both sides.
27. Remove the forward mounting nut on the radius rod on both sides. Then, pry the constant velocity joint out about ½ in. and pull the stub axle out of the transmission case. Repeat for other side.
28. Remove the six retaining bolts and remove the center beam.
29. On manual transmission cars only, drive out the pin retaining the shift linkage.
30. Disconnect the lower torque arm from the transmission.
31. On Hondamatic cars only, remove the bolt retaining the control cable stay at the transmission. Loosen the two U-bolt nuts and pull the cable out of its housing.
32. Disconnect the exhaust pipe at the manifold. Disconnect the retaining clamp also.
33. Remove the rear engine mount nut.
34. Attach a chain pulley hoist to the engine. Honda recommends using the threaded bolt holes at the extreme right and left ends of the cylinder head (with special hardened bolts) as lifting points, as opposed to wrapping a chain around the entire block and risk damaging some components such as the carburetor, etc.
35. Raise the engine enough to place a slight tension on the chain. Remove the nut retaining the front engine mount. Then, remove the three bolts retaining the front mount. While lifting the engine, remove the mount.
36. Remove the three retaining bolts and push the left engine support into its shock mount bracket to the limit of its travel.
37. Slowly raise the engine out of the vehicle.

1600 cc Accord CVCC

1. Disconnect the negative battery cable.
2. Remove the radiator cap, open the radiator drain cock, and drain the cooling system.
3. Drain the engine crankcase and transmission sump.
4. Unscrew the air cleaner wing nut and lift out the top cover and element. Loosen the air intake hose clamp. Disconnect the intake air door vacuum hose. Remove the phillips head screw at the bottom of the air cleaner housing retaining the PCV condensation chamber. Remove the two screws retaining the air cleaner housing to the valve cover. Lift up the air cleaner housing, disconnect any remaining hoses, and remove.
5. Disconnect the following wires and hoses:

a. Carburetor solenoid valve connector.

b. Power brake vacuum hose.

c. Engine ground cable.

d. Alternator harness connectors.

e. Starter leads and engine sub-harness connector.

f. Coil primary and high tension leads.

g. On Hondamatic models, transmission cooler lines.

6. Disconnect the carburetor fuel line at the three-way joint. Disconnect the evaporative canister hose.

7. Disconnect the choke and throttle cables by loosening their respective locknuts.

8. Disconnect the radiator hoses and heater hoses.

9. Label and disconnect all emission control vacuum hoses. Remove the "black box" connector for the hoses at the firewall.

10. Raise the front of the car and install jack stands beneath the front jacking points. Remove the front wheels.

11. Remove the clutch slave cylinder from the bell housing, leaving the fluid line connected. Disconnect the spring.

12. Disconnect the speedometer cable by removing the c-clip and separating the inner wire from the driven gear.

13. Attach a chain/pulley hoist to the engine. Raise the engine just enough to take the slack out of the chain.

14. Using a ball joint remover spoon, disconnect the lower control arm ball joints and tie rod end ball joints on both sides.

15. Lever the CV joint away from the transaxle and pry off the axle driveshaft snap ring. Then, grasp the knuckle and pull out the axle driveshaft. Remove the transaxle splash guard.

16. Remove the engine/transaxle support center beam.

17. Disconnect the shift rod positioner from the transmission case.

18. Drive out the shifter rod retaining pin at the linkage pivot.

19. On Hondamatic cars, disconnect the transmission control cable by removing the lever retaining clip and pin and loosening the cable pinch bolt.

20. Disconnect the exhaust pipe at the manifold and disconnect the pipe bracket from the engine.

21. Remove the three bolts retaining the left side (timing belt side) engine mount and push the left side support into the sheet metal tower of the body. Then remove the bolts for the front (spark plug side) and rear (carburetor side) engine mounts.

22. After making sure the engine is clear of all electrical lines or vacuum hoses, slowly raise the engine/transaxle unit out of the car, taking care not to damage the radiator.

23. Reverse the above procedure to install using the following installation notes:

a. Tighten the exhaust pipe-to-manifold nuts to 28–36 ft-lbs.

b. Tighten center beam attaching bolts to 13–17 ft-lbs.

c. Tighten shift rod positioner to 5–7 ft-lbs.

d. When installing axle driveshafts, push in until snap-ring snaps into position.

e. Tighten ball joint nuts to 28–35 ft-lbs.

f. When installing speedometer gear, place straight leg on groove side. Then, pull on cable to make sure gear is secure.

g. Adjust clutch free-play to 0.08–0.10 in.

h. Adjust choke and throttle cables.

i. Bleed cooling system.

Cylinder Head

Removal and Installation

NOTE: *You will need a 12 point socket to remove and install the head bolts on the CVCC engine.*

Removal Precautions

1. To prevent warping, the cylinder head should be removed when the engine is cold.

2. Remove oil, scale or carbon deposits accumulated from each part. When decarbonizing take care not to score or scratch the mating surfaces.

3. After washing the oil holes or orifices in each part, make sure they are not restricted by blowing out with compressed air.

4. If parts will not be reinstalled immediately after washing, spray parts with a rust preventive to protect from corrosion.

Civic and Accord

NOTE: *If the engine has already been removed from the car, begin with Step 12 in the following procedure.*

1. Remove the turn signals, grille, and hood. (Civic only). Disconnect the negative battery cable.

2. Drain the radiator.

3. Disconnect the upper radiator hose at the thermostat cover.

3a. On CVCC models, remove distributor cap, ignition wires and (blue) primary wire. Also, loosen the alternator bracket and remove the upper mounting bolt from the cylinder head.

4. Remove the air cleaner case.

5. Disconnect the tube running between the canister and carburetor at the canister.

6. Disconnect the throttle and choke control cables. Label and disconnect all vacuum hoses.

7. Disconnect the heater hose at the intake manifold.

8. Disconnect the wires from both thermoswitches.

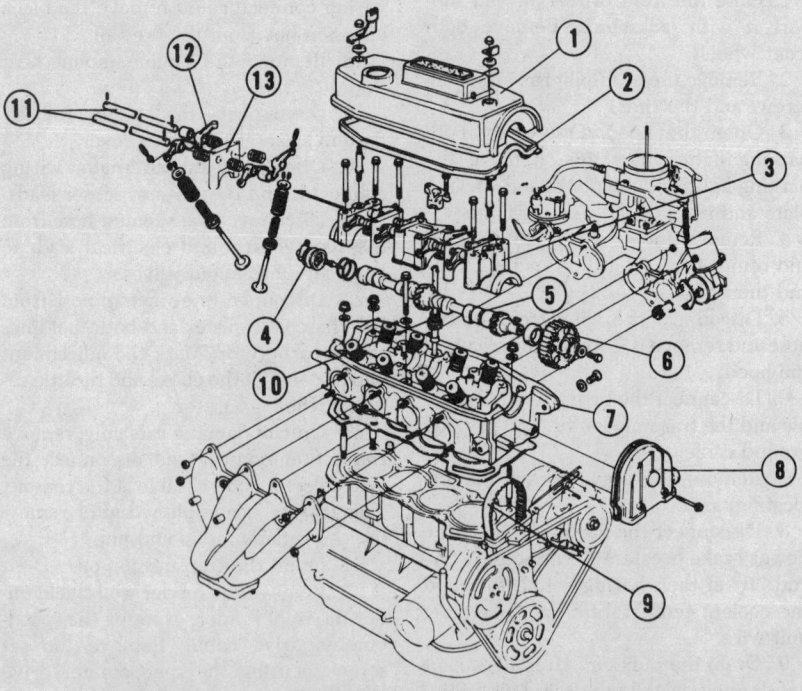

Exploded view of 1170, 1237 cc cylinder head and related parts

1. Head cover
2. Head cover gasket
3. Camshaft holder
4. Tachometer drive body
5. Camshaft
6. Timing belt driven pulley
7. Cylinder head
8. Timing belt upper cover
9. Timing belt
10. Oil pump drive gear
11. Rocker arm shafts
12. Rocker arm
13. Rocker arm shaft holder

18. On 1170 and 1237 cc models only, remove the oil pump gear holder and remove the pump gear and shaft.

19. Loosen and remove the cylinder head bolts in the *reverse* order given in the head bolt tightening sequence diagram.

20. Remove the cylinder head with the carburetor and manifolds attached.

21. Remove the intake and exhaust manifolds from the cylinder head.

NOTE: *After removing the cylinder head, cover the engine with a clean cloth to prevent materials from getting into the cylinders.*

22. To install, reverse the removal procedure, being sure to pay attention to the following points:

  a. Be sure that No. 1 cylinder is at top dead center before positioning the cylinder head in place;

  b. Use a new head gasket and make sure the head, engine block, and gasket are clean;

  c. The cylinder head aligning dowel pins should be in their proper place in the block before installing the cylinder head;

  d. Tighten the head bolts according to the diagram;

  e. After the head bolts have been tightened, install the woodruff key and camshaft pulley (if removed), and tighten the pulley bolt according to specification. Align the marks on the camshaft pulley so they are parallel with the top of the head and the woodruff key is facing up;

  f. After installing the pulley (if removed), install the timing belt. Be careful not to disturb the timing position already set when installing the belt.

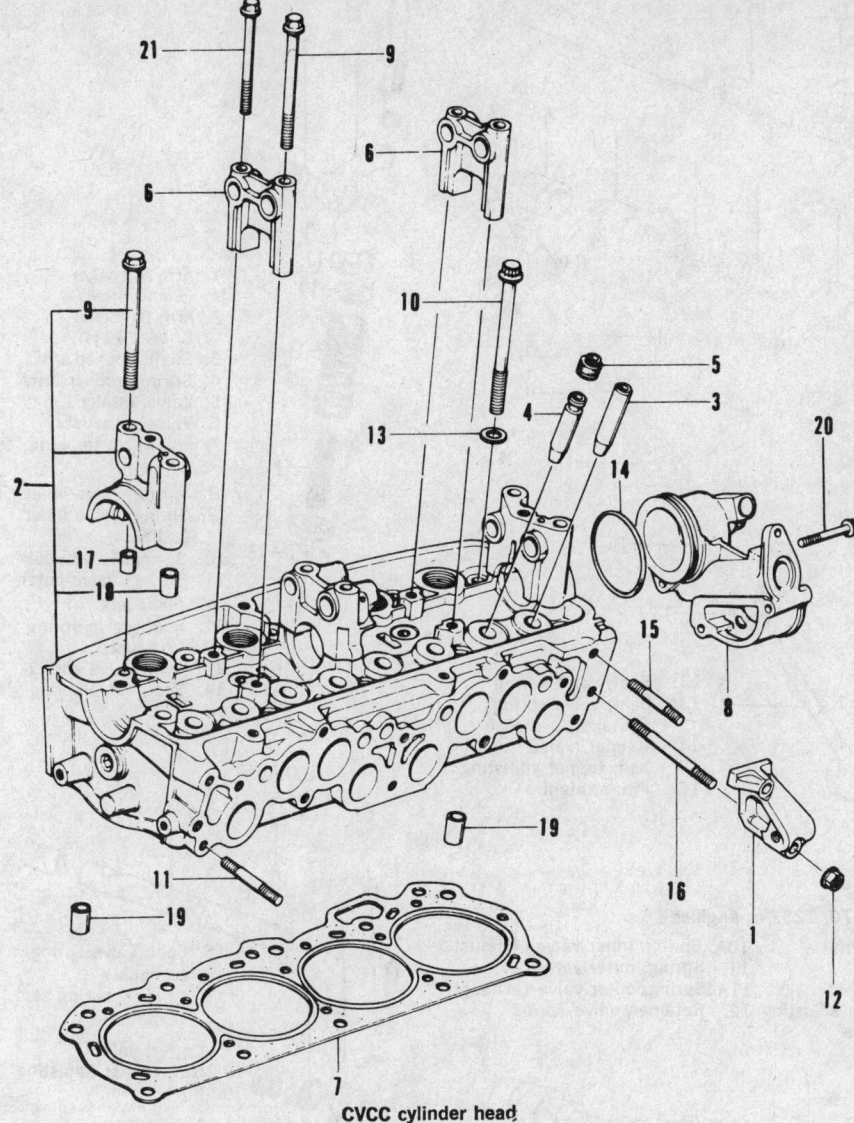

CVCC cylinder head

1. Torque rod bracket	12. Nut
2. Cylinder head assembly	13. Special washer
3. O/S exhaust valve guide	14. O-ring
4. O/S intake valve guide	15. Stud
5. Valve seal	16. Stud
6. Cam holder	17. Dowel pin
7. Gasket	18. Dowel pin
8. Distributor holder	19. Dowel pin
9. Bolt	20. Bolt
10. Bolt	21. Bolt
11. Stud	

9. Disconnect the fuel line.

9a. On CVCC models, disconnect the temperature gauge sending unit wire, idle cut-off solenoid valve, and primary-/main cut-off solenoid valve.

10. Disconnect the engine torque rod.

11. Disconnect the exhaust pipe at the exhaust manifold.

12. Remove the valve cover bolts and the valve cover.

13. Remove the two timing belt upper cover bolts and the cover.

14. Bring No. 1 piston to top dead center. Do this by aligning the notch next to the red notch you use for setting ignition timing, with the index mark on the timing belt cover (1170, 1237 cc) or rear of engine block (CVCC).

15. Loosen, but do not remove, the timing belt adjusting bolt and pivot bolt.

16. On 1170 and 1237 CC models only, remove the camshaft pulley bolt. Do not let the woodruff key fall inside the timing cover. Remove the pulley with a pulley remover (or special tool 07935–6110000).

CAUTION: *Use care when handling the timing belt. Do not use sharp instruments to remove the belt. Do not get oil or grease on the belt. Do not bend or twist the belt more than 90°.*

17. On 1170 and 1237 cc models only, remove the fuel pump and distributor.

When installing an 1170 or 1237 cc engine cylinder head, align the camshaft pulley marks so they are parallel with the top of the head

Camshaft and Rocker Shafts

Removal and Installation

NOTE: *To facilitate installation, make sure that No. 1 piston is at Top Dead Center before removal of camshaft.*

1. Follow the "Cylinder Head" removal procedure before attempting to remove the camshaft.

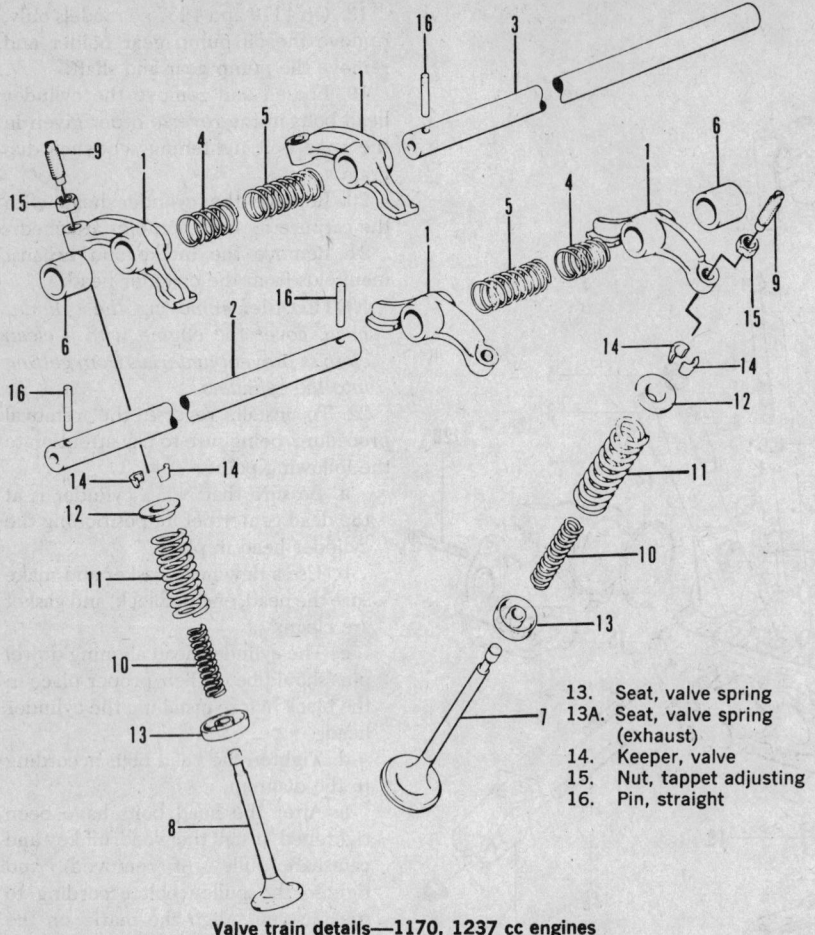

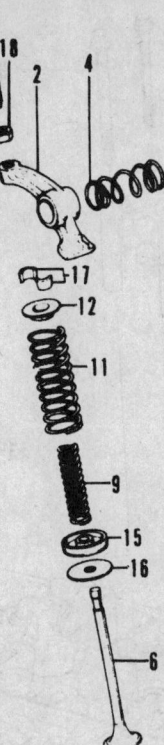

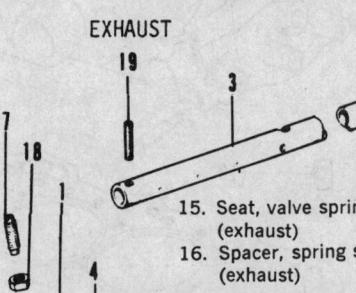

1. Arm A, rocker (1 and 4 cyl)
1. Arm A, rocker
   (1 and 4 cyl)
2. Arm B, rocker
   (2 and 3 cyl)
3. Shaft, rocker arm
4. Spring, rocker arm
5. Valve, intake
6. Valve, exhaust
7. Screw, rocker arm
   adjusting
8. Spring, valve inner
9. Spring, valve inner
   (exhaust)
10. Spring, valve outer
11. Spring, valve outer
    (exhaust)
12. Seat, valve spring
    (exhaust)
13. Seat, valve spring
14. Seat, valve spring

EXHAUST

15. Seat, valve spring
    (exhaust)
16. Spacer, spring seat
    (exhaust)
17. Cotter, valve
18. Nut, tappet adjusting
19. Pin

13.   Seat, valve spring
13A. Seat, valve spring
      (exhaust)
14.   Keeper, valve
15.   Nut, tappet adjusting
16.   Pin, straight

Valve train details—1170, 1237 cc engines

1. Arm, rocker
2. Shaft, intake rocker
3. Shaft, exhaust rocker
4. Spring A, rocker arm
5. Spring B, rocker arm
6. Spacer, rocker arm
7. Valve, intake
8. Valve, exhaust
9. Screw, rocker arm adjusting
10. Spring, inner valve
10A. Spring, inner valve (exhaust)
11. Spring, outer valve
11A. Spring, outer valve (exhaust)
12. Retainer, valve spring

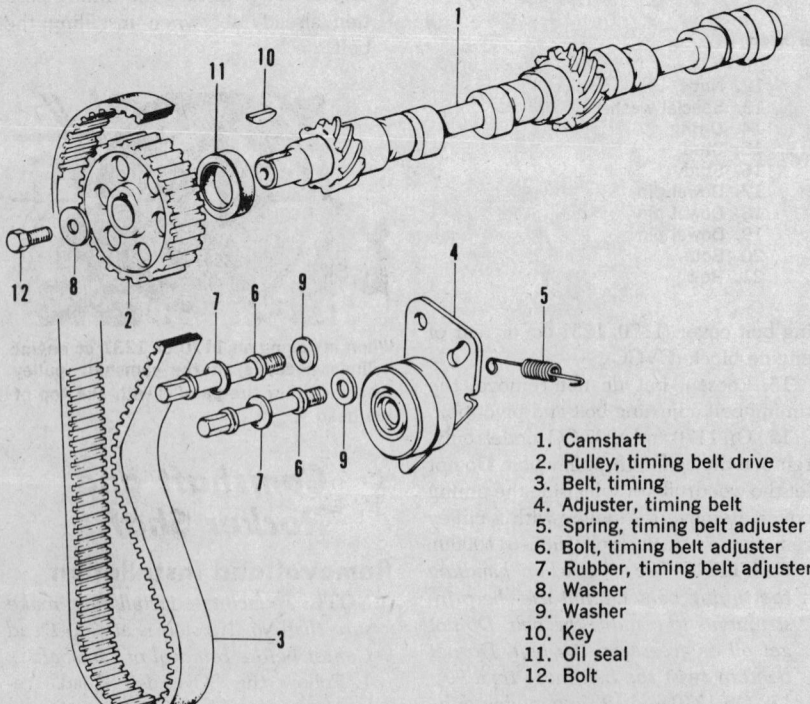

1. Camshaft
2. Pulley, timing belt drive
3. Belt, timing
4. Adjuster, timing belt
5. Spring, timing belt adjuster
6. Bolt, timing belt adjuster
7. Rubber, timing belt adjuster
8. Washer
9. Washer
10. Key
11. Oil seal
12. Bolt

INTAKE

Exploded view of camshaft and related parts—1170, 1237 cc engines

Details of intake and exhaust valve components—CVCC

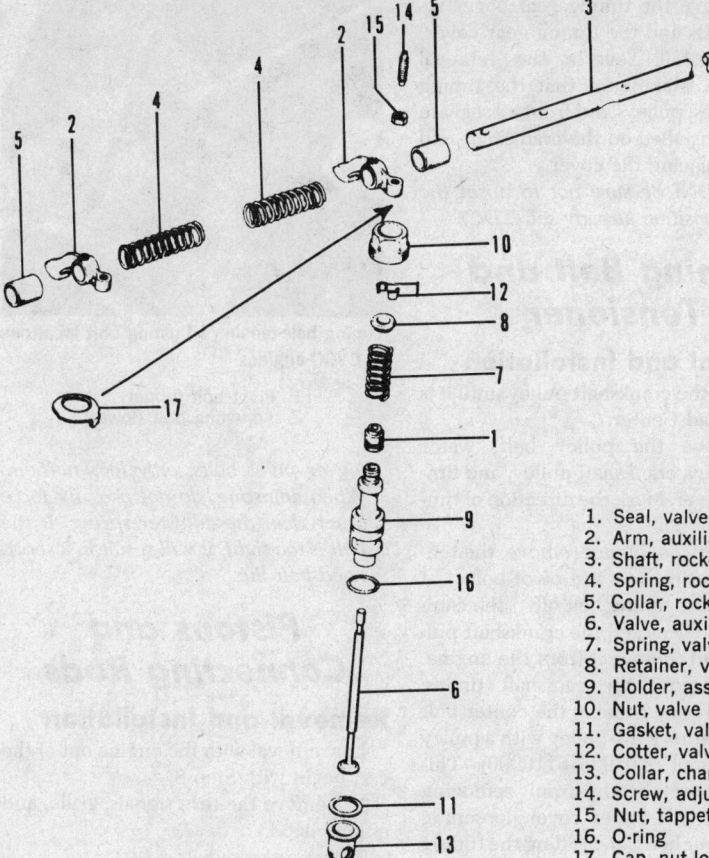

6. Remove the thermo-switch wires from the switches.

7. Remove the solenoid valve located next to the thermo-switch.

8. Remove the six (6) intake manifold attaching nuts in a crisscross pattern, beginning from the center and moving out to both ends. Then remove the manifold.

9. Clean all old gasket material from the manifold and the cylinder head.

10. If the intake manifold is to be replaced, transfer all necessary components to the new manifold.

11. To install, reverse the removal procedure, being sure to observe the following points:

    a. Apply a water-resistant sealer to the new intake manifold gasket before positioning it in place;

    b. Be sure all hoses are properly connected;

    c. Tighten the manifold attaching nuts in the reverse order of removal.

1. Seal, valve stem
2. Arm, auxiliary rocker
3. Shaft, rocker arm
4. Spring, rocker arm
5. Collar, rocker arm
6. Valve, auxiliary
7. Spring, valve
8. Retainer, valve spring
9. Holder, assy., valve
10. Nut, valve holder
11. Gasket, valve holder
12. Cotter, valve
13. Collar, chamber
14. Screw, adjusting
15. Nut, tappet adjusting
16. O-ring
17. Cap, nut lock

Details of auxiliary intake valve components—CVCC

Exhaust Manifold

Removal and Installation

1170, 1237 cc Models

CAUTION: *Do not perform this operation on a warm or hot engine.*

1. Remove the front grille.

2. Remove the three (3) exhaust pipe-to-manifold nuts and disconnect the exhaust pipe at the manifold.

2. Loosen the camshaft and rocker arm shaft holder bolts in a criss-cross pattern, beginning on the outside holder.

3. Remove the rocker arms, shafts, and holders as an assembly.

4. Lift out the camshaft and right head seal (or tachometer body if equipped).

5. To install, reverse the removal procedure, being sure to install the holder bolts in the reverse order of removal.

NOTE: *Back off valve adjusting screws before installing rockers. Then adjust valves as outlined earlier.*

Intake Manifold

Removal and Installation

1170, 1237 cc Models

1. Drain the radiator.

2. Remove the air cleaner and case.

3. Remove the carburetor from the intake manifold.

4. Remove the emission control hoses from the manifold T-joint. One hose leads to the condensation chamber and the other leads to the charcoal canister.

5. Remove the hose connected to the intake manifold directly above the T-joint and underneath the carburetor, leading to the air cleaner check valve.

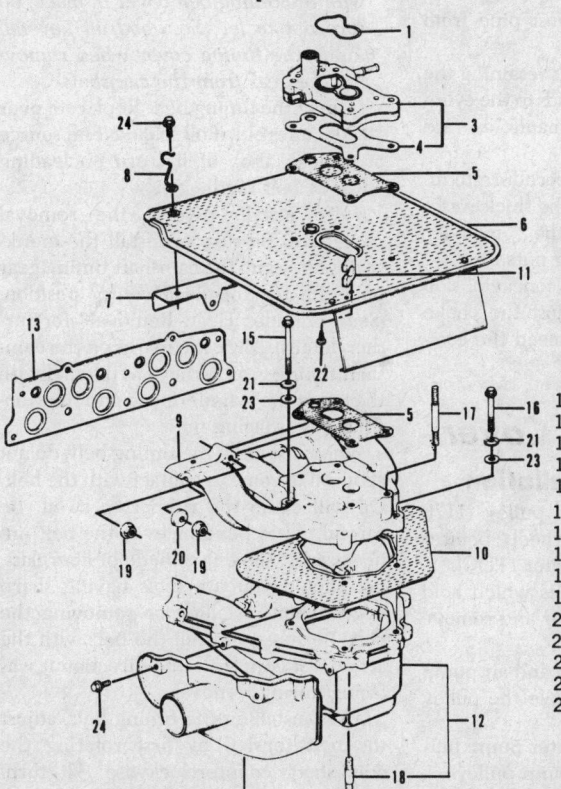

1. O-ring, insulator
2. O-ring, insulator
3. Insulator, carburetor
4. Gasket, heat insulator
5. Gasket, insulator lower
6. Plate, manifold insulator
7. Shroud, manifold
8. Clamp, clutch cable
9. Manifold, intake
10. Gasket, manifold riser
11. Clamp, tube
12. Manifold, exhaust
13. Gasket, manifold
14. Cover, hot air
15. Bolt
16. Bolt
17. Stud
18. Stud
19. Nut
20. Washer
21. Washer
22. Screw
23. Washer
24. Bolt

Intake, exhaust manifolds and related parts—1487 cc CVCC engine shown; 1600 cc engine similar

2a. On 1975–76 models, disconnect the air injection tubes from the exhaust manifold and remove the air injection manifold.

3. Remove the hot air cover, held by two bolts, from the exhaust manifold.

4. Remove the eight (8) manifold attaching nuts in a crisscross pattern starting from the center, and remove the manifold.

5. To install, reverse the removal procedure. Be sure to use new gaskets and be sure to tighten the manifold bolts in the reverse order of removal, and to the proper tightening torque.

Intake and Exhaust Manifold

Removal and Installation

CVCC Models

1. Drain the radiator. Disconnect manifold coolant hoses.

2. Remove the air cleaner assembly.

3. Label and disconnect all emission control vacuum hoses and electrical leads.

4. Disconnect the fuel lines, throttle, and choke linkage.

5. Remove the carburetor from the intake manifold.

6. Remove the upper heat shield. Loosen, but do not remove the four bolts retaining the intake manifold to the exhaust manifold.

7. Disconnect the exhaust pipe from the exhaust manifold.

8. Remove the nine nuts retaining the intake and exhaust manifolds to the cylinder head. The two manifolds are removed as a unit.

9. Reverse the above procedure to install, using new gaskets. The thick washers used beneath the cylinder head-to-manifold retaining nuts must be installed with the dished (concave) side toward the engine. Readjust the choke and throttle linkage and bleed the cooling system.

Timing Gear Cover

Removal and Installation

1. Align the crankshaft pulley (1170 and 1237 cc), or flywheel pointer (CVCC), at Top Dead Center (TDC).

2. Remove the two bolts which hold the timing belt upper cover and remove the cover.

3. Loosen the alternator and air pump (if so equipped), and remove the pulley belt(s).

4. Remove the three water pump pulley bolts and the water pump pulley.

5. Remove the crankshaft pulley attaching bolt. Use a two-jawed puller to remove the crankshaft pulley.

6. Remove the timing gear cover retaining bolts and the timing gear cover.

7. To install, reverse the removal procedure. Make sure that the timing guide plates, pulleys and front oil seal are properly installed on the crankshaft end before replacing the cover.

CAUTION: *Be sure not to upset the timing position already set (TDC).*

Timing Belt and Tensioner

Removal and Installation

1. Turn the crankshaft pulley until it is at Top Dead Center.

2. Remove the pulley belt, water pump pulley, crankshaft pulley, and timing gear cover. Mark the direction of timing belt rotation.

3. Loosen, *but do not remove,* the tensioner adjusting bolt and pivot bolt.

4. Slide the timing belt off the camshaft timing gear and the crankshaft pulley gear and remove it from the engine.

5. To remove the camshaft timing gear pulley, first remove the center bolt and then remove the pulley with a pulley remover (tool #07935–6110000). This can be accomplished by simply removing the timing belt upper cover, loosening the tensioner bolts, and sliding the timing belt off of the gear to expose the gear for removal.

NOTE: *If you remove the timing gear with the timing belt cover in place, be sure not to let the woodruff key fall inside the timing cover when removing the gear from the camshaft.*

Inspect the timing belt. Replace if over 10,000 miles old, if oil soaked (find source of oil leak also), or if worn on leading edges of belt teeth.

6. To install, reverse the removal procedure. Be sure to install the crankshaft pulley and the camshaft timing gear pulley in the top dead center position. (See "Cylinder Head Removal" for further details). Align the marks on the camshaft timing gear so they are parallel with the top of the cylinder head and the woodruff key is facing up.

When installing the timing belt, do not allow oil to come in contact with the belt. Oil will cause the rubber to swell. Be careful not to bend or twist the belt unnecessarily, since it is made of fiberglass; nor should you use tools having sharp edges when installing or removing the belt. Be sure to install the belt with the arrow facing in the same direction it was facing during removal.

After installing the timing belt, adjust the belt tension by first rotating the crankshaft counterclockwise ¼ turn. Then, retighten the adjusting bolt and finally the tensioner pivot bolt.

CAUTION: *Do not remove the adjust-*

Timing belt tension adjusting bolt locations —CVCC engines

1. Pivot bolt (upper)
2. Adjusting bolt (lower)

ing or pivot bolts, only loosen them. When adjusting, do not use any force other than the adjuster spring. If the belt is too tight, it will result in a shortened belt life.

Pistons and Connecting Rods

Removal and Installation

For removal with the engine out of the car, begin with Step 8.

1. Remove the turn signals, grille, and engine hood.

2. Drain the radiator.

3. Drain the engine oil.

4. Raise the front of the car and support it with safety stands.

5. Attach a chain to the clutch cable bracket on the transmission case and raise just enough to take the load off of the center mount.

NOTE: *Do not remove the left engine mount.*

6. Remove the center beam and engine lower mount.

7. Remove the cylinder head (see "Cylinder Head Removal and Installation").

8. Loosen the oil pan bolts and remove the oil pan and flywheel dust shield. Loosen the oil pan bolts in a criss-cross pattern beginning with the outside bolt. To remove the oil pan, lightly tap the corners of the oil pan with a mallet. It is not necessary to remove the gasket unless it is damaged.

CAUTION: *Do not pry the oil pan off with the tip of a screwdriver.*

9. Remove the oil passage block and the oil pump assembly.

NOTE: *As soon as the oil passage block bolts are loosened, the oil in the oil line may flow out.*

NOTE: *Before removing the pistons, check the top of the cylinder bore for carbon build-up or a ridge. Remove the carbon or use a ridge-reamer to remove the ridge before removing the pistons.*

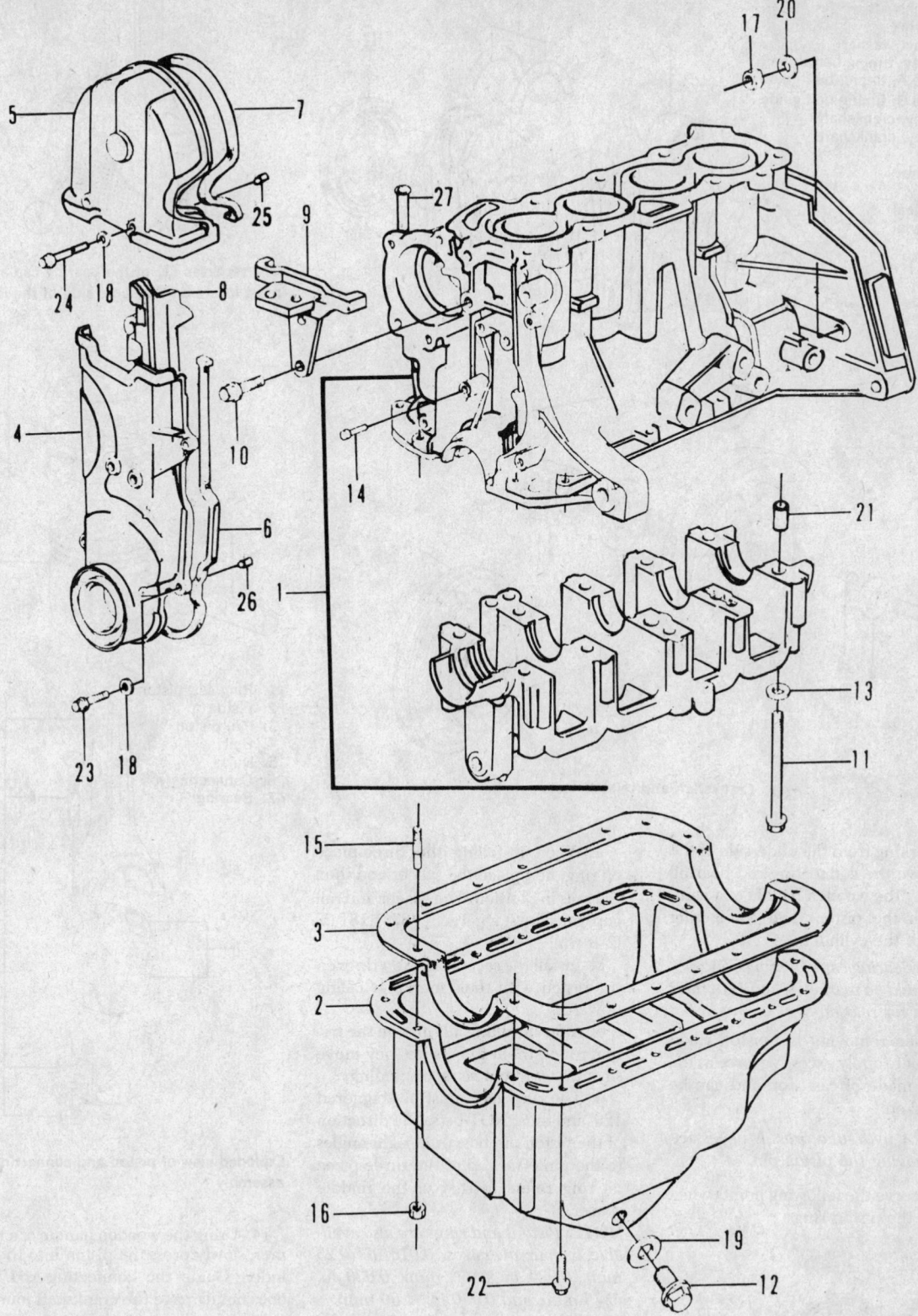

Cylinder block, crankcase and related parts, 1170, 1237 cc engines

1. Block assy., cylinder
2. Oil pan
3. Gasket, oil pan
4. Cover, timing belt lower
5. Cover, timing belt upper
6. Seal A
7. Seal B
8. Seal C
9. Bracket, engine mount

10. Bolt, hex
11. Bolt, flanged
12. Bolt, drain plug
13. Washer
14. Pin
15. Bolt
16. Nut
17. Nut
18. Washer

19. Washer
20. Washer
21. Pin
22. Bolt
23. Bolt
24. Bolt
25. Collar
26. Collar
27. Tube dipstick

Honda

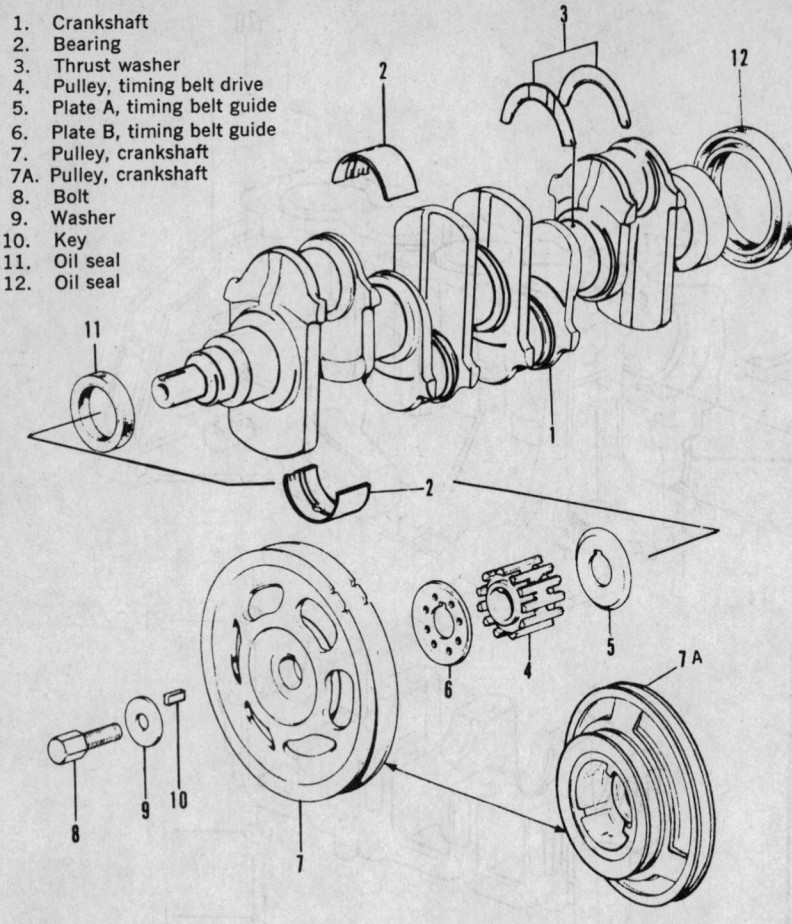

1. Crankshaft
2. Bearing
3. Thrust washer
4. Pulley, timing belt drive
5. Plate A, timing belt guide
6. Plate B, timing belt guide
7. Pulley, crankshaft
7A. Pulley, crankshaft
8. Bolt
9. Washer
10. Key
11. Oil seal
12. Oil seal

Crankshaft and related parts

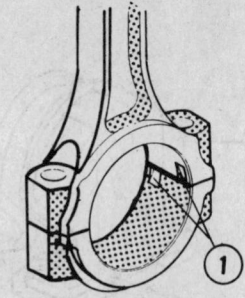

The recesses (1) of the bearing cap and rod must locate on the same side of the journal

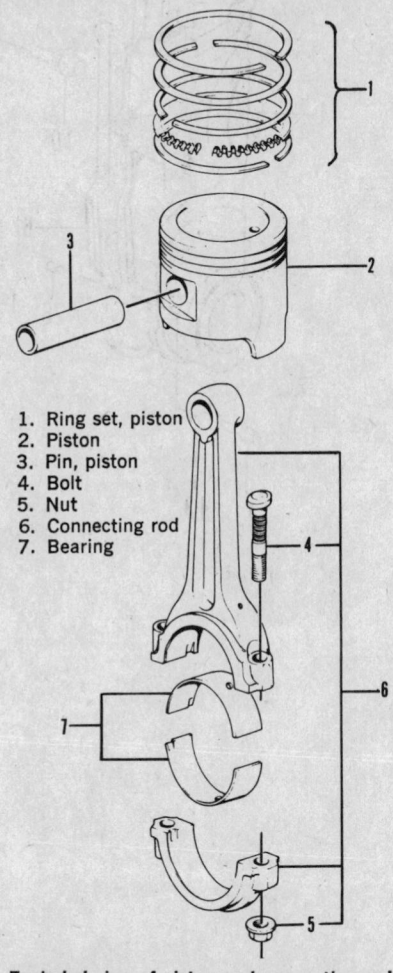

1. Ring set, piston
2. Piston
3. Pin, piston
4. Bolt
5. Nut
6. Connecting rod
7. Bearing

Exploded view of piston and connecting rod assembly

10. Working from the underside of the car, remove the connecting rod bearing caps. Using the wooden handle of a hammer, push the pistons and connecting rods out of the cylinders.

NOTE: *Bearing caps, bearings, and pistons should be marked to indicate their location for reassembly.*

11. When removing the piston rings, be sure not to apply excessive force as the rings are made of cast iron and can be easily broken.

NOTE: *A hydraulic press is necessary for removing the piston pin.*

12. Observe the following points when installing the piston rings:

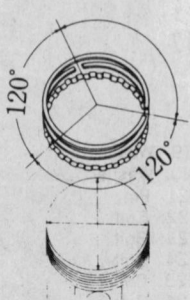

Piston ring positioning

a. When installing the three-piece oil ring, first place the spacer and then the rails in position. The spacer and rail gaps must be staggered 0.787–1.181 in. (2–3 cm);

b. Install the second and top rings on the piston with their markings facing upward;

c. After installing all rings on the piston, rotate them to be sure they move smoothly without signs of binding;

d. The ring gaps must be staggered 120° and must NOT be in the direction of the piston pin boss or at right angles to the pin. The gap of the three-piece oil ring refers to that of the middle spacer.

NOTE: *Pistons and rings are also available in four oversizes, 0.010 in. (0.25 mm), 0.020 in. (0.50 mm), 0.030 in. (0.75 mm), and 0.040 in. (1.00 mm).*

13. Using a ring compressor, install the piston into the cylinder with the skirt protruding about 1/3 of the piston height below the ring compressor. Prior to installation, apply a thin coat of oil to the rings and to the cylinder wall.

NOTE: *When installing the piston, the connecting rod oil jet hole or the mark on the piston crown faces the intake manifold.*

14. Using the wooden handle of a hammer, slowly press the piston into the cylinder. Guide the connecting rod so it does not damage the crankshaft journals.

15. Reassemble the remaining components in the reverse order of removal. Install the connecting rod bearing caps so that the recess in the cap and the recess in the rod are on the same side. After tightening the cap bolts, move the rod back and forth on the journal to check for binding. After tightening the crankshaft bearing cap bolts, rotate the crankshaft to check for smooth rotation.

ENGINE LUBRICATION

Oil Pan

Removal and Installation

1. Drain the engine oil.

2. Raise the front of the car and support it with safety stands.

3. Attach a chain to the clutch cable bracket (Civic) or slave Cylinder (Accord) on the transmission case and raise just enough to take the load off the center mount.

NOTE: *Do not remove the left engine mount.*

4. Remove the center beam and engine lower mount.

5. Loosen the oil pan bolts and remove the oil pan flywheel dust shield.

NOTE: *Loosen the bolts in a criss-cross pattern beginning with the outside bolt. To remove the oil pan, lightly tap the corners of the oil pan with a mallet. It is not necessary to remove the gasket unless it is damaged.*

6. To install, reverse the removal procedure. Apply a coat of sealant to the entire mating surface of the cylinder block, except the crankshaft oil seal, before fitting the oil pan. Tighten according to sequence.

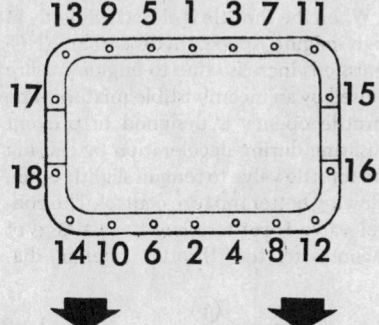

Oil pan tightening sequence

Rear Main Oil Seal

Replacement

The rear oil seal is installed in the rear main bearing cap. Replacement of the seal requires the removal of the transmission, flywheel and clutch housing, as well as the oil pan. Refer to the appropriate sections for the removal and installation of the above components.

Oil Pump

Removal and Installation

To remove the oil pump, follow the procedure given for oil pan removal and installation. After the oil pan has been

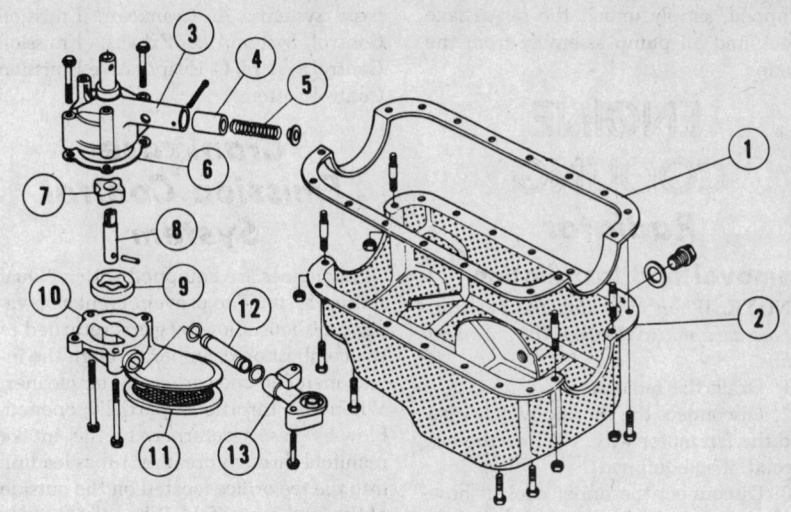

Oil pump and related parts—1170, 1237 cc engine

1. Oil pan gasket	6. Pump body gasket	10. Oil strainer rotor
2. Oil pan	7. Pump inner rotor	11. Oil pump filter screen
3. Oil pump body	8. Oil pump shaft	12. Oil pass pipe
4. Relief valve	9. Pump outer rotor	13. Oil pass block
5. Relief valve spring		

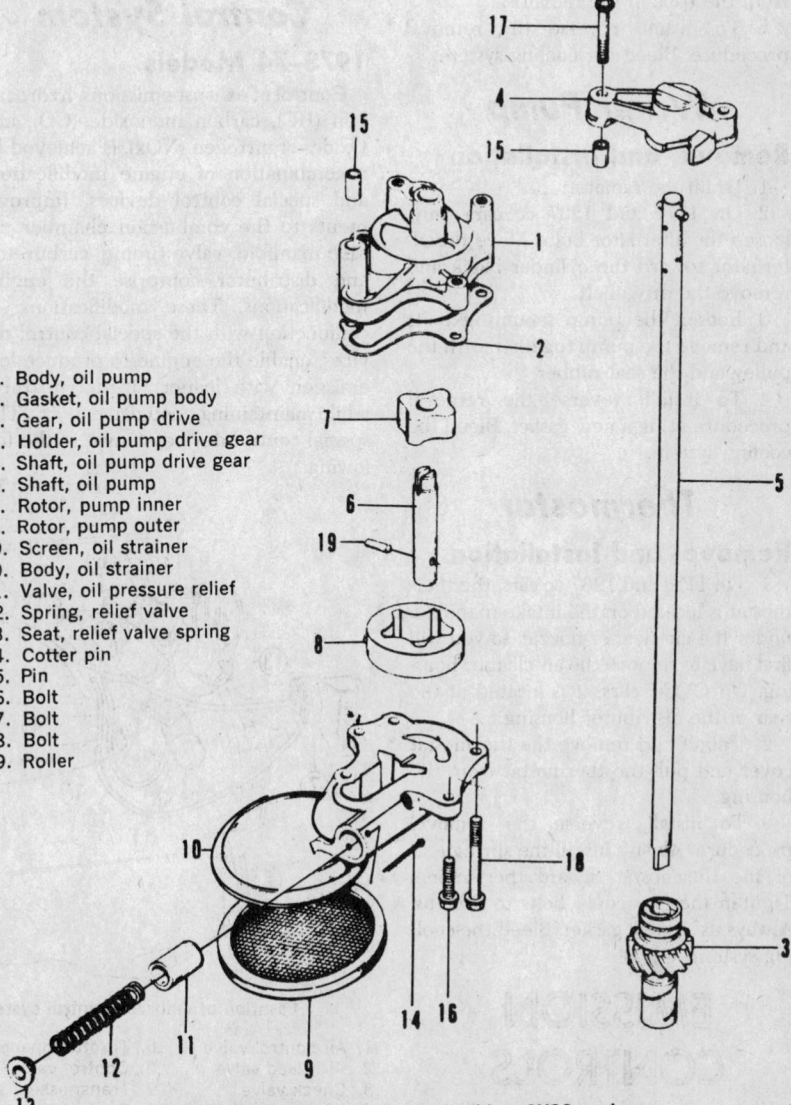

1. Body, oil pump
2. Gasket, oil pump body
3. Gear, oil pump drive
4. Holder, oil pump drive gear
5. Shaft, oil pump drive gear
6. Shaft, oil pump
7. Rotor, pump inner
8. Rotor, pump outer
9. Screen, oil strainer
10. Body, oil strainer
11. Valve, oil pressure relief
12. Spring, relief valve
13. Seat, relief valve spring
14. Cotter pin
15. Pin
16. Bolt
17. Bolt
18. Bolt
19. Roller

Exploded view of oil pump assembly—CVCC engine

dropped, simply unbolt the oil passage block and oil pump assembly from the engine.

ENGINE COOLING
Radiator

Removal and Installation

NOTE: *When removing the radiator, take care not to damage the core and fins.*

1. Drain the radiator.

2. Disconnect the thermo-switch wire and the fan motor wire. Remove the fan shroud, if so equipped.

3. Disconnect the upper coolant hose at the upper radiator tank and the lower hose at the water pump connecting pipe.

4. Remove the turn signals and front grille.

5. Detach the radiator mounting bolts and remove the radiator with the fan attached. The fan can be easily unbolted from the back of the radiator.

6. To install, reverse the removal procedure. Bleed the cooling system.

Water Pump

Removal and Installation

1. Drain the radiator.

2. On 1170 and 1237 cc cars only, loosen the alternator bolts. Move the alternator toward the cylinder block and remove the drive belt.

3. Loosen the pump mounting bolts and remove the pump together with the pulley and the seal rubber.

4. To install, reverse the removal procedure using a new gasket. Bleed the cooling system.

Thermostat

Removal and Installation

1. On 1170 and 1237 cc cars, the thermostat is located on the intake manifold, under the air cleaner nozzle, so you will first have to remove the air cleaner housing. On CVCC cars, it is located at the rear of the distributor housing.

2. Unbolt and remove the thermostat cover and pull the thermostat from the housing.

3. To install, reverse the removal procedure. Always install the spring end of the thermostat toward the engine. Tighten the two cover bolts to 7 ft lbs. Always use a new gasket. Bleed the cooling system.

EMISSION CONTROLS

Emission controls fall into one of three

basic systems: A. Crankcase Emission Control System, B. Exhaust Emission Control System, C. Evaporative Emission Control System.

Crankcase Emission Control System

All engines are equipped with a "Dual Return System" to prevent crankcase vapor emissions. Blow-by gas is returned to the combustion chamber through the intake manifold and carburetor air cleaner. When the throttle is partially opened, blow-by gas is returned to the intake manifold through breather tubes leading into the tee orifice located on the outside of the intake manifold. When the throttle is opened wide and vacuum in the air cleaner rises, blow-by gas is returned to the intake manifold through an additional passage in the air cleaner case.

Exhaust Emission Control System

1973–74 Models

Control of exhaust emissions, hydrocarbon (HC), carbon monoxide (CO), and Oxides of nitrogen (NOx), is achieved by a combination of engine modifications and special control devices. Improvements to the combustion chamber, intake manifold, valve timing, carburetor, and distributor comprise the engine modifications. These modifications, in conjunction with the special control devices, enable the engine to produce low emission with leaner air-fuel mixtures while maintaining good driveability. The special control devices consist of the following:

a. Intake air temperature control;

b. Throttle opener;

c. Ignition timing retard unit (1973 models only);

d. Transmission and temperature controlled spark advance (TCS) for the 4-speed transmission;

e. Temperature controlled spark advance for Hondamatic automatic transmission (1973 models only).

Intake Air Temperature Control

Intake air temperature control is designed to provide the most uniform carburetion possible under various ambient air temperature conditions by maintaining the intake air temperature within a narrow range. When the temperature in the air cleaner is below 100° F (approx.), the air bleed valve, which consists of a bimetallic strip and a rubber seal, remains closed. Intake manifold vacuum is then led to a vacuum motor, located on the snorkel of the air cleaner case, which moves the air control valve door, allowing only preheated air to enter the air cleaner.

When the temperature in the air cleaner becomes higher than approx. 100° F, the air bleed valve opens and the air control valve door returns to the open position allowing only unheated air through the snorkel.

Throttle Opener

When the throttle is closed suddenly at high engine speed, hydrocarbon (HC) emissions increase due to engine misfire caused by an incombustible mixture. The throttle opener is designed to prevent misfiring during deceleration by causing the throttle valve to remain slightly open, allowing better mixture control. The control valve is set to allow the passage of vacuum to the throttle opener dia-

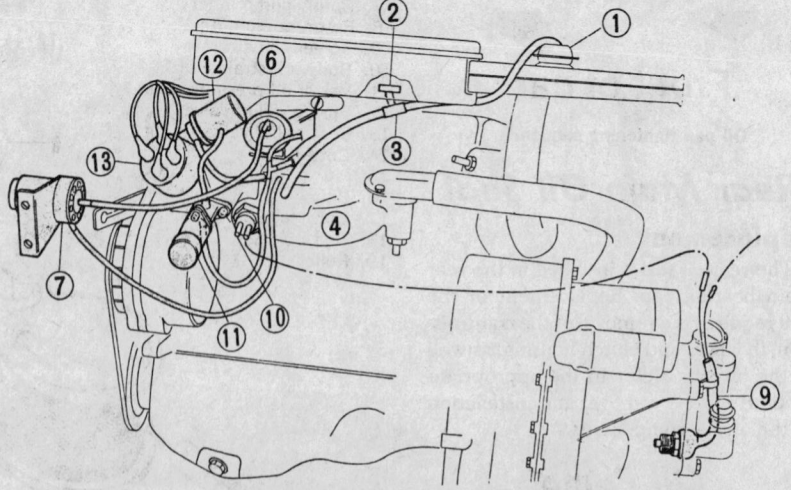

Location of emission control system components—1973 1170 cc engine

1. Air control valve	6. Throttle opener	11. Solenoid valve
2. Air bleed valve	7. Control valve	12. Spark advance/retard unit
3. Check valve	9. Transmission sensor	13. Distributor
4. Intake manifold	10. Coolant temperature sensor	

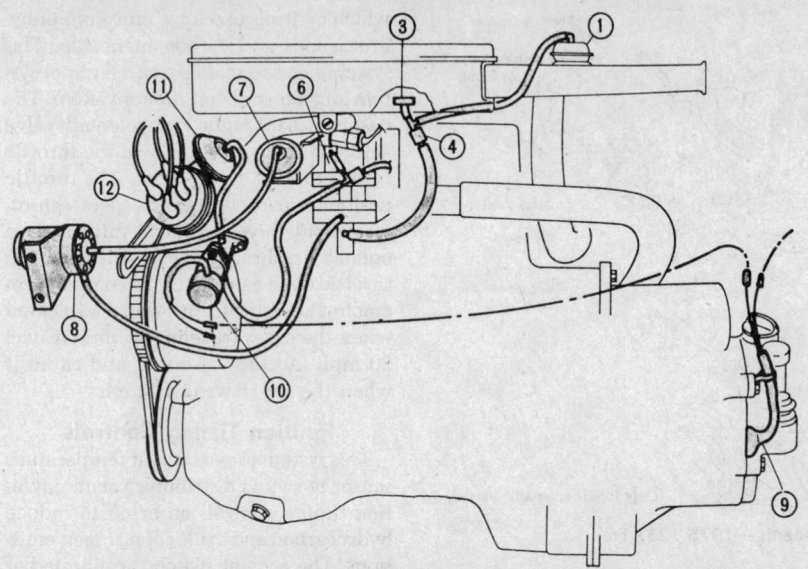

Location of emission control system components—1974 1237 cc models

1. Vacuum motor
3. Air bleed valve
4. Check valve
6. Carburetor
7. Throttle opener
8. Control valve
9. Transmission sensor (4-speed transmission only)
10. Solenoid valve (4-speed transmission only)
11. Spark advance unit (4-speed transmission only)
12. Distributor

phragm when the engine vacuum is equal to or greater than the control valve preset vacuum (21.6+1.6 in. Hg) during acceleration.

Under running conditions, other than fully closed throttle deceleration, the intake manifold vacuum is less than the control valve set vacuum; therefore the control valve is not actuated. The vacuum remaining in the throttle opener and control valve is returned to atmospheric pressure by the air passage at the valve center.

Ignition Timing Retard Unit

On 1973 models, when the engine is idling, the vacuum produced in the carburetor retarder port is communicated to the spark retard unit and the ignition timing, at idle, is retarded.

TCS System

The transmission and temperature controlled spark advance for 4-speed transmissions is designed to reduce NOx emissions during normal vehicle operation.

On 1973 models, when the coolant temperature is approximately 120° or higher, and the transmission is in First, Second, or Third gear, the solenoid valve cuts off the vacuum to the spark advance unit, resulting in lower NOx levels.

On 1974 models, the vacuum is cut off to the spark advance unit regardless of temperature when First, Second, or Third gear is selected. Vacuum advance is restored when Fourth gear is selected.

Temperature Controlled Spark Advance

Temperature controlled spark ad-

vance on 1973 cars equipped with Hondamatic transmission is designed to reduce NOx emissions by disconnecting the vacuum to the spark advance unit during normal vehicle operation. When the coolant temperature is approximately 120° or higher, the solenoid valve is energized, cutting off vacuum to the advance unit.

1975–76 1237 cc Models

Intake Air Temperature Control

Same as 1973–74 models.

Throttle Opener

Same as 1973–74 models.

Transmission Controlled Spark Advance

Same as 1974 models, with no coolant control override.

Ignition Timing Retard Unit

Same as 1973 models, but is used only on Hondamatic models and has no vacuum advance mechanism.

Air Injection System

Beginning with the 1975 model year, an air injection system is used to control hydrocarbon and carbon monoxide emissions. With this system, a belt-driven air pump delivers filtered air under pressure to injection nozzles located at each exhaust port. Here, the additional oxygen supplied by the vane-type pump reacts with any uncombusted fuel mixture, promoting an afterburning effect in the hot exhaust manifold. To prevent a reverse flow in the air injection manifold when exhaust gas pressure exceeds air supply pressure, a non-return check valve is used. To prevent exhaust afterburning or backfiring during deceleration, an anti-afterburn valve delivers air to the intake manifold instead. When manifold vacuum rises above the preset vacuum of the air control valve and/or below that of the air by-pass valve, air pump air is returned to the air cleaner.

1975–76 CVCC Models

Intake Air Temperature Control

Same as 1973–74 models.

Throttle Controls

This system controls the closing of the throttle during periods of gear shifting, deceleration, or anytime the gas pedal is released. In preventing the sudden closing of the throttle during these conditions, an overly rich mixture is prevented

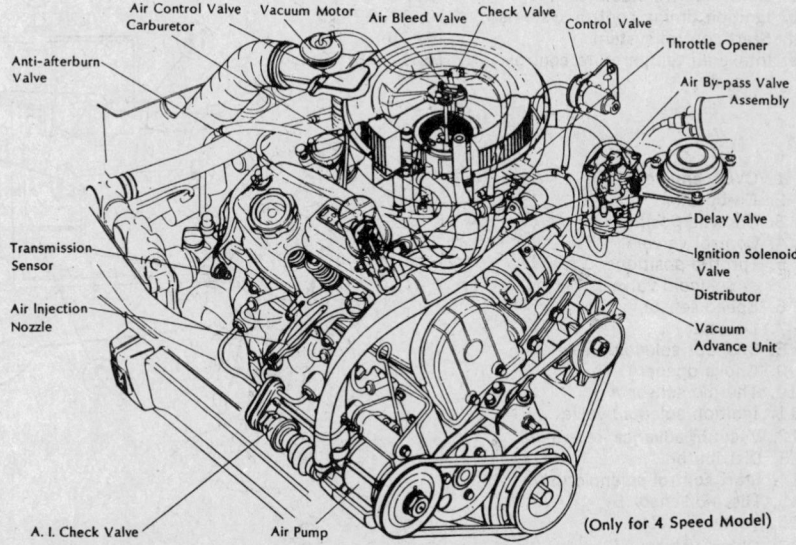

Air Control Valve
Carburetor
Vacuum Motor
Air Bleed Valve
Check Valve
Control Valve
Throttle Opener
Anti-afterburn Valve
Air By-pass Valve Assembly
Transmission Sensor
Air Injection Nozzle
Delay Valve
Ignition Solenoid Valve
Distributor
Vacuum Advance Unit
A. I. Check Valve
Air Pump
(Only for 4 Speed Model)

Location of emission control system components—1975 1237 cc models with Manual transmission

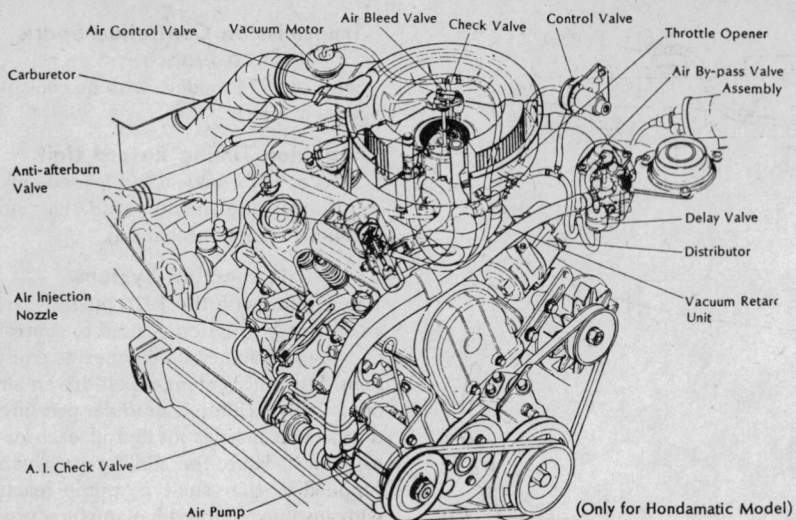

Location of emission control system components—1975 1237 cc with Hondamatic transmission

Labels on diagram: Air Control Valve, Vacuum Motor, Air Bleed Valve, Check Valve, Control Valve, Throttle Opener, Carburetor, Air By-pass Valve Assembly, Anti-afterburn Valve, Delay Valve, Distributor, Air Injection Nozzle, Vacuum Retard Unit, A. I. Check Valve, Air Pump, (Only for Hondamatic Model)

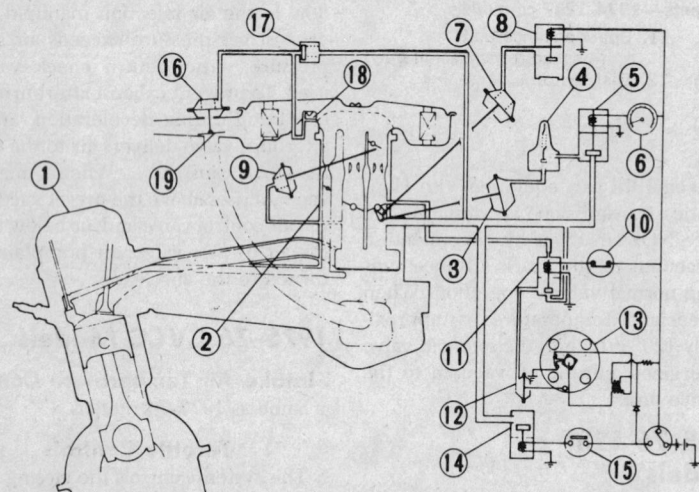

Emission control systems schematic—1975-76 1487 cc CVCC models with manual transmission

System	Item No.
a. Engine modification—HONDA CVCC	1
b. Carburetor related system	2, 3, 4, 5, 6, 7, 8, 9
c. Ignition timing control systems	10, 11, 12, 13
d. Start control system	14, 15
e. Intake air temperature control system	16, 17, 18, 19

1. CVCC engine
2. Carburetor
3. Throttle positioner
4. Control valve
5. Throttle positioner solenoid valve
6. Speed sensor
7. Dashpot
8. Dashpot solenoid valve
9. Choke opener
10. Thermo sensor A
11. Ignition solenoid valve
12. Vacuum advance/retard unit
13. Distributor
14. Start control solenoid valve
15. Thermo sensor B
16. Vacuum motor
17. Check valve
18. Air bleed valve
19. Air control valve

which controls excessive emissions of hydrocarbons and carbon monoxide. This system has two main parts; a dashpot system and a throttle positioner system. The dashpot diaphragm and solenoid valve act to dampen or slow down the throttle return time to 1–4 seconds. The throttle positioner part consists of a speed sensor, a solenoid valve, a control valve and an opener diaphragm which will keep the throttle open a predetermined minimum amount any time the gas pedal is released when the car is traveling 15 mph (Civic) 20 mph (Accord) or faster, and closes it when the car slows to 10 mph.

Ignition Timing Controls

This system uses a coolant temperature sensor to switch distributor vacuum ignition timing controls on or off to reduce hydrocarbon and oxides of nitrogen emissions. The coolant switch is calibrated at 149° F.

Hot Start Control

This system is designed to prevent an overrich mixture condition in the intake manifold due to vaporization of residual fuel when starting a hot engine. This reduces hydrocarbon and carbon monoxide emissions.

CVCC Engine Modifications

By far, the most important part of the CVCC engine emission control system is the Compound Vortex Controlled Combustion (CVCC) cylinder head itself. Each cylinder has three valves: a conventional intake and conventional exhaust valve, and a smaller auxiliary intake valve. There are actually *two* combustion chambers per cylinder: a pre-combustion or auxiliary chamber, and the main chamber. During the intake stroke, an extremely lean mixture is drawn into the

Emission control systems schematic—1975-76 1487 cc CVCC models with Hondamatic transmission

main combustion chamber. Simultaneously, a very rich mixture is drawn into the smaller precombustion chamber via the auxiliary intake valve. The spark plug, located in the precombustion chamber, easily ignites the rich pre-mixture, and this combustion spreads out into the main combustion chamber where the lean mixture is ignited. Due to the fact that the volume of the auxiliary chamber is much smaller than the main chamber, the overall mixture is very lean (about 18 parts air to one part fuel). The result is low hydrocarbon emissions due to the slow, stable combustion of the lean mixture in the main chamber; low carbon monoxide emissions due to the excess oxygen available; and low oxides of nitrogen emissions due to the lowered peak combustion temperatures. An added benefit of burning the lean mixture is the excellent gas mileage.

Evaporative Emission Control System

This system prevents gasoline vapors from escaping into the atmosphere from the fuel tank and carburetor and consists of the components listed in the illustration.

Fuel vapor is stored in the expansion chamber, in the fuel tank, and in the vapor line up to the one-way valve. When the vapor pressure becomes higher than the set pressure of the one-way valve, the valve opens and allows vapor into the charcoal canister. While the engine is stopped or idling, the idle cut-off valve in the canister is closed and the vapor is absorbed by the charcoal.

At partially opened throttle, the idle cut-off valve is opened by manifold vacuum. The vapor that was stored in the charcoal canister and in the vapor line is purged into the intake manifold. Any excessive pressure or vacuum which might build up in the fuel tank is relieved by the two-way valve in the filler cap (Civic) or in the engine compartment (Accord).

Maintenance and Service

Crankcase Emission Control System

1. On 1973–75 models, squeeze the lower end of the drain tube and drain any oil or water which may have collected. On 1976 models, remove the tube, invert, and drain it.

2. Make sure that the intake manifold T-joint is clear. Pass the shank end of a No. 65 (0.035 in. dia.) drill through both ends (orifices) of the joint on Non-CVCC

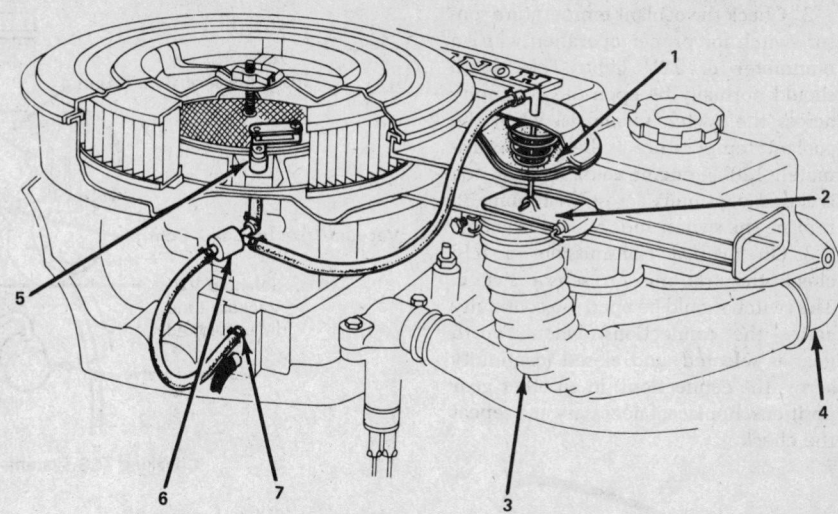

Details of air intake temperature control system—1973 1170 cc

1. Vacuum motor
2. Air control valve door
3. Hot air hose
4. To exhaust manifold
5. Air bleed valve
6. Check valve
7. Fixed orifice

models. On the CVCC, pass a No. 59 (0.041 in.) drill through the orifice.

3. Check for any loose, disconnected, or deteriorated tubes and replace if necessary.

Exhaust Emission Control System

Intake Air Temperature Control System (Engine Cold)

1. Inspect for loose, disconnected, or deteriorated vacuum hoses and replace as necessary.

2. Remove the air cleaner cover and element.

3. With the transmission in Neutral and the blue distributor wire disconnected, engage the starter motor for approximately two (2) seconds. Manifold vacuum to the vacuum motor should completely raise the air control valve door. Once opened, the valve door should stay open unless there is a leak in the system.

4. If the valve door does not open, check the intake manifold port by passing a No. 78 (0.016 in. dia.) drill or compressed air through the orifice in the manifold.

5. If the valve door still does not open, proceed to the following steps:

   a. Vacuum Motor Test—Disconnect the vacuum line from the vacuum motor inlet pipe. Fully open the air control valve door, block the vacuum motor inlet pipe, then release the door. If the door does not remain open, the vacuum motor is defective. Replace as necessary and repeat Steps 1–3;

   b. Air Bleed Valve Test—Unblock the inlet pipe and make sure that the valve door fully closes without sticking or binding. Reconnect the vacuum line to the vacuum motor inlet pipe. Connect a vacuum source (e.g. hand

vacuum pump) to the manifold vacuum line (disconnect at the intake manifold fixed orifice) and draw enough vacuum to fully open the valve door. If the valve door closes with the manifold vacuum line plugged (by the vacuum pump), then vacuum is leaking through the air bleed valve. Replace as necessary and repeat Steps 1–3;

   CAUTION: *Never force the air bleed valve (bi-metal strip) on or off its valve seat. The bi-metal strip and the valve seat may be damaged.*

   c. Check Valve Test—Again draw a vacuum (at the manifold vacuum line) until the valve door opens. Unplug the line by disconnecting the pump from the manifold vacuum line. If the valve door closes, vacuum is leaking past the check valve. Replace as necessary and repeat Steps 1–3.

6. After completing the above steps, replace the air cleaner element and cover and fit a vacuum gauge into the line leading to the vacuum motor.

7. Start the engine and raise the idle to 1500–2000 rpm. As the engine warms, the vacuum gauge reading should drop to zero.

NOTE: *Allow sufficient time for the engine to reach normal operating temperature—when the cooling fan cycles on and off.*

If the reading does not drop to zero before the engine reaches normal operating temperature, the air bleed valve is defective and must be replaced. Repeat Step 3 as a final check.

Temperature and Transmission Controlled Spark Advance (Engine Cold)—All Models

1. Check for loose, disconnected, or deteriorated vacuum hoses and replace as necessary.

Honda

2. Check the coolant temperature sensor switch for proper operation with an ohmmeter or 12V light. The switch should normally be open (no continuity across the switch terminals) when the coolant temperature is below approximately 120° F (engine cold). If the switch is closed (continuity across the terminals), replace the switch and repeat the check.

3. On manual transmission models, check the transmission sensor switch. The switch should be open (no continuity across the connections) when Fourth gear is selected, and closed (continuity across the connections) in all other gear positions. Replace if necessary and repeat the check.

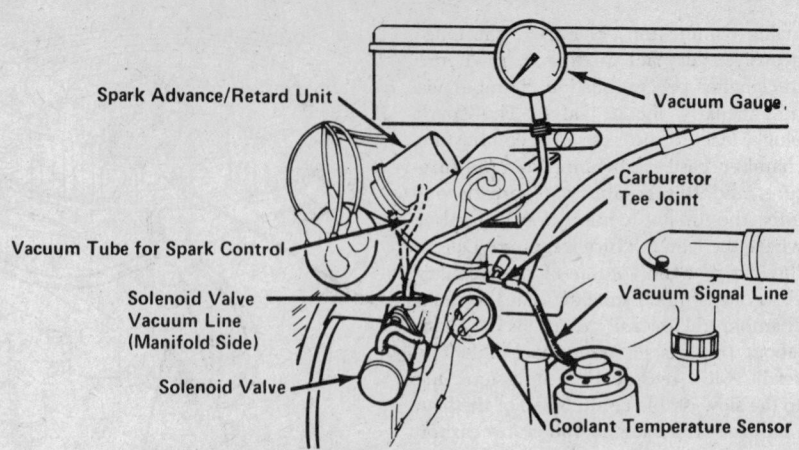

Checking TCS system—1973 1170 cc models

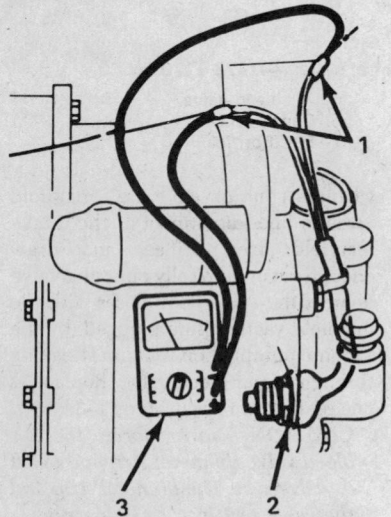

Testing coolant temperature switch for temperature controlled advance—1973 1170 cc models

1. Transmission sensor terminals
2. Transmission sensor
3. Ohmmeter

4. Remove the spark control vacuum tube, leading between the spark advance/retard unit and the solenoid valve, and connect a vacuum gauge to the now-vacant hole in the solenoid valve, according to the diagram.

5. Start the engine and raise the idle to 2000 rpm. With a cold engine, the vacuum gauge should read approximately 3 in./Hg or more. As the coolant temperature reaches 120° F (and before the radiator fan starts), the vacuum reading should drop to zero. On manual transmission models, vacuum should return when Fourth gear is selected (and the transmission switch is opened). If this is not the case, proceed to the following steps:

NOTE: *If the engine is warm from the previous test, disconnect the coolant temperature switch wires when making the following tests.*

6. If vacuum is not initially available, disconnect the vacuum signal line from the charcoal canister and plug the open

end, which will block a possible vacuum leak from the idle cut-off valve of the canister. With the line plugged, again check for vacuum at 2000 rpm. If vacuum is now available, reconnect the vacuum signal line and check the canister for vacuum leaks. (Refer to the "Evaporative Emission Control System" check.) If vacuum is still not available, stop the engine and disconnect the vacuum line from the solenoid valve (the line between the solenoid valve and the manifold T-joint) and insert a vacuum gauge in the line. If vacuum is not available, the vacuum port is blocked. Clear the port with compressed air and repeat the test sequence beginning with Step 3.

7. If vacuum is available in Step 5 after the engine is warm and in all ranges of the automatic transmission and in First, Second, and Third of the manual transmission, stop the engine and check for electrical continuity between the terminals of the coolant temperature sensor:

NOTE: *After completing the following steps, repeat the test procedure beginning with Step 4.*

a. If there is no continuity (and the engine is warm), replace the temperature sensor switch and recheck for continuity;

b. If there is continuity, check the battery voltage to the vacuum solenoid. If no voltage is available (with the ignition switch ON), check the wiring, fuses, and connections;

c. If there is battery voltage and the temperature sensor is operating correctly, check connections and/or replace the solenoid valve.

Evaporative Emission Control System (Engine at Normal Operating Temperature)

Charcoal Canister

1. Check for loose, disconnected, or deteriorated vacuum hoses and replace where necessary.

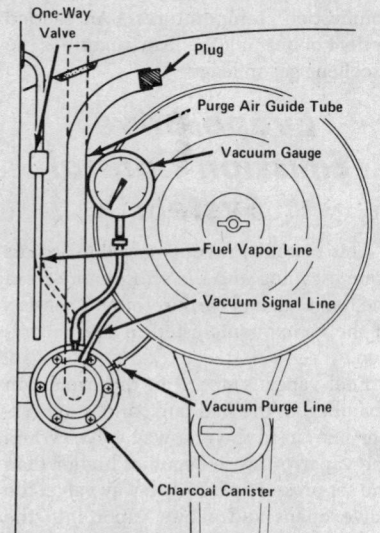

Checking evaporative control system idle cut-off valve operation—1973-74 models

2. Pull the free end of the purge air guide tube out of the body frame and plug it securely.

3. Disconnect the fuel vapor line from the charcoal canister and connect a vacuum gauge to the charcoal canister vapor inlet according to the diagram.

4. Start the engine and allow it to idle. Since the vacuum port in the carburetor is closed off at idle, the vacuum gauge should register no vacuum. If vacuum is available, replace the charcoal canister and recheck for no vacuum. A vacuum reading indicates that the charcoal canister idle cut-off valve is broken or stuck.

5. Open the throttle to 2000 rpm and make sure that the charcoal canister idle cut-off valve is opening by watching the vacuum gauge, which should indicate a vacuum. If vacuum is not available, proceed to the following steps:

a. Disconnect the vacuum signal line and connect the vacuum gauge to the carburetor T-joint orifice formerly occupied by the signal line. The vacuum reading at 2000 rpm should be greater than 3 in./Hg. If vacuum is now available (with the throttle open), replace the charcoal canister and repeat Steps 4 & 5. If vacuum is still not available, or is below 3 in./Hg, proceed to the next step;

b. If vacuum is less than 3 in./Hg (with the throttle open), the carburetor vacuum port or T-joint might be plugged. Clear the passages with compressed air. If vacuum is now available, repeat Steps 4 & 5. If vacuum is not available, or below 3 in./Hg, the carburetor vacuum port is blocked. Repair or replace as necessary and repeat Steps 4 & 5. If vacuum is *still* not available, proceed to the next step;

c. Plug the solenoid valve vacuum line (the other line to the carburetor T-joint) and recheck for vacuum. If vacuum is now available, the leak is in the advance/retard solenoid valve. Repair or replace as necessary and repeat Steps 4 & 5.

FUEL SYSTEM

1170 and 1237 cc models use a two-barrel downdraft Hitachi carburetor. Fuel pressure is provided by a camshaft-driven mechanical fuel pump. A replaceable fuel filter is located in the engine compartment in-line between the fuel pump and carburetor.

On the CVCC Civic and Accord a Keihin three-barrel carburetor is used. On this carburetor, the primary and secondary venturis deliver a lean air/fuel mixture to the main combustion chamber. Simultaneously, the third or auxiliary venturi which has a completely separate fuel metering circuit, delivers a small (in volume) but very rich air/fuel mixture to the precombustion chamber. Fuel pressure is provided by an electric fuel pump which is actuated when the ignition switch is turned to the "on" position. The electric pump is located under the rear seat beneath a special access plate on Civic sedan and hatchback models, and located under the rear of the car adjacent

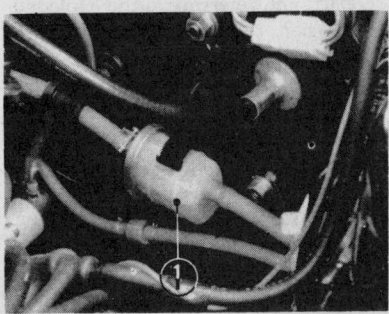

Fuel filter (1) location—1170, 1237 cc Civic

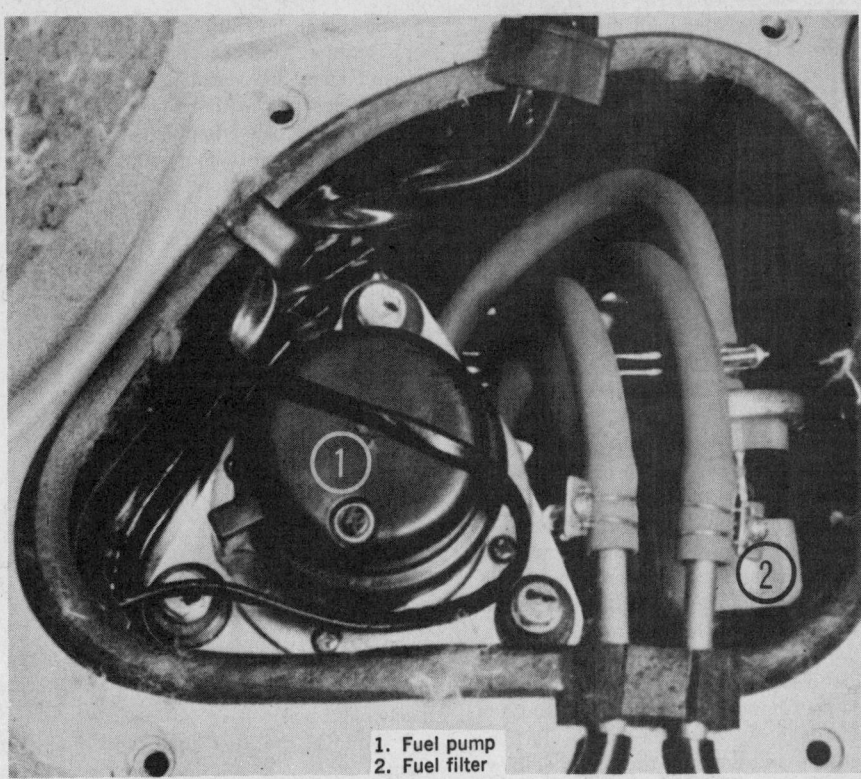

1. Fuel pump
2. Fuel filter

Fuel pump and filter location beneath the rear seat—Civic CVCC sedan and hatchback

to the fuel tank on station wagon models and the Accord. A replaceable in-line fuel filter located on the inlet side of the electric fuel pump is used on all CVCC models.

Fuel Filter

Replacement

CAUTION: *Before disconnecting any fuel lines, be sure to open the gas tank filler cap to relieve any pressure in the system. If this is not done, you may run the risk of being squirted with gasoline.*

All Civics use a disposable-type fuel filter which cannot be disassembled for cleaning. On 1973–74 models, the recommended replacement interval is 24,000 miles. On 1975–76 models, the filter is replaced after the first 15,000 miles, and every 30,000 miles thereafter.

On all 1973–74 Civics, as well as 1975–76 Civics with the 1237 cc engine, the filter is located in the engine compartment, inline between the fuel pump and carburetor. Replacement is a simple matter of pinching the lines closed, loosening the hose clamps and discarding the old filter.

On all 1975–76 CVCC Sedan models, the filter is located beneath a special access cover under the rear seat on the driver's side. The rear seat can be removed after removing the bolt at the rear center of the cushion and then pivoting the seat forward from the rear. Then,

remove the four screws retaining the access cover to the floor and remove the cover. The filter, together with the electric fuel pump, are located in the recess. Pinch the lines shut, loosen the hose clamps and remove the filter.

On all 1975–76 Wagon models, the filter is located under the car, in front of the spare tire, together with the electrical fuel pump. To replace the fuel filter, you must raise the rear of the car, support it with jackstands, and clamp off the fuel lines leading to and from the filter (or you will get a gasoline shampoo). Then, loosen the hose clamps and, taking note of which hose is the inlet and which is the outlet, remove the filter. Some replacement filters have an arrow embossed or printed on the filter body, in which case you want to install the new filter with the arrow pointing in the direction of fuel flow. After installing the new filter, remember to unclamp the fuel lines. Check for leaks.

Mechanical Fuel Pump

Removal and Installation

All Except CVCC

The fuel pump in the Civic is located in back of the engine, underneath the air cleaner snorkel.

1. Remove the air cleaner and cover assembly.

2. Remove the inlet and outlet fuel lines at the pump.

3. Loosen the pump nuts and remove the pump.

NOTE: *Do not disassemble the pump. Disassembly may cause fuel or oil leakage. If the pump is defective, replace it as an assembly.*

4. To install the fuel pump, reverse the removal procedure.

Inspection

1. Check the following items:
   a. Looseness of the pump connector.
   b. Looseness of the upper and lower body and cover screws.
   c. Looseness of the rocker arm pin.
   d. Contamination or clogging of the air hole.
   e. Improper operation of the pump.
2. Check to see if there are signs of oil or fuel around the air hole. If so, the diaphragm is damaged and you must replace the pump.
3. To inspect the pump for operation, first disconnect the fuel line at the carburetor. Connect a fuel pressure gauge to the delivery side of the pump. Start the engine and measure the pump delivery pressure.
4. After measuring, stop the engine and check to see if the gauge drops suddenly. If the gauge drops suddenly and/or the delivery pressure is incorrect, check for a fuel or oil leak from the diaphragm or from the valves.
5. To test for volume, disconnect the fuel line from the carburetor and insert it into a one quart container. Crank the engine for 64 seconds at 600 rpm, or 40 seconds at 3,000 rpm. The bottle should be half full (1 pint).

Mechanical Fuel Pump Specifications

Engine rpm	Delivery Pressure (lb/in²)	Vacuum (in. Hg.)	Displacement (in. ³/minute)
600	2.56	17.72	27
3,000	2.56	7.87-11.81	43
6,000	2.56	7.87-11.81	46

Electrical Fuel Pump
Removal and Installation
CVCC Models

1. Remove the gas filler cap to relieve any excess pressure in the system.
2. Obtain a pair of clothes pins or other suitable clamps to pinch shut the fuel lines to the pump.
3. Disconnect the negative battery cable.
4. Locate the fuel pump. On Civic sedan and hatchback models, you will first have to remove the rear seat by remov-

ing the bolt at the rear center of the bottom cushion and pivoting the seat forward from the rear. The pump and filter are located on the driver's side of the rear seat floor section beneath an access plate retained by four phillips head screws.

On station wagon models and the Accord, you will probably have to raise the rear of the car, or park it with two wheels up on a curb to obtain access. In all cases, make sure, if you are crawling under the car, that the car is securely supported. *Do do not venture beneath the car when it is supported only by the tire changing jack.*

5. Pinch the inlet and outlet fuel lines shut. Loosen the hose clamps. On station wagon and Accord models, remove the filter mounting clip on the left hand side of the bracket.
6. Disconnect the positive lead wire and ground wire from the pump at their quick disconnect.
7. Remove the two fuel pump retaining bolts, taking care not to lose the two spacers and bolt collars.
8. Remove the fuel lines and fuel pump.
9. Reverse the above procedure to install. The pump cannot be disassembled and must be replaced if defective. Operating fuel pump pressure is 2–3 psi.

Carburetor
Overhaul

Efficient carburetion depends greatly on careful cleaning and inspection during overhaul since dirt, gum, water, or varnish in or on the carburetor parts are often responsible for poor performance.

Overhaul your carburetor in a clean, dustfree area. Carefully disassemble the carburetor, referring often to the exploded views. Keep all similar and look-alike parts segregated during disassembly and cleaning to avoid accidental interchange during assembly. Make a note of all jet sizes.

When the carburetor is disassembled, wash all parts (except diaphragms, electric choke units, pump plunger, and any other plastic, leather, fiber, or rubber parts) in clean carburetor solvent. Do not leave parts in the solvent any longer than is necessary to sufficiently loosen the deposits. Excessive cleaning may remove the special finish from the float bowl and choke valve bodies, leaving these parts unfit for service. Rinse all parts in clean solvent and blow them dry with compressed air or allow them to air dry. Wipe clean all cork, plastic, leather, and fiber parts with a clean, lint-free cloth.

Blow out all passages and jets with compressed air and be sure that there are no restrictions or blockages. Never use

wire or similar tools to clean jets, fuel passages, or air bleeds. Clean all jets and valves separately to avoid accidental interchange.

Check all parts for wear or damage. If wear or damage is found, replace the defective parts. Especially check the following:

1. Check the float needle and seat for wear. If wear is found, replace the complete assembly.
2. Check the float hinge pin for wear and the float(s) for dents or distortion. Replace the float if fuel has leaked into it.
3. Check the throttle and choke shaft bores for wear or an out-of-round condition. Damage or wear to the throttle arm, shaft, or shaft bore will often require replacement of the throttle body. These parts require a close tolerance of fit; wear may allow air leakage, which could affect starting and idling.

NOTE: *Throttle shafts and bushings are not included in overhaul kits. They can be purchased separately.*

4. Inspect the idle mixture adjusting needles for burrs or grooves. Any such condition requires replacement of the needle, since you will not be able to obtain a satisfactory idle.
5. Test the accelerator pump check valves. They should pass air one way but not the other. Test for proper seating by blowing and sucking on the valve. Replace the valve if necessary. If the valve is satisfactory, wash the valve again to remove breath moisture.
6. Check the bowl cover for warped surfaces with a straightedge.
7. Closely inspect the valves and seats for wear and damage, replacing as necessary.
8. After the carburetor is assembled, check the choke valve for freedom of operation.

Carburetor overhaul kits are recommended for each overhaul. These kits contain all gaskets and new parts to replace those that deteriorate most rapidly. Failure to replace all parts supplied with the kit (especially gaskets) can result in poor performance later.

After cleaning and checking all components, reassemble the carburetor, using new parts and referring to the exploded view. When reassembling, make sure that all screws and jets are tight in their seats, but do not overtighten, as the tips will be distorted. Tighten all screws gradually, in rotation. Do not tighten needle valves into their seats; uneven jetting will result. Always use new gaskets. Be sure to adjust the float level when reassembling.

Removal and Installation
1170 and 1237 cc Models

1. Disconnect the following:
   a. Hot air tube.

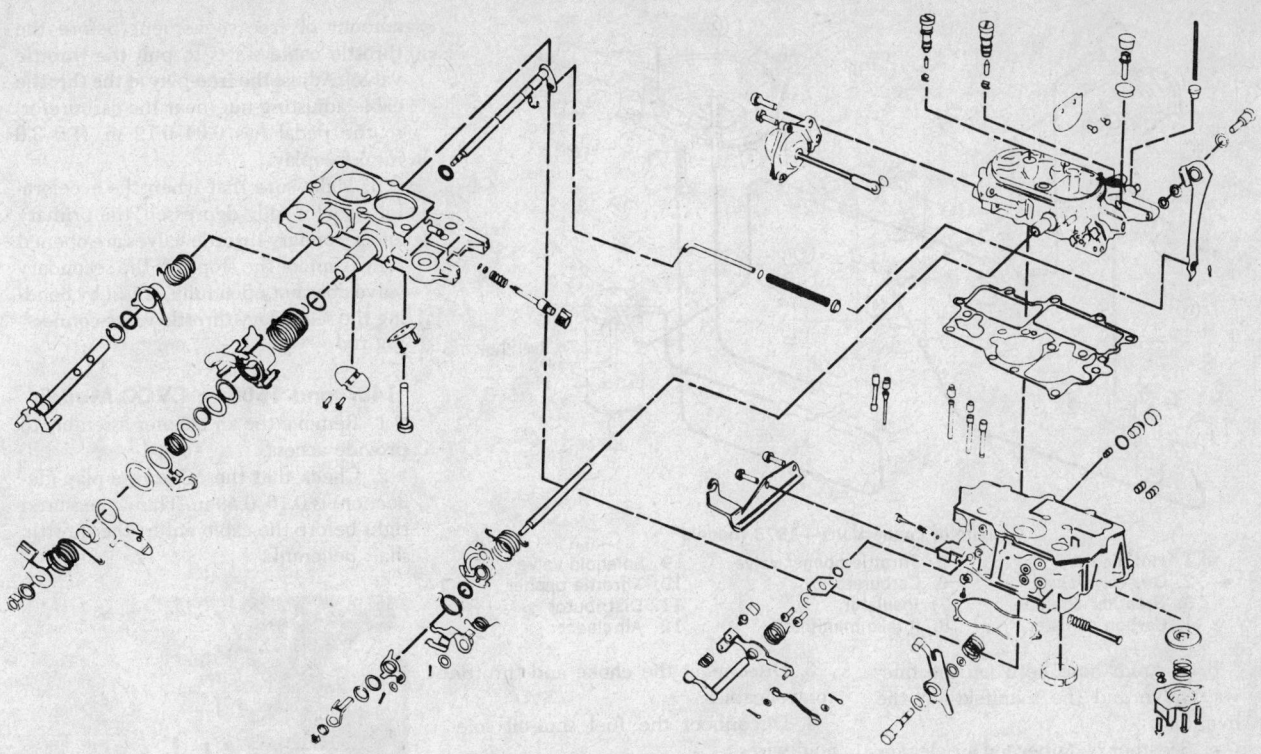

Keihin 3-bbl carburetor disassembled

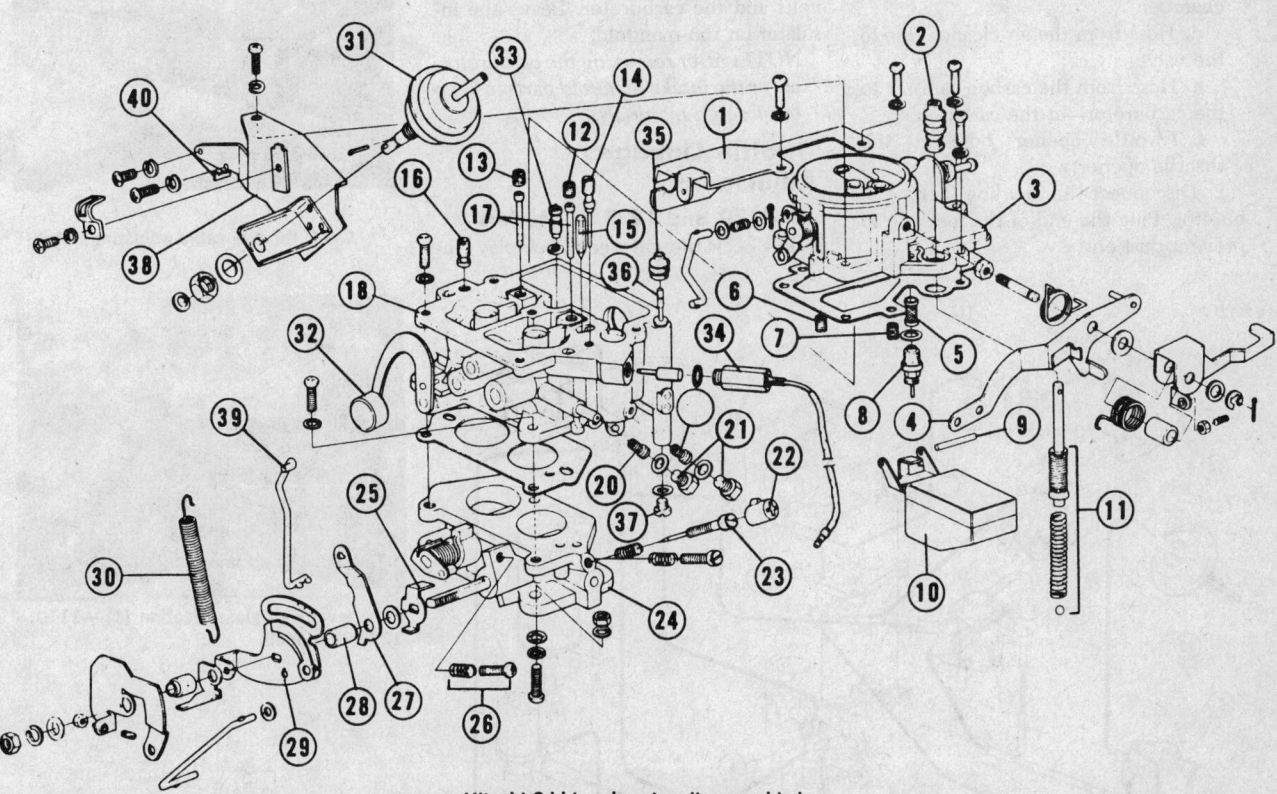

Hitachi 2-bbl carburetor disassembled

1. Spring hanger	11. Pump assembly	21. Drain plugs	31. Throttle opener
2. Pump cover	12. Primary main air jet	22. Limiter cap	32. Secondary air valve
3. Air horn	13. Secondary main air jet	23. Idle mixture screw	33. Economizer valve
4. Pump lever	14. Primary slow jet	24. Throttle body	34. Fuel shutoff solenoid
5. Filter	15. Pump needle	25. Adjusting plate	35. Secondary main jet valve cover
6. Secondary slow air jet	16. Secondary slow jet	26. Throttle adjusting screw	36. Secondary main jet valve needle
7. Primary slow air jet	17. Emission tubes	27. Choke connecting lever	37. Secondary main jet valve screw
8. Needle valve	18. Main body	28. Sleeve	38. Throttle opener bracket
9. Float pin	19. Primary main jet	29. Throttle control lever	39. Choke rod
10. Float	20. Secondary main jet	30. Throttle return spring	40. Reference tab

Honda

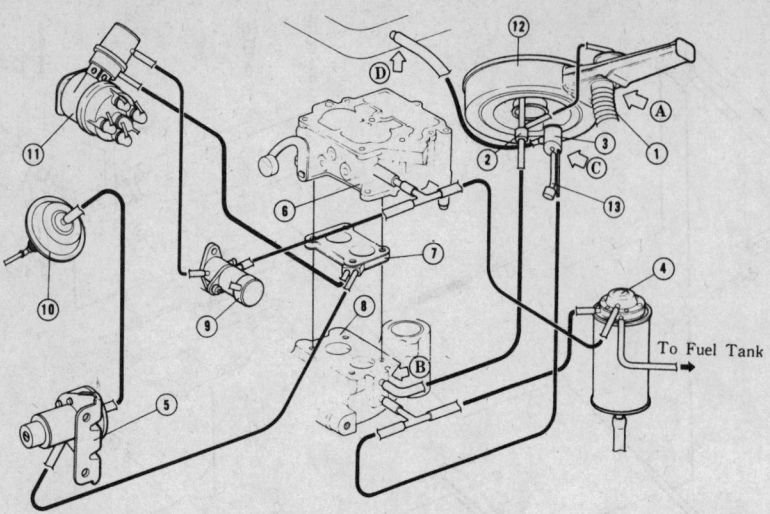

Carburetor connections—1973 models

1. Hot air tube
2. One-way valve
3. Breather chamber
4. Carbon canister
5. Throttle opener valve
6. Carburetor
7. Insulator
8. Intake manifold
9. Solenoid valve
10. Throttle opener
11. Distributor
12. Air cleaner

b. Vacuum hose between the one-way valve and the manifold—at the manifold.

c. Breather chamber (on air cleaner case) to intake manifold at the breather chamber.

d. Hose from the air cleaner case to the valve cover.

e. Hose from the carbon canister to the carburetor—at the carburetor.

f. Throttle opener hose—at the throttle opener.

2. Disconnect the fuel line at the carburetor. Plug the end of the fuel line to prevent dust entry.

3. Disconnect the choke and throttle control cables.

4. Disconnect the fuel shut-off solenoid wires.

5. Remove the carburetor retaining bolts and the carburetor. Leave the insulator on the manifold.

NOTE: *After removing the carburetor, cover the intake manifold parts to keep out foreign materials.*

Throttle Linkage Adjustment
1170 and 1237 cc Models

1. Check the gas pedal free-play (the amount of free movement before the throttle cable starts to pull the throttle valve). Adjust the free-play at the throttle cable adjusting nut (near the carburetor) so the pedal has 0.04–0.12 in. (1.0–3.0 mm) freeplay.

2. Make sure that when the accelerator pedal is fully depressed, the primary and secondary throttle valves are opened fully (contact the stops). If the secondary valve does not open fully, adjust by bending the secondary throttle valve connecting rod.

1487 and 1600 cc CVCC Models

1. Remove the air cleaner assembly to provide access.

2. Check that the cable free-play (deflection) is 0.16–0.40 in. This is measured right before the cable enters the throttle shaft bellcrank.

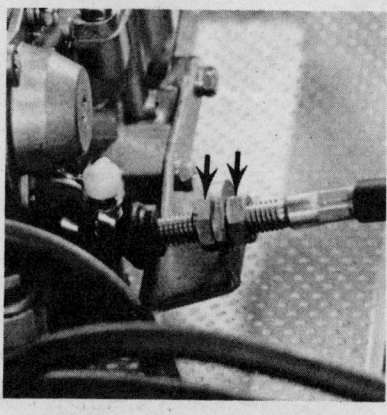

CVCC throttle cable adjusting nuts

Float level sightglass location (1)—1170, 1237 cc models

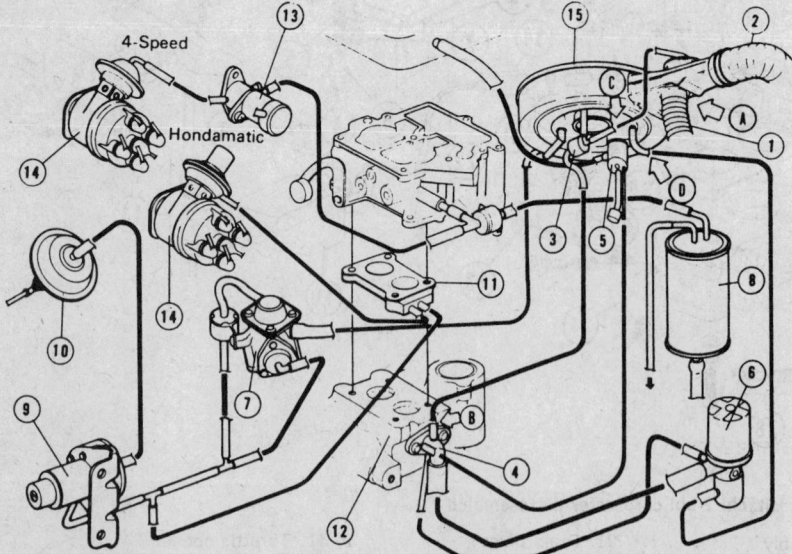

Carburetor connections—1975 1237 cc models

1. Hot air tube
2. Air intake pipe
3. One-way valve
4. 4-way joint
5. Breather chamber
6. Anti-afterburn valve
7. By-pass valve assembly
8. Carbon canister
9. Throttle opener valve
10. Throttle opener
11. Insulator
12. Intake manifold
13. Solenoid valve
14. Distributor
15. Air cleaner

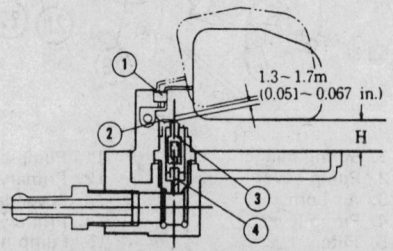

Float level adjustment—1170, 1237 cc models

1. Float stopper
2. Float seat
3. Valve stem
4. Needle valve

3. If deflection is not to specifications, rotate the cable adjusting nuts in the required direction.

4. As a final check, have a friend press the gas pedal all the way to the floor, while you look down inside the throttle bore checking that the throttle plates reach the wide open throttle (WOT) vertical position.

5. Install the air cleaner.

Float and Fuel Level Adjustment

1170 and 1237 cc Models

1. Check the float level by looking at the sight glass on the right of the carburetor. Fuel level should align with the dot on the sight glass. If the level is above or below the dot, the carburetor must be disassembled and the float level set.

NOTE: *Try to check float level with the dot at eye level.*

2. Remove the carburetor from the engine and disconnect the air horn assembly from the carburetor body.

NOTE: *When removing the air horn, do not drop the float pin.*

3. Invert the air horn and raise the float.

4. Now lower the float carefully until the float tang just touches the needle valve stem. The valve stem is spring loaded, so do not allow the float to compress the spring during measurement. Measure the distance between the float and the air horn flange (without gasket). The distance should be 0.44 in., or 11 mm. Adjust by bending the tang.

5. Raise the float until the float stop contacts the air horn body. Measure the distance between the float tang and the needle valve stem. The distance should be 0.051–0.067 in. (1.3–1.7 mm). Adjust by bending the float stop tang.

6. When the carburetor is installed, recheck the float level by looking into the carburetor float sight glass. Fuel level should be within the range of the dot on the glass.

1487 and 1600 cc CVCC Models

Due to the rather unconventional manner in which the Keihin 3-bbl carburetor float level is checked and adjusted, this is one job best left to the dealer, or someone with Honda tool no. 07501–6570000 (which is a special float level gauge/fuel catch tray/drain bottle assembly not generally available to the public). This carburetor is adjusted while mounted on a running engine. After the auxiliary and the primary/secondary main jet covers are removed, the special float gauge apparatus is installed over the jet apertures. With the engine running, the float level is checked against a red index line on the gauge. If adjustment proves necessary, there are adjusting

screws provided for both the auxiliary and the primary/secondary circuits atop the carburetor.

Fast Idle Adjustment

During cold engine starting and the engine warm-up period, a specially enriched fuel mixture is required. If the engine fails to run properly or if the engine over-revs with the choke knob pulled out in cold weather, the fast idle system should be checked and adjusted. This is accomplished with the carburetor installed.

1170 and 1237 cc Models

1973

1. Run the engine until it reaches normal operating temperature.

2. With the engine still running, pull the choke knob out to the first detent. The idle speed should rise to 1,500 to 2,000 rpm.

3. If the idle speed is not within this range, adjust by bending the choke rod. (See "Choke Adjustment" section below for further details.)

1974–76

1. Open the primary throttle plate and insert an 0.8 mm (0.032 in.), diameter drill bit between the plate and the bore.

2. With the throttle plate opened 0.8 mm, bend the reference tab so that it is midway between the two scribed lines on the throttle control lever.

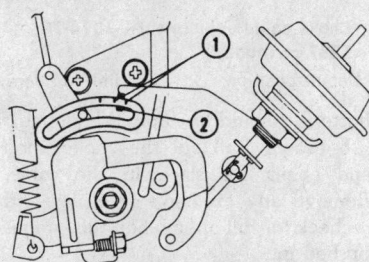

Fast idle adjustment—1974-76 1237 cc models

1. Scribe marks   2. Reference tab

1487 and 1600 cc CVCC Models

1. Run the engine until it reaches normal operating temperature.

2. Place the choke control knob in its second detent position (two clicks out from the dash). With the choke knob in this position, run the engine for 30 seconds and check that the fast idle speed is 3,000 rpm plus or minus 500 rpm.

3. To adjust, bend the slot in the fast idle adjusting link. Narrow the slot to lower the fast idle, and widen the slot to increase. Make all adjustments in small increments.

Choke Adjustment

1170 and 1237 cc Models

The choke valve should be fully open

Fast idle adjusting location—CVCC models

when the choke knob is pushed in, and fully closed with the choke knob pulled out. The choke valve is held in the fully closed position by spring action. Pull the choke knob to the fully closed position and open and close the choke valve by rotating the choke valve shaft. The movement should be free and unrestricted.

If adjustment is required, adjust the cable length by loosening the cable clamp bolt.

1. Using a wire gauge, check the primary throttle valve opening (dimension G1) when the choke valve is fully closed. The opening should be 0.050–0.066 in. (1.28–1.68 mm).

2. If the opening is out of specification, adjust it by bending the choke rod. After

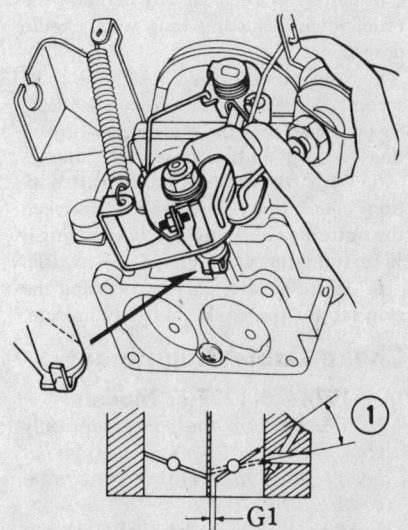

Precision choke adjustment—1170, 1237 cc models

Choke adjustment—CVCC models

1. Stop tab
2. Relief lever adjusting tang
3. Actuator rod
4. Choke opener diaphragm

installing, make sure that the highest fast idle speed is 2,500–2,800 rpm while the engine is warm.

NOTE: *When adjusting the fast idle speed, be sure the throttle adjusting screw does not contact the stop.*

1487 and 1600 cc CVCC Models

1. Push the choke actuator rod towards the diaphragm, so it does not contact the choke valve linkage.

2. Pull the choke knob out to the first detent (click) position from the dash. With the knob in this position, check the distance between the choke butterfly valve and the venturi opening with a 3/16 in. drill (shank end).

3. Adjust as necessary by bending the relief lever adjusting tang with needle nose pliers.

4. Now, pull out the choke knob to its second detent position from the dash. Again, make sure the choke actuator rod does not contact the choke valve linkage.

5. With the choke knob in this position, check that the clearance between the butterfly valve and venturi opening is ⅛ in. using the shank end of a ⅛ in. drill.

6. Adjust as necessary by bending the stop tab for the choke butterfly linkage.

Choke Cable Adjustment

1974–76 1237 cc Models

NOTE: *Perform the adjustment only after the throttle plate opening has been set as in the preceding procedure.*

1. Make sure that the choke cable is correctly adjusted.

   a. With the choke knob in, the choke

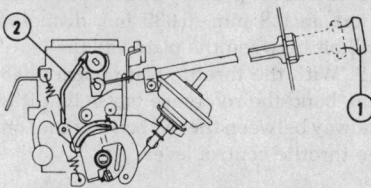

Choke cable adjustment—1974-76 1237 cc models

1. Detent position   2. Bend link rod here

butterfly should be completely open;

   b. Slowly pull out the choke knob and check for slack in the cable. Remove any excessive free-play and recheck for full open when the knob is pushed in.

2. Check the link rod adjustment by pulling the choke knob out to the first

detent. The two scribed lines on the throttle control lever should line up on either side of the reference tab. If not, adjust by bending the choke link rod.

1487 and 1600 cc CVCC Models

1. Remove the air cleaner assembly.

2. Push the choke knob all the way in at the dash. Check that the choke butterfly valve (choke plate) is fully open (vertical).

3. Next, have a friend pull out the choke knob while you observe the action of the butterfly valve. When the choke knob is pulled out to the second detent position, the butterfly valve should just close. Then, when the choke knob is pulled all the way out, the butterfly valve should remain in the closed position.

4. To adjust, loosen the choke cable locknut and rotate the adjusting nut so that with the choke knob pushed flush against the dash (open position), the butterfly valve just rests against its positioning stop tab. Tighten the locknut.

5. If the choke butterfly valve is notchy in operation, or if it does not close properly, check the butterfly valve and shaft for binding. Check also the operation of the return spring.

Throttle Valve Operation

1170 and 1237 cc Models

1. Check to see if the throttle valve opens fully when the throttle lever is moved to the fully open position. See if the valve closes fully when the lever is released.

2. Measure the clearance (G2) between the primary throttle valve and the chamber wall where the connecting rod begins to open the secondary throttle valve. The clearance should be 0.221–0.237 in. (5.63–6.03 mm).

3. If the clearance is out of specification, adjust by bending the connecting rod.

Choke cable adjustment—CVCC models

1. Choke butterfly valve   2. Adjusting nut   3. Locknut

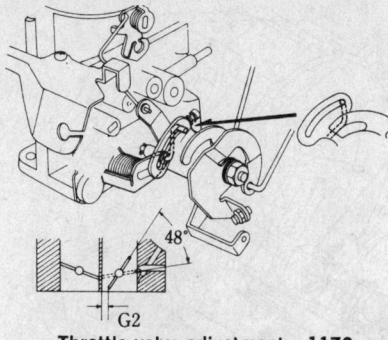

Throttle valve adjustment—1170, 1237 cc models

NOTE: *After adjusting, operate the throttle lever and check for any sign of binding.*

Accelerator Pump Adjustment

1170 and 1237 cc Models

Check the pump for smooth operation. See if fuel squirts out of the pump nozzle by operating the pump lever or the throttle lever. When the pump is operated slowly, fuel must squirt out until the pump comes to the end of its travel. If the pump is defective, check for clogging or a defective piston. Adjust the pump by either repositioning the end of the connecting rod arm in the pump lever, or the arm itself.

1487 and 1600 cc CVCC Models

1. Remove the air cleaner assembly.
2. Check that the distance between the tang at the end of the accelerator pump lever and the lever stop at the edge of the throttle body (distance "A") is 0.0311–0.0335 in. This corresponds to effective pump lever travel.
3. To adjust, bend the pump lever tang in the required direction.
4. Install the air cleaner.

Accelerator pump travel adjustment—CVCC models

MANUAL TRANSAXLE

Removal and Installation

Four and Five-Speed

1. Drain the transmission.
2. Raise the front of the car and support it with safety stands.
3. Remove the front wheels.
4. Disconnect the battery ground cable at the battery and the transmission case.
5. Remove the starter motor positive battery cable and the solenoid wire. Then remove the starter.
6. Disconnect the following cables and wires:
   a. Clutch cable at the release arm;
   b. Back-up light switch wires;
   c. TCS (Transmission Controlled Spark) switch wires;
   d. Speedometer cable.
CAUTION: *When removing the speedometer cable from the transmission, it is not necessary to remove the entire cable holder. Remove the end boot (gear holder seal), the cable retaining clip and then pull the cable out of the holder. In no way should you disturb the holder, unless it is absolutely necessary. For further details, see "Civic—Engine Removal" section.*
7. Disconnect the left and right lower ball joints at the knuckle, using a ball joint remover (tool no. 07941–6340000).
8. Pull on the brake disc and remove the left and right driveshafts from the differential case.
9. Drive out the gearshift rod pin (8 mm) with a drift (or tool no. 07944–6110200) and disconnect the rod at the transmission case.
10. Disconnect the gearshift extension at the clutch housing.
11. Screw in the engine hanger bolts (see the "Engine Removal" section) to the engine torque rod bolt hole and to the hole just to the left of the distributor. Hook a chain onto the bolts and lift the engine just enough to take the load off the engine mounts.
12. After making sure that the engine is properly supported, remove the two center beam-to-lower engine mount nuts. Next, remove the center beam, followed by the lower engine mount.
13. Reinstall the center beam (without mount) and lower the engine until it rests on the beam.
14. Place a jack under the transmission and loosen the 4 attaching bolts. Using the jack to support the transmission, slide it away from the engine and lower the jack until the transmission clears the car.
15. To install, reverse the removal procedure. Be sure to pay attention to the following points:

a. Tighten all mounting nuts and bolts to their specified torque (see the "Engine Removal" section);
b. Use a new shift rod pin;
c. After installing the driveshafts, attempt to move the inner joint housing in and out of the differential housing. If it moves easily, the driveshaft end clips should be replaced;
d. Make sure that the control cables and wires are properly connected;
e. Be sure the transmission is refilled to the proper level.

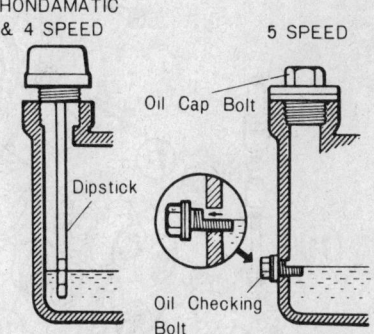

Checking manual transmission oil level

Overhaul

Civic

Disassembly

1. Remove the transmission end cover. Check the transmission mainshaft and countershaft end play. End play should be between 0.002–0.003 in. If the clearance is excessive, inspect the ballbearings after transmission disassembly.
2. Remove the locking tab from the mainshaft locknut. The mainshaft locknut has left hand threads. Place the transmission in gear and place the proper size wrench on countershaft to keep it from moving. Remove the mainshaft locknut.
3. Remove the mainshaft bearing and the large snap-ring.
4. Loosen the three shift detent lock ball screws. Remove the screws, springs and balls.
5. Remove the transmission case bolts. Lightly tap the case with a hammer and drift and separate case. Do not pry case apart with a screwdriver.
6. Remove the reverse idler gear and shaft. Remove the reverse shift fork.
7. Remove the shift selector assembly. If repair to the shift selector is necessary, disassemble as follows:
   a. Remove two screws and retaining plate. Stake screws when reinstalling.
   b. Push the shift arm into the reverse position (towards the large spring). Then release it.
   c. The pivot shaft holds a spring loaded detent. Do not lose the detent ball and spring when removing.

1. Needle roller bearing set
   plate
2. Needle roller bearing
3. Clutch case
4. Reverse gear shaft
5. Reverse idle gear
6. Reverse shift fork
7. Shift selector assembly
8. Countershaft gear assembly
9. Main shaft
10. First/second fork shaft
11. Reverse fork shaft
12. Third/fourth fork shaft
13. Steel ball

14. Ball set spring
15. Drain plug washer
16. Set ball spring screw
17. Ball bearing
18. Needle roller bearing
19. 48 mm snap ring
20. Ball bearing
21. 62 mm snap ring
22. 23 mm lock nut
23. 20 mm lock nut
24. Transmission rear cover
25. Speedometer gear

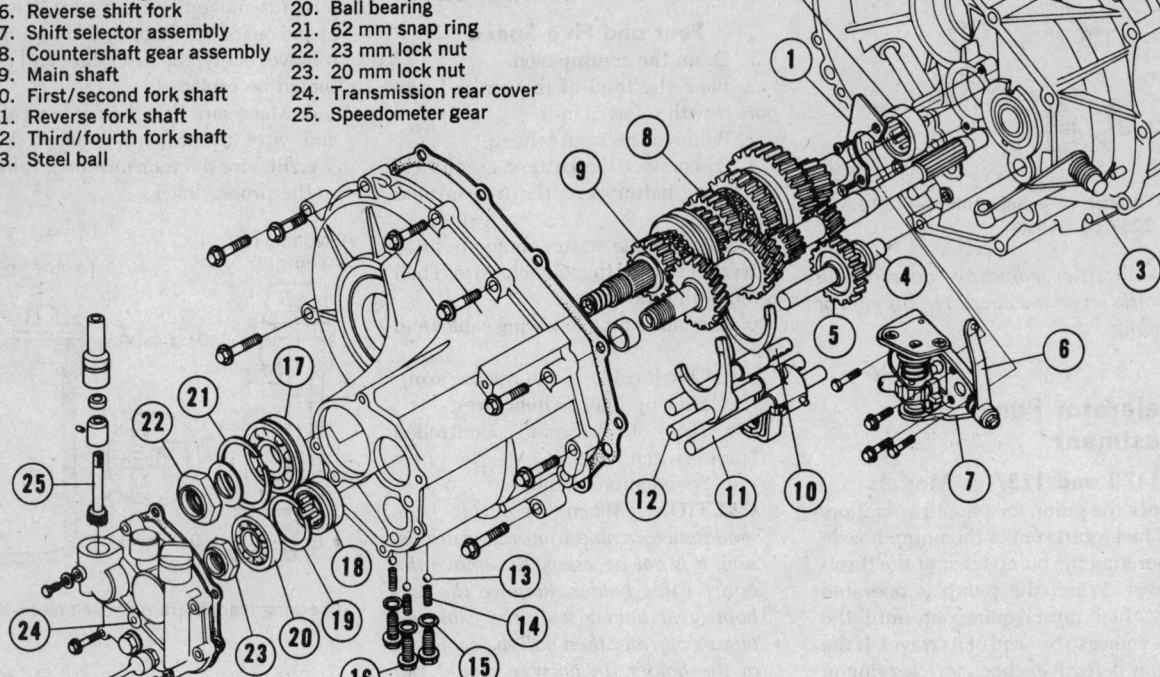

Civic standard transmission—exploded view

Remove the pivot shaft.

d. Remove the interlock bar and shift arms.

e. During reassembly, insert a screwdriver into the reverse side (large spring end) of the arm assembly to hold down the detent ball, while inserting the pivot shaft.

8. Remove the shift fork retaining bolts and pull the shift shafts up until they clear the case. Remove the forks and shafts.

NOTE: *When reinstalling the fork retaining bolts turn the shaft so the threaded portion of the hole is facing away from the bolt.*

9. Remove the mainshaft and countershaft at the same time by holding the two shafts and lightly tapping the flywheel end of the mainshaft with a brass hammer.

10. Remove the shift rod boot, shift arm, lock washer and bolt. Remove the shift rod and shift arm.

NOTE: *During installation of the shift arm retaining bolt, turn the shaft so that the threaded portion of the hole is facing away from the bolt.*

11. Measure the side clearance of the low gear with a feeler gauge, if the clearance is excessive, replace the thrust plate. Perform the same measurement on the

remaining gears, if the clearance is beyond the service limit, replace the bearing race (spacer). See chart for specifications.

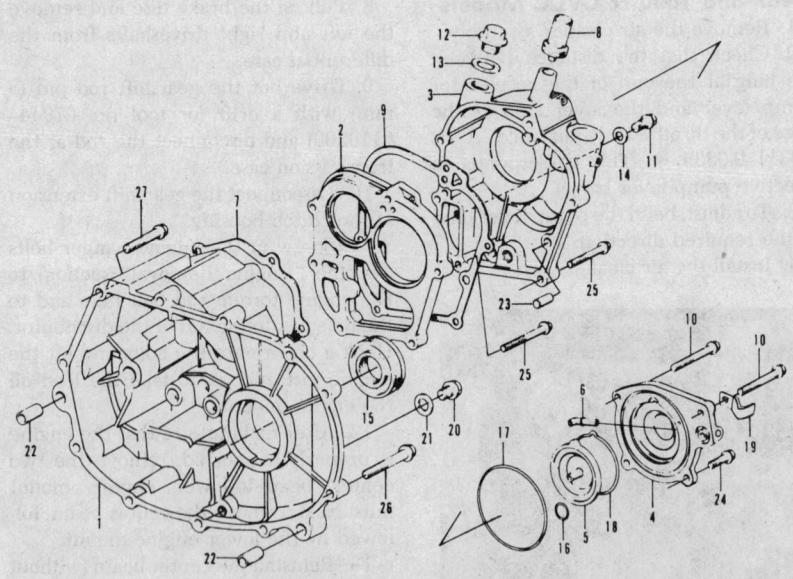

Exploded view of 5-speed transmission case

1 Housing, transmission
2 Spacer, transmission housing
3 Cover, transmission
4 Cover, right side
5 Plate, oil barrier
6 Tube, breather
7 Gasket, transmission housing
8 Cap, breather
9 Gasket, transmission case

10 Bolt, flanged, 6 x 85 mm
11 Bolt, oil check
12 Bolt, plug 25 mm
13 Washer, sealing, 25 mm
14 Washer, 8 mm
15 Oil seal, 35 x 56 x 9 mm
16 O-ring, 9.4 x 2.4
17 O-ring, 64.5 x 3
18 O-ring, 42 x 2.4

19 Bracket, wire harness
20 Bolt, drain plug, 14 mm
21 Washer, drain plug, 14 mm
22 Pin, dowel, 14 x 20 mm
23 Pin, dowel, 8 x 14 mm
24 Bolt, flanged, 6 x 20 mm
25 Bolt, flanged, 6 x 45 mm
26 Bolt, flanged, 8 x 40 mm
27 Bolt, flanged, 8 x 45 mm

Tap these locations to seperate transmission case—Civic

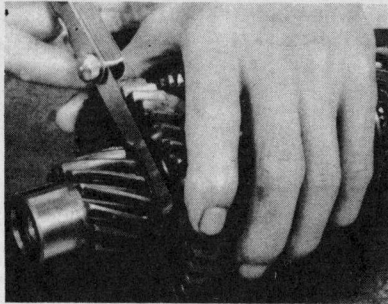

Measuring the clearance of low gear—Civic

Civic Transmission Specifications

	mm (in.)
Main Shaft	
Axial Play	0.09 (0.0035)
Needle Roller Bearing Journal O.D.	20-19.98 (0.7874-0.7866)
6304 Ball Bearing Journal O.D.	22-21.98 (0.8661-0.8654)
Runout	0.03 ((0.0012)
Countershaft	
Axial Play	0.09 (0.0035)
Runout	0.03 (0.0012)
Needle Roller Bearing Journal O.D.	31.98-32
Countershaft First and Fourth Gears	
I.D.	37.00-37.02 (1.4567-1.4575)
Axial Play	0.03 (0.0019)
Countershaft Second and Third Gears	
I.D.	37.00-37.02 (1.4567-1.4575)
Axial Play	0.03 (0.0019)
Spacers Between Gears	
O.D.	32-31.98 (1.2598-1.2590)
I.D.	25.98-25.99 (1.0228-1.0232)
Width	28.07-28.09 (1.105-1.106)
	28.05-28.07 (1.104-1.105)
Reverse Gear Shaft	
O.D.	14.98-14.97 (0.5898-1.5902)
Reverse Idle Gear	
I.D.	15.04-15.01 (0.5898-1.5909)
Gear to Shaft Clearance	0.07-0.03 (0.0028-0.0012)
Shift Fork	
Synchronizer Sleeve Sliding Surface Width	6.4-6.5 (0.2520-0.2559)
Fork-to-Synchronizer Sleeve Clearance	0.45-0.65 (0.0177-0.0256)

12. If the countershaft must be disassembled to adjust clearances, or replace gears, remove the locknut by installing the shaft in the case and holding the differential securely.

NOTE: *Place the end lugs of the holder in the case and center the lug in the hole of the differential carrier.*

13. Remove the two screws and retaining plate which hold the countershaft

1. Lever, gearshift
2. Knob, gearshift lever
3. Bolt, shift rod rear joint
4. Bushing, gearshift lever
5. O-ring, shift lever
6. Spacer, shift lever rear joint
7. Boot, gearshift lever
8. Seal, gearshift
9. Seat, shift lever ball
10. Stopper, shift lever bail
11. Clip, shift joint pin
12. Seal, gearshift lever dust
13. Rod, shift
14. Bar, change rod extension
15. Bushing, extension bar
16. Washer, extension bar
17. Retainer, extension bar
18. Seal, shift lever mounting
19. Bracket, console front
20. Nut
21. Nut
22. Bolt
23. Screw
24. Nut
25. Nut
26. Washer
27. Washer
28. Washer
29. Pin, spring
30. Snap-ring
31. Washer

bearing. Remove the countershaft bearing with a bearing puller.

Inspection

1. Clean all component parts thoroughly in solvent.

2. Inspect the surfaces of each gear and blocking ring for roughness or damage. Apply a thin coat of oil to the tapered surfaces of each gear and push them together with a rotating motion. Measure the distance between the ring and gear. Replace all necessary parts. Clearance should be between 0.120–0.139 in.

3. Measure the clearance between the shift forks and synchronizer sleeves. The clearance should be between 0.039–0.018. If clearances are excessive, replace the shift forks, synchronizers or both.

4. Ensure that there are no restrictions in the oil holes on the countershaft. Check the splines for wear.

5. Inspect the condition of the mainshaft and countershaft bearing surfaces. Check runout, gear tooth and spline condition.

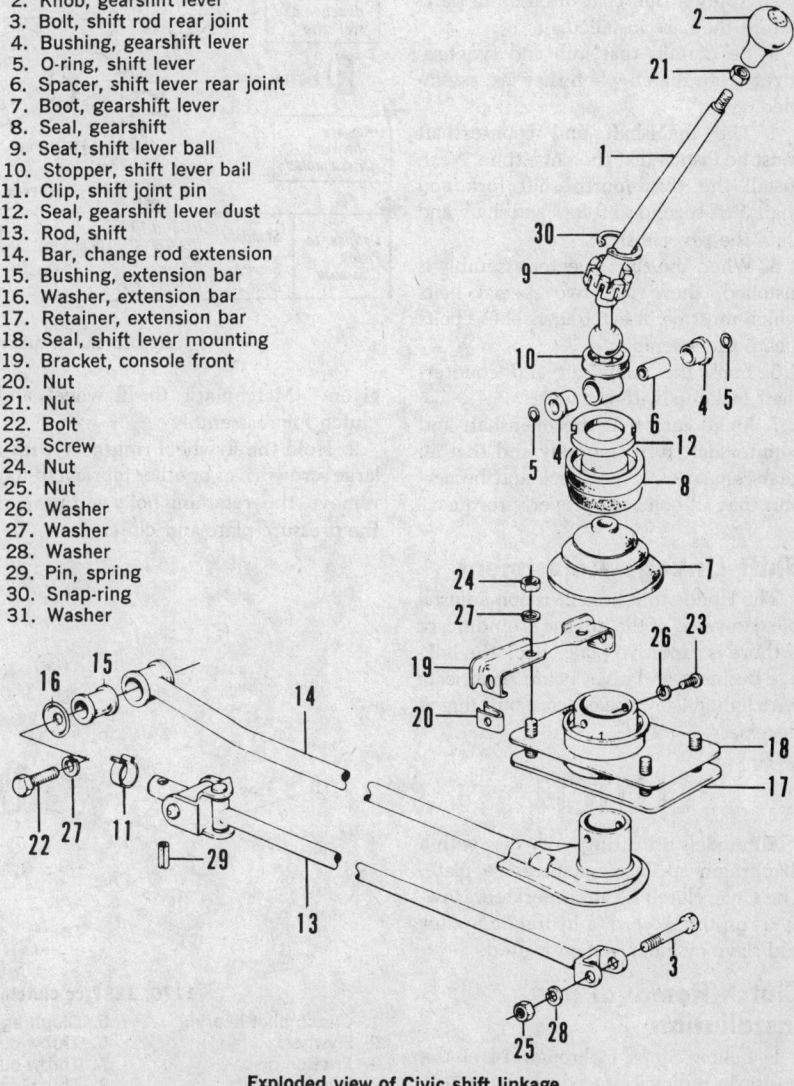

Exploded view of Civic shift linkage

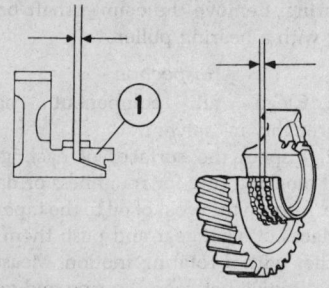

Measuring the clearance between the blocking ring and gear—Civic

1. Blocking ring

6. Check the condition of all the gears. Check the condition of all bearing surfaces.

7. Inspect the bearing race (spacer) of each gear.

8. Replace all questionable parts.

Assembly

Transmission should be assembled in the reverse order of disassembly. During assembly, note the following points:

1. Check the differential bearing clearance.

2. Apply a thin coat of oil to all parts before they are installed.

3. Be certain that hub and synchronizer teeth match when they are assembled.

4. The mainshaft and countershaft must be installed at the same time. Next, install the third-fourth shift fork and shaft, first-second shift fork and shaft, and then the reverse shaft.

5. When the shift selector assembly is installed, there are two special bolts which must be inserted first. These bolts locate the assembly.

6. Lock the mainshaft and countershaft locknuts with a punch.

7. Make sure that the mainshaft and countershaft turn smoothly and that all gears engage freely. Check and be certain that all bolts are properly torqued.

Shift Linkage Adjustment

The Honda shift linkage is non-adjustable. However, if the linkage is binding, or if there is excessive play, check the linkage bushings and pivot points. Lubricate with light oil, or replace worn bushings as necessary.

CLUTCH

All models use a single dry disc with a diaphragm spring type pressure plate. The Civic clutch is cable operated. However, on the Accord, a hydraulic master and slave cylinder system is used.

Clutch Removal and Installation

1. Follow Steps 1 through 14 of the transaxle removal procedure, previously

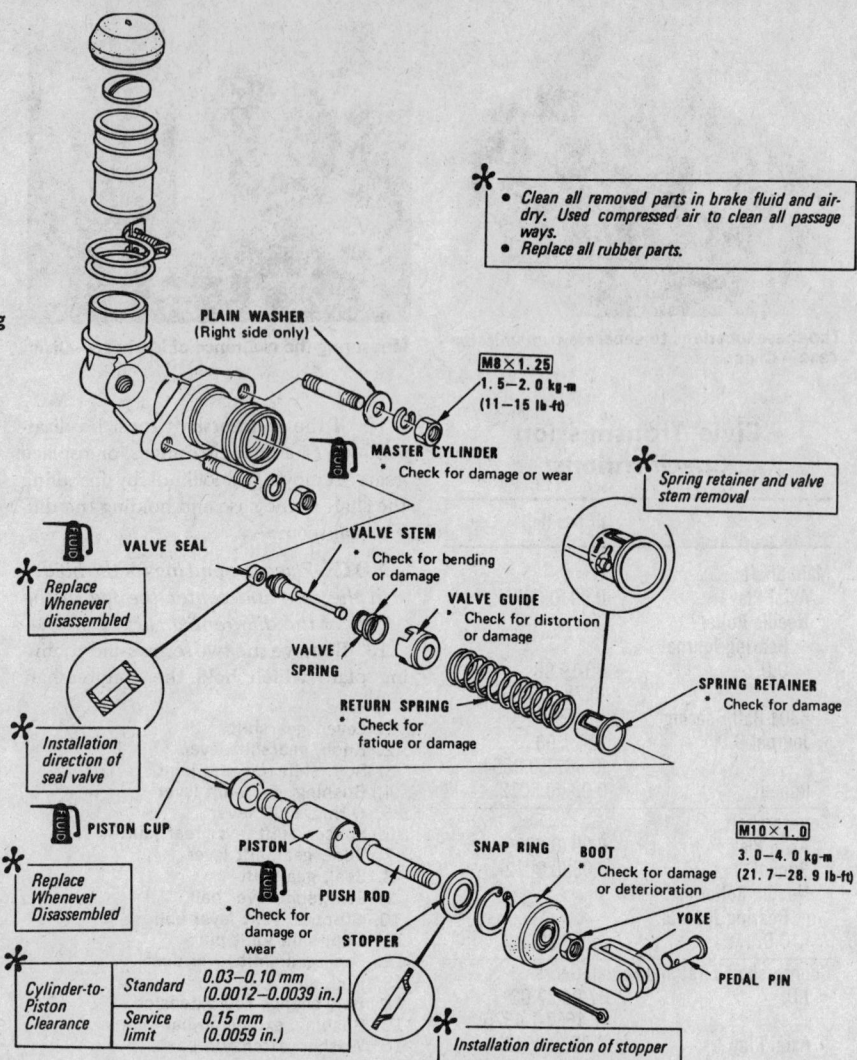

- Clean all removed parts in brake fluid and air-dry. Used compressed air to clean all passage ways.
- Replace all rubber parts.

PLAIN WASHER (Right side only)

M8×1.25
1.5—2.0 kg-m
(11—15 lb-ft)

MASTER CYLINDER
• Check for damage or wear

Spring retainer and valve stem removal

VALVE STEM
• Check for bending or damage

VALVE SEAL
Replace Whenever disassembled

VALVE GUIDE
• Check for distortion or damage

VALVE SPRING

SPRING RETAINER
• Check for damage

RETURN SPRING
• Check for fatique or damage

Installation direction of seal valve

PISTON CUP
Replace Whenever Disassembled

PISTON
• Check for damage or wear

PUSH ROD

STOPPER

SNAP RING

BOOT
• Check for damage or deterioration

M10×1.0
3.0—4.0 kg-m
(21.7—28.9 lb-ft)

YOKE

PEDAL PIN

Installation direction of stopper

Cylinder-to-Piston Clearance	Standard	0.03—0.10 mm (0.0012—0.0039 in.)
	Service limit	0.15 mm (0.0059 in.)

Accord clutch master cylinder disassembled

given. Matchmark the flywheel and clutch for reassembly.

2. Hold the flywheel ring gear with a large screwdriver or other fabricated tool remove the retaining bolts and remove the pressure plate and clutch disc.

NOTE: *Loosen the retaining bolts two turns at a time in a circular pattern. Removing one bolt while the rest are tight may warp the diaphragm spring.*

3. The flywheel can now be removed, if it needs repairing or replacing.

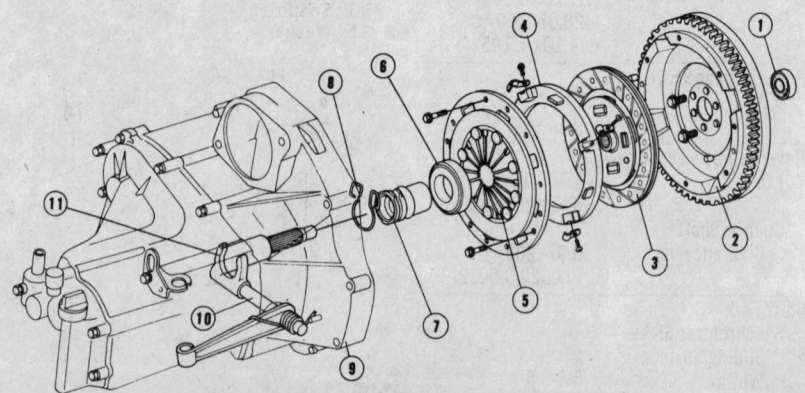

1170, 1237 cc clutch, flywheel and related parts

1. Clutch pilot bearing
2. Flywheel
3. Friction disc
4. Pressure plate
5. Diaphragm spring
6. Throw-out bearing
7. Throw-out bearing holder
8. Throw-out arm clip
9. Clutch case
10. Throw-out shaft
11. Clutch throw-out arm A

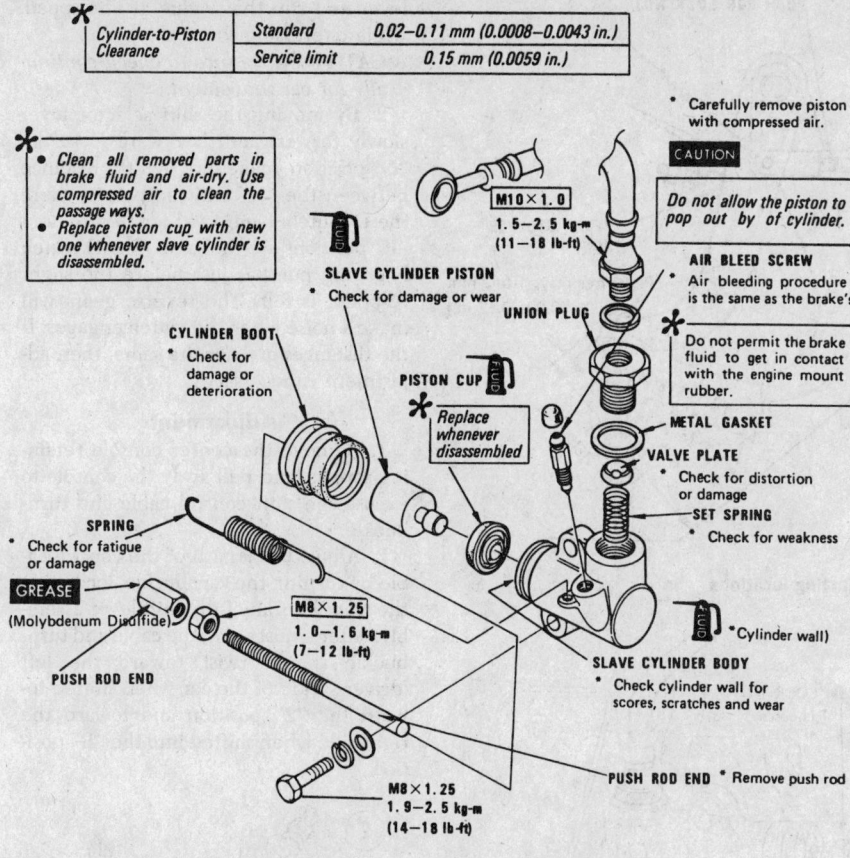

✱ Cylinder-to-Piston Clearance	Standard	0.02–0.11 mm (0.0008–0.0043 in.)
	Service limit	0.15 mm (0.0059 in.)

✱
- Clean all removed parts in brake fluid and air-dry. Use compressed air to clean the passage ways.
- Replace piston cup with new one whenever slave cylinder is disassembled.

• Carefully remove piston with compressed air.

CAUTION
Do not allow the piston to pop out by of cylinder.

M10×1.0
1.5–2.5 kg-m
(11–18 lb-ft)

AIR BLEED SCREW
Air bleeding procedure is the same as the brake's.

✱ Do not permit the brake fluid to get in contact with the engine mount rubber.

SLAVE CYLINDER PISTON
• Check for damage or wear

UNION PLUG

CYLINDER BOOT
• Check for damage or deterioration

PISTON CUP
✱ Replace whenever disassembled

METAL GASKET

VALVE PLATE
• Check for distortion or damage

SET SPRING
• Check for weakness

SPRING
• Check for fatigue or damage

GREASE
(Molybdenum Disulfide)

M8×1.25
1.0–1.6 kg-m
(7–12 lb-ft)

PUSH ROD END

(• Cylinder wall)

SLAVE CYLINDER BODY
• Check cylinder wall for scores, scratches and wear

M8×1.25
1.9–2.5 kg-m
(14–18 lb-ft)

PUSH ROD END • Remove push rod

Accord clutch slave cylinder disassembled

CAUTION: *Make sure that the upper and lower adjusting nuts are tightened after adjustment.*

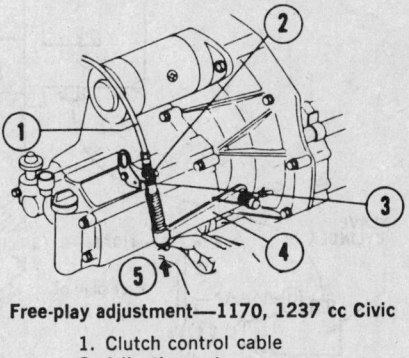

Free-play adjustment—1170, 1237 cc Civic

1. Clutch control cable
2. Adjusting nut
3. Locknut
4. Clutch release lever
5. Clutch release lever play

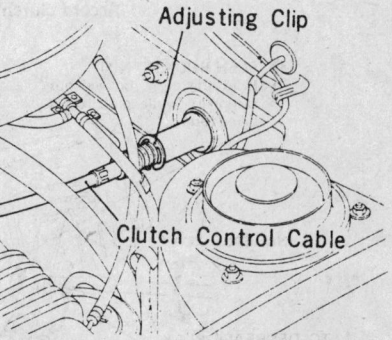

Free-play adjusting location—CVCC Civic

On CVCC models, the free-play adjustment is made on the cable at the firewall. Remove the C-clip and then rotate the threaded control cable housing until there is 0.12–0.16 in. free-play at the release lever.

4. To separate the pressure plate from the diaphragm spring, remove the 4 retracting clips.

5. To remove the release, or throw-out, bearing, first straighten the locking tab and remove the 8 mm bolt, followed by the release shaft and release arm with the bearing attached.

NOTE: *It is recommended that the release bearing be removed after the release arm has been removed from the casing. Trying to remove or install the bearing with the release arm in the case, will damage the retaining clip.*

6. If a new release bearing is to be installed, separate the bearing from the holder, using a bearing drift.

7. To assemble and install the clutch, reverse the removal procedure. Be sure to pay attention to the following points:

a. Make sure that the flywheel and the end of the crankshaft are clean before assembling;

b. When installing the pressure plate, align the mark on the outer edge of the flywheel with the alignment mark on the pressure plate. Failure to align these marks will result in imbalance;

c. When tightening the pressure plate bolts, use a pilot shaft to center the friction disc. The pilot shaft can be bought at any large auto supply store or fabricated from a wooden dowel. After centering the disc, tighten the bolts two turns at a time, in a circular pattern to avoid warping the diaphragm spring;

d. When installing the release shaft and arm, place a lock tab washer under the retaining bolt;

e. When installing the transmission, make sure that the mainshaft is properly aligned with the disc spline and the aligning pins are in place, before tightening the case bolts.

Pedal Height Adjustment— Civic

Check the clutch pedal height and if necessary, adjust the upper stop, so that the clutch and brake pedals rest at approximately the same height from the floor. First, be sure that the brake pedal freeplay is properly adjusted.

Free Play Adjustment— Civic

Adjust the clutch release lever so that it has 0.12–0.16 in. (3–4 mm) of play when you move the clutch release lever at the transmission with your hand. This adjustment is made at the outer cable housing adjuster, near the release lever on non-CVCC models. Less than ⅛ in. of freeplay may lead to clutch slippage, while more than ⅛ in. clearance may cause difficult shifting.

Pedal Release Height— Civic

You will probably need two people to perform this measurement; one to start and run the car, and the other to observe and measure.

To check the pedal release height:

a. Raise the front wheels off the ground and support the car with safety stands;

b. Place the transmission in Fourth gear;

c. Depress the clutch pedal and start the engine;

d. Release the clutch pedal until the front wheels begin to turn and measure the pedal height at this point, from the floor mat to the center of the pedal. The height should be over 1.18 in. (30 mm). If free-play and pedal height are properly adjusted, but the release height is not within specifications, then clutch components are damaged.

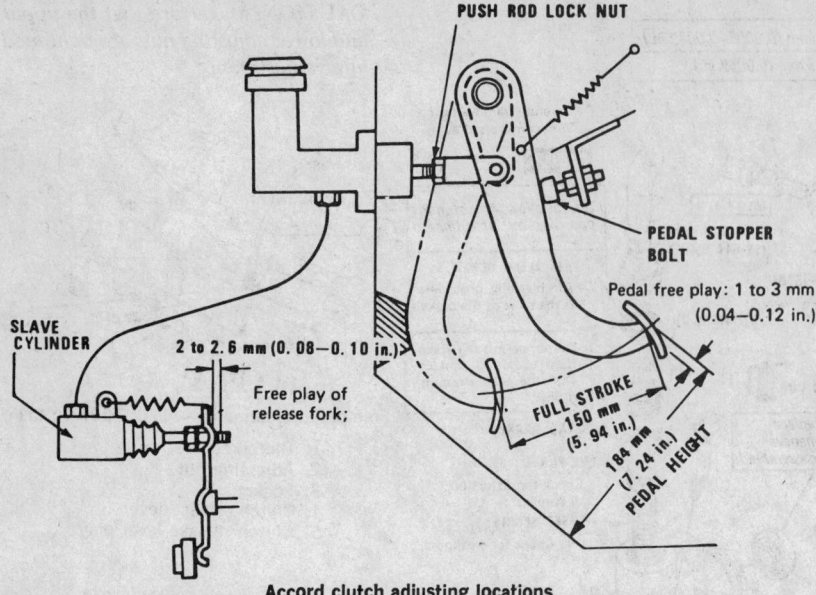

Accord clutch adjusting locations

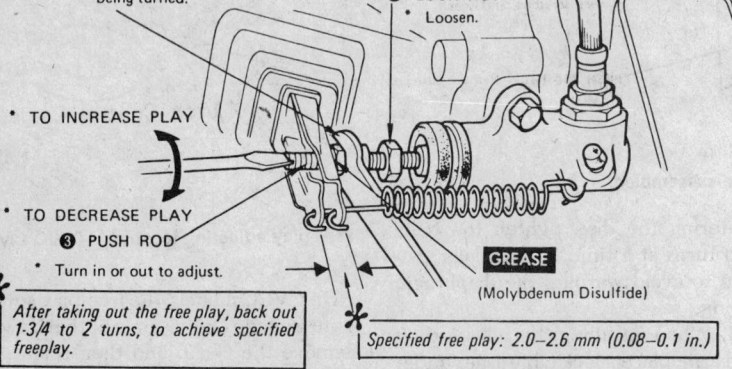

❷ PUSH ROD END NUT
• Hold the push rod end nut stationary while push rod is being turned.

❶ LOCK NUT
• Loosen.

• TO INCREASE PLAY

• TO DECREASE PLAY
❸ PUSH ROD
• Turn in or out to adjust.

GREASE
(Molybdenum Disulfide)

✳ After taking out the free play, back out 1-3/4 to 2 turns, to achieve specified freeplay.

✳ Specified free play: 2.0–2.6 mm (0.08–0.1 in.)

Adjusting release fork free-play—Accord

AUTOMATIC TRANSAXLE (Hondamatic)

Removal and Installation

Civic and Accord

The automatic transmission is removed in the same basic manner as the manual transmission (refer to Manual Transmission Removal and Installation). The following exceptions should be noted during automatic transmission removal and installation.

1. Remove the center console and control rod pin.

2. Remove the front floor center mat and control cable bracket nuts.

3. Jack and support the front of the car.

4. Remove the two selector lever bracket nuts at front side.

5. Loosen the bolts securing the control cable holder and support beam and disconnect the control cable.

6. Disconnect the transmission cooler lines at the transmission.

7. Remove the transmission together with the engine. Remove the engine mounts and torque converter case cover.

8. Remove the starter motor and separate the transmission from the engine.

9. Installation of the automatic transmission is the reverse of removal. Close attention should be paid to the following points.

10. Be sure that the stator hub is correctly located and moves smoothly. The stator shaft can be used for this purpose.

11. Align the stator, stator shaft, main shaft and torque converter turbine serrations.

12. After installation of the engine-transmission unit in car, make all required adjustments.

Shift Lever
Inspection

1. Pull up fully on the parking brake lever and run the engine at idle speed, while depressing the brake pedal.

CAUTION: *Be sure to check continually for car movement.*

2. By moving the shift selector lever slowly forward and backward from the "N" position, make sure that the distance between the "N" and the points where the D clutch is engaged for the "2" and "R" positions are the same. The D clutch engaging point is just before the slight response is felt. The reverse gears will make a noise when the clutch engages. If the distances are not the same, then adjustment is necessary.

Adjustment

1. Remove the center console retaining screws, and pull away the console to expose the shift control cable and turnbuckle.

2. Adjust the length of the control cable by turning the turnbuckle, located at the front bottom of the shift lever assembly. After adjustment, the cable and turnbuckle should twist toward the left (driver's) side of the car when shifted toward the "2" position and toward the right-side when shifted into the "R" position.

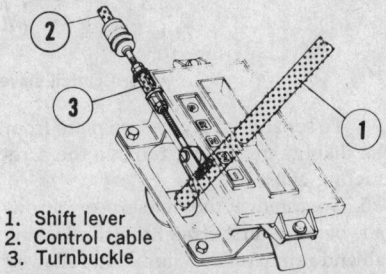

1. Shift lever
2. Control cable
3. Turnbuckle

Rotate the turnbuckle to adjust shift lever position

Differential

Differential Overhaul
Civic

1. Remove transmission as detailed in "Manual Transmission Removal and Installation".

2. Disassemble transmission as detailed in "Manual Transmission Overhaul", use steps 1 thru 9.

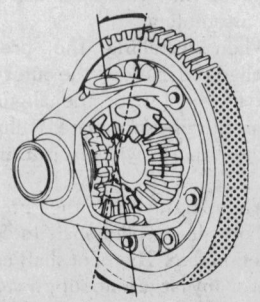

Differential pinion installation

1. Support, selector lever
2. Control assy., selector lever
3. Cover, lever
4. Seal, support
5. Gasket, control cable bracket
6. Guide, control cable
7. Clamp, control cable
8. Panel, shift indicator
9. Garnish, indicator panel
10. Bolt
11. Bolt
12. Screw
13. Nut
14. Nut
15. Washer
16. Washer
17. Washer
18. Switch assy., neutral/back-up light

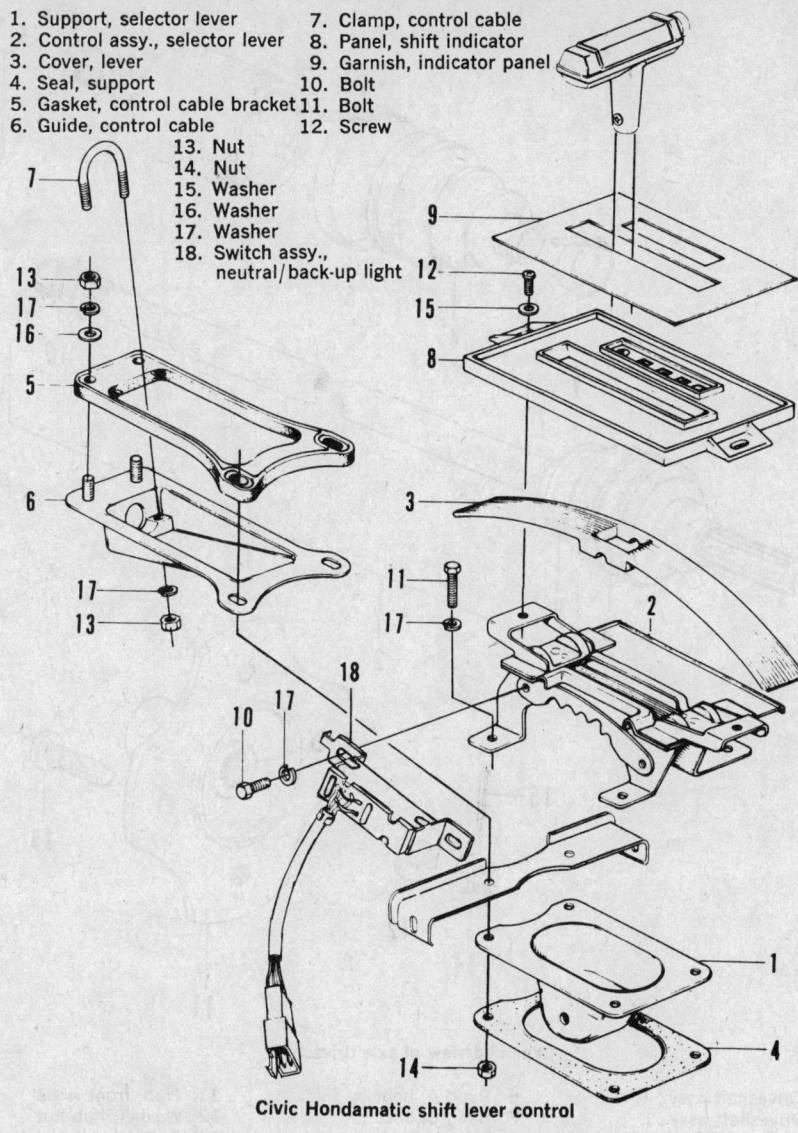

Civic Hondamatic shift lever control

3. Remove the differential assembly with a bearing driver.

4. Remove the differential carrier bearing, on the differential pinion side, with a standard bearing puller.

5. Place the differential carrier in a vice and loosen the ring gear retaining bolts. These bolts have a left-hand thread and must be loosened in a criss-cross pattern. Remove ring gear.

6. Remove the 4mm pin from the pinion shaft using a pin driver. The pin driver must be inserted from the side opposite the pinion gears.

7. Clean and inspect all parts. Replace any components that are worn or damaged.

8. Reassemble differential in the reverse order of disassembly. The following points should be followed during assembly:

a. Coat all parts with a thin covering of molybdenum disulfide before installation.

b. Install the differential pinions by placing the drive pinions in place first

then install the differential pinions and rotate them into position.

c. Torque the ring gear bolts in a criss-cross pattern.

Measure the backlash of the pinion gear. Backlash should be between 0.003–0.007 in. Thrust washers must be replaced in sets. If only one is replaced, the gear tooth will not mesh properly and will result in gear noise. Select the proper thrust washer from the following chart.

Pinion Gear Spacer Chart

Thickness (In.)	Part No.
0.028	41351-634
0.032	41352-634
0.035	41353-634

Differential clearance check—Civic
1. Feeler gauge

9. Measure the differential clearances in the following manner:

a. Remove the large snap ring-spacer on the engine side of the differential. Drive out the engine side differential seal.

b. Reinstall large snap ring-spacer in and differential in clutch case.

1. Final driven gear
2. Differential case
3. 72 mm set ring
4. Ball bearing
5. Drive pinion

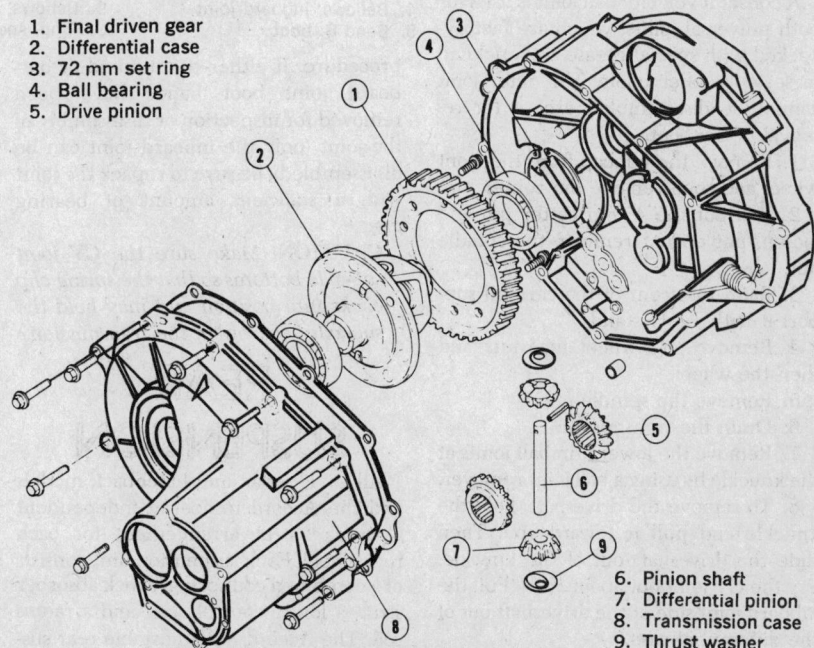

6. Pinion shaft
7. Differential pinion
8. Transmission case
9. Thrust washer

Exploded view of differential assembly

c. Install the transmission case in place (there is no need to have transmission assembled at this point) and torque the case bolts.

d. Tap the differential from the transmission case side with the bearing driver. This will seat the snap-ring spacer against the clutch case.

e. Using the same bearing driver, tap the differential from the clutch case side. This operation will align the differential assembly.

f. Using a feeler gauge, check the clearance between the snap-ring spacer and bearing race. Clearance should be 0.006 in. If the clearance is not correct, select a snap-ring spacer of the correct thickness from below:

Differential Side Gear Bearing Spacer Chart

Thickness-inches	Part No.
0.096	90414-634
0.100	90415-634
0.104	90416-634
0.108	90417-634
0.112	90418-634
0.116	90419-634

g. After selection of proper thickness spacer and installation, repeat measurement.

Axle Driveshafts

Halfshaft (Driveshaft) Removal and Installation

The front driveshaft assembly consists of a sub-axle shaft and a driveshaft with two universal joints.

A constant velocity ball joint is used for both universal joints, which are factory-packed with special grease and enclosed in sealed rubber boots. The outer joint cannot be disassembled except for removal of the boot.

1. Remove the hubcap from the front wheel and then remove the center cap.

2. Pull out the 4 mm cotter pin and loosen, but do not remove, the spindle nut.

3. Raise the front of the car and support it with safety stands.

4. Remove the wheel lug nuts and then the wheel.

5. Remove the spindle nut.

6. Drain the transmission.

7. Remove the lower arm ball joints at the knuckle by using a ball joint remover.

8. To remove the driveshaft, hold the knuckle and pull it toward you. Then slide the driveshaft out of the knuckle. Pry the CV joint out about ½ in. Pull the inboard joint side of the driveshaft out of the differential case.

9. To install, reverse the removal

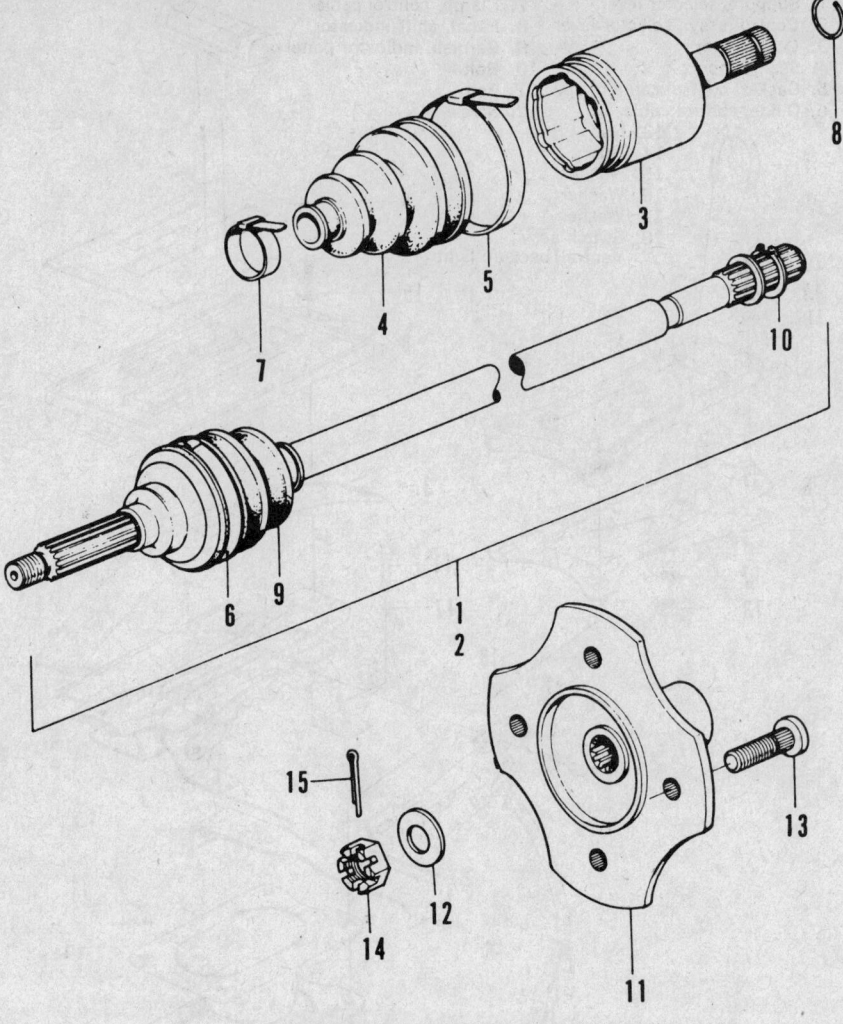

Exploded view of axle driveshaft

1. Driveshaft assy., R	6. Band A, boot	11. Hub, front wheel
2. Driveshaft assy., L	7. Band C, boot	12. Washer, hub nut
3. Joint, inboard joint	8. Ring set	13. Bolt, wheel mounting
4. Bellows, inboard joint	9. Bellows, inboard joint	14. Nut, spindle
5. Band B, boot	10. Ring, snap	15. Pin

procedure. If either the inboard or outboard joint boot bands have been removed for inspection or disassembly of the joint (only the inboard joint can be disassembled), be sure to repack the joint with a sufficient amount of bearing grease.

CAUTION: *Make sure the CV joint sub-axle bottoms so that the spring clip clicks into position and may hold the sub-axle securely in the transmission.*

REAR SUSPENSION

All Civic sedan and hatchback models and the Accord utilize an independent Chapman strut arrangement for each rear wheel. Each suspension unit consists of a combined coil spring/shock absorber strut, a lower control arm, and a radius rod. The Accord has adjustable rear suspension.

Station wagon models use a more conventional leaf spring rear suspension with a solid rear axle. The springs are three-leaf, semi-elliptic types located longitudinally with a pair of telescopic shock absorbers to control rebound. The solid axle and leaf springs allow for a greater load carrying capacity for the wagon over the sedan.

Strut Assembly

Removal and Installation

1. Raise the rear of the car and support it with safety stands.

2. Remove the rear wheel.

3. Disconnect the brake line at the shock absorber. Remove the retaining clip and separate the brake hose from the shock absorber.

4. Disconnect the parking brake cable at the backing plate lever.

5. Remove the lower strut retaining

bolt and hub carrier pivot bolt. To remove the pivot bolt, you first have to remove the castle nut and its cotter pin.

6. Remove the two upper strut retaining nuts and remove the strut from the car.

7. To install, reverse the removal procedure. Be sure to install the top of the strut in the body first. After installation, bleed the brake lines.

Disassembly

1. Use a coil spring compressor to disassemble the strut. When assembling the compressor onto the strut, the long studs should be installed so that they are flush with the bottom plate and also flush with the retaining nut on the top end. The adjustable plate in the center cup should be screwed all the way in.

2. Insert the strut in the compressor and compress the strut about 2 in. Then remove the center retaining nut.

3. Loosen the compressor and remove the strut.

4. Remove the top plate, rubber protector, spring and rubber bumper.

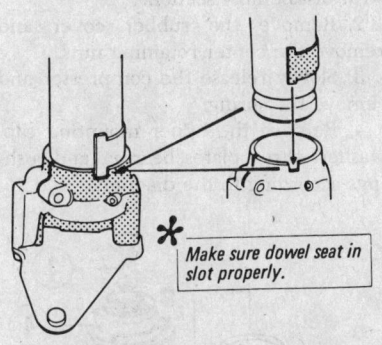

Make sure dowel seat in slot properly.

At the Accord lower strut attachment, install the dowel seat into its slot

1. Bushing, lower arm
2. Arm, rear lower
3. Bushing A, lower arm
4. Washer, lower arm
5. Bolt, rear lower through
6. Rod, radius
7. Spacer, radius
8. Washer, radius rod
9. Bushing A, radius rod
10. Bushing B, radius rod
11. Shock absorber assy., R rear
12. Shock absorber assy., L rear
13. Cap, rear shock absorber
14. Bolt, radius rod
15. Bolt, rear lower arm
16. Nut, self locking
17. Nut, radius rod
18. Bolt, rear lower arm
19. Nut, hex.
20. Nut, hex.
21. Nut, thin
22. Nut, castellated
23. Washer, spring
24. Washer, spring
25. Pin, cotter
26. Spring, rear damper
27. Damper, R rear
28. Damper, L rear
29. Washer, rear damper
30. Bushing, rear damper

31. Seat, spring
32. Guide, damper cover
33. Cover, damper
34. Bumper, rubber
35. Spacer, damper bushing
36. Rubber, spring seat
37. Nut

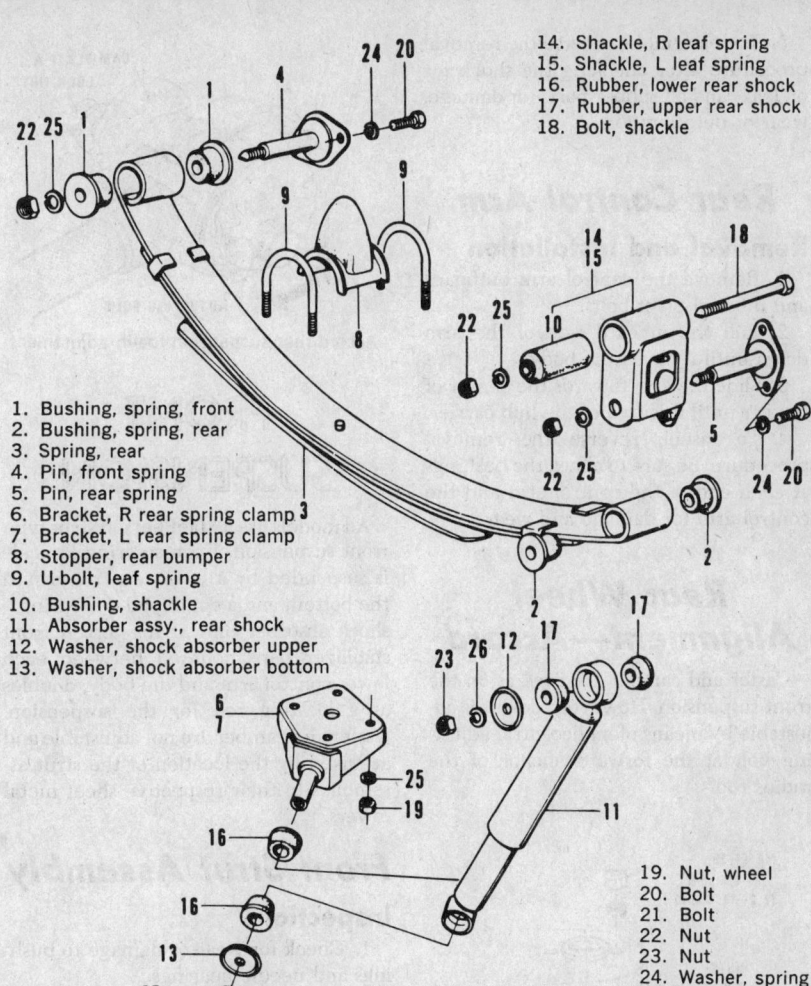

14. Shackle, R leaf spring
15. Shackle, L leaf spring
16. Rubber, lower rear shock
17. Rubber, upper rear shock
18. Bolt, shackle

1. Bushing, spring, front
2. Bushing, spring, rear
3. Spring, rear
4. Pin, front spring
5. Pin, rear spring
6. Bracket, R rear spring clamp
7. Bracket, L rear spring clamp
8. Stopper, rear bumper
9. U-bolt, leaf spring
10. Bushing, shackle
11. Absorber assy., rear shock
12. Washer, shock absorber upper
13. Washer, shock absorber bottom

19. Nut, wheel
20. Bolt
21. Bolt
22. Nut
23. Nut
24. Washer, spring
25. Washer, spring
26. Washer, spring

Exploded view of rear suspension—Civic wagon

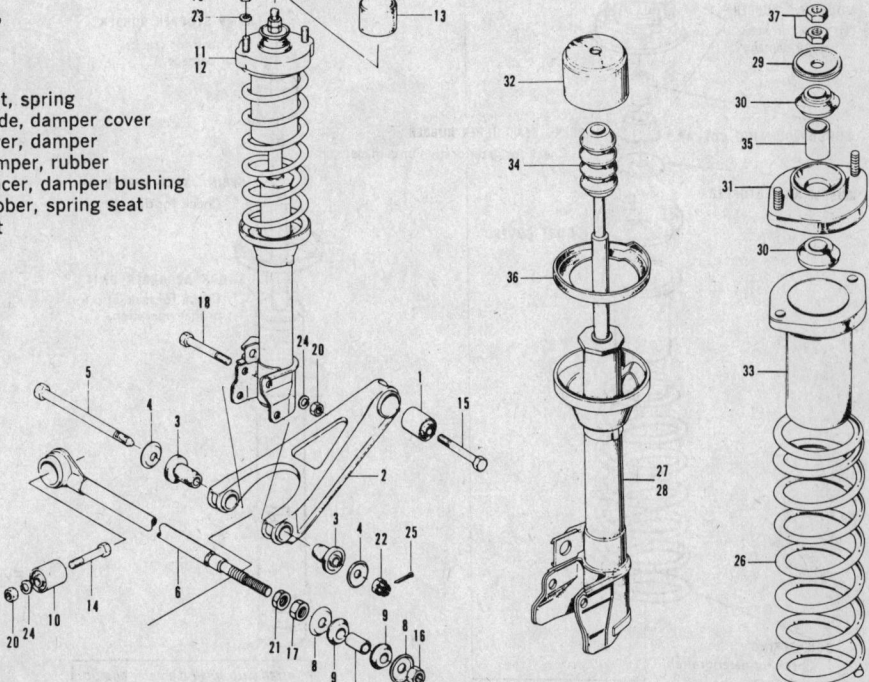

Exploded view of rear suspension—Civic sedan and hatchback

5. To reassemble, reverse the removal procedure after checking the shock for oil leaks and all rubber parts for damage, wear or deterioration.

Rear Control Arm

Removal and Installation

1. Remove the control arm outboard and inboard pivot bolts.

2. Pull the inboard side of the arm down until it clears the body.

3. Slide the arm towards the center of the car until it is free of the hub carrier.

4. To install, reverse the removal procedure. Be sure to check the bushings at each end of the control arm and the control arm for damage and wear.

Rear Wheel Alignment—Accord

Caster and camber are fixed as on the front suspension. However, toe-out is adjustable by means of an eccentric adjusting bolt at the forward anchor of the radius rod.

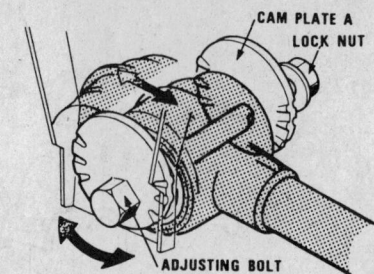

Accord rear suspension toe-in adjustment

FRONT SUSPENSION

All models use a MacPherson strut type front suspension. Each steering knuckle is suspended by a lower control arm at the bottom and a combined coil spring/shock absorber unit at the top. A front stabilizer bar, mounted between each lower control arm and the body, doubles as a locating rod for the suspension. Caster and camber are not adjustable and are fixed by the location of the strut assemblies in their respective sheet metal towers.

Front Strut Assembly

Inspection

1. Check for wear or damage to bushings and needle bearings.

2. Check for oil leaks from the struts.

3. Check all rubber parts for wear or damage.

4. Bounce the car to check shock absorbing effectiveness. The car should continue to bounce for no more than two cycles.

Removal and Installation

1. Raise the front of the car and support it with safety stands. Remove the front wheels.

2. Disconnect the brake pipe at the strut and remove the brake hose retaining clip.

3. Loosen the bolt on the knuckle that retains the lower end of the shock absorber. Push down firmly while tapping it with a hammer until the knuckle is free of the strut.

4. Remove the three nuts retaining the upper end of the strut and remove the strut from the car.

5. To install, reverse the removal procedure. Be sure to properly match the mating surface of the strut and the knuckle notch.

Disassembly

1. Disassemble the strut according to the procedure given in the above rear strut disassembly section.

2. Remove the rubber cover and remove the center retaining nuts.

3. Slowly release the compressor and remove the spring.

4. Remove the upper mounting cap, washers, thrust plates, bearings and bushings according to the diagrams.

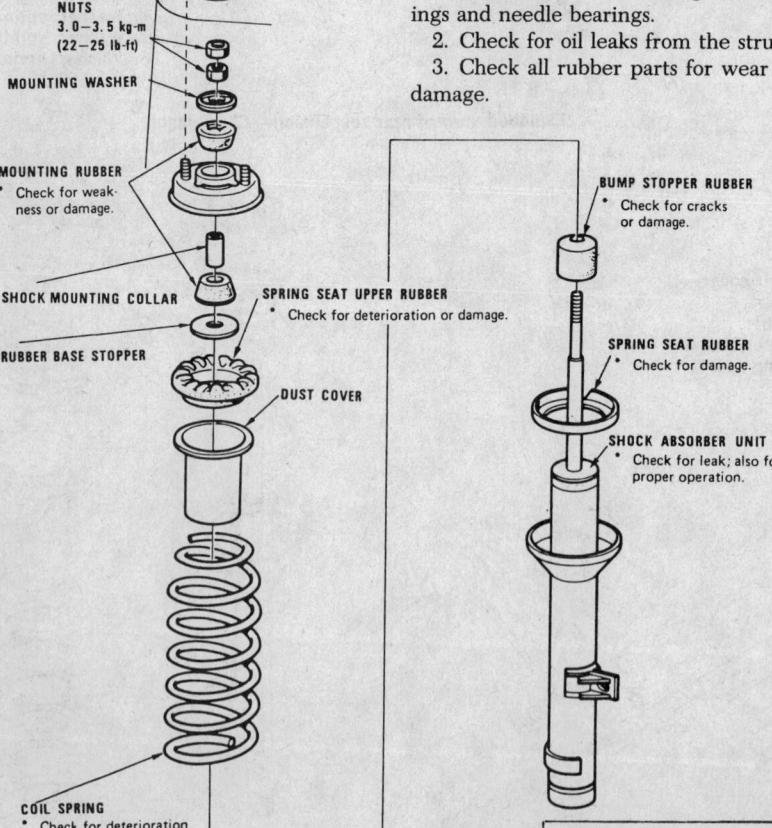

Accord rear shock absorber details

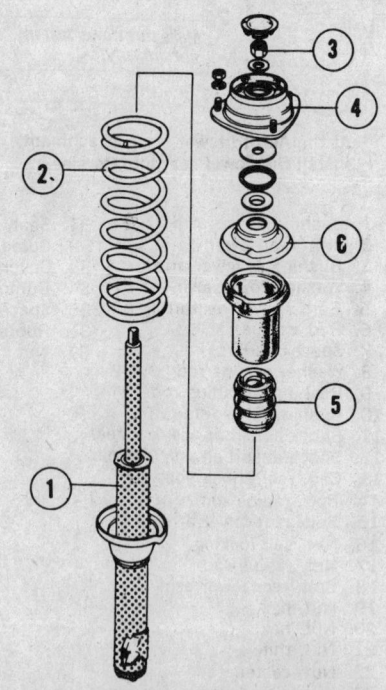

Exploded view of front strut assembly—Civic

1. Front shock absorber unit
2. Spring
3. Locknut
4. Top mount
5. Bump stopper rubber
6. Top plate

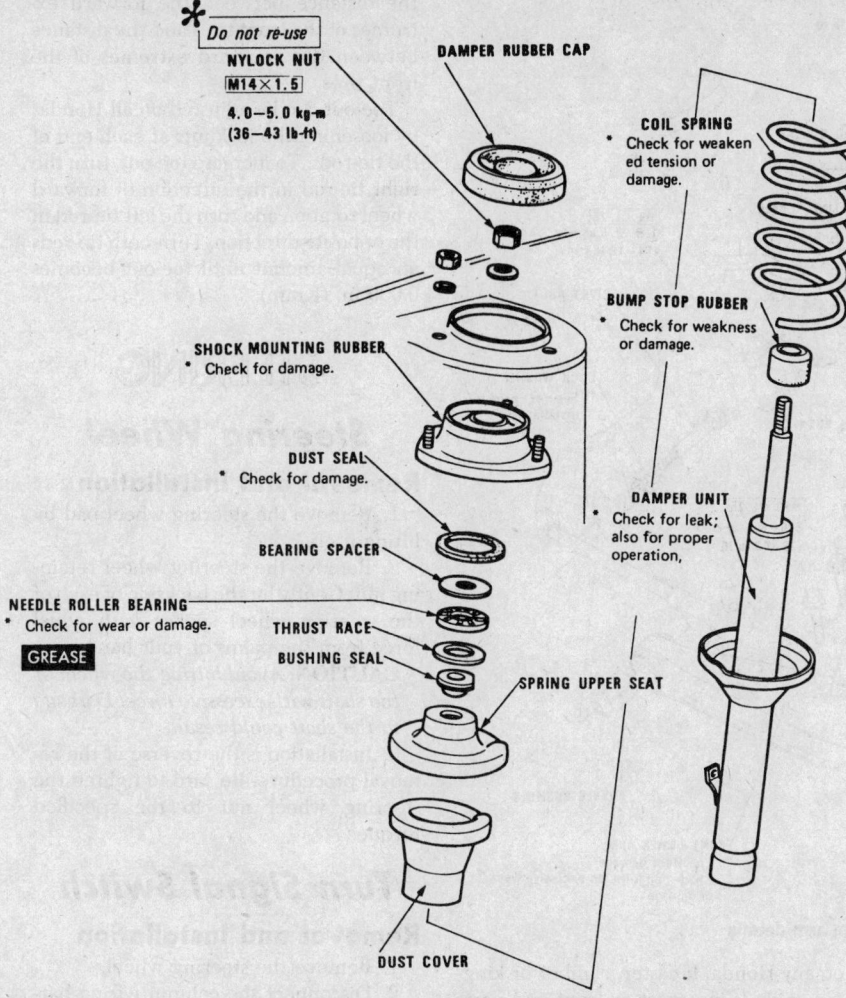

Do not re-use
NYLOCK NUT
M14×1.5
4.0—5.0 kg-m
(36—43 lb-ft)

DAMPER RUBBER CAP

COIL SPRING
* Check for weaken
ed tension or
damage.

BUMP STOP RUBBER
* Check for weakness
or damage.

SHOCK MOUNTING RUBBER
* Check for damage.

DUST SEAL
* Check for damage.

DAMPER UNIT
* Check for leak;
also for proper
operation,

BEARING SPACER

NEEDLE ROLLER BEARING
* Check for wear or damage.

GREASE

THRUST RACE

BUSHING SEAL

SPRING UPPER SEAT

DUST COVER

Accord front shock absorber

NOTE: *Before discarding any parts, check a parts list to determine which parts are available as replacements.*

5. To reassemble, first pull the strut shaft all the way out, hold it in this position and slide the rubber bumper down the shaft to the strut body. This should hold the shaft in the extended position.

6. Install the spring and its top plate. Make sure the spring seats properly.

7. Install the partially assembled strut in the compressor. Compress the strut until the shaft protrudes through the top plate about 1 in.

8. Now install the bushings, thrust plates, top mounting cap washers and retaining nuts in the reverse order of removal.

9. Once the retaining nut is installed, release the tension on the compressor and loosen the thumbscrew on the bottom plate. Separate the bottom plates and remove the compressor.

Lower Ball Joints

Inspection

Check ball joint play as follows:

a. Raise the front of the car and support it with safety stands.

b. Clamp a dial indicator onto the lower control arm and place the indicator tip on the knuckle, near the ball joint;

c. Place a pry bar between the lower control arm and the knuckle. Replace the ball joint if the play exceeds 0.020 in.

Removal and Installation

1. Raise the car and support it with safety stands.

2. Remove the front wheel.

3. Pull out the cotter pin holding the ball joint castle nut and remove the nut.

4. Remove the ball joint from the knuckle using a ball joint remover (special tool no. 07941-6340000.). This is done by hitting the end of the long wedge (07941-6340200), thus forcing the ball joint down and out.

5. To install, reverse the removal procedure. Tighten the ball joint nut to 29–35 ft lbs of torque. Be sure to grease the ball joint.

Lubrication

1. Remove the screw plug from the bottom of the ball joint and install a grease nipple.

2. Lubricate the ball joint with NLGI No. 2 multipurpose type grease.

3. Remove the nipple and reinstall the screw plug.

4. Repeat for the other ball joint.

Lower Control Arm and Stabilizer Bar

Removal and Installation

1. Raise the front of the car and support it with safety stands. Remove the front wheels.

2. Disconnect the lower arm ball joint as described above. Be careful not to damage the seal.

3. Remove the stabilizer bar retaining brackets, starting with the center brackets.

4. Remove the lower arm pivot bolt.

5. Disconnect the radius rod and remove the lower arm.

6. To install, reverse the removal procedure. Be sure to tighten the components to their proper torque.

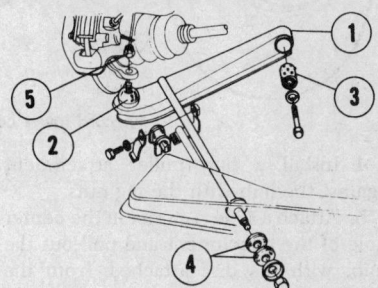

Civic lower control arm details—1973-75 models

1. Lower arm
2. Ball joint seal
3. Lower arm bushing
4. Radius rod bushing
5. Castle nut

Steering Knuckles

Removal and Installation

1. Raise the front of the car and support it with safety stands. Remove the front wheel.

2. Remove the spindle nut cotter pin and the spindle nut.

3. Remove the two bolts retaining the brake caliper and remove the caliper from the knuckle. Do not let the caliper hang by the brake hose, support it with a length of wire.

NOTE: *In case it is necessary to remove the disc, hub, bearings and/or outer dust seal, use Steps 4 and 5 given below. You will need a hydraulic press for this. If this is unnecessary, omit Steps 4 and 5.*

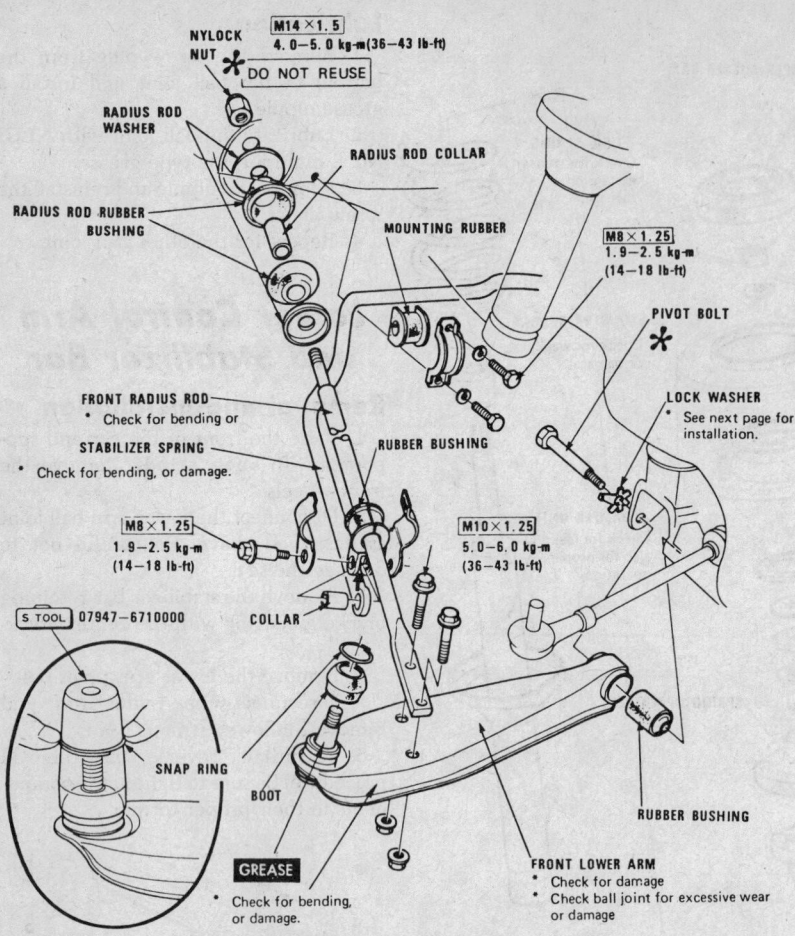

M14 ×1.5
4.0—5.0 kg-m(36—43 lb-ft)

NYLOCK NUT ✱ DO NOT REUSE

RADIUS ROD WASHER

RADIUS ROD COLLAR

RADIUS ROD RUBBER BUSHING

MOUNTING RUBBER

M8 × 1.25
1.9—2.5 kg-m
(14—18 lb-ft)

PIVOT BOLT ✱

LOCK WASHER
• See next page for installation.

FRONT RADIUS ROD
• Check for bending or

STABILIZER SPRING
• Check for bending, or damage.

RUBBER BUSHING

M8 × 1.25
1.9—2.5 kg-m
(14—18 lb-ft)

M10 × 1.25
5.0—6.0 kg-m
(36—43 lb-ft)

S TOOL 07947-6710000

COLLAR

SNAP RING

BOOT

GREASE
• Check for bending, or damage.

RUBBER BUSHING

FRONT LOWER ARM
• Check for damage
• Check ball joint for excessive wear or damage

Accord lower control arm details

4. Install a hub puller attachment against the hub with the lug nuts.

5. Attach a slide hammer in the center hole of the attachment and pull out the hub, with the disc attached, from the knuckle.

6. Remove the tie-rod from the knuckle using the ball joint remover (tool no. 07941-6340000). Use care not to damage the ball joint seals.

7. Remove the lower arm from the knuckle using the ball joint remover.

8. Loosen the lockbolt which retains the strut in the knuckle. Tap the top of the knuckle with a hammer and slide it off the shock.

9. Remove the knuckle and hub, if still attached, by sliding the driveshaft out of the hub.

10. To install, reverse the removal procedure. If the hub was removed, refer to Brake Disc Removal, for procedures with the hydraulic press. Be sure to visually check the knuckle for visible signs of wear or damage and to check the condition of the inner bearing dust seals.

Front End Alignment

Caster and Camber Adjustment

Caster and camber cannot be adjusted

on any Honda. If caster, camber or king-pin angle is incorrect or front end parts are damaged or worn, they must be replaced.

Toe-Out Adjustment

Toe-in (or toe-out) is the difference of

the distance between the forward extremes of the front tires and the distance between the rearward extremes of the front tires.

Toe-out can be adjusted on all Hondas by loosening the locknuts at each end of the tie-rods. To increase toe-out, turn the right tie-rod in the direction of forward wheel rotation and turn the left tie-rod in the opposite direction. Turn both tie-rods an equal amount until toe-out becomes 0.039 in. (1 mm).

STEERING

Steering Wheel

Removal and Installation

1. Remove the steering wheel pad by lifting it off.

2. Remove the steering wheel retaining nut. Gently hit the backside of each of the steering wheel spokes with equal force from the palms of your hands.
CAUTION: *Avoid hitting the wheel or the shaft with excessive force. Damage to the shaft could result.*

3. Installation is the reverse of the removal procedure. Be sure to tighten the steering wheel nut to the specified torque.

Turn Signal Switch

Removal and Installation

1. Remove the steering wheel.

2. Disconnect the column wiring harness and coupler.

3. Remove the four attaching bolts (remove the upper two bolts first), holding the steering column to the instrument panel and lower the column.

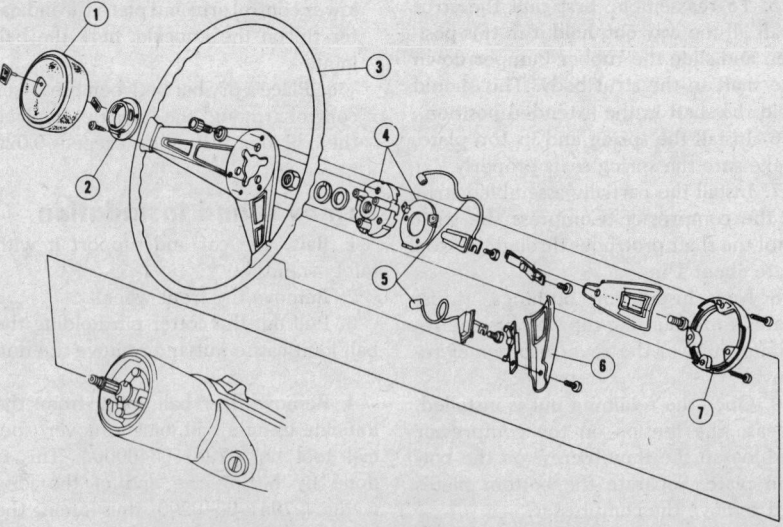

Exploded view of Civic steering wheel and related parts

1. Steering pad
2. Pad retainer
3. Steering wheel
4. Hub core
5. Horn wires
6. Horn wire cover
7. Steering pad lower retainer

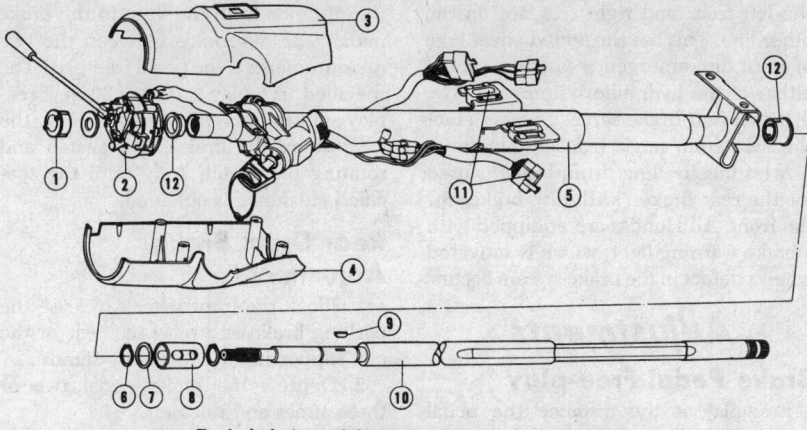

Exploded view of Civic steering shaft assembly

1. Cancelling cam
2. Turn signal switch
3. Upper cover
4. Lower cover
5. Steering column
6. Snap-ring
7. Spacer
8. Steering lock collar
9. Lock collar key
10. Steering shaft
11. Shear plates
12. Upper bushing
13. Lower bushing

CAUTION: *Be careful not to damage the steering column or shaft.*

4. Remove the upper and lower column covers.

5. Loosen the screw on the turn signal switch cam nut and lightly tap its head to permit the cam nut to loosen. Then remove the turn signal switch assembly and the steering shaft upper bushing.

6. To assemble and install, reverse the above procedure. When installing the turn signal switch assembly, engage the locating tab on the switch with the notch in the steering column. The steering shaft upper bushing should be installed with the flat side facing the upper side of the column. The alignment notch for the turn signal switch will be centered on the flat side of the bushing.

NOTE: *If the cam nut has been removed, be sure to install it with the small end up.*

Ignition Switch

Removal and Installation

1. Remove the steering shaft hanger retaining bolts and lower the steering shaft from the instrument panel to expose the ignition switch.

2. Remove the steering column housing upper and lower covers.

3. Disconnect the ignition switch wiring at the couplers.

4. The ignition switch assembly is held onto the column by two shear bolts. Remove these bolts, using a drill, to separate and remove the ignition switch.

5. To install, reverse the removal procedure. You will have to replace the shear bolts with new ones.

Steering Gear

Testing

1. Remove the dust seal bellows retaining bands and slide the dust seals off the left and right side of the gearbox housing.

2. Turn the front wheels full left and, using your hand, attempt to move the steering rack in an up-down direction.

3. Repeat with the wheel turned full right.

4. If any movement is felt, the steering gearbox must be adjusted.

Adjustment

1. Make sure that the rack is well lubricated.

2. Loosen the rack guide adjusting locknut.

3. Tighten the adjusting screw just to the point where the front wheels cannot be turned by hand.

4. Back off the adjusting screw 45 degrees and hold it in that position while adjusting the locknut.

5. Recheck the play, and then move the wheels lock-to-lock, to make sure that the rack moves freely.

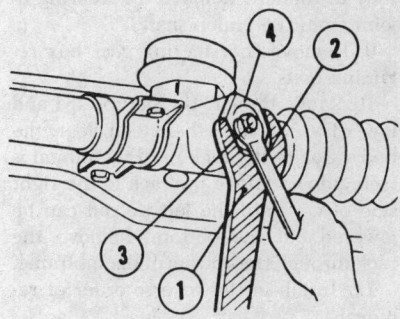

Steering gearbox adjustment

1. Special tool
2. 14 mm wrench
3. Rack guide screw
4. Rack guide screw locknut

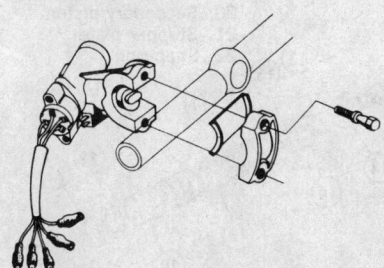

Ignition switch removal—Civic

Steering gearbox and linkage

1. Outer dust seal
2. Inner dust seal
3. Steering pinion dust seal
4. 45 mm internal snap-ring
5. External snap-ring
6. Ball bearing
7. Steering pinion washer
8. Steering pinion
9. Gearbox
10. Grease fitting
11. Ball joint seal
12. Circlip
13. Tie-rod end
14. Tie-rod dust seal
15. Bellow band
16. Tie-rod
17. Air tube
18. Tie-rod lockwasher
19. Tie-rod stop washer
20. Air tube clips
21. Gearbox bracket
22. Gearbox mounting cushion
23. Rack screw locknut
24. Rack guide O-ring
25. Rack guide screw
26. Rack guide pressure spring
27. Steering rack guide
28. Steering rack

6. Check the steering force by first raising the front wheels and then placing them in a straight-ahead position. Turn the steering wheel with a spring scale to check the steering force. Steering force on the Civic should be no more than 3.3 lbs.

Removal and Installation

1. Jack and support the front of the car.

2. Remove the front wheels.

3. Raise the engine off the mounts.

4. Remove the tie rod ends from the knuckles with a ball joint remover.

5. Disconnect the exhaust pipe at the manifold.

6. Disconnect the gear shift rod and extension at the engine.

7. Remove the center beam.

8. Position the steering wheel in the fully to the left. Remove the steering u-joint from the pinion shaft.

9. Remove the steering gear box retaining bolts.

10. Move the left tie rod upward and lower the rack until the pinion clears the body. Rotate the rack until the pinion is facing down. Move the rack to the right side of car until the left tie rod can be lowered out the bottom. Remove the rack through the bottom of the subframe.

11. Install in the reverse order of removal.

Tie-Rods

Removal and Installation

1. Raise the front of the car and support it with safety stands. Remove the front wheels.

2. Use the special ball joint remover (tool no. 07941–6340000) to remove the tie-rod from the knuckle on the Civic.

3. Remove the tie-rod dust seal bellows clamps and move the rubber bellows on the tie-rod and rack joints. On the Civic, you first have to disconnect the air tube at the dust seal joint.

4. Straighten the tie-rod lockwasher tabs at the tie-rod-to-rack joint and remove the tie-rod by turning it with a wrench.

5. To install, reverse the removal procedure. Always use a new tie-rod lockwasher during reassembly. Fit the locating lugs into the slots on the rack and bend the outer edge of the washer over the flat part of the rod, after the tie-rod nut has been properly tightened.

BRAKE SYSTEMS

Honda uses a dual hydraulic system, with the brakes connected diagonally. In other words, the right front and left rear brakes are on the same hydraulic line and

the left front and right rear are on the other line. This has the added advantage of front disc emergency braking, should either of the hydraulic systems fail. The diagonal rear brake serves to counteract the sway from single front disc braking.

A leading/trailing drum brake is used for the rear brakes, with disc brakes for the front. All Hondas are equipped with a brake warning light, which is activated when a defect in the brake system occurs.

Adjustments

Brake Pedal Free-play

Free-play is the distance the pedal travels from the stop (brake light switch) until the pushrod contacts the vacuum booster, which actuates the master cylinder.

To check free-play, first measure the distance (with the carpet removed) from the floor to the brake pedal. Then disconnect the return spring and again measure

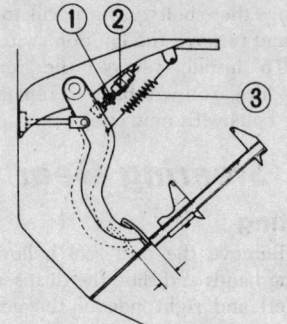

Brake pedal free-play adjustment
1. Locknut
2. Stop switch (adjuster)
3. Pedal return spring

the distance from the floor to the brake pedal. The difference between the two measurements is the pedal free-play. The specified free-play is 0.04–0.20 in. Free-play adjustment is made by loosening the locknut on the brake light switch and rotating the switch body until the specified clearance is obtained.

Rear Drum Brake Adjustment

1. Block the front wheels, release the parking brake and raise the rear of the car, supporting it with safety stands.

2. Depress the brake pedal two or three times and release.

3. The adjuster is located on the inboard side, underneath the control arm. Turn the adjuster clockwise until the wheel no longer turns.

4. Back off the adjuster two (2) clicks and turn the wheel to see if the brake shoes are dragging. If they are dragging, back off the adjuster one more click.

Rear brake adjustment
1. Adjuster wrench
2. Tighten
3. Loosen

1. Cap
2. Float
3. Reservoir tank
4. Reservoir tank clip
5. Master cylinder body
6. Check valve spring
7. Check valve
8. Check valve washer
9. Packing
10. Union cap
11. Primary spring
12. Piston cup
13. Primary piston
14. Wiper ring
15. Piston cup
16. Secondary stopper
17. Secondary spring
18. Piston cup
19. Secondary cup
20. Secondary piston
21. Stopper plate
22. Snap-ring

Exploded view of Civic master cylinder

Master Cylinder

Removal and Installation

CAUTION: *Before removing the master cylinder, cover the body surfaces with fender covers and rags to prevent damage to painted surfaces by brake fluid.*

1. Disconnect the brake lines at the master cylinder.

2. Remove the master cylinder-to-vacuum booster attaching bolts and remove the master cylinder from the car.

3. To install, reverse the removal procedure. Before operating the car, you must bleed the brake system (see below).

Disassembly and Overhaul

1. Remove the fluid reservoir caps and floats, and drain the reservoirs.

2. Loosen the retaining clamps and remove the reservoirs.

3. Remove the primary piston stop bolt.

4. Remove the piston retaining clip and washer, and remove the primary piston.

5. Wrap a rag around the end of the master cylinder, so that it blocks the bore.

Hold your finger over the stop bolt hole and direct a small amount of compressed air into the primary outlet. This should slide the primary piston to the end of the master cylinder bore, so that it can be removed.

6. Remove the two union caps, washers, check valves and springs.

7. For overhaul, check the following:

a. Clogged orifices in the pistons and cylinder;

b. Damage to the reservoir attaching surface;

c. Damage to the check valves;

d. Wear or damage to the piston cups;

e. The clearance between the master cylinder bore and the pistons. The clearance should be 0.0008–0.0050 in.

8. Assembly of the master cylinder is the reverse of the disassembly procedures. Be sure to check the following:

a. The check valves and piston cups should be replaced when the master cylinder is assembled, regardless of their condition;

b. Apply a thin coat of brake fluid to the pistons before installing. When installing the pistons, push in while rotating to prevent damage to the piston cups;

c. Tighten the union cap and stop bolts.

Bleeding

When it is necessary to flush the brake hydraulic system because of parts replacement or fluid contamination, the following procedure should be observed:

1. Loosen the wheel cylinder bleeder screw. Drain the brake fluid by pumping the brake pedal. Pump the pedal until all of the old fluid has been pumped out and replaced by new fluid.

2. The flushing procedure should be performed in the following sequence:

a. Bleed the left front brake;

b. Bleed the right rear brake;

c. Bleed the right front brake;

d. Bleed the left rear brake.

3. Bleed the back of the master cylinder before the front, through the two bleed valves. Fasten one end of a plastic tube onto the bleed valve and immerse the other end in a clear jar filled with brake fluid. When air bubbles cease to emerge from the end of the tubing, the bleeding is completed. Be sure to keep the fluid reservoir filled at all times during the bleeding process so air does not enter the system.

CAUTION: *Brake fluid is adversely affected by contamination from dirt, automotive petroleum products and water. Contaminants can plug parts of the hydraulic system, causing rapid wear or swelling of rubber parts and lower the boiling point of the fluid. KEEP FLUID CLEAN.*

Vacuum Booster

Inspection

A preliminary check of the vacuum booster can be made as follows:

a. Depress the brake pedal several times using normal pressure. Make sure that the pedal height does not vary;

b. Hold the pedal in the depressed position and start the engine. The pedal should drop slightly;

c. Hold the pedal in the above position and stop the engine. The pedal should stay in the depressed position for approximately 30 seconds;

d. If the pedal does not drop when the engine is started or rises after the engine is stopped, the booster is not functioning properly.

Removal and Installation

1. Disconnect the vacuum hose at the booster.

2. Disconnect the brake lines at the master cylinder.

3. Remove the brake pedal-to-booster

Check caps for restriction in vent holes.

FLUID LEVEL SENSOR
- Check operation of float and reed switch.

FILTER
- Remove sediment and any other foreign materials.

RESERVOIR TANK

METAL GASKET

STOP BOLT
M6 × 1.0
1.2 kg-m (9 lb-ft)

CHECK VALVE SPRING
* Note installation direction.

CHECK VALVE

M8 × 1.25 : 1.5–2.0 kg-m (11–15 lb-ft)

WASHER
METAL GASKET
BRAKE PIPE UNION

MASTER CYLINDER
- Check for wear or damage.

PISTON CUP
* Replace whenever disassembled

PISTON CUP
* Replace whenever disassembled

PRIMARY PISTON
- Check for clearance or sign of damage

SECONDARY PISTON
- Check for wear of damage.

SNAP RING
23 mm

RETURN STOP PLATE

* Cylinder-to-Piston Clearance	Standard	0.02–0.10 mm (0.0008–0.0039 in.)
	Service Limit	0.15 mm (0.0059 in.)

Exploded view of Accord master cylinder

link pin and the four nuts retaining the booster. The pushrod and nuts are located inside the car on the passenger side, under the dashboard.

4. Remove the booster with the master cylinder attached.

5. To install, reverse the removal procedure. Don't forget to bleed the brake system before operating the car.

FRONT DISC BRAKES
Disc Brake Pads
Removal and Installation
Civic

1. After removing the wheel, remove the pad retaining clip which is fitted in the holes of the pad retaining pins.

2. Remove the two retaining pins and fitting springs with pliers. When removing them, care must be taken to prevent the springs from flying apart.

3. The front brake pad can be removed, together with the shim, after removing the springs and pins. If the pads are difficult to remove, open the bleeder valve and move the caliper in the direction of the piston. The pads will become loose and can be easily removed.

NOTE: *After the pads are removed, the brake pedal must not be touched.*

To provide space for installing the pad, loosen the bleed valve and push the inner piston back into the cylinder. Also push

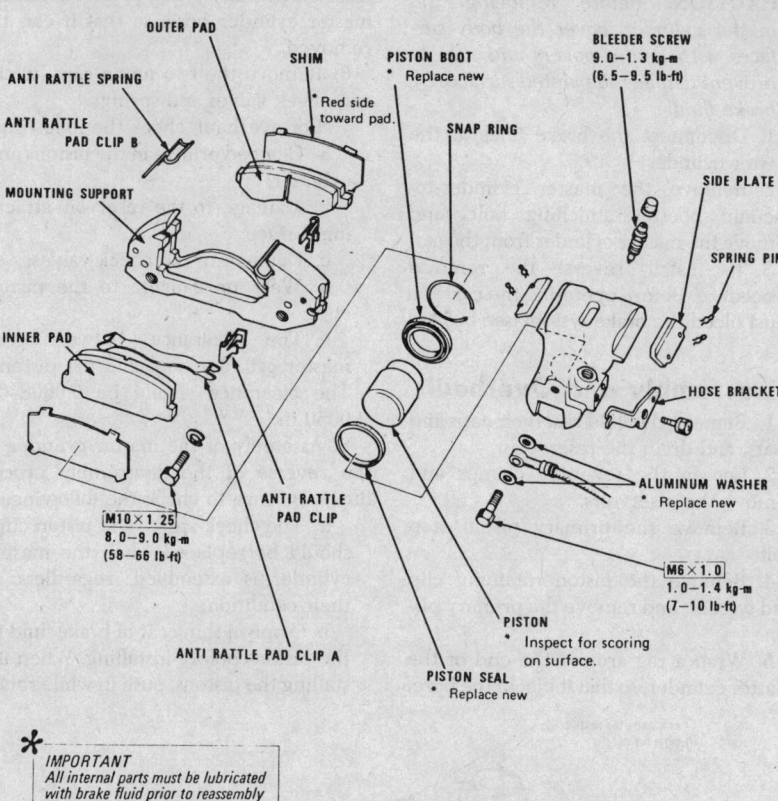

Caliper and mounting support must be reinstalled in same position.

* IMPORTANT
All internal parts must be lubricated with brake fluid prior to reassembly

Exploded view of Accord front disc brake assembly

back the outer piston by applying pressure to the caliper. After providing space for the pads, close the bleed valve and

insert the pad. Insert a shim behind each pad with the arrow on the shim pointing up. Incorrect installation of the shims can cause squealing brakes.

Accord

1. Remove the wheel.

2. With pliers, remove the four spring clips.

3. Slide out the upper and lower side plates.

4. Lift off the caliper piston body.

5. Remove the upper anti-rattle clip and lift out the pads.

6. Thoroughly clean the sliding surfaces of the caliper mounting support, caliper piston body, and side plates with a wire brush prior to assembly.

7. Reverse steps 1–5 to stall.

Disc Brake Calipers
Removal and Installation
Civic

1. Raise the front of the car and support it with safety stands. Remove the front wheels.

2. Loosen the brake line at the wheel cylinder.

3. The caliper housing is mounted to the knuckle with two bolts located behind the cylinder. Remove these bolts and the caliper.

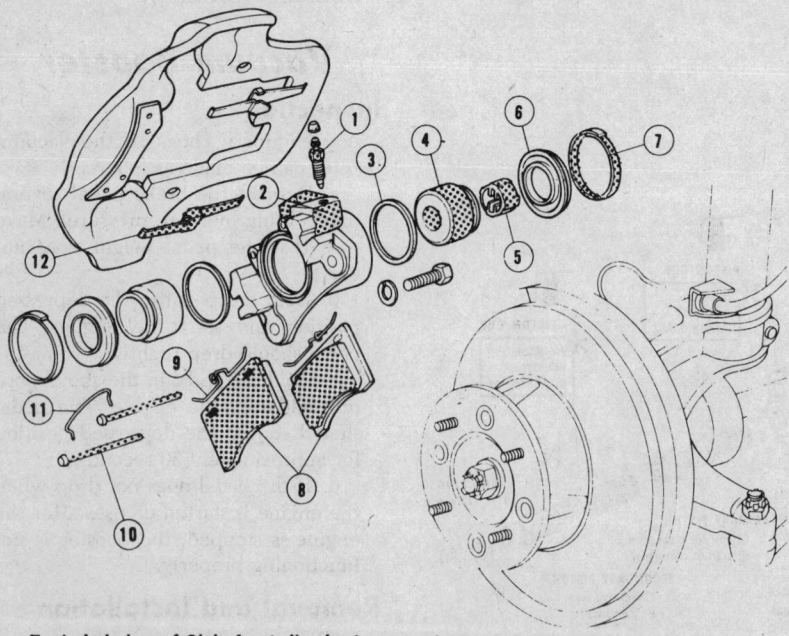

Exploded view of Civic front disc brake assembly—all models except 1976 wagon

1. Bleeder screw
2. Cylinder
3. Piston seal
4. Piston
5. Yoke guide
6. Dust cover
7. Retaining ring
8. Pad set
9. Pad spring
10. Pad retaining ring
11. Pad retaining clip
12. Yoke spring

To install, reverse the removal procedure. Be sure to inspect all parts before installing and bleed the brake system before operating the car.

Accord

1. Remove the brake pads as outlined above.

2. Remove the lower anti-rattle clip, and disconnect the brake hose.

3. Remove the two bolts retaining the caliper mounting support to the knuckle and lift off.

4. Reverse the above to install. Bleed the brakes.

Inspection and Overhaul

Civic

NOTE: *Wash all parts in brake fluid. Do not use cleaning solvent or gasoline.*

1. Remove the inner and outer pad springs and pin clips. Then remove the pins and pads.

NOTE: *The springs are different, so note the location and method of installation before removing.*

2. Push the yoke toward the rear (inboard side) of the cylinder, until it is free to separate the yoke from the cylinder. You may have to tap lightly with a plastic hammer (where the mounting bolts are located) to remove the cylinder. Exercise extreme care to avoid damaging the cylinder body. If only the cylinder body moves, without the outer piston, a gentle tap on the piston should loosen it.

3. To dismantle the cylinder, first remove the retaining rings at both ends of the cylinder with a screwdriver, being careful not to damage the rubber boot.

4. Both pistons can be removed from the cylinder body either by pushing through one end with a wooden rod or by blowing compressed air into the cylinder inlet port.

NOTE: *If the wheel cylinder pistons are removed for any reason, the piston seals must be replaced.*

5. Remove the piston seals, installed on the inside of the cylinder at both ends, with a screwdriver

6. Inspect the caliper operation. If the lining wear differs greatly between the inner and outer pads, the caliper may be unable to move properly due to rust and dirt on the sliding surfaces. Clean the sliding part of the caliper and apply brake grease.

NOTE: *All brake parts are critical items. If there is any question as to the service ability of any brake part—replace it.*

7. Check the piston-to-cylinder clearance. The specified clearance is 0.0008–0.005 in. Also check the pistons and cylinder bore for scuffing and scratching.

8. Check the dust covers, retaining rings, nylon retainers and all other parts for wear or damage.

9. To reassemble the caliper, reverse the removal procedure. After reassembly, measure the force necessary to slide the caliper from the neutral position with a spring scale. The specified force is 55 lbs. Bleed the brake system.

Accord

1. Remove the brake pads and caliper as outlined above.

2. Remove the snap-ring and piston boot from the caliper piston body.

3. Apply pressure through the brake hose hole and carefully force out the piston.

4. Using a screwdriver (or preferably a blunt plastic or wooden instrument) pry out the piston seal. Be sure not to scratch the piston bore.

5. Clean the piston and caliper bore with new brake fluid. Inspect for corrosion, scoring or other damage.

6. Install a new piston seal.

7. Coat the piston and caliper bore with clean, new brake fluid and press the piston into the bore by hand.

8. Install the piston boot and fit the snap-ring.

9. Wire brush the sliding surfaces of the caliper piston body and caliper mounting support.

10. Install the mounting support and torque the two bolts to 58–66 ft-lbs.

11. Connect the brake hose using new washers. Tighten to .7–10 ft-lbs.

12. Install the brake pads as outlined above.

13. Bleed the brakes and road-test.

Brake Disc

Removal and Installation

NOTE: *The following procedure for brake disc removal necessitates the use of a hydraulic press. You will have to go to a machine or auto shop equipped with a press. Do not attempt this procedure without a press.*

1. Raise the front of the car and support it with safety stands. Remove the front wheels.

2. Remove the center spindle nuts.

3. Remove the caliper assembly. Do not let the caliper assembly hang by the brake hose.

4. Use a slide hammer with a hub puller attachment (special tool no. 07934-6340100), or a conventional hub puller, to extract the hub with the disc attached.

5. Remove the four bolts and separate the hub and disc.

6. Remove the knuckle from the car.

7. Remove the wheel bearings from the knuckle (see below).

NOTE: *If, for any reason, the hub is removed, the front wheel bearings must be replaced.*

8. To install the disc, you have to use a hydraulic press for both the bearings and the hub. After installing the bearings (see below), install the front hub using the special base (tool no. 07965-6340300) and drifts (tool no. 07965-6340100 and 07965-6340200). Position the hub with the knuckle underneath on the base and press it down through the base.

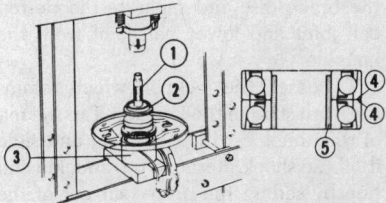

Using arbor press to install hub and bearings into knuckle
1. Driver handle
2. Driver attachment B
3. Front hub disassembly tool, base B
4. Product marking
5. Product marking

Inspection

1. The brake disc develops circular scores after long or even short usage when there is frequent braking. Excessive scoring not only causes a squealing brake, but also shortens the service life of the brake pads. However, light scoring of the disc surface, not exceeding 0.015 in. in depth, will result from normal use and is not detrimental to brake operation.

NOTE: *Differences in the left and right disc surfaces can result in uneven braking.*

2. Disc run-out is the movement of the disc from side-to-side. Place a dial indicator in the middle of the pad wear area and turn the disc, while checking the indicator. If disc run-out exceeds 0.006 in., replace the disc.

3. Disc parallelism is the measurement of variations in disc thickness at several locations on the disc circumference. To measure parallelism, place a mark on the disc and measure the disc thickness with a micrometer. Repeat this measurement at eight (8) equal increments on the circumference of the disc. If the measurements vary more than 0.0028 in., replace the disc.

NOTE: *Only the outer portion of the disc can be checked while installed on the car. If the installed parallelism check is within specifications, but you have reason to suspect that parallelism is the problem, then remove the disc and repeat the check using the center of pad wear for a checking point.*

Front Wheel Bearings

Removal and Installation

NOTE: *The following procedure for Civic wheel bearing removal and installation necessitates the use of an hydraulic press. You will have to go to a machine or auto shop equipped with a press. Do not attempt this procedure without a press.*

1. Raise the front of the car and support it with safety stands. Remove the front wheel.

2. Remove the caliper assembly from the brake disc and separate the tie-rod ball joint and lower ball joint from the knuckle.

3. Loosen the lockbolt which retains the front strut in the knuckle. Tap the top of the knuckle with a hammer and slide it off the shock. Remove the knuckle and hub by sliding the driveshaft out of the hub.

4. Remove the wheel bearing dust cover on the inboard side of the knuckle.

5. Remove the four bolts which hold the brake disc onto the hub. Remove the splashguard by removing the three retaining screws.

6. Remove the outer bearing retainer.

7. Remove the wheel bearings by supporting the knuckle in a hydraulic press, using two support plates (or special tool no. 07965-6340300). Make sure that the plates do not overlap the outer bearing race. Now use a proper sized driver (or tool no. 07947-6340400) and handle (tool no. 07949-6110000) to remove the bearings.

NOTE: *Whenever the wheel bearings are removed, always replace with a new set of bearings and outer dust seal.*

8. Pack each bearing with grease before installing (see below).

9. To install the bearings, press them into the knuckle using the same support plates as above, plus the installing base (tool no. 07965-634040). Use the same driver and handle you used to remove the bearing.

NOTE: *The front wheel bearings are the angular contact type. It is important that they be installed with the manufacturer's markings facing inward.*

10. Use the press to install the front hub (see above).

11. The rest of installation is the reverse of the removal procedure.

Cleaning and Repacking

1. Clean all old grease from the driveshaft spindles on the car.

2. Remove all old grease from the hub and knuckle and thoroughly dry and wipe clean all components.

3. When fitting new bearings, you must pack them with wheel bearing grease. To do this, place glob of grease in your left palm, then, holding one of the bearings in your right hand, drag the face of the bearing heavily through the

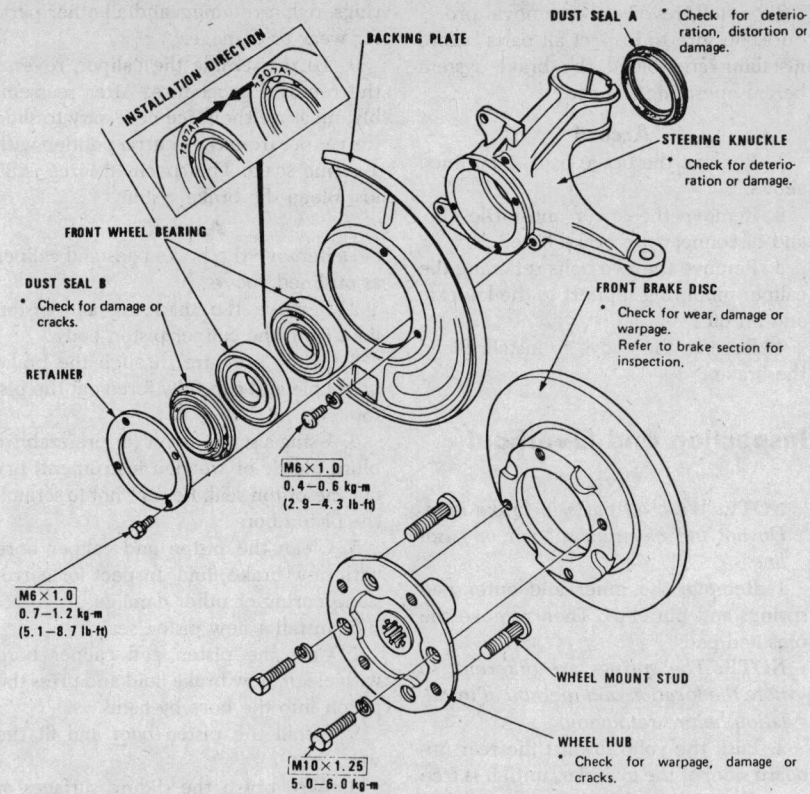

Exploded view of Accord front wheel bearings, disc rotor, knuckle and related parts—Civic similar

grease. This must be done to work as much grease as possible through the ball bearings and the cage. Turn the bearing and continue to pull it through the grease, until the grease is thoroughly packed between the bearing balls and the cage, all around the bearing. Repeat this operation until all of the bearings are packed with grease.

4. Pack the inside of the rotor and knuckle hub with a moderate amount of grease. Do not overload the hub with grease.

5. Apply a small amount of grease to the spindle and to the lip of the inner seal before installing.

6. To install the bearings, check the above procedures.

Checking and Adjusting

The front wheel bearings should be inspected and repacked (or replaced) every 30,000 miles. To check the wheel bearings for any play, jack up each wheel to clear the ground. Hold the wheel and shake it to check the bearings for any play. If any play is felt, tighten the castellated spindle nut to the specified torque (87–130 ft lbs) and reinspect. If play is still present, replace the bearing.

NOTE: *Overtightening the spindle nuts will cause excessive bearing friction and will result in rough wheel rotation and eventual bearing failure.*

REAR DRUM BRAKES

Brake Drums

Removal and Installation

1. Raise the rear of the car and support it with safety stands. Remove the rear wheels. Make sure that the parking brake is *off.*

2. Remove the bearing cap and the castle nut.

3. Pull off the rear brake drum. If the drum is difficult to remove, use a brake drum puller, or a front hub puller and slide hammer.

4. To install, reverse the removal procedures.

Inspection

Check the drum for cracks and the inner surface of the shoe for excessive wear and damage. The inner diameter (I.D.) of the drum should be no more than specifications, nor should the drum be more than 0.004 in. out-of-round.

Brake Shoes

Removal and Installation

1. Remove the brake drum (see above).

2. Remove the tension pin clips and the two brake return springs. Then remove the shoes. If you are installing new shoes, back off the adjusters.

CAUTION: *The upper and lower brake shoe return springs on the Civic sedan and hatchback are different and should not be interchanged. The upper spring is designed so that the spring coils are located on the outboard side of the shoe, while the lower spring is designed so that its coils are located on the inboard side of the shoe with the crossbar facing downward.*

3. To install, reverse the removal procedure. Be sure to check the brake lining thickness before assembly. If the thickness is less than specifications, replace the lining.

Wheel Cylinders

Removal and Installation

1. Remove the brake drum and shoes (see above).

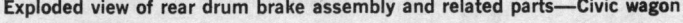

1. Plate, R rear backing	11. Cover, dust	21. Spring, shoe clamp
2. Plate, L rear backing	12. Adjuster assy., brake	22. Pin, tension
3. Shoe, rear brake	13. Ramp, brake adjuster	23. Spring, brake shoe return
4. Spring A, brake shoe return	14. Bolt, adjuster	24. Bolt
5. Spring B, brake shoe return	15. Cap, brake adjuster	25. Nut
6. Spring C, brake shoe return	16. Screw, bleed	26. Nut
7. Cylinder assy., rear wheel	17. Cap, bleed	27. Washer
8. Piston, wheel cylinder	18. Lever, R brake	28. Washer
9. Cup, wheel cylinder	19. Lever, L brake	
10. Spring, wheel cylinder	20. Seal, brake	

Exploded view of rear drum brake assembly and related parts—Civic wagon

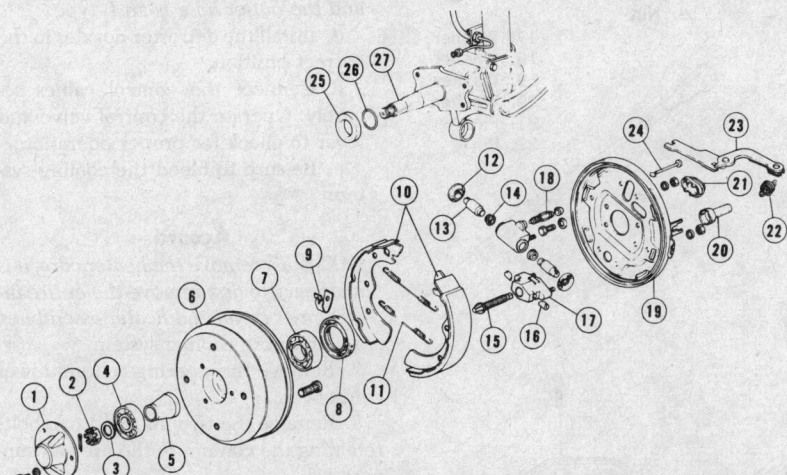

Exploded view of rear drum brake assembly and related parts—Accord and Civic sedan and hatchback

1. Rear wheel bearing cap	10. Rear brake shoes	19. Backing plate
2. Rear axle nut	11. Brake spring	20. Adjuster cap
3. Rear hub washer	12. Dust cover	21. Lever seal cap
4. Outer rear wheel bearing	13. Piston	22. Return spring
5. Hub carrier spacer	14. Piston cup	23. Lever
6. Rear brake drum	15. Adjuster bolt	24. Tension pin
7. Inner rear wheel bearing	16. Brake adjuster piston	25. Collar
8. Rear wheel bearing oil seal	17. Brake adjuster	26. O-ring
9. Shoe clamp spring	18. Bleeder screw	27. Hub carrier

2. Disconnect the parking brake cable and brake lines at the backing plate. Be sure to have a drip pan to catch the brake fluid.

3. Remove the two wheel cylinder retaining nuts on the inboard side of the backing plate and remove the wheel cylinder.

4. To install, reverse the removal procedure. When assembling, apply a thin coat of grease to the grooves of the wheel cylinder piston and the sliding surfaces of the backing plate.

Overhaul

Remove the wheel cylinder dust seals from the grooves to permit the removal of the cylinder pistons.

Wash all parts in fresh brake fluid and check the cylinder bore and pistons for scratches and other damage, replacing where necessary. Check the clearance between the piston and the cylinder bore, by taking the difference between the piston diameter and the bore diameter. The specified clearance is 0.0008–0.-004 in.

When assembling the wheel cylinder, apply a coat of brake fluid to the pistons, piston cups and cylinder walls.

Handbrake

Cable Removal and Installation

1. Remove the adjusting nut from the equalizer mounted on the rear axle and separate the cable from the equalizer.

2. Set the parking brake to a fully released position and remove the cotter pin from the side of the brake lever.

3. After removing the cotter pin, pull out the pin which connects the cable and the lever.

4. Detach the cable from the guides at the front and right side of the fuel tank and remove the cable.

5. To install. reverse the removal procedure, making sure that grease is applied to the cable and the guides.

Adjustment

Inspect the following items:

  a. Check the ratchet for wear;

  b. Check the cables for wear or damage and the cable guide and equalizer for looseness;

  c. Check the equalizer cable where it contacts the equalizer and apply grease if necessary;

  d. Check the rear brake adjustment. The rear wheels should be locked when the handbrake lever is pulled 1 to 5 notches on the ratchet. Adjustment is made by turning the nut located at the equalizer, between the lower control arms.

CHASSIS ELECTRICAL
Heater

Removal and Installation

NOTE: *These procedures do not apply to cars equipped with air conditioning. On cars equipped with air conditioning, heater removal may differ from the procedures listed below. Only a trained air conditioning specialist should tamper with A/C equipped units. Air conditioning units contain pressurized Freon which can be extremely dangerous (e.g. burns and/or blindness) to the untrained.*

Civic

1. Drain the radiator

2. Disconnect the right and left defroster hoses.

3. Disconnect the inlet and outlet water hoses at the heater assembly.

NOTE: *There will be a coolant leakage when disconnecting the hoses. Catch the coolant in a container to prevent damage to the interior.*

4. Disconnect the following items:

  a. Fre-Rec control cable;

  b. Temperature control rod;

  c. Room/Def. control cable;

  d. Fan motor switch connector;

  e. Upper attaching bolts;

  f. Lower attaching bolts;

  g. Lower bracket.

5. Remove the heater assembly through the passenger side.

6. To install the heater assembly, reverse the removal procedure. Pay attention to the following points:

  a. When installing the heater assembly, do not forget to connect the motor ground wire to the right side of the upper bracket;

  b. Connect the inlet and outlet water hoses SECURELY;

NOTE: *The inlet hose is a straight type, and the outlet hose is an L-type.*

  c. Install the defroster nozzles in the correct position;

  d. Connect the control cables securely. Operate the control valve and lever to check for proper operation;

  e. Be sure to bleed the cooling system

Accord

NOTE: *To remove the heater core, it is necessary to first remove the entire instrument panel and heater assemblies.*

1. Drain the cooling system.

2. Remove the steering column lower trim cover.

3. Remove the two nuts and two bolts retaining the column to the firewall support.

4. Remove the instrument wire harnesses from cabin wire harness couplers.

5. Reach behind the instrument cluster and disconnect the speedometer cable and four wiring harness connectors at rear of cluster. Pry out the lock tabs to disconnect.

6. Disconnect radio lead and antenna wire.

7. Remove the heater fan switch knob, heater lever knobs and heater control bezel. Remove heater control center panel.

1. Lever assy., parking brake
2. Knob, release
3. Spring, release knob
4. Pin, clevis
5. Switch, parking brake
6. Equalizer (w/parking brake secondary cable)
7. Pin, equalizer
8. Cable A, parking lever
9. Nut, brake adjusting
10. Spring, rear brake rod
11. Bracket, cable guide
12. Guide, cable
13. Dust seal, brake cable
14. Bolt
15. Bolt
16. Nut
17. Washer
18. Washer
19. Washer
20. Washer
21. Pin
22. Pin

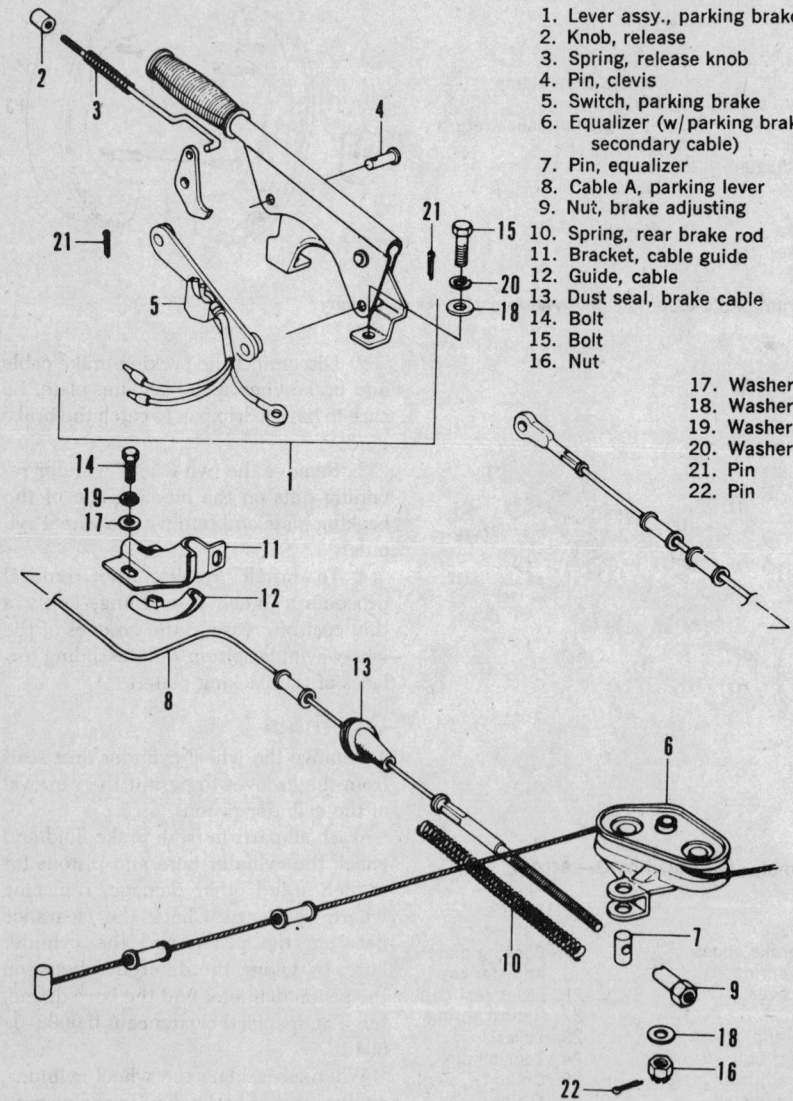

Civic parking brake assembly

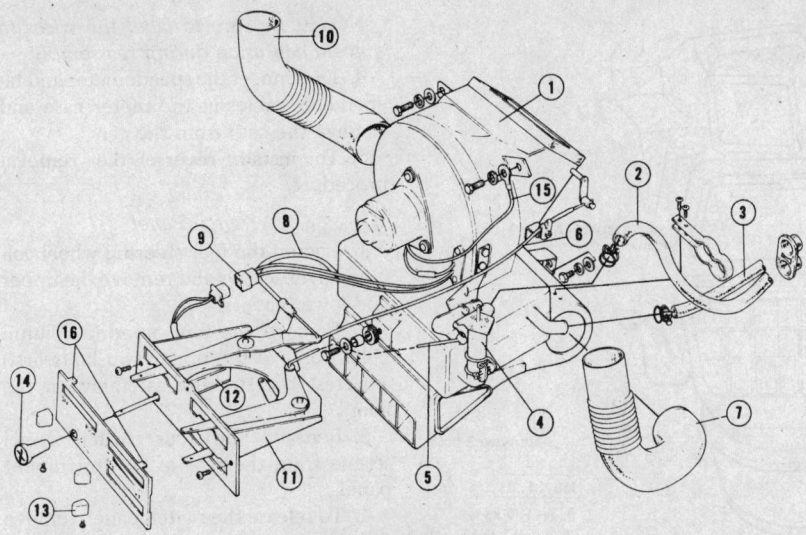

Civic heater

1. Heater assembly
2. Inlet hose
3. Outlet hose
4. Water valve
5. Temperature control rod
6. Fre-Rec control cable
7. Right defroster hose
8. Room/Def. control cable
9. Fan motor connector
10. Left defroster hose
11. Heater control assembly
12. Fan motor switch
13. Lever knob
14. Fan motor switch knob
15. Fan motor ground wire
16. Face plate retaining tabs

Disconnect cigarette lighter and blower motor leads.

8. Disconnect clock leads.

9. Remove the seven sheet metal screws retaining the instrument panel to the firewall. There are two at each end of the dash (adjacent to windshield pillar), two beneath the radio and one adjacent to the clock.

10. Pull out the instrument panel and support. Check for any wires still connected.

11. Inside the engine compartment, disconnect the two heater hoses at the firewall. Remove the nut retaining the heater unit to the firewall.

12. Disconnect the three heater control cables from the heater unit. Disconnect the cable clip from the heater valve.

13. Remove the heater unit lower mounting bolt and the right and left upper mounting bolts. Separate the blower hose from the heater.

14. Lay some towel underneath to catch residual coolant leakage. Remove the heater unit.

15. To service the heater core, separate the heater housing halves.

16. Reverse the above to install. Bleed the cooling system using the bleed bolt located near the ignition distributor.

Blower Motor

Removal and Installation
Accord

1. Remove the three lower retaining screws for the glovebox. Then, push

down and remove the glovebox. Remove the three screws for the glovebox ceiling and remove the ceiling.

2. Disconnect the fresh air control cable from the blower housing. Disconnect the blower leads.

3. Remove the three bolts retaining the blower housing to the firewall. Separate the heater duct hose from the blower housing, and remove the blower housing.

4. To service the blower motor, separate the blower housing halves.

5. Reverse the above to install.

Radio

Removal and Installation

CAUTION: *Never operate the radio without a speaker; severe damage to the output transistors will result. If the speaker must be replaced, use a speaker of the correct impedance (ohms) or else the output transistors will be damaged and require replacement.*

Civic

1. Remove the screw which holds the rear radio bracket to the back tray underneath the dash. Then remove the wing nut which holds the radio to the bracket and remove the bracket.

2. Remove the control knobs, hex nuts, and trim plate from the radio control shafts.

3. Disconnect the antenna and speaker leads, the bullet type radio fuse, and the white lead connected directly over the radio opening.

4. Drop the radio out, bottom first, through the package tray.

5. To install, reverse the removal procedure. When inserting the radio through the package tray, be sure the bottom side is up and the control shafts are facing toward the engine. Otherwise, you will not be able to position the radio properly through its opening in the dash.

Accord

1. Remove the center lower trim panel beneath the radio. Then, remove the three radio lower bracket retaining screws.

2. Pull off the radio knobs and remove the radio shaft nuts.

3. Remove the heater fan switch knob, the heater lever knobs, the heater control bezel, and the heater control center trim panel. Disconnect the cigarette lighter leads.

4. Pull out the radio from the front, and disconnect the power, speaker, and antenna leads.

5. Reverse the above to install.

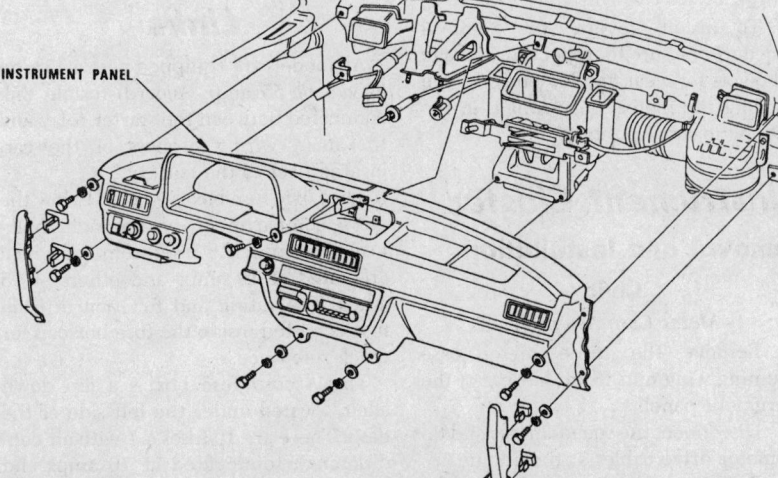

Removing Accord instrument panel

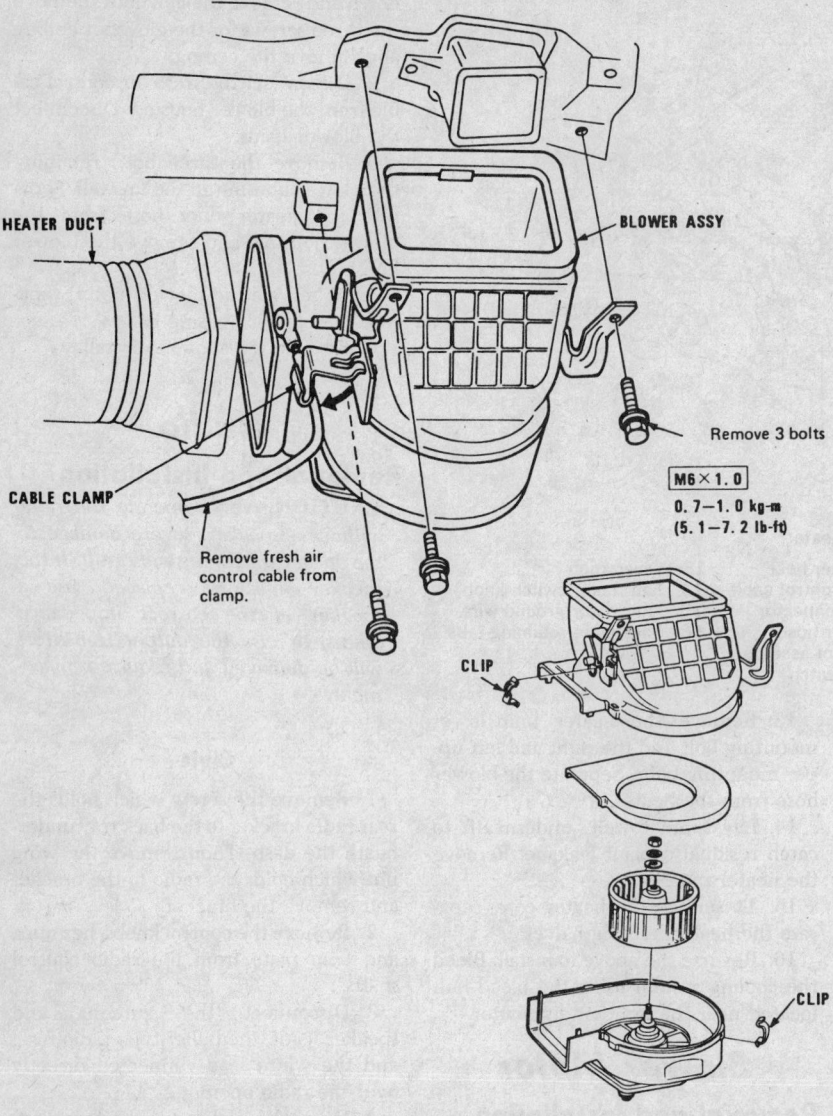

HEATER DUCT

BLOWER ASSY

Remove 3 bolts

M6×1.0
0.7—1.0 kg-m
(5.1—7.2 lb-ft)

CABLE CLAMP

Remove fresh air
control cable from
clamp.

CLIP

CLIP

Removing Accord heater blower motor

Windshield Wipers

Motor and Linkage

Removal and Installation

The wiper motor on all models is connected to the engine compartment wall, below the front windshield.

1. Remove the negative (−) cable from the battery.

2. Disconnect the motor leads at the connector.

3. Remove the motor water seal cover clamp, and the seal, from the motor.

4. Remove the special nut which holds the wiper arms to the pivot shafts and remove the arms.

5. Remove the left and right pivot nuts and push the pivots down.

6. Remove the three wiper motor mounting bolts and remove the wiper/-linkage assembly from the engine compartment.

7. Pull out the motor arm cotter pin

and separate the linkage from the motor.

8. Remove the three bracket bolts to remove the motor from its mounting bracket.

9. To install, reverse the removal procedure. Be sure to inspect the linkage and pivots for wear and looseness. When installing the motor, be sure it is in the "automatic stop" position.

Instrument Cluster

Removal and Installation

Civic

Meter Case Assembly

1. Remove the three meter case mounting wing nuts from the rear of the instrument panel.

2. Disconnect the speedometer and tachometer drive cables at the engine.

3. Pull the meter case away from the panel. Disconnect the meter wires at the connectors.

NOTE: *Be sure to label the wires to avoid confusion during reassembly.*

4. Disconnect the speedometer and tachometer cables at the meter case and remove the case from the car.

5. To install, reverse the removal procedure.

Switch Panel

1. Loosen the four steering wheel column cover screws and remove the upper and lower covers.

2. Remove the four steering column bolts (remove the upper two bolts first) and rest the steering assembly on the floor.

3. Remove the four switch panel screws from the rear of the instrument panel.

4. To release the switch panel, remove the switches in the following manner:

a. Remove the light switch by prying the cover off the front of the knob. Pinch the retaining tabs together and pull off the knob;

b. Remove the wiper switch by pushing the knob in and turning counterclockwise. Then remove the retaining nut;

c. Remove the choke knob by loosening the set screw. Then remove the retaining nut.

5. To install, reverse the removal procedure.

Accord

Meter Case

1. Disconnect the negative battery cable.

2. Follow steps 2–5 under "Accord Heater Removal".

3. Remove the two screws under the meter case (near the steering column support studs) and pull out the meter case

4. Reverse the above to install.

Fuses and Fusible Links

All models are equipped with a 45 amp (Civic) or 55 amp (Accord) fusible link connected between the starter relay and the main wiring harness of the car, located next to the battery.

The Civic fuse box is located below the glove compartment, on the right bulkhead. It contains 8 fuses, some of which are rated at 10 amps and others at 15 amps. The rating and function of each fuse is posted inside the fuse box cap for quick reference.

The Accord fuse box is a flip down affair, located under the left side of the dash. There are 10 fuses (11 with air conditioning), some rated at 10 amps and others at 15 amps. The rating and function of each fuse is posted inside the fuse box.

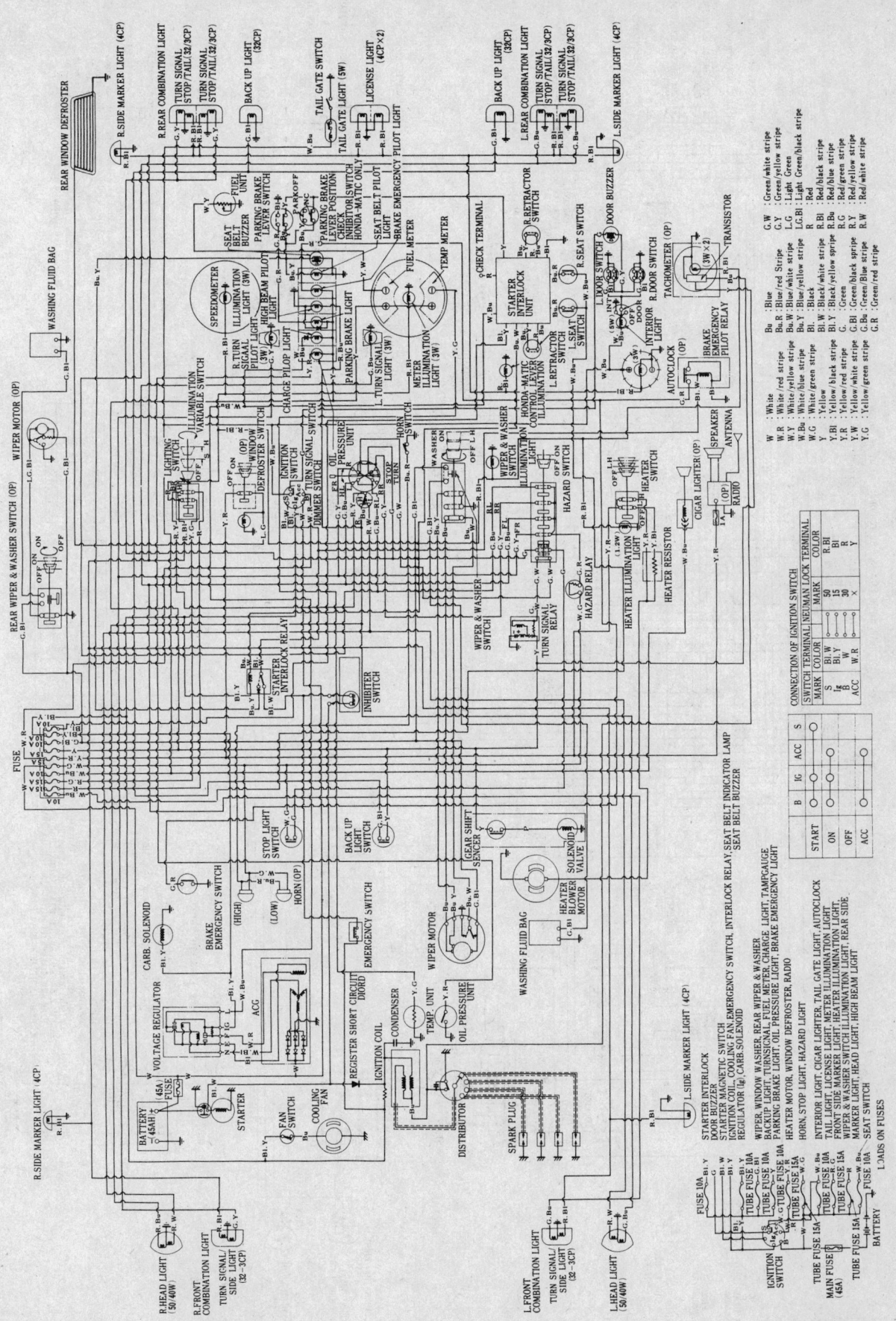

1974 Honda Civic

Wiring Circuits

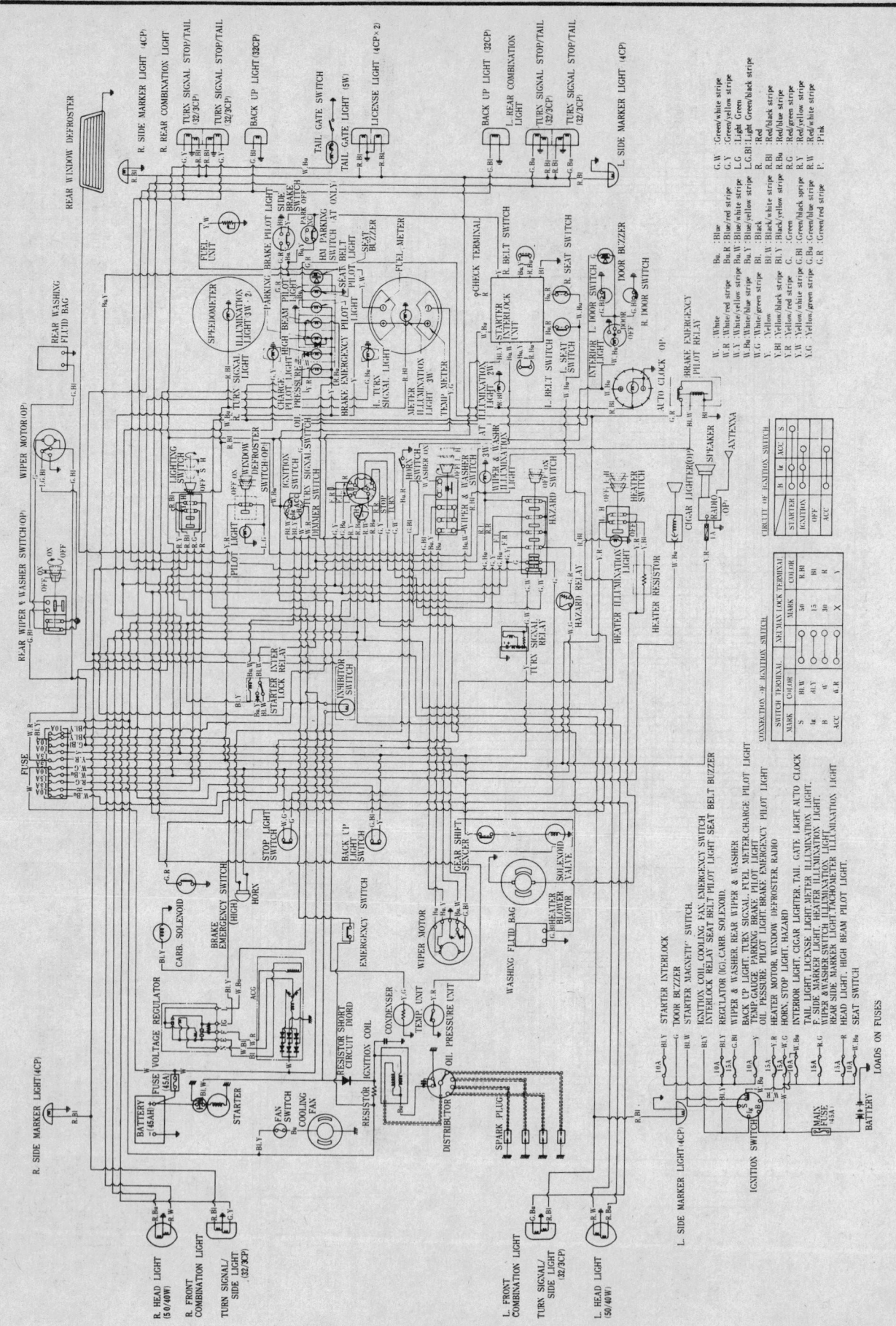

1975 Honda Civic (VIN 3300001-3319377)

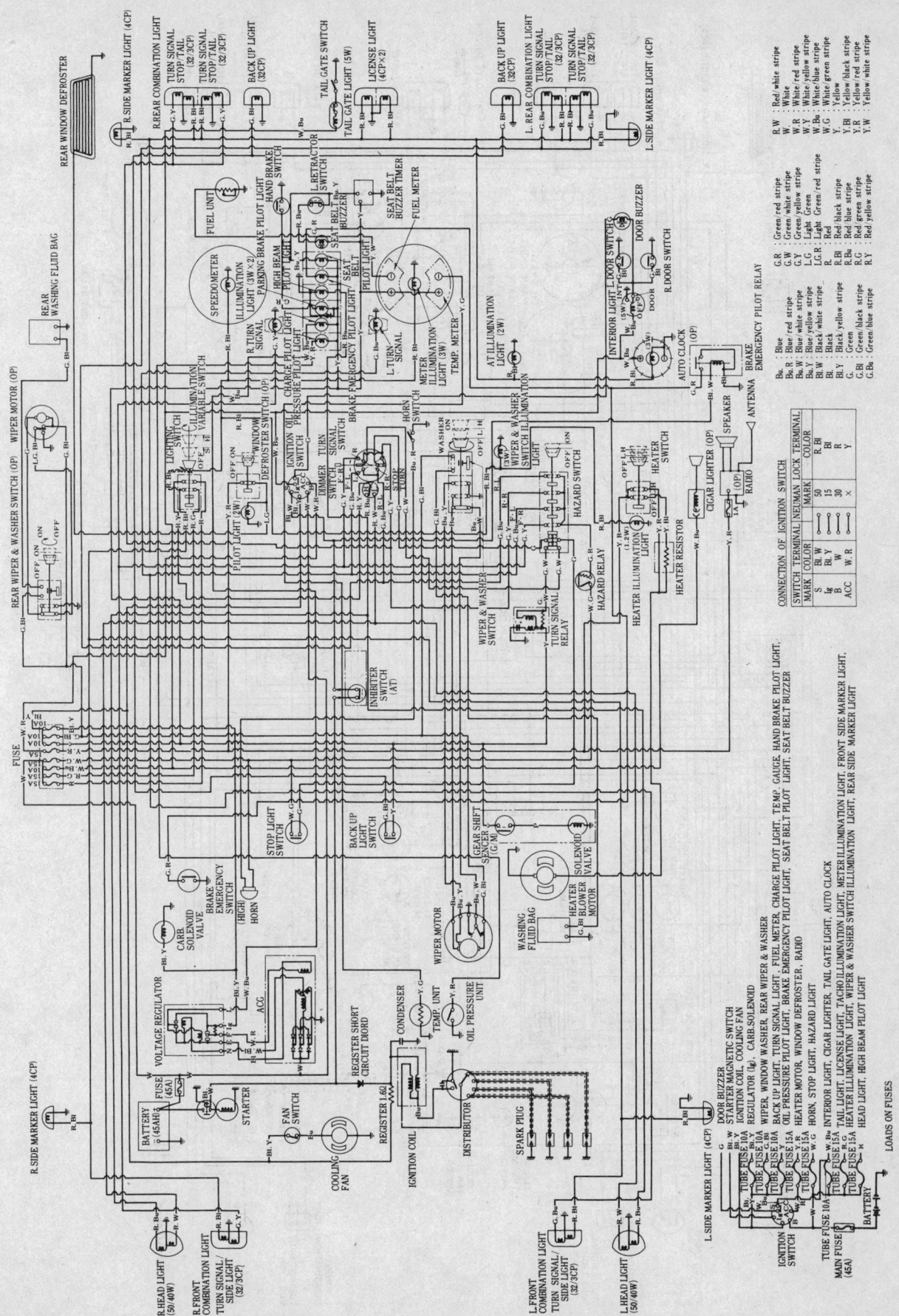

1975 Honda Civic (from VIN 3319378)

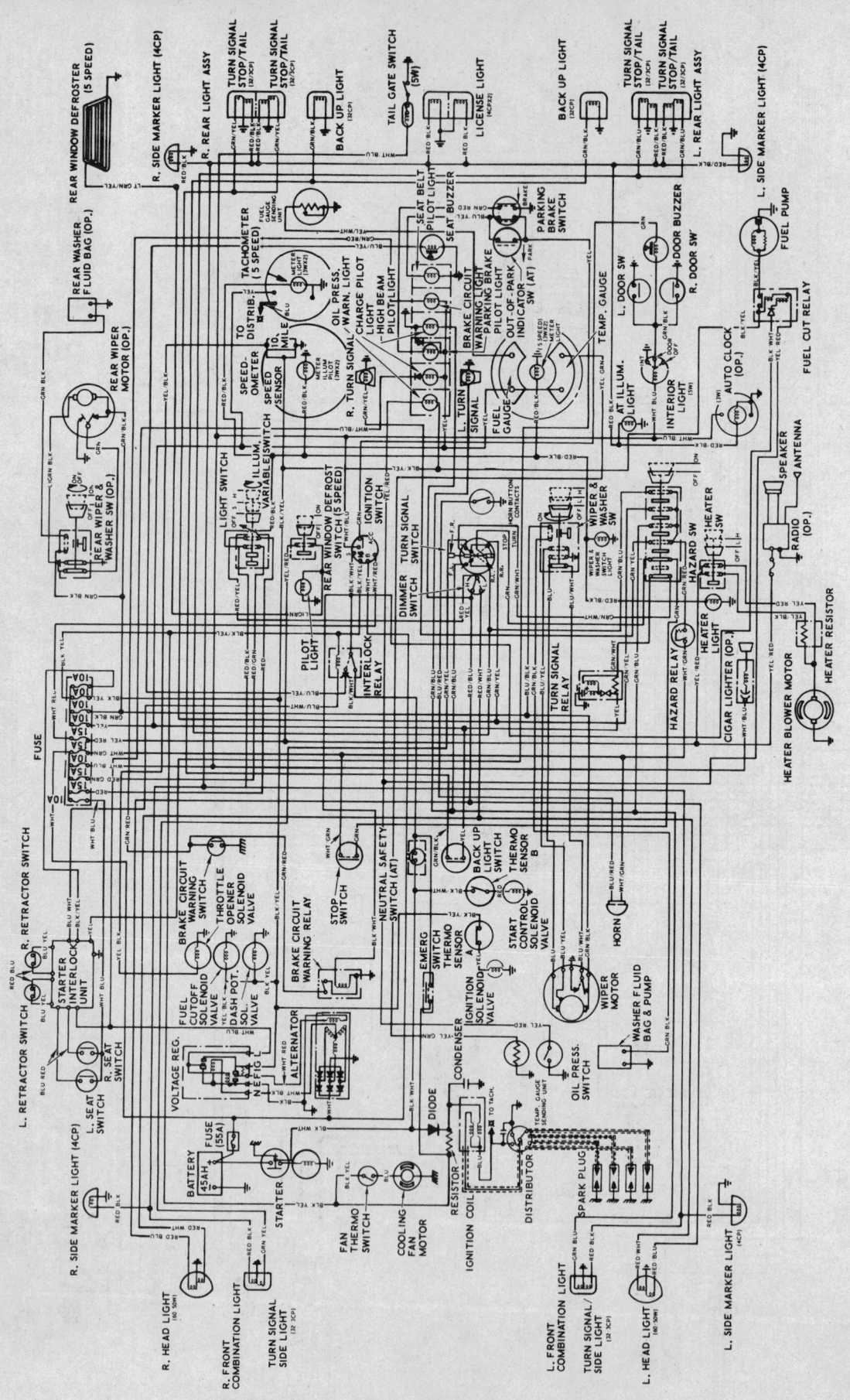

Early 1975 Honda CVCC

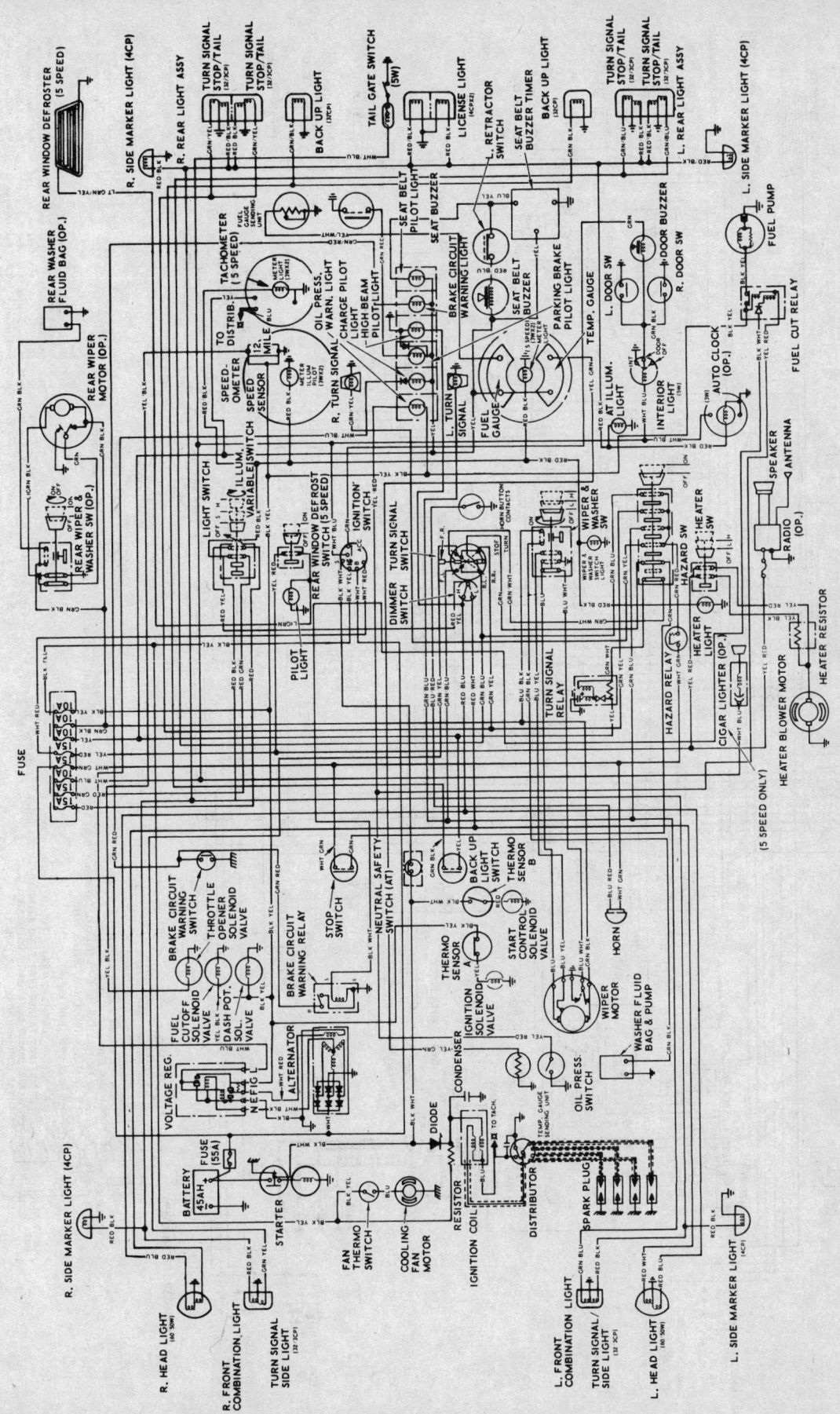

Late 1975 Honda CVCC

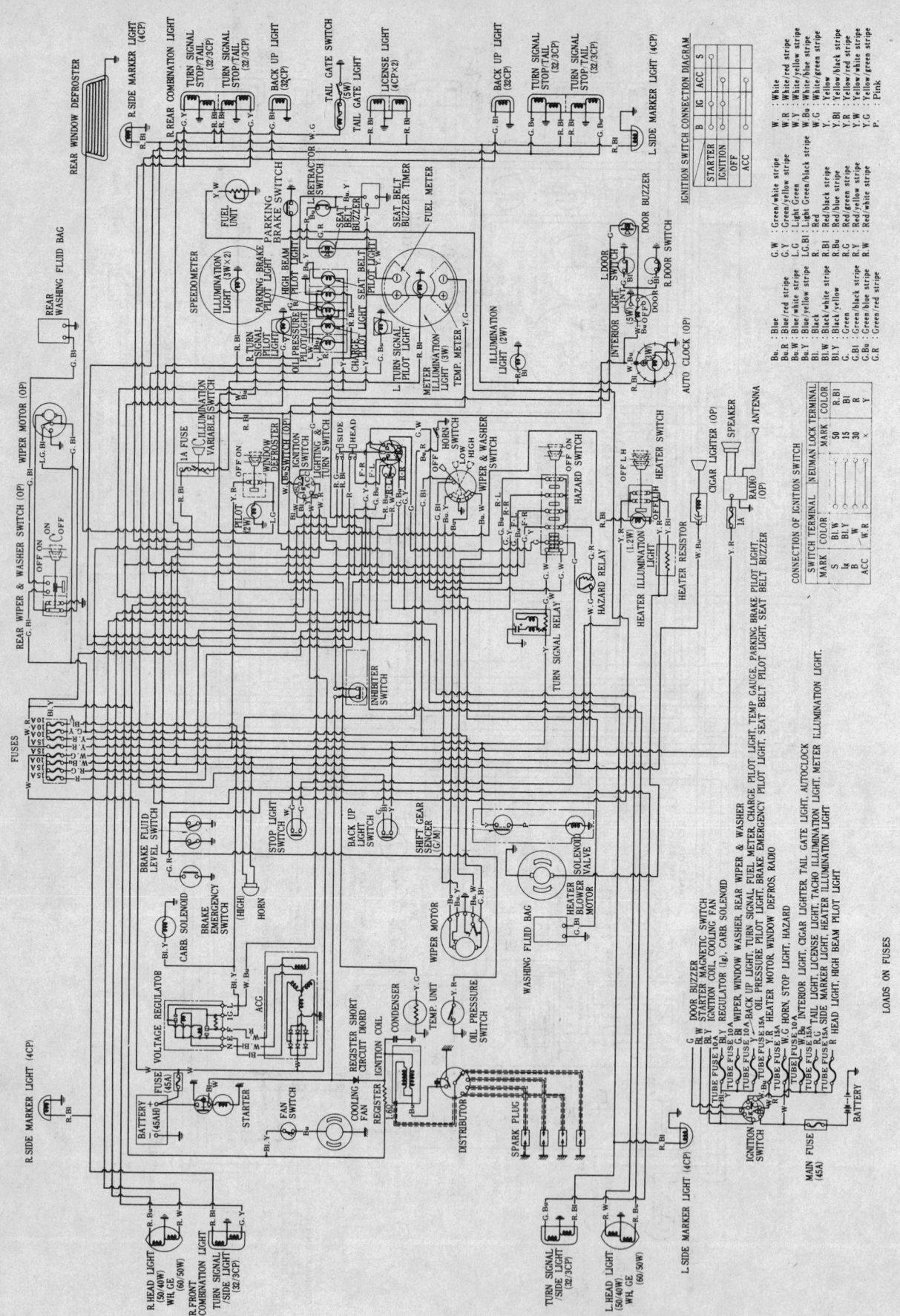

1976 Honda Civic

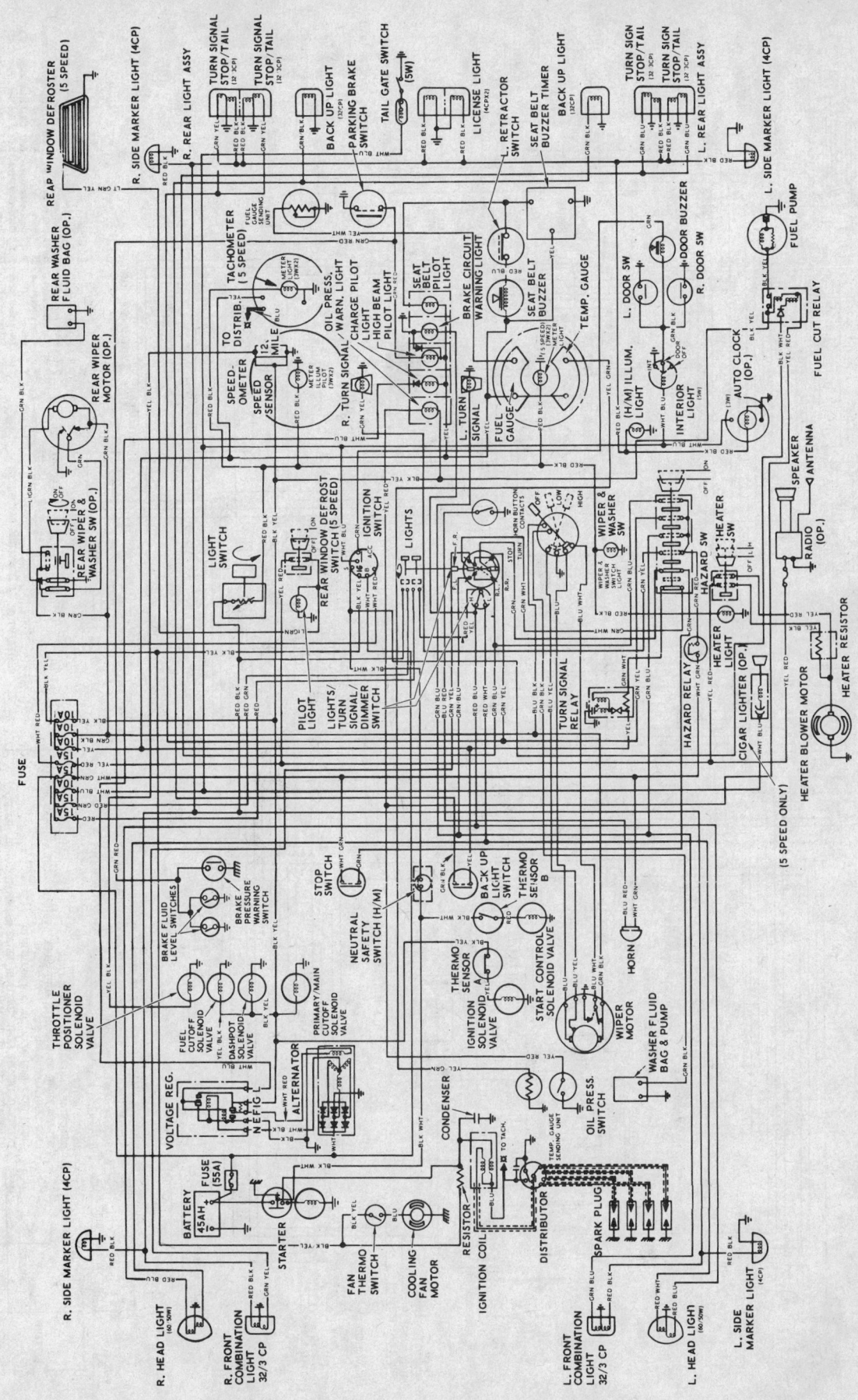

1976 Honda CVCC

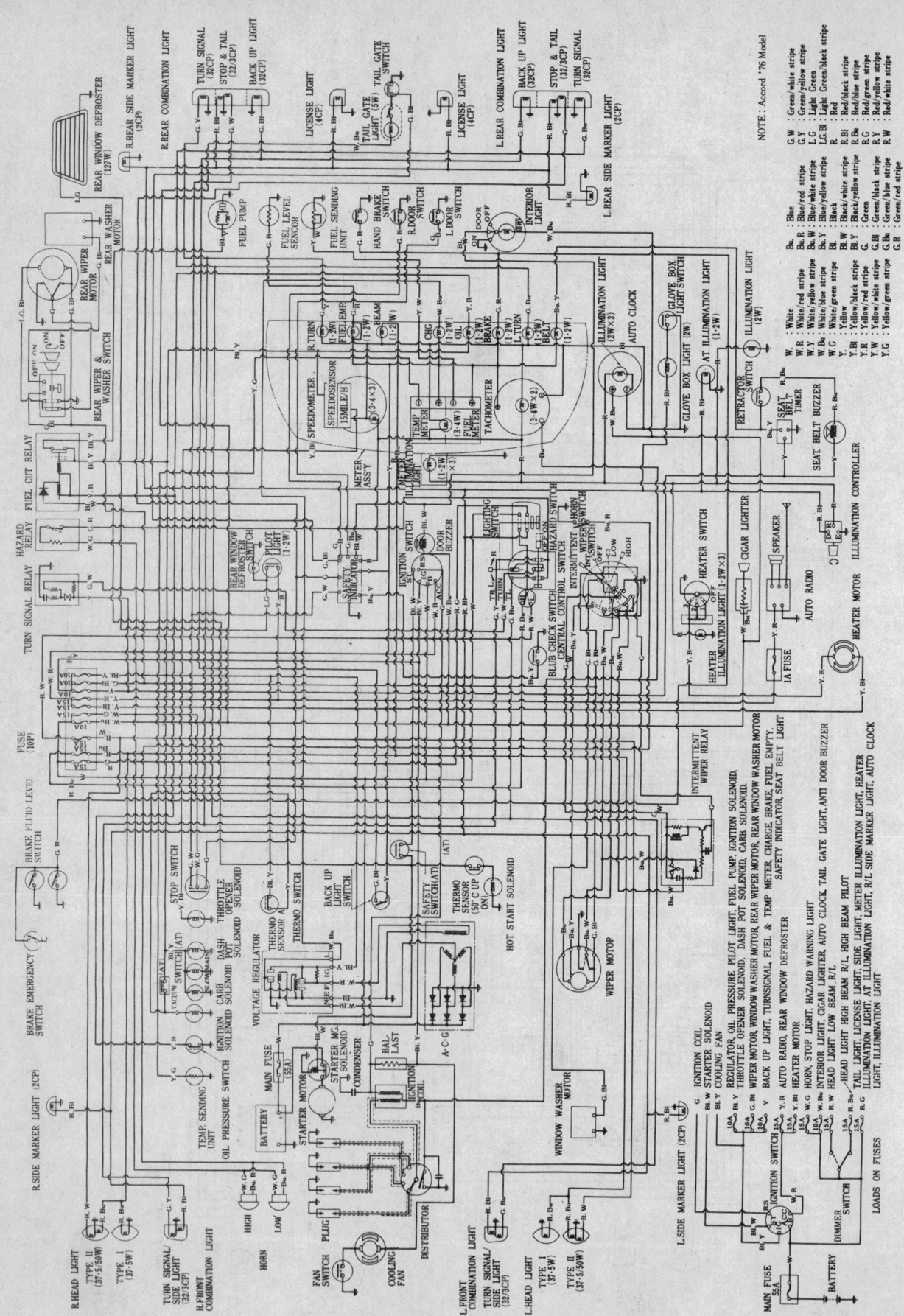

1976 Honda Accord

SPECIFICATIONS

INTRODUCTION

The Chevrolet Light Utility Vehicle (LUV) is exactly what the name implies. The LUV is a ½ ton mini-pickup truck, powered by a 4 cylinder engine with a 4-speed or automatic transmission

The LUV was introduced in 1972 (model year). Designed to compete with the Japanese imports, the LUV is made by a Japanese automobile manufacturer, Izuzu Motors of Tokyo, Japan, at Izuzu's Fujisawa plant.

MODEL IDENTIFICATION

There is only one model of the Chevy LUV: ½ ton conventional design powered by a water-cooled 110.8 cu in. (18 17 cc) 4 cylinder inline single over head camshaft gasoline engine with a 102.4 in. wheelbase and a 6 ft cargo bed. A Mikado version of the LUV is an added-on trim package.

Chevrolet LUV pickup

SERIAL NUMBER IDENTIFICATION

Vehicle

The chassis number plate is attached to the left-side rear door pillar within the cab. It has the date of manufacture and chassis number stamped on its face.

Engine

The engine number is stamped on the right upper center part of the cylinder block, adjacent to the distributor.

Location of the chassis number plate on the left-side rear door pillar

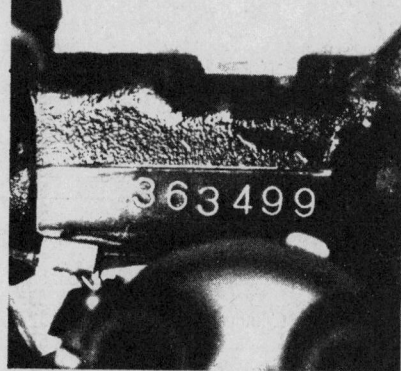

Location of the engine identification number on the center of the right-side of the cylinder block

GENERAL ENGINE SPECIFICATIONS

Year	Engine Displacement cu in. (cc)	Carb Type	Advertised Horsepower (@ rpm)	Advertised Torque @ rpm (ft lbs)	Bore and Stroke (in.)	Advertised Compression Ratio	Oil Pressure (psi)
1972-75	110.8 (1817)	2-bbl	75 @ 5000	88 @ 3000	3.31 x 3.23	8.2:1	57
1976-77	110.8 (1817)	2-bbl	80 @ 4800	95 @ 3000	3.31 x 3.23	8.5:1	64

CAPACITIES

Year	Engine No. Cyl. Displacement cu in. (cc)	Engine Crankcase (qts) With Filter	Engine Crankcase (qts) Without Filter	Transmission Pts to Refill After Draining 4-Speed	Transmission After Draining Auto	Drive Axle (pts)	Gas Tank (gals)	Cooling System (qts) With Heater	Cooling System (qts) Without Heater
1972-1977	4-110.8 (1817 cc.)	5.3	4.8	2.6	6	2.7	10①	6.4	5.3

① 13.2 gals. in 1974-77

TUNE-UP SPECIFICATIONS

When analyzing compression results, look for uniformity among cylinders, rather than specific pressures.

| Year | Engine No. Cyl. Displacement cu in. (cc) | Spark Plugs | | Distributor | | Ignition Timing (deg) | | Intake Valve Opens (deg) | Fuel Pump Pressure (psi) | Idle Speed (rpm) | | Valve Clearance (in.) | |
		Type	Gap (in.)	Point Dwell (deg)	Point Gap (in.)	MT	AT			MT	AT	In	Ex
1972-74	4-110.8 (1817)	BP-6ES④	0.030 ④	49-55	②	③	—	31	3-4.5	⑤	—	0.004	0.006
1975	4-110.8 (1817)	BP-6ES	0.030	49-55	0.018-0.022	12B	—	31	3-4.5	900	—	0.004	0.006
1976-77	4-110.8 (1817)	BPR-6ES	0.030	47-57	0.016-0.020	6B	6B	21	3-4.5	900	900	0.006	0.010

① See tune-up sticker in the engine compartment
② On 1972 and 1973 dual point distributor: Retarded points—0.016-0.024 in.; Advanced points—0.018-0.022 in. On 1974 single point distributor: 0.016-0.024 in.
③ 8°B @ 700 rpm—1972-73; 12°B @ 700 rpm—1974
④ Or AC-R42T with 0.035 in. gap—1972, or AC-44XLS with 0.035 in. gap—1974
⑤ 1,000 rpm—1972; 700 rpm—1973; 700 rpm w/o AC and 900 rpm w/AC—1974
— Not applicable
NOTE: The underhood specifications sticker often reflects tune-up specification changes made in production. Sticker figures must be used if they disagree with those in this chart.

FIRING ORDER

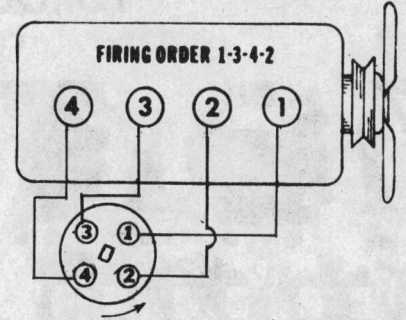

FIRING ORDER 1-3-4-2

CRANKSHAFT AND CONNECTING ROD SPECIFICATIONS
(All measurements given in in.)

| Year | Engine Displacement cu in. (cc) | Crankshaft | | | | Connecting Rod | | |
		Main Brg Journal Dia	Main Brg Oil Clearance	Shaft End-Play	Thrust on No.	Journal Dia	Oil Clearance	Side Clearance
1972-76	110.8 (1817)	2.2016-2.2022	0.0015-0.0047	0.0059-0.0120	3	1.9262-1.9268	0.0020-0.0047	0.0079-0.0130
1977	110.8 (1817)	2.2030-2.2050	0.0008-0.0025	0.0024-0.0094	3	1.8799-1.9290	0.0007-0.0030	0.0079-0.0130

VALVE SPECIFICATIONS

| Year | Engine Displacement cu in. (cc) | Seat Angle (deg) | Face (deg) Angle | Spring Test Pressure (lbs @ in.) | | Free Length (in.) | | Stem-to-Guide Clearance (in.) | | Stem Diameter (in.) | |
				Outer	Inner	Outer	Inner	Intake	Exhaust	Intake	Exhaust
1972-1977	110.8 (1817)	45	45	41.8-50.1 @ 1.58	15.4-19.0 @ 1.50	2.05-1.99	1.78-1.73	.0016-.0079	.0020-.0098	.3150-.3102	.3150-.3091

TORQUE SPECIFICATIONS
(All readings in ft lbs unless noted)

Year	Engine Displacement cu in. (cc)	Cylinder Head Bolts	Rod Bearing Bolts	Main Bearing Bolts	Crankshaft Pulley Bolt	Flywheel -to- Crankshaft Bolts
1972-77	11.08 (1817)	①	43	72	50	36②

① On 1972 models, tighten to 43 ft lbs first, then completely loosen and retighten to 58 ft lbs; On 1973 models, tighten, in sequence to 60 ft lbs; On 1974-75 models, tighten to 43 ft lbs first, then loosen completely and retighten 1, 2, 3, and 6 to 70 ft lbs, and the remaining bolts to 60 ft lbs.
On 1976-77 models, tighten to 61 ft lbs first, then retighten to 72 ft lbs.

② 69 ft. lbs in 1974-77

TORQUE SEQUENCES
Cylinder Head

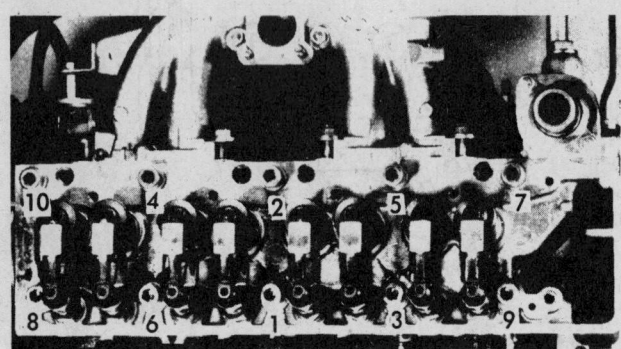

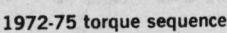

1972-75 torque sequence

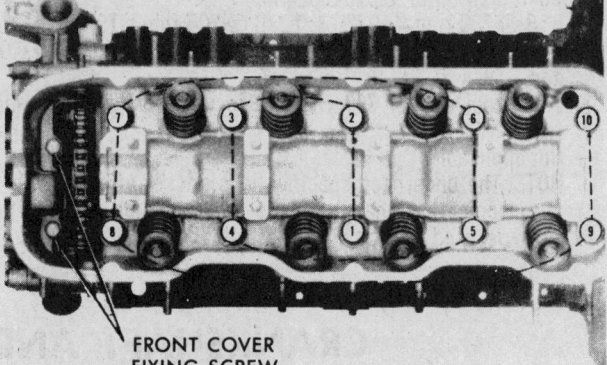

FRONT COVER
FIXING SCREW

1976-77 torque sequence

PISTON AND RING SPECIFICATIONS
All measurements in inches

Year	Engine Displacement Cu In. (cc)	Piston Clearance	RING GAP			RING SIDE CLEARANCE		
			Top Compression	Bottom Compression	Oil Control	Top Compression	Bottom Compression	Oil Control
1972-77	110.8 (1817)	0.0018-0.0026	0.008-0.016	0.008-0.016	0.012-①0.039	0.0012-0.0028	0.0012-0.0028	0.0008-0.0024

① 1977: .008-.035

BATTERY AND STARTER SPECIFICATIONS
All cars use 12 volt, negative ground electrical systems

Year	Model	Battery Amp Hour Capacity	Starter						Brush Spring Tension (oz)	Min. Brush Length (in.)
			Lock Test			No Load Test				
			Amps	Volts	Torque (ft/lbs)	Amps	Volts	RPM		
1972-77	All	50	330 or less	5.1	5:8	60 or less	12	6000 or more	56	0.49①

① 1977: 0.47

ALTERNATOR AND REGULATOR SPECIFICATIONS

| Year | ALTERNATOR | | | | REGULATOR | | | | | |
| | Part No. | Field Current @ 12 V (amps) | Output (amps.) | Part No. | Field Relay | | Regulator | | | |
					Core Gap (in.)	Point Gap (in.)	Core Gap (in.)	Point Gap (in.)	Volts @ 68°F
1972-76	LT 130-83	1.2-1.7	30	TL 12 66	.032-.039	.016-.024	.024-.039	.012-.016	13.5-14.5
1977	LT 135-30	N/A	35	TL 12 87	.032-.039	.016-.024	.024-.039	.012-.016	13.8-14.8

BRAKE SPECIFICATIONS
All measurements given are (in.) unless noted

Year	Model	Lug Nut Torque (ft/lb)	Master Cylinder Bore	Brake Disc Minimum Thickness	Brake Disc Maximum Run-Out	Brake Drum Diameter	Brake Drum Max. Machine O/S	Max. Wear Limit	Min Lining Front	Min Lining Rear
1972-77	All	65	0.875	0.668 (after refinishing) 0.653 (discard) ①	②	10.00	10.059	10.079	0.236	0.059

① Discard dimension stamped into disc.
② Maximum run-out—0.005 in. Rate of change must not exceed 0.001 in. in 30°
NOTE: Minimum lining thickness is as recommended by the manufacturer. Due to variations in state inspection regulations, the minimum allowable thickness may be different than recommended by the manufacturer.

WHEEL ALIGNMENT SPECIFICATIONS

Year	Model	CASTER Range (deg)	CASTER Preferred Setting (deg)	CAMBER Range (deg)	CAMBER Preferred Setting (deg)	Toe-in (in.)	Steering Axis Inclination (deg)
1972-77	All	0 to 1P	½P①	½P to 1½P	1P②	+ ⅛ ± 1/16③	7

① Caster should not vary more than ½° from side-to-side
② Camber should not vary more than ½° from side-to-side
③ Always adjust the toe-in after adjusting caster and camber

TUNE-UP PROCEDURES

Spark Plugs

Removal

1. Remove the wire from the end of the spark plug by grasping the wire by the rubber boot. If the boot sticks to the plug, remove it by twisting and pulling at the same time. Do not pull the wire itself or you will most certainly damage the delicate carbon core.

2. Use a 13/16 in spark plug socket to loosen all of the plugs about two turns.

3. If compressed air is available, blow off the area around the spark plug holes. Otherwise, use a rag or a brush to clean the area. Be careful not to allow any foreign material to drop into the spark plug holes.

4. Remove the plugs by unscrewing them the rest of the way from the engine.

Inspection

Check the plugs for deposits and wear. If they are not going to be replaced, clean the plugs thoroughly. Remember that any kind of deposit will decrease the efficiency of the plug. Plugs can be cleaned on a spark plug cleaning machine, or you can do an acceptable job of cleaning with a stiff brush.

Check the spark plug gap before installation. The ground electrode must be parallel to the center electrode and the specified size wire gauge should pass through the gap with a slight drag. If the electrodes are worn, it is possible to file them level.

Installation

1. Insert the plugs in the spark plug hole and tighten them hand-tight. Take care not to cross-thread them.

2. Tighten the plugs to 18–25 ft lbs.

3. Install the spark plug wires on their plugs. Make sure that each wire is firmly connected to each plug.

Breaker Points and Condenser

Never replace the points without replacing the condenser and vice versa.

Remember that a change in the point gap or dwell also changes the ignition timing. Therefore, if the points are adjusted, you must also correct the ignition timing.

NOTE: See "Emission Controls" for an explanation of the dual point distributor and how it works.

Inspection of the Points

1. Disconnect the high-tension wire from the top of the distributor.

2. Remove the distributor cap by prying off the spring clips on the sides of the cap.

3. Remove the rotor from the distributor shaft by pulling it straight up. Examine the condition of the rotor. If it is cracked or the metal tip is excessively worn or burned, it should be replaced. Clean the metal tip with fine emery paper.

4. Pry open the contacts of the points with a screwdriver and check the condition of the contacts. If they are excessively worn, burned or pitted, they should be replaced.

5. If the points are in good condition, adjust them and replace the rotor and the distributor cap. If the points need to be replaced, follow the replacement procedure given below.

Removal and Installation

NOTE: *Dual point distributors used in 1972–73 LUVs are serviced in a similar manner as single point units as far as replacement of the breaker points is concerned.*

1. Remove the coil high-tension wire from top of the distributor cap. Remove the distributor cap from the distributor and place it out of the way.

2. Loosen the screw that holds the condenser lead to the body of the breaker points and remove the condenser lead from the points.

3. Remove the screw that holds and grounds the condenser to the distributor body. Remove the condenser from the distributor and discard it.

4. Remove the points assembly attaching screws and adjustment lockscrews. A screwdriver with a holding mechanism will come in handy here, so that you don't drop a screw into the distributor and have to remove the entire distributor to retrieve it.

5. Remove the points by lifting them

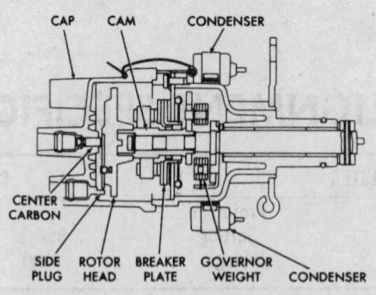

CAP   CAM   CONDENSER

CENTER CARBON

SIDE PLUG   ROTOR HEAD   BREAKER PLATE   GOVERNOR WEIGHT   CONDENSER

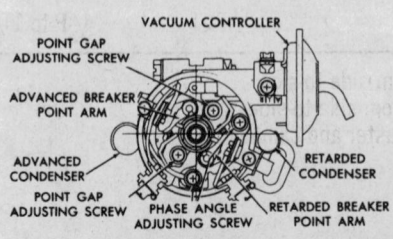

VACUUM CONTROLLER

POINT GAP ADJUSTING SCREW

ADVANCED BREAKER POINT ARM

ADVANCED CONDENSER

RETARDED CONDENSER

POINT GAP ADJUSTING SCREW   PHASE ANGLE ADJUSTING SCREW   RETARDED BREAKER POINT ARM

Dual point distributor

straight up and off the locating dowel on the plate. Wipe off the cam and apply new cam lubricant. Discard the old set of points.

6. Slip the new set of points onto the locating dowel and install the screws that hold the assembly onto the plate. Do not tighten them all the way.

7. Attach the new condenser to the plate with the ground screw.

8. Attach the condenser lead to the points at the proper place.

9. Apply a small amount of cam lubricant to the shaft where the rubbing block of the points touches.

Adjustment of the Breaker Points with a Feeler Gauge

Single Point Distributor

1. If the contact points of the assembly are not parallel, bend the stationary contact so that they make contact across the entire surface of the contacts. Bend only the stationary bracket part of the point assembly; not the moveable contact.

2. Turn the engine until the rubbing block of the points is on one of the high points of the distributor cam. You can do this by either turning the ignition switch to the start position and releasing it quickly ("bumping" the engine) or by using a wrench on the bolt that holds the crankshaft pulley to the crankshaft.

3. Place the correct size feeler gauge between the contacts. Make sure it is parallel with the contact surfaces.

4. With your free hand, insert a screwdriver into the notch provided for adjustment or into the eccentric adjusting screw, then twist the screwdriver to either increase or decrease the gap to the proper setting.

5. Tighten the adjustment lockscrew and recheck the contact gap to make sure that it didn't change when the lockscrew was tightened.

6. Replace the rotor and distributor cap, and the high-tension wire that connects the top of the distributor and the coil. Make sure that the rotor is firmly seated all the way onto the distributor shaft and that the tab of the rotor is aligned with notch in the shaft. Align the tab in the base of the distributor cap with the notch in the distributor body. Make sure that the cap is firmly seated on the distributor and that the retainer springs are in place. Make sure that the end of the high-tension wire is firmly placed in the top of the distributor and the coil.

Dual Point Distributor

The two sets of breaker points are adjusted with a feeler gauge in the same manner as those in a single point distributor. Check the "Tune-Up Specifications" chart for the correct setting for either set of points; they are not the same.

Adjustment of the Breaker Points with a Dwell Meter

Single Point Distributor

1. Adjust the points with a feeler gauge as previously described.

2. Connect the dwell meter to the ignition circuit as according to the manufacturer's instructions. One lead of the meter is connected to a ground and the other lead is connected to the distributor post on the coil. An adapter is usually provided for this purpose.

3. If the dwell meter has a set line on it, adjust the meter to zero the indicator.

4. Start the engine.

NOTE: *Be careful when working on any vehicle while the engine is running. Make sure that the transmission is in Neutral and that the parking brake is applied. Keep hands, clothing, tools and the wires of the test instruments clear of the rotating fan blades.*

5. Observe the reading on the dwell meter. If the reading is within the specified range, turn off the engine and remove the dwell meter.

NOTE: *If the meter does not have a scale for 4 cylinder engines, multiply the 8 cylinder reading by two.*

6. If the reading is above the specified range, the breaker point gap is too small. If the reading is below the specified range, the gap is too large. In either case, the engine must be stopped and the gap adjusted in the manner previously covered.

After making the adjustment, start the engine and check the reading on the dwell meter. When the correct reading is obtained, disconnect the dwell meter.

7. Check the adjustment of the ignition timing.

Dual Point Distributor

The breaker point dwell is set with a dwell meter in the same manner as for a single point distributor. However, the retard set of points is deenergized at curb idle and it will be necessary to energize the retard set of points in order to get a reading on a dwell meter. After adjusting the dwell of the advance set of points at curb idle speed, have an assistant depress the accelerator pedal at least 7° or move the throttle linkage enough to energize the accelerator switch, opening the accelerator relay-to-distributor relay circuit, thus energizing the retard set of breaker points, and getting retard breaker point dwell reading.

Ignition Timing

The timing marks are located at the front crankshaft pulley and consist of a pointer attached to the engine block and graduations on the crankshaft pulley.

1. Set the dwell angle to the proper specification.

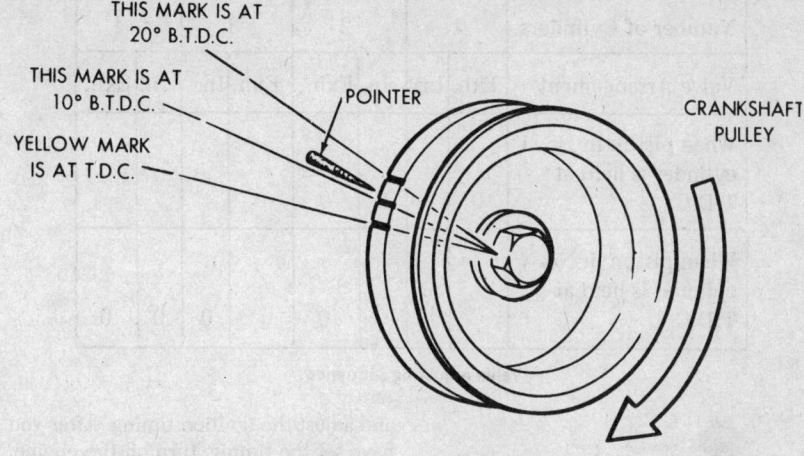

Timing marks—1972-75

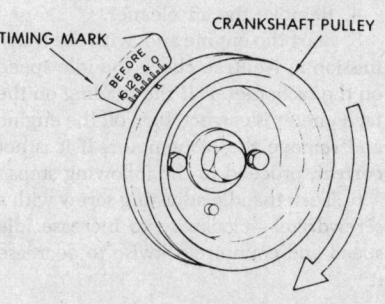

1976-77 timing marks

2. Locate the timing marks on the crankshaft pulley and the front of the engine.

3. Clean off the timing marks, so that you can see them.

4. Use chalk or white paint to color the mark on the crankshaft pulley that will indicate the correct timing, when aligned with the pointer. It is also helpful to mark the tip of the pointer with a small dab of color.

5. Attach a tachometer to the engine.

6. Attach a timing light to the engine according to the manufacturer's instructions. If the timing light has three wires, one, usually green or blue, is attached to the No. 1 spark plug with an adapter. The other wires are connected to the battery. The red wire goes to the positive side of the battery and the black wire is connected to the negative terminal of the battery.

7. Disconnect the vacuum line to the distributor at the distributor and plug the vacuum line. A golf tee does a good job.

8. Check to make sure that all of the wires clear the fan and then start the engine.

9. Adjust the idle to the correct setting.

10. Aim the timing light at the timing marks. If the marks that you put on the pulley and the engine are aligned when the light flashes, the timing is correct. Turn off the engine and remove the tachometer and the timing light. If the marks are not in alignment, proceed with

the following steps.

11. Turn off the engine.

12. Loosen the distributor lockbolt just enough so that the distributor can be turned with a little effort.

13. Start the engine. Keep the wires of the timing light clear of the fan.

14. With the timing light aimed at the pulley and the marks on the engine, turn the distributor in the direction of rotor rotation to retard the spark, and in the opposite direction of the rotor rotation to advance the spark. Align the marks on the pulley and the engine with the flashes of the timing light.

Valve Lash

NOTE: *While all valve adjustments must be made as accurately as possible, it is better to have the valve adjustment slightly loose than slightly tight, as a burned valve may result from overly tight adjustments.*

Adjustment

NOTE: *The valves are adjusted with the engine cold.*

1. Make sure that the cylinder head and camshaft retaining bolts are tightened to the proper torque.

2. Remove the camshaft carrier sidecover.

3. Turn the crankshaft with a wrench on the front pulley attaching bolt or by "bumping" the engine with the starter until the No. 1 piston is at TDC of the compression stroke. You can tell when the piston is coming up on the compression stroke by removing the spark plug and placing your thumb over the hole and you will feel air being forced out of the spark plug hole past your thumb. Stop turning the crankshaft when the TDC timing mark on the crankshaft pulley is directly aligned with the timing mark pointer.

4. With the No. 1 piston at TDC of the compression stroke, check the clearance between the rocker arm and the cam-

Number of Cylinders	1		2		3		4	
Valve Arrangement	Exh.	In.	In.	Exh.	Exh.	In.	In.	Exh.
When piston in No. 1 cylinder is held at T.D.C.	0	0	0		0			
When piston in No. 4 cylinder is held at T.D.C.				0		0	0	0

Valve adjusting sequence

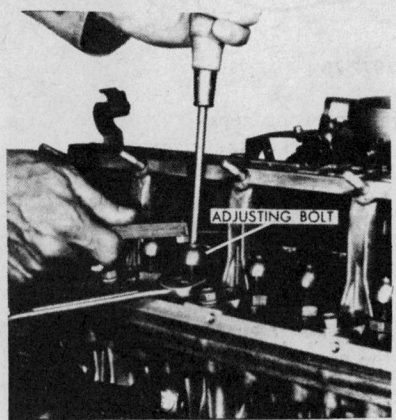

Adjusting the valves. The feeler gauge is placed between the rocker arm and the camshaft lobe

shaft with the proper thickness feeler gauge on Nos. 1 and 2, intake valves and Nos. 1 and 3 exhaust valves.

5. Adjust the clearance by loosening the locknut with an open-end wrench, turning the adjusting screw with a phillips head screwdriver and retightening the locknut. The proper thickness feeler gauge should pass between the camshaft and the rocker with a slight drag when the clearance is correct.

6. Turn the crankshaft one full turn to position the No. 4 piston at TDC of its compression stroke. Adjust the remaining valves: Nos. 2 and 4 exhaust and Nos. 3 and 4 intake in the same manner as outlined in Step 5.

7. Install the camshaft carrier side-cover.

Carburetor

This section contains only tune-up adjustment procedures for carburetors. Descriptions, adjustments, and overhaul procedures for carburetors can be found in the "Fuel System" section.

Idle Speed and Mixture Adjustment

1. Start the engine and run it until it reaches operating temperature.

2. If it hasn't already been done, check

and adjust the ignition timing. After you have set the timing, turn off the engine.

3. Attach a tachometer to the engine.

4. Remove the air cleaner.

5. Start the engine and, with the transmission in Neutral, check the idle speed on the tachometer. If the reading on the tachometer is correct, turn off the engine and remove the tachometer. If it is not correct, proceed to the following steps.

6. Turn the idle adjusting screw with a screwdriver—clockwise to increase idle speed and counterclockwise to decrease it.

7. If the vehicle is equipped with air conditioning:

1. Turn on the AC to maximum cold and high blower. Disconnect the vacuum line to the air cleaner housing air compensator and plug the inlet manifold;

b. Open the throttle approximately 1/3 and allow the throttle to close. This will allow the speed-up solenoid to reach full travel;

c. Adjust the speed-up controller adjusting screw to set the idle speed to 900 rpm;

d. Open the throttle about 1/3 and allow it to close. Read the idle rpm. If it is not at 900 rpm, repeat step c until the correct reading is obtained. Shut off the engine.

8. Turn the mixture adjusting screw all the way. Seat the needle tip *lightly* to avoid damaging the tip. Back the screw out 3½ turns.

9. Start the engine. Turn the mixture screw out until engine rpm starts to drop due to an overly rich mixture.

10. Turn the screw in past the starting point until the engine rpm start to drop because of a too lean mixture.

11. Turn the mixture screw back out to the point midway between the two extreme positions where the engine began losing rpm to achieve the fastest and smoothest idle.

12. Adjust the curb idle speed to the proper specification.

13. Reconnect the air cleaner hot idle compensator vacuum line.

Distributor

Removal and Installation

1. Remove the high-tension wires from the distributor cap terminal towers, noting their positions to assure correct reassembly.

2. Remove the primary lead from the coil terminal.

3. Disconnect the vacuum line.

4. Unlatch the two distributor cap retaining clips and remove the distributor cap.

5. Note the position of the rotor in relation to the base. Scribe a mark on the base of the distributor and on the engine block to facilitate reinstallation. Align the marks with the direction the metal tip of the rotor is pointing.

6. Remove the bolt which holds the distributor to the engine.

7. Lift the distributor assembly from the engine.

To install:

8. Insert the distributor into the engine. Line up the mark on the distributor and the one on the engine with the metal tip of the rotor. Make sure that the vacuum advance diaphragm is pointed in the same direction as it was pointed originally. This will be done automatically if the marks on the engine and the distributor are lined up with the rotor.

9. Install the distributor hold-down bolt and clamp. Leave the screw loose enough so that you can move the distributor with heavy hand pressure.

10. Connect the primary wire to the coil. Install the distributor cap on the distributor housing. Secure the distributor cap with the spring clips.

11. Install the spark plug wires. Make sure that the wires are pressed all the way into the top of the distributor cap and firmly onto the spark plug.

12. Adjust the point dwell and set the ignition timing.

NOTE: *If the crankshaft has been turned or the engine disturbed in any manner (i.e., disassembled and rebuilt) while the distributor was removed, or if the marks were not drawn, it will be necessary to initially time the engine. Follow the procedure given below.*

1. It is necessary to place the No. 1 cylinder in the firing position to correctly install the distributor. To locate this position, the ignition timing marks on the crankshaft front pulley are used.

2. Remove the No. 1 cylinder spark plug. Turn the crankshaft until the piston in the No. 1 cylinder is moving up on the compression stroke. This can be deter-

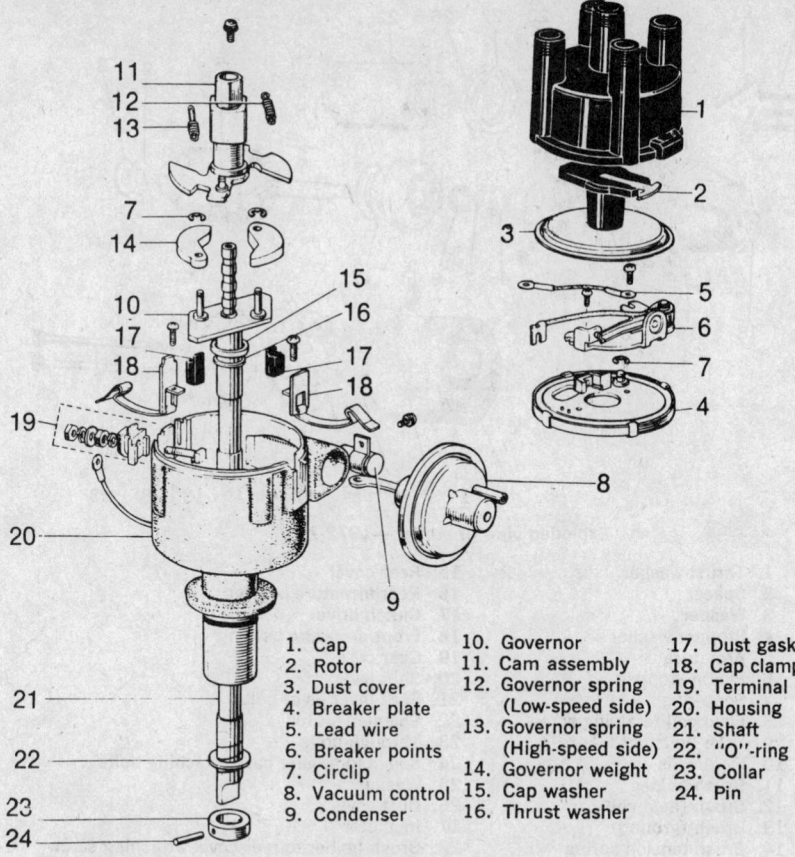

1. Cap
2. Rotor
3. Dust cover
4. Breaker plate
5. Lead wire
6. Breaker points
7. Circlip
8. Vacuum control
9. Condenser
10. Governor
11. Cam assembly
12. Governor spring (Low-speed side)
13. Governor spring (High-speed side)
14. Governor weight
15. Cap washer
16. Thrust washer
17. Dust gasket
18. Cap clamp
19. Terminal
20. Housing
21. Shaft
22. "O"-ring
23. Collar
24. Pin

Exploded view of distributor

mined by placing your thumb over the spark plug hole and feeling the air being forced out of the cylinder. Stop turning the crankshaft when the timing marks that are used to time the engine are aligned.

3. Oil the distributor housing lightly where the distributor bears on the cylinder block.

4. Install the distributor so that the rotor, which is mounted on the shaft, points toward the No. 1 spark plug terminal tower position when the cap is installed. Of course you won't be able to see the direction in which the rotor is pointing if the cap is on the distributor. Lay the cap on the top of the distributor and make a mark on the side of the distributor housing just below the No. 1 spark plug terminal. Make sure that the rotor points toward that mark when you install the distributor.

5. When the distributor shaft has reached the bottom of the hole, move the rotor back and forth slightly until the driving lug on the end of the shaft enters the slots cut in the end of the oil pump shaft and the distributor assembly slides down into place.

6. When the distributor is correctly installed, the breaker points should be in such a position that they are just ready to break contact with each other. This is accomplished by rotating the distributor

body after it has been installed in the engine. Once again, line up the marks that you made before the distributor was removed from the engine.

7. Install the distributor hold-down bolt.

8. Install the spark plug into the No. 1 spark plug hole and continue from Step 3 of the distributor installation procedure.

Alternator

1972–76 Chevrolet LUV vehicles are equipped with a 30 amp alternator with an electro-mechanical, adjustable voltage regulator. 1977 models use a similar 35 amp unit.

Alternator Precautions

To prevent damage to the alternator and regulator, the following precautionary measures must be taken when working with the electrical system.

1. Never reverse battery connections. Always check the battery polarity visually. This is to be done before any connections are made to be sure that all of the connections correspond to the battery ground polarity of the LUV.

2. Booster batteries for starting must be connected properly. Make sure that the positive cable of the booster battery is connected to the positive terminal of the battery that is getting the boost. This

applies to both negative and ground cables.

3. Disconnect the battery cables before using a fast charger; the charger has a tendency to force current through the diodes in the opposite direction for which they were designed. This burns out the diodes.

4. Never use a fast charger as a booster for starting the vehicle.

5. Never disconnect the voltage regulator while the engine is running.

6. Do not ground the alternator output terminal.

7. Do not operate the alternator on an open circuit with the field energized.

8. Do not attempt to polarize an alternator.

Removal and Installation

1. Remove the air pump.

2. Disconnect the battery ground cable before disconnecting the cable from the alternator "A" terminal. This is a hot cable connected directly to the battery.

3. Disconnect the alternator circuit at the connector and disconnect the cable from the "A" terminal.

4. Remove the mounting bolts on the lower part of the alternator and the fan belt adjusting bolt and remove the alternator.

5. Install the alternator in the reverse order of removal and tighten the fan belt and air pump belt tension.

Belt Tension Adjustment

Any engine V-belt is correctly tensioned when the longest span of belt between pulleys can be depressed about ¼ in. in the middle by moderate thumb pressure. To adjust, loosen the accessory's slotted adjusting bracket bolt. If the hinge bolt is very tight, it may be necessary to loosen it slightly to move the item.

CAUTION: *Be careful not to overtighten belts, as this will damage the bearings, particularly in air or water pumps and alternators.*

Regulator

Removal and Installation

1. Remove the negative battery cable from the battery.

2. Disconnect the electrical leads at the regulator, taking note to the positions in order to facilitate correct reconnection.

3. Remove the two mounting screws and remove the regulator.

4. Install the regulator in the reverse order of removal.

Adjustment

1. Remove the regulator from the vehicle and remove the regulator cover.

2. If the contact points are rough, dress them with fine sandpaper.

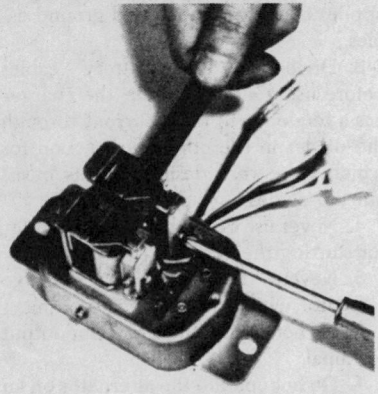

Adjusting the regulator core gap

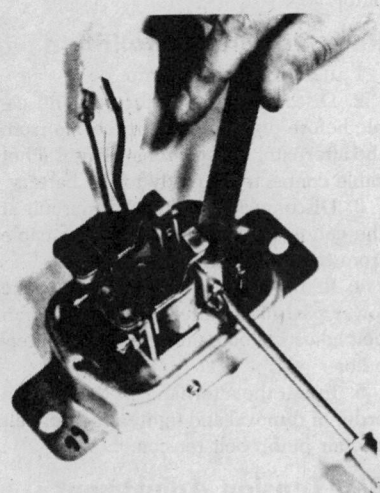

Adjusting the regulator point gap

Adjusting the regulator voltage

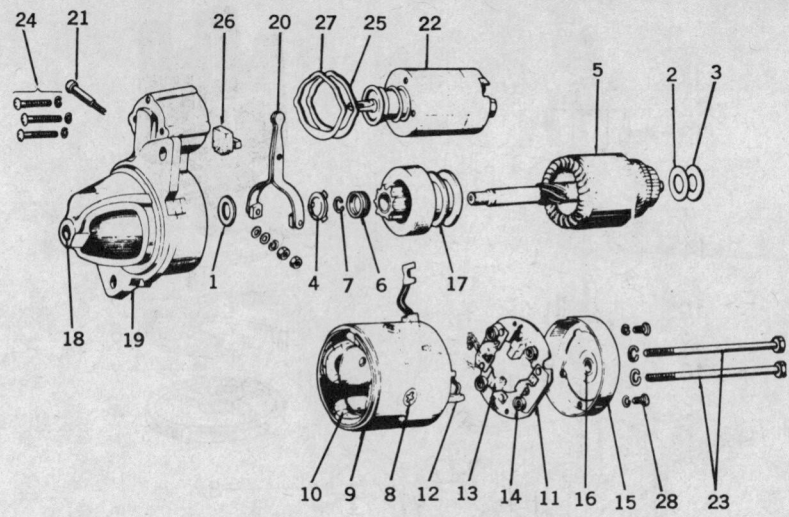

Exploded view of starter—1972-75

1. Thrust washer
2. Spacer
3. Washer
4. Stopper washer
5. Armature
6. Pinion stopper
7. Snap-ring
8. Field coil retaining screw
9. Yoke housing
10. Field coils
11. Brush holder
12. Brush (field coil)
13. Brush (ground)
14. Brush tension spring
15. Rear cover
16. Rear armature bearing
17. Clutch drive
18. Front armature bearing
19. Gear case
20. Shift lever
21. Shift lever pivot bolt
22. Solenoid switch
23. Through-bolts
24. Solenoid-to-gear case attaching bolts
25. Washer
26. Dust cover
27. Insulator
28. Brush holder-to-rear cover attaching screw

3. Check and adjust core gap first, and then the point gap. Adjustment of the yoke gap is unnecessary.

4. Adjust the core gap by loosening the screws attaching the contact set to the yoke. Move the contact set up or down as required. The standard core gap is 0.024–0.039 in. Tighten the attaching screw.

5. Adjust the point gap by loosening the screw attaching the upper contact. Move the upper contact up or down as required. The standard point gap is 0.012–0.016 in.

6. Adjust the regulated voltage by means of the adjusting screw. Turn the adjusting screw in to increase voltage and out to reduce voltage. When the correct

1. Armature
2. Snap-ring
3. Thrust washer
4. Thrust washer
5. Pinion stop
6. Pinion stop clip
7. Yoke
8. Field coil
9. Screw
10. Brush (+)
11. Rear cover
12. Rear cover bushing
13. Pinion
14. Gear case
15. Gear case bushing
16. Brush holder
17. Brush (−)
18. Brush spring
19. Shift lever
20. Torsion spring
21. Magnetic switch
22. Bolt
23. Adjusting plates
24. Dust cover
25. Dust cover
26. Bolt
27. Screw

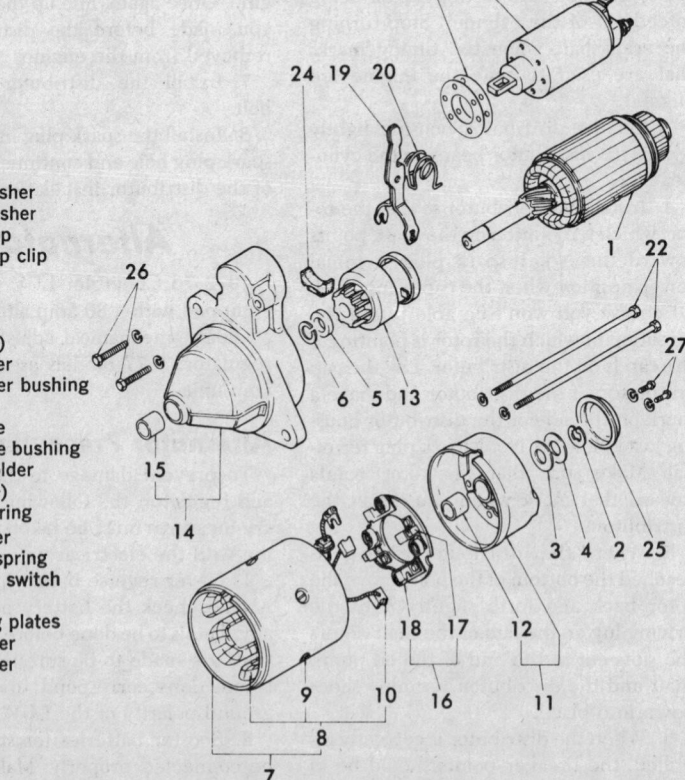

Exploded view of starter—1976-77

adjustment is obtained, secure the adjusting screw by tightening the locknut. The regulated voltage is 13.5–14.5 volts for 1972–76 models and 13.8–14.8 for 1977.

7. Install the regulator cover, reconnect the electrical leads and install the regulator.

Starter

Removal and Installation

1. Disconnect the negative battery cable from the battery.

2. Disconnect the starter wiring at the starter, taking note of the positions for correct reinstallation.

3. Remove the bolts attaching the starter to the engine and remove the starter from the vehicle.

4. Install the starter in the reverse order of removal.

Brush Replacement

1. With the starter out of the vehicle, remove the bolts holding the solenoid to the top of the starter and remove the solenoid.

2. To remove the brushes, remove the two thru-bolts and the two rear cover attaching screws and remove the rear cover.

3. Disconnect the brushes electrical leads and remove the brushes.

4. Install the brushes in the reverse order of removal.

Starter Drive Replacement

1. With the starter motor removed from the vehicle, remove the solenoid from the starter.

2. Remove the two thru-bolts and separate the gear case from the yoke housing.

3. Remove the pinion stopper clip and the pinion stopper.

4. Slide the starter drive off the armature shaft.

5. Install the starter drive and reassemble the starter in the reverse order of removal.

ENGINE MECHANICAL

Engine Removal and Installation

1. Disconnect the battery ground cable.

2. Prior to removing the hood, scribe a mark in the area of the hinges to ensure that the hood is reinstalled in its original position. Remove the hood.

3. Drain the cooling system through the drain cock on the radiator and on the cylinder block.

4. Drain the engine oil.

5. Disconnect the upper and lower hoses from the radiator and remove the radiator.

6. Disconnect the hoses from the air cleaner and remove the air cleaner assembly.

7. Remove the carburetor control cable.

8. Remove the choke control cable.

9. Disconnect the carburetor wiring.

10. Disconnect the exhaust pipe from the exhaust manifold at the flange.

11. Disconnect the alternator and starter wiring.

12. Disconnect the heater hose at the fender side.

13. Disconnect the vacuum hose.

14. Disconnect the spark plug wires from the distributor.

15. Disconnect the grounding cable between the cylinder head cover and the dashboard at the cylinder head cover side.

16. Disconnect the engine wiring at the two connectors.

17. Disconnect the oil pressure unit cord and temperature sending unit lead and the distributor ground wire; remove the wire from the three clips on the engine.

18. Disconnect the fuel line from the fuel pump.

19. Disconnect the ground cable on the timing gear case at the engine side.

20. Disconnect the two hoses from the fuel tank evaporative emission control check and relief valve.

21. Disconnect the driveshaft at the rear axle.

22. Remove the driveshaft from the transmission and install a plug in the end of the transmission to prevent loss of lubricant.

23. Disconnect the clutch slave cylinder.

24. Remove the exhaust pipe bracket from the clutch housing.

25. Disconnect the speedometer drive cable at the transmission.

26. Disconnect the body grounding cable between the transmission and the body at the floor side.

27. Remove the gearshift lever assembly.

28. Insert a lifting device into the engine hangers and lift the engine slightly.

29. Remove the engine rear mounts.

30. Check that the engine and auxiliary parts are separated completely from the chassis frame then, lift the engine out of position. When hoisting the engine, adjust the tension so that the front end of the engine is elevated slightly above the rear of the engine.

31. When the front of the engine clears the deflector, continue raising and move the engine toward the front of the truck.

32. Install the engine in the reverse order of removal. After the installation is complete, fill the crankcase with oil, the cooling system with coolant, adjust the clutch pedal free-play, and start the engine and check for leaks.

Cylinder Head

Removal and Installation

1972–75

1. Disconnect the negative battery cable, drain the cooling system and remove the air cleaner and hoses.

2. Remove the air pump.

3. Remove the alternator.

4. Disconnect the carburetor throttle linkage and fuel line together with the solenoid electrical lead.

5. Disconnect the exhaust pipe from the exhaust manifold.

6. Remove the six bolts retaining the camshaft carrier front cover and remove the front cover.

7. Remove the oil line from the secondary chain tensioner plug.

8. Remove the chain tensioner plug along with the tensioner spring.

9. Remove the bolt and plate washer retaining the timing (camshaft) sprocket.

Removing the camshaft carrier front cover

Removing the camshaft timing sprocket retaining bolt

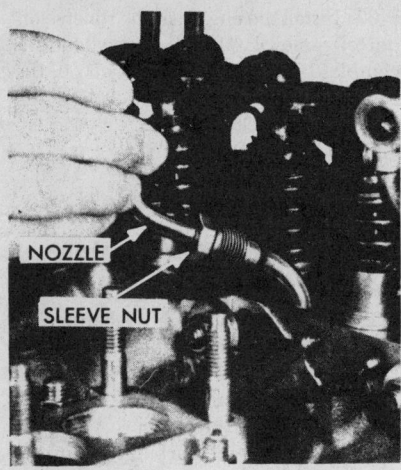

Removal of the air injection nozzle

10. Remove both upper secondary timing chain damper bolts, located in the front of the cylinder head.

11. Loosen both lower timing chain damper bolts.

12. Separate the timing (camshaft) sprocket from the camshaft, together with the chain.

13. Carefully separate the sprocket from the chain to prevent the timing sprocket pin from falling out.

NOTE: *When removing the camshaft from the timing sprocket, the pin should be positioned in the top. Mark the position of the pin on the timing sprocket prior to disassembling the parts.*

14. Hold the chain in position with a wire or cord.

15. Remove the 10 bolts retaining the camshaft cover and remove the cover.

16. Loosen the 12 camshaft carrier bolts evenly in progression and remove them. The camshaft carrier is under tension from the valve springs. Loosen all the bolts alternately in progression, so that a single bolt will not receive the tension of the valve springs. Care must be taken not to loosen the camshaft carrier locating dowel.

17. Loosen the sleeve nut on the air injection nozzle and remove the nozzle by turning it about 180°.

18. Remove the three bolts retaining the timing gear case to the cylinder head.

19. Loosen the cylinder head bolts in a progressional sequence.

20. Remove the cylinder head, gasket and O-rings.

Install the cylinder head in the reverse order of removal, as follows.

21. Position the cylinder head gasket on the block with the "Top" side up. Insert the O-rings into the oil ports.

22. Position a gear case-to-cylinder head gasket on the gear case, if necessary.

23. Install the cylinder head on the block and tighten the cylinder head bolts to specifications.

24. Tighten the three bolts attaching the timing gear case to the cylinder head.

25. Install the air injection nozzles. Do not tighten them securely at this time.

26. Align the setting mark on the camshaft thrust plate with the corresponding mark on the camshaft.

27. Position the O-rings to the camshaft carrier. Install these parts in position and lightly tighten the bolts retaining the dowels. Install the longest bolts in the position of the dowel.

28. Install the camshaft carrier bolts. Tighten the bolts alternately, in progression to 15 ft lbs to compress the valve springs evenly. Note that the camshaft carrier is also used to retain two portions of the air manifold bracket and PCV hose clips.

29. With the No. 4 cylinder at TDC of the compression stroke, check that the setting mark on the camshaft and on the thrust plate are correctly aligned. If the setting marks are not in good alignment, make the necessary adjustment as follows:

a. If the setting mark on the camshaft and the thrust plate are not in alignment, attach the camshaft sprocket to the camshaft, insert the pin into a hole in the camshaft timing sprocket and turn the crankshaft until the marks line up. Then, bring the camshaft into a free state by removing the camshaft timing sprocket from the camshaft and, set the piston in the No. 4 cylinder to TDC of the compression stroke. If the engine has been turned in reverse in the course of this adjustment, make a final adjustment by turning the engine in the normal direction of rotation so that the marks are lined up, with the chain properly tensioned on the correct side.

b. When installing the camshaft timing sprocket on the camshaft, keep

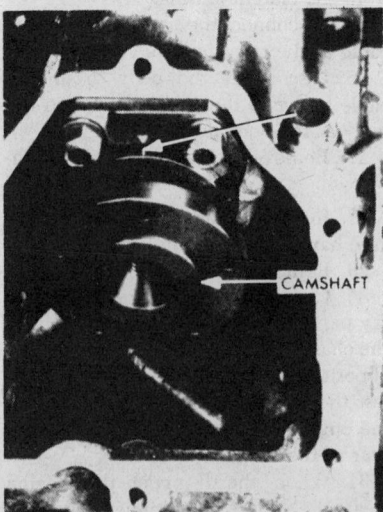

Camshaft timing marks

their mating faces free of foreign matter because the drive torque is relayed to the timing sprocket from the camshaft by means of frictional contact.

30. Bring the camshaft timing sprocket together with the timing chain, so that the punched mark on the sprocket is located at the 12 o'clock position. Assemble the sprocket to the camshaft.

31. Adjust the position of the camshaft timing sprocket, relative to the camshaft, so that the punched mark on the camshaft timing sprocket is turned up when the drive side of the timing chain is tensioned by pushing the chain tensioner shoe from the plug hole in the secondary chain tensioner. When the camshaft timing sprocket is correctly installed, the punched mark on the sprocket is brought to a position 6° 20′ from the top in the direction of rotation.

32. Hold the parts in their relative position. Look through each of the five holes in the camshaft timing sprocket to find a hole in alignment with the hole in the camshaft flange and insert the pin into that hole.

33. Tighten the camshaft timing sprocket attaching bolt, with the plate washer installed, to 33 ft lbs.

34. Install the camshaft carrier front cover.

35. Install the secondary chain tensioner.

36. Assemble the remaining components to the engine in the reverse order of removal, working backwards from Step 5.

37. Adjust the valves.

1976–77

1. Remove the cam cover.

2. Remove the EGR pipe clamp bolt at the rear of the cylinder head.

3. Raise the vehicle on a hoist and disconnect the exhaust pipe at the exhaust manifold.

4. Lower the vehicle from the hoist and drain the cooling system.

5. Disconnect the heater hoses at the inlet manifold and at the rear of the cylinder head.

6. Disconnect the accelerator linkage and fuel line at the carburetor, all necessary electrical connections, spark plug wires and vacuum lines.

7. Rotate the camshaft until the no. 4 cylinder is in the firing position. Remove the distributor cap and mark the rotor to housing relationship.

8. Lock the timing chain adjuster by depressing and turning the automatic adjuster slide pin 90° clockwise.

9. Removing the timing sprocket to camshaft bolt and remove the sprocket from the camshaft.

NOTE: *Keep the sprocket on the chain damper and chain.*

10. Disconnect the AIR hose and the

check valve at the exhaust manifold.

11. Remove the cylinder head to timing cover bolts.

12. Remove the cylinder head bolts in a progressional sequence, starting with the outer bolts.

13. Remove the cylinder head, intake and exhaust manifold as a unit.

14. To install reverse the removal procedure and tighten the bolts in the sequence and torque shown in the specifications table in the front of the section.

Valve Guide Replacement

1. With the cylinder head removed from the vehicle and the valves removed from the head, drive the guides out toward the upper face of the cylinder head with a suitable driver. The valve guides cannot be driven out downward because they are secured in place with a snap-ring.

2. Lubricate the outside of the new valve guide with oil. Press it all the way into position, from the upper face of the cylinder head, until it is brought in contact with the snap-ring. Allowable interference between the cylinder head and the valve guide is 0.0016 in.

Valve Rockers

Removal and Installation

1972–75

1. Remove the camshaft cover as outlined under "Cylinder Head Removal."

2. Remove the rocker spring from the pivot and lift the rocker from the cylinder head. Be careful not to lose the rocker guide resting on the top of each of the valves.

3. Install in the reverse order of removal.

1976–77

1. Remove the cam cover.

2. Loosen the rocker arm shaft bracket nuts a little at a time, in sequence, starting with the outer brackets.

3. Remove the nuts from the rocker arm shaft brackets.

Removing/installing the rocker retaining spring

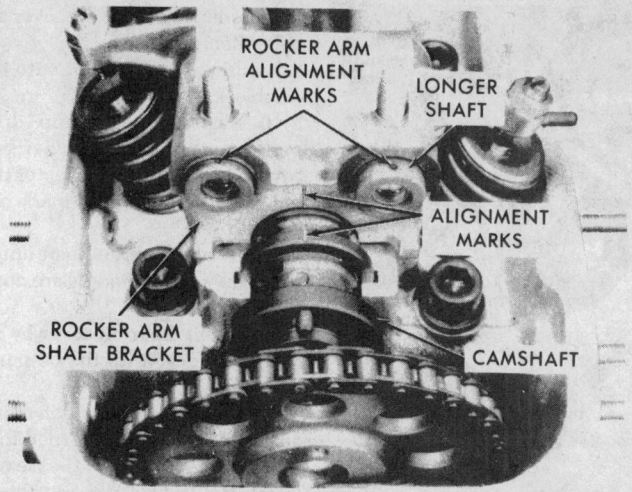

ROCKER ARM ALIGNMENT MARKS — LONGER SHAFT — ALIGNMENT MARKS — ROCKER ARM SHAFT BRACKET — CAMSHAFT

Rocker arm shaft installation—1976-77

4. Remove the spring from the rocker arm shaft and remove the rocker brackets and arms.

5. Before installing apply a generous amount of clean engine oil to the rocker arm shaft, rocker arms and valve stems.

6. Install the longer shaft on the exhaust valve side and the shorter shaft on the intake side, so that the aligning marks on the shafts are turned on the front side.

7. Assemble the rocker arm shaft brackets and rocker arms to the shafts so that the cylinder number that is on the upper face of the brackets is pointed toward the front of the engine.

8. Align the mark on the no. 1 rocker arm shaft bracket with the mark on the intake and exhaust valve side rocker arm shafts.

9. Make certain the amount of projection of the rocker arm shaft beyond the face of the no. 1 rocker arm shaft bracket is longer on the exhaust side shaft than on the intake shaft when the rocker arm shaft stud holes are aligned with the rocker arm shaft bracket stud holes.

10. Place the rocker arm shaft springs in position between the shaft bracket and rocker arm.

11. Check that the punch mark on the rocker arm shaft is turned upward, then install the rocker arm shaft bracket assembly onto the cylinder head studs. Align the mark on the camshaft with the mark on the no. 1 rocker arm shaft bracket.

12. Tighten the rocker arm shaft brackets stud nuts to 16 ft. lbs.

NOTE: *Hold the rocker arm springs with an adjustable wrench while torquing nuts to prevent damage to the spring. Start with the center nut and work outward.*

13. Adjust the valves and install the cam cover.

Combination Manifold

Removal and Installation

Although the intake and exhaust manifolds are separate pieces, they are removed and installed as a unit.

1. Remove the air cleaner with all of the hoses.

2. Disconnect all of the electrical leads, throttle linkage, fuel and vacuum lines from the carburetor.

3. The carburetor can be removed from the manifold at this point or can be removed as an assembly with the intake manifold.

4. Disconnect the exhaust pipe from the exhaust manifold.

5. Slightly loosen all of the manifold attaching nuts, and then remove them, working from the outside toward the center. Remove the two manifolds.

6. Install the manifolds in the reverse order of removal, making sure that the mating surfaces are clean before installation.

Timing Gear Cover

Removal and Installation

1972–75

1. Disconnect the negative battery cable, drain the cooling system, and remove the alternator and air pump with their respective mounting brackets and drive belts.

2. Remove the crankshaft pulley bolt and remove the pulley.

3. Remove the six bolts retaining the front cover and remove the front camshaft carrier cover.

4. Remove the 17 (11 bolts in 1972) bolts retaining the timing gear case.

5. Remove the access plug and take out the bolt on the inner face of the gear case.

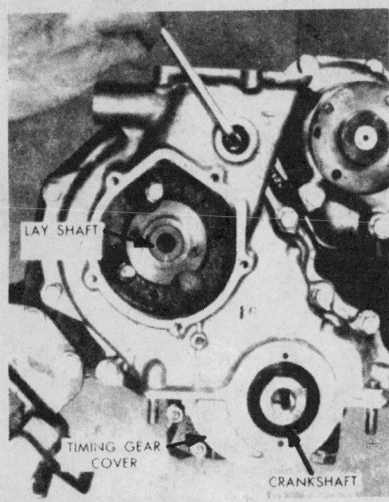

With the access plug removed, remove the bolt on the inner face of the gear cover. The layshaft in the illustration is the jack shaft referred to in the text

6. Insert the edge of a screwdriver into the cutaway portions on the outer rim of the timing gear case and pry it off the engine.

7. Install the timing gear case and the camshaft carrier front cover in the reverse order of removal and assemble the engine in the reverse order of disassembly.

1976–77

1. Remove the cylinder head.

2. Remove the oil pan.

3. Remove the oil pickup tube from the oil pump.

4. Remove the harmonic balencer. (See Timing Cover Seal—Removal and Installation)

5. Remove the air pump drive belt.

6. If equipped with air conditioning, remove the compressor and lay it to one side. Then remove the mounting brackets.

7. Remove the distributor cap and the distributor.

8. Removing the front cover attaching bolts then the cover

9. Install a new gasket onto the cylinder block.

10. Align the oil pump drive gear punch mark with the oil filter side of the cover; then align the center of the dowel pin with the alignment mark on the oil pump case.

11. Rotate the crankshaft until the no. 1 and the no. 4 cylinders are at top dead center.

12. Install the front cover by engaging the pinion gear with the oil pump drive gear on the crankshaft.

13. Check that the punch mark on the oil pump drive gear is turned to the rear side as viewed through the clearance between the front cover and the cylinder block.

14. Check that the slit at the end of the oil pump shaft is parallel with the front face of the cylinder block and is offset forward.

15. Reverse steps 1 thru 7.

Timing Cover Seal

Removal And Installation

1. Disconnect the negative battery cable.

2. Drain the cooling system.

3. Disconnect the radiator inlet and outlet hoses.

4. Remove the radiator assembly.

5. Remove the generator and compressor drive belts.

6. Remove the engine fan.

7. Remove the crankshaft pulley center bolt and remove the pulley and balencer assembly.

8. Pry out the timing cover seal using a suitable size screwdriver.

9. Using the appropriate tool install the new seal in the timing cover.

10. Reverse steps 1 thru 7.

Timing Chains, Sprockets, and Tensioner

Removal and Installation

1972–75

1. Disconnect the battery ground cable, drain the cooling system, and remove the alternator and air pump with their respective mounting brackets and drive belts. Remove the fan.

2. Remove the timing gear cover.

3. Remove the oil line from the secondary chain tensioner plug.

4. Remove the chain tensioner plug with the tensioner spring.

5. Remove the bolt and plate washer retaining the camshaft timing sprocket.

6. Remove both of the upper secondary timing chain damper bolts, located in the front of the cylinder head.

7. Loosen both of the lower timing chain damper bolts.

8. Separate the timing sprocket from the camshaft, together with the chain. Then, carefully remove the timing sprocket from the chain to prevent the timing sprocket pin from falling out. When removing the timing sprocket from the camshaft, the pin should be positioned at the top. Mark the position of the pin on the timing sprocket before disassembling the parts.

9. Remove the bolt retaining the secondary timing sprocket to the jackshaft. Remove the secondary sprocket by alternately screwing two bolts into the threaded holes in the timing sprocket one turn at a time.

10. Remove the secondary sprocket from the chain.

11. Remove the chain from the top, through the camshaft carrier front cover hole.

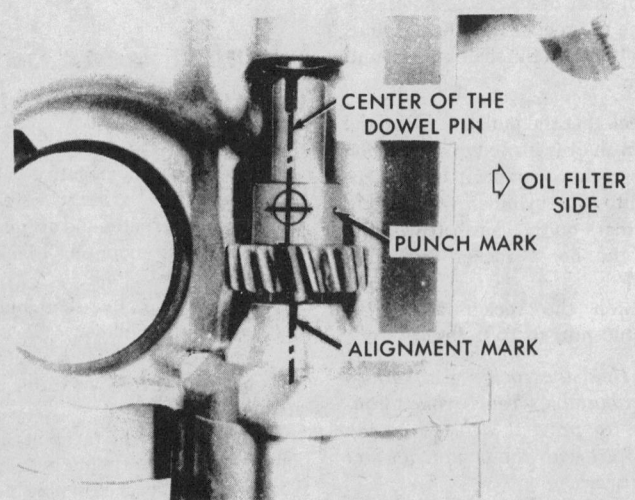

Oil pump alignment—1976-77

CENTER OF THE DOWEL PIN

OIL FILTER SIDE

PUNCH MARK

ALIGNMENT MARK

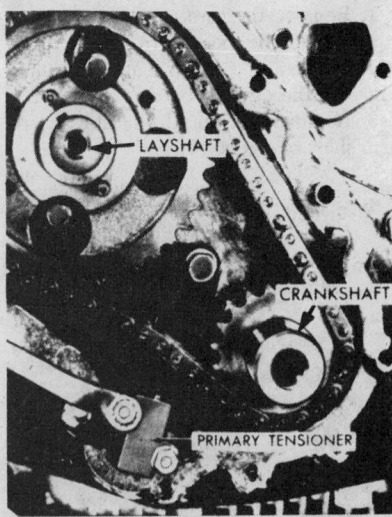

Removing the primary chain tensioner. The layshaft in the illustration is the jackshaft referred to in the text

LAYSHAFT

CRANKSHAFT

PRIMARY TENSIONER

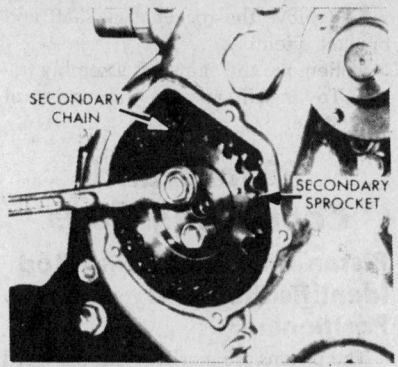

Removing the secondary timing sprocket from the jackshaft by installing two screws in the holes provided and turning them alternately

12. Remove the secondary chain tensioners from the cylinder head.

13. Remove the two nuts retaining the primary chain tensioner. Be careful to prevent the tensioner shoe from jumping out of position by the action of the spring. Remove the chain tensioner.

14. Remove the timing sprockets together with the chain, by inserting screws into the threaded holes in the jackshaft sprocket and turning them alternately and evenly until the sprockets are free.

To install the timing chains, tensioners and sprockets:

15. If the engine was not disturbed while the components were removed, then install everything in the reverse order of removal, using the procedure below as a guide. If, however, the crankshaft or camshaft was turned or the engine disassembled further, start the assembly procedure by bringing the No. 1 and No. 4 pistons to top dead center (TDC).

16. Check that the pistons are at TDC by positioning the timing gear cover on the locating dowels and place the crankshaft pulley in position. The TDC timing mark should be in direct line with the timing mark pointer.

17. Position the crankshaft and jackshaft timing sprocket into position with the primary chain attached to them. When installing the primary timing sprockets, the timing mark on the jackshaft sprocket must align with the timing mark on the crankshaft sprocket.

18. Align the keyway of the jackshaft with the key in the sprocket by turning the jackshaft, then set both sprockets in position by lightly tapping each sprocket alternately.

NOTE: *The jackshaft can be prevented from turning while driving the sprockets into position by holding it through the fuel pump opening.*

19. Install the primary chain tensioner.

20. Install a new oil seal in the timing gear case and fill the space between the

With the No. 1 and 4 pistons at TDC, install the crankshaft and jackshaft sprockets with the chain so timing marks on the sprockets are aligned

lips of the oil seal with grease. Position a new gasket to the mating face of the gear case with adhesive. Align the locating dowels with the proper holes and mount the gear case onto the engine. Install and tighten the retaining screws.

21. With the No. 4 piston at TDC on the compression stroke, check to make sure that the setting mark on the camshaft and on the camshaft thrust plate are aligned. If they are not aligned, go on to the next numbered step.

   a. Attach the camshaft sprocket to the camshaft, insert the pin into a hole in the camshaft sprocket and turn the crankshaft until the marks on the camshaft and the thrust plate align.

   b. Remove the camshaft sprocket from the camshaft and bring the No. 4 piston to TDC of the compression stroke.

NOTE: *If the engine has been turned in the opposite direction of normal rotation to align the marks on the thrust*

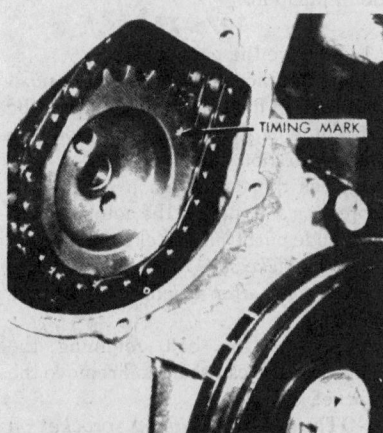

Install the jackshaft secondary timing sprocket so that the punched mark aligns with the key on the jackshaft

plate and the camshaft, make the final adjustment by turning the engine in the direction of normal rotation so that the marks are lined up and the chain is tensioned on the normal side.

22. Insert the timing chain into the gear case from the upper opening and hold it in position.

23. Bring the jackshaft timing sprocket together with the chain, and install it in position so that the punched mark on the sprocket is pointed to the key on the jackshaft. When the sprocket is correctly installed, the punched mark is located approximately at the 2 o'clock position.

24. Bring the camshaft timing sprocket together with the timing chain, so that the punched mark on the sprocket is located at the 12 o'clock position and assemble the sprocket to the camshaft.

25. Adjust the position of the camshaft timing sprocket, relative to the camshaft, so that the punched mark on the camshaft timing sprocket is turned up when the drive side of the timing chain is tensioned by pushing the chain tensioner shoe from the plug hole in the secondary chain tensioner.

NOTE: *When the camshaft timing sprocket is correctly installed, the punched mark on the sprocket is brought to a position 6° 20′ from the top in the direction of normal rotation.*

26. Hold all of the parts in position and look through each of the five holes in the camshaft timing sprocket to find a hole in alignment with the hole in the camshaft flange. Insert the pin into that hole.

27. Tighten the jackshaft timing sprocket attaching bolt to 33 ft lbs. Install the plate washer and tighten the camshaft timing sprocket attaching bolt to 33 ft lbs.

28. Install the gear case front cover and the camshaft carrier front cover.

29. Install the secondary chain tensioner.

30. Assemble the remaining components in the reverse order of removal.

1976–77

1. Remove the front cover assembly as previously described.

2. Remove the timing chain from the crankshaft sprocket.

3. Remove the sprocket and the pinion gear from the crankshaft using a puller.

4. Remove "E" clip and remove the automatic chain adjuster.

5. Remove "E" clip and remove the chain tensioner.

6. Check the timing chain for wear.

With a pull of approximately 22 lbs. as shown in the illustration the standard "L" distance is 15.00″; replace the chain if "L" is greater than 15.16″.

7. Check tensioner pins for wear or damage, and replace if necessary.

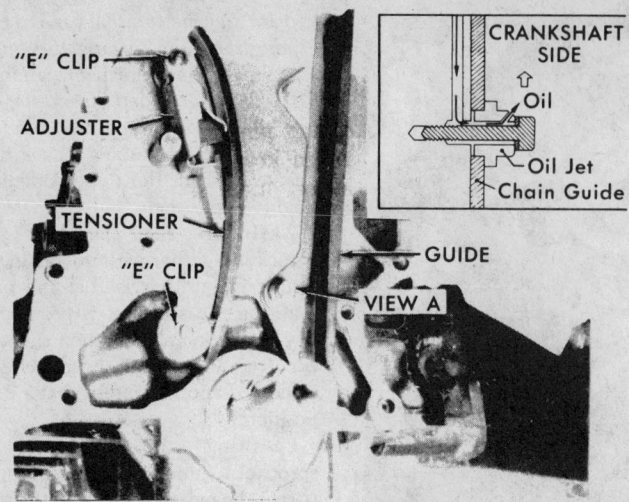

Timing chain adjuster—1976-77

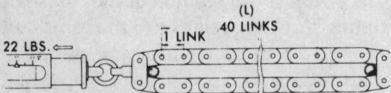

Checking timing chain wear—1976-77

8. Replace the chain tensioner and adjuster using the "E" clips.

9. Install the timing sprocket and pinion gear with the groove side toward the front cover. Align the key grooves with the key on the crankshaft, then drive into position using the appropriate tool.

10. Turn the crankshaft so that the key is turned toward the cylinder head side (#1 and #4 pistons at top dead center).

11. Install the timing chain by aligning the mark plate on the chain with the mark on the crankshaft timing sprocket. The side of the chain with the mark plate is on the front side and the side of the chain with the most links between the mark plates is on the chain guide side.

12. Install the camshaft timing sprocket so that the mark side of the sprocket faces forward and so that the triangular mark aligns with the chain mark plate.

NOTE: *Keep the timing chain engaged with the camshaft timing sprocket until the sprocket is installed on the camshaft.*

13. Install the front cover assembly.

Camshaft

Removal and Installation

1972-75

1. Remove the camshaft carrier as outlined under "Cylinder Head Removal and Installation".

2. Remove the two bolts retaining the thrust plate in position on the front of the camshaft carrier.

3. Remove the thrust plate and slide the camshaft out through the front of the carrier.

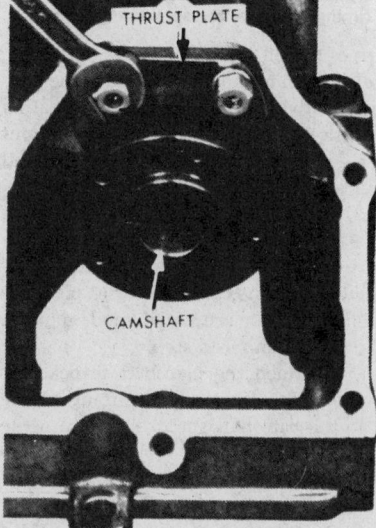

Removing the camshaft thrust plate

4. Install the camshaft in the carrier in the reverse order of removal, coating it liberally with engine oil before sliding it into position. Exercise care not to damage the camshaft bearing journals during the installation.

1976-77

1. Remove the cam cover.

2. Rotate the camshaft until the no. 4 cylinder is in firing position. Remove the distributor cap and mark the rotor to housing position.

3. Lock the timing chain adjuster by depressing and turning the automatic adjuster slide pin 90° in a clockwise position.

NOTE: *Make sure that the chain is in a free state, after locking the chain adjuster.*

4. Remove the bolt retaining the sprocket to the camshaft and remove the sprocket.

NOTE: *Keep the timing sprocket on the chain damper and tensioner without removing the chain from the sprocket.*

5. Remove the rocker arm, shaft and bracket assembly.

6. Remove the camshaft assembly.

7. To install reverse the removal procedure.

Pistons and Connecting Rods

Piston and Connecting Rod Identification and Positioning

The pistons are marked with the word "Front" and a notch in the piston head. When installed in the engine the "Front" and notch markings are to be facing the front of the engine. The connecting rods are numbered corresponding to the cylinders in which they are to be installed. Install the connecting rods in their correct cylinders with the marking to the right of the notch in the piston (looking from the rear of the engine), on the same side as the jackshaft.

ENGINE LUBRICATION

Oil Pan

Removal and Installation

1972–75

In 1972 the LUV engine had an oil pan made of two different sections: a cast aluminum crankcase attached to the cylinder block and a stamped steel oil pan attached to the crankcase. All other models have a one-piece stamped steel oil pan.

To remove the oil pan it may necessary to unbolt the motor mounts and jack the engine to gain clearance. Remove the attaching screws and remove the oil pan and/or crankcase. Install in the reverse order of removal, using new gaskets. Tighten the retaining bolts to 50 in. lbs. on models without the separate crank-

The two-piece crankcase-oil pan used on 1972 models

The tightening sequence for the oil pan used on 1973-75 models

case; 15 ft lbs on those with a separate crankcase.

1976–77

1. Raise the hood and disconnect the battery ground cable.
2. Raise the vehicle on a lift.
3. Drain the crankcase.
4. Remove the front splash shield.
5. Remove the front crossmember.
6. Disconnect the relay rod at the idler arm and lower the relay rod.
7. Remove the left hand bell housing brace.
8. Disconnect the vacuum line at the oil pan.
9. Remove the oil pan bolts and remove the oil pan.
10. To install reverse the removal procedure. Tighten the bolts evenly to 43 in. lbs.

Rear Main Oil Seal

Replacement

1972

1. Remove the crankshaft. It is advised that the engine be removed from the vehicle.
2. Remove the old oil seal from the cylinder block and the rear bearing cap.
3. Press the upper half of the seal evenly into position in the cylinder block with a large piece of smooth wooden dowel or similar tool. Trim the ends of the seal so that they are flush with the bearing cap mating surface. Also, trim

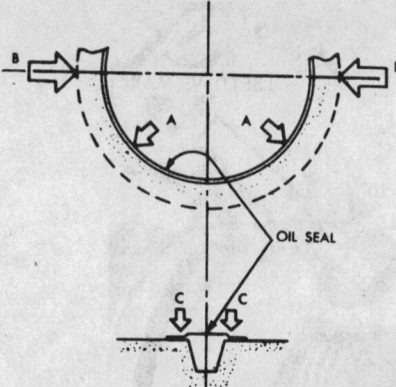

Installation of the rear main oil seal on 1972 models. Press areas "A" into the groove until smooth and even. Trim the excess material from areas "B" and "C"

any portion of the seal which overhangs the groove.

4. Install the lower half of the seal in the groove in the rear main bearing cap. Trim the ends of the seal so that they are flush with the mating surface of the cap.
5. Install and assemble in the reverse order of removal.

NOTE: *Install the thrust plates on either side of the No. 3 main bearing journal with the smooth side toward the crankshaft.*

1973–77

1. Remove the transmission.
2. Remove the oil pan and remove the rear main oil seal retainer from the cylinder block.
3. Fill the space between the lips of the oil seal with grease.
4. Position a new gasket on the mating surface of the cylinder block with adhesive.
5. Align the dowel holes with the locating dowels and mount the oil seal retainer to the cylinder block.
6. Install the oil pan.

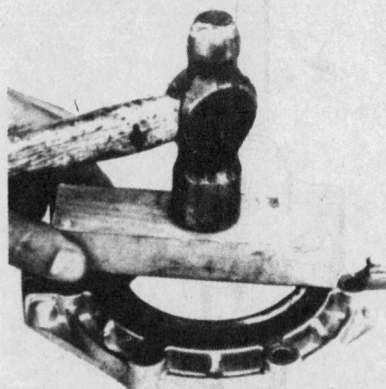

Installing the rear main oil seal retainer on 1973-77 models

Oil Pump

Removal and Installation

1972–75

1. Drain and remove the oil pan or crankcase.

2. Disconnect the oil feed pipe.
3. Remove the two bolts securing the oil pump to the cylinder block and remove the oil pump.

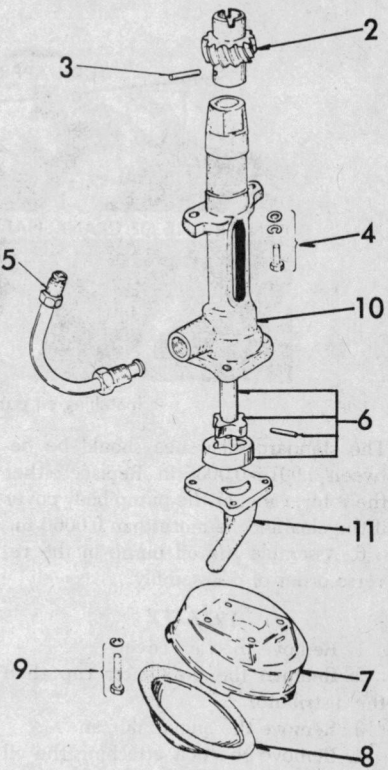

Exploded view of oil pump—1972-75

1. Pump assembly
2. Pinion
3. Pin
4. Bolt, lockwasher and plain washer
5. Pipe assembly
6. Rotor set
7. Case
8. Screen
9. Bolt and lockwasher
10. Body
11. Cover

4. Install in the reverse order of removal.

Checking Clearances

1. To disassemble the oil pump, first flatten out the tab bent to the case.
2. Remove the four bolts and remove the strainer case and pump body cover.
3. Measure the clearance between the tips of the rotor (center piece) and the high sections of the vane with a feeler gauge. The clearance should be between 0.0012–0.0059 in.
4. Measure the clearance between the vane and wall of the pump body with a feeler gauge. Replacement of either the vane or the pump body is necessary if the clearance is not within the limits of 0.-008–0.011 in.
5. Place a straight edge over the rotor and vane, resting the straight edge on the pump cover mating surface of the pump body. Measure the clearance between the straight edge and the rotor and vane.

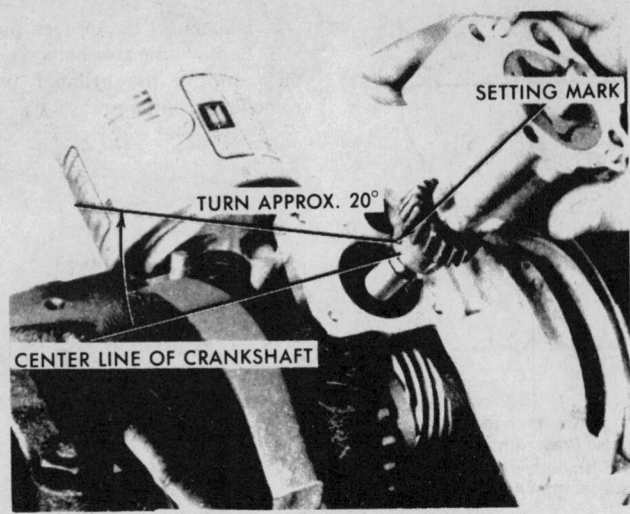

Installing oil pump—1976-77

The standard clearance should be between 0.0016–0.0035 in. Replace either the rotor, vane, or the pump body cover if the clearance is more than 0.0060 in.

6. Assemble the oil pump in the reverse order of disassembly.

1976–77

1. Remove the cam cover.
2. Remove the distributor cap then the distributor.
3. Remove the engine oil pan.
4. Remove the bolt attaching the oil pickup tube to the block and remove the tube from the oil pump.

1. Oil pump body
2. Driveshaft
3. Drive rotor
4. Rotor pin
5. Drive gear
6. Gear pin
7. Driven rotor
8. Cover assembly
9. Relief valve
10. Spring
11. Fitting
12. Gasket
13. Dowel pin

5. Remove the oil pump mounting bolts and remove the pump assembly.

6. To install align the mark on the cam-shaft with the mark on the no. 1 rocker arm shaft bracket. Align the notch on the crankshaft pulley with the "O" mark on the front cover. When the two sets of marks are aligned the no. 4 cylinder is at top dead center on the compression stroke.

7. Install the oil pump assembly by engaging the oil pump drive gear with the pinion gear on the crankshaft, so that the alignment mark on the drive gear is turned rearward and is away from the

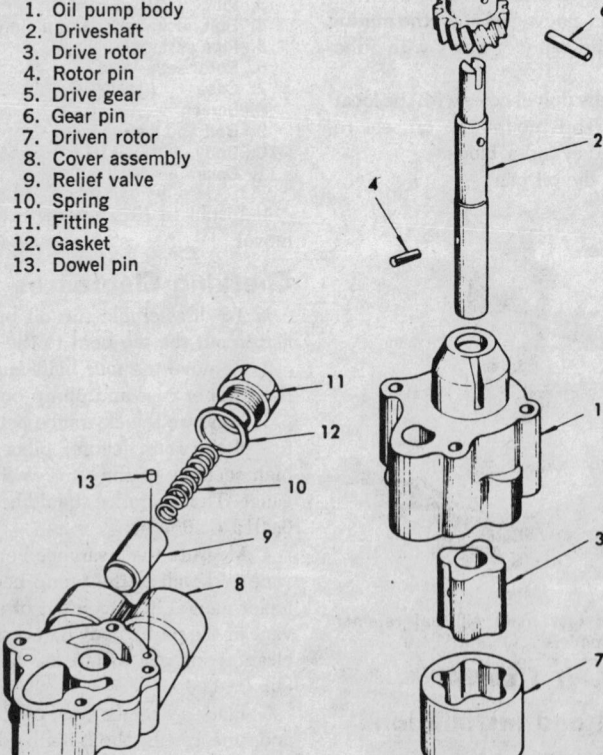

Exploded view of oil pump—1976-77

crankshaft by approximately 20° in a clockwise direction.

8. Install the oil pump mounting bolts.
9. Connect the oil pipe to the rubber hose and attach the oil pipe to the cylinder block.
10. Install the oil pan and cam cover.
11. Install the distributor by turning the distributor shaft, so that the boss on the shaft is fitted into the slit at the end of the oil pump drive shaft.
12. Install the distributor cap.

ENGINE COOLING
Radiator
Removal and Installation

1. Drain the radiator by opening the drain cock on the lower part of the radiator.
2. Disconnect the radiator upper and lower hoses.
3. Remove the four bolts retaining the radiator and remove the radiator assembly.
4. Install the radiator in the reverse order of removal.

Water Pump
Removal and Installation

1972–73

1. Disconnect the positive battery cable from the battery.
2. Remove the grille.
3. Drain the cooling system.
4. Disconnect the upper and lower radiator hoses.
5. Remove the radiator and shroud.
6. Remove the alternator and air pump belts.
7. Remove the fan, pulley and spacer.
8. Remove the camshaft access cover.
9. Bring the No. 4 piston to TDC of its compression stroke.
10. Remove the crankshaft pulley.
11. Remove the jackshaft access cover.
12. Remove the primary chain tensioner.
13. Remove the upper left and right chain dampener bolts.
14. Remove the camshaft gear bolt and gear.
15. Remove the jackshaft secondary sprocket bolt and remove the sprocket.
16. Remove secondary timing chain.
17. Remove the left chain dampener.
18. Remove the three cylinder head-to-timing cover attaching bolts.
19. Remove the timing case cover bolts.
20. Remove the timing case cover and gasket.
21. Remove the water pump assembly and gasket.

22. Remove the heater hose at the water pump.

23. Install in the reverse order of removal. Use new gaskets on the water pump and the timing covers.

1974–77

1. Disconnect the positive battery cable.

2. Drain the cooling system.

3. Disconnect the upper and lower radiator hoses.

4. Remove the radiator and shroud.

5. Remove the alternator and air pump drive belts.

6. Remove the fan, pulley and spacer.

7. Remove the water pump assembly and gasket.

NOTE: *When removing the water pump, loosen, but do not remove the bolt behind the timing gear cover.*

8. Remove the radiator lower hose and heater hose at the water pump.

9. Install the water pump in the reverse order of removal, using a new gasket.

Loosen, but do not remove the bolt behind the timing gear cover when removing the 1974-77 water pump.

Thermostat

Removal and Installation

1972–75

1. Drain the radiator by opening the drain petcock on the bottom of the radiator.

2. Disconnect the upper and lower radiator hoses.

3. Disconnect the water outlet from the engine.

4. Remove the thermostat.

5. Replace the thermostat in the reverse order of removal, using a new gasket under the outlet housing and making sure that the thermostat is placed so that the spring end is inside the engine.

1976–77

1. Remove the drain plug and drain the cooling system.

2. Disconnect the PCV, ECS, AIR, CCS hoses and remove the two bolts attaching the air cleaner, then loosen the clamp bolt.

3. Lift the air cleaner from the carburetor and disconnect the CCS hose from the air cleaner, then remove the air cleaner assembly.

4. Remove the two bolts attaching the outlet pipe and remove the outlet pipe and water hose.

5. Remove the thermostat from the intake manifold.

6. To install reverse the removal procedure.

EMISSION CONTROLS

There are three types of automotive pollutants; crankcase fumes, exhaust gases, and gasoline evaporation. The equipment that is used to limit these pollutants is commonly called emission control equipment.

Crankcase Emission Controls

The crankcase emission control equipment consists of a positive crankcase ventilation valve (PCV), a closed or open oil filler cap and hoses to connect this equipment.

Crankcase gases are recycled in the following manner: while the engine is running, clean filtered air is drawn into the crankcase through the carburetor air filter and then through a hose leading to the rocker cover. As the air passes through the crankcase it picks up the combustion gases and carries them out of the crankcase, up through the PCV valve and into the intake manifold. After they enter the intake manifold they are drawn into the combustion chamber and burned.

The most critical component in the system is the PCV valve. This vacuum controlled valve regulates the amount of gases which are recycled into the combustion chamber. At low engine speeds the valve is partially closed, limiting the flow of gases into the intake manifold. As engine speed increases, the valve opens to admit greater quantities of the gases into the intake manifold. If the valve should become blocked or plugged, the gases will be prevented from escaping from the crankcases by the normal route. Since these gases are under pressure, they will find their own way out of the crankcase. This alternate route is usually a weak oil seal or gasket in the engine. As the gas escapes by the gasket, it also creates an oil leak. Besides causing oil leaks, a clogged PCV valve also allows these gases to remain in the crankcase for an

extended period of time, promoting the formation of sludge in the engine.

Testing

Check the PCV system hoses and connections, to see that there are no leaks; then replace or tighten, as necessary.

To check the valve, remove it and blow through both of its ends.

When blowing from the side which goes toward the intake manifold, very little air should pass through it. When blowing from the crankcase (valve cover) side, air should pass through freely.

Replace the valve with a new one, if the valve fails to function as outlined.

NOTE: *Do not attempt to clean or adjust the valve; replace it with a new one.*

Removal and Installation

To remove the PCV valve, simply loosen the hose clamp and remove the valve from the manifold-to-crankcase hose and intake manifold. Install the PCV valve in the reverse order of removal.

Evaporative Emission Control System

When raw fuel evaporates, the vapors contain hydrocarbons. To prevent these nasties from escaping into the atmosphere, the fuel evaporative emission control system was developed.

The system consists of a sealed fuel tank, a vapor separator tank, check and relief valve and the hoses connecting these components, in the above order leading from the fuel tank, to the crankcase of the engine.

In operation, the vapor formed in the fuel tank passes through the vapor separator, which allows liquid fuel to flow back into fuel tank while allowing fuel vapor to pass into the check and relief valve and the crankcase. When the engine is not running, if the fuel vapor pressure in the vapor separator becomes as high as 1 to 1.4 in Hg, the check valve opens and allows the vapor to enter the engine crankcase. Otherwise the check valve is closed to the vapor separator while the engine is not running. When the engine is running, and a vacuum is developed in the fuel tank or in the engine crankcase and the difference of pressure between the relief side and the fuel tank or crankcase becomes 2 in. Hg, the relief valve opens and allows ambient air from the air cleaner into the fuel tank or the engine crankcase. This ambient air replaces the vapor within the fuel tank or crankcase, bringing the fuel tank or crankcase back into a neutral or positive pressure range.

Inspection and Service

Check the hoses for proper connections and damage. Replace as necessary. Check the vapor separator tank for fuel leaks, distortion and dents, and replace as necessary.

Remove the check valve and inspect it for leakage by blowing air into the ports in the check valve. When air is applied from the fuel tank side, the check valve is normal if air passes into the check side (crankcase side), but not leaking into the relief side (air cleaner side). When air is applied from the check side, the valve is normal if the passage of air is restricted. When air is applied from the relief side (air cleaner side), the valve is normal if air passes into the fuel tank side but not into the check side.

Removal and Installation

Removal and installation of the various evaporative emission control system components consists of disconnecting the hoses, loosening retaining screws, and removing the part which is to be replaced or checked. Install in the reverse order. When replacing hose, make sure that it is fuel and vapor resistant.

Exhaust Emission Control Systems

Air Injection Reactor System

In gasoline engines, it is difficult to burn the air/fuel mixture completely through normal combustion in the combustion chambers. Under certain operating conditions, unburned fuel is exhausted into the atmosphere.

The air injection reactor system is designed so that ambient air, pressurized by the air pump, is injected through the injection nozzles into the exhaust ports near each exhaust valve. The exhaust gases are at high temperatures and ignite when brought into contact with the oxygen of the ambient air. Thus, the unburned fuel is burned in the exhaust ports and manifold.

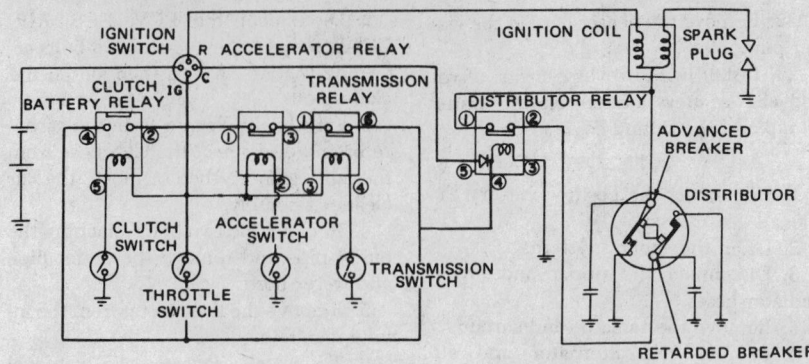

Electrical diagram of the dual point distributor system

To act against over-rich air/fuel mixture which occurs momentarily when the throttle plates in the carburetor are rapidly closed, additional ambient air is supplied intermittently into the intake manifold through the mixture control valve.

Dual Point Distributor (1972 and 1973)

The dual point distributor has two sets of breaker points which operate independently of each other and are positioned with a relative phase angle of 4° (1972) or 1° (1973) apart. This makes one set the advanced points and the other set the retarded points.

The two sets of points, which mechanically operate continuously, are connected in parallel to the primary side of the ignition circuit. One set of points controls the firing of the spark plugs and hence, the ignition timing, depending on whether or not the retarded set of points is energized.

When both sets of points are electrically energized, the first set to open (the advanced set, 4° or 1° sooner) has no control over breaking the ignition coil primary circuit because the retarded set is still closed and maintaining a complete circuit to ground. When the retarded set of points opens, the advanced set is still open, and the primary circuit is broken causing the electromagnetic field in the

coil to collapse and the ignition spark is produced.

When the retarded set of points is removed from the primary ignition circuit through the operation of a distributor relay inserted into the retarded points circuit, the advanced set of points controls the primary circuit.

The retarded set of points is energized under the following conditions:

1. Light throttle application in Low gears: the accelerator pedal is depressed to between 7° and 35° of throttle valve opening, the clutch is engaged, and the transmission is in either 1st or 2nd gear.

2. Light throttle application or coasting in High gears: the accelerator pedal is depressed up to 35° of throttle valve opening, the clutch is engaged, and the transmission is in either 3rd or 4th gear.

In any other mode of operation, for example, with the accelerator pedal depressed less than 7° in condition No. 1, or more than 35° in condition No. 1 or No. 2, or at anytime the clutch is disengaged, the circuit from any of the controlling switches is incomplete. This results in the distributor relay being energized which breaks the flow of current to the retarded set of points, and leaves the advance points in control of engine ignition timing.

There are four switches and relays which control the operation of the distributor relay. When the switches are On, their respective relays are energized and break an electrical circuit to the distributor relay, which in turn closes the electrical circuit to the retarded set of points, energizing them.

The switches are as follows:

1. The throttle switch: located on the carburetor primary throttle valve linkage and is turned On when the throttle valve is opened beyond 35°.

2. The transmission switch: located on the upper part of the transmission gearbox and is turned On when the transmission is shifted into 3rd or 4th gear.

3. The clutch switch: located on the clutch pedal arm and is turned on when the clutch pedal is depressed.

4. The accelerator switch: located on

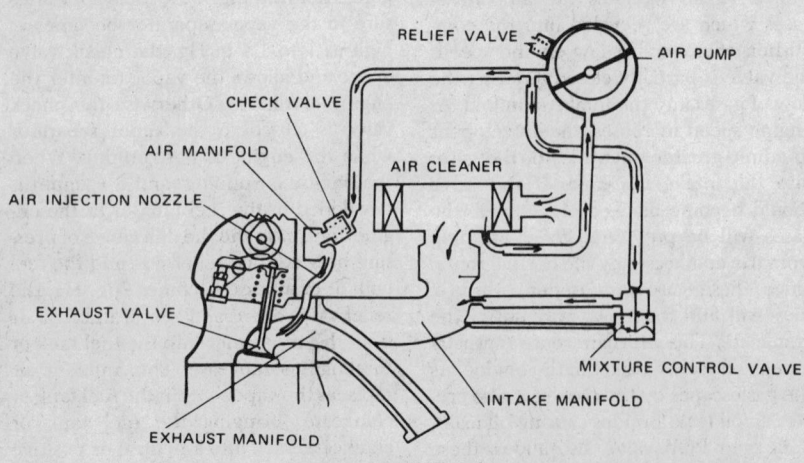

Diagram of the AIR system

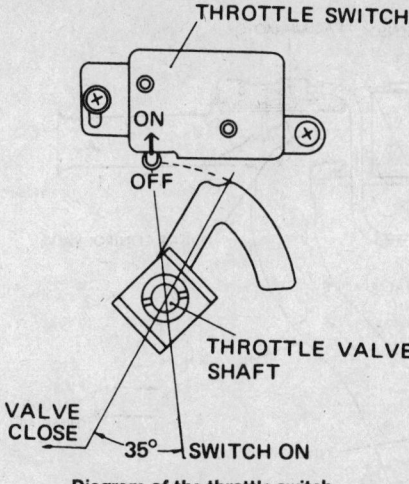

THROTTLE SWITCH

ON

OFF

THROTTLE VALVE SHAFT

VALVE CLOSE

35° — SWITCH ON

Diagram of the throttle switch

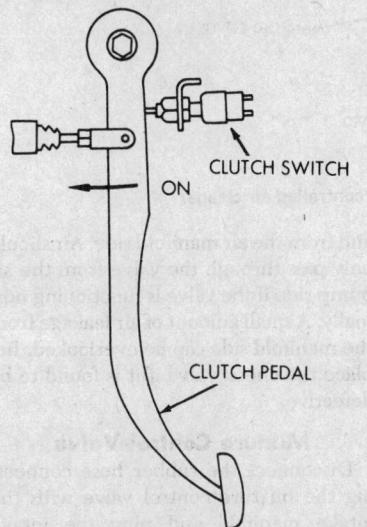

CLUTCH SWITCH

ON

CLUTCH PEDAL

Diagram of the clutch switch (1972-73). On 1974-75 models the clutch switch controls only the coasting richer solenoid and is Off when depressed

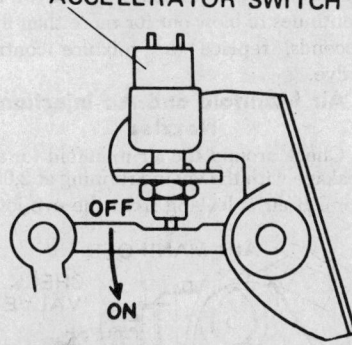

ACCELERATOR SWITCH

OFF

ON

ENGINE CONTROL LINK ROD

Diagram of the accelerator switch

the accelerator pedal linkage and is turned On when the throttle valve is opened to an angle of 7°.

The purpose of the dual point distributor is to allow ignition advance only when the vehicle is accelerating heavily, or when the engine is at idle.

The distributor vacuum advance mechanism produces a spark advance based on the amount of vacuum in the intake manifold. With a high vacuum, less air/fuel mixture enters the engine cylinders and the mixture is therefore less highly compressed. Consequently, this mixture burns more slowly and the advance mechanism gives it more time to burn. This longer burning time results in higher combustion temperatures at peak pressure and hence, more time for nitrogen to react with oxygen and form oxides of nitrogen (NO_x). At the same time, this advanced timing results in less complete combustion due to the greater area of cylinder wall (quench area) exposed at the instant of ignition. The "cooled" fuel will not burn as readily and hence, results in higher unburned hydrocarbons (HC). The production of NO_x and HC resulting from vacuum advance is highest during idle and moderate acceleration in lower gears.

Retardation of the ignition timing is necessary to reduce emissions. Various ways of retarding the ignition spark have been used in domestic automobiles, all of which remove vacuum to the distributor vacuum advance mechanism at different times under certain conditions. Another way of accomplishing the same goal is the dual point distributor system.

NOTE: *The transmission, clutch, and accelerator switches and relays also control the operation of the Coasting Richer System.*

Coasting Richer System

While the engine is coasting the air/fuel mixture remains lean, preventing efficient reburning of unburned exhaust gases which can only be done with the addition of more air. Therefore, it is necessary to enrich the air/fuel mixture while the engine is coasting to attain efficient reburning of exhaust gases.

However, enriching the air/fuel mixture with only the mixture adjusting screw will cause poor engine idle, or invite an increase in the CO content of the exhaust gases.

The coasting richer system consists of

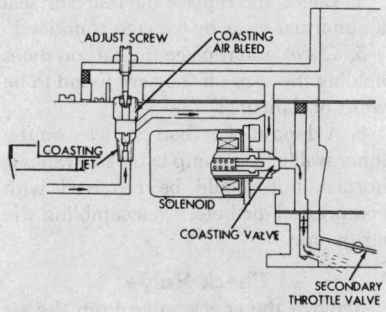

ADJUST SCREW

COASTING AIR BLEED

COASTING JET

SOLENOID

COASTING VALVE

SECONDARY THROTTLE VALVE

Diagram of the coasting richer system solenoid

an independent operative auxiliary fuel system. This system functions when the engine is coasting, to enrich the air/fuel mixture, which minimizes hydrocarbon content of the exhaust gases through efficient combustion. This is accomplished without adversely affecting engine idle and the carbon monoxide content of the exhaust gases.

A solenoid operated valve in the carburetor allows extra fuel to be drawn into the intake manifold. The solenoid valve is electrically connected in series to a transmission 4th/3rd gear switch, accelerator switch and a clutch switch, all of which are used to detect engine coasting conditions.

When all of these switches turn on or when the engine is coasting, the solenoid valve on the secondary side of the carburetor energizes and causes the valve to open. When the valve opens, fuel is drawn out of the float chamber by engine vacuum and metered via the coasting jet below the secondary throttle valve.

As a result of the operation of the coasting richer system, the air/fuel mixture becomes temporarily enriched to facilitate efficient reburning of exhaust gases in the exhaust manifold, thereby reducing hydrocarbon and carbon monoxide content in the exhaust gases exiting to the atmosphere.

When the engine coasting condition is halted (when the accelerator pedal is depressed, the clutch pedal depressed (1972–73 models) or when the transmission is placed in Neutral), the coasting richer circuit is opened and causes the coasting richer valve to close, shutting off the supply of extra fuel.

The solenoid switch is linked to the secondary side of the carburetor. The solenoid valve is electrically controlled by means of the accelerator switch, clutch switch, and the transmission switch.

The accelerator switch is connected to the engine accelerator linkage and is turned Off when the throttle valve is opened to an angle of 7°.

The clutch switch is installed in a position near the clutch pedal and turns Off when the clutch pedal is depressed.

The transmission switch is installed on the upper part of the transmission gearbox and turns On when the transmission is shifted into 4th or 3rd gear. The switch is Off in all other gear ranges and the coasting richer circuit is broken and the system deenergized.

Exhaust Gas Recirculation System (EGR)

Exhaust gas recirculation is used to reduce combustion temperatures in the engine, thereby reducing the oxides of nitrogen emissions.

An EGR valve is mounted on the center of the intake manifold. The recycled

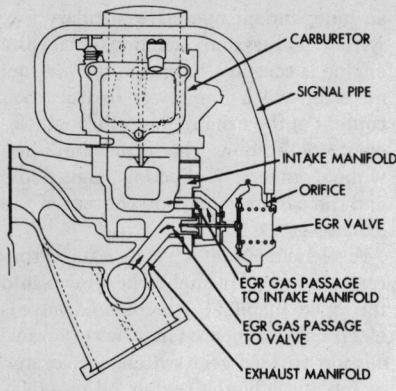

Diagram of the exhaust gas recirculation system

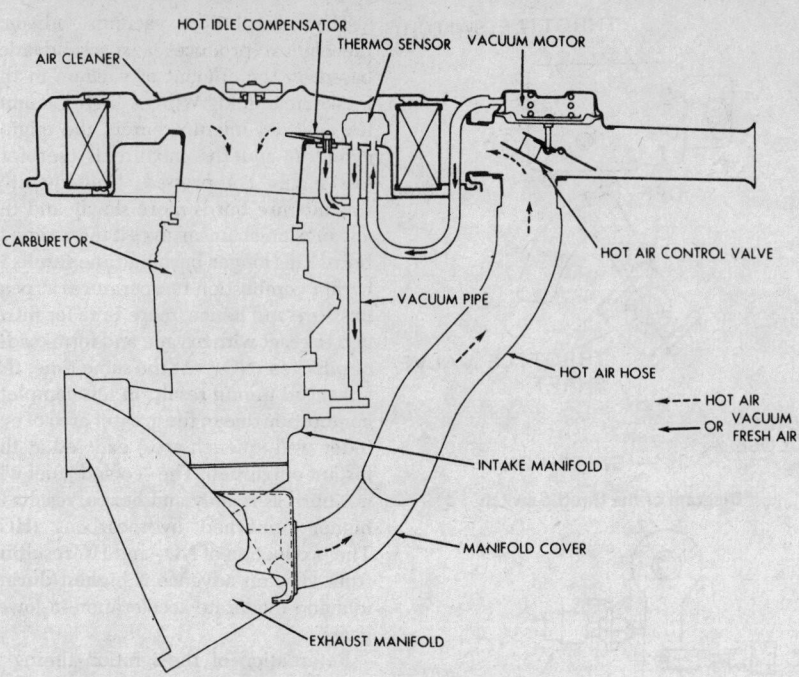

Diagram of the temperature controlled air cleaner

exhaust gas is drawn into the bottom of the intake manifold riser portion through the exhaust manifold heat stove and EGR valve. A vacuum diaphragm is connected to a timed signal port at the carburetor flange.

As the throttle valve is opened, vacuum is applied to the EGR valve vacuum diaphragm. When the vacuum reaches about 3.5 in. Hg, the diaphragm moves against spring pressure and is in a fully up position at 8 in. Hg of vacuum. As the diaphragm moves up, it opens the exhaust gas metering valve which allows exhaust gas to be pulled into the engine intake manifold. The system does not operate when the engine is idling because the exhaust gas recirculation would cause a rough idle.

Temperature Controlled Air Cleaner

The rate of fuel atomization varies with the temperature of the air that the fuel is being mixed with. The air/fuel ratio cannot be held constant for efficient fuel combustion with a wide range of air temperatures. Cold air being drawn into the engine causes a denser and more richer air/fuel mixture, inefficient fuel atomization, and thus, more hydrocarbons in the exhaust gas. Hot air being drawn into the engine causes a leaner air/fuel mixture and more efficient atomization and combustion for less hydrocarbons in the exhaust gases.

The automatic temperature controlled air cleaner is designed so that the temperature of the ambient air being drawn into the engine is automatically controlled, to hold the temperature of the air and, consequently, the fuel/air ratio at a constant rate for efficient fuel combustion.

A temperature sensing vacuum switch controls vacuum applied to a vacuum motor operating a valve in the intake snorkle of the air cleaner. When the engine is cold or the air being drawn into the engine is cold, the vacuum motor opens the valve, allowing air heated by the exhaust manifold to be drawn into

the engine. As the engine warms up, the temperature sensing unit shuts off the vacuum applied to the vacuum motor which allows the valve to close, shutting off the heated air and allowing cooler, outside (under hood) air to be drawn into the engine.

Inspection and Adjustments

Air Pump

If the air pump makes an abnormal noise and cannot be corrected without removing the pump from the vehicle, check the following in sequence:

1. Turn the pulley ¾ of a turn in the clockwise direction and ¼ of a turn in the counterclockwise direction. If the pulley is binding and if rotation is not smooth, a defective bearing is indicated.

2. Check the inner wall of the pump body, vanes and rotor for wear. If the rotor has abnormal wear, replace the air pump.

3. Check the needle roller bearing for wear and damage. If the bearings are defective, the air pump should be replaced.

4. Check and replace the rear side seal if abnormal wear or damage is noticed.

5. Check and replace the carbon shoes holding the vanes if they are found to be worn or damaged.

6. A deposit of carbon particles on the inner wall of the pump body and vanes is normal, but should be removed with compressed air before reassembling the air pump.

Check Valve

Remove the check valve from the air manifold. Test it for leakage by blowing air into the valve from the air pump side

and from the air manifold side. Air should only pass through the valve from the air pump side if the valve is functioning normally. A small amount of air leakage from the manifold side can be overlooked. Replace the check valve if it is found to be defective.

Mixture Control Valve

Disconnect the rubber hose connecting the mixture control valve with the intake manifold and plug the intake manifold side of the valve. If the mixture control valve is operating correctly, air will continue to blow out the mixture control valve for a few seconds after the accelerator pedal is fully depressed (engine running) and released quickly. If air continues to blow out for more than five seconds, replace the mixture control valve.

Air Manifold and Air Injection Nozzles

Check around the air manifold for air leakage with the engine running at 2,000 rpm. If air is leaking from the eye joint

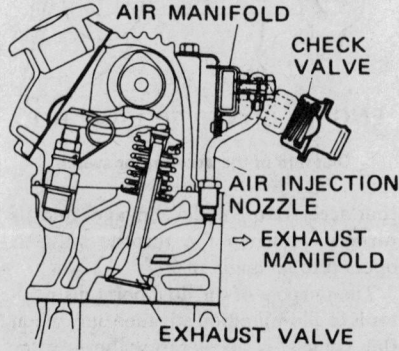

The air injection manifold and nozzles

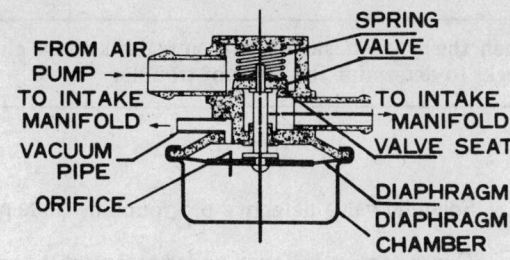

A cut-a-way diagram of the mixture control valve

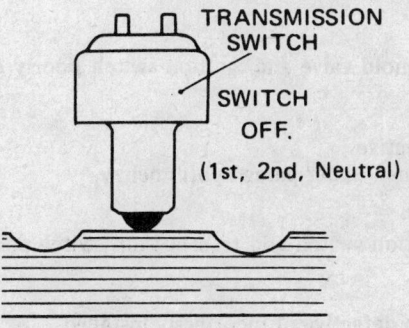

TRANSMISSION SWITCH

SWITCH OFF.

(1st, 2nd, Neutral)

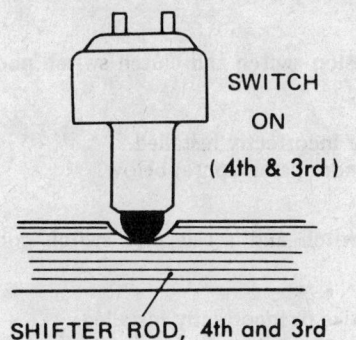

SWITCH ON

(4th & 3rd)

SHIFTER ROD, 4th and 3rd

Diagram of the transmission switch

bolt, retighten or replace the gasket. Check the air nozzles for restrictions by blowing air into the nozzles.

Hoses

Check and replace hoses if they are found to be weakened or cracked. Check all hose connections and clips. Be sure that the hoses are not in contact with other parts of the engine.

Coasting Richer System

Operation of the coasting richer system can be checked by carefully listening for the noise associated with the operation of the solenoid valve.

Check the setting of the accelerator switch and the clutch switch. The clearance between the switch plungers and the actuating surfaces of the accelerator pedal and clutch pedal are to be 0.04–0.05 in and 0.0197–0.0394 in. (1974–77 only), respectively. Test the operation of the switches with a test light connected to the electrical connectors. The switches are normally On when the pedals are released, and Off when the pedals are depressed. If the switches do not work in response to the movement of the pedals, replace the switches.

Check the operation of the transmission switch by moving the gearshift lever with the switch wiring disconnected and a test light connected to the switch terminals. The switch should only be On when the gearshift lever is shifted into either 3rd or 4th gear. Replace the switch if it is found to be defective.

EGR Valve

NOTE: *The EGR valve cannot be disassembled. No actual service is required except to determine proper operation of the valve.*

Check the valve shaft for proper movement by opening the throttle to give 2,-000–2,500 rpm. The shaft should move upward at these speeds and return to the downward position when the engine speed is reduced to normal idle speed.

Check the vacuum diaphragm function by applying an outside vacuum source to the vacuum supply tube at the top of the vacuum diaphragm. The diaphragm should not leak down and should move to the fully up position at about 8–10 in. Hg of vacuum.

Vacuum Switching Valve

Check the vacuum switching valve by carefully listening for the noise that is accompanied by electrically operating the plunger. The plunger can be operated electrically by connecting the connector terminals directly to the battery with suitable cables.

Air Switching Valve

The air switching valve is normal when air continues to blow out the air switch after the engine is started.

TROUBLESHOOTING COASTING RICHER SYSTEM

Checking Order	Ignition Switch	Transmission	Throttle	Clutch	Solenoid Valve		Defective Part or Check Point
					Normal Condition	Abnormal Condition	
1.	ON	4th or 3rd gear	When opening angle is 7° or less	Engage	ON	OFF	Check fuse then refer to checking order No. 6 if still not operating properly
2.	OFF	*	*	*	OFF	ON	Ignition Switch
3.	ON	1st, 2nd, Neutral, Reverse	*	*	OFF	ON	Transmission Switch
4.	ON	*	When opening angle is 7° or more	*	OFF	ON	Accelerator Switch
5.	ON	*	*	Dis-Engage	OFF	ON	Clutch Switch

*Operating condition is unimportant.

If the solenoid valve does not function properly when the ignition switch, transmission switch, clutch switch, and accelerator switch are turned ON, perform the following checks to determine the cause of trouble.

Check the solenoid valve terminal voltage.

a
- One terminal indicates 12V .... Solenoid valve defective or grounding cable poorly connected.

- Both terminals also indicate zero V .... Check parts mentioned under paragraph(b) below.

b Check voltage at ignition switch AM terminal and IG terminal.
- Both terminals indicate zero V .... Cable between solenoid valve and ignition switch poorly connected.

- AM terminal indicates 12 V and 1G terminal zero V .... Ignition switch defective
- Both terminals indicate 12 V .... Check parts mentioned under paragraph(c) below.

c Check voltage at transmission switch terminals.
- Both terminals indicate zero V .... Cable between ignition switch and transmission switch poorly connected.

- One of terminals indicates 12 V and the other zero V .... Transmission switch defective or incorrectly installed.
- Both terminals indicate 12 V .... Check parts mentioned under paragraph(d) below.

d Check voltage at clutch switch terminals.
- Both terminals indicate zero V .... Cables between transmission switch and clutch switch poorly connected.

- One of the terminals indicates 12 V, the other zero V .... Clutch switch defective or incorrectly installed.
- Both terminals indicate 12 V .... Check parts mentioned under paragraph(e) below.

e Check voltage at accelerator switch terminals
- Both terminals indicate zero V .... Cable between clutch switch and accelerator switch poorly connected.

- One of the terminals indicates 12 V and another zero V .... Accelerator switch defective or incorrectly installed.

Thermo Sensor

Run the engine at idle for a few minutes, then disconnect the thermo sensor wiring connector. Check for continuity between the terminals by using a tester. If no continuity exists, the thermo sensor is defective and should be replaced.

Thermo Controller

If the thermo controller is normal, the converter warning light and buzzer operate when the ignition switch is in the "ON" position, and go out automatically a few seconds later.

Engine Speed Sensor

Disconnect the engine speed sensor wiring connector and connect "B", "BR" and "BY" color-coded wiring terminals to each other with suitable cables. Then start the engine and check for the continuity between "LgB" color coded wiring terminals. When the engine runs over 1500–1700 rpm, the engine speed sensor is normal, if the continuity exists.

TCS SYSTEM TROUBLESHOOTING

1. Check the vacuum switching valve terminal voltage.

- One terminal indicates 12V .... Vacuum switching valve defective or grounding cable poorly connected.

- Both terminals also indicate zero V .... Check parts mentioned under test 2.

2. Check voltage at ignition switch AM terminal and IG terminal.

- Both terminals indicate zero V .... Cable between vacuum switching and ignition switch poorly connected.

- AM terminal indicates 12V and IG terminal zero V .... Ignition switch defective.

- Both terminals indicate 12V .... Check parts mentioned under test 3.

3. Check voltage at transmission switch terminals.

- Both terminals indicate zero V .... Cable between ignition switch and transmission switch poorly connected.

Catalytic Converter System —California Only

A 2.6 liter converter is used to control hydrocarbon and carbon monoxide emissions. The converter oxidizes hydrocarbons and carbon monoxide into water and carbondioxide.

Over-Temperature Control System

While the engine is coasting, the coasting richer system is operated to prevent catalyst over heating caused by poor combustion. The secondary air injection is operated simultaneously with the coasting richer system. When the catalyst temperature reaches 1350°F, due to high speed and/or high load driving, the secondary air is diverted to the atmosphere to reduce chemical reaction in the catalyst. When the catalyst temperature reaches 1830°F, due to engine malfunction or ignition system failure, the warning lamp and buzzer are turned on.

Vacuum Switching Valve

The vacuum switching valve has three ports, two of which are activated electrically by the solenoid plunger. The plunger is energized when the catalyst temperature exceeds 1350°F. It connects the diaphragm chamber of the air switching valve with the intake manifold permitting manifold vacuum to be applied to the diaphragm chamber.

Air Switching Valve

This valve diverts air flow from the pump and is operated by manifold vacuum and air pump pressure which are operated by the vacuum switching valve.

FUEL SYSTEM
Fuel Filter

A fuel filter is located in the fuel line leading from the fuel tank to the fuel pump. It is of the cartridge type with a paper filter element. If the fuel line is suspected of being clogged, check the fuel filter. Otherwise, the filter never has to be serviced.

Mechanical Fuel Pump

The fuel pump is a mechanically-operated, diaphragm-type driven by the fuel pump eccentric cam on the jackshaft.

Design of the fuel pump permits disassembly, cleaning and repair or replacement of defective parts.

Removal and Installation

1. Disconnect the rubber hose at the side of the fuel pump.

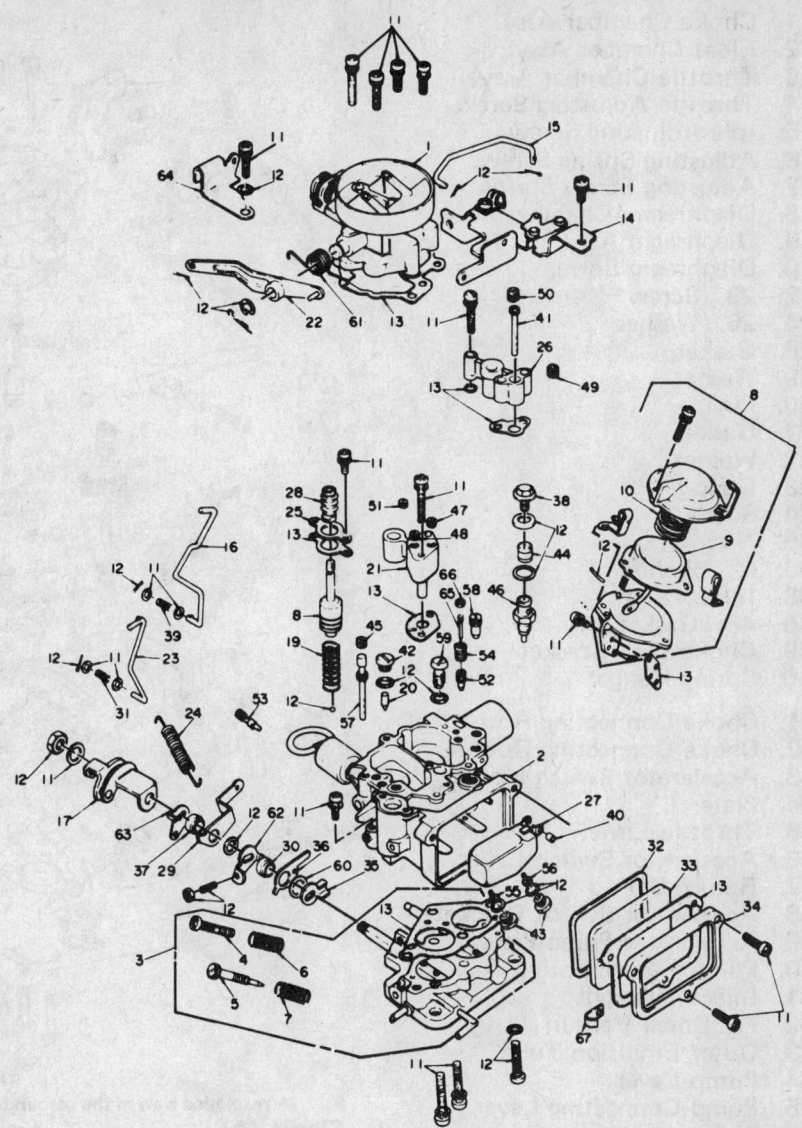

An exploded view of the carburetor used on 1974-75 models without air conditioning

1. Choke chamber assembly	24. Throttle return spring	47. Accel air bleed
2. Float chamber assembly	25. Plate	48. Main air bleed (Primary)
3. Throttle chamber assembly	26. Small venturi (Secondary)	49. Slow air bleed (Secondary)
4. Throttle adjust screw	27. Float	50. Main air bleed (Secondary)
5. Idle adjust screw	28. Dust cover	
6. Throttle adjust screw spring	29. Starting lever	51. Slow air bleed (Primary)
7. Idle adjust screw spring	30. Sleeve	52. Coasting jet
8. Diaphragm chamber assembly	31. Spring	53. Vacuum jet
9. Diaphragm	32. Rubber seal	54. Coasting air bleed
10. Diaphragm spring	33. Fuel level gage	55. Main jet (Primary)
11. Screw & washer kit, A	34. Cover	56. Main jet (Secondary)
12. Screw & washer kit, B	35. Adjust lever, B	57. Slow jet (Primary)
13. Gasket	36. Return plate	58. Slow jet (Secondary)
14. Choke control arm	37. Sleeve	59. Power valve
15. Choke connecting rod	38. Filter set screw	60. Thrust washer
16. Choke connecting rod	39. Spring	61. Pump lever return spring
17. Throttle lever (Primary)	40. Collar	62. Kick lever
18. Accelerator pump piston	41. Secondary emulsion tube	63. Crank
19. Piston spring	42. Plug	64. Choke control cable hanger
20. Injector weight	43. Drain plug	65. Coasting adjust screw
21. Small venturi (Primary)	44. Filter	66. Coasting adjust screw
22. Accelerator pump lever	45. Slow jet plug (Primary)	67. EGR vacuum pipe clip
23. Connecting rod	46. Needle valve	

1. Choke Chamber Assy.
2. Float Chamber Assy.
3. Throttle Chamber Assy.
4. Throttle Adjusting Screw
5. Idle Adjusting Screw
6. Adjusting Spring Screw
7. Adjusting Screw Spring
8. Diaphragm, Chamber Assy.
9. Diaphragm Assy.
10. Diaphragm Spring
12.–23. Screw
24.–26. Washer
28. Gasket
29. Washer
30. Pin
31. Gasket
32. Washer
33. Gasket
34. Screw
35. Nut
36. 37. Washer
38. Inlet Valve
40.–48. Gasket
49. Choke Wire Bracket
50. Spring Hanger

51. Choke Connecting Rod
52. Choke Connecting Rod
53. Accelerator Switch Holder
54. Plate
55. Throttle Lever
56. Accelerator Switch Lever
57. Return Spring
58. Accelerator Switch Bracket
59. Accelerator Pump Piston
60. Pump Return Spring
61. Injector Weight
62. Pri. Small Venturi
63. Outer Emulsion Tube
64. Pump Lever
65. Pump Connecting Lever
66. Return Spring

67. Piston Plate
68. Sec. Small Venturi
69. Float
70. Dust Cover
71. Choke Connecting Lever
72. Sleeve (B)
73. Spring
74. Rubber Seal
75. Level Gauge
76. Level Gauge Cover
77. Adjust Lever
78. Return Plate

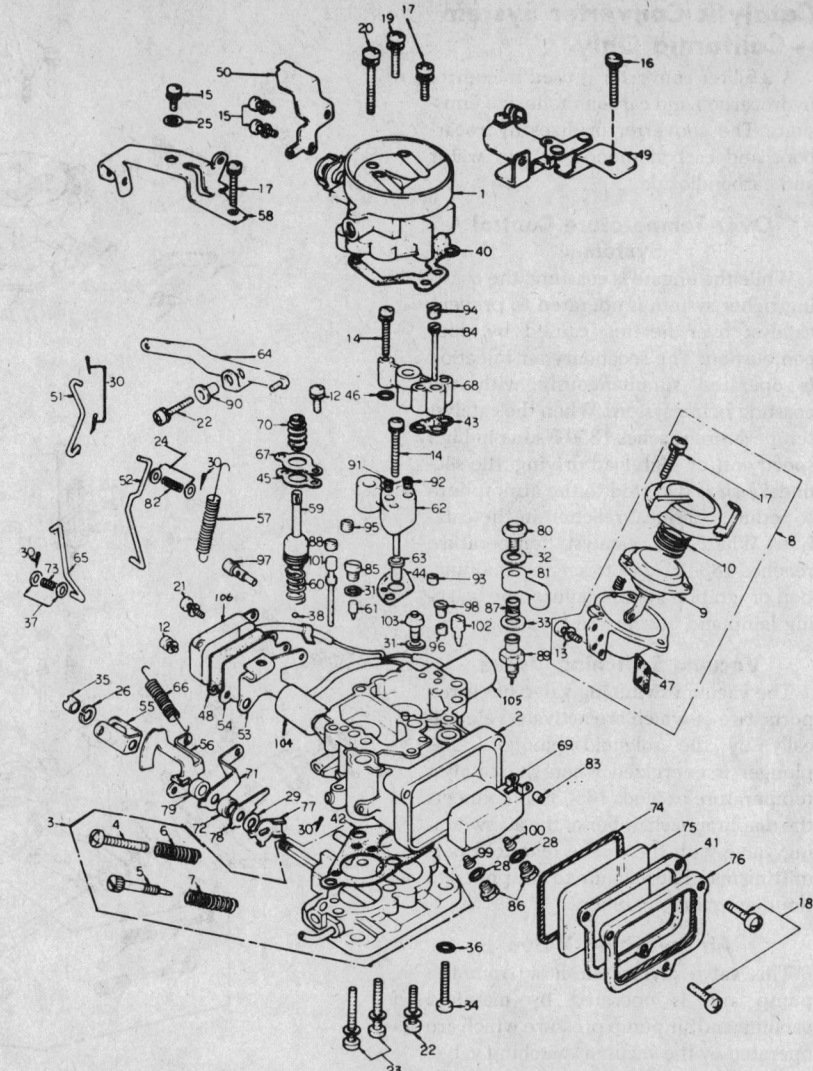

An exploded view of the carburetor used on 1972 and 1973 models

79. Sleeve (A)
80. Set Screw
81. Joint nipple
82. Spring
83. Float Collar
84. Sec. Emulsion Tube
85. Injector Weight Plug
86. Main Jet Plug
87. Strainer
88. Pri. Slow Jet Plug
89. Float Needle Valve Assy.
90. Collar
91. Pri. Main Air Bleed
92. Accelerator Air Bleed

93. Sec. Slow Air Bleed
94. Sec. Main Air Bleed
95. Pri. Slow Air Bleed
96. Coasting Jet
97. Vacuum Jet
98. Coasting Air Bleed
99. Pri. Main Jet
100. Sec. Main Jet
101. Pri. Slow Jet
102. Sec. Slow Jet
103. Power Valve
104. Anti Dieseling Solenoid
105. Coasting Valve Solenoid
106. Accelerator Switch

2. Remove the joint bolt and disconnect the fuel line at the side of the fuel pump. Be careful not to lose the joint bolt gaskets when removing the joint bolt.

3. Remove the two fuel pump mounting nuts and remove the fuel pump assembly from the side of the engine.

4. Install the fuel pump in the reverse order of removal, using a new gasket and sealer on the mating surface.

Electric Fuel Pump

The fuel pump is of the electro-magnetic type and is installed on the inner face of the third crossmember at the left hand side. This fuel pump is a totally enclosed type and cannot be disassembled.

Removal and Installation

1. Disconnect the hoses at the fuel pump side.

2. Remove the two bolts and one nut mounting the fuel pump and remove the fuel pump assembly.

Carburetor

The carburetor used on the Chevy LUV is a two-barrel downdraft type with a low-speed (primary) side and a high-speed (secondary) side.

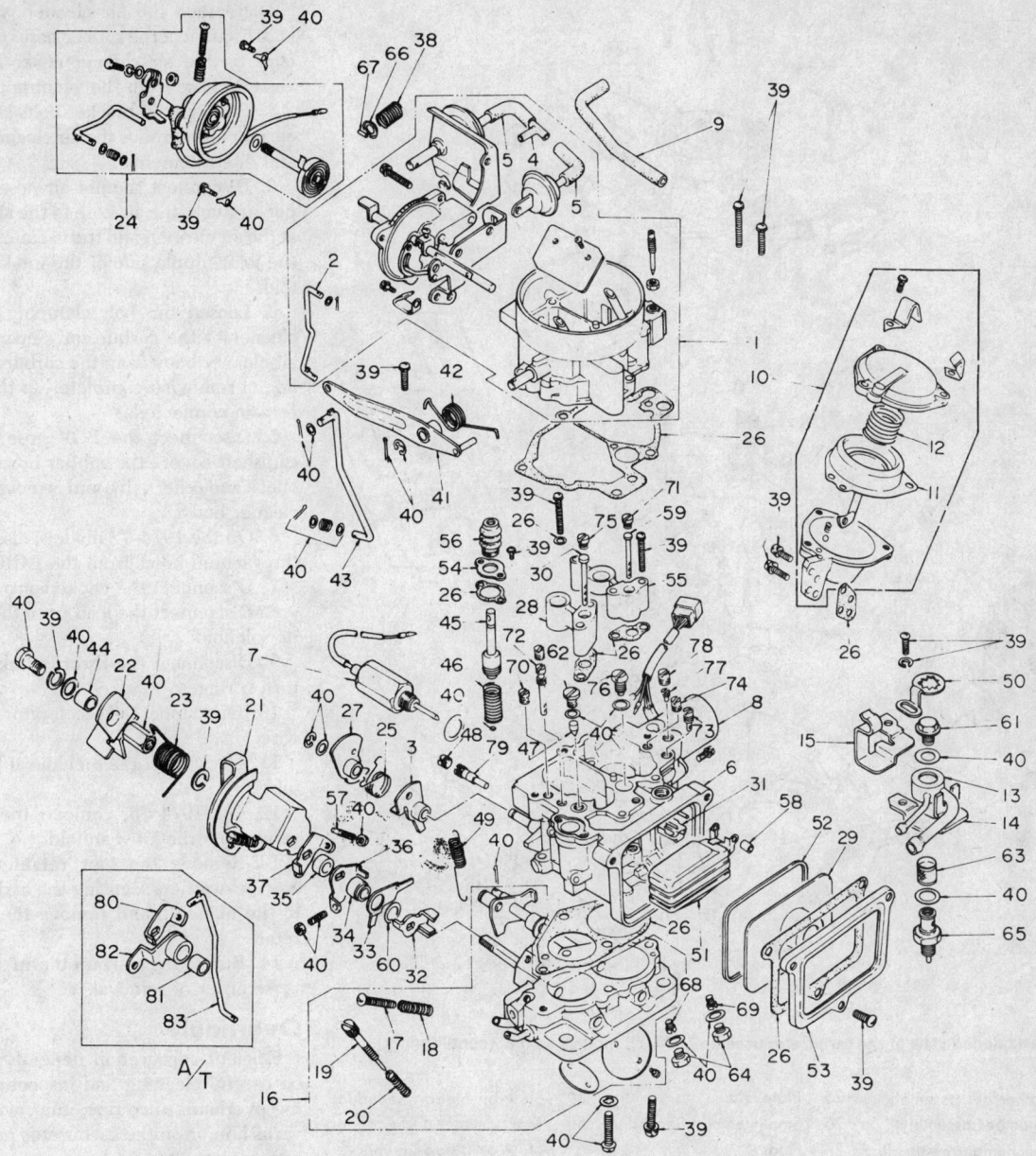

Exploded view of 1976-77 carburetor

1. Choke chamber assembly
2. Choke connecting rod
3. Counter lever
4. Nipple
5. Hose
6. Float chamber assembly
7. Anti-dieseling solenoid
8. Coasting richer solenoid
9. Hose
10. Diaphragm chamber assembly
11. Diaphragm
12. Diaphragm spring
13. Nipple
14. Nipple stop plate
15. EGR vacuum hose clip
16. Throttle chamber assembly
17. Throttle adjusting screw
18. Adjusting screw spring
19. Idle adjusting screw
20. Adjusting screw spring
21. Throttle lever (primary)

22. Fast idle lever
23. Fast idle lever spring
24. Thermostat cover assembly
25. Fast idle cam spring
26. Gasket kit
27. Fast idle cam
28. Small venturi (primary)
29. Fuel level gauge
30. Primary emulsion tube
31. Baffle plate
32. Throttle adjusting lever
33. Throttle return plate
34. Kick lever sleeve
35. Throttle lever sleeve
36. Kick lever
37. Fast idle lever
38. Auto choke piston spring
39. Screw & Washer kit, A
40. Screw & Washer kit, B
41. Accelerator pump lever
42. Pump lever return spring

43. Accelerator pump rod
44. Fast idle lever collar
45. Accelerator pump piston
46. Piston return spring
47. Injector weight
48. Vacuum jet plug
49. Throttle return spring
50. Lock lever
51. Float
52. Rubber seal
53. Cover
54. Plate
55. Small venturi (Secondary)
56. Dust cover
57. Fast idle adjusting screw
58. Collar
59. Secondary emulsion tube
60. Thrust washer
61. Filter set screw
62. Injector weight plug

63. Filter
64. Drain plug
65. Needle valve
66. Piston spring carrier
67. Piston spring stop pin
68. Main jet (Primary)
69. Main jet (Secondary)
70. Slow air bleed (Primary)
71. Main air bleed (Secondary)
72. Slow jet (Primary)
73. Slow jet (Secondary)
74. Slow air bleed (Secondary)
75. Main air bleed (Primary)
76. Power valve
77. Coasting jet
78. Coasting air bleed
79. Vacuum jet
80. Connecting lever
81. Collar A
82. Down shift lever
83. Pump rod

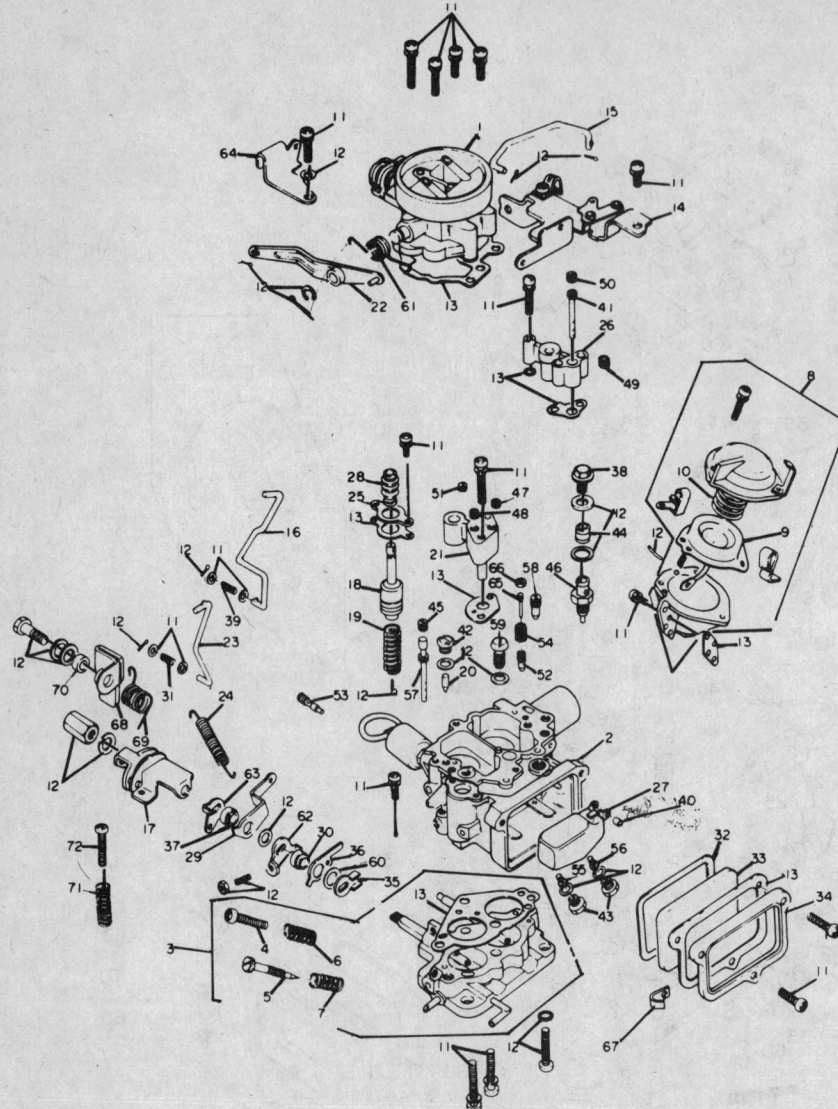

An exploded view of the carburetor used on 1974-75 models with air conditioning

1. Choke chamber assembly	25. Plate	49. Slow air bleed (Secondary)
2. Float chamber assembly	26. Small venturi (Secondary)	50. Main air bleed (Secondary)
3. Throttle chamber assembly	27. Float	51. Slow air bleed (Primary)
4. Throttle adjust screw	28. Dust cover	52. Coasting jet
5. Idle adjust screw	29. Starting lever	53. Vacuum jet
6. Throttle adjust screw spring	30. Sleeve	54. Coasting air bleed
7. Idle adjust screw spring	31. Spring	55. Main jet (Primary)
8. Diaphragm chamber assembly	32. Rubber seal	56. Main jet (Secondary)
9. Diaphragm	33. Fuel level gage	57. Slow jet (Primary)
10. Diaphragm spring	34. Cover	58. Slow jet (Secondary)
11. Screw & washer kit, A	35. Adjust lever, B	59. Power valve
12. Screw & washer kit, B	36. Return plate	60. Thrust washer
13. Gasket	37. Sleeve	61. Pump lever return spring
14. Choke control arm	38. Filter set screw	62. Kick lever
15. Choke connecting rod	39. Spring	63. Crank
16. Choke connecting rod	40. Collar	64. Choke control cable hanger
17. Throttle lever (Primary)	41. Secondary emulsion tube	65. Coasting adjust screw
18. Accelerator pump piston	42. Plug	66. Lock nut
19. Piston spring	43. Drain plug	67. EGR Vacuum pipe clip
20. Injector weight	44. Filter	68. Fast idle lever
21. Small venturi (Primary)	45. Slow jet plug (Primary)	69. Spring
22. Accelerator pump lever	46. Needle valve	70. Collar
23. Connecting rod	47. Accel air bleed	71. Fast idle adjust spring
24. Throttle return spring	48. Main air bleed (Primary)	72. Fast idle adjust screw

Removal and Installation

1. Remove the air cleaner wing nut and disconnect the rubber hoses from the clips on the air cleaner cover and the vacuum hose from the vacuum motor.

2. Remove the bracket bolts at the air cleaner and remove the air cleaner cover and filter element.

3. Disconnect the hot air hose (to the hot air duct), the air hose to the air pump at the air cleaner, and the vacuum hose at the joint nipple side of the intake manifold.

4. Loosen the bolt clamping the air cleaner to the carburetor. Separate the air cleaner body from the carburetor but do not remove it completely as the hoses remain connected.

5. Disconnect the PCV hose (to the camshaft cover), the rubber hoses to the check and relief valve and remove the air cleaner body.

6. On the 1974–77 models, disconnect the vacuum hoses from the EGR valve.

7. Disconnect the choke control wire.

8. Disconnect the lead from the throttle solenoid.

9. Disconnect the throttle linkage return spring.

10. Disconnect the accelerator linkage wire.

11. Disconnect the fuel line at the carburetor.

12. On 1974–75, remove the check valve from the air manifold.

13. Remove the four retaining nuts and lockwashers securing the carburetor to the manifold and remove the carburetor.

14. Install the carburetor in the reverse order of removal.

Overhaul

Efficient carburetion depends greatly on careful cleaning and inspection during overhaul, since dirt, gum, water, or varnish in or on the carburetor parts are often responsible for poor performance.

Overhaul your carburetor in a clean, dust-free area. Carefully disassemble the carburetor, referring often to the exploded views. Keep all similar and looka-like parts segregated during disassembly and cleaning to avoid accidental interchange during assembly. Make a note of all jet sizes.

When the carburetor is disassembled, wash all parts (except diaphragms, electric choke units, pump plunger, and any other plastic, leather, fiber, or rubber parts) in clean carburetor solvent. Do not leave parts in the solvent any longer than is necessary to sufficiently loosen the deposits. Excessive cleaning may remove the special finish from the float bowl and choke valve bodies, leaving these parts unfit for service. Rinse all parts in clean solvent and blow them dry with compressed air or allow them to air dry. Wipe clean all cork, plastic, leather with lint-free cloth.

Blow out all passages and jets with compressed air and be sure that there are no restrictions or blockages. Never use wire or similar tools to clean jets, fuel passages, or air bleeds. Clean all jets and valves separately to avoid accidental interchange.

Check all parts for wear or damage. If wear or damage is found, replace the defective parts. Especially check the following:

1. Check the float needle and seat for wear. If wear is found, replace the complete assembly.

2. Check the float hinge pin for wear and the float(s) for dents or distortion. Replace the float if fuel has leaked into it.

3. Check the throttle and choke shaft bores for wear or an out-of-round condition. Damage or wear to the throttle arm, shaft, or shaft bore will often require replacement of the throttle body. These parts require a close tolerance of fit; wear may allow air leakage, which would affect starting and idling.

NOTE: *Throttle shafts and bushings are not included in overhaul kits. They can be purchased separately.*

4. Inspect the idle mixture adjusting needles for burrs or grooves. Any such condition requires replacement of the needle, since you will not be able to obtain a satisfactory idle.

5. Test the accelerator pump check valves. They should pass air one way but not the other. Test for proper seating by blowing and sucking on the valve. Replace the valve if necessary. If the valve is satisfactory, wash the valve again to remove breath moisture.

6. Check the bowl cover for warped surfaces with a straightedge.

7. Closely inspect the valves and seats for wear and damage, replacing as necessary.

8. After the carburetor is assembled, check the choke valve for freedom of operation.

Carburetor overhaul kits are recommended for each overhaul. These kits contain all gaskets and new parts to replace those that deteriorate most rapidly. Failure to replace all parts supplied with the kit (especially gaskets) can result in poor performance later.

After cleaning and checking all components, reassemble the carburetor, using new parts and referring to the exploded view. When reassembling, make sure that all screws and jets are tight in their seats, but do not overtighten as the tips will be distorted. Tighten all screws gradually, in rotation. Do not tighten needle valves into their seats; uneven jetting will result. Always use new gaskets. Be sure to adjust the float level when reassembling.

Throttle Linkage Adjustment

When the primary throttle valve is opened to an angle of 50°—1972–75, 47°—1976–77 from its closed position, the adjust plate which is interlocked with the primary throttle valve, is brought into contact with portion A (see illustration) of the return plate. When the primary throttle valve is opened farther, the return plate is pulled apart from the stopper (B in the illustration), allowing the secondary throttle valve to open.

To adjust the linkage:

1. Measure the clearance between the primary throttle valve and the wall of the throttle chamber at the center of the throttle valve when the adjust plate is brought into contact with portion A of the return plate. Standard clearance is 0.26–0.32 in.—1972–75, 0.24–0.30 in.—1976–77.

2. If necessary, make the adjustment by bending the portion A of the return plate.

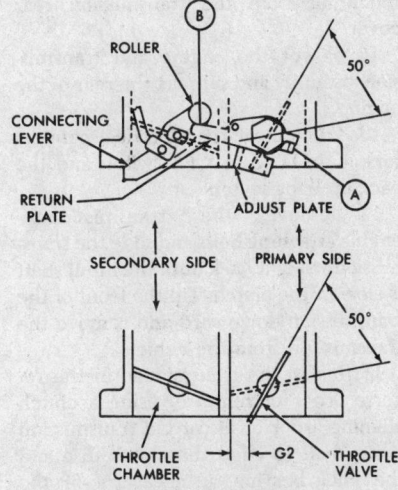

Throttle linkage adjustment

Float Level Adjustment

The fuel level is normal if it is within the lines on the window glass of the float chamber when the vehicle is resting on level ground and the engine is off.

If the fuel level is outside the lines, remove the float housing cover. Have an absorbent cloth under the cover to catch the fuel from the fuel bowl. Adjust the float level by bending the needle seat on the float.

The needle valve should have an effective stroke of about 0.059 in. When necessary, the needle valve stroke can be adjusted by bending the float stopper.

NOTE: *Be careful not to bend the needle valve rod when installing the float and baffle plate, if removed.*

Choke and Fast Idle Adjustment

When the choke is pulled completely

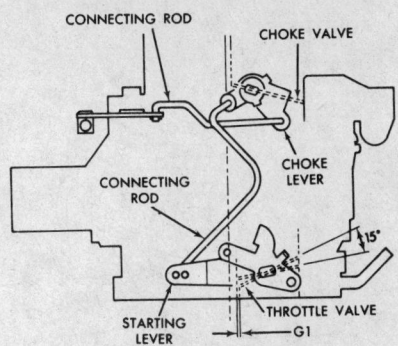

Choke and fast idle adjustment

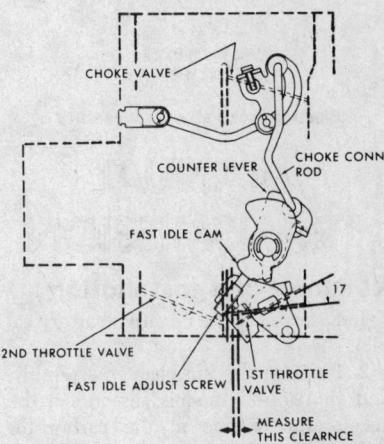

Choke and fast idle adjustment—1975-77

closed, the primary throttle valve is opened, by means of the choke connecting rod to an angle of 17.5°—1972–74, 17°—1975–77.

To check the opening angle of the primary throttle valve, close the choke valve completely and measure the clearance between the throttle valve and the wall of the throttle valve chamber at the center part of the throttle valve. The clearance should be 0.057–0.065 in.—1972–74, 0.047–0.051 in.—1975–77. If necessary, adjust the throttle valve opening angle by bending the connecting rod.

Make sure to turn the throttle stop screw all the way in before measuring the clearance.

Electric Choke Adjustment

Measure clearance (L) between the cover side stopper and the bimetal lever side stopper when the diaphragm (B) is fully stroked with negative pressure or finger pressure. If the measured value deviates from the standard clearance of 0.28–0.29 in. or the equivalent bimetal lever angle of 20 degrees adjust with the adjusting screw.

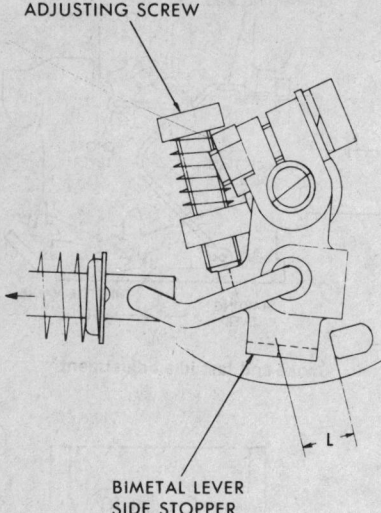

ADJUSTING SCREW

BIMETAL LEVER
SIDE STOPPER

Electric choke stopper clearance

MANUAL TRANSMISSION

Removal and Installation

1. Disconnect the negative battery cable.

2. Remove the air cleaner assembly, and on 1974–77 models, disconnect the accelerator linkage at the carburetor throttle lever.

3. Slide the gearshift lever boot upward on the lever, remove the two gearshift lever attaching bolts and remove the lever.

4. Remove the starter attaching bolts and lay the starter assembly aside.

5. Raise the vehicle on a hoist and disconnect the exhaust pipe at the flange and disconnect the exhaust pipe hanger at the transmission.

6. Disconnect the speedometer cable at the transmission and disconnect the driveshaft at the differential. Remove the driveshaft. At this point you will have to either drain the transmission lubricant or plug the output shaft opening to prevent spillage.

7. Disconnect the clutch slave cylinder and pushrod from the transmission case

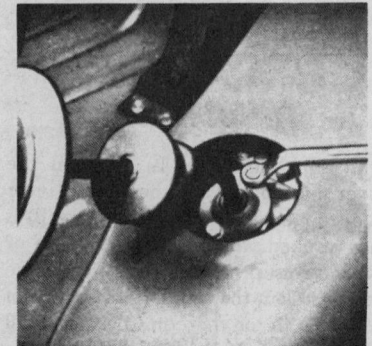

Removing the gearshift lever

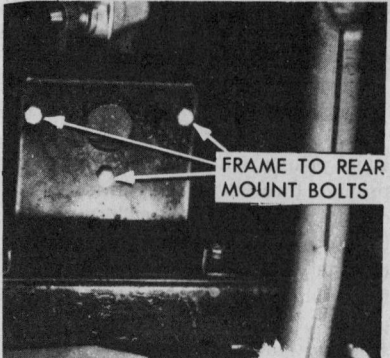

FRAME TO REAR MOUNT BOLTS

Removal of the three frame bracket-to-transmission rear mount bolts

and wire the slave cylinder to the frame.

8. On the 1973–77 models, remove the bolts attaching the stiffeners, then remove the stone shield (all models).

9. Remove the frame bracket-to-rear transmission mount attaching bolts.

10. Raise the engine and transmission as required and remove the four crossmember-to-frame bracket bolts.

11. On 1973–75 models, remove the mounting from the transmission rear cover.

12. Lower the engine and transmission assembly and support the rear of the engine.

13. Disconnect the electrical connectors at the TCS or CRS switch and the back-up light switch.

14. Remove the transmission-to-engine attaching bolts and slide the transmission straight back until the input shaft is clear of the clutch. Tip the front of the transmission downward and remove the transmission from the vehicle.

15. Install the transmission in the reverse order of removal, using a clutch aligning arbor or discarded transmission input shaft to align the clutch disc and the pilot bearing, if necessary (if the clutch was removed).

Overhaul

1972–75

1. Drain the transmission oil.

2. Remove the clutch fork, cover and release bearing.

3. Remove the five bolts from the front bearing retainer and the Belleville spring.

4. Remove the eight transmission top cover retaining bolts and remove the cover. Take care not to lose the three detent springs and balls.

5. Remove the four shift quadrant cover retaining bolts and remove the cover.

6. Remove the TCS or CRS switch and back-up lamp switch. Take care not to lose the back-up switch actuating pin and detent ball when removing the switch.

7. Remove the fulcrum bracket and the reverse idler gear control lever and the shift block.

8. Remove the three rollpins from the shift forks.

9. Remove the reverse shifter shaft through the front of the case and remove the shift fork. Be careful not to lose the three detent balls at the front of the case.

10. Remove the speedometer adapter from the transmission extension housing.

11. Remove the rear extension housing.

12. Remove the third and fourth gear shifter shaft through the rear of the case. Take care not to lose the two interlock balls at the front of the case.

13. Remove the first and second shifter shaft through the rear of the case. Avoid losing the interlock pin through the front of the shaft.

14. Remove the first and second, and the third and fourth gear shift forks through the top of the case.

15. Remove the lock plate at the rear of the case and remove the reverse idler gear shaft through the rear of the case.

16. Drive the countergear shaft through the rear of the case with a drift.

17. Remove the mainshaft from the rear of the transmission case. Remove the clutch gear pilot roller from the clutch gear. Remove the clutch gear and the bearing assembly from the front of the case. Press the front bearing from the clutch gear.

18. Remove the countergear and reverse idler gear from the transmission case.

19. Remove the snap-ring and remove the front bearing from the clutch gear shaft.

20. Remove the rear speedometer drive gear snap-ring, speedometer gear and drive key, and remove the front snap-ring.

21. Remove the rear bearing retainer nut and lockwasher and remove the rear bearing retainer.

22. Press the rear bearing from the retainer.

23. Remove the first gear rear thrust washer, gear, caged roller bearing, sleeve and blocker ring.

24. Remove the first and second gear synchronizer hub and gear assembly.

25. Remove the second speed gear, caged roller bearing and blocker ring.

26. Remove the third and fourth gear synchronizer hub snap ring and remove the synchronizer assembly, blocker ring, third speed gear and caged roller bearing.

To assemble the transmission:

27. Lightly oil the third gear bearing journal on the mainshaft. Install the caged roller bearing, the third gear blocker ring, and the third and fourth gear synchronizer hub assembly with the chamfer on the synchronizer hub toward the front of the transmission. Install the snap-ring.

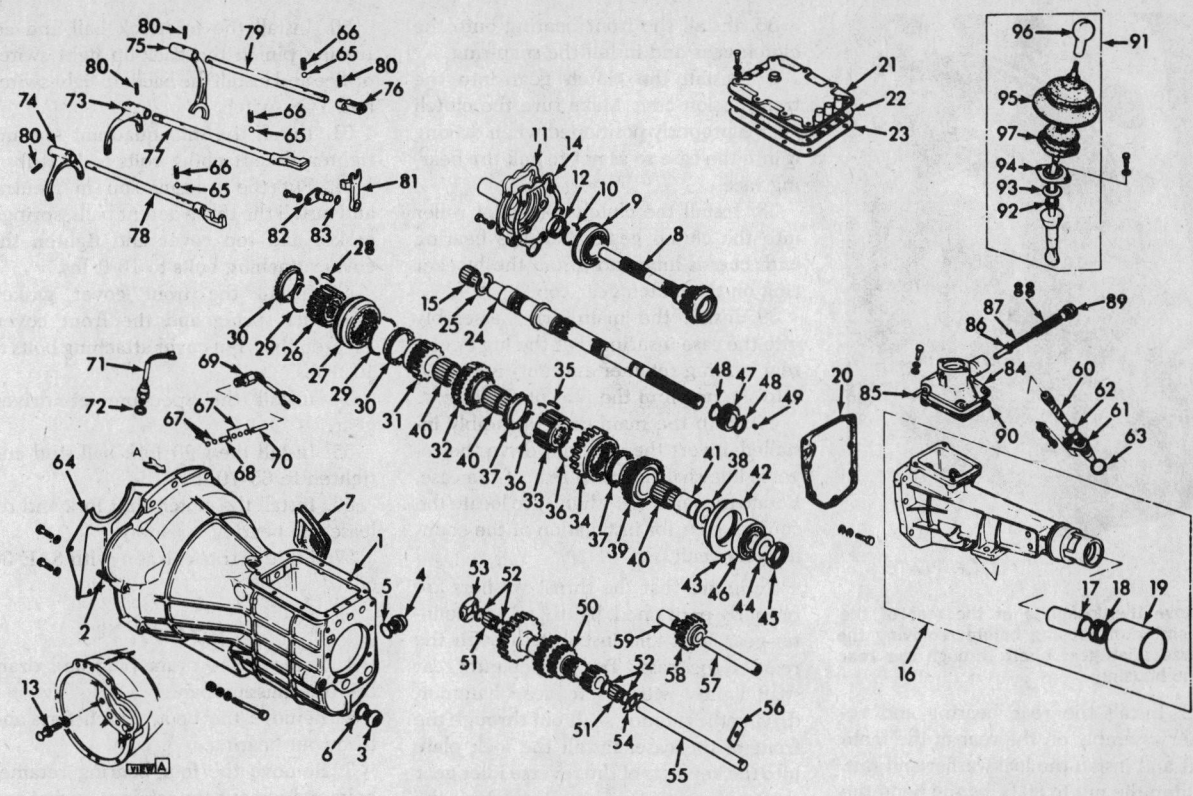

1972-75 LUV transmission

1. Transmission Case	34. Reverse Gear	66. Spring, Detent Ball, Gear
2. Stud; Starter to Case	35. Insert; Clutch Hub	67. Ball, Inner Lock, Gear Shift
3. Plug; Oil Filler	36. Spring; Insert	68. Pin, Lock, Inner Lock
4. Plug; Magnetic	37. Blocker Ring; 1-2	69. Switch Assy., Reverse Lamp
5. O-Ring; Drain Plug to Case	38. Thrust Washer	70. Plunger, Reverse Lamp Switch
6. Packing; Filler Plug	39. Low Gear	71. Switch Assy., Top - 3rd
7. Cover; Clutch Shift Fork	40. Bearing; Low, 2nd, 3rd	72. Gasket, Switch
8. Shaft; Clutch Gear	41. Collar; Low	73. Arm, Shift, top — 3rd
9. Bearing; Front	42. Adapter Asm.; Main Shaft	74. Arm, Shift Low — 2nd
10. Snap Ring; Bearing Top Gear	43. Pin; Adapter	75. Arm, Shift, Reverse
11. Cover Assy; Front	44. Spacer	76. Block, Shift, w/Pin, Reverse
12. Oil Seal; Front Cover	45. Nut; Main Shaft	77. Rod, Gear Shift, Top — 3rd
13. Support; Clutch Fork	46. Bearing; Main Shaft	78. Rod, Gear Shift, Low — 2nd
14. Gasket; Front Cover	47. Speedometer Drive Gear	79. Rod, Gear Shift, Reverse
15. Bearing; Main Shaft	48. Snap Ring; Speedometer Gear	80. Pin, Spring, Shift Arm
16. Extension Housing Asm.	49. Key; Speedometer Gear	81. Lever, Reverse, Idle Gear Control
17. Bushing; Prop Shaft Yoke	50. Counter Gear	82. Bracket, Fulcrum, Lever Control
18. Oil Seal; Rear Cover	51. Needle Roller	83. O-Ring, Fulcrum Bracket
19. Cover; Dust Rear Cover	52. Spacer; Countergear	84. Box, Quadrant
20. Gasket; Rear Cover	53. Thrust Washer	85. Pin, Quadrant Box
21. Cover Asm.	54. Thrust Washer	86. Plunger, Reverse Stop
22. Gasket; Top Cover	55. Gountergear; Shaft	87. Spring, Reverse Stop, Inner
23. Plate	56. Lock Plate	88. Spring, Reverse Stop, Outer
24. Main Shaft	57. Shaft; Reverse Idle	89. Cap, Reverse Stop, Spring
25. Snap Ring; Main Shaft	58. Gear; Reverse Idle	90. Gasket, Quadrant Box
26. Hub; 3-4	59. Bushing; Reverse Idle Gear	91. Lever Asm., Gear Shift Control
27. Sleeve; 3-4	60. Speedometer Driven Gear	92. Spring, Control Lever
28. Insert; Clutch Hub	61. W/O-Ring Bushing	93. Cage, Control Lever
29. Spring; Insert	62. O-Ring; Speedometer Gear Bush.	94. Cover, Control Lever
30. Blocker Ring; 3-4	63. O-Ring; Speedometer Gear	95. Grommet, Lever, Gear Shift
31. 3-rd Gear Asm.	64. Cover; Front Transmission Case	96. Knob, Lever, Gear Shift Control
32. 2-nd Gear Asm.	65. 71 Ball, Detent, Gear Shift	97. Cover, Dust, Control Lever
33. Hub; 1-2		

28. Hold the shaft in a vertical position so that the rearward end is up. Lightly oil the second speed journal on the main shaft. Install the clutch pilot roller bearing, second speed gear and blocker ring.

29. Install the first and second gear synchronizer hub and gear assembly. The toothed portion of the reverse sliding gear on the synchronizer assembly should be located toward the front of the transmission.

30. Install the first gear sleeve and lightly oil the sleeve. Install the caged roller bearing over the sleeve and install the blocker ring, first gear and the rear thrust washer. The thrust washer oil groove side faces first gear.

31. Press the rear bearing into the rear bearing retainer. The sealed portion of the bearing should be positioned toward the front of the retainer.

LOCK PLATE

Remove the lockplate at the rear of the transmission housing before removing the reverse idler gear shaft through the rear of the housing

32. Install the rear bearing and retainer assembly on the rear of the main shaft and install the lockwasher and nut. Tighten the nut to 80 ft lbs and bend the tab on the lockwasher over one flat portion of the nut. Be sure the notches of the blocker rings align with the keys on the synchronizer assemblies.

33. Insert the reverse idler gear into the case. The shift fork groove should be toward the rear of the transmission.

34. Install the inner thrust washers, of which there are 46 (23 on each side), the needle bearings and the outer thrust washers into the front and rear of the counter gear using chassis lube to retain the bearings. Install the dummy shaft.

35. Install the front and rear counter-gear thrust washers and install the countergear into the case locating the large diameter gear toward the front of the case.

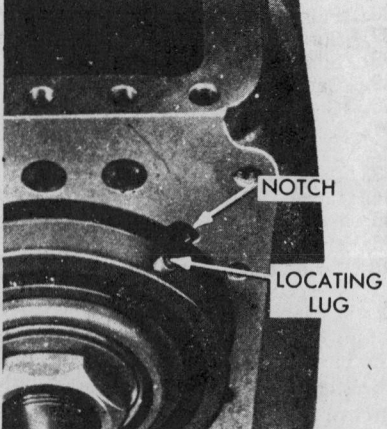

NOTCH

LOCATING LUG

Install the main drive assembly into the case insuring that the lug on the rear of the bearing retainer assembly is located into the notch in the rear of the case

36. Install the front bearing onto the clutch gear and install the snap-ring.

37. Install the clutch gear into the transmission case. Make sure the clutch gear is properly positioned when driving it into the case so as not to gall the bearing race.

38. Install the clutch gear pilot roller into the clutch gear, pack the bearing with chassis lube and install the blocker ring on the clutch gear cone.

39. Install the main drive assembly into the case insuring that the lug on the rear bearing retainer assembly is located into the notch in the rear of the case.

40. With the main drive assembly installed, invert the case and drive the reverse idle shaft into the rear of the case. Rotate the mainshaft slightly to locate the counter gear for installation of the counter gear shaft.

To insure that the thrust washers are properly positioned, lightly oil the counter-gear shaft and install it through the rear of the case. Tap the countergear shaft lightly with a soft faced hammer, driving the dummy shaft out through the front of the case. Install the lock plate into the key slots of the reverse idler gear shaft and counter gear shaft and drive the lock-plate against the rear of the case.

41. Install the shift forks into the case, positioning the shift forks into the grooves of the synchronizer sleeves on the first and second, and the third and fourth gear synchronizer assemblies. Install the reverse gear shift fork into the groove on the reverse idler gear.

42. Install the interlock pin into the first and second shifter shaft and install the shaft through the rear of the case, picking up the first and second gear shift fork.

43. Rotate the transmission case and install the two interlock balls into the front shifter shaft bosses. Install the third and fourth shifter shaft through the rear of the case, picking up the third and fourth shift fork and locate the shaft to the front of the case to retain the interlock balls.

44. Install the speedometer drive gear and snap rings.

45. Install the rear extension housing and tighten the attaching bolts and nut to 10 ft lbs. Install the extension housing seal.

46. Install the speedometer driven gear assembly.

47. Install the two interlock balls and insert the reverse shifter shaft through the front of the case, picking up the reverse shift fork.

48. Install the roll pins through the first and second, third and fourth, and the reverse shift forks into the shafts.

49. Install the reverse shift block, fulcrum bracket and reverse idler gear control lever and roll pin.

50. Install the interlock ball and actuating pin in the back-up light switch orifice and install the back-up light switch and TCS switch.

51. Install the shift quadrant top and tighten the attaching bolts to 10 ft lbs.

52. Put the transmission in Neutral and install the three detent balls, springs, gasket and top cover and tighten the cover attaching bolts to 10 ft lbs.

53. Install the front cover gasket, Belleville spring and the front cover. Tighten the front cover attaching bolts to 10 ft lbs.

54. Install the speedometer driven gear.

55. Install the shift fork ball stud and tighten to 65–70 ft lbs.

56. Install the clutch shift fork and release the bearing assembly.

57. Fill the transmission with SAE 30 oil.

1976–77

1. Remove the drain plug and drain the transmission pan.

2. Remove the boot, clutch fork and throwout bearing.

3. Remove the four bearing retainer bolts and remove the retainer, gasket and spring washer.

4. Remove the bolt holding the speedometer gear bushing and remove the speedometer driven gear assembly.

5. Remove the four bolts holding the shifter cover and remove the shifter cover and gasket.

6. Remove the back-up switch on California vehicles and both back-up and CRS switches on all others.

7. Remove the eight bolts holding the rear extension, then remove the rear extension and gasket.

8. Remove the thrust washers and reverse idler gear from the reverse idler gear shaft.

9. Remove the snap rings, speedometer drive gear and key from the mainshaft.

10. Remove the spring pin from the reverse shifter fork and reverse gear.

11. Remove the snap ring from the outer circumference of the clutch gear shaft ball bearing.

12. Remove the center support assembly from the transmission case.

13. Drive out the spring pins from the third and fourth and first and second shift forks.

NOTE: *When removing the spring pin, hold a round bar against the end of the shifter rods to prevent damage.*

14. Remove the detent spring plate from the center support, then remove the detent springs and balls.

15. Remove the first and second and the third and fourth shifter rods from the center support, then remove the shifter forks.

1. Case, w/center support
2. Pin, guide
3. Bearing, needle
4. Plug, shift rod
5. Stud.
6. Plug, oil filler
7. O-ring, oil filler
8. Dust cover, shift fork
9. Ring, snap, mainshaft
10. Ring, snap counter gear
11. Gasket, case and rear cover
12. Ball stud
13. Washer, lock
14. Washer, plain
15. Plug, screw
16. Gasket, plug (Calif. spec.)
17. Plug, screw (Calif. spec.)
18. Gasket, plug (Calif. spec.)
19. Shaft, clutch gear
20. Bearing, ball
21. Ring, snap
22. Ring, snap
23. Spring, belleville
24. Bearing, needle
25. Bearing retainer
26. Seal, oil, bearing retainer
27. Gasket, bearing retainer
28. Bolt
29. Extension Assy., rear, w/bushing and seal
30. Bushing
31. Seal, oil, rear extension
32. Breather assy.
33. Plug, oil drain
34. O-ring, oil drain
35. Bolt
37. Shaft main
38. Ring, snap

39. Hub, synchronizer, 3rd-4th
40. Sleeve, synchronizer
41. Key, synchronizer
42. Spring, synchronizer
43. Ring, blocker
44. Gear assy., 3rd
45. Gear assy., 2nd
46. Hub, synchronizer, 1st-2nd
47. Sleeve, synchronizer
48. Key, synchronizer
49. Spring, synchronizer
50. Ring blocker
51. Gear assy., 1st
52. Bearing, needle, 1st
53. Bearing, needle, 2nd
54. Collar, needle bearing
55. Washer, thrust, 1st
56. Bearing, mainshaft
57. Washer, lock, mainshaft
58. Nut, mainshaft
59. Gear, reverse
60. Gear, speed drive
61. Ring, snap, drive gear
62. Key
63. Gear, counter
64. Bearing, angular ball
65. Gear, counter reverse
66. Spacer
67. Washer, plain
68. Nut, self lock
69. Shaft, reverse idle
70. Plate, lock
71. Bolt, lock
72. Washer, spring
73. Gear, reverse idle
74. Washer, thrust
75. Synchronizer assy., 3rd-4th
76. Synchronizer assy., 1st-2nd

1976-77 LUV 4-speed transmission

16. Remove the reverse shifter rod forward as it is fitted with a stopper pin.

NOTE: *Be careful not to loose the detent interlock plugs located between the shifter rods in the center support.*

17. Move both synchronizers rearward to prevent turning of the mainshaft.

NOTE: *It may be necessary to tap the synchronizers with the hammer handle to get them engaged.*

18. Flatten out the lock washer and remove the lock nut and washer from the mainshaft.

19. Remove the self locking nut, washer, countershaft reverse gear and collar from the rear of the countergear.

20. Insert the nose of snap ring pliers into the countergear bearing snap ring hole in the center support and disengage the snap ring from the ring groove by tapping on the front face of the center support while expanding the countergear bearing snap ring.

21. Remove the center support by expanding the mainshaft rear bearing snap ring with the snap ring pliers.

22. Separate the clutch gear, needle bearings and blocker ring from the mainshaft assembly.

23. Press the rear bearing from the mainshaft.

24. Remove the thrust washer, 1st speed gear, needle roller bearing, a collar and blocker ring.

25. Remove the 1st and 2nd gear synchronizer assembly.

26. Remove the 2nd gear, blocker ring and needle roller bearing from the mainshaft.

27. Remove the snap ring 3rd and 4th synchronizer assembly and blocker ring from the mainshaft.

28. Remove the 3rd gear and needle bearings.

29. Remove the snap ring and press off the clutch bearing and countergear bearing from the shaft.

To assemble the transmission:

30. Stand the front of the mainshaft upward and install the 3rd speed gear and needle roller bearing with the tapered side of the gear facing the front of the mainshaft.

31. Install a blocker ring with the clutching teeth upward over the synchronizing surface of the 3rd speed gear.

31. If it is necessary to reassemble the synchronizer assembly turn the face of the synchronizer hub with the heavy boss to the face of the sleeve with the light chamfering on the outer rim.

32. Fit the keys into the key groove and position the synchronizer springs into the hole in the side face of the hub.

33. Install the 3rd and 4th synchronizer assembly on the mainshaft with the face of the sleeve with the light chamfer rearward.

34. Install the snap ring.

35. Now turn the rear of the mainshaft upward and install the 2nd speed gear and needle roller bearing on the mainshaft with the tapered surface of the gear facing the rear of the mainshaft.

36. Install a blocker ring with the clutching teeth downward over the synchronizing surface of the 2nd speed gear.

37. Install the 1st and 2nd synchronizer assembly with the chamfer on the sleeve facing the front of the mainshaft.

38. Install a blocker ring with the clutching teeth rearward.

39. Install the collar, needle roller bearing and 1st speed gear on the mainshaft.

NOTE: *The tapered side of the gear should be facing the front of the mainshaft.*

40. Install the 1st speed gear thrust washer on the mainshaft with the grooved side facing 1st gear.

41. Press the rear bearing on the mainshaft with the snap ring groove facing the front of the mainshaft.

42. If removed press the ball bearing on the clutch gear shaft with the snap ring groove on the bearing facing the front of the transmission. Install the snap ring on the clutch gear shaft.

43. Assemble the needle roller bearing, blocker ring and clutch gear to the front of the mainshaft.

44. If removed press on the countergear ball bearing with the snap ring groove facing the rear of the transmission.

45. If removed, install the snap rings in the snap ring groove in the inner circum-

ference of the mainshaft and countergear holes of the center support.

46. If removed, insert the idler gear shaft with the lock plate groove side into the center support from the rear, then install the lock plate into the groove and tighten the bolt to 14 ft. lbs.

47. Mesh the countergear with the mainshaft assembly and install a holding tool on the mainshaft and countergear.

48. Place the tool with mainshaft and countergear assembled into a vise, then install the center support.

49. Expand the mainshaft bearing snap ring in the center support and press the center support onto the shaft until the countergear bearing is brought into contact with its snap ring.

50. Expand the countergear bearing snap ring and press the center support further until the mainshaft and countergear snap rings are fitted into their grooves.

51. Remove the holding tool from the mainshaft and countergear and remove the assembly from the vise.

52. Move both synchronizers rearward to prevent turning of the mainshaft.

53. Install the collar, countershaft reverse gear, washer and self locking nut on the rear of the countergear; torque the nut to 100 ft. lbs.

NOTE: *New self-locking nuts should be used.*

54. Install the lock nut and lock washer on the mainshaft and torque the nut to 94 ft. lbs., then bend down the lock washer.

NOTE: *Install the lock nut so that the chamfered side is facing the lock washer.*

55. Apply grease to the two detent plugs and insert them into their detent holes from the middle hole of the center support.

56. Install the 1st and 2nd shifter forks and the 3rd and 4th into their grooves in the synchronizer assembly.

57. Install the 3rd and 4th shifter rod from the rear of the center support through the middle hole and into the 1st and 2nd, 3rd and 4th shifter forks. Align the spring pin hole in the shifter fork with the hole in the shifter rod.

NOTE: *Identify the 3rd and 4th shifter rod by the two detent grooves on the side of the rod.*

58. Install the 1st and 2nd shifter rod from the rear of the center support through the 1st and 2nd shifter fork and align the hole in the rod to the hole in the shifter fork.

59. If removed install the stopper pin in the reverse shifter rod and the front of the center support.

60. Install the two spring pins in the 1st/2nd and 3rd/4th shifter forks.

NOTE: *When installing the spring pins place a round bar against the end of the*

shifter rod to prevent damage.

61. Install the detent balls, spring, gasket and retainer on the center support and torque the bolts to 14 ft. lbs.

62. Place the transmission case upright on wooden blocks and install the center support assembly and gasket into the transmission case aligning the dowel pin holes with the dowel pins.

63. Assemble the reverse shifter fork to the reverse gear and install these parts into position from the rear side of the mainshaft, then connect them to the reverse shifter rod.

64. Install the spring pin in the reverse shifter fork.

65. Install the thrust washer and reverse idler gear on the idler shaft.

NOTE: *The reverse idler gear should be installed with undercut teeth forward.*

66. Install the speedometer drive gear snap ring and key on the mainshaft.

67. If removed install a new oil seal to the rear extension.

68. Apply grease to the outer thrust washer of the reverse idler shaft and insert it in the rear extension.

69. Install the rear extension and gasket to the transmission case aligning the dowel pin hole with the dowel pin. Torque the eight bolts to 27 ft. lbs.

70. Install the back-up lamp switch and CRS switch if removed.

71. Install the shifter cover and gasket and torque the bolts to 10 ft. lbs.

72. Install the oil "o" ring to the speedometer driven gear and install the gear to the rear extension.

73. Install the front bearing retainer seal.

74. Install a snap ring to the outer circumference of the clutch gear bearing.

75. Apply grease to the bearing retainer spring washer and place it in the bearing retainer with the dished face turned to the bearing outer race.

76. Install the bearing retainer to the front of the transmission case and torque the four bolts to 14 ft. lbs.

NOTE: *The shorter bolts are used on countergear front bearing side of the bearing retainer.*

77. Install the ball stud to the bearing retainer and torque to 30 ft. lbs.

78. Install the boot clutch fork and throwout bearing, then install the retaining spring.

79. Install the drain plug on the transmission case, then install the rear cover plug. Fill the transmission case to the specified level of 1.35 qt.

CLUTCH

The clutch is a hydraulically operated single-plate, dry friction disc, diaphragm spring type.

The clutch is operated by a clutch pedal which is mechanically connected to a clutch master cylinder. When the pedal is depressed, the piston in the master cylinder is moved in the master cylinder bore. This movement compresses the fluid in the master cylinder causing hydraulic pressure which is transfered through a tube to the slave cylinder. The slave cylinder is mounted to the clutch housing with its piston connected to the clutch release lever. The hydraulic pressure in the slave cylinder forces the slave cylinder piston to travel out the cylinder bore and move the clutch release lever, disengaging the clutch.

Removal and Installation

1. Raise the vehicle on a hoist.

2. Remove the transmission.

3. Mark the clutch assembly-to-flywheel relationship with paint or a center punch so that the clutch assembly can be reassembled in the same position from which it is removed.

4. Loosen the six clutch cover-to-flywheel attaching bolts, one turn at a time in an alternating sequence, until the spring tension is relieved to avoid distorting or bending the clutch cover.

5. Support the clutch pressure plate and cover assembly with a clutch aligning arbor, then remove the bolts and the clutch assembly.

6. Apply a thin coat of grease to the pressure plate wire ring, diaphragm spring, clutch cover grooves and the drive bosses on the pressure plate.

7. Apply a thin coat of Lubriplate to the splines in the driven plate.

8. Assemble the clutch cover and pressure plate and the driven plate on a clutch alignment arbor.

9. Align the marks made on the clutch cover and the flywheel and install the six clutch cover-to-flywheel attaching bolts. Tighten the bolts to 50 in. lbs. Remove the aligning arbor.

10. Install the transmission.

Pedal Height Adjustment
1972

1. Remove the clutch pedal return spring and disconnect the clutch pedal arm from the master cylinder pushrod.

2. Loosen the clutch switch locknut at the clutch pedal bracket and adjust the height of the clutch pedal until it is flush with the brake pedal. Then retighten the locknut.

3. Adjust the pushrod end-play by rotating the clevis until 25/32 in. of clutch pedal free-play is achieved then connect the pushrod clevis to the clutch pedal arm and tighten the through-bolt nut to 25 ft lbs and securely tighten the joint nut.

4. Install the clutch pedal return spring.

Clutch pedal height adjustment on the 1972 models

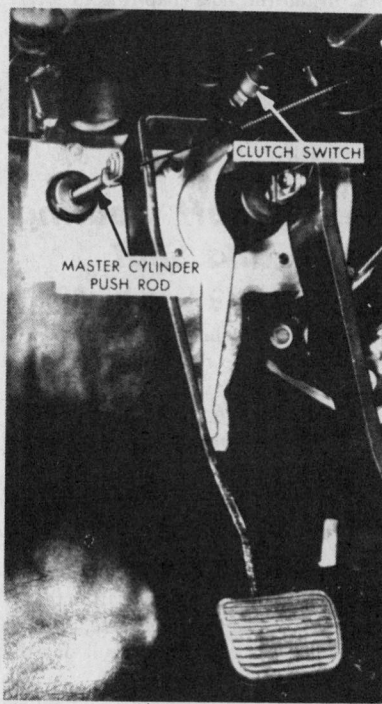

Clutch pedal height adjustment—1973-77

1973–77

1. Disconnect the battery ground cable.

2. Measure the clutch pedal height after making sure that the pedal is fully returned by the pedal return spring. The pedal height should be between 5.9 and 6.3 in.

3. To adjust the height, disconnect the clutch switch and remove it from its mounting bracket.

4. Loosen the locknut on the master cylinder pushrod.

5. Adjust the clutch pedal to the specified height by rotating the pushrod in the appropriate direction. Tighten the locknut when finished with the adjustment.

6. Install the clutch switch. Adjust the clearance between the switch housing (not the switch actuating pin) and the clutch pedal tab to 0.02–0.04 in. Tighten the switch locknut.

7. Connect the electrical leads to the clutch switch and connect the negative battery cable.

Clutch Release Fork Adjustment

1. Remove the clutch release fork return spring and move the release fork slightly rearward.

2. Loosen the adjusting nut and adjust the pushrod until it contacts the release fork.

3. Backoff the pushrod about 1¾ turns and tighten the locknut.

NOTE: *Excess clearance between the release (throwout) bearing and the diaphragm spring fingers will cause the clutch to drag while too little clearance can cause the clutch to slip.*

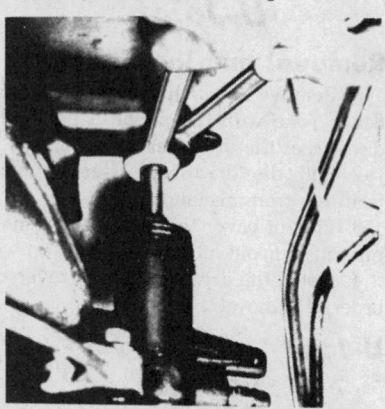

Clutch release fork adjustment

Clutch Master Cylinder

Removal and Installation

1. Disconnect the clutch pedal arm from the pushrod.

2. Disconnect the clutch hydraulic line from the master cylinder.

NOTE: *Take precautions to keep brake fluid from coming in contact with any painted surfaces.*

3. Remove the nuts attaching the master cylinder and remove the master cylinder and pushrod toward the engine compartment side.

4. Install the master cylinder in the reverse order of removal and bleed the clutch hydraulic system.

Overhaul

1. Remove the master cylinder from the vehicle.

2. Drain the clutch fluid from the master cylinder reservoir.

3. Remove the boot and circlip and remove the pushrod.

4. Remove the stopper, piston, cup and return spring.

5. Clean all of the parts in clean brake fluid.

6. Check the master cylinder and piston for wear, corrosion and scores and replace the parts as necessary. Light scoring and glaze can be removed with crocus cloth soaked in brake fluid.

7. Generally, the cup seal should be replaced each time the master cylinder is disassembled. Check the cup and replace it if it is worn, fatigued, or damaged.

8. Check the clutch fluid reservoir, filler cap, dust cover and the pipe for distortion and damage and replace the parts as necessary.

9. Lubricate all new parts with clean brake fluid.

10. Reassemble the master cylinder parts in the reverse order of disassembly, taking note of the following:

   a. Reinstall the cup seal carefully to prevent damaging the lipped portions;

   b. Adjust the height of the clutch pedal after installing the master cylinder in position on the vehicle;

   c. Fill the master cylinder and clutch fluid reservoir and then bleed the clutch hydraulic system.

Clutch Slave Cylinder

Removal and Installation

1. Remove the slave cylinder attaching bolts and the pushrod from the shift fork.

2. Disconnect the flexible fluid hose from the slave cylinder and remove the unit from the vehicle.

3. Install the slave cylinder in the reverse order of removal and bleed the clutch hydraulic system.

Overhaul

1. Remove the slave cylinder from the vehicle.

2. Remove the pushrod and boot.

3. Force out the piston by blowing compressed air into the slave cylinder at the hose connection.

NOTE: *Be careful not to apply excess air pressure to avoid possible injury.*

4. Clean all of the parts in clean brake fluid.

5. Check and replace the slave cylinder bore and piston if wear or severe scoring exists. Light scoring and glaze can be removed with crocus cloth soaked in brake fluid.

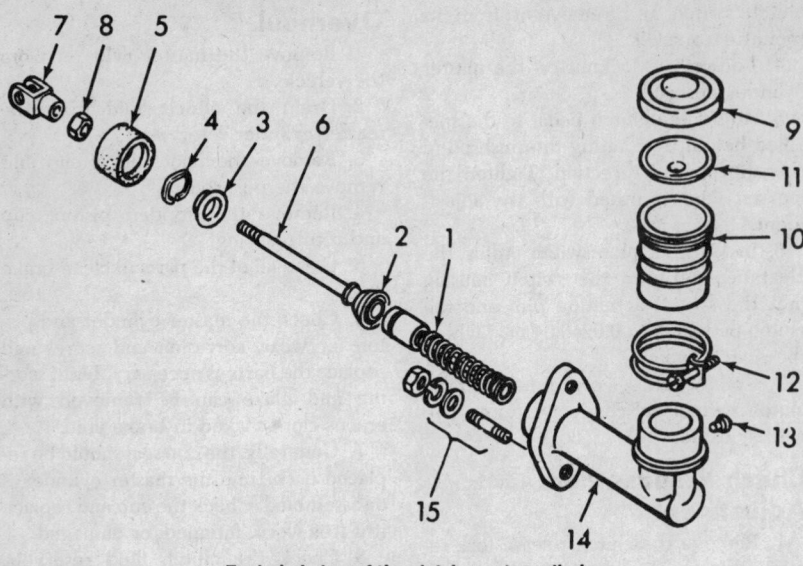

Exploded view of the clutch master cylinder

1. Piston Assembly
2. Cup, Piston
3. Retainer
4. Clip
5. Boot
6. Push Rod
7. Clevis
8. Lock Nut
9. Cap
10. Reservoir
11. Seal
12. Retaining Strap
13. Fitting
14. Body
15. Mounting Parts

6. Normally the piston cup should be replaced when the slave cylinder is disassembled. Check the piston cup and replace it if it is found to be worn, fatigued or scored.

7. Replace the rubber boot if it is cracked or broken.

8. Lubricate all of the new parts in clean brake fluid and reassemble in the reverse order of disassembly, taking note of the following:

a. Use care when reassembling the piston cup to prevent damaging the lipped portion of the piston cup;

b. Fill the master cylinder with brake fluid and bleed the clutch hydraulic system;

c. Adjust the clearance between the pushrod and the shift fork to 5/64 in.

DRIVE AXLES
Driveshaft and U-Joints
Removal and Installation

1. Remove the bolts connecting the flange yoke with the pinion flange and disconnect the driveshaft at the flange.

2. Pull the driveshaft assembly out from the transmission rear cover.

3. Plug or cover the end of the transmission to avoid lubricant loss.

4. Install the driveshaft in the reverse order of removal.

U-Joint
Overhaul

1. Remove the driveshaft from the vehicle.

2. Punch mating marks on both the yokes at either end of the driveshaft and

the driveshaft itself so that the driveshaft assembly can be reassembled in the same position.

3. Remove the snap-rings from the bearing hole of the yokes.

4. Place the yoke in a vise with a small socket positioned against one of the bearing cups and a larger socket placed against the yoke on the opposite side. The larger socket must be able to receive the bearing cap when it is pressed out of the yoke.

5. Tighten the vise until the bearing caps are free of the yoke.

6. Remove the two remaining bearings from the opposite yoke in the same manner and remove the spider bearing journal.

7. Make sure that the new spiders and needle bearings in the bearing caps are well lubricated.

8. Assemble the universal joint spider and bearing caps to the yoke in the reverse manner of removal, using the smaller socket to press the bearing caps into the yoke and the larger socket to bear against the yoke bearing cap hole at the opposite end. Use a vise to press the bearing caps in place.

9. Install the hole snap-ring to secure the bearing caps.

10. Assemble the slide yoke to the driveshaft, aligning the marks made prior to disassembly.

11. Install the driveshaft assembly on the vehicle.

Axle Shaft, Bearing and Seal
Removal and Installation

1. Raise the vehicle on a hoist.

2. Remove the rear wheel cover and the wheel and tire.

3. Remove the brake drum, brake shoes and disconnect the parking brake inner cable.

4. Disconnect the brake line at the wheel cylinder and plug the end of the line.

5. Remove the four nuts from the bearing holder through-bolts from the inside of the brake backing plate.

6. Using an axle puller, pull out the

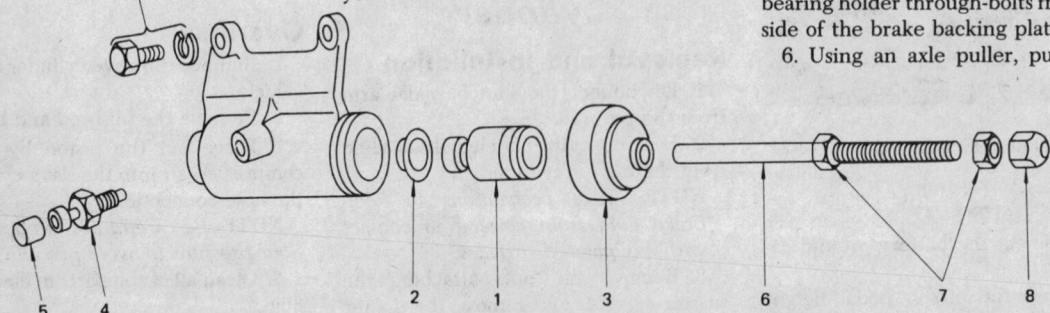

Exploded view of the clutch slave cylinder

1. PISTON
2. PISTON CUP
3. BOOT
4. BLEEDER SCREW
5. CAP
6. PUSH ROD
7. NUT
8. NUT
9. BOLT

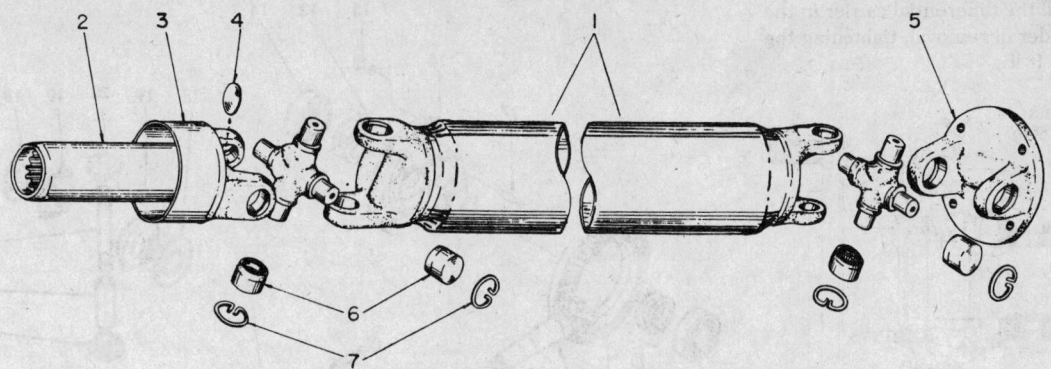

An exploded view of the driveshaft and U-joints

1. Driveshaft
2. Spline yoke
3. Cover
4. Plate plug
5. Flange yoke
6. Bearing caps
7. Snap-rings

axle shaft assembly. Never strike the brake backing plate with a hammer in an attempt to remove the axle shaft.

7. Install the axle shaft in the reverse order of removal, tightening the bearing holding plate attaching nuts to 55 ft lbs, bleeding the brake hydraulic system after installing the brakes and adjusting the parking brake cable as necessary.

Axle Shaft End-Play Adjustment

Tool J-24246 (or substitute) is necessary to break the locknut loose from the axle shaft. The locknut is torqued to 190 ft/lbs. Adjust the axle shaft end-play.

1. Remove the axle shaft.
2. Flatten the locktab and clamp the axle shaft nut in a vise.
3. Install tool J-24246 and clamp in place with two wheel nuts.
4. Turn the axle shaft nut loose from the locknut.
5. Press the backing plate, bearing and holder, locknut and washer from the axle shaft.
6. Remove the oil seal.
7. Install the bearing outer race and seal in the holder.
8. Install the bearing holder on the backing plate with the four through bolts. The oil seal side of the bearing holder goes against the backing plate.
9. Install the axle shaft through the backing plate and bearing holder.
10. Install a new lockwasher with dished side away from the bearing.
11. Clamp the locknut in a vise and using tool J-24246 tighten the axle shaft into the locknut to 190 ft/lbs. Bend the locktab.
12. Install the axle shaft.
13. To adjust the end-play:
If one shaft has been serviced, start with step B.
    A. Insert a .079 in. shim between bearing holder and axle tube flange. Install the axle shaft.
    B. Install the opposite axle shaft without shims until it contacts the diff-

Removing the axle shaft from brake backing plate

erential thrust block. Measure the clearance between the bearing holder and flange.
    C. The proper shim size is this measurement (Step B) plus 0.004 in.
    D. Remove the axle shaft, install shim pack and reinstall the axle shaft.

Differential

Removal and Installation

1. Raise the vehicle on a hoist.
2. Remove the wheels and brake drums.
3. Remove the axle shafts.
4. Remove the driveshaft.
5. Remove the ten attaching nuts retaining the differential carrier and case assembly to the axle housing and remove the carrier from the vehicle.

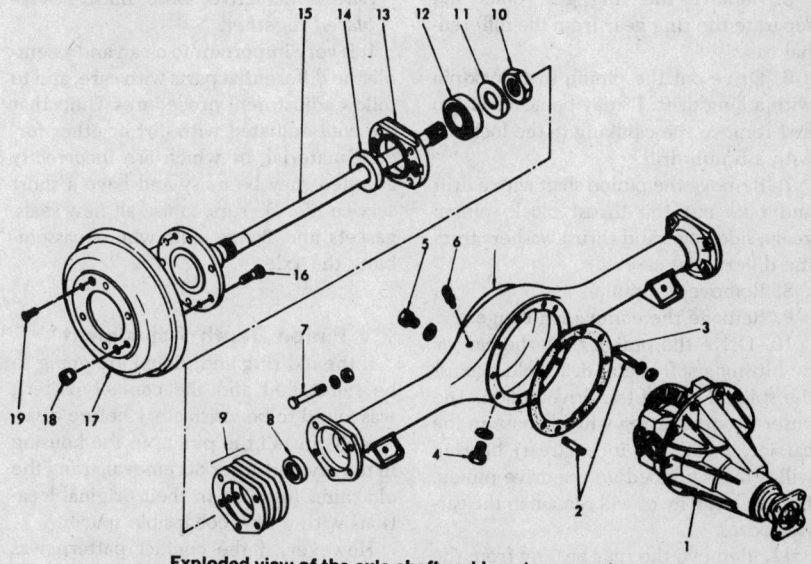

Exploded view of the axle shaft and housing assembly

1. Differential carrier and case assembly
2. Mounting bolt
3. Gasket
4. Drain plug
5. Filler plug
6. Vent
7. Through bolt
8. Oil seal
9. Shims
10. Locknut
11. Lockwasher
12. Axle shaft bearing
13. Bearing holder
14. Grease seal
15. Axle shaft
16. Wheel stud
17. Brake drum
18. Wheel nut
19. Drum-to-flange screw

6. Install the differential carrier in the reverse order of removal, tightening the nuts to 18 ft lbs.

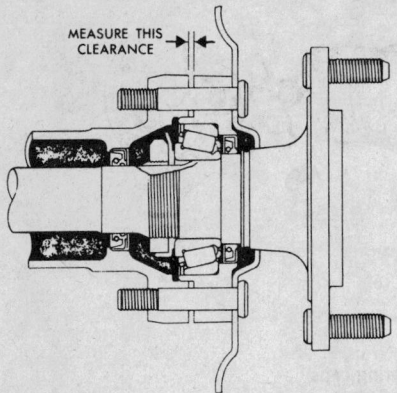

MEASURE THIS CLEARANCE

Axle shaft bearing holder to flange clearance. This dimension plus 0.004 in. equals the thickness of the shim pack.

Overhaul

Disassembly

1. Before disassembling the differential, make a pattern check of the ring gear.

2. Mark the side bearing caps so they can be reinstalled in the same positions.

3. Remove the nuts and the bearing caps, then remove the differential case and ring gear assembly. Keep left and right side bearing separate to avoid interchanging.

4. Remove the differential side bearings from the case. Carefully record the thickness of each side bearing and each shim pack removed and keep them separated.

5. Remove the ring gear bolts and separate the ring gear from the differential case.

6. Drive out the pinion shaft lock-pin with a long drift. It may be necessary to first remove the caulking in the lock-pin with a 5 mm drill.

7. Remove the pinion shaft with a drift and take out the thrust block, pinion gears, side gears and thrust washers from the differential case.

8. Remove the pinion nut.

9. Remove the companion flange.

10. Drive the pinion from the carrier by hitting a soft metal drift held against the splined end of the drive pinion. The outer (front) bearing will fall loose in the carrier, while the inner (rear) bearing will remain pressed on the drive pinion. Both bearing races will remain in the carrier bores.

11. Remove the rear bearing from the drive pinion by use of a press.

Wash all of the parts, being careful not to interchange any. Look for damaged excessively worn, or bent parts. Replace any defective parts.

NOTE: *Ring gears and drive pinions*

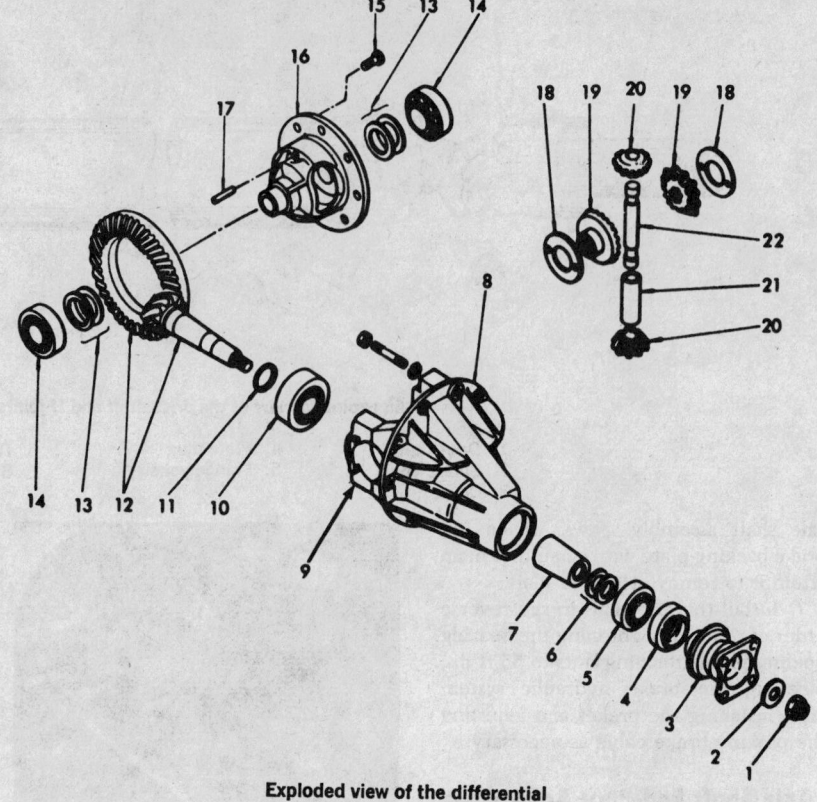

Exploded view of the differential

1. Pinion nut
2. Washer
3. Companion flange
4. Oil seal
5. Outer Bearing
6. Collapsible spacer
7. Bearing cap stud
8. Differential carrier
9. Bearing cap
10. Inner bearing
11. Depth shim
12. Ring and pinion
13. Side bearing shims
14. Side bearing
15. Ring gear-to-case bolt
16. Differential case
17. Pinion shaft lock pin
18. Thrust washer
19. Differential gear
20. Pinion gear
21. Thrust block
22. Pinion shaft

come only in matched sets. If either part is defective, both must be replaced together.

It is very important to clean and assemble the differential parts with care, and to follow adjustment procedures. Units that are contaminated with dirt or other foreign material, or which are incorrectly adjusted may be noisy and have a short service life. Be sure to use all new seals, gaskets and flange nuts when reassembling the axle.

Pinion Depth Adjustment

If the old ring and pinion are going to be reinstalled and the contact pattern was found to be satisfactory before disassembly, install the pinion in the housing in the reverse order of removal, using the old shims installed in their original locations with a new collapsible spacer.

However, if the contact pattern was found to be unsatisfactory due to assumed wear of a depth adjusting shim, measure the thickness of the shim(s) and install or subtract shims accordingly to gain a satisfactory contact pattern between the ring and pinion gear in regard to pinion depth.

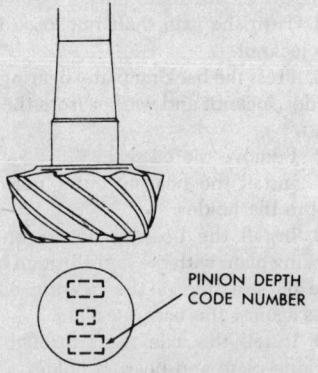

PINION DEPTH CODE NUMBER

Pinion depth code number location

NOTE: *Shims are available in sizes ranging from 0.086 in. to 0.101 in.*

If a new ring and pinion are being installed, compute the difference between the old and new pinions' depth code numbers then add or subtract shims accordingly as follows:

After installing a new ring and pinion together with the correct size shims conduct another gear tooth contact pattern check. If the pattern is satisfactory, install the differential in the housing. If the pattern must be changed, disassemble the

Pinion Shim Adjustment Chart

Pinion Depth Code Number	Thickness Shim Required
+10	Subtract 0.005 in.
+8	Subtract 0.004 in.
+6	Subtract 0.003 in.
+4	Subtract 0.002 in.
+2	Subtract 0.001 in.
0	No shim required
−2	Add 0.001 in.
−4	Add 0.002 in.
−6	Add 0.003 in.
−8	Add 0.004 in.
−10	Add 0.005 in.

differential, install different shims accordingly, and reassemble the differential with a new crush collar (collapsible spacer). Make another gear tooth contact pattern check.

Pinion Bearing Preload Adjustment

Upon installation of the drive pinion, it is necessary to tighten the companion flange-to-pinion attaching nut to the proper specification in order to place the right amount of preload on the drive pinion bearings.

1. Place the drive pinion and the crush collar into the carrier.

2. Lubricate, then position the front bearing into the carrier. Install a new oil seal.

3. Mount the companion flange to the drive pinion. Apply hypoid lubricant to the pinion threads. Install a new pinion nut and tighten it to 85 ft lbs.

4. Rotate the drive pinion to insure that the bearings are seated.

5. Wind a length of string around the pinion flange. Attach a pull scale to the loose end of the string. Note the scale reading required to rotate the pinion by pulling the scale.

6. Continue to tighten the pinion nut in small amounts until the pull required to rotate the drive pinion becomes 17 lbs for new bearings and 7–9 lbs for used bearings.

NOTE: *Tighten the drive pinion nut in small increments only, so as to be sure of not exceeding the preload specifications. If the preload specifications are exceeded, the crush collar will be compressed too far and will require replacement.*

Differential Case Reassembly

1. Install the side gears and thrust washers in the differential case.

2. Position the pinion gears 180° apart. Roll the gears into position, making sure they are in alignment, to allow installation of the pinion shaft.

3. Place the thrust block between the pinion gears, and drive the pinion shaft into position. Make sure that the lockpin hole in the cross shaft aligns with the hole in the case.

4. Measure the amount of backlash between the differential gears and the pinion gears. If the backlash is greater than 0.003 in., make the necessary adjustment with the thrust washers, available in thicknesses of 0.037 in., 0.041 in., and 0.045 in. Remember that increasing the thickness of the washers will decrease backlash and vice versa.

5. Install the lockpin into the cross-shaft and caulk its end to prevent loosening.

6. Clean the bolts. Apply thread locking compound to the threaded portion of the bolts. Install the ring gear in position on the differential case. Tighten the bolts in a diagonal sequence to 80–87 ft lbs.

Side Bearing Preload and Initial Backlash Adjustment

If the original side bearings, differential case, ring and pinion, and differential carrier are being reused, and if the pattern check taken before disassembly showed a satisfactory contact pattern, the original shims (or new shims of the same dimension) can be reinstalled in the same positions from which they were removed.

If you are going to install *new side bearings only,* and if the contact pattern was satisfactory, select the shims in the following manner:

1. Measure the new bearing with a micrometer, and compare its thickness with the original bearing.

2. If the new bearing is thicker, subtract the numerical difference between the new and old bearing from the original shim pack.

3. If the new bearing is thinner, add the numerical difference between the old and new bearing to the original shim pack.

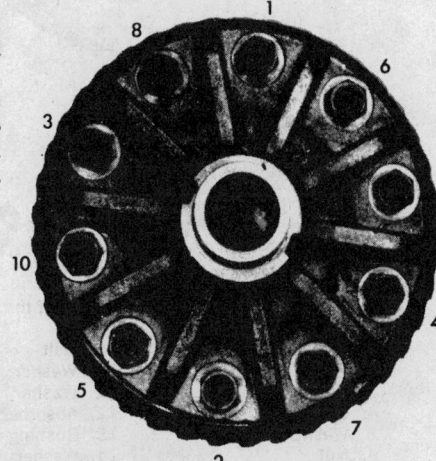

Ring gear tightening sequence

If new bearings *and/or* differential case, ring and pinion, or differential carrier are being installed, new shims will have to be selected for installation behind the side bearings for proper ring and pinion gear tooth contact.

1. Install the side bearings to be used in the final assembly onto the differential case. Do not install shims at this time.

2. Mount the case into the carrier bores.

3. Move the ring gear tightly against the carrier on the ring gear side, away from the drive pinion, and hold in this position. Using a feeler gauge just thick enough to produce a slight drag, carefully measure the clearance between the bearing and the differential carrier on the side opposite the ring gear. Record this measurement.

4. To determine the proper shims for installation, carry out the following procedure:

   a. A predetermined dimension of 0.002 in. is always needed to establish proper preload. Therefore, add 0.002 in. to the clearance measured in Step 3. This will give the necessary combined total thickness of both shim packs.

   b. Divide the total dimension into two shim packs, so that the numerical difference between the packs equals the numerical difference between the original shim packs.

5. Remove the case from the carrier. Carefully remove both side bearings. Install the shims as determined in Step 4 behind each bearing.

6. Install the case onto the carrier, tapping carefully into place. Install the side bearing caps in their original positions and tighten the attaching bolts to 75 ft lbs.

7. Measure the run-out of the ring gear. If the run-out exceeds 0.002 in., correct by cleaning or replacing parts.

8. Mount a dial indicator against the ring gear teeth with the indicator pin in-line with the direction of tooth travel. Measure the gear backlash in three locations. Backlash should be 0.005–0.007 in.

9. If backlash is not within the limits, the shims behind each side bearing will have to be adjusted.

NOTE: *In order to maintain the proper preload on the side bearings, the total thickness of the shim packs must not be changed. Therefore, if the thickness of one shim pack must be increased, the thickness of the opposite shim pack must be decreased by an equal amount.*

10. To increase backlash, the right side bearing shim must be increased, and the left side decreased. To decrease backlash, the right side shim must be decreased, while the left side is increased.

NOTE: *Backlash changed about 0.002 in. for each 0.003 in. shim change.*

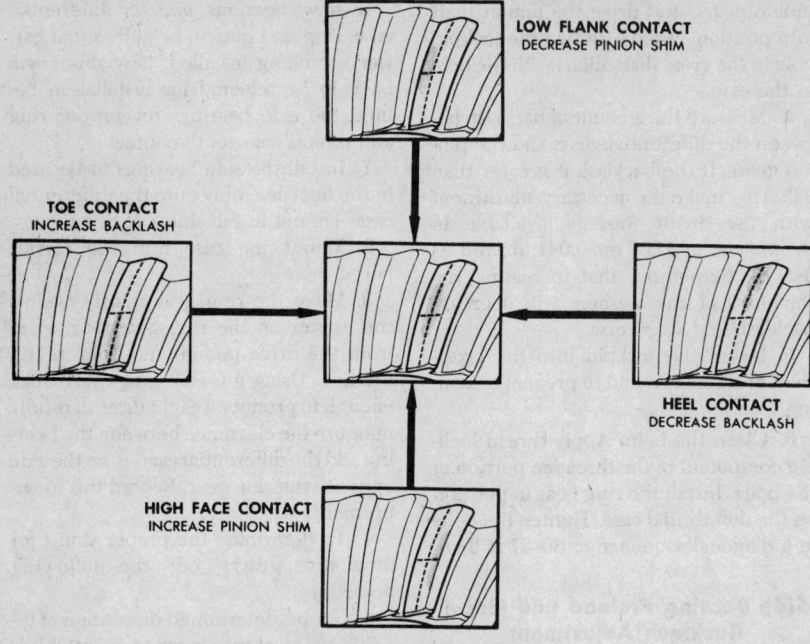

LOW FLANK CONTACT
DECREASE PINION SHIM

TOE CONTACT
INCREASE BACKLASH

HEEL CONTACT
DECREASE BACKLASH

HIGH FACE CONTACT
INCREASE PINION SHIM

Gear tooth contact patterns

Gear Tooth Contact Pattern Check

A gear tooth contact pattern check before final assembly is necessary to verify whether or not the drive pinion and the ring gear are meshed properly.

1. Wipe any oil out of the assembly and carefully clean each tooth of the ring gear.

2. Apply red lead gear marking compound sparingly to the ring gear teeth.

3. Rotate the drive pinion by hand ¼ of a turn in both directions so as to mark both the drive (convex) side and coast (concave) side of the ring gear teeth. Excessive turning of the ring gear is not recommended.

4. Observe the pattern made on the ring gear teeth and compare it with the illustration. Make the necessary adjustments recommended.

REAR SUSPENSION

The rear suspension consists of semi-elliptical leaf springs with hydraulic double-acting shock absorbers. There is a straight "helper" spring added to the bottom of the spring pack. When the semi-elliptical spring straightens out due to the vehicle being loaded, they come in contact with the helper spring which helps to support any additional weight.

Springs

Removal

1. Jack up the rear of the vehicle and place jackstands under the frame near the rear end of the rear spring brackets.

2. Remove the rear shock absorbers.

3. Remove the parking brake cable clips.

4. Remove the nuts from the U-bolts holding the springs to the axle housing.

5. Jack the rear axle up to remove the weight of the axle housing from the springs.

6. Remove the front and rear shackle pin nuts.

7. Drive out the rear shackle pin by using a hammer and drift and lower the rear end of the leaf spring assembly to the floor.

8. Drive out the front shackle pin and remove the leaf spring assembly rearward.

9. Remove the shackle pin from the rear spring bracket and remove the shackle.

Inspection

1. Check the leaf springs for cracks, wear and broken leaves. Replace any leaves found to be cracked, broken, fatigued or seriously worn.

2. Check the shackles for bending and the pins for wear.

3. Check the U-bolts for distortion or other damage.

Installation

1. Mount the shackle to the bracket.

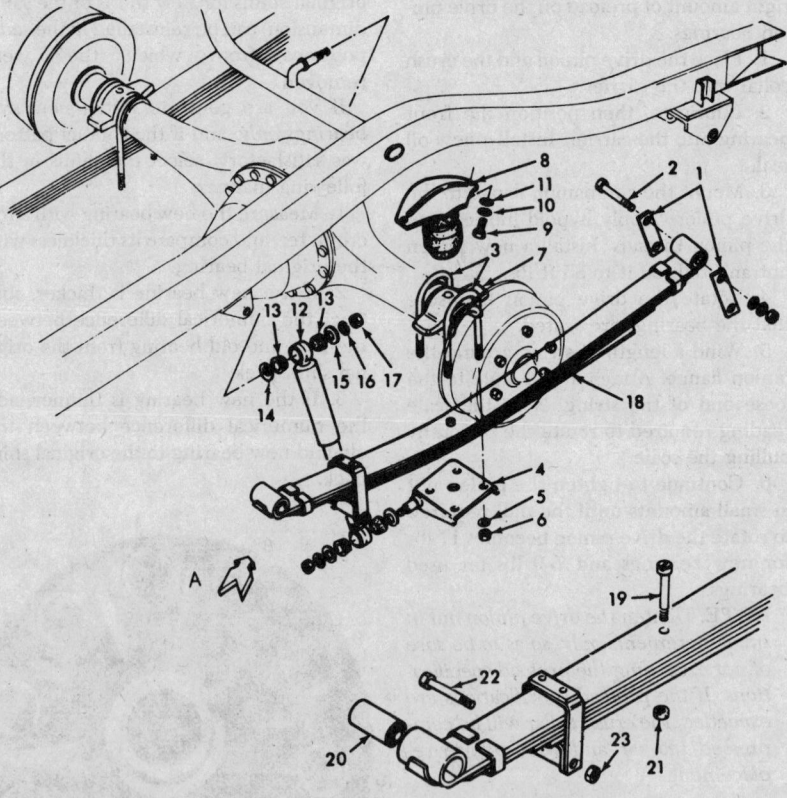

Exploded view of the rear suspension

1. Shackel	9. Bolt
2. Pin	10. Washer
3. U-bolt	11. Washer
4. Clamp	12. Absorber
5. Washer	13. Bushing
6. Nut	14. Washer
7. Seat	15. Washer
8. Rubber	16. Washer

17. Nut
18. Spring assembly
19. Bolt
20. Bush
21. Nut
22. Bolt
23. Nut

2. Align the front end of the leaf spring assembly with the front bracket and install the shackle pin.

3. Align the rear end of the leaf spring assembly with the shackle and install the shackle pin.

4. Loosely install the shackle pin nuts and install the U-bolts. Tighten the U-bolt nuts to 40 ft lbs.

5. Install the shock absorbers.

6. Clip the parking brake cable to the bracket.

7. Remove the jackstands and lower the vehicle so that the vehicle weight is on the leaf springs.

8. Tighten the shackle pin nuts to 130 ft lbs.

Shock Absorbers

Removal and Installation

Remove the rear shock absorbers by loosening and removing the upper and lower attaching nuts and pulling the shock absorber ends off the mounting studs, together with the washers and rubber bushings. Install the shock absorbers in the reverse order of removal, making sure that you use new rubber bushings and that they are installed correctly in the bevel shaped mounting holes in the end of the shock absorbers.

FRONT SUSPENSION

LUV trucks are equipped with the short and long arm type front suspension. The control arms are attached to the vehicle with bolts and bushings at their inner pivot points and to the steering knuckle, which is part of the front wheel spindle, at their outer points.

The front suspension is an independent type utilizing torsion bar springs. The torsion bar has splines on each end. Height control is provided on the third crossmember of the frame. Both upper and lower control arms are pressed steel and the torsion bar is supported at the ends by forged links. The links are bolted to the third frame crossmember in the rear and the lower control arms in front.

Fore and aft movement of the front suspension is controlled by strut bars bolted to the lower control arms at one end and mounted to the chassis frame, using a rubber bumper at the other end. A torsion bar type stabilizer is connected to the lower control arm by shackle rods.

Torsion Bars

Removal and Installation

1. Jack up the front of the vehicle and support it with jackstands.

2. Remove the adjusting bolt from the height control arm.

3. Mark the location and remove the height control arm from the torsion bar and the third crossmember.

4. Mark the location and withdraw the torsion bar from the lower control arm.

5. For installation, apply a generous amount of grease to the serrated ends of the torsion bars.

6. Hold the rubber bumpers in contact with the lower control arm. Jack the vehicle up under the lower control arm to accomplish this.

7. Insert the front end of the torsion bar into the control arm.

8. Install the height control arm in position so that its end is reaching the adjusting bolt. Be sure to lubricate the part of the height control arm that fits into the chassis with grease.

9. Install a new cotter pin in the height control arm.

10. Turn the adjusting bolt to the location marked before removal.

11. Lower the vehicle and check the vehicle height and trim attitude.

Shock Absorbers

Removal and Installation

1. Raise the vehicle and support it with jackstands.

2. Hold the upper stem of the shock absorber from turning with an open-end wrench, and then, remove the upper stem retaining nut, retainer and rubber grommet.

3. Remove the bolt retaining the lower shock absorber pivot to the lower control arm and remove the shock absorber from the vehicle.

4. Install the shock absorber by first installing the lower retainer and rubber grommet over the upper stem and then, installing the shock fully extended up through the upper control arm so that the upper stem passes through the mounting hole in the frame bracket.

5. Install the upper rubber grommet, retainer and attaching nut over the shock absorber upper stem.

6. Hold the upper stem of the shock absorber from turning with an open-end wrench and tighten the retaining nut.

7. Install the retainers attaching the shock absorber lower pivot to the lower control arm and tighten them.

8. Lower the vehicle.

Upper Control Arm and Ball Joint

Removal and Installation

NOTE: *The upper control arm and ball joint are replaced as an assembly.*

1. Raise the vehicle and support it on jackstands placed under the lower control arms.

2. Remove the wheel and tire assembly.

3. Remove the cotter pin nut fastening the upper control arm and upper ball joint assembly and disconnect the upper control arm from the steering knuckle.

NOTE: *Do not allow the steering knuckle to hang by the flexible brake line. Wire the steering knuckle up to the frame temporarily.*

4. Remove the two bolts from the upper pivot shaft and remove the upper control arm from the bracket. Be sure to note the position and number of shims used for adjusting the camber and caster angles when removing the upper control arm. This is to ensure that the shims are reinstalled in their original positions.

5. To remove the pivot shaft and bushings from the upper control arm assembly, remove the bushing nuts from the pivot shaft by loosening them alternately, then remove the pivot shaft.

6. To install the upper control arm and ball joint assembly, first install the pivot shaft boots to the pivot shaft.

7. Fill the internal part of the bushings with grease (molybdenum disulfide) and screw the bushings into the pivot shaft. Be sure to screw the right-side and the left-side bushings alternately into the pivot shafts carefully avoiding getting grease on the outer face of the bushings. Tighten the nuts to 250 ft lbs.

NOTE: *Be sure that the control arm and bushings are centered properly and that the control arm rotates with resistance but not binding on the pivot shaft when tightened to the proper torque.*

8. Install the grease fittings and lubricate the parts with grease through the grease fittings.

9. Install the ball joint stud through the steering knuckle. Install the castellated nut and tighten it to 75 ft lbs and just enough additional torque to install the cotter pin. Use a new cotter pin.

10. Mount the upper control arm to the chassis frame and install the shims in their original positions between the pivot shaft and bracket. Tighten the pivot shaft attaching nuts to 55 ft lbs.

NOTE: *Tighten the thinner shim pack's nut first for improved shaft-to-frame clamping force and torque retention.*

11. Install the dust cover.

12. Install the wheel and tire assembly and lower the vehicle to the floor.

Lower Ball Joint

Removal and Installation

1. Raise the front of the vehicle and support it with jackstands.

2. Remove the wheel and tire assembly.

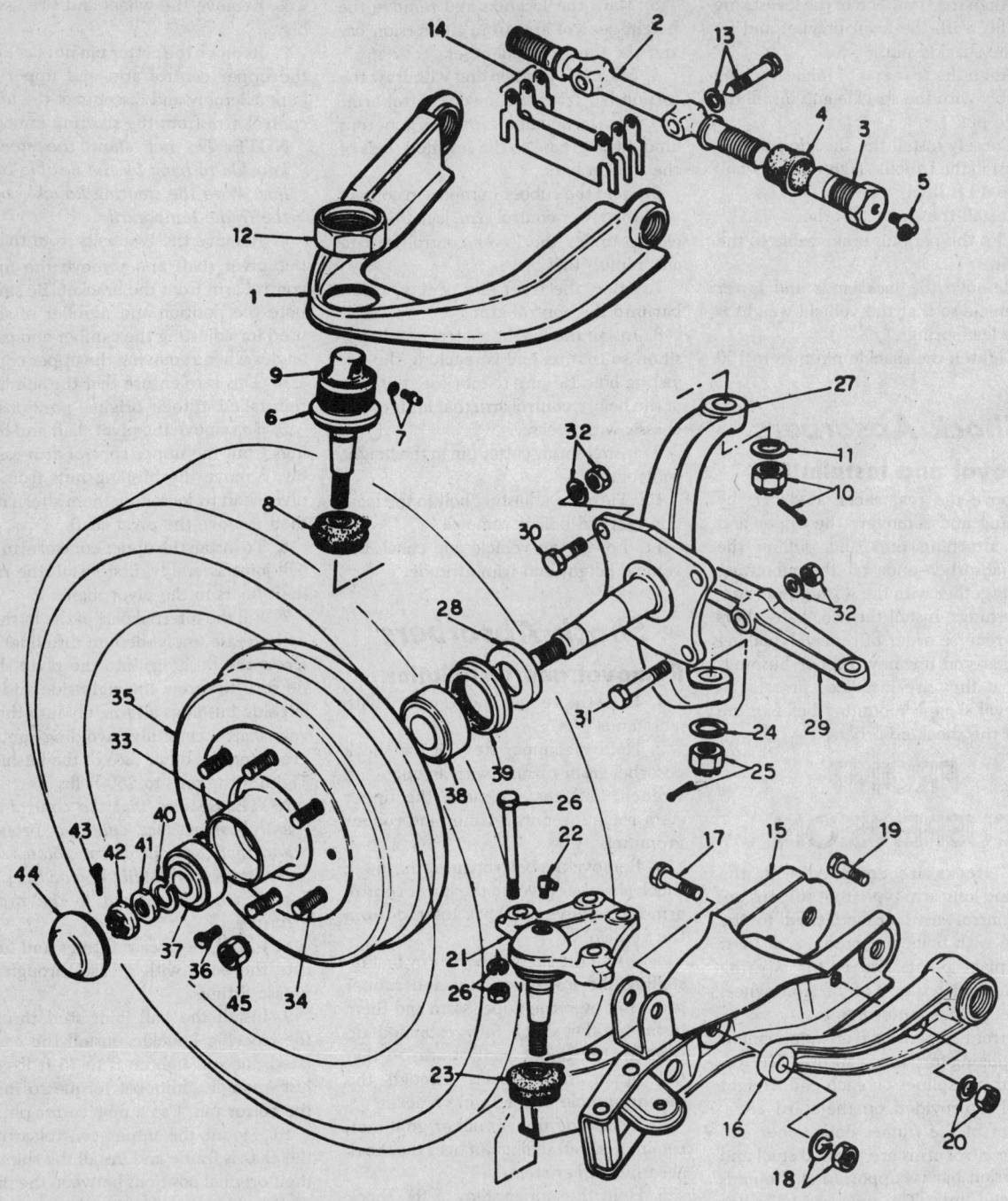

Exploded view of the upper and lower control arms, ball joints, spindle and hub assemblies

1. Upper Control Arm	16. Lower Control Arm Link	31. Bolt
2. Pivot Shaft	17. Bolt	32. Nut, Lock Washer
3. Bushing(2)	18. Nut, Lock Washer	33. Hub
4. Cover	19. Bolt	34. Wheel Stud
5. Grease Fitting	20. Nut, Lock Washer	35. Drum
6. Upper Ball Joint	21. Lower Ball Joint	36. Screw
7. Grease Fitting	22. Grease Fitting	37. Outer Wheel Bearing
8. Boot	23. Boot	38. Inner Wheel Bearing
9. Shim	24. Lock Washer	39. Grease Seal
10. Nut, Cotter Pin	25. Nut, Cotter Pin	40. Washer
11. Washer	26. Bolt, Nut, Lock Washer	41. Nut
12. Staked Nut	27. Knuckle	42. Nut Retainer
13. Bolt, Washer	28. Bearing Shoulder Piece	43. Cotter Pin
14. Shims	29. Tie Rod Link	44. Dust Cap
15. Lower Control Arm	30. Bolt	45. Wheel Stud Nut

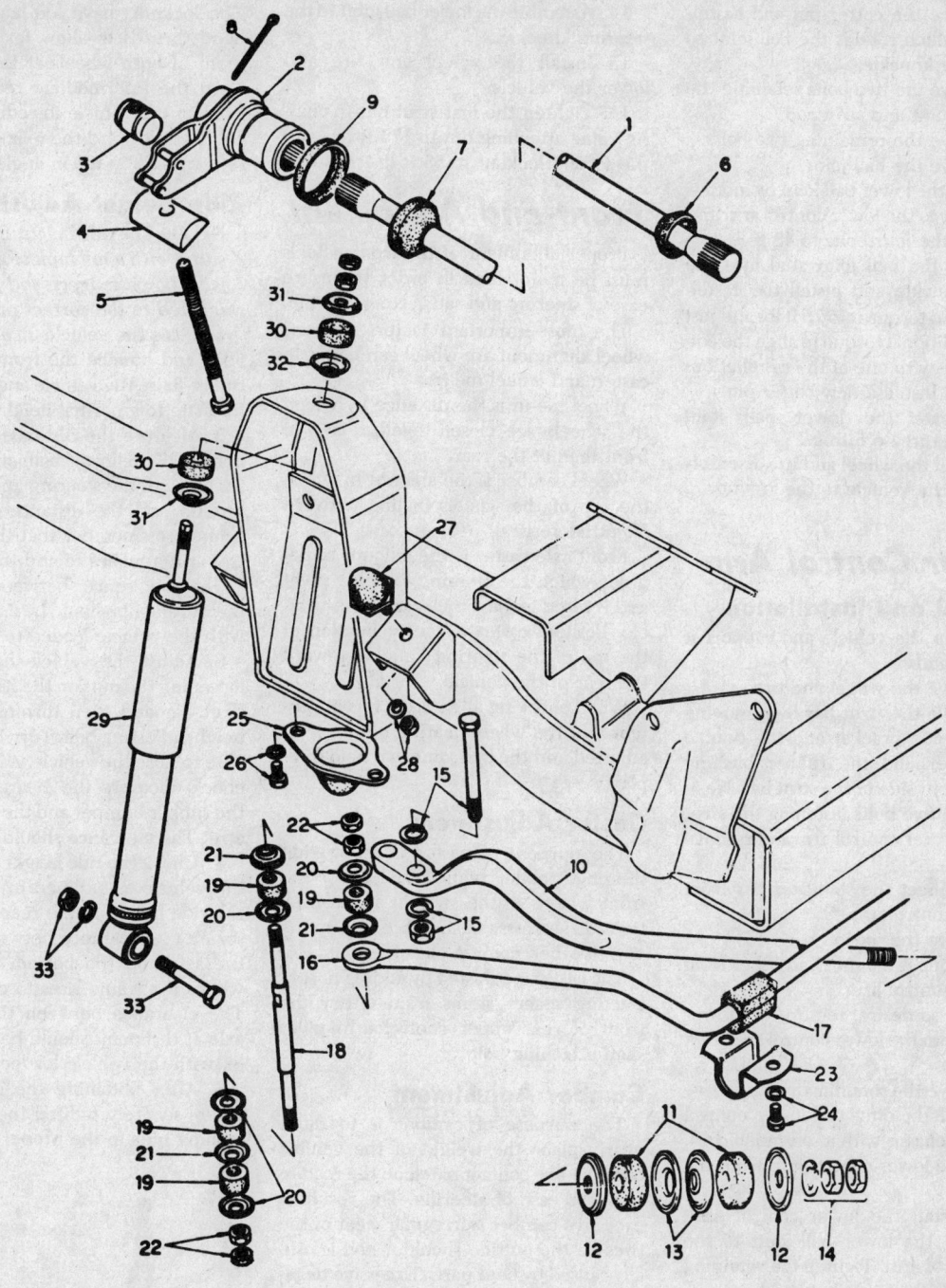

Exploded view of the stabilizer bar, strut rod, shock absorber, and torsion bar assemblies

1. Torsion Bar	12. Strut Rod Washer	23. Stabilizer Bar Bracket
2. Height Control Arm	13. Strut Rod Washer	24. Bolt and Washer
3. Pivot Nut	14. Nut, Lock Washer	25. Lower Control Arm Bumper
4. Height Control Seat	15. Bolt, Washer, Nut	26. Bolt, Washer
5. Height Control Bolt	16. Stabilizer Bar	27. Upper Control Arm Bumpers(2)
6. Boot	17. Stabilizer Bushings	28. Nut, Washer
7. Boot	18. Link Stud	29. Shock Absorber
8. Cotter Pin	19. Link Stud Bushings	30. Bushing
9. Seal	20. Stabilizer Link Stud Washers	31. Retainer
10. Strut Rod Assy.	21. Stabilizer Link Stud Washers	32. Retainer
11. Strut Rod Bushings	22. Nuts	33. Bolt, Lock Washer, Nut

3. Remove the cotter pin and castellated nut which retains the ball joint to the steering knuckle.

4. Remove the two bolts retaining the lower ball joint and strut rod.

5. Remove the remaining two bolts.

6. Remove the ball joint.

7. Install the lower ball joint by mounting the joint to the lower control arm and tightening the four bolts to 45 ft lbs.

8. Install the ball joint stud into the steering knuckle and install the castellated nut and torque it to 75 ft lbs and just enough additional torque to align the cotter pin hole with one of the castellations on the nut. Install a new cotter pin.

9. Lubricate the lower ball joint through the grease fitting.

10. Install the wheel and tire assembly and lower the vehicle to the ground.

Lower Control Arm

Removal and Installation

1. Jack up the vehicle and support it with jackstands.

2. Remove the wheel and tire.

3. Remove the strut bar by removing the frame side bracket and the double nuts, washer and the rubber bushing from the front side of the strut bar. Next, remove the two bolts fastening the strut bar to the lower control arm and remove the bar.

4. Disconnect the stabilizer bar from the lower control arm.

5. Remove the torsion bar.

6. Disconnect the shock absorber from the lower control arm.

7. If you so desire, remove the lower ball joint from the lower control arm joint at this time.

8. Remove the retaining nut and drive out the bolt holding the lower control arm to the chassis with a soft metal drift. Remove the lower control arm from the vehicle.

9. To install the lower control arm, first, install the lower ball joint to the lower control arm. Tighten the retaining nuts to 45 ft lbs.

10. Mount the lower control arm to the frame. Drive the bolt into position carefully with a soft metal drift. Use care not to damage the serrated portions. Tighten the nut on the end of the pivot bolt to 135 ft lbs.

11. Install the stabilizer bar to the lower control arm.

12. Place the washers and bushings on the strut rod and install it through the frame bracket. Install the second set of washers and bushings on the strut rod together with the lockwashers and nut. Leave the nut loose temporarily.

13. Install the strut rod to the lower control arm and tighten the bolts to 45 ft lbs.

14. Assemble the lower ball joint to the steering knuckle.

15. Install the wheel and tire and lower the vehicle.

16. Tighten the first strut bar-to-chassis frame attaching nut to 175 ft lbs, and the second locknut to 55 ft lbs.

Front End Alignment

Proper alignment of the front wheels must be maintained in order to ensure ease of steering and satisfactory tire life.

The most important factors of front wheel alignment are wheel camber, axle caster, and wheel toe-in.

Wheel toe-in is the distance by which the wheels are closer together at the front than at the rear.

Wheel camber is the amount in which the top of the wheels incline outward from the vertical.

Front axle caster is the amount in degrees which the steering knuckle pivot axis is tilted toward the rear of the vehicle. Positive caster is the inclination of the top of the steering knuckle toward the rear of the vehicle.

When checking alignment, it is important that the wheel bearing be properly adjusted and the ball joints have no freeplay.

Caster Adjustment

The purpose of caster is to provide steering stability which will keep the front wheels in the straight-ahead position and also assist in straightening up the wheels when coming out of a turn.

The caster is adjusted by adding or subtracting spacer shims from either the front or rear upper control arm pivot shaft attaching bolts.

Camber Adjustment

The purpose of camber is to more nearly place the weight of the vehicle over the tire contact patch on the road to facilitate ease of steering. The result of excessive camber is irregular wear of the tires on the outside shoulder and is usually caused by bent parts. Excessive negative camber will also cause hard steering and possibly wandering. The tires will wear on the inside shoulders.

The camber angle is adjusted by adding or subtracting spacer shims from both the front and rear upper control arm pivot shaft attaching bolts. The same amount of shims is added or subtracted to both of the bolts at the same time.

Toe-In

The toe-in measurement is the difference between the distances between the front and rear center of the tread of the two front tires.

The toe-in can be adjusted by turning the intermediate rod after loosening the locknuts on the intermediate rod ends.

The locknuts have left-hand and right-hand threads to allow for equal adjustment of both wheels at the same time. Turn the intermediate rod toward the front of the vehicle to reduce the toe-in angle and toward the rear of the vehicle to increase the toe-in angle.

Ride Height Adjustment

NOTE: *The ride height should be measured with a full tank of gas, spare tire, jack, no passengers, and with the tires inflated to the correct pressure.*

1. Place the vehicle on a smooth level floor and bounce the front end several times. Raise the vehicle and then allow it to settle to a normal height.

2. Measure the distance between the bottom of the lower ball joint stud which fits through the steering knuckle and the ground and the distance between the frame crossmember that the lower control arm attaches to and the ground.

The difference between these two measurements should be 2.52 in. (1.54 in. with the vehicle loaded to GVW).

3. Adjust the vehicle height by first loosening the nuts on the front end of the strut bar and then turning the vehicle height adjusting bolt. Turn the bolt clockwise to raise the vehicle. As an additional check, measure the clearance between the rubber bumper and the lower control arm. The clearance should be ⅞ in.

4. Check the ride height at the front of the vehicle as outlined in Step 2 above the ride height at the rear axle by measuring the clearance between the top of the axle and the bottom of the frame where the frame rises to clear the axle. The clearance between the frame and axle at this point should be 7.90 in. (6.26 in. with the vehicle loaded to GVW).

5. After obtaining the correct clearances, securely tighten the strut bar attaching nuts to the proper torque.

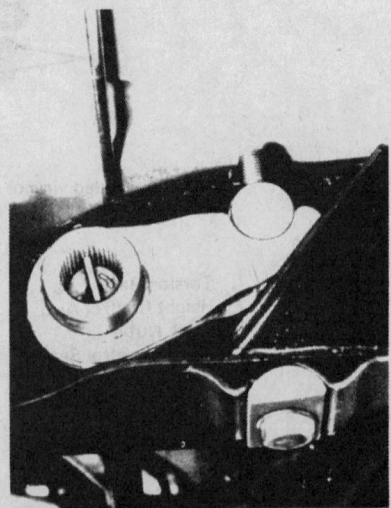

The vehicle ride height adjustment end of the torsion bar

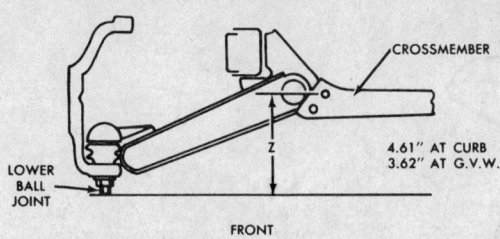

Ride height measurement at the front of the vehicle

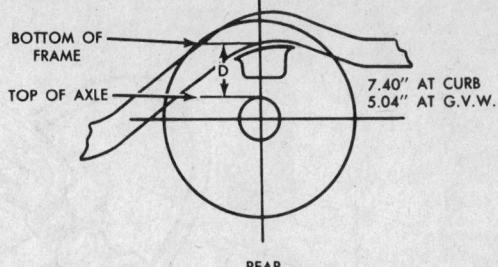

Ride height measurement at the rear of the vehicle

STEERING

Steering Wheel

Removal and Installation

1. Disconnect the battery ground cable.

2. Remove the horn shroud and spring by pushing and turning it counterclockwise. Remove the horn contact ring and wire.

3. Remove the steering wheel-to-steering shaft retaining nut, washer and lockwasher.

4. Mark the relative position of the steering wheel and shaft to each other.

5. Remove the steering column cowling by removing the four attaching screws and washers.

6. Remove the steering wheel from the shaft with a puller.

NOTE: *Under no circumstances is the steering shaft to be hammered upon; jarred, or leaned upon. The steering column is a collapsible, energy-absorbing type and can be easily damaged through mistreatment.*

7. Install the steering wheel in the reverse order of removal, aligning the marks made on the steering wheel and the shaft. Draw the steering wheel onto the shaft with the attaching nut.

Turn Signal and Dimmer Switch

Removal and Installation

1. Disconnect the battery ground cable.

2. Remove the four screws retaining the steering column cowling and remove the cowling.

3. Remove the wire connectors from the switch.

4. Remove the switch by removing the two screws which retain the switch clamp to the steering column mast jacket.

5. Replace the switch in the reverse order of removal.

Manual Steering Gear

Removal and Installation

1. Raise the vehicle on a hoist.

2. Remove the pitman arm nut and washer and mark the relationship of the shaft to the arm. Using a puller, remove the pitman arm from the pitman shaft.

3. Remove the engine stone shield.

4. Remove the two lower flexible coupling clamp bolts.

5. Remove the steering gear-to-frame bolts and remove the steering gear from the vehicle.

6. Install the steering gear in the reverse order of removal, installing the mounting bolts loosely at first and tightening the long bolts to 55 ft lbs and the short ones to 20 ft lbs only after the flexible coupling bolts have been tightened to 20 ft lbs.

BRAKE SYSTEMS

The Chevy LUV is equipped with vacuum assisted hydraulic self-adjusting type brakes.

On 1972–75 models the front brakes are of the two leading shoe type which incorporate two wheel cylinders at each wheel. The front wheel cylinder actuates the lower brake shoe and the rear cylinder the upper brake shoe. On 1976–77 models the front brakes are the floating disc brake type which incorporates a single piston actuating both inner and outer shoe and lining assemblies. The brake linings are molded and bonded to the brake shoes.

The rear brakes are the duo-servo type with a single wheel cylinder on each wheel. The wheel cylinder has two pistons, actuating both the secondary and primary brake shoes. The brake lining is also molded and bonded to the brake shoes. The primary lining is smaller than the secondary lining.

The self-adjusters on the front brakes operate during forward stops and the self-adjusters on the rear brakes adjust on reverse stops.

The parking brake is actuated by a ratchet type L-handle mounted to the dash at the right of the steering column. A cable connects the handle to the intermediate cable by means of a lever. The intermediate cable attaches to the two rear cables which operate the rear service brakes. Adjustment of the parking brake is provided at the equalizer.

Adjustment

Disc brakes require no adjustments. Drum brakes, although self-adjusting, may require an initial adjustment after the brakes have been replaced, or whenever the adjuster position has been changed. The final adjustment is made by using the self-adjusting mechanism.

1. With the brake drum removed, disengage the pullback springs from the adjuster plates on the front brakes, or the actuator from the starwheel on the rear brakes.

2. Using the brake drum as an adjustment gauge, adjust the upper and lower shoes an equal number of notches on the front brakes, or turn the starwheel on the rear brakes until the brake drum slides over the brake shoes with a slight drag.

3. Retract the upper and lower shoes of the front brakes two notches, or turn the starwheel on the rear brakes 1¼ turns to retract the shoes.

4. Install the brake drums and wheels and lower the vehicle.

NOTE: *If the backing place access plugs were removed on the front brakes, make sure that they are reinstalled before making the final adjustment. Also, the brake drums are to be installed in the same position from which they were removed. Make sure that you install the drum-to-flange locating screw.*

5. Perform the final adjustment by making a number of forward and reverse stops, applying the brakes with a firm pedal effort until a satisfactory brake pedal height, and straight-line braking is achieved.

Master Cylinder

Removal and Installation

1. Disconnect the battery ground cable.

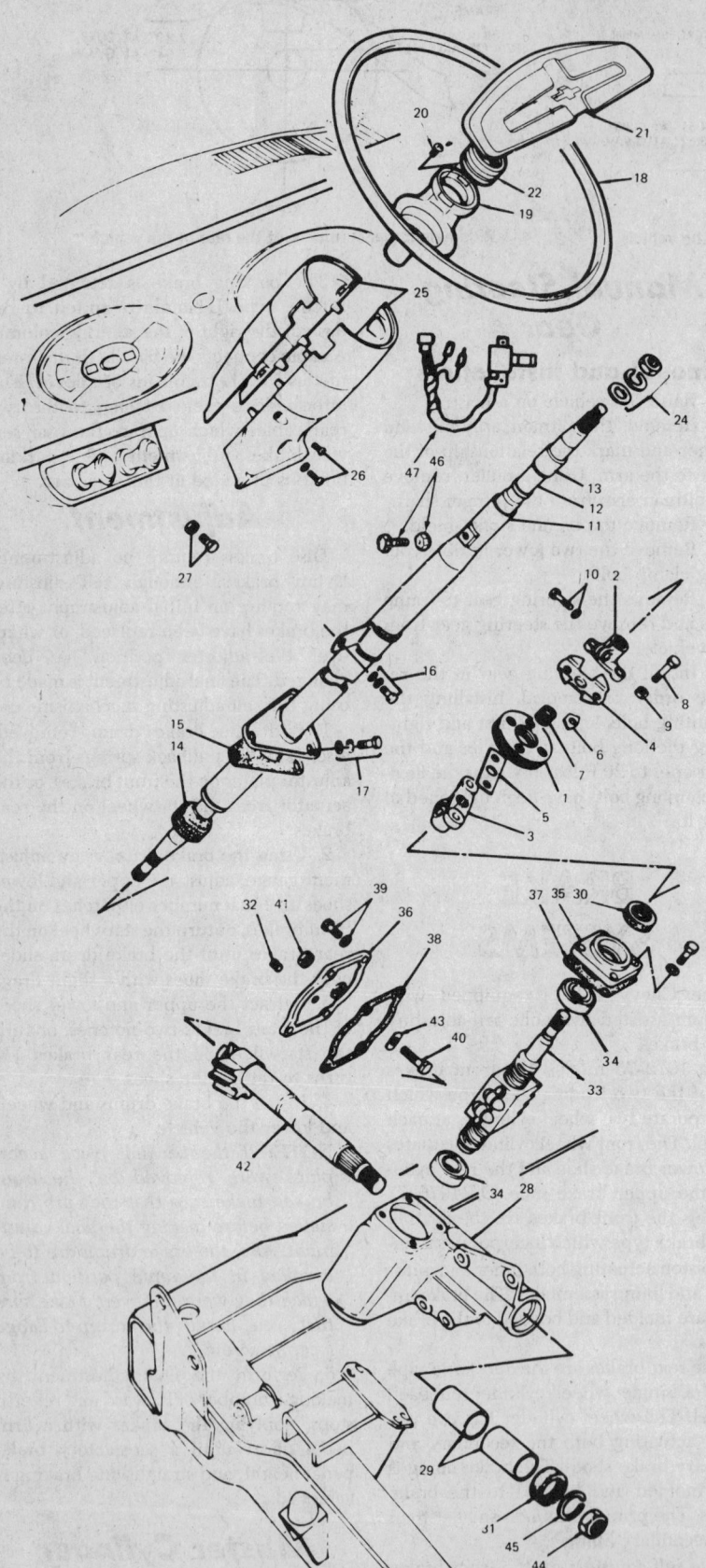

1. Coupling
2. Flange, Upper Coupling
3. Flange, Lower Coupling
4. Cross-Strap
5. Cross-Strap
6. Thrust Washer
7. Spring
8. Thru Bolt
9. Lock Nut
10. Pinch Bolt, Lock Washer
11. Mast Jacket
12. Shaft Assy.
13. Bushing
14. Grommet
15. Gasket
16. Bolt, and Washers
17. Screw, And Washers
18. Wheel Assembly
19. Horn Shroud Seat
20. Screw
21. Horn Shroud
22. Spring
23. Nut
24. Shaft Nut and Washers
25. Column Cowling
26. Cowling Screws and Washers
27. Bolt, Washer
28. Steering Gear Housing
29. Sector Shaft Bushings
30. Wormshaft Seal
31. Sector (Pitman) Shaft Seal
32. Filler Plug
33. Worm & Ball Nut Assy.
34. Wormshaft Bearing
35. End Cover
36. Top Cover
37. Worm Preload Shims
38. Gasket
39. Bolt, Lock Washer
40. Sector Adjuster Screw
41. Lock Nut
42. Sector Shaft
43. Adjusting Shim
44. Pitman Shaft Nut
45. Lock Washer
46. Bolt, Nut (Stopper)
47. Hazard Warning Switch Assm.

Exploded view of the steering system components

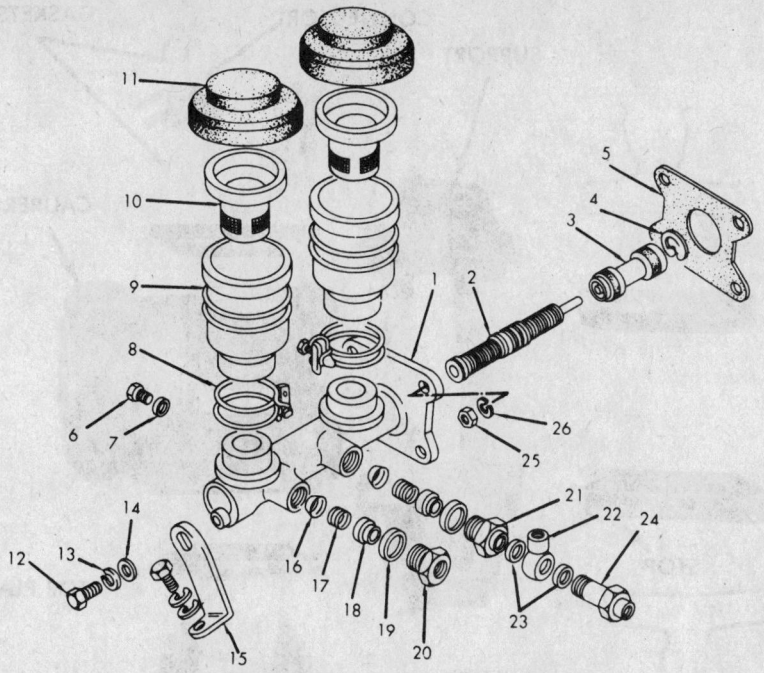

Exploded view of the brake master cylinder

1. Master Cylinder	10. Filter	19. Gasket*
2. Secondary Piston	11. Cover	20. Connector
3. Primary Piston	12. Bolt	21. End Plug
4. Snap Ring	13. Lock Washer	22. Connector
5. Gasket*	14. Washer	23. Gasket*
6. Stopper Bolt	15. Bracket	24. Connector Bolt*
7. Gasket*	16. Spring Seat	25. Nut
8. Clamp	17. Return Spring	26. Washer
9. Reservoir	18. Check Valve	

NOTE (*) Included in REPAIR KIT

2. Wipe the master cylinder and brake lines clean. Place absorbent cloths below the master cylinder area to absorb any fluid leakage.

3. Disconnect the hydraulic lines at the connections on the master cylinder. Cover the ends of the brake lines to prevent the entrance of dirt.

4. Remove the master cylinder bracket bolt at the front end of the master cylinder.

5. Remove the master cylinder-to-booster attaching nuts and lockwashers and remove the master cylinder and gasket from the booster.

6. Install the master cylinder in the reverse order of removal, and bleed the brake hydraulic system.

Overhaul

1. Remove the master cylinder from the vehicle.

2. Remove the fluid reservoir caps, plates and strainers and drain the fluid from the reservoirs.

3. Place the master cylinder in a vise.

4. Loosen the fluid reservoir clamp screws and remove the plastic reservoirs from the master cylinder body.

5. Remove the connector bolt, connector and gaskets from the front system side (rear outlet). Then, remove the end plug, gasket, check valve, return spring and spring seat.

6. Remove the connector, gasket, check valve, return spring and spring seat from the rear system side (front outlet).

7. Push the primary piston all the way in and then remove the stopper bolt and gasket on the right-side of the master cylinder.

8. Using snap-ring pliers, remove the primary piston snap-ring.

9. Remove the primary and secondary piston assemblies from the cylinder bore.

10. Clean all of the parts in clean brake fluid. Blow out all passages, orifices, and valve holes with compressed air.

11. Inspect the master cylinder bore and pistons for scoring, corrosion, and rust. Slight scoring and rust can be removed by polishing with crocus cloth or fine emery paper soaked with brake fluid.

12. Soak all new and old parts in clean brake fluid before reassembling.

13. Insert the secondary piston assembly into the master cylinder bore, so that the primary stem guide is projected slightly beyond the cylinder bore end.

14. Insert the primary piston into the master cylinder bore so that the secondary piston stem guide enters the hole in the primary piston.

15. Install the snap-ring into the groove in the master cylinder housing.

16. Depress the primary piston and install the piston stopper bolt and new gasket.

17. Install the spring seat, return spring, check valve, new gasket and end plug in the front system side of the master cylinder (rear outlet).

18. Install a new gasket on either side of the connector and secure it into position with the connector bolt.

19. Install the spring seat, return spring, check valve, new gasket and connector in the rear system side of the master cylinder (front outlet).

20. Install the clamps over the lower ends of the fluid reservoirs, place the reservoirs in position on the master cylinder body and then tighten the clamp bolts.

21. Install the reservoir filters, and fill the reservoirs with clean brake fluid. Push in on the primary piston to determine that it returns smoothly. Test the piston assembly two or three times to make sure that fluid comes out of the front and rear outlets.

22. Install the plates and covers.

23. Install plugs in all of the connector outlet ports.

24. Fill the reservoirs to the proper level with clean brake fluid.

25. Insert a rod with a smooth round end to the piston end and press it in to compress the piston return spring.

26. Release the pressure on the rod. Watch for air bubbles in the reservoir fluid.

27. Repeat Steps 25 and 26 as long as bubbles appear in the fluid.

28. Install the master cylinder on the vehicle and bleed the brake hydraulic system.

Bleeding

The brake hydraulic system must be bled after any line has been disconnected or air has somehow found its way into the system.

The bleeding operation should start with the wheel cylinder nearest the master cylinder and end with the one farthest away.

NOTE: *Do not bleed the brakes with the brake drums or calipers removed.*

1. Make sure that the master cylinder is full and kept at least ¾ full throughout the entire bleeding process. Check the fluid level in the master cylinder reservoirs frequently during the bleeding operation.

2. Remove the cap from the wheel cylinder or caliper bleeder valve. Position a wrench on the bleeder valve and place a rubber hose over the bleeder valve nipple.

3. Place the other end of the bleeder hose into a clear container containing enough brake fluid to ensure that the end of the bleeder hose will remain submerged.

4. Start the engine and allow it to run during the actual bleeding of each wheel cylinder. This is so to have vacuum applied to the brake booster during the bleeding process.

5. Open the wheel cylinder bleeder valve by turning the wrench counter-clockwise about ¾ of a turn. Have an assistant depress the brake pedal. Just before the brake pedal reaches the end of its travel, close the bleeder valve and allow the brake pedal to return slowly to the released position. Repeat this operation until the brake fluid being expelled is free from air bubbles, then close the bleeder valve tightly.

6. Remove the bleeder hose and the wrench from the bleeder valve and install them onto the next wheel cylinder or caliper to be bled. Repeat Step 5 on all of the remaining wheel cylinders. Don't forget to check and replenish the brake fluid in the master cylinder reservoirs.

7. After bleeding the brake hydraulic system, check the operation of the brakes. Depress the brake pedal several times then hold it depressed. Notice how far the pedal can be depressed. Release the pedal for about 10 seconds, then depress it again and hold it, taking notice of the distance which it can be depressed before it stops with the same amount of pedal pressure applied as before. If the pedal depresses further or can be "pumped up", then it can be assumed that there is still air in the hydraulic system and further bleeding is required.

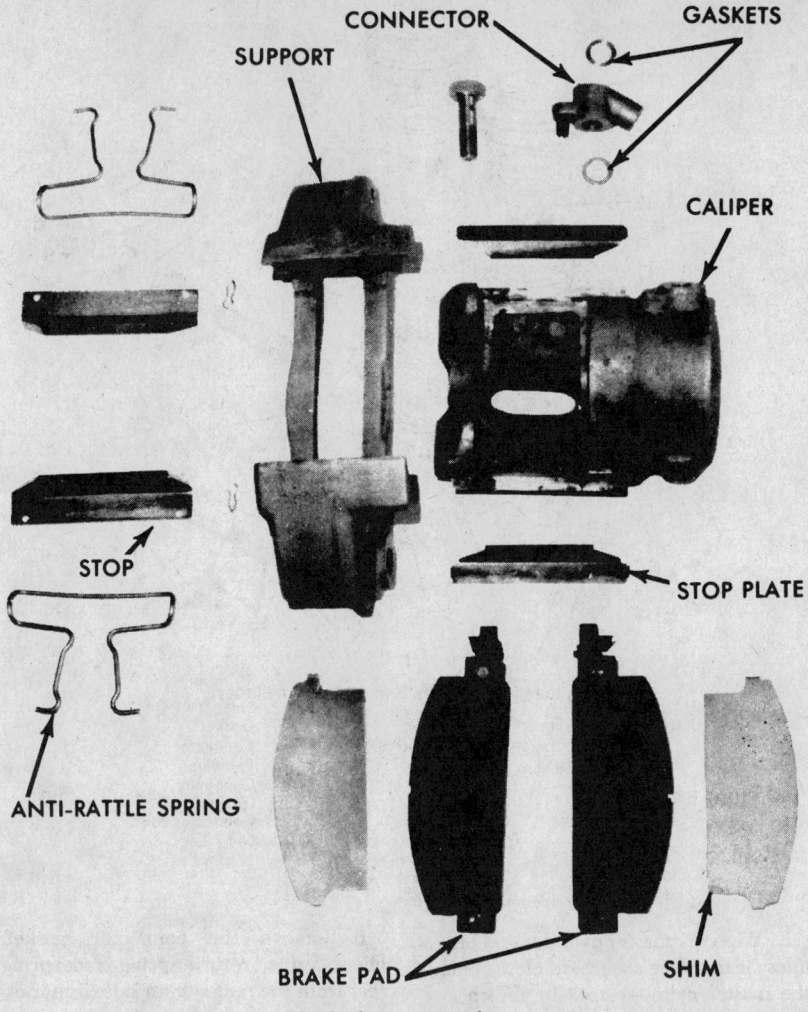

Disc brake components

FRONT DISC BRAKES

Disc Brake Pads

Inspection

Replace the front disc brake linings whenever the lining wear indicator makes a squeaking noise or when the lining is worn to within .039″ of the shoe table. All four brake linings should always be replaced at the same time.

Removal and Installation

1. Raise the vehicle on a lift.
2. Remove the wheel and tire assembly.
3. Remove the pins from the caliper stops and then remove the stops.
4. Remove the caliper from the support, remove the stop plates from the caliper then suspend the caliper assembly from the upper link or frame using a piece of heavy wire.
5. Remove the shoe and lining assemblies and shims and mark the locations if to be reinstalled.
6. Remove the anti-rattle springs from the support.

7. Wipe the inside of the caliper clean, including the exterior of the dust seal. Check to see that the dust seal is in good condition.
8. Install the anti-rattle springs, shims and the shoe and lining assemblies to the support.
NOTE: *If original linings are being reinstalled, they must be installed in the original position. Also position the wear indicators to the lower side of the support.*
9. Install new stop plates to the caliper, then install the caliper, stops and stop pins.
10. Install the wheel and tire assembly.

Disc Brake Calipers

Removal and Installation

1. Raise the vehicle on a lift.
2. Remove the wheel and tire assembly.
3. Remove the pins from the caliper stops and then remove the stops.
4. Disconnect the front flexible hose from the brake line.
NOTE: *To keep dirt from entering, cap or tape the openings of the flexible*

hose and brake line.
5. Remove the caliper from the support and remove the stop plates from the caliper.

Overhaul

1. Remove the flexible hose from the caliper.
2. Remove the dust seal from the caliper using a small screwdriver.
3. Insert a block of wood into the caliper and force out the piston by applying compressed air into the caliper at the flexible hose attachment. Remove and discard the piston square ring seal.
4. Clean all parts in clean brake fluid. Check the cylinder bore and pistons for wear, scuffing or corrosion and replace as necessary.
5. Apply a silicone lube to the caliper bore and the piston square ring seal and insert the piston seal into the caliper bore using finger pressure only.
6. Apply a silicone lubricant to the piston and assemble the dust seal to the piston and caliper. Install the seal ring into the dust seal.
7. Install the flexible hose to the caliper using new gaskets.

8. Lubricate the stop plates and the sliding surfaces of the caliper then install the new stop plates to the caliper, the caliper and the new stop pins.

9. Connect the flexible brake hose to the brake line.

10. Install the wheel and tire assembly.

Brake Disc Assembly

Removal and Installation

1. Raise the vehicle on a lift.

2. Remove the front tire and wheel assembly.

3. Remove the bolts attaching the caliper support to the adapter and then suspend the caliper and support from the upper link or frame using a piece of heavy wire.

4. Remove the hub grease cap, cotter pin, spindle nut retainer and nut and remove the hub and rotor assembly.

5. Replace the hub and disc as an assembly if either needs replacement.

NOTE: *All brake disc have a minimum thickness dimension cast into them. This dimension is the minimum wear dimension and not a refinish dimension.*

6. Install the dust shield and adapter to the steering knuckle and torque the long bolts to 55 ft. lbs. and the small bolts to 35 ft. lbs.

7. Install the front hub and disc assembly and adjust the wheel bearings.

8. Assemble the caliper and support assembly to the adapter and torque the bolts to 64 ft. lbs.

9. Install the front wheel and tire assembly.

FRONT DRUM BRAKES

Brake Drums

Removal and Installation

1. Jack up the vehicle and support it on jackstands.

2. Remove the wheel cover and remove the wheel and tire assembly.

3. Remove the brake drum and hub retaining screws and remove the drum. Identify the drum so that it can be reinstalled in the same position.

If the brake drums are worn considerably, it may be necessary to retract the brake shoes before the drum can be removed. Remove the rubber hole plugs in the backing plate and insert a screwdriver through the hole and into the hole in the brake shoe. Raise the end of the brake shoe return spring to release it from the serration and contact the brake shoe by moving it in toward the wheel cylinder.

NOTE: *Never depress the brake pedal while the brake drums are removed.*

4. Install the brake drums in the reverse order of removal.

Inspection

After removing the brake drum, remove any dirt and inspect the drum for cracks, deep grooves, roughness, scoring, or out-of-roundness. Replace any brake drum which is cracked completely through.

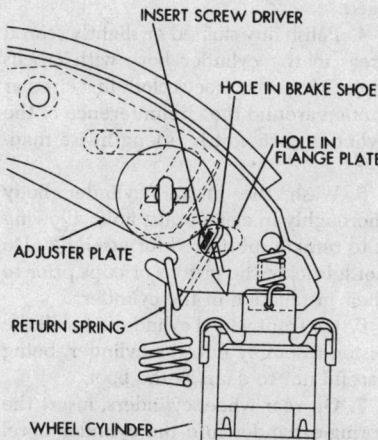

Insert the blade of a screwdriver through the hole in the backing plate and the brake shoe, raise and release the end of the return spring and move the brake shoe in toward the wheel cylinder

Smooth any slight scores by polishing the friction surface with fine emery cloth. Heavy or extensive scoring will cause excessive brake lining wear and should be removed from the brake drum through resurfacing of the brake drum friction surface. The maximum finished diameter of the brake drums must not exceed 10.059 in. The brake drum must be replaced if the diameter is 10.079 in. or greater.

Brake Shoes

Removal and Installation

The brake linings must be replaced when the lining thickness is 0.059 in. or less.

1. Remove the brake drum.

2. Disconnect the wheel cylinder piston springs from the pistons and shoes with a pair of pliers.

3. Depress and rotate the hold-down spring retainers 90° with a pair of pliers and then remove the springs and retainers.

4. Remove the upper and lower brake shoes.

5. Depress the self-adjusting spring retainers, rotate the shoe 90° while holding the retainer and then separate the self-adjuster retainer, washer, spring, pin, adjuster lever and the brake shoe from each other.

NOTE: *If the shoes, adjuster levers and return springs are to be reinstalled, be sure to mark their location so that they will be reinstalled in their original positions.*

6. Before you install the brake shoes, make sure that your hands and tools are free from grease and oil that could possibly contaminate the brake linings.

7. Place the brake shoe in an arbor press or similar tool and install the adjuster pivot pin, adjuster lever, washer, spring and retainers to each brake shoe. Compress the spring and rotate the retainer 90° while compressing the spring, making sure that the pin end is seated in the retainer groove.

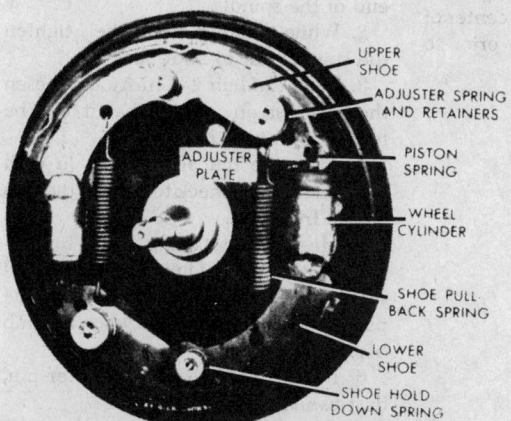

Front brake assembly components

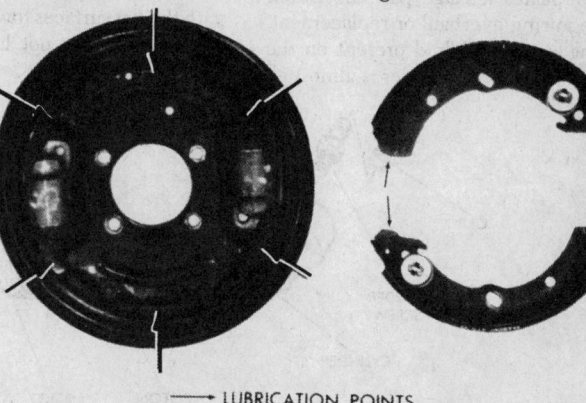

Lubrication points for the front brakes

NOTE: *Install the washer so that its lining side is facing the lever. Also, the left and right-side adjuster levers are not interchangeable and must be reinstalled in their original positions.*

8. Lubricate the brake shoe contact points on the backing plate and the wheel cylinder contact points on the brake shoes with Lubriplate.

9. Hook the return springs to the brake shoes. Be sure to install the left and right springs in their original positions as they are not interchangeable. The left springs are light blue; right springs are black.

10. Fit the grooved portion of the adjuster lever to the guide pin and install the brake shoes in position. Make sure that the shoes are fitted properly to the guide pin. If the end of the brake shoe is not inserted in the groove, it is an indication that the brake shoes are lifted off the ridged portion. Make sure that the return spring end is fitted properly to the adjuster lever.

11. Install the piston springs on the wheel cylinder piston ends.

12. Install the brake shoe hold-down springs and retainers. With a pair of pliers, compress the spring and rotate the retainer 90°, making sure that the pin end is seated in the retainer groove.

13. Reinstall the brake drum and adjust the brakes.

Wheel Cylinders

Removal and Installation

It is not necessary to remove the wheel cylinders from the backing plates to disassemble, inspect, and overhaul the cylinder. Removal is necessary only when the wheel cylinder is damaged beyond repair and must be replaced.

It is a good practice to inspect the wheel cylinders for leakage whenever the brake drums are removed. Simply pull the edge of the wheel cylinder boot carefully away from the cylinder and note whether or not the interior is wet with brake fluid. Excessive fluid at this point indicates leakage past the piston cup, requiring overhaul or replacement. A slight amount of fluid present on the inside of the wheel cylinder is almost al-

ways present and acts as a lubricant for the piston.

1. Remove the wheel and tire assembly, the brake drum and the brake shoes.

2. Disconnect the brake system hydraulic line from the wheel cylinder at the rear of the backing plate.

3. Remove the screws securing the wheel cylinder to the backing plate and remove the wheel cylinder from the backing plate.

4. Install the wheel cylinder in the reverse order of removal and bleed the brake hydraulic system.

Overhaul

1. Either with the wheel cylinder removed or still on the brake backing plate, remove the boot(s) from the cylinder end(s).

2. Remove the piston(s) and cup(s).

NOTE: *The front wheel cylinder pistons and cups are serviced as an assembly.*

3. Inspect the cylinder bore. Check for staining and corrosion. Discard any wheel cylinder which is excessively corroded. Inspect the piston and discard it if it is excessively pitted, scored or damaged.

4. Polish any stained or slightly scored areas in the cylinder bore with crocus cloth. Move the crocus cloth in a circular motion around the circumference of the cylinder bore, not in a lengthwise manner.

5. Wash the master cylinder body thoroughly in clean brake fluid, allowing it to remain lubricated for assembly. Do not lubricate the pistons or cups prior to their installation in the cylinder.

6. On front wheel cylinders, install the piston assembly into the cylinder, being careful not to damage the boot.

7. On rear wheel cylinders, insert the spring-expander into the cylinder bore. Install the new cups with the flat surface toward the outer ends of the cylinder. Be sure that the cups are lint-free. Do not lubricate the cups prior to installation. Install the new pistons into the cylinder with the flat surfaces toward the center of the cylinder. Do not lubricate prior to installation.

8. Press the new boot(s) onto the wheel cylinder.

9. Install the wheel cylinder onto the brake backing plate, if it was removed, assemble the brake shoes to the backing plate, install the brake drum and bleed the brake hydraulic system.

Front Wheel Bearings

Removal and Installation

1. Remove the hub Assembly.

2. Remove the outer roller bearing assembly from the hub. Pry out the inner bearing lip seal and remove the inner bearing assembly.

3. Wash all parts in a cleaning solvent and blow dry.

4. Check the bearings for pitting or scoring. Also check for smooth rotation and lack of noise.

5. Thoroughly lubricate the bearings with new wheel bearing lubricant.

6. Apply a light coat of lubricant to the spindle and inside surface of the hub.

7. Place the inner bearing in the race of the hub and install a new grease seal.

8. Install the hub assembly on the spindle.

9. Install the outer wheel bearing, washer and adjust nut.

10. Adjust the wheel bearings as outlined below.

11. Install the dust cap on the hub.

12. Install the brake caliper and support assembly.

13. Install the wheel and tighten the nuts.

Wheel Bearing Adjustment

1. With the wheel raised, remove the hub cap and dust cap and then remove the cotter pin and nut retainer from the end of the spindle.

2. While rotating the wheel, tighten the spindle nut to 22 ft. lbs.

3. Turn the hub 2–3 turns and loosen the nut just enough so that it can be turned with your fingers.

4. Turn the nut all the way in with your fingers and check to be sure the hub has no free play.

5. Measure the starting torque by pulling one of the wheel hub studs with a pull scale. Tighten the spindle nut so that the pull scale reads 1.1–2.6 lbs. when the hub begins to rotate.

6. Install the nut retainer, cotter pin, dust cap and hub cap.

7. Perform the same procedure for each wheel.

CAP

BLEEDER SCREW

CYLINDER

PISTON ASSEMBLY

BOOT

Exploded view of the front wheel cylinder

REAR DRUM BRAKES

Brake Drums

Removal and Installation

1. Raise the vehicle and support it on jackstands.

2. Remove the hub caps and remove the rear tire and wheel.

3. Loosen the check nuts at the parking brake equalizer sufficiently to remove all tension from the brake cable.

4. Remove the drum-to-hub retaining screws and remove the drum from the vehicle. Identify each brake drum so that it can be reinstalled in its original position. Never depress the brake pedal while any of the brake drums are removed.

5. Install the brake drums in the reverse order of removal.

Inspection

Inspect the rear brake drums in the same manner as is outlined for the front brake drums.

Brake Shoes

Removal and Installation

1. Remove the brake drums.

2. Unhook the brake return springs from the anchor pin using a brake tool and remove the springs.

3. Remove the brake shoe hold-down springs using pliers. Depress the spring retainer while rotating it 90° to align the slot in the retainer with the flanged end of the pin.

4. Remove the self-adjuster cable assembly by disconnecting the spring at the adjuster lever and removing the cable end from the anchor pin. Remove the guide plate from the anchor pin.

5. Remove the adjuster lever and the lever hold-down wire from the shoe pivot.

6. Separate the shoes from the wheel cylinder pushrods.

7. Separate the primary and secondary brake shoes, adjuster, return spring, and parking brake strut assemblies.

NOTE: *If the brake shoes are to be reinstalled, be sure to identify them so that they can be reinstalled in their original positions.*

8. Separate the parking brake lever and the rear cable. Remove the clip and washer and remove the parking brake lever from the secondary shoe.

9. Lubricate the parking brake cable with Lubriplate.

10. Assemble the parking brake lever to the secondary shoe and then assemble the parking brake cable to the lever.

11. Before installation, make sure that the adjusting screw is clean, lubricated and operable.

12. Connect the brake shoes together with bottom return spring and then place the adjuster screw into position. The adjuster screw is installed with the starwheel nearest to the secondary shoe.

13. Assemble the parking brake strut with the spring on the primary shoe end, and assemble the shoes to the wheel cylinder pushrods.

14. Install the shoe hold-down springs using a pair of pliers. Compress the springs and rotate the retainers 90°.

15. Install the guide plate on the anchor pin. Assemble the self-adjuster lever and the lever hold-down wire to the secondary shoe pivot pin. Place the adjuster cable over the anchor pin, route the cable around the shoe shield and then attach the spring at the opposite end to the adjuster lever.

16. Install the return springs using a brake tool.

17. Pry the shoes away from the backing plate and lubricate the shoe contact areas with a thin coat of Lubriplate.

18. Check the operation of the parking brake. *Do not step on the brake pedal.*

19. Install the brake drum and adjust the brake shoes.

Wheel Cylinders

Removal and Installation

Remove and install the rear wheel cylinders in the same manner as outlined for the front wheel cylinders.

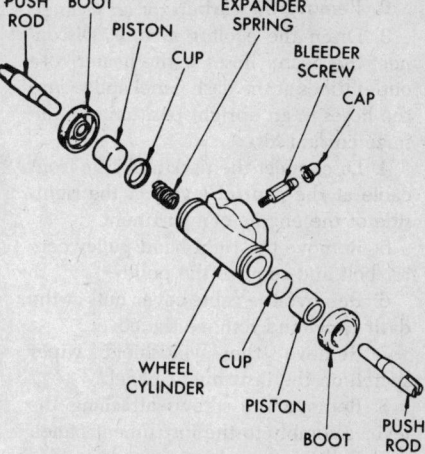

Exploded view of the rear wheel cylinder

Overhaul

Follow the procedure given for overhauling the front wheel cylinders to overhaul the rear wheel cylinders.

PARKING BRAKE

Adjustment

Since the rear brakes are utilized as service brakes and parking brakes, the service brake must be properly adjusted as a base for parking brake adjustment.

1. Raise the vehicle on a hoist.

2. Apply the parking brake two notches from the fully released position.

3. Loosen the equalizer check nut, and tighten or loosen the front jam nut until a light to moderate drag is felt when the rear wheels are rotated frontward.

4. Tighten the nuts securely. Hold the front nut while tightening the jam nut.

5. Fully release the parking brake and rotate the rear wheels. No drag should be present.

6. Lower the vehicle.

Front Cable

Removal and Installation

1. Disconnect the battery ground cable.

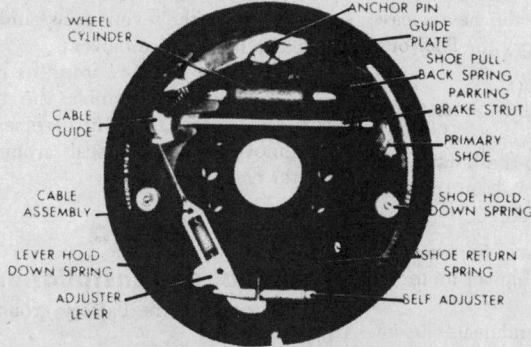

Rear brake assembly components

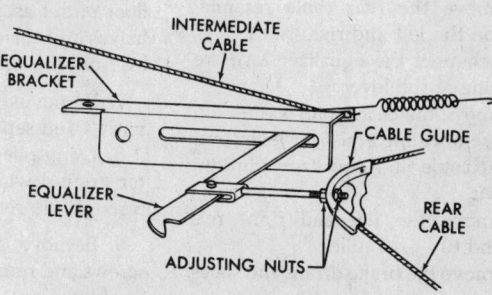

Parking brake adjusting mechanism

2. Remove the carburetor air cleaner.

3. Drain the cooling system. Disconnect the heater hoses at the heater core outlet tubes at the dash panel and secure the hoses in an upright position to minimize coolant loss.

4. Disconnect the parking brake front cable at the control lever on the right-side of the engine compartment.

5. Remove the right-hand pulley center bolt and remove the pulley.

6. Remove the cable cover nuts at the dash panel and remove the cover.

7. Remove the windshield wiper switch on the instrument panel.

8. Remove the screws attaching the lever assembly to the instrument panel.

9. Pull the assembly rearward and lay it on the floor.

10. Loosen the parking brake light switch bracket screw and rotate the switch and bracket 90°.

11. Manually release the ratchet and then depress the handle all the way in.

12. Remove the cotter pin, washer, pivot pin and the pulley. Remove the cable assembly.

13. To install the cable, install the cable to handle lower end and then pull the handle rearward several notches.

14. Rotate the parking brake light switch and bracket into position and tighten the bracket screw.

15. Install the pulley, pivot pin, washer and cotter pin.

16. For the remainder of the installation procedure follow the removal procedure in reverse starting with Step 8.

Intermediate Cable

Removal and Installation

1. Raise the vehicle on a hoist.

2. Disconnect the equalizer lever spring at the lever.

3. Loosen the cable guide nut and remove the cable assembly.

4. Install the intermediate cable in the reverse order of removal and adjust the parking brake.

Rear Cable

Removal and Installation

1. Raise the vehicle on a hoist.

2. Remove the rear cable retaining clamps on the left and right-sides.

3. Disconnect the equalizer lever return spring at the lever.

4. Remove the cotter pin, washer and pin and remove the equalizer lever from the front cable and equalizer adjusting bolt clevis.

5. Remove the left and right rear wheel and tire assemblies.

6. Remove the brake drums and shoes, disconnecting the rear cable from the brake lever.

7. Remove the rear cable spring cup using a box wrench.

8. Withdraw the cable ends from the backing plates on either side and remove the cable assembly.

9. Install the cable in the reverse order of removal and adjust the parking brake.

Removing the rear cable spring cup at the backing plate

CHASSIS ELECTRICAL
Heater Blower

Removal and Installation

1972 Only

1. Disconnect the battery ground cable.

2. Drain the cooling system.

3. Disconnect the heater hoses at the heater assembly. Cap or tape the open hoses and lines to prevent coolant spillage during removal.

4. Remove the two heater control-to-instrument panel screws (use the access holes in the lower flange of the control), the lower control and disconnect the blower switch electrical leads.

5. Remove the heater case-to-dash panel screws and lower the assembly to the floor. Disconnect the resistor electrical leads and remove the defroster door and air door bowden cables at the door bell cranks. Disconnect the defroster hoses at the floor outlet and remove the assembly from the vehicle.

6. Remove the six screws attaching the floor outlet assembly to the heater case halves and then gently pry the floor outlet from the case.

7. Remove the front-to-rear case screws and separate the case halves.

8. Using pliers, crimp the blower motor ground wire tab in half and push it through the rear case half.

9. Remove the blower-to-rear case screws and remove the blower motor assembly.

10. Install the motor and heater assembly in the reverse order of removal and refill the cooling system.

1973–77

1. Disconnect the battery ground cable.

2. Disconnect the blower motor electrical leads.

3. Remove the blower-to-heater core screws and remove the blower motor assembly.

4. Install in the reverse order.

Heater Core
Removal and Installation

1972

1. Remove the heater assembly as outlined under "Blower Motor Removal and Installation" for 1972, Steps 1 through 5.

2. Remove the blower motor.

3. Remove the core from the front half of the heater case.

4. Install in the reverse order of removal.

1973–77

1. Disconnect the battery ground cable.

2. Place a drain pan under the heater hoses at the heater and remove the heater hoses from the core tubes, securing the heater hoses in a raised position to prevent further loss of coolant. Plug or tape the heater core tubes to prevent spillage of coolant in the passenger compartment when removing.

3. Remove the five parcel shelf attaching screws and remove the shelf.

4. Loosen the air diverter and defroster door bowden cable clamps at the heater case and disconnect the cables from the doors.

5. Disconnect the blower resistor leads.

6. Remove the control assembly-to-instrument panel screws and swing the control to the left and lay it on the floor. Be careful not to kink the water valve bowden cable.

7. Remove the four heater-to-dash screws. Pull the heater rearward until the core tubes clear the dash opening, then remove the heater by moving it to the right and down.

8. Remove the core tube clamp screw and remove the clamp.

9. Remove the seven screws and separate the heater case halves.

10. Remove the core from the case.

11. Install and assemble the heater core and heater case in the reverse order of removal, using new seals around the heater core.

Radio
Removal and Installation

1. Disconnect the battery ground cable.

2. Remove the ash tray and ash tray plate.

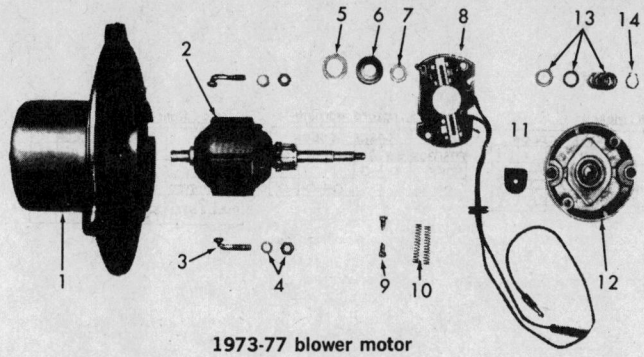

1973-77 blower motor

1. Stator-Shell Assy.
2. Armature-Shaft Assy.
3. Mounting Studs
4. Nuts and Washers
5. Felt Ring
6. Dust Seal
7. Spacer
8. Brushes and Plate
9. Screws
10. Brush Springs
11. Grommet
12. End Plate
13. Spacers and Washers
14. Snap Ring

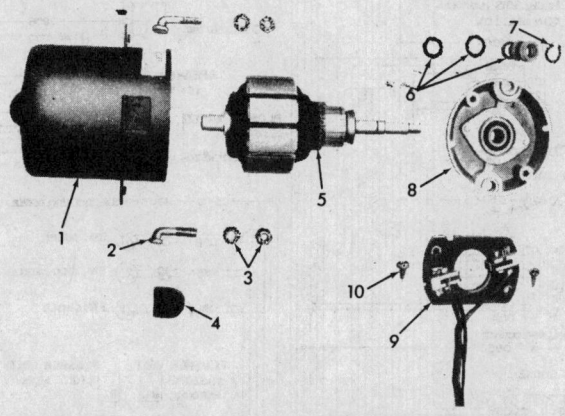

Exploded view of the heater blower motor for 1972 models

1. Stator Shell Assembly
2. Mounting Studs
3. Nuts and Lockwashers
4. Grommet
5. Armature Assembly
6. Spacers and Washers
7. Snap Ring
8. End Plate Assembly
9. Brushes and Plate
10. Screws

3. Remove the tuner and volume control knobs, jam nuts, plain washers and face panel.

4. Remove the screws from the front and rear mounting brackets.

5. Disconnect the electrical connec-

tions, antenna lead and remove the radio. Remove the front mounting brackets from the radio.

6. Install the radio in the reverse order of removal.

Windshield Wiper Motor and Linkage

Removal and Installation

1. Remove the wiper blades and arms.

2. Remove the two bolts attaching the pivot.

3. Remove the four wiper motor mounting bolts and remove the wiper motor and linkage.

4. To remove the motor independently, take out the motor shaft nut and three bolts and then pull off the connector and disconnect the ground cable.

5. Install and assemble in the reverse order of removal. Make sure to install the wiper motor linkage so that it is not twisted or touching any adjacent parts; otherwise, the wiper motor will be loaded and cause poor wiper action.

Instrument Cluster

Removal and Installation

1. Disconnect the speedometer cable.

2. Remove the wing nuts on the rear side of the instrument panel and pull the assembly part way out.

3. Disconnect the wiring harness at the connector and remove the instrument panel.

4. Install the panel in the reverse of removal.

Fuse Box Location

The fuse box is located under the hood, on the left inner fender panel, near the firewall, adjacent to the master cylinders. The fuse box contains ten fuses in use and four positions for spares.

SW; ig & starter
SW; wiper
SW; hazard warning
SW; lighting
HEAD LAMP; type 2 (37.5W/50W)
HEAD LAMP; type 1 (37.5W)
SIDE MARKER LAMP; front (8W~4CP)
TURN SIGNAL LAMP; front (23W~32CP)
PARKING LAMP (8W~3CP)
FUSIBLE LINK WIER
R H
BATTERY
FRAME
ENGINE
BODY
COMPRESSOR; magnet clutch
RELAY; fuel pump
EARTH ignition coil fixing
to CHASSIS HARNESS CONNECTION
RESISTOR
IGNITION COIL
WASHER TANK
SOLENOID VALVE ; T C S
SW; oil pressure
SOLENOIDEVALVE; idle speed control
AUTO CHOKE
RUN ON SOLENOID
COASTING RICHER
SPARK PLUG
THERMO UNIT
SW: 3rd
SW: back up lamp
SW: top 3rd
STARTER
AC GENERATOR
WIPER MOTOR
SW; thermo
SPEAKER (OPTION)
BLOWER MOTOR ; heater ; air conditioning
SW; parking brake
SW; accel
SW; stop lamp
SW; clutch
FLASHER UNIT ; hazard warning
FLASHER UNIT ; turn signal
L H
V REGULATOR
EARTH; regulator fixing
CONDENSER
FUSE BOX
RELAY; air conditioning
HORN
RELAY; horn
SIDE MARKER LAMP; front (8W~4CP)
MAGNET ANTENNA (OPTION)

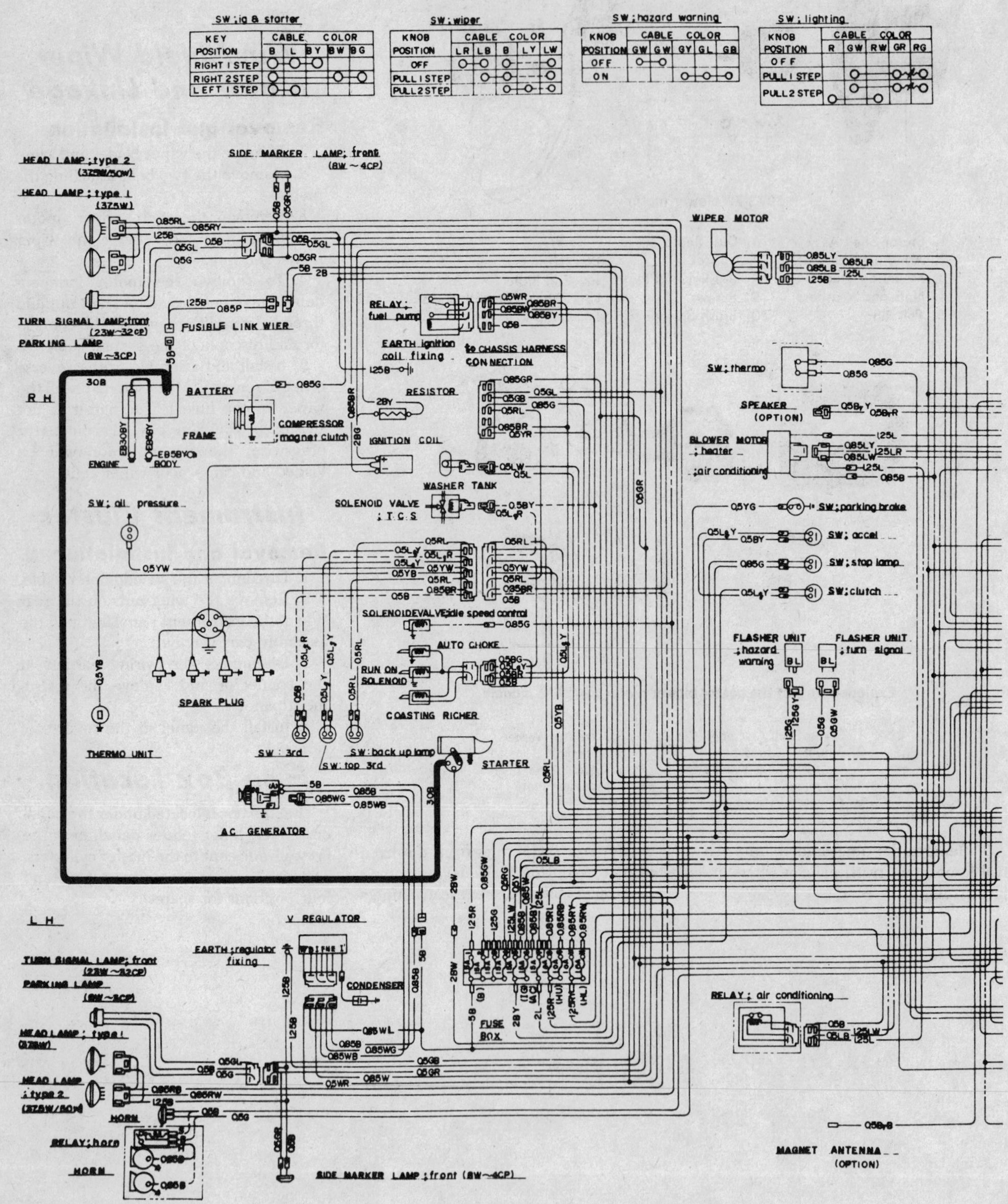

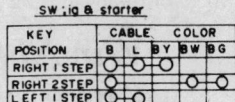

1975 LUV

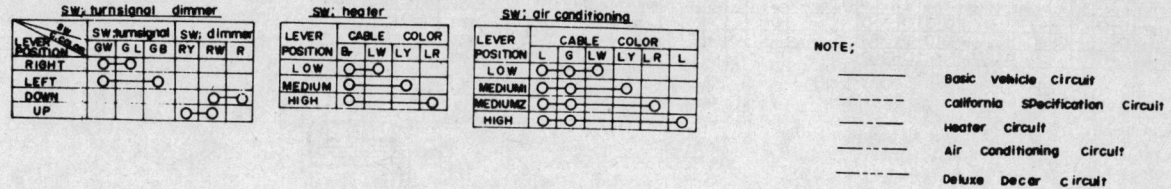

SW; turnsignal dimmer								
	SW; turnsignal			SW; dimmer				
LEVER POSITION	GW	G	GB	RY	RW	R		
RIGHT	O	O						
LEFT	O	O						
DOWN				O	O			
UP				O		O		

SW; heater					
	CABLE COLOR				
LEVER POSITION	Br	L	LW	LY	LR
LOW	O	O	O		
MEDIUM	O	O		O	
HIGH	O	O			O

SW; air conditioning							
	CABLE COLOR						
LEVER POSITION	L	G	LW	LY	LR	L	
LOW	O	O	O				
MEDIUM1	O	O		O			
MEDIUM2	O	O			O		
HIGH	O	O				O	

NOTE;

———————— Basic vehicle Circuit

– – – – – California SPecification Circuit

–·–·–·– Heater circuit

–··–··– Air conditioning Circuit

————— Deluxe Decor circuit

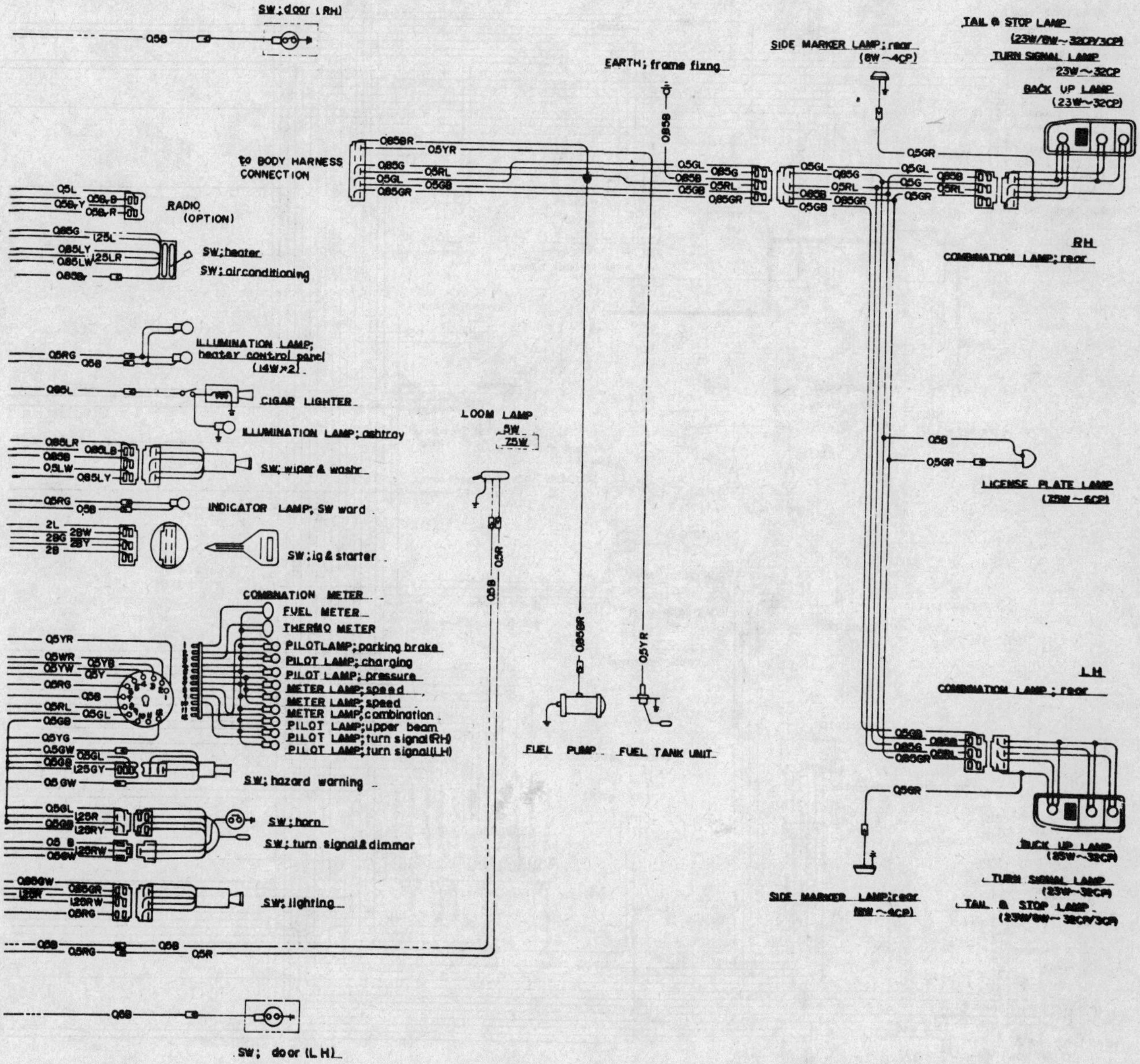

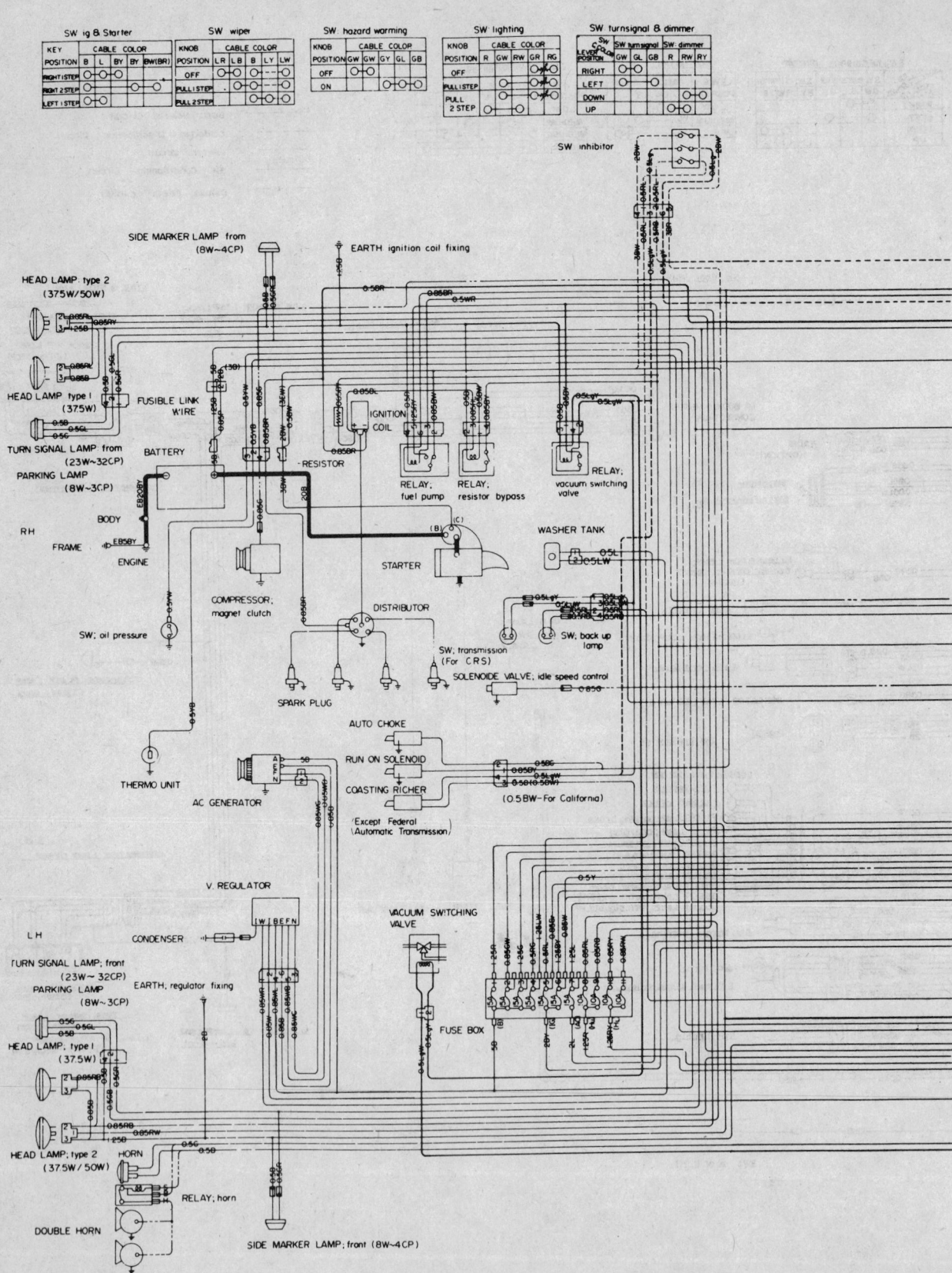

1976 LUV

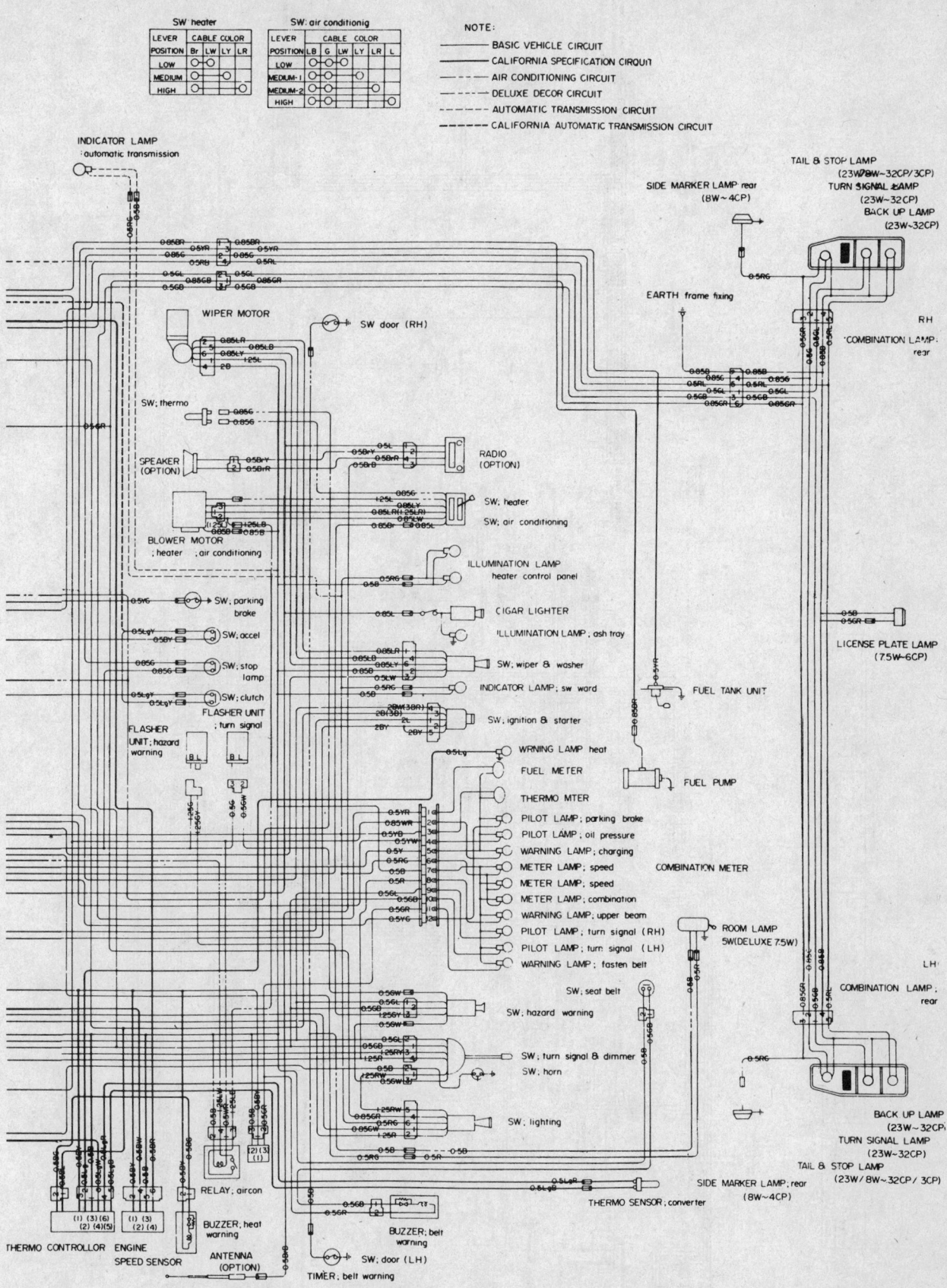

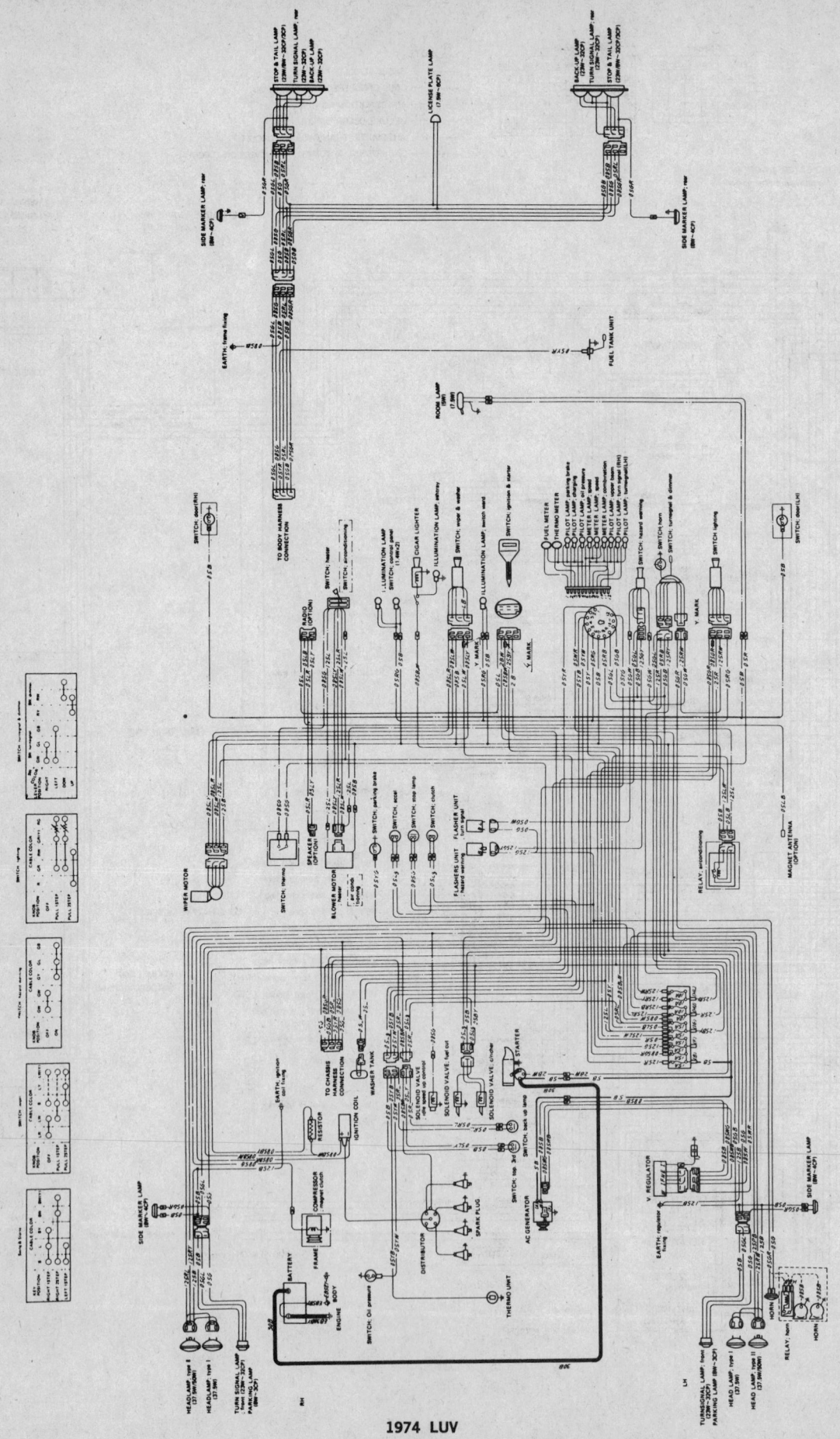

1974 LUV

SPECIFICATIONS

Mazda

INTRODUCTION

Toyo Kogyo Co., Ltd., Mazda's parent company, began manufacturing cork products over fifty years ago. In 1927, the company expanded into the machinery and tool business; by 1930 they were producing motorcycles under the Mazda name.

Their first three-wheeled trucks appeared in 1931. The first prototype automobile was built in 1940, but it was not until 1960 that the first Mazda R-360 coupe was sold.

In the interim, Toyo Kogyo produced light three-wheeled trucks, reaching, in 1957, a peak annual production of 20,000 units.

Shortly after automobile production began in 1960, Toyo Kogyo obtained a license from NSU-Wankel to develop and produce the rotary engine.

The first prototype car powered by this engine, the Mazda 110S—a two passenger sports car—appeared in August 1963. The car did not go on sale until it had been thoroughly tested. The first units were offered for sale in May 1967. The 110S was soon joined by smaller, cheaper model which put the rotary engine within the reach of the average consumer.

In 1970, Toyo Kogyo began exporting its Mazda cars (both rotary engined and conventional) to the United States. At first they were available only in the Pacific Northwest, but they have rapidly expanded their market to include all of the U.S.

MODEL IDENTIFICATION

1972-73 RX-3

1972-73 RX-2 (© Toyo Kogyo Co. Ltd.)

1974 RX-3

1974 RX-2

1974 RX-4

1974 Rotary Pick-Up

SERIAL NUMBER IDENTIFICATION

Vehicle

RX–3, RX–4

The serial number on RX–3 models is on a plate located on the driver's side windshield pillar and is visible through the glass.

A vehicle identification number (VIN) plate, bearing the serial number and other data, is attached to the cowl.

The serial number consists of a series identification number, followed by a six-digit production number.

RX–2

The VIN plate location and composition of the serial number for RX–2 models is the same as for RX–3 models, above. The only difference between models is the location of the RX–2 serial number plate: it is attached to the upper left-hand side of the instrument panel and is visible through the windshield.

Pick-Ups

The chassis number is stamped on the front of the left frame member, visible from the engine compartment.

Engine

Rotary Engine

The engine number is located on a plate which is attached to the engine housing, just behind the (upper) distributor.

The engine number consists of identification number (see chart), followed by a six-digit production number.

Engine Identification Codes

B1600 Pick-Up

The engine number is stamped on a machined pad on the the right, front side of the engine block.

Engine Identification Codes

Model	TRANSMISSION	
	Manual	Automatic
RX-3	12AH	12AQ
RX-2	12AJ	12AT
RX-4	13B	13B
Rotary Pickup	13B	13B

GENERAL ENGINE SPECIFICATIONS—ROTARY

Model	Engine Displacement Cu In. (cc)	Carburetor Type	Net Horsepower @ rpm	Net Torque @ rpm	Rotor Displacement (cu In.)	Compression Ratio	Oil Pressure @ rpm (psi)
RX-3	70 (1,146)	4-bbl	90 @ 6,000	96 @ 4,000	35	9.4:1	71.1 @ 3,000
RX-2	70 (1,146)	4-bbl	97 @ 6,500	98 @ 4,000	35	9.4:1	71.1 @ 3,000
RX-4 Cosmo and Pick-up	80 (1,308)	4-bbl	110 @ —	117 @ —	40	9.2:1	71.1 @ 3,000

GENERAL ENGINE SPECIFICATIONS—PISTON ENGINE

Year	Engine Displacement cu in. (cc)	Carb Type	Net Horsepower (@ rpm)	Net Torque @ rpm (ft lbs)	Bore and Stroke (in.)	Compression Ratio	Oil Pressure
1972-77	96.8 (1586)	2-bbl	70 @ 5000	82 @ 3400	3.07 x 3.27	8.6:1	50-64 @ 3000
1976-77	77.6 (1272)	2-bbl	N.A.	N.A.	2.87 x 2.99	9.2:1	50-64 @ 3000

TUNE-UP SPECIFICATIONS—ROTARY

Year	Model	SPARK PLUGS Type	SPARK PLUGS Gap	DISTRIBUTORS (both)▲ Point Gap (in.)	Point Dwell (deg)	IGNITION TIMING (deg) Leading Normal	Leading Retarded	Trailing Normal	IDLE SPEED (rpm) MT	AT
1971-73	All	N-80B	0.031-0.035	0.018	58 ± 3	TDC	10A	10A	900	750①
1974	All	N-80B	0.024-0.028	0.018	58 ± 3	5A	—	15A	900	750①
1975	All	N-80B	0.024-0.028	0.018	58 ± 3	TDC	20A	15A	800-850	750-800①

TUNE-UP SPECIFICATIONS—ROTARY

Year	Model	SPARK PLUGS Type	SPARK PLUGS Gap	DISTRIBUTORS (both)▲ Point Gap (in.)	DISTRIBUTORS (both)▲ Point Dwell (deg)	IGNITION TIMING (deg) Leading Normal	IGNITION TIMING (deg) Leading Retarded	IGNITION TIMING (deg) Trailing Normal	IDLE SPEED (rpm) MT	IDLE SPEED (rpm) AT
1976	All	RN278B	0.039-0.043	0.018	④	TDC	20A	15A	700-750	700-①750
1977	All	RN278B	0.039-0.043	0.018	58 ± 3	5A	—	25A	725-775	725-①775

▲ 1974-75 models have only one distributor
① Transmission in drive (D)
TDC Top dead center
A After top dead center
④ 1976 Leading 58 ± 3
         Trailing 53 ± 3

B Before top dead center
MT Manual transmission
AT Automatic transmission
deg degrees

TUNE-UP SPECIFICATIONS—PISTON ENGINE

Year	Engine Cu in. Displacement (cc)		Spark Plugs Type	Spark Plugs Gap (in.)	Distributor Point Dwell (deg)	Distributor Point Gap (in.)	Ignition Timing (deg) MT	Ignition Timing (deg) AT	Intake Valve Opens (deg)	Fuel Pump Pressure (psi)	Idle Speed (rpm) MT	Idle Speed (rpm) AT	Valve Clearance (in.)▲ In	Valve Clearance (in.)▲ Ex
1972-77	96.8	(1586)	BP-6ES	0.031	49-55	0.020	5B②	5B②	13B	2.8-3.6	①	650-③700	0.012-0.012	
1976-77	77.6	(1272)	BP-6ES	0.031	49-55		7B	—	13B	2.8-3.6		700-750	—	

▲ At the valve (warm engine)
— Not Applicable
① 1972: 775-825 rpm
    All others: 800-850 rpm
② 1976-77 Calif.: 8B
③ In drive
CO % at idle: 1972-75—1.5-2.5%
B—BTDC (Before Top Dead Center)

NOTE: The underhood specifications sticker often reflects tune-up specification changes made in production. Sticker figures must be used if they disagree with those in this chart.

FIRING ORDERS

The firing order for the Mazda rotary engine is 1–2, with the trailing spark plugs firing ten degrees after the leading.

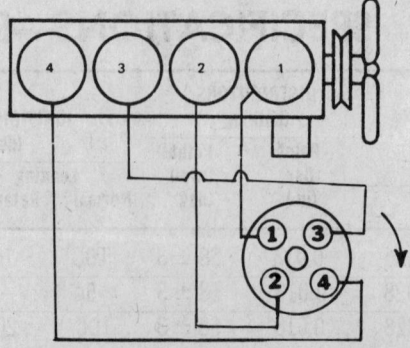

Piston engine (© Toyo Kogyo Co. Ltd.)

CAPACITIES

Year	Model	Engine Displacement Cu in (cc)	Engine Crankcase (qts)		Transmission (pts)			Drive Axle (pts)	Gasoline Tank (gals)	Cooling System (qts)	
			With Filter	Without Filter	Manual		Automatic			W/ AC	W/O AC
					4-spd	5-spd					
1972-73	RX-2	70 (1156)	5.80⑥	4.65⑥	3.20	—	11.62	2.60	16.9	—	8.45⑦
1972-73	RX-3	70 (1156)	5.50	4.45	3.20	—	11.62	3.00	15.6①	—	8.45
1974-75	RX-3	70 (1156)	4.80	3.65	3.20	—	11.62	3.00	15.6①	—	10.25④
1976	RX-3	70 (1156)	5.50	4.40	3.60	4.60	13.20	3.00	15.6①	—	9.8
1974-75	RX-4	80 (1308)	5.50	4.50	3.20	—	13.20	3.00	16.9②	—	10.50⑤
1976-77	RX-4	80 (1308)	6.80	5.30	3.60	4.60	13.20	2.80	16.9②	—	10.0
1977	Cosmo	80 (1308)	6.80	5.30	—	3.60	13.20	2.60	17.2	—	10.0
1975-77	808 (1600)	96.8 (1586)	3.80	—	3.20	3.60	11.60	3.00	11.9⑧	—	7.90
1976-77	808 (1300)	77.6 (1272)	3.20	—	2.80	—	—	2.20	11.7⑧	—	5.80
1972-75	B-1600	96.8 (1586)	4.00	3.00	3.00③	—	—	2.80	11.7	—	6.80
1974-75	Rotary Pick-up	80 (1308)	5.50	4.50	3.60	—	13.20	2.80	20.4	—	10.80
1976-77	Rotary Pick-up	80 (1308)	6.80	5.30	3.60	4.60	13.20	2.80	20.8	—	10.30

① Sta. Wgn. 14.3
② Sta. Wgn. 17.4
③ After #49825 3.20
④ 1975 10.9 qts
⑤ 1975 11.93 qts
⑥ 1974-75 4.80, 3.65
⑦ 1974-75 9.90
⑧ Sta. Wgn. 10.4

ECCENTRIC SHAFT SPECIFICATIONS—ROTARY
All measurements are given in inches.

Model	JOURNAL DIAMETER		OIL CLEARANCE		Eccentric Shaft End-Play		Min. Shaft Runout
	Main Bearing	Rotor Bearing	Main Bearing	Rotor Bearing	Normal	Limit	
All	1.6929	2.9134	0.0016-0.0028	0.0016-0.0031	0.0016-0.0028	0.0035	0.0008①

① RX-4/Rotary Pick-up—0.0024

CRANKSHAFT AND CONNECTING ROD SPECIFICATIONS—PISTON ENGINE
All measurements given in inches.

Year	Engine Displacement cu in. (cc)	Crankshaft				Connecting Rod		
		Main Brg Journal Dia	Main Brg Oil Clearance	Shaft End-Play	Thrust on No.	Journal Dia	Oil Clearance	Side Clearance
1972-77	96.8 (1586)	2.4804	0.001-0.002	0.003-0.009	4	2.0866	0.001-0.003	0.004-0.008
1976-77	77.6 (1272)	2.4804	0.0012-0.0024	0.003-0.009	4	1.7717	0.0011-0.0029	0.004-0.008

ROTOR AND HOUSING SPECIFICATIONS—ROTARY

All measurements are given in inches.

| Model | ROTOR | | | HOUSINGS | | | | | |
	Side Clearance	Standard Protrusion of Land	Limit of Protrusion of Land	Front and Rear Distortion Limit	Rear Wear Limit	Rotor Width	Distortion Limit	Intermediate Distortion Limit	Wear Limit
RX-3 and RX-2	0.0051-0.0067	0.004-0.006	0.003	0.002	0.004	2.7539	0.002	0.002	0.004
RX-4 Cosmo and Rotary Pick-up	0.0047-0.0083	0.004-0.006	0.003	0.002	0.004	3.1438	0.002	0.002	0.004

SEAL CLEARANCES—ROTARY

All measurements are given in inches.

| Model | APEX SEALS | | | | CORNER SEAL TO ROTOR GROOVE | | SIDE SEAL | | | |
| | To Side Housing | | To Rotor Groove | | | | To Rotor Groove | | To Corner Seal | |
	Normal	Limit	Normal	Limit	Normal	Limit	Normal	Limit	Normal	Limit
RX-3 and RX-2	0.0020-0.0028①	0.0039	0.0014-0.0029	0.0039	0.0008-0.0019	0.0031	0.0016-0.0028	0.0039	0.002-0.006	0.016
RX-4 Cosmo and Rotary Pick-up	0.0051-0.0067	0.012	0.0020-0.0035	0.006	0.0008-0.0019	0.0031	0.0016-0.0028	0.0040	0.0020-0.0059	0.016

① Arctic Specifications—0.0004-0.0020

SEAL SPECIFICATIONS—ROTARY

All measurements are given in inches.

| Model | APEX SEAL | | Corner Seal Width (OD) | SIDE SEAL | | OIL SEAL CONTACT WIDTH OF LIP | |
	Normal Height	Height Limit		Thickness	Width	Normal	Limit
RX-3 and RX-2	0.03937	0.03150	0.2756	0.0394	0.1378	0.008	0.031
RX-4 Cosmo and Rotary Pick-up	0.33500	0.27600	0.4331	0.0394	0.1378	0.008	0.031

VALVE SPECIFICATIONS—PISTON ENGINE

| Year | Engine Displacement cu in. (cc) | Seat Angle (deg) | Face Angle (deg) | Spring Test Pressure (lbs @ in.) | Spring Installed Height (in.) | Stem-to-Guide Clearance (in.) | | Stem Diameter (in.) | |
						Intake	Exhaust	Intake	Exhaust
1972-77	96.8 (1586)	45	45	①	②	0.0007-0.0021	0.0007-0.0023	0.3150	0.3150
1976-77	77.6 (1272)	45	45	③	④	0.0007-0.0021	0.0007-0.0023	0.3150	0.3150

① Outer: 31.4 @ 1.339
Inner: 20.9 @ 1.260

② Outer: 1.339
Inner: 1.260

③ Outer: 43.7 @ 1.319
Inner: 20.9 @ 1.260

④ Outer: 1.319
Inner: 1.260

TORQUE SPECIFICATIONS—ROTARY
(All figures in ft lbs)

Engine Displacement Cu In. (cc)	Front Cover	Bearing Housing	Rear Stationary Gear	Eccentric Shaft Pulley Bolt	Flywheel to Eccentric Shaft Nut	MANIFOLDS		Oil Pan	Tension Bolts
						Intake	Exhaust		
70 (1,156)	15	15	15	45	350	15	30	7	20
80 (1,308)	—	—	—	54-69	289-362	15	32-43	5-7	23-27

TORQUE SPECIFICATIONS—PISTON ENGINE
(All figures in ft lbs)

Engine Displacement Cu in. (cc)	Cylinder Head Bolts	Rod Bearing Bolts	Main Bearing Bolts	Crankshaft Pulley Bolt	Flywheel-to-Crankshaft Bolts	Manifold	
						Intake	Exhaust
All	56-60	36-40	61-65	101-108	112-118	14-19	12-17①

① 1300: 16-21

TORQUE SEQUENCES

Tension bolt loosening sequence—1974 (© Toyo Kogyo Co., Ltd.)

Tension bolt tightening sequence—1974 (© Toyo Kogyo Co., Ltd.)

Tension bolt loosening sequence—1972-73 (© Toyo Kogyo Co. Ltd.)

Tension bolt tightening sequence—1972-73 (© Toyo Kogyo Co. Ltd.)

Piston engine cylinder head torque sequence (© Toyo Kogyo Co. Ltd.)

PISTON AND RING SPECIFICATIONS

All measurements are given in inches.

Year	Engine Displacement Cu In. (cc)	Piston Clearance	RING GAP			RING SIDE CLEARANCE		
			Top Compression	Bottom Compression	Oil Control	Top Compression	Bottom Compression	Oil Control
1972-77	96.8 (1586)	0.0022-0.0028	0.008-0.016	0.008-0.016	0.008-0.016	0.0014-0.0028	0.0012-0.0025	0.008-0.016
1976-77	77.6 (1272)	0.0021-0.0026	0.008-0.016	0.008-0.016	0.008-0.016	0.0014-0.0028	0.0012-0.0025	0.008-0.016

BATTERY AND STARTER SPECIFICATIONS

All cars use 12 volt, negative ground electrical systems

Year	Model	Battery Amp Hour Capacity	STARTER						Brush Spring Tension (oz)	Min. Brush Length (in.)
			Lock Test			No Load Test				
			Amps	Volts	Torque (ft/lbs)	Amps	Volts	RPM		
1972-75	RX2, RX-3	70	600MT 1200AT	6.0MT 4.0AT	8.0MT 17.4AT	70MT 100AT	12.0	3600MT 5400AT	56.3	0.45
1976	RX-3	60	780MT 1100AT	5.0	8.0MT 17.4AT	75MT 100AT	11.5	4900MT 7800AT	49-63	0.45
1974-75	RX4 and Rotary Pickup	70	1100	5.0	17.0	100	11.5	7800	49-63	0.45
1976-77	RX-4 and Rotary Pickup	60MT 70AT	780MT 1100AT	5.0	8.0MT 17.4AT	75MT 100AT	11.5	4900MT 7800AT	49-63	0.45
1977	Cosmo	45MT 70AT	600MT 1050AT	5.0	6.9MT 15.9AT	50MT 100AT	11.5	5600MT 6600AT	49-63	0.45
1975-77	808	60	400	6.0	6.7	53	10.5	5000	49-63	0.45
1972-75	B1600	60	560	7.5	9.4	60	11.5	6000	35-46	0.45

ALTERNATOR AND REGULATOR SPECIFICATIONS

Year	Model	ALTERNATOR		REGULATOR			
		Field current @ 14 V	Output (amps)	Air Gap (in.)	Point Gap (in.)	Back Gap (in.)	Volts @-75°
1972-75	RX-2, RX-3	32	50	0.028-0.043	0.012-0.016	0.028-0.043	14.0
1976	RX-3	40	50	0.028-0.051	0.012-0.018	0.028-0.059	14.5
1974-75	Rotary Pickup, RX-4	40	50	0.028-0.051	0.012-0.018	0.028-0.059	14.5
1972-75	B1600	28	35	0.028-0.043	0.012-0.016	0.028-0.043	14.5
1976-77	RX-4, Cosmo, Rotary Pickup	56	63	0.028-0.051	0.012-0.018	0.028-0.059	14.0
1975-77	808	40	50	0.028-0.051	0.012-0.018	0.028-0.059	14.0

BRAKE SPECIFICATIONS

All measurements given are (in.) unless noted

| | | Brake Disc | | | Brake Drum | | | Minimum Lining Thickness | |
Model	Lug Nut Torque (ft/lb)	Master Cylinder Bore	Minimum Thickness	Maximum Run-Out	Diameter	Max. Machine O/S	Max. Wear Limit	Front	Rear
RX-2	65-72	0.875	0.433	0.003	7.874	7.90	7.9135	0.276	0.039
RX-3	65	0.875	0.394	0.003	7.874	7.90	7.9135	0.276	0.039
RX-4	65-72	0.875	0.433	0.004	9.0	9.025	9.0395	0.276	0.039
B1600	65-72	0.750	—	—	10.236③	10.276④	—	0.039	0.039
Rotary Pickup	65-72	0.875	0.433	0.004	10.236	10.275	—	0.276	0.039
808	65-72	0.8125	0.394	0.004	7.874	7.90	7.9135	0.256	0.039
Cosmo	65-72	0.875	0.6693①	0.0024②	—	—	—	0.276	0.276

① Rear: 0.354
② Rear: 0.004
③ Front: 10.236
④ Front: 10.276

NOTE: Minimum lining thickness is as recommended by the manufacturer. Due to variations in state inspection regulations, the minimum allowable thickness may be different than recommended by the manufacturer.

WHEEL ALIGNMENT SPECIFICATIONS

| | | CAMBER | | CASTER | | | |
Year	Model	Range (deg)	Preferred Setting (deg)	Range (deg)	Preferred Setting (deg)	Toe-in (in.)	Steering Axis Inclination (deg)
1972-74	RX-2	¼P-1¾P	1P	½N-1½P	½P	0-0.24	8¾P
1975	RX-3	1P-2P	1½P	½N-1½P	½P	0-0.24	8⁷/₁₀P
1976-77	RX-3	①	②	½N-1½P	½P	0-0.24	8⅔P
1975	RX-4	1½P-2½P	2P	0-2P	1P	0-0.24	9½P
1976	RX-4	1P-2P	1½P	③	④	0-0.24	9⅔P⑤
1975	Rotary pickup	⅔P-1½P	1⅙P	0-½P	¼P	0-0.24	8¾P
1976-77	Rotary pickup	1⅓P-2⅓P	1⅚P	0-½P	¼P	0-0.12	8¾P
1972-75	B-1600	½P-1½P	1P	1P-2P	1½P	0-0.24	7⅓P
1977	Cosmo	1½P-3P⑥	2¼P⑦	0-2P	1P	0-0.24	9¾P
1975	808	⅔P-2⅙P	1⅓P	½N-1½P	½P	0-0.24	8¾P
1976-77	808 (1300)	⑧	⑨	½N-1½P	½P	0-0.24	8⅔P
1976	808 (1600)	⑩	⑪	①-2P	½P	0-0.24	8½P
1977	808 (1600)	⑫	⑬	⑭	⑮	0-0.24	⑯

① Sedan & wagon ⅚N-1⅕P
  coupe: 1¹/₁₂P-2P
② Sedan & wagon: 1⅔P
  coupe: 1½P
③ Sedan & hardtop: 0-2P
  wagon: ⅓P-1⅓P
④ Sedan & hardtop: 1P
  wagon: ½P
⑤ Wagon: 9⅓P
⑥ Manual: 1P-2P

⑦ Manual: 1½P
⑧ Sedan: ⅔P-2⅙P
  coupe wagon: 1P-2⅓P
⑨ Sedan: 1⅓P
  coupe wagon: 1⅔P
⑩ Sedan: ⅚P-2⅓P
  coupe: 1P-2½P
  wagon: 1P-2⅓P
⑪ Sedan: 1½P
  coupe: 1⅚P
  wagon: 1⅔P

⑫ Sedan & wagon: 1P-2½P
  coupe: 1⅓P-2⅚P
⑬ Sedan & wagon: 1⅚P
  coupe: 2¹/₁₂P
⑭ Sedan & coupe: ¹/₁₂P-2½P
  wagon: ¼P-2¼P
⑮ Sedan & coupe: 1¹/₁₂P
  wagon: 1¼P
⑯ Sedan & coupe: 8⁵/₁₂P
  wagon: 8¼P

Mazda

TUNE-UP PROCEDURES

Spark Plugs

The spark plugs should be checked and adjusted every 4,000 miles or 4 months for rotary engine-models or every 6,000 miles for piston engine-models. New plugs should be installed every 12,000 miles or 12 months.

Rotary Engine

The Mazda rotary engine has four spark plugs. Each of the two combustion chambers uses two plugs. The leading bottom spark plug fires first, igniting the fuel/air mixture, as in conventional engines; the trailing top plug fires a short time afterward (10° later), igniting any unburned mixture. This aids in more complete combustion in the long narrow chamber, which helps to reduce exhaust emissions of unburned fuel.

The spark plugs are specially constructed and designed for use only in the Mazda rotary engine.

1. Remove the wire from one of the plugs. Use a spark plug wrench with a rubber insulator to remove the plug.

NOTE: *Both the distributor and the engine housing are marked to aid in identification of the spark plug and distributor connections. However, to avoid confusion, it is easier to remove one plug at a time.*

2. Check each plug for badly worn electrodes, black deposits, fouling, or cracked porcelain.
3. Clean the plug with a wire brush, if it is dirty.
4. Replace any plug which has a badly worn or burned electrode.
5. Measure the electrode gap with a *wire* gauge.
6. Adjust the gap to the specifications given in the "Tune-Up" Specifications Chart. Replace any plug which has a measured gap of 0.043 in. or more.
7. If the electrodes show signs of burning white or if the electrodes are burning rapidly, replace the plugs with cold range plugs.

NOTE: *When replacing spark plugs be sure all plugs are of the same manufacture and heat range. It is a good idea to replace plugs in sets of four, if possible.*

8. Replace the spark plug and torque it to 10 ft lbs.

Breaker Points

1972–73 Mazda RX-2 and RX-3 models are equipped with two distributors. One distributor operates the leading set of plugs and the other the trailing set.

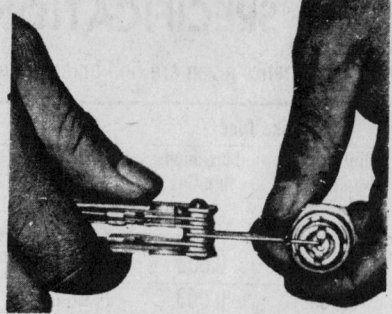

Checking the electrode gap; note dual electrodes
(© Toyo Kogyo Co., Ltd.)

When checking or replacing points, remember to service both distributors.

Adjustment—Models with Two Distributors (1972–73)

The points should be checked and adjusted every 4,000 miles.

To check the point gap and adjust it, proceed in the following manner:

1. Unfasten the clips and remove the cap from one of the distributors. Leave the leads attached to the cap.
2. Remove the rotor from the distributor.
3. Clean the points with a point file, if they are pitted. If they are badly pitted or burned, replace them, as detailed in the section below.
4. Rotate the engine by using a remote starter switch, or have someone inside the car operate the ignition key, until the rubbing block is at the top of the cam.
5. Check the point gap with a feeler gauge. The gap should be 0.018 in.
6. Adjust the point gap with a screwdriver.

NOTE: *The leading distributor on 1972–73 Mazdas has two sets of points.*

7. After completing adjustment, install the rotor and cap on the distributor.

Repeat steps 1–7 for the other distributor.

Adjustment—Single Point Distributors

There are two methods to adjust the breaker point gap. By far the more accurate is the method of measuring dwell angle electronically.

1. Check and adjust the breaker point alignment. Bend the fixed contact support only.
2. Crank the engine in short bursts until the rubbing block rests on a peak of a cam lobe.
3. Insert a feeler blade of the specified thickness between the breaker points. Adjust the gap until the feeler blade will slide through the gap with a slight drag, by loosening the adjustment screw and moving the point base. When the correct gap is obtained, tighten the adjustment screw.

4. Clean the breaker cam and apply a thin coating of distributor cam lubricant to the cam. Do not use engine oil.
5. After setting the breaker point gap, set the ignition timing.
6. Install the distributor rotor and cap.

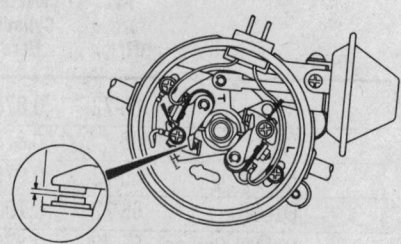

Adjusting the dual point distributor
(© Toyo Kogyo Co. Ltd.)

Adjustment—Dual Point Distributors (1974–77)

There are two methods to adjust the points. By far the most accurate and preferable, on used points, is the dwell meter method. (See below).

1. Remove the distributor high tension lead and the distributor cap and rotor.
2. Check the breaker point alignment. If necessary, align the points by bending the stationary contact. Never bend the movable contact.
3. Crank the engine in short bursts until the rubbing block on the breaker arm rests on the high point of the cam lobe. This is the maximum point opening.
4. Insert a feeler blade of the specified thickness between each set of breaker points in turn.
5. If adjustment is required, loosen the setscrews and move the stationary contact and base until the correct gap is obtained.
6. Tighten the setscrews and recheck the gap.
7. Install the rotor and distributor cap. Reconnect the high tension lead.

Removal and Installation

New points should be installed every 12,000 miles or once a year.

1. Repeat steps 1 and 2 of the adjustment procedure.
2. Unfasten the two screws which secure the point set and remove it.
3. Install the new set of points and fasten it with the two screws.

NOTE: *The leading distributor on 1972–73 rotary models has two sets of points.*

4. Adjust the point gap as detailed above and the dwell as detailed below.
5. Install the rotor and the cap on the distributor.
6. Repeat the procedure for the other distributor.

Condenser

The condenser should be replaced every time the points are replaced, i.e., every 12,000 miles.

If the condenser is suspect, the easiest way to check it is by replacing it with a new one. The condenser capacity is 0.27 mfd. To replace the condenser, perform the following steps:

1. Remove the distributor cap. Leave the wires connected. Withdraw the rotor.

2. Loosen the condenser lead retaining screw from inside the distributor and unfasten the clip.

3. Unfasten the condenser retaining screw which is located on the outside of the distributor housing.

NOTE: *The smaller condenser, mounted next to the ignition condenser, is for radio noise suppression. It need only be replaced if a clicking sound is heard over the radio.*

4. Remove the condenser.

Install the new condenser in the reverse order of removal.

Dwell Angle

Make separate checks of dwell angle for each distributor (two-distributor models), in the following manner:

1. Disconnect the vacuum line from the distributor and plug it.

2. Connect the dwell meter in accordance with its manufacturer's instructions.

3. Run the engine at idle, after it has been allowed to warm up.

4. Observe the dwell meter reading. It should be within the specifications in the "Tune-Up Specifications" chart.

5. If it is not within specifications, adjust the contact point gap as outlined above.

NOTE: *If dwell angle is above the specified amount, the point gap is too small; if it is below, the gap is too large.*

6. If both the dwell angle and the contact point gap cannot be brought to within specifications, check for one or more of the following:

a. Worn distributor cam
b. Worn rubbing block
c. Bent movable contact arm

Replace any of the parts, if necessary.

7. When the dwell angle check is completed, disconnect the meter and reconnect the vacuum line.

Ignition Timing

1972–73 Rotary

Normal Timing

As in other tune-up procedures involving the ignition system, both distributors must be adjusted separately. Begin with the *leading* distributor when checking timing:

1. Connect a timing light to the leading distributor spark plug cable which runs to the number one (front) rotor. Check the manufacturer's instructions for specific hook-up details.

2. Start the engine and run it at idle speed.

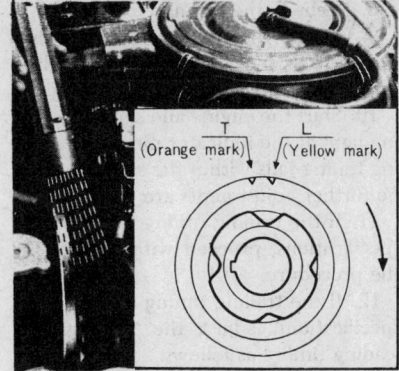

Ignition timing marks—1972-73 rotary engine (© Toyo Kogyo Co. Ltd.)

3. Loosen the distributor locknuts so that the distributor can be rotated.

4. Aim the timing light at the timing indicator pin in the front housing.

5. The *yellow* mark (TDC) should align with the pin on the housing.

6. If it does not, rotate the distributor until it aligns.

7. Tighten the locknuts and recheck the timing.

The ignition timing for the trailing distributor is checked and adjusted in the same manner, except that the timing light lead should be connected to the trailing distributor spark plug cable which runs to the number one rotor.

When the timing light is pointed at the eccentric shaft pulley, the *orange* mark (10°ATDC) should align with the timing pointer.

When the adjustment of normal timing has been completed for both distributors on 1972–73 models, proceed with the next section.

Retarded Timing

On 1972–73 Mazda RX–2 and RX–3 models, the leading distributor is equipped with dual points. One set of points is for normal ignition system operation, and the other is used for retarded operation during engine warm-up. To test and adjust retarded timing proceed in the following manner:

1. Disconnect both of the thermosensor connections. See "Emission Controls".

NOTE: *Disconnect the No. 2 thermosensor connection only on cars with manual transmissions only.*

2. Unfasten the idle and/or vacuum switch connections.

3. Detach the choke switch connector.

4. Connect the timing light to the number one (front) rotor, leading spark plug cable.

5. Check the timing at 900 rpm, (750 rpm in Drive—automatic) with the strobe, as above. The pointer should align with the *orange* mark on the timing pulley (10° ATDC ± 2°).

If the retarded timing setting is incorrect, adjust in the following manner:

1. Turn the engine off.

2. Unfasten the clips and remove the distributor cap. Withdraw the rotor.

3. Loosen the adjusting screws and move the point set base to correct the retarded timing setting.

NOTE: *Do not rotate the distributor housing.*

4. Assemble the distributor and check the retarded timing again with the strobe.

5. When the timing is satisfactory, disconnect the timing light and connect all of the leads.

NOTE: *If the timing cannot be brought to specification, check the components of the "air flow control system". See "Emission Controls".*

Piston Engine

1. Raise the hood and clean and mark the timing marks. Chalk or fluorescent paint makes a good, visible mark.

2. Disconnect the vacuum line to the distributor and plug the disconnected line. Disconnect the line at the vacuum source, not at the distributor.

3. Connect a timing light to the front (No. 1) cylinder, a power source and ground. Follow the manufacturer's instructions.

4. Connect a tachometer to the engine.

5. Start the engine and reduce the idle to 700–750 rpm to be sure that the centrifugal advance mechanism is not working.

6. With the engine running, shine the timing light at the timing pointer and observe the position of the pointer in relation to the timing mark on the crankshaft pulley.

7. If the timing is not as specified, adjust the timing by loosening the distributor hold-down bolt and rotating the distributor in the proper direction. When the proper ignition timing is obtained, tighten the hold-down bolt on the distributor.

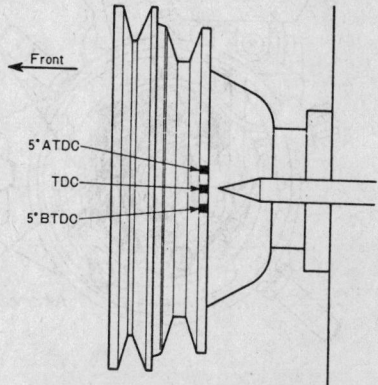

Ignition timing marks—Piston engine (© Toyo Kogyo Co. Ltd.)

Mazda

8. Check the centrifugal advance mechanism by accelerating the engine to about 2,000 rpm. If the ignition timing advances, the mechanism is working properly.

9. Stop the engine and remove the timing light.

10. Reset the idle to specifications.

11. Remove the tachometer.

1974–75 Rotary

1. Connect a tachometer to the engine.

2. Disconnect and plug the vacuum tube on the distributor.

3. Connect a timing light to the wire from the leading (lower) plug of the front rotor housing.

4. Start the engine and run it idle speed.

5. Shine the timing light on the indicator pin located on the front cover.

6. If the leading timing mark is not correctly aligned with the pointer, stop the engine.

7. Loosen the distributor locknut and rotate the distributor housing (with the engine running) until the timing marks align. Stop the engine and tighten the distributor locknut.

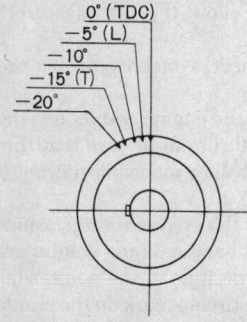

Ignition timing marks—1974-75 Rotary engine (ⓒ Toyo Kogyo Co., Ltd.)

8. Recheck the timing.

9. Change the connection of the timing light to the wire from the trailing (top) plug in the front rotor housing.

10. Start the engine and shine the timing light at the indicator pin. If the trailing timing falls within the specifications, no further adjustments are necessary.

11. If the trailing timing is not within specifications, proceed with the rest of the procedure.

12. If the trailing timing is not within specifications, adjust the trailing and leading timing as follows:

13. Adjust the trailing timing to specification by rotating the distributor body, as in Step 7.

14. Check the leading timing against and record how much it differs from specification.

15. Remove the distributor cap and rotor.

16. Loosen the breaker base setscrews (the ones directly opposite each other near the outside of the distributor body) and turn the distributor base plate until the correct leading plug timing is obtained again.

17. Recheck the timing. The leading and trailing plug timing marks should both be aligned (or within specifications). If not, repeat the procedure until they are.

1976 Rotary

1. Run the engine at normal operating temperature.

2. Connect a tachometer to the engine.

3. Connect a timing light to the leading spark plug.

4. Run engine at specified idle speed.

5. Aim the timing light at the timing indicator pin on the front cover.

6. If the timing is not correct, loosen the distributor locknut and rotate the dis-

tributor housing until the timing mark on the pulley aligns with the indicator pin.

7. Tighten the distributor locknut and recheck the lead timing.

8. Connect the timing light to the trailing spark plug.

9. Check the trailing timing with the timing light.

10. If the trailing timing is not correct, note the amount of error and stop the engine.

11. Remove the distributor cap and rotor.

12. Disconnect the primary wire from the leading point set.

13. Remove the breaker base plate and external lever for leading set.

14. Slightly loosen the breaker base set screws of the trailing side and turn the base plate as required. Install the leading breaker base assembly, rotor and cap.

15. Check the trailing and leading timing. If they are not correct, repeat the above steps.

16. Leave timing light connected to trailing plug of the front rotor housing.

17. Connect a jumper between both terminals in the coupler of the primary lead wires.

18. Check the leading retard timing. Adjust by moving the external adjusting lever.

1977 Rotary

1. Check the point gap for both leading and trailing sets. Adjust if necessary.

2. Warm-up engine and run it at specified idle speed.

3. Connect a timing light to the leading spark plug and aim it at the pointer on the front cover. If timing mark and pointer do not align as specified, adjust by loosening and rotating distributor body.

4. Tighten distributor body and switch timing light to trailing plug.

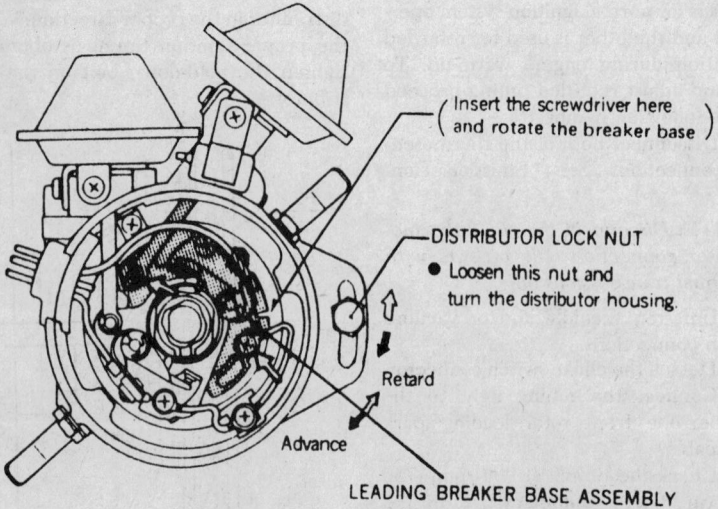

(Insert the screwdriver here and rotate the breaker base)

—DISTRIBUTOR LOCK NUT

● Loosen this nut and turn the distributor housing.

Retard

Advance

LEADING BREAKER BASE ASSEMBLY

● Slighly loosen two screws (shown with ⊃) and turn the breaker base

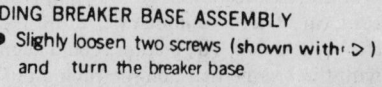

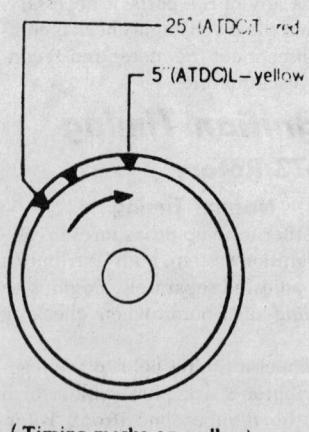

— 25° (ATDC)T—red

— 5° (ATDC)L—yellow

(Timing marks on pulley)

Ignition timing adjustment—1977 RX-4, Cosmo (ⓒ Toyo Kogyo Co. Ltd.)

5. Check trailing timing by pointing timing light at pointer on front cover. If not within specifications, adjust by loosening and rotating distributor body.

6. Adjust leading timing by loosening the breaker base set screws in the distributor body and rotating the breaker base. Then, tighten the base, replace the cap and rotor. Start the engine and check the timing. Adjust the timing to specifications by loosening and rotating the distributor body.

7. Recheck the trailing timing and adjust as above, if necessary.

Valve Lash

Piston Engine

1. Run the engine until normal operating temperature is reached.

2. Shut off the engine and remove the rocker cover.

3. Torque the cylinder head bolts to 70 ft lbs.

4. Rotate the crankshaft so that the No. 1 cylinder (front) is in the firing position. This can be determined by removing the spark plug from the No. 1 cylinder and putting your thumb over the spark plug port. When compression is felt, the No. 1 cylinder is on the compression stroke. Rotate the engine with a wrench on the crankshaft pulley and stop it a TDC of the compression stroke on the No. 1 cylinder.

5. Check the valve clearance with a feeler blade. The clearance can be checked at the camshaft or at the valve.

6. If the valve clearance is incorrect, loosen the adjusting screw locknut and adjust the clearance by turning the adjusting screw with the feeler blade inserted. Hold the adjusting screw in the correct position and tighten the locknut.

7. Rotate the crankshaft (in the normal direction of rotation), adjusting the valves for each cylinder at TDC of the compression stroke. Adjust the valves for each cylinder, in the firing order, 1–3–4–2.

8. Install the rocker arm cover and torque the nuts to 18 in. lbs.

Compression

Rotary Engine

Because of the unusual shape of the combustion chamber, the lack of valves and because there are three chambers for each rotor, a normal gauge is useless for the measurement of rotary engine compression.

Mazda makes a special recording compression tester which produces a separate graph for each of the three chambers.

This is an expensive piece of equipment and not one that most mechanics are likely to have. If low compression is

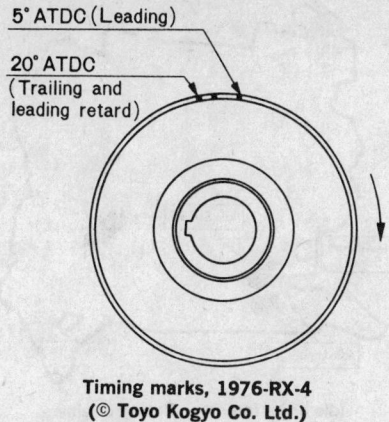

Timing marks, 1976-RX-4
(© Toyo Kogyo Co. Ltd.)

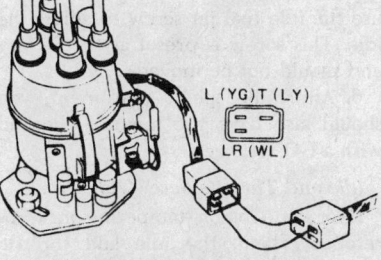

Connecting the distributor coupler with jumper—Rotary Engine
(© Toyo Kogyo Co. Ltd.)

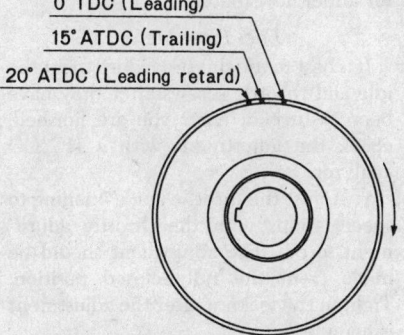

Timing marks 1976 RX-3 and Rotary Pick-up
(© Toyo Kogyo Co. Ltd.)

suspected, check with your local Mazda dealer.

Carburetor

NOTE: *For further carburetor adjustments, see the "Fuel System" section below.*

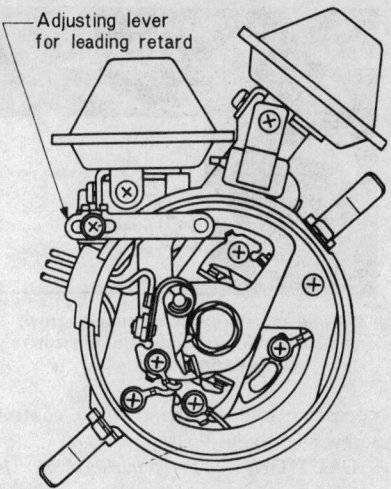

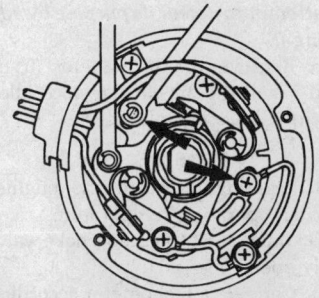

Adjusting ignition timing, 1975-77 rotary
(© Toyo Kogyo Co. Ltd.)

Idle Speed and Mixture

1972–73 Rotary

1. Start the engine and allow it to warm up. Remove the air cleaner assembly.

2. Operate the secondary throttle valve. Be sure that it returns fully.

3. Connect a tachometer to the engine in accordance with its manufacturer's instructions, or if none is available, have someone sit in the car and watch the tachometer on the instrument panel.

4. Adjust the mixture by seating the mixture control screw lightly and then unscrew it four to five turns.

5. Turn the idle screw until the specified idle speed obtained; it may be

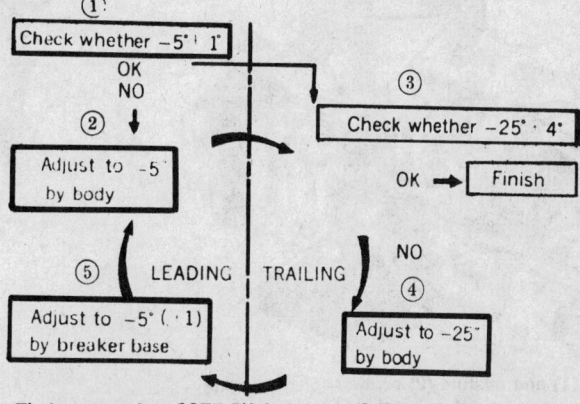

Timing procedure 1977 RX-4, Cosmo (© Toyo Kogyo Co. Ltd.)

Mazda

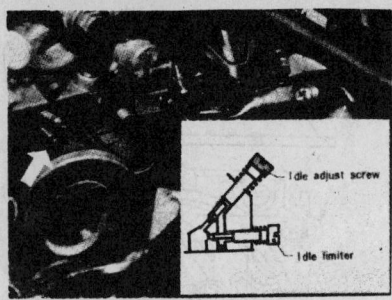

The idle adjustment screw (upper arrow)
and the idle limiter screw (lower arrow)
(© Toyo Kogyo Co., Ltd.)

necessary to turn the mixture control screw slightly, as well.

CAUTION: *The carburetor is equipped with an idle limiter screw as an aid in controlling emissions; do not attempt to defeat its purpose by adjusting it.*

6. Remove the tachometer (if used) and install the air cleaner once idle adjustments are completed.

Piston Engine

1. Thoroughly warm the engine to normal operating temperature.

2. Make sure that the choke valve is fully open.

3. Connect a tachometer according to the manufacturer's instructions.

4. Adjust the idle speed screw to specifications.

5. The mixture should be checked by, at least, a CO meter. The carbon monoxide percentage at idle should be 0.1%.

6. Disconnect the tachometer.

1974 Rotary

1. Warm the engine to normal operating temperature.

2. Be sure that the secondary throttle valve is fully returned.

3. Set the parking brake and block the front wheels.

4. Connect a tachometer according to the manufacturer's instructions.

5. Adjust the idle speed to specifications. The idle speed should ONLY be adjusted with the idle air screw. Never

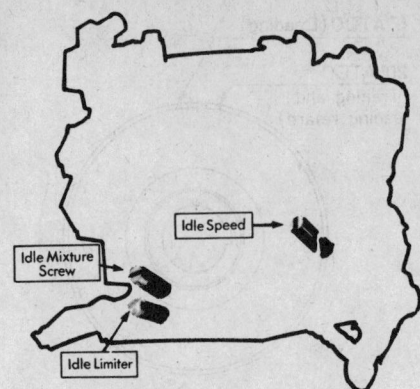

Idle adjustments—Rotary engine

use the idle fuel jet screw to adjust the idle. This screw is preset at the factory and should not be moved.

6. After idle speed adjustment, you should also have the mixture checked with a CO analyzer.

Idle and Throttle Screw Adjustment

If for some reason (tampering or carburetor overhaul) the idle and throttle screws need adjustment, use the following procedures. Two procedures are given; one for HC/CO analyzer and one for a fuel flow meter.

Fuel Flow Meter

It is best to use this procedure to set the idle and throttle screws after they have been disturbed. After you are finished, check the adjustment with a HC/CO analyzer.

1. Adjust the throttle angle opening to specifications with the throttle adjustment screw. The adjustment should be made from the fully closed position. Tighten the locknut after the adjustment is complete.

2. Connect a fuel flow meter.

3. Start the engine and set the approximate idle speed with the idle air screw.

4. Adjust the idle fuel flow to specifications with the idle fuel screw.

5. Use the idle air screw to set the idle speed again.

6. Repeat this procedure (Steps 4 & 5)

until both the idle fuel flow and the idle speed are within specifications.

7. Disconnect the fuel flow meter.

HC/CO Analyzer

1. If you have not already done so, adjust the throttle angle opening to specifications. Make the adjustment from the fully closed position.

2. Lock the nut after adjustment.

3. Start the engine and adjust the idle speed with the idle air screw.

4. Using the gas analyzer, check the HC (hydrocarbon) and CO (carbon monoxide) readings. If the HC is less than 200 ppm (parts per million) and the CO is between 0.1–2.0%, no further adjustment is needed.

5. If the HC and CO are not within specifications, adjust the CO reading to as close to 0.1% as possible, keeping the HC reading below 200 ppm. Use the idle fuel screw to make this adjustment.

6. Recheck the idle speed and adjust, if necessary, using the idle air screw.

7. Recheck the HC and CO readings to be sure that they are within limits. Repeat Steps 5 and 6 until the HC, CO and idle speed are all within specifications.

1975 Rotary

Idle speed changes with air temperature. It is suggested by Mazda that the idle adjustment be made indoors with a floor fan blowing through the radiator to assist in cooling. Whenever operating an engine indoors, make certain that provision is made for removal of exhaust gases. Idle speed should be adjusted with the engine at normal operating temperature, all accessories off and fuel tank cap removed.

1. Connect a tachometer to the engine.

2. Set idle speed to specification by turning the adjusting screw.

Mixture can be adjusted by:

1. Check the float level as described in the Fuel System Section.

2. Using a reliable CO meter, check the CO density at idle.

3. If density is not within 0.1%, adjust

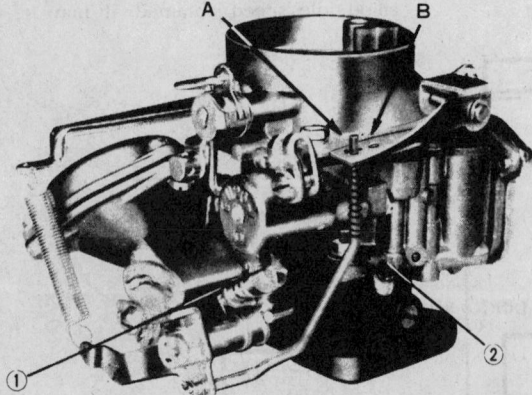

Idle speed (1) and mixture (2) screws—piston engine
(© Toyo Kogyo Co. Ltd.)

Adjusting idle speed, 1976-77 rotary-(1) air adjust screw;
(2) mixture adjust screw   (© Toyo Kogyo Co. Ltd.)

the idle mixture by turning the mixture screw.

4. Adjust the CO density to 0%, then turn the adjusting screw counterclockwise until the density is 0.5%.

5. Turn the screw clockwise until the density reaches 0.1%. Then turn screw an additional one quarter turn.

6. Check idle speed and reset if necessary.

1976–77 Rotary

As with 1975 models, the idle speed should be set indoors. See the starting paragraph under 1975 Rotary.

1. Disconnect the idle compensator tube at the air cleaner.

2. Run the engine at normal operating temperature and make sure that the choke is wide open.

3. Check the float level as described in the Fuel System Section.

4. Connect an exhaust gas analyzer and tachometer to the engine.

5. With engine at idle, check the CO density.

6. Adjust the idle speed to specification by turning the idle adjusting screw.

7. Turn the mixture adjusting screw clockwise until the engine lopes severely.

8. Turn the screw slowly counterclockwise until the CO density reaches 0.1%, then turn it an additional one quarter turn in the same direction.

ENGINE ELECTRICAL
Distributor
Removal and Installation
Rotary Engines—1972–1973

The removal procedure for both the leading and the trailing distributors is the same. To remove either or both of them, proceed in the following manner:

NOTE: *It is a good idea to remove and install the distributors separately to avoid confusion.*

1. Disconnect the vacuum advance line at the distributor.

2. Unfasten the vacuum advance switch connector (trailing distributor).

3. Disconnect the primary wire at the coil.

4. Note the letters and numbers identifying them, and remove the spark plug cables.

5. Matchmark the distributor housing and sockets. Also, matchmark the position of the rotor, relative to the distributor housing. These marks are an aid when installing the distributor in a properly timed engine.

6. Remove the distributor clamping screw and carefully lift the distributor

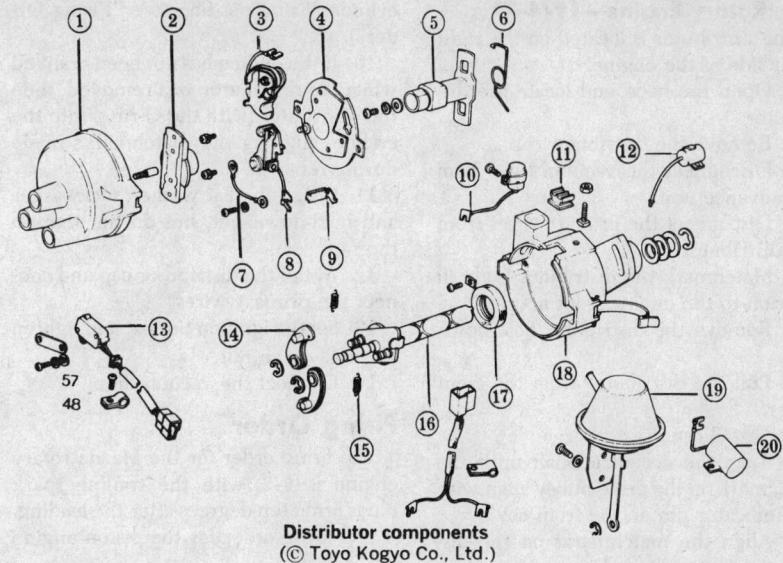

Distributor components
(© Toyo Kogyo Co., Ltd.)

1. Cap	8. Point set
2. Rotor	9. Felt
3. Point set	10. Ignition condenser
4. Breaker plate	11. Terminal
5. Cam	12. Radio supression condenser
6. Spring	13. Vacuum switch—trailing
7. Ground wire	distributor only

14. Governor
15. Governor spring
16. Shaft
17. Oil seal
18. Distributor housing
19. Vacuum advance unit
20. Ignition condenser

out of its socket.

NOTE: *Try to avoid rotating the engine while the distributors are removed. Unnecessary rotation of the engine under these conditions only means more work.*

If the engine has not been rotated with either of the distributors removed, their installation is performed in the reverse order of removal. Use the matchmarks made during removal to correctly position the distributors in their sockets.

NOTE: *If both distributors were removed at the same time, use care to see that they are returned to their proper sockets. Both the distributors and the front cover are marked to aid in correct installation.*

Once the distributors are installed, adjust the point gap, dwell angle, and timing, as detailed above.

If the engine was rotated or otherwise disturbed after either distributor was removed, installation is performed in the following manner:

1. Turn the engine until the white

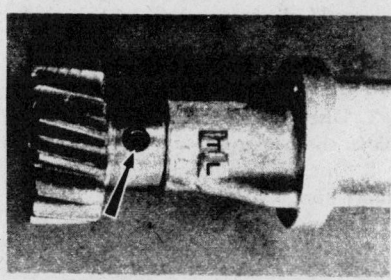

**Align the distributor identification marks
prior to installation**
(© Toyo Kogyo Co., Ltd.)

mark on the eccentric shaft pulley is aligned with the pointer on the front cover. This will always be top dead center (TDC) of the number one rotor's compression cycle, because each rotor makes only 1/3 of a turn for each full rotation of the eccentric shaft.

NOTE: *TDC cannot be found by feeling for compression at the number one spark plug hole, as in a conventional piston engine.*

2. Align the marks that are stamped on each distributor housing and driven gear.

3. Install either distributor so that the key on the end of its drive engages with the slot in the socket.

NOTE: *If both of the distributors were removed at the same time, be careful not to mix their parts or confuse them upon installation. Both the distributors and the front housing are marked with a "T" or an "L"; insert the distributor which has the same letter as the housing, into its proper socket.*

4. Rotate each distributor slightly until its points just start to open and then tighten its locknut.

5. Check the point gap (see above) and install the cap.

6. Carefully connect all of the vacuum lines and the wires to the proper distributor.

NOTE: *Spark plug position and leads are marked, as is each distributor cap, to aid installation.*

7. Check and adjust the dwell angle and ignition timing, using the procedures outlined above.

8. Connect the vacuum advance lines to the distributors.

Mazda

Rotary Engine—1974–77

The distributor is located on the right front side of the engine.

1. Open the hood and locate the distributor.
2. Remove the distributor cap.
3. Disconnect the vacuum tube from the advance unit.
4. Disconnect the primary wires from the distributor.
5. Matchmark the distributor body in relation to the engine front housing.
6. Remove the distributor hold-down bolt.
7. Pull the distributor from the front cover.

To install the distributor:

8. Turn the eccentric shaft until the TDC mark on the drive pulley align with the indicator pin on the front cover.
9. Align the matchmarks on the distributor housing and drive gear.
10. Install the distributor so that the distributor lockbolt is located in the center of the slot. Engage the gears.
11. Rotate the distributor clockwise until the leading contact point set starts to separate, and tighten the distributor lockbolt.
12. Install the distributor cap and connect the primary wires.
13. Set the ignition timing.
14. Connect the vacuum tube to the vacuum unit on the distributor.

Piston Engine

1. Matchmark the distributor cap and the body of the distributor. Remove the distributor cap.
2. Disconnect the vacuum hose from the diaphragm.
3. Scribe matchmarks on the distributor body and the cylinder block to indicate the relative positions.
4. Scribe another mark on the distributor body indicating the position of the rotor.
5. Disconnect the primary wires from the distributor.
6. Remove the distributor hold-down nut, lockwasher and flat washer.
7. Remove the distributor from the engine.

NOTE: *Do not crank the engine while the distributor is removed.*

To install the distributor:

8. Align the matchmarks on the distributor gear and body.
9. If the engine was cranked while the distributor was removed, turn the crankshaft until the No. 1 cylinder is at the top of the compression stroke. This can be determined by feeling compression with your thumb over the spark plug port. The 5° BTDC mark on the crankshaft pulley should also be aligned with the timing pointer. Slide the distributor into the engine with the rotor pointing to the No. 1

cylinder firing position (see "Firing Order").

10. If the engine has not been cranked while the distributor was removed, slide the distributor (with the O-ring) into the engine, aligning the matchmarks made during removal.
11. Install the flat washer, lockwasher and hold-down nut, but do not tighten the nut.
12. Install the distributor cap and connect the primary wires.
13. Set the ignition timing, and tighten the hold-down nut.
14. Connect the vacuum line.

Firing Order

The firing order for the Mazda rotary engine is 1–2, with the trailing spark plugs firing ten degrees after the leading.

The firing order for the piston engine is 1–3–4–2.

Alternator

Alternator Service Precautions

Because of the nature of alternator design, special care must be taken when servicing the charging system.

1. Battery polarity should be checked before making any connections such as jumper cables or battery charger leads. Reversed battery connections will damage the diode rectifiers.
2. The battery must never be disconnected while the alternator is running because the regulator will be ruined.
3. Always disconnect the battery ground cable before replacing the alternator.
4. Do not attempt to polarize an alternator.
5. Do not short across or ground any alternator terminals.
6. Always disconnect the battery ground cable before removing the alternator output cable whether the engine is running or not.
7. If electric arc welding equipment is to be used on the car, first disconnect the battery and alternator cables. Never operate the car with the electric arc welding equipment attached.
8. If the battery is to be "quick charged", disconnect the positive cable from the battery.

Removal and Installation

1. Disconnect the battery ground cable at the negative (−) terminal.
2. Disconnect all of the leads from the alternator.
3. Remove the alternator adjusting link bolt. Do not remove the adjusting link.
4. Remove the alternator securing nuts and bolts. Withdraw the drivebelt and remove the alternator.

Installation is performed in the reverse order of removal. Adjust the drivebelt tension as detailed below.

Belt Tension Adjustment

1. Check the drivebelt tension by applying about 22 lbs of thumb pressure to the belt, midway between the eccentric shaft and alternator pulleys. The belt should deflect to the following specifications:

Old belt—0.59–0.67 in.
New belt—0.47–0.55 in.

2. If belt deflection is not within specifications, loosen but do not remove the bolt on the adjusting link.
3. Push the alternator in the direction required to obtain proper belt deflection.

CAUTION: *Do not pry or pound the alternator housing.*

4. Tighten the adjusting link bolt to 20 ft lbs.

Regulator

Removal and Installation

1. Disconnect the battery ground cable at the negative (−) battery terminal.
2. Disconnect the wiring from the regulator.
3. Remove the regulator mounting screws.
4. Remove the regulator.

Installation is performed in the reverse order of removal.

Voltage Adjustments

Models With Ammeters Only

1. Remove the cover from the regulator.
2. Check the air gap, the point gap, and the back gap with a feeler gauge (see illustration).
3. If they do not fall within the specifications given in the "Alternator and Regulator" chart above, adjust the gaps by bending the stationary contact bracket.
4. Connect a voltmeter between the "A" and "E" terminal of the regulator.

NOTE: *Be sure that the car's battery is fully charged before proceeding with this test.*

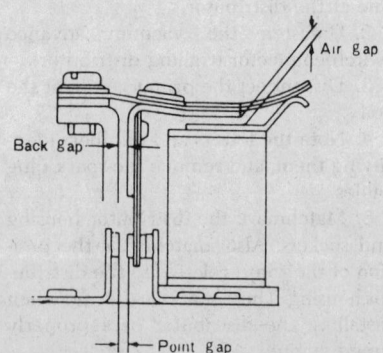

Regulator mechanical adjustments
(© Toyo Kogyo Co., Ltd.)

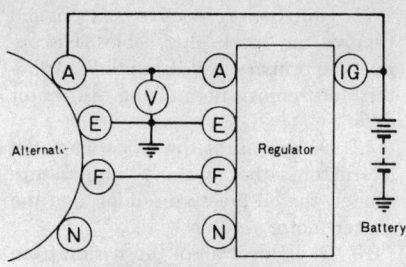

Testing the voltage regulator
(© Toyo Kogyo Co., Ltd.)

5. Start the engine and run it at 2,000 rpm (4,000 alternator rpm). The voltmeter reading should be 13.5–14.5 V.

6. Stop the engine.

7. Bend the upper plate *down* to decrease the voltage setting or *up* to increase the setting, as required.

8. If the regulator cannot be brought within specifications, replace it.

9. When the test is completed, disconnect the voltmeter and replace the regulator cover.

Regulator Test
Models With Warning Light

The alternator regulator is composed of two control units: a constant voltage relay and a pilot lamp relay.

Constant Voltage Relay

1. Use an almost fully charged battery and connect a voltmeter between the "A" and "E" terminals of the regulator.

2. Run the engine at 2,000 rpm and read the voltmeter. It should read from 14–15 volts.

3. If not, adjust the voltage relay.

Pilot Lamp Relay

1. Using a voltmeter and variable resistor, construct a circuit as shown.

2. Light the pilot lamp.

3. Slide the knob of the variable resistor so that the voltage gradually increases.

4. Read the voltage between the "N" and "E" terminals of the regulator. If the voltage is 3.7–5.7 volts, it is operating properly.

5. Slide the knob of the variable resistor to decrease the voltage. Note the point on the voltmeter where the light will light again. If the reading is less than 3.5 volts, the unit is working properly.

6. Disconnect the test instruments.

Regulator
Models With Warning Light

1. Check the air gap, back gap and point gap with a wire gauge. If they are not within specification, adjust the gap by bending the stationary bracket.

2. After the gaps are correctly set, adjust the voltage setting. Bend the upper plate down to increase the voltage setting, or bend it up to increase the voltage setting.

Constant Voltage Relay
Air Gap 0.028–0.043 in.
Point Gap 0.012–0.016 in.
Back Gap 0.028–0.043 in.

Pilot Lamp Relay
Air Gap 0.035–0.047 in.
Point Gap 0.028–0.043 in.
Back Gap 0.028–0.043 in.

Starter
Removal and Installation
Rotary Engine

NOTE: *There are two possible locations for the starter motor; one is on the lower right-hand side of the engine and the other is on the upper right-hand side.*

1. Remove the ground cable from the negative (−) battery terminal.

2. If the car is equipped with the lower mounted starter, remove the gravel shield from underneath the engine.

CAUTION: *Be extremely careful not to contact the hot exhaust pipe while working underneath the car.*

3. Remove the battery cable from the starter terminal.

4. Disconnect the solenoid leads from the solenoid terminals.

5. Remove the starter securing bolts and withdraw the starter assembly.

Installation is the reverse of the above steps.

Removal and Installation
Piston Engine

1. Raise the hood and disconnect the battery ground cable.

2. Remove the carburetor air cleaner and air intake tube.

3. Disconnect the battery cable from the starter solenoid battery terminal.

4. Pull the ignition switch wire from the solenoid terminal.

5. Raise and support the vehicle on jackstands.

6. Working under the vehicle, remove the two starter attaching bolts, washers and nuts.

7. Tilt the drive end of the starter and remove the starter by working it out below the emission system hoses.

8. Installation is the reverse of removal.

Solenoid Replacement

Perform solenoid replacement with the starter motor removed from the car.

1. Detach the field strap from the solenoid terminals.

2. Remove the solenoid securing screws.

3. Withdraw the solenoid spring and washers from the starter drive housing.

Solenoid installation is performed in the reverse order of removal.

Starter Drive Replacement

1. Perform the solenoid removal procedure as above.

2. Remove the plunger from the drive engagement fork.

3. Unfasten the nuts from the thru-bolts.

NOTE: *Unless further disassembly of the starter is desired, do not remove the thru-bolts.*

4. Remove the drive housing from the front of the starter.

5. Remove the engagement fork, spring, and spring seat.

6. Withdraw the over-running clutch from the armature shaft.

Assembly is performed in the reverse order of disassembly. Check the clearance between the pinion and the stop

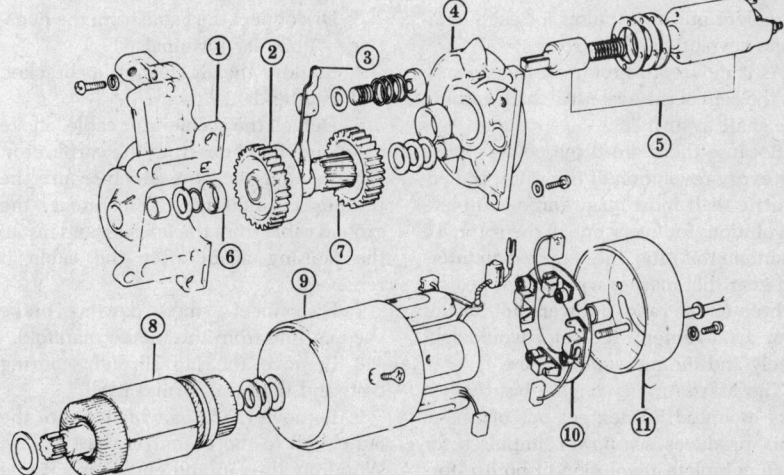

Starter components
(© Toyo Kogyo Co., Ltd.)

1. Front housing	5. Solenoid	
2. Overruning clutch	6. Stop	9. Field coil
3. Engagement fork	7. Idler gear	10. Brush holder
4. Center frame	8. Armature	11. End frame

collar with the solenoid closed. It should be 0.001–0.006 in.

ENGINE MECHANICAL
Rotary

NOTE: *Because of the unique design of the Mazda rotary engine, some procedures require the use of special factory tools. The text notes where these tools are necessary. If the tools are not available, the job should not be undertaken.*

Design

The Mazda rotary engine replaces conventional pistons with three-cornered rotors which have rounded sides. The rotors are mounted on a shaft which has eccentrics rather than crank throws.

The chamber which the rotor travels in is roughly oval-shaped, but with the sides of the oval bowed in slightly. The technical name for this shape is a two-lobe epitrochoid.

As the rotor travels its path in the chamber, it performs the same four functions as the piston in a traditional piston engine:

1. Intake
2. Compression
3. Ignition
4. Exhaust

But all four functions in a rotary engine are happening concurrently, rather than in four separate stages.

Ignition of the compressed fuel/air mixture occurs each time a side of the rotor passes the spark plugs. Since the rotor has three sides, there are three complete power impulses for each complete revolution of the rotor.

As it moves, the rotor exerts pressure on the cam of the eccentric shaft, causing the shaft to turn.

Because there are three power pulses for every revolution of the rotor, the eccentric shaft must make three complete revolutions for every one of the rotor. To maintain this ratio, the rotor has an internal gear that meshes with a fixed gear in a three-to-one ratio. If it were not for this gear arrangement, the rotor would spin freely and timing would be lost.

The Mazda rotary engine has two rotors mounted 60 degrees out of phase. This produces six power impulses for each complete revolution of both rotors and two power impulses for each revolution of the eccentric shaft.

Because of the number of power impulses for each revolution of the rotor, and because all four functions are concurrent, the rotary engine is able to produce a much greater amount of power for its size and weight than a comparable reciprocating piston engine.

Instead of using valves to control the intake and exhaust operations, the rotor uncovers and covers ports on the wall of the chamber as it turns. Thus, a complex valve train is unnecessary. The resulting elimination of parts further reduces the size and weight of the engine, as well as eliminating a major source of mechanical problems.

Spring-loaded carbon seals are used to prevent loss of compression around the rotor apexes and cast iron seals are used to prevent loss of compression around the side faces of the rotor. These seals are equivalent to compression rings on a conventional piston but must be more durable because of the high rotor rpm to which they are exposed.

Oil is controlled by means of circular seals mounted in two grooves on the side face of the rotor. These oil seals function to keep oil out of the combustion chamber and gasoline out of the crankcase, in a similar manner to the oil control ring on a piston.

The rotor housing is made of aluminum and the surfaces of the chamber are chrome plated for durability and the prevention of wear damage.

Engine Removal and Installation

CAUTION: *Be sure that the engine has completely cooled before attempting to remove it.*

1. Scribe matchmarks on the hood and hinges. Remove the hood from the hinges.
2. Working from underneath the car, remove the gravel shield; then drain the cooling system and the engine oil.
3. Disconnect the cable from the negative (−) battery terminal.
4. Remove the air cleaner, its bracket, and its attendant hoses.
5. Detach the accelerator cable, choke cable, and fuel lines from the carburetor.
6. Remove the nuts which secure the thermostat housing. Disconnect the ground cable from the housing and install the housing again after the cable is removed.
7. Disconnect the power brake vacuum line from the intake manifold.
8. Remove the fan shroud securing bolts and then the shroud itself.
9. Remove the bolts which secure the fan clutch to the eccentric shaft pulley. Withdraw the fan and clutch as a single unit.
   NOTE: *Keep the fan clutch in an upright position, so that its fluid does not leak out.*
10. Unfasten the clamps and remove both of the radiator hoses.
11. Note their respective positions and remove the spark plug cables. Disconnect the primary leads from the distributors and remove both of the distributor caps.
12. Detach all of the leads from the alternator, the water temperature sender, the oil pressure sender, and the starter motor.
13. Disconnect all of the wiring from the emission control system components. See "Emission Controls," below.
14. Detach the heater hoses at the engine.
15. Detach the oil lines from the front and the rear of the engine.
16. Disconnect the battery cable from the positive (+) battery terminal and from the engine.
17. Unfasten the nuts which secure the clutch slave cylinder and tie the cylinder up out of the way.
   NOTE: *Do not remove the hydraulic line from the slave cylinder.*
18. Remove the exhaust pipe and the thermal reactor.
   CAUTION: *Be sure that the thermal reactor has completely cooled; severe burns could result if it has not.*
19. Evenly and in two or three stages, remove the nuts and bolts which secure the clutch housing to the engine.
20. Support the transmission with a jack.
21. Remove the nuts from each of the engine mounts.
22. Attach a lifting sling to the lifting bracket on the rear of the engine housing.
23. Use a hoist to take up the slack on the sling.
   CAUTION: *Be sure that the hoist is secure to prevent possible personal injury or damage to the engine.*
24. Pull the engine forward until it clears the transmission input shaft. Lift the engine straight up and out of the car.
   NOTE: *Be careful not to damage any of the components which remain in the car.*
25. Remove the heat stove from the exhaust manifold.
26. Remove the thermal reactor as outlined below.
27. Mount the engine on a work stand.
   NOTE: *A special three part work stand, designed for the rotary engine, is manufactured by Mazda.*

Engine installation is performed in the reverse order of removal.

Rotary Engine Overhaul
Disassembly—1972–73

Engine disassembly should be performed in the following order, after it has been removed from the automobile and placed on a workstand:

1. Remove all of the components of the emission control system. See "Emission Controls," below.

2. Detach the metering oil pump linkage, oil lines, and vacuum sensing lines from the carburetor.

3. Remove the intake manifold securing nuts, evenly and in several stages.

4. Remove the intake manifold assembly complete with the carburetor.

5. Remove the alternator adjusting link bolt but do not remove the adjusting link itself.

6. Unfasten the alternator attaching bolts, then remove the alternator and its drive belt.

7. Remove the pulley from the water pump.

8. Unfasten the five nuts and two bolts which secure the water pump and remove the pump.

9. Remove the clamping nuts from both of the distributors and withdraw the distributors from their sockets.

10. Mark the distributor sockets for identification during assembly. Remove the nuts and withdraw the distributor sockets from the front housing.

11. Attach a brake to keep the ring gear from turning (Mazda part number 49 0820 060A).

12. Unfasten the eccentric shaft pulley bolt. Remove the pulley and the key from the eccentric shaft.

13. Unfasten the clutch cover attachment bolts.

14. Remove the clutch assembly from the flywheel.

15. Straighten the tabs on the flywheel nut lockwasher.

16. Remove the flywheel nut with a large wrench.

CAUTION: *Do not use locking pliers or a hammer and chisel to remove the flywheel nut.*

17. Remove the flywheel with a puller.
18. Invert the engine on the workstand.

19. Remove the oil pan bolts and take the oil pan off of the engine, complete with its gasket.

20. Remove the oil strainer bolts, the oil strainer, and its gasket.

21. Mark the front and rear rotor housings, which are identical in appearance, so that they will not be confused upon assembly.

22. With the front of the engine facing upward in the stand, unfasten the front engine mount nuts and remove the mounts.

23. Remove the front engine cover securing bolts. Lift off the cover and its gasket.

24. Withdraw the O-ring from the passage on the front of the housing.

25. Remove the oil pump drive chain

and related components in the following manner:

a. Slide the oil slinger, spacer, and distributor drive gear off of the eccentric shaft.

b. Remove the chain tensioner nuts and the chain tensioner.

c. Remove the locknut and washer from the oil pump sprocket.

d. Simultaneously slide the sprockets off of the eccentric shaft and oil pump driveshaft, complete with the chain.

e. Remove the key from the eccentric shaft.

26. Slide the oil pump balancing weight, thrust washer, and the first needle bearing off of the eccentric shaft.

27. Unfasten the bearing housing securing bolts.

28. Remove the bearing housing, second needle bearing, spacer, and thrust washer.

29. Turn the engine in the workstand so that the top side of it is facing upward.

30. Loosen the engine housing tension bolts in the order illustrated under "Torque Sequences".

CAUTION: *Loosen the bolts evenly and in two or three stages.*

31. With the front of the engine facing up, lift the front housing off the eccentric shaft.

32. Remove any side seals which are sticking to the surface of the front housing and place them in their original position on the rotor.

33. Remove the rotor seals and related components in the following order, after noting their original positions, so that they will not be confused during assembly:

a. Corner seals—3
b. Corner seal springs—3
c. Side seals—6
d. Side seal springs—6

NOTE: *Each seal has its own installation mark next to its groove on the rotor. Mazda has a special seal tray (part no. 49 0813 250) which uses the same marks, so that the seals will not be confused during storage and assembly.*

34. Remove the oil seals and O-rings from the grooves in the rotor face.

35. Hold the front rotor housing down while threading a nut and bolt of the proper *metric* size into each of the hollow dowels on the engine housing.

36. Remove the dowels by holding the bolt with a wrench while tightening the nut. Once the dowel contacts the nut, back off on the nut and insert a spacer between the nut and the housing. Continue tightening the nut and inserting spacers until each dowel is out of the housing.

37. Lift the front housing away from the rotor.

CAUTION: *When lifting the housing off the rotor, be careful that the apex seals do not fall off. If they strike a hard surface, they will shatter.*

38. Remove the air injection nozzles, the O-rings, and the rubber seals from the front housing.

39. Remove the apex seals and their springs from the front rotor. When removing each seal, place an identification mark on its *bottom,* with a felt tipped pen, so that it can be installed in the proper location and direction. If some of the seals have come off, be sure to note their proper location.

CAUTION: *When marking the seal, do not use a punch or scratch the surface of the seal.*

40. Remove the front rotor from the eccentric shaft and place it face down on a clean, soft cloth.

NOTE: *The internal gear side of the front rotor is marked with an "F" to ensure installation in the proper rotor housing.*

41. Remove the seals and springs from the rear side of the rotor in the same manner as detailed for the front side in step 38.

42. Hold the intermediate housing down and remove the hollow dowels, as outlined for the front rotor housing in steps 35–36.

43. Lift the intermediate housing off the eccentric shaft by sliding it beyond the front rotor journal while pushing up on the shaft. Be careful not to damage the eccentric shaft.

44. Withdraw the eccentric shaft.

45. Repeat steps 35–41 to remove the rear rotor housing and rotor.

NOTE: *The internal gear side of the rear rotor is marked with an "R" to ensure installation in the proper rotor housing.*

Inspection and Replacement

Front Housing

1. Check the housing for signs of gas or water leakage.

2. Remove the carbon deposits from the front housing with extra fine emery cloth.

NOTE: *If a carbon scraper must be used, be careful not to damage the mating surfaces of the housing.*

3. Remove any of the old sealer which is adhering to the housing, using a brush or a cloth soaked in Ke-tone®.

4. Check for distortion by placing a straightedge on the surface of the housing. Measure the clearance between the straightedge and the housing with a feeler gauge. If the clearance is greater than 0.002 in. at any point, replace the housing.

5. Use a dial indicator to check for wear on the rotor contact surfaces of the

housing. If the wear is greater than 0.004 in., replace the housing.

NOTE: *The wear at either end of the minor axis is greater than at any other point on the housing. However, this is normal and should be no cause for concern.*

Front Stationary Gear and Main Bearing

1. Examine the teeth of the stationary gear for wear or damage.

2. Be sure that the main bearing shows no signs of excessive wear, scoring, or flaking.

3. Check the main bearing-to-eccentric journal clearance by measuring the journal with a vernier caliper and the bearing with a pair of inside calipers.

The clearance should be between 0.-0018–0.0028 in. and the wear limit is 0.-0039 in. Replace either the main bearing or the eccentric shaft if it is greater than this. If the main bearing is to be replaced, proceed as detailed in the following section.

Main Bearing Replacement

1. Unfasten the securing bolts, if used. Drive the stationary gear and main bearing assembly out of the housing with a brass drift.

2. Press the main bearing out of the stationary gear.

3. Press a new main bearing into the stationary gear so that it is in the same position that the old bearing was.

4. Align the slot in the stationary gear flange with the dowel pin in the housing and press the gear into place. Install the securing bolts, if required.

NOTE: *To aid in stationary gear and main bearing removal and installation, Mazda manufactures a special tool, part number 49 0813 235.*

Intermediate and Rear Housings

Inspection of the intermediate and rear housings is carried out in the same manner as detailed for the front housing. Replacement of the rear main bearing and stationary gear (mounted on the rear housing) is given below.

Rear Stationary Gear and Main Bearing

Inspect the rear stationary gear and main bearing in a similar manner to the front. In addition, examine the O-ring, which is located in the stationary gear, for signs of wear or damage. Replace the O-ring, if necessary.

If required, replace the stationary gear in the following manner:

1. Remove the rear stationary gear securing bolts.

2. Drive the stationary gear out of the rear housing with a brass drift.

3. Apply a light coating of grease to a new O-ring and fit it into the groove on the stationary gear.

4. Apply sealer to the flange of the stationary gear.

5. Install the stationary gear on the housing so that the slot on its flange aligns with the pin on the rear housing.

CAUTION: *Use care not to damage the O-ring during installation.*

6. Tighten the stationary gear bolts evenly, and in several stages, to 15 ft lbs.

Rotor Housings

1. Examine the inner margin of both housings for signs of gas or water leakage.

2. Wipe the inner surface of each housing with a clean cloth to remove the carbon deposits.

NOTE: *If the carbon deposits are stubborn, soak the cloth in a solution of Ketone. Do not scrape or sand the chrome plated surfaces of the rotor chamber.*

3. Clean all of the rust deposits out of the cooling passages of each rotor housing.

4. Remove the old sealer with a cloth soaked in Ke-tone.

5. Examine the chromium plated inner surfaces for scoring, flaking, or other signs of damage. If any are present, the housing must be replaced.

6. Check the rotor housings for distortion by placing a straightedge on the axes.

7. Measure the clearance between the straightedge and the housing with a feeler gauge. If the gap exceeds 0.002 in., replace the rotor housing.

8. Check the widths of both rotor housings, at a minimum of eight points near the trochoid surfaces of each housing, using a vernier caliper.

If the difference between the maximum and minimum values obtained is greater than 0.0031 in. (RX–3 and RX–2) or 0.0024 in. (RX–4), replace the housing. A housing in this condition will be prone to gas and coolant leakage.

NOTE: *Standard rotor housing width is 2.7559 in.*

Rotors

1. Check the rotor for signs of blow-by around the side and corner seal areas.

2. The color of the carbon deposits on the rotor should be brown, just as in a piston engine.

NOTE: *Usually the carbon deposits on the leading side of the rotor are brown, while those on the trailing side tend toward black, as viewed from the direction of rotation.*

3. Remove the carbon on the rotor with a scraper or extra fine emery paper. Use the scraper carefully, when doing the seal grooves, so that no damage is done to them.

4. After removing the carbon, wash the rotor in solvent and blow it dry with compressed air.

5. Examine the internal gear for cracks or damaged teeth.

NOTE: *If the internal gear is damaged, the rotor and gear must be replaced as a single assembly.*

6. With the oil seal removed, check the land protrusions by placing a straightedge over the lands. Measure the gap between the rotor surface and the straightedge with a feeler gauge. The standard specification is 0.004–0.006 in. (RX–2 and RX–3) or 0.004–0.008 in. (RX–4); if it is less than this, the rotor must be replaced.

7. Check the gaps between the housings and the rotor on both of its sides:

a. Measure the rotor width with a vernier caliper. The standard rotor width is 2.7500 in.

b. Compare the rotor width against the width of the rotor housing which was measured above. The standard rotor housing width is 2.7559 in.

c. Replace the rotor, if the difference between the two measurements is not within 0.0051–0.0067 in.

8. Check the rotor bearing for flaking, wearing, or scoring and proceed as indicated in the next section, if any of these are present.

The rotors are classified into five lettered grades, according to their weight. A letter A and E is stamped on the internal gear side of the rotor. If it becomes necessary to replace a rotor, use one marked with a "C" because this is the standard replacement rotor, and it can be used in most balancing combinations.

Rotor Bearing Replacement

CAUTION: *The use of the special service tools, as indicated in the text, is mandatory, if damage to the rotor is to be avoided.*

Check the clearance between the rotor bearing and the rotor journal on the eccentric shaft. Measure the inner diameter of the rotor bearing and the outer diameter of the journal; the standard clearance is 0.0016–0.0031 in. The wear limit is 0.0039 in.; replace the bearing if it exceeds this.

To replace the bearing, proceed in the following manner:

1. Install the bearing expander (Mazda part number 49 0813 245) in the rotor bearing. If the expander is not used, bearing deformation will result when the holes are drilled.

2. Drill a 0.14 in. diameter hole, roughly 0.028 in. deep, into each of the lockscrews which secure the bearings to the rotor. Use a #28 drill.

3. Remove the bearing expander.

4. Support the rotor so that the internal gear is facing upward.

5. Using the rotor bearing remover (Mazda part number 49 0813 240), less the adaptor ring, press the bearing out of the rotor.

CAUTION: *Be extremely careful not to damage the internal gear. It cannot* be replaced separately from the rotor.

6. If the bore in which the bearing is installed is damaged, dress it with emery paper and blow it clean with compressed air.

7. With the rotor internal gear facing upward, press-fit a new bearing into the bore. Use the bearing replacer with the adaptor screws removed.

NOTE: *Be sure that the oil hole in the bearing is aligned with the hole in the apex side of the rotor. Once the bearing is installed, it should be flush with the rotor boss.*

8. Insert the rotor bearing expander into the new bearing, as in step 1.

9. Drill 0.14 in. holes, about 0.28 in. deep, within 0.28 in. of the original lockscrew holes (either to the left or right of them) with a #28 drill. The center of the holes must be 0.02 in. from the rotor bore.

NOTE: *The new holes should all be in the same direction from the original holes; e.g., if the first hole is drilled to the left of the original hole, drill the remaining holes to the left of the other lockscrew holes.*

10. Thread the holes with an M4, P–0.70 mm metric tap.

11. Install the bearing lockscrews and stake them with a punch so that they cannot work loose.

12. Wash the rotor and blow it dry with compressed air.

Oil Seal Inspection

NOTE: *Inspect the oil seal while it is mounted in the rotor.*

1. Examine the oil seal for signs of wear or damage.

2. Measure the width of the oil seal lip. If it is greater than 0.031 in., replace the oil seal.

3. Measure the protrusion of the oil seal; it should be greater than 0.020 in. Replace the seal, as detailed below, if it is not.

Oil Seal Replacement

NOTE: *Replace the rubber O-ring in the oil seal as a normal part of engine overhaul.*

1. Pry the seal out gently by inserting a screwdriver into the slots on the rotor. Do not remove the seal by prying it at only one point; seal deformation will result.

CAUTION: *Be careful not to deform the lip of the oil seal if it is to be reinstalled.*

2. Fit both of the oil seal springs into their respective grooves so that their ends are facing upward and their gaps are opposite each other on the rotor.

3. Insert a new rubber O-ring into each of the oil seals.

NOTE: *Before installing the O-rings into the oil seals, fit each of the seals into its proper groove on the rotor.*

Check to see that all of the seals move smoothly and freely.

4. Coat the oil seal groove and the oil seal with engine oil.

5. Gently press the oil seal into the groove with your fingers. Be careful not to distort the seal.

NOTE: *Be sure that the white mark is on the bottom side of each seal when it is installed.*

6. Repeat the installation procedure for the oil seals on both sides of each rotor.

Apex Seals

CAUTION: *Although the apex seals are extremely durable when in service, they are easily broken when they are being handled. Be careful never to drop them.*

1. Remove the carbon deposits from the apex seals and their springs. Do not use emery cloth on the seals as it will damage their finish.

2. Wash the seals and the springs in cleaning solution.

3. Check the apex seals for cracks and other signs of wear or damage.

4. Test the seal springs for weakness.

5. Use a micrometer to check the seal height. Replace any seal if its height is less than 0.3150 in. (RX–3 and RX–2) or 0.2750 in. (RX–4).

6. With a feeler gauge, check the side clearance between the apex seal and the groove in the rotor. Insert the gauge until its tip contacts the bottom of the groove. If the gap is greater than 0.004 in., replace the seal.

7. Check the gap between the apex seals and the side housing in the following manner:

a. Use a vernier caliper to measure the length of each apex seal.

b. Compare this measurement to the *minimum* figure obtained when the rotor housing width was being measured.

c. If the difference is more than 0.-0059 in. (RX–3 and RX–2) or 0.0118 in. (RX–4), replace the seal.

d. If, on the other hand, the seal is too long, sand the ends of the seal with emery cloth until the proper length is reached.

CAUTION: *Do not use the emery cloth on the faces of the seal.*

Side Seals

1. Remove the carbon deposits from the side seals and their springs with a carbon scraper.

2. Check the side seals for cracks or wear. Replace any seals found defective.

3. Check the clearance between the side seals and their grooves with a feeler gauge. Replace any side seals with a clearance of more than 0.0039 in. The standard clearance is 0.002–0.003 in.

4. Check the clearance between the side seals and the corner seals with both installed in the rotor.

a. Insert a feeler gauge between the end of the side seal and the corner seal.

NOTE: *Insert the gauge against the direction of the rotor's rotation.*

b. Replace the side seal if the clearance is greater than 0.016 in.

5. If the side seal is replaced, adjust the clearance between it and the corner seal as follows:

a. File the side seal on its reverse side, in the same rotational direction of the rotor, along the outline made by the corner seal.

b. The clearance obtained should be 0.002–0.006 in. If it exceeds this, the performance of the seals will deteriorate.

CAUTION: *There are four different types of side seals, depending upon location. Do not mix the seals up and be sure to use the proper type of seal for replacement.*

Corner Seals

1. Clean the carbon deposits from the corner seals.

2. Examine each of the seals for wear or damage.

3. Measure the clearance between the corner seal and its groove. The clearance should be 0.0008–0.0019 in. The wear limit of the gap is 0.0031 in.

4. If the wear between the corner seal and the groove is uneven, check the clearance with the special "bar limit gauge" (Mazda part number 49 0839 165). The gauge has a "go" end and a "no go" end. Use the gauge in the following manner:

a. If neither end of the gauge goes into the groove, the clearance is within specifications.

b. If the "go" end of the gauge fits into the groove, but the "no go" end does not, replace the corner seal with one that is 0.0012 in. oversize.

c. If both ends of the gauge fit into the groove, then the groove must be reamed out as detailed below. Replace the corner seal with one which is 0.-0072 in. oversize, after reaming.

NOTE: *Take the measurement of the groove in the direction of maximum wear, i.e. that of rotation*

Corner Seal Groove Reaming

NOTE: *This procedure requires the use of special tools; if attempted without them, damage to the rotor could result.*

1. Carefully remove all of the deposits which remain in the groove.

2. Fit the jig (Mazda part number 2113 99 900) (RX–3 and RX–2) or 49 2113 030 (RX–4) over the rotor. Tighten its adjusting bar, being careful not to damage the rotor bearing or the apex seal grooves.

3. Use the corner seal groove reamer

(Mazda part number 49 0839 170) to ream the groove.

4. Rotate the reamer at least 20 times, while applying engine oil as a coolant.

NOTE: *If engine oil is not used, it will be impossible to obtain the proper groove surfacing.*

5. Remove the reamer and the jig.

6. Repeat steps 1–5 for each of the corner seal grooves.

7. Clean the rotor completely and check it for any signs of damage.

8. Fit a 0.0079 in. oversize corner seal into the groove and check its clearance. Clearance should be 0.0008–0.0019 in.

Seal Springs

Check the seal springs for damage or weakness. Be exceptionally careful when checking the spring areas which contact either the rotor or the seal.

Eccentric Shaft

1. Wash the eccentric shaft in solvent and blow the oil passages dry with compressed air.

2. Check the shaft for wear, cracks, or other signs of damage. Make sure that none of the oil passages are clogged.

3. Measure the shaft journals with a vernier caliper. The standard specifications are:

Main journals—1.6929 in.

Rotor journals—2.9134 in.

Replace the shaft if any of its journals shows excessive wear.

4. Check eccentric shaft runout by placing the shaft on V-blocks and using a dial indicator. Rotate the shaft slowly and note the dial indicator reading. If runout is more than 0.0008 in. (RX–3 and RX–2) or 0.0024 in. (RX–4), replace the eccentric shaft.

5. Check the blind plug at the end of the shaft. If it is loose or leaking, remove it with an allen wrench and replace the O-ring.

6. Check the operation of the needle roller bearing for smoothness by inserting a mainshaft into the bearing and rotating it. Examine the bearing for signs of wear or damage.

7. Replace the bearing, if necessary, with the special bearing replacer (Mazda part numbers 49 0823 073 and 49 0823 072).

Engine Assembly—1972–73

1. Place the rear rotor on a rubber pad or a clean, thick cloth.

2. Install the oil seals on both sides of the rotor, if you have not already done so. Follow the procedure outlined in the appropriate section under "Inspection and Replacement".

3. Place the rear rotor, still using the pad or cloth, so that its internal gear is facing upward.

NOTE: *When installing the various seals, consult the marks made during engine disassembly in order to ensure installation of the seals in their proper location.*

4. Place each of the apex seals into their respective grooves, without fitting the springs.

5. Place each of the corner seal springs, followed by the corner seals, into the grooves on the rotor. Lubricate them with engine oil.

6. Check to see that the upper surface of the corner seal is 0.05–0.06 in. higher than the rotor. The corner seal should also move freely when finger pressure is applied to it.

7. Place the side seal springs into their grooves with both ends facing upward. Coat them with engine oil.

8. Install each of the side seals into its proper groove.

9. Be sure that each seal protrudes about 0.04 in. from the surface of the rotor. Test free movement of the seals by pressing them with your finger.

10. Lubricate all of the seals and the internal gear with engine oil.

11. Mount the rear housing in the workstand so that the top of it is facing upward.

12. Place the rotor on the rear housing so that both its rotor contact surface and the rotor are facing upward.

CAUTION: *Be sure that none of the seals falls off while the rotor is being moved.*

13. Mesh the rotor internal gear with the stationary gear on the housing, so that the apexes of the rotor are positioned as illustrated.

NOTE: *When positioning the rotor, be sure that none of the corner seals drops into the ports.*

14. Remove the three apex seals from the rotor and place them so that they are near their proper installation positions.

15. Lubricate the eccentric shaft rear rotor and main bearing journals with engine oil.

16. Insert the eccentric shaft into the rotor and rear housing using care not to damage any of the bearings or journals.

17. Fit the air injection nozzles into place. Apply sealer to the back of the rear rotor housing.

NOTE: *Use care not to get any sealer into the water or oil passages of the rear housing.*

18. Apply a small amount of rubber lubricant on new O-rings and rubber seals, then install them into the rear side of the rotor housing.

19. Invert the rear rotor housing. Fit it over the rotor and then onto the rear housing. Be sure that none of the O-rings or rubber seals falls out of the housing.

20. Coat the hollow dowels with engine oil. Fit the dowels through the holes in the rotor housing and into the holes on the rear housing.

21. Install the apex seals, complete with springs, in the proper position and in the proper direction within the rotor.

22. Position the corner and side seals, with their springs, in the proper grooves. Be sure that they are facing in the correct direction.

23. Lightly lubricate the rotor and the rotor contact surface of the rear housing with engine oil.

24. Apply sealer to the O-rings and rubber seals. Install them on the intermediate housing, in a similar manner to that outlined in steps 17–18 above.

25. Hold the back end of the eccentric shaft up so that the front end of the rear rotor journal does not extend beyond the front side of the rotor bearing.

26. Fit the intermediate housing onto the rear rotor housing, while holding the eccentric shaft, as explained in the step above.

27. Install the front rotor and rotor housing in the same manner outlined for the rear rotor and housing in steps 1–23.

NOTE: *The proper relationship between the timing of the front and rear rotors will be obtained when the front rotor is placed over the rotor journal on the eccentric shaft, and positioned as the rear rotor is in step 13.*

28. Apply engine oil to the front housing stationary gear and main bearing. Place the front housing over the front rotor housing. If necessary, turn the front rotor slightly to engage its internal gear with the front housing stationary gear.

29. Install the tension bolts in the following manner:

a. Fit each bolt through the housings and turn it two or three times.

b. Rotate the engine in the stand so that its top is facing upward.

c. Tighten the bolts evenly and in two or three stages. Use the sequence illustrated below and the torque figure listed in the torque specifications chart.

CAUTION: *Do not tighten the bolts one at a time.*

d. Rotate the eccentric shaft so that it operates lightly and smoothly.

30. Coat the rear oil seal with engine oil. Apply Loctite® to the threads on the eccentric shaft through the key.

31. Install the flywheel on the rear of the eccentric shaft with its keyway over the key on the shaft.

32. Coat both sides of the flywheel lockwasher with sealer, then fit the washer on the eccentric shaft.

33. Finger tighten the flywheel locknut. Use a brake on the flywheel to keep it from rotating while tightening the nut on the flywheel to 350 ft lbs.

34. Turn the engine on the workstand so that its front end is facing up.

35. Slip the thrust plate, spacer, and the rear needle bearing over the front of the eccentric shaft. Lubricate the parts

which were just installed with engine oil.

36. Install the bearing housing, tighten its securing bolts, and bend the lock-washer tabs upward.

37. Fit the front needle bearing and thrust washer on the shaft, then coat them with engine oil. Install the balance weight and the oil pump drive gear on the shaft.

38. Fit the oil pump drive chain over both of the sprockets. Install the sprocket and chain assembly over the eccentric

and oil pump shafts simultaneously. Place the key on the eccentric shaft.

NOTE: *Be sure that both of the sprockets are engaged by the chain before installing them over the shafts.*

39. Slip the distributor drive gear, the spacer, and the oil slinger over the eccentric shaft.

40. Align the keyway on the eccentric shaft pulley with the key on the shaft and install the pulley. Tighten the pulley securing bolt to 47 ft lbs while holding

the flywheel with the brake.

41. Check eccentric shaft end-play in the following manner:

a. Attach a dial indicator to the flywheel. Move the flywheel forward and backward.

b. Note the reading on the dial indicator; it should be 0.0016–0.0018 in.

c. If the end-play is not within specifications, adjust it by replacing the front spacer. Spacers come in four sizes, ranging from 0.3151–0.3181 in.

Mark the front and rear rotor housings to prevent confusion during assembly
(© Toyo Kogyo Co., Ltd.)

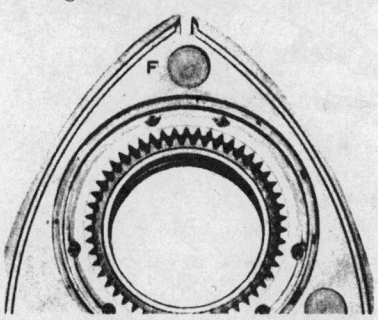

The front rotor is marked with an "F" on its internal gear side; The rear rotor is marked with an "R" in a similar manner.
(© Toyo Kogyo Co., Ltd.)

Measuring housing wear with a dial indicator
(© Toyo Kogyo Co., Ltd.)

Remove any side seals adhering to the front housing surfaces

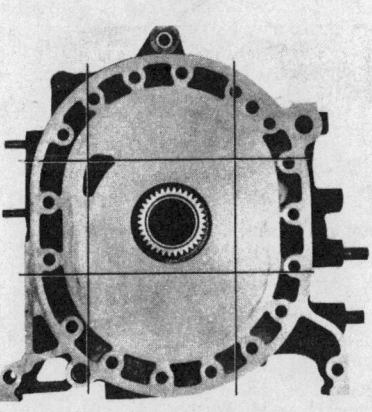

Measure the housing distortion along the axes indicated
(© Toyo Kogyo Co., Ltd.)

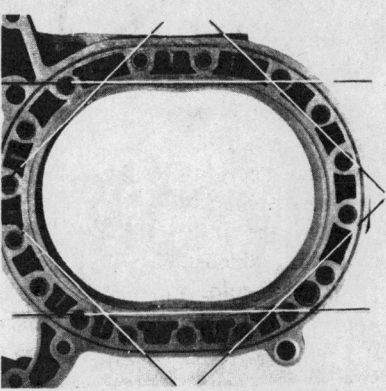

Measure the rotor housing distortion along the axes indicated
(© Toyo Kogyo Co., Ltd.)

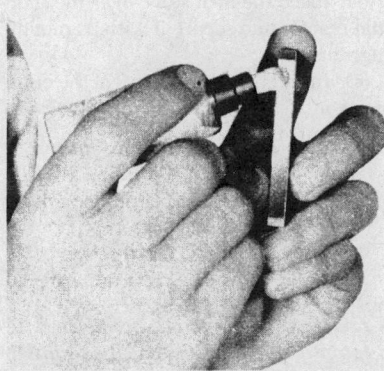

Use a felt-tipped pen to mark the bottom of each apex seal
(© Toyo Kogyo Co., Ltd.)

Align the slot in the stationary gear flange with the pin in the housing (arrow)
(© Toyo Kogyo Co., Ltd.)

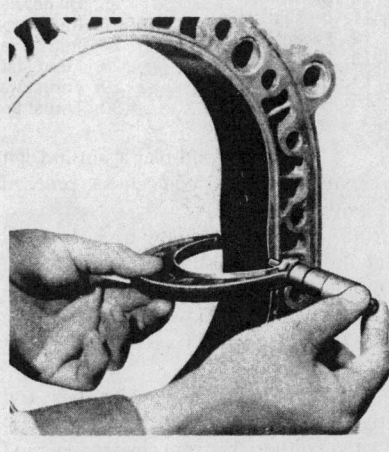

Check the rotor housing width at eight points near the trochold surface
(© Toyo Kogyo Co., Ltd.)

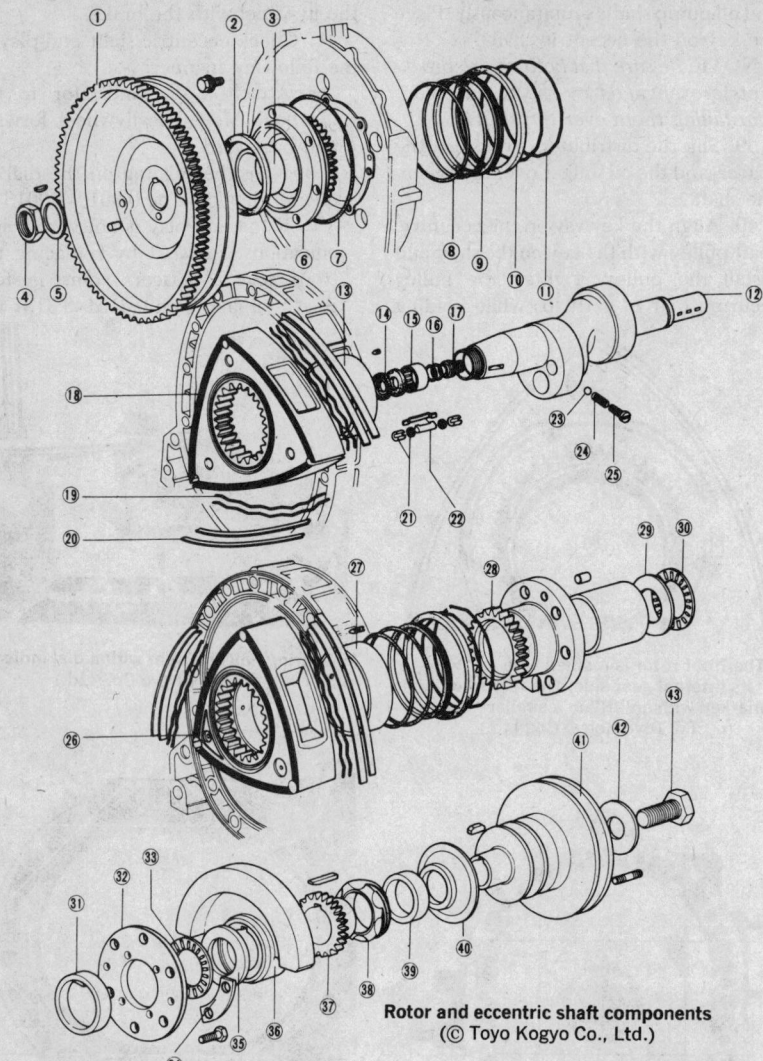

Rotor and eccentric shaft components
(© Toyo Kogyo Co., Ltd.)

1. Flywheel
2. Oil seal
3. Main bearing
4. Locknut
5. Washer
6. Rear stationary gear
7. O-ring
8. Oil seal O-ring
9. Oil seal
10. Oil seal
11. Oil seal spring
12. Eccentric shaft
13. Rotor bearing
14. Grease seal
15. Needle bearing
16. O-ring
17. Blind plug
18. Front rotor
19. Side seal spring
20. Side seal
21. Corner seal and spring
22. Apex seal and spring
23. Ball
24. Spring
25. Oil nozzle
26. Rear rotor
27. Rotor bearing
28. Front stationary gear
29. Thrust washer
30. Thrust bearing
31. Spacer
32. Bearing housing
33. Needle bearing
34. Washer
35. Thrust plate
36. Balance weight
37. Oil pump drive sprocket
38. Distributor drive gear
39. Spacer
40. Oil slinger
41. Eccentric shaft pulley
42. Washer
43. Pulley bolt

d. Check the end-play again and, if it is now within specifications, proceed with the next step.

42. Remove the pulley from the front of the eccentric shaft. Tighten the oil pump drive sprocket nut and bend the locktabs on the lockwasher.

43. Fit a new O-ring over the front cover oil passage.

44. Install the chain tensioner and tighten its securing bolts.

45. Position the front cover gasket and the front cover on the front housing, then secure the front cover with its attachment bolts.

46. Install the eccentric shaft pulley again. Tighten its bolt to 47 ft lbs.

47. Use a spare mainshaft or an arbor to hold the clutch disc in place.

48. Install the clutch cover and pressure plate assembly over the flywheel.

NOTE: *Align the O-mark on the clutch cover with the hole in the flywheel.*

49. Tighten the clutch cover bolts to 15 ft lbs while holding the ring gear with a brake. Install the self tapping bolt into the reamed hole.

50. With the bottom of the engine pointing upward in the workstand, cut the excess front cover gasket at the oil

pan mounting flange.

51. Install the oil strainer gasket and the strainer. Bolt them to the front housing.

52. Apply sealer to the oil pan and housing mounting flanges. Install the oil pan and gasket. Tighten the bolts evenly, and in several stages, to 7 ft lbs.

53. Align the white mark on the eccentric shaft pulley with the pointer on the front housing to obtain top dead center (TDC) of the number one rotor's compression cycle.

54. Place the distributor socket gaskets on the housing. Install the trailing distributor socket into the housing so that the driveshaft groove is inclined 34° to the right of the longitudinal axis of the engine.

55. Install the leading distributor socket in a similar manner, except that its driveshaft groove should be inclined 17° to the right of the longitudinal axis of the engine.

56. Install both of the distributors, as outlined under "Engine Electrical".

57. Install the water pump as detailed under "Cooling System".

58. Bolt the engine mounts onto the front housing.

59. Perform alternator installation and drivebelt tension adjustments as detailed under "Engine Electrical".

60. Position the intake manifold/carburetor assembly and gaskets onto the engine. Tighten the manifold securing nuts evenly, working in two or three stages, to the specifications in the "Torque Specifications" chart.

NOTE: *Start from the inside and work out when tightening the bolts.*

61. Attach the oil lines, the vacuum lines, and the metering oil pump linkage to the carburetor.

62. Remove the engine from the workstand.

63. Install the gaskets and the thermal reactor on the engine. Tighten its securing nuts evenly, working in two or three stages, to the specifications in the "Torque Specifications" chart.

64. Place the heat stove over the thermal reactor and secure it with its mounting nuts.

65. Install the components of the emission control system, as detailed in "Emission Controls".

66. Install the engine in the car.

Engine Disassembly —1974–77

NOTE: *Because of the design of the rotary engine, it is not practical to attempt component removal and installation. It is best to disassemble and assemble the entire engine, or, go as far as necessary with the disassembly procedure.*

Measure the rotor width at the point indicated
(© Toyo Kogyo Co., Ltd.)

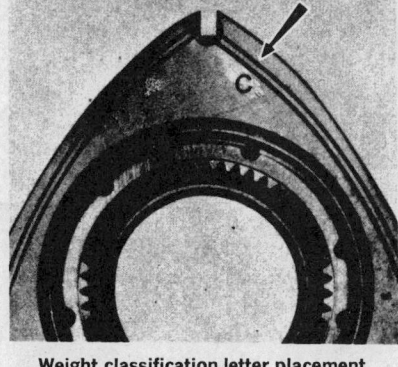

Weight classification letter placement (arrow)
(© Toyo Kogyo Co., Ltd.)

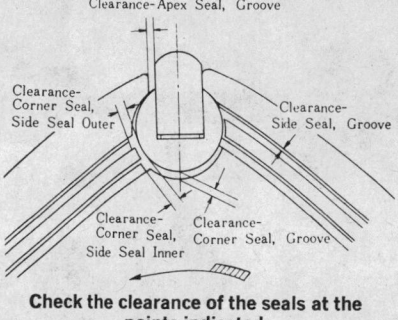

Check the clearance of the seals at the points indicated
(© Toyo Kogyo Co., Ltd.)

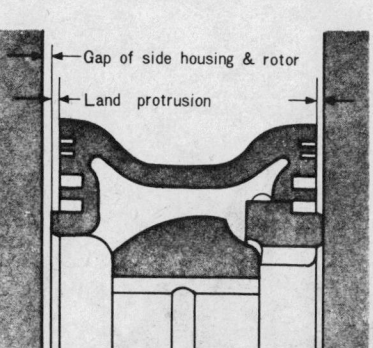

Oil seal protrusion
(© Toyo Kogyo Co., Ltd.)

Apex seal-to-side seal housing gap
(© Toyo Kogyo Co., Ltd.)

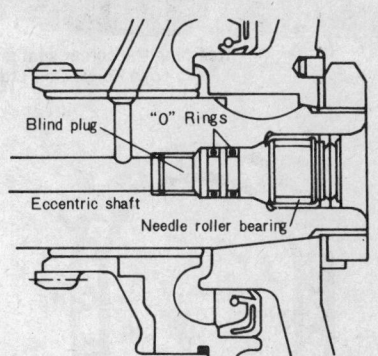

Eccentric shaft blind plug assembly
(© Toyo Kogyo Co., Ltd.)

Insert the special bearing expander into the rotor
(© Toyo Kogyo Co., Ltd.)

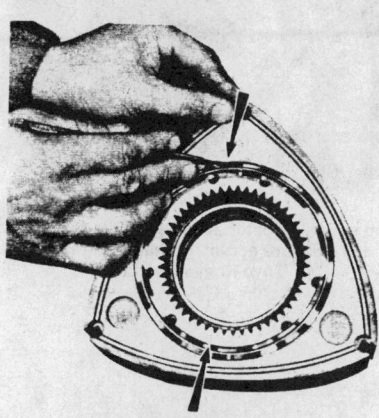

Position the oil seal spring gaps at arrows
(© Toyo Kogyo Co., Ltd.)

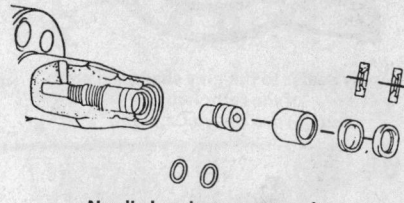

Needle bearing components
(© Toyo Kogyo Co., Ltd.)

Corner seal installation
(© Toyo Kogyo Co., Ltd.)

Installing a new rotor bearing
(© Toyo Kogyo Co., Ltd.)

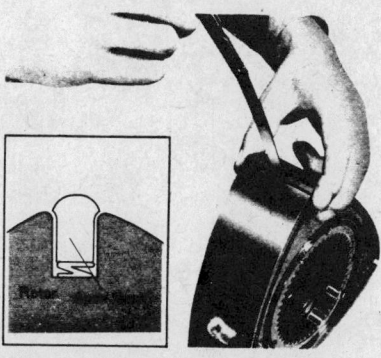

Check the gap between the apex seal and groove with a feeler gauge
(© Toyo Kogyo Co., Ltd.)

The rear rotor must be positioned as shown during engine assembly
(© Toyo Kogyo Co., Ltd.)

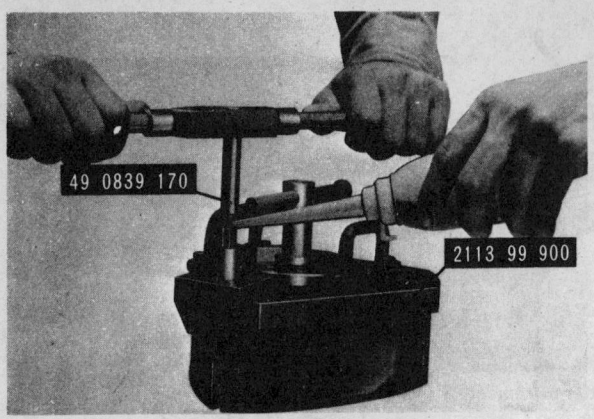

Reaming the corner seal groove
(© Toyo Kogyo Co., Ltd.)

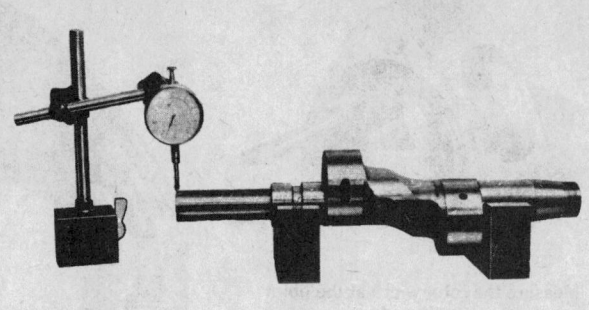

Position the dial indicator as shown, in order to measure shaft runout
(© Toyo Kogyo Co., Ltd.)

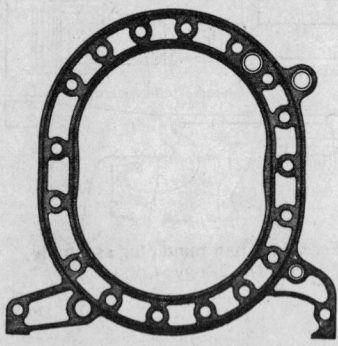

Apply sealer to the grey shadowed areas of the rotor housing
(© Toyo Kogyo Co., Ltd.)

Use a dial indicator attached to the flywheel to measure eccentric shaft end-play
(© Toyo Kogyo Co., Ltd.)

Installing oil pump
(© Toyo Kogyo Co., Ltd.)

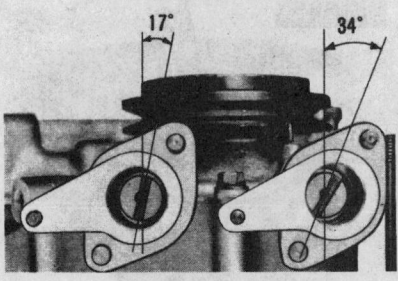

Position the slots in the distributor drive as shown
(© Toyo Kogyo Co., Ltd.)

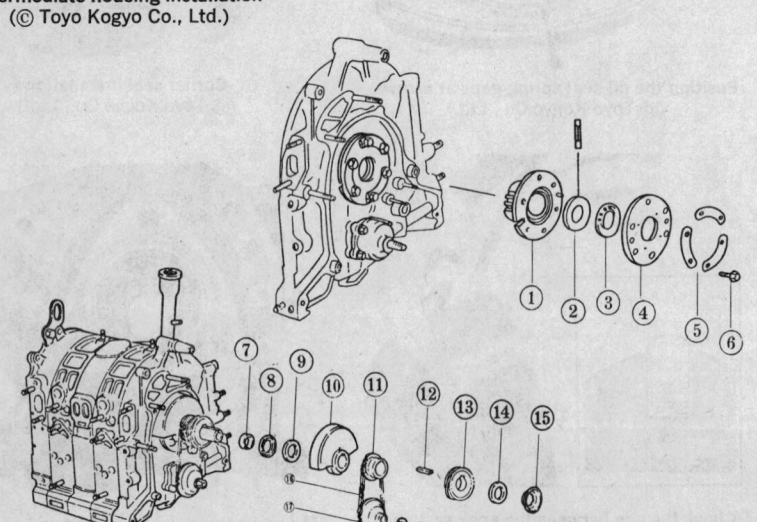

1. Stationary gear
2. Thrust plate
3. Needle bearing
4. Bearing housing
5. Lockwasher
6. Bolt

7. Spacer
8. Needle bearing
9. Thrust washer
10. Balance weight
11. Oil pump drive sprocket
12. Key

13. Distributor drive gear
14. Spacer
15. Oil thrower
16. Oil pump chain
17. Oil pump driven sprocket

Intermediate housing installation
(© Toyo Kogyo Co., Ltd.)

Bearing housing assembly—1972-73
(© Toyo Kogyo Co., Ltd.)

1. Mount the engine on a stand.

2. Remove the oil hose support bracket from the front housing.

3. Disconnect the vacuum hoses, air hoses and remove the decel valve.

4. Remove the air pump and drive belt. Remove the air pump adjusting bar.

5. Remove the alternator and drive belt.

6. Disconnect the metering oil pump connecting rod, oil tubes and vacuum sensing tube from the carburetor.

7. Remove the carburetor and intake manifold as an assembly.

8. Remove the gasket and two rubber rings.

9. Remove the thermal reactor and gaskets.

10. Remove the distributor from the front cover.

11. Remove the water pump and gasket.

12. Invert the engine on the stand.

13. Remove the oil pan and gasket.

14. Remove the oil pump screen and gasket.

15. Identify the front and rear rotor housings with a felt tip pen. These are common parts and must be identified to be reassembled in their respective locations.

16. Turn the engine on the stand so that the top of the engine is up.

17. Remove the engine mounting bracket from the front cover.

18. Hold the flywheel with a flywheel holder and remove the eccentric shaft pulley.

19. Turn the engine on a stand so that the front end of the engine is up.

20. Remove the front cover and gasket.

21. Remove the O-ring from the oil passage on the front housing.

22. Remove the oil slinger and distributor drive gear from the shaft.

23. Unbolt and remove the chain adjuster.

24. Remove the locknut and washer from the oil pump driven sprocket.

25. Slide the oil pump drive sprocket and driven sprocket together with the drive chain off the eccentric shaft and oil pump simultaneously.

26. Remove the keys from the eccentric and oil pump shafts.

27. Slide the balance weight, thrust washer and needle bearing from the shaft.

28. Unbolt the bearing housing and slide the bearing housing, needle bearing, spacer and thrust plate off the shaft.

29. Turn the engine on the stand so that the top of the engine is up.

30. If equipped with a manual transmission, remove the clutch pressure plate and clutch disc. Loosen the pressure plate bolts evenly in small stages to prevent distortion and possible injury

Position the O-ring in the groove on the stationary gear (arrow)
(© Toyo Kogyo Co., Ltd.)

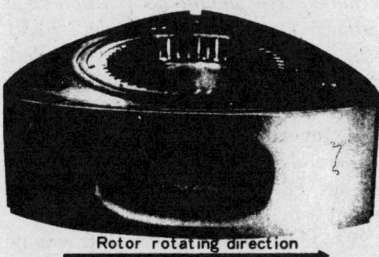

Normal shading of carbon deposits on rotor
(© Toyo Kogyo Co., Ltd.)

from the pressure plate flying off. Straighten the tab of the lockwasher and remove the flywheel nut. Remove the flywheel with a puller.

31. If equipped with an automatic transmission, remove the drive plate. Straighten the tab on the lockwasher and remove the counterweight nut, while holding the flywheel with a flywheel holder. Remove the counterweight using a puller.

32. Working at the rear of the engine, loosen the tension bolts in the sequence shown, and remove the tension bolts.

NOTE: *Do not loosen the tension bolts one at a time. Loosen the bolts evenly in small stages to prevent distortion.*

33. Lift the rear housing off the shaft.

34. Remove any seals that are stuck to the rotor sliding surface of the rear housing and reinstall them in their original locations.

35. Remove all the corner seals, corner seal springs, side seal and side seal springs from the rear side of the rotor. Mazda has a special tray which holds all the seals and keeps them segregated to prevent mistakes during reassembly. Each seal groove is marked to prevent confusion.

36. Remove the two rubber seals and two O-rings from the rear rotor housing.

37. Remove the dowels from the rear rotor housing.

38. Lift the rear rotor housing away from the rear rotor, being very careful not to drop the apex seals on the rear rotor.

39. Remove each apex seal, side piece and spring from the rear rotor and segregate them.

40. Remove the rear rotor from the eccentric shaft and place it upside down on a clean rag.

41. Remove each seal and spring from the other side of the rotor and segregate these.

42. If some of the seals fall off the rotor, be careful not to change the original position of each seal.

43. Identify the rear rotor with a felt tip pen.

44. Remove the oil seals and the springs. Do not exert heavy pressure at only one place on the seal, since it could be deformed. Replace the O-rings in the oil seal when the engine is overhauled.

45. Hold the intermediate housing down and remove the dowels from it.

46. Lift off the intermediate housing being careful not to damage the eccentric shaft. It should be removed by sliding it beyond the rear rotor journal on the eccentric shaft while holding the intermediate housing up and, at the same time, pushing the eccentric shaft up.

47. Lift out the eccentric shaft.

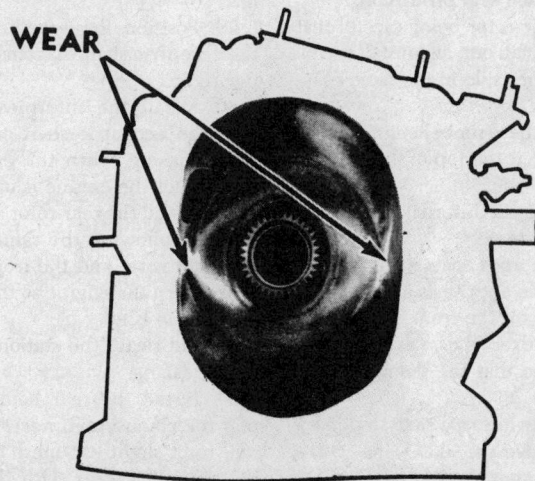

Most of the front and rear housing wear occurs at the end of the minor axis as shown

48. Repeat the above procedures to remove the front rotor housing and front rotor.

Engine Assembly—1974–77

1. Place the rotor on a rubber pad or cloth.

2. Install the oil seal rings in their respective grooves in the rotors with the edge of the spring in the stopper hole. The oil seal springs are painted cream or blue in color. The cream colored springs must be installed on the front faces of both rotors. The blue colored springs must be installed on the rear faces of both rotors. When installing each oil seal spring, the painted side (square side) of the spring must face upward (toward the oil seal).

3. Install a new O-ring in each groove. Place each oil seal in the groove so that the square edge of the spring fits in the stopper hole of the oil seal. Push the head of the oil seal slowly with the fingers, being careful that the seal is not deformed. Be sure that the oil seal moves smoothly in the groove before installing the O-ring.

4. Lubricate each oil seal and groove with engine oil and check the movement of the seal. It should move freely when the head of the seal is pressed.

5. Check the oil seal protrusion and install the seals on the other side of each rotor.

6. Install the apex seals without springs and side pieces into their respective grooves so that each side piece positions on the side of each rotor.

7. Install the corner seal springs and corner seals into their respective grooves.

8. Install the side seal springs and side seals into their respective grooves.

9. Apply engine oil to each spring and check each spring for smooth movement.

10. Check each seal protrusion.

11. Invert the rotor being careful that the seals do not fall out, and install the oil seals on the other side in the same manner.

12. Mount the front housing on a workstand so that the top of the housing is up.

13. Lubricate the internal gear of the rotor with engine oil.

14. Hold the apex seals with used O-rings to keep the apex seals installed and place the rotor on the front housing. Be careful not to drop the seals. Turn the front housing so that the sliding surface faces upward.

15. Mesh the internal and stationary gears and remove the old O-ring which is holding the apex seals in position.

16. Lubricate the front rotor journal of the eccentric shaft with engine oil and lubricate the eccentric shaft main journal.

17. Insert the eccentric shaft. Be careful that you do not damage the rotor bearing and main bearing.

18. Apply sealing agent to the front side of the front rotor housing.

19. Apply a light coat of petroleum jelly onto new O-rings and rubber seals (to prevent them from coming off) and install the O-rings and rubber seals on the front side of the rotor housing.

NOTE: *The inner rubber seal is of the square type. The wider white line of the rubber seal should face the combustion chamber and the seam of the rubber seal should be positioned as shown. Do not stretch the rubber seal.*

20. If the engine is being overhauled, install the seal protector to only the inner rubber seal to improve durability.

21. Invert the front rotor housing, being careful not to let the rubber seals and O-rings fall from their grooves, and mount it on the front housing.

22. Lubricate the dowels with engine oil and insert them through the front rotor housing holes and into the front housing.

23. Apply sealer to the front side of the rotor housing.

24. Install new O-rings and rubber seals on the front rotor housing in the same manner as for the other side.

25. Insert each apex spring seal, making sure that the seal is installed in the proper direction.

26. Install each side piece in its original position and be sure that the springs seat on the side piece.

27. Lubricate the side pieces with engine oil. Make sure that the front rotor housing is free of foreign matter and lubricate the sliding surface of the front housing with engine oil.

28. Turn the front housing assembly with the rotor, so that the top of the housing is up. Pull the eccentric shaft about 1 in.

29. Position the eccentric portion of the eccentric shaft diagonally, to the upper right.

30. Install the intermediate housing over the eccentric shaft onto the front rotor housing. Turn the engine so that the rear of the engine is up.

31. Install the rear rotor and rear rotor housing following the same steps as for the front rotor and the front housing.

32. Turn the engine so that the rear of the engine is up.

33. Lubricate the stationary gear and main bearing.

34. Install the rear housing onto the rear rotor housing. If necessary, turn the rear rotor slightly to mesh the rear housing stationary gear with the rear rotor internal gear.

35. Install a new washer on each tension bolt, and lubricate each bolt with engine oil.

36. Install the tension bolts and tighten them evenly, in several stages sequence. The specified torque is 23–27 ft lbs.

37. After tightening the bolts, turn the eccentric shaft to be sure that the shaft and rotors turn smoothly and easily.

38. Lubricate the oil seal in the rear housing.

39. On vehicles with manual transmission, install the flywheel on the rear of the eccentric shaft so that the keyway of the flywheel fits the key on the shaft.

40. Apply sealer to both sides of the flywheel lockwasher and install the lockwasher.

41. Install the flywheel locknut. Hold the flywheel SECURELY and tighten the nut to THREE HUNDRED AND FIFTY FT LBS (350 ft lbs) of torque.

NOTE: *350 ft lbs is a great deal of torque. In actual practice, it is practically impossible to accurately measure that much torque on the nut. At least a 3 ft bar will be required to generate sufficient torque. Tighten it as tight as possible, with no longer than 3 ft of leverage. Be sure the engine is held SECURELY.*

42. On vehicles with automatic transmission, install the key, counterweight, lockwasher and nut. Tighten the nut to 350 ft lbs. SEE STEP 41 AND THE NOTE FOLLOWING STEP 41. Install the drive plate on the counterweight and tighten the attaching nuts.

43. Turn the engine so that the front faces up.

44. Install the thrust plate with the tapered face down, and install the needle bearing on the eccentric shaft. Lubricate with engine oil.

45. Install the bearing housing on the front housing. Tighten the bolts and bend up the lockwasher tabs.

The spacer should be installed so that the center of the needle bearing comes to the center of the eccentric shaft and the spacer should be seated on the thrust plate.

46. Install the needle bearing on the shaft and lubricate it with engine oil.

47. Install the balancer and thrust washer on the eccentric shaft.

48. Install the oil pump drive chain over both of the sprockets. Install the sprocket and chain assembly over the eccentric shaft and oil pump shafts simultaneously. Install the key on the eccentric shaft.

NOTE: *Be sure that both of the sprockets are engaged with the chain before installing them over the shafts.*

49. Install the distributor drive gear onto the eccentric shaft with the "F" mark on the gear facing the front of the

engine. Slide the spacer and oil slinger onto the eccentric shaft.

50. Align the keyway and install the eccentric shaft pulley. Tighten the pulley bolt to 60 ft lbs.

51. Turn the engine top of the engine faces up.

52. Check eccentric shaft end-play in the following manner:

   a. Attach a dial indicator to the flywheel. Move the flywheel forward and backward.

   b. Note the reading on the dial indicator; it should be 0.0016–0.0028 in.

   c. If the end-play is not within specifications, adjust it by replacing the front spacer. Spacers come in four sizes, ranging from 0.3150–0.3181 in. If necessary, a spacer can be ground on a surface plate with emery paper.

   d. Check the end-play again and, if it is now within specifications, proceed with the next step.

Eccentric Shaft Spacer Thickness Chart

Marking	Thickness
X	8.08 ± 0.01 mm (0.3181 ± 0.0004 in)
Y	8.04 ± 0.01 mm (0.3165 ± 0.0004 in)
V	8.02 ± 0.01 mm (0.3158 ± 0.0004 in)
Z	8.00 ± 0.01 mm (0.3150 ± 0.0004 in)

53. Remove the pulley from the front of the eccentric shaft. Tighten the oil pump drive sprocket nut and bend the locktabs on the lockwasher.

54. Fit a new O-ring over the front cover oil passage.

55. Install the chain tensioner and tighten its securing bolts.

56. Position the front cover gasket and the front cover on the front housing, then secure the front cover with its attachment bolts.

57. Install the eccentric shaft pulley again. Tighten its bolt to 60 ft lbs.

58. Turn the engine so that the bottom faces up.

59. Cut off the excess gasket on the front cover along the mounting surface of the oilpan.

60. Install the oil strainer gasket and strainer on the front housing and tighten the attaching bolts.

61. Apply sealer to the joint surfaces of each housing.

62. Install the gasket and oil pan. Tighten the bolts evenly in two stages to 3.5 ft lbs.

63. Turn the engine so that the top is up.

64. Install the water pump and gasket on the front housing. Tighten the attaching bolts.

65. Rotate the eccentric shaft until the yellow mark (leading side mark) aligns with the pointer on the front cover.

66. Align the marks on the distributor gear and housing and install the distributor so that the lockbolt is in the center of the slot.

67. Rotate the distributor until the leading points start to separate and tighten the distributor locknut.

68. Install the gaskets and thermal reactor and tighten the attaching nuts.

69. Install the hot air duct.

70. Install the carburetor and intake manifold assembly with a new gasket. Tighten the attaching nuts.

71. Connect the oil tubes, vacuum tube and metering oil pump connecting rod to the carburetor.

72. Install the decel valve and connect the vacuum lines, air hoses and wires.

73. Install the alternator bracket, alternator and bolt and check the clearance. If the clearance is more than 0.006 in., adjust the clearance using a shim. Shims are available in three sizes: 0.0059 in., 0.0118 in., and 0.0197 in.

74. Install the alternator drive belt. Attach the alternator to the adjusting brace and adjust the belt tension to specification.

75. Install the air pump with the adjusting brace and install the air pump drive belt. Adjust the air pump drive belt to specifications.

76. Install the engine hanger bracket to the front cover.

77. Remove the engine from the stand.

78. Install the engine in the vehicle.

79, Fill the engine with fresh engine oil and install a new filter. Fill the engine with coolant. Start the engine, check the oil pressure, and warm it to normal operating temperature. Adjust the idle speed, timing and dwell. Recheck all capacities and refill if necessary. Check for leaks.

Intake Manifold
Removal and Installation

To remove the intake manifold and carburetor assembly with the engine remaining in the automobile, proceed in the following manner:

1. Perform steps 2, 3, 4, 5, 7, and 13 of "Engine Removal and Installation", above. Do not remove the engine. Do not drain the engine oil; merely remove the metering oil pump hose from the carburetor.

2. Then perform steps 1, 2, 3, and 4 of "Engine Disassembly" for 1972–73 models; perform steps 6 and 7 for 1974–77 models.

Install the intake manifold and carburetor assembly in the reverse order of removal. Tighten the manifold securing nuts, working from the inside out, and in two or three stages, to the torque specifications found in the "Torque Specifications" chart. Refill the cooling system.

Thermal Reactor
Removal and Installation

CAUTION: *The thermal reactor operates at extremely high temperatures. Allow the engine to cool completely before attempting to remove it.*

To remove the thermal reactor, which replaces the exhaust manifold, proceed in the following manner:

1. Remove the air cleaner assembly from the carburetor.

2. Unbolt and remove the air injection pump, as outlined in "Emission Controls".

3. Remove the intake manifold assembly, complete with carburetor. See the section above.

4. Remove the heat stove from the thermal reactor.

5. Unfasten the thermal reactor securing nuts, including those on the exhaust pipe flange.

NOTE: *The bottom nut is difficult to reach. Mazda makes a special wrench (part number 49 213 001) to remove it. If the wrench is unavailable, a flexible drive metric socket wrench may be substituted.*

6. Lift the thermal reactor away from the engine.

Installation of the thermal reactor is performed in the reverse order of removal.

ENGINE LUBRICATION
Rotary

A conventional pump, which is chain driven, circulates oil through the rotary engine. A full-flow filter is mounted on the top of the rear housing and an oil cooler is used to reduce the temperature of the engine oil.

An unusual feature of the rotary engine lubrication system is a metering oil pump which injects oil into the float chamber of the carburetor. Once there, it is mixed with the fuel which is to be burned, thus providing extra lubrication for the seals. The metering oil pump is designed to work only when the engine is working under a load.

Oil Pan
Removal and Installation

1. Raise the front of the car and support it with jackstands.

CAUTION: *Be sure that the car is supported securely.*

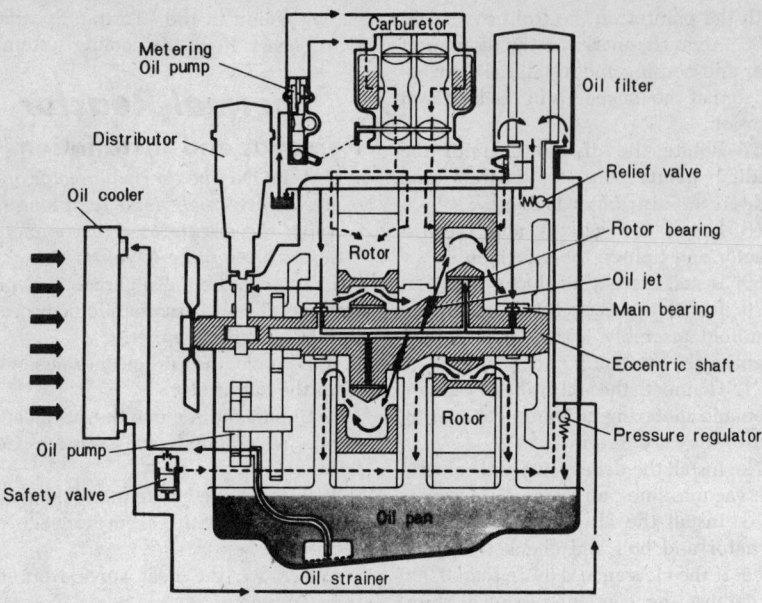

Lubrication circuits—1972-73 illustrated
(© Toyo Kogyo Co., Ltd.)

Labels: Metering Oil pump, Carburetor, Oil filter, Distributor, Relief valve, Rotor bearing, Oil cooler, Rotor, Oil jet, Main bearing, Eccentric shaft, Oil pump, Rotor, Pressure regulator, Safety valve, Oil pan, Oil strainer

2. Remove the drain plug and drain the engine oil.

3. Remove the nuts and bolts which secure the gravel shield and withdraw it from underneath the car.

4. Unfasten the retaining bolts and remove the oil pan with its gasket.

Oil pan installation is performed in the reverse order of removal. Coat both the oil pan flange and its mounting flange with sealer, prior to assembly.

Oil Pump

Removal and Installation

Oil pump removal and installation is contained in the engine overhaul section above. Perform only those steps needed to remove the oil pump.

Checking Clearances

1. Separate the halves of the oil pump housing.

2. Measure the clearance between the lobes of the rotors with a feeler gauge. The clearance should be 0.0004–0.0035 in. Replace both of the rotors if the clearance exceeds 0.006 in.

3. Check the clearance between the outer rotor and the housing with a feeler gauge. The clearance should be 0.008–0.010 in. If the clearance is greater than 0.012 in., replace both of the rotors.

4. Place a straightedge across the pump housing. Measure the gap between the straightedge and the housing with a feeler gauge. The gap should be 0.001–0.005 in. If the gap exceeds 0.012 in., replace the rotors or the pump housing.

Metering Oil Pump

Operation

A metering oil pump, mounted on the

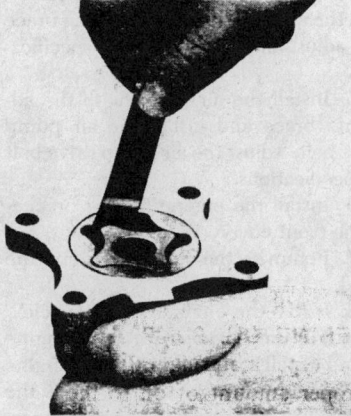

Measure the clearance between the rotors with a feeler gauge
(© Toyo Kogyo Co., Ltd.)

Measure the gap between the straightedge and the housing
(© Toyo Kogyo Co., Ltd.)

top of the engine, is used to provide additional lubrication to the engine when it is operating under a load. The pump provides oil to the carburetor, where it is mixed in the float chamber with the fuel to be burned.

The metering pump is a plunger type and is controlled by throttle opening. A cam arrangement, connected to the car-

buretor throttle lever, operates a plunger. The plunger, in turn, acts on a differential plunger, the stroke of which determines the amount of oil flow.

When the throttle opening is small, the amount of the plunger stroke is small; as the throttle opening increases, so does the amount of the plunger stroke.

Testing

1. At the carburetor, disconnect the oil lines which run from the metering oil pump to the carburetor.

2. Use a container which has a scale calibrated in cubic centimeters (cc) on its side to catch the pump discharge from the oil lines.

NOTE: *Such a container is available from a scientific equipment supply house.*

3. Run the engine at 2,000 rpm for six minutes.

4. At the end of this time, 2.4–2.9cc should be collected in the container. If not, adjust the pump as explained below.

Adjustments

Rotate the adjusting screw on the metering oil pump to obtain the proper oil flow. Clockwise rotation of the screw *increases* the flow; counterclockwise rotation *decreases* the oil flow.

If necessary, the oil discharge rate may be further adjusted by changing the position of the cam in the pump connecting rod. The shorter the rod throw, the more oil will be pumped. Adjust the throw by means of the three holes provided.

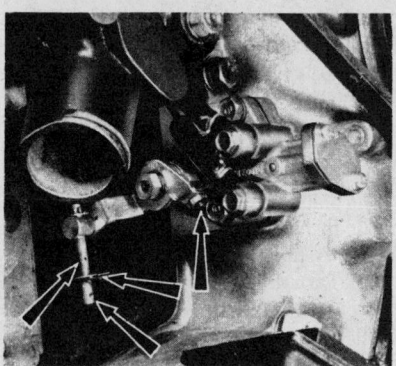

Arrow (right) indicates the metering oil pump adjusting screw. The 3 arrows (left) indicate the connecting rod adjusting holes (© Toyo Kogyo Co Ltd.)

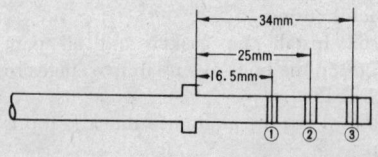

34mm
25mm
16.5mm
① ② ③

① : 248cc / 6,000rpm / Hr
② : 174cc / 6,000rpm / Hr
③ : 104cc / 6,000rpm / Hr

Connecting rod adjusting holes
(© Toyo Kogyo Co., Ltd.)

Oil Cooler

Removal and Installation

1. Raise the car and support it with jackstands.

CAUTION: *Be sure that the car is securely supported.*

2. Drain the engine oil.

3. Unfasten the screws which retain the gravel shield and remove the shield.

4. Unfasten the oil lines from the oil cooler.

5. Unfasten the nuts which secure the oil cooler to the radiator.

6. Remove the oil cooler.

Examine the oil cooler for signs of leakage. Solder any leaks found. Blow the cooler fins clean with compressed air.

Installation is performed in the reverse order of removal.

ENGINE COOLING

Rotary

Radiator

Removal and Installation

CAUTION: *Perform this operation when the engine has cooled completely.*

1. Drain the engine coolant into a large, clean container so that it may be reused.

2. Remove the nuts and bolts which attach the shroud to the radiator. Withdraw the shroud.

3. Remove the upper, lower, and expansion tank hoses from the radiator.

4. Unfasten the bolts which attach the radiator to its mounting bracket. Remove the oil cooler nuts and bolts.

5. Withdraw the radiator from the car.

Install the radiator in the reverse order of removal.

Water Pump

Removal and Installation

Passenger Cars

1. Drain the engine coolant into a large, clean container for reuse.

2. Remove the air cleaner assembly from the carburetor.

3. Loosen, but do not remove, the water pump pulley securing bolts.

4. Loosen the alternator adjusting link bolts and remove the drivebelt.

5. Unfasten the water pump pulley bolts and remove the pulley.

6. Unfasten the pump bolts from the front cover and withdraw the pump.

7. Separate the pump body from the casing, after removing the bolts.

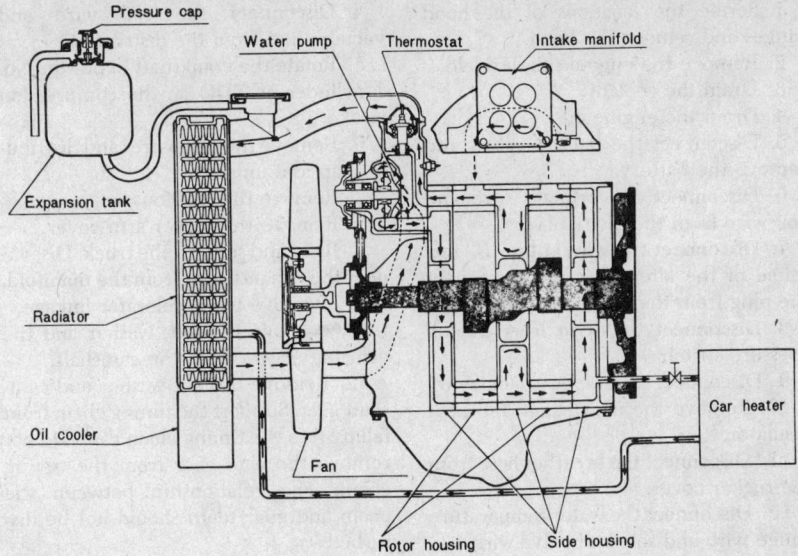

Cooling system
(© Toyo Kogyo Co., Ltd.)

Installation is performed in the reverse order of removal.

Rotary Pick-up

1. Drain the cooling system.

2. Remove the air cleaner.

3. Remove the bolts attaching the rear of the fan drive and remove the fan drive.

4. If necessary to disassemble the water pump, loosen the bolts attaching the water pump pulley to the water pump boss.

5. Remove the air pump and drive belt.

6. Remove the alternator and disconnect the drive belt.

7. If necessary, remove the water pump pulley and bolts.

8. Unbolt and remove the water pump.

9. Installation is the reverse of removal.

Thermostat

Removal and Installation

1. Drain the engine coolant into a large, clean container for reuse.

2. Remove the nuts which secure the thermostat housing to the water pump.

3. Lift out the thermostat.

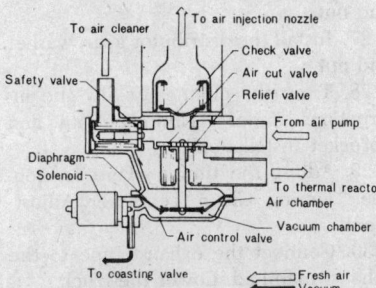

Thermostat installation and by-pass circuit
(© Toyo Kogyo Co., Ltd.)

Thermostat installation is performed in the reverse order of removal.

CAUTION: *The thermostat is equipped with a plunger which covers and uncovers a by-pass hole at its bottom. Because of this unusual construction, only the specified Mazda thermostat should be used for replacement. A standard thermostat will cause the engine to overheat.*

ENGINE MECHANICAL

Piston Engine

Mazda piston engines are 1586 cc (96.8 cu in.) and 1272 cc (77.6) single overhead camshaft, four-cylinder engines. Water cools the thin cast iron block and cast aluminum alloy cylinder head with multispherical type combustion chambers.

The camshaft bearing caps are machined with the cylinder head and are not interchangeable. The cylinder head bolts also retain the camshaft bearing caps and the rocker arm shaft supports.

Exhaust valves are free rotating to prevent uneven valve wear. Intake rocker arm shafts are a two-piece unit, while the exhaust rocker arm shafts are single piece units.

The timing chain is a dual cog type encircling the crankshaft and camshaft sprockets. The crankshaft sprocket also holds the rotor type oil pump drive chain.

Removal and Installation

The engine is removed through the engine compartment, leaving the transmission in place.

1. Scribe the locations of the hood hinges and remove the hood.

2. Remove the engine splash shield.

3. Drain the coolant.

4. Drain the engine oil.

5. Disconnect the battery cables and remove the battery.

6. Disconnect the primary wire and coil wire from the distributor.

7. Disconnect the wire at the "B" terminal of the alternator and disconnect the plug from the rear of the alternator.

8. Disconnect the wire from the oil pressure switch.

9. Disconnect the engine ground wire.

10. Remove the air cleaner and heat insulator.

11. Disconnect the breather hose from the rocker cover.

12. Disconnect the water temperature gauge wire and solenoid valve wire.

13. Disconnect the starter wires.

14. Remove the upper and lower radiator hoses.

15. Remove the bolts attaching the radiator cowling. The cowling can only be removed after the radiator has been removed.

16. Unbolt and remove the radiator and cowling (See below).

17. Disconnect the heater hoses from the intake manifold.

18. Disconnect the throttle cable from the carburetor and remove the throttle linkage from the rocker cover attaching point.

19. Disconnect the choke cable from the carburetor.

20. Disconnect the fuel ventilation hose from the oil separator.

21. Disconnect the fuel line at the carburetor and plug the fuel line.

22. Remove the starter.

23. Disconnect the exhaust pipe from the manifold.

24. Remove the clutch cover plate.

25. Support the transmission with a jack and remove the bolts attaching the engine to the transmission.

26. Unbolt the right and left engine mounts.

27. Attach a lifting sling to the engine and pull the engine forward until it clears the clutch shaft.

28. Lift the engine from the truck.

29. Installation is the reverse of removal. Be sure to check all fluid levels.

Cylinder Head

Removal and Installation

Be sure that the cylinder head is cold before removal. This will prevent warpage.

1. Drain the cooling system.

2. Scribe alignment marks around the hood hinges and remove the hood.

3. Remove the air cleaner.

4. Disconnect the coil wire and vacuum line from the distributor.

5. Rotate the crankshaft to put the No. 1 cylinder at TDC on the compression stroke.

6. Remove the plug wires and distributor cap as a unit.

7. Remove the distributor.

8. Remove the rocker arm cover.

9. Raise and support the truck. Disconnect the exhaust pipe from the manifold.

10. Remove the accelerator linkage.

11. Remove the nut, washer and the distributor gear from the camshaft.

12. Remove the nut, washer, and camshaft gear. Support the timing chain from falling into the timing chain case. Do not remove the cam gear from the timing chain. The relationship between the chain and gear teeth should not be disturbed.

13. Remove the cylinder head bolts and cylinder head-to-front cover bolt.

14. Remove the rocker arm assembly.

15. Remove the camshaft and camshaft gear.

16. Lift off the cylinder head.

17. Remove all tension from the timing chain.

To install the cylinder head:

18. Clean the rocker cover gasket surface at the head and the cover. Clean the head gasket surface at the head and the block. Clean the water pump gasket surface at the head gasket surface and the front cover.

19. Check the cylinder head flatness with a straightedge and feeler blades. It should not exceed 0.003 in. in any six in. span or 0.006 in. overall. If necessary, the cylinder head can be milled, not to exceed 0.008 in.

20. Clean the cylinder head bolt holes of oil and dirt.

21. Position a new head gasket on the cylinder block.

22. Install the cylinder head on the block using the guides at either end of the block.

23. Install the camshaft on the head and camshaft gear.

24. Install the rocker arm assembly.

25. Install the head bolts. Torque the bolts to specifications, in the sequence illustrated at the front of this section.

26. Install the camshaft gear washer and nut.

27. Install the distributor gear, washer and nut.

28. Time the engine. Follow the instructions under "Timing Chain and Sprocket Installation."

29. Adjust the timing chain tension. See "Timing Chain Tensioner Adjustment".

30. Connect the exhaust pipe to the exhaust manifold. Lower the truck.

31. Install the distributor, distributor cap and plug wires.

32. Install the lower intake bracket bolt.

33. Install the accelerator linkage.

34. Connect the vacuum line and coil wire.

35. Adjust the valve clearance cold.

36. Install the rocker arm cover. Fill the cooling system.

37. Run the engine until normal operating temperature is reached, and check for leaks. Adjust the valve clearance hot.

38. Adjust the carburetor and ignition timing. Install the air cleaner and install the hood.

Valve Guide Removal and Installation

Before attempting this, consult the "Engine Rebuilding" section for general procedures that will apply.

1. Remove the cylinder head.

2. Remove the deposits from the combustion chambers with a stiff wire brush and scraper before removing the valves. Do not scratch the cylinder head surface.

3. Compress the valve springs with a valve spring compressor. Remove the valve spring retainer locks and release the springs.

4. Keep the exhaust and intake valve retainers separate. They should be reassembled to the valve from which they were removed.

5. Remove the spring retainer, springs and valve.

6. Remove the valve stem seals. Identify all parts so that they can be reinstalled in their original locations.

7. Drive out the valve guides.

8. Check the cylinder head flatness as described under "Cylinder Head Removal and Installation".

Assemble the cylinder head using new parts where applicable:

a. Lubricate all valves, valve stems, and valve guides with heavy-duty oil (SE). The valve tips should be lubricated with Lubriplate or the equivalent. Apply this before installation.

b. Press new valve guides into each bore until the ring on the guide touches the cylinder head. Note that the intake and exhaust valve guides are different.

c. Install new valve seals on the valve guides.

d. Install each valve into the valve from which it was removed or fitted.

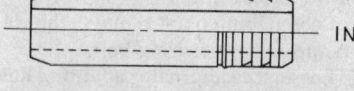

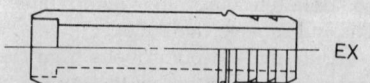

Intake (IN) and exhaust (EX) valve guides
(© Toyo Kogyo Co., Ltd.)

e. Install the valve springs over the valve. Install the spring retainer.

f. Compress the springs and install the retainer locks. Be sure that the exhaust and intake locks are assembled to the correct valves.

9. Install the cylinder head. See "Cylinder Head Installation". Adjust the valves (hot) and set the timing and carburetor.

Rocker Shafts

Removal and Installation

This operation should only be performed on a cold engine; the bolts which hold the rocker shafts in place also hold the cylinder head to the block.

1. Raise the hood and cover the fenders.

2. Disconnect the choke cable.

3. If equipped, disconnect the air by-pass valve cable.

4. Disconnect the spark plug wires. Remove the wires from the spark wire guides on the rocker covers and position them out of the way.

5. Remove the rocker cover and discard the gasket.

6. Remove the rocker arm shaft attaching bolts evenly and remove the rocker arm shafts.

To install the rocker shafts:

a. Install the rocker arm assemblies on the cylinder head. Install the balls on each rocker arm as shown. Temporarily tighten the cylinder head bolts to specifications and offset each rocker arm support 0.04 in. from the valve stem center. Torque the bolts to specifications.

7. Adjust the valves cold.

8. Clean the mating surfaces of the cylinder head and rocker cover.

9. Install the rocker cover with a new gasket.

10. Install the spark plug wires on the plugs. Place the wires in the clips on the rocker cover. Connect the choke and air by-pass valve cable.

11. Start the engine and check for leaks.

12. Allow the engine to reach operating temperature, torque the head bolts to specifications and adjust the valves hot.

Intake Manifold

Removal and Installation

1. Drain the cooling system.

2. Remove the air cleaner.

3. Remove the accelerator linkage.

4. Disconnect the choke cable and fuel line. Plug the fuel line.

5. Disconnect the PCV valve hose.

6. Disconnect the heater return hose and by-pass hose.

7. Remove the intake manifold-to-cylinder head attaching nuts.

8. Remove the manifold and carburetor as an assembly.

9. Installation is the reverse of removal.

Exhaust Manifold

Removal and Installation

1. Raise and support the truck.

2. Remove the two attaching nuts from the exhaust pipe at the manifold.

3. Remove the manifold attaching nuts.

4. Remove the manifold.

5. Installation is the reverse of removal.

Front Cover

Removal and Installation

1. Scribe alignment marks on the hood hinges and remove the hood.

2. Drain the cooling system.

3. Disconnect the upper and lower radiator hoses. Remove the radiator.

4. Remove the accessory drive belts.

5. Remove the crankshaft pulley and the water pump.

6. Remove the cylinder head-to-front cover bolt.

7. Raise and support the truck.

8. Remove the engine skid plate.

9. Disconnect the emission line from the oil pan. Drain the oil from the engine.

10. Remove the oil pan.

11. Remove the alternator and bracket and lay the alternator aside.

12. Remove the steel tube from the front of the engine.

13. Unbolt and remove the front cover.

14. Installation is the reverse of removal.

Front Cover Oil Seal

Removal and Installation

The front cover oil seal can be removed and a new one installed without removing the front cover.

1. Scribe alignment marks on the hood hinges and remove the hood.

2. Drain the cooling system.

3. Disconnect the upper and lower radiator hoses and remove the radiator.

4. Remove the drive belt(s).

5. Remove the crankshaft pulley.

6. Pry the front oil seal from the front cover.

To install a new oil seal:

7. Clean the pulley and seal area.

8. Press a new front seal into position (flush).

9. Install the crankshaft pulley and torque the bolt to specifications.

10. Install the drive belt(s) and adjust the tension.

11. Install the radiator and connect the upper and lower hoses. Fill the cooling system.

12. Start the engine and check for leaks.

13. Install the hood.

Timing Chain and Tensioner

Removal and Installation

1. Remove the cylinder head and front cover. It is not necessary that the intake and exhaust manifolds be removed from the head.

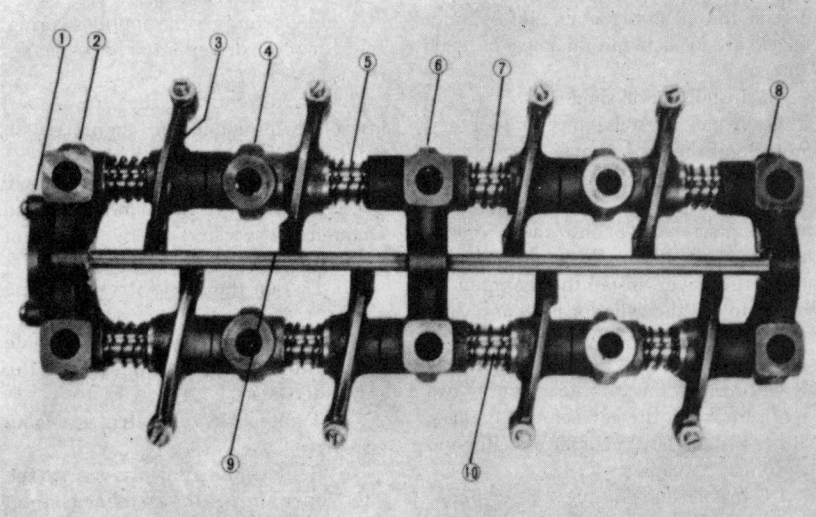

Rocker arm assembly—piston engine (© Toyo Kogyo Co. Ltd.)

1. Thrust plate
2. Front bearing cap
3. Rocker arm (Exhaust)
4. Support
5. Rocker arm shaft (Exhaust)
6. Center bearing cap
7. Spring
8. Rear bearing cap
9. Oil pipe
10. Rocker arm shaft (Intake)

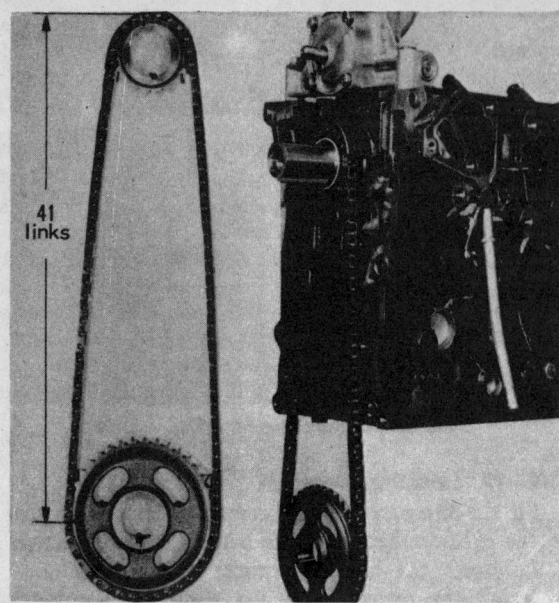

Installing the timing chain—piston engine (© Toyo Kogyo Co. Ltd.)

41 links

2. Remove the oil pump and chain.

3. Remove the timing chain tensioner.

4. Loosen the timing chain guide strip screws.

5. Remove the oil slinger.

6. Remove the oil pump gear and chain as an assembly.

7. Remove the timing chain, crankshaft gear and camshaft gears from the engine.

To install the timing chain, timing gears and tensioner:

8. Position the crankshaft gear in the timing chain.

9. Position the oil pump chain and gear on the crankshaft and oil pump. Check the oil pump drive chain slack. It should be 0.15 in. Adjusting shims (between the oil pump body and cylinder block) are available in thickness of 0.006 in.

10. Install the oil slinger.

11. Install the oil pump washer and nut. Bend the washer over the nut.

12. Install the timing chain tensioner. Fully compress the snubber spring and wedge a screwdriver into the tensioner release mechanism. Without removing the screwdriver, install the tensioner.

13. Install the cylinder head and camshaft. Be sure that the valve timing is as illustrated. It must be exact. You may have to move the cam gear one or two teeth to obtain the correct alignment.

14. Install the rocker arm shafts and cam bearing caps.

15. Install and torque the cylinder head bolts.

16. Adjust the timing chain tension. Press in on the chain guide strip. Tighten the guide strip attaching screws. Remove the screwdriver from the tensioner, allowing the snubber to take up the chain slack.

17. Replace the front cover.

18. Adjust the valve clearance cold. Run the engine. Torque the cylinder head bolts and adjust the valve clearance hot.

Timing Chain Tensioner

Removal and Installation

Front Cover Installed

1. Remove the water pump.

2. Remove the tensioner cover.

3. Remove the attaching bolts from the tensioner. Remove the tensioner.

To install the tensioner:

4. Fully compress the snubber spring. Insert a screwdriver into the tensioner release mechanism.

5. Without removing the screwdriver, insert the tensioner and align the bolt holes. Install and torque the bolts.

6. Adjust the chain tension as follows:

   a. Remove the two blind plugs and aluminum washers from the front cover.

   b. Loosen the guide strip attaching screws.

   c. Press the top of the chain guide strip through the adjusting hole in the cylinder head.

   d. Tighten the guide strip attaching screws.

   e. Remove the screwdriver from the tensioner and let the snubber take up the slack in the chain.

   f. Install the blind plugs and aluminum washers.

   g. Install the tensioner cover and gasket.

   h. Install a new gasket and water pump. Install the crankshaft pulley and

drive belt and adjust the tension. Check the cooling system level.

Timing Chain Tensioner Adjustment

Perform Steps 1 and 4 through 6 of the above procedure.

Camshaft

Removal and Installation

Perform this operation on a cold engine only.

1. Scribe alignment marks on the hood hinges and remove the hood.

2. Remove the water pump.

3. Disconnect the coil wire and vacuum line from the distributor.

4. Rotate the crankshaft to place the No. 1 cylinder on TDC of the compression stroke. This can be determined by removing the spark plug and feeling compression with your thumb. When compression is felt, rotate the crankshaft until the pointer aligns with the TDC mark on the pulley.

5. Remove the plug wires and distributor cap. Remove the distributor.

6. Remove the valve cover.

7. Release the tension on the timing chain.

8. Remove the cylinder head bolts. Only do this on a *cold* engine.

9. Remove the rocker arm assembly.

10. Remove the nut, washer and distributor gear from the camshaft.

11. Remove the nut and washer holding the camshaft gear.

12. Remove the camshaft. Do not remove the camshaft gear from the timing chain. Be sure that the gear teeth and chain relationship is not disturbed. Wire the chain and cam gear to a place so that they will not fall into the front cover.

To install the camshaft:

13. Clean all the gasket surfaces.

14. Clean the cylinder head bolt holes.

15. Install the camshaft on the head and install the camshaft gear.

16. Check the valve timing.

17. Install the rocker arm assembly.

18. Install and torque the head bolts.

19. Install the cam gear washer and nut.

20. Install the distributor gear, washer and nut.

21. Adjust the timing chain tension.

22. Check the camshaft end-play. It should be 0.001–0.007 in. If it exceeds 0.008 in., replace the thrust plate with a new one.

23. Install the distributor, distributor cap and plug wires.

24. Connect the vacuum line and coil wire.

25. Adjust the valve clearance cold. Install the valve cover and fill the cooling system.

26. Run the engine and check for

leaks. When normal operating temperature is reached, adjust the valve clearance hot.

27. Adjust the carburetor and ignition timing.

28. Install the air cleaner and hood.

Piston and Connecting Rod Positioning

Removal and Installation

Refer to the "Engine Rebuilding" section for general engine service.

ENGINE LUBRICATION

Piston Engine

Oil Pan

Removal and Installation

1. Raise and support the vehicle.
2. Remove the engine skid plate.
3. Drain the engine oil.
4. Remove the clutch release cylinder attaching nuts. Let the cylinder hang.
5. Remove the engine rear brace attaching bolts and loosen the bolts on the left-side.
6. Disconnect the emission line from the oil pan.
7. Remove the oil pan nuts and bolts and let the oil pan rest on the crossmember.
8. Remove the oil pump pickup tube from the pump.
9. Remove the oil pan.
10. Installation is the reverse of removal.

Rear Main Oil Seal

Replacement

If the rear main oil seal is being replaced independently of any other parts, it can be done with the engine in place. If the rear main oil seal and the rear main bearing are being replaced, together, the engine must be removed from the vehicle.

1. Remove the transmission.
2. Remove the clutch disc, pressure plate and flywheel.
3. Using an awl, punch two holes in the crankshaft rear oil seal. They should be punched on opposite sides of the crankshaft, just above the bearing cap-to-cylinder block split line.
4. Install a sheet metal screw in each hole. Pry against both screws at the same time to remove the oil seal. Do not scratch the oil seal surface on the crankshaft.

The "F" marks (arrow) face the front of the engine (© Toyo Kogyo Co., Ltd.)

5. Clean the oil recess in the cylinder block and bearing cap. Clean the oil seal surface on the crankshaft.
6. Coat the oil seal surfaces with oil. Coat the oil surface and the seal surface on the crankshaft with Lubriplate. Install the new oil seal and make sure that it is not cocked. Be sure that the seal surface was not damaged.
7. Install the flywheel. Coat the threads of the flywheel attaching bolts with oil-resistant sealer. Torque the bolts to specifications in sequence across from each other.
8. Install the clutch, pressure plate and transmission.

Oil Pump

Checking Oil Pump

1. Measure the clearance between the lobes of the rotors with a feeler gauge. If the clearance exceeds 0.010 in., replace both rotors.
2. Check the clearance between the outer rotor and the pump body with a feeler gauge. Clearance should be 0.006-0.010 in. If it exceeds 0.012 in., replace the pump.
3. Place a straight-edge across the pump body and measure the clearance between the rotor and the straight edge

1. Oil strainer
2. O-ring
3. Adjusting shim
4. Body
5. Adjusting shim
6. O-ring
7. Outer rotor
8. Inner rotor
9. Pin
10. Key
11. Cover
12. Shaft
13. Plunger
14. Spring
15. Spring seat
16. Cotter pin

with a feeler gauge. Then, place a straight-edge across the pump cover and measure the clearance between the straight-edge and the cover. The combined clearances is the rotor end float. If it is 0.006 in. or more, correct it by grinding the cover. End float should be 0.002–0.004 in.

Removal and Installation

1. Remove the oil pan.
2. Remove the oil pump gear attaching nut.
3. Remove the bolts attaching the oil pump to the block. Loosen the gear on the pump.
4. Remove the oil pump and gear. To install the oil pump:
5. Install the oil pump gear in the chain.
6. Prime the oil pump and install it on the gear and cylinder block. Install the bolts and torque them to specifications.
7. Install the washer, gear and nut. Bend the locktab on the washer.
8. Install the oil pan. Fill the engine with oil. Start the engine and check for oil pressure. Check for leaks.

Engine Cooling— Piston Engine

The completely sealed cooling system consists of a radiator with pressure cap, centrifugal water pump, thermostat and a fan.

Radiator

Removal and Installation

1. Drain the cooling system.
2. If equipped, remove the fan shroud.
3. Remove the fan. On California models, remove the fan clutch.

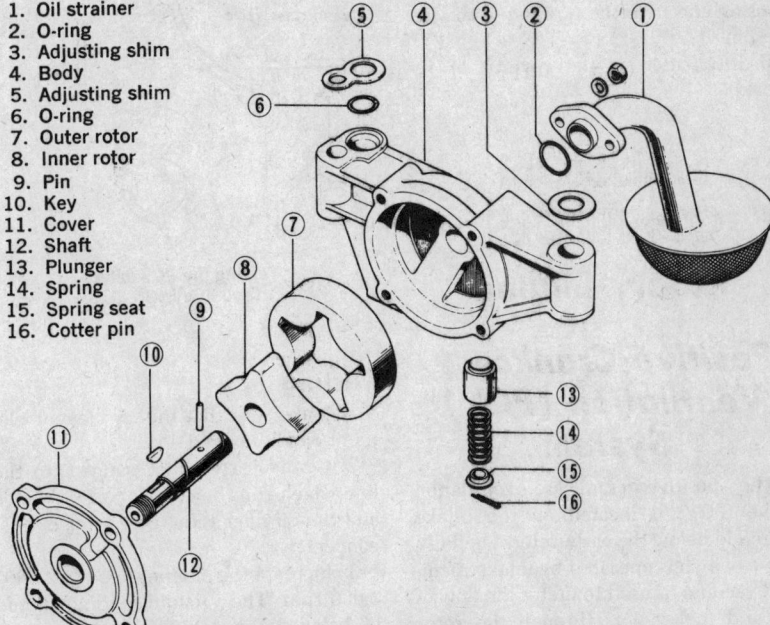

Oil pump components—piston engine (© Toyo Kogyo Co. Ltd.)

4. Disconnect the upper and lower radiator hoses.

5. Unbolt and remove the radiator.

6. Installation is the reverse of removal.

Water Pump

Removal and Installation

1. Scribe alignment marks on the hood hinges and remove the hood.

2. Drain the cooling system.

3. Remove the lower hose from the water pump.

4. Disconnect the upper radiator hose from the engine and the lower radiator hose at the radiator.

5. Remove the radiator.

6. Remove the drive belts.

7. Remove the fan and pulley. Remove the crankshaft pulley.

8. Unbolt and remove the water pump.

9. Installation is the reverse of removal.

Thermostat

Removal and Installation

1. Drain enough coolant to bring the coolant level down below the thermostat housing. The thermostat housing is located on the left front side of the cylinder block. Disconnect the temperature sending unit wire.

2. Remove the coolant outlet elbow. If so equipped, position the vacuum control valve out of the way. The vacuum control valve is not used on California cars.

3. Disconnect the coolant by-pass hose from the thermostat housing.

4. Remove the thermostat and housing from the engine.

5. Remove the thermostat from the housing and note the position of the jiggle pin.

6. Installation is the reverse of removal.

EMISSION CONTROLS
Rotary Engine

Positive Crankcase Ventilation (PCV) System

The positive crankcase ventilation valve (PCV) is located on the intake manifold below the carburetor. The PCV valve, which is operated by intake manifold vacuum, is used to meter the flow of air and fuel vapors through the rotor housing.

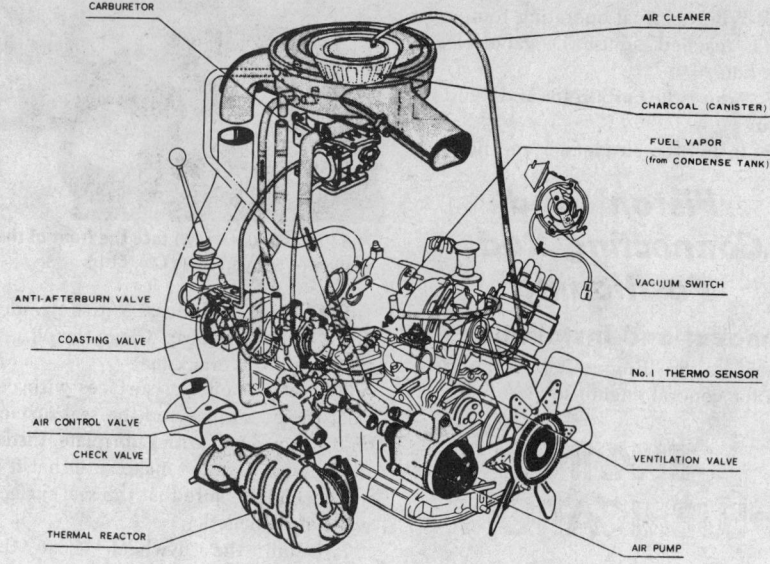

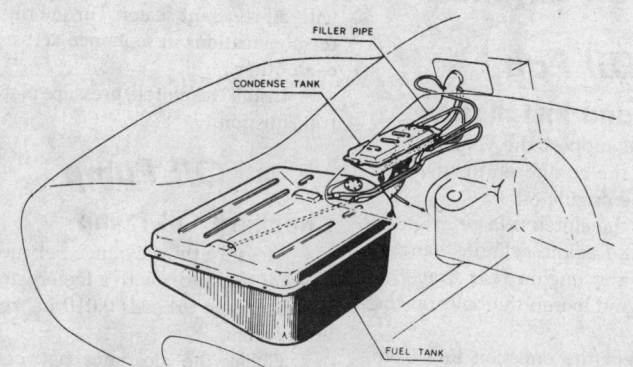

Components of the emission control system—1972 (other years are similar)
(© Toyo Kogyo Co., Ltd.)

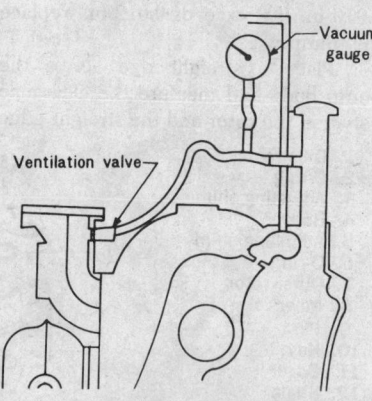

Testing the PCV valve
(© Toyo Kogyo Co., Ltd.)

Testing

1. Make sure that the air cleaner element is not clogged.

2. Connect a vacuum gauge into the line which runs between the PCV valve and the oil filler tube, by means of a T-connector.

3. Increase the engine speed to 2,500–3,000 rpm. The vacuum reading should be below 2.4 in. Hg. If it is not, replace the PCV valve.

PCV Valve Removal and Installation—1972–74

1. Remove the air cleaner assembly.

2. Remove the fuel return valve or the deceleration valve from the carburetor.

NOTE: *On RX–4 and Rotary Pickup models it may be necessary to remove the starter motor.*

3. Unfasten the distributor vacuum lines at the carburetor.

4. Disconnect the hose from the PCV valve.

5. Use a flexible drive metric socket wrench to remove the valve from the intake manifold.

NOTE: *If a flexible drive metric socket wrench is not available, the intake manifold must be removed in order to gain access to the PCV valve.*

Installation of a new PCV valve is performed in the reverse order of removal.

1975–77

1. Remove the air cleaner.

2. Disconnect the hose at the PCV valve.

3. Unscrew the valve from the manifold.

4. Installation is reverse of removal.

Air Injection System

The air injection system used on the Mazda rotary engine differs from one used on a conventional piston engine in two respects:

1. Air is supplied not only to burn the gases in the exhaust ports, it is also used to cool the thermal reactor.

2. A three-way "air control valve" is used in place of the conventional anti-backfire and diverter valves. It contains an air cut-out valve, a relief valve, and a safety valve.

Air is supplied to the system by a normal vane-type air pump. The air flows from the pump to the air control valve where it is routed to the air injection nozzles, to cool the thermal reactor or, in case of a system malfunction, to the air cleaner. A check valve, located beneath the air control valve seat, prevents the back-flow of hot exhaust gases into the air injection system, in case of loss of air pressure.

Air injection nozzles are used to feed air into the exhaust ports, just as in a conventional piston engine.

Component Testing

Air Pump

1. Check the air pump drive belt tension by applying 22 lbs of pressure halfway between the water pump and air pump pulleys. The belt should deflect 0.-28–0.35 in. Adjust the belt, if necessary, or replace it if it is cracked or worn.

2. Turn the pump by hand. If it has siezed, the drive belt will slip producing noise.

NOTE: *Disregard any chirping, squealing, or rolling sounds coming from inside of the pump; these are normal when it is being turned by hand.*

3. Check the hoses and connections for leaks. Hissing or a blast of air is indicative of a leak. Soapy water, applied around the area in question, is a good method for detecting leaks.

4. Connect a pressure gauge between the air pump and the air control valve with a T-fitting.

5. Plug the other hose connections (outlets) on the air control valve.

CAUTION: *Be careful not to touch the thermal reactor; severe burns will result.*

6. With the engine at normal idle speed, the pressure gauge should read 0.-93–0.75 psi for 1972–73; 0.48–0.68 psi for 1974–75 and more than 1.64 psi for 1976–77. Replace the air pump if it is less than this.

7. If the air pump is not defective, leave the pressure gauge connected but unplug the two connections at the air control valve and proceed with the next test.

Air Injection System Diagnosis Chart

Problem	Cause	Cure
1. Noisy drive belt	1a. Loose belt	1a. Tighten belt
	1b. Seized pump	1b. Replace
2. Noisy pump	2a. Leaking hose	2a. Trace and fix leak
	2b. Loose hose	2b. Tighten hose clamp
	2c. Hose contacting other parts	2c. Reposition hose
	2d. Air control or check valve failure	2d. Replace
	2e. Pump mounting loose	2e. Tighten securing bolts
	2g. Defective pump	2g. Replace
3. No air supply	3a. Loose belt	3a. Tighten belt
	3b. Leak in hose or at fitting	3b. Trace and fix leak
	3c. Defective air control valve	3c. Replace
	3d. Defective check valve	3d. Replace
	3e. Defective pump	3e. Replace
4. Exhaust backfire	4a. Vacuum or air leaks	4a. Trace and fix leak
	4b. Defective air control valve	4b. Replace
	4c. Sticking choke	4c. Service choke
	4d. Choke setting rich	4d. Adjust choke

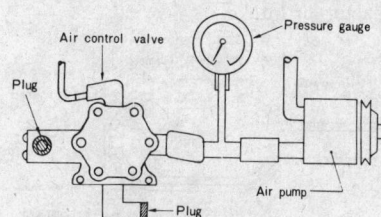

Testing the air pump
(© Toyo Kogyo Co., Ltd.)

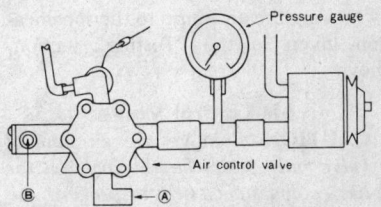

Testing the air control valve
(© Toyo Kogyo Co., Ltd.)

Air Control Valve

CAUTION: *When testing the air control valve, avoid touching the thermal reactor as severe burns will result.*

1. Test the air control valve solenoid as follows:

a. Turn the ignition switch off and on. A click should be heard coming from the solenoid. If no sound is audible, check the solenoid wiring.

b. If no defect is found in the solenoid wiring, connect the solenoid directly to the car's battery. If the solenoid still does not click, it is defective and must be replaced. If the solenoid is functioning, then check the components of the air flow control system, below.

2. Start the engine and run it at idle speed. The pressure gauge should read 0.37–0.75 psi. No air should leak from the two outlets which were unplugged.

3. Increase the engine speed to 3,500 rpm (3,000—automatic transmission). The pressure gauge should now read 2.-0–2.8 psi(1.2–2.8 psi—1974–77) and the two outlets still should not be leaking air.

4. Return the engine to idle.

5. Disconnect the solenoid wiring. Air should now flow from the outlet marked "A" but not from the outlet marked "B". The pressure gauge reading should remain the same as in step 2.

6. Reconnect the solenoid.

7. If the relief valve is faulty, air sent from the air pump will flow into the cooling passages of the thermal reactor when the engine is at idle speed.

8. If the safety valve is faulty, air will flow into the air cleaner when the engine is idling.

9. Replace the air control valve if it fails to pass any one of the above tests. Remember to disconnect the pressure gauge.

Check Valve 1972–74

1. Remove the check valve as detailed below.

2. Depress the valve plate to see if it will seat properly.

3. Measure the free length of the valve spring; it should be 1.22 in.

4. Measure the installed length of the spring; it should be 0.68 in.

NOTE: *The free length of the check valve spring should be 0.75 in. on models with automatic transmissions.*

Replace the check valve if it is not up to specifications.

Check Valve 1975–77

1. Run engine at operating temperature.

2. Disconnect air hose at air control valve.

3. Run engine at 1500 rpm. No exhaust leakage should be felt at the air inlet fitting of the air control valve.

Component Removal and Installation

Air Pump

1. Remove the air cleaner assembly from the carburetor.
2. Loosen, but do not remove, the adjusting link bolt.
3. Push the pump toward the engine to slacken belt tension and remove the drive belt.
4. Disconnect the air supply hoses from the pump.
5. Unfasten the pump securing bolts and remove the pump.

CAUTION: *Do not pry on the air pump housing during removal and do not clamp the housing in a vise once the pump has been removed. Any type of heavy pressure applied to the housing will cause it to distort.*

Installation is performed in the reverse order of removal. Adjust the belt tension by moving the air pump to the specification given in the "Testing" section, above.

Air Control Valve

CAUTION: *Remove the air control valve only after the thermal reactor has cooled sufficiently to prevent the danger of a serious burn.*

1. Remove the air cleaner assembly.
2. Unfasten the leads from the air control valve solenoid.
3. Disconnect the air hoses from the valve.
4. Loosen the screws which secure the air control valve and remove the valve.

Valve installation is performed in the reverse order of removal.

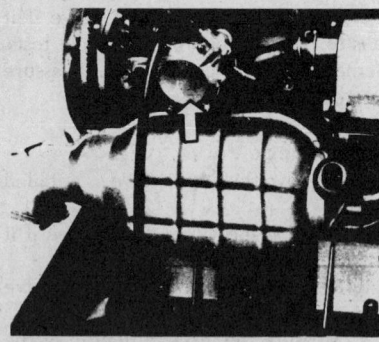

Arrow indicates position of the air control valve
(© Toyo Kogyo Co., Ltd.)

Check Valve

1. Perform the air control valve removal procedure, detailed above. Be sure to pay attention to the CAUTION.
2. Remove the check valve seat.
3. Withdraw the valve plate and spring.

Install the check valve in the reverse order of removal.

Air Injection Nozzle

1. Remove the gravel shield from underneath the car.

2. Perform the oil pan removal procedure, as detailed in "Engine Lubrication", above.
3. Unbolt the air injection nozzles from both of the rotor housings.

Nozzle installation is performed in the reverse order of removal.

Thermal Reactor

A thermal reactor is used in place of a conventional exhaust manifold. It is used to oxidize unburned hydrocarbons and carbon monoxide before they can be released into the atmosphere.

If the engine speed exceeds 4,000 rpm, or if the car is decelerating, the air control valve diverts air into passages in the thermal reactor housing in order to cool the reactor.

A one-way valve prevents hot exhaust gases from flowing back into the air injection system. The valve is located at the reactor air intake.

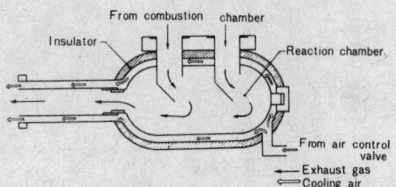

Thermal reactor cooling circuit
(© Toyo Kogyo Co., Ltd.)

Inspection

CAUTION: *Perform thermal reactor inspection only after the reactor has cooled sufficiently to prevent severe burns.*

1. Examine the reactor housing for cracks or other signs of damage.
2. Remove the air supply hose from the one-way valve. Insert a screwdriver into the valve and test the butterfly for smooth operation. Replace the valve if necessary.
3. If the valve is functioning properly, connect the hose to it again.

NOTE: *Remember to check the components of the air injection system which are related to the thermal reactor.*

Removal and Installation

Thermal reactor removal and installation procedures are given in the "Engine Mechanical" section, above.

Air Flow Control System

1972–73

The air flow control system for 1972–73 uses two thermosensors and control boxes, a thermo detector, and vacuum switch. A choke control switch is added as well.

The additional control box, choke

switch, and thermosensor are used to retard the timing of the leading distributor 10° when the engine is cold. The timing is retarded by means of an additional set of points in the leading distributor, which has no vacuum advance.

1974–77

Starting in 1974, the No. 2 control box and related components were dropped.

The functions of the leading and trailing distributor were combined into one unit which has four terminals and two sets of points.

The control box and thermodetector were moved: the control box is now located beneath the dash, next to the fuse box, and the thermodetector is behind the radiator grille.

Component Testing

No. 1 Thermosensor

NOTE: *Begin this test procedure with the engine cold.*

1. Remove the air cleaner.
2. Examine the No. 1 thermosensor, which is located next to the thermostat housing, for leakage around the boot and for signs of wax leakage.
3. Disconnect the multiconnector from the thermosensor and place the prods of an ohmmeter on the thermosensor terminals.

The ohmmeter should read over 7 k-ohms with the engine cold and less than 2.3 k-ohms after the engine has been warmed up.

4. Replace the thermosensor with a new one, if the reading on the ohmmeter is not within specifications.
5. If the No. 1 thermosensor is functioning properly, proceed with the appropriate test for the thermodetector below.

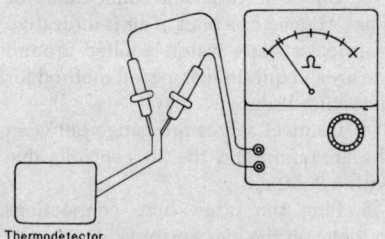

Testing the thermodetector
(© Toyo Kogyo Co., Ltd.)

Thermodetector

1. Unfasten the thermodetector connections.
2. Connect the test prods of an ohmmeter to the leads coming out of the thermodetector.
3. If the ohmmeter reading is below 200 k-ohms, the thermodetector is functioning satisfactorily.
4. Replace the thermodetector if it is defective and proceed with the vacuum switch if it is not.

Use the following chart to determine the correct ohmmeter reading for the ambient temperature at the time of the test.

Thermodetector Resistance Specifications

Ambient Temperature (°F)	Resistance (k-ohms ± 5%)
−4	10.0
+32	3.0
+68	1.2
+105	0.5

Vacuum Switch—1972–73 Manual Transmission Only

NOTE: *The vacuum switch is located in the trailing distributor on 1972–73 models.*

1. Remove the cap from the distributor that contains the vacuum switch.

2. Disconnect the vacuum lines from the same distributor's vacuum advance unit. Connect a vacuum gauge in its place, by means of a T-fitting.

3. Suck on the free end of the hose coming from the vacuum gauge. When the vacuum gauge reading is about 7 in. Hg, the vacuum switch should be heard to click from ON to OFF.

4. Reduce the vacuum level to 3–5 in. Hg, the vacuum switch should be heard to click ON.

5. Replace the distributor cap and remove the vacuum switch connector from the No. 1 thermosensor.

6. Connect a timing light to the *trailing* distributor, regardless of which distributor contains the vacuum switch.

7. The timing light should go off, i.e., the switch should go off, at 1,900 ± 300 rpm.

8. Check all of the vacuum lines and connections for leaks. If none are found, and the vacuum switch is not working properly, replace it. If the vacuum switch is not defective, proceed with the test for the No. 1 control box.

NOTE: *If the control box is to be tested, leave the timing light connected to the trailing distributor.*

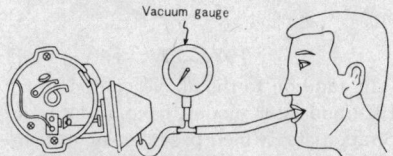

Testing the vacuum switch
(© Toyo Kogyo Co., Ltd.)

No. 1 Control Box

NOTE: *If all of the other components of the air flow control system are functioning properly and the system wiring*

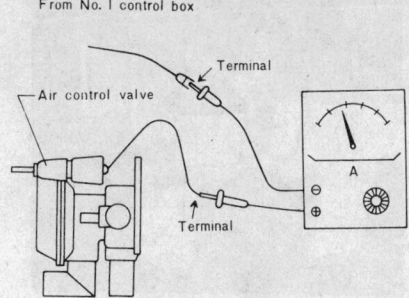

Testing the No. 1 control box
(© Toyo Kogyo Co., Ltd.)

and vacuum lines are in good condition, then the fault probably lies in the No. 1 control box. Perform the following tests to verify this.

1. Disconnect the No. 1 thermosensor. On 1973 models, disconnect the vacuum switch (manual transmission) and the idle switch multiconnectors (1973–77).

2. Start the engine and run it to the speeds specified below. The timing light should come on in these speed ranges:

12A Engine manual—3,800–4,200 rpm

12A Engine automatic—4,600–5,200 rpm

13B Engine manual—3,600–4,400 rpm

13B Engine automatic—4,320–5,280 rpm

NOTE: *These speeds should be held for an instant only.*

3. Connect an ammeter to the air control valve solenoid leads and to ground.

a. Current should flow when the engine speed is between 900–4,000±200 rpm (manual) or 750–5,200 (automatic) (1971–73 models).

b. Current flow should cease above 4,300–5,200 rpm (manual) or 3,600–4,400 rpm (automatic).

4. Short together the pins of the No. 1 thermosensor multiconnector with a jumper wire. Connect the timing light to the trailing distributor, if it is not already in place.

a. The timing light should go on when the engine is below 4,200 rpm (manual) or below 5,200 rpm (automatic).

b. On automatic transmission equipped models, connect an ammeter to the air control valve solenoid. Current should flow to the solenoid when the engine speed is below 3,400±200 rpm and should cease flowing above this speed.

5. Remove the jumper wire from the multiconnector and reconnect the No. 1 thermosensor. Reconnect the vacuum switch if it was disconnected.

6. Connect the prods of the ammeter to the coasting valve solenoid terminals.

NOTE: *For a further description of coasting valve operation, see "Deceleration Control Systems", below.*

7. No current should flow to the sole-

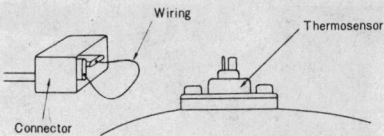

Short the pins of the No. 1 thermosensor multiconnector with a jumper wire
(© Toyo Kogyo Co., Ltd.)

noid with the engine at idle. Increase the engine speed; current should begin flowing between 1,250 and 1,550 rpm. Decrease engine speed; current should cease flowing between 1,300 and 1,100 rpm (1,400 rpm—automatic transmission).

If the No. 1 control box proves to be defective, replace it. Remember to disconnect all of the test equipment and reconnect the system components when the tests are completed.

No. 2 Thermosensor—1972–73 Manual

NOTE: *Begin this test with the engine cold.*

1. Check the terminal of the No. 2 thermosensor, which protrudes from the oil pan, for breakage.

2. Connect one ohmmeter prod to the terminal of the thermosensor and ground the other prod.

3. Take two ohmmeter readings:

a. With the air and water temperature below 86°F, the ohmmeter should register less than 5 k-ohms.

b. With the engine warmed up (water temperature above 158°F) the ohmmeter should register under 2 k-ohms.

If the thermosensor is defective, replace it; if not go on to the next test.

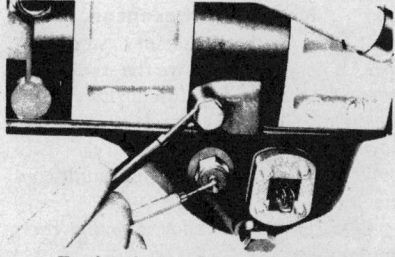

Testing the No. 2 thermosensor
(© Toyo Kogyo Co., Ltd.)

No. 2 Control Box—1972–73

1. Disconnect both of the thermosensors.

NOTE: *Only manual transmission equipped models have a No. 2 thermosensor.*

2. Unfasten the trailing vacuum switch connection (manual transmission only).

3. Connect a timing light to the leading distributor.

4. Start the engine and increase its speed, without placing a load on it, to 2,000–2,500 rpm.

5. Pull the choke switch, which is located underneath the dashboard, out

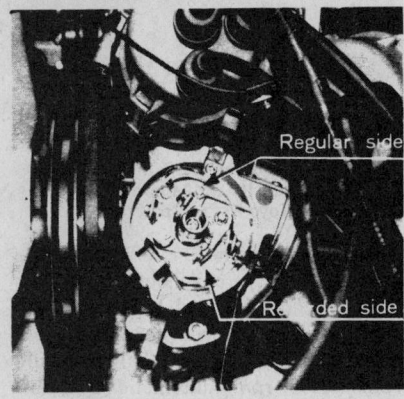

Dual-point leading distributor
(© Toyo Kogyo Co., Ltd.)

about 0.2–0.04 in. or 0.8–1.0 in. on automatic models. The engine speed should decrease by 200–300 rpm. If it does not, then test the choke switch to be sure that it's functioning correctly.

6. Disconnect the leading distributor at its negative (−) terminal so that only its retarded side is receiving power.

7. Start the engine and run it at idle.

8. Aim the timing light at the pointer on the front cover. The orange timing mark (10°ATDC) on the pulley should be seen to align with the pointer.

NOTE: *Be sure that the ignition timing is adjusted correctly before replacing the No. 2 control box with a new one.* Replace the No. 2 control box if it is defective. When finished, remove the test equipment and reconnect all of those components that were disconnected for this test.

Component Removal and Installation

No. 1 Thermosensor

1. Remove the air cleaner assembly.

2. If necessary, remove the starter motor as detailed under "Engine Electrical" or the deceleration control valve (see below).

3. Unplug the thermosensor multiconnector.

4. Withdraw the boot from the thermosensor.

Arrow indicates position of the No. 1 thermosensor
(© Toyo Kogyo Co., Ltd.)

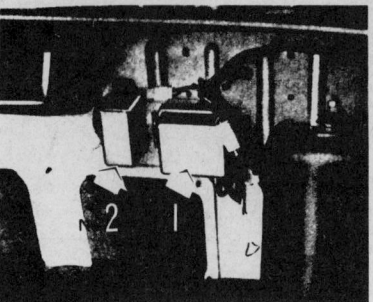

Both control boxes are located behind the luggage compartment trim panel—1972-73
(© Toyo Kogyo Co., Ltd.)

Thermodetector location
(© Toyo Kogyo Co., Ltd.)

5. Unfasten its securing nuts and remove the thermosensor.

Installation is performed in the reverse order of removal.

No. 1 Control Box—1972-73

CAUTION: *Be sure that the ignition is turned off to prevent damage to the control box.*

1. Open the luggage compartment.

2. Unfasten its screws and remove the panel from the back of the compartment.

3. Unfasten the control box multiconnector.

4. Loosen the control box securing nuts and remove the box.

Installation of the control box is performed in the reverse order of removal.

Control Box—1974–77

CAUTION: *Be sure that the ignition switch is turned off to prevent damage to the control box.*

1. Working from underneath the instrument panel, locate and disconnect the control box multiconnector.

2. Remove the screws which secure the control box.

3. Remove the control box.

Installation is performed in the reverse order of removal.

No. 2 Thermosensor

1. Drain the engine oil into a large, clean container for reuse.

2. Unfasten the connector from the No. 2 thermosensor.

3. Unscrew the thermosensor from the oil pan.

Installation is performed in the reverse order of removal.

No. 2 Control Box

The No. 2 control box is located in the luggage compartment next to the No. 1 control box. Its removal and installation are performed in the same manner as for the No. 1 control box (see above).

Other Components

Any of the other components used in the air flow control system are removed by unfastening their multiconnectors and removing the screws which secure them.

Deceleration Control System

1972–73

The deceleration control system uses an anti-afterburn valve, a coasting valve, and an air supply valve. In addition, an idle sensing switch is fitted to the carburetor. The No. 1 control box is shared with the air flow control system.

The anti-afterburn valve, which is located on the intake manifold, is used to supply fresh air to the manifold during deceleration or when the engine is shut off, in order to prevent afterburning.

A coasting valve, which functions in a similar manner, is used to prevent an overly rich mixture during deceleration. The coasting valve also vents the vacuum chamber of the air control valve during deceleration. The valve is operated by a solenoid which is controlled by the No. 1 control box and the idle sensing switch.

1972–77 models do not have a throttle positioner; they have an idle sensing switch attached to the carburetor in its place. When the throttle closes, its linkage contacts a plunger on the switch which completes the circuit from the No. 1 control box to the coasting valve thus causing the coasting valve to operate. On automatic transmission equipped models, it also determines trailing distributor operation.

A solenoid-operated air supply valve opens when the ignition is shut off to prevent the engine from dieseling (running on).

1974–77

In addition to the above components, 1974 and later models have an altitude compensator which provides air to lean out the overly rich mixture that accrues at high altitudes.

On 1974 and later models with an automatic transmission, a kick-down control system is used. Regardless of the gear selected, the transmission will not go above second gear when the choke knob is pulled out.

Component Testing

Anti-Afterburn Valve—All Models

1. Remove the air cleaner assembly.

2. Remove the hose from the air intake on the anti-afterburn valve.

3. With the engine idling, place your hand over the air intake. If a strong suction is felt, the valve is defective and should be replaced.

4. Increase the engine speed to 3,500–3,800 rpm. Release the throttle and allow it to snap shut. Air should be drawn in through the valve air intake for no longer than one second.

5. Keep the engine idling and disconnect the anti-afterburn valve solenoid wiring. Air should flow into the air intake while the solenoid is disconnected.

If the anti-afterburn valve fails to function properly, replace it with a new one. Remember to connect the air supply hose and the solenoid wiring after completing the test.

Coasting Valve—All Models 1972–73

1. Install a vacuum gauge in the line which runs from the coasting valve to the air control valve, by means of a T-fitting.

2. Start the engine and allow it to warm up.

3. With the engine at idle, the vacuum gauge should read at least 16 in. Hg.

4. Increase the engine speed to 2,500 rpm. Release the throttle valve so that it snaps shut. The vacuum reading should momentarily be 0–1 in. Hg and then return to 16 in. Hg when the engine speed drops below 1,300–1,100 rpm (manual) or 1,450–1,350 (automatic).

If the vacuum readings are within specifications, the vacuum valve is functioning correctly. If they are not, proceed with the rest of the test.

5. Check the circuit from the No. 1 control box to the coasting valve, as detailed in steps 8–9 of the no. 1 control box test procedure above.

6. Check the operation of the solenoid by connecting it directly to the car bat-

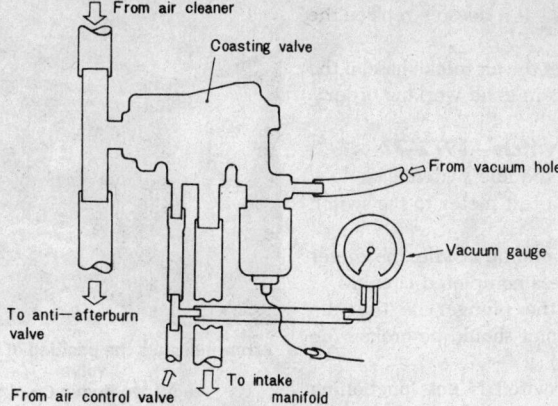

Testing the coasting valve
(© Toyo Kogyo Co., Ltd.)

tery. If it fails to click on and off, it is defective and must be replaced.

7. Examine the vacuum lines to see that they are not clogged or leaking.

8. Inspect the passage which runs between the air intake and the vacuum chamber of the coasting valve to be sure that it is not clogged.

9. Check the idle mixture; if it is not adjusted properly, it can affect valve operation.

If all of the checks above are positive, and the vacuum readings are incorrect, the valve is defective and must be replaced.

Combination Anti-Afterburn and Coasting Valve—1974–77

1. Disconnect the hose which runs from the air cleaner to the combination valve at the air cleaner end.

2. Start the engine and run it at curb idle.

3. There should be no vacuum present at the end of the hose which you disconnected in step 1.

4. Turn the engine off.

5. Disconnect the hose which runs from the coasting valve portion of the combination valve to the intake manifold from the coasting valve end and plug up the port.

6. Operate the engine at idle.

7. Disconnect the anti-afterburn valve solenoid connector.

8. Check for vacuum at the end of the hose which you disconnected in step 1; there should be vacuum present. If not, the anti-afterburn valve is defective.

9. Turn the engine off. Reconnect the anti-afterburn valve electrical leads and the hose to the coasting valve.

10. Disconnect the intake manifold-to-anti-afterburn valve vacuum line at the valve end, and plug the vacuum fitting on the valve.

11. Start the engine and allow it to idle.

12. Disconnect the coasting valve solenoid at the multiconnector.

13. Hold your hand over the end of the vacuum line which you disconnected in step 10. Vacuum should be felt; if not, replace the defective coasting valve.

14. Turn the engine off and reconnect the leads and hoses that were disconnected above.

Altitude Compensator—1975–77

1. Detach the air intake hose from the altitude compensator.

2. Start the engine and run it at idle.

3. Hold your finger over the altitude compensator air intake; the engine speed

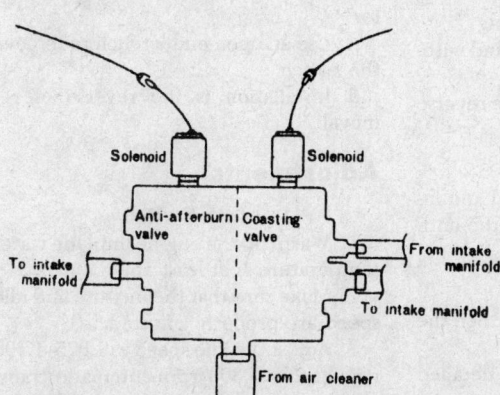

Combination anti-afterburn and coasting valve connections
(© Toyo Kogyo Co., Ltd.)

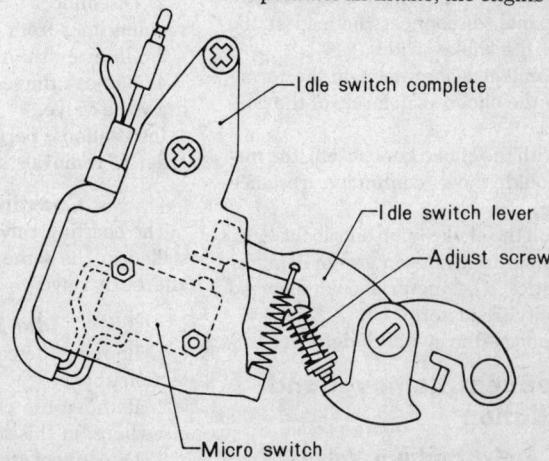

1972 idle switch—1973–77 use a multiconnector (© Toyo Kogyo Co. Ltd.)

Mazda

should decrease. If it doesn't, replace the compensator.

4. Reconnect the air intake hose, if the compensator is in good working order.

Idle Switch—1972-77

1. Unfasten the idle switch leads.
2. Connect a test meter to the switch terminals.
3. With the engine at idle, the meter should indicate a completed circuit.
4. Depress the plunger on the idle switch; the circuit should be broken (no meter reading).

If the idle switch is not functioning properly, replace it with a new one.

Air Supply Valve—1972

1. Remove the hose from the air supply valve air intake.
2. Start the engine and allow it to run at idle.
3. Block the air intake with your finger. The idle speed should be reduced by no more than 30 rpm.
4. Disconnect the air supply valve solenoid wiring. A large volume of air should be drawn into the air intake.

If the switch fails to function as outlined above, replace it with a new one.

Coolant Temperature Switch— 1974-77

Start this test with the coolant temperature below 68°F.
1. Disconnect the electrical lead from the temperature switch.
2. Connect a test light between one terminal of the switch and a 12 volt battery. Ground the other terminal.
3. The test light should light.
4. Start the engine and allow it to warm up. Once the engine reaches normal operating temperature, the test light should go out.
5. Replace the switch if it doesn't work as outlined.

Choke Switch (Semi-Automatic Choke)

1. Working underneath the instrument panel, disconnect the lead at the back of the choke switch.
2. Connect a ohmmeter to the terminals on the choke switch side of the connector.
3. With the choke knob *in* (off), the meter should show continuity (restance reading).
4. Pull the choke knob out, about ½ in. for manual transmission cars or 1 in. for automatics. The meter should show no continuity (read zero).
5. Replace the switch if defective.

Component Removal and Installation

Anti-Afterburn Valve

1. Remove the air cleaner assembly.

Arrow indicates the position of the coasting valve
(© Toyo Kogyo Co., Ltd.)

Arrow indicates the position of the anti-afterburn valve
(© Toyo Kogyo Co., Ltd.)

Idle switch position (arrow)
(© Toyo Kogyo Co., Ltd.)

2. Disconnect the air hoses and vacuum lines from the valve.
3. Unfasten the solenoid wiring.
4. Remove the securing nuts and withdraw the valve.
Installation is performed in the reverse order of removal.

Coasting Valve

The coasting valve is removed and installed in the same manner as the anti-afterburn valve.

Idle Switch

1. Remove the coasting valve. See the section above.
2. Remove the carburetor as detailed elsewhere, in this section.
3. Disconnect the wiring from the switch.

4. Unfasten the securing screws and remove the switch.
Installation is performed in the reverse order of removal. After installing the switch, adjust it as outlined under "Adjustments", below.

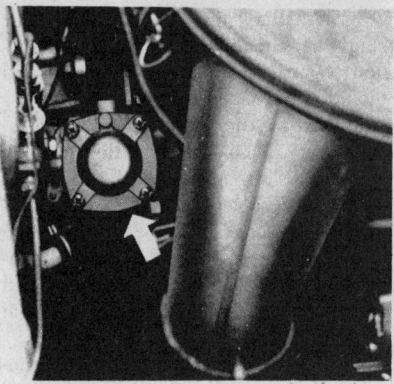

1972 air valve location (arrow). (© Toyo Kogyo Co. Ltd.)

Air Supply Valve

1. Remove the air cleaner and the hot air duct.
2. Disconnect the air hose, the vacuum lines, and the solenoid wiring from the valve.
3. Unfasten the screws which secure the valve and remove it.
Air supply valve installation is performed in the reverse order of removal.

Altitude Compensator

1. Disconnect both hoses from the altitude compensator. Be sure to note their positions for correct hook-up.
2. Unfasten the altitude compensator securing bolts.
3. Remove the compensator from its bracket.
Installation is the reverse of removal.

Coolant Temperature Switch

1. Drain the coolant from the radiator enough to bring the coolant level below the temperature switch.
2. Remove the alternator and drive belt if they are in the way.
3. Disconnect the switch multiconnector.
4. Use an open-end wrench to remove the switch.
5. Installation is the reverse of removal.

Adjustments

Idle Switch

1. Warm up the engine until the water temperature is at least 159°F.
2. Make sure that the mixture and idle speed are properly adjusted.
3. Adjust the idle speed to 1,075–1,100 rpm (1,200–1,300 rpm-automatic transmission) by rotating the throttle adjusting screw.
4. Rotate the idle switch adjusting

screw until the switch changes from OFF to ON position.

5. Slowly turn the idle switch adjusting screw back to the point where the switch just changes from ON to OFF.

6. Turn the throttle screw back so that the engine returns to idle.

NOTE: *Be sure that the idle switch goes on when the idle speed is still above 1,000 rpm.*

Evaporative Emission Control System

The vapors rising from the gasoline in the fuel tank are vented into a separate condensing tank which is located in the luggage compartment. There they condense and return to the fuel tank in liquid form when the engine is not running.

When the engine is running, the fuel vapors are sucked directly into the engine through the PCV valve and are burned along with the air/fuel mixture.

Any additional fuel vapors which are not handled by the condensing tank are stored in a filter which is incorporated into the air cleaner. When the engine is running, the charcoal is purged of its stored fuel vapor.

On 1973–77 models, a check valve vents the fuel vapor into the atmosphere if pressure in the fuel tank becomes excessive. The check valve is located in the luggage compartment, next to the condensing tank.

When the vehicle is parked for a short time following a long run, there is a tendency for the fuel in the float chamber to evaporate and enter the intake manifold through the air vent. To prevent this over-rich condition, an air vent solenoid valve is installed on 1977 models to divert the fumes to the canister filter.

Evaporative emission control system—1972
(© Toyo Kogyo Co., Ltd.)

System Testing

There are several things to check for if a malfunction of the evaporative emission control system is suspected.

1. Leaks may be traced by using an in-

Servo-diaphragm—B-1600 (© Toyo Kogyo Co., Ltd.)

frared hydrocarbon tester. Run the test probe along the lines and connections. The meter will indicate the presence of a leak by a high hydrocarbon (HC) reading. This method is much more accurate than a visual inspection which would indicate only the presence of a leak large enough to pass liquid.

2. Leaks may be caused by any of the following, so always check these areas when looking for them:

   a. Defective or worn lines;
   b. Disconnected or pinched lines;
   c. Improperly routed lines;
   d. A defective check valve.

NOTE: *If it becomes necessary to replace any of the lines used in the evaporative emission control system, use only those hoses which are fuel resistant or are marked "EVAP."*

3. If the fuel tank has collapsed, it may be the fault of clogged or pinched vent lines, a defective vapor separator, or a plugged or incorrect fuel filler cap.

EMISSION CONTROLS

Piston Engine B1600 Pickup

Throttle Positioner

The throttle positioner system consists of a servo-diaphragm connected to the throttle lever and a vacuum control valve which controls intake manifold vacuum through the servo-diaphragm.

Testing the System

Servo-Diaphragm

1. Start the engine and set the idle speed to 800 rpm. Stop the engine.

2. Disconnect the vacuum sensing tube between the servo-diaphragm and the vacuum control valve at the diaphragm.

The condensing tank is located in the luggage compartment
(© Toyo Kogyo Co., Ltd.)

3. Remove the intake manifold suction hole plug.

4. Connect the intake manifold and the servo-diaphragm with a tube so that the intake manifold vacuum goes directly to the servo-diaphragm.

5. Connect a tachometer and remove the vacuum sensing tube between the carburetor and distributor.

6. Start the engine and read the speed. If the engine is running 1300–1500 rpm, the servo-diaphragm is operating normally. If the engine speed is 800–1500, adjust the speed with the throttle opening screw. If the engine speed remains normal, about 800 rpm, the servo-diaphragm is defective and should be replaced.

7. Remove the test equipment and reconnect all the lines.

Service

Servo-Diaphragm

Removal and Installation

1. Remove the air cleaner.

2. Disconnect the vacuum sensing tube from the diaphragm.

3. Remove the cotter pin and link.

4. Loosen the locknut and remove the servo-diaphragm.

5. Installation is the reverse of removal. Adjust the servo-diaphragm.

PCV valve—B-1600 (© Toyo Kogyo Co., Ltd.)

Vacuum control valve—B-1600 (© Toyo Kogyo Co., Ltd.)

Vacuum Control Valve

Removal and Installation

1. Remove the air cleaner.
2. Disconnect the vacuum sensing tubes from the vacuum control valve.
3. Unbolt and remove the vacuum control valve.
4. Installation is the reverse of removal.

Adjustments

Throttle Opener

1. Install a tachometer on the engine.
2. Start the engine and set the idle speed.
3. Stop the engine.
4. Disconnect the vacuum sensing tube between the servo-diaphragm and the vacuum control valve from the servo-diaphragm.
5. Remove the plug from the intake manifold suction hole.
6. Attach a vacuum line between the intake manifold and the servo-diaphragm to route intake manifold vacuum directly to the servo-diaphragm.
7. Start the engine and note the speed.
8. Set the engine speed to 1400 rpm using the throttle opener screw. Turning the adjusting screw clockwise increases engine speed.
9. Stop the engine and disconnect the tachometer. Reconnect all lines.

Positive Crankcase Ventilation (PCV) System

The function of the PCV valve is to divert blow-by gases from the crankcase to the intake manifold to be burned in the cylinders. The system consists of a PCV valve, an oil separator and the hoses necessary to connect the components.

Ventilating air is routed into the rocker cover from the air cleaner. The air is then moved to the oil separator and from the separator to the PCV valve. The PCV valve is operated by differences in air pressure between the intake manifold and the rocker cover.

Testing the System

PCV Valve

Standard Test

1. Remove the hose from the PCV valve.
2. Start the engine and run it at approximately 700–1000 rpm.
3. Cover the end of the PCV valve with your finger. A distinct vacuum should be felt. If no vacuum is felt, replace the valve.

Alternate Test

Remove the valve from its fitting. Shake the valve. If a rattle is heard, the valve is probably functioning normally. If no rattle is heard, the valve is probably stuck (open or shut) and should be replaced.

Service

PCV Valve Removal and Installation

1. Remove the air cleaner.
2. Disconnect the hose from the PCV valve.
3. Remove the valve from the intake manifold fitting.

To install the valve, reverse the removal procedure.

Evaporative Emission Control System

The evaporative emission control system is designed to control the emission of gasoline vapors into the atmosphere. The system consists of a fuel tank, a condenser tank and a check valve.

When the engine is not running, fuel vapors are channeled to the condenser tank. The fuel returns to the fuel tank as the vapors condense. During periods of engine operation, fuel vapor that has not condensed in the condenser tank moves to the carbon canister. The stored vapors are removed from the charcoal by fresh air moving through the inlet hole in the bottom of the canister.

Service

Condenser Tank Removal and Installation

1. Raise and support the rear of the truck.
2. Disconnect the hoses from the condenser tank.
3. Unbolt and remove the condenser tank.

To install the tank:

4. Install the tank and tighten the bolts.
5. Connect the hoses to the tank.
6. Lower the truck.

Check Valve Removal and Installation

1. Disconnect the hoses from the check valve.
2. Unscrew and remove the valve from the crossmember.

Installation is the reverse of removal.

Emission Control System 808 Series

Positive Crankcase Ventilation System

Testing PCV Valve

1. Run engine at normal operating temperature.
2. Disconnect the hose from the valve and cover the end with your thumb. If engine speed decreases, the valve is working properly. If not, replace the valve.

Replacing the PCV Valve

1. Disconnect the hose from the valve.
2. Replace the valve.

Evaporative Emission Control System

Checking the Evaporative Line

1. Disconnect the Evap hose from the

Removing PCV valve—808 (© Toyo Kogyo Co. Ltd.)

Checking relief valve—808 (© Toyo Kogyo Co. Ltd.)

cannister to the check valve, at the cannister.

2. Connect this hose to a "U" type pressure gauge.

3. Apply pressure to the "U" gauge until the water level difference is 13.5–14.5 in. Seal the gauge inlet.

4. Let the gauge stand sealed for about 5 min. If the water level drops less than 1 in., the line is in good condition. If not, check the following:
   a. leak in hose
   b. leak in condensation tank
   c. leak in fuel tank
   d. leak in fuel line
   e. leak at fuel filler cap

Replacing Condensation Tank (Coupe or Sedan)

1. Open the trunk and remove the partition.

2. Disconnect the hoses from the tank.

3. Remove the rear seat and package tray trim.

4. Unbolt and remove the tank.

5. Install in reverse of the above.

Replacing the Condensation Tank (Station Wagon)

1. Open the rear door.

2. Remove the left trim panel.

3. Remove hoses from tank.

4. Unbolt and remove tank.

5. Installation is the reverse of removal.

Testing the Check Valve

1. Remove the valve as described below.

2. Connect a pressure gauge to the tank side port and cover the other port with your finger.

3. Blow through the valve. It should open at about 0.57 psi.

4. Remove the gauge and connect it to the vent side. Blow through the gauge. The valve should open at less than 0.14 psi. If these tests aren't met, replace the valve.

Replacing the Check Valve (Sedan and Coupe)

1. Open the trunk and remove the partition.

2. Disconnect the hoses from the valve.

3. Unbolt and remove the valve.

4. Installation is the reverse of removal.

Replacing the Check Valve (Station Wagon)

1. Open the rear door and remove the left side trim panel.

2. Disconnect and remove the valve.

3. Installation is the reverse of removal.

Checking the Canister

The canister is checked visually for leakage of the charcoal.

Replacing the Canister

1. Disconnect the hoses from the canister.

2. Unbolt and remove the unit.

Air Injection System

Checking the Air Pump

1. Disconnect the hose from the air pump outlet.

2. Connect a pressure gauge to the outlet.

3. Check the drive belt for proper tension and run engine at 1500 rpm. Gauge reading should be at least 1 psi. If not, replace the pump.

Testing the Relief Valve

1. Run the engine at idle.

2. At idle, no air should be felt at the relief valve. If air flow is felt, replace the valve.

3. Increase the idle to 2000 rpm. If air flow is felt, valve is working properly.

Pump Replacement

1. Disconnect the inlet and outlet hoses at the pump.

2. Remove the adjusting bolt and lift off the drive belt.

3. Support the pump and remove the mounting bolts. Lift out the pump.

4. Installation is the reverse of removal. Adjust drive belt to specification. Correct belt adjustment will give a .5" flex at the mid-point with a 22lb push.

Check Valve Replacement

Check valve is replaced by disconnecting the hose and unscrewing the valve from the manifold.

Air Control Valve Test

1. Start the engine and run it at idle.

2. Hold a finger over the relief valve port of the air control valve. Discharge air should be felt.

3. Disconnect the vacuum sensing tube from the air control valve and plug the tube. No air should be felt at the relief port.

Replacing Air Control Valve

1. Disconnect the vacuum lines from the valve.

2. Disconnect the wiring from the valve.

Check valve—808 (© Toyo Kogyo Co. Ltd.)

Mazda

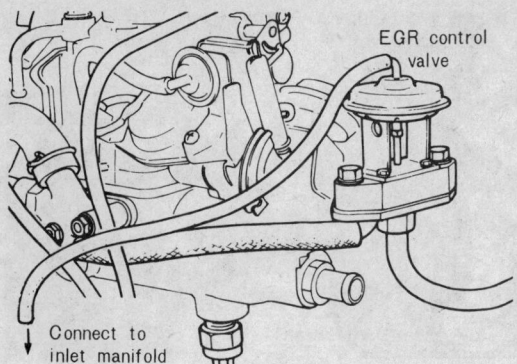

EGR control valve

Connect to inlet manifold

EGR control valve test—808 (© Toyo Kogyo Co. Ltd.)

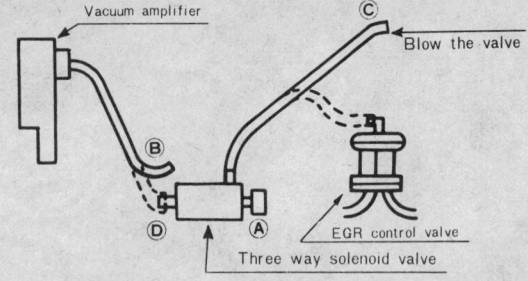

Checking the three-way solenoid valve—808 (© Toyo Kogyo Co. Ltd.)

3. Disconnect the air hoses from the valve.

4. Unbolt and remove the valve.

5. Install in reverse of removal.

Air Control Valve Check Valve Test

1. Disconnect the vacuum sensing tube from the air control valve solenoid.

2. Blow through the vacuum tube. Air should pass through the valve. Suck on the tube. No air should pass through the valve.

Exhaust Gas Recirculation System

EGR Control Valve Test

1. Remove the air cleaner.

2. Run the engine at idle.

3. Disconnect the vacuum sensing tube from the EGR control valve.

4. Disconnect the vacuum sensing tube from the intake manifold vacuum control valve.

5. Connect this vacuum tube to the EGR control valve. The engine should stop. If not, clean or replace the EGR control valve.

Replacing EGR Control Valve

1. Remove air cleaner.

2. Disconnect the vacuum sensing tube from the EGR control valve.

3. Disconnect the EGR control valve-to-exhaust manifold pipe.

4. Disconnect the pipe between the EGR control valve and the intake manifold.

5. Unbolt and remove the EGR control valve.

6. If old valve is to be reused, it should be cleaned with a wire brush before installation.

7. To install, reverse the above procedure.

Replacing and/or Testing the Water Temperature Switch

1. Drain the radiator until the coolant level is below the intake manifold.

2. Disconnect the wires from the switch.

3. Unscrew the switch from the manifold.

4. Suspend the switch in a container of water so that it does not touch the sides or bottom.

5. Heat the water to no more than 113°F. and check the switch with an ohmmeter. Continuity should exist between the terminals.

6. Heat the water until the temperature becomes 149°F or more.

7. No continuity should exist. If the switch fails either test, replace it.

8. To replace the switch, reverse removal procedure.

Testing the Three-Way Solenoid Valve

The valve is located at the top center of the firewall in the engine compartment.

1. Make sure that the engine coolant temperature is below 113°F.

2. Disconnect the vacuum sensing tube from the EGR control valve.

3. Blow into the tube through the three-way valve. Air should pass through the valve and out the filter.

4. Reconnect the tube.

5. Run the engine until the coolant temperature is at least 149°F.

6. Disconnect the vacuum sensing tube from the EGR control valve.

7. Disconnect the tube between the carburetor and the valve at the valve.

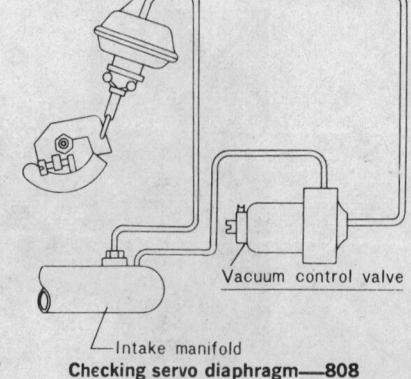

Checking servo diaphragm—808 (© Toyo Kogyo Co. Ltd.)

8. Turn the ignition switch on and blow through the EGR hose. Air should come out the port at which the carburetor hose was connected.

9. If the valve fails to operate properly, replace it.

Replacing the Three-Way Solenoid Valve

1. Disconnect the wiring from the valve.

2. Disconnect the hoses from the valve.

3. Remove the screws and replace the valve.

EGR Maintenance Warning System

Every 12,500 miles, the EGR warning light will come on when the ignition switch is turned on. When this occurs the valve should be removed and cleaned and checked for proper operation. When this is done reset the switch by taking off the cover from the switch and sliding the knob in the opposite direction.

Catalytic Converter

Periodically, the converter should be checked for excessive rust, cracks or corrosion. To replace the converter, raise and support the car and unbolt the converter from the flanges and body. A temperature sensor is located in the right side of the converter. To test its operation, remove a small plate under the floor mat on the passengers side. Remove the coupling and check across the terminals of the coupling with a circuit tester. If there is no current flow, replace the sensor.

Deceleration Control System

Checking Anti-Afterburn Valve

1. Disconnect the inlet hose from the valve at the air cleaner.

2. Run the engine at idle and close off the inlet hose with your finger. There should be no change in engine speed.

3. Raise the engine speed and hold your finger over the inlet hose. Quickly

release the accelerator linkage. Air should be sucked in for a few seconds. If air is sucked in for longer than three seconds or not at all, replace the valve.

Replacing the Anti-Afterburn Valve

1. Remove the air cleaner.
2. Disconnect all hoses from the valve and unbolt and remove the valve.

Throttle Opener System

Checking Servo Diaphragm

1. Start the engine and set the idle to specification.
2. Stop the engine and remove the air cleaner.
3. Disconnect the vacuum hose between the diaphragm and the vacuum control valve at the diaphragm.
4. Disconnect the vacuum tube between the intake manifold and the control valve at the valve.
5. Connect the last hose to the diaphragm.
6. Disconnect the distributor vacuum hose at the distributor.
7. Connect a tachometer to the engine.
8. Start the engine. If engine speed is between 1300 and 1500 rpm the diaphragm is normal. If not, turn the throttle opener screw to adjust. If the adjustment cannot be made, replace the diaphragm.

Replacing the Servo Diaphragm

1. Remove the air cleaner.
2. Disconnect the vacuum sensing tube from the diaphragm.
3. Remove the two bolts attaching the diaphragm to the intake manifold.
4. Disconnect the cotter pin and washer from the servo diaphragm link and remove the diaphragm and bracket assembly.
5. Installation is the reverse of removal.

Checking the Vacuum Control Valve

1. Remove the air cleaner.
2. Remove the vacuum hose between the control valve and the manifold at the manifold.
3. Connect a vacuum gauge between the hose and the manifold.
   NOTE: *the tube to the vacuum gauge must be at least 0.12 inner diameter and not more than 6ft long.*
4. Start the engine and maintain 3000 rpm.
5. Release the accelerator and check the gauge.
6. The gauge reading, after reaching its highest point, should hesitate at 22.4"

on its way down to idle level. The above test was determined at a mean atmospheric pressure of 29.9 inHg. Correct the reading as necessary. If the reading is not within specifications, loosen the setscrew and turn the adjuster as necessary.

Checking the Spark Delay Valve

1. Disconnect the vacuum tube between the valve and the distributor, at the distributor.
2. Connect this tube directly to the intake manifold.
3. Disconnect the vacuum tube between the valve and the carburetor at the carburetor and connect a vacuum gauge between the tube and the carburetor.
4. Run the engine at idle and note the gauge reading.
5. Disconnect the vacuum tube from the manifold and note the time it takes for the gauge reading to drop by 12 inHg. The time should be 2–10 seconds. If not, replace the valve.

FUEL SYSTEM

Electric Fuel Pump

Location and Type

The electric fuel pump is located in the luggage compartment of the coupes and sedans. On station wagons, it is located behind the left-hand trim panel in the luggage compartment.

Removal and Installation

Sedans and Coupes

1. Open the luggage compartment lid.
2. Remove the rear inside trim panel, after unfastening its two securing screws.
3. Disconnect the wiring and the fuel lines from the pump.
4. Unfasten the nuts and bolts which secure the pump assembly. Remove the pump.
   Installation is performed in the reverse order of installation.

Station Wagon

1. Remove the left-hand cargo compartment trim panel.
2. Disconnect the wiring and fuel lines from the pump.
3. Unfasten the nuts which secure the pump and remove the pump.
   Installation is performed in the reverse order of removal.

Pick-Up Trucks

An external electric fuel pump is mounted on the left frame rail adjacent to the fuel tank. Current is supplied to the pump through the ignition circuit and the pump will operate with the key in the RUN position.

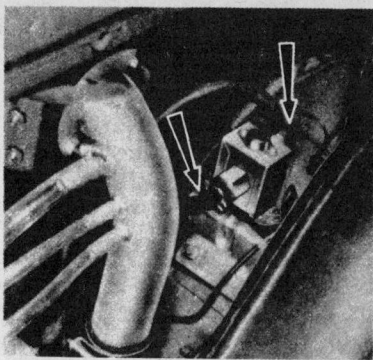
Fuel pump location on the RX-3 wagon
(© Toyo Kogyo Co., Ltd.)

1. Remove the fuel pump shield from the frame. Disconnect the electrical leads from the pump.
2. Disconnect the inlet and outlet lines from the pump. Plug the lines.
3. Unbolt and remove the pump from its mounting bracket.
   To install the fuel pump:
4. Position the fuel pump on the mounting bracket and install the bolts. Be sure that both mounting surfaces are clean.
5. Connect the inlet and outlet hoses.
6. Connect the electrical leads to the pump.
7. Install the fuel pump shield.

Carburetor

Removal and Installation

Rotary Engine

1. Remove the air cleaner assembly complete with its hoses and mounting bracket.
2. Detach the choke and accelerator cables from the carburetor.
3. Disconnect the fuel and vacuum lines from the carburetor.
4. Remove the oil line which runs to the metering oil pump, at the carburetor.
5. Remove all electrical wiring from carburetor.
6. Remove the carburetor attaching nuts and/or bolts, gasket or heat insulator, and remove the carburetor.
   Installation is performed in the reverse order of removal. Use a new gasket. Fill the float bowl with gasoline to aid in engine starting.

Piston Engine

1. Remove the air cleaner and duct.
2. Disconnect the accelerator shaft from the throttle lever.
3. Disconnect and plug the fuel supply and fuel return lines and plug these.
4. Disconnect the leads from the throttle solenoid and deceleration valve at the quick-disconnects.
5. Disconnect the carburetor-to-distributor vacuum line.
6. Disconnect the throttle return spring.

7. Disconnect the choke cable.

8. Remove the carburetor attaching nuts from the intake manifold studs and remove the carburetor.

To install the carburetor:

9. Install a new carburetor gasket on the manifold.

10. Install the carburetor and tighten the carburetor attaching nuts.

11. Connect the throttle return spring.

12. Connect the accelerator shaft to the throttle shaft.

13. Connect the electrical leads to the throttle solenoid and deceleration valve.

14. Connect the distributor vacuum line.

15. Connect the fuel supply and fuel return lines.

16. Connect and adjust the choke cable.

17. Install the air cleaner and duct.

18. Start the engine and check for fuel leaks.

Overhaul

Efficient carburetion depends greatly on careful cleaning and inspection during overhaul since dirt, gum, water, or varnish in or on the carburetor parts are often responsible for poor performance.

Overhaul your carburetor in a clean, dust-free area. Carefully disassemble the carburetor, referring often to the exploded views. Keep all similar and look-alike parts segregated during disassembly and cleaning to avoid accidental interchange during assembly. Make a note of all jet sizes.

When the carburetor is disassembled, wash all parts (except diaphragms, electric choke units, pump plunger, and any other plastic, leather, fiber, or rubber parts) in clean carburetor solvent. Do not leave parts in the solvent any longer than is necessary to sufficiently loosen the deposits. Excessive cleaning may remove the special finish from the float bowl and choke valve bodies, leaving these parts unfit for service. Rinse all parts in clean solvent and blow them dry with compressed air or allow them to air dry. Wipe clean all cork, plastic, leather, and fiber parts with a clean, lint-free cloth.

Blow out all passages and jets with compressed air and be sure that there are no restrictions or blockages. Never use wire or similar tools to clean jets, fuel passages, or air bleeds. Clean all jets and valves separately to avoid accidental interchange.

Check all parts for wear or damage. If wear or damage is found, replace the defective parts. Especially check the following:

1. Check the float needle and seat for wear. If wear is found, replace the complete assembly.

2. Check the float hinge pin for wear and the float(s) for dents or distortion. Re-

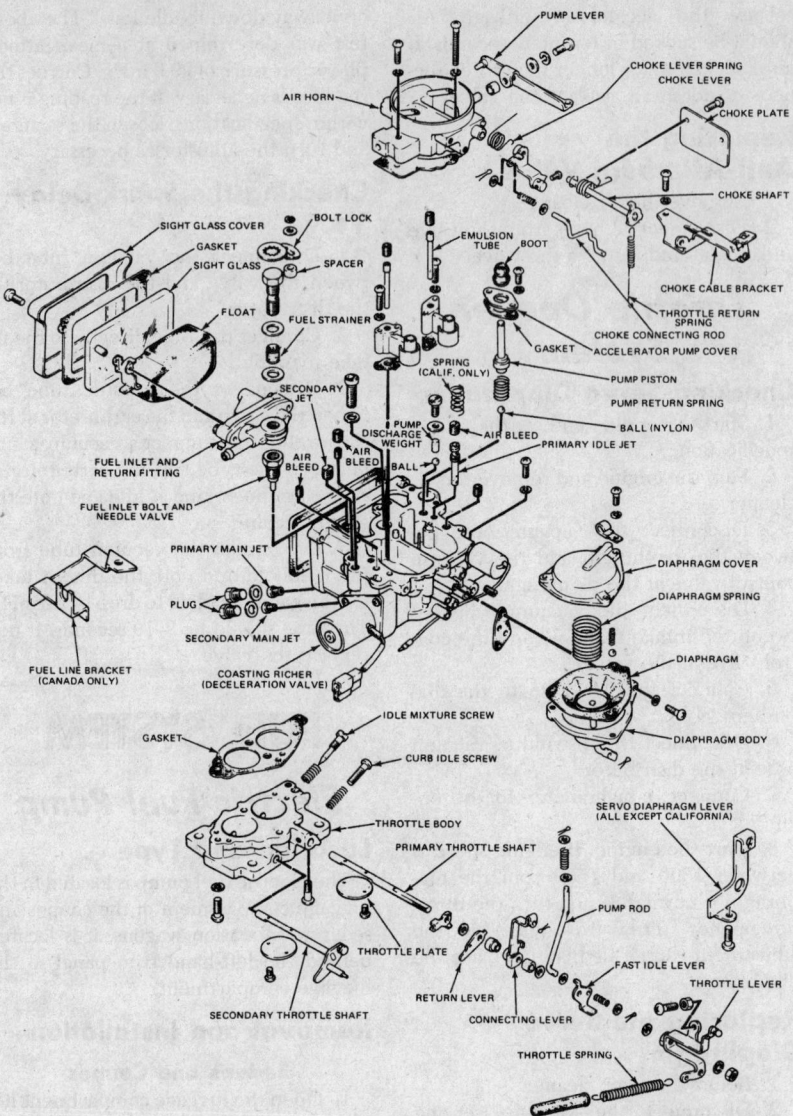

Carburetor exploded view—piston engine (© Toyo Kogyo Co. Ltd.)

place the float if fuel has leaked into it.

3. Check the throttle and choke shaft bores for wear or an out-of-round condition. Damage or wear to the throttle arm, shaft, or shaft bore will often require replacement of the throttle body. These parts require a close tolerance of fit; wear may allow air leakage, which could affect starting and idling.

NOTE: *Throttle shafts and bushings are not included in overhaul kits. They can be purchased separately.*

4. Inspect the idle mixture adjusting needles for burrs or grooves. Any such condition requires replacement of the needle, since you will not be able to obtain a satisfactory idle.

5. Test the accelerator pump check valves. They should pass air one way but not the other. Test for proper seating by blowing and sucking on the valve. Replace the valve if necessary. If the valve is satisfactory, wash the valve again to remove breath moisture.

6. Check the bowl cover for warped surfaces with a straightedge.

7. Closely inspect the valves and seats for wear and damage, replacing as necessary.

8. After the carburetor is assembled, check the choke valve for freedom of operation.

Carburetor overhaul kits are recommended for each overhaul. These kits contain all gaskets and new parts to replace those that deteriorate most rapidly. Failure to replace all parts supplied with the kit (especially gaskets) can result in poor performance later.

After cleaning and checking all components, reassemble the carburetor, using new parts and referring to the exploded view. When reassembling, make sure that all screws and jets are tight in their seats, but do not overtighten, as the tips will be distorted. Tighten all screws gradually, in rotation. Do not tighten needle valves into their seats; uneven jet-

1. Air horn
2. Choke valve lever
3. Clip
4. Choke lever shaft
5. Screw
6. Setscrew
7. Spring
8. Choke valve
9. Connector
10. Connecting rod
11. Spring
12. Fuel return valve
13. Hanger
14. Screw
15. Ring
16. Bolt
17. Carburetor body
18. Bolt
19. Diaphragm cover
20. Screw
21. Diaphragm
22. Accelerator pump arm
23. Float
24. Gasket
25. Connecting rod
26. Spring
27. Spring
28. Small venturi
29. Small venturi
30. Bolt
31. Check ball plug
32. Steel ball
33. Flange
34. Throttle shaft
35. Throttle shaft
36. Throttle lever
37. Spring washer
38. Nut
39. Lock
40. Adjusting arm
41. Starting lever
42. Arm
43. Screw
44. Gasket
45. Valve
46. Screw
47. Throttle valve
48. Throttle lever link
49. Ring
50. Throttle return spring
51. Arm
52. Retainer
53. Metering pump lever
54. Metering pump arm

55. Screw
56. Pin
57. Union bolt
58. Cover
59. Diaphragm spring
60. Diaphragm lever
61. Diaphragm pin
62. Diaphragm chamber
63. Screw
64. Diaphragm
65. Gasket
66. Connecting rod
67. Pin
68. Ring
69. Washer
70. Diaphragm stop ring
71. Diaphragm stop ring

72. Screw
73. Level gauge screw
74. Gasket
75. Gasket
76. Stop ring
77. Float pin
78. Needle valve seat
79. Gasket
80. Collar
81. Throttle adjusting screw
82. Idle adjusting screw
83. Spring
84. Main jet
85. Main jet
86. Gasket
87. Plug
88. Gasket
89. Air bleed
90. Air bleed
91. Slow jet
92. Step jet
93. Air bleed screw
94. Air bleed step
95. Cover
96. Diaphragm
97. Spring
98. Gasket
99. Washer
100. Shim
101. Jet
102. Bleed plug
103. Retainer
104. Pin
105. Screw
106. Gasket
107. Plug
108. Gasket
109. Gasket
110. Bolt
111. Nut
113. Cover
114. Gasket
115. Sight glass
116. Gasket
117. Filter
118. Accelerator nozzle
119. Gasket
120. Plug
121. Cover
122. Coasting valve bracket
123. Clip
124. Screw
125. Spring
126. Screw
127. Spring
128. Shim
129. Throttle positioner
130. Nut
131. Rod
132. Collar
133. Shim
134. Collar
135. Arm
136. Plate
137. Retaining spring
138. Lever
139. Setscrew
140. Ring

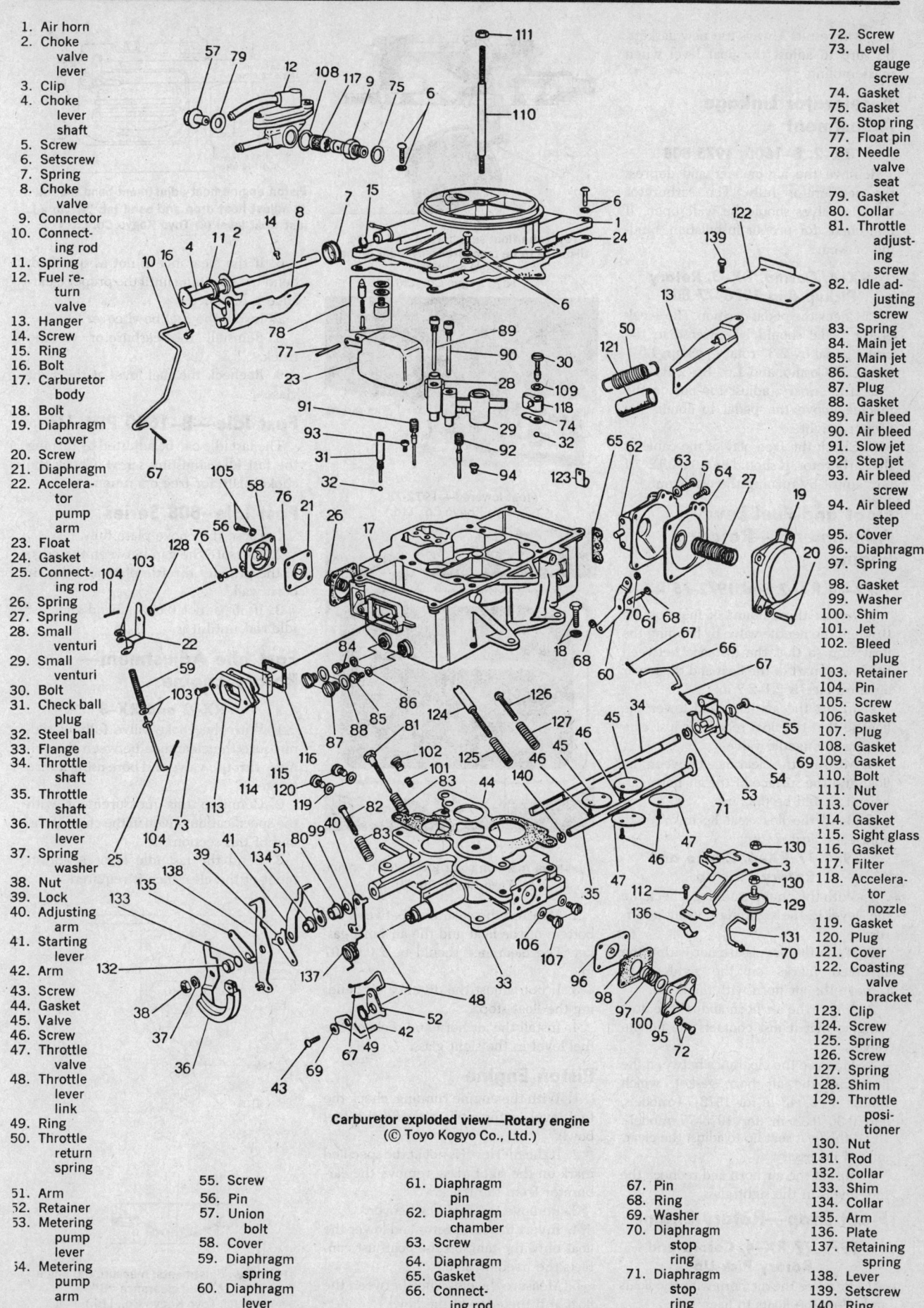

Carburetor exploded view—Rotary engine
(© Toyo Kogyo Co., Ltd.)

ting will result. Always use new gaskets. Be sure to adjust the float level when reassembling.

Accelerator Linkage Adjustment

RX-2, B-1600, 1975 808

Remove the air cleaner and depress the accelerator fully. The carburetor throttle valves should be wide open. If not, check for proper installation, binding or wear.

RX-4, Cosmo, RX-3, Rotary Pickup and 1976-77 808

1. Check the pedal position. The accelerator pedal should be lower than the brake pedal by 2.3"-rotary pickup, 1.0"-808, 2.2"-Cosmo, and 1.6"-Rx-3, Rx-4.
2. If necessary, adjust the nut on the linkage above the pedal to obtain the proper height.
3. Check the free-play of the cable at the carburetor. It should be 0.04-0.12". If not, adjust by turning the clevis nut.

Float and Fuel Level Adjustments—Rotary Engine

1972-74 RX-2 and 1972-75 RX-3

1. Adjust the amount of fuel coming through the needle valve by bending the float stop so that the distance between the lowest part of the float and the lower air horn face is 2.1-2.2 in.
2. Invert the air horn and lower the float so that the float seat lip is just contacting the needle valve.
3. Measure the clearance between the float and the surface of the air horn gaskets; it should be 0.22 in.
4. Bend the float seat lip in order to adjust the float setting.

1974-77 RX-4, Cosmo and Rotary Pick-Up

1. With the engine running, check the fuel level in the sight glass, using a mirror.
2. If the fuel levels are not within the specified marks on the sight glass, remove the air horn with the floats.
3. Invert the air horn and let the float hang so that it just contacts the needle valve.
4. Measure the clearance between the float and the air horn gasket, which should be 0.043 in for 1972-74 models, and 0.30-0.38 in. for 1975-77 models. Bend the float seat lip to adjust the clearance if necessary.
5. Install the air horn and recheck the fuel levels in the sight glass.

Float Drop—Rotary Engine

1974-77 RX-4, Cosmo and Rotary Pick-Up

1. Remove the air horn with the floats and allow the floats to hang free.

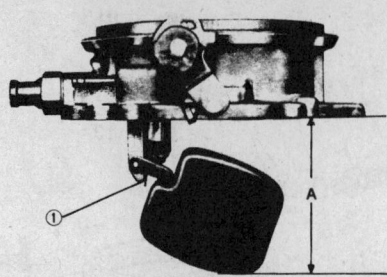

(1) is the float seat lip and "A" is the distance to be measured with float in the raised position
(© Toyo Kogyo Co., Ltd.)

(With gasket)

Float lowered—1972-73
(© Toyo Kogyo Co., Ltd.)

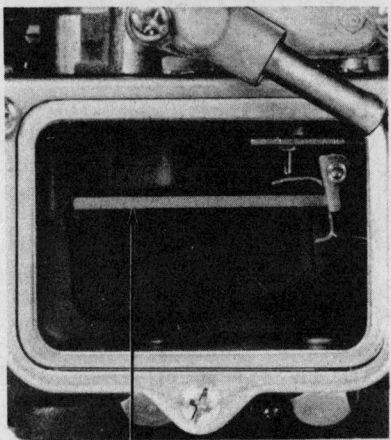

FUEL LEVEL MARK

Fuel level mark on sight glass piston engine
(© Toyo Kogyo Co. Ltd.)

2. Measure the clearance between the bottom of the float and the air horn gasket. The clearance should be 2.03-2.07 in.
3. If not, adjust the distance by bending the float stop.
4. Install the air horn and recheck the fuel level in the sight glass.

Piston Engine

1. With the engine running, check the fuel level in the sight glass (in the fuel bowl).
2. If the fuel level is not at the specified mark on the sight glass, remove the carburetor from the truck.
3. Remove the fuel bowl cover.
4. Invert the carburetor and lower the float until the tang on the float just contacts the needle valve.
5. Measure the clearance between the float and the edge of the bowl.

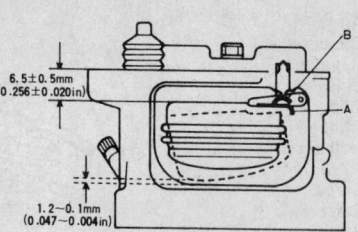

6.5±0.5mm (0.256±0.020in)

1.2—0.1mm (0.047—0.004in)

Piston engine float adjustment-bend tab "A" to adjust float drop and bend tab "B" to adjust float level (© Toyo Kogyo Co. Ltd.)

6. If the clearance is not as specified, bend the float tang until the proper clearance is obtained.
7. Install the fuel bowl cover.
8. Reinstall the carburetor on the truck.
9. Recheck the fuel level at the sight glass.

Fast Idle—B-1600 Pick-Up

The fast idle can be adjusted by turning the fast idle adjusting screw. Check the choke plate for free operation.

Fast Idle—808 Series

1. Close the choke plate fully.
2. Measure the gap between the edge of the primary throttle plate and the air horn wall.
3. If it is not 0.052", bend the fast idle rod until it is.

Fast Idle Adjustment— Rotary Engine

RX-2 and RX-3

1. With the choke valve fully closed, measure the clearance between the primary throttle valve and bore using a wire gauge.
2. Compare this measurement with the specifications given in the chart at the end of this section.
3. Bend the fast idle lever if adjustment of the clearance is required

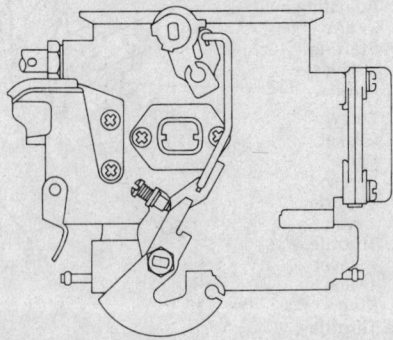

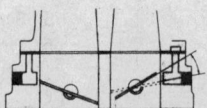

Fast idle adjustments: measure the angle "A" and clearance "B"
(© Toyo Kogyo Co., Ltd.)

4. Test the choke valve to make sure that it operates freely.

5. Open the choke valve all the way. The throttle valve should be opened less than one degree, when measured with a protractor.

6. Close the choke valve to an angle of 35°. The throttle valve should just begin to open at this point.

7. Start the engine and run it at idle. The choke diaphragm rod should be pulled all the way out. If it is not, check for a clogged or an improperly connected vacuum line.

Fast Idle

Year	Throttle Valve Clearance (in.)
1972-73 (M/T)	0.045
1973 (A/T)	0.055
1974-75	0.069-0.085

1973–75 RX–4 and Rotary Pick-Up

1. Warm the engine and pull the choke knob all the way out.

2. Measure the clearance between the primary throttle plate and the wall of the primary throttle bore. The clearance can be measured with a suitable drill bit.

3. The clearance should be 0.0398-0.-0524 in. (#61-#55 drill) for cars with manual transmission, or 0.0480-0.0618 in. (#55-#53 drill) for cars with automatic transmission.

4. If the clearance is not as specified, adjust the fast idle by bending the connecting rod to obtain the proper clearance.

1976–77 RX–4, Cosmo & Rotary Pickup

1. Remove the carburetor.

2. Close the choke and measure the gap between the primary throttle valve and the throttle wall. Clearance should be 0.067–0.079 in.

3. Bend the fast idle rod to adjust.

Accelerator Pump Adjustment—Rotary Engine

1. Remove the air cleaner assembly.

2. Move the primary throttle valve and check pump discharge.

3. If there is no discharge, check for a clogged pump nozzle or a binding pump lever.

4. If it is binding, dress the sliding surface of the lever with sandpaper and lubricate it with oil.

5. If pump discharge is still unsatisfactory, adjust the pump lever by selecting one of the two other adjusting holes in the connecting rod.

MANUAL TRANSMISSION

Removal and Installation

Passenger Cars 4 Speed or 5 Speed

1. Remove the knob from the gearshift lever.

2. Unfasten the screws which secure the center console to the floor and remove the console over the shift lever.

3. Remove the floor mat.

4. Unfasten the screws which attach the shift lever boot and withdraw the boot over the shift lever.

5. Unbolt the cover and remove it from the gearshift lever retainer.

6. Pull the gearshift lever, complete with its shims and bushings, straight up and out of its retainer.

7. Detach the ground lead from the negative (−) battery terminal.

8. Unfasten the nuts which secure the clutch release cylinder and tie the cylinder up out of the way. Do not disconnect the hydraulic line from the clutch release cylinder. On RX-4 models, remove the starter motor upper bolt and loosen the 3 upper engine-to-transmission bolts.

9. Detach the back-up light switch multiconnector which is located near the clutch release cylinder. On RX-4s, remove the brake booster vacuum line bracket from the clutch housing.

10. Raise the car and support it with jackstands.

CAUTION: *Be sure that the car is securely supported.*

11. Unscrew the transmission drain plug and drain the oil. Wipe the drain plug clean and install it.

12. Remove the driveshaft, as described below, and plug up the transmission extension housing.

NOTE: *An old U-joint yoke makes an excellent plug. Or, lacking this, secure a plastic bag over the opening with rubber bands.*

13. Detach the exhaust pipe from the thermal reactor flange. On RX-4 models, remove the heat insulators first.

CAUTION: *Be sure that the reactor and exhaust pipe have cooled sufficiently to prevent severe burns.*

14. Unfasten the speedometer cable from the extension housing.

15. Detach the starter motor wiring. Remove its securing nuts and bolts and withdraw the starter motor.

16. Support the transmission with a block of wood mounted on a jack.

17. Remove the nuts which attach the transmission support to the frame members.

18. Evenly, and in several stages, remove the bolts which retain the bell housing on the engine.

19. Carefully slide the transmission assembly rearward until the input shaft has cleared the clutch disc.

20. Gently lower the transmission from the car.

Transmission installation is performed in the reverse order of removal. Align the clutch plate with an arbor or an old input shaft. Adjust the clutch and shift linkage as detailed elsewhere. Refill the transmission with gear oil:

Below 0°F—SAE EP 80

Above 0°F—SAE EP 90

B–1600 Pick-Up 4 Speed

1. Raise and support the truck. Drain the lubricant from the transmission.

2. Disconnect the ground wire from the battery.

3. Remove the gearshift lever boot.

4. Unbolt the cover plate from the gearshift lever retainer.

5. Pull the gearshift lever, shim and bushing straight up and away from the gearshift lever retainer.

6. Disconnect the wires from the starter motor and back-up light switch.

7. Disconnect the speedometer cable from the extension housing.

8. Remove the driveshaft.

9. Unbolt the exhaust pipe from the bracket on the transmission case.

10. Disconnect the exhaust pipe at the exhaust manifold.

11. Unhook the clutch release fork return spring and remove the clutch release cylinder from the clutch housing.

12. Remove the starter.

13. Support the transmission with a jack.

14. Unbolt the transmission from the rear of the engine.

15. Place a jack under the engine, protecting the oil pan with a block of wood.

16. Unbolt the transmission from the crossmember.

17. Unbolt and remove the crossmember.

18. Lower the jack and slide the transmission rearward until the mainshaft clears the clutch disc.

19. Remove the transmission from under the truck.

20. Installation is the reverse of removal.

Rotary Pick-Up 4 Speed or 5 Speed

1. Remove the knob from the gearshift lever.

2. Remove the gearshift lever boot.

3. Unbolt the retainer cover from the gearshift lever retainer.

4. Pull the gearshift lever, shim and bushing straight up and away from the gearshift lever retainer.

5. Disconnect the battery ground wire.

6. Remove the bolt attaching the power brake vacuum pipe to the clutch housing.

7. Disconnect the ground strap from the transmission case.

8. Remove the clutch release cylinder.

9. Remove the one upper bolt holding the starter and the three upper bolts and nuts securing the transmission to the engine.

10. Raise and support the truck.

11. Disconnect the wires from the starter motor and the back-up light switch wires.

12. Unbolt and remove the heat insulator from the front exhaust pipe.

13. Disconnect the exhaust pipe from the brackets.

14. Disconnect the exhaust pipe front flange from the exhaust manifold. Remove the front exhaust pipe.

15. Remove the driveshaft.

16. Insert a transmission oil plug into the extension housing.

17. Remove the starter.

18. Install a jack under the engine and support the engine.

19. Unbolt the transmission support from the body.

20. Remove the two lower bolts holding the transmission to the engine.

21. Slide the transmission rearward until the mainshaft clears the clutch disc and remove the transmission from under the truck.

22. Installation is the reverse of removal.

Overhaul

Disassembly—RX–3 and RX–2

1. Remove the clutch throwout bearing, spring, and fork.

2. Unfasten the bolts which secure the bellhousing to the transmission case. Remove the bellhousing assembly.

3. Remove the shift lever tower from the extension housing.

4. Withdraw the spring seat and spring from the end of the intermediate lever.

5. Unfasten the nuts which secure the extension housing to the transmission case. Slide the extension housing off of the mainshaft.

NOTE: *Turn the intermediate lever end as far to the left as it will go, while sliding the extension housing off.*

6. Remove the spring cap bolt, the spring, and contact piece from the extension housing. On models with seatbelt interlocks, remove the neutral switch.

7. Remove the intermediate lever assembly from the extension housing.

8. Remove its setscrew and then the speedometer driven gear from the extension housing.

9. Remove the bottom cover and the two upper covers from the transmission case.

10. Remove the shift fork rod lockballs and springs; then remove the interlock pins.

11. Unfasten the shift fork retaining bolts. Remove the shift forks along with the reverse idler gear from the transmission case.

12. Slide the speedometer drive gear off the mainshaft and remove the lockball, after first withdrawing the snap-ring at the rear of the speedometer drive gear.

13. Check the synchronizer key clearance in the following manner:

   a. Shift the transmission into third gear.

   b. Use a feeler gauge to check the clearance between the synchronizer key and the opposite edge of the synchronizer ring. The clearance should be 0.0295–0.0787 in.

   c. If the measurement is greater than 0.0787 in., use a thicker thrust washer between first gear and the mainshaft bearing. Selective fit thrust washers are available in three sizes, ranging from 0.0984 to 0.1387 in.

14. Hold the mainshaft to prevent it from turning.

CAUTION: *Be careful when holding the mainshaft not to bend it or damage its surface.*

15. Unfasten the reverse gear locknut. Remove the lockwasher, reverse gear, and the key.

16. Remove the snap-ring from the counter gear and remove the reverse countergear.

17. Remove the bearing retainer and reverse idler gear shaft.

18. Use a bearing puller to remove the ball bearing on the mainshaft and the roller bearing on the countershaft.

19. Remove the snap-rings from the ball bearings on the front side of the transmission case. Then, using the puller, remove the bearings from the input gear and the countergear.

20. Withdraw the input gear, the countergear, and the mainshaft assembly from the case.

21. Remove these parts from the mainshaft in the following order:

   a. Thrust washer

   b. First gear and sleeve assembly

   c. Synchronizer ring

   d. First/second gear clutch hub

   e. Synchronizer ring

   f. Second gear

22. Remove the snap-ring on the front end of the mainshaft; then remove these parts in the following order:

   a. Third/fourth clutch hub

   b. Synchronizer ring

   c. Third gear

Inspection—RX–3 and RX–2

Clean the transmission case thoroughly with solvent and blow it dry with compressed air. Inspect the case for cracks or other signs of damage.

Inspect all of the bearings for wear or roughness.

Examine each of the gears. Replace any gears that have chipped or missing teeth, or gears that show signs of excessive wear.

Check the operation of the synchronizers. Replace any which are worn or damaged.

Place the mainshaft on V-blocks, and measure its runout with a dial indicator. If runout exceeds 0.0012 in., replace the mainshaft.

Assembly—RX–3 and RX–2

1. Assemble the first/second and the third/fourth clutch hubs, with their sleeves. Be careful not to mix up any of the components of the two assemblies.

2. Install the following items, working

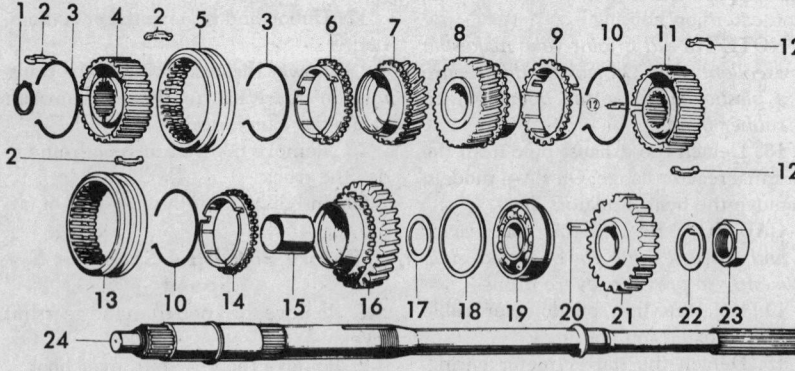

Mainshaft—RX-2 and RX-3

1. Snap-ring
2. Key
3. Spring
4. First and second clutch hub
5. Clutch hub sleeve
6. Third gear synchronizer ring
7. Third gear
8. Second gear
9. Second gear synchronizer ring
10. Spring
11. Third and fourth clutch hub
12. Key
13. Third and fourth clutch hub sleeve
14. Low synchronizer ring
15. Low gear sleeve
16. Low gear
17. Thrust washer
18. Adjusting shim
19. Ball bearing
20. Key
21. Reverse gear
22. Lockwasher
23. Locknut
24. Mainshaft

from the rear side of the mainshaft, in the order listed:

a. Second gear
b. Synchronizer ring
c. First/second clutch hub
d. Synchronizer ring
e. First gear sleeve
f. First gear
g. Thrust washer

3. Working from the front side of the mainshaft, install these items in the following order:

a. Third gear
b. Synchronizer ring
c. Third/fourth clutch hub
d. Snap-ring

4. Install the needle roller bearing and the synchronizer ring on the input shaft.

5. Temporarily place the input shaft-/mainshaft assembly into the transmission case without using the ball bearings.

6. Fit the first/second and third-/fourth shift forks into their respective grooves on the clutch sleeves.

7. Place the countergear assembly in the transmission case.

8. Install the needle roller bearing on the rear side of the countershaft. Install the roller bearing, using the same number of adjustment shims, as were removed, on the front of the countershaft. Fit its snap-ring in place.

9. Install the roller bearings, shims, and snap-rings on the input shaft and on the mainshaft in the same order as outlined in step 8.

10. Fit the reverse gear and snap-ring onto the countershaft.

11. Install the bearing retainer and the reverse idler gearshaft in the transmission case. Torque the bearing retainer bolts to 7 ft lbs.

12. Install the reverse gear and key on the mainshaft.

13. Hold the mainshaft to keep it from turning. Install its lockwasher and locknut. Tighten the lockwasher to 170 ft lbs and then bend up the tabs on the lockwasher.

14. Fit the first/second shift rod into the transmission case and lock it to the first/second shift fork with its set screw.

15. Place the shift rod in Neutral and insert the interlock pin.

16. Install the third/fourth shift rod and interlock pin in the same manner detailed in steps 14 and 15.

17. Install the reverse shift rod and reverse idler gear in the case.

18. Place the shift lockballs and springs into the grooves on the shift rods and install the spring caps.

19. Install the bottom cover and the top covers on the transmission case.

20. Use the lockball to hold the speedometer drive gear on the mainshaft and retain it with the snap-ring.

21. Carefully drive the oil seal into the rear side of the extension housing.

22. Insert the intermediate lever into the extension housing. Install the end onto it and secure it with the setbolt.

23. Fit the contact piece and spring into the extension housing. Secure them with the spring cap bolt.

24. Screw the back-up light switch into the extension housing.

25. Install the speedometer driven gear assembly into the housing, then secure them with the lockplate.

26. Place the gasket on the rear of the transmission case. Bolt the extension housing to the case.

NOTE: *Turn the intermediate lever end as far to the left as it will go, while performing step 26.*

27. Check the operation of the intermediate lever for smoothness.

28. Insert the selector lever interlock over the return spring and install both into the shift tower.

29. Install the lockball and spring so that they align with the groove on the interlock. Screw the spring cap in place and the setscrew into the tower.

30. Install the spring and seat in the intermediate lever end.

31. Place the shift tower gasket on the extension housing and bolt the tower in place.

32. Place a gasket on the front of the transmission case. Install the bellhousing over the gasket.

33. Fit the throwout bearing, spring, and fork into the bellhousing.

34. Remove the transmission from the workstand and intall it in the car.

Disassembly—RX–4, 808 and Rotary Pick-Up—4 Speed

1. Install the transmission in a workstand.

2. Drain the oil from the transmission, if you haven't already done so. Clean any metal chips off the drain plug and reinstall it.

3. Pull outward on the release fork, until it becomes disengaged from the ball stud. Slide the fork and throwout bearing out of the housing.

4. Remove the bellhousing nuts and remove the housing, complete with gasket.

5. Withdraw the adjusting shim from the bellhousing bearing bore.

6. Unfasten the nuts which secure the shift lever tower to the extension housing. Remove the tower and gasket.

7. Remove the extension housing securing nuts, set the control lever end in the neutral position, press the control lever end as far left as possible, and slide the extension housing off the transmission.

8. Remove the neutral switch from the transmission (models with seat belt interlock).

9. Unfasten the gearshift control lever yoke bolt and remove the yoke from the central lever.

10. Remove the speedometer sleeve lockplate. Withdraw the sleeve and driven gear from the extension housing. Remove the back-up light switch, also.

11. Unfasten the speedometer drive gear snap-ring, slide the drive gear off of the output shaft, and remove the lockball.

12. Loosen the bottom cover bolts evenly, and in several stages; then remove the bottom cover and gasket.

13. Remove the cap bolts, the detent springs, and detent balls from the transmission case.

14. Remove the blind covers and gaskets from the transmission case.

15. Remove the Reverse shift rod and idler gear from the rear of the transmission case. Unfasten the Reverse shift fork securing bolt and remove the fork.

16. Unfasten Third/Fourth shift fork securing bolt and remove the Third-/Fourth shift rod from the rear of the case.

17. Repeat step 16 for the First-/Second shift rod.

18. Straighten out the output shaft lockwasher. Hold the output shaft to keep it from turning, and loosen the locknut. Slide the reverse gear and key off the end of the output shaft.

19. Remove the countershaft snap-ring (rear) and remove the Reverse countergear.

20. Unfasten the bearing cover bolts and remove the cover.

21. Remove the reverse idler gear.

22. Hold the fourth synchronizer ring and gear on the output shaft.

23. Remove the countershaft front bearing snap-ring. Using a puller remove the front bearing. Withdraw the adjusting shim from the case bearing bore.

24. Remove the countershaft rear bearing with the puller. Remove the adjusting shim from the case bearing bore.

25. Remove the input shaft bearing snap-ring and remove the bearing with the puller.

26. Lift the countershaft out of the case.

27. Separate the input and output shafts. Remove the input shaft. Remove the fourth synchronizer ring and needle bearing from the input shaft.

28. Lift the output shaft gear assembly out of the case.

29. Remove First/Second and Third-/Fourth shift forks from the case. Withdraw the shift interlock pins from the case.

30. Remove the Third/Fourth clutch hub snap-ring, then slide the clutch hub sleeve, third synchronizer ring and Third gear off the front of the output shaft. Be careful not to mix-up the synchronizer rings.

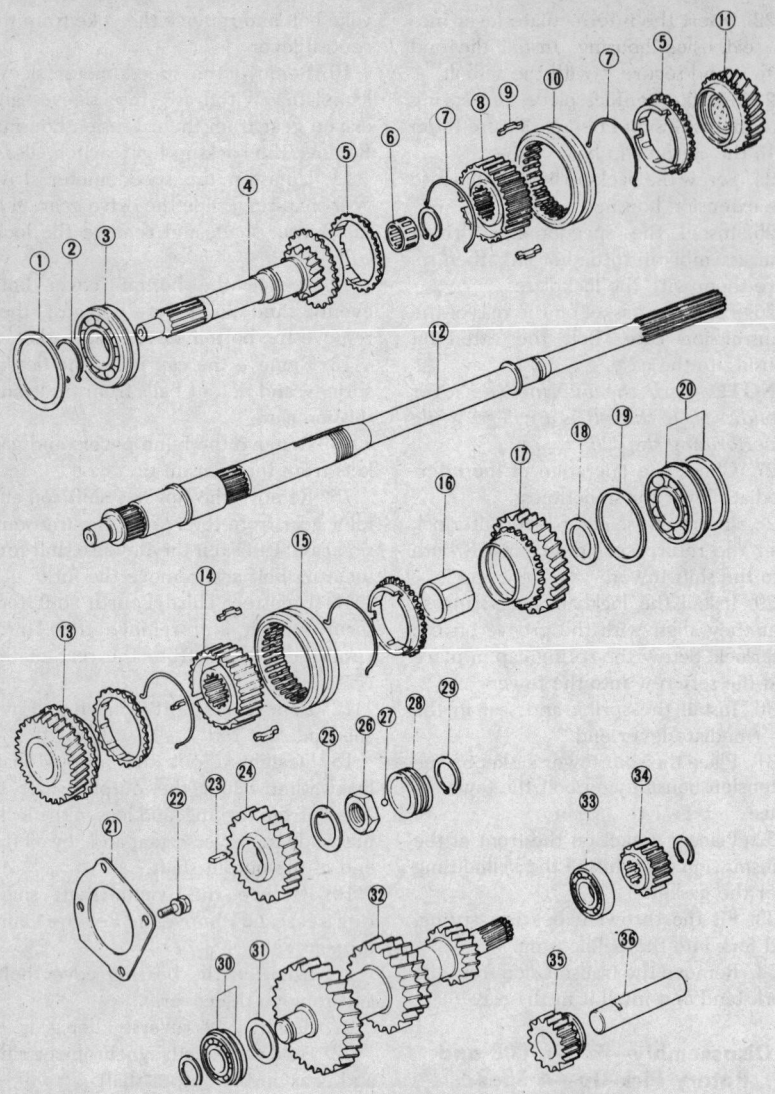

Transmission gears—RX-4, 808 and Rotary Pick-Up 4-speed

1. Adjusting shim
2. Snap-ring
3. Input shaft bearing
4. Input shaft
5. Synchronizer ring
6. Needle bearing
7. Synchronizer key spring
8. Third-and-Fourth clutch hub
9. Synchronizer key
10. Clutch hub sleeve
11. Third gear
12. Output shaft
13. Second gear
14. First-and-Second clutch hub
15. Clutch hub sleeve
16. Gear sleeve
17. First gear
18. Thrust washer
19. Adjust shim
20. Ball bearing and clip
21. Bearing stop
22. Bolt
23. Key
24. Reverse gear
25. Lockwasher
26. Locknut
27. Steel ball
28. Speedometer drive gear
29. Snap-ring
30. Ball bearing and clip
31. Adjusting shim
32. Countershaft
33. Needle bearing
34. Reverse countergear
35. Reverse idler gear
36. Reverse idler gear shaft

31. Slide the First gear and synchronizer ring off the rear of the output shaft.

32. Slide the First gear sleeve, Second gear, second synchronizer ring and First-/Second clutch hub/sleeve assembly off the output shaft.

Inspection—RX-4, 808 and Rotary Pick-Up 4 Speed

The inspection procedures for this transmission are identical to those outlined for the RX-3 and RX-2 above.

Assembly—RX-4, 808 and Rotary Pick-Up 4 Speed

1. Install the First/Second clutch hub on its sleeve, place the three shift keys in the clutch hub key slots, and install the key springs. Be sure to keep the open ends of the key springs 120° apart.

2. Perform step 1 for the Third-/Fourth synchronizer assembly.

3. Place the synchronizer ring on Second gear and then slide Second gear on the output shaft, so that the synchronizer ring faces the rear of the shaft.

4. Slide the First/Second clutch hub and sleeve on the output shaft so that the clutch oil grooves face forward. Be sure that the three synchronizer keys engage the notches on the Second gear synchronizer ring.

5. Install the First gear sleeve in the

output shaft.

6. Fit the synchronizer ring in the First gear and install the gear on the output shaft so that the ring faces the front of the shaft.

7. Install the same thrust washer on the output shaft that you removed during disassembly.

8. Perform step 6 for Third gear.

9. Install the Third/Fourth clutch hub and sleeve on the output shaft, being sure to engage the three synchronizer keys with the notches in the ring.

NOTE: *The larger boss on the Third-/Fourth clutch hub goes toward the front.*

10. Install the snap-ring on the front of the output shaft. Install the output shaft-/gear set assembly in the case. Fit the needle bearing on the front of the output shaft.

11. Place the synchronizer ring on the input shaft gear (Fourth) and install the gear on the front of the output shaft. Be sure that the synchronizer keys engage the notches in the synchronizer ring.

12. Position the First/Second and Third/Fourth shift forks in groove on the clutch hub/sleeve assembly.

13. Install the countergear assembly in the case, being careful to engage each countergear with its respective output shaft gear.

14. Check the output shaft bearing end-play as follows:

  a. Measure the depth of the transmission case output shaft bearing bore.

  b. Measure the height of the bearing.

  c. The difference of these two measurements indicates the correct thickness of the adjusting shim to be used. The amount of end-play permitted is 0–0.0039 in.

  d. Shims are available in thicknesses of 0.0039 or 0.0118 in.

15. Hold the Fourth synchronizer ring off the input shaft synchronizer gear.

16. Install the input and output shaft bearings in their respective bores with a press.

17. Install the input shaft bearing snap-ring.

18. Check the countershaft bearing end-play, as outlined in step 14 for the input shaft. The amount of end-play allowed and available shim size are the same for both bearings.

19. Perform step 15 again.

20. Press the countershaft front and rear bearings into their respective bores. Install the snap-ring on the front bearing.

21. Install the Reverse countergear on the rear of the countershaft and secure with its snap-ring.

22. Fit the reverse gear idler shaft in the transmission case.

23. Install the bearing cover on the case.

24. Secure the reverse gear on the output shaft with its key.

25. Hold the output shaft to keep it from turning and tighten its locknut 150–180 ft lbs. Secure the locknut by bending the tabs on the lockwasher.

26. Fit the first/second shift rod into the case and secure it to the shift fork with the lockbolt. Place the shift rod in Neutral. Drift the interlock pin into its bore.

27. Perform step 26 for the Third-/Fourth shift rod.

28. Slide the Reverse shift rod, complete with the Reverse idler gear, in from the rear of the case. Secure the shift rod to the Reverse fork with its lockbolt.

29. Install the detent balls and springs in their bores and secure them with their cap bolts.

30. Check the synchronizer key-to-exposed edge of the synchronizer ring clearance with a feeler gauge; it should be 0.026–0.079 in. If the clearance is greater, the synchronizer key could pop out. If the clearance is greater than specified, replace the selective-fit thrust washer with one of the three available sizes.

31. Install the blind covers over their gaskets.

32. Fit the lockball, speedometer drive gear, and snap-ring, in that order, on the rear of the output shaft.

33. Install the gearshift control lever through the holes in the front of the extension housing. Fit the Woodruff key on the control lever and install the yoke over it. Secure the yoke with its setbolt.

34. Thread the Neutral switch (for seat belt interlock) into the extension housing.

35. Fit the spring and plunger in the extension housing and secure them with the cap bolt.

36. Install the back-up light switch.

37. Secure the speedometer driven gear in its extension housing bore with the lockplate and bolt.

38. Push the gearshift control lever over to the left as far as possible. Place a gasket on the rear of the transmission case and install the extension housing over it. Secure the extension housing with its bolts. Check the operation of the gearshift control lever.

39. Install the bottom cover on the case. Secure it with its bolts.

40. Insert the select lockpin and spring in the shift tower. Align the slot in the pin with the lockball bore. Drop the lock ball and spring into the bore; secure with the cap bolt.

41. Install the shift tower on the extension housing and secure it with its bolts.

42. Perform step 14 for the input shaft bearing and clutch housing bore. The end-play and shim thickness are the same as in step 14.

43. Lubricate the lip of the bellhousing oil seal.

44. Put a gasket on the front of the transmission case, install the bellhousing on the case, and secure it with the nuts.

45. Install the throwout bearing, release fork and boot in the bellhousing.

Disassembly—RX4, 808, Cosmo, Rotary Pickup 5 Speed

NOTE: *The use of special tools is required for the following procedure.*

1. Pull the release fork outward until the spring clip of the fork releases from the ball pivot.

2. Remove the fork and release bearing from the clutch housing.

3. Remove the nuts attaching the clutch housing and remove the housing, shim and gasket.

4. Remove the bolts attaching the gearshift lever retainer to the extension housing and remove the retainer and gasket.

5. Remove the spring and steel ball, select lock spindle and spring from the gearshift lever retainer.

6. Unbolt and remove the extension housing with the control lever end down to the left as far as it will go.

7. Unbolt and remove the control lever end, key and control rod.

8. Remove the lock plate and speedometer gear assembly from the extension housing.

9. Remove the back-up light switch from the extension housing.

10. Remove the snap ring and slide the speedometer drive gear from the mainshaft.

11. Remove the bottom cover and gasket.

12. Unbolt and remove the shift rod ends.

13. Remove the rear bearing housing from the intermediate housing.

14. Remove the snap ring and remove the mainshaft rear bearing, thrust washer and race. A puller may be necessary.

15. Using the puller, remove the washer and countershaft rear bearing.

16. Remove the counter fifth gear.

17. Remove the intermediate housing from the case.

18. Unbolt and remove the springs and shift locking balls.

19. Remove the two blind covers and gaskets from the case.

20. Unbolt and remove the reverse/fifth shift rod, fork and interlock pin.

21. Unbolt and remove the first/second and third/fourth shift forks, rods and interlock pins.

22. Remove the snap ring and slide the washer, fifth gear and synchronizer ring from the main shaft. Also, remove the steel ball and needle bearing.

23. Lock the rotation of the mainshaft with second and reverse.

24. Remove the locknut and slide the reverse/fifth clutch hub and sleeve assembly, synchronizer ring, reverse gear and the needle bearing from the mainshaft.

25. Remove the spacer and counter reverse gear from the countershaft.

26. Remove the reverse idler gear, thrust washers and shaft from the transmission case.

27. Remove the bearing rear cover plate.

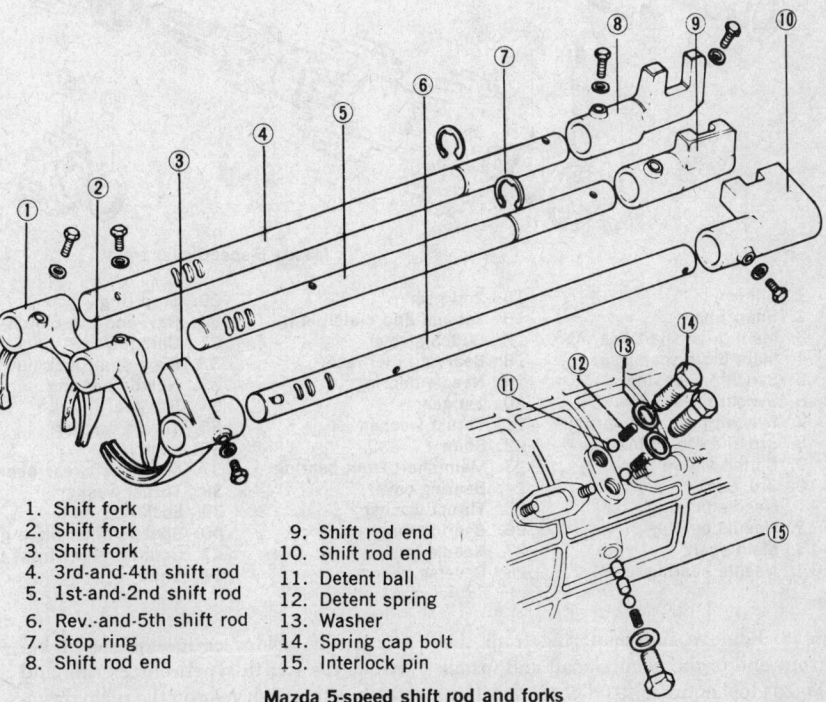

1. Shift fork	9. Shift rod end
2. Shift fork	10. Shift rod end
3. Shift fork	11. Detent ball
4. 3rd-and-4th shift rod	12. Detent spring
5. 1st-and-2nd shift rod	13. Washer
6. Rev.-and-5th shift rod	14. Spring cap bolt
7. Stop ring	15. Interlock pin
8. Shift rod end	

Mazda 5-speed shift rod and forks

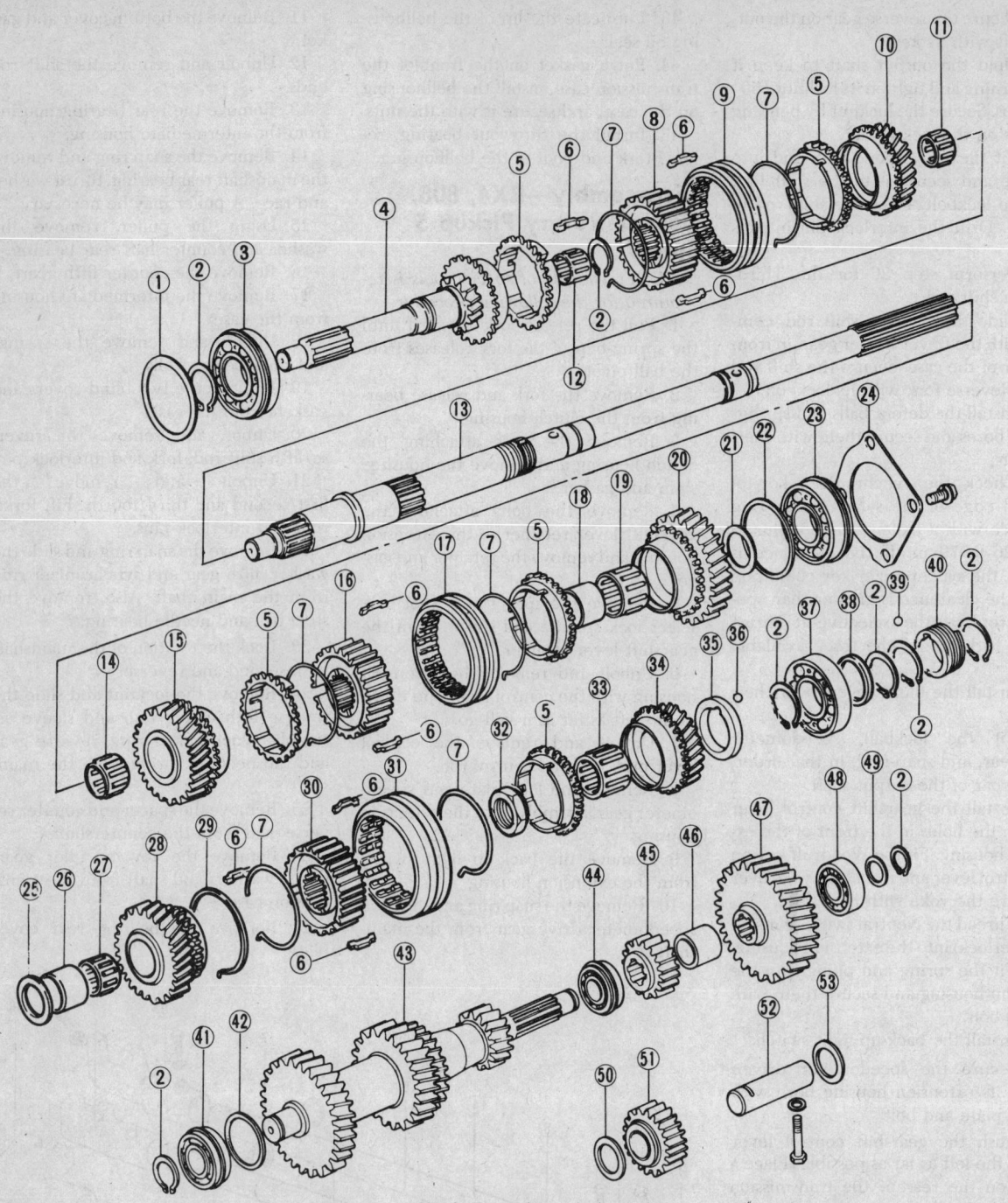

Mazda 5-speed gear train

1. Shim
2. Snap ring
3. Main drive shaft bearing
4. Main drive shaft gear
5. Synchronizer ring
6. Synchronizer key
7. Synchronizer key spring
8. 3rd-and-4th clutch hub
9. Clutch sleeve
10. 3rd gear
11. Needle bearing
12. Needle bearing
13. Main shaft
14. Needle bearing

15. 2nd gear
16. 1st-and-2nd clutch hub
17. Clutch sleeve
18. Bearing inner race
19. Needle bearing
20. 1st gear
21. Thrust washer
22. Shim
23. Main shaft front bearing
24. Bearing cover
25. Thrust washer
26. Bearing inner race
27. Needle bearing
28. Reverse gear

29. Stop ring
30. Rev.-and-5th clutch hub
31. Clutch sleeve
32. Main shaft lock nut
33. Needle bearing
34. 5th gear
35. Thrust washer
36. Lock ball
37. Main shaft rear bearing
38. Thrust washer
39. Lock ball
40. Speedometer drive gear
41. Counter shaft front bearing
42. Shim

43. Counter shaft
44. Counter shaft center bearing
45. Counter reverse gear
46. Spacer
47. Reverse gear
48. Counter shaft rear bearing
49. Thrust washer
50. Thrust washer
51. Reverse idler gear
52. Idler gear shaft
53. Thrust washer

28. Remove the snap ring from the front end of the countershaft and install Mazda tool number 49 0839 445 synchronizer ring holder or its equivalent between the fourth synchronizer ring and the synchromesh gear on the main drive shaft.

29. Using a bearing puller, remove the countershaft front bearing.

30. Remove the adjusting shim from the countershaft front bearing bore.

31. With the puller, remove the countershaft center bearing outer race.

32. With a special puller and attachment, remove the mainshaft front bearing, thrust washer, and inner race along with the adjusting shim front the mainshaft front bearing bore.

33. Remove the snap ring, and using the puller, remove the main drive shaft bearing.

34. Remove the countershaft center bearing inner race with the puller.

35. Separate the input shaft from the mainshaft and remove the input shaft from the case.

36. Remove the synchronizer ring and needle bearing from the input shaft.

37. Remove the mainshaft assembly from the case.

38. Remove the first/second and third/fourth shift forks from the case.

39. Remove the snap ring and slide the third/fourth clutch hub and sleeve assembly, synchronizer ring and third gear from the mainshaft.

40. Remove the thrust washer, first gear and needle bearing from the rear of the mainshaft.

41. Press out the needle bearing inner race, synchronizer ring, first and second clutch hub, sleeve assembly, synchronizer ring and second gear from the mainshaft.

Inspection—5 speed

Inspection of components is carried out in the same manner as described in Rx–2, Rx–3.

Assembly

1. Install the third/fourth clutch hub into the sleeve, place the three keys into the clutch hub slots and install the springs onto the hub.

2. Assemble the first/second and reverse/fifth clutch hub and sleeve as described in step 1.

3. Install the needle bearing, second gear, synchronizer ring, and first/second clutch assembly on the rear section of the mainshaft.

4. Press on the first gear needle bearing inner race.

5. Install the third gear and synchronizer ring onto the front section of the mainshaft.

6. Install the third/fourth clutch assembly onto the mainshaft.

7. Fit the snap ring on the mainshaft.

8. Install the needle bearing, synchronizer ring, first gear and thrust washer on the mainshaft.

9. Install the mainshaft assembly in the case.

10. Install the needle bearing on the front end of the mainshaft.

11. Install the first/second and third-/fourth shift forks in their respective clutch sleeves.

12. Press the countershaft center bearing inner race on the countershaft.

13. Position the countershaft in the case.

14. Check the mainshaft bearing end play. Check the depth of the mainshaft bearing bore in the case. Measure the mainshaft bearing height. The difference indicates the required adjusting shim to give a total end play of less than 0.0039″.

15. Install the synchronizer ring holder tool between the fourth synchronizer ring and the synchromesh gear on the input shaft.

16. Position the shims and mainshaft bearing in the bore and install with a press.

17. Install the input shaft bearing in the same way.

18. Check the countershaft front bearing end play in the same way as the mainshaft bearing end play.

19. Install the front bearing snap ring.

20. Press the countershaft center bearing into position.

21. Install the bearing cover plate.

22. Install the reverse idler gear shaft, thrust washers and reverse idler gear in the case.

23. Install the counter reverse gear and spacer on the rear end of the countershaft.

24. Install the thrust washer and press the needle bearing inner race of the reverse gear on the mainshaft.

25. Install the needle bearing, reverse gear, synchronizer ring, reverse/fifth clutch assembly and new mainshaft lock nut on the mainshaft.

26. Lock the mainshaft with the second and reverse gears. Tighten the locknut to 115–173 ftlb. Bend the tabs of the locknut.

27. Install the needle bearing, synchronizer ring and fifth gear on the mainshaft.

28. Install the thrust washer, steel ball and snap ring on the mainshaft.

29. Check the thrust washer-to-snap ring clearance. Clearance should be 0.-0039–0.0118″.

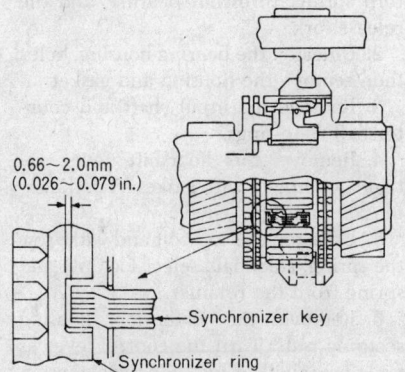

0.66~2.0mm
(0.026~0.079 in.)

Synchronizer key

Synchronizer ring

Checking synchronizer clearance

30. Install the first/second shift rod through the holes in the case and fork.

31. Install the interlock pin with a special installer and guide.

32. Install the third/fourth shift rod through the holes in the case and fork.

33. Align the holes and install the lock bolts of each shift fork and rod.

34. Install the interlock pin as above.

35. Position the reverse/fifth shift fork on the clutch sleeve and install the shift rod.

36. Tighten the lock bolt.

37. Install the three shift locking balls, springs and cap bolts.

38. Place the third/fourth clutch sleeve in third gear.

39. Check the clearance between the synchronizer key and the exposed edge of the synchronizer ring with a feeler gauge. The gap should be 0.026–0.079″. Adjust by varying thrust washers.

40. Install the two blind covers and gaskets.

41. Install the undercover and gasket. Torque to 4–7ftlb.

42. Apply a thin coat of sealer to the mating edges and install the intermediate housing on the transmission case. Align the lock bolt holes of the housing and reverse idler gear shaft, install and tighten the lock bolt.

43. Position the counter fifth gear and bearing to the rear end of the countershaft and install with a press.

44. Install the thrust washer and snap ring.

45. Check the clearance between the washer and snap ring. Clearance should be less than 0.0039″.

45. Install the mainshaft rear bearing with a press.

46. Install the thrust washer and snap ring.

47. Check the thrust washer-to-snap ring clearance. Clearance should be less than 0.0059″.

48. Apply a thin coat of sealing agent to the mating surfaces and install the bearing housing on the intermediate housing.

49. Install the shift rod ends on their respective rods.

50. Install the speedometer drive gear and steel ball on the mainshaft. Secure it with a snap ring.

51. Install a speedometer driven gear assembly on the extension housing and secure it with the bolt and lock plate.

52. Insert the control rod through the holes from the front side of the extension housing.

53. Align the key and insert the control lever end in the control rod.

54. Install the bolt and tighten it to 20–30ftlb.

55. Install the back-up light switch and tighten to 20–30 ftlb.

56. Place the gasket on the case and

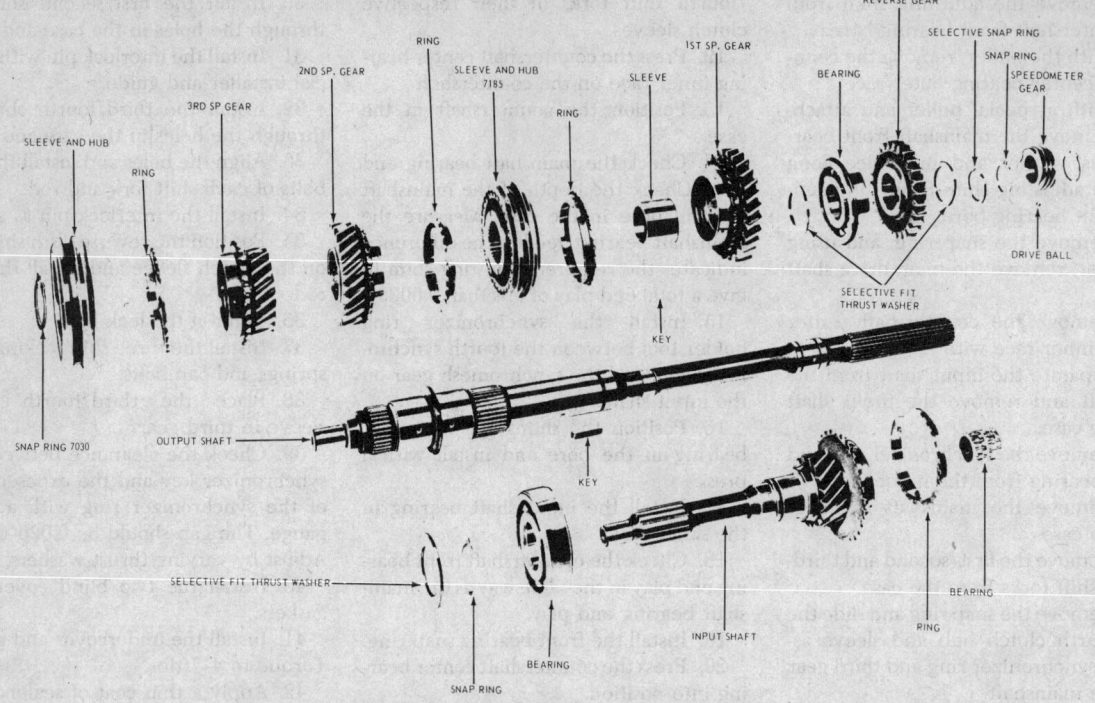

Input and output shafts—B-1600 (© Toyo Kogyo Co., Ltd.)

Labels on diagram: SLEEVE AND HUB, RING, 3RD SP GEAR, 2ND SP. GEAR, RING, SLEEVE AND HUB 7185, RING, 1ST SP. GEAR, SLEEVE, REVERSE GEAR, BEARING, SELECTIVE SNAP RING, SNAP RING, SPEEDOMETER GEAR, DRIVE BALL, SELECTIVE FIT THRUST WASHER, KEY, SNAP RING 7030, OUTPUT SHAFT, KEY, SELECTIVE FIT THRUST WASHER, SNAP RING, BEARING, INPUT SHAFT, RING, BEARING

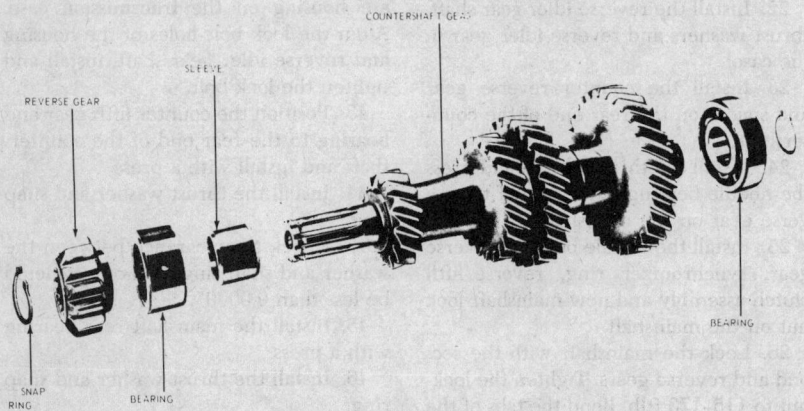

B-1600 countershaft (© Toyo Kogyo Co., Ltd.)

Labels on diagram: REVERSE GEAR, SLEEVE, COUNTERSHAFT GEARS, BEARING, SNAP RING, BEARING

install the extension housing with the control lever end down and as far to the left as it will go.

57. Tighten the bolts.

58. Check for proper operation of the gear shift lever.

59. Insert the select lock spindle and spring from the underside of the shift lever retainer.

60. Install the steel ball and spring in alignment with the spindle groove and install the spring cap bolt.

61. Install the gearshift lever retainer and gasket on the extension housing.

62. Check the bearing end play. Measure the depth of the bearing bore in the housing. Measure the height of the bearing protrusion. The difference indicates the thickness of the shim needed. The end play should be less than 0.0039″.

63. Place the gasket on the front side of the case. Apply lubricant to the lip of

the oil seal and install the clutch housing on the case.

64. Install the release bearing and fork on the clutch housing.

Disassembly—B-1600 Pick-Up

1. Remove the throwout bearing return spring, throwout bearing, and the release fork.

2. Unfasten the bearing housing, bolts, then remove the housing and gasket.

3. Remove the input shaft and countershaft snap-rings.

4. Remove the floorshift lever retainer, complete with gasket from the extension housing.

5. Unfasten the cap bolt and withdraw the spring, steel ball, select lock pin and spring from the retainer.

6. Remove the extension housing securing nuts. Turn the control lever as far left as it will go and slide the extension housing off the output shaft.

7. Remove the spring seat and spring from the end of the shift control lever.

8. Loosen the spring cap and withdraw the spring and plunger from their bore.

9. Unfasten the bolt from the control rod yoke, then remove the control rod and boss from the extension housing.

10. Loosen the setscrew and remove the speedometer driven gear. Remove the back-up light switch.

11. Remove the speedometer drive gear snap-ring, slide the gear off the output shaft and take off the lockball.

12. Tap the front ends of the input shaft and countershaft with a plastic hammer; then remove the intermediate housing assembly from the transmission case.

13. Remove the three cap bolts; then withdraw the springs and lockballs.

14. Unfasten the shift lever securing nut. Remove the reverse shift rod. Reverse idler gear, and shift lever from the intermediate housing.

15. Remove the setscrews from all the shift forks and push the shift rods rearward to remove them. Remove the shift forks as well.

16. Withdraw the Reverse shift rod lockball, spring, and interlock pins from the intermediate housing.

17. Keep the output shaft from turning; straighten the tabs on its lockwasher, and remove its locknut. Remove Reverse gear and key from the output shaft.

18. Remove the snap-ring from the rear of the countershaft and slide the reverse countergear off.

19. Using a plastic hammer, tap the rear of the output shaft and countershaft

Remove the Reverse shift lever from the intermediate housing—B-1600 (ⓒ Toyo Kogyo Co., Ltd.)

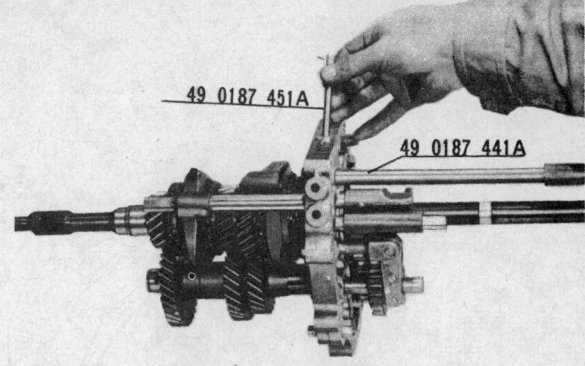

Input shaft, output shaft, and countershaft assembled to the intermediate housing—B-1600 (ⓒ Toyo Kogyo Co., Ltd.)

in turn, being careful not to damage them. Remove both shafts from the intermediate housing.

20. Remove the bearings from the intermediate housing and transmission case.

21. Remove the snap-ring from the output shaft.

22. Slide the Third/Fourth clutch hub, sleeve, synchronizer ring, and Third gear off the output shaft.

23. Remove the thrust washer, First gear, sleeve, synchronizer ring, and second gear from the rear of the output shaft.

Inspection—B-1600 Pick-Up

The inspection procedures for this transmission are identical to those outlined for the RX-2 and RX-3, above.

Assembly—B-1600 Pick-Up

1. Install the Third/Fourth synchronizer clutch hub on the sleeve. Place the three synchronizer keys in the clutch hub key slots. Install the key springs with their open ends 120° apart.

2. Install Third gear and the synchronizer ring on the front of the output shaft. Install the Third/Fourth clutch hub assembly on the output shaft. Be sure that the larger boss faces the front of the shaft.

3. Secure the gear and synchronizer with the snap ring.

4. Perform step 1 to the First/Second synchronizer assembly.

5. Position the synchronizer ring on second gear. Slide Second gear on the output shaft so that the synchronizer ring faces the rear of the shaft.

6. Install the First/Second clutch hub assembly on the output shaft so that its oil grooves face the front of the shaft. Engage the keys in the notches on the Second gear synchronizer ring.

7. Slide the First gear sleeve onto the output shaft. Position the synchronizer ring on First gear. Install the First gear on the output shaft so that the synchronizer ring faces frontward. Rotate the First gear as required to engage the notches in

the synchronizer ring with the keys in the clutch hub.

8. Slip the thrust washer on the rear of the output shaft. Install the needle bearing on the front of the output shaft.

9. Install the synchronizer ring on Fourth gear and install the input shaft on the front of the output shaft.

10. Press the countershaft rear bearing and shim into the intermediate housing; then press the countershaft into the rear bearing.

11. Keep the thrust washer and First gear from falling off the output shaft by supporting the shaft. Install the output shaft on the intermediate housing. Be sure that each output shaft gear engages with its opposite number on the countershaft.

12. Tap the output shaft bearing and shim into the intermediate housing with a plastic hammer. Fit the cover on the housing.

13. Install Reverse gear on the output shaft and secure it with its key. Keep the output shaft from turning while tightening its locknut. Secure the nut by bending the tabs on the lockwasher.

NOTE: *The chamfer on the teeth of both the Reverse gear and the Reverse countergear should face rearward.*

14. Install the Reverse countergear and secure it with its snap-ring.

15. Install the lockball and spring into the bore in the intermediate housing. Depress the ball with a screwdriver.

16. Install the Reverse shift rod, lever, and idler gear at the same time. Tighten the nut which secures the shift lever to the intermediate housing. Place the Reverse shift rod in the neutral position.

17. Align the bores and insert the shift interlock pin.

18. Install the Third/Fourth shift rod into the intermediate housing and shift bores. Place the shift rod in Neutral.

19. Install the next interlock pin in the bore.

20. Install the First/Second shift rod.

21. Install the lockballs and springs in their bores. Install the cap bolt.

22. Fit the speedometer drive gear and lockball on the output shaft, and install its snap-ring.

23. Apply sealer to the mating surfaces of the intermediate housing. Install the intermediate housing in the transmission case.

24. Install the input shaft and countershaft front bearings in the transmission case. Fit the snap-ring on the input shaft bearing.

25. Secure the speedometer driven gear to the extension housing with its set-screw.

26. Install the control rod through the holes in the front of the extension housing.

27. Align the key with the keyway and install the yoke on the end of the control rod. Install the yoke lockbolt.

28. Fit the plunger and spring into the extension housing bore and secure with the spring cap.

29. Turn the control rod all the way to the left, install the extension housing on the intermediate housing, and tighten its securing nuts. Check control rod operation.

30. Insert the spring and select lockpin inside the gearshift retainer. Align the steel ball and spring with the lockpin slot, and secure it with the spring cap.

31. Install the spring and spring seat in the control rod yoke.

32. Install the gearshift lever retainer over its gasket on the extension housing.

33. Lubricate the lip of the front bearing cover oil seal and secure the cover on the transmission case.

34. Check the clearance between the front bearing cover and bearing. It should be less than 0.006 in. If it is not within specifications insert additional adjusting shims. The shims are available in 0.006 in. or 0.012 in. sizes.

35. Install the throwout bearing, return spring and release fork.

Shift Lever Adjustment

The shift lever may be adjusted during transmission installation by means of the

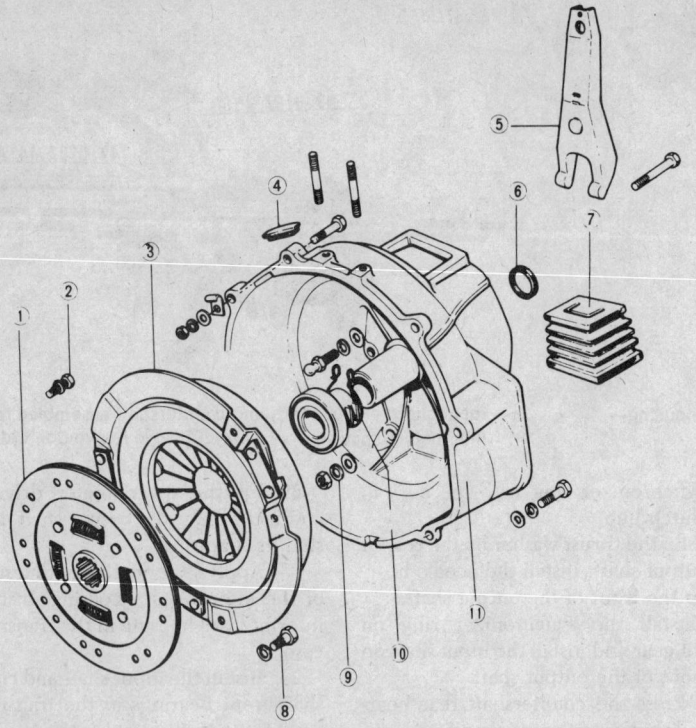

Clutch components
(© Toyo Kogyo Co., Ltd.)

1. Clutch disc
2. Bolt
3. Clutch cover and
   pressure plate
   assembly
4. Service hole cover
5. Release fork
6. Oil seal
7. Dust boot
8. Reamer bolt
9. Release bearing
10. Spring
11. Clutch housing

adjusting shims on the three bolts between the cover plate and the packing. The force required to move the shift knob should be 4.4–8.8 lbs.

CLUTCH

Removal and Installation

1. Remove the transmission as detailed above.
2. Attach a brake to the flywheel.
3. Install a clutch arbor to hold the clutch in place. An old input shaft makes an excellent arbor.
4. Unfasten the bolts (4 securing and 2 pilot) which secure the clutch cover, one turn at a time in sequence, until the clutch spring tension is released. Remove the bolts evenly.
5. Remove the clutch disc.
   CAUTION: *Be careful not to get grease or oil on the surface of the clutch disc.*
6. Unfasten the nut which secures the flywheel to the eccentric shaft, using a suitably large wrench.
7. Remove the flywheel with a puller.
8. Unhook the return spring from the throwout bearing and remove the bearing.
9. Pull out the release fork until the retaining spring frees itself from the ball

stud. Withdraw the fork from the housing.

Clutch installation is performed in the following order:

1. Clean the flywheel and pressure plate surfaces with fine sandpaper. Be sure that there is no oil or grease on them. Grease the eccentric shaft needle bearing.
2. Apply Loctite® (RX–2 and RX–3 only) on the eccentric shaft threads. Install the flywheel with its keyway over the key on the eccentric shaft.
3. Apply sealer to both sides of the flywheel lockwasher and position the lockwasher on the eccentric shaft.
4. Install the flywheel locknut(s) and tighten it to 350 ft lbs (112–118 ft lbs— 808 and B–1600 Pick-Up); then bend the tabs of the lockwasher up around it.
5. Use an arbor to center the clutch disc during installation. Install the clutch disc with the long end of its hub facing the transmission.

   NOTE: *Use an old input shaft to center the clutch disc, if an arbor is not available.*

6. Align the O-mark on the clutch cover with the reamed hole or the O-mark on the flywheel.
7. Tighten the clutch cover bolts evenly, and in two or three stages, to 13–20 ft lbs.

CAUTION: *Do not tighten the bolts one at a time.*

8. Grease the pivot pin. Insert the release fork through its boot so that its retaining spring contacts the pivot pin.
9. Lightly grease the face of the throwout bearing and its clutch housing retainer.
10. Install the throwout bearing and return spring. Check the operation of the release fork and throwout bearing for smoothness.
11. Install the transmission.

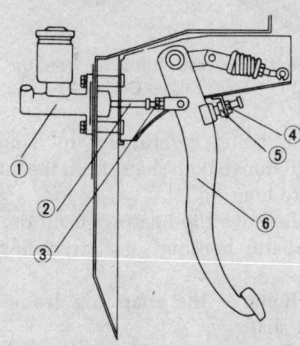

Clutch pedal height adjustment
(© Toyo Kogyo Co., Ltd.)

1. Master cylinder
2. Rod
3. Locknut
4. Adjusting bolt
5. Locknut
6. Clutch pedal

Pedal Height Adjustment

1. Loosen the locknut on the adjusting bolt.
2. Turn the adjusting bolt until the clearance between the pedal pad and the floormat is 7.28 in.
3. Carefully tighten the locknut.

Pedal Free-Play Adjustment

RX–2 and RX–3

1. Loosen the locknut on the master cylinder pushrod.
2. Rotate the pushrod until the clutch pedal has a travel of 0.8–1.2 in. before clutch disengagement.
3. Carefully tighten the locknut.

RX–4, Cosmo, 808 and Pick-Ups

The free-play of the clutch pedal before the pushrod contacts the piston in

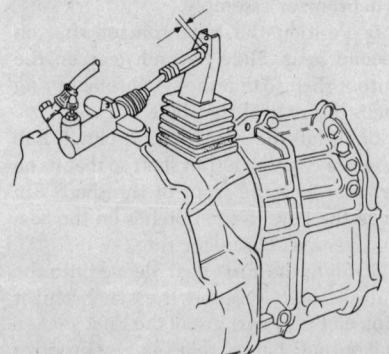

Release fork free-play is measured at arrows
(© Toyo Kogyo Co., Ltd.)

the master cylinder should be 0.02–0.12 in.

To adjust the free-play, loosen the locknut and turn the pushrod until the proper adjustment is obtained. Tighten the locknut after the adjustment is complete.

Release Fork Free-Play Adjustment

1. Unfasten the return spring from the release fork.
2. Loosen the locknut on the release rod.
3. Turn the adjusting nut on the release rod until the proper release fork free-play is obtained:
RX–3, RX–4 and Cosmo—0.12–0.16 in.
RX–2—0.16–0.20 in.
Pick-Ups—0.14–0.18 in.
4. Carefully tighten the locknut and hook the return spring back on the release fork.

Clutch Master Cylinder

Removal and Installation

1. Unfasten the hydraulic line from the master cylinder outlet and plug the outlet.
   CAUTION: *Use care not to drip any hydraulic fluid on the car's painted surfaces, as it is an excellent paint remover.*
2. Remove the nuts which secure the master cylinder assembly to the firewall.
3. Withdraw the master cylinder straight out and away from the firewall.
   Installation is performed in the reverse order of removal. Bleed the hydraulic system as detailed below.

Overhaul

1. Thoroughly clean the outside of the master cylinder.

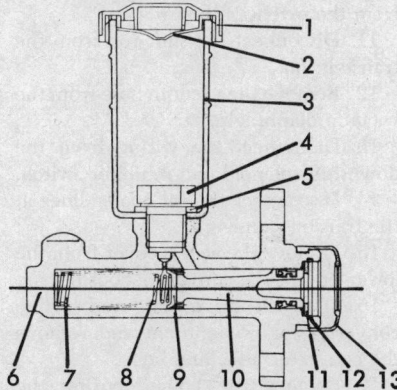

Cutaway view of the master cylinder
(© Toyo Kogyo Co., Ltd.)

1. Cap	8. Compensating
2. Baffle	port
3. Reservoir	9. Primary cup
4. Bolt	10. Piston
5. Washer	11. Stop washer
6. Cylinder	12. Stop wire
7. Return spring	13. Boot

2. Drain the hydraulic fluid from the cylinder. Unbolt the reservoir from the cylinder body.
3. Remove the boot from the cylinder.
4. Release the wire piston stopring with a screwdriver and withdraw the stop washer.
5. Withdraw the piston, piston cups, and return spring from the cylinder bore.
6. Wash all of the parts in clean hydraulic (brake) fluid. Do not use mineral spirits.
7. Examine the piston cups. If they are damaged, softened, or swollen, replace them with new ones.
8. Check the piston and bore for scoring or roughness.
9. Use a wire gauge to check the clearance between the piston and its bore. Replace either the piston or the cylinder if the clearance is greater than 0.006 in.
10. Be sure that the compensating port in the cylinder is not clogged.
    Assembly of the master cylinder is performed in the following order:
1. Dip the piston and cups in clean hydraulic (brake) fluid.
2. Bolt the reservoir up to the cylinder body.
3. Fit the return spring into the cylinder.
4. Insert the primary cup in the bore so that its flat side is facing the piston.
5. Place the secondary cup on the piston and insert them in the cylinder bore.
6. Install the stop washer and the wire piston stop.
7. Fill the reservoir half-full of hydraulic fluid. Operate the piston with a screwdriver until fluid spurts out of the cylinder outlet.
8. Fit the boot on the cylinder.

Clutch Release Cylinder

Removal and Installation

1. Unscrew the hydraulic line from the release cylinder and plug it.
2. Unhook the release fork return spring from the cylinder.
3. Unfasten the nuts which secure the release cylinder to the transmission.
   Installation is performed in the reverse order of removal. Bleed the hydraulic system, as detailed below, and adjust the release fork free-play, as detailed above.

Overhaul

Consult the master cylinder overhaul section above for release cylinder overhaul procedures.

System Bleeding

1. Remove the rubber cap from the bleeder screw on the release cylinder.
2. Place a bleeder tube over the end of the bleeder screw.

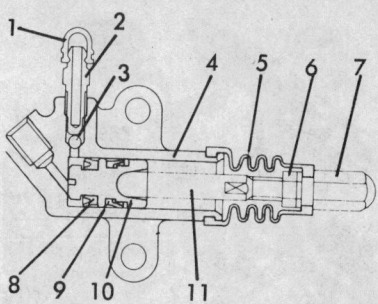

Cutaway view of the release cylinder
(© Toyo Kogyo Co., Ltd.)

1. Cap	7. Adjusting nut
2. Bleeder screw	8. Primary cup
3. Valve	9. Secondary cup
4. Cylinder	10. Piston
5. Boot	11. Push rod
6. Lock nut	

3. Submerge the other end of the tube in a jar half-filled with hydraulic (brake) fluid.
4. Depress the clutch pedal fully and allow it to return slowly.
5. Keep repeating step 4, while watching the hydraulic fluid in the jar. As soon as the air bubbles disappear, close the bleeder screw.
   NOTE: *During the bleeding procedure the reservoir must be kept at least ¾ full.*
6. Remove the tube and refit the rubber cap. Fill the reservoir with hydraulic fluid.

AUTOMATIC TRANSMISSION

Removal and Installation

RX–2 and RX–3

1. Remove the ground cable from the negative battery terminal.
2. Jack up the vehicle and securely support it with jackstands.
3. Remove the heat shroud. Unfasten the exhaust pipe bracket on the right-hand side of the torque converter housing.
4. Unfasten the bolts which secure the exhaust pipe to the rear side of the front muffler. Detach the exhaust pipe.
   CAUTION: *The exhaust system on rotary engine-equipped Mazda's gets considerably hotter than a conventional system; be sure to allow enough time for it to cool before performing steps 3–4.*
5. Unfasten the four bolts from the driveshaft flange and withdraw the driveshaft from the extension housing. Plug up the hole in the extension housing so that fluid does not leak out.
6. Detach the speedometer cable at the extension housing.
7. Remove the control rod.

Mazda

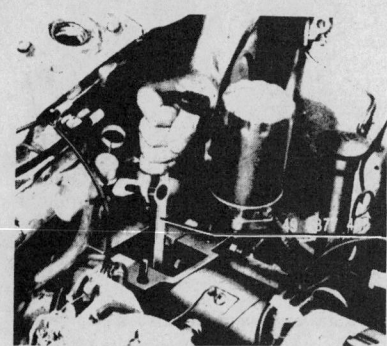

Loosening the torque converter bolts
(© Toyo Kogyo Co., Ltd.)

8. Unfasten the vacuum lines from the vacuum modulator.

9. Unfasten the multiconnector from the downshift solenoid and the neutral safety switch. Remove the wires from the bracket.

10. Disconnect the lines which run to the oil cooler on the left-hand side of the transmission.

11. Attach a brake to the ring gear.

12. Remove the starter motor. See the appropriate section under "Engine Electrical" for details.

13. Matchmark the torque converter and the flex-plate.

14. Working through the starter motor mounting hole, unfasten the four bolts which secure the torque converter to the flex-plate.

15. Support the transmission with an automatic transmission jack.

16. Unfasten the nuts which secure the transmission support member and remove the member.

17. Lower the transmission jack to increase the gap between the transmission and the underbody of the car.

18. Unfasten evenly, and in several stages, the bolts which secure the torque converter housing to the top of the engine.

19. Raise the transmission so that it is level again.

20. Use a screwdriver to carefully apply pressure between the torque converter and the flex-plate.

21. Slide the transmission rearward and lower it from the car.

CAUTION: *Do not rest the weight of the transmission on the torque converter splines.*

Automatic transmission installation is performed in almost the reverse order of removal. There are several points which should be noted, however:

1. Before installing the transmission, use a dial indicator to measure flex-plate runout. Runout should be around 0.012 in. If runout exceeds 0.020 in., the flex-plate must be replaced.

2. Hand-tighten the four torque converter installation bolts and then lock the flex-plate with a brake. Next, tighten the four bolts evenly, and in several stages, to 29–36 ft lbs.

3. After completing transmission installation, rotate the eccentric shaft to be sure that there is no interference in the transmission.

4. Fill the transmission with type F transmission fluid. Converter capacity is 5.7 qts.

5. Check and adjust the following items, after completing installation:
    a. Shift linkage
    b. Neutral safety switch
    c. Engine idle speed
    d. Kickdown switch and downshift solenoid.

6. Check the fluid level again and road test the car.

RX–4, Cosmo and Rotary Pick-Up

1. Disconnect the cable from the negative (−) battery terminal.

2. Remove the power brake vacuum line bracket from the converter housing.

3. Remove the converter access hole cover. Lock the flex-plate by holding the drive pulley lockbolt with a wrench.

4. Matchmark the converter and flex-plate. Unfasten the four converter-to-flex-plate securing bolts.

5. Perform steps 2 through 4 of the RX–2 and RX–3 automatic transmission removal procedure. Be sure to observe the "CAUTION".

6. Unfasten the bolts from the driveshaft flange and center bearing. Push the driveshaft out of the extension housing. Plug the hole in the extension housing, so that fluid doesn't leak out.

7. Perform steps 6 and 7 of the RX–2 and RX–3 removal procedure.

8. Disconnect the starter wiring. Remove the starter motor securing bolts and separate the starter from the converter housing.

9. Remove the bottom cover from the converter housing.

10. Perform steps 15 through 17 of the RX–2 and RX–3 removal procedure.

11. Remove the vacuum fitting from the intake manifold. Unfasten the vacuum line from the converter housing, transmission case, and extension housing. Disconnect the hose from the vacuum modulator and remove the vacuum line.

12. Disconnect the downshift solenoid wiring and separate the wires from the clip.

13. Disconnect the lines which run to the oil cooler at the left-hand side of the transmission. Remove the clips for these lines from the converter housing and transmission case.

14. Perform steps 18 through 21 of the RX–2 and RX–3 automatic transmission removal procedures. Be sure to observe the "CAUTION."

Automatic transmission installation is performed in almost the reverse order of removal. There are several points which should be noted, however:

1. Before installing the transmission, use a dial indicator to measure flex-plate runout. Runout should be about 0.012 in. If runout exceeds 0.020 in., the flex-plate must be replaced.

2. Hand-tighten the four torque converter installation bolts and then lock the flex-plate with a brake. Next, tighten the four bolts evenly, and in several stages, to 27–40 ft lbs.

3. After completing transmission installation, rotate the eccentric shaft to be sure that there is no interference in the transmission.

4. Fill the transmission with type F transmission fluid. Converter capacity is 6.6 qts.

5. Check and adjust the following items, after completing installation:
    a. Shift linkage
    b. Neutral safety switch
    c. Engine idle speed
    d. Kickdown switch and downshift solenoid

6. Check the fluid level again and road test the car.

808

1. Disconnect the battery.

2. Raise and support the vehicle.

3. Place a drain pan under the transmission.

4. Starting at the rear and working toward the front, loosen the attaching bolts at the pan and allow the fluid to drain.

5. After the fluid has drained, replace the pan using one bolt at each corner.

6. Remove the heat insulator.

7. Disconnect the exhaust pipe.

8. Disconnect the drive shaft at the rear axle flange.

9. Lower the drive shaft and remove it from the vehicle.

10. Disconnect the speedometer cable from the extension housing.

11. Disconnect the shift rod from the transmission.

12. Remove the vacuum hose from the vacuum diaphragm.

13. Disconnect the wiring from the downshift solenoid and inhibitor switch.

14. Disconnect the oil cooler lines at the transmission.

15. Remove the access cover from the lower end of the converter housing.

16. Mark the drive plate and torque converter for realignment and remove the converter attaching bolts.

17. Remove the bolts securing the transmission rear support to the crossmember.

18. Support the transmission with a jack and remove the crossmember.

19. Secure the transmission to the jack with a safety chain.

20. Lower the transmission enough to loosen the attaching bolts.

21. Remove the converter housing-to-engine bolts.

22. Remove the filler tube.

23. Insert a pry bar between the flex plate and the converter to prevent the converter from disengaging the transmission as the assembly is moved rearward.

24. Remove the transmission and converter as an assembly.

25. To install the transmission, reverse the removal procedure. Tighten the converter-to-drive plate bolts to 33 ftlb.

26. Fill the transmission with Type F fluid only.

NOTE: *Do not use any other fluid except Type F.*

Check the following and adjust if necessary:

    a. Manual linkage
    b. inhibitor switch
    c. engine idle
    d. kick-down switch
    e. downshift solenoid

Shift Linkage Adjustment

1972–75

1. Unfasten the T-joint on the intermediate lever.

2. Place the range selector lever, which is mounted on the side of the transmission case, in Neutral (N); i.e., so that the slot in the selector shaft is pointing straight up and down.

3. Adjust the console-mounted gear selector lever by turning the T-joint until it indicates Neutral (N).

4. Reconnect the T-joint. Check the gear selector operation in all other ranges and to see that the linkage has no slack.

1976–77

1. Place the transmission selector lever in N.

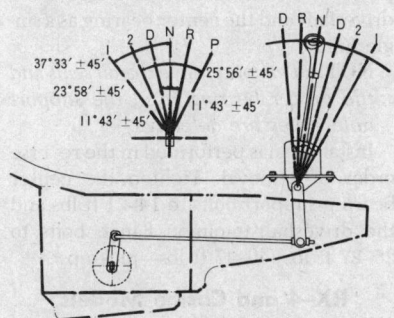

Transmission linkage adjustment
(© Toyo Kogyo Co., Ltd.)

2. Raise the vehicle and disconnect the clevis from the lower end of the selector arm.

3. Move the manual lever to the N position.

NOTE: *The N position is the third detent from the back.*

4. Loosen the two clevis retaining nuts and adjust the clevis so that it freely enters the lever hole.

5. Tighten the retaining nuts.

6. Connect the clevis to the lever and secure with the spring washer, flat washer and retaining clip.

Neutral Safety Switch Adjustment

RX–3 and RX–2

1. Check the shift linkage, as detailed above, before adjusting the neutral safety switch.

2. Remove the nut which secures the gear selector lever and the neutral safety switch attaching bolts.

3. Unfasten the screw which is located underneath the switch body.

4. Place the selector shaft in Neutral by using the gear selector lever.

NOTE: *If the linkage is adjusted properly, the slot in the selector shaft should be vertical.*

5. Move the switch body so that the screw hole in the case aligns with the hole in the internal rotor.

6. Check their alignment by inserting an 0.009 in. diameter pin or a No. 53 drill through the holes.

7. Once the proper alignment is obtained, tighten the switch mounting bolts. Remove the pin or drill and insert the screw back into the hole.

8. Tighten the nut which secures the gearshift selector lever.

9. Check the operation of the neutral safety switch again. If it still is not operating properly, i.e., the car starts in positions other than P (Park) or N (Neutral) or the back-up lights come on in gears other than R (Reverse), replace the switch.

RX–4, Cosmo and Rotary Pick-Up

1. Remove the housing from the shift lever.

2. Adjust the shift lever so that there is 0.–0.012 in. clearance between the pin and the guide plate, when the lever is in Neutral.

3. Adjust the neutral safety switch so that the pin hole in the switch body is aligned with the pin hole of the sliding plate when the shift lever is in Neutral.

4. Check the adjustment by trying to start the engine in all gears. It should only start in Park or Neutral.

5. Reinstall the housing on the shift lever.

808

1. Place the manual lever in N. N is the third detent from the back.

2. Remove the manual lever.

3. Loosen the two neutral switch attaching bolts and remove the screw from the alignment hole at the bottom of the switch.

4. Rotate the switch so that the hole in the switch aligns with the hole in the internal rotor. The pin should be inserted while tightening switch.

Align the neutral safety switch by inserting a drill through the holes on it
(© Toyo Kogyo Co., Ltd.)

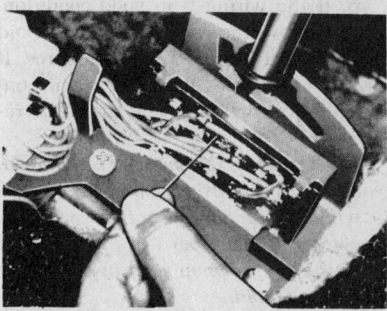

Adjusting the RX-4, Cosmo and Rotary Pickup neutral safety switch
(© Toyo Kogyo Co. Ltd.)

5. Install the alignment hole screw and manual lever.

Pan Removal and Installation

1. Raise and support the vehicle.

2. Place a drain pan under the transmission pan.

3. Remove the pan attaching bolts (except the two at the front). Loosen the two at the front slightly. Allow the fluid to drain.

4. Remove the pan.

5. Remove and discard the gasket.

6. Install a new pan gasket and install the pan on the transmission.

7. Lower the vehicle and fill the transmission with fluid. Check the transmission operation.

Kickdown Switch and Downshift Solenoid Adjustment

1. Check the accelerator linkage for smooth operation.

2. Turn the ignition on but do not start the engine.

3. Depress the accelerator pedal fully to the floor. As the pedal nears the end of its travel, a light "click" should be heard from the downshift solenoid.

4. If the kickdown switch operates too soon, loosen the locknut on the switch shaft. Adjust the shaft so that the accelerator linkage makes contact with it when the pedal is depressed 7/8–15/16 of the way to the floor. Tighten the locknut.

5. If no noise comes from the solenoid at all, then check the wiring for the solenoid and the switch.

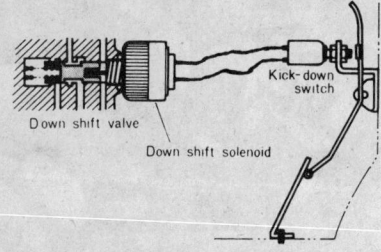

Kickdown switch and downshift solenoid circuit
(© Toyo Kogyo Co., Ltd.)

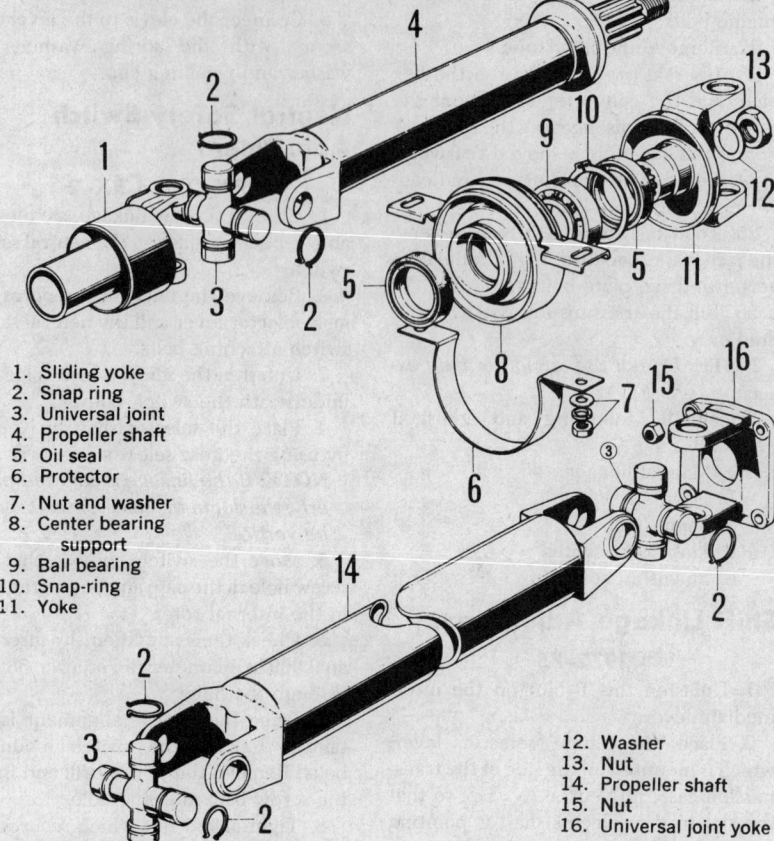

1. Sliding yoke
2. Snap ring
3. Universal joint
4. Propeller shaft
5. Oil seal
6. Protector
7. Nut and washer
8. Center bearing support
9. Ball bearing
10. Snap-ring
11. Yoke

12. Washer
13. Nut
14. Propeller shaft
15. Nut
16. Universal joint yoke

Components of the RX-2 driveshaft
(© Toyo Kogyo Co., Ltd.)

6. If the wiring is in good condition, then remove the wire from the solenoid and connect it to a 12V power source. If the solenoid does not click when connected, it is defective and should be replaced.

NOTE: *When the solenoid is removed, about two pints of transmission fluid will leak out; have a container ready to catch it. Remember to add more fluid to the transmission after installing the new solenoid.*

DRIVE AXLES

Driveshaft and U-Joints

Removal and Installation

RX–3 and 808 Models

1. Raise the rear end of the car and support it using jackstands.

CAUTION: *Be sure that the car is securely supported. Remember, you will be working underneath it.*

2. Matchmark the flanges on the driveshaft and pinion so that they may be installed in their original position.

3. Remove the four bolts which secure the driveshaft to the pinion flange.

4. Lower the back end of the driveshaft and slide the front end out of the transmission.

5. Plug up the hole in the transmission to prevent it from leaking.

NOTE: *Use an old U-joint yoke; or, if none is available, place a plastic bag, secured with rubber bands, over the hole.*

Driveshaft installation is performed in the reverse order of removal. Tighten the driveshaft-to-pinion flange bolts to 22 ft lbs.

1. Yoke
2. Spider and bearing cup assembly
3. Snap ring
4. Shaft
5. Yoke

Components of the RX-3 driveshaft
(© Toyo Kogyo Co., Ltd.)

RX–2 and Pick-up Models

The driveshaft used on these models is removed in a manner similar to that outlined for RX–3 models above. The only difference in the removal procedure is that the center bearing must be unbolted prior to driveshaft removal. Remove the driveshaft and the center bearing as a single unit.

NOTE: *Do not remove the oil seals and the center bearing from the support unless they are defective.*

Installation is performed in the reverse order of removal. Tighten the center bearing support bolts to 14–21 ft lbs and the driveshaft-to-pinion flange bolts to 25–27 ft lbs (40–47 ft lbs—pick-ups).

RX–4 and Cosmo Models

Perform this operation only when the exhaust system is *cold.*

Raise the rear of the car and support it securely with jackstands.

2. Unfasten the nuts, bolts, and screws which secure the front heat insulator to the downpipe. Remove the insulator.

3. Remove the nuts which secure the downpipe to the thermal reactor flange.

4. Unfasten the downpipe from the main muffler flange.

5. Remove the heat insulator from the underbody.

6. Matchmark the pinion and drive-

shaft flange to aid in installation. Remove the driveshaft-to-pinion flange bolts.

7. Unfasten the center bearing securing bolts.

8. Lower the driveshaft, slide it rearward, and remove it.

9. Plug the hole in the transmission with an old U-joint yoke, or cover it with a plastic bag secured by rubber bands, to keep the oil from leaking out.

Driveshaft installation is performed in the reverse order of removal. Tighten the yoke-to-front driveshaft locknut to 116–130 ft lbs.

U-Joint Overhaul

Perform this procedure with the driveshaft removed from the car.

1. Matchmark both the yoke and the driveshaft so that they can be returned to their original balancing position during assembly.

2. Remove the bearing snap-rings from the yoke.

3. Use a hammer and a brass drift to drive *in* one of the bearing cups. Remove the cup which is protruding from the other side of the yoke.

4. Remove the other bearing cups by pressing them from the spider.

5. Withdraw the spider from the yoke. Examine the spider journals for rusting or wear. Check the bearings for smoothness or pitting.

Measure the spider diameter. The standard diameter is 0.5746 on the 808, 0.-5795 on the RX–2 and RX–3 or 0.6516 in. on RX–4, Cosmo and Pick-Up. If the spider wear exceeds 0.0040 in. on RX–2, RX–4, Cosmo and Pick-Up models or 0.-0079 in. on RX–3 models, replace the spider.

NOTE: *The spider and bearing are replaced as a complete assembly only.*

Check the seals and rollers for wear or damage.

Assembly of the U-joint is performed in the following order:

1. Pack the bearing cups with grease.

2. Fit the rollers into the cups and install the dust seals.

3. Place the spider in the yoke and then fit one of the bearing cups into its bore in the yoke.

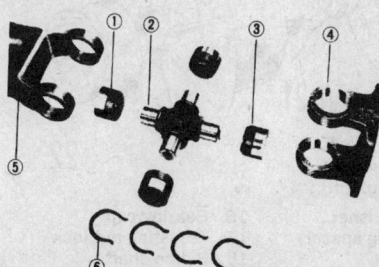

Components of the U-joint
(©Toyo Kogyo Co., Ltd.)

1. Roller bearing (cup) 4. Yoke
2. Spider   5. Driveshaft
3. Oil seal   6. Snap-ring

4. Press the bearing cup home, while guiding the spider into it so that a snap-ring can be installed.

5. Press-fit the other bearings into the yoke.

6. Select a snap-ring to obtain minimum end-play of the spider. Use snap-rings of the same thickness on both sides to center the spider.

NOTE: *Selective fit snap-rings are available in sizes ranging from 0.048 to 0.054 in.*

7. Install the spider/yoke assembly and bearings to the driveshaft in the same manner as the spider was assembled to the yoke.

8. Test the operation of the U-joint assembly. The spider should move freely with no binding.

Axle Shafts

Removal and Installation

Passenger Cars

NOTE: *The left and the right rear axle shafts are not interchangeable, as the left shaft is shorter than the right.*

1. Remove the wheel cover and loosen the lug nuts.

2. Raise the rear of the car and support the axle with jackstands.

3. Unfasten the lug nuts and remove the wheel.

4. Remove the brake assembly as detailed below.

5. Unfasten the nuts which secure the brake backing plate and the bearing retainer to the axle housing.

6. Withdraw the axle shaft with a puller.

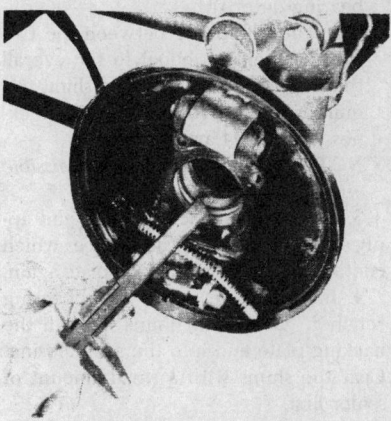

Measure the depth of the bearing seat
(© Toyo Kogyo Co., Ltd.)

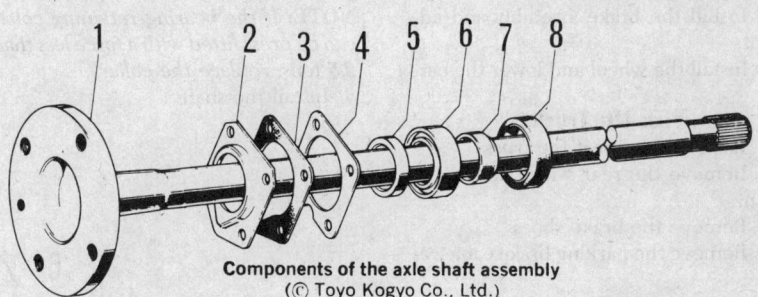

Components of the axle shaft assembly
(© Toyo Kogyo Co., Ltd.)

1. Rear axle shaft   4. Shim   7. Bearing collar
2. Bearing retainer   5. Spacer   8. Oil seal
3. Gasket   6. Bearing

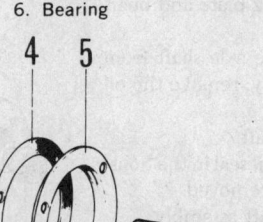

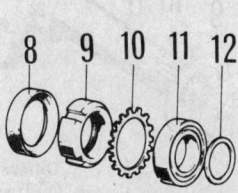

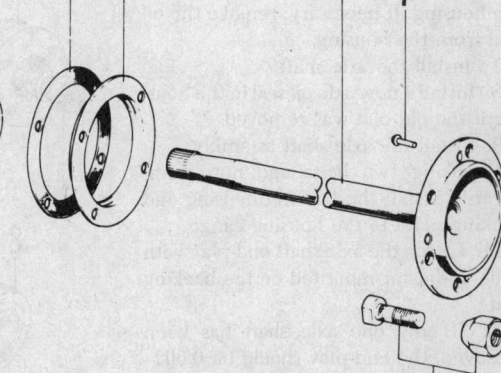

Components of the axle shaft assemblies—pick-up trucks (© Toyo Kogyo Co., Ltd.)

1. Shims   8. Oil seal (Inner)
2. Bearing housing   9. Locknut
3. Oil seal (Outer) 10. Lockwasher
4. Gasket   11. Bearing
5. Baffle   12. Spacer
6. Axle shaft   13. Hub bolt and nut
7. Rivet

Axle shaft installation is performed in the following order:

1. Apply grease to the oil seal lips and then insert the oil seal into the axle housing.

2. Check the axle shaft end-play in the following manner:

a. Temporarily install the brake backing plate on the axle shaft.

b. Measure the depth of the bearing seat and then measure the width of the bearing outer race.

c. The difference between the two measurements is equal to the overall thickness of the adjusting shims required. Shims are available in thicknesses of 0.004 and 0.016 in.

NOTE: *The maximum permissible end-play is 0.004 in.*

3. Remove the backing plate and apply sealer to the rear axle surfaces which contact it. Install the backing plate again.

4. Install the rear axle shaft, bearing retainer, gasket, and shims through the backing plate and into the axle housing. Coat the shims with a small amount of sealer first.

5. Engage the splines on the differential side gear with those on the end of the axle shaft.

6. Install the brake assembly and adjust it.

7. Install the wheel and lower the car.

Pick-Up Trucks

1. Raise and support the truck.

2. Remove the rear wheel and brake drum.

3. Remove the brake shoes.

4. Remove the parking brake cable retainer.

5. Disconnect and plug the hydraulic brake lines at the wheel cylinders.

6. Unbolt the backing plate and bearing housing.

7. Slide the complete axle shaft from the housing. If necessary, remove the oil seal from the housing.

To install the axle shaft:

8. Install a new axle oil seal in the housing if the old one was removed.

9. Install the axle shaft assembly.

10. Using two bolts and nuts, temporarily install the bearing housing and backing plate to the housing flange.

11. Check the axle shaft end-play with a dial indicator mounted on the backing plate.

12. If only one axle shaft has been removed, the end-play should be 0.002–0.006 in. If both axle shafts have been removed, check the end-play after the first shaft is installed. It should be 0.026–0.033 in. The end-play of the second shaft should then be 0.002–0.006 in. Shims are available to adjust the end-play.

13. After adjusting the end-play, install all bolts and torque them to 12–16 ft lbs.

14. Install the brake shoes.
15. Install the brake drum and wheel.
16. Connect the brake lines.
17. Bleed the brakes.
18. Lower the truck and road-test it.

Axle Shaft Bearing and Seal Replacement

1. Remove the rear axle shaft as described above.

2. Using a suitable press, press the axle shaft out of the collar and bearing.

NOTE: *If the pressure needed to press out the shaft exceeds 10 tons, grind off part of the bearing retaining collar and cut it with a cold chisel, taking care not to damage the shaft surface.*

3. Remove the bearing retainer from the shaft.

4. Clean all parts and inspect the condition of the collar, spacer and shaft.

5. Install the retainer and spacer on the shaft.

6. Position the bearing on the shaft with the sealed side toward the shaft flange. Press it on until the spacer comes in contact with the shoulder of the shaft.

7. Press the bearing retaining collar onto the shaft until it contacts the bearing inner race.

NOTE: *If the bearing retaining collar can be press fitted with a force less than 2.5 tons, replace the collar.*

8. Install the shaft.

Differential

Removal and Installation

1. Raise the vehicle and support it with jackstands.

2. Remove the drain (lower) plug from the axle housing and drain the lubricant into a suitable container. Clean and reinstall the plug.

3. Remove the driveshaft as detailed in the appropriate section above.

4. Remove both of the axle shafts as detailed in the section immediately above.

5. Unfasten the nuts which secure the differential carrier to the axle housing and withdraw the carrier assembly from the housing.

Installation is performed in the reverse order of removal. Tighten the carrier-to-housing bolts to 14.5 ft lbs. Fill the axle housing to the level just below the filler plug with one of the following:

Above 0°F-HP SAE 90
Below 0°F-HP SAE 80

Overhaul

NOTE: *Differential overhaul requires the use of special tools and equipment. Proper overhaul cannot be performed without them. The following procedures apply to all Mazda differentials as they are all similar in design.*

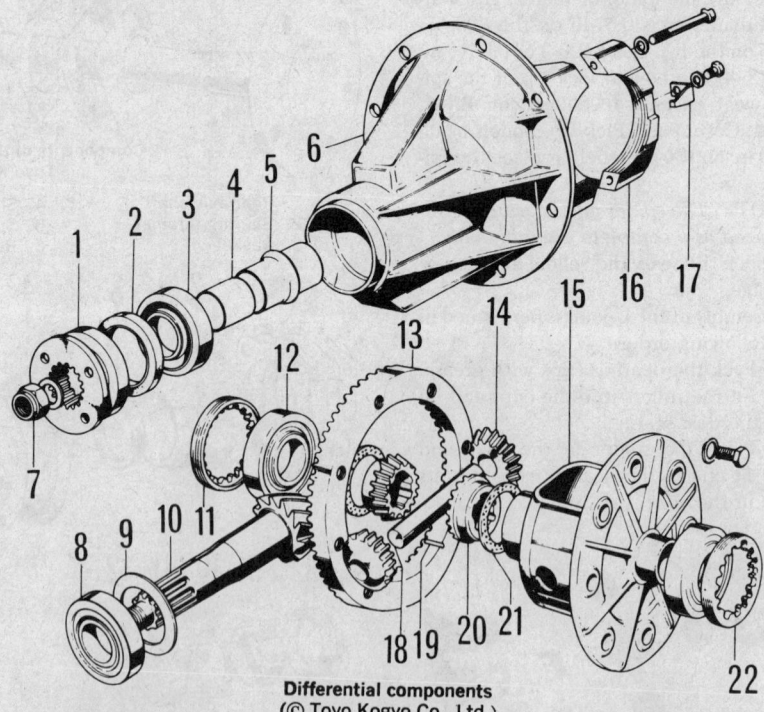

Differential components
(© Toyo Kogyo Co., Ltd.)

1. Pinion flange
2. Pinion oil seal
3. Pinion front bearing
4. Pinion bearing collar
5. Collapsible pinion bearing spacer
6. Carrier
7. Pinion nut
8. Pinion rear bearing
9. Adjusting washer (Adjusting spacer)
10. Drive pinion
11. Pinion side adjusting nut
12. Side bearing
13. Ring gear
14. Pinion gear
15. Differential gear case
16. Bearing cap
17. Adjusting nut lock
18. Pinion shaft
19. Pinion shaft lock pin
20. Side gear
21. Thrust washer
22. Ring gear side adjusting nut

Disassembly

1. Mount the carrier on a workstand.
2. Apply identification marks to the carrier, bearing caps, and adjuster, to aid in installation.
3. Unfasten the bolts which secure adjusting nut lockplates and then remove the lockplates.
4. Loosen, but do not remove, the bearing cap securing nuts and then back off on the adjuster, just enough to remove bearing preload.
5. Remove the differential assembly, complete with the outer bearing races.
   CAUTION: *Be sure that each bearing outer race remains with its bearing.*
6. Remove the differential bearings from the gear case with a puller.
   NOTE: *Use care not to mix up the bearings when setting them aside.*
7. Unfasten the bolts which secure the ring gear to the gear case and remove their washers. Separate the ring gear from the case.
8. Straighten out the punched portion of the gear case, then drive the pinion gear shaft locking pin out of the case with a brass drift.
9. Withdraw the pinion gear shaft.
10. Rotate each of the pinion (spider) gears 90° and remove them, complete with thrust washers.
11. Remove the side gears and thrust washers.
12. Hold the pinion flange by screwing two bolts into it and grabbing them with a pipewrench. Remove the pinion nut.
13. Remove the pinion from the carrier.
    NOTE: *If the pinion is difficult to remove, tap it with a plastic hammer while guiding it out by hand.*
14. Remove the collar, if so equipped, and the collapsible spacer from the pinion.
15. Press out the rear bearing and remove the adjustable shim. Save the shim for later reference.
16. Withdraw the oil seal and the front bearing from the carrier.
17. If necessary, the pinion bearing outer races can be driven out with a brass drift placed in the slots which are provided for this purposes.
    NOTE: *Do not remove the outer races unless they are worn or damaged. If they are replaced, the bearing cones must be replaced as well.*

Inspection

1. Check all of the gears for chipping, broken teeth, wear, or other signs of damage. Replace any gears, as required.
2. Examine the carrier and pinion flange for cracks, wear, and other signs of damage. Replace these parts as necessary.
3. Check the clearance between the splines on the side gears and the rear axle shafts. If it is greater than 0.012 in., replace either the side gears or the axle shafts.
4. Inspect the oil seal for wear and/or damage; replace it if either are present.

Assembly and Adjustment

NOTE: *Start out with a handful of collapsible spacers and different sizes of pinion adjusting shims.*

1. If the old pinion/ring gear assembly and rear bearing are being used, replace the shim with a new one of the same size (identification marking) as was removed. Use a new collapsible spacer.
2. If a new pinion/ring gear assembly or rear bearing is being used, determine the correct adjustment shim size in the following manner:

   a. Look at the identification markings on the old pinion and shim which were removed. Record their markings.
   NOTE: *Pinion markings are given in plus (+) or minus (−) millimeter measurements while the shim has a numbered identification code. Consult the chart below for proper shim identification.*

Pinion Shim Identification

Marking	Thickness (mm)	Marking	Thickness (mm)
08	3.08	29	3.29
11	3.11	32	3.32
14	3.14	35	3.35
17	3.17	38	3.38
20	3.20	41	3.41
23	3.23	44	3.44
26	3.26	47	3.47

   b. Look at the identification measurement stamped on the new pinion and note its value.
   c. Calculate the difference between the measurements of the new and old pinions by adding or subtracting, as necessary.
   d. If the value on the new pinion is *less* than the value on the old, *add* the difference to the thickness of the old shim (in millimeters). Use a new shim of the total thickness.
   e. If the value on the new pinion is *greater* than the value on the old, *subtract* the difference from the thickness of the old shim (in millimeters). Use a new shim having a thickness of the difference.
   f. If the rear pinion bearing was replaced, measure the difference (in millimeters) between the new and the old bearing. Add or subtract the difference between the two bearings from the size of the adjusting shim.
   g. Select the proper size adjusting shim, as determined in the steps above,

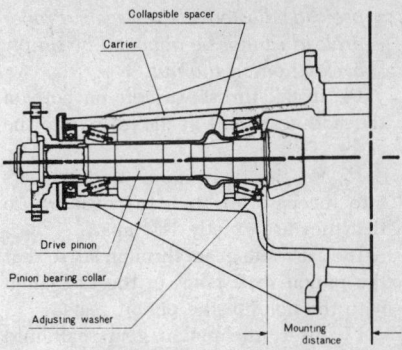

Proper pinion positioning
(© Toyo Kogyo Co., Ltd.)

from one of the following:

3. Position the adjusting shim, of the size as determined in steps 1 or 2, and install the rear pinion bearing on the pinion.
4. If they were removed, install the pinion bearing outer races in the carrier. Be sure that they are properly seated.
5. Place the pinion assembly through the collapsible spacer and into the carrier.
   NOTE: *Use a new collapsible spacer.*
6. Position the front bearing on the pinion. Hold the pinion as far forward as it will go and drive the front bearing on to the pinion until it is fully seated.
7. Coat the lips of the pinion oil seal with grease and fit the seal into the carrier.
8. Tap the pinion flange home on the pinion with a rubber mallet.
9. Install the pinion washer and nut but do not tighten the nut.
10. With the nut still loose, i.e., with no preload on the pinion, check the amount of force required to turn the pinion with a torque wrench that is calibrated in inch pounds; this will measure the amount of drag produced by the oil seal.
11. Install two bolts on the pinion flange and hold it with a spanner or pipe wrench to keep it from rotating. Tighten the pinion nut to 94 ft lbs—RX–2, 808 and RX–3, to 101 ft lbs—RX–4 and Cosmo or to 145 ft lbs—pick-ups.
    CAUTION: *Use care not to overtighten the pinion, as the spacer will collapse and have to be replaced.*
12. Release the pinion flange and measure the amount of preload obtained using the inch/pound torque wrench.
13. Continue tightening the pinion nut, if necessary, a little at a time. Check the preload after each small amount of tightening, until the final preload figure of 7.8–12.2 ft lbs—RX–2, RX–3, 808, RX–4 and Cosmo; or 11.3–15.6 ft lbs—pick-ups plus the oil seal drag measured in step 10, is obtained.
    CAUTION: *If the preload is exceeded, the collapsible spacer will be compressed too much. A new spacer will have to be installed and the bearing*

preload adjusted all over again. Proper preload cannot be obtained by simply backing off on the nut.

14. Install thrust washers on both of the side gears and fit the gears into the case.

15. Fit the two pinion (spider) gears into the case, through the opening, so that they are exactly 180° apart.

16. Turn the gears through 90° so that the pinion shaft holes in the case align with the holes in the pinion gears.

17. Insert the pinion gear shaft into the holes in the case and through the holes in the pinion gears.

NOTE: *Align the pinion shaft so that the lockpin holes in it align with the holes in the case.*

18. Check the backlash between the side gears and the pinion gears with a dial indicator. The backlash between the gear teeth should be 0–0.004 in. If backlash exceeds 0.008 in., adjust it to specifications by selecting one of the following side gear thrust washers:

Thrust Washer Identification

Marking	Thickness (in.)
0	0.0787
1	0.0827
2	0.0866

NOTE: Use the same thickness thrust washers for both side gears.

NOTE: *Use the same thickness thrust washers for both side gears.*

19. Install and stake the lockpin onto the pinion shaft.

20. Bolt the ring gear up to the gear case. Torque the bolts evenly, and in sequence, to 40–47 ft lbs—RX–2, RX–3, 47–54 ft lb—808, and B–1600 or 65–80 ft lbs RX–4, Cosmo and Rotary Pick-Up. Lock the bolts in place with their lockplates.

21. Install the gear bearings in the gear case hub and fit each of the outer races into its respective bearing.

22. Place the differential gearset in the carrier.

NOTE: *Be sure that the marks used for backlash adjustment, which are stamped on the faces of the ring gear and pinion teeth, are aligned.*

23. Install the adjusters on their respective sides by consulting the identification marks made during their removal.

24. Install the bearing cups properly by consulting the identification marks made on them during removal.

25. Rotate the adjusters until the bearings are properly positioned in their outer races and their end-play is eliminated.

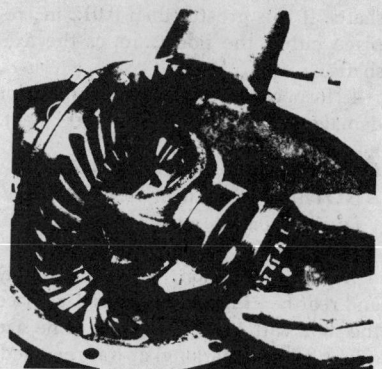

Installing the differential bearing adjuster
(© Toyo Kogyo Co., Ltd.)

Ring Gear Contact Patterns

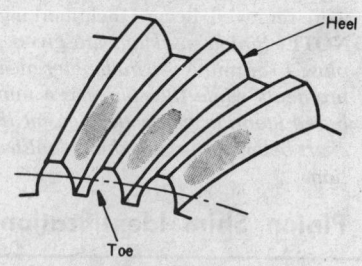

Correct contact pattern
(© Toyo Kogyo Co., Ltd.)

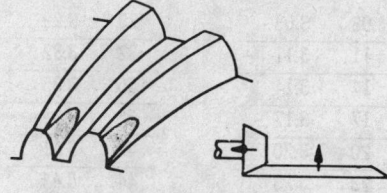

Too much toe contact
(© Toyo Kogyo Co., Ltd.)

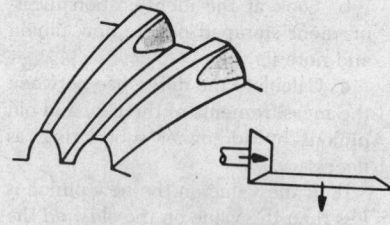

Too much heel contact
(© Toyo Kogyo Co., Ltd.)

26. Finger tighten one of the bearing cap bolts on each bearing.

27. Attach a dial indicator to the flange on the carrier so that its plunger comes into contact with the ring gear at right angles to its teeth.

28. Check the backlash between the pinion and the ring gear teeth:

a. If backlash is *more* than specified, loosen the adjusting nut on the pinion side one notch and tighten the ring gear adjusting nut on notch.

b. If the backlash is *less* than specified, loosen the adjusting nut on the

ring gear side one notch and tighten the pinion adjusting nut one notch.

c. Repeat the procedure until the specified backlash of 0.0067–0.0075 in. —passenger cars or 0.0075–0.0083 in. —pick-ups is obtained.

29. Tighten the adjusting nut on the differential bearings to obtain proper preload. Proper preload is determined when the distance between the pilot sections of the bearing caps is 7.3033 in.— passenger cars or 8.0485–8.0513 in.— pick-ups. Measure the distance with a vernier caliper.

NOTE: *Be careful not to disturb the backlash between the pinion and the ring gear teeth while adjusting the bearing preload.*

30. Tighten the bearing cap securing bolts to 30 ft lbs—passenger cars or 47–56 ft lbs—pick-ups. Install the lockplate on the bearing adjuster so that they cannot loosen.

31. Coat both sides of about six to eight ring gear teeth with red lead. Move the ring gear back and forth several times and then examine the contact pattern made. Compare it to the illustrations below. Adjust the preload or backlash, as required to obtain proper tooth contact.

32. Install the carrier in the axle housing, as outlined above.

REAR SUSPENSION
Springs
Removal and Installation
RX–3, RX–4 and 808

1. Remove the wheel cover and loosen the lug nuts.

2. Raise the back end of the car and support it with jackstands.

CAUTION: *Be sure that the car is securely supported.*

3. Remove the lug nuts and the wheel.

4. Support the rear axle housing with jackstands.

5. On RX–4 and 808 models, disconnect the lower end of the shock from the spring clamp. On all models, unfasten the nuts which secure the U-bolts. Withdraw the U-bolt seat, rubber pad, plate, and the U-bolt itself.

6. Unfasten the two bolts and the nut that secure the spring pin to the front end of the rear spring.

7. Pry the spring pin out with a large, flat screwdriver inserted between the spring pin and its body bracket.

8. Unfasten the nuts and the bolts which attach the rear shackle to the car's body.

9. Withdraw the rear spring assembly, complete with its shackle.

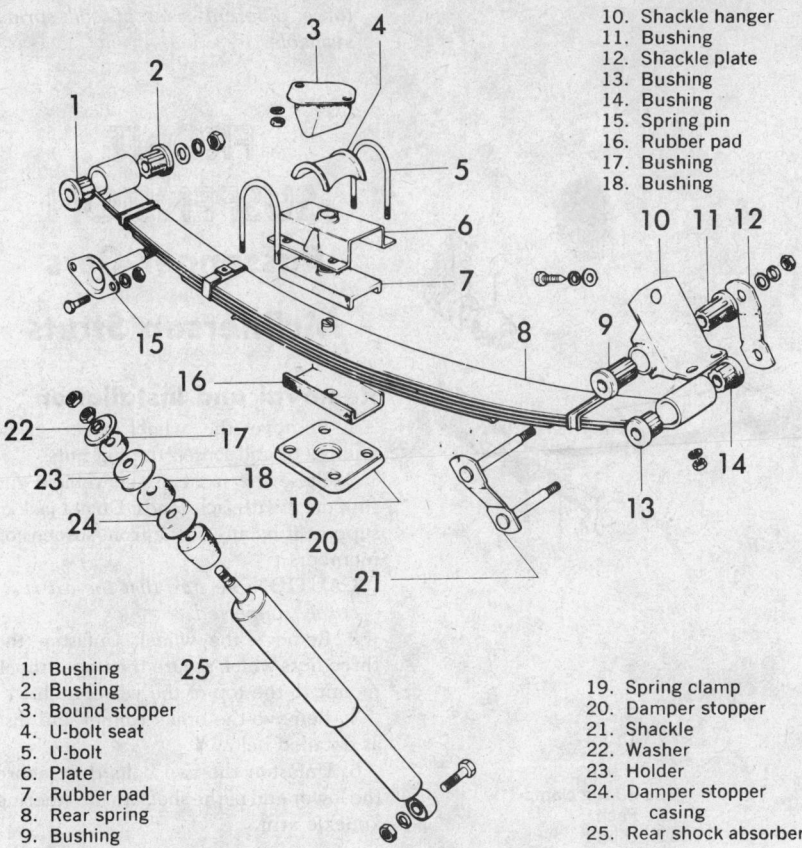

10. Shackle hanger
11. Bushing
12. Shackle plate
13. Bushing
14. Bushing
15. Spring pin
16. Rubber pad
17. Bushing
18. Bushing

1. Bushing
2. Bushing
3. Bound stopper
4. U-bolt seat
5. U-bolt
6. Plate
7. Rubber pad
8. Rear spring
9. Bushing

19. Spring clamp
20. Damper stopper
21. Shackle
22. Washer
23. Holder
24. Damper stopper casing
25. Rear shock absorber

RX-3 sedan and coupe rear suspension—wagon and RX-4 similar
(© Toyo Kogyo Co., Ltd.)

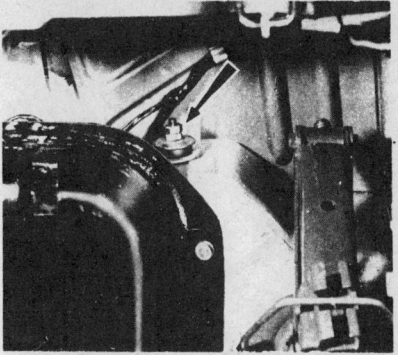

Arrow shows the location of the upper rear shock nut on RX-3 coupes and sedans
(© Toyo Kogyo Co., Ltd.)

Removing the rear shock upper mounting bracket on RX-3 wagons
(© Toyo Kogyo Co., Ltd.)

10. Remove the shackle assembly from the end of the spring.

11. Pull the rubber bushings out from both ends of the spring.

Rear spring installation is performed in the reverse order of removal. When installing the rubber bushings, do not lubricate them. Tighten the U-bolt securing nuts to 30 ft lbs and both the spring and the shackle pins to 14 ft lbs.

Cosmo

1. Raise and support car on stands under the frame side rails.

2. Remove the rear wheels.

3. Support the lower arms with a jack.

4. Remove the pivot bolt and nut which secures the rear end of the lower arm to the axle housing.

5. Slowly and carefully lower the jack to relieve the spring pressure on the lower arm and remove the spring.

6. If replacing one spring only, a suitable adjusting plate will be necessary to give equal road clearance on each side.

7. Install spring in reverse order of removal, but do not tighten bolts while car is on stands. Lower car to rest on wheels and torque the lower arm pivot bolt to 87 ftlb.

RX-2

Rear coil spring removal is performed as part of the shock absorber removal operation. See the appropriate section below for the combined procedure.

Pick-Ups

1. Raise and support the truck, allowing the spring to hang freely.

2. Support the rear axle with jackstands.

3. Disconnect the rear shock absorber at the lower mount.

4. Remove the spring clip nuts and the spring plate.

5. Remove the spring pin nut and remove the two bolts and nuts attaching the spring pin to the frame bracket.

6. Remove the spring pin and remove the front end of the spring from the truck.

7. Remove the shackle plate nuts and the shackle plate.

8. Remove the spring from the truck.

9. Installation is the reverse of removal.

Shock Absorbers

Removal and Installation

RX-3, RX-4 808 Coupes and Sedans and Cosmo

1. Remove the trim panel from the rear of the luggage compartment. On RX-4 models it will be necessary to remove the rear seat first.

2. Unfasten the nuts, then remove the washers and rubber bushings from upper shock absorber mounts.

3. Unfasten the nut and bolt which secure the end of the rear shock to the axle housing.

4. Withdraw the shock from underneath the car.

Installation is performed in the reverse order of removal. Tighten the upper shock mount to 15 ft lbs. on all except 808.

On 808 models, tighten the upper nuts until 6.5 mm exists between the top of the shock absorber rod and the top of the top nut.

RX-3, RX-4 and 808 Wagons

1. Raise the back end of the vehicle and support it with jackstands.

2. Remove the locknuts, washers, and rubber bushings from the bottom shock absorber mount.

3. Install a compressor on the shock and compress it.

4. Unfasten the bolts which secure the upper shock absorber mount to the body.

5. Withdraw the shock, with the compressor still attached, from underneath the car.

6. Slowly remove the compressor from the shock.

Shock absorber installation is performed in the reverse order of removal. Tighten the upper shock mount to 15 ft lbs. on all but the 808. On 808 models, tighten the top nuts until 6.5 mm exists

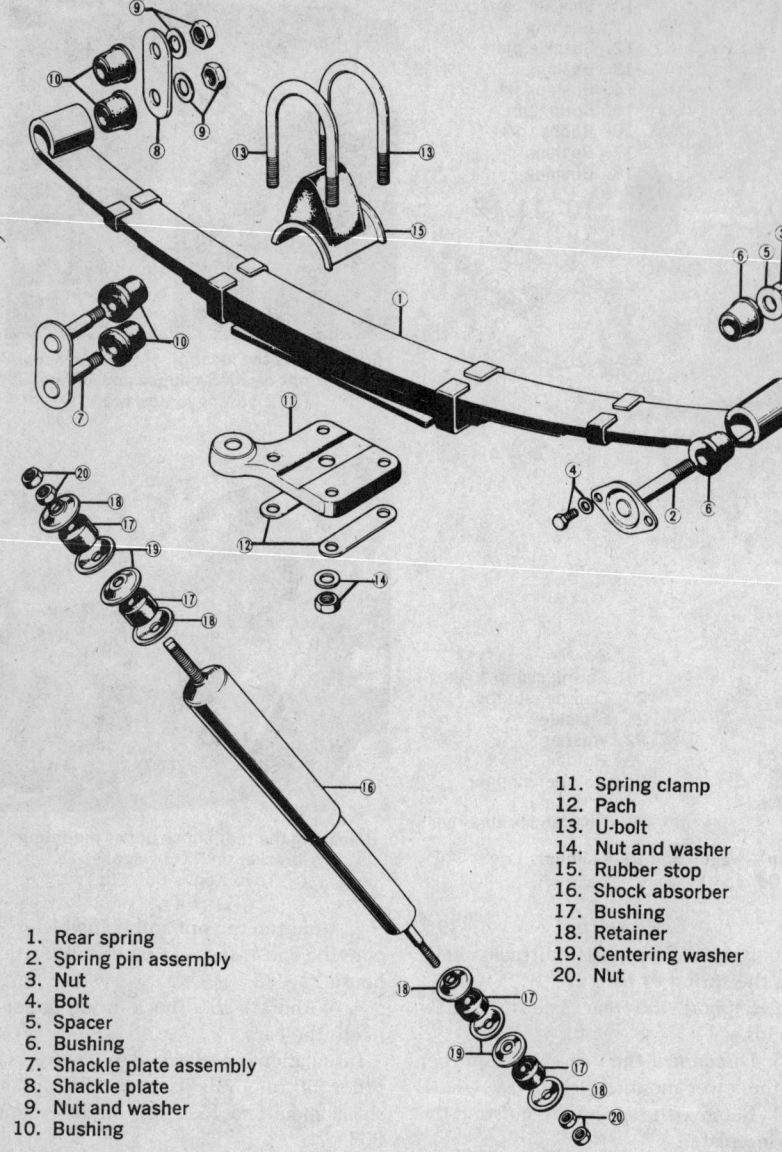

1. Rear spring
2. Spring pin assembly
3. Nut
4. Bolt
5. Spacer
6. Bushing
7. Shackle plate assembly
8. Shackle plate
9. Nut and washer
10. Bushing

11. Spring clamp
12. Pach
13. U-bolt
14. Nut and washer
15. Rubber stop
16. Shock absorber
17. Bushing
18. Retainer
19. Centering washer
20. Nut

Rear suspension—pick-ups (© Toyo Kogyo Co., Ltd.)

between the top of the shock absorber rod and the top of the top nut. Tighten the bottom nut until a gap of 5.0 mm exists.

RX-2 Models

1. Working from inside the luggage compartment, unfasten the nuts which secure the upper end of the shock absorber.

2. Unfasten the nut and bolt at the lower end of the shock absorber.

3. Place a jack underneath the axle housing and raise the car.

4. Place jackstands underneath the frame side rails.

CAUTION: *Be sure that the jackstands are properly placed under the side rails.*

5. Slowly lower the jack to take the load off the springs.

6. Withdraw the shock/coil spring assembly from underneath the car.

7. Mark the shock for identification during assembly and secure the bottom of the shock in a vise.

8. Fit a spring compressor on the spring.

9. Unfasten the locknuts from the upper end of the shock.

10. Remove the washers, bushings, setplate, spring seat, rubber pad, adjusting plate, and bumper from the top of the shock.

Installation of the rear shock is performed in the reverse order of removal. Be sure to mount the shock with its stone guard facing toward the front of the car. Tighten the bolt and nut which secure the lower end of the shock, to 72–87 ft lbs.

NOTE: *If a new coil spring is being fitted, match it with an adjusting plate of the correct thickness to obtain equal road clearance on both sides. There are*

three different sizes of coil springs available.

FRONT SUSPENSION
Passenger Cars
McPherson Struts

Removal and Installation

1. Remove the wheel cover (if so equipped) and loosen the lug nuts.

2. Raise the front of the vehicle and support it with jackstands. Do not jack or support it by any of the front suspension members.

CAUTION: *Be sure that the car is securely supported.*

3. Remove the wheel. Unfasten the three nuts which secure the upper shock mount to the top of the wheel arch.

4. Remove the brake caliper and disc as detailed below.

5. Unfasten the two bolts that secure the lower end of the shock to the steering knuckle arm.

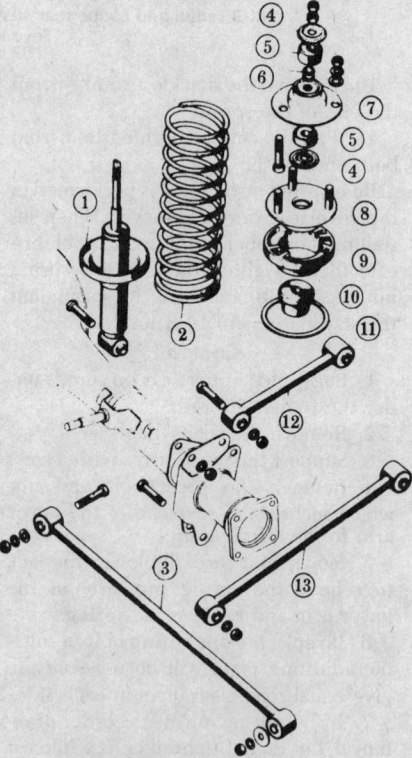

RX-2 rear suspension assembly
(© Toyo Kogyo Co., Ltd.)

1. Shock absorber
2. Coil spring
3. Lateral rod
4. Retainer
5. Rubber insulator
6. Gromet
7. Set plate
8. Spring seat (upper)
9. Rubber seat
10. Bound stopper
11. Adjusting plate
12. Upper link
13. Lower link

6. Remove the shock and coil spring as a complete assembly.

7. Mount the strut (shock/spring) assembly in a vise. Compress the coil spring with a spring compressor.

8. Hold the upper end of the shock piston rod with a pipe wrench and remove the locknut.

9. Remove the following parts from the top of the shock absorber in the order listed:

    a. Rubber mount

    b. Bearing

    c. Rubber seat

    d. Adjusting plate(s)

    e. Sealing ring

    f. Dust boot

    g. Coil spring

    h. Lower seat

CAUTION: *When removing the spring compressor from the coil spring, do so gradually so that spring tension is not released all at once.*

Installation of the McPherson strut is performed in the reverse order of removal. Tighten the nut on the top of the piston rod to 10 ft lbs.

NOTE: *If a new coil spring is being fitted, match it with an adjusting plate of the correct thickness to obtain equal road clearance on both sides. Do not use more than two adjusting plates on a side.*

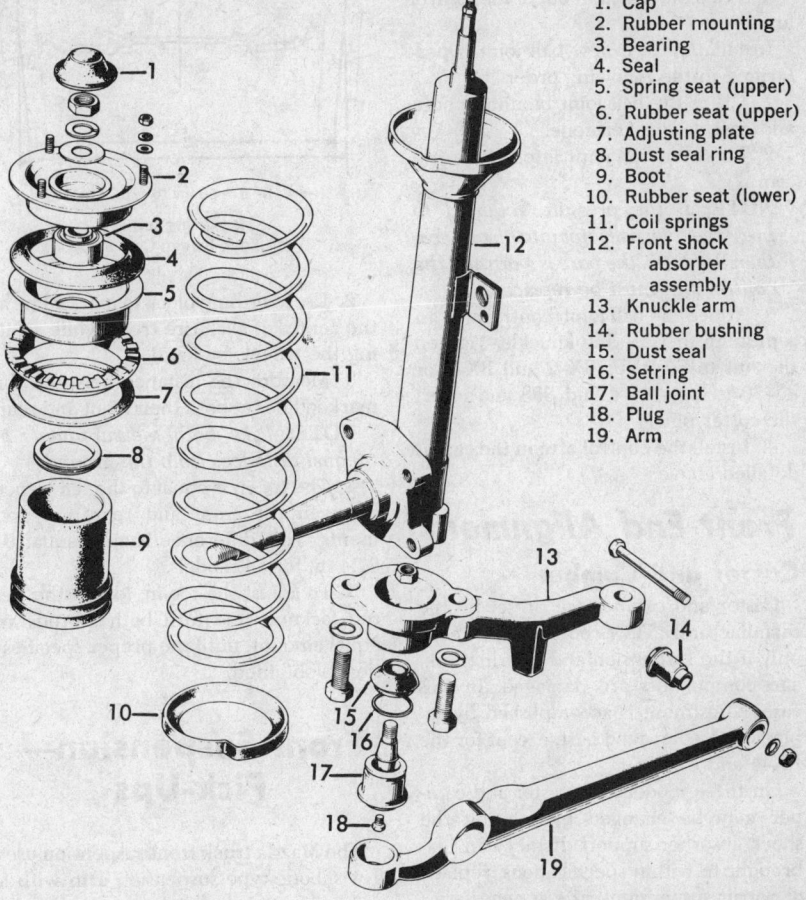

1. Cap
2. Rubber mounting
3. Bearing
4. Seal
5. Spring seat (upper)
6. Rubber seat (upper)
7. Adjusting plate
8. Dust seal ring
9. Boot
10. Rubber seat (lower)
11. Coil springs
12. Front shock absorber assembly
13. Knuckle arm
14. Rubber bushing
15. Dust seal
16. Setring
17. Ball joint
18. Plug
19. Arm

McPherson strut front suspension (© Toyo Kogyo Co., Ltd.)

Control Arm

Removal and Installation

1. Perform the first two steps of the McPherson strut removal procedure.

2. Remove the cotter pin and nut, which secure the tie-rod end, from the knuckle arm; then use a puller to separate them.

3. Unfasten the bolts which secure the lower end of the shock absorber to the knuckle arm.

4. Remove the nut, then withdraw the rubber bushing and washer which secure the stabilizer bar to the control arm.

5. Unfasten the nut and bolt which secure the control arm to the frame member.

6. Push outward on the strut assembly while removing the end of the control arm from the frame member.

7. Remove the control arm and steering knuckle arm as an assembly.

8. Install the assembly in a vise. Remove its cotter pin and unfasten the ball joint nut; then separate the knuckle arm from the control arm with a puller.

Installation of the control arm is performed in the reverse order of its removal. Torque the control arm-to-crossmember nut and bolt to 34 ft lbs on the RX–3, 51–65 ft lbs on the RX–2, or 29–40 ft lbs on the 808, RX–4, and Cosmo.

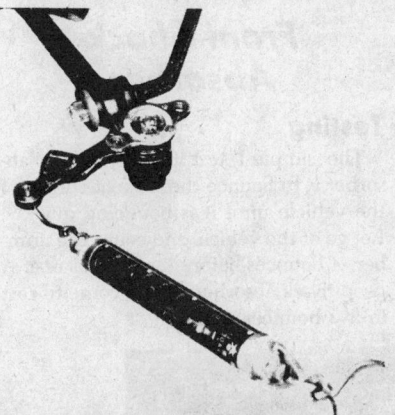

Checking the ball stud rotational torque with a spring scale (© Toyo Kogyo Co., Ltd.)

Ball Joints

Inspection

1. Perform steps 1–5 of the control arm removal procedure.

2. Check the ball joint dust boot condition. Replace the boot if it will allow water or dirt to enter the ball joint assembly.

3. Check the amount of pressure required to turn the ball stud, by hooking a pull scale into the tie-rod hole in the knuckle arm. Pull the spring scale until the arm just beings to turn; this should

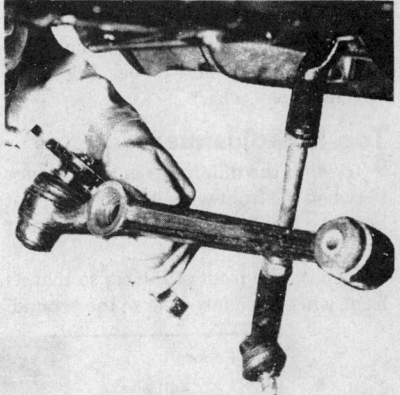

Removing the control arm (© Toyo Kogyo Co., Ltd.)

require 13–24 ft lbs—RX–2 and RX–3 or 27–40 ft lbs—RX–4 and Cosmo, or 17.-6–30 ft lbs.—808.

4. Replace the ball joint, as detailed in the following section, if it is not up to specification.

Removal and Installation

1. Complete the control arm removal procedure, as detailed above.

2. Remove the set-ring and the dust boot from the ball joint.

3. Clean the ball joint and control arm assembly.

4. Press the ball joint out of the control arm.

Installation of a new ball joint is performed in the following order:

1. Clean the ball joint mounting bore and coat it with kerosene.

2. Press the ball joint into the control arm.

NOTE: *If the pressure required to press the new ball joint into place is less than 3,300 lbs, the bore is worn and the control arm must be replaced.*

3. Attach the ball joint/control arm assembly to the steering knuckle. Tighten the nut to 60 ft lbs RX–2 and RX–3 or 43–50 ft lbs—RX–4 and 808 and insert the cotter pin.

4. Install the control arm in the car, as detailed above.

Front End Alignment

Caster and Camber

Caster and camber are preset by the manufacturer. They require adjustment only if the suspension and steering linkage components are damaged. In this case, adjustment is accomplished by replacing the damaged part, except for the RX–4 and Cosmo.

On these models, the caster and camber may be changed by rotating the shock absorber support. If they can't be brought to within specifications, replace or repair suspension parts as necessary.

To check caster and camber, use an alignment checking machine by following its manufacturer's instructions. Compare the results obtained against the specifications in the "Wheel Alignment Specifications" chart.

Toe-In Adjustment

Toe-in is the difference in the distance between the front wheels, as measured at both the front and the rear of the front tire.

1. Raise the front of the car so that its front wheels are just clear of the ground.

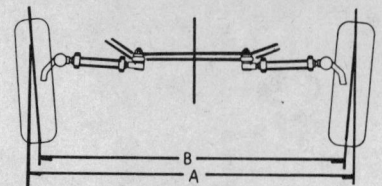

A–B= 0 ~ 6 mm (0 ~ 0.24 in)
Measuring toe-in
(© Toyo Kogyo Co., Ltd.)

2. Use a scribing block to mark a line at the center of each tire tread while rotating the wheels by hand.

3. Measure the distance between the marked lines at both their front and rear.

NOTE: *Take both measurements at equal distances from the ground.*

4. The toe-in is equal to the difference between the front and rear measurements. This difference should equal 0–0.24 in. for all models.

5. To adjust the toe-in, loosen the tie-rod locknuts and turn both tie-rods an equal amount, until the proper specification is obtained.

Front Suspension— Pick-Ups

The Mazda truck front suspension uses a wishbone-type suspension arm with a coil spring. Shock absorbers are hydraulic double-action.

Front Shock Absorber

Testing

The simplest test for any shock absorber is to bounce the suspect corner of the vehicle until it is bouncing quickly. Let go of the vehicle and count the number of bounces before it comes to rest. A good shock absorber should come to rest in 2–3 bounces at the most.

Caster and camber adjustment—RX-4 (© Toyo Kogyo Co., Ltd.)

As an alternative:

1. Remove the shock absorber.

2. Hold the shock in an upright position and work it up and down 4–5 times through its full travel.

3. If strong resistance is felt, the shock is functioning properly. If no resistance is felt, or, if there is a sudden free movement in the stroke, replace the shock absorber with a new one. It is also a good idea to replace a shock absorber if an *excessive* amount of oil is visible on its exterior.

Removal and Installation

1. Raise and support the truck.

2. Remove the nuts attaching the upper end of the shock absorber to the crossmember.

3. Remove the rubber bushings and washers.

4. Remove the bolts attaching the lower end of the shock absorber to the lower control arm.

5. Remove the shock from under the lower control arm.

6. Installation is the reverse of removal. Tighten the nuts as shown.

7. Lower the truck.

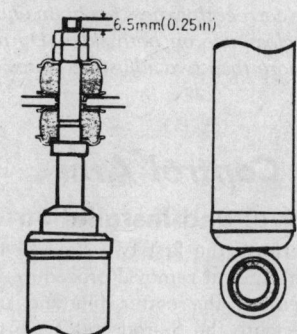

6.5mm(0.25in)

Tighten the front shock nut as illustrated— Rotary Pick-Up (© Toyo Kogyo Co., Ltd.)

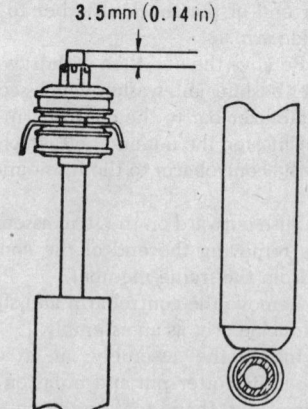

3.5mm (0.14 in)

Tighten the front shock nut as illustrated— B-1600 (© Toyo Kogyo Co., Ltd.)

Upper Control Arm

Removal and Installation

1. Raise and support the truck.

2. Position jackstands under the lower control arm.

3. Lower the vehicle on the jackstands until the upper control arm is off the bumper stop.

4. Remove the wheel. Install a chain around the coil spring as a safety measure.

5. Remove the cotter pin and nut retaining the upper ball joint.

6. Break the tapered fit loose by striking it with a hammer and separate the ball joint from the spindle.

7. From under the hood, remove the two upper arm retaining bolts and remove the arm from the vehicle. Note the number and position of shims.

8. Remove the three ball joint retaining bolts and remove the ball joint from the upper arm.

To install the upper control arm:

9. Install the ball joint in the upper control arm.

10. Position the upper control arm in the truck and install the alignment shims from where they were removed. Install the retaining nuts and bolts on the shaft and torque them to 62–76 ft lbs.

11. Position the spindle on the ball joint and install the retaining nut and cotter pin.

12. Remove the safety chain.

13. Install the wheel.

14. Remove the jackstands and lower the truck. Have the front end alignment checked.

Lower Control Arm

Removal and Installation

1. Raise the front of the truck and position jackstands under both sides of the frame just behind the lower control arms.

2. Remove the wheel.

3. Remove the lower shock absorber retaining bolts and push the shock up into the spring.

4. Remove the front stabilizer bar retaining bolt, nut and bushings and disconnect the stabilizer bar from the lower control arm.

5. Position a floor jack under the lower control arm and raise the arm to take the spring pressure off. Install a safety chain on the spring.

6. Unbolt the ball joint from the lower control arm.

7. Pull the spindle and ball joint away from the lower arm.

8. If necessary, the lower ball joint can be removed by removing the cotter pin and nut and loosening the ball joint with a hammer.

9. Carefully lower the control arm on the jack, being careful that the spring does not fly out.

10. Remove the three lower control arm retaining bolts and remove the lower control arm.

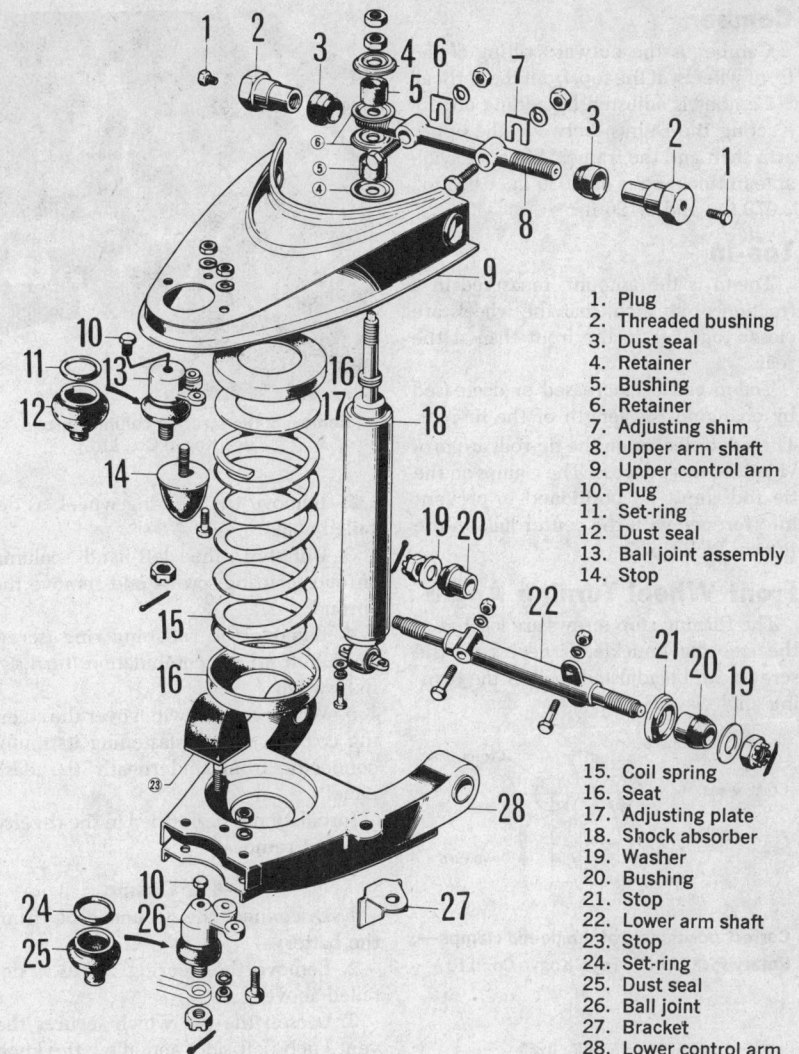

1. Plug
2. Threaded bushing
3. Dust seal
4. Retainer
5. Bushing
6. Retainer
7. Adjusting shim
8. Upper arm shaft
9. Upper control arm
10. Plug
11. Set-ring
12. Dust seal
13. Ball joint assembly
14. Stop
15. Coil spring
16. Seat
17. Adjusting plate
18. Shock absorber
19. Washer
20. Bushing
21. Stop
22. Lower arm shaft
23. Stop
24. Set-ring
25. Dust seal
26. Ball joint
27. Bracket
28. Lower control arm

Front suspension components—pick-ups (© Toyo Kogyo Co., Ltd.)

To install the lower control arm:

11. Position the lower control arm in place and install the three retaining bolts and nuts. Do not tighten. If removed, install the ball joint.

12. Position the spring on the lower control arm and in the upper frame retaining pocket.

13. Use a C-clamp to clamp the spring to the lower control arm.

14. Raise the lower control arm with a floor jack and position the ball joint and spindle in the lower arm.

15. Loosely install the three lower arm-to-ball joint bolts. Remove the safety chain from the spring, and remove the floor jack and C-clamp.

16. Torque the three ball joint retaining nuts to 60–70 ft lbs.

17. Pull the shock absorber down and install the bolts and nuts.

18. Install the stabilizer bar on the lower control arm.

19. Install the front wheel. Lower the truck and have the front wheel alignment checked.

Ball Joints

Checking

1. Check the ball joint dust seals and replace them if they are defective.

2. Check the end-play of the upper and lower ball joints. If the end-play exceeds 0.039 in., replace the ball joint.

Replacement

Use the applicable procedures under "Upper Control Arm Removal and Installation", or "Lower Control Arm Removal and Installation".

Front End Alignment

Caster

Caster is the forward or rearward tilt of the upper ball joint. Rearward tilt is referred to as positive caster, while forward tilt is referred to as negative caster.

Caster is adjusted by changing the shim(s) between the upper arm shaft and the frame, or, by turning the shaft until the correct angle is obtained.

Mazda

Camber

Camber is the outward tilting of the front wheels, at the top, from the vertical.

Camber is adjusted by adding or subtracting the shim(s) between the upper arm shaft and the frame. Shims are available in thicknesses of 0.039 in., 0.063 in., 0.079 in., and 0.126 in.

Toe-In

Toe-in is the amount, measured in a fraction of an inch, that the wheels are closer together in the front than at the rear.

Toe-in can be increased or decreased by changing the length of the tie-rods. Threaded sleeves on the tie-rods are provided for this purpose. The clamps on the tie rods must be positioned to prevent interference with the center link on the Rotary Pick-Up.

Front Wheel Turning Angle

The turning stop screws are located at the steering knuckle. If necessary, the screws can be adjusted to alter the turning angle.

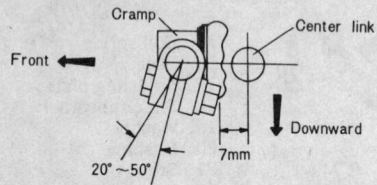

Correct positioning of the tie-rod clamps—Rotary Pick-Up (© Toyo Kogyo Co., Ltd.)

STEERING

Steering Wheel

Removal and Installation

1. Remove the screws which secure the crash pad/horn button assembly to the steering wheel. Remove the assembly. On four-spoke steering wheels, pull the center cap toward the wheel top.
2. Punch matchmarks on the steering wheel and steering shaft.
3. Unfasten the steering wheel hub nut and remove the steering wheel with a puller.

CAUTION: *The steering column is collapsible; pounding on it or applying excessive pressure to it may cause it to deform, in which case, the entire column will have to be replaced.*

Installation of the steering wheel is performed in the reverse order of removal. Tighten the steering wheel nut to 25 ft lbs.

Combination (Turn Signal) Switch Replacement

RX–2, 808, RX–3 and Pick-Ups

1. Disconnect the ground cable from the battery.

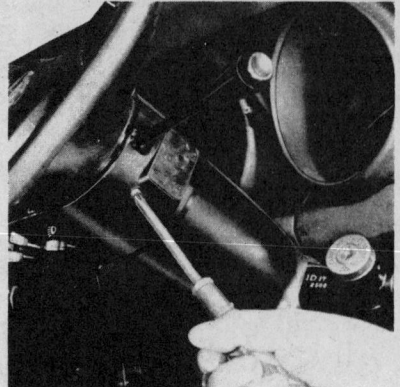

Removing the steering column shroud (© Toyo Kogyo Co., Ltd.)

2. Remove the steering wheel, as detailed above.
3. Unfasten the left-hand column shroud securing screws and remove the shroud.
4. Remove the retaining ring (screw on 808) from the combination (turn signal) switch.
5. Withdraw the switch over the steering column, after unfastening its multiconnector from underneath the dash panel.

Installation is performed in the reverse order of removal.

RX–4 & Cosmo

1. Disconnect the ground cable from the battery.
2. Remove the steering wheel as detailed above.
3. Loosen the nut which secures the vent knob (left side) and allow the knob assembly to drop away from its mounting bracket.
4. Remove choke knob by loosening its set screw. Remove the choke retaining nut and separate the choke from the panel.
5. Unfasten the upper column cover retaining screws and remove the cover.
6. Disconnect the panel light dimmer switch wiring.
7. Disconnect the exhaust temperature warning light wiring.
8. Loosen, but don't remove the screws at either end of the lower panel cover.

NOTE: *The left-hand screw is located in the hole which was covered by the upper column cover and the right-hand screw is above the ashtray opening (ashtray removed).*

9. Pull the upper column cover away from the instrument panel.
10. Disconnect the combination switch connector.
11. Remove the retaining ring from the steering column.
12. Unfasten the combination switch retaining screw and remove the switch.

Installation is the reverse of removal.

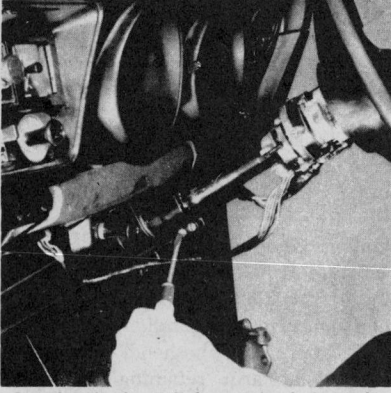

Cut slots in the switch securing bolts and remove them with a screwdriver (© Toyo Kogyo Co., Ltd.)

Ignition Lock/Switch Assembly

Removal and Installation

RX–3, RX–2 and 808

1. Disconnect the ground cable from the battery.

NOTE: *For 808 models, follow procedure for removing combination switch, then skip to #5 below.*

2. Remove the light switch knob.
3. Remove the left and right steering column shrouds by unfastening their retaining screws.
4. Disconnect the multiconnector from the switch assembly.
5. Use a file or a hacksaw to make slots in the switch securing bolts. Remove the bolts with a screwdriver.
6. Withdraw the switch assembly.

To install the switch, follow the removal procedure in reverse order. After tightening the switch securing bolts, break their heads off, in order to make the switch difficult for a thief to remove.

RX–4 and Cosmo

1. Follow steps under Combination Switch Replacement.
2. Remove the instrument frame brace.
3. Disconnect the switch wires.
4. Remove the switch.
5. Installation is the reverse of removal.

Steering Linkage

Manual or Power Steering

Removal and Installation

All exc. 808

1. Turn the steering wheel so that the front wheels are pointing straight ahead. Then raise the front end of the vehicle and support it with jackstands.

CAUTION: *Be sure that the vehicle is securely supported. Remember, you will be working underneath it.*

2. Remove the cotter pins and the castellated nuts which secure the ends of the tie-rods to the center link and the steering knuckle.

3. Use a ball joint puller to disconnect the tie-rods from the center link and steering knuckle. Remove the tie-rods.

4. Remove the cotter pin and the castellated nut which secure the idler arm to the center link.

5. Use the ball joint puller to detach the idler arm from the center link.

6. Unfasten the nuts at the other end of the idler arm and remove the arm from its bracket.

7. Perform steps 4–5 for the pitman arm. Remove the center link. On RX–4 models, remove steering damper first.

8. Unfasten the nut which secures the pitman arm to the sector shaft and use a puller to separate them.

Installation is performed in the reverse order of removal. Align the marks on the pitman arm and the sector shaft to ensure proper steering linkage alignment.

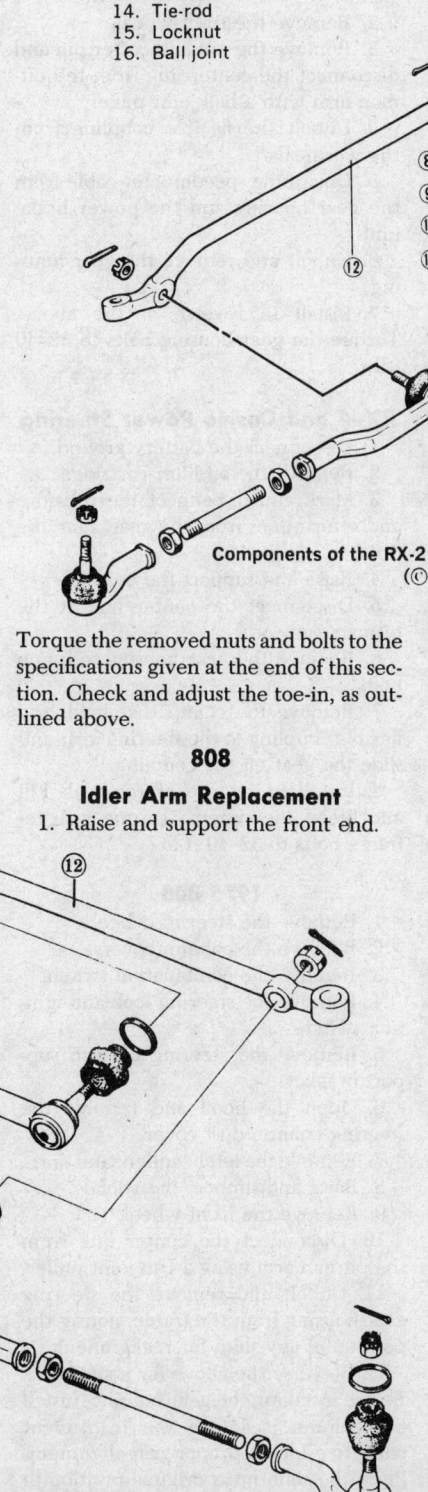

1. Idler bracket
2. Seal
3. Bushing
4. Plug
5. Spring
6. Idler arm
7. Rubber bushing
8. Rubber bushing
9. Washer
10. Nut
11. Cotter pin
12. Center link
13. Ball joint
14. Tie-rod
15. Locknut
16. Ball joint

Components of the RX-2 steering linkage—RX-3 and RX-4 similar
(© Toyo Kogyo Co., Ltd.)

1. Plug
2. Idler arm bracket
3. Spring
4. Grease seal
5. Idler arm
6. Insulator
7. Pin
8. Nut
9. Dust seal set ring
10. Ball joint dust seal
11. Ball joint
12. Center link
13. Tie rod
14. Lock nut
15. Ball joint

Steering linkage—808 (© Toyo Kogyo Co. Ltd.)

Torque the removed nuts and bolts to the specifications given at the end of this section. Check and adjust the toe-in, as outlined above.

808
Idler Arm Replacement

1. Raise and support the front end.

2. Remove the front wheels.

3. Disconnect the center link from the idler arm by removing the cotter pin and nut and applying a puller.

4. Unbolt the idler arm bracket from the frame and remove the bracket and arm assembly.

5. Hold the assembly in a vise and remove the arm from the bracket by turning the arm counterclockwise.

6. Check all parts for wear and replace as necessary.

7. Insert the spring into the bracket and screw the idler arm into the bracket until the distance between the lip edge on the idler arm and the leading edge of the bracket is 0.157–0.236 in.

8. Check the revolving torque of the arm with a spring scale. If the torque is less than 0.2 lb, screw in the arm until the correct reading is obtained. If the torque is greater than 6.6 lb, unscrew the arm until the correct torque is obtained.

9. If the correct torque cannot be obtained, replace the spring.

10. Grease the assembly through a nipple replacing the plug in the end of the bracket.

11. Attach the idler arm and bracket assembly to the frame and torque the bolts to 32–40ftlb.

12. Connect the idler arm to the center link and tighten the nut to 18–25ftlb. Install a new cotter pin.

Replacing the Pitman Arm

1. Raise and support the front end.
2. Remove the wheels.
3. Disconnect the center link at the pitman arm.
4. Remove the nut attaching the pitman arm to the sector shaft and remove the arm with a puller.
5. Install the pitman arm onto the sector shaft, aligning the identification marks. Tighten the nut to 94–123ftlb.
6. Connect the center link to the pitman arm and torque the nut to 22–32 ftlb. Install a new cotter pin.

Replacing the Tie-Rod

1. Raise and support the front end.
2. Disconnect the tie-rod from the center link and knuckle arm. A puller will be necessary.
3. Install the tie-rod to the center link and knuckle arm. Tighten the nuts to 22–32 ftlb. and install new cotter pins.

Replacing the Center Link

1. Raise and support the front end.
2. Remove the center link from both tie-rods, pitman arm and idler arm by removing the cotter pins and nuts. A puller will also be necessary.
3. Install the center link and tighten the nuts to 22–32 ftlb. Install new cotter pins.

Steering Gear
Removal and Installation
RX–2

1. Loosen the bolt securing the worm-shaft to the steering joint.
2. Jack up the vehicle, support it and remove the front wheel.
3. Remove the split pin and nut and disconnect the center link from the pitman arm by using a puller.
4. Unbolt the steering gear from the frame. Note the position of any shim for realigning the gear and column shaft.
5. Install in reverse of removal. Place shim in its original position. Torque gear-to-frame bolts to 32–40 ftlb.

RX–3

1. Remove the steering wheel.
2. Remove the column covers.
3. Remove the combination switch assembly.
4. Remove the steering lock and ignition switch assembly.
5. Remove the steering column support bracket.
6. Raise and support the front end.
7. Remove the front wheel.
8. Remove the cotter pin and nut and disconnect the center link from the pitman arm using a ball joint puller.
9. Unbolt the steering gear from the frame, taking note of the presence of any shim for realigning the gear with the shaft.

10. Remove the steering column dust cover and remove the gear housing, column jacket and aligning shim.
11. Reverse the removal for installation. Place the shim in its original position for realignment. Gear housing-to-frame bolt torque is 32–40 ftlb.

RX–4, Cosmo and Rotary Pickup Manual Steering

1. Raise the vehicle and support on stands.
2. Remove the front wheel.
3. Remove the nut and cotter pin and disconnect the center link from the pitman arm with a ball joint puller.
4. Unbolt the flexible coupling from the worm shaft.
5. Unclip the speedometer cable from the gear housing and the power brake unit.
6. Unbolt and remove the gear housing.
7. Install in reverse of the above. Torque the gear housing bolts to 32–40 ftlb.

RX–4 and Cosmo Power Steering

1. Disconnect the battery ground.
2. Remove the oil filter cartridge.
3. Mark and disconnect the pressure and return lines from the gear. Plug the lines.
4. Raise and support the vehicle.
5. Disconnect the center link at the pitman arm.
6. Remove the gear housing-to-frame bolts.
7. Remove the clamp that holds the flexible coupling to the steering gear and slide the gear off the coupling.
8. Install in reverse of removal. Fill and bleed the system. Torque gear-to-frame bolts to 32–40 ft.lb.

1975 808

1. Remove the steering wheel.
2. Remove the column covers.
3. Remove the combination switch.
4. Remove the steering lock and ignition switch.
5. Remove the steering column support bracket.
6. Open the hood and remove the steering column dust cover.
7. Remove the left headlight and horn.
8. Raise and support the vehicle.
9. Remove the front wheel.
10. Disconnect the center link from the pitman arm using a ball joint puller.
11. Unbolt and remove the steering gear housing from the frame, noting the position of any shim for realignment.
12. Reverse the above for installation. Before installing the gear housing, install the column jacket to the instrument panel to establish proper gear alignment. Place the shim in its original position to establish proper shaft alignment.

1976–77 808

1. Remove the steering wheel.
2. Remove the column covers.
3. Remove the combination switch assembly.
4. Remove the steering lock and ignition switch assembly.
5. Remove the steering column support bracket.
6. Raise and support the front end.
7. Disconnect the center link from the pitman arm using a ball joint puller.
8. Remove the steering gear retaining bolts and check for the existence of a shim. Note its position for realignment.
9. Remove the steering column dust cover.
10. Remove the gear housing, column jacket and aligning shim.
11. Installation is the reverse of removal.
12. Place shim in its original position. Torque gear-to-frame bolts to 32–40 ftlb.

B–1600 Pickup

1. Remove the steering wheel.
2. Remove the column covers.
3. Remove the combination switch.
4. Remove the column support bracket.
5. Remove the column jacket.
6. Remove the column dust cover.
7. Raise and support the vehicle.
8. Remove the front wheel.
9. Remove the nuts and bolts that attach the upper arm shaft to the support bracket. Note the number and position of adjusting shims for correct alignment.
10. Temporarily remove the left upper arm.
11. Disconnect the center link from the pitman arm using a ball joint puller.
12. Unbolt and remove the steering gear from the frame. Note the position of any shim for realignment.
13. Install in reverse of the above. Place the shim in its original position. Torque the gear-to-frame bolts to 32–40 ftlb.

Steering Gear Adjustment

Worm Bearing Preload

1. Remove the gear from the vehicle.
2. Rotate the worm shaft with a torque wrench and check the torque. Rotating torque should be 5–7 inlb. for RX–2; 7.–8–13 inlb. for RX–3; 8–10 inlb. for RX–4 and rotary pickup; 5–11 inlb for Cosmo; 8–13 inlb for 808 and 5–7 inlb. for B–1600. If not, adjust as follows:
3. Remove the end cover and shims.
4. If the preload was too light, remove shims; if too heavy, add shims.
5. Install the end cover.

Sector Gear and Ball Nut Backlash

The sector shaft adjusting screw, located in the cover, raises or lowers the sector shaft to provide proper mesh with the sector gear and rack. Adjust as follows:

1. Turn the wormshaft gently and stop it at the center position.

2. Loosen the locknut and turn the adjusting in or out. The standard backlash is 0–0.0039″.

3. Tighten the adjusting screw.

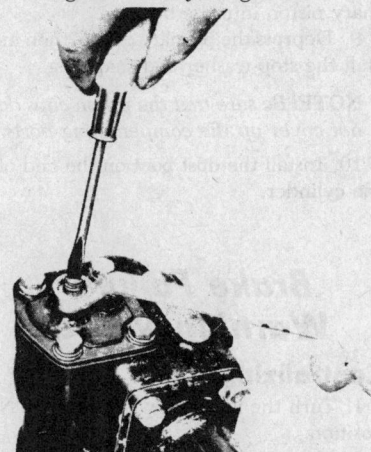

Adjusting backlash (© Toyo Kogyo Co. Ltd.)

Power Steering Pump

Removal and Installation

1. Disconnect the fluid hoses from the pump.

2. Loosen the pump belt adjusting bolt, slide the pump to one side and remove the belt.

3. Support the pump, remove the mounting bolts and lift out the pump.

Installation is the reverse of removal. Adjust belt to give a ½″ deflection at the mid-point of its longest straight stretch. Fill the reservoir and bleed the system.

BRAKE SYSTEMS

Adjustments

Front or Rear Discs

The front disc brakes are self-adjusting by design. As the brake pads and discs wear, fluid pressure compensates for the amount of wear. Because this action causes the fluid level to go down, the level should be checked and replenished as often as is necessary.

Front Drum Brakes

B–1600 Only

The brake shoes should be at normal room temperature. Adjust each front brake shoe as follows:

1. Raise and support the truck. The wheels must be free to turn freely.

2. Remove the adjusting slot covers from the brake backing plate.

3. Insert a brake adjusting spoon (a screwdriver will do in a pinch) to grab the starwheel of the wheel cylinder.

4. Rotate the starwheel of one wheel cylinder toward the inside of the brake drum until the wheel is locked. Then back off the starwheel five notches.

5. Repeat step 4 for each wheel cylinder of each wheel.

6. Install the adjusting slot covers.

7. Check the brake adjustment by spinning the wheel by hand. There should be no drag.

8. Lower the truck.

Rear Drum Brakes

1. Block the front wheels, raise the car, and support it with jackstands.

2. Release the parking brake completely. On pick-ups, disconnect the equalizer clevis pin.

3. Remove the adjusting hole plugs from the backing plate.

4. Engage the adjuster with a screwdriver. Turn the adjuster in the direction of the arrow stamped on the backing plate until the brake shoes are fully expanded, i.e., the wheel will not turn.

5. Pump the brake pedal several times to be sure that the brake shoe contacts the drum evenly.

NOTE: *If the wheel turns after you remove your foot from the brake pedal, continue turning the adjuster until the wheel will no longer rotate.*

6. Back off on the adjuster about five notches (2–3 notches—RX-4). The wheel should rotate freely, without dragging. If it does not, turn the adjuster an additional notch.

7. Pump the brake pedal several times and check wheel rotation again.

8. Fit the plug into the adjusting hole and then repeat the adjusting procedure for the three other rear brake shoes.

Brake Pedal

Passenger Cars and Rotary Pick-Up

1. Detach the wiring from the brake light switch terminals.

2. Loosen the locknut on the switch.

3. Turn the switch until the distance between the pedal and the floor is 7.3 in.

4. Tighten the locknut on switch.

5. Loosen the locknut located on the push rod.

6. Rotate the pushrod, until a pedal free travel of 0.2–0.6 in. is obtained.

7. Tighten the pushrod locknut.

B–1600

There should be 0.02–0.12 in. of brake pedal free-travel before the pushrod contacts the piston.

1. Loosen the locknut on the master cylinder pushrod at the clevis, which attaches the pushrod to the pedal.

2. Turn the master cylinder pushrod either in or out to obtain the specified clearance.

3. When the adjustment is complete, tighten the locknut to 8–13 ft lbs.

HYDRAULIC SYSTEMS

Master Cylinder

Removal and Installation

1. Detach all of the hydraulic lines from the master cylinder.

NOTE: *On models which have a fluid reservoir located separately from the master cylinder, remove the lines which run between the two and plug the lines to prevent leakage.*

2. Unfasten the nuts which secure the master cylinder to the power brake unit or firewall.

3. Withdraw the master cylinder assembly straight out and away from the

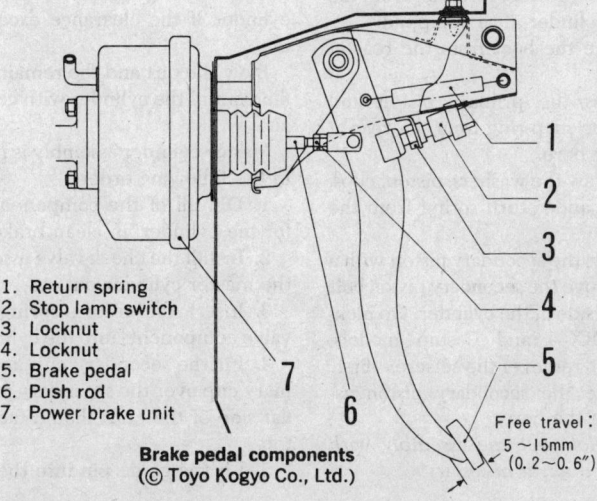

1. Return spring
2. Stop lamp switch
3. Locknut
4. Locknut
5. Brake pedal
6. Push rod
7. Power brake unit

Free travel:
5 ~ 15mm
(0.2 ~ 0.6″)

Brake pedal components
(© Toyo Kogyo Co., Ltd.)

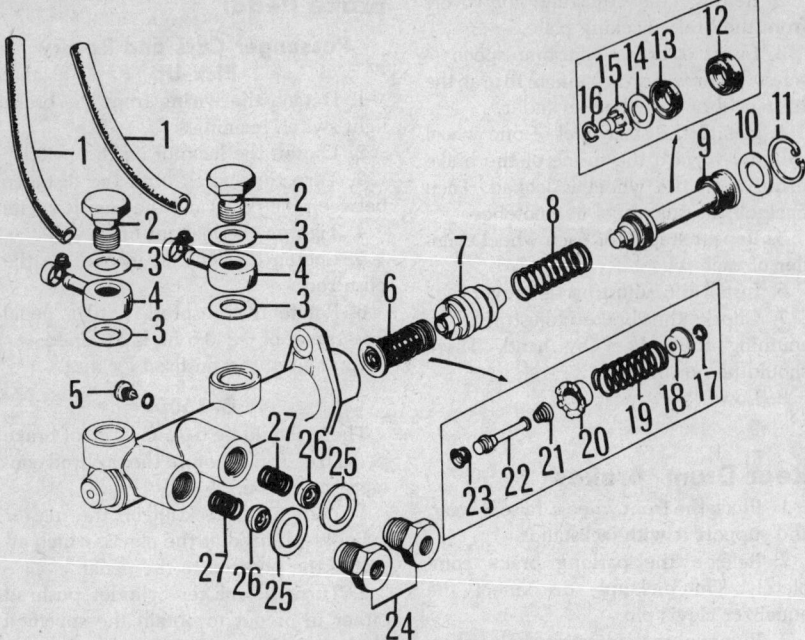

Components of the master cylinder
(© Toyo Kogyo Co., Ltd.)

1. Hydraulic line
2. Connector bolt
3. Washer
4. Union
5. Stop bolt
6. Valve and spring
7. Secondary piston
8. Return spring
9. Primary piston
10. Washer
11. Retaining ring
12. Secondary cup
13. Primary cup
14. Spacer
15. Spring seat
16. Stop ring
17. Stop ring
18. Spring seat
19. Return spring
20. Valve case
21. Spring
22. Valve rod
23. Valve
24. Outlet fitting
25. Washer
26. Check valve
27. Spring

power brake unit or the firewall and pushrod.

CAUTION: *Be careful not to spill brake fluid on the painted surfaces of the car, as it makes an excellent paint remover.*

Installation of the master cylinder is performed in the reverse order of its removal. Fill up its reservoir and bleed the brake system, as detailed below.

Overhaul

1. Clean the outside of the master cylinder and drain any brake fluid remaining in it.
2. Remove the fluid reservoir from the top of the cylinder, if so equipped.
3. Remove the boot from the rear of the cylinder.
4. Depress the primary piston and withdraw the snap-ring from the rear of the cylinder bore.
5. Withdraw the washers, piston, cups, spacer, seat and return spring from the cylinder bore.
6. Depress the secondary piston with a rod and remove the secondary piston bolt from the outside of the cylinder. On pickups, 808, RX–4 and Cosmo models, loosen (don't remove) the setscrew first.
7. Remove the secondary piston assembly from the bore.

NOTE: *Blow out the assembly with compressed air, if necessary.*

8. Unfasten the hydraulic line fittings from the master cylinder outlet.
9. Withdraw the check valves and springs from the outlets.
10. Wash all of the components in clean brake fluid.

CAUTION: *Never use kerosene or gasoline to clean the master cylinder components.*

Examine all of the piston cups and replace any that are worn, damaged, or swollen.

Check the cylinder bore for roughness or scoring. Check the clearance between the piston and cylinder bore with a feeler gauge. Replace either the piston or the cylinder if the clearance exceeds 0.006 in.

Blow the dirt and the remaining brake fluid out of the cylinder with compressed air.

Master cylinder assembly is performed in the following order:

1. Dip all of the components, except for the cylinder, in clean brake fluid.
2. Install the check valve assemblies in the master cylinder outlets.
3. Insert the return spring and the valve components into the cylinder bore.
4. Fit the secondary cup and the primary cup over the secondary piston. The flat side of the cups should face the piston.
5. Fit the guide pin into the stop-bolt

hole. Place the secondary piston components into the cylinder bore.

6. Depress the secondary piston as far as it will go and withdraw the guide pin. Screw the stop bolt into the hole.
7. Place the primary cups on the primary piston with the flat side of the cups facing the piston.
8. Insert the return spring and the primary piston into the bore.
9. Depress the primary piston, then install the stop-washer and snap-ring.

NOTE: *Be sure that the piston cups do not cover up the compensating ports.*

10. Install the dust boot on the end of the cylinder.

Brake Failure Warning Valve

Centralizing

1. Turn the ignition switch to the ON position.
2. Make sure that the fluid level in the master cylinder is at the ¾ mark.
3. Depress the brake pedal and the piston will center itself causing the light to go off.
4. Turn the switch to OFF and check the fluid level. Check for a firm pedal.

Bleeding

Disc Brakes

NOTE: *Keep the master cylinder reservoir at least ¾ full during the bleeding operation.*

1. Remove the cap from the bleeder screw on that wheel cylinder which is furthest from the master cylinder.
2. Install a vinyl tube over the bleeder screw. Submerge the other end of the tube in a jar half-full of clean brake fluid.
3. Open the bleeder valve. Fully depress the brake pedal and allow it to return slowly.
4. Repeat this operation until air bubbles cease flowing into the jar.
5. Close the valve, remove the tube, and install the cap on the bleeder valve.

Drum Brakes (Front and Rear)

1. Repeat steps 1–2 of the disc brake bleeding procedure.
2. Depress the brake pedal rapidly several times.
3. Keep the brake pedal depressed and open the bleeder valve. Close the valve without releasing the pedal.
4. Repeat this operation until bubbles cease to appear in the jar.
5. Remove the tube and install the cap on the bleeder valve.

FRONT DISC BRAKES

Disc Brake Pads

Removal and Installation

All Models—Front

1. Raise the front of the vehicle and securely support it with jackstands.
2. Remove the hub cap and the wheel.
3.
   a. On all except RX–2 models, unfasten the retainer and withdraw the locating pins.
   b. On RX–2 models, remove the securing clips, the stop plates, the caliper assembly, and the anti-rattle spring.

CAUTION: *Do not disconnect the hydraulic line from the caliper when only pad removal is being performed.*

4. Remove the return spring and withdraw the pad.
5. Take the rubber cap off of the bleeder screw and fit a vinyl tube over the screw. Submerge the other end of the tube in a jar half-filled with brake fluid.
6. Open the bleeder screw. Use a screwdriver with its blade wrapped in electrical tape, to depress the piston in the cylinder.
7. Tighten the bleeder screw. Remove the vinyl tube and the screwdriver. Fit the rubber cap back on the bleeder screw.
8. Install new pads with shims in the caliper.
9. Install all of the parts which were removed during disassembly.
10. Bleed the brake system, as outlined below.

CAUTION: *Replace all of the front brake pads at the same time. Do not use pads of different materials for replacement.*

Cosmo—Rear

1. Raise the vehicle and support it on stands.
2. Remove the rear wheel.
3. Remove the locking clips and pull out the stopper plates.
4. Remove the caliper and anti-rattle spring.
5. Remove the brake shoes and shims.
6. When installing new shoes, some fluid will have to be removed from the master cylinder to allow the new shoes to be positioned. Take care not to take too much fluid from the cylinder. When shoes are replaced, replace both sets of front shoes at once. Never replace only one side. A light coating of chassis lube should be applied to the stopper plates.

Disc Brake Calipers

Removal and Installation

All Models exc. RX–2

1. Perform the disc brake pad removal procedure, as detailed above.
2. Detach the hydraulic line from the caliper. Plug the end of the line to prevent the entrance of dirt or the loss of fluid.
3. Unfasten the bolts which secure the caliper to the support and remove the caliper.

Follow the caliper removal procedure in reverse order for installation. Bleed the hydraulic system after completing installation.

RX–2 Models

Perform steps 1–3 of the disc brake pad removal procedure, as outlined above. In addition, disconnect and plug the hydraulic line at the caliper.

Caliper installation is performed in the reverse order of removal. Bleed the hydraulic system after completing installation.

Overhaul

1. Thoroughly clean the outside of the caliper.
2. Remove the dust boot retainer and the boot.
3. Place a piece of hardwood in front of the piston.
4. Gradually apply compressed air through the hydraulic line fitting and withdraw the piston.

NOTE: *If the piston is frozen and cannot be removed from the caliper, tap lightly around it while air pressure is being applied.*

5. Withdraw the piston and seal from the caliper bore.
6. If necessary, remove the bleeder screw.
7. Wash all of the parts in clean brake fluid. Dry them off with compressed air.

CAUTION: *Do not wash the parts in kerosene or gasoline.*

Examine the caliper bore and piston for scores, scratches, or rust. Replace either part as required. Minor scratches, rust, or scoring can be corrected by dressing with crocus cloth.

NOTE: *Discard the old piston seal and dust boot. Replace them with new ones.*

Apply clean brake fluid to the piston and bore. Assemble the caliper in the reverse order of disassembly. Install it on the car and bleed the brake system.

Brake Disc

Front Removal and Installation

1. Remove the caliper assembly, as detailed in the appropriate section above.

NOTE: *It is unnecessary to completely remove the caliper from the vehicle. Leave the hydraulic line wired to it and wire the caliper to the underbody of the car so that it is out of the way.*

2. Check disc runout, as detailed below, before removing it from the vehicle.
3. Withdraw the grease cap cotter pin, nut-lock, adjusting nut, and washer from the spindle.
4. Take the thrust washer and outer bearing off of the hub.
5. Pull the brake disc/wheel hub assembly off of the spindle.
6. Unbolt and separate the brake disc from the hub after matchmarking them for proper installation.

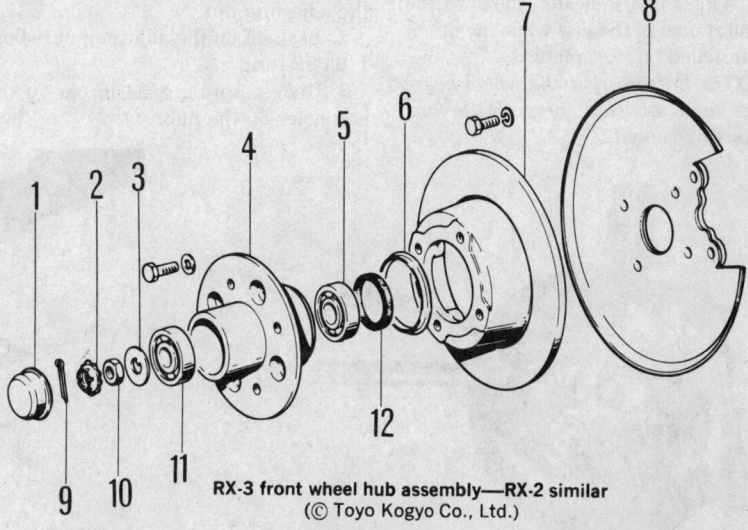

RX-3 front wheel hub assembly—RX-2 similar
(© Toyo Kogyo Co., Ltd.)

1. Grease cap	5. Inner bearing
2. Nut lock	6. Dust ring
3. Flat washer	7. Brake disc
4. Hub	8. Backing plate
9. Cotter pin	
10. Adjusting nut	
11. Outer bearing	
12. Grease seal	

Mazda

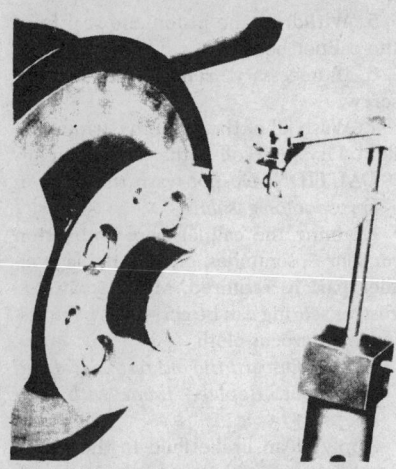

Checking the front brake disc runout
(© Toyo Kogyo Co., Ltd.)

CAUTION: *Do not drive the disc off of the hub.*

Installation of the disc and hub is performed in the reverse order of removal. Adjust the bearing preload, as detailed below.

Rear

Removal and Installation

1. Raise the vehicle and support it on stands.
2. Remove the wheel.
3. Remove the caliper and bracket assembly and suspend it by a wire from the frame rail.
4. Make certain that the parking brake is fully released.
5. Remove the disc attaching screws and fit them into the tapped holes. Screw them in evenly to force the disc off the flange.
6. Installation is the reverse of the above.

Inspection

1. With a dial indicator, measure the lateral runout of the disc while the disc is still installed on the spindle.

NOTE: *Be sure that the wheel bearings are adjusted properly before checking runout.*

2. If runout exceeds more than 0.004 in., replace or resurface the disc.
3. Inspect the surface of the disc for scores or pits and resurface it, if necessary.
4. If the disc is resurfaced, its thickness should be no less than the following:
   808 and RX–3—0.394 in.
   RX–2, RX–4, and Rotary Pick-Up—0.433 in.
   Cosmo—0.6693 front, 0.354 rear

Wheel Bearings

Removal and Installation

1. Remove the brake disc/hub assembly and separate them, as detailed above.
2. Drive the seal out and then remove the inner bearing from the hub.
3. Drive the outer bearing races out with a brass drift applied to the slots provided for this purpose.
4. Clean the inner and outer bearings, completely.

CAUTION: *Do not use compressed air to spin the bearings dry.*

5. Clean the spindle and the hub cavity with solvent.

Installation is performed in the reverse order of removal. However, the following points should be noted:

1. Repack the bearings and the hub cavity with lithium grease.

CAUTION: *Do not over pack them.*

2. Install the wheel hub-to-brake disc bolts to 36 ft lbs torque.
3. Adjust the bearing preload, as described below.

Preload Adjustment

NOTE: *This operation is performed with the wheel, grease cap, nut lock, and cotter pin removed.*

1. To seat the bearings, back off on the adjusting nut three turns and then rotate the hub/disc assembly while tightening the adjusting nut.
2. Back off on the adjusting nut about 1/6 of a turn.
3. Hook a spring scale in one of the bolt holes on the hub.

4. Pull the spring scale squarely, until the hub just begins to rotate. The scale reading should be 0.9–2.2 lbs—passenger cars; or 1.3–2.4 lbs Rotary Pick-Up. Tighten the adjusting nut until the proper spring scale reading is obtained.
5. Place the castellated nut lock over the adjusting nut. Align one of the slots on the nut-lock with the hole in the spindle and fit the cotter pin into place.

FRONT DRUM BRAKES

Brake Drum

Removal and Installation

1. Raise and support the truck.
2. Remove the wheel.
3. Remove the brake drum attaching screws and install them in the tapped holes in the brake drum.
4. Turn these screws in evenly to force the brake drum away from the wheel hub.
5. Remove and inspect the brake drum. See "Inspection".

To install the brake drum:

6. Install the brake drum with the attaching screw holes aligned with the holes in the hub.
7. Transfer the attaching screws from the tapped holes in the brake drum to the attaching holes in the hub.
8. Tighten the screws evenly to secure the hub.
9. Install the wheel.
10. Lower the truck and check the brake adjustment.

Inspection

1. Brush all dust from the inside of the brake drum.
2. Check the brake drum diameter with a brake drum gauge. Replace any drums which have a diameter greater than 10.28 in.

Checking front wheel bearing preload
(© Toyo Kogyo Co., Ltd.)

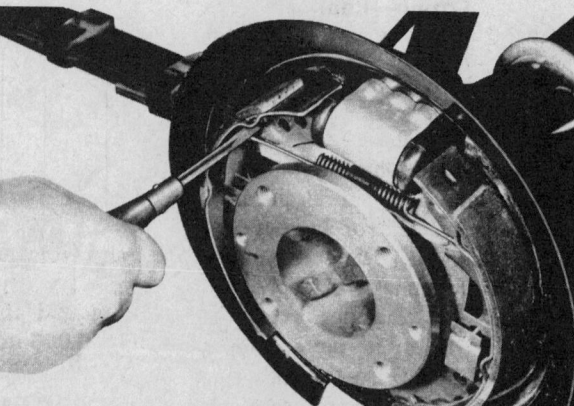

Shoe return spring removal
(© Toyo Kogyo Co., Ltd.)

3. Inspect the brake drums for cracks. Replace any cracked drums.

4. Look carefully for any scoring of the drums. If the drums are scored, have them reground.

Brake Shoes

Inspection

1. If compressed air is available, blow out the accumulated dust and grit.

2. Inspect for excessive lining wear or shoe damage. Replace any cracked shoes.

3. If the lining is worn to within 0.039 in. of the shoe or if the shoes are damaged, they must be replaced.

4. Replace any linings that are contaminated with grease or brake fluid from leaking wheel cylinders. Replace linings in axle sets only.

5. Check the condition of the shoes, retracting springs and hold-down springs for signs of overheating. If the shoes have a slight blue color, this indicates overheating and replacement of the springs as well as the linings is recommended.

6. If signs of overheating are present, the wheel cylinders should be rebuilt as a precaution against future problems.

Removal and Installation

1. Raise and support the truck.

2. Remove the wheel.

3. Remove the brake drum.

4. Remove the brake shoe retracting springs.

5. Remove the shoe retaining spring guide pin and the retaining spring, by holding the guide pin to the backing plate and compressing and turning the spring 90°. Use a brake spring tool to do this.

6. Remove the brake shoes, noting their positions.

To install new brake shoes:

7. Lubricate the threads of the adjusting screw with brake paste and one or two spots on the adjuster wheel inside threads. Lubricate the backing plate shoe pads.

8. Position each brake shoe on the brake backing plate so that the slot in the shoe web is toward the starwheel in the wheel cylinder.

9. Install the shoe retaining spring guide pin. Install the retaining spring over the guide pin, hold the guide pin in place and depress the retaining spring. Turn it 90° to lock the spring in place.

10. Install the brake shoe retracting spring. Be careful not to bend the springs or stretch the hooks.

11. Install the brake drum.

12. Install the wheel.

13. Adjust the brakes.

14. Bleed the brakes.

15. Lower the truck and check for proper operation.

Wheel Cylinder

Removal and Installation

1. Raise and support the truck.

2. Remove the wheel.

3. Remove the brake drum and brake shoes.

4. Disconnect and plug the brake line at the wheel cylinder.

5. Remove the stud nuts and bolt attaching the wheel cylinder to the backing plate and remove the wheel cylinder.

To install the wheel cylinder:

6. Install the wheel cylinder on the backing plate.

7. Clean the end of the brake line and attach it to the wheel cylinder. Tighten the tube fitting nut.

8. Install the links in the end of the wheel cylinder.

9. Install the shoes and adjuster assemblies.

10. Install the brake drum and wheel.

11. Adjust the brakes.

12. Bleed the brakes.

13. Lower the truck.

Overhaul

1. Remove the wheel cylinder.

2. Remove the piston and adjusting screw with the boot attached to the cylinder. Separate the adjuster and boot from the adjuster.

3. Using compressed air (if possible), blow the piston cup, cup expander and spring. Lay the cylinder face down and apply air pressure to the brake line port.

4. Wash all parts in isopropyl alcohol, except the rubber boot.

5. Examine the cylinder bore, piston and adjuster for wear, roughness or damage. Check the clearance between the piston and cylinder bore. If the clearance is greater than 0.006 in., replace with new parts. Discard the piston cups.

To assemble the wheel cylinder:

6. Lubricate the cylinder bore, adjuster and new piston cup with clean brake fluid.

7. Position the piston return spring in the piston cup expander. Install the return spring, piston cup expander and piston cup in the cylinder. The flat side of the piston cup goes toward the piston.

8. Install the piston boot to the piston adjuster (smaller lip of the boot in the groove of the piston adjuster.)

9. Insert the piston adjuster into the cylinder and install the larger lip of the boot in the groove on the cylinder body.

10. Install the adjusting screw in the piston adjuster.

11. Install the wheel cylinder.

Front Wheel Bearings

Adjustment

The front wheel bearings should be adjusted if the wheel is loose on the spindle or if the wheel does not rotate freely.

1. Raise and support the truck.

2. Remove the wheel and tire.

3. Attach a spring scale onto a hub bolt.

4. Pull the spring scale squarely and read the pull as the hub begins to turn. It should be 1.3–2.4 lbs.

5. If the reading is not correct, remove the grease cap and cotter pin. Adjust the bearings with the large nut on the end of the spindle until the proper reading is obtained.

6. Align the holes of the adjusting nut and spindle and install a new cotter pin.

7. Install the grease cap, wheel and tire.

8. Lower the truck.

Alternate Procedure

If a spring scale is not available, the following procedure can be used.

1. Raise and support the truck.

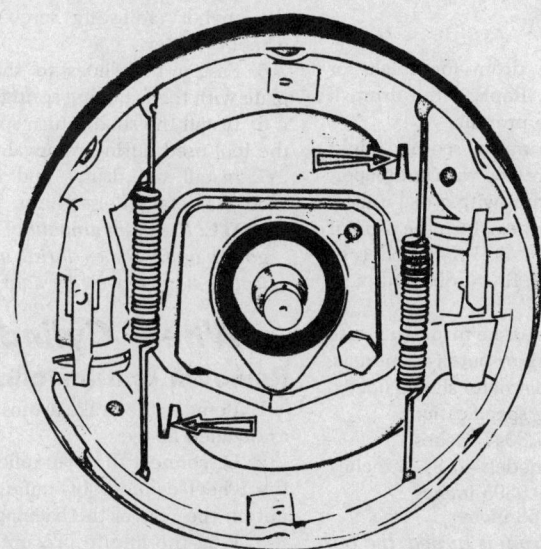

Front brake shoe installation—B-1600 (© Toyo Kogyo Co., Ltd.)

2. Remove the wheel and tire and the grease cap.

3. Remove the cotter pin.

4. Rotate the hub and tighten the adjusting nut until the hub binds.

5. Back the adjusting nut off 1/6 turn. Be sure that the hub rotates freely with no side-play.

6. Align the holes of the nut and spindle and install a new cotter pin.

7. Install the grease cap, wheel and tire.

8. Lower the truck.

Removal, Installation and Packing

1. Raise and support the truck.

2. Remove the wheel cover.

3. Remove the wheel and tire.

4. Remove the grease cap from the hub. Remove the cotter pin, nut lock, adjusting nut and flat washer from the spindle.

5. Remove the hub and drum from the wheel spindle.

6. Remove and discard the old grease retainer. Remove the inner bearing cone and roller from the hub.

7. Clean the grease from the inner and outer bearing cups with solvent and inspect the cups for scratches, pits, or wear.

8. If the cups are worn or damaged, remove them with a drift.

9. Thoroughly clean the inner and outer bearing cones and rollers. DO NOT SPIN THE BEARINGS TO DRY THEM. Allow them to air dry.

10. Inspect the cones and rollers for wear and replace as necessary. The cone and roller assemblies should be replaced as a set. Do not use new bearings or cups with old bearings or cups.

11. Clean the spindle and the inside of the hub with solvent to remove all of the old grease.

12. Cover the spindle with a cloth and clean the dirt from the dust shield. Remove the cloth carefully. Do not get dirt on the spindle.

13. If the inner or outer bearing cups were removed, install the new replacement cups in the hub. Be sure that they are seated squarely and properly.

14. Pack the inside of the hub with wheel bearing grease. Add grease to the hub until grease is flush with the inside diameter of both bearing cups.

NOTE: *It is important that all the old grease is removed, because the more popular lithium base grease is not compatible with the sodium base grease that was originally installed.*

15. Pack the bearing cone and roller with wheel bearing grease. Work as much grease as possible between the cone and rollers. Lubricate the outside cone surfaces with grease.

16. Installing the inner bearing cone and roller in the inner cup. Apply a light film of grease to the grease seal and install the seal. Be sure that the seal is properly seated.

17. Install the hub and drum on the spindle. Keep the hub centered on the spindle to prevent damaging the grease seal.

18. Install the outer bearing cone and roller and the flat washer on the spindle. Install the adjusting nut.

19. Install the wheel and tire.

20. Adjust the wheel bearings.

21. Install the hub cap.

22. Before driving the truck, pump the brake pedal several times to restore normal brake lining-to-drum clearance and normal brake pedal pressure.

REAR DRUM BRAKES

Brake Drums

Removal and Installation

1. Remove the wheel disc and loosen the lug nuts.

2. Raise the rear of the vehicle and securely support it with jackstands.

3. Remove the lug nuts and the rear wheel.

4. Be sure that the parking brake is fully released.

5. Remove the bolts which secure the drum to the rear axle shaft flange.

6. Pull the brake drum off of the flange.

NOTE: *If the drum will not come off easily, screw the drum securing bolts into the two tapped holes in the drum. Tighten the bolts evenly in order to force the drum away from the flange.*

Rear brake drum installation is performed in the reverse order of removal. Adjust the shoes after installation is completed.

Inspection

1. Examine the drum for cracks or overheating spots. Replace the drum if either of these are present.

2. Check the drum for scoring. Light scoring can be corrected with sandpaper.

3. Check the drum with a dial indicator for out-of-roundness; turn the drum if it exceeds 0.0393 in. on RX–3 models or 0.0059 in. on RX–2, RX–4, 808 and pick-up models.

4. If the drum must be turned because of excessive scoring or out-of-roundness, the drum's inside diameter should not exceed the following specifications:

RX–3 models—7.8347 inches

RX–2 and 808 models—7.9135 inches

RX–4 models—9.0395 inches

Pick-ups—10.2758 inches

NOTE: *If one drum is turned, the opposite drum should also be turned to the same size.*

Brake Shoes

Removal and Installation

1. Perform the brake drum removal procedure, as detailed above.

2. Remove the return springs from the upper side of the shoe with a brake spring removal tool.

3. Remove the return springs from the lower side of the shoes in the same manner, as in step 2.

4. Remove the shoe retaining spring:

  a. On RX–3 and RX–4 models, by removing the retaining pin with pliers.

  b. On RX–2, 808 and pick-up models, by compressing the retaining spring while turning the pin 90°.

5. Withdraw the primary shoes and the parking brake link.

6. Disengage the parking brake lever from the secondary shoes by unfastening its retaining clip.

7. Remove the secondary shoe.

CAUTION: *Be careful not to get oil or grease on the lining material.*

Inspect the linings; replace them if they are badly burned or if worn 0.039 in. beyond the specification for a new lining. (See "Brake Specification" chart).

Replace the linings if they are saturated with oil or grease.

Brake shoe installation is performed in the following manner:

1. Lubricate the threads of the adjusting screw, the sliding surfaces of the shoes, and the backing plate flanges with a small quantity of grease.

CAUTION: *Be careful not to get grease on the lining surfaces.*

2. Install the eye of the parking brake cable through the parking brake lever which has previously been installed on the secondary shoe and secured with its retaining clip.

3. Fit the link between the shoes.

4. Engage the shoes with the slots in the anchor (adjusting screw) and the wheel cylinder.

5. Fasten the shoes to the backing plate with the retaining springs and pins.

6. Install the shoe return springs with the tool used during removal.

7. Install the drums and adjust the shoes, as detailed elsewhere.

NOTE: *If a slight amount of grease has gotten on the shoes during installation, it may be removed by light sanding.*

Wheel Cylinders

Removal and Installation

1. Remove the brake drums and shoes, as detailed above.

2. Disconnect the hydraulic line from the wheel cylinder by unfastening the nut on the rear of the backing plate.

3. Plug the line to prevent dirt from entering the system or brake fluid from leaking out.

4. Unfasten the nuts which secure the wheel cylinder to the backing plate and remove the cylinder.

Installation of the wheel cylinder is performed in the reverse order of removal. Bleed the hydraulic system and adjust the brake shoes after installation is completed.

Overhaul

Passenger Cars

1. Remove the boots at either end of the wheel cylinder.

2. Withdraw the pistons, piston cups, push rods, and return spring.

3. Wash all of the components in clean brake fluid.

CAUTION: *Never use kerosene or gasoline to clean wheel cylinder components.*

Check the cylinder bore and piston for roughness or scoring. Use a wheel cylinder hone, if necessary.

Measure the clearance between the cylinder and the piston with a feeler gauge. If the clearance is greater than 0.006 in., replace either the piston or the cylinder.

Examine the piston cups for wear, softening, or swelling; replace them if necessary.

Assembly is performed as follows:

1. Apply clean brake fluid to the cylinder bore, pistons, and cups.

2. Fit the steel ball into the bleed hole and install the screw, if removed.

3. Insert the parts into the cylinder bore in the reverse order of removal.

NOTE: *Install the piston cups so that their flat side is facing outward.*

4. Fit the boots over both ends of the cylinder.

Pick-Up Trucks

1. Remove the wheel cylinder from the backing plate.

2. Remove the piston and adjusting screw with the boot attached to the adjuster.

3. Separate the adjuster screw and boot from the adjuster.

4. Remove the other piston and boot and separate the boot from the piston.

5. Press in on either piston cup and force the piston cups, cup expanders, and return spring from the cylinder.

6. Wash all parts (except the boots) in clean isopropyl alcohol. Examine the cylinder bore for roughness or scoring.

7. Check the piston-to-cylinder bore clearance. If it exceeds 0.006 in., replace with new parts.

To assemble the wheel cylinder:

8. Lubricate the cylinder bore, adjuster and new piston cups with clean brake fluid, before assembly. Always use new piston cups.

9. Install the piston return spring in a piston cup expander. Place the other piston cup expander and new piston cup on the return spring. Install the return spring, piston cup expanders and piston cups into the cylinder.

10. Install the piston boot to the piston

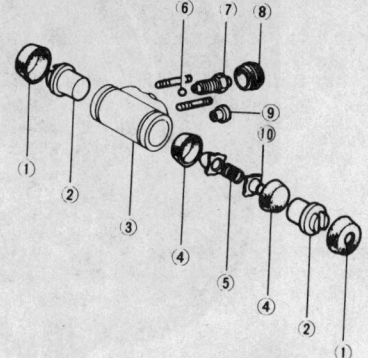

Rear wheel cylinder components
(Ⓒ Toyo Kogyo Co., Ltd.)

1. Boot
2. Piston
3. Cylinder body
4. Piston cup
5. Return spring
6. Steel ball
7. Bleeder screw
8. Bleeder screw cap
9. Hydraulic line seat
10. Push rod

adjuster with the smaller lip of the boot on the groove of the piston adjuster.

11. Insert the piston adjuster into the cylinder assembly and install the larger lip of the boot in the groove of the cylinder.

12. Install the adjusting screw in the piston adjuster.

13. Install the wheel cylinder as detailed above.

PARKING BRAKE

Adjustment

Passenger Cars

1. Adjust the rear brake shoes, as outlined above.

2. Adjust the front cable with the nut located at the rear of the parking brake handle. The handle should require 3–7 notches for RX–3, RX–4 and Cosmo models, 3–4 notches for 808 and 2–3 notches for RX–2 models to apply the parking brake.

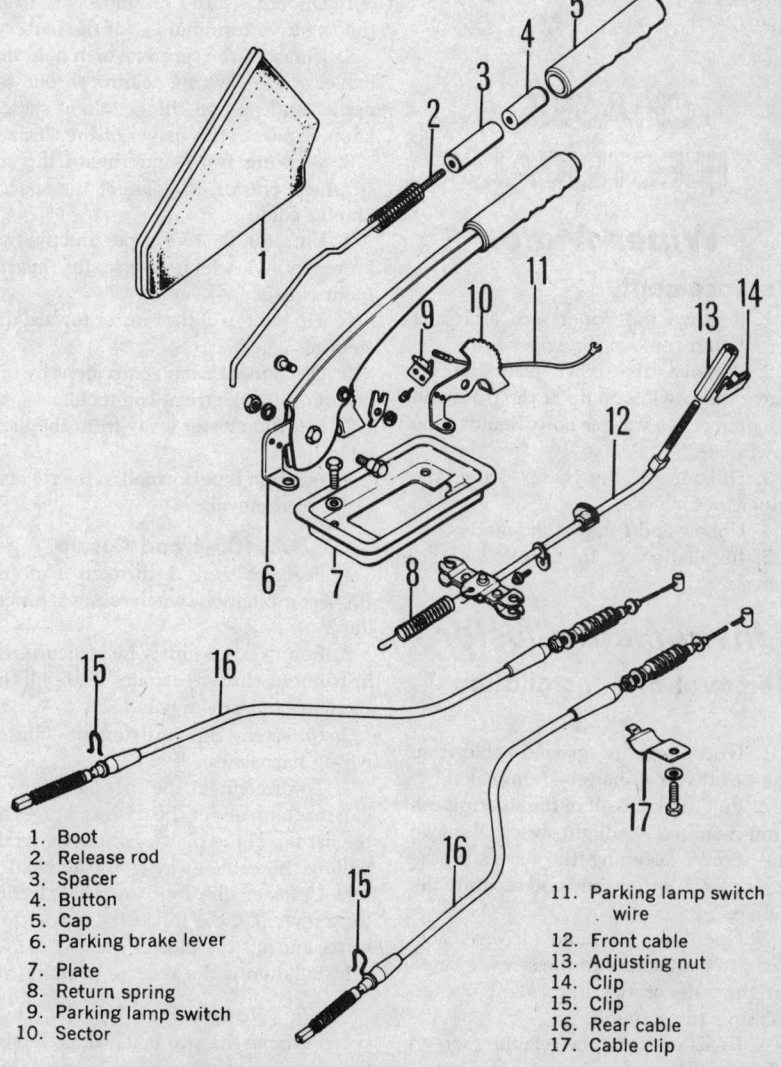

1. Boot
2. Release rod
3. Spacer
4. Button
5. Cap
6. Parking brake lever
7. Plate
8. Return spring
9. Parking lamp switch
10. Sector
11. Parking lamp switch wire
12. Front cable
13. Adjusting nut
14. Clip
15. Clip
16. Rear cable
17. Cable clip

RX-3 parking brake components—RX-2 and RX-4 similar
(Ⓒ Toyo Kogyo Co., Ltd.)

3. Operate the parking brake several times; check to see that the rear wheels do not drag when it is fully released.

Pick-Up Trucks

1. Adjust the service brakes before attempting to adjust the parking brake.

2. Use the adjusting nut to adjust the length of the front cable so that the rear brakes are locked when the parking brake lever is pulled out 5–10 notches.

3. After adjustment, apply the parking brake several times. Release the parking brake and make sure that the rear wheels rotate without dragging. If they drag, repeat the adjustment.

Parking Brake Shoes

Replacement

Cosmo Only

1. Remove the brake disc.

2. Remove the brake shoe return springs.

3. Remove the secondary brake shoe retaining spring and guide pin by compressing the retaining pin and turning the guide pin 90°. Then remove the brake shoe.

CHASSIS ELECTRICAL

Wiper Motor

Replacement

1. Remove the wiper arm attaching screws and remove the wiper arms.

2. Remove the cowl plate screws, move the cowl plate up at the front and disconnect the washer hose. Remove the cowl plate.

3. Disconnect the wires from the wiper motor.

4. Unbolt and remove the motor.

5. Installation is the reverse of removal.

Instrument Cluster

Removal and Installation

RX–3

1. Disconnect the ground cable from the negative (−) battery terminal.

2. Pull the knob off of the steering column-mounted headlight switch. Remove the screws fastening the halves of the steering column shroud and separate the halves.

3. Open the left-hand (driver's side) door, to gain access to the screw located on the side of the instrument cluster. Remove the screw.

4. Unfasten the three retaining screws which are located underneath the instrument cluster.

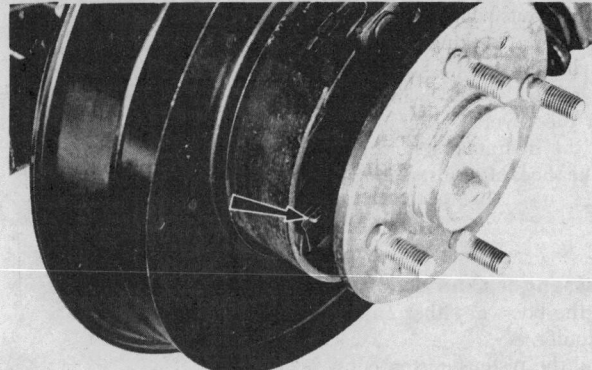

Removing shoe hold-down spring—Cosmo parking brake (© Toyo Kogyo Co. Ltd.)

5. Tip the top of the cluster toward the steering wheel.

6. Disconnect the wiring and the speedometer cable from the back of the instrument cluster.

7. Remove the cluster assembly completely.

Installation is performed in the reverse order of removal.

RX–2

1. Disconnect the ground cable from the negative terminal (−) of the battery.

2. Unfasten the screws which hold the halves of the steering column shroud together and pull off the headlight switch knob. Separate the halves of the shroud.

3. Working from underneath the instrument cluster, disconnect the speedometer cable.

4. Unfasten the two upper and the two lower screws which secure the instrument cluster.

5. Tip the top of the cluster toward the steering wheel.

6. Disconnect each component by unfastening its electrical connector.

7. Lift the cluster away from the dash panel.

Installation is performed in the reverse order of removal.

808, RX–4 and Cosmo

1. Perform steps 1 through 9 of the RX–4 combination switch removal procedure.

2. Remove the nuts which secure the instrument cluster surround and pull the surround out of the panel.

3. Unfasten the instrument cluster wiring harness(es).

4. To disconnect the speedometer cable, reach up under the dash and press on the flat tab of the plastic connector while pulling the cable away from the head.

5. Unfasten the four instrument cluster screws. Tilt the top of the cluster forward, and lift the cluster out.

Installation is the reverse of removal.

Rotary Pick-Up

1. Remove the two bolts which secure the steering column bracket to the instrument panel.

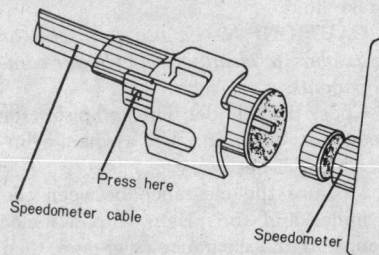

Speedometer cable removal—all models
(© Toyo Kogyo Co., Ltd.)

2. Unfasten the four instrument cluster securing screws.

3. To disconnect the speedometer cable, reach up under the dash and depress the flat plastic connector tab while pulling the cable away from the head.

4. Unfasten the wiring harness from the instrument cluster.

5. Lift the instrument cluster out.

Installation is performed in the reverse order of removal.

B–1600 Pick-Up

1. Disconnect the cable from the negative (−) battery terminal.

2. Remove the four instrument cluster securing screws.

3. Move the cluster rearward, so that you can gain access to the back of it.

4. To disconnect the speedometer cable, reach up under the dash and depress the flat plastic connector tab while pulling the cable away from the head.

5. Disconnect the cluster wiring harness from the printed circuit. Note the position of the ammeter leads and disconnect them as well.

6. Remove the screw which secures the ground lead to the cluster. On models with air injection, unfasten the two speedometer sensor lead connectors.

7. Remove the cluster.

Installation is the reverse of removal.

Fuses

Fuse Box Location

RX–3 and RX–2

The fuse boxes on both the RX–3 and the RX–2 models are located underneath the right-hand (passenger's) side of the dash.

On the RX–3 models, the box is located just above the lower parcel shelf, and uses a back-hinged cover.

On RX–2 models, the box is located underneath the leading edge of the dash and is equipped with a sliding cover.

Both of the covers have the location, amperage, and the circuit protected by each individual fuse, stamped on them.

The cable running from the positive side of the battery is equipped with a fusible link on both models.

CAUTION: *Do not replace the fusible link with a regular wire if it burns out. If it must be replaced, use the proper Mazda part.*

RX–4

The main fuse and secondary fuse block are located next to the battery in the engine compartment. An additional fuse box is located beneath the glove compartment. The amperage of each fuse is printed on the fuse box lids.

Rotary Pick-Up

The main fuse block is mounted behind the seat at the right side of the cab. Another fuse box is attached to the firewall at the left, rear corner of the engine compartment. Fuse amperage and location are printed on the inside of the fuse box cover.

B–1600 Pick-Up

The main fuse is located behind the battery. The fuse box is located at the left, rear corner of the engine compartment. Fuse amperage and location are printed on the inside of the cover.

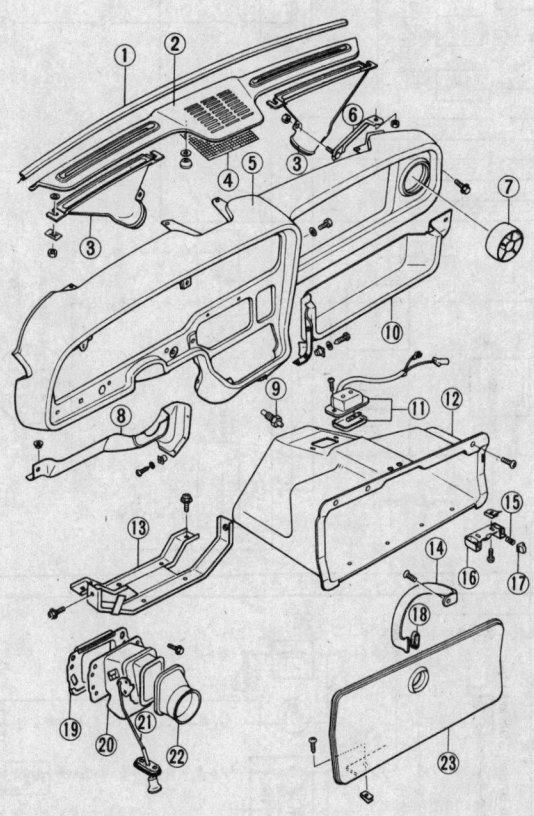

1. Seaming welt
2. Garnish
3. Defroster nozzle
4. Cloth cover
5. Instrument panel pad
6. Defroster nozzle bracket
7. Louver
8. Instrument panel lower
9. Glove box switch
10. Instrument panel lower
11. Glove box lamp
12. Glove tray
13. Instrument panel center bracket
14. Stopper
15. Spring
16. Striker
17. Spring plate
18. Cushion
19. Gasket
20. Ventilator
21. Control wire
22. Duct
23. Glove box lid

Cosmo instrument panel

Wiring Circuits

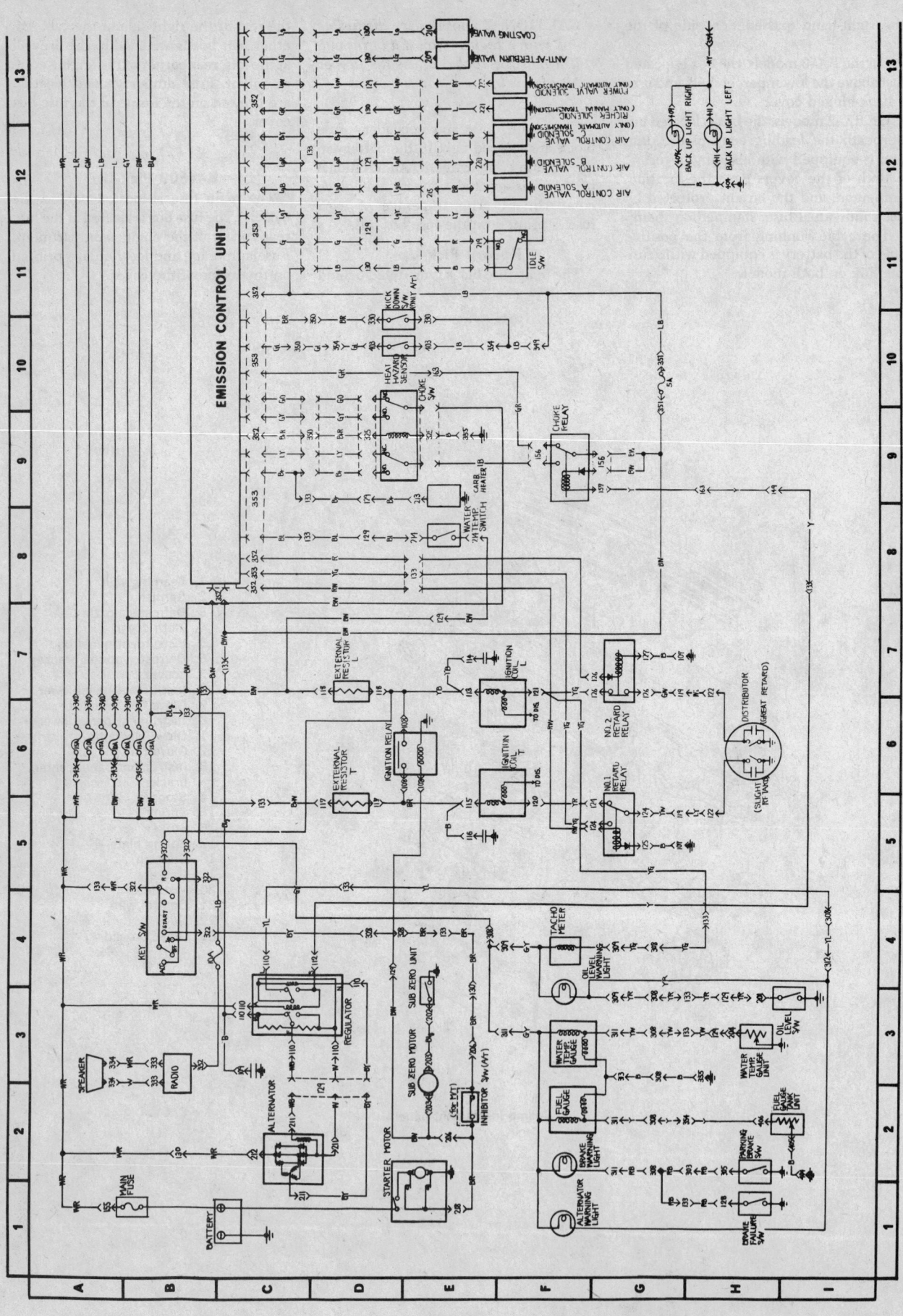

1975 RX-3

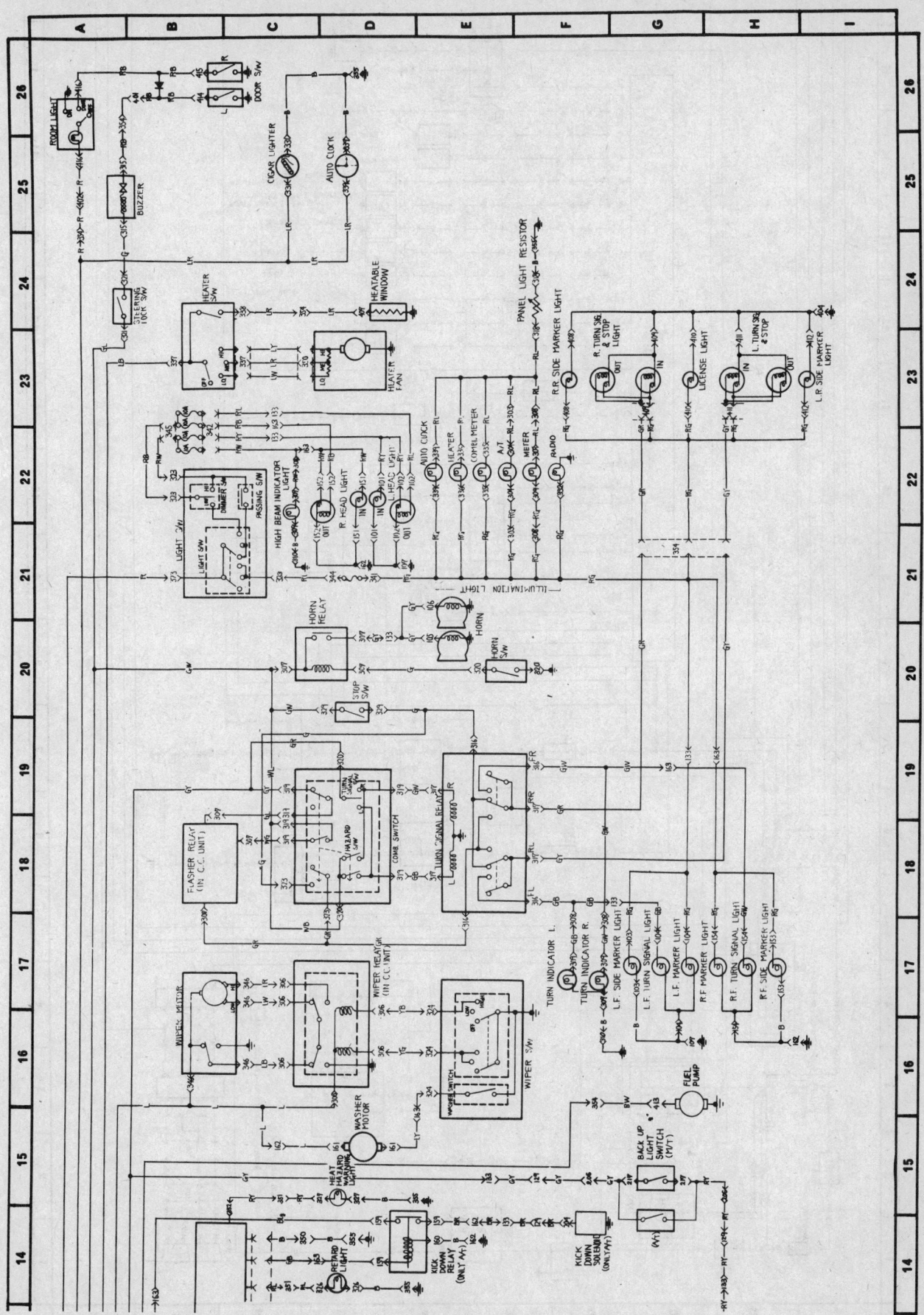

1975 RX-3

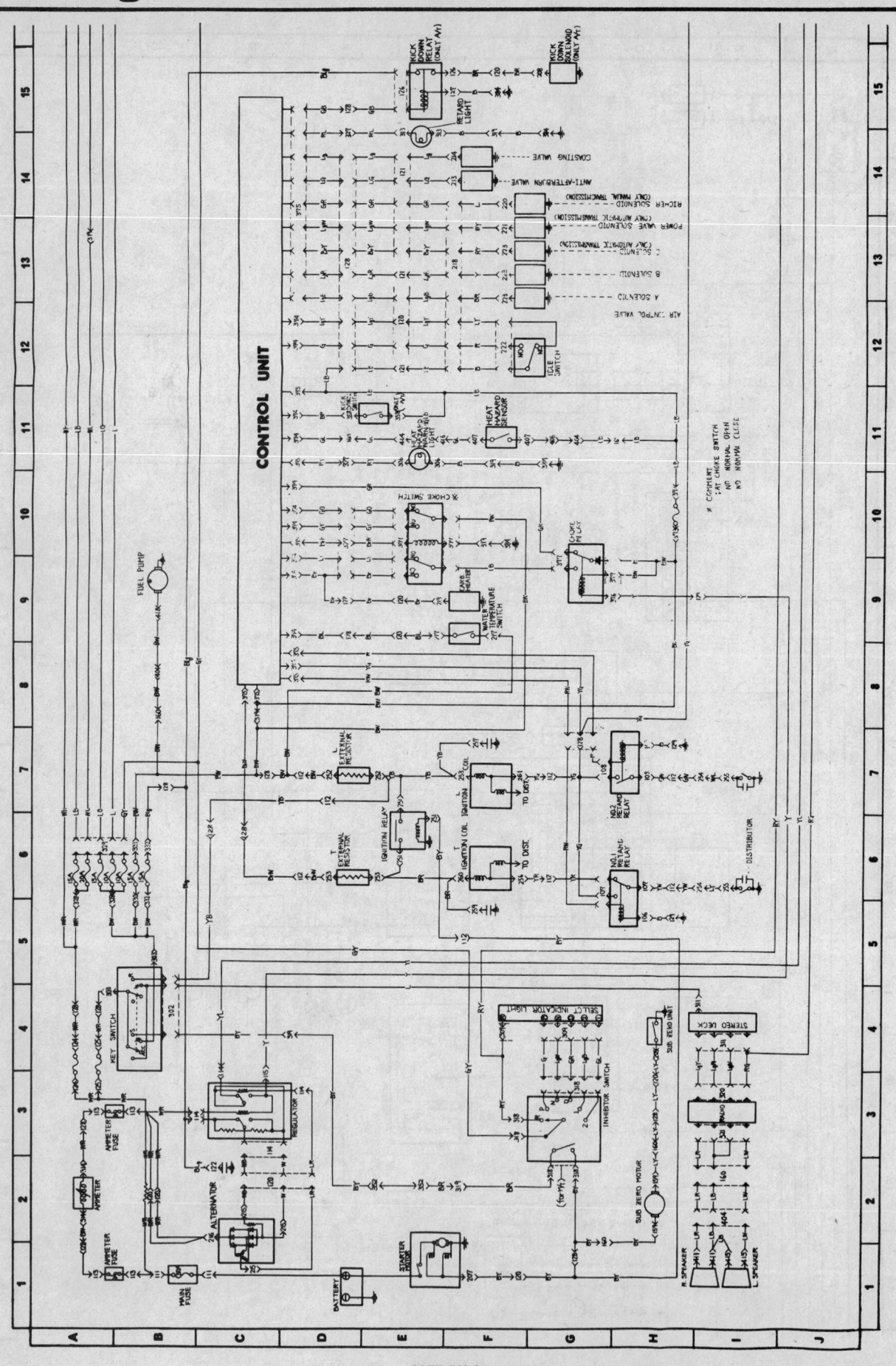

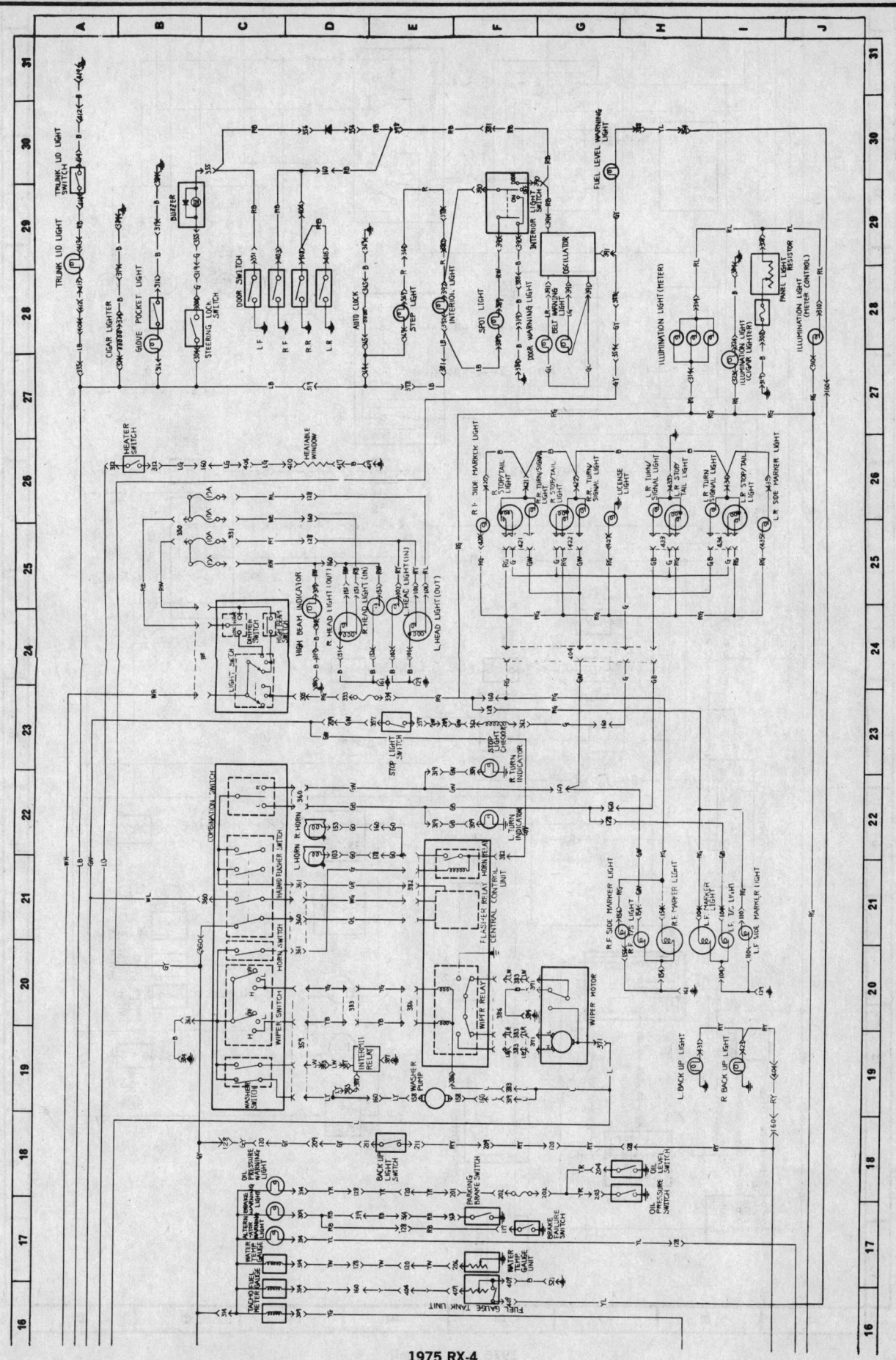

1975 RX-4

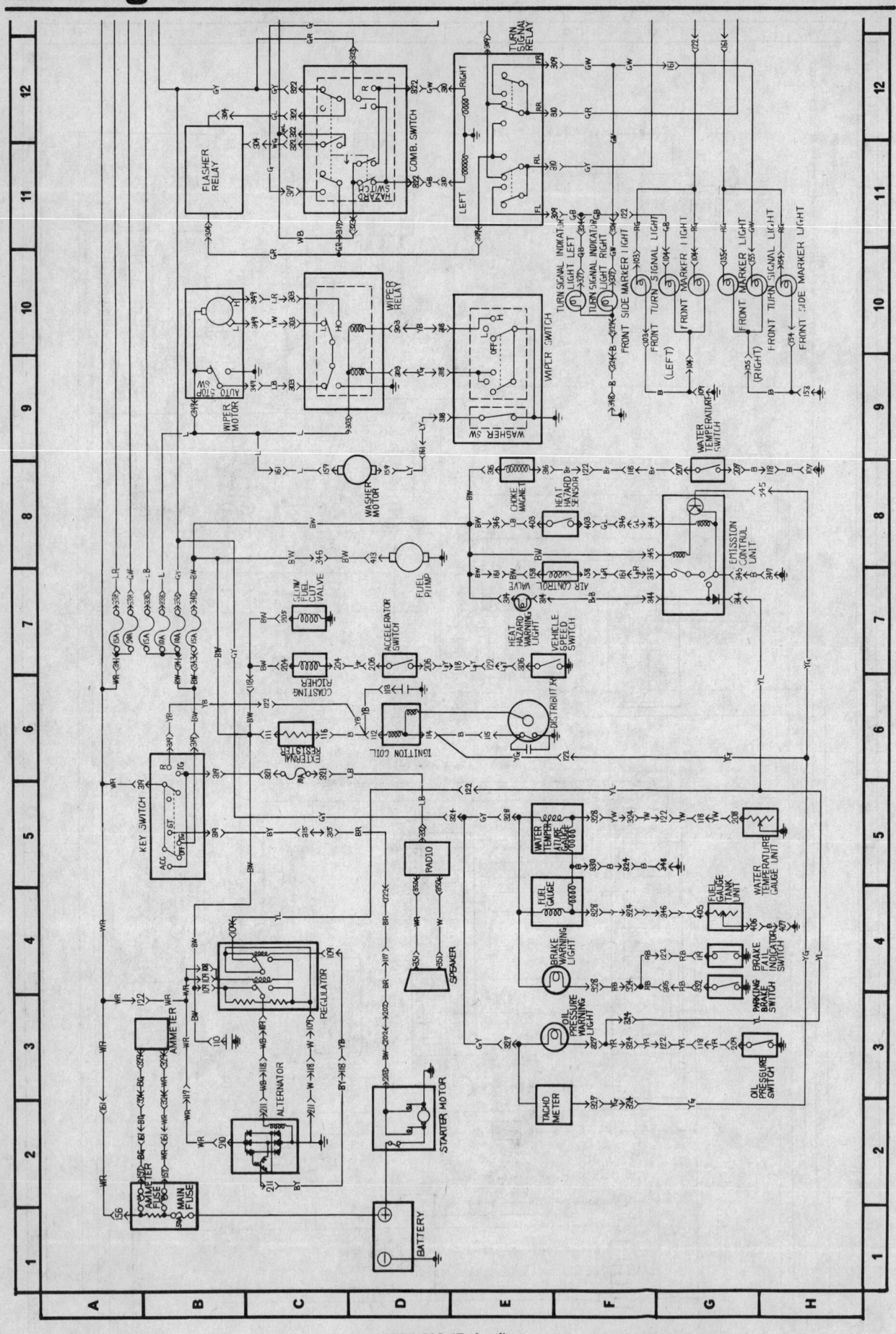

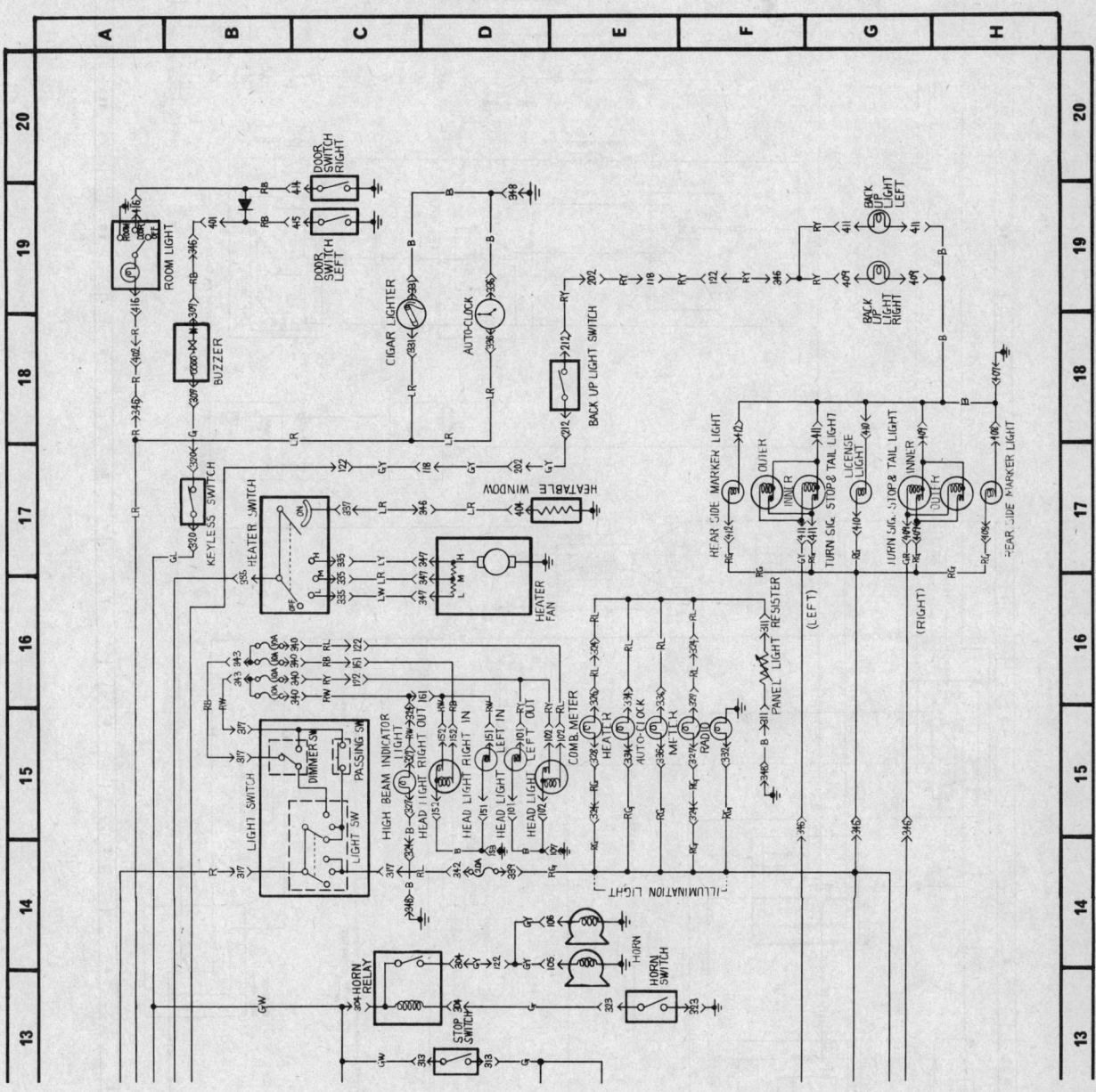

1975 808 (Federal)

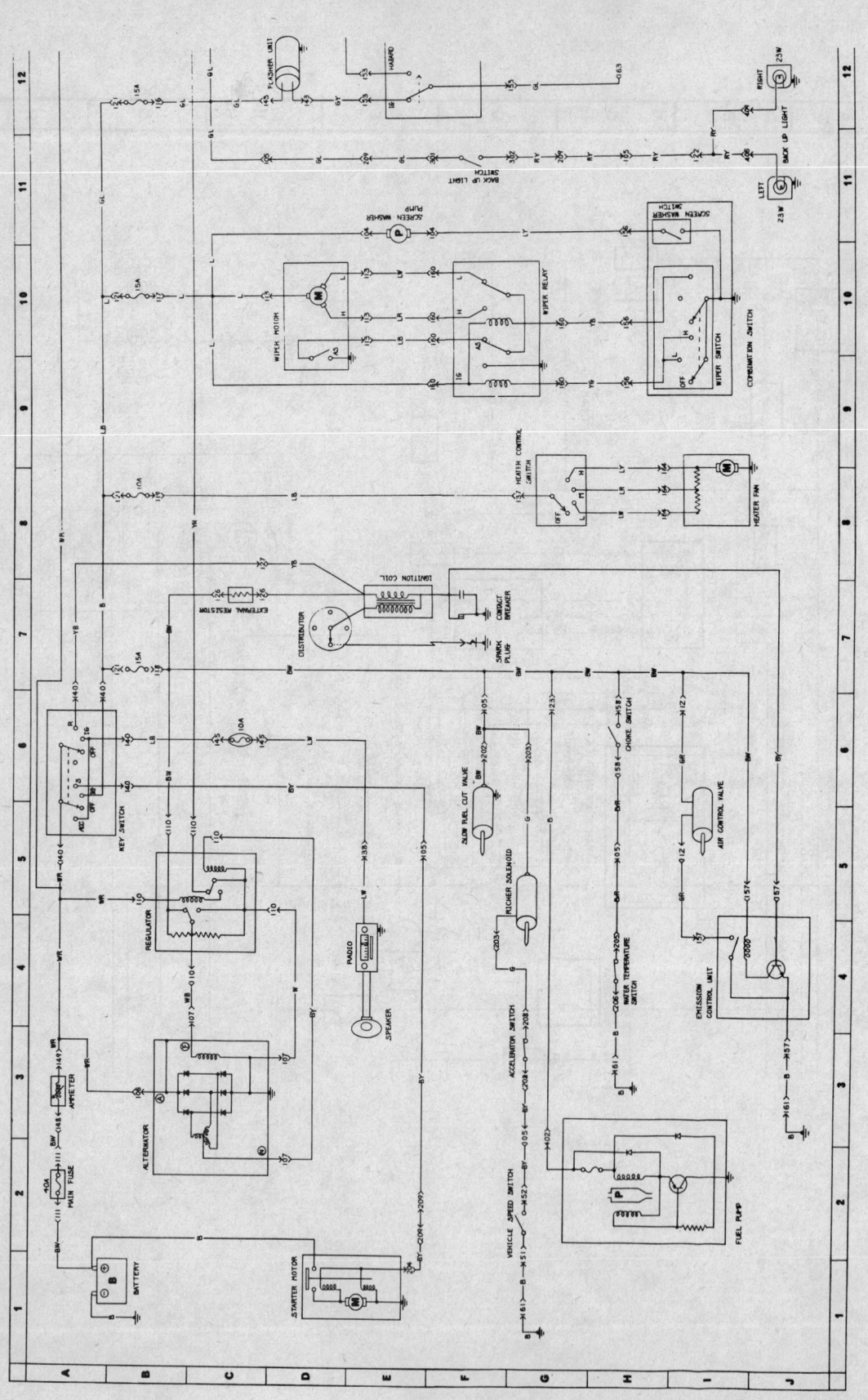

1975 B1600

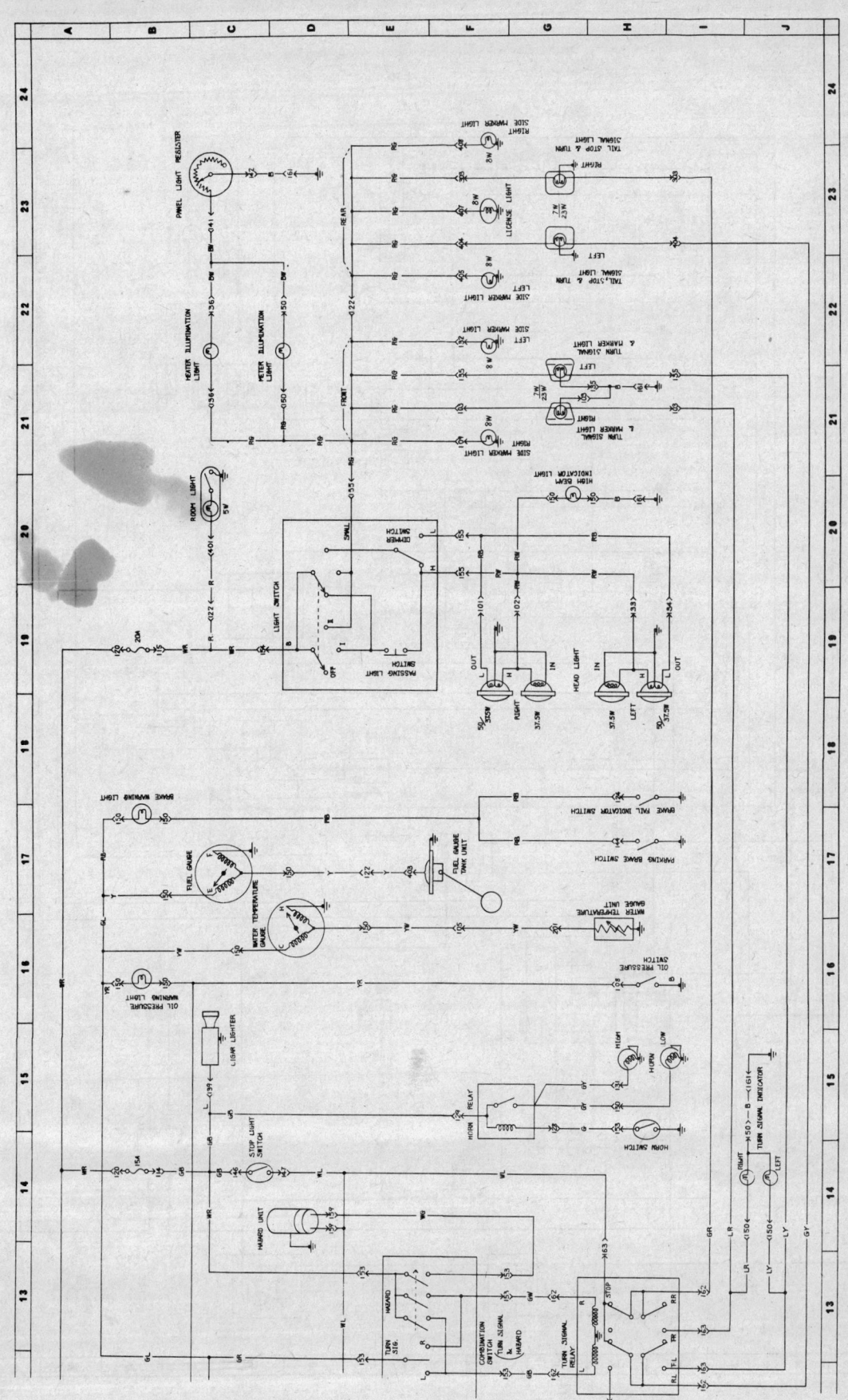

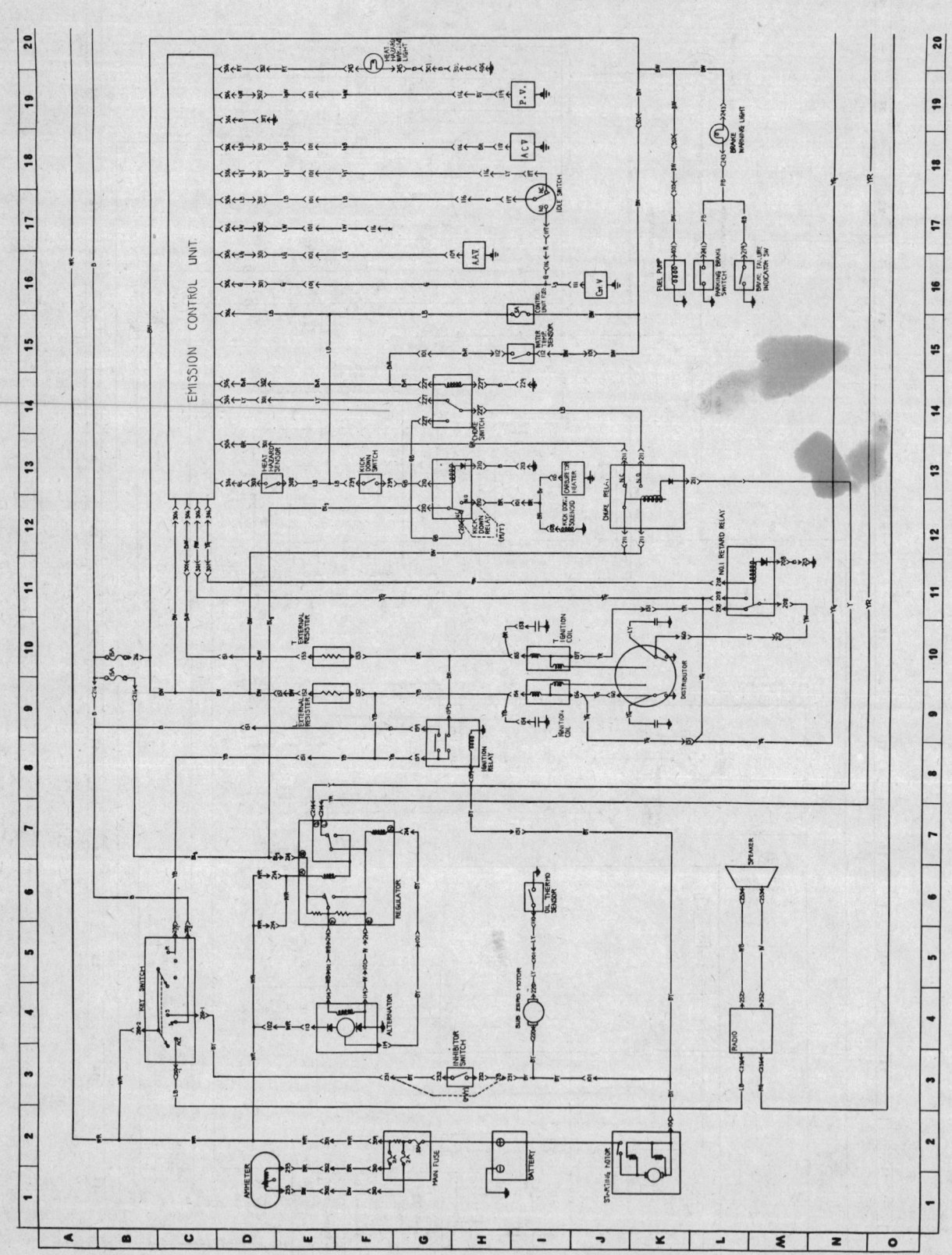

1975 Rotary Pick-Up

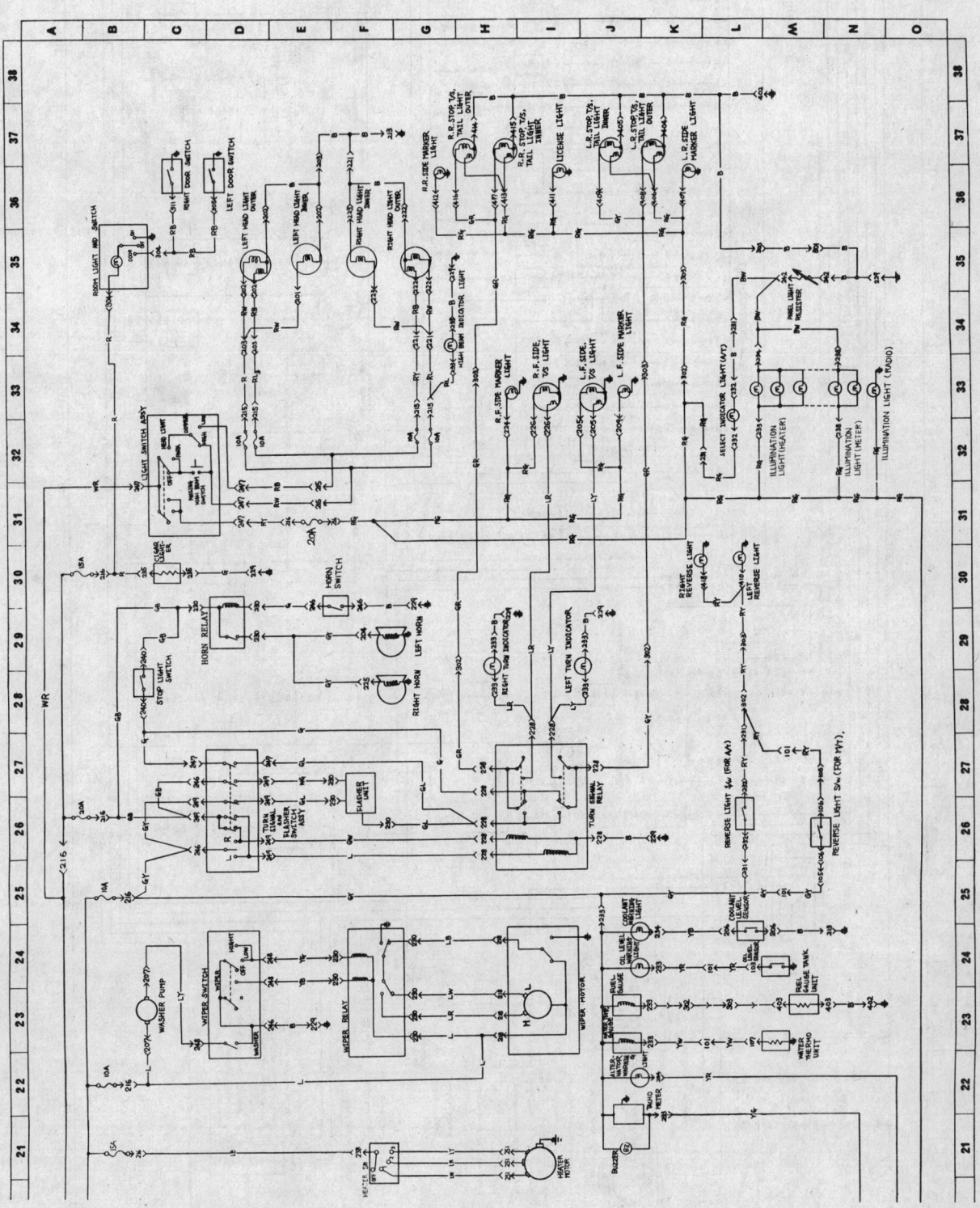

1975 Rotary Pick-Up

Wiring Circuits

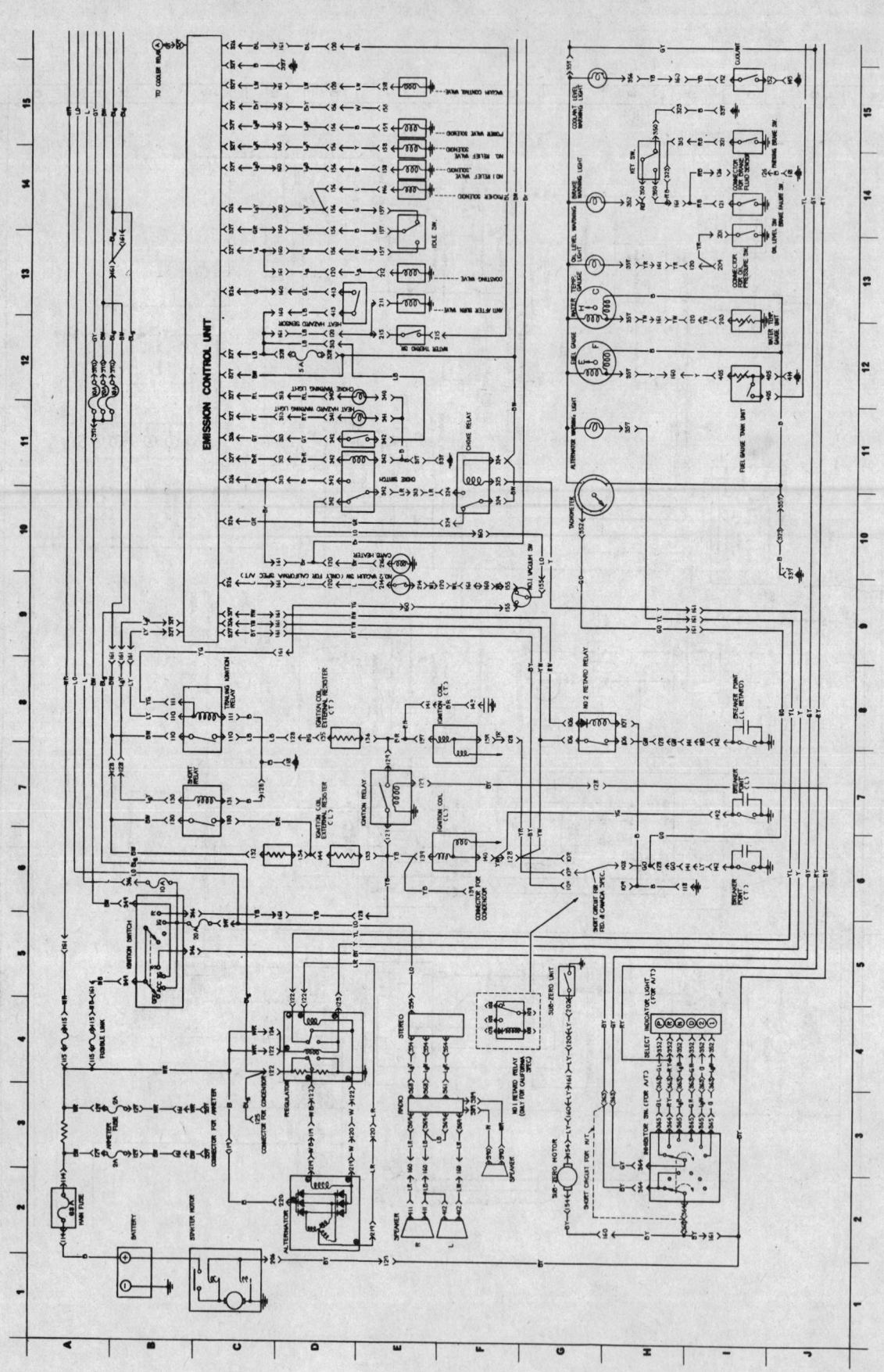

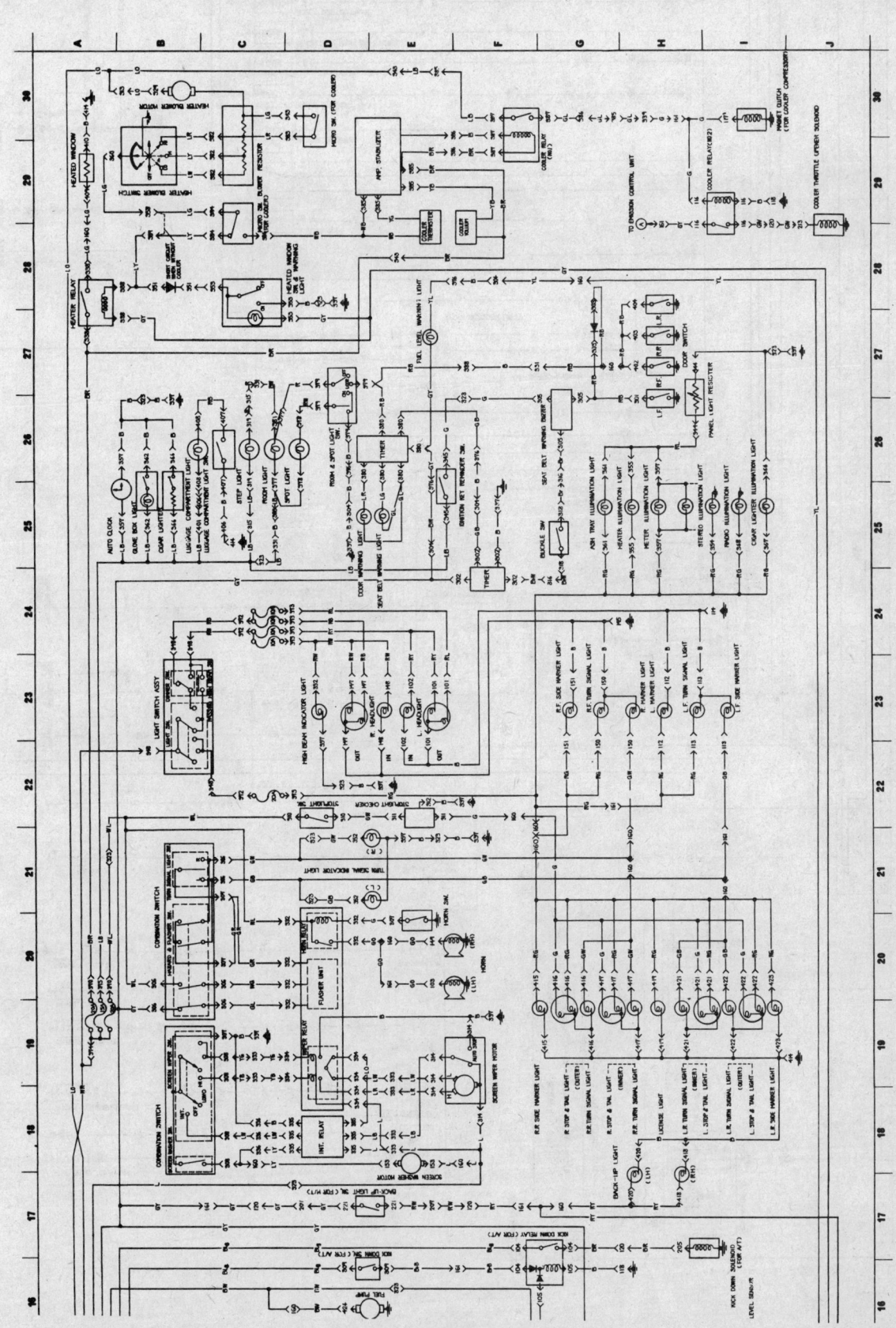

1976 RX-4

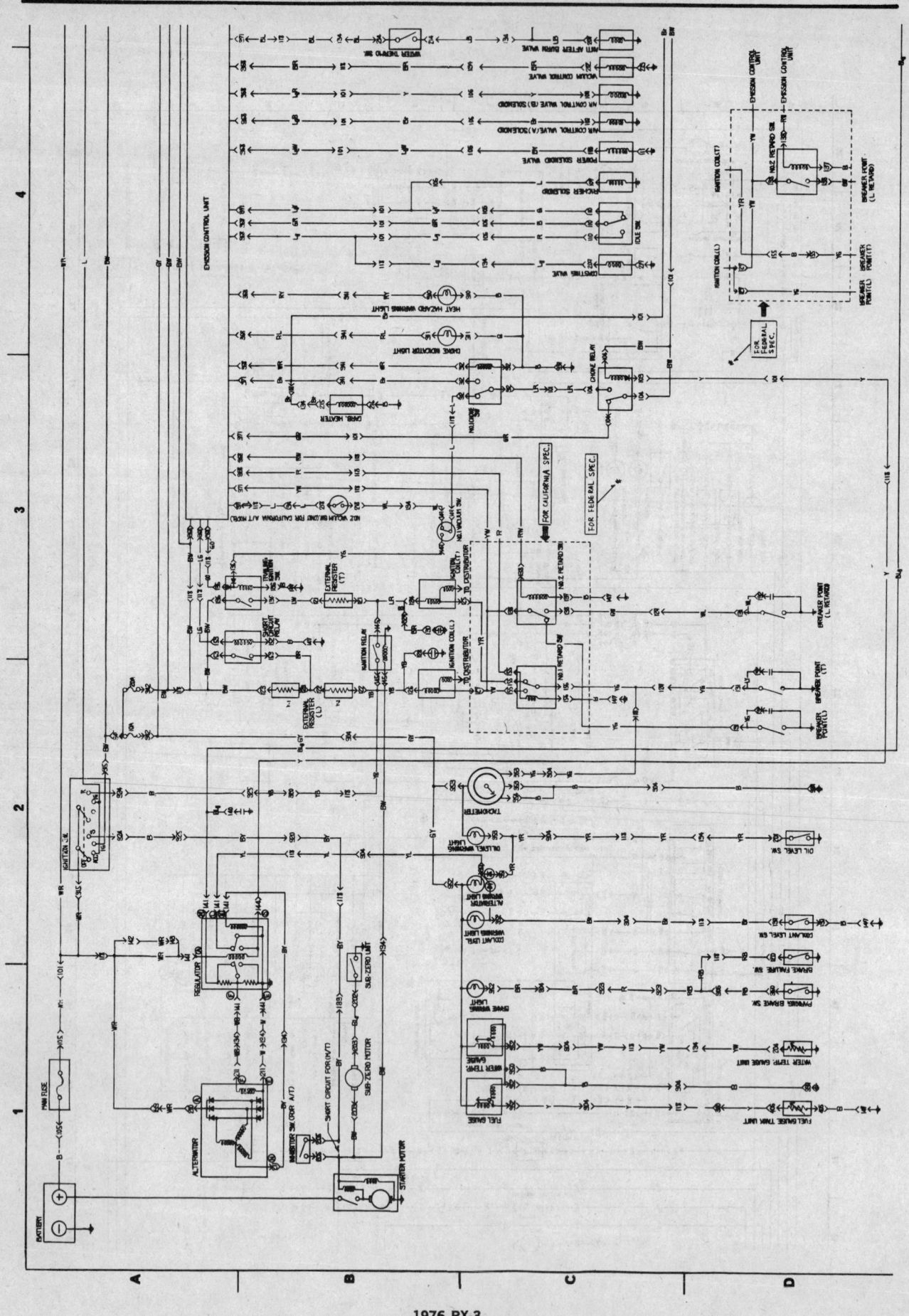

1976 RX-3

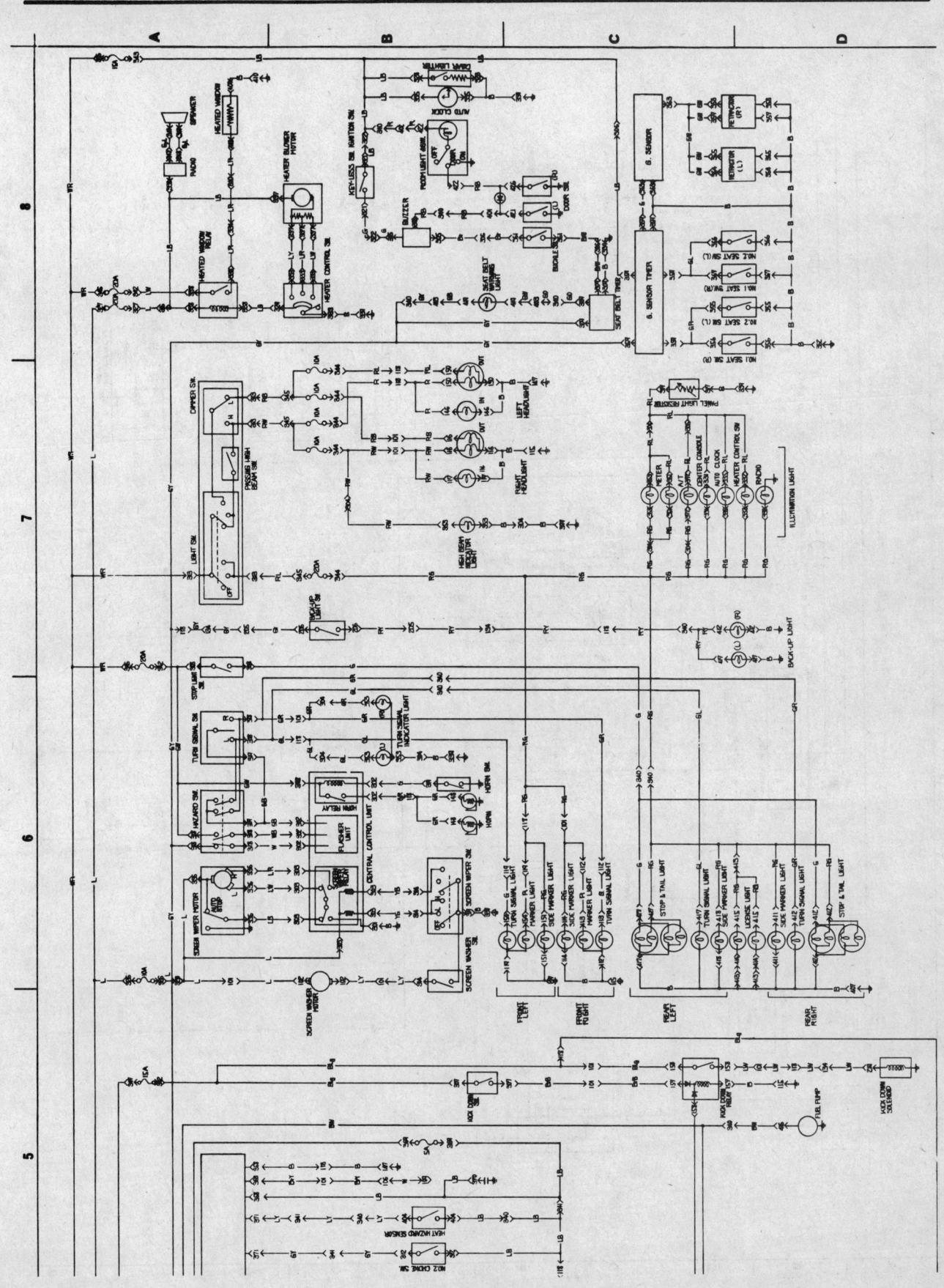

1976 RX-3

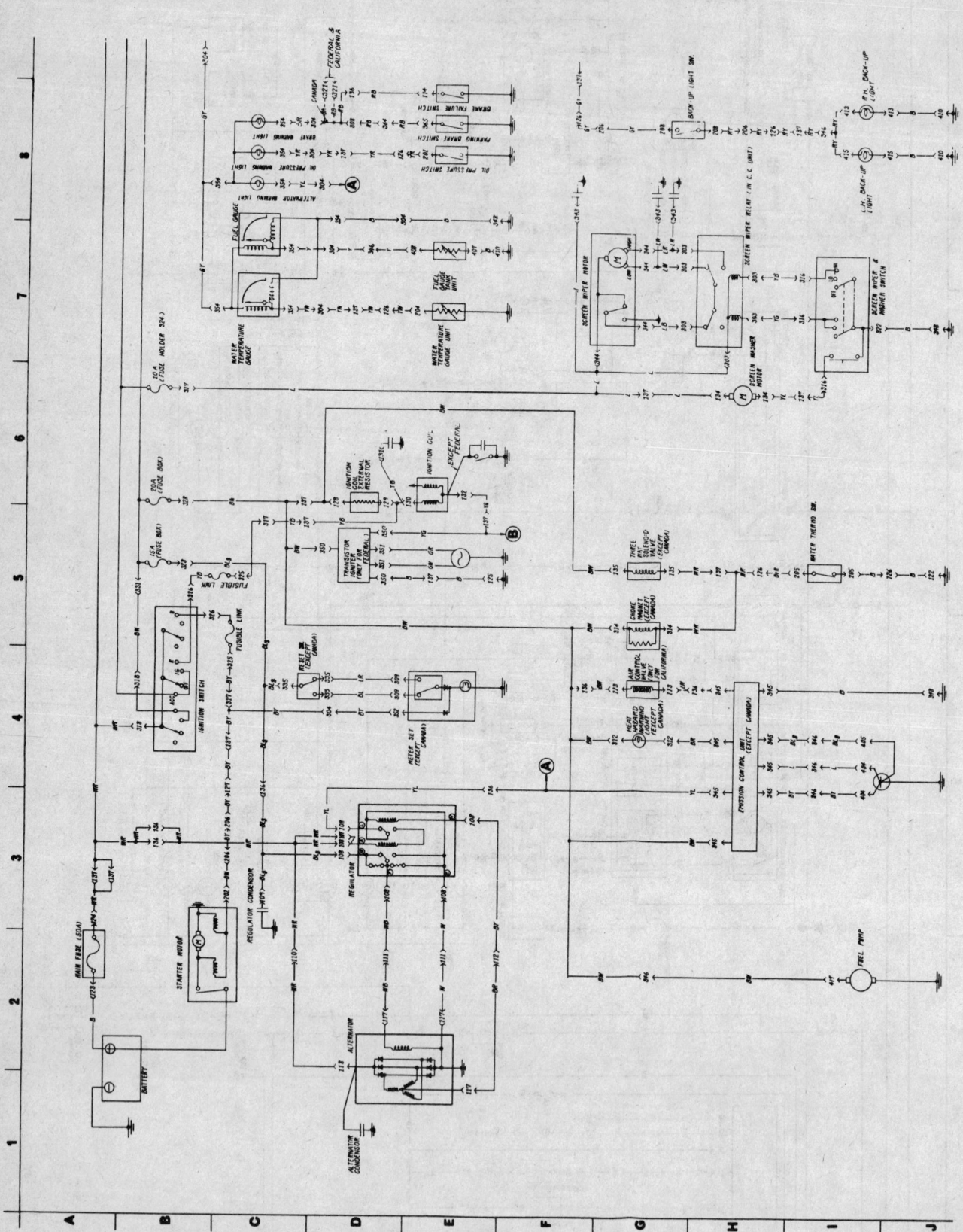

1976 808

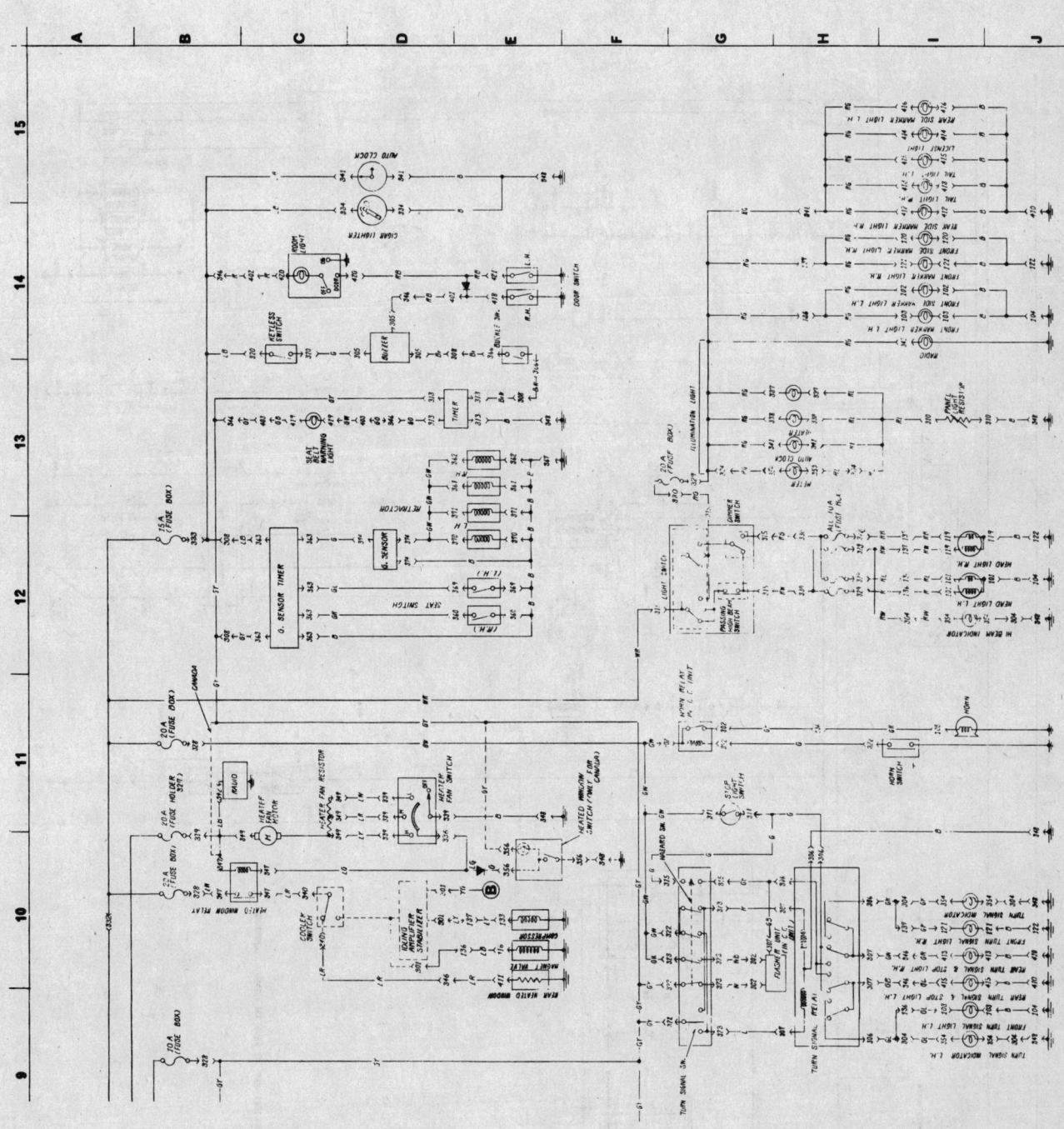

1976 808

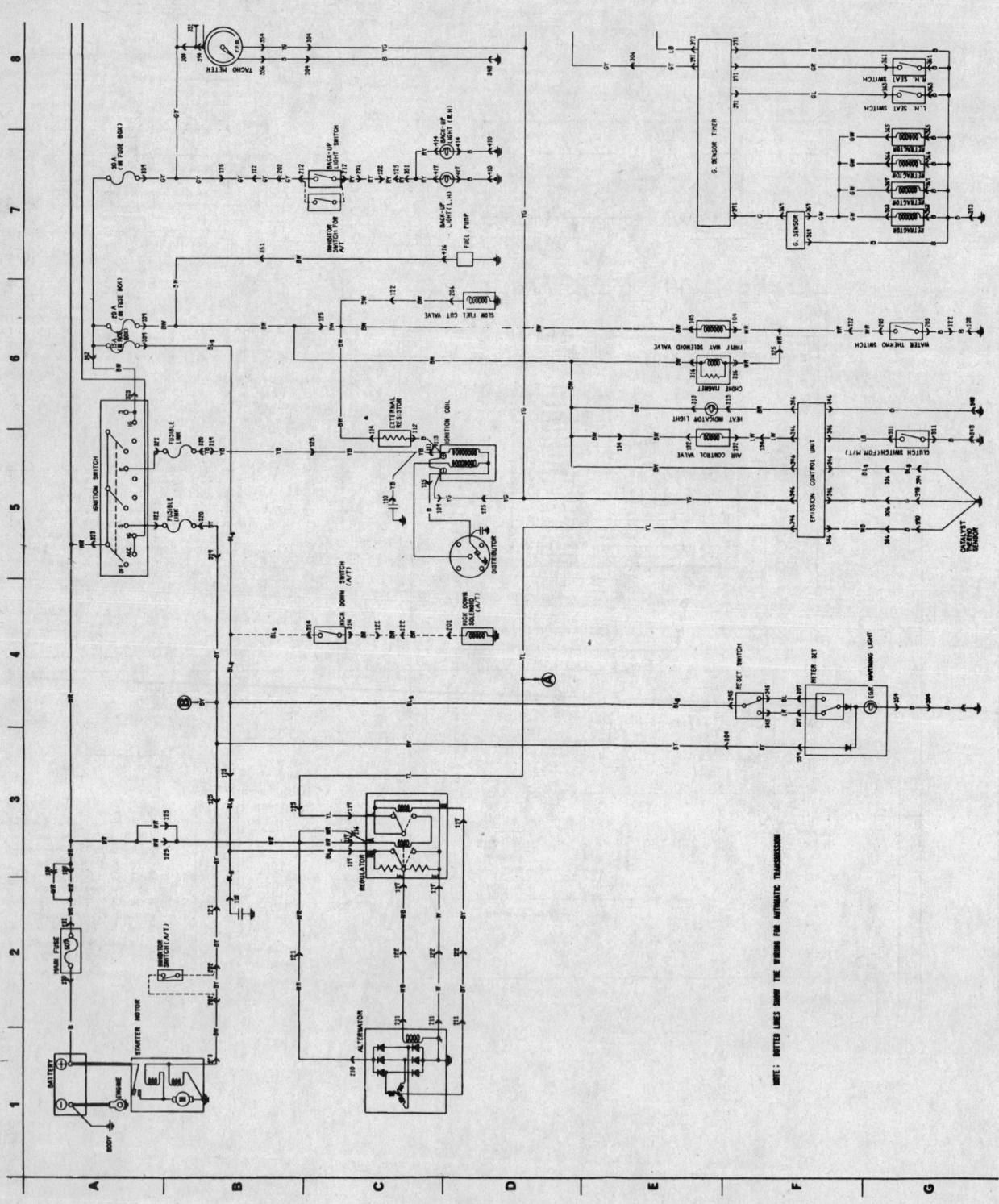

NOTE: DOTTED LINES SHOW THE WIRING FOR AUTOMATIC TRANSMISSION

1976 808 (1600)

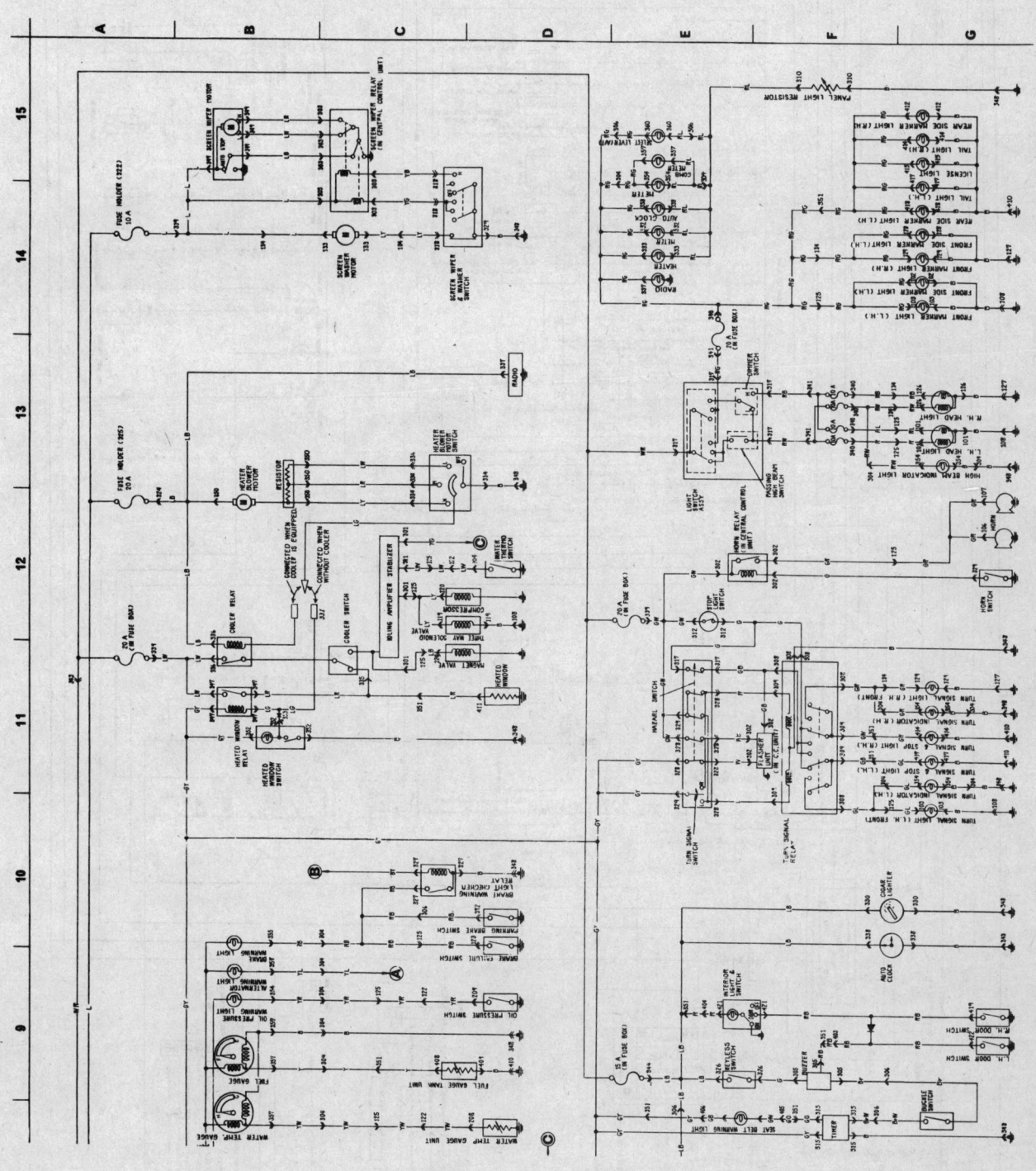

1976 808 (1600)

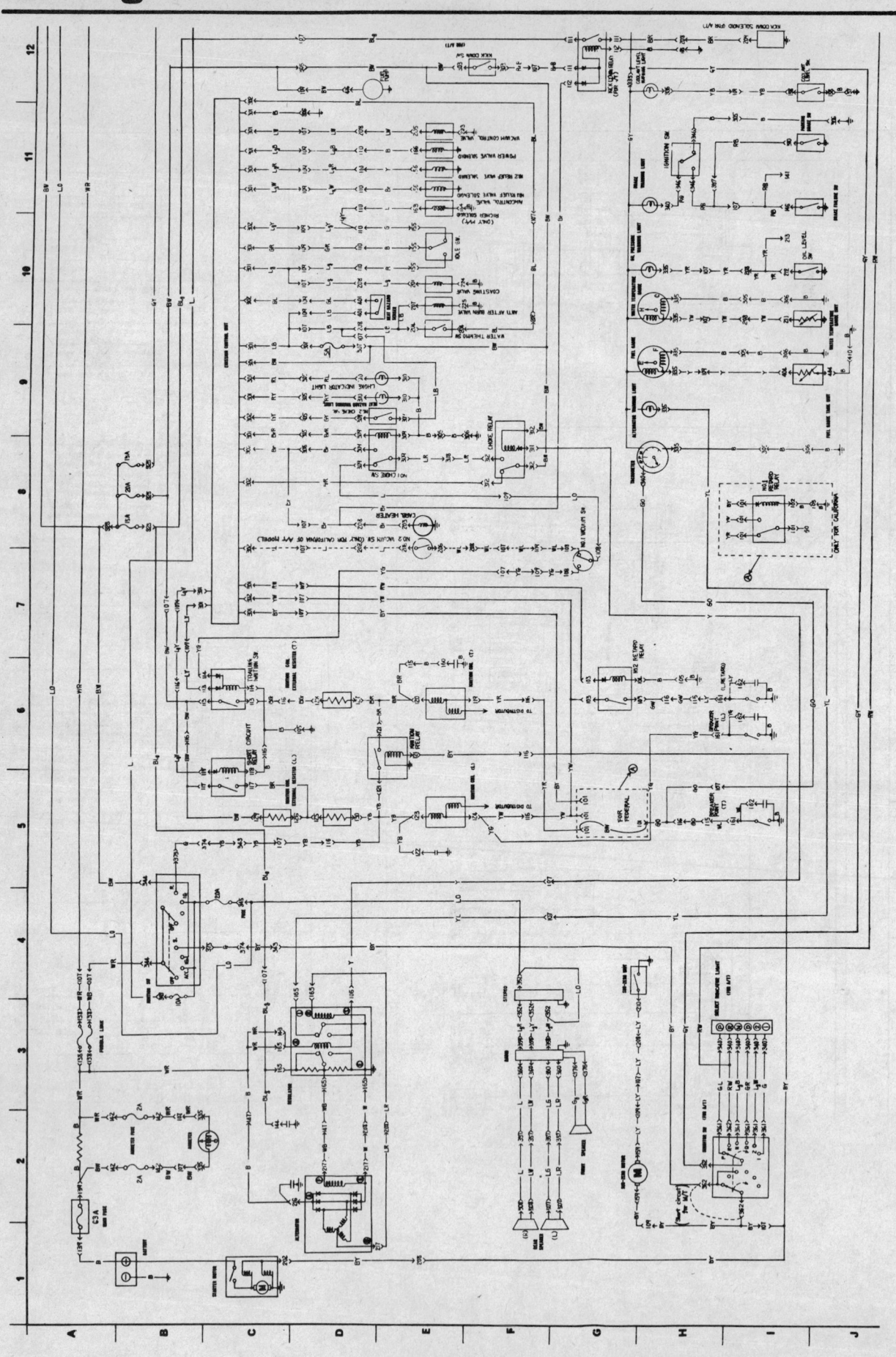

Cosmo

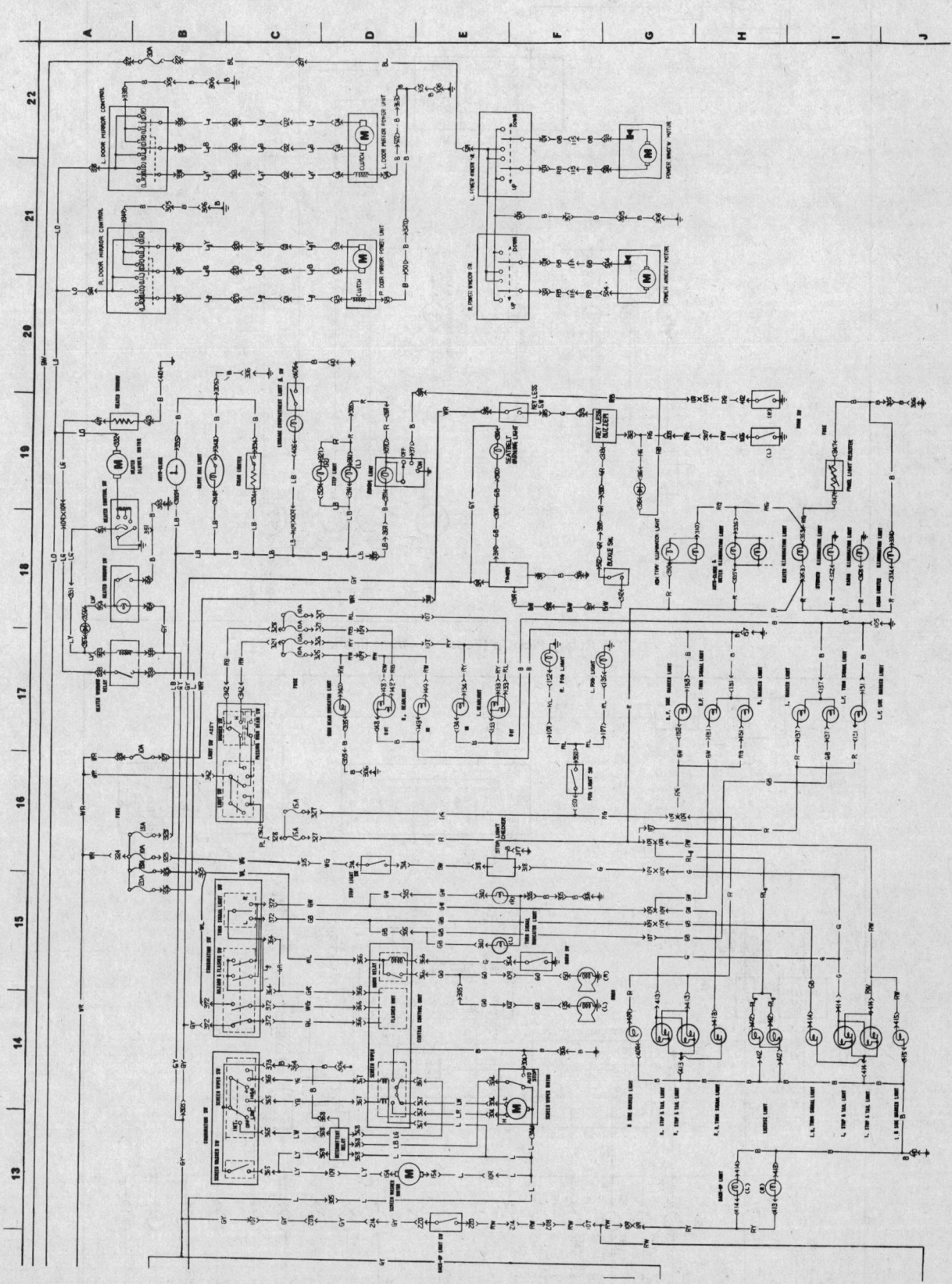

Cosmo

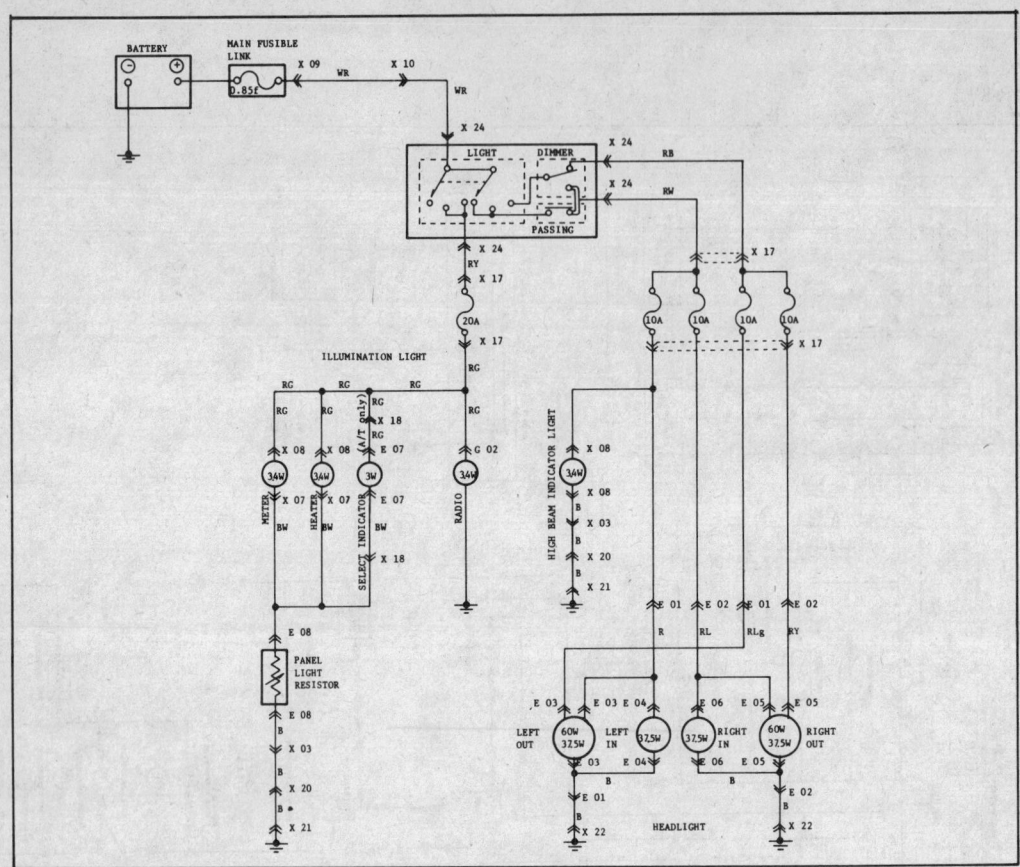

1976 Rotary Pick-Up (Federal)—front lighting

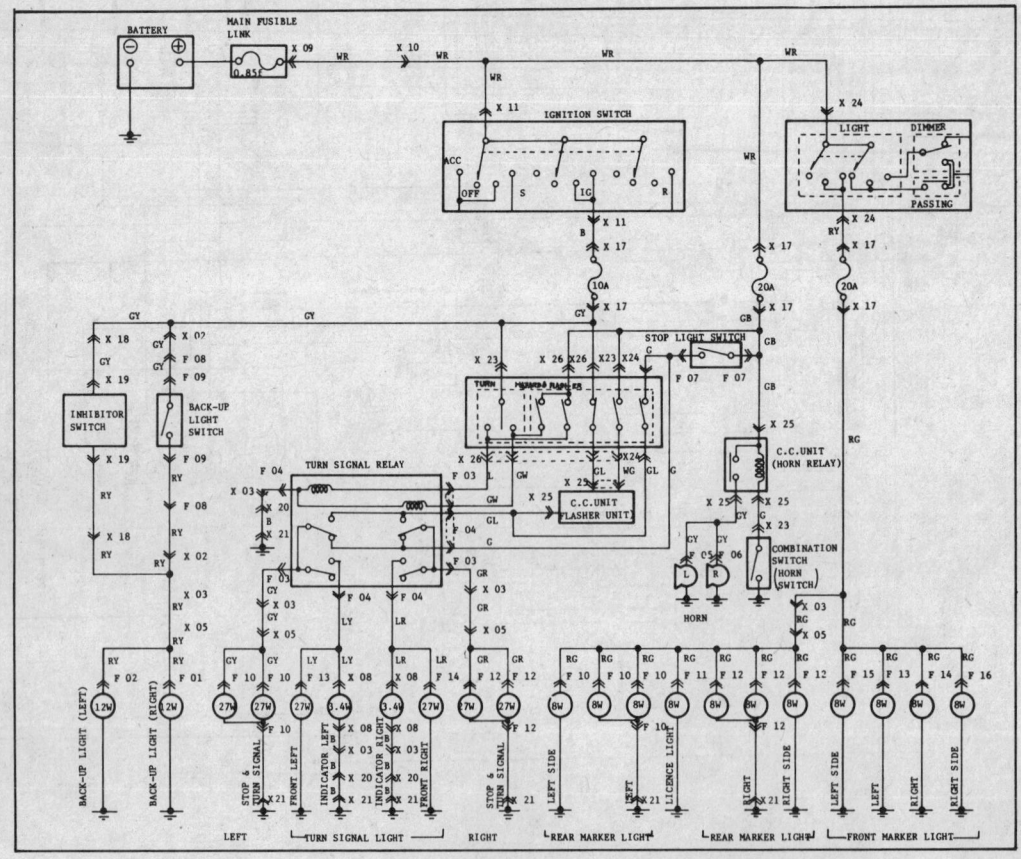

1976 Rotary Pick-Up (Federal)—rear lighting

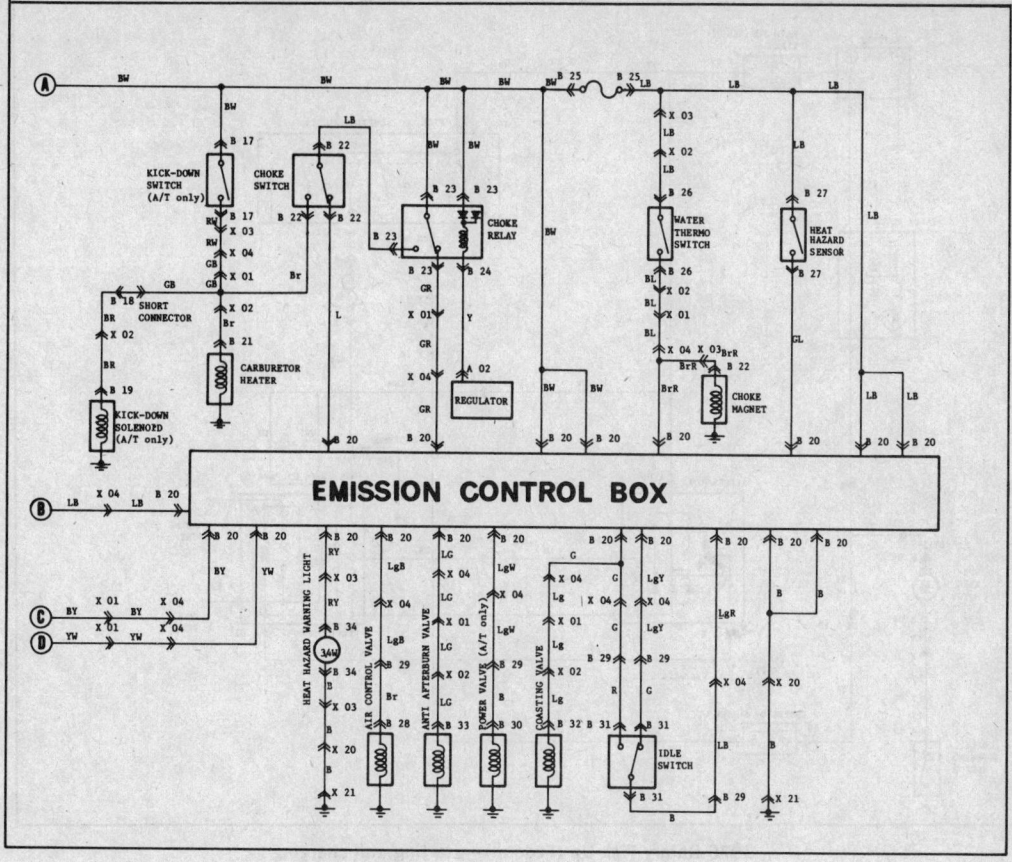

1976 Rotary Pick-Up (Federal)—emission controls

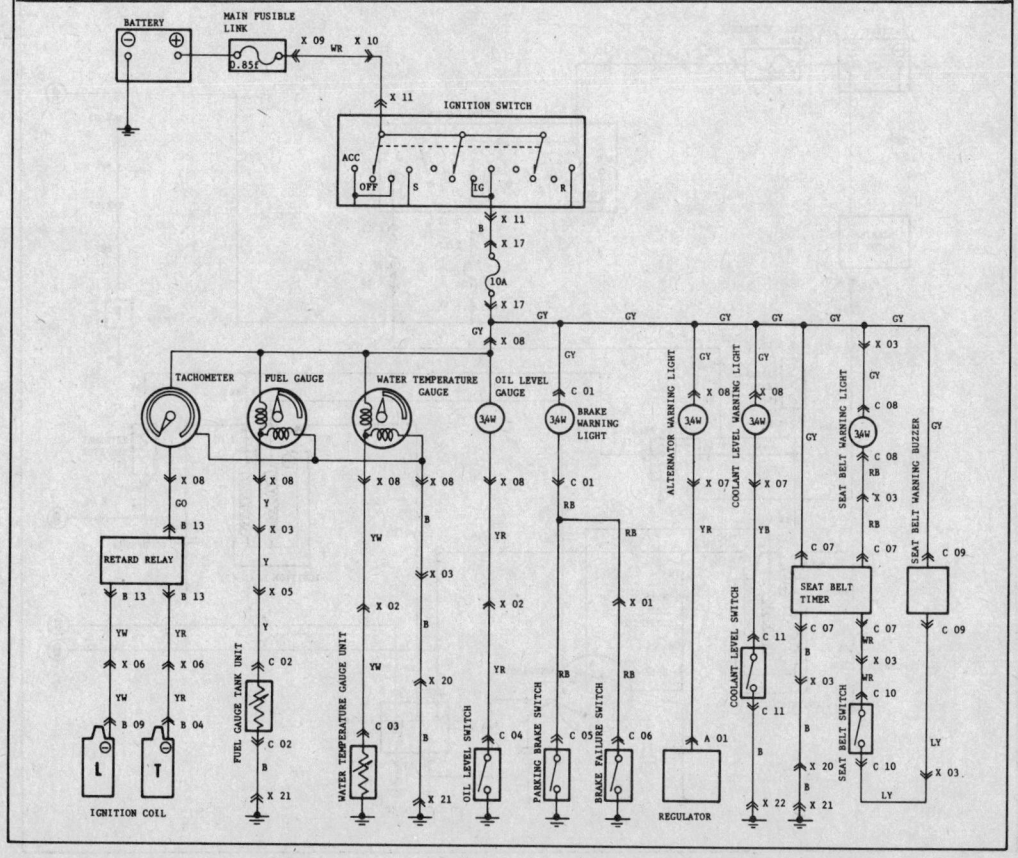

1976 Rotary Pick-Up (Federal)—gauges and seat belt system

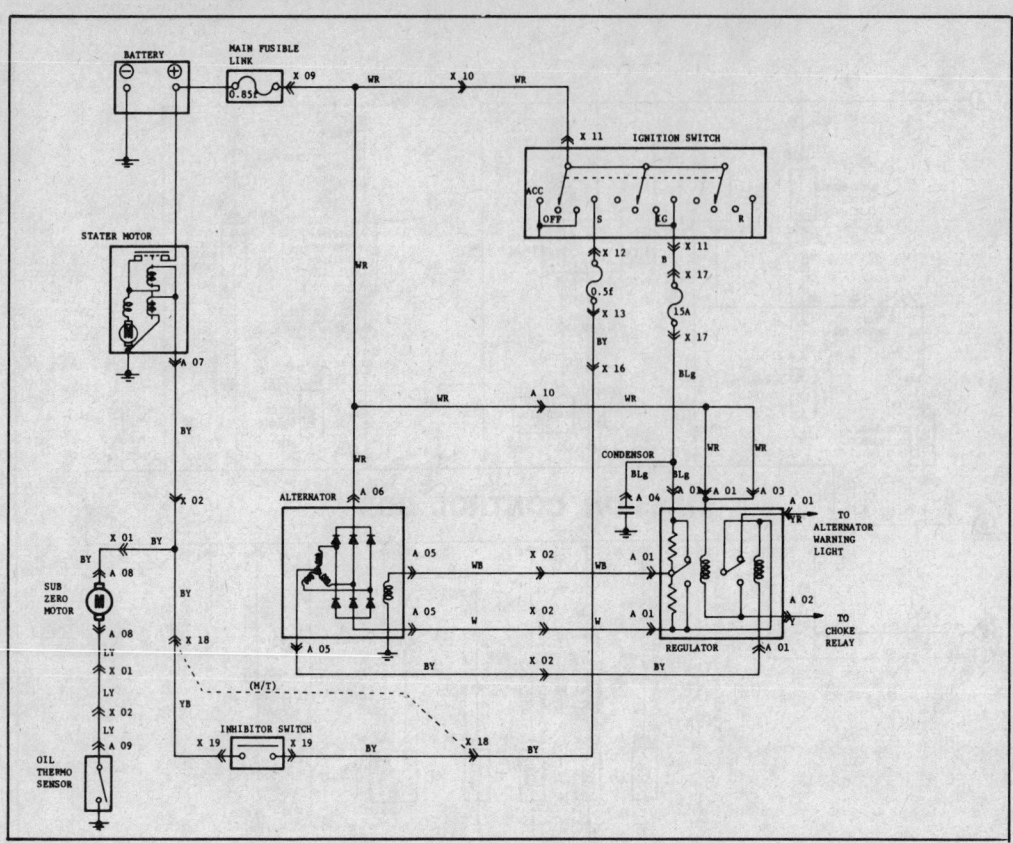

1976 Rotary Pick-Up (Federal)—starting and charging

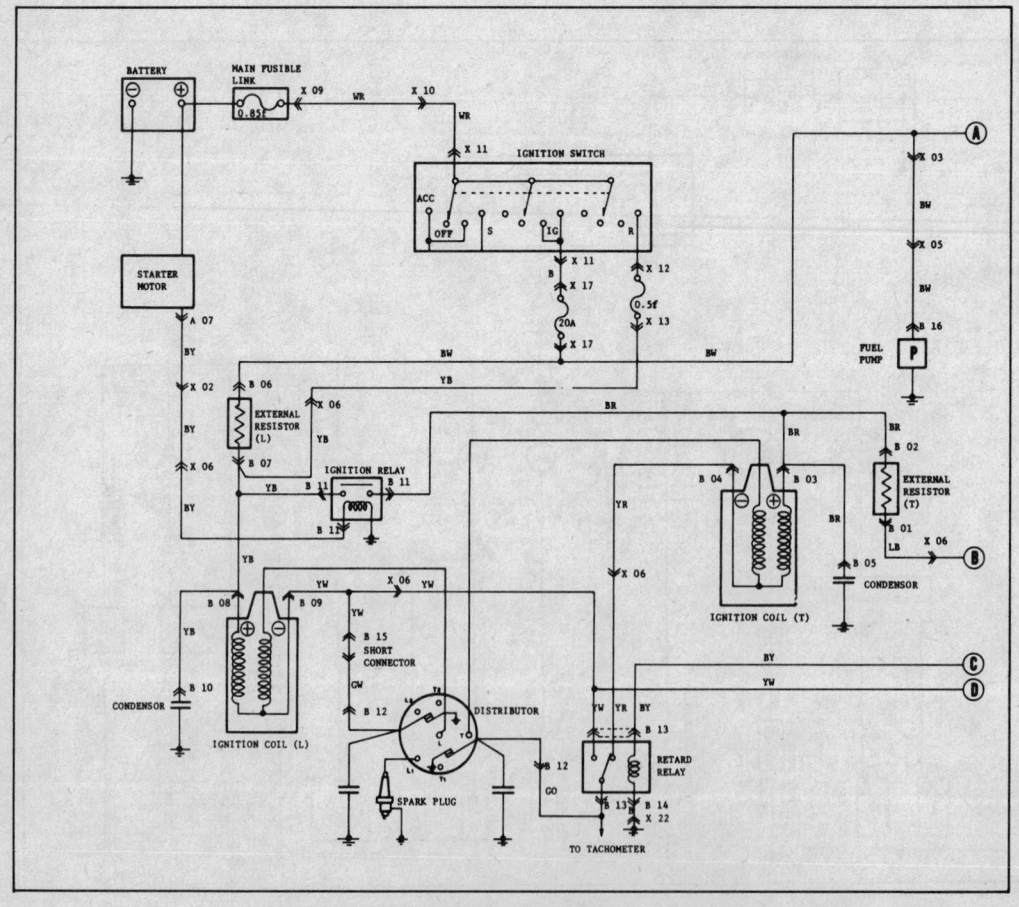

1976 Rotary Pick-Up (Federal)—ignition and fuel pump

SPECIFICATIONS

INTRODUCTION

While the name Mercedes-Benz is familiar to most Americans, few are aware that the founders of Mercedes-Benz share credit for inventing the automobile. Two mechanical engineers, Gottlieb Daimler and Karl Benz, brought their revolutionary machines to life in 1886, 22 years before Henry Ford's Model T.

In addition to pioneering such technical advances as fuel injected engines and the first diesel powered car, Mercedes-Benz has played a prominent role in racing. No other car manufacturer can match Mercedes' record of over 4000 competition victories: a long string stretching back to history's first auto race from Paris to Rouen in 1894. In the pursuit of land speed records, Mercedes-Benz has been equally successful. The legendary Blitzen Benz was the world's fastest automobile from 1911 to 1924; and a 1938 Mercedes-Benz record of 271.5 mph still stands as the highest speed ever recorded on a highway.

In 1968, Mercedes-Benz introduced the "New Generation" of Mercedes-Benz cars. These new sedans, the 220D/8, 220/8, 230/8 and the 250/8, share the same new body style and represent a nine year advance in automotive design (the preceding models were first introduced in 1959). The new bodies featured a sharply sloping hood with decreased frontal area, to insure a smoother flow of air over the car, greater glass area and a squared off rear deck. These new features combine to give the cars a look that is clean and simple, and at the same time, classic. The smaller sedans were followed by the 280 series and the 300 series, all the way up to the 300SEL 6.3 in 1970. All bodies share the same basic concept of clean and timeless styling. Such features as independent suspension and four wheel disc brakes are notable safety features of Mercedes-Benz cars.

The 350 SLC (450SLC in 1973) marks an important change in the coupe design philosophy of Mercedes-Benz. Previous coupe designs were derived from the contemporary sedan models but the 350 and 450SLC models are based on the 350SL coupe/roadster, resulting in a vehicle which combines sports car performance with luxurious looks and comfort. The 350 and 450SLC replace the coupe and convertible models which were built until 1971. The introduction of the 350 and 450SL and SLC models was followed by the introduction of the 450SE and 450SEL in 1973. These cars share the wedge body design with the newer SL and SLC series. The 450SE and 450SEL use the 4.5 liter DOHC V-8 used in the 450SL and 450SLC. The front axle is a modified design taken from the rotary engined test vehicle, the C-111.

In 1975, the 280S was introduced, basically a 450SE/SEL body with the DOHC 6-cylinder engine from the 1973–75 280, 280C.

This was followed by the 1977 280SE, 280E and the 240D, 300D and 230 which also share the new wedge body.

The 280 and 280C were introduced in 1973, using the body originally introduced in 1968.

The 240D, introduced in 1974 is basically a larger engine than the 220D. A major improvement in 1975 was the 300D, using the same body as the 220D and 240D, but with a 3 liter, 5 cylinder diesel, giving greatly improved performance, even though the engine is a larger version of the 240D engine.

MODEL IDENTIFICATION

Identification plate locations

1. Vehicle name plate with safety certification
2. Chassis number (left front door past and front stiffening)
3. Body number and paintwork number
4. Engine number on engine-block, rear
5. Emission control information

Identification plate locations

1. Vehicle name plate with safety certification
2. Chassis number (left front door post and front stiffening)
3. Body number and paintwork number
4. Engine number on rear of engine block
5. Emission control information

Identification plate location

1. Certification tag (left door pillar)
2. Identification tag (left window post)
3. Chassis no.
4. Body no. and paintwork no.
5. Engine no. on engine block, rear
6. Emission control information

Type plate

Chassis number

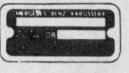

Body and paint

Engine number

Identification plates

1. Type plate
2. Chassis number plate
3. Body and paint number plate
4. Engine number plate

280S/8 (1972), 280SE/8

230 (1974-76), 280 and 280C

350SL, 450SL (introduced 1972)

450SLC (1973-75)

220/8, 220D/8, 240D and 300D

250/8 sedan

Mercedes-Benz

450SE, 450SEL and 280S

250C (coupe)

1977 280E, 230, 240D and 300D—280E shown

ENGINE/VEHICLE IDENTIFICATION

Model	Chassis Type	Engine Model	No. of Cyls.	Engine Type	Engine Description (Fuel, Fuel Delivery, Valve Gear, Displacement)	Production Years
220D/8	115.110	OM615	4	615.912	Diesel (2197 cc)	1968-73
240D	115.117	OM616	4	616.916	Diesel (2404 cc)	1974-76
240D	W123	OM616	4	N.A.	Diesel (2404 cc)	1977
300D	115.114	OM617	5	617.910	Diesel (3005 cc)	1975-76
300D	W123	OM617	5	N.A.	Diesel (3005 cc)	1977
220/8	115.110	M115	4	115.920	Gas, Carb., OHC, (2197 cc)	1968-73
230	115.017	M115	4	115.951	Gas, Carb., OHC, (2307 cc)	1974-76
230	W123	M115	4	N.A.	Gas, Carb., OHC, (2307 cc)	1977'
250/8	114.011	M130V	6	130.923	Gas, Carb., OHC, (2778 cc)	1971-72
250C	114.023	M130V	6	130.923	Gas, Carb., OHC, (2778 cc)	1970-72
280S/8	108.016	M130E	6	130.980	Gas, Fuel Inj., OHC, (2778 cc)	1968-72
280SE/8	111.024 (cvt)	M130E	6	130.980	Gas, Fuel Inj., OHC, (2778 cc)	1968-72
(cpe/cvt)	111.025 (cpe)	M130E	6	130.980	Gas, Fuel Inj., OHC, (2778 cc)	1968-72
280SE 4.5	108.067	M117	8	117.984	Gas, Fuel Inj., OHC, (4520 cc)	1972-73
280SEL 4.5	108.068	M117	8	117.984	Gas, Fuel Inj., OHC, (4520 cc)	1972-73
280	114.060	M110	6	110.921	Gas, Carb., DOHC, (2746 cc)	1975-76
280C	114.073	M110	6	110.921	Gas, Carb., DOHC, (2746 cc)	1973-76
280S	116.020	M110	6	110.922	Gas, Carb., DOHC, (2746 cc)	1975-76
280E	W123	M110	6	N.A.	Gas, Fuel Inj., OHC, (2778 cc)	1977
280SE	W116	M110	6	N.A.	Gas, Fuel Inj., OHC, (2778 cc)	1977
300SEL 4.5	109.057	M117	8	117.981	Gas, Fuel Inj., OHC, (4520 cc)	1972-73
450SE	116.032	M117	8	117.983	Gas, Fuel Inj., OHC, (4520 cc)	1973-75
450SEL	116.033	M117	8	117.983	Gas, Fuel Inj., OHC, (4520 cc)	1973-75
350SL	107.044	M117	8	117.982	Gas, Fuel Inj., OHC, (4520 cc)	1972
450SL	107.044	M117	8	117.982	Gas, Fuel Inj., OHC, (4520 cc)	1973-75
450SLC	107.044	M117	8	117.982	Gas, Fuel Inj., OHC, (4520 cc)	1973-75
450SE	116.032	M117	8	117.986	Gas, Fuel Inj., OHC, (4520 cc)	1976
450SEL	116.033	M117	8	117.986	Gas, Fuel Inj., OHC, (4520 cc)	1976-77
450SL	107.044	M117	8	117.985	Gas, Fuel Inj., OHC, (4520 cc)	1976-77
450SLC	107.024	M117	8	117.985	Gas, Fuel Inj., OHC, (4520 cc)	1976-77

cvt convertible   cpe coupe   NOTE: Production years are given from inception, but only 1972-77 models are covered.

TRANSMISSION APPLICATIONS

Model	Vehicle Type	TRANSMISSION Manual	TRANSMISSION Automatic
220D/8	115.110	G76/18	K4C 025
240D	115.117	G76/18	W4B 025
300D	115.114	—	W4B 025
220/8	115.110	G76/18	K4C 025
230	115.017	—	W4B 025
250/8 (1972)	114.011	G76/18	K4C 025
250C	114.023	G76/18	K4C 025
280S/8	108.016	G76/27	K4A 025
280SE/8 (sedan)	108.018	G76/27	K4A 025
280SE/8 (cpe-cvt)	111.024-111.025	—	K4A 025
280SE 4.5	108.067	—	W34 040
280SEL 4.5	108.068	—	W34 040

Model	Vehicle Type	TRANSMISSION Manual	TRANSMISSION Automatic
280 (1973)	114.060	—	K4C 025
280 (1974-76)	114.060	—	W4B 025
280C (1973-76)	114.073	—	K4C 025
280C (1974-76)	114.073	—	W4B 025
280S	116.020	—	W4B 025
280E	W123	—	W4B 025
280SE	W123	—	W4B 025
300SEL 4.5	109.057	—	W3A 040
350SL	107.044	—	K4B 040
450SE	116.032	—	W3A 040
450SEL	116.033	—	W3A 040
450SL	107.044	—	W3A 040
450SLC	107.044	—	W3A 040

— Not applicable

AUTOMATIC TRANSMISSION FLUIDS

Transmission Type	Model Application	Type A Suffix A	Type B Dexron B
K4A 025 2 planetary gearset	280S/8, 280SE/8	X	
K4C 025 3 planetary gearset	220D/8, 220/8, 250C, 280S/8, 280, 280C		X
W3A 040 torque converter	280SE 4.5, 280SEL 4.5, 300SEL 4.5, 350SL, 450SL, 450SLC, 450SE, 450SEL		X
W4B 025 torque converter	230, 240D, 300D, 280S (1975-76), 280E, 280SE (1977)		X

AUTOMATIC TRANSMISSION IDENTIFICATION

Transmission Type	Model Application
K4A 025 2 planetary gearset	280S/8, 280SE/8
K4C 025 3 planetary gearset	220D/8, 220/8, 250C, 280S/8, 280, 280C
W3A 040 torque converter	280SE 4.5, 280SEL 4.5, 300SEL 4.5, 350SL, 450SL, 450SLC, 450SE, 450SEL
W4B 025	230, 240D, 300D, 280S (1975-76), 280E, 280SE (1977)

Transmission Identification

Since 1968, Mercedes-Benz cars for the U.S. market have been equipped with either a 4-speed manual transmission or with a fully automatic 3 or 4-speed unit. In 1973, the automatic transmissions were equipped with a torque converter.

Serial numbers on the manual transmission are located on a pad on the side cover of the transmission (left side).

Automatic transmission serial numbers are located on a metal plate which is attached to the driver's side of the transmission.

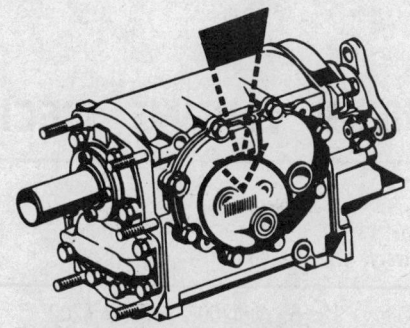

Transmission identification number—side cover transmission.

Special Lubricants

Automatic Level Control

Mercedes-Benz recommends that only the following fluids be used in the automatic level control unit:

Aral 1010
Gasolin 1010
Shell Tellus T 17
Shell Aero Fluid 4

Recommended Diesel Engine Oils

While there are many high quality diesel engine oils, the following are particularly suitable for the 220D/8 240D and 300D. These provide the greatest engine life and best serivce.

Castrol (HD)
Esso Engine Oil (HD)
Valvoline Super HP HDM
Veedol High Detergency HD900

GENERAL GASOLINE ENGINE SPECIFICATIONS

Year Model	Engine Model	Engine Displacement (cc)	Carburetor Type	Horsepower @ rpm (SAE)	Torque @ rpm (ft lbs) (SAE)	Bore x Stroke (mm)	Compression Ratio	Firing Order
220/8	M115	2197	1 Stromberg 175 CDT	116 @ 5200	142 @ 3000	87.00 x 92.40	9.0:1	1 3 4 2
230	M115	2307	Stromberg 175 CDT	95 @ 4800 ③	128 @ 2500 ④	93.75 x 83.6	8.0:1	1 3 4 2
250/8, 250C	M130V	2778	2 Zenith 35/40 INAT	157 @ 5400	181 @ 3100	86.50 x 78.80	9.0:1	1 5 3 6 2 4
280S/8	M130E	2778	Fuel Injection	180 @ 5750	193 @ 4500	86.50 x 78.80	9.5:1	1 5 3 6 2 4
280S (1975-76)	M110	2746	Solex 4-bbl	120 @ 4800	143 @ 2800	86.00 x 78.80	8.0:1	1 5 3 6 2 4
280SE 4.5 280SEL 4.5 300SEL 4.5	M117	4520	Fuel Injection	230 @ 5000	232 @ 4200	92.00 x 85.00	8.0:1	1 5 4 8 6 3 7 2
280, 280C (1973-76)	M110	2746	Solex 4-bbl	120 @ 4800	143 @ 2800	86.00 x 78.80	8.0:1	1 5 3 6 2 4
280E (1977) 280SE (1977)	M110	2746	Fuel Injection	142 @ 5150	149 @ 4600	86.00 x 78.80	8.0:1	1 5 3 6 2 4
350SL, 450SL, 450SLC	M117	4520	Fuel Injection	230 @ 5000	232 @ 4200	92.00 x 85.00	8.0:1	1 5 4 8 6 3 7 2
1974-77 450SE 450SEL 450SL 450SLC	M117	4520	Fuel Injection	190 @ 4750 ①	240 @ 3000 ②	92.00 x 85.00	8.0:1	1 5 4 8 6 3 7 2
1975-77 450SE 450SEL 450SL 450SLC	M117	4520	Fuel Injection	180 @ 4750	220 @ 3000	92.00 x 85.00	8.0:1	1 5 4 8 6 3 7 2

① California—180 @ 4750
② California—232 @ 3000
③ 1975 California—85 @ 4500
④ 1975-77 California—122 @ 2500

GENERAL DIESEL ENGINE SPECIFICATIONS

Car Model	Engine Model	Engine Displace. (cc)	Fuel Delivery	Horsepower @ rpm (SAE)	Torque @ rpm (ft lbs) (SAE)	Bore x Stroke (mm)	Compression Ratio	Firing Order
220D/8	OM615	2197	Fuel Injection	65 @ 4200	65 @ 4200	87 x 92.4	21:1	1 3 4 2
240D	OM616	2404	Fuel Injection	62 @ 4000	97 @ 2400	91.0 x 92.4	21:1	1 3 4 2
300D (5-cylinder)	OM617	3005	Fuel Injection	77 @ 4000	115 @ 2400	91.0 x 92.4	21:1	1 2 4 5 3

GASOLINE ENGINE TUNE-UP SPECIFICATIONS

When analyzing compression results, look for uniformity among cylinders rather than specific pressures.

Car Model	Engine Type	SPARK PLUGS		Distributor Point Dwell (deg)	Ignition Timing	Intake Valve Opens (deg)	Fuel Pump Pressure (psi) @ Idle	Idle Speed (rpm)	VALVE CLEARANCE (in.) ▲	
		Type	Gap (in.)						In (cold)	Ex (cold)
220/8	115.920	①	①	50 ± 2	②	11B	2-3	750-850	0.003	0.008
230 (1974)	115.951	①	①	47-53⑦	②	14B	2-3	750-950	0.004	0.008
230 (1975-77)	115.951	①	①	47-53⑦	②	14B	2-3	800-900	0.004	0.008
250/8 (1972)	130.920	①	①	40 ± 1	②	11B	2-3	800-900	0.003	0.007
250C	130.920	①	①	40 ± 1	②	11B	2-3	800-900	0.003	0.007
280S/8	130.920	①	①	40 ± 1	②	11B	2-3	800-900	0.003	0.007
280S (1975-76)	110.922	①	①	34-40⑦	②	7B	3.5-5.0	800-900	0.004	0.010
280SE/8, 280SEL/8	130.980	①	①	40 ± 1	②	11B	30③	④	0.003	0.007
280SE 4.5 280SEL 4.5	117.984	①	①	32 ± 2	②	27B	30③	700-800	0.003	0.007
280,280C (1973)	110.921	①	①	42 ± 1	②	11A	3.5-5.0	750-900	0.004	0.008
280, 280C (1974)	110.921	①	①	34-40⑦	②	11B⑧	3.5-5.0	750-950 ⑩	0.004	0.010
280, 280C (1975-76)	110.921	①	①	34-40⑦	②	7B	3.5-5.0	800-900	0.004	0.010
300SEL 4.5	117.981	①	①	32 ± 1	②	27B	30③	700-800	0.003	0.007
350SL	116.982	①	①	32 ± 2	②	27B	30③	700-800	0.003	0.007
450SL, 450SLC	117.982	①	①	32 ± 2	②	27B	30③	700-800	0.003	0.007
450SE, 450SEL (1974) 450SL, 450SLC (1974)	117.983 117.982	①	①	30-34⑦	②	4B	30③	700-800	0.004	0.008
450SE, 450SEL (1975) 450SL, 450SLC (1975)	M117 M117	①	①	30-34⑦	②	5B⑨	30③	700-800	0.004	0.008
450SE, 450SEL (1976-77) 450SL, 450SLC (1976-77)	M117 M117	①	①	Electronic	②	5B	75-84	700-800	Hyd.	Hyd.

CAUTION: If the specifications listed above differ from those on the tune-up decal in the engine compartment, use those listed on the tune-up decal.

NOTES:
1. On transistor ignitions, only a transistorized dwell meter can be used. Transistor ignitions are recognizable by the "Blue" ignition coil, 2 series resistors and the transistor switchgear.
2. On dual point distributors, check each set separately by inserting an insulator between each set in turn. Dwell values given are total both sets.
3. To counteract wear of the fiber contact block, adjust the dwell to the lower end of the range.

① See the spark plug chart for recommendations.
A ATDC
B BTDC
Electronic—Electronic ignition not adjustable.
▲ On all engines with intake valve clearance of .003 in., it is better to set the values at .003 in. "loose" (closer to 0.004 in.).
② See "Ignition Timing Specifications"
③ Injection pump pressure
④ 1972-73—700-850

⑤ Total dwell
⑥ Left bank—5B; Right bank—7B
⑦ When installing new points or adjusting used points, adjust the dwell to the lesser figure ± 1°.
⑧ 6B—California
⑨ With a new engine (under 12,500 miles) or with a new timing chain, valve timing is 3A with camshaft coded 57. The camshaft code number is stamped into the rear of the camshaft.
⑩ 700-900—California

IGNITION TIMING SPECIFICATIONS

Car Model	Engine Type	IGNITION TIMING				
		1972 @ 800 rpm w/vacuum	1973 @ 800 rpm w/vacuum	1974 @ 800 rpm w/vacuum	1975 @ 800 rpm w/vacuum	1976 w/vacuum @ idle
220/8	115.920	5A	10B	—	—	—
230	115.951	—	—	10B	10B	10B
250/8 (1971-72)	130.923	4A	—	—	—	—
250C	130.923	4A	—	—	—	—
280S	110.922	—	—	—	7B	7B
280SE/8, 280SEL/8	130.980	6A	—	—	—	—
280SE 4.5, 280SEL 4.5	117.984	5A	5A	—	—	—
280, 280C	110.921	—	4A	4A	7B	7B
300SEL 4.5	117.981	5A	5A	—	—	—
350SL	117.982	5A	—	—	—	—
450SL, 450SLC	117.982	—	5A	5A	TDC	TDC
450SE, 450SEL	117.983	—	5A	5A	TDC	TDC

—   Not Applicable   w/   with (vacuum connected)
B   BTDC   ① 32B @ 3000 rpm—cylinder no. 1
A   ATDC   56-60A @ 3000 rpm—cylinder no. 5 (total)

CAUTION: Do not run the engine at high RPM speeds (3000-4500) for more than an instant. Severe engine damage can result.

SPARK PLUG RECOMMENDATIONS
All measurements in inches

Car Model	Engine	1972		1973		1974		1975		1976		1977	
		Type	Gap	Type	Gap	Type	Gap	Type	Gap	Type	Gap	Type	Gap
220/8	115.920	N9Y	0.024	N9Y	0.024	—	—	—	—	—	—	—	—
230	115.951	—	—	—	—	N9Y	0.024	N9Y	0.024	N9Y	0.024	N9Y	0.024
250/8 (1971-72)	130.923	N8Y	0.024	—	—	—	—	—	—	—	—	—	—
250C	130.923	N8Y	0.024	—	—	—	—	—	—	—	—	—	—
280S/8	130.920	N8Y	0.024	—	—	—	—	—	—	—	—	—	—
280S	110.922	—	—	—	—	—	—	N9Y	0.024	N9Y	0.024	N9Y	0.024
280SE/8 280SEL/8	130.980	N7Y	0.024	—	—	—	—	—	—	—	—	—	—
280SE 3.5	116.980	N12Y	0.024	—	—	—	—	—	—	—	—	—	—
280SE 4.5 280SEL 4.5	117.984	N12Y	0.024	—	—	—	—	—	—	—	—	—	—
280, 280C	110.921	—	—	N9Y	0.024	N9Y	0.024	N9Y	0.024	N9Y	0.024	N9Y	0.024
280E, 280SE	M110	—	—	—	—	—	—	—	—	—	—	N9Y	0.024
300SEL/8	130.981	—	—	—	—	—	—	—	—	—	—	—	—
300SEL 4.5	117.981	N12Y	0.024	N9Y	0.024	—	—	—	—	—	—	—	—
350SL	117.982	N12Y	0.024	—	—	—	—	—	—	—	—	—	—
450SL, 450SLC	117.982	—	—	N9Y	0.024	N9Y	0.024	N9Y	0.024	N9Y	0.024	N9Y	0.024
450SE, 450SEL	117.983	—	—	N9Y	0.024	N9Y	0.024	N9Y	0.024	N9Y	0.024	N9Y	0.024

— Not applicable

IDLE SPEED EXHAUST GAS VALUES

(% CO at Idle)
NOTE: For Gasoline Engines Only

Model Year Engine	1972 Speed (rpm)	1972 Exhaust Gas Value % CO	1973 Speed (rpm)	1973 Exhaust Gas Value % CO	1974 Speed (rpm)	1974 Exhaust Gas Value % CO	1975-77 Speed (rpm)	1975-77 Exhaust Gas Value % CO
114	—	—	—	—	—	—	—	—
115	750-850	2.0-3.5	750-800	Up to 1.5	800-900	Max. 1.5	800-900	0.4-1.5③
130.920	—	—	—	—	—	—	—	—
130.923	800-900	1.0-1.5	—	—	—	—	—	—
180.954	—	—	—	—	—	—	—	—
100	560-620	1.0-4.0	—	—	—	—	—	—
116	—	—	—	—	—	—	—	—
117 (to 1975)	700-800	0.5-2.0	700-800	0.5-2.0	700-800	0.5-2.0②	700-800	Max. 1.5③
M117 (1976-77)	—	—	—	—	—	—	800-900	0.2-1.5
M110	—	—	750-950	Up to 1.5	750-950①	Max. 1.5	800-900	Max. 1.0③

① 700-900 California   ② Maximum 1.0   ③ Without air injection   — Not applicable

NOTE: If the values on the tune-up decal in the engine compartment, differ from those listed above, use the values on the tune-up decal.

CAPACITIES

Model	Fuel Tank (gals)	CRANKCASE (qts) Max	CRANKCASE (qts) Min	Radiator (qts)	Rear Axle (pts)	Oil Filter (pts)	TRANSMISSION (pts) Manual	TRANSMISSION (pts) Automatic	Power Steering (pts)	Manual Steering (pts)
220D/8	17.25	4.25⑦	2.5	11.25	2.5	2.0	3.0	9.75①	3.0	5/8
240D	17.2④	6.8	5.3	10.5	2.1	1.0	3.4	10.1⑨	3.0	—
300D	17.2④	7.8	6.3	11.7	2.1	1.6	—	10.1⑨	3.0	—
220/8	17.25	4.25	2.5	11.0	2.5	1.0	3.5	8.75②	3.0	5/8
230 (1974-77)	17.2⑩	5.8	5.0	10.5	2.1	1.0	—	10.1⑨	3.0	—
250/8 (1972)	17.25	5.75⑧	3.75	11.0	2.5	1.0	3.5	9.75①	3.0	5/8
250C	21.5	5.75⑧	3.75	11.0	2.5	1.0	3.5	9.75①	3.0	5/8
280S/8	21.5	5.75⑧	3.75	11.0	5.25	1.0	3.0	8.0③	3.0	5/8
280SE/8	21.5	5.75⑧	3.75	11.25	5.25	1.0	3.0	8.0③	3.0	5/8
280SE 4.5 280SEL 4.5	25.0	8.0	6.0	14.75	6.0	1.5	—	19.0⑤	3.0	5/8
280, 280C, 280S, 280E, 280SE	19.5	7.0	5.5	11.5	2.1	1.5	—	11.6⑥	3.0	—
300SEL 4.5	25.0	8.0	6.0	14.75	6.0	1.5	—	19.0⑤	3.0	—
350SL	27.5	8.0	6.0	16.0	3.0	1.5	—	17.0⑤	3.0	—
450SL 450SLC	27.5	8.0	6.0	16.0	3.0	1.5	—	17.0⑤	3.0	—
450SE, 450SEL	28.9	8.0	6.0	16.0	3.0	1.5	—	17.0	3.0	—

— Not applicable
① Initial filling—11.5
② Initial filling—11.75
③ Initial filling—10.0
④ 20.6—1976-77
⑤ Initial filling—19.0
⑥ Initial filling—9.5
⑦ Oil filter added after chassis no. 052 894; add 1 pt extra
⑧ With oil cooler—6.25
⑨ Initial filling—12.9
⑩ 20.6 gallon fuel tank—1975-77

Mercedes-Benz

DIESEL TUNE-UP SPECIFICATIONS

Model	VALVE CLEARANCE (cold) ①		Intake valve opens (deg)	Injection pump setting (deg)	INJECTION NOZZLE PRESSURE (psi)		Idle speed (rpm) ③	Cranking compression pressure (psi)
	Intake (in.)	Exhaust (in.)			New	Used		
220D/8	0.004②	0.016	12.5B	24B	1564-1706	1422-1706	750-800	284-327
240D	0.004	0.016	13.5B	24B	1564-1706	1422-1706	750-800	284-327
300D (5-cylinder)	0.004	0.012	13.5B ⑤	24B	1635-1750 ④	1422	700-800	284-327

① Hot: Intake—0.008 in.   Exhaust—0.018 in.
② In cold weather (below 5° F.), increase valve clearance 0.002 in.
③ Manual transmission in Neutral; Automatic in Drive.
④ Difference in opening pressure on injection nozzles should not exceed 71 psi.
⑤ The injection pump is in start of delivery position when the mark on the pump camshaft is aligned with the mark on the injection pump flange.
B Before Top Dead Center

FIRING ORDERS

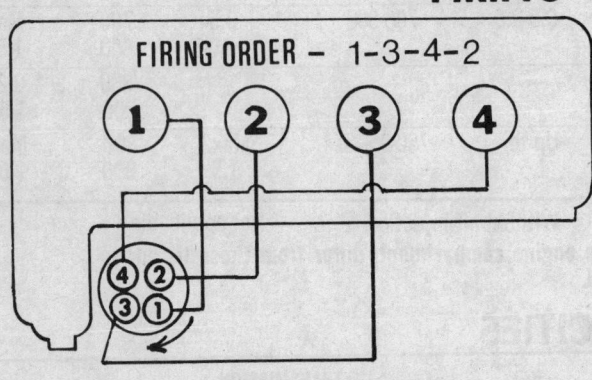

220/8, 220D/8, 240D

FIRING ORDER – 1-3-4-2

FIRING ORDER 1-5-3-6-2-4

6 cylinder engines (except 280, 280C and 280S).

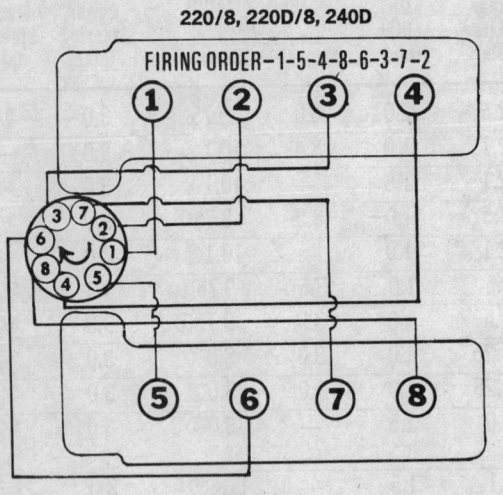

FIRING ORDER–1-5-4-8-6-3-7-2

4.5 V-8

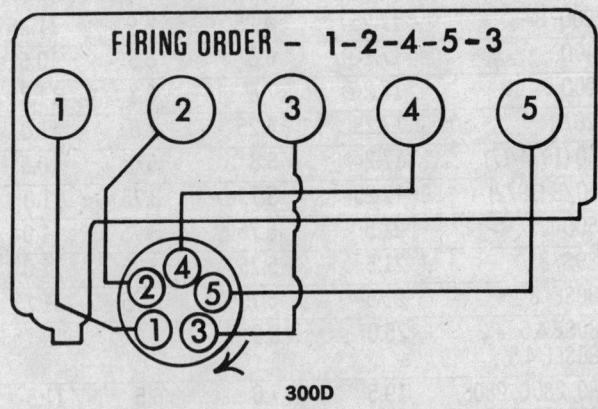

FIRING ORDER – 1-2-4-5-3

300D

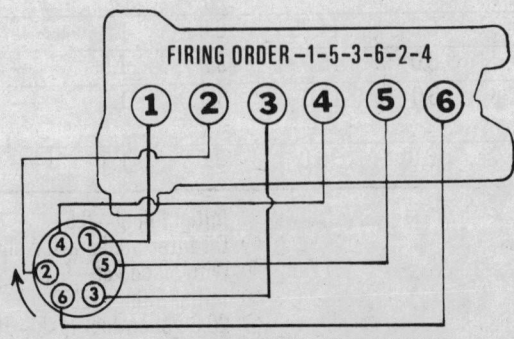

FIRING ORDER–1-5-3-6-2-4

280, 280C, 280S, 280E, 280SE (1977)

CRANKSHAFT AND CONNECTING ROD SPECIFICATIONS

All measurements are given in millimeters

Car Model	Engine Displace. (cc)	Engine Model	Main Brg. Journal Dia.	CRANKSHAFT Main Brg. Oil Clearance	Shaft End-Play	Thrust on No.	CONNECTING ROD Journal Diameter	Oil Clearance	Side Clearance
220/8 220D/8	2197 2197	M115 OM615	69.955- 69.965	0.045- 0.065	0.100- 0.240	①	51.955- 51.965	0.035- 0.055	0.110- 0.260
240D	2404	OM616	69.955- 69.965	0.045- 0.065	0.100- 0.240	①	51.955- 51.965	0.035- 0.055	0.110- 0.260
300D (5-cylinder)	3005	OM617	69.955- 69.965	0.045- 0.065	0.100- 0.240	①	51.955- 51.965	0.035- 0.055	0.110- 0.260
230	2307	M115	69.955- 69.965	0.045- 0.065	0.100- 0.240	①	51.955- 51.965	0.035- 0.055	0.110- 0.260
250/8 250/C 280S/8 280SE/8	2778	M130	59.955- 59.965	0.045- 0.065	0.100- 0.240	①	47.965 47.955-	0.055 0.035-	0.260 0.110-
280SE 3.5 300SEL 3.5	3499 3499	M116	63.955- 63.965	0.035- 0.075	0.100- 0.240	①	51.955- 51.965	0.035- 0.065	0.220- 0.380
280SE 4.5 280SEL 4.5 300SEL 4.5 350SL 450SL 450SLC 450SE 450SEL	4520	M117	63.955- 63.965	0.035- 0.075	0.100- 0.240	①	51.955- 51.965	0.035- 0.065	0.220- 0.380
28C 280C 280S 28E 280SE	2746	M110	N.A.	N.A.	N.A.	①	N.A.	N.A.	N.A.

N.A. Not Available
① Center main on 5 main bearing engines; rear main on 7 main bearing engines; 3rd from front on 300D (5-cylinder)

VALVE SPECIFICATIONS

Car Model	Engine Displacement (cc)	Seat Angle (deg)	Spring Test Pressure (mm @ KP)	Spring Installed Height (mm)	STEM DIAMETER (mm) Intake	Exhaust
220D/8	2197	30 + 15′	38.4 @ 23-26.4	29.9	9.920-9.905	9.918-9.940
240D	2404	30 + 15′	38.4 @ 23-26.4	29.9	9.920-9.905	9.918-9.940
300D	3005	30 + 15′	38.4 @ 23-26.4	29.9	9.920-9.905	9.918-9.940
220/8	2197	45 + 15′	39 @ 36①	30.0①	8.948-8.970	10.918-10.940
230	2307	45 + 15′	39 @ 36①	30.0①	8.948-8.970	10.918-10.940
250/8 250/C 280S/8 280SE/8	2778	45 + 15′	42 @ 29.5-32.5①	30.5①	8.955-8.970	10.918-10.940
280SE 4.5 280SEL 4.5 300SEL 4.5 350SL 450SL 450SLC 450SE 450SEL	4520	45 + 15′	42 @ 29.5-32.5①	30.5①	8.955-8.970	10.928-10.950

VALVE SPECIFICATIONS

Car Model	Engine Displacement (cc)	Seat Angle (deg)	Spring Test Pressure (mm @ KP)	Spring Installed Height (mm)	STEM DIAMETER (mm)	
					Intake	Exhaust
280 280C 280S 280E 280SE	2746	45 + 15′	N.A.	N.A.	N.A.	N.A.

① Outer spring—The spring should be installed so that the close coils are in contact with the cylinder head

VALVE TIMING SPECIFICATIONS

Model	Camshaft Code Number	INTAKE VALVE		EXHAUST VALVE	
		Opens BTDC	Closes ABDC	Opens BBDC	Closes ATDC
220/8	61	11	47	48	16
220D/8	18	12.5	41.5	45	9
240D	02	13.5	15.5	19	17
300D	00	13.5	15.5	19	17
230 (1974-77)	05	14	20	22	12
280S/8 280SE/8	0835	11	47	48	16
280SE 4.5 280SEL 4.5 300SEL 4.5	52/53①	27	43	61	13
350SL (1972) 450SL (1973) 450SLC (1973)	48/49①	22	48	47	17
450SE (1974) 450SEL (1974) 450SL (1974) 450SLC (1974)	52/54③	4	14	30	16
450SE (1975-76)③ 450SEL (1975-77)③ 450SL (1975-77)③ 450SLC (1975-77)③	56/57③	5	21	25	5
300SEL 6.3	L-16 R-17	L-5 R-7	L-50 R-48	L-40 R-42	L-15.5 R-13.5
280 280C	30/33②	11	15	22	14
280, 280C (1974) Federal	30/33②	11	15	22	24
280, 280C (1974) California	25/24②	6	21	30	13
280, 280C, 280S, 280E, 280SE	57/25	7	21	30	12

① Camshafts with identification number 46, 48, or 52 are for the left bank of cylinders (5-8). Camshafts with identification code number 47, 49 or 53 are for the right bank of cylinders (1-4).
② Code number 30 for exhaust camshaft
 Code number 33 for intake camshaft
③ New engine with new timing chain

L   Left
R   Right
BTDC Before Top Dead Center
ABDC After Bottom Dead Center
BBDC Before Bottom Dead Center

TORQUE SPECIFICATIONS
All readings in ft lbs

Car Model	Engine Model	Cylinder Head Bolts ②	Rod Bearing Bolts	Main Bearing Bolts	Crankshaft Pulley Bolt	Flywheel To Crankshaft Bolts	Cam Sprocket Bolt(s)	Exhaust Manifold Bolts
220D/8	OM615	65	①	65	151-158	①	18	18-21
240D	OM616	65	①	65	151-158	①	18	18-21
300D	OM617	65	①	65	195-240	①	18	18-21
220/8 230 (1974-77)	M114	58	①	58③	151-158	①	18	18-21
250/8 280S/8 280SE/8	M130	72	①	58	151-158	①	18	18-21
280SE 4.5 280SEL 4.5 300SE 4.5 350SL 450SL 450SLC 450SE 450SEL	M116 M117	36	①	④	180-194	①	36	18-21
280 280C 280S 280E 280SE	M110	58	①	58	206-226	①	58	N.A.

① See text
② With cold engine; cylinder head bolts should be tightened in at least 3 stages
③ 65 on M115 engines

④ M 10 bolts—37 ft lbs
  M 12 bolts—72 ft lbs
N.A. Not available

TORQUE SEQUENCES

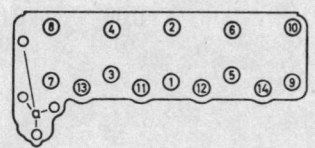

220/8, 230 (1974-77) cylinder head

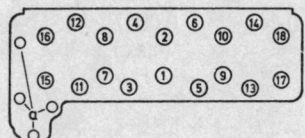

220D/8 and 240D cylinder head

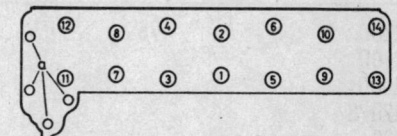

Cylinder head—250/8, 250C, 280S/8, 280SE/8,

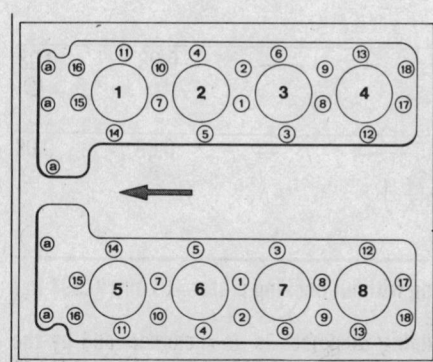

V8 cylinder head

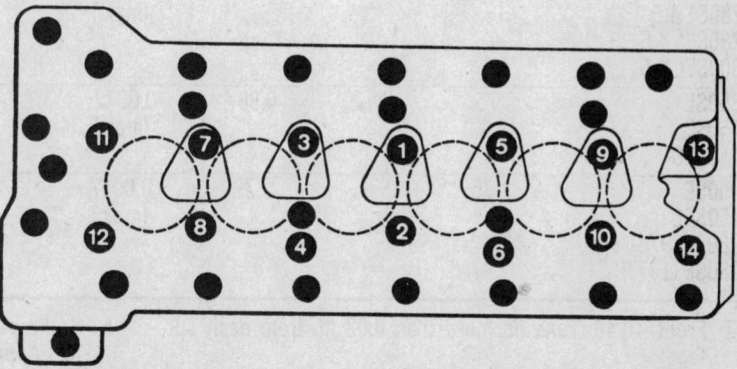

Tighten ●   Concealed, cannot be tightened

280, 280C, 280S, (1975-76), 280E and 280SE (1977)

TORQUE SEQUENCES

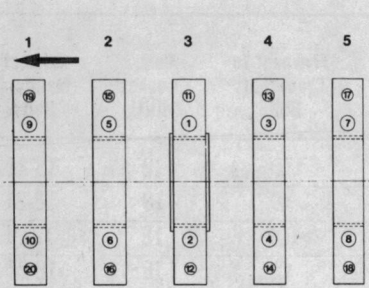

V8 main bearing caps

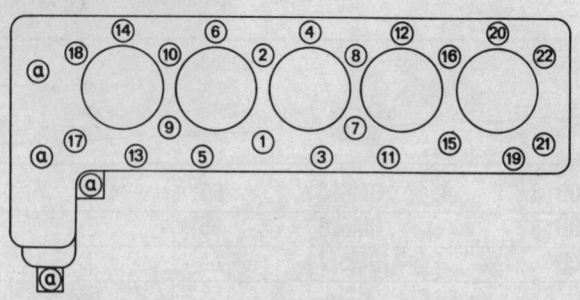

300D—Bolts marked "a" are tightened with a hex socket bit

BATTERY AND STARTER SPECIFICATIONS

All cars use 12 volt, negative ground electrical systems

Engine Model	Battery Amp Hour Capacity	Starter							Brush Spring Tension (oz)	Min. Brush Length (in.)
		Lock Test			No Load Test					
		Amps	Volts	Torque (ft/lbs)	Amps	Volts	RPM			
All w/Diesel Engine	88	650-750	9.0	1000-1200	80-95	12	7500-8500		N.A.	N.A.
All w/Gas Engine	66	290-300	9.0	1600-1800	50-70	12	9000-11000		N.A.	0.5

N.A. Not specified by manufacturer

BRAKE SPECIFICATIONS

All measurements given are (in.) unless noted

Model	Lug Nut Torque (ft/lb)	Master Cylinder Bore	Brake Disc		Brake Drum			Minimum Lining Thickness	
			Minimum Thickness	Maximum Run-Out	Diameter	Max. Machine O/S	Max. Wear Limit	Front ▲	Rear ▲
220D 240D 300D 220/8 230 280 280C 280E	75	¹⁵/₁₆	0.44	0.0047 (max.)	—	—	—	0.08 ②	0.08 ②
280SE/8 280SE 4.5 280SEL 4.5 300SEL 4.5	75	¹⁵/₁₆	①	0.0047 (max.)	—	—	—	0.08 ②	0.08 ②
350SL 450SL 450SLC	75	¹⁵/₁₆	0.36	0.0047 (max.)	—	—	—	0.08 ②	0.08 ②
450SE 450SEL 280S (1975-76) 280SE (1977)	75	¹⁵/₁₆	0.79	0.0047 (max.)	—	—	—	0.08 ②	0.08 ②

① Front—0.46 (Take no more than 0.02 in. from each surface)
Rear—0.37 (Take no more than 0.01 in. from each surface)

② 1976-77 brake pads are equipped with electric pad wear indicators

▲ Brake pad lining without backing plate—10 mm (0.394 in.)
— Not Applicable

NOTE: Minimum lining thickness is as recommended by the manufacturer. Due to variations in state inspection regulations, the minimum allowable thickness may be different than recommended by the manufacturer.

WHEEL ALIGNMENT SPECIFICATIONS

| Car Model | FRONT WHEELS | | | | | REAR WHEELS | |
| | Camber (deg) | Caster (deg) | | Toe-in (mm) | | Camber (deg) | Toe-in (mm) |
		Mech. Steer.	Power Steer.				
220D/8 240D (to 1976) 300D (to 1976)	0°15' + 10' − 20'	2°40' ± 20'	3°40' ± 20'	2-4		See Chart 1	See Chart 2
220/8	0°15' + 10' − 20'	2°40' ± 20'	3°40' ± 20'	2-4		See Chart 1	See Chart 2
230 (1974-77)	0°15' + 10' − 20'	2°40' ± 20'	3°40' ± 20'	2-4		See Chart 1	See Chart 2
250C	0°15' + 10' − 20'	2°40' ± 20'	3°40' ± 20'	2-4		See Chart 1	See Chart 2
280S/8	0°30' − 20'	3°30' ± 15'	4° ± 15'	1-3		0° ± 30'	0 ± 2
280S (1975-76)	(−) 20' − 0° ①	—	9°30' − 10°30'	2-4		See Chart 1	See Chart 3
280SE/8	0°30' − 20'	3°30' ± 15'	4° ± 15'	1-3		0° ± 30'	0 ± 2
280SE 4.5	0°30' − 20'	3°30' ± 15'	4° ± 15'	1-3		0° ± 30'	0 ± 2
280SEL 4.5	0°30' − 20'	3°30' ± 15'	4° ± 15'	1-3		0° ± 30'	0 ± 2
280, 280C (to 1976)	0°15' + 10' − 20'	—	3°40' ± 15'	1-3		See Chart 1	0 ± 2
300SEL 4.5	0°20' − 20'	—	4° ± 15'	1-3		−0°45' ± 15'	0 ± 2
350SL 450SL 450SLC	0° ± 10' − 20'	—	3°40' ± 20'	1-3		See Chart 1	See Chart 2
450SE 450SEL	(−) 20' − 0°	—	9°30' − 10°30'	2-4		See Chart 3	See Chart 4

① A 0° 10' change in a minus or plus direction, yields a 0° 10' change in caster in a corresponding minus or plus direction.

② A 0° 30' change in caster in a minus or plus direction, yields a 0° 10' change in camber in a corresponding minus or plus direction.

Wheel Alignment Chart 1

| Control Arm Position (mm) | Corresponds to Rear Wheel Camber on: | | Control Arm Position (mm) | Corresponds to Rear Wheel Camber on: | |
	220D/8, 240D, 300D, 220/8, 250/8, 250C, 230 (1974-77), 450SE, 450SEL, 280S	350SL, 450SL, 450SLC		220D/8, 240D, 300D, 220/8, 250/8, 250C, 230 (1974-77), 450SE, 450SEL, 280S	350SL, 450SL, 450SLC
			+ 30	0° ± 30'	− 0°10' ± 30'
+ 80	+ 2°30' ± 30'	—	+ 25	− 0°15' ± 30'	− 0°25' ± 30'
+ 75	+ 2°15' ± 30'	—	+ 20	− 0°30' ± 30'	− 0°40' ± 30'
+ 70	+ 2° ± 30'	—	+ 15	−0°45' ± 30'	− 0°55' ± 30'
+ 65	+ 1°45' ± 30'	—	+ 10	− 1° ± 30'	− 1°10' ± 30'
+ 60	+ 1°30' ± 30'	—	+ 5	− 1°15' ± 30'	− 1°25' ± 30'
+ 55	+ 1°15' ± 30'	—	0	− 1°30' ± 30'	− 1°40' ± 30'
+ 50	+ 1° ± 30'	+ 0°50' ± 30'	− 5	− 1°45' ± 30'	− 1°55' ± 30'
+ 45	+ 0°45' ± 30'	+ 0°35' ± 30'	− 10	− 2° ± 30'	− 2°10' ± 30'
+ 40	+0°30' ± 30'	+ 0°20' ± 30'	− 15	− 2°15' ± 30'	− 2°25' ± 30'
+ 35	+ 0°15' ± 30'	+ 0°05' ± 30'	− 20	− 2°30' ± 30'	− 2°40' ± 30'

Mercedes-Benz

Wheel Alignment Chart 2
220D/8, 220/8, 250C, 350SL, 450SL, 450SLC

Rear Wheel Control Arm Position (mm)	Corresponds to Rear Wheel Toe-in of:
0 to +35 mm	1 $^{+2}_{-1}$ mm or 0°10′ $^{+20′}_{-10′}$
+35 to +50 mm	1.5 $^{+2}_{-1}$ mm or 0°15′ $^{+20′}_{-10′}$
+50 to +60 mm	2 $^{+2}_{-1}$ mm or 0°20′ $^{+20′}_{-10′}$
+60 to +70 mm	2.5 $^{+2}_{-1}$ mm or 0°25′ $^{+20′}_{-10′}$
+70 to +80 mm	3.0 $^{+2}_{-1}$ mm or 0°30′ $^{+20′}_{-10′}$

Wheel Alignment Chart 3

Rear Wheel Camber		Refer to Wheel Alignment Chart 1 Control arm position—Rear wheel camber
Toe-in of rear wheels	at rear control arm position 0 to +35 mm	1 $^{+2}_{-1}$ mm or 0° 10′ $^{+20′}_{-10′}$
	at rear control arm position +35 to +50 mm	1.5 $^{+2}_{-1}$ mm or 0° 15′ $^{+20′}_{-10′}$
	at rear control arm position +50 to +60 mm	2 $^{+2}_{-1}$ mm or 0° 20′ $^{+20′}_{-10′}$

TUNE-UP PROCEDURES
Spark Plugs

Spark plugs should be checked frequently (approximately 5000 miles) depending on use. Mercedes-Benz recommends that the spark plugs be renewed at least every 10,000 miles; if heavily leaded fuels are used, they should be replaced every 5000 miles.

NOTE: *Some Mercedes-Benz automobiles are equipped with platinum spark plugs. These spark plugs must be regapped more carefully than "normal" types, and, while their lifespan may be longer, they are also subject to the "once only" regapping rule.*

To regap a platinum plug, the body electrode is bent slightly forward by light strokes applied at the arrowed portion of its outer casing. If in doubt concerning spark plug substitution, consult a Mercedes-Benz dealer.

To gap the spark plugs, remove each one in turn and measure the gap with a round feeler gauge of the appropriate thickness. Prior to removing the plugs, blow dirt away with compressed air. This is especially necessary on 6 cylinder DOHC engines. Insert the round feeler gauge between the center and side electrode. To adjust the gap, bend the side electrode with the tool on the end of the feeler gauge until the specified gap is obtained.

Reinstall and tighten the spark plugs to 18–21 ft lbs and install the spark plug wires on their respective plugs.

Check the spark plug wires and replace any that are cracked or brittle.

Bend the wires into a loop to check for cracks.

Breaker Points and Condenser

NOTE: *1976 V8 and some 1977 models are equipped with electronic ignition and have no points.*
NOTE: *Some 6-cylinder engines may be equipped with a flyweight in the distributor rotor to limit maximum rpm.*

Replacement

NOTE: *Transistor ignitions can be recognized by the blue ignition coil, 2 series resistors and transistor switchgear.*

1. Remove the rubber or plastic cover from the distributor.
2. Release the clips on the side of the distributor cap and remove the cap. Lay it aside.
3. Remove the rotor and plate from the distributor shaft.
4. Remove the distributor contact holder by removing the screw or screws. Some models also have a snap-ring on the bearing contact lever, which must also be removed. Pry the wire from the connecting terminal or loosen the screw at the terminal and remove the wire from the connecting terminal.
5. On models with 2 sets of points, remove the snap-rings from the bearing pins and unscrew the setscrews and screw at the connecting terminal. Pull both contact sets off the bearing pins and remove the wire from the connector.
6. Disconnect the condenser wire and remove the condenser from its bracket.
7. Before installing new points, clean the contact surfaces by squeezing them against a clean matchbook cover. This will remove any film or condensate.
8. Lightly coat the slide piece of the contact breaker with high temperature multipurpose grease.
9. Check to be sure that the contacts are parallel and at the same level with each other when closed. Misalignment can be corrected by bending the fixed contact support. Never bend the movable contact support.
10. On distributors with 2 sets of points, clean the connecting cable and insulating plate.
11. Install a new condenser and connect the wire.
12. Install a new contact set or sets into the distributor.
13. Install the hold-down screw(s) and-/or the snap-rings on the bearing pins of the contact plate.
14. Connect the wire to the terminal and tighten the nut, if necessary.
15. Install the plate and rotor on the shaft.
16. Install the cap.
17. Check the dwell angle and ignition timing. Adjust if necessary.

Dwell Angle

Adjustment

When setting ignition contact points, it is advisable to observe the following general rules:

1. If the points are old, they should not be adjusted using a feeler gauge. The gauge will not give an accurate reading on a pitted surface.
2. Never file the points—this removes their protective coating and results in rapid pitting.

3. When using a feeler gauge to set new points, be certain that the points are fully open. The fiber rubbing block must rest on the highest point of the cam lobe.

4. Always make sure the feeler gauge is free of oil or grease before setting points.

5. Make sure the points are properly aligned and that the feeler gauge is not tilted. If points are misaligned, bend the fixed contact support only, never the movable breaker arm.

A dwell meter virtually eliminates errors in point gap caused by distributor cam lobes being unequally worn, or human error. In any case, point dwell should be checked as soon as possible after setting with a feeler gauge, because it is a far more accurate check of point operation under normal operating conditions.

Because the fiber block wears down gradually in service, it is good practice to set the dwell on the low side of any dwell range (smaller number of degrees) given in specifications. As the block wears, the dwell becomes greater (toward the center of the range) and point life is increased between adjustments.

All Gasoline Engines Without Electronic Ignition

1. The dwell angle should be measured at idle speed.

2. Raise the hood and connect a dwell meter and tachometer.

3. Start the engine and allow it to reach normal idle speed. Read the dwell angle from the meter on the appropriate scale.

4. If the dwell varies by 5 or more degrees from the specifications, the points should be replaced.

NOTE: *On normal coil ignitions, the dwell angle should not be adjusted on worn contact points. It is also possible that a given dwell meter will not work satisfactorily on transistor ignitions. This depends on the construction of the individual meter used.*

5. If the dwell angle is not according to specifications, remove the distributor cap and adjust the dwell angle. Reduce the point gap if the dwell angle is too small, or increase the contact point gap if the dwell angle is too large.

6. To actually adjust the point gap, loosen the hold-down screw and insert a screwdriver between the lugs on the breaker plate and move the plate to the desired location. Tighten the hold-down screw. On some models the point gap is adjusted with the eccentric screw in the breaker plate.

7. Recheck the dwell angle and adjust the gap again if it is still not satisfactory. Repeat the process until the dwell angle is as specified.

All Gas Engines With Electronic Ignition

It is not possible to adjust the dwell angle on Mercedes-Benz electronic ignitions.

Ignition Timing

Adjustment

Before setting the ignition timing, be sure that the point gap (dwell angle) is set to the proper specifications since this will influence the timing, while timing will have no influence on the dwell angle.

Before attempting to set the timing, read the "Ignition Timing Specifications" chart carefully and determine at what speed the timing should be set. The vacuum should be connected on all models.

NOTE: *It is a good idea to paint the appropriate timing mark with dayglow or white paint to make it quickly and easily visible.*

On engines with transistorized coil ignition, the timing light may or may not work depending on the construction of the light. If in doubt, consult a Mercedes-Benz dealer.

All Gas Engines

1. Raise the hood and connect a tachometer.

2. Connect a timing light as specified by the manufacturer.

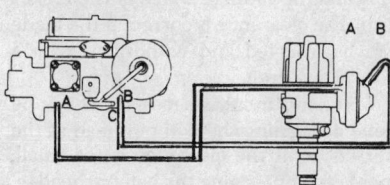

Vacuum connections—280, 280C, 280S (1975-76)

(a)—Vacuum connection (retard) (white)
(b)—Vacuum connection (advance) (red)
(c)—Vacuum connection to vacuum governor and fuel return valve

3. On 280S/8 models, the cable plug on the temperature switch in the thermostat housing must also be disconnected to eliminate the possibility of the engine switching from retard to advance while adjusting the timing.

4. Run the engine at the specified speed and read the firing point on the balancing plate or vibration damper while shining the light on it.

NOTE: *The balancer on some 6-cylinder engines has 2 timing scales. The front degree scale (in driving direction) is for use with the old (9 mm wide) pointer. The rear scale (in driving direction) is for use with the new (triangular) pointer. If in doubt as to which scale to use, rotate the crankshaft (in the direction of rotation only) until the distributor rotor is aligned with the notch on the distributor housing (No. 1 cylinder). In this position, the timing*

pointer should be at TDC on the proper timing scale.

5. Adjust the ignition timing by loosening the distributor clamp bolt and rotating the distributor. To advance the timing, rotate the distributor in the opposite direction of normal rotation. To retard the timing, rotate the distributor in the direction of normal rotation.

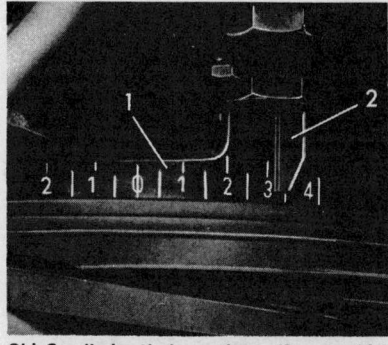

Old 6 cylinder timing pointer (9 mm wide)

1. TDC mark and degree scale
2. Pointer (9 mm wide)

New 6 cylinder timing pointer (triangular)

1. Front degree scale
2. Rear degree scale
3. Triangular pointer

CAUTION: *When setting the timing at high rpm (3000) do not try to adjust the timing while the engine is running. Run the engine to the specified rpm (for an instant) and read the timing on the scale. Shut the engine off and adjust the timing by rotating the distributor in the proper direction slightly. Repeat the process of adjusting the timing slightly and reading the timing on the scale until the timing is adjusted correctly.*

6. On 280S/8 models, install the temperature switch cable plug after the timing is set satisfactorily. Check the operation of the changeover switch by connecting the temperature switch on the thermostat housing to ground. The speed should increase from approximately 800 rpm to approximately 1300–1500 rpm.

7. Once the timing has been adjusted, recheck the timing once more to be sure that it has not been disturbed.

8. Remove the timing light and tachometer and connect any wires that were removed.

Valve Clearance

Adjustment

The valve clearance of all gasoline engines should be checked and, if necessary, adjusted when the engine is cold.

Carbureted Engines (Except 280, 280C and 1975-76 280S)

The valve clearance is measured between the sliding surface of the rocker arm and the heel of the camshaft lobe. The highest point of the camshaft lobe should be at a 90° angle to the sliding surface of the rocker arm.

1. Remove the air vent hose from the valve cover. Remove the spark plugs.

2. Remove the valve cover and gasket. On 250/8 engines, remove the air cleaner also.

3. Note the position of the intake and exhaust valves.

4. Rotate the crankshaft, by means of a socket wrench on the crankshaft pulley bolt, until the heel of the camshaft lobe is perpendicular to the sliding surface of the rocker arm.

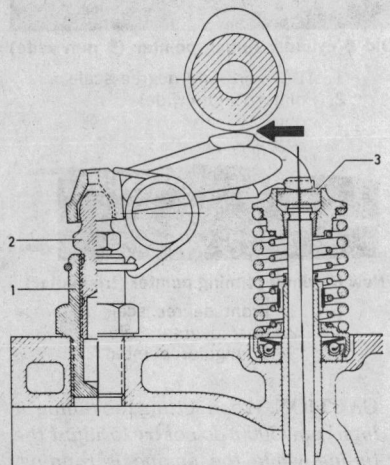

Measure the valve clearance between the sliding surface of the rocker arm and the heel of the camshaft lobe (all engines except V8 and DOHC 6-cylinder)

1. Threaded bushing
2. Adjusting screw
3. Pressure piece

Adjusting the valve clearance

(a)—Position of cam when adjusting valve clearance
1. Feeler gauge strip
2. Valve clearance wrench
3. Torque wrench

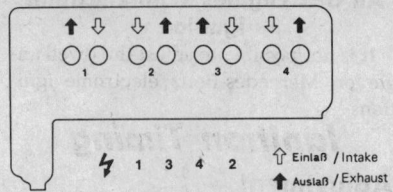

Valve location—4-cylinder engines

⇧ Einlaß / Intake
⬆ Auslaß / Exhaust

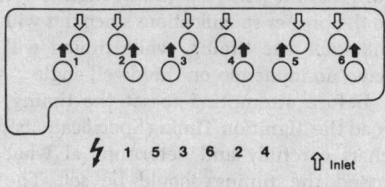

Valve location—6 cylinder except DOHC

⇧ Inlet
⬆ Exhaust

NOTE: *Do not rotate the engine using the camshaft sprocket bolt. The strain will distort the timing chain tensioner rail.. Always rotate the engine in the direction of normal rotation only.*

5. Some models have holes in the vibration damper plate to assist in crankshaft rotation. In this case, a screwdriver can be used to carefully rotate the crankshaft.

6. To measure the valve clearance, insert a feeler blade of the specified thickness between the heel of the camshaft lobe and the sliding surface of the rocker arm. The clearance is correct if the blade can be inserted and withdrawn with a very slight drag.

7. If adjustment is necessary, it can be done by turning the ball pin head at the hex collar. If the clearance is too small, increase it by turning the ball pin head in. If the clearance is too large, decrease it by turning the ball pin head out.

NOTE: *This adjustment is ideally made with a special adapter and a torque wrench. By using it, the torque wrench can be directly aligned with the ball pin head.*

8. When the ball pin head is turned, the adjusting torque should be 14-25 ft lbs. If the torque is less than 14 ft lbs, the ball pin head will vibrate and the clearance will not remain as set. If the valve clearance is too small, and the ball pin head cannot be screwed in far enough to correct it, a thinner pressure piece should be installed in the spring retainer. The standard thickness of the pressure piece is 0.177 in. Pressure pieces are available in thicknesses of 0.137 in., and 0.0985 in. To replace the pressure piece, the rocker arm must be removed.

9. After all the valves have been checked and adjusted in the manner described above, install the valve cover. Be sure that the gasket is seated properly. It

is best to use a new gasket whenever the valve cover is removed.

10. Install the spark plugs.

11. Reconnect the air vent line to the valve cover and install the air cleaner, if removed.

12. Run the engine and check for leaks at the rocker arm cover.

Fuel Injected Engines (6-Cylinder, 1972–75 V8)

NOTE: *1976–77 V8 engines use hydraulic valve lifters and require no periodic adjustment.*

The valve clearance is measured between the sliding surface of the rocker arm and the heel of the camshaft lobe. The highest point of the camshaft lobe should be at a 90° angle to the sliding surface of the rocker arm.

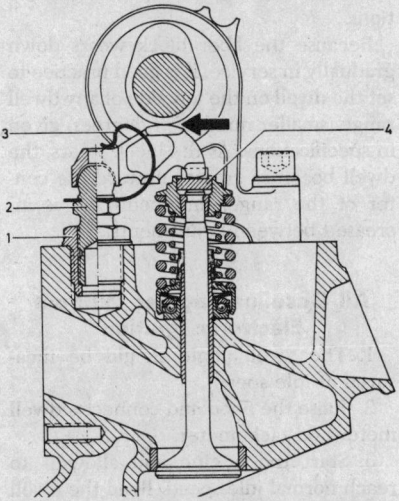

Valve clearance measurement—V8 engines

1. Threaded bushing
2. Adjuster
3. Spring
4. Pressure piece

1. Loosen the venting line and remove the regulating linkage. Remove the valve cover.

2. On V8 engines, disconnect the cable from the ignition coil.

3. Identify all of the valves, as intake or exhaust.

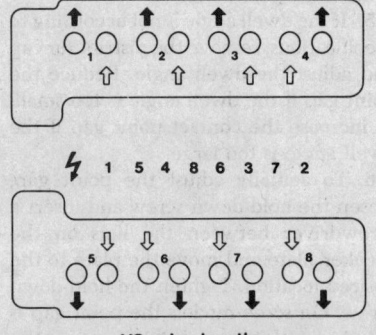

V8 valve location

4. Beginning with No. 1 cylinder, crank the engine with the starter to position the heel of the camshaft approximately over the sliding surface of the rocker arm.

5. Rotate the crankshaft by means of a socket wrench on the crankshaft pulley bolt until the heel of the camshaft lobe is perpendicular to the sliding surface of the rocker arm.

NOTE: *Do not rotate the engine using the camshaft sprocket bolt. The strain will distort the timing chain tensioner rail. Always rotate the engine in the direction of normal rotation only.*

6. Some models have holes in the vibration damper plate to assist in crankshaft rotation. In this case, a screwdriver can be used to carefully rotate the crankshaft.

7. To measure the valve clearance, insert a feeler blade of the specified thickness between the heel of the camshaft lobe and the sliding surface of the rocker arm. The clearance is correct if the blade can be inserted and withdrawn with a very slight drag.

8. If adjustment is necessary, it can be done by turning the ball pin head at the hex collar. If the clearance is too small, increase it by turning the ball pin head in. If the clearance is too large, decrease it by turning the ball pin head out.

NOTE: *This adjustment is ideally made with a special adapter and a torque wrench. By using it, the torque wrench can be directly aligned with the ball pin head.*

9. When the ball pin head is turned, the adjusting torque should be 14–29 ft lbs. If the torque is lower, either the adjusting screw, the threaded bolt, or both will have to be replaced. If the valve clearance is too small, and the ball pin head cannot be screwed in far enough to correct it, a thinner pressure piece should be installed in the spring retainer. The standard thickness of the pressure piece is 0.177 in. Pressure pieces are available in thicknesses of 0.137 in., and 0.0985 in. To replace the pressure piece, the rocker arm must be removed. (See the Engine Mechanical Section.)

10. Install the regulating linkage, valve cover gasket. and valve cover. Be sure the gasket is seated properly.

11. Connect the cable to the coil and the venting line. Run the engine and check for leaks at the valve cover.

280 and 280C

The valve clearance is measured between the sliding surface of the rocker arm and the heel of the camshaft lobe. The highest point of the camshaft lobe should be at a 90° angle to the sliding surface of the rocker arm.

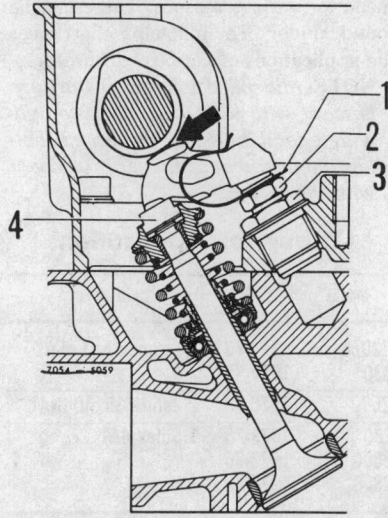

Check the valve clearance between the sliding surface of the rocker arm and the heel of the camshaft lobe on DOHC—6-cylinder engines

1. Tension spring   3. Threaded bushing
2. Adjusting screw   4. Pressure piece

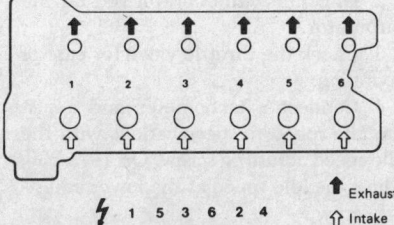

1 5 3 6 2 4

Exhaust
Intake

Valve location—DOHC 6-cylinder engine

Turning the engine with a screwdriver (arrow) inserted in the hole in the balancer.

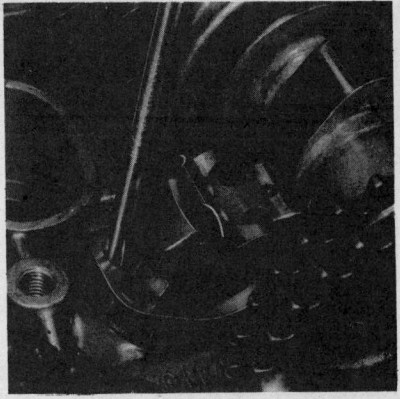

Removing the tension springs

1. Loosen the venting line and remove the valve cover.

2. Remove the tension springs and rubber gaskets.

3. Identify all of the valves as to intake or exhaust.

4. Beginning with No. 1 cylinder, crank the engine with the starter to position the heel of the camshaft lobe approximately over the sliding surface of the rocker arm.

5. Rotate the crankshaft, by means of a socket wrench on the crankshaft pulley, until the heel of the camshaft lobe is perpendicular to the sliding surface of the rocker arm.

NOTE: *Do not rotate the engine using the camshaft sprocket bolt. The strain will distort the timing chain tensioner rail. Always rotate the engine in the direction of normal rotation only.*

6. To measure the valve clearance, insert a feeler blade of the specified thickness between the heel of the camshaft lobe and the sliding surface of the rocker arm. The clearance is correct if the blade can be inserted and withdrawn with a very slight drag.

7. If adjustment is necessary, it can be done by turning the ball pin head at the hex collar. If the clearance is too small, increase it by turning the ball pin head in. If the clearance is too large, decrease it by turning the ball pin head out.

Adjusting the valve clearance on DOHC 6-cyinder engine

Mercedes-Benz

NOTE: *This adjustment is ideally made with a special adapter and a torque wrench. By using it, the torque wrench can be directly aligned with the ball pin head.*

8. When the ball pin head is turned the adjusting torque should be 14–29 ft lbs. If the torque is lower, either the adjusting screw, the threaded bolt, or both will have to be replaced. If the valve clearance is too small, and the ball pin head cannot be screwed in far enough to correct it, a thinner pressure piece should be installed in the spring retainer. The standard thickness of the pressure piece is 0.177 in. Pressure pieces are available in thicknesses of 0.137 in., and 0.0985 in. To replace the pressure piece, the rocker arm must be removed.

9. After all the valves have been adjusted as described above, push the tension springs into the grooves on the adjusting screws.

10. Check and, if necessary, replace the rubber gaskets before installing the valve cover.

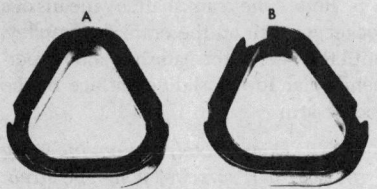

Two versions of rubber gaskets

(a)—Spark plug holes 1, 3 and 5
(b)—Spark plug holes 2 and 4

CAUTION: *Two types of rubber gaskets are used.*

11. Install the valve cover gasket and valve cover. Be sure that the gasket is seated properly to prevent leaks. If necessary, install a new valve cover gasket.

12. Connect the cable to the coil and connect the venting line to the valve cover.

13. Run the engine and check for leaks at the valve cover.

Idle Speed

Engines with Catalytic Converters

With the exception of the 230 (1975–76), all 1975–77 Mercedes-Benz cars are equipped with catalysts. The following points should be adhered to:

1. Use only unleaded gas.
2. Maintain the engine at the specified intervals.
3. Avoid running the engine with an excessively rich mixture. Do not run the engine excessively on fast idle.
4. Prolonged warm-up after a cold start should be avoided.

5. Do not check exhaust emissions over a long period of time without air injection.
6. Do not alter the emission control system in any way.

Carbureted Engines

The adjustments given here are intended to include only those which would be performed in the course of a normal tune-up, after the spark plugs, dwell angle, and ignition timing have been adjusted. Obviously, there are other adjustments which can and should be made for various reasons. These can be found under . The following chart gives the applications of various carburetors.

NOTE: *Idle speed and fuel mixture are best set with a CO meter to comply with federal emission regulations. Follow the instructions that are packaged with the meter.*

Carburetor Applications

Model	Year	Carburetor
220/8	1970-73	1 Stromberg 175 CDT
230	1974-77	
250C	1970-72	2 Zenith 35/40 INAT
280	1973-76	1 Solex 4A1
280C	1973-76	
280S	1975-76	

Stromberg 175 CDT

1. Turn off the heater and run the vehicle to normal operating temperature. Remove the air intake and air cleaner from cars equipped with air conditioning.
2. Disconnect the control rod on the carburetor.
3. Check the throttle valve for ease of operation.
4. Connect a tachometer and adjust the idle speed to specifications with the idle speed adjusting screw. On 1975 230, adjust the idle speed at the lower adjusting screw.

Adjust the idle speed with the lower adjusting screw (8) on the 230

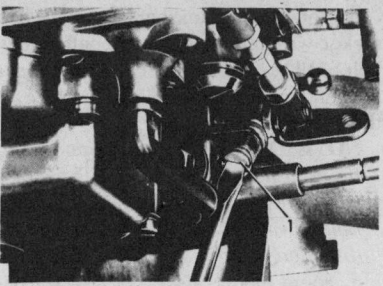

Adjust the idle speed on Stromberg 175 CDT carburetors with the idle speed adjusting screw (1).

5. See whether the idle speed stop is resting against the throttle valve lever and not against the vacuum governor. Set the vacuum governor back if required.
6. If an exhaust gas analyzer (CO meter) is available, check the exhaust gas for percentage of CO. On 1975 and later 230, disconnect and plug the blue/purple vacuum line.
7. If required, adjust the gas rating by means of the fuel mixture screw or idle shut-off valve on the 1975 and later 230. Loosen the locknut while simultaneously holding the nozzle screw and turning the fuel shut-off valve. Accelerate a brief instant after each adjustment of the idle speed and fuel control screw, to stabilize the mixture.

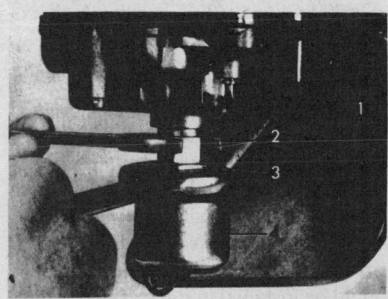

Adjust the fuel mixture on Stromberg 175 CDT carburetors with the fuel mixture screw (4).

1. Idle speed adjusting screw
2. Holding screw
3. Stop nut
4. Fuel control screw (idle speed shut-off valve)

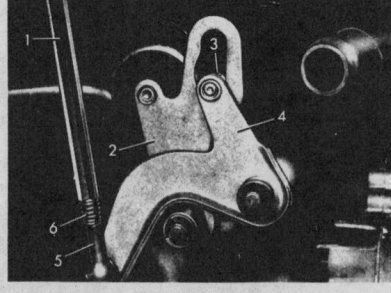

Adjusting the Stromberg 175 CDT control linkage on manual transmission vehicles.

1. Control rod
2. Gate lever
3. Roller
4. Bellcrank
5. Ball joint
6. Compression spring

Adjusting the Stromberg 175 CDT control linkage on automatic transmission vehicles.

7. Pull rod
8. Ball socket
9. Intermediate lever
10. Control rod
11. Ball socket
12. Control rod

8. Check the idle speed again and adjust with the idle speed adjusting screw, if required.

9. Adjust the control linkage as follows:

a. On vehicles with manual transmission, attach the control rod and adjust it so that the roller rests in the gate lever without binding. The control lever is equipped with right and left-hand threads.

b. On vehicles with automatic transmission, run the engine at idle speed. Set the control rod so that it can be attached with no binding.

Zenith 35/40 INAT

1. Run the engine to normal operating temperature.

2. Remove the air cleaner.

3. Disconnect the connecting rod and regulating rod.

4. Check the throttle levers for ease of operation.

5. Be sure that both throttle valve levers are resting against the idle speed stop. Turn back the adjusting screw on vehicles with a vacuum regulator.

6. Connect a tachometer and adjust the idle speed to specifications with the idle adjusting screws.

7. Synchronize both carburetors. See Balancing Multiple Carburetor Installations which follows in this section.

8. Adjust the mixture regulating screws with a CO meter (if available) to the specified figure. If no CO meter is available, adjust the regulating screws to maximum engine rpm or to maximum vacuum.

9. Check the idle and synchronization again.

10. Attach the connecting rod so that it does not bind; check it with a synchronization tester to be sure that both carburetors are opening simultaneously. Raise the actuating lever of the front carburetor to obtain a speed of approximately 1200–1500 rpm. Check the synchronization of both carburetors and adjust the connecting rod if necessary.

11. Adjust the regulating rod as follows:

a. On cars with manual transmission, adjust the regulating rod so that

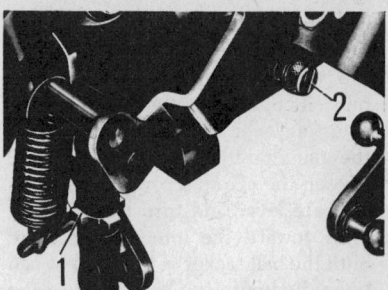

Adjusting screws on Zenith 35/40 INAT carburetors.

1. Idling speed adjusting screw
2. Mixture adjusting screw

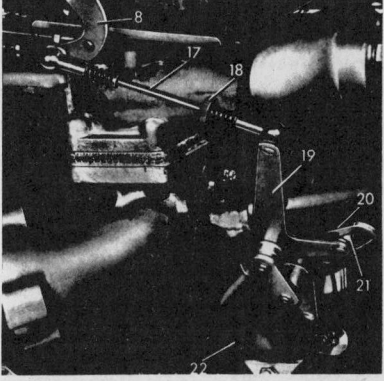

Regulating rod adjustment on manual transmission vehicles.

8. Actuating lever
17. Regulating rod
18. Adjusting nut
19. Bellcrank
20. Cam lever
21. Roller
22. Bearing bracket

Zenith 35/40 INAT dual installation

1. Idle adjustment screw
2. Throttle valve lever
3. Test joint
4. Pump lever
5. Idle stop screw
6. Float chamber vent valve
7. Idle mixture adjustment screw
8. Actuating lever
9. Hexagon bolt
10. Adjustment nut
11. Connecting rod
12. Adjustment screw
13. Return valve lever
14. Fuel return valve
15. Nut
16. Control rod
17. Lever
18. Lever
19. Adjustment screw

the roller in the cam lever rests against the end stop with no binding.

b. On vehicles with automatic transmissions, disconnect the pull rod on the adjusting lever and push the pull rod to the idling position of the transmission. Loosen the clamp screw on the intermediate lever and turn the adjusting lever toward the intermediate lever until the ball socket of the pull rod can be pushed onto the ball socket of the adjusting lever with no binding. Adjust the regulating rod so that with the engine running, the regulating rod can be connected without binding (when fully extended). The actuating lever should rest against the idle speed stop screw.

12. Install the air cleaner and check the idle speed and CO content of the exhaust.

13. Reconnect the cable plug to the temperature switch on the thermostat housing.

Solex 4 A 1

1. The idle speed adjustment on this carburetor is made with the air cleaner installed and the crankcase breather connected.

2. Warm the engine to normal operating temperature. Do not adjust the idle after the engine has been driven very far because the engine will be too hot.

3. On 1975-76 280, 280C and 280S models with catalytic converter, disconnect the blue/purple vacuum line, to prevent air injection.

Solex 4A 1 carburetor linkage

  61. Adjusting nut
  62. Locknut
  63. Adjusting screw
      (vacuum governor)
  68. Idling speed adjusting
      screw
 119. Guide lever
 120. Angle lever
 130. Regulating rod
 140. Slide rod
 144. Connecting rod

4. Disconnect the regulating rod on the carburetor.

5. Check the throttle valve shaft for binding.

6. Adjust the idle speed to specifications with the idle speed adjusting screw. This should be done with a tachometer installed. Be sure that the idle speed stop is on the throttle valve lever and not on the vacuum governor. Loosen the spring of the vacuum governor, if necessary, by

Solex 4A 1 idle speed adjustment

  61. Adjusting nut
  68. Idling speed adjusting screw
 130. Regulating rod

Solex 4A 1 mixture control screws (arrows).

altering the setting of the adjusting nut.

7. Check the CO content of the exhaust gas. Follow the manufacturer's directions. If necessary, turn both mixture control screws to the right against the stop. Turn both screws simultaneously to the left until the CO percentage is within specifications. Turning the screws out will give a richer mixture and turning the screws in will give a leaner mixture.

On 1974 California cars, disconnect the center hose (arrow)

On 1974 California cars, check the CO% with and without air injection. Disconnect the center hose from the air filter. A noticeable air stream should escape. The CO% without air injection should be 6–8%. Connect the center hose and adjust the CO% to maximum of 1.-5%.

8. Check the idle speed once again until both the idle speed and CO percentage of the exhaust gas are as specified.

9. On 1975-76 280, 280C and 280S, reconnect the blue/purple vacuum line.

Balancing Multiple Carburetor Installations

Carburetor synchronization is greatly simplified by use of one of the various devices made for the purpose. A Moto Meter unit is discussed, but a similar device is available in this country under the name Uni-Syn.

To use this unit, warm up the engine, then remove the air cleaner and disconnect the linkage between the carburetors. Adjust the idle speed as previously described, then place the synchronizing device on the air venturi of one of the carburetors. Adjust the air intake on the measuring unit until the ball float is somewhere in the center of the tube. Now simply transfer the unit to the other carburetor and note how far the ball rises. Adjust carburetors until the ball rises equally for both.

NOTE: *A grease pencil is handy for marking the ball position in the tube. The tube must be vertical to allow free movement of the ball.*

Fuel Injected Engines

Mercedes-Benz passenger cars use several types of fuel injection. All U.S.A. version passenger cars with 6-cylinder engines (except the 280, 280C and 280S) use mechanical injection units. All 1972–75 U.S.A. cars with the 4.5 liter engine use electronically controlled injection units. 1976-77 450 series use the Bosch K-Jetronic (air flow controlled) system.

The injection pump and its attendant linkage can only be accurately tested and adjusted using special test equipment and tools which are not readily available. For this reason it is recommended that all but the simplest service operations concerning the fuel injection system be referred to a Mercedes-Benz dealer. Even when adjusting idle speed on fuel-injected engines, be very careful. The system is extremely sensitive.

Mechanical Fuel Injection (1972 6 Cyl. Engines)

1. Run the engine until it has warmed to normal operating temperature. Do not adjust the idle speed when the engine is extremely hot.

2. Check to be sure that the throttle valve is closing completely without binding.

3. Under firm pressure, the throttle valve should exert a slight pressure on the idle speed stop screw without binding. If necessary, adjust this with the stop screw.

4. Be sure that the regulating levers on

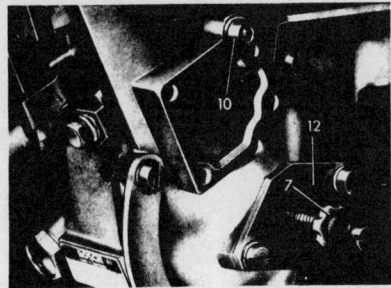

Idle speed air adjustment on mechanical fuel injection.

7. Idling speed adjusting screw
10. Closing screw—full load adjustment
12. Closing flange partial load adjustment

the injection pump and the venturi control unit are seated against the idle speed stops.

5. Connect a tachometer and adjust the idle speed to specifications by turning the idle speed air screw.

NOTE: *It must be emphasized that adjustments of this nature are extremely critical in light of emission control regulations. For best results it is necessary to use a CO meter. See the specifications or the tune-up decal for CO percentages.*

6. If the emission values must be adjusted, stop the engine. Turn the idle speed adjusting screw (on the pump) to the left if the mixture is too rich, or to the right if the mixture is too lean. Note that the pump idle screw is turned from notch to notch. It should not be turned more than three notches in either direction.

7. Start the engine and check the idle speed; readjust with the idle speed air screw if necessary. Repeat this procedure until the idle speed and emissions content are satisfactory.

8. If no CO meter is available, idle speed can be adjusted as follows:

a. Connect a vacuum gauge to the vacuum pressure test connection on the venturi control unit.

b. Open the idle speed air screw slightly until the vacuum falls off. Close the idle speed air screw until the vacuum falls off again. From this point, adjust the idle speed air screw until maximum rpm is obtained.

c. Read the idle speed on a tachometer. If the speed is too high, the mixture is too rich. If the speed is too low, the mixture is too lean.

d. Adjust the mixture as required on the idle speed adjusting screw on the injection pump. Note that the adjusting screw is adjusted from notch to notch. It should not be adjusted more than three notches in either direction.

e. Repeat the adjustment of the idle speed air screw and, if necessary, the

idle speed adjusting screw on the injection pump.

Electronic Fuel Injection (V8)—1972–75

1. Run the engine to normal operating temperature. The idle speed should not be adjusted when the engine is extremely hot.

2. Remove the air cleaner.

3. Disconnect the connecting rod from the valve connection and check to be sure that the throttle valve closes completely without binding.

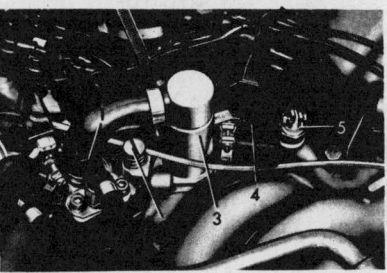

Idle speed adjustment on electronic fuel injection.

1. Starting valve
2. Idling speed air screw
3. Supplementary air valve
4. Water temperature sensor
5. Thermal time switch

4. Re-attach the connecting rod so that it does not bind.

5. Connect a tachometer and adjust the idle speed to specifications with the idle speed air screw.

6. Check the exhaust gas content with a CO meter. On 1975 models with catalytic converter, disconnect the 63°F temperature switch, located in the right-front of the engine compartment. Connect the switch lead to ground, to prevent air injection. If necessary, adjust the CO content with the adjusting screw on the control unit. Turning the screw clockwise will give a richer mixture while turning the screw counterclockwise will give a leaner mixture.

7. The control unit can be reached after removing the inner lining below the glovebox.

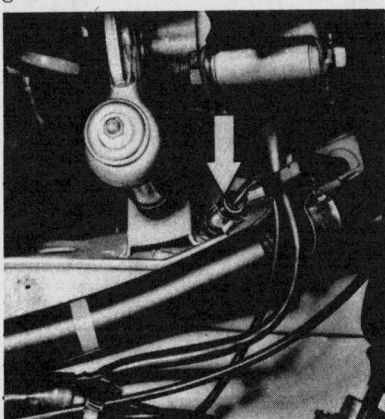

Disconnect the 63°F. temperature switch (arrow) on 1975 V-8 engines

Fuel mixture adjustment (arrow) on electronic fuel injection control box.

8. Check and, if necessary, readjust the idle speed.

9. Install the air cleaner. Check the idle speed and exhaust emissions values and readjust if necessary.

10. Remove the tachometer.

11. Reconnect the 63°F temperature switch.

Electronic Fuel Injection (V8)—1976–77

Idle speed adjustment is made with the A/C off. A special wrench and CO meter are necessary.

1. Remove the air filter.

2. Disconnect the control rod at the bellcrank.

3. The throttle lever should rest against the idle stop.

4. Adjust the control rod so that the roller rests tension free in the slot of the gate lever.

1976-77 V8 fuel injection idle speed adjusting screw (10)

Adjusting the CO with a special wrench on 1976-77 V8 fuel injection

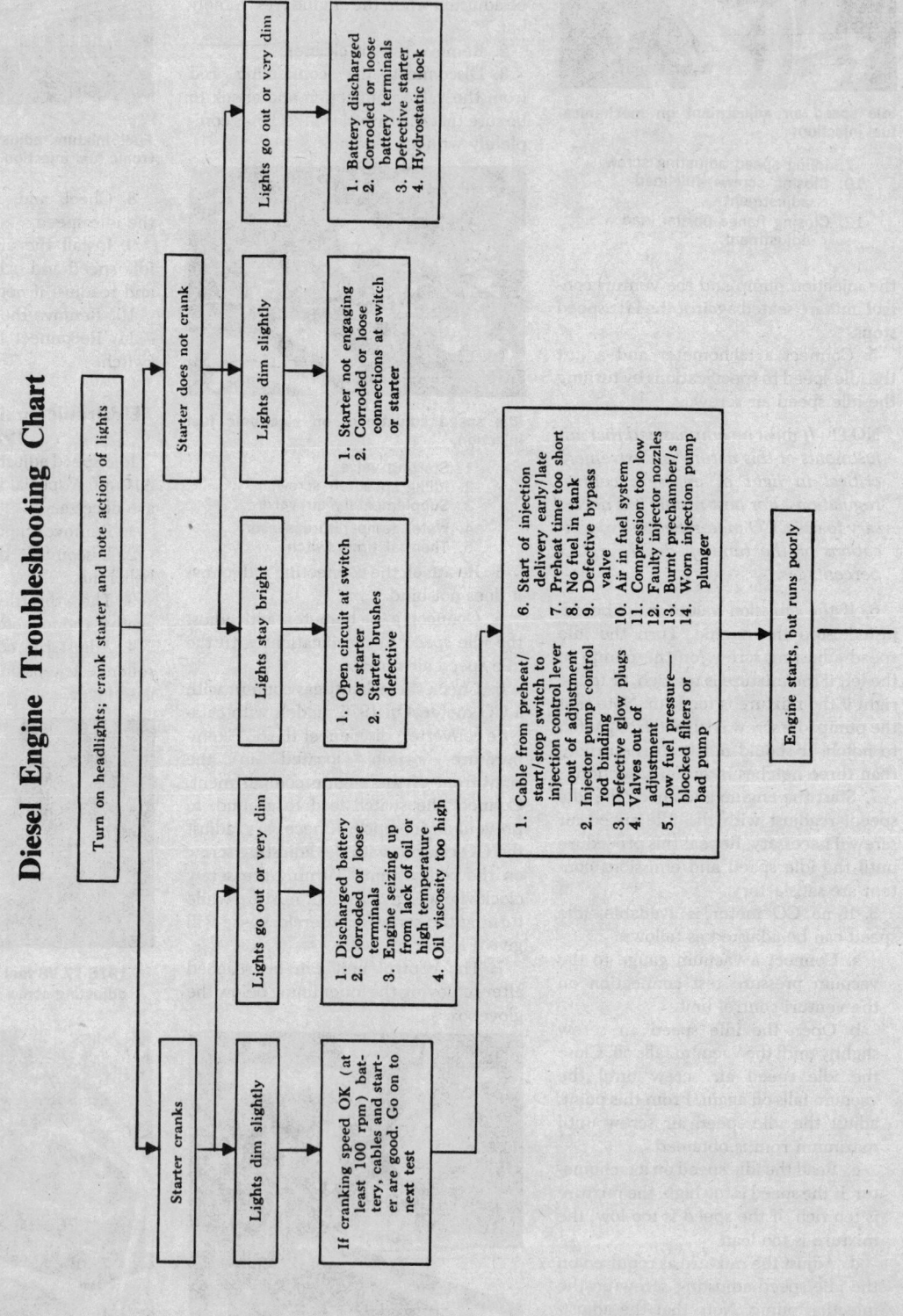

Diesel Engine Troubleshooting Chart

Turn on headlights; crank starter and note action of lights

Starter cranks

Lights dim slightly

If cranking speed OK (at least 100 rpm) battery, cables and starter are good. Go on to next test

Lights go out or very dim

1. Discharged battery
2. Corroded or loose terminals
3. Engine seizing up from lack of oil or high temperature
4. Oil viscosity too high

Starter does not crank

Lights stay bright

1. Open circuit at switch or starter
2. Starter brushes defective

Lights dim slightly

1. Starter not engaging
2. Corroded or loose connections at switch or starter

Lights go out or very dim

1. Battery discharged
2. Corroded or loose battery terminals
3. Defective starter
4. Hydrostatic lock

---

1. Cable from preheat/start/stop switch to injection control lever—out of adjustment
2. Injector pump control rod binding
3. Defective glow plugs
4. Valves out of adjustment
5. Low fuel pressure—blocked filters or bad pump

6. Start of injection delivery early/late
7. Preheat time too short
8. No fuel in tank
9. Defective bypass valve
10. Air in fuel system
11. Compression too low
12. Faulty injector nozzles
13. Burnt prechamber/s
14. Worn injection pump plunger

Engine starts, but runs poorly

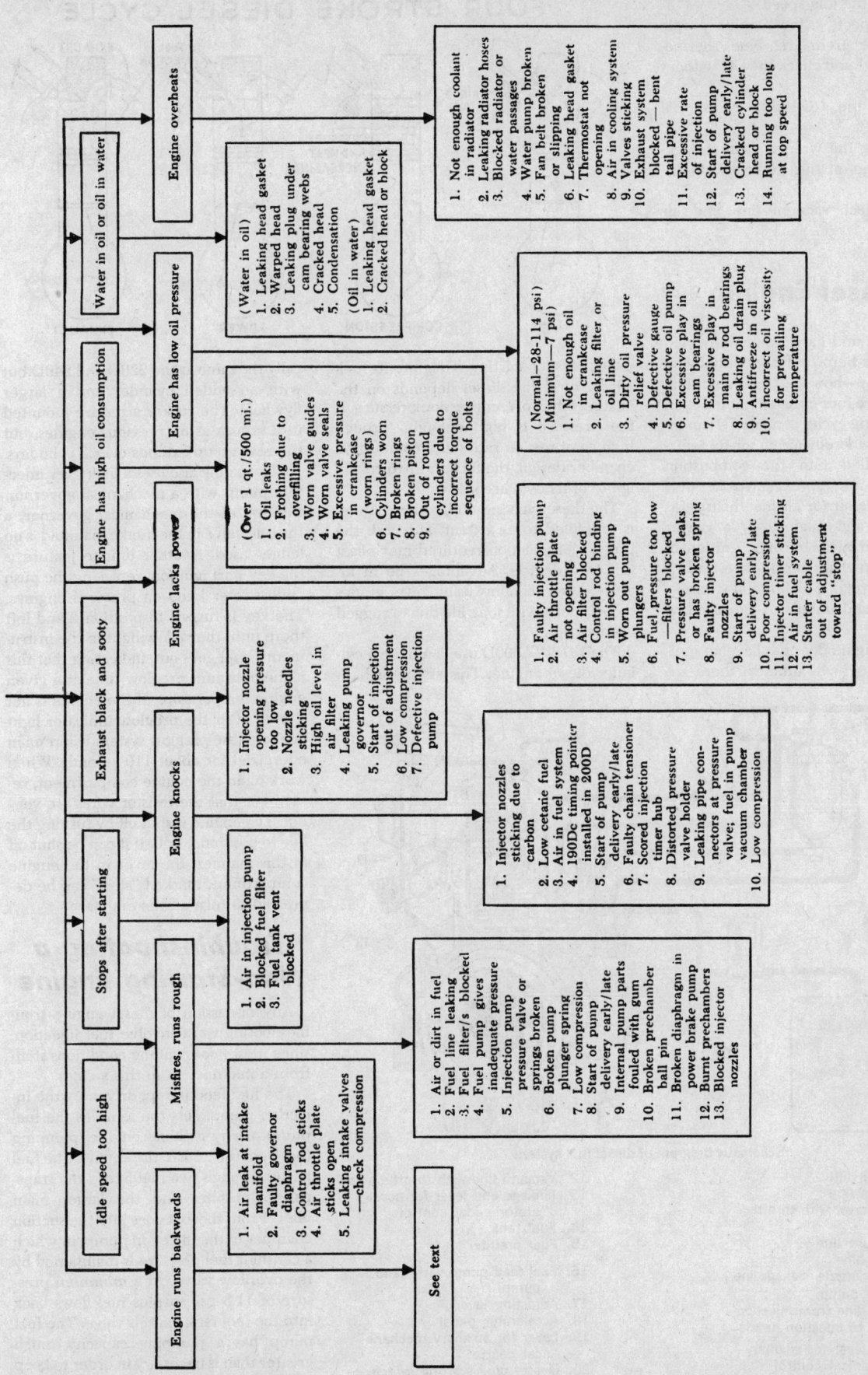

Engine overheats

1. Not enough coolant in radiator
2. Leaking radiator hoses
3. Blocked radiator or water passages
4. Water pump broken
5. Fan belt broken or slipping
6. Leaking head gasket
7. Thermostat not opening
8. Air in cooling system
9. Valves sticking
10. Exhaust system blocked — bent tail pipe
11. Excessive rate of injection
12. Start of pump delivery early/late
13. Cracked cylinder head or block
14. Running too long at top speed

Water in oil or oil in water

(Water in oil)
1. Leaking head gasket
2. Warped head
3. Leaking plug under cam bearing webs
4. Cracked head
5. Condensation
(Oil in water)
1. Leaking head gasket
2. Cracked head or block

Engine has high oil consumption

(Over 1 qt./500 mi.)
1. Oil leaks
2. Frothing due to overfilling
3. Worn valve guides
4. Worn valve seals
5. Excessive pressure in crankcase (worn rings)
6. Cylinders worn
7. Broken rings
8. Broken piston
9. Out of round cylinders due to incorrect torque sequence of bolts

Engine has low oil pressure

(Normal—28-114 psi)
(Minimum—7 psi)
1. Not enough oil in crankcase
2. Leaking filter or oil line
3. Dirty oil pressure relief valve
4. Defective gauge
5. Defective oil pump
6. Excessive play in cam bearings
7. Excessive play in main or rod bearings
8. Leaking oil drain plug
9. Antifreeze in oil
10. Incorrect oil viscosity for prevailing temperature

Engine lacks power

1. Faulty injection pump
2. Air throttle plate not opening
3. Air filter blocked
4. Control rod binding in injection pump
5. Worn out pump plungers
6. Fuel, pressure too low —filters blocked
7. Pressure valve leaks or has broken spring
8. Faulty injector nozzles
9. Start of pump delivery early/late
10. Poor compression
11. Injector timer sticking
12. Air in fuel system
13. Starter cable out of adjustment toward "stop"

Exhaust black and sooty

1. Injector nozzle opening pressure too low
2. Nozzle needles sticking
3. High oil level in air filter
4. Leaking pump governor
5. Start of injection out of adjustment
6. Low compression
7. Defective injection pump

Engine knocks

1. Injector nozzles sticking due to carbon
2. Low cetanic fuel
3. Air in fuel system
4. 190Dc timing pointer installed in 200D
5. Start of pump delivery early/late
6. Faulty chain tensioner
7. Scored injection timer hub
8. Distorted pressure valve holder
9. Leaking pipe connectors at pressure valve; fuel in pump vacuum chamber
10. Low compression

Stops after starting

1. Air in injection pump
2. Blocked fuel filter
3. Fuel tank vent blocked

Misfires, runs rough

1. Air or dirt in fuel
2. Fuel line leaking
3. Fuel filter/s blocked
4. Fuel pump gives inadequate pressure
5. Injection pump pressure valve or springs broken
6. Broken pump plunger spring
7. Low compression
8. Start of pump delivery early/late
9. Internal pump parts fouled with gum
10. Broken prechamber ball pin
11. Broken diaphragm in power brake pump
12. Burnt prechambers
13. Blocked injector nozzles

Idle speed too high

Engine runs backwards

1. Air leak at intake manifold
2. Faulty governor diaphragm
3. Control rod sticks
4. Air throttle plate sticks open
5. Leaking intake valves —check compression

See text

5. Adjust the idle speed.

6. Disconnect the blue/purple vacuum line from the blue thermo-vacuum valve and check the CO without air injection.

7. Adjust the CO with the special wrench.

8. Turning the wrench counterclockwise leans the mixture and clockwise richens it.

9. Reconnect vacuum line and air cleaner.

Diesel Engine

The diesel and gasoline engines used by Mercedes-Benz differ essentially in only one way—how the fuel is ignited. Both types are four cycle engines; that is, their operating cycles consist of (1) an intake stroke, whereby air (or air-fuel mixture) is pulled into the combustion chamber, (2) a compression stroke, during which the air (or air-fuel mixture) is compressed and heated, (3) a power stroke, caused by the burning (ignition) of the injected fuel and air mixture, and (4) an exhaust stroke, which literally pushes the burned and unburned gases out of the engine.

A diesel engine does not have an ignition system as such, although there are

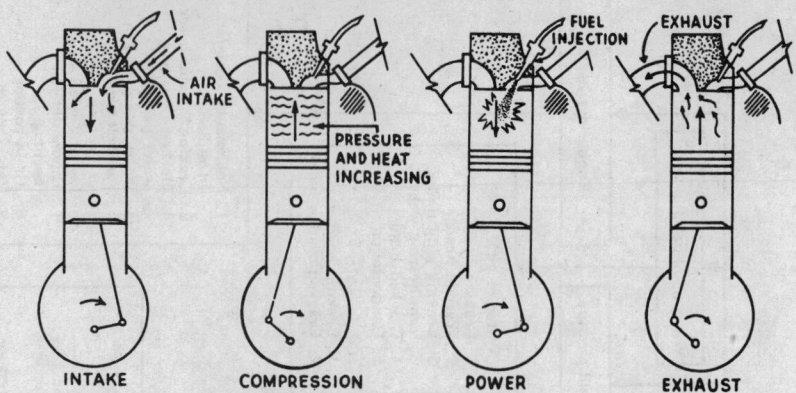

FOUR STROKE DIESEL CYCLE

INTAKE — COMPRESSION — POWER — EXHAUST

glow plugs for starting. To ignite its fuel-air mixture, the diesel depends on the heating effect of compression pressure. If the pressure is high enough, through high compression ratios and combustion chamber design, the fuel-air mixture will ignite of its own accord.

The diesel, having no ignition system, is simplified to an extent, although the timed fuel injection required may offset this to a degree. Advantages lie in increased fuel economy using lower grades of fuel, along with long life due to rugged construction.

The 1975–77 300D uses a unique 5-cylinder diesel engine. This engine is basi-cally the same as the 220D and 240D but with an added cylinder and a larger flywheel. The rocker arms are mounted in 2 groups as on previous engines, but the rear group extends over 3 cylinders.

This engine also uses a 5 plunger injection pump with a mechanical governor. Because of the mechanical governor, a throttle valve in the intake manifold is no longer used. Another unique feature is the key start ignition, replacing the push/pull starter knob on previous engines. The key is turned to position 2 and left there until the yellow light in the instrument panel goes out, indicating that this is the optimum preglow time at a given engine temperature. If the engine is not started after the preglow indicator light goes out, the preglow system will remain energized for about 110 seconds. When working in the engine compartment, remember that the resistor wires are very hot. The engine is shut off by turning the key to position 1 or 0. If it can be shut off in this manner, the lever in the engine compartment marked "stop" can be depressed to turn off the engine.

Troubleshooting a Non-Starting Engine

Any discussion of diesel engine troubleshooting must involve fuel injection, since most poor running conditions stem from a malfunction in this system.

The fuel feed pump, driven by the injection pump, acts the same as the fuel pump of any gasoline engine, pumping fuel from the tank to the engine. The fuel passes through two fuel filters, the transparent prefilter and the larger main filter. From there it goes into the suction chamber of the injection pump, in which a constant fuel pressure is maintained by the overflow valve. At a *minimum* pressure of 11.8 psi, surplus fuel flows back into the fuel tank via this valve. The fuel pump has a pumping capacity much greater than is necessary in order to keep the chamber always full of bubble-free fuel.

Schematic diagram of diesel fuel system

1. Main fuel filter
2. Vent screw
3. Hollow screw with throttle screw
4. Fuel return line
5. Overflow line
6. Injection nozzle leakage line
7. Injection pump
8. Pressure line from injection pump to injection nozzle
9. Angular lever for auxiliary mechanical control
10. Injection nozzle
11. Venturi control unit
12. Vacuum line with throttle screw
13. Linkage and lever for accelerator pedal control
14. Fuel tank
15. Fuel prefilter
16. Fuel feed pump with hand pump
17. Adjusting lever
18. Accelerator pedal
19. Lever for auxiliary mechanical control
20. Heater plug starting switch with starting and stopping cable

The injection pump plungers force the fuel from the suction chamber through the pump pressure valves into the injection lines—thence to the injection nozzles, at a spray pressure of 1564–1750 psi. The spray must pass through the prechamber before reaching the main combustion chamber. Surplus fuel at the injectors is passed through leakage lines into the fuel tank.

The fuel volume is influenced by the accelerator pedal position, engine load and speed, and controlled by the pneumatic governor on the rear of the injection pump.

If the engine will not start, as usually happens in cold weather with a poorly maintained car, try turning the idle speed adjuster knob all the way counterclockwise, pre-glow for a full minute, push the clutch all the way in, and the accelerator pedal halfway down. Then try to start the engine. If the engine does not start after 10–15 seconds, pre-glow again and repeat the procedure. If the engine fires a few times but just won't catch, hold the starter on for a longer period.

NOTE: *The 1975 and later 5-cylinder diesel uses a key start system, eliminating the glow plug knob.*

This assumes, of course, that the starter motor turns the engine over at all. The most common cause of the starter not working, or working sluggishly, is a low battery, sometimes in combination with "summer" oil. The diesel, having such a high compression ratio (21:1) is difficult to turn over with high viscosity oil working against it.

If, after checking the battery, starter, cables, and oil, the engine still will not start, a check of one, or all, of the following areas is in order:

1. Cable from pre-glow/start-stop switch to injection control lever.

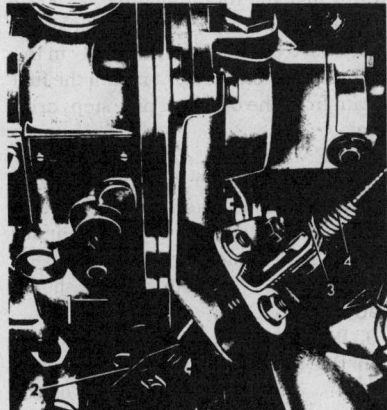

Starting cable adjustment

1. Adjusting lever (starting and stopping cable lever)
2. Eye with rubber molding of starting and stopping cable
3. Angle bracket
4. Coil spring

2. Injection pump control rod.
3. Compression pressure (including valve adjustment).
4. Glow plugs.
5. Fuel pressure.
6. Start of injection pump delivery.

Cable

1. To adjust the cable, first disconnect the ground cable from the negative battery post. Push the control knob all the way in to the STOP position. In this position, the adjusting lever on the injection pump will be pushed completely forward.

2. Next, pull the knob to the START position. In this position, the pin of the adjusting lever should rest against the end of the eye.

3. Now release the knob. The adjusting lever should return to the DRIVING position. In both this and the pre-glow position, the adjusting lever pin must clear the eye end by at least 0.080 in. If not, adjust the cable by loosening the bolt and moving the coil spring outer housing with relation to the angle bracket. Also, make sure the adjusting lever is firmly attached to the pump shaft by tightening the clamp screw.

4. Check the cable and adjusting lever for free movement and make sure that the lever is pulled all the way back when the knob is pulled to the starting position.

5. Reconnect the battery cable and try to start the engine.

NOTE: *If both the start and stop positions cannot be adjusted properly, it is best to sacrifice a little starting delivery to gain a full stop position on the lever.*

Control Rod

The control rod runs through the center of the injection pump, one end protruding from the end housing, covered with a protective cap. If this rod is binding in the stop position, no fuel is delivered to the injectors and the engine will not start. Remove the end cap and check the rod for binding.

Compression

The section on compression testing found in the "Tune-Up" charts applies to diesel engines as well. The only differ-

Testing glow plugs

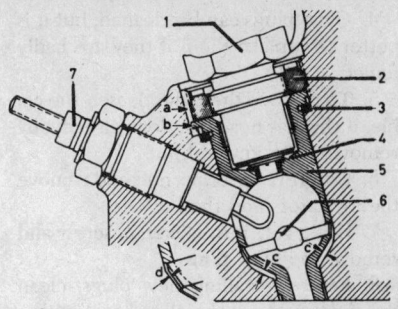

Glow plug and prechamber

(a)—Groove in cylinder head
(b)—Lug securing prechamber
(c)—Distance between prechamber and cylinder head
(d)—Max. permissible measure of a retracted ball pin with respect to the outer dia. of the prechamber (.020")
1. Nozzle holder
2. Threaded ring
3. Seal ring between prechamber and cylinder head
4. Seal ring between prechamber and nozzle holder (nozzle plate)
5. Prechamber (ball pin version)
6. Ball pin in the prechamber
7. Glow plug

ence in testing is that the glow plugs instead of the spark plugs are removed for the test. Individual cylinder pressures should not vary more than 45 psi.

Don't forget, valve clearances set too close will result in poor compression readings for the diesel, also.

Some engines have a valve rotator installed. If this rotator fails, compression will be low. Usually, the replacement of the rotator will bring compression back up to normal.

Glow Plugs

The glow plugs provide a means for ignition during starting and perform the same function as normal spark plugs, although they do so in a different manner.

The light on the dashboard which indicates when the glow plugs are hot enough to fire can also serve as a troubleshooting aid. If the light does not glow, it usually indicates a faulty plug.

1. Test the plugs by having an assistant hold the starting knob or key (1975 and later 5-cylinder) in the preheat position while shorting the plugs to ground, in turn, with a screwdriver. Each plug should produce a spark if working properly. While bridging the connections, the light on the dashboard should light.

2. If, after disconnecting the ground lead of the preheating system, the light still stays lit, a short circuit in the system is indicated. This is usually caused by a carbon-fouled plug electrode or by a lead touching the cylinder head. Check the leads first.

3. If they seem satisfactory pull the knob or turn the key to the preheat position and disconnect one plug power lead at a time, starting from the ground end, until the light goes out, indicating the faulty plug.

4. Glow plugs can be cleaned, but it is better to replace them if they are badly fouled.

5. To remove the plugs, loosen the cable, if this has not been done already, by removing the knurled nut.

6. Unscrew the other nuts and remove the insulators and the bus bars.

7. Using a 21 mm socket, unscrew and remove the glow plugs.

8. Before installing new plugs, clean the ducts and prechamber bores with a stiff bristle brush or a small scraper. The ball pin in the prechamber is easy to break, so don't go much deeper than 2 in. into the plug hole.

9. Crank the engine a few times to blow out any carbon particles loosened by the scraping, then insert the plugs. Do not exceed 35 ft lbs torque.

10. It might be a good idea to recheck these new plugs to ensure that all connections are tight and not grounded and that the plugs are not faulty.

Fuel Pressure

The fuel pump is mounted on the side of the fuel injection pump and can be easily identified by the hand priming pump. Its job, like that of the gasoline engine fuel pump, is to deliver a constant fuel volume, at adequate pressure, to the injection pump. With the diesel engine it is extremely important that the fuel is airfree, without bubbles. A fuel bypass valve is located in the injection pump to maintain constant fuel pressure for the engine load. This valve opens at a pressure of 14.7–22 psi, sending excess fuel back into the supply system.

Pressure valve components
1. Pipe joint
2. Rubber sealing ring
3. Coil spring
4. Sealing ring
5. Pressure valve plate with pressure valve

As with most things mechanical, accurate testing is possible only with the proper instruments. A general check of fuel pressure can be made, however, if one assumes that the bypass valve is functioning properly.

1. Disconnect the return line at the fitting and hold the line over an open coffee can.

2. Start the engine and watch the line. If fuel comes out, it can be assumed that the fuel pressure is sufficient, as a pressure of at least 14.7 psi is required to open a good bypass valve.

3. It is also a good practice to check the discharge line from the fuel filter, as a blocked filter will deliver no fuel.

4. Check the tank before assuming the worst about a fuel pump. Gauges have been known to be wrong. It may be a good idea to disconnect the input line from the fuel tank and blow back through it with low-pressure compressed air. A line free of debris will allow the air to bubble in the tank.

CAUTION: *High pressure air will blow out the fuel tank filter.*

5. Defective fuel pumps should be replaced, as it is not really feasible to rebuild them without the proper tools.

6. To check the pump, unscrew the hand pump and remove the suction valve. Unscrew the plug which covers the pressure valve and remove the valve. Worn valve seats can be reground sometimes, but it is better to replace them.

7. To check the plunger, remove the plug and pull the plunger and spring. If it is badly scored or worn, the pump must be replaced. If the pump is only clogged with gum, it is possible to clean it with lacquer thinner or carbon tetrachloride but a new rubber O-ring should be used on the hand pump during reassembly.

Start of Injection Pump Delivery

As the piston comes up on the compression stroke, there is a delay caused by the fuel having to come from the pump to the injector nozzle. For example, if injection takes place too early, temperatures may not yet be high enough for ignition (piston has not come up far enough to compress the air). To compensate for this lag, the injection pump begins to deliver fuel to the nozzle before the piston reaches TDC.

1. To check the start of delivery, remove the negative battery cable and set the piston of No. 1 cylinder at top dead center by lining up the TDC mark on the crankshaft pulley with the pointer. If TDC is achieved, both intake and exhaust valves of No. 1 cylinder will be closed (springs not compressed).

2. This can be checked by removing the camshaft cover and observing the relationship of the rockers to the valve stems.

3. Using a wrench on the crankshaft pulley nut (never use the camshaft pulley nut, as the timing chain rails will be damaged), turn the engine over 1¾ turns, in the normal direction of rotation.

4. Unscrew the injection line at the pipe union of the first pump cylinder. Remove the pipe union, rubber O-ring,

Measuring the start of pump delivery
1. Adjustment lever of injection pump
2. Hand-operated fuel pump
3. Jaws for locking two pipe unions
4. Tachometer drive
5. Overflow pipe
6. Bleed screw
7. Fuel container
8. Fuel return lines

spring, and the pressure valve. Replace the union and screw on an overflow pipe.

5. Detach the starting cable from the lever at the injection pump and make sure that the lever is in the full delivery position. If this is not done, the test may be inaccurate.

6. Either connect an auxiliary fuel container to the injection pump or fill the main fuel filter by operating the hand pump and cranking the bleed screw to ensure that the fuel is air-free.

7. With the wrench on the crankshaft pulley, turn the engine over slowly in the normal direction of rotation until the fuel stream from the overflow pipe stops dripping.

NOTE: *Another drop may follow 10–15 seconds later, but this is normal.*

8. At this point, the pump piston covers the intake core in the pump cylinder and the start of delivery point has been reached. The crankshaft pointer should read 24° BTDC.

9. Repeat the test by continuing to turn the crankshaft in the direction of rotation—two turns. At the end of the second revolution, the fuel should cease dripping again at the proper point.

10. To adjust the start of delivery, loosen the bolts of the front flange and rotate the pump toward the engine to begin delivery earlier, or away from the engine to delay delivery. It may be neces-

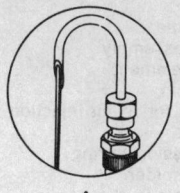 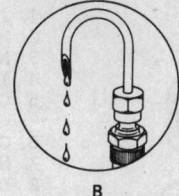 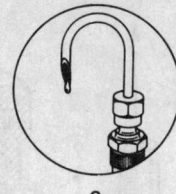

Overflow pipe during test

(a)—Solid fuel stream   (c)—One drop follows 10-15
(b)—Fuel begins to drip   seconds later

sary to disconnect the injector tubes so that the pump will be free enough to rotate.

11. Remove all test equipment and reassemble, using a new seal in the pressure valve assembly. The pressure valve assembly pipe union must be tightened to exactly 25 ft lbs with the threads coated with petroleum jelly.

12. Bleed the fuel system by opening the bleed screw and pumping the hand pump to evacuate any air.

13. Re-attach the starting cable and adjust as previously detailed.

Troubleshooting a Poorly Running Engine

A careful study of the troubleshooting chart will reveal most of the symptoms of poor running associated with diesel engines of this type, along with their probable causes. You will also note that many items are found in more than one column because the breakdown or malfunctioning of one component part could cause any number of problems, depending on whether other components are involved in this breakdown. For instance, a blocked fuel filter could cause the engine to stop immediately after starting, cause it to misfire or run badly, or even not start at all.

Many of the problems listed have been covered elsewhere. Compression testing, for example, is explained, as are the causes of poor compression. Many of the other items have obvious corrective measures.

In order to eliminate repetition, the most common testing and repair procedures follow in no particular order or sequence. Simply consult the troubleshooting chart and find the associated test.

Engine Runs Backward

Under the proper conditions the diesel engine can run backward (although poorly) accompanied by smoke issuing from the air cleaner. This is not a common condition but one that can be damaging to the engine.

For example, if reverse gear is accidentally engaged while coasting forward, or if the engine stalls under load and restarts itself, the engine can run backward. To stop it, engage a gear and let out the clutch suddenly, or block the exhaust pipe with a rag. This can also happen if an attempt is made to start the engine without preheating. If the switch is moved from the start to the preheat position, the beginning of preheat may coincide with engine revolutions, causing extremely early ignition. If this happens, the air filter will quickly catch fire and the engine can seize due to lack of oil, so quick action is necessary.

Since 1962, diesel engines have had a check throttle valve installed to prevent this situation, so a check of that valve will usually isolate the problem. Lubricate the valve every 5,000 miles with engine oil.

Engine Stops After Starting

This can be caused by a blocked fuel tank, fuel filter, or an air-locked injection pump. Remove the tank filler cap and try starting the engine. Remove the fuel line to the injection pump and crank the engine. Check the fuel volume. Bleed the fuel system.

Idle Speed Too High

Air leaks at the intake manifold can be located by squirting some soapy water at any suspected joints, with the engine running. The solution will be sucked in or bubble if a leak exists.

The injection pump governor diaphragm cannot be checked accurately unless the pump is placed on a test stand. It is possible, however, to determine roughly whether or not the governor is operating. First, with the engine idling,

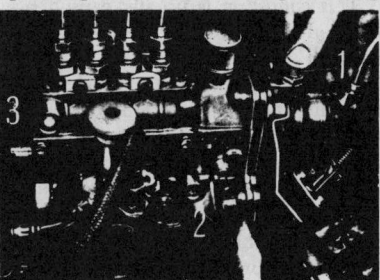

Checking the vacuum cleaner
1. Vacuum union   3. Protector sleeve
2. Control lever   over control rod

squirt a soapy water solution over the intake manifold, vacuum line, governor housing, and air venturi housing joints to check for leakage. An old squirt type oil can works well to avoid soaking the engine.

1. Remove the starting cable from the control lever of the injection pump and remove the sleeve over the control rod.

2. Unscrew the vacuum line and actuate the control lever, making sure the control rod goes to its full stop position, while holding your thumb over the fitting.

3. Release the control lever and observe the control rod. If the diaphragm of the pump governor is functioning, the control rod will move slightly, but will be restrained by vacuum produced in the housing. Removing your thumb should allow the control rod to move. If this test indicates the diaphragm to be faulty, remove the four bolts and take out the diaphragm for inspection.

4. It is possible, although not the best procedure, to replace the diaphragm with the injection pump in place, but care must be taken in assembly. For example, it is easy to lose the compensator mechanism components. It is also necessary to use a dial indicator to measure the maximum compensator travel.

5. To measure this travel, obtain a pin 6 mm in diameter (approximately 0.235 in.) and insert it through the sleeve of the old diaphragm and compensator pin. Place the assembly on a large socket for stability. Set up the gauge as illustrated, with the prod tip on the end of the compensator pin, slightly preloaded. Press down on the prod and measure existing travel (maximum travel is 0.043–0.105 in.)

6. Disassemble the old diaphragm and insert the shims into the new one. Now measure maximum travel of the diaphragm. The difference in readings

Checking the diaphragm
1. Prod of dial indicator
2. Sleeve of diaphragm
3. Piece of tubing
4. Pin, 6 mm. in diameter
5. Compensator pin

should not exceed 0.0024 in. Shims are available to make corrections.

Uneven Running, Metallic Noise, Blue Smoke

The usual cause of this condition is a broken ball pin in the prechamber, a jammed injection nozzle, or a leaky vacuum pump system.

With the car stationary, rev the engine a few times and note the exhaust. If intermittent clouds of black smoke are emitted, it indicates one or more of the injection nozzles is faulty.

1. To determine which nozzle is malfunctioning, allow the engine to idle.

2. Loosen the cap nuts of each injection tube, one at a time, about ½ turn, then retighten. If there is no change in the rough idle, it indicates a faulty nozzle. A good nozzle will be indicated by a further roughening of the idle when the cap nut is unscrewed.

3. To remove the nozzle, take off the cap nut and unscrew the nut that holds the banjo fitting.

4. Remove the bolt and the overflow line.

5. Then, unscrew the nozzle assembly and seal.

6. Examine the prechamber for carbon deposits and clean it if necessary.

7. To disassemble the nozzle holder, remove the cap nut with a 27 mm box wrench, then pull out the nozzle assembly and jet needle.

8. Remove the nozzle element, thrust pin, and spring from the nozzle holder. It is very easy to crush or distort the nozzle holder, therefore do *not* clamp it in a vise to disassemble. Individual nozzle components are run-in together and never should be interchanged.

9. Nozzle testing requires special equipment capable of producing accurately measured pressure while allowing observation of the spray pattern. Since this equipment is not readily available and jury-rigged setups do not produce good results, it is recommended that the dealer do any nozzle testing.

10. In any case, malfunctioning nozzles are usually only fouled and, if care is exercised, they can be hand-cleaned.

11. Brush any carbon away using a brass-bristle brush or a piece of kerosene-soaked wood. Never use a steep scraper, because any burrs will ruin the injector. Using a sharpened brass rod, scrape any deposits from the grooves and orifices, then soak in solvent and blow out with compressed air.

12. Examine for burrs or scratches and out-of-round injection holes, then make sure that the jet needle moves freely in the nozzle.

13. Immerse the assembly in diesel fuel and pull the jet needle about one-

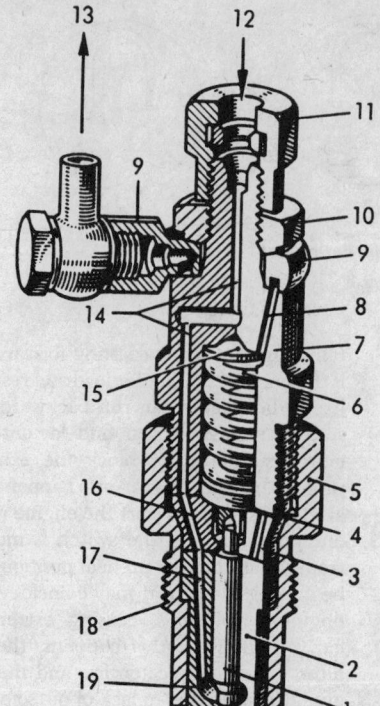

1. Jet needle
2. Nozzle assembly
3. Nozzle element
4. Thrust pin
5. Cap nut for fixing injection nozzle
6. Compression spring
7. Nozzle holder
8. Drain hole in the nozzle holder
9. Through-way jointing piece with annular canal for leak-off oil union
10. Hexagon nut for fixing the through-way jointing piece
11. Cap nut for fixing the injection pipe
12. Fuel feed
13. Leak-off drain back to fuel tank
14. Pressure canal in the nozzle holder
15. Special washers belonging to compression spring (machined steel disks)
16. Annular groove and feed bores in nozzle element
17. Annular groove and pressure canal in nozzle assembly
18. Mounting thread
19. Pressure chamber in nozzle assembly

Nozzle holder injection assembly

third out of the nozzle, then release it. The jet should fall of its own weight.

14. In emergency situations only, burrs keeping the jet from sliding may be removed by lapping with fine valve grinding compound. Damaged seating surfaces, however, usually will not be restored by lapping. It is best to replace such damaged units.

15. Assemble the unit carefully, checking the illustrations for correct parts assembly. Any dirt will prevent free operation of the jet.

16. When tightening the cap nut, do not exceed 50 ft lbs—excessive torque may distort the nozzle and cause the jet needle to bind.

CAUTION: *Always use new seals when reassembling and installing injectors and never try to stop leaks by overtightening connections.*

Uneven Running, Droning Noise, Very Heavy Blue Smoke

This condition is usually caused by a cracked diaphragm in the power brake vacuum pump. Engine oil is sucked through the crack into the vacuum hose, then into the intake manifold. The result can be burned prechambers if not corrected in time, as well as general carbon build-up in the combustion chamber.

1. Remove the hose from the vacuum pump to the intake manifold. If it is filled with oil, the prechambers must be examined for damage. If the prechamber is scorched badly or burnt away, it must be replaced. Unfortunately, special tools are

required for this job. In light of the difficulty sometimes encountered in removal even *with* the special tools, it is almost certain that any substitute will not work and may even damage the cylinder head. Leave this job to the dealer and confine activity to general scraping and cleaning of the chamber. This usually will be sufficient if the condition was caught in time. To alleviate the cause of the problem, the vacuum pump diaphragm must be replaced.

2. To check the diaphragm, detach the vacuum hose between the pump and the power brake and, using a T-fitting connector, connect a vacuum gauge into the line. With the engine running at 2,000 rpm, the gauge should show a little over 21 in. Hg. (vacuum) after about 10 seconds.

Engine Knocks

"Knocking" of the engine falls into four general categories:

1. Knocking during idling.
2. Knocking under partial load at low speed.
3. Knocking under partial load at high speed.
4. Hard knocking, engine shaking on mounts.

Unless the noise has some mechanical cause, for instance, worn connecting rod bearings, diesel knock can be considered harmless to everything but the driver's ears.

Diesel "knock" was once a characteristic of the type of engine. Mercedes-Benz has made great strides in eliminating "knock" from the diesel, and newer engines in a good state of time exhibit little or no "knock".

Knocking at Partial Load at Low Speed

This usually occurs with a cold engine and becomes less as the engine heats up. The most common cause of this is use of diesel fuel with too low a cetane rating (equivalent to "octane" for gasoline). Try mixing about a quart of engine oil with each tank of fuel or change fuel brands.

Often air in the fuel system will cause this problem as well. Check all fuel lines and hoses, from the tank all the way up. The fuel filter and hand pump can also develop leaks. Bleed the fuel system, as described previously in this section, and check the fuel pump vacuum (idle speed=6–12 in. Hg.) and pressure (open pressure of relief valve at idle=11–21 psi).

Knocking at Partial Load at Higher Speeds

This type of knocking usually happens in third gear traveling at 30–45 mph. It can be distinguished by the fact that it gets louder as the engine heats up.

This is often caused by a faulty timing chain tensioner. When the chain loses tension it vibrates, causing a rattle. In addition, the injection timer hub can be scored to such a degree that injection timing is retarded.

1. To accurately check the chain tensioner requires special test equipment. However, if the tensioner is bad enough to cause chain rattle, it will suffice to remove it, clamp it down, fill it with oil and bleed it, then push down slowly.

2. If the tensioner is good, it will require quite high pressure to compress and will compress very slowly.

3. To remove the tensioner, first take off the camshaft cover and drain the radiator to a level below the thermostat housing.

4. Remove the housing and the idler pulley bracket. The tensioner now can be easily removed.

5. Check the tensioner and, if necessary, replace it. Parts are available separately, but the pressure pin and housing must be replaced together for proper operation.

6. To bleed the tensioner after installation, fill the oil case in the cylinder head with engine oil and, using a screwdriver, push the tension sprocket bearing as far as it will go.

7. Slowly release the tensioner, making sure the oil case is filled with oil at all times.

8. Repeat the procedure until no air bubbles appear and there is no free-play on the tensioner.

The injection timer can be removed and checked in the following manner:

1. Remove the radiator.

2. Detach the vacuum and pressure hoses from the vacuum pump. Remove the vacuum pump.

3. Remove the cover screws and cover. Remove the hex nut and washer from the shaft.

4. Remove the camshaft cover.

5. Remove the hex screw and holder.

6. Remove the camshaft sprocket bolt.

7. Turn the crankshaft, using a wrench on the pulley nut, in the direction of rotation until the TDC mark coincides with the pointer.

8. Matchmark the position of the chain with the injection timer. (Use paint dots.)

9. Matchmark the position of the chain on the camshaft sprocket.

10. Remove the chain tensioner.

11. Remove the screw and the inner and outer sliding rails.

12. Pull the camshaft sprocket, making sure the thrust washers are not lost.

13. Unscrew the locking screw and pull the upper guide rail pivot pin.

14. Using a strip of sheet metal or cardboard between the chain and the gear teeth, remove the chain from the intermediate sprocket.

15. Pry off the injection timer, being careful not to turn the engine or camshaft.

16. Inspect the timer. If badly scored or broken internally, replace it, remembering to transfer matchmarks from the old timer.

17. When reassembling, follow the removal procedure in reverse, being careful to align or stiffwire the matchmarks. A bent piece of brazing rod will hold the guide rail in place while inserting the pivot pin. Don't forget to bleed the chain tensioner.

Hard Knocking and Shaking of Engine

The main cause of this is a sticking injector nozzle. These can be tested as described earlier in this section, as well as the pressure valve holders, another cause of the problem.

Leaks between the pipe connectors and pressure valve holders can cause fuel to leak into the governor vacuum chamber. Replacement of the seals will stop the problem, but the fuel must be drained from the vacuum chamber. Unscrew the oil level plug and loosen the governor housing bolts. Drain the fuel by pulling the housing away.

Injection Pump

In many cases of poor running, the injection pump itself is at fault. Fuel that is extremely gritty will cause wear of the pump plungers and plunger springs can break in service. Accurate testing of the pump must be carried out on a test stand. Aside from testing the governor vacuum and control rod, little else other than visual inspection for broken or worn parts can be accomplished.

1. To remove the pump for service, unscrew all the injection lines, the vacuum line and fuel lines.

2. Plug the lines, then detach the connecting rod for the auxiliary mechanical control and the starting cable at the adjusting lever.

3. Turn the crankshaft, in the normal direction of rotation, to align the 45° BTDC mark with the pointer (No. 1 piston on compression stroke).

4. Matchmark the pump and flange.

5. Unscrew the nut at the bell-shaped support, then the front flange hold-down nuts. Pull the pump from the crankcase, then remove the coupling sleeve from the pump drive collar or driveshaft. New pumps do not come with the splined drive collar, therefore the old one must be removed if the pump is to be exchanged.

6. Using a puller, carefully remove the collar and woodruff key.

7. To install the pump, be sure that the crankshaft has not moved from the 45° BTDC position, then insert the Woodruff key into its groove in the driveshaft, making sure the shaft is dirt free.

8. Install the drive collar and hex nut, using a pair of pliers wrapped in tape to hold the collar while tightening the nut. It is extremely important that the splines are not damaged in any way during this operation.

9. Try sliding the coupling sleeve onto the drive collar. If it slides on easily, it can be pressed onto the driveshaft. Remove the oil overflow pipe plug at the rear of the injection pump and adjust start of delivery position by aligning the marks. Apply light finger pressure to the follower in a direction opposite normal direction of rotation (left). This pressure should cause the drive collar to jump two teeth.

10. Grease the paper gaskets with petroleum jelly and install them to side of crankcase, then install pump, finger-tightening the bolts in the slotted holes.

11. Turn the crankshaft in the direc-

Bleeding the timing chain tensioner

tion of rotation to 24° BTDC and check the start of delivery, as outlined previously.

Diesel Engine Tune-Up

Some of the tune-up procedures have been covered in the "Diesel Engine Troubleshooting" section. For those who are not having any problems and wish to tune their engines as part of normal maintenance procedure, these tune-up jobs are listed below. (Starred items have been covered previously.)

1. Adjust idle speed.
*2. Check pneumatic governor for leakage.
3. Adjust idle control cable.
4. Adjust additional mechanical control (Stupser).
5. Adjust no-load maximum speed (governor).
6. Adjust full-load maximum speed (governor).
7. Adjust for minimum exhaust smoke.
8. Adjust valves.
*9. Check start of delivery.
*10. Check glow plugs and prechamber.
*11. Check and adjust start/stop cable.

While not a regular tune-up procedure, checking and adjustment of valve timing should be done, as it can affect performance to a considerable degree. It is also a good practice to check this if the chain tensioner has been removed or replaced to rectify a noise condition.

Idle Speed Adjustment

220D/8, 240D

1. To adjust idle speed, start the engine and allow it to come to normal operating temperature.
2. Turn the idle control knob on the dashboard to the extreme right to get enough slack in the cable. It may be necessary to readjust the cable bracket to get the required free-play.
3. Since there is no electronic ignition system, a mechanical tachometer take-off drive is provided. (If such a tachometer is not available, adjust the idle speed by ear to specifications, manual transmission in Neutral and automatic in Drive, with the parking brake on fully and the wheels chocked.) The ammeter light will go out when sufficient speed is reached.
4. To adjust the idle speed, turn the idle screw on the air intake in or out. If the vacuum line is leaking, the idle speed will not drop when the screw is turned, so make sure both the line connections and the pneumatic governor are good before proceeding.
5. Drain any fuel that might have leaked into the governor housing by unscrewing the oil level plug and loosening the governor housing bolts.

Air venturi and linkage

1. Full-load stop screw
2. Front control valve
3. Connecting rod from front control valve lever to angle lever for injection pump butt bolt operation
4. Idle stop screw
5. Vacuum line to injection pump
6. Check valve lever with stop for automatic opening and rubber damping (in this position the check valve is open)
7. Follower on rear control valve lever for automatic opening of check valve
8. Rear control valve lever
9. Connecting rod (approx. 250 mm. long) to reversing lever, pushrod, control shaft, pedal lever, foot-plate
10. Power brake line to vacuum pump

300D

1. Check the control linkage for freedom of movement.
2. Run the engine to normal operating temperature.
3. Turn the idle speed regulator knob clockwise as far as it will go and check the distance between the collar and spring, which should be 0.040 in. If necessary, adjust this dimension.

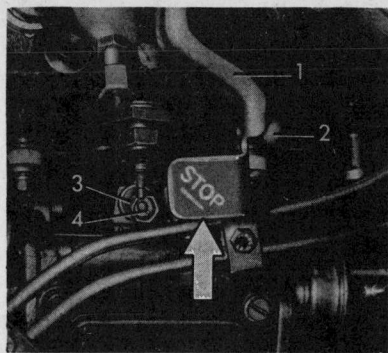

Idle speed adjustment—300D

1. Bell crank lever
2. Control rod
3. Lock nut
4. Idle adjusting screw

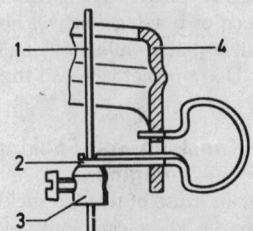

Bowden cable adjustment—300D

1. Bowden cable for idle increase
2. Spring
3. Collar
4. Bell crank

4. Disconnect the control rod at the bell crank.
5. With the engine off, depress the accelerator pedal and simultaneously turn the idle regulator knob counterclockwise as far as it will go.
6. With the engine running, the idle speed should be a maximum of 1000–1100 rpm. If necessary adjust the screw on the bowden cable. If the engine speed is above 1100 rpm, it will be above the range of the governor.

Idle Control Cable

1. Turn the idle control knob on the dashboard to the extreme right and adjust the cable to provide 0.004–0.008 in. clearance between the adjusting ring and the relay lever. The cable must be checked for binding as well and lubricated if necessary.

Additional Mechanical Control

1. This control mechanism helps to eliminate idle speed variations, i.e., "hunting".
2. With the idle speed properly adjusted, detach the connecting rods and measure their length, center to center between ball sockets.

Connecting rod No. 2—310 mm (12.1 in.)
Connecting rod No. 6—205 mm (8.1 in.)
Connecting rod No. 9—250 mm (9.8 in.)

With the rods adjusted, detach connecting rod No. 6 from the relay lever and push it down until it rests against the idle stop. In this position, clearance between the ball socket and head should be 0.04 in. If it requires more than 0.04 in. lift to reattach the connecting rod, unscrew the ball socket.

Maximum Speed Adjustment, No-Load Conditions

This adjustment must be made using a tachometer. The purpose of this adjustment is to limit the maximum engine revolutions so that the engine will never exceed its design speed in service.

1. First, warm up the engine and press the accelerator to the floor.

CAUTION: *Under no circumstances should the engine be revved to 5,000 rpm for more than an instant (split-second). Running the engine for any longer than a split-second at high no-load rpm is extremely dangerous and could result in engine damage. The full-load stop at the air venturi should be contacted by the linkage and the engine speed should not exceed 5,000 rpm.*

2. The speed can be adjusted by turning the full-load stop screw.

3. If the throttle plate is already all the way open and the speed is not up to par, the injection pump control spring tension may be increased by shimming. A 0.004 in. shim will usually increase the engine speed by about 120–150 rpm, depending on the original tension of the spring.

CAUTION: *At first glance, this appears to be an easy way to increase the engine speed range, thus the power output. Unfortunately, the power output decreases sharply above 5,000 rpm, and the reliability of the engine suffers as well, to the point of almost certain bearing failure or crankshaft destruction.*

Maximum Speed at Full-Load

If all aspects of engine and chassis performance have been checked and/or adjusted to produce optimum power and the car will not reach its maximum speed, the full-load stop screw can be adjusted further, or the injection pump control spring tension can be increased slightly. However, under no circumstances should the engine speed under no-load conditions be allowed to go over 5,000 rpm. If no-load engine speed is satisfactory check the speedometer for accuracy, using a stopwatch and a turnpike measured mile.

Model	Max. speed in second gear (mph)	Max. speed in third gear (mph)	Top speed (mph*)
190 Dc	34	54	77
200 D	34	54	80
220 D/8	35	57	83

*Depends on transmission power drain.

NOTE: *The best full-load engine speed is 4,350 rpm.*

Exhaust Smoke Emission

If the emission of black exhaust smoke seems excessive, test in the following manner: make all engine checks and adjustments and, with the engine fully tuned, road test the car on a slight grade.

1. Accelerate in third gear from about 15 mph to the third-gear shift point mark on the speedometer. Have a passenger watch the exhaust smoke while doing this. If the smoke remains black and can be seen extending three or four feet behind, the maximum fuel delivery rate is too high.

2. Adjust by screwing in the full-load stop screw on the *injection pump governor* about ¼ turn. Repeat the road test and adjust in small increments until the smoke disappears.

CAUTION: *Do not exceed ½ turn total.*

3. If the smoke level is still objectionable, the full-load stop screw on the *air venturi* can be adjusted to reduce max-

imum speed slightly, or the injection pump start of delivery can be retarded 2°.

Valve Adjustment

Valve adjustment for diesel engines is basically the same as that given for 220/8 gasoline engines. On the diesel, however, the feeler gauge must be inserted between the rocker arm and the cap nut.

Adjusting the valves

6. Rocker arm pad. 14. Holding wrench
7. Cap nut 15. Feeler Blade
8. Locknut 16. Adjusting wrench

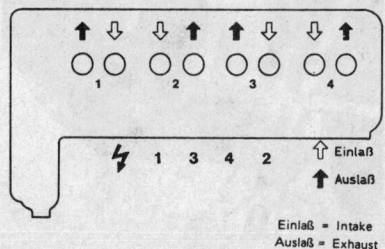

Valve locations—Diesel engines. On 5-cylinder models, the fifth cylinder front valve is exhaust, and the rear, intake

1. Remove the camshaft cover and turn the engine, using a wrench on the crankshaft pulley nut (22 mm), until the TDC mark and the pointer are aligned.
2. This job can be accomplished easily if someone helps. First, a wrench must be placed on the valve spring retainer hex nut.
3. The hex nut then must be loosened with another open end wrench (bent to fit) while the cap nut is held with another wrench.
4. Turn the cap nut to adjust, then tighten the locknut and recheck. Go on

to the other cylinders turning the crankshaft to TDC position for each adjustment.

ENGINE ELECTRICAL
Distributor

Removal and Installation

The removal and installation procedures for all distributors on Mercedes-Benz vehicles are basically similar. However, certain minor differences may exist from model to model.

1. The distributor is usually located on the front of the engine.
2. Remove the dust cover, distributor cap, cable plug connections, and vacuum line.
3. Rotating the engine in the normal direction, crank it around until the markings on the distributor rotor and distributor housing are aligned.
4. The engine can be cranked with a socket wrench on the balancer bolt or with a screwdriver inserted in the balancer.
5. Matchmark the distributor body and the engine so that the distributor can be returned to its original position. White paint can be used for this purpose.
6. Remove the distributor hold-down bolt and withdraw the distributor from the engine.

NOTE: *Do not crank the engine while the distributor is removed.*

7. To install the distributor, reverse the removal instructions. Insert the distributor so that the matchmarks on the distributor and engine are aligned.
8. Tighten the clamp bolt and check the dwell angle and ignition timing.

Electronic Ignition Distributor

Testing

1. Check the screw type plug terminals and the plug wires.
2. With the ignition ON, a primary current of about 8 amps will flow continuously through the system.
3. Check the input voltage at the ter-

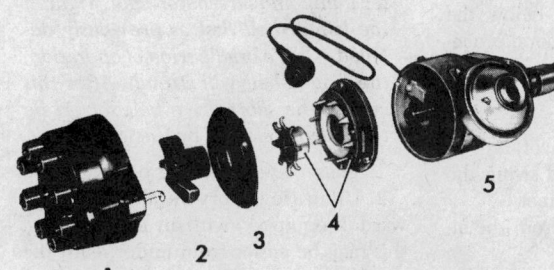

1. Distributor cap
2. Rotor
3. Dust cover
4. Armature and pick-up assembly
5. Distributor housing with pick-up connection

Breakerless ignition distributor—1976 shown

minal block. Terminal 15 should show 4.5 volts and terminal 1 should show 0.5–2.0 volts. If the voltage at terminal 1 is excessive, replace the switching unit.

4. If there is no spark but terminal 1 voltage is OK, check the armature resistance (terminal 7 and 31 d). Resistance should be 450–750 ohms.

5. Test the pick-up coil resistance. There should be infinite resistance between terminal 7 and ground.

6. Check the armature and pick-up coil for mechanical damage. An air gap should exist between them.

7. Check the dwell angle. Even though it cannot be adjusted, it should be 25–39° at 1400–1500 rpm.

8. If the armature and pick-up coil are functioning, replace the switching unit. If the armature and pick-up coil indicate no damage, replace the switching unit. If the armature or pick-up coil are defective, replace the distributor.

Alternator

All Mercedes-Benz cars covered in this book use 12 volt electrical systems with alternators, sometimes in conjunction with the transistor ignition system.

Alternator Precautions

Some precautions that should be taken into consideration when working on this, or any other, AC charging system are as follows:

1. Never switch battery polarity.
2. When installing a battery, always connect the grounded terminal first.
3. Never disconnect the battery while the engine is running.
4. If the molded connector is disconnected from the alternator, do not ground the hot wire.
5. Never run the alternator with the main output cable disconnected.
6. Never electric weld around the car without disconnecting the alternator.
7. Never apply any voltage in excess of battery voltage during testing.
8. Never "jump" a battery for starting purposes with more than 12 volts.

Removal and Installation

Viewing the engine from the front, the alternator is located on the left or right-hand side, usually down low. Because of the location, it is generally easier to remove the alternator from below the vehicle. The following is a general procedure for all models.

1. Locate the alternator and disconnect and tag all wires.
2. Loosen the adjusting (pivot) bolt or the adjusting mechanism and swing the alternator in toward the engine.
3. Remove the drive belt from the alternator pulley.
4. The alternator can now be removed from its mounting bracket or the bracket

and alternator can be removed from the engine.

5. Installation is the reverse of removal.
6. Tighten all of the drive belts that were loosened.

Belt Tension Adjustment

All alternator drive belts should be tensioned to approximately ½ in. deflection under thumb pressure at the middle of its longest span.

All Vehicles Except 6-Cylinder Engines with 55 Amp. Alternator and Double Groove Pulley

1. Loosen the counternut and the attaching bolt.
2. Adjust the drive belt tension with the tensioning nut.
3. Tighten the attaching bolt and counternut.

Adjusting the alternator belt tension—all models except 6 cylinder engines with 55 amp. alternator and double groove pulley.

1. Locknut
2. Pivot bolt
3. Adjusting nut

6-Cylinder Engines with 55 Amp. Alternator and Double Groove Pulley

NOTE: *Observe the following when tensioning new drive belts on vehicles equipped with 55 amp. alternators. The 2 drive belts are of different lengths; one encircles the crankshaft, alternator and water pump pulleys while the shorter one encircles the water pump and alternator only. Tighten the longer belt first as previously detailed. After a brief period of operation, the long V-belt will stretch. After this occurs, the short drive belt should be tensioned, followed by the longer belt.*

1. Loosen the attaching bolt.
2. Using a lever, pry the alternator outward. If equipped with air conditioning, this may be easier from underneath the vehicle.
3. Tighten the attaching bolts.

Adjusting alternator belt tension—6 cylinder engines with 55 amp alternator and double groove pulley.

1. Adjusting bolt
2. Outer attaching bolt
3. Inner attaching bolt

Starter

All Mercedes-Benz passenger cars are equipped with 12-volt Bosch electric starters of various rated outputs. The starter is actuated and the pinion engaged by an electric solenoid mounted on top of the starter motor.

When removing the starter, note the exact position of all wires and washers since they should be installed in their original locations. Also, on some models it may be necessary to position the front wheels to the left or right to provide working clearance.

Removal and Installation

1. Remove all wires from the starter and tag them for location.

Starter installed (typical installation)

1. Terminal 30
2. Terminal 50
3. Solenoid
4. Hex head screw
5. Hex nut
6. Exhaust manifold
7. Hex nut
8. Holding bracket
9. Holding bracket

2. Disconnect the battery cable.
3. Unbolt the starter from the bell housing and remove the ground cable.
4. Remove the starter from underneath the car.
5. Installation is the reverse of removal. Be sure to replace all wires and washers in their original locations.

ENGINE MECHANICAL

All engines are of overhead valve design, operating the valves through individual rocker arms. The smallest of the engines is the 2197 cc gasoline engine installed in the 220/8. A diesel engine of the same displacement is also available in the 220D/8. The 230 engine (2307 cc) replaced the 220/8 in 1974. In the same year the 220D/8 engine was enlarged 2404 cc and installed in the 240D. In 1975, the 5-cylinder diesel was introduced. Basically, it is a 5th cylinder added to the 2404 cc engine giving a displacement of 3005 cc. Six-cylinder, OHC cam engines are available in displacements from 2292 to 2778 cc's. The exception to the six-cylinder engine family is the DOHC engine installed in the 280, 280C and 280E. All other cars use a 4.5 liter V-8 except the 1975–76 280S, and 1977 280SE, which uses the 280/280C engine. All V-8 s are OHC models with one camshaft per head.

NOTE: *Care should be taken when working on Mercedes-Benz engines since there are many aluminum parts which can be damaged if carelessly handled.*

CAUTION: *Before attempting any service on a Mercedes-Benz engine with mechanical fuel injection, read each procedure carefully. The mechanical fuel injection is very sensitive. Anytime the linkage is disconnected, the possibility exists that it will have to be readjusted. This is a complicated procedure requiring very special instruments and should not be attempted by anyone other than a trained Mercedes-Benz mechanic. It is possible, however, to disconnect and reassemble the linkage without disturbing the adjustment, providing that great care is taken throughout the procedure and that components are match marked whenever possible. It should be pointed out however, that there is no guarantee of satisfactory adjustment once the linkage has been disturbed.*

Engine Removal and Installation

NOTE: *In all cases, Mercedes-Benz engines and transmissions are removed as a unit.*

220/8, 220D/8, 240D, 300D, 230 (1974–77), 250/8

1. First, remove the hood, then drain the cooling system and disconnect the battery. While not strictly necessary, it is better to remove the battery completely to prevent breakage by the engine as it is lifted out.

2. Remove the fan shroud, radiator, and disconnect all heater hoses and oil cooler lines.

3. Remove the air cleaner and all fuel, vacuum and oil hoses (e.g., power steering and power brakes). Plug all openings to keep out dirt.

CAUTION: *Air conditioner lines should not be indiscriminately disconnected without taking proper precautions. It is best to swing the compressor out of the way while still connected to its hoses. Never do any welding around the compressor—heat may cause an explosion. Also, the refrigerant, while inert at normal room temperature, breaks down under high temperature into hydrogen fluoride and phosgene (among other products), which is highly poisonous.*

4. Remove the viscous coupling and fan and, on applicable engines, disconnect the carburetor choke cable.

5. On diesel engines, disconnect the idle control and starting cables.

6. On all engines, disconnect the accelerator linkage.

7. On six-cylinder engines with a three-groove crankshaft pulley, remove the heater pipe on the firewall.

8. Disconnect all ground straps and electrical connections. It is a good idea to tag each wire for easy reassembly.

9. Detach the gearshift linkage and the exhaust pipes from the manifolds.

10. Loosen the steering relay arm and pull it down out of the way, along with the center steering rod and hydraulic steering damper.

11. The hydraulic engine shock absorber should be removed.

12. Remove the hydraulic line from the clutch housing and the oil line connectors from the automatic transmission.

13. Unbolt the clutch slave cylinder from the bellhousing after removing the return spring.

14. Remove the exhaust pipe bracket attached to the transmission and place a wood-padded jack under the bellhousing, or place a cable sling under the oil pan, to support the engine.

15. Mark the position of the rear engine support and unbolt the two outer bolts, then remove the top bolt at the transmission and pull the support out.

16. Disconnect the speedometer cable and the front driveshaft U-joint. Push the driveshaft back and wire it out of the way.

17. Unbolt the engine mounts on both sides and, on four-cylinder engines, the front limit stop.

18. Unbolt the power steering fluid reservoir and swing it out of the way; then, using a chain hoist and cable, lift the engine and transmission upward and outward. An angle of about 45° will allow the car to be pushed backward while the

engine is coming up.

19. Reverse the procedure to install, making sure to bleed the hydraulic clutch, power steering, power brakes and fuel system.

280SE/8 (1972) and 280S/8

1. Remove the engine hood.

2. Remove the air cleaner and loosen the engine damper.

3. On all models except the 280S/8, disconnect the hose for the air cleaner and idle speed line.

4. Detach the vacuum line for the brakes.

5. Loosen the cable connections on the cold start valve, idle switch, solenoid switch, injection pump solenoid, time switch, automatic choke, alternator, ignition coil, and oil sender.

6. Unscrew the temperature switch.

7. Disconnect the heater hoses.

8. Disconnect the line to the oil pressure gauge.

9. Lay the windshield washer bag aside.

10. Drain the power steering reservoir.

11. Unscrew and plug the high pressure and return lines on the power steering pump.

12. Disconnect and plug the fuel line at the fuel filter.

13. Remove the ground strap from the body.

14. Remove the exhaust pipes from the exhaust manifolds.

15. Disconnect the speedometer shaft, shift linkage, and control linkage.

16. Remove the bracket from the exhaust pipe support on the transmission, loosen the clamp, and push the holder down.

17. Support the transmission with a jack.

18. Disconnect the driveshaft and slide it toward the rear of the car.

19. Mark the position of the rear engine support and remove it.

20. Remove the splash shield.

21. Loosen the front engine mounting bolts.

Rear engine mount removal—280S/8, 280SE/8

1. Rear engine carrier
2. Engine mount
3. Exhaust pipe support (automatic transmission)

22. Connect a hoist to the engine and take up all the slack.

23. Remove the front engine mount bolts and remove the engine and transmission by pulling it out at a 45° angle.

24. Installation is the reverse of removal. Fill the engine with water, check the oil level in the engine and transmission, and fill the power steering system with the proper fluid. Bleed the steering system. Start the engine and check for leaks.

4.5 Liter V8

1. Remove the hood.

2. Drain the cooling system and remove the radiator.

3. Remove the cable plug from the temperature switch.

4. Remove the battery.

5. Drain the power steering reservoir.

6. Disconnect and plug the high pressure and return lines on the power steering pump.

7. On vehicles with air conditioning, swing the compressor out of the way without disconnecting the pressurized lines. The air conditioner lines should not be indiscriminately disconnected because of the possibility of physical harm from the pressurized gases.

8. Detach the fuel lines from the fuel filter, pressure regulator, and pressure sensor.

9. Loosen the line to the supply and anti-freeze tanks.

10. Disconnect the cables from the ignition coil and transistor ignition switchbox.

11. Disconnect the brake vacuum lines.

12. Detach the cable connections for the following:
    a. venturi control unit
    b. temperature sensor
    c. distributor
    d. temperature switch
    e. cold starting valve

13. Remove the regulating shaft by pushing it in the direction of the firewall.

14. Disconnect the thrust and pull-rods.

15. Disconnect the heater lines.

16. Detach the lines to the oil pressure and temperature gauges.

17. Remove the ground strap from the vehicle.

18. Detach the cables from the alternator, terminal bridge, and battery. Remove the battery.

19. Position a lifting sling on the engine and take up the slack in the chain.

20. Remove the left-hand engine mount and loosen the hex nut on the right-hand mount.

21. Remove the exhaust system. Remove the connecting rod chain on the rear level control valve and loosen the torsion bar slightly. Raise the vehicle

Supporting the transmission—3.5 and 4.5 V-8's.

1. U-Joint flange   4. U-Joint plate
2. Front driveshaft   5. Wooden block
3. Hex bolt

slightly at the rear and remove the exhaust system in a rearward direction.

22. Disconnect the handbrake cable.

23. Remove the shield plate from the transmission tunnel.

24. Loosen the driveshaft intermediate bearing and the driveshaft slide.

25. Support the transmission with a jack.

26. Mark the installation of the crossmember and remove it.

27. Unbolt the front U-joint flange on the transmission and push it back.

28. Disconnect the speedometer shaft, shift rod, control pressure rod, regulating linkage (on automatic transmissions), kickdown switch cable, starter lockout switch cable, and the cable for the backup light switch.

29. On manual transmissions, loosen the hydraulic clutch lines.

30. Remove the front engine mounting bolt and remove the engine at approximately a 45° angle. On 450SE and

450SEL, unbolt the engine on the mount from below, after removing the battery frame.

31. Installation is the reverse of removal. Lower the engine until it is behind the front axle carrier. Place a jack under the transmission and lower the engine into its compartment. While lowering the engine, install the right-hand shock mount.

Fill the engine with all required fluids and start the engine. Check for leaks.

280, 280C, 280S, 280E, 280SE

1. Scribe alignment marks on the hood hinges and remove the hood. Drain the coolant from the radiator and block.

2. Remove the radiator.

3. Disconnect the lines from the vacuum pump.

4. On vehicles with air conditioning, remove the compressor and place it aside.

CAUTION: *Do not remove the refrigerant lines from the compressor. Physical harm could result.*

5. Disconnect and tag all electrical connections from the engine.

6. Disconnect all coolant and vacuum lines from the engine.

7. Disconnect and plug the pressure oil lines from the power steering pump after draining the pump reservoir.

8. Remove the accelerator linkage control rod by pulling off the lock-ring and pushing the shaft in the direction of the firewall.

9. Loosen and remove the exhaust pipes from the manifold and transmission supports.

10. Disconnect the transmission linkage and all other connections.

11. Loosen the front right (driving direction) shock absorber from the front axle carrier.

Engine removal—280, 280C, 280E, 280S, 280SE. Inset shows lift attaching points.

12. Remove the left-hand engine shock absorber from the engine mount.

13. Attach a lifting device to the engine and tension the cables.

14. Unbolt the engine and transmission mounts and remove the engine at a 45° angle.

15. Installation is the reverse of removal. Be sure to check all fluids and fill or top up as necessary. Check all adjustments on the engine.

Cylinder Head

Removal and Installation

4 and 6-Cylinder Engines (Except 280, 280C, 280E, 280SE)

While cylinder head removal and installation may seem fairly straightforward, some precautions must be observed to ensure that valve timing is not disturbed.

1. Drain the radiator and remove all hoses and wires.

2. Remove the camshaft cover and associated throttle linkage, then press out the spring clamp from the notch in the rocker arm.

3. Push the clamp outward over the ball cap of the rocker, then depress the valve with a large screwdriver, and lift the rocker arm out of the ball pin head.

4. Remove the rocker arm supports and the camshaft sprocket nut.

5. On diesels, the rockers and their supports must be removed together.

6. Using a suitable puller, remove the camshaft sprocket after having first marked the chain, sprocket, and cam for ease in assembly.

7. Remove the sprocket and chain and wire it out of the way.

CAUTION: *Make sure the chain is securely wired so that it will not slide down into the engine.*

8. Unbolt the manifolds and exhaust header pipe and push them out of the way.

9. Loosen the cylinder head holddown bolts in the reverse order of that shown in torque diagrams for each model. The engine should be cold to prevent distortion. It is good practice to loosen each bolt a little at a time, working around the head, until all are free. This

prevents unequal stresses on the metal.

10. Reach into the engine compartment and gradually work the head loose from each end by rocking it. Never, under any circumstances, use a screwdriver between the head and block to pry, as the head will be scarred badly and may be ruined.

NOTE: *Four studs for attaching the rocker cover are screwed into the cylinder head on the 300D.*

11. Installation is the reverse of removal.

4.5 Liter V8 Engines

1. Drain the cooling system.

2. Remove the battery.

3. Remove the air cleaner.

4. Pull the cable plug from the temperature sensor.

5. Detach the vacuum hose from the venturi control unit.

6. Remove the following electrical connections:

    a. injection valves

    b. distributor

    c. venturi control unit

    d. temperature sensor and temperature switch

    e. starting valve

    f. temperature switch for the auxilliary fan.

7. Loosen the ring line on the fuel distributor.

The fuel feed system must be disconnected to remove the V8 cylinder head

1. Injection valve holding screws
2. Pressure regulator
    Arrows—disconnect ring line at arrows
3. Ring line
    Arrows—disconnect ring line at arrows

8. Loosen the screws on the injection valves and pressure regulator. Remove the ring line with the injection valves and pressure regulator.

9. Plug the holes for the injection valves in the cylinder head.

10. Remove the regulating shaft by disconnecting the pull-rod and the thrust rod.

11. Remove the ignition cable plug.

12. Loosen the heating connection on the intake manifold.

13. Loosen the vacuum connection for the central lock at the transmission.

14. Remove the oil filler tube from the right-hand cylinder head and remove the temperature connector.

15. Remove the oil pressure gauge line from the left-hand cylinder head.

16. Loosen the coolant connection on the intake manifold.

17. Remove the intake manifold.

18. Loosen the alternator belt and remove the alternator and mounting bracket.

19. Remove the electrical connections from the distributor and electronic ignition switchgear.

20. Drain some fluid from the power steering reservoir and disconnect and plug the return hose and high pressure supply line.

21. Disconnect the exhaust system.

22. Loosen the right-hand holder for the engine damper.

23. Remove the right-hand chain tensioner.

24. Matchmark the camshaft, camshaft sprocket, and chain. Remove the camshaft sprocket and chain after removing the cylinder head cover. Be sure to hang the chain and sprocket to prevent it from falling into the timing chain case.

25. Remove the upper slide rail.

26. Unscrew the cylinder head bolts. This should be done with a cold engine. Unscrew the bolts in the reverse order of the illustrated torque sequences. Unscrew all the bolts a little at a time and proceed in this manner until all the bolts have been removed.

27. Remove the cylinder head. Do not pry on the cylinder head.

28. Remove the cylinder head gasket.

29. Clean the cylinder head and cylinder block joint faces.

30. To install, position the cylinder head gasket.

31. Do not confuse the cylinder head gaskets. The left-hand head has two at-

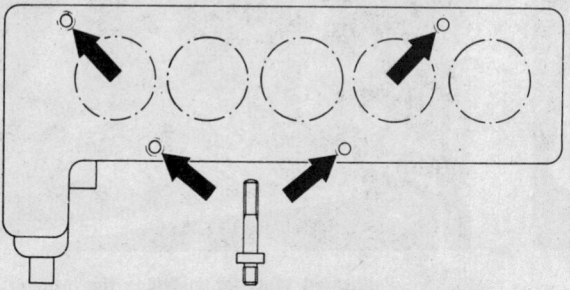

Studs (arrows) on the 300D are for attaching the rocker cover

Remove the bottom row of camshaft support bolts on V8

taching holes in the timing chain cover while the right-hand head has three.

32. Install the cylinder head and torque the bolts according to the illustrated torque sequence.

33. Further installation is the reverse of removal. Check the valve clearance and fill the engine with oil. Top up the power steering and bleed the power steering.

34. Run the engine and check for leaks.

280, 280C, 280S, 280E, 280SE

1. Completely drain the cooling system.

2. Remove the air filter.

3. Remove the radiator.

4. Remove the rocker arm cover.

5. Remove the battery. Remove the idler pulley and the holding bracket for the compressor.

6. Remove the compressor and bracket and lay them aside without disconnecting any of the lines.

CAUTION: *Disconnecting any of the refrigerant lines could result in physical harm.*

7. Unbolt the cover from the camshaft housing.

8. Disconnect the heater water line from the carburetor, the vacuum line on the starter housing, and the distributor vacuum line.

9. Disconnect all electrical connections, water lines, fuel lines, and vacuum lines which are connected to the cylinder head. Tag these for reassembly.

10. Remove the regulating linkage shaft.

11. Remove the EGR line between the exhaust return valve and the exhaust pipe.

12. Disconnect and plug the oil return line at the cylinder head.

13. At the thermostat housing, loosen the hose which passes between the thermostat housing and the water pump. Unscrew the bypass line on the water pump.

14. Loosen the oil dipstick tube from the clamp and bend it slightly sideward.

15. Unbolt the exhaust pipes from the exhaust manifolds and from the bracket on the transmission.

16. Force the tension springs out of the rocker arm with a screwdriver.

17. Remove all of the rocker arms.

18. Crank the engine to TDC. This can be done with a socket wrench on the crankshaft pulley bolt. The marks on the camshaft's sprockets and bearing housings must be aligned.

19. Hold the camshafts and remove the bolts which hold each camshaft gear to the camshaft.

20. Remove the upper slide rail. Knock out the bearing bolts with a puller.

21. Remove the chain tensioner.

22. Push both camshafts toward the rear and remove the camshafts' sprockets.

23. Remove the spacer sleeves on both camshafts. The sleeves are located in front of the camshaft bearings.

24. Remove the guide wheel by unscrewing the plug and removing the bearing bolt.

25. Lift off the timing chain and suspend the chain from the hood with a piece of wire. Pull out the guide gear.

26. Remove the slide rail in the cylinder head by removing the bearing pin with a puller.

27. Loosen the cylinder head bolts in small increments, using the reverse order of the tightening sequence. This should be done on a cold engine to prevent the possibility of head warpage.

28. Pull out the two bolts in the chain case with a magnet. Be careful not to drop the washers.

29. Pull up on the timing chain and force the tensioning rail toward the center of the engine.

30. Lift the cylinder head up in a vertical direction.

NOTE: *Mercedes-Benz recommends two men for this job.*

31. Remove the cylinder head gasket and clean the joint faces of the block and head.

32. To install, cut 2 pieces of wood ½ in. × 1 ½ in. × 9 ½ in. Lay one piece between cylinders 1 and 2 in the upright position and the other flat between cylinders 5 and 6.

33. Install the cylinder head in an inclined position so that the timing chain and tensioning rail can be inserted.

34. Lift the cylinder head at the front and remove the front piece of wood toward the exhaust side. Carefully lower the cylinder head until the bolt holes align.

35. Lift the head at the rear so that the board can be removed toward the exhaust side. Carefully lower the cylinder head until all of the bolt holes align.

36. Tighten the cylinder head bolts in gradual steps until they are fully tightened. Follow the torque sequence illustrated.

37. Check to be sure that both camshafts rotate freely after the bolts are tight.

38. The remainder of installation is the reverse of removal. Be sure that the spacer for the camshaft gear, with the engaging lugs for the vacuum pump drive gear, is installed on the exhaust side. Also, the washers for the bolts attaching the camshaft gears to the camshafts must be installed with the domed side against the head of the bolt.

39. Note that the attaching bolt for the exhaust camshaft gear is 0.2 in. shorter.

40. Be sure to adjust the valve clearance and fill the cooling system. Run the engine and check for leaks.

Overhaul

Overhaul procedures for cylinder heads are contained in the "Engine Rebuilding" section of this book. Consult this section for detailed overhaul procedures.

The marks on the camshaft and bearing housings must align on DOHC 6-cylinder engines when the engine is at TDC

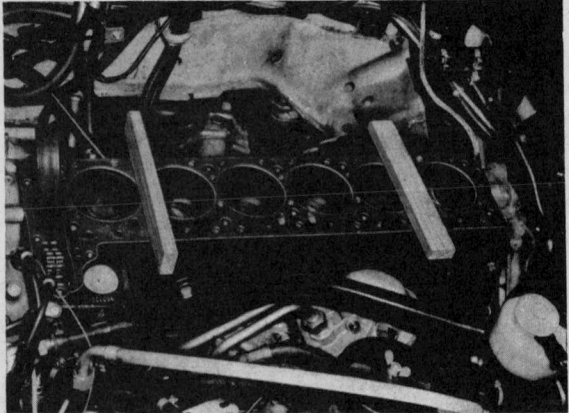

Fabricated tools for installing the cylinder head on DOHC 6-cylinder engines

Valve Guides
Removal and Installation

1. Remove the cylinder head.
2. Clean the valve guide with a brush, knocking away all loose carbon and oil deposits.
3. Knock out the old valve guide with a drift.
4. Check the bore in the cylinder head and clean up any rough spots. Use a reamer for this purpose. If necessary, the valve guide bore can be reamed for oversize valve guides.
5. Clean the basic bores for the valve guides.
6. Heat the cylinder head in water to approximately 176–194°F.
7. If possible cool the valve guides slightly.
8. Drive the valve guides into the bores with a drift. Coat the bores in the cylinder head with wax prior to installation and be sure that the circlip rests against the cylinder head.
9. Let the head cool and try to knock the valve guide out with light hammer blows and a plastic drift. If the guide can be knocked out, try another guide with a tighter fit.
10. Install the cylinder head.

Rocker Arms

Removal and Installation

Diesel Engines

Rocker arms on diesel engines can only be removed as a unit with the respective rocker arm blocks.

1. Detach the connecting rod for the venturi control unit from the bearing bracket lever and remove the bearing bracket from the rocker arm cover.
2. Remove the air vent line from the rocker arm cover and remove the rocker arm cover.
3. Remove the stretchbolts from the rocker arm blocks and remove the blocks with the rocker arms. Turn the crankshaft in each case so that the camshaft does not put any load on the rocker arms.
NOTE: *Turn the crankshaft with a socket wrench on the crankshaft pulley bolt. Do not rotate the engine by turning the camshaft sprocket.*
4. Before installing the rocker arms, check the sliding surfaces of the ball cup and rocker arms. Replace any defective parts.
5. To install, assemble the rocker arm blocks and insert new stretchbolts.
6. Tighten the stretchbolts. In each case, position the camshaft so that there is no load on the rocker arms. See the previous NOTE.
7. Check to be sure that the tension clamps have engaged with the notches of the rocker arm blocks.

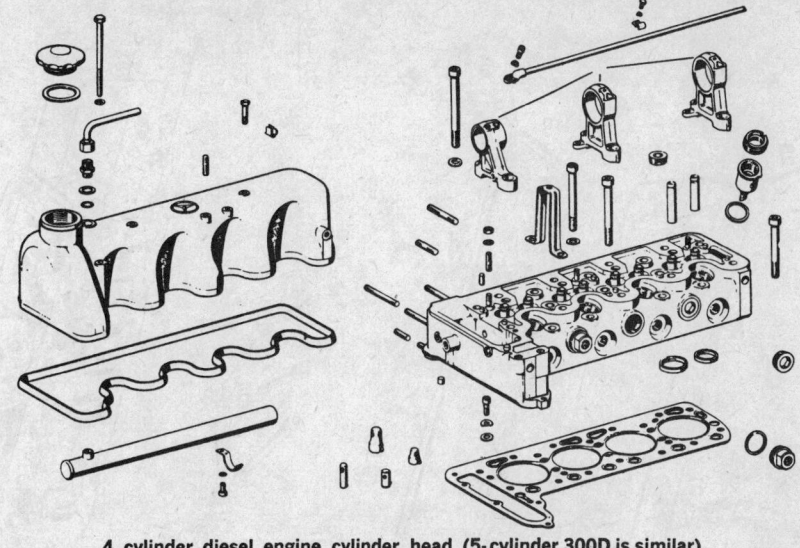

4 cylinder diesel engine cylinder head (5-cylinder 300D is similar).

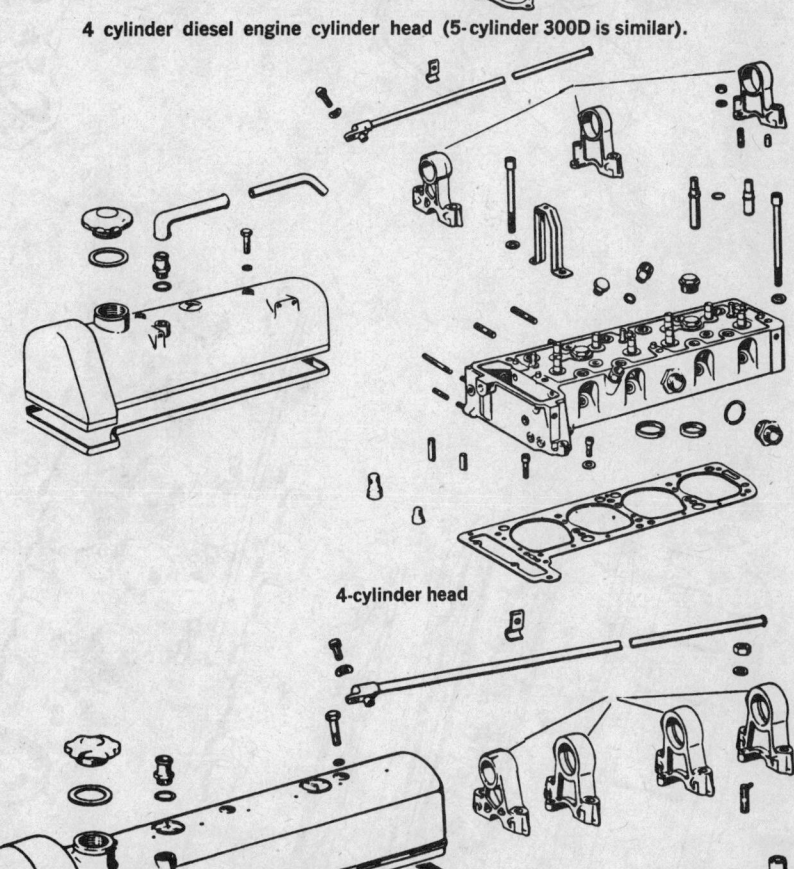

4-cylinder head

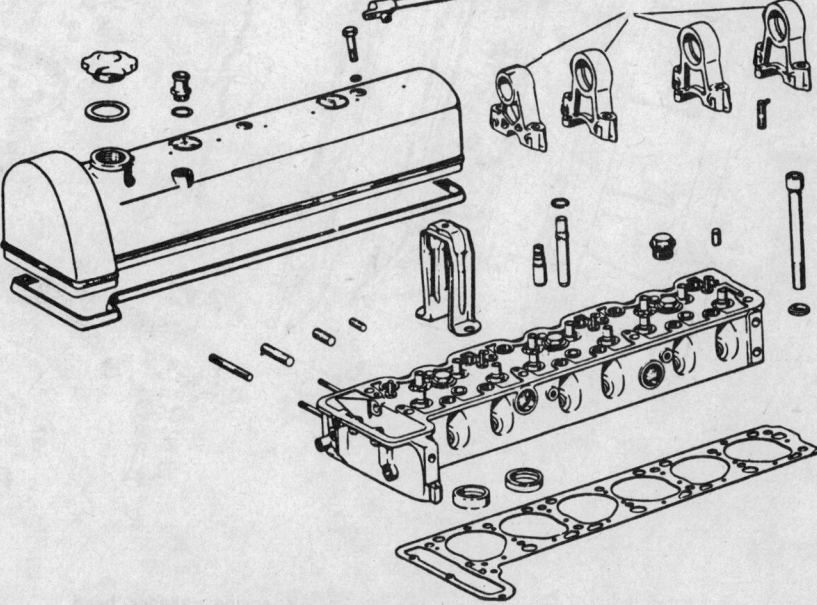

SOHC cylinder head

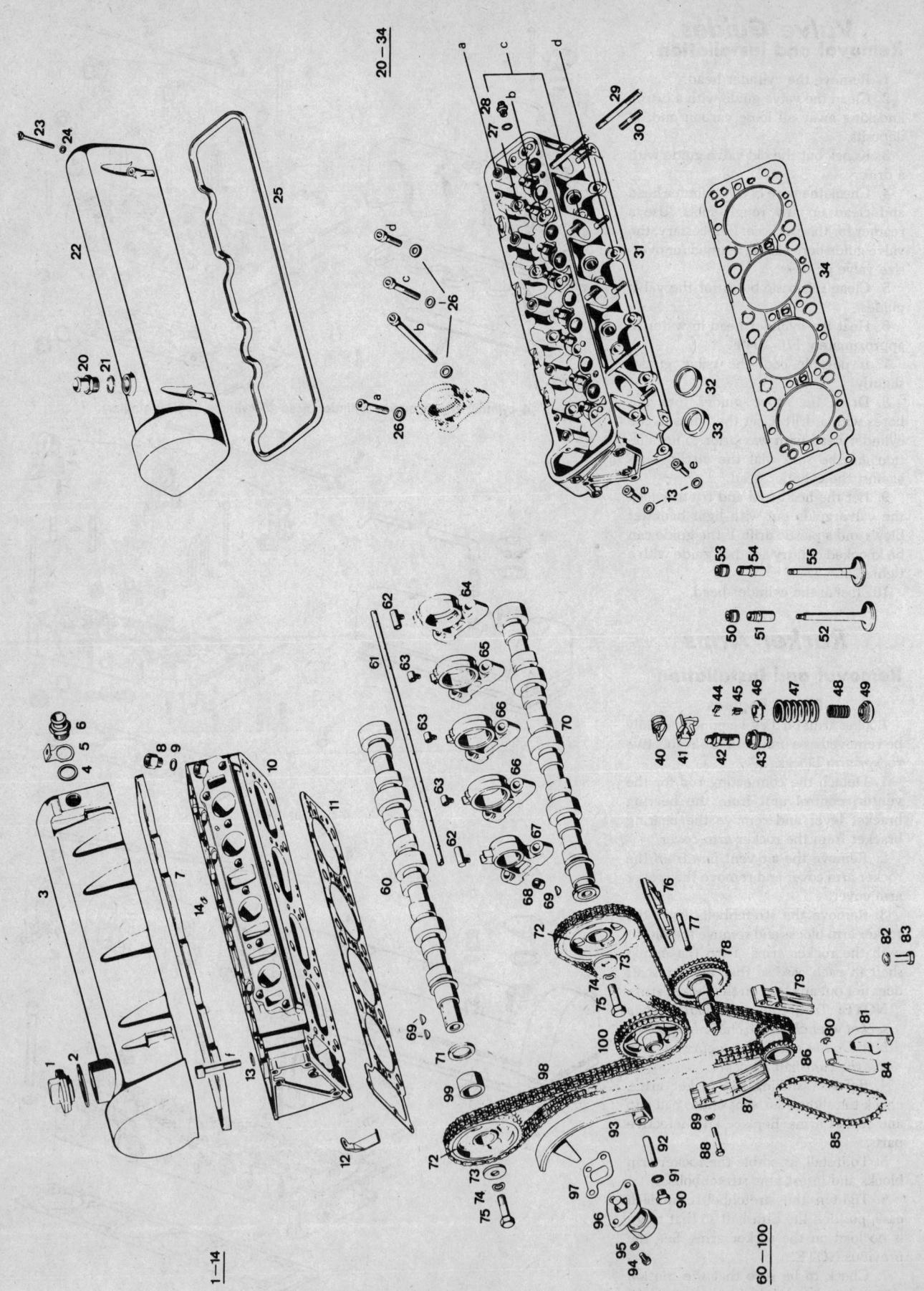

V-8 engine cylinder head

Cylinder head right 1-14

1. Filler plug
2. Sealing ring
3. Cylinder head cover
4. Sealing ring
5. Holder for cable to injection valves
6. Connection
7. Valve cover gasket
8. Connection to temperature sensor
9. Sealing ring
10. Cylinder head
11. Cylinder head gasket
12. Cable holder
13. 5 Washers
14. Hollow dowel pins

Cylinder head left 20-34

20. Connection
21. Sealing ring
22. Cylinder head cover
23. 8 Screws
24. 8 Sealing rings
25. Cylinder head cover gasket
26. 36 Washers
27. Sealing ring
28. Screw connection oil pressure gauge
29. 3 Studs
30. 13 Studs
31. Cylinder head
32. Valve seat ring—intake
33. Valve seat ring—exhaust
34. Cylinder head gasket

Cylinder head bolts

(a)—10 M 10 x 50chrauben)

(camshaft bearing fastening bolts)
(b)—10 M 10 x 155
(c)—18 M 10 x 80
(d)—8 M 10 x 55
(e)—4 M 8 x 30
(f)—1 M 8 x 70

Valve arrangement 40-55

40. Tensioning spring
41. Rocker arm
42. Adjusting screw
43. Threaded bushing
44. Thrust piece
45. Valve cone piece
46. Valve spring retainer
47. Outer valve spring
48. Inner valve spring
49. Rotator
50. Intake valve seal
51. Exhaust valve guide
52. Intake valve
53. Exhaust valve seal
54. Exhaust valve guide
55. Exhaust valve

Engine timing 60-100

60. Camshaft-right
61. Oil pipe (external lubrication)   Oil pipe to
62. Connecting piece   camshaft
63. Connecting piece   bearing
64. Camshaft bearing-flywheel end
65. Camshaft bearing 4

66. Camshaft bearing 2 and 3
67. Camshaft bearing-cranking end
68. 5 Hollow dowel pins
69. Spring washer
70. Camshaft-left
71. Compensating washer
72. Camshaft gear
73. Washer-camshaft gear
74. Spring washer
75. Bolt
76. 3 Slide rails
77. 6 Bearing bolts
78. Drive gear ignition distributor
79. Guide rail
80. Lockwasher
81. Spring—chain tensioner, oil pump
82. Washer
83. Screw
84. Clamp
85. Single roller chain (oil pump drive)
86. Crankshaft gear
87. Slide rail
88. 4 Screws
89. 4 Spring washers
90. Plug
91. Sealing ring
92. Bearing bolt
93. Tensioning lever
94. 2 Bolts
95. 2 Spring washers
96. Chain tensioner
97. Gasket
98. Double roller chain
99. Spacer ring
100. Idler gear

V-8 engine cylinder head

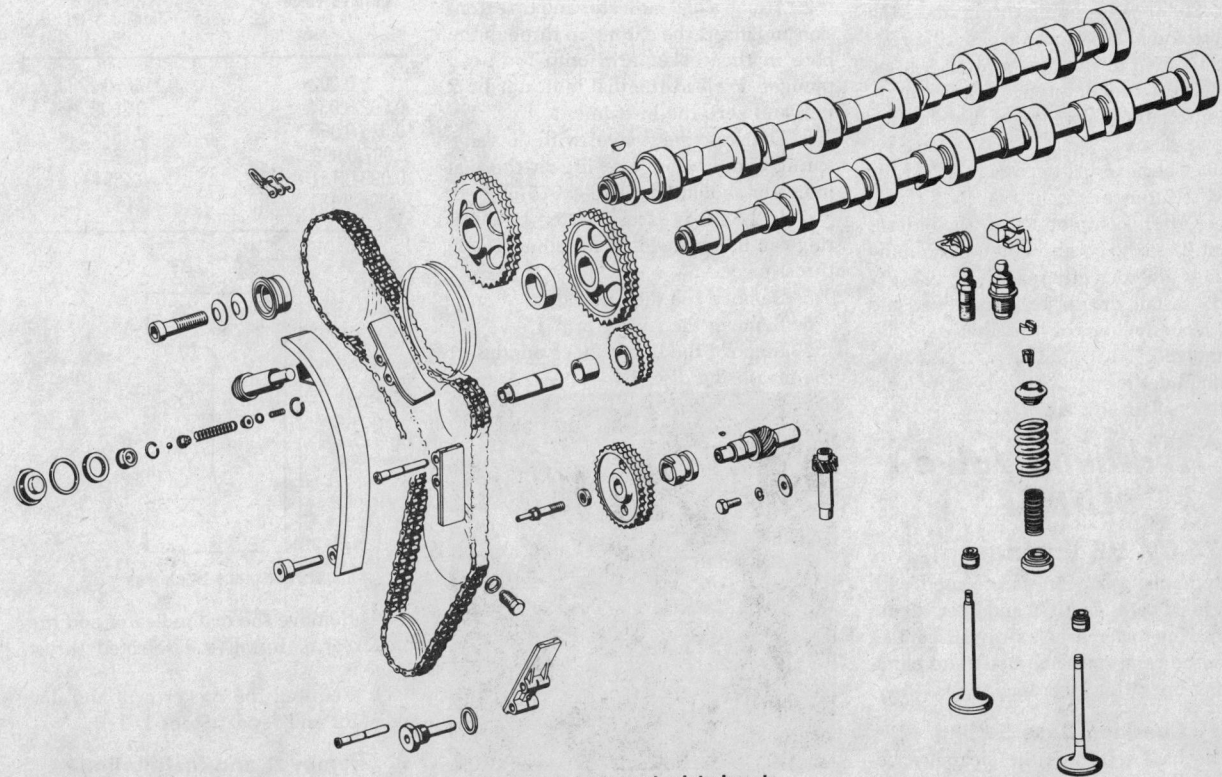

DOHC camshafts and related parts

8. Adjust the valve clearance.

9. Reinstall the rocker arm cover, air vent line, and bearing bracket for the reverse lever. Attach the connecting rod for the venturi control unit to the reversing lever.

10. Make sure that during acceleration, the control cable can move freely without binding.

11. Start the engine and check the rocker arm cover for leaks.

Gasoline Engines

Before removing the rocker arm(s), be sure that they are identified by their position relative to the camshaft lobe. They should be installed in the same place as they were before assembly.

1. Remove the rocker arm cover or covers.

2. Force the clamping spring out of the notch in the top of the rocker arm. Slide it in an outward direction across the ball socket of the rocker arm.

NOTE: *Turn the engine over each time to relieve any load from the rocker arm.*

3. On 4.5 models, the clamping spring must be forced from the adjusting screw with a screwdriver.

4. Force the valve down to remove load from the rocker arm.

5. Lift the rocker arm from the ball pin and remove the rocker arm.

6. To install the rocker arm(s), force the rocker arm down until the rocker arm and its ball socket can be installed in the top of the ball pin.

7. Install the rocker arms.

8. Slide the clamping spring across the ball socket of the rocker arm until it rests in the notch of the rocker arm.

9. On 4.5 models, engage the clamping spring into the recess of the adjusting screw.

10. Check and, if necessary, adjust the valve clearance.

11. After completion of the adjustment, check to be sure that the clamping springs are correctly seated.

12. Install the rocker arm cover and connect any hoses or lines that were disconnected.

13. Run the engine and check for leaks at the rocker arm cover.

Hydraulic Valve Lifters

1976–77 V8 Engines

Hydraulic valve lifters are used with overhead cams on 1976 and later V8 engines. The rocker arm is always in contact with the cam, reducing noise and eliminating operating clearance.

Checking Base Setting

The base setting is the clearance between the upper edge of the cylindrical

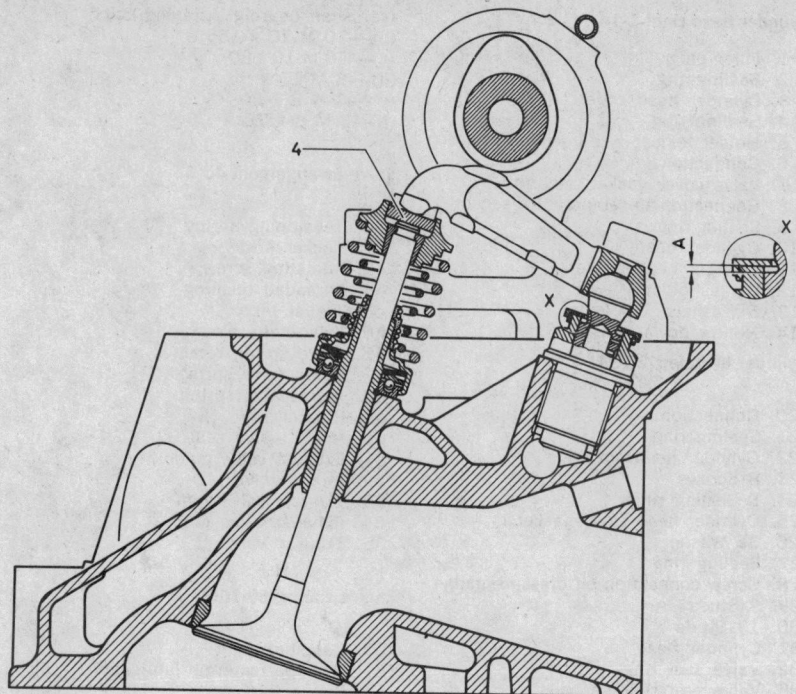

Cutaway view of hydraulic valve lifter

part of the plunger and the lower edge of the retaining cap (dimension A) when the cam lobe is vertical.

NOTE: *A dial indicator with an extension and a measuring thrust piece (MBNA # 100 589 16 63 00, 0.187 in. thick are necessary to perform this adjustment.*

1. Turn the cam lobe to a vertical position.

2. Attach a dial indicator and tip extension and insert the extension through the bore in the rocker arm onto the head plunger. Preload the dial indicator by 2 mm and zero the instrument.

3. Depress the valve with a valve spring compressor. The lift on the dial indicator should be 0.028–0.075 in.

4. If the lift is excessive, the base setting can be changed by installing a new thrust piece.

5. Remove the dial indicator.

6. Remove the rocker arm.

7. Remove the thrust piece and insert the measuring disc.

Measuring base setting

8. Install the rocker arm and repeat Steps 1–3.

9. Select a thrust piece according to the table. If the measured value was 0–0.002 in. and the 0.2146 in. thrust piece will not give the proper base setting, use the 0.2283 in. thrust piece.

Selective Thrust Pieces

Measured Value (in.)	Thrust Piece Thickness (S) (in.)
0-0.002	0.2146/0.2283
0.002-0.034	0.2008
0.035-0.066	0.1870
0.067-0.099	0.1732
0.099-0.131	0.1594
above 0.131	0.1457

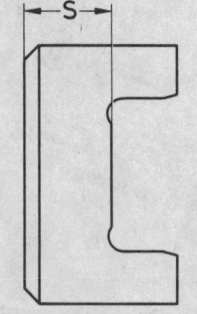

Thrust piece thickness

10. Remove the dial indicator and the rocker arm. Install the selected thrust piece.

11. Reinstall the rocker arm and dial indicator and repeat Steps 1–3.

Removal and Installation

Temporarily removed valve lifters

must be reinstalled in their original locations. When replacing worn rocker arms, the camshaft must also be replaced. If the rocker arm, or hydraulic lifter is replaced, check the base setting.

Remove the rocker arm and unscrew the valve lifter with a 24 mm socket.

Engine Disassembly

NOTE: *This procedure is general and intended to apply to all Mercedes-Benz engines. It is suggested, however, that you be entirely familiar with Mercedes-Benz engines and be equipped with the numerous special tools before attempting an engine rebuild. If at all in doubt concerning any procedure, refer the job to a qualified dealer. While this may be more expensive, it will probably produce better results in the end. If you attempt the rebuild yourself, refer often to the "Engine Rebuilding" section, and read the procedure carefully before beginning.*

1. Remove the engine and support it on an engine stand or other suitable support.

2. Set the engine at TDC and matchmark the timing chain and timing gear(s). Remove the cylinder head(s) and gasket(s).

3. Remove the oil pan bolts and the pan and, on most models, the lower crankcase section.

4. Remove the oil pump.

5. Matchmark the connecting rod bearing caps to identify the proper cylinder for reassembly. Matchmark the sides of the connecting rod and side of the bearing cap for proper alignment. Pistons should bear an arrow indicating the front. If not, mark the front of the piston with an arrow using a magic marker. Also identify pistons as to cylinder so they may be replaced in their original location.

6. Remove the connecting rod nuts, bearing caps, and lower bearing shells.

7. Place small pieces of plastic tubing on the rod bolts to prevent crankshaft damage.

8. Inspect the crankshaft journals for nicks and roughness and measure diameters.

9. Turn the engine over and ream the ridge from the top of the cylinders to remove all carbon deposits.

10. Using a hammer handle or other piece of hardwood, gently tap the pistons and rods out from the bottom.

11. The cylinder bores can be inspected at this time for taper and general wear.

12. Check the pistons for proper size and inspect the ring grooves. If any rings are cracked, it is almost certain that the grooves are no longer true, because broken rings work up and down. It is best to replace any such worn pistons.

13. The pistons, pins and connecting rods are marked with a color dot assembly code. Only parts having the same color may be used together.

14. If the cylinders are bored, make sure the machinist has the pistons beforehand-cylinder bore sizes are nominal, and the pistons must be individually fitted to the block. Maximum piston weight deviation in any one engine is 4 grams.

15. The flywheel and crankshaft are balanced together as a unit. Matchmark the location of the flywheel relative to the crankshaft, then remove the flywheel. Stretch bolts are used on some newer flywheels and can be identified by their "hourglass" shape. Once used, they should be discarded and replaced at assembly.

16. Remove the water pump, alternator, and fuel pump, if not done previously.

17. Unbolt and remove the vibration

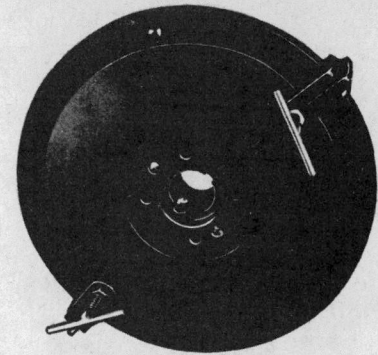

Clamping the vibration damper

damper and crankshaft pulley. On certain models, it is necessary to clamp the vibration damper with C-clamps before removing the bolts. Otherwise, the vibration damper will come apart.

18. Remove the timing chain tensioner and chain cover.

19. Matchmark the position of the tim-

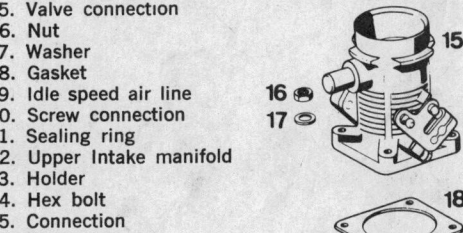
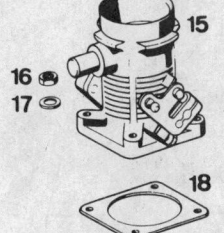

15. Valve connection
16. Nut
17. Washer
18. Gasket
19. Idle speed air line
20. Screw connection
21. Sealing ring
22. Upper intake manifold
23. Holder
24. Hex bolt
25. Connection
26. Sealing ring

27. Gasket
28. Screw connection
29. Sealing ring
30. Screw connection
31. Sealing ring
32. Bottom intake manifold
33. Rubber connecting piece
35. Hex bolt
34. Hex bolt
36. Sealing ring
37. Plug
38. Hose

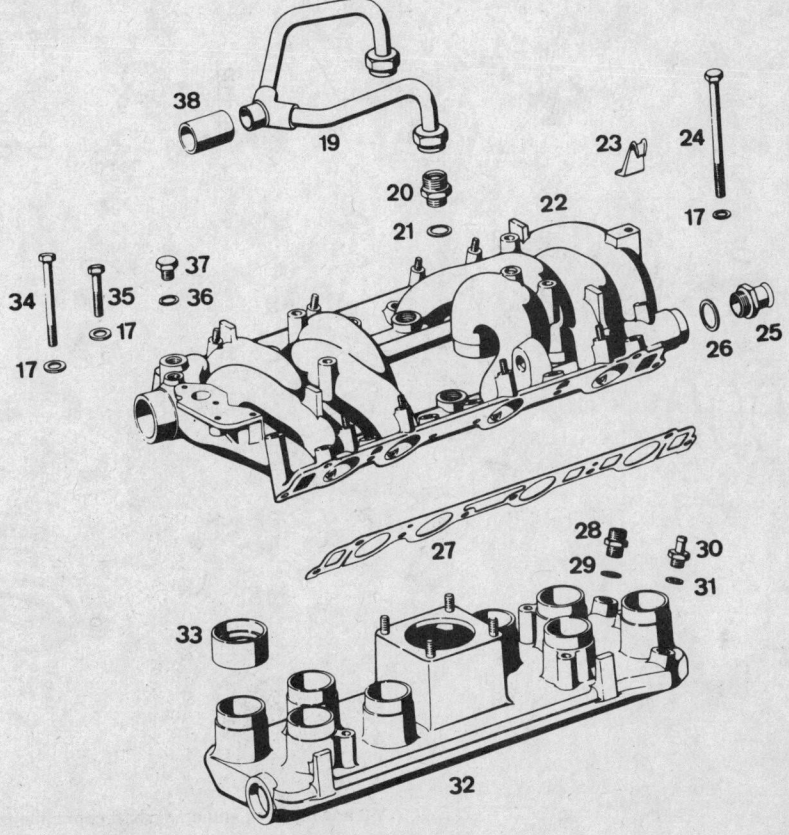

V8 intake manifold

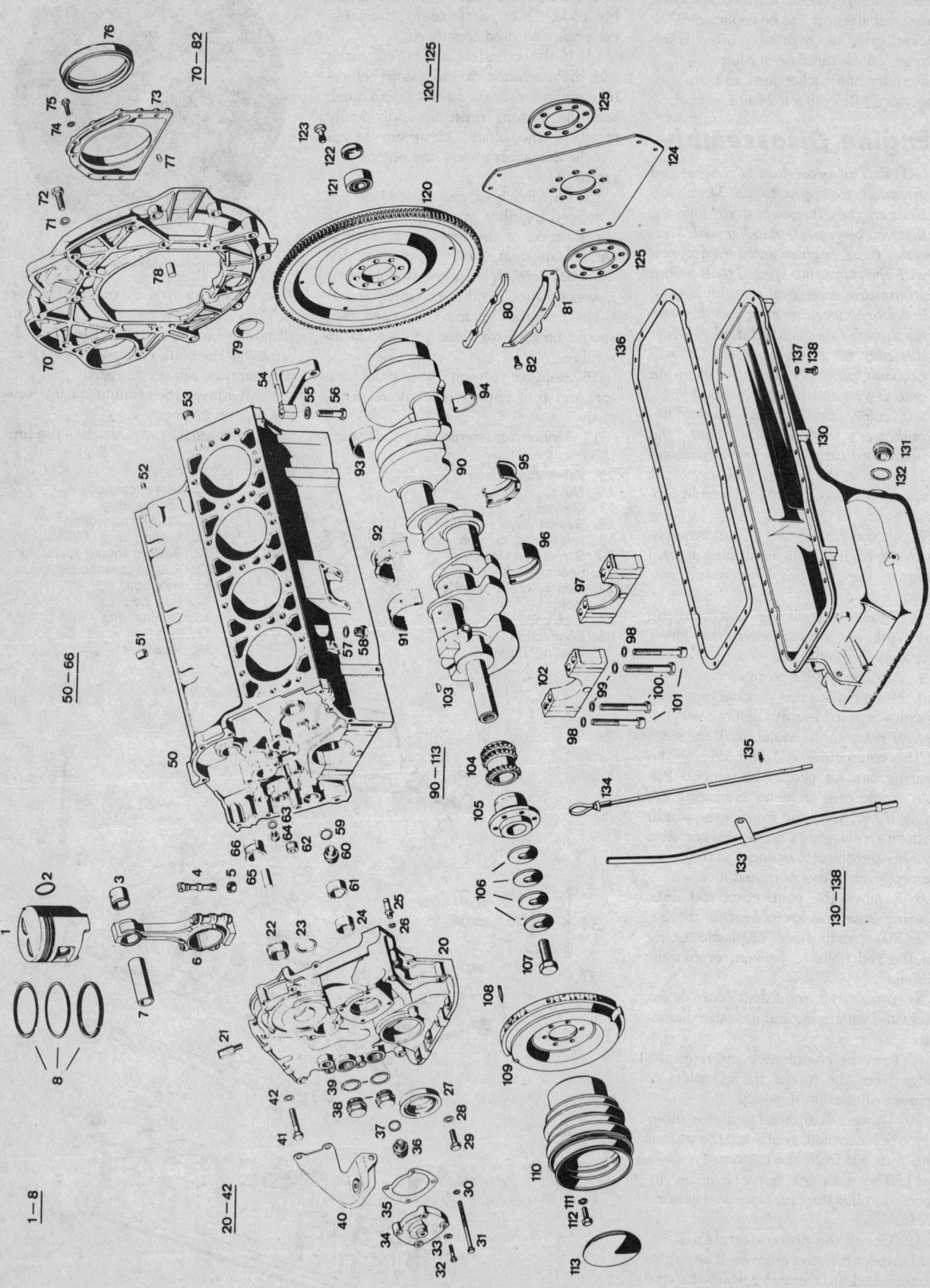

V-8 engine block and crankshaft components

Piston and connecting rod 1-8

1. Piston
2. Circlip
3. Connecting rod bearing
4. Connecting rod bolt
5. Nut
6. Connecting rod
7. Wrist pin
8. Piston rings

Timing housing cover 20-42

20. Timing housing cover
21. Threaded bolts for adjusting lever of ignition distributor
22. Bearing bushing (guidewheel bearing)
23. 2 O-rings
24. Bearing bushing (intermediate gear shaft)
25. Bolt
26. Spring plate
27. Crankshaft sealing ring (front)
28. Washer
29. Screw
30. Washer
31. Screw
32. 4 Screws
33. 4 Washers
34. End cover
35. Gasket
36. Screw connection
37. Sealing ring
38. Plug
39. Sealing ring
40. Holder-engine damper
41. 6 Screws
42. 6 Washers

Cylinder crankcase 50-66

50. Cylinder block
51. 4 Hollow dowel pins
52. 3 Plugs (oil duct)
53. Plug (rear main oil duct)
54. 2 Supporting angle pieces
55. 2 Washers
56. 2 Screws
57. 2 Sealing rings
58. 2 Plugs
59. Sealing ring
60. Screw connection
61. Bearing bushing intermediate gear shaft rear
62. Plug (front main oil duct)
63. Sealing ring
64. Plug
65. 2 Cyl. pins
66. Idler gear bearing

Intermediate flange 70-82

70. Intermediate flange
71. 4 Spring washers
72. 4 Screws
73. Cover (crankcase sealing ring, rear)
74. 8 Washers
75. 3 Screws
76. Crankshaft sealing ring (rear)
77. 2 Cyl. pins
78. 2 Set pins
79. Cover
80. Sealing strip
81. Cover plate
82. 3 Screws

Crankshaft 90-113

90. Crankshaft
91. Main bearing shell (top)
92. Fitted bearing shell (top)
93. Connecting rod bearing shell (top)
94. Connecting rod bearing shell (bottom)
95. Fitted bearing shell (bottom)
96. Main bearing shell (bottom)
97. Crankshaft bearing cap (fitted bearing)

98. 10 Washers
99. 10 Washers
100. 10 Hex bolts
101. 10 Hex socket bolts
102. Crankshaft bearing cap (main bearing)
103. Key
104. Crankshaft gear
105. Vibration damper pulley
106. Plate springs
107. Bolt
108. Indicating needle
109. Vibration damper
110. Pulley
111. 6 Circlips
112. 6 Screws
113. Pulley cover

Flywheel and driven plate 120-125

120. Flywheel

121. Ball bearing 6202
122. Closing ring
123. 8 bolts
124. Driven plate
125. Spacers

Oil pan 130-138

130. Oil pan
131. Oil drain plug
132. Sealing ring
133. Guide tube (oil dipstick)
134. Oil dipstick
135. Stop-ring (oil dipstick)
136. Oil pan gasket
137. 30 washers
138. 30 Screws

V-8 engine block and crankshaft components

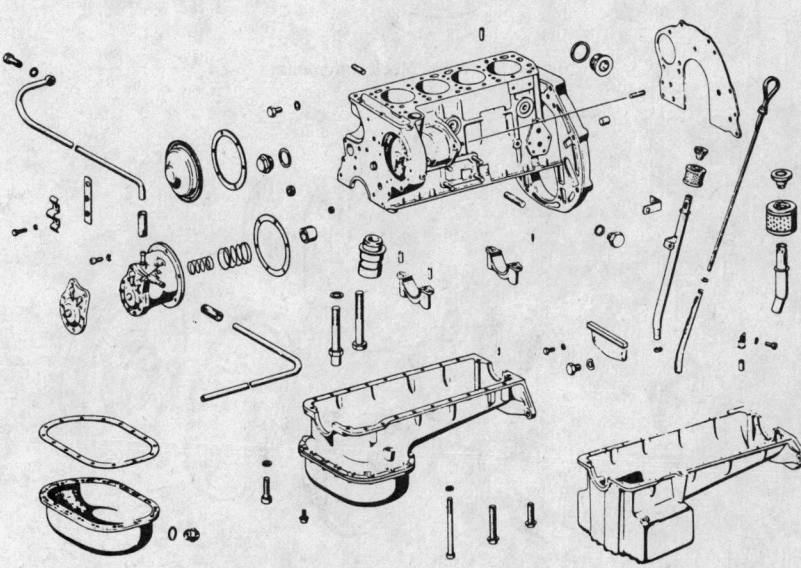

4-cylinder Diesel engine cylinder block components. (5-cylinder 300D is similar).

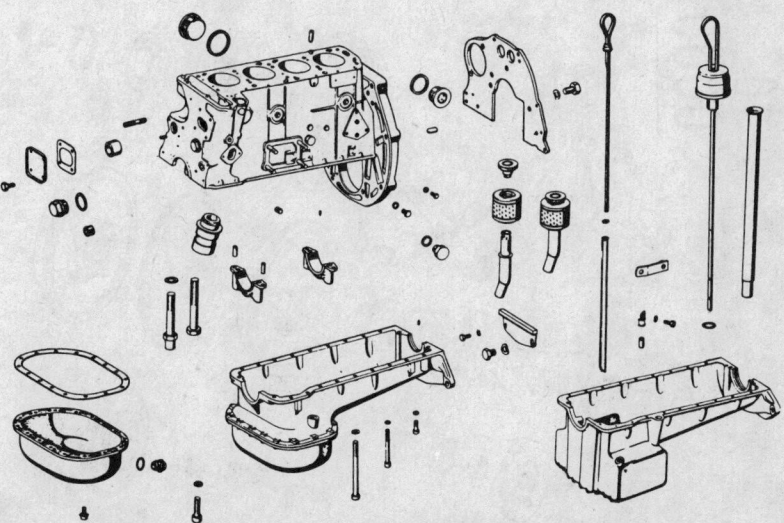

4-cylinder gasoline engine cylinder block components.

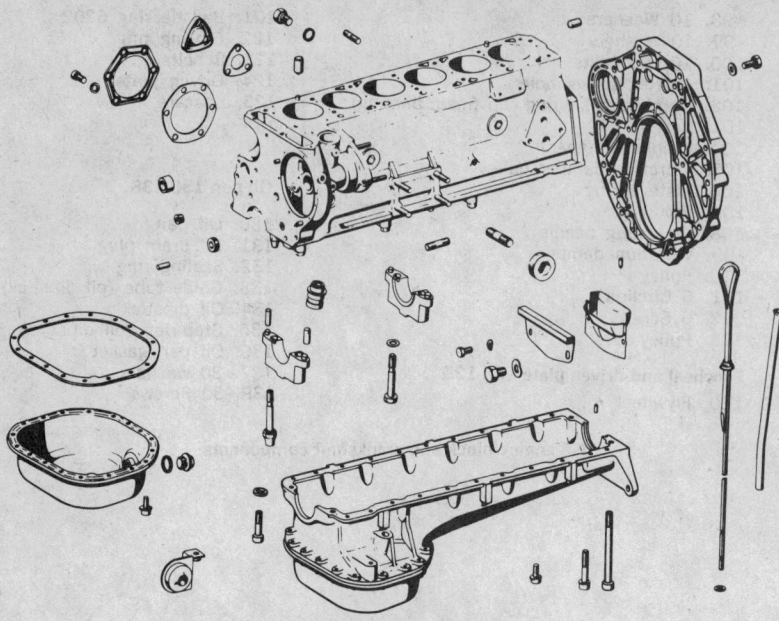

6-cylinder engine block components

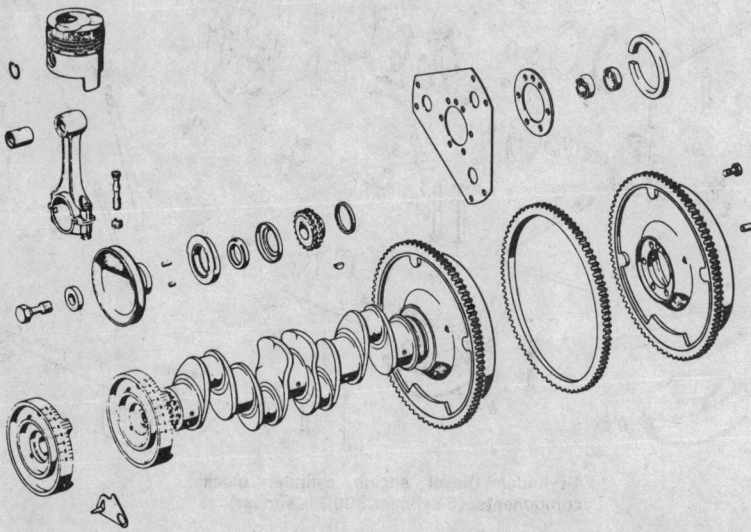

4-cylinder diesel engine crankshaft components (5-cylinder 300D is similar)

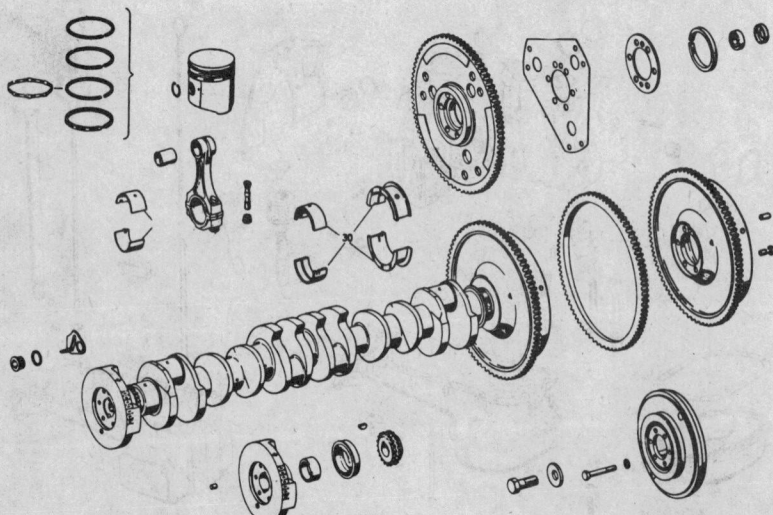

6-cylinder crankshaft and components (4- cylinder engine is similar).

ing chain on the timing gear of the crank-shaft.

20. Matchmark the main bearing caps for number and position in the block. It is important that they are installed in their original positions. Most bearing caps are numbered for position. Remove the bearing caps.

21. Lift the crankshaft out of the block in a forward direction.

22. With the block completely disassembled, inspect the water passages and bearing webs for cracks. If the water passages are plugged with rust, they can be cleaned out by boiling the block at a radiator shop.

CAUTION: *Aluminum parts must not be boiled out. They will be eroded by chemicals.*

23. Measure piston ring end-gap by sliding a new ring into the bore and measuring. Measure the gap at top, bottom, and midpoint of piston travel and correct by filing or grinding the ring ends.

24. To check bearing clearances, use Plastigage® inserted between the bearing and the crankshaft journal. Blow out all crankshaft oil passages before measuring; torque the bolts to specification. Plastigage® is a thin plastic strip that is crushed by the bearing and cap and spreads out an amount in proportion to clearance. After torquing the bearing cap, remove the cap and compare the width of the Plastigage® with the scale.

NOTE: *Do not rotate the crankshaft. Bearing shells of various thicknesses are available, and should be used to correct clearance; it may be necessary to machine the crankshaft journals undersize to obtain the proper oil clearance.*

CAUTION: *Use of shim stock between bearings and caps to decrease clearance is not a good practice.*

25. Check crankshaft end-play using a feeler gauge.

26. When installing new piston rings, ring grooves must be cleaned out, preferably using a special groove cleaner, although a broken ring will work as well. After installing the rings, check ring side clearance.

Engine Assembly

1. Assemble the engine using all new gaskets and seals and make sure all parts are properly lubricated. Bearing shells and cylinder walls must be lubricated with engine oil before assembly. Make sure no metal chips remain in the cylinder bores or crankcase.

NOTE: *1975 V-8 s use camshafts coded 56 and 57. These cams have an oil groove in the 5th bearing journal and are not interchangeable with previous designs.*

2. To install pistons and rods, turn the engine right side up and insert the rods

into the cylinders. Clamp the rings to the piston, with their gaps equally spaced around the circumference, using a piston ring compressor. Gently tap the piston into the bore, using a hammer handle or similar hard wood, making sure the rings clear the edge.

3. Torque the rod and main caps to specification and try to turn the crankshaft by hand. It should turn with moderate resistance, not spin freely or be locked up.

4. Disassemble the oil pump and check the gear backlash. Place a straightedge on the cover and check for warpage. Deep scoring on the cover usually indicates that metal or dirt particles have been circulating through the oil system. Covers can be machined, but it is best to replace them if damaged.

5. Install the oil pump.

6. Install the oil pan and lower crankcase and tighten the bolts evenly all around, then turn the engine right side up and install the cylinder head gasket and head. Make sure the gasket surfaces are clean before installation; a small dirt particle could cause gasket failure. Tighten the cylinder head bolts in sequence, in stages, to insure against distortion. Don't forget the small bolts at the front of the head.

7. Install the engine into the vehicle. **NOTE:** *It is a good practice to retighten all bolts after about 500 miles of running, although this is not absolutely necessary. The cylinder head is the only exception to this and should be retightened to specifications after 500 miles. It is also a good practice to use a good break-in oil after an engine overhaul. Be sure that all fluids have been replaced and perform a general tune-up. Check the valve timing.*

8. Some models may use connecting rod stretch bolts. These bolts are tightened by angle of rotation rather than by use of a torque wrench. Make sure the stretch section diameter is greater than 0.35 in. (−0.003 in.). Remove the bolt from the rod and measure the diameter at the point normally covered by the rod; it should be at least 0.31 in. For reasons of standardization, the angle of rotation for all the screw connections tightened ac-

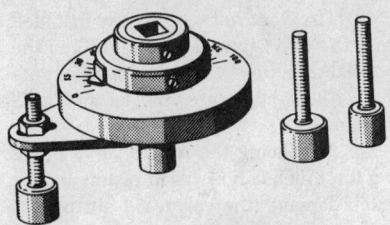

Preferred tools for torqueing by angle rotation. Torque wrench also needed

cording to angle of rotation has been set to 90° + 10°. The initial torque for connecting rod bolts has been increased to 22–35 ft lbs.

Valve Timing

Ideally, this operation should be performed by a dealer who is equipped with the necessary tools and knowledge to do the job properly.

Checking valve timing is too inaccurate at the standard tappet clearance, therefore timing values are given for an assumed tappet clearance of 0.4 mm. The 280, 280C, 280E, 280S and 280SE engines are not measured at 0.4 mm. but rather at 2 mm.

1. To check the timing, remove the rocker arm cover and spark plugs. On 4.5 liter V-8 s, 280, 280C, 280E, 280SE and 280S models, remove the tensioning springs. On the 280, 280C, 280S, 280E and 280SE engine install the testing thrust pieces. Eliminate all valve clearance.

2. Install a degree wheel.

3. A pointer must be made out of a bent section of 3/16 in. brazing rod or

coathanger wire, and attached to the engine.

NOTE: *If the degree wheel is attached to the camshaft as shown, values read from it must be doubled.*

4. With a 22 mm wrench on the crankshaft pulley, turn the engine, in the direction of rotation, until the TDC mark on the vibration damper registers with the pointer and the distributor rotor points to the No. 1 cylinder mark on the housing.

5. Turn the loosened degree wheel until the pointer lines up with the 0° (OT) mark, then tighten it in this position.

6. Continue turning the crankshaft in the direction of rotation until the camshaft lobe of the associated valve is vertical (e.g., points away from the rocker arm surface). To take up tappet clearance, insert a feeler gauge (thick enough to raise the valve slightly from its seat) between the rocker arm cone and the pressure piece.

7. Attach the indicator to the cylinder head so that the feeler rests against the valve spring retainer of No. 1 cylinder intake valve. Preload the indicator at least 0.008 in. then set to zero, making sure the feeler is exactly perpendicular on the valve spring retainer. It may be necessary to bleed down the chain tensioner at this time to facilitate readings.

8. Turn the crankshaft in the normal direction of rotation, again using a wrench on the crankshaft pulley, until the indicator reads 0.016 in. less than zero reading.

9. Note the reading of the degree

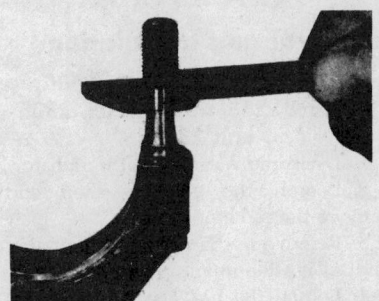

Checking stretchbolts (connecting rod stretchbolt illustrated).

Engine set up for checking valve timing

1. Pointer for graduation on crankshaft
2. TDC mark or graudation on degree wheel of crankshaft
3. Degree wheel from endpaper
4. Pointer on camshaft
5. Dial micrometer with feeler and holder
6. Bracket for camshaft cover
7. Distributor rotor arm
8. Mark on distributor housing for cylinder No. 1

Dial indicator installed for checking valve timing.

1. Feeler gauge
2. Valve spring retainer
3. Dial indicator prod
4. Dial indicator holder
5. Dial indicator

wheel at this time, remembering to double the reading if the wheel is mounted to the camshaft sprocket.

10. Again turn the crankshaft until the valve is closing and the indicator again reads 0.016 in. less than zero reading. Make sure, at this time, that preload has remained constant, then note the reading of the degree wheel. The difference between the two degree wheel readings is the timing angle (number of degrees the valve is open) for that valve.

11. The other valves may be checked in the same manner, comparing them against each other and the opening values given in "Tune-up Specifications." It must be remembered that turning the crankshaft contrary to the normal direction of rotation results in inaccurate readings.

12. If valve timing is not to specification, the easiest way of bringing it in line is to install an offset woodruff key in the camshaft sprocket. This is far simpler than replacing the entire timing chain and it is the factory-recommended way of changing valve timing provided the timing chain is not stretched too far or worn out. Offset keys are available in the following sizes:

Valve Timing Offset Keys

Offset	Part No.	For a correction at crankshaft of
2° (0.7)	621 991 04 67	4°
3°20′ (0.9)	621 991 02 67	6½°
4° (1.1)	621 991 01 67	8°
5° (1.3)	621 991 00 67	10°

13. The woodruff key must be installed with the offset toward the "right", in the normal direction of rotation, to effect advanced valve opening; toward the "left" to retard.

14. Advancing the intake valve opening too much can result in piston and/or valve damage (the valve will hit the piston). To check the clearance between the valve head and the piston, the crankshaft must be positioned at 5° ATDC (on intake stroke). The procedure is essentially the same as for measuring valve timing.

15. As before, the dial indicator is set to zero after being preloaded, then the valve is depressed until it touches the top of the piston. As the normal valve head-to-piston clearance is approximately 0.-035 in., you can see that the dial indicator must be preloaded at least 0.042 in. so there will be enough movement for the feeler.

If the clearance is much less than 0.035 in., the cylinder head must be removed and checked for carbon deposits. If none exist, the valve seat must be cut deeper into the head. Always set the ignition timing after installing an offset key.

Diesel Engines Only

1. After valve timing is checked, measure the distance between the exhaust valve and the piston at 5° BTDC as well as the intake valve to piston clearance at 5° ATDC. (All measurements taken at the top of the exhaust stroke.) The clearance must be at least 0.050 in., intake and exhaust.

ENGINE COOLING

Mercedes-Benz passenger car engines are all equipped with closed, pressurized, water cooling systems. Care should be exercised when dealing with the cooling system. Always turn the radiator cap to the first notch and allow the pressure to decrease before completely removing the cap.

Radiator

Removal and Installation

1. Remove the radiator cap.
2. Unscrew the radiator drain plug and drain the coolant from the radiator. If all of the coolant in the system is to be drained, move the heater controls to WARM and open the drain cocks on the engine block.
3. If the car is equipped with an oil cooler, drain the oil from the cooler.
4. If equipped, loosen the radiator shell.
5. Loosen the hose clips on the top and bottom radiator hoses and remove the

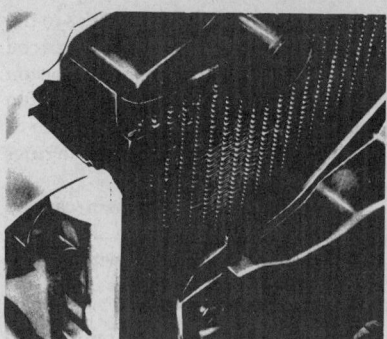

Radiator retaining springs on 350SL, 450-SL, 450SLC, 450SE, 450SEL.

hoses from the connections on the radiator.

6. Unscrew and plug the bottom line on the oil cooler.
7. If the car is equipped with an automatic transmission, unscrew and plug the lines on the transmission cooler.
8. Disconnect the right-hand and left-hand rubber loops and pull the radiator up and out of the body. On 350 and 450 SL and SLC and 280S models, push the retaining springs toward the fenders to remove the radiator from the shell.
9. Inspect and replace any hoses which have become hardened or spongy.
10. Install the radiator shell and radiator (if the shell was removed) from the top and connect the top and bottom hoses to the radiator.
11. Bolt the shell to the radiator.
12. Attach the rubber loops or position the retaining springs, as applicable.
13. Position the hose clips on the top and bottom hoses.
14. Attach the lines to the oil cooler.
15. On cars with automatic transmissions, connect the lines to the transmission cooler.
16. Move the heater levers to the WARM position and slowly add coolant, allowing air to escape.
17. Check the oil level and fill if necessary. Run the engine for about one minute at idle with the filler neck open.
18. Add coolant to the specified level. Install the radiator cap and turn it until it seats in the second notch. Run the engine and check for leaks.

Water Pump

Removal and Installation

220/8, 220D/8, 250/8, 250C, 280SE/8, 280, 280C, 280S, 280E and 280SE

1. Drain the water from the radiator.
2. Loosen the radiator shell and remove the radiator.
3. Remove the fan with the coupling and set it aside in an upright position.
4. Loosen the belt around the water pump pulley and remove the belt.
5. Remove the bolts from the har-

monic balancer and remove the balancer and pulley.

6. Unbolt and remove the water pump.

7. Installation is the reverse of removal. Tighten the belt and fill the cooling system.

280SE 4.5, 280SEL 4.5, 300SEL 4.5, 350SL, 450SL, 450SLC, 450SE and 450SEL

1. Drain the water from the radiator and block.

2. Remove the air cleaner.

3. Loosen and remove the drive belt.

4. Disconnect the upper water hose from the radiator and thermostat housing.

5. Remove the fan and coupling.

6. On 3.5 engines, remove the bottom water hose from the water pump housing.

7. Remove the hose from the intake (top) connection of the water pump.

8. Set the engine at TDC. Matchmark the distributor and engine and remove the distributor. Crank the engine with a socket wrench on the crankshaft pulley bolt or with a screwdriver inserted in the balancer. Crank in the normal direction of rotation only.

9. Turn the balancer so that the recesses provide access to the mounting bolts. Remove the mounting bolts. Rotate the engine in the normal direction of rotation only.

10. Remove the water pump.

11. Clean the mounting surfaces of the water pump and block.

12. Installation is the reverse of removal. Always use a new gasket. Set the engine at TDC and install the distributor so that the distributor rotor points to the notch on the distributor housing. Fill the cooling system and check and adjust the ignition timing.

Thermostat

Removal and Installation

220/8, 220D/8, 250/8, 250C, 280S/8, 280SE/8

The thermostat housing is a light metal casting attached directly to the cylinder head.

1. Open the radiator cap and de-pressurize the system.

2. Open the radiator drain cock and partially drain the coolant. Drain enough coolant to bring the coolant level below the level of the thermostat housing.

3. Remove the four bolts on the thermostat housing cover and remove the cover.

4. Note the installation position of the thermostat and remove it.

5. Installation is the reverse of removal. Be sure that the thermostat is positioned with the ball valve at the highest

point and that the 4 bolts are tightened evenly against the seal.

6. Refill the cooling system and check for leaks.

280SE 4.5, 280SEL 4.5, 300SEL 4.5, 450SE, 450SEL, 450SL and 450SLC

1. Drain the coolant from the radiator and block.

2. Remove the air cleaner.

3. Disconnect the battery and remove the alternator. Usually this need not be done on 450SL, 450SLC, 450SE or 450SEL.

4. Unscrew the housing cover on the side of the water pump and remove the thermostat. Note that the thermostat used on 4.5 liter V-8 models differs from the one used on other models due to a different positioning of the ball valve.

5. If a new thermostat is to be installed, always install a new sealing ring.

6. Installation is the reverse of removal. Be sure to tighten the screws on the housing cover evenly to prevent leaks. Refill the cooling system and check for leaks.

280, 280C, 280S, 280E and 280SE

1. Drain the coolant from the radiator.

2. Remove the vacuum pump and put the pump aside.

3. Remove the three bolts on the thermostat housing.

4. Remove the cover and the thermostat.

5. Installation is the reverse of re-

moval. Install the thermostat so that the ball valve is at the highest point. Refill the cooling system.

EMISSION CONTROLS *1972*

Various modifications were made to the previous years system. The engine compression ratio was reduced to 8.0:1 on all engines except the diesel. The shift

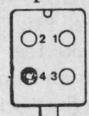

Terminals on 4 pole relay box (all models)

Terminals on 6 pole relay box (all models)

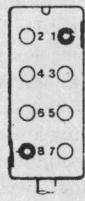

Terminals on 8 pole relay box (all models)

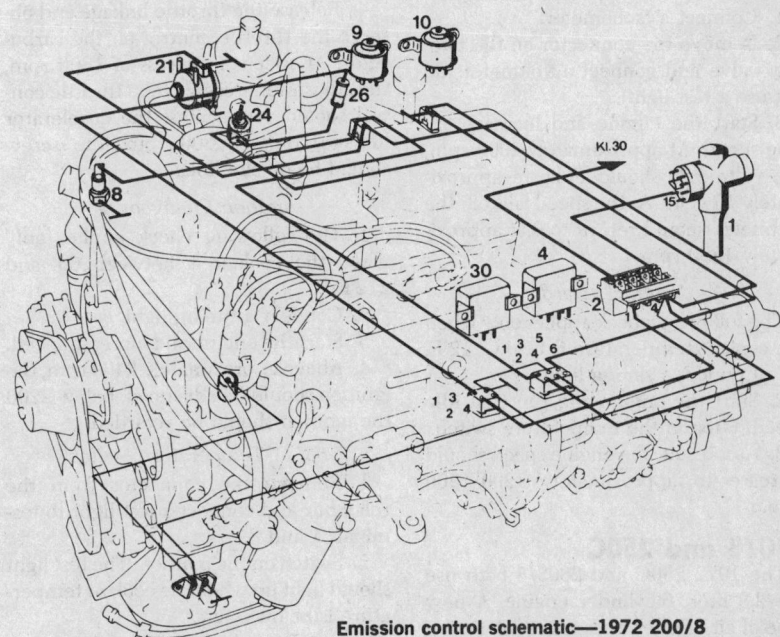

Emission control schematic—1972 200/8

1. Ignition starter switch
2. Fuse box
3. Ignition coil
4. RPM switch
8. Temperature switch (212° F)
9. Two-way valve
   (ignition changeover)
10. Two-way valve
    (Throttle positioner lift)
21. Heating element for
    automatic choke
24. Idling speed shutoff valve
26. Connector
30. Delay switch

points of the automatic transmission on the 250, 250C, and 280SE were modified. The fuel evaporation control system remains unchanged, but the evaporation valve unit was improved and relocated under the vehicle in the rear seat area.

220/8

An ignition retard device was installed in conjunction with a temperature switch in the thermostat housing. At idle speed, manifold vacuum is ported to the distributor via a two-way valve and this retards the timing. When coolant temperatures reach 212°F., the temperature switch breaks the connection of manifold vacuum and prevents the retard device from functioning.

While decelerating, a throttle positioner is operated by the two-way valve and an rpm switch, which functions above 2000 rpm. At speeds below 1800 rpm, the throttle positioner is deactivated and manifold vacuum takes over.

Checking the System

Throttle Positioner

1. Connect a tachometer to the engine.

2. Start the engine and increase the speed to approximately 2500 rpm.

3. Release the accelerator linkage and observe the tachometer. At speeds above 1800 rpm, the adjusting screw should rest against the actuating lever. At speeds below 1800 rpm, the adjusting screw should be off the actuating lever.

RPM Switch

1. Connect a tachometer.

2. Remove the connector on the two-way valve and connect a voltmeter (do not use a test light).

3. Start the engine and increase engine speed. At approximately 2000 rpm, the voltmeter should indicate approximately 13 volts. As the speed falls off, the voltmeter should return to 0 at approximately 1800 rpm.

Ignition Retard

The following check applies only when the coolant temperature is below 212°F.

1. Connect a timing light.

2. Start the engine and run it at idle speed. Ground the temperature switch.

3. As a result, the engine speed should increase to approximately 1200–1500 rpm.

250/8 and 250C

The 1972 250C and 280S/8 both use the 2.8 liter, 6-cylinder engine. A new type of air cleaner is used in conjunction with the 32/40 INAT carburetor. The distributor also has a modified advance curve and the 63°F. temperature switch has been relocated to the oil filter housing. Ignition changeover is accomplished by a three-way valve in the distributor vacuum line. The valve is controlled by a

1972 250/8 and 250C 3-way valve (11), 2-way valve (10), and relay (5).

relay from the 63°F. switch, the 212°F. switch in the thermostat housing, and by the rpm relay. The ignition will be retarded at speeds below 2200 rpm, when the oil temperature is above 63°F. and the coolant temperature is above 212°F. The ignition is advanced when the engine speed is above 2500 rpm and when the temperatures are below the rated values of the switches.

A throttle positioner is also installed to slightly open the throttle valves depending on coolant and oil temperatures and engine speed.

Testing the System

Throttle Positioner

1. Make this test with the oil temperature above 63°F. and the coolant temperature above 212°F.

2. Connect a tachometer.

3. Start the engine and increase engine speed to approximately 2500 rpm.

4. Release the throttle linkage and observe the throttle control on the carburetor. At speeds in excess of 1800 rpm, the adjustment screw of the throttle control should rest against the accelerator linkage. Below 1800 rpm, the screw should be off the linkage.

Ignition Changeover

1. The following check applies only when the coolant is between 63° and 212°F.

2. Connect a timing light.

3. Start the engine and increase speed.

4. Above approximately 2400 rpm, the ignition should be advanced; below 2200 the ignition should be retarded.

63° F. Temperature Switch

1. Remove the connector from the relay box and connect a test light to terminals 1 and 8.

2. Switch on the ignition. The test light should light up when the coolant temperature is below 63°F.

212°F. Temperature Switch

1. Remove the connector from the relay box and connect a test light to terminals 6 and 8.

2. Switch on the ignition. The test light should light up only if the coolant temperature is above 212°F.

RPM Switch

The rpm switch is actually two switches. Use only a voltmeter to test the rpm switch.

1. Remove the connector from the three-way valve and connect a voltmeter.

2. Start the engine and increase rpm.

3. At speeds between approximately 1800–2000 rpm, the voltmeter should indicate about 13 volts.

4. At speeds above approximately 2500 rpm, the voltmeter should read approximately 0 volts.

280SE/8

The following modifications have been made to the system for 1972:

1972 280SE/8 idle solenoid (12)

1. The injection pump has a modified cam.

2. The advance curve of the distributor is changed.

3. The 63°F. temperature switch is relocated to the oil filter housing.

4. When the ignition is shut off, the fuel shut-off solenoid is activated for a short time to prevent dieseling.

Basically, the function of the system has not changed except for the idle solenoid. The idle solenoid is activated under the following conditions:

1. The engine speed drops below 600 rpm due to increased load from the air conditioner or other power equipment.

2. The selector lever of the transmission indicates Slope or Drive.

Testing the System

Ignition Changeover

1. Connect a timing light and tachometer.

2. Start the engine and increase speed.

3. At approximately 2400 rpm, the distributor should switch from retard to advance.

Gulp Valve

1. Because the gulp valve must be checked either on the road or on a dynamometer, testing the mechanical function of the gulp valve should be sufficient.

1972 280SE/8 gulp valve (20) and valve for ignition retard (9)

2. Disconnect the air hose between the air cleaner and the gulp valve.

3. At engine speeds above 2900 rpm under deceleration, suction should be felt at the gulp valve.

Idle Solenoid

CAUTION: *To perform this test, the parking and service brakes must be firmly set.*

1. Connect a test lamp to the idle solenoid and run the engine at idle.

2. Switch on the air conditioner, turn the power steering to full lock, and engage reverse gear.

3. Should the idle drop below 600 rpm, the test lamp should light and the solenoid energize.

4. At speeds above approximately 1000 rpm, the test light should go out.

5. Place the transmission selector lever in Slope and Drive. At speeds up to approximately 2600 rpm, the test lamp should light. At speeds above approximately 2900 rpm, the test lamp should go out.

63°F. Temperature Switch

1. Remove the connector from the relay box and connect a test light to terminals 6 and 8.

2. Switch on the ignition.

3. The test light should light only below 63°F. oil temperature.

212°F. Temperature Switch

1. Remove the connector from the relay box and connect a test light to terminals 5 and 8.

2. Switch on the ignition.

3. The test lamp should light when coolant temperature is above 212°F.

Idle Switch on Throttle Valve Housing

1. Remove the connector from the relay box and connect a test lamp to terminals 1 and 8. Ground terminal 6.

2. Turn on the ignition.

3. The test light should go out immediately when the throttle is depressed.

RPM Switch

1. Use a voltmeter to test the rpm

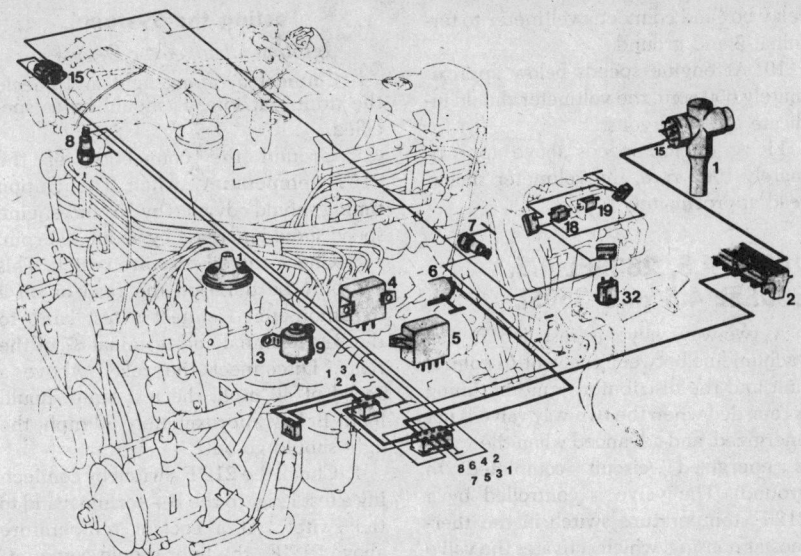

Emission control schematic—1972 280SE/8 w/manual transmission (see text also)

1. Ignition starter switch
2. Fuse box
3. Ignition coil
4. RPM switch
5. Relay box
6. Shut-off solenoid
7. Temperature switch 17° C (63° F)

8. Temperature switch 100° C (212° F)
9. Two-way valve
15. Idling speed switch
18. 3rd gear switch
19. 4th gear switch
32. Clutch pedal switch

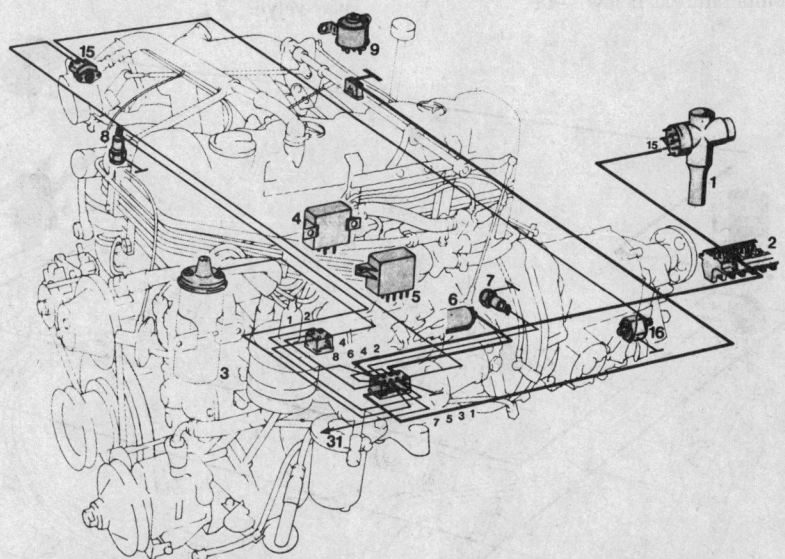

Emission control schematic—1972 280SE/8 w/automatic transmission (see text)

1. Ignition starter switch
2. Fuse box
3. Ignition coil
4. RPM switch
5. Relay box
6. Shut-off solenoid

7. Temperature switch 17° (63° F)
8. Temperature switch 100°C (212° F)
9. Two-way valve
15. Idling speed switch
16. Oil pressure switch
31. To relay for supplementary fan

switch. Use of a test light may damage the switch.

2. Remove the connector from the two-way valve. Connect a voltmeter.

3. Start the engine and increase speed.

4. Above approximately 2400 rpm, the voltmeter should indicate approximately 13 volts. Below approximately 2200 rpm, the voltmeter should indicate approximately 0 volts.

In addition, perform the following test.

5. Remove the cable connector from the relay box.

6. Connect a voltmeter to terminal 4 and to ground.

7. Below approximately 2600 rpm, the voltmeter should indicate about 13 volts.

8. Above approximately 2900 rpm, the voltmeter should indicate about 0 volts.

9. Remove the connector from the

relay box and connect a voltmeter to terminal 2 and ground.

10. At engine speeds below approximately 600 rpm, the voltmeter should indicate about 13 volts.

11. At engine speeds above approximately 1000 rpm, the voltmeter should read approximately 0 volts.

280SE 4.5, 280SEL 4.5, 300SEL 4.5 and 350SL

A two-way valve is installed in the vacuum line between the venturi control unit and the distributor. Ignition timing is retarded when the two-way valve is not energized, and advanced when the valve is energized (circuit completed to ground). The valve is controlled by a 212°F. temperature switch in the thermostat housing, which activates the valve above coolant temperatures of 212°F.

A fuel shut-off solenoid cuts off the delivery of fuel under the following conditions:

1. Accelerator pedal is in the idling position.

2. Engine speed is above 1500 rpm, determined by an electronic control unit. There is no fuel shut-off when coolant temperature is below −4°F.

Testing the System

Ignition Changeover Device

1. Connect a timing light and check the timing at idle. It should be as specified.

2. Ground the connection of the 212°F. temperature switch. The ignition timing should advance by 15° and engine speed should increase by about 300 rpm.

3. Check the oil pressure switch. This can only be done on the road or on a dynamometer. Connect a test lamp to the B+ terminal and terminal 87 of the relay. Disconnect the relay. Above a speed of 40 mph, the test lamp should light. Below approximately 30 mph, the light should go out.

4. Check the 212°F. switch by connecting a test lamp to the B+ terminal and to the switch. At a coolant temperature above 212°F., the light should come on.

5. If there is no ignition changeover and the oil pressure switch is working, check the following:

a. Fuse no. 6 in the main fuse box.

b. All vacuum and electrical connections on the two-way valve.

c. The two-way valve. Switch on the ignition and ground the oil pressure switch. This should energize the two-way valve.

d. The relay. Connect a test lamp to the plug of the two-way valve. Switch on the ignition and ground the 212°F. temperature switch. The relay is working if the lamp lights.

1973

The fuel evaporation control system remains unchanged for 1973.

Beginning in 1973, the two-way valves used previously are replaced with switchover valves that are externally identical. When new valves are installed, it is important that the vacuum line always be connected to the center connection, whether it is on the top or the bottom. To be able to distinguish the function of the individual valves, the covers are color coded according to valve function, as follows:

WHITE—advanced ignition valve
RED—retarded ignition valve
GREY—throttle opening valve
BROWN—exhaust gas recycling (EGR) valve

220/8

Ignition changeover is accomplished through vacuum and oil temperature. Vacuum retard is only activated during acceleration, while vacuum advance is

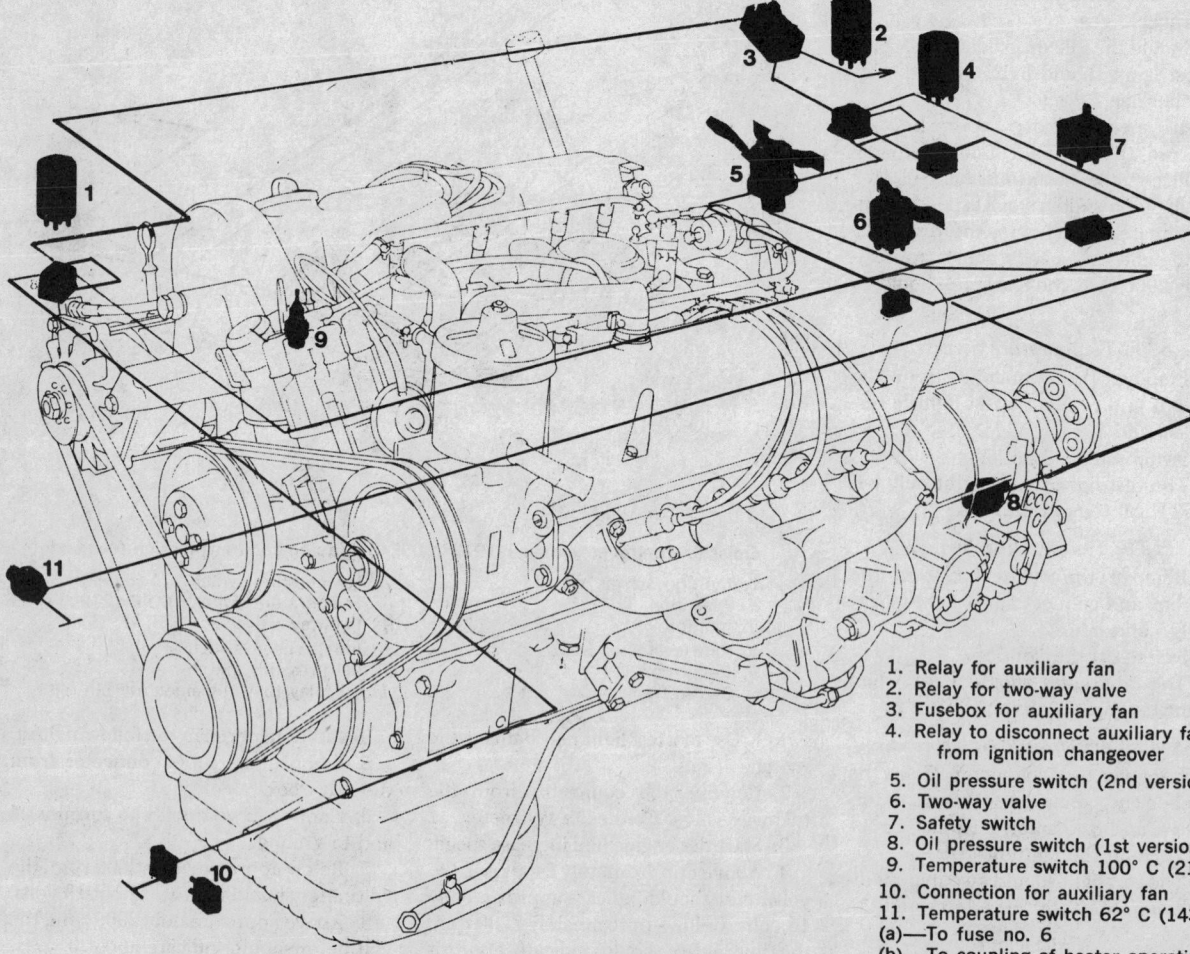

1. Relay for auxiliary fan
2. Relay for two-way valve
3. Fusebox for auxiliary fan
4. Relay to disconnect auxiliary fan from ignition changeover
5. Oil pressure switch (2nd version)
6. Two-way valve
7. Safety switch
8. Oil pressure switch (1st version)
9. Temperature switch 100° C (212° F)
10. Connection for auxiliary fan
11. Temperature switch 62° C (143° F)
(a)—To fuse no. 6
(b)—To coupling of heater operating device

Emission control schematic—1972 V8 (see text also)

activated under the following conditions:
1. Oil temperature below 77°F.
2. Oil temperature above 77°F. and engine speed above 2000 rpm.
The throttle valve is also opened slightly during coasting, through a vacuum governor on the carburetor.
Exhaust gas is being recycled by the EGR valve under the following conditions:

1. Oil temperature above 77°F. up to 3600 rpm.
Exhaust gas recirculation is not effective under the following conditions:
1. Oil temperature below 77°F.

Part No.		Dead	Live	Operation
001 540 04 97	white			When de-energized, the air connection B is closed and the vacuum connections A and E are interconnected. When energized, the connection E is closed and only connection A is supplied with air.
001 540 07 97	grey			
001 540 08 97	brown			
001 540 09 97	red			The connections E and A must under no circumstances be confused.
001 540 00 97	no color coding			When de-energized, the air connection B is closed and the vacuum connections A and E are interconnected. When energized, the connections A and E are supplied with air. Air is taken in via the air cap B. The connections may be interchanged.
001 540 05 97	white			When de-energized, connection A is supplied with air and connection E is closed. When energized, connection A is connected to E and air connection B is closed.
001 540 11 97	brown			The connections E and A must under no circumstances be confused.

1973 switch valves

1973 220/8

9. Switch-over valve (ignition)
10. Swtch-over valve (throttle positioner)
12. Switch-over valve (exhaust recycling)

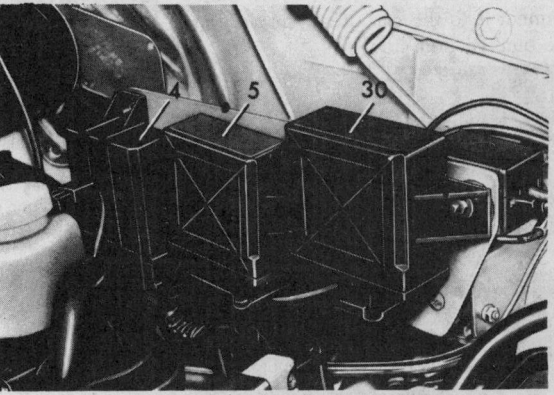

1973 220/8 EGR rpm switch (4)

4. RPM relay with two rpm switches
5. Relay box
30. Delay relay for idle cut-off valve

2. Speed above 3600 rpm.

Testing the System
Ignition Timing

1. Check the ignition timing. It should be as specified earlier.

2. If not, check all vacuum connections and the 77°F. temperature switch before adjusting the timing.

77°F. Temperature Switch

1. Remove the plug from the relay.

2. Connect a test lamp to terminals 5 and 8.

3. The test lamp should light when the oil temperature exceeds 77°F.

RPM Switch

Use only a voltmeter to check the rpm switch.

1. Disconnect the plug on the switch-over valve and connect a voltmeter.

2. Start the engine and increase speed.

3. Up to approximately 2000 rpm, the voltmeter should read about 13 volts. The voltage should be approximately 0 volts above 2000 rpm.

Ignition Switchover Valve

1. Connect the plug to the valve and increase rpm. At about 2000 rpm, the piston in the valve will be audibly heard to switch over.

EGR Switch Valve

1. Connect a tachometer, start the engine, and increase speed. The switchover valve should be heard to switch over at approximately 3600 rpm.

EGR RPM Switch

1. Disconnect the plug on the switch valve and connect a voltmeter (do not use a test lamp).

2. Start the engine and increase speed.

3. The voltmeter should indicate about 13 volts up to 3600 rpm and should drop to 0 volts above 3600 rpm.

EGR Valve

1. Start the engine and run it at idle.

2. Remove the lower, brown vacuum line from the EGR switchover valve and connect it to the carburetor in place of the blue vacuum line.

1973 220/8 EGR valve (31)

3. If the EGR valve is working, the engine will idle roughly or stop running. If the engine does not do one or the other, replace the EGR valve.

4. Do not forget to replace the vacuum lines.

280 and 280C

An ignition changeover is installed to retard or advance the ignition. Ignition is retarded under the following conditions:

1. When the oil temperature is above 62°F. and coolant temperature is below 212°F.

2. Engine speed is below 3200 rpm. Ignition retard is negated under the following conditions:

1. Oil temperature below 62°F.

2. Coolant temperature above 212°F.

3. Engine speed above 3200 rpm and oil temperature above 62°F, and coolant temperature below 212°F.

4. When shifting into fourth gear.

5. When switching on the air conditioner.

6. With vacuum between 0 and 2.8 psi.

A throttle positioner is installed which will open the throttle slightly when the oil temperature is above 62°F., when the coolant temperature is below 212°F., and when engine speed exceeds 200 rpm.

Exhaust gases are recycled when engine oil temperature is above 62°F., when coolant temperature is below 212°F., and when manifold vacuum is between 0 and 2.8 psi, up to 3200 rpm.

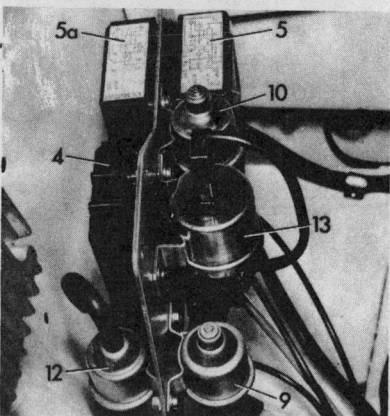

280 and 280C switch valves (1973-74)

5. Relay box 8-prong plug
5a. Relay box 12-prong plug
4. RPM relay with two rpm switches
9. Switch-over valve (ignition switch-over)
10. Switch-over valve (throttle positioner)
12. Switch-over valve (exhaust recycling)

Testing the System
Ignition Timing

1. Check the ignition timing. It should be as specified.

2. If not, check all vacuum connections and the temperature switches before adjusting the timing.

62°F. Temperature Switch

1. Disconnect the plug of the relay box.

2. Connect a voltmeter to terminals 5 and 8.

3. The voltmeter should indicate 0 volts when the oil temperature is above 62°F.

212°F. Temperature Switch

1. Disconnect the plug from the relay box.

2. Connect a test lamp to terminals 4 and 8.

3. Switch on the ignition.

4. The test lamp should light when coolant temperature is above 212°F.

Throttle Positioner

See the test for the throttle positioner under "1972 220/8".

RPM Switch

Use only a voltmeter to test the rpm switch.

1. Disconnect the plug of the switch valve and connect a voltmeter.

2. Start the engine and increase speed.

3. The voltmeter should indicate about 13 volts, above 2000 rpm.

4. Decrease speed below about 1800 rpm and the voltmeter should read approximately 0 volts.

EGR Switch Valve

1. Disconnect the plug from the switch valve and connect a tachometer.

2. Connect a voltmeter and increase rpm.

3. The voltmeter should read about 13 volts up to 3200 rpm.

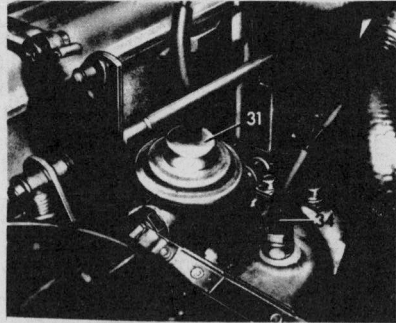

1973-74 280 and 280C 149° F. temperature switch (32).

149°F. Temperature Switch

1. Disconnect the plug from the relay box and connect a voltmeter to terminals 6 and 8.

2. The voltmeter should indicate approximately 13 volts above 149°F.

Vacuum Switch

1. Disconnect the plug from the relay box and connect a voltmeter to terminals 7 and 8.

2. Idle the engine.

3. The voltmeter should indicate 0 volts.

4. Disconnect the vacuum line from

the switch. The voltmeter should now indicate about 13 volts.

EGR rpm Switch

1. Disconnect the plug from the relay box.

2. Connect a voltmeter to terminals 1 and 3.

3. Start the engine and increase speed.

4. The voltmeter should indicate 0 volts up to approximately 3200 rpm. Beyond that, voltage should be about 13 volts.

5. When rpm decreases, the voltmeter should return to 0 volts at about 2800 rpm.

EGR Valve

See this test under "1973 220/8".

1973-74 280 and 280C EGR valve (31)

280SE 4.5, 280SEL 4.5, 300SEL 4.5, 450SL, 450SLC, 450SE and 450SEL

The emission system used on these vehicles functions in the same manner as that used on 1972 4.5 engines. All tests are performed in a similar manner to those given under 1972 for 4.5 engines.

1974

Design and function of the emission control system is basically unchanged except for the addition of an air pump on 280, 280C and 450 California models.

It is impossible to list test procedures for all the various switches and valves in this book, so only basic tests and results appear here.

The following tests should be performed on a warm engine at normal operating temperature, and should be performed in the sequence listed. Be sure to check the fuses if a malfunction is suspected.

230

The design of this system is similar to 1973 220/8 models.

Testing the System

77°F. Temperature Switch

1. Disconnect the plug to the temperature switch in the oil filter housing and ground it. The engine rpm should increase, indicating that vacuum advance is present.

2. Increase the engine speed to about 2500 rpm and remove the red vacuum line at the distributor. The engine rpm should drop slightly, indicating that vacuum advance is no longer present.

If the results are not as specified, check the connections of the vacuum lines. The blue line from the carburetor should go to the center port of the red switchover valve and the red line should go from the outer port of the switchover valve to the distributor.

EGR Switchover Valve

1. Place your hand over the brown EGR switchover valve. It may be necessary to remove the valve to isolate its operation. Increase the engine speed. The valve should be felt to switch.

2. If it does not function, check the voltage at the plug. If no voltage is measured at the plug, below 3600 rpm, replace the rpm relay.

EGR Valve

1. Connect the EGR valve directly to intake manifold vacuum with the blue vacuum line. The engine should run poorly or stall, indicating that the valve is open.

2. If the speed does not change, remove the valve and connect it to vacuum. The valve stem should lift from its seat. Remove exhaust deposits from the valve with a 10 mm drill and blow it clean with compressed air.

Vacuum Governor

1. Connect a tachometer and increase engine speed to about 2500 rpm and release the throttle slowly. The vacuum governor should pop out above 2000 rpm and retract below 1800 rpm.

If not, check the vacuum lines. The blue line should connect the center port of the gray switchover valve. The gray line should connect the vacuum governor and the outer port of the switchover valve.

2. If the vacuum lines are connected properly, remove the relay box plug and connect terminals 2 and 8. With the ignition ON, the switchover valve should click. If the switchover valve functions properly, the relay box is defective.

280 and 280C (Federal)

The emission control system for these cars is unchanged from 1973.

280 and 280C (California Only)

The California system for these cars is a modification of the Federal system. A Saginaw air pump is used and a reactor

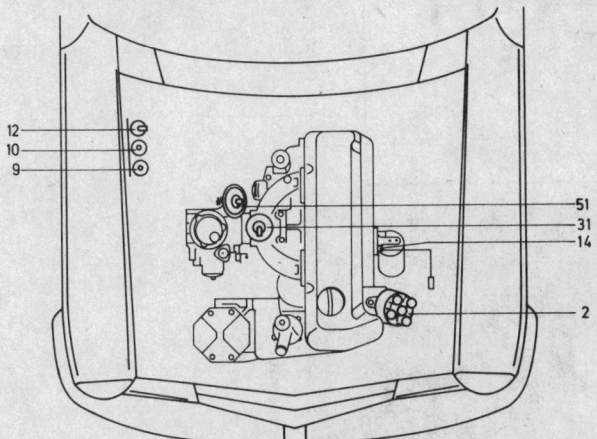

1974 230 emission control component location

2. Ignition distributor
9. Switch-over valve, ignition
10. Switch-over valve, throttle valve lift
12. Switch-over valve, EGR
14. 77° F temperature switch
31. EGR valve
51. Vacuum governor

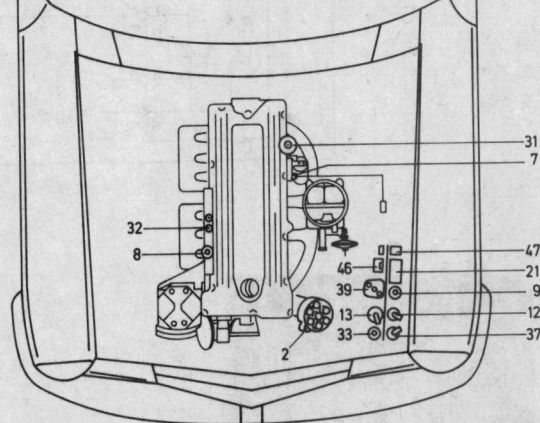

1974 280, 280C (California) emission control component location

2. Distributor
7. 62° F temperature switch
8. 212° F temperature switch
9. Switchover valve, ignition
12. Switchover valve, EGR
13. Vacuum switch
21. Relay box
31. EGR valve

32. 149° F temperature switch
33. Switchover valve, air injection
37. Switchover valve, fuel evaporation system
39. Charcoal canister
46. Resistor for automatic choke
47. Relay for resistor, automatic choke

Mercedes-Benz

⑧ 100°C (212°F) temperature switch

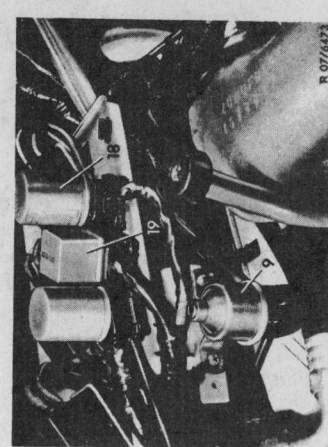

⑨ 2-way valve

⑲ Relay 2-way valve.

㉑ Auxiliary fan

Connection of test instruments shown with dotted lines.

Color code

ws = white	ge = yellow	rt = red
gn = green	rs = pink	sw = black
br = brown	bl = blue	li = violet

Emission schematic—1973 280SE 4.5 280SEL 4.5 300SEL 4.5, 350SL

① Relay
Auxiliary fan

③ 62°C (144°F) temperature switch

704

⑨ 2-way valve

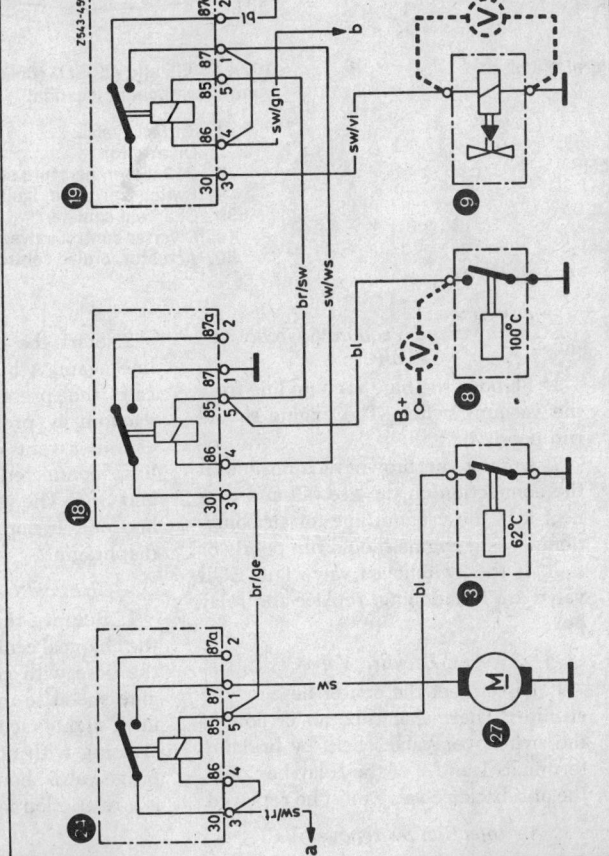

Connection of test instruments shown with dotted lines.

Color code

ws = white	ge = yellow	rt = red
gn = green	rs = pink	sw = black
br = brown	bl = blue	li = violet

Emission schematic—1973 450SL and 450SLC

⑱ Relay

⑲ Relay 2-way valve.
㉔ Relay Auxiliary fan
㉗ Auxiliary fan

③ 62°C (144°F) temperature switch

⑧ 100°C (212°F) temperature switch

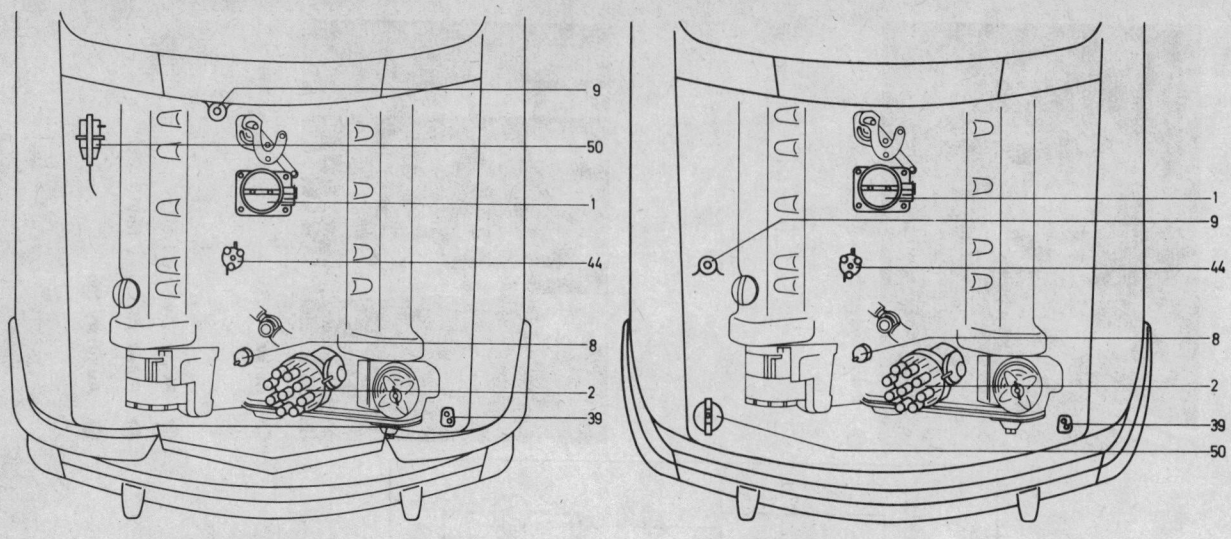

1974 450SE and 450SEL (California) emission control component location

1. Throttle valve
2. Distributor
8. 212° F temperature switch
9. Switchover valve, ignition
39. Charcoal canister
44. Diverter control valve
50. Actuator, cruise control

1974 450SL and 450SLC (California) emission control component location

1. Throttle valve
2. Distributor
8. 212° F temperature switch
9. Switchover valve, ignition
39. Charcoal canister
44. Diverter control valve
50. Actuator, cruise control

with injection tubes is used in place of an exhaust manifold.

Testing the System

62°F. Temperature Switch

1. Disconnect and ground the plug to the switch in the oil filter housing. The engine rpm should increase. If not disconnect the relay box plug and connect terminals 2 and 10. With the ignition ON the valve should click. If the valve clicks, replace the relay box.

212°F. Temperature Switch

1. Unplug and ground the temperature switch. The engine speed should increase and the auxiliary fan should run. If not, replace the relay box.

Relay Box Voltage

1. Turn the air conditioner ON. The engine speed should not drop. If the engine speed decreases, remove the relay box plug and connect a voltmeter to terminals 3 and 8 of the plug. If less than 13 volts is present, replace the relay box, or, if no voltage is present, check the air conditioner circuit.

Vacuum Switchover Valve

1. Remove the vacuum line from the top of the switchover valve and remove the blue line from the vacuum switch. The engine speed should increase. A voltmeter should read 13 volts between terminals 11 and 2 of the relay box plug with the engine running. Remove the vacuum line from the vacuum switch. No voltage should be present. If both readings are correct, replace the relay box.

EGR Valve and Vacuum Switchover Valve

1. Remove the blue vacuum line from the vacuum switch. The engine should run poorly or stall.

2. Unplug the brown vacuum line at the connection on the firewall and connect it to the vacuum line for air conditioning. The engine should run poorly or stall. If the switchover valve and EGR valve are functioning, replace the relay box.

Anti-Backfire Valve

1. Disconnect the center hose on the air filter. There should be no air flow. If the switchover valve clicks by bridging terminals 1 and 2 of the relay box plug, the anti-backfire valve must be replaced.

Air Injection Switchover Valve

1. Increase engine speed slowly to above 3450 rpm. The air flow should stop in the injection line at about 3450 rpm.

Automatic Choke Relay

1. Disconnect the plug to the 62° F. temperature switch in the oil filter housing and ground the switch. The automatic choke resistor relay should click. Voltage at the switch should be about 13 volts. If none is present, replace the relay box.

Float Chamber Vent Valve

1. Shut the engine OFF. Disconnect the gray vacuum line at the float chamber vent valve on the carburetor. No vacuum should be present. Reconnect the line.

2. Start the engine and remove the line again. A hissing sound should indicate the presence of vacuum. If no vacuum is present, remove the float chamber vent valve. With the vacuum lines connected, turn the ignition ON and OFF. The valve stem should move in and out. If not, replace the vent valve diaphragm.

Charcoal Canister Purge Valve

1. Remove the thin center hose from the charcoal canister and close the end of the hose with your finger. Increase engine speed to more than 2000 rpm. At idle, slight vacuum should be felt, increasing with engine speed. If not, the purge valve should be replaced, or there is a restriction in the line.

450SL, SLC and 450SE, SEL (Federal)

This system is the same as for 1973.

450SL, SLC and 450SE, SEL (California Only)

The California system is a refinement of the Federal System and closely resembles it, with an added air pump.

Testing the System

212° F. Temperature Switch

1. Unplug the temperature switch and ground it. The engine rpm should increase and the auxilliary fan should run on the 450SE and 450SEL. If not connect terminals 3 and 4 of the relay box plug. With the ignition ON, the switchover

valve should click. If not, replace the relay.

2. Switch ON the air conditioning. The engine rpm should rise slightly. If the engine rpm does not increase, check the air conditioning. If the air conditioning works, replace the relay.

EGR

1. Remove the air filter top cover and check that exhaust gas is emitted from the recirculation line in the throttle valve housing. If no exhaust is emitted into the throttle valve housing, clean the throttle housing and EGR line.

Diverter Control Valve

1. Remove the air filter housing and lay it aside without unplugging the warm air sensor. Disconnect the brown vacuum line at the diverter control valve. Increase the rpm to over 2000 and release the throttle linkage. Vacuum should be present at the port of the diverter valve only when the throttle linkage is released. A hissing sound should be heard.

2. If no vacuum is present, replace the diverter valve.

CO Content

1. Check the CO content of the exhaust gas. It should be a maximum of 1.0% WITH OR WITHOUT air injection. To check the CO, remove the air filter housing and lay it aside without unplugging the warm air sensor. Disconnect the brown vacuum line at the diverter valve and connect this to the vacuum supply line for the cruise control actuator.

2. If the CO content varies with or without air injection, check the brown vacuum line to the diverter valve for tightness. Also check the diverter valve.

Charcoal Canister Purge Valve

See this test under 280 and 280C (California Only).

1975

The 1975 emission control equipment closely resembles that for 1974. The 230 (California only) and all other gasoline engines are equipped with catalysts. These models must be operated only with unleaded gasoline.

All of the following tests should be made in the specified sequence with the engine at operating temperature.

As of 1975, the base color of vacuum lines for emission control is white. Lines originating at a vacuum source have only one color stripe. These lines are connected to the center connection of the switchover valve of the same color. Lines terminating at a vacuum operated device have 2 color stripes. Purple is always the second color. The lines are connected to the outer connection of the switchover valve of the same color.

Switchover valve filter caps are color coded as follows:

Red—Valve for ignition advance
Grey—Valve for throttle lift
Brown—Valve for EGR
Blue—Valve for air injection

230

Testing the System

77° F. Temperature Switch

1. Disconnect the temperature switch plug and ground the switch. The engine rpm should increase.

2. If not, check the vacuum line connections.

3. Unplug the relay box and connect terminals 7 and 1; an audible click should be heard. If not, replace the relay box.

4. Disconnect and ground the temperature switch. Place your hand over the air pump muffler. A light air flow should be present.

5. If no air flow is present, check the vacuum line connections (see Step 2).

6. Disconnect the plug from the relay box and connect terminals 6 and 7. The blue switchover valve should click. If not, replace the switchover valve. If the valve does click, the relay is defective.

RPM Switch

1. Increase engine speed to about 2500 rpm and remove the red/purple vacuum line from the distributor. The engine speed should drop slightly. Below about 2000 rpm, there should be 13 volts at the switch. If there is less than 11 volts, temporarily replace the rpm relay or relay box and repeat the test.

EGR Switchover Valve

1. Disconnect the brown vacuum line at the carburetor and brown/purple vacuum line at the carburetor. Blow into the brown vacuum line and simultaneously increase the rpm to about 3600. At idle, air can be blown through the line, while above 3600, no air should pass.

EGR Valve

1. Connect the EGR valve to intake manifold vacuum. Disconnect the red line at the carburetor and the brown-/purple line at the carburetor. Connect both lines together. The engine should run poorly or stall. If not be sure that the valve stem is moving and if not, replace the valve. If the valve works, clean the EGR valve with a 10 mm drill.

Vacuum Governor

1. Increase the engine speed to about 2500 rpm and release the throttle slowly. At the same time watch the vacuum control on the carburetor. It should pop out above 2000 rpm and retract below 1800 rpm. If not, remove the plug from the relay box and connect terminals 2 and 7. With the ignition ON, the valve should click audibly. If it does, replace the relay box.

280, 280C and 280S

The system remains basically un-

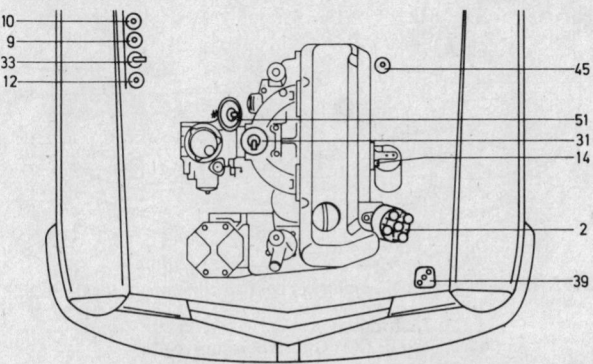

1975-76 230 emission control component location

2. Distributor
9. Switchover valve, ignition (red)
10. Switchover valve, throttle lift (grey)
12. Switchover valve, EGR (brown)
14. 77° F temperature switch
31. EGR valve
33. Switchover valve, air injection (blue)
45. Muffler (air filter for noise suppression)
51. Vacuum control, throttle lift

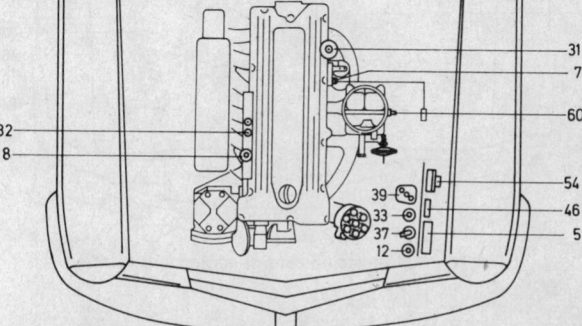

1975-76 280 and 280C emission control component location

5. Relay box
7. 62° F temperature switch
8. 212° F temperature switch
12. Switchover valve, EGR (brown)
31. EGR valve
32. 149° F temperature switch
33. Switchover valve, air injection (blue)
37. Switchover valve, fuel evaporation control system (green)
39. Charcoal canister
46. Resistor, automatic choke cover
54. Vacuum booster
60. Venturi connection

Mercedes-Benz

changed except for different color coding of vacuum lines and addition of a catalytic converter in all states.

Testing the System

EGR

1. Remove the brown/purple vacuum line from the EGR valve and turn the ignition ON. Blow air into the line. Place the gear selector in a driving position (not N or P). The line should be closed.

2. Remove the brown vacuum line on the carburetor and the green line on the carburetor. Connect the brown line in place of the green line. Start the engine and place the gear selector in a driving position (not N or P).

3. The engine should run roughly or stall. If not, either the vacuum booster or the EGR valve is at fault.

Air Injection

1. Remove the air injection hose at the air filter (center hose) and run the engine at idle. There should be no air flow present. If air is discharged at idle, replace the diverter valve.

62° F. Temperature Switch

1. Disconnect the plug from the switch in the oil filter housing and ground the switch. Air flow in the injection line should cease. If it does not, disconnect the plug from the blue switchover valve and connect a voltmeter. Disconnect and ground the temperature switch. Turn the ignition ON; the voltmeter should read

about 12 volts. If no voltage is present, replace the relay box.

Automatic Choke Resistor

1. Connect a voltmeter to the resistor

outlet (top connection) and to ground. Disconnect the plug of the 62°F. temperature switch and connect it ground. Disconnect the plug of the 149° F.

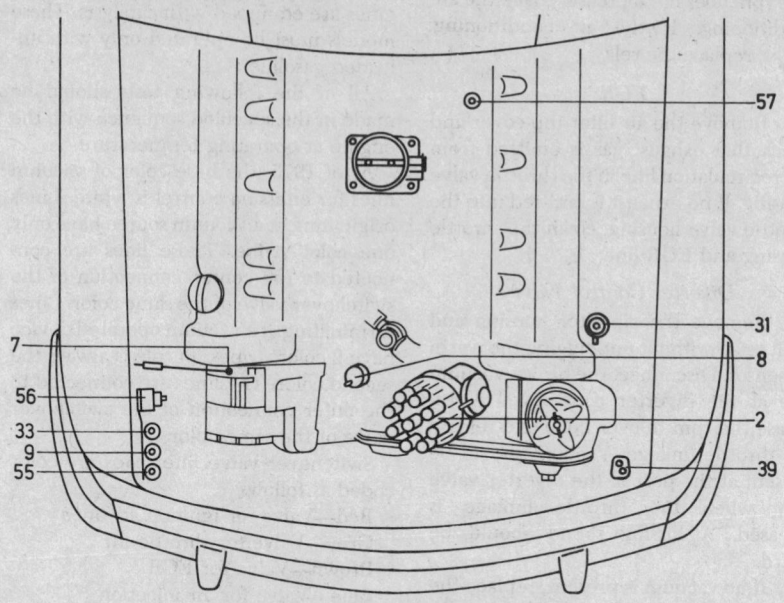

1975 450SL and 450SLC emission control component location

2. Distributor
7. 62° F (17° C) temperature switch
8. 212° F (100° C) temperature switch
9. Switch-over valve, ignition retard (yellow)
31. EGR valve
33. Switch-over valve, air injection (blue)
39. Charcoal canister
55. Switch-over valve, EGR/ ignition advance (red)
56. Vacuum control switch
57. 104° F (40° C) temperature switch

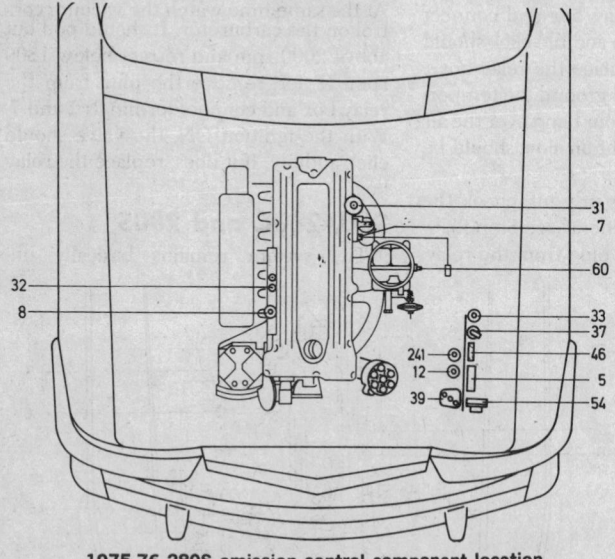

1975-76 280S emission control component location

5. Relay box
7. 62° F temperature switch
8. 212° F temperature switch
12. Switchover valve, EGR (brown)
31. EGR valve
32. 149° F temperature switch
33. Switchover valve, air injection (blue)
37. Switchover valve, fuel evaporation control system (green)
39. Charcoal canister
46. Resistor, automatic choke cover
54. Vacuum booster
60. Venturi connection

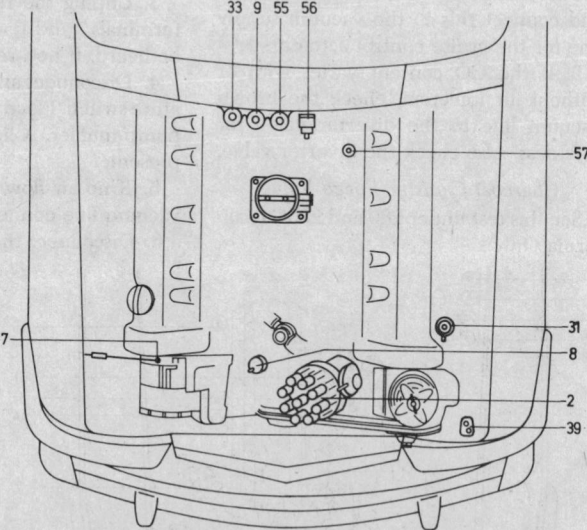

1975 450SE and 450SEL emission control component location

2. Distributor
7. 62° F (17° C) temperature switch
8. 212° F (100° C) temperature switch
9. Switch-over valve, ignition retard (yellow)
31. EGR valve
33. Switch-over valve, air injection (blue)
39. Charcoal canister
55. Switch-over valve, EGR/ ignition advance (red)
56. Vacuum control switch
57. 104° F (40° C) temperature switch

temperature switch and turn the ignition ON. With the 62° switch grounded the voltmeter should read about 7–8 volts. If the ground is interrupted, it should read about 12 volts.

2. If the voltage is not as specified, check the relay box. Connect a voltmeter to the input of the resistor (lower connection) and to ground. Ground the plug of the 62° temperature switch and the voltmeter should read about 12 volts. If not, replace the relay box.

Float Chamber Vent Valve

1. Connect a vacuum gauge to the green/purple vacuum line to the float chamber vent valve. Start the engine and briefly accelerate. The vacuum should build up and remain constant. With the ignition OFF, the vacuum should drop to zero.

2. If no vacuum is present, connect a voltmeter to the switchover valve. About 13 volts should be present, and the valve should click audibly.

If vacuum does not remain constant, unscrew the float chamber vent valve. With the vacuum line connected run the engine at idle. The valve rod should move. If necessary, replace the valve vacuum diaphragm.

Charcoal Canister Purge Valve

See this test under 1974 280 and 280C (California Only). The test is the same.

450SL, SLC and 450SE, SEL

This system is basically the same as the 1974 system with the addition of a dual diaphragm distributor and catalytic converter.

Testing the System

212° F. Temperature Switch

See this test under 1974 450SL, SLC and 450SE, SEL. It is identical, except for color coding.

Vacuum Control Unit

1. Remove the yellow/purple and red/purple vacuum lines from the vacuum control on the distributor. The engine rpm should increase slightly. Connect the yellow/purple vacuum line to the upper connection of the vacuum control unit. The engine speed should increase slightly. If not, replace the vacuum control unit.

EGR Switchover Valve

1. Remove the red/purple vacuum line at the EGR valve. Connect a vacuum gauge to the red/purple line and to the red connection of the EGR valve. Run the engine at idle and increase the rpm to 2500. At idle the gauge should show no vacuum. At higher rpm, there should be some vacuum.

2. If not, shut the engine OFF and turn the ignition to ON. Remove the plug from the 104°F. temperature switch. The

switchover valve should click. If it does not click, replace the switchover valve with a new one and repeat the test. If it still does not click, replace the relay.

EGR Vacuum Control Switch

1. Remove the brown/purple vacuum line from the EGR valve. Connect a vacuum gauge to the brown/purple line and to the bottom of the EGR valve. Start the engine and increase speed to 2500 rpm. At idle, the gauge should show no vacuum. During acceleration, vacuum should be present for a brief period until engine rpm stabilizes at a higher speed.

2. If no vacuum can be measured and the vacuum lines are correctly attached, the vacuum control switch is defective.

EGR Valve

1. Remove the yellow/purple vacuum line from the vacuum control unit on the distributor. Disconnect the vacuum lines from the EGR valve. With a vacuum test line, connect the yellow/purple line with the upper, and then the lower connection of the EGR valve. The engine should run roughly or stall in both operating phases of the EGR valve.

2. If the engine does not run roughly or stall, the EGR valve should be replaced.

CO Exhaust Gas Content

1. Run the engine at idle. Test the CO content of the exhaust gas. Disconnect the plug for the 62° F. temperature

switch and ground it with a test cable. Measure the CO again without air injection. The CO content should change noticeably.

2. If it does not change noticeably, disconnect and ground the 62° temperature switch. The blue switchover valve should click. If it doesn't, replace the switchover valve.

3. If the switchover valve functions, remove the air filter on the diverter valve. Disconnect and ground the 62° temperature switch. Air should exit from the diverter valve. If there is no air flow, replace the diverter valve and repeat the test. Also, check the air pump and air pump drive belt tension.

Charcoal Canister Purge Valve

See this test under 1974 280 and 280C (California Only).

1976

The 1976 emission control system is close to the system used in 1975. Catalytic converters are used on all engines, but the 450 series cars have the catalysts installed on the exhaust manifold. Due to Federal regulations, the routing of the fuel evaporation lines has been changed.

230

See the 1975 230 Emission Control System.

280, 280C, 280S

See the 1975 280, 280C and 280S Emission Control System.

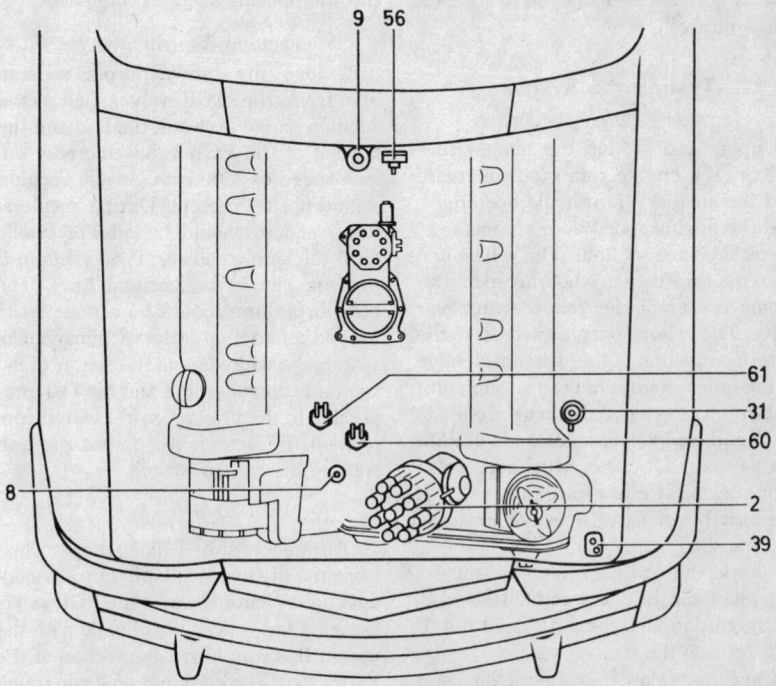

1976 450SE, 450SEL, 450SL and 450SLC emission control component location

2. Distributor
8. 212° F temperature switch
9. Switch-over valve, ignition retard (yellow)
31. EGR valve
39. Charcoal canister
56. Vacuum control switch
60. 104° F thermo-vacuum valve (black)
61. 63° F thermo-vacuum valve (blue)

450SE, 450SEL, 450SL, 450SLC

These cars with the M117 engine use one emission system for the entire U.S. market, including California.

The base color of the vacuum lines is opaque (white). Lines originating at a vacuum source have only one color stripe; lines terminating at a vacuum source have 2-color stripes. Purple is always the second color.

Thermo vacuum valves are used to control the ignition changeover, EGR and air injection. They are color coded:

Black—104°F. valve
Blue—63°F. valve

The retard side of the vacuum control unit is only activated when the coolant is below 212°F., during deceleration with the A/C off. The advance side of the vacuum control unit is activated when temperatures at the thermo-valve are 104°F. or above and the advance is determined by the position of the throttle plate.

The EGR valve works in 2 stages. The first stage (small amount) takes place with coolant temperature above 104°F. There is no EGR with coolant temperature below 86°F.

The second (larger) stage of EGR occurs during acceleration with coolant temperature above 140°F. and vacuum less than 7.9 in./Hg.

Air injection takes place above 62°F. and is cancelled below 50°F. (coolant temperatures).

Testing the System

Ignition Changeover Switch

Unplug and ground the temperature switch. The engine rpm should increase and the auxiliary fan should operate.

If the engine speed does not increase, check the vacuum lines. The yellow line from the throttle valve housing should go to the center of the yellow switchover valve. The yellow/purple line goes to the outer connection of the switchover valve to the inner chamber of the vacuum unit (retard). Disconnect the plug from the relay and bridge terminals 3 and 4. With the ignition ON, the switchover valve should click. If not, replace the relay. If the switchover valve does not function, replace the valve.

Check the auxiliary fan. Disconnect the relay and bridge terminals 1 and 3. With ignition ON, the fan should run. If not, replace the fan.

Check the relay. Remove the plug and bridge terminals 1 and 3. With the ignition ON, the fan should run. If so, replace the relay.

Ignition Retard Relay

Switch on the A/C. The engine rpm should increase slightly. If not, check that the A/C is operating. If the A/C is operating, replace the relay.

Ignition Advance

Remove the yellow/purple and red/-purple vacuum lines from the distributor. The engine speed should increase slightly. Connect the yellow/purple vacuum line to the upper connection at the vacuum diaphragm. The engine speed should increase.

If not, replace the 2-way vacuum diaphragm.

EGR Switchover Valve

Remove the red/purple vacuum line at the EGR valve. Connect a vacuum gauge to the red/purple line and run the engine at idle. Increase speed to 2500 rpm. At idle, the gauge should show no vacuum; at 2500 rpm, vacuum should be present.

If no vacuum is indicated, check the line connections. The red line from the red connection at the throttle valve housing should go to the angular connection of the thermo-vacuum valve. The red/-purple line should be attached to the vertical connection at the thermo-vacuum valve, to the red connection of the vacuum control switch and red connection of the EGR valve.

Check the 104°F. thermo-vacuum valve. It should open if the surrounding temperature is above 104°F. It should close below 86°F. If the valve is not functioning properly, check the bore of the throttle housing vacuum connection.

Vacuum Control Switch

Remove the brown/purple vacuum line from the EGR valve. Connect a vacuum gauge between the line and the bottom of the EGR valve. Increase engine speed to 2500 rpm. At idle vacuum should not be present. During acceleration, vacuum should be present briefly until the rpm stabilizes. If no vacuum is present, check the vacuum lines. The red/purple line should be connected to the red connection at the vacuum control switch, the white line to the center of the vacuum control switch and the red/purple line to the brown control switch connection. If vacuum still is not present, replace the control switch.

EGR Valve

Disconnect the yellow/purple line from the distributor diaphragm. Disconnect both vacuum lines at the EGR valve. Connect the yellow/purple line with the upper, then the lower connection of the EGR valve. The engine should run rough or stall in both cases. If not, replace the EGR valve.

Diverter Valve

Run the engine at idle. Connect a CO tester. Note the reading. Remove the blue/purple vacuum line from the blue thermo-valve and note reading again. It should change noticeably.

If not, check the vacuum lines. The blue line runs to the angular connection on the blue thermo-vacuum valve. The blue/purple line goes to the vertical connection of the same valve.

Check the diverter valve. Remove the muffler on the valve. Disconnect the blue/purple vacuum line at the blue thermo-vacuum valve. Air should flow from the diverter valve. If there is no air flow, replace the diverter valve. If necessary, check the drive belt tension.

Charcoal Canister

Remove the thin hose from the charcoal canister. Cover the hose opening with finger or connect vacuum gauge. Slowly increase rpm to 2500. At idle a small amount of vacuum should be present, and vacuum should increase with engine speed.

If no vacuum is present at idle, check the purge line to the intake manifold. Disconnect the charcoal canister hose at the purge valve and clean it by blowing through with compressed air in the direction of the intake manifold. Replace the purge valve if necessary.

If vacuum does not increase at idle, check the vacuum at the purge valve. Disconnect the white vacuum line at the purge valve. Connect a vacuum gauge or close the line with a finger. Increase engine speed. At idle, there should be no vacuum. With increasing engine speed, vacuum should increase. If vacuum is present replace the purge valve. If no vacuum is present, blow through the line towards the throttle valve housing.

FUEL SYSTEM
Fuel Filter

Replacement

V 8 In line in Engine Compartment

1. Unclamp hoses from each side of filter.
2. Remove filter.
3. Replace filter, install hoses and check for leaks.

V 8 Between Rear Axle and Fuel Tank

1. Remove cover box.
2. Remove hoses.
3. Remove filter retaining clamp.
4. Install new filter in direction of flow.
5. Check for leaks.

6 Cylinder with Mechanical Injection

1. Loosen retaining screw and remove lower housing.
2. Remove filter element and clean housing.

3. Install new filter element and new seal ring in filter cover.

4. Check for leaks.

Diesel-Prefilter

1. Remove hose clamps and remove filter from line.

2. Install new filter with the hex head stamped "Austritt" toward the pump.

Diesel-Main Filter

1. Drain fuel from housing.

2. Remove element and blow through it with compressed air, from inside out.

3. Wash the filter element in clean fuel.

4. Replace the seal ring in the filter cover.

5. Install the filter, bleed the filter and check for leaks.

6 Cylinder—1973–76 Only

1. Remove the fuel return valve and plug at the carburetor.

2. Remove and clean the fuel filter.

3. Use a new gasket and replace the filter and plug.

4. Check for leaks.

4 Cylinder Gasoline Engine

1. Remove hoses and remove filter.

2. Install new filter in direction of flow.

3. Check for leaks.

Mechanical Fuel Pump

All Mercedes-Benz carbureted engines use a diaphragm type fuel pump, which is mounted on the side of the block. It is operated by a gear driven eccentric shaft through a rocker arm on the fuel pump.

Removal and Installation

1. Clean the joint around the fuel pump base and cylinder block.

2. One at a time, remove and plug the intake and outlet lines from the fuel pump.

3. Unbolt the retaining bolts and remove the fuel pump and gasket from the cylinder block.

4. Clean the mating surfaces of the engine and cylinder block.

5. Install a new gasket.

6. Insert the fuel pump into the block and install the retaining bolts. Be sure that the bolts are tightened evenly.

7. Reconnect the intake and outlet lines to the fuel pump.

8. Run the engine and check for leaks.

Testing Delivery Pressure

1. Remove the wire from the coil to prevent starting.

2. Connect a pressure gauge into the output line of the fuel pump.

3. Crank the engine and read the delivery pressure on the pressure gauge. The pressure should be a constant 1.5–2.5 psi.

4. If the pressure is not within specifications or is erratic, remove the pump for service or for replacement with a new or rebuilt unit. No adjustment is provided.

Electric Fuel Pump

NOTE: *Do not confuse the electric fuel pump with the injection pump.*

All Mercedes-Benz fuel injected engines are equipped with electric fuel pumps. The electric fuel pump is located underneath the rear floor panel. The fuel return line was also eliminated and a check ball installed in its place.

Two types of fuel pumps have been used. One, the large pump, has been replaced with a new small design which has a bypass system to prevent vapor lock.

Removal and Installation

1. Jack the left rear of the car and support it on jackstands. This will provide sufficient working clearance.

2. Remove and plug the intake, outlet, and bypass lines from the pump.

3. Disconnect the electrical leads.

4. Unbolt and remove the fuel pump and vibration pads.

5. Install the fuel pump in the reverse order of removal. Be sure that the electrical leads are connected to the proper terminals. The negative wire (brown) is connected to the negative terminal (brown plastic plate) and the positive wire (black/red) is connected to the positive terminal (red plastic plate). If the terminals are reversed, the pump will operate in the reverse direction of normal rotation and will deliver no fuel.

Testing Fuel Pump Delivery Pressure

1. Reduce the pressure in the ring line by pulling the plug on the starting valve. Connect the terminals of the starting valve to the positive and negative terminals of the battery for about 20 seconds. Reconnect the plug to the starting valve.

2. Remove the air filter and connect a pressure gauge at the branch connection of the ring line.

3. Run the engine at idle speed and measure the pressure in the ring line. The pressure should be 28.0–29.5 psi.

4. Stop the engine. The pressure may drop to 25 psi. Wait another five minutes and the pressure may drop to 22 psi. This is normal.

5. The pressure may drop uniformly to 0 psi. This indicates that there is a leak somewhere in the system.

Carburetors

Removal and Installation

Stromberg 175CDT (220/8 and 1974–77 230)

1. Remove the air cleaner.

Carburetor Applications

Model	Year	Carburetor
220/8	1970-73	1 Stromberg 175 CDT
230	1974-77	
250C	1970-72	2 Zenith 35/40 INAT
280	1973-76	1 Solex 4A1
280C	1973-76	
280S	1975-76	

2. Remove and plug the fuel lines.

CAUTION: *Do not pull off the fuel lines. They should be pried off along with the securing discs.*

3. Disconnect the control linkage.

4. Remove the vacuum lines.

5. Disconnect the water hoses for the automatic choke.

6. Disconnect the leads for the automatic choke and fuel shut-off valve.

7. Remove the carburetor retaining nuts and remove the carburetor.

8. Installation is the reverse of removal. Adjust the carburetor. See "Tune-Up".

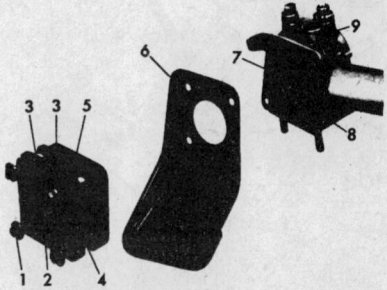

Gasket installation on Stromberg 175CDT

1. Carburetor retaining screw
2. Paper gasket
3. Rubber flange
4. Rubber flange fastening screw
5. Insulating flange
6. Deflector plate
7. Paper gasket
8. Intake manifold
9. Water separator

Zenith 35/40 INAT (250/8, 250C, 280S/8)

1. Remove the air cleaner.

2. Pull the cable from the starter cover.

3. Unscrew and plug the fuel lines.

4. Detach the carburetor linkage from the carburetor body.

5. Remove any water lines and electric choke leads. Remove the vacuum line.

6. Loosen and remove the carburetor retaining nuts. Lift the carburetors from the manifolds.

7. Installation is the reverse of removal.

8. Place the insulating flanges and screening plate on the intake manifold.

9. Install the rubber rings on the carburetors. Slide the rubber ring on the water separator located at the bottom of the air cleaner.

10. Install the air cleaner so that the water separator empties into the funnel.

11. Tighten the retaining nuts and install the hot air line and engine vent line.

Solex 4 A 1 (280, 280C and 280S)

1. Remove the air filter.

2. Remove the electric cable from the starter cover and cut-off valves.

3. Remove the vacuum lines.

4. To prevent corrosion from leaked coolant, cover the starter housing with a rag. Release the pressure in the cooling system by cracking the radiator cap until

pressure has escaped. Install and tighten the radiator cap. Remove and plug the coolant water hoses from the carburetor.

5. Remove and plug the fuel lines.

6. Remove the retaining nuts and remove the carburetor from the manifold.

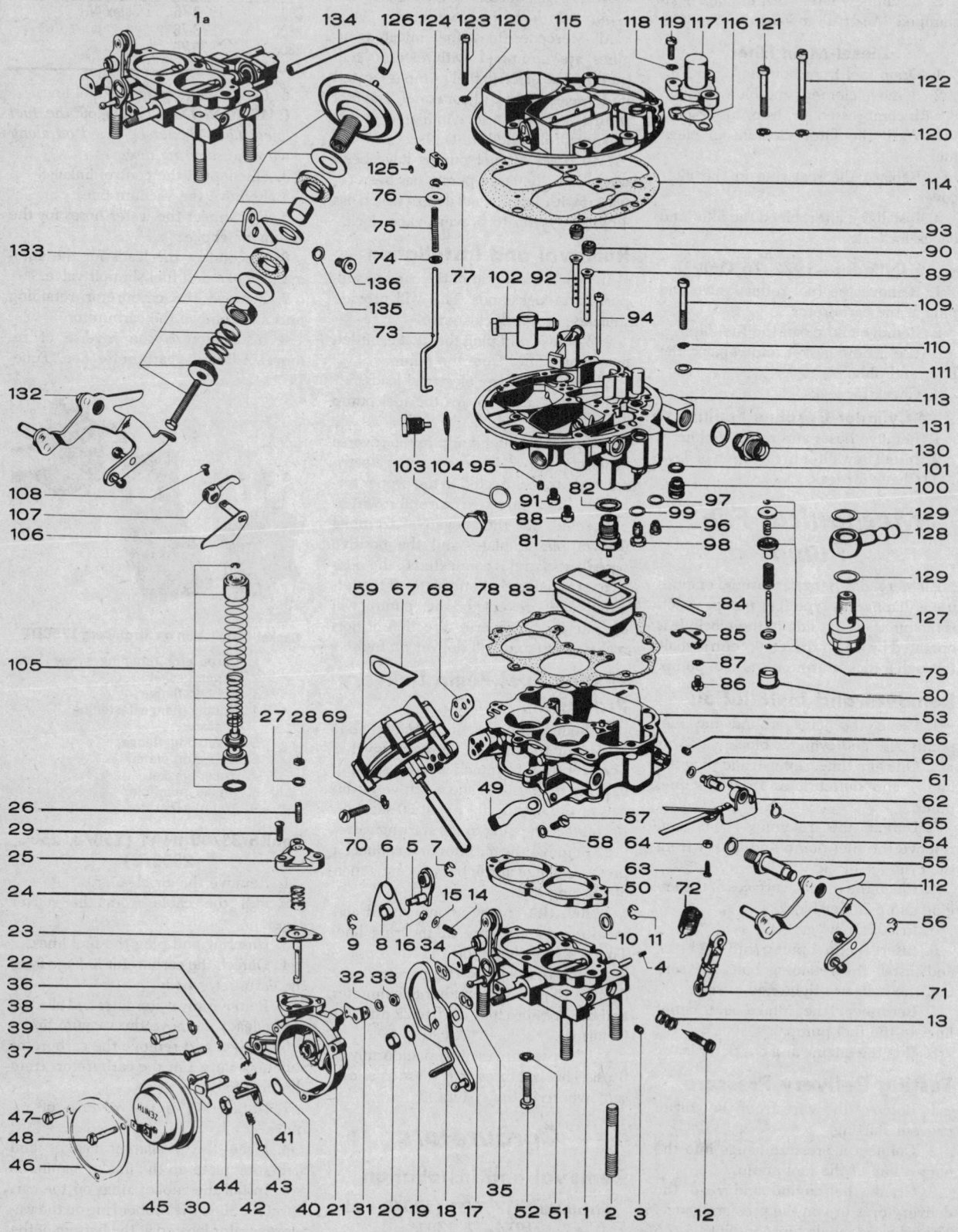

Zenith 35/40 INAT carburetor

2. Pin screw
3. Screw
5. Joint lever
6. Return spring
7. Safety washer
8. Roller
9. Safety washer
10. Flat washer
11. Safety washer
12. Idle mixture screw
13. Pressure spring
14. Adjustment screw
15. Spring washer
16. Hex head nut
17. Flat washer
18. Throttle lever
19. Safety washer
20. Spacer
21. Choke body
22. Return spring
23. Diaphragm spring
24. Pressure spring
25. Valve cover
26. Screw
27. Seal ring
28. Hex head nut
29. Countersunk screw
30. Operating lever
31. Transfer lever

32. Spring washer
33. Hex head nut
34. Gasket
35. Gasket
36. Star washer
37. Countersunk screw
38. Spring washer
39. Screw
40. Safety washer
41. Stop lever
42. Pressure spring
43. Stop screw
44. Hex head nut
45. Choke cover
46. Stop ring
47. Hex head nut
48. Hex head nut
49. Clamp
50. Isolation flange
51. Spring washer
52. Screw
53. Float bowl
54. Spring washer
55. Bearing bolt
56. Safety washer
57. Screw
58. Spring washer
59. Vacuum chamber
60. Seal ring

69. Spring washer
70. Screw
71. Connecting rod
72. Return spring
73. Connecting rod
74. Flat washer
75. Pressure spring
76. Washer
77. Tension ring
78. Seal ring
79. Air valve
80. Bushing
81. Needle valve
82. Seal ring
83. Float
84. Shaft
85. Bracket
86. Cheesehead screw
87. Spring washer
88. Main jet
89. Mixture tube
90. Air correction jet
94. Idle jet
95. Jet
96. Pump suction valve

97. Seal ring
98. Pump pressure valve
99. Seal ring
100. Jet
101. Seal ring
102. Sprayer
103. Pressure screw
104. Seal ring
105. Pump piston
106. Pump lever
107. Inner pump lever
108. Countersunk screw
109. Screw
111. Spring washer
110. Lockwasher
114. Carburetor body gasket
115. Carburetor top
116. Seal ring
117. Cover
118. Lockwasher
119. Screw
120. Lockwasher
122. Screw
121. Screw
123. Screw
124. Joint piece
125. Safety washer
126. Cheesehead screw

1. Throttle valve
60. Lockwasher
61. Bearing bolt
62. Operating lever

63. Cheesehead screw
64. Hex head nut
65. Expansion ring
112. Complete operating lever

113. Complete platin block
127. Fuel return valve

128. Ring hose piece
129. Seal ring
130. Threaded fitting
131. Seal ring

Additional parts for carburetor 000.120-13 DB 16

1. Throttle valve
4. Screw
66. Threaded pin
67. Cable holder

112. Complete operating lever
113. Platin block

Additional parts for carburetor 000.120-14 DB 17

1. Throttle valve
67. Cable holder
113. Platin block
132. Operating lever

133. Vacuum regulator
134. Rubber hose
135. Lockwasher
136. Cheesehead screw

Additional parts for carburetor 000.120-23 DB 27

1a. Throttle valve
60. Lockwasher
61. Bearing bolt
62. Operating lever

63. Cheesehead screw
64. Hex head nut
65. Expansion ring
67. Cable holder

112. Complete operating lever
113. Platin block
127. Fuel return valve

128. Ring hose piece
129. Seal ring
130. Threaded fitting
131. Seal ring

Zenith 35/40 INAT carburetor

Install the gasket on a Solex 4 A 1 carburetor with the mark as shown (lower left corner).

7. Installation is the reverse of removal. Install the insulating flange on the intake manifold as shown. The paper side of the insulating flange must face UP. In 1974, a new style insulating flange was used, which can be installed on previous engines.

8. Install the retaining nuts and tighten evenly, torquing the nuts in a crossing pattern. Torque the nuts to 7–11 ft lbs.

9. Be sure to adjust the idle speed. See "Tune-Up".

Overhaul

Efficient carburetion depends greatly on careful cleaning and inspection during overhaul. Since dirt, gum, water, or varnish in or on the carburetor parts are often responsible for poor performance.

Overhaul your carburetor in a clean, dust-free area. Carefully disassemble the carburetor, referring often to the exploded views. Keep all similar and lookalike parts segregated during disassembly and cleaning to avoid accidental interchange during assembly. Make a note of all jet sizes.

When the carburetor is disassembled, wash all parts (except diaphragms, electric choke units, pump plunger, and any other plastic, leather, fiber, or rubber parts) in clean carburetor solvent. Do not leave parts in the solvent any longer than is necessary to sufficiently loosen the deposits. Excessive cleaning may remove the special finish from the float bowl and choke valve bodies, leaving these parts unfit for service. Rinse all parts in clean solvent and blow them dry with compressed air or allow them to air dry. Wipe clean all cork, plastic, leather, and fiber parts with a clean, lint-free cloth.

Blow out all passages and jets with compressed air and be sure that there are no restrictions or blockages. Never use wire or similar tools to clean jets, fuel passages, or air bleeds. Clean all jets and valves separately to avoid accidental interchange.

Check all parts for wear or damage. If wear or damage is found, replace the defective parts. Especially check the following:

Mercedes-Benz

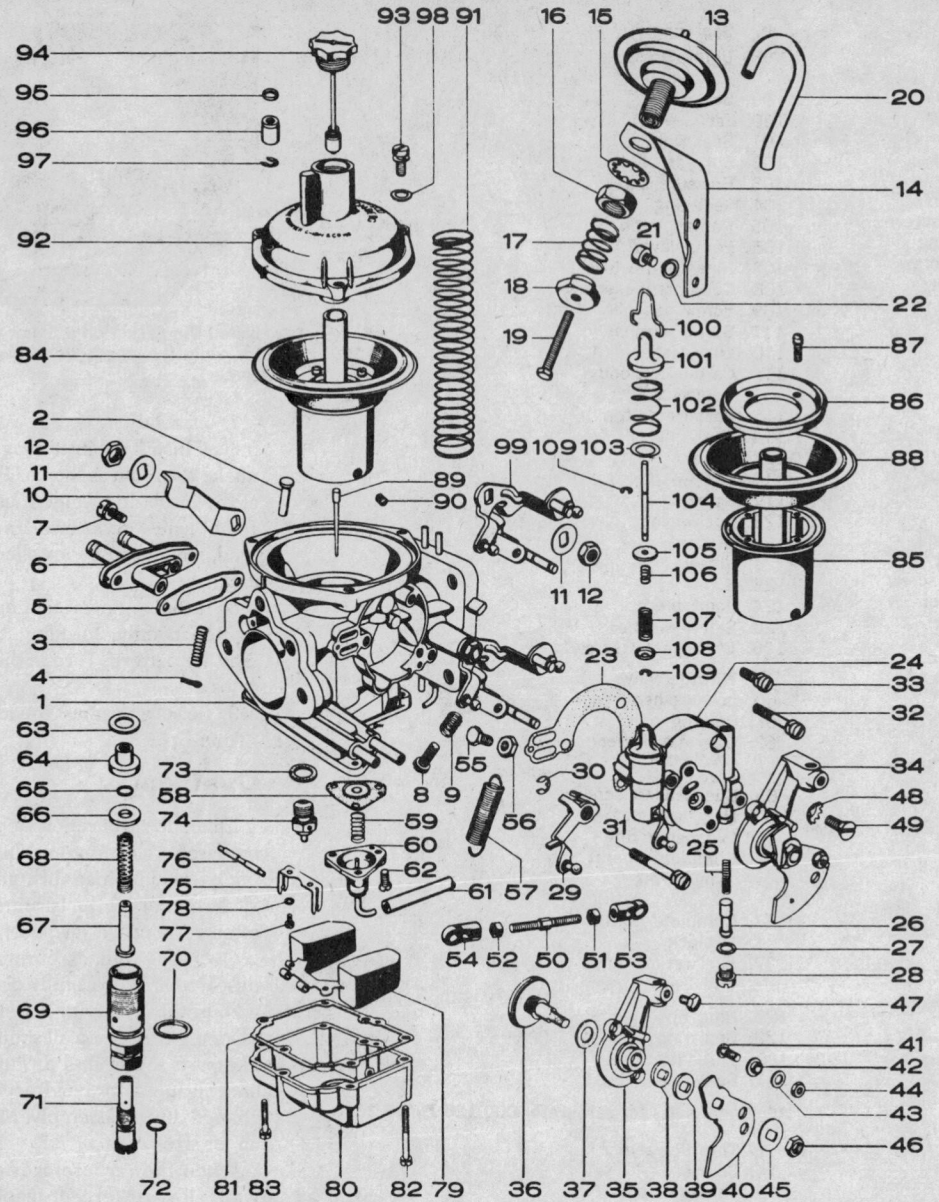

Stromberg 175CDT carburetor

1. Carburetor housing
2. Carburetor tickler
3. Compression spring
4. Locking spring
5. Gasket
6. Connecting cover
7. Screw
8. Idle adjustment screw
9. Spring
10. Control rod
11. Locking plate
12. Nut
13. Vacuum control
14. Bracket
15. Lockwasher
16. Hex nut
17. Spring
18. Adjustment nut
19. Screw
20. Vacuum hose
21. Screw
22. Lockwasher
23. Gasket
24. Starter housing
25. Spring
   (not installed)
26. Vacuum piston
27. Sealing ring

28. Plug
29. Starter lever
30. Circlip
31. Screw
32. Screw
33. Screw
34. Starter cover, compl.
35. Starter cover
36. Rotary slide valve
37. Gasket
38. Stop
39. Spacer
40. Starter lever
41. Clamp bolt
42. Bushing
43. Washer
44. Hex nut
45. Lock plate
46. Hex nut
47. Clamping bolt
48. Lockwasher
49. Countersunk screw
50. Connecting rod
51. Hex nut
52. Hex nut
53. Ball socket
54. Ball socket
55. Hex screw

56. Hex nut
57. Spring
58. Vacuum diaphragm
59. Spring
60. Valve cover
61. Vacuum hose
62. Countersunk screw
63. Sealing ring
64. Guide tube
65. Rubber ring
66. Washer
67. Needle valve
68. Spring
69. Lockscrew
70. Rubber ring
71. Idle mixture adjustment
   screw
72. Rubber ring
73. Sealing ring
74. Float needle valve
75. Bracket
76. Float spindle
77. Screw
78. Lockwasher
79. Dual float
80. Float chamber cover
81. Gasket

82. Screw
83. Screw
84. Air piston with diaphragm
85. Air piston
86. Retaining disc
87. Screw
88. Diaphragm
89. Nozzle needle
90. Clamping bolt
91. Compression spring
92. Carburetor cover
93. Screws
94. Damping element
95. Sleeve
96. Piston
97. Circlip
98. Washer
99. Throttle lever
100. Clamping spring
101. Cap
102. Spring
103. Washer
104. Rod
105. Valve disc
106. Spring
107. Spring
108. Spring retainer
109. Circlip

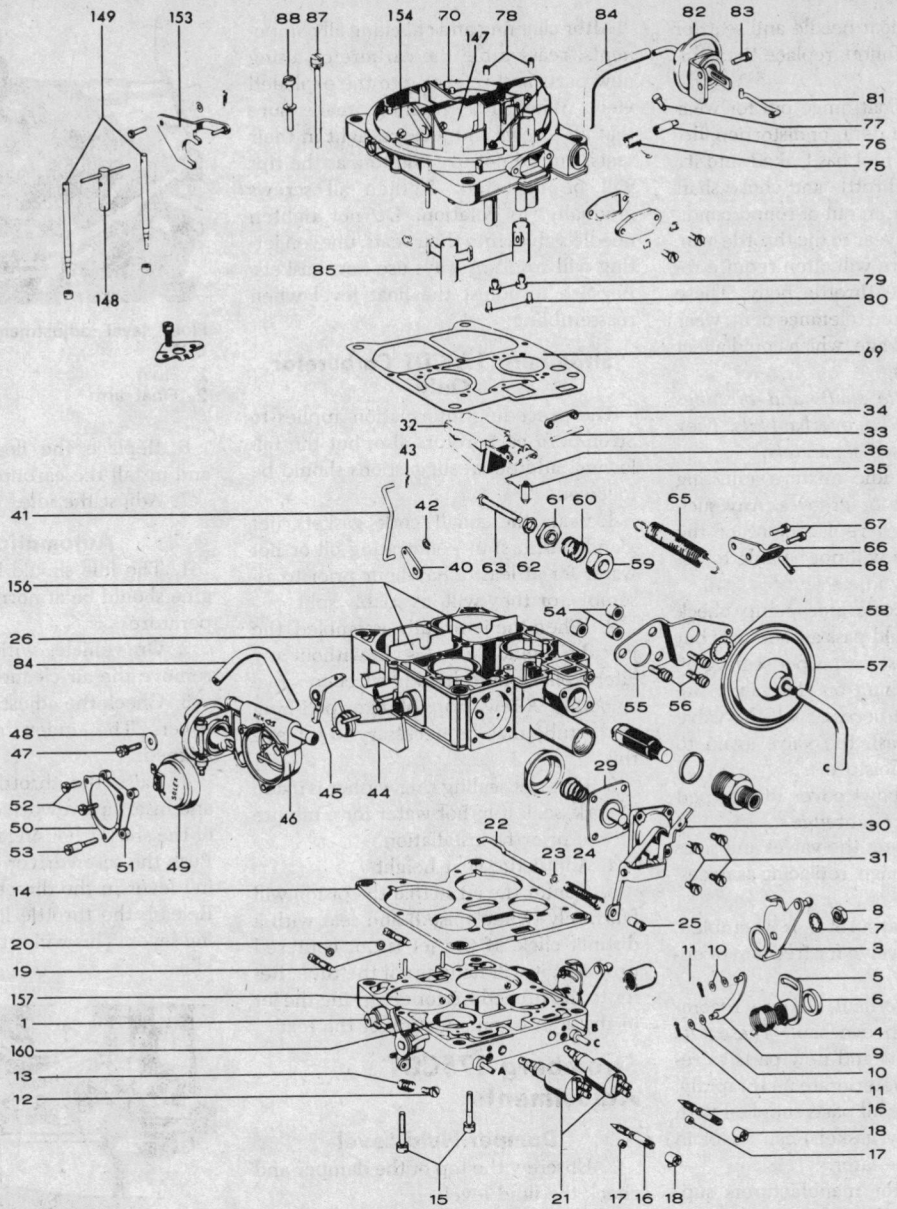

Solex 4 A 1 carburetor

1. Throttle valve housing
3. Bracket
4. Spring
5. Cam lever
6. Bushing
7. Washer
8. Nut
9. Secondary connecting rod
10. Washer
11. Cotter pin
12. Screw
13. Spring
14. Plate
15. Screw
16. Idle mixture adjusting screws
17. Idle mixture adjusting screws
18. Idle mixture adjusting screws
19. Secondary jets
20. Secondary jets
21. Idle speed solenoid
22. Actuating levers for accelerator pump
23. Actuating levers for accelerator pump
24. Actuating levers for accelerator pump
25. Actuating levers for accelerator pump
26. Float housing
29. Diaphragm
30. Accelerator pump cover
31. Screws

32. Float
33. Float shaft
34. Hold-down clamp
35. Float needle
36. Float needle
40. Choke connecting rod
41. Choke connecting rod
42. Circlip
43. Cotter pin
44. Cam lever
45. Step lever
46. Thermostat housing
47. Screw
48. Washer
49. Thermostat cover
50. Attaching plate
51. Bushing
52. Screws (short)
53. Screw (long)
54. Vacuum regulator with bracket
55. Vacuum regulator with bracket
56. Vacuum regulator with bracket
57. Vacuum regulator with bracket
58. Vacuum regulator with bracket
59. Nut
60. Spring
61,62. Nut
63. Screw

65. Throttle return spring
66. Idle stop screw with bracket
67. Idle stop screw with bracket
68. Idle stop screw with bracket
69. Gasket
70. Carburetor cover
75. Spring
76. Eccentric pin
77. Clamp screw
78. Primary idle air jets
79. Main jets
80. Screws
81. Vacuum diaphragm connecting rod
82. Vacuum diaphragm
83. Screw
84. Vacuum line
85. Emulsion Tube
87. Screw
88. Screw
147. Choke plate
148. Guide pin
149. Secondary needle valve
153. Lever
154. Secondary choke plate
156. Secondary baffle plates
157. Throttle valve (primary)
160. Throttle valve (secondary)

1. Check the float needle and seat for wear. If wear is found, replace the complete assembly.

2. Check the float hinge pin for wear and the float(s) for dents or distortion. Replace the float if fuel has leaked into it.

3. Check the throttle and choke shaft bores for wear or an out-of-round condition. Damage or wear to the throttle arm, shaft, or shaft bore will often require replacement of the throttle body. These parts require a close tolerance of fit; wear may allow air leakage, which could affect starting and idling.

NOTE: *Throttle shafts and bushings are not included in overhaul kits. They can be purchased separately.*

4. Inspect the idle mixture adjusting needles for burrs or grooves. Any such condition requires replacement of the needle, since you will not be able to obtain a satisfactory idle.

5. Test the accelerator pump check valves. They should pass air one way but not the other. Test for proper seating by blowing and sucking on the valve. Replace the valve if necessary. If the valve is satisfactory, wash the valve again to remove breath moisture.

6. Check the bowl cover for warped surfaces with a straightedge.

7. Closely inspect the valves and seats for wear and damage, replacing as necessary.

8. After the carburetor is assembled, check the choke valve for freedom of operation.

Carburetor overhaul kits are recommended for each overhaul. These kits contain all gaskets and new parts to replace those that deteriorate most rapidly. Failure to replace all parts supplied with the kit (especially gaskets) can result in poor performance later.

Some carburetor manufacturers supply overhaul kits of three basic types: minor repair; major repair; and gasket kits. Basically, they contain the following:

Minor Repair Kits:
All gaskets
Float needle valve
Volume control screw
All diaphragms
Spring for the pump diaphragm
Major Repair Kits:
All jets and gaskets
All diaphragms
Float needle valve
Volume control screw
Pump ball valve
Main jet carrier
Float
Complete intermediate rod
Intermediate pump lever
Complete injector tube
Some cover hold-down screws and washers
Gasket Kits:
All gaskets

After cleaning and checking all components, reassemble the carburetor, using new parts and referring to the exploded view. When reassembling, make sure that all screws and jets are tight in their seats, but do not overtighten, as the tips will be distorted. Tighten all screws gradually, in rotation. Do not tighten needle valves into their seats; uneven jetting will result. Always use new gaskets. Be sure to adjust the float level when reassembling.

Stromberg 175CDT Carburetor Only

The preceding information applies to Stromberg carburetors also, but the following, additional suggestions should be followed.

1. Soak the small cork gaskets (jet gland washers) in penetrating oil or hot water for at least a half-hour prior to assembly, or they will invariably split.

2. When the jet is fully assembled, the jet tube should be a close fit without any lateral play, but it should be free to move smoothly. A few drops of oil or polishing of the tube may be necessary to achieve this.

3. If the jet sealing ring washer is made of cork, soak it in hot water for a minute or two prior to installation.

4. Adjust the float height.

5. Center the jet so that the piston will fall freely (when raised) and seat with a distinct click. If the jet is not centered properly, it will hang up in the tube. Refer to the procedure for centering the jet in the adjustments section of the text.

Stromberg 175CDT Adjustments

Damper Fluid Level

1. Unscrew the top of the damper and check the fluid level.

2. If necessary, top up the reservoir with engine oil, or in cold weather, automatic transmission fluid (ATF). 1974–77 models use only ATF.

3. The fluid level should be to the top edge of the piston ring or on 1974–77 models, to the lower edge of the filler plug threads.

4. Replace the top on the reservoir.

Float Adjustment

1. Remove the carburetor.

2. Remove the float chamber cover.

3. Do not loosen the lock screw from the needle, or the needle will have to be recentered.

4. Measure the distance between the edge of the carburetor housing and the upper edge of the float; it should be 15–17 mm.

5. To correct the float level, bend the float arm at the tang over the needle valve. The float arm must always remain perpendicular to the needle valve.

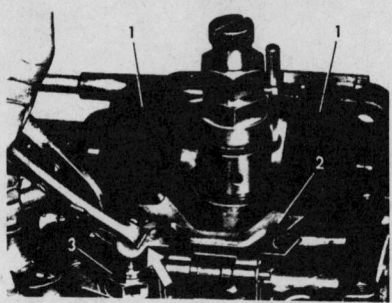

Float level adjustment—Stromberg 175-CDT.
1. Float
2. Float arm
3. Needle valve
4. Sealing ring

6. Replace the float chamber cover and install the carburetor.

7. Adjust the idle.

Automatic Choke

1. The idle should be set and the engine should be at normal operating temperature.

2. On vehicles with air conditioning, remove the air cleaner and air intake.

3. Check the adjustment of the choke cover. The index marks should be aligned.

4. Raise the throttle linkage slightly and insert a screwdriver through the slot of the starter housing on the carburetor. Push the screwdriver against the engaging lever in the direction of the engine. Release the throttle linkage and engaging lever. This will set the engine at fast idle.

Stromberg 175CDT automatic choke adjustment.
1. Connecting rod
2. Hex nut
3. Threaded bolt
4. Hex nut
5. Actuating lever
6. Venting valve

5. The fast idle speed should be 3300–3600 rpm. If the speed requires adjustment, loosen both locknuts on the connecting rod and turn the threaded bolt. ½ turn of the bolt will change the engine rpm by about 200–300 rpm. Decreasing the length of the bolt will decrease rpm and increasing the length will increase rpm.

Fast Idle (1975–77 Only)

The fast idle adjustment is done with the cam on the second step.

1. Run the engine to normal operating temperature.

Fast idle adjusting screw (114) on 1975-77 Stromberg 175 CDT

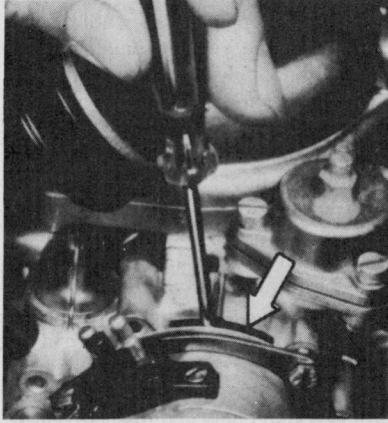

Access slot (arrow) on 1975-77 Stromberg 175 CDT

2. With the engine idling, raise the throttle linkage slightly.

3. At the same time, push the engaging lever with a small screwdriver, through the slot of the choke housing in the direction of the engine, against the stop on the pull down diaphragm rod. Do not force it past the stop.

4. Raise the throttle linkage, while holding the engaging lever against the stop.

5. Check the CO and fast idle.

6. Adjust the fast idle speed with the upper adjusting screw to 1600–1800 rpm.

7. Adjust the CO with the mixture adjusting screw to 5–8%. To check the CO, the center vacuum line for the air injection switchover valve must be disconnected and plugged.

Full Throttle Stop (1975–77 California Only)

1. With the accelerator pedal fully depressed, adjust the full throttle stop screw so that a clearance of .02 in. exists between the throttle valve lever and carburetor housing.

Thermo Air Valve

1. Disconnect the hoses from the thermo air valve and blow into one hose.

Full throttle stop adjusting screw and clearance (arrow) on 1975-77 Stromberg 175 CDT

If the valve is cold, no air can pass through the valve. If the valve is warm (slightly above room temperature) air should pass through the valve.

Zenith 35/40 INAT Adjustments

Float Level

1. Remove the carburetor.

2. Remove the float chamber cover with the float attached.

3. Measure the distance from the edge of the float housing to the top edge of the float.

4. The distance in Step 3 should be 21–23 mm if the float level is correct. If the float level requires adjustment, install a sealing ring, of the appropriate thickness, under the needle valve.

5. Install the carburetor cover using new gaskets; tighten the cover screws evenly.

6. Install the carburetor and adjust the idle and balance the carburetors.

Accelerator Pump

1. Be sure that the pump and lever are working smoothly.

2. Check the start of injection. As the throttle valve is opened, a powerful jet of

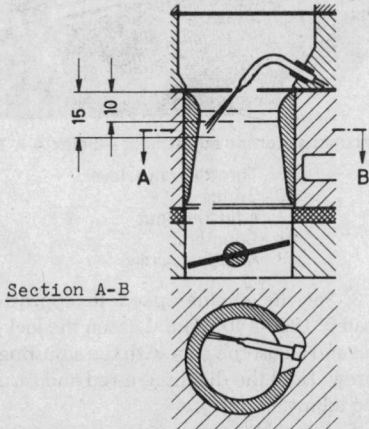

Section A-B

Fuel spray pattern—Zenith 35/40 INAT

fuel must emerge from the injection tube. It may be necessary to check the injection tube and the accelerator diaphragm for blockage.

3. The fuel jet must be sprayed against the wall of the air horn, 10–15 mm below the upper edge of the float chamber cover.

Dashpot

NOTE: *Apply the parking brake and chock the wheels.*

1. If the car is equipped with automatic transmission, place the selector lever in a drive range and, with the engine not running, back out the hex bolt until the vent valve is raised 0.020–0.040 in.

2. Then start the engine and adjust the compression spring by turning the nut to obtain the specified idle speed.

3. Place the selector lever in Neutral and make sure that the lever is against the idle stop.

4. If the lever touches the hex bolt, back out the bolt and readjust the spring with the car in Drive.

5. If the car is equipped with manual transmission, start the engine, make sure all accessories are turned off, and adjust the nut to give 0.004 in. clearance between the hex bolt and the actuating lever.

Dashpot adjustment—Zenith 35/40 INAT

1. Idle stop screw
2. Vent valve
3. Vacuum hose to valve
4. Vacuum hose connecting valve and control unit
5. Spring
6. Knurled nut
7. Adjustment screw
8. Actuating lever

Automatic Choke

1. Make sure that the choke butterflies operate without binding, then check the choke housing cover; the marks must align.

NOTE: *The spring is preloaded 0.20 in.*

2. Turn on the ignition switch and make sure the throttle butterflies open after a few minutes (engine cold).

3. To adjust the pilot throttle gap with the engine running, lift the accelerator linkage and insert a screwdriver between the choke housing and the throttle lever. Press the relay lever upward until it touches the stop on the diaphragm rod, then release the linkage.

4. Measure the clearance between the choke butterfly and the carburetor bore; it should be 0.096 in. If necessary, adjust by turning the screw on the starter valve.

5. Start the engine and allow it to warm up.

Automatic choke and fast idle adjustment —Zenith 35/40 INAT.
1. Starter cover
2. Starter housing
3. Adjustment screw

6. Shut off the engine, raise the accelerator linkage and insert a screwdriver between the starter housing and the throttle lever of one carburetor. Press the relay lever upward and release the linkage. This should cause the adjustment screw inside the choke housing to come to rest on the top notch of the cam. The adjustment screw should only be turned with the engine off.

7. Hook up a tachometer and start the engine; adjust the screw to obtain the proper fast idle. Adjust the other carburetor in the same manner.

Solex 4 A 1 Adjustments

Fuel Level

1. There is no provision for measuring the fuel level, other than with the special Mercedes-Benz tool. It is a measuring rod which is inserted through the bore of the carburetor cover, and can be purchased from a dealer or fabricated.

2. Run the engine briefly at fast idle and shut off the ignition.

3. Insert the measuring gauge through the bore of the carburetor cover as far as it will go.

Measuring fuel level on Solex 4 A 1 with gauge (1).

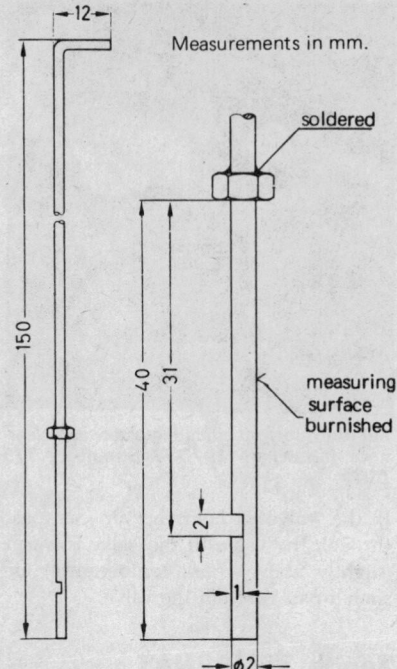

Measurements in mm.

Fabricated tool for measuring fuel level on Solex 4 A 1 carburetor

4. Remove the gauge and read the fuel level. The reading should be within the tolerance range marked on the stick.

5. To adjust the level, remove the carburetor cover and adjust the float by bending it on the hinge.

6. Reinstall the cover and test the level again.

Vacuum Governor

1. Set the idle speed and make sure that the engine is at normal operating temperature.

2. Run the engine at idle and pull the vacuum hose from the governor.

Vacuum governor adjustment—Solex 4 A 1
3. Throttle valve lever
60. Spring
61. Adjusting nut
62. Counternut
63. Adjuting screw

3. Set the engine speed to approximately 1200–1400 rpm. Loosen the locknut and adjust the rpm with the adjusting screw. Hold the diaphragm rod and turn the adjusting nut.

4. Adjust the compression spring with the transmission in gear.

5. The speed should be 600–700 rpm. If necessary, adjust the compression spring with the adjusting nut.

6. Turn on the air conditioning, and turn the wheels to full lock. The engine should keep running. If it does not, adjust the speed with the adjusting nut again. See Step 3.

Automatic Choke

1. Check the choke for ease of operation.

2. Switch on the ignition and check to be sure that the choke opens after a minute or so.

3. Check the adjustment on the choke cover. The markings on the housing and cover should be aligned.

Choke Gap

1. Run the engine at idle until the diaphragm in the vacuum unit has been pulled completely against the stop.

2. Then clamp the hose to block all vacuum.

3. Be sure that the diaphragm is still against the stop and slightly raise the throttle valve lever. Position the stepped disc upward against the top stop. Release the throttle valve lever.

4. Push the lever of the bi-metallic spring until the stop is felt. The connecting rod will now be against the stop in the slot of the lever.

5. Measure the choke gap with a # 53 drill (0.060 in.) between the choke plate and the wall of the air horn.

6. To adjust the gap, remove the coolant hose from the choke housing. Cover the choke housing with a rag and release the pressure in the radiator. Tighten the radiator cap again. Remove the coolant hose and clamp it shut.

Automatic choke adjustment—Solex 4 A 1. If the choke gap is too large, push the bend apart; if the choke gap is too small, push the bend together.

7. Hold the connecting rod with a screwdriver. Bend the connecting rod with a second screwdriver.

8. While making the adjustment, be sure that the diaphragm in the vacuum unit is still against its stop.

Fast Idle

1. Adjust the idle speed and be sure that the engine is at normal operating temperature.

2. Run the engine at idle speed.

3. Raise the throttle valve lever slightly and position the stepped disc completely upward against the top stop.

4. Release the throttle valve lever.

5. Connect a tachometer and measure the engine speed. It should be 2400–2600. If required, adjust the fast idle with the fast idle speed adjusting screw.

Solex 4 A 1 fast idle adjustment screw (12)

Accelerator Pump

1. Move the throttle valve lever several times. A strong jet of fuel should be forced out of the fuel outlets.

2. If not, remove the accelerator pump cover and check the diaphragm. Blow out the ducts with compressed air.

3. Install the accelerator pump cover.

4. If there still is no fuel from the injection tube, remove the carburetor cover.

5. Actuate the accelerator pump. If fuel emerges from the ball valves, blow out the injection holes in the carburetor cover with compressed air.

6. Install the carburetor cover. Tighten the screws evenly to 11 ft lbs.

Fuel Return Valve

1. Pull the fuel return hose from the connection to the return line below the fuel pump.

2. Hold the return hose in a container and check whether a strong fuel jet comes from the line with the automatic transmission in Drive and the air conditioning on.

Fuel Injection

Several types of fuel injection are used on Mercedes-Benz gasoline engines. All 6-cylinder engines except the 280E and 280SE use mechanical fuel injection, while the 280E and 280SE use the CIS fuel injection. 1972–75 V-8 s are equipped with electronic fuel injection. 1976–77 V-8 s use the Bosch K-Jetronic mechanical injection. Due to the sensitive nature of these systems, and the numerous special tools required, it is best to refer any service or adjustment, other than idle speed adjustment, to a qualified Mercedes-Benz service facility.

CAUTION: *Even a seemingly minor adjustment, such as idle speed, can necessitate adjustments to other portions of the fuel injection system. Be extremely careful when adjusting the idle. If any difficulty at all is experienced, immediately refer the vehicle to a Mercedes-Benz dealer. Further attempts at adjustment will only upset the balance of an already delicate system.*

Mechanical Fuel Injection—280SE/8 (1972) and 280S/8 (1972)

This system is a mechanical system used on 6-cylinder engines. The injection pump is a 6-cylinder type with mechanical linkage.

Adjustments

Regulating Linkage

NOTE: *Do not change the idle speed and full load stop on the injection pump.*

1. Disconnect the regulating rod.

2. Check the linkage for freedom of operation. There should be no play.

3. When checking the adjusting lever on the injection pump, it will not return to idling position each time. It is sufficiently free if it jumps back to idle position when the starter is activated for a few seconds.

4. Disconnect regulating rod from venturi control unit.

5. The throttle valve in the venturi should close completely with no binding.

6. Adjust the idle stop screw so that when the throttle valve lever is pressed tightly against the stop screw it will grip slightly without binding.

7. Loosen the regulating shaft ball-head.

8. If there is no bolt hole on six-cylinder models adjust the length of the regulating linkage to 233 mm between the center of the 2 ball heads.

9. Make the same adjustment on the regulating rod toward the venturi control unit so that the throttle valve lever rests against the idle speed stop.

10. Slowly move the regulating shaft and adjust the levers on the injection pump and throttle valves so that they are lifted simultaneously.

11. Connect the regulating rod.

12. On engines with progressive regulating linkage, adjust the regulating rod so that the roller is just resting against the end stop in the cam lever.

13. If equipped with regulating damper, the closing damper stroke should be 4–5 mm.

14. On automatic transmission cars, disconnect the control thrust rod on the guide lever. Disconnect the pull rod and connect it free of any tension. Push the control rod back to the idle position and connect the ball socket free of tension.

15. Step on the accelerator pedal. The adjusting lever on the injection pump should be against the full load stop with the pedal floored. Adjust the regulating shaft if necessary.

Mechanical fuel injection components

1. Throttle valve lever
2. Full load stop
3. Idling speed stop screw
4. Regulating rod
5. Regulating lever
6. Regulating rod
7. Regulating shaft
8. Regulating rod
9. Adjusting lever
10. Idling speed and full load stop

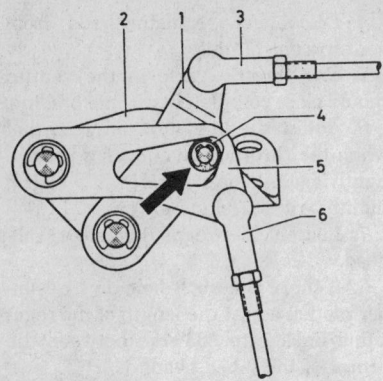

Mechanical fuel injection—progressive regulating linkage adjustment

1. Regulating lever
2. Holder
3. Pull rod
4. Roller
5. Cam lever
6. Thrust rod

Constant Speed

On those engines with a solenoid to keep the engine rpm steady, set the adjusting nut on the solenoid so that idle is maintained (either in Drive or with A/C ON).

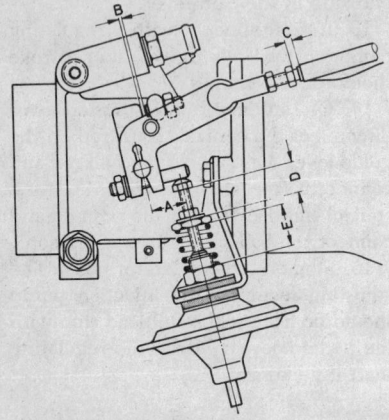

Mechanical fuel injection—vacuum governor solenoid adjustment

A. Shaft distance = 17 mm (±0.5 mm)
B. Throttle valve opening = 1.0-1.5 mm with gear engaged
C. Idle travel of sliding rod
D. Length of thrust bolt = 14.5-15.5 mm
E. Spring length = 19.5 mm

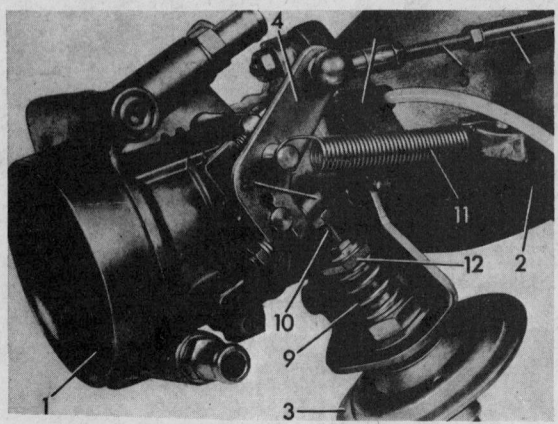

1. Venturi control unit
2. Intake manifold
3. Vacuum box
4. Throttle valve lever
5. Sliding rod
6. Sliding sleeve
7. Vacuum tap
8. Clamping bolt
9. Compression spring
10. Adjusting screw
11. Return spring
12. Adjusting nut

Mechanical fuel injection—vacuum governor adjustment

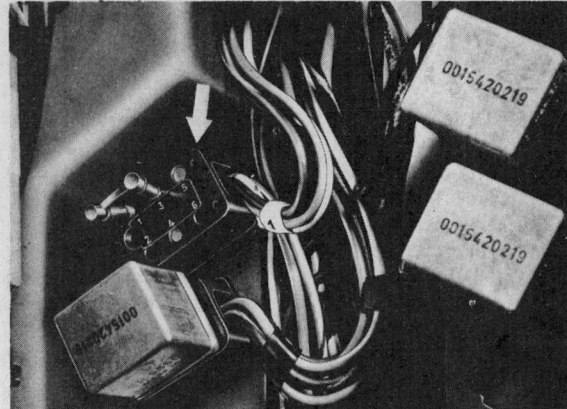

Bridge terminals 1 and 3 of the fuel pump relay

1. At idle, in Neutral, the adjusting screw should barely rest against the clamp bolt.

2. Engage Drive. The throttle valve should open 1–1.5 mm. Check the adjusting screw again.

3. Check the clamp bolt. It should not bind. Maintain dimension A as shown.

4. On cars with A/C, run the engine at idle, in Drive, with A/C ON. Adjust the solenoid so that the idle travel on the regulating rod is cancelled.

Delivery Pressure

The engine is stopped for this test; merely switch on the ignition. Disconnect the fuel line from the starting valve and connect it to a pressure gauge. Delivery pressure should be 11–15.5 psi.

Bosch Electronic Fuel Injection—1972–75 V8 Engines

This system is a constant pressure, electronically controlled unit. The "brain" of the system, actually a small computer that senses the determining factors for fuel delivery, is located behind the passenger kick panel on the right-hand side.

A Bosch tester is necessary to accurately test the solid state circuitry and components, but there are a few checks that can be carried out independently of the tester.

Tests

Delivery Pressure

Temporarily reduce the pressure in the ring line by unplugging the connection at the starting valve. Connect the terminals of the starting valve to the battery for approximately 20 seconds. Reconnect the starting valve.

1. Remove the air filter and connect a pressure gauge at the branch connection at the ring line.

2. Run the engine and measure the pressure. It should be 26.5–29.5 psi.

3. Stop the engine. The fuel pressure may drop to 21 psi, after approximately 5 minutes. If the fuel pressure drops uniformly to 0, check the following points for leaks:

Starting valve—Switch on ignition and disconnect hose at starting valve. If there is no drop in pressure, the valve leaks.

Pressure regulator—Switch on the ignition and disconnect the fuel return hose, as soon as the fuel pump stops. If there is no drop in pressure, the regulator leaks.

Ball valve in delivery connection of fuel pump—Switch on the ignition and disconnect the fuel hose in front of the ring line the moment the fuel pump stops. If there is no drop in pressure, replace the fuel pump.

Injection Valves—remove the kick panel and bridge terminals 1 and 3 of the relay shown. This will energize the fuel pump with the engine stopped, and ignition ON. Check the valves for leaks.

4. Before removing the gauge, reduce the pressure in the ring line.

Adjustments

Fuel Pressure

The fuel pressure can be adjusted on the regulator with the adjusting screw. Adjust to 28 psi. If a slight turn of the screw shows no change of pressure replace the regulator.

Electronic fuel injection pressure regulator adjusting screw

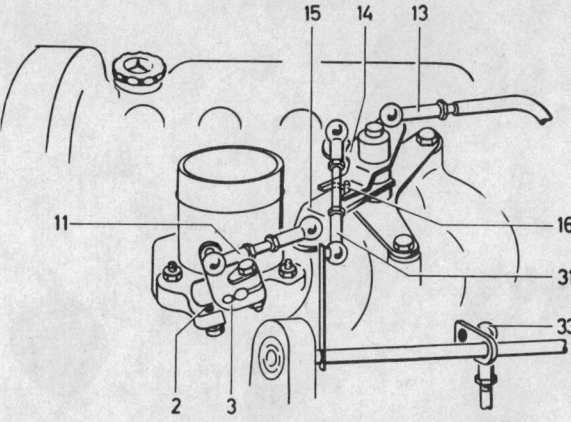

Electronic fuel injection regulating linkage

2. Idling speed stop
3. Throttle valve level
11. Connecting rod
13. Control pushrod
14. Regulating lever
15. Regulating lever
16. Stop pin
31. Connecting rod
33. Pushrod

Before replacing the regulator or removing the pressure gauge, reduce the pressure in the ring line by unplugging the starting valve and connecting it to battery voltage for 20 seconds.

Regulating Shaft

Step on the accelerator pedal up to the kickdown. The regulating lever should rest against the fuel throttle stop of the valve.

Loosen the hex bolt and push the linkage up to the full throttle stop if adjustment is required.

Regulating Linkage

1. Check the linkage for ease of operation.

2. Check that the throttle valve closes completely. Disconnect the regulating rods.

3. Adjust the pushrod to a length of 4 in. from the center of the rubber mount to the center of the ball socket and attach.

On vehicles with manual transmission:

4. Adjust the connecting rod to a length of 3.5 in. (4.1 in. for cars with gate shift lever with bore next to ball head) and attach it.

5. Push the throttle lever against the idle speed stop. Adjust the connecting rod so that the regulating lever rests with the roller against the end stop of the gate shift lever.

On cars with automatic transmission and no gate shift lever:

6. Adjust the connecting rod (31) to 4.2 in. and the connecting rod (11) to 2.7 in. and attach.

7. Push the control rod to the rear against the stop and attach it tension free. During adjustment of the control pushrod, the ball socket must be held next to the ball head.

On cars with automatic transmission and gate shift lever:

8. Adjust the connecting rod to 4.2 in. and attach.

9. Push the throttle valve lever against the idle speed stop. Adjust the connect-

Electronic fuel injection regulating linkage—manual transmission with gate valve shown; automatic transmission with gate valve similar

2. Idling speed stop
3. Throttle valve lever
4. Full throttle stop
7. Roller
9. Gate shift lever
10. Regulating lever
11. Connecting rod
12. Bearing bracket

ing rod so that the regulating lever rests with the roller against the end stop of the gate lever. Push the regulating lever to the rear against the stop pin.

10. Push the control pushrod against the stop and connect it tension free. The ball socket must be held next to the ball head.

Mechanical Fuel Injection (Air Flow Controlled)— 1976–77 V8 Engines

This system replaces the electronic system of earlier years. In contrast to the intermittent type fuel injection, this system measures air volume through and air flow sensor and injects fuel continuously in front of the intake valves, regardless of firing position.

Testing

Delivery Capacity

Remove the fuel return hose from the fuel distributor. Connect a fuel line and hold the end in a measuring cup. Disconnect the plug from the safety switch on the mixture regulator and turn on the ignition for 30 seconds. If the delivery

rate is less than 1 liter in 30 seconds, check the voltage at the fuel pump (11.5) and the fuel lines for kinks.

Disconnect the leak off line between the fuel accumulator and the suction damper. Check the delivery rate again. If it is low replace the accumulator.

Replace the fuel filter and test again. If still low, replace the fuel pump.

Cold Start Valve

1. Disconnect the plugs from the safety switch and mixture control regulator.

2. Remove the cold start valve with fuel line connected.

3. Hold the cold start valve in a container.

4. Turn on the ignition. Connect the valve to battery voltage. It should emit a cone shaped spray.

5. Dry the nozzle off. No fuel should leak out.

Hot Start System

Perform the test at coolant temperature 104°–122° F.

1. Remove the coil wire.

2. Connect a voltmeter to hot-start terminal 3 and ground.

3. Actuate the starter. In approximately 3–4 seconds, the voltmeter should

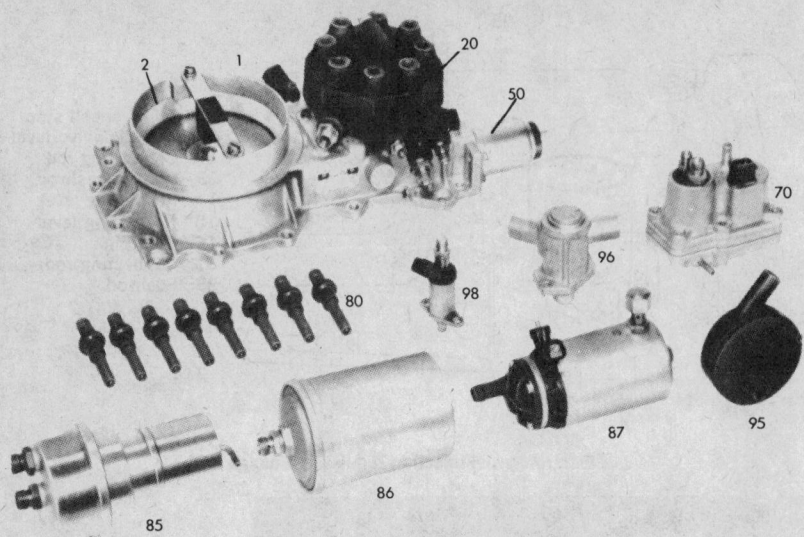

Adjusting control rod linkage (arrow)

Air Flow Controlled injection system components

1. Mixture regulator assembly	70. Warm-up/full-load enrichment compensator	86. Fuel filter
2. Airflow sensor		87. Fuel pump
20. Fuel distributor	80. Injection nozzles	95. Suction damper
50. Hot-start solenoid	85. Fuel accumulator	96. Auxiliary air valve
		98. Cold-start valve

read about 11 volts for 3–4 seconds.

4. If 11 volts are not indicated, check fuse 10. Connect the plug of the 104°F. temperature switch and ground and repeat the test. If 11 volts are now indicated, replace the temperature switch. If 11 volts are not indicated, or if the time periods are wrong, replace the hot start relay.

Fuel Pump Safety Circuit

The pump will only run if the starter motor is actuated or if the engine is running.

1. Remove the air filter.

2. Turn on the ignition and briefly depress the sensor plate.

3. Remove the coil wire from the distributor.

4. Connect a voltmeter to the positive fuel pump terminal and ground.

5. Actuate the starter. Voltmeter should indicate 11 volts.

6. If the fuel pump runs only when the sensor plate is depressed or only when the engine is cranked, replace the fuel pump relay. If the pump is already running when the ignition is turned ON, replace the safety switch.

Adjustments

Control Linkage

1. Check the control linkage for ease of operation.

2. Disconnect the control rod. The throttle valve should rest against the idle stop. Reconnect the control rod.

3. Adjust the control rod so that the roller rests tension free in the gate lever slot.

Full Throttle Stop

1. With the engine stopped, press the accelerator pedal until it rests against the kickdown switch.

2. The throttle valve lever should rest against the full throttle stop. If necessary, adjust the throttle valve lever.

3. If the full throttle stop is not reached, adjust the control rod (bell crank lever to accelerator pedal) to 4.8 in. (from center to center of ball sockets).

4. Adjust the accelerator pedal linkage if necessary with the fastening screw.

5. Adjust the control pressure rod (at idle) by compressing the adjusting clip, and moving the rod completely to the rear against the stop.

MANUAL TRANSMISSION
Removal and Installation

The transmission can be removed with the engine as a unit or it can be removed

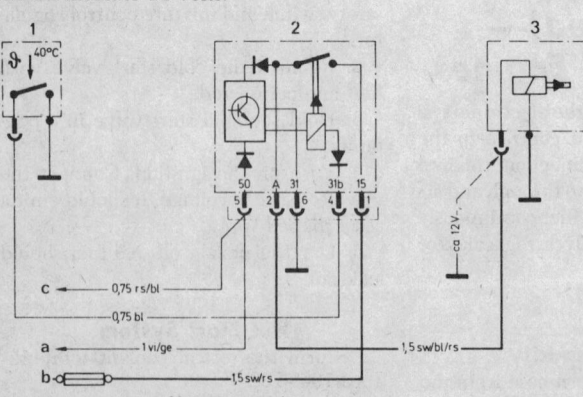

Hot start wiring schematic

1. Temperature switch 104° F (40° C)
2. Hot-start relay
3. Hot-start solenoid

a. Terminal 50 (starter lockout switch)
b. Fuse No. 10 (15/54)
c. To thermo-time switch

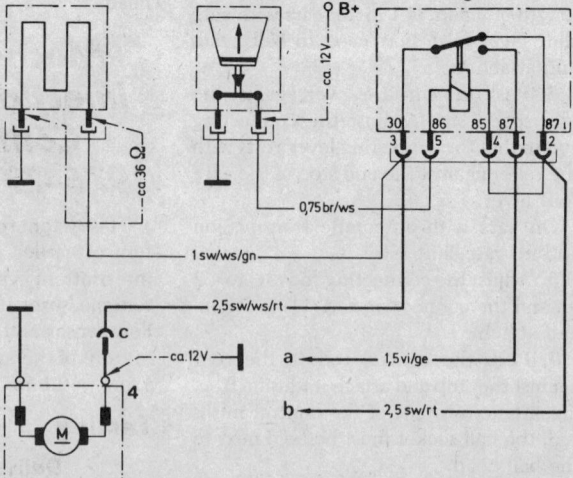

Safety circuit wiring schematic

1. Heating coil, warm-up/full-load enrichment compensator
2. Safety switch, sensor plate
3. Relay, fuel pump
4. Fuel pump

a. To terminal 50 (starter)
b. To terminal 15/54 (ignition)
c. To plug connection, tail light harness

separately, whichever appears easiest. See the procedures under "Engine Removal and Installation" or those following for separate Removal and Installation. Once the engine/transmission unit has been removed from the vehicle, the transmission and bell housing must be separated from the engine, as follows:

Removal and Installation— with Engine

1. After removing the engine/transmission unit, unbolt the bellhousing from the engine. The bolts which hold the transmission to the bellhousing cannot be reached except from inside the bell housing.

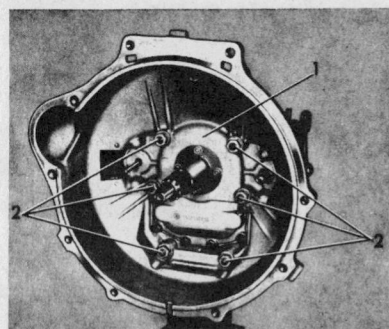

Clutch housing (1) and clutch housing attaching bolts (2) which can only be reached from inside the clutch housing.

2. Remove the starter from its mounting position and pull the transmission and bellhousing from the engine.

3. The bolts which secure the bellhousing to the transmission are now visible and can be removed to separate the bellhousing and transmission.

4. To install, connect the engine, bellhousing, and transmission, after coating the splines of the mainshaft with grease.

5. Install the starter.

6. Further installation is the reverse of removal.

Removal and Installation— Without Engine

1. First jack up the car at all four corners and place it on axle stands. Remove the negative battery cable and disconnect all shift rods.

2. With a column-mounted gearshift lever, remove the rods at the relay arm from under the hood.

3. On floorshift models, unhook the rods at the transmission side cover by prying upward on the clips from the open end using a screwdriver.

4. On models having a top cover shift mechanism, the floor tunnel must be removed to reach the shift rods.

5. On older models having the clutch slave cylinder held to the clutch housing with two bolts, remove the cylinder completely and swing it out of the way. On newer models it is sufficient to remove the hose and plug it to prevent fluid loss.

6. Remove the speedometer cable and the exhaust pipe bracket and wire them out of the way.

7. If equipped, disconnect the back-up light switch.

8. Disconnect the driveshaft by holding one nut with a wrench; loosen the other, then unbolt the shaft from the transmission tailshaft. Remove the center bearing support.

NOTE: *It is a good idea to scribe marks on the center bearing support bracket for ease in assembly.*

9. Mark the position of the rear crossmember and slightly jack up the engine with a block of wood between the jack and the oil pan. This serves to take the weight off the crossmember bolts during removal and prevents stripped threads.

10. Unscrew all crossmember bolts that hold it to the body and transmission and remove the crossmember.

11. Unbolt the bellhousing and starter bolts and pull the transmission straight backward, while rotating clockwise 90° to clear obstructions. *Make absolutely sure the mainshaft is out of the clutch before lowering the transmission, otherwise the clutch hub will be damaged.*

12. The reason for removing both the transmission and bellhousing together is immediately obvious when the unit is out: the transmission hold-down bolts can be reached only from the inside. Bolt configurations vary slightly with the different models, but, in general, removal procedure is identical.

13. To remove the housing, pull off the throwout bearing, then the throwout fork. The non-anchored end of the fork must be pulled outward, then to the left to disengage the ball socket pivot.

14. Unscrew the bolts that hold the transmission to the housing, then tap the housing lightly with a fiber hammer to separate it from the transmission nose piece. The housing is easily distorted, so never use a steel hammer.

15. Installation is the reverse of removal except that the rear U-joint must be split on some models and the driveshaft pushed further back for clearance.

16. Always coat the mainshaft splines and pilot bushing surfaces with Vaseline or Molykote grease before installing. Don't forget the ground cables under the nuts, and make sure that all bolts are tightened evenly. The center bearing support must not be cocked or it will soon disintegrate under torque loads, so tighten its mounting bolts finger tight until everything else is torqued, then tighten them.

17. The driveshaft double clamp nuts get torqued to about 140 ft lbs.

18. Bracing the hold-down wrench on the body pan is not recommended without some insulation to distribute the load. Use a 24 in. section of pipe on the wrench handle, but don't put full weight on it or the nut might be distorted.

CAUTION: *On all Allen-head bolts, use the proper size key with a short extension. Use of too small American keys may round the bolt heads to such a degree that removal without drilling is impossible. Unfortunately, Allen bolts are extremely hard, and almost impossible to drill out with any success if they are in an awkward position. Grinding an oversize American key to fit is alright if the grinding is done slowly so as not to destroy the temper of the steel from frictional heating.*

Overhaul

The G 76/18, G 76/18A, G 76/18B, G 76/27 and G 76/27A 4–speed manual transmissions are all very much alike. Overhaul is predominantly given for the G 76/18 since only minor modifications have been made.

Transmission Modification Chart

Transmission Type	Application	Modification
G 76/18	220D/8, 220/8, 230, 250/8, To March 1972	—
G 76/18A	250/8, 220D, 240D, 300D, 220/8 From March 1972	Wider helical 1st gear and revised countershaft
G 76/18B	280, 280C	Wider helical 1st gear and revised counter shaft
G 76/27	280S/8, 280SEL/8, 300SEL/8, 280SE 3.5 280SE 4.5 From March 1972	The countershaft, countershaft reverse gear and the rear cover were modified to match type G 76/18B
G 76/27A	300SEL 3.5, 300SEL 4.5 From April 1972	The countershaft, countershaft reverse gear and the rear cover were modified to match type G 76/18B

NOTE: Due to differing dimensions and varying surface finishes, do not attempt to use parts from differing transmissions.

NOTE: *Internal parts of both side cover and top cover transmissions are basically similar.*

1. Locked-up transmissions or shifting problems may be caused by defective parts in the shifting mechanism of the transmission itself.

2. After making sure that the shift rods are all in proper adjustment, check the first and second gear shift yoke needle bearings and the shift detent mechanism.

3. Drain the transmission oil and remove the clamp bolt and reverse shift lever at the transmission.

4. Remove the lock tab from the reverse shift shaft and unscrew the cover hold-down bolts.

5. Tap the cover with a fiber hammer to loosen it, while driving the reverse shift shaft upward with another fiber hammer.

6. When the cover is off about ¾ in. reach in and slide the shift forks out of the shift yokes, then pull the cover downward and upward.

7. The transmission gears are now visible for inspection, as is the shift mechanism. When inspecting gear teeth, rotate all the gears to make sure no part has been missed. A chipped tooth is as bad as a broken tooth, for it weakens the entire gear and can lead to transmission failure.

8. Work the gears by hand and check the synchronizers.

9. Badly burred or worn synchronizing rings usually cause grinding during shifting.

10. To disassemble the shift mechanism, loosen the clamp bolts and remove the shift levers from the outside of the cover.

11. Going to the inside, remove the circlips from the shafts and pull out shift yokes and the reverse detent lever.

12. Using a screwdriver, bend back the locktab on the bolt and unbolt the detent cage and locating pin.

13. The detent balls should not be scarred and should move in and out easily, although under spring tension. If they are immovable even under pressure, or if they flop in and out with ease, the detent cage should be replaced.

14. The shift yokes then must be checked for wear, as a burred shift yoke will more than likely ruin a new detent cage in a short time.

15. Check the bearings where the shift rods pass through the cover. If the caged needle bearings are scored or broken, new ones must be pressed into place. Use of an arbor press is recommended, although some ingenuity and a large bench vise can be utilized in an emergency.

16. Don't forget to replace the O-rings, because they will almost always leak after once being disturbed. Adjustment of the levers is described later.

Replacing Front and Rear Seals

1. Fluid leaking from the front seal is usually visible in the clutch housing and can cause clutch slippage if allowed to progress too far. In any case, it is good practice to replace the front and rear seals while the transmission is out, just on general principles.

2. After the clutch housing is removed, unscrew the front cover bolts and remove the cover.

3. The thrust washers must be replaced in exactly the same position, so note their order when removing.

4. Unbolt the nose piece from the front cover, then press the old seal out. It is recommended that an arbor press with a 1 ¾ in. adapter be used, but a slide hammer with a screw attachment can be used for this job.

5. It is important, however, that the new seal is *pressed* into the cover, not hammered.

6. The thrust washers can be held in place with wheel bearing grease during installation of the cover.

NOTE: *Use nonhardening Permatex on the cover and bolt threads to prevent leaks.*

7. To remove the rear seal, insert a bar through the rear flange and remove the locktab and nut.

8. Remove the flange, then remove the cover bolts and cover.

9. The gear train can now be inspected for wear and the seal replaced.

CAUTION: *When installing, the reverse shaft must be properly aligned with the keyed portion of the cover or the cover will break.*

1. Remove the throwout bearing and fork.

2. Remove the clutch housing with the slave cylinder.

3. Remove the reverse shift lever clamp.

4. Remove the reverse shift lever.

5. Remove the side cover.

6. Remove the shift forks.

7. Disassemble the side cover and forks.

8. Unbolt and remove the transmission front cover.

9. Remove the bearing housing.

10. Remove the rear transmission cover.

11. Press out the speedometer drive gear.

12. Remove the tach drive seal.

13. Remove the reverse gear from the mainshaft.

14. Remove the reverse sliding gear shaft from the housing while holding the sliding gear.

15. Unlock the nut on the rear of the countershaft.

16. Remove reverse gear from the countershaft.

17. Knock the pin from reverse shifter shaft and move the shaft as far forward as possible.

18. Remove the shift rod from the housing.

19. Unlock the slotted nut.

20. Remove the front countershaft bearing. On G 76/27A transmissions, the bearing is beveled and is removed toward the inside of the case.

21. Remove the rear countershaft bearing.

22. Lift the mainshaft at the rear and pull the input shaft out of the housing.

23. Push the mainshaft completely rearward and remove it at an angle.

24. Remove the countershaft from the housing.

25. Disassemble the mainshaft, if necessary.

26. If necessary, disassemble the countershaft.

27. Assembly is basically the reverse of disassembly. Try to obtain 0 end-play on the main and input shafts.

Linkage Adjustment

Column Mounted Shift Lever

Proper adjustment of the column shift linkage is dependent on both the position of the levers at the transmission and the length of the shift rods.

1. Check the positioning of the shift levers at the transmission (see illustration) and correct by loosening the clamp bolts. The diagram shows the levers in neutral.

2. Next, go to the lower steering column and lock the three levers by inserting a 0.2156 in. rod (a No. 3 drill will do or other tool of approximately the same diameter) through the levers and the hole in the bearing block.

3. With the shift levers at the lower steering column locked and the levers at the transmission adjusted, try hooking the shift rods into their respective levers. If they are too long or short, adjust their

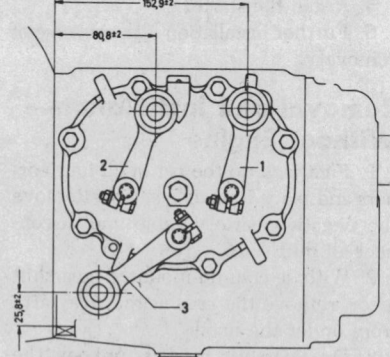

Side cover transmission shift levers

1. 1st and 2nd gear lever
2. 3rd and 4th gear lever
3. Reverse lever

length by loosening the locknuts and turning the ball socket ends. Remove the locking rod and try shifting through the gears. Very slight further adjustments may clear up any binding.

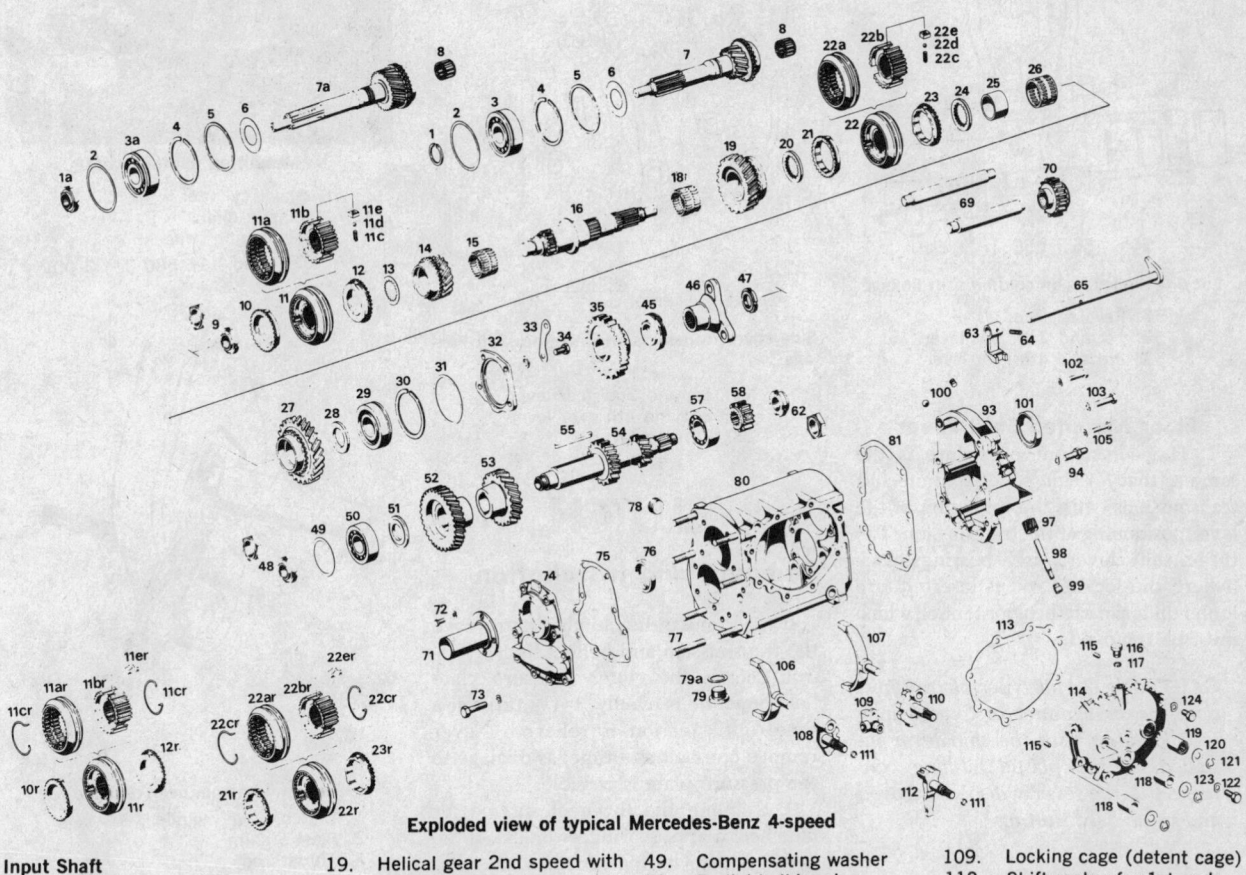

Exploded view of typical Mercedes-Benz 4-speed

Input Shaft
1. Circlip
1a. Slot nut for input shaft
2. Compensating washer
3. Radial ball bearing
3a. Radial ball bearing with split inner race G 76/27 A
4. Circlip
5. Spacer ring
6. Oil thrower disc
7. Input shaft with synchronizing cone
7a. Input shaft with synchronizing cone for transmission G 76/27 A
8. Needle cage

Main Shaft
9. Slot nut or hex. nut main shaft, front
10. Synchronizing rings for 4th speed
11. Synchronizing body with sliding sleeve for 3rd and 4th speed
11a. Sliding sleeve
11b. Synchronizing body
11c. Compression spring—synchronizing body
11d. Steel ball
11e. Driver member
12. Synchronizing ring for 3rd speed
13. Thrust washer for 3rd speed
14. Helical gear 3rd speed
15. Needle cage for 3rd speed gear
16. Main shaft
18. Needle cage for 2nd speed gear

19. Helical gear 2nd speed with synchronizing cone
20. Thrust washer
21. Synchronizing ring for 2nd speed
22. Synchronizing body with sliding sleeve 1st and 2nd speed
22a. Sliding sleeve
22b. Synchronizing body
22c. Compression spring—synchronizing body
22d. Steel ball
22e. Drive member
23. Synchronizing ring for 1st speed
24. Thrust washer
25. Race, 1st speed gear
26. Needle cage for 1st speed gear
27. Helical gear for 1st speed
28. Thrust washer
29. Radial ball bearing (for G 76/27 A the same as 3a)
30. Circlip
31. Compensating washer
32. Holding ring, rear bearing, main shaft
33. Lock washer or spring washer
34. Hex. bolt
35. Reversing gear, main shaft
45. Helical gear, speedometer drive
46. Universal flange
47. Lock nut, universal flange on main shaft

Countershaft
48. Slot nut or hex. nut

49. Compensating washer
50. Radial ball bearing
51. Spacing washer (for constant countershaft gear)
52. Countershaft helical gear, constant gear
53. Countershaft helical gear 3rd speed
54. Countershaft with helical teeth for 2nd and 1st speed
55. Woodruff key
57. Grooved ball bearing
58. Reversing gear—countershaft
62. Slot nut or hex. nut

Shift Members for Reverse Gear
63. Shifter for reverse gear
64. Clamping sleeve for shifter on shift rod
65. Shift rod for reverse gear
69. Reversing shaft
70. Reversing slide gear

Rear transmission cover
93. Tranmission housing cover rear
94. Flange screw
97. Drive pinion for speedometer
98. Shaft drive for speedometer
99. Radial sealing ring
100. Plug or steel ball
101. Radial sealing ring for main shaft

Transmission shift cover
106. Shift fork 3rd and 4th speed
107. Shift fork 1st and 2nd speed
108. Shift rocker for 3rd and 4th speed

109. Locking cage (detent cage)
110. Shift rocker for 1st and 2nd speed
111. O-ring
112. Shift finger for reverse speed
113. Gasket
114. Transmission shift cover
115. Pin
116. Breather
117. Circlip
118. Bushing (bearing gear shifting shaft for 3rd/4th or reverse speed)
119. Needle sleeve (bearing shifting shaft 1st/2nd speed)

Annual Spring Synchronization
10r. Synchronizing spring for 4th speed
11r. Synchronizing body with sliding sleeve for 3rd and 4th
11ar. Sliding sleeve
11br. Synchronizing body
11cr. Annual spring
11er. Drive member
12r. Synchronizing ring for 3rd speed
21r. Synchronizing ring for 2nd speed
22r. Synchronizing body with sliding sleeve for 1st and 2nd speed
22ar. Sliding sleeve
22br. Synchronizing body
22cr. Annual spring
22er. Drive member
23r. Synchronizing ring for 1st speed

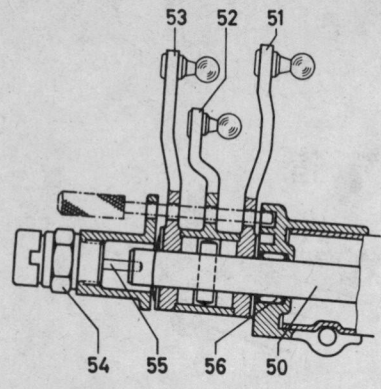

Locking the levers on column shift linkage

51. Reverse lever
52. 1st and 2nd gear lever
53. 3rd and 4th gear lever

Floor Mounted Shift Lever

1. The adjustment procedure is the same as that for side cover column shift transmissions, with the exception of the lever positioning at the transmission. The three shift levers and bearing block (where the locking rod is inserted) are found underneath the floor tunnel, which must be removed.

CAUTION: *On all types of transmissions, never hammer or force a new shift knob on with the shift lever installed, as the plastic bushing connected to the lever will be destroyed and cause hard shifting.*

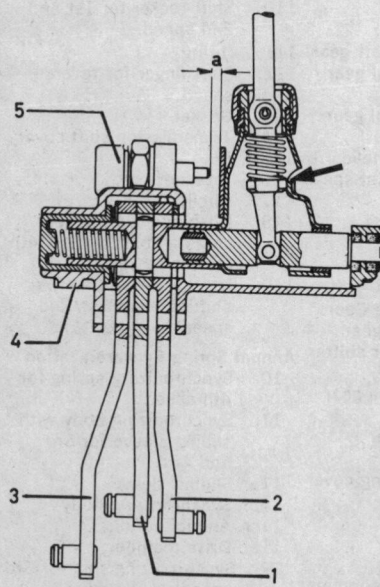

Floorshift levers with side cover transmission.

1. Shift lever for 1st and 2nd gear
2. Shift lever for 3rd and 4th gear
3. Shift lever for reverse gear
4. Bearing block
5. Backup light switch
6. Adjusting dimension for reversing light switch, 4±1 mm.—gearshift lever in shifting plane 1st or 2nd gear

726

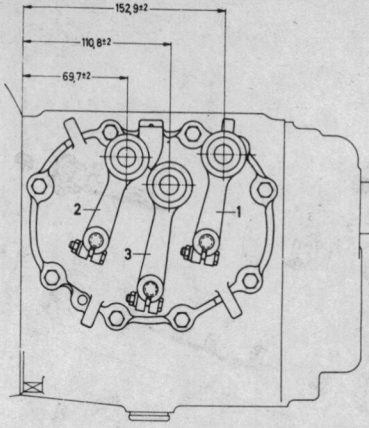

Side cover transmission with floorshift linkage.

1. 1st and 2nd gear lever
2. 3rd and 4th gear lever
3. Reverse lever

CLUTCH

Removal and Installation

1. To remove the clutch, first remove the transmission and bellhousing.
2. Loosen the clutch pressure plate hold-down bolts evenly, 1–1½ turns at a time, until tension is relieved. Never remove one bolt at a time, as damage to the pressure plate is possible.
3. Examine the flywheel surface for blue heat marks, scoring, or cracks. If the flywheel is to be machined, always machine both sides.
4. To reinstall, coat the splines with high temperature grease and place the clutch disc against the flywheel, centering it with a clutch pilot shaft. A wooden shaft, available at automotive jobbers, is satisfactory, but an old transmission mainshaft works best.
5. Tighten the pressure plate hold-down bolts evenly 1–1½ turns at a time until tight, then remove the pilot shaft.

CAUTION: *Most clutch plates have the flywheel side marked as such (Kupplungsseite). Do not assume that the pressure springs always face the transmission.*

Checking Clutch Plate Wear

Apart from the usual slippage which accompanies severe wear of the clutch plate or disc, Mercedes-Benz has a simple tool, which can be purchased from a dealer that measures the amount of wear on the clutch plate. Actually, it is a simple "go-no go" gauge.

1. A plastic shim is installed between the slave cylinder and the bellhousing.
2. The shim is provided with two flat grooves running diagonally from bottom to center. When the shim is installed, these grooves appear as slots. Use groove

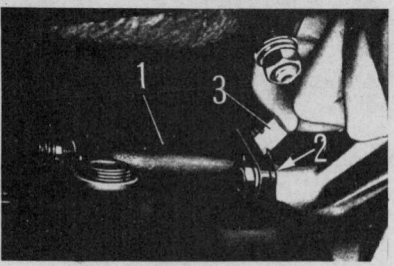

Measuring clutch wear

1. Slave cylinder
2. Plastic shim
3. Measuring gauge
   (Part No. 115 580 07 23 00)

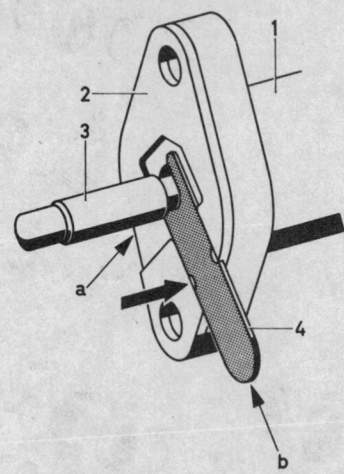

Wear limit has not been reached

1. Clutch slave cylinder
2. Plastic shim
3. Thrust rod
4. Measuring gauge
   (Part No. 115 589 07 23 00)
(a)—Direction of measuring on lefthand drive vehicle with steering wheel and center shift, as well as on righthand drive vehicles with center shift
(b)—Direction of measuring on righthand drive vehicles with steering wheel shift

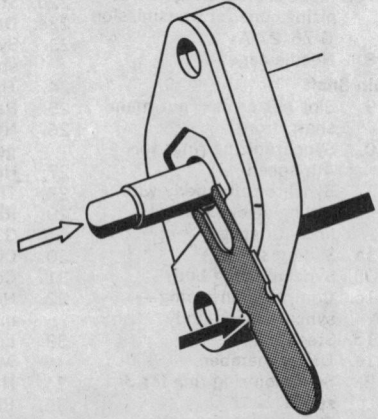

Wear limit has been reached

(a) for left-hand drive vehicles and groove
(b) for right-hand drive vehicles.

3. The clutch slave cylinder pushrod has two different diameters. The jaw width of the test device corresponds to

the smaller diameter of the pushrod. If the notches on the test device disappear when the test device is inserted as far as it will go, the clutch plate is still operational.

4. If, however, the notches on the test device remain visible, this is an indication that the clutch plate is worn severely and should be replaced.

Clutch Slave Cylinder

Removal and Installation

1. Detach and plug the pressure line from the slave cylinder.

2. Remove the attaching screws from the slave cylinder.

3. Remove the slave cylinder, pushrod, and spacer.

4. To install, place the grooved side of the spacer in contact with the housing and hold it in position.

5. Install the slave cylinder and pushrod into the housing. Be sure that the dust cap is properly seated.

6. Install the attaching screws.

7. Connect the pressure line to the slave cylinder.

8. Bleed the slave cylinder.

AUTOMATIC TRANSMISSION

Removal and Installation

Mercedes-Benz automatic transmissions are removed as a unit with the engine. Consult the "Engine Mechanical" section for removal and installation procedures concerning a given engine.

In-Car Service

Because automatic transmission work is mainly done by specialty shops, only in-car service procedures are given here.

Before doing any work on the automatic transmission, consult the transmission identification chart to determine which transmission you are dealing with.

Pan and Filter Replacement

1. Drain the transmission of all fluid.

2. Remove the transmission pan.

3. Remove the bolt or bolts which retain the filter to the transmission.

4. Remove the filter and replace it with a new one.

5. Install the transmission pan, using a new gasket.

6. Refill the transmission to the proper level with the specified brand of fluid.

Selector Rod Linkage Adjustment

NOTE: *Before performing this adjustment on any Mercedes-Benz vehicle, be sure that the vehicle is resting on its wheels. No part of the vehicle may be jacked for this adjustment.*

Column Mounted Linkage

K4C 025 and W3A 040

1. Loosen the counternut on the ball socket.

2. Disconnect the selector rod from the shift lever bracket.

3. Set the transmission selector lever and the selector rod in Neutral.

4. Adjust the length of the selector rod until the ball socket aligns with the end of the ball on the intermediate lever.

5. Attach the ball socket to the intermediate lever, making sure that the play in the selector lever in position Three (D) and Four (S) is about equal.

6. Tighten the counternut on the ball socket.

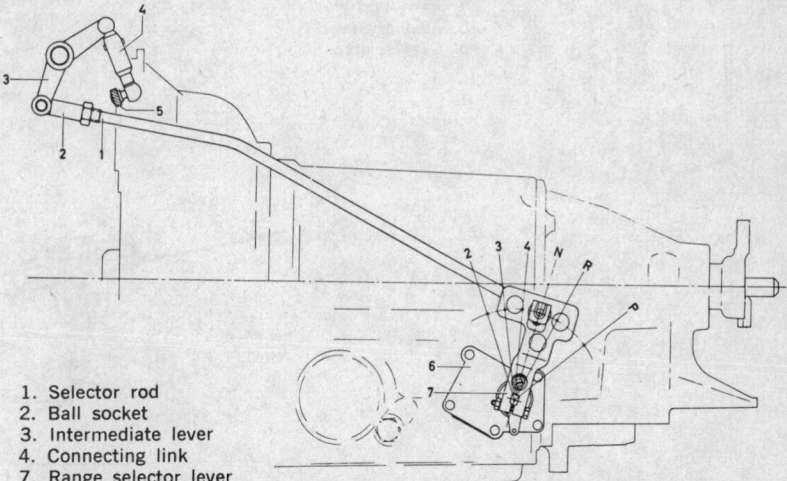

1. Selector rod
2. Ball socket
3. Intermediate lever
4. Connecting link
7. Range selector lever

Column mounted selector rod linkage—K4C 025 and W3A 040

K4A 025

1. Disconnect the selector rod from the intermediate lever.

2. Loosen the counternut on the ball socket.

3. Set the range selector lever on the column in position N and the selector lever on the transmission in Neutral.

4. Adjust the length of the selector rod until the ball socket aligns with the ball end on the intermediate lever.

5. Attach the selector rod to the intermediate lever and tighten the counternut.

6. Set the selector lever in position Neutral.

7. Adjust the knurled nut after loosening the counternut on the bowden cable.

8. After adjusting the nut, tighten the counternut on the bowden cable.

W3A 040 (450SE and 450SEL Only) and W4B 025

1. Loosen the counternut on the rear selector rod while holding both recesses

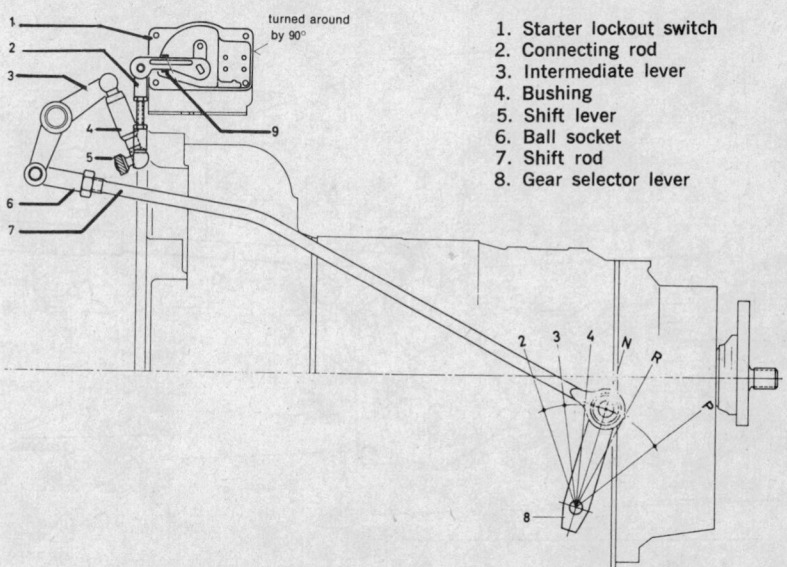

1. Starter lockout switch
2. Connecting rod
3. Intermediate lever
4. Bushing
5. Shift lever
6. Ball socket
7. Shift rod
8. Gear selector lever

Column mounted selector rod linkage—K4A 025

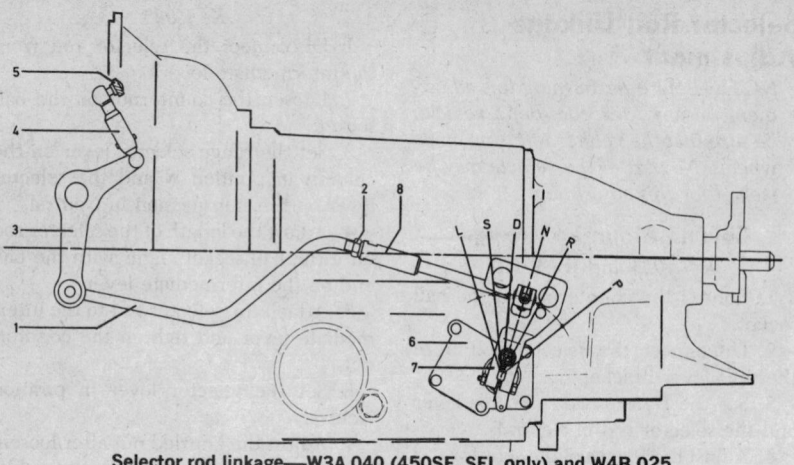

Selector rod linkage—W3A 040 (450SE, SEL only) and W4B 025

1. Front selector rod
2. Counternut
3. Intermediate lever
4. Elastic intermediate piece
5. Bearing bracket
6. Starter and backup light switch
7. Selector lever
8. Rear selector rod

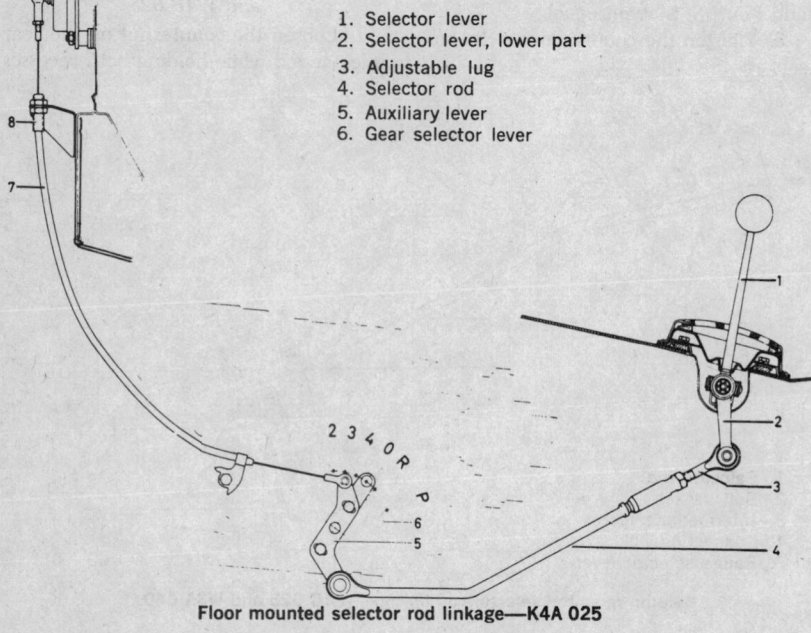

1. Selector lever
2. Selector lever, lower part
3. Adjustable lug
4. Selector rod
5. Auxiliary lever
6. Gear selector lever

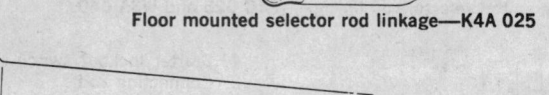

Floor mounted selector rod linkage—K4A 025

of the front selector rod with an open end wrench.

2. Disconnect the selector rod from the selector lever.

3. Set the selector lever on the transmission and on the column to Neutral.

4. Adjust the selector rod until the bearing pin is aligned with the bearing bushing in the selector lever.

5. Connect the rear selector lever to the selector rod and secure it with the lock. Be sure that the clearance of the selector lever in D and S is equal.

6. Tighten the locknut on the rear selector rod while holding the front selector rod as in Step 1.

Floor Mounted Linkage

NOTE: *The vehicle must be standing with the weight normally distributed on all four wheels. No jacks may be used.*

K4C 025, W3A 040, W4B 025

1. Disconnect the selector rod from the selector lever.

2. Set the selector lever in Neutral and make sure that there is approximately 1 mm clearance between the selector lever and the N stop of the selector gate.

3. Adjust the length of the selector rod so that it can be attached free of tension.

4. Retighten the counternut.

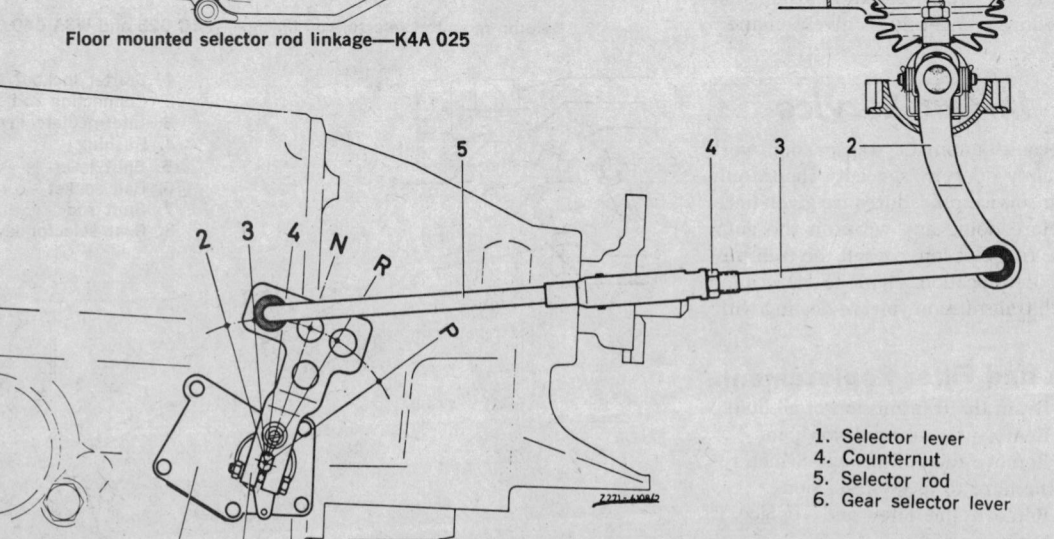

1. Selector lever
4. Counternut
5. Selector rod
6. Gear selector lever

Floor mounted selector rod linkage—K4C 025 and W3A 040

1. Selector range lever
2. Washer
3. Adjusting screw
4. Shaft
5. Locating pin
6. Clamping screw

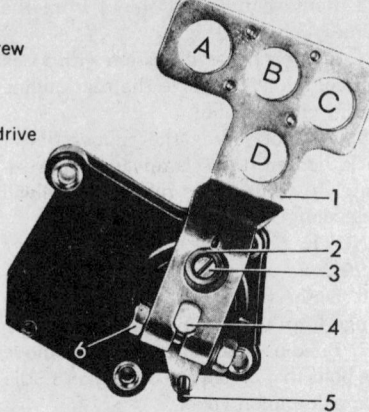

(a)—Column shift for left-hand and right-hand drive vehicles 220/8, 220 D/8, 230/8, 280 S/8, 280 SE/8 and 300 SEL/8.

(b)—Steering wheel shift for left-hand drive vehicles (220/8, 220 D/8, 230/8, 250/8)

(c)—Steering wheel shift for right-hand drive vehicles (220/8, 220 D/8, 230/8, 250/8)

(d)—Steering wheel shift for left-hand drive vehicles (280S/8, 280 SE/8, 300 SEL/8, 280 SE/3.5 and 300 SEL/3.5)

Starter lockout and backup light switch adjustment—K4C 025 and W3A 040

K4A 025

1. Disconnect the selector rod from the lower part of the selector lever.

2. Set the selector lever on the linkage, and the selector lever on the transmission, at Neutral.

3. Adjust the lug or the selector rod so that it aligns with the pivot pin on the lower part of the selector lever.

4. A finer adjustment can be made at the 2 slots in the auxilliary lever.

5. Press the selector rod onto the lower part of the selector lever and tighten the counternut.

Starter Lockout and Back-Up Light Switch Adjustment

K4C 025, W3A 040 and W4B 025

1. Disconnect the selector rod and move the selector lever on the transmission to position Neutral.

2. Tighten the clamping screw prior to making adjustments.

3. Loosen the adjusting screw and insert the locating pin through the driver into the locating hole in the shift housing.

4. Tighten the adjusting screw and remove the locating pin.

5. Move the selector lever to position N and connect the selector rod so that there is no tension.

6. Check to be sure that the engine cannot be started in Neutral or Park.

K4A 025

1. The bowden cable, which actuates the neutral starter lockout and the back-up light switch, should be adjusted so that the engine can be started only in Neutral or Park.

2. In all other positions, the starter lockout should be activated.

3. In addition, the back-up lights should light up in Reverse.

4. Any adjustment should be made at the adjusting stop on the other end from the transmission linkage.

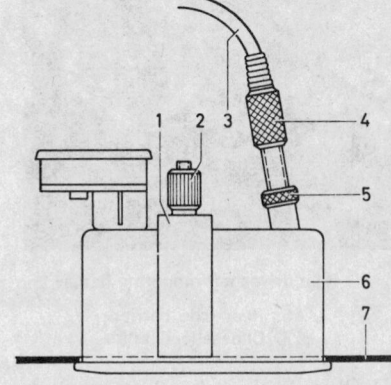

Adjust the knurled nut on the Bowden cable

1. Clamp
2. Clamp nut
3. Bowden cable
4. Knurled nut
5. Counternut
6. Housing
7. Instrument panel

Kickdown Switch

W3A 040 and W4B 025

1. The kickdown position of the solenoid valve is controlled by the accelerator pedal.

2. Push the accelerator pedal against the kickdown limit stop. In this position the throttle lever should rest against the full load stop of the venturi control unit.

Kickdown switch adjustment—W3A 040 and W4B 025

3. Adjustments are made by loosening the clamping screw on the return lever on the accelerator pedal shaft and turning the shaft. Tighten the clamping screw again.

Control Pressure Rod

1975–77 230 (California)

1. Remove the vacuum control unit from the carburetor.

2. Disconnect the automatic choke connecting rod so the throttle valve rests against the idle stop.

3. Loosen the screw and turn the levers against each other so the control rod rests against the idle stop.

4. Tighten the screw and depress the accelerator to the kickdown position. The throttle valve must rest against the full throttle stop. If necessary adjust the full throttle stop (see Fuel System).

5. Install the vacuum control unit on the distributor and connect the automatic choke rod.

DRIVE AXLES

Mercedes-Benz automobiles use either two or three piece driveshafts to connect the transmission to a hypoid independent rear axle. All models covered in this book use independent rear suspension with

Control pressure rod adjustment—1975-77 230

1. Control pressure rod
2. Bellcrank
3. Screw
4. Bellcrank

open or enclosed driveshafts to the rear wheels.

Driveshaft and U-Joints

Removal and Installation

220D/8, 240D, 300D, 220/8, 230, 250/8, 250C, 280, 280C, 280E

1. Remove the equalizer and disconnect the parking brake cables.

2. Remove the bolts which secure the two brackets to the chassis at the front and rear and remove the brackets. It may be necessary to lower the exhaust system slightly to allow access to the left-hand bolts on the rear bracket.

3. a. 1972 models: On three piece driveshafts, back off the nut on the front clamp only. On both two and three piece driveshafts, push back the rubber sleeve on the clamp nut.

3. b. 1973–77 models: Loosen the nut on the driveshaft about 2 turns without pushing the rubber sleeve back (it slides along). On a two-piece shaft, only loosen the front clamp nut.

4. Remove the nuts which secure the attaching plate to the transmission flange and rear axle.

5. Remove the bolts which secure the intermediate bearing(s) to the chassis. Push the driveshaft together and slightly down, and remove the driveshaft from the vehicle.

NOTE: *If possible, do not separate the parts of the driveshaft since each driveshaft is balanced at the factory. If separation is necessary, all parts must be marked and reassembled in the same relative positions to assure that the driveshafts will remain reasonably well balanced.*

6. Installation is the reverse of removal.

7. Pack the cavities of the two centering sleeves with special Mercedes-Benz grease.

8. Install the driveshaft and attach the intermediate bearing(s) to the chassis.

9. Rock the car backward and forward several times to be sure that the driveshaft is properly centered without forcing.

10. Prior to tightening the clamp nuts on a three piece driveshaft, be sure that the intermediate shaft does not contact either the front or rear intermediate bearing. The clearance between the intermediate shaft and the bearing should be the same at both ends.

All Other Models

NOTE: *Steps 1–3 apply to V 8 models.*

1. Fold the torsion bar down after disconnecting the level control linkage (if equipped).

2. Remove the exhaust system.

3. Remove the heat shield from the frame.

4. Support the transmission with a jack and completely remove the rear engine mount crossmember.

5. Without sliding the rubber sleeve back. loosen the clamp nut approximately two turns (the rubber sleeve will slide along).

NOTE: *On 3 piece driveshafts, only the front clamp nut need be loosened.*

6. Unscrew the U-joint mounting flange from the U-joint plate.

7. Bend back the locktabs and remove the bolts that attach the driveshaft to the rear axle pinion yoke.

Rear driveshaft mounting flange

16. Rear axle carrier
17. Cheesehead bolts

8. Remove the bolts which attach the intermediate bearing(s) to the frame. Push the driveshaft together slightly and remove it from the vehicle.

9. Try not to separate the driveshafts. If it is absolutely necessary, matchmark all components so that they can be reassembled in the same order.

10. Installation is the reverse of removal. Always use new self-locking nuts. After the driveshaft is installed, rock the car back and forth several times to settle the driveshaft. Make sure that neither intermediate shaft is binding against either intermediate bearing, and that the clearance between the intermediate bearing and the driveshaft is the same at both ends.

Axle Shaft

Removal and Installation

220D/8, 240D, 300D, 220/8, 230, 250/8, 250/C, 280, 280C, 280E and all 450 models and 280S and 280SE without torque compensator.

NOTE: *On the 280, 280C and 280E only axle shafts identified with a yellow paint dot or part no. 107 350 07 10 (left) or part no. 107 350 0810 (right) can be installed.*

1. Jack up the rear of the car and remove the wheel and center axle hold-down bolt (in hub).

2. Remove the brake caliper and suspend it from a hook.

3. Drain the differential oil and place a jack under the differential housing.

4. Unbolt the rubber mount from the chassis and the differential housing, then remove the differential housing cover to expose the ring and pinion gears.

5. Press the shaft from the axle flange. If necessary, loosen the shock absorber.

6. Using a screwdriver, remove the axle lock ring inside the differential case.

Removing the lock-ring (26) from the axle shaft with pliers (1) or a screwdriver.

7. Pull the axle from the housing by pulling the splined end from the side gears, with the spacer.

NOTE: *Axle shafts are stamped R and L for right and left units. Always use new lock-rings.*

8. Installation is the reverse of removal. Fill the rear axle.

CAUTION: *Check end-play of the lock-ring in the groove. If necessary, install a thicker lock ring or spacer to eliminate all end-play, while still allowing the lock-ring to rotate. Do not allow the joints in the axleshaft to hang free or the joint bearing may be damaged and leak.*

280S/8, 280SEL/8, 280SE and SEL 4.5, 300SEL 4.5

1. Jack up the rear of the car and remove the wheel, brake caliper, and disc.

2. Remove the parking brake shoes.

3. Unbolt the backing plate and dust cover and pull the axle from the housing using a puller or slide hammer.

NOTE: *Axle bearings must be removed with a special puller or slide hammer only. Never hammer on the bearings.*

NOTE: *The grooved nut is threaded to the shaft; bearings must be removed and replaced using an arbor press. Use a punch, as previously described, to anchor the sliding joint during axle installation.*

4. Installation is the reverse of removal.

350SL, all 450, 280S, 280SE, 1977 280E with Torque Compensation

1. Drain the oil from the rear axle.
2. Disconnect and plug the brake lines.
3. Remove the torsion bar.
4. Lower the shock absorber.
5. Remove the bolt which attaches the rear axle shaft to the rear axle shaft flange.
6. Disconnect the brake cable control. Remove the bracket from the wheel carrier, remove the rubber sleeve, and push back the cover.
7. Force the rear axle shaft out of the flange with a suitable tool.
8. Support the rear axle with a jack.
9. Remove the rear rubber mount.
10. Clean the axle housing and remove the cover from the housing.

NOTE: *The axle shafts are the floating type and can be compressed in the constant velocity joints.*

11. Remove the locking ring from the end of the axle shafts which engage the side gears in the differential.
12. Disengage the axle shaft from the side gear and remove the axle shaft together with the spacer.

CAUTION: *Do not hang the outer constant velocity joint in a free position (without any support) as the shaft may be damaged and the constant velocity joint housing may leak.*

13. Installation is the reverse of removal.

Axle shaft markings (R)

14. If either axle shaft is replaced, be sure that the proper replacement shaft is installed. Axle shafts are marked L and R for left and right.
15. Check the end-play between the lock-ring on the axle shaft and the side gear. There should be no noticeable end-play, but the lock-ring should be able to turn in the groove.
16. Be sure to bleed the brakes and fill the rear axle with the proper quantity and type of lubricant.

Differential

Removal and Installation

Models With Enclosed Axle Shafts

1. Jack up the rear of the car and remove the rear wheels.
2. If equipped with air suspension, remove the sway bar.
3. Remove the rear exhaust pipe and the two mufflers, then loosen the parking brake adjuster wingnut and disconnect the brake cables.

Differential attaching points

42. Rear rubber mounting
43. Hexagon socket bolt
45. Breather
46. Filler plug
47. Drain plug

4. Disconnect the rear universal joint and push the driveshaft forward, then remove the compensating spring.
5. Remove the rear coil springs.
6. On cars with air suspension, disconnect the spring piston from the torque arm.

NOTE: *Do not remove it from the bellows.*

7. Disconnect the hoses from the lines at the calipers.
8. Remove the front link from the cross strut by loosening the bolts. Push the strut out of the way.
9. Remove the trailing arm brackets from the chassis.

NOTE: *Tape any shims found beneath the plate to the appropriate trailing arm.*

10. If equipped with air suspension, disconnect the brake support chassis mount by removing the rear seat and unscrewing the castle nut thus exposed.
11. Pull the bolt out from beneath the car.
12. Jack up the axle tubes slightly to unload the shock absorbers, then disconnect the lower shock mounts.
13. Raise the axle tubes to a horizontal position.
14. Place a 24 in. section of 2 × 4 (wood) over the top of the differential

housing, the long axis lined up with the axle tubes, then, using short sections of chain or rope, fasten the axle tubes to the ends of the 2 × 4 so that the axle tubes remain in a horizontal position and do not sag at their ends. This is to prevent damage to the inner constant velocity joint of the axle shafts.

15. From inside the trunk, unbolt the differential housing from the chassis, then gradually lower the entire rear differential housing and axle tube assembly to the floor.
16. Installation is the reverse of removal. Bleed the brakes.

Models With Exposed Axle Shafts

1. Jack up the rear of the car as high as possible.
2. Support the rear axle subframe on jackstands (both sides).
3. Drain the oil from the differential housing.

Loosening or tightening the axle shaft bolt

4. Remove the hubcaps and the two bolts (one per side) that hold the axle to the axle flange.
5. The rear axle splined shaft then must be pressed from the axle flange.
6. Place a jack under the differential housing and jack up the housing slightly. Then unscrew the Allen bolt.

NOTE: *This bolt is tightened to 87–115 ft lbs.*

7. From inside the trunk, remove the four plugs and unbolt the differential housing from the subframe (17 mm socket).
8. Loosen the driveshaft center bearing support bracket, push back the rubber dust cover, and loosen the locknut.
9. Disconnect the rear universal joint from the flange and push the driveshaft forward out of the way.
10. Lower the entire rear differential housing assembly and axle shafts to the floor.
11. Installation is the reverse of removal.

1973–77 240D, 300D, 230, 280, 280C, 280E, 280S, 280SE, 450SL, 450SLC, 450SE and 450SEL

1. Drain the oil from the rear axle.
2. On cars without torque compensa-

Mercedes-Benz

**Axle housing removal (with axle shafts)
—1973-77 240D, 300D, 230, 280, 280C,
280E, 280S, 280SE, 450SL, 450SE,
450SLC and 450SEL**

tion, remove the brake caliper and suspend it on a hook.

3. On cars with torque compensation, disconnect the brake cable control, unbolt the holding bracket on the wheel carrier, remove the rubber sleeve and push the cover back.

4. Remove the bolt from both sides that holds the rear axle shaft to the flange.

5. Press the rear axle shaft out of the flange.

6. If required, loosen the right-hand rear shock absorber and lower it to the stop.

7. Remove the exhaust system, if necessary.

8. On the 450 series and 280S, remove the heat shield.

9. Loosen the clamp nut and remove the intermediate bearing from the floor pan. On 3-piece driveshafts, only remove the front nut.

10. Unbolt the driveshaft and remove it.

11. Support the rear axle housing.

12. Unbolt the rear rubber mount from the frame floor.

13. On the 450 series and 280S, lower the jack until the self-locking nuts are accessible.

14. Unbolt the rear axle center housing from the rear axle carrier.

15. On the 240D, 300D, 230, 280 and 280C, remove the bolt from the rubber mount on the cover of the rear axle housing. Fold back the rubber mat in the trunk and remove the rubber plugs; unbolt the rear axle center housing from the rear axle carrier.

16. Lower the rear axle center housing and remove it with the axle shafts. Do not allow the axle shafts to hang free, or the seals will be damaged, resulting in leaks.

17. Installation is the reverse of removal. Install new self-locking nuts, adjust the parking brake and fill the rear axle with the correct fluid.

REAR SUSPENSION

Springs

Removal and Installation

**220D/8, 240D, 300D, 220/8, 230,
250/8, 250C, 280, 280C, 280E,
350SL, 450SL, and 450 SLC**

1. Jack up the rear of the car.

2. Remove the rear shock absorber.

3. With a floor jack, raise the control arm to approximately a horizontal position. Install a spring compressor to aid in this operation.

4. Carefully lower the jack until the control arm contacts the stop on the rear axle support.

5. Remove the spring and spring compressor with great care.

6. Installation is the reverse of removal. For ease of installation, attach the rubber seats to the springs with masking tape.

**280S/8, 280SEL/8, 280SE 4.5,
280SEL 4.5, 300SEL 4.5**

1. Jack up the rear of the vehicle.

2. Support the trailing arm (thrust rod) with a floor jack or other jack.

NOTE: *For safety's sake, install a spring compressor on the rear spring and take up some of the tension.*

3. Loosen the fastening plate on the chassis and swing it aside.

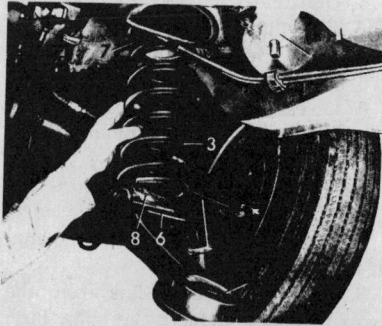

**Coil spring removal—280 and 300 series
cars (except 280, 280C, 280E, 280S and
280SE)**

2. Thrust rod   7. Rubber mount (top)
3. Rear spring   8. Rubber mount (bottom)
6. Spring disc 13. Cup

4. Carefully lower the trailing arm (thrust rod) and remove the spring.

5. Installation is the reverse of removal. Be sure to have the camber of the rear wheels checked.

450SE, 450SEL, 280S, 280SE

1. Jack and support the rear of the car and the trailing arm.

2. Remove the rear shock absorber.

3. Be sure that the upper shock absorber attachment is released first.

4. Compress the spring with a spring compressor.

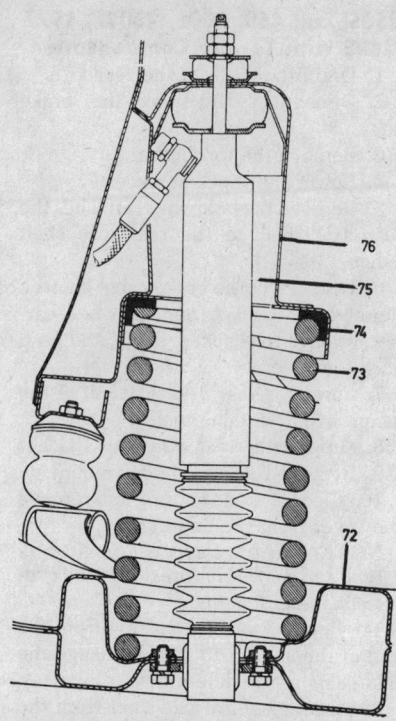

**Rear coil spring—450SE, 450SEL, 280S
and 280SE**

  72. Semi-trailing arm
  73. Rear spring
  74. Rubber mounting
  75. Shock absorber or spring
      strut
  76. Dome on frame floor

5. Remove the rear spring with the rubber mount.

6. Installation is the reverse of removal. When installing the shock absorber, tighten the lower mount first.

Shock Absorbers

Removal and Installation

**220D/8, 240D, 300D, 220/8, 230,
250/8, 250C, 280, 280C, 280E,
450SL, and 450SLC**

1. Jack up the rear of the car and support the control arm.

2. From inside the trunk (sedans), remove the rubber cap, locknut, and hex nut from the upper mount of the shock absorber. On 350SL, 450SL, and 450SLC, the upper mount of the rear shock absorber is accessible after removing the top, top flap, rear seat, backrest, and lining.

3. Unbolt the mounting for the rear shock absorber at the bottom and remove the shock absorber.

4. Installation is the reverse of removal.

**280S/8, 280SE 4.5, 280SEL 4.5,
300SEL 4.5**

1. Jack up the rear of the vehicle.

2. Support the trailing arm (thrust rod) or axle tube with a floor jack or other jack.

3. On vehicles with air suspension,

leave the pull knob for the valve in the driving position.

4. On sedans, open the trunk and remove the nut, washer, and rubber disc from the upper mount of the rear shock absorber. On the 280SL/8, these pieces are accessible from the top box when the roadster top is closed or when the coupe top is removed.

5. Loosen the lower shock absorber mounting bolt and remove the shock absorber.

6. Installation is the reverse of removal. With load on the wheels, jack the axle up to the level of the shock absorber lower mount and install the bolt.

450SE, 450SEL, 280S, 280SE

1. Remove the rear seat and backrest.
2. Remove the cover from the rear wall.
3. Jack and support the car and the trailing arm.

Rear upper shock absorber mount (75)—450SE, 450SEL and 280S

4. Loosen the nuts on the upper mount. Remove the washer and rubber ring.

5. Loosen the lower mount and remove the shock absorber downward.

6. Installation is the reverse of removal. Tighten the upper mounting nut to the end of the threads.

Independent Rear Suspension Adjustments

Suspension adjustments should only be checked when the vehicle is resting on a level surface and is carrying the required fluids (full tank of gas, engine oil, etc.).

Camber

220D/8, 240D, 300D, 220/8, 230, 250/8, 250C, 280, 280C, 280E, 350SL, 450SL, 450SLC, 450SE, 450SEL, 280S and 280SE

Rear wheel camber is determined by the position of the control arm. The difference in height (a) between the axis of

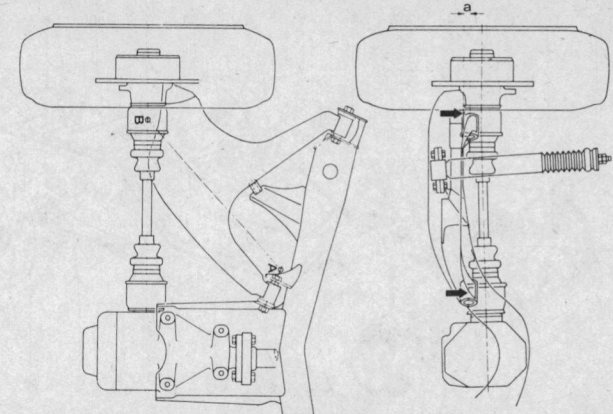

Rear wheel camber measurement on 220D/8, 240D, 300D, 220/8, 230, 250/8, 250C, 280, 280C, 280E, 280S, 280SE, 350SL, 450SL, 450SLC, 450SE and 450SEL—control arm position (difference in height between the axis of the rear control arm mount (A) and the lower edge of the cup on the outer constant velocity joint (B)

the control arm mounting point on the rear axle subframe and the lower edge of the cup on the constant velocity joint is directly translated in degrees of camber.

280S/8, 280SEL/8, 280SE 4.5, 280SEL 4.5, 300SEL 4.5

The rear wheel camber, measured with the vehicle ready for the road, is the result of the installation height of the rear springs and of the compensating spring. On vehicles with a hydroneumatic compensating spring, only the basic pressure of the compensating spring is effective.

Toe-In

Toe-in, on the rear wheels, is dependent on the camber of the rear wheels.

Rear Wheel Camber
350SL, 450SL, and 450SLC

Control Arm Position (mm)	Corresponds to Rear Wheel Camber of: (deg)
+ 50	+ 0°50′ ± 30′
+ 45	+ 0°35′ ± 30′
+ 40	+ 0°20′ ± 30′
+ 35	+ 0° 5′ ± 30′
+ 30	− 0°10′ ± 30′
+ 25	− 0°25′ ± 30′
+ 20	− 0°40′ ± 30′
+ 15	− 0°55′ ± 30′
+ 10	− 1°10′ ± 30′
+ 5	− 1°25′ ± 30′
0	− 1°40′ ± 30′
− 5	− 1°55′ ± 30′
− 10	− 2°10′ ± 30′
− 15	− 2°25′ ± 30′

Air Suspension System

NOTE: Service of this system should be

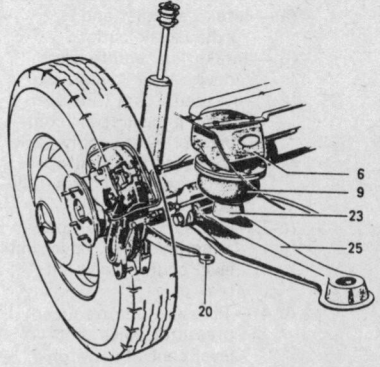

Schematic of air suspension system on the rear wheel.

6. Air chamber
9. Bellows
20. Lever for brake support
23. Air piston
25. Strut rod

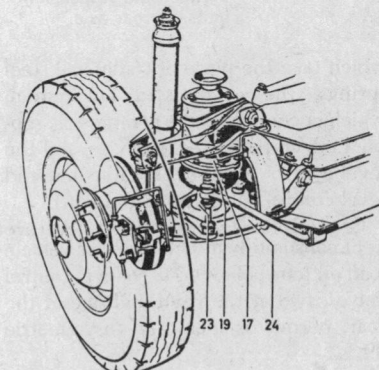

Schematic of air suspension system on the front wheel.

17. Air chamber
19. Bellows
23. Air piston
24. Lower control arm

left to a qualified Mercedes-Benz dealer.

The air suspension consists of three basic systems; the air suspension units (chambers, bellows, and air pistons)

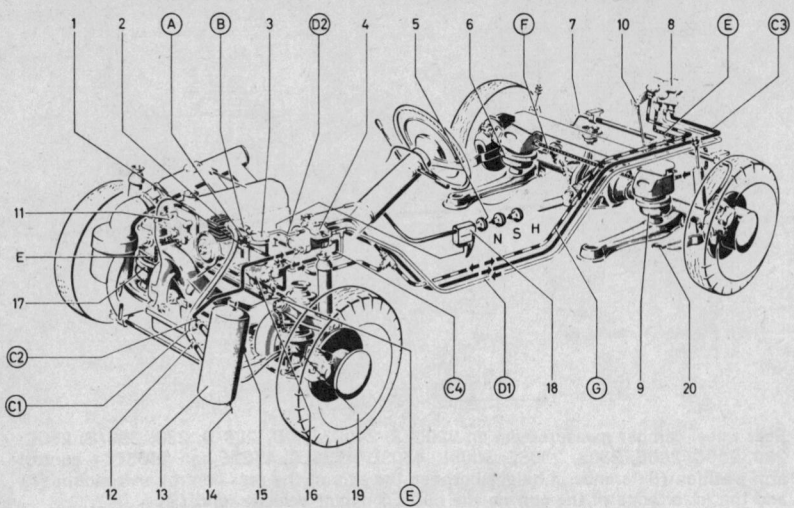

Air suspension system schematic

Front coil spring removal—cars with pivot pins.

- (a)—Intake air inlet and exhaust air outlet
- (b)—Intake line anti-freeze device—air compressor
- (c 1)—Pressure line (full operating pressure) air compressor—air supply tank
- (c 2)—Pressure line (full operating pressure) air supply tank—valve unit
- (c 3)—Pressure line (full operating pressure) valve unit—level control valve on rear axle
- (c 4)—Pressure line (reduced) pressure) valve unit—level control valve on front axle
- (d 1)—Return line to level control valve—valve unit
- (d 2)—Return line valve unit—anti-freeze device
- (e)—connecting line to level control valves—air suspension units
- (f)—Compensating line between air suspension units on rear axle

- (g)—pressure control line for higher level valve unit—level control valves
1. Air cleaner
2. Air compressor
3. Anti-freeze device
4. Valve unit
5. Warning light
6. Air chamber on rear axle
7. Torsion bar on rear axle
8. Level control valve on rear axle
9. Bellows on rear axle
10. Connecting rod for level control valve
11. Level control valve—right front
12. Check valve
13. Air supply tank
14. Drain valve
15. Filling valve
16. Level control valve—left front
17. Air chamber on front axle
18. Cable control for valve unit
19. Bellows on front axle
20. Lever for brake support

1. Front axle carrier
3. Lower control arm
4. Upper control arm
5. Steering knuckle
6. Kingpin
7. Steering knuckle carrier
10. Front spring
11. Front shock absorber
12. Torsion bar
18. Brake caliper
27. Torsion bar connecting linkage
30. Cam bolt
31. Leaf spring
33. Bearing bolt
44. Center brake cable control
45. Brake lever

which take the place of traditional steel springs, the compressed air system, which encompasses the compressor, supply tank and anti-freeze device, and the level control equipment (valve unit and level control valves front and rear).

Ground clearance and vehicle level are kept constant by distributing the vehicle load on four bellows. Three level control valves, two at the front and one at the rear, permit balancing of unsymmetric loads.

FRONT SUSPENSION
Springs
Removal and Installation

All Models except 450SE, 450SEL, 280S, 280SE and 1977 240D, 300D, 230, 280E

NOTE: *Be extremely careful when attempting to remove front springs as*

they are compressed and under considerable load.

1. Jack up the front of the car, put up jackstands and remove the front wheels.
2. Remove the front shock absorber and disconnect the sway bar.
3. On cars having pivot pins and threaded bushings (all 280 and 300 series sedan except 280 and 280C), unscrew the two outer bolts that attach the pivot pin to the frame.
3a. Place a jack under the inner control arm, then remove the two inner bolts and gradually lower the jack and arm.
3b. When the spring tension is relieved, remove the spring and its rubber bumpers.
4. On cars having eccentric adjusters (all others), first punchmark the position of the adjusters, then loosen the hex bolts.
4a. Support the lower control arm with a jack.
4b. Then knock out the eccentric pins and gradually lower the arm until spring tension is relieved.

4c. The spring can now be removed. **NOTE:** *Check caster and camber after installing a new spring.*
5. Installation is the reverse of removal.
6. For ease of installation, tape the rubber mounts to the springs.
7. If the eccentric adjusters were not matchmarked, install the eccentric bolts as illustrated under "Front End Alignment".

450SE, 450SEL, 280S, 280SE and 1977 240D, 300D, 230, 280E

1. Jack and support the front of the car and support the lower control arm.

Front coil spring removal—cars with eccentric adjusters.

3. Lower control arm
4. Upper control arm
6. Guide joint
7. Suspension joint
10. Front spring
11. Front shock-absorber
12. Torsion bar
29. Rubber mounting
44. Jack cradle
47. Angled intermediate brace

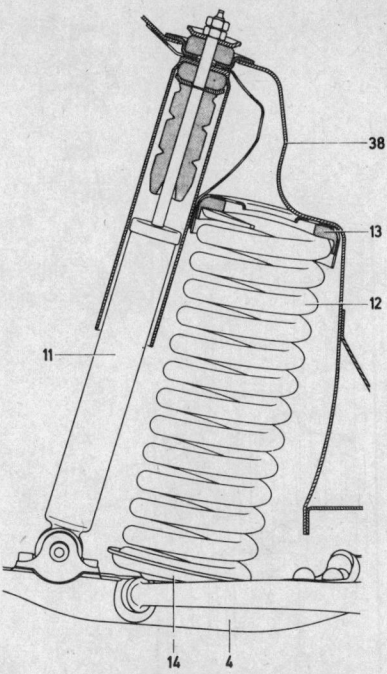

Front spring—450SE, 450SEL, 280S, 280SE and 1977 280E, 240D, 300D and 230

4. Lower control arm
11. Front shock absorber
12. Front spring
13. Rubber mount for front spring
14. Retainer for front spring
38. Front end

2. Remove the wheel. Unbolt the upper shock absorber mount.

3. Install a spring compressor and compress the spring.

4. Remove the front spring with the lower mount.

5. Installation is the reverse of removal. Tighten the upper shock absorber suspension.

Shock Absorbers

Removal and Installation

All Models except 450SE, 450SEL, 280S, 280SE, and 1977 240D, 300D, 230, 280E

Shock absorbers are normally replaced only if leaking excessively (oil visible on outside cover) or if worn internally to a point where the car no longer rides smoothly and rebounds after hitting a bump. A good general test of shock absorber condition is made by bouncing the front of the car. If the car rebounds more than two or three times it can be assumed that the shock absorbers need replacement.

1. For removal and installation of shock absorbers, it is best to jack up the front of the car until the weight is off of the wheels and support the car securely on jackstands.

2. When removing the shock absorbers, it is also wise to draw a simple diagram of the location of parts such as lock-rings, rubber stops, locknuts, and steel plates, since many shock absorbers require their own peculiar installation of these parts.

3. Raise the hood and locate the upper shock absorber mount.

4. Support the lower control arm with a jack.

5. Unbolt the mount for the shock absorber at the top. On 350SL, 450SL, and 450SLC, remove the coolant expansion tank to allow access to the right front shock absorber.

6. Remove the nuts which secure the shock absorber to the lower control arm.

7. Push the shock absorber piston rod in, install the stirrup, and remove the shock absorber.

8. Remove the stirrup, since this must be installed on replacement shock absorbers.

NOTE: *220D/8 through 250C sedans, use both Bilstein and F&S shock absorbers. On Bilstein shock absorbers, never re-use the upper or lower cups.*

9. Installation is the reverse of removal. Always use new bushings when installing replacement shock absorbers.

450SE, 450SEL, 280S, 280SE, and 1977 240D, 300D, 280E and 230

1. Jack and support the front of the car. Support the lower control arm.

2. Loosen the nuts on the upper shock absorber mount. Remove the plate and ring.

3. Place the shock absorber vertical to the lower control arm and remove the lower mounting bolts.

4. Remove the shock absorber.

5. Installation is the reverse of removal. On Bilstein shocks, do not confuse the upper and lower plates.

Steering Knuckle and Ball Joints/Kingpins

Mercedes-Benz cars 220D/8, 240D, 300D, 220/8, 230, 250/8, 250C, 280, 280C, 280E, 350SL, 450SL, 450SLC, 450SE, 450SEL, 280S and 280SE use steering knuckles with ball joints. All other models covered here use steering knuckles with kingpins.

Checking Ball Joints/Kingpins

1. To check the steering knuckles or ball joints, jack up the car, placing a jack directly under the front spring plate. This unloads the front suspension to allow the maximum play to be observed.

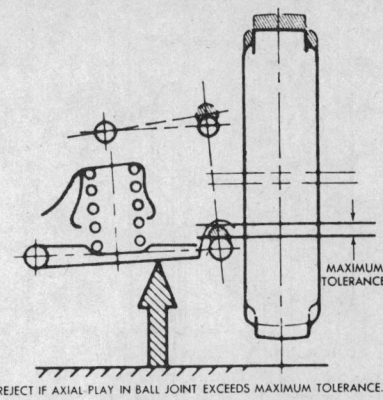

REJECT IF AXIAL PLAY IN BALL JOINT EXCEEDS MAXIMUM TOLERANCE.

2. On older models having kingpins, the maximum allowable play between the kingpin and bearing bushing is 0.016 in. The kingpin end-play is the same.

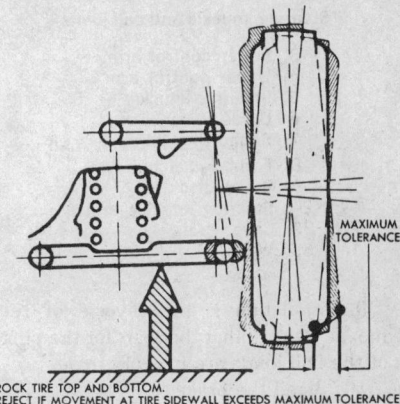

ROCK TIRE TOP AND BOTTOM.
REJECT IF MOVEMENT AT TIRE SIDEWALL EXCEEDS MAXIMUM TOLERANCE, BUT DO NOT CONFUSE WHEEL BEARING LOOSENESS WITH BALL JOINT WEAR.

3. Late model ball joints need be replaced only if dried out with plainly visible wear and/or play.

Removal and Installation

Steering Knuckle and Ball Joints except 450SE, 450SEL, 280S, 280SE and 1977 240D, 300D, 230 and 280E

1. This should only be done with the front shock absorber installed. If, however, the front shock absorber has been removed, the lower control arm should be supported with a jack and the spring should be clamped with a spring tensioner. In this case, the hex nut on the guide joint should not be loosened without the spring tensioner installed.

2. Jack up the front of the car and support it on jackstands.

3. Remove the wheel.

4. Remove the brake caliper.

5. Unbolt the steering relay lever from the steering knuckle. For safety, install spring clamps on the front springs.

6. Remove the hex nuts from the upper and lower ball joints.

7. Remove the ball joints from the steering knuckle with the aid of a puller.

8. Remove the steering knuckle.

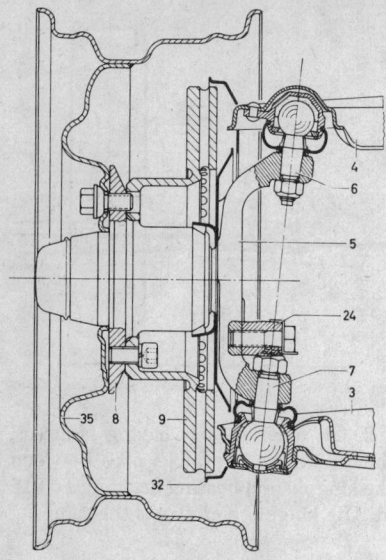

Steering knuckle and ball joints

3. Lower control arm
4. Upper control arm
5. Steering knuckle
6. Guide joint
7. Supporting joint
8. Front wheel hub
9. Brake disc
24. Steering knuckle arm
32. Cover plate
35. Wheel

9. Installation is the reverse of removal. Be sure that the seats for the pins of the ball joints are free of grease.

10. Bleed the brakes.

Steering Knuckle and Kingpins

1. Jack the vehicle and support it with jackstands.

2. Remove the wheel.

3. Remove the brake caliper.

4. On vehicles with air suspension, perform the following:

a. Leave the pull knob for the valve in the driving position.

b. Completely evacuate the compressed air from the compressor.

c. Open the plug on the valve unit and plug it again after evacuating the air.

5. Remove the front shock absorber.

6. On vehicles with air suspension, disconnect the connecting rod for the front level control valve on the bottom of the control arm. Unscrew the ball pin.

7. Lift the lower control arm and attach the special holding tool to the upper and lower shock absorber mounts.

8. Remove the brake caliper. Remove the brake line from the steering knuckle and plug the line.

9. Loosen and remove the track rod from the steering knuckle arm.

10. Loosen and remove the cam bolt from the upper bearing of the steering knuckle.

11. Remove the steering knuckle by unscrewing the threaded bolt and castle

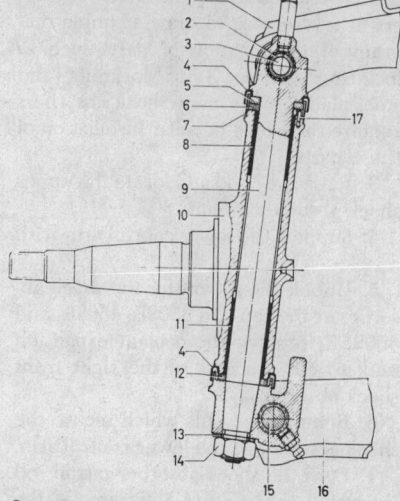

Cross-section of steering knuckle and king-pin.

1. Upper control arm
2. Threaded bolt
3. Cam bolt
4. Dust cap
5. Thrust washer (top)
6. Thrust washer (bottom)
7. Dust sleeve
8. Upper bearing bushing
9. Kingpin
10. Steering knuckle
11. Bottom bearing bushing
12. Compensating washer
13. Lockwasher
14. Hex nut
15. Steering knuckle carrier with threaded bolt
16. Lower control arm
17. Pin

nut from the bottom bearing of the steering knuckle.

12. Installation is the reverse of removal. Use new rubber rings throughout. The threaded bolt must be screwed in from the rear of the control arm so that the steering knuckle will not contact the castle nut at full lock. Be sure that the adjusting lug of the adjusting disc correctly enters the groove on the threaded bolt in the steering knuckle carrier.

450SE, 450SEL, 280S, 280SE, and 1977 240D, 300D, 230, 280E

1. Jack and support the car. Position jackstands at the outside front against the lower control arms.

2. Remove the wheel.

3. Remove the steering knuckle arm from the steering knuckle.

4. Remove and suspend the brake caliper.

5. Remove the front wheel hub.

6. Loosen the brake hose holder on the cover plate.

7. Loosen the nut on the guide joint and remove the joint from the steering knuckle.

8. Loosen the nut on the support joint.

9. Swivel the steering knuckle outward and force the ball joint from the lower control arm.

10. Remove the steering knuckle.

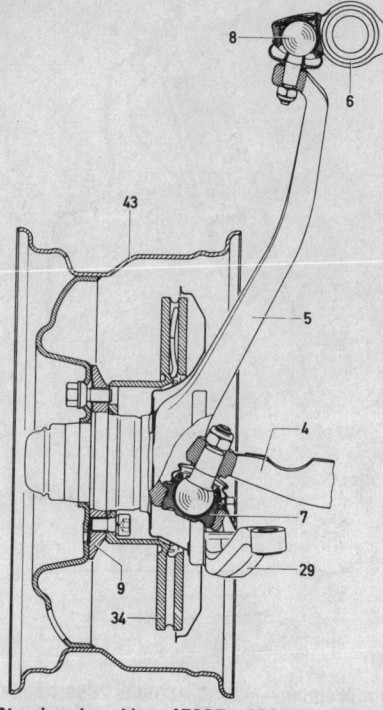

Steering knuckle—450SE, 450SEL, 280S, 280SE and 1977 230, 240D, 300D, 280E

4. Lower control arm
5. Steering knuckle
6. Upper control arm
7. Support joint
8. Guide joint
9. Front wheel hub
29. Steering knuckle arm
34. Brake disc
43. Wheel

11. If necessary, remove the cover plate from the steering knuckle.

12. Installation is the reverse of removal. Use self-locking nuts and adjust the wheel bearings.

Upper Control Arm

Removal and Installation

220D/8, 240D, 300D, 220/8, 230, 250/8, 250C, 280, 280C, 350SL, 450SL, and 450SLC

1. The front shock absorbers should remain installed. Never loosen the hex nuts of the ball joints with the shock absorber removed, unless a spring clamp is installed.

2. Jack the front of the car and remove the wheel.

3. Support the front end on jackstands.

4. Remove the steering arm from the steering knuckle.

5. Separate the brake line and brake hose from each other and plug the openings.

6. Support the lower control arm and unscrew the nuts from the ball joints.

7. Remove the ball joints from the steering knuckle.

8. Loosen the bolts on the upper control arm and remove the upper control arm.

Right-hand view of 450SE, 450SEL, 280S
and 1977 230, 240D, 300D and 280E front
suspension

2. Frame cross member
3. Cross yoke
4. Lower control arm
5. Steering knuckle
6. Upper control arm
11. Front shock absorber
12. Front spring

9. Installation is the reverse of removal.

CAUTION: *Mount the front hex bolt from the rear in a forward direction, and the rear hex bolt from the front in a rearward direction.*

10. Bleed the brakes.

All 280 and 300 Series Cars (except 280 and 280C)

1. On models having threaded control arm supports, first remove the steering knuckle, then unscrew the threaded bushings and the pivot pin.

2. Remove the rubber seals and the control arm.

3. On models having hex bolt supports, support the control arm with a jack, then disconnect the sway bar and shock absorber.

4. Remove the front coil spring, then disconnect the brake hose from the steel line, plug the line to prevent fluid loss and unscrew the hex bolts.

NOTE: *The bolts are installed from the inside—the nut always goes on the outside of the control arm.*

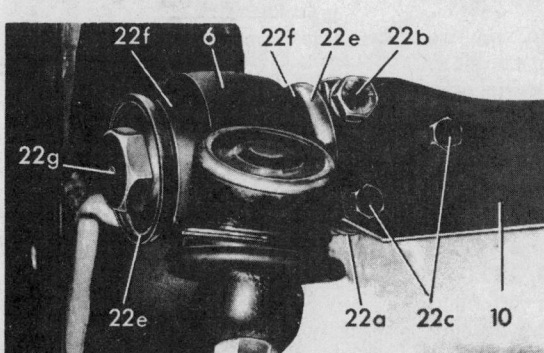

6. Upper control arm
10. Torsion bar
22a. Clamp
22b. Clamping screw
22c. Bolts with washers and self-locking nuts
22e. Cup washers
22f. Rubber mount
22g. Screw

Upper control arm and torsion bar attachments—450SE, 450SEL, 280S and 1977 230, 240D, 300D, 280E

5. To install, reverse the removal procedure. On models having threaded bushings, make sure the bushing rotates freely on the pivot pin.

450SE, 450SEL, 280S and 1977 240D, 300D, 230 and 280E

1. Jack and support the car. Position jackstands at the outside front against the lower control arms.

2. Remove the wheel.

3. Loosen the nut on the guide joint.

4. Remove the guide joint from the steering knuckle.

5. Secure the steering knuckle with a hook on the upper control arm stop to prevent it from tilting.

6. Loosen the clamp screw and separate the upper control arm from the torsion bar.

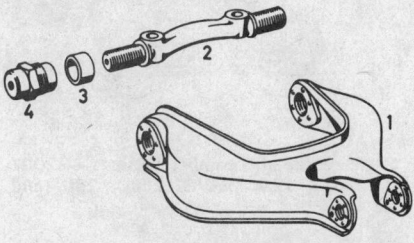

Upper control arm and pivot shaft

1. Upper control arm
2. Pivot pin
3. Rubber sealing ring
4. Threaded bushing

Front axle half—450SE, 450SEL, 280S and 1977 230, 240D, 300D, 280E

7. Loosen the upper control arm bearing at the front and remove the upper control arm.

8. Installation is the reverse of removal. Use new self-locking nuts and check the front wheel alignment.

Lower Control Arm
Removal and Installation
220D/8, 240D, 300D, 220/8, 230, 250/8, 250C, 280, 280C, 350SL, 450SL, and 450SLC

1. Since the front shock absorber acts as a deflection stop for the front wheels, the lower shock absorber attaching point should not be loosened unless the vehicle is resting on the wheels or unless the lower control arm is supported.

2. Jack up the front of the vehicle and support it on jackstands.

3. Support the lower control arm.

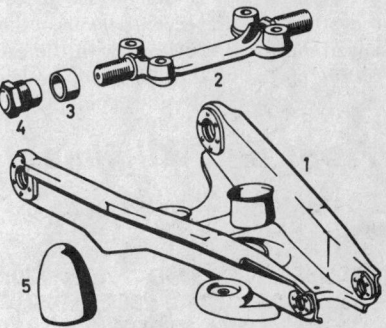

Lower control arm and pivot shaft

1. Lower control arm
2. Pivot pin
3. Rubber sealing ring
4. Threaded bushing
5. Additional rubber buffer

4. Loosen the lower shock absorber attachment.

5. Unscrew the steering arm from the steering knuckle.

6. Separate the brake line and brake hose and plug the openings.

7. Remove the front spring.

8. Unscrew the hex nuts on the ball joints.

9. Remove the lower ball joint and remove the lower control arm.

10. Installation is the reverse of removal. Bleed the brakes and check the front end alignment.

450SE, 450SEL, 280S, and 1977 240D, 300D, 230 and 280E

The lower control arm is the same as the front axle half.

1. Remove the front shock absorber. Loosen the top mount first.

2. Jack and support the front of the car and remove the wheels.

3. Remove the front springs.

4. Separate and plug the brake lines.

5. Remove the track rod from the steering knuckle arm.

6. Matchmark the position of the eccentric bolts on the bearing of the lower control arm in relation to the frame crossmember.

7. Remove the shield from the cross-yoke.

8. Support the front axle half.

9. Loosen the eccentric bolt on the front and rear bearing of the lower control arm and knock them out.

10. Remove the bolt from the cross-yoke bearing.

11. Loosen the screw at the opposite end of the cross-yoke bearing.

12. Pull the cross-yoke bearing down slightly.

13. Loosen the support of the upper control arm on the torsion bar. Remove the clamp screw from the clamp.

14. Remove the upper control arm bearing on the front end.

15. Remove the front axle half.

16. Installation is the reverse of removal. Tighten the eccentric bolts of the lower control arm bearing with the car resting on the wheels. Bleed the brakes and check the front end alignment.

Front End Alignment

Caster and Camber Adjustment

220D/8, 240D, 300D, 220/8, 230, 250/8, 250C, 280, 280C, 350SL, 450SL, 450SLC

Caster and camber are dependent upon each other and cannot be adjusted independently. They can only be adjusted simultaneously.

Caster is adjusted by turning the lower control arm around the front mounting, using the eccentric bolt.

Camber is adjusted by turning the

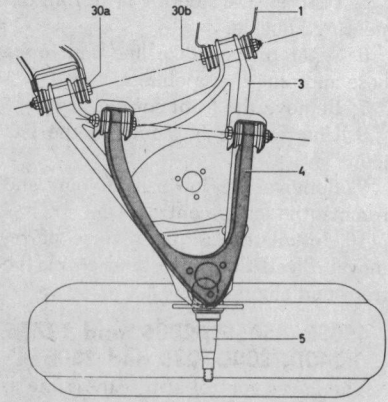

Caster and camber adjustment points on 220D/8, 220/8, 230/8, 250/8, 250C, 280, 280C, 350SL, 450SL, and 450SLC.

1. Front axle carrier
3. Lower control arm
4. Upper control arm
5. Steering knuckle
30a. Cam bolt front (caster)
30b. Cam bolt rear (camber)

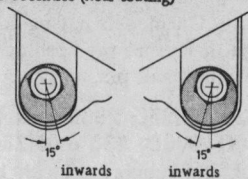

Camber eccentric (Rear seating)

inwards   inwards

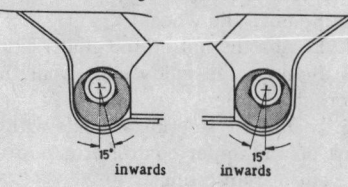

Caster eccentric (front seating)
Mechanical steering

inwards   inwards

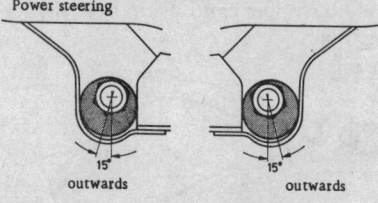

Caster eccentric (front seating)
Power steering

outwards   outwards

Basic caster and camber settings—220D/8, 220/8, 230, 250/8, 250C, 280, and 280C.

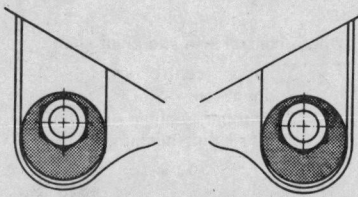

Basic adjustment of rear cams (camber) on 350SL, 450SL, and 450SLC.

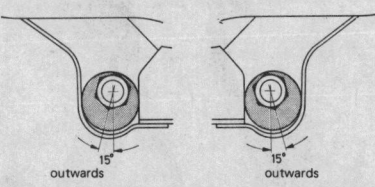

outwards   outwards

Basic adjustment of front cams (caster) on 350SL, 450SL, and 450SLC.

lower control arm about the rear mounting, using the eccentric bolt. Bear in mind that caster will be changed accordingly.

When camber is adjusted in a positive direction, caster is changed in a negative direction, and vice versa. Adjustment of camber by 0° 15' results in a caster change of approximately 0° 20'. Adjustment of caster by 1° results in a camber change of approximately 0° 7'.

450SE, 450SEL, 280S, and 1977 240D, 300D, 280E, 230, 280SE

The front axle provides for caster and camber adjustment, but both wheel adjustments can only be made together. Adjustments are made with cam bolts on the lower control arm bearings.

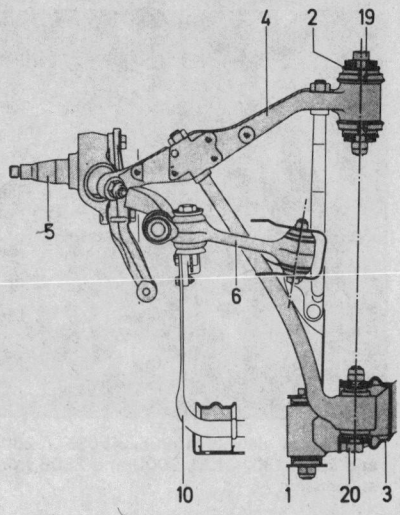

450SE, 450SEL, 1976 280S, 1977 280SE, 280E, 1977 230, 1977 240D, 1977 300D caster and camber adjusting bolts

1. Frame side member
2. Frame cross member for front axle
3. Cross yoke
4. Lower control arm
5. Steering knuckle
6. Upper control arm
10. Torsion bar
19. Cam bolt of front bearing (camber adjustment)
20. Cam bolt of rear bearing (caster adjustment)

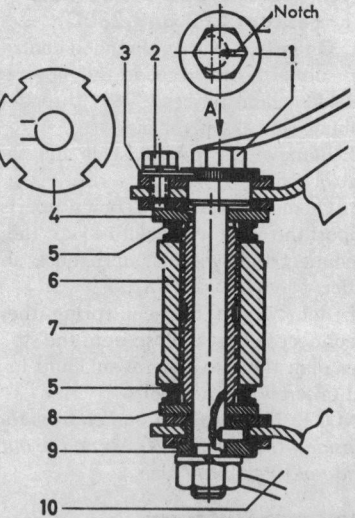

Caster and camber adjustment—280 and 300 series except 280, 280C, 280E, 280S, and 280SE (1977) and 300D

1. Eccentric bolt for camber adjustment
2. Hex screw with lockwasher
3. Locking plate
4. Adjusting washer for caster adjustment
5. Rubber sealing ring
6. Kingpin
7. Threaded bolt
8. Eccentric bushing with drive pin
10. Upper control arm

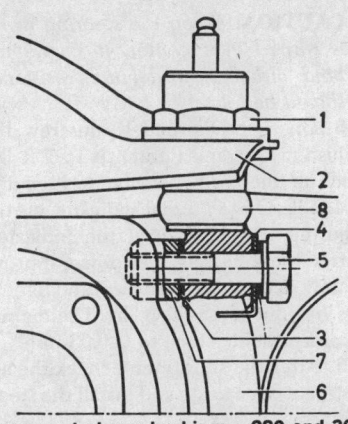

Upper control arm bushings—280 and 300 series cars except 280, 280C, 280E, 280S, and 280SE (1977) and 300D

1. Threaded bushing
2. Upper control arm
3. Shim
4. Lockplate
5. Bolt
6. Pivot pin
7. Front axle support
8. Rubber seal

The front bearing cam bolt is used to set caster, while the rear bearing cam bolt is used for camber.

Caster Adjustment

All 280 and 300 Series Vehicles (Except 280, 280C, 450SE, 450SEL, 280S and 1977 240D, 300D, 280E, 230, 280SE)

Caster is adjusted by swivelling the front axle carrier by means of the eccentric bolts. Caster should be adjusted equally on the left and right, so as not to distort the rubber front axle mounts. Before adjusting the caster, the four hex bolts which attach the rear engine mount carrier to the front axle carrier should be loosened to prevent any distortion. Tighten the nuts after adjustment.

Small differences in caster between the left and right can be adjusted (within minor limits) on the upper steering knuckle bearing at the bolt.

Camber Adjustment

All 280 and 300 Series Vehicles (Except 280, 280C)

Camber is adjusted at the upper steering knuckle bearing by turning the cam bolt. In special cases, if adjustment cannot be obtained at the bolt, camber can be adjusted by adding or removing some of the washers between the upper control arm bearing bolt and the front axle carrier. Washers should be added between the hex bolt and the lockwasher. One washer should always be used with each bolt.

Toe-In Adjustment

Toe-in is the difference of the distance between the front edges of the wheel rims and the rear edges of the wheel rims.

To measure toe-in, the steering should be in the straight ahead position and the marks on the pitman arm and pitman shaft should be aligned.

Toe-in is adjusted by changing the length of the two tie-rods (track rods on 450SE, 450SEL or 280S) with the wheels in the straight ahead position. Some older models have a hex nut locking arrangement rather than the newer clamp, but adjustment is the same.

NOTE: *Install new tie-rods so that the left-hand thread points toward the left-hand side of the car.*

STEERING

Steering Wheel

Removal and Installation

All Models Except 350SL, 450SL, 450SLC and 1973–77 Models

1. In general, the steering wheel is removed from the steering column shock absorber, while the shock absorber remains on the steering column. If work on the steering column jacket is required, the shock absorber and wheel must be removed.

2. Pry the three-pointed star trademark out of the center padding.

3. To remove only the steering wheel, unscrew the five hex nuts and lift off the steering wheel. Be careful because the cable is connected to the wheel.

4. To remove the wheel and shock absorber, leave the five nuts intact and remove the center hex nut.

5. Remove the steering wheel and shock absorber carefully because the cable is still connected.

6. Installation is the reverse of removal, no matter which part was removed.

Steering wheel (only) removal—all models except 350SL, 450SL, 450SLC and 1973-77 models.

2. Steering wheel   4. Hex nut

350SL, 450SL, 450SLC, and 1973–77 Models

1. Pry the three-pointed star trademark from the center padding.

2. Unscrew the hex nut from the steering shaft and remove the spring washer and the steering wheel.

3. Installation is the reverse of removal. Be sure that the alignment mark on the steering shaft is pointing upward and be sure that the slightly curved spoke of the steering wheel is down.

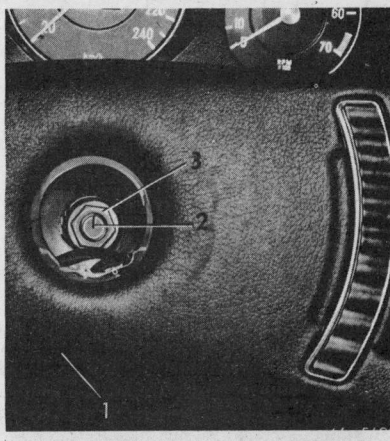

Align the marks on the wheel and shaft— 350SL, 450SL and 450SLC and 1973-77 models.

1. Steering wheel
2. Steering spindle
3. Hex nut with spring washer

Manual Steering Gear

Removal and Installation

CAUTION: *The telescopic steering tube must be fixed in position with an assembly pin inserted through the hole as illustrated, otherwise the tube will be shifted out of position when the steering box is installed.*

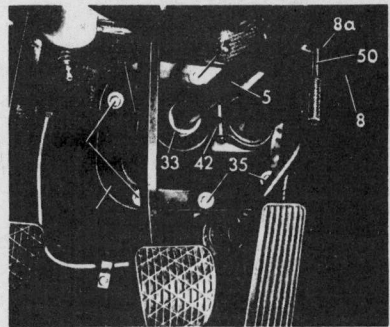

Assembly tool inserted in telescopic steering column.

5. Steering tube
8. Steering column jacket
8a. Assembly hole in steering column jacket
33. Rubber boot
34. Cover plate
35. Hexagon screw with washer
41. Rubber grommet
42. Fixing screw
50. Assembly pin

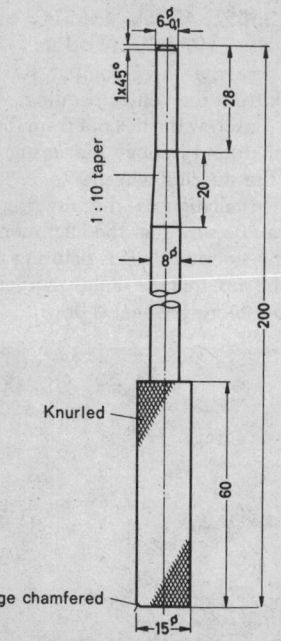

Dimensions for fabricating assembly tool

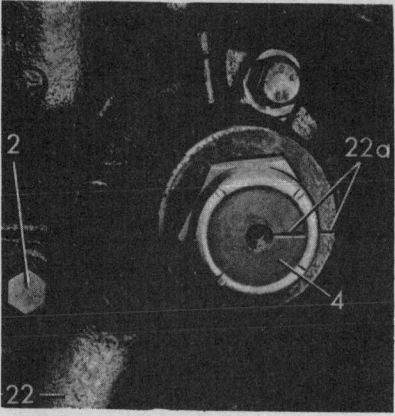

The steering is centered when the marks are aligned.

2. Closing plug in steering gear housing
4. Steering shaft
22. Pitman arm
22a. Assembly mark for pitman arm

1. Remove the socket screw from the upper flange of the steering coupling.

2. Detach the tie-rod and center tie-rod from the pitman arm.

3. Remove the pitman arm from the gear box using a puller. The pitman arm can be removed from the gear box with the two tie-rods still attached if desired. In any case, the pitman arm must be removed from the gear box before the box will come out of the car.

4. Detach the steering shock absorber from the bracket on the chassis, then remove the three hex-head bolts that secure the gear box to the frame side member.

5. Press the steering worm shaft off the coupling and remove the gear box from underneath the car.

6. To install, attach the pitman arm

(observing matchmarks) to the gear box, then remove the oil fill plug and fill the box with the required lubricant.

7. Place the steering box in its centered position (this can be found by observing the steering worm shaft while looking down through the bore in the housing cover). Center the steering wheel and install the gear box from beneath the car.

8. Insert the steering shaft of the box into the lower coupling.

9. Install the three chassis-to-gear box bolts and tighten.

10. Tighten the lower clamp bolt, after making sure the steering wheel and gear box are both in centered positions.

11. Reattach the center tie-rod to the pitman arm.

Adjustment

Steering Worm

1. Remove the steering gear from the vehicle and clamp it in a vise between two pieces of wood.

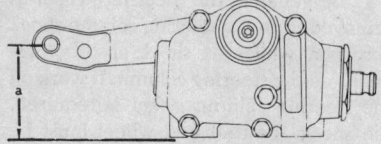

Dimension (a) can be altered by changing the position of the pitman arm on the shaft.

2. Remove the hex nut from the adjusting screw.

3. Remove the steering housing cover and at the same time unscrew the adjusting screw.

4. Remove the steering shaft from the housing.

5. Measure the torque necessary to rotate the steering shaft.

6. The torque should be 4–5 in. lbs. To adjust the torque, unscrew the ring and remove the snap-ring. Tighten or loosen the adjusting ring until the specified torque is obtained.

7. Install the threaded ring and snap-ring and check the torque again.

8. Assembly is the reverse of disassembly. Adjust the pressure block.

Pressure Block

1. Center the steering gear.

2. Unscrew the plug from the steering housing and turn the steering worm until the center of the steering nut is exactly below the threaded bore for the plug.

3. Measure the torque needed to turn the steering worm beyond the center position. If necessary, adjust the torque using the directions below:

4. On 220D/8, 240D, 300D, 220/8, 230, 250/8, and 250C models, screw in the adjusting screw to increase the torque and screw out the screw to decrease the torque. Lock the adjusting screw.

CAUTION: *When the steering worm is turned over center, it should not bind although a definite resistance should be felt.*

5. On all other models, unscrew the adjusting bolt and tighten it to 7 ft lbs. Back off the bolt ¼ turn and tighten it to 3–4 ft lbs. Install a dial indicator on the adjusting bolt and zero the indicator. Screw the adjusting bolt down approximately ⅛ turn (0.1–0.15 mm) and tighten the hex nut to 18–22 ft lbs. The dial indicator should return to 0–0.03 mm.

6. After the adjustment, check the adjustment once again and install the steering gear.

7. Check the steering in the vehicle.

Power Steering Gear

Removal and Installation

1. Suck the oil from the power steering reservoir using a syringe.

2. Detach the high-pressure hose and oil return hose from the steering assembly.

3. Cap both lines to prevent entry of dirt, then remove the clamp screw from the lower part of the coupling flange.

4. Remove the rubber plug from the cover plate and remove the U-joint socket screw. On LS90 power steering used on 1973–77 230, 220/8, 220D/8, 240D, 300D, 450SE, 450SEL, and 280S, remove the steering spindle. Pull the steering spindle up only until the coupling is no longer engaged with the worn gear.

5. On 1973 and later cars, the tailpipe and left side exhaust pipe may have to be removed for access.

6. Detach the tie-rod and center tie-rod (or drag link and track rod) from the pitman arm, using pullers or a tie-rod splitter.

7. Remove the hex-head bolts that hold the gear box to the frame, then press the worm shaft stub from the steering coupling and remove the gear box from underneath the car.

8. To install, first install the pitman arm (if it has been removed) aligning the matchmarks. Tighten the pitman arm nut to 110 ft lbs and install the cotter pin. Use new self-locking nuts to attach the gear to the frame.

9. Remove the screw plug from the steering box. Turn the worm shaft until the center of the power piston is directly below the bore in the housing. Check dimension (a) which can be altered by changing the position of the pitman arm on its shaft.

10. Center the steering wheel.

11. Press the worm shaft stub into the steering shaft coupling, making sure not to damage the serrations.

NOTE: *Install assembly pin as for manual steering.*

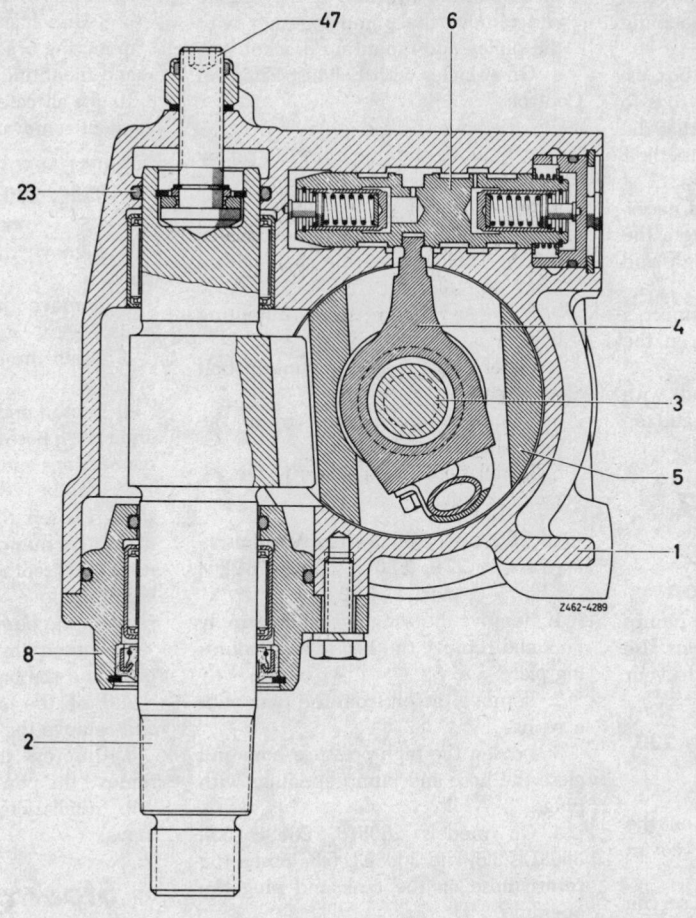

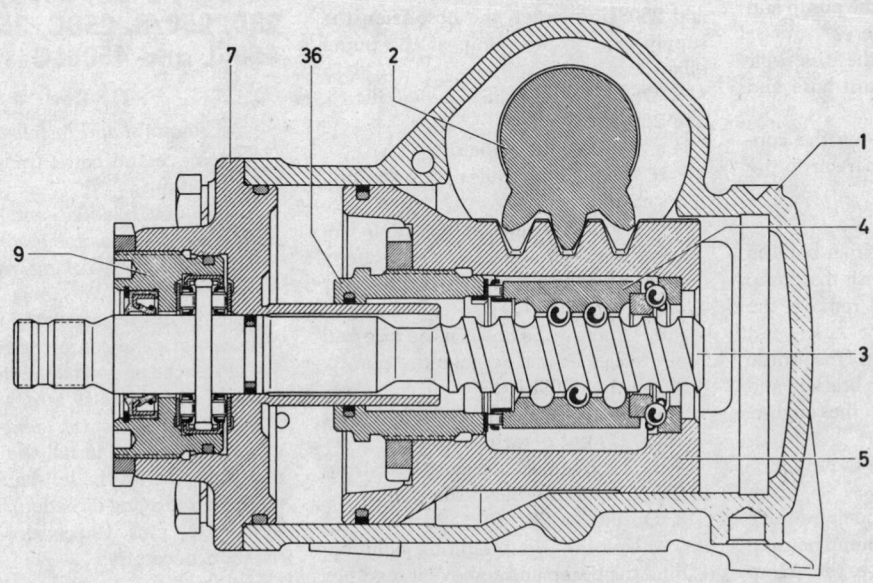

Cross Section of Power Steering Gear.

1 Steering case	4 Steering nut	7 Bearing cap	23 O-ring
2 Pitman shaft	5 Working piston	8 Housing cover	36 Screw cover
3 Steering worm	6 Control valve	9 Bearing insert	47 Adjusting screw

12. Install and tighten the hex-head screws that hold the gear box to the chassis, then install and tighten the coupling clamp screw.

13. Install the plug in the gear box, using a new gasket; attach the tie-rods to the pitman arm and make sure that the steering knuckle arms rest against their stops at full left and right lock.

14. Check toe-in and correct if necessary. Remove the dust covers from the fluid lines, then reconnect the high- and low-pressure lines.

15. Fill the reservoir and connect a hose between the bleed screw on the steering and the reservoir.

16. Open the bleed screw and, with engine running, bleed the system and top up.

Power Steering Pump

Removal and Installation

Many types of power steering pumps are used on Mercedes-Benz vehicles. Use only the instructions that apply to your vehicle.

220D/8, 240D, 300D, 220/8, 230, 250/8, and 250C

1. On all models:
   a. Remove the wing nut on the reservoir and remove the cover, spring, and damping plate.
   b. Suck the fluid from the reservoir with a syringe.
   c. Loosen the hose on the pump and plug both pump and hose.
   d. On pumps with the reservoir attached, loosen the return hose and plug it.
   e. On other types, loosen the connecting hose from the reservoir to the pump.
2. On 4 cylinder models:
   a. On 220/8, loosen the four bolts on the mounting bracket, push the pump toward the engine, and remove the belt.
   b. On 220D/8, loosen the three screws on the mounting bracket and push the pump toward the engine. Remove the belt.
   c. On 220D/8, remove the supporting strut.
   d. On all 4 cylinder models, remove the screws between the pump housing and the bracket. Remove the pump and pulley.
3. On 6 cylinder models:
   a. Loosen the screws that are hidden by the pulley (mounting bracket) and the nuts on the clamp screw.
   b. Loosen the rear screw and remove it together with the spacer. Push the pump toward the engine and remove the belt.

c. Remove the screws which attach the mounting bracket to the engine and remove the pump together with the pulley and mounting bracket.
4. On vehicles with Exhaust Emission Control:
   a. Remove the radiator.
   b. Remove the nut from the pulley shaft. On pumps with cylindrical shafts, remove the pulley.
   c. On pumps with tapered shafts, pull the pulley from the shaft with a jaw type puller.
   d. Unscrew both front mounting bolts.
   e. Remove the rear mounting bolt with spacer.
   f. Remove the pump from the mounting bracket.
5. Installation, in all cases, is the reverse of removal.

All 280 and 300 Series Vehicles (Except 280, 280C, 280S, 280E and 280SE)

1. Remove the wing nut on the supply tank and remove the spring and mounting plate.
2. Remove the oil from the tank with a syringe.
3. Loosen the high-pressure hose and close the hose and pump openings with plugs.
4. On models 280S/8, 280SE 3.5, 300SEL 3.5, and 300SEL 6.3, loosen the return hose on the tank and plug the openings.
5. On 280SE/8, 280SEL/8, 300SEL/8, and 280SL/8, loosen the hose from the supply tank to the pump at the pump elbow.
6. On 280S/8, 280SE/8, 280SEL/8, and 280SL/8:
   a. Remove the radiator.
   b. Remove the pulley from the pulley shaft.
   c. Loosen the nuts on the clamp. Unscrew the bolt and note the arrangement of bolt and spacer on the rear mounting bolt.
   d. Unscrew the bolts on the face end of the carrier and remove the pump.
7. On the 300SEL/8:
   a. Remove the compressor and lay it aside. Do not detach the lines.
   b. Remove the mounting bolts from the pump and remove the pump.
8. On the 300SEL 6.3:
   a. Unscrew the mounting bolts behind the pump and remove it together with the spacers.
   b. Remove the bolt which attaches the bracket to the cylinder head.
   c. Remove the bolts which hold the pump to the air compressor and remove the pump.
9. On the 280SE 3.4 and 300SEL 3.5:
   a. Remove the nuts from the attaching plate and from the support.

b. Push the pump toward the engine and remove the belt from the pulley.
   c. Unbolt and remove the pump and mounting bracket. Separate the pump and mounting bracket.
10. In all cases, installation is the reverse of removal.

350SL, 450SL, 450SLC, 450SE, 450SEL, 280, 280C, 280S, 280E and 280SE

1. Remove the nut from the supply tank.
2. Remove the spring and damping plate.
3. Drain the oil from the tank with a syringe.
4. Loosen and remove the expanding and return hoses from the pump. Plug all connections and pump openings.
5. On the 280S, loosen the radiator shell. Loosen the mounting bolts, and move the pump toward the engine by using the toothed wheel. Remove the belt. Remove the pulley, and then remove the pump.
6. Loosen the nut on the attaching plate and the bolt on the support.
7. Push the pump toward the engine and remove the belts from the pulley.
8. Unscrew the mounting bolts and remove the pump and carrier.
9. Installation is the reverse of removal.

Steering Linkage

220D/8, 240D, 300D, 200/8, 230, 250/8, 250C, 350SL, 450SL and 450SLC

Tie-Rod

Removal and Installation

1. Remove the cotter pins from the castellated nuts.
   NOTE: *350SL, 450SL and 450SLC do not use cotter pins and castellated nuts, but do use self-locking nylon insert nuts.*
2. Remove the castellated nuts.
3. Remove the center tie-rod.
4. Press the tie-rod off the steering arm and the steering relay arm.
5. Installation is the reverse of removal. Be sure to install the tie-rods so that the rod with the left-hand thread is on the left (driving direction). Always use new cotter pins. Check and adjust the toe-in, if necessary.

Center Tie-Rod

Removal and Installation

1. Disconnect the steering damper from the center tie-rod.
2. After removing the cotter pins, remove the castellated nuts from the center tie-rod joints.
3. Press the center tie-rod off the steering gear and steering relay arm.

4. Installation is the reverse of removal. Use new cotter pins and adjust the toe-in if necessary. Install new plastic rings and plastic caps on the ball pins.

All 280 and 300 Series Vehicles (Except 280 and 280C)

Tie-Rod

Removal and Installation

1. Remove the cotter pins and remove the castellated nuts.
2. Press the tie-rod from the steering knuckle arm.
3. Press the tie-rod from the steering lever.
4. Installation is the reverse of removal. Always use new cotter pins. Be sure that the tie-rod with the left-hand threads is installed on the left (driving direction). Adjust the toe-in if necessary.

Center Tie-Rod

Removal and Installation

See this procedure under "Center Tie-Rod Removal and Installation for 220D/8 through 450SLC."

450SE, 450SEL, 280S and 1977 240D, 300D, 280E and 280SE

Track Rod

Removal and Installation

1. Remove the castle nuts from the track rod joints.
2. Remove the track rod from the steering arms with a puller.
3. Installation is the reverse of removal. Install the track rods so that the end with the left-hand threads is on the left side.

Drag Link

Removal and Installation

1. Remove the castle nuts from the drag link joints.
2. Unbolt the steering damper and force it from the bracket.
3. Remove the drag link with a puller.
4. Installation is the reverse of removal.
5. Check the front wheel alignment.

BRAKE SYSTEMS

All Mercedes-Benz cars imported into the United States since 1968 are equipped with four wheel disc brakes. The disc brake systems are basically similar on all models, although removal and installation procedures may vary slightly. In addition, caliper bore sizes differ, depending upon application. The bore size (in millimeters) is represented by the number stamped on the outside of the caliper. Usually the number is the bore size, but occasionally a code is used. For

instance, a 14 on a Teves caliper is a 57 mm. bore caliper. Obviously, it isn't a 14 mm. caliper. On late production cars, both Teves and Bendix calipers are used, but the same manufacturer is installed on each axle. For service, install calipers of only one firm on the front axle. On the rear, calipers of both firms can be installed.

Adjustment

Since disc brakes are used at all four wheels, no adjustments are necessary. Disc brakes are inherently self-adjusting. The only adjustment possible is to the handbrake, which is covered at the end of this section.

Master Cylinder

Removal and Installation

The dual master cylinder has a safety feature which the single unit lacks—if a leak develops in one brake circuit (rear wheels, for example), the other circuit will still operate.

Failure of one system is immediately obvious—the pedal travel increases appreciably and a warning light is activated. This warning light is operated by a simple switch attached to a float in the reservoir/s. When the fluid falls below a certain level, the switch activates the circuit.

CAUTION: *This design was not intended to allow driving the car for any distance with, in effect, a two-wheel brake system. If one brake circuit fails, braking action is correspondingly lower. Front circuit failure is the more serious, however, since the front brakes contribute up to 75% of the braking force required to stop the car.*

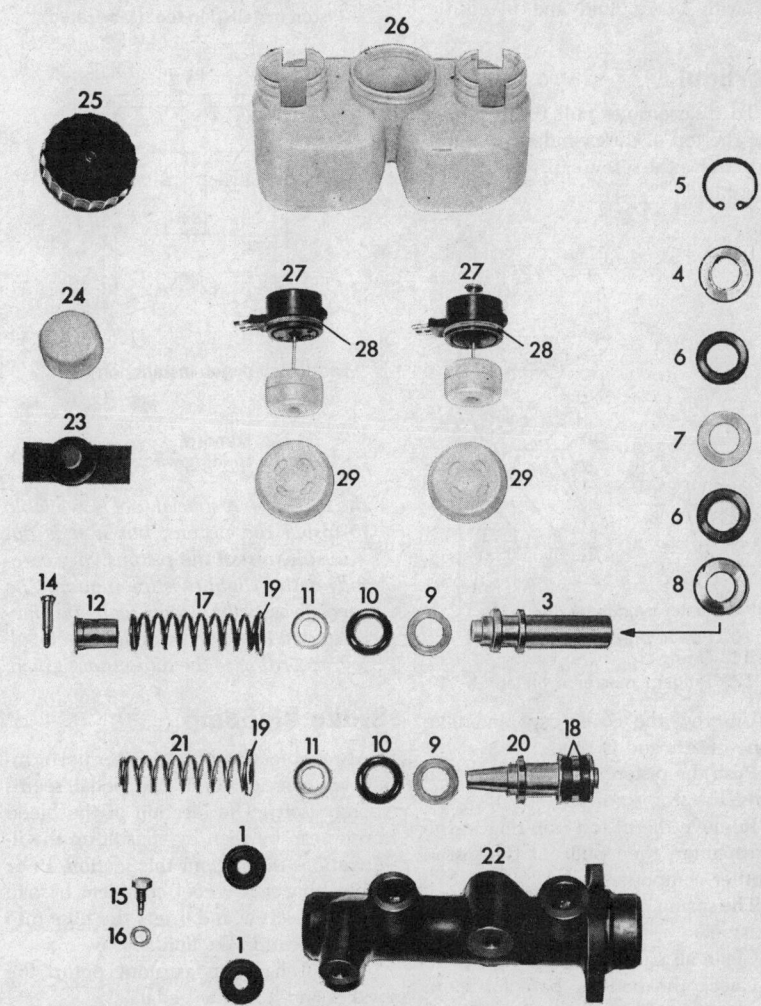

Exploded view of tandem master cylinder

1. Container plug	11. Supporting ring	21. Compression spring
3. Piston (push rod circuit)	12. Spring retainer	22. Housing
4. Stop washer	14. Connecting screw	23. Splash guard
5. Lock ring	15. Stop-screw	24. Strainer
6. Vacuum seal	16. Sealing ring (copper)	25. Closing cover
7. Intermediate ring	17. Compresion spring	26. Compensating tank
8. Bearing ring	18. Ring sleeve	27. Contact insert
9. Filler	19. Spring plate	28. O-ring
10. Primary sleeve	20. Intermediate piston	29. End cover

Mercedes-Benz

1. To remove the master cylinder, first open a bleed screw at one front, and one rear, wheel.

2. Pump the pedal to empty the reservoir completely. Make sure both reservoirs are completely drained.

3. Disconnect the switch connectors using a small screwdriver. Disconnect the two brake lines to the front brakes and the brake line to the rear brakes. Plug the ends with bleed screw caps or the equivalent.

4. Unbolt the master cylinder from the power brake unit and remove. Be careful you do not lose the O-ring in the flange groove of the master cylinder.

5. Installation is the reverse of removal. Be sure to replace the O-ring between the master cylinder and the power brake unit, since this must be absolutely tight. Torque the nuts to 12–15 ft lbs. Be sure that both chambers are completely filled with brake fluid and bleed the brakes.

Overhaul

1. To disassemble, pull the reservoir out of the top of the cylinder.

2. Remove the screw cap, strainer, and splash shield.

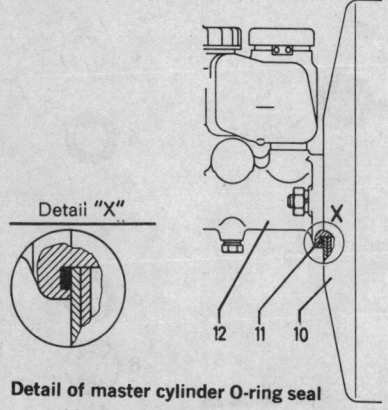

Detail of master cylinder O-ring seal
10. Power brake
11. O-ring
12. Tandem master cylinder

3. Unscrew the cover caps and take out the inserts and O-rings.

4. Push the piston inward slightly and remove the stop screws.

5. Remove the piston stop-ring in the same manner, then pull out the piston and other components.

6. The spring must be unscrewed from the piston.

7. Clean all parts in clean brake fluid.

8. Check the housing bore for score marks and rust. Do not hone the cylinder bore. If slight rust marks do not come out with crocus cloth, replace the housing.

9. Assembly is the reverse of disassembly. Before installing the pistons, coat the sleeves of both pistons with ATE brake fluid paste or with brake fluid in the absence of the special paste.

NOTE: *Do not force the pistons into*

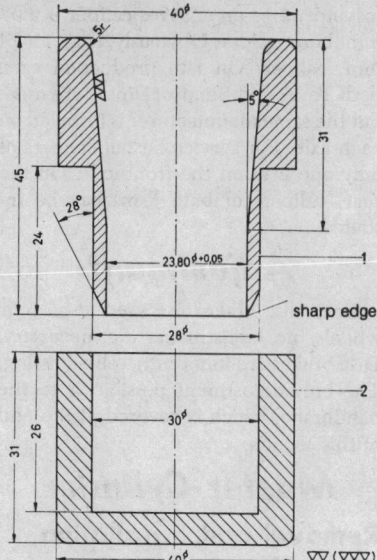

Piston installation tool (fabricated)

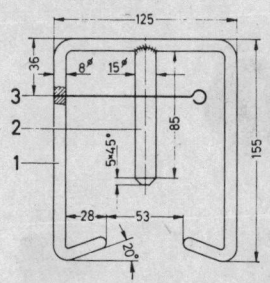

Fabricated piston installation tool

1. Clip
2. Mandrel
3. Holding wire

the housings. A special tool is available to install the pistons, but if it is not available, install the pistons very carefully with a slight twisting motion. The special assembly tools can be fabricated in the shop from light metal alloy, according to the dimensions given.

Brake Bleeding

Always bleed the brakes after performing any service, or if the pedal seems spongy (soft). The location of the bleed screws can be seen by consulting the illustrations throughout this section. Prior to bleeding each wheel, connect a hose to the bleed screw and insert the hose into a jar of clean brake fluid.

1. First have an assistant pump the brakes and hold the pedal.

2. Then, starting at the point farthest from the master cylinder, slightly open the bleed screw.

3. When the pedal hits the floor, close the bleed screw before allowing the pedal to return (to prevent air from being sucked into the system).

4. Continue this procedure until no more air bubbles exit from the bleed

screw hole, then go to the next wheel. Fluid, which has been bled from the system, is filled with microscopic air bubbles after the bleeding process is completed, therefore it should be discarded.

NOTE: *On dual master cylinders, bleed only the circuit that has been opened. If both circuits have been opened, first bleed the circuit connected to the pushrod bore starting with the wheel farthest from the master cylinder, then bleed the other circuit.*

Front Disc Brakes

Disc Brake Pads

Removal and Installation

All Models

The disc brake pads should be replaced when the lining thickness has worn down to 2 mm.

NOTE: *The 2 mm (approx. 0.08) minimum lining thickness figure specified is the manufacturer's specification. State laws may vary on this subject. Consult your state authorities for any conflict in minimum acceptable lining (pad) thickness.*

Use only approved quality brake pads and always install pads as a set. Be sure that the calipers on the front and rear wheels are equipped with the same type of pads.

NOTE: *This procedure also applies to replacement of rear disc brake pads.*

1. Remove the cover plate (front calipers only) and drive the retaining pins out of the caliper, using a drift.

2. Remove the anti-rattle spring.

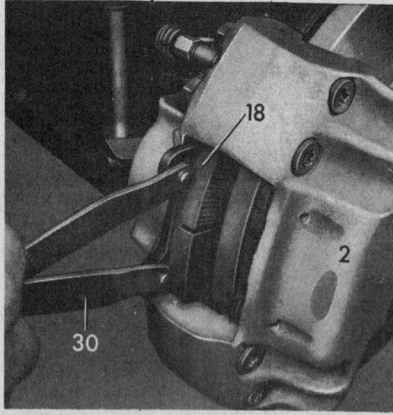

Removing one brake pad

2. Brake caliper
18. Brake pad   30. Removal tool

3. Then remove one pad only by pulling out on both tabs with bent pieces of welding rod. Always leave one brake pad in the caliper.

4. Blow off the brake assembly with compressed air and clean the pad guide in the caliper.

5. Check the dust covers for cracks. If

Mercedes-Benz

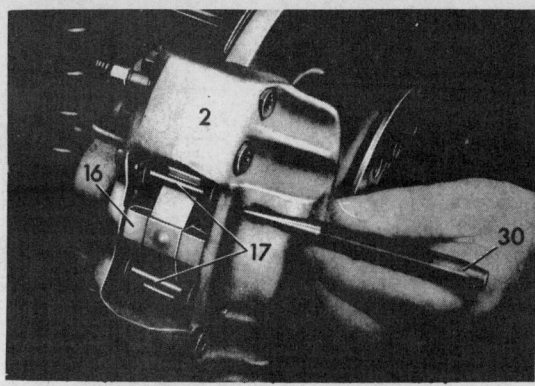

Drive out the retaining pins

2. Brake caliper	17. Retaining pin
16. Anti-rattle spring	30. Drift

cracks exist, the caliper must be disassembled (not separated) and the cover replaced.

6. Press one piston back into its bore, using special pliers or a flat piece of steel bent to fit. Do not scratch the surface of the piston.

NOTE: *Fluid may be displaced from the master cylinder reservoir. It is wise to siphon off a small amount of fluid to avoid damaging the paint.*

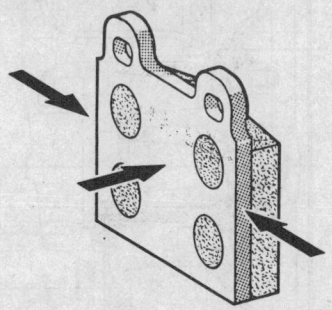

Lubricate the new pad at the areas indicated.

7. Install one friction pad. Before installing the pad, grease the area illustrated with special grease (Molykote® Paste "U".)

NOTE: *One pad must always remain in the caliper, because pushing one piston back would bring the other forward too far.*

8. Replace the other pad using the same procedure.

9. Install the anti-rattle spring and retaining pins, then seat the pads by pumping the brake pedal a few times.

10. Hard stopping for the first few hundred miles could ruin the new pads by causing heat glazing.

11. Refill the master cylinder and bleed the brakes.

Disc Brake Calipers

Removal and Installation

1. Drain brake fluid from the front brake circuit through an open bleeder screw.

2. Disconnect the brake hose from the brake line (or, on some models, disconnect the brake line from the caliper).

3. Immediately plug the lines and openings to prevent loss of fluid.

4. On models where the brake line does not connect directly to the caliper, remove the hose from the caliper.

5. Remove the brake hose from the bracket.

6. Plug the connection at the brake caliper.

7. Unlock the lockwasher and remove the hex mounting bolts.

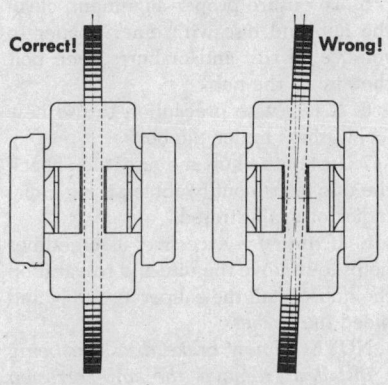

Correct! **Wrong!**

Uneven brake pad wear will result from misaligned calipers and discs.

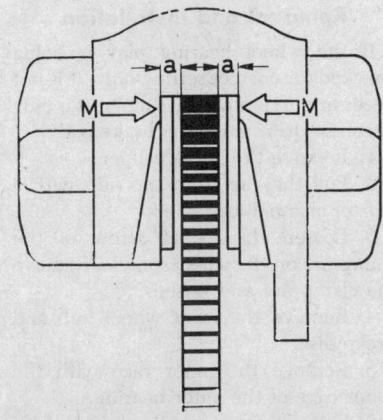

Measure the clearance (a) on each side of the disc at point (M).

CAUTION: *The caliper mounting bolts should not be removed unless the calipers are at approximately room temperature.*

8. Remove the calipers from the steering knuckle. As the caliper is removed, take note of any shim that may be installed and tape these (if any) in their original position.

9. To install, use a new lockplate and attach the brake caliper to the steering knuckle. The proper torque for the mounting bolts is 82 ft lbs.

It is extremely important that the brake disc be parallel to the caliper. Using a feeler gauge, measure the clearance at the top and bottom of the caliper (between disc and caliper) and on both sides of the disc. The clearance should not vary more than 0.15 mm. If the clearance varies, position the brake caliper by adding or subtracting shims as required. This procedure only applies to models equipped with shims, usually on the rear brake calipers.

10. On all 280 and 300 series cars (except 280, 280C, 280S, 280SE), the following mounting bolts are used:

   a. On vehicles with solid brake discs, use a 34 mm bolt, part no. 111 421 00 71.

   b. On vehicles with vented discs, use a 31.5 mm bolt, part no. 109 421 00 71. This bolt is identified with notches on the hex head.

11. Insert the brake hose into the bracket, making sure that the grommet is not damaged, or connect the brake line to the calipers. If applicable, connect the brake hose to the brake line. Make sure that the hose is not twisted.

12. On some models (220D/8, 240D, 300D, 220/8, 230, 250/8, 250C, 280, 280C, 350SL, 450SL, and 450SLC) a locking disc is attached to the brake line bracket. Install the brake hose into the disc so that the disc or hose does not bind.

13. Turn the steering lock-to-lock to make sure that the brake hose or lines do not bind.

14. Fill the master cylinder and bleed the brake system.

15. Before driving the car, depress the brake pedal hard, several times, to seat the pads.

Piston Seal Replacement (Front Brake Caliper)

CAUTION: *Do not unbolt the two caliper halves for any reason. Remove the brake caliper for easier service.*

1. Remove the friction pads, brake line, and dust cap, then pry the clamp ring from the housing.

2. Using a rubber-backed piece of flat steel, hold one piston in place while blowing the other one out with compressed air (7–8 psi).

745

NOTE: *If a piston is stuck, clamp the other piston in place and pump the brake pedal. The hydraulic pressure will force the piston out. This is a messy operation, so protect exterior paint from splashing brake fluid.*

3. Remove the piston seals from the cylinder bores and examine the bores.

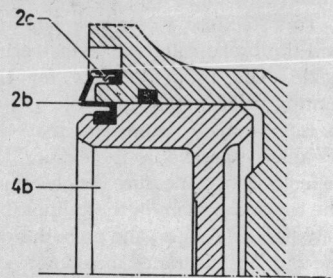

Piston seal and dust cover.

2b. Dust cap
2c. Closed clamp ring
4b. Piston

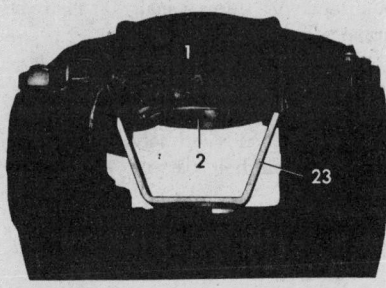

Piston holding fixture installed

1. Brake caliper
2. Piston
23. Holding fixture

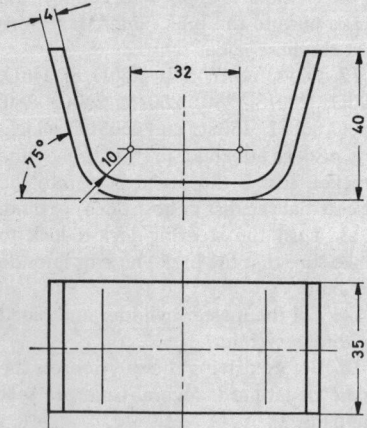

Dimensions for fabricating the piston holding fixture. (given in mm.)

Scored bores necessitate replacement of the entire caliper, since the inner surface is chrome plated and cannot be honed.

4. Clean the bores with crocus cloth only, never emery paper.

5. Install the new seals, coating them with brake fluid beforehand, then install the (front) piston so that the projection points downward. The rear caliper pis-

tons must be installed with the projection facing downward.

NOTE: *If the projection is in any other position, the brakes may squeal badly.*

6. Install the dust cap, clamp ring and heat shield.

7. The recess in the heat shield must fit the piston projection, but be above the shield level by about 0.004 in.

NOTE: *The heat shields differ for inner and outer pistons.*

8. Install the friction pads and the caliper assembly, then bleed the brakes.

Brake Disc

Removal and Installation

1. Removal for the various types is similar.

2. First, remove the brake caliper, then the front hub. The hub and disc can be removed by prying off the dust cap, removing the socket screw and clamp nut, and pulling off the wheel hub.

3. Fasten the hub in a vise or holding fixture (be careful not to distort the housing), matchmark the disc and hub, then unbolt the brake disc.

4. Inspect the disc for burning (blue color), cracks and scoring. The disc becomes scored slightly in normal service; therefore, replace it only if the depth of individual scores exceeds 0.020 in.

5. To ensure proper alignment, clean the hub and disc with emery paper to remove all rust and/or burrs, then bolt the disc to the hub.

6. It is a wise precaution to use new lockwashers under the bolts.

7. Install the hub and disc, then check the disc for runout (wobble), using a dial indicator as illustrated.

8. If runout is excessive, it sometimes helps to remove the disc and reseat it on the hub. Install the caliper assembly and bleed the brakes.

NOTE: *If new brake discs are being installed, remove the anti-corrosion paint before installing it.*

Wheel Bearings

Removal and Installation

If the wheel bearing play is being checked for correct setting only, it is not necessary to remove the caliper. It is only necessary to remove the brake pads.

1. Remove the brake caliper.

2. Pull the cap from the hub with a pair of channel-lock pliers.

3. Loosen the socket screw of the clamp nut on the wheel spindle. Remove the clamp nut and washer.

4. Remove the front wheel hub and brake disc.

5. Remove the inner race with the roller cage of the outer bearing.

6. Using a brass or aluminum drift, carefully tap the outer race of the inner

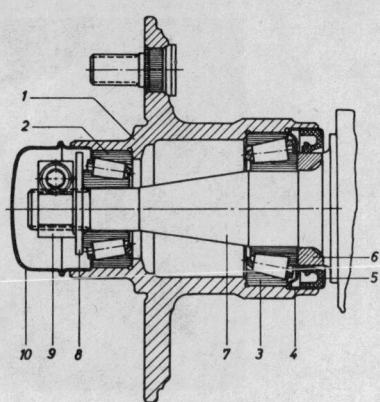

First version wheel bearings

1. Front wheel hub
2. Outer bearing
3. Inner bearing
4. Puller ring
5. Seal
6. Spacer
7. Wheel spindle
8. Washer
9. Clamp nut
10. Dust cap

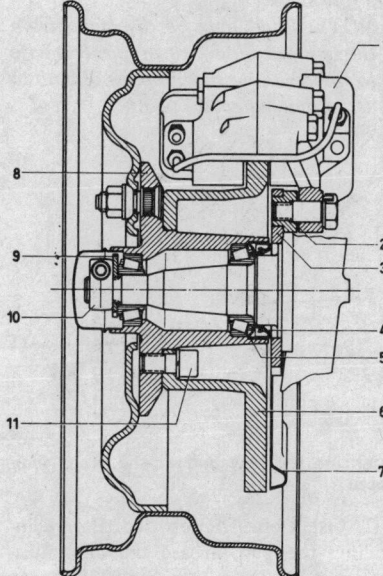

Second version wheel bearings

1. Brake caliper
2. Shim
3. Caliper bracket
4. Seal
5. Puller ring
6. Brake disc
7. Cover plate
8. Wheel hub
9. Washer
10. Clamp nut
11. Screw and lockwasher

bearing until it can be removed with the inner race, bearing cage, and seal.

7. In the same manner, tap the outer race of the bearing out of the hub.

8. Separate the front hub from the brake disc.

9. To assemble, press the outer races into the front wheel hub.

10. Pack the bearing cage with bearing grease and insert the inner race with the bearing into the wheel hub.

11. Coat the sealing ring with sealant and press it into the hub.

12. Pack the front wheel hub with 45–55 grams of wheel bearing grease. The races of the tapered bearing should be well packed and also apply grease to the front faces of the rollers. Pack the front bearings with the specified amount of grease. Too much grease will cause overheating of the lubricant and it may lose its lubricity. Too little grease will not lubricate properly.

13. Coat the contact surface of the sealing ring on the wheel spindle with Molykote®paste.

14. Press the wheel hub onto the wheel spindle.

15. Install the inner race and cage of the outer bearing.

16. Install the steel washer and the clamp nut.

Adjustment

1. Tighten the clamp nut until the hub can just be turned.

Loosening the Allen screw in the clamp nut
1. Brake disc
2. Brake caliper
10. Front wheel hub
12. Washer
13. Clamping nut
13a. Allen screw

2. Slacken the clamp nut and seat the bearings on the spindle by rapping the spindle sharply with a hammer.

3. Attach a dial indicator, with the pointer indexed, onto the wheel hub. Preload the dial indicator approximately 2 mm.

4. Check the end-play of the hub by pushing and pulling on the flange. The end-play should be approximately 0.0008 in. (0.0004–0.0008 in. 1973–75).

5. Make an additional check by rotating the washer between the inner race of the outer bearing and the clamp nut. It should be able to be turned by hand.

6. Check the position of the suppressor pin in the wheel spindle and the contact spring in the dust cap.

7. Pack the dust cap with 20–25 grams of wheel bearing grease and install the cap.

8. Install the brake caliper and bleed the brakes.

Rear Disc Brakes
Disc Brake Pads

Removal and Installation

The procedure for removing the rear disc brake pads is the same as for front disc brake pads. Use the instructions given under "Front Disc Brake Pad Removal and Installation", with the accompanying illustrations.

Disc Brake Calipers
Removal and Installation

Use the procedure given under "Front Brake Caliper Removal and Installation". Some rear brake calipers have no disc run-out compensating feature. These calipers can only be installed on vehicles where the rear axle shaft is supported on

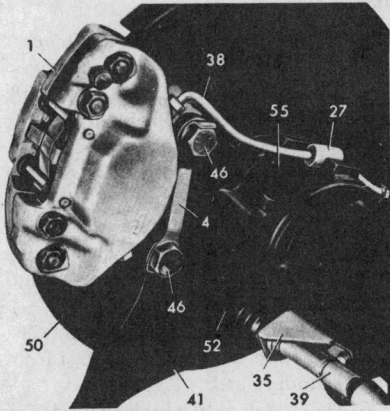

Rear wheel disc brake caliper (models with enclosed axle shafts and brake hold-down).
1. Brake caliper
4. Lockwasher
27. Rubber ring
35. Holder for brake cable control
38. Brake line
39. Brake cable control
41. Lever for brake holddown
46. Bolt
50. Cover plate
52. Rubber sleeve
52. Bearing body

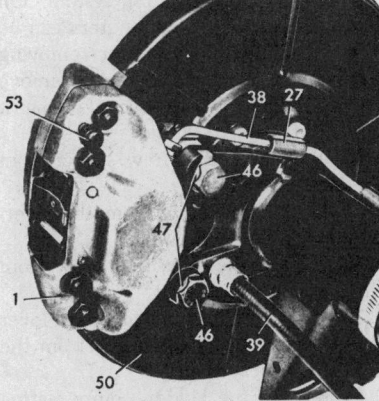

Rear wheel disc brake caliper (models with enclosed axle shafts and no brake hold-down).
1. Brake caliper
27. Rubber ring
38. Brake line
39. Brake cable control
46. Hex bolt
47. Lockwasher
50. Cover plate
53. Bleed screw with rubber cap

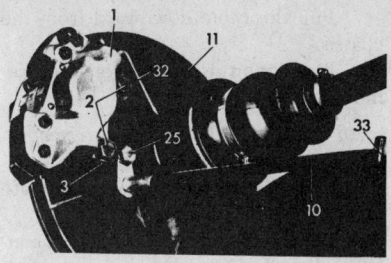

Rear wheel disc brake caliper (models with exposed axle shafts).
1. Brake caliper
2. Hexagon screw
3. Locking plate
10. Brake cable
11. Cover plate
25. Hexagon scrw
32. Brake line
33. Bracket for brake cable with rubber grommet

grooved ball bearings. Calipers with a compensating feature may be installed on axles with grooved ball bearings or self-aligning bearings.

Overhaul

Rear disc brake caliper overhaul procedures are the same as those given for front disc brake caliper overhaul.

Brake Discs
Removal and Installation

1. Remove the brake caliper.

2. Remove the brake disc from the rear axle shaft flange. Jammed brake discs can be loosened from the axle shaft flanges by light taps with a plastic hammer. Be sure that the parking brake is fully released.

3. The air ducts on the vented discs used on the 300SEL 6.3 are provided with spring clips which serve as balancing weights. These should never be removed.

4. Installation is the reverse of removal.

5. Inspection procedures are the same as those for front brake discs.

Handbrake
Front Cable

Removal and Installation
220D/8, 240D, 300D, 230, 220, 250/8, 280, 280C, 280E

1. Remove the spring from the equalizer.

2. Back off the adjusting screw completely.

3. Detach the relay lever from the bracket on the frame and from the adjusting shackle.

4. Detach the cable from the relay lever by pulling the cotter pin out of the bolt.

5. Remove the clip from the cable guide. Remove the clips from the chassis.

6. Detach the brake cable from the parking brake link. Remove the clip from the cable guide and detach the brake cable from the parking brake.

7. Pull the cable downward from the chassis.

8. Installation is the reverse of removal.

All 280 and 300 Series Cars (Except 280, 280C and 280E)

1. Loosen the nut on the intermediate lever.

2. Remove the flange bolt from the intermediate lever.

3. Pull the cotter pin from the brake cable guide of the brake lever. Remove the brake cable control.

4. Installation is the reverse of removal.

350SL, 450SL, 450SLC

1. Remove the exhaust system.

2. Disconnect the return spring.

3. Remove the bolts which attach the guide to the intermediate lever.

4. Remove the adjusting screw from the adjusting bracket.

5. Loosen the brake control cables on the intermediate lever and pull the cotter pin from the flange bolt. Remove the flange bolt.

6. Remove the spring clamp from the cable guide and remove the cable control from the bracket.

7. Remove the tunnel cover.

8. Disconnect the brake control from the parking brake and remove the spring clamp from the cable guide. Remove the cable control from the parking brake.

9. Remove the brake control cable out of the frame toward the rear.

10. Installation is the reverse of removal.

450SE, 450SEL, 280S and 280SE

1. Remove the floor mat.

2. Remove the legroom cover (upper and lower).

3. Remove the air duct.

4. Disconnect the 4 rubber rings and lower and support the exhaust system.

5. Remove the shield above the exhaust pipes.

6. Disconnect the return spring from the bracket.

7. Back off the adjusting screw on the bracket.

8. Disconnect the intermediate lever from the adjusting bracket.

9. Loosen the brake cable controls on the intermediate lever while pulling the cotter pin from the flange bolt. Remove the flange bolt.

10. Remove the spring clip from the cable guide on the floor pan.

11. Disconnect the brake cable control from the parking brake bracket.

12. Remove the spring clip from the cable guide and remove the cable control from the parking brake.

13. Pull the cable away upward.

14. Installation is the reverse of removal. Adjust the parking brake.

Rear Brake Cable

Removal and Installation

220D/8, 240D, 300D, 220/8, 230, 250/8, 250C, 280, 280C, 280E

1. Remove the parking brake shoes after removing the wheel.

2. Remove the screw from the wheel support and detach the brake cable.

3. Back off the adjusting screw from the adjusting shackle.

4. Remove the spring clips, detach the cable, and remove the equalizer.

5. Installation is the reverse of removal.

All 280 and 300 Series Cars (Except 280, 280C and 280E)

1. On all models except 280SL/8, loosen the nut on the intermediate lever and disconnect the return spring.

2. On 280SL/8 s, loosen the capstan nut on the brake lever.

3. Loosen the flange nut which attaches the cable to the bracket. Remove the cable control from the bracket and compensating lever.

4. Remove the parking brake shoes.

5. Disconnect the brake control from the expanding lock.

6. On models with a brake hold-down, loosen the holder on the support tube and remove the brake cable together with the rubber sleeve.

7. On models without a brake hold-down, remove the safety from the brake cable and remove the brake cable from the carrier plate.

350SL, 450SL, 450SLC

1. Remove the parking brake shoes.

2. Remove the bolt from the wheel carrier and remove the cable.

3. Remove the exhaust system. On some models the exhaust system can be lowered and supported after removing the rubber rings. If equipped, remove the heat shield from above the exhaust pipes.

4. Disconnect the draw spring from the holder.

5. Detach the guide from the intermediate lever.

6. Remove the adjusting screw from the bracket.

7. Disconnect the intermediate lever on the bearing and remove it from the adjusting bracket.

8. Remove the holder, compensating lever, cable control plates, and intermediate lever from the tunnel.

9. Remove the spring clamps and disconnect the cable from the plate.

10. Installation is the reverse of removal.

Adjustment

All Models

1. If the floor pedal can be depressed more than two notches before actuating

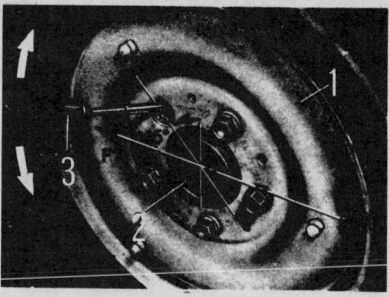

Parking brake adjustment with wheel installed—all models.

1. Disc wheel
2. Rear axle shaft
3. Screwdriver
(f)—Direction of travel

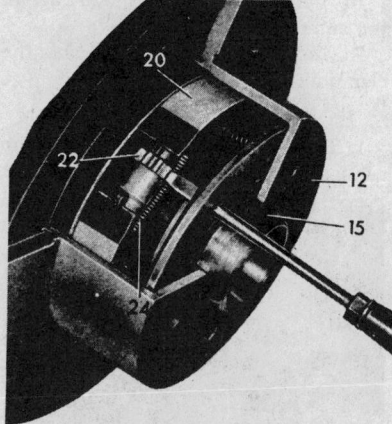

Parking brake adjustment with wheel removed—all models expect 280SL/8.

12. Brake disc
15. Rear axle shaft flange
20. Brake shoes
22. Adjustment device
24. Upper return spring

the brakes, adjust by jacking up the rear of the car, then removing one lug bolt and adjusting the star wheel with a screwdriver.

2. Move the screwdriver upward on the left (driver's)side, downward on the right (passenger's) side to tighten the shoes.

3. When the wheel is locked, back off about 2–4 clicks.

4. With this type system, the adjusting bolt on the cable relay lever only serves to equalize cable length; therefore, do not attempt to adjust the brakes by turning this bolt.

Parking Brake Shoes

Removal and Installation

1. Remove the brake caliper.

2. Remove the brake disc.

3. Disconnect the lower spring with brake pliers.

4. Turn the rear axle shaft flange so that one hole faces the spring. With brake

spring removal pliers, disconnect and remove the spring from the cover plate.

5. Remove the spring on the other brake shoe in a similar manner.

6. Pull both brake shoes apart so that they can be removed past the rear axle shaft flange.

7. Disconnect the upper return spring from the brake shoes and remove the adjuster.

8. Force the pin out of the expanding lock and remove the expanding lock from the brake cable.

9. Remove the brake shoes.

10. Installation is the reverse of removal. Coat all bearing and sliding surfaces with Molykote® prior to installation. Attach the lower spring with the small eye to the brake shoes.

11. Adjust the parking brakes.

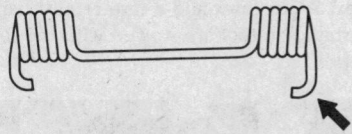

Install the lower parking brake shoe spring with the small eye to the brake shoes.

CHASSIS ELECTRICAL
Heater Blower

Removal and Installation

220D/8, 240D, 300D, 220/8, 230, and 250/8

1. Remove the heater box.

2. Back out the three retaining screws.

3. Slightly pull out the blower and remove the electrical plug and the blower.

4. Installation is the reverse of removal. To prevent leaks, install the three screws with three new special washers exactly like those removed.

350SL, 450SL and 450SLC

1. Remove the panel which covers the heater blower.

2. Loosen the blower retaining nuts.

3. Pull the plug from the series resistance that is located on the firewall.

4. Remove the series resistance.

5. Lift the cable and remove the blower.

6. Installation is the reverse of removal. Be sure that the sealing frame is not damaged.

450SE, 450SEL and 280S

1. Unplug the resistor on the firewall, located just above the automatic transmission and dipstick.

2. Unscrew the resistor.

3. Remove the air intake grille.

4. Remove the glove compartment.

5. Remove the cover under the right-hand instrument panel.

6. Remove the hose between the center air duct and right-hand outlet.

7. Remove the clip and disconnect the wire control from the lever.

8. Unbolt and remove the blower.

9. Installation is the reverse of removal.

Instrument Cluster

Removal and Installation

350SL, 450SL, 450SLC, 450SE, 450SEL and 280S

1. Remove the padding from the steering wheel.

2. Remove the steering wheel.

3. The instrument cluster is held in place by a rubber ring which fits into a groove. Remove the ring and pull the instrument cluster slightly forward.

4. Loosen and disconnect the speedometer shaft, the electrical plug connections, and the oil pressure line.

5. Completely remove the instrument cluster.

CAUTION: *Do not bend the oil pressure line.*

6. Installation is the reverse of removal. Be sure that the speedometer is not bent excessively or it will vibrate when running.

All Other Models

1. Remove the cover plate from the left side underneath the dashboard.

2. On vehicles with automatic transmission, disconnect the Bowden cable for the gear selector lever, after engaging Park.

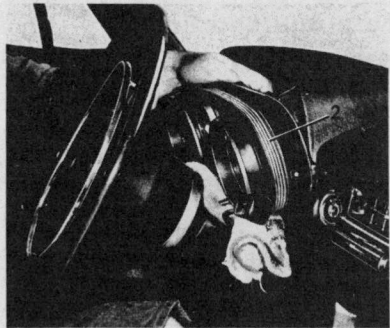

Instrument panel removal showing rubber retaining strip (2).

3. Remove the bracket holding the handbrake.

4. Unscrew the knurled nut and pull the instrument cluster slightly forward.

5. Disconnect the tachometer drive.

6. Cover the steering column to prevent scratches.

7. If only bulb replacement is desired, this is sufficient. To remove the entire cluster, continue with the remaining steps.

8. Disconnect the oil pressure line.

9. Remove the electrical plug connections.

10. Release the excess pressure in the cooling system and install the cap afterward.

11. Remove the temperature sensor from the cylinder head and plug the hole.

12. Carefully remove the instrument cluster with the capillary tube and temperature sensor.

CAUTION: *Do not bend the capillary tube.*

13. Installation is the reverse of removal.

Ignition Switch

Removal and Installation

All Models with Ignition Switch in Dashboard

1. Remove the instrument cluster.

2. Remove the right-hand cover plate under the dashboard.

3. Remove the plug connection from the ignition switch.

4. Remove the screws which hold the ignition switch to the rear of the lock cylinder and remove the ignition switch.

5. To install the ignition switch, attach the plug connection, after fastening the switch to the steering lock.

6. Install the instrument cluster.

7. Check the switch for proper function and install the lower cover.

Lock Cylinder Key Can Be Removed in Position 1

Removal and Installation

All Models Equipped as Above

1. Turn the key to position 1 and remove the key.

2. Pry the cover sleeve from the lock cylinder with a small screwdriver.

3. Using a bent paper clip, hook onto the cover sleeve and remove the sleeve. Be sure that you do not remove the rosette in the dashboard also.

4. Insert the paper clip between the rosette and the steering lock and push in

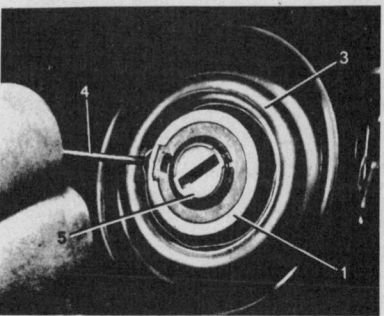

Ignition lock cylinder removal from the instrument panel (both types).

1. Steering lock   4. Steel wire (paper clip)
3. Rosette   5. Locking cylinder

the lock pin. Remove the lock cylinder slightly with the key.

5. Insert the paper clip into the locking hole and pull the lock cylinder completely out.

6. Installation is the reverse of removal. Turn the lock cylinder to position 1 and insert it into the steering lock, making sure that the lock pin engages. Push the cover sleeve into position 1.

7. Make sure that the cylinder operates properly.

Lock Cylinder Key Cannot Be Removed in Position 1

Removal and Installation

Because of legal requirements, the lock was changed from the previous version, so that the key can only be removed in position 0.

1. Turn the key to position 1.

2. Lift the cover sleeve to the edge of the key and turn the key to position 0.

3. Remove the key and cover sleeve.

4. Insert the key into the lock cylinder and turn to position 1 (90° to the right), push in the lock pin and remove the lock cylinder.

5. To install the lock cylinder, turn the lock cylinder to position 1 and insert the lock cylinder, making sure that the locking pin engages.

6. Turn the key to position 0 and remove the key.

7. Place the cover sleeve on the steering lock, insert and turn the key, and push in the cover sleeve at position 1.

8. Check the locking cylinder for proper function.

Steering Lock

Removal and Installation

All Models With Ignition Switch in Dashboard

1. Disconnect the ground cable from the battery.

2. Remove the instrument cluster.

3. Remove the plug connection from the ignition switch behind the dashboard.

4. Pull the ignition key to position 1.

5. Loosen the attaching screw for the steering lock.

6. Remove the cover sleeve from the steering lock.

7. On vehicles with the latest version of the steering lock, pull the connection for the warning buzzer.

8. Push in the lock pin with a small punch.

9. Turn the steering lock and remove it from the holder in the column jacket. Be sure that the rosette is not damaged.

CAUTION: *The lock pin can only be pushed in when the cylinder is in position 1.*

10. To install the steering lock, connect the warning buzzer if so equipped.

11. Place the steering lock in position 1 and insert the lock into the steering column while pushing the lockpin in. Be sure that the lockpin engages.

12. Tighten the attaching clamp screw.

13. Attach the plug connection to the ignition switch.

14. Push the cover sleeve onto the lock in position 1.

15. Install the instrument cluster.

16. Check to be sure that the steering lock works properly.

Fuses

Fuse Box Location

220D/8, 240D, 300D, 220/8, 230, 250/8 and 250C, 450SE, 450SEL, 280S, 280SE

The main fuse box is located in the engine compartment, on the fender, next to the master cylinder. The amperage of the fuses and protected circuits is stamped on the cover of the fuse box. In addition, various other electrical equipment is fused separately. The additional fuse boxes are also located in the engine compartment. Replacement fuses are located in the fuse box.

280S/8, 280SEL/8, 280SEL 4.5, 300SEL 4.5, 280, 280C, and 280E

The fuse box is located in the kick panel on the driver's side. Protected circuits and amperage of fuses is contained on the cover of the fuse box. Separate fuse boxes for additional equipment are located in the engine compartment.

350SL, 450SL and 450SLC

The fuse box is located in the kick panel on the right-hand (passenger) side. The protected circuits and fuse amperage are printed on the cover of the fuse box. Spare fuses and a fuse removal and installation tool are stowed with the tool kit.

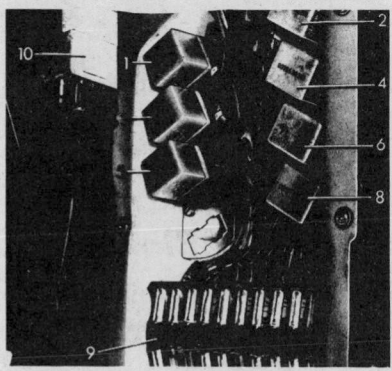

Fuse box and relays—350SL, 450SL and 450SLC

1. Relay for fuel pump
2. Relay for starting valve automatic choke
3. Relay for electronic control unit
4. Relay for starter (terminal 50)
5. Relay for 2-way valve (exhaust emission control)
6. Relay for air conditioning (fan)
8. Relay for disconnecting electric fan when ignition is retarded
when ignition is retarded
9. Fuse box
10. Time switch for heated rear window

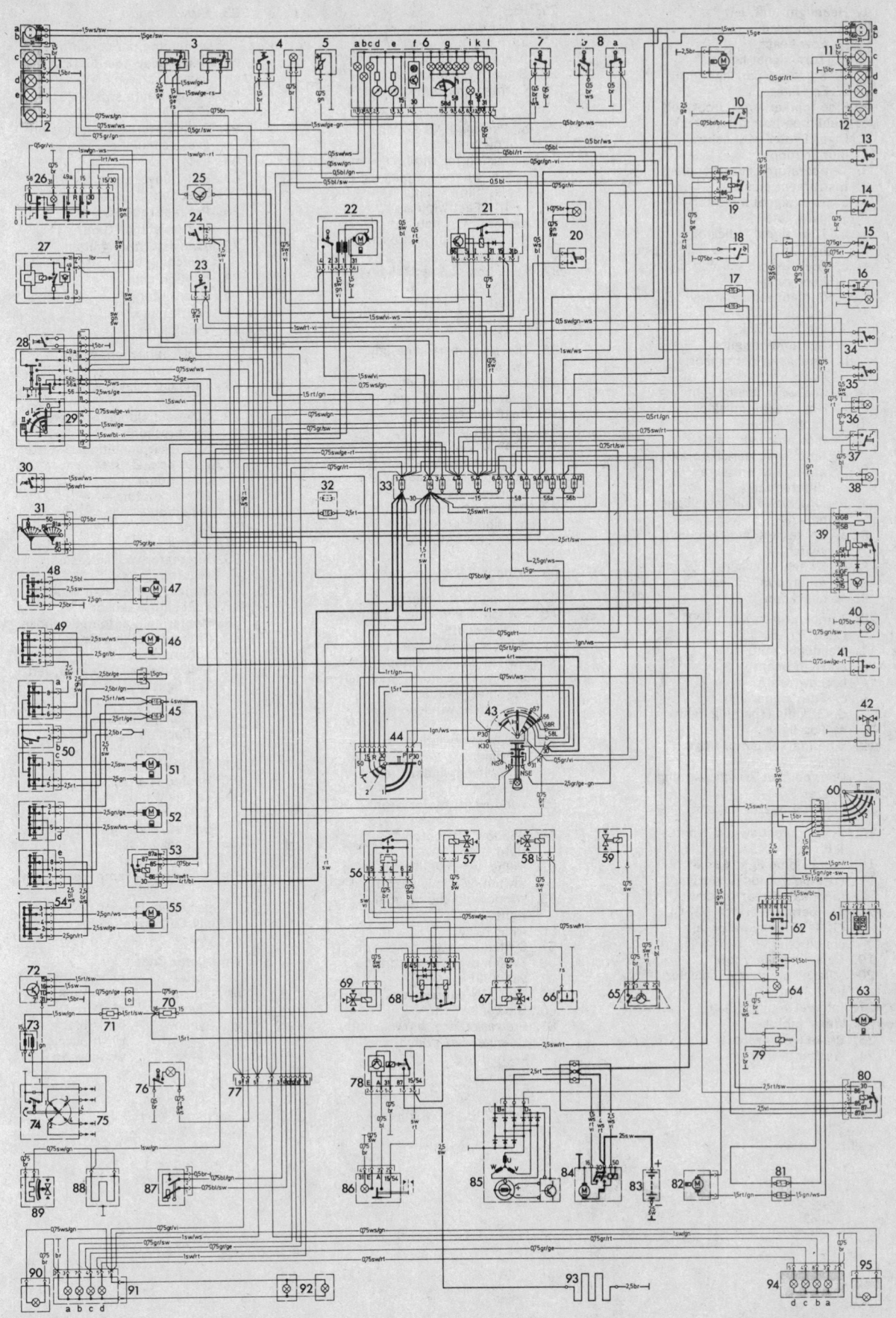

1975 230 (1976 similar)

Wiring Circuits

1. Headlight unit, left
   a. High beam
   b. Low beam
   c. Turn signal light
   d. Standing/parking light
   e. Fog light
2. Side marker lamp, front, left
3. Dual-tone horns (fanfares)
4. Cigar lighter with ashtray illumination
5. Temperature sensor, coolant
6. Instrument cluster
   a. Turn signal indicator light, left
   b. Turn signal indicator light, right
   c. Fuel reserve warning light
   d. Fuel gauge
   e. Coolant temperature gauge
   f. Electric clock
   g. Instrument lights
   h. Rheostat, instrument lights
   i. Charge indicator light
   k. High beam indicator light
   l. Indicator light, brake fluid level, parking brake and brake pressure differential
7. Parking brake indicator light switch
8. a. Brake fluid indicator light switch
8. b. Switch, pressure differential indicator light
9. Auxiliary fan
10. Temperature switch 100° C (212° F)
11. Headlight unit, right
    a. High beam
    b. Low beam
    c. Turn signal light
    d. Standing/parking light
    e. Fog light
12. Side marker lamp, front, right
13. Door contact switch, warning buzzer
14. Warning buzzer contact
15. Door contact switch, front, left
16. Front dome light w/switch
17. Fuse box, 2 fuses, auxiliary fan/heated rear window
18. Temperature switch 52° C (124° F) dehydrator, air conditioner
19. Relay, auxiliary fan*
20. Mileage counter / indicator light / catalyst**
21. Interval wiping timer
22. Wiper motor
23. Brake light switch
24. Washer switch

25. Radio*
26. 4-way warning flasher switch
27. Turn signal and warning flasher relay
28. Signal system contact
29. Combination switch
    a. Turn signal light switch
    b. Passing light switch
    c. Low beam
    d. Switch for wiping speed
       I. Interval wiping
       II. Slow wiping
       III. Fast wiping
30. Kick-down switch
31. Starter-lockout and back-up light switch
32. Fuse box, 2 fuses, sliding roof*
33. Fuse box
34. Door contact switch, front, right
35. Glove compartment light switch
36. Glove compartment light
37. Rear dome light switch*
38. Rear dome light*
39. Warning device
40. Seat-belt warning light
41. Driver's belt buckle switch
42. Solenoid valve, automatic transmission
43. Rotary light switch
44. Ignition starter switch
45. Fuse box, 2 fuses, window lift*
46. Window lift motor, rear, left*
47. Sliding roof motor*
48. Switch, electrically operated sliding roof*
49. Switch, window, rear, left*
50. Switch cluster, window lifts
    a. Switch, window, rear, left
    b. Safety switch
    c. Switch, window, front, left
    d. Switch, window, front, right
    e. Switch, window, rear, right
51. Window lift motor, front, left*
52. Window lift motor, front, right*
53. Relay, window lifts*
54. Switch, window, rear, right*
55. Window lift motor, rear, right*
56. RPM relay
57. Switch-over valve, ignition
58. Switch-over valve, throttle valve lift
59. Idle fuel cut-out valve
60. Blower switch
61. Pre-resistance, blower motor
62. Change-over switch, cooling — heating*

63. Blower motor
64. Temperature control w/lighting, air conditioner*
65. Delay relay, idle fuel cut-out valve
66. Temperature switch 25° C (77° F)
67. Switch-over valve, emission gas recirculation
68. Relay box
69. Switch-over valve, air injection
70. Pre-resistance 0.4 Ω
71. Pre-resistance 0.6 Ω
72. Transistorized ignition switching unit
73. Ignition coil
74. Distributor
75. Spark plugs
76. Trunk light
77. Plug connection, cable to rear components
78. Time-lag relay, heated rear window
79. Solenoid clutch, refrigerant compressor*
80. Relay, air conditioner/starter
81. Fuse box, 2 fuses, air conditioner*
82. Blower motor, air conditioner*
83. Battery
84. Starter
85. Alternator w/electronic regulator
86. Switch, heated rear window
87. Fuel gauge sensor
88. Heater coil, automatic choke
89. Thermo-switch-over valve, automatic choke
90. Side marker lamp, rear, left
91. Tail light unit, left
    a. Turn signal light
    b. Tail/parking light
    c. Back-up light
    d. Brake light
92. License plate light
93. Heated rear window
94. Tail light unit, right
    a. Turn signal light
    b. Tail/parking light
    c. Back-up light
    d. Brake light
95. Side marker lamp, rear, right

* Special equipment
** Only California

Wire Color Code

bl = blue	nf = neutral
br = brown	rs = pink
el = ivory	rt = red
ge = yellow	sw = black
gn = green	vi = purple
gr = grey	ws = white

1975 230 (1976 similar)

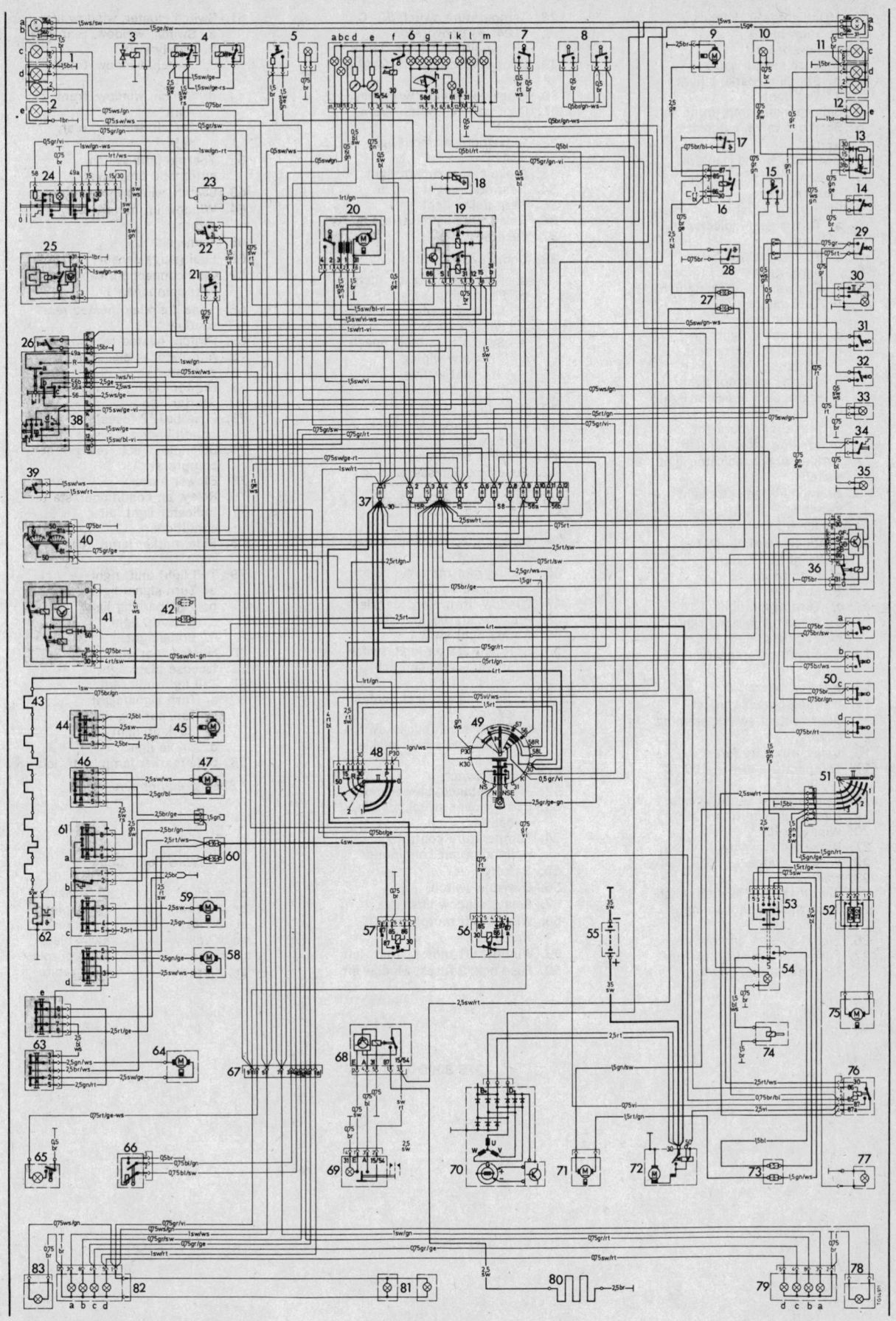

1975 300D

1. Headlight unit, left
   a. High beam
   b. Low beam
   c. Turn signal light
   d. Standing/parking light
   e. Fog light
2. Side marker lamp, front, left
3. Solenoid valve, automatic transmission
4. Dual-tone horns (fanfares)
5. Cigar lighter with ashtray illumination
6. Instrument cluster
   a. Turn signal indicator light, left
   b. Turn signal indicator light, right
   c. Fuel reserve warning light
   d. Fuel gauge
   f. Electric clock
   g. Instrument lights
   h. Rheostat, instrument lights
   i. Charge indicator light
   k. High beam indicator light
   l. Brake fluid and parking brake indicator light
   m. Preglow indicator light
7. Parking brake indicator light switch
8. Brake fluid indicator light switch
9. Auxiliary fan
10. Seat-belt warning light
11. Headlight unit, right
    a. High beam
    b. Low beam
    c. Turn signal light
    d. Standing/parking light
    e. Fog light
12. Side marker lamp, front, right
13. Warning buzzer
14. Warning buzzer contact
15. Door contact switch, warning buzzer
16. Relay, auxiliary fan
17. Temperature switch 100° C (212° F)
18. Temperature sensor, coolant
19. Interval wiping timer
20. Wiper motor
21. Brake light switch
22. Washer switch
23. Radio
24. 4-way warning flasher switch
25. Turn signal and warning flasher relay
26. Signal system contact
27. Fuse box, 2 fuses, auxiliary fan/heated rear window

28. Temperature switch 52° C (124° F) dehydrator, air conditioner
29. Door contact switch, front, left
30. Front dome light w/switch
31. Door contact switch, front, right
32. Glove compartment light switch
33. Glove compartment light
34. Rear dome light switch
35. Rear dome light
36. Relay, seat-belt starter-logic
37. Fuse box
38. Combination switch
    a. Turn signal light switch
    b. Passing light switch
    c. Dimmer switch
    d. Wiper switch
    e. Switch for wiping speed
       I. Slow wiping
       II. Fast wiping
       III. Interval wiping
39. Kick-down switch
40. Starter-lockout and back-up light switch
41. Preglow time relay
42. Fuse box, 2 fuses, sliding roof*
43. Glow plugs and series resistor
44. Switch, electrically operated sliding roof*
45. Sliding roof motor*
46. Switch, window, rear, left
47. Window lift motor, rear, left
48. Preglow/starter switch
49. Rotary light switch
50. Seat-belt starter-logic switch
    a. Driver's seat contact switch
    b. Passenger's seat contact switch
    c. Driver's belt buckle switch
    d. Passenger's belt buckle switch
51. Blower switch
52. Pre-resistance, blower motor
53. Change-over switch, cooling —heating
54. Temperature control w/lighting, air conditioner
55. Battery
56. Override switch
57. Relay, window lifts
58. Window lift motor, front, right
59. Window lift motor, front, left
60. Fuse box, 2 fuses, window lift

61. Switch cluster, window lifts
    a. Switch, window, rear, left
    b. Safety switch
    c. Switch, window, front, left
    d. Switch, window, front, right
    e. Switch, window, rear, right
62. Thermo time switch, automatic preglower
63. Switch, window, rear, right
64. Window lift motor, rear, right
65. Trunk light
66. Fuel gauge sensor
67. Plug connection, cable to rear components
68. Time-lag relay, heated rear window
69. Switch, heated rear window
70. Alternator w/electronic regulator
71. Blower motor, air conditioner
72. Starter
73. Fuse box, 2 fuses, air conditioner
74. Solenoid clutch, refrigerant compressor
75. Blower motor
76. Relay, air conditioner/starter
77. Indicator light, air conditioner
78. Side marker lamp, rear, right
79. Tail light unit, right
    a. Turn signal light
    b. Tail/parking light
    c. Back-up light
    d. Brake light
80. Heated rear window
81. License plate light
82. Tail light unit, left
    a. Turn signal light
    b. Tail/parking light
    c. Back-up light
    d. Brake light
83. Side marker lamp, rear, left

* Special equipment

Wire Color Code

bl	= blue	nf	= neutral
br	= brown	rs	= pink
el	= ivory	rt	= red
ge	= yellow	sw	= black
gn	= green	vi	= purple
gr	= grey	ws	= white

1975 300D

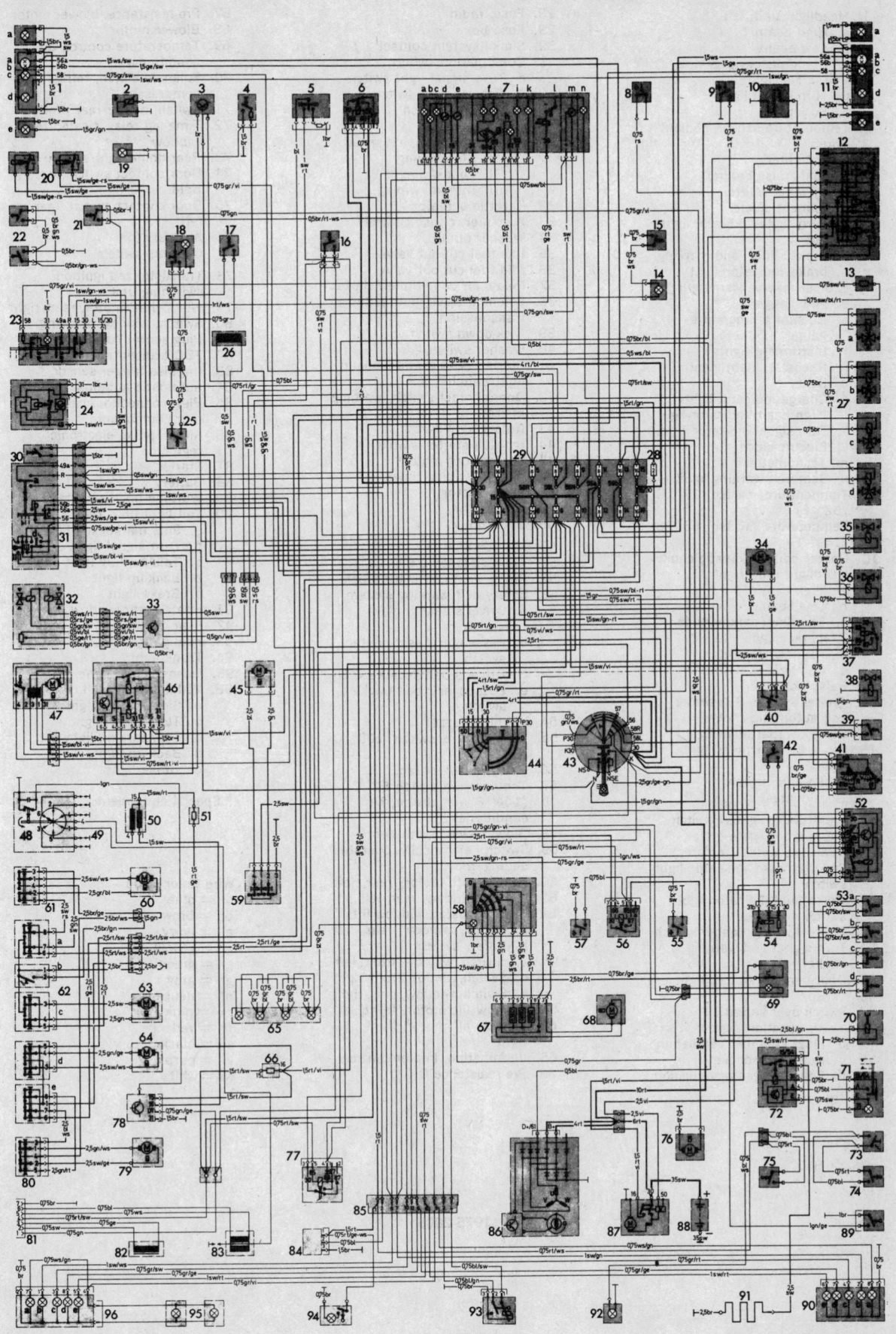

1975 280S

Wiring Circuits

1. Headlight unit, left
   a. High beam
   b. Low beam
   c. Standing/parking/side marker light
   d. Turn signal light
   e. Fog light
2. Temperature sensor, coolant
3. Radio
4. Cigar lighter
5. Switch, cruise control
6. Relay window lifts
7. Instrument cluster
   a. Turn signal indicator light, left
   b. Brake fluid and parking brake indicator light
   c. Fuel reserve warning light
   d. Fuel gauge
   e. Coolant temperature gauge
   f. Instrument lights
   g. Rheostat, instrument lights
   h. Charge indicator light
   i. High beam indicator light
   k. Turn signal indicator light,
   l. Electric clock
   m. Tachometer
   n. Seat-belt warning light
8. Temperature switch 17° C (62° F)
9. Temperature switch 65° C (149° F)
10. Heater coil, automatic choke
11. Headlight unit, right
    a. High beam
    b. Low beam
    c. Standing/parking/side marker light
    d. Turn signal light
    e. Fog light
12. Relay box
13. Pre-resistance, 8 Ω heater coil automatic choke
14. Glove compartment light
15. Glove compartment light switch
16. Brake light switch
17. Door contact switch, left
18. Front dome light w/switch
19. Illumination, gate plate
20. Dual-tone horns (fanfares)
21. Parking brake indicator light switch
22. Brake fluid indicator light switch
23. 4-way warning flasher switch
24. Turn signal and warning flasher relay
25. Door contact switch, right
26. Sensor
27. Switch-over valves
    a. Air injection
    b. Float chamber ventilation
    c. Automatic choke
    d. Emission gas recirculation

28. Fuse, radio
29. Fuse box
30. Signal system contact
31. Combination switch
    a. Turn signal light switch
    b. Passing light switch
    c. Dimmer switch
    d. Wiper switch
    e. Switch for wiping speed
       I. Slow wiping
       II. Fast wiping
       III. Interval wiping
32. Throttle actuator
33. Amplifier, cruise control
34. Washer pump
35. Idle fuel cut-out valve
36. Idle fuel cut-out valve
37. Relay, air conditioner/starter
38. Solenoid valve, automatic transmission
39. Kick-down switch
40. Washer switch
41. Starter-lockout and back-up light switch
42. Door contact switch, warning buzzer
43. Rotary light switch
44. Ignition starter switch
45. Sliding roof motor*
46. Interval wiping timer
47. Wiper motor
48. Distributor
49. Spark plugs
50. Ignition coil
51. Pre-resistance 0.6 Ω
52. Relay, seat-belt starter-logic
53. Safety belt warning system
    a. Driver's seat contact switch
    b. Passenger's seat contact switch
    c. Driver's belt buckle switch
    d. Passenger's belt buckle switch
54. Warning buzzer
55. Temperature switch 100° C (212° F)
56. Relay, auxiliary fan
57. Temperature switch 62° C (144° F dehydrator, air conditioner
58. Blower switch with light
59. Switch, electrically operated sliding roof*
60. Window lift motor, rear, left
61. Switch, window, rear, left
62. Switch cluster, window lifts
    a. Switch, window, rear, left
    b. Safety switch
    c. Switch, window, front, left
    d. Switch, window, front, right
    e. Switch, window, rear, right
63. Window lift motor, front, left
64. Window lift motor, front, right
65. Illumination, heater controls
66. Pre-resistance 0.4 Ω

67. Pre-resistance, blower motor
68. Blower motor
69. Temperature control, air conditioner
70. Solenoid clutch, refrigerant compressor
71. Switch, heater rear window
72. Time-lag relay, heated rear window
73. Rear dome light switch
74. Door contact switch, rear, right
75. Door contact switch, rear, left
76. Auxiliary fan
77. Override switch
78. Transistorized ignition switching unit
79. Window lift motor, rear, right
80. Switch, window, rear, right
81. Plug socket (diagnosis
82. TDC transmitter
83. Impulse trigger sensor
84. Automatic antenna
85. Plug connection, cable to rear components
86. Alternator w/electronic regulator
87. Starter
88. Battery
89. Warning buzzer contact
90. Tail light unit, right
    a. Side marker light
    b. Turn signal light
    c. Tail/parking light
    d. Back-up light
    e. Brake light
91. Heated rear window
92. Rear dome light
93. Fuel gauge sensor
94. Trunk light
95. License plate light
96. Tail light unit, left
    a. Side marker light
    b. Turn signal light
    c. Tail/parking light
    d. Back-up light
    e. Brake light

* Special equipment

Wire Color Code
bl = blue
br = brown
el = ivory
ge = yellow
gn = green
gr = grey
nf = neutral
rs = pink
rt = red
sw = black
vi = purple
ws = white

1975 280S

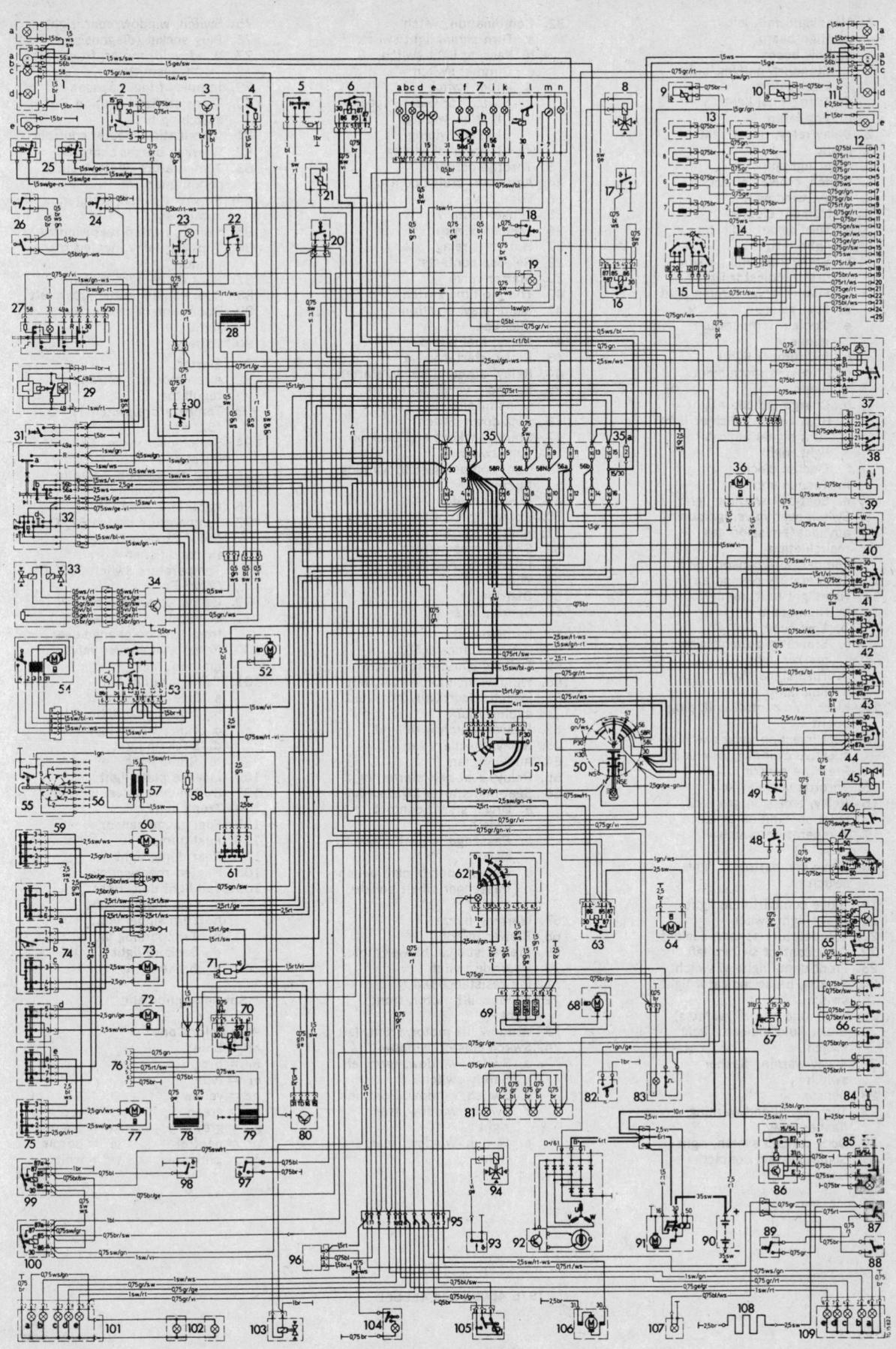

1975 450SE and 450SEL

Wiring Circuits

1. Headlight unit, left
   a. High beam
   b. Low beam
   c. Standing/parking/side marker light
   d. Turn signal light
   e. Fog lamp
2. Delay relay, dome light
3. Radio
4. Cigar lighter
5. Switch, cruise control
6. Relay, window lifts
7. Instrument cluster
   a. Turn signal indicator light, left
   b. Brake fluid and parking brake indicator light
   c. Fuel reserve warning light
   d. Fuel gauge
   e. Coolant temperature gauge
   f. Instrument lights
   g. Rheostat, instrument lights
   h. Charge indicator light
   i. High beam indicator light
   k. Turn signal indicator light, right
   l. Electric clock
   m. Tachometer
   n. Seat-belt warning light
8. Switch-over valve, ignition advance/emission gas recirculation
9. Temperature sensor, water
10. Temperature sensor, air
11. Headlight unit, right
    a. High beam
    b. Low beam
    c. Standing/parking/side marker light
    d. Turn signal light
    e. Fog lamp
12. Electronic control unit, plug board
13. Fuel injection valves with respective cylinder designation
14. Pressure sensor
15. Throttle valve switch
16. Relay, emission gas recirculation/ignition advance
17. Temperature switch 40° (104° F)
18. Glove compartment light switch
19. Glove compartment light
20. Brake light switch
21. Temperature sensor, coolant
22. Door contact switch, left
23. Front dome light w/switch
24. Parking brake indicator light switch
25. Dual-tone horns (fanfares)
26. Brake fluid indicator light switch
27. 4-way warning flasher switch
28. Sensor
29. Turn signal and warning flasher relay
30. Door contact switch, right
31. Signal system contact

32. Combination switch
    a. Turn signal light switch
    b. Passing light switch
    c. Dimmer switch
    d. Wiper switch
    e. Switch for wiping speed
       I. Slow wiping
       II. Fast wiping
       III. Interval wiping
33. Throttle actuator
34. Amplifier, cruise control
35. Fuse box
35a. Fuse, radio
36. Washer pump
37. Hot start relay
38. Release contacts
39. Starter valve
40. Thermo-time switch
41. Main relay, electronic injection
42. Relay, fuel pump
43. Relay, starter valve
44. Relay, air conditioner/starter
45. Solenoid valve, automatic transmission
46. Kick-down switch
47. Starter-lockout and back-up light switch
48. Door contact switch, warning buzzer
49. Washer switch
50. Rotary light switch
51. Ignition starter switch
52. Sliding roof motor*
53. Interval wiping timer
54. Wiper motor
55. Distributor
56. Spark plugs
57. Ignition coil
58. Pre-resistance 0.6 Ω
59. Switch, window, rear, left
60. Window lift motor, rear, left
61. Switch, electrically operated sliding roof*
62. Blower switch with light
63. Relay, auxiliary fan
64. Auxiliary fan
65. Relay, seat-belt starter-logic
66. Seat-belt starter-logic switch
    a. Driver's seat contact switch
    b. Passenger's seat contact switch
    c. Driver's belt buckle switch
    d. Passenger's belt buckle switch
67. Warning buzzer
68. Blower motor
69. Pre-resistance, blower motor
70. Override switch
71. Pre-resistance 0.4 Ω
72. Window lift motor, front, right
73. Window lift motor, front, left
74. Switch cluster, window lifts
    a. Switch, window, rear, left
    b. Safety switch
    c. Switch, window, front, left
    d. Switch, window, front, right
    e. Switch, window, rear, right

75. Switch, window, rear, right
76. Plug socket (diagnosis)
77. Window lift motor, front, left
78. TDC transmitter
79. Impulse trigger sensor
80. Transistorized ignition switching unit
81. Illumination, heater controls
82. Warning buzzer contact
83. Temperature control, air conditioner
84. Solenoid clutch, refrigerant compressor
85. Switch, heated rear window
86. Time-lag relay, heated rear window
87. Rear dome light switch
88. Door contact switch, rear, left
89. Door contact switch, rear, right
90. Battery
91. Starter
92. Alternator w/electronic regulator
93. Temperature switch 17° C (62° F)
94. Switch-over valve, air injection
95. Plug connection, cable to rear components
96. Automatic antenna
97. Temperature switch 62° C (144° F) dehydrator, air conditioner
98. Temperature switch 100° C (212° F)
99. Relay, separation air conditioner (auxiliary fan) from ignition change-over
100. Relay, switch-over valve, ignition
101. Tail light unit, left
     a. Side marker light
     b. Turn signal light
     c. Tail/parking light
     d. Back-up light
     e. Brake light
102. License plate light
103. Switch-over valve, ignition
104. Trunk light
105. Fuel gauge sensor
106. Fuel pump
107. Rear dome light
108. Heated rear window
109. Tail light unit, right
     a. Side marker light
     b. Turn signal light
     c. Tail/parking light
     d. Back-up light
     e. Brake light

* Special equipment

Wire Color Code

bl = blue
br = brown
el = ivory
ge = yellow
gn = green   rt = red
gr = grey   sw = black
nf = neutral   vi = purple
rs = pink   ws = white

1975 450SE and 450SEL

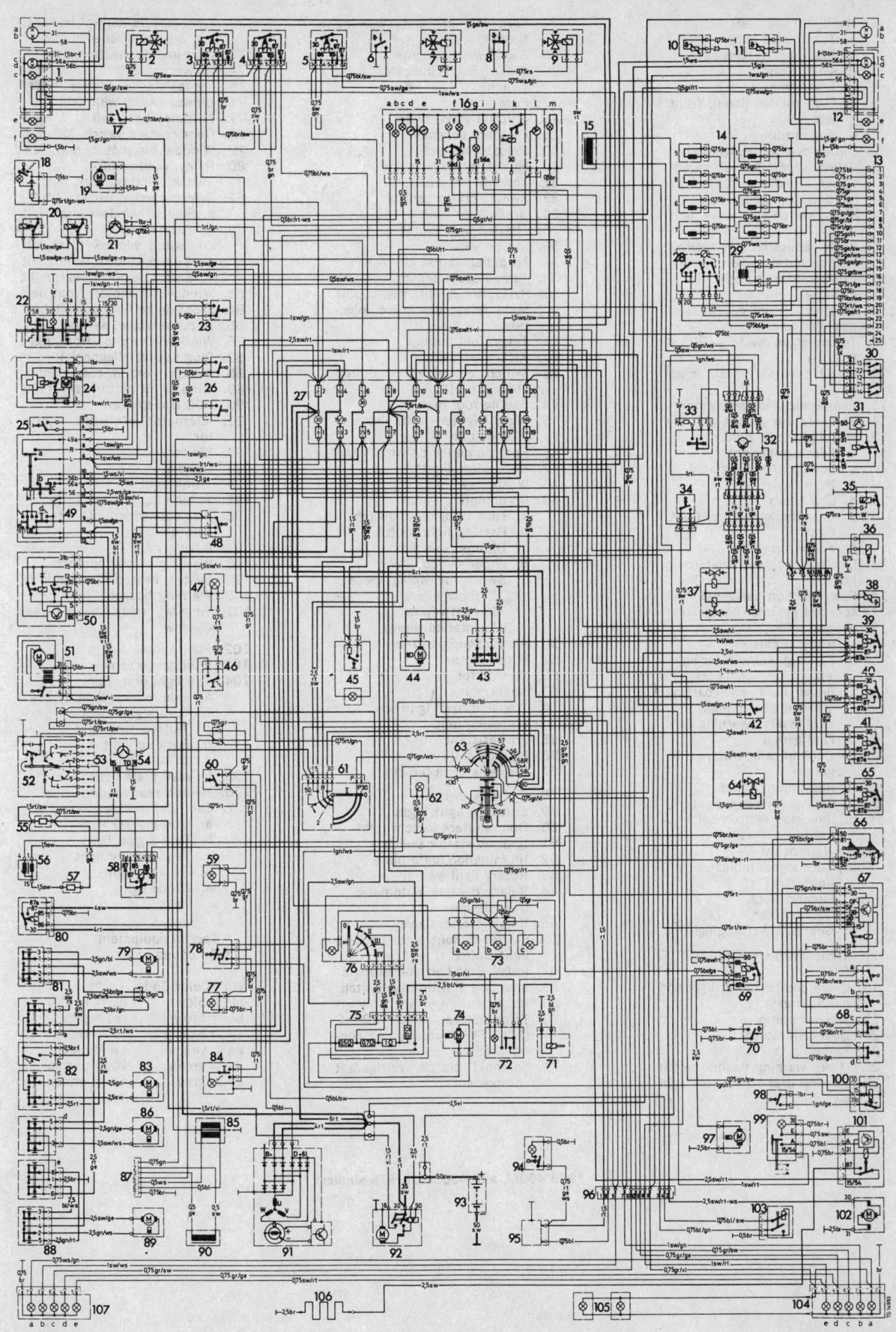

1975 450SL and 450SLC (1976 similar)

Wiring Circuits

1. Headlight unit, left
   a. Turn signal light
   b. Standing/parking light
   c. High beam
   d. Low beam
   e. Side marker lamp, front, left
   f. Fog lamp
2. Switch-over valve, ignition
3. Relay, separation air conditioner (auxiliary fan) from ignition change-over
4. Relay, switch-over valve, ignition
5. Relay, emission gas recirculation/ignition advance
6. Temperature switch 40° C (104° F)
7. Switch-over valve, emission gas recirculation
8. Temperature switch 170° C (62° F)
9. Switch-over valve, air injection
10. Temperature sensor, water
11. Temperature sensor, air
12. Headlight unit, right
    a. Turn signal light
    b. Standing/parking light
    c. High beam
    d. Low beam
    e. Side marker, lamp, front, right
    f. Fog lamp
13. Electronic control unit, plug board
14. Fuel injection valves with respective cylinder designation
15. Sensor
16. Instrument cluster
    a. Turn signal indicator light, left
    b. Brake fluid and parking brake indicator light
    c. Fuel reserve warning light
    d. Fuel gauge
    e. Coolant temperature gauge
    f. Instrument lights
    g. Charge indicator light
    h. Rheostat, instrument lights
    i. High beam
    j. Turn signal indicator light, right
    k. Electric clock
    l. Tachometer
    m. Seat-belt warning light
17. Temperature switch 100° C (212° F)
18. Glove compartment light and hand lamp
19. Washer pump
20. Dual-tone horns
21. Radio
22. 4-way warning flasher switch
23. Parking brake indicator light switch

24. Turn signal and warning flasher relay
25. Signal system contact
26. Brake fluid indicator light switch
27. Fuse box
28. Throttle valve switch
29. Pressure sensor
30. Release contacts
31. Hot start relay
32. Throttle actuator
33. Switch, cruise control
34. Brake light switch
35. Thermo-time switch
36. Starter valve
37. Amplifier, cruise control
38. Temperature sensor, coolant
39. Relay, air conditioner/starter
40. Main relay, electronic injection
41. Telay, fuel pump
42. Kick-down switch
43. Switch electrically operated sliding roof*
44. Sliding roof motor*
45. Cigar lighter with ashtray illumination
46. Rear dome light switch**
47. Rear dome light**
48. Washer switch
49. Combination switch
    a. Turn signal light switch
    b. Passing light switch
    c. Dimmer switch
    d. Wiper switch
    e. Switch for wiping speed
       I. Slow wiping
       II. Fast wiping
       III. Interval wiping
50. Interval wiping timer
51. Wiper motor
52. Distributor
53. Spark plugs
54. Transistorized ignition switching unit
55. Pre-resistance
56. Ignition coil
57. Pre-resistance 0.6 Ω
58. Override switch
59. Entrance light, right
60. Door contact switch, right
61. Ignition starter switch
62. Illumination, gate plate
63. Rotary light switch
64. Solenoid valve, automatic tranmission
65. Relay, starter valve
66. Starter-lockout and back-up light switch
67. Relay, seat-belt starter-logic
68. Seat-belt starter-logic switch
69. Relay, auxiliary fan
70. Temperature switch 52° C (124° F) dehydrator, air conditioner
71. Solenoid clutch, refrigerant compressor

72. Temperature control w/lighting, air conditioner
73. Illumination, heater control
74. Blower motor
75. Pre-resistance, blower motor
76. Blower switch with light
77. Entrance light, left
78. Door contact switch, left
79. Window lift motor, rear, left
80. Relay, window lifts
81. Switch, window, rear, left
82. Switch cluster, window lifts
    a. Switch, window, rear, left
    b. Safety switch
    c. Switch, window, front, left
    d. Switch, window, front, right
    e. Switch, window, rear, right
83. Window lift motor, front, left
84. Front dome light w/switch**
85. Impulse trigger sensor
86. Window lift motor, front, right
87. Plug socket (diagnosis)
88. Switch, window, rear, right
89. Window lift motor, rear, right
90. TDC transmitter
91. Alternator w/electric regulator
92. Starter
93. Battery
94. Trunk light
95. Automatic antenna
96. Plug connection, cable to rear components
97. Auxiliary fan
98. Warning buzzer contact
99. Switch, heated rear window
100. Warning buzzer
101. Time-lag relay, heated rear window
102. Fuel pump
103. Fuel gauge sensor
104. Tail light unit, right
    a. Side marker light
    b. Turn signal light
    c. Tail/parking light
    d. Back-up light
    e. Brake light
105. License plate light
106. Heated rear window
107. Tail light unit, left
    a. Side marker light
    b. Turn signal light
    c. Tail/parking light
    d. Back-up light
    e. Brake light

* Special equipment
** On coupe only

Wire Color Code

bl = blue	nf = neutral
br = brown	rs = pink
el = ivory	rt = red
ge = yellow	sw = black
gn = green	vi = purple
gr = grey	ws = white

1975 450SL and 450SLC (1976 similar)

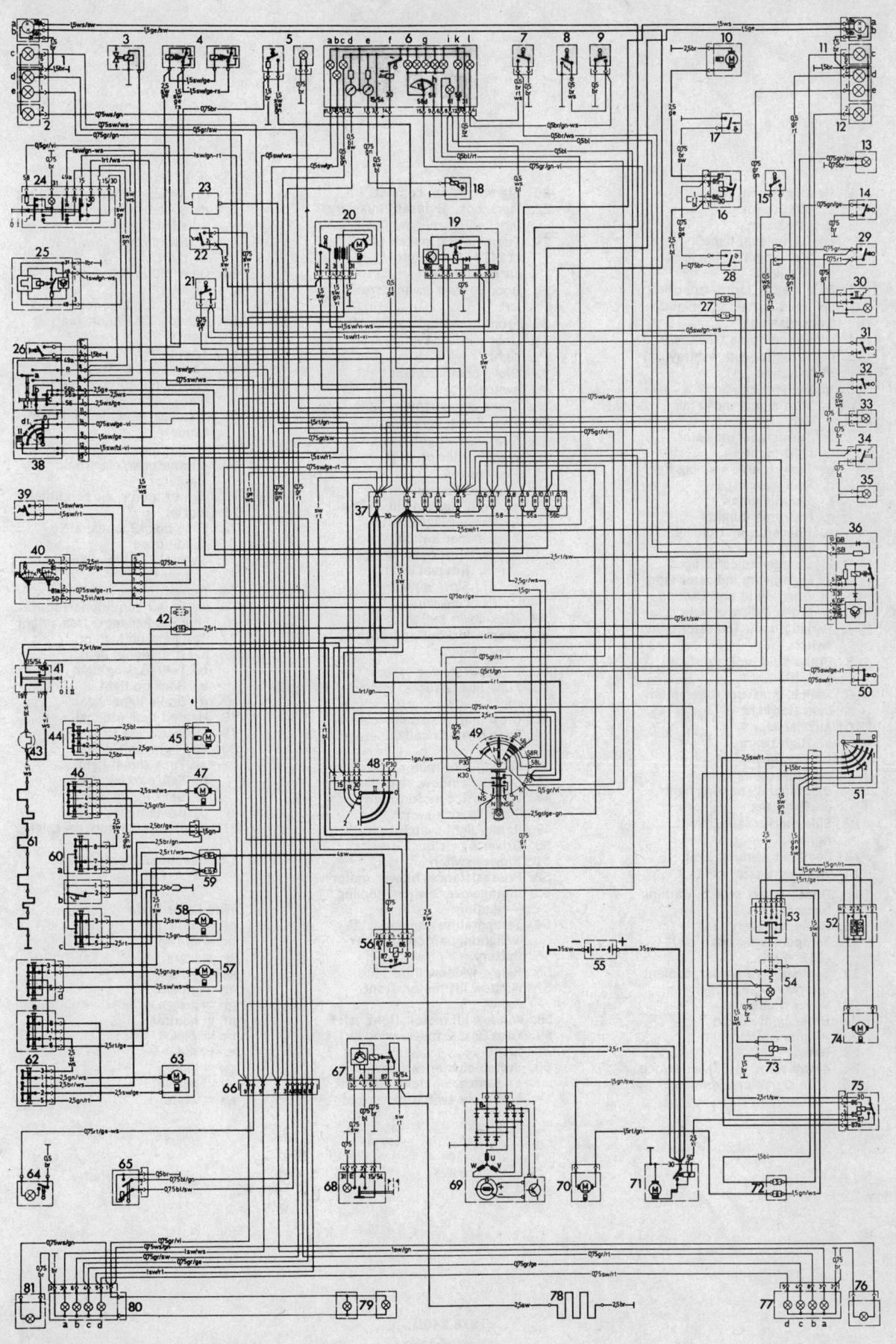

1976 240D

1. Headlight unit, left
   a. High beam
   b. Low beam
   c. Turn signal light
   d. Standing/parking light
   e. Fog light
2. Side marker lamp, front, left
3. Solenoid valve, automatic transmission*
4. Dual-tone horns (fanfares)
5. Cigar lighter with ashtray illumination
6. Instrument cluster
   a. Turn signal indicator light, left
   b. Turn signal indicator light, right
   c. Fuel reserve warning light
   d. Fuel gauge
   f. Electric clock
   g. Instrument lights
   h. Rheostat, instrument lights
   i. Charge indicator light
   k. High beam indicator light
   l. Brake fluid and parking brake indicator light
7. Parking brake indicator light switch
8. Brake fluid indicator light switch
9. Switch, pressure differential indicator light
10. Auxiliary fan*
   a. High beam
   b. Low beam
   c. Turn signal light
   d. Standing/parking light
   e. Fog light
12. Side marker lamp, front, right
13. Seat-belt warning light
14. Warning buzzer contact
15. Door contact switch, warning buzzer
16. Relay, auxiliary fan*
17. Temperature switch 100° C (212° F)*
18. Temperature sensor, coolant
19. Interval wiping timer
20. Wiper motor
21. Brake light switch
22. Washer switch
23. Radio*
24. 4-way warning flasher switch
25. Turn signal and warning flasher relay

26. Signal system contact
27. Fuse box, 2 fuses, auxiliary fan/heated rear window
28. Temperature switch 52° C (124° F) dehydrator, air conditioner*
29. Door contact switch, front, left
30. Front dome light w/switch
31. Door contact switch, front, right
32. Glove compartment light switch
33. Glove compartment light
34. Rear dome light switch
35. Rear dome light
36. Warning device
37. Fuse box
38. Combination switch
   a. Turn signal light switch
   b. Passing light switch
   c. Dimmer switch
   d. Switch for wiping speed
      I. Interval wiping
      II. Slow wiping
      III. Fast wiping
39. Kick-down switch
40. Starter-lockout and back-up light switch
41. Preglow/starter switch
42. Fuse box, 2 fuses, sliding roof*
43. Glow plug resistance control
44. Switch, electrically operated sliding roof*
45. Sliding roof motor
46. Switch, window, rear, left*
47. Window lift motor, rear, left
48. Steering lock switch
49. Rotary light switch
50. Driver's belt buckle switch
51. Blower switch
52. Pre-resistance, blower motor
53. Change-over switch, cooling —heating*
54. Temperature control w/lighting, air conditioner
55. Battery
56. Relay, window lifts*
57. Window lift motor, front, right*
58. Window lift motor, front, left*
59. Fuse box, 2 fuses, window lift*
60. Switch cluster, window lifts
   a. Switch, window, rear, left
   b. Safety switch

   c. Switch, window, front, left
   d. Switch, window, front, right
   e. Switch, window, rear, right
61. Glow plugs and series resistor
62. Switch, window, rear, right*
63. Window lift motor, rear, right*
64. Trunk light
65. Fuel gauge sensor
66. Plug connection, cable to rear components
67. Time-lag relay, heated rear window
68. Switch, heated rear window
69. Alternator w/electronic regulator
70. Blower motor, air conditioner
71. Starter
72. Fuse box, 2 fuses, air conditioner*
73. Solenoid clutch, refrigerant compressor*
74. Blower motor
75. Relay, air conditioner/starter
76. Side marker lamp, rear, right
77. Tail light unit, right
   a. Turn signal light
   b. Tail/parking light
   c. Back-up light
   d. Brake light
78. Heated rear window
79. License plate light
80. Tail light unit, left
   a. Turn signal light
   b. Tail/parking light
   c. Back-up light
   d. Brake light
81. Side marker lamp, rear, left

* Special equipment

Wire Color Code
bl = blue
br = brown
el = ivory
ge = yellow
gn = green
gr = grey
nf = neutral
rs = pink
rt = red
sw = black
vi = purple
ws = white

1976 240D

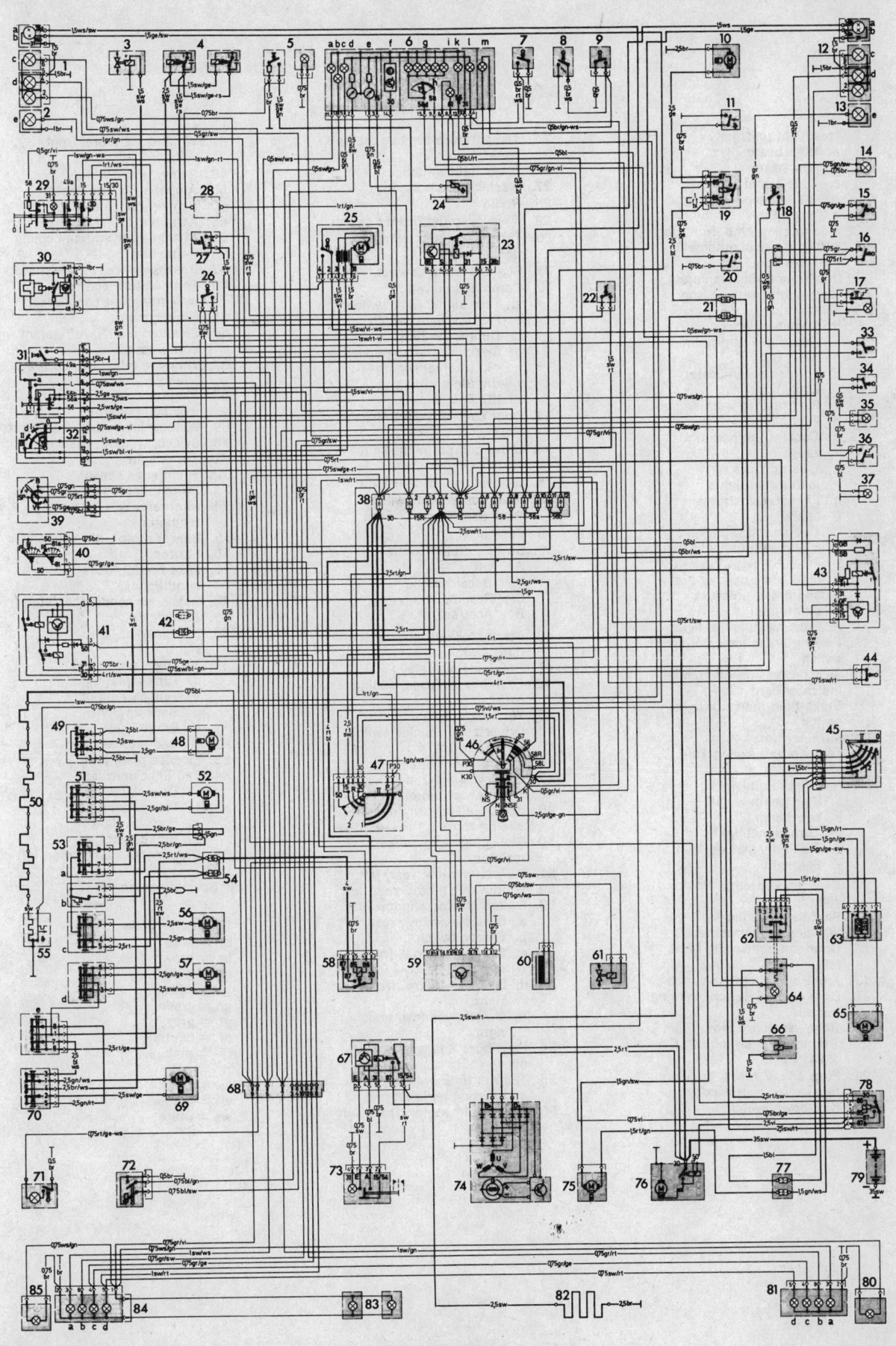

1976 300D

1. Headlight unit, left
   a. High beam
   b. Low beam
   c. Turn signal light
   d. Standing/parking light
   e. Fog light
2. Side marker lamp, front, left
3. Solenoid valve, automatic transmission
4. Dual-tone horns (fanfares)
5. Cigar lighter with ashtray illumination
6. Instrument cluster
   a. Turn signal indicator light, left
   b. Turn signal indicator light, right
   c. Fuel reserve warning light
   d. Fuel gauge
   e. Coolant temperature gauge
   f. Electric clock
   g. Instrument lights
   h. Rheostat, instrument lights
   i. Charge indicator light
   k. High beam indicator light
   l. Indicator light, brake fluid level, parking brake and brake pressure differential
   m. Preglow indicator light
7. Parking brake indicator light switch
8. Switch pressure differential indicator light
9. Brake fluid indicator light switch
10. Auxiliary fan
11. Temperature switch 100° C (212° F)
12. Headlight unit, right
    a. High beam
    b. Low beam
    c. Turn signal light
    d. Standing/parking light
    e. Fog light
13. Side marker lamp, front, right
14. Seat-belt warning light
15. Warning buzzer contact
16. Door contact switch, front, left
17. Front dome light w/switch
18. Door contact switch, warning buzzer
19. Relay, auxiliary fan
20. Temperature switch 52° C (124° F)
21. Fuse box, 2 fuses, auxiliary fan/heated rear window
22. Kick-down switch
23. Interval wiping timer

24. Temperature sensor, coolant
25. Wiper motor
26. Brake light switch
27. Washer switch
28. Radio
29. 4-way warning flasher switch
30. Turn signal and warning flasher relay
31. Signal system contact
32. Combination switch
    a. Turn signal light switch
    b. Passing light switch
    c. Dimmer switch
    d. Switch for wiping speed
       I. Interval wiping
       II. Slow wiping
       III. Fast wiping
33. Door contact switch, front, right
34. Glove compartment light switch
35. Glove compartment light
36. Rear dome light switch
37. Rear dome light
38. Fuse box
39. Switch, cruise control
    A. Off
    V. Decel/set
    SP. Resume
    B. Acel/set
40. Starter-lockout and back-up light switch
41. Preglow time relay
42. Fuse box, 2 fuses, sliding roof*
43. Warning device
44. Driver's belt buckle switch
45. Blower switch
46. Rotary light switch
47. Preglow/starter switch
48. Sliding roof motor*
49. Switch, electrically operated sliding roof*
50. Glow plugs and series resistor
51. Switch, window, rear, left
52. Window lift motor, rear, left
53. Switch cluster, window lifts
    a. Switch, window, rear, left
    b. Safety switch
    c. Switch, window, front, left
    d. Switch, window, front, right
    e. Switch, window, rear, right
54. Fuse box, 2 fuses, window lift
55. Thermo time switch, automatic preglower
56. Window lift motor, front, left

57. Window lift more, front, right
58. Relay, window lifts
59. Amplifier, cruise control
60. Sensor, cruise control
61. Actuator, cruise control
62. Change-over switch, cooling —heating
63. Pre-resistance, blower motor
64. Temperature control w/lighting, air conditioner
65. Blower motor
66. Solenoid clutch, refrigerant compressor
67. Time-lag relay, heated rear window
68. Plug connection, cable to rear components
69. Window lift motor, rear, right
70. Switch, window, rear, right
71. Trunk light
72. Fuel gauge sensor
73. Switch, heated rear window
74. Alternator w/electronic regulator
75. Blower motor, air conditioner
76. Starter
77. Fuse box, 2 fuses, air conditioner
78. Relay, air conditioner/starter
79. Battery
80. Side marker lamp, rear, right
81. Tail light unit, right
    a. Turn signal light
    b. Tail/parking light
    c. Back-up light
    d. Brake light
82. Heated rear window
83. License plate light
84. Tail light unit, left
    a. Turn signal light
    b. Tail/parking light
    c. Back-up light
    d. Brake light
85. Side marker lamp, rear, left

* Special equipment

Wire Color Code
bl = blue
br = brown
el = ivory
ge = yellow
gn = green
gr = grey
nf = neutral
rs = pink
rt = red
sw = black
vi = purple
ws = white

1976 300D

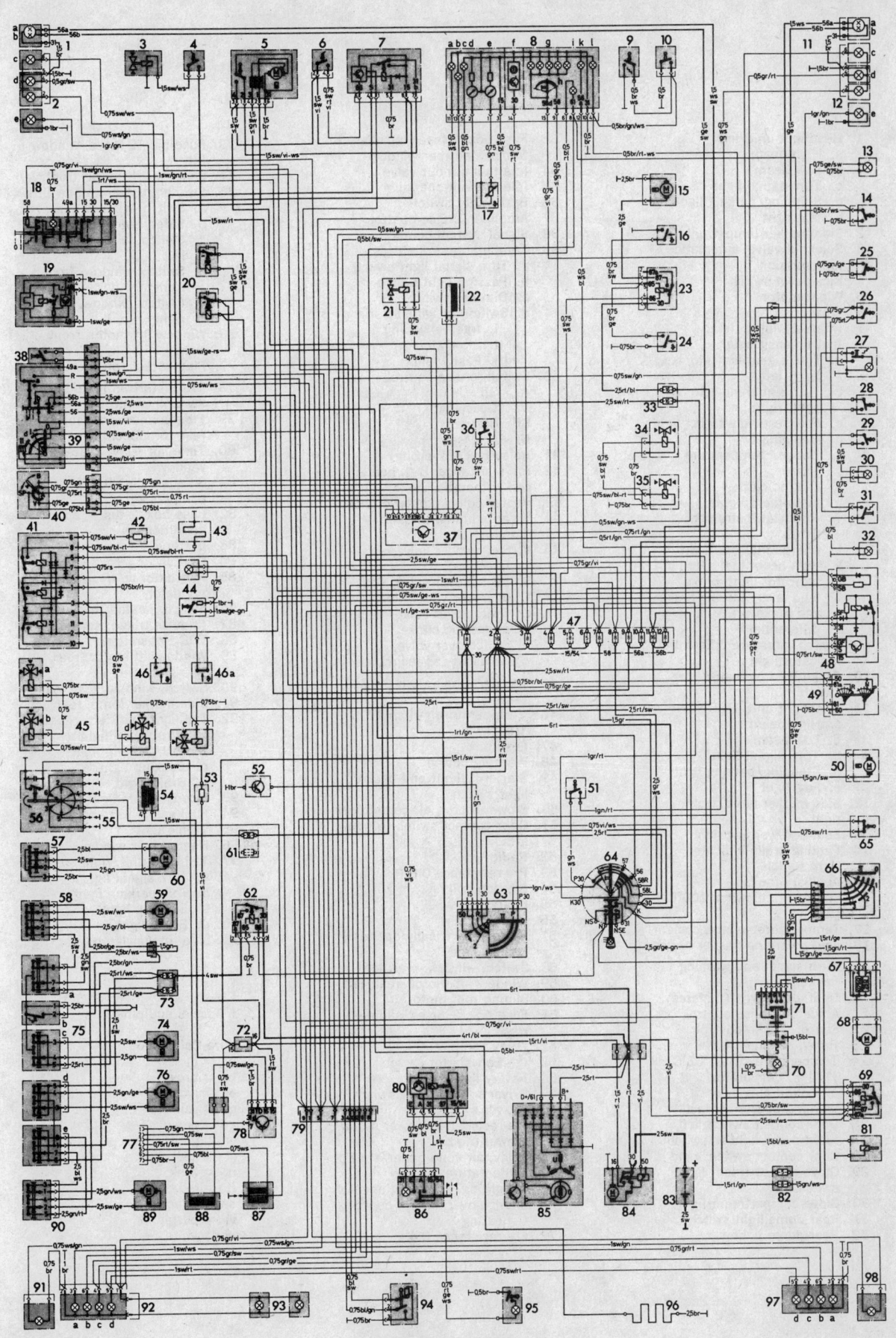

1976 280 and 280C

1. Headlight unit, left
   a. High beam
   b. Low beam
   c. Turn signal light
   d. Standing/parking light
   e. Fog light
2. Side marker lamp, front, left
3. Solenoid valve, automatic transmission
4. Kick-down switch
5. Wiper motor
6. Washer switch
7. Interval wiping timer
8. Instrument cluster
   a. Turn signal indicator light, left
   b. Turn signal indicator light, right
   c. Fuel reserve warning light
   d. Fuel gauge
   e. Coolant temperature gauge
   f. Electric clock
   g. Instrument lights
   h. Rheostat instrument lights
   i. Charge indicator light
   k. High beam indicator light
   l. Indicator light, brake fluid level, parking brake and brake pressure differential
9. Switch, pressure differential indicator light
10. Brake fluid indicator light switch
11. Headlight unit, right
    a. High beam
    b. Low beam
    c. Turn signal light
    d. Standing/parking light
    e. Fog light
12. Side marker lamp, front, right
13. Seat-belt warning light
14. Parking brake indicator light switch
15. Auxiliary fan
16. Temperature switch 100°C (212°F)
17. Temperature sensor, coolant
18. 4-way warning flasher switch
19. Turn signal and warning flasher relay
20. Dual-tone horns (fanfares)
21. Actuator, cruise control
22. Sensor, cruise control
23. Relay, auxiliary fan
24. Temperature switch 62°C (144°F) dehydrator, air conditioner
25. Warning buzzer contact
26. Door contact switch, left
27. Front dome light w/switch
28. Door contact switch, right
29. Glove compartment light switch
30. Glove compartment light
31. Rear dome light switch
32. Rear dome light

33. Fuse box, 2 fuses, auxiliary fan/heated rear window
34. Idle fuel cut-out valve
35. Idle fuel cut-out valve
36. Brake light switch
37. Amplifier, cruise control
38. Signal system contact
39. Combination switch
    a. Turn signal light switch
    b. Passing light switch
    c. Dimmer switch
    d. Switch for wipping speed
       I. Interval wiping
       II. Slow wiping
       III. Fast wiping
40. Switch, cruise control
    A. Off
    V. Decel/set
    SP. Resume
    B. Acel/set
41. Relay box (11 prong)
42. Pre-resistance, 8 Ω, heater coil automatic choke
43. Heater coil, automatic choke
44. Cigar lighter with ashtray illumination
45. a. Switch-over valve, air injection
    b. Switch-over valve, float chamber ventilation
    c. Switch-over valve, automatic choke
    d. Switch-over valve, emission gas recirculation
46. Temperature switch 65°C (149°F)
46a. Temperature switch 17°C (62°F)
47. Fuse box
48. Warning device
49. Starter-lockout and back-up light switch
50. Blower motor, air conditioner
51. Door contact switch, window lifts
52. Radio*
53. Pre-resistance 0.6 Ω
54. Ignition coil
55. Spark plugs
56. Distributor
57. Switch, electrically operated sliding roof*
58. Switch, window, rear, left
59. Window lift motor, rear, left
60. Sliding roof motor*
61. Fuse box, 2 fuses, sliding roof*
62. Relay window lifts
63. Ignition starter switch
64. Rotary light switch
65. Driver's belt buckle switch
66. Blower switch
67. Pre-resistance, blower motor
68. Blower motor
69. Relay, air conditioner/starter
70. Temperature control w/lighting, air conditioner
71. Change-over switch, cooling —heating
72. Pre-resistance 0.4 Ω

73. Fuse box, 2 fuses, window lift
74. Window lift motor, front, left
75. Switch cluster, window lifts
    a. Switch, window, rear, left
    b. Safety switch
    c. Switch, window, front, left
    d. Switch, window, front, right
    e. Switch, window, rear, right
76. Window lift motor, front, right
77. Plug socket (diagnosis)
78. Transistorized ignition switching unit
79. Plug connection, cable to rear components
80. Time-lag relay, heated rear window
81. Solenoid clutch, refrigerant compressor
82. Fuse box, 2 fuses, air conditioner
83. Battery
84. Starter
85. Alternator w/electronic regulator
86. Switch, heated rear window
87. Impulse trigger sensor
88. TDC transmitter
89. Window lift motor, rear, right
90. Switch, window, rear, right
91. Side marker lamp, rear, left
92. Tail light unit, left
    a. Turn signal light
    b. Tail/parking light
    c. Back-up light
    d. Brake light
93. License plate light
94. Fuel gauge sending unit
95. Trunk light
96. Heated rear window
97. Tail light unit, right
    a. Turn signal light
    b. Tail/parking light
    c. Back-up light
    d. Brake light
98. Side marker lamp, rear, right

* Special equipment

Wire Color Code
bl = blue
br = brown
el = ivory
ge = yellow
gn = green
gr = grey
nf = neutral
rs = pink
rt = red
sw = black
vi = purple
ws = white

1976 280 and 280C

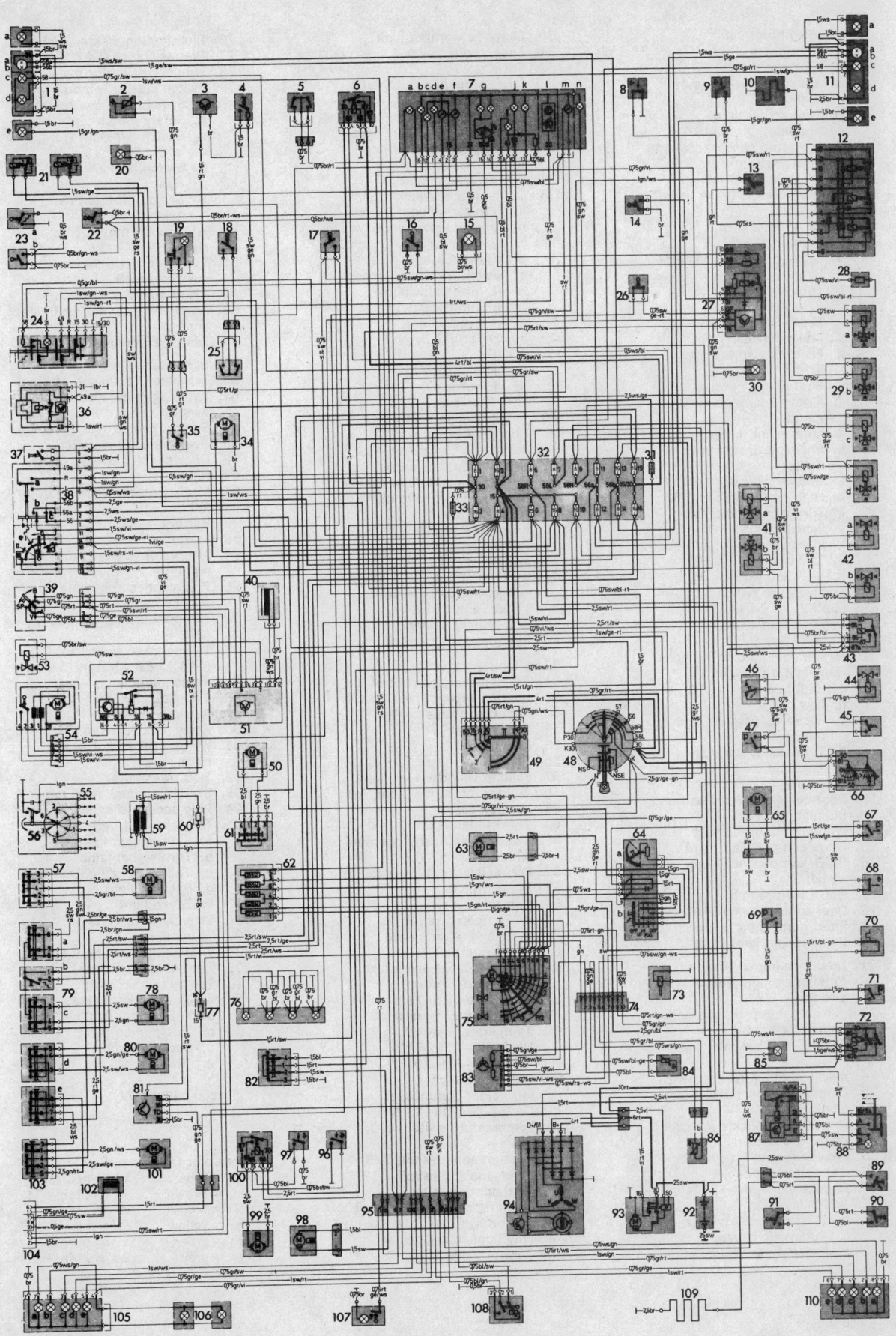

Wiring Circuits

1. Headlight unit, left
   a. High beam
   b. Low beam
   c. Standing/parking/side marker light
   d. Turn signal light
   e. Fog light
2. Temperature sensor, coolant
3. Radio*
4. Cigar lighter
5. Contact sensor, brake pads, front, left
6. Relay, window lifts
7. Instrument cluster
   a. Brake pad wear indicator light
   b. Turn signal indicator light, left
   c. Brake fluid and parking brake indicator light
   d. Fuel reserve warning light
   e. Fuel gauge
   f. Coolant temperature gauge
   g. Instrument lights
   h. Rheostat, instrument lights
   i. Charge indicator light
   j. High beam indicator light
   k. Turn signal indicator light, right
   l. Electronic clock
   m. Tachometer
   n. Seat-belt warning light
8. Temperature switch 17°C (62°F)
9. Temperature switch 65°C (149°F)
10. Heater coil, automatic choke
11. Headlight unit, right
    a. High beam
    b. Low beam
    c. Standing/parking/side marker light
    d. Turn signal light
    e. Fog light
12. Relay box
13. Door contact switch, warning buzzer
14. Warning buzzer contact
15. Glove compartment light
16. Glove compartment light switch
17. Brake light switch
18. Door contact switch, left
19. Front dome light w/switch
20. Illumination, gate plate
21. Dual-tone horns (fanfares)
22. Parking brake indicator light switch
23a. Switch, pressure differential indicator light
23b. Brake fluid indicator light switch
24. 4-way warning flasher switch
25. Contact sensor, brake pads, front, right
26. Driver's belt buckle switch
27. Warning device
28. Pre-resistance, 8 Ω, heater coil automatic choke
29. Change-over valve
    a. Air injection
    b. Float chamber ventilation
    c. Automatic choke
    d. Exhaust gas recirculation

30. Seat-belt warning light
31. Fuse, radio
32. Fuse box
33. Fuse, amplifier, automatic climate control
34. Washer pump
35. Door contact switch, right
36. Turn signal and warning flasher relay
37. Signal system contact
38. Combination switch
    a. Turn signal light switch
    b. Passing light switch
    c. Dimmer switch
    d. Washer switch
    e. Switch for wiping speed
       I. Interval wiping
       II. Slow wiping
       III. Fast wiping
39. Switch, cruise control
    A. Off
    V. Decel/set
    SP. Resume
    B. Acel/set
40. Sensor cruise control
41. Change-over valve, automatic climate control
42. Idle fuel cut-out valve
43. Relay, air conditioner/starter
44. Solenoid valve, automatic transmission
45. Kick-down switch
46. Refrigerant compressor switch, on/off
47. Vacuum switch, 78.5 mbar, refrigerant compressor "FOG" and "DEF"
48. Rotary light switch
49. Ignition starter switch
50. Sliding roof motor*
51. Amplifier, cruise control
52. Interval wiping timer
53. Actuator, cruise control
54. Wiper motor
55. Spark plugs
56. Distributor
57. Switch, window, rear, left
58. Window lift motor, rear, left
59. Ignition coil
60. Pre-resistance 0.6 Ω
61. Switch, electrically operated sliding roof*
62. Pre-resistance, blower motor
63. Blower motor
64. Control unit
    a. Temperature slector
    b. Push-button switch
65. Water pump
66. Starter-lockout and back-up light switch
67. Vacuum switch, 78.5 mbar, refrigerant compressor
68. Temperature switch, On 16°C—Off 26°C (On 61°F—Off 79°F)
69. Pressure switch, refrigerant compressor, On 2.8 bar, Off 0.7 bar
70. Temperature switch, 2°C (36°F)
71. Vacuum compressor, 175 mbar, master switch
72. Dual contact relay
73. Solenoid clutch, refrigerant compressor
74. Plug connection, tester
75. Control valve

76. Illumination, heater controls
77. Pre-resistance 0.4 Ω
78. Window lift motor, front, left
79. Switch cluster, window lifts
    a. Switch, window, rear, left
    b. Safety switch
    c. Switch, window, front, left
    d. Switch, window, front right
    e. Switch, window, rear, right
80. Window lift motor, front, right
81. Transistorized ignition switching unit
82. Electric antenna switch
83. Amplifier, automatic climate control
84. Temperature sensor, external
85. Rear dome light
86. Temperature sensor, internal
87. Time-lag relay, heated rear window
88. Switch, heated rear window
89. Rear dome light switch
90. Door contact switch, rear, right
91. Door contact switch, rear, left
92. Battery
93. Starter
94. Alternator w/electronic regulator
95. Plug connection, cable to rear components
96. Temperature switch 100°C (212°F)
97. Temperature switch 62°C (144°F) dehydrator, air conditioner
98. Electric antenna
99. Auxiliary fan
100. Relay, auxiliary fan
101. Window lift motor, rear, right
102. TDC transmitter
103. Switch, window, rear, right
104. Plug socket (diagnosis)
105. Tail light unit, left
    a. Side marker light
    b. Turn signal lgiht
    c. Tail/parking light
    d. Back-up light
    e. Brake light
106. License plate light
107. Trunk light
108. Fuel gauge sending unit
109. Heated rear window
110. Tail light unit, right
    a. Side marker light
    b. Trun signal light
    c. Tail/parking light
    d. Back-up light
    e. Brake light

* Special equipment

Wire Color Code

bl	= blue	nf	= neutral
br	= brown	rs	= pink
el	= ivory	rt	= red
ge	= yellow	sw	= black
gn	= green	vi	= purple
gr	= grey	ws	= white

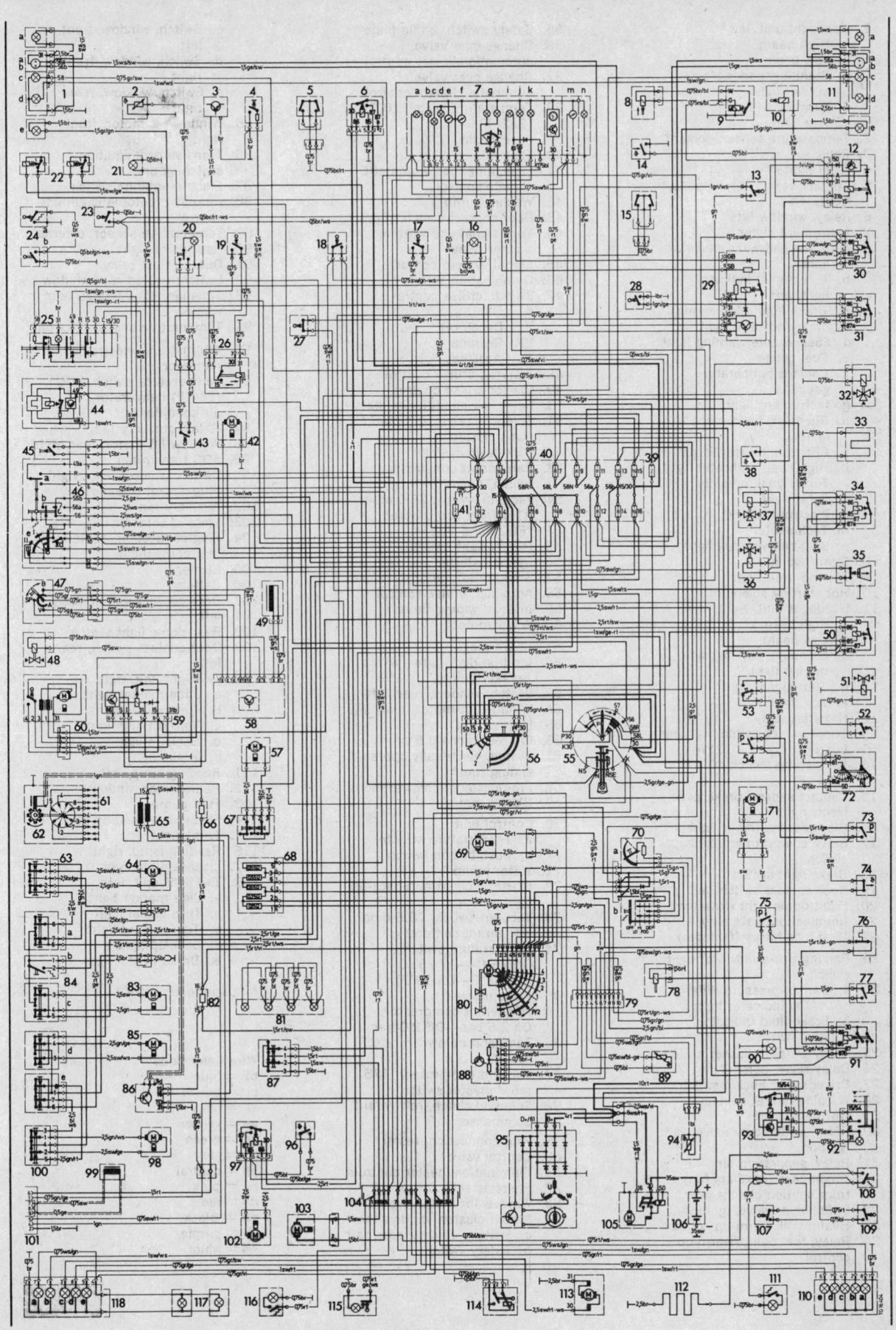

1976 450SE and 450SEL

Wiring Circuits

1. Headlight unit, left
   a. High beam
   b. Low beam
   c. Standing/parking/side marker light
   d. Turn signal light
   e. Fog light
2. Temperature sensor, coolant
3. Radio
4. Cigar lighter
5. Contact sensor, brake pads, front, left
6. Relay, window lifts
7. Instrument clster
   a. Brake pad wear indicator, light
   b. Turn signal indicator light, left
   c. Brake fluid and parking brake indicator light
   d. Fuel reserve warning light
   e. Fuel gauge
   f. Coolant temperature gauge
   g. Instrument light
   h. Rheostat, instrument lights
   i. Charge indicator light
   j. High beam indicator light
   k. Turn signal indicator light, right
   l. Electronic clock
   m. Tachometer
   n. Seat-belt warning light
8. Starter valve
9. Thermo-time switch
10. Hot starting solenoid
11. Headlight unit, right
    a. High beam
    b. Low beam
    c. Standing/parking/side marker light
    d. Turn signal light
    e. Fog light
12. Hot start relay
13. Door contact switch, warning buzzer
14. Temperatre switch 40° C (104° F)
15. Contact sensor, brake pads, front, right
16. Glove compartment light
17. Glove compartment light switch
18. Brake light switch
19. Door contact switch, left
20. Front dome light w/switch
21. Illumination, gate plate
22. Dual-tone horns (fanfares)
23. Parking brake indicator light switch
24. a. Switch, pressure differential indicator light
    b. Brake fluid indicator light switch
25. 4-way warning flasher switch
26. Delay relay, dome light
27. Driver's belt buckle switch
28. Warning buzzer contact
29. Warning device
30. Relay, switch-over valve, ignition
31. Relay, separation air conditioner (auxiliary fan) from ignition change-over
32. Switch-over valve, ignition
33. Heater coil, warm-up control
34. Relay, fuel pump/warm-up control

35. Safety switch, baffle plate
36. Change-over valve, automatic climate control
37. Change-over valve, automatic climate control
38. Temperature switch 100° C (212° F)
39. Fuse, radio
40. Fuse box
41. Fuse, amplifier, automatic climate control
42. Washer pump
43. Door contact switch, right
44. Turn signal and warning flasher relay
45. Signal system contact
46. Combination switch
47. Switch, cruise control
    A. Off
    V. Decel/set
    SP. Resume
    B. Acel/set
48. Acuator, cruise control
49. Sensor cruise control
50. Relay, air conditioner/starter
51. Solenoid valve, automatic transmission
52. Kick-down switch
53. Refrigerant compressor switch, on/off
54. Vacuum switch, 78.5 mbar refrigerant compressor "FOG" and "DEF"
55. Rotary light switch
56. Ignition starter switch
57. Sliding roof motor*
58. Amplifier, cruise control
59. Interval wiping timer
60. Wiper motor
61. Spark plugs
62. Ignition distributor, w/o breaker points
63. Switch, window, rear, left
64. Window lift motor, rear, left
65. Ignition coil
66. Pre-resistance 0.6 Ω
67. Switch, electrically operated sliding roof*
68. Pre-resistance, blower motor
69. Blower motor
70. Control unit
    a. Temperature selector
    b. Push-button switch
71. Water pump
72. Starter-lockout and back-up light switch
73. Vacuum switch, 78.5 mbar, refrigerant compressor
74. Temperature switch, On 16°C—Off 26° C (On 61°F—Off 79°F)
75. Pressure switch, refrigerant compressor, On 2.6 bar—Off 2.0 bar
76. Temperature switch, 2°C (36°F)
77. Vacuum compressor, 175 mbar master switch
78. Solenoid clutch, refrigerant compressor
79. Plug connection, tester
80. Control valve
81. Illumination, heater controls
82. Pre-resistance 0.4 Ω
83. Window lift motor, front, left
84. Switch cluster, window lifts
    a. Switch, window, rear, left
    b. Safety switch

   c. Switch, window, front, left
   d. Switch, window, front, right
   e. Switch, window, rear, right
85. Window lift motor, front, right
86. Transistorized ignition switching unit
87. Electric antenna switch
88. Amplifier, automatic climate control
89. Temperature sensor, external
90. Rear dome light
91. Dual contact relay
92. Switch, heated rear window
93. Time-lag relay, heated rear window
94. Temperature sensor, internal
95. Alternator w/electronic regulator
96. Temperature switch 62°C (144°F) dehydrator, air conditioner
97. Relay, auxiliary fan
98. Window lift motor, rear, right
99. TDC transmitter
100. Switch, window, rear, right
101. Plug socket (diagnosis)
102. Auxiliary fan
103. Electric antenna
104. Plug connection, cable to rear component
105. Starter
106. Battery
107. Door contact switch, rear, left
108. Rear dome light switch
109. Door contact switch, rear, left
110. Tail light unit, right
     a. Slide marker light
     b. Turn signal light
     c. Tail/parking light
     d. Back-up light
     e. Brake light
111. Reading lamp, left
112. Heated rear window
113. Fuel pump
114. Fuel gauge sending unit
115. Trunk light
116. Reading lamp, right
117. License plate light
118. Tail light unit, left
     a. Side marker light
     b. Turn signal light
     c. Tail/parking light
     d. Back-up light
     e. Brake light

* Special equipment

Wire Color Code
bl = blue
br = brown
el = ivory
ge = yellow
gn = green
gr = grey
nf = neutral
rs = pink
rt = red
sw = black
vi = purple
ws = white

SPECIFICATIONS

MODEL IDENTIFICATION

1971-74 MGB

1971-74 MGB GT

1971-74 Midget

1975 MGB

1975 MGB-GT

1975 Midget

SERIAL NUMBER IDENTIFICATION

Vehicle

The Vehicle Serial Number can be found stamped on a plate located on the inner fender panel of the engine compartment. Late model cars have this plate located on the top of the dashboard, visible through the windshield.

Vehicle Identification— Midget

Year	Model	Commencing Serial Numbers	
1972-73	Midget	G-AN5	105501
1973-74	Midget	G-AN5	123731
1975	Midget	GAN-6UF	154101
1976	Midget	GAN-6UG	166301G

Vehicle Identification—MGB

Year	Model		Commencing Serial Numbers
1972	Conv.	G-HN5	219021-258001
1972-73	Conv.	G-HN5	258001-294251
1973-74	Conv.	G-HN5	294251-328101
1971-72	GT	G-HD5	219355-298004
1972-73	GT	G-HD5	298004
1973-74	GT	G-HD5	296001
1975	GT	GHN-5UF	367901G
1976	GT	GHN-5UG	386601G

Engine

The engine serial number is located on a plate riveted to the engine block on the distributor side.

Engine Identification— Midget

No. of Cyl- inders	Dis- place- ment (cc.)	Year	Engine Code
4	1275	1972	12CJ
4	1275	1973-74	12V
4	1275	1975-76	PE94J

Engine Identification— MGB

No. of Cyl- inders	Dis- place- ment (cc.)	Year	Engine Code
4	1798	1972-76	18V

GENERAL ENGINE SPECIFICATIONS

Model/Year	Engine Code	Displacement	Carburetor Type	Advertised Horsepower @ RPM	Advertised Torque @ RPM	Bore and Stroke (in.)	Comp. Ratio	Oil Pressure
Midget Mk. III								
1972	12CJ	1,275 cc.	HS2 (2)	62 @ 6,000	72 @ 3,000	2.78 x 3.20	8:1	40-70
1973-74	12V	1,275 cc.	HS2 (2)	62 @ 6,000	72 @ 3,000	2.78 x 3.20	8:1	40-70
1975-76	PE94J	1,500 cc.	CD4 (1)	50 @ 5,000	N.A.	2.90 x 3.44	7.5:1	40-60
MGB								
1972-74	18V	1,798 cc.	HIF4 (2)	92 @ 5,200	110 @ 3,000	3.16 x 3.50	8:1	50-80
1975-76	18V	1,798 cc.	CD5 (1)	92 @ 5,200	105 @ 3,000	3.16 x 3.50	8:1	50-80
MGB GT								
1972-74	18V	1,798 cc.	HIF4 (2)	92 @ 5,200	110 @ 3,000	3.16 x 3.50	8:1	50-80

① Exhaust Emission Control System fitted.
② Exhaust Emission Control and Evaporative Loss Control Systems fitted.
③ Exhaust Emission Control, Evaporative Loss Control, and NOx Systems fitted.

TUNE-UP SPECIFICATIONS

Model/Year	Engine Code	SPARK PLUGS Cham- pion	Gap (in.)	DISTRIBUTOR Dwell (deg.)	Gap (in.)	Timing (deg.)	Com- pression pres- sure (psi)	VALVES Clearance (in.) Intake	Exhaust	In- take Opens (deg.)	Idle Speed (rpm)
Midget											
1972	12V	N9Y	0.025	60	0.015	9B②	120	0.012C	0.012C	5B	1,000
1973-74	12V	N9Y	0.025	60	0.015	9B②	120	0.012C	0.012C	5B	700
1975-76	PE94J	N12Y	0.025	①	①	2A	120	0.010C	0.010C	16B	800
1977	PE94J					See Underhood Specifications Sticker					
MGB											
1972	18V	N9Y	0.025	60	0.015	16B②	160	0.015H	0.015H	16B	850
1973-74	18V	N9Y	0.025	60	0.015	11B②	160	0.015C	0.015C	16B	850
1975-76	18V	N9Y	0.025	①	①	12B②	160	0.013H	0.013H	16B	850
1977	18V					See Underhood Specifications Sticker					

B Before Top Dead Center
H Engine Hot
C Engine Cold

① Factory installed electronic ignition with fixed dwell. If adjustment is needed, use brass or plastic feeler. Pick-up air gap should be:
Midget 0.014-0.016 in.
MGB 0.010-0.017 in.
② @ 1500 rpm
For catalytic converter equipped models—½% ± 1% CO (max.) disconnect air pump and plug injector pipe.

NOTE: The underhood specifications sticker often reflects tune-up specification changes made in production. Sticker figures should be used if they disagree with this chart.

MG

FIRING ORDERS

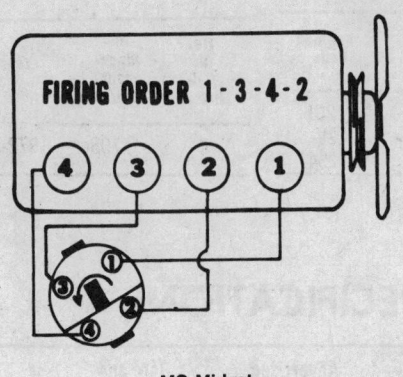

MG Midget

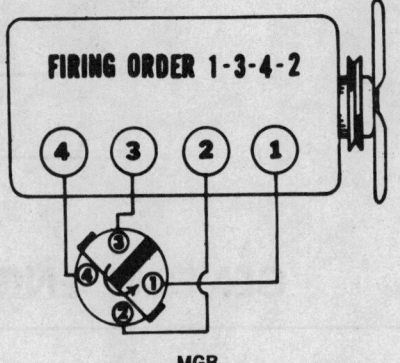

MGB

CAPACITIES AND PRESSURES

Model & Engine	CRANKCASE (qts.) With Filter	CRANKCASE (qts.) Without Filter	TRANSMISSION 4-Speed	TRANSMISSION Auto.	Drive Axle (pts.)	Fuel Tank (gals.)	Coolant with Heater (qts.)	Fuel Pressure (psi)	Coolant Pressure (max. psi)
Midget									
12CJ/12V	4.0	3.5	2.7	—	2.1	7.2①	6.3	2.5-3.0	15
PE94J	4.8	4.2	3.0	—	2.1	7.2	6.3	2.5-3.0	15
MGB									
18V	4.5	4.5	6.0	—	2.0	12.0	6.0	2.5-3.0	10

① 12CJ—6.0 gallons.

CRANKSHAFT SPECIFICATIONS

Model & Engine	MAIN BEARING JOURNALS (in.) JOURNAL DIAMETER New	MAIN BEARING JOURNALS (in.) JOURNAL DIAMETER Minimum	Oil Clearance	Shaft End-Play	Thrust On No.	CONNECTING ROD BEARING JOURNALS (in.) JOURNAL DIAMETER New	CONNECTING ROD BEARING JOURNALS (in.) JOURNAL DIAMETER Minimum	Oil Clearance	End-Play
Midget									
12CJ/12V	2.0005-2.0010	—0.010①	0.001-0.0027	0.002-0.003	2	1.6254-1.6259	—0.010①	0.001-0.0025	0.006-0.010
PE94J	2.3115-2.3120	—0.010①	0.0005-0.0025	0.006-0.014	3	1.8750-1.8755	—0.030	0.001 0.003	—
MGB									
18V	2.1262-2.1270	—0.040	0.001-0.0027	0.004-0.005	3	1.8759-1.8764	—0.040	0.001-0.0027	0.008-0.012

① Maximum permissible without heat treatment.   — Not available

VALVE SPECIFICATIONS

Model & Engine	Seat Angle (deg.)	VALVE LIFT (in.) Intake	VALVE LIFT (in.) Exhaust	VALVE HEAD DIAMETER (in.) Intake	VALVE HEAD DIAMETER (in.) Exhaust	VALVE SPRING FREE LENGTH (in.) Inner	VALVE SPRING FREE LENGTH (in.) Outer	SPRING PRESSURE (lbs.)① Intake	SPRING PRESSURE (lbs.)① Exhaust	STEM DIAMETER (in.) Intake	STEM DIAMETER (in.) Exhaust	STEM TO GUIDE CLEARANCE (in.) Intake	STEM TO GUIDE CLEARANCE (in.) Exhaust	Guide Height Above Head (in.)
Midget														
12CJ	45	0.318	0.318	1.307-1.312	1.152-1.156	1.703	1.828	131	131	0.2793-0.2798	0.2788-0.2793	0.0015-0.0025	0.0015-0.0025	19/32②

774

VALVE SPECIFICATIONS

Model & Engine	Seat Angle (deg.)	VALVE LIFT (in.)		VALVE HEAD DIAMETER (in.)		VALVE SPRING FREE LENGTH (in.)		SPRING PRESSURE (lbs.)①		STEM DIAMETER (in.)		STEM TO GUIDE CLEARANCE (in.)		Guide Height Above Head (in.)
		Intake	Exhaust	Intake	Exhaust	Inner	Outer	Intake	Exhaust	Intake	Exhaust	Intake	Exhaust	
12V	45	0.318	0.318	1.307-1.312	1.515-1.565	1.703	1.828	131	131	0.2793-0.2798	0.2788-0.2793	0.0015-0.0025	0.0015-0.0025	.540
PE94J	44.5	0.318	0.318	1.377-1.383	1.168-1.172	1.52	—	123	123	0.3107-0.3113	0.3100-0.3105	0.0007-0.0023	0.0015-0.0030	¾
MGB 1972-on	45.5	0.318	0.318	1.625-1.630	1.343-1.348	1.92	2.141	142	142	0.3429-0.3434	0.3417-0.3422	0.0008-0.0018	0.002-0.003	¾

① Combined pressure of inner and outer valve springs with valve fully open.
— Not available

② 12CD and 12CJ engines should only use valve guides having an identification groove machined 0.187 in. from the guide top.

PISTON AND RING SPECIFICATIONS

Model & Engine	PISTON SPECIFICATIONS (in.)		SKIRT CLEARANCE		RING SPECIFICATIONS (in.)			
	Oversize Maximum	Wrist Pin Diameter	Top	Bottom	COMPRESSION End-Gap	Side Clearance	OIL CONTROL End-Gap	Side Clearance
Midget 12CJ/12V	+.020	0.8123-0.8125	0.0029-0.0037	0.0015-0.0021	0.008-0.013①	0.0015-0.0035	0.012-0.028	0.0015-0.0035
PE94J	+.030	0.8124-0.8126	0.002-0.003	0.0002-0.0016	0.012-0.022	0.0015-0.0035	0.015-0.055	0.0016-0.0036
MGB 18V	+.040	0.8125-0.8127	0.0021-0.0033	0.0006-0.0012	0.012-0.022	0.0015-0.0035	0.015-0.045	0.0016-0.0036

① Top compression ring—0.011-0.011 in.

TORQUE SPECIFICATIONS
(ft. lbs.)

Model & Engine	Cylinder Head Bolts	Main Bearing Bolts	Rod Bearing Bolts	Crankshaft Damper Bolt(s)①	Flywheel to Crankshaft Bolt(s)	MANIFOLD NUTS Intake	Exhaust
Midget 12CJ/12V	42②	60	45③	70	40	15	15
PE94J	50	65	50	70	40	14	14
MGB All Engine Series	45-50	70	35-40	70	40	15	15

① Torque figure given applies to crankshaft pulley on cars not equipped with damper.

② Studs stamped 22 or with small drill point—50.
③ Nylon-type locknut—32-34.

TIGHTENING SEQUENCES

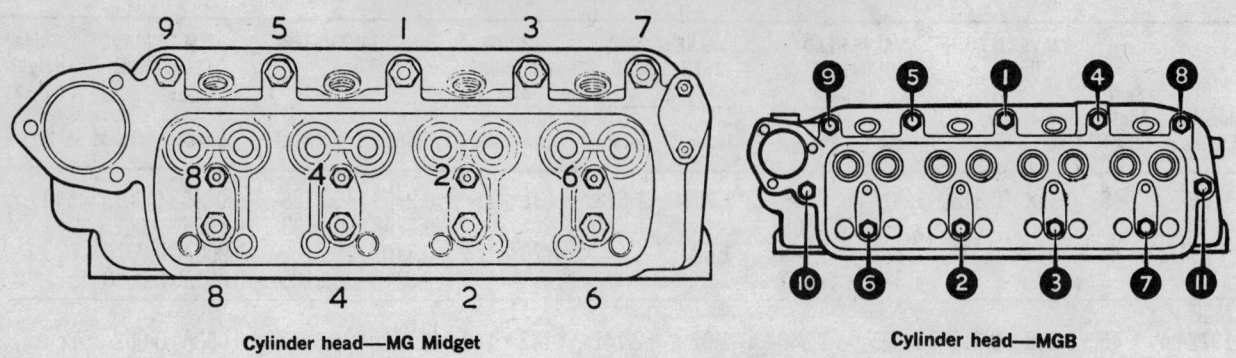

Cylinder head—MG Midget

Cylinder head—MGB

ELECTRICAL SPECIFICATIONS

All cars use 12 volt, negative ground electrical systems

| Model & Engine | BATTERY | | STARTER (LUCAS) | | | | | | | |
| | Capacity (amp. hrs.) | Type | LOCK TEST | | | NO LOAD TEST | | | Brush Spring Tension (oz.) |
			Amps	Volts	Torque (ft. lb.)	Amps	Volts	Rpm	
Midget									
12CJ/12V	50	M35J	250-375	7	7.0	65	11.5	8,000-10,000	28
PE94J	50	M35J	250-375	7	4.4	65	11.5	8,000-10,000	28
MGB									
18V	60	2 M100	463	7	14.4	40	11.5	6,000	36

| Model & Engine | GENERATOR (LUCAS) | | | | REGULATOR (LUCAS) CUT-OUT RELAY | | | | | |
	Type	Output (amps)	Brush Pressure (oz.)	Resistance (ohms)	Type	Points Close (volts)	Reverse Current (amps)	Points Air Gap (in.)	Maximum Current (amps)	Points Air Gap (in.)
Midget										
12CJ	C40/1	22	22-25	6.0	RB340	12.7-13.3	5.0	①	22	①

① The settings of the points should never need adjustment. See text for further explanation.

| Model & Engine | ALTERNATOR (LUCAS) | | | | | REGULATOR (LUCAS) FIELD RELAY | | | | | |
| | Type | OUTPUT @ ENGINE RPM (amps) | | Field Current Draw (amps @ 12V) | Brush Tension (oz.) | Type | Air Gap (in.) | Point Gap (in.) | Points Close (volts) | Air Gap (in.) | Volts @ 125 deg. |
		850	3,300								
MGB											
18V	16ACR	12-15	34	3	7-10	8TR 11TR	Integral with alternator, transistor type—no adjustment				14.0-14.4 14.0-14.4
Midget											
12V from 1972 PE94J	16ACR	12-15	34①	3	9-13		Integral with alternator, transistor type—no adjustment				14.0-14.4

① 34 amps at 6000 **Alternator** RPM, 3000 **engine** rpm

WHEEL ALIGNMENT SPECIFICATIONS

Model & Engine	CASTER (deg.) Range	Ideal	CAMBER (deg.) Range	Ideal	Toe-In (in.)	Kingpin Inclination (deg.)	WHEEL PIVOT RATIO (deg.) Inner	Outer
Midget 12CJ/12V/PE94J	—	3P	—	¾N	⅛	6¾	20	19¾
MGB All Engine Series	5P-7¼P	7P	¼N-1¼P	1P	1/16	8	20	19

P—Positive
N—Negative

BRAKE SPECIFICATIONS

All measurements given are (in.) unless noted

Model	Lug Nut Torque (ft/lb)	Master Cylinder Bore	Brake Disc Minimum Thickness	Maximum Run-Out	Brake Drum Diameter	Max. Machine O/S	Max. Wear Limit	Minimum Lining Thickness Front	Rear
Midget 12CJ/12V	45	1 1/16	.300-.305	0.006	7.0	0.015	0.030	1/16	40%②
PE94J	45	¾	0.29	0.006	7.0	0.015	0.030	1/16	40%②
MGB 12V	60-65	¾①	.340-.350	0.003	10.0	0.015	0.030	1/16	40%②

① 13/16 in. from vehicle number G-HD3/138, 401 (GT only)
② If riveted; 25% if bonded
NOTE: Minimum lining thickness is as recommended by the manufacturer. Due to variations in state inspection regulations, the minimum allowable thickness may be different than recommended by the manufacturer.

CARBURETOR SPECIFICATIONS

Model/Engine	Type	Throat Diameter (in.)	Main Jet Size (in.)	JET NEEDLE② IDENTIFICATION NO. Standard	Rich	Lean	Piston Spring Strength (Color identification)
Midget 12CJ	HS2	1.25	.090	AAC①	—	—	blue
12V	HS2	1.25	.090	AAT④	—	—	blue
PE94J	CD4	1.50	0.100	44A	—	—	blue
MGB 18V	HIF4	1.50	.090	AAU③	—	—	red
18V	CD5	1.50	0.100	45H	—	—	blue

① Fixed needle—AN.
② Most emission control engines are fitted with spring-loaded jet needles.
③ ABD—1973
④ ABC—1973

TUNE-UP PROCEDURES

Spark Plugs

Number each spark plug wire by placing a piece of tape on the wire indicating the cylinder number. Grasp each spark plug wire by the rubber boot on the end of the wire and remove the wire from the plug.

Using a socket and a ratchet remove the spark plugs. Before installing new plugs, gap each plug according to specification in the "Tune-up Specification Chart." Install the new plugs by hand then tighten them snugly with the wrench.

Breaker Points and Condenser

NOTE: *This section applies only to MGs with conventional ignition systems. The 75 and later MG's are equipped with an electronic ignition system which does not require servicing.*

Removal and Installation

1. Remove the distributor. See the "Engine Electrical" section for distributor removal.

2. Lift the rotor from the distributor shaft. Make a careful note of the positions of the components so that they may be reassembled correctly.

3. Unscrew the nut from the moving contact return-spring locating pin and remove the plastic insulating sleeve and the condenser and low tension lead wires.

4. Remove the screw and washers holding the contact breaker plate and lift out the plate.

5. Remove the condenser screw and lift out the condenser.

6. Thoroughly clean the distributor body and base plate, making sure that the base plate is left without an oily film that could insulate the contact breaker plate from the distributor base plate and pre-

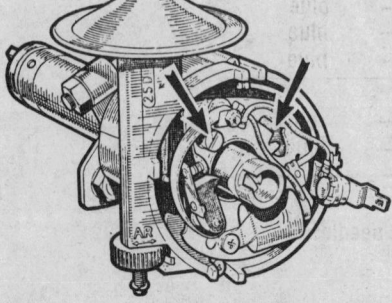

Location of the breaker points adjusting notch and screw.

vent the ground circuit from being completed. The vacuum advance diaphragm may be checked by applying a suction where the line connects and watching for movement of the base plate.

7. Install the contact breaker points and condenser in reverse order of removal. Clean the surfaces of the contact points with a non-oily solvent such as alcohol to remove any preservative coating or dirt, and set the points gap to specification (see "Tune-Up Specifications").

CAUTION: *The order of installation of components on the moving contact return-spring locating pin must be followed exactly or the ignition spark will be short-circuited to ground. The fiber insulating washer must be installed first, followed by the return-spring end loop, the low-tension and condenser lead wires, the insulating sleeve (which slides down between the pin and the return-spring and wire end loops), and the nut.*

8. Apply one or two drops of engine oil to the felt in the top of the distributor shaft (if applicable). Lightly smear the distributor cam with engine oil or distributor cam lubricant.

Adjustment

Rotate the distributor camshaft until the points are fully open. Loosen the attaching nut on the securing plate and insert a screwdriver between the notches in the fixed plate. Turn the screwdriver until the gap between the two contacts is 0.15 in., using a feeler gauge. Tighten the attaching nut.

Dwell Angle

Dwell angle is the angle that the distributor cam rotates when the breaker points are closed. The dwell angle on all 1975–77 MG's is factory set, due to electronic ignition,

This is a more accurate way of adjusting point gap than using a feeler gauge.

1. Remove the distributor cap and connect a dwell meter between the primary lead and the ground.

2. Crank the engine and observe the degree of dwell on the meter. Refer to the "Tune-Up Specifications Chart" for the proper dwell angle. If it is necessary to adjust this angle, adjust the points as previously described.

Ignition Timing

Dynamic (engine running) timing is done with a timing light. Connect the light as per manufacturer's instructions. Mark the notch in the crankshaft pulley with a bright color that will be easily visible (such as yellow crayon). Disconnect and plug the vacuum advance line from the intake manifold.

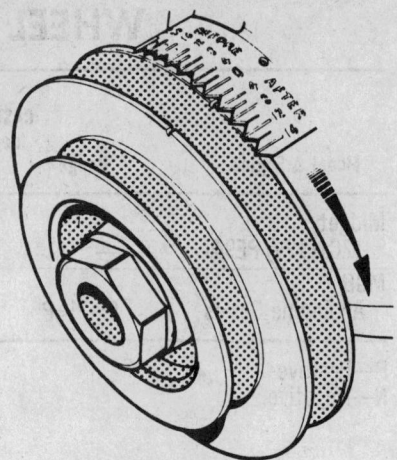

MG Midget timing marks

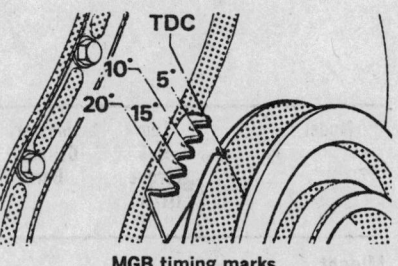

MGB timing marks

The engine should be warm and running steadily at the correct rpm when the timing check is made. If the timing is no more than 5 degrees off, correction can usually be made with the vernier adjustment knob on the vacuum advance unit of the distributor. Otherwise, the distributor clamp pinch-bolt will have to be loosened and the distributor rotated to the correct position. Check the timing once again after the pinch-bolt has been tightened, and reconnect the vacuum advance line after final adjustment is made to check operation of the vacuum advance unit.

Valve Adjustment

Valve clearances for the different MG models can be found in "Tune-Up Specifications." Adjustment procedures for all models are the same. Valve adjustment should be carried out at every engine tune-up or whenever excessive valve train noise is noticed. Loose valve clearance will generally only cause a metallic thrashing sound, while over-tight adjustment can cause rough running and burnt valves.

To adjust the valves, remove the rocker cover and provide a means of turning the engine over slowly. Although the engine may be turned over by hand or with the ignition switch, the best method is connecting an auxiliary starter wire to the solenoid. An auxiliary starter wire can be either a two-position switch with one lead connected to the battery

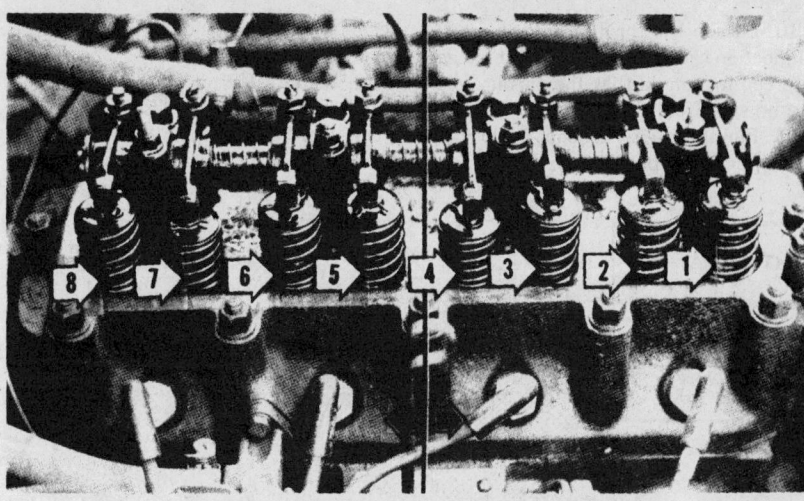

Valves No. 4 and 7 Open, Valves No. 5
and 2 Positioned for Adjustment.

Measuring Valve Lash

cable terminal at the solenoid and the other lead connected to the small gauge wire at the separate solenoid terminal, or simply a short length of wire connected momentarily in the above manner to turn the engine over.

Valve Adjustment Chart

Valve Open	Adjust this Valve
1	8
2	7
3	6
4	5
5	4
6	3
7	2
8	1

Valve rocker clearance adjusting sequence for four cylinder engines.

CAUTION: *Make sure that the transmission is in Neutral before turning the engine over while outside the vehicle.*

In order to adjust an individual valve, it must be in a certain relationship to the camshaft; i.e., it must be on the low side of the camshaft lobe. Because the relationship of one valve to the action of another is known (through camshaft configuration), it is possible to position one of the valves in its fully opened position (valve spring compressed) and thus know that another valve is correctly positioned for adjustment. If a line is drawn at the midpoint of the head separating the valves into two equal groups, then this relationship is symmetrical. In other words, if one of the end valves is open, then the valve at the opposite end can be adjusted; if the second valve in from one end is open, the second valve in from the other end can be adjusted, etc.

When a valve is correctly positioned for adjustment, check the clearance between the valve stem and the rocker arm. If clearance is incorrect, loosen the adjusting screw locknut and turn the screw (clockwise to decrease clearance,

counterclockwise to increase clearance) until the feeler gauge blade slides in and out with some resistance. To double check adjustment, try inserting the next size thinner and next size thicker feeler blade. If, for example, desired clearance is 0.010 in., the 0.009 in. blade should fit quite easily, while the 0.011 or 0.012 in. blade should be too thick to fit. When correct clearance has been obtained, hold the adjusting screw from turning and tighten the locknut. Recheck clearance in case the adjustment screw turned slightly when the locknut was tightened.

When all valves have been adjusted, reinstall the rocker cover. Make sure that the cover gasket is in good condition or an oil leak will develop. Breather hose connections at the rocker cover (if any) should be tight.

Carburetors

Idle Speed and Fuel Mixture, Balancing Dual Carburetors

Before the carburetors are adjusted, there are several preliminary checks that should be made.

HS/HIF Series

1. Start the engine and spray a solvent such as an aerosol-type carburetor cleaner on the carburetor bodies where the throttle spindles pivot. If the engine speed varies, there is an indication of an air leak at those points and adjustments of the carburetor will prove to be futile. The carburetors should be rebuilt and the throttle spindles and bushings replaced if the carburetors are expected to respond to adjustment.

2. On HIF types, unscrew the throttle adjusting screws until they are just clear of the throttle lever, with the throttle closed, then turn the screw clockwise two full turns.

3. Check the carburetor pistons for sticking by lifting them all the way and letting them fall. Their descent should be steady, and a metallic click should be heard when they hit bottom. If there is evidence of sticking, remove and clean the pistons in solvent. Do not lubricate any part of the piston except the rod.

4. HIF only. Lift and support the piston clear of the bridges so that the jet is visible; if not possible because of the position of the carburetor, remove the suction piston chamber.

5. HIF only: turn the jet adjusting screw counterclockwise until the jet is flush with the bridge, or as high as possible without exceeding the bridge height. Be sure that both jets in each carburetor are in the same position.

6. HIF only. Check that the needle guides are flush with the bottom of the piston groove. Turn the jet adjusting screws clockwise two full turns.

7. HIF only. Turn the fast idle adjusting screws counterclockwise until they are clear of the cam. Reinstall the suction piston chamber if it has been removed and check that the pistons fall freely onto the bridge.

8. Check that the piston damper chambers have the proper amount of oil. On carburetors with vented damper caps the level should be ½ in. above the piston rod, and with non-vented caps the level should be ½ in. below the rod.

A dirty air filter will affect the carburetors quite noticeably. If the carburetor adjustment is made with the air filters off, the engine will run badly when they are replaced, unless they are clean. MG uses replaceable paper filter elements.

The carburetor bodies and throttle linkage should be cleaned before adjustments are made. Check the manifold and carburetor nuts for looseness which could cause an air leak.

9. Start the engine and warm it to normal operating temperature.

MG

10. Loosen the throttle linkage interconnection clamps and the choke linkage interconnection so that the carburetors can be synchronized.

11. Run the engine at about 3,000 rpm (HS type) 2,500 rpm (HIF type) for a few seconds to clear it out, and let it drop back to idle.

12. Using a Unisyn ® or other carburetor balance meter, adjust the idle (see "Tune-Up Specifications") via the throttle adjusting screws so that when the correct speed is obtained both carburetors register the same draw on the Unisyn ®.

The carburetors are now synchronized at idle, and must be set also for off-idle operation. Set the throttle interconnec-

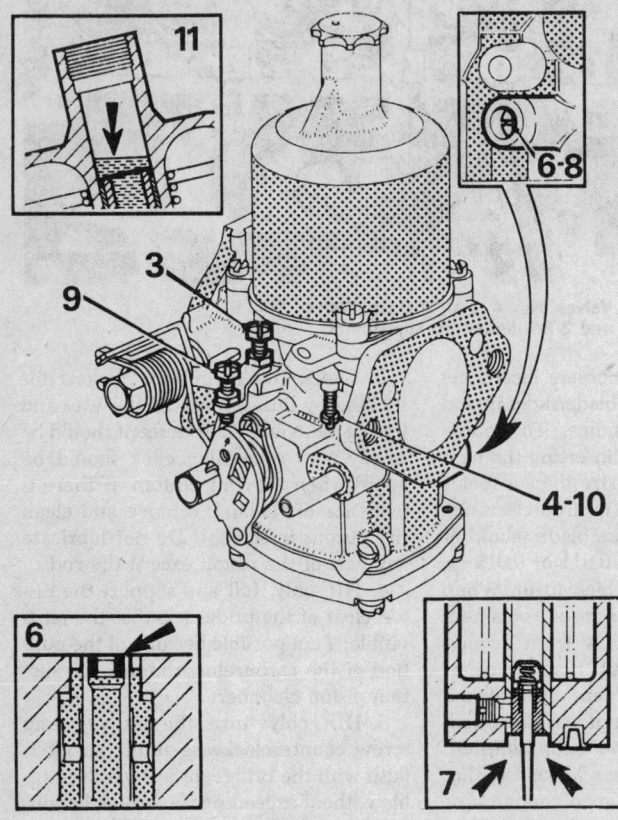

Type HIF carburetor

3. Throttle adjusting screw
9. Fast idle adjusting screw
4-10. Lifting pin
11. Reservoir oil level
6-8. Jet adjusting screw
6. Jet adjusting screw, flush with bridge
7. Needle guide

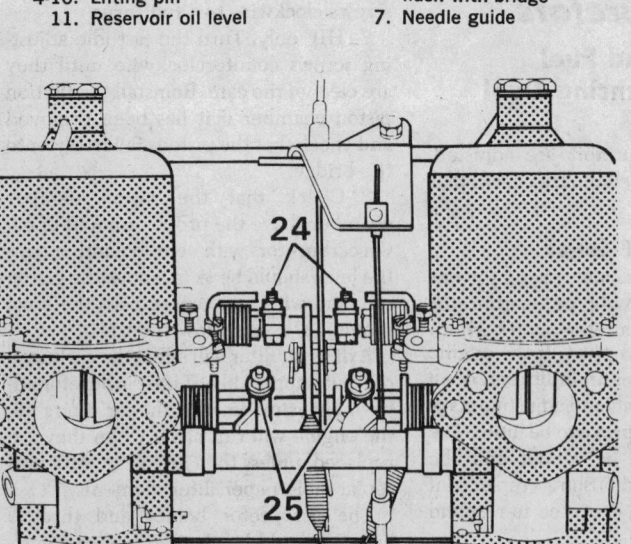

HIF carburetor interconnection screws

24. Throttle spindle interconnection bolts
25. Choke clamping bolts

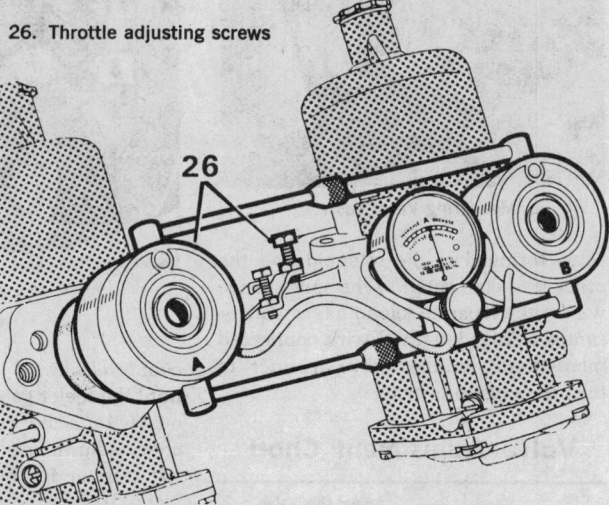

26. Throttle adjusting screws

Balance Meter on HIF carburetors

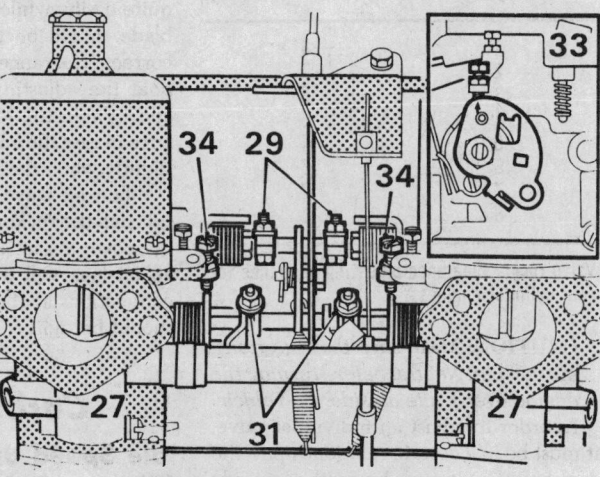

Adjusting screws—HIF carburetor

34. Fast idle adjusting screws
29. Throttle interconnection clamping lever
33. Choke
27. Jet adjusting screw
31. Choke interconnection screws

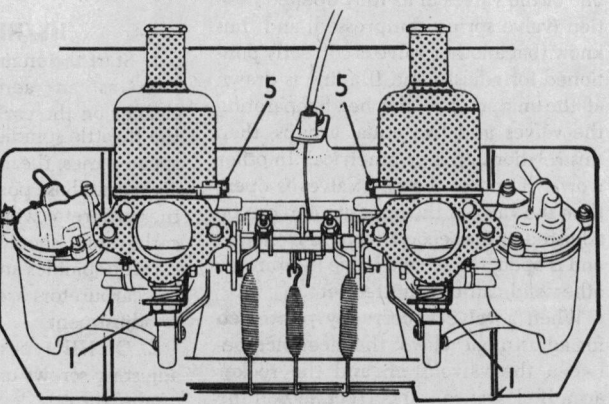

Idle Adjusting Screw (5), Jet Adjusting Nuts (1)

tion clamps so that the link pin is 0.012 in. away from the lower edge of the fork (see illustration), and tighten the clamps. Open the throttles by pulling on the accelerator cable until the engine is just above idle speed, and check carburetor balance at this point with the Unisyn. If there is a balance difference of more than ½ in. on the meter, loosen one of the interconnection clamps and position it so that the carburetor drawing less in the meter will open slightly sooner than the other one. Tighten the clamp and recheck balance. Repeat the operation, if necessary, until balance is satisfactory.

Carburetor mixture strength is adjusted by turning the jet adjusting nut up to lean the mixture and down to richen it. Mixture strength is checked for the individual carburetors by lifting the piston very slightly (about 1/32 in.) and listening for a change in engine speed. If the engine slows down and remains at the lowered speed, the mixture is too lean. If the engine speeds up slightly and then returns to its original idle, the mixture is correct. If the engine speeds up and remains at the higher speed, the mixture is too rich. If jet adjustment is necessary, turn the adjusting nut one flat at a time and pause to check for any change in engine response.

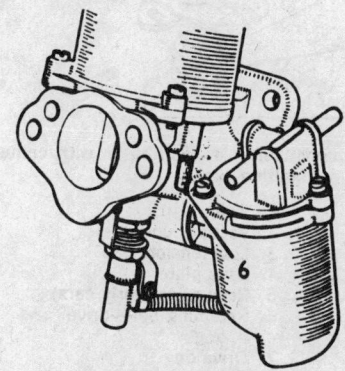

Piston Lifting Pin (6)

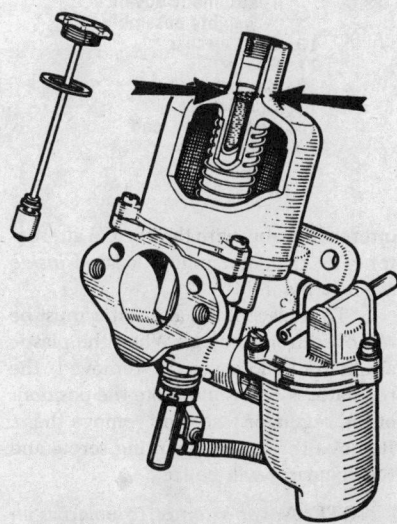

Oil level 1/2 inch below the tube

On Emission Control System carburetors with jet adjusting nut restrictors, it will not be possible to adjust the mixture in the preceding manner because of the limited range of adjustment.

1. Turn the jet adjusting nut on both carburetors over the full range of adjustment, selecting the setting where maximum idle speed is consistent with smoothness. Do not remove or reposition the jet adjusting nut restrictors, as the adjusting range permitted is in the range of minimum exhaust emissions.

2. Altering the mixture strength will have altered the engine speed in either case, and the idle will have to be reset. Both of the throttle screws should be turned an equal amount so that carburetor synchronization will not be upset.

3. With throttle synchronization and mixture strength set, the choke (jet lifting) linkage can be adjusted.

4. Set the linkage interconnection clamps so that both jets are lifted simultaneously.

5. Adjust the choke cable so that when the jets are just beginning to lift, the choke knob is pulled out ¼ in. (HS) or 1/16 in. (HIF)

6. Set the engine idle at 1200 rpm (HS) and 1500 rpm (HIF) with the fast idle screws at this point. The Unisyn® may be used to set up the choke linkage as it was used to balance throttle openings.

If the carburetors will not respond to jet adjustments and the engine cannot be made to idle or respond smoothly, it is probable that jet tube and jet needle wear is excessive and the carburetors should be overhauled.

1975–77 Midget 1500 cc engine

Carburetor Adjustments

There are three permissible adjustments on the CD4 Carburetor attached to the 1975 Midget. These are: Idle speed, fast idle and mixture. After these adjustments have been made, it is necessary that an exhaust gas test be made to ensure that the adjustments have not raised the level of pollution permissible for the car.

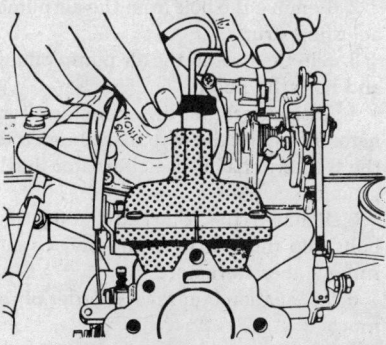

**Carburetor mixture adjustment
1975 Midget**

Idle Speed Adjustment

1. Remove the air cleaner by removing the two bolts.

2. Start the engine and warm it up to normal operating temperature; make sure the choke knob is pushed all the way in.

3. Adjust the engine speed to between 800–850 RPM by turning the idle screw.

Fast Idle Adjustment

1. Remove the air cleaners and start the engine.

2. Pull out the choke knob until the cam is turned at an angle where the cam pivot, cable clamp screw and fast idle screw are in alignment. Adjust the fast idle by turning the fast idle adjusting screw until the engine reaches between 1100–1300 RPM.

3. Push the choke knob back in and check the exhaust gas emissions.

Mixture Adjustment

1. Remove the air cleaner and the carburetor damper.

2. Slowly insert an allen wrench of the proper size into the dashpot until it fits into the hexagon in the needle adjuster plug.

3. Turn the wrench clockwise to richen and counterclockwise to lean the mixture, until a smooth idle is obtained.

4. Check the exhaust gas reading, and readjust if necessary.

5. Add oil to the dashpot if necessary, replace the damper.

6. Recheck the idle speed and replace the air cleaner assembly.

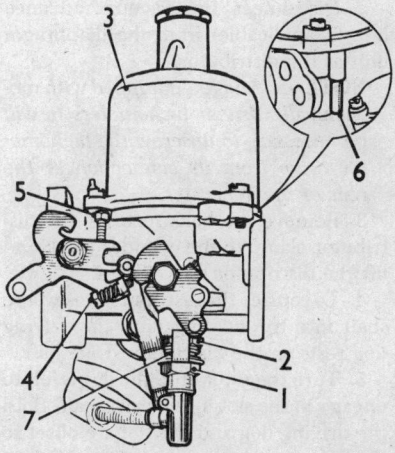

Emission control carburetor adjusting points.

1. Jet adjusting nut
2. Jet assembly locknut
3. Piston-chamber
4. Fast idle adjusting screw (actuated by the choke)
5. Throttle (idle) adjusting screw
6. Piston lifting pin
7. Jet adjustment restrictor (Emission Control System only)

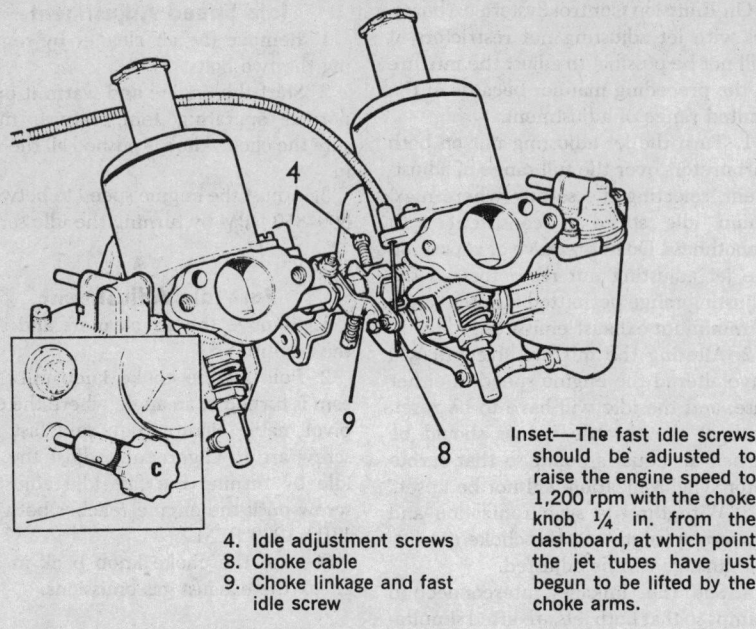

4. Idle adjustment screws
8. Choke cable
9. Choke linkage and fast idle screw

Inset—The fast idle screws should be adjusted to raise the engine speed to 1,200 rpm with the choke knob ¼ in. from the dashboard, at which point the jet tubes have just begun to be lifted by the choke arms.

Idle Adjustment Points

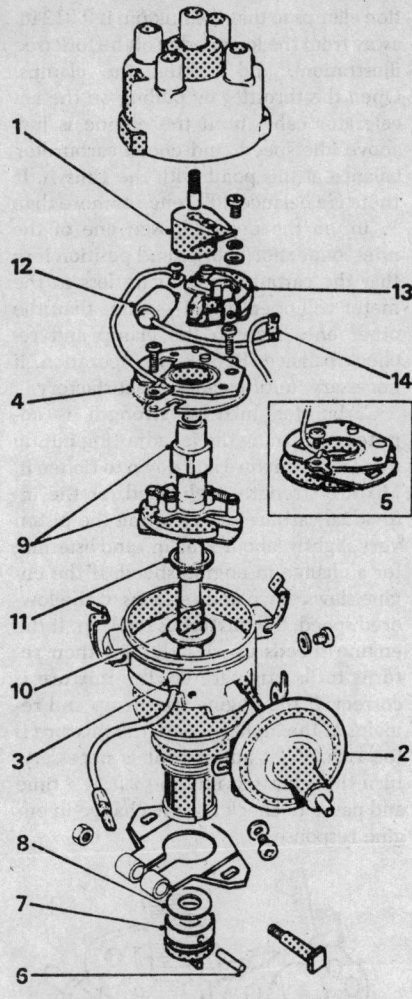

Exploded view of distributor with conventional ignition

1. Rotor arm
2. Vacuum unit
3. Low tension lead
4. Base plate
5. Base plate (early cars)
6. Retaining pin—drive dog
7. Drive dog
8. Thrust washer
9. Cam spindle and automatic advance weights assembly
10. Steel washer
11. Spacer
12. Capacitor
13. Contact set
14. Low tension lead connector

ENGINE ELECTRICAL

Distributor

Removal and Installation

The distributor can be removed and replaced without disturbing the ignition timing, provided the pinch-bolt on the clamp that positions the distributor is not loosened.

1. Remove the distributor cap and disconnect the low tension lead from the terminal on the distributor.

2. Disconnect the vacuum advance line (if applicable) from the diaphragm unit at the distributor.

NOTE: *On Midgets equipped with mechanically driven tachometers it will be necessary to unscrew the tachometer drive from its connection at the rear of the generator.*

3. Remove the bolts securing the distributor clamp to the cylinder block and lift the distributor out.

4. To replace the distributor, insert the shaft into the housing until the driving dog rests on the distributor driveshaft.

5. Turn the rotor until the dog is felt to engage in the slot in the driveshaft. Both the driving dog and the slot are offset so that the distributor will not fall into place until it is properly positioned.

6. Turn the distributor body to align the clamp and housing bolt holes and replace the bolts.

7. Replace the distributor cap, the vacuum advance line, the low tension lead from the coil, and reconnect the tachometer drive to the generator (if applicable).

Alternator

Alternator Precautions

1. Do not run the engine with the batteries out of the circuit or any of the charging circuits wires disconnected (except as given in test procedures). All charging circuit electrical connections must be clean and tight, and the drive belt properly adjusted.

2. Correct battery and alternator polarity (negative ground) must be maintained or the alternator will be destroyed. If arc welding equipment is used on the car the alternator and regulator leads must be disconnected.

Alternator and Regulator

Removal and Installation

16ACR Alternators

To remove the alternator disconnect the hoses from the air pump outlets.

1. Loosen the air pump mounting bolt.

2. Remove the bolt from the air pump adjusting strut.

3. Slip the belt off the air pump pulley and raise the pump.

4. Disconnect the wires from the alternator (do not let the wire that connects to the B+ terminal on the alternator touch ground).

5. Remove the alternator mounting bolts, slip the belt from the pulley, and remove the alternator.

6. Installation is in reverse order of removal.

8TR, and 11TR Regulators

The 8TR and 11TR regulators are used interchangeably with the 16ACR alternator. The regulator unit is located *inside the alternator.*

1. To replace it the alternator must be removed from the car. When the plastic alternator end-cover is removed the regulator is accessible. Note the positions of the regulator leads and remove them. Remove the lower mounting screw and the regulator will be free.

NOTE: *Never attempt to polarize an alternator or alternator regulator.*

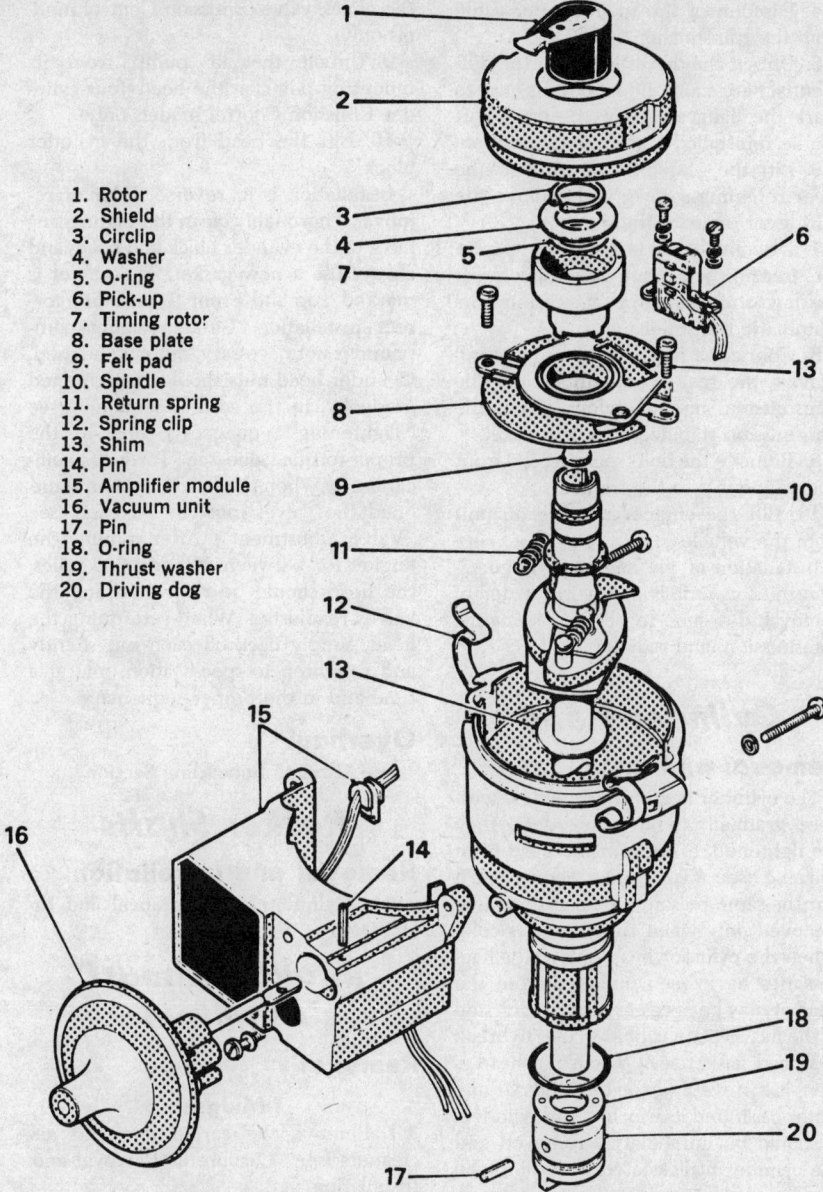

1. Rotor
2. Shield
3. Circlip
4. Washer
5. O-ring
6. Pick-up
7. Timing rotor
8. Base plate
9. Felt pad
10. Spindle
11. Return spring
12. Spring clip
13. Shim
14. Pin
15. Amplifier module
16. Vacuum unit
17. Pin
18. O-ring
19. Thrust washer
20. Driving dog

Exploded view of distributor with electronic ignition

ENGINE MECHANICAL
Engine Removal and Installation

MG Midget

The engine of the Midget can be removed with or without the transmission. Either way, the preliminary steps are:

1. Drain the crankcase.

2. Disconnect the battery.

3. Remove the hood.

4. Disconnect the radiator and heater hoses and oil cooler lines (late models only), and remove the radiator.

5. Disconnect the choke and throttle cables and tachometer cable.

6. Disconnect the oil pressure gauge pipe from the engine.

7. Disconnect and tag all electrical connections to the engine.

8. Disconnect the high tension wires from the coil and spark plugs, and remove the distributor cap.

9. Unbolt the exhaust header pipe from the manifold and tie the pipe out of the way.

10. Remove the air cleaners and disconnect the fuel line.

At this point, the engine can be removed either with or without the transmission. If it is desired to remove only the engine:

1. Remove the starter motor.

2. Remove the fuel filter bowl (only).

3. Support the transmission with a jack, and remove the bell housing bolts.

4. Connect a hoist to the engine and unbolt the right-side engine mount from the chassis bracket.

5. Disconnect the left-side engine mount from the front engine plate and lift the engine from the vehicle, taking care not to damage the transmission mainshaft.

If it is desired to remove the engine and the transmission as a unit:

1. Drain the transmission oil and disconnect the back-up light switch lead (later models only).

2. Remove the gearshift lever cover, and remove the spring cap, spring, and plunger.

3. Unbolt the shift lever retaining plate and lift out the lever.

4. With the carpet turned back, remove the rear transmission mount bolts.

5. From underneath the car, unscrew the speedometer cable from the transmission housing and release the cable support bracket from the bell housing.

6. Unbolt the clutch slave cylinder from the bell housing.

7. Unbolt the driveshaft from the diff-

Starter

Removal and Installation

1. Disconnect the battery. Remove the distributor (MGB and Midget only).

2. On the Midget, remove the skid plate. Remove the top starter bolt.

3. Disconnect and tag the starter wires.

4. Remove the lower starter bolt and remove the starter.

5. Installation is the reverse of removal.

Starter Drive Replacement

1. Disconnect the cable from the terminal on the solenoid marked "STA".

2. Remove the solenoid attaching nuts.

3. Remove the solenoid from the starter case and disengage it from the drive lever.

4. Remove the brush cover and remove the brushes.

5. Remove the through-bolts from the end bracket.

6. Remove the lever pivot pin from the drive gear.

7. Separate the drive end bracket from the yoke and remove the drive gear engagement lever.

8. Remove the armature and separate the commutator plate from the yoke.

9. Remove the thrust washers from the shaft.

10. Remove the drive gear. Reverse the procedure to install.

erential flange and slide it out. Be sure to mark the flanges so that the driveshaft can be reinstalled correctly.

8. Connect a hoist to the engine and remove the remaining transmission mounting bolts.

9. Unbolt the right-side engine mount from the chassis bracket and disconnect the left-side mount from the front engine plate.

10. Lift the engine/transmission unit from the vehicle.

Installation of the engine or engine/-transmission unit is in reverse order of removal. Be sure to refill the engine, transmission, and radiator.

MGB

The engine of the MGB can be removed with or without the transmission, but it is recommended that the engine/transmission be removed as a unit. This will avoid possible damage to the clutch when separating and installing the transmission.

Either way, the preliminary steps are:
1. Drain the crankcase.
2. Disconnect the batteries.
3. Remove the hood.
4. Disconnect the oil cooler and pressure gauge lines from the engine.
5. Disconnect the heater and radiator hoses, and unbolt and remove the radiator, radiator shroud, and oil cooler as a unit.
6. Disconnect and tag all electrical connections to the engine.
7. Disconnect the high tension leads from the coil and spark plugs, and remove the distributor cap.
8. Disconnect the choke and throttle cables and the tachometer cable (early models only).
9. Unbolt the exhaust header pipe from the manifold, and disconnect the bell housing bracket.
10. Remove the air cleaners and disconnect the fuel line.

At this point, the engine can be removed either with or without the transmission. If it is desired to remove only the engine:
1. Support the transmission with a jack, and remove the bell housing bolts.
2. Remove the bolts holding the front engine mounts to the frame.
3. Connect a hoist to the engine and lift it from the chassis, taking care not to damage the transmission mainshaft or the oil pan.

If it is desired to remove the engine and transmission as a unit:
1. Drain the transmission oil and disconnect the back-up light switch lead (later models only).
2. Disconnect the overdrive solenoid wire.
3. Unbolt the clutch slave cylinder from the bell housing.

4. Disconnect the speedometer cable from the transmission.
5. Unbolt the driveshaft from the differential flange and slide it out. Be sure to mark the flanges so that the driveshaft can be reinstalled in its original position.
6. Lift the gearshift boot, unbolt the lever retaining screws, and remove the shift lever (manual transmission).
7. Disconnect the gearshift lever from the transmission shaft, and disconnect the downshift cable from the carburetors (automatic transmission).
8. Connect a hoist to the engine and remove the rear crossmember and the transmission mounts, along with the transmission stabilizer rod or bracket.
9. Remove the bolts securing the front engine mounts to the frame.
10. Lift the engine/transmission unit from the vehicle.

Installation of the engine or engine/-transmission unit is in reverse order of removal. Be sure to refill the engine, transmission, and radiator.

Cylinder Head

Removal and Installation

The cylinder head nuts should be loosened, gradually, in the same order as they are tightened, to prevent the head from warping (see "Tightening Sequences"). For the same reason, the head should be removed only when the engine is cold. When the cylinder head nuts and all accessories have been unbolted from the head, it may be necessary to tap each side of the head with a rubber mallet to break the head gasket seal. When the head is free, lift it evenly over the studs. If any water has found its way into the cylinders it should be immediately removed and the cylinder walls coated with oil. If the head is not to be reinstalled for a day or more, it is a good idea to stuff towels into the cylinders to protect them.

The cylinder head removal procedure for all models is as follows:
1. Drain the radiator.
2. Disconnect the radiator and heater hoses from the cylinder head.
3. Remove the heater control valve and unbolt the top radiator bracket.
4. Remove the carburetors and air cleaners, and unbolt the manifolds and pull them back out of the way.
5. Remove the rocker cover and remove the cylinder head nuts in the proper order (see "Tightening Sequences").
6. Lift the rocker shaft assembly off and remove the pushrods, keeping them in order.
7. Remove the spark plugs and disconnect the water temperature sending unit from the head.
8. Disconnect the air supply hose from

the check valve (Emission Control models only).
9. Unbolt the air pump from its mounting point on the head (four-cylinder Emission Control models only).
10. Lift the head from the cylinder block.

Installation is in reverse order of removal. Thoroughly clean the mating surfaces of the cylinder block and head, and always use a new gasket. The gasket is marked Top and Front to facilitate correct installation. Gasket sealing compound is not necessary, but may be used. Cylinder head nuts should be tightened gradually, in the correct sequence (see "Tightening Sequences"), and to the proper torque value (see "Torque Specifications"). When the head has been tightened the valves must be adjusted (see "Valve Adjustment"). After running the engine for between 200 and 500 miles, the head should be retorqued and the valves readjusted. When retorquing the head, simply back off each nut slightly and retighten to specification, one at a time and in the proper sequence.

Overhaul

See "Engine Rebuilding Section".

Rocker Shafts

Removal and Installation

See Cylinder Head Removal and Installation

Intake/Exhaust Manifold

Removal

Midget

1. Remove the carburetors and air cleaners (see "Carburetor Removal and Installation").
2. Unbolt the exhaust pipe from the exhaust manifold.
3. Unbolt the heater pipe clamps from the intake manifold.
4. Unscrew the PCV valve hose from the manifold connection (if applicable).
5. Disconnect the vacuum advance and gulp valve lines from the intake manifold (if applicable).
6. Unbolt and remove the manifolds.

MGB

1. Remove the carburetors and air cleaners (see "Carburetor Removal and Installation").
2. Disconnect the distributor vacuum advance line and the gulp valve line (if applicable).
3. Unscrew the PCV valve hose from the intake manifold connection (if applicable).
4. Unbolt the exhaust header pipes from the exhaust manifold.
5. Unbolt and remove the manifolds.

Installation—All Models

Manifold installation in all cases is in reverse order of removal.

1. Thoroughly clean the mating surfaces and use new gaskets. The perforated metal face of the gasket should face the manifold.

2. New exhaust header ring gaskets should be used on the MGB, and Midget models. It may be necessary to use a new exhaust pipe clamp on the early Midget. Be sure to tighten the manifold studs evenly (see "Torque Specifications").

Timing Gear Cover and Oil Seal

Removal and Installation

MG Midget

To remove the timing gear cover:
1. Remove the radiator.
2. Loosen the generator adjustment bolts and remove the fan belt.

NOTE: *On 1968 and later Midgets it is necessary to unbolt the engine mounts and exhaust pipe in order to raise the front of the engine to provide clearance for removal of the pulley.*

3. Bend the locktab back and unscrew the crankshaft pulley nut.
4. Carefully pry the pulley from the crankshaft.
5. Unbolt and remove the timing gear cover.

To replace the timing gear cover oil seal:
1. Pry the old seal out of the cover.
2. Lubricate the new seal and install it evenly into the cover in the same position as the old one, taking care not to damage it.
3. If the seal is made of rubber, fill the groove between the seal lips with grease. Felt seals do not need to be lubricated in this manner.
4. Make sure that the oil thrower behind the crankshaft pulley is installed with the face marked F away from the engine.

The cover and pulley are installed together to ensure that the oil seal is centered correctly. To reinstall:
1. Lubricate the hub of the pulley and insert it into the oil seal, turning the pulley in a clockwise direction to avoid damaging the seal.
2. Align the pulley keyway with the crankshaft key and push the pulley (with the cover and cover gasket) onto the crankshaft.
3. Replace the cover bolts and tighten them evenly.
4. Tighten and lock the crankshaft pulley nut.
5. Reinstall the fan belt, and replace and fill the radiator.

MGB

Timing gear cover removal and installation and oil seal replacement procedures for the MGB are the same as for the Midget, with one exception: on 18GB and later engines, the steering rack must be unbolted from the body and moved forward to provide clearance for removal of the crankshaft pulley. It is not necessary to raise the front of the engine to remove the pulley on the MGB.

Timing Gear and Chain

Removal and Installation

The camshafts in all MG engines are driven by a chain from the crankshaft. The Midget models up to and including 1974, have an endless, single-row timing chain without a tensioner, while the MGB has an endless, duplex chain and a chain tensioner. Chain tensioner removal and service procedures can be found under "Timing Chain Tensioner Service—MGB."

The crankshaft and camshaft timing gears and the timing chain usually do not require service or replacement unless, due to high mileage or improper lubrication, gear tooth wear is noticeable. If wear is evident, replace all three components. Worn gears or chain stretch as isolated problems almost never occur.

MGB and Pre-1975 Midget

1. To remove the chain and gears, first remove the timing gear cover (see preceding section). On the MGB, remove the chain tensioner or retract and lock the rubbing block by removing the plug from the tensioner body and turning the adjusting bolt clockwise (see following section).

2. Bend the locktab back and remove the camshaft timing gear nut. The camshaft and crankshaft timing gears may now be removed together with the chain by easing the gears off the shafts simultaneously, using a puller or suitable levers.

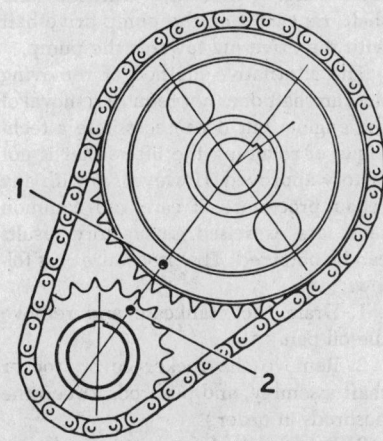

Timing Gear Marks—Midget, MGB

3. When replacing the timing chain and gears, set the crankshaft with its keyway at twelve o'clock and the camshaft with its keyway at one o'clock as seen from the front. The washers behind the crankshaft gear are spacers to align the two gears properly.

4. When reassembling, the same number of washers should be installed as were removed *unless* any of the following components have been replaced: crankshaft, crankshaft main bearings and thrust washers, crankshaft timing gear, camshaft, camshaft timing gear, or camshaft locating plate. If any of the above components have been replaced, timing gear alignment can be checked and adjusted by placing a straightedge across the gear sides and adding or subtracting washers to eliminate any gaps between the gear side surfaces and the straightedge (after the gears have been installed).

5. To install the timing gears and chain, assemble the chain onto the gears with the gear marks facing each other so that a line drawn through them would pass through the camshaft and crankshaft axes. Keeping the gears in this position, start the crankshaft gear onto the crankshaft (with the gear keyway and crankshaft key aligned).

6. Install the camshaft gear onto the camshaft, turning the camshaft to align the key with the keyway if necessary.

7. Make a final check of alignment of the timing gears and gear marks, and install the camshaft gear lockwasher and nut. Replace the timing cover.

1975–77 Midget 1500 cc

Removal and Installation

1. Remove the timing gear cover as outlined in the applicable "Timing Gear Cover Removal and Installation" procedure.

2. Remove the oil thrower.

3. Check timing chain wear by placing a straightedge along the slack length of chain. If the free-play between the straightedge and the chain at a point midway between the two sprockets exceeds 0.4 in., the chain must be discarded and replaced.

4. Rotate the crankshaft until the crankshaft key is at 12 o'clock and the sprocket dots align.

5. Pry back the locking tabs and remove the bolts which retain the camshaft sprocket to the camshaft.

6. Taking care not to disturb the crankshaft or camshaft, remove both sprockets with the timing chain.

7. To check alignment of the sprockets, remove the crankshaft drive key and temporarily install both sprockets. Place a straightedge across the teeth of both

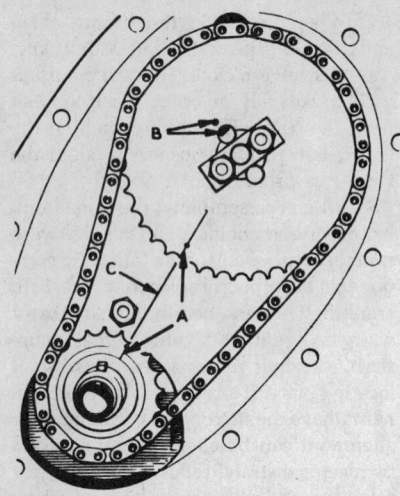

Position of timing marks on sprockets Midget

sprockets. Correct any misalignment by placing shims behind the crankshaft sprocket.

8. After checking the alignment, remove the sprockets, install the crankshaft drive key, and place the sprocket and chain assembly into position, aligned dot to dot, and install the camshaft sprocket retaining bolts using a new lockplate.

9. Install the oil thrower.

10. Install the timing gear cover as outlined in the applicable "Timing Gear Cover Removal and Installation" procedure.

Timing Chain Tensioner

Removal Installation, and Adjustment

1. To remove the tensioner (after the timing gear cover has been removed), first unscrew the plug from the tensioner body. Using a ⅛ in. Allen wrench, turn the tension adjusting bolt clockwise until the rubbing block is fully retracted and locked behind the limit peg.

2. Unbolt and remove the tensioner and its backing plate.

3. Withdraw the rubbing block and plunger from the tensioner body, and turn the tension adjusting bolt clockwise until the piston and spring are released.

4. Clean the components in solvent and blow out the oil passages with compressed air.

5. Check the bore of the tensioner body for ovality. If the diameter of the bore at or near the mouth varies more than 0.003 in., the complete tensioner unit should be replaced. If within the limit given, it is acceptable to replace just the rubbing block.

6. To reassemble the tensioner, insert

the spring and piston into the bore and compress the spring.

7. Turn the piston clockwise until the inner end is below the peg. Install the rubbing block plunger into the bore.
CAUTION: *Do not attempt to turn the tension adjusting bolt counterclockwise.*

8. Bolt the backing plate and tensioner onto the cylinder block and lock the mounting bolts with the locktab.

9. Release the rubbing block for operation by turning the adjusting bolt clockwise until the block contacts the chain under spring pressure.

10. Check the rubbing block for freedom of movement and make sure that it does not bind against the backing plate.

11. Replace and lock the plug in the tensioner body.

Camshaft

Removal

Midget Mk. III

The 1,275 cc. engine does not have lifter covers on the side of the cylinder block; therefore, some method of holding the lifters all the way up in their bores must be employed so that the camshaft can be withdrawn without the cam lobes hanging up on them. There are two ways to accomplish this. The factory recommended method is to:

1. Drain the crankcase and remove the engine.

2. Remove the rocker cover and unbolt and remove the rocker shaft assembly and pushrods (keeping the pushrods in order).

3. Remove the timing cover and gears.

4. Remove the oil pan.

5. Remove the distributor.

6. Remove the camshaft locating plate.

7. Invert the engine to allow the lifters to fall into their bores.

8. Withdraw the camshaft, rotating it slowly to assist removal. If the oil pump drive flange comes away with the camshaft, replace it on the pump driveshaft with the drive lug towards the pump.

The alternative method of removing the camshaft does not require removal of the engine, but does necessitate a technique of retaining the lifters that is not factory approved. However, as with any repair procedure, if care and common sense are exercised, satisfactory results can be obtained. The procedure is as follows:

1. Drain the crankcase and remove the oil pan.

2. Remove the rocker cover, rocker shaft assembly, and pushrods. (Keep the pushrods in order.)

3. Remove the timing cover and camshaft gear.

4. Remove the distributor.

5. Remove the camshaft locating plate.

6. From underneath the car, coat the lifters with a thick lubricant such as a petroleum base grease and push them up into their bores. They should remain in this position long enough to remove and replace the camshaft.

7. Withdraw the camshaft while rotating it slowly. If the oil pump drive flange comes out with the cam, replace it on the pump driveshaft with the drive lug toward the pump.
NOTE: *Removal procedures for individual units such as the timing gear cover can be found under appropriate subheads in the "Engine" section.*

MGB and 1975–77 Midget

Removal of the camshaft from the MGB can be accomplished without removing the engine from the chassis. The following procedure can, however, be used whether the engine is in or out of the car.

1. Drain the crankcase and remove the oil pan from the engine.

2. Remove the rocker cover from the head and unbolt and remove the rocker shaft assembly and pushrods, keeping pushrods in order.

3. Remove the intake and exhaust manifolds.

4. Remove the lifter covers from the side of the cylinder block.

5. Remove the lifters, and, as with the pushrods, keep them in order.

6. Remove the timing cover and gears.

7. Remove the oil pump.

8. Remove the distributor.

9. Remove the camshaft locating plate.

10. Pull the camshaft from the front of the engine, rotating it slowly to assist removal.
NOTE: *Removal procedures for individual units such as the oil pump, timing gear cover, etc. can be found under appropriate subheads in the "Engine" section.*

Installation

All Models

Camshaft installation in all cases is in reverse order of removal. Camshaft bearings, except in cases of insufficient lubrication, almost never need replacement. Clearance can be checked with a feeler gauge. Replacement of bearings requires special pullers and machine tools (for align-boring) and should be left to a machine shop.

Camshaft end-play can be checked before installation by assembling the locating plate and timing gear onto the camshaft and measuring fore and aft play. If it exceeds specification, the locating plate should be replaced.

Camshaft Specifications
(in.)

Model	End Play	Oil Clearance
Midget	0.003-0.007	0.001-0.002
PE94J	0.0045-0.0085	0.0016-0.0036
MGB	0.003-0.007	0.001-0.002

NOTE: Valve lift for the different engine models can be found under VALVE SPECIFICATIONS. Intake valve opening timing (deg. BTDC) can be found under TUNE-UP SPECIFICATIONS.

Pistons and Connecting Rods

NOTE: *On engines with floating or press-fit type wrist pins, the pistons are select-fitted to the bores, and the piston crowns and cylinders are marked with identification numbers.*

Piston and connecting rod installation position for all models is indicated in the accompanying illustrations. Unmarked pistons must be identified with regard to cylinder and installation position prior to removal so that they may be reinstalled in the same position. Select-fitted pistons are identified by a number enclosed in a diamond stamped on the piston crown and block. Oversize dimensions are stamped on the piston crown, enclosed in some cases in an ellipse.

Oversize Piston Markings

ENGINE LUBRICATION
Oil Pan

Removal and Installation

Midget

1. Drain the oil and unbolt and lower the oil pan.

2. Always replace the two pan gaskets and the two main bearing cork seals when the pan has been removed. It may be necessary to soak the cork seals in hot water to keep them from breaking when installing them.

MGB

1. Drain the oil. Drain the radiator and disconnect the hoses.

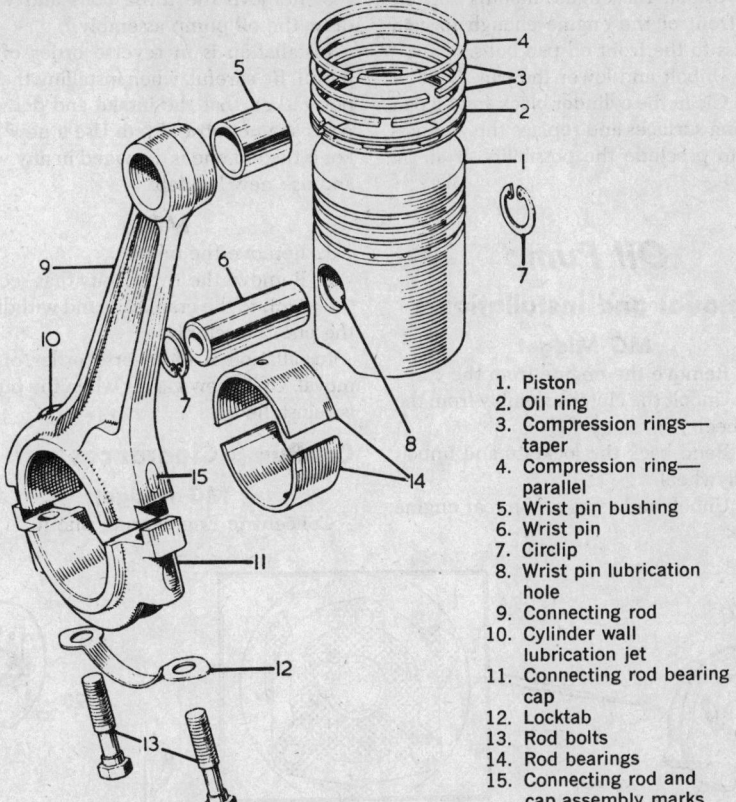

1. Piston
2. Oil ring
3. Compression rings—taper
4. Compression ring—parallel
5. Wrist pin bushing
6. Wrist pin
7. Circlip
8. Wrist pin lubrication hole
9. Connecting rod
10. Cylinder wall lubrication jet
11. Connecting rod bearing cap
12. Locktab
13. Rod bolts
14. Rod bearings
15. Connecting rod and cap assembly marks

Piston and Connecting Rod Components

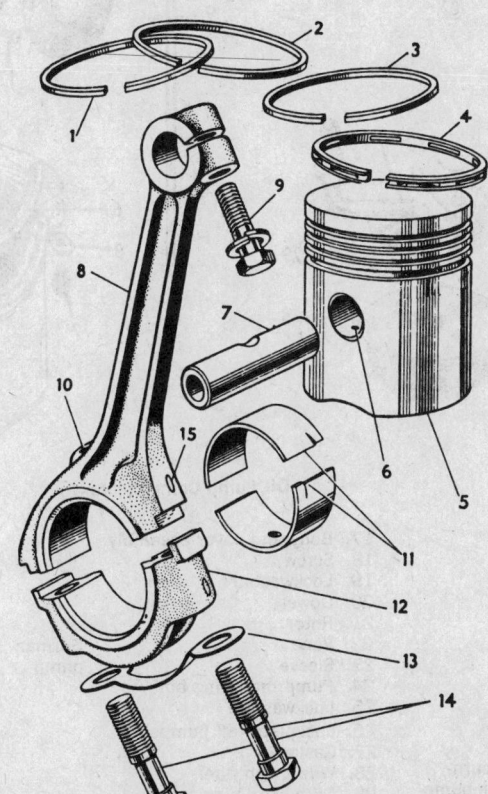

1. Piston ring—parallel
2. Piston ring—taper
3. Piston ring—taper
4. Piston ring—scraper
5. Piston
6. Piston pin lubricating hole
7. Piston pin
8. Connecting rod
9. Clamping screw and washer
10. Cylinder wall lubricating jet
11. Connecting rod bearings
12. Connecting rod cap
13. Lock washer
14. Bolts
15. Connecting rod and cap marking

Piston and Connecting Rod Components— Midget.

2. Unbolt the engine mounts and lift the front of the engine enough to gain access to the front oil pan bolts.

3. Unbolt and lower the pan.

4. Clean the cylinder block and oil pan mating surfaces and replace the pan gasket to preclude the possibility of an oil leak.

Oil Pump

Removal and Installation

MG Midget

1. Remove the engine from the car.
2. Unbolt the clutch assembly from the flywheel.
3. Bend back the locktabs and unbolt the flywheel.
4. Unbolt and remove the rear engine plate.

5. Remove the three bolts and withdraw the oil pump assembly.

Installation is in reverse order of removal. Be careful, when installing the paper gasket, that the intake and delivery ports are not obstructed. Use a new gasket if the old one is damaged in any way, and use new locktabs.

MGB

1. Remove the oil pan.
2. Remove the three nuts that secure the pump to the crankcase and withdraw the pump assembly.

Installation is in reverse order of removal. Use a new gasket when the pump is reinstalled.

Oil Pump Clearances

MG Midget

Concentric Engineering pump:

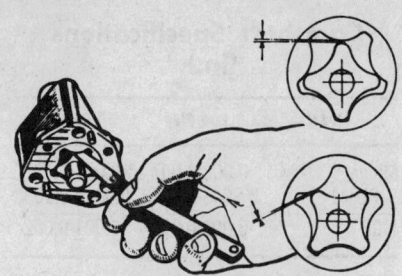

Oil Pump Rotor Position

The concentric pump is replaceable as a unit only; parts are not available.

Burman pump:

1. Remove the pump cover and withdraw the rotor and vane assembly. Remove the sleeve from the end of the rotor and remove the vanes.
2. Replace any worn or galled parts.

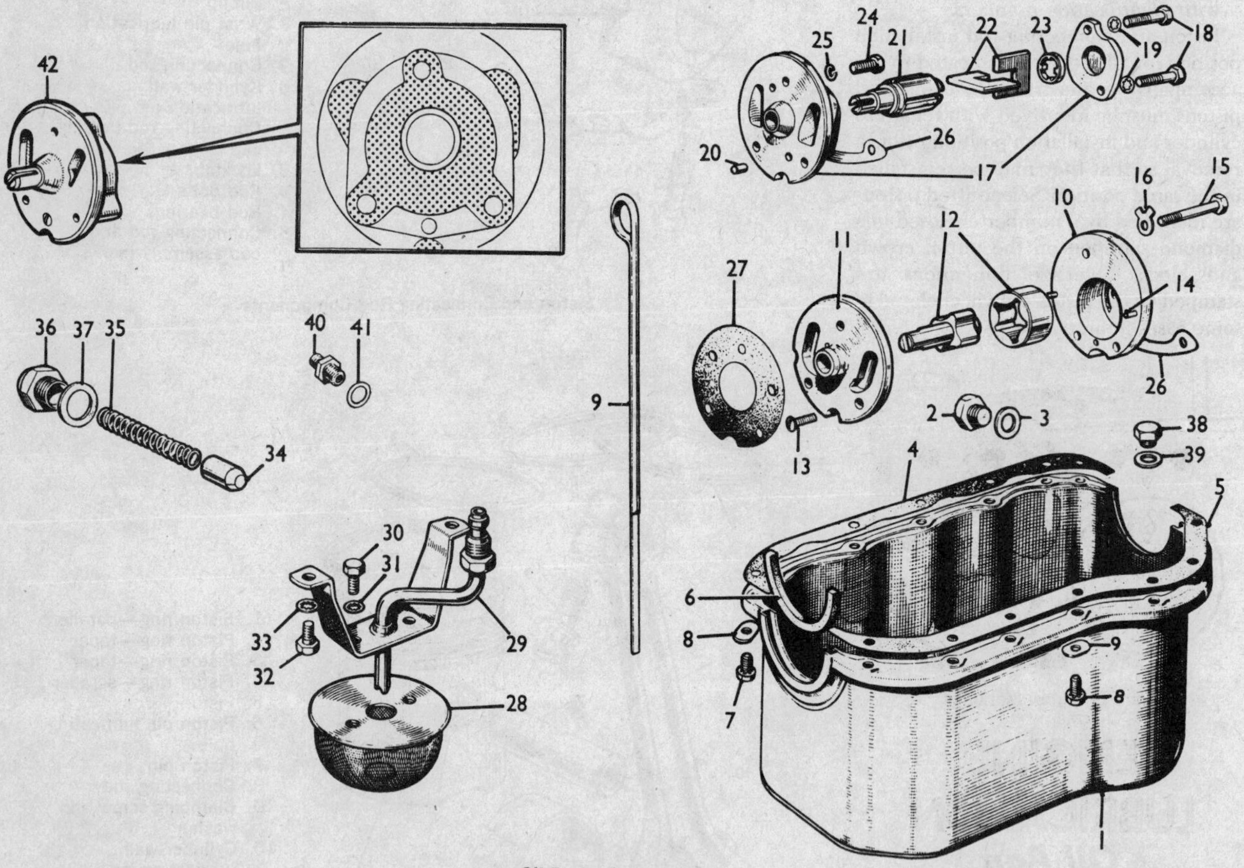

Oil Pump Components

1. Oil pan
2. Drain plug
3. Washer
4. Oil pan gasket
5. Oil pan gasket
6. Main bearing cork seal
7. Oil pan bolt
8. Washer
9. Dip stick
10. Oil pump body
11. Cover
12. Inner and outer rotors — Hobourn-Eaton pump
13. Cover screws
14. Dowel
15. Pump mounting bolt
16. Lockwasher

17. Body and cover assembly
18. Screw
19. Lockwasher
20. Dowel
21. Rotor
22. Vane — Burman pump
23. Sleeve
24. Pump mounting bolt
25. Lockwasher
26. Lockplate (all pumps)
27. Gasket
28. Wire mesh filter
29. Oil pickup pipe
30. Screw
31. Lockwasher
32. Screw

33. Lockwasher
34. Oil relief valve
35. Spring
36. Cap-nut
37. Washer
38. Oil priming plug
39. Copper washer
40. Oil pressure feed connection
41. Fiber washer
42. Pump assembly—Concentric Engineering type

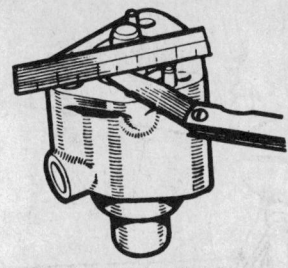

Checking Rotor End Play

3. Coat all parts with motor oil before assembly.

Hobourn-Eaton pump:

4. Remove the pump cover and lift out the inner and outer rotors.

5. Check clearance between the outer rotor and the pump body. If the clearance exceeds 0.010 in., the complete pump assembly should be renewed.

6. Check clearance between the rotor lobes.

7. Replace the rotors if clearance exceeds 0.006 in.

8. Check the rotor end float. If the clearance exceeds 0.005 in., remove the dowels from the pump body mating surface and mill or lap the surface until clearance is within specification.

9. Coat all parts with fresh motor oil before assembling. Install the outer rotor in the pump body with the beveled end at the drive end of the pump body.

10. Check the pump for freedom of movement after assembly.

MGB

MGB oil pump service procedures are identical to those of the Hobourn-Eaton pump on the Midget.

Oil Cooler

Removal and Installation

On all models equipped with oil coolers, disconnect the oil cooler pipes from the oil filter, cylinder block, and oil cooler connections. Next, remove the oil cooler attaching bolts and remove the cooler. Withdraw the oil cooler pipes from the radiator diaphragm grommets. When replacing, start the line fittings onto the connections by hand to avoid crossing the threads. Tighten the fittings, check the engine oil, and start the engine. Let the engine idle until the oil pressure is developed, and check the oil lines for leaks. Shut off engine and recheck oil level.

ENGINE COOLING
Radiator

Removal and Installation
MG Midget

1. Drain the cooling system by opening the radiator tap.

2. Remove the radiator grille.

3. Disconnect the upper and lower hoses from the radiator.

4. Remove the nuts securing the top and bottom radiator cowl plates to the body.

5. Disconnect the oil cooler lines on cars so equipped.

6. Remove the radiator retaining bolts and lift the radiator out (complete with shroud, Mk. III).

7. Installation is in reverse order of removal.

MGB

1. Open the radiator tap and drain the coolant.

2. Disconnect the upper and lower radiator hoses.

3. If the car is not equipped with an oil cooler, remove the shroud bolts and remove the radiator and shroud as an assembly.

4. If the car has an oil cooler, loosen the shroud mounting bolts, remove the overflow hose clamp, and remove the radiator-to-shroud bolts. Withdraw the radiator from the shroud.

5. Installation is in reverse order of removal.

Water Pump

MG Midget—Removal

1. Remove the radiator.
2. Remove the fan retaining bolts and remove the fan.
3. Loosen the air pump mounting bolts, remove the adjusting strut bolt, remove the belt and swivel and pump up out of the way (Emission Control models only).
4. Loosen the generator mounting bolts, remove the belt, remove the top mounting bolts and lower the generator out of the way.
5. Disconnect the by-pass hose and lower radiator hose from the water pump.
6. Remove the water pump mounting bolts and remove the pump.

MGB—Removal

1. Remove the radiator.
2. Remove the generator or alternator.
3. Remove the fan and pulley retaining bolts and remove the fan.
4. Remove the water pump mounting bolts and remove the pump.

All Models—Installation

Installation in all cases is a reversal of removal procedures. Make sure that the mating surface of the cylinder block is cleaned of pieces of the old gasket that may remain. Always use a new gasket, and torque the mounting bolts evenly.

Thermostat
Removal and Installation

The thermostat on all MGs is located in the aluminum housing, bolted to the cylinder head, that connects to the upper radiator hose.

1. Replacement involves simply unbolting the housing and lifting out the thermostat.

2. Before unbolting the housing, drain (and save) about half of the coolant from the radiator to prevent loss when the housing is removed. Thermostats of three different opening temperatures are available: 160° F., 180° F., and 190° F. The 180° thermostat is suitable for all around use in most climates, while the 160° and 190° thermostats can be used in very hot or cold weather, respectively.

3. The thermostat should always be installed with the bellows or spring facing downward toward the block.

4. Use a new gasket between the thermostat housing and the cylinder head. If the gasket is made of cork, as some replacements are, be careful not to overtighten the housing nuts or the cork will be completely crushed out and will not seal.

NOTE: *Never remove the thermostat in an attempt to cure overheating, as this may cause a blown head gasket, burnt valves, etc. due to localized overheating. Instead, install a restricting washer or a gutted thermostat body.*

EMISSION CONTROLS
Emission Control Applications

Model/ Year	Engine Code	Emission Control System Type
Midget		
1972-74	12CJ①	EAI/ELC
1972-74	12V	EAI/ELC/NOx
1975-76	PE94J	EAI/ELC/EGR/CC
MGB		
1972-74	18V	EAI/ELC/NOx
1975-76	18V	EAI/ELC/EGR/CC

EAI Exhaust Air Injection.
ELC Evaporative Loss Control.
NOx Nitrogen Oxide Control.
CC Catalytic converter
① Some 12CJ engines also incorporate the NOx modifications.

NOTE: Models equipped with the Evaporative Loss Control system are provided with a crankcase ventilation system integral with the ELC. The only service required is to replace the oil filler cap at 12,000 mile intervals.

Positive Crankcase Ventilation

The PCV system prevents crankcase

fumes from venting to the atmosphere by routing them back to the intake manifold and reburning them in the combustion chambers. A non-operational PCV system can cause sludge formations and overheating. The only components in the system are the PCV valve and one-way breather type oil filler cap. To test the efficiency of the valve, remove the oil filler cap while the engine is idling. If the engine speed does not rise slightly (about 200 rpm), the valve is not operating properly and should be replaced. Valve components should be cleaned and inspected at 6,000 mile intervals, and the oil filler cap replaced every 12,000 miles.

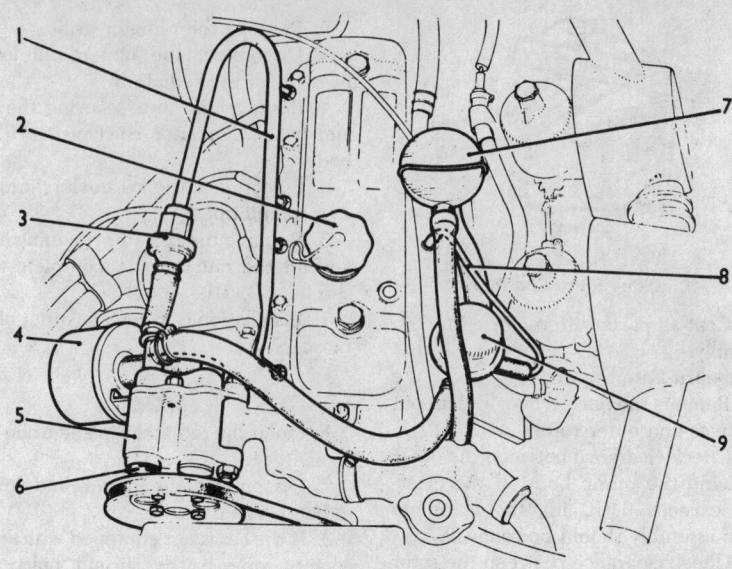

Exhaust Air Injection System

1. Air manifold	4. Air pump air filter	7. PCV valve
2. Oil filler cap	5. Air pump	8. Vacuum sensing line
3. Check valve	6. Relief valve	9. Gulp valve

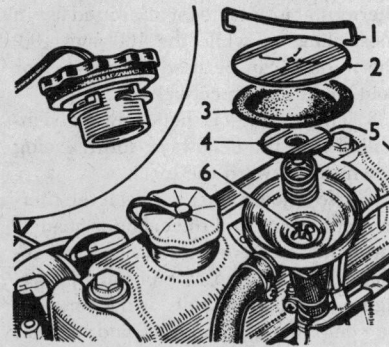

PCV Valve and Components
1. Retaining clip
2. Cover
3. Diaphragm
4. Metering valve
5. Spring
6. Guides (later type valves)

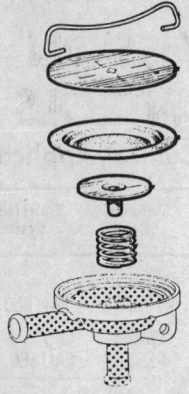

A gulp valve, located in the pump output line to the intake manifold, leans out the rich fuel/air mixture that develops when the engine is decelerating (engine overrun). A line between the intake manifold and the gulp valve allows the valve to be activated by changes in manifold vacuum. On some engines a restrictor is located in the output line between the pump and valve to prevent engine surge when the valve is operating.

In addition to the air pump and its attendant equipment, all vehicles with emission control systems are equipped with the distributor and carburetors modified to meet emission standards. These units are covered separately in the "Engine Electrical" and "Fuel System" sections, as well as in the "Specifications" section.

The efficient and trouble-free operation of the emission control system depends to a large extent upon the engine being correctly tuned. Proper tuning specifications given for a particular engine should be strictly adhered to (see "Tune-Up Specifications").

Maintenance

At the time of an engine tune-up (6,000 miles recommended), the entire exhaust air injection system should be inspected. Clean or replace the air pump air filter element. Check the air hoses and connections for any evidence of leaking. (This is very important, because an air leak can cause overheating, resulting in burnt valves, a blown head gasket, etc.) Check the air pump drive belt tension and adjust it if necessary. Properly adjusted, the

Exhaust Air Injection

Operation

The EAI system consists of a belt driven air pump that forces air into the exhaust port of each cylinder, causing a reburning of exhaust gases in order to reduce the number of harmful emissions.

Air is drawn into the pump through a replaceable paper filter.

A relief valve in the pump vents excessive air pressure, created by high rpm operation, to the atmosphere.

A check valve, located in the pump output line to the injection manifold, protects the pump from exhaust gas backflow.

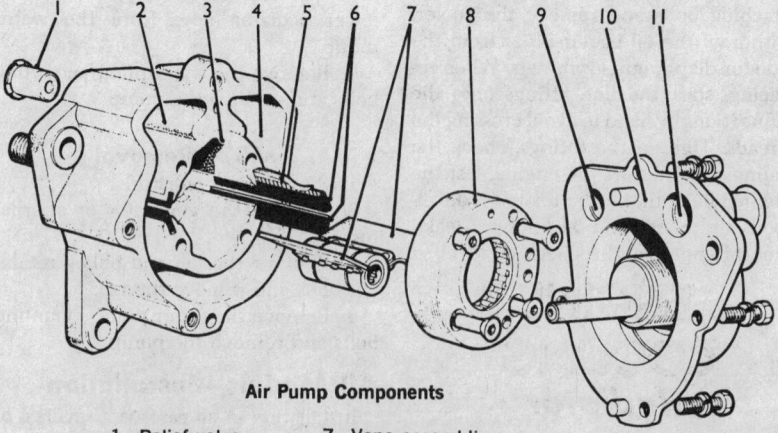

Air Pump Components

1. Relief valve	7. Vane assemblies
2. Intake chamber	8. Rotor bearing support
3. Rotor	plate
4. Output chamber	9. Output port
5. Spring	10. End-cover
6. Carbons	11. Intake port

belt should have a total defection of ½ inch midway between the pulleys. Adjustment is made by loosening the mounting bolt and adjusting strut bolts, in the same manner as generator adjustment.

Component Testing

1. To check the air pump and relief valve, first make sure that the pump drive belt is properly adjusted and that the air filter is clean.

2. Disconnect and plug the air supply hose to the gulp valve. Disconnect the injection manifold air hose at the check valve, and connect a pressure gauge to the hose.

3. At an engine speed of 1,000 rpm (Midget—1,200 rpm), the pressure gauge should not read less than 2.75 lb./sq. in. If a lower reading is obtained, tape the relief valve shut and repeat the test. If the reading is now satisfactory, replace the relief valve (it can be removed by prying with a screwdriver or with a gear puller).

4. If the reading is still low, replace or overhaul the air pump unit.

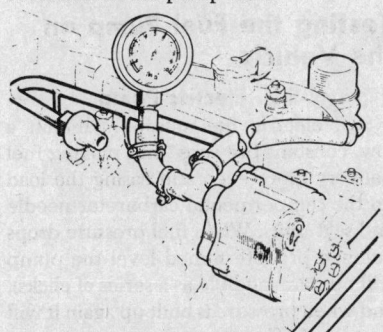

Air pressure check

NOTE: *If the pump is removed for service, do not hold it in a vise. Even a small amount of pressure will distort the pump body.*

5. To test the check valve, disconnect the air supply hose from the valve and unscrew it from the injection manifold. Blow through the valve at each connection (do not use compressed air). Air should pass through the valve only from the air supply side (from the air pump) to the manifold connection. If air passes in the opposite direction or not at all, the valve must be replaced.

6. To test the gulp valve, disconnect the valve air supply hose from the air pump connection.

7. Start the engine and let it idle for a few seconds.

8. With the engine still idling, connect a vacuum gauge to the end of the gulp valve air hose that is disconnected from the air pump. The gauge should read zero for approximately fifteen seconds. If a vacuum is registered, the gulp valve should be replaced.

9. If the valve passes the test, snap the

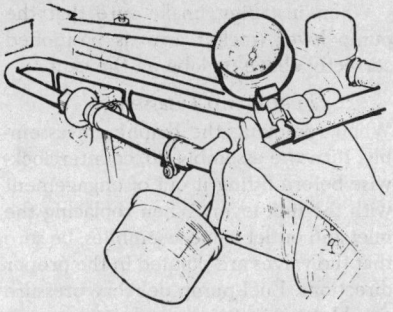

Vacuum Gauge Connected to Gulp Valve

throttle open once and let it spring shut.

10. Repeat this test several times, breaking the connection between the vacuum gauge and the gulp valve hose before each operation of the throttle to return the gauge to zero. In every case the gauge should register a vacuum. If it does not, replace the gulp valve.

11. To check the intake manifold vacuum limit valve (integral with the carburetor throttle butterfly), disconnect the gulp valve sensing line from the intake manifold.

12. Connect a vacuum gauge to the sensing line connection at the manifold.

13. With the engine at normal operating temperature, increase the engine speed to 3,000 rpm and let the throttle snap shut. The vacuum gauge reading should immediately rise to between 20.5 and 22.0 in. vacuum. If the reading is outside these limits, the carburetors must be removed and the throttle butterflies replaced. Make sure, in each carburetor, that the butterfly is centered in the bore before the securing screws are tightened. Carburetor removal and tuning procedures can be found in the "Fuel System" section.

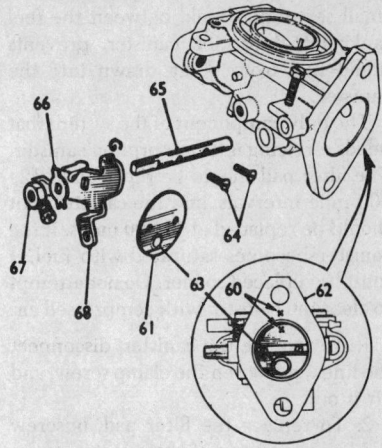

Throttle Butterfly and the Vacuum Limit Valve.

60. Alignment marks (scribed in)
61. Throttle butterfly
62. Carburetor body
63. Intake manifold vacuum limit valve
64. Butterfly retaining screws
65. Throttle shaft
66. Locktab
67. Spindle nut
68. Throttle lever

Evaporative Loss Control System

The system is designed to collect fuel vapor from the fuel tank and carburetor float chambers. The vapor is stored in the absorption canister while the engine is stopped, and when the engine is restarted it passes through the crankcase ventilation system and into the combustion chambers. Vapors are drawn into the engine directly when the engine is running. An air bleed chamber is located in the fuel tank to prevent overfilling, and a

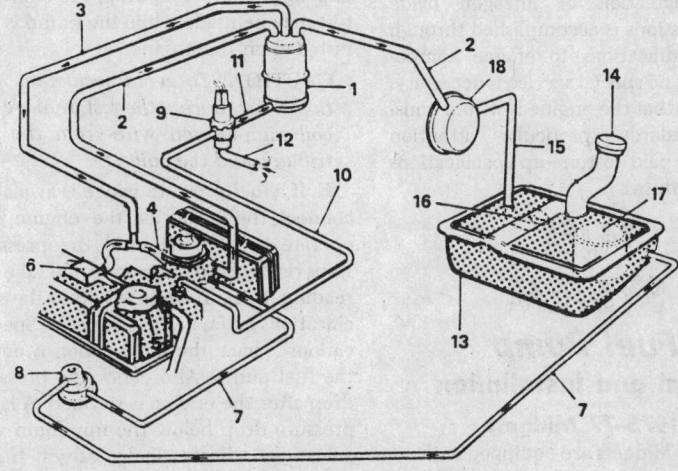

Evaporative Loss Control System

1. Charcoal adsorption canister
2. Vapor lines
3. Purge lines
4. Restricted connection
5. Sealed oil cap
6. Oil flame trap
7. Fuel pipe
8. Fuel pump
9. Break in control valve
10. Running-on control pipe
11. Running-on control hose
12. Air vent pipe
13. Fuel tank
14. Sealed filler cap
15. Vapor line
16. Vapor tube
17. Capacity limiting tank
18. Separation tank

small separation tank, between the fuel tank and absorption canister, prevents liquid fuel from being drawn into the canister.

The only component of the system that needs servicing is the absorption canister. The filter pad should be replaced at 12,-000 mile intervals, and the canister unit should be replaced at 50,000 miles. If the canister becomes saturated with fuel, it must be replaced sooner. Do not attempt to clear the canister with compressed air.

1. To remove the canister, disconnect the lines and loosen the clamp screw, and lift it out.

2. To replace the filter pad, unscrew the lower end cap of the canister.

3. Remove the filter, clean the cap, install a new filter, and replace the end cap.

4. To pressure check the fuel system for leaks, first make sure that there is fuel in the tank and that the fuel system is primed.

5. Disconnect the fuel tank ventilation line from the absorption canister.

6. Connect a low scale pressure gauge between the fuel tank ventilation line and a low pressure air supply (such as a tire pump). Pressurize the system to 1 psi. *Do not exceed this pressure at any time.* The pressure should not fall below ½ psi over a period of ten seconds. If there is evidence of a leak, check all fuel system components and connections beginning with the fuel filler cap. The cap is not vented and should not allow any pressure loss. When the test is completed, remove the fuel filler cap and check that the gauge returns to zero. Reconnect the fuel tank ventilation line to the canister.

NO~x~ Control System

The regulation of nitrogen oxide (NO_x) emissions is accomplished through slight modifications to engine components, and no special service is necessary. To ensure that the engine is within emission standards, particular attention should be paid to tune-up specifications and procedures.

FUEL SYSTEM
Fuel Pump
Removal and Installation

1975–77 Midgets

All 1975 Midgets are equipped with an AC mechanical diaphragm type fuel pump on the left side of the engine.

To remove the fuel pump, disconnect fuel inlet and outlet lines.

NOTE: *Gasoline will spill on the engine unless precautions are taken.*

Unscrew the attaching nuts. The pump will now be free and can be removed.

When installing, make sure that the pump lever (rocker arm) is positioned correctly above its lobe on the cam.

Fuel Pump Disassembly

When removing the diaphragm assembly, turn the assembly 90° counterclockwise before lifting it out of engagement with the link lever. When replacing the inlet and outlet valve assemblies, be sure that the valves are pointed in the proper directions. Fuel pump delivery pressure should be 1½–2½ pounds per square inch (psi).

CAUTION: *Be certain that the fuel lines are snug to the pump, but do not overtighten them.*

Fuel Pump Cleaning

Every 12,000 miles the fuel pump should be serviced. This may be accomplished by:

1. Removing the top bolt and domed cover.

2. Removing the gauze filter and thoroughly washing it in a safe solvent.

3. Cleaning out the sediment in the fuel bowl with a small screwdriver. The preferred method for removing loosened sediment is compressed air. Wipe out the interior of the fuel bowl with a soft, clean rag.

CAUTION: *The interior of the fuel bowl must be absolutely free of grease or lint.*

4. Renewing the cork gasket if it is cracked or brittle. Fuel pump parts are delicate; use caution. When reassembling, be sure that the filter gauze is facing down.

Testing and Adjustment

No adjustments may be made to the fuel pump. Before removing and overhauling the old fuel pump, the following test may be made while the pump is still installed on the engine.

CAUTION: *To avoid accidental ignition of fuel during the test, remove the coil high-tension wire from the distributor and the coil.*

1. If a fuel pressure gauge is available, connect the gauge to the engine and operate the engine until the pressure stops rising. Stop the engine and take the reading. If the reading is within the specifications given in the "Tune-Up Specifications" chart, the malfunction is not in the fuel pump. Also check the pressure drop after the engine is stopped. A large pressure drop below the minimum specification indicates leaky valves. If the pump proves to be satisfactory, check the tank and inlet line.

2. If a fuel pressure gauge is not available, disconnect the fuel line at the pump outlet, place a vessel beneath the pump outlet, and crank the engine. A good pump will force the fuel out of the outlet in steady spurts. A worn diaphragm

spring may not provide proper pumping action.

3. As a further test, disconnect and plug the fuel line from the tank at the pump, and hold your thumb over the pump inlet. If the pump is functioning properly, a suction should be felt on your thumb. No suction indicates that the pump diaphragm is leaking, or that the diaphragm linkage is worn.

4. Check the crankcase for gasoline. A ruptured diaphragm may leak fuel into the engine.

MGB and Midgets through 1974

1. Disconnect the electrical supply and ground wires from the pump, and insulate the supply wire against grounding.

2. Disconnect the fuel lines and the breather pipe (later cars) from the pump and cap the fuel lines.

3. Remove the pump bracket bolts and remove the pump.

4. When installing the pump, make sure that the ground wire makes a good connection and that the breather pipe is correctly routed.

Testing the Fuel Pump on the Vehicle

S.U. Electric Pump

S.U. electric fuel pumps maintain a low, constant pressure, thus making fuel delivery more even and easing the load on the tempermental carburetor needle and seat units. When fuel pressure drops below a predetermined level the pump will operate (audible as a series of clicks), and when pressure is built up again it will shut itself off.

1. To check pump operation, disconnect the fuel line at the carburetors and switch the ignition on.

2. The pump should be heard to operate and fuel should flow readily from the line.

If it does not, disconnect the output line at the pump and switch the ignition on again. If the pump now operates, the fuel line to the carburetors is blocked and should be cleared with compressed air. If the pump does not operate, disconnect the fuel intake line from the pump and check for a free flow of gasoline from the tank.

3. The line may be cleared, if necessary, with compressed air by pressurizing the gas tank through the tank filler tube.

CAUTION: *Never blow compressed air through the fuel pump, and on vehicles equipped with Evaporative Loss Control systems the fuel lines must never be pressurized unless the absorption canister is disconnected.*

If the fuel lines are clear and the pump will not operate, the electrical connections at the pump should be checked.

4. Switch on the ignition and connect

a test light between the supply (battery) wire and ground. If it does not light, the pump is not being supplied with electricity. If it does light, check the ground wire continuity by connecting a jumper wire between the ground terminal on the pump and a good chassis ground.

5. If the pump still does not operate, the fault lies in the pump unit itself. Refer to the following section.

Servicing the Fuel Pump
S.U. Electric Pump

If the pump unit is not operating correctly, remove it from the vehicle.

1. Remove the intake and outlet line fittings from the pump body and remove the small fuel filter (if fitted).

2. Examine the ports for any foreign matter that may be lodged inside.

3. Clean the ports, if necessary, and clean and replace the filter and line fittings.

4. Remove the plastic end-cover by removing the electrical terminal retaining nut and the rubber or tape joint seal.

5. Examine the contact points for burning, and check the contact rotor assembly movement. If the end-cover was not sealed properly, the contact and

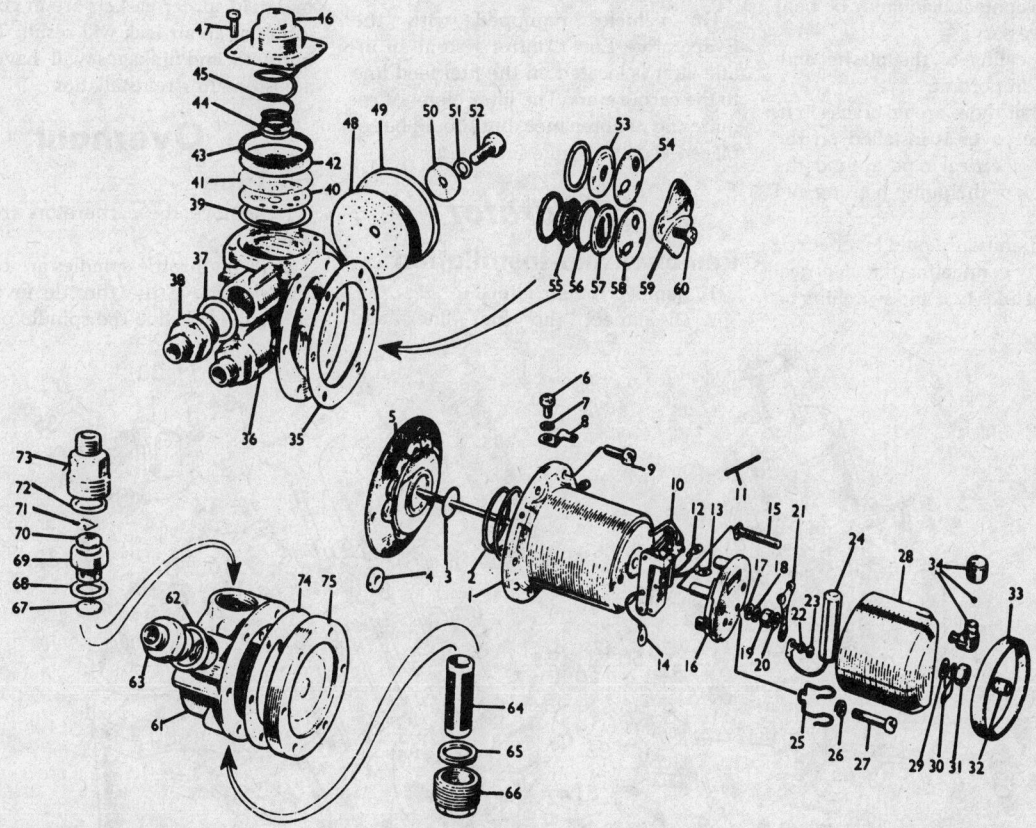

Electric Fuel Pump—Exploded View

1. Coil housing
2. Armature spring
3. Impact washer
4. Armature centralizing roller
5. Diaphragm and spindle assembly
6. Set screw
7. Spring washer
8. Ground connector
9. Set screw
10. Rocker mechanism
11. Rocker pivot pin
12. Terminal tag
13. Terminal tag
14. Ground tag
15. Terminal stud
16. Pedestal
17. Spring washer
18. Lead washer
19. Terminal nut
20. End cover seal washer
21. Contact blade
22. Washer
23. Contact blade screw
24. Condenser
25. Condenser clip

26. Spring washer
27. Pedestal screw
28. End cover
29. Shakeproof washer
30. Lucar connector
31. Nut
32. Insulating sleeve
33. Sealing band
34. Vent valve
35. Gasket
36. Pump body
37. Fiber washer
38. Outlet connection
39. Sealing washer
*40. Diaphragm plate
41. Plastic diaphragm barrier — AUF
*42. Rubber diaphragm — 300
43. Rubber "O" ring — type
*44. Spring end cap
*45. Diaphragm spring
†46. Delivery flow smoothing device cover
47. Set screw
48. Gasket
49. Inlet air bottle cover
50. Dished washer

51. Spring washer
52. Set screw
53. Outlet valve
54. Valve cap — AUF
55. Filter — 300
56. Sealing washer — type
57. Inlet valve
58. Valve cap
59. Clamp plate
60. Set screw
61. Pump body
62. Fiber washer
63. Outlet connection
64. Filter
65. Washer
66. Plug
67. Inlet valve — HP
68. Thin fiber washer — type
69. Outlet valve cage
70. Outlet valve
71. Spring clip
72. Medium fiber washer
73. Outlet connection
74. Gasket
75. Sandwich plate

* Early pumps
† Delivery air bottle (later pumps)

rocker assemblies will have been exposed to water and dirt and should be thoroughly cleaned or replaced.

If the contacts are not badly burnt, they may be smoothed with fine sandpaper and cleaned with a non-oily solvent such as an aerosol-type carburetor cleaner.

6. When adjusting the points, make sure that when the outer rocker is pressed onto the pump housing, the contact blade rests on the narrow rib of the pedestal. The contact blade may be bent slightly if necessary.

7. Proper sealing of the plastic end-cover is very important.

8. Check that there are no cracks in it, and, after the cover is installed on the pump, wrap electrical tape around the mating surface of the pump housing and cover.

9. Pump operation should be checked by temporarily connecting the electrical wires and fuel lines to it and switching on the ignition.

10. Allow a few seconds for the pump to prime itself, and check fuel flow at the carburetors.

11. At this point, if the pump is still not operating correctly, the pump unit will have to be replaced. Do not discard the pump, as most MG dealers carry factory rebuilt S.U. fuel pumps instead of new ones (at a considerable savings), and will allow some trade-in on the old unit.

Fuel Filter

On vehicles equipped with the Evaporative Loss Control system an in-line filter is located on the fuel feed line to the carburetors. The filter element requires no maintenance, but should be replaced at 12,000 mile intervals.

Carburetor

Removal and Installation

1. Remove the air filters.
2. Disconnect the fuel lines and remove the overflow tubes from the float chamber.

3. Disconnect the accelerator and choke cables.

4. Disconnect the vacuum advance line and remove the throttle return springs.

5. Unbolt the carburetor retaining nuts and remove the carburetors, being careful not to bend the throttle linkage.

6. Installation is in reverse order of removal. Make sure that the carburetor and manifold spacer gaskets are in good condition or an air leak will result. The carburetors and linkages will have to be adjusted after reinstallation.

Overhaul

HS Type

1. Remove the carburetors from the vehicle.

2. If the throttle spindles are to be replaced remove the throttle levers and butterfly, and slide the spindle out.

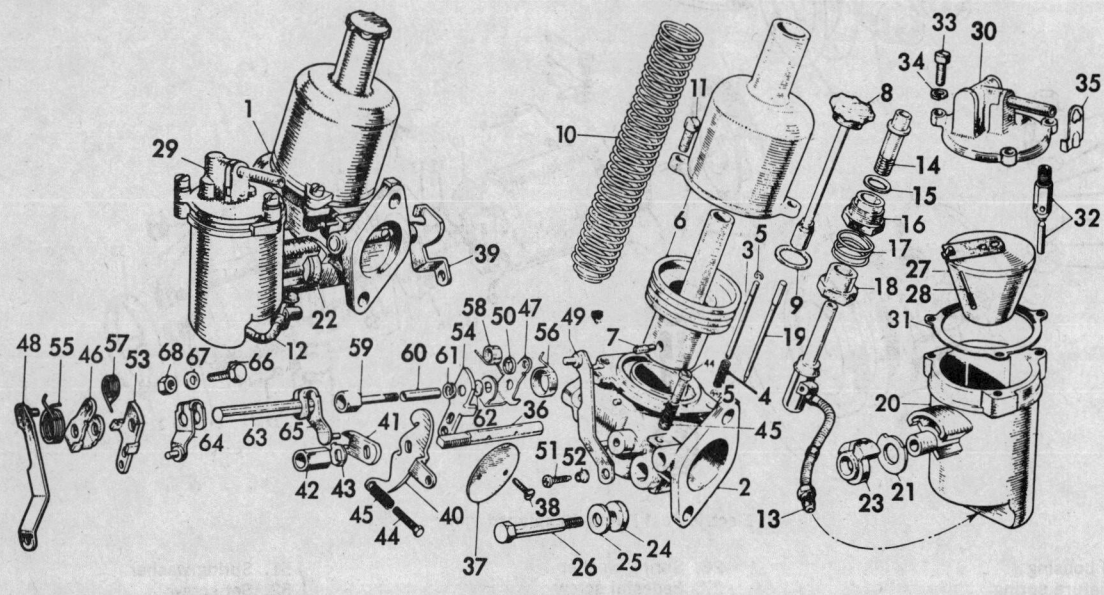

Dual Carburetor Set-up

1. Carburetor body (left)
2. Carburetor body (right)
3. Piston lifting pin
4. Spring
5. Circlip
6. Piston chamber assembly
7. Screw
8. Cap and damper assembly
9. Fibre washer
10. Piston spring
11. Screw
12. Jet assembly (left carburetor)
13. Jet assembly (right carburetor)
14. Bearing
15. Washer
16. Screw
17. Spring
18. Screw
19. Needle
20. Float-chamber
21. Support washer
22. Rubber grommet (left carburetor)
23. Rubber grommet (right carburetor)
24. Washer (rubber)

25. Washer (steel)
26. Bolt
27. Float assembly
28. Lever pin
29. Float-chamber lid (left carburetor)
30. Float-chamber lid (right carburetor)
31. Washer
32. Needle and seat assembly
33. Screw
34. Spring washer
35. Baffle plate
36. Throttle spindle
37. Throttle disc
38. Screw
39. Throttle return lever (left carburetor)
40. Throttle return lever (right carburetor)
41. Lost motion lever
42. Nut
43. Tab washer
44. Throttle screw stop
45. Spring
46. Pick-up lever (left carburetor)
47. Pick-up lever (right carburetor)
48. Link (left carburetor)

49. Link (right carburetor)
50. Washer
51. Screw
52. Bush
53. Cam lever (left carburetor)
54. Cam lever (right carburetor)
55. Pick-up lever spring (left carburetor)
56. Pick-up lever spring (right carburetor)
57. Cam lever spring (left carburetor)
58. Cam lever spring (right carburetor)
59. Bolt
60. Tube
61. Spring washer
62. Distance piece
63. Jet rod
64. Lever and pin assembly (left carburetor)
65. Lever pin assembly (right carburetor)
66. Bolt
67. Washer
68. Nut

3. Remove the retaining screws and lift the piston-chamber straight off.

4. Remove the spring and carefully lift the piston out. Unscrew the piston damper from the top of the piston-chamber.

5. Unscrew the fuel transfer line from the bottom of the float chamber.

6. Unbolt and remove the float chamber from the carburetor body.

7. Remove the float cover and remove the float by pressing out the hinge pin with an ice pick or small drift.

8. Unscrew the needle and seat from the cover.

9. Remove the pivot pin from the jet lifting (choke) arm at the bottom of the jet assembly.

10. Unscrew the jet assembly locknut and withdraw the jet assembly.

11. Pull the jet tube out and lift the top jet bearing off. The small spring, washers, and gaskets can now be removed. Unscrew the jet adjusting nut from the bottom jet bearing and remove the gaskets, the spring, and the washer.

12. All carburetor components except the float and seals should be soaked in acid-type carburetor cleaner for about an hour, then washed thoroughly with solvent and air dried. Components included in good carburetor rebuilding kits should include jet tubes, jet needles, needle and seat assemblies, and all gaskets and seals. If throttle spindles or bushings or any other carburetor parts are needed they will have to be purchased separately. The small cork gaskets (jet gland washers) should be soaked in hot water or penetrating oil for at least half an hour before they are assembled onto the jet, or they will invariably split.

13. Assembly is in reverse order of disassembly. When the jet is fully assembled the jet tube should be a close fit without any lateral play, but it should be free to move smoothly up and down in the jet assembly. A few drops of oil or polishing the tube lightly may be necessary to achieve this. If the jet sealing ring washer is made of cork, it should be soaked in hot water for a minute or two before installation. Float height should be adjusted. Install the jet needle so that the shoulder is even with the bottom of the piston (see illustrations for fixed and spring-loaded type needles). Do not lubricate any part of the piston except the surface of the damper tube.

14. After the jet assembly is fitted into the carburetor body and before it is fully tightened, the jet will have to be centered so that the needle will fit into it evenly and without binding.

15. With the piston removed, look down into the bore and center the top of the jet in the hole by moving the bottom of the jet assembly. Partially tighten the jet assembly locknut.

16. Insert the piston, with the needle installed, into the bore. Push the jet tube all the way up in the jet assembly.

17. Temporarily install the piston-chamber over the piston. Lift the piston all the way and let it fall. It should fall smoothly and seat with a distinct click. If the jet is not centered properly the needle will hang up in the jet tube and the piston will not fall all the way. Several tries will probably be needed before the piston falls freely. Be sure to check it once more after the jet assembly locknut is fully tightened.

18. The jet restrictor on Emission Control System carburetors cannot be accurately repositioned without the aid of an exhaust gas analyzer. If an analyzer is available, lock the restrictor in the range where carbon dioxide emissions from the engine are just inside the maximum allowable level. If an analyzer is not available, adjust the jet as for an earlier engine without emission controls and have the emissions level checked at the earliest possible date.

19. Carburetor synchronization and jet adjustment should be carefully performed when the units have been rebuilt. Refer to the preceding section.

HIF Type

1. Remove the carburetors from the car.

2. Thoroughly clean the outside of the carburetor.

3. Unscrew the suction piston chamber retaining screws and remove the identity tag.

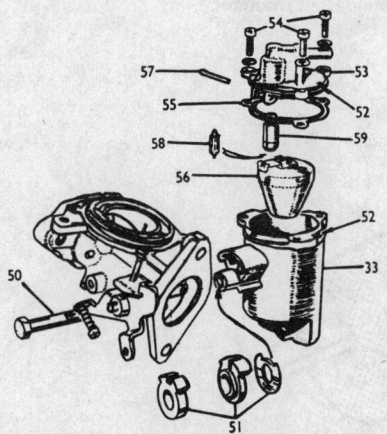

Float bowl components

33. Float bowl
50. Mounting bolt
51. Mounting washers
52. Alignment marks—to be scribed in upon removal
53. Float bowl cover
54. Retaining screws
55. Gasket
56. Float
57. Float hinge pin
58. & 59. Needle and seat assembly

4. Lift the chamber vertically from the body without tilting it.

5. Remove the piston spring and lift out the piston assembly. Empty the oil from the piston rod.

6. Unscrew and withdraw the needle guide locking screw, the needle, guide, and screw.

7. Mark the bottom cover plate and body to ensure correct reassembly; remove retaining screws and cover with sealing ring.

8. Remove the jet adjusting screw with "O" ring; remove jet adjusting lever retaining screws and spring.

9. Withdraw the jet complete with adjusting lever and disengage the lever.

10. Remove the float pivot spindle, washer, and float.

11. Remove the needle valve and unscrew the valve seat.

12. Unscrew the jet bearing locking nut and remove bearing and washer.

13. Note the location of the ends of the fast idle cam lever return spring.

14. Unlock and remove the cam lever retaining nut and lockwasher.

15. With the return spring held toward the carburetor body, pry off the cam lever and remove the return spring.

16. Unscrew the starter retaining screws and remove the cover plate; withdraw assembly and remove gasket.

17. Withdraw the valve spindle, and remove "O" ring, seals, dust cap.

18. Remove throttle lever return spring. Remove the throttle lever nut and washer and remove the throttle levers.

19. Remove the throttle disc retaining screws. Open the throttle and withdraw the throttle from the throttle spindle.

20. Withdraw the throttle spindles and remove their seals.

Assembly is the reverse of removal with these exceptions:

1. The throttle spindle must be fitted with the threaded end at the piston lifting pin side of the body.

2. Fit the throttle disc so that the overrun valve is at the top of the bore and its spring toward the inside when the throttle is closed.

3. New throttle disc retaining screws must be used when reinstalling the disc. Make sure that the throttle disc is correctly positioned before tightening.

4. Position the throttle spindle end seals just below the spindle housing flange.

5. The starter unit valve is installed with the cut-out towards the top retaining screw hole, and its retaining plate is positioned with the slotted flange towards the throttle spindle.

6. After installing the float and valve, invert the carburetor so that the needle valve is held in the shut position by the weight of the float alone. Check that the

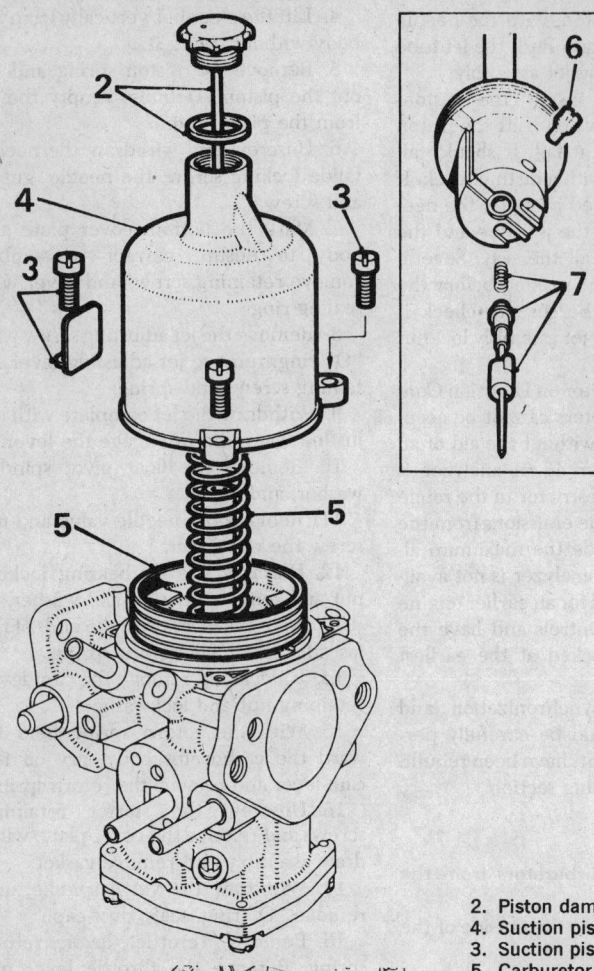

2. Piston damper and washer
4. Suction piston chamber
3. Suction piston chamber screws
5. Carburetor body
6. Jet adjusting screw
7. Needle assembly
8. Bottom cover plate

Exploded view—top section HIF carburetor

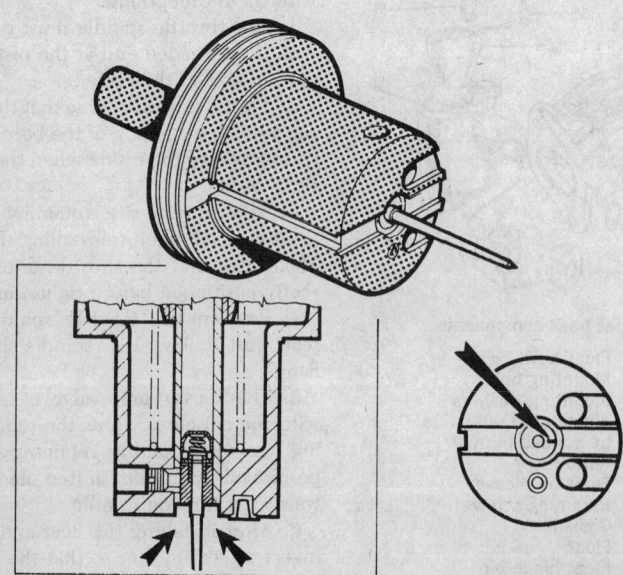

Replacing the needle assembly

point indicated on the float is 0.04 +/− 0.02 in. below the level of the float chamber.

7. Check that the small diameter of the jet adjusting screw engages the slot in the adjusting lever and set the jet flush with the bridge of the body.

8. Use a new retaining screw when reinstalling the needle and ensure that the needle guide etch mark aligns correctly with the piston transfer holes. After installing the needle assembly, check that the shoulder of the needle aligns the full face of the piston.

Zenith-Stromberg (1975–77 Midget)

1. Remove the carburetor(s).
2. Remove the damper.
3. Lever out the bottom plug.
4. Drain the carburetor of oil and fuel.
5. Remove the O-ring from its plug.
6. Remove the six screws which secure the float chamber to the body.
7. Remove the float chamber.
8. Remove the float assembly by gently prying the spindle from the clip of each end.
9. Remove the needle valve.
10. Remove the four screws which secure the top cover to the body.
11. Remove the top cover.
12. Remove the spring.
13. Remove the air valve assembly.
14. Remove the four screws which secure the diaphragm and retaining ring to the air valve assembly.
15. Remove the diaphragm and retaining ring.
16. Slacken the set screw in the side of the air valve.
17. Insert tool S353 or an allen wrench of the proper diameter into the stem of the air valve, turn it counterclockwise approximately two turns, and withdraw the needle and housing by pulling firmly and straight with your fingers.
18. Remove the two screws which secure the starter box to the body.
19. Remove the starter box.
20. Remove the two screws which secure the temperature compensator to the body.
21. Remove the temperature compensator and two rubber washers of different diameters.
22. Remove the three (slotted) screws which secure the by-pass valve to the body.
23. Remove the by-pass valve and gasket.
24. Remove the two screws which secure the butterfly to the spindle.
25. Turn the spindle return spring.
26. Release the spindle return spring.
27. Withdraw the spindle and spring.
28. Remove the spindle seals from the body by hooking them out with a small screwdriver.

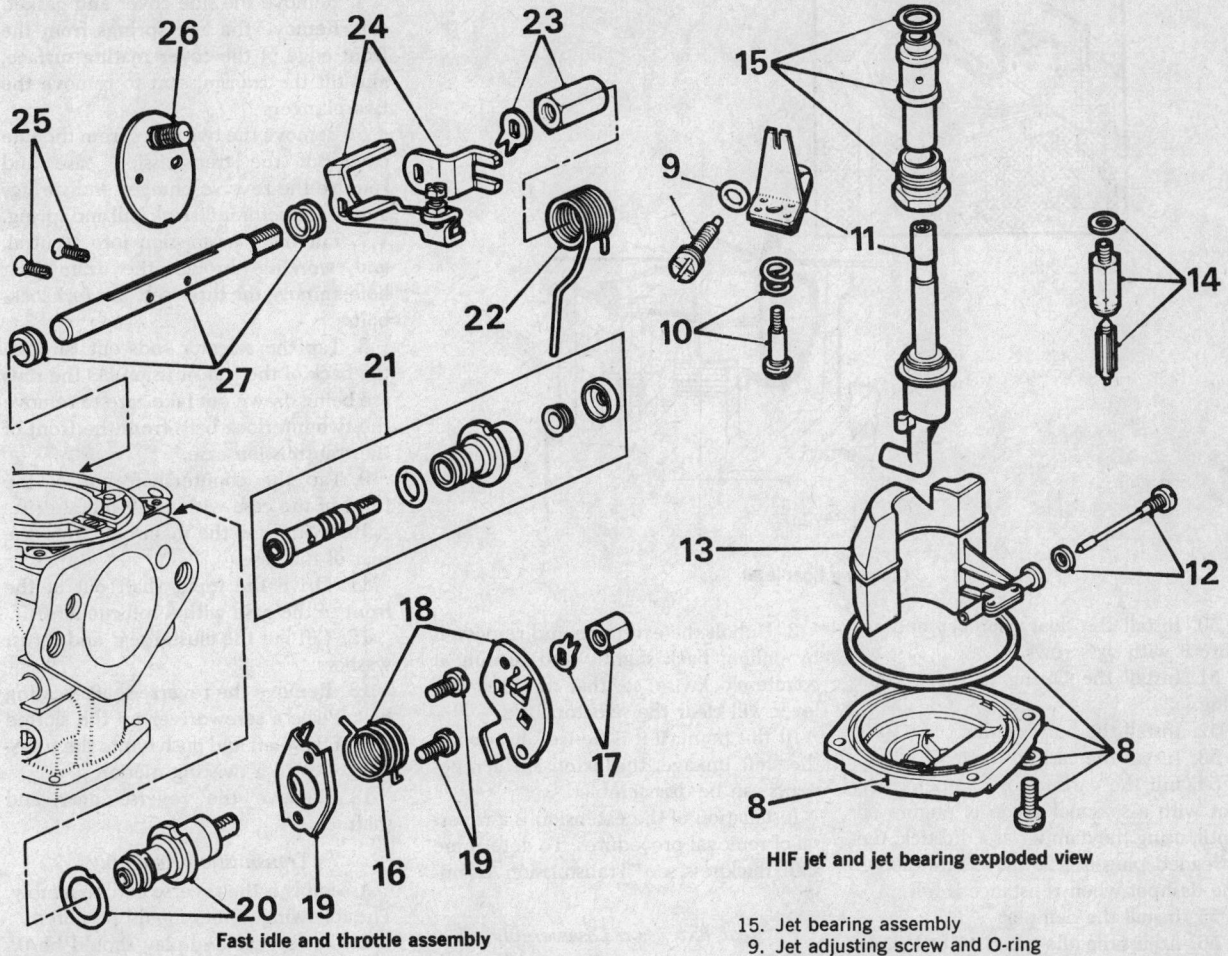

Fast idle and throttle assembly

HIF jet and jet bearing exploded view

25. Throttle disc screws
26. Throttle disc
24. Throttle and throttle actuating lever
23. Throttle lever nut
27. Throttle spindle
21. Valve spindle assembly

22. Throttle lever return spring
18. Fast idle cam
19. Starter unit cover
16. Fast idle cam lever spring
19. Starter unit screws
17. Cam lever retaining nut

15. Jet bearing assembly
9. Jet adjusting screw and O-ring
9. Jet adjusting assembly with lever
10. Jet adjusting lever retaining screw and spring
14. Needle valve assembly
12. Float pivot spindle
13. Float
8. Bottom cover plate and screws

29. Wash all components in clean fuel. Allow them to air dry or use compressed air. Place all components on a clean surface. Discard all seals and gaskets. Scrape all old gasket material from the mating surfaces.

30. Examine the condition of all components for wear, paying special attention to the needle and seat and the air valve and diaphragm which should be replaced unless in exceptionally good condition.

31. Use clean compressed air to blow through all ports, needle valve, and starter box.

32. Fit the spindle seals to the body, tapping them gently into position, with the metal casing of the seals flush with the body of the carburetor.

33. Insert the spindle, loading and locating the spindle return spring while doing so.

34. Insert the butterfly with the two protruding spots facing outboard and below the spindle. Tighten the screws.

35. Install the starter box and tighten the screws.

36. Install the by-pass valve and gasket and tighten the screws.

37. Install the temperature compensator and tighten the screws.

38. Insert the needle housing assembly into the bottom of the air valve.

39. Install tool S353 or an allen wrench of the proper diameter, turning it clockwise to engage the threads of the needle valve assembly with the adjusting screw. Then, continue turning until the slot in the needle housing is aligned with the set screw.

40. Tighten the set screw.

NOTE: *The set screw does not tighten on the needle housing but locates into the slot. This ensures that during adjustment the needle will remain in its operating position, i.e. biased by a spring in the needle housing toward the air cleaner side of the carburetor.*

41. Install the diaphragm, locating the inner tag into the recess in the air valve.

42. Install the diaphragm retaining ring and secure it with four screws.

43. Install the air valve assembly, locating the outer tag and rim of the diaphragm in the complementary recesses in the carburetor body.

44. Install the carburetor top cover with the bulge on the housing neck toward the air intake.

45. Install and evenly tighten the top cover screws.

46. Install the needle valve and sealing washers and tighten them.

47. Install the float assembly by levering the pivot pin gently into the piston.

48. Check the float height by measuring the distance between the carburetor gasket face and the highest point of the floats.

NOTE: *The float heights must be equal and set to 0.625–0.672 in (16–17 mm). Adjust by bending the tabs while ensuring that the tab sits on the needle valve at right angles.*

49. Install the float chamber gasket.

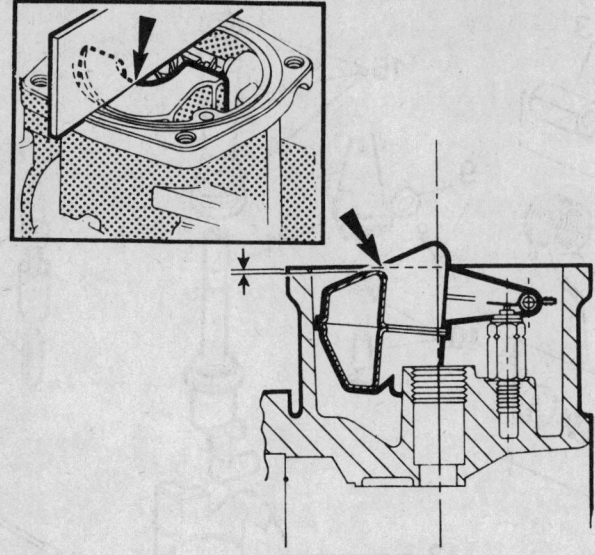

Checking float level

50. Install the float chamber and secure it with six screws.

51. Install the O-ring to the bottom plug.

52. Install the bottom plug.

53. Install the carburetor(s).

54. Fill the carburetor damper dashpot with a seasonal grade of engine oil until, using the damper as a dipstick, the threaded plug is 0.25 in. (6 mm) above the dashpot when resistance is felt.

55. Install the damper.

56. Adjust the idle speed, throttle linkage, and choke.

MANUAL TRANSMISSION

Removal and Installation

On all models the engine and transmission are removed as a unit (see "Engine Removal and Installation"). On the Midget, MGB, the transmission can be unbolted from the engine by simply removing the bell housing bolts.

Installation in all cases is in reverse order of removal. On the Midget, MGB, the clutch disc will have to be centered if the clutch assembly has been removed (see "Clutch Removal and Installation").

Overhaul

Midget 4-Speed Manual

After the transmission is removed from the vehicle and separated from the engine, disassembly begins with:

Rear Extension Removal and Installation

1. Unbolt and remove the speedometer drive from the extension.

2. Unbolt and remove the shift linkage housing.

3. Unbolt the extension and remove it by pulling back slightly and turning it counterclockwise so that the selector lever will clear the selector forks.

At this point, if it is desired to rebuild the shift linkage, the extension components can be disassembled.

Installation of the extension is a reversal of removal procedures. To determine shim thickness, see "Transmission Assembly."

Rear Extension Disassembly

1. Unscrew the guide shaft locating bolt and remove the shaft.

2. Remove the selector lever nylon bushing.

3. Remove the bottom cover from the extension.

4. Remove the shift lever locating bolt and spring retaining cap, and remove the springs and plungers.

5. Unbolt the shift lever retaining plate and remove the lever, O-ring, pivot bushing, and spring.

6. Unscrew the bolts from the front and rear selector levers, remove the core plugs at either end of the housing, and drive out the selector shaft.

7. Remove the selector levers.

8. Remove the reverse plunger cap and remove the spring, ball, and pin.

Rear Extension Assembly

Assembly is in reverse order of disassembly. Replace any worn parts, and lubricate all moving parts in the linkage housing with grease (paying particular attention to the shift lever pivot bushing).

Transmission Disassembly

1. Remove the clutch release bearing.

2. Unscrew the locknut and pivot bolt, and remove the clutch release lever.

3. Unbolt and remove the front cover, and remove the gasket and shim.

4. Remove the side cover and gasket.

5. Remove the two springs from the front edge of the cover mating surface, and tilt the transmission to remove the two plungers.

6. Remove the two plugs from the side cover of the transmission case and remove the reverse plunger and springs and the selector interlock ball and spring.

7. Put the transmission into Neutral, and, working through the drain plug hole, remove the three selector fork lockbolts.

8. Tap the selector rods out through the back of the transmission. As the rods are being drawn out take care to remove the two interlock balls from the front of the transmission case.

9. Tap the countershaft out of the front of the case with a soft-metal drift.

10. Withdraw the mainshaft from the rear of the case.

11. Drive the input shaft out of the front of the case with a soft-metal drift.

12. Lift out the clustergear and thrust washers.

13. Remove the reverse shaft locating bolt. Place a screwdriver on the slotted end of the shaft and push it into the transmission with a twisting motion.

14. Remove the reverse gear and shaft.

Transmission Assembly

Assembly is the reverse of disassembly. The following points should be noted:

1. Clustergear end-play should be 0.-003–0.005 in. (Mk. III). If end-play exceeds these limits, the thrust washers should be replaced. Several thicknesses are available.

2. Determine shim thickness for the front and rear covers, when any mainshaft or input shaft components have been replaced, as follows: Measure the depth of the cover recess and the amount by which the bearing outer race protrudes from the case. Install and tighten the cover with the gasket in place to allow it to be compressed. Take off the cover and measure the gasket thickness. Add this measurement to the depth of the cover recess and subtract the amount by which the bearing protrudes. The result gives the thickness of shims to be used.

Gear Train Component Replacement

1. When rebuilding a transmission, all bearings should be replaced as a matter of course. Gear and synchronizer assemblies, if worn or broken, should be replaced as assembly units.

2. When disassembling the mainshaft components, do not disassemble the third and fourth gear synchronizer assembly or first gear assembly. A special tool is needed to install the spring-loaded balls that are released from the hub when the unit is taken apart. British Leyland can

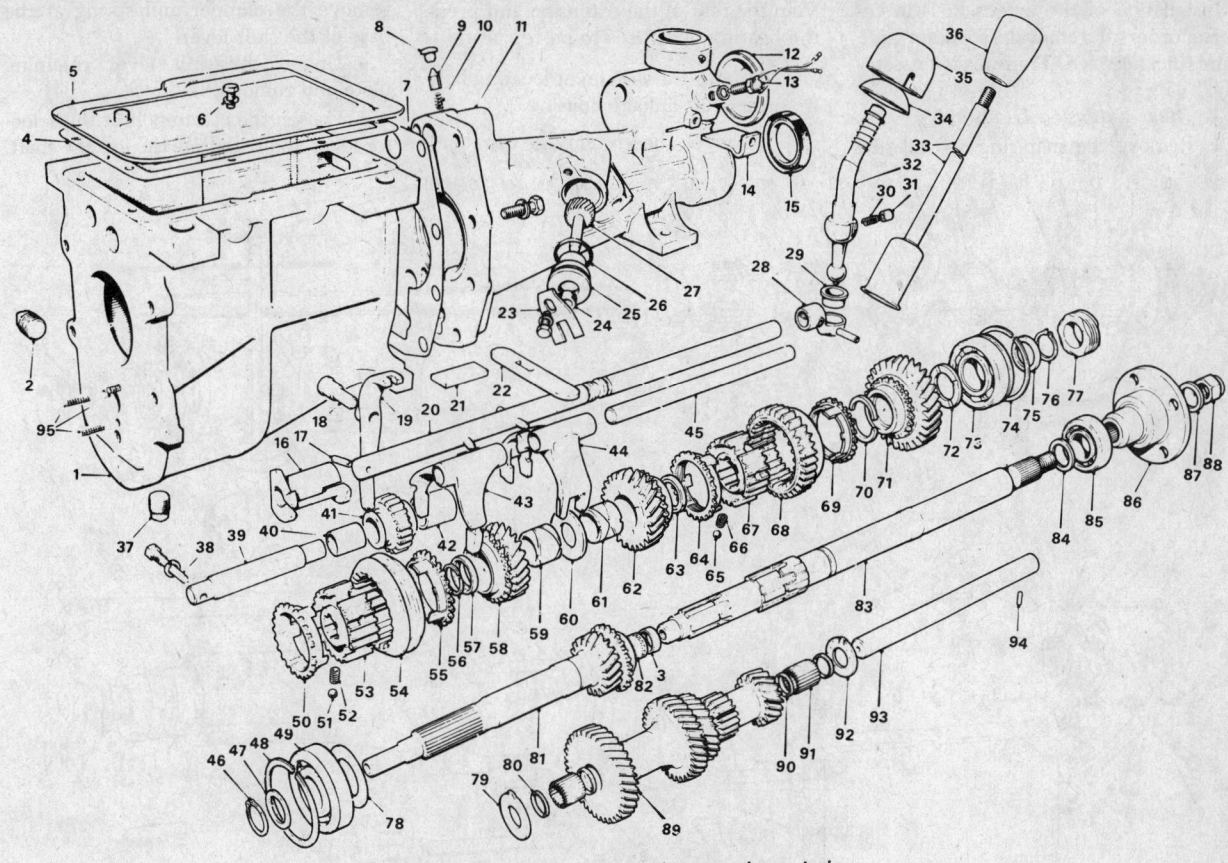

1975-77 MG Midget 4-speed case and gear train

1. Gearbox case	27. Speedometer pinion
2. Oil filter level plug	28. Gear lever yoke
3. Spacer	29. Seat
4. Joint gaskets	30. Spring
5. Top cover	31. Anti-rattle plunger
6. Top cover bolt	32. Lower gear-change lever
7. Joint gasket	33. Upper gear-change lever
8. Plug	34. Dust cover washer
9. Detent plunger	35. Dust cover
10. Detent spring	36. Knob
11. Rear extension	37. Drain plug
12. End cover	38. Reverse idler spindle locating screw
13. Reverse light switch	39. Reverse idler spindle
14. Reverse lift plate	40. Reverse idler gear bushing
15. Oil seal	41. Reverse idler gear
16. Interlock spool	42. Reverse idler spacer
17. Selector shaft roll pin	43. 3rd and 4th speed selector forks
18. Reverse operating lever pin	44. 1st and 2nd speed selector forks
19. Reverse operating lever	45. Selector fork shaft
20. Gear selector shaft	46. Circlip
21. Magnet	47. Backing washer
22. Interlock spool plate	48. Snap-ring
23. Retaining clip	
24. Seal	
25. Housing	
26. "O"-ring	

49. Ball bearing	71. 1st speed gear
50. Synchromesh cup	72. Thrust washer
51. Ball	73. Mainshaft center bearing
52. Spring	74. Snap-ring
53. 3rd and 4th speed synchromesh hub	75. Selective washer
54. 3rd and 4th speed operating sleeve	76. Circlip
55. Synchromesh cup	77. Speedometer wheel
56. Mainshaft circlip	78. Oil flinger
57. 3rd speed gear thrust washer	79. Front thrust washer
58. 3rd speed gear	80. Bearing outer retaining ring
59. Gear bushing	81. 1st motion shaft
60. Selective washer	82. Needle-roller bearing
61. Gear bushing	83. Mainshaft
62. 2nd speed gear	84. Washer
63. Thrust washer	85. Ball bearing
64. Synchromesh cup	86. Drive flange
65. Ball	87. Washer
66. Spring	88. Self-locking nut
67. 1st and 2nd operating sleeve	89. Countershaft gear cluster
68. Mainshaft reverse gear	90. Bearing inner retaining ring
69. Synchromesh cup	91. Needle rollers
70. Split collar	92. Rear thrust washer
	93. Layshaft
	94. Layshaft dowel
	95. Laygear pre-load springs

supply the tool (part number 18G 144), or a piece of pipe with an inside diameter slightly larger than the hub diameter can be used. A hole must be drilled in the pipe through which the springs and balls can be loaded.

3. When assembling components onto the countershaft on early models, the uncaged needle bearings can be held in place with grease.

On later models, make sure that the first and second gear assembly is correctly positioned on the mainshaft. The plunger in the hub must align with the cut-away tooth in the gear, and the cone end of the hub and tapered side of the gear teeth must be on opposite sides of the assembly. If the gears are not assembled in this manner, it will be impossible to engage second gear.

MGB 4-Speed Manual

After the transmission is removed from the vehicle and separated from the engine, disassembly begins with:

Rear Extension Removal and Installation

1. Remove the driveshaft flange.
2. Unbolt and remove the shift linkage housing.
3. Withdraw the selector interlock arm and plate assembly.
4. Unbolt and remove the extension and mainshaft shims.

At this point, if it is desired to rebuild the shift linkage, the extension components can be disassembled.

Installation of the extension is in reverse order of removal. To determine shim thickness, see "Transmission Assembly."

Rear Extension Disassembly

1. Remove the snap-ring and oil seal from the rear of the extension and press the bearing out if it is to be replaced.

2. Remove the shift lever locating bolt from the shift linkage housing.

3. Remove the retaining cap and remove the damper and spring at the base of the shift lever.

4. Unbolt the shift lever retaining plate and remove the lever.

5. Loosen the clamp bolt at the selector lever and withdraw the linkage shaft.

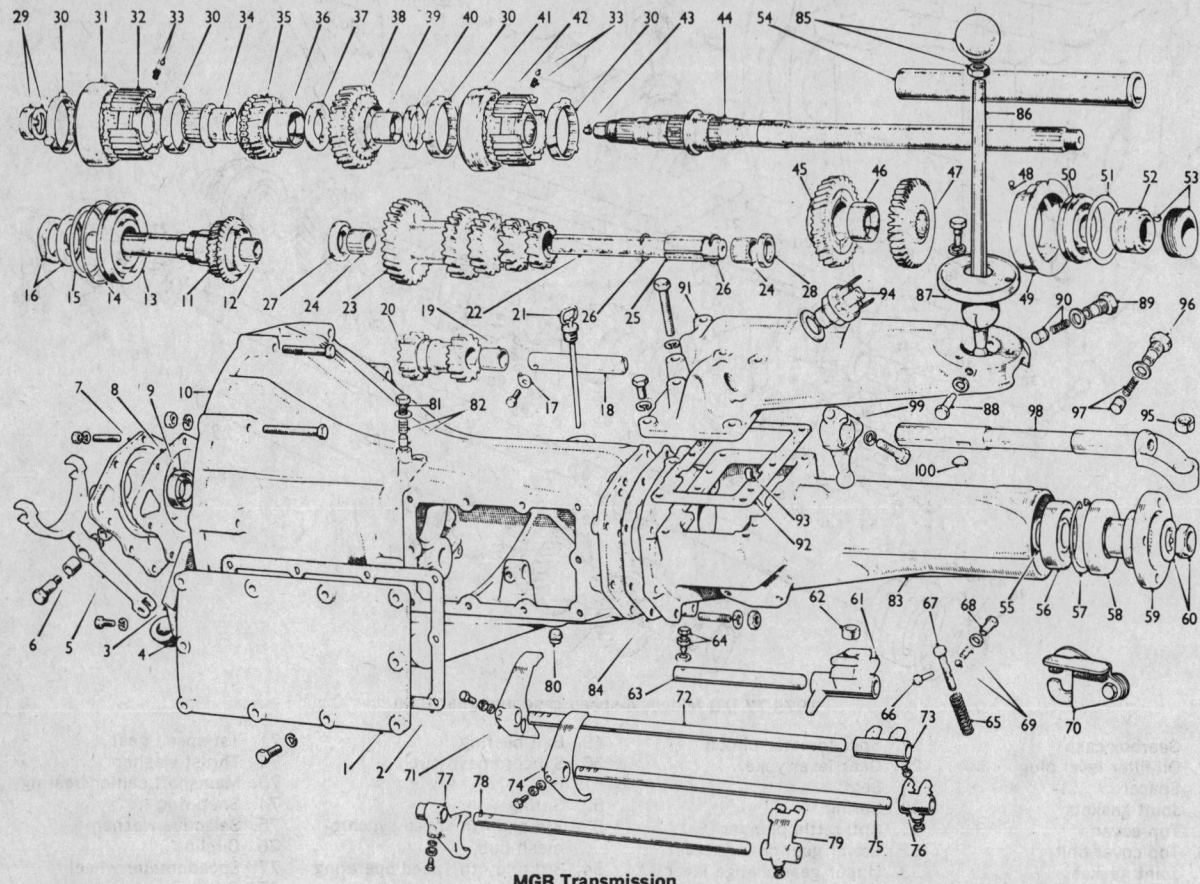

MGB Transmission

1. Side cover
2. Gasket for side cover
3. Stone guard
4. Dust cover
5. Clutch release lever
6. Bushing
7. Front cover
8. Gasket for front cover
9. Oil seal
10. Gearbox main casing
11. Input shaft
12. Needle roller bearing
13. Bearing
14. Snapring
15. Shim
16. Lockwasher and nut
17. Screw and lockwasher
18. Reverse idler shaft
19. Bushing
20. Reverse idler gear
21. Oil level indicator
22. Countershaft
23. Clustergear
24. Needle roller bearing
25. Spacer
26. Snapring
27. Front thrust washer
28. Rear thrust washer
29. Nut and lockwasher
30. Synchronizer ring
31. Sliding coupling for first and second gear
32. Synchronizer
33. Ball and spring
34. Sleeve

35. Third gear
36. Bushing
37. Interlocking thrust washer
38. Second gear
39. Bushing
40. Thrust washer
41. Sliding coupling for third and fourth gear
42. Synchronizer
43. Oil restrictor
44. Mainshaft
45. First gear
46. Bushing
47. Reverse gear
48. Locating peg
49. Bearing housing
50. Bearing
51. Shim
52. Spacer
53. Speedometer gear and driving gear
54. Spacer
55. Shim
56. Bearing
57. Circlip
58. Oil seal
59. Driving flange
60. Nut and lockwasher
61. Selector
62. Bushing
63. Selector levershaft
64. Locating bolt and locknut for selector shaft
65. Spring for reverse plunger
66. Locating pin for reverse plunger

67. Reverse plunger
68. Plug
69. Detent plunger and spring
70. Interlock arm
71. First and second selector fork
72. First and second selector rod
73. First and second selector
74. Third and fourth selector fork
75. Third and fourth selector rod
76. Third and fourth selector
77. Reverse selector fork
78. Reverse selector rod
79. Reverse selector
80. Drain plug
81. Plug
82. Detent spring and plunger
83. Rear extension
84. Gasket for rear extension
85. Knob
86. Shift lever
87. Retainer plate
88. Locating pin
89. Plunger retaining cap
90. Plunger and spring
91. Shift linkage housing
92. Gasket for remote control housing
93. Dowel
94. Back-up light switch
95. Bushing
96. Damper retaining cap
97. Damper and spring
98. Linkage shaft
99. Selector lever
100. Key for selector lever

Rear Extension Assembly

Assembly is in reverse order of disassembly. The nylon shift lever pivot bushing should be replaced and lubricated with motor oil.

Transmission Disassembly

1. Remove the clutch release bearing and release lever.

2. Unbolt and remove the front cover and bearing shims.

3. Unbolt and remove the side cover.

4. Remove the selector detent plunger plugs and springs.

5. Remove the selector fork and selector lever retaining bolts.

6. Withdraw the selector rods and remove the selector forks.

7. Bend back the locktab on the reverse shaft retaining bolt and remove the bolt. Remove the shaft and withdraw the gear.

8. Carefully drive the countershaft out of the transmission case.

9. Drive the input shaft assembly forward out of the case, making sure it is clear of the clustergear.

10. Remove the spacer and shims from the mainshaft.

11. Remove the rear extension mounting studs from the rear of the transmission case.

12. Check that the mainshaft components are clear of the clustergear teeth, and press the mainshaft assembly out the back of the transmission. Remove the clustergear.

Transmission Assembly

Transmission assembly is in reverse order of disassembly. The following points should be noted:

1. When the rear extension housing or any mainshaft components have been replaced, the shim thickness for the rear extension must be checked. Temporarily install the extension with the gasket, to allow the gasket to be compressed. Remove the extension and measure the amount that the bearing is recessed from the transmission case mating surface, and add to this the thickness from the extension bearing surface to the extension mating surface. Use the number of shims required to make the second distance equal to or 0.001 in. less than the first distance.

2. If the front cover or any of the input shaft components have been replaced, the shim thickness for the front cover must be checked. Temporarily install the cover with the gasket, to allow the gasket to be compressed. Measure the amount that the bearing protrudes from the transmission case. Measure the distance from the cover mating surface to the face of the cover bearing surface and add to this the thickness of the gasket. Use the number of shims required to make the

second distance equal to or 0.001 in. less than the first distance.

Gear Train Component Replacement

Gear train replacement notes for the earlier non-synchromesh first gear transmission are applicable to the later type. See the preceding section.

CLUTCH

Removal and Installation

All Models

1. Remove the engine from the car, and, if the engine and transmission are removed as a unit, separate them. On the Midget, remove the starter motor.

2. Loosen the clutch pressure plate bolts gradually until the spring pressure is released, and remove the pressure plate and disc from the flywheel.

3. Examine the flywheel surface for scoring and signs of overheating. If scored at all, the flywheel should be turned down on a lathe or replaced. If it appears to have been overheated (blue discoloration), the surface should be checked for warpage and turned down if necessary. If disc wear is evident, the pressure plate and release bearing, as well as the disc, should be replaced. The pilot bushing in the end of the crankshaft should be checked for wear and replaced if galled or elongated. Lubricate the

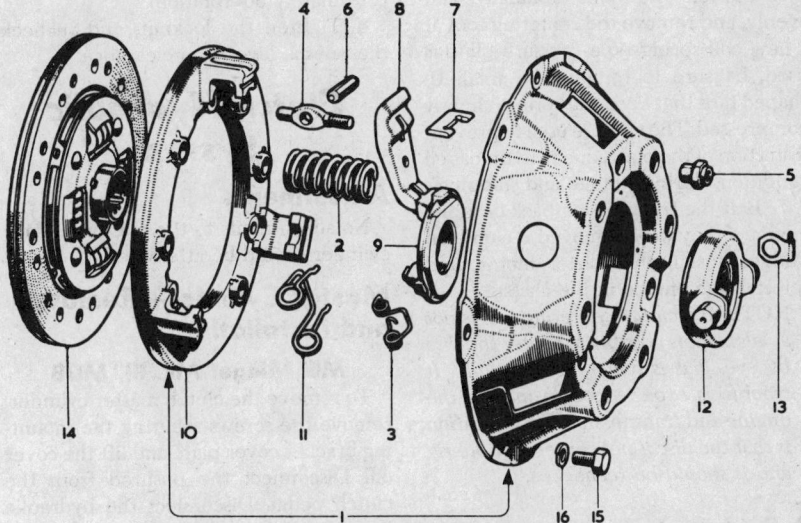

MG Midget Clutch Components

1. Pressure plate assembly
2. Spring
3. Release fork retainer
4. Eyebolt
5. Eyebolt nut
6. Release fork pin
7. Strut
8. Release fork
9. Thrust plate
10. Pressure plate
11. Anti-rattle spring
12. Release bearing
13. Retainer
14. Disc
15. Pressure plate mounting bolt
16. Lockwasher

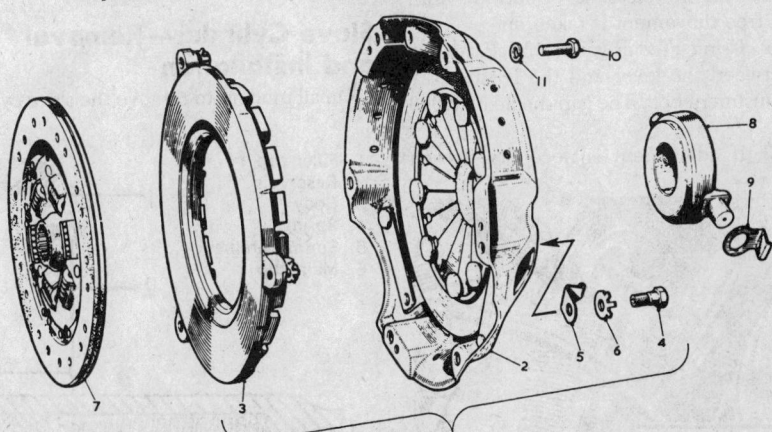

MGB clutch components

1. Pressure plate assembly
2. Cover with driving struts and springs
3. Pressure plate
4. Strut bolt
5. Clip
6. Locktab
7. Disc
8. Release bearing
9. Bearing retainer clip
10. Pressure plate mounting bolt
11. Lockwasher

bushing with a graphite base grease or white grease such as *Molykote*.

4. Upon reinstallation of the disc and pressure plate, the disc must be centered so that the transmission mainshaft will engage the pilot bushing as well as the disc splines. To accomplish this, install the disc and pressure plate on the flywheel with the bolts only finger tight so that the disc can be moved.

5. At this point a dummy transmission mainshaft or clutch aligning tool (available from most tool manufacturers and from MG dealers) should be inserted through the disc hub and into the pilot bushing to hold the disc in position while the pressure plate bolts are tightened.

6. Tighten the bolts gradually and evenly, and remove the centering tool. If a new coil spring type pressure plate is used, be sure to remove the small U-shaped tabs that keep the springs slightly compressed. The tabs are used to prevent distortion of the plate, due to its unloaded condition, during storage and shipping.

7. Bolt the transmission back onto the engine if they were removed as a unit; on Midget, install the starter motor, and reinstall the engine in the chassis.

NOTE: *If a clutch centering tool is not available it is possible to center the disc by eye, if it is done very carefully. If trouble is experienced in mating the engine and transmission, the indication is that the disc is not centered properly and it should be rechecked.*

Adjustments

When the clutch has been replaced, it will be necessary to adjust the release lever stop and the release bearing stop. The lever stop should be adjusted first, and the procedure is as follows:

1. Pull the release lever outward until all free movement is taken up.

2. Using a feeler gauge, check the gap between the lever and the head of the adjustment bolt. The gap should be 0.020 in.

3. If adjustment is necessary, loosen

the locknut and turn the adjustment bolt in the required direction until the proper clearance is obtained. Tighten the locknut.

Periodic adjustment of the release lever may be necessary as wear occurs; however, the release bearing stop should need adjustment only when the clutch is replaced. To adjust the bearing stop:

1. Screw the stop and locknut away from the clutch cover housing to the limit of travel.

2. Have a helper fully depress and hold the clutch pedal. Screw the stop in until it contacts the housing.

3. Release the clutch pedal, and turn the stop in a further 0.002–0.005 in. (approximately 30° rotation).

4. Tighten the locknut, and recheck the release lever stop clearance.

Clutch Hydraulic System

Adjustments

No adjustments to the master or slave cylinder should be attempted.

Master Cylinder—Removal and Installation

MG Midget Mk. III, MGB

To remove the clutch master cylinder, remove the screws securing the mounting bracket cover plate and lift the cover off. Disconnect the pushrod from the clutch pedal. Disconnect the hydraulic line from the clutch master cylinder and cap it. Remove the cylinder mounting bolts and lift the cylinder out.

Installation is in reverse order of removal. When the hydraulic line has been reconnected the clutch hydraulic system must be bled.

Slave Cylinder—Removal and Installation

On all models, to remove the slave cyl-

inder simply disconnect and cap the hydraulic line, disconnect the pushrod from the clutch release lever, and unbolt and remove the cylinder.

Installation is in reverse order of removal. When the hydraulic line has been reconnected, the clutch hydraulic system must be bled.

Master and Slave Cylinder Rebuilding

Rebuilding kits are available, and usually contain the rubber seals and metal washers. Pistons and springs are available as individual pieces.

When the piston assembly has been removed from the cylinder, examine the bore. If it is pitted or scored the entire cylinder assembly should be replaced. If bore damage is light it may be honed, but in most cases the repair will not be lasting and the cylinder may begin to leak again after a short time. When honing a cylinder, occasionally dip the hone in clean brake fluid for lubrication.

Whenever a cylinder is disassembled for inspection or rebuilding, the rubber seals should be replaced as a matter of course. Before installing the seals lubricate them thoroughly with brake fluid or the special lubricant that is included in some rebuilding kits. All internal components of the cylinder, especially the bore, must be completely free of dirt and grit or the cylinder may leak or fail to operate properly. When installing the piston and seals into the bore make sure that the seal lips are not turned back as they enter the cylinder. Once the cylinder has been installed on the car the clutch hydraulic system must be bled.

Bleeding the Clutch Hydraulic System

The purpose of bleeding the hydraulic system is to expel air that is trapped in the cylinders and lines. Air in the system is what gives the pedal a spongy feel, be-

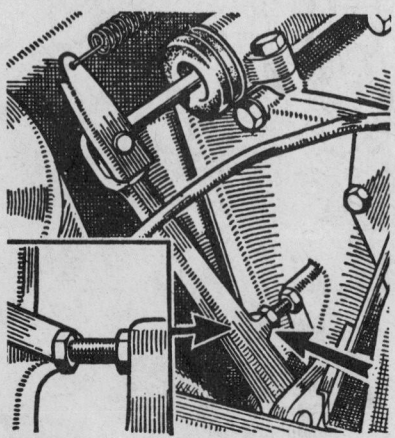

Clutch Release Lever Adjustment

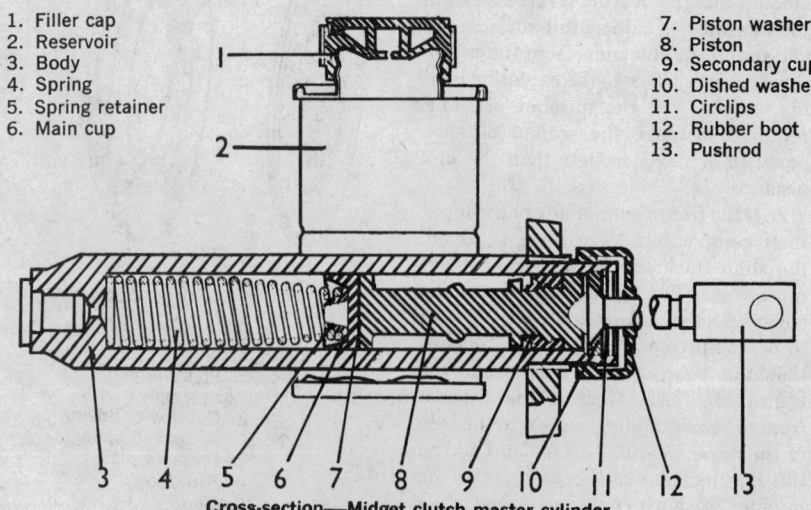

1. Filler cap
2. Reservoir
3. Body
4. Spring
5. Spring retainer
6. Main cup
7. Piston washer
8. Piston
9. Secondary cup
10. Dished washer
11. Circlips
12. Rubber boot
13. Pushrod

Cross-section—Midget clutch master cylinder

cause air can be compressed while a liquid, for all practical purposes, cannot be. Bleeding is accomplished in the following manner:

1. Fill the master cylinder with brake fluid. (Recheck the fluid level often during bleeding.)

2. Attach a rubber tube to the slave cylinder bleed valve and immerse the other end of the tube in a jar or can containing a small amount of clean brake fluid.

3. With a helper in the car pump the clutch pedal several times until some resistance can be felt, hold the pedal down, and open the bleed valve about ½ turn.

4. With the bleed valve still open, pump the pedal slowly through its full travel several times. Close the bleed valve and check the pedal for firmness and proper free-play (about 0.5–1.0 in. free-play before the release bearing contacts the pressure plate).

5. If sponginess or excessive free-play indicates that some air is still in the system, it may be necessary to repeat Step 3 until the fluid running from the bleed valve is clear and free of air bubbles.

DRIVE AXLES

Driveshaft

Removal and Installation

To remove the driveshaft on the Midget, MGB, mark the U-joint flanges and the transmission and differential flanges (for assembly purposes). Remove the nuts and bolts from the flanges and lower the driveshaft assembly. When reinstalling the driveshaft make sure that the alignment marks on the flanges are positioned correctly.

Universal Joint
Removal, Installation and Overhaul

MG Midget, MGB

NOTE: *If only the rear U-joint is to be replaced, unbolt the differential flange from the driveshaft flange and pull the driveshaft out toward the rear of the car to separate the driveshaft at the spline.*

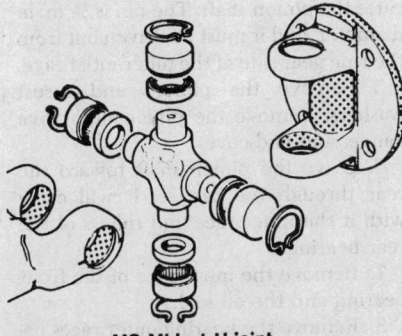

MG Midget U-joint

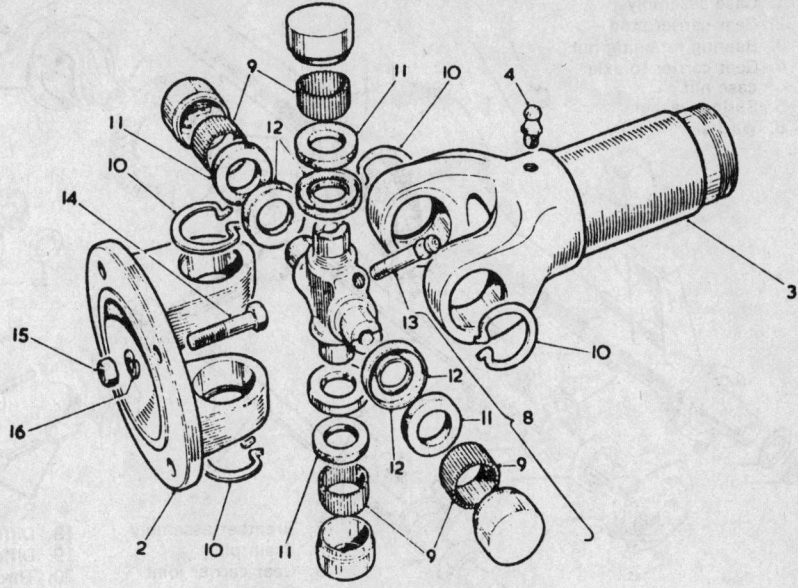

MGB U-joint

2. Flange yoke
3. Sleeve assembly—yoke
4. Lubricator
8. Journal assembly
9. Bearing assembly —needle
10. Circlip
11. Gasket
12. Retainer—gasket
13. Lubricator journal
14. Bolt—shaft to pinion flange
15. Nut for bolt
16. Spring washer

After the driveshaft has been removed and the outside surfaces of the U-joints have been cleaned:

1. Remove all four snap-rings retaining the bearing cups. If the ring does not come out, tap the bearing cup lightly to relieve pressure on the ring.

2. Tap the flange and driveshaft yokes with a hammer until one of the bearings begins to come out. If difficulty is experienced, use a small screwdriver to tap the bearings out from the inside. Repeat this operation until all four bearing cups and their rollers have been removed.

3. Thoroughly clean the flange and driveshaft yokes.

4. Fill the reservoir holes in the spider journals with grease (sealed joints without grease fittings).

5. Fill the bearing cups to a depth of ⅛ in. with grease and install the needle rollers in the cups.

6. Install the seals on the spider journals (sealed joints).

7. Position the spider inside the flange yoke and install the bearings and snap-rings. Place the spider inside the driveshaft yoke and install the remaining two bearings and snap-rings.

NOTE: *Make sure that the grease fittings on joints so equipped face away from the flanges, toward the center of the driveshaft.*

8. Lubricate the joint with a grease gun (early type with grease fitting).

9. Check the joint for freedom of movement. If it binds, tap it lightly with a soft-metal or wooden hammer to re-

lieve pressure from the bearing cups on the ends of the journals.

10. Remove any surplus grease from the joint and replace the driveshaft.

Axle Shaft
Removal and Installation

Midget

1. Raise the rear of the vehicle and support it under the springs.

2. Release the parking brake and back off the brake adjusters if the wheel does not spin freely.

3. Remove the brake drum retaining screws and remove the drum.

Wire Wheels:

4. Remove the nuts which secure the axle hub to the splined wheel hub.

5. Remove the splined wheel hub, and withdraw the axle shaft, gasket, and O-ring.

Disc Wheels:

4. Remove the axle shaft retaining screws and withdraw the axle and gasket.

5. Installation is in reverse order of removal. Always use a new gasket and O-ring (wire wheels). Adjust the brakes if necessary after the wheels have been installed.

MGB/MGB-GT Tube type Axle

The tube-type axle has been used on the MGB since 1967, and on the MGB-GT since its introduction. The tube-type axle is semi-floating, with hypoid ring and pinion gearset. The axle shafts and the

1. Case assembly
2. Gear carrier stud
3. Bearing retaining nut
4. Gear carrier to axle case nut
5. Spring washer
6. Washer

35. Pinion nut
36. Spring washer
37. Hub assembly
38. Wheel stud
39. Nut
40. Oil seal
41. Hub bearing
42. Oil seal ring
43. Hub shaft joint
44. Axle shaft
45. Screw
46. Bumper
47. Axle shaft
48. Hub assembly Wire
49. Wheel stud   wheels
50. Hub extension only
51. Welch plug

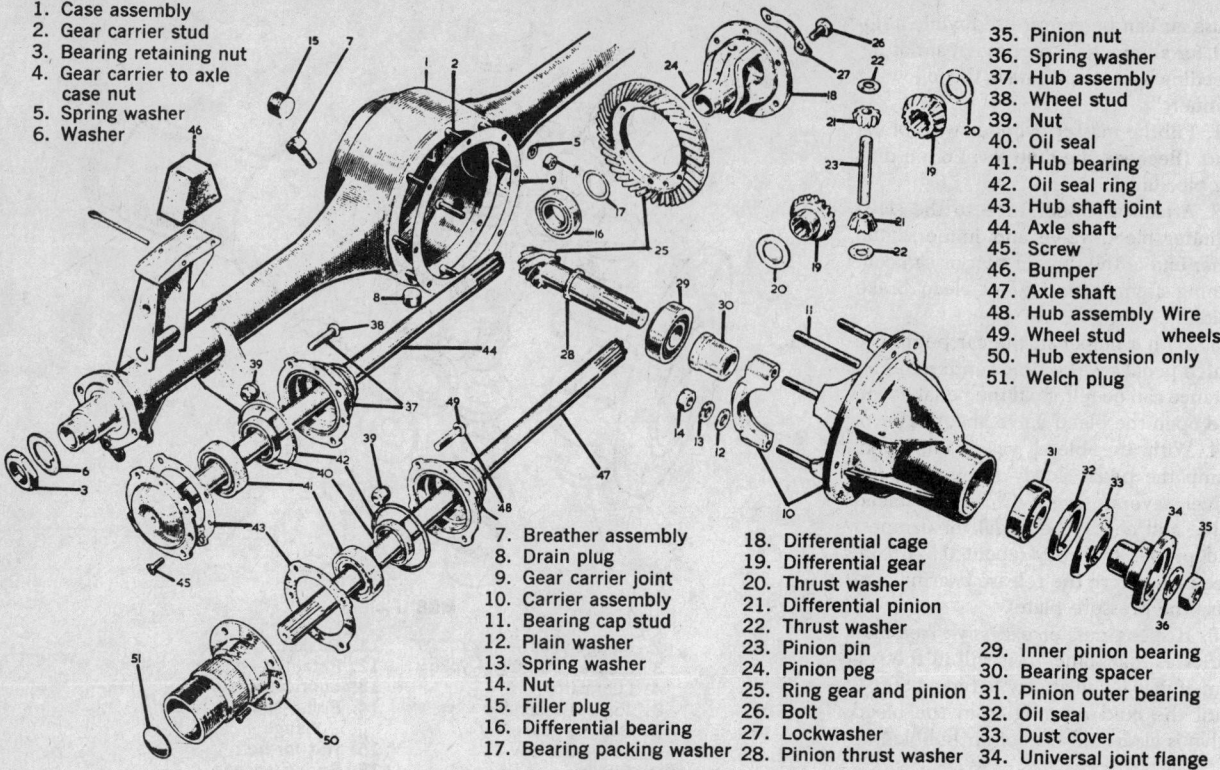

7. Breather assembly
8. Drain plug
9. Gear carrier joint
10. Carrier assembly
11. Bearing cap stud
12. Plain washer
13. Spring washer
14. Nut
15. Filler plug
16. Differential bearing
17. Bearing packing washer

18. Differential cage
19. Differential gear
20. Thrust washer
21. Differential pinion
22. Thrust washer
23. Pinion pin
24. Pinion peg
25. Ring gear and pinion
26. Bolt
27. Lockwasher
28. Pinion thrust washer

29. Inner pinion bearing
30. Bearing spacer
31. Pinion outer bearing
32. Oil seal
33. Dust cover
34. Universal joint flange

Rear axle components—Midget

pinion oil seal can be removed with the drive axle in place.

NOTE: *The GT uses stronger springs which should not be used on the convertible except in axle pairs.*

Axle Shaft and Pinion Oil Seal Removal

1. Raise the rear of the car and remove the wheel.

2. Back off the brake adjuster if the brake drum will not spin freely, and remove the drum.

3. Remove the cotter pin and unscrew the axle shaft nut. Remove the wheel hub.

4. Disconnect the parking brake cable and hydraulic line, and remove the backing plate. Plug the hydraulic line.

5. Remove the oil seal collar, bearing cap, and oil seal from the axle shaft.

6. Attach a slide hammer to the hub and remove it. Remove the axle shaft.

7. Installation is the reverse of removal. The oil seal should be replaced at this time; also the brakes should be bled and adjusted after the drums have been installed.

Differential

Removal and Installation

Midget

1. Drain the drive axle.

2. Remove the axle shafts as previously described.

3. Mark the flanges and disconnect the driveshaft from the differential.

4. Remove the nuts securing the diff-

erential assembly to the drive axle and withdraw the complete assembly.

5. Installation is in reverse order of removal. Always use a new gasket, and make sure that the differential and drive axle mating surfaces are clean.

Disassembly

1. Mark and remove the housing caps, and withdraw the differential cage.

2. Remove the bearings and shims from the cage.

3. Bend back the locktabs, remove the ring gear bolts, and remove the ring gear.

4. Drive out the dowel pin which locates the pinion shaft. The pin is ⅛ in. in diameter, and it must be driven out from the ring gear side of the differential cage.

5. Remove the pinions and thrust washers. Remove the pinion nut, drive flange, and end-cover.

6. Drive the pinion shaft toward the rear through the carrier. It will carry with it the inner race and rollers of the rear bearing.

7. Remove the inner race of the front bearing and the oil seal.

8. Remove the bearing outer races using a puller.

9. Slide off the pinion sleeve and shims.

10. Remove the rear bearing inner race, the spacer, and the bearing outer race.

Assembly

If no components other than the oil seal have been replaced, assembly is in reverse order of disassembly. Note that

the thrust face of the differential bearings are marked with the word THRUST.

If any gears or bearings have been replaced, see "Differential Gear Adjustment."

MGB/MGB-GT

The removal of the differential unit requires a special tool to stretch the axle case and even with this tool it is very easy to permanently damage the case while using the tool. For these reasons, removal and installation of the differential should be left to an MG dealer.

Overhaul

Midget

1. Mark and remove the housing caps, and withdraw the differential cage.

2. Remove the bearings and shims from the cage.

3. Bend back the locktabs, remove the ring gear bolts, and remove the ring gear.

4. Drive out the dowel pin which locates the pinion shaft. The pin is ⅛ in. in diameter, and it must be driven out from the ring gear side of the differential cage.

5. Remove the pinions and thrust washers. Remove the pinion nut, drive flange, and end-cover.

6. Drive the pinion shaft toward the rear through the carrier. It will carry with it the inner race and rollers of the rear bearing.

7. Remove the inner race of the front bearing and the oil seal.

8. Remove the bearing outer races using a puller.

1.	Case assembly	3.	Plain washer	5.	Dust cover	7.	Outer pinion bearing
2.	Nut	4.	Universal joint flange	6.	Oil seal	8.	Bearing spacer

9. Inner pinion bearing
10. Pinion thrust washer
11. Pinion
12. Ring gear
13. Differential cage
14. Bolt
15. Thrust washer
16. Differential pinions
17. Pinion pin
18. Roll pin
19. Thrust washer
20. Differential wheels
21. Differential bearing
22. Spacers
23. Bearing cap
24. Bolt
25. Joint washer
26. Axle case cover
27. Spring washer
28. Set-screws
29. Compensating lever bracket
30. Spring washer
31. Set-screw
32. Spring washer
33. Set-screw

34. Filler and level plug
35. Drain plug
36. Axle shaft
37. Driving flange — Wire wheels only
38. Stud
39. Nut
40. Bearing spacer
41. Bearing
42. Bearing hub cap
43. Oil seal
44. Oil seal collar
45. Axle shaft
46. Driving flange — Disc wheels only
47. Wheel stud
48. Wheel nut
49. Axle shaft collar
50. Axle shaft nut
51. Cotter pin

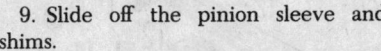

Rear axle components—MGB

9. Slide off the pinion sleeve and shims.

10. Remove the rear bearing inner race, the spacer, and the bearing outer race.

If no components other than the oil seal have been replaced, assembly is in reverse order of disassembly.

Adjustments

Pinion Depth Adjustment

Pinion depth adjustment is an adjustment of the pinion mounting distance D. In the absence of special factory tools for measuring this distance the pinion can be accurately positioned by taking note of the markings on the original and replacement pinions and using suitable shims behind the pinion head. A number with a plus or minus sign is etched into the pinion head C, which is the deviation (in thousandths of an inch) of pinion head thickness from nominal. If there is not an etched number on the pinion head the pinion is of nominal thickness. If, for example, the old pinion is marked −2 and the new pinion is marked −2, the same shims may be used behind the pinion head. If, however, the new pinion is marked −5 a shim or combination of shims 0.003 in. thick must be added as compensation. Therefore, if the new pinion is undersize as compared to the old

one, shims must be added, and if the new pinion is oversize shim thickness must be decreased proportionately.

Pinion Bearing Preload

Preload adjustment is automatically made by the collapsible spacer when the differential drive flange nut is tightened. *It is of extreme importance that the nut is not overtightened.* See "Pinion Oil Seal Replacement" under the applicable model section for tightening procedures and torque values. The collapsible spacer should be replaced whenever the differential is disassembled.

Differential Bearing Preload and Ring Gear Mesh Adjustment

Bearing preload and mesh adjustment can be made simultaneously by first measuring total differential end-play, using a dial indicator to determine shim thickness needed. Either the ring or pinion must be removed to accurately measure end-play. To this measurement must be added 0.004 in., which is the amount of pinch needed to properly preload the bearings (all models).

1. With both gears in position, shift the differential assembly to one side so that the gap at Y is reduced to zero, and measure ring gear backlash with a dial indicator.

2. From the measurement obtained, subtract the correct backlash figure, which is etched into the rear face of the ring gear. This will give the shim thickness required at Y. Subtract this figure from A + 0.004 in., and the remainder will be shim thickness required.

Example:

End-float A	0.060
Plus 0.004 in. preload	0.004
Total shim thickness required	0.064

Shim thickness at Y:
Backlash with zero gap at Y	0.020
Subtract specified backlash (Marked on ring gear.)	0.005
Shim thickness needed	0.015

Shim thickness at X:
Total shim thickness	0.064
Subtract shims needed at Y	0.015
Shim thickness needed	0.049

If the above calculations have been done correctly, backlash should be within specification and the ring gear should be meshing properly with the pinion gear.

3. Gear mesh can be checked by painting the ring gear teeth with red lead or machinist's blue dye and rotating the gear to obtain a mesh pattern. If correction is necessary do not alter the total number of shims (total thickness), but increase or decrease thickness as needed.

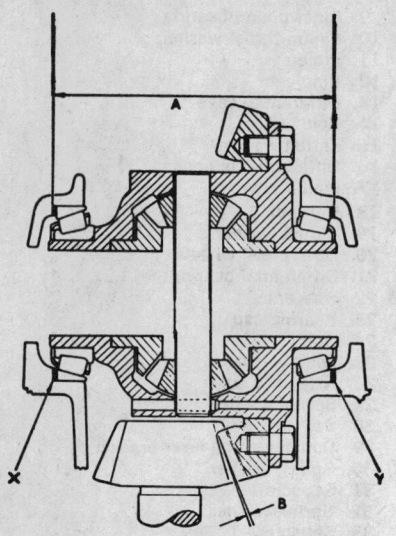

Preload and Ring Gear Mesh Adjustment

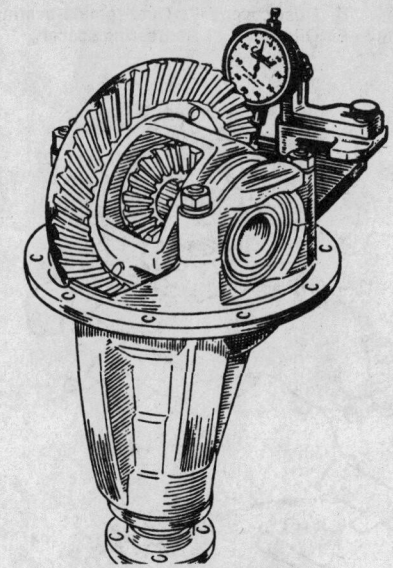

Checking Ring Gear Backlash

REAR SUSPENSION
Springs
Removal and Installation
Midget

1. Raise and support the car as above.
2. Remove the wheels.
3. From inside the car remove the bolts which secure the spring anchor bracket to the body.
4. From beneath the car remove the two front bracket bolts.
5. Remove the four U-bolt nuts and the shock absorber anchor plate.
6. Remove the rear shackle nuts, pins, and plates, and remove the spring.
7. Installation is in reverse order of removal. The axle limit strap may be removed to facilitate U-bolt installation.

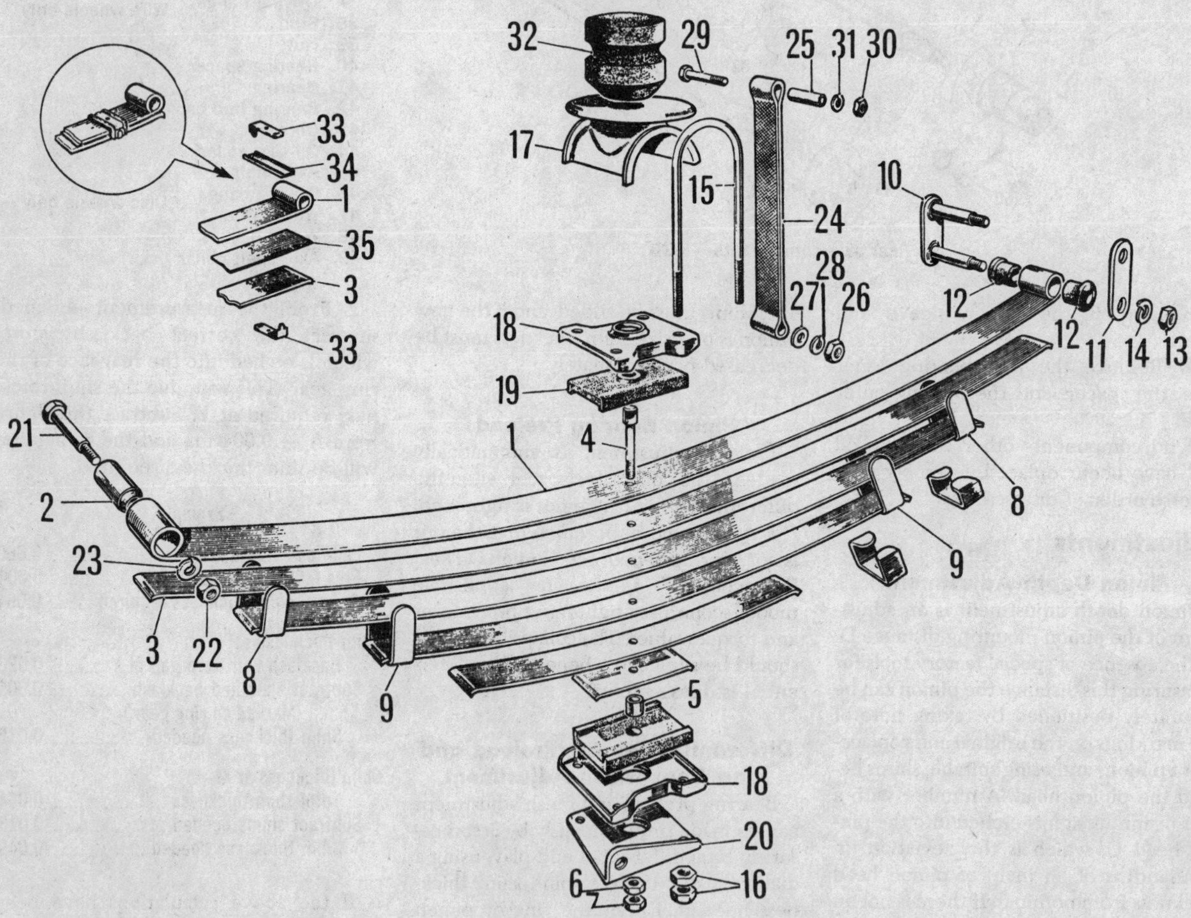

Rear Suspension Components

1. Main leaf assembly	10. Plate	19. Pad	28. Washer
2. Bushing	11. Plate	20. Bracket	29. Bolt
3. Second leaf	12. Bushing	21. Bolt	30. Nut
4. Locating bolt	13. Nut	22. Nut	31. Washer
5. Spacer	14. Washer	23. Washer	32. Bumper
6. Nut	15. Clip	24. Strap	33. Clip
7. Locknut	16. Nut	25. Spacer	34. Pad
8. Clip	17. Pedestal	26. Nut	35. Strip
9. Clip	18. Plate	27. Washer	

Tighten the spring bolt fully after the car is lowered and the spring is loaded.

MGB-MGB-GT

1. Remove the wheel adjacent to the spring that is to be removed.

2. Raise and support the body and support the axle with a hydraulic jack to enable the axle to be lowered to relieve tension in the spring.

3. Disconnect the shock absorber link from its bracket and the rebound strap from the rebound spindle.

4. Remove the nuts and spring washers from the eyebolt and shackle plate pins and take off the outer shackle plate.

5. Using a small screwdriver, tap each shackle plate pin alternately until the plate and pins are free of the spring and mounting bracket.

6. Remove the eyebolt from the front of the spring.

7. Remove the locknuts and nuts from the two "U" bolts. Remove the shock absorber bracket, locating plate, and pad which will fall from the under side of the spring.

8. Remove the spring, the upper locating plate pad, pedestal, and "U" bolts.

9. Installation is the reverse of removal.

Shock Absorber

Removal and Installation

1. To remove a rear shock absorber simply disconnect the connecting link arm from the shock lever and unbolt the unit. Shock absorbers should be replaced in axle sets (pairs).

2. If a new shock absorber appears to operate erratically, allow the hydraulic fluid a few minutes to become de-aerated.

FRONT SUSPENSION

Springs

Removal and Installation

MG Midget and MGB

1. Removal of a front spring requires a spring compressor. Once the spring is slightly compressed the spring seat can be unbolted and the spring withdrawn. If a spring compressor is not available, remove two of the spring seat mounting bolts as shown and substitute two long slave bolts that will allow the spring to expand slowly when unbolted evenly (Midget only).

2. Installation is in reverse order of removal.

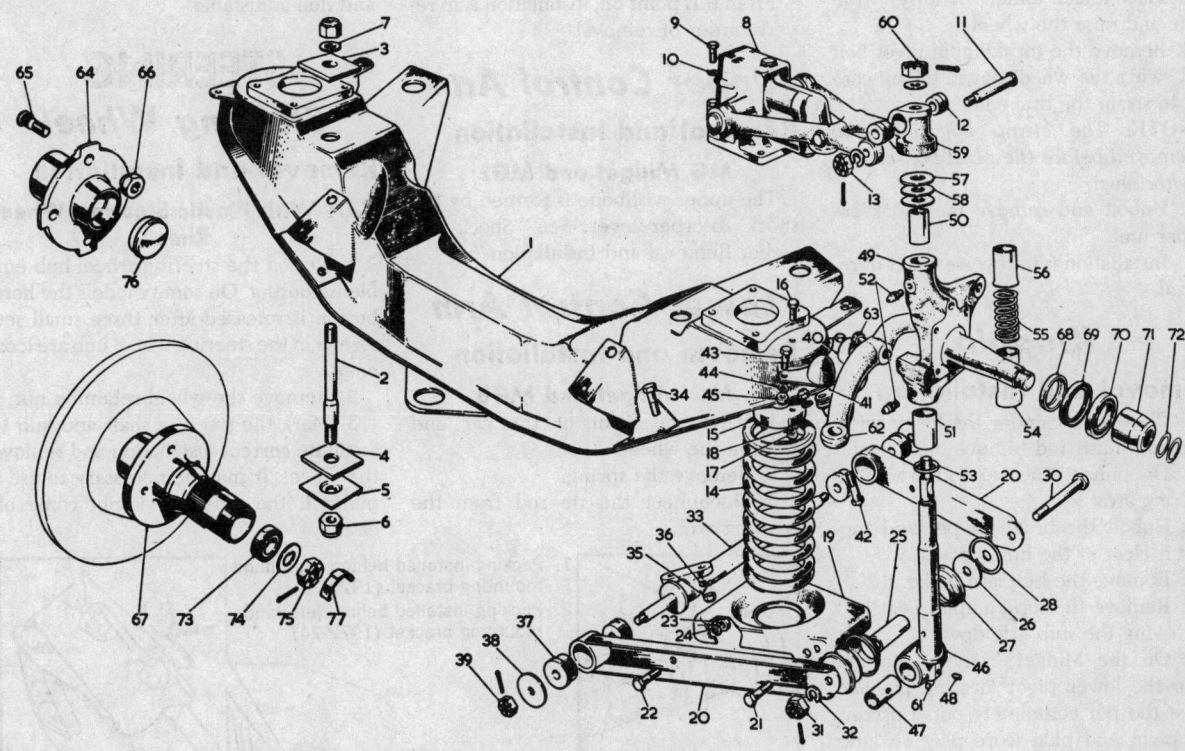

MGB Front Suspension

1. Crossmember	41. Spacer	60. Nut
2. Bolt	42. Bolt	61. Grease fitting
3. Pad	43. Bolt	62. Steering arm
4. Pad	44. Lockwasher	63. Bolt
5. Plate	45. Nut	64. Hub assembly
6. Nut	46. Kingpin	65. Stud
7. Washer	47. Bushing	66. Nut
8. Shock absorber	48. Setscrew	67. Hub assembly
9. Bolt	49. Stub axle assembly	68. Collar
10. Lockwasher	50. Bushing	69. Oil seal
11. Pivot bolt	51. Bushing	70. Bearing
12. Bushing	52. Grease fitting	71. Spacer
13. Nut	53. Seal	72. Shim—.003 in.
14. Spring	54. Spacer	73. Bearing
15. Plate	55. Spring	74. Washer
16. Bolt	56. Spacer	75. Nut
17. Nut	57. Thrust washer	76. Grease cap
18. Lockwasher	58. Floating thrust washer—.052 to	77. Collar
19. Spring pan assembly	.057 in.	
20. Wishbone assembly	59. Trunnion—suspension link.	

21. Bolt	31. Nut
22. Bolt	32. Lockwasher
23. Nut	33. Pivot bracket
24. Lockwasher	34. Bolt
25. Spacer	35. Nut
26. Thrust washer	36. Lockwasher
27. Seal	37. Bushing
28. Support	38. Washer
29. Nut	39. Nut
30. Bolt	40. Buffer

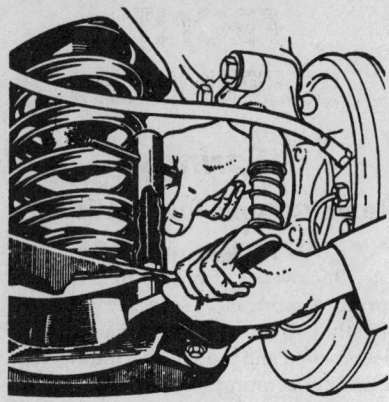

Spring Removal

Shock Absorbers

Removal and Installation

MG Midget and MGB

1. Place a jack under the lower wishbone and raise the wheel.

2. Remove the top kingpin pivot bolt and swing the wheel down, taking care not to strain the brake line.

NOTE: *The clamp bolt must be removed before the pivot bolt can be withdrawn.*

3. Unbolt and remove the shock absorber unit.

4. Installation is in reverse order of removal.

Kingpin

Removal and Installation

1. Place a jack under the lower wishbone and raise and remove the wheel.

2. Disconnect the tie rod from the steering arm.

3. Unbolt the brake caliper and support it clear of the hub.

4. Remove the hub and brake disc.

5. Remove the top kingpin pivot bolt and swing the stub axle down.

6. On the Midget, remove the nut from the lower pivot locating pin and drive the pin completely out. Unscrew the pivot end plug (core plug on later models) and unscrew the pivot using a screwdriver.

7. On the MGB, unscrew the nut from the lower pivot bolt and remove the bolt.

8. Withdraw the stub axle and kingpin assembly from the lower control arm.

9. Unscrew the nut from the top of the stub axle and kingpin assembly and remove the kingpin, washers, and seals.

10. Press the bushings out from the bottom of the axle.

11. Install the new bushings, taking care that the open end of the oil groove enters first and that the hole in the bushing is in line with the lubrication channel in the axle.

12. On the MGB the bushings must be line-bored after installation. (Most ma-

chine shops can perform this operation.) The bushings should be machined to these dimensions:

MGB—top bushing: 0.7815–0.7820 in.; bottom bushing: 0.9075–0.9080 in.

13. On the Midget the kingpin bushings do not require reaming. However, the kingpin should be lubricated and installed to check the fit. If it takes excessive effort to rotate the kingpin, the bushing surfaces may be refinished using a brake cylinder hone.

14. Install the kingpin in the axle body along with the washers and seals, as removed, and tighten the nut.

15. Lubricate the bushings via the grease fittings using a high pressure grease gun, and check the resistance of the kingpin to rotation. If it is excessively stiff, remove the nut and substitute a thinner floating thrust washer (MGB) or a thicker adjustment washer (Midget).

From this point on, installation is in reverse order of removal.

Upper Control Arm

Removal and Installation

MG Midget and MGB

The upper wishbone is formed by the shock absorber lever. See "Shock Absorber Removal and Installation."

Lower Control Arm

Removal and Installation

MG Midget and MGB

1. Raise the front of the car and remove the wheel.

2. Remove the spring.

3. Disconnect the tie rod from the steering arm.

4. Remove the lower kingpin pivot. On the Midget it is necessary to remove the locating pin and pivot bolt end cap before the pivot can be unscrewed.

5. Swivel the stub axle and hub assembly up slightly and support it.

6. Unbolt the wishbone pivot bracket and remove the wishbone.

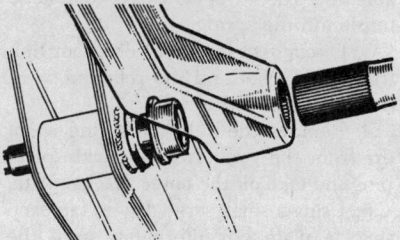

Rear Half of the Control Arm

Adjustments

Front suspension geometry is pre-set and non-adjustable.

STEERING
Steering Wheel

Removal and Installation

Cars With Plastic Steering Wheel Rims

1. Pry off the steering wheel hub emblem housing. On some models the horn button is released after three small setscrews in the steering wheel hub are loosened.

2. Remove the wheel retaining nut.

3. Mark the steering shaft and hub to facilitate correct installation and remove the wheel. It may be necessary to use a puller if the wheel does not come off easily.

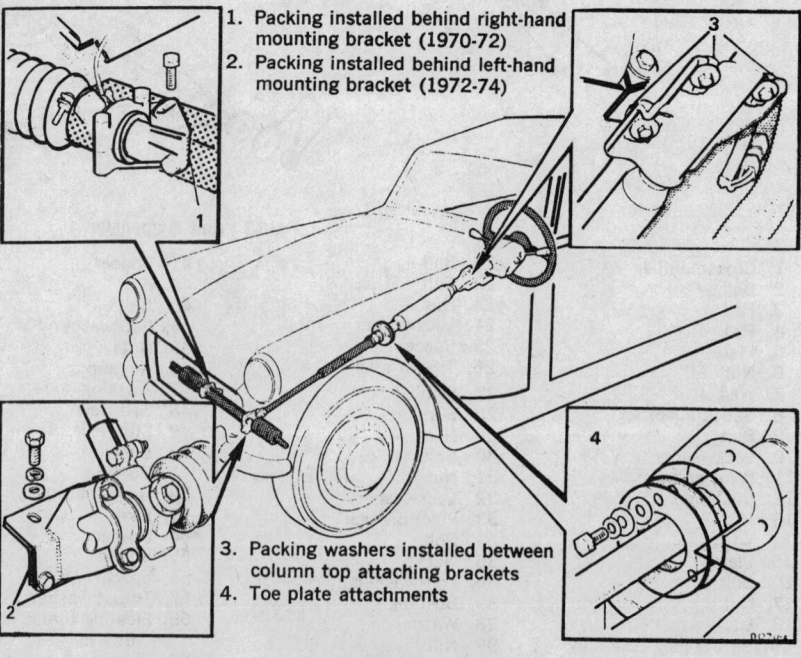

1. Packing installed behind right-hand mounting bracket (1970-72)
2. Packing installed behind left-hand mounting bracket (1972-74)
3. Packing washers installed between column top attaching brackets
4. Toe plate attachments

Steering alignment—Midget

4. Installation is in reverse order of removal. Make sure that the steering wheel is centered when the front wheels are straight ahead. The steering wheel nut in all cases should be tightened to 40 ft lbs.

Cars With Leather Covered or Wood Steering Wheel Rims

1. Pry off the steering wheel hub emblem housing.

2. Bend back the locktabs, remove the wheel retaining bolts, and remove the wheel.

3. Installation is in reverse order of re-

moval. The retaining bolts should be tightened to 12–17 ft lbs.

Turn Signal Switch

Unfasten the screws that hold the halves of the steering column shroud together. Remove both halves, except on the late MGB models, on which it is

necessary only to remove the left (turn signal side) of the shroud.

Disconnect the snap connector (underneath the instrument panel), and remove the screws that mount the switch. Remove the switch assembly.

Installation is the reverse of removal.

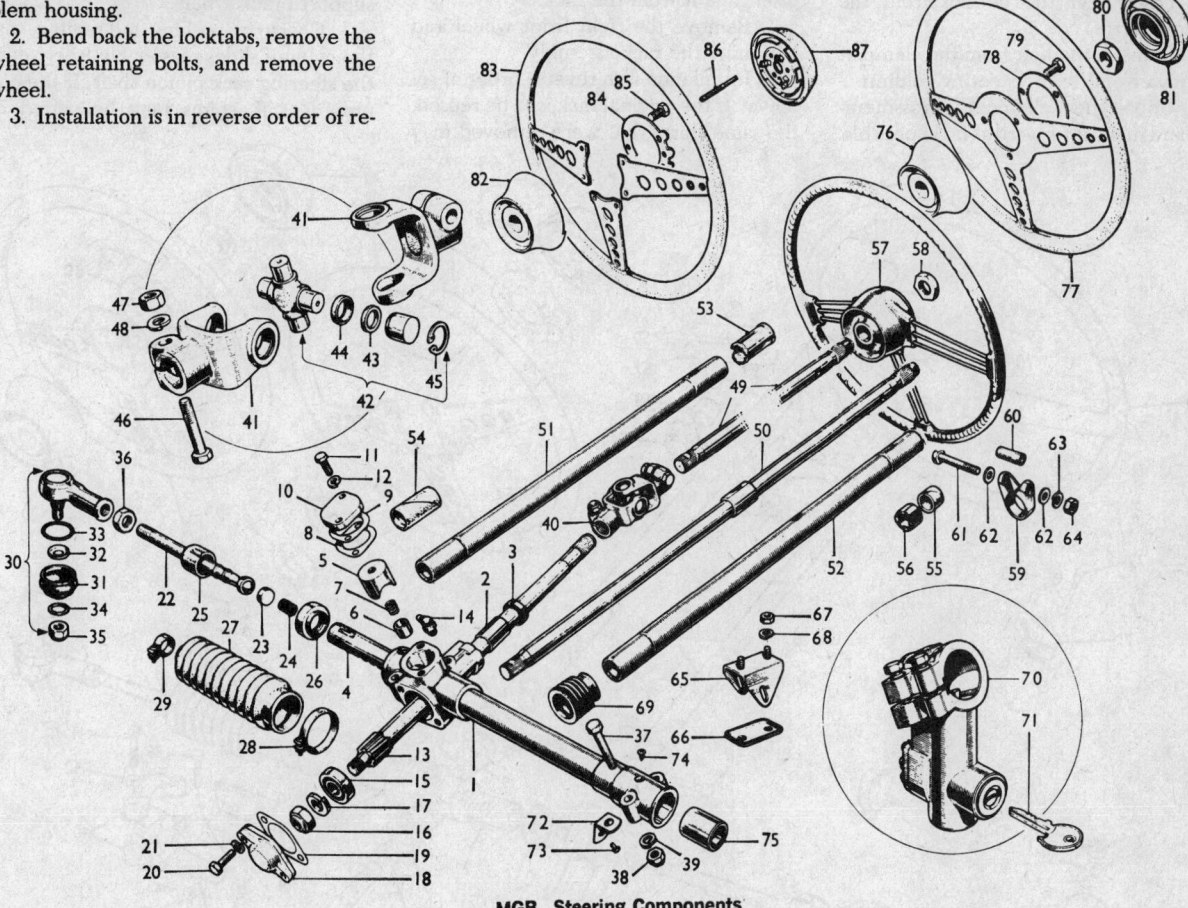

MGB Steering Components

1. Housing assembly
2. Bushing
3. Seal
4. Rack
5. Yoke
6. Damper
7. Spring
8. Shim
9. Gasket
10. Cover plate
11. Bolt
12. Lockwasher
13. Pinion
14. Grease fitting
15. Pinion bearing
16. Nut
17. Lockwasher
18. End cover
19. Gasket
20. Bolt
21. Lockwasher
22. Tie-rod
23. Ball seat
24. Thrust spring
25. Housing
26. Locknut
27. Seal
28. Clip
29. Clip
30. Socket assembly
31. Boot
32. Retainer
33. Spring
34. Washer
35. Nut
36. Locknut
37. Bolt
38. Nut
39. Lockwasher
40. Steering column U-joint
41. Yoke
42. Journal assembly
43. Seal
44. Retainer
45. Circlip
46. Bolt
47. Nut
48. Lockwasher
49. Column assembly—inner
50. Column assembly—inner—R.H.D.
51. Coumn tube
52. Column tube—R.H.D.
53. Bearing
54. Bearing
55. Bushing (felt)
56. Clip
57. Steering wheel
58. Nut
59. Clamp
60. Spacer
61. Bolt
62. Washer
63. Lockwasher
64. Nut
65. Bracket
66. Plate
67. Nut
68. Lockwasher
69. Boot
70. Lock assembly—steering and ignition
71. Key
72. Shim
73. Rivet
74. Bushing locating screw
75. Bushing
76. Wheel hub
77. Steering wheel
78. Ring
79. Bolt
80. Nut
81. Emblem housing
82. Wheel hub
83. Steering wheel
84. Ring
85. Bolt
86. Horn push contact
87. Horn push
When steering lock is fitted.
1970 and later cars.

Steering Gear

Removal and Installation

MG Midget—1972

1. Remove the radiator.
2. Disconnect the tie-rods from the steering arms.
3. Remove the bolt from the clamp at the lower end of the steering column.
4. Unbolt the rack from the crossmember and move it forward as far as possible.

Note the number of shims used under the rack.

5. Remove the three bolts from the steering column retaining plate near the firewall.
6. Loosen the three steering column support bracket bolts from inside the car and pull the column back far enough to disengage it from the rack.
7. Remove the right front wheel and withdraw the rack assembly.
8. Installation is in reverse order of removal. If the original rack is to be reused, the same shims that were removed may

be used also and steering column alignment should be correct. If a new rack is to be used, alignment should be carried out as follows:

1. Push the steering column forward as far as it will go (after the rack is in position).
2. Tighten the three steering column support bracket bolts.
3. Check, by pushing and pulling, that the column slides reasonably freely over the steering rack pinion shaft. If the column is stiff, shims may be added or

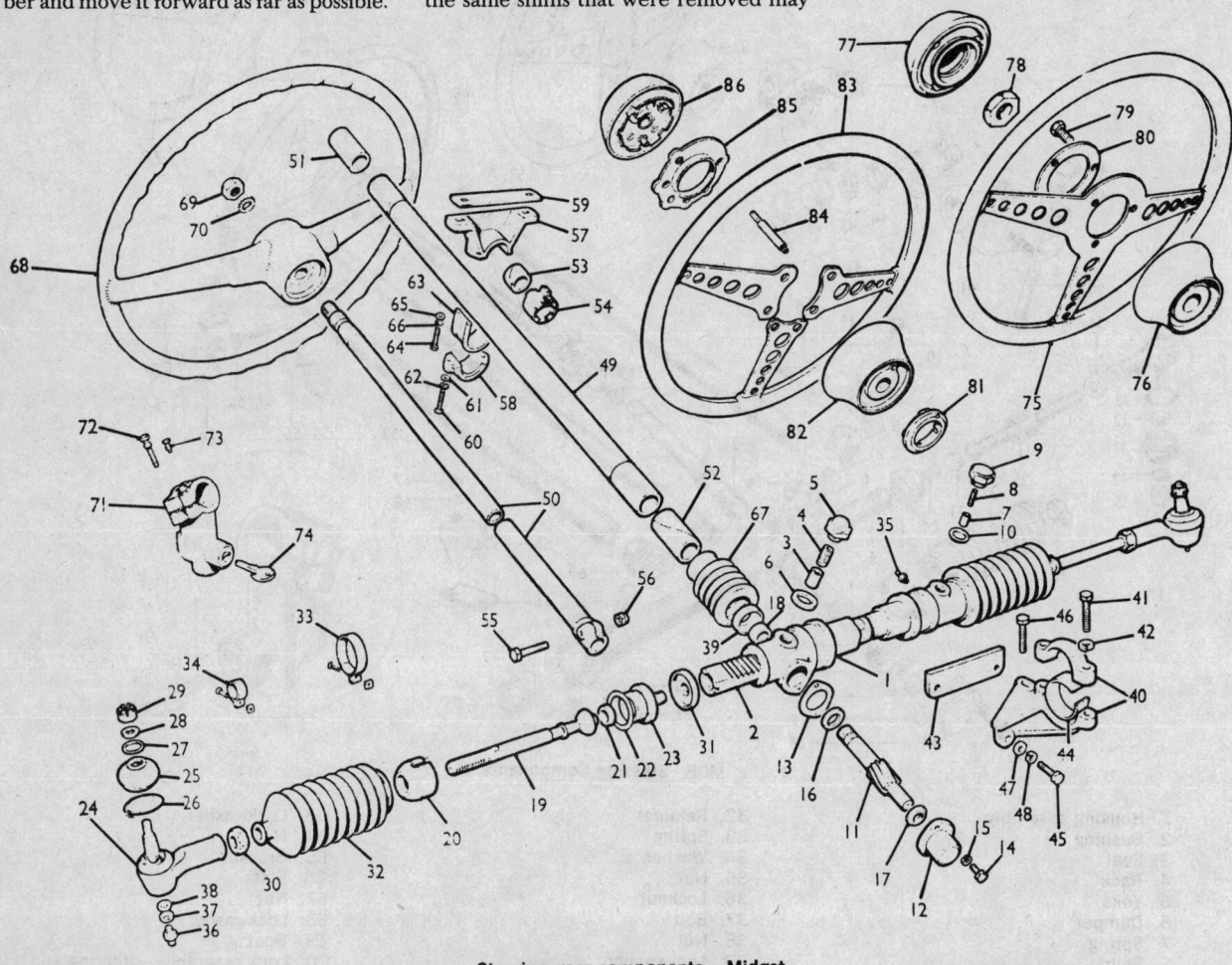

Steering gear components—Midget

1. Rack housing	23. Ball housing (male)	45. Setscrew	67. Draught excluder
2. Rack	24. Ball socket assembly	46. Setscrew	68. Steering wheel
3. Damper pad	25. Boot	47. Plain washer	69. Nut
4. Damper pad spring	26. Clip	48. Spring washer	70. Lockwasher
5. Damper pad housing	27. Ring	49. Outer column	71. Steering column lock
6. Shim	28. Plain washer	50. Inner column tube	72. Shear bolt
7. Secondary damper pad	29. Nut	51. Felt bearing (top)	73. Locating screw
8. Secondary damper spring	30. Locknut	52. Felt bearing (bottom)	74. Lock key
9. Secondary damper housing	31. Lock washer	53. Felt bearing (bottom)	75. Steering wheel
10. Housing washer	32. Seal	54. Clip	76. Steering wheel nut
11. Pinion	33. Clip (inner)	55. Bolt	77. Badge Midget Mk. III (GAN5)
12. Pinion tail bearing	34. Clip (outer)	56. Nut	78. Nut
13. Shim	35. Lubricator	57. Bracket	79. Set screw
14. Setscrew	36. Lubricator	58. Bracket cap	80. Locking ring
15. Spring washer	37. Dished washer	59. Shim	81. Slip-ring
16. Pinion thrust washer (top)	38. Fiber washer	60. Setscrew	82. Steering wheel boss
17. Pinion thrust washer (bottom)	39. Retainer	61. Plain washer	83. Steering wheel From car number
18. Pinion seal	40. Bracket and cap assembly	62. Spring washer	84. Horn contact Midget Mk. III (GAN5)
19. Tie-rod	41. Setscrew	63. Seating	85. Lock-ring 89515
20. Ball housing (female)	42. Spring washer	64. Setscrew	86. Horn push
21. Ball seat	43. Seating	65. Plain washer	
22. Shim	44. Packing	66. Spring washer	

removed from behind the rack or the column support bracket.

MG MIDGET—1973 on:

1. Remove the radiator and turn the steering wheel to the straight ahead position with the slot of the column clamp uppermost. Remove the wheels.

2. Remove the nuts from the tie rod assemblies and detach the tie rod assemblies from the steering levers.

3. Remove the steering column "U" bolt and the three toe plate bolts.

4. Loosen the three steering column upper retaining bolts and pull the column back enough to disengage the sleeve from the pinion.

5. Mark the steering rack housing in relation to the mounting bracket to assist when replacing.

6. Remove the clamps and bolts from the mounting brackets and withdraw the steering rack assembly.

To install:

7. Position the rack on the mounting brackets and install the clamps, but do not tighten the clamp bolts.

8. Make sure that the rack is in the straight ahead position with the pinch bolt flat on the top of the pinion shaft.

9. Check that the column is in the straight ahead position with the slot of the clamp at the top.

10. Slide the column over the pinion shaft as far as it will go; then tighten the three toe plate bolts.

11. Turn the steering wheel one complete turn to the left and right; check that the marks made in the removal section, step 5, are aligned, and tighten the clamp bolts.

12. Tighten the steering column "U" bolt to 9–12 ft lbs.

13. Reverse the procedure in steps 1 and 2.

MGB

1. Disconnect the batteries and take the air cleaners off the carburetors.

2. Turn the steering wheel so that the wheels point straight ahead.

3. Mark the inner steering column and the universal joint to ensure correct alignment when reinstalling.

4. Remove the pinch bolt and nut securing the universal joint to the steering column.

5. Disconnect the multi-connector block; disconnect the wiring from the ignition switch.

6. Remove the bolts retaining the steering column upper and lower support clamp brackets; note the location, quantity, and thickness of the packing washers between the column upper fixing flanges and the body brackets. Remove the washers.

NOTE: *If the packing washers are mislaid or their installed positions not re-*

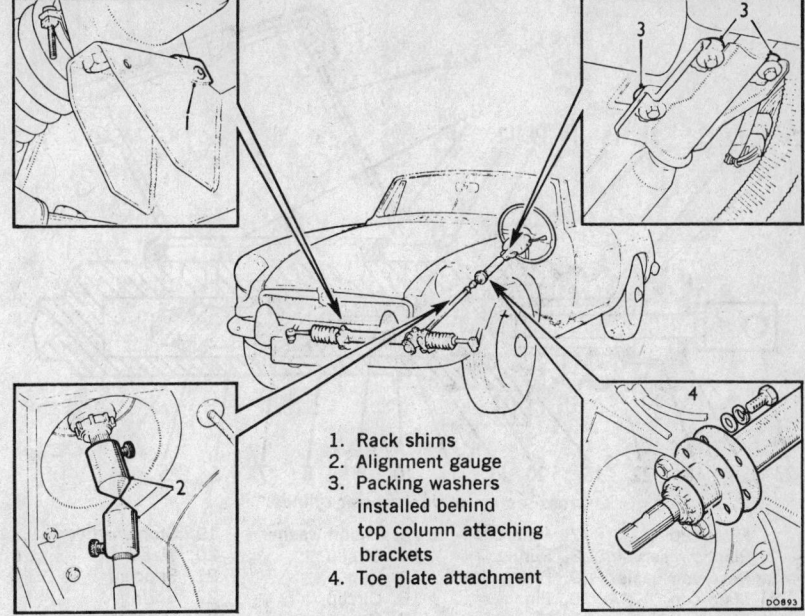

1. Rack shims
2. Alignment gauge
3. Packing washers installed behind top column attaching brackets
4. Toe plate attachment

Steering alignment—MGB

corded, the steering must be aligned when the column is refitted.

7. Remove the steering column complete with outer tube, steering wheel, direction indicator and ignition/steering lock switch.

Installation is the reverse of removal but note the following:

8. Check that the steering rack is in the straight ahead position.

9. Check that the steering column is in the straight ahead position.

10. Note that in steps 1 and 4–8, the outer tube is installed to the steering column with the gaitered end towards the floor board. In step 3, ensure that the marks align when installing the inner column to the universal joint.

To align the steering column:

11. Remove the three bolts from the steering column retaining plate near the firewall.

12. Install the rack assembly with the shims that were originally removed and check, by pushing and pulling, that the column slides reasonably freely over the steering rack pinion shaft. If the column is stiff, shims may be added or removed from behind the rack or the steering column support bracket.

Adjustments

No adjustments are possible.

Steering/Ignition Lock Switch

Removal and Installation— All Models

1. Disconnect the battery(s).
2. Mark and disconnect the wires from the ignition switch.

3. Insert the key and unlock the steering.

4. Unbolt the lock bracket through the access hole in the upper surface. On some models it will be necessary to use an *easy-out* to remove the bolts.

5. Loosen the steering column support bracket to aid in removal, and withdraw the lock switch assembly.

6. Installation is in reverse order of removal.

BRAKE SYSTEMS
Adjustment

While turning wheel, rotate adjuster clockwise until shoes lock the drum, then turn back slightly until wheel rotates freely.

Master Cylinder
Removal and Installation
MG Midget Mk. III, MGB

To remove the brake master cylinder, remove the screws which secure the mounting bracket cover plate and lift the cover off. Disconnect and cap the hydraulic line(s) from the cylinder. Remove the mounting bolts and lift the cylinder out.

Installation is in reverse order of removal. When the hydraulic lines have been reconnected, the brakes must be bled.

Overhaul

Rebuilding kits are available, and usually contain the check valve, rubber seals,

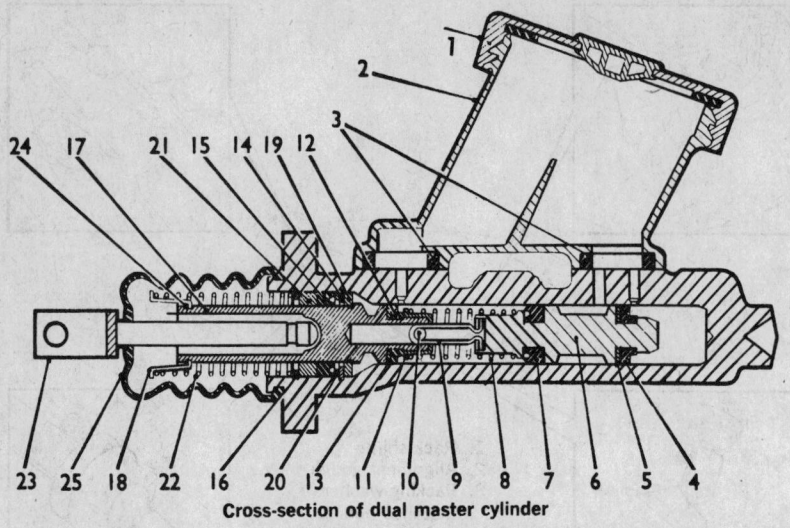

Cross-section of dual master cylinder

1. Filler cap	7. Main cup	13. Pinion washer	19. Stop washer
2. Plastic reservoir	8. Spring	14. Circlip	20. Washer
3. Reservoir seals	9. Piston link	15. Cup	21. Spacer
4. Main cup	10. Pin	16. Circlip	22. Spring
5. Piston washer	11. Pin retainer	17. Piston	23. Pushrod
6. Piston	12. Main cup	18. Spring retainer	24. Retainer ring

and metal washers. Pistons and springs are available as individual pieces.

When the piston assembly has been removed from the cylinder, examine the bore. If it is pitted or scored the entire cylinder assembly should be replaced. If bore damage is light, it may be honed; but in most cases the repair will not be lasting and the cylinder may begin to leak again after a short time. When honing a cylinder, occasionally dip the hone in clean brake fluid for lubrication.

Whenever a cylinder is disassembled for inspection or rebuilding, the rubber seals should be replaced as a matter of course. Before installing the seals lubricate them thoroughly with brake fluid or the special lubricant that is included in some rebuilding kits. All internal components of the cylinder, especially the bore, must be completely free of dirt and grit or the cylinder may leak or fail to operate properly. When installing the piston and seals into the bore, make sure that the seal lips are not turned back as they enter the cylinder. Once the cylinder has been installed on the car the brakes must be bled.

Brake Bleeding

There are two methods of accomplishing this. The quickest and easiest of the two is pressure bleeding, but special pressure equipment is needed to externally pressurize the hydraulic system. The other, more commonly used method is gravity bleeding.

NOTE: *Only brake fluid conforming to SAE specification J1703 should be used.*

Gravity Bleeding Procedure

1. Clean the bleed valve at each wheel.
2. Attach a small rubber hose to the bleed valve on one of the rear wheel cylinders and place the other end in a container of brake fluid.
3. Top up the master cylinder with brake fluid (check often during bleeding).
4. Open the bleed valve about one-quarter turn, have assistant press the brake pedal to the floor and slowly release it. Continue until no more air bubbles are forced from the cylinder on application of the brake pedal.

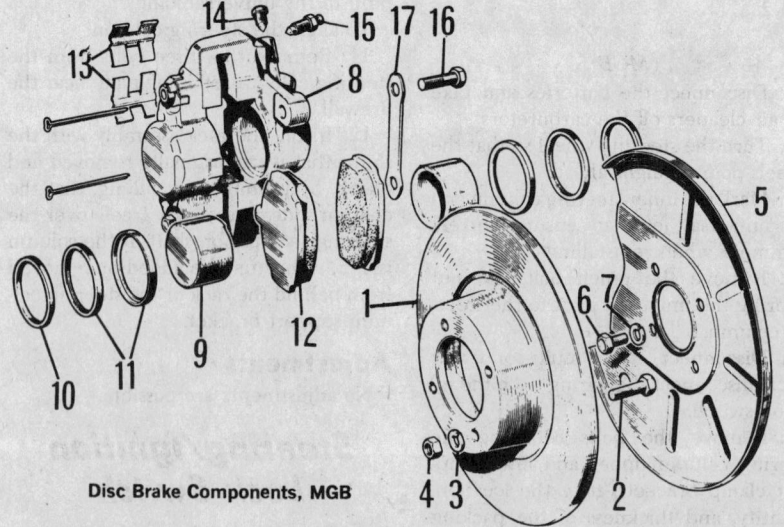

Disc Brake Components, MGB

1. Disc	7. Lockwasher	13. Retaining springs
2. Bolt	8. Caliper	14. Plug
3. Lockwasher	9. Piston	15. Bleed valve
4. Nut	10. Piston seal	16. Bolt
5. Dust cover	11. Dust seal and retainer	17. Locktab
6. Bolt	12. Pad	

5. Repeat for each of the remaining wheel cylinders, beginning with the other rear wheel.

FRONT DISC BRAKES
Disc Brake Pads
Removal and Installation

1. Raise the front of the car and remove the wheel.
2. Remove the two cotter pins that locate the pad retaining spring(s).
3. Remove the retaining spring and pull the pads and anti-squeal shims from the caliper.
4. Installation is in reverse order of removal. It may be necessary to push the pistons back into the caliper so that the new pads will fit. Be careful not to mar the disc in doing so. Install the anti-squeal shims in their original positions or they will not function properly. Pads should never be allowed to wear to a thickness of less than 1/16 in. Replace pads in axle sets (two pair).

Disc Brake Calipers
Removal and Installation

1. Remove the friction pads.
2. Disconnect the hydraulic line retaining plate and disconnect the line from the caliper.
3. Bend back the locktabs and unbolt and remove the caliper.
4. Installation is in reverse order of removal. Tighten the bolts to 40–45 ft lbs. It will be necessary to bleed the brakes after the hydraulic line is reconnected.

Overhaul

1. Remove the caliper and clean the exterior.

2. Temporarily reconnect the hydraulic line to the caliper and press the brake pedal until the pistons protrude far enough to be removed by hand.

3. Remove the dust seals and retainers, taking care not to damage the piston bores.

4. Remove the seals from the pistons using a non-metallic instrument.

NOTE: *It is not normally necessary to separate the caliper halves. If the separation is necessary the fluid transfer hole seal, bridge bolts, and bolt locktabs must be replaced with new parts. Only use bolts obtained from an MG dealer that are supplied for this special application. Torque the bolts to 34–37 ft lbs.*

5. Clean all components in solvent and dry thoroughly with compressed air.

6. Examine the pistons and bores for wear or damage. Damaged pistons should be replaced. Slight bore roughness can be removed with crocus cloth or a brake cylinder hone. Remove all traces of grit from the bore after refinishing. Badly pitted or damaged bores cannot be refinished; the caliper must be replaced.

7. Coat the pistons and piston seals with brake fluid and install the seals on the pistons.

8. Loosen the bleed valve one turn and install the pistons in the bores with the piston cut-away facing inward. Press the piston in until approximately ⅜ in. of the piston is protruding from the bore.

9. Install the dust seals on the pistons.

10. Install the caliper(s) and bleed the brakes.

Brake Disc

Removal and Installation

1. Remove the caliper.

2. Remove the grease cap and cotter pin, and remove the hub retaining nut. Withdraw the hub assembly.

3. Unbolt and remove the disc from the hub.

4. Installation is in reverse order of removal.

Any disc that is badly scored should be replaced. Light scoring is not detrimental to the operation of the brakes, but friction pad life will be reduced. Runout is measured at the outer edge of the disc friction surface with a dial indicator or runout gauge. Parallelism refers to variations in the thickness of the disc. The disc should be measured for parallelism at four equally spaced points around the friction surface.

Wheel Bearings

Removal, Installation and Adjustment

Midget

1. Raise and support the front of the car.

2. Remove the wheel.

3. Remove the brake pads.

4. Remove and support the caliper out of the way.

5. Remove the grease cap, cotter pin and hub nut.

6. Cars using pressed (solid) wheels, remove the hub with tool 18G304 and adapters. Cars with wire wheels, use tool 18G1032.

7. Remove the outer bearing from the hub and hammer out the race with a drift. Remove the inner bearing and race in a like manner.

8. Pack the new bearings with grease so that the grease protrudes from the bearings.

9. Drive the races into place and install the bearings and grease seal.

10. Pack the hub recess with grease and install the hub on the spindle.

11 Tighten the hub bolt to 46 ftlb and align the cotter pin hole by tightening, if necessary, the nut.

12. Assemble remaining parts in reverse of removal.

MGB

1. Raise and support the front of the car.

2. Remove and support the caliper out of the way.

3. Remove the grease cap, cotter pin and nut.

4. On cars with solid wheels, remove the hub with tool 18G304 and adapters. On cars with wire wheels, use tool 18G363.

5. From the hub, remove the bearing retaining washer, outer bearing, shims, spacer, inner bearing, oil seal collar and oil seal.

6. If necessary, the races may be hammered out with a drift.

7. Install new races, if necessary.

8. Pack each bearing with grease until it squeezes out.

9. Fill the cavity between the bearing and the oil seal with grease and lightly grease the spacer.

10. Assemble hub parts, minus the shims, and install hub on spindle.

11. Install the retaining washer and nut and tighten the nut until the bearings bind.

12. Remove the nut and hub and pull the outer race.

13. Install enough shims to produce excessive end play, install the parts and hub and check the end play with a dial gauge. Reduce the number of shims to give an end play of 0.0020.004".

14. When desired end play is attained, tighten the nut to 40-70 ftlb., aligning the cotter pin hole.

15. Install a new cotter pin. Install remaining parts.

Drum Brake Shoes

Removal and Installation

Brake shoes should always be replaced in axle sets. Replace riveted shoe assemblies or linings when they have less than 40% of original thickness left at the thinnest point, and bonded shoe assemblies or linings when they have less than 25% of original thickness left at the thinnest point. Examine the linings for signs of cracking and oil or brake fluid contamination.

With the drum off, examine the wheel cylinders for leakage. Check the brake springs for stretching and clean the backing plate after the shoes have been removed. Lightly lubricate the brake shoe contact points on the backing plate before installing the new shoes. Adjust the brakes after installation.

Brake Drums

Removal and Installation

1. Raise the car and remove the wheel.

2. Back off the brake adjuster if the drum will not spin freely.

3. Remove the drum retaining screws or nuts and pull the drum off the hub.

4. Installation is in reverse order of removal. Adjust the brakes when the drum has been replaced on the hub.

Wheel Cylinders

Ideally, wheel cylinder assemblies should be replaced when they begin to leak. However, seal kits are available and a rebuilt cylinder should function well if it has been rebuilt carefully. Use the illustrations at the beginning of the brake section for disassembly and assembly, and refer to "Master Cylinder Rebuilding" for inspection and rebuilding notes. It is possible to rebuild a wheel cylinder without removing it from the backing plate. In any case, cleanliness is of extreme importance. Adjust and bleed the brakes after the drum has been reinstalled.

Parking Brake

Cable

Adjustment

Adjustment can be made at the brake balance lever where the main parking brake cable splits into separate cables for each rear wheel, underneath the car near the axle. Adjust the cable so that the brake is fully applied when the lever is pulled up four or five notches. Some cars have grease fittings on the cables and balance lever pivot, and these points must be lubricated regularly to prevent brake drag.

Removal and Installation
Midget

1. Raise and support the rear of the car at the axle.
2. Disconnect the battery ground.
3. Remove the driver's seat.
4. Unbolt the handbrake lever from the mounting plate.
5. Remove the warning switch wires.
6. Unbolt the mounting plate from the tunnel and rotate it 180°.
7. Pull the handbrake lever away from the tunnel and remove the cotter pin and clevis.
8. Remove and separate the handbrake lever and mounting plate.
9. Remove the cotter pin, washer and clevis pin from the equalizer lever.
10. Free the cable rear adjustment nut and slide it along the cable.
11. Remove the threaded sleeve and cable from the equalizer.
12. Remove the cable front lock nut and remove the cable from the front bracket and tunnel.
13. Installation is the reverse of removal. Use new cotter pins.

MGB

1. Raise and support the car.
2. Remove the adjusting nut and remove the cable end from the lower end of the lever.
3. Remove the nut securing the lever to the spindle and remove the spring washer, forked lever and plain washer. Remove the lever.
4. Remove the right side seat.
5. Disconnect the brake switch wiring.
6. Unbolt the ratchet plate from the tunnel.
7. Remove the nut and spring washer securing the outer cable front bracket.
8. Remove the clips securing the cable assembly to the body and axle.

9. Remove the bolt, nut and spring washer securing the two halves of the compensating lever.
10. Completely loosen the self-locking nut securing the lever to the axle bracket and release the cable bracket trunnion from the lever.
11. Remove the cotter pins and clevis pins to release the cable yokes from the levers on the backing plates.
12. Replacement is the reverse of removal.

CHASSIS ELECTRICAL
Heater Blower
Removal and Installation
Midget—1970–72

The heater blower is adjacent to the heater box, on the right-hand side of the engine compartment. To remove the blower, loosen both hose clamps which retain the ducts to the unit, and pull off the ducts. Disconnect the ground and hot leads, remove the sheet metal mounting screws, and remove the blower.

Install in the reverse order of removal.

72–77

1. Disconnect and remove the battery and tray.
2. Disconnect the blower motor cables from the wiring harness at the snap connectors.
3. Remove the three screws and withdraw the blower motor complete with fan from the heater unit cover.

4. Drive the motor spindle out of the fan to release the fan from the motor.
5. Installation is the reverse of removal.

MGB

The heater blower is part of the heater assembly, mounted in the rear of the engine compartment, adjacent to the firewall. To remove the blower, disconnect the batteries, separate the leads at the snap connectors, and remove the three blower mounting bolts.

Install in the reverse order of removal.

Heater Core
Removal and Installation
Midget

The heater core is located in the heater box, mounted directly in front of the battery in the engine compartment. To remove the core, it is necessary to drain the cooling system and proceed as follows:

1. Disconnect the battery cables, and the heater valve control cable. Remove the screws which retain the heater box to the tray.
2. Separate the water hoses and the blower duct from the heater box. Disconnect the air hose from the heater air intake tube.
3. Lift the heater box out of the car as a unit.

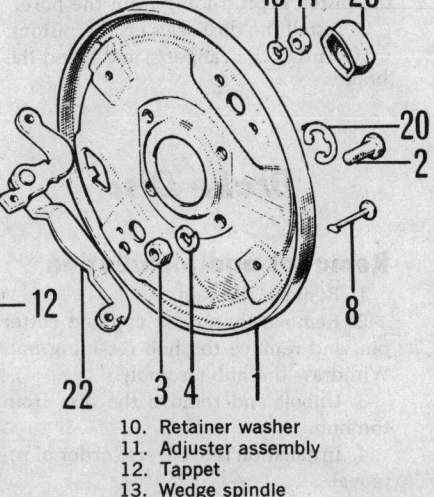

10. Retainer washer
11. Adjuster assembly
12. Tappet
13. Wedge spindle
14. Nut
15. Washer
16. Wheel cylinder assembly
17. Piston
18. Piston seal
19. Piston boot
20. Wheel cylinder retaining clip
21. Bleed valve
22. Parking brake lever
23. Parking brake lever boot
24. Brake drum
25. Drum retaining screw
26. Drum retaining nut
(wire wheels)

1. Backing plate
2. Bolt
3. Nut
4. Lockwasher
5. Shoe assembly
6. Spring
7. Spring
8. Shoe retaining pin
9. Brake-shoe retaining spring

Rear Brake Components

4. The heater core may be removed from the heater box by removing the retaining sheet and metal screws.

5. Install in the reverse order of removal.

6. Bleed the system, if necessary, by removing the return hose from its connector, and extending it with an additional piece of hose, so that water may be returned to the radiator filler.

7. Plug the open connection, and run the engine until water flow into the radiator is free of bubbles.

8. Reconnect the hose as quickly as possible.

MGB

The heater core is located in the heater box, in the rear of the engine compartment, adjacent to the firewall.

1. To remove the heater core, it is necessary to remove the heater assembly as follows:

2. Disconnect the heater valve control cable (if the valve is mounted on the heater box).

3. Separate the blower motor leads at the snap connectors.

4. Drain the cooling system, and remove the water hoses from the heater unit.

5. Remove the screws which retain the heater box in the engine compartment.

6. Remove the center console (speaker panel).

7. Remove the defroster hose plate and pull the defroster tubes out of the heater box.

8. Remove the heater trim panel and loosen the clip which retains the air control cable.

9. Remove the heater air control from the dash panel, disconnect the control cable from it, and lift out the heater assembly.

10. To remove the core from the heater box, pry off the spring clips which retain the front panel to the assembly.

11. Assemble and install in the reverse order of disassembly and removal. Following installation, bleed the heater in the same manner as described for the Midget.

Radio

The radios used in MGs are dealer installed or aftermarket units. It is therefore impossible to give specific procedures for these radios. The following information applies generally to all radios installed in MGs.

Care should be exercised during installation to prevent reversing the ground and power leads. Reversal of the leads will result in serious damage to the radio. The power lead may be identified by an in-line fuse holder. The ground lead is not fused.

Should the speaker require replacement, it must be replaced with one of the same impedance. A speaker of the proper impedance must also be used during initial radio installation (consult the radio manual). Failure to observe proper impedance can result in rapid transistor failure. When installing a second speaker, it is also necessary to maintain impedance at the proper level by using a fader control or altering the entire system to maintain the specified load.

CAUTION: *Never operate a radio without load (no speaker), or with the speaker leads shorted together. This will result in transistor failure.*

Windshield Wiper Motor

Removal and Installation

1. Disconnect the electrical wires from the wiper motor.

2. Remove the wiper arms and wiper arm pivot nuts.

3. Unbolt the motor and withdraw the motor complete with drive cables and wiper arm pivots and gearboxes.

4. Loosen the cover screws in each wiper arm gearbox and remove the rack housings.

5. Remove the wiper motor gearbox cover and disconnect the cross-head and rack from the motor.

Installation is in reverse order of removal. Do not kink or bind the drive cable in any way, and make sure that the wiper arm gearboxes are aligned correctly.

Instrument Cluster

Removal and Installation

Instruments are mounted individually in the panel and are removed by unbolting the panel and releasing the instrument brackets.

Fuse Box Location

The fuse box is located under the dash panel on the right-hand side.

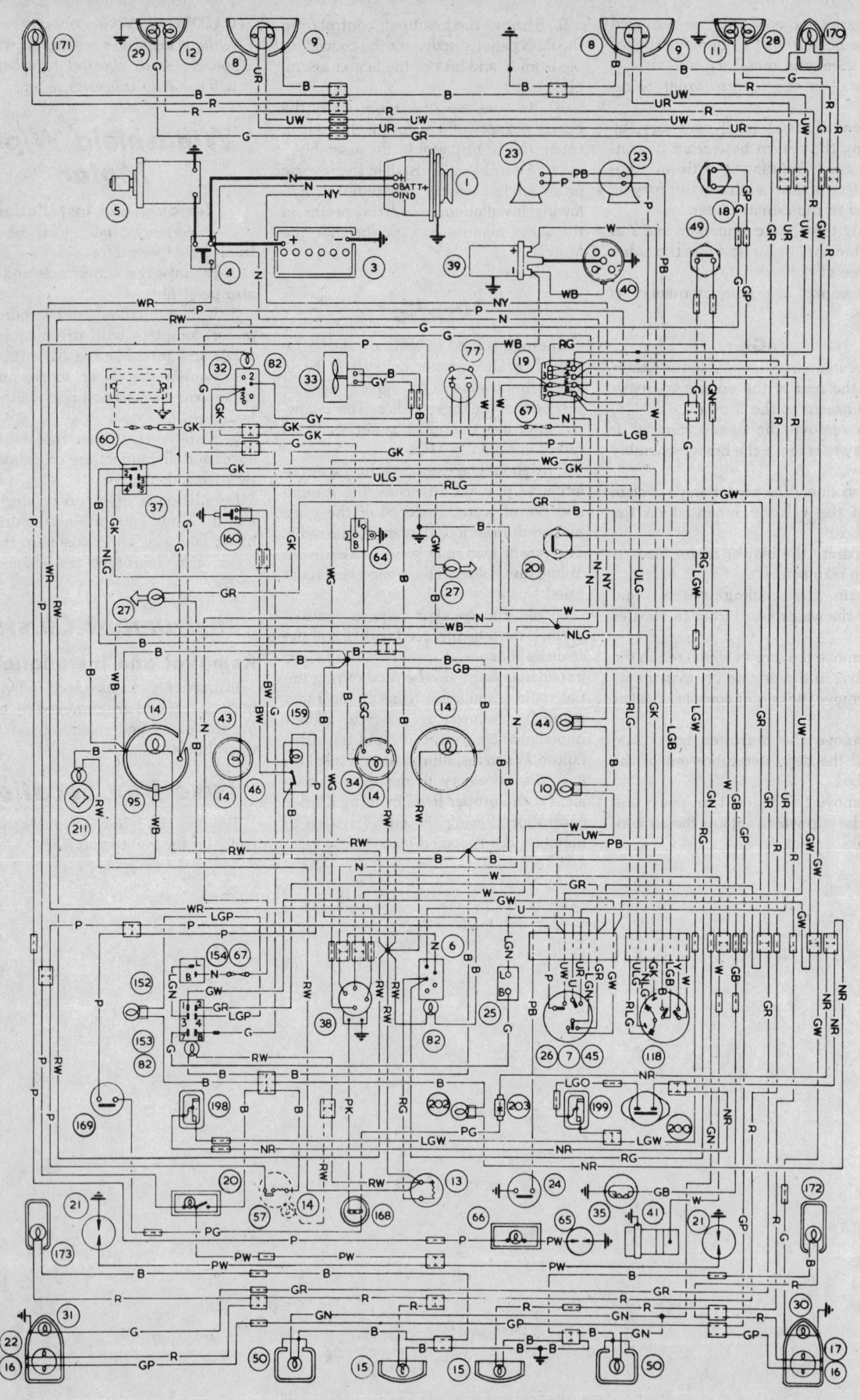

1973-74 Midget (Car No. 123731-138800)

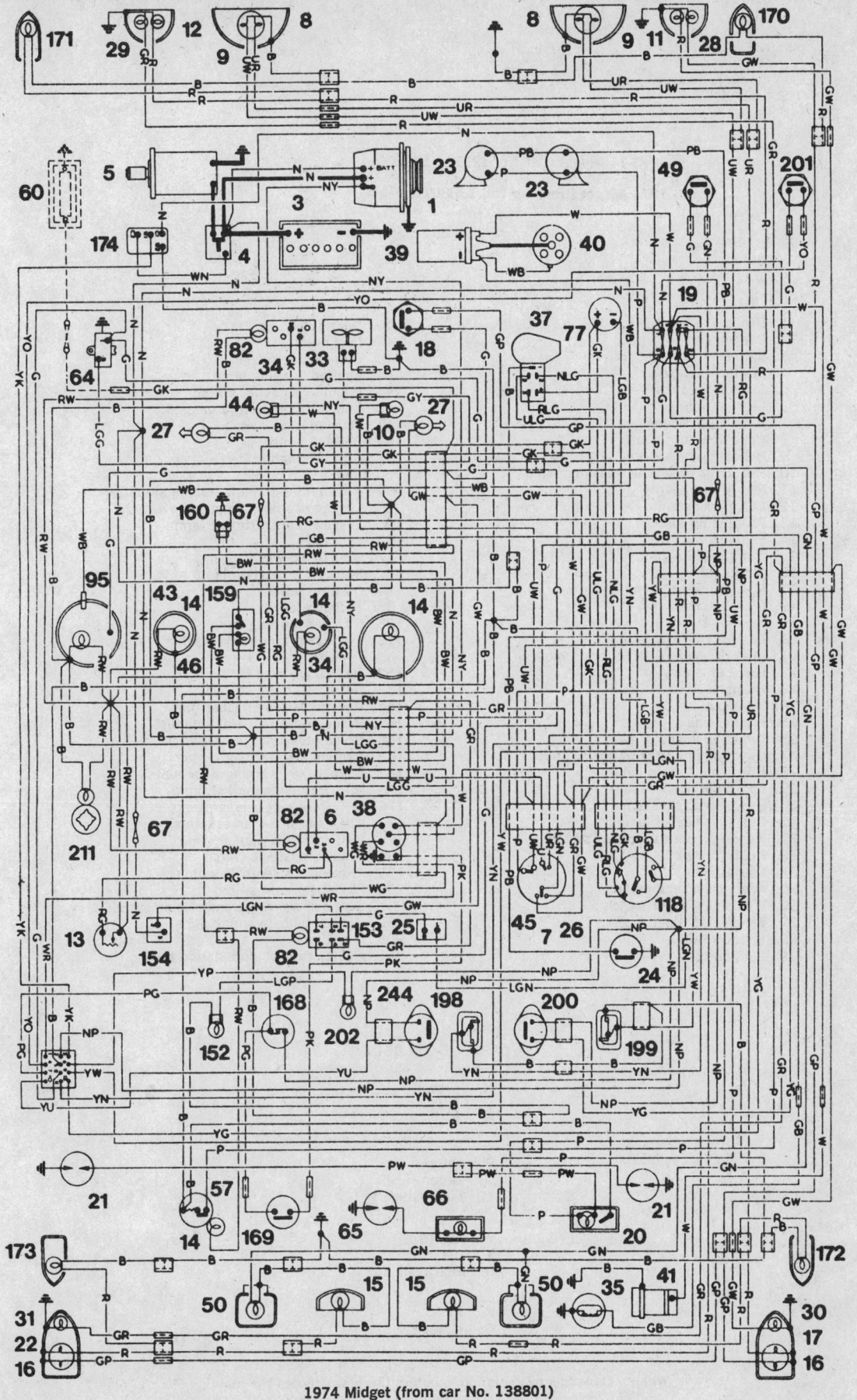

1974 Midget (from car No. 138801)

Wiring Circuits

1973-74 Midget (Car No. 123731-138800)

1974 Midget (from car No. 138801)

1. Dynamo
2. Control box
3. Battery
4. Starter solenoid
5. Starter motor
6. Light switch
7. Headlamp dimmer switch
8. Headlamp low beam
9. Headlamp high beam
10. Headlamp high beam warning lamp
11. R.H. parking lamp
12. L.H. parking lamp
13. Panel lamp switch
14. Panel lamps
15. Number-plate light
16. Stop light
17. R.H. tail lamp
18. Stop lamp switch
19. Fuse unit
20. Interior courtesy lamp
21. Interior courtesy lamp door switch
22. L.H. tail lamp
23. Horns
24. Horn button
25. Flasher unit
26. Direction indicator switch
27. Direction indicator warning lamp
28. R.H. front flasher lamp
29. L.H. front flasher lamp
30. R.H. rear flasher lamp
31. L.H. rear flasher lamp
32. Heater or fresh-air motor switch
33. Heater motor
34. Fuel gauge
35. Fuel gauge sending unit
36. Windshield wiper switch
37. Windshield wiper motor
38. Ignition switch
39. Ignition coil
40. Distributor
41. Fuel pump
43. Oil pressure gauge
44. Ignition warning lamp
45. Headlamp flasher switch
46. Coolant temperature gauge
49. Reverse lamp switch
50. Reverse lamp
57. Cigarette lighter
60. Radio
64. Bi-metal instrument voltage stabilizer
65. Luggage compartment lamp switch
66. Luggage compartment lamp
67. Line fuse
77. Windshield washer pump
82. Switch illumination lamp
94. Oil filter switch
95. Tachometer
105. Oil filter warning lamp
118. Combined windshield washer and wiper switch
152. Hazard warning lamp
153. Hazard warning switch
154. Hazard warning flasher unit
159. Brake pressure warning lamp
160. Brake pressure failure switch
168. Ignition key warning buzzer
169. Ignition key warning door switch
170. R.H. front side-marker lamp
171. L.H. front side-marker lamp
172. R.H. rear side-marker lamp
173. L.H. rear side-marker lamp
198. Driver's seatbelt switch
199. Passenger's seatbelt switch
200. Passenger seat switch
201. Seat belt warning transmission switch
202. 'Fasten belts' warning light
203. Line diode
211. Heater control illumination bulb

CABLE COLOR CODE

N. Brown
U. Blue
R. Red

P. Purple
G. Green
LG. Light Green.s

W. White
Y. Yellow
B. Black

K. Pink
O. Orange

When a cable has two color-code letters the first denotes the main
color and the second denotes the tracer color

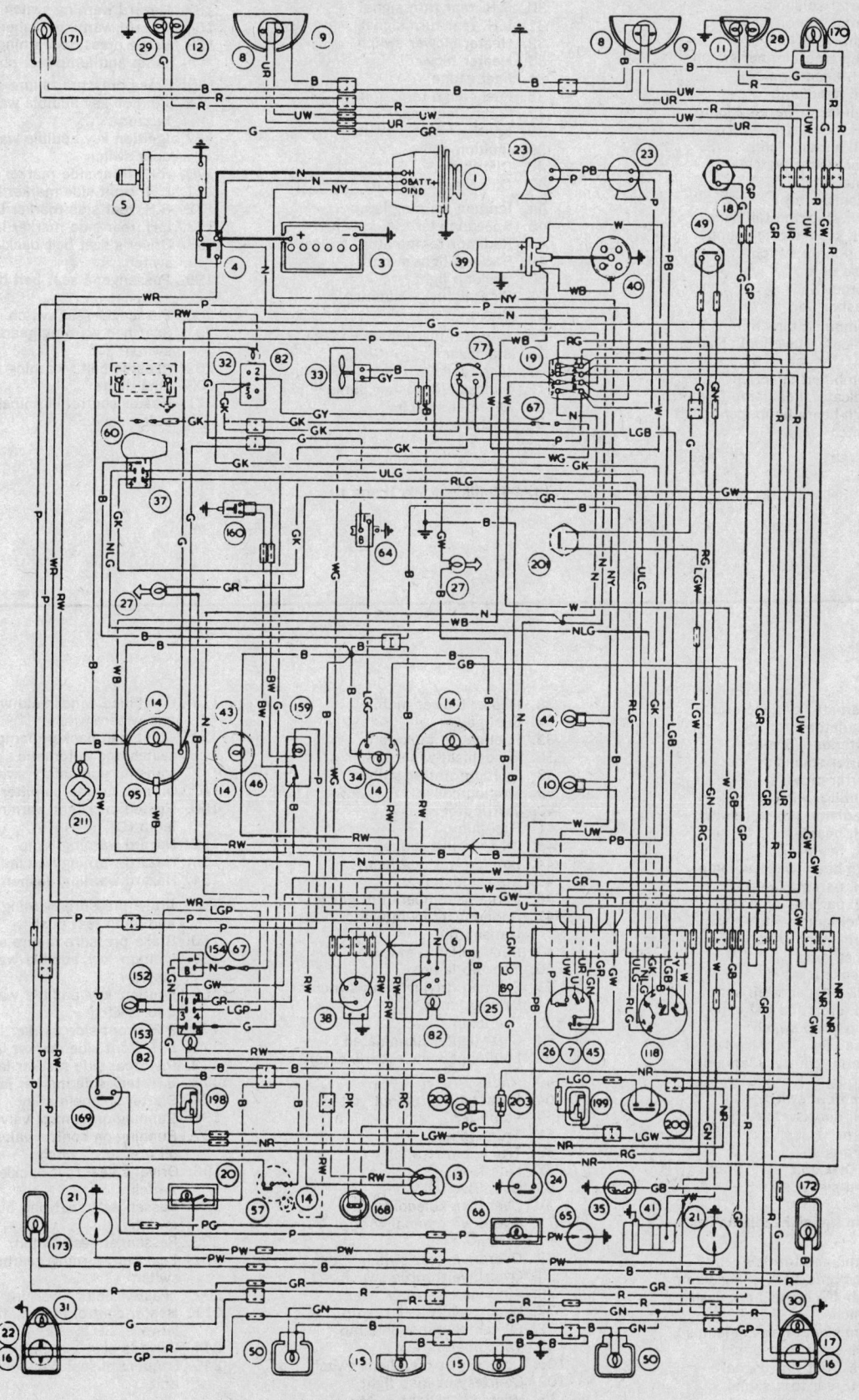

1974-75 Midget Mk. II and III

Wiring Circuits

1. Generator
2. Regulator
3. Battery
4. Starter solenoid
5. Starter motor
6. Lighting switch
7. Headlamp dimmer switch
8. R.H. headlamp
9. L.H. headlamp
10. High-beam warning lamp
11. R.H. parking lamp
12. L.H. parking lamp
13. Panel lamp switch
14. Panel lamps
15. License lamp
16. R.H. stop and tail lamp
17. L.H. stop and tail lamp
18. Stop lamp switch
19. Fuse unit
23. Horns
25. Flasher unit
26. Combined direction indicator/headlamp flasher
   or
26. Combined direction indicator/headlamp flasher/ high-beam lamp/horn-push switch

27. Turn signal warning lamp
28. R.H. front turn signal
29. L.H. front turn signal
30. R.H. rear turn signal
31. L.H. rear turn signal
32. Heater blower switch
33. Heater blower
34. Fuel gauge
35. Fuel gauge tank unit
37. Windshield wiper motor
38. Ignition/starter switch
39. Ignition coil
40. Distributor
43. Oil pressure gauge
44. Ignition warning lamp
45. Speedometer
46. Radiator temperature gauge
49. Back-up light switch
50. Back-up light
57. Cigar-lighter—illuminated
60. Radio
64. Bi-metal instrument voltage stabilizer
67. Line fuse
77. Windshield washer pump
94. Oil filter switch
95. Tachometer

118. Combined windshield washer and wiper switch
152. Hazard warning lamp
153. Hazard warning switch
154. Hazard warning flasher unit
159. Brake pressure warning lamp and lamp test push
160. Brake pressure failure switch
168. Ignition key audible warning buzzer
169. Ignition key audible warning door switch
170. R.H. front side marker lamp
171. L.H. front side marker lamp
172. R.H. rear side marker lamp
173. L.H. rear side marker lamp
198. Driver's seat belt buckle switch
199. Passenger's seat belt buckle switch
200. Passenger seat switch
201. Seat belt warning gearbox switch
202. "Fasten belt" warning light
203. Line diode
211. Heater control illumination bulb

1974-75 Midget Mk. II and III

---

1. Alternator or generator
2. Regulator
3. Batteries—6-volt
4. Starter solenoid
5. Starter motor
6. Lighting switch
7. Headlamp dimmer switch
8. R.H. headlamp
9. L.H. headlamp
10. High-beam warning lamp
11. R.H. parking lamp
12. L.H. parking lamp
13. Panel lamp switch or rheostat switch
14. Panel lamp
15. License lamp
16. R.H. stop and tail lamp
17. L.H. stop and tail lamp
18. Stop lamp switch
19. Fuse unit
20. Interior courtesy lamp or map light (early cars)
21. R.H. door switch
22. L.H. door switch
23. Horns
24. Horn-push
25. Flasher unit
26. Turn signal switch
   or
26. Turn signal/headlamp flasher
   or
26. Combined turn signal/ headlamp flasher/headlamp high-low beam/horn-push switch
27. Turn signal warning lamps
28. R.H. front turn signal
29. L.H. front turn signal
30. R.H. rear turn signal
31. L.H. rear turn signal
32. Heater blower motor switch

33. Heater blower motor
34. Fuel gauge
35. Fuel gauge tank unit
36. Windshield wiper switch
38. Ignition/starter switch
39. Ignition coil
40. Distributor
41. Fuel pump
43. Oil pressure gauge
44. Ignition warning lamp
45. Speedometer
46. Radiator temperature gauge
47. Radiator temperature transmitter
49. Back-up lamp switch
50. Back-up lamp
53. Fog and driving lamp switch
54. Driving lamp
55. Fog lamp
57. Cigar-lighter illuminated
59. Map light switch (early cars)
60. Radio
64. Bi-metal instrument voltage stabilizer
65. Trunk lamp
65. Trunk lamp switch
67. Line fuse
68. Overdrive relay unit
71. Overdrive solenoid
72. Overdrive manual control switch
73. Overdrive gear switch
74. Overdrive throttle switch
76. Automatic gearbox gear
77. Windshield washer lamp
82. Switch illumination lamp
95. Tachometer
101. Courtesy or map light switch
102. Courtesy or map light
115. Heated backlight switch ⎫ GT
116. Heated backlight ⎭ only

118. Combined windshield washer and wiper switch
131. Combined back-up lamp switch and automatic transmission safety switch
147. Oil pressure transmitter
150. Heated backlight warning lamp (GT only)
152. Hazard warning lamp
153. Hazard warning switch
154. Hazard warning flasher unit
159. Brake pressure warning lamp and lamp test push
160. Brake pressure failure switch
168. Ignition key audible warning buzzer
169. Ignition key audible warning door switch
170. R.H. front side marker lamp
171. L.H. front side marker lamp
172. R.H. rear side marker lamp
173. L.H. rear side marker lamp
174. Starter solenoid relay
196. Running-on control valve
197. Running-on control valve oil pressure switch
198. Driver's seat belt buckle switch
199. Passenger's seat belt buckle switch
200. Passenger seat switch
201. Seat belt warning gearbox switch
202. "Fasten belts" warning light
211. Heater control illumination lamp
244. Driver's seat switch
245. Sequential seat belt control unit

MGB convertible (from GHN5/328101) and GT (from GHD5/328101)

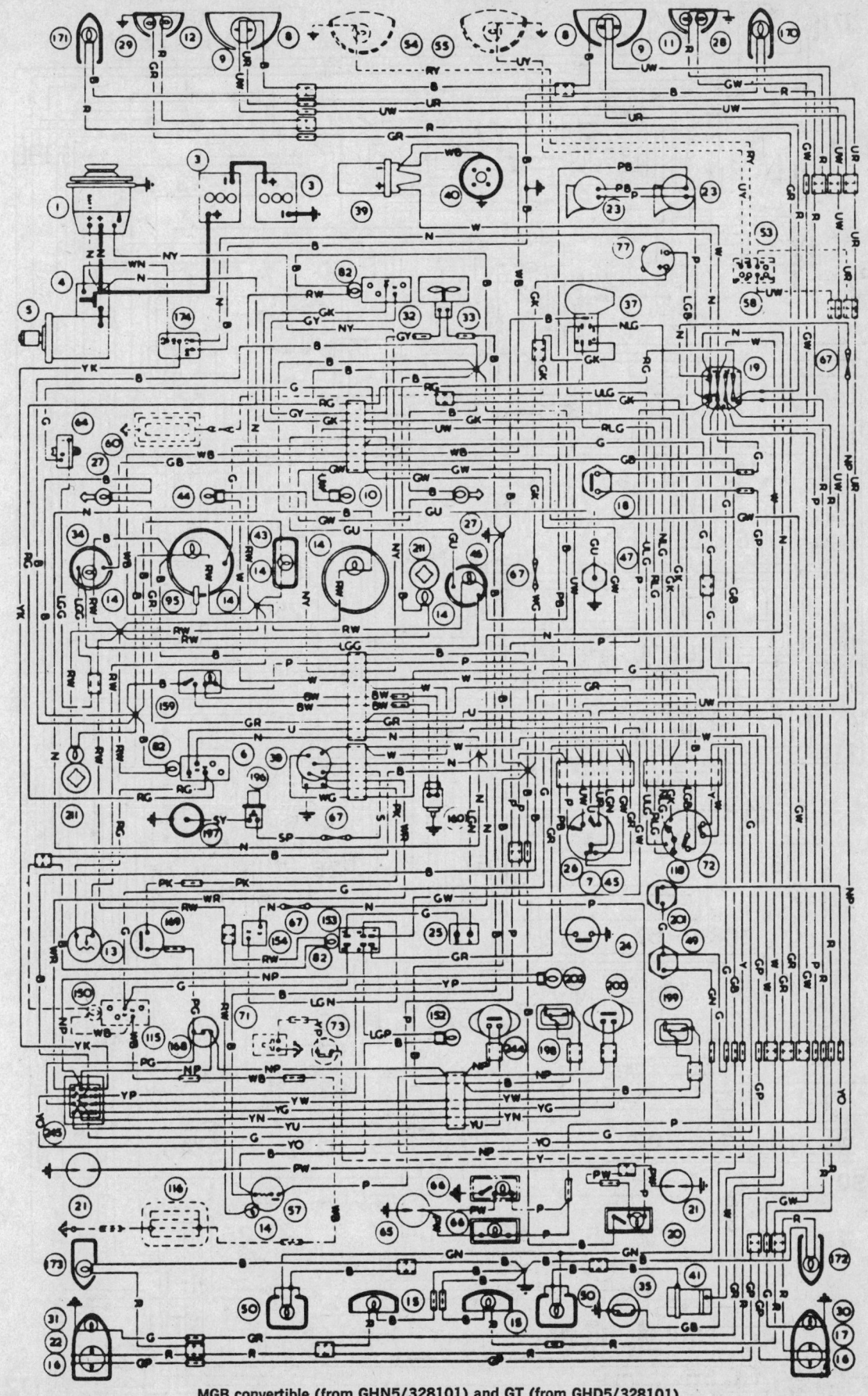

MGB convertible (from GHN5/328101) and GT (from GHD5/328101)

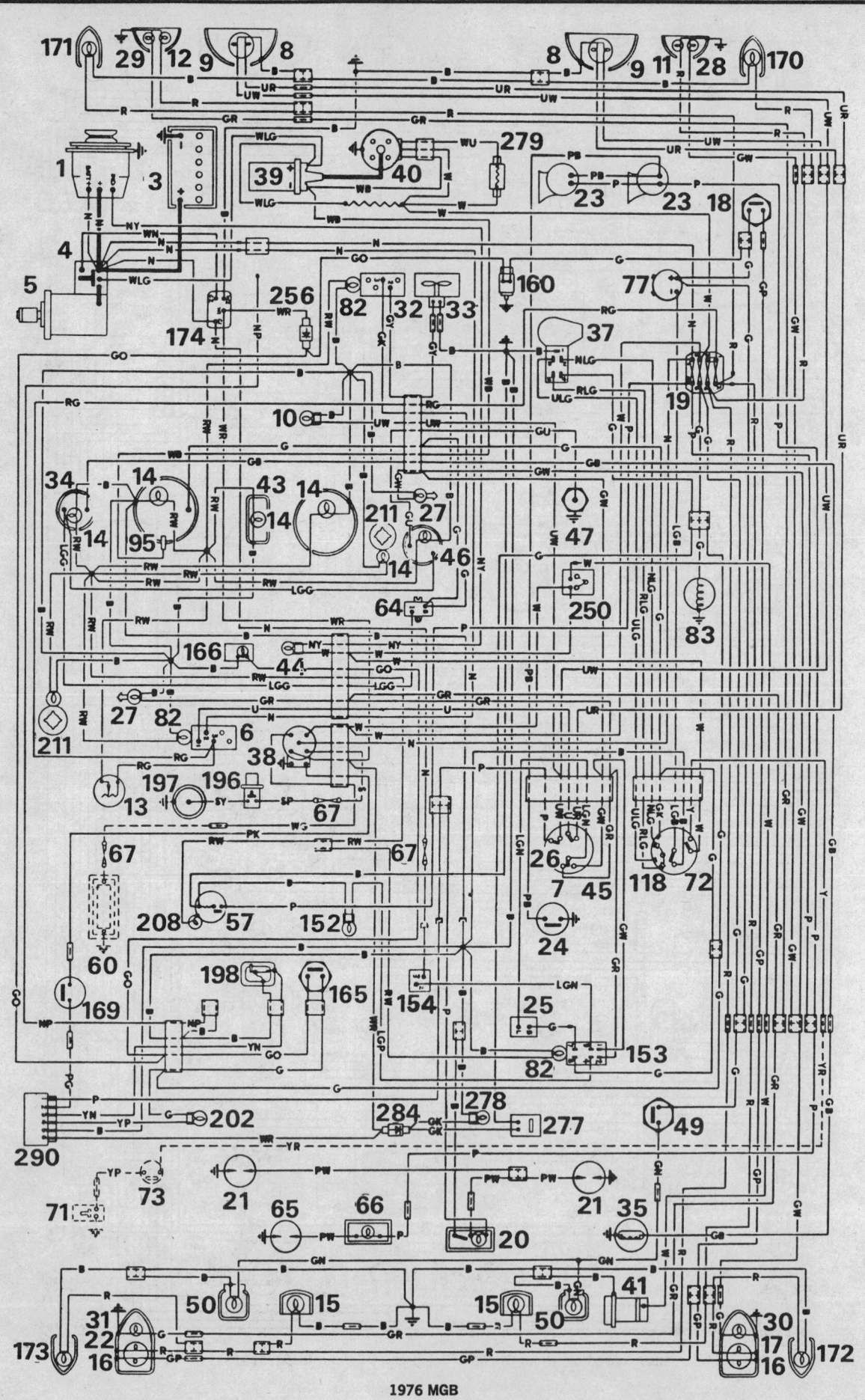

1976 MGB

1. Alternator
3. Battery
4. Starter solenoid
5. Starter motor
6. Lighting switch
7. Headlamp dimmer switch
8. Headlamp dimmer beam
9. Headlamp high beam
10. Headlamp high beam
    warning lamp
11. R.H. parking lamp
12. L.H. parking lamp
13. Panel lamp rheostat switch
14. Panel illumination lamp
15. License plate illumination
    lamps
16. Stop lamp
17. R.H. tail lamp
18. Stop lamp switch
19. Fuse unit (4-way)
20. Interior courtesy lamp
21. Interior lamp door switch
22. L.H. tail lamp
23. Horn
24. Horn button
25. Flasher unit
26. Turn signal switch
27. Turn signal warning lamp
28. R.H. front turn signal lamp
29. L.H. front turn signal lamp
30. R.H. rear turn signal lamp
31. L.H. rear turn signal lamp
32. Heater motor switch
33. Heater motor
34. Fuel gauge
35. Fuel gauge tank unit
37. Windshield wiper motor
38. Ignition/starter switch
39. Ignition coil
40. Distributor

41. Fuel pump
43. Oil pressure gauge
44. Ignition warning lamp
45. Headlamp flasher switch
46. Coolant temperature gauge
47. Coolant temperature switch
49. Reverse lamp switch
50. Reverse lamp
57. Cigar lighter—illumination
    lamp
60. Radio*
64. Instrument voltage stabilizer
65. Luggage compartment lamp
    switch
66. Luggage compartment lamp
67. Line fuse
71. Overdrive solenoid*
72. Overdrive manual control
    switch*
73. Overdrive gear switch*
77. Windshield washer pump
82. Switch illumination lamp
83. Induction heater
95. Tachometer
118. Combined windshield washer
    and wiper switch
152. Hazard warning lamp
153. Hazard warning switch
154. Hazard warning flasher unit
160. Brake pressure failure switch
165. Hand brake switch
166. Hand brake warning lamp
169. Ignition key audible warning
    door switch
170. R.H. front side-marker lamp
171. L.H. front side-marker lamp
172. R.H. rear side-marker lamp
173. L.H. rear side-marker lamp
174. Starter solenoid relay
196. Running-on control valve

197. Running-on control valve
    oil pressure switch
198. Driver's seat belt buckle
    switch
202. Seat belt warning light
208. Cigar lighter
211. Heater control illumination
    lamp
250. Inertia switch
256. Diode for brake warning
277. Service interval counter
278. Service interval counter
    warming lamp
279. Resistor—distributor
284. Diode for service interval
    counter
290. Time delay buzzer unit

* Optional equipment circuits
  shown dotted

CABLE COLOR CODE
N. Brown
U. Blue
R. Red
P. Purple
G. Green
LG. Light Green
W. White
Y. Yellow
B. Black
K. Pink
O. Orange
S. Gray
When a cable has two color code
letters the first denotes the main
color and the second denotes the
tracer color.

1976 MGB

1. R.H. front side marker lamp
2. Reverse lamp switch
3. Stop lamp switch
4. R.H. front turn signal lamp
5. Horn button
6. Horn
7. Service interval counter for
   EGR valve
8. Diode for EGR valve service
   interval counter
9. Diode for brake warning
10. Diode for catalytic converter
    service interval counter—
    if installed
11. Service interval counter
    for catalytic converter—
    if installed
12. R.H. rear side-marker lamp
13. R.H. rear turn signal lamp
14. R.H. tail lamp
15. Stop lamp
16. R.H. parking lamp
17. Headlamp light beam
18. Headlamp dimmer low beam
19. Turn signal switch
20. Headlamp dimmer switch
21. Headlamp flasher switch
22. Windshield washer pump
23. Running-on control valve
    oil pressure switch
24. Running-on control valve
25. Line fuse for running-on
    control valve
26. Flasher unit
27. Brake pressure failure switch
28. Time delay buzzer
29. Fuel gauge tank unit
30. "Catalyst" warning light—
    if installed
31. Reverse lamp

32. Combined windshield washer
    and wiper switch
33. Instrument voltage stabilizer
34. Hazard warning switch
35. Parking brake
36. Interior courtesy lamp door
    switch
37. EGR warning light
38. License plate lamp
39. Windshield wiper motor
40. Fuse unit
41. Turn signal warning lamp
42. Parking brake warning lamp
43. Ignition starter switch
44. Switch illumination lamp
45. Driver's seat belt buckle
    switch
46. Interior courtesy lamp
47. Distributor
48. Alternator
49. Resistor—distributor
50. Ignition warning lamp
51. "Fasten belts" warning lamp
52. Luggage compartment lamp
53. Ignition coil
54. Panel lamp
55. Fuel gauge
56. Lighting switch
57. Luggage compartment lamp
    switch
58. L.H. parking lamp
59. L.H. front turn signal lamp
60. Starter solenoid
61. Headlamp high beam
    warning lamp
62. Oil pressure gauge
63. Temperature gauge
64. Hazard warning flasher unit
65. Ignition key audible warning
    door switch

66. Cigar lighter
67. Cigar lighter illumination
    lamp
68. L.H. front side-marker lamp
69. Battery
70. Starter motor
71. Heater motor
72. Heater motor switch
73. Tachometer
74. Heater control illumination
    lamp
75. Panel lamp switch
76. Line fuse for hazard warning
77. Line fuse for radio*
78. Radio*
79. L.H. rear turn signal lamp
80. L.H. tail lamp
81. L.H. rear side-marker lamp

* Optional equipment circuits
  shown dotted

CABLE COLOR CODE
N. Brown
U. Blue
R. Red
P. Purple
G. Green
LG. Light Green
W. White
Y. Yellow
B. Black
K. Pink
O. Orange
S. Gray
When a cable has two color code
letters the first denotes the main
color and the second denotes the
tracer color.

1976 Midget

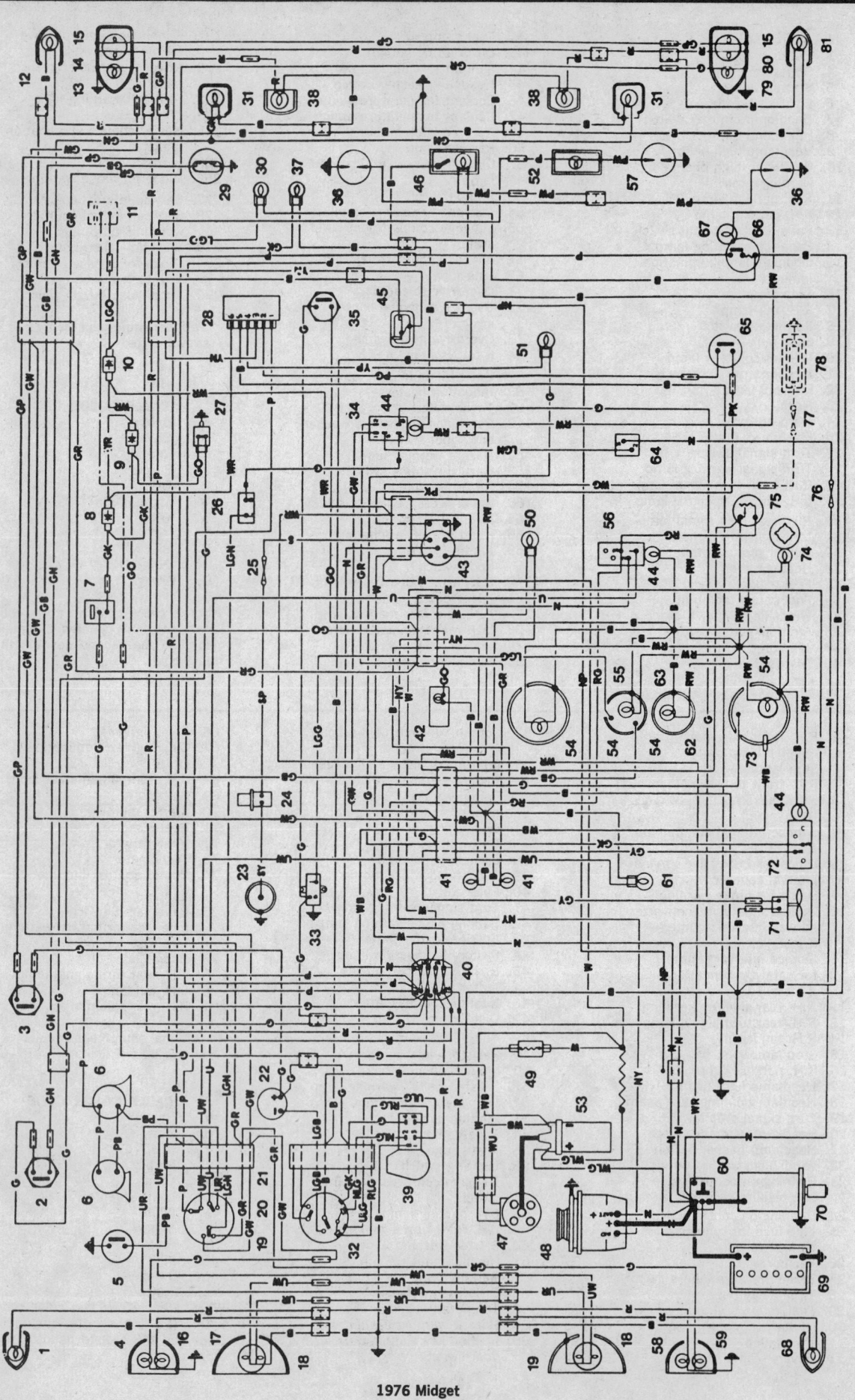

1976 Midget

SPECIFICATIONS

INTRODUCTION

Opel A.G., owned by General Motors since 1929, began importing and selling the Opel Rekord through the Buick Motor Division dealer network in 1958. In 1964, the Opel line was expanded to include the Kadett Models, a sedan, a coupe and a station wagon. Since then the Opel has become more Americanized, adding such options as a fully automatic 3-speed transmission in 1969. A sport version of the Kadett, the Rallye, with improved performance and special trim, was introduced in 1967, followed by the Opel GT, a two seat sports coupe based on the Kadett Rallye running gear, in 1969.

In 1971, Opel introduced the 1900 series. It incorporates an all new sheet metal and interior design.

1975 was the final year for the "German" Opel. It was replaced by the Opel Izuzu.

MODEL IDENTIFICATION

1972-73 Opel Wagon

1972-75 1900 Coupe

1972-73 GT

1972-73 Opel Sedan

SERIAL NUMBER IDENTIFICATION

Vehicle

Opel, 1900 and Manta

Opel vehicle-identification numbers run consecutively from the first Kadett produced in 1964. The first two digits of the serial number (reading from the left) indicate the model. The other numbers indicate production sequence. The identification plate is located in the engine compartment either on the right fender wall or on the left side of the fire wall.

GT

The GT is numbered in an identical manner to the Kadett. Identification plates are located on the right side of the cowl and on the left side of the instrument panel at the base of the windshield.

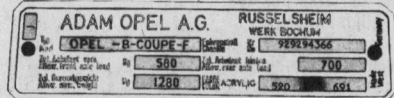

Model identification plate

Engine

Opel and GT

The engine number, stamped on the upper left center of the engine block, is prefixed with numbers and letters to indicate engine displacement and power.

Reading from the left, the first two digits represent engine identification. Engines with an "S" designation are designed to run on premium gas.

GENERAL ENGINE SPECIFICATIONS

Year	ENGINE Model	Cu. In. Displacement	Carburetor Type	Horsepower @ rpm	Torque @ rpm (ft lbs)	Bore x Stroke (in.)	Compression Ratio
1972	1.9	115.8	1-Solex 2 Bbl w/automatic choke	90 @ 5200	111 @ 3400	3.66 x 2.75	7.6:1
1973	1.9	115.8	1-Solex 2 Bbl w/automatic choke	75 @ 4800	92 @ 2800①	3.66 x 2.75	7.6:1
1974	1.9	115.8	1-Solex 2 Bbl w/automatic choke	75 @ 4800	92 @ 2800①	3.66 x 2.75	7.6:1
1975	1.9	115.8	Electronic Fuel Injection	81 @ 5000	96 @ 2200	3.66 x 2.75	7.6:1

① 92 @ 3400 with automatic transmission

TUNE-UP SPECIFICATIONS

Year	Engine Model	SPARK PLUGS Type	Gap (in.)	DISTRIBUTOR Point Dwell (deg)	Point Gap (in.)	Ignition Timing (deg)	Intake Valve Opens (deg)	Fuel Pump Pressure (psi)	IDLE SPEED (rpm) MT	AT (Neutral)	Valve Clearance (in.) In	Ex
1972	1.9	42FS①	0.030	48-52	0.018	②	—	3.1-3.8	850	850	HYD.	HYD.
1973	1.9	42FS①	0.030	48-52	0.018	②	—	3.1-3.7	925	875	HYD.	HYD.
1974	1.9	42FS①	0.030	48-52	0.018	②	—	3.1-3.7	900	850	HYD.	HYD.
1975	1.9	42FS①	0.030	50	0.016	②	—	3.1-4.4	925	925	HYD.	HYD.

① If carbon fouling occurs, use AC43FS
② Align the timing marks. No timing scale is used. Vacuum hose to be disconnected and plugged.
— Not Available
NOTE: The underhood specifications sticker often reflects tune-up specification changes made in production. Sticker figures must be used if they disagree with those in this chart.

FIRING ORDER

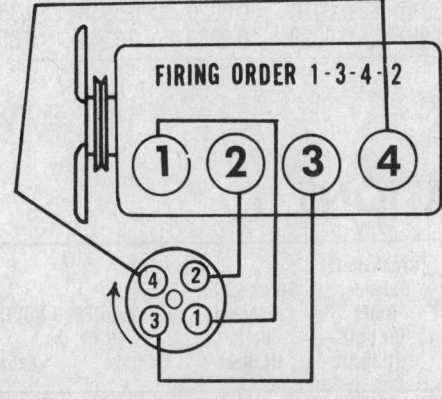

FIRING ORDER 1-3-4-2

1.9 liter engines

ALTERNATOR AND REGULATOR SPECIFICATIONS

Year	ALTERNATOR Part No. or Manufacturer	Field Current Resistance (ohms)	Test Output (amps.) @ 2500 RPM	REGULATOR Part No. or Manufacturer	Volts @ 2500 RPM
1972	K114V35A20 (all)	4-4.4	30 min.	AD 1/14 V	13.5-14.5
1973-1975	K114V35A20 (all)	4-4.4	23①	AD1/14 V	13.5-14.5

① @ 2000 engine rpm

CAPACITIES

| Year | Model | Engine Displacement (liters) | ENGINE CRANKCASE (qts) | | TRANSMISSION (pts) | | Drive Axle (pts) | Gasoline Tank (gals) | Cooling System (qts) Wo/AC |
			With Filter	Without Filter	Manual 4-spd	Automatic			
1972-75	GT & 1900	1.9	3¼	3	2½	10½③	2½	13¼①②	6

① All 1900s use a gasoline tank of 11¾ gallons capacity.
② 71-73 GTs use a gasoline tank of 14½ gallons capacity.
③ Includes converter

CRANKSHAFT AND CONNECTING ROD SPECIFICATIONS

Year	Engine Displacement (liters)	Main Brg. Journal Dia.	CRANKSHAFT Main Brg. Oil Clearance	Shaft End-Play	Thrust on No.	Journal Diameter	CONNECTING ROD Oil Clearance	Side Clearance
1972-1975	1.9	2.2829-2.2835	0.0009-0.0025	0.0017-0.0061	5	2.0461-2.0467	0.0004-0.0025	0.0043-0.0095

PISTON AND RING SPECIFICATIONS
All measurements in inches

Year	Engine Displace. (liters)	Piston Clearance	Top Compression	RING GAP Bottom Compression	Oil Control	Top Compression	RING SIDE CLEARANCE Bottom Compression	Oil Control
1972	1.9	0.0012	0.0118-0.0216	0.0118-0.0216	0.0098-0.0157	0.0024-0.0034	0.0013-0.0024	0.0013-0.0024
1973-1975	1.9	0.0014	0.0140-0.0220	0.0140-0.0220	0.0150-0.0550	0.0024-0.0034	0.0013-0.0024	0.0013-0.0024

VALVE SPECIFICATIONS

Year	Engine Displace. (liters)	Seat Angle (deg)	Face Angle (deg)	SPRING TEST PRESSURE (lb @ in.) Closed Intake	Exhaust	Open Intake	Exhaust	STEM TO GUIDE CLEARANCE (in.) Intake	Exhaust	STEM DIAMETER (in.) Intake	Exhaust
1972	1.9	45	44	81.6 @ 1.57	71.7 @ 1.36	153.2 @ 1.18	157 @ 0.96	0.0014-0.0025	0.002-0.0039	0.3538-0.3543	0.3524-0.3528
1973-75	1.9	45	44	93 @ 1.57	97 @ 1.36	182 @ 1.18	180 @ 0.96	0.0010-0.0029	0.0020-0.0039	0.3538-0.3543	0.3524-0.3528

— Not Applicable
N.A. Information not available

TORQUE SPECIFICATIONS

Year	Model	Engine Displace. (liters)	Cylinder Head Bolts (ft. lbs.)	Main Bearing Bolts (ft. lbs.)	Rod Bearing Bolts (ft. lbs.)	Crankshaft Balancer Bolts (or nut) (ft. lbs.)	Flywheel to Crankshaft Bolts (ft. lbs.)	MANIFOLD BOLTS (ft. lbs.) Intake	Exhaust
1972-75		1.9	72 cold 58 warm	72	36	72	43	33	33

TORQUE SEQUENCES

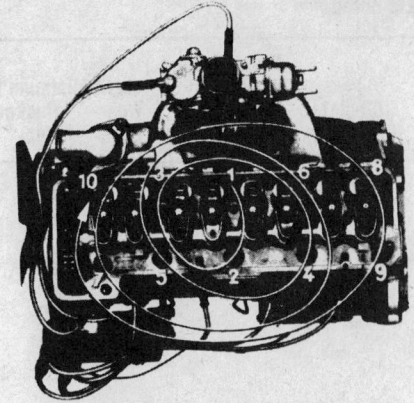

Cylinder head (1.9 Engines)

Combination manifolds (1.9 Engine)

CARBURETOR SPECIFICATIONS

Year	Engine	Carburetor	Main Metering Jets Primary	Secondary	High Speed Air Jets Primary	Secondary	Idle Jets Primary	Secondary	Float Needle Valve
1972	1.9②	1 Solex 2 bbl	X112.5③	X150④	120	100	g52.5	—	2
	1.9⑤	1 Solex 2 bbl	X115⑥	X135⑦	120	150	g47.5	—	2
1973	1.9②	1 Solex 2 bbl	X122.5	X155	120	80	47.5	—	2
	1.9⑤	1 Solex 2 bbl	X120	X137.5	110	120	45	—	2
1974	1.9	1 Solex 2 bbl	X125	X160	130	80	55	—	2

② Opel 1900
③ X115 with automatic transmission
④ X155 with automatic transmission
⑤ Opel GT

⑥ X112.5 with automatic transmission
⑦ X130 with automatic transmission
— Not Applicable

BATTERY AND STARTER SPECIFICATIONS
All cars use 12 volt, negative ground electrical systems

Year	Model	Battery Amp Hour Capacity	Amps	Lock Test Volts	Torque (ft/lbs)	Starter Amps	No Load Test Volts	RPM	Brush Spring Tension (oz)	Min. Brush Length (in.)
1972	All	44	280-320	6 (or more)	—	35-45	12	6400-7900	40-46	0.28
1973-75	All	44	280-320	6 (or more)	—	30-50	10.6	7300-8500	40-46	0.28

— Not available

BRAKE SPECIFICATIONS

All measurements given are (in.) unless noted

Year	Model	Lug Nut Torque (ft/lb)	Master Cylinder Bore	Brake Disc Minimum Thickness	Brake Disc Maximum Run-Out	Diameter	Brake Drum Max. Machine O/S	Max. Wear Limit	Minimum Lining Thickness Front	Rear
1972-75	All	65	0.813	0.394	0.004	9.06	9.09	9.09	0.280	1/32 in. above rivets

NOTE: Minimum lining thickness is as recommended by the manufacturer. Due to variations in state inspection regulations, the minimum allowable thickness may be different than recommended by the manufacturer.

WHEEL ALIGNMENT

Year	Model	CASTER① Range (deg)	Pref. Setting (deg)	CAMBER Range (deg)	Pref. Setting (deg)	Toe-in (in.)	WHEEL PIVOT RATIO (deg) Inner Wheel	Outer Wheel
1972	Opel	1P-3P	2P	½P-1½P	1P	1/32-1/8	20	18½
1972-73	GT	2P-4P	3P	½P-1½P	1P	1/32-1/8	20	18½
	1900	3½P-6½P	5P	1½N-½N	1N	1/8-3/16	20	19¼
1974	All	3P-6P	5P	1½N-½N	1N	1/8-3/16	20	19¼
1975	All	3P-6P	5P	¼P-1¼N	1N	1/8-3/16	20	19¼

① Permissible deviation from left to right wheel is 1 degree maximum

DIFFERENTIAL PINION BEARING PRELOAD SPECIFICATIONS

	(Average)	(Range)
New bearings	9 in. lbs.	7-12 in. lbs.
Original bearings	6 in. lbs.	5-7 in. lbs.

Pinion depth setting (from pinion marking) +0.002 to −0.001 in.

Shims for Setting Pinion Depth

Notches in shim	Shim thickness (in.)
One side flattened	0.0016-0.0024
0	0.0094-0.0102
1	0.0104-0.0112
2	0.0114-0.0122
3	0.0124-0.0132
4	0.0134-0.0142
5	0.0144-0.0152

Clearance from differential side gears to case max 0.006 in.

Shims for Setting Preload

Notches in shim	Shim thickness (in.)
0	0.0056-0.0062
1	0.0066-0.0072
2	0.0076-0.0082
3	0.0085-0.0092
4	0.0094-0.0102
5	0.0104-0.0112
6	0.0193-0.0201
7	0.0386-0.0398

Shims for Setting Clearance

Notches in shim	Shim thickness (in.)
0	0.019-0.020
1	0.023-0.024
2	0.027-0.028
3	0.031-0.032

Maximum runout, axle shaft bearing-seat   0.002 in.
Maximum lateral runout, rear axle shaft-flange (at largest flange diameter)   0.004 in.
Maximum lateral runout, ring gear   0.003 in.
Lash, ring gear to drive pinion   0.004-0.008 in.
Differential side baring preload
     New bearings: 20-30 ft lbs.
     Old bearings   10-20 ft lbs.

TUNE-UP PROCEDURES

Engine tune-up is performed to restore engine performance which has deteriorated due to normal wear and loss of adjustment. The three major areas considered in a routine tune-up are compression, ignition, and carburetion, although valve adjustment may be included.

Spark Plugs

1. Remove all spark plugs, noting the cylinder in which they were installed. Evaluate the spark plugs according to the spark plug chart in the troubleshooting section. If any of these conditions exist, the plug must be replaced.

2. Check the plug gap on both new and used plugs before installing them in the engine. If the air gap between the two electrodes is not correct, open or close the ground electrode, with the proper tool, to bring it to specifications. Such a tool is usually provided with a gap gauge.

NOTE: *Be sure to clean the seats before installing the plugs. After the correct gap is obtained, reinstall the plug.*

Breaker Points and Condenser

1. Remove the distributor cap, and inspect it inside and out for cracks and/or carbon tracks, and for excessive wear or burning of the rotor contacts. If any of these faults are evident, the cap must be replaced.

2. Remove and inspect the rotor. If the contacts are burned or worn, or if the rotor is excessively loose on the distributor shaft, the rotor must be replaced.

3. Check the breaker points for burning, pitting or wear, and the contact heel which rests on the distributor cam for excessive wear. If defects are noted, remove the original points and condenser, and wipe out the inside of the distributor housing with a clean, dry rag.

NOTE: *A magnetic or locking screwdriver should be used to remove the points and attaching screws from the distributor.*

Lightly lubricate the contact heel and pivot point and install the new points and condenser. The points should then be set with a feeler gauge, (0.018) and rechecked with a dwell meter after the rotor and cap have been replaced.

Dwell Angle

Point gap can be set by using a feeler gauge or a dwell meter. Accurate measurements with a feeler gauge require careful, precise usage of the feelers.

1. A dwell meter should be calibrated first, switched to the four-cylinder position, and connected between the distributor primary terminal and ground.

2. Remove the distributor cap and rotor.

3. Loosen the breaker set screw approximately ⅛ turn. With a feeler gauge, check the gap between the contact point and correct it if necessary.

4. With a dwell meter, turn the reset screw of the stationary contact to obtain specified dwell angle.

5. Tighten set screw and recheck dwell.

6. Install rotor and cap, start engine, and make a final dwell angle check.

Ignition Timing

1.9S engines have timing marks in the form of a steel ball embedded in the flywheel and a pointer in a window on the right side of the flywheel housing. 1975 timing marks are located at the lower left front of the engine. The pointer is part of a bracket attached to the engine block. A timing mark is located on the crankshaft pulley. Timing is correct when the timing marks are aligned at the moment No. 1 cylinder

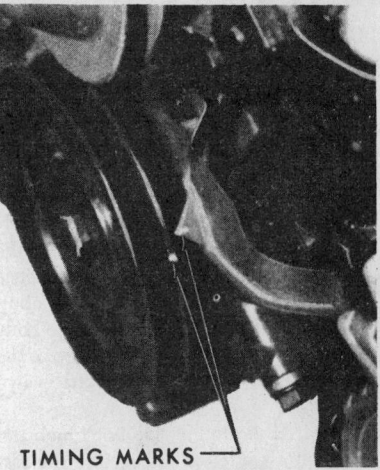

TIMING MARKS

Ignition timing mark—1975

reaches top dead center (TDC).

Basic timing is set by rotating distributor housing counterclockwise slightly until contact points just start to open. Timing marks must line up at this point. Install distributor cap, and connect spark plugs.

Adjust ignition timing after setting point gap. A fast and easy way to adjust timing is with a stroboscope or timing light.

1. Connect timing light to No. 1 spark plug.

2. Disconnect all vacuum hoses from distributor and plug the hoses.

3. Start engine and reduce idle speed below 500 rpm for 1.1 liter engine and 700 rpm for 1.9 liter engines. Idle performance must be smooth. Slowing the idle is essential to keep the centrifugal advance, in distributor, from engaging.

4. Rotate distributor as necessary to align timing marks with strobe light pulses.

CAUTION: *When working on a vehicle with the engine running, the following precautions must be observed: Work only in a well-ventilated area. Be certain the transmission is in neutral and the parking brake firmly applied. Always keep your hands, clothing, and tools clear of the moving radiator fan.*

Carburetor

NOTE: *See "Fuel Systems" for further adjustments.*

1972

1. Connect a tachometer to the engine. Run the engine until it reaches operating temperature. Make sure the automatic choke valve is fully open.

2. Remove the hose leading from the rear of the carburetor to the charcoal canister and plug the hose.

3. Adjust the idle air speed screw and mixture screw to obtain the best idle at 820 to 870 rpm on vehicles with automatic transmissions and 870 to 920 rpm on vehicles with manual transmissions.

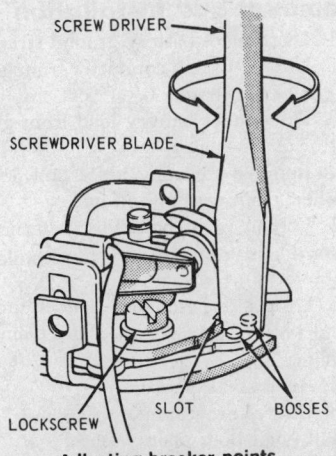

SCREW DRIVER

SCREWDRIVER BLADE

LOCKSCREW   SLOT   BOSSES

Adjusting breaker points

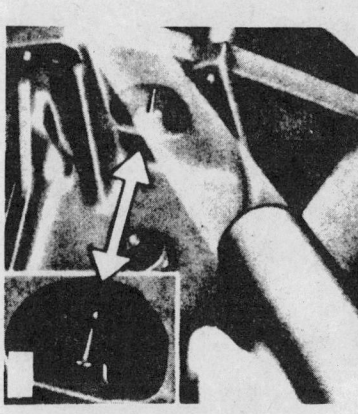

Ignition timing mark—1972-74

4. Make the final adjustment by screwing the mixture screw in to reduce the idle speed 20 to 50 rpm. Always lean out the mixture. Poor driveability, rough hot idle, and incorrect emission control may result if the idle mixture screw is not leaned 20 to 50 rpm.

5. Reconnect the charcoal canister.

6. To adjust the fast idle speed, fully open the throttle and fully close the choke valve. Now release the throttle linkage and the choke valve. The abutment lever in the automatic choke body should now rest on the highest step of the fast idle cam, opening the throttle valve slightly.

7. Start the engine. Do not touch the accelerator pedal or linkage, or the fast idle mechanism will be released. If not already done so, allow the engine to reach operating temperature.

8. The engine should operate at between 2500 and 2900 rpm.

9. Adjust the fast idle speed by turning the nuts on the throttle connecting link. Shorten the linkage to decrease engine speed and lengthen the linkage to increase engine speed.

1973–74

1. With the air cleaner installed, run the engine until normal operating temperature is reached.

2. Adjust the idle speed to the proper specification by turning the air speed screw.

3. Check the exhaust gas with an exhaust gas anylizer. The reading should be 1%–2% on the CO meter on 1974 models.

Adjust the CO reading by turning the idle mixture screw. After adjusting the idle mixture, adjust the idle speed to the proper specification by turning the idle air speed screw.

4. If CO measuring equipment is not available, and the mixture requires adjustment, alternately adjust the idle mixture screw and then the idle air screw to obtain the best idle at 50 rpm above the specified idle speed on 1973 models and 80–100 rpm above the specified idle speed on 1974 models.

Next, lean the idle mixture by turning the idle mixture screw in (clockwise) and reduce the idle speed to the proper specification.

1975

All 1975 Opels are equipped with an electronic fuel injection system.

1. Run the engine to its normal operating temperature.

2. Connect a tachometer to the engine.

3. Adjust the idle air adjustment screw located on the throttle body to 925–975 rpm.

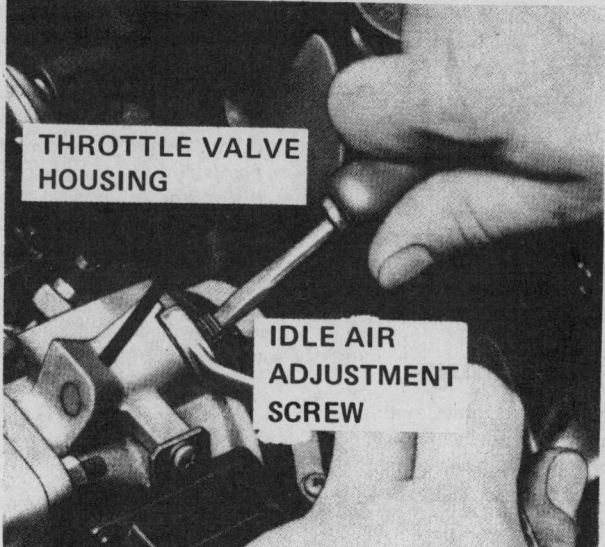

Idle air adjustment screw—1975 fuel injection

ENGINE ELECTRICAL

Distributor

Removal and Installation

1. Remove the fuel pump on 1972–74 models.

2. Remove the distributor cap and turn the crankshaft of the engine until the tip of the rotor points to the notch on the lip of the distributor housing. The ball imbedded in the flywheel should be approximately aligned with the pointer in the flywheel housing.

3. Remove the distributor hold-down clamp and remove the distributor. While the distributor is removed, cover the hole in the timing case to prevent the entry of dirt.

4. Install the distributor with the tip of the rotor and the mark on the distributor housing aligned in the reverse order of

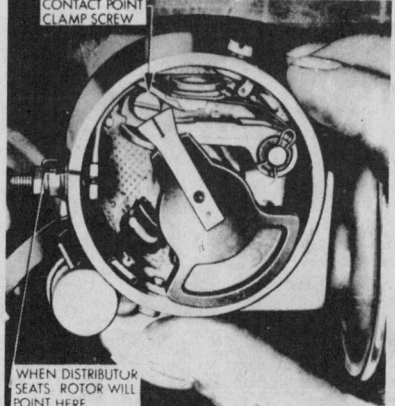

Distributor installation alignment marks

removal if the engine was not disturbed while the distributor was removed from the engine. If the crankshaft was turned while the distributor was removed, it will be necessary to bring the piston in no. 1 cylinder to TDC of its compression stroke (align the timing marks on the flywheel and the flywheel housing) and install the distributor with the tip of the rotor and the mark on the distributor housing aligned.

5. Install the fuel pump on 1970–74 models.

Alternator

Alternator Precautions

If the alternator will not meet output specifications when supplied with full field current, the assembly must be replaced. If the voltage regulator does not limit maximum voltage within specifications, adjust the voltage regulator. If steady voltage regulation, within specifications, cannot be achieved, the voltage regulator assembly must be replaced.

Removal and Installation

1. Disconnect battery ground strap.

2. Unplug wiring connector from generator or alternator.

3. Disconnect battery lead from generator or alternator.

4. Remove adjusting brace bolt, lockwasher, plain washer and nut.

5. Loosen pivot bolt. Push alternator inward and remove belt from pulley.

6. Drop alternator down and remove pivot bolt, nut, lockwasher and plain washer.

7. Remove alternator.

8. Hold alternator in position and install pivot bolt, plain washer, lockwasher and nut finger tight.

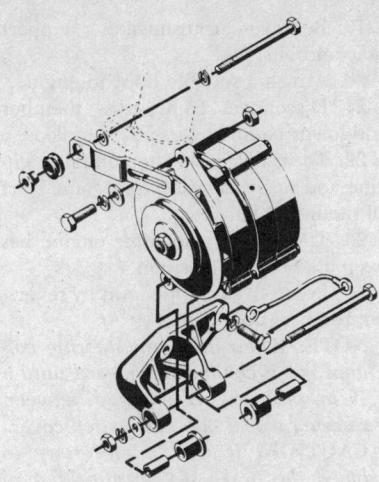

Alternator installation

9. Install the belt.

10. Install adjusting brace bolt, lockwasher, plain washer and nut finger tight.

11. Position a belt tension gauge on belt. Pull alternator outward until gauge reads 45 lbs, then tighten adjusting brace bolt.

12. Tighten alternator pivot bolt.

13. Connect battery lead to alternator.

14. Plug three-way wiring connector into alternator and engage safety catch.

15. Connect battery ground strap.

Belt Tension Adjustment

Any engine V-belt is correctly tensioned when the longest span of belt between pulleys can be depressed about ½ in. in the middle by moderate thumb pressure. To adjust, loosen the accessory's slotted adjusting bracket bolt. If the hinge bolt is very tight, it may be necessary to loosen it slightly to move the item.

CAUTION: *Be careful not to overtighten belts, as this will damage the bearings, particularly in air or water pumps and alternators.*

Alternator and Regulator Tests

Current Output

1. Check alternator belt condition and tension. Adjust to 45 lbs.

2. Install a battery post adapter at the positive post of the battery.

3. Connect ammeter leads to adapter with red lead toward alternator and black lead toward battery positive post. Connect ground lead to battery negative post.

4. Connect voltmeter across the battery: red lead at alternator side of battery post adapter and black lead to battery negative post.

5. Connect a tachometer to ignition system.

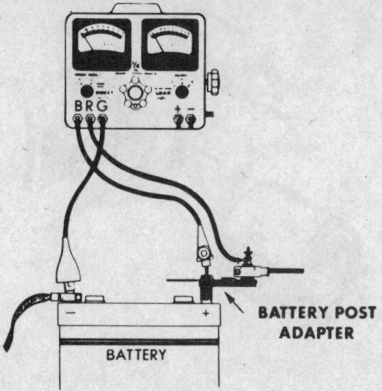

Connecting ammeter leads

6. Make sure all electrical accessories are turned off. Start engine with battery post adapter switch closed; open switch as soon as engine is started.

7. Adjust engine speed to 2500 RPM.

8. Turn tester control knob to "LOAD" position and adjust knob to obtain highest possible ammeter reading. Output must be 30 amperes minimum. If output is okay, proceed to voltage regulator test below.

9. If output is low, defect may be in alternator or in regulator. To eliminate regulator, supply field current direct to cause full alternator output. unplug three-way connector from regulator, and plug in a jumper between the red and black leads.

NOTE: *Retest as described in Steps 7 and 8. In either charging system, if output is still low,* alternator *is faulty and must be replaced.*

10. If output (using field jumper) is now okay, defect is in the regulator or wiring harness. Check all wiring connections. If all wiring is okay, try replacing regulator; if output now tests okay (without using field jumper), you have found the trouble.

NOTE: *Always follow-up with a voltage regulator test.*

Adjusting Voltage Regulator

1. Always test alternator output first. Leave all test instruments connected, but make sure field jumper is removed, if used.

2. With engine speed at 2500 RPM, turn tester control knob to "¼ OHM" position. Make sure all electrical accessories are turned off. After voltage reading stabilizes, any reading between 13.5 and 14.5 volts is okay.

3. If voltage reading is out of limits, remove regulator cover and adjust voltage regulator armature spring tension to obtain a middle reading of 14.0 volts. If reading fluctuates, voltage contacts are dirty.

4. Replace regulator cover and recheck voltage setting. A steady voltage

reading between 13.5 and 14.5 volts means voltage regulator is okay.

5. Adjust engine speed to specified idle.

Starter

Removal and Installation

1. Disconnect battery and starter wiring.

2. Unbolt and remove starter support bracket.

3. Remove starter bolts and nuts.

4. To remove starter, you must drive out stud.

5. To install the starter, reverse the removal steps.

Removing starter stud

Starter Drive Replacement

1. Remove the field connecting nut from terminal on the solenoid.

2. Remove screws which hold solenoid to the drive housing.

3. Remove two thru-bolts and the solenoid shift lever pivot bolt.

4. Remove the armature and drive assembly, with the shift lever, from the drive housing.

5. To remove the drive assembly from the armature, tap the pinion stop retainer toward the armature to uncover the snap ring.

6. Remove snap-ring from shaft, then slide pinion drive assembly from the shaft.

7. Clean all parts by wiping with a clean dry cloth.

NOTE: *Do not use any degreaser or high temperature solvents. This will damage the insulation and will cause shorts in windings.*

8. Carefully inspect all parts for wear or damage and replace all unserviceable parts.

NOTE: *When soldering use resin flux only.*

9. Reassemble the starter by reversing the previous steps. Make sure that the pinion stop retainers and assist spring are in proper position.

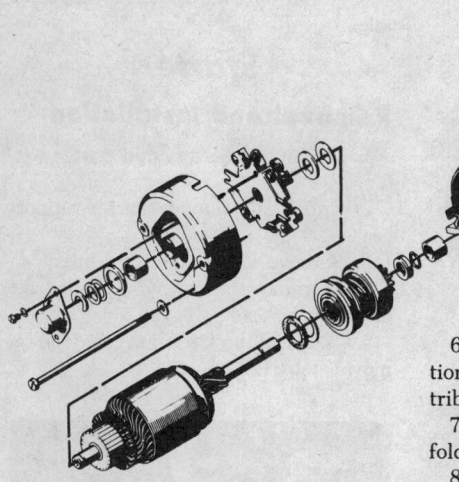

Starter motor exploded view

Battery

Opels use a 12 volt, 44 amp-hour Delco battery. The electrical system requires that the battery produce at least 9 volts while starter is cranking the engine.

Batteries should be checked periodically for proper output and good, clean connections. Inspect the case for cracks and weakness. Check the density (specific gravity) with a hydrometer.

NOTE: *All readings for each cell should produce a nearly equal charged condition. If one or two cell readings are sharply lower, the battery is defective.*

When jump starting, make sure that the cable polarity is correct. Disconnect cables as soon as engine starts in order to avoid damage to the charging system.

ENGINE MECHANICAL

Engine Removal and Installation

1972

NOTE: *This engine assembly removal is only possible by lowering the engine out through the bottom of the car.*

1. Mark hood hinge location and remove hood.

2. Disconnect battery cables.

3. Drain radiator. Disconnect and remove radiator, radiator hoses, and heater hoses.

4. Remove shift lever by removing snap ring and lifting lever out of position.

5. Detach throttle linkage from carburetor and remove the rear support, fuel lines, vacuum lines, heater control cables, and oil pressure lines.

6. Disconnect all electrical connections at the generator, starter, and distributor.

7. Remove T-fitting from intake manifold.

8. Disconnect exhaust pipe from manifold.

NOTE: *To facilitate reinstallation, do not completely unscrew the exhaust flange bolts on inboard side.*

9. Raise vehicle, both front and back, and support it safely.

10. Disconnect clutch cable, speedometer cable, and back-up lights.

11. Remove drive shaft.

12. Remove tailpipe and hangers.

13. Remove ground strap from engine to side rail.

14. Disconnect brake lines at hoses.

15. Remove steering shaft clamp pinch bolt and mark location of shaft on flange.

16. Remove steering mast guide sleeve stop bolt from mast jacket bracket. Move steering column out of way.

17. Attach front suspension to a hoist to keep it from tilting when assembly is lowered.

18. Disconnect shock absorbers at upper mounting bracket.

19. Remove transmission support bracket bolts.

20. Attach a suitable hoist to engine.

21. Disconnect front cross member and lower complete assembly to floor.

22. To install, raise the complete engine and suspension into place and start all mounting bolts.

23. Tighten all bolts after engine has been aligned into position.

24. Reinstall all components by reversing removal operation.

NOTE: *When installing steering column, push column downward until a ⅛ in. clearance is obtained between steering wheel hub and switch cover.*

CAUTION: *It will be necessary to bleed the brake system after system has been installed in car.*

1973–75 1900 and Manta

NOTE: *The engine can be removed together with the transmission through the top of the engine compartment .*

1. Scribe marks on the hood hinge and the hood mounting location to help install the hood in the proper location and then remove the hood.

2. Disconnect the negative battery cable.

3. Drain the engine coolant at the lower radiator hose.

4. Remove the upper and lower radiator hoses.

5. Remove the radiator and fan shroud.

6. Disconnect the heater hoses.

7. Disconnect the brake booster vacuum hose.

8. Remove the air cleaner assembly and the evaporative emissions canister lines if applicable.

9. Disconnect the electrical connections and accelerator linkage.

10. Remove the console.

11. Remove the shift lever boot, plate, and shift lever.

12. Raise the car on a hoist.

13. Disconnect the fuel line at the fuel pump.

14. Remove the front stone shield.

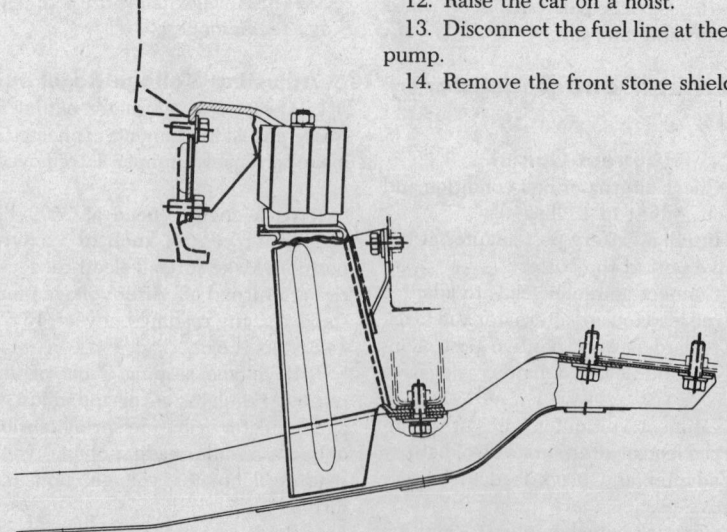

Right side engine support bracket with crossmember—GT

15. Disconnect the speedometer cable, back-up light switch, and the clutch cable.

16. Remove the driveshaft.

17. Disconnect the bell housing support, the EGR line to the exhaust pipe, and the exhaust pipe.

18. Disconnect the transmission support.

19. Remove the engine mount bolts.

20. Attach an engine lifting device.

21. Lift the engine and transmission assembly up, forward and out of the vehicle.

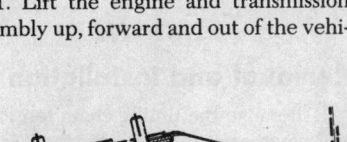

Left side engine support bracket with crossmember—GT

22. Install the engine in the reverse order of removal.

1973 GT

NOTE: *The engine is removed and installed from below the car.*

1. Disconnect the negative battery cable.

2. Remove the air cleaner.

3. Drain the engine coolant by disconnecting the lower radiator hose. Disconnect the upper radiator hose. The radiator need not be removed.

4. Disconnect all electrical connections:

   a. The coil to distributor wires,

   b. Wires from the alternator, then remove the alternator and bracket,

   c. The positive battery cable from the starter switch,

   d. The oil pressure switch wires from the cylinder block, and

   e. The wires from the starter solenoid.

5. Remove the vacuum hoses at the T-fitting mounted to the intake manifold. Remove the T from the manifold to avoid interference and possible damage during removal of the engine.

6. Remove the throttle linkage and the carburetor.

7. Disconnect the heater hoses.

8. Disconnect the water valve bracket from the manifold.

9. Remove the gear shift lever.

10. Jack the engine enough so that the front engine mounts are somewhat relieved.

11. Raise the front and rear of the vehicle enough for the engine to clear from under the vehicle.

12. Disconnect the fuel line at the fuel pump and plug the fuel line. Make sure the fuel line is disconnected from any

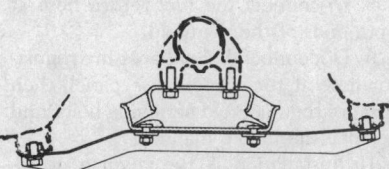

Transmission support bracket—1900 and Manta

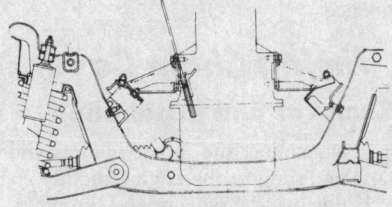

Engine mounting in the 1900 and Manta—1.9 engine

clips fastening it to the engine or transmission.

13. Disconnect the speedometer cable from the transmission.

14. Disconnect the clutch cable.

15. Disconnect the driveshaft at the rear universal joint and remove the driveshaft.

16. Disconnect the exhaust pipe at the exhaust manifold.

17. Remove the tailpipe and muffler hangers.

18. Disconnect the ground strap from the engine.

19. Remove the transmission crossmember from the transmission and frame.

20. Remove the engine crossmember from the engine and frame.

21. Carefully lower the engine and transmission and remove from under the vehicle.

22. Install in the reverse order of removal.

Cylinder Head
Removal and Installation

1972–74

1. Drain radiator and cylinder block. The plug for block is located on right side in front of motor mount.

2. Disconnect radiator hoses, heater hoses, fuel lines, vacuum lines, and throttle linkage from manifolds.

3. Remove spark plug and cap along with any electrical connection.

4. Remove rocker arm cover and rocker arms.

5. Remove plate which is attached to front of cylinder head. Then remove the bolts from end of camshaft.

6. Unbolt cylinder head in proper sequence (reverse of tightening sequence).

7. Disconnect camshaft sprocket from cylinder head. Slide sprocket off camshaft and remove cylinder head.

CAUTION: *Never place cylinder head, with installed camshaft and valves, on its machined surface on work bench.*

8. Clean piston tops and combustion chamber. Thoroughly clean all gasket surfaces on the cylinder head and block.

9. Lubricate cylinder walls with engine oil and clean all foreign matter from machined surfaces.

10. Coat cylinder head gasket with grease or gasket cement on both sides.

11. Install coolant passage rubber gasket ring in timing case.

12. Place gasket on cylinder block and install cylinder head into position.

NOTE: *Rotate camshaft to align recesses for installation of left row of bolts.*

Coolant passages rubber gasket ring in timing case.

1. Timing chain
2. Camshaft sprocket
3. Sprocket timing mark
4. Timing case
5. Support timing mark
6. Support
7. Cylinder block
8. Rubber gasket ring

13. Install head bolts and tighten to specified torque. (72 ft lbs)

14. Slide camshaft sprocket and chain onto camshaft and guide pin, then bolt them together. Install nylon adjusting screw. After sprocket is attached, recheck alignment to see that chain has not slipped.

15. Reinstall cover plate and procede to install in reverse of removal.

1975

1. Remove the air flow meter and air cleaner assembly to gain access to the intake and exhaust manifold bolts.

2. Remove the EGR valve hold down bolt from the thermostat housing.

3. Disconnect all hoses and electrical connections from the thermostat housing and auxiliary air valve.

4. Follow steps 1–15 of the 1971–74 procedure.

Combination Manifolds

1972–74
Removal and Installation

1. Disconnect battery.

2. Remove air cleaner and disconnect throttle linkage, vacuum lines, and fuel lines from carburetor.

3. Drain radiator and remove water hoses to automatic choke.

4. Remove positive crankcase ventilation valve (PCV valve) at rocker arm cover. Disconnect E.G.R. lines from carburetor and intake manifold.

5. Disconnect exhaust pipe.

6. Remove (6) bolts which attach the manifold assembly to cylinder head, and remove complete assembly.

NOTE: *To separate intake and exhaust manifolds, remove carburetor and the bolts which attach them together. Always replace gasket between the manifolds.*

7. Clean all surfaces where new gaskets are to be installed.

NOTE: *Never reuse old gaskets when replacing manifolds onto the engine.*

8. Place manifold assembly into position and install bolts.

9. Tighten bolts in proper sequence. Torque bolts to 33 ft lbs.

10. Reinstall vacuum lines, fuel lines, and throttle linkage.

11. Replace everything that was removed from engine.

1975

1. Cover the fender with a heavy shop cloth to prevent damage.

2. Disconnect the wires at the cold start injector, the four fuel injectors, the throttle valve switch, temperature sensor, thermo time switch, auxiliary air valve, and the airflow meter.

3. Loosen the air outlet hose clamp and remove the hose at the airflow meter. Loosen the airflow meter retaining nut and the air cleaner top clips; remove the air cleaner top and flow meter.

4. Disconnect the throttle body housing inlet hose and move it aside.

5. Disconnect the Bowden wire from the accelerator linkage, and then disconnect the hoses from the auxiliary air valve, distributor vacuum hose at the "T" fitting, the air conditioning hose at the "T" fitting and the EGR vacuum hose at the carburetor.

6. Disconnect the fuel injection ground at the rear of the intake manifold, and the EGR pipe at the throttle body.

7. Disconnect the vacuum brake hose and remove the two accelerator linkage springs.

8. Disconnect the fuel return hose at both ends of the manifold.

9. Disconnect the fuel pressure regulator hose at the wheelhouse panel, then remove the manifold attaching bolts, and remove the intake manifold.

10. Installation is the reverse of removal, but remember to apply a sealing compound to the mounting bolt threads and to torque the bolts in the proper sequence.

Timing Chain Cover
Removal and Installation

1. Disconnect the motor mounts and raise and support the engine slightly.

2. Remove the radiator and shroud assembly.

3. Remove the cylinder head.

4. Remove the alternator belt and remove the alternator mounting bracket.

5. Remove the fuel pump.

6. Remove the distributor.

7. Remove the timing chain tensioner assembly out of the timing chain cover.

8. Remove the crankshaft pulley bolt and remove the pulley.

9. Remove the water pump assembly.

BOLT BEHIND WATER PUMP COVER – MUST BE REMOVED BEFORE TIMING CHAIN COVER CAN BE REMOVED

There is a timing case cover attaching bolt behind the water pump

10. Remove the oil pan.

11. Remove the timing chain cover bolts. One bolt is covered by the water pump.

12. Remove the timing chain cover.

13. Clean the mating surfaces of both the cover and the engine block, install a new gasket and install the cover in the reverse order of removal.

Timing Chain and Tensioner
Removal and Installation

1. Remove the timing chain tensioner and cover as outlined under the Timing Chain Cover, Removal and Installation headings.

2. Pull off the timing chain sprockets with the chain attached. Mark the timing chain and a sprocket with paint so the chain can be reinstalled in its original position.

3. To install the timing chain, first, turn the crankshaft so that the key for the sprocket is on top and vertical. Install the crankshaft sprocket.

4. Assemble the chain with the camshaft sprocket to the crankshaft sprocket. Be sure the paint mark on the chain and camshaft sprocket are facing outward and aligned.

Make sure the camshaft sprocket mark is in alignment with the mark on the sup-

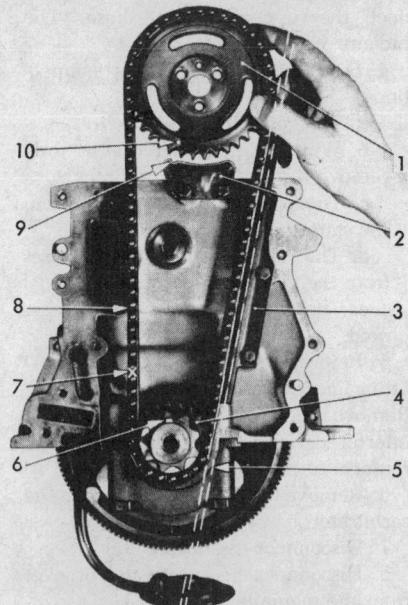

Valve timing marks

1. Camshaft sprocket
2. Camshaft sprocket support
3. Long damper block
4. Crankshaft sprocket
5. Chain and damper block in parallel
6. Crankshaft key
7. Paint mark on front of chain
8. Timing chain
9. Mark on camshaft sprocket support
10. Mark on camshaft sprocket

port and the chain is in parallel with the damper block.

5. Install a new timing case crankshaft oil seal. Install a new timing case rubber gasket to the cylinder block. The gaskets will overlap with the oil pan gasket slightly.

6. Position the timing cover onto the guide pin in the upper left corner of the cylinder block and insert the centering bolt through the cover into the lower right corner of the cylinder block.

7. Install the cylinder head.

8. Attach the camshaft sprocket to the camshaft. Recheck the alignment of the paint marks to make sure the chain has not slipped.

9. At this point both No. 4 and No. 1 pistons will be at TDC. No. 4 piston will be on the compression stroke and No. 1 on the exhaust stroke. To time the engine, rotate the crankshaft 360° to position the camshaft sprocket timing mark 180° from the original alignment of the camshaft sprocket timing mark and mark on the camshaft sprocket support. Also, the piston in No. 1 cylinder will be at TDC on its compression stroke with both the intake and exhaust valves completely closed. The timing mark on the flywheel and the flywheel housing will be aligned at this time.

10. Assemble remaining components in the reverse order of removal.

Tensioner Adjustments

A non-adjustable curved spring plate timing chain tensioner with a wear resistant, oil-proof synthetic rubber slipper pad is provided on the right side (non-driving side) of the timing chain.

There is a self-adjusting chain tensioner above the crankshaft sprocket, also located on the right side, which has a plunger head which is pressed against the chain by both spring and oil pressure. No adjustment is necessary.

A long timing chain damper block is provided on the driving side of the timing chain (left). This, also is not adjustable.

Timing Cover Crankshaft Seal Replacement

1. Remove the fan belts.

2. Remove the crankshaft pulley bolt and remove the pulley.

3. Insert a screwdriver behind the seal and rest the screwdriver on the crankshaft pin. Pry out the seal.

4. Lubricate the new oil seal and install the seal into the timing chain cover.

5. Install the crankshaft pulley and the fan belts.

Camshaft

Removal and Installation

1. Remove cylinder head. Follow

procedures outlined in that section.

2. Loosen rocker arms, swing arms off of the valve lifters and remove lifters.

NOTE: *The lifters must be installed in same position if not being replaced.*

3. Remove cover from access hole on left side of cylinder head.

4. Pull camshaft toward front, while supporting it with one hand through access hole. Be careful not to damage bearing surfaces or cam journals.

5. Before installing camshaft into head, lubricate journals liberally.

6. Reinstall valve lifters, push rods, and rocker arms.

7. Replace head gasket and reinstall head.

8. Reinstall other parts by reversing removal procedures.

Piston and Connecting Rods

Removal and Installation

(See "Engine Rebuilding" section)

1. Remove engine from car and support it safely.

2. Drain crankcase oil and remove oil pan.

3. Remove cylinder head assembly.

4. Check top of cylinder bore for a ridge above ring travel. If a ridge exists, remove it with ridge reamer.

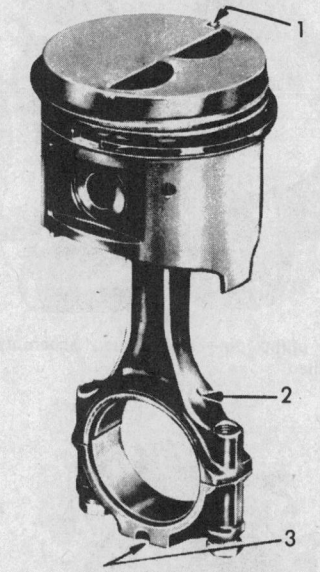

1. NOTCH IN PISTON HEAD POINTING TOWARD THE FRONT
2. OIL HOLE IN CONNECTING ROD POINTING TOWARD THE RIGHT (MANIFOLD SIDE)
3. NOTCH IN CONNECTING ROD CAP POINTING TOWARD THE REAR

Proper positioning of installed piston and connecting rod

CAUTION: *Don't try to remove pistons before removing ridge. This is to avoid damage to the rings and ring lands during removal.*

5. Remove cap and bearing shell and push the piston-rod assembly out through the top of the block. Replace cap onto rod to prevent loss.

NOTE: *Mark piston assemblies to show from which cylinder they were removed.*

6. Remove other pistons and rods in same manner.

7. To install, reverse removal procedure.

NOTE: *After replacing worn or damaged pistons or rings, a ring compressor must be used to reinstall pistons into block.*

ENGINE LUBRICATION

Oil Pan

Removal and Installation

1900 and Manta

1. With chains attached to the alternator support rear bolt on the left side of the engine and to the existing threaded hole at the lower right front of the engine, use a lifting device to raise the engine enough to remove the weight of the engine from the motor mounts.

2. Remove the two motor mount bracket-to-motor mount retaining nuts.

3. Remove the two front suspension-to-frame rail bolt retaining nuts.

4. Remove the nut and bolt at the lower end of the steering shaft U-joint.

5. With a floor jack under the center of the front suspension crossmember, raise the car high enough for the wheels and suspension assembly to be rolled from under the car.

6. Position jackstands under both of the front jack brackets on the under body to support the car in this position.

7. Remove both front crossmember support-to-frame attaching bolts.

8. Remove the brake pipe-to-brake hose retaining clips at the frame rails and disconnect the brake hose from the brake pipes.

9. Lower the front suspension assembly and remove the assembly from under the vehicle.

10. Drain the oil and remove the oil pan and gasket from the engine.

11. To install the oil pan, first clean the mating surfaces of both the oil pan and the engine block and then apply a light bead of sealer to the mating surfaces together with a new oil pan gasket.

12. Bolt the oil pan to the engine block.

13. Roll the front suspension and floor jack under the car and raise the assembly into position. Be careful to guide the crossmember-to-frame rail attaching bolts and the steering shaft to their proper locations.

14. Install the crossmember support-to-frame attaching bolts and tighten to 22 ft lbs.

15. Connect the brake hoses to the brake fluid pipes and install the retaining clips.

16. Bleed the front brake system.

17. Remove the jackstands and lower the car.

18. Install the suspension-to-frame rail bolt retaining nuts.

19. Lower the engine and remove the lifting device.

20. Install the motor mount bracket-to-motor mount retaining nuts.

21. Install the steering shaft U-joint lower bolt and nut.

22. Refill the crankcase with oil.

GT

In order to remove the oil pan from the 1.9 liter engine installed in the GT model, the engine must be raised slightly off of the engine mounts to gain the necessary clearance. Opel has a special tool for this purpose (Tool J-23375) which is a bracket that attaches to the motor mount and rests on the frame rail with the engine in the raised position.

The front suspension need not be removed.

After the engine is raised to give enough clearance, simply remove the oil pan attaching bolts (after draining the oil) and remove the oil pan.

Install the oil pan in the reverse order of removal, installing a new gasket between the two cleaned mating surfaces.

Rear Main Oil Seal

Replacement

1. Remove transmission and bell housing.

2. Remove the clutch and flywheel.

3. Punch a hole into oil seal, screw in a sheet metal screw, and then pull out old seal.

4. Lubricate new seal to assure proper sealing. Place seal on crankshaft flange and move lip of seal over rear of crankshaft.

Removing rear main seal

5. Drive seal into position. Be careful not to tilt seal or it will not seal properly.

6. Reinstall flywheel, clutch, bell housing, and transmission.

NOTE: *When replacing flywheel, use new bolts and torque to 43 ft lbs.*

Oil Pump

Removal and Installation

1. Unbolt oil pump cover from timing chain cover.

2. Slide gears out of housing.

3. Clean and inspect gears and cover for scoring. Replace any part found unserviceable.

NOTE: *If pump housing or distributor shaft bushings are worn, the timing case and all pump parts must be replaced.*

NOTE: *In isolated cases, timing cases have been installed at the factory with 0.008 in. oversize bores for pump gears and shafts. Oversize bores may exist either for one or both gears. Timing cases with oversize bores are identified by the number 0.2 stamped into the pump flange on the left and/or right side. Oversize parts must be replaced with identically oversized parts.*

Oil pump pipe and screen assembly installed

Checking Clearances

1. Disassemble the oil pump as outlined under Oil Pump Removal and Installation.

2. Measure the end clearance of the pump gears with the gears installed in a clean dry housing. Place a straight edge across the face of the housing and ends of the gears and measure the clearance between the straight edge and the machined surface of the housing. The clearance should be no more than 0.004 in.

3. With a feeler gauge placed between the gear teeth where they mesh, measure

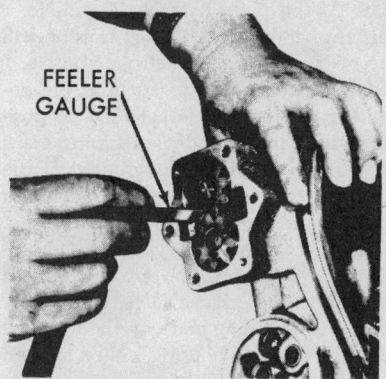

Checking gear backlash

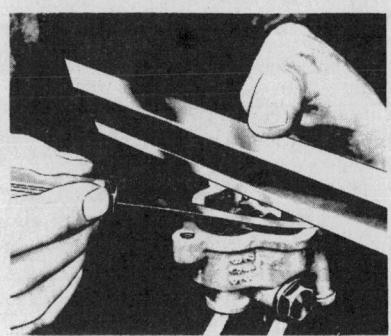

Checking gear end clearance

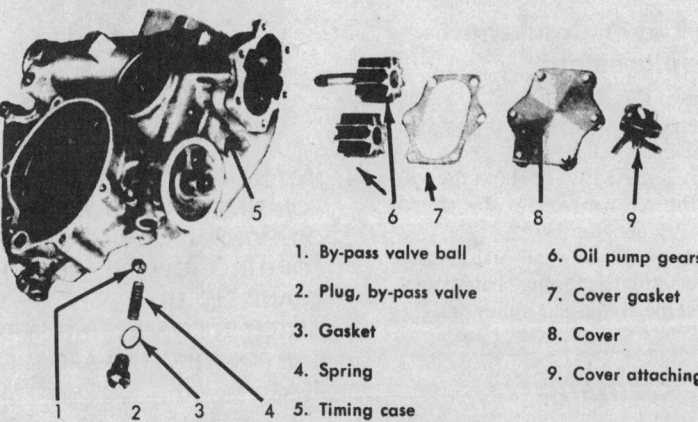

1. By-pass valve ball
2. Plug, by-pass valve
3. Gasket
4. Spring
5. Timing case
6. Oil pump gears
7. Cover gasket
8. Cover
9. Cover attaching screws

Exploded view of oil pump

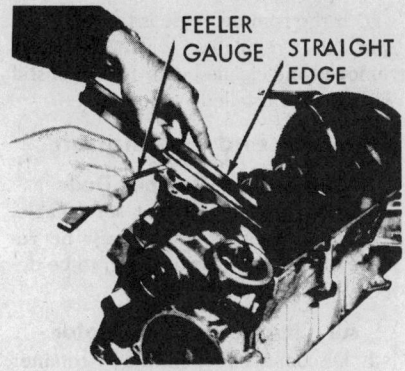

Checking oil pump gear end clearance

the gear backlash. It should be between 0.004 and 0.008 in.

4. Unscrew the plug and check the spring and relief valve plunger in the oil pump cover for dirt particles and free operation. If necessary, carefully clean the plunger and seat. Sticking of the pressure relief valve as a result of foreign material or sludge build-up in the oil pump cover can cause loss of oil pressure.

5. Reassemble the oil pump.

ENGINE COOLING

Radiator

Removal and Installation

1. Drain system of all fluid.
2. Disconnect upper and lower radiator hoses at radiator.
3. Disconnect and plug the oil lines from the bottom of the radiator on those vehicles with automatic transmissions.
4. Remove lower attaching nuts and slide radiator out of compartment.
5. Install by reversing removal process.

NOTE: *Be sure to add the proper amount of anti-freeze solution when filling the system with fluid.*

Water Pump

Removal and Installation

1. Drain radiator of coolant.
NOTE: *Remove radiator and shroud on cars equipped with overhead cam engines.*
2. Loosen alternator and remove fan belt.
3. Unbolt fan and pulley from water pump shaft.
4. If equipped with a clutch fan, remove it along with the fan. The clutch fan retaining bolt has a *left-hand* thread.
5. Remove the radiator and/or heater hoses from the water pump.
6. Remove water pump.
7. Before reinstalling pump,

thoroughly clean old gasket material from the block and pump mating surfaces.

8. Install in reverse of removal.

Thermostat

1972–74

Removal and Installation

1. Drain radiator.
2. Unbolt thermostat housing from block.
3. Remove thermostat from block.
4. Thoroughly clean old gasket material from the mating surfaces and reinstall thermostat.
CAUTION: *Be sure to place the thermostat right side up to allow fluid to flow properly.*

1975

1. Partially drain the radiator, and remove the airflow meter and air cleaner. (See "Intake Manifold Removal and Installation").
2. Remove the throttle lever spring and the accelerator linkage springs.
3. Disconnect the EGR pipe and accelerator linkage at the throttle body housing.
4. Remove the thermostat.

EMISSION CONTROLS

Applications

1972

The 1972 exhaust emission control system is designed to reduce unburned hydrocarbons and carbon monoxide through the use of: (1) leaned out carburetion, (2) heated air (except 1972–74 GT), and (3) tuned spark timing.

The exhaust manifold provides heated air for a stable intake temperature and accurate mixture by means of a "stove" mounted on the exhaust manifold. This heated air is drawn through the heated air pipe into the snorkel of the air

cleaner. The temperature control air cleaner has a sensor that is designed to mix the heated air with colder outside air so the carburetor inlet air temperature averages about 115±20°F. This is done with the sensor, two doors in the air cleaner, and a vacuum motor. The motor operates the doors so that as one opens the other closes, mixing heated and cold air to keep temperature constant. The doors are spring loaded, so that when there is no vacuum from the engine the cold air door is open. When the engine is running, the amount of vacuum delivered to the motor is regulated by the sensor and the amount of vacuum available from the engine. Thus when underhood temperature rises above 135°F., the sensor allows no vacuum to the motor and the door for the heated air closes completely, admitting only cold air. When accelerating hard, manifold vacuum drops and the motor gets no vacuum regardless of the temperature, so again the cold air door is open. When decelerating, the manifold vacuum is high and, if the underhood temperature is less than 135°F., the cold air door closes and only heated air is admitted. The hot air door opens fully at 9 in. of vacuum and the cold air door opens fully below 5 in. of vacuum.

1973

The basic components of the OECS (Opel Emission Control System) on the 1.9 liter engine are; a leaned out carburetor, heated carburetor intake air (except on the GT), and tuned spark timing.

The new addition to the emission control system on Opel in 1973 is Exhaust Gas Recirculation (EGR).

The EGR system consists of a pipe connected to the center of the front exhaust pipe, an EGR valve, a short pipe from the valve to the intake manifold and a short vacuum hose from the EGR valve to the base of the carburetor.

During acceleration and part throttle with sufficient vacuum applied to the EGR valve to open the valve, exhaust gases are siphoned from the exhaust pipe,

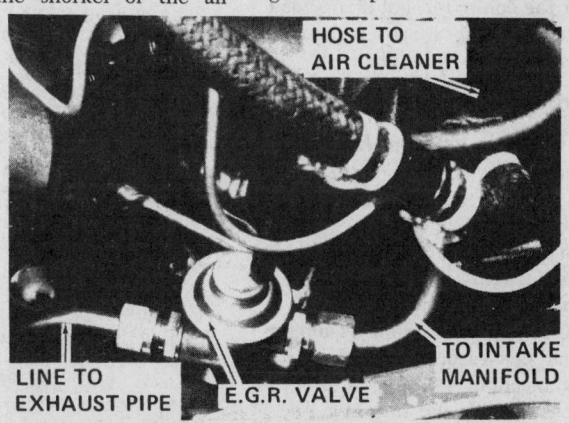

EGR components—1973-75

through the EGR valve and into the intake manifold. The system does not operate at idle speeds.

1974

The OECS changed in 1974 to become known as the controlled combustion system (CCS).

The EGR system was retained in 1974 for use on cars sold in California only. The system was modified however, and now contained two EGR valves connected in series.

The first valve, connected to the exhaust manifold by a pipe, is a shut-off valve, and the second valve is a regulating valve. The regulating valve is operated by manifold vacuum (which varies with engine load) and shut-off valve operates on vacuum present at the base of the carburetor.

The regulating valve begins to open at 3.5 in. of vacuum and is fully open at 9.8 in. of vacuum. The shut-off valve opens at 2.8 in. of vacuum and closes to a smaller gap at 11.8 in. of vacuum. The smaller gap under high vacuum conditions (deceleration and partial load) allows only a small amount of exhaust gas to be recirculated. There is no EGR during idle. There is maximum EGR at all other times.

1975

The EGR system continues on the 1975 models to reduce oxides of nitrogen (NOx) in the exhaust gas. The exhaust gas is fed back into intake manifold after the throttle valve. A vacuum diaphragm in the EGR valve opens and closes the port that recirculates exhaust gas. The vacuum source for the EGR valve is ported vacuum at the throttle valve. As a result, the valve only functions during part throttle. The valve remains closed at idle because of port location in the throttle valve. The valve is also closed during full throttle operation because of low vacuum.

All 1975 Opels are equipped with a catalytic converter to control exhaust emissions. There is no scheduled maintenance for the converter, but it is a good idea to check it for exterior damage whenever the car is on a lift.

Testing

Air Cleaner Vacuum Motor

1. Check hoses for looseness, kinks, plugs, or damage.
2. With engine off, damper door should be open, if it isn't check for binding of the linkage.
3. Apply at least nine (9) in. HG of vacuum to diaphragm assembly. Damper door should be closed. Check linkage for proper connection.
4. Apply vacuum and trap in system, damper door should remain closed.

Check diaphragm assembly for vacuum leakage.

Air Cleaner Sensor Check

1. Observe, the position of the air door before starting the engine. It should be open to outside cold air.
2. Start engine. The cold air door should close to outside air immediately.
3. As engine warms up, the cold air door should start to open, and the air cleaner should become warm.

EGR System—1973

1. With the engine at operating temperature, connect a tachometer to the engine and note the rpm at idle.
2. Disconnect the vacuum hose at the intake manifold that leads to the air cleaner.
3. Disconnect the vacuum hose for the EGR valve from the throttle valve and connect it to the intake manifold where the vacuum hose to the air cleaner was connected.
4. Engine speed should decrease between 100–240 rpm from the previously noted reading.
5. If the rpm decreased less than 100 rpm, the EGR valve and fitting leading into the intake manifold must be removed, cleaned with a piece of stiff wire, and reinstalled.

EGR System—1974–75

1. With the engine at operating temperature, connect a tachometer to the engine and note the rpm at idle.
2. Disconnect the vacuum hose for the air cleaner from the fitting on the intake manifold.
3. Connect the vacuum hose for EGR shut-off valve to the intake manifold fitting where the vacuum hose to the air cleaner was connected. The EGR regulating valve remains connected to its normal fitting on the intake manifold.
4. The engine rpm should drop 270–300 rpm.

5. If the rpm decrease is less than 270 rpm, the regulating valve must be removed and cleaned with a piece of stiff wire, and reinstalled.

Removal and Installation

Air Cleaner Damper Door

The damper door is not serviceable. The air cleaner assembly must be replaced if damper door is found to be defective.

Air Cleaner Vacuum Motor

1. Disconnect vacuum motor retainer spring clamp.
2. Remove vacuum lines, lift motor, and unhook vacuum motor control linkage at damper door.
3. Install in the reverse order of removal.

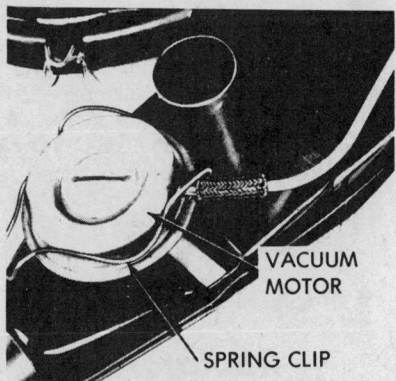

Vacuum motor assembly installed in air cleaner.

Air Cleaner Sensor

1. Disconnect vacuum lines from sensor.
2. Remove retaining clips from sensor, and remove them from air cleaner.

NOTE: *Before removal of sensor, mark position of old sensor to assure installation of new sensor into same position.*

3. Reinstall retaining clip and vacuum lines.

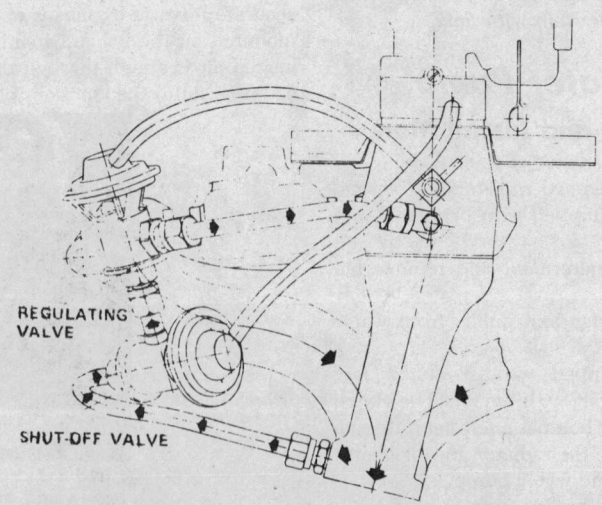

EGR components—1974-75 California only

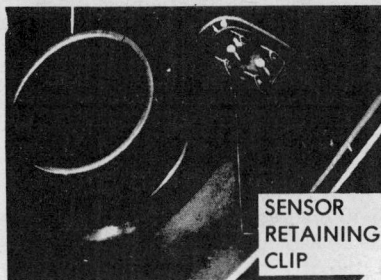

Sensor assembly installed in air cleaner

Air Cleaner Control Valve

1. Remove air cleaner and detach rubber hoses, air bleeder lines, and vacuum lines.

2. Remove attaching bolts and then remove control valve from bracket.

3. Reinstall by reversing removal procedures.

FUEL SYSTEM
Fuel Filter

1972–74

The fuel filter is located in the engine compartment in the line from the fuel pump to the carburetor.

Removal

1. Loosen the hose clamps and pull the filter from the hoses.

1975

The filter is located directly in front of the fuel tank and must be reached from underneath the car.

Removal

1. Remove the support bracket, disconnect the hose clamps and pull the filter from the hoses.

Mechanical Fuel Pump

Removal and Installation

1. Remove fuel lines from pump and plug them.

CAUTION: *Because the fuel tank is higher than the pump, fuel will flow freely when the fuel line is disconnected.*

2. Unbolt the fuel pump from the engine block.

3. Reinstall fuel pump by reversing the removal procedures.

NOTE: *When replacing the fuel pump, be sure to use a new gasket to prevent leakage between pump and block assemblies.*

Testing and Adjustments

1. Disconnect fuel lines at carburetor.

2. Connect a pressure testing gauge to

1972-74 fuel pump

that end of the fuel line that comes directly from the pump.

3. Start the engine. The pressure should read 3.1–3.7 PSI at 1950 rpm. Defective pumps should be replaced.

Electric Fuel Pump

All 1975 Opels are equipped with an electric fuel pump located near the left front corner of the gas tank.

Removal and Installation

1. Disconnect the negative battery cable and raise the car.

2. Disconnect the fuel pump electrical connector. Using a 10 mm socket, remove the pump lower bracket bolt.

3. Open the bracket and remove the pump and insulator.

4. Loosen the hose clamps and remove the hoses. Some fuel will escape as the system is under pressure.

5. Remove the pump insulator. Replace the components in the reverse order of removal. The fuel pump is nonserviceable; it must be replaced if defective.

Carburetors

Removal and Installation

1972

1. Remove the air cleaner and remove the fuel lines and all vacuum hoses from the carburetor.

2. Drain radiator and remove the water hoses from the choke housing. (Automatic chokes only)

3. Disconnect the choke cable (where applicable) and the throttle control rods.

4. Unbolt the mounting nuts and remove the carburetor.

NOTE: *Before reinstalling the carburetor, adjust the automatic choke by rotating the choke housing so that the choke plate is nearly closed at room temperature.*

5. To install, reverse the removal procedures.

1973–74

1. Remove the air cleaner.

2. Remove the fuel and vacuum hoses from the carburetor fittings.

3. Remove the choke wire.

4. Disconnect the throttle linkage by removing the lock pin and unsnapping the ball socket from the ball on the end of the throttle shaft.

5. Remove the carburetor by removing the 4 attaching nuts and washers.

6. Prior to reinstalling the carburetor, install a new gasket on the intake manifold.

7. Install the carburetor and tighten the attaching nuts securely.

8. Connect the choke wire, the throttle linkage, vacuum hoses and the fuel line.

9. Install the air cleaner.

Overhaul

Efficient carburetion depends greatly on careful cleaning and inspection during overhaul, since dirt, gum, water, or varnish in or on the carburetor parts are often responsible for poor performance.

Overhaul your carburetor in a clean, dust-free area. Carefully disassemble the carburetor, referring often to the exploded views. Keep all similar and look-alike parts segregated during disassembly and cleaning to avoid accidental interchange during assembly. Make a note of all jet sizes.

When the carburetor is disassembled, wash all parts (except diaphragms, electric choke units, pump plunger, and any other plastic, leather, fiber, or rubber parts) in clean carburetor solvent. Do not leave parts in the solvent any longer than is necessary to sufficiently loosen the deposits. Excessive cleaning may remove the special finish from the float bowl and choke valve bodies, leaving these parts unfit for service. Rinse all parts in clean solvent and blow them dry with compressed air or allow them to air dry. Wipe clean all cork, plastic, leather, and fiber parts with a clean, lint-free cloth.

Blow out all passages and jets with compressed air and be sure that there are no restrictions or blockages. Never use wire or similar tools to clean jets, fuel passages, or air bleeds. Clean all jets and valves separately to avoid accidental interchange.

Check all parts for wear or damage. If wear or damage is found, replace the defective parts. Especially check the following:

1. Check the float needle and seat for wear. If wear is found, replace the complete assembly.

2. Check the float hinge pin for wear and the float(s) for dents or distortion. Replace the float if fuel has leaked into it.

3. Check the throttle and choke shaft bores for wear or an out-of-round condition. Damage or wear to the throttle arm, shaft, or shaft bore will often require re-

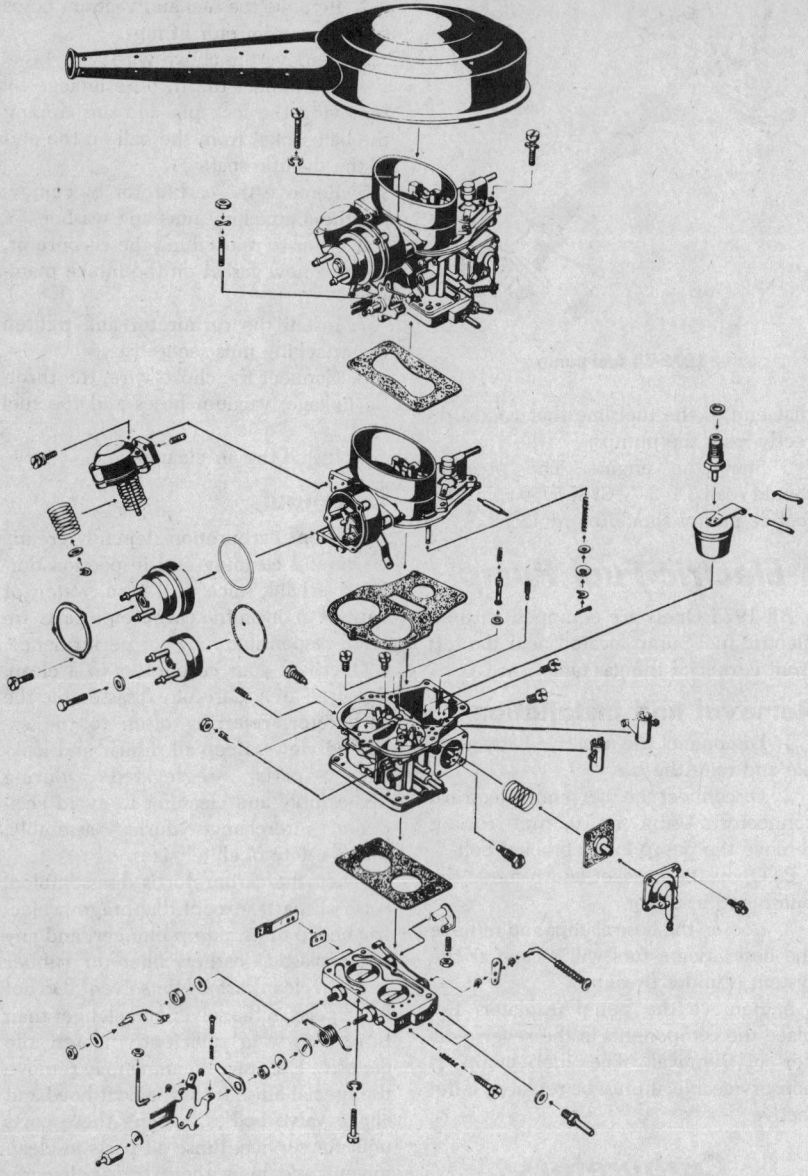

Exploded view of 2-bbl Solex carburetor

placement of the throttle body. These parts require a close tolerance of fit; wear may allow air leakage, which could affect starting and idling.

NOTE: *Throttle shafts and bushings are not included in overhaul kits. They can be purchased separately.*

4. Inspect the idle mixture adjusting needles for burrs or grooves. Any such condition requires replacement of the needle, since you will not be able to obtain a satisfactory idle.

5. Test the accelerator pump check valves. They should pass air one way but not the other. Test for proper seating by blowing and sucking on the valve. Replace the valve if necessary. If the valve is satisfactory, wash the valve again to remove breath moisture.

6. Check the bowl cover for warped surfaces with a straight edge.

7. Closely inspect the valves and seats

for wear and damage, replacing as necessary.

8. After the carburetor is assembled, check the choke valve for freedom of operation.

Carburetor overhaul kits are recommended for each overhaul. These kits contain all gaskets and new parts to replace those that deteriorate most rapidly. Failure to replace all parts supplied with the kit (especially gaskets) can result in poor performance later.

After cleaning and checking all components, reassemble the carburetor, using new parts and referring to the exploded view. When reassembling, make sure that all screws and jets are tight in their seats, but do not overtighten as the tips will be distorted. Tighten all screws gradually, in rotation. Do not tighten needle valves into their seats; uneven jetting will result. Always use new gaskets.

Be sure to adjust the float level when reassembling.

Throttle Linkage Adjustments

1972 Opels, All GT Models

To determine whether or not adjustment is necessary, have a helper depress the accelerator pedal to the floor and see if the throttle valves are completely open. If they are not and adjustment is necessary, proceed in this manner:

1. Unhook the accelerator pedal return spring.

2. Remove the lock spring at the upper end of the vertical control rod and detach the rod.

3. Lengthen or shorten the control rod so that wide open throttle is obtained when the accelerator pedal is about ¼ in. from the floor.

4. Reinstall the control rod, lock spring, and pedal return spring.

Opel 1900 and Manta Series

The carburetor bowden control wire is properly adjusted when the ball of the carburetor bowden control wire (A) rests against the accelerator pedal lever and the accelerator pedal is at an angle of 25° to the vertical plane with the engine at operating temperature at idle speed. Adjustment is as follows:

1. The accelerator pedal must be positioned at an angle of 25°. To do this, loosen the lock nut of the adjusting bolt and unscrew the bolt a few turns. Push a wood block measuring about 1⅜ in. between the accelerator pedal and the dash panel. Screw in the adjusting bolt until the accelerator pedal lever releases the wood block; then tighten the lock nut.

2. Adjust the engine idle speed.

3. Adjust the bowden wire at the adjuster located in the engine compartment. Set the bowden wire so that the ball rests against the accelerator pedal lever and the wire core between the adjuster bracket and the segmental disc on the carburetor is not sagging.

4. Depress the accelerator pedal to the floorboard and check to see that the throttle valves are completely open.

Float and Fuel Level Adjustments

The float level is fixed on both the Solex 1 bbl and 2 bbl carburetors. There is not provision for adjustment. Compare the shape of the old float to that of a new one. If the one being checked is damaged, it must be replaced.

The float level is established by the thickness of the copper seal ring on the float needle valve. The correct seal ring thickness for the Solex 1 bbl is 0.06 in.; for the Solex 2 bbl, 0.08 in. If any other thickness gasket is used, the float level will be changed.

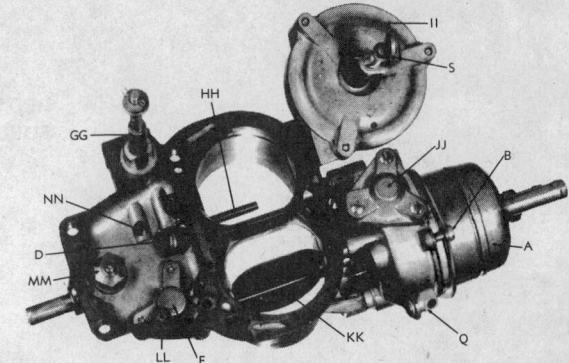

Solex 2 barrel carburetor with an automatic choke

(a)—Automatic choke cover (water temp)
(b)—Choke adjustment screws
(c)—Cover of choke control mechanism
(d)—Float chamber vent tube
(e)—Enrichment diaphragm chamber
(f)—Fuel inlet
(g)—Float cover screws
(h)—Idle jet
(i)—Accelerator pump screws
(j)—Vacuum pipe for distributor advance
(k)—Idle air (speed) adjusting screw
(l)—Accelerator pump adjustment
(m)—Connection for A.I.R.
(n)—Idle mixture (volume) adjustment
(o)—Throttle stop screw
(p)—Throttle lever
(q)—Choke-throttle connecting rod
(r)—Venturi set screw
(s)—Secondary throttle control rod

(t)—Hot water hose connections
(u)—Enrichment air jet
(v)—Check valve carrier for accelerator pump
(w)—Injection nozzle for accelerator pump

(x)—Main nozzle bleed (emulsion tube underneath)
(y)—Primary venturi (choke tube)
(aa)—Air channel of progression circuit for secondary venturi

(bb)—Control arm for outside ventilation channel to float bowl
(cc)—High speed air bleed (main air jet)
(dd)—Primary main metering jet (secondary main metering jet not visible)
(ee)—Fuel inlet to check valve
(ff)—Enrichment fuel inlet
(gg)—Control rod for the inside-outside ventilator for the float bowl
(hh)—Enrichment tube
(ii)—Secondary-throttle diaphragm chamber
(jj)—Vacuum-choke diaphragm chamber
(kk)—Choke valve
(ll)—Vacuum passage to enrichment chamber
(mm)—Needle valve carrier
(nn)—Float bowl ventilation passage

Fast Idle Adjustments

It is best to perform this operation when the engine has been run to operating temperature. The actual adjustment should be made initially with the engine OFF.

1. Operate the throttle linkage by hand until the throttle valve is half open. With your other hand, completely close the choke valve. Release the throttle valve first and then the choke valve.

2. By performing this operation the abutment lever in the automatic choke body has come to rest on the highest step of the fast idle cam and the throttle valve is partially open.

3. Start the engine but do not touch the accelerator pedal. The slightest touch will release the position of the fast idle mechanism.

4. With a tachometer connected to the engine, check the fast idle speed. It should be within 200 rpm of the specified speed.

5. Adjustments to the fast idle speed are made by lengthening or shortening the throttle connecting link.

6. Shorten the rod to decrease engine speed by loosening the lower nut and tightening the upper.

7. Lengthen the rod to increase engine speed by loosening the upper nut and tightening the lower.

Automatic Choke Adjustments

NOTE: *To adjust automatic choke, the engine must be cold.*

1. Remove the air cleaner. Check vacuum lines for cracks and loose connections.

Decreasing fast idle speed—solex 2 bbl

Increasing fast idle speed—solex 2 bbl

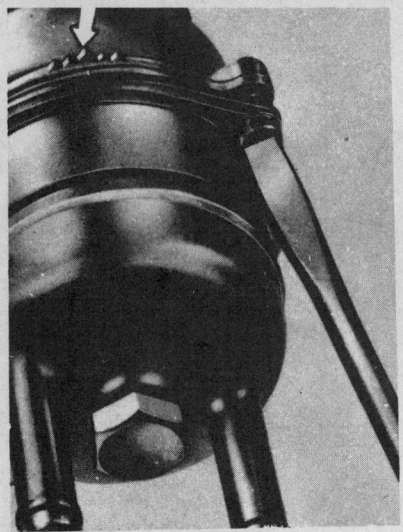

Alignment marks on the choke housing—Solex 2 bbl

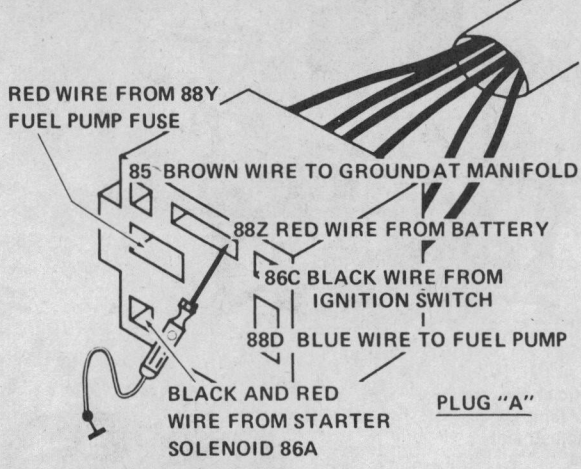

RED WIRE FROM 88Y FUEL PUMP FUSE

85 BROWN WIRE TO GROUND AT MANIFOLD

88Z RED WIRE FROM BATTERY

86C BLACK WIRE FROM IGNITION SWITCH

88D BLUE WIRE TO FUEL PUMP

BLACK AND RED WIRE FROM STARTER SOLENOID 86A

PLUG "A"

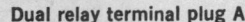

Dual relay terminal plug A

2. Check choke plate for freedom of movement.

3. The choke plate should be nearly closed.

4. To adjust, loosen choke cover and rotate assembly until choke plate is nearly closed.

5. Tighten cover assembly and start engine. When operating temperature has been reached, the choke plate should be completely open.

Electronic Fuel Injection

All 1975 Opels use electronic fuel injection to meter fuel to the cylinders. Information is fed to the control unit (the "brain" of the system), from various engine sources; the control unit constantly computes the proper fuel and air mixture for all operating conditions. The computer also controls the pulse time of the injectors so that the right mixture can be achieved. Most testing operations involve specialized testing equipment and should be left to a qualified dealer, but there are some checks that you can make.

1. First, make sure that the ignition system is in good working order.

2. Vacuum leaks in the manifold system, or between the airflow meter and the combustion chambers can cause misfiring, a rough idle, hard starting, or stalling. If a leak is suspected, correctly torque the intake manifold bolts, then check all vacuum hoses for condition and poor connections.

3. Disconnect the brake booster hose at the intake manifold and apply a soapy water solution around all fittings and gaskets. Apply about 5 psi of air to the hose. Air leaks will produce bubbles.

4. If improper operation is suspected, such as high idle RPM at all times, or no

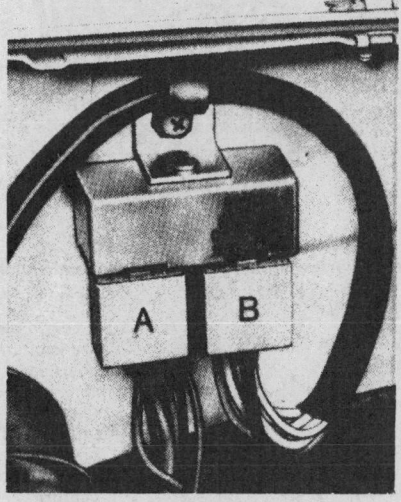

Dual relay terminal connectors

high idle following cold starts in low ambient temperature check the auxiliary air valve as follows:

a. Remove the valve from the engine.

b. Look through the air passage. The rotary disc will be slightly open at room temperature. Use a jumper wire and connect the positive terminal of a 12 volt battery to one electrical contact of the auxiliary air valve and negative terminal to the other electrical contact. This will heat the valve, and in approximately five minutes the rotary slide should cover the passage completely.

Dual Relay Checks

The dual relay is made up of two relays which control current to the entire fuel injection system. One relay provides current to the control unit and pre-resistors; the other provides current to the electric fuel pump.

1. Disconnect plug "A" from the dual relay, and hook up a test light.

2. Insert the probe into terminal 88Z. If the plug does not light, there is a short between the plug and the battery.

3. Insert the probe into terminal 88Y. If it does not light, the fuel pump fuse is blown. The fuel pump fuse is in its own holder next to the fuse box.

4. Turn the ignition switch on; insert the probe into terminal 86C. If it does not light, there is a short between the plug and the ignition switch.

5. With the ignition switch on, insert the probe into terminal 86A and crank the starter. If the light does not come on, check the black and red wire connected to the starter solenoid.

6. With an ohmmeter, check for continuity between terminal 85 and ground. If there is no continuity, the brown wire between the terminal plug and intake manifold connection is broken.

Fuel Supply Checks

1. Install a fuel pressure gauge to the fuel feed line of the cold start injector. Take readings while cranking and with the engine running; the pressure should be between 31–44 psi.

2. If there is no pressure, check the fuse. If it is OK, remove the "A" plug from the dual relay and connect a jumper between terminals 88D and 88Y of the plug. If the pump does not run, check for current at the fuel pump. If you are getting current and the ground is good, and the pump still will not work, replace the pump. If the pump works with the jumper wire installed, replace the dual relay. If the problem still exists with the new relay, repeat the dual relay checks.

3. If you get normal fuel pressure readings while cranking, but it drops off when the engine is running, the airflow meter circuit has to be checked. Remove the electronic fuel injection wiring harness plug and connect a jumper between terminals 36 and 39 of the plug. Turn the

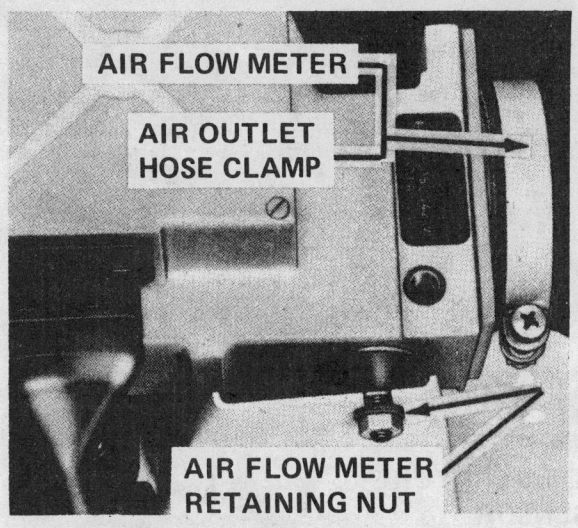

Removing the air flow meter

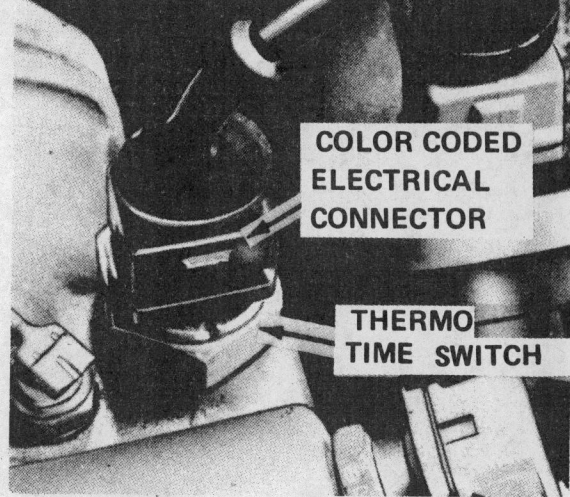

Removing the thermo time switch

ignition switch on; if the pump operates, the wiring harness and dual relay are OK, and the problem is in the airflow meter.

Connect an ohmmeter to terminals 36 and 39 of the airflow meter. Disconnect the hose at the front of the airflow meter and operate the baffle plate by hand. You must register continuity when the baffle plate is moved from the closed position.

4. If the fuel pump is operating, but you are reading no pressure, check for obstruction and restrictions in the fuel lines.

5. If you are registering pressure, and it is over 44 psi, check for a restricted fuel return line from the pressure regulator valve to the fuel tank. If it is not restricted, the pressure regulator valve is faulty. If the pressure does not vary with intake manifold vacuum, either the pressure regulator valve is not receiving vacuum or the valve itself is bad. If the pressure you are registering is low, check the pressure regulator valve, the fuel pump, and the fuel lines.

6. If you are not getting enough fuel flow, remove the fuel line from the cold start injector. Run a hose from the line to a container and insert a jumper wire between terminals 88D and 88Y on terminal plug "A". If the volume pumped is not at least 1.5 qts in a minute, check the lines for restrictions; if there are none, replace the fuel pump.

Air Flow Meter

Removal and Installation

1. Disconnect the electrical connector from the air flow meter.

2. Loosen the air outlet hose clamp and remove the hose at the air flow meter.

3. Remove the air cleaner top and the air flow meter together as a unit after loosening the retaining nut and clips.

4. Remove the four air cleaner to air flow meter bolts and remove the gasket and air flow meter.

5. Clean the flap and chamber with a lint-free cloth.

6. Use an ohmmeter between terminals 36 and 39 of the air flow meter to determine if the electrical circuits are operating correctly. When the baffle plate is closed, the ohmmeter should show no continuity, infinite reading. When the flapper valve is moved from the closed position the ohmmeter should show 0 ohms indicating continuity.

7. To install reverse the removal procedure.

Auxiliary Air Valve

Removal and Installation

1. Loosen both hose clamps and remove both the throttle valve hose and the manifold adapter hose.

2. Disconnect the auxiliary air valve color coded electrical connector.

3. Remove the two hold down bolts and remove the valve from the thermostat housing.

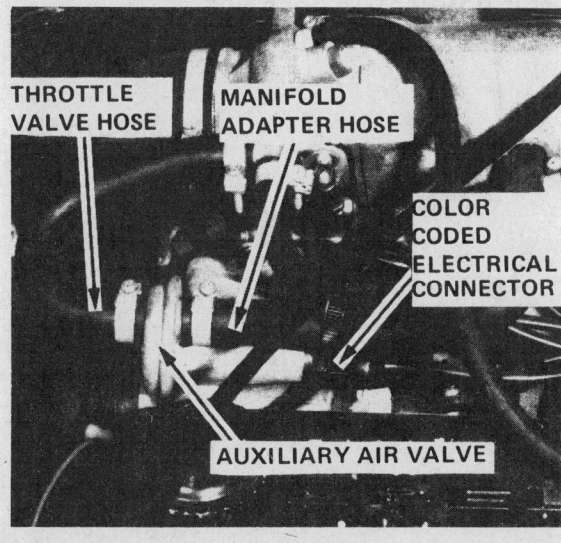

Removing the auxiliary air valve

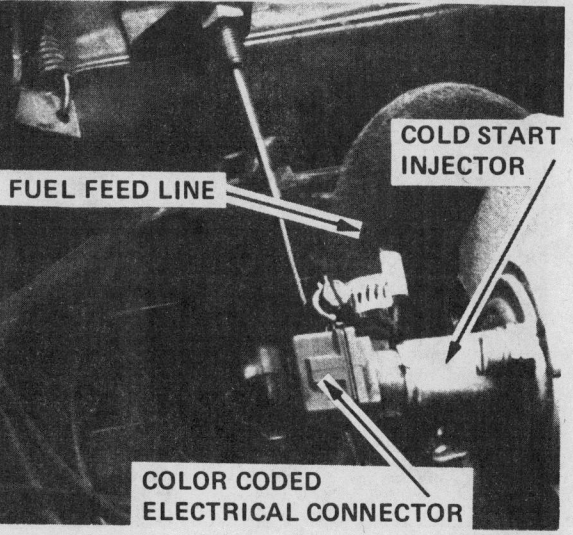

Removing the cold start injector

Removing the dual relay

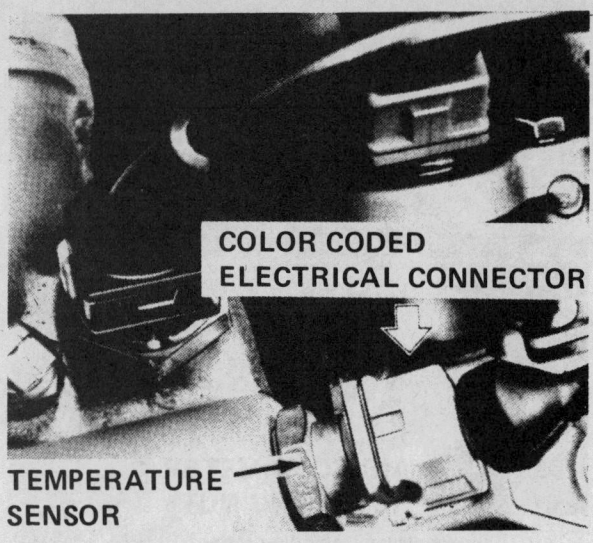

Removing the temperature sensor

4. To install reverse the removal procedure. Torque the retaining bolts to 2.5 ft lbs.

Cold Start Injector

Removal and Installation

1. Disconnect the color coded electrical connector from the cold start injector.

2. Loosen the clamp and disconnect the fuel feed line.

3. Remove the two injector retaining screws.

4. Remove the injector and gasket.

5. To install reverse the removal procedure. Torque the two retaining screws to 2.5 ft lbs.

Thermo Time Switch

Removal and Installation

1. Rotate the radiator cap counter clockwise until the first stop is reached and release the pressure.

2. Disconnect the color coded electrical connector at the thermo time switch.

3. Use a deep socket and remove the switch.

4. To install reverse the removal procedure. Make sure the metal sealing ring is used and torque the switch to 21.7 ft lbs.

Dual Relay

Removal and Installation

1. Disconnect the two electrical connectors from the relay.

2. Remove the hold down screw and the harness bracket.

3. To install reverse the removal procedure.

Temperature Sensor

Removal and Installation

1. Rotate the radiator cap counter clockwise until the first stop is reached and release the pressure.

2. Loosen the clamp and remove the hose between the auxiliary air valve and the manifold hose.

3. Disconnect the electrical connector from the sensor.

4. Remove the sensor using a 20 mm wrench.

6. To install reverse the removal procedure. Torque the sensor to 10.8 ft lbs.

Control Unit

Removal and Installation

1. Loosen the right door edge beading rearward.

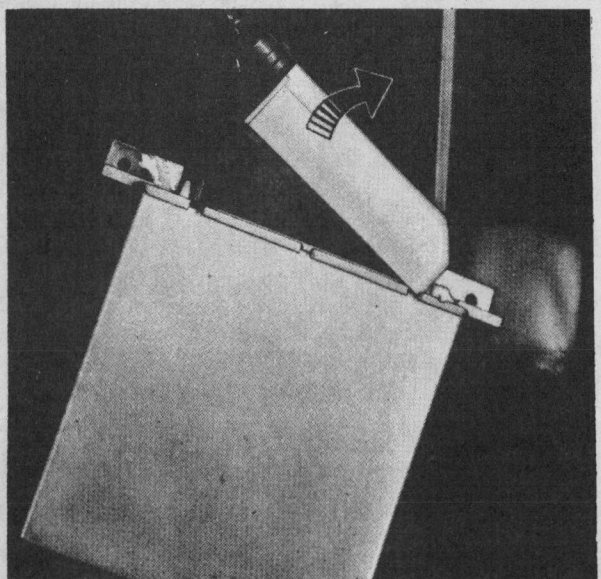

Removing the control unit wiring connector

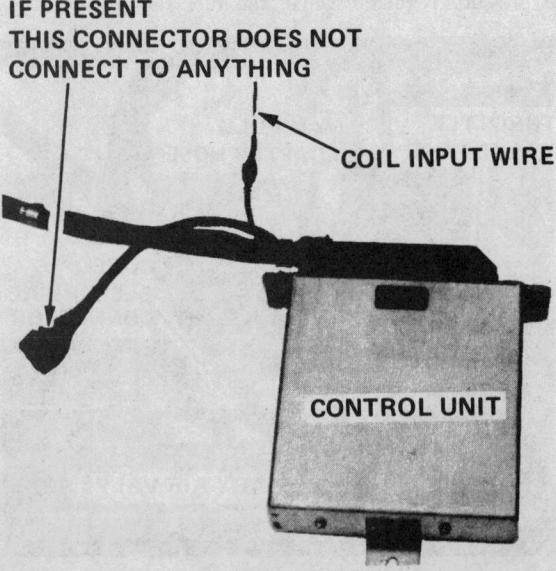

Coil input wire

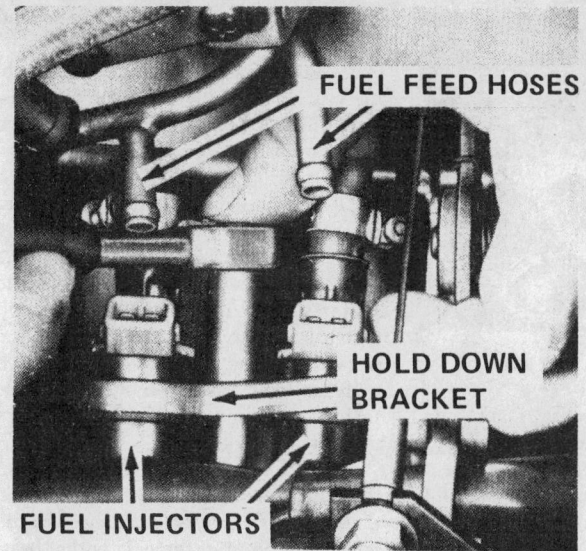

Removing fuel injectors

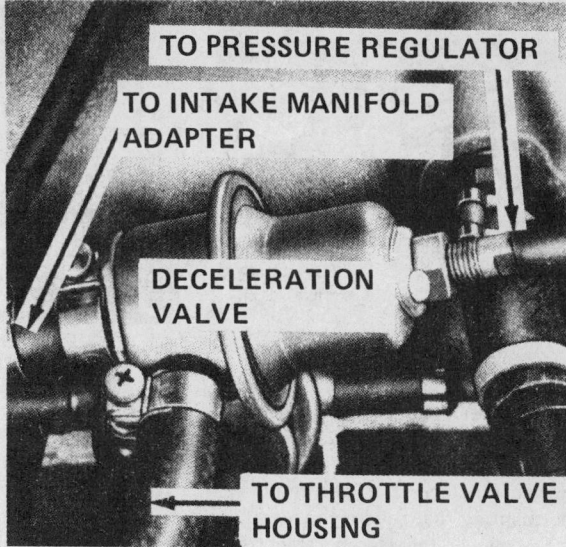

Removing the deceleration valve

2. Remove the right kick pad by pulling the kick pad rearward and toward the inside.

3. Remove the three control unit retaining screws.

4. Disconnect the electrical connector from the control unit. To release the connector push the front edge of the connector forward then upward.

5. To install reverse the removal procedure. Make sure the coil in put wire is connected which may inadvertently become disconnected during the removal procedure.

Fuel Pressure Regulator Valve

Removal and Installation

1. Remove the rear injector hold down bracket bolt from the injector insulator.

2. Remove the vacuum hose coming from the fuel pressure regulator valve "T".

3. Loosen the two fuel feed hose clamps and remove the fuel hoses.

4. Loosen the fuel return hose clamp and remove the pressure regulator valve.

5. To install reverse the removal procedure.

Injector (Pair)

Removal and Installation

1. Disconnect the electrical connectors from the injectors.

2. Remove the center hold down bolt.

3. Loosen the clamp and disconnect the injector from the fuel feed pipe.

4. Remove the injectors from the hold down clamp being careful not to damage the injector needle.

5. To install reverse the removal procedure. Make sure to install the seal rings on the injector and torque the hold down bracket bolt to 2.9 ft lbs.

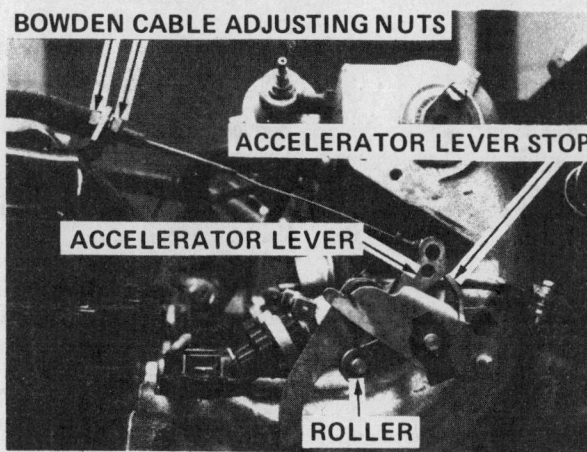

Adjusting the Bowden cable

NOTE: *Do not over torque since the hold down bolt is secured to a plastic insulator.*

Deceleration Valve

Removal and Installation

1. Loosen the two hose clamps at the valve.

2. Remove the three hoses connected to the valve and remove the valve.

3. To install secure the unclamped hose coming from the pressure regulator "T" to the threaded fitting at the end of the deceleration valve.

4. Secure the clamped hose coming from the intake manifold adapter to the welded fitting at the end of the valve.

5. Secure the clamped hose coming from the throttle valve housing to the welded fitting on the side of the deceleration valve.

Accelerator Linkage Adjustment

1. Adjust the bowden cable at the rocker arm cover so that the accelerator lever touches the accelerator lever stop, and slack in the bowden cable is minimal.

2. The clearance between the roller and lever should be as small as possible and still allow the roller to turn easily. If the clearance between the roller and accelerator lever is incorrect adjust the accelerator rod. Loosen the lock nuts and lengthen or shorten the rod as required then retighten the lock nuts. When everything is correctly adjusted, the throttle valve lever should rest against the throttle valve lever stop screw.

MANUAL TRANSMISSION

Removal and Installation

1. Remove the air cleaner and throttle rod from the engine.

2. Remove the standard shift lever by

Opel

Removing standard shift lever

Removing sports shift lever

pulling up the boot, pushing the lock cap down and turning it counterclockwise.

a. The sport shift lever is removed by removing the boot, and removing the snapring that retains the lever.

3. Disconnect the clutch cable from the clutch fork, the speedometer cable from the speedometer drive housing, and the wires from the backup lamp switch.

4. Unhook the parking brake cable return spring, and remove the cable adjusting nut, equalizer, and spacer.

5. Mark the relative positions of the driveshaft U-joint flange and the drive pinion extension shaft flange at the central joint.

6. Support the vehicle at its rear jack brackets, loosen · the bolt locks and remove the flange bolts. Work the driveshaft slightly forward, swing the rear end of the shaft down, and remove the shaft rearward and remove thrust spring.

NOTE: *Plug the end of the transmission to prevent fluid loss.*

7. Remove the lower bolt on each side of the crankcase, and install guide pins to prevent clutch disc warpage when removing the transmission.

8. Support the engine from below, and unbolt the right engine mount.

9. Remove one rear transmission mounting bolt, loosen the other, and raise the front of the engine to provide clearance for removal of the transmission.

10. Remove the remaining transmission to crankcase bolts, and the rear mounting bolt, and slide the transmission back and out of the vehicle.

11. Installation is the reverse of removal.

Overhaul

1. Remove the cotter pins that secure each end of the shifter shaft.

2. Remove the shifter shaft with the washer and spring washer at each end.

3. Drive out the pin securing the selector lever to the transmission extension bolt with a suitable punch.

4. Remove the 2 bolts and spring washers from the transmission case extension housing which secure the selector lever bracket.

5. Remove the selector lever and bracket. The selector lever will simply slip off the selector ring.

6. Remove the locknut and selector ring.

7. Remove the transmission case extension bolt.

8. Remove the 10 transmission case cover bolts, and remove the cover and its gasket.

9. Invert the transmission and drain the oil.

10. Remove the remaining 3 transmission case extension housing-to-case attaching bolts and spring washers.

11. Turn the transmission case extension housing until the gear unit countershaft is exposed.

12. Drive out the countershaft from the front of the transmission. There is a lock ball inserted in the rear of the countershaft. Do not lose the ball.

13. Remove the countershaft gear assembly from the transmission case. Remove both of the thrust washers from either end.

14. Drive out the reverse intermediate lever bedding bolt and remove the reverse speed shifter intermediate lever.

15. With the selector shaft turned so that the lockpins are in a vertical position, drive the lockpins out of the third and fourth speed intermediate lever and then out of the first and second speed intermediate lever. Use a ⅛ in. pin punch to remove all of the lockpins.

16. Push the selector shaft out of the case and remove the intermediate levers.

17. With a screwdriver, pry out the selector shaft oil seals on the transmission case.

18. Pull out both of the lock ball plugs from the bottom of the transmission, using a sheet metal screw installed in the end of a slide hammer. Remove the thrust springs and balls.

19. With the transmission in first gear, drive the lock pins out of the shifter yokes and the shifter shaft cam.

20. Turn the extension housing until the shifter shaft is exposed. Drive out the first and second speed shifter shaft from the rear of the transmission with a brass drift.

21. Remove both the first and second speed shifter yoke and shifter cam.

22. Pull the main drive gear and needle bearing assembly out of the transmission through the front. It may be necessary to rock the main drive gear to remove it.

23. Pull the mainshaft assembly and the transmission case extension housing out of the transmission from the rear. The gear shifter sleeve will be pulled off the shifter sleeve carrier by the third and fourth speed shifter yoke. Remove the sleeve from the yoke and keep the sleeve with the mainshaft assembly. Make sure that the third and fourth speed shoes are not lost.

24. With the mainshaft assembly out of the transmission case, drive the third and fourth gear shifter shaft out through the hole in the front of the case with a brass drift from the rear of the transmission through the mainshaft assembly hole in the case.

25. Remove the third and fourth speed yoke.

26. Using the brass drift and from the front of the transmission, drive out the reverse gear shifter shaft and plug. The reverse speed shifter yoke will remain in the transmission case.

27. Push the reverse idler gear shaft from the front of the transmission toward the rear. Make sure the lock ball is not lost. The reverse idler gear shaft is removed from the mounting boss in the center of the case with special tool J-22923 or a suitable substitute.

28. Take the reverse idler gear shaft, gear, and reverse speed shifter yoke out of the transmission case.

29. To disassemble the mainshaft assembly, remove the mainshaft bearing snap-ring from the transmission case extension housing groove and remove the mainshaft assembly from the housing.

30. Remove the loose parts such as the mainshaft needle bearing, the mainshaft front ring, synchronizer cover, gear shifter sleeve, shoes, and the front synchronizer spring.

The gear shifter sleeve carrier and the first and second speed sliding gear guide unit and their respective gear shifter sleeve and first and second gear sliding gear are selected assemblies and should be kept together as originally assembled.

31. Remove the snap-ring from in front of the clutch hub.

32. Remove the snap-ring from behind the speedometer drive gear, and remove the speedometer drive gear spring washer and the gear.

33. Remove the speedometer drive gear lock ball from the mainshaft.

34. Press the mainshaft inner bearing from the mainshaft. Remove all of the loose parts from the mainshaft, such as the mainshaft washer, transmission case

1. Case, transmission
2. Gasket, trans. case to clutch housing
3. Cap, ventilator
4. Gear, w/bushings, reverse idler
5. Shaft, reverse idler gear
6. Cluster gear, countershaft
7. Washer, trans. counter gear thrust
8. Roller, trans. counter gear bearing
9. Countershaft, cluster gear
10. Gear, main drive
11. Spacer ring, trans. counter gear bearing roller
12. Bearing, trans. main shaft pilot
13. Ring, trans. main drive gear ball bearing lock
14. Seal ring, main drive gear to clutch
15. Shaft, main
16. Ring, trans. main shaft snap—front
17. Needle bearing, 1st speed gear on main shaft
18. Sliding gear, 1st and 2nd speed
19. Guide unit, 1st and 2nd speeding sliding gear
20. Gear, 3rd speed
21. Gear, 1st.speed
22. Gear, 2nd speed
23. Sleeve, trans. gear shifter
24. Carrier, trans. gear shifter sleeve
25. Snap ring, trans. gear shifter sleeve
26. Cone, trans. 3rd and 4th speed syncronizer
27. Cone, trans. 1st and 2nd speed syncronizer
28. Spring, synchronizer (1st and 2nd speed)
29. Spring, syncronizer
30. Shoe, 1st and 2nd speed shifter
31. Shoe, 3rd and 4th speed shifter
32. Bearing, trans. main shaft—R.R.
33. Snap ring, trans. main shaft ball bearings
34. Washer, main shaft—between inner ball bearing and 1st speed gear
35. Bearing, trans. main shaft needle—right
36. Gear, speedometer drive
37. Washer, speedo—drive gear
38. Ring, speedo—drive gear snap
39. Retainer, R.R. bearing
40. Oil seal, R.R.
41. Gasket, R.R. bearing retainer
42. Bushing, trans. main shaft—R.R.

43. Clip, speedo—gear
44. Guide, speedo—drive
45. Gear, speedo—driven
46. Seal, speedo—shaft sleeve
47. Bracket, speedo and guide on trans.
48. Seal ring, speedo drive guide
49. Cover, trans. case
50. Gasket, trans. case cover
51. Shifter shaft, 1st and 2nd speed
52. Shifter shaft, 3rd and 4th speed

53. Shaft, reverse speed shifter
54. Intermediate lever, 1st and 2nd speed shifter
55. Lever, reverse shifter intermediate
56. Lever, intermediate 3rd, 4th and reverse
57. Seal, shifter shaft oil in trans.
58. Cam on shifter shaft
59. Shifter shaft, intermediate lever reverse
60. Shaft, w/lever and bolt, in trans.

61. Fork (yoke), reverse speed shifter
62. Yoke, trans. shifter (1st and reverse)
63. Fork (yoke), trans. 2nd and 3rd speed
64. Spring, trans. gearshift interlock thrust
65. Detent spring, reverse speed gearshift interlock
66. Plug, gearshift interlock detent

1972-75 Opel manual transmission

extension housing snap-ring, first speed gear, first speed needle bearing, synchronizer cover, first and second gear sliding gear, shoes, and the rear synchronizer spring.

35. Press out the gear shifter sleeve carriers below the third and second speed gears respectively.

To assemble the transmission:

36. Start to assemble the mainshaft by first installing the third speed gear onto the mainshaft from the front of the main-

shaft. The gear must turn freely on the mainshaft.

37. Install the third speed synchronizer cover onto the third speed gear cone.

38. Install the rear synchronizer sleeve into the rear side of the gear shifter sleeve carrier so that the hooked spring end rests in one of the slots.

39. Press the gear shifter sleeve carrier onto the mainshaft so that the original tooth contact is obtained. The rear side of

the gear shifter sleeve carrier with the spring installed should be toward the third speed gear. This rear side of the carrier is recessed more than the front side to allow the carrier to be pressed almost flush with the synchronizer cover.

40. Using a pair of snap-ring pliers, secure the gear shifter sleeve carrier on the mainshaft with the snap-ring.

41. Slide the second speed gear onto the mainshaft from the rear of the mainshaft. The gear must turn freely on the

GUIDE UNIT   SYNCHRONIZER SPRING

Install both synchronizer springs into the first and second speed sliding gear guide with the hooks of both springs in the same shoe slot.

mainshaft.

42. Place the second speed synchronizer cover onto the second speed gear cone.

43. Install both synchronizer springs into the first and second speed sliding gear guide unit so that the hooks of both springs rest in the same guide unit shoe slot and the other spring ends are positioned opposite to each other.

44. Press the first and second speed sliding gear guide unit onto the mainshaft so that the original tooth contact is made.

45. Press the first speed gear needle bearing inner sleeve onto the mainshaft.

46. Install the first and second speed shoes (long style) and install the first and second gear sliding gear with the forked groove to the rear, onto the first and second speed sliding gear guide unit.

47. Slide the first speed gear needle bearing, synchronizer cover, first speed gear, mainshaft washer with the chamfer toward the rear, and the mainshaft bearing snap-ring onto the mainshaft.

48. Press on the mainshaft inner bearing.

49. Insert the lock ball in place in the mainshaft and place the speedometer drive gear and the speedometer drive gear spring washer on the mainshaft. Secure the assembly with the speedometer drive gear snap ring.

50. Place the mainshaft assembly into the transmission case extension housing up to its stop. Secure the mainshaft with the mainshaft bearing snap-ring.

51. Place the front synchronizer spring in the gear shifter sleeve carrier. Install the 3 third and fourth speed shoes (short design) and gear shifter sleeve over

the gear shifter sleeve carrier along with the synchronizer cover. The arrows on the shoes point toward the rear of the mainshaft. The gear shifter sleeve yoke groove should be toward the front.

52. Install a new gasket onto the transmission case extension housing and install the housing.

53. Lightly oil the reverse idler gear and the reverse gear shifter shaft with transmission oil. Place the lock ball into the reverse idler gear shaft and push the shaft through the hole in the rear of the case and on through the reverse idler gear which should have the groove end toward the front. Continue to drive the reverse idler gear shaft forward with a rubber hammer until the rear end of the shaft is flush with the rear face of the transmission case.

54. Position the reverse speed shifter yoke in the groove of the reverse idler gear and install the reverse gear shifter shaft from the rear of the case with the notches facing up, pushing it through the reverse speed shifter yoke.

55. Install the spiral pin to secure the yoke to the shifter shaft and drive a plug

into the hole in the rear of the case.

56. Slide the mainshaft assembly into the transmission case from the rear.

57. Slide the mainshaft front ring and the mainshaft needle bearing onto the mainshaft from the front.

58. Install the main drive gear through the front of the transmission case until the main drive snap-ring is flush with the case.

59. Position the third and fourth speed yoke onto the gear shifter sleeve.

60. Insert the third and fourth gear shifter shaft through the hole in the front of the case with the notches facing down, pushing it through the third and fourth speed yoke. The third and fourth speed yoke should be positioned with the rounded notch at the shaft hole portion of the yoke toward the rear.

61. Install the spiral pin, allowing 1/16 in. to 5/64 in. of the pin to protrude.

62. Lightly coat the first and second gear shifter shaft with transmission oil and insert the shaft through the hole in the rear of the case with the 3 notches facing down and toward the rear of the transmission. Push the shaft first through first and second gear shifter yoke, which should be positioned on the first and second gear sliding gear with the shoulder toward the front of the case. To position the first and second gear shifter yoke on the first and second gear sliding gear, push the reverse idler gear forward, engaging the idler gear with the first and second gear sliding gear. This will make room for positioning the first and second gear shifter yoke.

63. Continue to drive the first and second gear shifter shaft through the shifter shaft cam until properly positioned. The "L" shaped selector dog on the shifter shaft should point toward the rear extension housing.

64. Install the spiral pins to secure the shifter yoke and the shifter shaft cam to the first and second gear shifter.

65. Insert new selector shaft oil seals in the holes on both sides of the transmission case. Lightly oil the selector shaft with transmission oil and insert the shaft into the case and through the third, fourth, and reverse intermediate lever.

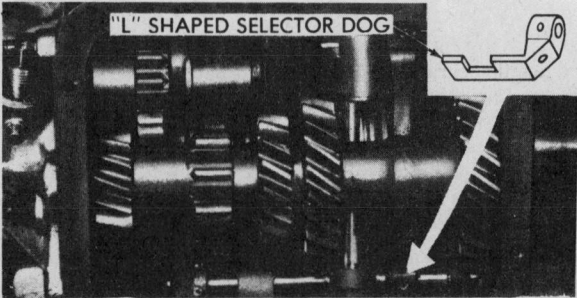

"L" SHAPED SELECTOR DOG

Positioning the "L" shaped selector dog on the first and second gear shifter shaft

66. Continue to push the selector shaft through the first and second intermediate lever and through the other side of the case. Rotate the selector shaft counterclockwise (looking from the lever end of the selector shaft) from its working position to vertically align the spiral pin holes in the shaft with the pin holes in the intermediate levers. To rotate the selector shaft in this manner. the reverse gear shifter shaft and its reverse speed shifter yoke must be pushed rearward so that the reverse idler gear is against the rear of the case.

67. Install the spiral pins to secure both the intermediate levers to the selector shaft. The spiral pins should not be flush with the lever surface, but should extend up between 1/16 in. and 5/64 in.

68. Engage the reverse speed shifter intermediate lever with the third, fourth, and reverse intermediate lever and also in the slot in the reverse gear shifter shaft, and install the bedding bolt through the reverse speed shifter intermediate lever and into the case. The reverse speed shifter intermediate lever end play on the bolt should be between 0.004 in. and 0.012 in.

69. Insert both of the interlock balls and then the springs, and drive plugs into the case holes until they bottom in the interlock plug hole seats. The grooves in the plugs will be showing when installed.

70. Coat the countershaft gear assembly thrust washers with wheel bearing grease and stick them in position in the transmission case. The lugs of the thrust washers must fit into the transmission case slots.

71. Turn the transmission case extension housing until the gear assembly countershaft bore is completely exposed.

72. Place the lock ball into the shaft and from the rear of the transmission insert the shaft so that the thrust washer is held in position. Hold the opposite thrust washer in position by using a short drift.

73. Insert the countershaft gear assembly into the transmission case. Be sure all of the needle bearings and both needle bearing washers are in place.

74. Insert the gear assembly countershaft into the gear assembly and drive the shaft into the transmission case. Make sure that the lock ball is properly positioned when the countershaft is fully installed.

75. Align the transmission case extension housing and gasket and tighten the 3 bolts with their spring washers to 21 ft lbs.

76. Install the gearshift interlock ball into the top of the transmission bore and then install the gearshift thrust spring.

77. Install the case cover gasket cover, and tighten the attaching screws.

78. Install the selector ring and the lock nut onto the selector shaft.

79. Tighten the 2 bracket bolts and spring washers to 14.5 ft lbs while holding the selector lever and support in place.

80. Install the pin securing the selector lever to the transmission case extension bolts.

81. Install the shifter shaft with the spring washers on the inside of the shifter shaft ends and the flat washers on the outside of the shaft.

82. Secure each end of the shifter shaft and washers with new cotter pins.

Shift Linkage Adjustment

The shift linkage is attached directly to the transmission and no linkage adjustment is possible.

CLUTCH

Removal and Installation

1. Remove the transmission.

2. Remove the bolts from the engine support brackets on both sides. Let the brackets hang by the front bolts.

3. Remove the flywheel cover pan.

4. Remove the flywheel housing-to-engine attaching bolts and pry the housing from the locating pins. Be sure to pry evenly from side to side to avoid breaking the housing.

To remove the release bearing from the clutch fork, slide the lever off the ball stud against the spring action. Remove the ball stud lock nut and remove the stud from the housing.

5. Provide alignment marks on the flywheel and clutch housing with either paint or a center punch so that they can be reassembled in their original positions.

6. Loosen the clutch cover-to-flywheel attaching bolts one turn at a time to avoid having unevenly applied clutch spring pressure bending the clutch cover.

7. Support the pressure plate and cover assembly while removing the last bolt and remove the pressure plate and disc.

8. Install the clutch in the reverse order of removal, using an aligning tool to align the disc (driven plate) with the spline in the flywheel. Tighten the 4 attaching bolts finger tight, then tighten them alternately one turn at a time to 36 ft lbs. Tighten the flywheel housing attaching bolts to 36 ft lbs.

Clutch Linkage Adjustment
GT

Clutch pedal free play should be adjusted to between ¾ and 1¾ in., by turning the ball stud located on the right side of the clutch housing. Cable length is not adjustable. Turning the ball stud clockwise decreases, and counterclockwise increases, pedal travel.

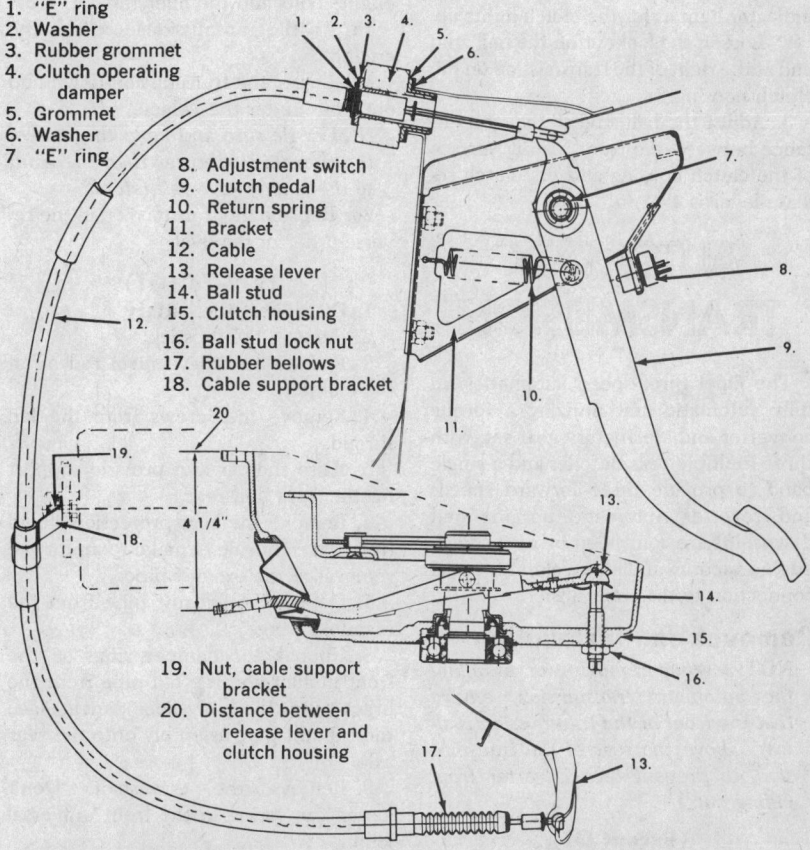

1. "E" ring
2. Washer
3. Rubber grommet
4. Clutch operating damper
5. Grommet
6. Washer
7. "E" ring
8. Adjustment switch
9. Clutch pedal
10. Return spring
11. Bracket
12. Cable
13. Release lever
14. Ball stud
15. Clutch housing
16. Ball stud lock nut
17. Rubber bellows
18. Cable support bracket
19. Nut, cable support bracket
20. Distance between release lever and clutch housing

4 1/4"

Clutch pedal and components parts on 1900 and Manta—others similar.

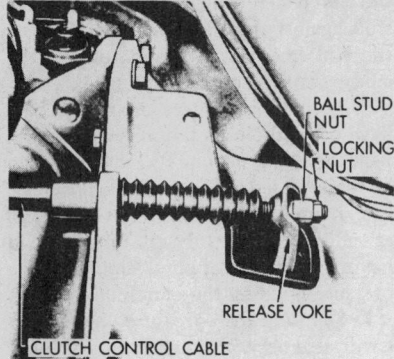

Clutch cable and attaching parts

1900 and Manta

Clutch operation is accomplished without any clutch pedal free play. Adjustment of the clutch is required only when the clutch adjustment warning light in the instrument panel starts to glow.

As the clutch disc lining wears, the upward limit of the travel of the clutch pedal moves upward toward the driver. When the clutch disc lining has worn to the point necessitating adjustment and proper clutch operation, the clutch pedal will rest against a switch, lighting the warning lamp.

1. If the parking brake is provided with an indicator lamp, the parking brake has to be disengaged, as the same indicator light as for the clutch lights up.

2. Loosen the locknut on the ball stud end at the right of the transmission on the clutch housing.

3. Adjust the ball stud so that the distance between the front mating surface of the clutch housing and the clutch release lever is 4–¼ in.

AUTOMATIC TRANSMISSION

The Opel three-speed automatic is a fully automatic unit utilizing a torque converter and a planetary gear set, with three multiple disc clutches and a single band to provide three forward speeds and reverse. Automatic upshifts and downshifts are controlled by road speed, engine vacuum and an accelerator pedal connection to the transmission.

Removal and Installation

NOTE: *When removing or installing the automatic transmission, ensure that the front of the transmission is always above the rear of the transmission, to prevent the converter from falling out.*

(Except GT)

1. Disconnect the battery.
2. Remove the dipstick.

3. Remove the screws from the fan shroud.
4. Remove the two upper starter bolts.
5. Raise the car and provide support for the front and rear.
6. Remove the bolts from the engine support brackets on both sides and allow the brackets to hang by the front bolts.
7. Remove the flywheel cover pan.
8. Remove the exhaust pipe from the manifold and unhook the rubber tailpipe suspension.
9. Remove the driveshaft. Be sure not to loosen the thrust spring in the spline.
10. Disconnect the transmission oil cooler lines at the flexible hoses.
11. On 1900 models, detach both stabilizer supports from the crossmember-to-body supports and loosen the stabilizer bolts in the lower control arms.
12. Place a suitable jack under the transmission and remove the transmission support bolts.
13. Lower the transmission enough to remove the detent cable and modulator vacuum line.
14. Remove the speedometer cable.
15. Remove the selector lever.
16. Mark the flywheel and the converter so that they can be reassembled in the same position from which they are removed and remove the converter-to-flywheel attaching bolts.
17. Remove the converter housing-to-engine bolts and the filler tube.
18. Pry the transmission loose from the engine.
19. Lower the transmission down and out from under the vehicle.

NOTE: *Be sure and keep the rear of the transmission lower than the front so the converter won't fall off.*

20. Replace the transmission in the reverse order of removal.

1972–75 (GT)

1. Disconnect the battery.
2. Remove the dipstick.
3. Pull the throttle control rod off of the ball pin.
4. Remove the screws from the fan shroud.
5. Raise the car and provide support for the front and rear.
6. Remove the heat protection shield from the right side to make room for the removal of the exhaust pipe.
7. Detach the exhaust pipe from the manifold flange.
8. Unhook the damper rings on the front muffler and the tail pipe from the brackets on the body floor panel. Place the exhaust pipe assembly onto the rear axle.
9. Remove the driveshaft. Don't loosen the spring in the front universal joint.
10. Disconnect the rear engine support from the transmission crossmember.

11. Support the transmission below the oil pan with a suitable jack.
12. Unscrew the transmission crossmember from the side members.
13. Lower the transmission as far as possible.
14. Drain the transmission oil.
15. Disconnect the selector rod from the ball pin of the outer transmission selector lever on the right side of the transmission.
16. Unscrew the oil cooler lines from the transmission. Plug the oil lines to prevent the entrance of dirt.
17. Pull the vacuum line off the modulator diaphragm.
18. Unscrew the detent cable retainer from the transmission, pull the cable out of the transmission, and unhook the cable from the detent valve.
19. Pry the detent cable and the oil cooler pipes out of the retainers on the transmission oil pan.
20. Unscrew the speedometer cable and pull it out of the speedometer driven gear housing.
21. Unscrew the engine support brackets from the torque converter housing on both sides of the engine. Loosen the front attaching bolt.
22. Remove the torque converter housing cover plate.
23. Mark the flywheel and the converter with paint or a center punch so they can be reassembled in the same position.
24. Unscrew the 3 torque converter-to-flywheel attaching bolts.
25. Pry the transmission loose from engine.
26. Move the transmission rearward away from the flywheel sufficiently to lower the transmission down and out of the vehicle.

NOTE: *Keep the rear of the transmission lower than the front so the torque converter does not fall off the front of the transmission.*

27. Install the transmission in the reverse order of removal, aligning the marks on the converter with the ones made on the flywheel. Tighten the flywheel-to-converter attaching bolts to 30 ft lbs and the converter housing-to-engine attaching bolts to 35 ft lbs.

Pan Removal and Installation

1. Raise the car and drain the oil.
2. Remove the twelve bolts which hold the pan to transmission.
3. Remove pan and gasket.
4. Installation is the reverse of removal.

NOTE: *Always replace old gasket and be careful not to over-tighten pan bolts.*

Filter or Strainer Service

1. Raise car and support it safely.
2. Drain fluid from pan.
3. Remove pan and gasket. Discard gasket.
4. Remove strainer assembly, strainer gasket and discard the gasket.
5. Install a new strainer gasket. Install new strainer assembly.
6. Install a new gasket on pan and install pan. Tighten attaching bolts to 7–10 ft lbs.
7. Lower car and add approximately three (3) pints of transmission fluid through filler tube.
8. With manual control lever in Park position, start engine. DO NOT RACE ENGINE. Move manual control lever through each range.
9. Immediately check fluid level with selector lever in Neutral, engine running, and vehicle on a LEVEL surface.
10. Add additional fluid to bring level to ¼ in. below the ADD mark on the dipstick. Do not overfill.

Servo Adjustment

1. Drain fluid from transmission and remove pan.
2. Use a 3/16 in. hex head wrench on servo adjusting bolt. Adjust servo apply rod by tightening adjusting bolt to 40 in. lbs. Back off bolt exactly five (5) turns.
3. Tighten lock nut while holding adjusting bolt and sleeve firmly with a hex-head wrench.

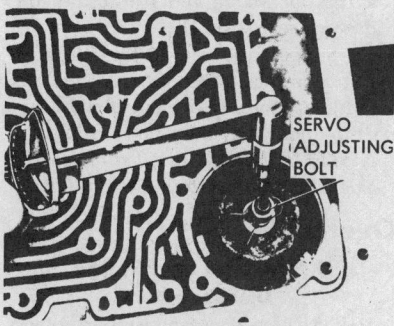

Servo adjusting bolt

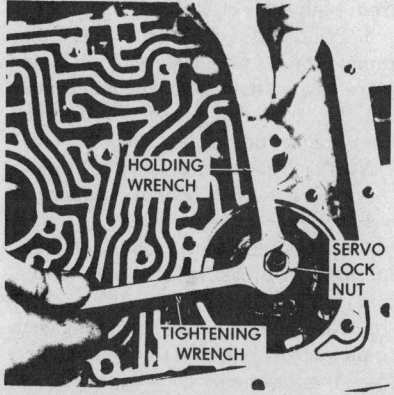

Locking servo into position

4. Reinstall pan, using a new gasket, and refill transmission.

Shift Linkage Adjustment

1. Remove the lock clip which holds the control rod to the selector lever.
2. Remove the control rod from the selector lever and place both the selector lever and the transmission shift lever in the drive position.
3. Adjust the control rod by turning until it slides freely over the pin on the selector lever, and install the lock clip.

Throttle Linkage Adjustments

Adjustments are made using the threaded end of the throttle rods. The throttle should be adjusted so that it operates freely and permits the throttle plates of the carburetor to close fully.

Detent Cable Adjustments

NOTE: *Before adjusting the detent ca-*

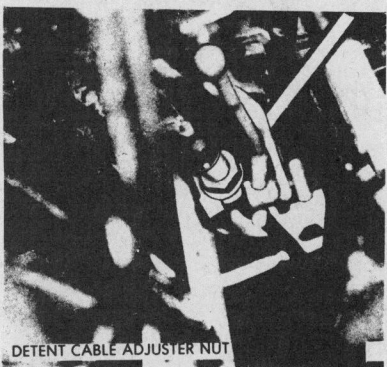

Detent cable adjusting points (Lower)

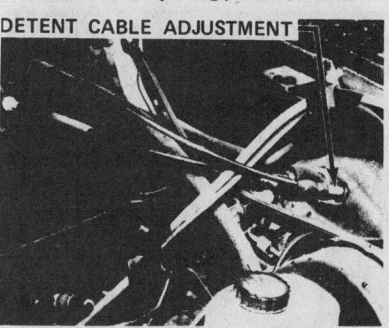

Detent cable adjusting point (Upper)

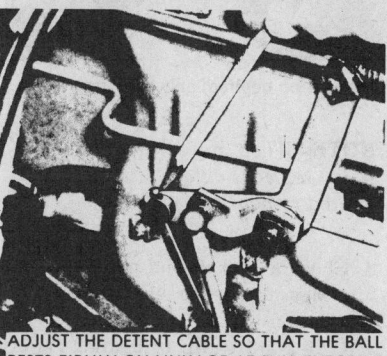

Detent cable ball position at full throttle

ble (downshift cable) it is essential that the throttle linkage be adjusted first.

1. Place throttle in full open position.
2. Loosen and tighten upper and lower adjustor nuts of the detent cable until ball end of the cable rests firmly against selector lever.
3. Measure length of exposed detent inner cable. The detent cable should measure approximately ⅜ in.

Neutral Safety Switch Adjustment

The neutral safety switch has no adjustments on its mounting position. If switch needs an adjustment, adjust shift linkage to center neutral starting position in transmission.

DRIVE AXLES

Driveshaft and U-Joints

Removal and Installation

1. Raise the rear of the car and support it on jackstands.
2. Disconnect the parking brake cable equalizer from the rod.
3. On the 1900 and Manta, unhook the parking brake cable from the floor pan.
4. On the 1900 and Manta, disconnect the exhaust system.
5. Make mating marks on the U-joint and the drive pinion extension shaft flange.
6. Loosen the bolt locks and remove the bolts or nuts from the U-bolts.
7. Work the driveshaft slightly forward, lower the rear end of the shaft and slide it rearward and out of the end of the transmission. Remove the thrust spring from the front of the driveshaft. Plug the rear of the transmission to avoid loss of lubricant.
8. Install the driveshaft in the reverse order of removal.

Center Joint Assembly

Removal and Installation

1. Remove driveshaft. Follow the procedure outlined in that section.
2. Support torque tube and remove center joint bracket.
3. Lower torque tube and disconnect it from differential carrier.
4. Install pinion flange holder and remove self-locking nut.
5. Pull pinion shaft from extension housing using a soft mallet.
6. Remove the ball bearing from the cushion and then remove support bracket-to-support cushions.

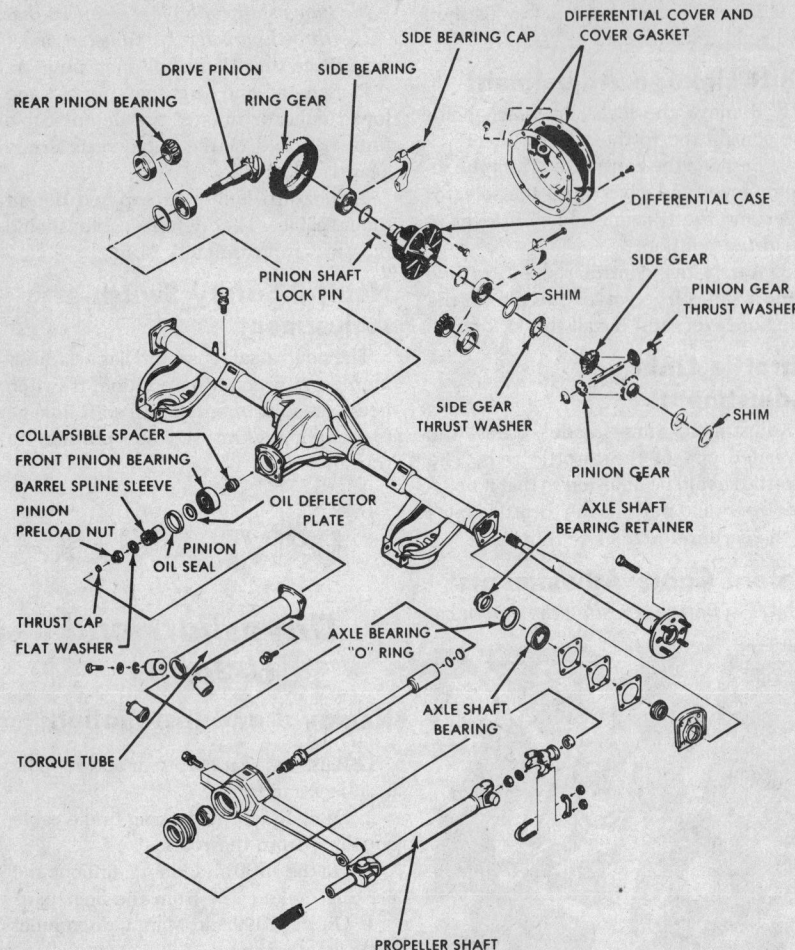

REAR PINION BEARING
DRIVE PINION
RING GEAR
SIDE BEARING
SIDE BEARING CAP
DIFFERENTIAL COVER AND COVER GASKET
DIFFERENTIAL CASE
PINION SHAFT LOCK PIN
SIDE GEAR
SHIM
PINION GEAR THRUST WASHER
COLLAPSIBLE SPACER
FRONT PINION BEARING
BARREL SPLINE SLEEVE
PINION PRELOAD NUT
OIL DEFLECTOR PLATE
PINION OIL SEAL
SIDE GEAR THRUST WASHER
PINION GEAR
SHIM
THRUST CAP
FLAT WASHER
AXLE SHAFT BEARING RETAINER
AXLE BEARING "O" RING
AXLE SHAFT BEARING
TORQUE TUBE
PROPELLER SHAFT

Exploded view of drive axle

7. Installation is the reverse of removal.

NOTE: *Check the support cushions and replace if necessary. The fasteners which hold the center joint should be replaced when overhauled. Also, use a new selflocking nut for pinion flange and torque to 87 ft lbs.*

Axle Shaft Assembly

Removal and Installation

1. Raise and support rear of the car.
2. Remove wheel and brake drum from the side to be removed.
3. Unscrew axle shaft retaining plate and pull axle from housing.
4. Installation is the reverse of removal.

Overhaul

1. Check radial runout (0.002 in.) and lateral runout (0.004 in.) of the axle shaft. If these tolerances are exceeded, the shaft must be replaced.
2. Press a new bearing onto shaft so that oil seal groove faces shaft splines.

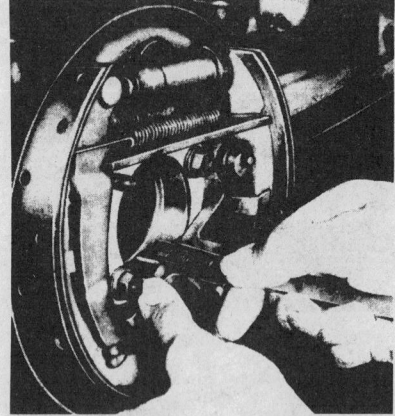

Measuring depth of axle shaft bearing

NOTE: *When replacing bearing, always replace outer race which is located in housing.*

3. Check axle shaft end play.
   a. Measure depth of axle bearing seat in housing.
   b. Measure width of bearing outer race. The maximum end play is 0.002–0.006 in.

Differential

Removal and Installation

1. Raise the rear of the vehicle and support it with jack stands at the jack brackets.
2. Remove both rear wheels and one rear brake drum.
3. Disconnect the parking brake rod from the equalizer, and the cable from the actuating lever on the side with the drum removed.
4. Separate the cable from the lower control arm brackets and hang the free end over the exhaust pipe.
5. Unbolt the shock absorbers, the track rod, and (if so equipped) the stabilizer shackles, from the rear axle brackets.
6. Mark the mating parts of the driveshaft-to-pinion extension flange, separate the flange, and tie the driveshaft out of the way.
7. Disconnect and cap the brake hoses at the differential.
8. Lower the axle enough to remove load from the springs, and remove the springs.
9. Unbolt the central joint bracket from the under pan and the lower control arms from the axle brackets, and roll the axle out from under the vehicle.
10. Install in the reverse order of removal.

NOTE: *When installing the central joint to the underpan, place a load of approximately 350 lbs. in the trunk of a 1900 or Manta and 150 lbs. on the driver's seat of a GT.*

11. Support the vehicle by the differential housing (raise off of the jack stands), and torque the central joint support-to-underbody bolts to 33 ft lbs.

NOTE: *Following installation of the axle, the brake system must be bled.*

Overhaul

Differential and Pinion Disassembly

1. Raise rear of car and support it with jackstands.
2. Remove wheels and brake drums from both sides of the car.
3. Prior to draining differential, remove brake pipe assembly, including pipes which attach wheel cylinder, junction block at differential housing, and hose bracket on torque tube.

NOTE: *It is not necessary to remove brake hardware to remove differential assembly.*

4. Loosen differential bolts and drain lubricant by breaking loose cover at bottom. Remove cover.
5. Next, check pinion depth, ring gear-to-pinion backlash, and side bearing preload. If adjustments meet specifications, it is not necessary to disassemble pinion and differential.

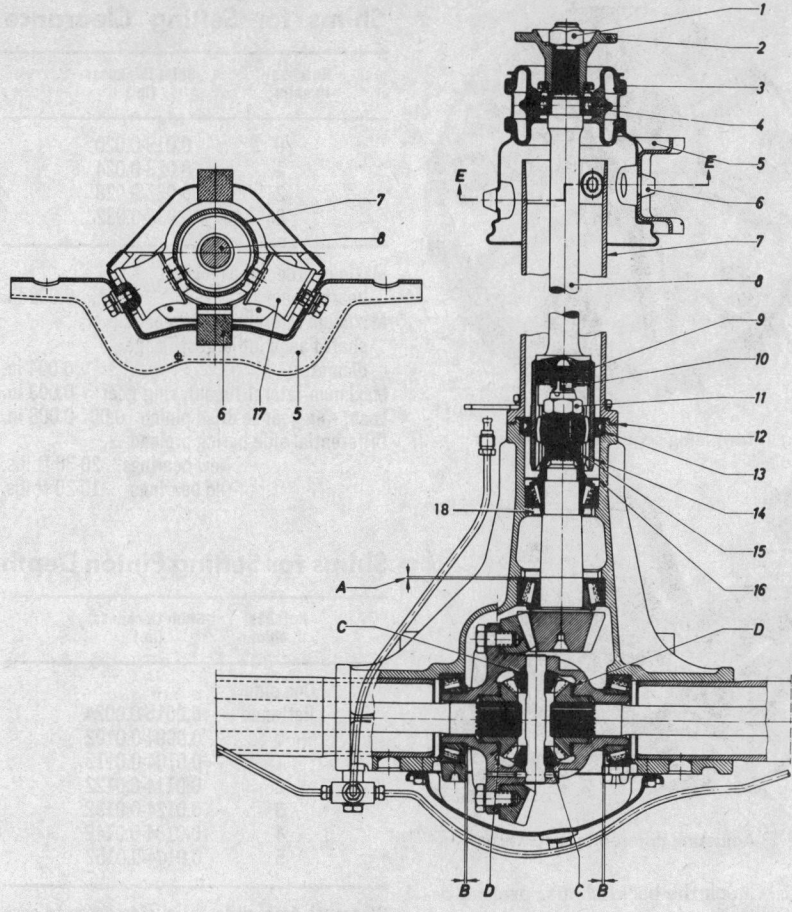

Cross-section of differential assembly

1. Self-locking nut
2. Drive-pinion-shaft extension flange
3. Rubber cushion
4. Ball bearing with sheet metal casing
5. Central joint support
6. Rubber cushion on central joint support
7. Torque tube
8. Drive pinion extension
9. Hard rubber disc
10. Thrust cap
11. Hex. nut
12. Paper gasket
13. Oil seal
14. Slip joint
15. Splined sleeve
16. Oil deflector
17. Rubber cushion
18. Collapsible spacer
(a)—Shims for drive-pinion height adjustment
(b)—Shims for ring gear and pinion backlash adjustment
(c)—Spherical washer
(d)—Shim for differential side gears

To remove the differential assembly proceed as follows:

1. Mark side-bearing caps and housing with a punch for proper reinstallation.

2. Remove the side bearing attaching bolts and caps. Using suitable wood levers (such as hammer handles), pry out differential assembly. Do not drop or interchange bearing outer races.

3. Remove both differential side bearings with a bearing puller.

NOTE: *Do not interchange bearings or shims.*

4. Remove bolts which attach the ring gear to differential case.

5. Evenly tap ring gear off of case with a brass drift and a hammer.

6. On 1.9 engine cars, remove the differential pinion shaft retaining pin using a ⅛ in. drift. Remove the pinion shaft, pinion gears, differential side gears and thrust washers.

To remove the drive pinion from the housing, proceed as follows:

1. With driveshaft disconnected and central joint disassembled, remove bolts which attach the rear torque tube to axle housing and break the flange seal with a block of wood.

2. Withdraw pinion-shaft extension and torque tube from axle housing.

3. Remove pinion-shaft extension from torque tube using a soft mallet against shaft at central-joint end.

4. Remove ball bearing from its cushion.

5. Remove self locking nut on pinion-shaft (immobilize flange with a wrench which can be clamped in a vise).

6. Pull off pinion flange with a puller, taking care to protect threads.

7. Using a suitable sharp-pointed tool, pry pinion oil seal from its seat.

NOTE: *To prevent damage to the flange, lay a screwdriver against the flange as a base for prying.*

8. Place a wrench on preload adjusting nut and grip barrel splines to hold pinion from turning while removing pinion nut.

Remove the barrel spline from the drive pinion. Use a long armed gear puller or special tool #5-22937.

10. Tap pinion from housing with a soft-face hammer.

11. Tap out pinion bearing races, noting shims behind inner bearing outer race.

12. Press off pinion inner bearing.

Assembly and Installation of the Drive Pinion

1. Install the front pinion bearing outer race.

2. Install the rear pinion bearing outer race with the proper number and size shims behind it to provide the proper pinion depth.

3. Lubricate the pinion bearings and assemble the drive pinion, collapsible spacer, front pinion bearing, oil deflector plate and the barrel spline sleeve in the differential carrier.

4. Draw the barrel spline onto the drive pinion until there are sufficient threads of the pinion protruding to install the pinion preload nut. Special tool J-22938 is used to install the barrel spline onto the pinion.

5. Tighten the drive pinion preload nut until drive pinion end play is eliminated, which indicates the bearing preload specification is being approached. If the preload nut is tightened past this point, replace the collapsible spacer.

6. Hold the barrel spline from turning and tighten the preload nut until a preload of 9 in. lbs. within a range of 6–13 in. lbs. for new bearings or 6 in. lbs. within a range of 5–8 in. lbs. for used bearings is reached.

7. Install a new pinion oil seal that has been soaked in differential lubricant.

Assembly and Installation of the Differential Case— 1900 and Manta

1. Install the side gears in the differential case with the proper number and size of shims to give ±0.002 in. end-play. The pinion gear thrust washers are installed with the concave side toward the differential case. Install the differential case pinion shaft and then the pinion shaft lockpin.

2. In order to check the torque required to turn the gears in the differential, mount an axle shaft in a vice and then place the differential onto the axle shaft with the splines meshed.

3. Turn the differential with a torque wrench inserted in the opposite side. The

torque required to turn the gears should be between 14-½ and 17-½ ft lbs. If the torque is not correct, it will be necessary to reshim the differential gears.

4. Install the ring gear on the case making certain their mating surfaces are clean. Tighten the bolts to 47 ft lbs. Maximum lateral runout of the installed ring gear is 0.003 in.

5. Install the side bearings.

6. Position the case assembly and the outer races in the carrier with the proper number and size of shims to provide 0.-004–0.008 in. of ring gear-drive pinion gear backlash and 0.002 in. shims added to each side after zero side-to-side end play is established to provide the correct side bearing preload. Use a soft faced hammer to drive the differential case into the carrier until the side bearing outer races bottom in their bores.

7. Install the side bearing caps in their original location and tighten the bolts to 33 ft lbs.

8. Rotate the case assembly several times to seat the bearings. Check the backlash and preload using a torque wrench on a ring gear attaching bolt. The torque required to turn the case should be 20–30 in. lbs. for new bearings and 10–20 in. lbs. for used bearings. If the torque is not correct, it will be necessary to reshim the side bearings.

9. Install the torque tube assembly.

10. Install the axle shafts.

Assembly and Installation of the Differential Case—GT

1. Lubricate the thrust washers, side and pinion gears and install the side gears with their thrust washers into the differential case with the proper number and size of shims to provide 0.003–0.006 in. of side clearance between the side gears and the case.

2. Install the differential pinion shaft so that the lockpin hole in the shaft aligns with the lockpin hole in the case. Install the pinion shaft lockpin.

3. Install the ring gear to the case. Make sure the mating surfaces are free of dirt, etc. Tighten the bolts to 47 ft lbs. Maximum lateral runout of the installed ring gear is 0.003 in.

4. Install the side bearings.

5. Install the differential case and outer side bearing races into the carrier with the proper number and size shims to provide 0.004–0.008 in. of ring gear-drive pinion gear backlash and 0.002 in. shims added to each side after zero side-to-side end-play is established to provide the correct side bearing preload. Use a soft hammer to drive the case into the carrier until the side bearing outer races bottom in their bores.

6. Install the side bearing caps in their original location and tighten the bolts to 33 ft lbs.

Torqueing sequence on ring gear

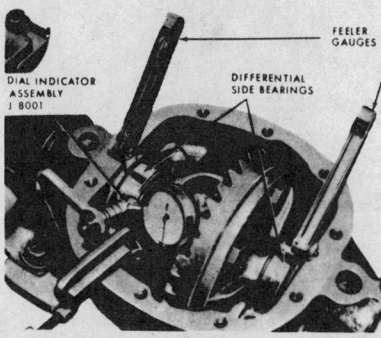

Adjusting differential tolerances

7. Check the backlash and preload using a torque wrench on a ring gear attaching bolt. The torque required to turn the case should be 20–30 in. lbs. for new bearings and 10–20 in. lbs. for used bearings. If the torque is not correct, it will be necessary to reshim the side bearings.

8. Install the torque tube assembly.

9. Install the axle shafts.

Shims for Setting Preload

Notches in shim	Shim thickness (in.)
0	0.0056-0.0062
1	0.0066-0.0072
2	0.0076-0.0082
3	0.0085-0.0092
4	0.0094-0.0102
5	0.0104-0.0112
6	0.0193-0.0201
7	0.0386-0.0398

	(Average)	(Range)
New bearings	9 in. lbs.	7-12 in. lbs.
Original bearings	6 in. lbs.	5-7 in. lbs.

Pinion depth setting (from pinion marking) +0.002 to −0.001 in.

Shims for Setting Clearance

Notches in shim	Shim thickness (in.)
0	0.019-0.020
1	0.023-0.024
2	0.027-0.028
3	0.031-0.032

Maximum runout, axle shaft bearing-seat 0.002 in.
Maximum lateral runout, rear axle shaft-flange (at largest flange diameter) 0.004 in.
Maximum lateral runout, ring gear 0.003 in.
Lash, ring gear to drive pinion 0.004-0.008 in.
Differential side baring preload
New bearings: 20-30 ft lbs.
Old bearings 10-20 ft lbs.

Shims for Setting Pinion Depth

Notches in shim	Shim thickness (in.)
One side flattened	0.0016-0.0024
0	0.0094-0.0102
1	0.0104-0.0112
2	0.0114-0.0122
3	0.0124-0.0132
4	0.0134-0.0142
5	0.0144-0.0152

Clearance from differential side gears to case max 0.006 in.

REAR SUSPENSION
Spring

Removal and Installation

1. Raise the vehicle and support it at its rear jack brackets.

2. Remove the wheels and disconnect the shock absorbers and (if equipped) the stabilizer and shackles from the rear axle brackets.

3. Lower the rear axle as far as possible and remove the springs.

NOTE: *When lowering rear axle, do not stress brake hose. If necessary, tilt the rear axle assembly to remove the rear springs. Note the upper and lower rubber damper rings.*

4. Install the springs, checking to ensure that they are properly seated in the damper rings and seats.

5. Jack up the rear axle at the differential housing, compressing the springs in their seats.

6. Attach the shock absorbers to the rear axle, torquing the nuts to 15 ft lbs on the GT and 47 ft lbs for the 1900 and Manta.

7. Attach stabilizer and torque bolts to 25 ft lbs.

8. Install the rear wheels and lower the vehicle.

Shock Absorber

Removal and Installation

1. Raise the vehicle and support it at its rear jacking brackets.

2. The trim panel under the spare tire on the 1973–74 GT must be removed to gain access to the attaching nuts.

3. Remove the upper attaching nut, retainer and rubber grommet.

4. Remove the lower attaching nut and rubber grommet retainer, compress the shock absorber and remove it from the lower mounting pin.

5. Install the shock absorber in the reverse order of removal, tightening the retaining nuts to 15 ft lbs on the GT and 47 ft lbs on the 1900 and Manta.

FRONT SUSPENSION

GT

The GT uses a maintenance-free independent front wheel suspension with unequal length control arms and a transverse 3 leaf spring. The entire front suspension assembly is attached to the front crossmember and can be removed as a unit if necessary.

The engine in the GT is not supported by the mounting brackets but rests on a separate crossmember. The front suspension crossmember is reinforced in the area where it is attached to the frame. A one-piece damper plate is installed between the frame and the crossmember.

Ball joints are used to provide pivoting joints between the control arms and the steering knuckles. Upward travel of the suspension is limited by a rubber bumper mounted on each side of the crossmember which contacts the lower control arm.

Direct acting shock absorbers and a transverse double or triple steel band spring dampen road shock. The shock absorbers also limit the downward travel of the control arms.

1900 and Manta

The front suspension on the 1900 and Manta features coil springs and unequal length control arms.

The front stabilizer also acts as a tie strut. The end is supported in a rubber bushing located in a piece of tubing welded into the longer control arm.

To minimize torque caused by braking,

the horizontal shafts of the upper and lower control arms are not parallel.

A ball joint is used to connect the steering knuckle to the lower control arm.

The 2 body-to-crossmember supports are attached to the horizontal part of the crossmember with 2 bolts. The outer bolt also serves as a support for the lower control arm. Since the bolts are inserted from the front, the body-to-crossmember support can be removed without the lower control arm. The inner bolt simultaneously attaches to the steering.

The complete front suspension assembly is attached to the body in 4 places.

Removal and Installation as a Unit

GT

1. Block and brake wheels, jack up front end (place block of wood between jack and cross member to prevent damage), and support car with stands at rear of front frame rails.

2. Support the engine at rear of transmission with a stand; loosen the clamp at the lower universal joint and take out the clamp bolt.

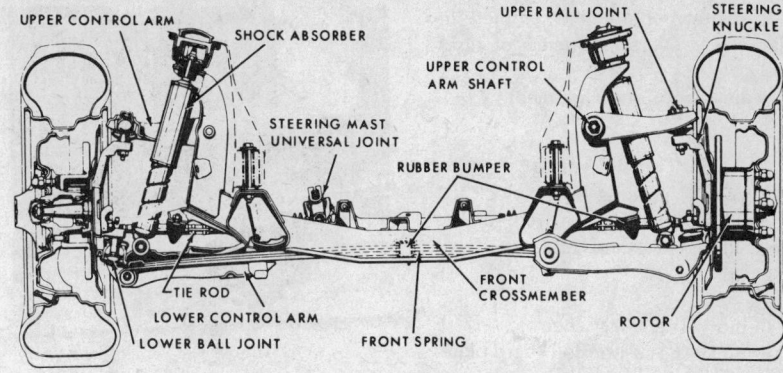

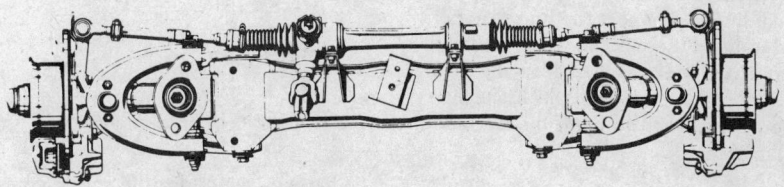

GT Front suspension (disc brakes)

3. Loosen the clamp at the upper universal joint and lift the steering mast upward until it is free of the lower universal joint.

4. Remove the air cleaner. Disconnect brake hoses, front engine support bolts, rubber mounts, clutch cable at engine mount, shock-absorber plastic cover, and upper shock-absorber attaching nuts.

5. Detach the radiator from the crossmember. Remove cross-member attaching nuts and lower the cross member. Make sure that the engine mounting bracket does not interfere with starter cables.

6. Installation is easier if rubber dampening block is lubricated to reduce friction of mounting brackets.

7. Slide engine mounting bracket over rubber block, attach cross member to front frame rail with new nuts, and torque to 30 ft lbs.

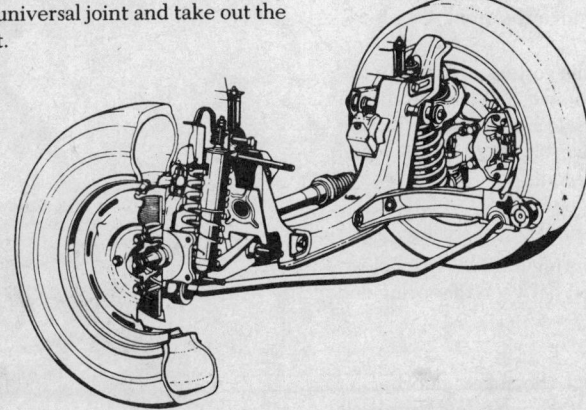

The front suspension on a 1900 and Manta

8. Bolt down engine and complete installation in reverse sequence of disassembly.

9. Adjust front end alignment.

1900 and Manta

1. Apply the parking brake, block the rear wheels and raise the front of the vehicle. Place jack stands under the front of the car.

2. Remove the front wheels.

3. Remove the suspension guard plate.

4. Remove the clips retaining the brake line, disconnect the brake calipers and suspend them in the wheel well with heavy wire hooks. Do not allow the calipers weight to hang on the brake line. There is no need to open the hydraulic brake system.

5. Suspend the engine with a suitable lifting device.

6. Unscrew the lower steering mast clamp bolt out of the pinion flange.

7. Unscrew the front left and right engine mounts from the damper blocks.

8. From the top, unscrew the front suspension assembly at the crossmember-to-body support from the frame and let it down onto a jack. Remove the suspension assembly from the vehicle.

9. Install the suspension in the reverse order of removal. When the assembly is raised into position, the lower steering mast must be inserted into the pinion flange.

Springs
Removal and Installation
GT

1. Raise the car and support it at the rear of the front frame rails with jackstands and remove the front wheels.

2. Remove the cotter pin from the castle nut on the lower ball joint studs and back off the castle nut 2 turns. Give the ball stud a sharp blow to break it loose. Do not remove the nut.

3. Install a spring compressor and compress the spring until 3⅛ in. of clearance is obtained between the spring and compressor.

4. Disconnect the shock absorbers at their lower attachment and compress them.

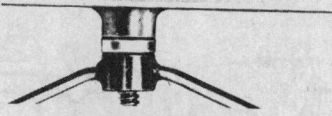

Leaf spring compresser installed

5. Raise a jack under the spring compressor and the spring. Remove the lower control arm to crossmember attaching nuts and bolts.

6. Remove the lower ball joint stud nuts and lower the jack slightly so that the spring and the lower control arm assemblies are removed from the front crossmember and steering knuckles.

7. Lower the jack, spring compressor, and front spring and control arm assemblies. Remove the lower control arm-to-spring attaching nuts.

8. Relieve the tension on the spring compressor and remove the control arm attaching bolts and the control arms.

9. Install the spring in the reverse order of removal, compressing the spring after the lower control arms are installed to the appropriate length. Torque the lower ball joint castle nuts to 54 ft lbs and the lower shock absorber attaching nuts to 30 ft lbs.

1900 and Manta

1. Before raising the car, upper control arm hooks J-23697 or a spring compressor must be installed.

2. Raise the car and support the front end with stands. The hoist should be left in the raised position to maintain pressure on the lower control arm.

3. Remove the front wheel.

4. Disconnect both of the stabilizer supports from the crossmember-to-body support.

5. Remove the shock absorber.

6. Remove the castle nut cotter pin and castle nut from the lower control arm ball joint.

7. Disconnect the lower control arm ball joint from the steering knuckle with a suitable drift. Be careful not to damage the threads.

8. Loosen the nut that retains the lower control arm to the front crossmember.

9. Slowly lower the hoist to release the spring tension.

10. Swing the lower control arm downward and remove the front spring.

11. Install the spring in the reverse order of removal. Tighten the lower ball joint castle nut to 54 ft lbs, the lower control arm-to-crossmember bolt to 43 ft lbs, and the lower shock absorber attaching nut to 30 ft lbs.

Shock Absorber
Removal and Installation

1. Remove plastic cover from shock absorber upper attaching point on the GT.   Remove the air cleaner on a GT.

2. Raise the vehicle and remove upper attaching nuts from shocks.

3. Remove lower attaching nuts and

Upper control arm hooks used to keep the control arm in a level position

compress shocks.

4. Remove shock absorber from car.

5. Installation is the reverse of removal.

NOTE: *Always replace old bushings and lock washers.*

Ball Joints

Removal and Installation

Upper

1. Place a jack under the spring eye and raise the car. Remove the wheel.

2. Remove the cotter pin and castle nut from the upper ball joint stud.

3. Remove the ball stud from the steering knuckle using a gear puller, and remove the 2 bolts attaching the ball joint to the upper control arm.

NOTE: *If the dust cap on the upper ball joint is damaged or missing, the ball joint should be replaced.*

4. Install the upper control arm ball joint with the off center holes in the flange showing toward the steering knuckle spindle.

5. Install the 2 bolts that attach the ball joint to the upper control arm. Tighten the bolts to 29 ft lbs.

6. Install the upper ball joint stud in the steering knuckle and torque the castle nut to 29 ft lbs on the Opel and GT and 40 ft lbs on the 1900 and Manta.

7. Install a new cotter pin and install the wheel. Lower the vehicle.

8. Check the caster and camber.

Lower

NOTE: *Maximum axial play of all Opel vehicle lower ball joints is .080 inches. Greater play or worn parts require replacement of joint. New lower ball joints have axial play of .020 inches or less.*

1. When removing lower ball joint, back off castle nut only two turns.

2. Strike the ball stud to break it loose. Do not remove nut.

3. Compress transverse spring or coil spring 3⅛ in. from lower spring pad.

4. Disconnect shock absorber-to-lower control arm attachment, compress it and swing it aside.

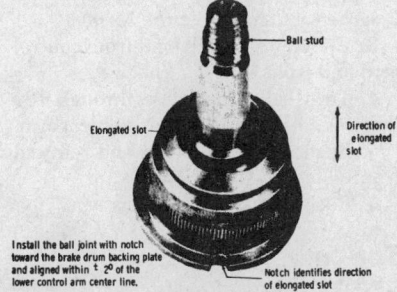

Lower ball joint assembly

5. Then remove castle nut from ball-joint stud.

NOTE: *Prior to the removal of the lower ball joint from the control arm, note the position of the locating notch, in the rim of the balljoint housing. Scribe or mark the control arm to facilitate realignment of the replacement ball joint.*

6. Pry off dust-cap retainer and dust cap carefully and press ball stud out of lower control arm.

7. When reinstalling lower ball joint, the notch in the ball joint bottom plate (identifying the direction of the elongated slot) must point toward the brake drum backing plate.

8. Alignment must be within 2° of lower control-arm centerline. Improper positioning of the ball joint will cause binding and fracture.

If the ball joint does not have a marking notch, the joint is completely symmetrical and may be installed in any position.

NOTE: *Do not press ball joint onto bottom plate, but only onto joint housing.*

9. Install dust cap on lower ball joint and fill with chassis lubricant. Attach dust cap retainer.

10. Press ball joint into steering knuckle.

11. Install castle nut and torque it to 45 ft lbs. Use new cotter pin.

1900 and Manta

1. Before raising the vehicle, install the upper control arm hooks J-23697 or a spring compressor which hold the upper control arm up at a predetermined height by attaching the control arm to the crossmember.

2. Raise the car and support it at the rear of the front fram rails.

3. Remove the castle nut cotter pin and slacken the back nut of the lower control arm ball joint so that the thread can no longer be damaged.

4. Drive the ball joint from the steering knuckle with a suitable drift. Lift the lower control arm with a jack and unscrew the castle nut. Remove the upper control arm hooks.

5. Unscrew the upper control arm ball joint and suspend the front wheel hub and brake caliper in the wheel well with a length of heavy wire. Do not turn the upper control arm ball joint flange, as this would change the camber setting.

6. Press the lower control arm ball joint from the lower control arm.

7. Press the new ball joint into the lower control arm. Do not strike the bottom plate of the ball joint. Make sure that the marking groove in the housing bottom is in alignment with the axis of the lower control arm. A deviation of ±2° is permissible.

8. Connect the steering knuckle, front wheel hub and brake caliper to the lower

control arm ball joint. Tighten the castle nut to 54 ft lbs.

9. Attach the ball joint to the upper control arm and tighten the nut to 29 ft lbs.

10. Install the wheel, lower the vehicle and check the caster and camber.

Upper Control Arm

Removal and Installation

Opel and GT

1. Raise front of car and support it securely.

2. Remove front wheel from the side to be worked on.

NOTE: *The front shock absorber must be disconnected and front spring must be compressed as described under "Spring Removal and Installation".*

3. Remove cotter pin from upper ball joint and separate it from steering knuckle (spindle) with tie rod removal tool.

4. Support brake drum assembly to relieve tension on brake hose.

5. Remove nut from upper control arm shaft and remove it from car.

NOTE: *If rubber bushings on control arms are worn, they should be replaced.*

6. Reinstall all parts in reverse order of removal.

NOTE: *After installation, the front end alignment should be checked and corrected if necessary.*

1900 and Manta

1. Raise the car and support it at the rear of the front frame rails and remove the front wheel.

2. Remove the upper control arm-to-crossmember attaching nut.

3. Unscrew the ball joint from the upper control arm. Do not turn the upper control arm ball joint flange, as this will change the camber adjustment.

4. Support the hub assembly so that the brake hose is not stressed.

5. Pull out the upper control arm shaft-to-crossmember attaching bolt and remove the control arm. The shims must be reinstalled in their original position to maintain the proper caster setting.

6. Upon installation of the upper control arm, make sure that the damper bushing with the rubber shoulder on both sides is always located in the rear.

7. Attach the upper control arm to the crossmember and tighten the attaching bolt to 40 ft lbs. The upper control arm must be tightened only in the horizontal position. This position exists if the hooks J-23697 are used.

8. Attach the ball joint to the upper control arm and tighten to 29 ft lbs.

9. Install the wheel and lower the vehicle.

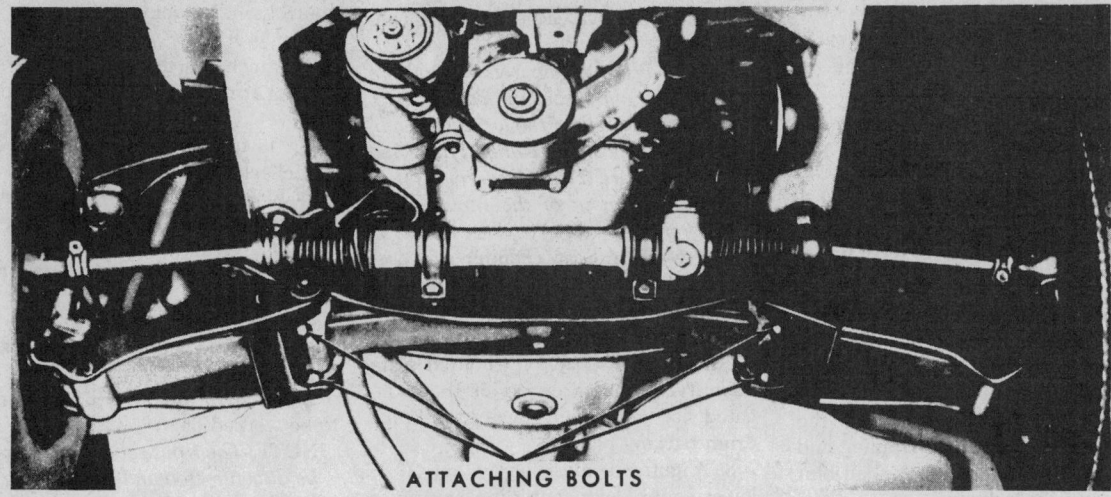

ATTACHING BOLTS

Lower control arm attaching points

Lower Control Arm

Removal and Installation

1. Raise front of car and support it securely.

2. Remove front wheels.

3. Using a spring compressor, compress the spring to relieve tension.

4. Disconnect lower shock absorber attaching bolts to cross member. Shocks do not have to be removed from position.

5. Remove cotter pins from the lower ball joint stud. Use a tie rod removal tool to release the ball joint from the steering knuckle (spindle).

6. Support the brake drum assembly to relieve the tension on the brake hose.

7. Slightly lower the car to remove the bolt which holds the front spring to the control arm.

8. Remove lower control arm to crossmember attaching bolts.

9. Remove the control arm from the car.

10. Installation is the reverse of removal.

NOTE: *After installation, the front end alignment should be checked and corrected if necessary.*

1900 and Manta

1. Before raising the vehicle, install the upper control arm hooks J-23697 or a spring compressor.

2. Raise the car and support it with jack stands. The jack should be left in position to maintain pressure on the lower control arm.

3. Remove the front wheel.

4. Disconnect both stabilizer supports from the crossmember-to-body support.

5. Remove the self-locking hex head bolt from the stabilizer support in the lower control arm and remove the washer.

6. Pry the stabilizer bar out of the lower control arm support.

7. Remove the shock absorber.

8. Remove the lower control arm ball joint castle nut and drive the ball joint from the steering knuckle.

9. Loosen the nut that retains the lower control arm to the front crossmember.

10. Slowly lower the hoist to release the spring tension.

11. Swing the lower control arm downward and remove the front spring.

12. Remove the nut that secures the lower control arm to the front crossmember and remove the lower control arm.

13. To install the lower control arm, loosely attach the lower control arm to the front crossmember.

14. Seat the spring between the lower control arm and the crossmember.

15. Raise the jack and place the lower control arm in position.

16. Attach the lower control arm ball joint to the steering knuckle and tighten the nut to 54 ft lbs.

17. Tighten the lower control arm-to-crossmember bolt to 43 ft lbs.

18. Attach the stabilizer bar to the lower control arm and tighten to 87 ft lbs.

19. Attach the stabilizer bar to crossmember to body support.

20. Install the shock absorber, the wheel and lower the vehicle.

Front End Alignment

Caster Adjustment

1900 and Manta

NOTE: *To change caster either add or remove the toothed washers from the front and rear of the lower control arm shafts.*

1. Raise vehicle and support it at lower control arms.

2. Remove front wheels.

NOTE: *On some models it will be necessary to remove the shock absorber and compress the spring.*

3. Unbolt upper control arm shaft from cross-member and remove shaft from control arm.

4. Adjust caster by adding or subtracting the tooth washers from the front and rear of the shaft, between the upper control arm and the shock absorber supports.

5. Replace shaft into the upper control arm from front to rear and torque to 40 ft lbs. using new lock nuts.

6. Reinstall upper control arm to crossmember and reinstall the wheel.

7. Recheck caster setting after installation.

GT

To change the caster, 3 washers are available; one with a 0.12 in. thickness, one 0.24 in. thick, and one 0.36 in. thick.

To increase caster, place *one* of the thin washers at the front of the control arm shaft and *one* of the thick washers at the rear. To decrease caster, place *one* of the thick washers at the front of the control arm shaft and *one* thin washer at the rear.

Camber

NOTE: *Camber is adjusted by turning the upper ball joint flange 180 degrees.*

1. Raise car and support it below lower control arms.

2. Remove front wheels.

NOTE: *On some models it will be necessary to remove the shock absorber and compress the spring.*

3. Unbolt upper ball joint from control arm and front steering knuckle.

4. Turn ball joint flange through 180 degrees and reinstall it onto control arm.

5. Reattach the ball joint and reinstall front wheels.

6. Recheck camber settings.

Toe-In

NOTE: *To adjust toe-in, rotate the tie rod sleeves to lengthen or shorten the tie rod.*

1. Recheck caster and camber before adjusting toe-in.

2. Align wormshaft-to-steering gear high point (center the steering).

3. Loosen wire clamps on tie rod ends and push back bellows.

4. Loosen clamp bolt on tie rod ends.

5. Unbolt tie rod from steering knuckle and disconnect tie rod.

6. Rotate tie-rod end to gain the correct settings. The toe-in should be 1/32–⅛ in. for all Opels and GT, and ⅛–3/16 in. for 1900's and Manta's.

7. Tighten clamp on tie-rod end and reinstall end onto steering knuckle.

8. Install wheels and recheck the complete front end alignment.

STEERING

Steering Wheel

Removal and Installation

1. Disconnect the ground strap from the battery, pry out the horn cap, and disconnect the horn wires.

2. Bend the lockplate tabs down, and remove the steering wheel nut and washer.

3. Mark the relative position of the steering wheel and shaft.

4. Install a conventional steering wheel puller, and remove the steering wheel.

5. Prior to installation, lightly lubricate the sliding parts of the turn signal mechanism with lubriplate.

6. Ensure that the match marks align, and install in the reverse order of removal.

Turn Signal Switch Replacement

GT

1. Remove steering wheel. Follow steps in that section.

2. Remove directional signal lever by

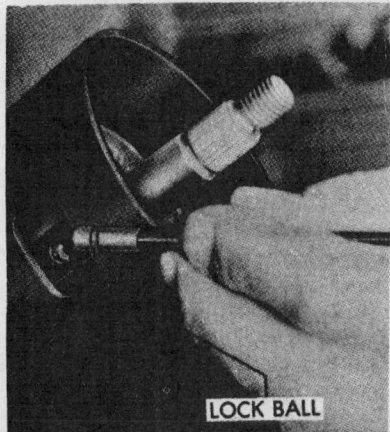

LOCK BALL

Removing directional signal lever

pulling on lever to unlock ball seat.

3. Unbolt all caps and attaching screws.

NOTE: *Some models have attaching screws that hold the switch housing cover halves together.*

4. Remove switch housing cover and switch from the steering column.

NOTE: *Be careful not to lose guide ring on top of bearing housing.*

5. Disconnect wires from switch and remove switch from column.

6. Install turn signal switch in reverse order of removal.

1900 and Manta

1. Remove the steering wheel.

2. Disconnect the signal switch, steering and ignition lock wire set.

3. Pull the turn signal lever out of its seat. The lever is held in place by a lock ball.

4. Unscrew the lower half of the turn signal switch housing cover.

5. Remove the nut from the steering mast jacket attachment at the front of the dash panel.

6. Unscrew the slide-off base from the under side of the instrument panel and remove the upper part of the signal switch housing cover.

7. Place a thick piece of wood onto the front seat and let the steering mast jacket assembly down. When doing this, the front seat must be in its full forward position.

8. Center-punch the tear-off bolt for the steering and ignition lock bracket attachment. Drill a 0.12 in. (3 mm or about ⅛ in.) diameter hole in the tear-off bolt and remove the bolt with a bolt remover with a left-hand twist screw.

9. Remove the steering and ignition lock, as well as the signal switch from steering mast jacket and loosely attach

Drilling out the steering and ignition lock tear-off bolt on a 1900 and Manta

the slide-off base below the instrument panel.

10. Before replacing the turn signal switch, install a new bearing and snapring in the switch assembly.

11. Install the turn signal switch and the steering and ignition lock to the steering mast jacket. Screw on the steering and ignition lock bracket using a new tear-off bolt. The head of the bolt should tear off when the proper tightening torque is reached.

12. Disconnect the slide-off base, install the upper half of the signal switch housing cover, and loosely reattach the slide-off base.

13. Attach the steering mast jacket at the front of the dash panel.

14. Tighten the slide-off base attaching nuts to 11 ft lbs.

15. Install the lower half of the signal switch housing cover and connect the signal switch and ignition lock wire set.

16. Install the steering wheel and tighten the nut to 11 ft lbs. Use a new lock plate.

Steering Column

Removal and Installation

1900 and Manta

1. Disconnect the battery.

2. Remove the clamp screw of the upper steering mast out of the universal joint flange. This must be accomplished from underneath the car.

3. Remove the steering mast jacket attaching nut at the floor panel.

4. Disconnect the turn signal switch wire and the steering and ignition lock wire.

5. Unscrew the slide-off base from the underside of the instrument panel and remove the steering column assembly from the vehicle.

NOTE: *Carefully put down the column assembly. The column should never be subjected to any impacts or blows. Any impact to the exposed ends of the shaft, leaning on the steering column or dropping it may loosen or shear off the plastic components that provide the rigidity of the assembly.*

6. Carefully insert the steering mast into the universal joint flange, making sure the steering wheel spokes point downwards and steering gear is in its high point (wheels straight ahead).

7. Loosely attach the slide-off base attaching nuts at the underside of the instrument panel.

8. Attach the steering mast jacket at the front of the dash.

9. Tighten the nuts at the slide-off base to 11 ft lbs.

10. Tighten the screw at the steering mast clamp to 22 ft lbs.

11. Connect the wires to the turn sig-

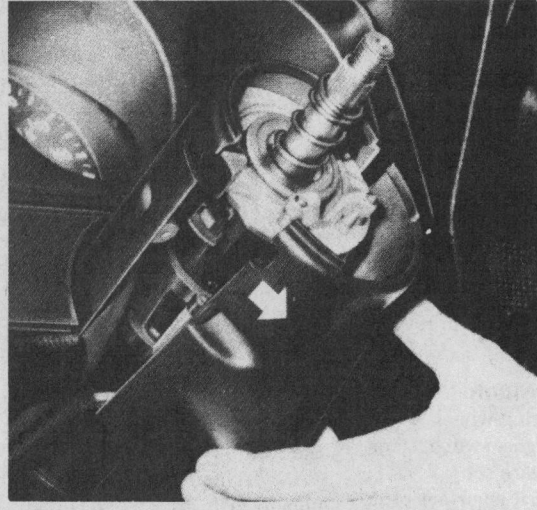

Removing the lower half of the signal switch housing on the 1900 and Manta

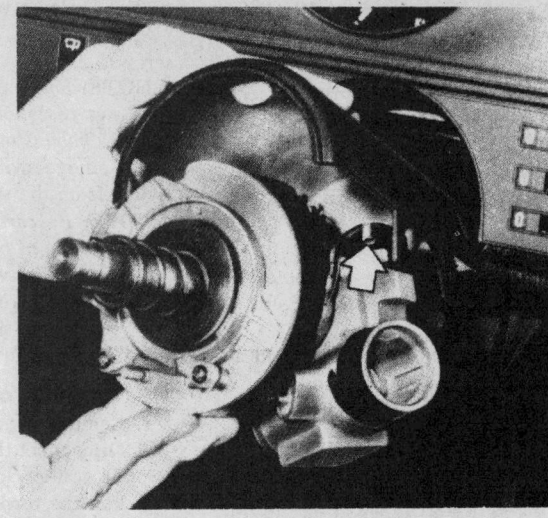

Removing the upper half of the signal switch housing on the 1900 and Manta

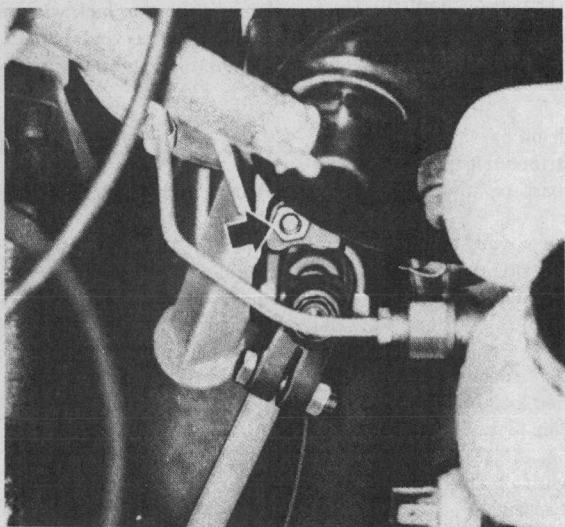

Upper steering mast clamp screw—1900 and Manta

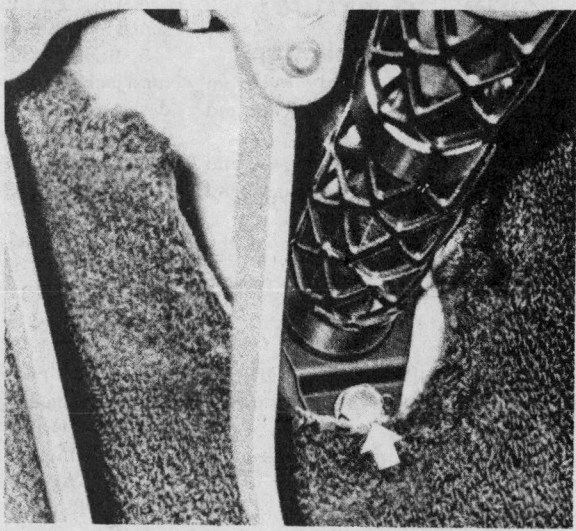

The steering mast jacket attaching nut at the floor panel of the 1900 and Manta

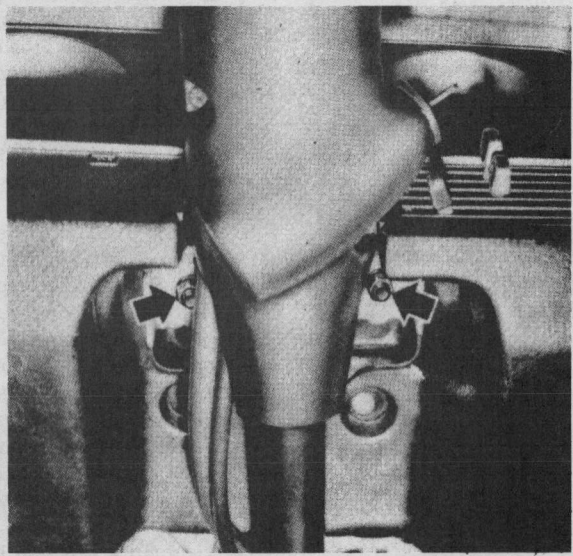

The slide-off base on the 1900 and Manta

nal and ignition switch.

12. Connect the battery.

Ignition Lock Switch

Removal and Installation

GT

1. Disconnect battery, remove the steering wheel and turn ignition switch to the ON position.

2. Insert a rod into stop pin hole on the side of the ignition lock switch and remove cylinder assembly.

3. Remove screws which hold the electrical switch to ignition lock housing.

4. Remove switch from housing.

5. Install switch into steering and ignition lock housing and rotate switch. The assembly will lock itself into proper position.

1900 and Manta

1. Disconnect battery, remove the steering wheel and turn ignition switch

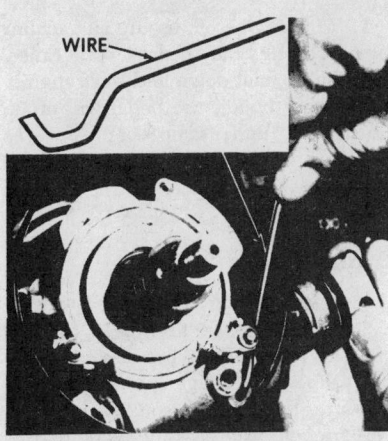

Removing ignition cylinder lock assembly GT.

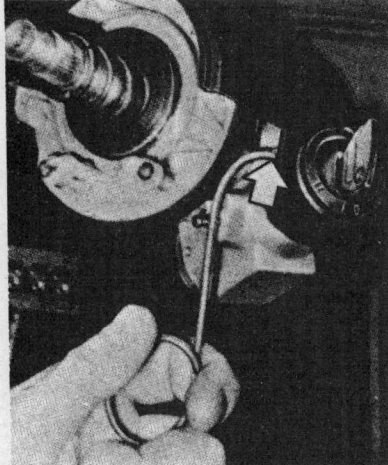

Removing ignition cylinder lock assembly (1900 & Manta).

to the LOCK position.

2. Unscrew split signal switch housing covers and remove lower half.

3. Remove lock cylinder by pushing in lock spring of the cylinder.

4. To install, insert lock cylinder into housing and install lower half of the signal switch housing.

Steering Gear

Removal and Installation

Opel and GT

1. Remove flexible-coupling bolt above gear box and the stop bolt located below steering wheel in steering mast jacket.

2. Lift out steering column from mast about three in. and position it with a block of wood.

3. Detach tie rod ends, pressing ball studs out of steering arms.

4. Unfasten steering gear assembly from suspension cross member and lift it off with tie rods.

5. Installing the steering gear, position steering gear on front suspension cross member and tighten bolts to 25 ft lbs.

6. Position tie-rod ball studs on steering arm; install castle nuts and torque to 30 ft lbs.

7. Lock it into position with new cotter pins.

8. Set steering wheel so that flat, lower portion of steering mast is parallel to ring-coupling bolt hole.

9. Position the mast in the flexible coupling and set clearance between steeringwheel hub and directional signal housing between 3/32 and 1/8 in.

10. Tighten flexible coupling to 23 ft lbs. Reinstall stop bolt in steering mast jacket.

11. Turn steering wheel 1/2 turn both right and left. If any resistance is noticeable, remove the steering mast and find the cause.

NOTE: *Do not over-tighten stop bolt in plastic bushing.*

1900 and Manta

1. Remove the splash shield from the lower deflector panel and both side members.

2. Remove the clamp bolt securing the flexible coupling to the steering shaft.

3. Remove the cotter pin located on both of the tie rod ends and unscrew the nuts.

4. Press the tie rod ends out of the steering arms.

5. Disconnect the steering gear housing from the front suspension crossmember and remove the steering gear with the tie rods.

6. Install the steering gear in the reverse order of removal, being sure to position the gear to the high point (centered) the steering wheel spokes pointing downward and the elongated cutout of the lower steering mast coinciding with the clamp bolt hold of the pinion flange. Tighten the steering gear attaching bolts and the tie rod end attaching nuts to 29 ft lbs. Tighten the flexible coupling bolt to 22 ft lbs.

Steering Gear Adjustment

1. Set steering gear to high point by positioning front wheels straight ahead with center steering wheel spoke pointing directly downward.

2. Flexible-coupling bolt hole will

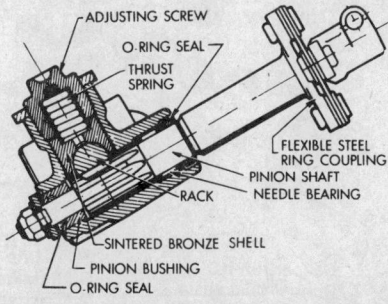

Steering gear assembly

thereby be positioned parallel to the rack.

3. Thread adjusting screw into steering gear housing until resistance is felt. (The screw pushes the sintered bronze shell against the rack).

4. Back off adjusting screw 1/12 of a turn (a quarter turn = 3/12) and check for free movement of rack, left and right. If not free, delicately back off screw further until rack does move freely.

5. Hold adjuster screw in position and tighten lock nut to 43 ft lbs.

6. Fill area under pinion shaft rubber boot with steering gear lubricant and slide boot into position.

BRAKE SYSTEM

Adjustment

1. The drum brakes are adjusted using two eccentrics mounted on the backing plate.

2. Turning the eccentrics in the direction of the arrows stamped on the backing plate increases shoe-to-drum contact.

3. When adjusting the front shoes, turn the eccentrics, while turning the wheel forward, until the wheel locks. Then back off the eccentric until the wheel is just free to turn.

Master Cylinder

The drum-type brake system requires a minimum static pressure of 4¼ psi on the brake fluid at all times to hold the wheel cylinder cups firmly against the cylinder walls, preventing loss of fluid or entrance of air. Disc brakes, on the other hand, require that all pressure be released to disengage brake pistons.

Removal and Installation

1. Disconnect the 2 brake pipes from the master cylinder. Be prepared to absorb any brake fluid that will flow out of the pipes and master cylinder with a cloth.

2. On the GT, remove the front support-to-fender skirt attaching bolts.

3. Remove the 4 master cylinder-to-booster attaching nuts and remove the master cylinder from the vehicle.

4. Install in the reverse order of removal, and bleed the hydraulic system.

Overhaul

1. Screw static pressure valve out of housing.

2. Push piston into cylinder to a point where a rod 1/10 in. thick will slip into the feed port to hold piston in this position.

3. Remove stop screw at bottom and circlip at booster end of housing and take

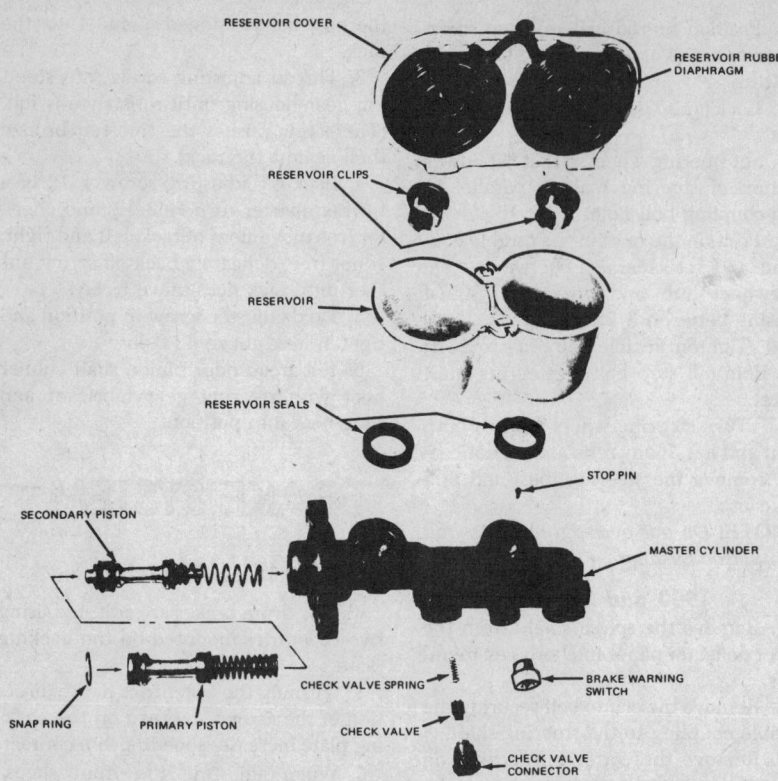

An exploded view of the dual type master cylinder used on 1973-75 1900 and Manta

out both pistons together with springs.

4. Unscrew stop screw from rear-brake-circuit piston. Remove remaining parts.

5. Clean master cylinder parts with brake fluid and dry with compressed air. Clean the compensating and feed ports. Polish cylinder bore and pistons.

Maximum piston diameter: 0.82 in.
Minimum piston diameter: 0.81 in.

7. Replace rubber seals and static pressure valve.

8. Coat all parts with brake fluid for reassembly.

9. Assemble intermediate piston and insert it into cylinder bore with thrust spring and spring seat. The smaller diameter of the tapered thrust spring must face piston.

10. With a drift, push piston into housing and insert a rod into feed port.

11. Install stop screw with a new seal ring.

12. Insert preassembled piston for rear brake circuit into cylinder bore and install circlip into groove in housing.

13. Check piston for free movement.
NOTE: *If required, place washers under the head of the stop screw.*

14. Push piston partly into housing and remove rod from feed port.

15. Screw in new static pressure valves.

16. Coat new sealing plugs thinly with brake fluid and insert them into housing.

17. Push twin brake fluid container into sealing plugs.

Brake Booster

The brake booster available on Opels reduces required foot pressure for braking by approximately 25%, as compared to non-booster assisted brakes. The booster is mechanically controlled by the foot pedal and conveys this pressure along with an engine vacuum assistance to the dual master cylinder. A vacuum control valve prevents air from flowing back into booster when engine is not running. The valve must be replaced when defective.

Checking Brake Booster Operation

The operation of the brake booster can be checked easily.

1. With engine off, use up all vacuum by depressing brake pedal several times.

2. Hold pedal down and start engine. As vacuum builds, the pedal will move farther (held under same foot pressure) as power is developed by booster.

Disc Brakes

Brake Pads

Inspection and Replacement

1. Disc brake friction pads can be checked for wear without disassembling the caliper if a gauge is available that measures the distance from the inside of one friction pad backing plate to the other when the brake is engaged.
NOTE: *Both brake friction pads must be replaced if either pad is worn down to a thickness of 0.08 in. or less.*

2. If no gauge is available, tap dowel pins from brake caliper toward center of car after pin retainer has been removed.

3. Mark friction pads for later reassembly and pull pads from caliper.
NOTE: *Oily, cracked, or defaced pads need replacement.*

4. Pads themselves must measure at all times greater than 0.280 in. thick.

5. Remove high spots on friction pads with a cut stone file before reinstalling.

6. *If installing new friction pads,* force both caliper pistons into their caliper bores completely with a clamp.
NOTE: *Open bleeder valve on caliper to prevent brake reservoir overflow.*

7. Replace friction pad retaining spring.

8. Press brake pedal several times to seat pads. Bleed and add brake fluid.

9. Avoid forceful braking for 125 miles to break in pads.

Disc Brake Calipers

Removal and Installation

1. Remove caliper from wheel backing

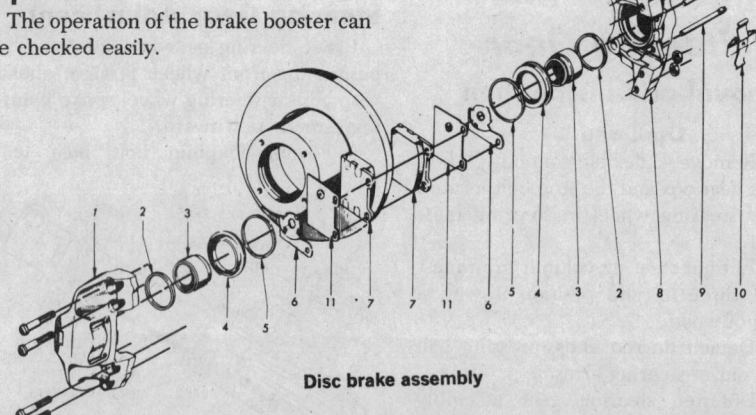
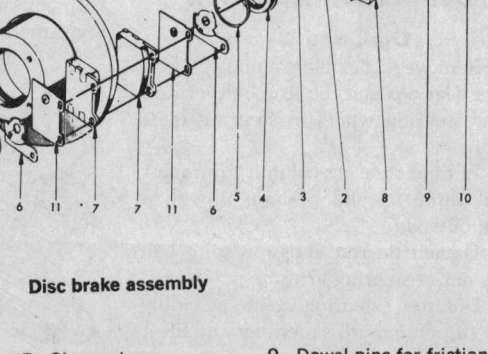

Disc brake assembly

1. Caliper rim half
2. Rubber fluid seals
3. Hollow pistons
4. Rubber seals
5. Clamp rings
6. Retainer plates
7. Friction pads
8. Caliper mounting half
9. Dowel pins for friction pads
10. Cross-shaped retaining spring
11. Pad backing plate

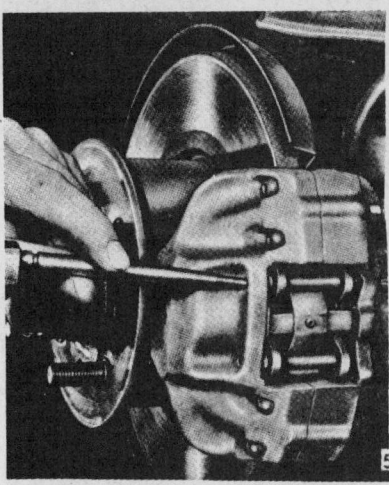

Removing dowel pins from calipers

Removing friction pads from caliper

plate.

2. Loosen brake line at union, unfasten caliper and brake hose bracket and remove brake pipe (plugging hose at union) on their collars and clamp rings are correctly positioned on the seals.

4. Push retainer plates into pistons with handle of a screwdriver.

Overhaul

NOTE: *Caliper halves are not disassembled for repair work.*

1. From opening for friction pads, lift retainer plates from each piston.

2. Next, pry clamp rings from rubber seals and remove seals. Keep twin parts from the two halves separated.

3. Check caliper piston seals and clamp rings for deterioration or damage. Clean ring recesses with *denatured* alcohol.

NOTE: *A special clamp (J-22429) is recommended for forcing pistons from caliper halves.*

4. New rubber seals are recommended for reinstallation with cleaned clamp rings.

5. Make sure that seals are securely seated.

6. Attach brake pipe and caliper to front end, making sure that mating surfaces of caliper and steering knuckle are

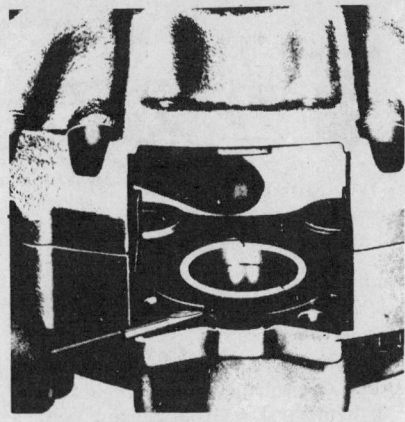

Removing rubber seal clamp ring

Checking brake disc for lateral runout

clean and smooth.

7. Tighten caliper attaching bolts to 50 ft lbs.

Brake Disc (Rotor)

Removal and Installation

1. Unbolt the caliper and suspend it on a piece of heavy wire.

NOTE: *Do not stress the brake hose.*

2. Remove the wheel hub.

3. Support the wheel backing plate in a vise, and unbolt the disc hat from the hub using a star wrench.

4. The disc may now be pulled from the hub.

CAUTION: *Do not drive the hub out of the disc.*

5. The disc is installed in the reverse order of removal.

6. When installing the disc on the hub, ensure that the mating surfaces are free of dirt, and torque the star bolts to 36 ft lbs.

7. Before installing the disc on the car, repack the wheel bearings.

Disc Inspection

The discs should be inspected visually for scratches, nicks, or scoring. The discs may be checked for lateral runout using a dial indicator, mounted perpendicular to the disc, ½ in. from its circumference.

Disc parallelism is checked with a micrometer.

Minimum thickness of brake disc: 0.-394 in.

Maximum unevenness: 0.002 in.

Maximum lateral runout: 0.004 in.

If runout or parallelism exceed the above specifications, the disc should be machined or replaced.

NOTE: *In no case should the disc be machined beyond the minimum thickness. If it is impossible to true disc without exceeding this figure, the disc must be replaced.*

Wheel Bearings

Removal and Installation

1. Remove front wheels.

2. Remove front wheel bearing hub cap and spindle nut.

3. Pull rotor hub assembly off of the spindle. Be careful not to drop the outer bearing.

NOTE: *On cars equipped with disc brakes, it will be necessary to remove the caliper assembly before removing the rotor and hub assembly.*

4. Thoroughly clean bearings of old lubricant and press fresh grease into bearing.

NOTE: *Both inner and outer front bearings should be repacked with grease. For best results, both sides of the car should be repacked at the same time.*

5. Place hub assembly on spindle and install spindle nut in reverse order of removal.

Adjustments

When reinstalling the hub assembly onto the spindle, it is important to set the free play in bearing to prevent damage.

1. Install hub assembly onto spindle.

2. Place outer bearing into position together with the washer and install spindle nut.

3. Tighten spindle nut to 18 ft lbs or until all free play is removed from the wheel bearing.

NOTE: *Do not overtighten nut. This will cause binding of the bearing on its race, and will cause excessive wear.*

4. If the spindle nut was tightened to 18 ft lbs, back off the nut ¼ of a turn and install the cotter pin. Back off the spindle nut 1/12 additional turn if necessary to install the cotter pin. Do not tighten the nut any further to install the cotter pin.

5. Reinstall bearing hub cap and recheck free play.

Drum Brakes

Brake Drums

Removal and Installation

1. Support rear of car and remove rear

wheels.

2. Remove rear drums by pulling them off of hub.

3. Install in the reverse order of removal.

Inspection

1. The drums should be checked for cracks, scoring and concentricity.

2. Slight scores may be polished out using emery cloth. Eccentricity or serious scores should be removed by turning the drum providing the maximum diameter is not exceeded.

Maximum eccentricity of drum: 0.-004 in.

NOTE: *Eccentricity is measured by comparing the diameter of the inner and outer edge of the machined surface in two places, 90° apart.*

Standard drum inner diameter: 9.060 in.

Maximum diameter after turning: 9.090 in.

3. To regain center contact with brake shoes, grind linings to 0.02 in. under drum diameter.

4. Before reinstalling brake drum, inspect all brake pipe and hose connections for fluid leakage. Tighten these connections and apply heavy pressure to brake pedal to recheck seal.

5. Inspect rear wheel backing plate for leaks from wheel bearing oil seals. Replace seals if needed.

6. Check all backing plate bolts for tightness.

7. Clean away all dirt from assemblies and repack wheel bearings.

8. If rear wheel backing plate was removed, use new gaskets lightly coated with grease. Torque plate to 43 ft lbs.

9. Seal the outside of the backing plate near the brake shoe hold-down springs with body sealing compound.

Brake Shoes

Removal and Installation

1. Raise car and support it safely.

2. Remove wheels and drum as-

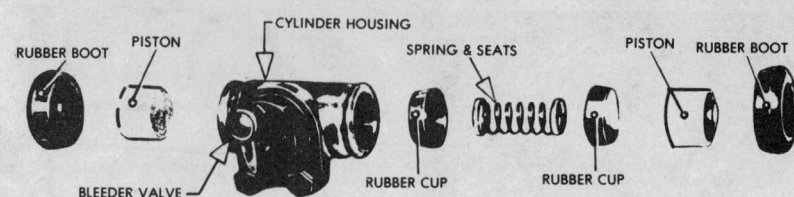

Exploded view of wheel cylinder

semblies.

3. Remove upper and lower brake shoe return springs.

4. Remove brake shoe hold down springs and retainers.

5. Remove shoes from backing plate.

6. Clean all dirt from drum and backing plate and inspect all fittings and parts.

7. Installation is reverse of removal.

Wheel Cylinders

Removal and Installation

1. Remove wheels, drums, and brake shoes from backing plates.

2. Disconnect brake lines from back of wheel cylinder.

3. Unbolt wheel cylinder and remove it from backing plate.

4. Installation is the reverse of removal.

NOTE: *After installation be sure to bleed system of all air.*

Overhaul

1. Carefully pull lower edges of wheel cylinder boots away from cylinders and note if interior is wet—an indication of brake fluid seepage past the piston cup. If so, cylinder overhaul is required.

2. Clean dirt from all surrounding surfaces and then disconnect and seal off brake line (tape is often satisfactory for sealing).

3. Remove cylinder from backing plate.

4. Dismantle boots, pistons, cups and spring from cylinder.

5. Remove bleeder valve.

6. Discard boots and cups; clean other parts with fresh brake fluid.

NOTE: *Use no fluid containing even a trace of mineral oil.*

7. Light scratches and corrosion can be polished from pistons and bore with fine emery cloth or steel wool.

8. Dip all parts in brake fluid and reassemble.

9. After installation, adjust brakes and road test for performance.

Parking Brake

Cable

Removal and Installation

1. Raise car and support it securely.

2. Release parking brake and disconnect return spring.

3. Remove adjusting nut from parking brake equalizer.

4. Disconnect parking brake cable at rear connections.

5. Remove cable from car.

6. Install in reverse order of removal.

Adjustment

1. Lift the rear of the vehicle, and support it with jackstands.

2. Release the parking brake lever and loosen the nut in front of the equalizer.

3. Pull the brake lever up three notches (clicks), and tighten the nut behind the equalizer until the rear brakes begin to bind.

4. Tighten the nut in front of the equalizer.

5. Lubricate the cable in the area of the equalizer to ensure proper operation.

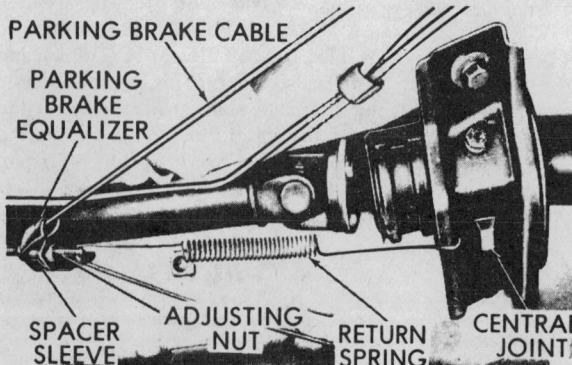

Parking brake assembly

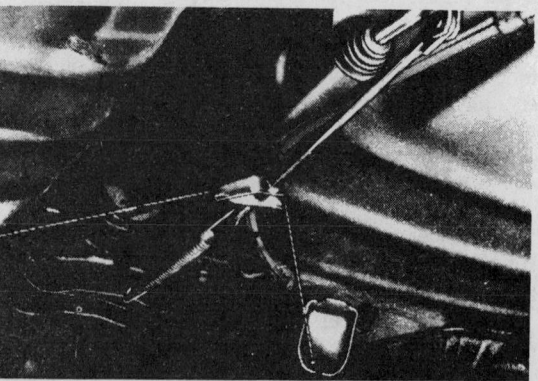

Parking brake equalizer assembly

CHASSIS ELECTRICAL

Heater Blower

Removal and Installation

GT

1. Drain the coolant by removing the lower radiator hose, then remove the hoses from the heater in the engine compartment.

2. Disconnect the hood lock control cable from the lock bar.

3. Remove the console by removing two screws under the ash tray, two screws which retain the headlamp lever handle, and prying the console up to release four retaining snaps.

4. Lower the steering column, and separate the two plug connectors from it.

5. Remove the two plugs from the sides of the instrument panel, adjacent to the heater control, and remove the screws through the openings.

6. Detach the speedometer cable from the speedometer, and remove the flasher unit, located adjacent to the hood release.

7. Disconnect five plug connectors from the left underside of the instrument panel.

8. Remove two retaining screws from the radio bracket, and one nut from the left side of the instrument panel, and pull the panel out from the top.

9. If so equipped, mark for identification and remove the wires from the ammeter.

10. Unbolt the heater control panel, and the heater support bracket, located at the upper right corner of the radio bracket.

11. Remove all screws from the dash panel padding, and remove it from the dash.

12. Disconnect all duct hoses, remove one bolt from the top and two nuts from the bottom of the case, and remove the heater assembly.

13. Install in the reverse order of removal, checking all connections such as hoses to ensure that they are airtight.

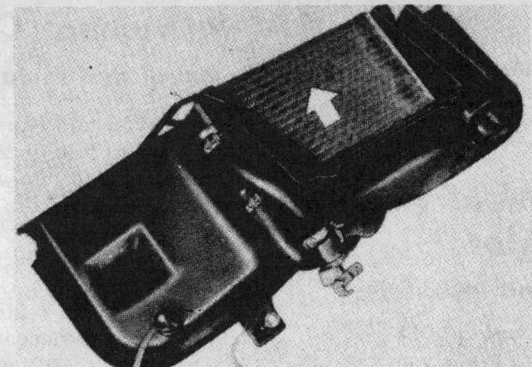

The heater assembly of the 1900 and Manta, showing the location of the heater core

14. Correct any leaks with body sealer.

1900 and Manta

1. Remove the 5 shroud cover attaching screws; accessible from the engine compartment.

2. Remove the cover carefully.

3. Pull the water hose off the windshield wiper jet.

4. Disconnect the electrical multiple plug connection on the left side of the shroud.

5. Remove the 3 heater motor attaching screws and remove the motor.

6. Installation is the reverse of removal.

Heater Core

Removal and Installation

GT

See "Heater Blower Removal and Installation".

1900 and Manta

1. Unscrew the hood lock together with the ground wire which is only on vehicles with radio interference suppression.

2. Unscrew the heater housing cover.

3. Pull the hose off the windshield washer system off the jet and take the jet out of the housing cover.

4. Unscrew the bowden control wire from the heater valve.

5. Unscrew the heater housing from the dash panel and pull it off carefully.

6. Remove the water hoses from the heater core and pull the heater core out of the heater housing.

7. Install the heater core and the housing in the reverse order of removal.

Radio

Removal and Installation

NOTE: *When installing the radio, the antenna trimmer should be adjusted as follows: extend the antenna to a height of 31 in. tune the radio to a barely audible station around 1400 KC, and turn the trimmer screw (on the bottom of the receiver) until maximum volume is achieved.*

1900 and Manta

1. Disconnect the battery ground cable and the antenna and speaker connectors from the radio.

2. Remove the knobs from the radio and unbolt the mounting nuts.

3. Remove the receiver bracket lower screw from the receiver, loosen the upper bolt approximately three turns, and slide out the radio.

4. Install in the reverse order of removal.

GT

1. Disconnect the battery.

2. Remove the access trim plug from the right side of the console.

3. Remove the hex head screw with an 8 mm socket through the access hole.

4. Remove the access trim cover on the left side of the console.

5. Remove the tear-lock bolts by first drilling a 3/16 in. hole in the bolt and then using a ¼ in. bolt extractor.

6. Disconnect the white ignition and black turn signal wire set plugs.

7. Support the steering column assembly and remove the two attaching bolts.

8. Disconnect the speedometer cable.

9. Remove the 6 instrument cluster retaining screws and pull the panel straight out.

10. Disconnect the radio harness plug and antenna lead from the back of the radio.

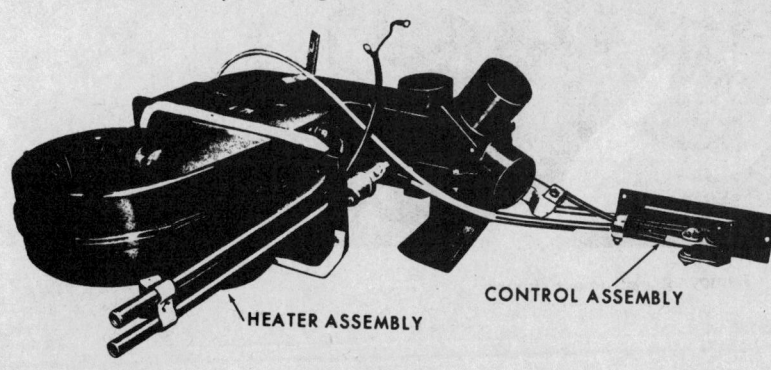

CONTROL ASSEMBLY

HEATER ASSEMBLY

Heater assembly-GT

11. Remove the knobs from the radio.

12. Remove the radio control shaft retaining nuts while supporting the radio and then remove the radio.

13. Install the radio in the reverse order.

Windshield Wiper Motor

Removal and Installation

1900 and Manta

1. Remove the crank arm nut and crank arm from the wiper motor drive shaft, located above the clutch and brake pedals.

2. Unbolt the three nuts which attach the motor and drive to the firewall and remove the wiper motor.

3. Install in the reverse order of removal.

GT

1. Unbolt the retaining nuts, and remove the wiper arms.

2. Remove the three bolts which retain the wiper posts to the deflector panels, and allow the posts to drop out of the panels.

3. Unscrew the left and center deflector panels, and remove the left panel, including the motor and linkage.

4. Remove the crank arm nut from the wiper drive, and separate the linkage from the motor.

5. Unbolt the three retaining nuts, and remove the motor from the deflector panel.

6. Install in the reverse order of removal.

NOTE: *When installing the wiper arms, ensure that they are in the proper position at rest.*

Instrument Cluster

Removal and Installation

1900 and Manta

1. Disconnect battery cable.

2. Remove headlight switch knob by depressing retaining clip and pulling knob out.

3. Disconnect two plugs and screws behind plugs on front of cluster.

4. Remove heater control knob and pull cover from instrument panel.

5. Disconnect speedometer cable by turning coupling counterclockwise.

NOTE: *If equipped with a rear defogger or fog lamps, disconnect switch and remove it from panel.*

6. Remove two screws for lower attaching point and remove cluster partially. Disconnect wires from back of cluster.

7. Remove cluster from car.

8. Install by reversing removal procedures.

GT

1. Disconnect the battery cable.

2. Remove right and left access covers and remove screws.

3. Remove flasher unit and position wheels so they are pointed straight ahead.

4. Pull heads off of both rear bolts, drill a 3/16 in. hole, and then remove rear bolts by using a stud extractor.

5. Disconnect ignition and directional signal wire set plugs.

6. Remove steering column support bolts and drop column to floor.

7. Disconnect speedometer cable.

8. Remove six attaching screws and pull instrument cluster back from the top.

Removing lower cluster attaching screws

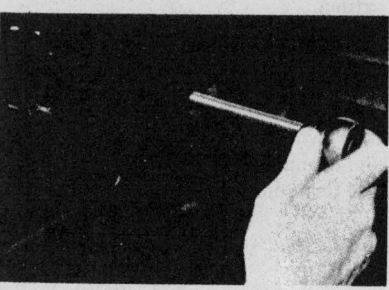

Removing right access cover and attaching bolts.

9. Unplug wires from the radio and other instruments, gauges, and switches.

10. Pull instrument cluster out and turn it sideways to remove any gauge or switch.

11. Install in reverse order of removal.

Fuse Box Location

The fuse box is located below the instrument panel to the left of the steering column on the inner cowl panel. The fuse for the heated glass back window is located in the relay switch.

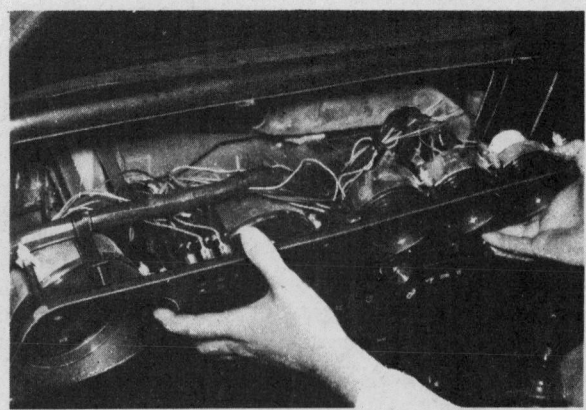

Removing instrument cluster

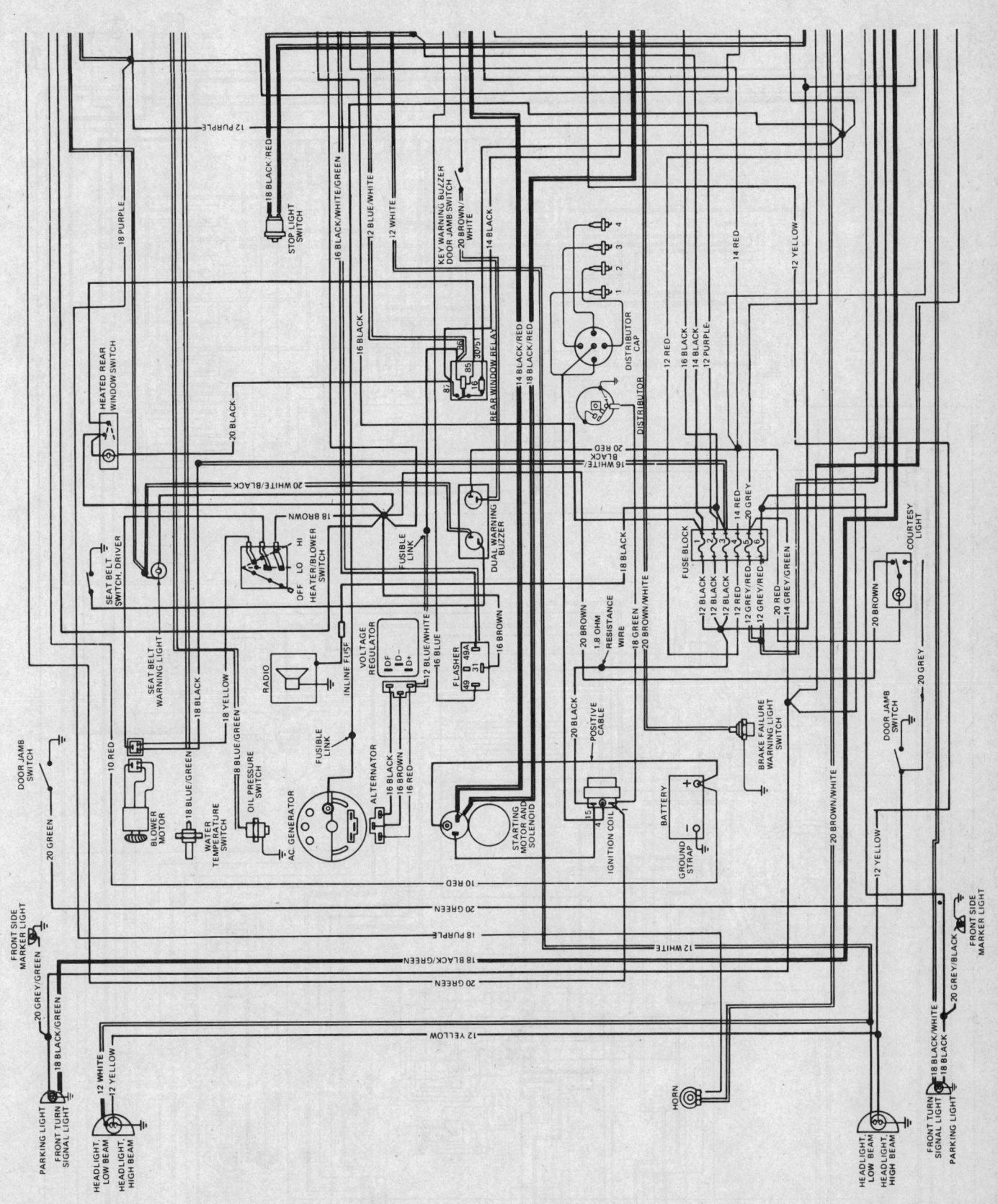

1975 2-dr. Coupe

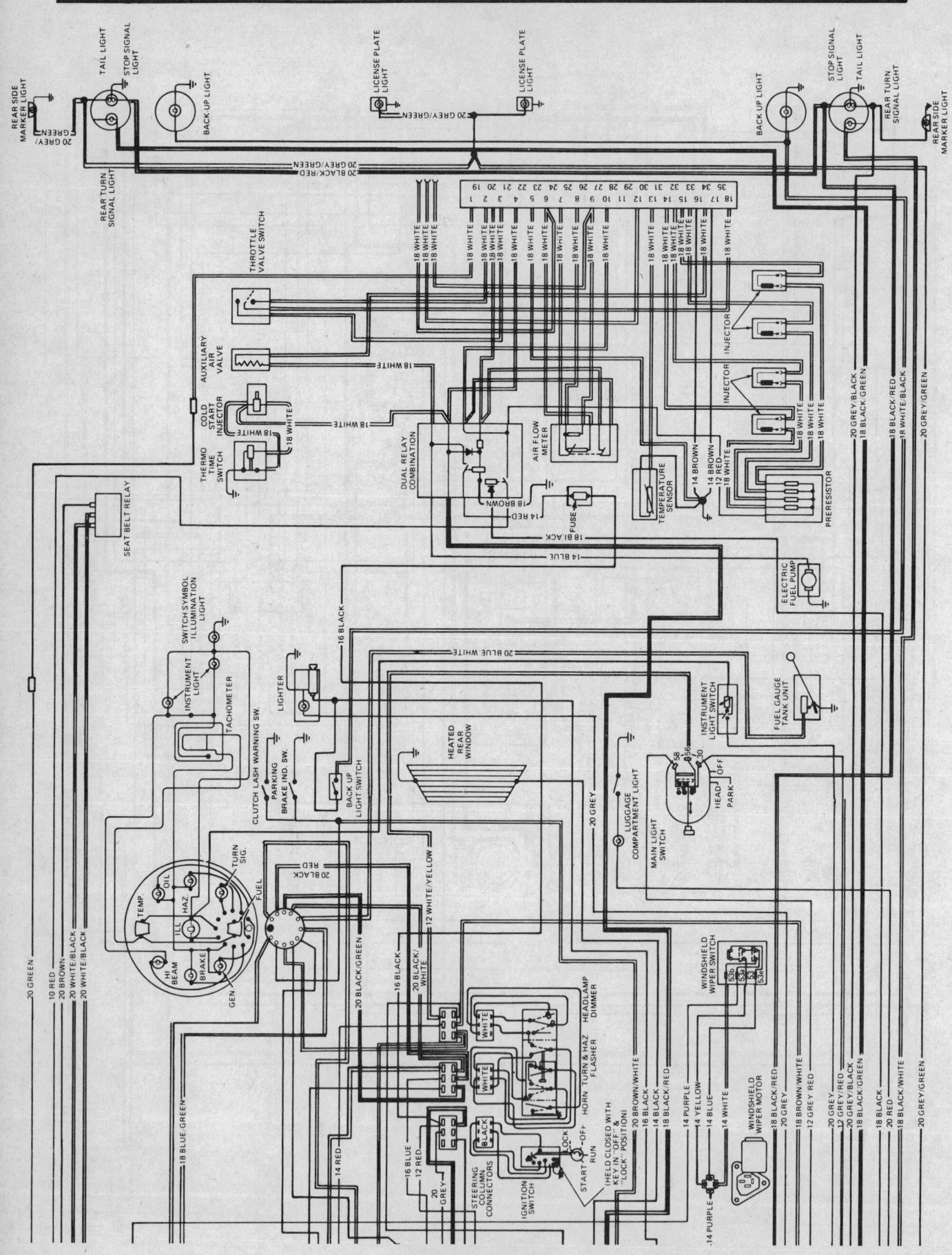

1975 2-dr. Coupe

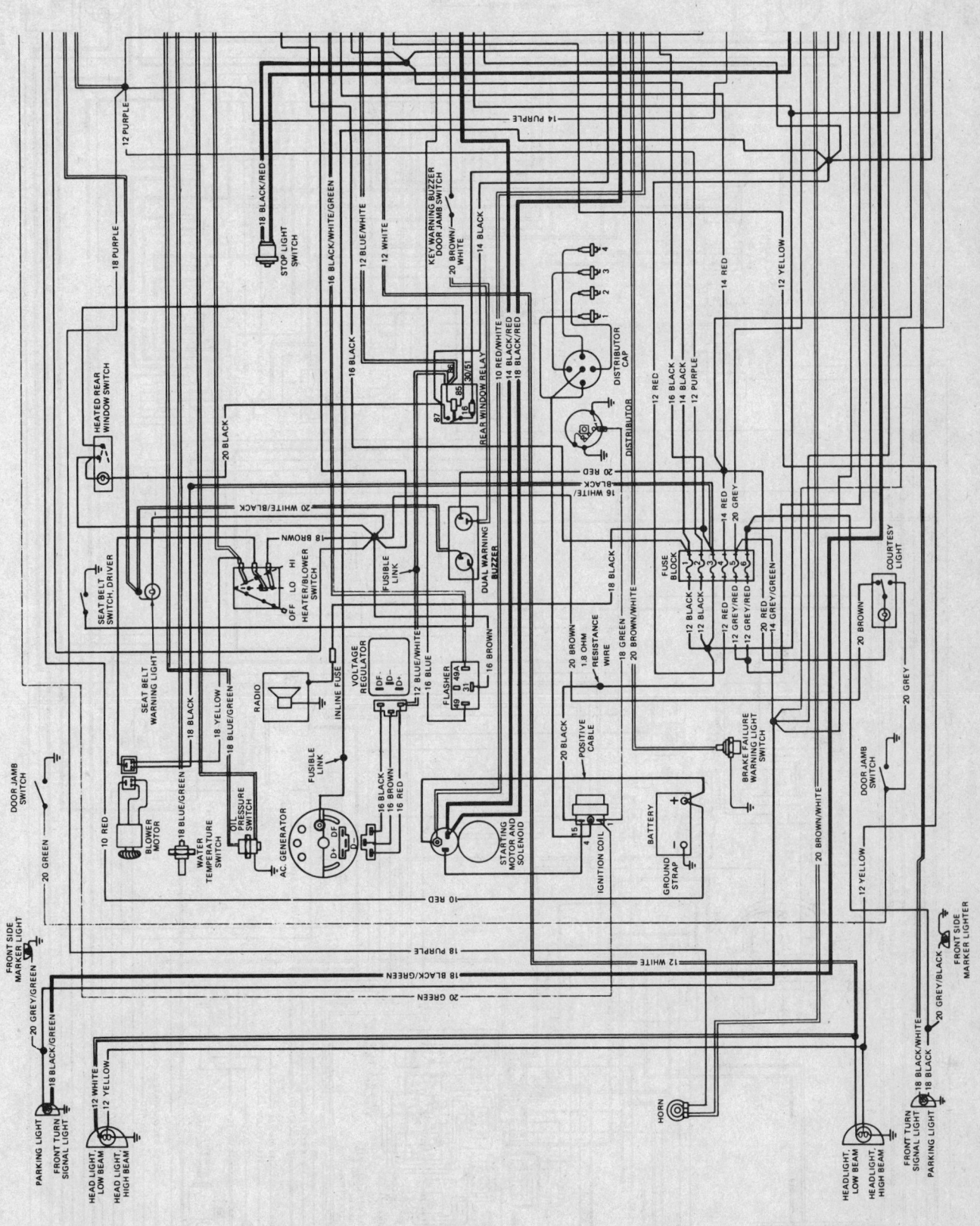

1975 Station wagon

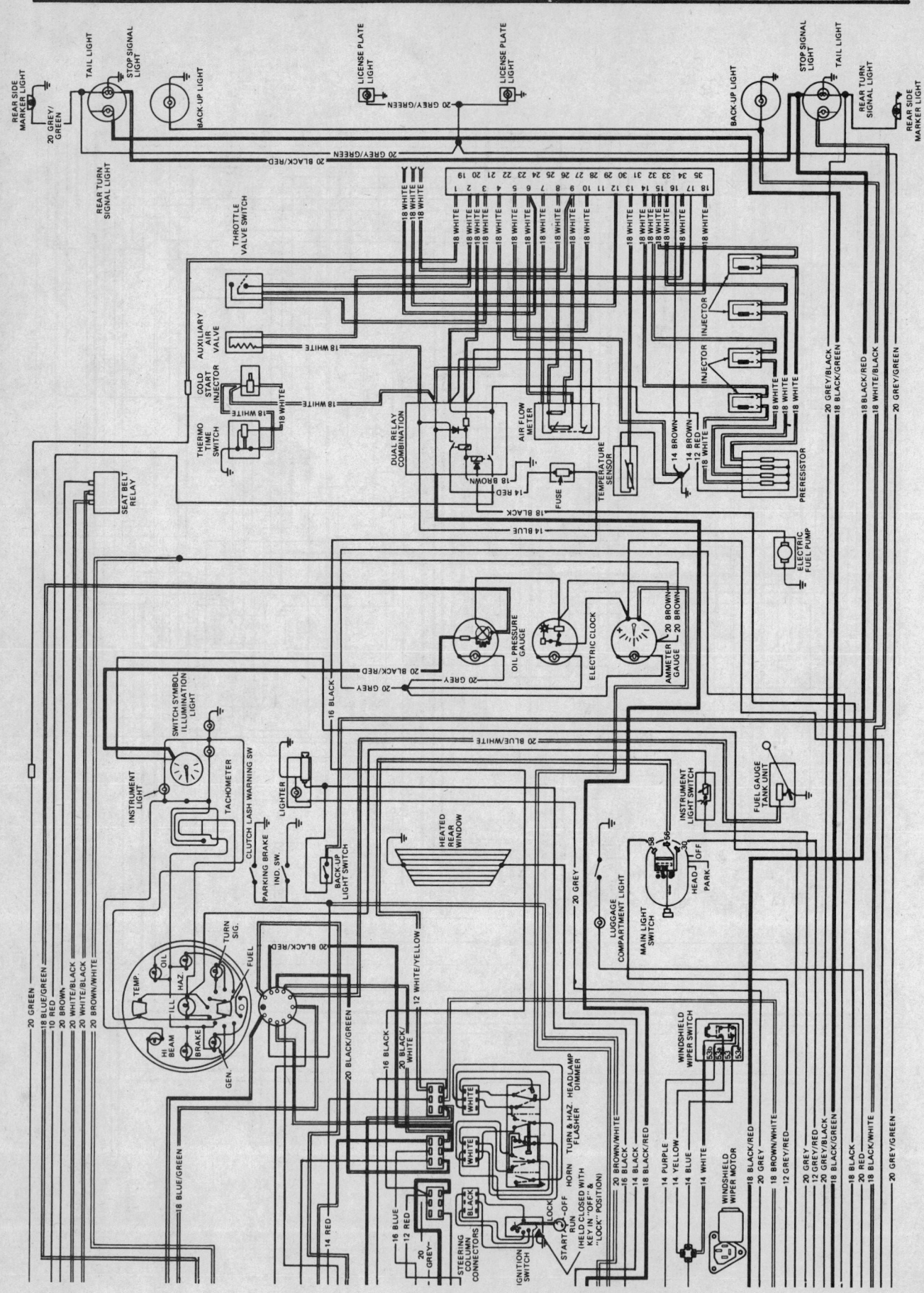

1975 Station wagon

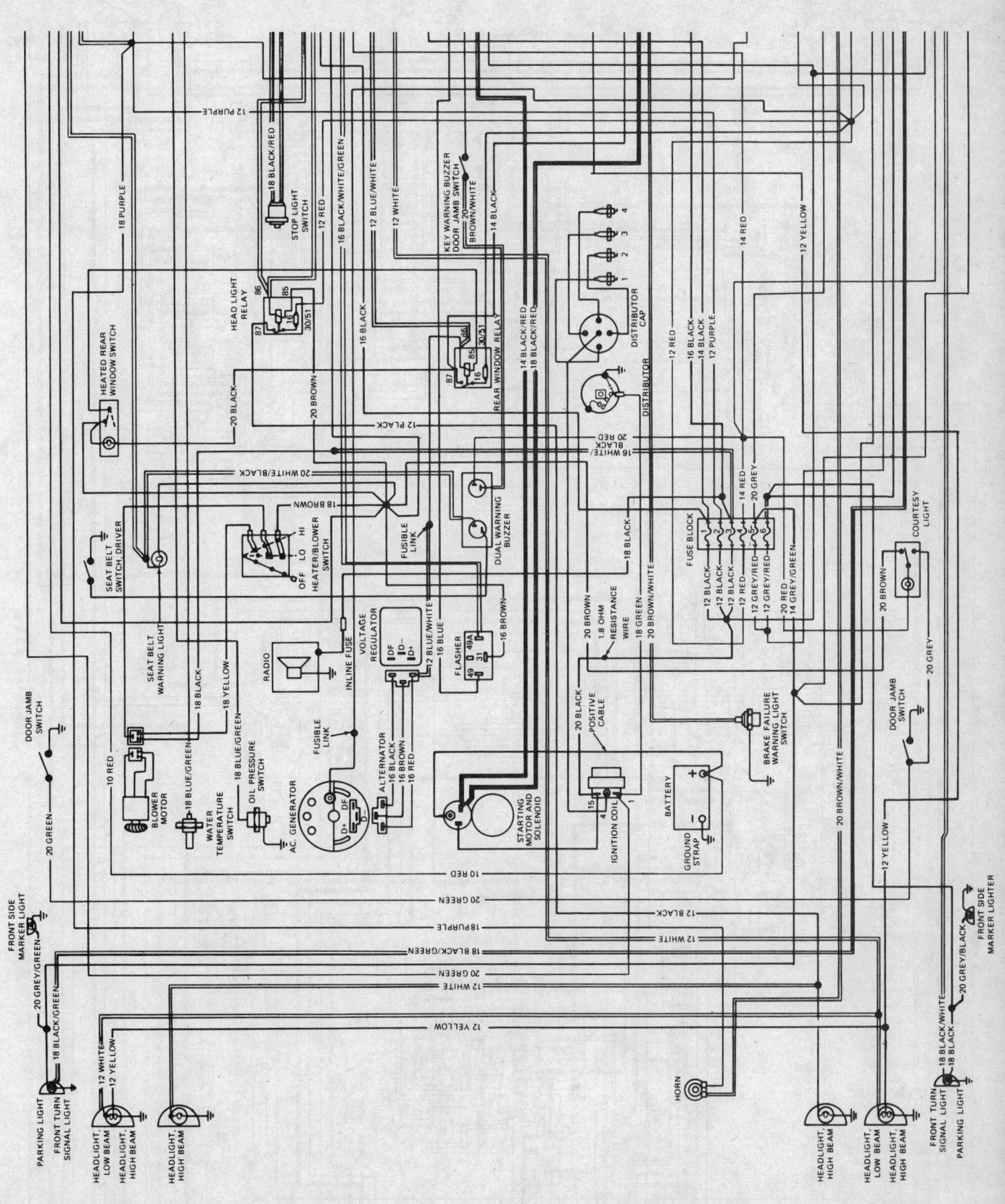

1975 Sedan

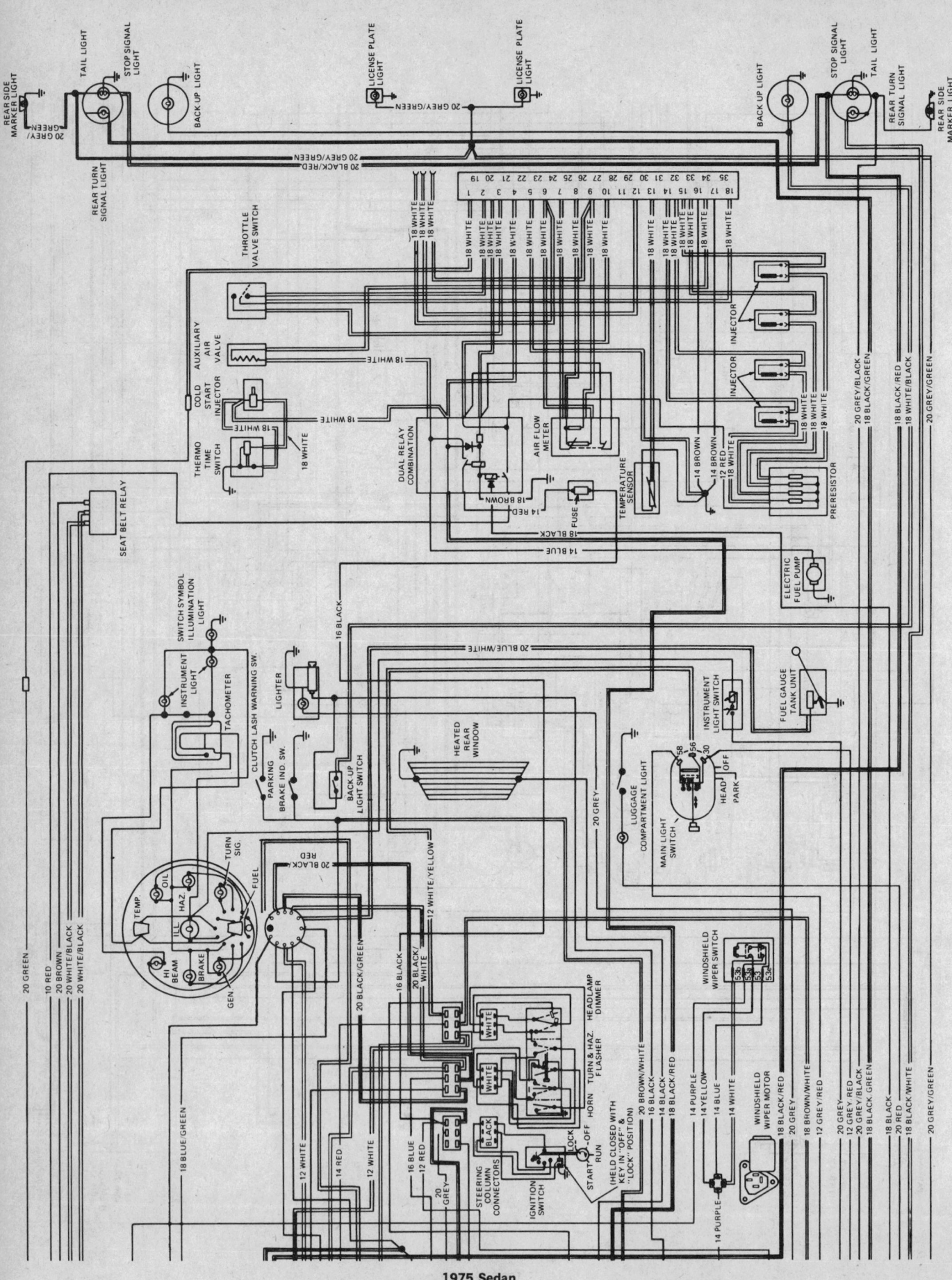

1975 Sedan

SPECIFICATIONS

Opel Isuzu

INTRODUCTION

The Opel by Isuzu fits somewhere in the marketing plans of General Motors between the original GM import, the Opel Kadett, and the Chevette. Slotted as a replacement for the Opel Manta (German produced), the Japanese Isuzu sports a 4-cylinder, single-overhead-cam engine displacing 1817cc (110.8 cu. in.).

This is the same engine under the hood of Chevrolet's "Luv."

The Isuzu sports a 4-speed manual transmission, or an extra cost 3-speed Turbo-Hydramatic, installed in a conventional, front-engine, rear-drive power train. The engine is slightly smaller than the 1975 Manta (1817cc to 1897cc) and

only develops one less horsepower with its carburetor, rather than the Manta's fuel-injection.

The suspension is independent in the front, employing unequal length wishbones and a live rear axle is supported by an unusual 3-link system.

MODEL IDENTIFICATION

1976 Isuzu

SERIAL NUMBER IDENTIFICATION

Vehicle

The vehicle identification number is carried on an embossed plate attached the top, left end of the instrument panel as seen from the driver's seat.

Vehicle Identification Number

Refer to the Vehicle Identification Number interpretation shown.

Engine

The engine serial number is stamped on the top, right front corner of the engine block.

Transmissions

The Isuzu is either equipped with a 4-speed manual transmission, or the 3-speed Turbo Hydramatic.

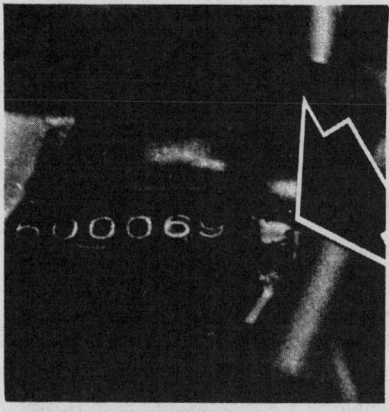

Engine serial number

Vehicle identification number

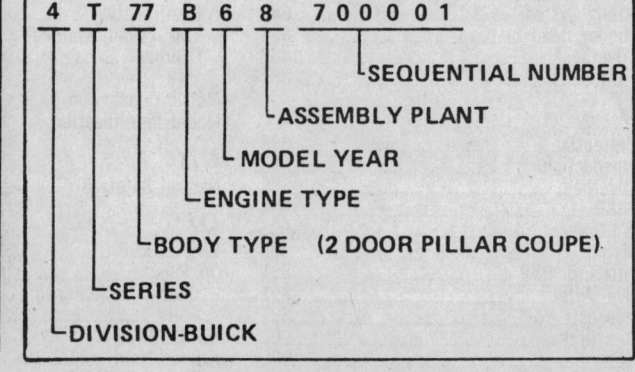

Vehicle Identification Breakdown

GENERAL ENGINE SPECIFICATIONS

Year	Engine Displacement Cu. In.	Carburetor Type	Horsepower (@ rpm)	Torque @ rpm (ft lbs)	Bore x Stroke (in.)	Compression Ratio	Oil Pressure @ rpm (psi)
1976	110.8	Nikki-2V	80 @ 4,800	95 @ 3,000	3.31 x 3.23	8.5:1	56.88 @ 1,400

TUNE-UP SPECIFICATIONS

When analyzing compression test results, look for uniformity among cylinders, rather than specific pressures

Year	Engine Displace. (Cu In.)	SPARK PLUGS Type	SPARK PLUGS Gap (in.)	DISTRIBUTOR Point Dwell (deg)	DISTRIBUTOR Point Gap (in.)	IGNITION TIMING (deg) MT	IGNITION TIMING (deg) AT	Intake Valve Opens (deg)	Fuel Pump Pressure (psi)	Idle Speed (rpm)	VALVE CLEAR (in) In	VALVE CLEAR (in) Ex
1976	110.8	BPR6ES	0.030	52	0.018	6B	6B	—	3.3	700	0.006	0.010

NOTE: The underhood specifications sticker often reflects tune-up specification changes made in production. Sticker figures must be used if they disagree with this chart.

B   Before top dead center
—   Not available

FIRING ORDERS

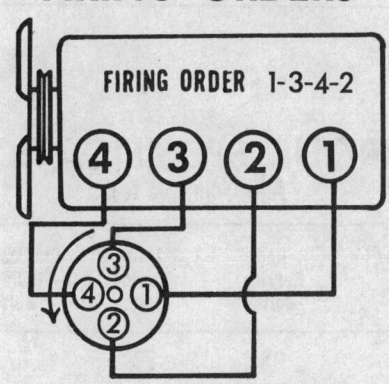

FIRING ORDER 1-3-4-2

CAPACITIES

Year	Model	Engine Displacement Cu in	Engine Crankcase (qts) With Filter	Engine Crankcase (qts) Without Filter	Transmission (pts) Manual 3-spd	Transmission (pts) Manual 4-spd	Transmission (pts) Automatic	Drive Axle (pts)	Gasoline Tank (gals)	Cooling System (qts) W/ AC	Cooling System (qts) W/O AC
1976	All	110.8	4.7	5.7	—	2.3	10½	2½	13.7	6½	6½

—Not applicable

CRANKSHAFT AND CONNECTING ROD SPECIFICATIONS

All measurements are given in inches

Year	Engine Displacement Cu. in.	CRANKSHAFT Main Brg Journal Dia	CRANKSHAFT Main Brg Oil Clearance	CRANKSHAFT Shaft End-Play	CRANKSHAFT Thrust on No.	CONNECTING ROD Journal Diameter	CONNECTING ROD Oil Clearance	CONNECTING ROD Side Clearance
1976	110.8	2.205	0.0008-0.0025	0.0024-0.0094	3	1.929	0.0007-0.0030	0.0079-0.013

VALVE SPECIFICATIONS

Year	Engine Displacement Cu. In.	Seat Angle (deg)	Face Angle (deg)	Spring Test Pressure (lbs. @ in.)	Spring Installed Height (in.)	STEM TO GUIDE CLEARANCE (in.)		STEM DIAMETER (in.)	
						Intake	Exhaust	Intake	Exhaust
1976	110.8	①	45	outer-34.5 inner-20	outer-1.61 inner-1.51	0.009-0.0022	0.0015-0.0031	0.315	0.315

① Because of the aluminum head and valve seat inserts, cut the valve seat with 15, 45 or 75 degree cutters. Use the minimum necessary to remove dents or damage, leaving the contact width inside the 0.0472—0.063 range.

PISTON AND RING SPECIFICATIONS

Year	Engine Displacement Cu. in.	Piston Clearance	RING GAP			RING SIDE CLEARANCE		
			Top Compression	Bottom Compression	Oil Control	Top Compression	Bottom Compression	Oil Control
1976	110.8	0.001-0.0026	0.008-0.016	0.008-0.016	0.008-0.035	0.0010-0.0024	0.0010-0.0024	0.0008

TORQUE SPECIFICATIONS
All readings in ft lbs

Year	Engine Displacement Cu In.	Cylinder Head Bolts	Rod Bearing Bolts	Main Bearing Bolts	Crankshaft Pulley Bolt	Flywheel-to Crankshaft Bolts	MANIFOLDS	
							Intake	Exhaust
1976	110.8	72①	33	72	87	60	17	17

① Initially install the bolts, according to pattern, to 61 ft lbs. Then torque to 72 ft lbs.

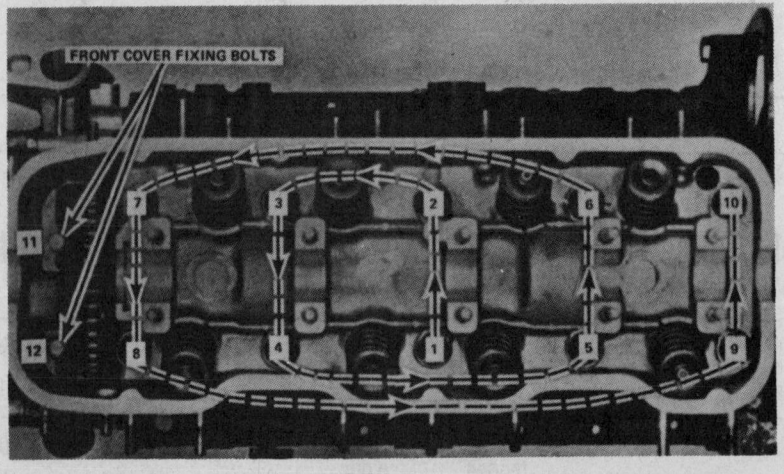

Cylinder head torque sequence

BATTERY AND STARTER SPECIFICATIONS
All cars use 12 volt, negative ground electrical systems

| Year | Model | Battery Amp Hour Capacity | Lock Test | | | Starter No Load Test | | | Brush Spring Tension (oz) | Min. Brush Length (in.) |
			Amps	Volts	Torque (ft/lbs)	Amps	Volts	RPM		
1976	All	50	280-320	6 Min.	—	30-50	10.6	7300-8500	56	0.472

— Not available

ALTERNATOR AND REGULATOR SPECIFICATIONS

| Year | Model | ALTERNATOR | | | | REGULATOR | | | | | |
| | | Part No. or Manufacturer | Field Current @ 12v | Output (amps) | Part No. or Manufacturer | Field Relay | | | Regulator | | |
						Air Gap (in.)	Point Gap (in.)	Volts to Close	Air Gap (in.)	Point Gap (in.)	Volts @ 75°
1976	All	Hitachi	—	40	—	.012	.030	4.9	.012	.015	14

BRAKE SPECIFICATIONS
All measurements given are (in.) unless noted

| Model | Lug Nut Torque (ft/lb) | Master Cylinder Bore | Brake Disc | | Brake Drum | | | Minimum Lining Thickness | |
			Minimum Thickness	Maximum Run-Out	Diameter	Max. Machine O/S	Max. Wear Limit	Front	Rear
Isuzu	50	0.875	.339	.067	8.98	9.04	9.06	.067	.040

WHEEL ALIGNMENT SPECIFICATIONS

| Year | Model | CASTER | | CAMBER | | Toe-in (in.) |
		Range (deg)	Preferred Setting (deg)	Range (deg)	Preferred Setting (deg)	
1976	All	4P-6P	5P	½N-½P	0	⅛

TUNE-UP PROCEDURES

Following is the information needed to properly tune the Isuzu. The purpose is to restore performance lost through normal operation. It is not advisable to replace or correct only one thing at a time. Money will be saved and the results will be better if the entire process is done thoroughly.

The Isuzu automobile comes equipped with a tune-up label in the engine compartment. This label has information developed during production. Should the information in any way disagree with the specifications given here, follow the label.

Spark Plugs

Removal and Installation

It is a good idea to remove and inspect the spark plugs every six months or 6,000 miles. Driving habits vary and geographical location can affect the condition of the plugs. It is wise to remove them after six months, no matter how far the car was driven during that time.

Remember to label each plug and wire as it is removed so you will know the exact operating condition of the cylinder involved, should a problem develop later.

Remove each spark Plug wire by grasping it on the boot, pulling back, and twisting at the same time. Remove the plugs by using a 13/16" plug socket (deep) and turning them counterclockwise. Be careful, during both removal and installation, that you do not crack the porcelain (white part), because this will render the plug useless (it's a good idea to have an extra set available, just in case). Also, when removing and installing the plug, try not to bump the block with the wrench or your hand. It may cause dirt to get into the cylinder through the spark plug hole.

If after inspecting the plugs for cracks in the porcelain, and badly corroded electrodes, and you determine if they are reusable (refer to the inspection examples in the Troubleshooting Section), and clean them with a wire brush or sandblasting unit. Before re-gapping them, file off any uneven spots on the electrode flats. Trying to do this after gaping will change the setting.

Using a feeler gauge, set the gap at 0.030 by feeling a slight drag on the feeler as it is pulled through.

To make installation easier and removal much easier next time, coat the threads of each plug with a light covering of oil. Turn them, being careful not to crossthread, by hand until tight, rocking them slightly as you go. Using a reliable torque wrench, tighten each plug to 19 ft.

lbs. Too tight an installation can permanently damage the engine's cylinder head. Reinstall the correctly numbered ignition wire to the plugs and this step is over.

Breaker Points and Condenser

Removal and installation

Electricity doesn't constantly flow through the engine. The breaker points, or "points" as they are more commonly called, cause a slight and necessary hesitation between one spark Plug firing and the next. This allows the coil to build up the needed voltage to provide a strong spark.

Release the two clamps on either side of the distributor with a screwdriver. Be careful not to exert too much pressure, because you may slip and break the distributor cap.

After the cap is removed there will be a black bakelite piece with a brass "T" on one end. This is the rotor. Pull it straight up to remove. Under that will be a dustproof cover. Lift it out to expose the points.

Remove the two retaining screws and disconnect the wire leads and take out the point set. Examine them. If they are pitted, corroded, the contacts black or excessively worn, replace them. Check the tension on the breaker arm. If this seems loose it also indicates replacement. A slightly gray coating is alright, just take a small file (point file) and remove it.

The condenser is located just behind the vacuum control assembly and is removed by loosening the screw holding it to the distributor and disconnecting its lead wire (note the order of removal of the insulators and washers).

To reassemble, reverse the procedure. Put the point set in the distributor and loosely tighten retaining screws. Plug the lead wire into the terminal assembly. At this point turn the crankshaft pulley until the heel of the point set rubbing block is in contact with a high point on the cam lobe.

Using flat feeler gauges and a screwdriver, adjust the point gap to 0.018 and tighten the retaining screws all the way. Install the dust shield, rotor and the distributor cap.

Dwell Angle

The dwell angle is the amount of degrees of distributor rotation when the points are closed. Setting the angle requires the use of a dwell meter and should only be attempted if you have one. A change of 1° in your dwell angle causes a 2° change in your ignition timing it is imperative that you be properly equipped for these two operations.

Adjustment

Connect the dwell meter to the primary lead and ground. Start the engine and observe the reading. It should be 52°. If it is less, reduce the point gap. If the reading is more than 52°, increase the point gap.

Ignition Timing

As was mentioned, a change in dwell angle will affect timing. This could affect the operation of the automobile, the gas mileage and comfort.

Adjustment

After making sure that the point gap is set correctly and the engine is idling smoothly at 900 RPM, clean the crankshaft pulley with a rag and you will notice a notched line. Mark it with chalk. On the block is a series of numbers and lines. Mark the one labeled "6."

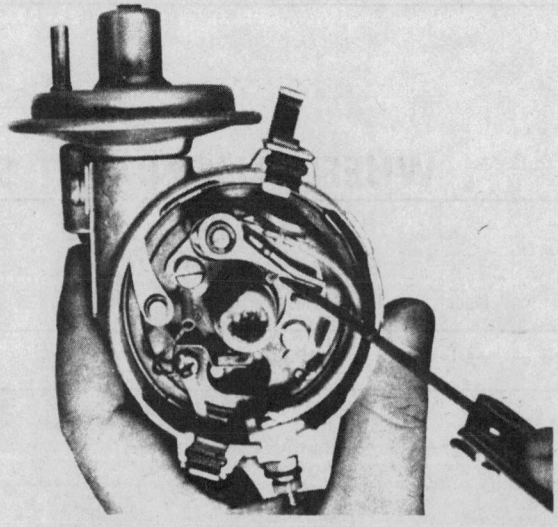

Measuring point gap with a feeler gauge

Connect the timing light and start the engine. Once the engine has leveled and is idling at 900 RPM, aim the light at the marks and observe their positions relative to each other.

If the two marks do not align, loosen the distributor mounting bolts (on either side of the distributor, at the engine block) and adjust the timing by turning the distributor. If the timing is behind where it should be (retarded) turn the unit clockwise. If it is forward of 6°, turn the distributor counterclockwise. Remember to refer to the tune-up sticker under the hood for the factory requirements. They may have been changed during production and, if they differ in any way from the information given here, follow the manufacturer's instructions.

Valve Lash

The valves in the Isuzu are driven by a single, overhead camshaft, directly to the rocker arms. There are no pushrods in the engine and, therefore, fewer adjustments and more efficient operation.

Adjustment

Valve adjustment should be carried out at every tune-up or whenever excessive valve noise is noticed. An important fact to remember is that the intake valves are on the LEFT side of the engine, looking from the front, and the exhaust valves on the RIGHT.

The first step is to turn the crankshaft pulley until the notched line is opposite the "O" mark on the front cover. This will put either the No. 1 or No. 4 piston at Top Dead Center. Once this is done, half the valves will be compressed and the other half, free.

With a flat feeler gauge set the free (uncompressed) valves on the intake (left) side of the engine to 0.006 in. If correctly done, there will be a slight drag on the gauge as it is pulled through. On the exhaust (right) side of the engine set the valves to 0.010 in.

Rotate the crankshaft pulley one complete turn and align the notched mark with the "O" timing indicator. This will decompress the compressed valves and compress the "free" ones. Adjust the clearances to 0.006 for the intake and 0.010 for the exhaust.

Carburetor

The engine is equipped with a Nikki, down-draft, 2-barrel carburetor.

The primary venturi operates at relatively low speed and load. The secondary side opens when engine load and speed are increased. The unit is equipped with an electric automatic choke for easier starting at low temperatures.

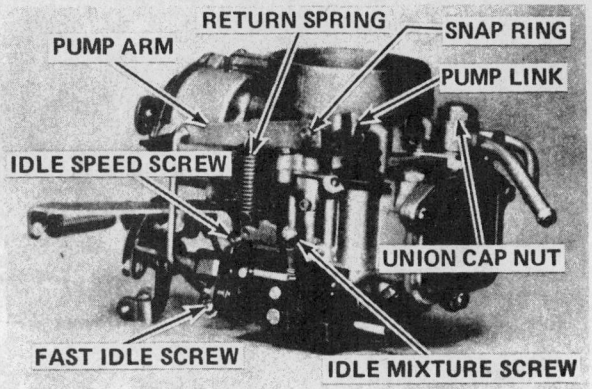

Carburetor adjustments

Idle Speed and Mixture

As with all adjustments made with the engine running, set the parking brake, block the drive wheels and put the transmission in neutral. Warm the engine to operating temperature, check to make sure the choke is open, turn off the air conditioner (if installed), install the air cleaner and disconnect the distributor and idle compensator vacuum line and plug them.

1. Turn the idle mixture adjusting screw all the way in and back it out three (3) turns.

2. Adjust the throttle adjusting screw to 900 RPM.

3. Go back to the idle mixture screw and turn it in and out, until reaching a point where the idle is the highest. Reset the throttle adjusting screw to 900 RPM.

4. Turn the idle mixture adjusting screw clockwise (lean) until down to 850 RPM. Then turn the screw ½ turn clockwise (rich).

5. Reset the throttle adjusting screw to 900 RPM.

6. Reconnect the vacuum lines.

NOTE: *If equipped with air conditioning, add the following steps.*

7. Turn the air conditioning on to maximum and set the blower on high. Open the throttle about 1/3 and allow it to close (this opens the speed-up solenoid).

8. Set idle to 900 RPM with the speed-up controller adjusting screw.

ENGINE ELECTRICAL

Distributor

Removal and Installation

The first step in removing the distributor is to release the cap retaining clips and remove it. At this point you should make note of the position of the rotor, in relation to the engine block, to make installation easier.

Disconnect the hose from the vacuum advance and remove the distributor clamp bolt and clamp. After you have finished these steps you may remove the distributor by lifting it straight out.

The steps to reinstall the unit are just the reverse of removal with a few exceptions.

Rotate the rotor to the same relative position as when you removed it and put the shaft through the hole in the engine block making sure it is aligned with the slot in the oil pump drive shaft. When this is done, install the distributor clamp and bolt, turning it finger tight. Put the distributor cap back on and check for correct dwell and timing as outlined in Tune-up procedures.

Alternator

Precautions

An alternator is a precise piece of equipment and certain precautions must be taken to lessen the possibility of permanent damage.

When making connections always insure against mistakenly reversing the polarity (hooking a "+" wire to a "−" pole) this will cause a short and burn out the diodes.

Do not connect the alternator "B" terminal to a ground. This terminal is connected to the battery and this will cause it to short, burning out the wires.

Whenever charging the battery, always remove the negative cable. Not doing so can burn out the diodes due to the pulse voltage of the charger.

Keep the alternator dry.

Removal and Installation

1. Disconnect the negative cable from the battery.

2. Remove the stone shield and two lower attaching bolts.

3. Remove the horn and disconnect all wiring from the alternator.

4. Remove the top bolt and take off the belt, the adjusting bracket and bolt. You can now remove the alternator.

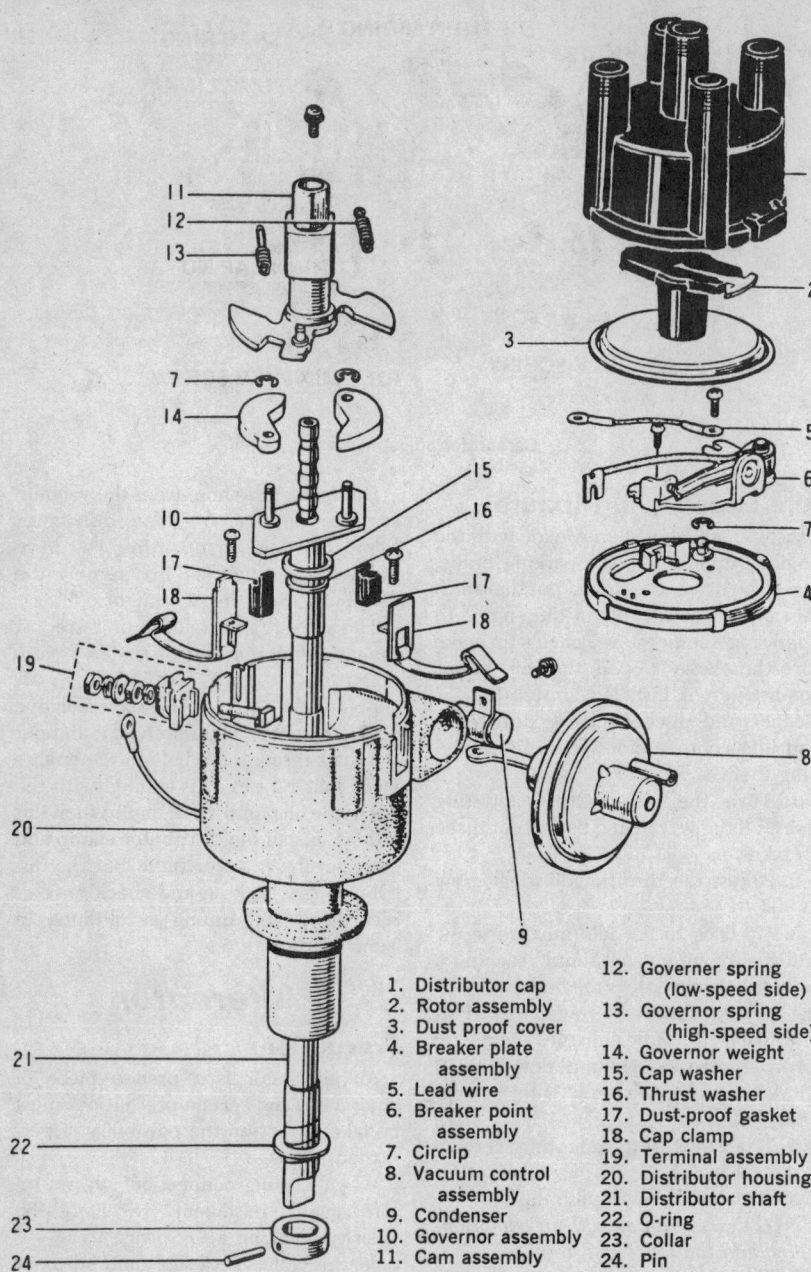

1. Distributor cap
2. Rotor assembly
3. Dust proof cover
4. Breaker plate assembly
5. Lead wire
6. Breaker point assembly
7. Circlip
8. Vacuum control assembly
9. Condenser
10. Governor assembly
11. Cam assembly
12. Governer spring (low-speed side)
13. Governor spring (high-speed side)
14. Governor weight
15. Cap washer
16. Thrust washer
17. Dust-proof gasket
18. Cap clamp
19. Terminal assembly
20. Distributor housing
21. Distributor shaft
22. O-ring
23. Collar
24. Pin

Exploded view of distributor

Air Gap Voltage Adjustment

Connect a voltmeter between the condenser lead and the ground with all electrical loads disconnected including the blower relay connector.

Start the engine and increase engine speed gradually. The voltage should climb with the RPMs up to 1400–1850 RPM. A normal condition is indicated when the voltage is between 13.5 and 14.5 volts.

If the voltage is too high, bend core arm "D" down. If too low, bend the arm up.

If bending the core arm does not correct the voltage difference, go on to a point gap adjustment.

Disconnect the battery ground cable and depress the armature until the moving point contacts "E" side point. Bend point arm "E" to get a gap of 0.012 or more.

Release the pressure and by bending point arm "F" set a distance of 0.012–0.018. After the adjustments are made, recheck the voltage. Repeat, if necessary.

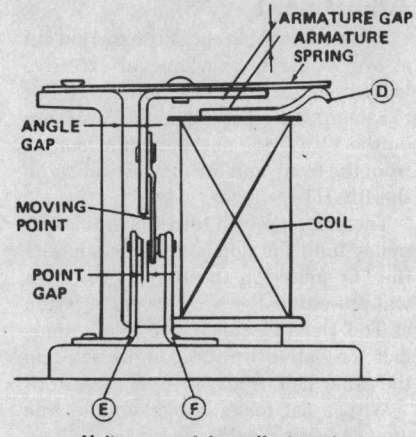

Voltage regulator adjustment

5. Installation is the reverse of this procedure, but you must remember to check the belt tightness by pushing on it with your finger about halfway along its length. The belt should dip about ½ in. where you apply pressure.

Belt Tension Adjustment

If you should notice that your V-belt driving the alternator is slipping you can easily adjust it.

Loosen all attaching bolts and, using your hand or a lever, apply enough pressure to the alternator housing to give the belt about ½ in. play halfway along its length. Before loosening, check the condition of the belt for hardening and cracking. If you find it, replace the belt.

Regulator

The voltage regulator in this installation is a separate unit and not attached to the alternator. The unit actually contains two parts: the voltage regulator and a voltage relay.

Removal and Installation

You will find the voltage regulator protective box behind the windshield washer tank. Removing the two sheet metal screws holding it to the inside of the fender-well will allow you to remove it. Unplug the unit from the harness. Installation is just the reverse.

Starter

Removal and Installation

Without air conditioning, the entire starter removal process may be done through the engine compartment. With air conditioning, you will have to jack the car and, using U-joint and extensions, reach from underneath and over the crossmember and behind the solenoid to remove the starter-to-flywheel-housing nut and washer. Otherwise:

1. Disconnect the negative cable from the battery and the wiring to the solenoid.

2. Remove the starter-to-flywheel-housing top retaining nut and washer and the lower retaining bolt. This will allow you to lift the starter forward, to clear the stud, and remove it from the engine compartment.

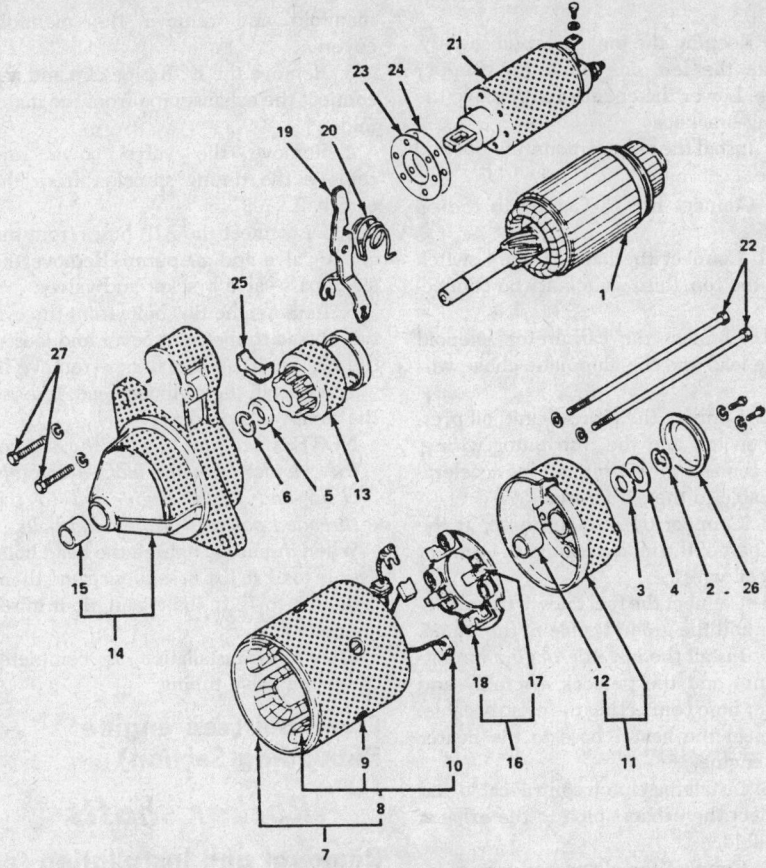

Exploded view of starter

1. Armature assembly
2. Snap ring
3. Thrust washer
4. Thrust washer
5. Retainer
6. Snap ring
7. Yoke assembly
8. Field coil assembly
9. Screw
10. Brush (+)
11. Rear cover assembly
12. Rear cover bushing
13. Pinion assembly
14. Gear case assembly
15. Gear case bushing
16. Brush holder assembly
17. Brush (−)
18. Brush spring
19. Shift lever
20. Torsion spring
21. Magnetic switch
22. Through-bolt
23. Adjustment plate
24. Adjustment plate
25. Dust cover, gear case
26. Dust cover, rear cover
27. Bolt

3. Reverse steps 1 and 2 for installation.

Starter Drive

Removal and Installation

1. Remove solenoid.
2. Pry off dust cover, remove snap ring and washer.
3. Remove the two through bolts.
4. Remove the cover assembly.
5. Separate the yoke and gear case.
6. Remove the armature shift lever.
7. Remove drive assembly snap ring and retainer.
8. Slide drive assembly from shaft.
9. Assembly is the reverse of remove.

NOTE: *when installing armature, set shift lever on lever guide of pinion assembly. Do not turn armature after installation as shift lever may come off guide.*

ENGINE MECHANICAL
Removal and Installation

There are several basic precautions you must take if you plan on removing the engine and transmission.

1. Handle all aluminum alloy parts with extreme care. They are easily damaged.

2. Keep the nut and bolt combinations in separate locations to prevent mixing them. They vary in design and composition, depending on their position and use.

3. Remove and install the engine and transmission as a unit.

Removal

1. Remove the battery cables.
2. Outline the position of the mounting hinges on the hood and remove it.
3. Remove the engine under-cover and drain the cooling system by opening the drains on the radiator and block.
4. Drain the oil from the crankcase.
5. Disconnect all hoses connected to the air cleaner and remove the air cleaner.
6. Disconnect the CCS hose and remove the manifold cover.
7. Unplug the alternator wiring.
8. Disconnect the exhaust pipe from the manifold.
9. Free the clutch control cable by turning the adjusting unit.
10. Disconnect the heater hoses from the engine, and the heater.
11. Remove the cable from the water petcock and remove the petcock and hose.
12. Attach the engine lift brackets to the exhaust manifold stud bolts.
13. Disconnect the ground cable from the frame.
14. Remove fuel hoses from the carburetor.
15. Disconnect all ignition wires.
16. Remove the vacuum hose from the rear part of the intake manifold.
17. Remove the accelerator cable and all wiring from the carburetor.
18. Disconnect the starter motor connections.
19. Disconnect the thermo-unit, and oil pressure switch.
20. Unplug the back-up light switch

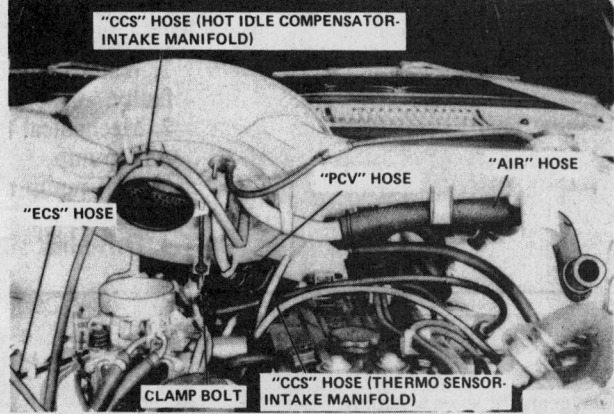

Air cleaner hose connections

and top/third switch (neutral switch wiring for California models) at the rear part of the engine.

21. Remove the ECC hose from the oil pan.

22. Remove the engine mounting nut and stopper plate.

23. Install engine lift brackets using one intake manifold stud bolt and one engine hanger mounting stud.

24. Raise the engine slightly and remove the left side engine mounting stopper plate.

25. Remove the top and lower water hoses from the outlet pipe and radiator, respectively.

26. Remove the nuts holding the radiator and remove it by pulling upwards.

27. From inside the car, remove the bolts holding the gearshift lever and remove the unit.

28. Remove the parking brake return spring.

29. Unbolt the driveshaft at the axle flange and remove it from the vehicle.

20. Remove the clutch cable heat protector.

31. Remove the clutch return spring.

32. Disconnect the clutch cable from the lever and engine torque rod.

33. Remove the exhaust pipe bracket from the transmission.

34. Remove the speedometer cable.

35. Slightly lift the engine and remove the four rear engine mounting bolts.

36. Check to make sure that all connections to the frame have been removed.

37. Lift the engine forward and out of the car.

Installation

Before installing the engine, perform the following steps:

1. Check the electrical harness for damage.

2. Check the engine mount bushings for damage or looseness.

The installation of the engine is basically the reverse of removal.

1. Carefully lower the engine into the engine compartment as shown in the illustration.

2. Keeping the weight off, install the four rear engine mounting bolts.

3. Connect the speedometer cable and install the front side exhaust pipe by connecting the front and rear sides at the joint. Install the front side exhaust pipe bracket to the transmission.

4. Install the clutch control cable. Reconnect the clutch return spring and install the clutch cable heat protector.

5. Install the drive shaft and parking brake spring.

6. Install the gearshift lever assembly, the radiator, and the top and lower water hoses.

7. Keeping the engine raised slightly, install the left side mounting stopper plate. Lower the engine and remove the lifting brackets.

8. Install the engine mounting nut and plate.

9. Connect the ECC hose to the oil pan.

10. Connect the back-up light switch and the top/third switch at the connector.

11. Connect the carburetor solenoid valve lead and the automatic choke wiring.

12. Connect the thermo-unit, oil pressure switch and the distributor wiring. Also connect the starter and the accelerator cable to the carburetor.

13. Connect the vacuum hose, at the rear part of the intake manifold. Connect the coil wires.

14. Connect the fuel lines to the carburetor and the ground cable to the frame.

15. Install the left side engine mounting nut and the petcock assembly and heater hose connecting the control cable. Connect the heater hose to the heater and engine.

16. Install the clutch control cable and connect the exhaust pipe to the exhaust manifold.

17. Connect the alternator wiring, install the manifold cover and reconnect the CCS hot air hose.

18. Connect the CCS hose to the air cleaner. Install the air cleaner. Connect the CCS hose to the manifold and connect the AIR hose to the air pump.

19. Connect the ECS hose to the air cleaner and the PCV hose to the valve cover.

20. Install the under-cover, the hood and connect the battery.

Cylinder Head

Removal and Installation

1. Drain the cooling system and remove the air cleaner.

2. Remove all parts from the intake manifold and remove the manifold cover.

3. Remove the EGR pipe clip and disconnect the exhaust pipe from the manifold.

4. Remove the valve cover and remove the timing sprocket from the camshaft.

5. Disconnect the AIR hoses from the check valve and air pump. Remove the air bypass valve bracket and valve.

6. Remove the two bolts from the cylinder head to the front cover and loosen the head bolts. You may now remove it.

To reinstall the cylinder head, reverse the removal procedures.

NOTE: *Make sure to wipe the faces of the cylinder head and block absolutely clean and apply engine oil to the threaded portions of the head bolts.*

When installing, tighten the head bolts evenly to 61 ft. lbs. in sequence and then, retighten to 72 ft. lbs. Again, do it in sequence.

After the installation is complete, check the valve timing.

Overhaul (see engine Rebuilding Section)

Rocker shafts

Removal and Installation

1. Remove the air cleaner.

2. Disconnect the accelerator control cable from the carburetor.

3. Pull out the clips and ignition wires from the valve cover.

4. Disconnect the AIR hose from the intake manifold and remove the PCV hose. Remove the valve cover.

5. Bring the mark on the camshaft into alignment with the mark on the No. 4 rocker arm shaft by turning the crankshaft.

6. Lock the automatic chain adjuster in position by depressing the slide pin and rotating it 90 degrees.

7. Remove the timing sprocket from the cam along with the chain. Make sure to hold the timing sprocket to the chain,

Aligning marks for camshaft installation

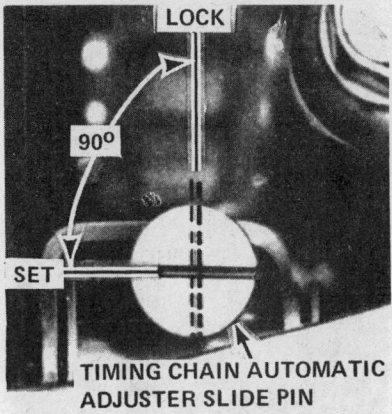

TIMING CHAIN AUTOMATIC ADJUSTER SLIDE PIN

Locking the chain adjuster

keeping it in position.

8. Loosen the nuts holding the rocker arm shaft a little at a time. Loosen them in sequence, starting on the outside. Remove the nuts and rocker assembly.

To install:

1. Apply a good amount of new oil to the cam and bearing faces before attempting installation. Do the same with the rocker arms and shaft.

2. Align the rocker arm shaft brackets with the stud bolts on the head.

NOTE: *Make sure the punch mark at the end of the rocker shaft is pointed upward.*

3. Make sure the mark on the cam and the mark on the No. 4 rocker shaft align.

Tightening bracket nuts

4. Snug-down the rocker arm shaft nuts evenly and then tighten them fully to 16 ft. lbs. Hold the rocker arm springs with an adjustable wrench.

5. Install the timing sprocket by aligning the dowel pin hole and tighten to 58 ft. lbs.

6. Apply liquid gasket to the arched portion of the plugs and install them.

7. Set the automatic chain adjuster by turning the slide pin back 90 degrees (counterclockwise).

NOTE: *After chain adjuster is set, check for proper chain tension.*

8. Adjust the valve clearances and reinstall the remaining parts by reversing their removal.

Intake Manifold
Removal and Installation

1. Remove clips and disconnect water hose.

2. Disconnect accelerator control cable from carburetor.

3. Disconnect vacuum hose from carburetor.

4. Remove PCV hose from cylinder head valve cover.

5. Remove the eight assembly mounting nuts and remove the manifold with the carburetor.

6. Installation is the reverse of removal. Tighten nuts snugly.

Exhaust manifold

1. Disconnect the EGR pipe from the EGR valve and exhaust manifold.

2. Remove the ignition wires from the sparkplugs and pull them away from the engine block, along with the holding clips.

3. Holding the manifold, remove the seven nuts and pull the manifold away from the block.

4. Assembly installation is the reverse of removal. Refer to torque specifications for proper torque amounts.

Crankshaft Pulley and Front Cover

The Isuzu is equipped with a chain-driven, single, over-head cam and the front cover covers almost the entire front of the engine block.

Removal and Installation

1. Remove the fan.

2. Remove the under-cover and remove the crankshaft pulley bolt from under the engine. Remove the pulley together with the pulley boss.

3. Remove the oil filter and the dis-

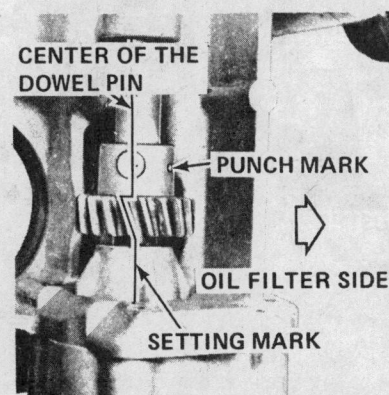

CENTER OF THE DOWEL PIN — **PUNCH MARK**

OIL FILTER SIDE

SETTING MARK

Oil pump alignment for installation of front cover

tributor.

4. Remove the nine cover bolts and pull off the cover, together with the water and oil pumps.

To install:

1. Install a new gasket on the cylinder block.

2. Turn the punch-marked side of the oil pump drive gear to the filter side of the engine. Align the center of the dowel pin with the alignment mark on the oil pump case.

3. Bring pistons No. 1 and 4 to top dead center by aligning the "O" timing mark with the pulley keyway.

4. Attach the front cover by engaging the pinion gear with the oil pump drive gear.

PUNCH MARK

Punch mark in correct position

5. Make sure that the punch mark on the drive gear is turned to the rear, as seen through the gap between the front cover and block.

6. Check that the slit at the end of the oil pump shaft is parallel with the front face of the block and that it is offset forward.

7. After checking for the exact settings, secure the front cover assembly.

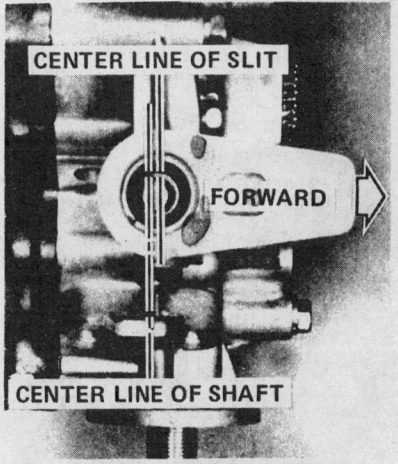

CENTER LINE OF SLIT

FORWARD

CENTER LINE OF SHAFT

Shaft in correct position

Front Cover Oil Seal Replacement

1. Remove the fan, belts and crank

pulley.

2. Pry off the old oil seal.

3. Fill the gap between the lips of the new seal with grease and install the seal to the front cover, using an installer or other suitable tool.

4. Apply oil to the oil seal fitting face of the crank pulley and install, tightening the pulley bolt to 87 ft. lbs.

Timing Chain and Tensioner
Removal

1. Remove front cover.

2. Pull out the crankshaft pinion gear and remove the chain with the camshaft timing sprocket.

3. Remove the two chain guide bolts and remove the guide.

4. Remove the snap rings from both the chain adjuster and tensioner and remove.

Installation

1. Install the guide by aligning the groove in the guide with the cutaway portion of the oil jet.

NOTE: *Check that the oil port in the jet is free of restrictions. The oil jet should be installed so the oil port is pointed in toward the crankshaft.*

2. Assemble the chain tensioner to the set pin and secure it with a snap ring.

3. Assemble the automatic adjuster locking plate with the curved arm as shown in the illustration.

NOTE: *If these parts are not properly assembled, the chain tensioner will not contact the curved arm smoothly.*

4. Connect the automatic adjuster slide pin with the pivot pin so that the slide pin head is turned toward the cylinder head side. Secure with a snap ring.

Sprocket and Chain Installation

1. Turn the crankshaft key to the cylinder head side. Install the timing chain and align the mark plate on the chain

with the aligning mark on the crankshaft sprocket as follows:

a. The side of the chain with the plate must be on the front side of the engine.

b. The part of the chain with the most links between the mark plates, must be positioned toward the chain guide side.

2. Install the camshaft sprocket so the aligning mark side is on the front side of the engine. Align the aligning mark (triangle) with the mark plate.

3. Install the pinion gear to the crankshaft so the groove faces the front cover. Reassemble the front cover, belts and fan.

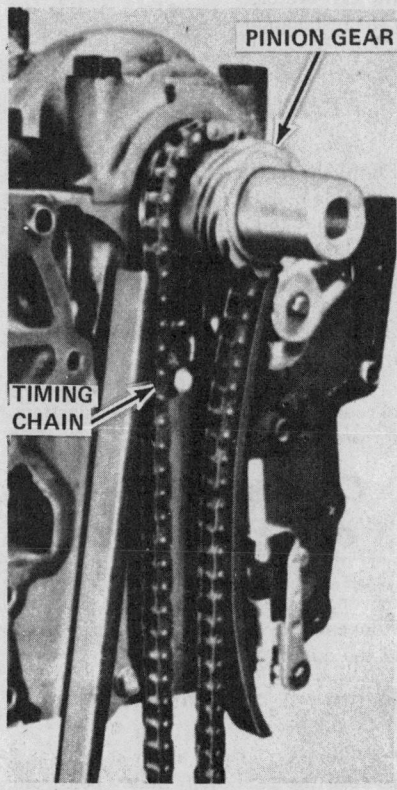

Crankshaft Gear and Timing Chain

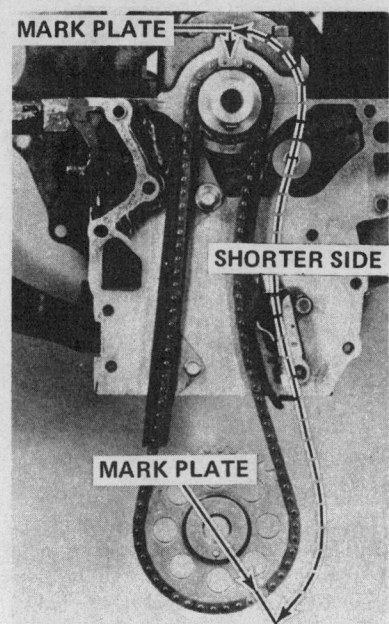

Sprocket and chain installation

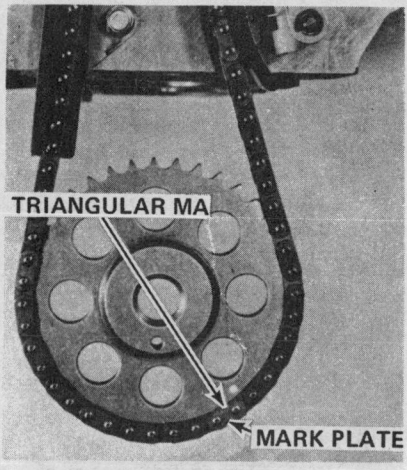

Timing sprocket installation

Camshaft
Removal

1. Remove the air cleaner.

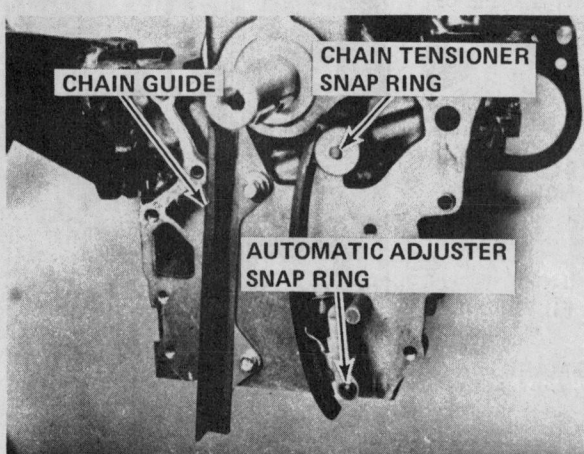

Chain tensioner and adjuster

Chain guide position

2. Disconnect the accelerator control cable.

3. Remove all wires and hoses connected to the valve cover.

4. Disconnect the AIR vacuum hose from the intake manifold.

5. Disconnect the PCV hose, take out the four bolts and remove the valve cover.

6. Turn the crankshaft so that the mark on the camshaft aligns with the mark on the #4 rocker arm shaft.

7. Lock the automatic chain adjuster by depressing the slide pin downward and turning it clockwise 90°.

8. Remove the timing sprocket and chain. Keep the timing chain in position on the sprocket.

9. Loosen the rocker arm bracket bolts a little at a time, starting with the outer ones, and remove the rocker arm assemblies.

10. Remove camshaft from head.

Installation

1. Thoroughly coat all parts with clean engine oil before assembly.

2. Position camshaft on head.

3. Install rocker arm assemblies. Check that the punch mark at the end of the shaft is turned upward.

4. Bring the camshaft mark into alignment with the mark on the #4 rocker bracket by turning the camshaft.

5. Tighten rocker shaft bolts evenly to 16 ft. lb.

6. Align the dowel pin hole and install the timing sprocket and chain on the camshaft. Torque bolt to 58 ft. lb.

7. Apply sealer to the arched portion of the plug and install it in the front of the head.

8. Set the timing chain adjuster by turning the slide pin 90° counterclockwise.

9. Check valve adjustment.

10. Install remaining parts in reverse order of removal.

Pistons and Connecting Rods

Piston and Ring Positions

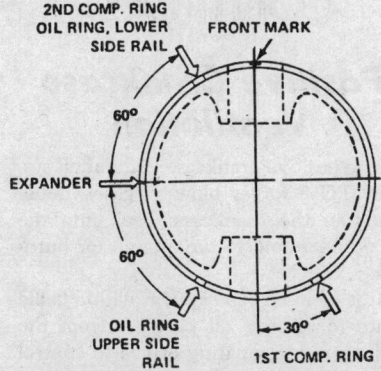

Position of piston rings

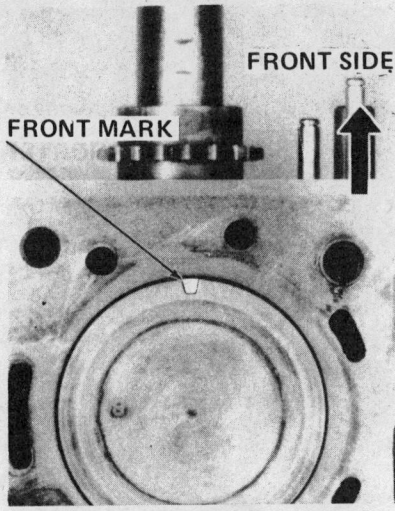

Position of correctly installed piston

ENGINE LUBRICATION
Oil Pan

Removal

1. Remove the oil pressure switch from the block.

NOTE: *If you have an oil pressure gauge, remove the pressure unit and switch, together with the adapter.*

2. Remove the 14 bolts and six nuts in the pan edge and remove. This will expose the two dust cover bolts. Remove them and drop the undercover.

Installation

1. Apply a thin coating of gasket sealer to the areas shown in the illustration.

2. Align the gasket with the bolt holes and install the pan. Tighten the bolts and nuts evenly to 3.6 ft. lbs. Check the edge of the gasket to see it is set correctly.

Rear Main Oil Seal

Replacement

1. Remove the clutch pressure plate assembly.

2. Flatten the flywheel bolt lockplates and remove the flywheel.

3. Using a screwdriver, pry off the oil seal from the retainer.

4. Fill the gap between the lips of the new seal with grease and apply engine oil to the seal fitting face of the crank. Apply a thin coat of oil to the fitting face of the seal, and install the new seal with a setting tool.

NOTE: *After installation, check the flanged part of the seal is properly seated on the retainer.*

5. Install the remaining parts in reverse of removal and, using new lock plates, tighten the flywheel bolts to 60 ft. lbs.

Oil Pump

Removal

Follow procedures for front cover removal, above. Remove pump from cover.

For installation, follow procedure under front cover installation.

NOTE: *When oil pump is installed, the aligning mark on the drive gear is turned rearward and away from the crankshaft by about 20° in a clockwise direction.*

Checking Clearances

1. Measure the tip clearance between the drive rotor and the driven rotor with a feeler gauge. If it exceeds 0.0079 in., replace the unit.

2. Check the clearance between the driven rotor and the wall of the pump body. Replace the assembly if the clearance is 0.0098 in. or more.

3. Using a straight-edge and a feeler gauge, measure the clearance between the drive rotor, the driven rotor and the pump cover. Again, replace the oil pump if the clearance is greater than 0.0079 in.

4. Measure the outside diameter of the drive shaft and the inside diameter of the shaft hole in the pump cover. Compare the two values to get the clearance. If it is more than 0.0098 in., replace the unit.

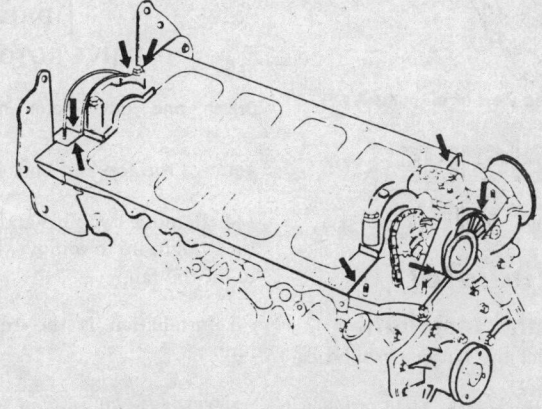

Liquid gasket application points

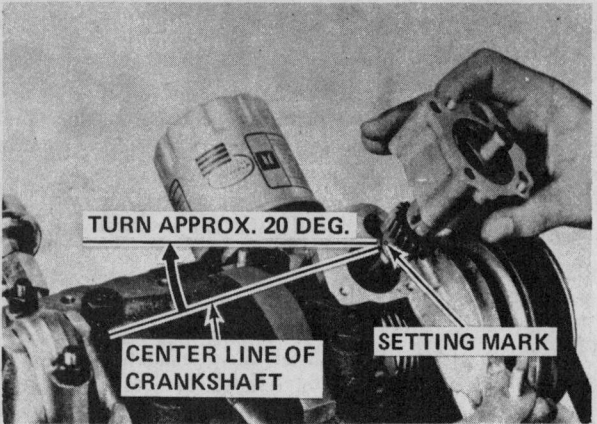

Installing oil pump

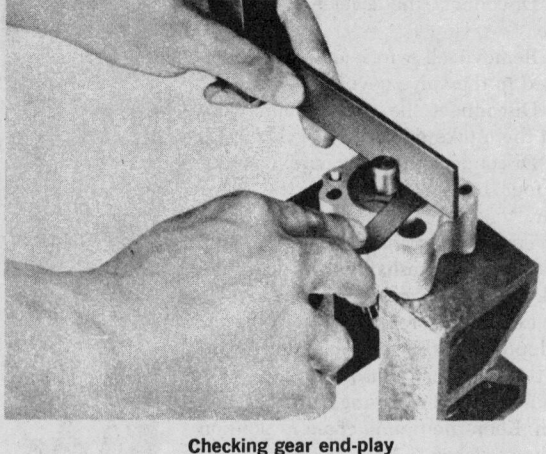

Checking gear end-play

1. Oil pump body
2. Oil pump shaft
3. Drive rotor
4. Straight pin
5. Oil pump gear
6. Straight pin
7. Driven rotor
8. Oil pump cover
9. Relief valve
10. Spring
11. Plug
12. Packing
13. Knock pin

Exploded view of oil pump

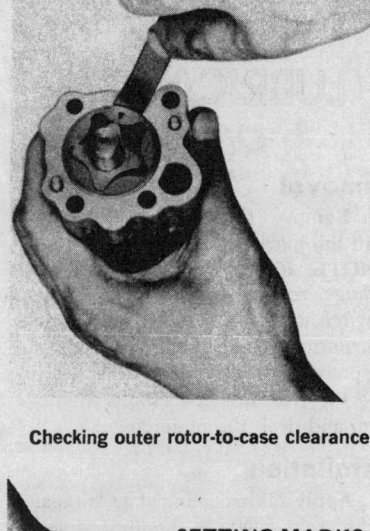

Checking outer rotor-to-case clearance

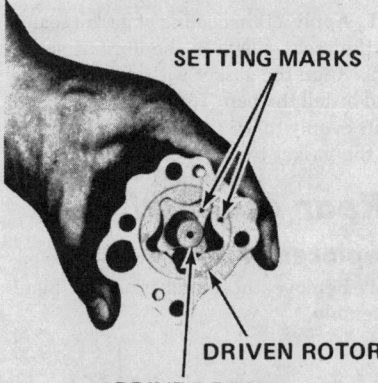

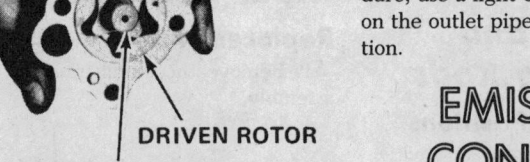

Driven and drive rotor marks aligned

ENGINE COOLING

Radiator

Removal and Installation

1. Disconnect the battery ground cable at the battery.
2. Remove the splash shield (4 bolts).
3. Drain the radiator and loosen and remove the top and bottom hoses.

4. Remove two nuts and lift the radiator straight up to remove. Be careful not to hit the fan.

5. Installation is the reverse procedure.

NOTE: *To fill cooling system, use a 50% water to antifreeze solution.*

Water Pump

Removal and Installation

1. Disconnect battery ground cable.
2. Remove the splash shield (4 bolts).
3. Drain the cooling system and remove the fan (4 nuts).
4. Remove air pump and generator bolts and both drive belts.
5. Remove the fan pulley.
6. Remove the water pump.
7. Installation is the reverse of removal; use a new gasket. Be sure mating surfaces are clean.
8. Adjust belt to give a ½" deflection at the mid-point of its longest straight stretch.

Thermostat

Removal and Installation

1. Remove splash shield and drain cooling system.
2. Remove the air cleaner.
3. Remove the thermostat outlet pipe and water hose and remove the thermostat from the intake manifold.
5. Installation is the reverse procedure; use a light coating of gasket sealer on the outlet pipe gasket before installation.

EMISSION CONTROLS

Positive Crankcase Ventilation

The positive crankcase ventilation system (PCV) forces blow-by gases, generated in the crankcase, back into the intake manifold to the engine for burning.

It is a closed-type system with a baffle plate to remove oil particles from the gases and a regulating orifice to control the amount of suction needed to draw the gases off.

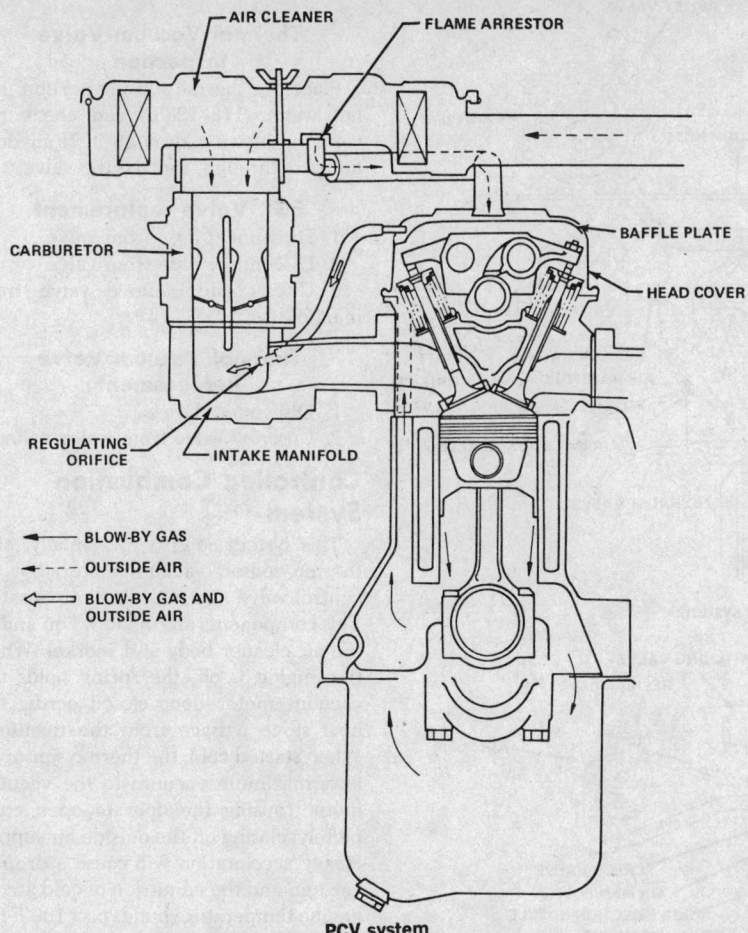

PCV system

The PCV system has no moving parts and any replacement of materials would differ from car to car.

Service

Servicing the Isuzu system is simple. Clean all hoses, inside and out, with detergent oil and blow away any dirt with compressed air.

Check the hoses for cracks, fatigue and swelling. Replace if necessary.

Evaporative Emissions Control System

The evaporative emission control system takes gasoline vapors from the fuel tank into the crankcase for mixture with blow-by gases and burning. The system consists of a vapor separator tank, check and relief valves and the tubes connecting these parts.

The separator tank separates fuel from its vapors and allows it to return to the tank, while moving the vapors to the crankcase.

The check and relief valve serves two purposes. When the engine is not running, the valve opens at a pressure of .2 to .6 in. and allows the vapors into the crankcase.

When the engine is running, the valve keeps a vacuum from building up in the tank by allowing outside air in and, at the same time, moving the vapors along.

Service

Remove check valve and inspect for leaks by blowing air into the ports.

a. When air is forced from the tank side, the valve should allow air to pass into the pan side, but not allow it into the air cleaner side.

b. If air is applied to the pan side it should be restricted.

c. If applied from the air cleaner side, air should pass into the fuel tank side, but not into the crankcase side.

Check rubber hoses for cracks or fatigue and look at the separator tank to see about fuel leaks, distortion or dents. Replace parts as necessary.

Exhaust Emission Control

The Air Injector Reactor (AIR) system is designed to pressurize outside air and inject it through a series of nozzles to a location near the exhaust valves. Because of the temperature of the gases leaving the exhaust chambers, the added air causes a re-ignition and further burning of any unused portions of fuel remaining.

Air Pump

The air pump is equipped with a relief valve and a check valve. The pump should be checked for excess noise and replaced if found to be malfunctioning.

Check Valve

The check valve allows air to enter only from one direction. This protects the air pump and hoses if a belt breaks or in the case of a backfire.

The valve may be checked by removing it from the manifold and blowing air into it from the air pump side. If working properly, air will pass only from the pump side. If air passes from anywhere else, replace valve.

Air Bypass Valve

This valve controls the air flow between the air pump and the manifold. It prevents afterburning and, therefore, backfires, because of rich fuel mixtures.

If the air bypass valve is working normally, excess air continues to blow out of the valve for a few seconds after the accelerator is depressed and released. If air

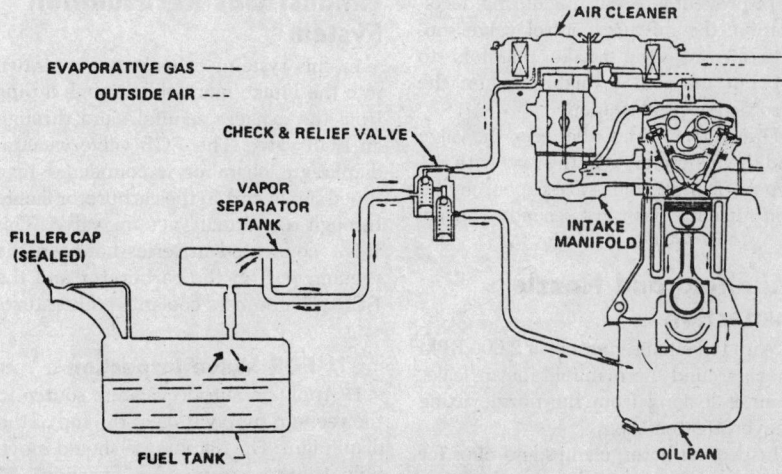

Evaporative emission control system

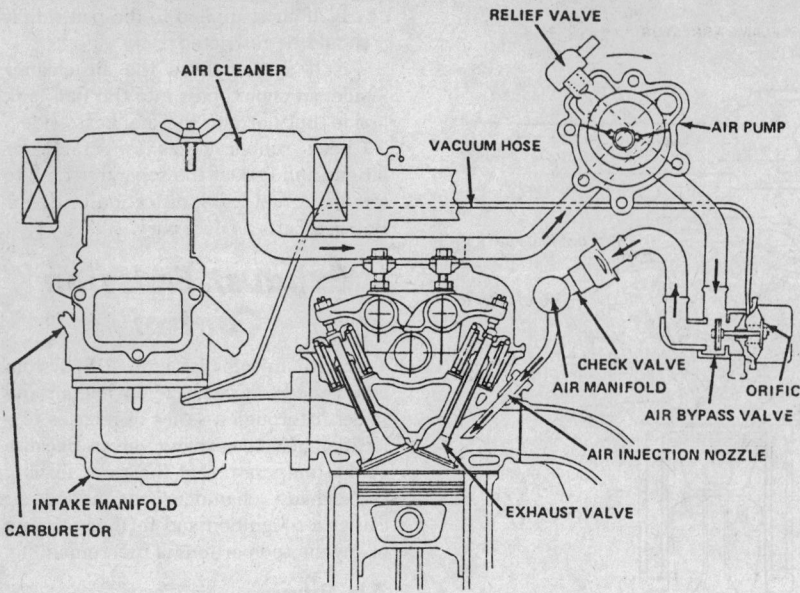

Air Injector Reactor system

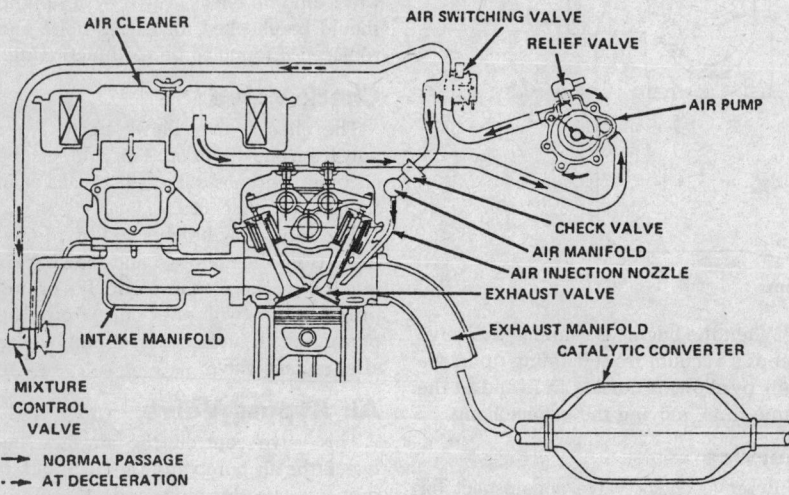

→ NORMAL PASSAGE
⇢ AT DECELERATION

Air Injector Reactor system (California)

should continue to escape for five seconds or more, replace the valve.

Mixture Control Valve

To prevent afterburning during deceleration, the mixture control valve supplies air into the intake manifold to prevent too rich a mixture when the throttle is closed suddenly.

Disconnect the hose between the valve and the manifold. As in the case with the bypass, if air continues to escape from the unit for more than five seconds, replace it.

Manifold and Nozzle Inspection

With the engine running at 2,000 RPM check around the manifold for air leaks. If air is leaking from the nozzle fixing sleeves, tighten them.

Inspect all hoses, clamps and clips for cracks and fatigue. Make sure the hoses do not contact any other parts.

Exhaust Emission Control

Exhaust Gas Recirculation System

In this system, exhaust gas is drawn into the intake manifold through a pipe from the exhaust manifold and through an EGR valve. The EGR valve vacuum diaphragm chamber is connected to a timed signal port in the carburetor flange through a thermal vacuum valve. This valve, connected in series between the vacuum port in the carburetor and the EGR valve, senses coolant temperature.

EGR Valve Inspection

1. Apply an outside vacuum source to the vacuum supply tube at the top of the diaphragm. The diaphragm should move fully to the up position at about 8" vacuum.

Thermal Vacuum Valve Inspection

Place the thermo sensing portion into hot water (118–126°F) and check the valve by blowing through it. If air does not pass through, replace the valve.

EGR Valve replacement

1. Disconnect hose from valve.
2. Disconnect pipe from valve.
3. Unbolt and remove valve from manifold.

Thermal Vacuum Valve Replacement

1. Disconnect hoses.
2. Unscrew valve from water gallery.

Controlled Combustion System

This system consists, principally, of a thermo sensor, vacuum motor, hot air control valve and hot idle compensator. This components are mounted on and in the air cleaner body and snorkel. When the engine is off, the spring holds the vacuum motor door closed across the heat stove passage from the manifold. When started cold, the thermo sensor allows maximum vacuum to the vacuum motor causing the door to open completely, closing off the outside air supply. Heavy acceleration will cause a drop in vacuum and the admission of cold air. As engine temperature builds past 100°F the door will begin to close over the heat stove passage. At 111°F, the door should be completely closed. During heat build-up, excessive fuel vapors will enter the intake manifold. To prevent rough idle and increased emissions, the air cleaner is equipped with a hot idle compensator. The compensator opens to feed cold air into the manifold to temporarily lean out the mixture.

Inspection

Little maintenance is necessary other than checking and cleaning, if necessary, the viscous type air filter element. This should be done every 30,000 miles.

Coasting Richer System

This system allows for enrichment of the fuel mixture during engine coasting. It consists of a solenoid valve coupled with one of the following equipment groups:

Non-California manual transmission—accelerator switch, clutch switch, transmission 4th/3rd gear switch.

California manual transmission—accelerator switch, clutch switch, transmission neutral switch, engine speed sensor.

California automatic transmission—accelerator switch, inhibitor switch, engine speed sensor. The system is not used on non-California automatic transmission models.

When all the switches in a system are on, the solenoid valve and magnet on the secondary side of the carburetor become energized and cause the valve to open. Fuel is drawn out of the float bowl and is metered through the coasting jet and mixed with air through the coasting bleed. The mixture is supplied, through the coasting valve into the secondary part of the throttle valve.

Inspection

Engine Speed Sensor

Disconnect the speed sensor wiring and, using jumpers, connect terminals B BR and BY to each other. Start the engine and check for continuity among the terminals. Continuity should exist at between 1500 and 1700 rpm.

Accelerator Switch and Clutch Switch

1. Check setting of accelerator switch and clutch switch. A clearance of 0.04" should exist between the accelerator switch and the accelerator pedal. A clearance of 0.02–0.04" should exist between the clutch switch and the clutch pedal.

2. Operate the pedals. Both switches are normal if they are on when the pedal is released and off when the pedal is depressed.

Transmission Switch (non-Cal.) or Neutral Switch (Cal.)

1. Disconnect the switch wiring and connect a test light.

2. Move the lever to 4th or 3rd gear (non-Cal.) or neutral (Cal.). The switch is normal if it turns on in either of these positions.

Catalyst Over-heat Control System

When the catalyst temperature reaches 1350°F due to high speed or high load driving, the secondary air from the air injection system is diverted to the atmosphere to reduce chemical reaction in the catalyst. When the catalyst temperature exceeds 1850°F, due to a system malfunction, a warning lamp and buzzer are turned on.

The system consists of a vacuum switching valve, an air switching valve and a thermo sensor and thermo controller.

Inspection

Vacuum Switching Valve

Using jumpers, connect the switch directly to a power source. Listen for the plunger to move while energizing the switch.

Air Switching Valve

Energize the vacuum switching valve as in the previous test. If the air switching valve is normal, secondary air will blow from the air switching valve.

Thermo Sensor

Run the engine at idle for a few minutes, then disconnect the switch wiring. Check for continuity across the terminals of the switch. If no continuity exists, replace the switch.

Thermo Controller

If the converter warning light and buzzer operate for a few seconds when the key is turned to ON, the controller is normal.

Throttle Closing Dashpot (Non-Cal. Manual Trans.)

The dashpot is a diaphragm device used to prevent the throttle from closing too rapidly on deceleration.

Inspection and Adjustment

Check for smooth operation of the shaft and for cracks or deterioration of the rubber boot.

To adjust:

1. Loosen the lock nut and screw the unit all the way in a counterclockwise direction.

2. Start engine and run at 2600–3000 rpm. Turn the dashpot clockwise until the shaft comes into contact with the throttle lever. Tighten the lock nut.

FUEL SYSTEM

Fuel Filter Replacement

The filter should be replaced every 15,-000 miles of operation. Disconnect the inlet and outlet fuel lines from the filter and replace it with a new one.

Electric Fuel Pump

The fuel pump is located near the bottom of the tank to insure proper fuel delivery during hard cornering. It is a motor-driven, centrifugal type.

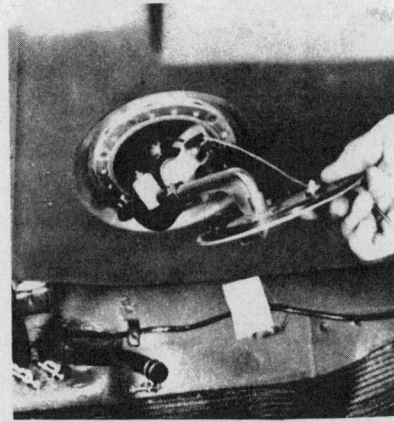

Removing fuel pump

Removal and Installation

1. Disconnect the fuel return hose from pipe and drain.

2. Remove the fuel tank and fuel pipe covers.

3. Disconnect the fuel hose and the pump wiring. Remove the attaching screws (9) and take out the assembly.

4. Installation is the reverse of removal.

Adjustments

Repair or adjustments are not possible. Replace if defective.

Testing

NOTE: *Do not run pump when disconnected from fuel supply.*

To test for pressure of delivery, you should:

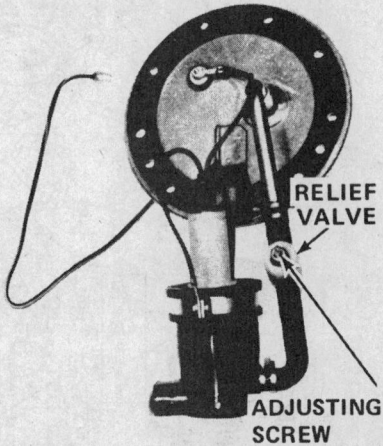

Fuel pump relief valve and adjusting screw

1. Disconnect main fuel line at the carburetor and connect a fuel pump tester with a three-way connector.

2. Start the engine and read the tester.

3. Fuel pump pressure should be 3.3 psi. If it deviates from this, remove the pump and adjust the relief valve.

   a. Loosen the locknut and turn the screw clockwise to increase the pressure and counterclockwise to decrease.

Carburetor

Removal and Installation

1. Remove the air cleaner and CCS hose from carburetor.

2. Disconnect the fuel lines at both the main and return side joints and disconnect the vacuum advance and EGR vacuum hoses.

3. Disconnect the accelerator cable from the throttle lever and disconnect the automatic choke and solenoid valve wiring at connector.

4. Remove the clip from the water outlet pipe. An angled wrench will be necessary to remove the carburetor mounting nuts.

5. Installation is the reverse of re-

Opel Isuzu

An angled wrench is necessary to remove the carburetor nuts

moval.

NOTE: *After installation, check for leaks and check that the accelerator cable is within specifications. Adjust engine idle after warm up.*

Overhaul

All Types

Efficient carburetion depends greatly on careful cleaning and inspection during overhaul, since dirt, gum, varnish, water in or on the carburetor parts are mainly responsible for poor performance.

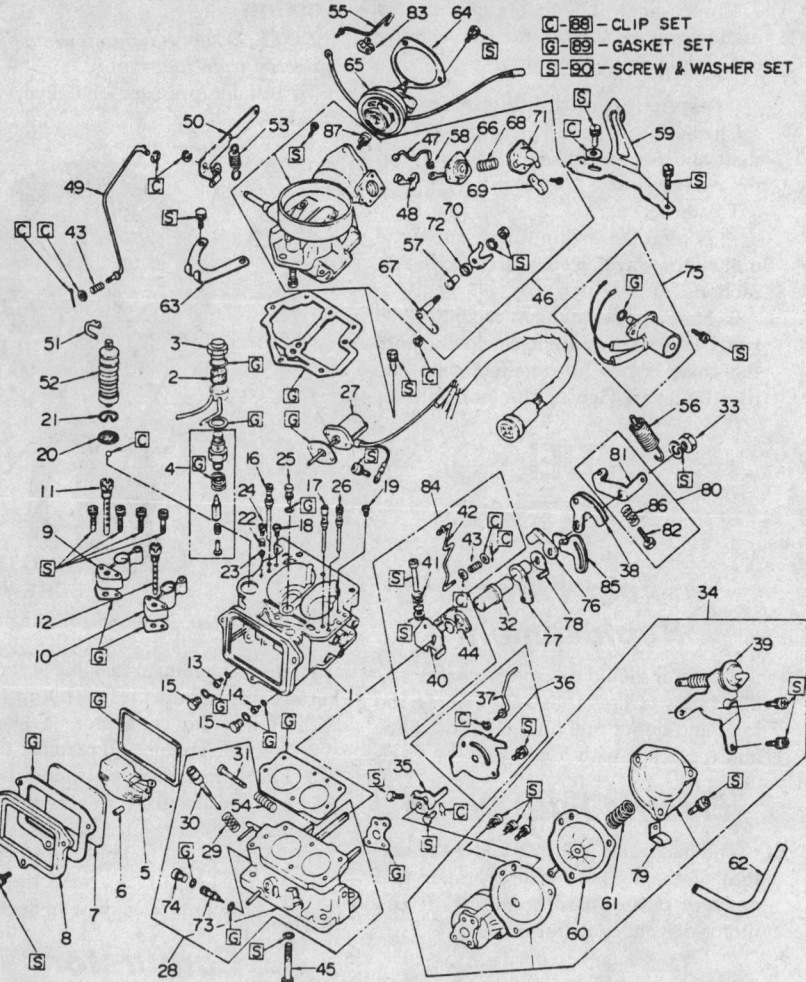

Exploded view of the Nikki carburetor

45. Bolt
46. Air horn assembly
47. Choke diaphragm rod
48. Link holder
49. Pump connecting rod
50. Pump arm
51. Pump link
52. Accelerator pump plunger
53. Pump arm return spring
54. Throttle adjust screw spring
55. Choke piston link
56. Throttle return spring
57. Tape bearing bushing
58. Teflon bushing
59. Throttle return spring hanger
60. Diaphragm
61. Diaphragm spring
62. Automatic choke vacuum hose
63. Clamp
64. Thermostat case cover
65. Thermostat case
66. Automatic choke diaphragm
67. Select arm lever
68. Automatic choke diaphragm spring
69. Lead wire clip
70. Select arm
71. Automatic choke diaphragm cover
72. Washer
73. Idle nozzle
74. Idle nozzle plug
75. Coasting richer solenoid (except federal, A/T)
76. Dash pot arm (only for M/T)
77. Throttle valve cable lever (only for A/T)
78. Throttle valve cable stopper (only for A/T)
79. Lead wire clip
80. Fast idle lever assembly
81. Fast idle lever
82. Speed up controller adjusting screw
83. Link holder
84. Throttle adjust arm assembly
85. Primary throttle arm
86. Speed up controller adjusting spring
87. Screw & washer
88. Clip set
89. Gasket set
90. Screw & washer set

1. Body assembly
2. Strainer
3. Union cap nut
4. Float valve
5. Float assembly
6. Float pin collar
7. Glass
8. Float chamber cover
9. Primary small venturi
10. Secondary small venturi
11. Primary main air bleed
12. Secondary main air bleed
13. Primary main jet
14. Secondary main jet
15. Main passage plug
16. Slow jet
17. Step jet
18. Slow air bleed
19. Step air bleed
20. Accelerator pump strainer
21. Strainer clip
22. Discharge check valve spring
23. Discharge check valve
24. Outlet valve plug
25. Power valve jet
26. Coasting jet (except federal, A/T)
27. Anti-dieseling solenoid
28. Flange assembly
29. Idle adjust screw spring
30. Idle adjust screw
31. Throttle adjust screw
32. Throttle shaft sleeve
33. Throttle shaft nut
34. Diaphragm chamber assembly
35. Secondary throttle shaft arm
36. Secondary throttle return arm
37. Throttle link
38. Throttle wire lever
39. Choke piston assembly
40. Choke piston arm
41. Fast idle adjust spring
42. Select lever rod
43. Select lever rod spring
44. Select lever

NOTE:
A/T . . . . . Automatic Transmission Models
M/T . . . . . Manual Transmission Models

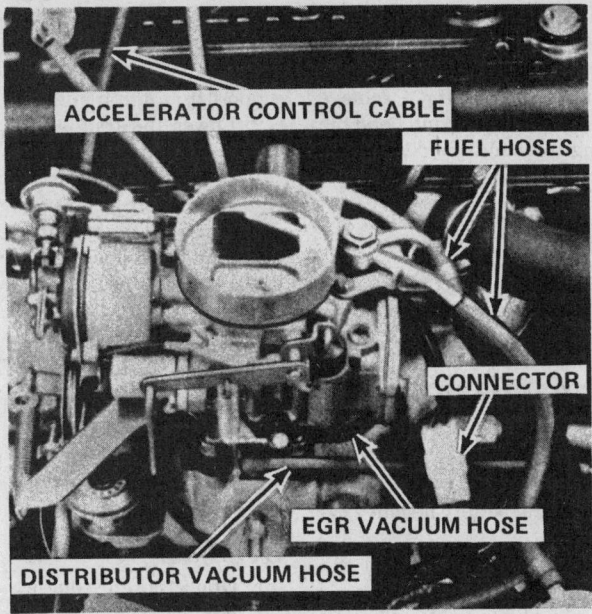

Carburetor removal

Carburetor overhaul should be performed in a clean, dust-free area. Carefully disassemble the carburetor, keeping look-alike parts segregated. Note all jet sizes.

Once the carburetor is disassembled, wash all parts (except diaphragms, electric choke units, pump plunger and any other plastic, leather or fiber parts) in clean carburetor solvent. Do not leave the parts in solvent any longer than necessary to sufficiently loosen the deposits. Excessive cleaning may remove the special finish from the float bowl and choke valve bodies, leaving them unfit for service. Rinse all parts in clean solvent and blow dry with compressed air. Wipe all plastic, leather or fiber parts with a clean, lint-free cloth.

Blow out all passages and jets with compressed air and be sure there are no restrictions or blockages. Never use wire to clean jets, fuel passages or air bleeds.

Check all parts for wear or damage. If wear or damage is found, replace the complete assembly. Especially check the following:

1. Check the float and needle seat for wear. If any is found, replace the assembly.

2. Check the float hinge pin for wear and the floats for distortion or dents. Replace the float if fuel has leaked into it.

3. Check the throttle and choke shaft bores for out-of-round. Damage or wear to the throttle arm, shaft or shaft bore will often require replacement of the throttle body. These parts require close tolerances and air leaking here can cause poor starting and idling.

4. Inspect the idle mixture adjusting needles for burrs or grooves. Burrs or grooves will usually require replacement of the needles since a satisfactory idle cannot be obtained.

5. Test the accelerator pump check valves. They should pass air one way but not the other. Test for proper seating by blowing and sucking on the valve. If the valve is satisfactory, wash the valve again to remove breath moisture.

6. Check the bowl cover for warping, with a straightedge.

7. Closely inspect the valves and seats for wear or damage, replacing as necessary.

8. After the carburetor is assembled, check the choke valve for freedom of operation.

Carburetor overhaul kits are recommended for each overhaul. These kits contain all gaskets and new parts to replace those that deteriorate most rapidly. Failure to replace all parts supplied with the kit (especially gaskets) can result in poor performance later.

Some carburetor manufacturers supply overhaul kits of three types—minor repair, major repair and gasket kits. They basically consist of:

Minor Repair Kits:
  All gaskets

  Float needle valve
  Volume control screw
  All diaphragms
  Pump diaphragm spring
Major Repair Kits:
  All jets and gaskets
  All diaphragms
  Float needle valve
  Volume control screw
  Pump ball valve
  Main jet carrier
  Float
  Complete intermediate rod
  Intermediate pump lever

Complete injector tube
Assorted screws and washers
Gasket Kits:
  All gaskets.

After cleaning and checking all components, reassemble the carburetor using new parts and using the exploded views if necessary. Make sure that all screws and jets are tight in their seats, but do not overtighten, or the tips will be distorted. Do not tighten needle valves into their seats or uneven jetting will result. Always use new gaskets and adjust the float.

Fuel Level

Fuel level in the Nikki carburetor can be seen through an access window on the float bowl. The fuel should always be at the level mark, whether the engine is running or not.

To adjust the level, you must add gaskets to increase, or remove them to decrease.

Fast Idle Adjustment

To adjust the fast idle you must use a gauge constructed as indicated in the illustration. Use it to check the opening angle of the trotle valve when the choke is closed. If the angle is wrong, adjust with the fast idle adjusting screw.

Throttle Plate Angles

To check the relative angles between the primary and secondary throttle

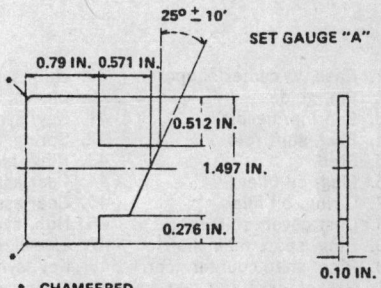

Dimensions of set gauge "A"

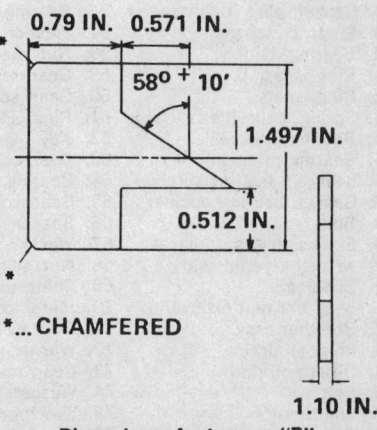

Dimensions of set gauge "B"

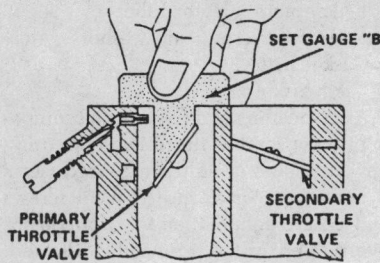

Checking relative angles of throttle valves

PRIMARY THROTTLE VALVE

SECONDARY THROTTLE VALVE

SET GAUGE "B"

valves you must use a set gauge, labeled "B". Construct it as shown.

Gradually open the primary throttle valve until the secondary begins to open. Check the angle of the primary valve with "B" and, if the angle is incorrect, adjust by bending the throttle link.

Automatic Choke Adjustment

1. Align the mark on the choke cover with the mark on the choke case, then tighten the three retaining screws.

2. With the bimetal lever held against the stopper, check that the choke piston stroke is within range of 3/16–7/32". If not, adjust by bending the piston link.

Choke Unloader Adjustment

1. Open throttle valve fully while holding down on choke valve.

2. Choke valve should be forced open part way.

3. Using a wire or drill gauge, measure the distance between the air horn wall and the lower edge of the choke valve. The gap should be 0.215". If not, remove the choke heater coil cover and bend the unloader tang to obtain the correct setting.

MANUAL TRANSMISSION
4-Speed Transmission

Removal

1. Disconnect the battery negative cable.

2. From inside the car, remove the shift lever assembly.

3. Loosen the clutch cable adjusting nuts at the left side of the engine compartment.

4. Remove the upper starter bolt and disconnect the wiring.

5. Remove the drive shaft and disconnect the speedometer cable.

6. Remove the clutch cable heat shield and cable. Remove the lower starter bolt and remove the unit.

7. Disconnect the exhaust pipe from the manifold and remove the flywheel inspection cover.

8. Remove the transmission rear support mounting bolt. Supporting the transmission under the case, remove the rear support from the frame.

9. Lower the transmission, leaving it about four inches lower than mounted.

10. Disconnect the backup light and CRS switch wires.

11. Remove the transmission housing-to-engine block bolts and move the unit straight back and lower away from the car.

Installation

Lubricate drive gear shaft with light coating of grease and reverse steps 1 through 11 of the removal procedure. Adjust the clutch and fill transmission with SAE 30 engine oil.

Overhaul

1. Drain transmission.

2. Remove the release bearing and yoke.

3. Remove the drive gear bearing retainer and the Belleville spring.

4. Remove the bolt, retainer and speedometer gear and remove the shift lever quadrant from the housing.

5. Remove the CRS (Coasting Richer System) switch and backup light switch from the quadrant.

6. Remove the extension housing and then the reverse idler gear and thrust washers.

1. Case, w/center support
2. Pin, guide
3. Bearing, needle
4. Plug, shift rod
5. Stud.
6. Plug, oil filler
7. O-ring, oil filler
8. Dust cover, shift fork
9. Ring, snap, mainshaft
10. Ring, snap counter gear
11. Gasket, case and rear cover
12. Ball stud
13. Washer, lock
14. Washer, plain
15. Plug, screw
16. Gasket, plug (Calif. spec.)
17. Plug, screw (Calif. spec.)
18. Gasket, plug (Calif. spec.)
19. Shaft, clutch gear
20. Bearing, ball
21. Ring, snap
22. Ring, snap
23. Spring, belleville
24. Bearing, needle
25. Bearing retainer
26. Seal, oil, bearing retainer
27. Gasket, bearing retainer
28. Bolt
29. Extension Assy., rear, w/bushing and seal
30. Bushing
31. Seal, oil, rear extension
32. Breather assy.
33. Plug, oil drain
34. O-ring, oil drain
35. Bolt
37. Shaft main
38. Ring, snap
39. Hub, synchronizer, 3rd-4th
40. Sleeve, synchronizer
41. Key, synchronizer
42. Spring, synchronizer
43. Ring, blocker
44. Gear assy., 3rd
45. Gear assy., 2nd
46. Hub, synchronizer, 1st-2nd
47. Sleeve, synchronizer
48. Key, synchronizer
49. Spring, synchronizer
50. Ring blocker
51. Gear assy., 1st
52. Bearing, needle, 1st
53. Bearing, needle, 2nd
54. Collar, needle bearing
55. Washer, thrust, 1st
56. Bearing, mainshaft
57. Washer, lock, mainshaft
58. Nut, mainshaft
59. Gear, reverse
60. Gear, speed drive
61. Ring, snap, drive gear
62. Key
63. Gear, counter
64. Bearing, angular ball
65. Gear, counter reverse
66. Spacer
67. Washer, plain
68. Nut, self lock
69. Shaft, reverse idle
70. Plate, lock
71. Bolt, lock
72. Washer, spring
73. Gear, reverse idle
74. Washer, thrust
75. Synchronizer assy., 3rd-4th
76. Synchronizer assy., 1st-2nd

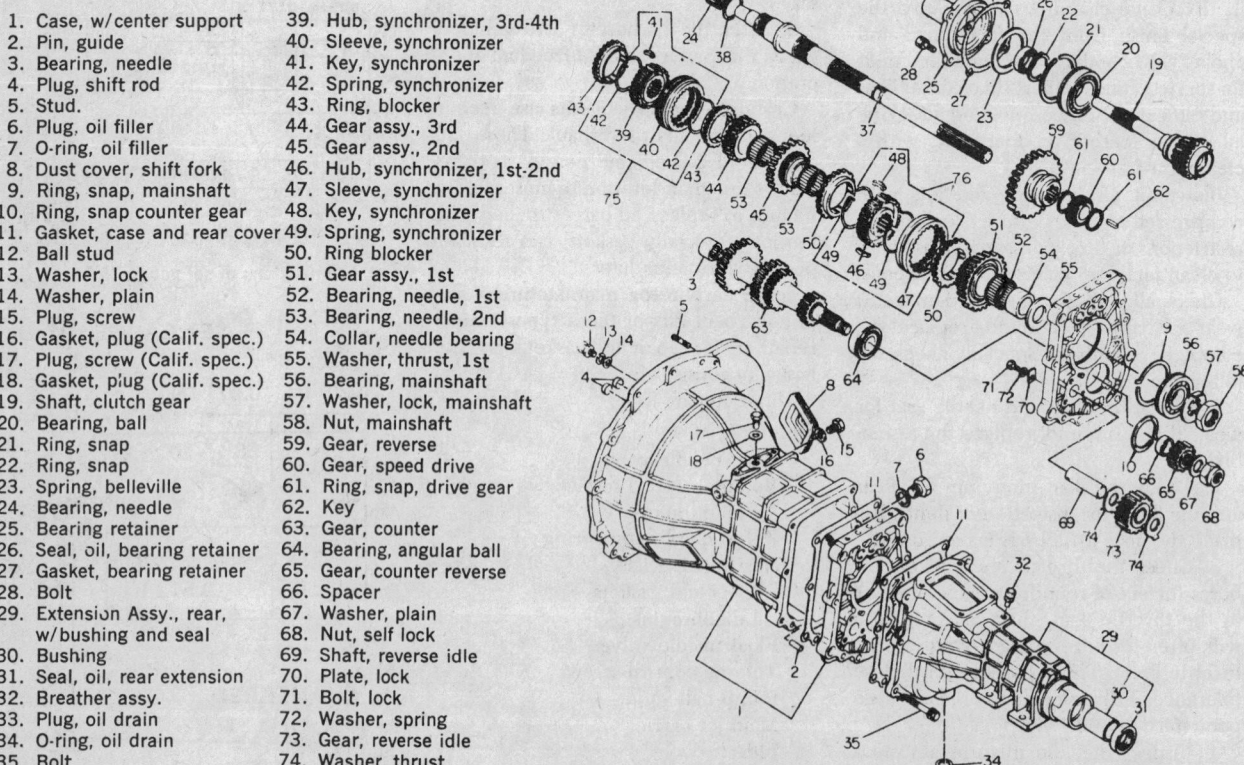

Izuzu 4-speed manual transmission

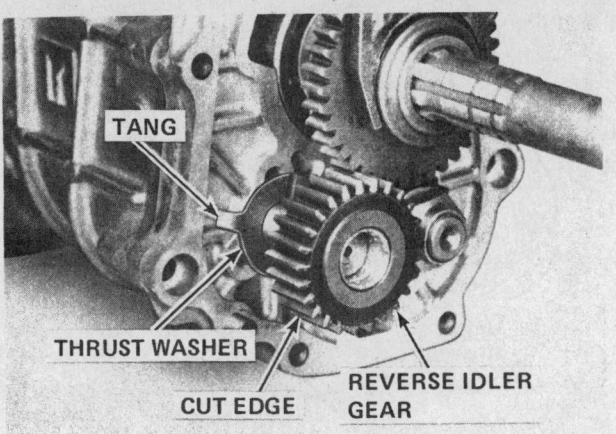

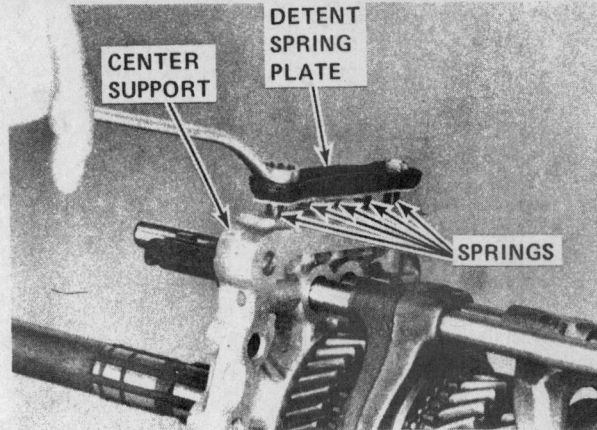

Remove reverse idler gear after removing the extension housing

Removing the detent plate

7. Remove the snap ring, speedometer drive gear and key and, using a punch, drive the retaining pin from the reverse shift fork and remove from the shaft.

8. Remove the center support, along with the mainshaft, countergear, and drive gear. Drive the retaining pins from the 1st, 2nd, 3rd and 4th shift yokes. Support the end of the shafts with a bar or a block of wood.

9. Remove the detent spring and remove the plate, gasket, three springs and detent balls.

10. Remove the shifter shafts from the center support and remove the shift forks and interlock pins.

11. Put the 1st and 2nd synchronizer in 1st. And the 3rd and 4th in 3rd. This step is necessary to prevent the mainshaft and countergear from turning and allows the lock nuts to be removed.

12. Hold the end of the drive gear shaft and bend the locking retainer back to remove the mainshaft nut and retainer.

13. Remove the nut, washer, counter-reverse gear and spacer from the shaft.

14. Put the synchronizers back to the neutral position and remove the drive gear, needle bearing and blocker ring from the mainshaft.

15. Expand the countergear bearing snap ring and tap on the front of the center support and remove. Expand the mainshaft bearing snap ring and move the shaft inward to remove the countergear and shaft.

16. Press out the mainshaft rear bearing. Remove the thrust washer, 1st speed gear, needle bearings, blocker ring and spacer.

17. Remove 1st and 2nd synchronizer, 2nd gear and needle bearings.

18. Remove the snap ring at the front of the 3rd and 4th synchronizer and remove the synchronizer. Remove the 3rd gear and needle bearing.

19. Remove the snap ring from the drive shaft, and, using a press, remove the drive gear bearing.

20. Press out the counterbearing in the same way as the drive gear.

21. To remove the extension housing rear seal, pry with a screwdriver.

22. Remove the drive gear retainer seal in the same way.

Assembly

1. Install the 3rd gear with coned side towards the front of the transmission and the needle bearings on the front of the mainshaft.

2. Put the 3rd and 4th synchronizer on the mainshaft with the large end towards the front. Put in the snap ring.

3. Install 2nd gear with the coned end toward the rear and the needle bearings on the rear of the mainshaft.

4. Put the 1st and 2nd synchronizer on the mainshaft with the large end toward the front and install the spacer, blocker ring needle bearings and 1st gear in the same direction.

5. Press the bearing (rear) onto the mainshaft with the groove toward the front.

6. If the countergear, mainshaft snap rings, and the reverse idler shaft and retainer were removed from the center support, install them and tighten the bolt to 14 ft. lbs.

7. Put the drive gear on the mainshaft and engage it with the countergear. Place the center support onto the mainshaft.

8. Hold the end of the drive gear shaft and countergear. Position the center support along the mainshaft and put a snap ring into the bearing groove.

9. Put the 1st and 2nd synchronizers into 1st gear and the 3rd and 4th into 3rd. This will stop the mainshaft and countergear from turning while you install the locking nuts.

10. Install the spacer, counter-reverse gear washer and nut to the countergear shaft. Tighten the nut to 108 ft. lbs.

11. Install the locking retainer and the mainshaft nut. The chamfered side of the nut should be towards the front of the transmission. Tighten the nut to 94 ft. lbs. and lock into place.

12. Install the stop pin on the reverse shaft so the pin is equally exposed on both sides. Then install the reverse shifter from the front of the center support.

13. Grease the interlock pins and install them. Place the shift fork into position on the synchro sleeves. Install the 3rd and 4th shifter shaft from the rear of the center support through the shift fork. Then install the 1st-2nd shaft in the same way, through the 1st and 2nd shift fork.

14. Install the detent balls, springs, gasket and detent spring plate in the center support. Tighten the bolts to 14 ft. lbs.

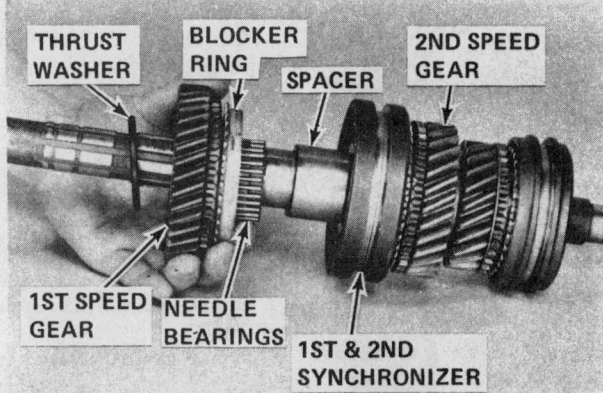

Assembled view of the mainshaft

15. Install the retaining pins in the 3rd, 4th, 2nd and 1st shift forks into the shafts. Make sure to support the ends of the shafts with a bar or a block of wood.

16. Lubricate the countergear bearing and install it. Use the proper-sized socket to contact the outer race. Place a gasket on the transmission case and install the center support into the case. Put a snap ring on the drive gear shaft bearing.

17. Install the fork on the reverse gear and place them on the main and reverse shafts. Install the retaining pin in the reverse shift fork and shifter shaft.

18. Install the front reverse idler thrust washer, with tang inward, in position on the center support.

19. Install the speedometer drive gear snap ring and key. Align the groove in the speedometer gear with the key and push on. Then install the rear snap ring.

20. Install the reverse idler gear thrust washer in the extension housing with the tang inward. Retain the washer with grease. Install a gasket on the center support and install the housing on the support and case. Tighten the bolts to 27 ft. lbs.

21. Put in a new gasket and install the shift lever quadrant to the housing. Tighten the bolts to 10 ft. lbs. Install the speedometer-driven gear.

22. Install the CRS and back-up light switches and the Belleville spring with the dished side toward the gear bearing.

23. Put in a bearing retainer gasket and the retainer. Tighten the bolts to 14 ft. lbs. Seal the lower left bolt with Permatex. Install the release bearing and yoke assembly.

Bolt Tightening Specifications

Countergear to Center Support 108 ft. lb.

Reverse Idler Shaft to Center Support .... 14 ft. lb.

Mainshaft to Center Support 94 ft. lb.

Extension Housing to Case.... 27 ft. lb.

Shift Quadrant to Extension Housing 10 ft. lb.

Drive Gear Retainer to Case 14 ft. lb.

Detent Spring Plate to Center Support .... 14 ft. lb.

Shift Linkage Adjustment

1. Remove the nut and lever from the manual shaft.

2. Place the transmission in neutral.

3. Place the shifter in neutral.

4. Loosen the locknut on the shift rod and adjust the lever until it lines up with the shaft.

5. Install the lever on the shaft and tighten the locknut. Check shift patterns.

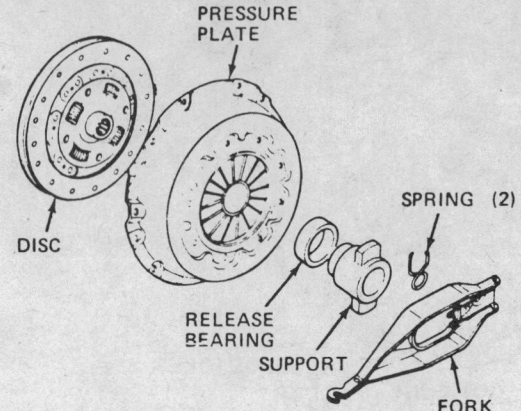

Exploded view of the clutch

CLUTCH

Removal and Installation

1. Remove the transmission.

2. Loosen the clutch pressure plate bolts gradually until all pressure is released and slip the pressure plate and disc from the flywheel.

3. Check over the surface of the flywheel for scoring and signs of overheating. If scored, the flywheel should be resurfaced or replaced. If overheating is indicated, check for warpage and reface as needed.

4. If disc wear is indicated, the pressure plate, release bearing and disc should be replaced.

5. To install you must be sure that the disc is centered so the transmission mainshaft will engage the pilot bushing as well as the disc splines. A dummy mainshaft or a clutch aligning tool should be inserted through the disc hub and into the pilot bushing while tightening pressure plate bolts.

6. Tighten the bolts gradually and evenly and reassemble the transmission to the engine.

Free-play Adjustment

1. Loosen the lock and adjusting nuts on the clutch cable.

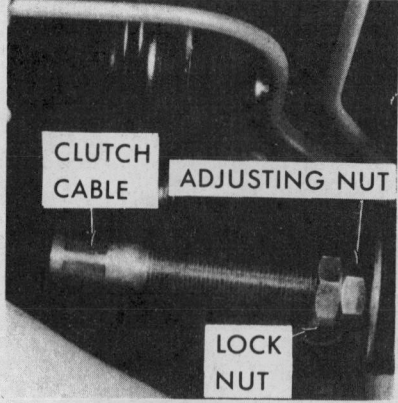

Clutch cable adjusting and lock nuts

2. Pull the cable toward the front of the car to take up the slack and turn the adjusting nut until the clutch pedal free travel is approximately ⅝ inch. Tighten the locknut.

AUTOMATIC TRANSMISSION

Removal and Installation

1. Disconnect the battery negative cable.

2. Disconnect the throttle valve cable at right side of carburetor.

3. Disconnect the exhaust pipe from the manifold.

4. Disconnect the wiring and remove the starter.

5. Remove the flywheel inspection cover, converter bolts and mark for reassembly in the same position.

6. Mark the driveshaft and flange, and remove the driveshaft.

7. Remove the rear transmission mount pad bolts.

8. Raise the transmission and remove the crossmember support and mount.

9. Lower the transmission still holding its weight at the lowest position.

10. Disconnect the shift linkage and speedometer cable, as well as the throttle valve cable and cooler lines.

11. Remove the transmission-to-engine bolts and filler pipe and move the transmission back and lower away from the car. You must use a holding tool to hold the converter in place.

The installation of the transmission is the reverse, except for these reminder steps:

1. Torque transmission-to-engine bolts to 35 ft. lbs.

2. Install the drive shaft in the original position.

3. Connect converter and flywheel in the original position and torque bolts to 30 ft. lbs.

4. If transmission was disassembled,

Removing the automatic transmission filter

add 6 pints (9 if converter was replaced) of transmission fluid.

5. With shift lever in the "Park" position, start engine. DO NOT RACE ENGINE. Apply parking brake and move shift lever through each gear.

6. With selector lever in "Park," check fluid level. Make sure the engine is running.

7. Add additional fluid to bring level to between the two small dimples below the "add" mark on the dipstick. This is the correct reading for room temperature.

Pan Removal and Installation

Remove the bolts around the outside edge of transmission pan. Discard gasket.

Installation is the reverse of removal and all bolts should be tightened to 12 ft. lbs.

Fluid Change and Filter Service

1. Remove pan and discard gasket.
2. Remove the screen and discard the surrounding gasket.
3. Clean the screen in clean transmission fluid and blow dry with compressed air.
4. Assembly is the reverse of removal. Make sure all gaskets seat firmly. Hold the gaskets in place by using a light coating of petroleum jelly. Torque all bolts (screen and pan) to 12 ft. lbs.

Neutral Safety Switch

The neutral safety switch (located on top of transmission) prevents the engine from starting in any position other than park or neutral. Should the engine start in any other gear, check the connection and replace if there is a malfunction. There is no adjustment on this unit.

Shift Linkage Adjustment

1. Remove lever from transmission manual shaft and put the transmission in neutral.

2. Place the shift indicator in neutral and loosen the locking nut. Adjust lever until it lines up with the manual shaft.

3. Install the lever on the manual shaft and tighten the locking nut. Recheck shift patterns.

Throttle Linkage Adjustment

1. Loosen cable adjusting nuts on right side of carburetor.

2. Move the carburetor lever to wide open and adjust the cable until a play of approximately 0.040 is reached above the adjusting nuts. Tighten the nuts.

DRIVE AXLES

Driveshaft and U-Joints

Removal and Installation

1. Raise the rear of the car and support on jack stands. Disconnect the parking brake return spring from rod.

2. Mark mating parts for reassembly and remove bolts and nuts.

3. Push the driveshaft slightly forward to clear the rear attachment and lower rear joint slightly; pull toward the back at the same time. Remove the thrust spring from the front of the driveshaft.

4. Install a plug in the transmission extension housing to prevent the loss of oil.

NOTE: *Do not replace fasteners with an inferior grade. They must be replaced with one of the same part number or an equivalent. Torque values must be followed to assure proper retention of the parts.*

To install the driveshaft:

1. Remove the plug from the rear of the transmission.

2. Slide the thrust spring onto the transmission output shaft and slide the driveshaft through the oil seal. Make sure not to damage the rear seal.

3. Align the pinion flange with the locating marks and install bolts and lock plates. Tighten bolts to 18 ft. lbs. Connect the parking brake spring to the rod.

U-joint Overhaul

1. Remove the driveshaft.

2. Remove the snap rings (4) on each assembly and tap on flange with hammer until one of the bearing caps starts to come out. Remove this cap with a pliers. Remove the remaining caps in a similar fashion.

3. After removing the bearing caps, bearings and spider, thoroughly clean the flange and yoke.

4. Fill the holes in the journals with grease and put about ⅛ in. of grease in the bearing caps.

5. If reusing old joint, put the needle bearings into the caps and, putting the spider inside the flange, slip the caps into the yoke. Caps may be pressed into position with a strong vise. Take care not to lose any needle bearings. Install the snap rings.

Axle Shafts

Removal and Installation

1. Raise and support and rear of the car.

2. Remove the wheel and brake drum.

3. Unscrew the rear axle shaft retaining plate and, using an axle shaft puller, coupled with a slide hammer, on flange, remove the shaft.

To install the shafts:

1. Coat shaft splines with hypoid gear lubricant and insert into housing.

2. Using a mallet, drive the shaft completely in and install the lock washers and nuts. Torque to 28 ft. lbs.

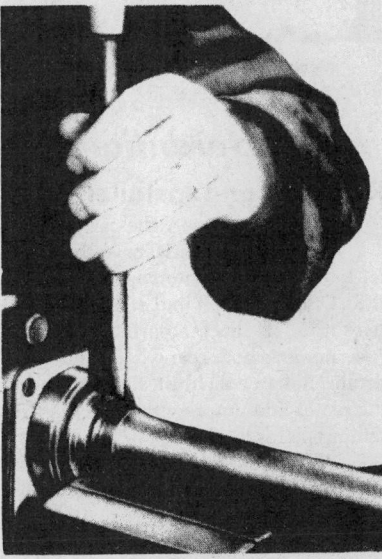

Removing axle bearing retaining ring

3. Install the brake drum and wheel and lower the car.

Bearing and Seal Replacement

1. Remove axle shaft.

2. Remove the bearing retaining ring by cutting with a cold chisel.

3. Press off the bearing using a rear pinion bearing remover.

To check for end play, measure the depth of the rear axle bearing seal with the backing plate and gaskets in place.

Next, measure the width of the bearing outer race. The difference between the two measurements indicates the required thickness of the shims.

The maximum permissable end play is 0.002 in. If necessary to reduce it, add 0.004 in. shims behind the bearing as necessary. A slight crush fit is desirable.

After shim depth has been determined, install the grease-coated bearing in place. Reinstall the axle, the wheels and lower the car.

Measuring for axle bearing depth

Differential

Removal and Installation

1. Raise and support the car.

2. Remove differential cover bolts and let lubricant drain into container.

3. Disconnect left end of track rod and wire it to left shock absorber.

4. Remove both rear wheels and brake drums. Remove the dust shield and backing plates and unscrew the axle shaft retaining plates.

5. Pull axles and be careful not to damage oil seals. Remove the differential cover and discard gasket.

6. Using a dial indicator, check and record the ring gear backlash.

7. Mark side bearing caps with a punch for reassembly to the original position, and remove.

8. Using two wooden handles, pry the differential case assembly from the housing. Be careful not to drop or confuse the bearing outer races.

To install the differential to the carrier:

1. Position the differential and outer races in the carrier. Use a soft faced hammer to drive the case into the carrier until the side bearing outer races bottom in their bores. Install the bearing caps to their original position as marked and torque the bolts to 35 ft. lbs.

2. Rotate the case assembly several times to seat the bearings and check the backlash with a dial indicator and preload by using a torque wrench on a ring gear bolt. Torque should be 25 ft. lbs. for new bearings and 15 ft. lbs. for used. If not correct, it will be necessary to add, or subtract from, the shims at the side bearings.

3. Install the torque tube assembly and insert the axle shafts.

Overhaul

1. Remove the differential case from the carrier and remove the side bearings.

2. Remove the differential case-to-ring gear bolts and tap off the case using a soft hammer.

3. Remove the differential pinion shaft retaining pin using a ⅛ in. punch and remove the pinion shaft, pinion gears, differential side gears and thrust washers.

To remove and disassemble the Drive Pinion:

1. Remove the torque tube assembly.

2. Hold barrel spline and remove the bearing preload nut.

3. Using a barrel spline sleeve remover remove spline from pinion.

4. Remove pinion by tapping rearward with a soft hammer. Remove the pinion bearing with a press.

5. Remove the bearing outer races using a brass drift.

To assemble and Install The Drive Pinion:

Make sure all parts are thoroughly cleaned before starting assembly. Check each part for imperfections.

1. Install front pinion bearing outer race using an installer and driver handle.

2. Install the rear pinion bearing outer race using an installer and driver handle.

This next procedure requires a special tool called a gauge plate to determine the correct pinion depth setting.

NOTE: *Front pilot J–23597–21, Stud J–21772–43, Rear pilot J–23597–12 and Gauge plate J–23597–22 or their equivalents are the needed pieces.*

3. Make sure all gauge parts are clean, lubricate the new front and rear bearings and position them in their races.

4. Thread the stud into gauge plate and intall on the rear pinion inner race. Put the pilot on front pinion bearing.

5. Install the nut on the stud and hold the stud stationary with a wrench and tighten the nut with a torque wrench until there is a reading of 20 in. lbs.

6. Clean differential side bearing support bores. Make sure there are no burrs.

7. Install the discs on the gauge shaft.

8. Position the gauge shaft in the carrier so the dial rod is centered on the gauging area of the gauge block and the discs are fully seated in the bearing bores. Install the bearing caps and torque to 35 ft. lbs.

9. Set the dial to "O" and contact the indicator pad with the button on the shaft. Push the dial down until the needle goes about ¾ the way around the dial. Lock in position and reset.

10. Rotate the gauge shaft back and forth until the dial reaches its greatest point of deflection. At this point, set the dial to "0" and repeat to verify.

11. Rotate the shaft until the dial rod does not touch the block. Record the reading.

NOTE: *Example: if the dial reading showed .003, this would indicate a shim thickness of .003.*

Use this procedure to select the proper shim.

12. Examine the head of the drive pinion. The depth code is stamped by chemical ink. The number indicates the change necessary in the mounting distance. A "Plus" number indicates the need for greater mounting distance (decrease shim thickness) and a "−" indicates the need for smaller (increase shim thickness).

If there is no code the pinion is "nominal."

13. If the figure is plus, convert it from millimeters to inches and subtract from step 11. If the figure is minus, convert and add to 11. Use the chart to determine the proper variation to use to compensate.

14. Place the shim on the drive pinion and install the pinion bearing.

To set or check the bearing preload:

1. Lubricate pinion bearings and assemble the drive pinion, collapsible spacer, front pinion bearing, oil deflector plate and barrel spline sleeve in the carrier.

2. Pull the spline sleeve through the pinion far enough to engage the pinion nut.

3. Install the nut, and, holding the spline barrel, tighten the preload nut until 9 in. lbs. are required to rotate the pinion on new bearings. A spring scale should be used to determine preload. For used bearings, the setting is 6 in. lbs.

4. Install a new oil seal that has been soaked in differential lubricant.

To assemble the differential case:

1. Install the side gears and thrust washers. Put them into the case.

2. Lubricate and install pinion gears 180 degrees apart and rotate the gears as an assembly until the pinion gear bores are aligned with the shaft bores in the case.

3. Install the pinion shaft and use a dial indicator to measure the amount of backlash between the gears. One gear must be held stationary while making this check. If backlash is greater than .003 in., make the adjustments with thrust washers. Increasing thickness will decrease backlash and decreasing thickness will increase backlash.

4. Install the lock pin into the pinion shaft and caulk to prevent loosening. Install the ring gear after making sure there are no burrs or dirt. Tighten bolt to 47 ft. lbs.

5. Check the lateral runout of the ring gear. Maximum allowable is .003 in. If the runout is greater, make sure there are no burrs holding the gear in a cocked position and that the bolts are evenly torqued.

Check for side bearing preload and backlash by:

1. Install side bearings. Make sure to support the opposite side of the case on the pilot to prevent bearing damage.

2. Put the case assembly into the carrier, less the side bearing shims. Using two sets of feeler gauges, insert enough feeler thickness to remove all end play. Make sure the feelers are pushed to the bottom of the bearing bores.

3. Mount a dial gauge, as illustrated, at right angles to a tooth on the ring gear. Adjust feeler thickness from side to side until ring gear backlash is .005 in. to .007 in.

4. Remove the feeler gauges and determine the amount of thickness needed. Add .002 in. to each shim pack for side bearing preload.

5. Remove the case assembly and both side bearings and install shim packs with respective side bearing.

6. Put the case assembly and races into the carrier. Use a soft-faced hammer to drive it in until the side bearing races bottom in their bores. Install the side bearing caps in their original location and torque the bolts to 35 ft. lbs.

7. Rotate the case several times to seat

Removing pinion shaft lock pin

1. Rear axle housing assembly
2. Rear axle case
3. Bolt; axle housing to lateral rod
4. Nut
5. Washer
6. Bolt; bearing cap to axle housing
7. Rear axle breather assembly
8. Pinion bearing shim
9. Pinion bearing (inner)
10. Collapsible distance spacer
11. Shim; distance piece
12. Pinion bearing (outer)
13. Oil thrower
14. Sliding sleeve oil seal
15. Barrel spline sleeve
16. Final pinion washer
17. Pinion nut
18. Pressure cap
19. Differential case
20. Ring gear and pinion
21. Ring gear setting bolt
22. Side gears
23. Pinion gears
24. Side gear thrust washer
25. Differential pinion pin
26. Lock pin
27. Side bearing
28. Side gear shim
29. Rear axle housing rear cover
30. Rear axle housing gasket
31. Brake pipe union bracket
32. Union bracket bolt
33. Wheel nut
34. Oil filler plug
35. Oil filler gasket
36. Rear axle shaft
37. Axle shaft bearing retainer
38. Axle shaft bearing
39. Axle shaft sleeve
40. Wheel pin
41. Axle shaft shim
42. Bolt; brake to axle case
43. Spring washer
44. Nut
45. Rear brake drum

Exploded view of the rear axle

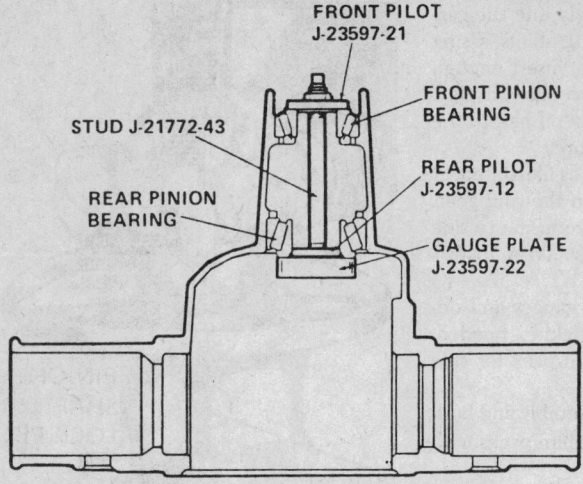

Gauge plate set-up for determining pinion depth

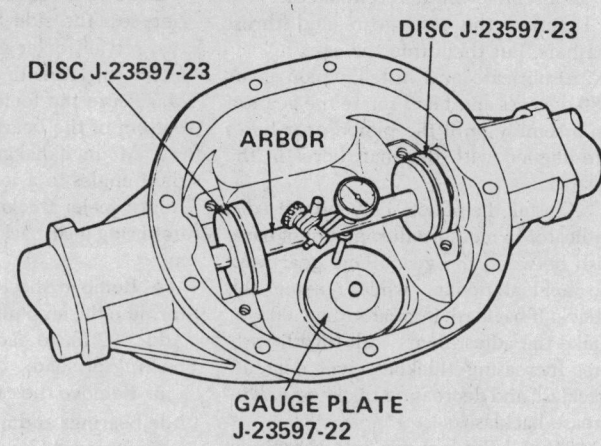

Dial gauge set-up to measure pinion depth

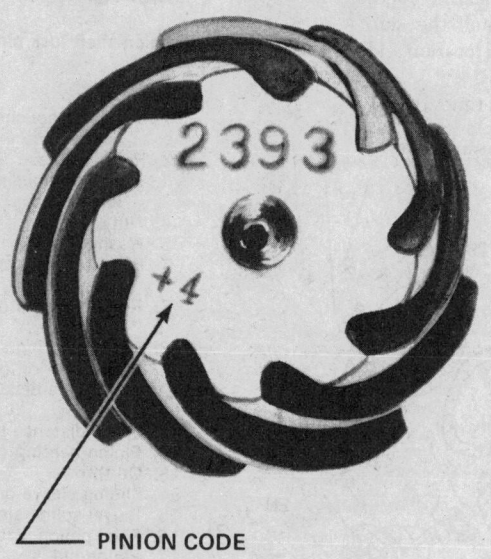

PINION CODE

Pinion depth code

PINION DEPTH CODE NUMBER	ALTER SHIM THICKNESS AS DETERMINED BY DIAL INDICATOR AS FOLLOWS:	
+20	SUBTRACT	0.20 MM (0.0079 IN.)
+18	"	0.18 MM (0.0071 IN.)
+16	"	0.16 MM (0.0063 IN.)
+14	"	0.14 MM (0.0055 IN.)
+12	"	0.12 MM (0.0047 IN.)
+10	"	0.10 MM (0.0039 IN.)
+ 8	"	0.08 MM (0.0032 IN.)
+ 6	"	0.06 MM (0.0024 IN.)
+ 4	"	0.04 MM (0.0016 IN.)
+ 2	"	0.02 MM (0.0008 IN.)
0	USE DIAL INDICATOR READING	
- 2	ADD	0.02 MM (0.0008 IN.)
- 4	"	0.04 MM (0.0016 IN.)
- 6	"	0.06 MM (0.0024 IN.)
- 8	"	0.08 MM (0.0032 IN.)
-10	"	0.10 MM (0.0039 IN.)
-12	"	0.12 MM (0.0047 IN.)
-14	"	0.14 MM (0.0055 IN.)
-16	"	0.16 MM (0.0063 IN.)
-18	"	0.18 MM (0.0071 IN.)
-20	"	0.20 MM (0.0079 IN.)

the bearings and check the backlash and preload using a torque wrench on a ring gear bolt. The torque required to turn the case should be 25 in. lbs. for new bearings and 15 in. lbs for used. If torque is not correct, it will be necessary to re-shim the side bearings.

8. Install the torque tube assembly and put in the axle shafts.

Differential Specifications

Axle Bearing Radial Runout—.002 in.
Axle Flange Lateral Runout—.004 in.
Lateral Ring Gear Runout—.003 in.
Ring Gear and Pinion Backlash—.005–.007 in.

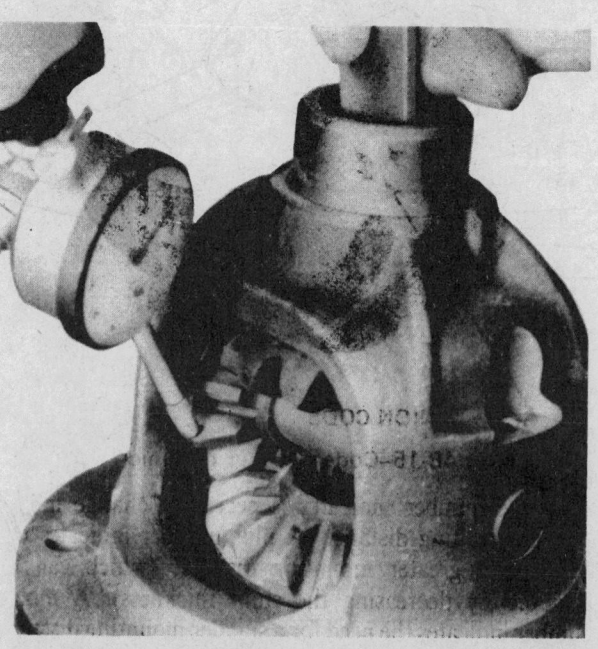

Checking ring gear backlash

REAR SUSPENSION

Springs

Removal and Installation

1. Raise car and remove wheels. Raise the rear axle with another jack.
3. Disconnect lower end of shock absorber from the rear axle.
4. Lower jack holding rear axle until spring can be removed by hand.

Installation is the reverse procedure. Torque shock absorber-to-axle nut to 29 ft. lbs. Lug nut torque is 50 ft. lbs.

Shock Absorbers

Removal and Installation

1. Raise car and remove the wheel.
2. Disconnect the lower end of absorber from the axle.
3. Remove the fuel tank cover from inside the trunk and disconnect the upper end of the shock.

Installation is the reverse procedure. Torque shock-to-axle nut to 29 ft. lbs. and lug nuts to 50 ft. lbs.

FRONT SUSPENSION

Springs

Removal and Installation

1. Raise the car and remove the wheel.
2. Remove the tie-rod cotter key and castle nut. Disconnect the tie-rod end from the steering knuckle.
3. Remove the lower shock bolt and collapse the shock. Remove the stabilizer bar bolt and grommet assembly from lower control arm.
4. Remove the upper brake caliper bolt and slide hose clip back ½ in.
5. Compress spring with a reliable spring compressor. Raise the lower control arm until level and support it with a jackstand.
6. Loosen the lower ball joint castle nut until the top of the nut is flush with the top of the ball joint. Disconnect the lower ball joint from the steering knuckle. A ball joint remover is necessary.
7. Remove the hub assembly and steering knuckle from lower ball joint and support it out of the way with a piece of wire.
8. Remove the support from under the control arm and loosen the compressor while prying the control arm down.

To Install the spring:

1. Seat the spring between the lower

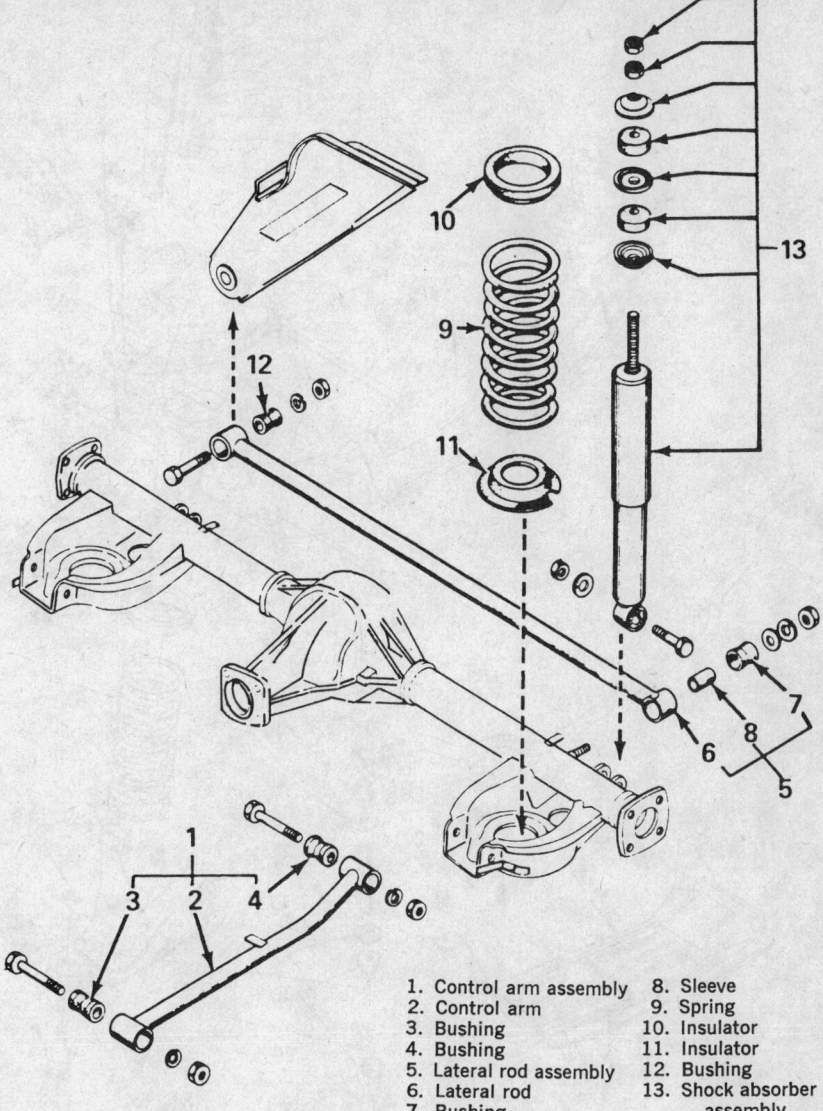

1. Control arm assembly	8. Sleeve
2. Control arm	9. Spring
3. Bushing	10. Insulator
4. Bushing	11. Insulator
5. Lateral rod assembly	12. Bushing
6. Lateral rod	13. Shock absorber
7. Bushing	assembly

Exploded view of rear suspension

control arm and crossmember. Compress it until the control arm can be moved to a level position.
2. Replace the support under the control arm and remove the compressor.
3. Attach the hub assembly and steering knuckle to the joint and torque castle nut to 72 ft. lbs.
4. Attach the upper ball joint to steering knuckle and torque to 40 ft. lbs.
5. Install the stabilizer bar bolt and grommet to the lower control arm and tighten the nut to the end of the threads on the bolt.
6. Install the lower shock bolt and torque to 29 ft. lbs. Slide the hose clip in place and install the upper caliper bolt. Torque to 36 ft. lbs.
7. Attach the tie-rod end to the steering knuckle and torque castle nut to 29 ft. lbs. Put in a NEW cotter pin.
8. Install the wheels and torque lug nuts to 50 ft. lbs.

Shock Absorbers

Removal and Installation

1. Raise the car and remove the wheel.
2. Disconnect the shock from from the upper control arm.
3. From inside the engine compartment, remove the shock nuts and take out the shock.

To install:

1. Install the shock absorber.
2. Install grommets and washers and tighten thicker nut to the end of the threads and install lock nut.
3. Connect shock to upper control arm and torque to 29 ft. lbs. Replace wheel and torque lug nuts to 50 ft. lbs.

Upper Ball Joint

Removal and Installation

To remove the upper ball joint:

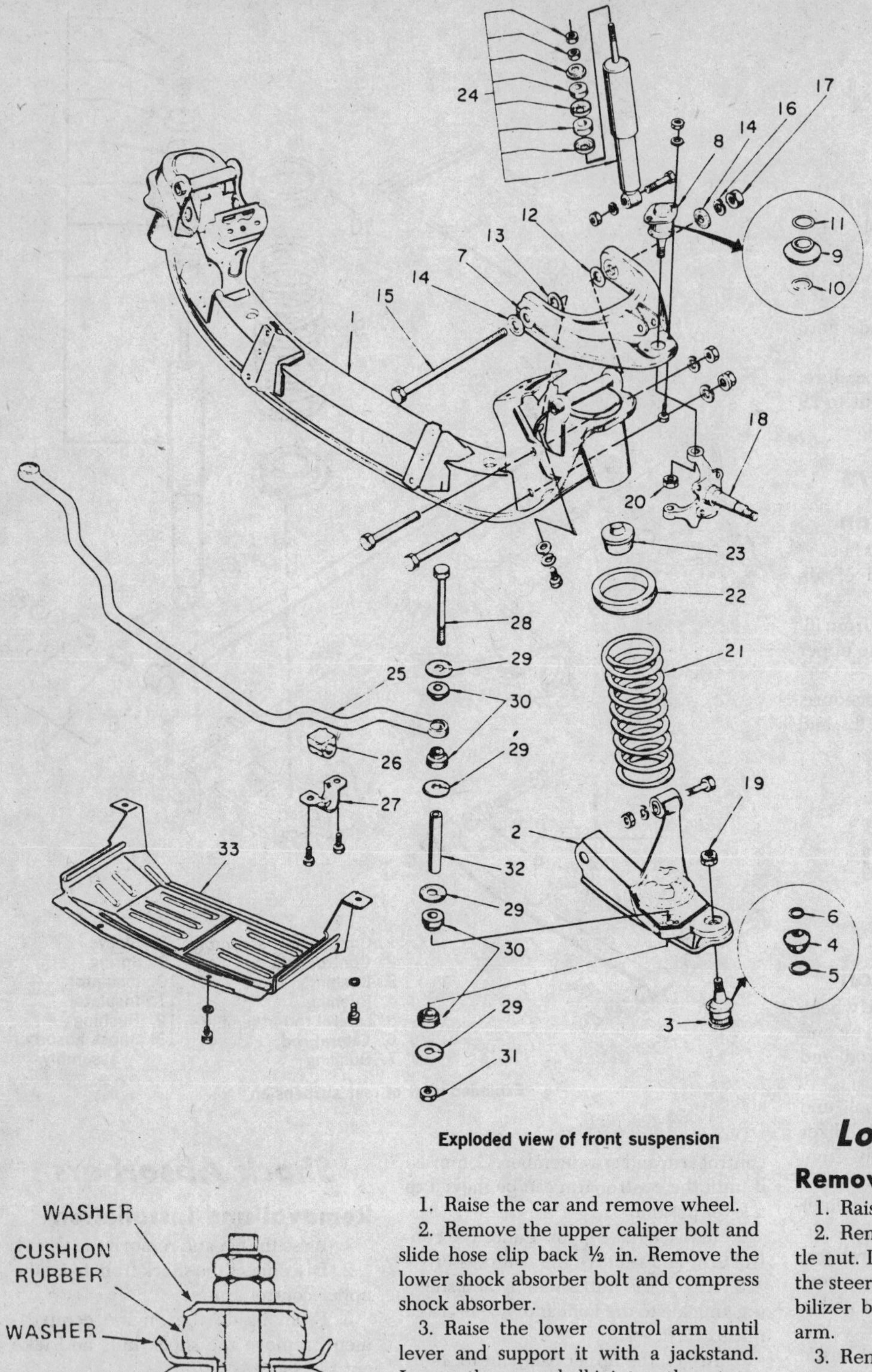

1. Crossmember assembly
2. Lower link assembly
3. Lower link end
   assembly
4. Boot
5. Clamp ring
6. Clamp ring
7. Upper link assembly
8. Upper link end
   assembly
9. Boot
10. Clamp ring
11. Clamp ring
12. Washer
13. Washer
14. Washer
15. Bolt
16. Spring washer
17. Nut
18. Knuckle
19. Nut
20. Nut
21. Front coil spring
22. Damper rubber
23. Bumper rubber
24. Shock absorber
25. Stabilizer bar
26. Rubber bush
27. Clamp
28. Bolt
29. Retainer
30. Buffer
31. Nut
32. Distance tube
33. Under cover

Exploded view of front suspension

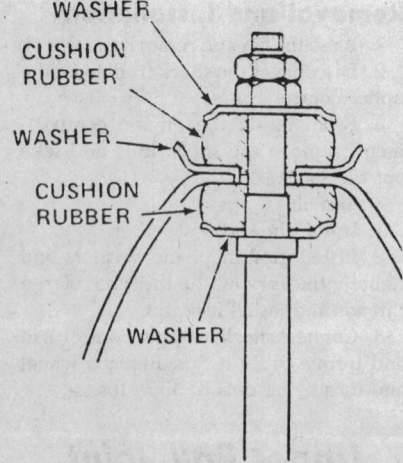

WASHER
CUSHION RUBBER
WASHER
CUSHION RUBBER
WASHER

Front shock absorber installation

1. Raise the car and remove wheel.
2. Remove the upper caliper bolt and slide hose clip back ½ in. Remove the lower shock absorber bolt and compress shock absorber.
3. Raise the lower control arm until lever and support it with a jackstand. Loosen the upper ball joint castle nut until the top of the nut is flush with the top of the ball joint. Disconnect the ball joint from the steering knuckle with a ball joint remover.
4. Remove the two bolts holding the ball joint to the control arm.
5. Installation is the reverse procedure. Torque control arm bolts to 29 ft. lbs. and the upper castle nut to 40 ft. lbs.
6. The shock absorber should be torqued to 29 ft. lbs and the upper brake caliper bolt to 36 ft. lbs. Torque the lug nuts to 50 ft. lbs.

Lower Ball Joint

Removal and Installation

1. Raise the car and remove wheel.
2. Remove tie-rod cotter pin and castle nut. Disconnect the tie-rod end from the steering knuckle and remove the stabilizer bar bolt from the lower control arm.
3. Remove the upper caliper bolt and slip hose clip back ½ in. Remove the lower shock absorber bolt and compress the shock absorber.
4. Put the spring compressor over the upper control arm and let it hang. Place a support under the lower control arm and loosen lower ball joint castle nut until the top of the nut is flush with the top of the ball joint.
5. Disconnect the ball joint from the steering knuckle with a ball joint remover. Remove the hub assembly and steering knuckle from the ball joint and tie them to the side with wire.

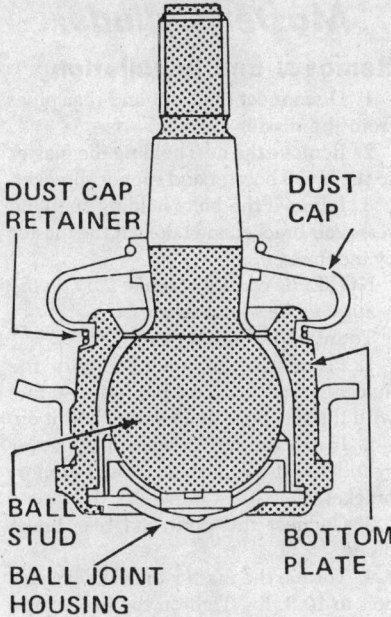

DUST CAP RETAINER

DUST CAP

BALL STUD

BALL JOINT HOUSING

BOTTOM PLATE

Lower ball joint

6. Put the spring compressor between the first exposed coil of the spring, tighten and remove the jackstand from under the control arm.

7. Remove the lower ball joint from the control arm.

To install the ball joint:

1. Install the new ball joint using a reliable ball joint installer. DO NOT STRIKE the ball joint bottom during installation.

2. Place the jackstand under the lower control arm and remove the compressor. Attach the hub and steering knuckle and torque nut to 72 ft. lbs.

3. Slide the hose clip back and install the upper caliper bolt. Tighten to 36 ft. lbs.

4. Install the stabilizer bar bolt and grommet to control arm. Tighten the nut to the end of the threads. Attach the tie-rod end to the steering knuckle and torque the nut to 29 ft. lbs. Put in a cotter pin.

5. Install the lower shock bolt and torque to 29 ft. lbs. Torque the lug nuts to 50 ft. lbs.

Upper Control Arm

Removal and Installation

1. Raise the car and remove the wheel.

2. Remove the upper caliper bolt and slide the hose clip back ½ in. Remove the lower shock absorber bolt and compress the shock absorber.

3. Raise the lower control arm until lever and place a jackstand under it.

4. Loosen the upper ball joint castle nut until the top of the nut is flush with the top of the ball joint. Disconnect the ball joint from the steering knuckle with a ball joint remover.

5. Remove the through bolt connect-

ing the upper control arm to the frame.

To install the upper control arm:

1. Install the ball joint to the upper control arm (refer to Ball Joint Installation).

2. Install the control arm; make sure the smaller washer is on the inner face of the front arm and the larger washer on the rear arm.

3. Attach the upper control arm to the crossmember. Do not tighten bolt. Attach the upper ball joint to the steering knuckle and torque the nut to 40 ft. lbs. Torque the through bolt-to-crossmember to 43 ft. lbs.

4. Install the lower shock bolt and torque to 29 ft. lbs. Slide the hose clip back and install the caliper bolt to 36 ft. lbs. Install wheel and torque lug nuts to 50 ft. lbs.

NOTE: *Always check caster and camber when working on upper control arm area.*

Lower Control Arm

Removal and Installation

1. Raise the car and remove the wheel.

2. Remove the tie-rod end cotterpin and castle nut. Disconnect the tie-rod end from the steering knuckle.

3. Remove the lower shock bolt and push it up. Remove the stabilizer bar bolt and assembly from the lower control arm.

4. Remove the upper caliper bolt and slide the hose clip back ½ in. Place a spring compressor over the upper control arm and let it hang.

5. Raise the lower control arm level and place a jackstand under the extreme end of the arm.

6. Loosen the ball joint castle nut until the nut is flush with the top of the ball joint. Disconnect the ball joint from the steering knuckle using a reliable ball joint remover.

7. Remove the hub assembly and steering knuckle from the lower ball joint and tie them to the side with a wire. Put the spring compressor between the first exposed coil of the spring.

8. Compress the spring until it clears the lower spring seat and remove the jackstand from under the control arm.

9. Take out the bolts connecting the control arm to the crossmember and body and remove the arm.

To install the lower control arm:

1. Install the ball joint to the lower control arm using a reliable ball joint installer. Put in the bolts connecting the front of the control arm to the crossmember and body. Do not tighten bolts.

2. Raise the control arm until level and place a jackstand under it. Remove the spring compressor.

3. Attach the hub assembly and steering knuckle to control arm and torque

the nut to 72 ft. lbs.

4. Attach the upper ball joint to the steering knuckle and torque the nut to 40 ft. lbs. Then torque the bolts from control arm to crossmember and body to 43 ft. lbs.

5. Install the stabilizer bar bolt and assembly to the control arm and tighten the nut to the end of the threads.

6. Install the lower shock bolt and torque to 29 ft. lbs. Slide the hose clip back and put in the caliper bolt. Torque it to 36 ft. lbs.

7. Attach the tie-rod end to steering knuckle and torque the nut to 29 ft. lbs. Install a new cotterpin.

8. Install the wheels and torque to 50 ft. lbs.

NOTE: *Always check caster and camber when working in the lower control arm area.*

Adjustments

Caster

Change the caster angle by realigning the washers located between the legs of the upper control arm.

Camber

Camber angle can be increased about 1 degree by removing the upper ball joint, rotating it ½ turn and reinstalling it with the flat of the upper flange on the inboard side of the control arm.

Toe-in

Toe-in is controlled by the position of the tie-rod. Rotating the tie-rod end will make the adjustment.

STEERING

Steering Wheel

Removal and Installation

1. From the rear of the wheel, remove the screws holding the horn button and, from the front, disconnect the horn contacts.

2. Using a steering wheel puller, turn with a wrench until loose. Installation is the reverse.

Turn Signal Switch Replacement

The turn signal switch is a combination unit, housing turn signals, headlight dimmer and hazard warning switch.

1. Remove the steering wheel and the screws holding the upper and lower column covers.

2. Remove the switch (left side) by taking out the four retaining screws and unplugging wiring.

3. Installation is the reverse of removal.

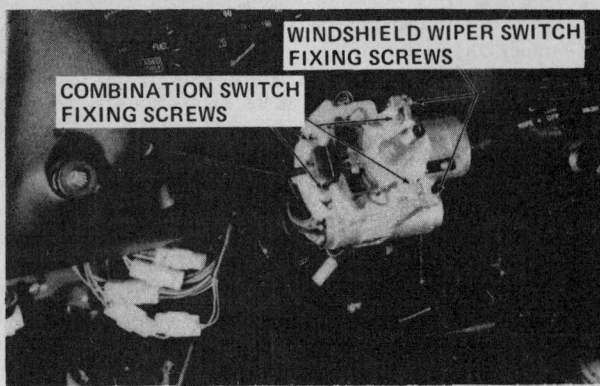

Switch removal locations

Ignition Lock Switch

Removal and Installation

The ignition lock switch is located on the right side of the steering column, near the windshield wiper switch.

1. Remove steering wheel and column covers.

2. Remove the snap ring and the three bolts holding the switch to the column. Unplug the wiring.

3. Installation is the reverse of removal.

Manual Steering Gear

Removal and Installation

1. Raise the front of the car and remove the undercover.

2. Remove the steering shaft coupling bolt and remove both tie-rod end castle nut.

3. Disconnect the tie-rod ends from the steering knuckles.

4. Expand the steering shaft coupling and remove the assembly. Remove the tie-rods from the steering gear.

To install:

1. Attach tie-rod ends to steering gear.

2. Before installing the steering gear, set the steering gear to the high point by putting the front wheels straight ahead, with steering wheel centered.

3. Attach steering coupling to steering wheel and attach the steering gear housing to the crossmember. Torque bolts to 29 ft. lbs.

4. Install the steering shaft coupling bolt and torque it to 19 ft. lbs.

5. Attach both tie-rod ends to the steering knuckles and torque the castle nuts to 29 ft. lbs. Install new cotterpins.

6. Check and adjust toe-in, install undercover and lower the car.

Adjustments

1. Set the wheels straight ahead, with the steering wheel centered.

2. Loosen the locknut around the adjusting screw and turn the screw in until resistance is felt.

3. Back out the screw ⅛ to ¼ of a turn and tighten the locknut to 49 ft. lbs.

BRAKES

Adjustment

Both front and rear brakes are self-adjusting.

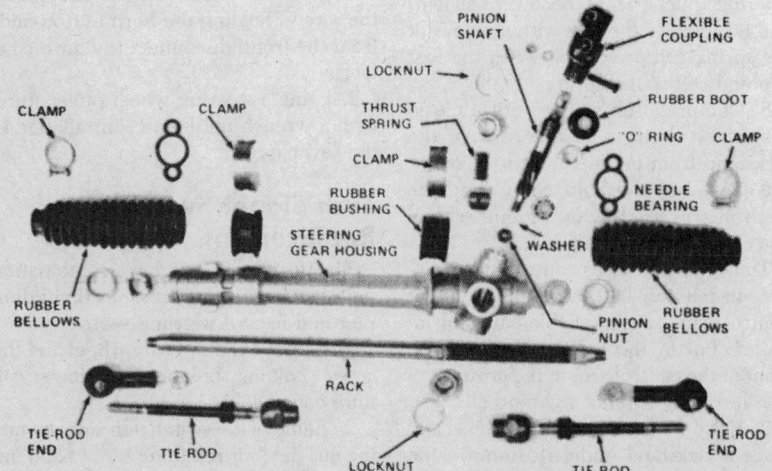

Exploded view of steering gear

Master Cylinder

Removal and Installation

1. Disconnect the front and rear pipes from the master cylinder.

2. Remove the nuts holding the master to the brake booster and support bracket.

3. Remove the bolts holding the fluid reservoir bracket and take out the master cylinder assembly.

NOTE: *Be careful of brake fluid on the automobile's painted surfaces.*

To install the master cylinder:

1. Place the unit, together with the fluid reservoir (with rubber hoses) in line with the reservoir bracket and bolt it on.

2. Install the nuts holding the master cylinder to the brake booster and support bracket.

3. Connect the front and rear brake pipes.

4. Torque the master-to-brake booster bolt to 10 ft. lbs. Tighten the brake pipe flare to 12 ft. lbs. Bleed the brake system.

Overhaul

1. Remove the master cylinder.

2. Pour the fluid out of the reservoir.

3. Place the master cylinder in a vise and remove the pipe connectors. Remove the check valves, springs and retainers.

4. Push in the primary piston with a screwdriver and remove the secondary piston stop bolt and snap ring.

5. Remove the primary and secondary piston assemblies from the cylinder.

6. Clean the parts with brake fluid. *Do Not* use any other type of solvent. Dry with compressed air.

7. Using a good caliper measure the cylinder bore diameter and outside diameter of the primary and secondary pistons. Compare the two to determine the clearance. Replace the master cylinder assembly if clearance is beyond 0.006 in.

8. Check the master cylinder inner wall for damage. Replace if necessary. Check the pistons for wear or damage. Replace if necessary.

9. Always replace the piston cups as their condition affects the performance of the system. Piston must also be replaced if damaged. They are not repairable.

10. Check the front and rear check valves for poor contact or damage. Check the fluid reservoir and rubber hoses for damage, cracking or bulging. Check the snap rings and gaskets for fatigue and replace if necessary.

To Assemble:

1. Check for dirt in the cylinder bore, or any parts going into it. Lubricate the brake parts with clean brake fluid.

2. Assemble the retainer, spring, check valve, gasket and pipe connector to the cylinder body and semi-tighten the

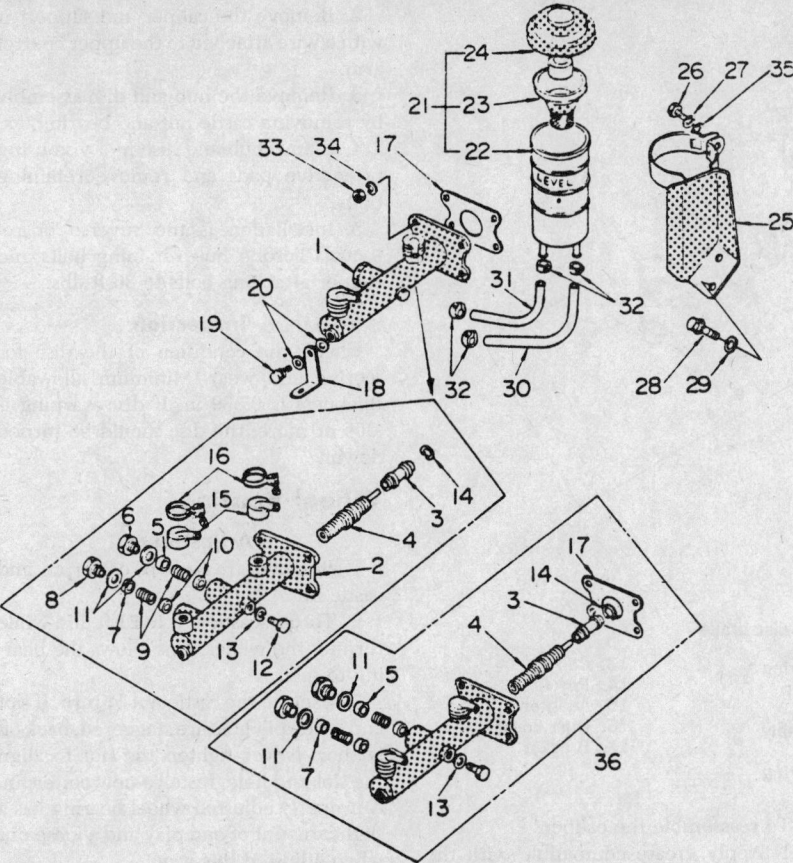

Exploded view of master cylinder

1. Tandem master cylinder assembly	8. Connector	18. Bracket	28. Bolt
2. Cylinder body	9. Check valve spring	19. Bolt	29. Washer
3. Primary piston assembly	10. Check valve spring retainer	20. Washer	30. Rubber hose, front
4. Secondary piston assembly	11. Gasket	21. Fluid reservoir assembly	31. Rubber hose, rear
5. Primary check valve	12. Stopper bolt	22. Body	32. Clip
6. Connector	13. Gasket	23. Filter	33. Nut
7. Secondary piston assembly	14. Snap ring	24. Cover	34. Washer
	15. Connector	25. Bracket	35. Washer
	16. Clip	26. Screw	36. Tandem master cylinder repair kit
	17. Gasket	27. Washer	

connector. The check valve in the front has a hole. Install the one without the hole in the rear.

3. Clamp the cylinder body in a soft-jawed vise and tighten the connector to 87 ft. lbs. Install the secondary piston assembly.

4. Install the primary piston assembly and secure with snap ring. Note the direction of setting when assembling. Do not force the piston as damage to the cups may result.

5. Press the primary piston all the way in with a screwdriver and hold. Install the secondary piston stop bolt with gasket on the cylinder body. Tighten the bolt to 14 ft. lbs.

6. Install the master cylinder.

Brake System Indicator Light

The brake system light is connected in parallel with the parking brake switch. The sending unit is located on the master cylinder and cannot be adjusted. Any malfunction of the unit requires replacement.

Bleeding

1. Check the fluid level in the reservoir and refill as necessary.

2. Clean all dirt from around the bleeder valves and remove caps.

3. Push a bleeder hose over the valve and the other end into a jar. A length of ⅛" vacuum hose will work.

4. Pump up pressure on the brake pedal and hold. Crack the bleeder valve open and allow the brake pedal to travel to the floor. Close the bleeder valve and release the brake.

Pump brake up again, hold and crack the valve open. Repeat this procedure at each bleeder valve until all air is out of the system.

5. Remove bleeder hose and install caps.

6. When the bleeding is finished, make sure to bring the fluid level in the reservoir up to full.

NOTE: *During the bleeding process, constantly check the fluid level in the reservoir. Allowing it to go too low could draw air into the system. Also, do not try to save the bled brake fluid. Discard it.*

Front Disc Brakes

Disc Brake Pads

Inspection

1. Remove brake pads.
2. Check their condition. Minimum pad thickness allowable is .067 in.

Removal and Installation

1. Raise the front of the car, support and remove the wheels.
2. Remove clips, pins, "M" type spring, pad shims and friction pads.
3. Remove any dirt from friction pad recess and visually inspect piston seals for leakage.
4. Apply grease compatible with caliper seals (included in pad repair kit) to the small areas on the pad.
5. Push the pistons into bores and while holding, open bleeder valves slightly to keep from overflowing the reservoir. Tighten valve when pistons bottom.
6. Put anti-rattle shims on brake pads with arrows pointing in the direction the disc rotates. Install caliper.
7. Install the "M" type spring, pins and clips. Install the wheels and lower the car.

Disc Brake Calipers

Removal and Installation

1. Raise front of car, support, and remove wheel.
2. Disconnect the brake pipe from hose and cap or tape ends to protect from dirt.
3. Remove the caliper bolts and remove the caliper.
4. Installation is the reverse. Torque the caliper bolts to 36.2 ft. lbs and the brake flare nut to 11.6 ft. lbs.

Pad lubrication points

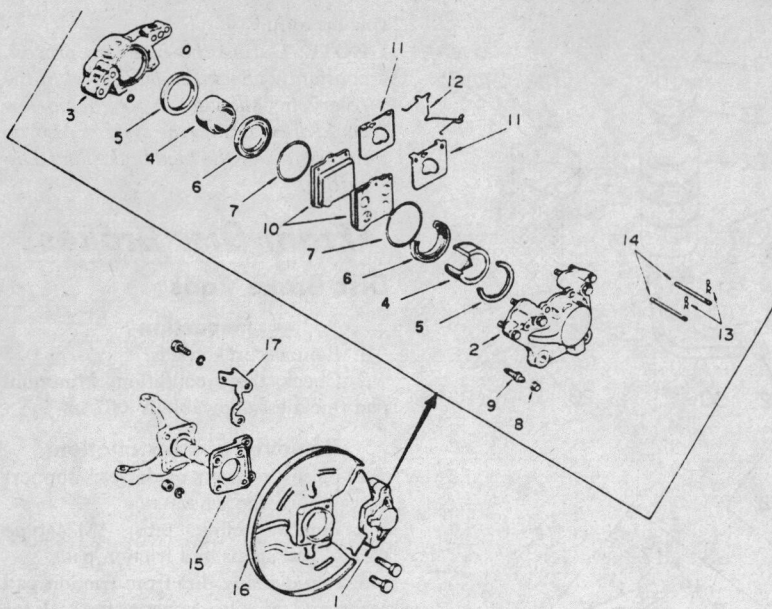

Exploded view of front disc brake

1. Caliper assembly	7. Dust seal ring	13. Clip
2. Inner caliper	8. Bleeder cap	14. Pin
3. Outer caliper	9. Bleeder	15. Adapter
4. Piston	10. Pad assembly	16. Dust cover
5. Piston seal	11. Pad shim	17. Bracket
6. Dust seal	12. M type spring	

Overhaul

1. Remove caliper and brake pads.
2. Remove the dust seal ring and take out dust seals from each piston.
3. Install clamp on mounting half of caliper and remove rim half piston by applying compressed air at the brake line connection.
4. Install the clamp on the rim half to remove the mounting half piston.
5. Remove fluid seals from annular grooves in caliper piston bores.

NOTE: *The caliper is integral in design and cannot be taken apart. If fluid is leaking from a joint, replace the entire unit. NEVER disturb any of the bridge bolts.*

To reassemble the caliper:

1. Apply grease compatible with the seals to the seal and cylinder wall. Insert new piston.
2. Carefully install the piston in the bottom of the bore using only finger pressure to avoid scratching.
3. Install the dust seal and seal ring. Insert pads as outlined in the Disc Brake Pads section.
4. Put the caliper on the disc and knuckle assembly and connect the brake hose to the pipe. Bleed the brakes.

Brake Disc

Removal and Installation

1. Raise the front of the car and support. Remove the wheel.

2. Remove the caliper and support it with a wire attached to the upper control arm.
3. Remove the hub and disc assembly by removing castle nut and bearing.
4. Clamp hub and disc in a vise using protective pads and remove retaining bolts.
5. Installation is the reverse of removal. Torque hub retaining bolts and caliper attaching bolts to 36 ft. lbs.

Inspection

Check the condition of the disc for scoring and wear. Minimum allowable thickness is 0.339 in. If disc warping is .006 or more, the disc should be turned down.

Wheel Bearings

Adjustment

1. Remove grease cap, cotterpin and castle nut.
2. Torque castle nut to 21 ft. lbs. while turning the wheel. This allows the bearing to seat.
3. Back off the castle nut ¼ turn. If slot and cotterpin hole are staggered, back off farther. Never tighten the nut to align the slot and hole. Install a new cotterpin. A properly adjusted wheel bearing has a slight amount of end play and a loose nut when adjusted this way.

Rear Drum Brakes

Brake Drums

Inspection

1. Jack up the rear of the car, support, and remove the wheels.
2. Tap the outside of the drum lightly with a hammer and pull the brake drum straight off. Tap the outside edge of the drum on the ground to knock out any loose dirt. Never blow out drum or brake part with compressed air. Asbestos particle are dangerous when inhaled. Clean the drum in solvent.
3. Look the inside of the drum over for scoring or evidence of heat. Keep your fingers off the contact surface as much as possible.
4. The original diameter for the drum is 8.980 inches and the maximum machined diameter is 9.040 inches.

Should the drum have an inside diameter of 9.060 inches, it must be discarded and replaced. If the drum is out of round by .003 or more, the drum should be turned.

Installation

Check the linings for any oil or grease. Align the holes in the drum with the adjustment holes in the axle flange and gently push the drum onto the wheel lugs. Install the wheel and torque lug nuts to 50 ft. lbs.

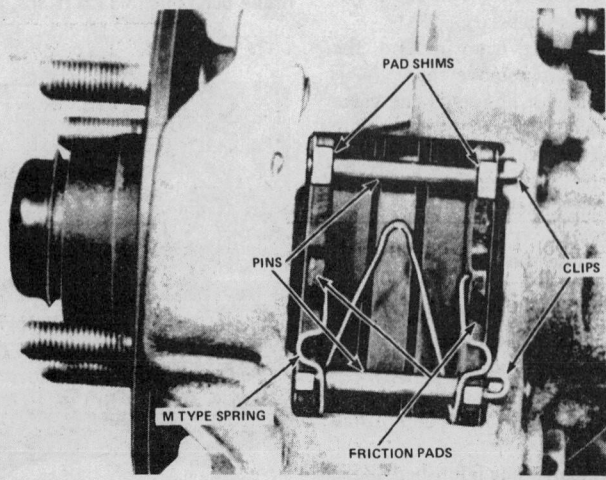

PAD SHIMS

PINS

CLIPS

M TYPE SPRING

FRICTION PADS

Caliper and brake pad

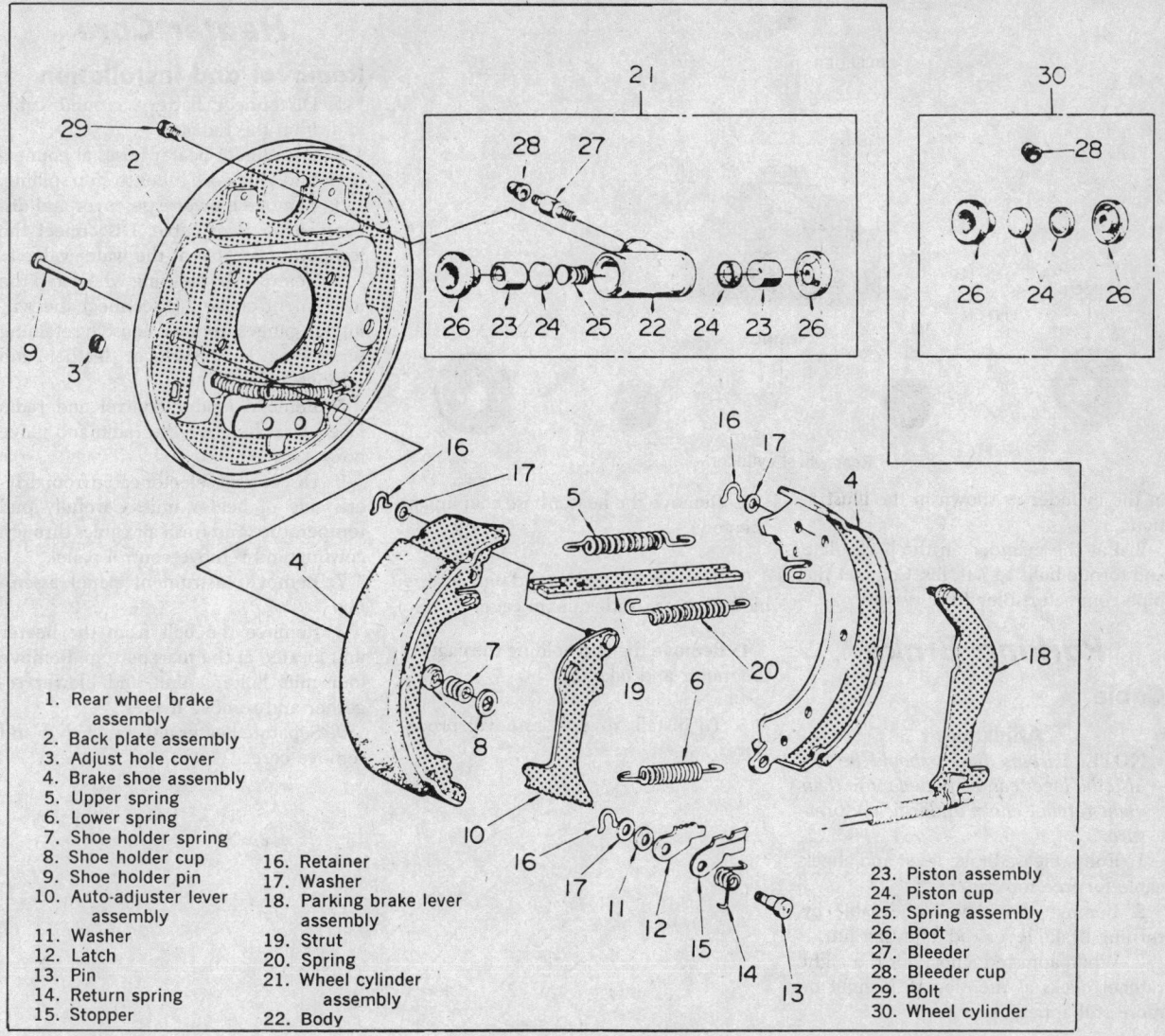

1. Rear wheel brake
   assembly
2. Back plate assembly
3. Adjust hole cover
4. Brake shoe assembly
5. Upper spring
6. Lower spring
7. Shoe holder spring
8. Shoe holder cup
9. Shoe holder pin
10. Auto-adjuster lever
    assembly
11. Washer
12. Latch
13. Pin
14. Return spring
15. Stopper

16. Retainer
17. Washer
18. Parking brake lever
    assembly
19. Strut
20. Spring
21. Wheel cylinder
    assembly
22. Body

23. Piston assembly
24. Piston cup
25. Spring assembly
26. Boot
27. Bleeder
28. Bleeder cup
29. Bolt
30. Wheel cylinder

Exploded view of rear brakes

Brake Shoes

Removal and Installation

1. Raise the rear of the car, support, and remove the wheels and drums.

2. Remove the return springs, shoe holding pins, cups and springs.

3. Move the adjuster lever in the direction of expansion and disconnect the strut. Remove the primary shoe.

4. Disconnect the parking brake cable from the lever and remove the secondary shoe.

At this point, look over the shoes for wear or contamination with grease or oil.

Should the brakes show 0.040 or less, they must be replaced.

To install:

NOTE: *When installing the brakes, make sure not to scratch the wheel cylinder boots.*

1. Install the secondary shoe and the parking brake cable to the lever.

2. Install the primary shoe, the strut and the automatic adjusting lever.

3. Install the return springs, shoe holding pins, cups and springs.

4. Install the wheel and drum assembly.

Wheel Cylinders

Removal and Installation

1. Remove brake shoes.

2. Pry on the spring cup and pull out the cable from the rear face of the back plate.

3. Take out the cylinder mounting bolts and disconnect the brake pipe. Cap or tape the ends of the brake pipe and wheel cylinder to keep out dirt.

To install:

1. Remove the tape and install the cylinder assembly and connect the brake pipe. Torque the bolts to 7 ft. lbs.

2. Install the parking brake cable through the back plate.

3. Assemble the shoes and install the wheel and drum assembly. Bleed the system.

Overhaul

1. Remove the brakes and wheel cylinder.

2. Pry (carefully) the boot away from the cylinder bore and see if the interior is wet. If it is, it indicates a leak past the pistons and the cylinder must be rebuilt.

3. Pry the boots off the cylinders and remove the pistons, cups and spring. Inspect the cylinders carefully.

4. Wash out the interior of the bore with clean brake fluid and blow out with compressed air.

5. Measure the wheel cylinder bore, and the outside diameter of the pistons. Compare to determine the clearance. Should the clearance equal .006 or more, replace the entire wheel cylinder assembly.

NOTE: *Always discard the old piston cups and boots whenever the wheel cylinder is disassembled.*

1. Soak the sliding parts of the assembly in clean brake fluid. Assemble them

Rear wheel cylinder

in the cylinder as shown in the illustration.

2. Put the cylinder on the back plate and torque bolts to 7 ft. lbs. Connect the pipe connector. Bleed the system.

Parking Brake

Cable

Adjustment

NOTE: *Parking brake should be adjusted if lever can be pulled more than eight ratchet clicks under heavy pressure.*

1. Fully release brake lever and check cable for free movement.

2. Remove the play in the cable by turning brake lever rod adjusting nut.

3. When adjusted, check for the eight ratchet clicks as mentioned. If eight or more still appear, readjust.

Removal and Installation

1. Remove the driver's seat and take off the sill plate.

2. Disconnect the return spring and remove the nut connecting the lever rod with the cable.

3. Loosen the nut holding the cable and remove.

4. Peel back the floor mat and remove the bolts holding the lever. Disconnect the wiring and remove the assembly.

5. Jack up the rear of the car and remove the wheels and brakes. Pull the cable from the rear of the back plate.

Installation is the reverse of removal.

CHASSIS ELECTRICAL

Heater Blower

Removal and Installation

1. Disconnect the battery ground cable and disconnect the wiring at the blower.

2. Remove the heater hose coupling at the cowl.

3. Remove the screws and pull out the blower motor and squirrel cage.

4. Remove the clip holding the cage to the motor and take off.

5. To install, reverse removal procedures.

Heater Core

Removal and Installation

1. Disconnect battery ground cable and drain the radiator.

2. Disconnect heater hoses at connections and plug core tubes to stop spilling.

3. Remove blower case cover and disconnect air door cable. Disconnect the temperature cable at the water valve.

4. Remove the steering wheel and the instrument cluster. Disconnect the wiring for gauges, remove console retaining screws, untie shift lever leather and remove.

5. Remove heater control and radio face plate. Remove the radio and glove box.

6. Disconnect selector cable from driver's side of heater unit. Carefully pull temperature and fresh air cables through cowling and remove control panel.

7. Remove instrument panel assembly.

8. Remove the bolt from the heater unit located at the rear, bottom. Remove four nuts holding unit and blower together and remove heater.

9. Separate heater unit case halves and remove core.

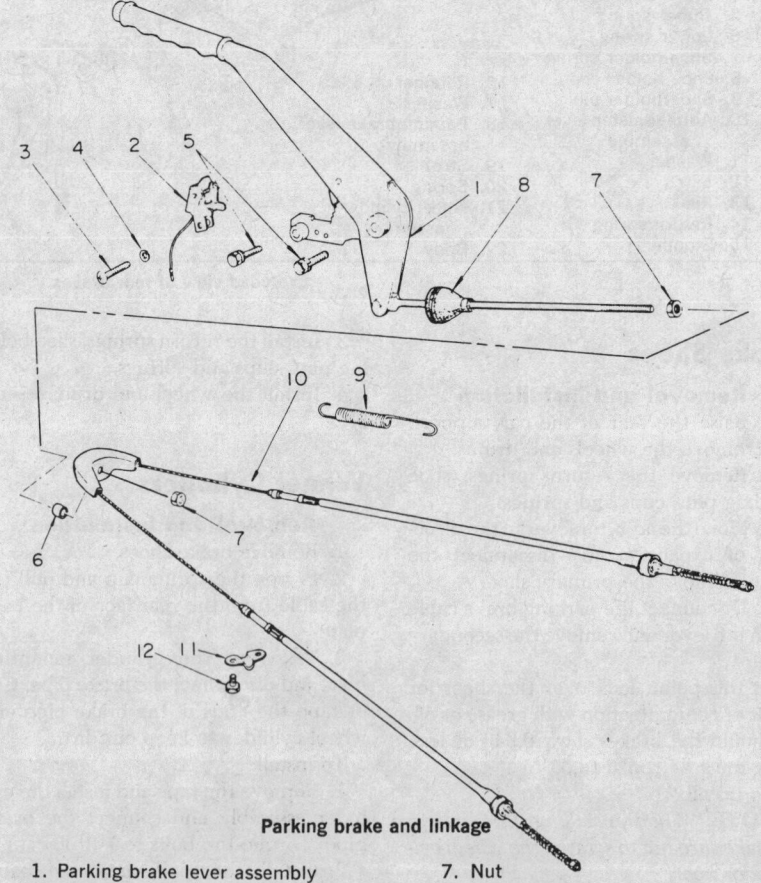

Parking brake and linkage

1. Parking brake lever assembly
2. Parking brake switch assembly
3. Bolt
4. Washer
5. Bolt
6. Sleeve
7. Nut
8. Grommet
9. Return spring
10. Parking brake cable assembly
11. Clip
12. Bolt

10. Installation is the reverse procedure

Radio

Removal and Installation

Disconnect negative battery cable.

1. Remove ash tray and tray support. Remove radio knobs by pulling off.

2. Remove the radio shaft nuts and trim panel.

3. Remove retainer screws from under dash.

4. Disconnect electrical connectors and lead-in cable and take the radio out through the back of the dash.

5. To install, reverse removal procedures.

Windshield Wiper Motor

Removal and Installation

1. Disconnect negative battery cable.

2. Remove nut, washer and crank arm from under the instrument panel.

3. Disconnect wiring at connector.

4. Remove the rubber boot, three screws and the motor assembly.

5. Installation is the reverse of removal.

Instrument Cluster

Removal and Installation

1. Disconnect the negative battery cable.

2. Remove the steering wheel and disconnect the speedometer cable and wing nut.

3. Remove cluster screws, rotate the cluster outward to disconnect the 6 and 12 pole connectors and remove the cluster assembly.

4. Remove the glove box and door.

5. Release instrument panel harness from clips and disconnect at connectors.

6. Disconnect the heater control, control cables at the heater unit and water valve assembly in the engine compartment.

7. Pull out the control lever knobs and remove the panel. Remove the screws and the control assembly.

8. Through the glove box opening, remove instrument panel and loosen the bracket. Disconnect the heater air hoses.

9. Remove the three nuts holding the upper portion of instrument panel and remove the bolts at each end of the inside panel.

10. Remove the bolts holding the steering column bracket to the instrument panel and remove the panel.

11. Reverse the procedures for installation.

Fuse Box Location

The fuse box is located under the instrument panel, along the side wall of the passenger's side of the compartment.

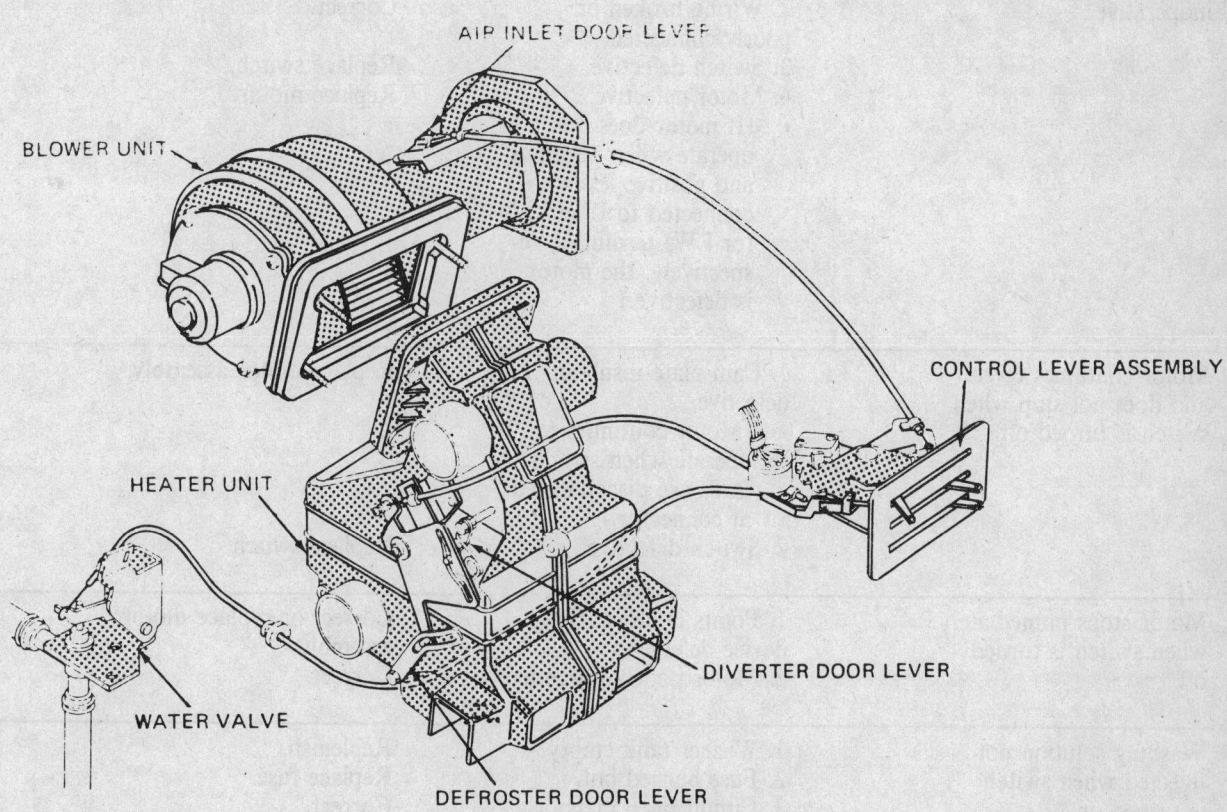

Exploded view of heater and blower assembly

WASHERS AND WIPERS DIAGNOSIS

NOTE: When testing the windshield wiper, keep the windshield wet with water or washing solution.

Complaint	Cause	Correction
Poor wiping action.	1. Blade(s) defective. 2. Wiper link distorted or joint worn.	Replace blade(s). Correct or replace link.
Wiping action sluggish.	1. Circuit poorly connected or grounded. 2. Resistance increased due to twisting of link. (Check operation of link with motor disconnected.) 3. Motor defective. (Disconnect linkage from motor and make a test on motor.)	Correct. Correct link. Replace motor.
Wiper circuit inoperative.	1. Fuse burned out. 2. Wiring broken or poorly connected. 3. Switch defective. 4. Motor defective. (If motor does not operate when negative and positive leads are connected to L and LY (or LW) terminals, respectively, the motor is defective.)	Replace Fuse Correct. Replace switch. Replace motor.
Motor continues to run and does not stop when switch is turned off.	1. Cam plate insulator defective. (Motor continues to operate when switch leads are disconnected at connector.) 2. Switch defective.	Replace motor assembly. Replace switch.
Motor stops immediately when switch is turned off.	1. Points in self-parking device defective. 2. Motor poorly grounded.	Correct or replace motor assembly. Correct.
Washing solution not injected when switch is turned on.	1. Washer tank empty. 2. Fuse burned out. 3. Circuit open or poorly connected. 4. Washer pump defective. 5. Nozzle or pipes clogged.	Replenish. Replace fuse. Correct. Replace washer tank assembly. Clean.
Injection pressure insufficient.	1. Restrictions in nozzle or piping. 2. Washer pump defective.	Clean. Replace washer tank assembly.

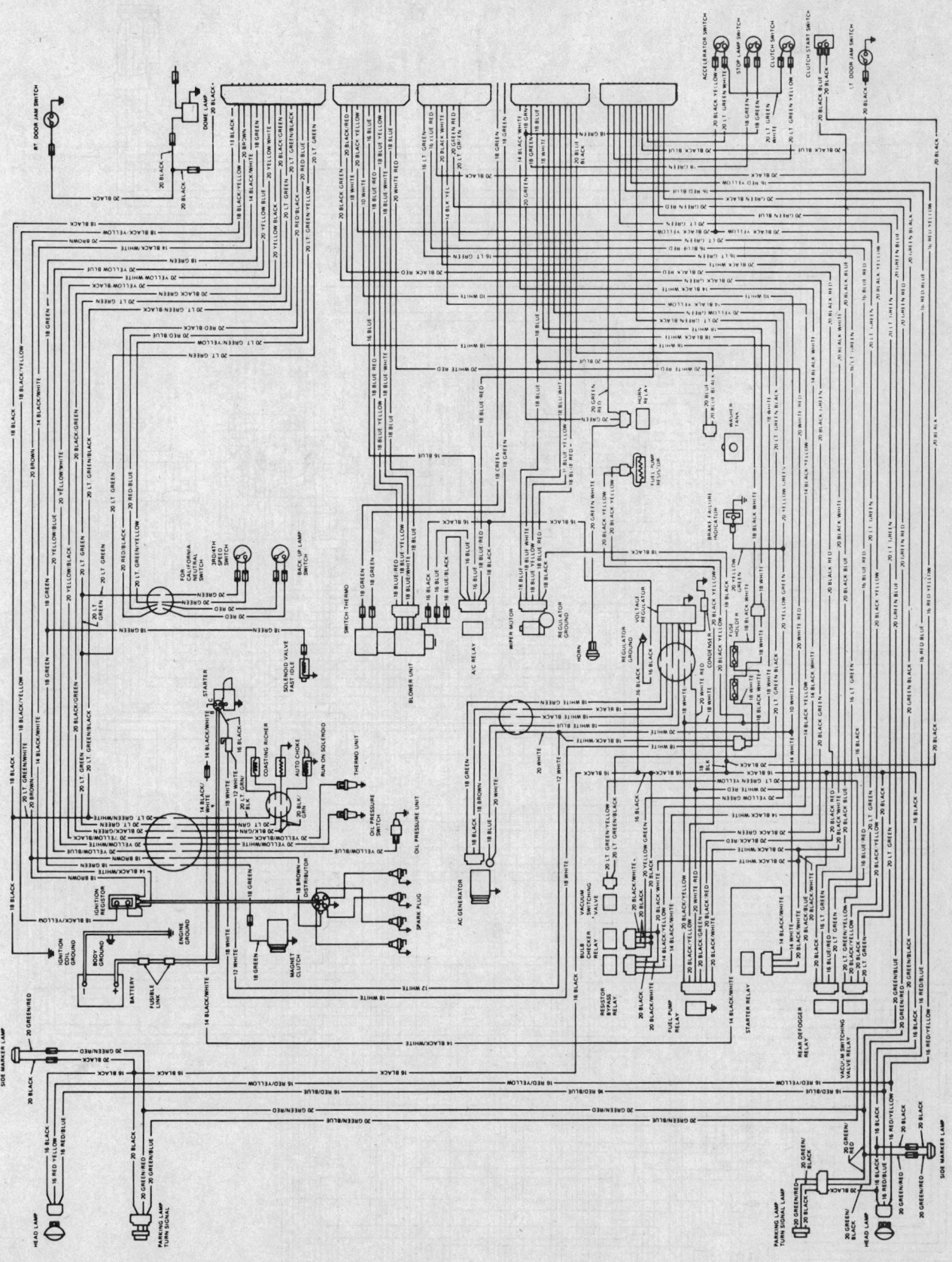

1976-77 Opel Isuzu

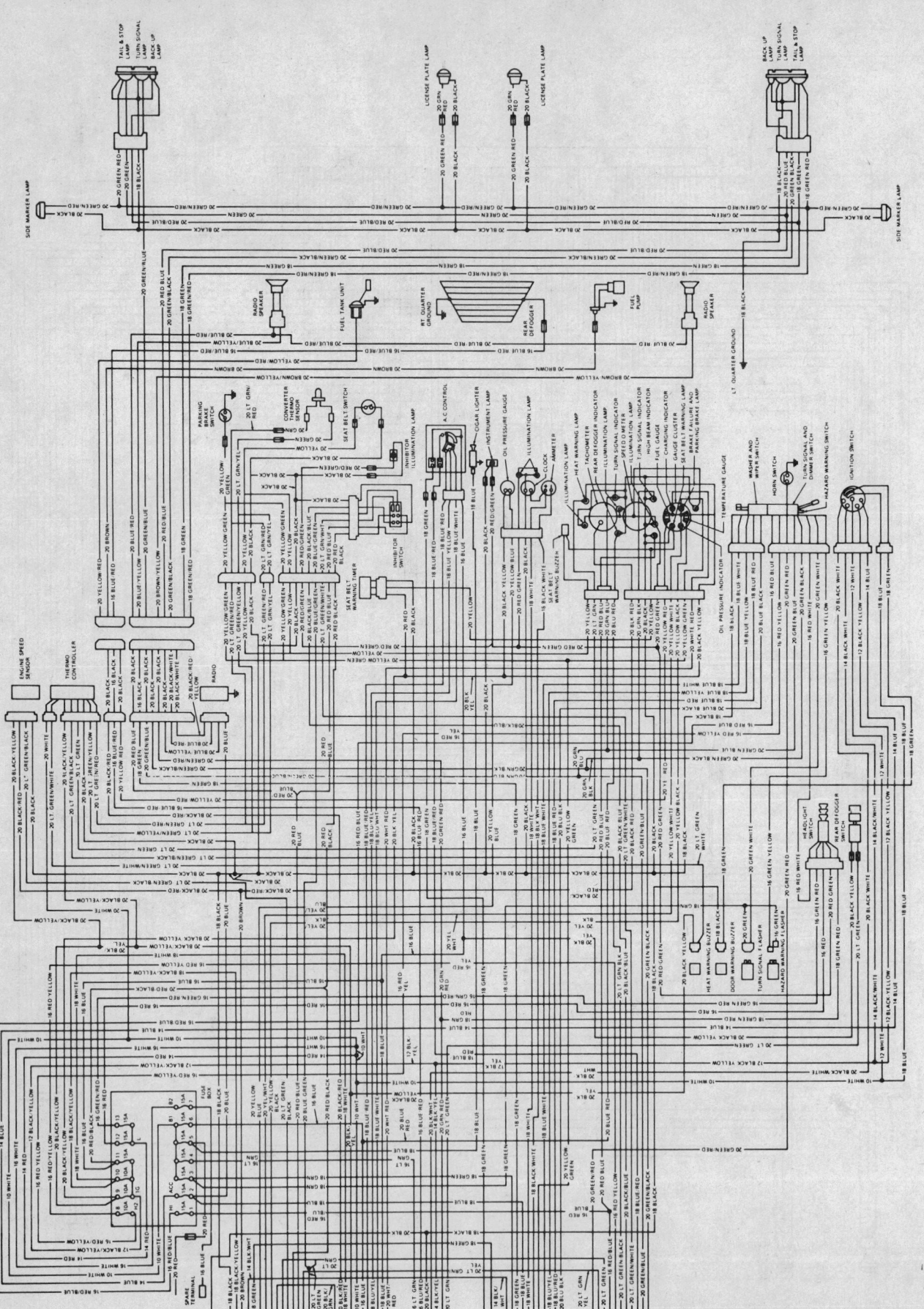

1976-77 Opel Isuzu

SPECIFICATIONS

Porsche

INTRODUCTION

The name Porsche and the term sports car have always been synonymous. The current 911 and 914 series have continued the Porsche tradition of performance and reliability. Myriad competition victories in endurance racing, such as the 24 Hours of Le Mans and the Targa Florio, and in Sports Car Club of America production class racing have kept the marque in the vanguard of the high-performance car ranks. Remarkably, Porsche cars have been in production for only twenty-four years, which is difficult to comprehend in view of the legendary reputation and the legion of enthusiasts that the car has attracted. The first Porsches were built in Gmund, Austria, since, at that time, Professor Porsche was denied entrance to Germany. The factory was eventually moved to its present location near Stuttgart, Germany. Porsche has since grown into a multimillion dollar concern, but the painstaking attention to detail, inherited from the small group of men who produced the first cars, was not lost in the transition from workshop to large factory.

MODEL IDENTIFICATION

1972 911

Front view of 1973 911 E and S models (spoiler optional on T)

1972 914

1973 914 front view

1974 914

1974 911

1975 914

1976 911S

SERIAL NUMBER IDENTIFICATION

Chassis

The chassis number on all models is located on the drivers side windshield post and is visible from the outside of the car. The chassis number on 911 912E models is also found in the luggage compartment under the rug and on the identification plate near the front hood lock catch. The 914 chassis number is stamped on the right front wheel well and on the identification plate on the right headlight housing inside the luggage compartment.

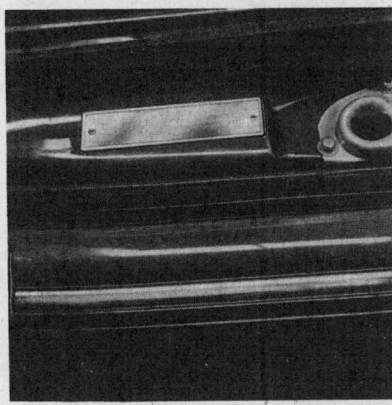

911 identication plate location

911 chassis serial number location

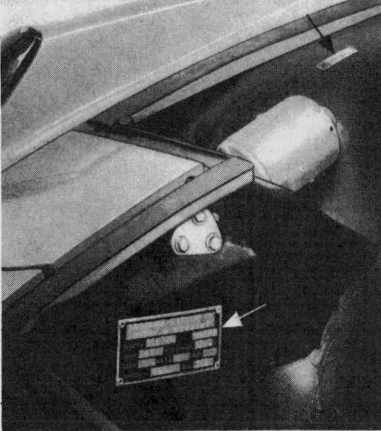

914 identification plate (bottom) and chassis serial number (top) location

The 911 and 912E series chassis identification number breaks down in the following manner:

	911 2 2 1 0001
Series type	911, 911S or 930 (Turbo)
Model year	2 = 1972
	3 = 1973
	4 = 1974
	5 = 1975
Engine type	1 = T
	2 = E or 2.7S
	3 = S
	4 = Carrera
	8 = Tubo
Body type	0 = Porsche coupe
	1 = Targa
	2 = Karmann coupe
Four-digit sequential number	

The 914 series chassis identification number is broken down as follows:

	47 12 000001
Series type	47 914 series
Model year	2 = 1972
	3 = 1973
	4 = 1974
	5 = 1975
	6 = 1976
Factory number 29	
Five-digit sequential number	

Porsche

Chassis Identification Chart

Year	Model	Starting Number
1972	911T	9112100001
	911T Targa	9112110001
	911E	9112200001
	911E Targa	9112210001
	911S	9112300001
	911S Targa	9112310001
	914	4722900001
1973	911T	9113100001
	911T Targa	9113110001
	911E	9113200001
	911E Targa	9113210001
	911S	9113300001
	911S Targa	9113310001
	914	4732900001

(P) Porsche body
(K) Karmann body

Engine Identification Chart

Year	Model	Starting Number
1972	911T	6120001
	911E	6220001
	911S	6320001
	914	W0000001
1973	911T	6130001
	911E	6230001
	911S	6330001
	914 (1.7 except Calif.)	EA0057001
	914 (1.7 Calif.)	EB0000001
	914 (2.0)	GA0000001

914 1.7 liter engine serial number

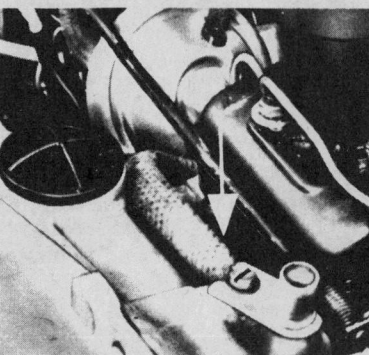

914 2.0 liter engine serial number

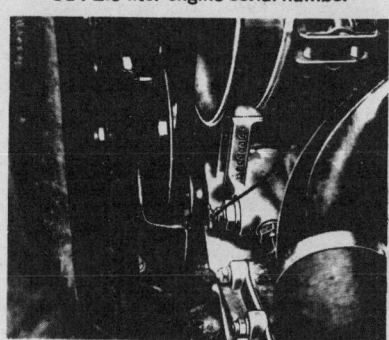

911 identification plate location

Engine

The engine number for the 911 model is located on the right side of the crankcase adjacent to the blower. The 1.7 liter, 914 engine number is stamped on the upper right of the crankcase, below the air intake runners. The 2.0 liter, 914 engine number is stamped on the upper part of the crankcase between the oil filler and the blower housing. The 912E engine number is stamped in the crankcase on the left side, near the mount for the air pump.

911 engine numbers are divided as follows:

```
              6 3 2 0001
Engine type   6 = cylinder
Engine model  1 = T
              2 = E
              3 = S
              4 = Carrera
              8 = Turbo
Model year    2 = 1972
              3 = 1973
              4 = 1974
              5 = 1975
              6 = 1976
              7 = 1977
Four-digit sequential number
```

914 engine numbers are divided as follows:

```
              W 0 000 001
Engine type   W = 1.7 liter, 4 cylinder
              EA = 1.7 liter, 4 cylinder
                   (except California)
              EB = 1.7 liter, 4 cylinder
                   (California)
              GA = 2.0 liter, 4 cylinder
              EC = 1.8 liter AFC
Seven-digit sequential number
```

GENERAL ENGINE SPECIFICATIONS

Year	Model	Engine Displacement cc (Cu in.)	Carburetor Type	Horsepower @ rpm ①	Torque @ rpm (ft lbs) ①	Bore x Stroke (in.)	Compress. Ratio (to 1)
1972	911T	2341 (142.8)	Fuel Injection	134 @ 5600	140 @ 4000	3.31 x 2.77	7.5
	911E	2341 (142.8)	Fuel Injection	157 @ 6200	147 @ 4500	3.31 x 2.77	8.0
	911S	2341 (142.8)	Fuel Injection	181 @ 6500	154 @ 5200	3.31 x 2.77	8.5
	914	1679 (102.5)	Fuel Injection	85 @ 5000	98 @ 2700	3.54 x 2.60	8.2
1973	911T	2341 (142.8)	Fuel Injection	134 @ 5600	140 @ 4000	3.31 x 2.77	7.5
	911E	2341 (142.8)	Fuel Injection	157 @ 6200	147 @ 4500	3.31 x 2.77	8.0
	911S	2341 (142.8)	Fuel Injection	181 @ 6500	154 @ 5200	3.31 x 2.77	8.5
	914	1679 (102.5)	Fuel Injection	76 @ 4900 ②	92 @ 2700 ③	3.54 x 2.60	8.2 ④
	914 2.0	1971 (120.3)	Fuel Injection	91 @ 4900	105 @ 3500	3.70 x 2.80	7.6
1974	911	2687 (164)	Fuel Injection	143 @ 5700	168 @ 3800	3.54 x 2.77	8.0
	911S/ Carrera	2687 (164)	Fuel Injection	167 @ 5800	168 @ 4000	3.54 x 2.77	8.5
	914 1.8	1795 (109.5)	Fuel Injection	76 @ 4900	92 @ 2700	3.66 x 2.60	7.3

GENERAL ENGINE SPECIFICATIONS

Year	Model	Engine Displacement cc (Cu in.)	Carburetor Type	Horsepower @ rpm [1]	Torque @ rpm (ft lbs) [1]	Bore x Stroke (in.)	Compress. Ratio (to 1)
	914 2.0	1971 (120.3)	Fuel Injection	91 @ 4900	105 @ 3500	3.70 x 2.79	7.6
1975	911S/ Carrera	2687 (164)	Fuel Injection	157 @ 5800	166 @ 4000	3.54 x 2.77	8.5
	914 1.8	1795 (109.5)	Fuel Injection	72.5 @ 4900	89 @ 4000	3.66 x 2.60	7.3
	914 2.0	1971 (120.3)	Fuel Injection	84 @ 4900	97 @ 4000	3.70 x 2.79	7.6
1976	911S	2687 (164)	Fuel Injection	157 @ 5800[5]	166 @ 4000	3.54 x 2.77	8.5
	Turbo	2994 (183)	Fuel Injection[6]	234 @ 5500	245 @ 4000	3.74 x 2.77	6.5
	912E	1971 (120.3)	Fuel Injection	86 @ 4900	98 @ 4000	3.70 x 2.79	7.6
	914 1.8	1795 (109.5)	Fuel Injection	72.5 @ 4900	89 @ 4000	3.66 x 2.60	7.3
	914 2.0	1971 (120.3)	Fuel Injection	84 @ 4900	97 @ 4000	3.70 x 2.79	7.6
1977	911S	2687 (164)	Fuel injection	157 @ 5800	168 @ 4000	3.54 x 2.77	8.5
	Turbo	2994 (183)	Fuel Injection [6]	234 @ 5500	245 @ 4000	3.70 x 2.77	6.5

[1] 1972 and later horsepower and torque ratings are SAE net values.
[2] California: 69 @ 5000
[3] California: 87 @ 2700
[4] California: 7.3
[5] California: 152 @ 5800
[6] Turbocharged

TUNE-UP SPECIFICATIONS

Year	Model	Engine Displace. cc (Cu in.)	Spark Plugs Type *	Spark Plugs Gap (in.)	Distributor Point Dwell (deg)	Distributor Point Gap (in.)	Ignition Timing (deg) Basic	Ignition Timing (deg) Dynamic @ rpm	Intake Valve Opens (deg)	Compress. Press. (psi)	Idle Speed (rpm)	Valve Clearance (in.) In	Valve Clearance (in.) Ex
1972	911T	2341 (142.8)	W265-P21	0.024	37 ± 3	0.016	5A	32-38B @ 6000	15B	[1]	850-950	0.004	0.004
	911E	2341 (142.8)	W265-P21	0.024	37 ± 3	0.016	5A	32-38B @ 6000	20B	[1]	850-950	0.004	0.004
	911S	2341 (142.8)	W265-P21	0.024	37 ± 3	0.016	5A	32-38B @ 6000	38B	[1]	850-950	0.004	0.004
	914	1679 (102.5)	W175-T2	0.028 [3]	50 ± 3	0.016	5B	27B @ 3500	11°30'	[1]	850-950	0.006	0.006
1973	911T	2341 (142.8)	W235-P21	0.022	37 ± 3	0.016	5A	32-38B @ 6000	16B	[1]	850-950	0.004	0.004
	911E	2341 (142.8)	W265-P21 5 [4]	0.022	37 ± 3	0.016	5A	32-38B @ 6000	18B	[1]	850-950	0.004	0.004
	911S	2341 (142.8)	W265-P21	0.022	37 ± 3	0.016	5A	32-38B @ 6000	38B	[1]	850-950	0.004	0.004
	914 1.7	1679 (102.5)	W175-T2	0.028	47 ± 3	0.016	5B [5]	27B @ 3500	12B	[1]	850-950	0.006	0.006
	914 2.0	1971 (120.3)	W175-T2	0.028	47 ± 3	0.016	5B [5]	27B @ 3500	12B	[1]	850-950	0.006	0.008
1974	911	2687 (164)	W215-P21	0.022	38 ± 3 [6]	0.016	5A	—	1A	[1]	850-950	0.004	0.004
	911S/ Carrera	2687 (164)	W235-P21	0.022	38 ± 3 [6]	0.016	5A	—	6A	[1]	850-950	0.004	0.004
	914 1.8	1795 (109.5)	W175-T2	0.028	47 ± 3	0.016	7½B	—	12B	[1]	850-950	0.006	0.006
	914 2.0	1971 (120.3)	W175-T2	0.028	47 ± 3	0.016	—	27B @ 3500	12B	[1]	850-950	0.006	0.008

Porsche

TUNE-UP SPECIFICATIONS

Year	Model	Engine Displace. cc (Cu in.)	SPARK PLUGS Type *	SPARK PLUGS Gap (in.)	DISTRIBUTOR Point Dwell (deg)	DISTRIBUTOR Point Gap (in.)	IGNITION TIMING (deg) Basic	IGNITION TIMING (deg) Dynamic @ rpm	Intake Valve Opens (deg)	Compress. Press. (psi)	IDLE SPEED (rpm)	VALVE CLEARANCE (in.) In	VALVE CLEARANCE (in.) Ex
1975	911S/ Carrera	2687 (164)	W235-P21	0.022	38 ± 3	0.016	5A	—	6A	①	850-950	0.004	0.004
	914 1.8	1795 (109.5)	W175-T2	0.028	47 ± 3	0.016	7½B	—	12B	①	850-950	0.006	0.006
	914 2.0	1971 (120.3)	W175-T2	0.028	47 ± 3	0.016	—	27B @ 3500	12B	①	850-950	0.006	0.008
1976	911S	2687 (164)	W235-P21	0.022	38 ± 3 ⑥	0.016	5A	—	6A	①	850-950	0.004	0.004
	Turbo	2994 (183)	W280-P21	0.024	Electronic		7A	29B @ 4000	3A	①	950-1050	0.004	0.004
	912E	1971 (120.3)	W175-M3	0.028	47 ± 3	0.016	—	27B @ 3500	12B	①	925	0.006	0.008
	914 1.8	1795 (102.5)	W175-M3	0.028	47 ± 3	0.016	7½B	—	12B	①	850-950	0.006	0.006
	914 2.0	1971 (120.3)	W175-M3	0.028	47 ± 3	0.016	—	27B @ 3500	12B	①	850-950	0.006	0.008
1977	911S	2687 (164)	W235-P21	0.024	38 ± 3 ⑥	0.016	TDC ⑦	—	6A	①	900-1000	0.004	0.004
	Turbo	2994 (183)	W280-P21	0.024	Electronic		7A	29B @ 4000	3A	①	950-1050	0.004	0.004

*   Bosch spark plugs
B   Before top dead center
A   After top dead center
MT   Manual transmission
AT   Automatic transmission

② With Bosch distributor, 40° ± 3° with Marelli distributor
③ 0.016-0.020 in. for cold weather setting
④ W260T2 gapped at 0.028 in.
⑤ Static, 5°A at idle speed
⑥ With Bosch distributor, 37° ± 3° with Marelli distributor
⑦ California: 15ATDC

① All cylinders should be within 22 psi of the highest reading. Compression test to be performed with engine warmer than 140°F

NOTE: The underhood specifications sticker often reflects tune-up specification changes made in production. Sticker figures must be used if they disagree with those in this chart.

FIRING ORDER

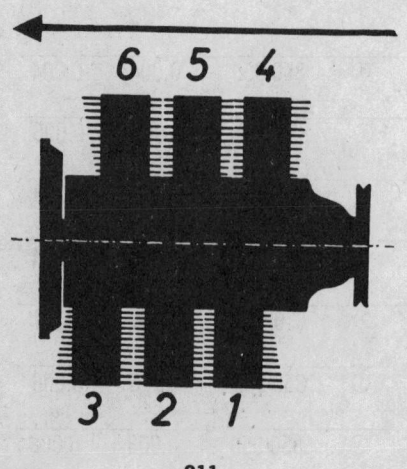

911

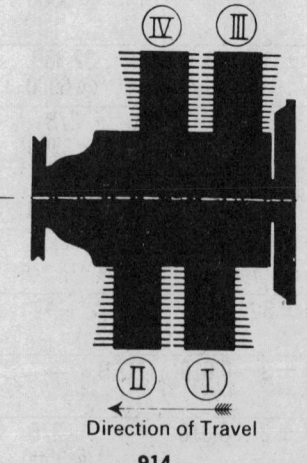

Direction of Travel

914

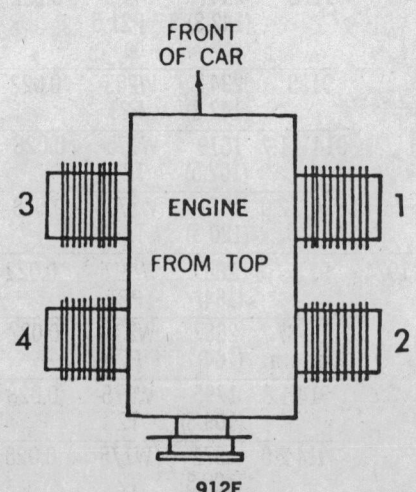

912E

CAPACITIES

Year	Model	Engine Displacement cc (Cu in.)	Engine Crankcase (qts)	Transaxle (qts)	Gasoline Tank ① (qts)
1972	911T	2341 (142.8)	9.5⑤	3.17	16.4
	911E	2341 (142.8)	9.5⑤	3.17	16.4
	911S	2341 (142.8)	10.5⑥	3.17	16.4
	914	1679 (102.5)	3.7④	2.6	16.4
1973	911T	2341 (142.8)	11.6⑦	3.17	16.4
	911E	2341 (142.8)	11.6⑦	3.17	16.4
	911S	2341 (142.8)	11.6⑦⑧	3.17	16.4
	914	1679 (102.5)	3.7④	2.6④	16.4
	914	1971 (120.27)	3.7④	2.6④	16.4
1974	911	2687 (164)	11.6⑦	3.17	21.13
	911S/Carrera	2687 (164)	11.6⑦⑧	3.17	21.13
	914	All	3.7	2.6	16.4
1975	911S/Carrera	2687 (164)	11.6⑦⑧	3.17	21.13
	914	All	3.7④	2.6	16.4

Year	Model	Engine Displacement cc (Cu in.)	Engine Crankcase (qts)	Transaxle (qts)	Gasoline Tank ① (qts)
1976	911S	2687 (164)	11.6⑦⑧	3.17	21.13
	Turbo	2994 (183)	13	3.91	21.13
	912E	1971 (120.3)	3.7④	3.17	21.13
	914	All	3.7④	2.6	16.4
1977	911S	2687 (164)	13⑨	3.17	21.13
	Turbo	2994 (183)	13	3.91	21.13

① Including 1.6 gal reserve
② Initial filling including oil cooler is 10.5 qts
③ Total capacity with Sportomatic is 11.6 qts; however, only 9.5 qts are added when refilling
④ With filter, 3.2 qts refill without filter
⑤ Total capacity with Sportomatic is 12.1 qts; however, only 9.5 qts are added when refilling
⑥ Total capacity with Sportomatic is 13.2 qts; however, only 9.5 qts are added when refilling
⑦ Total capacity with Sportomatic is 13.6 qts; however, only 10.4 qts are added when refilling
⑧ Total capacity of 14.2 qts with optional oil cooler. Capacity with oil cooler and Sportomatic is 16.9 qts. Normal refill for all models is 10.4 qts.
⑨ 15 qts with Sportomatic

CRANKSHAFT AND CONNECTING ROD SPECIFICATIONS
All measurements are given in millimeters

Model	Engine Displacement cc (Cu in.)	CRANKSHAFT				CONNECTING ROD		
		Main Brg① Journal Dia	Main Brg. Oil Clearance	Shaft End-Play	Thrust on No.	Journal① Diameter	Oil Clearance	Side Clearance
911	All	56.970-② 56.990	0.010- 0.072	0.010- 0.195	1	51.971- 51.990	0.030- 0.088	0.200- 0.400
914	1679 (102.5)	59.971-③ 59.990	0.050-④ 0.100	0.070- 0.130	1	39.984- 40.000	0.020- 0.070	0.100- 0.400
914/912E	1971 (120.3)	59.971-③ 59.990	0.050-④ 0.100	0.070- 0.130	1	49.983- 49.996	0.020- 0.070	0.100- 0.400

① Undersize bearings available in 0.25, 0.50, and 0.75 mm sizes
② Journal diameter for bearings 1 through 7, journal 8 is 30.980-30.993 mm
③ Journal diameter for bearings 1 through 3, journal 4 is 39.984-40.000 mm
④ Clearance on bearing 2 is 0.03-0.09 mm

VALVE SPECIFICATIONS

Model	Engine Displacement cc (Cu in.)	Face Angle (deg)	Spring Test Pressure (lbs @ in.)	Spring Installed Height (mm)	STEM TO GUIDE CLEARANCE (mm)		STEM DIAMETER (mm)	
					Intake	Exhaust	Intake	Exhaust
911	All	45	176.4 @ 1.21①	35③	0.030-0.057	0.050-0.077	8.97	8.95
914/912E	All	45②	168-186 @ 1.14	30	0.45	0.45	7.94	8.91

① Intake; 165.3 @ 1.25 for exhaust
② 30° for intake valves on 1.7 and 1.8 engines
③ 35.5 mm for exhaust

PISTON AND RING SPECIFICATIONS
All measurements in millimeters

Model	Engine Displacement cc (Cu. in.)	Piston Clearance	RING GAP			RING SIDE CLEARANCE		
			Top Compression	Bottom Compression	Oil Control	Top Compression	Bottom Compression	Oil Control
911	All	0.025-0.045	0.074-0.107	0.058-0.071	0.025-0.051	0.300-0.450	0.300-0.450	0.249-0.399
914/912E	All	0.020-①0.050	0.061-0.089	0.041-0.071	0.020-0.051	0.350-0.551	0.300-0.551	0.249-0.399

① 1.7 engine: 0.04-0.06

TORQUE SPECIFICATIONS
All readings in ft lbs

Model	Engine Displacement cc (Cu in.)	Cylinder Head Bolts	Rod Bearing Bolts	Main Bearing Bolts	Crankshaft Pulley Bolt	Flywheel To Crankshaft Bolts
914/912E	All	23	24	24	43	80
911	All	24	36	25	58	109

TORQUE SEQUENCE

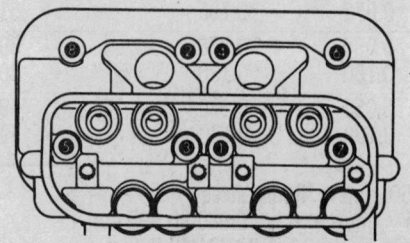

Four cylinder engine cylinder head torque sequence

BATTERY AND STARTER SPECIFICATIONS
All cars use 12 volt, negative ground electrical systems

Model	Battery Amp Hour Capacity	Starter							Brush Spring Tension (oz)	Min. Brush Length (in.)
		Lock Test			No Load Test					
		Amps	Volts	Torque (ft/lbs)	Amps	Volts	RPM			
911/912E	(2) 36①	160-200	9	1100-1400	33-50	11.5	6400-7900		42.3	0.5
914	45	170-205	9	900-1300	35-45	12	7400-9100		42	N.A.

① 1974-77 uses 1 66 ah battery

ALTERNATOR AND REGULATOR SPECIFICATIONS

Model	ALTERNATOR		REGULATOR						
	Part No. or Manufacturer	Output (amps.)	Part No. or Manufacturer	Air Gap (in.)	Field Relay Point Gap (in.)	Volts to Close	Air Gap (in.)	Regulator Point Gap (in.)	Volts @ 75°
911/912E	Bosch	55	Bosch			— Not Adjustable —			
914	Bosch	50	Bosch			— Not Adjustable —			

BRAKE SPECIFICATIONS
All measurements given are (in.) unless noted

Year	Model	Lug Nut Torque (ft/lb)	Master Cylinder Bore	Brake Disc		Brake Drum			Minimum Lining Thickness	
				Minimum Thickness	Maximum Run-Out	Diameter	Max. Machine O/S	Max. Wear Limit	Front	Rear
1972-77	911/912E①	94	0.75	③	0.008	—	—	—	0.08	0.08
1972-76	914	94	0.687	0.35②	0.008	—	—	—	0.08	0.08

— Not Applicable; 4 wheel disc brakes used on all models
① Solid discs on 912E; ventilated on all 911 models
② Wear limit—0.335 in.
③ 912E (front)—0.45 in.
   912E (rear)—0.37 in. (wear limit) 0.35
   911 (front/rear)—0.725 (refinish limit) or 0.70 (wear limit)

NOTE: Minimum lining thickness is as recommended by the manufacturer. Due to variations in state inspection regulations, the minimum allowable thickness may be different than recommended by the manufacturer.

WHEEL ALIGNMENT

Year	Model	CASTER		CAMBER		Toe-in (deg)
		Range (deg)	Pref Setting (deg)	Range (deg)	Pref Setting (deg)	
1972	911	6°20'-7°20'	6°50'	—50'-(+)10'	0°②	0°①
1973-77	911/912E	5°50'-6°20'	6°5'	—50'-(+)10'	0°②	0°③
1972-76	914	5°30'-6°30'	6°	—40'-(+)20'	0°④	+20' ± 10'⑤

① Front and rear wheels
② Rear wheels —1 ± 10'
③ Rear wheels: 0° ± 20'
④ Rear wheels: —30' ± 20'
⑤ Rear wheels: 0° ± 15'

TUNE-UP PROCEDURES
Spark Plugs

In addition to performing their basic function of igniting the air-fuel mixture, spark plugs can also serve as very useful diagnostic tools. Once removed, compare your spark plugs with the samples in the "Troubleshooting" section. Typical plug conditions are illustrated along with their causes and remedies. Plugs which exhibit only normal wear and deposits can be cleaned, gapped, and reinstalled.

Before removing the spark plug leads, number the towers on the distributor cap with tape. Grasp each spark plug boot and pull it straight out. Check the condition of the rubber boot and/or shroud seals and replace them if necessary. Install the spark plug socket on the plug's hex and remove it. If removal is difficult, loosen the plug only slightly and drip some light oil onto the threads. Allow the oil to penetrate and then unscrew the spark plug. Proceeding this way will prevent damaging the threads in the cylinder head. Be sure to keep the socket straight to avoid breaking the ceramic insulator. Most spark plug sockets are lined with rubber for this reason. Inspect the plugs using the "Troubleshooting" section illustrations and then clean or discard them according to their condition. Recommended spark plug gap is given in the "Tune-Up Specifications Chart." Use a spark plug wire gauge for checking the gap. The wire should pass through the electrodes with just a slight drag. Using the electrode bending tool on the end of the gauge, bend the side electrode to adjust the gap. Never attempt to adjust the center electrode. Lightly oil the threads of the replacement plug and install it hand-tight. The spark plugs in all engines should be tightened to a torque of 18–21 ft lbs. Install the ignition wire boots firmly on the spark plugs. On the 914 models, be sure that the cooling shroud seals are snug or cooling efficiency will be lost.

Breaker Points and Condenser

Snap the two retaining clips off the distributor cap. Remove the cap and examine it for cracks, deterioration, or carbon tracks. Replace the cap, if necessary, by transferring one wire at a time from the old cap to the new one. Some 911 models have a dust cover which must be removed to service the points. Examine the rotor for corrosion or wear and replace it if necessary. **NOTE:** *Marelli rotors are retained by a screw.* Check the points for pitting and burning. Slight im-

perfections on the contact surface may be filed off with a point file (fine emery paper will also do), but it is usually wise to replace the breaker point set when tuning. Replace the condenser when you replace the point set. All Porsches are equipped with externally mounted condensers mounted on the body of the distributor. To replace the condenser, disconnect its lead from the distributor primary terminal and unscrew it from the mounting on the body. Reverse the removal procedure to install a replacement condenser.

Breaker Point Removal and Installation

911

911 distributor showing breaker point retaining screws

NOTE: *Porsche recommends removing the distributor to replace the breaker points on these models. The problem is one of access and working space. Some mechanics find they are able to remove the points with the distributor in the car; however it is much easier to do it out of the car. Follow the directions in the "Engine Electrical" section to remove the distributor and then remove the points as outlined below.*

The 1976–77 Turbo is equipped with pointless, electronic ignition and requires only distributor cap and wire condition checks.

1. Undo the retaining screw(s), if so equipped, and remove the rotor.

2. Remove the breaker point retaining screw(s), disconnect the primary lead from the terminal, and lift out the breaker point set.

NOTE: *When removing the points in the car, it is best to use a magnetic screwdriver to prevent dropping the screws.*

3. Install the replacement point set, but leave the adjustment screw hand-tight.

4. Turn the engine until the rubbing block of the breaker arm rests on the highest point of a cam lobe.

5. Insert a 0.016 in. feeler gauge between the two contact points. The gauge should pull through the points with just a slight drag.

6. When the gap is adjusted, tighten the retaining screw. Lightly lubricate the cam with silicone grease.

7. Install the rotor.

8. Install the distributor cap. Check the dwell angle and ignition timing as outlined in the following sections.

914 and 912E

The 914, in addition to resistor spark plugs, is equipped with a resistor rotor. The rotor may be checked with an ohmmeter. If a resistance greater than 10k ohms is indicated, the rotor should be replaced.

1. Remove the breaker point retaining screw.

2. Unclip the wire lead and remove the point set.

3. Install the replacement point set, tightening the retaining screw only hand-tight.

4. Turn the engine (with a remote starter switch or by having an assistant "bump" the starter) until the rubbing block of the point set is on the high point of a cam lobe.

5. Using a 0.016 in. feeler gauge, adjust the point gap and then tighten the retaining screw.

6. Place a few drops of engine oil on the pivot bearing of the breaker arm and the felt in the center of the distributor shaft.

7. Install the rotor and distributor cap.

8. Check the dwell angle and ignition timing as outlined in the following sections.

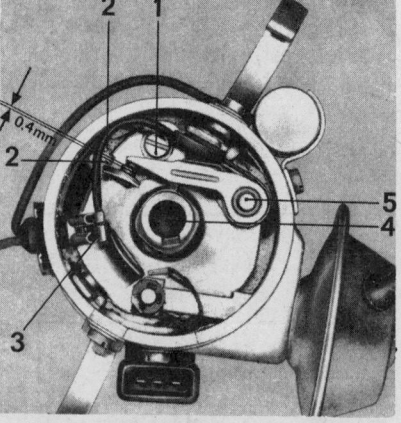

914 distributor
1. Retaining screw
2. Breaker plate
3. Primary connection
4. Distributor shaft felt
5. Breaker arm pivot (place a few drops of oil on 4 and 5)

Dwell Angle

The dwell angle or cam angle is the number of degrees that the distributor cam rotates while the points are closed. There is an inverse relationship between dwell angle and point gap. Increasing the point gap will decrease the dwell angle and vice versa. Checking the dwell angle with a meter is a far more accurate method of measuring point opening than the feeler gauge method.

After setting the point gap to specification with a feeler gauge, check the dwell angle with a meter. Hook-up the dwell meter according to the maker's instruction sheet. The negative lead is grounded and the positive lead connected to the primary wire (terminal no. 1 on 911 models) that runs from the coil to the distributor. Start the engine, let it idle and reach operating temperature, and observe the dwell. The reading should fall within the allowable range. If it does not, the gap will have to be reset or the breaker points will have to be replaced.

911 dwell meter hook-up

1. Ground connection
2. Primary connection

Ignition Timing

CAUTION: *When performing this or any other adjustment with the engine running, be very careful of the fan belt and pulley.*

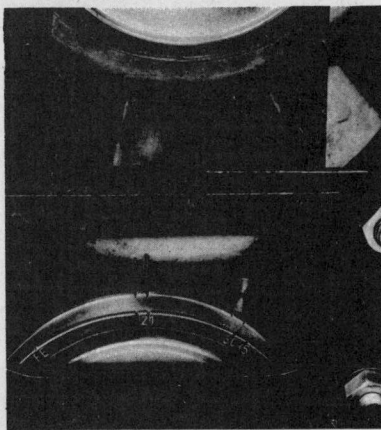

1972-1973 911 timing marks

Ignition timing should always be checked as part of any tune-up. Timing is checked after the points have been adjusted or replaced. A stroboscopic timing light is a necessity for timing any Porsche and, in addition, a static 12 V timing light is necessary for the 911, and the 914.

1972–76 911

These models are equipped with a vacuum retard unit which retards the ignition to 5° ATDC at idle. Ignition timing is checked both at idle and at 6000 rpm with a stroboscopic timing light. Leave the vacuum hose on. The crankshaft pulley has a TDC notch ("Z1"), a 5° ATDC notch directly to the left of the "Z1" notch, a 30° BTDC notch, and a 35° notch. The 1972–75 911 distributor has a slotted mounting flange on its base. The retaining nut is loosened and the distributor swivels on the mounting stud to make timing changes.

1. Start the engine and allow it to reach normal operating temperature.
2. Stop the engine and attach a timing light to no. 1 spark plug according to the manufacturer's instructions.
3. Restart the engine. Make sure that the idle speed is according to specifications and that the vacuum advance hose is connected.
4. When the timing light flashes, the 5° ATDC notch in the pulley should be aligned with the reference notch in the blower housing.
5. If the notches do not align, loosen the retaining nut and slowly rotate the distributor as necessary until they line up. Ignition timing is now correct at idle.
6. Dynamic timing is checked at this point. Total advance at 6000 rpm should be between 32° and 38°.
7. While you stand at the rear with the timing light aimed at the timing notches on the crankshaft pulley, have an assistant accelerate the engine to 6000 rpm for an instant.

CAUTION: *Do not hold the engine at this high speed for an extended period.*

8. The pulley has a 30° and 35° notch, so 32–38° would start to the right of the 30° notch and end just to the right of the 35° notch. The blower housing reference notch should be aligned with the desired timing area on the crankshaft pulley when the light flashes.
9. If the timing is incorrect, loosen the nut and slowly rotate the distributor to adjust it.
10. Stop the engine and remove the timing light.

1977 911S and Turbo

Ignition timing is done with the vacuum hose on. Use the same basic procedure given for earlier models. Timing for the 49 states 911S is TDC at normal idle (Z1 notch). California 911S models get 15° ATDC at idle speed (15° notch to the left of Z1). The centrifugal advance timing check is no longer performed on these models. Basic timing for the Turbo is 7° ATDC at idle. Full centrifugal advance should be 29° BTDC and come in at 4000 rpm.

1972–73 914

Basic timing is set at 5° BTDC and checked with a static timing light. Dy-

914 timing marks

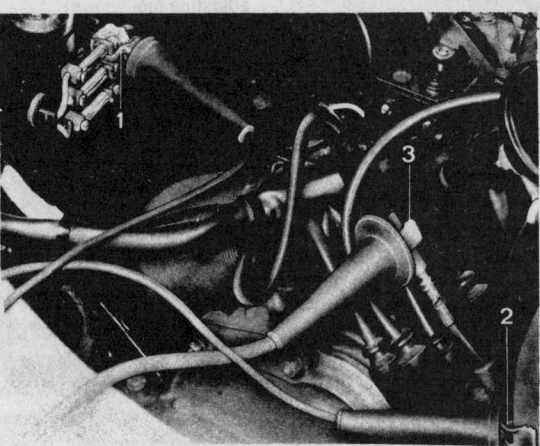

911 timing light hook-up

1. Positive connection
2. Ground connection
3. No. 1 terminal

namic timing is set at 3500 rpm and checked with a stroboscopic timing light. 1973 models are equipped with vacuum retard ignition timing which should be checked dynamically at idle (5° A) in addition to 3500 rpm.

1. Loosen the clamp on the right hand heater hose, and pull the hose from the heater blower. Position the hose out of the way.

2. Unscrew the inspection hole cover from the cooling shroud.

3. Turn the engine until the black notch in the crankshaft pulley aligns with V-shaped notch in the blower housing. Remove the distributor cap and rotor.

4. Attach one lead of a 12 V static timing to terminal no. 1 (primary) on the distributor and the other lead to ground. Switch on the ignition.

5. Loosen the distributor clamp and rotate the distributor clockwise until the light is out. The points will be closed.

6. Slowly turn the distributor counterclockwise until the breaker points open and the light just comes on. Tighten the distributor clamp.

7. Install the rotor and distributor cap.

8. Disconnect both vacuum hoses from the vacuum unit on the distributor. Install a stroboscopic timing light according to the manufacturer's instructions.

9. Start the engine and allow it to reach normal operating temperature.

10. On 1973 models, check the timing at idle speed first (5° A). While you aim the timing light through the inspection hole, have an assistant accelerate the engine to 3500 rpm for an instant.

11. The red notch (27°) on the crankshaft pulley should be aligned with the V-shaped notch in the blower housing.

12. If the notches are not in alignment, loosen the distributor clamp and slowly rotate the distributor until they do align.

13. Tighten the retaining clamp, stop the engine, and remove the timing light.

1974–76 914

1. Hook up the timing light.

2. Disconnect the distributor vacuum hose(s).

3. Unscrew the inspection hole cover from the cooling shroud.

4. Start the engine and bring it to normal operating temperature.

5. Advance should be 7.5° BTDC at idle speed on 1.8 engine models.

6. On 2.0 models, accelerate the engine to 3500 rpm. Timing should be at 27° BTDC (red notch aligned with V-shaped notch in blower housing).

7. If the timing is off specifications, loosen the distributor clamp and slowly rotate the distributor until it is correct.

8. Shut the engine off and connect the vacuum hose(s).

1976 912E

This engine is essentially the same as

the 2.0 liter engine used in the 914. Timing is checked in the same manner as the 2.0 914. The only difference is in the location of the timing marks. The air injection pump made it necessary to move the timing marks. The TDC marker is located on the fanbelt pulley. The timing scale is on a bracket attached to the intake housing.

Valve Lash

Adjustment

1. The engine must be cold when adjusting the valves on any Porsche. Remove the rocker arm covers, two per head in the case of the 911.

2. The valves of each cylinder are adjusted with that piston at the top of its compression stroke. Both the intake and exhaust valves will be closed at this point. Turn the engine to align the TDC mark ("Z1" for the 911 and the black notch on 914 models) with the reference mark.

3. Using a feeler gauge (thickness equal to a figure given in the "Valve Clearance" column of the "Tune-Up Specifications Chart"), check the clearance between the valve stem and the rocker arm. The feeler gauge should just slip through; if it has to be forced the clearance will be incorrect.

914 valve clearance adjustment (special adjusting tool shown)

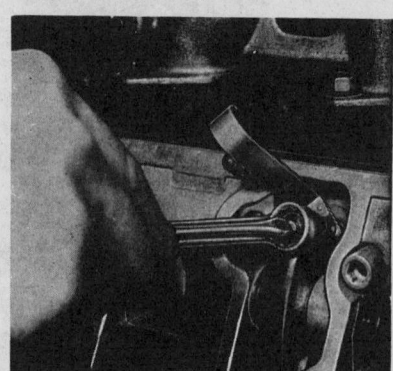

911 and 914/6 valve clearance adjustment

4. If the clearance is not within specifications, loosen the locknut with a box wrench and, using a screwdriver, turn

the rocker arm adjusting screw while holding the locknut. A tool to simplify this procedure is available from automotive suppliers. It has a screwdriver bit which can be turned while the locknut is held with a socket.

5. Tighten the locknut while holding the adjusting screw. Recheck the valve clearance to ensure that it wasn't changed when the locknut was tightened. Repeat this procedure on the other valve of no. 1 cylinder.

6. Proceed to adjust the valves of the remaining cylinders in an order of 1–2–3–4 for four-cylinder engines or 1–6–2–4–3–5 for six-cylinder engines. The piston of the cylinder on which the valves are being adjusted must be at TDC. Turn the engine until both valves of the cylinder being adjusted are closed. Six-cylinder engines have TDC marks for each cylinder on the crankshaft pulley. Adjust the valves in the same manner as no. 1 cylinder.

7. Install the rocker arm or camshaft housing covers with new gaskets. Start the engine and check for leaks.

Fuel Injection

Idle Speed

911

On the mechanical fuel injection used on 1972 models and 1973 911E, S, and early T models, the idle speed adjustment screw is located on the rear of the fuel injection pump. The adjuster is a spring loaded screw. Using a mirror, it is possible to adjust the idle speed without removing the air cleaner. All other adjustments require the Porsche special tools.

The idle speed adjustment on the CIS system used on all later models is done with the bypass screw on the throttle valve housing. The engine should be at normal operating temperature.

1972–73 914 1.7 and 1973–76 2.0

1. Remove the air filter and connect a tachometer to the engine.

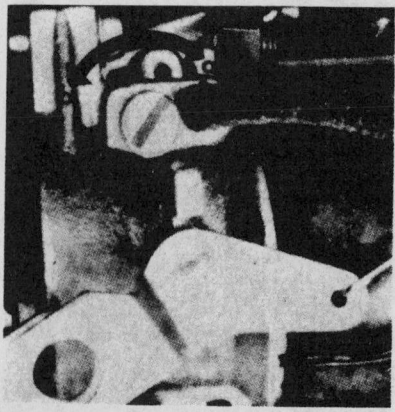

914 idle speed screw

2. Start the engine and set the idle speed to specifications. Turning the adjustment screw clockwise, in the direction of (a) increases the idle speed. Turning the screw in the direction of (b), or counterclockwise, decreases the idle speed.

1974–76 914 1.8 and 1976 912E

1. Make sure all hoses are tight. Connect a tachometer to the engine.
2. Start the engine and bring it to normal operating temperature.
3. The idle speed adjustment screw is located on the throttle housing. Do not touch the idle mixture screw which is covered with a plastic plug.

ENGINE ELECTRICAL
Distributor

Removal and Installation

911

1. Remove the heated air intake duct.
2. Unsnap and remove the distributor cap. Position it out of the way.
3. Mark the direction in which the rotor is pointing on the body of the distributor.

NOTE: *Some models have a scribe mark indicating the correct rotor positioning for no. 1 cylinder. On these models it will be more convenient to turn the engine so that the rotor points to this mark before removing the distributor.*

4. Detach the distributor leads. Remove the vacuum line.
5. Loosen and remove the retaining nut from the base of the distributor. Pull the distributor straight out of the engine. Check and, if necessary, replace the sealing ring on the distributor housing.
6. Insert the distributor into the engine. Turn the rotor back and forth to engage the distributor and crankshaft gears. If the engine has been turned while the distributor was out, bring no. 1 cylinder to TDC as described below under "Ignition Timing".
7. Adjust the static and dynamic timing as described below.

914

1. Remove the air cleaner.
2. Loosen the clamp on the right-hand heater hose and pull it from the heater. Position the hose out of the way.
3. Screw the inspection hole cover out of the cooling shroud.
4. Turn the engine until the black notch in the crankshaft pulley aligns with v-shaped notch in the blower housing.
5. Remove the distributor cap and check that the rotor is, indeed, pointing towards the no. 1 cylinder position.

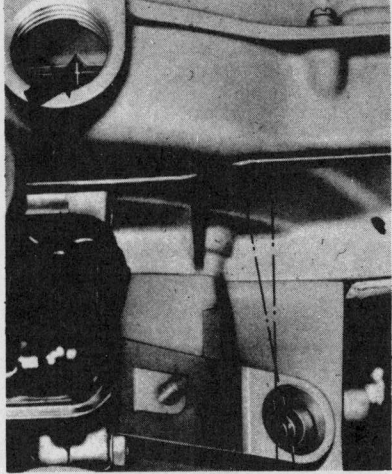

914 distributor drive gear positioning

6. Detach the two electrical leads and vacuum hoses from the distributor.
7. Loosen the retaining nut on the base of the distributor and pull it out of the engine.

To install the distributor with the engine undisturbed:

8. Ensure that the spring is in place in the center bore of the drive gear. A length of wire may be used to install the spring if it has been removed.
9. Insert the distributor, making sure that the dog on the distributor engages the slot in the drive gear. Turning the rotor a few times will ease installation.
10. Push the distributor in firmly. Tighten the clamp nut.
11. Install the distributor leads and vacuum hoses. Install the distributor cap.
12. Check the ignition timing as described below. Install the inspection cover, heater hose, and air cleaner.

Install the distributor in the following manner if the engine has been disturbed:

13. Turn the engine to bring no. 1 cylinder up to TDC. At this point, the black notch in the crankshaft pulley should be aligned with the V-shaped notch in the blower housing and the slot in the distributor drive gear should be at approximately a 12° angle to the engine centerline. The slot should be pointing toward the rear retaining screw of the air filter support and the smaller side of the gear should be facing the center of the engine.
14. Install the distributor using steps 8 through 12.

Alternator

Alternator Precautions

A few precautions should be observed when servicing an electrical system that uses an alternator. Failure to do so can result in serious damage to the charging system. The negative terminal(s) of the battery(ies) is (are) always grounded. Al-

ways connect the correct battery terminals when attaching a battery charger or replacing a battery. Never operate the alternator on an open, uncontrolled circuit. Never ground or short across any regulator or alternator terminals. Never attempt to polarize the alternator. Remove the battery cables from the terminals when charging the battery in the car.

Removal and Installation

911

The alternator is located in the blower housing.

1. Disconnect the battery ground straps.
2. Remove the air cleaner assembly.

911 alternator pulley nut removal

911 alternator removal

3. Remove the upper shroud retaining bolts.
4. Hold the alternator pulley and remove the pulley nut.
5. Remove the drive belt.
6. Remove the blower housing strap retaining bolts.
7. Pull the blower housing/alternator towards the rear until there is enough clearance to disconnect the wiring.
8. Remove the alternator.
9. Install the alternator in a reverse order of the removal. Be sure that the blower housing is seated on the dowel in the crankcase.
10. Tighten the pulley nut to 29 ft lbs.

Porsche

Belt Tension Adjustment
911

A correctly tensioned belt can be deflected ½–¾ in. by light hand pressure. If the tension is not within specifications, follow the steps below to adjust or replace the belt.

1. Remove the pulley nut as outlined above in "Alternator Removal and Installation".

2. Remove the outside half of the pulley.

3. Remove adjustment spacers to increase belt tension. Add spacers to decrease belt tension.

4. When the correct spacer grouping is achieved, install the belt, pulley half, spacers, and nut.

911 fan belt pulley adjustment spacers

5. Tighten the nut to 29 ft lbs.

NOTE: *If you have removed spacers, install the extra spacers on the outside of the pulley so they won't become lost or misplaced.*

6. Recheck the belt tension after about 60 miles of driving.

914

A correctly tensioned belt will be able to be deflected approximately ½ in. by light hand pressure. If the tension is not within specification, follow the steps below to adjust or replace the belt.

1. Remove the small cover plate from the alternator cover.

2. Loosen the socket screw and slide the alternator left or right as necessary.

3. Tighten the screw and replace the cover.

Regulator
Removal and Installation
911, 912E and 914

1. Disconnect the ground cable from the battery.

2. Disconnect the wiring from the regulator.

3. Remove the mounting screws and remove the regulator.

4. Install the regulator. Do not overtighten the screws. An alternator system requires no polarization.

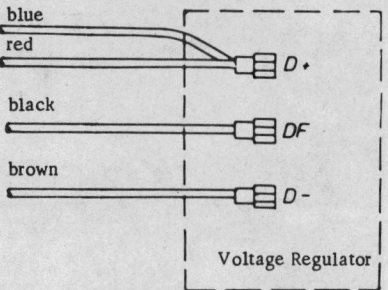

911 voltage regulator wiring schematic

Starter
Removal and Installation
911

1. Disconnect the battery(ies) ground strap(s).

2. Jack up the rear of the car and support it with jack stands.

3. Note their locations (tag to be sure) and then remove the starter electrical connections.

4. Loosen the retaining bolts, support the starter, remove the bolts, and then pull out the starter.

5. Install the starter using a reverse order of the removal procedure. Ensure that the terminal connections are correctly installed and tight.

6. Lower the car and connect the battery(ies) ground strap(s).

914

1. Open the engine compartment lid. Disconnect the battery ground cable.

2. The top retaining bolt is accessible from within the engine compartment. Remove the nut.

3. Jack up the starter side of the car and support it with jack stands.

4. Remove the bottom bolt and pull out the starter.

5. Install the starter into the transaxle housing and the long top bolt into the mounting bracket hole. Install and tighten the bottom bolt.

6. Connect the electrical leads to the correct terminals.

7. Install and tighten the nut on the top bolt.

8. Seal the mounting bracket and transaxle housing with a suitable self-adhesive sealer.

9. Lower the car and connect the battery cable.

Overrun Clutch and Drive
Replacement

1. Remove starter.

2. Press clutch operating sleeve against drive pinion.

3. Pull both off shaft by turning slightly.

4. Hold armature in vise and push pinion and sleeve on shaft until detent locks.

Battery

The 911 batteries are located in the front luggage compartment. One battery is located in each fender well behind the headlights.   The 914 battery is located in the engine compartment. 1974–77 911 and 1976 912E models are equipped with a single battery located in the luggage compartment.

ENGINE MECHANICAL
Engine Removal and Installation

All Porsche engines are removed and installed with the transaxle attached. The recommended method for removal is to raise the rear of the car high enough for working clearance and then support it on jack stands. A hydraulic transmission/-differential jack or service jack of at least 800 lbs. capacity is required for lowering the engine/transaxle and raising it back into the chassis. Have an assistant steady the engine/transaxle during removal. Strap the engine to the jack so that it doesn't slide off. Proceed slowly and carefully as the engine/transaxle combination is both heavy and delicate.

911 and 912E

1. Disconnect the battery. Drain the engine and transaxle oil.

2. Open the engine compartment lid and detach the hot air ducts from the air gates and exhaust manifold heat exchangers.

3. Detach the two heater control cables.

4. Remove the hot air ducts from the T-union between the air cleaners and then remove the T-union from the blower housing.

5. Remove the tops of the air cleaners.

6. Tag for installation and then remove the electrical cables from the generator and blower housing.

7. Tag for installation and remove the wires from the coil.

8. Remove the connections from the oil temperature and pressure sending units.

9. Remove the fuel line from the fuel pump and detach its clip from the engine shield.

10. Remove the allen bolts retaining the axle shaft flange to the transaxle. Free the axle shaft from the transaxle and drop them out of the way.

11. Remove the starter electrical leads.

12. Disconnect the clutch cable from the control lever.

13. Remove the ground strap.

14. Detach the back-up light lead.

912 and 911 rear engine-to-body mounts

15. Disconnect the throttle linkage from the cross-shaft at the transaxle.

16. Remove the cover in the center of the rear floor.

17. Detach the rubber shift lever cover from the flange on the body and pull it forward on the control lever.

18. Remove the safety wire from the square-headed from the joint. Loosen the screw and slide the shift rod off its base.

19. Position the jack, including the flat support plate, under the engine/transaxle. The jack should be under the point of balance of the powertrain.

20. Raise the jack a slight amount.

21. Remove the body mounting bolts on either side of the engine compartment.

22. Remove the body mounting bolts from the short transaxle crossmember. The engine is removed with this crossmember attached.

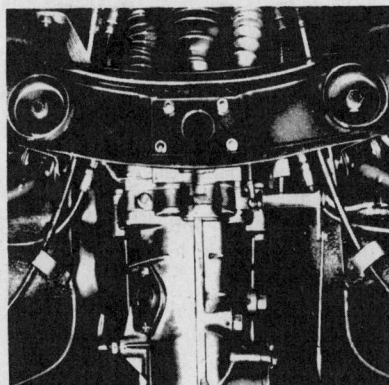

912 and 911 transaxle crossmember mounting

Releasing throwout bearing tension

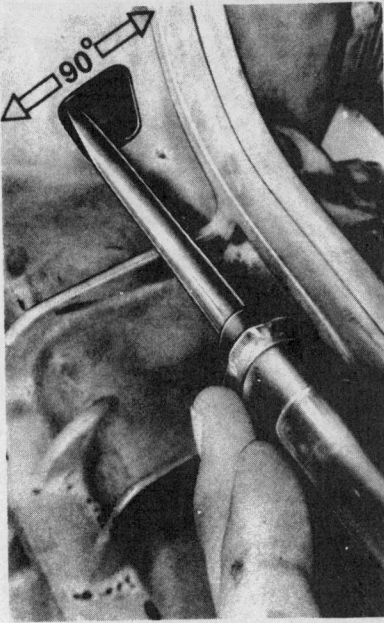

Sliding the fork past the throwout bearing

23. Very carefully lower the engine, while your assistants help balance it.

24. Roll the engine/transaxle out from under the car.

Follow steps 25 through 30 for engine and transaxle separation.

Remove the starter. Release the throwout fork tension by disconnecting the return spring if one is used.

After releasing throwout bearing tension it is necessary to slide the throwout fork past the bearing. To do this, insert a screwdriver in the opening in the transaxle and turn the bearing 90°. Slide the fork past the bearing. The transaxle may now be separated from the engine.

25. Remove the engine-to-transaxle bolts and nuts. Carefully pull the transaxle away from the engine. Be sure that the full weight of the transaxle is supported, so as not to damage the pilot bushing, throwout bearing, clutch disc, or pressure plate.

26. Whichever component you are repairing, rebuilding, or replacing may now be moved to a suitable workbench, dolly, or engine stand.

27. Before reinstalling the transaxle, fill the pilot bushing in the gland nut with a small amount of graphite grease (no more than 3cc, or 1/10 oz).

28. Lightly grease the transmission input shaft splines, starter shaft bushing, and the starter and flywheel gear teeth.

29. Carefully attach the transaxle to the engine. Remember the transmission input shaft will be passing through the throwout bearing, pressure plate, clutch disc, and pilot bushing, so give it ample support during the attachment procedure.

NOTE: *If the clutch disc splines and the input shaft splines don't line up, as*

they so often won't, have an assistant turn the crankshaft pulley until they do.

30. Push the transaxle home so that the mounting flanges are flush. Align the bottom holes and install the bolts. Install the top bolts, and then tighten all of the retaining bolts evenly.

31. The engine/transaxle is installed by following the removal steps in reverse order.

32. After the engine is installed, check the clutch adjustment as described in below.

33. Refill the engine and transaxle with the correct lubricant. Lower the car.

34. Start the engine and check for leaks.

914

1. Scribe the hinge positioning, and then remove the engine compartment lid.

2. Disconnect the battery cables.

3. Remove the air cleaner and attendant hoses.

4. Tag each of the eleven cables for the fuel injection (for correct reinstallation) and then disconnect them. Tape the cables to the engine compartment sides so that they are out of harm's way.

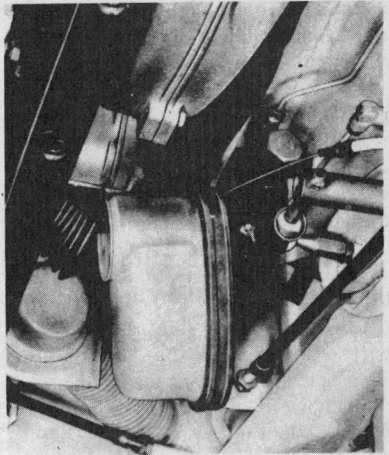

914 shift rod retainer

5. Disconnect the throttle cable and push it through the front engine firewall.

6. Open the fuel line retaining clip: Disconnect and plug the fuel lines near the pressure regulator.

7. Remove the top retaining nut for the starter (accessible from the engine compartment).

8. Jack up the car and support it safely with stands.

9. Remove the muffler shrouding. Drain the engine and transaxle.

10. Remove the lower heater components.

11. Detach the dust cover and then unscrew the shift rod retainer.

12. Remove the protective cover, unscrew the retaining nuts, and remove the rear shift rod.

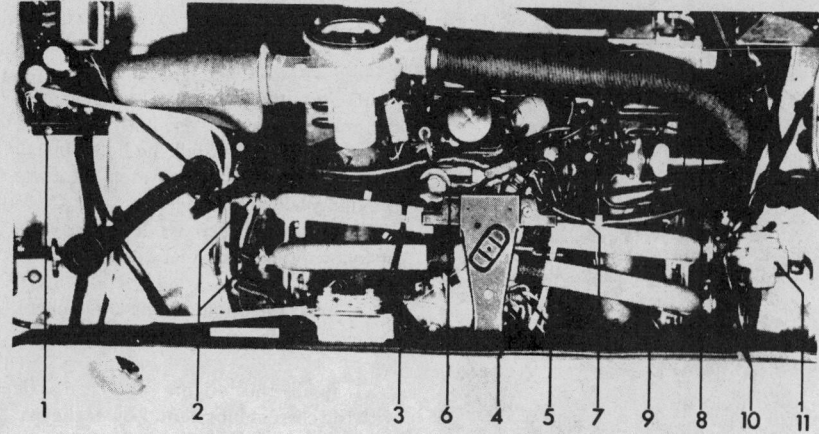

914 fuel injection connections

1. Voltage supply relay
   4-pole
2. Two injection valves
   left 2-pole
3. One throttle valve
   switch 4-pole
4. Temperature feeler
   1-pole
5. Mass connections
   3-pole
6. Cold starting valve
   2-pole

7. Thermal switch
   1-pole
8. Ignition distributor
   release contact
   3-pole
9. Temperature feeler
   1-pole
10. Two injection valves
    right 2-pole
11. Pressure feeler
    4-pole

13. Remove the heater box, hoses, and control cables.

14. Loosen the cable pulley adjusting nut and retaining nut. Bend the retaining bracket and pull the clutch cable towards the front.

15. Loosen the speedometer cable and pull it forward.

16. Remove the starter. Detach the ground strap from the underbody.

17. Detach the axle driveshafts from the transaxle as described below. Wire the driveshafts out of the way.

18. Position the jack and plate under the engine/transaxle and raise it slightly.

19. Unscrew the four transaxle support retaining nuts. Remove the two allen bolts on the front engine mount.

20. Lower the engine/transmission down and out of the car.

21. Engine/transaxle separation is similar to that given for the 912 and 911, with exception of step 25.

22. Installation is essentially a reverse of the removal procedure, with the addition of the following steps.

23. Be especially careful that the injector valve fuel lines aren't squashed when repositioning the engine. The parking brake cables go above the engine mount.

24. Torque the engine mount allen bolts to 22 ft lbs. The transmission mount nuts are tightened to 15 ft lbs. Tighten the axle driveshaft bolts to 33 ft lbs.

25. Adjust the clutch as described later.

26. Adjust the throttle cable.

27. Refill the engine and transaxle with lubricant.

28. Lower the car. Start the engine and check for leaks.

Cylinder Head

For removal and installation, see the engine Disassembly and Assembly Section.

Rocker Shafts

Removal and Installation
911

Each rocker arm has an individual shaft on this single overhead camshaft engine. One or all of the shafts and rocker arms may be removed with the engine in the chassis.

1. Remove the camshaft housing cover nuts and spring washers. Remove the covers.

911 rocker arm removal

2. Scribe the rocker arms being removed so that they can be returned to the same position.

3. Unscrew the allen bolt in the rocker shaft. Push the shaft out of its bore and remove it along with the rocker arm.

NOTE: *If the rocker is under pressure, you won't be able to push the shaft out.*

Turn the camshaft until the rocker rests on the heel of the cam lobe.

4. Check the rocker arm and shaft for excessive wear or damage. Replace any suspect pieces.

NOTE: *End rockers are installed with the allen screw heads facing towards cylinders no. 2 and 5 respectively.*

5. Place the rocker arm on its shaft.

6. The rocker arm shaft should be centered in its bore so that each grodve is recessed 0.059 in (1.5mm).

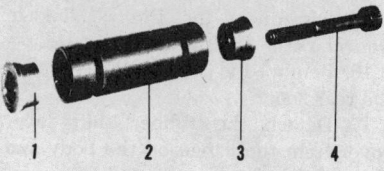

911 rocker arm shaft assembly

1. Allen nut cone
2. Shaft
3. Bushing cone
4. Allen bolt

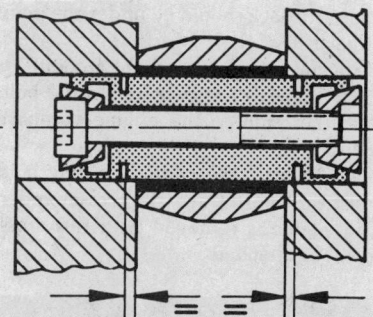

Correct rocker arm shaft positioning

a. Insert a 0.06 in. feeler gauge in the groove on one side of the shaft. Push the shaft in until the feeler gauge is held tight against the edge.

b. Carefully remove the gauge and push the shaft in approximately 0.06 in. more, using the feeler gauge to judge the distance.

7. Tighten the allen bolt to 156 in lbs.

8. Install the camshaft cover.

914 and 912E

Each cylinder head mounts two rocker assemblies, each one consisting of a shaft and two rocker arms. Each shaft is mounted in two bearings which are positioned on studs and retained by nuts. The rocker arm shaft assemblies can be removed with the engine in the car.

1. Remove the rocker arm cover.

2. Unscrew the retaining nuts and lift the rocker arm assemblies off the cylinder head.

3. When installing the rocker arm assemblies, the open slots of the bearings must face down.

4. With the rocker assemblies mounted on the head, tighten the retaining nuts to 120 in. lbs.

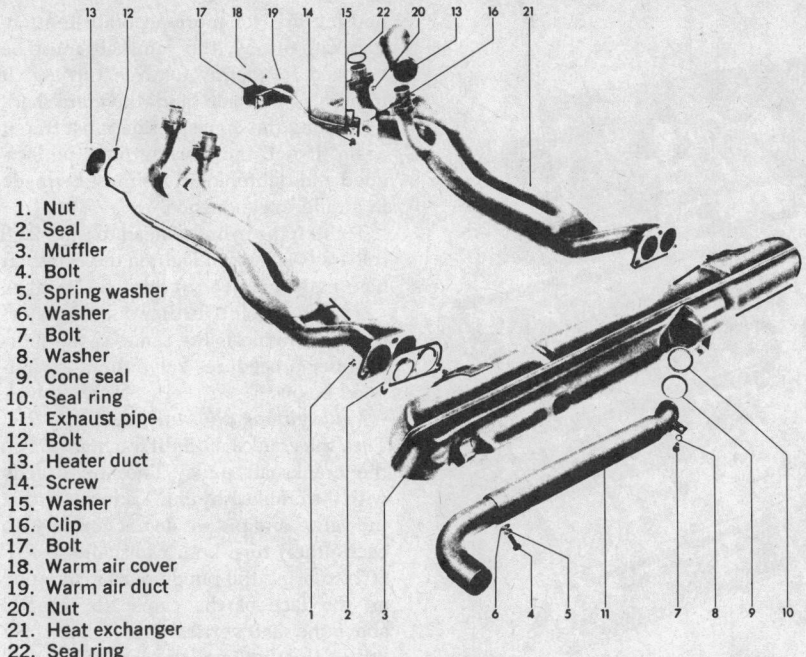

1. Nut
2. Seal
3. Muffler
4. Bolt
5. Spring washer
6. Washer
7. Bolt
8. Washer
9. Cone seal
10. Seal ring
11. Exhaust pipe
12. Bolt
13. Heater duct
14. Screw
15. Washer
16. Clip
17. Bolt
18. Warm air cover
19. Warm air duct
20. Nut
21. Heat exchanger
22. Seal ring

914 exhaust system

Removing the camshaft housing and cylinder heads as a unit

Exhaust Pipe and Muffler

Removal and Installation

911 and 912E

1. Remove the flange nuts and bolts.
2. Loosen the retaining clamps and detach the muffler from its support.
3. Position the muffler on its support and then fit the clamps.
4. Install new gaskets between the muffler and exhaust manifold/heat exchanger.
5. Install and alternately tighten the flange nuts and bolts.

914

To remove only the exhaust pipe:
1. Remove the two tailpipe-to-muffler retaining bolts.
2. Pull the tailpipe out of the muffler.
3. Install the tailpipe using two new gasket rings. Tighten the two retaining bolts.
To remove the tailpipe and muffler:
1. Remove the three flange nuts on each side.
2. Pry the muffler loose and remove it.
3. Use new flange gaskets when installing the muffler. Tighten the six flange retaining nuts alternately.

Exhaust Manifold/Heat Exchanger

Removal and Installation

911, 912E and 914

1. Remove the muffler as previously outlined. Detach and remove the connecting hose from the heat exchanger to the heater valve chamber.
2. Detach the heater hose from the heat exchanger.
3. Remove the three sunken bolts from the bottom of the heat exchanger.
4. Remove the six cylinder head-to-heat exchanger nuts using a universal socket set-up.

NOTE: *For 914 models, skip steps 3 and 4 and loosen the four retaining clamps.*

5. Remove the heat exchanger.
6. Examine the heat exchanger for damaged flanges or cracks. Replace it, if necessary.
7. Install the heat exchanger in a reverse order of the removal procedure. Use new flange gaskets and tighten the retaining nuts and bolts alternately.

Engine Disassembly and Assembly

Further component removal and installation requires engine removal and disassembly. Follow the steps of engine disassembly and then assembly for the part being replaced. A general engine rebuilding section is included at the end of the book.

911

Follow the disassembly procedure for four cylinder Porsche engines up to the rocker carriers and the cylinder heads. Further disassembly of the 911 engine is as follows:

Removal of the cylinder heads on the 911 involves removing the overhead camshafts. All three cylinder heads on each bank can be removed as a unit complete with the camshaft and rockers or each cylinder head can be removed individually. For access to the cylinder heads and valves, the camshaft housing must be disassembled and removed.

Rockers. Scribe a mark on the rockers for later installation. Remove the 5 mm allen retaining screws in the rocker shafts, holding the cone-nut that is released on the other end of the shaft. Push out the shafts and lift away the rockers. *Position the camshaft so that the cam lobe does not press against the rocker being improved.*

Camshaft. Remove the timing chain cover at each camshaft. Unbolt the chain tensioner and the intermediate wheel, using tools P 202 and P 203. Withdraw the dowel pin from the camshaft wheel with tool P 212. Remove the sliding wedges and withdraw the wheel and flange. Take the key from the camshaft, unscrew the three sealing ring screws, and remove the sealing ring together with the O-ring and the gasket. Withdraw the camshaft toward the rear. Note that both camshafts turn in the same direction and therefore require that the cam lobes be positioned differently.

Cam housing. Unscrew the hex nuts and the three allen screws to lift off the camshaft housing. Each housing fits either cylinder bank.

Cylinder head. Loosen the cylinder head securing nuts (using tool P 119) and remove the cylinder head. Cylinders are numbered from the crankshaft pulley on the left bank as 1, 2 and 3 (left when facing the front of the car), and on the right bank as 4, 5 and 6.

The upper and lower sealing surfaces of the cylinder head (between the head and the camshaft and between the head and the cylinder) should not be machined. Permitted distortion at the cylinder seating surface must not exceed 0.15 mm (0.0059 in.). Examine the mating surfaces to ensure that they are in good condition.

When installing the cylinder heads, use

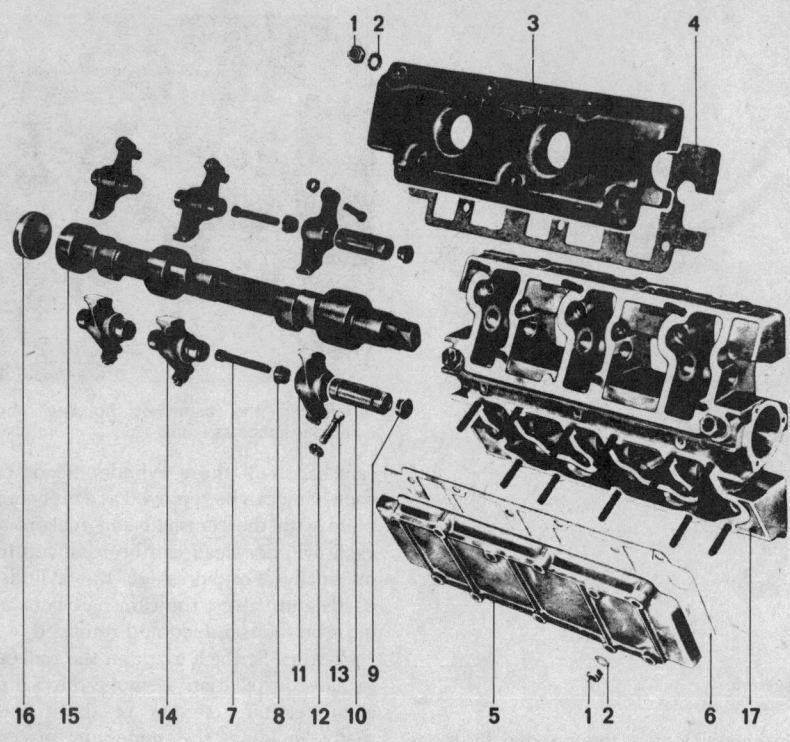

Six cylinder camshaft housing assembly

1. Nut	7. Bolt
2. Aluminum washer	8. Bushing
3. Cover	9. Nut
4. Gasket	10. Rocker arm shaft
5. Cover	11. Rocker arm
6. Gasket	12. Nut

13. Adjusting screw
14. Rocker arm assembly
15. Camshaft
16. Cover
17. Housing

housing first for more accurate tensioning. Either way, the camshaft must be checked frequently for free turning. If tightening one side binds the crankshaft, tightening the opposite side must free it again. If not, the housing must be loosened and tightening steps must be made in a different sequence.

Tighten the cylinder head to 21.6–23.8 ft lbs (3.0–3.3 mkg). Tighten the camshaft housing to 15.9–18.1 ft lbs (2.2–2.5 mkg).

From this point, further disassembly of the 911 engine is the same as the four-cylinder procedure. Valve timing is outlined below.

Valve timing adjustment for the 911. Turn the crankshaft until the mark Z1 on the crankshaft pulley lines up exactly with the crankcase joint. Taking care that the valves and pistons do not collide with each other, turn both camshafts (tool P 202) to bring the punch marks, stamped on the face of the camshafts, exactly above the shaft vertical center. Back off a little if the slightest resistance is felt during the turn. Then turn the free shaft to bring the valves and pistons into proper harmony before continuing with the first shaft.

With the crankshaft timing marks aligned and the camshaft punch marks exactly on the top, the engine is timed at the firing point in cylinder No. 1 with

Six cylinder valve timing positioning

new cylinder head gaskets with the perforations set toward the cylinder. Carefully position each head, insert the washers and tighten the hex nuts lightly.

The camshaft housing is sealed to the cylinder heads only with sealing compound. Assemble the camshaft housing

and oil return pipes on the cylinder heads, but only handtighten.

The Porsche factory workshop manual suggests that at this point in reassembly, the cylinder head be torqued down first and then the camshaft housing. Some mechanics prefer to torque the camshaft

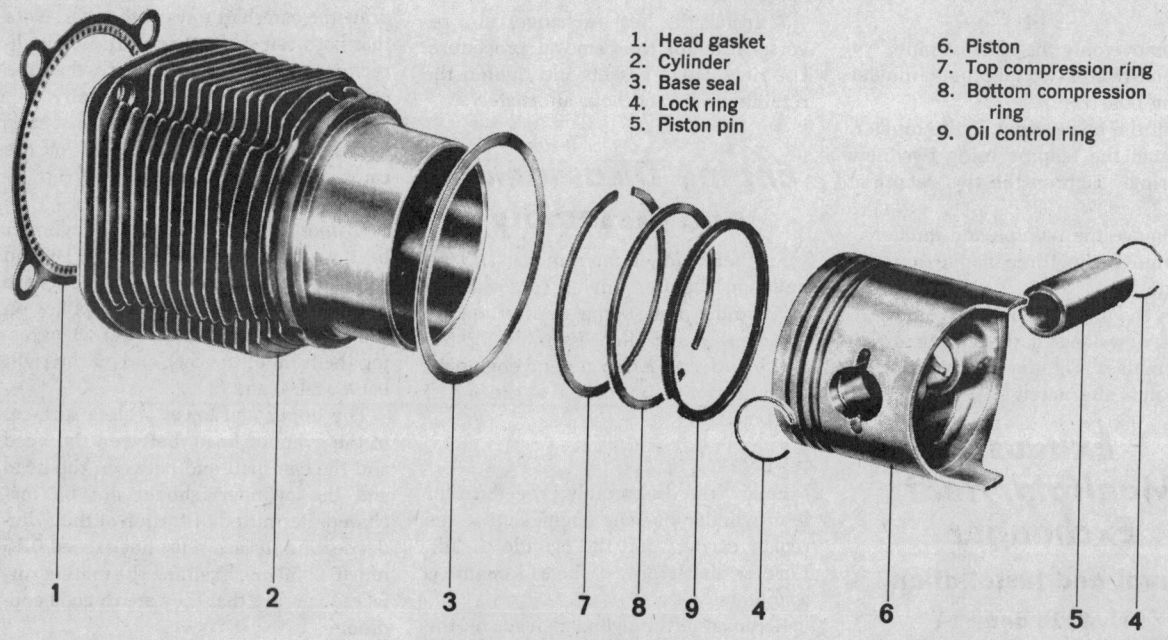

1. Head gasket	6. Piston
2. Cylinder	7. Top compression ring
3. Base seal	8. Bottom compression ring
4. Lock ring	9. Oil control ring
5. Piston pin	

911 cylinder and piston assembly

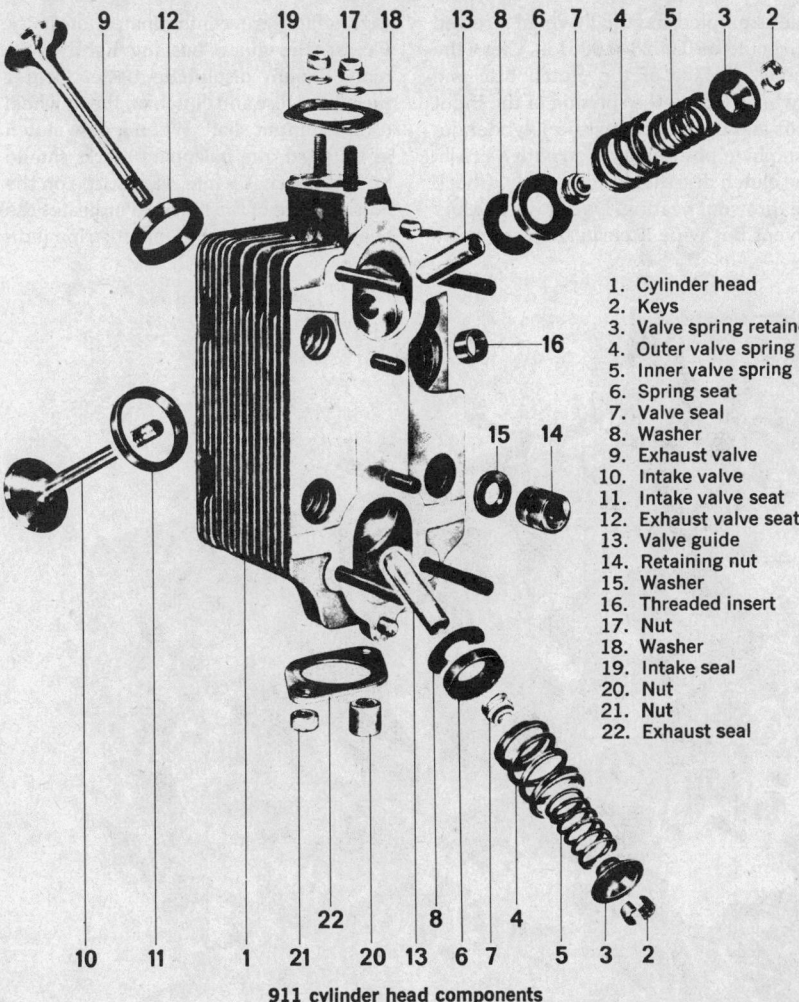

1. Cylinder head
2. Keys
3. Valve spring retainer
4. Outer valve spring
5. Inner valve spring
6. Spring seat
7. Valve seal
8. Washer
9. Exhaust valve
10. Intake valve
11. Intake valve seat
12. Exhaust valve seat
13. Valve guide
14. Retaining nut
15. Washer
16. Threaded insert
17. Nut
18. Washer
19. Intake seal
20. Nut
21. Nut
22. Exhaust seal

911 cylinder head components

ets with the warm air guides. Remove the oil cooler, oil filter and oil pump. Remove the rocker arm shafts with the protective tubes, pushrods and tappets. Remove the cylinder heads, cylinders and pistons. Remove the clutch and flywheel. Disassemble the crankcase, being careful not to score any of the mating surfaces by trying to pry the halves apart. Remove the camshaft and crankshaft with the connecting rods.

Assembly is the reverse of disassembly, noting the following procedures. Check the riveting of the camshaft gear and the camshaft. Check the camshaft for out-of-true using V-blocks. The maximum allowable wear is 0.0016 in. Check the end-play of the guide bearing which should be 0.0016–0.0051 in. The oil holes in the crankshaft bearing journals and bearings should have no sharp edges. Carefully remove any metallic foreign substances. Install the crankshaft and connecting rods. Install the camshaft and gear so that the tooth marked with a 0 is located between the two teeth of the crankshaft gear which are identified with a punch mark (see illustration). Coat the

Four cylinder engine timing marks

overlapping in cylinder No. 4. Find which hole in the camshaft sprocket lines up with a corresponding hole in the sprocket flange and insert the aligning dowel pin.

Slip on the washer and tighten the retaining nut to 101 ft. lbs. (14.7 mkg.).

Adjust cylinder No. 1 intake valve clearance to 0.10 mm (0.004 in.) and attach a dial gauge. The gauge sensor must be positioned exactly on the edge of the valve spring retaining collar. Adjust the gauge to a preload of 10 mm (0.39 in.) to provide for sensor travel when the cam lobe depresses the valve. Depress the chain tensioner with a screwdriver to tighten the chain (on the side to be measured) and turn the crankshaft one complete turn until the timing marks are aligned again. The dial gauge should read between 4.2 and 4.6 mm (0.165–0.181 in.). A preferred range is 4.25 to 4.45 mm.

If the gauge shows a lower or higher reading, the camshaft has to be readjusted as follows:

1. Remove the sprocket retaining nut, spring washer and aligning dowel pin.

2. Make sure that the crankshaft pulley mark is still aligned with the crankcase joint.

3. Depress the tensioner to tighten the chain and turn the camshaft until the dial gauge indicates 4.4 to 4.45 mm (0.173–0.175 in.).

4. Find the hole in the camshaft sprocket which lines up with the sprocket flange and insert the dowel pin. Replace the spring washer and nut and tighten.

5. Turn the crankshaft two complete turns to the right and read the dial gauge. If the specified value is still not obtained, repeat the steps above.

When the valves overlap in cylinder No. 1, cylinder No. 4 is at firing point (TDC). Repeat the procedure for cylinder No. 4 valve timing adjustment.

914 and 912E

Mount the engine on a stand. Drain the engine oil and remove the muffler and heat exchanger. Remove the rear engine cover plate. Remove the intake distributor and intake pipe with the injection valves (on fuel injection engines). Remove the ignition distributor and the front engine cover plate. Remove the cooling blower impeller. Remove the cooling blower housing with the alternator attached. Remove the engine mount. Remove the front and rear cylinder jack-

mating surfaces of the housing halves with a thin coat of sealing compound. Be sure that no sealing compound enters the oil ducts. Assemble the crankcase halves and lightly tighten the screw for the oil intake pipe. Screw on the sealing nuts with the sealing ring on the outside and tighten to the specified torque. Rotate the crankshaft to ensure free rotation. Grease the needle bearing in the flywheel with a small amount of multipurpose grease. Moisten the felt ring with engine oil, wiping off any excess. Install the flywheel and adjust the axial play of the crankshaft. Measure the axial play by installing the flywheel with two spacing washers but without the sealing rings. Using a dial gauge, measure the play by rotating the flywheel. The thickness of the third spacer can be computed by subtracting 0.0039 in. from the measured re-

Porsche

sult. Remove the flywheel and install the sealing ring, felt ring, and three spacers. Three spacers must always be installed for the required thickness. Spacers are available in the following sizes: 0.0094, 0.0118, 0.0126, 0.0134, 0.0142 and 0.-0150 in. Each spacer is marked for proper identification. The axial play of the crankshaft, measured with the en-gine assembled and the flywheel screwed on, should be 0.0028–0.0051 in. Clean the contact surface of the clutch disc and flywheel. Check the splining of the input shaft and coat lightly with molybdenum disulphide powder, applied with a brush. The clutch disc should slide easily. Check the throwout bearing. Do not wash in any solvent but wipe it clean. Replace bear-ings which are contaminated or noisy. Grease the guide bushing lightly with molybdenum disulphide paste. Center the clutch disc and clutch on the flywheel using an input shaft. When a new clutch in installed, the balancing marks should be 180° apart. A white paint stripe on the outside edge of the flywheel indicates the heavy end, and a white paint stripe indi-

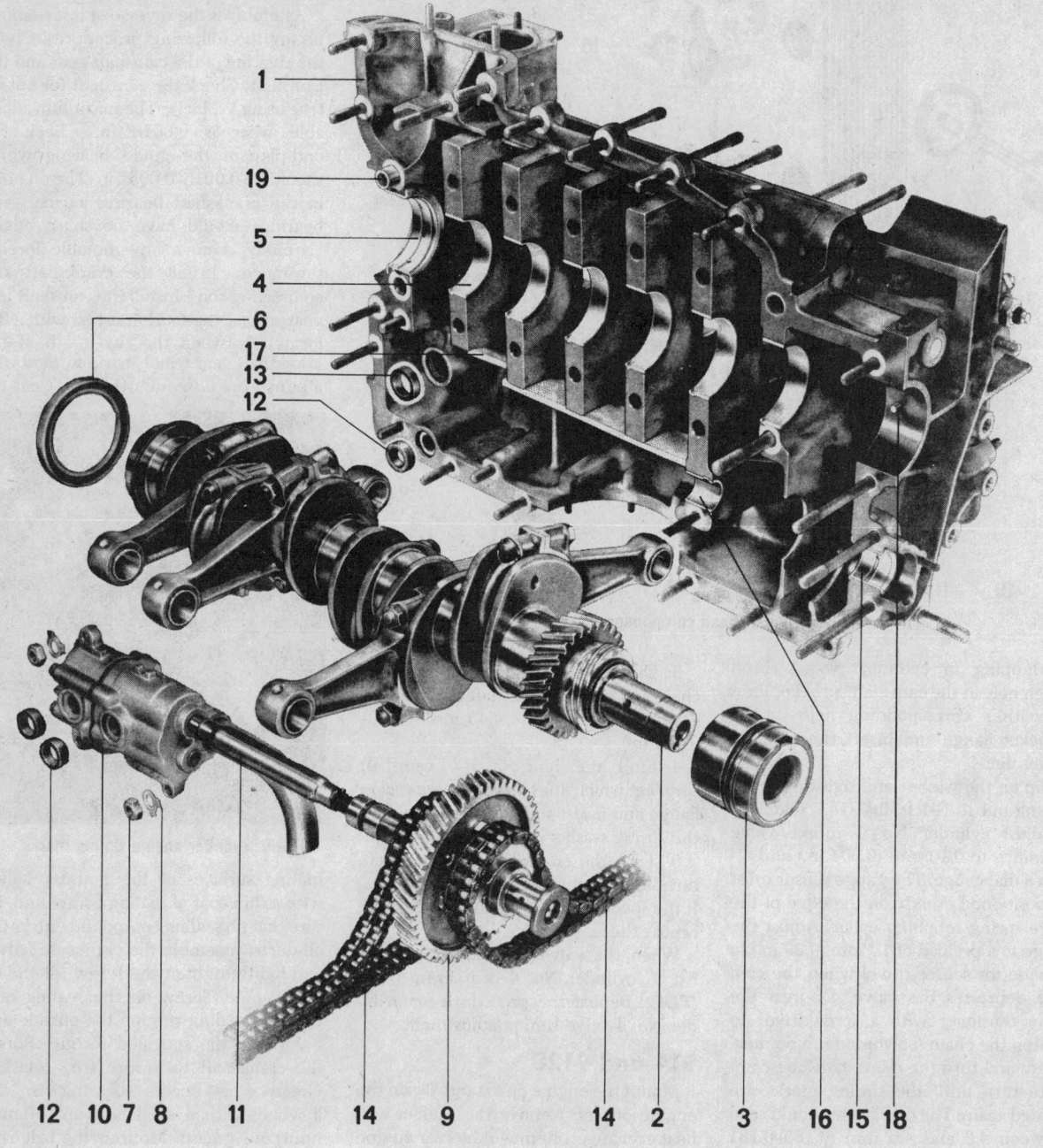

Six cylinder crankcase assembly

1. Crankcase half
2. Crankshaft assembly
3. No. 8 bearing
4. Bearing shell
5. Thrust bearing shell
6. Seal
7. Nut
8. Lock washer
9. Intermediate shaft
10. Oil pump assembly
11. Connecting shaft
12. Seal
13. Seal
14. Camshaft chain
15. Intermediate shaft thrust bearing
16. Intermediate shaft bearing
17. Oil strainer
18. pin
19. bushing

cates the heavy end of the clutch. Tighten the bolts to 14.5 ft lbs. Clean all pistons and check for wear. Check the marking of the pistons according to the following designations:

A.—The letter next to the arrow is the index of the spare parts number.

B.—The punched in arrow indicates that the piston must be installed with the arrow facing the flywheel.

C.—The color dot (blue, pink or green) indicates the paired size of the piston.

D.—A statement of weight class (+ or −) is punched in or printed.

E.—The weight class is indicated by a color dot (brown equals (−) weight and grey equals (+) weight).

F.—Number indicates the piston size in mm.

Fit the compression and oil scraper rings. The designation TOP should face up. Insert the locking rings of pistons 1 and 2 on the side facing the flywheel. The

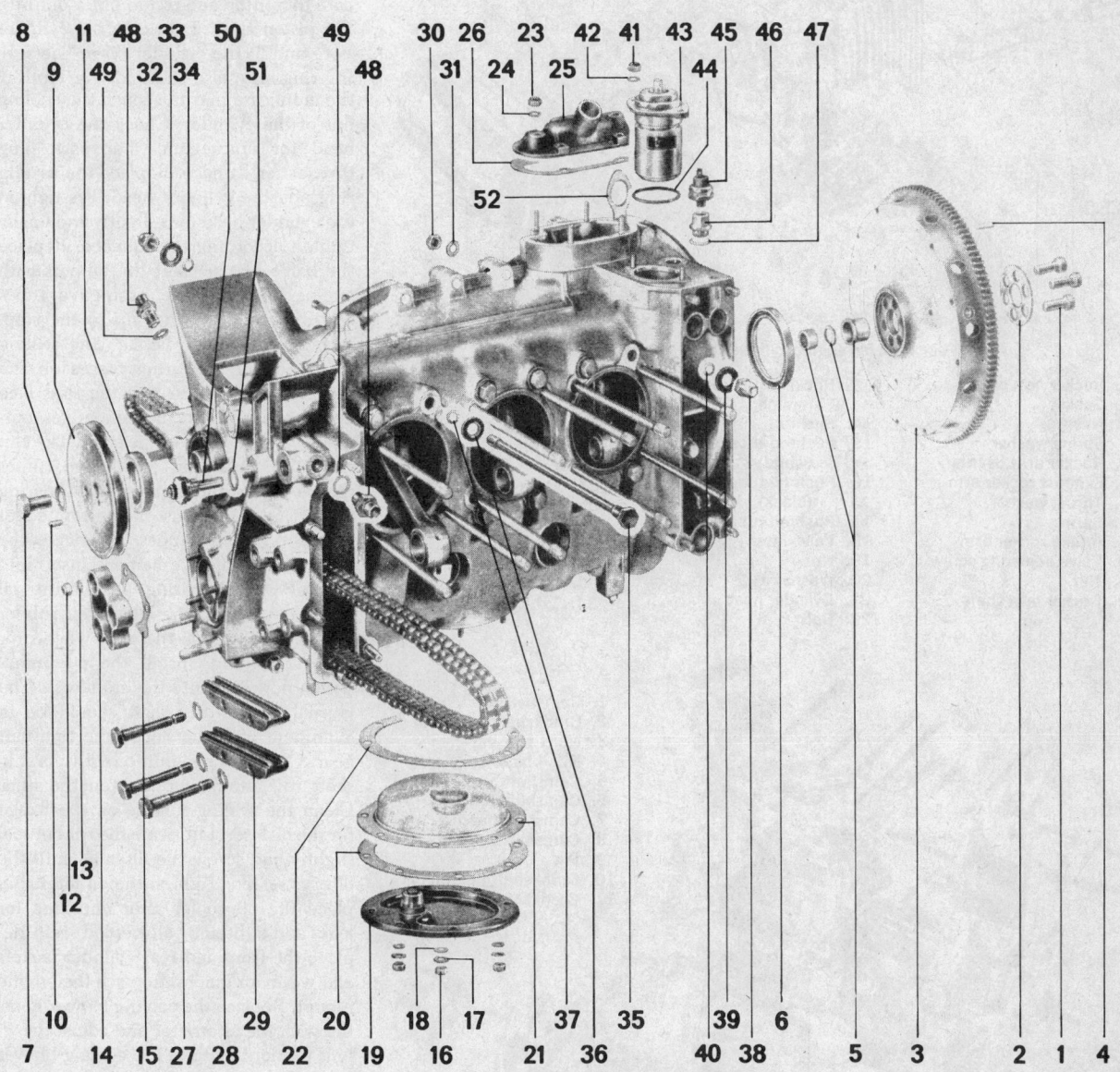

Six cylinder crankcase assembly

1. Bolt	17. Spring washer	32. Nut
2. Washer	18. Washer	33. Washer
3. Flywheel	19. Cover	34. Seal
4. Pin	20. Seal	35. Crankcase bolt
5. Bushing	21. Oil strainer	36. Washer
6. Seal	22. seal	37. Seal
7. Bolt	23. Nut	38. Nut
8. Spring washer	24. Washer	39. Washer
9. Pulley	25. Breather cover	40. Seal
10. Pin	26. Seal	41. Nut
11. Seal	27. Slide rail bolt	42. Spring washer
12. Nut	28. Seal	43. Thermostat
13. Washer	29. Slide rail	44. Seal
14. Cover	30. Nut	45. Oil pressure switch
15. Seal	31. Washer	
16. Nut		

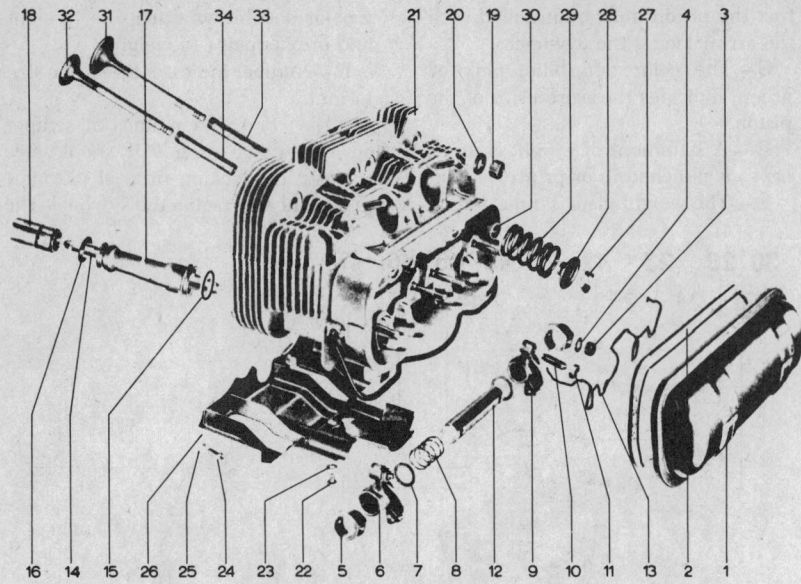

Four cylinder engine cylinder head components

1. Rocker arm cover
2. Gasket
3. Nut
4. Spring washer
5. Rocker arm bearing
6. Exhaust rocker arm
7. Thrust washer
8. Spring
9. Intake rocker arm
10. Valve adjusting screw
11. Nut
12. Rocker arm shaft

13. Rocker arm cover retainer
14. Pushrod
15. Pushrod tube seal (white)
16. Pushrod tube seal (black)
17. Pushrod tube
18. Valve lifter
19. Nut
20. Washer
21. Cylinder head
22. Bolt

23. Washer
24. Bolt
25. Washer
26. Baffle plate
27. Valve keys
28. Valve spring retainer
29. Valve spring
30. Valve stem seal
31. Intake valve
32. Exhaust valve
33. Intake valve guide
34. Exhaust valve guide

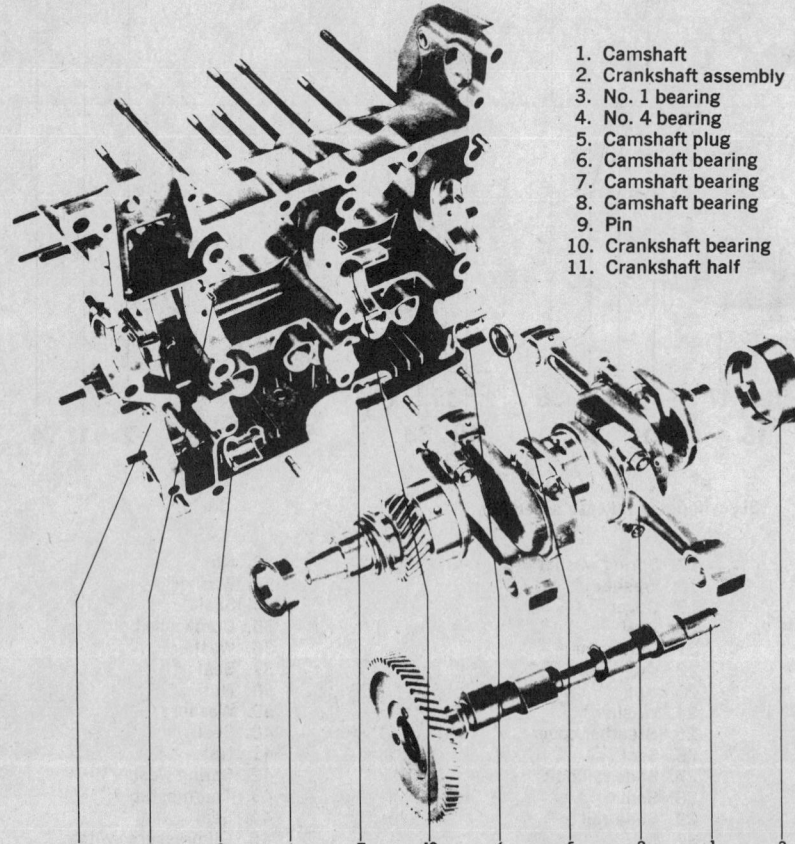

1. Camshaft
2. Crankshaft assembly
3. No. 1 bearing
4. No. 4 bearing
5. Camshaft plug
6. Camshaft bearing
7. Camshaft bearing
8. Camshaft bearing
9. Pin
10. Crankshaft bearing
11. Crankshaft half

Four cylinder engine crankcase and crankshaft assembly

locking rings of pistons 3 and 4 should be fitted on the impeller side. Fit the piston pin. The piston pin may slide in easily by hand, which is normal. Should the pin not fit easily, heat the piston to approximately 176°F. and slide in the piston pin without bottoming the pin on the locking ring. Seat the second locking ring. Lubricate the piston and piston pin. Compress the piston rings. Lubricate the cylinder bore and fit the cylinder bore. The sealing ring must also be fitted. The studs of the crankcase may not touch the cooling fins of the cylinder. Check the cylinder head for cracks and the spark plug threads for damage. Replace the sealing ring and the cylinder head. Pre-tighten the cylinder head nuts slightly and finally tighten according to sequence. Replace the baffle plate. Insert the tappets with engine oil. Slide the protective tubes with new sealing rings up to the stop, taking care not to damage the sealing rings. Slide the bearing pieces on the rocker arm shafts so that the slots face downward and the broken edges outward when settling on the studs. The clip which secures the protective tubes should enter the slots of the bearing pieces and rest against the bottom edges of the protective tubes. Lubricate the gear wheel and driveshaft and insert into the oil pump housing. Install the oil pump cover with the lubricated rubber sealing ring. Check the gear wheels for proper running. Install the oil pump, with a new seal, into the crankcase. The journal of the driveshaft should be in alignment with the slot in the camshaft gear. Center the oil pump by two crankshaft revolutions and tighten the nuts. Clean the sealing surface on the flange for the oil filter. Lubricate the rubber seal slightly and screw the filter in until the filter is seated. Tighten the oil filter. Replace the oil cooler after checking for leaks and tightening all welded seats. Replace the front and rear cylinder jackets and warm air guides. Replace the engine mount. Replace the cooling blower housing with the alternator and adjust the V-belt tension. Replace the cooling blower

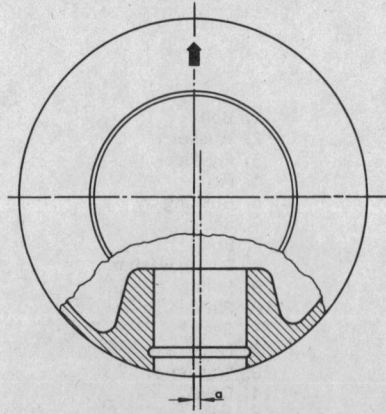

Four cylinder engine piston positioning

impeller and the front engine cover plate. Replace the ignition distributor. Bring cylinder No. 1 to the firing point. The black notch should be in alignment with the reference mark. The center off-set slot in the head of the ignition distributor driveshaft should be at an angle of approximately 12° in relation to the longitudinal axis of the engine. Turn the distributor rotor to the mark for cylinder No. 1 on the distributor housing. Insert the ignition distributor. Replace the oil filler neck with the oil vent. Replace the intake distributor with the intake pipes and injection valves. Mount the rear engine cover plate. Replace the exhaust muffler and heat exchanger. Fill the engine with oil and replace the engine in the car. Adjust the ignition timing.

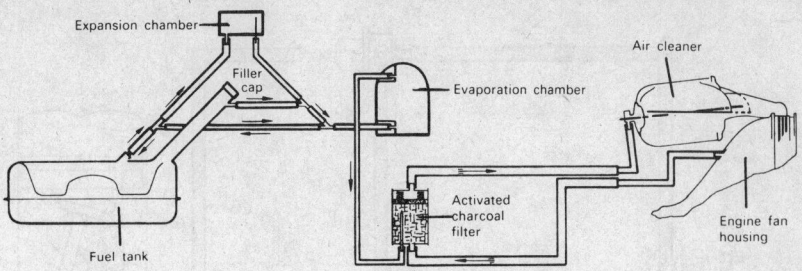

911 evaporative emission control system

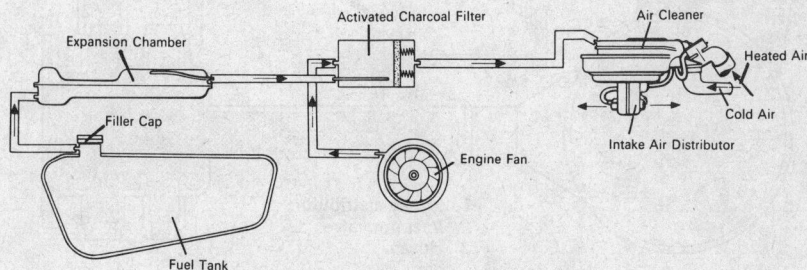

914 evaporative emission control system

EMISSION CONTROLS

Crankcase Ventilation System

All models are equipped with a crankcase ventilation systems. The purpose of the crankcase ventilation system is twofold. It keeps harmful vapors from escaping into the atmosphere and prevents the buildup of pressures within the crankcase which could cause oil leaks.

The 911 system carries vapors from the crankcase to the oil tank and then to the air cleaner. The crankcase emissions are then burned along with the air/fuel mixture. The ventilation system on 914 models supplies fresh air from the air cleaner to the rocker arm covers, where it mixes with crankcase vapors and continues through the pushrod tubes and into the crankcase. The mixture of fresh air and crankcase vapors is then released through the oil breather and a regulator

valve into the intake air distributor to be burned with the air/fuel mixture. The only maintenance required on the crankcase ventilation system is a periodic check. At every tune-up, examine the hoses for clogging or deterioration. Clean or replace the hoses as required.

Evaporative Emission Control System

Required by California in 1970 and nationwide in 1971, this system has been standard equipment on Porsches imported to the United States since 1970. Fuel vapors are no longer vented into the atmosphere. The systems used on the 911 and 914 are basically similar and consist of an expansion chamber, evaporation chamber, and an activated charcoal filter.

Fuel vapors which reach the filter deposit hydrocarbons on the surface of the charcoal element. The engine fan forces fresh air into the charcoal filter when the engine is running. The air purges the filter and the hydrocarbons are sent into the air cleaner where they become part of the air/fuel mixture and are burned.

Maintenance on this system consists of checking the condition of the various connecting lines and the charcoal filter at 10,000 mile intervals. The charcoal filter, which is located in the front luggage compartment on all models, should be replaced at 50,000 mile intervals.

Dual Diaphragm Distributors

The purpose of the dual diaphragm distributor is to improve exhaust emissions during idling. The distributor has a vacuum retard diaphragm, in addition to a vacuum advance diaphragm. The 911 series was equipped with the vacuum retarding distributor in 1972 and the 914 in 1973. Both models retard the ignition advance to 5° ATDC at idle speed.

Testing

All Models

1. Connect a timing light to the engine. Check the ignition timing.
2. Remove the retard hose from the distributor and plug it. Increase the engine speed. The ignition timing should advance. If it doesn't, then the vacuum unit is faulty and must be replaced.

Deceleration Valve

On 1972-73 models, the 914 is equipped with a vacuum deceleration

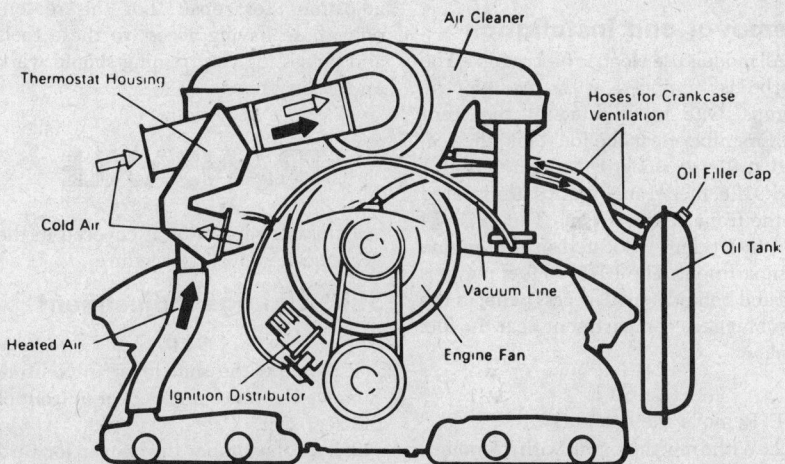

911 crankcase ventilation schematic

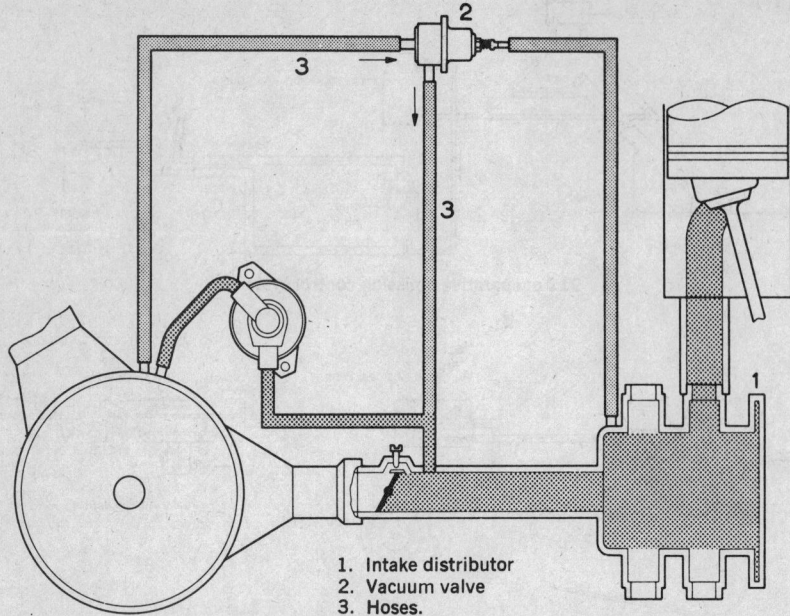

1. Intake distributor
2. Vacuum valve
3. Hoses.

Vacuum deceleration valve system

911 fuel pump removal

valve. On deceleration, with the throttles closed and engine speeds high, the valve opens and allows additional air from the air cleaner to flow into the intake air distributor. The mixture is leaned out and the exhaust emissions lowered.

Testing
1972–1973 914
1. Disconnect the vacuum valve hose at the air cleaner.
2. Start the engine and increase the speed momentarily to 3000 rpm. Close the throttle.
3. A suction should be evident at the end of the hose removed from the air cleaner. If there is no suction, replace the valve.

Air Injection System

All 1975 914 models and some 911 models are equipped with this system. A belt driven air pump supplies air to the exhaust ports. Injection of air at this point causes combustion of unburned hydrocarbons in the exhaust manifold rather than allowing them to escape into the atmosphere.

Exhaust Gas Recirculation

California 914 models and some 911 models are equipped with EGR. This system directs a portion of the exhaust gases back into the intake where they combine with the incoming mixture. This diluting of the mixture lowers peak combustion temperatures and reduces NO_x.

Thermal Reactor

A thermal reactor is used on certain 911 models and the 912E. The thermal reactor is used to reduce HC and CO emissions by supplying an improved location for exhaust combustion. 911s with the thermal reactor are equipped with an additional heater blower.

Catalytic Convertor

California delivered 1975–76 914 models are equipped with a catalytic convertor in the exhaust system. When the hot exhaust gases mix with air in the presence of the catalyst, HC, CO and NO_X are reduced to harmless gases.

FUEL SYSTEM

Electric Fuel Pump
Removal and Installation

All models use electric fuel pumps. The Turbo is equipped with two electric pumps. One is mounted at the front crossmember near the fuel tank, the second at the rear near the engine. All 911 and 912E model fuel pumps are located at the front near the tank. The 1972–74 914 fuel pump is located in the engine compartment. The 1975–76 fuel pump is located behind a small access panel in the front luggage compartment near the fuel tank.

911
1. Remove the cap nuts.
2. Withdraw the pump with its mounting bracket.
3. Loosen the hose clamp and remove the pump from the bracket.

4. Loosen the hose clamps and remove the three fuel lines from the pump.
5. Install the pump using a reverse of the removal procedure. Coat both electrical terminals with grease and make sure that the rubber boot is firmly seated.

914
1. Pinch the fuel hoses to prevent spillage and remove the cable plug.
2. Cut the hose clamps and pull the hoses from the pump, catching any fuel with a rag.
3. Raise the fuel pressure hose to prevent draining any fuel.
4. Unscrew the retaining nuts and remove the pump.
5. Fit the hoses to the pump. Use new hose clamps.
6. Mount the pump on its supports and remove the clamps used to pinch the hoses.
7. Replace the cable plug, ensuring that the protective cap is correctly installed.

Fuel Injection

The 911 mechanical fuel injection and the 914 electronic fuel injection systems require special tools and training for any adjustment or repair. For this reason, only those having access to these tools and possessing this training should work on these systems.

TRANSAXLE

Transaxle separation is covered in the "Engine Removal" procedure.

Shift Linkage Adjustment
911
1. Position the shift lever in Neutral. Remove the rear tunnel cover in front of the rear seat.
2. Pull the rubber dust cover forward on the shift rod.
3. Loosen the clamp bolt on the shift rod.

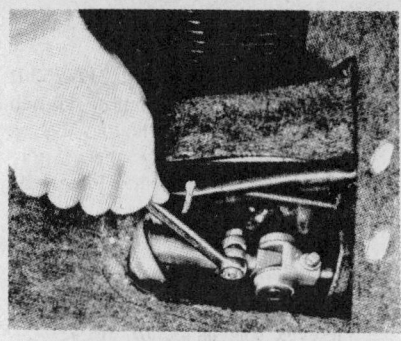

911 and 912 linkage adjustment

4. Move the transmission selector shaft all the way to its left stop, keeping it in Neutral.

5. With the transmission still in Neutral, move the gearshift rod to the right to its stop.

6. Tighten the clamp bolt to 18 ft lbs.

7. Test the shift lever. Play should be the same in all gears in all directions.

1972 914

1. Place the shift lever in Neutral.

2. Loosen the clamp between the front rod and the center rod.

3. The bottom of the shift lever should be straight up and down.

4. Set the shift lever against the left stop.

5. Loosen the dust cap clamp and remove the cap.

6. Place the transmission selector lever into Neutral and center the selector lever by moving the rear shift rod.

7. Tighten the front and center rod clamps.

8. Shift the lever into Third gear. Make sure that the transmission selector lever is correctly engaged.

9. Adjust the linkage again, if necessary.

1973–76 914

For 1973, the transaxle was modified for a side shift configuration. This change eliminated the inner selector levers and selector shaft in the rear transmission cover. The linkage goes straight back to the side shift lever without the twists of the older models.

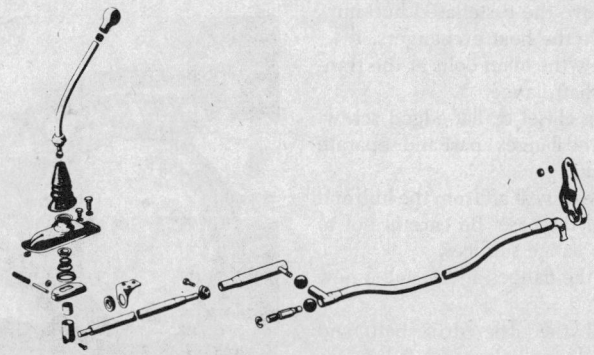

1972 914 shift linkage

1. Loosen the shift linkage retaining bolt on the shift mount.

2. Place the shift lever in Neutral and to the right (toward the Fourth and Fifth gear side).

3. Remove the rear tunnel cover in the passenger compartment.

4. Rotate the shift rod clockwise (facing toward the front of the car).

5. Tighten the mounting screw hand tight.

6. Shift lever travel must be the same for Second, Third, Fourth, and Fifth gears. Make sure that First and Reverse are easily engaged.

7. Finally tighten the mounting bolt to 18 ft lbs.

CLUTCH
Removal and Installation

Each Porsche covered in this section is equipped with single dry disc clutch and diaphragm pressure plate. Clutch actuation is controlled by a cable.

1. Separate the engine/transaxle.

2. Gradually loosen the pressure plate bolts one or two turns at a time in a criss-cross pattern to prevent distortion.

3. Remove the pressure plate and clutch disc.

4. Check the clutch disc for uneven or excessive lining wear. Examine the pressure plate for cracking, scorching, or scoring. Replace any questionable components.

Clutch disc centering

5. On 912 and 911 models, fill the pilot bearing with about 2 cc of grease.

6. Install the clutch disc and pressure plate. Use a pilot shaft or an old transaxle input shaft to keep the disc centered.

7. Gradually tighten the pressure plate-to-flywheel bolts in a criss-cross pattern. Torque the bolts to 25 ft lbs on the 912, models.

Tighten the bolts on the 914 to 15 ft lbs. On 911s, tighten the bolts to 18 ft lbs.

8. Install the throwout bearing.

9. Install the transaxle on the engine.

Free Play Adjustment
1972–76 911 and 912E

This adjustment is made at the throwout arm on the transaxle. Free play should be between ¾ in. and 1 in.

1. Jack up the rear of the car and support it on stands.

2. On older models, loosen the locknut on the clevis and turn the adjusting nut as necessary to obtain the correct free play.

Free-play adjustment

3. A threaded cable extension is provided on later models. While holding the flats on the cable end to prevent it from turning, screw the self-locking nut in or out for the correct free play.

1977 911S and Turbo

These models are equipped with an auxiliary spring to reduce pedal effort. Free play is no longer checked at the pedal. Play is checked by measuring the distance between the adjusting bolt and the positioning lever. The distance should be 1mm (0.04 in.).

1. Release the cable.

2. Adjust clutch play to 1.2mm (0.047 in.).

3. Tighten the cable at the holder until play is reduced to 1mm (0.04 in.).

4. Adjust the stop on the pedal floor plate so that the release travel is 25mm (0.984 in.) for the S or 27mm (1.063 in.) when the clutch pedal is depressed.

914

1. Raise the rear of the car and support it on jack stands.

2. Hold the threaded cable end with

pliers and turn the self-locking adjustment nut in or out until the free play is ½ in. to ¾ in.

Pedal Travel Adjustment

1. Pull the front carpeting back.
2. Loosen the two retaining bolts on the pedal stop.
3. Move the pedal up or down until reverse can be engaged with only a slight amount of gear clash.
4. Tighten the pedal stop bolts.
5. Double check the adjustment by shifting into reverse several times. Reinstall the floor carpeting.

911 and 912 pedal travel adjustment

DRIVE AXLES
Axle Driveshaft
Removal and Installation
911 and 912E

1. Jack up the rear of the car and support it on stands.
2. Remove the wheels. Remove the brake caliper and disc.
3. Raise the trailing arm with a hydraulic jack.
4. Remove the lower shock absorber mounting.
5. Install a fixture similar to Porsche tool P36b to hold the hub.
6. Remove the cotter pin and using a long ratchet handle extension, remove the hub nut.
7. Remove the allen bolts at the axle driveshaft/transaxle flange.

Hub nut removal (Porsche tool P36b shown)

Disconnecting inner driveshaft joint at transaxle

8. Use a flat chisel to pry the flanges apart.
   CAUTION: *Don't damage the flanges when separating them.*
9. Check the axle driveshaft joints for excessive play and replace them if necessary.
10. Use a new gasket on the transaxle flange. Ensure that the flanges are clean and free from burrs.
11. Pack the joints with a moly grease.
12. Install the axle drive-shaft using a reverse of the removal procedure.
13. Tighten the flange bolts to 60 ft lbs. The hollow side of the lock washer should face the spacer slate.
14. Using a long extension handle wrench, tighten the castellated nut to 217–253 ft lbs and install a new cotter pin.
   NOTE: *Be prepared to apply considerable force on this nut.*
15. Tighten the shock absorber bolt to 54 ft lbs.
16. Install the brake caliper and disc.
17. Install the wheels and lower the car.

914

1. Raise the rear of the car and support it on jack stands.
2. Remove the wheels.
3. Remove the brake caliper and disc as described in the brake section.
4. Using a ratchet handle with a long extension (a pipe will provide more leverage), remove the castellated hub nut.
5. Remove the heat exchangers.
6. Unscrew the allen bolts at the transaxle/driveshaft flange.
7. Using a chisel or flat-edged screwdriver, pry the flanges apart and separate the driveshaft.
8. Pull the driveshaft from the hub and down out of the case. Be careful not to damage the flange surfaces.
9. Clean the flanges and install a new gasket.
10. Install the axle driveshaft and tighten the flange bolts to 31 ft lbs. Use new lock washers and install them so that

their hollow ends are against the spacer plate.
12. Tighten the hub nut to 217–253 ft lbs, using a long extension on the wrench handle and plenty of muscle.
13. Install the brake disc and caliper.
14. Install the wheels and lower the car.

REAR SUSPENSION

All models covered in this section have independent rear suspension. The 911 rear suspension is a semi-trailing arm de-

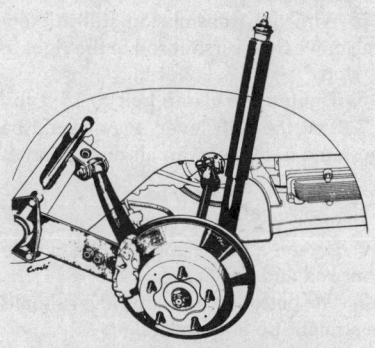

911 and 912 rear suspension

sign. Springing is provided by transverse torsion bars located forward of each trailing arm. Telescopic shock absorbers at each wheel provide dampening. A rear stabilizer bar is standard equipment on the 911S Turbo and Carrera and optional on the other two 911 models.

The 914 is also equipped with trailing arms, but they are one piece arms as opposed to the two piece arms on the 911. Telescopic strut/shocks with concentric coil springs support the weight of the car. A rear stabilizer bar is optionally available on later models.

Torsion Bars
Removal and Installation
911 and 912E

1. Jack up the rear of the car and support it safely with stands.

Raising the trailing arm

2. Remove the wheel on the side where the torsion bar is being removed.

3. Fabricate a fixture similar to the one shown. The fixture is necessary to hold the trailing arm while it is raised and lowered. The special Porsche tool for this purpose is number P 289.

4. Using a hydraulic jack under the holding fixture, raise the trailing arm.

5. Remove the lower shock absorber bolt.

6. Remove the trailing arm retaining bolts. Remove the toe and camber adjusting bolts.

7. Remove the four retaining bolts from the trailing arm cover. Withdraw the spacer.

8. Using two screwdrivers, pry off the trailing arm cover.

9. Remove the holding fixture.

10. Knock out the round body plug and remove the trailing arm.

11. Paint a reference mark on the torsion bar support, matching the location of the "L" or "R" side identification letter, so that the torsion bar may be installed in the same position.

NOTE: *The torsion bars are splined to allow adjustment of the rear riding height.*

12. Remove the torsion bar. Do not scratch the protective paint on the torsion bar, or it will corrode and possibly develop fatigue cracks.

NOTE: *If you are removing a broken torsion bar, the inner end can be knocked from its seat by removing the opposite torsion bar and tapping through with a steel rod. Torsion bars are not interchangeable from side-to-side and are marked "L" and "R" for identification.*

13. Check the torsion bar splines for damage and replace it if necessary. If any corrosion is present on the bar, replace it.

14. Coat the torsion bar lightly with a multi-purpose grease. Carefully grease the splines.

15. Apply glycerine or another rubber preservative to the torsion bar support.

16. Install the torsion bar, matching the "L" or "R" with the paint mark you made before removal.

17. Install the trailing arm cover into position and start the three accessible bolts.

18. Raise the trailing arm into place with the holding fixture (or special tool P 289) until the spacer and the fourth bolt can be installed.

19. Assemble the remaining components in a reverse order of their removal.

20. Tighten the trailing arm cover bolts to 34 ft lbs. Tighten the trailing arm retaining bolts to 65 ft lbs.

21. Tighten the camber adjusting bolt to 43 ft lbs. and the toe-in adjusting bolt to 36 ft lbs. Tighten the shock absorber bolt to 54 ft lbs.

22. Adjust the rear wheel camber and toe-in.

Spring Strut

Removal and Installation

914

1. Jack up the rear of the car and support it safely with stands.

2. Support the wheel on the side where the spring strut is being removed.

3. Loosen and remove the bottom through-bolt and nut from the trailing arm.

4. Loosen and remove the nut at the top of the strut. Hold the strut shaft while loosening the nut.

5. Remove the strut by pulling it down and out of the car.

6. When reinstalling the strut, use a nut at the top. Install the bottom nut and bolt.

7. Tighten the top nut to 36–43 ft lbs. Torque the bottom bolt to 72–87 ft lbs.

8. Lower the car.

Disassembly

914

1. Remove the strut as outlined above.

2. Install the strut in a vise. Grip at the bottom spring retainer.

3. Install a compressor on the coil spring.

4. Alternately tighten the compressor bolts to hold the spring.

CAUTION: *Be sure that the lips of the compressor are gripping the coils firmly.*

5. Remove the two threaded bushings and remove the top spring retainer.

6. Gradually release the spring compressor. When the spring tension is fully released, remove the spring, bushing, and washer.

7. Using a drift, drive the cap off the shock absorber.

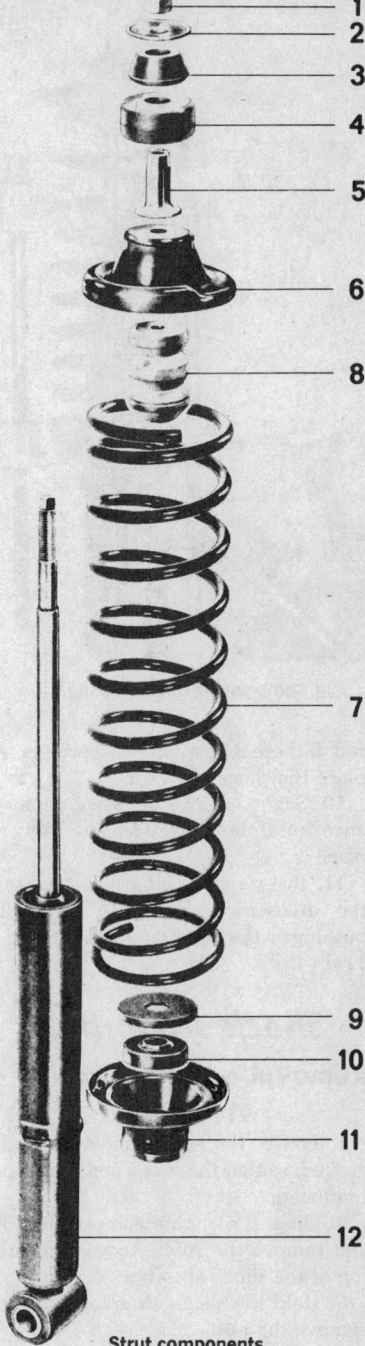

Strut components

1. Nut
2. Washer
3. Bushing
4. Bushing
5. Threaded bushing
6. Top spring retainer
7. Coil spring
8. Bumper
9. Stop washer
10. Cap
11. Bottom spring retainer
12. Shock absorber

8. Remove the bottom spring retainer by pulling over the top of the shock absorber.

9. Check the shock absorber for correct action by pushing and pulling on the

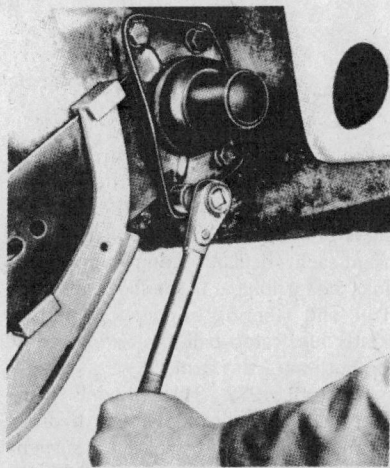

Installing the trailing arm cover

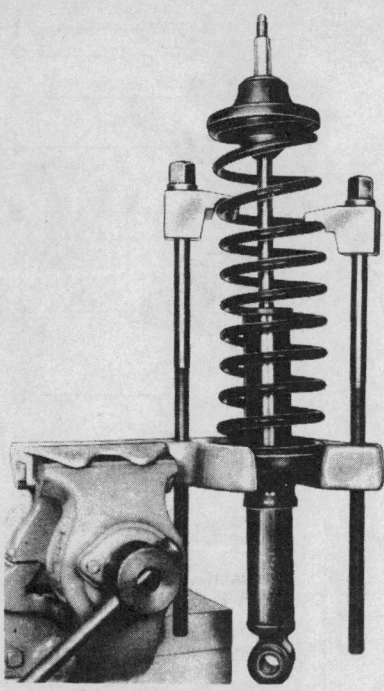

Compressing the coil spring

rod. If there is any sloppiness present, replace the shock absorber.

10. Slight oil leakage is within tolerance, but if the shock is leaking badly replace it.

11. Reassembly is basically a reverse of the disassembly steps. The threaded bushing on the top should be tightened to 11–14 ft lbs.

Shock Absorbers

Removal and Installation

911 and 912E

1. Leave the car standing on the ground, so that the shock absorber is not tensioned.

2. Open the engine compartment lid and remove the rubber cover from the top of the shock absorber.

3. Hold the shock absorber shaft and remove the nut.

4. On the bottom, remove the retaining nut and bolt.

5. Remove the shock absorber.

Top shock absorber mounting

Bottom shock absorber mounting

6. If the shock exhibits excessive free travel or is leaking, replace it.

7. Install the shock up through the body and screw the nut on hand-tight.

8. Align the shock absorber eye with the hole in the trailing arm and install the nut and bolt.

9. Tighten the top nut and install the rubber cover.

10. Tighten the bottom retaining bolt to 54 ft lbs.

Stabilizer

Removal and Installation

911 and 912E

1. Jack the rear of the car and safely support it with stands.

2. Using a large screwdriver, pry the upper eyes of the stabilizer bar off the studs in the trailing arm.

3. Remove the body mounting brackets.

4. Remove the stabilizer.

5. Check the rubber bushings for wear or damage and, if necessary, replace them.

6. Install the stabilizer bar using a reverse of the removal steps.

Adjustments

Camber Adjustment

911 and 912E

The rearmost of the two allen bolts on the trailing arm provides camber adjustment. Tighten the bolt to 43 ft lbs. after the camber is adjusted to specifications.

914

Camber is adjusted by removal or insertion of shims under the trailing arm bearing plate. Scribe the plate's position, so the toe-in setting isn't lost, and then remove the center bolt and loosen the two end bolts. Each 1 mm shim results in a 10' change in camber. Tighten the bolts

911 and 912 rear wheel alignment adjustment points

1. Camber
2. Toe-in

914 rear wheel alignment adjustment point

to 18 ft lbs after the correct camber is reached.

Toe-in Adjustment

911 and 912E

The front allen bolt on the trailing arm adjusts the toe-in. Tighten the bolt to 36 ft lbs after toe-in is adjusted to specification.

914

Loosen all three bolts on the trailing arm bearing plate and push the arm forward or backward as necessary to correct the toe-in. Tighten the bolts to 18 ft lbs when the adjustment is complete.

FRONT SUSPENSION

Front suspension is similar in design on all models; but parts are not interchangeable from one type to the other. Springing is provided by a longitudinal torsion bar at each wheel. A triangular lower arm links the torsion bar to the shock absorber strut and steering knuckle. A permanently lubricated ball joint is located at the bottom of the strut.

Up until 1972, 911E models were equipped with self-leveling hydropneumatic suspension struts. This suspension package was optionally available on the T and S, but few were so equipped. In this design, the strut acts as shock absorber, spring, and locating member and the torsion bars are replaced by a shaft in the lower arm.

Torsion Bars

Removal and Installation

911 and 912E

1. Jack up the front of the car and support it safely with stands.

2. Remove the torsion bar adjusting screw.

3. Take the adjusting lever off the torsion bar and withdraw the seal.

4. Unscrew the retaining bolts from the front mount cover bracket and remove the bracket.

5. Using a drift, carefully drive the torsion bar out of the front of the arm.

6. Check the torsion bar for spline damage and rust. If necessary, replace the bar.

7. Give the torsion bar a light coating of grease before installing it.

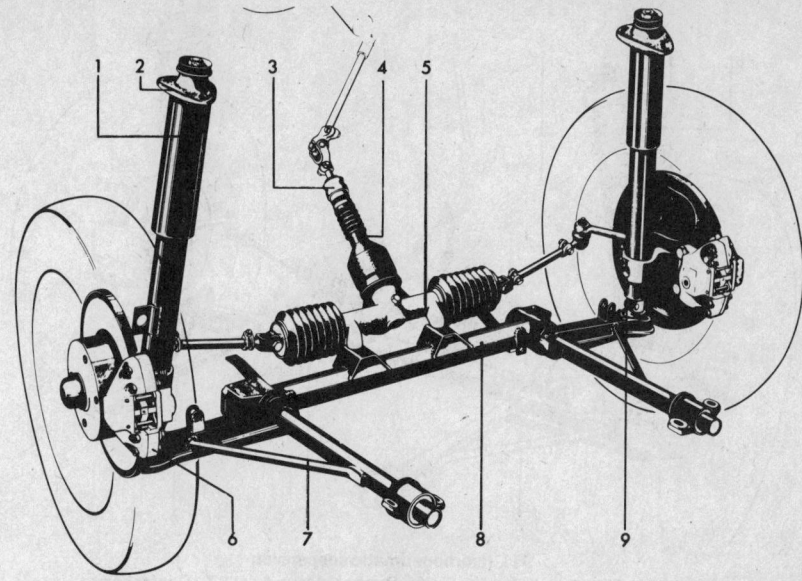

914 front suspension and steering

1. Strut
2. Strut support bracket
3. Steering shaft
4. Dust boot
5. Steering gear
6. Brake caliper
7. Control arm
8. Crossmember
9. Ball joint

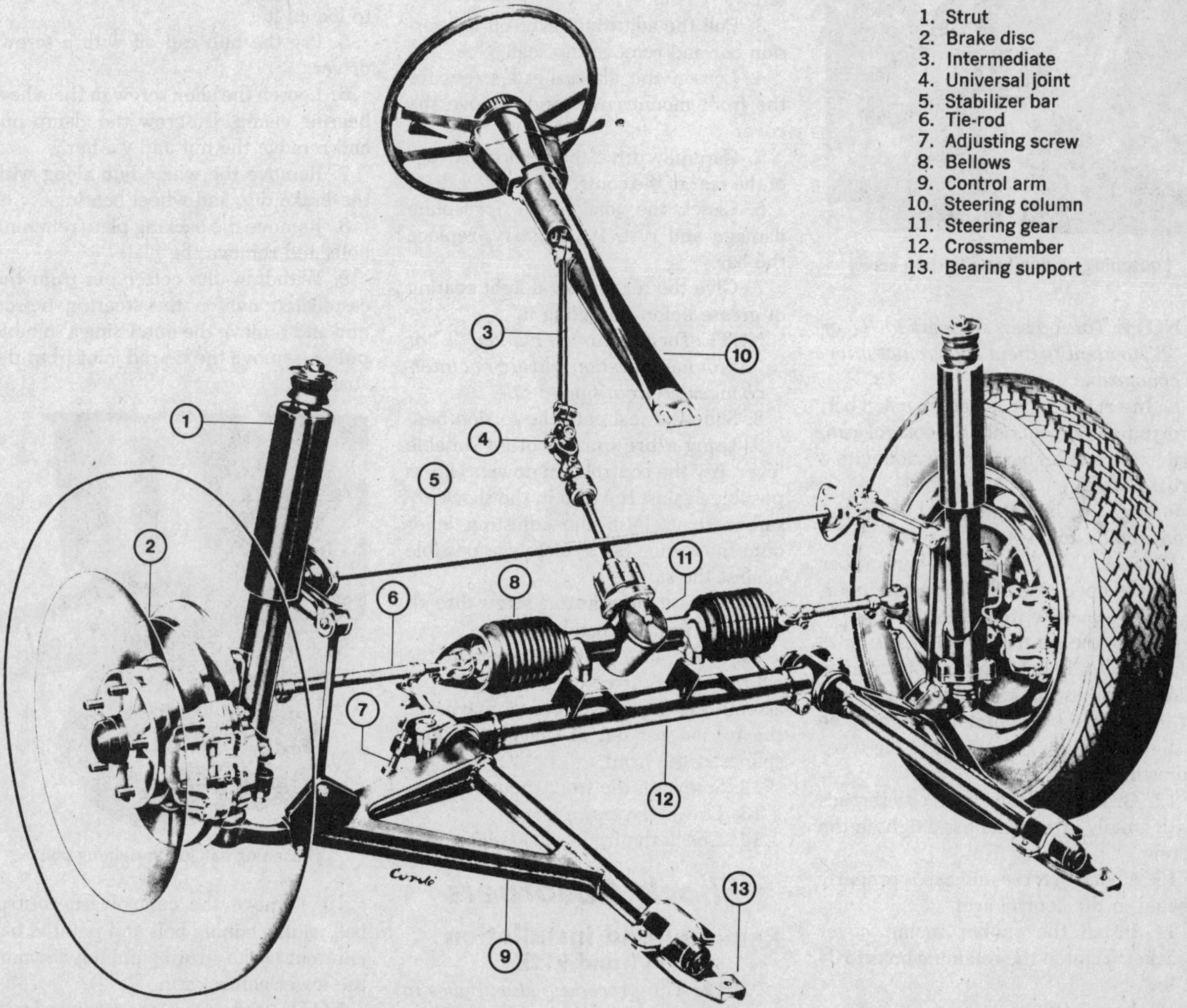

1. Strut
2. Brake disc
3. Intermediate
4. Universal joint
5. Stabilizer bar
6. Tie-rod
7. Adjusting screw
8. Bellows
9. Control arm
10. Steering column
11. Steering gear
12. Crossmember
13. Bearing support

911 and 912 front suspension and steering

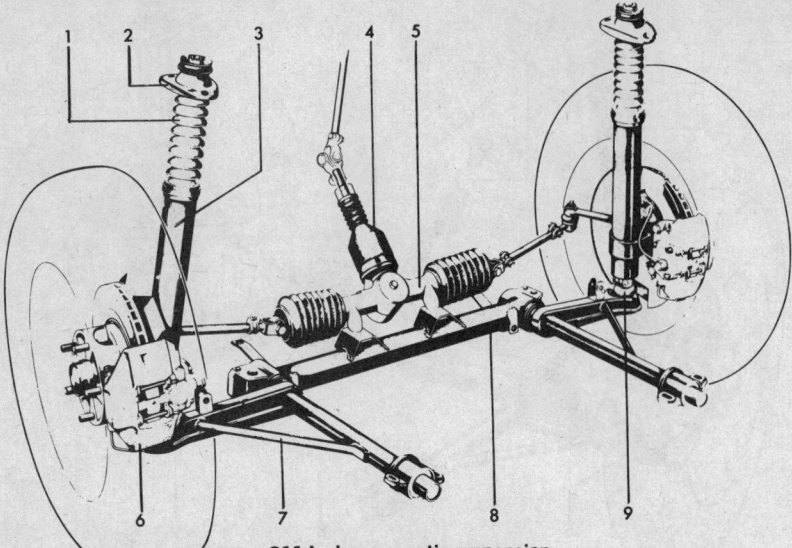

911 hydropneumatic suspension

1. Rubber spring	4. Rubber sleeve	7. Control arm
2. Step bearing	5. Steering gear	8. Crossmember
3. Hydropneumatic strut	6. Brake caliper	9. Ball joint

Top mounting nut removal

Loosening torsion bar adjusting screw

NOTE: *Torsion bars are marked "L" or "R" to identify them and are not interchangeable.*

8. Insert the end cap of the torsion bar, protruding side out, into the control arm. Drive the torsion bar into position with a drift. Carefully.

9. Tighten the retaining bolts on the front mount to 34 ft lbs.

10. Slide the seal onto the torsion bar from the open side of the crossmember.

11. Using a tire iron, or other suitable lever, pry the control arm down as far as possible. While holding the control arm, slide the adjusting lever onto the splines of the torsion bar. There should only be a slight amount of clearance at the lever adjusting point.

12. Grease the adjusting screw threads with a moly grease and hand tighten the screw.

13. Check that the end cap is properly seated in the control arm.

14. Install the rubber mount cover bracket. Tighten the retaining bolts to 34 ft lbs.

15. Lower the car.

16. Check the front wheel alignment.

914

1. Jack up the front of the car and support it safely with stands.

2. Unscrew the torsion bar adjusting screw.

3. Pull the adjusting lever off the torsion bar and remove the seal.

4. Loosen the cheesehead screw for the front mount cover and remove the cover.

5. Carefully drive the torsion bar out of the rear of the control arm with a drift.

6. Check the torsion bar for spline damage and rust. If necessary, replace the bar.

7. Give the torsion bar a light coating of grease before installing it.

NOTE: *Torsion bars are marked "L" or "R" for identification and are not interchangeable from side-to-side.*

8. Slide the seal onto the torsion bar.

9. Using a tire iron, or other suitable lever, pry the control arm down as far as possible against the stop in the shock absorber strut. Push the adjusting lever onto the torsion bar as closely as possible against the stop.

10. Grease the adjusting screw threads and then install it hand-tight.

11. Make sure that the cover in the control arm is correctly seated. Improper assembly of the adjusting lever may force the torsion bar out of the control arm splines at the front.

12. Screw on the front mount cover.

13. Lower the car.

14. Check the front wheel alignment.

Shock Absorbers

Removal and Installation
911 and 912E

NOTE: *This procedure also applies to cars equipped with hydropneumatic struts.*

1. Jack up the front of the car and support it safely on stands. Remove the wheels.

2. Remove the brake line from the clip on the suspension strut. A small amount of brake fluid will run out of the line, plug it so that dirt cannot enter the system.

3. Unscrew the retaining bolts and remove the caliper.

4. Using a soft mallet, tap the hub cap to loosen it.

5. Pry the hub cap off with a screwdriver.

6. Loosen the allen screw in the wheel bearing clamp. Unscrew the clamp nut and remove the nut and washer.

7. Remove the wheel hub along with the brake disc and wheel bearing.

8. Remove the backing plate retaining bolts and remove the plate.

9. Withdraw the cotter pin from the castellated nut on the steering tie-rod end and remove the nut. Using a suitable puller, remove the tie-rod joint from the strut.

Loosening ball joint retaining bolt

10. Remove the control arm-to-strut ball joint retaining bolt and pull the ball joint out of the strut by pulling down on the lower control arm.

NOTE: *If the car is not equipped with hydropneumatic struts, the torsion bar* *adjusting screw will have to be loosened and the adjusting arm removed.*

11. Remove the keeper for the nut on the top of the strut. Unscrew the nut and remove it, the keeper plate, and washer.

12. Remove the strut from the bottom. It will be necessary to loosen and pull the side of the luggage compartment out for clearance.

13. Check the shock absorber strut for excessive free travel and leaking. Replace the shock absorber if it is at all suspect.

14. Install the strut in a reverse order of the removal.

15. Tighten the top nut to 58 ft lbs. Use a new keeper plate and ensure that the peg on the plate is pointing up.

16. Tighten the ball joint bolt to 47 ft lbs.

NOTE: *Remember to install the washer between the ball joint seal and strut.*

17. On non-hydropneumatic strut equipped cars, install the torsion bar adjusting lever as described in "Torsion Bar Removal and Installation".

18. Tighten the tie-rod nut to 33 ft lbs and install a new cotter pin.

19. Torque the backing plate bolts to 18 ft lbs.

20. Install and adjust the wheel bearings as outlined in the "Brake" section.

21. Tighten the caliper retaining bolts to 50 ft lbs.

22. Bleed the hydraulic system as outlined in the "Brake" section.

23. Install the wheels and lower the car.

24. Check the wheel alignment.

914

1. Jack up the front of the car and support it safely with stands. Remove the wheels.

2. Remove the brake line from its retainer on the shock absorber strut.

3. Remove the retaining bolts and detach the caliper.

4. Carefully pry the hub cap off.

5. Loosen the screw in the wheel bearing clamp nut. Unscrew the clamp nut and remove the washer.

6. Remove the brake disc and the wheel bearings.

7. Remove the retaining bolt and remove the splash shield.

8. Remove the cotter pin and nut and remove the tie-rod joint from the strut with a suitable puller.

9. Loosen the torsion bar adjusting screw and remove the adjusting lever.

10. Loosen the ball joint retaining bolt on the strut. Pull the control arm down to free the strut from the ball joint.

11. Open the front luggage compartment lid. Remove the strut retaining nut, lock washer, and tab washer.

12. Pull the strut down and out of the car.

13. Check the shock absorber strut for excessive free travel and leaking and replace it, if necessary.

14. Installation of the strut is essentially a reverse order of the removal. Remember to install the washer on the ball joint before attaching the strut.

15. Tighten the top nut to 58 ft lbs. Use a new lock washer and ensure that its tab points up. Torque the ball joint bolt in the strut to 47 ft lbs.

16. Reinstall the torsion bar adjusting lever as outlined in "Torsion Bar Removal and Installation".

17. Tighten the tie-rod end nut to 33 ft lbs and install a new cotter pin. Torque the three splash shield bolts to 18 ft lbs.

18. Install and adjust the wheel bearings as described in the "Brake" section.

19. Install new lock washers on the caliper retaining bolts. Tighten both bolts to 51 ft lbs.

20. Bleed the brake system.

21. Install the wheels and lower the car.

22. Check the wheel alignment.

Control Arm and Ball Joint

914

Removal

1. Remove torsion bar adjusting screw and pull adjusting lever from torsion bar. Remove seal.

2. Loosen ball joint hex bolt, push control arm downward and pull ball joint from shock absorber strut.

3. Remove control arm and auxiliary carrier hex bolt.

4. Unbolt and remove front control arm bearing protective cap.

5. Remove control arm bearing bolts.

6. Push control arm together with torsion bar out of auxiliary carrier and remove.

NOTE: *If both control arms are to be removed, first remove one arm and tighten the control arm and carrier hex bolt so that the carrier is supported.*

7. Clamp the control arm in a soft-jawed vise and unlock the ball joint nut, removing the ball joint.

Installation

1. Position ball joint in control arm and tighten nut to 108 ftlbs.

2. Coat torsion bar lightly with lithium grease, paying attention to the serrations, and insert torsion bar into control arm.

3. Position control arm and torsion in carrier.

NOTE: *Torsion bars are not interchangeable. They are marked R and L for identification.*

4. Torque control arm bolts (front) to 34 ftlb.

5. Torque hex bolt for ball joint to 34 ftlb.

6. Slide seal across torsion bar and push control arm, with shock absorber connected, down against stop in strut. Slide the adjusting lever as closely as possible against the stop of the auxiliary carrier for the adjusting screw on the torsion bar.

7. Grease the threads of the adjusting screw with molybdenum di-sulfide grease and slightly tighten the adjusting screw.

8. Check the closing cover in the control arm for a good seal.

9. Attach the control arm protective cap.

10. Check front end height.

Stabilizer Bar
Removal and Installation
911 and 912E

1. Jack up the front of the car and safely support it on stands.

2. Loosen the stabilizer clamp bolts and pry the lever ends off their mounts.

3. Remove the stabilizer bar along with the levers.

4. Check the rubber bushings for deterioration and, if necessary, replace them. Lubricate the bushings with glycerine or some other rubber preservative.

5. Install the stabilizer bar in a reverse order of the removal.

6. The square end of the stabilizer should protrude slightly above the clamp. Tighten the clamp nuts to 18 ft lbs.

Adjustments
Camber Adjustment

Camber is adjusted at the top of the strut. Pull back the luggage compartment rug to expose the three mounting bolts. Scrape the undercoating from the bolts and plates. Scribe the positions of the two plates under the bolts. Loosen the bolts and move the strut in or out as necessary to correct the camber angle.

Caster and camber adjustment location

Caster Adjustment

Caster is adjusted in the same manner as camber, except that the strut is moved forward or backward to change the caster angle.

Toe-in Adjustment

Toe-in is set with the front wheels straight ahead. Tie-rod length is adjusted by loosening the tie-rod clamps and moving them an equal amount in or out to obtain the correct toe-in.

STEERING

All models are equipped with rack and pinion type steering gear. No maintenance is required on the steering system. It is filled with a special lubricant at the time of manufacture and does not require checking or filling.

Steering Wheel
Removal and Installation

1. Disconnect the battery(ies). Place the wheels in a straight ahead position.
2. Twist the center cover to the left and remove it.

Steering wheel center cover removal

3. Remove the horn contact pin.
4. Remove the steering wheel nut.
5. Mark the steering wheel and the shaft so that it can be reinstalled in the same position.
6. Remove the steering wheel. Catch the bearing support ring and spring.
7. Install the spring and bearing support ring on the wheel hub.
8. Lightly grease the horn contact ring.
9. Install the wheel. Make sure that you align the match marks made before removal.
10. Tighten the steering wheel nut to 58 ft lbs on 911 models, and 36–43 ft lbs on 914s.

11. Twist the center cover back on to the right to snap it into place.

Turn Signal/Headlight Flasher Switch
Removal and Installation
911 and 912E

The combination turn signal, headlight dimmer, and flasher switch is located in the steering column housing. The wiper/washer switch removal and installation procedure is identical.

1. Remove the steering wheel as outlined above.
2. Reach under the instrument panel and disconnect all wiring to the switch.
3. Remove the two horn contact ring screws, disconnect the wire, and remove the ring.
4. Remove the two upper housing retaining nuts. Pull the entire assembly off the column, leading the switch wires through the hole in the housing.
5. Remove the three retaining screws and remove the switch.
6. Reverse the removal steps to reinstall the switch.

914

Both the turn signal/headlight dimmer and wiper/washer switches are located within the steering column cover halves.

1. Remove the steering wheel as previously outlined.
2. Unscrew and remove the horn contact ring.
3. Remove the screw retaining the horn ground wire and remove the wire.
4. Remove the retaining screw from the top and bottom covers. Detach the covers.
5. Remove the switch attaching screws and remove the switch.
6. Installation is a reverse of the removal procedure. Make sure that the turn signal switch is in neutral, or the cancelling cams will be damaged.

Ignition Switch/Steering Lock
Removal and Installation
911 and 912E

1. Remove the ignition switch cover.
2. Drill out the two shear bolts which retain the switch.
3. Remove the steering lock and spacer.
4. Disconnect the electrical wiring and remove the switch.
5. Place the steering lock into position.
6. Insert the protective plate.
7. Install and evenly tighten the shear bolts until their heads break off.

Steering Gear
Removal and Installation
911 and 912E

1. Remove the front luggage compartment carpeting. Jack up the front of the car and support it safely with stands.
2. Remove the auxiliary heater duct from the steering post and position it to one side.
3. Open the access door and the intermediate steering shaft cover by prying the spring clips off with a screwdriver.
4. Remove the three heater fuel pump retaining bolts and position the pump to one side.
5. Remove the cotter pin from the lower universal joint bolt and loosen the castellated nut. Pull the universal joint off the steering shaft.
6. Remove the allen bolts from the steering shaft bushing bracket. Remove the bracket and pull the bushing and dust cover.

Disconnecting steering coupling

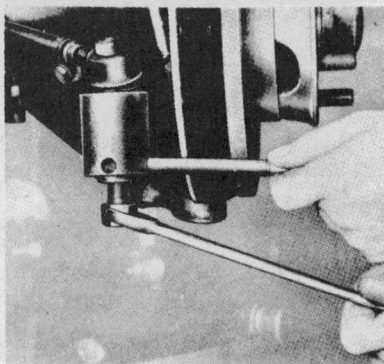

Removing tie-rod ends

7. Loosen and remove the steering coupling bolts.
8. Remove the retaining bolts and remove the bottom shield.
9. Remove the cotter pins and nuts, and then pull the tie-rod ends out of the suspension struts with a suitable puller.
10. Remove the two rack and pinion housing retaining bolts.
11. Remove the right side crossmember brace.
12. Pull the steering assembly out the right side of the car.

Rack and pinion retaining bolts

13. Remove the retaining bolts from the tie-rod yokes.

14. Installation is the reverse of the removal procedure.

15. Tighten the yoke bolts to 34 ft lbs.

16. Make sure that the crossmember brace mounts without binding. Tighten the nuts to 47 ft lbs and the bolts to 34 ft lbs.

17. Install the steering housing bolts with new lockwashers and tighten to 34 ft lbs.

18. Tighten the tie-rod end nuts to 33 ft lbs and install new cotter pins.

19. Tighten the steering bushing bracket allen bolts to 18 ft lbs.

20. Install new washers on the steering coupling bolts and tighten them to 18 ft lbs.

21. Lower the car.

914

1. Raise the front of the car and support it safely on stands.

2. Remove the nut and bolt from the bottom universal joint.

3. Remove the cotter pins and castellated nuts from the tie-rod ends. Using a suitable puller, remove the tie-rod ends from the struts.

4. Remove the front shield.

5. Loosen the crossmember retaining bolts for the steering gear.

6. Loosen the torsion bar adjusting screws.

7. Remove the adjusting levers and seals from the torsion bars.

8. Remove the crossmember and control arm retaining bolts and remove the crossmember.

9. Remove the steering gear and tie-rods.

10. Detach the tie-rods from the steering gear by removing the yoke bolts.

11. Installation is essentially a reverse of the removal procedure. Reinstall the torsion bar adjusting levers as described in "Torsion Bar Removal and Installation".

12. The tie-rod yoke bolts are tightened to 34 ft lbs, the steering housing mounting bolts to 34 ft lbs, and the crossmember mounting bolts to 65 ft lbs.

13. Torque the tie-rod end nuts to 33 ft lbs. Tighten the steering coupling bolts and universal shaft nut to 18 ft lbs.

BRAKE SYSTEMS

All models are equipped with four wheel disc brakes. Fixed, two-piston calipers are utilized on each system. The discs on the 914 are solid. 911 are equipped with internally vented discs at each wheel. Disc brakes on all of these models are self-adjusting and require no periodic adjustment

HYDRAULIC SYSTEMS

Each car has a tandem master cylinder, remote reservoir (mounted in the front luggage compartment for convenience), and separate hydraulic circuits for the front and rear brakes. The 914 rear circuit includes a pressure regulator which maintains maximum rear brake pressure at a predetermined level to prevent rear wheel lockup under hard braking. The 1977 911S and Turbo models are equipped with power brakes. A vacuum booster is mounted in tandem with the master cylinder. It is located under the luggage compartment carpet.

Master Cylinder
Removal and Installation

1. Pull the accelerator back and out of its pushrod. Pull back the driver's side carpeting.

2. Unscrew the floorboard retainer(s) under the brake and clutch pedals.

3. Remove the master cylinder dust cover.

4. Jack the front of the car up and support it with stands.

5. Siphon the brake fluid out of the reservoir. Discard the fluid, don't save it for reuse.

Master cylinder removal

6. Unbolt the front splash shield.

7. Remove the brake lines from the master cylinder. Disconnect the brake failure warning light sending unit wire.

8. Remove the two master cylinder mounting nuts.

9. Disconnect the reservoir lines and remove the master cylinder.

10. Before installing the master cylinder, apply body sealer around the mounting flange.

11. Install the cylinder, making sure that the piston pushrod is correctly posi-

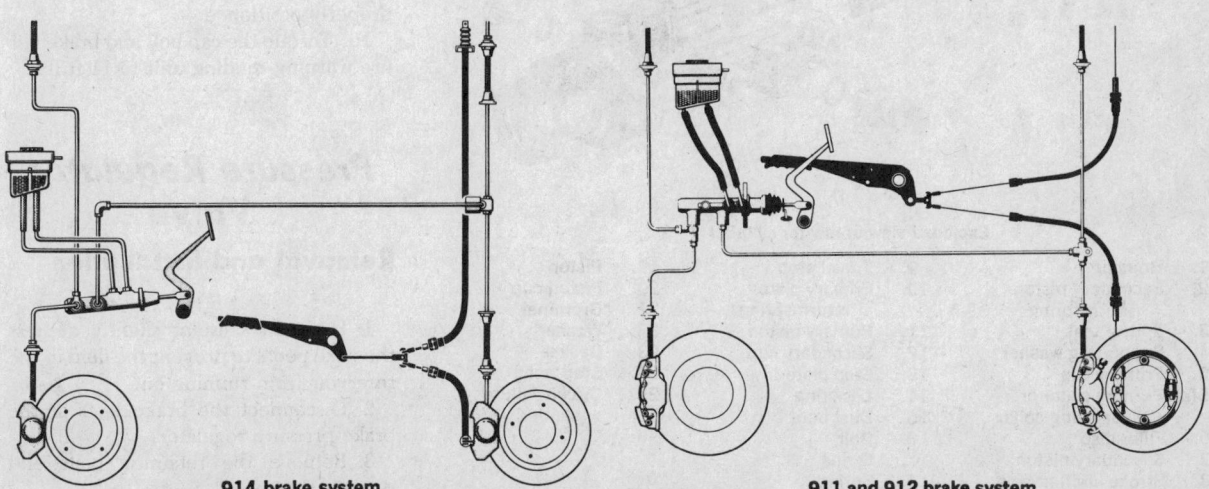

914 brake system

911 and 912 brake system

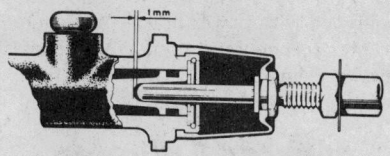

Correct piston pushrod clearance

tioned. Torque the mounting nuts to 18 ft lbs.

12. The piston pushrod should have 0.04 in. (1 mm) clearance between it and the piston. Loosen the piston rod nut and turn the rod to adjust the clearance.

13. Refill the system with new brake fluid. Bleed the brakes as outlined below.

14. Tighten the splash shield bolts to 34 ft lbs (larger bolt) and 18 ft lbs (smaller bolt).

15. Test the brake failure warning light.

a. Switch on the ignition. The hand-

brake warning light will go on. If it doesn't, replace the bulb.

b. Start the engine. While you depress the brake pedal, have an assistant open a bleeder valve on one of the wheels to simulate a brake failure. The light should go on.

c. When your assistant closes the valve, the light should go out.

d. Repeat the test on the other brake circuit.

If the light fails to light during one of the tests, check the circuit failure sender which screws into the master cylinder.

Overhaul

1. Mount the master cylinder in a vise. Use cloths to protect the cylinder from the vise jaws.

2. Using a small screwdriver, carefully pry out the lock ring in the end of the master cylinder.

3. Remove the stop plate and the complete primary piston assembly.

4. Unscrew the secondary piston stop bolt and blow the piston out with compressed air.

5. Remove the spring, spring seat, and the support washer.

6. Carefully clamp the primary piston in a vise. Slightly compress the spring and screw out the stroke limiting bolt.

7. Remove the primary piston stop sleeve, stop-bolt, spring, spring seat, and support washer.

8. Replace the used parts with those supplied in the overhaul kit.

9. Clean all metal parts in denatured alcohol and dry them with compressed air.

10. Check every part you are reusing. Pay close attention to the cylinder bores. If there is any scoring or rust, replace the master cylinder.

11. Lightly coat the bores and cups with brake fluid. Assemble the cylinder components in the sequence shown in the illustration.

12. Insert the secondary piston into the cylinder, along with the filler disc, primary cup, supporting washer, spring seat, and the spring.

NOTE: *The large coil of the spring must face the bottom of the housing.*

13. Using a plastic rod or other non-metallic tool, push the secondary piston into the housing until the stop-bolt and washer can be screwed in and tightened (7–9 ft lbs).

NOTE: *Check the stop-bolt seating. It must be ahead of the secondary piston and the piston must move freely to the bottom of the housing.*

14. Assemble the filler disc, primary cup, and supporting washer onto the primary piston. Fasten the spring, spring seat, and stop sleeve to the piston with the stroke limiting bolt.

15. Assemble the remaining master cylinder components in a reverse order of disassembly. Ensure that the lock ring is fully seated and that the piston cups are properly positioned.

16. Torque the cap bolt and brake failure warning sending unit to 11 ft lbs.

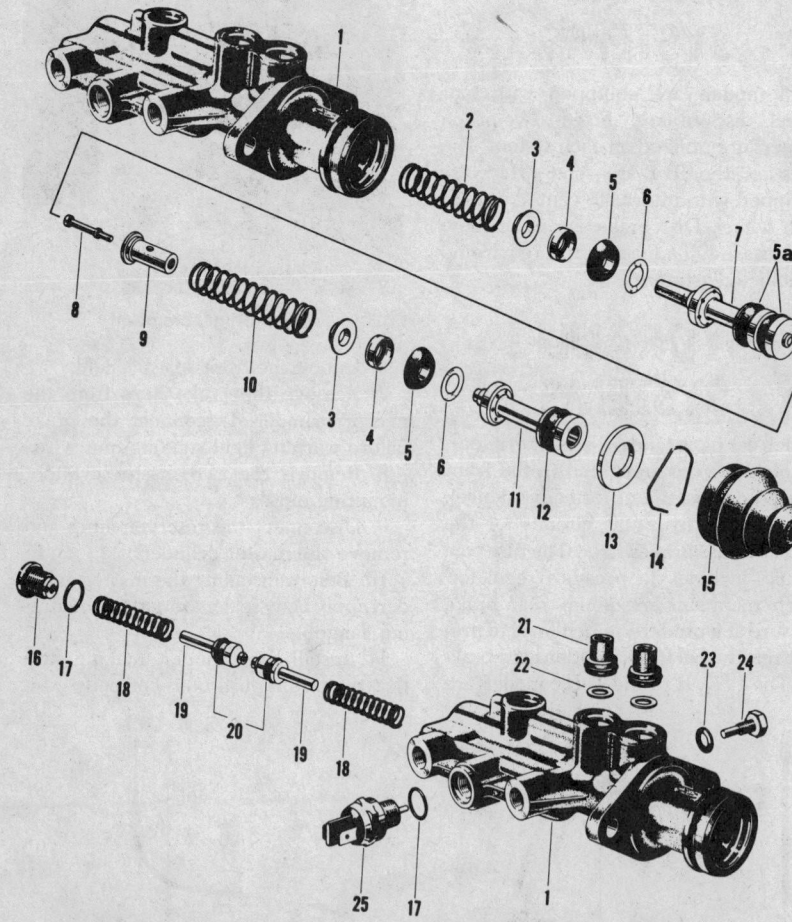

Exploded view of master cylinder

1.	Housing	9.	Travel stop	19.	Piston
2.	Secondary piston return spring	10.	Primary piston return spring	20.	Piston cup
				21.	Grommet
3.	Spring seat	11.	Primary piston	22.	Washer
4.	Supporting washer	12.	Secondary cup	23.	Gasket
5.	Primary cup	13.	Stop plate	24.	Stop bolt
5(a)	Primary collar or separating collar	14.	Lock ring	25.	Circuit failure sender
		15.	Dust boot		
6.	Filler disc	16.	Bolt		
7.	Secondary piston	17.	O-ring		
8.	Stroke limiting bolt	18.	Spring		

Pressure Regulator Valve

Removal and Installation

914

1. Have an assistant slightly depress the rake pedal to prevent the fluid in the reservoir from running out.

2. Disconnect the brake lines at the brake pressure regulator.

3. Remove the retaining bolts and remove the valve.

914 brake pressure regulator

4. Install the regulator valve.
5. Bleed the brakes.

Checking and Adjustment
914

The brake pressure regulator is not repairable and must be replaced if defective. To check if the valve is operating, have an assistant depress the brake pedal while you hold your hand on the valve. When your assistant releases the brake pedal, you should feel a slight knock in the regulator. High pressure gauges are required to thoroughly check and adjust the valve. If you suspect the valve, replace it.

Bleeding

Anytime a brake line has been disconnected, the hydraulic system should be bled. The brakes should also be bled when the pedal travel becomes unusually long ("soft pedal") or the car pulls to one side during braking. You will require one assistant to bleed the brakes. The proper bleeding sequence for 911 and 912E models is: left rear wheel (outer bleeder valve and then the inner), right rear wheel (outer bleeder valve and then the inner), right front wheel, and then left front wheel. 914 models use the following sequence: right rear, left rear, left front, and then right front.
NOTE: *If the system has been drained, first refill it with fresh brake fluid. Following the above sequence, open each*

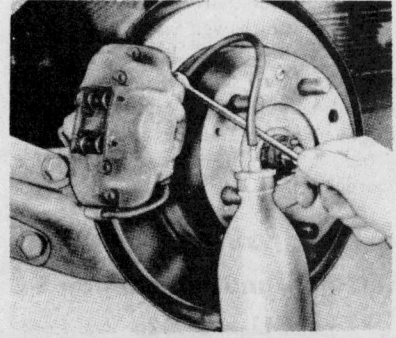

Brake bleeding

bleeder valve ½ to ¾ of a turn and pump the brake pedal until fluid runs out of the valve. Proceed with the bleeding as outlined below.

1. Remove the bleeder valve dust cover and install a rubber bleeder hose.
2. Insert the other end of the hose into a container about 1/3 full of brake fluid.
3. Have your assistant pump the brake pedal several times until the pedal pressure increases.
4. Hold the pedal under pressure and then start to open the bleeder valve about ½ to ¾ of a turn. At this point, have your assistant depress the pedal all the way and then quickly close the valve. The helper should allow the pedal to return slowly.
NOTE: *Keep a close check on the brake fluid in the reservoir and top it up as necessary throughout the bleeding process.*
5. Keep repeating this procedure until no more air bubbles can be seen coming from the hose in the brake fluid.
6. Remove the bleeder hose and install the dust cover.
7. Continue the bleeding at each wheel in sequence.

FRONT DISC BRAKES
Brake Disc Pads

Removal and Installation

Brake pads should be replaced when there is no visible clearance between the pads and the cross-spring or when they are worn to a thickness of 0.08 in. (2 mm) or less.

Brake pad wear indication

1. Jack up the front of the car and support it on stands. Remove the wheels.
2. Using pliers, pull out the pin retaining clips.

Retaining pin removal

3. While pressing down on the cross-spring, push the pad retaining pins out with a drift or small screwdriver.
4. Reference mark the positions of the brake pads if they are being reused.
5. Remove the brake pads from the caliper.
NOTE: *Porsche has a special tool for this purpose, P 86, but using a small drift or punch you can pry the pad out of the caliper until it can be gripped by a pair pliers and removed.*
6. Siphon out half of the brake fluid in the reservoir to prevent it from overflowing when the pistons are pushed in and new thicker pads are inserted.
7. Using a flat, smooth piece of hardwood, push the pistons back into the caliper. Do this carefully so that you don't damage either the piston or the brake disc.
8. Clean the brake pad slots in the caliper with alcohol. On 914 models, remove the piston anti-rotation plate. Blow out any foreign matter dislodged by the cleaning.

914 piston anti-rotation plate positioning

9. Examine the piston boots for damage or deterioration. Any questionable parts should be replaced.
10. Dress any ridges on the disc edge with crocus cloth.
11. On 914 models, install the anti-rotation plate onto the piston.

12. Install the brake pads into the caliper. Pads must be free in their slots, there should be no binding.

NOTE: *Replace used pads in the side of the caliper from which they were removed. When installing new pads, always replace the pads on the opposite wheel at the same time.*

13. Position a new cross-spring in the caliper, and then carefully tap the pad retaining pins into place with a small hammer. Install the pin clips. If the clips are rusty, replace them.

14. New brake pads must be run-in for approximately 100 miles. During this period, try not to apply the brakes extremely hard. Use them moderately and gradually during break-in.

Brake Calipers

Removal and Installation

1. Jack up the front of the car and support it on stands.
2. Remove the brake pads as outlined above.
3. Disconnect and plug the brake line at the caliper.
4. Remove the retaining bolts and remove the caliper.
5. Install the caliper using a reverse of the removal procedure. Tighten the two retaining bolts to 50 ft lbs.
6. Bleed the brakes.

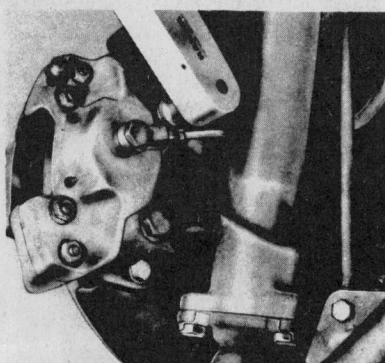

Removing caliper retaining bolts

Overhaul

1. Remove the caliper from the car.
2. Screw out the bleeder valve and apply air pressure to clean out any brake fluid.
3. Mount the caliper in a soft-jawed vise or place cloths over the jaws to protect the caliper.
4. Remove the anti-rotation plate on 914 models.
5. Using a screwdriver, pry out the retaining ring and remove the boot from one piston.
6. Depress the other piston with a C-clamp and a flat piece of wood or metal. This setup will do the same job as Porsche tool P83.

Removing piston retaining ring

7. Insert another flat piece of wood or metal in the caliper to protect the piston which is being removed. Apply an initial air pressure of 30 psi to the bleeder valve to force the piston from its bore in the caliper.

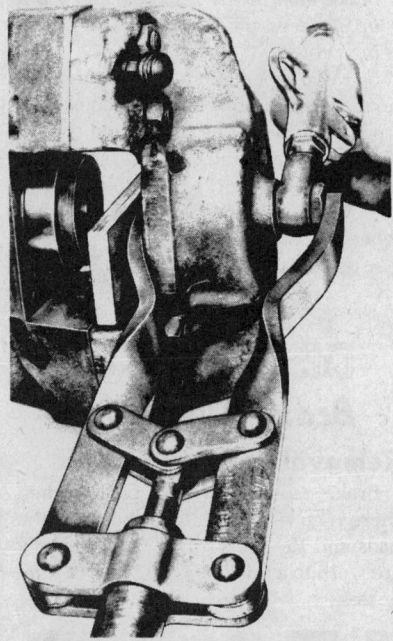

Forcing the piston out of the caliper

CAUTION: *Keep your hands away from the inside of the caliper. Air pressure of 147 psi produces an equivalent pressure of 550 lbs.*

8. When the piston pops out of the caliper, remove the rubber seal with a wood or plastic pin to avoid damaging the seal groove.
9. Clean all metal parts with denatured alcohol. Never use any mineral based solvents such as gasoline, kerosene, acetone, or the like. These solvents deteriorate rubber parts. Inspect the pistons and bores. They must be free of scoring and pitting. Replace the caliper if there is any damage.
10. Discard all rubber parts. Caliper rebuilding kits include new boots and seals which should be used as the caliper is reassembled.
11. Lightly coat the cylinder bore, piston, seals with a brake cylinder assembly paste.

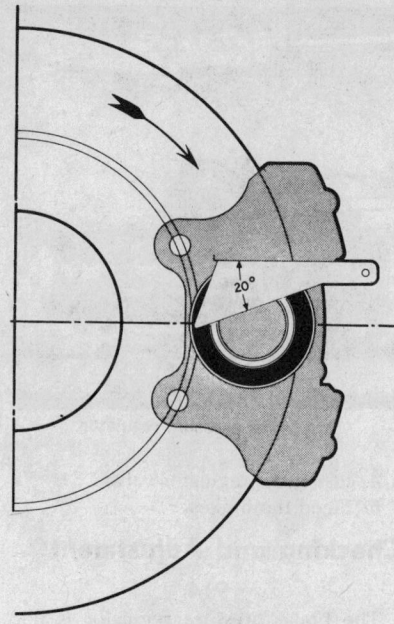

Piston alignment gauge

12. Install the piston seal in the cylinder groove. Install the piston into its bore.
13. Fabricate a 20° piston alignment gauge, similar to the one in the illustration, from heavy cardboard. Using the gauge, position the step-down on the piston so that it faces the direction of brake disc rotation.
14. Wipe off any excess assembly paste on the piston and install the boot and retaining ring. Install the anti-rotation plate on 914 models.
15. Repeat the above operation on the second piston. Overhaul is complete at this point, unless the caliper half O-rings are leaking. In this case, the caliper must be split.

NOTE: *Light alloy calipers on some 911S models are one piece and cannot be disassembled. Do not remove the caliper side cover on these models.*

16. Remove the four caliper assembly bolts.
17. Remove the caliper cover housing. Remove the spacer plate on vented disc models.
18. Install two fresh O-rings in the fluid passages. Replace the assembly bolts and nuts. The outside bolts are shorter.
19. Align the halves and place the caliper in a soft-jawed vise. On 914 models, tighten the bolts to 7 ft lbs in the sequence shown. 911 models use the same tightening sequence, but are first torqued to 12.5 ft lbs and then final torqued to 25 ft lbs (6.5 and 13 ft lbs for rear calipers).

Brake Disc

Removal and Installation

911 and 912E

1. Jack up the front of the car and

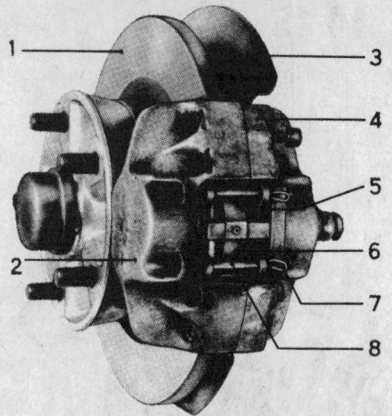

912 and 911 front disc brake components

1. Brake disc
2. Caliper cover
3. Disc shroud
4. Caliper base housing
5. Brake pad segment
6. Cross-spring
7. Pin retainer
8. Retaining pin

place it on stands. Remove the wheels.

2. Remove the brake caliper as outlined above.

3. Using two screwdrivers, pry off the hub cap.

4. Loosen the screw in the hub clamp nut. Unscrew the clamp nut and thrust washer.

5. Grip the disc with both hands and give it a sharp pull to remove it. A stubborn disc should be removed with a puller. Never strike the disc with a hammer.

6. Match mark the hub and disc, if the disc is being reused, and separate them.

7. The disc is installed in a reverse order of removal. Install the disc-to-hub bolts from the inside out and tighten the nuts to 17 ft lbs.

8. Install the disc/hub assembly on the spindle. Install the thrust washer and clamp nut.

9. Install the brake caliper.

10. Adjust the wheel bearings as outlined below.

11. Bleed the brakes.

914

1. Jack up the front of the car and support it safely on stands. Remove the wheels.

2. Remove the brake caliper as described above.

3. Pry off the hub cap.

4. Loosen the screw in the hub clamp nut and unscrew the clamp nut.

5. Pull off the brake disc along with the inner and outer wheel bearings.

6. Installation is the reverse of removal.

7. Adjust the wheel bearings as outlined below.

8. Bleed the hydraulic system.

Inspection and Checking

Brake discs may be checked for lateral runout while installed on the car. This check will require a dial indicator gauge

and stand to mount it on the caliper. Porsche has a special tool for this purpose which mounts the dial indicator in the brake pad slots of the caliper, but a dial indicator can also be mounted on the shaft of a C-clamp attached to the outside of the caliper.

1. Adjust the front wheel bearings.

2. Mount the dial indicator using either of the above methods. The feeler should touch the disc about ½ in. below the outer edge.

3. Rotate the disc and observe the gauge. Lateral runout (wobble) must not exceed 0.008 in. (0.2 mm). A disc which exceeds this specification must be replaced or refinished.

4. Brake discs which have excessive lateral runout, sharp ridges, or scoring

Dial indicator set-up for determining lateral disc run-out

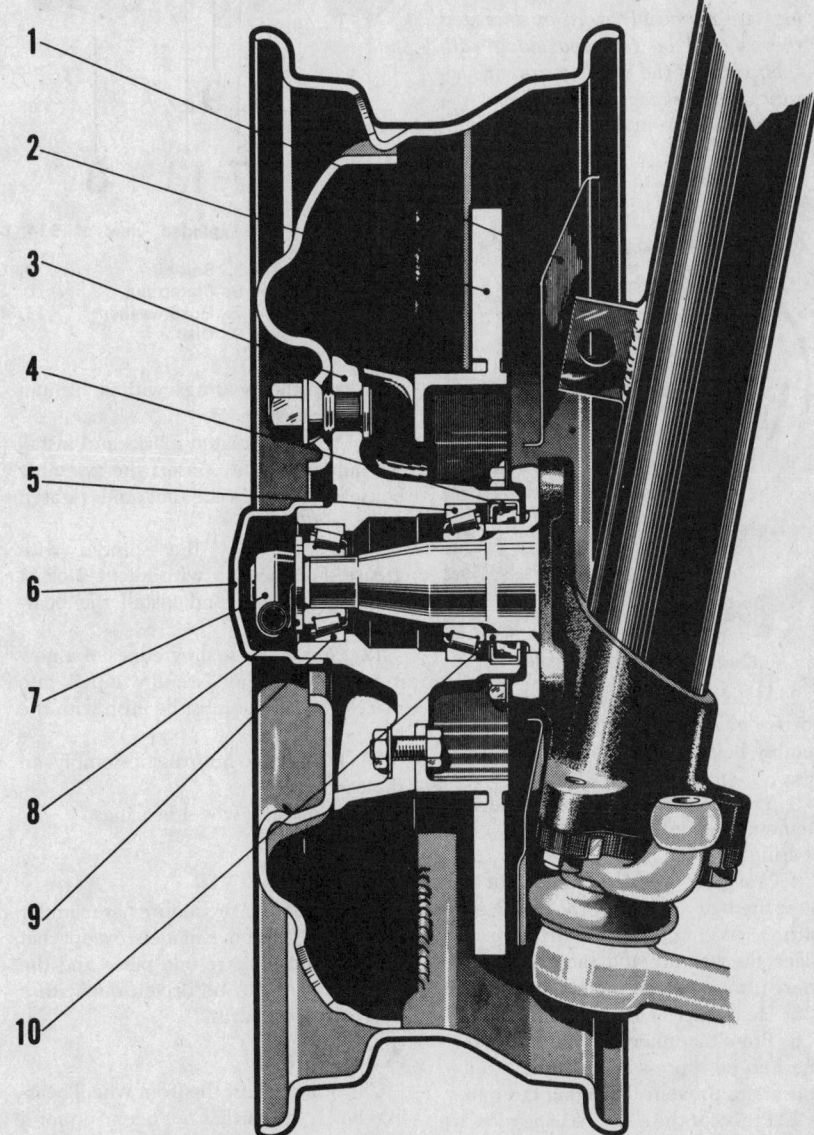

Cross-section of 911 and 912 brake disc/hub assembly

1. Cover shroud
2. Brake disc
3. Front wheel hub
4. Seal
5. Tapered roller bearing
6. Grease cap
7. Clamping nut
8. Washer
9. Tapered roller bearing
10. Distance ring

Porsche

can be refinished. Final grinding must be done on both sides of the disc to prevent squeaking and vibrating. Discs which have only light grooves and are otherwise acceptable can be used without refinishing.

NOTE: *Ventilated brake discs (911) are balanced by special clips inserted into the vent fins of the disc. Do not remove the clips or the original balance will be lost.*

Wheel Bearings
Removal and Installation
911 and 912E
NOTE: *The inner bearing, seal, and outer bearing may be removed and lubricated once the hub/disc assembly is off the car. If after cleaning, the bearings are noticeably worn or damaged they should be replaced along with their races. If the bearings are satisfactory, skip the race removal steps.*

1. Remove the brake disc/hub assembly.

Checking wheel bearing play

2. Match mark the hub and disc for correct reassembly, remove the five assembly bolts, and separate the hub and disc.

3. Pry the inner seal out of the hub. Remove the inner bearing and outer bearing.

4. Wash the bearings in solvent and blow them dry. Examine the bearings for pitting, scoring, or other damage. Replace the bearing and race as a unit if there is any question as to their condition.

5. Heat the wheel hub to 250°–300° F.

6. Press the inner bearing race out of the hub on a press table, using suitable spacers to prevent damaging the hub.

7. Press out the outer bearing race, using suitable spacers and a support fabricated from the accompanying drawing.

8. Press a new inner bearing race into the hub and then press in a new outer bearing race.

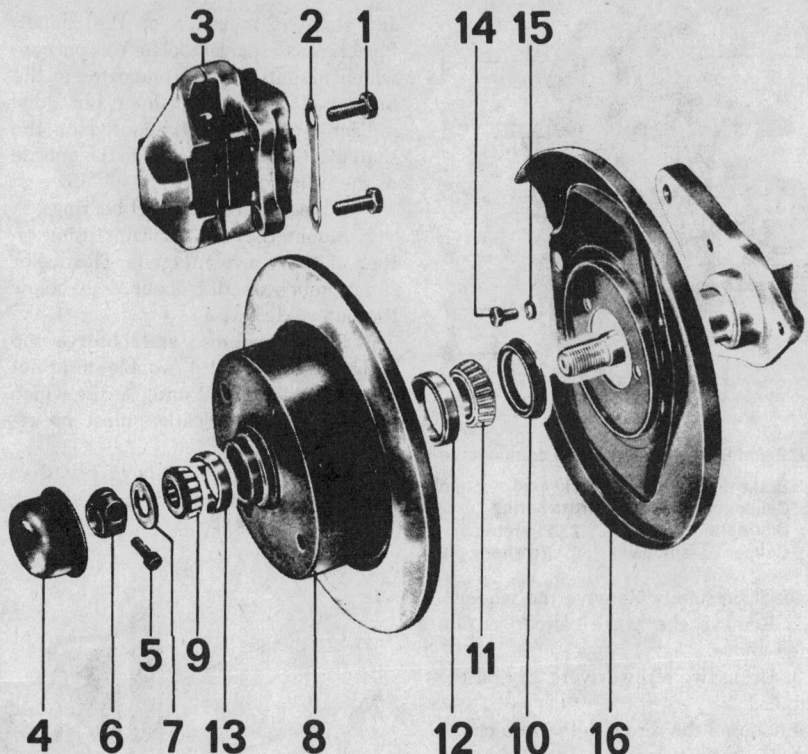

Exploded view of 914 brake disc/hub assembly

1. Bolt
2. Lockplate
3. Caliper
4. Hub cap
5. Bolt
6. Clamp nut
7. Hose washer
8. Disc
9. Outer bearing
10. Seal
11. Inner bearing
12. Inner bearing race
13. Outer bearing race
14. Bolt
15. Lock washer
16. Rear shroud

9. Pack the bearings with a lithium multipurpose grease.

10. Align the match marks and install the hub on the disc. Insert the assembly bolts from the inside out and tighten them to 17 ft lbs.

11. Lightly coat the spindle with grease. Fill the hub with about 2 oz of grease. Lubricate and install the bearings.

12. Grease the sealing edges of a new inner oil seal and carefully tap it into place. The oil seal must be flush with the hub.

13. Install the hub/disc assembly on the car.

14. Adjust the wheel bearings.

914
Wheel bearing procedures are similar to those for the above models, except that the hub and disc are one piece and the bearing races can be driven out with a brass or copper drift.

Adjustment
Check and adjust the front wheel bearings when the car has not been run for a few hours, the bearings will be cold then.

1. The front wheel bearings are correctly adjusted when the thrust washer can be moved slightly sideways under light pressure from a screwdriver, but no

Final tightening of the wheel clamp nut–check play again before installing hub cap

bearing play is evident when the wheel hub is shaken axially.

2. Jack up the front of the car, support it on stands, and remove the wheels. Turn the hub several times to seat the bearings.

3. Pry the hub cap off with a screwdriver and perform the check described in step 1.

NOTE: *Don't press the screwdriver against the hub. Hold it lightly in your hand so you get a better feel.*

4. If the bearings require an adjust-

ment, loosen the allen screw and turn the clamp nut in or out as necessary.

5. Tighten the clamp nut allen screw to 11 ft lbs without altering the adjusted position of the clamp nut.

6. Double check the adjustment and readjust, if necessary.

7. Give the clamp nut and thrust washer a light coating of lithium grease. Tap the hub cap into place with a plastic or rubber mallet.

8. Install the wheels and lower the car.

REAR DISC BRAKES
Disc Brake Pads
Removal and Installation
911 and 912E

Brake pad removal and installation is identical to that for front pads.

914

Removal of the rear brake pads is the same as that for the front pads. Installation, however, differs due to the automatic adjuster mechanism necessary for the handbrake.

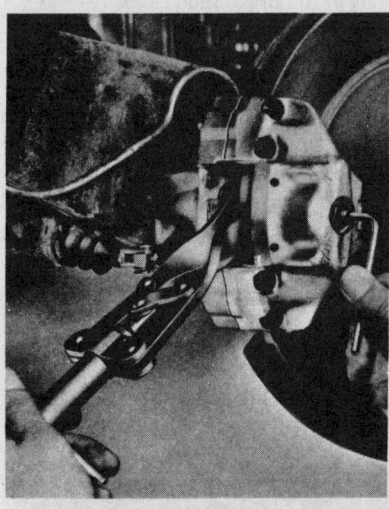

Setting the outer piston back (special Porsche tool shown)

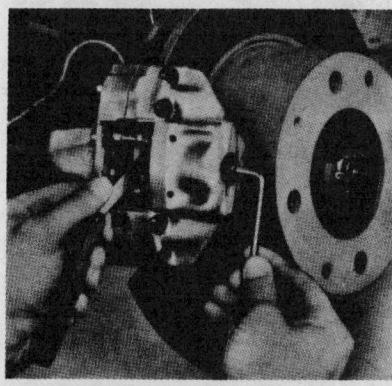

Adjusting pad and disc clearance

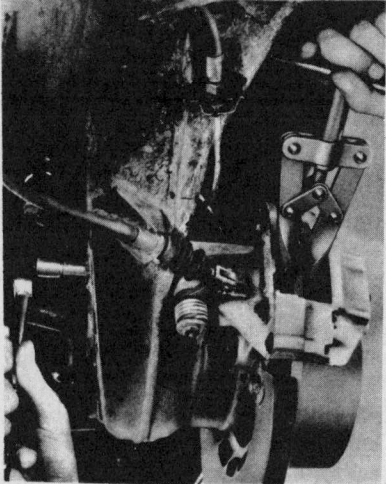

Setting the inner piston back

1. Using two flat pieces of hardwood, or Porsche tool P 83, lightly pre-load the pistons. Unless you have four hands, an assistant becomes just about a necessity at this point.

2. Have your assistant remove the cover screw on the outside of the caliper. Loosen the locknut and insert a 4 mm allen key into the adjusting screw.

3. Set the piston back by turning the allen key clockwise, all the while maintaining tension on the pistons with the flat boards.

4. Remove the cover bolt on the inside caliper half. Insert a 4 mm allen socket (an extension handle will be necessary) through the trailing arm access hole. Set the piston back by turning the adjusting screw counterclockwise, again maintaining constant pressure on the piston with the flat board.

5. Install the brake pads with retaining pins, but without the cross-spring.

6. Insert a 0.08 in. (0.2 mm) feeler gauge between the pad and the disc. Adjust the pistons for that much clearance by turning the allen screws on both sides as necessary.

7. Remove the retaining pins and install them again with the cross-spring. Install the pin clips.

8. Install the wheel and lower the car.

Disc Brake Caliper
Removal and Installation
911 and 912E

Remove the shields from the rear of the brake and then use the same procedure as the front calipers. Tighten the caliper retaining bolts to 44 ft lbs and the shield bolts to 18 ft lbs.

914

Disconnect the handbrake cables and then proceed as outlined in the front caliper section.

Overhaul

Overhaul is exactly the same as the front calipers, except that the 914 rear calipers should not be split as there is a possibility of damaging the automatic adjuster. If the O-ring seals are leaking, replace the caliper.

Brake Discs
Removal and Installation

1. Remove the rear shroud on 911 models. Detach the handbrake cables on 914 and 914/6 models.

2. Remove the brake caliper.

3. Remove both countersunk screws from the disc and pull it off the car.

4. Installation is the reverse of the removal procedure.

Inspection and Checking

The rear brake disc procedure is similar to that for the front, except that the disc must be fastened to the hub. Install the wheel nuts on 911, models and tighten them in a criss-cross pattern to 72 ft lbs. On 914 models, install the wheel bolts and tighten them to 80 ft lbs.

PARKING BRAKE

The 911 and 912E models are equipped with a separate handbrake system. The center, pull-up lever mechanically operates a pair of brake shoes inside each rear disc, which act as drums through a pot-shaped center section.

The 914 handbrake mechanically applies the rear service brakes. The rear calipers are equipped with automatic adjusting mechanisms.

Cable
Adjustment
911 and 912E

1. Jack up the rear of the car and support it on stands. Remove the wheels.

2. Release the handbrake lever.

3. Push the brake pads away from the disc so that it can be turned by hand.

Adjusting the handbrake

4. Loosen the cable adjusting nuts to release tension.

5. Insert a screwdriver into the disc access hole and rotate the handbrake star wheel until the disc can no longer be turned by hand.

6. Repeat this operation on the other side.

7. Readjust the cable nuts to take up the slack.

8. Pull up the center tunnel cover and handbrake lever boot at the rear. By looking through the two inspection holes, see if the cable equalizer is exactly perpendicular to the car's centerline.

9. If the equalizer positioning is off, correct it by loosening or tightening the cable adjusting nuts. Tighten the locknuts after the adjustment is correct.

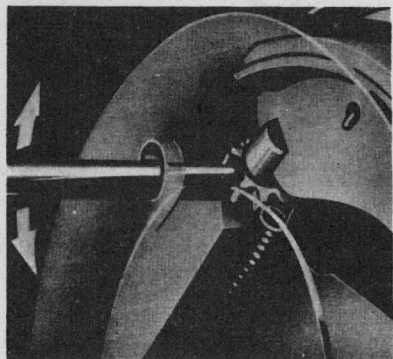

Handbrake star wheel adjustment

10. Back off each brake star wheel by four or five teeth until the disc can be turned by hand.

11. Check the handbrake lever clearance. There should be a slight clearance at the lever. The handbrake should be set when the lever is pulled up.

12. After completing the handbrake adjustment, depress the brake pedal several times to reposition the rear caliper pistons. Check the fluid level in the reservoir and top it up, if necessary.

Removal and Installation

1. Jack up the rear of the car and support it on stands. Remove the wheels.

2. Remove the center tunnel cover and handbrake lever boot.

3. Remove the heater control knob.

4. Undo the handbrake support housing bolts.

5. Unscrew the heater control lever nut. Remove the cup spring, discs, and the lever.

6. Slightly raise the handbrake support housing. Snap off the retaining clip and pull out the cable equalizing stud.

7. Disconnect the handbrake light switch wire.

8. Remove the handbrake support housing.

9. Detach the cables from the cable equalizer.

10. Remove the rear brake calipers.

11. Remove the rear brake discs and spacer rings.

12. Remove the cotter pin, castellated nut, and disc from each cable. Pull the cables toward the center of the car.

13. Pull the cables out from the center tunnel in the passenger compartment.

14. Lubricate the replacement cables with multipurpose grease and then feed them into the tube.

15. Place a washer between the spacer sleeve and the brake expander. Place another washer under the castellated nut.

16. Tighten the nut until a new cotter pin can be inserted. Make sure that the brake expander is correctly seated.

17. Install the brake discs and calipers.

18. Connect the handbrake light wire to the switch.

19. Insert the heater control lever into the handbrake support housing.

20. Install and clip the equalizer stud. Ensure that the handbrake cables are correctly seated.

21. Torque the handbrake support housing bolts to 18 ft lbs.

22. Install a friction disc, the heater control lever, another friction disc, pressure disc, cup spring, and the nut.

23. Tighten the nut so that the lever doesn't slip back when the heater is on full, and yet isn't too tight to operate.

24. Bleed the brakes.

25. Check the handbrake adjustment.

26. Install the wheels and lower the car.

Brake Shoes

Removal and Installation

911 and 912E

1. Jack up the rear of the car and support it on stands. Remove the wheels.

2. Remove the brake calipers.

3. Detach the brake discs.

4. Remove the cotter pin, castellated nut, and washer from the brake cable.

5. Pull the cable out toward the center of the car.

6. Remove the expander and spring.

7. Depress the upper spring and twist

Star wheel assembly removal

the holddown cup to remove it and the spring.

8. Pull the brake shoe outward and remove the pin through the rear.

9. Using a screwdriver, raise the upper brake shoe and remove the star wheel assembly. Unhook the spring.

10. Repeat steps 7 and 8 for the bottom shoe.

11. Unhook the front return spring and remove both shoes.

NOTE: *Complete the brake shoe removal and installation one side at a time, so the opposite side can be used as a reference.*

12. Clean all metal parts in alcohol. Contaminated or worn brake shoes should be replaced.

13. Insert the brake cable from the back and slide the inner part of the expander onto the cable. Don't forget to install a washer between the spacer tube and the expander.

14. Install the front return spring (two coils) so that the coils point towards the center of the axle.

15. Install the upper and lower brake shoes.

16. Install the pins, springs, and holddown cups.

17. Insert the inner expander into the seats in the brake shoes.

18. Raise the upper brake shoe with a screwdriver and install the star wheel assembly so that the adjusting sprocket is on both brakes shoes.

19. Install the other brake return spring.

20. Turn the cable adjusting nut in the tube all the way back.

21. Install the spring, second expander half, washer, and castellated nut. Tighten the nut until a new cotter pin can be installed.

22. Install the brake discs and calipers.

23. Bleed the hydraulic system.

24. Adjust the handbrake.

25. Install the wheels and lower the car.

Correct handbrake lining and spring installation

CHASSIS ELECTRICAL

Heater

The primary heating system in all models uses fresh air drawn in by the engine cooling fan, directs it to heat exchangers around the exhaust pipes, through a muffler, and distributes warm air into the passenger compartment via a system of ducts. A variable speed blower, located in the front luggage compartment on all models, speeds the circulation of heated and/or fresh air. 914 models are equipped with a blower motor in the engine compartment. An auxiliary, gas-fired heater is an option on 911 models.

Blower

Removal and Installation

911 and 912E

1. Disconnect the battery cables.
2. Remove the front luggage compartment carpeting.
3. Open the blower compartment lid. Remove the steering shaft cover.
4. Disconnect the electrical wiring.
5. Loosen the hose clamps and disconnect the hoses from the blower.
6. Pull the blower off the air intake stack and remove it from the car.
7. Install the blower on the intake stack. Make sure that the sealing ring is correctly seated.
8. Fasten the hoses on the blower and tighten the hose clamps.
9. Connect the electrical wiring.
10. Install the steering shaft cover and close the blower compartment lid.
11. Cement the carpeting to the right front side panel.
12. Connect the battery cables.

914

1. Remove the front luggage compartment lid.
2. Remove the fuel tank.
3. Unscrew the mounting bolt on each end of the fresh air intake box.
4. Loosen the hose clamps on the two air hoses and pull them from the blower.

Correct blower cable installation

5. Squeeze the corbin clamps on the two water drain hoses and pull them from the fresh air box.
6. Loosen the cable clamp nut and detach the cable from the blower by pushing the retaining clip off. Be careful not to bend the cable.
7. Disconnect the electrical wiring.
8. Remove the fresh air box and blower as an assembly.
9. Unscrew the attaching bolts and separate the fresh air box and blower.
10. Install the blower in the fresh air box.
11. Install the cable on the blower. The cable casing should protrude from the retaining clip by about ¼ in.
12. Install the fresh air box/blower assembly in a reverse manner of removal. Adjust the cable, if necessary.

Auxiliary Heater

The 911 auxiliary heater assembly is mounted in the front luggage compartment in the place of the standard blower.

Removal and Installation

1. Jack up the front of the car and support it on stands.
2. Disconnect the battery cables.
3. Remove the luggage compartment lid.
4. Open the heater compartment lid.
5. Loosen the clamp on the hot air hose and pull the hose off the heater unit.
6. Remove the three mixture pump retaining bolts and remove them from the bracket.
7. Disconnect the fuel lines and wiring from the pump.
8. Working under the car, loosen the front muffler clamp. Disconnect the exhaust pipe and bend it down and out of the way.
9. Remove the muffler clamp and slide the white collar onto the heater unit.
10. Disconnect all wiring to the heater and carefully lift it out of the car.
11. Installation is the reverse of the removal procedure. Ensure that the wiring is correctly reinstalled.

Windshield Wipers

Motor and Linkage

Removal and Installation

911 and 912E

The windshield wiper motor and linkage are located in front of the instrument panel.

1. Pull back the front luggage compartment carpeting. Disconnect the battery cables.

2. Remove the retaining clip and air duct. Remove the fresh air box.
3. Disconnect the blower motor wires.
4. Remove the wiper arms. Remove the rubber bushings under the arms and unscrew the shaft retaining nuts.
5. Pull the motor and linkage down as a unit. Separate the motor and linkage.
6. Installation is the reverse of the removal procedure.

914

The windshield wiper motor and linkage are mounted on a common frame.

1. Disconnect the battery.
2. Unscrew the retaining nut on each wiper arm.
3. Remove the rubber bearing cap.
4. Unscrew the retaining nut and remove the washers and seals.
5. Remove the fuel tank.
6. Remove the evaporative emission charcoal canister.
7. Remove the fresh air box and blower as previously described.
8. Remove the anti-vibration bearing retaining nut from under the instrument panel. Make sure that the bearing isn't twisted.
9. Pull the windshield wiper assembly down and out.
10. Disconnect the electrical wires.
11. To separate the motor and linkage:
    a. Remove the wiper motor shaft nut and washer.
    b. Using a puller, remove the linkage drive crank from the motor shaft.
    c. Remove the three retaining bolts and remove the motor.
12. To install the motor onto the linkage:
    a. The motor must be in the park position. Ground the motor and connect terminals 53 and 53a to a positive battery wire.
    b. Run the motor for a few seconds and then disconnect terminal 53. The motor will be parked.
    c. Position the drive crank parallel to the drive rod.
    d. Attach the motor with a washer and nut. Install the three retaining bolts.
13. Connect the electrical wiring.
14. Install the wiper arms in a reverse order of removal. Ensure that they are in the parked position.
15. Install the fresh air box/blower assembly.
16. Connect the battery.

911 Rear Window Wiper

1. Pull the wiper arm from the rear window.
2. Open the engine compartment lid.
3. Disconnect the wiper motor electrical wiring.
4. Disconnect the wiper arm linkage at the bellcrank.

5. Remove the three wiper motor bracket bolts and remove the motor/linkage assembly.

6. Install the wiper motor/linkage assembly in a reverse order of removal.

7. Adjust the linkage at the bellcrank for correct wiper operation.

Instrument Panel

Removal and Installation

911 and 912E

The gauges are mounted in individual rubber rings.

1. Pry the gauge out until you can grip it firmly, and then pull it out of the instrument panel.

2. Disconnect the wiring and/or cable and remove the gauge.

3. Connect the wiring or cable and position the gauge in its opening.

4. Align the gauge and then push it into place.

914

1. Disconnect the battery.

2. Remove the steering wheel as outlined in the "Steering" section.

911 and 912 instrument removal

3. Remove the four phillips retaining screws.

4. Disconnect the speedometer cable and the trip odometer cable.

5. Pull the instrument panel out.

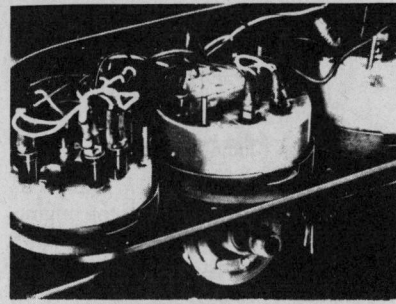

914 instrument panel service

6. Individual gauges are retained by rubber rings. Push the gauge out towards the front to remove it.

7. Be sure that the wires are correctly reinstalled on the gauge.

8. Install the instrument panel in a reverse order of removal.

Fuse Box Location

The 911 and 912E fuse box is located in the left front of the luggage compartment. The 914 fuse box is located under the instrument panel to the left of the steering column.

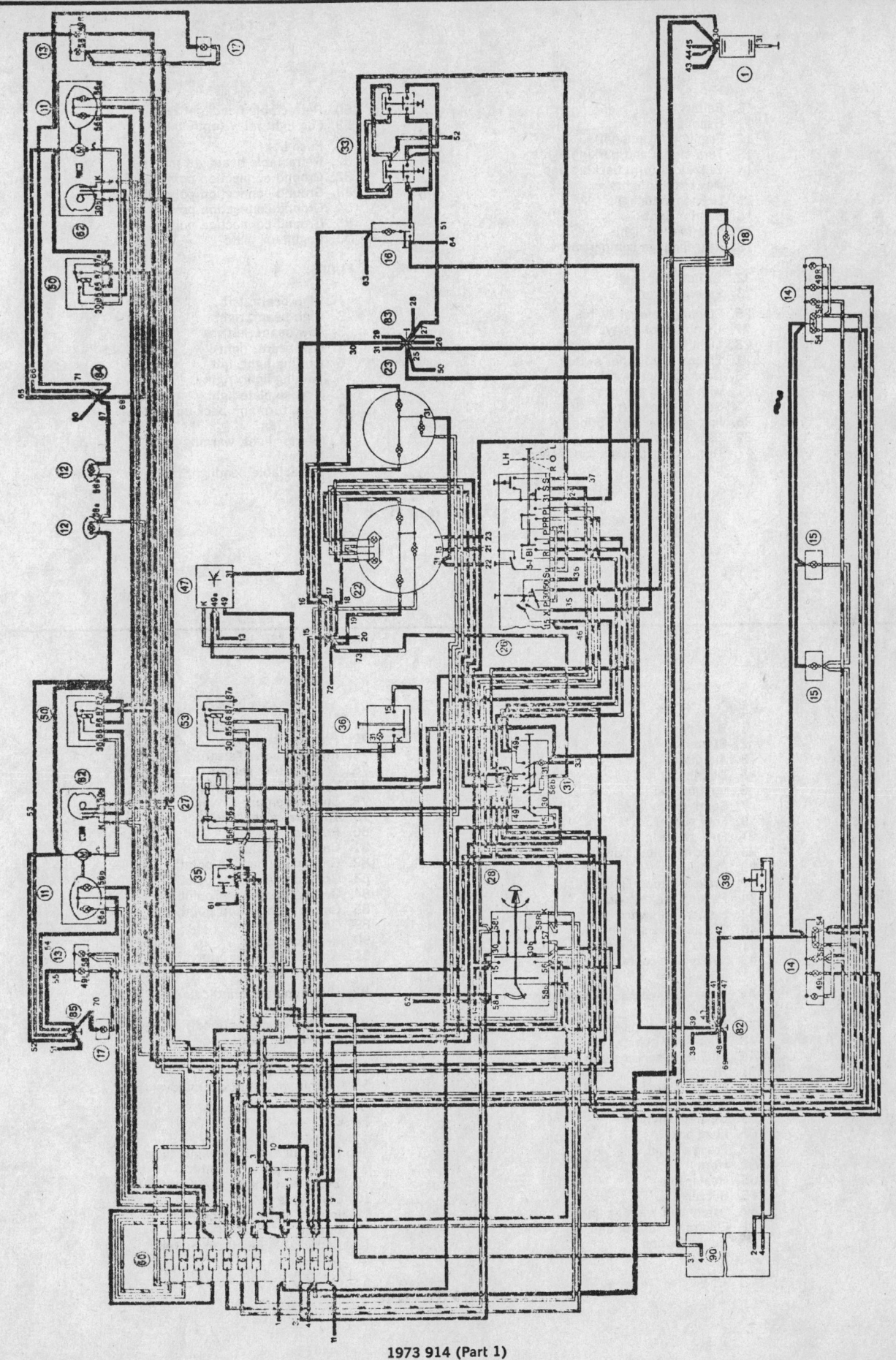

1973 914 (Part 1)

Wiring Circuits

1. Battery
11. Headlights
12. Fog lights (optional)
13. Turn signal and parking lights
14. Tail, stop, turn, back-up and side marker lights
15. License plate light
16. Interior light
17. Side marker lights
18. Rear luggage compartment light
22. Tachometer
23. Speedometer
26. Steering column switch
27. Combination relay
28. Light switch
31. Emergency flasher switch
33. Door contact switch with buzzer contact
35. Stop light switch
36. Fog light switch (optional)
39. Back-up light switch
47. Turn signal/emergency flasher unit

50. Retractable headlight relay
53. Fog light relay (optional)
60. Fuse box
62. Retractable headlight motor
82. Ground connection point A
83. Ground connection point B
84. Ground connection point C
85. Ground connection point D
90. Regulator plate

FUSES:

1. High beam, left
2. High beam, right
3. Low beam, left
4. Low beam, right
5. Parking light, left
6. Parking light, right
7. License plate light
9. Stop, turn and back-up lights
10. Fog lights
11. Interior light, warning light, buzzer
12. Retractable headlight motor

1973 914 (Part 1)

---

1. Battery
2. Starter
3. Alternator
5. Distributor
6. Ignition coil
7. Spark plugs
9. Fuel pump
21. Fuel gauge
26. Steering column switch
30. Fan switch
32. Brake warning light switch
34. Parking brake contact
37. Heater fan switch
40. Oil pressure switch
41. Diode
43. Safety belt contact, driver side
44. Safety belt contact, passenger side
46. Seat contact, passenger side
48. Thermo-switch
49. Fuel level sending unit
51. Horn relay
54. Relay for fresh air fan
56. Wiper motor
59. Cigarette lighter
60. Fuse box
63. Fresh air fan
64. Horn
65. Heater fan
66. Buzzer
67. Safety belt warning light
71. Electronic control unit (fuel injection)

72. Pressure sensor
73. Injection valve (electric)
76. Temperature sensor I
77. Temperature sensor II
78. Supplementary air valve
79. Throttle valve switch
80. Resistor
81. Cold start valve
82. Ground connection point A
83. Ground connection point B
84. Ground connection point C
85. Ground connection point D
89. Optional horn
90. Regulator plate
91. Windshield wiper interval relay (optional)
92. Oil temperature indicator (optional)
93. Electric clock (optional)
94. Oil temperature gauge dial (optional)
95. Voltmeter (optional)
96. Illumination for heating lever

FUSES:

8. Fresh air fan, horn, windshield wipers, cigarette lighter
9. Stop, turn and back-up lights
10. Fog lights
11. Interior light, warning light, buzzer
12. Retractable headlight motor

1973 914 (Part 2)

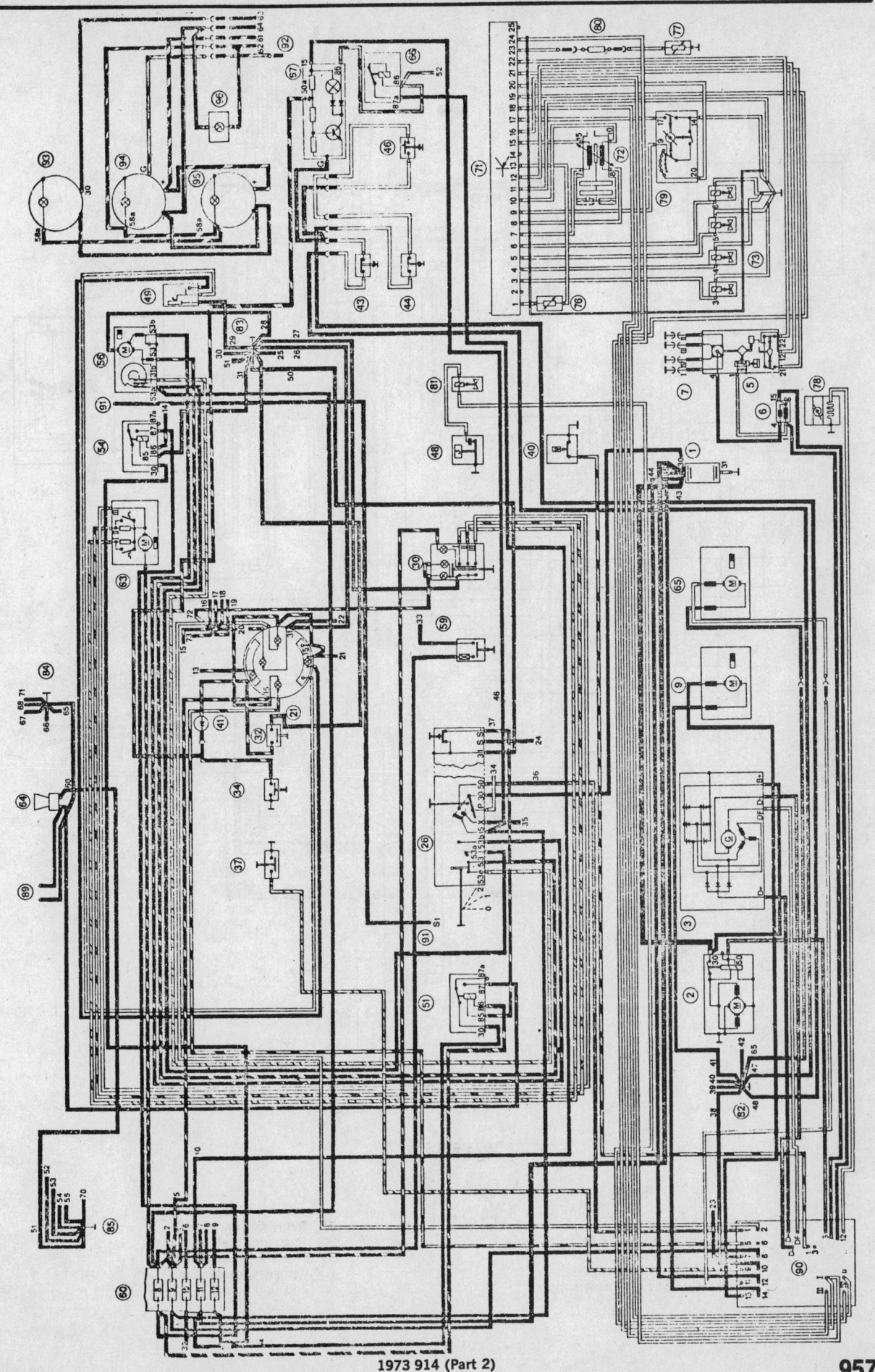

1973 914 (Part 2)

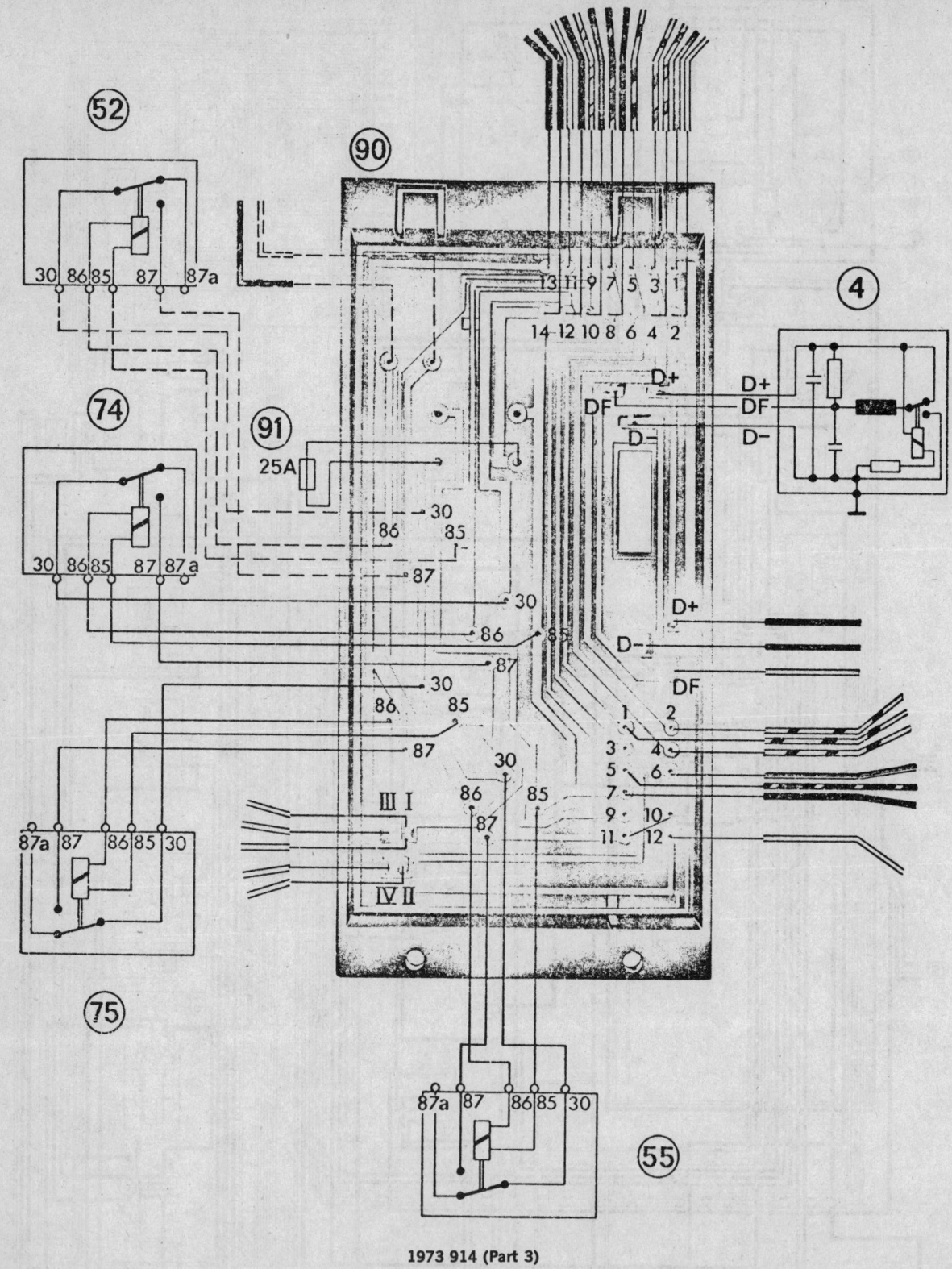

1973 914 (Part 3)

4. Govérnor
52. Rear window defogger relay (optional)
55. Relay for heater fan
74. Relay for power supply

75. Relay for fuel pump
90. Regulator plate
91. Fuses for rear window defogger, heater fan and fuel pump

SPECIFICATIONS

INTRODUCTION

The Porsche 924 is powered by a four cylinder, inline, watercooled engine. The engine, located at the front drives the rear wheels through a torque tube. The transmission and differential are located in the rear. The 924 was introduced in mid-year 1976 and carried over with little change as a 1977 model. Only one model, a two door sport coupe, is available.

MODEL IDENTIFICATION

SERIAL NUMBER IDENTIFICATION

Vehicle

The chassis serial number is located on the left windshield post and can be viewed from the outside. The vehicle identification plate is in the engine compartment near the battery.

Engine

The engine serial number is stamped on the left of the crankcase near the clutch housing.

GENERAL ENGINE SPECIFICATIONS

Year	Engine Displacement cc (Cu. In.)	Carburetor Type	Horsepower (@ rpm)	Torque (@ rpm) (ft lbs)	Bore x Stroke (in.)	Compression Ratio	Oil Pressure (@ rpm) Kp/cm²
1976-77	1984 (121.06)	Fuel Injection	95 @ 5500	109.2 @ 3000	3.41 x 3.32	8.0:1	7 @ 5500

TUNE-UP SPECIFICATIONS

When analyzing compression test results, look for uniformity among cylinders, rather than specific pressures

Year	Engine Displace. cc (Cu. In.)	SPARK PLUGS Type	SPARK PLUGS Gap (in.)	DISTRIBUTOR Point Dwell (deg)	DISTRIBUTOR Point Gap (in.)	IGNITION TIMING (deg)[1] MT	IGNITION TIMING (deg)[1] AT	Intake Valve Opens (deg)	Idle Speed (rpm)	VALVE CLEAR MM[2] (in.) In	VALVE CLEAR MM[2] (in.) Ex
1976-77	1984 (121.06)	W200T30	0.028-0.032	Electronic		10A	10A	5B	900-1000	0.10 (0.004)	0.40 (0.016)

[1] Vacuum hose(s) connected
co at Idle: 49 states 1.5±0.5% (air pump disconnected)
California 0.7% (in front of converter)
[2] Cold, hot clearance 0.20 (0.008 in.) intake and 0.45 (0.018 in.)

NOTE: The underhood specifications sticker often reflects tune-up specification changes made in production. Sticker figures must be used if they disagree with those in this chart.

FIRING ORDER

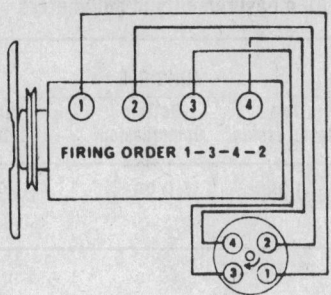

FIRING ORDER 1—3—4—2

CAPACITIES

| Year | Engine Displacement cc (Cu. In.) | Engine Crankcase (qts) | | Transaxle (qts) | | Gasoline Tank (gals) | Cooling System (qts) |
		With Filter	Without Filter	Manual	Automatic		
1976-77	1984 (121.06)	4.75	4.23	2.75①	3.17②	16.4	7.4

① SAE 80 or 80W 90 gear oil
② ATF Dexron®, differential 1.06 qt. SAE 90 gear oil

CRANKSHAFT AND CONNECTING ROD SPECIFICATIONS
All measurements are given in millimeters

| Year | Engine Displacement cc (Cu. In.) | CRANKSHAFT | | | | CONNECTING ROD | | |
		Main Brg Journal Dia	Main Brg Oil Clearance	Shaft End-Play	Thrust on No.	Journal Diameter	Oil Clearance	Side Clearance
1976-77	1984 (121.06)	60.00	0.05-0.10	0.08-0.18	3	48.001	0.02-0.08	0.10-0.23

VALVE SPECIFICATIONS

| Year | Engine Displacement cc (Cu. In.) | Seat Angle (deg) | Face Angle (deg) | STEM TO GUIDE CLEARANCE (mm) | | STEM DIAMETER (mm) | |
				Intake	Exhaust	Intake	Exhaust
1976-77	1984 (121.06)	45	45°15′	0.02	0.05	8.908	8.888

PISTON AND RING SPECIFICATIONS
All measurements in millimeters

| Year | Engine Displacement cc (Cu. In.) | Piston Clearance | RING GAP | | | RING SIDE CLEARANCE | | |
			Top Compression	Bottom Compression	Oil Control	Top Compression	Bottom Compression	Oil Control
1976-77	1984 (121.06)	0.02	0.99	0.99	0.99	0.15	0.15	0.15

TORQUE SPECIFICATIONS
All readings in ft lbs

| Year | Engine Displacement cc (Cu. In.) | Cylinder Head Bolts | Rod Bearing Bolts | Main Bearing Bolts | Crankshaft Pulley Bolt | Flywheel to Crankshaft Bolts | MANIFOLDS | |
							Intake	Exhaust
1976-77	1984 (121.06)	56①	34-42	58②	18	65	15	15

① Cold; 63 ft lbs warm
② Allen head bolts on cap #5: 47 ft. lbs.

TORQUE SEQUENCE

BATTERY AND STARTER SPECIFICATIONS
All cars use 12 volt, negative ground electrical systems

| Model | Battery Amp Hour Capacity | STARTER | | | | | | Brush Spring Tension (oz) | Min. Brush Length (in.) |
| | | Lock Test | | | No Load Test | | | | |
		Amps	Volts	Torque (ft/lbs)	Amps	Volts	RPM		
1976-77	63	250-300	7	N.A.	N.A.	N.A.	N.A.	N.A.	0.47

ALTERNATOR AND REGULATOR SPECIFICATIONS

| | ALTERNATOR | | REGULATOR | | | | | | |
| | | | | Field Relay | | | Regulator | | |
Year	Part No. or Manufacturer	Output (amps)	Part No. or Manufacturer	Air Gap (In.)	Point Gap (in.)	Volts to Close	Air Gap (in.)	Point (in.) Gap	Volts @ 75°
1976-77	Bosch	75	Bosch			— Sealed unit—not adjustable —			

BRAKE SPECIFICATIONS
All measurements given are in millimeters unless noted. Inches given in parentheses.

Year	Lug Nut Torque (ft/lb)	Master Cylinder Bore	Brake Disc			Brake Drum			Minimum Lining Thickness	
			Minimum Thickness	Maximum Run-Out	Diameter	Max. Machine O/S	Max. Wear Limit	Front	Rear
1976-77	80①	20.64 (0.81)	1.04 (0.41)	NA.	230 (9.06)	0.76 (0.30)	N.A.	2.0 (0.078)	2.5 (0.098)

① Standard wheel; alloy wheel 94 ft lbs. Note that lugs are not interchangeable between the standard steel wheel and optional alloy wheel.

N.A. Not given by manufacturer

WHEEL ALIGNMENT SPECIFICATIONS

Year	CASTER		CAMBER		Toe-in	Steering Axis Inclination (deg)
	Range	Preferred Setting	Range	Preferred Setting		
1976-77	2°15'—3°15'	2°45'	(—)30'—(—)10'	—20'	0	N.A.

TUNE-UP PROCEDURES

Spark Plugs

Spark plugs are located on the passenger side of the engine and are removed with a standard 13/16 in. spark plug socket. Spark plug tightening torque is 22 ft lb (3 mkg).

Ignition

The ignition is fully electronic, using no breaker points. A CD unit is located at the front of the engine compartment. The coil and two ballast resistors are located on the firewall. Tune-up maintenance is limited to checking: ignition wires, distributor cap and rotor condition, and rotor resistance (5000 ohms). The distributor cap is retained by two snap clips. When replacing the cap, be sure to reinstall the shield over the cap.

Ignition Timing

The timing light is attached in the usual way, the timing marks are not on the crankshaft pulley however, but on the flywheel. They can be seen through a small access hole in the clutch housing. Loosen the distributor hold-down bolt, if adjustment is necessary. Basic timing at idle should be 10° ATDC with vacuum hose(s) left connected.

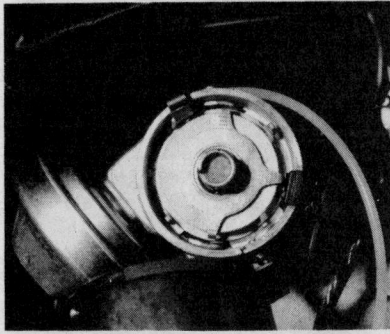

Electronic ignition rotor and sensor

ATTENTION. HAUTE TENSION
Danger de mort en cas de travaux sur l'allumage et compte-tours.

The CD ignition control unit. Never touch this unit or any other ignition terminals with the ignition ON. There is danger of a high voltage shock.

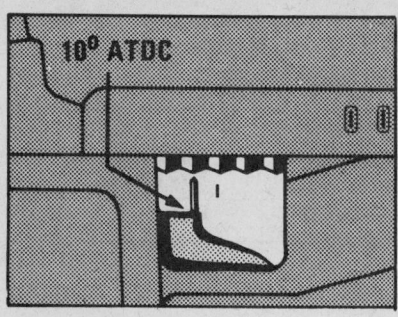

10° mark should line up with timing window ledge in clutch housing opening

Valve Lash

CAUTION: *When turning the engine over for valve adjustment, do not turn it with the camshaft pulley. Use the crankshaft pulley or bump the starter. The timing belt can be damaged by turning the camshaft pulley.*

Adjustment is made possible by means of an adjustment screw which is flat on one side. This side rides directly on the valve stem. Four different diameter adjustment screws are available to compensate for wear. Adjustment is made by inserting an allen wrench through the hole in the cam follower. Adjustment is made in full turns. If more than several turns are necessary to correct the clearance, the adjustment screw will probably have to be replaced with the next larger size. Always start with the smallest adjustment screws (white) after a valve job.

1. Remove the camshaft cover.
2. Turn the crankshaft pulley until No. 1 cylinder is at TDC compression stroke (both cam lobes pointing up).
3. Insert the correct feeler gauge be-

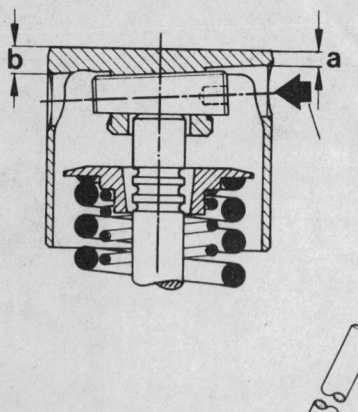

Valve adjustment is made by turning the screw one full turn at a time

tween the cam follower and the camshaft heel.

4. If adjustment is necessary, insert an allen wrench and turn the adjustment screw until clearance is correct.
5. Proceed to adjust valve clearance for each cylinder in the same way.

Valve Adjustment Screws

White	6.6 mm diameter
Blue	6.9 mm diameter
Red	7.2 mm diameter
Yellow	7.5 mm diameter

Fuel Injection

The 924 uses CIS fuel injection. The system operates in the same way as the system used on 911s.

Idle Speed

Idle speed is adjusted by means of the bypass screw located on the throttle housing. Turn the screw in or out as necessary to obtain an idle speed of 900–1000 rpm.

Idle Mixture

Idle mixture can be adjusted with the CO adjuster located between the fuel dis-

Idle speed screw

tributor and the sensor plate, remove the plug for access. Special tool P377 is needed for this adjustment. On 49 state cars, HC/CO readings are taken with the air pump disconnected. On California cars, take the sample before the converter.

ENGINE ELECTRICAL

Distributor

Removal and Installation

1. Remove the distributor cap and place it out of the way. Turn the engine so that the rotor points to No. 1 in the cap and the timing marks on the flywheel align.
2. Disconnect the primary wire at the distributor. Matchmark the distributor base and the distributor mount housing.
3. Loosen the holdown bolt and remove the distributor clamp.
4. Pull the distributor from the engine.
5. Installation is the reverse of removal. Use a new distributor base gasket. Check the ignition timing after installation.

Alternator

Removal and Installation

The 924 alternator and voltage regulator are combined in one housing. No voltage adjustment can be made with this unit. The regulator can be replaced without removing and disassembling the alternator, just unbolt it from the rear.

1. Disconnect the battery cables.
2. Remove the cooling shroud and scoop from the alternator. The scoop is retained by a snap clip.

CO adjuster is located under this plug

Distributor hold-down

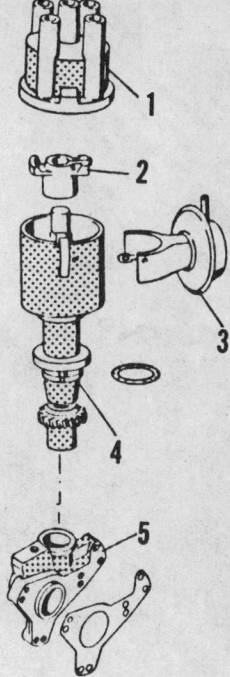

Exploded view of dstributor

1. Cap
2. Rotor
3. Vacuum advance unit
4. Distributor
5. Mounting housing

3. Disconnect the multi-connector from the rear of the alternator.

4. Loosen and remove the two allen head retaining bolts.

5. Remove the fan belt. Remove the alternator.

6. Installation is the reverse of removal. Properly tension the fan belt. Deflection of the belt midway between the pulleys should be about ⅜ in.

Starter

Removal and Installation

1. Disconnect the battery ground cable.

2. Jack up the right front of the car and support it with a stand.

3. Disconnect the two small wires from the starter solenoid. One wire connects to the ignition coil and the second to the ignition switch through the wiring harness.

4. Disconnect the large cable, which is the positive battery cable, from the solenoid.

5. Remove the two starter retaining bolts.

6. Pull the starter straight out and to the front, then drop it out of the car.

7. Installation of the starter is carried out in reverse order of removal.

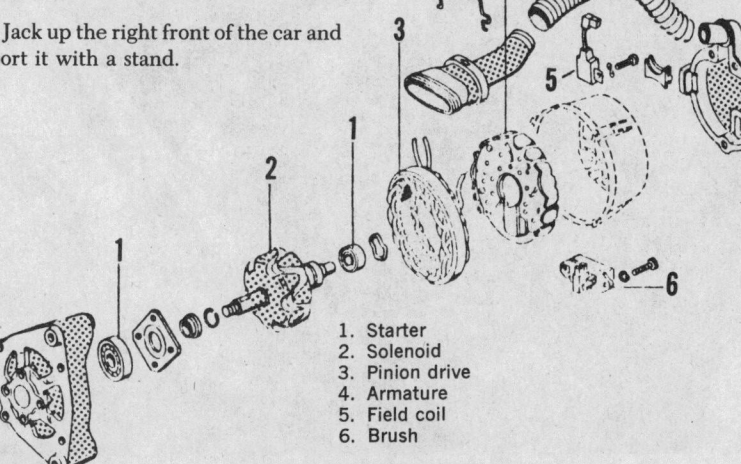

1. Starter
2. Solenoid
3. Pinion drive
4. Armature
5. Field coil
6. Brush

Exploded view of alternator

Overhaul

Use the following procedure to replace brushes or starter drive.

1. Remove the solenoid as outlined below.

2. Remove the end bearing cap.

3. Loosen both of the long housing screws.

4. Remove the lockwasher and spacer washers.

5. Remove the long housing screws and remove the end cover.

6. Pull the two field coil brushes out of the brush housing.

7. Remove the brush housing assembly.

8. Loosen the nut on the solenoid housing, remove the sealing disc, and remove the solenoid operating lever.

9. Loosen the large screws on the side of the starter body and remove the field coil along with the brushes.

NOTE: *If the brushes require replacement, the field coil and brushes and/or the brush housing and its brushes must be replaced as a unit. Turn the armature if it is out-of-round, scored, or grooved.*

10. If the starter drive is being replaced, push the stop ring down and remove the circlip on the end of the shaft. Remove the stop ring and remove the drive.

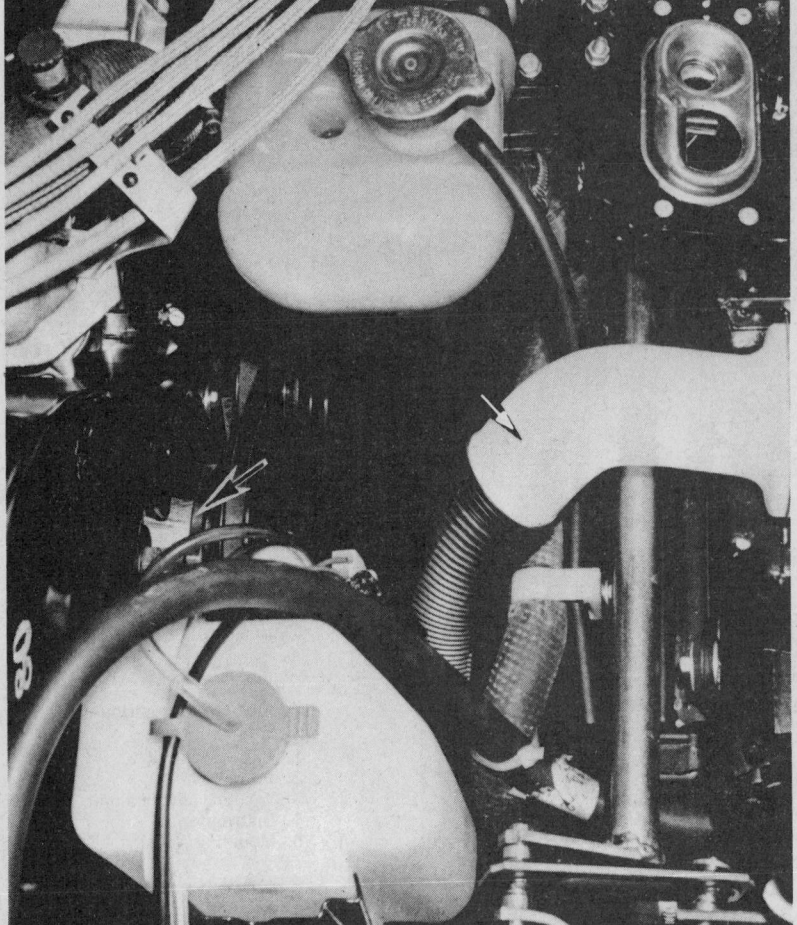

Alternator (white arrow) is buried under passenger side of engine. Scoop (black arrow) and air hose keep alternator cool

Engine Removal and Installation

1. Disconnect the battery cables. Raise the car and support it on jack stands.

2. Support the engine. Use an overhead hoist, if using a jack under the engine be careful not to damage the aluminum oil pan. Use a wooden block between the jack and pan.

3. Remove the splash panel. Remove the windshield washer tank and bracket and place it behind the right headlight.

4. Disconnect the clutch cable. Remove the bottom clutch adjustment lock nut and detach the cable from the lever.

5. Remove the access plate from the bottom of the clutch housing.

6. Have an assistant turn the engine with the crankshaft pulley. Remove the pressure plate bolts gradually until all pressure is released.

7. Remove the exhaust pipe flange bolts.

8. Remove the bracket at the rear of the transaxle.

9. Remove the entire exhaust system.

10. Remove the back up light switch from the transaxle.

11. Disconnect the axle driveshafts at the transaxle and let them hang down out of the way.

NOTE: *If the car is going to be moved around with the engine out of the car, wire the driveshafts up so that they don't become damaged.*

11. Assembly of the starter is carried out in the reverse order of disassembly. Use a gear puller to install the stop ring in its groove. Use a new circlip on the shaft.

Solenoid Replacement

1. Remove the starter.

2. Remove the nut which secures the connector strip on the end of the solenoid.

3. Take out the two retaining screws on the mounting bracket and withdraw the solenoid after it has been unhooked from the operating lever.

4. Installation is the reverse of removal. In order to facilitate engagement of the lever, the pinion should be pulled as far as possible when inserting the solenoid.

ENGINE MECHANICAL

The 924 engine is based on an Audi cylinder block. It is a watercooled, inline four with a belt driven overhead cam. The engine is inclined 40° to the right.

The heat shield must be removed before the starter.

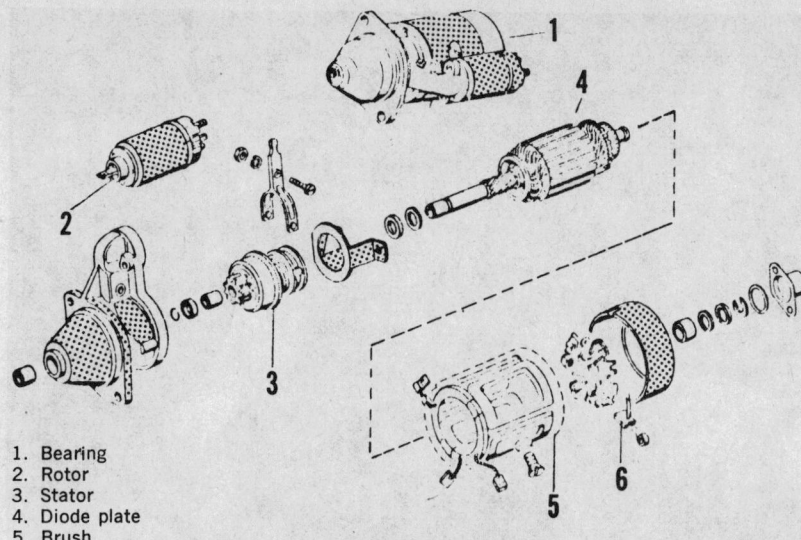

1. Bearing
2. Rotor
3. Stator
4. Diode plate
5. Brush
6. Voltage regulator

Exploded view of starter

10. Remove the throttle valve housing and intake manifold as a unit.

11. Disconnect the air pump lines on models so equipped.

12. Remove the timing belt cover. Loosen the tensioner and remove the belt.

13. Loosen the bolts according to the sequence and remove the bolts.

14. Carefully lift off the cylinder head.

15. Installation is the reverse of removal. Be sure to correctly position the new cylinder head gasket. Align the timing marks and install the timing belt and properly tension it. This procedure is under "Timing Belt". Tighten the cylinder head bolts to 58 ft. lbs. in the sequence shown.

NOTE: *Cylinder head bolts should be retorqued after 600 miles. Loosen the bolts ¼ turn and then tighten to 65 ft. lbs.*

12. Remove the clutch housing-to-engine bolts.

13. Place a wooden block under the front tunnel reinforcement to support the transaxle tube.

14. Remove the transaxle mounting bolts and slide the transaxle toward the rear.

15. Remove the air cleaner. Disconnect the brake booster vacuum line.

16. Disconnect and plug the fuel line.

17. Disconnect the accelerator cable.

18. Drain the cooling system.

19. Disconnect the radiator hoses. Remove the electric cooling fan.

20. Remove the hood. Detach the air conditioning compressor and place it out of the way. Do not disconnect the lines.

21. Remove the radiator and expansion tank. Disconnect the heater hoses from the engine.

22. Disconnect the starter wiring.

23. Attach the engine lift chains to the hoist points on the engine. Disconnect the steering at the rack universal joint.

24. Disconnect the two side mounts on the engine block. Remove the left side mount from the car.

25. Lift the engine from the car.

26. Installation is basically the reverse of removal. Tighten the pressure plate bolts to 24 ft. lbs., the clutch housing bolts to 60 ft. lbs (12mm bolt), 36 ft. lbs (10mm bolt) and 20 ft. lbs. (8mm bolt).

Cylinder Head

Removal and Installation

1. Disconnect the battery cables.
2. Drain the cooling system.
3. Remove the air cleaner.
4. Disconnect the radiator and heater hoses.
5. Disconnect all electrical wires from the cylinder head.
6. Detach the spark plug wires.

Remove the distributor.

7. Disconnect the exhaust manifold from the exhaust pipe.

8. Disconnect the EGR line. Remove the exhaust manifold.

9. Remove the fuel injection lines from the cylinder head.

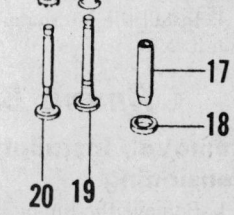

1. Camshaft cover
2. Gasket
3. Cylinder head bolt
4. Cover plate
5. Cylinder head gasket
6. Cylinder head
7. Camshaft oil seal
8. Camshaft sprocket
9. Timing belt
10. Tensioner
11. Timing belt cover
12. Camshaft
13. Cam follower
14. Outer valve spring
15. Inner valve spring
16. Valve seal
17. Valve guide
18. Valve seat
19. Intake valve
20. Exhaust valve

Exploded view of cylinder head

Porsche 924

Overhaul

Valve guides and valve seats are replaceable. A solid valve spring seat is used on intake valves, a rotator valve seat is used on exhaust valves. Umbrella type oil seals are used on all valves. Remember to use the smallest diameter valve adjuster screws (white) after a valve grind or replacement.

Intake Manifold

Removal and Installation

1. Remove the air cleaner.
2. Disconnect the accelerator cable.
3. Disconnect the EGR connections.
4. Detach all electrical leads.
5. Disconnect the auxiliary air regulator hose.
6. Remove all vacuum hoses attached to the intake manifold.
7. Remove the eight retaining nuts and remove the throttle valve housing and intake manifold as a unit.
8. Installation is the reverse of removal. Tighten the nuts to 15 ft. lbs.

Exhaust Manifold

Removal and Installation

1. Disconnect the EGR line from the manifold.
2. On models so equipped, remove the air pump connections.
3. Disconnect the exhaust pipe from the manifold, there are five nuts at this flange.
4. Remove the eight retaining nuts and remove the manifold.
5. Clean the cylinder head and manifold mating surfaces.
6. Using new gaskets (there are four), install the exhaust manifold.
7. Tighten the nuts to 15 ft. lbs. Work from the inside out.
8. Install the remaining components in the reverse order of removal. Use a new manifold flange gasket if the old one is deteriorated.

Timing Belt Cover

Removal and Installation

1. Loosen the alternator mounting bolts, pivot the alternator over, and slip the drive belt off the pulleys.
2. Unscrew the cover retaining bolts and remove the cover. Keep the washers and spacers together.
3. Reposition the spacers and then install the washers and bolts.
4. Install the alternator belt and tension it.

Timing Belt

Removal, Installation, and Tensioning

1. Remove the timing belt cover.

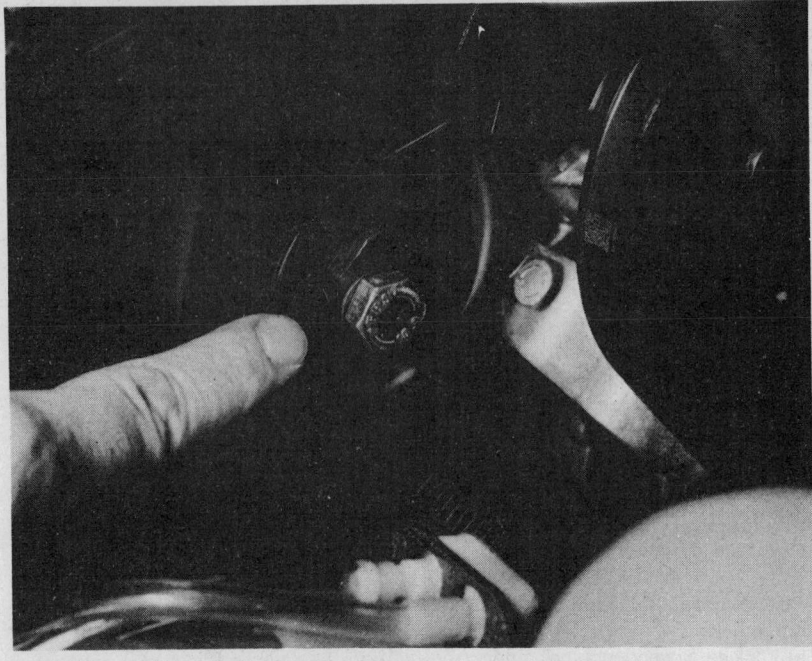

Timing belt tension

2. While holding the large hex on the tensioner pulley, loosen the pulley locknut.
3. Release the tensioner from the timing belt.
4. Slide the belt off the two toothed pulleys and remove it.
5. Using the large center bolt on the crankshaft pulley, turn the engine until the No. 1 cylinder is at TDC of the compression stroke. At this point, both valves will be closed and the timing marks at the flywheel will be aligned.
6. Check that the timing dot on the rear face of the camshaft pulley is aligned with the camshaft cover as shown in the illustration. If it's not, turn the pulley so that it does.
7. Check that the V-notch in the crankshaft pulley aligns with the adjusting lug on the oil pump housing as shown. If they don't, turn the crankshaft until they do.

CAUTION: *If the timing marks are not correctly aligned with the No. 1 piston at TDC of the compression stroke and the belt is installed, valve timing will be incorrect. Poor performance and possible engine damage can result from improper valve timing.*

8. Install the belt on the pulleys.
9. Adjust the tensioner by turning the large hex on the pulley to the left until the belt can be twisted 90° with the thumb and forefinger at the midpoint between the camshaft pulley and the crankshaft pulley. Tighten the locknut to 30 ft. lbs.
10. Install the timing belt cover and check the ignition timing.

Timing Gears

Removal and Installation

The camshaft and crankshaft pulleys (gears) are located by keys on their respective shafts and each is retained by a bolt. To remove either or both of the pulleys, first remove the timing belt cover and belt and then use the following procedure.

NOTE: *When removing the crankshaft pulley, don't remove the four bolts which retain the outer belt pulley to the timing belt pulley.*

1. Remove the center bolt.
2. Gently pry the pulley off the shaft. If the pulley is stubborn, use a gear puller. Don't hammer on the pulley.
3. Remove the pulley and the key.
4. Install the pulley in the reverse order of removal.
5. Tighten the center bolt on the crankshaft pulley to 58 ft. lbs. Tighten the camshaft pulley retaining bolt to 15 ft lbs.
6. Install the timing belt, check valve timing, tension belt, and install the cover.

Camshaft

Removal and Installation

1. Remove the timing belt.
2. Remove the camshaft sprocket.
3. Remove the air cleaner.
4. Remove the camshaft cover.
5. Remove the distributor and mounting housing.
6. Remove the oil injection tube and then reinstall the retaining nuts hand tight.

7. Unscrew and remove the Nos. 1, 3, and 5 bearing caps (No. 1 is at the front of the engine).

8. Unscrew the Nos. 2 and 4 bearing caps, diagonally and in increments.

9. Lift the camshaft out of the cylinder head.

10. Lubricate the camshaft journals and lobes with assembly lube or gear oil before installing it in the cylinder head. Bolts are tightened to 8 ft. lbs. and nuts to 20 ft. lbs.

11. Tighten bearing caps Nos. 2 and 4 carefully in a diagonal pattern.

12. Install bearing caps Nos. 1, 3, and 5.

13. Install the oil injection tube. You will have to loosen the nuts on Nos. 2 and 4 again.

14. Install the camshaft cover using new gaskets and seals.

15. Install the camshaft pulley and the timing belt.

16. Check the valve clearance.

ENGINE LUBRICATION

The 924 full pressure lubrication system consists of a wet sump, crankshaft driven oil pump, oil temperature gauge with sender in the oil pan, and a disposable type oil filter on the passenger side of the block.

Oil Pan

Removal and Installation

1. Drain the oil. Remove the engine splash shield.

2. Disconnect the temperature sending unit wire.

3. Disconnect the side engine mounts and raise the engine for pan removal clearance.

4. Remove the pan retaining bolts and lower the pan from the car.

5. Install the pan using the reverse of

the removal procedure. Use new gaskets and seals.

Rear Main Seal

Replacement

The rear main oil seal is located in the back of the cylinder block and so replacement involves disconnecting the torque tube and pulling the transaxle back, removing the clutch housing, and then removing the flywheel.

1. Carefully pry the seal out with a screwdriver.

2. Lightly oil the replacement seal with engine oil and carefully tap it into place. Do not damage the seal or score the flywheel.

3. Install the flywheel, clutch housing and torque tube and transaxle. Tighten the flywheel-to-crankshaft bolts to 65 ft. lbs.

Oil Pump

Removal and Installation

The oil pump is driven directly by the crankshaft.

1. Remove the oil pan.

2. Remove the timing belt cover.

3. Remove the timing belt.

4. Remove the crankshaft pulley.

5. Unbolt and remove the oil pump. Remove the oil pickup.

6. Clean and then install the oil pickup to the replacement oil pump.

7. Install the oil pump. Tighten the

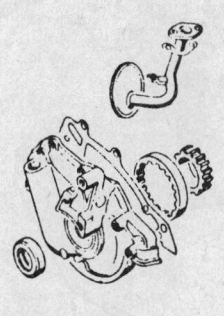

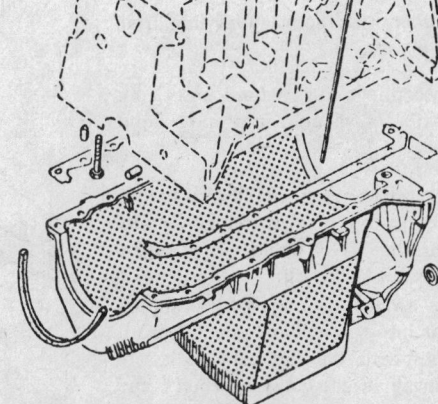

Oil pump and oil pan

pump-to-crankcase bolts to 8 ft. lbs.

8. Install the remaining components in reverse order of removal.

ENGINE COOLING

The 924 cooling system consists of a radiator, belt driven water pump, expansion tank, electric thermostatically controlled fan, and a conventional thermostat.

Radiator

Removal and Installation

1. Drain the cooling system.

2. Remove the electric fan and radiator shroud.

3. Remove the radiator hoses.

4. Disconnect the expansion tank and move it out of the way.

5. Unbolt the radiator and remove it.

6. Installation is the reverse of removal. Refill the cooling system as follows: set the heater on the hot position, remove the vent plug on the radiator hose, fill the cooling system, start the engine and run it for one minute at fast idle, replace the vent plug when no more air bubbles appear at the plug opening.

Water Pump

Removal and Installation

1. Drain the cooling system.

2. Remove the timing belt cover.

3. Remove the fan belt.

4. Disconnect the radiator hoses from the pump.

5. Unbolt and remove the water pump.

6. Clean the crankcase and pump mating surfaces.

7. Install the water pump using a new gasket.

8. Install the remaining components in the reverse order of removal. Refill the cooling system using the previously outlined procedure.

Thermostat

The thermostat is located in the upper radiator hose neck on the engine.

1. Drain the cooling system.

2. Don't disconnect the radiator hose, unbolt the neck and lift out the thermostat.

3. Clean the mating surfaces and install the new thermostat (spring down) using a new gasket.

4. Refill the cooling system.

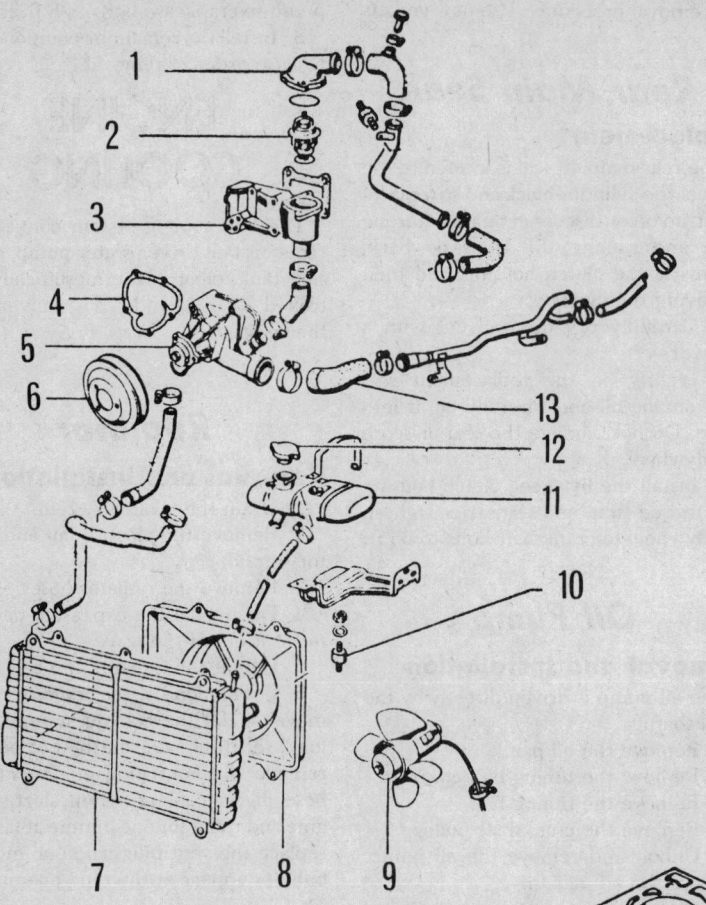

Exploded view of the cooling system

EMISSION CONTROLS

Positive Crankcase Ventilation

The 924 uses a conventional crankcase ventilation system. A PCV valve, located on the driver's side of the engine, meters blow-by gases into the air intake.

Service

The PCV valve should be replaced at the recommended intervals. Check hoses for plugging and cracking and replace where necessary.

Exhaust Gas Recirculation

All 924s are equipped with this system which lowers NOx emissions. Metered amounts of cooled exhaust gases are added to the air/fuel mixture. The recirculated gas lowers the peak flame temperature during combustion to cut the output of oxides of nitrogen. Exhaust gas from the exhaust pipe passes through a filter where it is cleaned. The vacuum operated EGR valve controls the amount of exhaust gas which enters the intake.

Testing

1. Disconnect the vacuum line from the EGR valve.

2. Disconnect the vacuum hose from the distributor vacuum unit and extend the hose.

3. Start the engine and allow it to idle.

4. Connect the distributor vacuum hose to the EGR valve. The engine should stumble or stall.

reduces exhaust emissions by pumping fresh air into the exhaust port. There it combines with the hot exhaust gas to burn away excess hydrocarbons and reduce carbon monoxide. The system consists of a belt driven pump, air filter, diverter valve and check valve.

5. If the idle speed stays even, the EGR line is clogged or the EGR valve is defective.

Service

The only required maintenance is that the EGR filter be replaced at the recommended intervals. The filter is located on the right side of the engine block under the intake housing.

1. Disconnect the line fittings at each end of the filter.

2. Unbolt the bracket retaining screws and remove the filter.

3. Install the replacement filter using the reverse order of removal.

Removal and Installation

EGR Valve

The EGR valve is located on the rear of the intake housing.

1. Disconnect the vacuum line from the EGR valve.

2. Unbolt the EGR line fitting on the opposite side of the valve.

3. Remove the two retaining bolts and lift the EGR valve from the intake housing.

4. Install the EGR valve in the reverse order of removal. Use a new gasket.

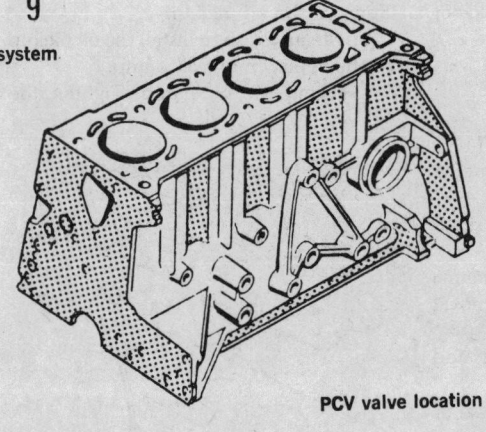

PCV valve location

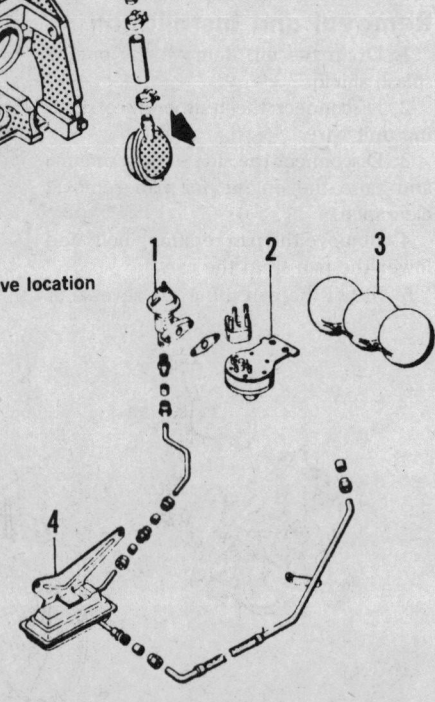

EGR system

1. EGR valve
2. Vacuum amplifier
3. Vacuum reservoir
4. EGR filter

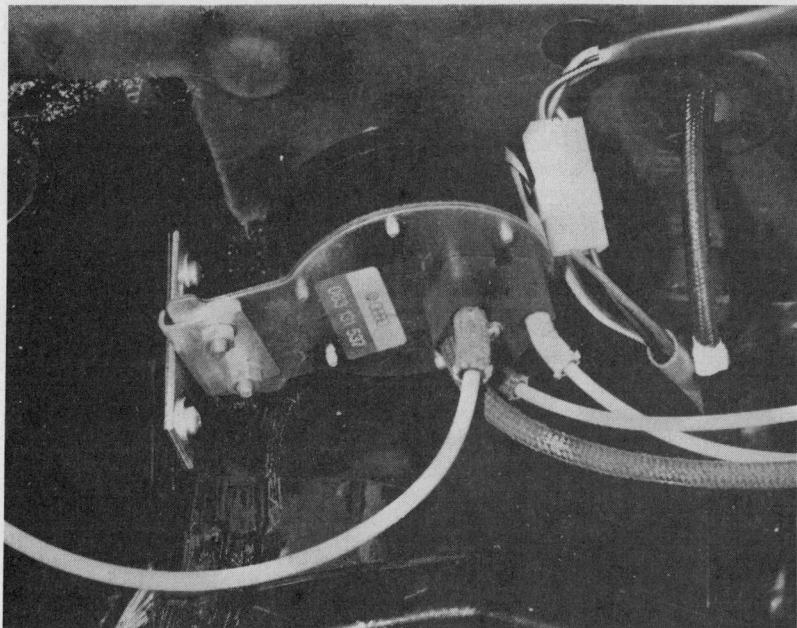

The EGR vacuum amplifier is located on the passenger side inner fender

The EGR filter is located on the driver's side of the engine

bilize on either side of the diaphragm.

2. When you release the line, the sudden surge of vacuum will make the valve work. If it's operating properly, you should be able to hear it open and exhaust air.

Check Valve

The check valve is located on the intake housing. It keeps hot exhaust gases from flowing back into the pump and hoses and destroying them.

To test the valve:

1. With the engine off and cool enough so that there is no danger of being burned, disconnect the hose and use mouth pressure to blow through it.

2. You should be able to easily blow through the valve towards the intake housing, but the valve should seal tightly when you suck back. Replace the valve if it doesn't seal.

Air Pump

1. Disconnect a hose at the diverter valve.

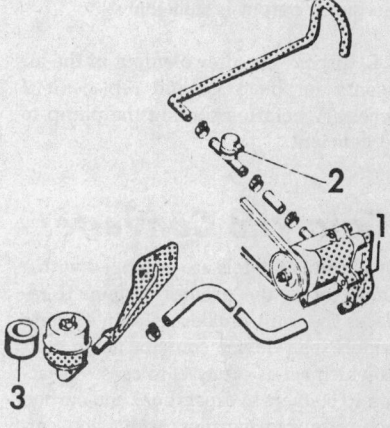

Air injection system

1. Air pump
2. Check valve
3. Air filter

Air Injection

Testing

Diverter Valve

The diverter valve is located between the air pump and the check valve on the intake housing. The diverter valve also houses a relief valve, so that it serves two functions. The valve diverts air during deceleration to prevent backfiring and relieves excess pressure during high rpm to prevent damage to the hoses and air pump.

To test the valve:

1. Pinch the vacuum line closed and wait a few seconds for the vacuum to sta-

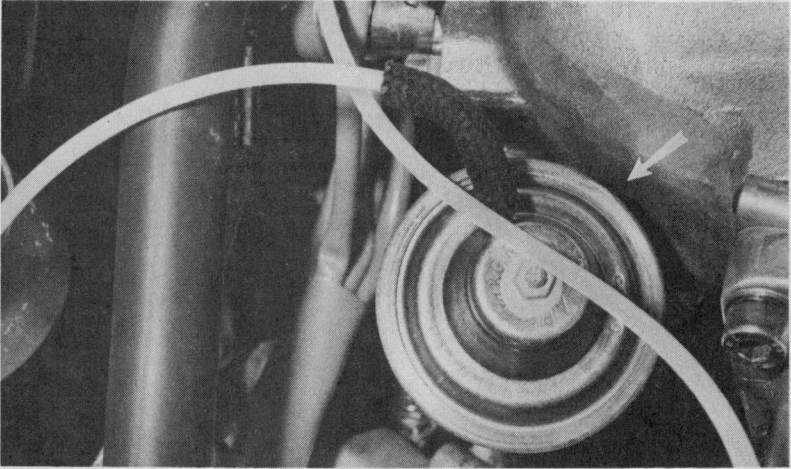

The EGR valve is located on the rear of the intake housing.

Porsche 924

Air injection filter is under the expansion tank

2. With the engine idling, check the flow of air by feeling at the hose with your hand.

3. Increase the engine speed to about 1500 rpm and again check the air flow. If it increases as the engine is accelerated, the pump output is sufficient.

4. Inspect the filter element in the air cleaner for blockage and replace it if necessary before assuming the pump to be deficient.

Catalytic Converter

California models are equipped with a converter in the exhaust system. It replaces the front muffler used on 49 state models. This device contains noble metals which act as catalysts to cause a reaction to convert hydrocarbons and carbon monoxide into harmless water and carbon dioxide. Service on the converter consists of replacing it when it malfunctions.

Evaporative Emission Control System

This system prevents the escape of raw fuel vapors into the atmosphere. The system consists of a charcoal canister and an expansion chamber. Vapors from the fuel tank are trapped in the canister. When the engine is running, fresh air is drawn in through the charcoal filter. The fresh air cleans the canister and routes the unburned hydrocarbons through the air cleaner to be burned during combustion. The fuel tank is vented to an expansion chamber which prevents fuel vapors from entering the atmosphere.

FUEL SYSTEM

The 924 is equipped with a Bosch continuous flow fuel injection system.

Fuel Filter

Replacement

The fuel filter is located in the fuel line on the driver's side of the engine compartment.

1. Place a shop rag under the filter.
2. Using a line wrench, unscrew both line connections from the filter.

3. Remove the filter.
4. Install the replacement filter in the line and tighten both fittings.

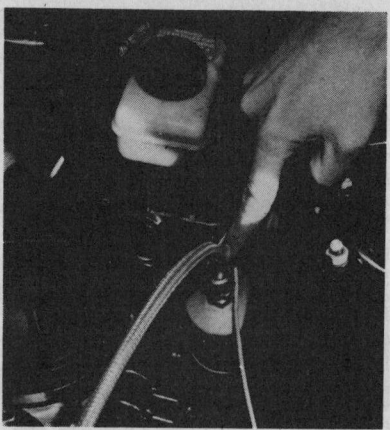

Fuel filter location

Electric Fuel Pump

Removal and Installation

The fuel pump is located near the fuel tank behind the right rear wheel.

1. Disconnect the battery ground cable.
2. Unplug the electrical connections at the pump.
3. Disconnect the fuel lines.
4. Unscrew the retaining clamp and remove the pump.
5. Install the new pump. Clean the electrical connections to ensure continuity.

Testing

1. Disconnect the fuel line from the fuel distributor to fuel pump and hold into a container.
2. Switch the ignition on and disconnect the electrical plug at the air sensor.
3. The fuel pump should deliver at least one quart of fuel in 40 seconds. Replace the pump or check for blockage in the fuel lines, if fuel flow is less.

CLUTCH

The 924 uses a conventional, dry clutch and a diaphragm spring pressure plate. Clutch actuation is by cable.

Free-Play Adjustment

Clutch pedal free-play should be ¾–1 in. (20–25mm). Pedal free-play is the distance the pedal can be depressed before the linkage starts to act on the throwout bearing.

1. Adjust the clutch pedal free-play by loosening the two nuts on the cable near the intake housing.
2. After obtaining the correct free-play at the pedal, tighten the adjusting nuts.

Removal and Installation

To gain access to the clutch disc and

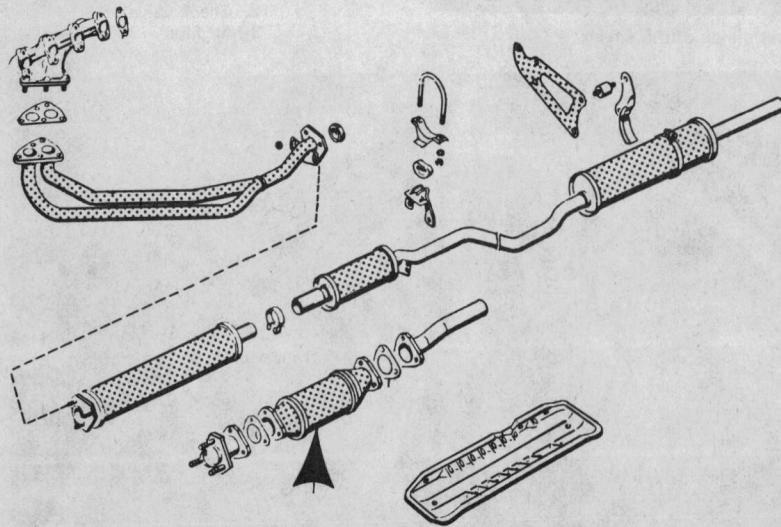

Exhaust system showing catalytic converter and heat shields

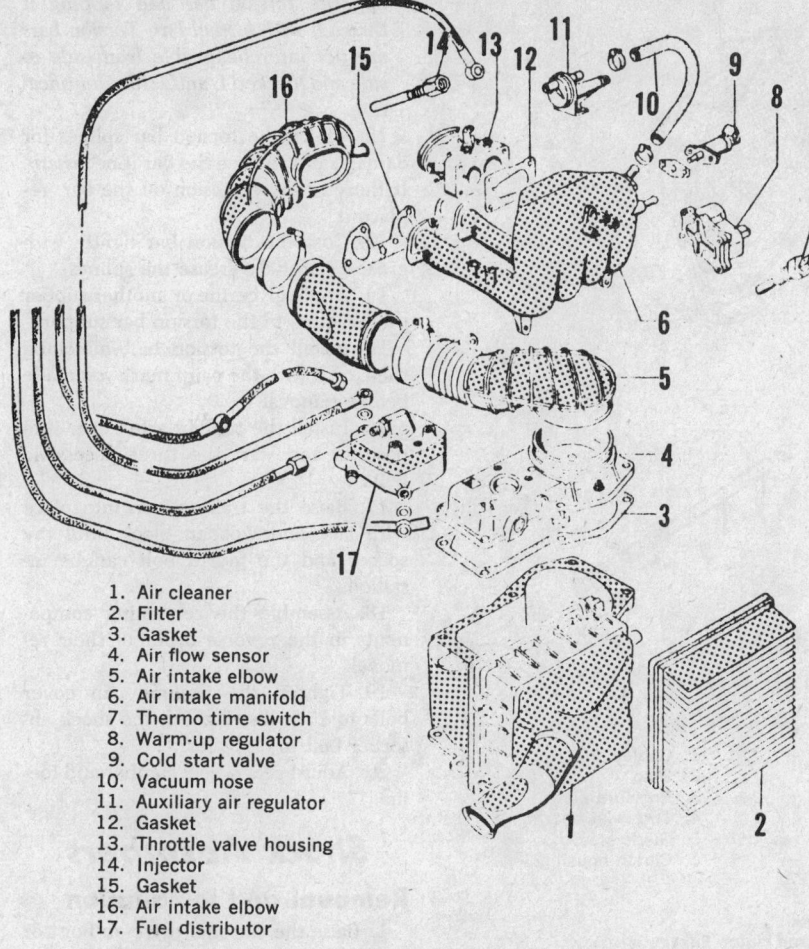

1. Air cleaner
2. Filter
3. Gasket
4. Air flow sensor
5. Air intake elbow
6. Air intake manifold
7. Thermo time switch
8. Warm-up regulator
9. Cold start valve
10. Vacuum hose
11. Auxiliary air regulator
12. Gasket
13. Throttle valve housing
14. Injector
15. Gasket
16. Air intake elbow
17. Fuel distributor

Fuel injection system

pressure plate assembly, the transaxle, torque tube, and clutch housing must be dismounted and pulled back out of the way.

1. Disconnect the battery ground cable. Raise the car and support it on jack stands.

2. Support the engine with an over-head hoist or a jack and cradle under the engine.

3. Remove the engine splash shield.

4. Disconnect the clutch cable.

5. Remove the bottom clutch adjustment lock nut and detach the cable from the lever.

6. Remove the access plate from the bottom of the clutch housing.

7. Have an assistant turn the engine with the crankshaft pulley. Remove the pressure plate bolts gradually until all pressure is released.

8. Remove the exhaust pipe flange bolts.

9. Remove the bracket at the rear of the transaxle.

10. Remove the entire exhaust system.

11. Remove the back up light switch from the transaxle.

12. Disconnect the axle driveshafts at the transaxle and let them hang down out of the way.

13. Remove the clutch housing-to-engine bolts.

14. Place a wooden block under the front tunnel reinforcement to support the transaxle tube.

15. Remove the transaxle mounting bolts and slide the transaxle towards the rear.

16. Remove the pressure plate and clutch disc.

17. Install the pressure plate and clutch disc onto the driveshaft in the clutch housing.

18. Push the transaxle, torque tube, and clutch housing assembly forward to the engine.

19. Install the clutch housing-to-engine bolts. Tighten the 12mm bolts to 60 ft. lbs., the 10mm bolts to 36 ft. lbs. and the 8mm bolts to 20 ft. lbs.

20. Tighten the pressure plate-to-flywheel bolts to 24 ft lbs. in a gradual diagonal pattern.

21. Install the remaining components in the reverse order of removal. Adjust the clutch.

TRANSAXLE

The 924 4-speed transmission and differential are mounted in a single transaxle housing mounted at the rear of the car.

Removal and Installation

Remove the transaxle as outlined in clutch removal and installation. Disconnect the torque tube from the transaxle for servicing.

Axle Driveshafts

Power is transferred to the rear wheels by independent axle driveshafts. These are similar to the ones used on the VW Type 2. Each shaft has a constant velocity joint at either end.

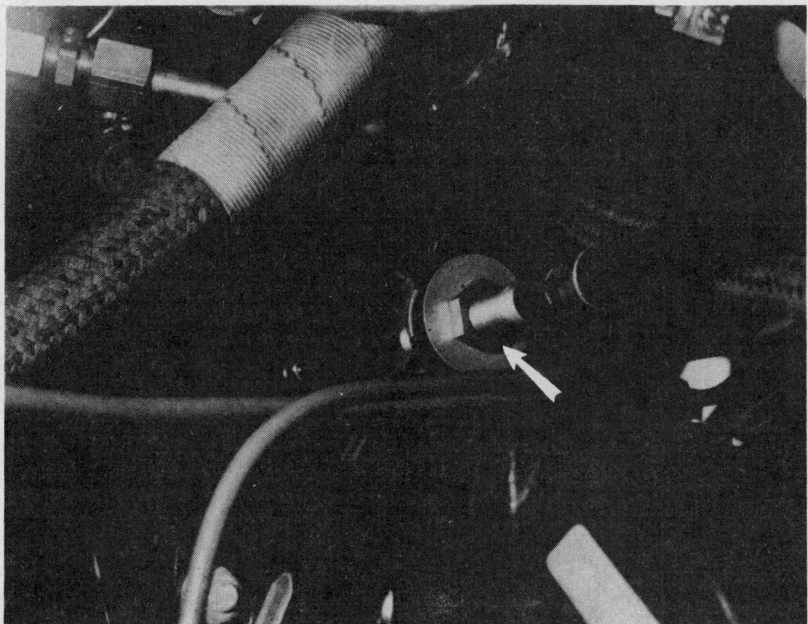

Clutch adjusting nuts

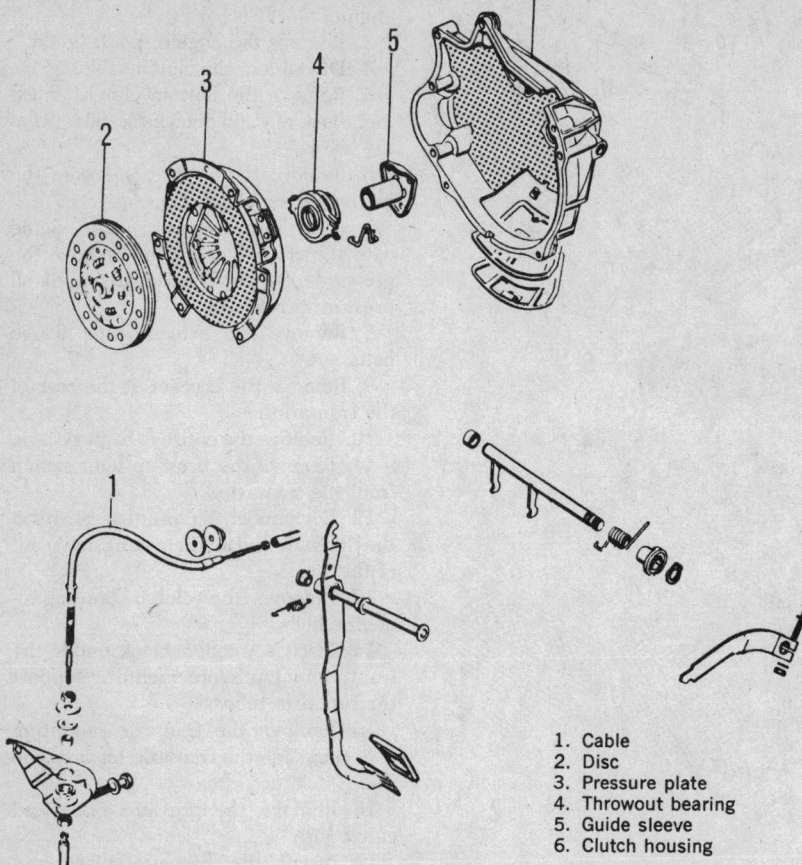

1. Cable
2. Disc
3. Pressure plate
4. Throwout bearing
5. Guide sleeve
6. Clutch housing

Exploded view of the clutch and clutch linkage

Removal and Installation

1. Jack the rear of the car up and support it on jack stands.

2. Remove the six star bolts on the inside joint at the transaxle.

3. Remove the six star bolts at the stub axle. Use a wide, flat bladed screwdriver to pry the flanges apart.

4. Drop the axle driveshaft down and out of the car.

5. Pack the constant velocity joints with grease before installation.

6. Installation is the reverse of removal. Tighten the bolts to 30 ft. lbs.

REAR SUSPENSION

Rear suspension is by lateral torsion bars, trailing arms and conventional shock absorbers.

Torsion Bars

Removal and Installation

NOTE: *This procedure requires that the rear wheel camber and toe-in be checked and adjusted as the final step.*

1. Jack up the rear of the car and support it on stands.

2. Remove the wheel on the side where the torsion bar is being removed.

3. Using a hydraulic jack and a block of wood with a slot cut in it, raise the trailing arm.

4. Remove the lower shock absorber bolt.

5. Remove the trailing arm retaining bolts. Remove the toe and camber adjusting bolts.

6. Remove the four retaining bolts from the trailing arm cover.

7. Using two screwdrivers, pry off the trailing arm cover.

8. Lower the jack.

9. Remove the round body plug and remove the trailing arm.

10. Paint a reference mark on the torsion bar support, matching the location of the L or R side identification letter, so that the torsion bar may be installed in the same position.

NOTE: *The torsion bars are splined to allow adjustment of the rear riding height.*

11. Remove the torsion bar. Do not scratch the protective paint on the torsion bar, or it will corrode and possibly develop fatigue cracks.

NOTE: *If you are removing a broken torsion bar, the inner end can be knocked from its seat by removing the*

opposite torsion bar and tapping it through with a steel bar. Torsion bars are not interchangeable from side to side and marked L and R for identification.

12. Check the torsion bar splines for damage and replace the bar if necessary. If there is any corrosion on the bar, replace it.

13. Coat the torsion bar lightly with grease. Carefully grease the splines.

14. Apply glycerine or another rubber preservative to the torsion bar support.

15. Install the torsion bar, matching the L or R with the paint mark you made before removal.

16. Install the trailing arm cover into position and start the three accessible bolts.

17. Raise the trailing arm into place with jack and wooden block until the spacer and the fourth bolt can be installed.

18. Assemble the remaining components in the reverse order of their removal.

19. Tighten the trailing arm cover bolts to 25 ft lbs. Tighten the shock absorber bolt to 50 ft. lbs.

20. Adjust rear wheel camber and toe-in.

Shock Absorbers

Removal and Installation

1. Raise the car on a drive-on hoist or support the wheels on stands for this procedure.

2. Remove the bottom retaining bolt and nut.

3. Remove the top bolt.

4. Remove the shock absorber.

5. Install the replacement shock in the reverse order of removal. Tighten the retaining bolts to 50 ft lbs.

Wheel Alignment Adjustments

Camber

Rear wheel camber is adjusted by changing the trailing arm spring plate setting. To increase positive camber, loosen the spring plate-to-trailing arm bolts (with the wheels on the ground). To increase negative camber, do so with car on hoist. Tighten bolts after adjustment.

Toe-In

Rear wheel toe-in is adjusted by moving the control arm in the slots of the spring plates.

FRONT SUSPENSION

The 924 front suspension is a MacPherson strut design. The strut consists of the

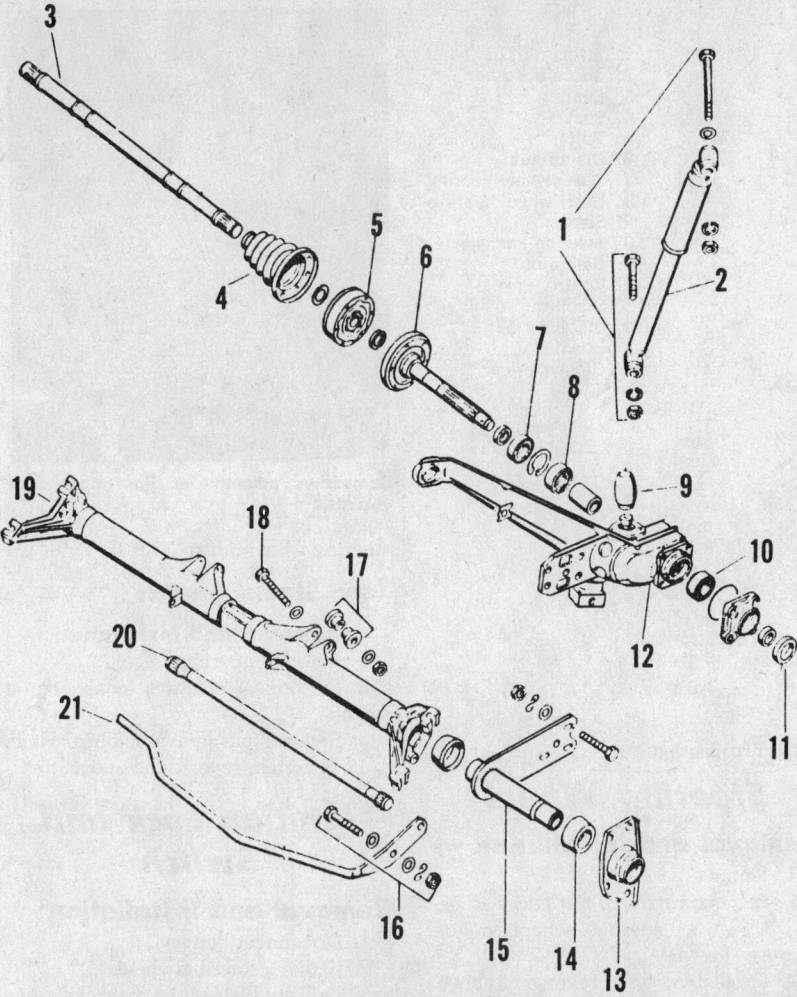

Exploded view of the rear suspension and axle driveshaft

1. Shock absorber mounting
2. Shock absorber
3. Driveshaft
4. Boot
5. CV joint
6. Stub axle
7. Seal
8. Inner wheel bearing
9. Bumper
10. Outer wheel bearing
11. Seal
12. Control arm
13. Torsion bar cover
14. Bearing
15. Trailing arm (spring plate)
16. Stabilizer mounting
17. Bushings
18. Bolt
19. Torsion bar housing
20. Torsion bar
21. Stabilizer bar

Rear wheel alignment is adjusted at the trailing arm-to-spring plate bolts

strut housing, a shock absorber insert in the housing, and a concentric coil spring. The steering knuckle is bolted to the strut assembly. A lower control arm locates the strut at the bottom. A ball joint is riveted to the control arm and bolted to the steering knuckle.

Strut

Removal and Installation

1. Jack up the front of the car and support it on stands.
2. Remove the brake line from the bracket on the strut.
3. Remove the two through bolts that retain the strut to the steering knuckle.
4. Remove the four retaining nuts from the inner fender in the engine compartment.
5. Pry the lower control arm down and remove the strut from the car.
6. To replace either the spring or shock absorber, place the strut in a spring compressor and remove the large retaining nut at the top.
7. Installation is the reverse of removal. Front wheel alignment must be reset after a strut is removed.

Lower Control Arm

Removal and Installation

1. Jack up the front of the car and support it on stands.
2. Remove the through bolt at the front that retains the control arm to the suspension crossmember.
3. Detach the stabilizer bar from the control arm.
4. Remove the two bolts that retain the control arm bracket at the rear.
5. Remove the ball joint pinch bolt at the steering knuckle.
6. Pry the control arm down and remove it from the car.
7. Installation is the reverse of removal. Caster must be reset after the control arm has been removed.

Ball Joint

1. Remove the lower control arm.
2. Drill out the three rivets retaining the ball joint to the control arm.
3. Install the replacement ball joint using the bolts and nuts supplied in the kit.
4. Reinstall the control arm and align the wheels.

Wheel Alignment Adjustments

Camber

Camber is adjusted at the upper strut-to-steering knuckle retaining bolt.

Caster

Caster is adjusted by loosening the two

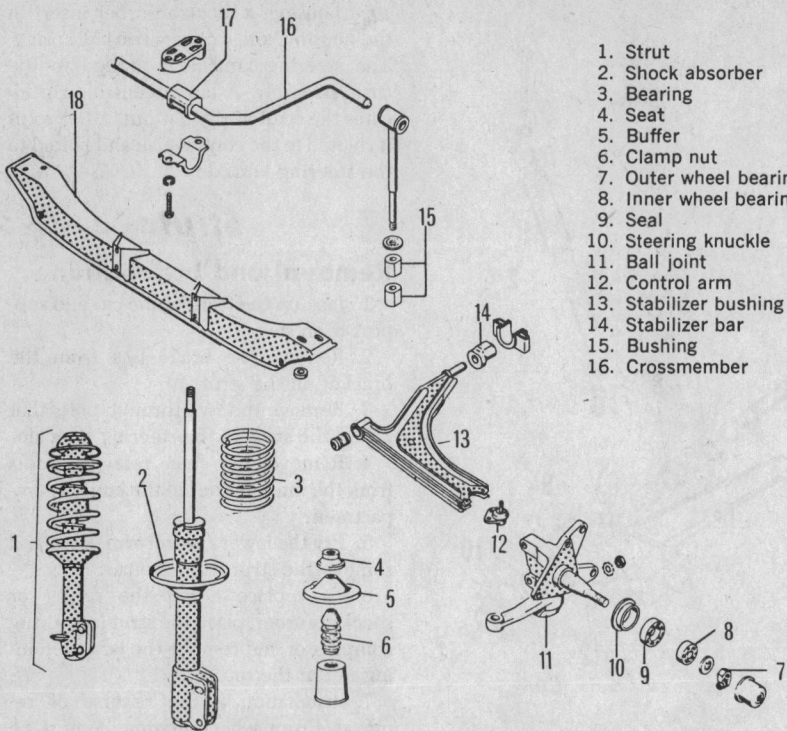

1. Strut
2. Shock absorber
3. Bearing
4. Seat
5. Buffer
6. Clamp nut
7. Outer wheel bearing
8. Inner wheel bearing
9. Seal
10. Steering knuckle
11. Ball joint
12. Control arm
13. Stabilizer bushing
14. Stabilizer bar
15. Bushing
16. Crossmember

Exploded view of the front suspension

Camber is adjusted at the upper strut eccentric

control arm to crossmember bolts and moving the control arm laterally.

Toe-In

Toe-in is set by loosening the locknuts on the tie-rod ends and turning them in or out as necessary.

Steering Wheel

Removal and Installation

1. Remove horn pad.
2. Remove retaining nut and washer.
3. Using a steering wheel puller, remove the wheel.
4. Installation is the reverse of above. Make sure road wheels are straight ahead and steering wheel is centered. Torque steering wheel nut to 33 ft lb.

Turn Signal Switch

Removal and Installation

1. Remove steering wheel.
2. Disconnect electrical connector at switch.
3. Remove four screws holding switch.
4. To install, reverse the above.

Ignition Lock and Switch

Removal and Installation

1. Disconnect battery.
2. Remove steering wheel.
3. Drill out casing tube sheer bolts, disconnect electrical connectors, and pull column and casing out of car.
4. Remove casing from steering column.
5. Remove pinch bolt holding switch housing to column.
6. Remove retaining screw and pull ignition switch from rear of casing.
7. Depress lock cylinder retainer with an ice pick or similar tool and remove lock cylinder.
8. Installation is the reverse of removal. Make sure road wheels are straight ahead and steering wheel is centered when installing. Torque steering wheel nut to 33 ftlb. Torque sheer bolts to 23 ftlb.

Steering Gear

Removal and Installation

1. Remove bolt connecting gear box to steering column drive shaft.
2. Press out tie rod ends
3. Remove steering gear and tie rods from car.
4. Remove tie rods from steering gear.
5. To install, reverse the above. Center steering gear with VW tool 9116 or its equivalent. Be sure that both tie rod

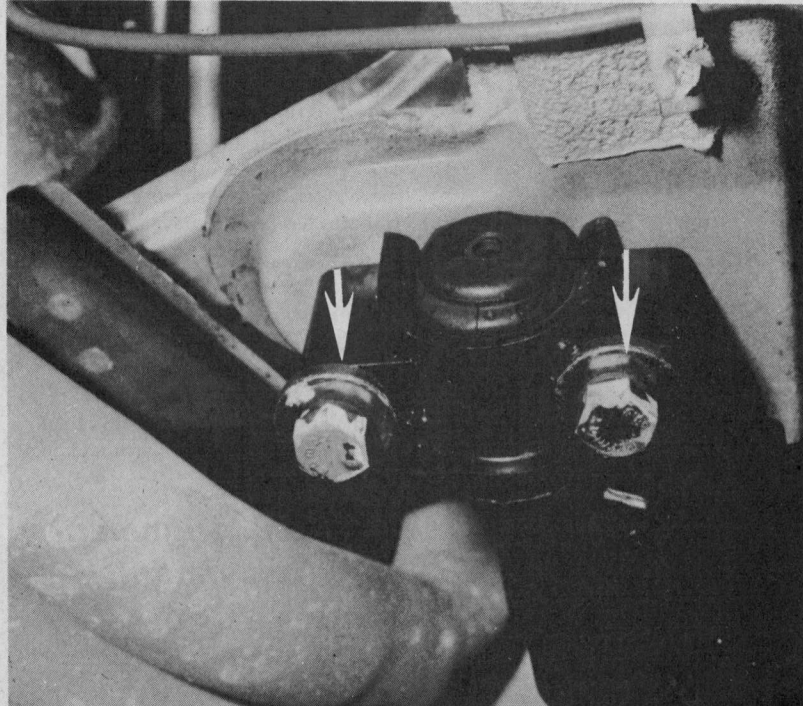

Adjust caster at the lower control arm mounting

Tie-rod ends are adjustable for toe-in.

lengths are equal (68–68.5mm). Tighten tie rod counter nuts to 29 ftlb. and gear box to driveshaft bolt to 23 ftlb.

Steering Gear Adjustment

1. Tighten adjusting screw (on front of gear box) until it just touches the washer.
2. Hold adjusting screw tightly and tighten lock nut.

BRAKE SYSTEMS

The 924 is equipped with power assisted front disc brakes and drum rear brakes.

Adjustment

The front disc brakes require no adjustment, as disc brakes automatically adjust themselves to compensate for pad wear. The rear drum brakes must be periodically adjusted, or whenever free travel is one third or more of the total pedal travel.

1. Raise the rear of the car.
2. Block the front wheels and release the parking brake. Step on the brake pedal hard to center the linings.
3. Remove the rubber plugs from the rear of the backing plate on each wheel.
4. Insert a brake adjusting tool or wide-blade screwdriver and turn the adjuster wheel until the brakes drag as you turn the tire/wheel.

5. Turn the adjuster in the opposite direction until you just pass the point of drag.
6. Repeat on the other wheel.
7. Lower the car and road-test. Readjust, if necessary.

Master Cylinder

The hydraulic system is a dual circuit type which has the advantage of retaining 50% braking effectiveness in the event of failure in one system. The circuits are arranged so that you always have one front and one rear brake for a more controlled emergency stop. The right front and left rear are one circuit; the left front and right rear the second circuit. The dual master cylinder is attached to the brake booster which is in turn bolted to the firewall. The booster uses intake manifold vacuum to provide pedal assist.

Removal and Installation

1. To prevent brake fluid from spilling out and damaging the paint, place a protective cover over the fender.
2. Disconnect and plug the brake lines.
3. Disconnect the electrical plug from the sending unit for the brake failure switch.
4. Remove the two master cylinder mounting nuts.
5. Lift the master cylinder and reservoir out of the engine compartment be-

Rear brake adjusters are behind rubber plugs.

ing careful not to spill any fluid on the fender. Empty out and discard the brake fluid.

CAUTION: *Do not depress the brake pedal while the master cylinder is removed.*

6. Position the master cylinder and reservoir assembly onto the studs for the booster and install the washers and nuts. Tighten the nuts to no more than 10 ft lbs.

7. Remove the plugs and connect the brake lines.

8. Bleed the entire brake system as explained further on in this chapter.

Overhaul

1. Remove the master cylinder from the booster.

2. Firmly mount the master cylinder in a vise. Use clean rags to protect the cylinder from the vise jaws.

3. Grasp the plastic reservoir and pull it out of the rubber plugs. Remove the plugs.

4. In the center of the cylinder there is a stop screw, remove it. Discard the stop screw seal, a new one is in the kit.

5. At the end of the master cylinder is a snap-ring (circlip), remove it, using snap-ring pliers.

6. Shake out the secondary piston assembly. If the primary piston remains lodged in the bore, it can be forced by applying compressed air to the open brake line fitting.

7. Disassemble the secondary piston. The two secondary rings will be replaced with those in the rebuilding kit. Save the washers and spacers.

8. Carefully clamp the secondary piston, slightly compress the spring and screw out the stroke limiting bolt.

9. Remove the secondary piston stop sleeve bolt, spring, spring seat, and support washer.

10. Replace all parts with those supplied in the overhaul kit.

11. Clean all metal parts in denatured alcohol and dry them with compressed air.

12. Check every part you are reusing. Pay close attention to the cylinder bores. If there is any scoring or rust, have the master cylinder honed or replace it.

13. Lightly coat the bores and cups with brake fluid. Assemble the cylinder components.

14. Install the primary piston assembly, notice that the primary spring is conically shaped. Be sure that you aren't using the secondary spring.

15. Using a plastic rod or other non-metallic tool, push the primary piston assembly into the housing until the stop bolt (with a new seal) can be screwed in and tightened.

16. Assemble the secondary piston. Fasten the spring, spring seat, primary cup, and stop sleeve to the piston with the stroke limiting bolt.

17. Assemble the remaining master cylinder components in the reverse order of disassembly. Ensure that the snap-ring is fully seated and that the piston cups are properly positioned.

18. Install and tighten the brake failure warning sending unit.

Bleeding

Anytime a brake line has been disconnected the hydraulic system should be bled. The brakes should also be bled when the pedal travel becomes unusually long ("soft pedal") or the car pulls to one side during braking. The proper bleeding sequence is: right rear wheel, left rear wheel, right front caliper, and left front caliper. You'll need a helper to pump the brake pedal while you open the bleeder valves.

NOTE: *If the system has been drained, first refill it with fresh brake fluid. Following the above sequence, open each bleeder valve by ½ to ¾ of a turn and pump the brake pedal until fluid runs out of the valve. Proceed with the bleeding as outlined below.*

1. Remove the bleeder valve dust cover and install a rubber bleeder hose.

2. Insert the other end of the hose into a container about 1/3 full of brake fluid.

3. Have your assistant pump the brake pedal several times until the pedal pressure increases.

4. Hold the pedal under pressure and then start to open the bleeder valve about ½ to ¾ of a turn. At this point, have your assistant depress the pedal all the way and then quickly close the valve. The helper should allow the pedal to return slowly.

NOTE: *Keep a close check on the brake fluid in the reservoir and top it up as necessary throughout the bleeding process.*

5. Keep repeating this procedure until no more air bubbles can be seen coming from the hose in the brake fluid.

6. Remove the bleeder hose and install the dust cover.

7. Continue the bleeding at each wheel in sequence.

FRONT DISC BRAKES

The 924 uses single piston, floating caliper disc brakes. In this design, the single piston forces one pad against the rotating brake disc. Counter pressure forces against the floating frame and the frame then pushes the second pad into the disc. The advantages of the floating

Drive the pad retaining pins out in the direction shown. Use new pins on installation

caliper are, better heat dissipation, simpler repairs, fewer leaks, and less sensitivity to variance in disc thickness and parallelism.

Brake Pads

Removal and Installation

Brake pads should be replaced when there is no visible clearance between the pads and the cross-spring or when they are worn to a thickness of 0.08 in.

1. Jack up the front of the car and support it on stands. Remove the wheels.

2. Pry the clip out of both retaining pins.

3. While pressing down on the cross-spring, push the pad retaining pins out with a drift or small screwdriver.

4. Reference mark positions of the brake pads if they are being reused.

5. Remove the cross-spring from the caliper.

6. Remove the inner brake pad. A special tool is available for this purpose, but by using a small drift or punch you can pry the pad out of the caliper until it can be gripped by a pair of pliers and removed.

7. The outer brake pad is positioned in a notch. Use a flat, smooth piece of hardwood or metal to press the floating caliper frame and piston cylinder outward.

8. Grip the outer pad and remove it. Press the piston back into the cylinder with the flat piece of wood or metal.

9. Siphon out about half of the brake fluid in the reservoir to prevent it from overflowing when the piston is pushed in and new thicker pads are inserted.

10. Check that the piston is at the proper 20° angle. Make a gauge out of stiff cardboard.

11. Install the brake pads into the caliper.

NOTE: *Replace used pads in the side of the caliper from which they were removed. When installing new pads always replace the pads on the opposite wheel at the same time.*

12. Position the cross-spring in the caliper and then carefully tap the pad retaining pins into place with a small hammer. Install the pin clip.

Calipers

Removal and Installation

1. Jack up the front of the car and support it on stands.
2. Remove the brake pads as previously outlined.
3. If you are removing the caliper for overhaul, disconnect and plug the brake line at the caliper. If not, do not remove the hose—hang it by a wire.
4. Remove the two caliper-to-strut retaining bolts and remove the caliper.
5. Install the caliper using the reverse of the removal procedure. Tighten the two retaining bolts to 43 ft lbs.
6. Bleed the brakes.

Overhaul

1. Remove the caliper as outlined above.
2. Mount the caliper in a soft-jawed vise or place cloths over the jaws to protect the caliper.
3. Pry the fixed mounting frame off the floating frame.
4. Separate the caliper cylinder from the floating frame by prying it and the guide spring off the frame. Use a brass drift to lightly tap on the cylinder and place a piece of wood under the piston to protect it.
5. Using pliers remove the piston clamp ring. Remove and discard the rubber dust cover, a new one is supplied with the rebuilding kit.
6. Remove the piston from the cylinder. If it is stubborn, remove the bleeder screw and blow it out with compressed air.
   CAUTION: *Hold the piston over a block of wood when doing this as the piston will fly out with considerable force.*
7. When the piston pops out of the caliper, remove the rubber seal with a wood or plastic pin to avoid damaging the seal groove.
8. Clean all metal parts in denatured alcohol. Never use a mineral based solvent such as gasoline, kerosene, acetone or the like. These solvents deteriorate rubber parts. Inspect the pistons and their bores. They must be free of scoring and pitting. Replace the cylinder if there is any damage.
9. Discard all rubber parts. The caliper rebuilding kit includes new boots and seals which should be used as the caliper is reassembled.

10. Lightly coat the cylinder bore, piston, and seal with brake assembly paste or fresh brake fluid.
11. Using a vise, install the piston into the cylinder.
12. Position the guide spring in the groove of the brake cylinder and, using a brass drift, install the cylinder on the floating frame.
13. Place the mounting frame in the guide spring and slip it onto the floating frame. The fixed frame has two grooves which position it over the raised ribs of the floating frame.
14. Install pads, caliper, and bleed the brakes.

Brake Disc Replacement

1. Remove caliper and suspend from a suspension member by means of a wire.
2. Remove the dust cap and loosen and remove adjusting clamp.
3. Pull the disc and hub assembly from the spindle, taking care not to drop the outer wheel bearing.
4. When installing, turn wheel while tightening adjusting clamp. Proper adjustment is achieved when flat washer can be just moved by finger pressure on a screwdriver.

Wheel Bearing Adjustment

See procedures under Brake Disc Replacement.

REAR DRUM BRAKES

Brake Drums

Removal and Installation

1. With the wheels still on the ground, remove the cotter pin from the slotted nut on the rear axle and remove the nut from the axle.
   CAUTION: *Make sure the emergency brake is now released.*
2. Jack up the car and remove the wheel and tire.
3. The brake drum is splined to the rear axle and the drum should slip off the

axle. However, the drum sometimes rusts on the splines and it is necessary to remove the drum using a puller.
4. Before installing the drum, lubricate the splines. Install the drum on the axle and tighten the nut on the axle to 220–290 ft lbs. Line up a slot in the nut with a hole in the axle and insert a cotter pin. Never loosen the nut to align the slot and hole.

Brake Shoes

Removal and Installation

1. Remove the brake drum.
2. Remove both shoe retaining springs.
3. Disconnect the lower return spring.
4. Disconnect the hand brake cable from the lever attached to the rear shoe.
5. Remove the upper return spring and clip.
6. Remove the brake shoes and connecting link.
7. Remove the emergency brake lever from the rear shoe.
8. Lubricate the adjusting screws and the star wheel against the head of the adjusting screw.
9. Reverse Steps 1–7 to install the shoes.
10. Adjust the brakes.

Wheel Cylinders

Removal and Installation

Remove the brake drum and brake shoes. Disconnect the brake line from the cylinder and remove the bolts which secure the cylinder to the backing plate. Remove the cylinder from the vehicle.

Overhaul

1. Remove the wheel cylinder.
2. Remove the brake adjusters and remove the rubber boot from each end.
   NOTE: *The Type 2 cylinder has only one rubber boot, piston, and cup. The rebuilding procedures are the same.*
3. Push in on one of the pistons to force out the opposite piston and rubber cup.
4. Wash the pistons and cylinder in clean brake fluid or alcohol.
5. Inspect the cylinder bore for signs of pitting, scoring, and excessive wear. If it is badly scored or pitted, the whole cylinder should be replaced. It is possible to

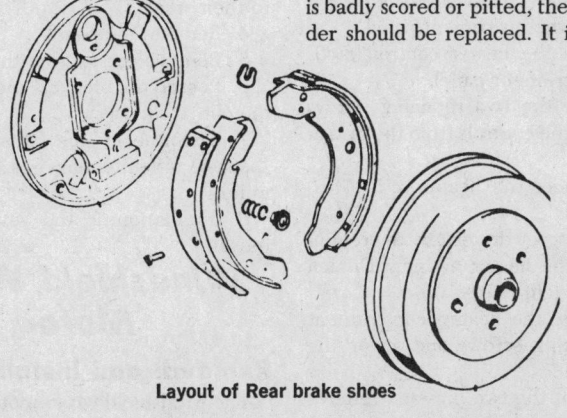

Layout of Rear brake shoes

remove the glaze and light scores with crocus cloth or a brake cylinder hone. Before rebuilding the cylinder, make sure the bleeder screw is free. If the bleeder is rusted shut or broken off, replace the entire cylinder.

6. Dip the new pistons and rubber cups in brake fluid. Place the spring in the bore and insert the rubber cups into the bore against the spring. The concave side of the rubber cup should face inward.

7. Place the pistons in the bore and install the rubber boot.

8. Install the cylinder and bleed the brakes after the shoes and drum are in place. Make sure that the brakes are adjusted.

PARKING BRAKE

Cable

Adjustment

1. Raise the rear wheels and support on stands. Adjust the brakes.

2. Remove the parking brake handle boot.

3. Pull the lever up two teeth.

4. Tighten the adjusting nut until both wheels can just barely be turned by hand.

CHASSIS ELECTRICAL

Heater Assembly

Removal and Installation

The heater core and blower are contained in the heater assembly which is removed and disassembled to service either component. The heater assembly is located under the center of the instrument panel.

1. Disconnect the battery ground cable.

2. Drain the cooling system.

3. Disconnect the two hoses from the heater core connections at the firewall.

4. Unplug the heater electrical connector.

5. Detach the center console and the right side of the instrument panel.

6. Remove the heater control knobs from the instrument panel.

7. Remove the two retaining screws and remove the controls from the instrument panel.

8. Disconnect the heater control cables.

9. Using a screwdriver, pry the retaining clip off the heater housing. Detach the left and right hoses.

10. Remove the heater-to-instrument panel mounting screws and lower the heater.

11. Pull out the two pins and remove

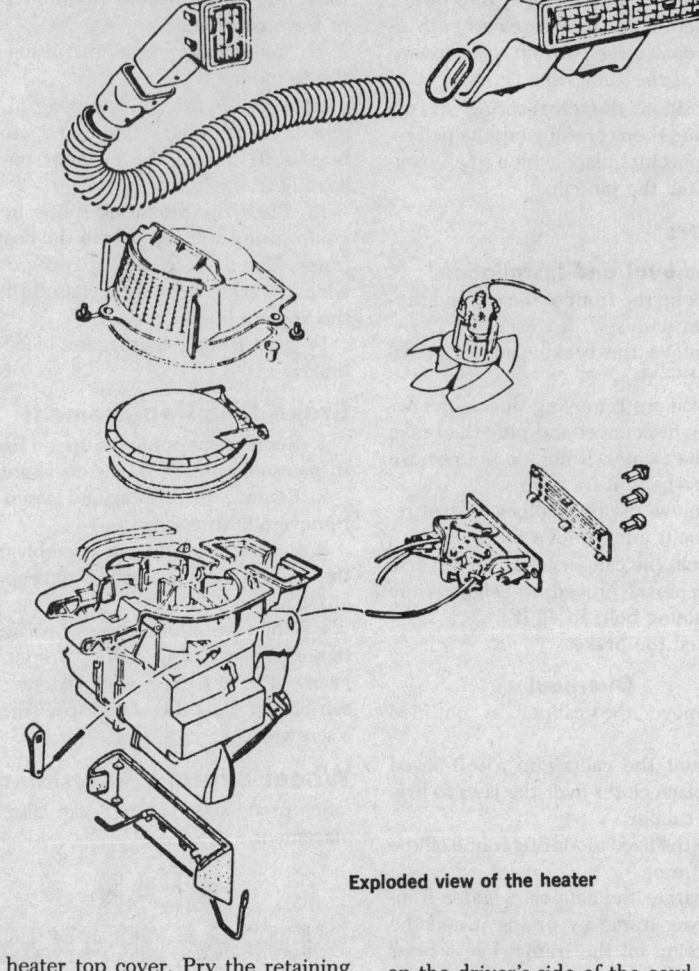

Exploded view of the heater

the heater top cover. Pry the retaining clips off and separate the two heater halves.

12. Remove the heater core and/or blower.

13. Installation is the reverse of removal. Refill the cooling system.

Radio

Removal and Installation

1. Disconnect the battery ground cable.

2. Remove the radio knobs.

3. Release the radio bezel by pressing the springs in the shaft openings outward to their stops.

4. Remove the bezel.

5. Remove the nuts on the shafts.

6. Loosen the brackets and pull the radio out.

7. Disconnect the fuse, ground, speaker, and antenna wires. Remove the radio.

8. Installation is the reverse of removal.

Windshield Wiper Motor

Removal and Installation

The windshield wiper motor is located

on the driver's side of the cowl under a plastic cover.

1. Remove the cover.

2. Disconnect the battery ground cable.

3. Unscrew the wiper linkage, disconnect the plugs, unscrew the motor, remove the mounting screw on the frame, lift frame slightly, and remove motor.

4. Installation is the reverse of removal. Connect the plug and turn on the ignition before fastening the linkage.

5. Move the wiper arms to the off position and mount the linkage.

Instruments

Removal and Installation

The three main instruments can be removed by pushing them out from behind the instrument panel. They are mounted in rubber rings. Push them back into place to install.

To remove the center instrument cluster, disconnect the battery ground cable, remove the two phillips screws at the top, lift the bottom slightly and pull the cluster out.

SPECIFICATIONS

Subaru

INTRODUCTION

In 1971, the model 1300 G was introduced with a 1300 cc engine. In 1972 the DL sedan, the DL station wagon, and the GL coupe were introduced. These had the 1300 cc engine, also. Engine size was increased to 1400 cc in 1973 and 1600 cc in 1976. The four wheel drive station wagon was introduced in 1975.

Notable features of Subaru automobiles include four-wheel independent suspension, a horizontally-opposed flat four watercooled engine, front-wheel drive, and a parking brake operating on the front wheels.

Year	Model (displacement)	Body Style	Vehicle Identification Number Code
1972	1300 G (1300)	Sedan	A15L
		Station Wagon	A44L
1972	1300 GL	Sedan and Coupe	A23L
	1300 DL	Station Wagon	A63L
1973-75	1400 GL	Sedan, Coupe, Hardtop	A22L
	1400 DL	Station Wagon	A62L
1975	4 wheel drive	Station Wagon	A64L
1976	1400, 1600 DL	Sedan, Coupe (M.T.)	A22L
	1400, 1600 DL	Sedan (A.T.)	A26L
	1400, 1600 DL	Station Wagon (M.T.)	A62L
	1400, 1600 DL	Station Wagon (A.T.)	A66L
	1400, 1600 GF	Hardtop (M.T.)	A22L
	1400, 1600 GF	Hardtop (A.T.)	A26L
	4 wheel drive	Station Wagon	A64L
1977	1600 DL	Sedan, Coupe	A26L
	1600 DL	Station Wagon	A66L
	1600 GF	Hardtop	A26L
	4WD	Station Wagon	A67L

MODEL IDENTIFICATION

DL Sedan

1300 G Sedan

DL Station Wagon

GL Coupe

1977 Subaru

SERIAL NUMBER IDENTIFICATION

The Vehicle Identification Number is stamped on a tab located on the top of the dashboard on the driver's side, visible through the windshield. The Vehicle Identification Plate is on the bulkhead in the engine compartment. The engine number is stamped on the crankcase, behind the distributor. The 1300 cc engine code is EA62. The engine code of the 1400 engine is EA63 and the 1600 cc engine code is EA71.

GENERAL ENGINE SPECIFICATIONS

Year	Type	Displacement Cu. In. (cc.)	Carburetor	Horsepower @ rpm (SAE)	Torque @ rpm (SAE)	Bore and Stroke (in.)	Comp. Ratio	Normal Oil Pressure (psi)
1972	4 cylinder horizontally opposed	77.3 (1,267)	2 bbl	61 @ 5,600	65 @ 4,000	3.23 x 2.36	9.0:1	36-57
1973-74	4 cylinder horizontally opposed	83.2 (1,361)	2 bbl	61 @ 5,600	69 @ 3,600	3.35 x 2.36	9.0:1	36-57
1975	4 cylinder horizontally opposed	83.2 (1,361)	2 bbl	58 @ 5,200	68 @ 2,400	3.35 x 2.36	9.0:1	36-57
1976	4 cylinder horizontally opposed	83.2 (1,361)	2 bbl.	58 @ 5,200	68 @ 2,400	3.35 x 2.36	8.5:1	36-57
	4 cylinder horizontally opposed	97 (1,600)	2 bbl.	67 @ 5,200	81 @ 2,400	3.62 x 2.36	8.5:1	36-57
1977	4 cylinder horizontally opposed	97 (1,600)	2 bbl.	67 @ 5,200	81 @ 2,400	3.62 x 2.36	8.5:1	36-57

TUNE-UP SPECIFICATIONS

Year	Engine Displacement (cc)	SPARK PLUGS		DISTRIBUTOR		Ignition Timing (deg)	Intake Valve Opens (deg)	Cranking Compression Pressure (psi)	IDLE SPEED (rpm)	VALVE CLEARANCE (in)	
		Type	Gap (in.)	Point Dwell (deg)	Point Gap (in.)					In	Ex
1972	1300	BP-6ES	0.032	49-55	0.020	6B @ 800	24B	178	800	0.011-0.013	0.011-0.013
1973-74	1400	BP-6ES	0.032	49-55	0.020	6B @ 800	24B	178	800	0.011-0.013	0.011-0.013
1975	1400	BP-6ES	0.030	49-55	0.020	8B @ 800M, 8B @ 900A	24B	178	①	0.012	0.014
1976	1400	BP-6ES	0.032	49-55	0.018	8B @ 900	24B	156	①	0.011	0.015
	1600	BP-6ES	0.032	49-55	0.018	8B @ 900	24B	156	①	0.011	0.015
1977	1600	BP-6ES	0.032	49-55	0.018	8B @ 850②	24B	156	①	0.010	0.014

B   Before Top Dead Center
TDC Top Dead Center
M—Manual, A—Automatic
NOTE: The underhood specifications sticker often reflects tune-up specification changes made in production. Sticker figures must be used if they disagree with those in this chart.

① See Engine Compartment Sticker
② Calif. 900

Subaru

FIRING ORDER

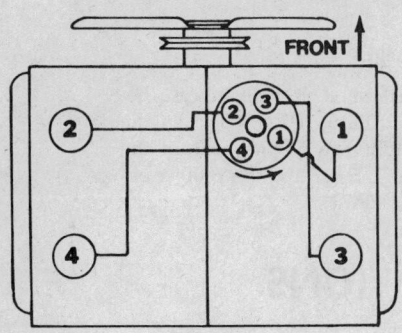

Firing order is 1-3-2-4

TORQUE SEQUENCE

Cylinder head 1972-75

Cylinder head 1976-77

CAPACITIES

Year	Model	Engine Crankcase (qts) with filter	Engine Crankcase (qts) without filter	Transaxle (pts)	Automatic Transmission (pts)	Fuel Tank (gals)	Cooling System (qts)
1972	1300 G	3.4	3.2	5.3	—	11.9 car, 9.5 wagon	6
1972	1300 GL, DL	3.4	3.2	5.4	—	13.2 car, 9.5 wagon	6.5
1973	1400 GL, DL	3.5	3.2	5.4	—	13.2 car, 9.5 wagon	6.5
1974-75	1400 GL, DL	3.5	3.2	5.4①②	11.8-12.7	13.2 car, 11.8 wagon	6.5
1976-77	1400, 1600	3.8	3.5	5.4①②	11.8-12.7	13.2 car, 11.9 wagon	6.5

① 1.7 to 2.5 with automatic transmission
② 4 WD rear differential—1.7 pts.

CRANKSHAFT AND CONNECTING ROD SPECIFICATIONS

All measurements are given in inches

Year	Engine	CRANKSHAFT Main Brg. Journal Dia.	CRANKSHAFT Main Brg. Oil Clearance	CRANKSHAFT Shaft End-Play	CRANKSHAFT Thrust On No.	CONNECTING ROD Journal Diameter	CONNECTING ROD Oil Clearance	CONNECTING ROD Side Clearance
1972	1300 (in 1300 G)	1.9665-1.9669	0.001-0.002	0.002-0.005	2	1.8900-1.8960	0.001-0.003	0.004-0.007
1972	1300 (in DL, GL)	1.9668-1.9692	0.001-0.002	0.002-0.005	2	1.8912-1.8918	0.001-0.003	0.003-0.012
1973	1400	1.9688-1.9692	0.001-0.002	0.002-0.005	2	1.8912-1.8918	0.001-0.003	0.003-0.012
1974-75	1400	1.9688-1.9692	0.001-0.002	0.002-0.005	2	1.8898-1.8905	0.001-0.003	0.003-0.012
1976	1400, 1600	1.9667-①1.9673	0.0004-②0.0020	0.002-0.005	2	1.8898-1.8905	0.0012-0.0029	0.0028-0.0130
1977	1600	1.9667-①1.9673	0.0004-③0.0016	0.002-0.005	2	1.8898-1.8905	0.0008-0.0025	0.0028-0.0130

① Center—1.9673-1.9677   ② Center—0-0.0014   ③ Center—0-0.008

VALVE SPECIFICATIONS

| Year | Engine | Seat Angle (deg) | Face Angle (deg) | Spring Test Pressure (lbs @ in.) | | STEM TO GUIDE CLEARANCE (in.) | | STEM DIAMETER | |
				Inner	Outer	Intake	Exhaust	Intake	Exhaust
1972 (GL, DL)	1300	45	45	40-47 @ 1.85	101-116 @ 1.91	0.001-0.002	0.002-0.003	0.3134-0.3140	0.3128-0.3134
1972 (G)	1300	45	45	40-47 @ 1.01	91-105 @ 1.16	0.001-0.002	0.002-0.003	0.3130-0.3136	0.3124-0.3130
1973-75	1400	45	45	40-47 @ 1.01	91-105 @ 1.16	0.001-0.003	0.002-0.003	0.3130-0.3136	0.3124-0.3130
1976-77	1400, 1600	45	45	39-45 @ 1.16	88-101 @ 1.25	0.001-0.003	0.002-0.003	0.3130-0.3136	0.3124-0.3130

PISTON AND RING SPECIFICATIONS
All measurements in inches

| Year | Engine | Piston Clearance | RING GAP | | | RING SIDE CLEARANCE | | |
			Top Compression	Bottom Compression	Oil Control	Top Compression	Bottom Compression	Oil Control
1972	1300 (in 1300 G)	0.001-0.002	0.008-0.020	0.008-0.020	0.012-0.035	0.001-0.003	0.001-0.003	None
1972	1300 (in GL, DL)	0.001-0.003	0.008-0.020	0.008-0.020	0.012-0.035	0.001-0.003	0.001-0.003	None
1973	1400	0.001-0.002	0.008-0.020	0.008-0.020	0.012-0.035	0.001-0.003	0.001-0.003	None
1974-77	1400, 1600	0.001-0.002	0.012-0.020	0.012-0.020	0.012-0.035	0.001-0.003	0.001-0.003	None

TORQUE SPECIFICATIONS
All readings in ft lbs

| Year | Engine | Cylinder Head Bolts | Rod Bearing Bolts | Crankcase Halves | Crankshaft Pulley Bolt | Flywheel To Crankshaft Bolt | MANIFOLD | |
							Intake	Exhaust
1972	1300	37-43①	35-38	11 mm bolts 15-29 10 mm nuts 27-31 8 mm nuts 3-4 6 mm nuts 3-4	39-42	30-33	13-16	7-9
1973	1400	37-43①	29-32①	11 mm bolts 15-29 10 mm nuts 27-31 8 mm nuts 17-19 6 mm nuts 3-4	39-42	30-33	13-16	7-9
1974-77	14,00 1600	37-43①	29-31① ②	10 mmbolts 29-35 8 mm bolts 17-19 6 mm bolts 3-4	39-42	30-33	13-16	12-15

① Nuts and studs
② 1976-77—36

985

BATTERY AND STARTER SPECIFICATIONS

All cars use 12 volt, negative ground electrical systems

| Year | Model | Battery Amp Hour Capacity | Lock Test | | | Starter No Load Test | | | Brush Spring Tension (oz) | Min. Brush Length (in.) |
			Amps	Volts	Torque (ft/lbs)	Amps	Volts	RPM		
1972	1300G	35	470	7.7	9.4	50	11	5,000	35-54	0.41
1972-74	GL, DL	50	470	7.7	9.4	50	11	5,000	35-54	0.47
1975	All	60	470	7.7	9.4	50	11	5,000	35-54	0.47
1976-77	All	60	470①	7.7②	9.4③	50④	11	5,000	35-54	0.47

— Not Available
① 600 w/Auto. Trans.
② 7 Volts w/Auto. Trans.
③ 13 w/Auto. Trans.
④ 60 Amps w/Auto. Trans.

ALTERNATOR AND REGULATOR SPECIFICATIONS

| YEAR | ALTERNATOR | | | REGULATOR | | | | | | | | |
| | | | | Charge Relay | | | | Voltage Regulator | | | |
	Model	Part No.	Output (amps.)	Part No.	Yoke Gap (in.)	Core Gap (in.)	Point Gap (in.)	Volts to Open	Yoke Gap (in.)	Core Gap (in.)	Point Gap (in.)	Volts @ 1,200 rpm
1972	1300 G	LT13059A	30	TL1Z54	0.035	0.032-0.039	0.016-0.020	8-10	0.035	0.024-0.039	0.012-0.016	13.7
1972-73	DL, GL	LT13520	35	TL1Z64	0.035	0.032-0.039	0.016-0.020	8-10	0.035	0.024-0.039	0.012-0.016	14.0
1974	DL, GL	LT13520	35	TL1Z74	0.035	0.032-0.039	0.016-0.020	8-10	0.035	0.024-0.039	0.012-0.016	14.0
1975	All	—	50	TL1Z74	0.035	0.032-0.039	0.016-0.024	8-10	0.035	0.024-0.039	0.012-0.016	14.0
1976	All	—	50	TL1Z90	0.035	0.032-0.039	0.016-0.024	8-10	0.035	0.024-0.039	0.012-0.016	14.0
1977	All	—	50	TL1Z94	0.035	0.032-0.039	0.016-0.024	8-10	0.035	0.024-0.039	0.012-0.016	14.0

BRAKE SPECIFICATIONS

All measurements given are (in.) unless noted

| Model | Lug Nut Torque | Master Cylinder Bore | Brake Disc | | Brake Drum | | | Minimum Lining Thickness | |
			Minimum Thickness	Maximum Run-Out	Diameter	Max. Machine O/S	Max. Wear Limit	Front	Rear
1972-77 Sedan, Sta. Wag.	40-54①	¾"	—	—	9-F, 7.09-R	9.08-F 7.17-R	9.08-F 7.17-R	0.04-P 0.06-S	7.17
1972-77 Coupe	40-54①	¾"	0.33	0.33	7.09	7.17	7.17	0.06	7.17

F—Front
R—Rear
P—Primary
S—Secondary
① 1975-77—58-72

WHEEL ALIGNMENT

Year	Model	CASTER Range (deg)	CASTER Pref. Setting (deg)	CAMBER Range (deg)	CAMBER Pref. Setting (deg)	Toe-in (in.)	Steering Axis Inclination (deg.)	WHEEL PIVOT RATIO (deg) Inner Wheel	WHEEL PIVOT RATIO (deg) Outer Wheel
1972	FF-1, 1300G	1½-2P	2P	1¼P-1¾P	1¾P	0.20	2⅓	36¼	34½
1972	GL, DL	0-1½P	1P	¾P-1¾P	1¼P	0.08-0.32	12½	36	35
1973-74	GL, DL	0-1½P	¾P	—	1½P	0.09-0.32	12½	36	35
1975-77	All	0-1½P	¾P	0-2P	—	0.00	12½	36	35

NOTE: Caster and camber are not adjustable on DL and GL models.

TUNE-UP PROCEDURES

Spark Plugs

1. Using a plug wrench, remove all of the spark plugs.
2. Check them for damage or wear and clean or replace them.
3. Set the gap between the two electrodes, using a spark plug gap gauge.
4. Install the spark plugs in the engine, tightening to 13–17 ft lbs.

Breaker Points and Condenser

It is not necessary to remove the spark plug wires from the top of the distributor cap when removing the cap from the top of the distributor. After removing the cap, pry open the points with a screwdriver. Inspect the condition of the points. If they are excessively pitted or worn they must be replaced.

1. To replace the points, remove the hold down screws, the ground lead and the condenser lead.
2. Lift out the point assembly and insert the new assembly.
NOTE: *Always replace the condenser when replacing the points.*
3. Install the hold down screws and the leads in their proper positions. Do not tighten the attaching screws, just leave them snug so the point gap can be adjusted.
4. Adjust the gap by placing the proper size feeler gauge between the contacts and turning the adjusting eccentric with a screwdriver.
5. The breaker point arm must be on the high point of the cam lobe. Turn the eccentric screw until there is a slight drag when the gauge is drawn through the gap.
6. Lubricate the cam surface with cam lube.

Checking the breaker point gap

7. Replace the distributor cap, making sure that the spark plug wires are installed tightly in the top of the cap.

Dwell Angle

1. Hook-up a dwell meter according to the manufacturer's instructions. Start the engine and read the dwell on the meter. If the dwell is correct, then shut off the engine and remove the dwell meter.
2. If the dwell must be adjusted, shut off the engine, remove the distributor cap and adjust the point gap.
3. Open the points to decrease the dwell, close them to increase the dwell.
4. Replace the cap and start the engine. Check the dwell. If it is correct, shut off the engine and remove the dwell meter. If the dwell is not correct, repeat the above steps.

Ignition Timing

The ignition timing marks are located on the edge of the flywheel, graduated in 2° increments from 0° to 16°. The marks are visible through a port in the flywheel housing, just behind the dipstick. There is usually a plastic cap in the opening. Set the timing with the engine at normal operating temperature.

1. After cleaning the timing marks, hook a timing light to the positive battery terminal and the number one spark plug.

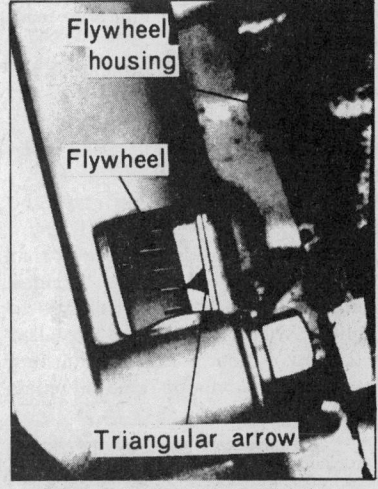

Ignition timing marks

Disconnect and plug the distributor vacuum retard line.

2. Start the engine and aim the timing light at the timing marks on the flywheel.
3. Adjust the ignition timing by loosening the bolt on the retaining plate, and rotating the distributor clockwise to advance the timing or counterclockwise to retard the timing. There is a small bolt and scale on the distributor for minor adjustments on 1972–73 models.

Valve Lash

1. Before adjusting the valves, make sure that the cylinder head bolts are torqued to the proper specifications. The adjusting sequence for the valves is the firing order which is 1–3–2–4.
2. Position No. 1 piston at TDC of the compression stroke, and adjust the valves for that cylinder. The 0° mark on the flywheel should align with the timing pointer and the distributor rotor should point to the No. 1 spark plug wire location. The valves are adjusted with the engine cold. Use a feeler gauge between the rocker arm and the valve stem.
3. Adjust the gap by loosening the

locknut and turning the adjusting bolt.

4. When the proper gap is reached, tighten the adjusting locknut and the adjusting bolt.

5. Turn the engine 180° (indicated on the flywheel) in the normal direction of rotation for each cylinder's valves thereafter. 180° rotation at the flywheel corresponds to 90° at the distributor rotor. This places the next cylinder to be adjusted at TDC.

Carburetor

Idle Speed and Mixture Adjustment

The idle adjustment is made when the engine is at operating temperature.

1. Disconnect the vacuum hose leading to the distributor.

2. Adjust the ignition timing to the proper specification.

3. By turning the throttle adjusting screw, adjust the engine idle speed to the proper specification.

4. Replace the vacuum hose onto the distributor.

5. Adjust the idle mixture screw so that the highest RPM reading is obtained after the throttle has been adjusted to 850 RPM. There is a limiter cap installed on the top of the idle mixture adjusting screw that should not be removed unless

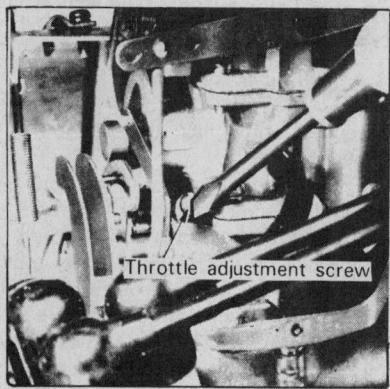

Throttle adjustment

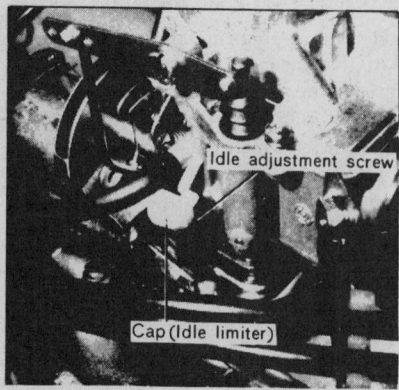

Idle mixture adjustment

the proper carbon monoxide reading on a CO meter cannot be obtained.

6. After adjusting the idle mixture to the best idle speed or the proper CO reading on a CO meter, (replace the limiter cap) adjust the throttle adjustment screw to the proper idle speed. See "Fuel System" for further adjustments.

ENGINE ELECTRICAL

Distributor

Removal and Installation

1. Disconnect the distributor primary wire from the coil, and the vacuum hose from the distributor.

2. Remove the distributor cap, and mark the position of the rotor in relation to the distributor body. On 1970–73 models, note the position of the octane selector pointer on the octane selector scale.

3. Remove the bolt which retains the distributor at the octane selector and remove the distributor, retainer plate, and the octane selector pointer.

4. If the engine has not been disturbed since removal of the distributor, align the marks on the distributor rotor and body, and insert the distributor so that the octane selector is positioned as it was prior to removal.

5. Install the distributor cap, connect the primary wire at the coil, and check the ignition timing.

6. If the engine was disturbed while the distributor was removed, position the No. 1 cylinder on its compression stroke, and align the housing with the TDC (0°) mark on the flywheel.

7. Insert the distributor so that the rotor points toward the number one tower

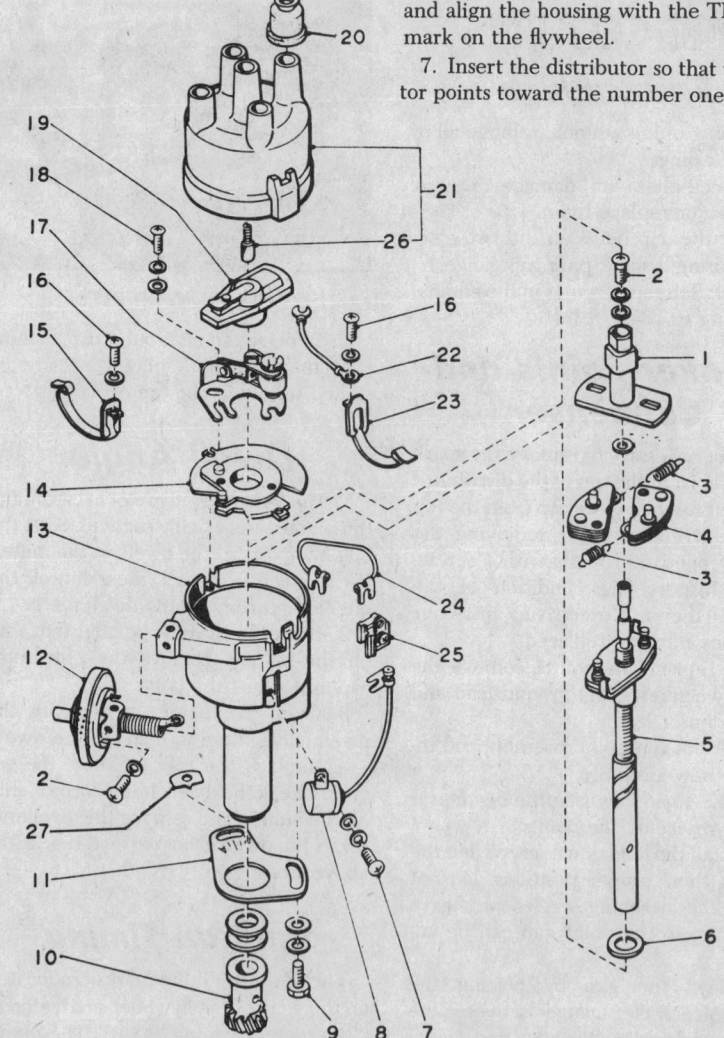

Exploded view of the distributor

1. Cam	8. Condenser	15. Clamp	21. Cap
2. Screw	9. Bolt	16. Screw	22. Ground wire
3. Governor spring	10. Gear	17. Breaker points	23. Clamp
4. Governor weight	11. Plate	18. Breaker point set	24. Lead wire
5. Shaft	12. Vacuum unit	screw	25. Terminal
6. Washer	13. Housing	19. Rotor	26. Carbon brush
7. Screw	14. Breaker plate	20. Boot	27. Pointer

in the distributor cap, and the points are just beginning to open.

8. Center the octane selector between A and R, and tighten the retaining bolt.

9. Install the distributor cap, connect the primary wire, and check the ignition timing.

Alternator

Alternator Precautions

1. Pay particular attention to the polarity connections of the battery when connecting the battery cables. Make sure that you connect the correct cable to the corresponding terminal.

2. If a jumper battery is used to start the vehicle, make sure that the cables leading from the jumper battery are matched with the terminals on the battery being jumped, positive to positive and negative to negative.

3. When testing or adjusting the alternator, install a condensor between the alternator output terminal and the ground. This is to prevent the diode from becoming damaged by a spark which occurs due to testing equipment with a defective connection.

4. Do not operate the alternator with the output terminals disconnected. The diode would be damaged by the high voltage generated.

5. When recharging the battery by a quick charge or any other charging apparatus, disconnect the alternator output terminal before hooking up the charging leads.

6. When installing a battery, always connect the grounded terminal first.

7. Never disconnect the battery while the engine is running.

8. Never electric weld on the car without disconnecting the alternator.

9. Never apply any voltage in excess of the battery voltage during testing.

10. Never jump a battery for starting purposes with more than the battery voltage.

Removal and Installation

1. To remove the alternator from the vehicle, first disconnect the negative battery terminal.

1. Nut
2. Spring washer
3. Washer
4. Pulley
5. Fan
6. Washer
7. Spacer
8. Front cover
9. Packing
10. Retainer
11. Ball bearing
12. Bearing retainer
13. Rotor assembly
14. Ball bearing
15. Stator assembly
16. Diode
17. Insulator
18. Cover
19. Through bolt
20. Brush (E)
21. Brush holder
22. Brush (F)
23. Brush cover
24. Insulator tube
25. Lead wire
26. Clip
27. Thru-bolt
28. Rear cover
29. Terminal bolt set

Exploded view of the alternator

2. Disconnect the wiring to the alternator.

3. Remove the alternator attaching bolts and nuts.

4. Remove the drive belt and take out the alternator.

5. Install in the reverse order of removal.

Belt Tension Adjustment

1. To adjust the belt tension, first loosen the adjusting bolt on the right of the alternator (looking from the rear).

2. Lift up on the alternator to increase the tension on the belt. When it takes 22 lbs of force to move the belt ½ in., the tension adjustment is correct.

3. Tighten the adjusting bolt so that the alternator will not move in the adjusting bracket.

Regulator

Removal and Installation

1. Disconnect the negative battery cable from the battery.

2. Disconnect the wires leading to the regulator.

3. Remove the screws which attach the regulator to the fender well.

4. Install the regulator in the reverse order of removal.

Core Gap Adjustment

Loosen the screw securing the contact set to the yoke and adjust the core gap.

Point Gap Adjustment

Loosen the screw securing the upper contact and adjust to the proper specifications by shifting the upper contact up and down.

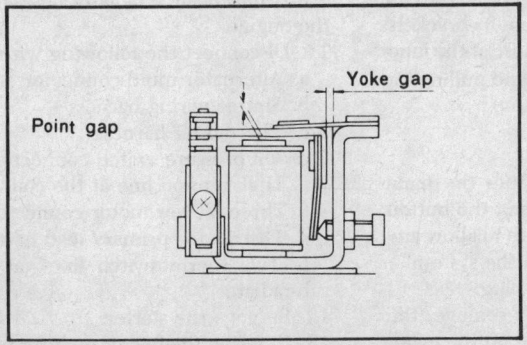

Adjusting points for the voltage

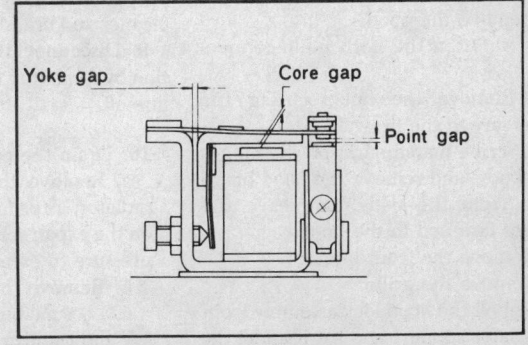

Adjusting points for the charge relay

Starter

Removal and Installation

1. Disconnect the battery ground terminal.

2. Disconnect the lead wires to the starter.

3. Remove the starter from the engine after removing the two nuts which attach the starter to the flywheel housing.

4. When reinstalling the starter, make sure that the mating surfaces of the flywheel housing and the starter fit flush against each other.

5. Install the starter in the reverse order of removal.

Starter Drive Replacement

1. Remove the starter from the engine. Remove the two thru-bolts that run through the length of the starter housing.

2. Remove the pinion housing from the end of the starter. Using a length of pipe the same diameter as the armature shaft, tap the pinion stop collar down toward the starter drive so that it is off the snap ring. Use a pair of snap ring pliers to remove the snap ring from the armature shaft.

3. Remove the starter drive from the threaded spline, taking care not to damage the threaded spline.

4. To install the starter drive, slip the starter drive onto the armature shaft and install the snap ring into position. Drive the pinion stop collar down onto the snap ring with the length of pipe. Assemble and install the starter in the reverse order of disassembly and removal.

ENGINE MECHANICAL

Engine Removal and Installation

1300 G

The engine and transaxle must be removed as an assembly.

1. Disconnect the battery cables, ground (−) first.

2. Remove the spare tire.

3. Remove the hood:

   a. Unfasten the horn multi-connector.

   b. Remove the nut securing the hood stay to the firewall.

   c. Scribe matchmarks on the hinges and body, and remove the hood hinge bolts from the body, but leave the hinges fastened to the hood.

4. Remove the front bumper.

5. Remove the grille.

6. Unbolt the hood lock assembly from the radiator support and set it aside.

7. Remove the front roll pan.

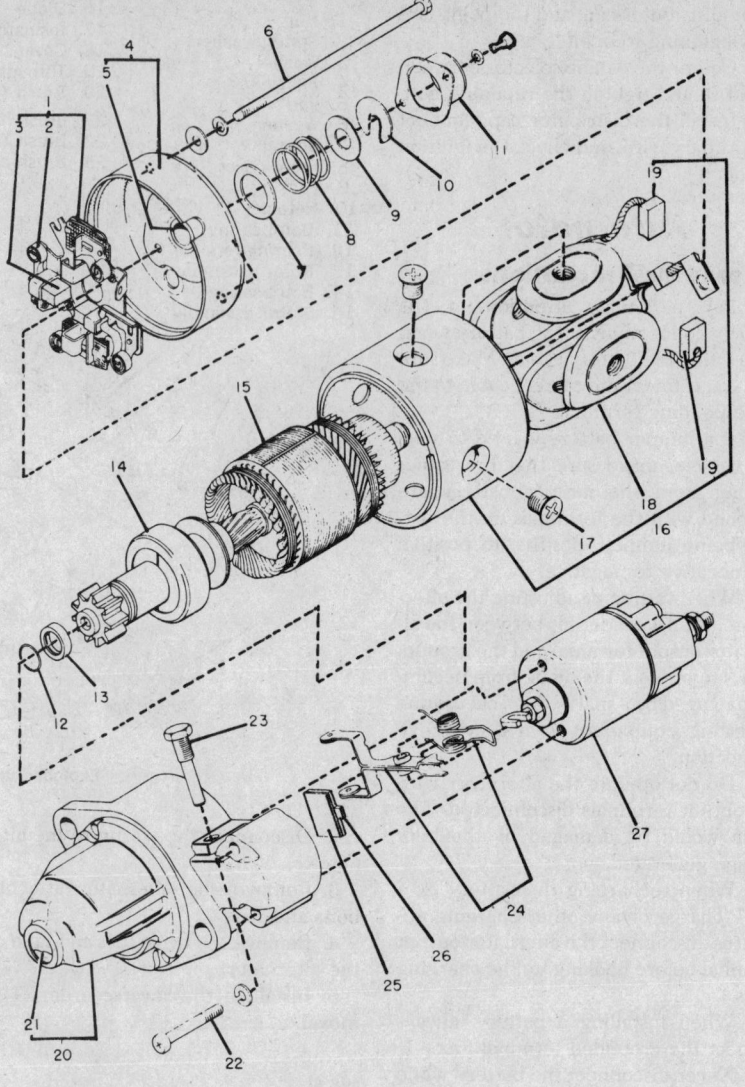

An exploded view of the starter

1. Brush holder plate assembly
2. Spring type brush holder
3. Brush
4. Commutator frame assembly
5. Bushing
6. Thru-bolt
7. Rubber parts
8. Spring
9. Washer
10. Lock plate
11. End frame cap
12. Snap ring
13. Pinion stop collar
14. Over running clutch assembly
15. Armature assembly
16. Yoke assembly
17. Pole core screw
18. Field coil assembly
19. Brush
20. Housing assembly
21. Housing bushing
22. Screw
23. Lever set bolt
24. Drive lever assembly
25. Plate
26. Rubber parts
27. Magnet switch assembly

8. Remove the hoses from the air cleaner and unfasten it from its brackets.

9. Disconnect the fuel hose at the junction by removing the clip and pulling the line off.

10. Drain the coolant:

   a. Remove the cap from the main radiator, after first pushing the button on the expansion tank cap to allow any pressure to escape from the system.

   b. Remove the drain plug.

   c. Loosen, but do not remove, the left and right drain plugs on the cylinder head.

d. Unfasten all 3 radiator hoses from the engine.

11. Disconnect the following wiring:

   a. Alternator multi-connector

   b. Starter wiring harness

   c. Thermostat harness

   d. Oil pressure switch connector

   e. High-tension line at the coil

   f. Three blower motor connectors

   g. Distributor primary lead harness

   h. Two thermoswitch lines (at the sub-radiator)

12. Remove the starter.

13. Unfasten the heater duct from the blower housing.

14. Remove the clip which secures the inner and outer control cables, and then detach the cables from the blower housing.

15. Remove the front radiator support with the main radiator, sub-radiator, shroud, blower motor and expansion tank as an assembly:

a. Unfasten the two 8 mm bolts which secure the blower housing.

b. Remove the 4 screws and two bolts which secure the radiator support to the headlamp bracket.

NOTE: *Do not remove the center bolt.*

c. Slowly withdraw the assembly from the front of the car.

16. Remove the hoses and leads from the windshield washer reservoir, and then lift the reservoir out of its bracket.

17. Disconnect both double offset joints (DOJ) in the following manner:

a. Apply the parking brake so that the drums can't turn.

b. Remove the brake drum-to-double offset joint retaining bolts.

c. Gently lower the joint and the axle shaft.

d. Repeat for the other side.

18. Disconnect the brake lines from both sides.

19. Disconnect the following cable and linkages:

a. Loosen, but don't remove, the screw on the carburetor throttle lever. Detach the end of the cable, and pull the cable out.

b. Remove the nut which secures the choke cable from its lever and loosen the bracket retaining nut.

c. Disconnect the speedometer cable from the speedometer head (from behind the instrument cluster) and pull it out, working from the engine compartment.

d. Disconnect the gear selector rod from inside the car.

e. Disconnect the left and right parking brake cables from the turnbuckles inside the car.

f. Remove the clutch torque rod (ball stud) bolts on the side of the crossmember.

20. Remove the bolts from the manifold pipe flanges and separate the downpipes from the left and right manifolds. Unfasten the brackets which secure the exhaust pipe to the floor pan and remove the bolts which secure the exhaust pipe to the muffler hanger. Remove the exhaust pipe.

21. Disconnect the engine mount in the following order:

a. Remove the securing nut from the shaft while holding the adjustment nut.

b. Withdraw the washer, cushion, pipe and tube.

c. Unscrew the two retaining bolts and remove the bracket.

22. Remove the left and right bolts from the rear support cushion which is located on the transaxle housing. Leave the cushion attached to the transaxle case.

23. Remove the nut, spring washer, and washer from the front support cushion. Leave the cushion attached to the engine.

24. On station wagons, remove the horizontal damper by unfastening the front nut and pulling the shaft rearward.

25. Attach a chain hoist to the front and rear engine lifting hooks (hangers).

26. Hoist the engine/transaxle assembly straight up, high enough so that the brake drums clear the crossmember. Then carefully move the engine forward so that the exhaust manifolds clear the crossmember and torsion bars.

27. Support the engine and transaxle in a suitable workstand.

Engine/transaxle installation is the reverse of removal. However, be sure to observe the following:

1. Tighten the engine mounts to the following specifications:

Engine mount bolts—18–20 ft lbs
Front cushion bolts—18–25 ft lbs
Rear cushion bolts (3)—18–25 ft lbs
Rear cushion side bolt—22–29 ft lbs

2. When installing the engine mount, temporarily raise the adjusting nut so that it is positioned about 1/5 in. below the nut above it. After installing the body bracket, lower the adjusting nut until the middle cushion can be turned by hand, then hold the adjusting nut so that it cannot be turned, while tightening the bottom nut.

3. On station wagons, when installing the horizontal damper, be sure that the larger of the two rubber cushions is compressed to 0.55 in.

4. Prior to installing the double offset joints, install the parking brake cable and apply the parking brake.

DL, GL, GF, 4WD

NOTE: *On these models, the engine can be removed separately from the transaxle.*

1. Open the hood as far as possible and secure it with the stay.

2. Disconnect the ground cable from the negative (−) battery terminal.

3. Unbolt the ground cable from the intake manifold.

4. On 1972–77 models, remove the spare tire.

5. Remove the emission control system hoses from the air cleaner. Unfasten the air cleaner brackets, remove the wing nut, and lift the air cleaner assembly off the carburetor.

6. Disconnect the fuel hoses at the union, by removing the clip and pulling the hose off.

7. Drain the coolant and disconnect the radiator hoses:

a. Loosen the drain plug on the radiator and turn it so that its slot faces downward.

b. Disconnect both of the hoses at the radiator, leaving them connected to the engine.

c. Disconnect the heater hoses from the side of the engine.

8. Disconnect the following electrical wiring:

a. Alternator multi-connector

b. Oil pressure sender connection

c. Three engine cooling fan connectors

d. Temperature switch harness

e. Primary distributor lead

f. Secondary ignition leads (ignition side)

g. Starter wiring harness

h. Anti-dieseling solenoid lead

i. Automatic choke lead (1974)

j. EGR vacuum solenoid (1974—Calif.)

k. EGR coolant temperature switch (1974—Calif.)

l. Disconnect the 4WD selector switch harness (4WD only).

9. Loosen the two radiator securing bolts, remove the ground lead from the upper side of the radiator, and lift the radiator out.

a. On 4WD vehicles, disconnect the engine fan from the pulley.

10. Remove the horizontal engine damper rod:

a. Unfasten the front nut from the damper.

b. Remove the nut on the body bracket and remove the damper.

c. Pull the damper rearward away from the engine lifting hook.

11. Remove the starter.

12. Disconnect the following cables and linkages:

a. Loosen, but don't remove the screw in the carburetor throttle lever. Unfasten the outer end of the accelerator cable and pull it out.

b. On 1972–73 models, loosen the nut which secures the cable to the manual choke lever, loosen the retaining bracket nut, and detach the choke cable from the carburetor.

c. Unfasten the return spring from the clutch release lever and the intake manifold.

d. Disconnect the speedometer cable.

e. Drain the automatic transmission fluid.

f. Remove the inlet and outlet cooler hoses connected to the transmission, from the pipes attached on the body (auto. trans only).

13. Unfasten the two upper nuts which retain the clutch housing to the engine. Working from the engine compartment (top) side, remove the lower

clutch housing-to-engine nuts.

14. Unfasten the exhaust pipe-to-manifold flange securing nuts and separate the exhaust pipe from the manifold. Repeat for the other side.

15. Remove the 4 bolts which attach the front mount to the engine. Leave the cushion mounted to the crossmember.

16. Place a jack under the transaxle housing with a block of wood on the lifting pad. Raise the jack to support the transaxle.

17. Install a hoist on the front and rear engine lifting hooks. 1974 models don't have lifting hooks.

18. Raise the engine slightly while keeping it level, and move it forward, off the transaxle input shaft.

CAUTION: *Do not raise the engine more than 1 in. If it is raised more than this, too much force is applied to the driveshaft double offset joints.*

19. Remove the engine.

Engine installation is the reverse of removal. However, be sure to observe the following:

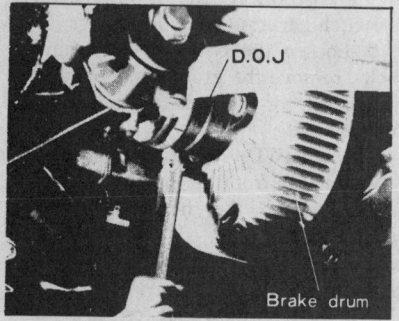

Unbolting the double offset joint on a model with inboard brakes.

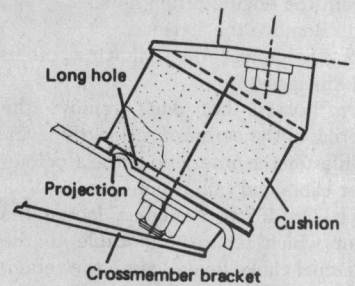

Engine mount alignment

1. Use the following torque specifications, when installing the engine:
Horizontal damper—5–8 ft lbs
Engine-to-clutch housing—30–40 ft lbs
Exhaust flange-to-pipe—12–14 ft lbs
Engine mount—15–22 ft lbs
Radiator mounts—6–10 ft lbs

2. Use care not to damage the input shaft splines or the clutch spring while lowering the engine in place.

3. Adjust the horizontal engine damper rod:
  a. Tighten the body bracket nut.
  b. Turn the front nut, until the clear-

ance between the front washer and rubber cushion is zero.
  c. Insert the bushing and tighten the front nut.

Cylinder Head
Removal and Installation

The engine must be removed from the vehicle to remove the cylinder heads. Although it is physically possible (on some models) to remove the cylinder heads with the engine installed, head gasket failure will result upon installation, due to misalignment of the cylinders. The cylinder heads should be removed with the engine cold to prevent warpage.

1. Remove the engine from the vehicle and mount it on a work stand.

2. Unbolt and remove the intake and exhaust manifolds.

3. Remove the spark plugs.

4. Disconnect the crankcase ventilation hose(s) and remove the valve covers.

5. Loosen the alternator adjusting bolts, and unbolt the alternator bracket from the cylinder head.

6. Remove the air injection distributor tubes from the cylinder heads by unscrewing the fittings.

7. Gradually loosen the head bolts or nuts in the reverse of the tightening sequence, and remove the cylinder heads and pushrods.

8. Install the heads in the reverse order of removal.

The cylinder heads must be installed with the cylinders vertical, to avoid misalignment, and to permit the head gasket to crush evenly around the cylinder. Prior to installation of the heads, cylinder liner projection must be checked. It must be 0.003–0.004 in. Liner projection is adjusted by varying the size of the liner gaskets.

NOTE: *Liner projection must be checked whenever a head gasket has failed.*

Torque in the specified sequence, in stages, using a spacer in place of the rocker shaft support. After the head is torqued to specifications, remove the rocker shaft bolts (or nuts) and the spacers, and install the rocker shafts.

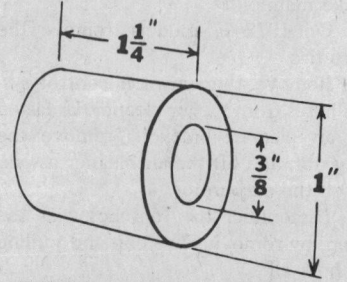

Cylinder head installation spacer

Service, 4WD

Using a straight edge, check the cylinder heads for warpage. Should warpage exceed 0.002 in., the cylinder head must be resurfaced (grinding limit 0.020 in. for 1300 G and 0.0157 in. for 1400, 1600.) Should the valve sink exceed approximately 0.040 in., the seats must be replaced. The valve guides are pressed in, and should be replaced if clearance exceeds specifications. On the 1300, 1400 and 1600, the intake valve guide should extend 0.71 and the exhaust 0.71 in. from the spring seat.

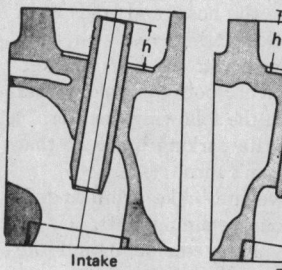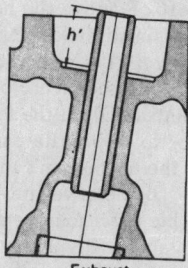

Valve guide installed height

Rocker Shafts

With the engine removed from the vehicle, remove the rocker arm covers and gaskets from the cylinder heads. Unscrew the nuts which hold the rocker arm assemblies to the cylinder heads and lift the rocker arm assemblies from the engine. Identify the push rods so they can be replaced in their original positions. Install in the reverse order of removal.

Intake Manifold
Removal and Installation
1972–74

1. On 1972–73 models, remove the spare tire from the engine compartment.

2. Disconnect the emission control system hoses, remove the mounting bracket screws and remove the air cleaner assembly.

3. Drain the cooling system and detach all of the water hoses from the thermostat housing.

4. Unfasten the thermoswitch connector.

5. On models with a distributor vacuum control valve, disconnect the hoses and leads from it. Disconnect the anti-dieseling solenoid leads, as well.

6. On models which have an air injection system:
  a. Disconnect the lines from the anti-afterburn valve.
  b. Unbolt the air injection manifold mounting brackets from the intake manifold.

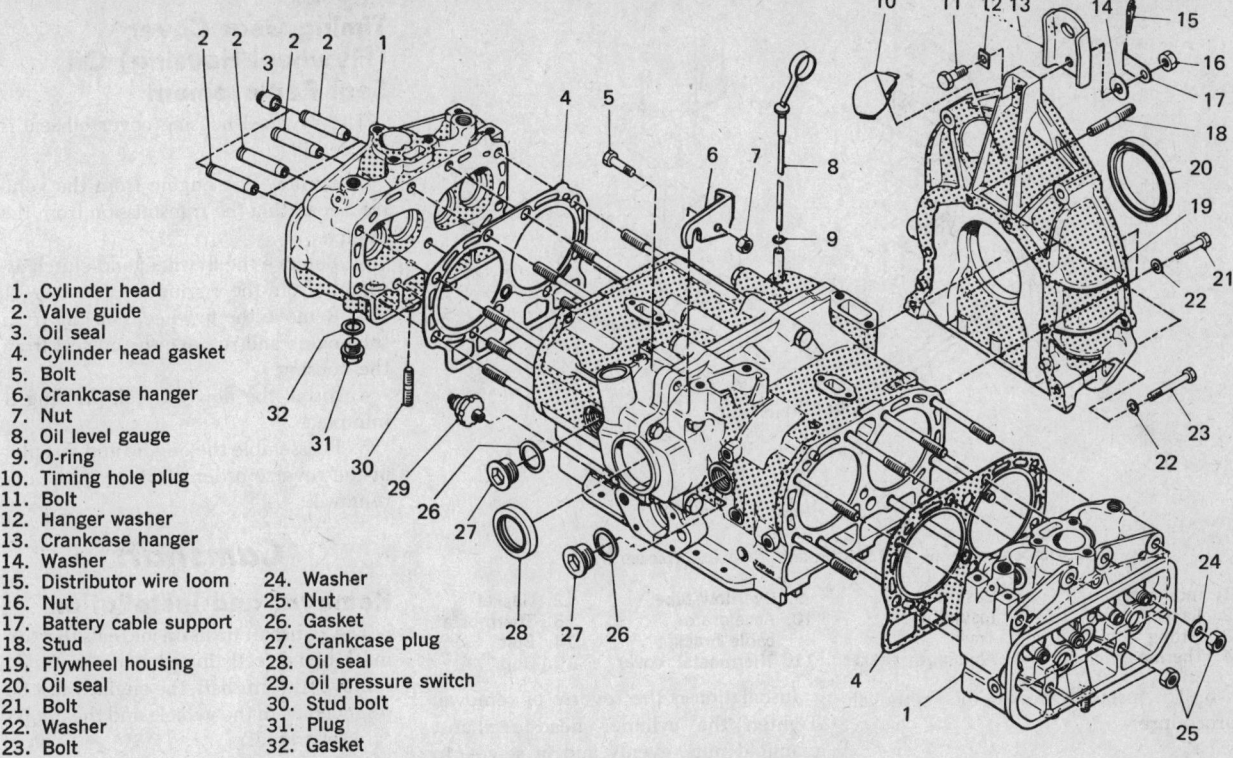

1. Cylinder head
2. Valve guide
3. Oil seal
4. Cylinder head gasket
5. Bolt
6. Crankcase hanger
7. Nut
8. Oil level gauge
9. O-ring
10. Timing hole plug
11. Bolt
12. Hanger washer
13. Crankcase hanger
14. Washer
15. Distributor wire loom
16. Nut
17. Battery cable support
18. Stud
19. Flywheel housing
20. Oil seal
21. Bolt
22. Washer
23. Bolt
24. Washer
25. Nut
26. Gasket
27. Crankcase plug
28. Oil seal
29. Oil pressure switch
30. Stud bolt
31. Plug
32. Gasket

Cylinder heads, flywheel housing (typical)

c. Remove the by-pass valve.

7. On 1974 models, disconnect:

a. Automatic choke-to-voltage regulator wire at the connector.

b. EGR solenoid wiring.

c. The EGR pipe, by removing the nuts which secure it to the intake manifold and the cylinder head.

8. On all models, disconnect the throttle and manual choke cables and their brackets. Disconnect the fuel line from the carburetor.

9. Unbolt the intake manifold from the cylinder heads and remove the manifold assembly. Be careful not to lose any of the gaskets.

Installation is the reverse of removal.

Be sure to use new gaskets. Tighten the bolts evenly, in stages, to the specifications in the "Torque Specifications" chart.

1975

1. Remove the air cleaner assembly.
2. Disconnect the air distributor connector.
3. Disconnect the radiator hose from the thermostat case cover.
4. Disconnect the water by-pass hose, master Vac vacuum hose, clutch return spring and the EGR pipe from the intake manifold (Calif. models).
5. Disconnect the vacuum hose from the solenoid valve.
6. Disconnect the accelerator cable and fuel hose.
7. Remove the wires for the carburetor anti-dieseling valve and automatic choke heater, thermometer and coolant temperature switch.
8. Remove the six bolts and remove the intake manifold.
9. To install reverse the removal procedure.

1976–77

1. Remove the EGR pipe from the manifold.
2. Remove the water by-pass hose from the intake manifold.
3. Disconnect the wiring harness lead from the oil pressure switch.
4. Disengage the harness from the clip on the water pipe.
5. Remove the six bolts and remove the intake manifold.

1. Screw
2. Spring washer
3. Accelerator cable clamp
4. Bolt
5. Spring washer
6. Accelerator cable bracket
7. Washer
8. Thermostat cover
9. Thermostat cover gasket
10. Thermostat
11. Hose clamp
12. Water bypass hose
13. Water bypass connector
14. Gasket
15. Water bypass connector
16. Bolt
17. Bolt
18. Intake manifold gasket
19. Intake manifold
20. Stud
21. Plug
22. Temperature sending unit
23. Carburetor gasket
24. Spring washer
25. Nut

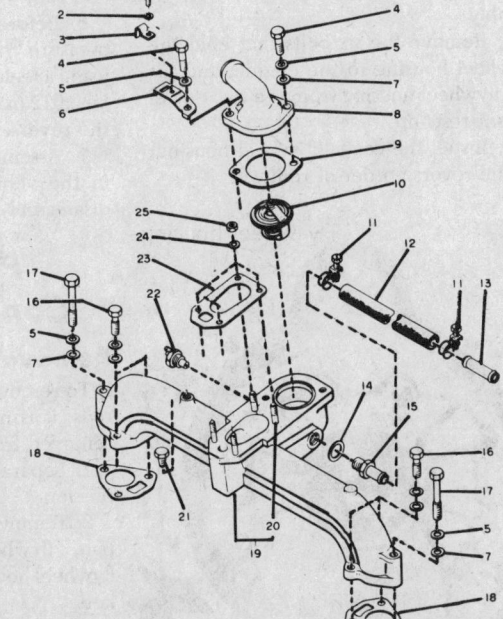

Exploded view of a 1400 intake manifold

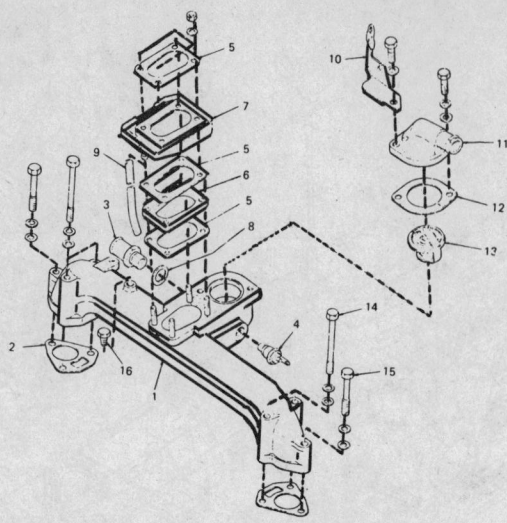

Exploded view of a 1300 intake manifold (Model G).

1. Intake manifold
2. Gasket
3. Fitting
4. Thermoswitch
5. Gasket
6. Insulator
7. Tray
8. Aluminum gasket
9. Overflow tube
10. Accelerator cable bracket
11. Thermostat cover
12. Gasket
13. Thermostat
14. Bolt
15. Bolt

6. To install reverse the removal procedure.

Exhaust Manifolds
Removal and Installation

1300 G

1. Loosen, but do not remove, the brass exhaust manifold-to-cylinder head retaining nuts.

2. Unfasten the exhaust pipe from the manifold flange.

3. Remove the band which secures the exhaust pipe to the left-side of the transaxle.

4. Move the manifold around until the mounting slots permit its removal.

5. Pull the manifold downward, in order to remove it.

6. Repeat for the other side.

Installation is the reverse of removal. Torque the nuts evenly and in stages, to the figure in the "Torque Specifications" chart. Use a new insulator in the exhaust pipe-to-transaxle securing band. Replace any damaged gaskets.

DL, GL, GF, 4WD

1. Separate the exhaust pipe from the exhaust manifold by unfastening the flange nuts.

2. Loosen, but do not remove, the nuts which secure the exhaust manifold to the cylinder head.

3. Then do one of the following, whichever is most convenient:

    a. Loosen the front engine mounting bolt and raise the engine slightly.

    b. Remove the valve cover.

4. Remove the exhaust manifold by lifting it upward, after working it off the mounting studs.

5. Repeat the procedure for the other side.

Installation is the reverse of removal. Tighten the cylinder head-to-exhaust manifold nuts, evenly and in stages, to the figure in the "Torque Specifications" chart. Tighten the exhaust pipe-to-manifold flange nuts to 12–15 ft lbs. Replace any damaged gaskets. Check for exhaust leaks.

Timing Gear Cover
Removal and Installation

The flywheel housing covers the timing gears. In order to remove it, the engine has to be removed from the vehicle.

1. Separate the engine from the transmission.

2. Remove the flywheel and clutch assembly.

3. Remove the six bolts that hold the flywheel housing to the engine, and lift the flywheel housing from the two dowel pins it rests on.

4. Install the cover (flywheel housing) in the reverse order of removal.

Fly wheel housing

The flywheel housing covers the timing gears

Timing Gear Cover (Flywheel Housing) Oil Seal Replacement

The flywheel housing cover oil seal is pressed in.

1. Remove the engine from the vehicle, separating the transmission from the engine.

2. Remove the flywheel and clutch assembly from the engine.

3. Remove the flywheel housing from the engine and remove the oil seal from the housing.

4. Install the new oil seal, pressing it into place.

5. Reassemble the engine and install it in the reverse order of disassembly and removal.

Camshaft
Removal and Installation

The camshaft turns on journals that are machined directly into the crankcase. To remove the camshaft, the engine must be removed from the vehicle and the crankcase separated.

1. Remove the engine from the vehicle, separating the transmission from the engine.

2. Remove the clutch and flywheel assembly.

3. Remove the flywheel housing.

4. Straighten the lockwashers and remove the bolts that hold the camshaft retaining plate to the crankcase. The lockwashers are straightened and the bolts removed through the access holes in the camshaft gear.

5. Remove the intake manifold and separate the two halves of the crankcase and remove the camshaft.

6. Before installing the camshaft, measure the end play of the camshaft, using a feeler gauge. The end-play should be 0.012 in. or less. Install the camshaft in the reverse order of removal.

7. Assemble the engine and reinstall it in the vehicle in the reverse order of disassembly and removal.

Pistons and Connecting Rods
Removal and Installation

To remove the pistons and connecting rods, it is necessary that the engine be removed from the vehicle.

1. Separate the engine and the transmission.

2. Remove the intake manifold, oil pan, flywheel and clutch assembly, flywheel housing, cylinder heads and gaskets.

3. Unscrew and remove the two bolts and lockwashers that hold the camshaft retaining plate in place. The bolts and

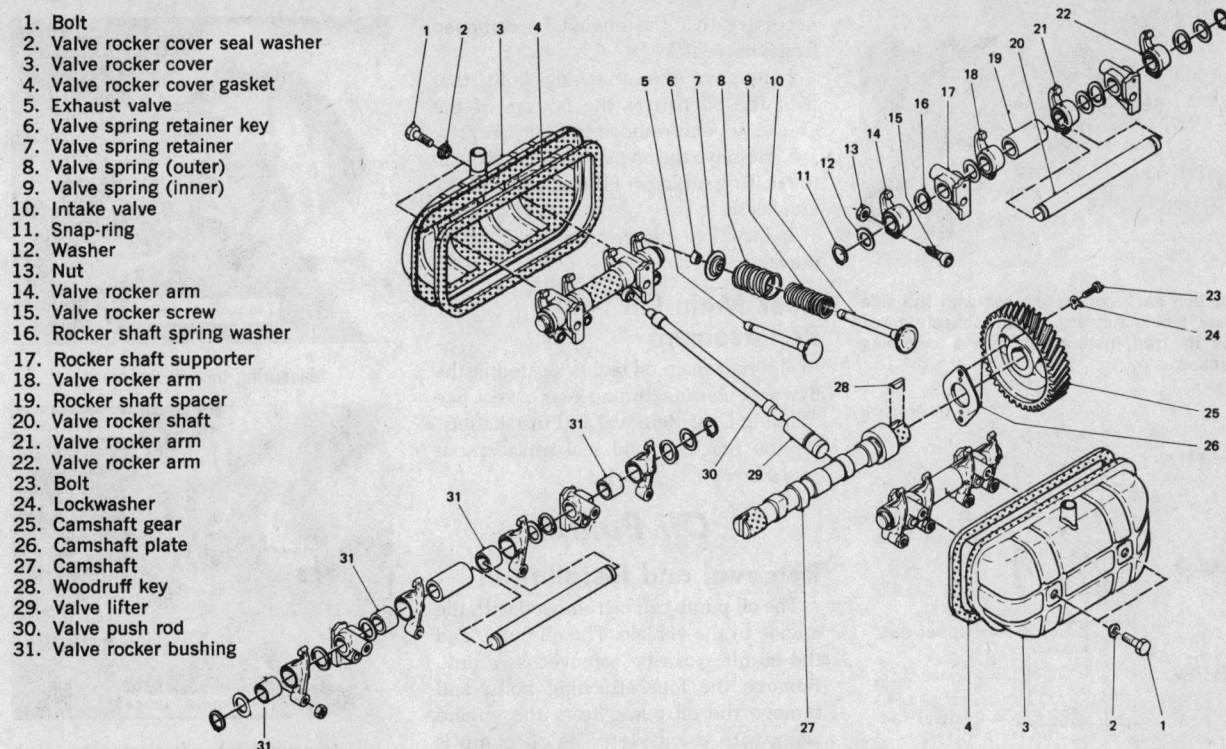

1. Bolt
2. Valve rocker cover seal washer
3. Valve rocker cover
4. Valve rocker cover gasket
5. Exhaust valve
6. Valve spring retainer key
7. Valve spring retainer
8. Valve spring (outer)
9. Valve spring (inner)
10. Intake valve
11. Snap-ring
12. Washer
13. Nut
14. Valve rocker arm
15. Valve rocker screw
16. Rocker shaft spring washer
17. Rocker shaft supporter
18. Valve rocker arm
19. Rocker shaft spacer
20. Valve rocker shaft
21. Valve rocker arm
22. Valve rocker arm
23. Bolt
24. Lockwasher
25. Camshaft gear
26. Camshaft plate
27. Camshaft
28. Woodruff key
29. Valve lifter
30. Valve push rod
31. Valve rocker bushing

Camshaft and rocker arm assembly (typical)

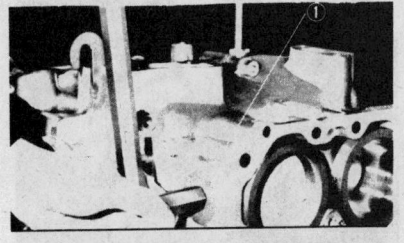

Removing the crankcase access plugs

lockwashers are removed through two access holes in the camshaft gear.

4. Remove the crankcase plug from

1. Bolt
2. Washer
3. Crankshaft pulley
4. Drive belt
5. Distributor drive gear
6. Woodruff key
7. Crankshaft
8. Woodruff key
9. Needle bearing
10. Oil seal
11. Crankshaft gear
12. Flywheel (MT)
13. Starter ring gear
14. Bolt
15. Bolt
16. Drive plate (AT)
17. Connecting rod
18. Nut
19. Connecting rod bolt
20. Connecting rod bearing
21. Piston rings
22. Piston
23. Piston pin
24. Circlip

the crankcase by using an Allen wrench.

5. Remove the cylinder liners by using a cylinder liner puller.

6. Remove the cylinder liner gaskets, keeping the cylinder liners and the gaskets of each cylinder together. The flanges of the liner should be marked so that they can be reinstalled in the correct positions.

7. Remove the circlips that hold the wrist pins in the pistons by inserting the piston circlip pliers through the crankcase plug holes.

8. Remove the wrist pins by inserting the wrist pin remover through the crankcase plug holes. Keep the pistons and the

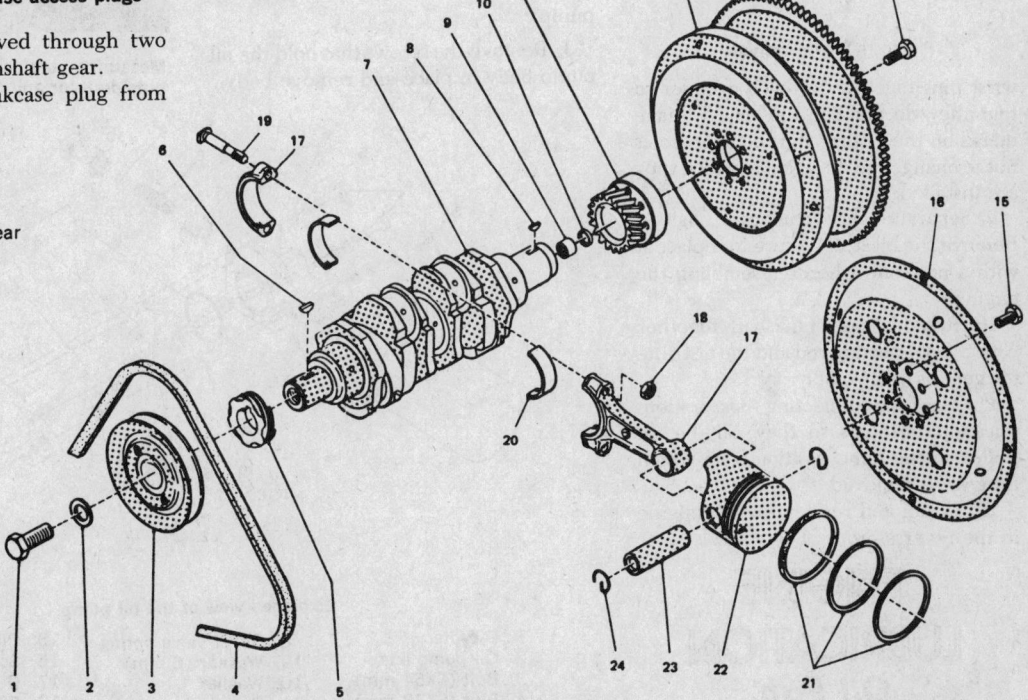

Crankshaft, piston, and connecting rod assembly

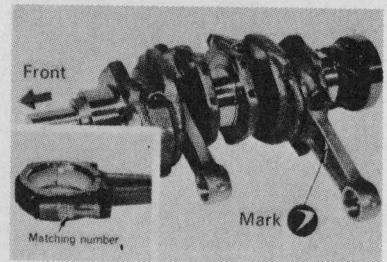

Position each connecting rod with the side mark facing forward. Each connecting rod has its own mating cap with a matching number.

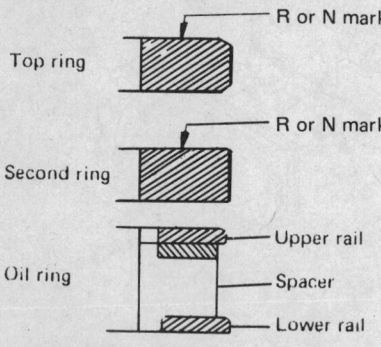

Installation of piston rings. The top and second rings are provided with "R" or "N" mark. Install the rings with the mark facing upward.

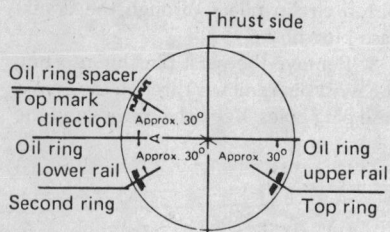

Piston ring gap position

wrist pins together for each cylinder so that they do not become mixed. Make marks on the pistons and the liners so as not to change the direction in which they are installed.

9. Separate the crankcase halves. Remove the oil seal. Be sure to replace it with a new one when reassembling the engine.

10. Remove the crankshaft together with the connecting rod and the distributor gear as an assembly.

11. Mark the connecting rods for identification purposes so they can be installed in the same position from which they were removed.

12. Install and reassemble the engine in the reverse order of removal.

ENGINE LUBRICATION
Oil Pan
Removal and Installation

1. To remove the oil pan, it is not necessary that the engine be removed from the vehicle.

2. Remove the attaching bolts that hold the oil pan to the bottom of the crankcase, and remove the oil pan.

3. Remove the oil pan gasket and clean the mating surfaces of the oil pan and the crankcase.

4. Install in the reverse order of removal.

Rear Main Oil Seal Replacement

The rear main oil seal is located in the flywheel housing (timing gear cover). See "Timing Gear Removal and Installation" for the rear main oil seal replacement procedures.

Oil Pump
Removal and Installation

The oil pump can be removed with the engine in the vehicle. The oil pump and the oil filter can be removed as a unit. Remove the four attaching bolts, and remove the oil pump from the engine along with the gasket. The oil pump is driven directly by the camshaft. The oil pump shaft fits into a slot in the end of the camshaft. When the oil pump is reinstalled, make sure that the oil pump shaft fits into the slot in the end of the camshaft and that the mating surfaces are flush. Install in the reverse order of removal.

Checking Clearances

1. Remove the oil pump from the engine.

2. Remove the oil filter from the oil pump.

3. Remove the screws that hold the oil pump body in place and remove body.

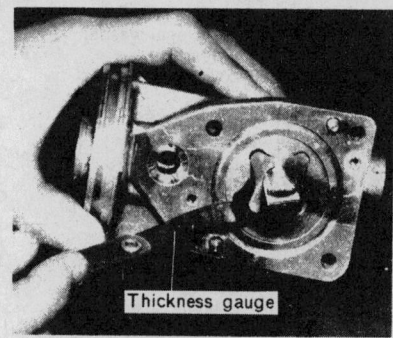

Measuring the tip clearance

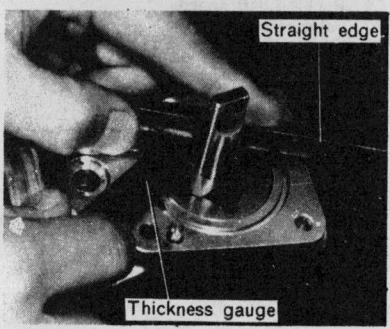

Measuring the side clearance

Measuring the clearance between the outside rotor and the pump body.

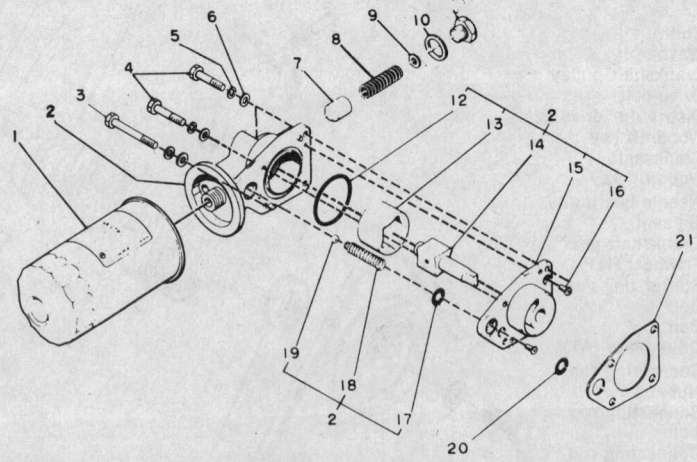

Exploded view of the oil pump

1. Oil filter	8. Relief valve spring	15. Oil pump holder
2. Oil pump body	9. Washer (6 mm)	16. Screw
3. Bolt (6X54 mm)	10. Washer	17. O ring
4. Bolt (6X32 mm)	11. Plug	18. Bypass valve spring
5. Spring washer	12. O ring	19. Ball
6. Washer	13. Rotor	20. O ring
7. Oil relief valve	14. Gear	21. Gasket

4. With a feeler gauge, measure the tip clearance between the inner and outer rotor, when one of the lobes of the inner rotor is on the very top of one of the lobes of the outer rotor. The tip clearance should be between 0.001 in. and 0.008 in. If the clearance is more than this, the oil pump should be replaced.

5. Measure the side clearance by placing a straightedge across the top of the pump body and the inner and outer rotors and measuring the gap between the straight edge and the rotors. The clearance should be between 0.002 in. and 0.008 in. If the clearance is more than allowed, either the rotors or the pump housing must be replaced.

6. Measure the radial clearance between the outer rotor and the pump housing with a feeler gauge. The clearance should be between 0.006 in. and 0.010 in.

ENGINE COOLING

Radiators

Removal and Installation

1300 G

A main radiator, sub-radiator, and reservoir tank are utilized. They can be removed individually or as an assembly. To remove as an assembly proceed as follows:

1. Remove the grille.
2. Remove the drain plug, and drain the coolant.
3. Disconnect the radiator hoses from the top of the main and sub-radiators, and from the bottom of the main radiator (water pump side).

When removing the engine:

4. Disconnect the heater control cable, by removing the circlip which retains the inner cable, and the nut which retains the sheath to the bracket. Loosen the clamp that retains the heater duct to the blower casing, and remove the blower casing mounting bolts.

When not removing the engine:

4. Remove the bolts that retain the sub-radiator shroud to the blower casing.
5. Remove the four screws and two bolts that retain the radiator bracket, and remove the radiator assembly.

NOTE: *Do not remove the bolt between the radiators.*

To remove only the main radiator proceed as follows:

1. Remove the grille.
2. Remove the drain plug and drain the coolant.
3. Disconnect all hoses from the main radiator.
4. Remove the center and right-hand radiator mounting bolts, and the four

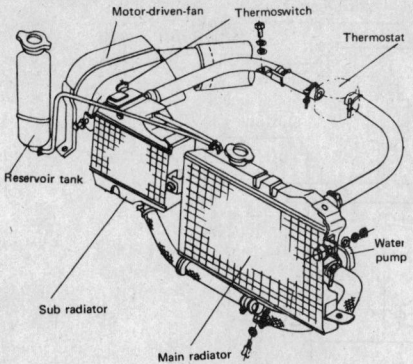
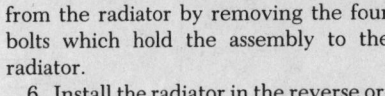

The dual radiator cooling system

screws which retain the radiator bracket.

5. Remove the main radiator and bracket, leaving the sub-radiator suspended on the left-hand mounting bolt and the blower motor casing.

To remove only the sub-radiator:

1. Remove the grille.
2. Remove the drain plug and drain the coolant.
3. Disconnect the radiator shroud from the blower casing.
4. Remove the center and left-hand radiator retaining bolts, and remove the sub-radiator.

Install in the reverse order of removal.

DL, GL, GF, 4WD

1. Drain the cooling system by removing the drain plug in the bottom of the radiator. After loosening the drain plug, remove the radiator cap, which will allow the coolant to drain faster.
2. Loosen the hose clamps and remove the inlet (upper) and outlet (lower) hoses from the radiator.
3. Remove the two radiator mounting bolts.
4. Before removing the radiator from the vehicle, disconnect the wiring harness of the following items: thermostat and thermoswitch wiring, oil pressure switch wiring, fan motor wiring, and secondary terminal of the distributor.
5. Remove the fan and motor assembly

from the radiator by removing the four bolts which hold the assembly to the radiator.

6. Install the radiator in the reverse order of removal.

Water Pump

Removal and Installation

A centrifugal water pump, mounted on the front of the engine, is utilized. To remove, drain the coolant, and remove the radiator hose from the pump. Remove the drive belt, unbolt and lift out the pump.

Install in the reverse order of removal.

Thermostat

Removal and Installation

A wax pellet type thermostat is used. It is removed by removing the air cleaner assembly and the thermostat cover, which is adjacent to the carburetor.

Install in the reverse order of removal.

NOTE: *It is essential to the proper operation of the cooling system that the thermostat be installed in the proper direction.*

EMISSION CONTROLS

Crankcase Emission Control System

The sealed crankcase emission control system takes blow-by gas emitted from the crankcase and routes the gas through the air cleaner and into the intake manifold for recombustion.

The system consists of a sealed oil filler cap, a rocker cover with an outlet pipe,

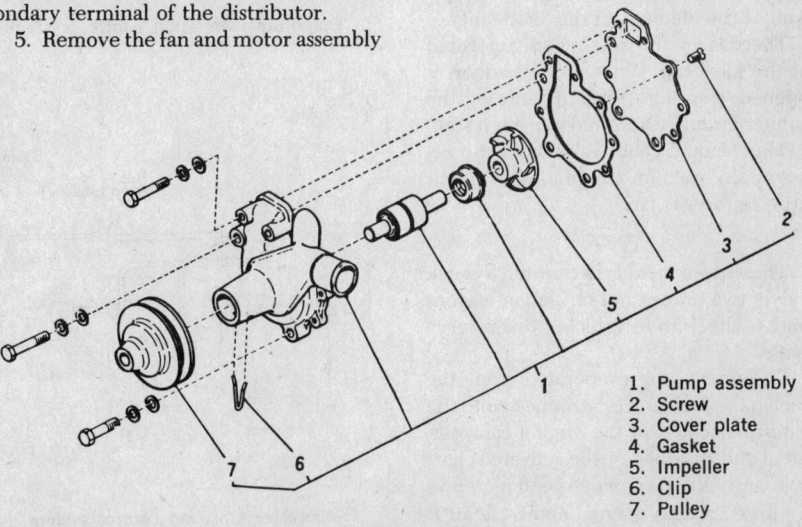

1. Pump assembly
2. Screw
3. Cover plate
4. Gasket
5. Impeller
6. Clip
7. Pulley

Exploded view of water pump

Subaru

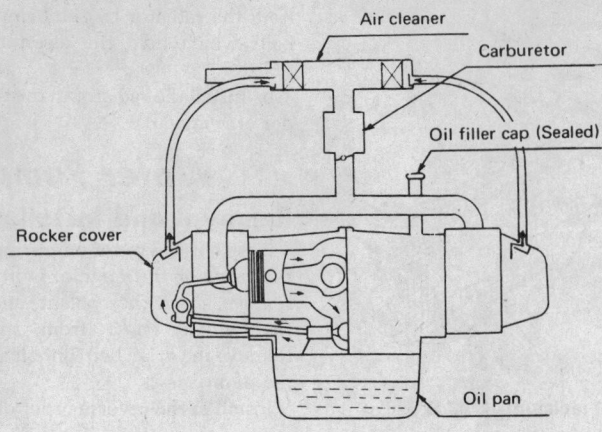

Diagram of the crankcase emission control system

canister purging the absorbed vapor from the activated charcoal.

Service

Keep all of the lines in good repair and free from cracks and blockage. The system should be relatively air tight. On 1977 models replace the canister filter every 25,000 miles.

Air Injection System

A belt-driven air pump is used to supply air, under pressure, to air distribution manifolds which have openings at each exhaust port. Injection of air at this point causes combustion of the unburned hydrocarbons in the exhaust manifolds. An

an air cleaner with an inlet pipe to receive the connecting hoses and the connecting hoses and clamps.

There are no tests to insure operation of the system other than making sure that the system is kept clean.

Evaporative Emission Control System

1972–76

Evaporative gas from the fuel tank is not discharged into the atmosphere but conducted to the air cleaner unit and then burned in the combustion chamber. No absorbent is used.

The system consists of a sealed fuel tank and filler cap, two reservoir tanks on the station wagon, an air breather valve or a restriction, breather hoses, breather pipe and the air cleaner.

While the engine is running, evaporative gas is absorbed into the intake manifold due to the suction pressure of the manifold, and never discharged directly into the atmosphere. While the engine is stopped, the gases collect on the inner wall of the element of the air cleaner.

There is an air breather valve located at the filler cap. When the flap (door) is opened, a spring exerts pressure on the rubber breather hose and pinches it shut.

The vacuum relief valve filler cap relieves any vacuum condition that might arise in the gas tank.

1977

This system includes a canister, a check valve, two orfices and on station wagons and 4-wheel drive vehicles, two reserve tanks.

Gasoline vapor evaporated from the fuel in the fuel tank is introduced into the canister located in the engine compartment and absorbed by the activated charcoal particles. As engine speed increases a purge valve is opened and fresh air is sucked in through the bottom filter of the

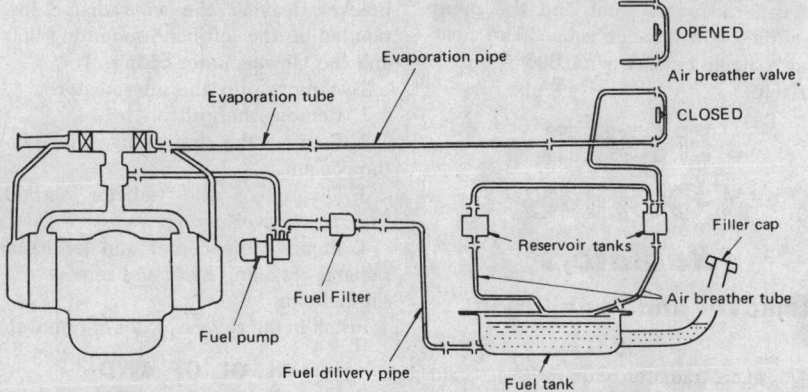

Diagram of evaporative emission control system for 1972 and some 1973 station wagons, sedans and coupes don't have the reservoir tanks

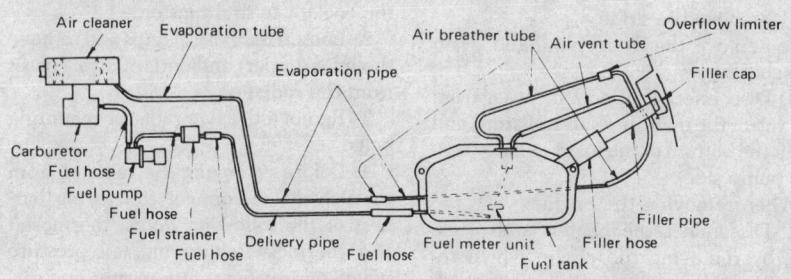

Evaporative emission control system for 1973 and later sedan and coupe

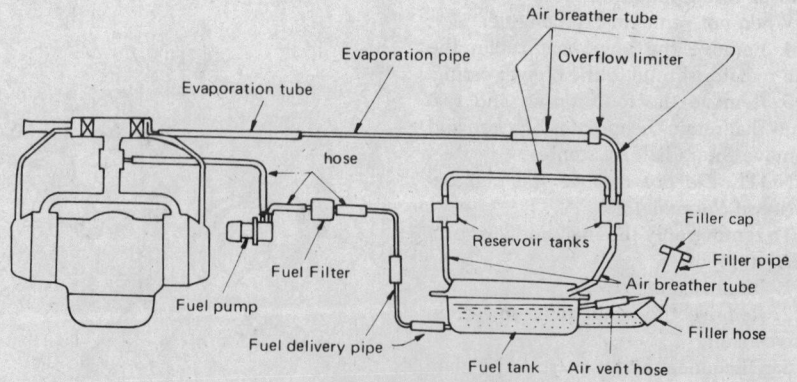

Evaporative emission control system used on some 1973 and all 1974 and later wagons. The 1973 models don't have the air vent hose

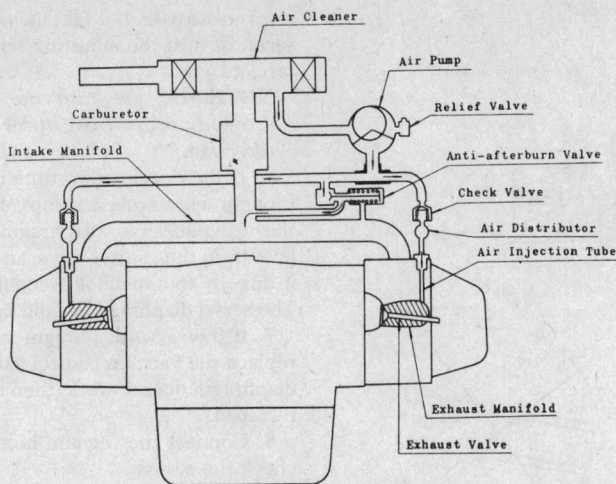

Air injection system

anti-backfire valve controls the flow of air from the pump to prevent backfiring resulting from an overly rich mixture under deceleration.

Check valves prevent hot exhaust gas backflow into the pump and hoses in case of pump or anti-backfire valve failure.

The air pump has a relief valve to discharge excess pressure at high engine speed.

On the 1300 G, an additional air by-pass valve is used. When the manual choke is pulled out, the air by-pass causes the air from the pump to flow into the air cleaner rather than the exhaust manifolds to prevent manifold overheating.

Removal and Installation

Air Pump

1. Disconnect the air hoses from the pump.
2. Loosen the bolt on the adjusting link and remove the drive belt.
3. Remove the mounting bolts and the pump.

Installation is the reverse of removal. Adjust the drive belt tension after installation. Belt deflection should be ⅜ in. with 22 lbs pressure.

Anti-Backfire Valve

1. Detach the air hoses from the valve.
2. Remove the valve securing bolt.
3. Remove the valve.

Installation is the reverse of removal.

Check Valves

1. Detach the intake hoses from the valves.
2. Use an open-end wrench to remove the valve from its mounting. Save the aluminum gasket.

Installation is the reverse of removal.

Relief Valve

1. Remove the air pump from the car.
2. Support the pump so that it cannot rotate.

CAUTION: *Never clamp the pump in a vise, the aluminum case will be distorted.*

3. Use a puller to remove the relief valve from the top of the pump.
4. Position the new relief valve over the opening in the pump.
NOTE: *The air outlet should be pointing toward the left.*
5. Gently tap the relief valve into place using a block of wood and a hammer.
6. Install the pump on the engine.

Air Injection Manifold

1. Remove the check valve.
2. Loosen the air injection manifold attachment nuts and remove the manifold.

Air By-pass Valve—1300 Engine

1. Disconnect the hoses from the air by-pass valve.
2. Detach the cable from the valve butterfly operating lever.
3. Remove the valve.

Installation is the reverse of removal.

Testing

Air Pump

CAUTION: *Do not hammer, pry, or bend the pump housing while tightening the drive belt or testing the pump.*

Belt Tension and Air Leaks

1. Before proceeding with the tests, check the pump drive belt tension.
2. Turn the pump by hand. If it has seized, the belt will slip, making a noise. Disregard any chirping, squealing, or rolling sounds from inside the pump; these are normal when it is turned by hand.
3. Check the hoses and connections for leaks. Hissing or a blast of air is indicative of a leak. Soapy water, applied lightly around the area in question, is a good method for detecting leaks.

Air Output

1. Disconnect the air supply hose at the antibackfire valve.
2. Connect a pressure gauge, using an adapter, to the air supply hose.
NOTE: *If there are two hoses, plug the second one.*
3. With the engine at normal operating temperature, increase the idle speed and watch the gauge.
4. The air flow from the pump should be steady and fall between 1½ and 6 psi. If it is unsteady or falls below this, the pump is defective and must be replaced.

Pump Noise Diagnosis

The air pump is normally noisy, as engine speed increases, the noise of the pump will rise in pitch. The rolling sound the pump bearings make is normal. But if this sound becomes objectionable at certain speeds, the pump is defective and will have to be replaced.

A continual hissing sound from the air pump pressure relief valve at idle, indicates a defective valve. Replace the relief valve.

If the pump rear bearing fails, a continual knocking sound will be heard.

Anti-Backfire Valve

1. Detach the air supply hose which runs between the pump and the gulp valve.
2. Connect a tachometer and run the engine to 1,500–2,000 rpm.
3. Allow the throttle to snap closed. This should produce a loud sucking sound from the valve.
4. Repeat this operation several times. If there is no sound, the valve is not working, or the vacuum connections are loose.

Check Valve Test

1. Before starting the test, check all of the hoses and connections for leaks.
2. Detach the air supply hose from the check valve.
3. Insert a probe into the check valve and depress the plate. Release it; the plate should return to its original position against the valve seat. If binding is evident, replace the valve.
4. With the engine running at normal operating temperature, gradually increase its speed to 1,500 rpm. Check for exhaust gas leakage. If there is any replace the valve assembly.

Air By-Pass Valve—1300 Engine

Check the air by-pass valve to be sure that it is open when the choke is closed.

If it is not open, adjust its operating cable.

Engine Modification System

This system is used on the DL and GL, beginning 1972. The principle of this system is not only to obtain correct air/fuel mixture while the vehicle is decelerating,

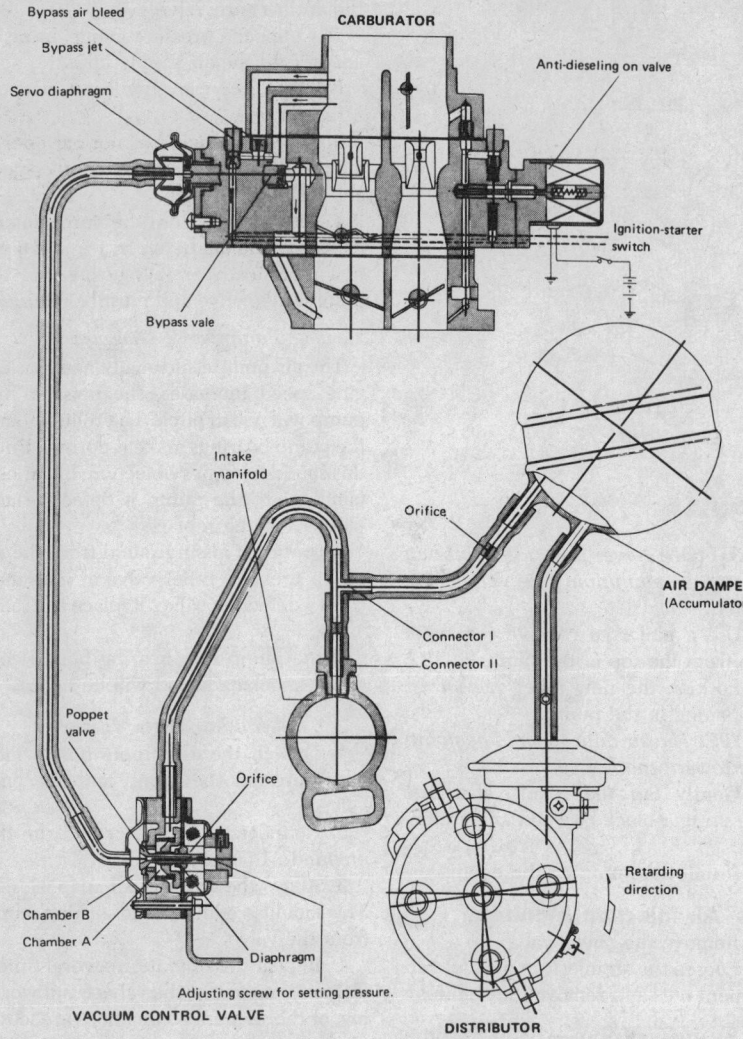

Engine modification system

but also to promote complete combustion by retarding the ignition timing, thus reducing the amount of emissions released into the atmosphere.

While the vehicle is decelerating, the primary throttle valve is closed, causing a high vacuum in the intake manifold. This vacuum is conducted through a vacuum control valve and on to the carburetor where a by-pass jet is opened and extra mixture is allowed to enter the venturi below the throttle plates. This richens the mixture and promotes cleaner combustion.

The vacuum is also routed to the distributor vacuum retard unit. After passing through an air damper (1972–73 only) which regulates the vacuum for smooth application, the vacuum unit retards the ignition spark in order to promote complete combustion in the cylinders.

There is an anti-dieseling solenoid mounted opposite the float bowl on the carburetor. This switch prevents the engine from dieseling when the ignition switch is turned off. When the ignition switch is turned off, an electromagnet in

the switch is also cut off. A spring inside the housing forces a plunger into position, blocking the fuel passages leading to the opening below the throttle plates. When the ignition switch is turned on, it energizes the electromagnet in the switch and pulls the plunger out of the fuel passage, allowing fuel to reach the opening below the throttle plates.

Vacuum Control Valve and Servo Diaphragm Adjustment

1. Start the engine and allow it reach normal operating temperature.
2. Connect a tachometer to the engine.
3. Increase the engine speed to 3000 rpm (no load); release the throttle immediately.
4. Note the time it takes for the engine speed to decrease from 3000 to 1000 rpm.
5. It should take from 3–5 seconds for the engine speed to decrease. If it takes *less* than 3 seconds, remove the cover and turn the vacuum valve adjusting

screw *clockwise*. If it takes *longer* than 5 seconds, turn the adjusting screw *counterclockwise*.

NOTE: *Do not turn the adjusting screw more than two turns in either direction.*

6. If the deceleration time cannot be brought within specifications, disconnect the valve-to-servo diaphragm vacuum hose from the control valve, and connect it directly to a manifold vacuum source. The servo diaphragm should operate.
7. If the servo diaphragm is working, replace the vacuum control valve. If the diaphragm doesn't work, then it must be replaced.
8. Connect the vacuum hoses and recheck the system.

Electrically Assisted Automatic Choke

Starting 1974, a vacuum-operated automatic choke replaces the manual choke previously used. The automatic choke uses a choke cap containing a heating element to speed up choke valve opening and reduce CO emissions during warm-up. The heating element gets its power from a special tap on the voltage regulator, when the ignition is on and the engine running.

Testing

1. Disconnect the choke lead from the voltage regulator.
2. Connect an ohmmeter between the lead that you just disconnected and a good ground. The ohmmeter should read about 9 ohms.
3. Replace the choke cap if the reading shows an opened (no resistance) or shorted (infinite resistance) heating coil.

Carburetor Dashpot

Adjustment

1. Be sure that the throttle valve is in the idle (closed) position.
2. The dashpot stem should be able to move about 0.16 in. beyond the throttle lever's idle position.
3. If the stem does not move the correct distance, adjust the dashpot, by loosening its locknut and rotating the dashpot until the correct amount of movement is obtained.
4. Tighten the locknut and recheck dashpot stem movement.

Exhaust Gas Recirculation (EGR) System

An exhaust gas recirculation (EGR) system is used on 1974–76 California models and all 1977 models to reduce NO_x (oxides of nitrogen) emissions by lowering

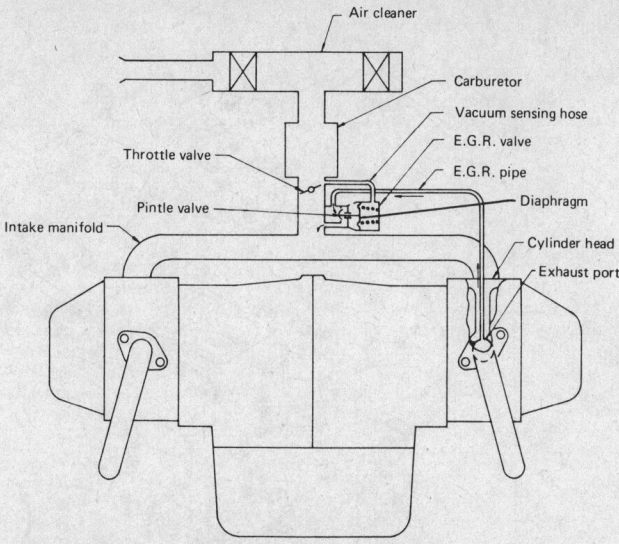

Exhaust gas recirculation system

peak flame temperature during combustion. A small portion of the exhaust gases are routed into the intake manifold via a vacuum-operated EGR control valve.

A solenoid vacuum valve controls the flow of vacuum from a port on the carburetor (above the primary throttle valve) to the EGR valve vacuum diaphragm. The solenoid, in turn, is operated by a coolant temperature switch.

When the coolant temperature is above 122°F, the temperature switch breaks the current flow to the vacuum solenoid valve. The valve closes, permitting the throttle port vacuum to operate the EGR valve diaphragm. This causes the EGR valve to open under conditions other than idle or wide-open throttle.

Below 122°F, the vacuum solenoid valve is energized to vent the vacuum from the throttle port into the atmosphere through a filter. By preventing exhaust gas recirculation from occurring before the engine has warmed-up, cold driveability is greatly improved.

Testing

EGR System

1. Start the engine and allow it to reach normal operating temperature.

2. Increase the engine speed to 3000–3500 rpm (no load). The valve shaft should move upward.

3. Decrease the engine speed to idle, the valve shaft should go down.

4. If the valve shaft fails to raise in Step 2, check the vacuum lines, connections, and the carburetor throttle vacuum port. Replace any clogged or damaged hoses, and clean the throttle port if it is clogged.

5. Connect the EGR valve vacuum hose directly to the throttle port on the carburetor. Speed the engine up and return it to idle as in Steps 2 and 3. If the valve works, the fault lies in the vacuum

solenoid valve or the temperature switch.

6. If the EGR valve doesn't work, perform the following EGR valve checks:

a. Remove the EGR valve from the intake manifold.

b. Plug the vacuum inlet on the top of the valve diaphragm.

c. Depress and release the pintle (valve plunger) several times.

d. The pintle should remain depressed as long as the vacuum inlet is plugged. If it doesn't, the diaphragm is leaking and the valve assembly must be replaced.

e. If the valve stem appears to be stuck, clean the pintle with a wire brush or spark plug cleaning machine.

f. Install the valve and retest it.

Vacuum Solenoid Valve and Coolant Temperature Switch

1. Disconnect the vacuum solenoid leads.

2. Connect the solenoid directly to a 12-volt power source. The solenoid should click.

3. If the solenoid is working properly and everything else in the system is in proper operating order, replace the coolant temperature switch.

Hot Air Control System

The hot air control system consists of the air cleaner, the air stove on the exhaust pipe and the air intake hose connecting the air cleaner and air stove. The air cleaner is equipped with an air control valve which maintains the temperature of the air being drawn into the carburetor at 100°–127° F to reduce HC emission when the underhood temperature is below 100° F. This system should be inspected every 12,000 miles.

Temperature Sensor

Removal and Installation

1. Using pliers, flatten the clip securing the vacuum hose to the sensor vacuum pipe.

2. Disconnect the hose from the sensor.

3. Remove the clip from the sensor vacuum pipe and remove the sensor body from the air cleaner.

NOTE: *The gasket is glued to the air cleaner and should not be removed.*

4. To install reverse the removal procedure.

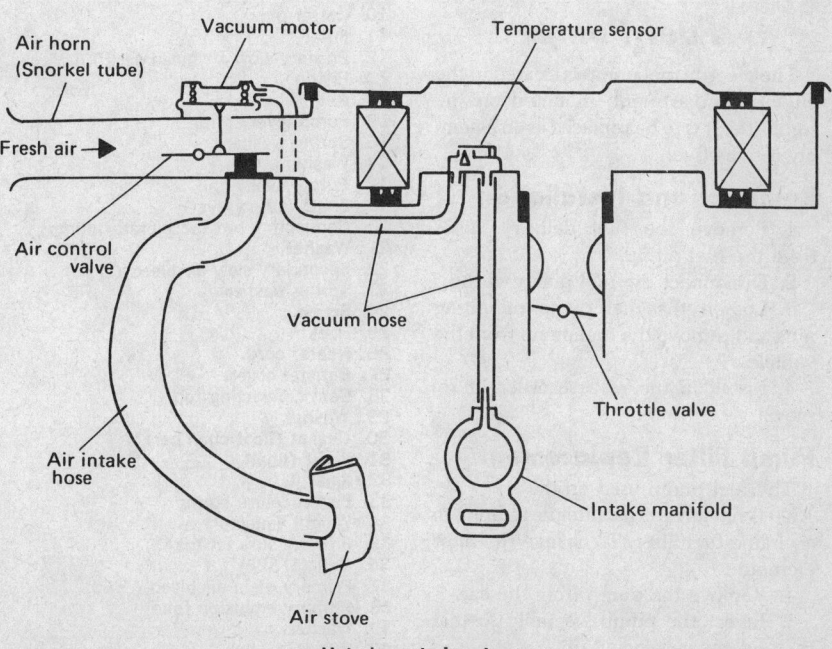

Hot air control system

Vacuum Motor

Removal and Installation

1. Remove the screws securing the vacuum motor to the air cleaner.

2. Disconnect the valve shaft, attached to the vacuum motor diaphragm, at the air control valve, and remove the vacuum motor from the air cleaner.

3. To install reverse the removal procedure.

FUEL SYSTEM

Fuel Filter

Replacement

All Subarus use a cartridge fuel filter, located in the fuel pump-to-carburetor fuel line. The filter is the disposable type which cannot be cleaned. It should be replaced every 12 months/12,000 miles, whichever occurs first.

To replace the filter cartridge, proceed in the following manner:

1. Loosen, but do not remove, the nuts which secure the two hose clamps located at either end of the filter.

2. Work the hoses off the filter necks.

3. Snap the filter out of its mounting bracket, if so equipped.

4. Throw the old filter away.

NOTE: *When removing the old filter, be careful not to allow any fuel from it to drip onto hot engine components.*

Installation of a new filter is performed in the reverse order of removal. Be sure that the hose clamps are tightened securely.

Fuel Pump

The electric fuel pump is located in the engine compartment, mounted on the right side. It is to be replaced as an assembly if defective.

Removal and Installation

1. Remove the fuel delivery hoses from the fuel pump.

2. Disconnect the fuel pump wiring.

3. Loosen the fuel pump mounting nuts and remove the fuel pump from the vehicle.

4. Install in the reverse order of removal.

Pump Filter Replacement

The fuel pump used on the 1300 G has an internal filter in addition to an inline fuel filter. To change the filter element:

1. Remove the pump from the car.

2. Invert the pump assembly so that the end cover is facing up.

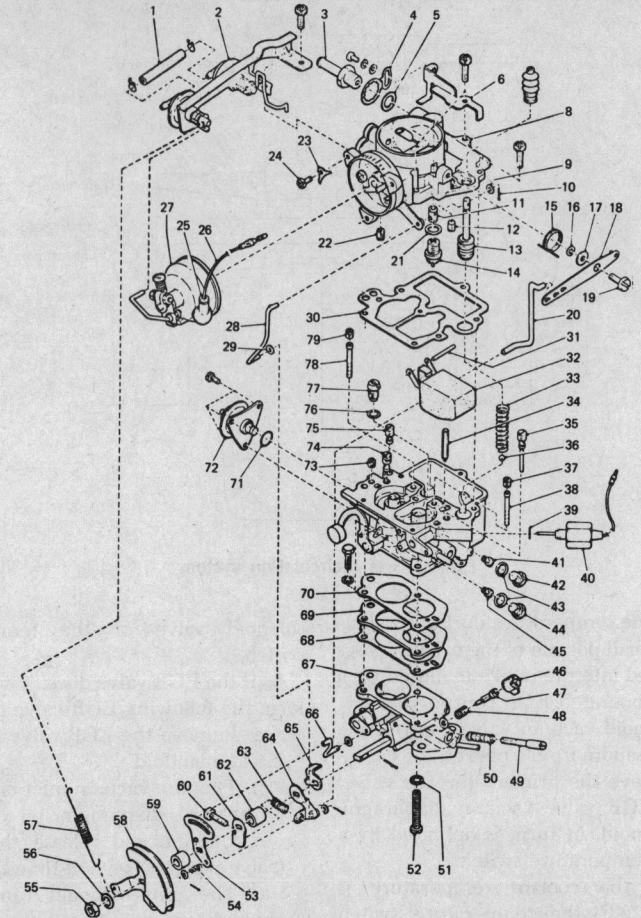

Exploded view of the 1974-77 GL and DL carburetor with automatic choke

1. Vacuum hose
2. Vacuum diaphragm assembly
3. Nipple (fuel inlet)
4. Stopper
5. Washer
6. Nipple guide
7. Pump cover
8. Choke chamber
9. Washer
10. Cotter pin
11. Filter
12. Primary slow air bleed (#200)
13. Piston
14. Needle valve
15. Pump lever spring
16. Spring washer
17. Washer
18. Pump lever
19. Shaft (pump lever)
20. Connecting rod (accelerator pump)
21. Washer
22. Secondary slow air bleed (#70)
23. Spring washer
24. Screw
25. Boot
26. Heater cord
27. Bimetal cover
28. Cam connecting rod
29. Washer
30. Gasket (float chamber)
31. Shaft (float)
32. Float
33. Piston return spring
34. Weight (injector)
35. Primary slow jet (#43)
36. Ball (5/32")
37. Primary main air bleed (#60)
38. Primary emulsion tube
39. Washer
40. Solenoid valve

41. Primary main jet (#95, #93)
42. Drain plug (primary)
43. Washer
44. Drain plug (secondary)
45. Secondary main jet (#155)
46. Idle limiter cap
47. Idle adjust screw
48. Spring (idle adjust screw)
49. Throttle adjusting screw
50. Spring (throttle adjusting screw)
51. Washer
52. Screw
53. Connecting lever
54. Spring
55. Nut
56. Spring washer
57. Throttle return spring
58. Throttle lever
59. Sleeve
60. Fast idle adjust screw
61. Lever A (fast idle)
62. Sleeve
63. Spring (throttle adjusting screw)
64. Lever B (fast idle)
65. Plate
66. Connecting rod
67. Throttle chamber
68. Gasket (throttle chamber)
69. Insulator
70. Gasket (throttle chamber)
71. O-ring
72. Servo diaphragm
73. Air bleed (coasting)
74. Secondary slow jet (#60)
75. Slow jet (coasting) (#50)
76. Washer
77. Power valve (#45)
78. Secondary emulsion tube
79. Secondary main air bleed (#90)

Subaru

3. Remove the ground lead screw from the end cover.

4. Carefully remove the end cover from the pump body by turning the cover.

5. Remove the gasket and filter element from the pump.

6. Insert a new filter element and reassemble the end cover to the pump.

CARBURETORS

All models use a two-barrel Zenith-Stromberg carburetor manufactured under license by Hitachi Ltd. in Japan.

The carburetor uses progressive linkage between the primary and secondary circuits. For optimum performance plus fuel economy, the secondary circuit of the carburetor is used only at high engine speed. Normal low speed operation is handled by the primary circuit. All 1970–73 models have a manual choke; 1974–77 models have an automatic choke system.

Removal and Installation

1. Unbolt and remove the air cleaner assembly.

2. Disconnect the fuel and distributor vacuum lines from the carburetor.

3. On 1970–73 models disconnect the choke cable from the choke lever and the spring hanger, and the throttle cable from the throttle lever.

4. On 1974–77 models disconnect the anti-dieseling switch wire and the heater wire for the automatic choke.

5. Remove the four carburetor mounting bolts and remove the carburetor.

NOTE: *Cover the intake manifold while the carburetor is removed to prevent dirt from entering.*

6. Install the carburetor in the reverse order of removal.

Overhaul

Efficient carburetion depends greatly on careful cleaning and inspection during overhaul since dirt, gum, water, or varnish in or on the carburetor parts are often responsible for poor performance.

Overhaul the carburetor in a clean, dust-free area. Carefully disassemble the carburetor, referring often to the exploded views. Keep all similar and look-alike parts segregated during disassembly and cleaning to avoid accidental interchange during assembly. Make a note of all jet sizes.

When the carburetor is disassembled, wash all parts (except diaphragms, electric choke units, pump plunger, and any other plastic, leather, fiber, or rubber parts) in clean carburetor solvent. Do not leave parts in the solvent any longer than is necessary to sufficiently loosen the deposits. Excessive cleaning may remove

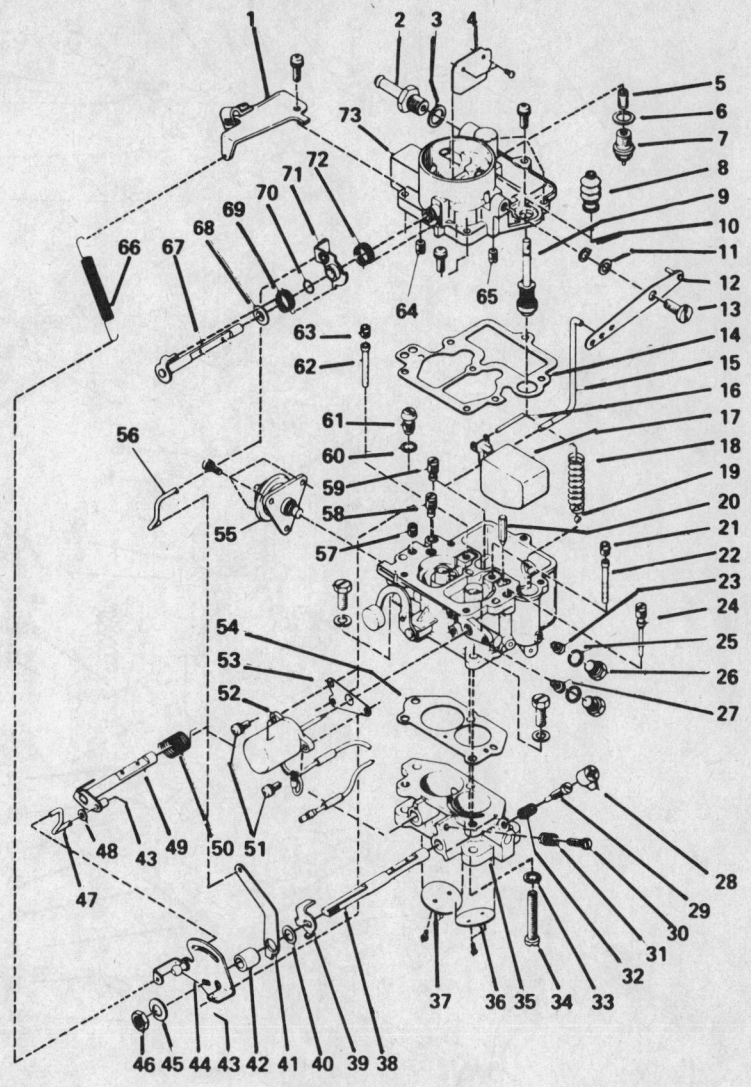

1300G carburetor

1. Spring hanger
2. Nipple
3. Washer (12ϕ)
4. Choke valve
5. Filter
6. Washer (10ϕ)
7. Needle valve (1.5ϕ)
8. Cover (Pump)
9. Piston
10. Spring washer
11. Washer
12. Lever (Pump)
13. Shaft (Pump lever)
14. Gasket (Float chamber)
15. Connecting rod (Pump)
16. Shaft (Float)
17. Float
18. Piston return spring
19. Ball (5/32")
20. Weight A (Injector)
21. Primary main air bleed (#60)
22. Primary emulsion tube
23. Primary main jet (#95)
24. Primary slow jet (#43)
25. Washer (9ϕ)
26. Drain plug (Float chamber)
27. Secondary main jet (#155)
28. Cap (Idle limiter)
29. Idle adjustment screw
30. Throttle adjustment screw
31. Spring (Throttle adjustment screw)
32. Spring (Idle adjustment screw)
33. Washer
34. Screw
35. Throttle chamber
36. Primary throttle valve
37. Secondary throttle valve
38. Primary throttle shaft
39. Adjusting plate
40. Washer
41. Connecting lever
42. Sleeve
43. Cotter pin
44. Throttle lever
45. Spring washer
46. Nut
47. Connecting rod
48. Washer
49. Secondary throttle shaft
50. Spring (Secondary throttle)
51. Screw
52. Anti-dieseling switch
53. Anti-dieseling switch gasket
54. Gasket (Throttle chamber)
55. Servo diaphragm
56. Connecting rod (Choke)
57. Bypass air bleed (#320)
58. Secondary slow jet (#60)
59. Bypass slow jet (#55)
60. Washer
61. Power valve (#45)
62. Secondary emulsion tube
63. Secondary main air bleed (#90)
64. Secondary slow air bleed (#70)
65. Primary slow air bleed (#200)
66. Throttle return spring
67. Choke shaft
68. Sleeve (A)
69. Choke valve spring
70. Clip
71. Choke lever
72. Choke spring
73. Choke chamber

1003

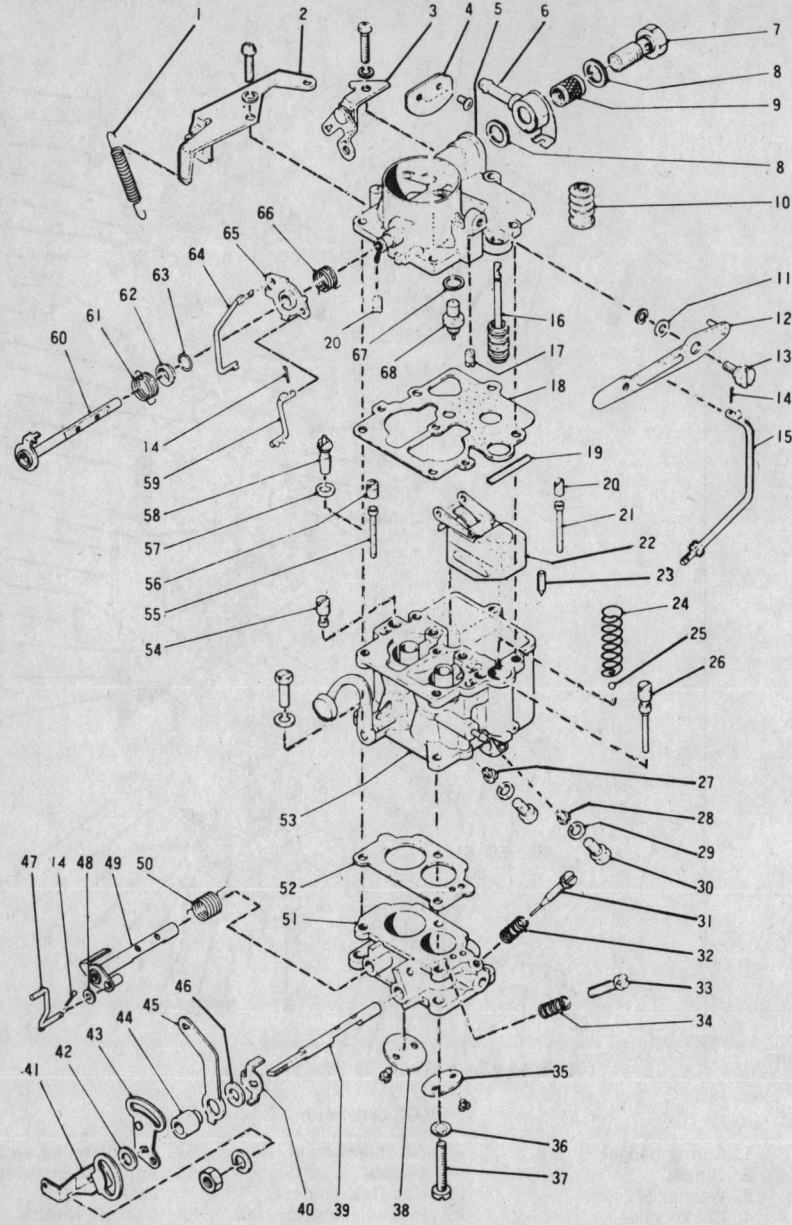

1. Throttle return spring
2. Spring hanger
3. Bell crank
4. Choke plate
5. Air horn
6. Banjo
7. Banjo bolt
8. Gasket
9. Filter
10. Pump cover
11. Washer
12. Pump arm
13. Pump arm pivot
14. Cotter pin
15. Pump rod
16. Pump shaft
17. Idle air bleed (primary)
18. Gasket
19. Float pivot
20. Idle air bleed (secondary)
21. Emulsion tube
22. Float
23. Pump needle
24. Pump return spring
25. Ball
26. Idle jet (primary)
27. Main jet (secondary)
28. Main jet (primary)
29. Washer
30. Drain plug
31. Idle mixture screw
32. Spring
33. Idle speed screw
34. Spring
35. Throttle plate (primary)
36. Washer
37. Screw
38. Throttle plate (secondary)
39. Throttle shaft (primary)
40. Throttle stop
41. Throttle lever
42. Washer
43. Secondary actuating arm
44. Sleeve
45. Choke unloader
46. Washer
47. Secondary link
48. Washer
49. Throttle shaft (secondary)
50. Spring
51. Throttle body
52. Gasket
53. Body
54. Idle jet (secondary)
55. Emulsion tube (secondary)
56. High speed air bleed (secondary)

DL, GL and GF carburetor (1972-73 shown)

the special finish from the float bowl and choke valve bodies, leaving these parts unfit for service. Rinse all parts in clean solvent and blow them dry with compressed air or allow them to air dry. Wipe clean all cork, plastic, leather, and fiber parts with a clean, lint-free cloth.

Blow out all passages and jets with compressed air and be sure that there are no restrictions or blockages. Never use wire or similar tools to clean jets, fuel passages, or air bleeds. Clean all jets and valves separately to avoid accidental interchange.

Check all parts for wear or damage. If wear or damage is found, replace the defective parts. Especially check the following:

1. Check the float needle and seat for

wear. If wear is found, replace the complete assembly.

2. Check the float hinge pin for wear and the float(s) for dents or distortion. Replace the float if fuel has leaked into it.

3. Check the throttle and choke shaft bores for wear or an out-of-round condition. Damage or wear to the throttle arm, shaft, or shaft bore will often require replacement of the throttle body. These parts require a close tolerance of fit; wear may allow air leakage, which could affect starting and idling.

NOTE: *Throttle shafts and bushings are usually not included in overhaul kits. They can be purchased separately.*

4. Inspect the idle mixture adjusting needles for burrs or grooves. Any such condition requires replacement of the

needle, since you will not be able to obtain a satisfactory idle.

5. Test the accelerator pump check valves. They should pass air one way but not the other. Test for proper seating by blowing and sucking on the valve. Replace the valve if necessary. If the valve is satisfactory, wash the valve again to remove breath moisture.

6. Check the bowl cover for warped surfaces with a straightedge.

7. Closely inspect the valves and seats for wear and damage, replacing as necessary.

8. After the carburetor is assembled, check the choke valve for freedom of op-

eration.

Carburetor overhaul kits are recommended for each overhaul. These kits contain all gaskets and new parts to replace those that deteriorate most rapidly. Failure to replace all parts supplied with the kit (especially gaskets) can result in poor performance later.

After cleaning and checking all components, reassemble the carburetor, using new parts and referring to the exploded view. When reassembling, make sure that all screws and jets are tight in their seats, but do not overtighten, as the tips will be distorted. Tighten all screws gradually, in rotation. Do not tighten needle valves into their seats; uneven jetting will result. Always use new gaskets. Be sure to adjust the float level when reassembling.

Primary/Secondary Throttle Linkage Adjustment

1. With the carburetor removed from the engine, operate the linkage so that the connecting rod contacts the groove on the end of the secondary actuating lever.

2. Measure the clearance between the lower end of the primary throttle valve and its bore. It should be about 0.24 in. for all models.

3. Adjust the clearance by bending the connecting rod.

4. Check that the linkage operates smoothly.

Float and Fuel Level Adjustment

On models with a sight glass on the carburetor float bowl, the fuel should be level (within 1/16 in) with the dot on the glass when the engine is running.

The float level may be adjusted with the carburetor installed on the engine:

1. Disconnect the accelerator pump actuating rod from the pump lever.

2. Remove the throttle return spring.

3. Disconnect the choke cable from the choke lever, and remove it from the spring hanger.

4. Remove the spring hanger, the choke bellcrank, and the remaining air horn retaining screws.

5. Lift the air horn slightly, disconnect

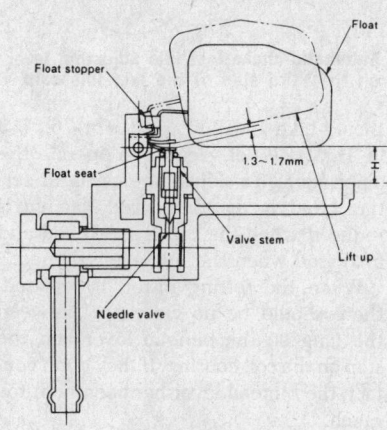

Float adjustment

the choke connecting rod, and remove the air horn.

6. Invert the air horn (float up), and measure the distance between the surface of the air horn and the float.

7. Bend the float arm until the clearance is approximately 0.41 in.

8. Invert the air horn to its installed position, and measure the distance between the float arm and the needle valve stem. This dimension should be 0.050–0.065 in., and is adjusted by bending the float stops.

Fast Idle

1972–73

1. With the carburetor removed from the engine, make sure that the choke valve is fully closed.

2. Measure the clearance between the upper edge of the primary throttle valve and its bore.

Fast Idle Clearance

Engine	Primary throttle to bore clearance (in.)
1100	0.038
1300	0.046
1400	0.054

Fast Idle Clearance

3. If the clearance is incorrect, adjust it by bending the choke adjusting rod.

4. Check the operation of the linkage for smoothness.

1974–77

1. With the carburetor removed from the engine, set the fast idle cam adjusting lever on the fourth step of the fast idle cam.

2. Check to be sure that the choke valve is fully closed.

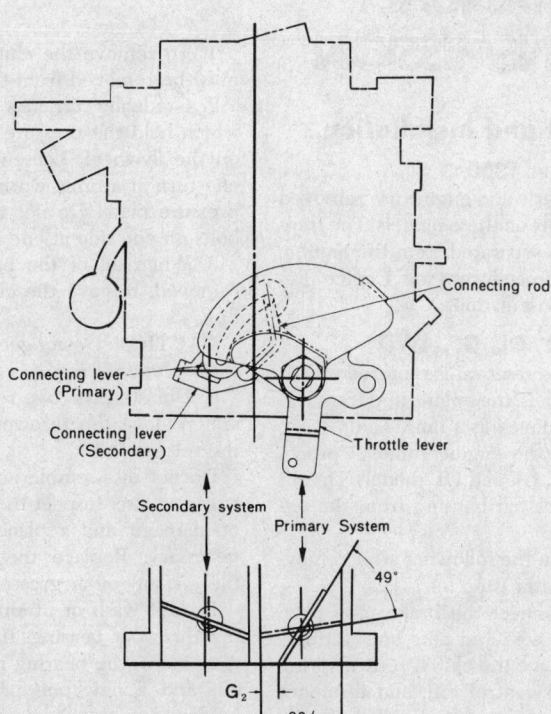

G₂ = 6.0mm when primary throttle valve opening is 49° from full close.
(EA63A)

Throttle linkage adjustment

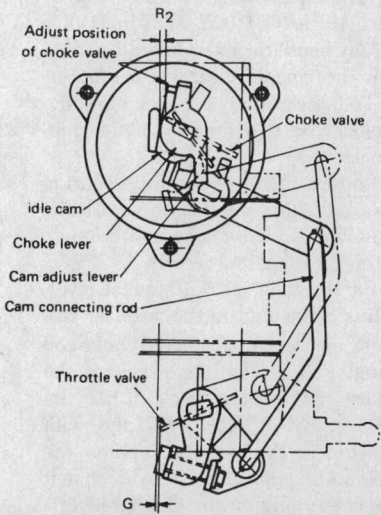

Fast idle adjustment on the 1974-77 carburetor. "G" is the angle to be measured.

3. Measure the clearance between the lower edge of the primary throttle valve and its bore. The clearance should be 0.047–0.052 in. (1974), 0.043–0.060 in. (1975–77).

4. If the clearance is incorrect, turn the fast idle adjusting screw to bring it within specifications. Turning the screw *in* increases the throttle clearance.

Manual Choke Adjustment

1972–73

1. Pull the choke knob on the instrument panel out all the way. Remove the air cleaner and check the position of the choke valve. If the choke valve is fully closed, the cable is adjusted properly.

2. If the choke valve is not fully closed, adjust the cable by loosening its retaining nut and pulling on the cable lightly to take up any slack.

3. Tighten the retaining nut.

4. Check to see that the choke valve is now fully opened when the choke knob is pushed all the way in.

Automatic Choke Adjustment

1974–77

1. Adjust the fast idle first.

2. Pull the main choke diaphragm lever as far as it will go to the left and measure the clearance between the upper end of the choke valve and its bore. The clearance should be 0.046–0.055 in. Adjust, as necessary, by bending the diaphragm-to-choke connecting rod.

3. Apply vacuum to the main diaphragm, it should operate the choke valve. If it does not, replace the diaphragm.

4. Place the fast idle cam adjusting lever on the *third* step of the fast idle cam. Measure the clearance between the upper end of the choke valve and its bore. The clearance should be 0.063–0.074 in. (1974–76), 0.025–0.037 in. (1977). Carefully bend (turn) the fast idle cam to obtain the correct clearance, as necessary. To increase the clearance bend the cam clockwise; to decrease it, bend counterclockwise.

5. Loosen the 3 choke cap securing screws, and align the line on it with the longest line on the choke coil housing. Tighten the retaining screws.

6. Fit the tang on the bimetal lever, which is connected to the auxiliary diaphragm, against the stop in the choke coil housing. Pull the setting piston of the auxiliary diaphragm back 0.197 in. (1974–76), 0.36–0.39 in. (1977) and, with the piston in this position, tighten the compensator adjusting screw so that it contacts the tang on the bimetal lever.

7. Apply vacuum from an outside source to the auxiliary diaphragm. It

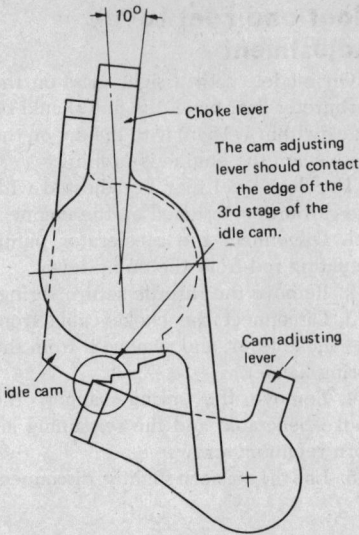

Automatic choke fast idle adjusting lever on the third step of the fast idle cam

should take 10–12 in. Hg (1974–76), 7–9 in. Hg. (1977) of vacuum to operate the diaphragm. To adjust the vacuum setting, bend the diaphragm rod. Vacuum is reduced when the rod is shortened and increased when the rod is lengthened.

When the setting piston is released, there should be no clearance between the tang on the bimetal lever and the stop on the coil housing. If they don't contact, the bimetal lever has been bent too much.

MANUAL TRANSMISSION

Removal and Installation

1300 G

The transaxle and engine are removed as an assembly on these models. The transaxle is then separated from the engine. For these procedures, see Engine Removal and Installation.

DL, GL, GF, 4WD

If transaxle removal is required on GL and DL models, the engine and transaxle must be removed as a unit. To do so:

1. Follow the engine removal procedure for GL, GF and DL models. Do not unbolt the clutch housing from the engine (step 13).

2. Perform the following after removing the radiator (step 9):

a. Disconnect the brake pipe from the brake hose and plug both fittings.

b. Remove the clutch return spring and pedal control rod, and dismount the clutch cross-shaft bracket on the body side. Remove the transmission side ball stud.

c. Lock the handbrake, and separate the double-offset joints from the drive-

shafts by removing the 3 retaining bolts, or driving out the spring pins. Lower the joints by turning the steering wheel to full lock.

d. Release the handbrake, and disconnect the cable so that it may be removed with the power train.

e. Remove the carpeting and cover plate from the front floorboard center hump. Loosen the clamp, and slide the shift rod cover tube rearward. Separate the shifter shaft from the shift rod by tapping the roll pin out of the shaft.

f. Detach the speedometer cable from the speedometer and pull it into the engine compartment, to be removed with the power train.

3. Perform the following after removing the engine horizontal damper (step 10):

a. Detach the exhaust pipe from its mount on the bottom of the transaxle.

b. Unbolt the right and left-hand engine mounts, leaving the rubber mounting pads bolted to the engine. Unbolt the transaxle rear mount. Support the power train with a chain hoist attached to the front and rear hangers.

c. Slowly lift the engine, until there is clearance for the brake drums to clear the crossmember, and pull the power train forward and out of the vehicle.

Reverse the removal procedure for installation.

CLUTCH

1. To remove the clutch, the engine must be removed from the vehicle.

2. Gradually unscrew the six bolts which hold the pressure plate assembly on the flywheel. Loosen the bolts only one turn at a time, working around the pressure plate. Do not unscrew all the bolts on one side at one time.

3. When all of the bolts have been removed, remove the clutch plate and disc.

CAUTION: *Do not get oil or grease on the clutch facing.*

4. Unfasten the two retaining springs and remove the throwout bearing and the release fork.

Do not disassemble either the clutch cover or disc. Inspect the parts for wear or damage and replace any parts as necessary. Replace the clutch disc if there is any oil or grease on the facing.

Do not wash or attempt to lubricate the throwout bearing. If it requires replacement, the bearing may be pressed out and a new one pressed into the holder.

Installation is as follows:

1. Fit the release fork boot on the front of the transmission housing. Install the release fork.

2. Insert the throwout bearing assembly and secure it with the two springs. Coat the inside diameter of the bearing holder and the fork-to-holder contact points with grease.

3. Insert a pilot shaft through the clutch cover and disc, then insert the end of the pilot into the needle bearing.

4. Gradually tighten the pressure plate retaining bolts one turn at time, working around the cover, to 7–9 ft lbs.

NOTE: *When installing the clutch pressure plate assembly, make sure that the 0 marks on the flywheel and the clutch pressure plate assembly are at least 190° apart. This is for purposes of balance. Also, make sure that the clutch disc is installed properly, noting the FRONT and REAR markings.*

5. After installation, adjust the pedal free-play and height.

Pedal Height

Adjust the pedal with the return stop bolt, so that its pad is at the same height as the brake pedal pad. The stroke of the pedal should be 5.04–5.43 in. The clutch release fork stroke should be 0.67 in.

Cable Adjustment

The clutch cable can be adjusted at the cable bracket where the cable is attached to the side of the transmission housing. To adjust the length of the cable, remove the circlip and clamp, slide the cable end in the direction desired and then replace the circlip and clamp. The cable should not be stretched out straight nor should it have right angle kinks in it. Any curves should be gradual.

Free-Play Adjustment

1. Remove the clutch fork return spring and loosen the locknut on the fork adjusting nut.

2. Turn the adjusting nut until a release fork free-play of 0.14–0.18 in. is obtained.

3. Tighten the locknut.

4. Check the pedal free-play. It should be:

    1300 G—1.20–1.50 in.

GL, GF, DL—0.94–1.18 in.

5. Adjust the pedal free-play with the pedal adjusting bolt.

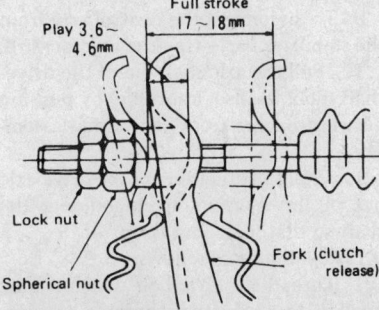

Clutch linkage free-play adjustment at the release fork

AUTOMATIC TRANSMISSION

Removal and Installation

The usual procedure is to remove the transmission and engine from the car together.

1. Support the car and release the handbrake.

2. Prop the hood open as far as possible.

3. Disconnect the battery ground cable from the battery and the engine.

4. Remove the air cleaner and cover the carburetor to keep out dirt.

5. Disconnect the fuel line.

6. Drain the coolant from the radiator. Remove the radiator hoses.

7. Detach all the engine to body wires.

8. Remove the radiator.

9. Remove the engine pitching damper.

10. Remove the starter.

11. Detach the accelerator, choke, and speedometer cables.

12. Drain the transmission pan.

13. Detach the oil cooler lines. Plug the openings to exclude dirt.

14. Detach the exhaust pipe flange.

15. Remove the pin holding the shifting lever.

16. Unbolt the front mounting bracket from the engine.

17. Attach a hoist to the engine and take up the slack.

18. Remove the spring pins from the axle shaft double offset joints.

19. Unbolt the rear crossmember from the body.

20. Lower the transmission to rest lightly on the stabilizer bar.

21. Remove the double offset joints from the transmission. You may have to move the rear of the transmission from side to side.

22. Remove the rear crossmember.

23. Lift the engine, tilting the transmission down slightly. Guide the transmission pan over the stabilizer and remove the engine/transaxle assembly.

24. Separate the engine from the transmission:

    a. Unbolt the torque converter from the engine, working through the timing hole.

    b. Unbolt the engine from the transmission.

    c. Pull the transmission back, making sure that the torque converter stays on the transmission.

25. Assemble the engine to the transmission, torquing the torque converter bolts to 17–20 ft lbs and the transmission to engine bolts to 34–40 ft lbs.

26. When installing the engine/transaxle assembly into the car, guide the transmission pan over the stabilizer bar.

27. When connecting the double offset joints with the drive shafts, align the joint paint marking with the pin hole in the shaft and insert the spring pin.

28. To connect the shifting lever to the shifting rod, place the selector lever in the Neutral position. Place the shifting lever shaft hole slot at right angles to the pan surface.

29. Tighten the front mounting bracket to engine bolts to 14–22 ft lbs, the rear crossmember to rubber mount to 14–22 ft lbs, the crossmember to body to 14–22 ft lbs, and the engine pitching damper rod to 5–9 ft lbs.

30. Put in four quarts of Dexron transmission fluid before starting the engine. Check the level with the engine idling.

Second Gear Band Adjustment

1. Hold the adjusting screw above the pan on the left side of the transmission.

2. Loosen the locknut.

3. Tighten the screw ¼ turn or less clockwise.

4. Tighten the locknut, while holding the screw.

Neutral Safety Switch Adjustment

This switch is mounted on the transmission shift lever shaft, bolted to the transmission. It also operates the backup lights.

1. Remove the shift lever shaft nut.

2. Remove the shift lever from the shaft.

3. Make sure that the slot in the shaft is vertical (Neutral position).

4. Remove the switch mounting bolts, but leave the switch in place.

5. Remove the setscrew from the lower face of the switch.

6. Insert a 0.059 in. drill bit through the setscrew hole. Turn the switch slightly so that the bit passes through into the back part of the switch.

7. Bolt the switch down.

8. Remove the bit and replace the setscrew.

9. Replace the lever and tighten the shaft nut.

10. Check that the engine can start only in Park or Neutral, and that the backup lights go on in Reverse.

Shift Linkage Adjustment

1. Loosen the clamp nuts on the shifting rod at the bottom of the shift lever on the transmission.

2. Put the selector lever in Neutral and hold it forward against the detent.

3. Check that the transmission shift lever is in the Neutral position (pull it all the way back into Park and push it forward two positions).

4. Tighten the clamp nuts.

Subaru

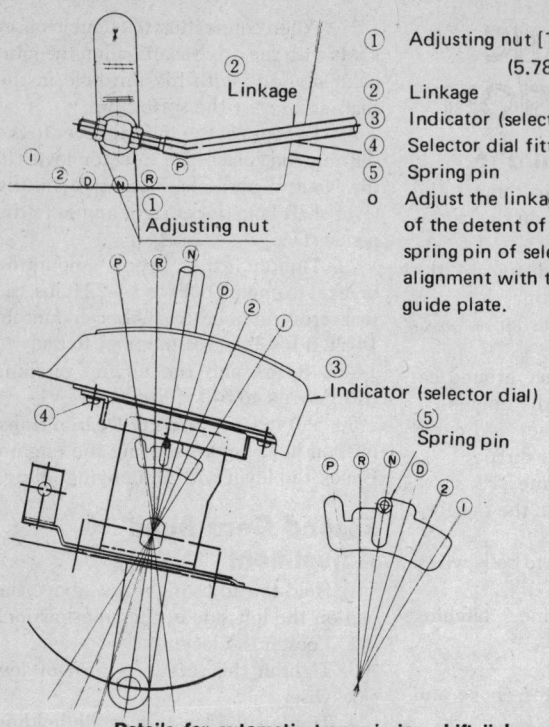

① Adjusting nut [Tightening torque: (5.78 to 8.68 ft-lb)
② Linkage
③ Indicator (selector dial)
④ Selector dial fitting screw
⑤ Spring pin
o Adjust the linkage so that the position "N" of the detent of the manual valve and the spring pin of selector lever will come in alignment with the position "N" of the guide plate.

Details for automatic transmission shift linkage adjustment

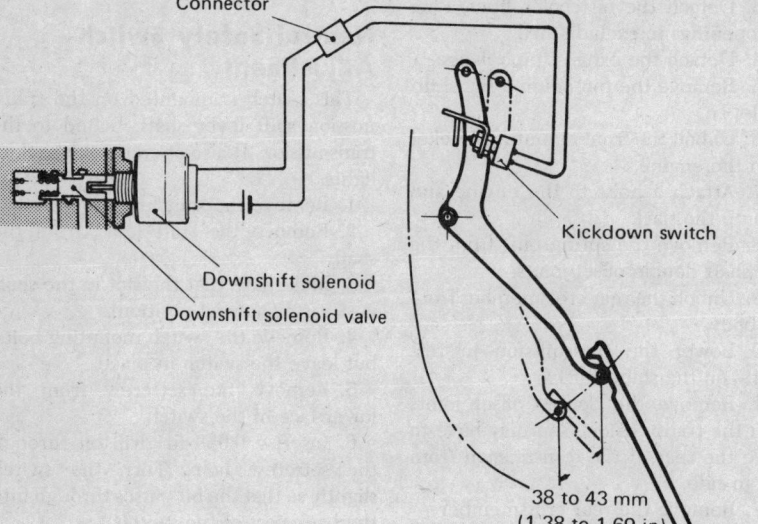

Automatic transmission kickdown system

Kickdown Solenoid

An audible click should be heard from the solenoid on the right side of the transmission, when the accelerator pedal is pushed down all the way with the engine off and the ignition switch on. The switch is operated by the upper part of the accelerator lever inside the car. The position of the switch can be varied to give quicker or slower kickdown response.

Front Drive Axle

The drive axle consists of a double-offset joint (DOJ) at the inner end, an axle shaft, a constant velocity joint at the outer end, and a stub axle.

Removal and Installation

1300 G

1. Engage the parking brake. Remove the wheel cover and loosen the lug nuts. Flatten the lockplate and loosen the hubnut.
2. Raise the car and support it with jackstands.
3. Remove the lug nuts, wheel and tire.
4. Remove the hub nut.

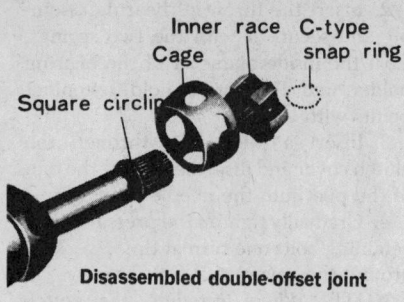

Disassembled double-offset joint

5. Unfasten the 3 retaining bolts and separate the double-offset joint from the brake drum.
6. Unfasten the inner panel from the wheel well.
7. Turn the steering knuckle to full lock and pull the stub axle out of the hub.
8. Slide the drive axle assembly out of the wheel well.

Installation is the reverse of removal. Tighten the hub nut to 87–101 ft lbs and secure it by bending the tabs of the lockplate up around it.

DL, GL, GF, 4WD

1. Engage the parking brake. Remove the wheel cover (sedans and wagon), and loosen the lug nuts. Loosen the hub nut. Later models have the hub nut staked in place; unstake it with a thin chisel or a punch.
2. Raise the car and support it with jackstands.
3. Remove the lug nuts, wheel and tire. Remove the hub nut.
4. Remove the drum brake or disc brake assembly.
5. On drum brakes, remove the 4 backing plate installing bolts and wire the backing plate to the suspension without disconnecting the hydraulic line.
6. Drive out the spring (roll) pin, which fastens the double-offset joint end of the axle shaft to the driveshaft, by lightly tapping with a hammer. Throw the old pin away; do not reuse it.
7. Remove the self-locking nuts which attach the ends of the control arm to the stabilizer bar and the crossmember inner pivot.
8. Separate the control arm from the crossmember pivot by prying it rearward with a suitable lever.
9. To disconnect the control arm from the stabilizer bar, swing the link forward.
10. Pull the axle shaft out of the driveshaft (double-offset joint side) by pushing outward on the front suspension assembly.
11. Pull the other end of the drive axle out of the housing, while holding the shaft so that it doesn't drop.

Installation is as follows:
1. Thread a metric bolt which is long enough to fit through the axle housing, into the end of the stub axle.
2. Fit the bolt through the axle hous-

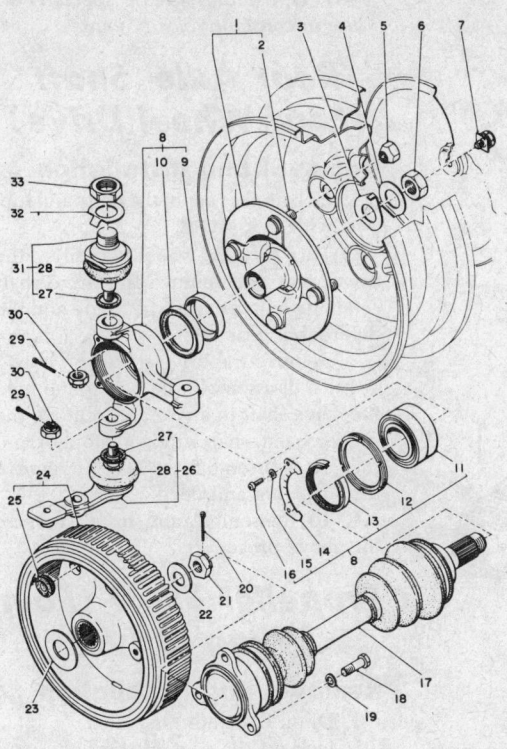

1. Hub
2. Hub bolt
3. Washer
4. Lock plate
5. Wheel nut
6. Hub nut
7. Bolt (wheel cap)
8. Knuckle assembly
9. Spacer
10. Oil seal
11. Bearing assembly
12. Nut
13. Oil seal
14. Lock plate
15. Spring washer
16. Bolt
17. Axle shaft assembly
18. Bolt
19. Spring washer
20. Cotter pin
21. Castle nut
22. Washer
23. Buffer plate
24. Brake drum
25. Brake adjusting port cover (brake drum)
26. Ball joint assembly (lower)
27. Clip
28. Boot
29. Cotter pin
30. Castle nut
31. Ball joint assembly (upper)
32. Lock plate
33. Nut

Drive axle and inboard brakes—1300G

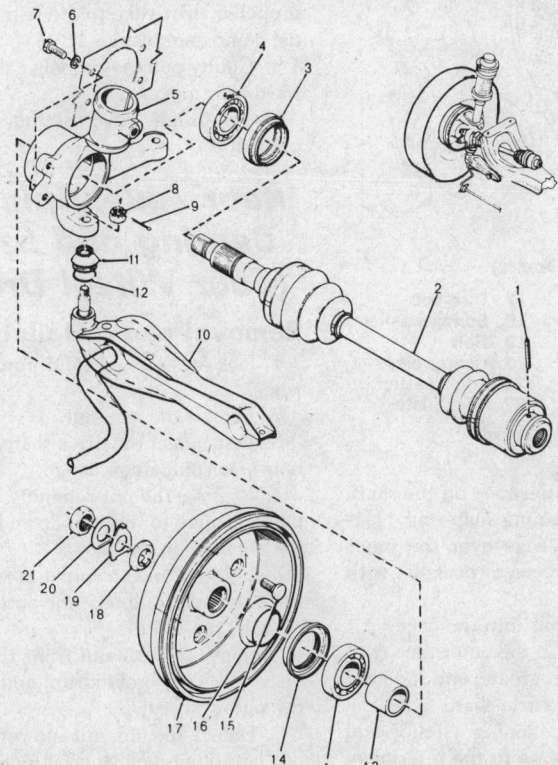

Exploded view of the DL front axle assembly (drum brakes)

1. Spring pin
2. Axle shaft
3. Oil seal (in.)
4. Bearing
5. Housing
6. Spring washer
7. Bolt
8. Castle nut
9. Cotter pin
10. Transverse link
11. Dust seal (Ball joint)
12. Circlip
13. Spacer
14. Oil seal (out)
15. Hub bolt
16. Sleeve
17. Brake drum
18. Center piece
19. Lock washer
20. Lock plate
21. Nut

ing, using care not to damage the oil seal, splines, or bearing. Draw the drive axle assembly into place by grasping the end of the bolt with a puller.

3. On disc brakes, install the brake disc and hub.

4. On drum brakes, do the following:

a. Secure the backing plate with its 4 bolts. Tighten the bolts to 22–37 ft lbs.

b. Install the brake drum assembly.

5. Install the hub nut:

a. On 1972–73 models, install the spacer, lockwasher, and hub nut. Tighten the nut to 145–181 ft lbs and secure it with the lockwasher.

b. On 1974–77 models, install the spacer, conical spring washer and the hub nut. Tighten the nut to 160–180 ft lbs (174 ft lbs preferred). Secure the hub nut to the axle shaft by using a punch to stake the flange on the nut to the groove in the end of the axle shaft.

6. Connect the double-offset joint side of the axle shaft to the driveshaft and secure them with a new spring pin.

7. Fit the washer and bushing over the end of the stabilizer bar and then connect the transverse link to the end of the stabilizer.

Install the remaining washer and bushing and temporarily secure them with a new self-locking nut.

8. Install the control arm to the crossmember pivot. Temporarily secure them with another new self-locking nut.

9. On disc brakes, install the dust cover, caliper, and parking brake cable.

10. Install the wheel and remove the jackstands.

11. Tighten the new self-locking nuts used at each end of the transverse link to 72–87 ft lbs with the car resting on its wheels.

U-Joint Overhaul

1. Remove the bands from the boots at both the constant velocity and double-offset joints, and slide the boots away from the joints.

2. Pry the circlip out of the double-offset joint, and slide the outer race of the joint off the shaft.

3. Remove the balls from the cage, rotate the cage slightly, and slide the cage inward on the axle shaft.

4. Using snap-ring pliers, remove the outer snap-ring which retains the inner race to the shaft.

5. Slide the inner race, cage, and boot off the axle shaft.

NOTE: *Exercise care to avoid damaging the boot on the inner snap-ring.*

6. Pull back the constant velocity joint boot and pivot the stub axle around the joint far enough to expose a ball.

7. Remove the exposed ball, and continue this procedure until all balls are removed, at which time the outer race

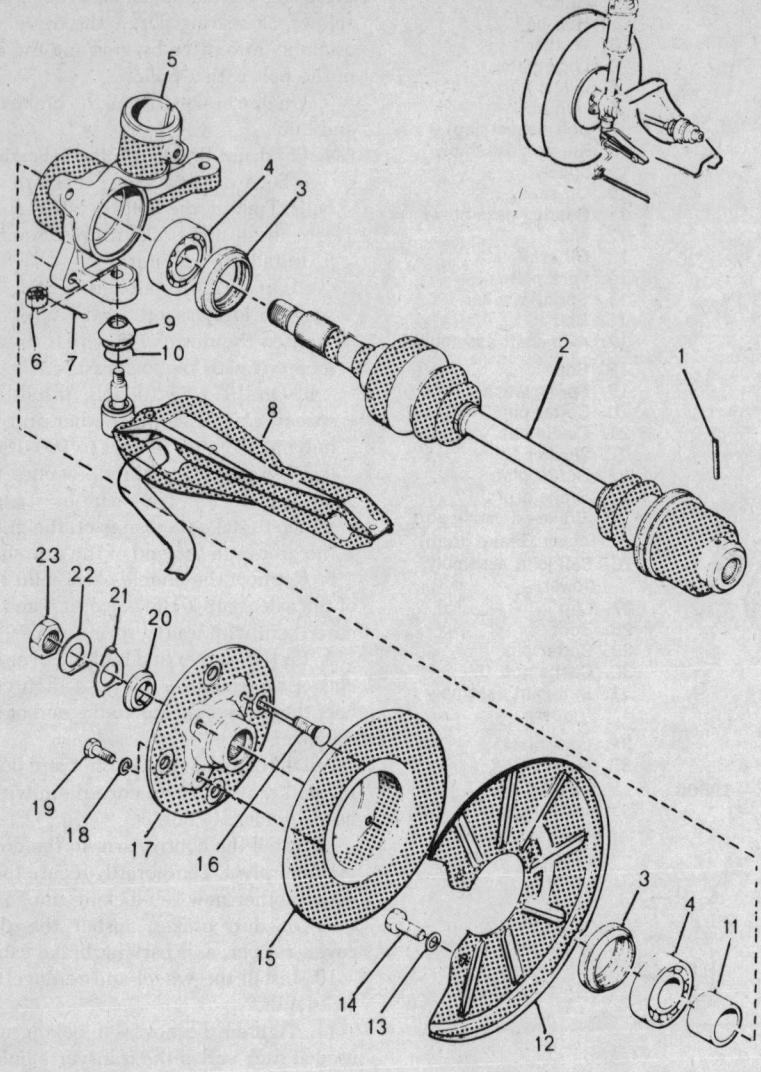

Exploded view of the GL front axle assembly (disc brakes)

1. Spring pin
2. Axle shaft
3. Oil seal
4. Bearing
5. Housing
6. Castle nut
7. Cotter pin
8. Transverse link
9. Dust seal (Ball joint)
10. Circlip
11. Spacer
12. Disc cover
13. Spring washer
14. Bolt
15. Disc
16. Hub bolt
17. Disc hub
18. Spring washer
19. Bolt
20. Center piece
21. Lock washer
22. Lock plate
23. Nut

(stub axle) may be removed from the axle shaft.

8. Remove the retaining snap-ring, and slide the inner race off the shaft.

9. Inspect the parts of both joints for wear, damage, or corrosion, and replace if necessary. Examine the axle shaft for bending or distortion, and replace if evident. Should the boots be dried out, cracked, or distorted, they must be replaced.

10. Install the constant velocity joint inner race on the axle shaft, and retain with a snap-ring.

11. Assemble the joint in the opposite order of disassembly.

12. Slide the double-offset joint cage onto the shaft, with the counterbore toward the end of the shaft.

13. Install the inner race on the shaft, and install the retaining snap-ring.

14. Position the cage over the inner race, and fill the cage pockets with grease.

15. Insert the balls into the cage.

16. Fill the well in the outer race with approximately 1 oz. grease, and slide the outer race onto the axle shaft.

17. Install the retaining circlip, and add 1 oz. more grease to the interior of the joint. Fill the boot with approximately 1 oz. grease, and slide it into position over the double-offset joint.

18. Fill the constant velocity joint boot with 3 oz. grease, and install the boot over the joint.

19. Band the boots on both joints tightly enough that they cannot be

turned by hand.

NOTE: *Use only grease specified for use in constant velocity joints.*

Rear Axle Shaft (Four Wheel Drive)

Removal and Installation

1. Jack up the rear of the body and support with jack stands.

2. Turn the rear wheel to position the drive shaft and remove the drive shaft retaining bolts on the wheel side and the differential gear side.

3. Remove the drive shaft assembly.

4. To disassemble the ball spline hold the drive shaft in a vise, and remove the rubber band, snap ring and stopper.

5. To disassemble the U-joint remove the snap ring and needle bearing.

6. To reassemble and install reverse the above procedure.

Propeller Shaft (Four Wheel Drive)

Removal and Installation

1. Drain the transmission oil.

2. Jack up the rear of the body, and support with jack stands.

3. Remove the bolts connecting the propeller shaft yoke to the rear differential companion flange.

4. Gently pull the propeller shaft rearward to remove.

5. To install reverse the removal procedure.

Rear Axle, Spindle, Bearing and Seals (Four Wheel Drive)

Removal and Installation

1. Jack up the car and remove the wheel.

2. Loosen the axle nut.

3. Disconnect the drive shaft from the rear axle companion flange.

4. Remove the nut retaining the companion flange to the spindle and remove the companion flange.

5. Pull the brake drum and spindle to the outer side, and take the outer oil seal off with the spindle.

6. Remove the axle nut from the spindle disconnect the brake drum and pull out the outer oil seal.

7. Unlock the link nut and remove the nut with a wrench (special tool.)

8. Remove the inner race.

9. New seals may be pressed into place at this time or if the bearing is to be replaced proceed as follows.

10. Dismount the rear suspension including the rear brake back plate.

11. Use a press and remove the bearing.

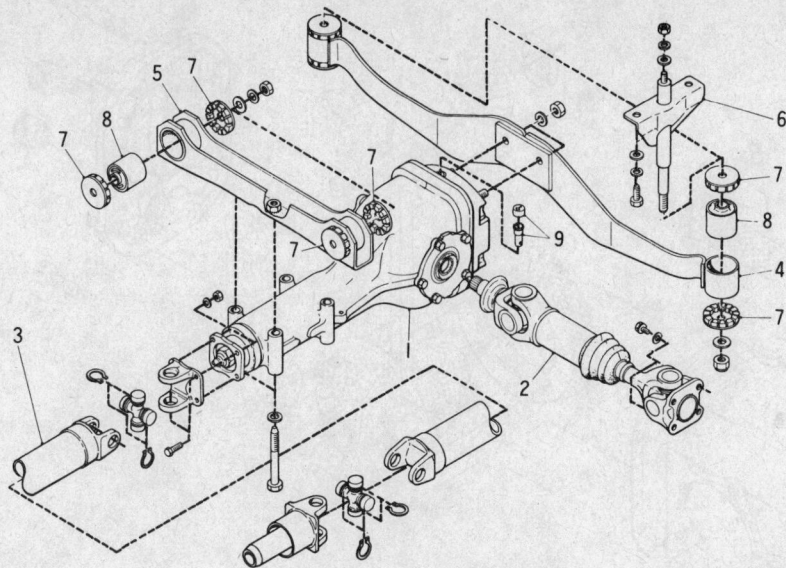

Rear drive assembly (4 WD vehicles)

1. Differential assembly
2. Driveshaft assembly
3. Propeller shaft assembly
4. Mounting member
5. Mounting bracket
6. Bracket
7. Stoppper
8. Bushing
9. Breather cap

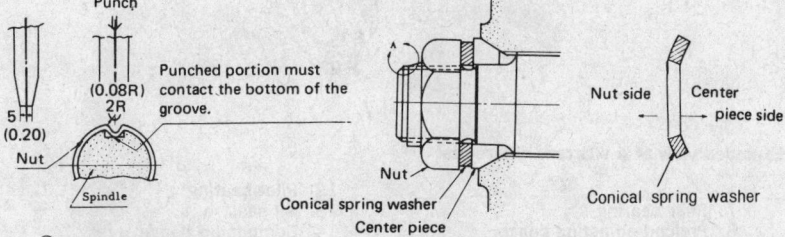

A. ◯ Axial direction view

Installing the axle nut

Unit : mm (in.)

Removing the link nut using special tool

12. When replacing the inner and outer seals place the inner and outer side of the housing on a V-block and press the seals into place.

13. Hold the trailing arm in a vise and lightly tighten the link nut in the housing with the special wrench. Torque the nut to 130–166 ft lbs.

14. Lock the link nut.

15. Install the rear trailing arm to the body.

16. Fit the back plate (22–35 ft. lbs) and connect the brake pipe (11–14 ft. lbs.).

17. Temporarily fit the brake drum to the spindle.

18. Bleed the brake system.

19. Position the companion flange to the spindle inner end and tighten the lock nut to 145–181 ft. lbs.

NOTE: *When tightening, apply the foot brake to produce reaction force.*

20. Make sure the bearing rotates smoothly and stake the lock nut.

21. Fit the center piece, conical spring washer and retaining nut onto the axle shaft and tighten the retaining nut to 174 ft. lbs.

NOTE: *Punch the flange portion of the retaining nut toward the groove of the front axle after tightening.*

22. Connect the axle shaft and companion flange and tighten the retaining nuts to 29–36 ft. lbs.

23. Install the spindle and wheel assembly. Tighten the wheel nuts to 58–72 ft. lbs.

REAR SUSPENSION

Early models utilize full trailing arms, mounted to transverse torsion bars, with an auxiliary center spring. Shock absorbers mount to the trailing arm, close to the stub axle.

Late models use semi-trailing arms mounted to torque tubes, which act on an internal torsion bar. Shock absorbers are mounted to the trailing arm, close to the stub axle.

Torsion Bars

Removal and Installation

1300 G Wagon

1. Raise the rear of the vehicle and remove the wheel.

2. Using a hex key (8 mm), loosen the center arm and spring to relax the torsion bars.

3. Remove the nut and retaining plate from the crossmember mounting bracket.

4. Back out the lock bolts at each end of the torsion bar to be removed, thread a bolt into the bar, and pull it out of the crossmember.

Torsion bars are marked R or L, and must be installed on the correct side.

Install in the reverse order of removal, and adjust ride height.

1300 G Sedan, GL, GF, DL, 4WD

1. Remove the shock absorber lower retaining nut, and separate the shock absorber from the trailing arm.

2. Raise the vehicle and remove the rear wheel.

3. Index mark the splines on the outside and inside of the torsion bar, to indicate mounting position for installation.

4. Remove the lockbolt from the outer torsion bar bushing.

5. Position the trailing arm so as to remove all load from the torsion bar, and tap the torsion bar out.

6. Install the torsion bars in the reverse order of removal. Each torsion bar is marked R or L, on the outer end, to indicate on which side it is installed.

Index the splines according to the marks made during removal, install the wheel and check ride height. If necessary, adjust ride height. Remount the shock absorber after the vehicle has been lowered.

Shock Absorbers

Removal and Installation

1. Remove the wheel cover and loosen the lug nuts. Raise the rear of the car and support it with jackstands, after setting

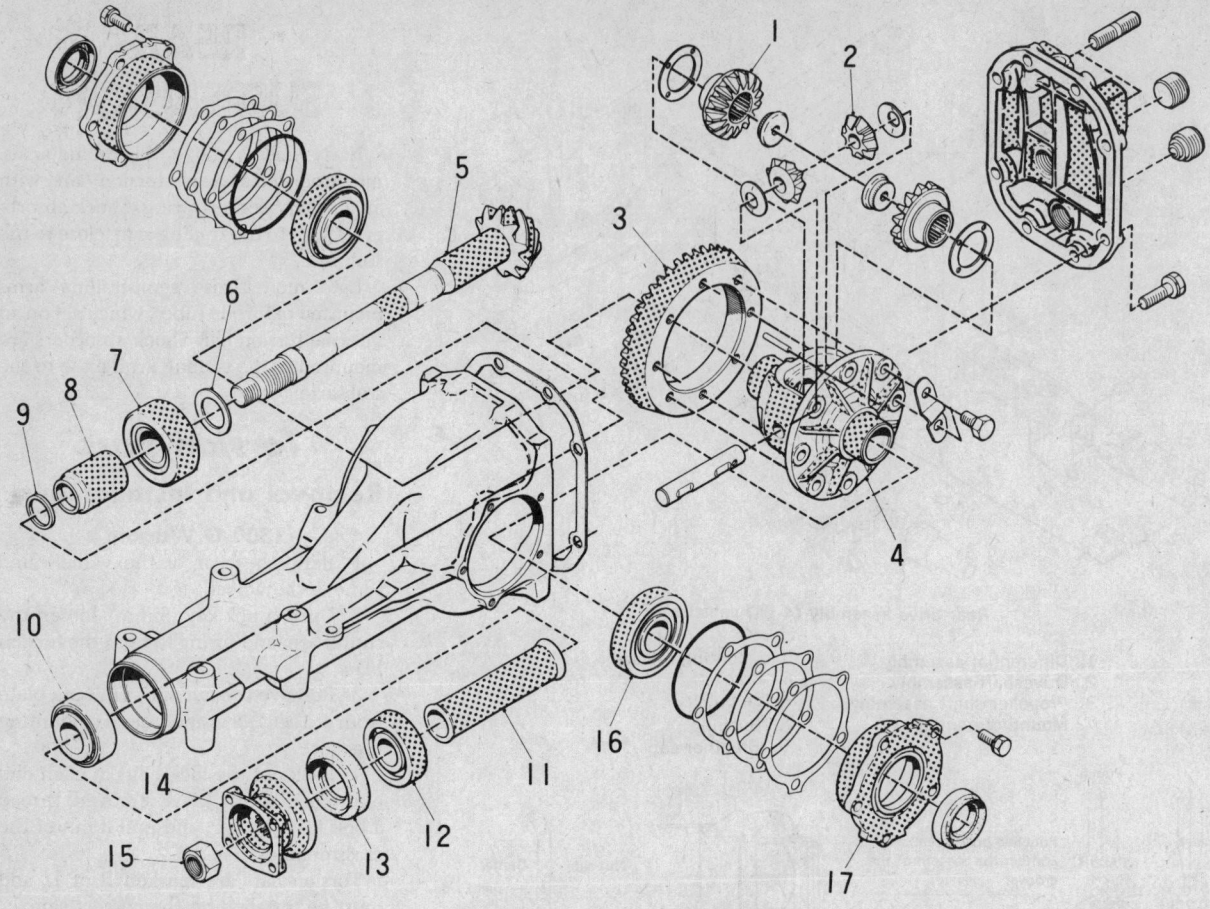

Exploded view of 4 WD rear differential

1. Side gear
2. Pinion mate gear
3. Drive gear
4. Differential case
5. Drive pinion
6. Pinion height adjusting washer
7. Rear bearing
8. Preload adjusting spacer
9. Preload adjusting washer
10. Front bearing
11. Spacer
12. Pilot bearing
13. Oil seal
14. Companion flange
15. Pinion nut
16. Side bearing
17. Side bearing retainer

the parking brake and blocking the front wheels.

2. Remove the lug nuts and the rear wheels.

3. Fully loosen the ride height adjustment bolt on all 1300 G station wagons.

4. Loosen the two upper shock absorber mounting nuts. Remove the washer and the bushing, being sure to note their correct assembly sequence for installation.

5. Unfasten the nut on the trailing arm pin and remove the shock absorber. Note the installing positions of the washers.

Installation is the reverse of removal. Do not fully tighten the upper mounting nuts until the lower shock nut has been installed with the washer and the pin shoulder contacting each other. Tighten the upper nuts to 22–32 ft lbs. Adjust the ride height bolt.

Rear End Alignment

Camber

Rear wheel camber is adjusted by changing the number of shims mounted between the inner torsion bar bushing assembly and the body. Each shim corresponds to ¼° of change. Adding shims decreases the camber; removing shims increases it.

Toe-In

Rear wheel toe-in is changed by loosening the inner torsion bar bushing assembly bolts and sliding the bushing assembly forward or backward. Forward movement decreases toe-in and back-

REAR END ALIGNMENT

Year	Model	Ride* Height (in.)	Camber (deg)	Toe-In (in.)
1972	FF-1, 1300 G Sedan	12.1-12.6	½P to 1½P	0.04-0.20
	FF-1, 1300 G Wagon	13.0-13.4	½P to 1½P	0.04-0.20
1972	GL	11.1-11.7	¼P to 1½P	0.04-0.20
	DL	11.3-11.9	½P to 1½P	0.04-0.20
1973-74	GL, DL Coupe, Sedan	11.3-11.9	¼P to 1½P	0.04-0.20
	DL Wagon, except 4 wd	11.2-12.0	¼P to 1½P	0.04-0.20
1975-77	Coupe, Sedan	11.3-11.9	¼P to 1½P	0.08-0.24
	Sta. Wag.	12.2-12.8	1P to 2P	0.04-0.20
	4 wd	14.1-14.8	1⅓P to 2⅓P	0.08-0.24

P Positive
* Measured from outer center of torsion bar

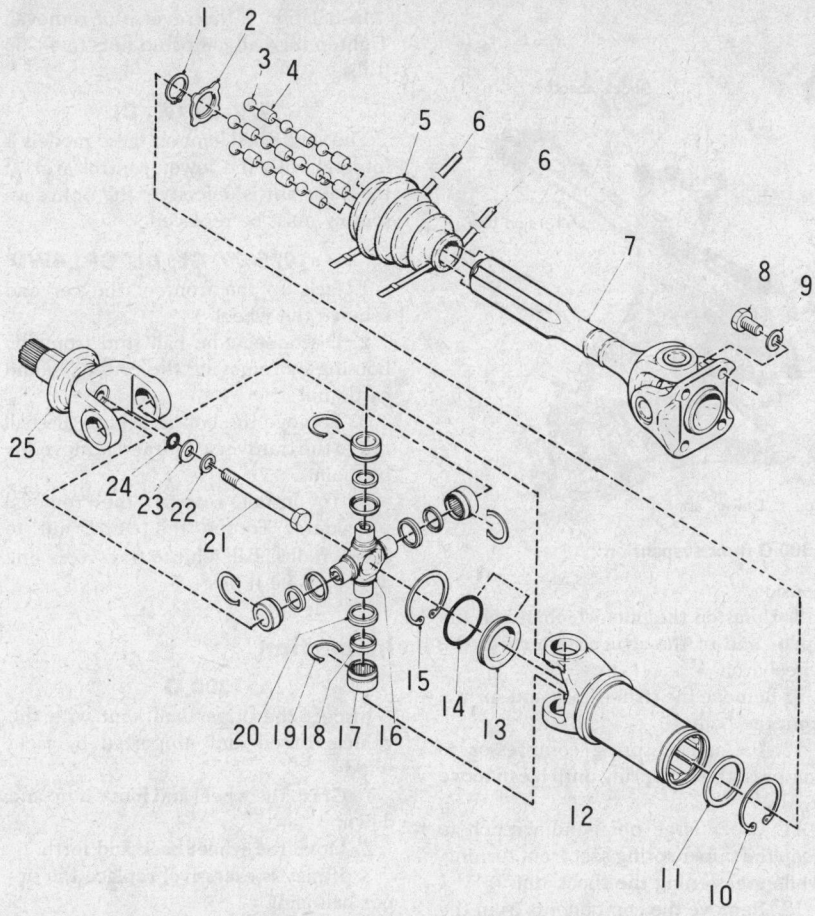

Exploded view of 4 WD rear axle shaft

1. Snap-ring
2. Stopper
3. Ball
4. Ball spacer
5. Rubber boot
6. Boot band
7. Yoke
8. Bolt
9. Spring washer
10. Snap-ring
11. Stopper
12. Sleeve yoke
13. Plug
14. O-ring
15. Snap-ring
16. Spider
17. Bearing race
18. Oil seal
19. Snap-ring
20. Dust cover (oil seal)
21. Bolt
22. Spring washer
23. Washer
24. O-ring
25. Side yoke

ward movement increases it. Tighten the bolts after completing the adjustment.

Ride Height

1300 G Wagon

Adjust rear ride height by turning a socket head bolt (8 mm), clockwise to raise, and counterclockwise to lower the vehicle. The bolt is accessible through a port in the trunk.

1300 G Sedan, GL, GF, DL, 4WD

No routine ride height adjustment is provided. Should it be necessary to adjust ride height, the torsion bar(s) must be removed. To increase ride height, turn the outer end of the torsion bar in the direction of the arrow (on the end of the bar), and the inner end in the opposite direction an equal number of teeth. Decrease ride height by reversing the

above. Shifting the torsion bar one tooth will alter ride height approximately 0.2 in.

FRONT SUSPENSION

Torsion Bars

Removal and Installation

1300 G

1. Raise the vehicle, and loosen the ride height adjusting cam retainer.
2. Remove the shock absorber upper retaining nuts.
3. Flatten the locktab, and remove the upper ball joint upper nut.
4. Remove both torsion bar lockbolts and nuts, at the adjuster arm and the upper control arm.

5. Rotate the upper control arm away from the ball joint, and then down, to fully relax the torsion bar.
6. Remove the adjuster arm, and slide the torsion bar out.

Installation is the reverse of removal.
CAUTION: *Do not interchange torsion bars side-to-side.* Index the missing tooth on the torsion bar splines with the double tooth on the anchor arm. Following installation, adjust ride height.

McPherson Strut Assembly

Removal and Installation

DL, GL, GF, 4WD

NOTE: *Use this procedure to remove the entire suspension assembly. If only shock and/or spring removal are desired, use the procedure given under "Shock Absorbers".*
Raise and support.

1. Remove the battery cable from the negative terminal of the battery.
2. Remove the hub caps, loosen the lug nuts, jack up the vehicle until the tire clears the ground and remove the lug nuts and the wheel/tire assembly. Place the jackstands under the vehicle and remove the jack. Perform this operation on the opposite side if the suspension is to be removed from both sides of the vehicle.
3. Remove the hand brake cable bracket and the hand brake cable hanger from the transverse link and the tie-rod end. Remove the hand brake cable end.
4. Remove the axle nut, lockplate, washer, and center piece and remove the front brake drums by using a puller.
5. Disconnect the brake hoses from the brake fluid pipes.
6. Remove the backing plates with the brake assemblies attached.
7. On cars equipped with front disc brakes, remove the hand brake cable end from the caliper lever. Remove the outer cable clip from the cable-end support bracket at the caliper. Remove the hand brake cable bracket from the housing mount by loosening the nuts.
8. Drive out the spring pins of the double offset joint by using a drift pin and a hammer. The double offset side of the axle is the side closest to the transaxle.
9. Remove the lower control arm by loosening the self-locking nut which holds it to the inner pivot shaft of the crossmember. Loosen and remove the nuts which clamp the control arm to the stabilizer. Remove the stabilizer rearward from the crossmember by using a lever and pulling the control arm out from the end of the stabilizer.
10. Remove the cotter pin from the castle nut and remove the nuts and ball

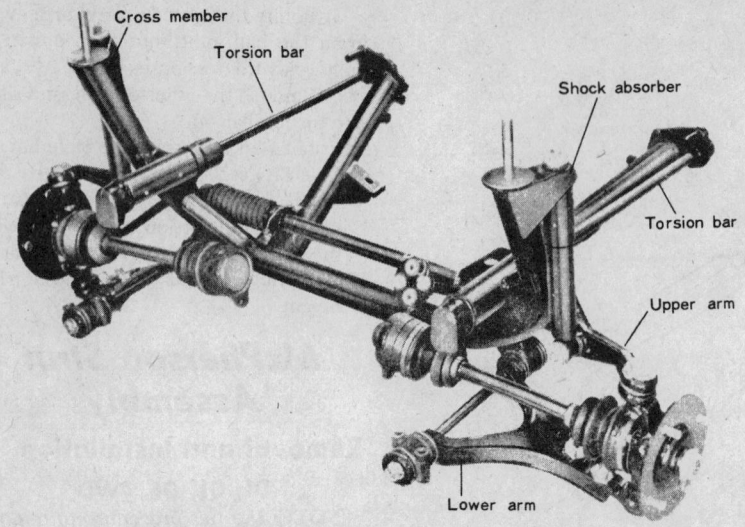

Exploded view of FF-1 and 1300 G front suspension

stud from the knuckle arm of the tie-rod end ball joint housing. Take care not to bend the housing.

11. Remove the nuts which hold the strut mount to the body (suspension assembly upper mounting nut-top of the shock absorber tower).

12. Pull the double offset joint out of the driveshaft and then remove the suspension assembly from the body.

Install the suspension assembly in the reverse order of removal.

Shock Absorbers

Removal and Installation

1300 G

The front shock absorber is removed and installed in the same way as the rear shock absorber.

NOTE: *Prior to shock removal, loosen the ride height adjusting cam, and adjust ride height after shock absorber installation is completed.*

Check the shock for leaks, binding, external damage, defective bushings, and wear. Replace the shock, as necessary.

DL, GL, GF, 4WD

NOTE: *Use this procedure if only shock absorber (strut) or spring removal is desired.*

1. Remove the wheel cover and loosen the lug nuts.

2. Raise the front of the car and support it on jackstands.

3. Remove the lug nuts and wheels.

4. Unfasten the bolts which secure the bottom of the strut assembly to the axle housing.

5. Remove the bolts which attach the strut bracket to the axle housing.

6. Detach the end of the tie-rod from the axle housing in order to prevent ball joint damage.

7. Remove the strut from the housing, gradually and carefully, by lowering the housing.

8. Unfasten the nuts which attach the upper end of the strut assembly to the wheel arch.

9. Remove the strut (shock and spring) from the body.

10. Use a coil spring compressor to compress the coil spring until it can move freely.

11. Use a large open-end wrench to keep the upper spring seat from turning, while unfastening the shock nut.

12. Remove the components from the top of the shock, being careful to note their order, and remove the compressed spring.

Test the operation of the shock absorber by placing it in an upright position; push and pull on the shock, if it presents little resistance or binds, replace it with a new shock.

Examine the shock for leaks, a bent mounting stud, or other signs of wear or damage.

Installation is the reverse of removal. Be sure to assemble the components on the top of the shock in the correct order. Lubricate the oil seal lips and the thrust washers with a light coating of grease. Tighten the shock absorber-to-mount self-locking nut to 43–54 ft lbs.

Ball Joints

Removal and Installation

1300 G

In order to remove the ball joints, it will be necessary to remove the steering knuckle/hub assembly from the car first. See "Wheel Bearings" for the knuckle/-hub removal and installation procedure. After removal, do the following:

1. Remove the cotter pin from the castellated nut. Unfasten the nut.

2. Extract the ball joint with a puller.

3. Repeat for the other ball joint.

Installation is the reverse of removal. Tighten the ball joint stud nuts to 43–65 ft lbs.

1972–74 GL, DL

The single ball joint on these models is integral with the lower control arm. If the ball joint is defective, the entire assembly must be replaced.

1975–77 GL, DL, GF, 4WD

1. Jack up the front of the car and remove the wheel.

2. Disconnect the ball stud from the housing by removing the cotter pin and castle nut.

3. Remove the bolt attaching the ball nut to the transverse link and remove the ball joint.

4. To install reverse the removal procedure. Torque the castle nut to 35–40 ft. lbs., ball joint to transverse link nut to 80–94 ft. lbs.

Inspection

1300 G

Inspect the upper ball joint with the vehicle raised and supported by jackstands.

1. Grasp the wheel and move it up and down.

2. Move the wheel back and forth.

3. If play is excessive, replace the upper ball joint.

NOTE: *Excessive wheel play may also be caused by a worn wheel bearing or an improperly installed bearing nut.*

Inspect the upper ball joint next, with the vehicle still raised and supported, as follows:

1. Separate the ball stud from the steering knuckle.

2. Move the stud with your finger.

3. If there is excessive play replace the lower ball joint.

Check the ball joint boots for tears or other damage. Repack with a long-lasting chassis grease, if the boots are being replaced. Apply grease to the stud neck, to the boot interior, and to the inner lip of the boot.

1972–74 GL, DL

The lower control arm must be removed from the vehicle, in order to check the ball joint.

1. Use a spring scale to apply a force of 154 lbs to the ball joint stud.

2. The ball joint should have no more than 0.12 in. play when this force is applied.

3. Replace the entire control arm assembly if the ball joint is defective.

4. Check the boot for wear, tears, or other damage.

5. Lubricate the ball stud chassis grease and also apply grease to the inside of the boot.

8. Push the upper control arm downward, in order to release the tension from the torsion bar.

9. Pull on the upper anchor arm in order to disengage the upper control arm from the torsion bar. Remove the control arm.

Installation is the reverse of removal. Adjust the ride height after installation.

Lower Control Arm

Removal and Installation

1300 G

1. Perform Steps 1–3 of the upper control arm removal procedure.

2. Remove the nut which secures the lower control arm shaft to its front crossmember bracket.

3. Disconnect the lower control arm from the front crossmember.

4. Separate the arm from the ball joint and remove the arm from the steering knuckle.

5. Remove the nuts and spring washers which attach the control arm to the body mounting bracket.

Installation is the reverse of removal. Tighten the nuts which secure the arm to the body bracket to 26–32 ft lbs. and the lower arm shaft nut to 33–43 ft lbs.

DL, GL, GF, 4WD

GL and DL models have only one control arm. To remove and install it, proceed as follows:

1. Remove the wheel cover and loosen the lug nuts.

2. Jack up the car and support it with jackstands. Block the rear wheels.

3. Remove the lug nuts and the wheel.

4. Remove the parking brake cable clamp from the control arm by unfastening its nut.

5. Unfasten the self-locking nut which attaches the control arm to the crossmember. Be sure to note the installation sequence of the washers.

6. Unfasten the self-locking nut which secures the stabilizer bar to the control arm. Again, note the installation sequence of the washers.

7. Pry the control arm off the crossmember.

8. Push the control arm forward and detach it from the end of the stabilizer bar.

9. Remove the cotter pin from the castellated nut. Unfasten the nut and remove the ball joint from the axle housing with a puller.

10. Remove the control arm from under the car.

Installation is the reverse of removal. Do not grease the upper ball joint stud which fits into the axle housing. Tighten the castellated nut to 30–40 ft lbs. Use *new* self-locking nuts on the crossmember and stabilizer bar mounts. Tighten

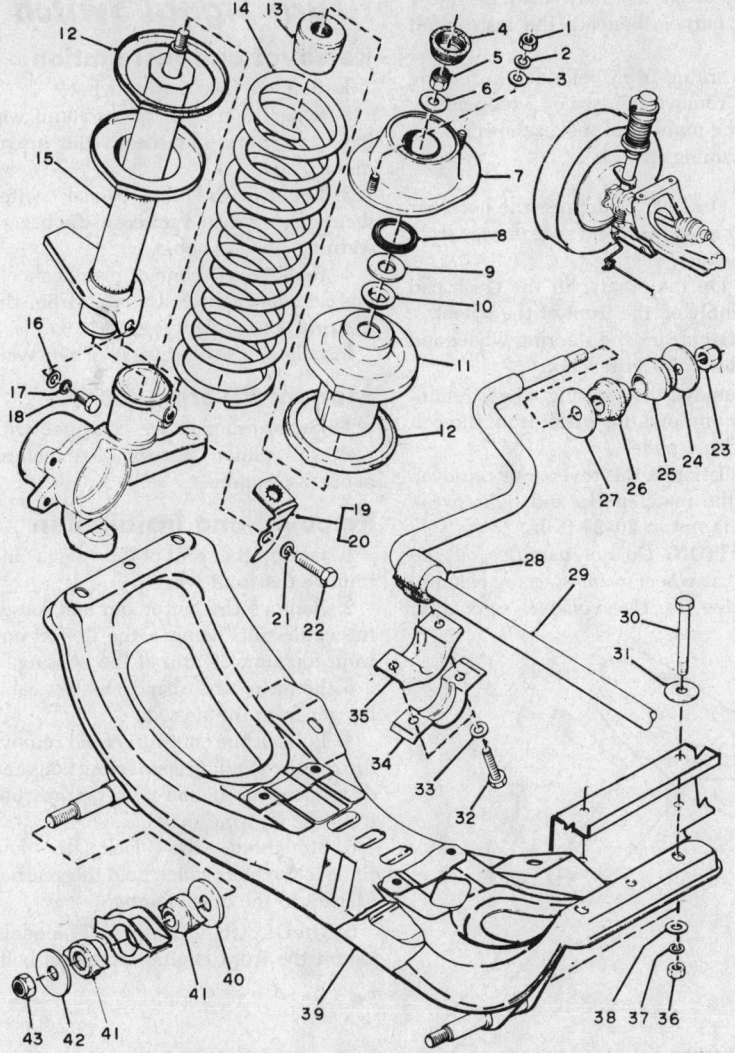

Exploded view of the 1972-75 DL and GL suspension. The 1976-77 models have a similar suspension.

1. Nut	16. Washer	30. Bolt
2. Spring washer	17. Spring washer	31. Washer
3. Washer	18. Bolt	32. Bolt (10 x 40)
4. Cap (strut mount)	19. Bracket compl. (brake hose: RH)	33. Washer
5. Self locking nut	20. Bracket compl. (brake hose: LH)	34. Lock plate
6. Washer	21. Spring washer	35. Bracket (stabilizer)
7. Strut mount	22. Bolt	36. Nut
8. Oil seal (strut mount)	23. Self locking nut	37. Spring washer
9. Washer (thrust bearing)	24. Washer (transverse link inner)	38. Washer
10. Thrust washer	25. Bushing (link outer)	39. Crossmember compl. (F)
11. Spring retainer (upper)	26. Bushing (link outer)	40. Washer (transverse link inner)
12. Rubber seat (coil spring)	27. Washer (transverse link outer)	41. Bushing (inner pivot)
13. Helper	28. Bushing (stabilizer)	42. Washer (transverse link outer)
14. Coil spring	29. Stabilizer	43. Self locking nut
15. Shock absorber complete		

Upper Control Arm

Removal and Installation

1300 G

1. Remove the wheel cover and loosen the lug nuts.

2. Raise the car and support it with jackstands. Block the rear wheels.

3. Remove the lug nuts and wheels.

4. Remove the end bolt on the ride height adjusting cam, in order to loosen the cam.

5. Remove the two nuts and washers from the shock absorber upper mounting stud.

6. Straighten out the lockwasher on the upper ball joint securing nut and remove the nut.

7. Remove the dust cover and the locknut from the upper arm.

the new self-locking nuts to 73–87 ft lbs with the vehicle resting on the wheels.

Front End Alignment

Caster and Camber

1300 G

Caster and camber are controlled by hexagonal cams which control the position of the lower ball joint on the control arm. Rotating the inner (caster) or outer (camber) cam by two flats changes caster or camber by 1°.

DL, GL, GF, 4WD

Caster and camber are not adjustable on these models. If either of these specifications is not within the factory recommended range, this would indicate bent or damaged parts that must be replaced.

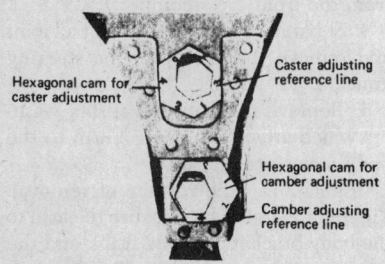

Caster and camber adjustment cams (1300G)

Toe-In

Toe-in is adjusted by loosening the locknuts on the tie-rods, and turning the tie-rods.

NOTE: *Before performing the toe-in adjustment, be sure that the steering gear is centered by aligning the marks on it, and that the wheels are straight-ahead.*

Tighten the locknuts after the toe-in adjustment is completed.

Ride Height

1300 G

Ride height is measured from the center of the lower control arm to the ground. It should be 8.94–9.33 in. Adjust it by turning the adjustment cam on the front of each torsion bar. Turning the cam clockwise raises, and counterclockwise lowers ride height. Each notch in the cam corresponds to a 0.32 in. change in height.

Access to the cams is through the cooling slots on either side, below the grille.

STEERING

Steering Wheel

Removal and Installation

1. Disconnect the negative battery cable.

2. Unfasten the horn lead from the wiring harness beneath the instrument panel.

3. Working from behind the steering wheel, remove the two or 3 (depending upon the number of spokes) horn assembly retaining screws.

4.
  a. On 1300 G, depress the horn bar as far as you can, and slide it away from the wheel.
  b. On the others, lift the crash pad assembly off the front of the wheel.

5. Matchmark the steering wheel and the column for installation.

6. Remove the steering wheel retaining nut and pull the wheel from the column with a puller.

Installation is the reverse of removal. Index the matchmarks and tighten the retaining nut to 20–29 ft lbs.

CAUTION: *Do not hammer on the steering wheel or the steering column; damage to the collapsible column could result.*

Turn Signal Switch

Removal and Installation

1. Remove the steering wheel.

2. Separate the steering column wiring connectors underneath the instrument panel.

3. Remove the turn signal switch securing screws and unscrew the hazard warning switch knob.

4. Remove the contact plate, cancelling cam, and switch assembly from the steering column housing.

Installation is the reverse of removal.

Manual Steering Gear

All Subaru models are equipped with rack and pinion steering. No maintenance is required.

Removal and Installation

1. Jack up the front of the vehicle and remove the front wheels.

2. Remove the cotter pin and loosen the castle nut. Remove the tie-rod end from the knuckle arm of the housing.

3. Remove the hand brake cable hanger from the tie-rod.

4. Pull out the cotter pins and remove the rubber coupling connecting bolts and disconnect the pinion with the gearbox from the steering shaft.

5. Straighten the lockplate and remove the bolts which hold the gearbox bracket to the crossmember.

6. On DL, GF, GL, and 4WD models, loosen the front engine mounting bolts

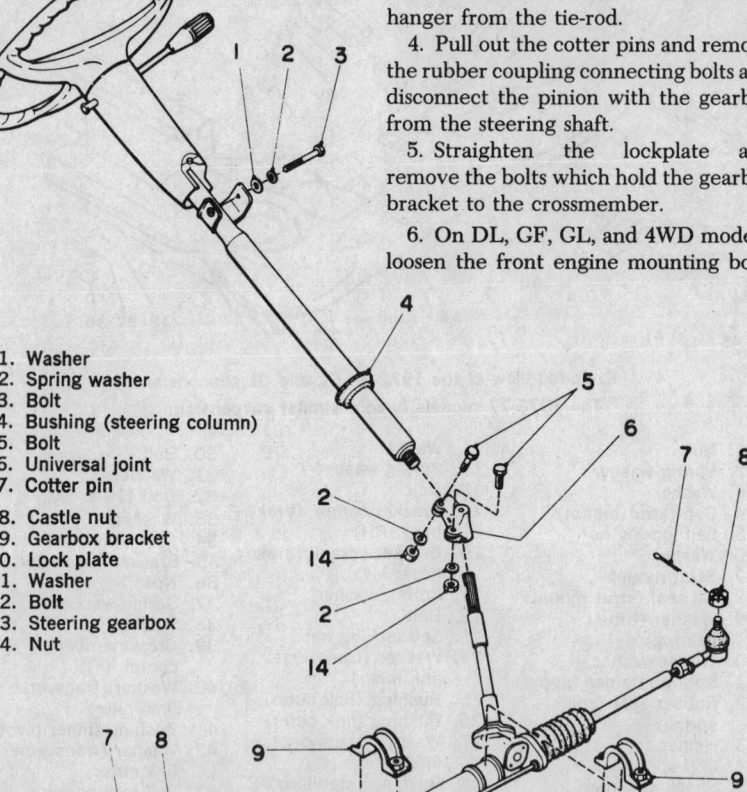

1. Washer
2. Spring washer
3. Bolt
4. Bushing (steering column)
5. Bolt
6. Universal joint
7. Cotter pin
8. Castle nut
9. Gearbox bracket
10. Lock plate
11. Washer
12. Bolt
13. Steering gearbox
14. Nut

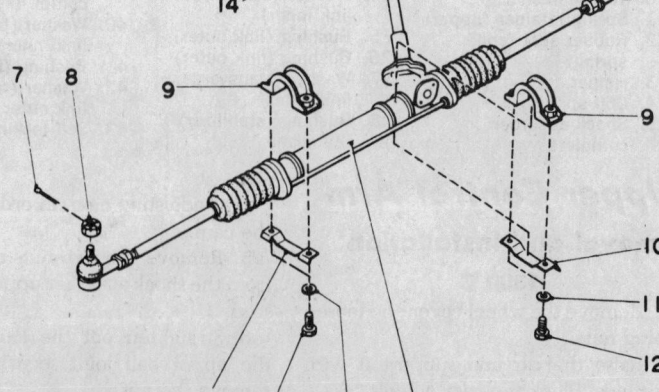

DL, GL, GF steering system

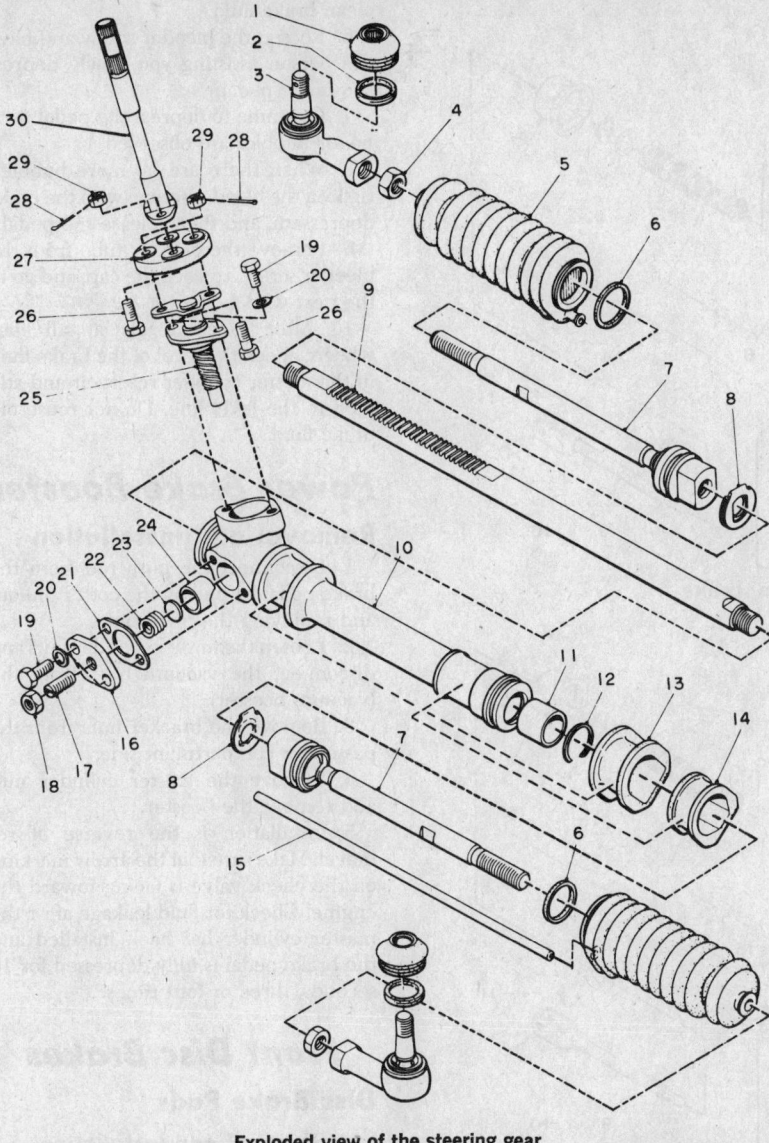

Exploded view of the steering gear

1. Dust seal
2. Snap ring
3. Tie rod end
4. Lock nut
5. Boot
6. Snap ring (boot)
7. Ball joint ass'y
8. Lockwasher
9. Rack
10. Gear box unit
11. Bushing-A
12. Clip
13. Adapter-A
14. Adapter-B
15. Air vent tube
16. Cap (steering gear box)
17. Adjusting screw
18. Lock nut
19. Bolt
20. Spring washer
21. Packing
22. Spring (sleeve)
23. Plate (sleeve)
24. Sleeve
25. Pinion
26. Bolt
27. Rubber coupling
28. Cotter pin
29. Castle nut
30. Torque rod

and lift up the engine by about 0.2 in. to avoid touching the gearbox with the engine. Remove the gearbox from the vehicle.

NOTE: *On 4WD models remove the fan protector on top of the radiator and remove the pitching stopper before lifting the engine.*

Installation is the reverse of removal. Tighten the rack and pinion assembly securing bolts to 33–40 ft lbs. Tighten the rubber coupling castellated nut to 4–5 ft lbs. Tighten the tie-rod end castellated nuts to 18–22 ft lbs. Adjust the toe-in after completing installation.

NOTE: *Check the collapsible steering shaft for straightness or looseness and always replace with a new one if found damaged.*

BRAKES

Adjustment

The front drum brakes are self-adjusting and seldom, if ever, require manual adjustment. For this reason, prior to manual adjustment, ensure that the self-adjuster is functioning, and that brake linings are not excessively worn. To adjust the front brakes, remove the rubber inspection plug, insert a tool through the hole, and turn the star wheel to adjust the brakes. Pushing the handle of the tool will reduce shoe-to-drum clearance. Front disc brakes have no provision for manual adjustment.

The rear brakes are adjusted by turning a bolt at the bottom of the backing plate. Turn the wedge clockwise to lock the brake, and back off 180°. Secure the bolt with its locknut.

Master Cylinder

Removal and Installation

1. Remove the brake line from the master cylinder.
2. Remove the nuts which connect the master cylinder to the pedal bracket.
3. Pull the master cylinder assembly forward and out.
4. Install in the reverse order of removal.

Overhaul

Disassembly

1. Remove the boot from the cylinder body.
2. Remove the stop ring and the stop plate.
3. Remove the stop pin and the gasket.
4. Pull out the primary and the secondary piston assembly.
5. Pull out the return spring.
6. Loosen and remove the screw, the retainer, return spring and secondary cup.

Inspection

Make sure that the bore of the master cylinder is smooth and perfectly round. If the bore is worn or scarred, replace the master cylinder. It is not advisable to repair the bore by honing with emery cloth. The sliding parts used in the cylinder should be washed in clean brake fluid before assembling. Do not allow dust or other foreign matter to enter the cylinder.

The inside diameter of the master cylinder should be 0.7489 in. to 0.7501 in.

The outside diameter of the piston should be 0.7476 in. to 0.7491 in.

The cylinder-to-piston clearance should be within the following limits: 0.-0008 in. to 0.0058 in.

Check the master cylinder rubber cup for scars, splits, wear, and other damage.

Replace the return spring if it is excessively worn. The length of the primary spring should be 2.32 in. with no load. The length of the secondary spring should be 1.99 in. with no load.

Check the fluid reservoir for cracks.

Assembly

1. Insert the return secondary spring.

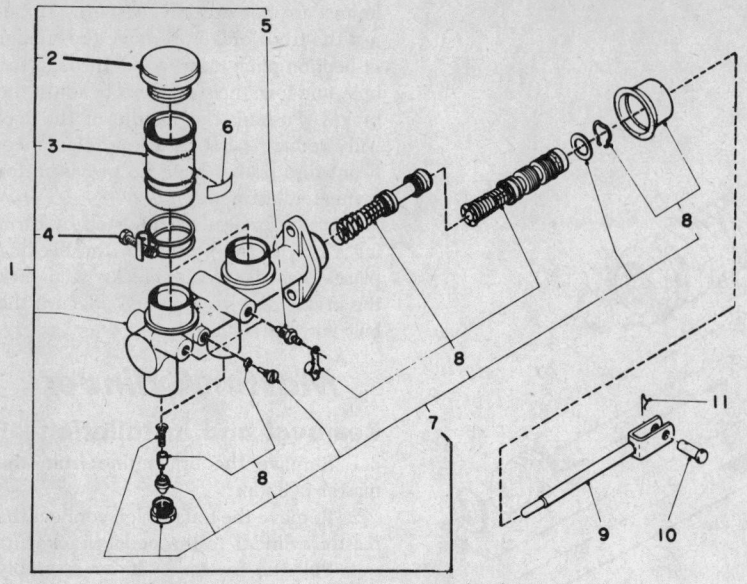

For drum brake

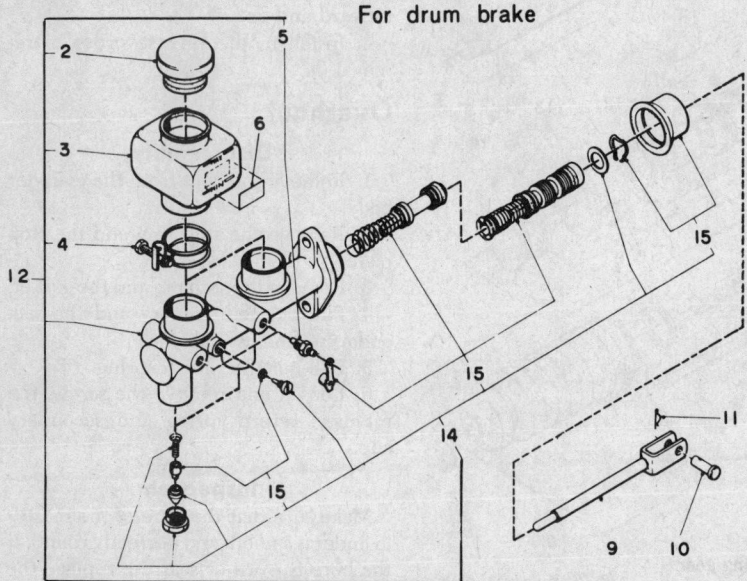

Exploded view of master cylinders

1. Master cylinder ass'y
2. Cap complete (reservoir)
3. Brake fluid reservoir (master cylinder)
4. Reservoir band (master cylinder)
5. Breeder screw
6. Lavel (brake oil tank)
7. Master cylinder repair kit (B)
8. Master cylinder repair kit (A)
9. Push rod
10. Head pin
11. Cotter pin (master cylinder)
12. Master cylinder ass'y
13. Brake fluid reservoir
14. Master cylinder repair kit (B)
15. Master cylinder repair kit (A)

2. Assemble the primary cup, spring and retainer.

3. Insert the secondary piston and the primary piston assembly into the cylinder body.

4. Assemble the gasket and stopper and tighten it.

5. Install the stop plate and stop-ring in the cylinder.

6. Install the boot on the cylinder body.

Bleeding

1. Before beginning to bleed the air from the brake lines, check the pedal play and the level of the brake fluid in the master cylinder. Fill the master cylinder with brake fluid.

2. Begin bleeding the brake lines at the wheel farthest away from the master cylinder.

3. During the bleeding process, fill the reservoir with brake fluid and keep it full during the process.

4. Remove the bleeder screw cap and wipe away any dirt. Then attach the end of a bleeder tube to the bleeder screw end.

5. Insert the other end of the bleeder tube in a glass receptacle containing clean brake fluid.

6. Loosen the bleeder screw and have the person assisting you slowly depress the brake pedal.

7. Continue to depress the pedal until no air bubbles are observed.

8. When there are no more bubbles, tighten the bleeder screw (with the pedal depressed), and then release the pedal.

9. Remove the bleeder tube from the bleeder screw, replace the cap, and go to the next wheel.

10. After bleeding air at all four wheels, check the level of the brake fluid in the master cylinder reservoir and add fluid to the level line. Do not reuse old brake fluid.

Power Brake Booster

Removal and Installation

1. Disconnect the push rod from the brake pedal by pulling the cotter pin out and removing the pivot pin.

2. Loosen the master cylinder nuts and disconnect the vacuum hose from the (vacuum booster).

3. Remove the bracket nuts from the passenger compartment side.

4. Remove the master cylinder nut, and remove the booster.

5. Installation is the reverse of removal. Make sure that the arrow marking on the check valve is facing toward the engine. Check for fluid leakage after the master cylinder has been installed and the brake pedal is fully depressed for 10 seconds, three or four times.

Front Disc Brakes

Disc Brake Pads

Removal and Installation

1. Jack up the front of the vehicle and support it with jackstands. Remove the wheel and tire.

2. Remove the hand brake cable by removing the outer cable clip.

3. Remove the four pins from the caliper.

4. Fit the tip of a screwdriver on the guide and tap lightly to drive it out. When one is removed, the other one can be easily removed.

NOTE: *It is not necessary to remove the brake pipe.*

Remove the caliper by firmly holding the caliper body and pulling the lower part out while pushing the upper part in.

5. Remove the pad.

6. Check the pads for wear and replace them if the thickness is less than 0.060 in. Replace all four brake pads.

7. Check the disc for wear or damage. Have it resurfaced if it is excessively worn or grooved. The standard thickness is 0.39 in. Do not remove more than 0.06 in. of metal during resurfacing. The disc

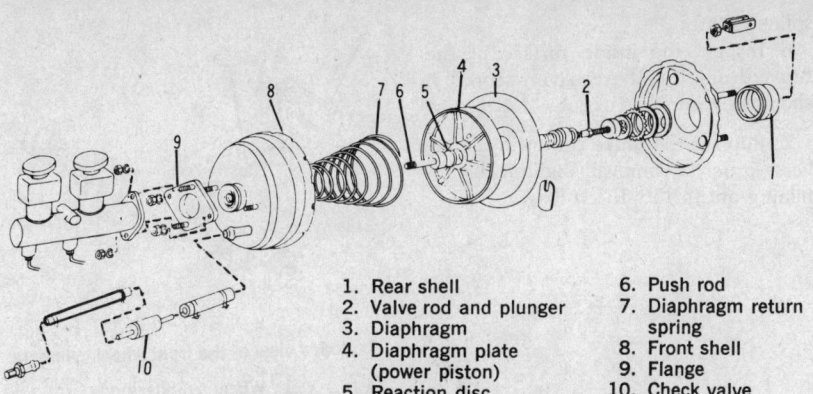

1. Rear shell
2. Valve rod and plunger
3. Diaphragm
4. Diaphragm plate (power piston)
5. Reaction disc
6. Push rod
7. Diaphragm return spring
8. Front shell
9. Flange
10. Check valve

Exploded view of the power brake booster

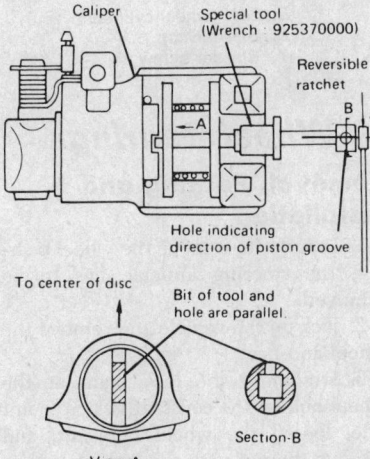

Caliper

Special tool (Wrench 925370000)

Reversible ratchet

Hole indicating direction of piston groove

To center of disc

Bit of tool and hole are parallel.

Section-B

View-A

Special tool to seat the piston in the caliper

must be replaced when the thickness is less than 0.33 in.

8. Installation can be done in the reverse order of removal.

NOTE: *(1972–75) Before installing the brake pads, seat the piston in the caliper by pushing it into its cylinder with a screwdriver.*

(1976–77) A special tool is needed to push the piston into the caliper by turning it clockwise.

Disc Brake Calipers

Removal and Installation

The calipers are removed part of the disc brake pad removal procedure.

Brake Disc

Removal and Installation

1. Jack up the vehicle and remove the front wheel, hand brake cable, guides, and caliper as in the brake pad removal and installation procedure.

2. Remove the two bolts that hold the caliper bracket to the housing and remove the bracket from the housing.

3. Pull the disc out of the axle shaft with a puller.

4. Remove the four bolts that hold the disc to the hub.

5. Installation is the reverse of removal.

Inspection

See "Disc Brake Pad Removal and Installation".

Wheel Bearings

Removal and Installation, Packing

1. Jack up the vehicle and remove the front tire and wheel.

2. Remove the hand brake cable from the lever of the caliper body and disconnect the brake line from the caliper.

3. Remove the stopper (plug) from the caliper bracket.

4. Remove the caliper bracket (mounting) from the disc hub by loosening the

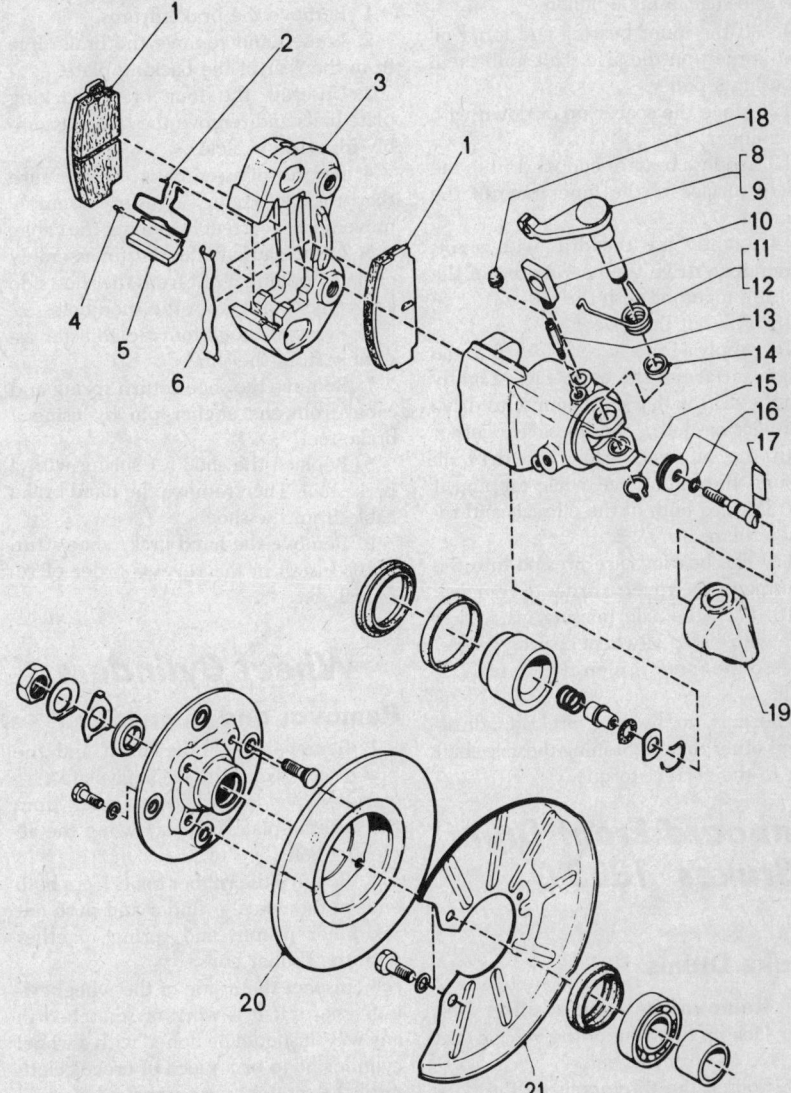

Exploded view of the disc brake assembly

1. Pad (disc brake F)
2. Spring (caliper)
3. Bracket (mounting)
4. Pin (caliper)
5. Stopper (plug)
6. Spring (pad)
7. Body caliper ass'y
8. Lever & spindle ass'y (LH)
9. Lever & spindle ass'y (RH)
10. Bracket (hand brake)
11. Spring (hand brake lever return LH)
12. Spring (hand brake lever return RH)
13. Bleeder screw (wheel cylinder)
14. Bushing (hand brake)
15. Retaining spring
16. Spindle ass'y
17. Connecting link
18. Cap (air bleeder)
19. Cap (lever)
20. Brake disc (F)
21. Cover (disc)

two bolts which hold it to the backing plate.

5. Remove the bolts which connect the suspension strut to the housing.

6. Remove the hand brake hanger on the tie rod end. Remove the cable bracket from the housing.

7. Remove the tie rod ball joint from the housing knuckle by using a puller.

8. Carefully pull the housing downward and out to separate the suspension strut from the housing.

9. Remove the control arm ball joint from the housing. Loosen the castle nut and pry the castle nut by using a lever with the hub as the base.

10. Pull the rotor and rotor hub out of the axle shaft using a puller.

11. If the inner bearing and inner oil seal are left on the axle shaft, pull them off using a puller.

12. Move the spacer up or down with your finger.

13. Apply a brass or copper drift to the inside surface of the inner race of the bearing.

14. Lightly tap the drift with a soft hammer to drive the bearing out of the housing together with the oil seal.

15. Pull out the spacer.

16. Apply a brass or copper drift to the inside surface of the outer race. Lightly tap the drift with a soft hammer to drive the bearing out of the housing together with the oil seal. Apply the drift all around the outer race while tapping it out. Discard both of the oil seals and replace them.

17. The bearings are pressed into the housing in the reverse order of removal.

18. Pack the axle housing inside surface with ½ oz. of wheel bearing grease. Grease the inner lips on the oil seals, as well.

There is no bearing preload adjustment other than tightening the axle shaft nut to the correct torque.

Inboard Front Drum Brakes 1300 G

Brake Drums

Removal and Installation

1. Jack up the front of the vehicle and remove the front wheels.

2. Loosen the three bolts on the double offset joint (DOJ) side, and remove the DOJ from the drum.

3. Remove the drum cover attached to the brake assembly.

4. Remove the interior portion of the hand brake cable assembly into the engine compartment.

5. Straighten the brake drum locking cotter pin and remove it. Unscrew the nut and remove the drum from the

splined shaft.

6. Inspect the inside surface of the brake drum. If it is excessively scored, it should be resurfaced or cut.

7. Replace the brake drums in the reverse order of removal. Tighten the retaining nut to 116–134 ft lbs.

Brake Shoes

Removal and Installation

1. Remove the brake drums.

2. Loosen and remove the brake line from the rear of the backing plate.

3. Unscrew the four brake backing plate bolts and remove the brake assembly from the vehicle.

4. Before disassembling, make sure that the automatic adjuster assembly movement is correct by pulling the cable.

5. Lift the automatic adjuster assembly cable by pulling it out from the shoe side and removing it from the shoe hole.

6. Remove the automatic adjuster assembly from the shoe.

7. Remove the shoe return spring and cable from the anchor pin by using a brake tool.

8. Replace the shoe set spring with a brake tool. Then remove the hand brake cable from the shoe.

9. Remove the hand brake shoe strut.

10. Install in the reverse order of removal.

Wheel Cylinders

Removal and Installation

1. Remove the brake drum and the brake shoes from the backing plate.

2. Remove the wheel cylinder from the backing plate by unscrewing the attaching bolts.

3. Remove the rubber boots from both ends of the wheel cylinder and push out the inner pistons and spring together with the rubber cups.

4. Inspect the inside of the wheel cylinder bore. If it is worn or scratched in any way, it should be honed with a wheel cylinder hone or a piece of crocus cloth until the scratches are removed.

5. Replace the rubber cups with new ones. The internal replacement parts are usually supplied in a wheel cylinder rebuilding kit.

6. Reassemble the wheel cylinder and replace it on the backing plate in the reverse order of removal.

7. After reinstalling the brake line and the brake assembly, together with the brake drum, bleed the brake system.

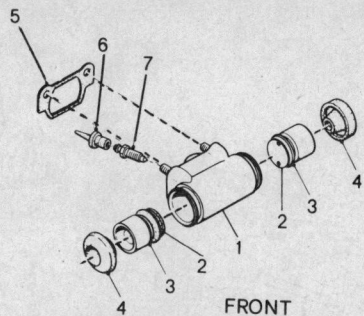

Exploded view of the front wheel cylinders

1. Wheel cylinder body
2. Cup
3. Piston
4. Boot
5. Seal (wheel cylinder)
6. Bleeder cap
7. Bleeder screw

Wheel Bearings

Removal, Packing and Installation

1. In order to remove the wheel bearing, the steering knuckle has to be removed.

2. Jack up the vehicle and remove the wheel and tire.

3. Straighten the lock plate at the wheel hub on the constant velocity joint side, loosen the wheel hub nut, and remove the nut with the lock plate.

4. Remove the tie rod end from the knuckle arm.

5. Remove the two cotter pins, castle nuts, spring washers, and the lower arm ball joint.

NOTE: *When the camber and caster adjusting cams are removed, remember the setting number for reassembly.*

6. After flattening the lock washer, remove the nut and lock plate which joins the upper arm and the upper arm joint.

7. Remove the hub and knuckle assembly from the splined section of the axle shaft constant velocity joint side.

8. Separate the hub from the knuckle.

9. Remove the upper and lower ball joints and then remove the steering knuckle from the vehicle.

10. Straighten out the lock plate, loosen the bolt, and remove the bolt to-

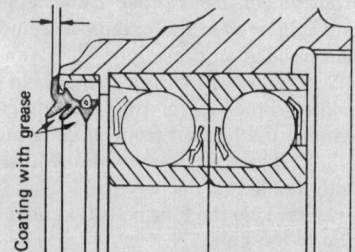

Installation of the outer oil seal

gether with the spring washer and the lock plate.

11. Remove the inner oil seal from the bearing nut.

12. Remove the nut from the knuckle.

13. Remove the spacer.

14. Remove the outer oil seal from the knuckle.

15. Remove the bearing from the knuckle by pressing it out with a press.

NOTE: *The bearing race cannot be removed because of its peculiar construction.*

16. The wheel bearing is in two parts. If the bearing has to be replaced, make sure that both halves are replaced at the same time. Never just replace one half of the bearing without replacing the other half. Make sure that the bearings are put together in the same position as they were removed.

17. Before installing the bearing, clean and inspect it for damage. Repack the bearing with wheel bearing grease.

18. Press the outer oil seal into the knuckle. Insert the outer oil seal so that it protrudes from the knuckle end surface about 0.04 in. Coat the outer seal lip with grease when installing.

19. Insert the spacer making sure that the lip of the oil seal is not tucked up.

20. Tighten the bearing nut to 115–133 ft lbs.

21. Align the lock plate groove with the nut groove and bend the lock plate and lock the nut.

22. Press the inner oil seal into the nut. Be careful not to damage the side lip of the oil seal. Coat the inner oil seal lip surface with grease when installing.

23. Assemble the steering knuckle to the vehicle in the reverse order of removal.

Outboard Front Drum Brakes (DL Sedans and Wagons, 4WD)

Brake Drums

1. Apply the parking brake. Remove the wheel cover and loosen the lug nuts.

2. Either straighten out the locktabs with pliers or straighten the staked portion of the axle shaft nut with a chisel, depending upon the year. Loosen, but do not remove the axle shaft nut.

3. Jack up the front of the car and support it with jackstands.

4. Remove the lug nuts and the wheel.

5. Unfasten the axle shaft nut, and release the parking brake.

6. Remove the brake drum with a puller.

Installation is the reverse of removal.

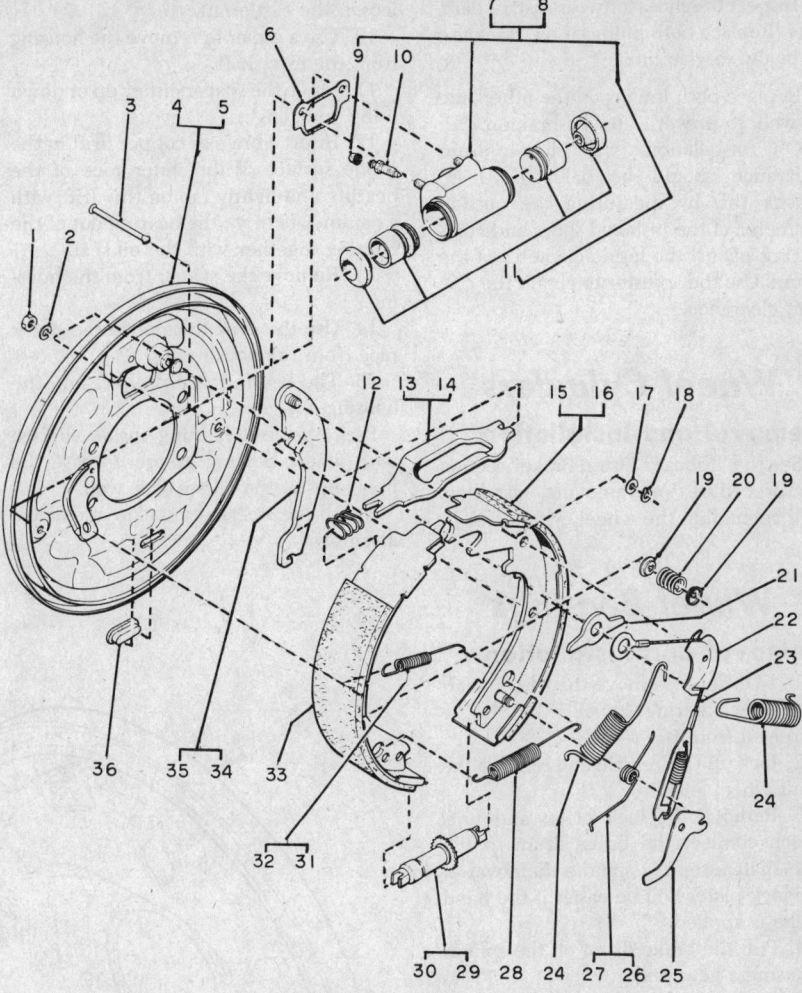

DL front drum brakes

1. Nut	19. Cup
2. Lock washer	20. Spring (shoe hold down)
3. Pin (shoe hold down)	21. Stopper
4, 5. Backing plate assembly	22. Cable guide
6. Seal	23. Cable assembly
7, 8. Wheel cylinder assembly	24. Spring (shoe return, upper)
9. Bleeder cap	25. Lever (auto adjuster)
10. Bleeder screw	26, 27. Spring (auto adjuster)
11. Wheel cylinder repair kit	28. Spring (shoe return lower)
12. Spring (strut)	29, 30. Auto adjuster assembly
13, 14. Strut	31, 32. Spring
15, 16. Brake shoe	33. Brake shoe
17. Lock washer	34, 35. Lever assembly
18. Retainer	36. Cover

Install the axle nut and torque to 145–181 ft lbs for 1972–73 and 170 ft lbs for 1974 and later.

Secure the nut with either the nut lock (1972–73) or by staking it (1974–77).

Inspection

After removing the brake drum, inspect the inner braking surface for excessive wear or damage. If it is unevenly worn, streaked or cracked, either have it resurfaced or replaced.

Brake Shoes

Removal and Installation

1. Jack up the vehicle then remove the wheel and tire and the brake drum.

2. Remove the automatic adjuster spring with a screwdriver and then remove the automatic adjuster lever.

3. Remove the lower shoe return spring and the automatic adjuster.

4. Remove the hand brake cable end from the hand brake lever. Remove the clamp nut with a box wrench. Remove the washer and pull the hand brake cable out.

5. Remove the upper shoe return springs from the anchor pin with a brake tool and remove the automatic adjuster.

6. Remove the shoe set springs with the brake tool and free the brake shoes.

7. Install in the reverse order of removal.

Inspect the shoes for wear rust, or damage. Replace both linings if the thickness is below service limits:

Replace both linings on the other side as well, to prevent uneven braking.

On installation, the shoe-to-drum clearance should be 0.004–0.010 in. Check this by measuring the outside diameter of the installed shoes and comparing against the inside diameter of the drum. Use the adjuster to obtain the correct clearance.

Wheel Cylinders

Removal and Installation

See the "Inboard Drum Brake" section for procedures on removing, installing, and rebuilding the wheel cylinders.

Wheel Bearings

Removal and Installation

1. In order to remove the wheel bearings, the steering knuckle has to be removed from the vehicle.

2. Jack up the vehicle and remove the front wheel and tire.

3. Remove the lock plates and nuts which connect the brake drum to the axle shaft assembly spindle. Removal of the lock plates will be easier if the hand brake is applied.

4. Pull the brake drum off the splines by using a gear puller.

5. Remove the backing plate with the brake assembly by removing the four attaching bolts.

6. Remove the bolts which connect the suspension strut to the housing.

7. Remove the tie rod ball joint from the housing knuckle by using a puller.

8. Carefully pull the housing downward to separate the suspension strut from the housing.

9. Remove the control arm ball joint from the housing. Install a spacer between the housing and the castle nut and loosen the castle nut.

10. Use a puller to remove the housing from the axle shaft.

11. Move the spacer either up or down using your finger.

12. Insert a brass or copper drift in the inside surface of the inner race of the bearing and lightly tap on the drift with a hammer to drive the bearing out of the housing together with the oil seal.

13. Remove the spacer from the housing.

14. Use the drift to remove the outer race from the housing.

15. The bearings are pressed into the housing.

Pack the axle housing inside surface with wheel bearing grease. Grease the inner lips of the oil seals, as well.

Install the steering knuckle and brake assembly.

There is no bearing preload adjustment, other than tightening the axle shaft nut to the proper specifications.

Rear Drum Brakes

Brake Drums

Removal and Installation

1. Jack up the vehicle and remove the wheel and tire.

2. Remove the three cap installing bolts, spring washers, cap, and bearing retainer plate.

3. Remove the cotter pin and loosen the castle nut taking care not to damage the bearing seal.

4. Remove the brake drum with a puller.

5. Install in the reverse order of removal.

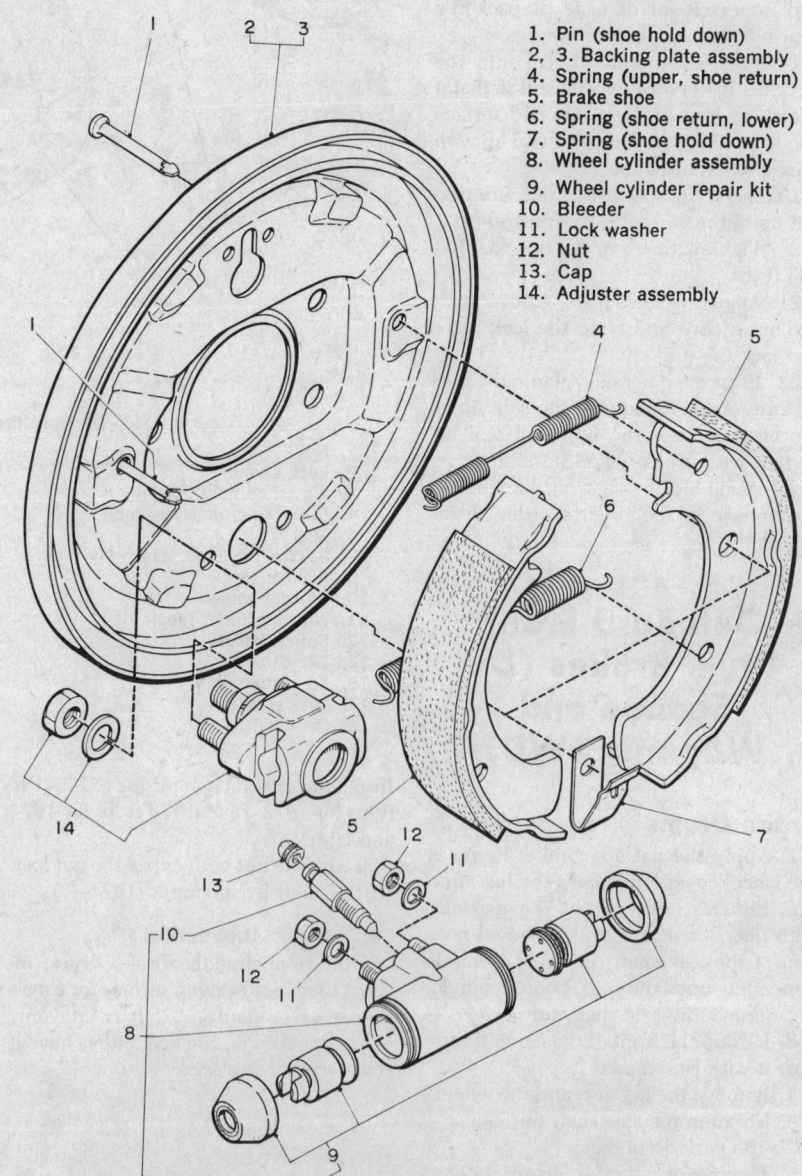

1. Pin (shoe hold down)
2, 3. Backing plate assembly
4. Spring (upper, shoe return)
5. Brake shoe
6. Spring (shoe return, lower)
7. Spring (shoe hold down)
8. Wheel cylinder assembly
9. Wheel cylinder repair kit
10. Bleeder
11. Lock washer
12. Nut
13. Cap
14. Adjuster assembly

DL and GL rear drum brakes

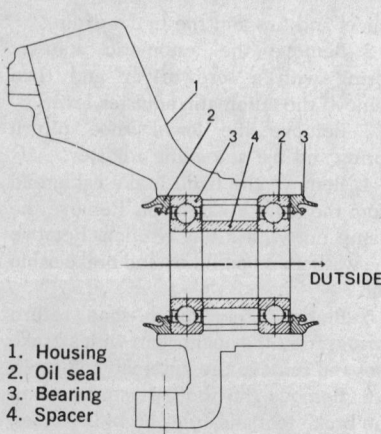

1. Housing
2. Oil seal
3. Bearing
4. Spacer

Bearing and oil seal arrangement

Installation is the reverse of removal. On models through 1973, tighten the axle shaft castle nut to 80–145 ft lbs. On all 1974–77 models except 4WD and on 1300 G station wagons, do not tighten the bearing adjusting nut; instead perform the bearing preload adjustment. 4WD rear bearing service is covered under Rear Axle Spindle, Bearing, and Seals Removal and Installation.

Inspection

After removing the brake drum, inspect the inner braking surface for excessive wear or damage. If it is unevenly worn, streaked, or cracked, have it resurfaced or replaced.

Bearing Preload Adjustment

1974–77 GL and DL, 1970–72
1300 G Wagon

1. Tighten the rear bearing adjusting nut enough to seat the bearing. The bearing is seated properly when the brake drum has no side-play but still rotates freely. Do not overtighten.
2. Back off on the nut ⅛ turn.
3. Check the nut starting torque with a torque wrench; it should be 6–9 ft lbs. Be careful not to tighten the nut.
4. Complete installation in the reverse order of removal.

Brake Shoes

Removal and Installation

1. Jack up the vehicle and remove the wheels.
2. Remove the brake drums.
3. Remove the shoe retaining spring with a pair of pliers.
4. Remove the anchor side of the shoe first by removing the return springs on the bottom.
5. Remove the cylinder side of the shoe by removing the upper return springs.
6. Remove the brake shoes from the backing plate.
7. Measure the lining thickness. Replace the linings if they are below the minimum service thickness limits:

Replace the leading and trailing shoes on both sides at the same time. Replacement of the shoes one side or one shoe at a time, will cause uneven braking.

Installation is as follows:

1. Assemble the shoes and the return springs. The upper spring (wheel cylinder side) is thin; the lower spring (anchor side) is thick.
2. Apply brake grease to the backing plate where the brake shoes make contact.
3. Install the shoe and spring assembly to the wheel cylinder first and then to the anchor. Secure the shoes with their retaining springs.

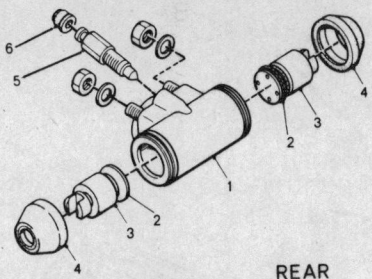

REAR

Exploded view of the rear wheel cylinders

1. Wheel cylinder body
2. Cup
3. Piston
4. Boot
5. Bleeder screw
6. Bleeder cap

CAUTION: *Do not allow grease to get on the surface of the lining.*

4. Install the drum and adjust the brakes.

Wheel Cylinders

See the "Inboard Front Drum Brake" section for removal, installation, and rebuilding of the wheel cylinders.

PARKING BRAKE

Cable

Removal and Installation

1300 G

1. Loosen the cable turnbuckle locknut.
2. Separate the halves of the cable.
3. Remove the clip, pin, pulley, and the cable.
4. Loosen the nut and remove the cable from its bracket. Remove the nut, washer, bushing, and turnbuckle from the cable.
5. Remove the cable boot from the engine compartment.
6. Remove the brake cable.

Installation is the reverse of removal.

DL, GL, GF, 4WD

1. Jack up the vehicle and remove the wheel and tire.
2. Remove the brake drum (drum brake type).
3. Remove the hand brake cover and console.
4. Loosen the cable adjusting nut.

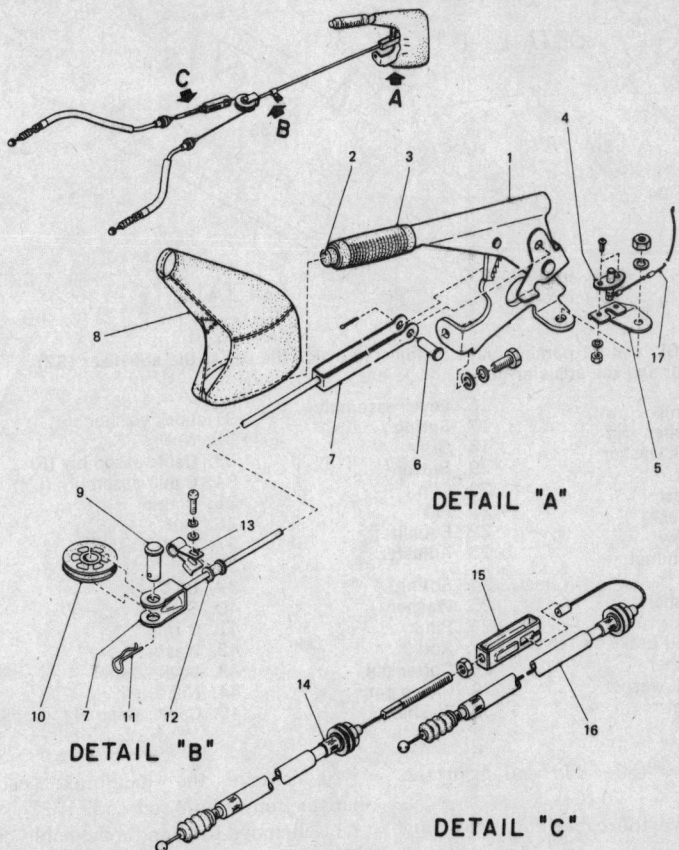

DETAIL "A"

DETAIL "B"

DETAIL "C"

1300G parking brake is adjusted inside the car at the cable turnbuckle

1. Lever Assembly	6. Clevis Pin	12. Bushing
2. Button	7. Rod assembly	13. Clip
3. Grip	8. Boot	14. Cable
4. Switch	9. Pin	15. Turnbuckle
5. Warning light	10. Pulley	16. Cable
switch bracket	11. Clip	17. Wire

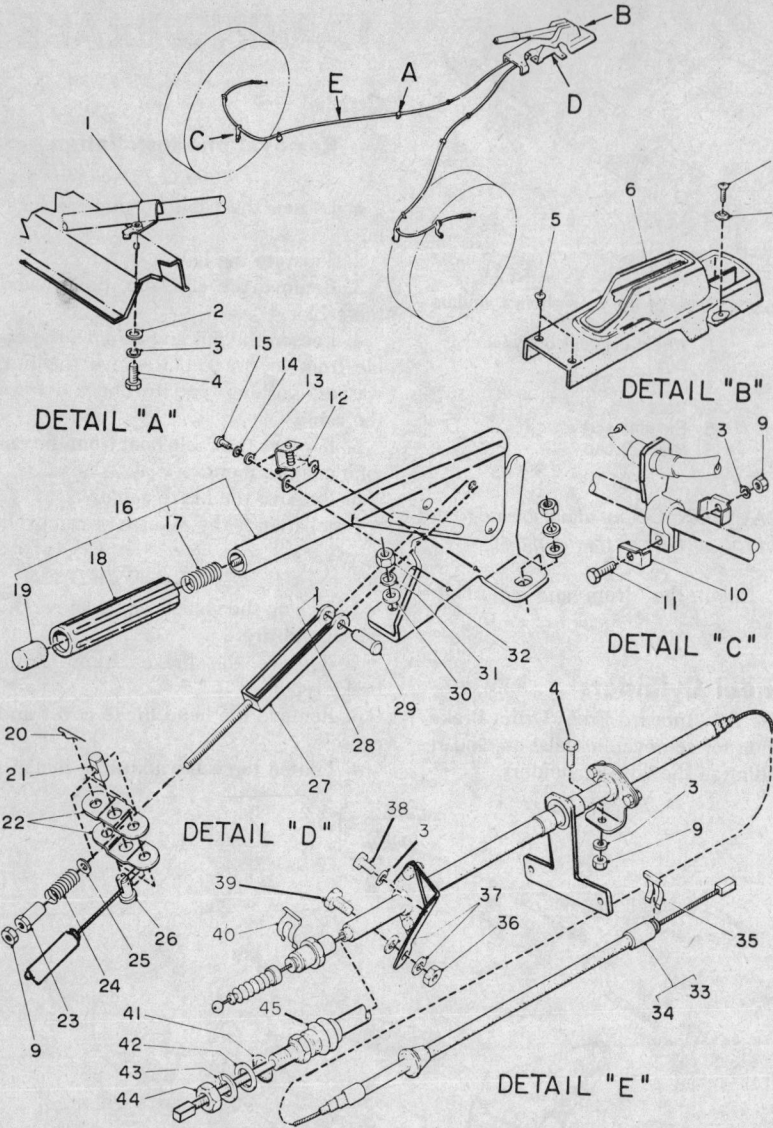

DETAIL "A"

DETAIL "B"

DETAIL "C"

DETAIL "D"

DETAIL "E"

DL, GL, and GF parking brake is adjusted inside the car at the equalizer (22) by turning the adjuster (23).

1. Clamp	16. Lever assembly	31. Lock washer
2. Washer	17. Spring	32. Nut
3. Lock washer	18. Grip	33. Cable assembly (RH)
4. Bolt	19. Button	34. Cable assembly (LH)
5. Screw	20. Clip	35. Clamp
6. Cover	21. Pin	36. Nut
7. Screw	22. Equalizer	37. Lock washer
8. Grommet	23. Adjuster	38. Bolt
9. Nut	24. Spring	39. Bolt
10. Washer	25. Washer	40. Clamp
11. Bolt	26. Pin	41. O ring
12. Hand brake switch	27. Rod	42. Washer
13. Washer	28. Cotter pin	43. Lock washer
14. Lock washer	29. Clevis pin	44. Nut
15. Screw	30. Washer	45. Cable assembly

5. Remove the cable end from the equalizer.

6. Remove the cable end tightening clip.

7. Remove the service hole cover on the tunnel.

8. Remove the cable clamp from the cross-member.

9. Remove the cable installing bracket from the control arm.

10. Remove the handbrake cable hanger from the tie-rod end.

11. Remove the handbrake cable end from the hand brake lever by removing the secondary shoe.

12. Remove the cable end nut, washer, and spring washer from the inside of the backing plate and pull the hand brake cable out from the backing plate (drum brakes).

13. Pull the brake hose clamp out and remove the hand brake cable end from the lever and spindle assembly (disc brakes).

14. Pull the handbrake cable assembly from the engine compartment and remove it from the body together with the grommet.

15. Reinstallation is the reverse order of removal.

Adjustment
1300 G

1. Pull the parking brake lever up forcefully. Release it and repeat several times.

2. It should take 7–8 notches to apply the parking brake.

3. Loosen the locknut on the turnbuckle and adjust the length of the cable.

4. Tighten the locknut.

GL, DL, GF, 4WD

The parking brake adjusting procedure is similar to that for 1300 G models. The brake should be fully engaged when the lever is pulled up 9–10 notches on the 1972–73 GL and DL, and 6–7 notches beginning 1974.

Adjust the cable by loosening the locknut and turning the cable adjusting nut.

CHASSIS ELECTRICAL
Heater Blower
Removal and Installation
1300 G

1. Disconnect the negative battery cable.

2. Detach the heater control cable at the blower housing in the front of the engine compartment, by removing the cable retaining clip and the sheath securing nut.

3. Unfasten the blower motor connections at the motor.

4. Remove its clamps and take the hot air duct off the blower housing.

5. Unbolt the sub-radiator shroud at the housing.

6. Remove the bolts which secure the housing and lift it out of the car.

7. To remove the motor and fan assembly from the housing, remove the motor securing screws.

Installation is the reverse of removal.

Heater Core
Removal and Installation
1300 G

The sub-radiator also functions as the heater core. Sub-radiator removal and installation are given under "Engine Cooling".

Heater Unit

Removal and Installation

1972–73 DL, GL

The blower motor and the heater core are in the heater unit. In order to service either of these components, the heater unit must be removed from the vehicle. In order to remove the heater unit from the vehicle, the entire instrument panel has to be removed.

1. Disconnect the negative terminal of the battery.

2. Unscrew the nuts which retain the instrument panel to the body at both ends.

3. Remove the screws which hold the upper panel face of the instrument panel to the body bracket which is attached to the firewall.

4. After removing the bolts which retain the steering bracket and the steering shaft, loosen the nuts which hold the lower side of the instrument panel to the steering bracket.

5. Disconnect the defroster hoses.

6. Disconnect the heater control rod and wiring harness.

7. Disconnect the following wiring and cables and label them for identification when reinstalling.

8. Remove the speedometer cable hanger spring.

9. Disconnect the speedometer cable from the speedometer.

10. Disconnect all of the electrical wiring connected to the instrument panel.

11. Disconnect the antenna lead.

12. Remove the instrument panel from the vehicle being careful of interference between the side end of the instrument panel and the front pillars.

13. Drain the coolant from the radiator.

14. Disconnect the heater hoses on the engine side, both the inlet and the outlet hoses.

15. Remove the console by removing the six attaching screws.

16. Disconnect the heater control assembly and the heater unit by disconnecting the shutter cable and the two air inlet control rods.

17. Disconnect the wiring harnesses of the fan motor, the main harness, and the motor control switch wirings.

18. Remove the heater unit mounting bolts.

19. Lift the assembly to the side being careful of the stopper at the bottom of the unit. Remove the grommet on the firewall at this time.

20. Remove the unit assembly.

21. Remove the blower fan, motor, and the heater core. There is no set procedure other than removing other components that are in the way of removal of the motor and the core.

22. Install in the reverse order of removal.

1974 GL, DL

The heater unit contains the core and blower. The entire assembly must be removed from the car before either the blower or core can be serviced. To remove the heater unit:

1. Disconnect the cable from the negative battery terminal.

2. Drain the coolant from the radiator.

3. Disconnect the heater water hoses at the engine.

4. Remove the console by unfastening its screws and lifting it out.

5. Remove the screws which secure the parcel shelf and remove it from under the instrument panel.

6. Remove the instrument cluster.

7. Pull the knob off the ventilator lever. Remove the ventilator grille by unfastening the two screws at each end.

8. Disconnect the control cables from the heater valve by unfastening the cable clamp and retaining nut.

9. Detach the control rod from the heater shutter (door).

10. Disconnect the heater blower multiconnector.

11. Unfasten the heater housing securing bolts and remove the housing from underneath the dash.

12. Unfasten the two housing screws and spring, then remove the housing.

13. Separate the defroster duct from the heater assembly.

14. Remove the water hoses.

15. Unfasten the two heater valve screws and remove the valve.

16. Remove the shutter control rod from the link, unfasten the link screws, and remove the link.

17. Withdraw the heater core assembly.

18. Disconnect the fan motor wiring harness, loosen its 3 retaining screws, and separate it from the core, complete with blower.

Installation is the reverse of removal. Adjust the shutter control rod as follows:

1. Loosen the screw which attaches the air intake shutter (door) control rod to its link.

2. Push the link down as far as it will go.

3. Slide the heater control lever to "CIRC".

4. Fasten the shutter control rod and link securing screw.

Adjust the heater valve cable as follows:

1. Slide the temperature control lever to "COOL".

2. Pull the lever on the heater valve toward the driver's side and secure the control cable to it with the clamp.

3. Slide the temperature control to "WARM" and push the heater valve lever outward.

4. Fasten the outer cable to the heater valve cable with the clamp.

1975–77

The heater unit contains the core and blower. The entire assembly must be removed from the car before either the blower or core can be serviced. To remove the heater unit:

1. Disconnect the ground cable from the battery.

2. Remove the console, luggage shelf, meter and visor assembly, and center ventilation grill.

3. Drain the coolant and disconnect the two heater hoses in the engine compartment.

4. Disconnect the heater control cable, fan motor harness, and the control rod connecting the air flow fan switch control lever on the instrument panel to the heater unit, on the right side.

Remove the two mounting bolts and remove the heater unit.

5. To install reverse the removal procedure.

6. To reconnect the control rod push up the link provided at the side of the heater unit to its full stroke, set the air/fan switch control lever to vent and then connect the rod to the link.

7. To reconnect the heater control cable set the temperature control lever to cold, the heater control lever on the heater unit to off then connect the cock cable.

Radio

Removal and Installation

1300 G

1. Disconnect the negative battery cable.

2. Pull the two radio knobs off their shafts and remove the nuts from the shafts.

3. Unfasten the two bezel retaining screws and remove the radio bezel.

4. Remove the lower heater duct cover and the ash tray, then unfasten the radio securing screw which is underneath them.

5. Pull the radio out of the dash, after disconnecting its power, speaker, and antenna leads.

Installation is the reverse of removal.

1972–73 GL, DL

1. Remove the center panel of the instrument panel by first removing the radio installing nut. Remove the bolt which holds the center panel to the instrument panel. It can be reached by removing the ash tray. Remove the light switch and the wiper switch knobs by loosening the screw and removing the nut. Remove the heater control knobs by loosening the screws. Remove the hanger spring of the speedometer cable. Disconnect the

speedometer cable from the back side of the instrument cluster. Disconnect the junction block from the back side of the instrument cluster. Disconnect the wiring harness from the cigar lighter. Remove the center panel from the instrument panel.

2. Remove the speaker grille by loosening the two attaching screws.

3. Pull out the feeder cord from the radio plug.

4. Loosen the radio mounting bolt.

5. Loosen the radio mounting screws.

6. Disconnect the radio wiring and remove the radio.

7. Install in the reverse order of removal.

1974–77

1. Disconnect the negative battery cable.

2. Use a phillips screwdriver with a short shank to remove the screws holding the speaker grille down. Remove the grille.

3. Disconnect the speaker lead from the radio connector.

4. Remove the instrument cluster bezel screws at the radio end.

5. Unfasten its screws and lift out the console.

6. Pull the knob off the fresh air lever, unfasten the two securing screws at either end, and remove the center outlet grille.

7. Pull both knobs off the radio shafts.

8. Remove the ash tray. Pull the knobs off the heater controls.

9. Remove the nuts from the radio control shafts.

10. Unfasten the screws which secure the radio surround panel. Remove the panel.

11. Unfasten the radio bracket screws.

12. Disconnect the radio leads and pull the radio out of the dash.

Installation is the reverse of removal.

Windshield Wiper Motor

Removal and Installation

1300 G

The wiper linkage is attached to the wiper motor, and the two are removed as a complete assembly.

1. Unfasten the phillips screws retaining the arms, and remove the arms.

2. Remove the pivot installing nuts, rubber boots, and washers.

3. Remove the instrument cluster. Disconnect the wiper motor wiring.

4. Unfasten both windshield wiper assembly retaining bolts and slide the motor and linkage assembly out from behind the dash.

Installation is the reverse of removal.

DL, GL, GF 4WD

1. Disconnect the negative battery cable.

2. Remove the windshield washer reservoir.

3. Unfasten the 3 screws which secure the motor to the firewall.

4. Remove the wiper arms and cowl by unfastening their respective securing nuts (2) and screws (6).

5. Disconnect the wiper motor wiring.

6. Unfasten the clip which attaches the motor to the link, and remove the motor.

Installation is the reverse of removal.

Instrument Cluster

Removal and Installation

1972 FF-1, 1300 G

1. Disconnect the negative battery cable.

2. Disconnect the speedometer cable by reaching up behind the dash panel and loosening its securing nut.

3. Carefully pull the instrument cluster wiring connector straight back, away from the cluster.

4. Loosen the cluster retaining springs and pull the cluster forward, out of the dash panel.

Installation is the reverse of removal.

1972–73 GL, DL

1. Disconnect the negative battery cable.

2. Pull the knobs off the radio shafts and unfasten the shaft securing nuts.

3. Remove the ash tray and unfasten the instrument panel securing nut which is located behind it.

4. Remove the set screws which secure the light switch (GL Coupe only) and the wiper switch (all models) knobs. Pull the knob(s) off and unfasten the retaining nut(s) from the switch(es).

5. Working underneath the dash, remove the speedometer cable securing spring. Push the hook on the speedometer up, while pulling the cable back, in order to disengage it.

6. Disconnect the junction block at the back of the instrument cluster.

7. Unfasten the lighter wiring connectors.

8. Remove the complete instrument panel assembly from the car and separate the cluster from it, by unfastening the cluster securing screws.

9. On GL models only, remove the tachometer as follows:

    a. Remove the tachometer panel by loosening its two attaching screws.

    b. Unfasten the tachometer securing screws.

    c. Disconnect the tachometer leads.

    d. Remove the tachometer from the dash.

Installation is the reverse of removal.

1974–77 DL, GL, GF, 4WD

1. Disconnect the negative battery cable.

2. Detach the driver's side fresh air vent duct by loosening its securing clamp.

3. On GL Coupe models, do the following working underneath the dash:

    a. Disconnect the rear window defogger switch leads.

    b. Unfasten the tachometer lead.

    c. Loosen the trip odometer reset knob setscrew and pull the knob off.

4. On all models, reach up underneath the dash and disconnect the speedometer cable and the junction block.

5. Unfasten the screws which secure the instrument cluster bezel.

6. On GL Coupes, pull the cluster/bezel assembly out just far enough to disconnect the following electrical leads:

    a. Clock

    b. Brake warning lamp

    c. Seat belt warning lamp

7. Pull the cluster/bezel assembly out, away from the dash and lift it out of the car. Separate the cluster from the bezel by removing its attaching screws.

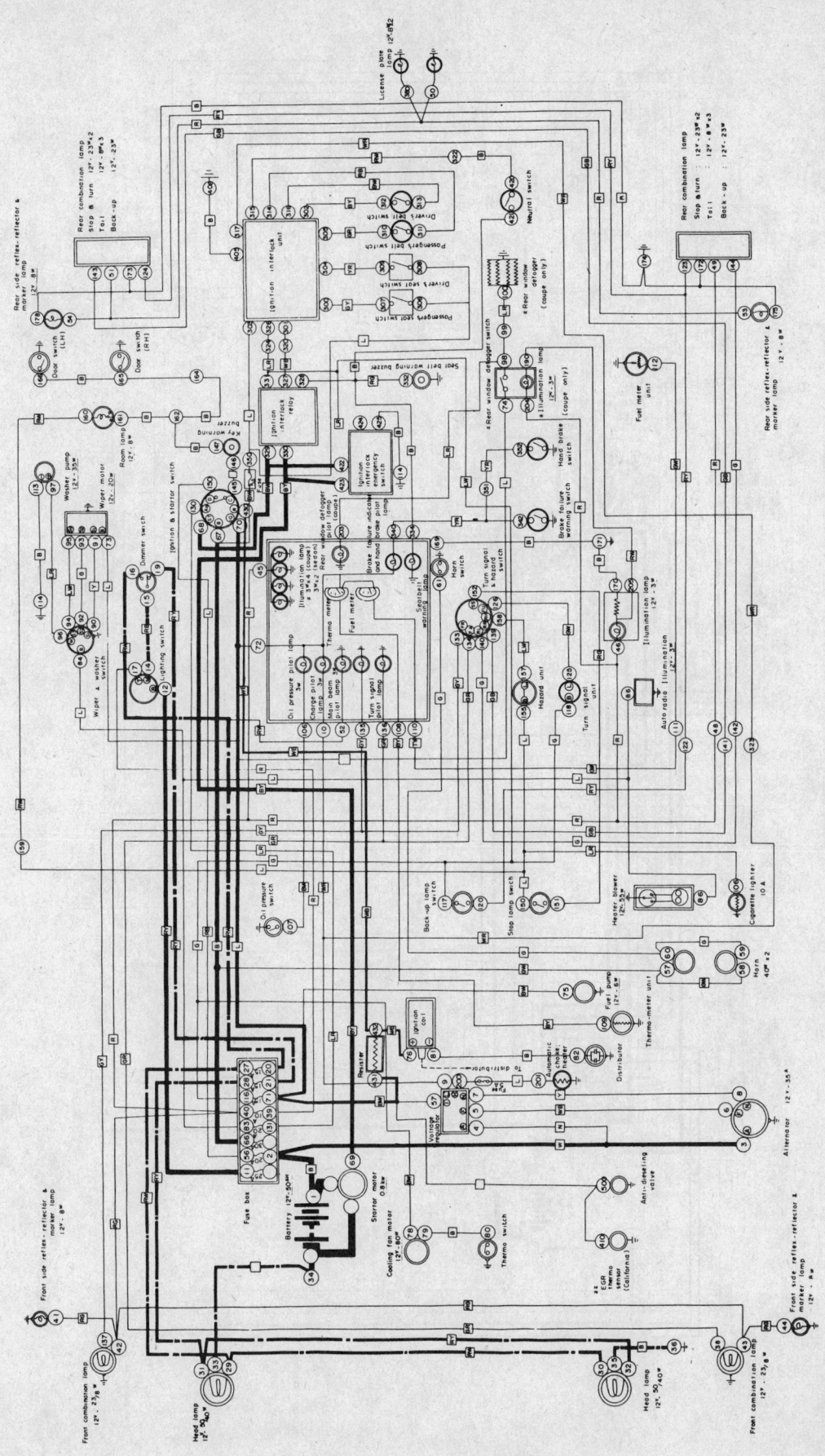

1974 GL and DL, except wagon

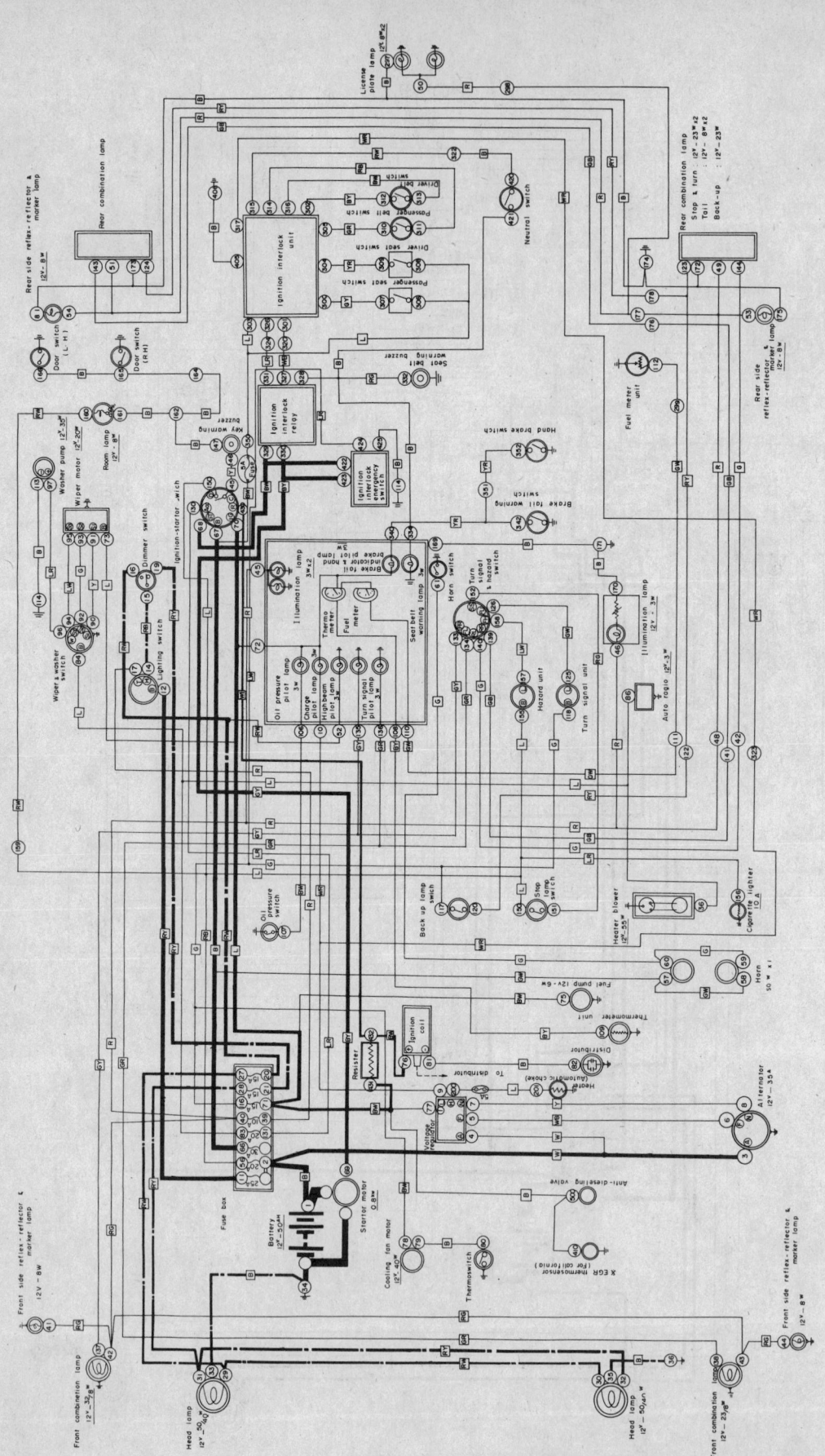

1974 DL wagon

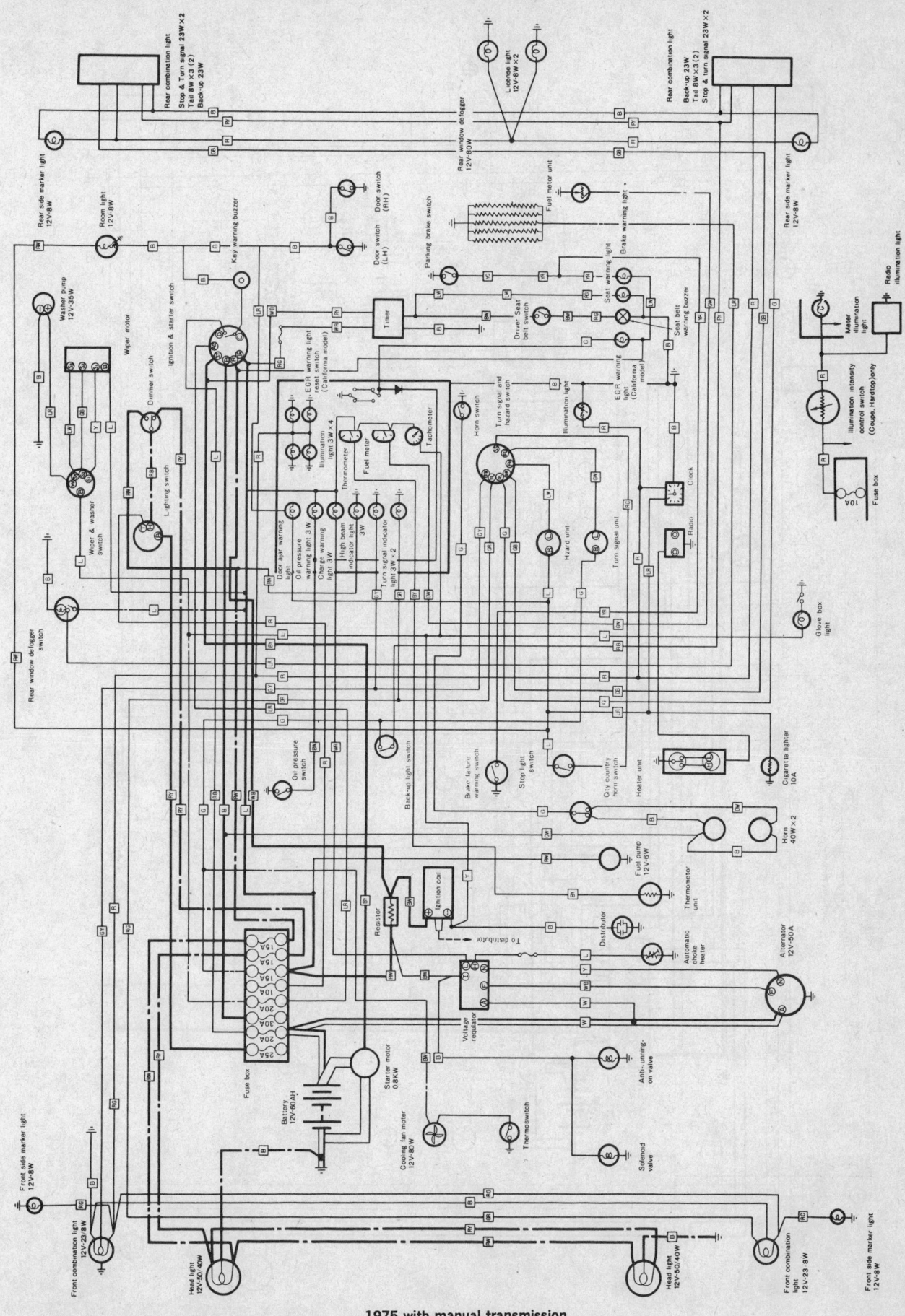

1975 with manual transmission

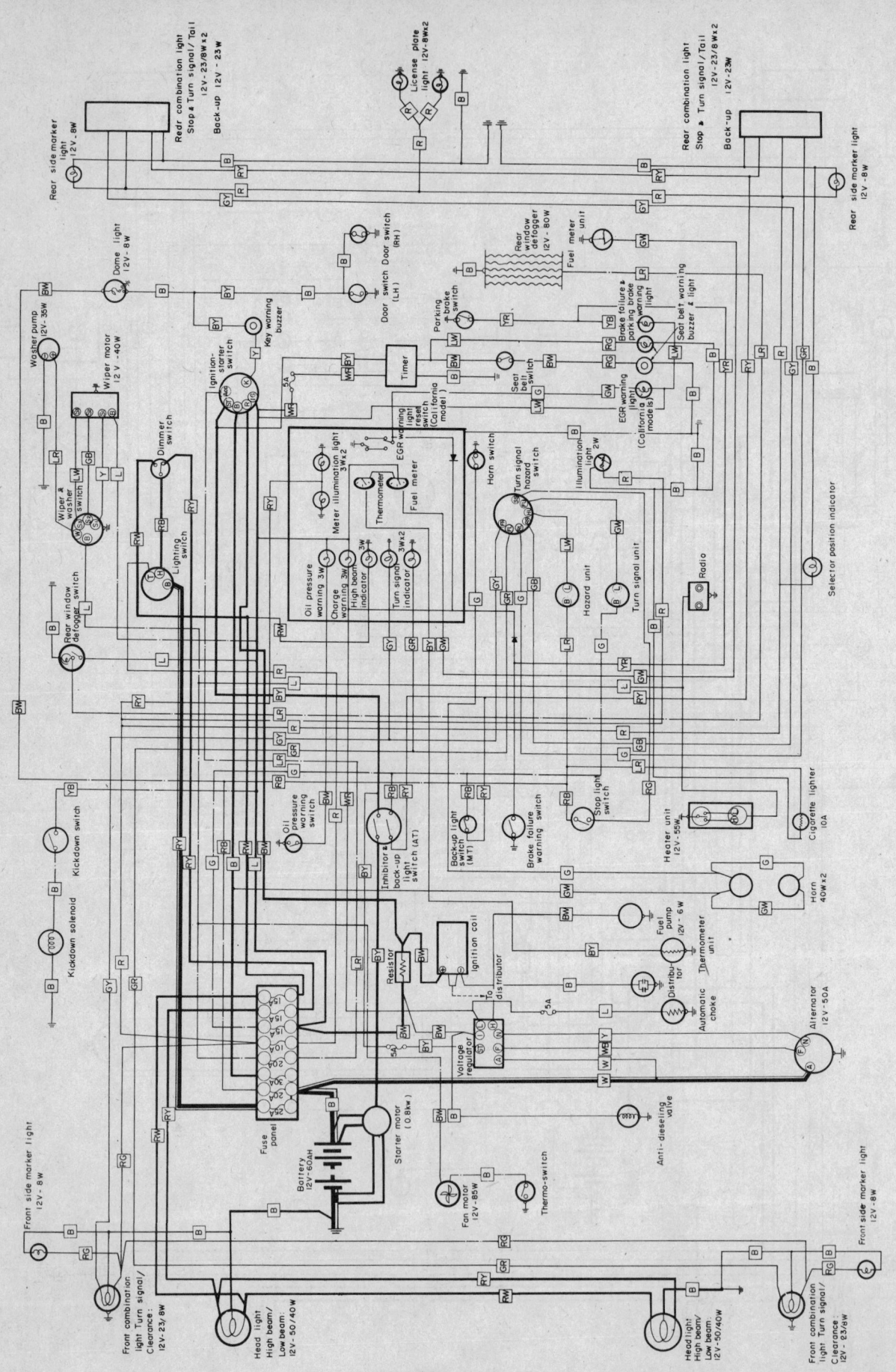

1975 Station wagon

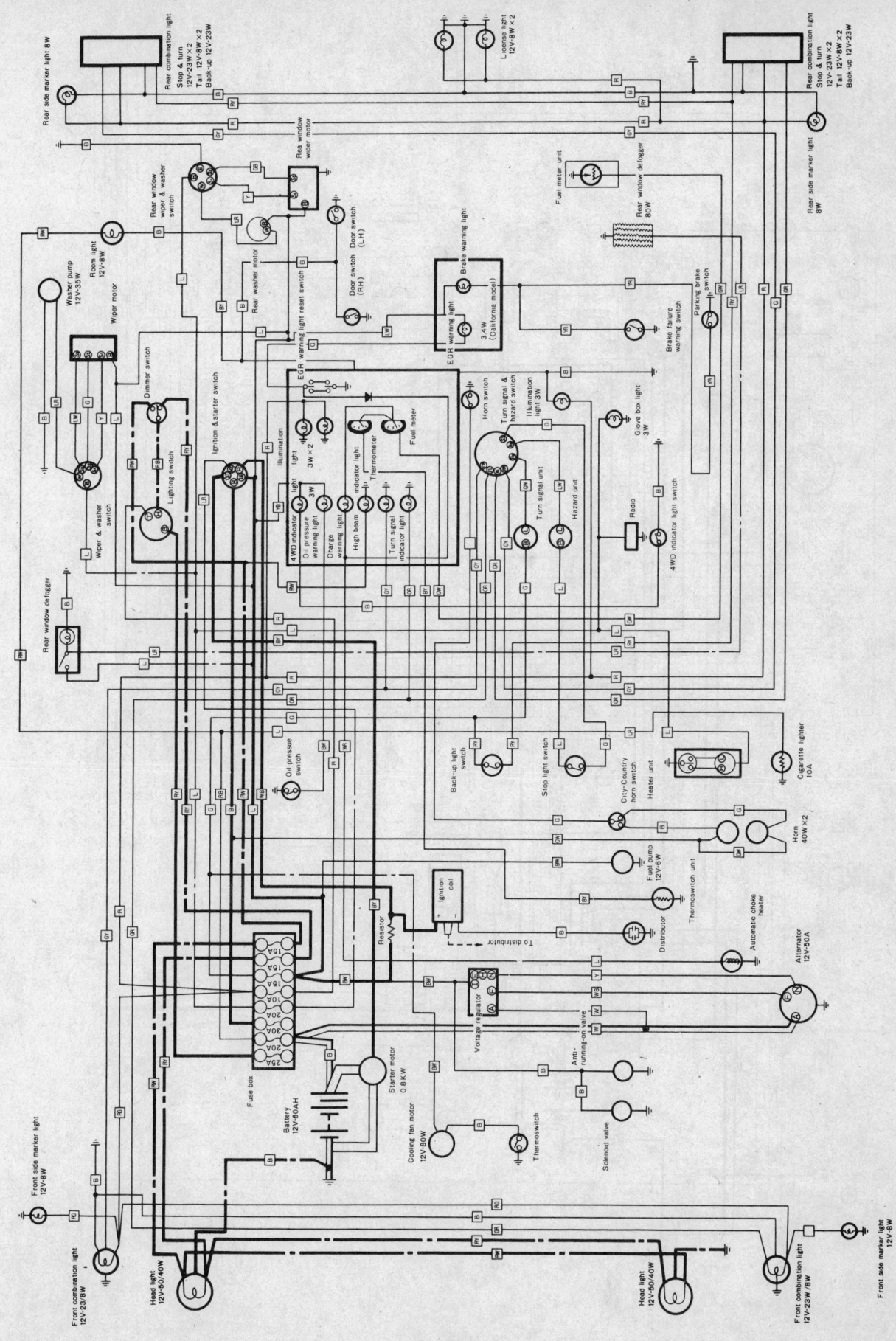

1975 4 WD

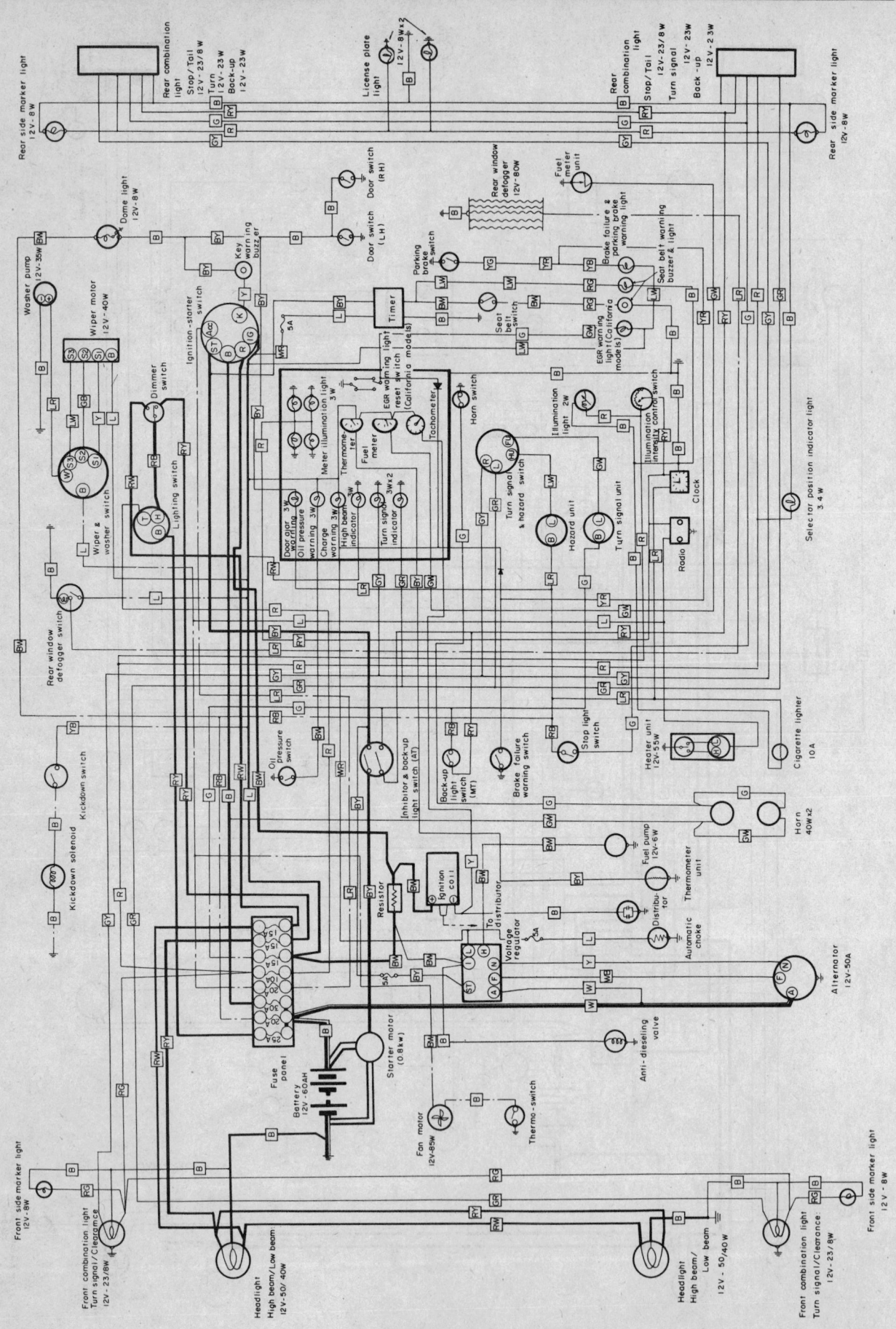

1976 Hardtop

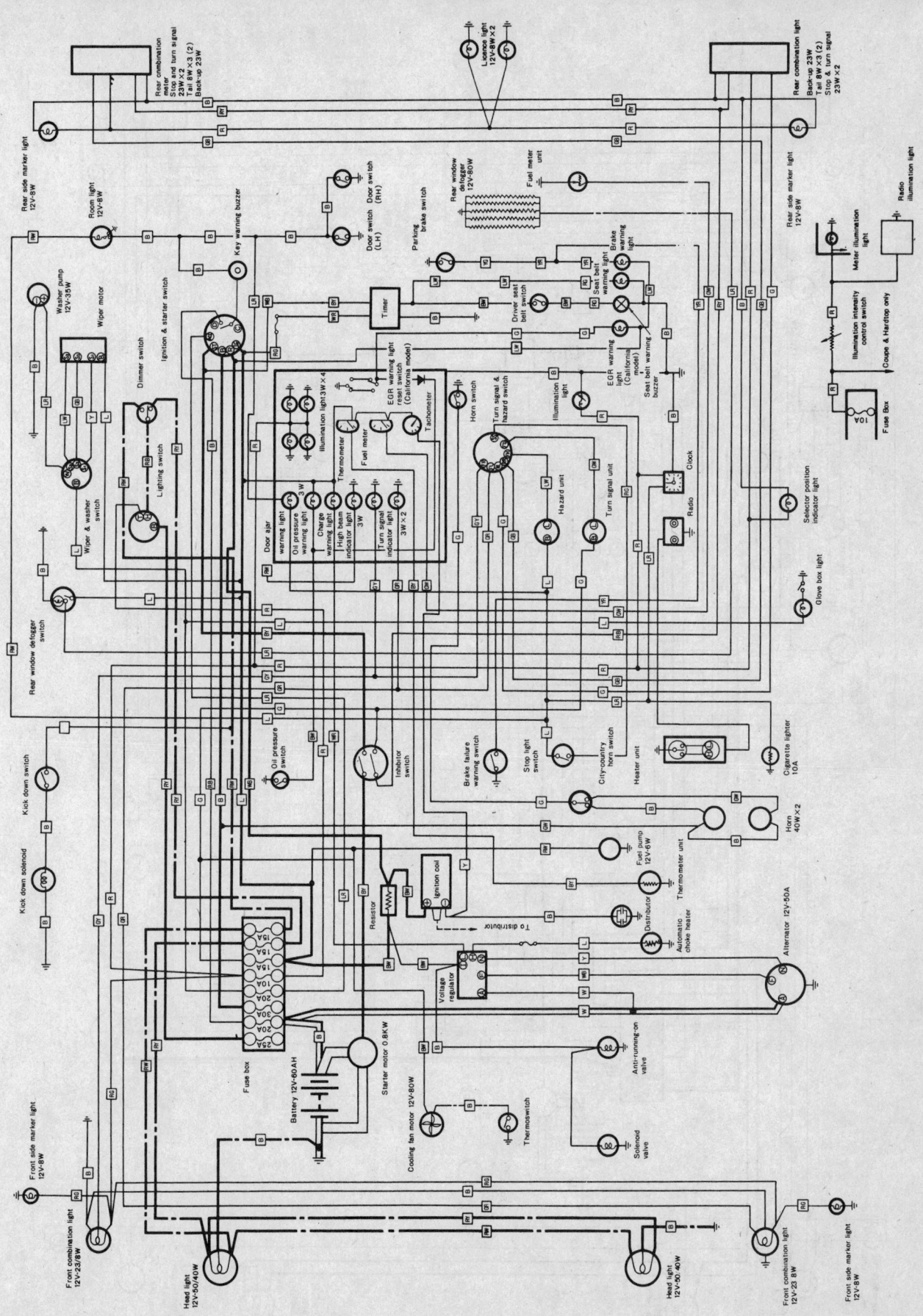

1976 sedan and coupe

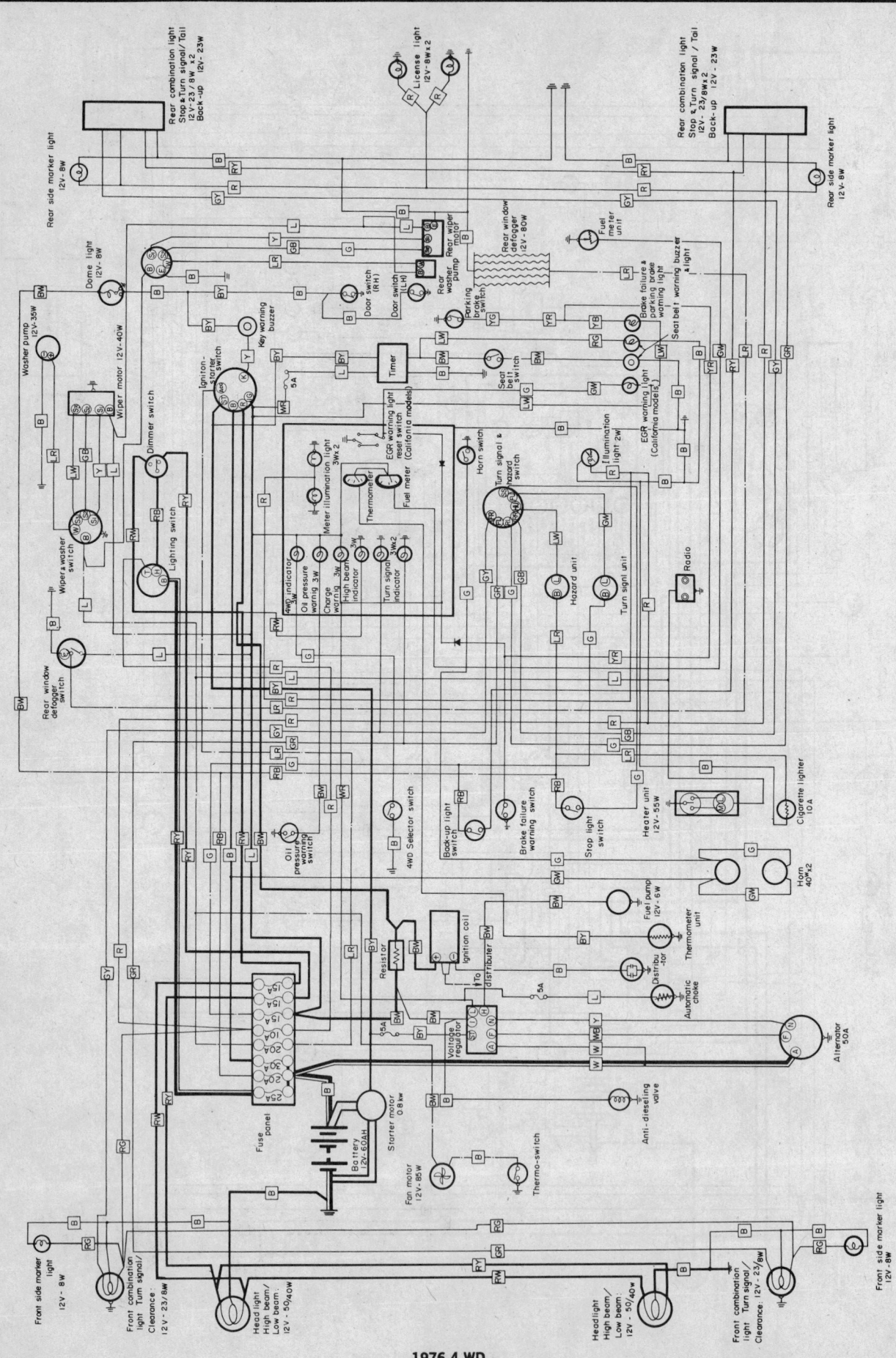

1976 4 WD

SPECIFICATIONS

INTRODUCTION

In 1933, the Toyoda Automatic Loom Works started an automobile division. Several models, mostly experimental, were produced between 1935 and 1937. Automobile production started on a large scale in 1937 when the Toyota Motor Co. Ltd. was founded. The name for the automobile company was changed from the family name, Toyoda, to Toyota, because a numerologist suggested that this would be a more auspicious name to use for this endeavor. It must have been; by 1947, Toyota had produced 100,000 vehicles. Today Toyota is Japan's largest producer of motor vehicles and ranks third largest in world production.

It was not until the late 1950s, that Toyota began importing cars to the United States. Public reception of the "Toyopet" was cool. The car was heavy and under-powered by U.S. standards. Several other models were imported, including the almost indestructible Land Cruiser. It was not until 1965, however, with the introduction of the Corona sedan, that Toyota enjoyed a real success on the U.S. market. Since that time, Toyota sales have risen at a steady rate, to make the Toyota the second largest-selling import in the U.S.

Continual product improvement, a good dealer network, and an ability to blanket the economy end of the market are responsible for this success. Today, Toyota produces a full range of models, from the economical Corolla to the luxurious Corona Mark II, for the U.S. market. Toyota's primary emphasis has been on economy sedans but in 1971 the sporty Celica coupe was introduced, putting Toyota into the "mini ponycar" business.

MODEL IDENTIFICATION

1972 Corolla 1200 and 1600

1973 – 74 Corolla

1975 Corolla

1972 – '73 Carina

Hi-Lux

1972 Corona 2000

1973 Corona 2000

1974-76 Corona

1976 Corona

1971 Mark II 1900

1972-73 Mark II 6 cyl.

1972 Mark II 2000

1975 Celica

1974-75 Mark II 6 cyl.

Toyota

1972-77 Land Cruiser

1972-77 Land Cruiser station wagon

SERIAL NUMBER IDENTIFICATION

Vehicle

All models have the vehicle identification number (VIN) stamped on a plate which is attached to the left side of the instrument panel. This plate is visible through the windshield.

The serial number consists of a series identification numbers followed by a six-digit production number.

VEHICLE IDENTIFICATION

Model Type	Year	Series Identification Number*
Corolla 1200		
Sedan	1972-74	KE20L
Coupe	1972-74	KE25L
Corolla 1600		
Sedan	1972-74	TE21L
Coupe	1972-74	TE27L
Station Wagon	1972-74	TE28LV
Corolla 1600		
Sedan	1975-77	TE31L
Hardtop	1975-77	TE37L
Station Wagon	1975-77	TE38LV
Carina		
Sedan	1972-73	TA12L
Corona 2000		
Sedan	1972-73	RT85L
Hardtop	1972-73	RT95L
Station Wagon	1973	RT89L
Corona 2000		
Sedan	1974	RT104L
Hardtop	1974	RT114L
Station Wagon	1974	RT118L
Corona 2200		
Sedan	1975-77	RT105L
Hardtop	1975-77	RT115L
Station Wagon	1975-77	RT119L
Mark II 2000		
Sedan	1972 (early)	RT63L
Hardtop	1972 (early)	RT73L
Station Wagon	1972 (early)	RT79L

Model/Type	Year	Series Identification Number*
Mark II 2300		
Sedan	1972 late)	MX12L
Hardtop	1972 (late)	MX22L
Station Wagon	1972 (late)	MX28L
Mark II 2600		
Sedan	1973-77	MX13L
Hardtop	1973-77	MX23L
Station Wagon	1973-77	MX29L
Celica 2000		
Hardtop	1972-74	RA21L
Celica 2200		
Hardtop	1975-77	RA22L
Crown 2600		
Sedan	1972	MS65L
Hardtop	1972	MS75L
Station Wagon	1972	MS63L
Hi-Lux 2000	1972	RN14L
Hi-Lux 2000		
Standard Wheelbase	1973-74	RN22L
Long Wheelbase	1973-74	RN27L
Hi-Lux 2200		
Standard Wheelbase	1975-77	RN23L
Long Wheelbase	1975-77	RN28L
Land Cruiser		
2-door	1972-74	FJ40LV
Station Wagon	1972-74	FJ55LV
Land Cruiser		
2-door	1975-77	N.A.
Station Wagon	1975-77	N.A.

* The suffixes, L, V, KA, etc, may not appear in the serial number; a typical Toyota serial number would appear: MS55-132246
N.A. Not Available

Engine

The engine serial number consists of an engine series identification number, followed by a six-digit production number.

The location of this serial number varies from one engine type to another. Serial numbers may be found in the following locations:

1200 cc (3K-C)

The serial number on the K-C and 3K-C engine is stamped on the right side of the engine, below the spark plugs.

1600 cc(2T-C)

The serial number is stamped on the left side of this engine, behind the dipstick.

2000 cc(18R-C)

The serial number is stamped on the left side of the engine, behind the dipstick.

2200 cc (20R)

The serial number is stamped on the left side of the engine, behind the alternator.

2600 cc (4M)

The serial numbers on both of these engines are stamped on the right side of the cylinder block, below the oil filter.

Land Cruiser (F and 2F)

The serial number is located on the front, right side of the engine.

ENGINE IDENTIFICATION

Model	Year	Displacement Cu in. (cm³)	Number of cylinders	Type	Engine Series Identification
Corolla					
1200	1972-74	71.2 (1166)	4	OHV	3K-C
1600	1972-76	96.9 (1588)	4	OHV	2T-C
Carina	1972-73	96.9 (1588)	4	OHV	2T-C
Corona					
2000	1972-74	120.0 (1980)	4	OHC	18R-C
2200	1975-77	133.6 (2189)	4	OHC	20R
Mark II					
2000	1972	120.0 (1980)	4	OHC	18R-C
2300	1972 (late)	137.5 (2258)	6	OHC	2M
2600	1973-76	156.4 (2563)	6	OHC	4M
Celica					
2000	1972-74	120.0 (1980)	4	OHC	18R-C
2200	1975-77	133.6 (2189)	4	OHC	20R
Crown					
2600	1972	156.4 (2563)	6	OHC	4M
Hi-Lux					
2000	1972-74	120.0 (1980)	4	OHC	18R-C
2200	1975-77	133.6 (2189)	4	OHC	20R
Land Cruiser	1972-74	236.7 (3878)	6	OHV	F
	1975-77	256.00 (4200)	6	OHV	2F

OHV—Overhead valve
OHC—Overhead cam

GENERAL ENGINE SPECIFICATIONS

Year	Engine Type	Engine Displacement Cu in. (cc)	Carburetor Type	Horsepower @ rpm ▲	Torque @ rpm (ft lbs) ▲	Bore x Stroke (in.)	Compression Ratio
1972-74	3K-C	71.8 (1166)	2-bbl	65 @ 6000	67 @ 3800	2.95 x 2.60	9.0:1
	2T-C	96.9 (1588)	2-bbl	88 @ 6000	91.3 @ 3800	3.35 x 2.76	8.5:1
	18R-C	123.0 (1980)	2-bbl	97 @ 5500	106 @ 3600	3.48 x 3.15	8.5:1
	2M②	137.5 (2253)	2-bbl	109 @ 5200	120 @ 3600	2.95 x 3.35	8.5:1
	4M	156.4 (2563)	2-bbl	122 @ 5200	141 @ 3600	3.15 x 3.35	8.5:1
	F	236.7 (3878)	2-bbl	135 @ 4000	213 @ 2000	3.54 x 4.00	7.8:1

GENERAL ENGINE SPECIFICATIONS

Year	Engine Type	Engine Displacement Cu in. (cc)	Carburetor Type	Horsepower @ rpm ▲	Torque @ rpm (ft lbs) ▲	Bore x Stroke (in.)	Compression Ratio
1975-77	2T-C	96.9 (1588)	2-bbl	75 @ 5800③	83 @ '3800	3.35 x 2.76	9.0:1
	20R	133.6 (2189)	2-bbl	96 @ 4800⑧	120 @ 2800	3.48 x 3.50	8.4:1
	4M*	151.4 (2563)	2-bbl	108 @ 5000	130 @ 2800	3.15 x 3.35	8.5:1
	2F	257.9 (4200)	2-bbl	125 @ 3600	200 @ 1800	3.70 x 4.00	7.8:1
	3K-C	71.8 (1166)	2-bbl	65 @ 6000	67 @ 3800	2.95 x 2.60	9.0:1

▲ Horsepower and torque ratings given in SAE net figures in 1972-77
① 2T-C engines were introduced in 1971
② Not available in 1973-74

③ 73 @ 5800—California
④ 90 @ 4800—California
* Not available in 1977

TUNE-UP SPECIFICATIONS

Year	Engine Type	SPARK PLUGS Type (ND)	Gap (in.)	DISTRIBUTOR Point Dwell (deg)	Point Gap (in.)	Ignition Timing (deg) ▲ MT	AT	Compression Press. **	Fuel Pump Press.	IDLE SPEED (rpm) ▲ MT	AT	VALVE CLEARANCE (in.) Intake	Exhaust
1972-73	3K-C	W20EP	0.031	52	0.018	5B	—	171①	2.8-4.3	650	—	0.008	0.012
	2T-C	W20EP	0.031	52	0.018	5B	5B	170①	2.8-4.3	750	650	0.008	0.013
	18R-C	W20EP	0.031	52	0.018	7B	7B	164①	2.8-4.3	650	650	0.008	0.014
	2M	W16EP	0.030	41	0.018	7B	7B	149	3.4-4.6	700	600	0.007	0.010
	4M	W14EP	0.031	41	0.018	7B	5B	156①	4.2-5.4	700	650	0.007	0.010
	F	W17ES	0.030	41	0.018	7B	—	145①	3.4-4.8	600②	—	0.008	0.014
1974	3K-C	W20EP	0.031	52	0.018	5B	—	156	2.8-4.3	750	—	0.008	0.012
	2T-C③	W20EP	0.031	52	0.018	5B	5B	149	2.8-4.3	750	800	0.008	0.013
	2T-C④	W20EP	0.031	52	0.018	10B	10B	149	2.8-4.3	850	850	0.008	0.013
	18R-C	W20EP	0.031	52	0.018	7B	7B	156	2.8-4.3	650	800	0.008	0.014
	4M	W16EP⑧	0.031	41	0.018	5B	5B	156	4.2-5.4	700	750	0.007	0.010
	F	W14ES⑨	0.030	41	0.018	7B	—	149	3.4-4.8	650	—	0.008	0.014
1975-77	2T-C	W16EP	0.030	52⑤	0.018	10B⑥	10B⑥	171	2.8-4.3⑦	850	850	0.008	0.013
	20R	W16EP	0.030	52	0.018⑩	8B	8B	156	2.2-4.2	850	850	0.008	0.012
	4M③*	W16EP	0.030	41	0.018	10B	10B	156	4.2-5.4	800	750	0.007	0.010
	4M④*	W16EP	0.030	41	0.018	5B	5B	156	4.2-5.4	800	750	0.007	0.010
	2F	W14EX	0.037	41	0.018	7B	—	149	3.4-4.7	650	—	0.008	0.014
	3K-C	W20EP	0.031	52	0.018	5B	—	156	2.8-4.3	750	—	0.008	0.012

NOTE: If the information given in this chart disagrees with the information on the engine tune-up decal, use the specifications on the decal—they are current for the engine in your car.

▲ With manual transmission in Neutral and automatic transmission in Drive (D) (1972-73) or Neutral (1974-77).
** Difference between cylinders should not exceed 14 psi, however, look for uniformity among cylinders rather than specific pressures
‡ Valve clearances checked with engine HOT
① 1973 compression specifications:
 3K-C—156 psi   4M—156 psi
 2T-C—149 psi   F—149 psi
 18R-C—156 psi
② 1973—650 rpm
③ USA—except Calif.
④ California only

⑤ Dual point—main 57°; sub 52°
⑥ Dual point—main 12B; sub 19-25°B.
⑦ Electric pump (Calif.)—2.4-3.8
⑧ California 18R-C engines with EGR—W16EP
⑨ California F engines—W14EX
⑩ California model Celica GT equipped with transistorized ignition
MT Manual transmission
AT Automatic transmission
TDC Top Dead Center
B Before top dead center
A After top dead center
* Not available in 1977

FIRING ORDERS

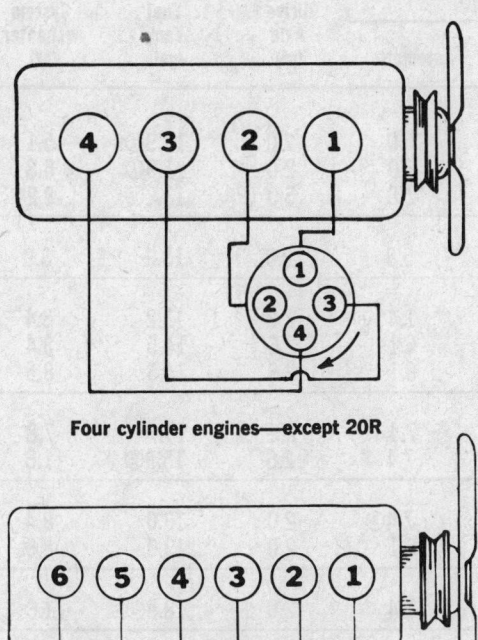

Four cylinder engines—except 20R

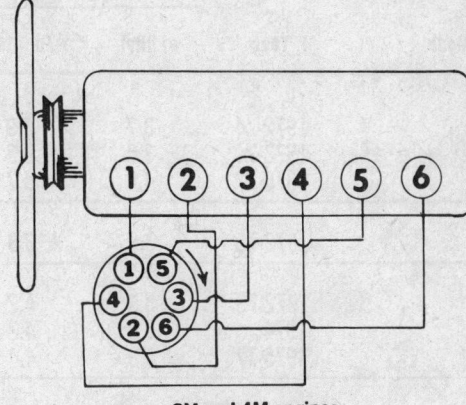

2M and 4M engines

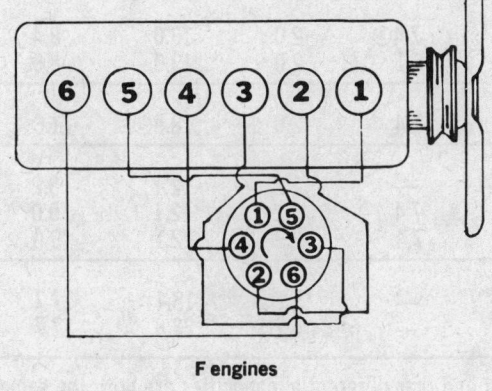

F engines

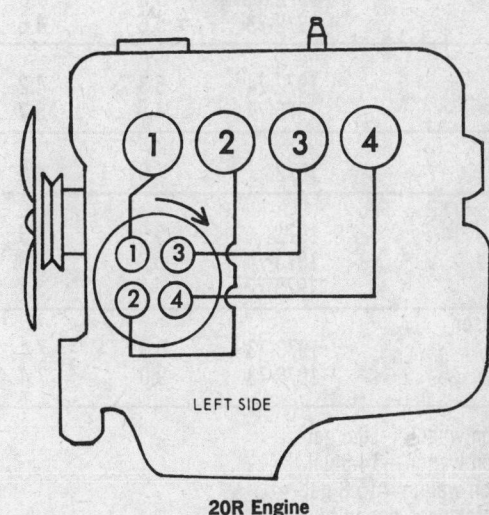

LEFT SIDE

20R Engine

VALVE SPECIFICATIONS

Engine Type	Seat Angle (deg)	Face Angle (deg)	SPRING TEST PRESSURE (lbs)		SPRING INSTALLED HEIGHT (in.)		STEM TO GUIDE CLEARANCE (in.) ▲		STEM DIAMETER (in.)	
			Inner	Outer	Inner	Outer	Intake	Exhaust	Intake	Exhaust
3K-C	45	45	—	55.1	—	1.512	0.0010-0.0020	0.0020-0.0030	0.3140	0.3140
2T-C	45	45	—	58.4	—	1.484	0.0012-0.0022	0.0012-0.0024	0.3142	0.3140
18R-C	45	45	15.2	50.6	1.480	1.640	0.0010-0.0022	0.0014-0.0030	0.3140	0.3136
20R	45	45	—	60.0	—	1.594	0.0006-0.0024	0.0012-0.0026	0.3141	0.3140
2M	45	45	11.9	68.0①	1.535	1.654②	0.0006-0.0018	0.0014-0.0030	0.3153	0.3121
4M	45	45	25.7	63.1③	1.504	1.642④	0.0006-0.0018	0.0010-0.0024	0.3146	0.3140
F	45	45	—	132.0	—	1.324	0.0010-0.0026	0.0014-0.0028	0.3141	0.3137
2F	45	45	—	71.6	—	1.693	0.0012-0.0024	0.0016-0.0028	0.3140	0.3147

▲ Valve guides are removable
① Exhaust valve spring test pressure: inner—11.5 lbs; outer —66.6 lbs
② Exhaust valve installed height: inner—1.535 in.; outer— 1.661 in.
③ Exhaust valve spring test pressure: inner—24.6 lbs; outer —59.4 lbs
④ Exhaust valve installed height: inner—1.520 in.; outer— 1.657 in.

CAPACITIES

Model	Year	CRANKCASE (qt)		TRANSMISSION (qt)		Drive Axle (pt)	Fuel Tank (gal)	Cooling System w/heater (qt)
		w/filter	w/o filter	Manual	Automatic			
Corolla								
1200	1972-74	3.7	2.9	2.9	5.0	2.0	11.9①	5.1
1600	1972-74	3.6	3.3	1.6	5.0	2.0	11.9①	6.8
1600	1975-77	4.6	3.7	1.6	1.6	5.0	13.2⑧	8.2
Carina								
1600	1972-73	3.9	3.3	1.6	5.0	2.0	13.2	6.9
Corona								
2000	1972-73	5.3	4.2	2.1	1.4	2.2	13.2	8.4
2000	1974	5.3	4.2	2.9⑧	6.1	2.6	14.5	8.4
2200	1975-77	5.3	4.4	2.9⑧	6.1	2.6	14.5	8.5
Mark II								
2000	1972 (early)	5.6	4.6	2.1	7.4	2.2	13.7	7.8
6 cyl	1972-73	5.6	4.6	1.8	7.4	2.6	15.9②	11.6
Celica								
2000	1972-74	5.3	4.2	2.1	7.4⑥	2.0	13.0	8.4
2200	1975-77	4.5	3.7	2.1	6.1	2.0	13.0	8.5
Crown								
2600	1972	5.6	4.6	1.8	7.4	2.6	18.5③	11.6
Hi-Lux								
2000	1972	5.3	4.3	1.8	—	2.2	12.1	8.2
2000	1973-74	5.3	4.3	1.8	7.4	2.2	12.1	9.0
2200	1975-77	4.5	3.7	1.8	7.4	2.2	12.1	9.0
Land Cruiser								
2-dr	1970-73	9.0	7.4	1.8④	—	5.2⑤	18.4	17.7
4-dr	1970-73	9.0	7.4	1.8④	—	5.2⑤	23.8	17.7

① Station wagon—10.6 gal
② Station wagon—14.5 gal
③ Station wagon—15.8 gal
④ Transfer case capacity—1.8 qts
⑤ Front and rear differential capacities are both the same
⑥ Automatic available in 1973
⑦ 5-speed—2.7 qts
⑧ Wagon—12.4 gal

CRANKSHAFT AND CONNECTING ROD SPECIFICATIONS
All measurements in inches.

Engine Type	CRANKSHAFT				CONNECTING ROD		
	Main Brg. Journal Dia.	Main Brg. Oil Clearance	Shaft End-Play	Thrust on no.	Journal Diameter	Oil Clearance	Side Clearance
3K-C	1.9675-1.9685	0.0005-0.0015	0.0020-0.0090	3	1.6525-1.6535	0.0006-0.0015	0.0040-0.0080
2T-C	2.2827-2.2834	0.0012-0.0024	0.0030-0.0070	3	1.8889-1.8898	0.0008-0.0020	0.0063-0.0102
18R-C	2.3613-2.3622	0.0008-0.0020	0.0008-0.0080	3	2.0857-2.0866	0.0010-0.0021	0.0060-0.0100
20R	2.3614-2.3622	0.0010-0.0022	0.0008-0.0079	3	2.0862-2.0866	0.0010-0.0022	0.0063-0.0102
2M	2.3616-2.3622	0.0007-0.0017	0.0020-0.0017	4	2.0466-2.0472	0.0006-0.0020	0.0040-0.0100
4M	2.3617-2.3627	0.0012-0.0021	0.0020-0.0100	4	2.0463-2.0472	0.0008-0.0021	0.0020-0.0100
F	2.6366-2.6378	0.0012-0.0018	0.0024-0.0065	3	2.1252-2.1260	0.0008-0.0024	0.0040-0.0090
2F	①	0.0008-0.0017	0.0024-0.0063	3	2.1252-2.1260	0.0008-0.0024	0.0043-0.0091

Dia. Diameter   Brg. Bearing
① No. 1—2.6367-2.6376   No. 3—2.7548-2.7557
No. 2—2.6957-2.6967   No. 4—2.8139-2.8148

PISTON AND RING SPECIFICATIONS
All measurements in inches

Engine Type	Piston Clearance	RING GAP			RING SIDE CLEARANCE		
		Top Compression	Bottom Compression	Oil Control	Top Compression	Bottom Compression	Oil Control
3K-C	0.0010-0.0020	0.006-0.014	0.006-0.014	0.006-0.014	0.0011-0.0027	0.0007-0.0023	0.0006-0.0023
2T-C	0.0024-0.0031	0.008-0.016	0.004-0.012	0.004-0.012	0.0008-0.0024	0.0008-0.0024	0.0008-0.0024
18R-C	0.0020-0.0030	0.004-0.012	0.004-0.012	0.004-0.012	0.0012-0.0028	0.0012-0.0028	0.0008-0.0028
20R	0.0012-0.0020	0.004-0.012	0.004-0.0012	N.A.	0.008	0.008	N.A.
2M and 4M	0.0010-0.0020	0.006-0.014	0.006-0.014	0.008-0.020	0.0012-0.0028	0.0008-0.0024	N.A.
F	0.0012-0.0020	0.006-0.018	0.006-0.016	①	0.0016-0.0031	0.0016-0.0031	②
2F	0.0012-0.0020	0.0079-0.0157	0.0079-0.0157	—	0.0012-0.0024	0.0008-0.0024	—

① Oil control gap:
   Top—0.006-0.018 in.
   Bottom—0.006-0.016 in.
N.A. Not Available

② Control clearance
   Top—0.0016-0.0031 in.
   Bottom—0.0016-0.0033 in.

TORQUE SPECIFICATIONS
All readings in ft lbs

Engine Type	Cylinder Head Bolts	Rod Bearing Bolts	Main Bearing Bolts	Crankshaft Pulley Bolt	Flywheel to Crankshaft Bolts	MANIFOLD	
						Intake	Exhaust
3K-C	39-48	29-38	39-46	29-43	39-48	7-12	14-22
2T-C	52-63	28-36	52-63	29-43	42-48	7-12	7-12
18R-C	72-82	39-48	69-83	43-51	51-58		30-35①
20R	52-64	39-48	69-83	80-94	62-69	11-15	29-36
2M	②	25-30	72-79	43-51	41-46③	22-29④	18-25⑤
4M	⑥	30-36	72-78	69-76	41-46⑦	17-21④	12-17⑤
F	83-98	35-55	90-108⑧	—	43-51		14-22①
2F	83-98	35-55	90-108⑧	116-145	59-62	28-37	28-37

① Intake and exhaust manifolds combined
② 8mm bolts—11-15 ft lbs
   13mm bolts—54-61 ft lbs
③ Flex-plate (automatic) 14-22 ft lbs
④ Intake manifold stud bolt—14-18 ft lbs
⑤ Exhaust manifold stud bolt—6-7 ft lbs
⑥ 8mm bolts—7-12 ft lbs
   10mm bolts—54-61 ft lbs
⑦ Flex-plate (automatic) 11-16 ft lbs
⑧ Rear bearing—76-94 ft lbs

TORQUE SEQUENCES
Cylinder Head

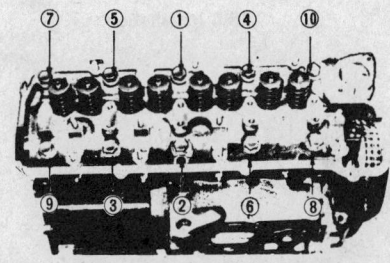

8R-C and 18R-C installation

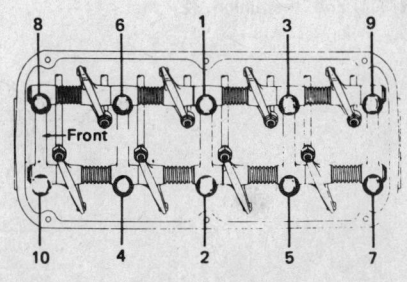

2T-C installation

TORQUE SEQUENCES
Cylinder Head

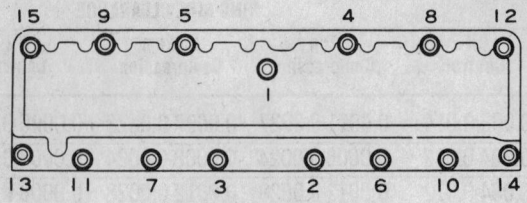

F and 2F installation

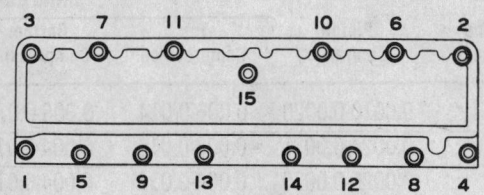

F and 2F removal

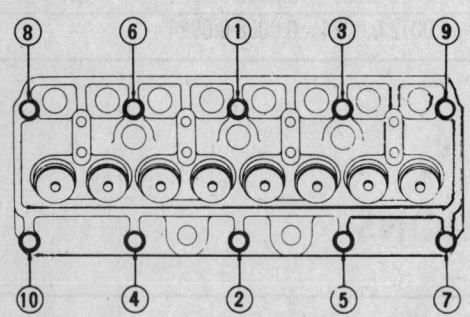

3K-C installation

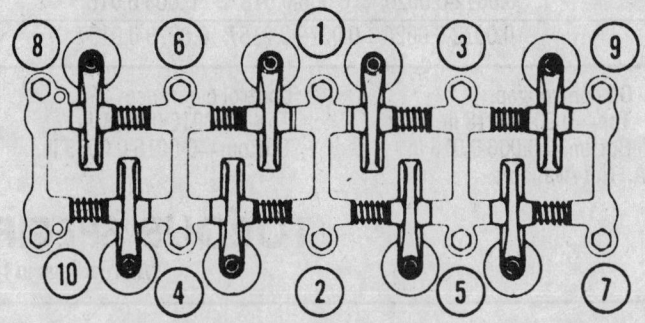

20R cylinder head installation sequence

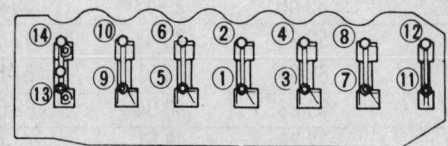

2M and 4M installation

Rocker Arms

2M and 4M removal—remove the union
bolt (1) and the union (2) first.

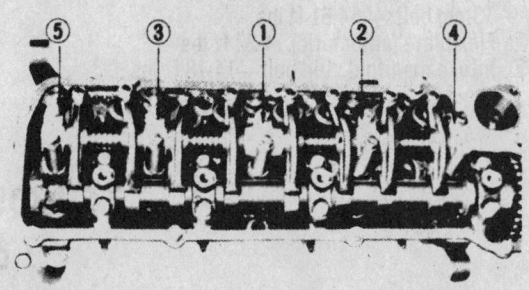

18R-C installation

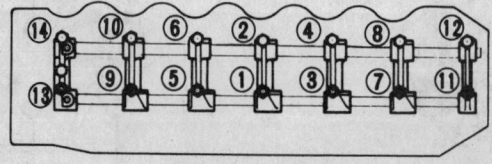

2M and 4M installation

BATTERY AND STARTER SPECIFICATIONS

All models use 12-volt, negative ground electrical systems

| Engine Type | Battery Amp. Hour Capy. | STARTERS | | | | | | Brush Minimum Tension (oz) | Brush Minimum Length (in.) |
| | | Lock Test | | | No-Load Test | | | | |
		Amps	Volts	Torque (ft lbs)	Amps	Volts	Rpm		
3K-C	48	450	8.5	8	55	11	3,500	21	0.51
2T-C	50	—— Not Recommended ——			—— Not Recommended ——			21	0.47
8R-C and 18R-C	40①④	550	7.7	10	45	11	6,000	21	0.47
2M	60②	600	7.0	13	50	11	5,000	21	0.47
4M and 20R	50③②	600	7.0	13	50	11	5,000	21	0.47
F	50	430	7.3	11	45	11	3,500	21	0.51
2F	50	—— Not Recommended ——			Less than 50	11.5	More than 5,000	21	0.51
2T-C, 20R Optional HD	60	—— Not Recommended ——			80	11.5	3,500	41	0.39
4M Optional HD	70	—— Not Recommended ——			90	11.5	4,000	21	0.33

① 50 AH—Celica and Hi-Lux
② 70 AH—Mark 11/6
③ 60 AH—with air conditioning
④ 1974 Corona—50 AH; cold weather areas 60 AH

AH Amp Hour
Neg Negative
HD Heavy duty

NOTE: On Corona models with "ESP" a replacement battery with separate caps must be used, so the low electrolyte sender can be installed in one of the cells.

ALTERNATOR AND REGULATOR SPECIFICATIONS

| Engine Type | ALTERNATOR | | REGULATOR | | | | | | | |
| | | | | Field Relay | | | Regulator | | |
	Manufacturer	Output (amps)	Manufacturer	Contact Spring Deflection (in.)	Point Gap (in.)	Volts to Close	Air Gap (in.)	Point Gap (in.)	Volts
3K-C	Nippondenso	25	Nippondenso	0.008-0.024	0.016-0.047	4.5-5.8	0.012	0.010-0.018	13.8-14.8
2T-C	Nippondenso	40	Nippondenso	0.008-0.024	0.016-0.047	4.5-5.8	0.012	0.012-0.018	13.8-14.8
18R-C	Nippondenso	40②	Nippondenso	0.008-0.018	0.016-0.047	4.5-5.8	0.008	0.010-0.018	13.8-14.8
2M	Nippondenso	40	Nippondenso	0.008-0.024	0.016-0.047	4.5-5.8	0.012	0.012-0.018	13.8-14.8
2M①	Nippondenso	45	Nippondenso	0.008-0.018	0.016-0.047	4.5-5.8	0.012	0.012-0.018	13.8-14.8
4M	Nippondenso	55	Nippondenso	0.008-0.024	0.016-0.047	4.5-5.8	0.012	0.008-0.024	13.8-14.8
F	Nippondenso	38	Nippondenso	—	—	4.5-5.8	—	0.001-0.018	13.6-14.8
2F	Nippondenso	45	Nippondenso	—— Not Adjustable ——					13.8-14.8

① Mark II/6—1972
② 1974-75 Corona 45 amps

BRAKE SPECIFICATIONS

All measurements given are (in.) unless noted

Model	Lug Nut Torque (ft/lb)	Master Cylinder Bore	Brake Disc		Brake Drum			Minimum Lining Thickness	
			Minimum Thickness	Maximum Run-Out	Diameter	Max. Machine O/S	Max. Wear Limit	Front	Rear
Corolla									
1200	65-86	0.626	0.35	0.006	7.9	7.94	7.95	0.22	0.04
1600	65-86	0.813	0.35	0.006	9.0	9.07	9.08	0.22	0.04
Carina, Celica	65-86	0.813	0.35	0.006	9.0	9.07	9.08	0.22	0.04
Corona									
2000 (1972-73)	65-86	0.876	0.35	0.006	9.0	9.07	9.09	0.35	0.06
2000/2200 (1974-77)	65-86	0.876	0.45	0.006	9.0	9.07	9.09	0.04	0.04
Mark II									
2000 (4 cyl.)	65-86	0.873	0.37	0.006	9.0	9.07	9.08	0.08	0.06
2300/2600 (6 cyl.)	65-86	0.937	0.45	0.006	9.0	9.07	9.08	0.28	0.06
Crown 2600	65-86	0.937	0.45	0.006	10.0	10.07	10.08	0.27	0.06
Hi-Lux									
1972	65-86	1.001	—	—	9.1	9.13	9.15	0.06	0.06
1973-77	65-86	1.001	0.45	0.006	10.0	10.07	10.08	0.27	0.06
Land-Cruiser									
1972-75	65-86	0.997	—	—	11.4	11.54	11.54	0.16	0.16
1976-77	65-86	0.997	0.74	0.005	11.4	11.54	11.54	0.04	0.06

NOTE: Minimun lining thickness is as recommended by the manufacturer. Due to variations in state inspection regulations, the minimum allowable thickness may be different than recommended by the manufacturer.

WHEEL ALIGNMENT

Model	CASTER		CAMBER		Toe-in (in.)	Steering Axis Inclination	WHEEL PIVOT RATIO (deg)	
	Range (deg)	Pref Setting (deg)	Range (deg)	Pref Setting (deg)			Inner Wheel	Outer Wheel
Corolla								
1200	1½P-2⅓P	—	½P-1½P	½P	0.04-0.20	7½P-8½P	38½-41½	30-36
1600	1⅓-2P②	—	½P-1½P	½P	0.04-0.20	7½P-8½P	38½-41½③	27½-33½
Carina & Celica	½P-1½P	1P	0-1½P	1P	0.20-0.28	7½P	—	—
Corona (1972-73)	0-1P	½P	1P-2P	1½P	0.16-0.24①	7P	38½	31
Corona (1974-75)	½P-1½P	1P	0-1P	½P	0.05-0.12	7P	—	—
Corona (1976-77)	⅓P-1⅓P	—	0-1P	½P	0.04-0.12	7P	37½	31
Mark II/4	1P-2P	1½P	1P-2P	1P	0.16-0.24	7P	40	32½
Mark II/6	0-1P	½P	½P-1½P	1P	0.16-0.24	7P	36½	32½
Crown 2600	1N-½P	½N	0-1P	½P	0.12-0.20	7½P	38	29
Hi-Lux	1N-0	½N	½P-1½P	1P	0.24	7P	39	31½
Land Cruiser								
2 door	½P-1½P	1P	½P-1½P	1P	0.12-0.20	9½P	32	27
Wagon	½P-1½P	1P	½P-1½P	1P	0.12-0.20	9½P	30*	23*

P   Positive
N   Negative
① 1966-69 Corona—0.04-0.12 in.

*   1976-77 Inner—32; Outer—30
② 1975 Wagon—¾P-1½P
③ 1975 Inner—37-39°

TUNE-UP PROCEDURES

NOTE: *The procedures outlined below are the specific procedures for Toyota vehicles; general tune-up procedures may be found in the section at the end of this book.*

Spark Plugs

Check, clean, and adjust the spark plugs every 6,000 miles. Replace them every 12,000 miles.

Clean any foreign material from around the spark plugs before removing them. Use the spark plug wrench supplied in the tool kit.

Clean any plugs which appear to be dirty and file their electrodes flat. Adjust the gap to the figure given in the "Tune-up Specifications" chart, above, using a wire feeler gauge.

NOTE: *Do not use a flat gauge; an inaccurate reading will result.*

Inspect the spark plug hole threads for rust and, if necessary, use a 14 mm plug tap to clean them.

Examine the condition of the spark plugs and check them against the diagnosis guide at the end of the book.

Lightly oil the threads and torque the plugs to 11–14 ft lbs. Use caution when tightening the plugs, as most Toyota models use aluminum heads.

Breaker Points and Condenser

Loosen the clips which attach the distributor cap to the distributor body and lift the cap straight up. Leave the leads connected to the cap. Remove the rotor and dust cover.

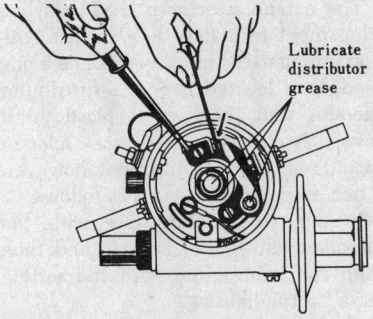

Lubricate distributor grease

Point gap : 0.018 inch

Adjustment of the points and lubrication of the distributor.

Clean the distributor cap and rotor with alcohol. Inspect them for cracks and other signs of wear or damage. Polish the points with a point file.

NOTE: *Do not use emery cloth or sandpaper; these may leave particles on the points, causing them to arc. On 1975–77 models with electronic igni-*

tion use only pure alcohol to clean the points; shop solvent, gasoline, or an oily rag will cause the system to misfire.

If the points are badly pitted or worn, replace them as follows:

1. Unfasten the point lead connector.
2. Remove the point retaining clip and remove the point hold-down screw.
3. Remove the point set.
4. Installation is the reverse of removal.

After replacing the points, or as routine maintenance, adjust the points to the specifications given in the tune-up chart at the beginning of this section as follows:

1. Rotate the engine by hand or by using a remote starter switch, so that the rubbing block is on the high point of the cam lobe.
2. Insert a 0.018 in. feeler gauge between the points; a slight drag should be felt.
3. If no drag is felt or if the feeler gauge cannot be inserted at all, loosen, but do not remove, the point hold-down screw.
4. Insert a screwdriver into the adjustment slot. Rotate the screwdriver until the proper point gap is attained. The point gap is increased by rotating the screwdriver counterclockwise and decreased by rotating it clockwise.
5. Tighten the point hold-down screw.

Lubricate the cam lobes, breaker arm, rubbing block, arm pivot, and distributor shaft with special high-temperature distributor grease.

Check the operation of the centrifugal advance mechanism by moving the rotor clockwise. Release the rotor; it should return to its original position. If it does not, check it for binding.

Check the vacuum advance unit by removing the cap and pressing in on the octane selector. Release the octane selector. It should snap back to its original position. Check for binding if it fails to do so.

Replace the condenser if it is suspect or as routine maintenance during the point replacement operation, in the following manner:

1. Remove the nut and washer from the condenser lead terminal.
2. Remove the condenser mounting screw and withdraw the condenser.
3. Installation is the reverse of removal.

NOTE: *The condenser is mounted on the outside of the distributor body on all models, except the Land Cruiser, which has it mounted inside the body.*

Install the dust cover, rotor, and distributor cap on the distributor. Adjust the dwell and timing, as outlined below.

Dwell Angle

Connect a dwell/tachometer, in accordance with its manufacturer's instruc-

tions, between the distributor primary lead and a ground.

CAUTION: *On models with electronic ignition, hook the dwell meter or tachometer to the negative (−) side of the coil, not to the distributor primary lead; damage to the ignition control unit will result.*

With the engine warmed up and running at the specified idle speed (see the tune-up chart), take a dwell reading.

If the point dwell is not within specifications, shut the engine off and adjust the point gap, as outlined above.

NOTE: *Increasing the point gap decreases the dwell angle and vice versa.*

Install the dust cover, rotor, and cap. Check the dwell reading again.

Ignition Timing

Single Point

1. Warm up the engine. Connect a tachometer and check the engine idle speed to see that it is within specifications. Adjust it as outlined below if it is not.

CAUTION: *On models with electronic ignition, hook the dwell meter or tachomater to the negative (−) side of the coil, not to the distributor primary lead; damage to the ignition control until will result.*

If the timing mark is difficult to see, use chalk or a dab of paint to make it more visible.

2. Connect a timing light to the engine, as outlined in the instructions supplied by the manufacturer of the light.
3. Disconnect the vacuum line from the distributor vacuum unit and plug the line.
4. Allow the engine to run at the specified idle speed with the gear shift in neutral for cars with manual transmissions, and in Drive (D) for cars with automatic transmissions.

CAUTION: *Be sure that the parking brake is firmly set and that the wheels are chocked.*

5. Point the timing light at the timing marks indicated in the chart below. With the engine at idle, timing should be at the specification given in the tune-up chart at the beginning of this section. If it is not, loosen the pinch bolt at the base and rotate the distributor to advance or retard the timing, as required.
6. Stop the engine and tighten the pinch bolt. Start the engine and recheck the timing.
7. Stop the engine and disconnect the timing light and the tachometer. Connect the vacuum line to the vacuum advance unit.

Dual Point Distributor

A dual point distributor is offered as an option on some Corolla models, sold outside of California, starting in 1975.

To adjust the dual point system, proceed as follows:

1. Adjust the timing for the main set of points as outlined in the "Single Point" section above.

2. Use a jumper wire to ground the terminal on the thermoswitch connector after removing the connector from the thermoswitch. The thermoswitch is threaded into the intake manifold and is connected to the dual point system relay. Be careful not confuse it with any of the emission control system switches which are connected to the computer.

3. Check the timing with a light as described above, the timing should be 22° before top dead center (BTDC).

4. If the timing is off, connect a dwell meter to the *negative* side of the coil, and adjust the sub-points so that the dwell angle is 52°. The sub-points are adjusted in the same manner as the main points.

5. Remove the test equipment, and reconnect the thermoswitch.

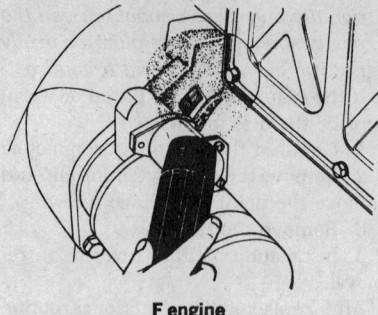

F engine

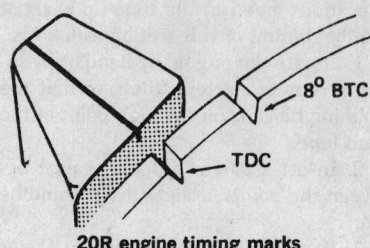

20R engine timing marks

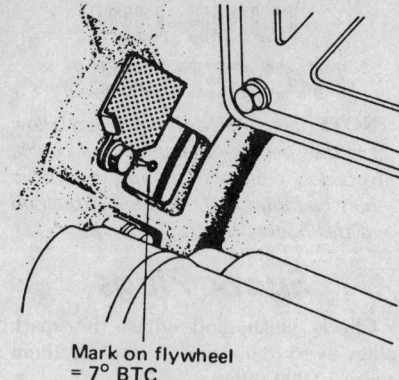

Mark on flywheel = 7° BTC

2F Engine timing mark

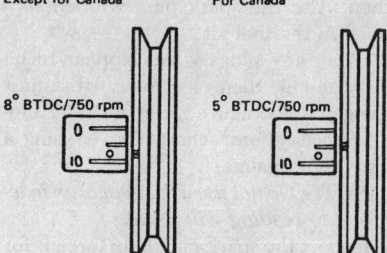

3K-C Engine timing marks

Timing Marks

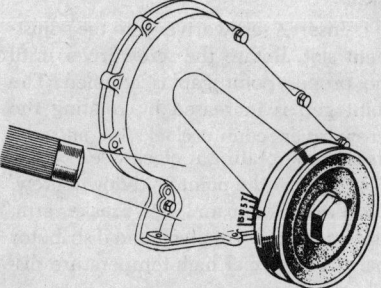

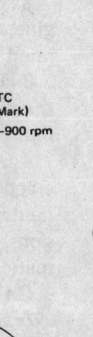

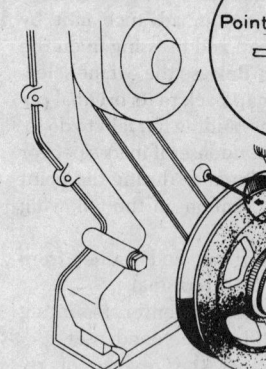

2T-C

18R-C

A 099 2M

2M and 4M

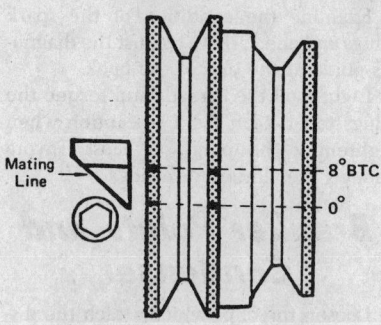

20R Timing marks (w/o HAC)

20R Timing marks (with HAC)

Octane Selector

The octane selector is used as a fine adjustment to match the vehicle's ignition timing to the grade of gasoline being used. It is located near the distributor vacuum unit, beneath a plastic dust cover. Normally the octane selector should not require adjustment, however, if necessary, adjustment is as follows:

1. Align the setting line with the threaded end of the housing and then align the center line with the setting mark on the housing.

TIMING MARK LOCATIONS

Engine Type	Location	Type of mark
3K-C and 2T-C	Crankshaft pulley	Notch and number scale
18R-C, 20R	Crankshaft pulley	Pointer and painted slot
2M and 4M	Crankshaft pulley	Slot and number scale
F, 2F	Flywheel	Ball and pointer

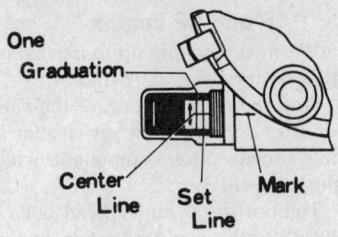

One Graduation · Center Line · Set Line · Mark

Passenger car and Hi-Lux octane selector

NOTE: *Land Cruiser models have no setting mark on the housing. 1973 and later Land Cruiser models do not have octane selectors.*

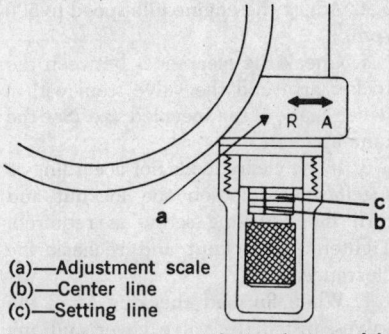

(a)—Adjustment scale
(b)—Center line
(c)—Setting line

Land Cruiser octane selector (not used in 1973-77).

2. Drive the car to the speed specified on the chart below, in high gear, on a level road.

3. Depress the accelerator pedal all the way to the floor. A slight "pinging" sound should be heard. As the car accelerates, the sound should gradually go away.

4. If the pinging sound is loud or if it fails to disappear as the vehicle speed increases, retard the timing by turning the knurled knob toward "R" (Retard).

5. If there is no pinging sound at all, advance the timing by turning the knob toward "A" (Advance).

6. When the adjustment is completed, replace the plastic dust cover.

NOTE: *One graduation of the octane selector is equal to about ten degrees of crankshaft angle.*

Octane Selector Test Speeds

Engine Type	Test Speed (mph)
3K-C	19-21
2T-C and 18R-C	16-22
2M and 4M	25
F and 2F	20

Valve Lash

3K-C and 2T-C Engines

1. Start the engine and allow it to reach normal operating temperature (165–185°F).

2. Stop the engine. Remove the air cleaner assembly, its hoses, and its bracket. Remove any other hoses, cables, etc. attached to the valve cover. Remove the valve cover.

3. On 3K-C engines tighten the cylinder head bolts, in the proper sequence to the following values:
3K-C—35–48 ft lbs

4. Next, on the 3K-C engines, tighten the valve rocker support bolts to 13–17 ft lbs.

CAUTION: *Tighten all of the above bolts in the proper sequence and in three stages.*

5. Install a suitable oil tray on the 3K-C engine, to prevent hot engine oil from being splashed out.

NOTE: *The tray may be ordered from a dealer or fabricated from sheet metal. (See illustration.)*

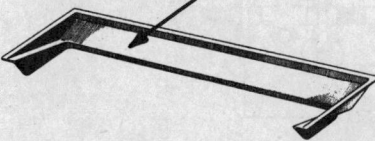

Special oil splash tray for 3K-C engines

6. Start the engine. Check the clearance between the rocker arm and the valve stem with a feeler gauge, for each valve. The clearance specifications are given in the tune-up chart at the beginning of this section.

7. If the valves require adjustment, loosen the locknut and turn the adjustment screw to obtain the proper clearance.

8. Tighten the locknut. Check the valve clearance to be sure that it was not disturbed when the locknut was tightened.

9. When the valve inspection and adjustment are completed, replace the valve cover and all of the other components which were removed.

18R-C Engine

1. Start the engine and allow it to reach normal operating temperature (above 175°F).

2. Stop the engine. Remove the air cleaner assembly, its hoses, and bracket. Remove any other cables, hoses, wires, etc. which are attached to the valve cover. Remove the valve cover.

3. Check the torque of the valve rocker shaft bolts and the camshaft bearing bolts; they should be 12–17 ft lbs.

4. Check the torque specification of the bearing cap union bolts. They should be torqued to 11–16 ft lbs.

5. Set the number one cylinder to TDC on its compression stroke. Remove the spark plug from the number one cylinder and place a finger over the hole. Crank the engine until a pressure is felt, then line the V-notch on the crankshaft

pulley with the pointer on the timing chain cover. The number one cylinder is now at TDC.

NOTE: *Do not start the engine. Valve clearances are checked with the engine stopped to prevent hot oil from being splashed out by the timing chain.*

6. Check the clearances (see the tune-up chart) and adjust valves 1, 2, 3, and 5 to the proper specifications, if necessary.

NOTE: *The clearance is measured with a feeler gauge between the valve stem and the adjusting screw.*

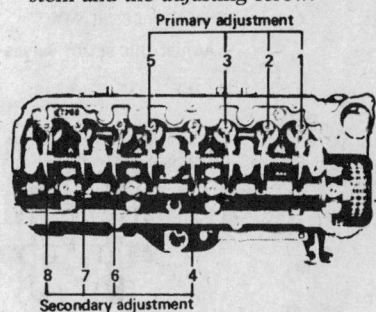

18R-C Valve adjustment sequence

7. To adjust the valve clearance, loosen the locknut and turn the adjusting screw until the specified clearance is obtained. Tighten the locknut and check the clearance again.

8. Crank the engine one revolution (360°) and perform steps 6 and 7 for valves 4, 6, 7, and 8 in the illustration.

9. Install the spark plug in the number one cylinder. Install the valve cover, air cleaner assembly, and any other components which were removed.

20R Engine

1. Start the engine and allow it to reach normal operating temperature (above 180°F).

2. Stop the engine. Remove the air cleaner assembly, its hoses, and bracket. Remove any other cables, hoses, wires, etc., which are attached to the valve cover. Remove the valve cover.

3. Set the no. 1 cylinder at top dead center (TDC) of its compression stroke, with the TDC notch aligned with the pointer.

4. Measure the clearance between the valve stem and the rocker arm with a feeler gauge for the valves shown in the first illustration. See the tune-up chart for the correct clearance.

5. To adjust the valve clearance, loosen the locknut and turn the adjusting screw until the proper clearance is obtained. Tighten the locknut and check the clearance again.

6. Crank the engine *one* revolution (360°) and perform steps 4 and 5 for the set of valves shown in the second illustration.

7. Install the spark plug in the no. 1 cylinder and reconnect the coil lead. Install the valve cover, air cleaner assem-

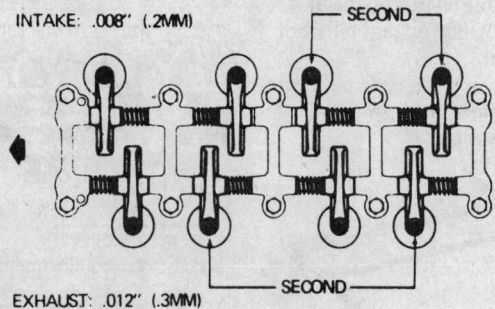

INTAKE: .008" (.2MM)

FIRST

FIRST

EXHAUST: .012" (.3MM)

Adjust this set of valves first on the 20R engine

INTAKE: .008" (.2MM)

SECOND

SECOND

EXHAUST: .012" (.3MM)

Turn the crankshaft one full turn and then adjust this set of valves on the 20R engine

bly, and any other components that were removed.

2M and 4M Engines

1. Allow the engine to reach normal operating temperature. Stop the engine.

2. Remove the air cleaner assembly, air cleaner braket, spark plug cable guides, and any other components attached to the valve cover. Remove the valve cover.

3. Crank the engine until the number one cylinder is at TDC of its compression stroke. To determine this, remove the spark plug from the number one cylinder and place a screwdriver over the spark plug hole. Crank the engine until pressure is felt against the screwdriver and the slot in the crankshaft pulley aligns with the "O" (TDC) on the timing scale.

4. Check and adjust the clearance of the intake valves on 1, 2, and 4 cylinders and of the exhaust valves on 1, 3, and 5 cylinders.

5. Measure the clearance between the valve stem and the adjusting screw with a feeler gauge of the proper size. (See the

specification chart at the beginning of this section.)

6. If the valves require adjustment, loosen the locknut and turn the adjusting screw until the proper clearance is obtained. Tighten the locknut. Check the clearance again.

7. Crank the engine one revolution (360°) and repeat Steps 5 and 6 for the remaining valves.

8. Install the cylinder head cover, spark plug cable guides, air cleaner bracket, air cleaner assembly and any other components removed. Replace the number one spark plug as well.

F and 2F Engine

1. Warm the engine up to normal operating temperature (167–185°F).

2. Stop the engine. Remove the valve cover after removing the air cleaner assembly and any other components which might be in the way.

3. Tighten the cylinder head bolts to 83–98 ft lbs; the manifold retaining nuts to 14–22 ft lbs; and the rocker support nuts or bolts to 25–30 ft lbs (10 mm) and 14–22 ft lbs (8 mm).

NOTE: *See above for the proper tightening sequences. Tighten in three stages.*

4. Adjust the engine idle speed to 500 rpm.

5. Check the clearances between the rocker arm and the valve stem with a feeler gauge of the specified size. (See the tune-up chart.)

6. If the clearance is not according to specifications, loosen the locknut and turn the adjusting screw as required. Tighten the locknut and recheck the clearance.

7. When finished checking all of the valves, install the valve cover and any other components which were removed.

8. Adjust the idle speed to specification, as outlined in the appropriate section below.

Carburetor

NOTE: *See "Fuel System," above, for other carburetor adjustments.*

Idle Speed and Mixture

1972–74

NOTE: *Perform the following adjustments with the air cleaner in place. While adjusting the idle speed and mixture the gear selector should be placed in Drive (D) range on models equipped*

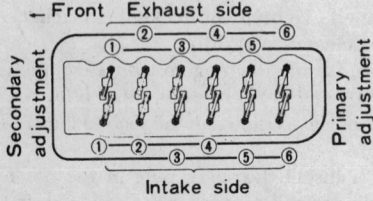

2M and 4M valve adjustment sequence

CARBURETOR ADJUSTMENTS

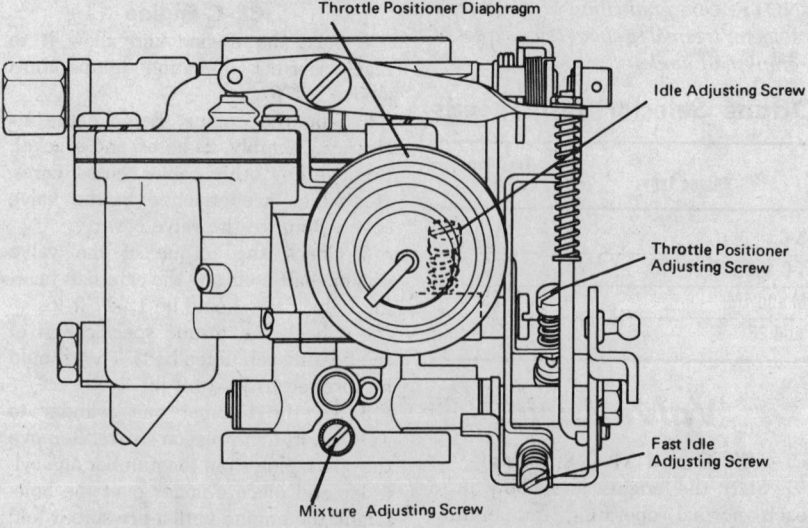

3K-C

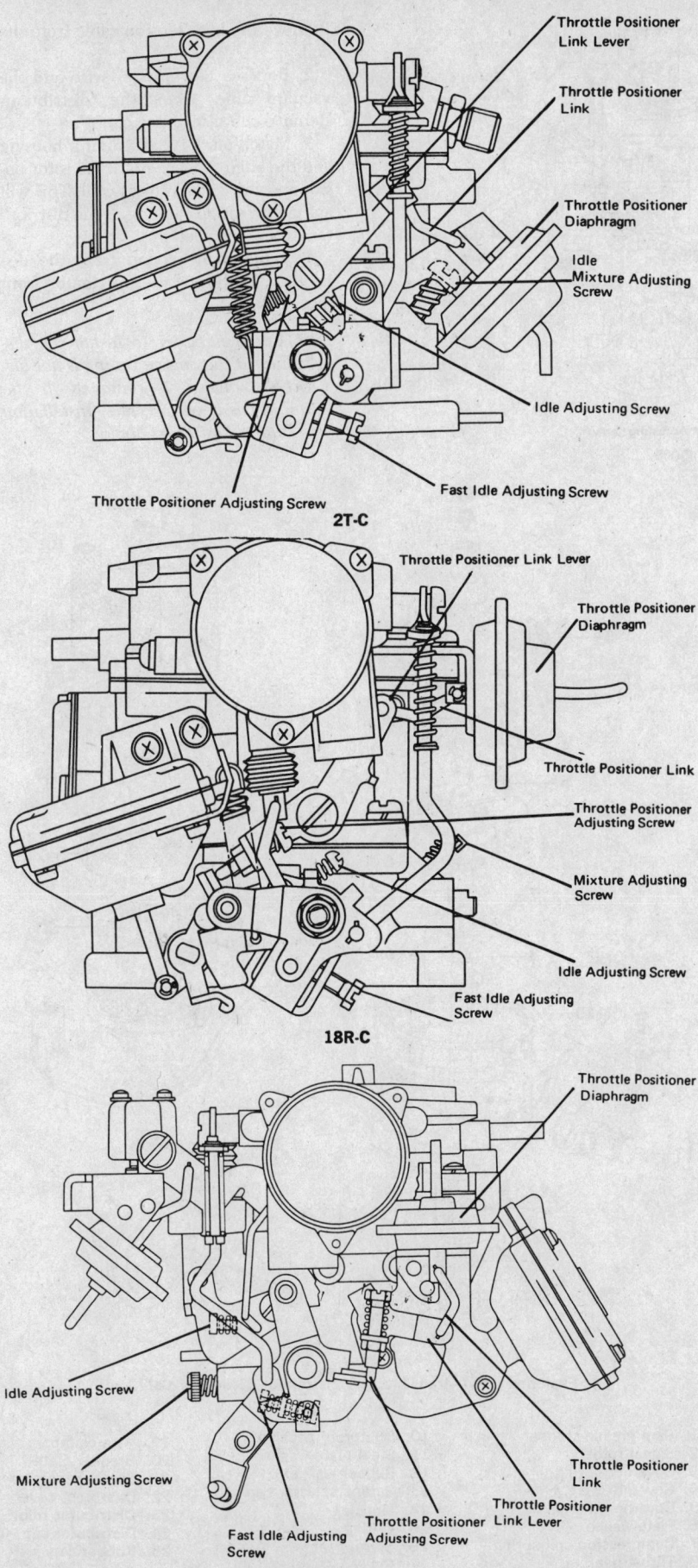

2T-C

18R-C

Throttle Positioner
Diaphragm

Idle Adjusting Screw

Mixture Adjusting Screw

Fast Idle Adjusting Screw

Throttle Positioner Link Lever

Throttle Positioner Adjusting Screw

Throttle Positioner Link

2M and 4M

with automatic transmissions. Be sure to block the front wheels.

1. Run the engine until it reaches normal operating temperature. Stop the engine.

2. Connect a tachometer to the engine, as detailed in its manufacturer's instructions.

CAUTION: *On models with electronic ignition, do not connect the tachometer to the distributor side of the coil, instead hook it up to the negative (−) side of the coil to prevent damage to the ignition control unit.*

3. Remove the plug and install a vacuum gauge in the manifold vacuum port by using a suitable metric adaptor.

4. Start the engine and allow it to run at idle speed.

5. Turn the mixture screw in or out, until the engine runs smoothly at the lowest possible engine speed without stalling.

6. Turn the idle speed screw until the vacuum gauge indicates the highest specified reading (see the chart below) at the specified idle speed. (See the tune-up chart at the beginning of the section.)

7. Tighten the idle speed screw to the point just before the engine rpm and vacuum readings drop off.

8. Remove the tachometer and the vacuum gauge. Install the plug back in the manifold vacuum port. Road-test the vehicle.

Vacuum at Idle

Engine	Year	Minimum Vacuum gauge (in. Hg)
3K-C	1972-74	16.5
	1975-77	15.7
2T-C	1972-73	16.0 MT
		14.0 AT
2T-C	1974	16.9①
18R-C	1972-74	17.7
2M	1972	16.0
4M	1972-73	18.9 MT
		13.8 AT
4M	1974-77	16.3 MT
		13.8 AT
F and 2F	1972-77	16.5

① 1974 California and 1975-77 2T-C—15.7 in. Hg
AT—Automatic Transmission
MT—Manual Transmission

1975–77

The idle speed and mixture should be adjusted under the following conditions: the air cleaner must be installed, the choke fully opened, the transmission should be in Neutral (N), all accessories should be turned off, all vacuum lines should be connected, and the ignition timing should be set to specification.

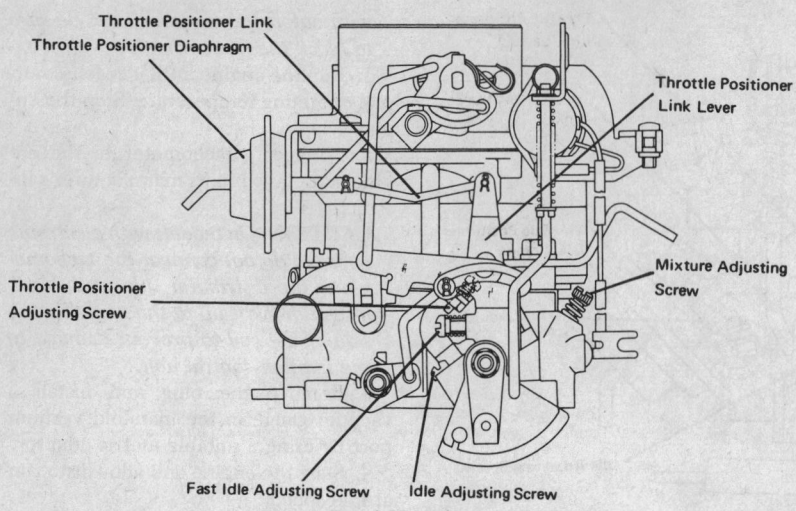

Throttle Positioner Link
Throttle Positioner Diaphragm

Throttle Positioner
Link Lever

Throttle Positioner
Adjusting Screw

Mixture Adjusting
Screw

Fast Idle Adjusting Screw   Idle Adjusting Screw

F and 2F engines

1. Start the engine and allow it reach normal operating temperature 180°F).

2. Check the float setting; the fuel level should be just about even with the spot on the sight glass. If the fuel level is too high or low, adjust the float level. (See the float adjustment procedure, below).

3. Connect a tachometer in accordance with its manufacturer's instructions. However, connect the tachometer positive (+) lead to the coil Negative (−) terminal. Do NOT hook it up to the distributor side; damage to the transistorized ignition could result.

4. Turn the idle speed adjusting screw to obtain one of the following initial idle speeds:

2T-C—930 rpm
20R—900 rpm
4M—820 rpm
2F—690 rpm

5. Turn the idle mixture adjusting screw to increase the idle speed as much as is possible.

6. Next, turn the idle speed screw to again obtain the same idle speed figure given in step 4.

7. If possible, turn the idle mixture screw to increase the idle speed again.

8. Keep repeating steps 6 and 7 until the idle mixture adjusting screw will no longer increase the idle speed above the figure specified in step 4.

9. Slowly turn the idle mixture screw *clockwise,* until the idle speed specified in the "Tune-Up Specifications" chart is reached. (This makes the mixture leaner.)

10. Disconnect the tachometer.

ENGINE ELECTRICAL
Distributor

Removal

1. Unfasten the cables from the spark plugs, after marking the wiring order.

Remove the high tension cable from the coil.

2. Remove the primary wire and the vacuum line from the distributor. Remove the distributor cap.

3. Match-mark the distributor housing and the engine block; mark the rotor position in the distributor as well. This will aid in correct positioning of the distributor during installation.

4. Remove the clamp from the distributor. Withdraw the distributor from the block.

NOTE: *It is easier to install the distributor if the engine timing is not disturbed while it is removed. If the timing has been lost, see "Installation—Timing Disturbed" below.*

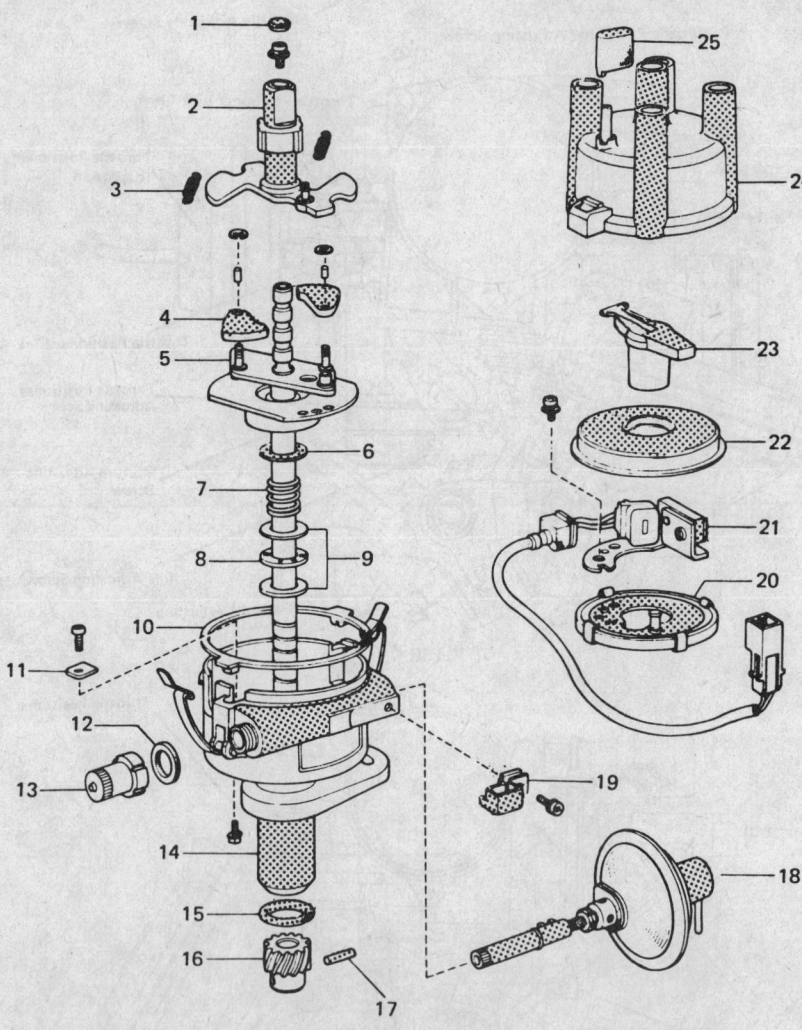

Exploded view—transistorized distributor (Celica GT-Calif.)

1. Cam grease stopper
2. Signal rotor
3. Governor spring
4. Governor weight
5. Governor shaft
6. Plate washer
7. Compression coil spring
8. Thrust bearing
9. Washer
10. Dustproof packing
11. Steel plate washer
12. Rubber washer
13. Octane selector cap
14. Housing
15. O-Ring
16. Spiral gear
17. Pin
18. Vacuum diaphragm
19. Wire clamp
20. Breaker plate
21. Signal generator
22. Dustproof cover
23. Distributor rotor
24. Distributor cap
25. Rubber cap

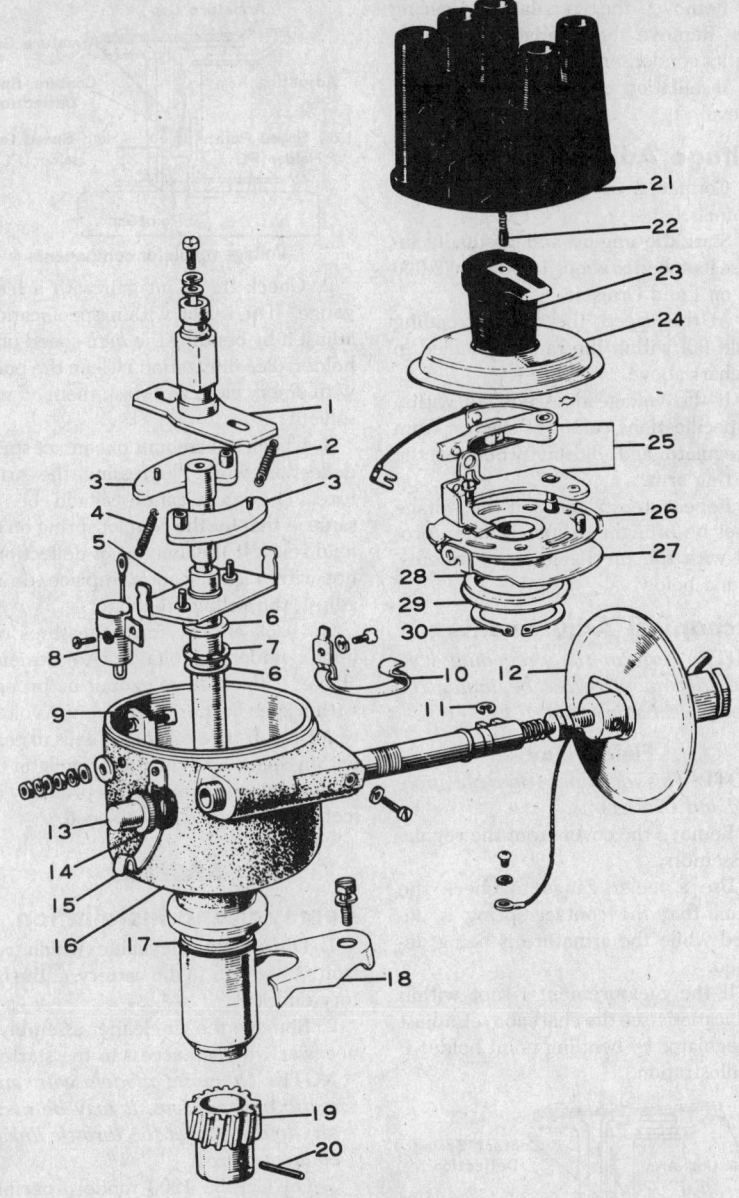

cranking the engine until the timing marks indicate TDC (or 0°).

2. Next, align the timing marks to the specifications given in the "Ignition Timing" column of the tune-up chart at the beginning of the Toyota section.

3. Temporarily install the rotor in the distributor without the dust cover. Turn the distributor shaft so that the rotor is pointing toward the number one terminal in the distributor cap. The points should just be about to open.

4. Use a small screwdriver to align the slot on the distributor drive (oil pump driveshaft) with the key on the bottom of the distributor shaft.

5. Install the distributor in the block by rotating it slightly (no more than one gear tooth in either direction) until the driven gear meshes with the drive.

NOTE: *Oil the distributor spiral gear and the oil pump driveshaft end before distributor installation.*

6. Rotate the distributor, once it is installed, so that the points are just about to open. Temporarily tighten the pinch bolt.

7. Remove the rotor and install the dust cover. Replace the rotor and the distributor cap.

8. Install the primary wire and the vacuum line.

9. Install the no. 1 cylinder spark plug. Connect the cables to the spark plugs in the proper order by using the marks made during removal. Install the high tension wire on the coil.

10. Start the engine. Adjust the ignition timing and the octane selector, as outlined above.

Electronic Distributor (Calif.)

Celica GT

The Celica GT for California is equipped with a fully electronic ignition system.

Points and rotor in the California model are replaced with a magnetic signal rotor and pickup coil.

Setting the points (in this case and air gap) is accomplished almost the same as in a conventional system, but for a few things.

The air gap should be set using a brass or plastic feeler gauge and *extreme* care must be taken to eliminate the possibility of mixed wiring.

Set the air gap to 0.008–0.012 in.

Alternator

Alternator Precautions

1. Always observe proper polarity of the battery connections; be especially careful when jump-starting the car.

2. Never ground or short out any alternator or alternator regulator terminals.

Distributor components

1. Cam
2. Governor spring
3. Governor weight
4. Governor spring
5. Distributor shaft
6. Metal washer
7. Bakelite washer
8. Condenser
9. Insulator
10. Cap spring clip
11. Snap ring
12. Vacuum advance unit
13. Octane selector assembly
14. Rubber washer
15. Cap spring clip
16. Distributor housing
17. O-ring
18. Distributor clamp
19. Spiral gear
20. Pin
21. Distributor cap
22. Spring
23. Rotor
24. Dust cover
25. Breaker point assembly
26. Movable plate
27. Stationary plate
28. Adjusting washer
29. Wave washer
30. Snap ring

Installation—Timing Not Disturbed

1. Insert the distributor in the block and align the matchmarks made during removal.

2. Engage the distributor drive with the oil pump drive shaft.

3. Install the distributor clamp, cap, high tension wire, primary wire, and vacuum line.

4. Install the wires on the spark plugs.

5. Start the engine. Check the timing and adjust the octane selector.

Installation—Timing Disturbed

If the engine has been cranked, dismantled, or the timing otherwise lost, proceed as follows:

1. Determine top dead center (TDC) of the number one (no. 1) cylinder's compression stroke by removing the spark plug from the no. 1 cylinder and placing a finger or a compression gauge over the spark plug hole.

Crank the engine until compression pressure starts to build up. Continue

3. Never operate the alternator with any of its or the battery's leads disconnected.

4. Always remove the battery or disconnect its output lead while charging it.

5. Always disconnect the ground cable when replacing any electrical components.

6. Never subject the alternator to excessive heat or dampness if the engine is being steam-cleaned.

7. Never use arc-welding equipment with the alternator connected.

Removal and Installation

NOTE: *On some models the alternator is mounted very low on the engine. On these models it may be necessary to remove the gravel shield and work from underneath the car in order to gain access to the alternator.*

1. Unfasten the starter-to-battery cable at the battery end.

2. Remove the air cleaner, if necessary, to gain access to the alternator.

3. Unfasten the bolts which attach the adjusting link to the alternator. Remove the alternator drive belt.

4. Unfasten and tag the alternator wiring connection.

5. Remove the alternator attaching bolt and then withdraw the alternator from its bracket.

6. Installation is the reverse order of removal. After installing the alternator, adjust the belt tension.

Belt Tension Adjustment

Inspection and adjustment to the alternator drive belt should be performed every 3,000 miles or if the alternator has been removed.

1. Inspect the drive belt to see that it is not cracked or worn. Be sure that its surfaces are free of grease or oil.

2. Push down on the belt halfway between the fan and the alternator pulleys, (or crankshaft pulley) with thumb pressure. Belt deflection should be ⅜–½ in.

3. If the belt tension requires adjustment, loosen the adjusting link bolt and move the alternator until the proper belt tension is obtained.

CAUTION: *Do not overtighten the belt; damage to the alternator bearings could result.*

4. Tighten the adjusting link bolt.

Regulator

Removal and Installation

1. Disconnect the battery-to-starter cable at the battery end.

2. Disconnect the wiring harness connector from the regulator.

NOTE: *On Land Cruisers disconnect the leads from their screw terminals after noting their positions for installation.*

3. Remove the regulator securing bolts. Remove the regulator, complete with its condenser.

4. Installation is the reverse order of removal.

Voltage Adjustment

1. Connect a voltmeter to the battery terminals.

2. Start the engine and gradually increase its speed to about 1,500 rpm (2,000 rpm on Land Cruisers).

3. At this speed, the voltage reading should fall within the range specified in the chart above.

4. If the voltage does not fall within the specifications, remove the cover from the regulator and adjust it by bending the adjusting arm.

5. Repeat steps 2 and 3; if the voltage cannot be brought to specification, proceed with the mechanical adjustments, outlined below.

Mechanical Adjustments

NOTE: *Perform the preceding voltage adjustment before beginning the mechanical adjustments.*

Field Relay

NOTE: *This adjustment does not apply to Land Cruisers.*

1. Remove the cover from the regulator assembly.

2. Use a feeler gauge to check the amount that the contact spring is deflected while the armature is being depressed.

3. If the measurement is not within specifications (see the chart above), adjust the regulator by bending point holder P (See illustration.)

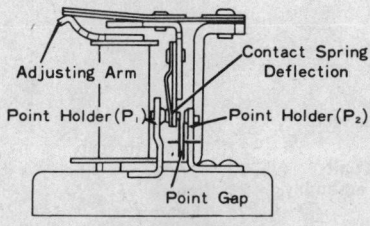

Field relay components

4. Check the point gap with a feeler gauge against the specifications in the chart.

5. Adjust the point gap, as required, by bending the point holder P (See illustration.)

6. Clean off the points with emery cloth if they are dirty and wash them with solvent.

Voltage Regulator

NOTE: *Step 1 does not apply to Land Cruisers.*

1. Use a feeler gauge to measure the air (armature) gap. If it is not within the specifications (see chart), adjust it by bending the *low*-speed point holder. (See illustration.)

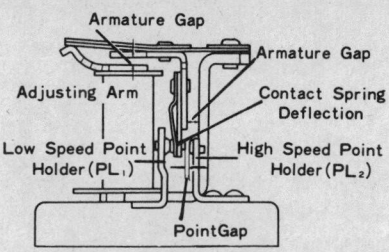

Voltage regulator components

2. Check the point gap with a feeler gauge. If it is not within specifications, adjust it by bending the *high*-speed point holder. (See illustration.) Clean the points with emery cloth and wash them off with solvent.

3. Check the amount of contact spring deflection while depressing the armature. The specification should be the same as that for the contact spring on the field relay. If the amount of deflection is not within specification, replace, do not adjust, the voltage regulator.

Go back and perform the steps outlined under "Voltage Adjustment," above. If the voltage cannot be brought within specifications, replace the voltage regulator. If the voltage still fails to come within specifications after regulator replacement, the alternator is probably defective and should be replaced.

Starter

Removal and Installation

1. Disconnect the cable which runs from the starter to the battery, at the battery end.

2. Remove the air cleaner assembly, if necessary, to gain access to the starter.

NOTE: *On some models with automatic transmissions, it may be necessary to disconnect the throttle linkage connecting rod.*

3. On Corolla 1200 models, perform the following:

a. Disconnect the manual choke cable and the accelerator cable from the carburetor.

b. Unbolt the front exhaust pipe flange from the manifold and then remove the complete manifold assembly. (See the appropriate section below for details.)

4. Disconnect all of the wiring at the starter.

5. Remove the starter toward the front of the car.

6. Installation is in the reverse order of removal.

Starter Drive Replacement

1. Disconnect wiring and remove starter from engine.

2. Remove solenoid from starter.

3. Remove through bolts and take off end plate.

4. Slide armature shaft far enough out to disengage clutch forks.

5. Remove retaining clip and washer from shaft.

6. Slide starter drive assembly from shaft.

7. Install in reverse of removal. Always use a new retaining clip.

Starter Solenoid and Brush Replacement

Direct Drive Starter

NOTE: *The starter must be removed from the car in order to perform this operation.*

1. Remove the field coil lead from the solenoid terminal.

2. Unfasten the solenoid retaining screws. Remove the solenoid by tilting it upward and withdrawing it.

3. Remove the end frame bearing cover screws and remove the cover.

4. Remove the thru-bolts. Remove the commutator end-frame.

5. Withdraw the brushes from their holder if they are to be replaced.

6. Check the brush length against the specification in the "Battery and Starter Specifications" chart, above. Replace the brushes with new ones if required.

7. Dress the new brushes with emery cloth so that they will make proper contact.

8. Use a spring scale to check the brush spring tension against the specification in the chart. Replace the springs if they do not meet specification.

Assembly is the reverse of disassembly. Pack the end bearing cover with multipurpose grease before installing it.

Gear Reduction Type

NOTE: *The starter must be removed*

from the car, in order to perform this operation.

1. Disconnect the solenoid lead.

2. Loosen the two bolts on the starter housing and separate the field frame from the solenoid. Remove the O-ring and felt dust seal.

3. Remove the two screws and separate the starter drive from the solenoid.

4. Withdraw the clutch and gears. Remove the ball from the clutch shaft bore or solenoid.

5. Remove the brushes from the holder.

6. Measure brush length and compare it to the specification given in the "Battery and Starter Specifications" chart. Replace the brushes if they are too short.

7. Check the gears for wear or damage. Replace as required.

Assembly is the reverse of disassembly. Lubricate all bearings and gears with high temperature grease. Grease the ball before inserting in the clutch shaft bore. Align the tab on the brush holder with the notch on the field frame. Check the positive (+) brush leads to see that they aren't grounded. Align the mark on the solenoid with the bolt anchors on the field frame.

ENGINE MECHANICAL
Engine Removal and Installation

CAUTION: *Be sure that the car is supported securely, during engine removal.*

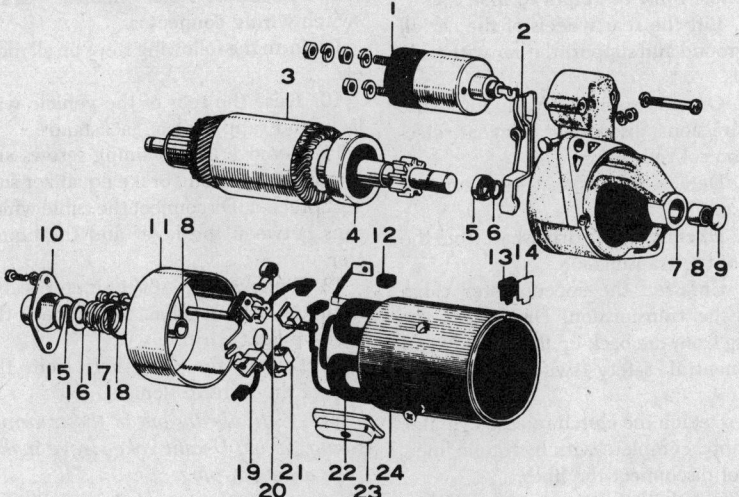

Direct-drive starter components

1. Solenoid	9. Bearing cover	17. Brake spring
2. Engagement lever	10. Bearing cover	18. Gasket
3. Armature	11. Commutator end frame	19. Brush
4. Overrunning clutch	12. Rubber bushing	20. Brush spring
5. Clutch stop	13. Rubber grommet	21. Brush holder
6. Snap ring	14. Plate	22. Field coil
7. Drive housing	15. Lock plate	23. Pole shoes
8. Bushing	16. Washer	24. Field yoke

3K-C Engine

1. Drain the entire cooling system.

2. Unfasten the cable which runs from the battery to the starter at the battery terminal.

3. Scribe marks on the hood and hinges to aid in hood alignment during assembly. Remove the hood.

4. Unfasten the headlight bezel retaining screws and remove the bezels. Remove the five radiator grille attachment screws and remove the grille.

5. Remove the hood lock assembly after detaching the release cable.

6. Unfasten the nuts from the horn retainers and disconnect the wiring. Remove the horn assembly.

7. Remove the air cleaner from its bracket after unfastening the hoses from it.

8. Remove the windshield washer tank from its bracket but first drain its contents into a clean container.

9. Remove both the upper and lower radiator hoses from the engine after loosening the hose clamps.

NOTE: *On models with automatic transmissions, disconnect the oil lines from the oil cooler.*

10. Detach the radiator mounting bolts and remove the radiator.

11. Remove the accelerator cable from its support on the cylinder head cover. Unfasten the cable at the carburetor throttle arm. Disconnect the choke cable from the carburetor.

12. Detach the water hose retainer from the cylinder head.

13. Disconnect the bypass and heater hoses at the water pump. Disconnect the other end of the heater hose from the water valve. Remove the heater control cable from the water valve.

14. Disconnect the wiring harness multiconnectors.

15. Detach the downpipe from the exhaust manifold.

16. Detach the wires from the water temperature and oil pressure sending units.

17. Remove the nut from the front left-hand engine mount.

18. Remove the fuel line from the fuel pump.

19. Detach the battery ground cable from the cylinder block.

20. Remove the nut from the front right-hand engine mount.

21. Remove the clip and detach the cable from the clutch release lever.

22. Remove the primary and high-tension wires from the coil.

23. Detach the back-up light switch wire at its connector on the right side of the extension housing.

The following steps apply to Corolla models with manual transmissions:

24. Remove the carpet from the trans-

mission tunnel. Remove the boots from the shift lever.

25. Remove the snap-ring from the gearshift selector lever base. Withdraw the selector lever assembly.

The following steps apply to Corolla models with automatic transmissions:

26. Disconnect the accelerator linkage torque rod at the carburetor.

27. Disconnect the throttle linkage connecting rod from the bellcrank lever.

28. Drain the oil from the transmission oil pan.

29. Detach the transmission gear selector shift rod from the control shaft.

The following steps apply to Corollas with both manual and automatic transmissions:

30. Raise the rear wheels of the car. Support the car with jackstands.

31. Disconnect the driveshaft from the transmission.

NOTE: *Drain the oil from the manual transmission, first, to prevent it from leaking out.*

32. Detach the exhaust pipe support bracket from the extension housing.

33. Remove the insulator bolt from the rear engine mount.

34. Place a jack under the transmission and remove the four bolts from the rear (engine support) crossmember.

35. Install lifting hooks on the engine lifting brackets. Attach a suitable hoist.

36. Lift the engine slightly; then move it toward the front of the car. Bring the engine the rest of the way out at an angle.

Engine installation is the reverse order of removal. Adjust all transmission and carburetor linkages, as detailed in the appropriate section. Install and adjust the hood. Refill the engine, radiator, and transmission to capacity.

2T-C Engine

1. Drain the radiator, cooling system, transmission, and engine oil.

2. Disconnect the battery-to-starter cable at the positive battery terminal.

3. Scribe marks on the hood and its hinges to aid in alignment during installation.

4. Remove the hood supports from the body. Remove the hood.

NOTE: *Do not remove the supports from the hood.*

5. On Carina models, remove the headlight bezels. Disconnect the hood release cable then remove the grille, lower grille molding, hood lock base, and base support.

6. On Corolla models, perform steps 4–6 as detailed in the 3K-C engine removal section above.

7. Detach both the upper and lower hoses from the radiator. On cars with automatic transmissions, disconnect the lines from the oil cooler. Remove the radiator.

8. Unfasten the clamps and remove the heater and bypass hoses from the engine. Remove the heater control cable from the water valve.

9. Remove the wiring from the coolant temperature and oil pressure sending units.

10. Remove the air cleaner from its bracket, complete with its attendant hoses.

11. Unfasten the accelerator torque rod from the carburetor. On models equipped with automatic transmissions, remove the transmission linkage as well.

12. Remove the emission control system hoses and wiring, as necessary.

13. Remove the clutch hydraulic line support bracket.

14. Unfasten the high-tension and primary wires from the coil.

15. Mark the spark plug cables and remove them from the distributor.

16. Detach the right-hand front engine mount.

17. Remove the fuel line at the pump.

18. Detach the downpipe from the exhaust manifold.

19. Detach the left-hand front engine mount.

20. Disconnect all of the wiring harness multiconnectors.

21. On cars equipped with manual transmissions, remove the shift lever boot and the shift lever cap boot.

22. Unfasten the four gear selector lever cap retaining screws, remove the gasket and withdraw the gear selector lever assembly from the top of the transmission.

NOTE: *On all Carina models and on Corolla five-speed models, the floor console must be removed first.*

23. Lift the rear wheels of the car off the ground and support the car with jackstands.

24. On cars equipped with automatic transmissions, disconnect the gear selector control rod.

25. Detach the exhaust pipe support bracket.

26. Disconnect the driveshaft from the rear of the transmission.

27. Unfasten the speedometer cable from the transmission. Disconnect the wiring from the back-up light switch and the neutral safety switch (automatic only).

28. Detach the clutch release cylinder assembly, complete with hydraulic lines. Do not disconnect the lines.

29. Unbolt the rear support member mounting insulators.

30. Support the transmission and detach the rear support member retaining bolts. Withdraw the support member from under the car.

31. Install lifting hooks on the engine lifting brackets. Attach a suitable hoist to the engine.

32. Remove the jack from under the transmission.

33. Raise the engine and move it toward the front of the car. Use care to avoid damaging the components which remain on the car.

34. Support the engine on a workstand. Install the engine in the reverse order of removal. Adjust all of the linkages as detailed in the appropriate section. Install the hood and adjust it. Replenish the fluid levels in the engine, radiator, and transmission.

20R and 18R-C Engines

1. Perform steps 1–4 of the 2T-C engine removal procedure.

2. Remove the headlight bezel and the radiator grille.

3. Remove the fan shroud, the hood lock base and the base support.

4. Perform steps 7–20 of the 2T-C engine removal procedure.

Perform the following steps on 1972–75 models with manual transmissions:

5. Remove the center console if so equipped.

6. Remove the shift lever boot(s).

7. Unfasten the four shift lever cap retaining screws. Remove the cap and withdraw the shift lever assembly.

Perform the following steps on models equipped with automatic transmissions:

8. Remove the transmission selector linkage:

   a. On models equipped with a floor-mounted selector, disconnect the control rod from the transmission.

   b. On column-mounted gear selector models, remove the shifter rod.

9. Disconnect the neutral safety switch wiring connector.

Perform the following steps on all models:

10. Raise the rear of the vehicle with jacks and support it on jackstands.

11. Remove the retaining screws and remove the parking brake equalizer support bracket. Disconnect the cable which runs between the lever and the equalizer.

12. Remove the speedometer cable from the transmission. Disconnect the back-up light wiring.

13. Detach the driveshaft from the rear of the transmission.

NOTE: *If oil runs out of the transmission, an old U-joint yoke sleeve makes an excellent plug.*

14. On pre-1971 vehicles which are equipped with manual transmission, unfasten the gearshift cross-shaft from the transmission.

15. Perform steps 28–34 of the 2T-C engine removal procedure.

Installation of the engine is the reverse order of removal. Refer to the appropriate chapters for transmission and carburetor adjustments. Refill the engine oil, coolant, and transmission oil to the proper levels.

2M and 4M Engines

1. Disconnect the battery cables and remove the battery.

2. Scribe aligning marks on the hood and hinges to aid in their assembly. Remove the hood.

3. Remove the fan shroud and drain the cooling system.

4. Disconnect both the upper and lower radiator hoses. Disconnect and plug the oil lines from the oil cooler on cars with automatic transmissions.

5. Detach the hose which runs to the thermal expansion tank at the tank. Remove the expansion tank from its mounting bracket.

6. Remove the radiator.

7. Disconnect the heater and bypass hoses from the engine.

8. Disconnect the oil pressure light sender wiring, the alternator multiconnector, and the back-up light switch wiring.

9. Disconnect the power brake unit vacuum lines.

10. Disconnect the engine oil cooler hoses at the oil filter, if so equipped.

11. Disconnect the power steering fluid cooler hose, if so equipped.

12. Remove the air cleaner assembly from its bracket, complete with hoses.

13. Detach the emission control system wires and hoses, as required.

14. Unfasten the distributor primary wire and the high tension wire from the coil.

15. Disconnect the wiring from the starter and temperature gauge sender.

16. Remove the fuel line from the fuel pump.

17. Disconnect the heater control cable from the water valve. Unfasten the heater control vacuum hose.

18. Remove the accelerator linkage from the carburetor.

19. Detach the clutch hydraulic line from its master cylinder connections (manual transmission only). Install a cap on the master cylinder fitting to keep the hydraulic fluid from running out.

20. Detach the pressure-feed lines from the steering gear housing on models equipped with power steering.

21. Raise both the front and the rear of the car with jacks. Support the car with jackstands.

22. Detach the exhaust pipe from the downpipe and remove the exhaust pipe hangers.

23. Disconnect the speedometer cable from the right side of the transmission.

The following steps apply to models with manual transmission only:

24. On 1972–74 models:

a. Remove the center console securing screws, the gearshift knob, the gearshift boot, and then unfasten the console wiring multiconnector. Lift the console over the gearshift lever.

b. Remove the four screws which attach the shift lever retainer to the shift tower and withdraw the shift lever assembly.

The following steps apply to models with automatic transmissions:

25. On models equipped with a floor-mounted gear selector, unfasten the connecting rod swivel nut and detach the control rod from the gear selector lever.

26. On models equipped with a column-mounted gear selector:

a. Disconnect the control rod and cross-shaft.

b. Remove both of the throttle link connecting rods.

27. Disconnect the parking brake lever rod, return spring, intermediate rod, and the cable from the equalizer.

28. Disconnect the driveshaft from the end of the transmission.

NOTE: *If oil runs out from the transmission, an old U-joint yoke makes a good plug.*

29. Remove the left-hand gravel shield and then the front engine mounts.

30. Support the transmission with a jack.

31. Remove the rear engine mounts and the rear crossmember.

32. Attach a hoist to the engine and lift it up and forward, so that it clears the car.

Installation is in the reverse order of removal. Adjust the transmission and carburetor linkages, as detailed in the appropriate sections. Bleed the clutch as outlined below. Install the hood and adjust it. Replenish the fluid levels.

F and 2F Engine

1. Scribe marks on the hood and hinges to aid in alignment during installation. Remove the hinge bolts from the hood and then remove the hood.

2. Drain the cooling system and engine oil.

3. Unfasten the radiator grille mounting bolts and remove the grille.

NOTE: *On station wagon models, remove the parking light assembly and wiring first.*

4. Remove the hood latch support rod. Detach the hood latch assembly from the radiator upper bracket. Remove the bracket.

5. Disconnect the heater hose from the radiator.

6. Detach the upper radiator hose at the water outlet housing and the lower hose at water pump.

7. Remove the six bolts which secure the radiator and lift the radiator out of the vehicle.

8. Remove the heater hoses from the water valve and heater box. Disconnect the temperature control cable from the water valve.

9. Detach both of the battery cables and remove the battery.

10. Remove the wires from the starter solenoid terminal.

11. Detach the fuel lines from the pump and remove the fuel filter assembly.

12. Disconnect the primary wire from the ignition coil.

13. Detach both of the intermediate rods from the shifter shafts (column-shift models only).

14. Remove the air cleaner assembly complete with hoses, from its bracket.

15. Remove the emission control system cables and hoses as necessary.

16. Disconnect the alternator multiconnector.

17. Disconnect the hand throttle, accelerator, and choke linkages from the carburetor.

18. On Land Cruisers with vacuum assisted 4WD engagement, remove the control unit vacuum hose from its manifold fitting.

19. Disconnect the oil pressure and water temperature gauge sender's wiring.

20. Unfasten the downpipe from the exhaust manifold.

21. Detach the parking brake cable from the intermediate lever.

22. Unbolt the front driveshaft from the flange on the transfer case output shaft.

23. Remove both the left and right engine stone shields. Remove the transmission skid-plate.

24. Remove the cotter pin and disconnect both the high- and low-range shifter rods from their respective inner levers.

25. Remove the high/low range shifter link lever and the high/low shift rod.

26. Disconnect the clutch release fork spring. Remove the clutch release cylinder from its mounting bracket at the rear of the engine.

27. Unfasten the clamp screws and withdraw the vacuum lines from the transfer case control unit vacuum chamber (only on models with vacuum-assisted 4WD engagement).

28. Remove the 4WD indicator switch assembly.

29. Unfasten the speedometer cable from the transmission.

30. Disconnect the rear driveshaft from the transmission.

31. Detach the gearshift rod and gear selector rod from the shift outer lever and the gear selector outer lever, respectively.

32. Unbolt the rear engine mounts from the frame.

33. Perform Step 32 to the front engine mounts.

34. Install lifting hooks on the engine lift-points and connect a hoist.

35. Lift the engine slightly and toward the front, so the engine/transmission assembly clears the front of the vehicle.

Engine removal is performed in the reverse order of its installation. Refill the engine with coolant and lubricant, as specified above. Check and adjust all linkages, as outlined in the appropriate section. Install the hood and align the matchmarks.

Cylinder Head

CAUTION: *Do not perform this operation on a warm engine. Remove the head bolts in the sequence and in several steps. Loosen the head bolts evenly, not one at a time. Keep the pushrods in their original order. Do not attempt to slide the cylinder head off of the block, as it is located with dowel pins. Lift the head straight up and off the block.*

Removal and Installation

3K-C

1. Disconnect the battery and drain the cooling system.

2. Remove the air cleaner assembly from its bracket, complete with its attendant hoses.

3. Disconnect the hoses from the air injection system or the vacuum switching valve lines (1972–73).

4. Detach the accelerator cable from its support on the cylinder head cover and also from the carburetor throttle arm.

5. Remove the choke cable and fuel lines from the carburetor.

6. Remove the water hose bracket from the cylinder head cover.

7. Unfasten the water hose clamps and remove the hoses from the water pump and the water valve. Detach the heater temperature control cable from the water valve.

8. Disconnect the PCV line from the cylinder head cover.

9. Unbolt and remove the valve cover.

10. Remove the valve rocker support securing bolts and nuts. Lift out the valve rocker assembly.

11. Withdraw the pushrods from their bores.

12. Unfasten the hose clamps and remove the upper radiator hose from the water outlet.

13. Remove the wires from the spark plugs.

14. Disconnect the wiring and the fluid line from the windshield washer assembly. Remove the assembly.

NOTE: *Use a clean container to catch the fluid from the windshield washer reservoir when disconnecting its fluid line.*

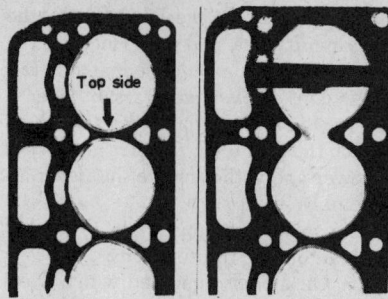

Identification of the top side of the 3K-C head gasket.

15. Unfasten the exhaust pipe flange from the exhaust manifold.

16. Remove the head assembly retaining bolts and remove the head from the engine.

17. Place the cylinder head on *wooden* blocks to prevent damage to it.

Installation is essentially the reverse order of removal. Clean both the cylinder head and block gasket mounting surfaces.

Always use a new head gasket.

NOTE: *Be sure that the top side of the gasket is facing upward. (See illustration.)*

When installing the head on the block, be sure to tighten the bolts in the sequence shown (see "Torque Sequences"), in several stages, to the specified torque.

The valve rocker assembly nuts and bolts should be tightened to 13–16 ft lbs.

NOTE: *The valve clearance should be adjusted to specification with each piston at top dead center (TDC) of its compression stroke.*

2T-C Engine

1. Perform steps 1–2 of the 3K-C head removal procedure.

2. Disconnect the vacuum lines which run from the vacuum switching valve to the various emission control devices mounted on the cylinder head.

3. Disconnect the mixture control valve hose which runs to the intake mani-

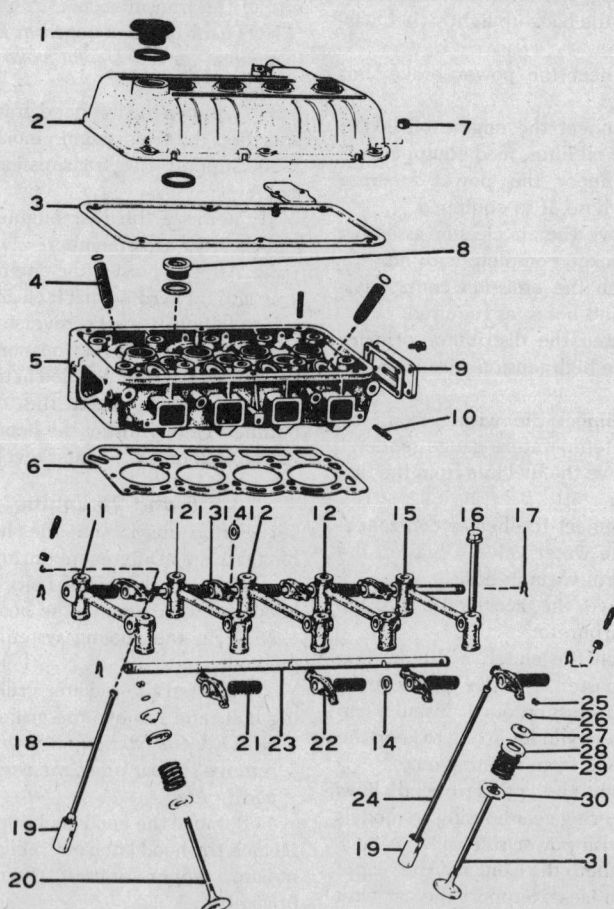

2T-C cylinder head components

1. Oil filler cap	11. Valve rocker support
2. Valve cover	12. Valve rocker support
3. Valve cover gasket	13. Valve rocker arm
4. Valve guide (intake)	14. Washer
5. Cylinder head	15. Valve rocker support
6. Cylinder head gasket	16. Bolt
7. Nut	17. Retainer spring
8. Screw plug	18. Pushrod
9. Cylinder head rear cover	19. Valve lifter
10. Stud	20. Intake valve

21. Compression spring
22. Valve rocker arm
23. Valve rocker shaft
24. Pushrod
25. Lock spring
26. O-ring
27. Valve spring retainer
28. Oil splash shield
29. Compression spring
30. Plate washer
31. Exhaust valve

fold and remove the valve from its mounting bracket (1972–74).

4. Perform step 7 of the K–C and 3K–C head removal procedure.

5. Detach the water temperature sender wiring.

6. Remove the choke stove pipe and its intake pipe.

7. Remove the PCV hose from the intake manifold.

8. Disconnect the fuel and vacuum lines from the carburetor.

9. Remove the clutch hydraulic line bracket from the cylinder head.

10. Raise the car and support it with jackstands. Unfasten the exhaust pipe clamp. Remove the exhaust manifold from the cylinder head. (See below.)

11. Remove the valve cover.

12. Remove the cylinder head bolts in the sequence illustrated under "Torque Sequences."

13. Perform steps 10–11 of the K–C and 3K–C cylinder head removal procedure.

14. Remove the cylinder head, complete with the intake manifold.

15. Separate the intake manifold from the cylinder head.

Install the cylinder head in the following order:

1. Clean the gasket mounting surfaces of the cylinder head and the block completely.

NOTE: *Remove oil from the cylinder head bolt holes, if present.*

2. Place a *new* gasket on the block and install the head assembly.

3. Install the pushrods and the valve rocker assembly.

4. Tighten the cylinder head bolts *evenly,* in stages, as illustrated in the "Torque Sequence" diagrams. See the "Torque Specifications" chart, above, for the proper tightening torque.

5. Install the intake manifold, using a new gasket and tighten it to specifications.

6. The rest of the installation procedure is the reverse of removal. Adjust the valve clearances.

18R–C Engine

1. Perform steps 1–2 and then steps 4–8 of the 3K–C engine cylinder head removal procedure.

2. Remove the vacuum lines from the distributor vacuum unit. Remove the lines which run from the vacuum switching valve to the various emission control system components on the cylinder head.

3. Remove the fuel and vacuum lines from the carburetor.

4. Remove the pipes from the automatic choke stove.

5. Unfasten the wires from the spark plugs. Remove the spark plugs.

6. Remove the cylinder head cover retaining bolts and withdraw the cover.

NOTE: *Use a clean cloth, placed over the timing cover opening, to prevent anything from falling down into it.*

7. Remove the upper radiator hose from the cylinder head water outlet.

8. Remove the outlet elbow and thermostat.

9. Unfasten the downpipe clamp from the exhaust manifold. Remove the manifold from the head.

10. Remove the valve rocker assembly mounting bolts and the oil delivery pipes. Withdraw the valve rocker shaft assembly.

CAUTION: *When removing the rocker shaft securing bolts, loosen them in two or three stages and in the proper sequence.*

11. Remove the timing gear from the camshaft. Support it so that the chain does not fall down into the cover.

12. Remove the camshaft bearing caps and withdraw the camshaft. Remove the camshaft bearings.

NOTE: *Temporarily assemble the bearings and caps to keep them with their mates. Be sure to keep the bearings in proper order.*

13. Remove the gear from the timing chain. Support the timing chain so that it does not fall into the cover.

14. Loosen the head bolts in two or three stages; in the sequence illustrated. Lift the head assembly off the block.

Installation is in the following order:

1. Remove any water from the cylinder head bolt holes.

2. Clean the mating surfaces of the cylinder head and block. Use liquid sealer around the oil holes on the head and cylinder block. Do not get sealer in the holes.

3. Lower the cylinder head on to the block.

4. Tighten the cylinder head bolts in the proper sequence (see diagrams, above) and in three or four stages. Tighten them to specifications.

5. Install each lower bearing half into the seat from which it was removed.

6. Place the camshaft in the cylinder head.

7. Install each bearing into the cap from which it was removed.

8. Install the camshaft bearing caps on the head, in their numbered sequence, with the numbers facing forward. Tighten to 12–17 ft lbs.

9. First, check the camshaft bearing clearance using Plastigage®, and end-play.

NOTE: *For the procedure see "Engine Rebuilding".*

The oil clearance should be 0.001–0.002 in.; the end-play should be 0.0017–0.0066 in.

10. Crank the engine so that no. 1 piston is at TDC of its compression stroke.

11. Align the mark on the timing chain with the dowel hole on the camshaft timing gear and the stamped mark on the camshaft.

NOTE: *All three marks should be aligned so that they are facing upward.*

Alignment of marks on the 8R–C and 18R–C sprocket and timing chain

12. Install the valve rocker assembly. Tighten its securing bolts to 12–17 ft lbs, in the sequence illustrated, and in two or three stages.

13. Attach the oil delivery pipe to the valve rocker assembly and camshaft bearing caps. Tighten their securing bolts to 11–16 ft lbs.

14. Adjust the valve clearance as outlined above to the following *cold* specifications:

Intake—0.007 in.
Exhaust—0.013 in.

15. The rest of installation is performed in the reverse order of removal.

20R Engine

1. Disconnect the battery.

2. Remove the three exhaust pipe flange nuts and separate the pipe from the manifold.

3. Drain the cooling system (both radiator and block). Save the coolant to be re-used.

4. Remove the air cleaner, complete with hoses, from the carburetor.

NOTE: *Cover the carburetor with a clean rag so that nothing can fall into it.*

5. Mark all vacuum hoses to aid installation, and disconnect them. Remove all linkages, fuel lines, etc. from the carburetor, cylinder head, and manifolds. Remove the wire supports.

6. Mark the spark plug leads and disconnect them from the plugs.

7. Matchmark the distributor housing and block. Disconnect the primary lead and remove the distributor. Installation will be easier if you leave the cap leads in place.

8. Remove the valve cover.

9. Remove the rubber camshaft seals. Use a 19mm wrench to remove cam sprocket bolt. Slide the distributor drive gear off of the cam and wire the cam sprocket in place.

10. Remove the timing chain cover 14mm bolt at the front of the head. This

must be done before the head bolts are removed.

11. Remove the cylinder head bolts in the order shown under "Torque Sequences". Improper removal could cause head damage.

12. Using pry bars applied evenly at the front and the rear of the valve rocker assembly, pry the assembly off of its mounting dowels.

13. Lift the head off of its dowels. Do NOT pry it off. Support the head on a workbench.

14. Drain the engine oil from the crankcase *after* the head has been removed, because the oil will become contaminated with coolant while the head is being removed.

Installation is in the following order:

1. Apply liquid sealer to the front corners of the block and install the head gasket.

2. Lower the head over the locating dowels. Do not attempt to slide it into place.

3. Rotate the camshaft so that the sprocket aligning pin is at the top. Remove the wire and hold the cam sprocket. Manually rotate the engine so that the sprocket hole is also at the top. Wire the sprocket in place again.

4. Install the rocker arm assembly over its positioning dowels.

5. Tighten the cylinder head bolts evenly, in three stages, and in order to 52–63 ft lbs.

6. Install the timing chain cover bolt and tighten it to 7–11 ft lbs.

7. Remove the wire and install the sprocket over the camshaft dowel. If the chain won't allow the sprocket to reach, rotate the crankshaft back and forth, while lifting up on the chain and sprocket.

8. Install the distributor drive gear and tighten the crankshaft bolt to 51–65 ft lbs.

9. Set the no. 1 piston at TDC of its compression stroke and adjust the valves.

10. After completing valve adjustment, rotate the crankshaft one turn, so that 8°BTDC mark on the pulley aligns with the pointer.

11. Install the distributor, as outlined above.

12. Install the spark plugs and leads.

13. Make sure that the oil drain plug is installed. Fill the engine with oil after installing the rubber cam seals. Pour the oil over the distributor drive gear and the valve rockers.

14. Install the rocker cover and tighten the bolts to 8–11 ft lbs.

15. Connect all the vacuum hoses and electrical leads that were removed during disassembly. Install the spark plug lead supports. Fill the cooling system. Install the air cleaner.

16. Tighten the exhaust pipe to manifold flange bolts to 25–33 ft lbs.

17. Reconnect the battery. Start the engine and allow it to reach normal operating temperature. Check and adjust the timing and valve clearance. Adjust the idle speed and mixture. Road test the vehicle.

2M and 4M Engines

1. Perform steps 1–4 and 6–8 of the 3K-C cylinder head removal procedure. Skip step 5.

2. Remove the fuel and vacuum lines from the carburetor. Remove the carburetor.

3. Remove the spark plug wires from their supports on the cylinder head cover and from the spark plugs themselves.

4. Remove the distributor assembly.

5. Take off the automatic choke stove hoses.

6. Remove the exhaust manifold and the oil pressure light sender.

7. Remove the intake manifold assembly.

8. Unfasten the retaining bolts and remove the valve cover assembly.

NOTE: *Place a cloth over the timing gear to prevent anything from falling into the timing gear cover.*

9. Remove the valve rocker shaft assembly retaining bolts in the sequence illustrated. Loosen the bolts in two or three stages. Remove the rocker shaft assembly.

10. Remove the timing chain tensioner.

11. Straighten out the lockplate and unfasten the timing gear retaining bolt (left-hand thread). Withdraw the timing gear from the camshaft.

12. Perform steps 12–14 of the 8R-C and 18R-C cylinder head removal procedure.

Installation is performed in the following order:

1. Perform steps 1–10 of the 8R-C and 18R-C cylinder head removal procedure.

NOTE: *Apply liquid sealer around each cylinder block oil hole but be careful not to get any in the hole itself. Also, apply sealer to the timing chain cover and cylinder block.*

2. Align the V-notch on the camshaft with the 5/32 in. hole on the no. 1 camshaft bearing.

NOTE: *Be sure that the V-notch is also*

aligned with the mark on the timing chain cover.

3. Install the camshaft timing gear, with the chain, on the end of the camshaft. Align the pin on the camshaft flange with the hole in the gear.

4. Install the timing gear bolt and lockplate. Fasten the bolt with the lockplate. **NOTE:** *The bolt has a left-hand thread. Tighten it to 47–54 ft lbs.*

5. Install the chain tensioner, complete with shim. Tighten it to 22–29 ft lbs.

6. Turn the crankshaft two complete revolutions while checking to see that valve timing is correct. If, at the end of the two revolutions, the timing marks do not align, repeat Steps 2–4.

7. Apply pressure to the chain tensioner arm. If its movement is less than 3/16 in., add additional shims.

8. Install the valve rocker assembly and tighten the bolts to 22–29 ft lbs, in the sequence illustrated, and in three or four stages.

NOTE: *The stud bolt should only be tightened to 11–14 ft lbs.*

9. Install the union on the No. 1 rocker support and the No. 1 camshaft bearing cap. Tighten the union bolts to 6–9 ft lbs.

10. Adjust the valve clearance, as outlined above, to the following *cold* specifications:

Intake—0.006 in.
Exhaust—0.008 in.

11. The rest of the installation procedure is the reverse of removal.

F and 2F Engine

1. Perform steps 1–2 and 4–8 of the 3K-C cylinder head procedure. Skip step 3.

2. Disconnect the vacuum lines, which run from the vacuum switching valve, at the various components of the emission control system.

3. Drain the engine oil. Unfasten the oil lines from the oil filter and remove the filter assembly from the manifold.

4. Detach the vacuum valve solenoid wire from the coil.

5. Disconnect any remaining lines from the carburetor and remove the carburetor from the manifold.

6. Unfasten the alternator adjusting link and then remove the drivebelt and the alternator.

7. Disconnect the distributor vacuum line from the distributor. Remove the wire from its supports on the head.

8. Disconnect the carburetor fuel line from the fuel pump. Remove the line.

9. Disconnect the spark plug and coil cables, after marking their respective locations.

10. Unfasten the primary wire from the distributor. Remove the distributor clamp bolts and withdraw the distributor.

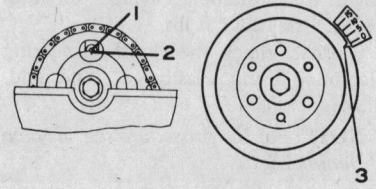

1. Valve timing mark (5/32 in. hole)
2. V-notch—camshaft flange
3. V-notch—crankshaft pulley

Alignment of the timing marks on the crankshaft and camshaft for 2M and 4M engines

11. Remove the oil gauge sending unit.

12. Remove the coil from its bracket on the cylinder head.

13. Remove the fuel pump.

14. Remove the oil filler tube clamping bolt from the valve lifter (side) cover. Drive the oil filler tube out of the cylinder block.

15. Remove the combination intake/exhaust manifold from the cylinder block.

16. Take off the cylinder head cover and its gasket.

17. Unfasten the oil delivery union, spring, and sleeve from the valve rocker shafts.

18. Unfasten the securing nuts and bolts from the valve rocker shaft supports. Withdraw the rocker assembly.

19. Withdraw the pushrods from their bores. Be sure to keep them in the same order in which they were removed.

20. Remove the valve lifter (side) cover and gasket.

21. Withdraw the valve lifters from the block.

NOTE: *The valve lifters should be kept, with their respective pushrods, in the sequence in which they were removed.*

22. Unfasten the oil delivery union from the oil feed pipe.

23. Loosen the cylinder head bolts in two or three stages and in the order illustrated above.

24. Lift off the cylinder head and the gasket.

Installation of the cylinder head is performed in the following order:

1. Clean the gasket mounting surfaces of both the cylinder head and block.

2. Place a *new* head gasket over the dowels on the block.

3. Lower the cylinder head on to the block with the air cleaner mounting bracket attached.

4. Tighten the bolts, in stages, and in the sequence illustrated, to the specified torque.

5. Install the oil feed pipe.

6. Place each valve lifter in the original position from which it came.

NOTE: *Do not interchange valve lifters.*

7. Perform step 6 for the pushrods, being careful to mate each pushrod with its original lifter.

8. Install the valve rocker assembly, oil delivery union, spring, and connecting sleeve in the head. Tighten the rocker assembly support nuts and bolts to the following torque specifications, in several stages:

10mm nuts and bolts—25–30 ft lbs
8mm bolts—14–22 ft lbs

9. Adjust the valves, as outlined above, to the following *cold* specifications (each piston TDC of its compression stroke):

Intake—0.008 in.
Exhaust—0.014 in.

NOTE: *Adjust the valve clearance again after the engine is assembled and warmed up.*

10. The rest of cylinder head installation is performed in the reverse order of the removal procedure.

Overhaul

NOTE: *General cylinder head overhaul procedures are given in the "Engine Rebuilding" section. The operations which differ greatly from those at the end of the book are detailed below.*

Valve Guide Replacement—2M, 4M, and 3K-C Engines

1. Heat the cylinder head to 176–212°F, evenly, before beginning the replacement procedure.

2. Use a brass rod to break the valve guide off above its snap-ring. (See illustration.)

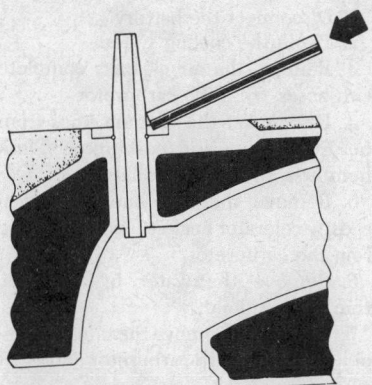

Use a brass drift to break off the valve guide.

3. Drive out the valve guide, toward the combustion chamber. Use a tool fabricated as described in "Engine Rebuilding," at the end of this book.

4. Install a snap-ring on the new valve guide. Apply liquid sealer. Drive in the valve guide until the snap-ring contacts the head. Use the tool described above.

5. Measure the guide bore; if the stem-to-guide clearance is below specification, ream it out, using a valve guide reamer.

Rocker Arm Shafts

Removal and Installation

18R-C, 3K-C Engines

1. Remove air cleaner.

2. Remove PCV valve.

3. Remove spark plug wires.

4. Remove valve cover.

5. Loosen rocker shaft bolts, alternating front to rear.

6. Remove shaft assembly and oil tube.

7. Install in reverse of removal. Torque bolts in alternating, front to rear sequence, to 14–16 ftlb. Torque oil pipe bolts to 14 ftlb. Check valve clearance.

F Engine

1. Remove the PCV valve.

2. Remove the air cleaner.

3. Remove the spark plug wires.

4. Remove the valve cover.

5. Disconnect the rocker shaft oil delivery joint, spring and the oil connection sleeve from the rocker shaft.

6. Remove the rocker shaft bolts and lift off the shaft assembly.

7. Install in reverse of removal. Torque rocker shaft bolts, in front to rear sequence to: 10mm–30 ftlb., 8mm–22 ftlb. Check valve clearance.

2M, 4M Engine

1. Remove the air cleaner assembly.

2. Remove the choke stove outlet and inlet hose.

3. Remove the valve cover.

4. Remove the two front clamp bolts.

5. Loosen the rocker arm shaft bolts in a rotating order starting at the ends and working toward the center.

6. Remove bolts and lift off rocker shaft assemblies.

7. Install in reverse of removal. Tighten rocker shaft bolts, in a rotating order from the center to the ends, to 25 ftlb. Torque the front end clamp bolts to 9 ftlb. Check valve clearance.

2T-C Engine

1. Remove the air cleaner.

2. Remove the PCV valve.

3. Remove the spark plug wires.

4. Disconnect the fuel inlet from the carburetor.

5. Remove the valve cover.

6. **NOTE:** *the cylinder head bolts also serve as the rocker arm shaft bolts. Remove these a little at a time in circular rotation from the ends toward the center.*

7. Lift off the shaft assemblies.

8. Install in reverse of removal. Install and tighten the cylinder head bolts in a circular rotation from the center toward the ends. Torque to 63 ftlb. Check valve clearance.

20R Engine

1. Remove air cleaner.

2. Disconnect all hoses and linkage clipped to the valve cover.

3. Remove the spark plug wires.

4. Remove the carburetor.

5. Remove the valve cover.

6. Remove the distributor.

7. Set the #1 piston at TDC of the compression stroke.

8. Paint mating marks on the timing chain and sprocket, and drive gear.

9. Remove the distributor drive gear, leaving the chain and sprocket in position.

10. Remove the one 14mm chain cover bolt in the front of the head. This must be done before the head bolts, which also serve as rocker shaft bolts, are removed.

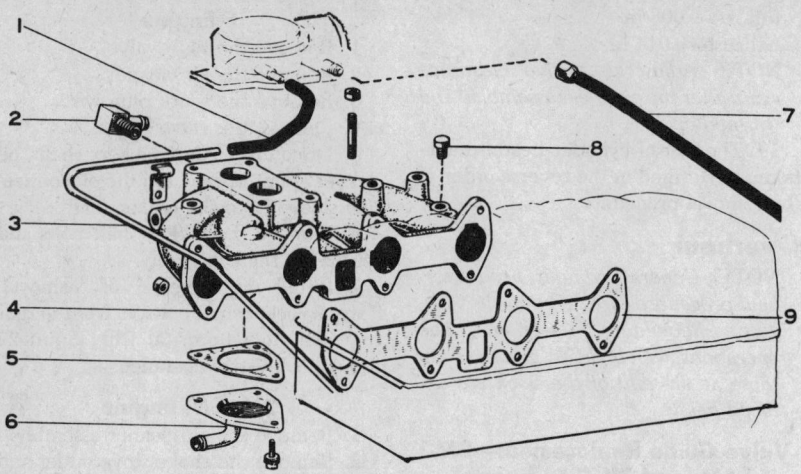

2T-C intake manifold assembly

1. Choke stove intake hose	4. Intake manifold	7. Choke stove outlet
2. Elbow	5. Gasket	8. Plug
3. Choke stove intake	6. Water by-pass outlet	9. Intake manifold gasket

11. Remove the head bolts in a diagonal pattern. Start at the front, carburetor side. This must be done to prevent head warpage.

12. Remove the shaft assemblies from the head. It may be necessary to use a pry bar to evenly lift the assemblies from the dowels.

13. Install in reverse of removal. Torque the head bolts, in a diagonal pattern, starting at the center. Tighten in three, equal stages to 64 ftlb. Torque the chain cover bolt to 12 ftlb. Torque drive gear bolt to 65 ftlb.

Intake Manifold

Removal and Installation

2T-C Engine

1. Drain the cooling system.
2. Remove the air cleaner assembly, complete with hoses, from its bracket.
3. Remove the choke stove hoses, fuel lines, and vacuum lines from the carburetor. Unfasten the emission control system hoses and the accelerator linkage from it.
4. Unfasten the four nuts which secure the carburetor to the manifold and remove the carburetor.
5. Remove the mixture control valve line from its intake manifold fitting (1971–74).
6. Disconnect the PCV hose.
7. Disconnect the water bypass hose from the intake manifold.
8. Unbolt and remove the manifold.

Installation is performed in the reverse order of removal. Remember to use *new* gaskets. Tighten the intake manifold bolts to specifications.

NOTE: *Tighten the bolts, in several stages, working from the inside out.*

20R Engine

1. Disconnect the battery.
2. Drain the cooling system.
3. Remove the air cleaner, complete with hoses, from the carburetor.
4. Disconnect the vacuum lines from the EGR valve and carburetor. Mark them first, to aid in installation.
5. Remove the fuel lines, electrical leads, accelerator linkage, and water hose from the carburetor.
6. Remove the water by-pass hose from the manifold.
7. Unbolt and remove the intake manifold, complete with carburetor and EGR valve.

8. Cover the cylinder head ports with clean rags to keep anything from falling into the cylinder head or block.

Installation is the reverse of removal. Replace the gasket with a new one. Torque the mounting bolts to specifications. Tighten the bolts in several stages working, from the inside bolts outward. Refill the cooling system.

2M and 4M Engines

1. Drain the cooling system.
2. Remove the air cleaner assembly, complete with hoses, from its mounting bracket.
3. Remove the distributor cap.
4. Remove the upper radiator hose from the elbow.
5. Remove the wiring from the temperature gauge sending unit.
6. Remove the following from the carburetor; fuel lines; vacuum line; choke stove hoses; emission control system hoses; accelerator torque rod; and automatic transmission linkage (if so equipped).
7. Remove the emission control system lines and wiring from the manifold when equipped with a vacuum switching valve. Remove the EGR pipe from the intake manifold (1974–75).
8. Remove the water bypass hose from the manifold.
9. Unbolt and remove the manifold, complete with the carburetor.

Installation is in the reverse order of removal. Remember to replace the gaskets with new ones. Torque the mounting bolts to specifications.

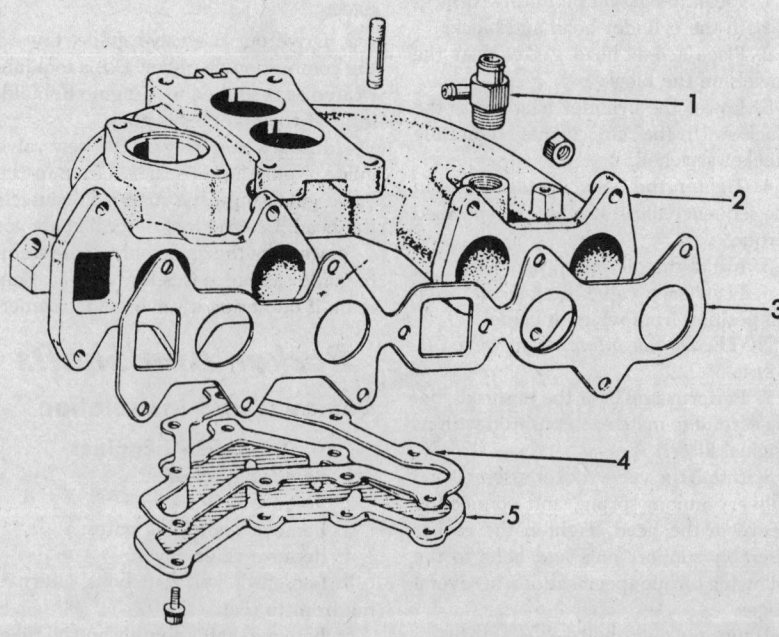

Intake manifold—20R engine

1. Vacuum hose fitting	4. Gasket (bottom)
2. Intake manifold	5. Bottom cover
3. Gasket (to head)	

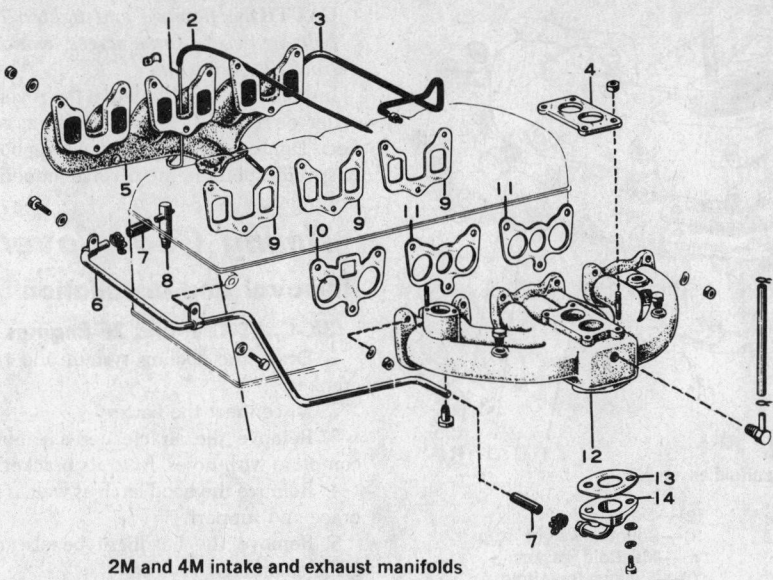

2M and 4M intake and exhaust manifolds

1. Automatic choke stove intake pipe
2. Automatic choke stove intake hose
3. Automatic choke stove outlet pipe
4. Carburetor heat insulator
5. Exhaust manifold
6. Water by-pass line
7. Water by-pass hose
8. Water hose joint
9. Exhaust manifold gasket
10. Intake manifold gasket (1)
11. Intake manifold gasket (2)
12. Intake manifold
13. Gasket
14. Water by-pass outlet

NOTE: *Tighten the bolts, in stages, working from the inside out.*

Exhaust Manifold

Removal and Installation

CAUTION: *Do not perform this operation on a warm or hot engine.*

2T-C Engine

1. Detach the manifold heat stove intake pipe.
2. Unfasten the nut on the stove outlet pipe union.
3. Remove the wiring from the emission control system thermo sensor.

4. Unfasten the U-bolt from the downpipe bracket.
5. Unfasten the downpipe flange from the manifold.
6. In order to remove the manifold, unfasten the manifold retaining bolts.
CAUTION: *Remove the bolts in two or three stages and working from the inside out.*
Installation of the manifold is performed in the reverse order of removal. Remember to use a *new* gasket.

20R Engine

1. Remove the three exhaust pipe flange bolts and disconnect the exhaust pipe from the manifold.

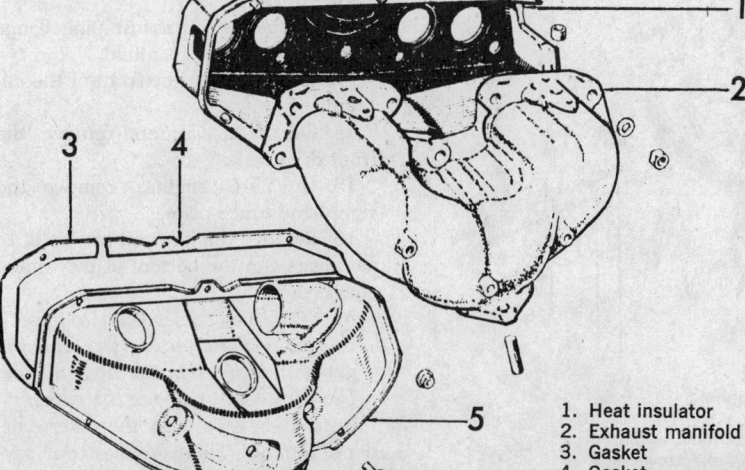

1. Heat insulator
2. Exhaust manifold
3. Gasket
4. Gasket
5. Manifold heat stove

Exhaust manifold—20R engine

2. Disconnect the spark plug leads.
3. Matchmark the distributor rotor, housing and the engine block. Remove the distributor.
4. Remove the air cleaner tube from the heat stove. Remove the outer part of the heat stove.
5. Remove the manifold (14mm nuts), complete with air injection tubes and the inner portion of the heat stove.
6. Separate the inner portion of the heat stove from the manifold.
Installation is the reverse of removal. Tighten the retaining nuts to 29–36 ft lbs, working from the inside out. Install the distributor and set the timing. Tighten the exhaust pipe flange nuts to 25–32 ft lbs.

2M and 4M Engines

1. Raise the front and the rear of the car and support it with jackstands.
2. Remove the right-hand gravel shield from beneath the engine.
3. Remove the downpipe support bracket.
4. Unfasten the bolts from the flange and detach the downpipe from the manifold.
5. Remove the automatic choke and air cleaner stove hoses from the exhaust manifold. Remove the EGR valve, if so equipped.
6. Remove, or move aside, any of the air injection system components which may be in the way when removing the manifold.
7. In order to remove the manifold, unfasten the manifold retaining bolts.
CAUTION: *Remove and tighten the bolts in two or three stages and, starting from the inside, working out.*
Installation is performed in the reverse order of removal. Always use a new gasket. Tighten the retaining bolts to specifications in two or three stages.

Combination Manifold

Removal and Installation

CAUTION: *Do not perform this procedure on a warm engine.*

3K-C and F Engines

1. Remove the air cleaner assembly, complete with hoses.
2. Disconnect the accelerator and choke linkages from the carburetor, as well as the fuel and vacuum lines. On F engines, remove the hand throttle linkage.
3. Remove, or move aside, any of the emission control system components which are in the way.
4. On F engines, disconnect the oil filter lines and remove the oil filter assembly from the intake manifold. Unfasten the solenoid valve wire from the

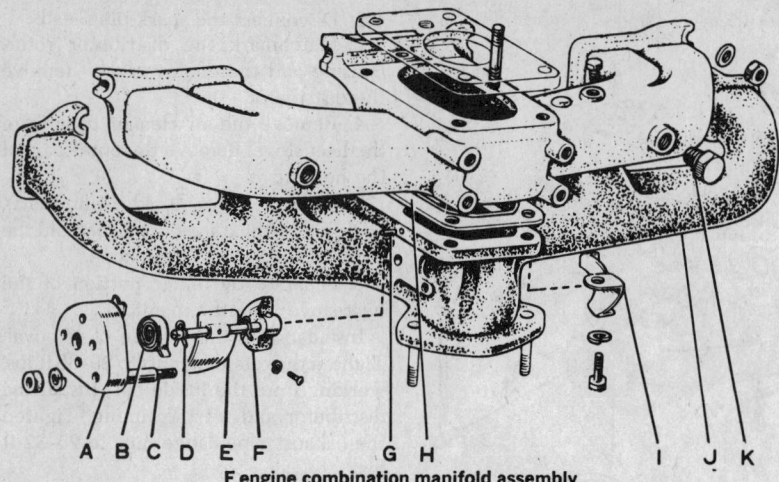

F engine combination manifold assembly

(a)—Heat control valve bimetal case	(g)—Dowel
(b)—Valve coil	(i)—Counter weight stop
(c)—Bolt	(h)—Manifold gasket
(d)—Retaining spring	(j)—Exhaust manifold
(e)—Heat control valve	(k)—Screw plug
(f)—Heat control valve shaft	

ignition coil terminal. Remove the EGR pipes from the exhaust gas cooler, if so equipped.

5. Unfasten the retaining bolts and remove the carburetor from the manifold.

6. Loosen the manifold retaining nuts, working from the inside out, in two or three stages.

7. Remove the intake/exhaust manifold assembly from the cylinder head as a complete unit.

Installation is performed in the reverse order of removal. Always use *new* gaskets. Tighten the bolts, working from the inside out.

NOTE: *Tighten the bolts in two or three stages.*

18R-C Engines

1. Remove the air cleaner assembly, complete with hoses, from its mounting bracket.

2. Remove the fuel line, vacuum line, automatic choke stove hoses, PCV hose, and accelerator linkage from the carburetor.

3. Unfasten the carburetor securing nuts. Remove the torque rod support, carburetor, and heat insulator.

4. Use a jack to raise the front of the car. Support the car with jackstands.

5. Unfasten the bolts which attach the downpipe flange to the exhaust manifold.

6. In order to remove the manifold assembly, unfasten the manifold retaining bolts.

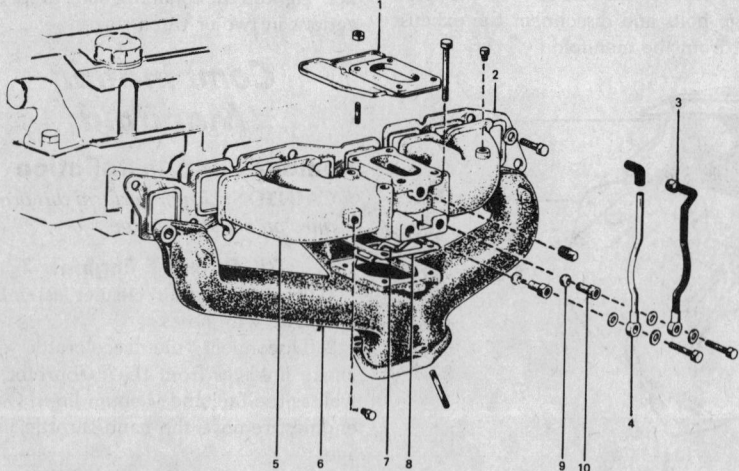

18R-C combination manifold

1. Heat insulator	6. Exhaust manifold
2. Manifold gasket (manifold-to-car)	7. Choke stove pipe
3. Choke stove outlet pipe	8. Manifold gasket (intake-to-exhaust)
4. Choke stove intake pipe	9. Sleeve
5. Intake manifold	10. Union

CAUTION: *Remove and tighten the bolts in two or three stages, working from the inside out.*

Installation is performed in the reverse order of removal. Always use *new* gaskets. Tighten the manifold securing bolts to specifications, in the reverse sequence of removal.

Timing Gear Cover

Removal and Installation

3K-C, 2T-C, F and 2F Engines

1. Drain the cooling system and the crankcase.

2. Disconnect the battery.

3. Remove the air cleaner assembly, complete with hoses, from its bracket.

4. Remove the hood latch as well as its brace and support.

5. Remove the headlight bezels and grille assembly.

6. Unfasten the upper and lower radiator hose clamps and remove both of the hoses from the engine.

7. Unfasten the radiator securing bolts and remove the radiator.

NOTE: *Take off the shroud first, if so equipped.*

8. Loosen the drive belt adjusting link and remove the drive belt. Unfasten the alternator multiconnector, withdraw the retaining bolts, and remove the alternator.

9. Perform step 8 to the air injection pump, if so equipped. Disconnect the hoses from the pump before removing it.

10. Remove the fan and water pump as an assembly.

11. Unfasten the crankshaft pulley retaining bolt (except F engines). Remove the crankshaft pulley with a gear puller.

12. Remove the gravel shield from underneath the engine.

13. The following steps apply to the 3K-C engine only:

　　a. Remove the nuts and washers from both the right and left front engine mounts.

　　b. Detach the exhaust pipe flange from the exhaust manifold.

　　c. Slightly raise the front of the engine.

14. On Land Cruisers remove the front driveshaft.

15. On 2T-C engines, remove the right-hand brace plate.

16. Remove the front oil pan bolts, to gain access to the bottom of the timing chain cover.

NOTE: *It may be necessary to insert a thin knife between the pan and the gasket in order to break the pan loose. Use care not to damage the gasket.*

Installation is basically the reverse order of removal. There are, however, several points to remember:

1. Apply sealer to the two front corners of the 2T-C engine's oil pan gasket.

2. Tighten the crankshaft pulley to specifications.

3. Adjust the drivebelts.

18R-C, 20R, 2M, and 4M Engines

1. Perform the cylinder head removal procedure as detailed in the appropriate section.

2. Remove the radiator.

3. Remove the alternator.

4. On engines equipped with air pumps, unfasten the adjusting link bolts and the drivebelt. Remove the hoses from the pump; remove the pump and bracket from the engine.

NOTE: *If the car is equipped with power steering, see below for its pump removal procedure.*

5. Remove the fan and water pump as a complete assembly.

CAUTION: *To prevent the fluid from running out from the fan coupling, do not tip the assembly over on its side.*

6. Unfasten the crankshaft pulley securing bolt and remove the pulley with a gear puller.

CAUTION: *Do not remove the 10 mm bolt from its hole, if installed, as it is used for balancing.*

7. Loosen the bolts which secure the front of the oil pan, after draining the engine oil. Lower the front of the oil pan.

8. Remove the bolts which secure the timing chain cover. Withdraw the cover.

Installation is performed in the reverse order of removal. Apply sealer to the gaskets for both the timing chain cover and the oil pan.

NOTE: *The 2M and 4M engines use two gaskets on the timing chain cover.*

Tighten the timing chain cover bolts to the specifications below:

18R-C engines:
All bolts—11–15 ft lbs
20R engines
All bolts—8–11 ft lbs.
2M and 4M engines:
8 mm bolts—7–12 ft lbs
10 mm bolts—14–22 ft lbs

Timing Chain Cover Oil Seal Replacement

1. Remove the timing chain cover, as detailed in the appropriate section above.

2. Inspect the oil seal for signs of wear, leakage, or damage.

3. If worn, pry the old oil seal out, using a large flat-bladed screwdriver. Remove it toward the *front* of the cover.

NOTE: *Once the oil seal has been removed, it must be replaced.*

4. Use a socket, pipe, or block of wood and a hammer to drive the oil seal into place. Work from the *front* of the cover.

CAUTION: *Be extremely careful not to damage the seal.*

5. Install the timing chain cover as outlined above.

Timing Chain and Tensioner

Removal and Installation

3K-C Engine

1. Remove the timing chain cover.

2. Unbolt and remove the chain tensioner.

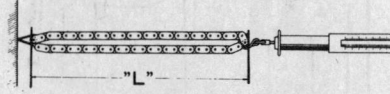

Measure timing chain stretch along "L"—K-C, 3K-C, and 2T-C

3. Remove the camshaft chain sprocket and then the chain itself.

4. Check the timing chain for wear, cracks, or loose links.

5. Secure one end of the chain to a fixed hook and pull on the other end with a spring scale. When the scale indicates 11 lbs, the chain should be no longer than 10.7 in. Replace the chain if it exceeds this specification.

Installation is in the following order:

1. Install the crankshaft chain sprocket. Align the sprocket O mark with the straight pin on the crankshaft, as illustrated.

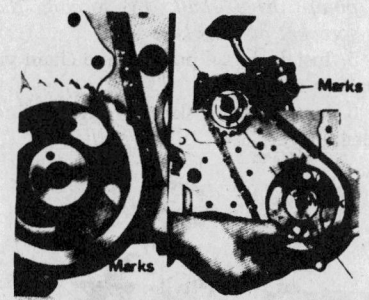

Aligning the marks on the timing chain and sprocket—3K-C

2. Fit the timing chain on the crankshaft sprocket.

3. Align the mating marks on the timing chain with the O-marks on both sprockets, as illustrated.

4. Align the camshaft sprocket O mark with the one on the crankshaft.

5. Tighten the camshaft timing sprocket securing bolt to 16–22 ft lbs.

6. Install the chain tensioner assembly and chain vibration damper. Tighten their bolts to 4–6 ft lbs.

7. Install the timing chain cover as detailed above.

2T-C Engine

1. Perform steps 1–3 of the 3K-C timing chain removal procedure.

2. Perform steps 4–5 of the 3K-C timing chain removal procedure (chain inspection). The chain should stretch no

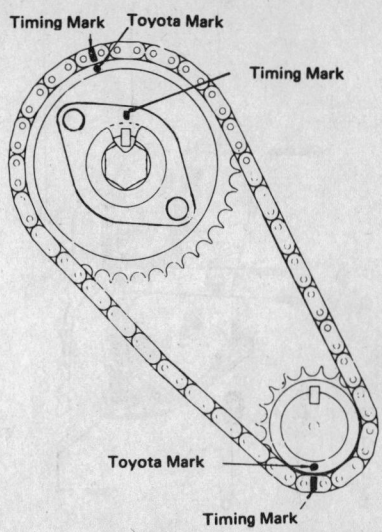

Proper alignment of the marks on 2T-C timing chain and sprocket

more than 11.47 in. at 11 lbs on the spring scale.

Installation is performed in the following order:

1. Rotate the crankshaft so its key points straight up.

NOTE: *The no. 1 and no. 4 pistons should be at TDC.*

2. Rotate the camshaft so its key is aligned with the timing mark on the thrust plate.

3. Install the chain on the camshaft and crankshaft timing sprockets so the marks on the timing chain align with the "Toyota" trademarks on each of the sprockets.

NOTE: *The above step is performed with the sprockets off the engine.*

4. Being careful to keep all the parts in proper alignment, install the timing chain/sprocket assembly to the engine. When assembled, the marks should align as in the illustration.

5. Torque the camshaft timing gear bolt to 50–79 ft lbs.

6. Fill the chain tensioner with engine oil and install it. Install the chain damper.

7. Install the timing chain cover as outlined above.

18R-C Engines

1. Remove the cylinder head and timing chain cover as detailed above.

2. Remove the timing chain (front) together with the camshaft drive sprocket.

3. Remove the crankshaft sprocket and oil pump jack shaft, complete with the pump drive chain (rear). Remove the chain vibration damper.

CAUTION: *Both timing chains are identical; tag them for proper identification during installation.*

4. Inspect the chains and sprockets for wear or damage. Clean the chains with solvent.

5. Use a vernier caliper to measure the amount of stretch of both chains. Meas-

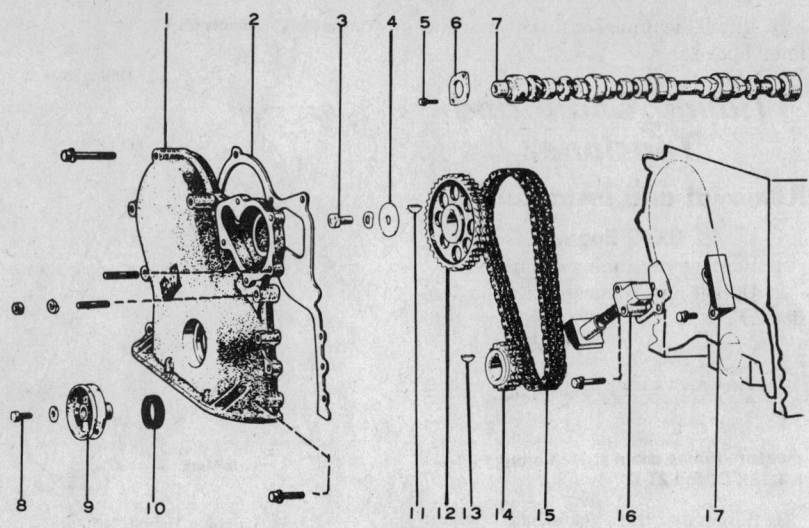

Timing chain covers, timing chain and camshaft—2T-C engine

1. Timing chain cover
2. Timing chain cover gasket
3. Bolt
4. Plate washer
5. Bolt
6. Plate
7. Camshaft
8. Bolt
9. Crankshaft pulley
10. Front oil seal
11. Woodruff key
12. Camshaft sprocket
13. Woodruff key
14. Crankshaft sprocket
15. Timing chain
16. Chain tensioner
17. Chain vibration damper

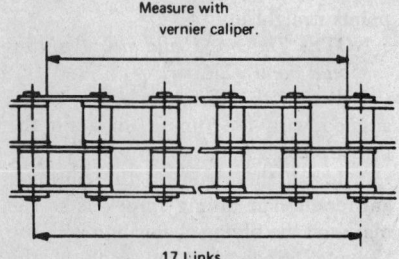

Measure with vernier caliper.

17 Links

Timing chain stretch measurement—18R-C engine

ure any 17 links while pulling the chain that is being measured taut.

6. Repeat step 5 at two other places on each chain. Replace either of the chains if any of the 17 link measurements exceed 5.792 in. or if the difference between the minimum and maximum readings is more than 0.0078 in., on any one chain.

7. Remove the plunger and spring from one of the chain tensioners. Inspect all of the parts of the tensioner for wear or damage. Fill it with oil and assemble it if it is not defective.

8. Repeat step 7 for the other tensioner.

CAUTION: *Do not mix the parts of the two chain tensioners together.*

Installation is performed in the following manner:

1. Position the No. 1 piston at TDC by having the crankshaft keyway point straight up (perpendicular to), toward the cylinder head.

2. Align the oil pump jackshaft, with its keyway pointing straight up as well.

3. Align the marks on the timing sprocket and the oil pump drive sprocket with each of the marks on the chain.

4. Install the chain and sprocket assembly over the keyways, while retaining alignment of the chain/sprocket timing marks.

CAUTION: *Use care not to dislodge the welch plug at the rear of the oil pump drive shaft, by forcing the sprocket over its keyway.*

5. Install the oil pump drive chain vibration damper.

6. Install the gasket for the timing chain cover.

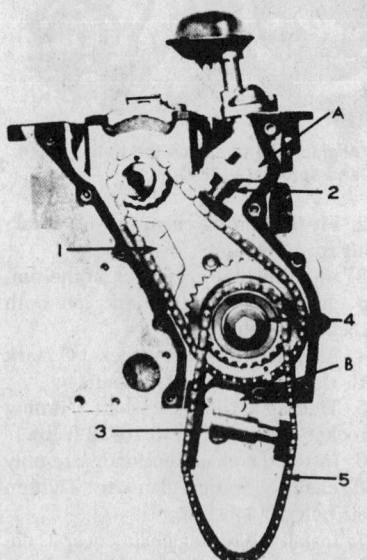

Installing the 18R-C timing chain

(a)—Chain tensioner bolt
(b)—Chain tensioner bolt
1. Chain vibration damper
2. Chain tensioner (oil pump drive chain)
3. Chain tensioner (Camshaft timing chain)
4. Camshaft drive sprocket
5. Camshaft timing chain

NOTE: *Use liquid sealer on the gasket before installation.*

7. Install both of the chain tensioners in their respective places, being careful not to mix them up. Tighten their securing bolts to 12–17 ft lbs.

CAUTION: *Use care when installing the chain tensioner bolts; they have oil holes tapped in them.*

8. Fit the camshaft drive sprocket over the keyway on the oil pump drive shaft. Tighten its securing nut to 58–72 ft lbs.

9. Install the camshaft drive chain over the camshaft drive sprocket. Align the mating marks on the chain and sprocket.

10. Apply tension to the chain by tying it to the chain tensioner. This will prevent it from falling back into the timing chain cover once it is installed.

11. Install the timing chain cover and cylinder head as outlined above.

20R Engine

1. Remove the cylinder head and timing chain cover as outlined above.

2. Separate the chain from the damper, and remove the chain, complete with the camshaft sprocket.

3. Remove the crankshaft sprocket and the oil pump drive with a puller.

4. Inspect the chain for wear or damage. Replace it, if necessary.

5. Inspect the chain tensioner for wear. If it measures less than 0.43 in., replace it.

6. Check the dampers for wear. If they measure are below specification replace them:

Upper damper—0.20 in.
Lower damper—0.18 in.

Installation is performed in the following order:

1. Rotate the crankshaft until its key is at TDC. Slide the sprocket in place over the key.

2. Place the chain over the sprocket so that its *single* bright link aligns with the mark on the crank sprocket.

3. Install the cam sprocket so that the timing mark falls between the *two* bright links on the chain.

4. Fit the oil pump drive spline over the crankshaft key.

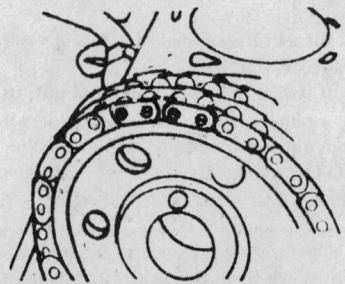

Align the timing marks between the two bright links of the chain—20R engine

5. Install the timing cover gasket on the front of the block.

6. Rotate the camshaft sprocket counter-clockwise to remove the slack from the chain.

7. Install the timing chain cover and cylinder head, as outlined above.

2M and 4M Engines

1. Remove the cylinder head and timing chain cover, as outlined above.

2. Remove the chain tensioner assembly (arm and gear).

3. Unfasten the bolts which retain the chain damper and damper guide and withdraw the damper and guide.

4. Remove the oil slinger from the crankshaft.

Removing the timing chain from the 2M or 4M engine.

1. Timing chain tensioner gear
2. Timing chain tensioner arm
3. Damper guide
4. Vibration damper
5. Vibration damper
6. Crankshaft oil slinger

5. Withdraw the timing chain.

6. Inspect the chain for wear or damage. Replace it if necessary.

Installation is performed in the following manner:

1. Position the no. 1 cylinder at TDC.

2. Position the crankshaft sprocket O mark downward, facing the oil pan.

3. Align the "Toyota" trademarks on the sprockets as illustrated.

4. Fit the tensioner gear assembly on the block.

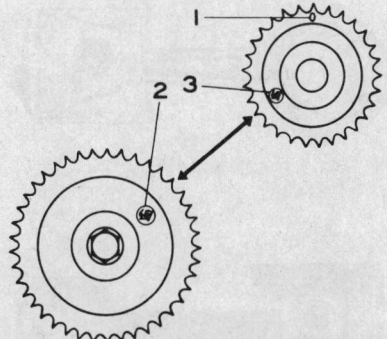

Proper alignment of the 2M or 4M timing marks.

1. Crankshaft sprocket O-mark
2. Camshaft sprocket "Toyota" mark
3. Crankshaft sprocket "Toyota" mark

NOTE: *Its dowel pin should be positioned 1.5 in. from the surface of the block.*

5. Install the chain over the two gears while maintaining tension.

6. Install both of the vibration dampers and the damper guide.

7. Fit the oil slinger to the crankshaft.

8. Tie the chain to the upper vibration damper, to keep it from falling into the chain cover, once the cover is installed.

9. Install the timing chain cover, as detailed above.

10. Perform the cylinder head installation procedure as detailed above.

NOTE: *If proper valve timing cannot be obtained, it is possible to adjust it by placing the camshaft slotted pin in the second or third hole on the camshaft timing gear, as required. If the timing is out by more than 15°, replace the chain and both of the sprockets.*

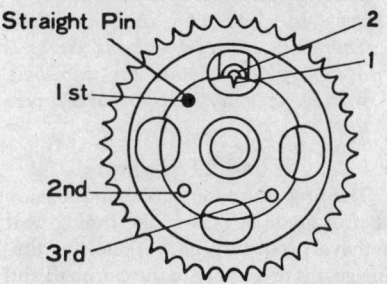

Camshaft sprocket showing normal timing

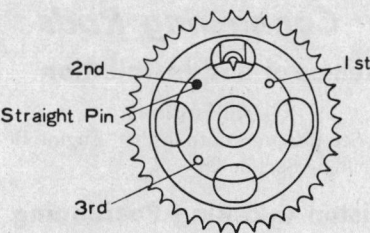

Camshaft sprocket installation—valve timing retarded 3-9°.

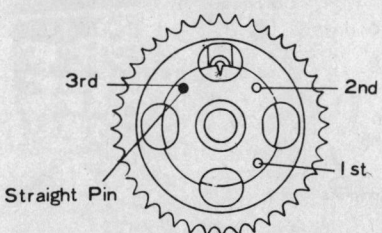

Camshaft sprocket installation—valve timing retarded 9-15°.

Timing Gears

Removal and Installation

F and 2F Engines

NOTE: *This procedure contains camshaft removal and installation.*

1. Perform the cylinder head and timing cover removal procedures, outlined above.

2. Slip the oil slinger off the crankshaft.

3. Remove the camshaft thrust plate retaining bolts by working through the holes provided in the camshaft timing gear.

4. Remove the camshaft through the front of the cylinder block. Support the camshaft while removing it, so as not to damage its bearings or lobes.

NOTE: *The timing gear is a press-fit and cannot be removed without removing the camshaft.*

5. Inspect the crankshaft timing gear. Replace it if it has worn or damaged teeth.

6. To remove it, remove the sliding key from the crankshaft. Withdraw the timing gear with a gear puller.

Installation is performed in the following order:

1. Use a large piece of pipe to press the timing gear onto the crankshaft. Lightly and evenly tap the end of the pipe until the gear is in its original position.

2. Apply a coat of engine oil to the camshaft journals and bearings.

3. Insert the camshaft into the block.

CAUTION: *Use care not to damage the camshaft lobes, bearings, or journals.*

4. Align the mating marks on each of the gears as illustrated.

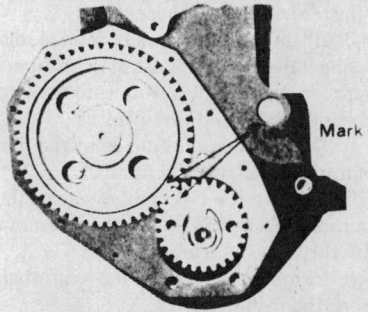

Alignment of the F engine timing marks

5. Slip the camshaft into position. Tighten the camshaft thrust plate bolts to 14.5 ft lbs.

6. Check the gear backlash with a feeler gauge, inserted between the crankshaft and the camshaft timing gears. The backlash should be no more than 0.002–0.005 in.; if it exceeds this, replace one or both of the gears, as required.

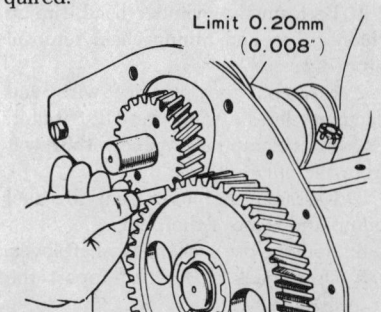

Checking timing gear backlash with a feeler gauge.

7. Check the gear run-out with a dial indicator. Run-out, for both gears, should not exceed 0.008 in.; if it does, replace the gear.

8. Install the oil nozzle, if it was removed, by screwing it in place with a screwdriver and punching it in two places, to secure it.

NOTE: *Be sure that the oil hole in the nozzle is pointed toward the timing gear before securing it.*

9. Install the oil slinger on the crankshaft.

10. Install the timing gear cover and cylinder head, as outlined above.

Camshaft

Removal and Installation

3K-C Engines

1. Perform the timing chain cover and timing chain removal procedure, above.

2. Perform steps 1–11 of the 3K-C engine cylinder head removal procedure.

NOTE: *It is unnecessary to remove the cylinder head.*

3. Unfasten the spark plug wires and remove the spark plugs.

4. Remove the valve lifters in sequence.

NOTE: *Keep the valve lifters in their proper sequence, so that they go back into their original bores.*

5. If you have not already done so, disconnect the vacuum line and the primary wire from the distributor, loosen its clamping bolt, and remove it.

6. Detach the fuel lines from the fuel pump and remove the pump.

7. Remove the bolts which secure the camshaft thrust plate and then remove the thrust plate, itself.

8. Carefully remove the camshaft from the cylinder block.

CAUTION: *Use care not to damage the camshaft lobes, journals, or bearings.*

Installation of the camshaft is performed in the reverse order of removal. Coat the camshaft bearings and journals lightly with engine oil. The camshaft thrust plate attaching bolt should be tightened to 4–6 ft lbs.

2T-C Engine

1. Perform the cylinder head, timing chain cover, and timing chain removal procedures.

2. Unfasten the primary wire and vacuum lines from the distributor. Loosen its clamping bolt and withdraw it from the engine block.

3. Unfasten the lines from the fuel pump and remove the pump.

4. Remove the gear shifter shaft lever.

5. Use a jack to *lightly* support the transmission.

6. Remove the engine rear supporting crossmember.

7. Carefully lower the jack from beneath the transmission.

8. Unbolt and remove the camshaft thrust plate.

9. Ease out the camshaft, being careful not to damage the camshaft lobes or bearings.

Installation is performed in the reverse order of removal. Lubricate the camshaft journals and bearings lightly with engine oil prior to camshaft installation. Tighten the camshaft thrust plate attaching bolts to 7–11 ft lbs.

18R-C, 20R, 2M, and 4M Engines

All of these engines utilize a chain-driven overhead camshaft (OHC). Therefore, the procedure for removing the camshaft is given as part of the cylinder head removal procedure. Consult the appropriate section, above, for details.

NOTE: *It will not be necessary to completely remove the cylinder head in order to remove the camshaft. Therefore, proceed only as far as is necessary, to remove the camshaft, with the cylinder head removal procedure.*

F and 2F Engine

The procedure for removing the camshaft is given as part of the timing gear removal procedure, above; since the timing gear is press-fit onto the camshaft and cannot be removed separately from it.

Pistons and Connecting Rods

Removal and Installation

All Engines

See the procedure in the "Engine Rebuilding Section".

Piston and Ring Positioning

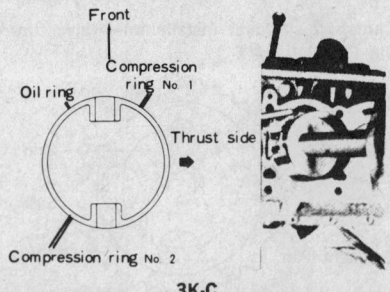

3K-C

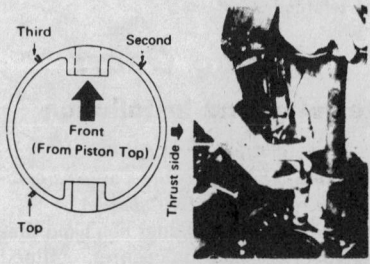

2T-C

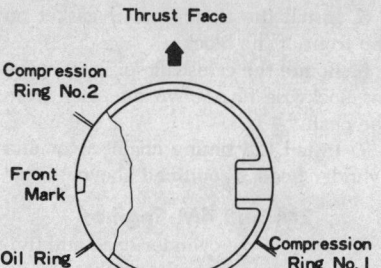

20R and 18R-C (2M and 4M are similar with no "Front" mark)

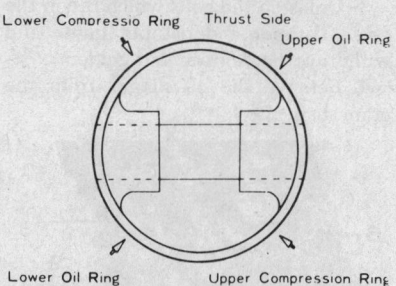

F engine

Piston and Connecting Rod Positioning

3K-C and 2TC

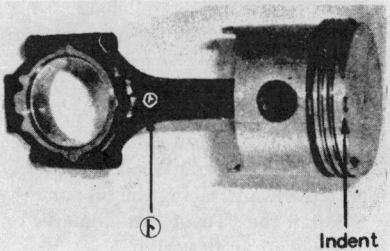

18R-C

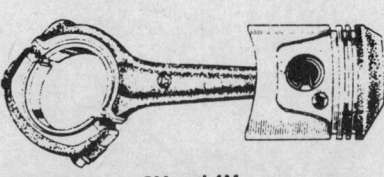

2M and 4M

F engine—piston marking

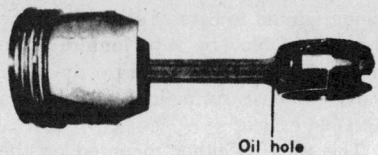

F engine—connecting rod oil hole

ENGINE LUBRICATION

Oil Pan

Removal and Installatin

Corolla 1200/1600 and 1974–77 Corona

1. Open the engine compartment hood.
2. Raise the front end of the car and support it with jackstands.
3. Remove the splash shield from underneath the engine.
4. Place a jack under the transmission to support it.
5. Unfasten the bolts which secure the engine rear supporting crossmember to the chassis.
6. Raise the jack under the transmission, *slightly*.
7. Unbolt the oil pan and work it out from underneath the engine.

NOTE: *If the oil pan does not come out easily, it may be necessary to unbolt the rear engine mounts from the crossmember.*

Installation is performed in the reverse order of removal. On Corolla models equipped with the 2T-C (1600cc) engine and Corona models with 20R engines, apply liquid sealer to the four corners of the oil pan. Tighten the oil pan securing bolts to the following specifications:

3K-C engine:
  2–3 ft lbs
2T-C engine:
  4–6 ft lbs
18R-C engine:
  3.0–5.0 ft lbs
20R engine:
  3.0–6.0 ft lbs

Apply sealer to the 20R and 2T-C oil pan gasket as shown.

Carina, Corona (1972–73), Mark II, Celica, and Hi-Lux

1. Drain the oil.
2. Raise the front end of the car with jacks and support it with jackstands.

CAUTION: *Be sure that the car is supported securely. Remember, you will be working underneath it.*

3. Detach the steering relay rod and the tie rods from the idler arm, pitman arm, and steering knuckles, as detailed below.
4. Remove the engine stiffening plates.
5. pRemove the splash shields from underneath the engine.
6. Support the front of the engine with a jack and remove the front engine mount attaching bolts.
7. Raise the front of the engine *slightly* with the jack.
8. Unbolt and withdraw the oil pan.

Installation is performed in the reverse order of removal. Apply liquid sealer to the four corners of the oil pan gasket used on 2T-C engines. Torque the oil pan securing bolts to the following specifications:

2T-C engine:
  4–6 ft lbs
18R-C engines:
  3–5 ft lbs

Crown 2600

NOTE: *It is far easier to remove the engine on Crown models, in order to remove the oil pan, than to attempt to remove it with the engine installed in the car.*

1. Remove the engine.
2. Remove the oil pan securing bolts and withdraw the oil pan.

Installation is the reverse of removal. Use a new oil pan gasket. Tighten the oil pan securing bolts to 3–5 ft lbs.

Land Cruiser

1. Remove the engine skid plates.
2. Remove the flywheel side cover and skid plate.
3. Disconnect the front driveshaft from the engine.
4. Drain the engine oil.
5. Remove the bolts which secure the oil pan; remove the pan and its gasket.

Installation is performed in the reverse order from removal. Always use a new pan gasket.

Real Main Oil Seal

Replacement

All Engines

1. Remove the transmission.
2. Remove the clutch cover assembly and flywheel.
3. Remove the oil seal retaining plate, complete with the oil seal.
4. Use a screwdriver to pry the old seal from the retaining plate. Be careful not to damage the plate.
5. Install the new seal, carefully, by using a block of wood to drift it into place.

CAUTION: *Do not damage the seal; a leak will result.*

6. Lubricate the lips of the seal with multipurpose grease.

Installation is the reverse of removal.

Oil Pump
Removal and Installation

All Engines (except 20R)

1. Remove the oil pan, as outlined in the appropriate section above.
2. On passenger cars and High-Lux trucks, unbolt the oil pump securing bolts and remove it as an assembly.
3. On Land Cruisers:
  a. Remove the oil strainer and unfasten the union nuts on the oil pump pipe.
  b. Remove the lock wire and the oil pump retaining bolt and pipe from the engine.

Installation is the reverse of removal.

20R Engine

1. Remove the oil pan.
2. Remove the three bolts which secure the oil strainer.
3. Remove the drive belts, the pulley bolt, and the crankshaft pulley.
4. Unfasten the bolts which secure the oil pump housing and remove the pump assembly.

OIL PUMP CLEARANCE SPECIFICATIONS (IN.)

Engine	Tip clearance	Side Clearance	Body Clearance	Relief valve spring installed length
3K-C	0.008	0.006	0.008	1.45
2T-C	0.010	0.006	0.010	1.45
18RC	0.008	0.006	0.008	1.45
2M/4M	0.016	0.006	0.008	1.89
20R	0.012	0.006	0.008	——
F/2F	0.012	0.002	0.002	——

5. Remove the oil pump drive spline and the rubber O-ring.

Installation is the reverse of removal. Apply sealer to the top oil pump housing bolt. Use a new oil strainer gasket.

Checking Clearance

Wash the pump thoroughly and allow to air dry. Check for shiny spots which indicate wear and scuffling. Check backlash of gears and measure free length of relief valve spring, then check play between gears and housing, gears and pump cover and between gears themselves. See specification chart for toleracnes.

ENGINE COOLING
Radiator
Removal and Installation

1. Drain the cooling system.
2. Unfasten the clamps and remove the radiator upper and lower hoses. If equipped with an automatic transmission, remove the oil cooler lines.
3. Detach the hood lock cable and remove the hood lock from the radiator upper support, except on pre-1970 Corona and all Celica models.

NOTE: *It may be necessary to remove the grille in order to gain access to the hood lock/radiator support assembly.*

4. Remove the fan shroud, if so equipped.
5. On models equipped with the a closed cooling system, disconnect the hose from the thermal expansion tank and remove the tank from its bracket.
6. Unbolt and remove the radiator upper support.
7. Unfasten the bolts and remove the radiator.

Installation is performed in the reverse order of removal. Remember to check the transmission fluid level on cars with automatic transmissions.

Fill the radiator to the specified level.

Water Pump
Removal and Installation

1. Drain the cooling system.
2. Unfasten the fan shroud securing bolts and remove the fan shroud, if so equipped.
3. Loosen the alternator adjusting link bolt and remove the drive belt.
4. Repeat step 3 for the air pump, air conditioning compressor, or power steering pump drive belts, if so equipped.
5. Detach the bypass and radiator hoses from the water pump.

6. Unfasten the water pump retaining bolts and remove the water pump and fan assembly, using care not to damage the radiator with the fan.

CAUTION: *If the fan is equipped with a fluid coupling, do not tip the fan/-pump assembly on its side, as the fluid will run out.*

Installation is the reverse of removal. Always use a new gasket between the pump body and its mounting. Check for leaks after installation is completed.

Thermostat
Removal and Installation

1. Drain the cooling system.
2. Unfasten the clamp and remove the upper radiator hose from the water outlet elbow.
3. Unbolt and remove the water outlet (thermostat housing).
4. Withdraw the thermostat.

Installation is performed in the reverse order of the removal procedure. Use a new gasket on the water outlet.

CAUTION: *Be sure that the thermostat is installed with the spring pointing down.*

EMISSION CONTROLS
Positive Crankcase Ventilation (PCV) System

A positive crankcase ventilation (PCV) system is used on all Toyotas sold in the United States. Blow-by gases are routed from the crankcase to the carburetor, where they are combined with the fuel-/air mixture and burned during combustion.

A (PCV) valve is used in the line to prevent the gases in the crankcase from

being ignited in case of a backfire. The amount of blow-by gases entering the mixture is also regulated by the PCV valve, which is spring-loaded and has a variable orifice.

The valve is either mounted on the valve cover or in the line which runs from the intake manifold to the crankcase.

Removal and Installation

Remove the PCV valve from the cylinder head cover on 3K-C and 18R-C engines. Remove the hose from the valve.

On the remainder of the engines, remove the valve from the manifold-to-crankcase hose.

Installation is the reverse of removal.

Testing

Check the PCV system hoses and connections, to see that there are no leaks; then replace or tighten, as necessary.

To check the valve, remove it and blow through both of its ends.

When blowing from the side which goes toward the intake manifold, very little air should pass through it. When blowing from the crankcase (valve cover) side, air should pass through freely.

Replace the valve with a new one, if the valve fails to function as outlined.

NOTE: *Do not attempt to clean or adjust the valve; replace it with a new one.*

Air Injection System

A belt-driven air pump supplies air to an injection manifold which has nozzles in each exhaust port. Injection of air at this point causes combustion of unburned hydrocarbons in the exhaust manifold rather than allowing them to escape into the atmosphere. An antibackfire valve controls the flow of air from the pump to prevent backfiring which results from an overly rich mixture under closed throttle conditions.

A check valve prevents hot exhaust gas backflow into the pump and hoses, in case

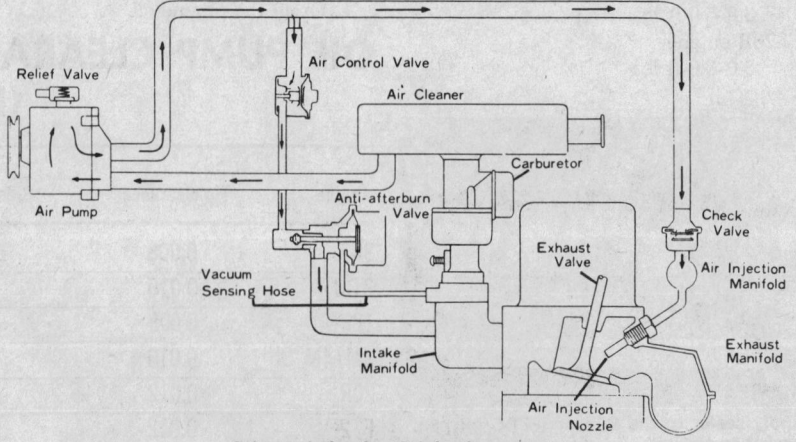

Schematic for the air injection system

of a pump failure, or when the antibackfire valve is working.

In addition newer engines have an air switching valve. On engines without catalytic converters, the ASV is used to stop air injection under a constant heavy engine load.

On engines with catalytic converters the ASV is used to protect the catalyst from overheating, by blocking the air necessary for the reaction.

On all engines, except the 2F, the relief valve is built into the ASV.

Removal and Installation

Air Pump

1. Disconnect the air hoses from the pump.
2. Loosen the bolt on the adjusting link and remove the drive belt.
3. Remove the pump.

CAUTION: *Do not pry on the pump housing; it may be distorted.*

Installation is in the reverse order of removal. Adjust the drive belt tension to ½–¾ in. under thumb pressure.

Antibackfire Valve and Air Switching Valve

1. Detach the air hoses from the valve.
2. Remove the valve securing bolt.
3. Withdraw the valve.

Installation is performed in the reverse order of removal.

Check Valve

1. Detach the intake hose from the valve.
2. Use an open-end wrench to remove the valve from its mounting.

Installation is the reverse of removal.

Relief Valve

1. Remove the air pump from the car.
2. Support the pump so that it cannot rotate.

CAUTION: *Never clamp the pump in a vise; the aluminum case will be distorted.*

3. Use a jaw-type puller to remove the relief valve from the top of the pump.

Removing the relief valve from the air pump.

4. Position the new relief valve over the opening in the pump.

NOTE: *The air outlet should be pointing toward the left.*

5. Gently tap the relief valve home, using a block of wood and a hammer.

6. Install the pump on the engine, as outlined above.

Air Injection Manifold

1. Remove the check valve, as outlined above.
2. Loosen the air injection manifold attachment nuts and withdraw the manifold.

NOTE: *On 20R, 2M and 4M engines, it will first be necessary to remove the exhaust manifold.*

Installation is in the reverse order of removal.

Air Injection Nozzles

1. Remove the air injection manifold as outlined above.
2. Remove the cylinder head, as detailed in the appropriate section, above.
3. Place a new nozzle on the cylinder head.
4. Install the air injection manifold over it.
5. Install the cylinder head on the engine block.

Testing

Air Pump

CAUTION: *Do not hammer, pry, or bend the pump housing while tightening the drive belt or testing the pump.*

Belt Tension and Air Leaks

1. Before proceeding with the tests, check the pump drive belt tension to see if it is within specifications.
2. Turn the pump by hand. If it has seized, the belt will slip, making a noise. Disregard any chirping, squealing, or rolling sounds from inside the pump; these are normal when it is turned by hand.

3. Check the hoses and connections for leaks. Hissing or a blast of air is indicative of a leak. Soapy water, applied lightly around the area in question, is a good method for detecting leaks.

Air Output

1. Disconnect the air supply hose at the antibackfire valve.

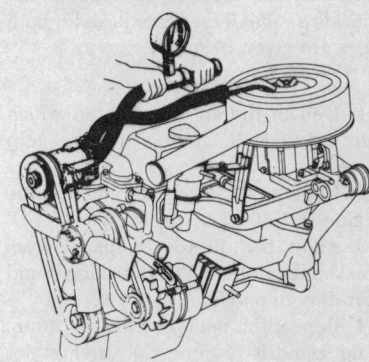

Checking the air pump output

2. Connect a pressure gauge, using a suitable adaptor, to the air supply hose.

NOTE: *If there are two hoses, plug the second one.*

3. With the engine at normal operating temperature, increase the idle speed to 1,000–1,500 rpm (1,950 rpm-2T-C) and watch the vacuum gauge.

4. The air flow from the pump should be steady and fall between 2 and 6 psi. If it is unsteady or falls below this, the pump is defective and must be replaced.

Pump Noise Diagnosis

The air pump is normally noisy; as engine speed increases, the noise of the pump will rise in pitch. The rolling sound the pump bearings make is normal. But if this sound becomes objectionable at certain speeds, the pump is defective and will have to be replaced.

A continual hissing sound from the air pump pressure relief valve at idle, indicates a defective valve. Replace the relief valve.

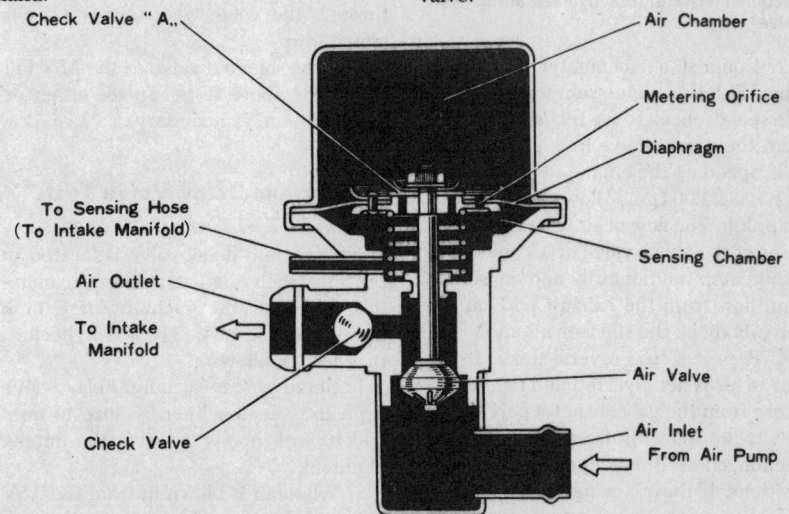

Check Valve "A"

To Sensing Hose
(To Intake Manifold)

Air Outlet

To Intake
Manifold

Check Valve

Air Chamber

Metering Orifice

Diaphragm

Sensing Chamber

Air Valve

Air Inlet
From Air Pump

Sectional view of the gulp-type antibackfire valve.

If the pump rear bearing fails, a continual knocking sound will be heard.

Antibackfire Valve Tests

There are two different types of antibackfire valve used with air injection systems. A bypass valve is used on 1972–77 engines, while 1974 F engines for California use a gulp type of antibackfire valve. Test procedures for both types are given below.

Gulp Valve

1. Detach the air supply hose which runs between the pump and the gulp valve.

2. Connect a tachometer and run the engine to 1,500–2,000 rpm.

3. Allow the throttle to snap closed. This should produce a loud sucking sound from the gulp valve.

4. Repeat this operation several times. If no sound is present, the valve is not working or else the vacuum connections are loose.

5. Check the vacuum connections. If they are secure, replace the gulp valve.

Bypass Valve

1. Detach the hose, which runs from the bypass valve to the check valve, at the bypass valve hose connection.

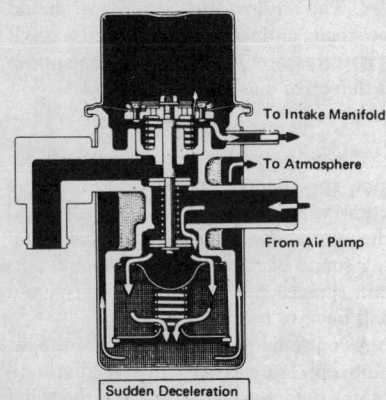

Sectional view of the by-pass antibackfire valve.

2. Connect a tachometer to the engine. With the engine running at normal idle speed, check to see that air is flowing from the bypass valve hose connection.

3. Speed up the engine so it is running at 1,500–2,000 rpm. Allow the throttle to snap shut. The flow of air from the bypass valve at the check valve hose connection should stop momentarily and air should then flow from the exhaust port on the valve body or the silencer assembly.

4. Repeat step 3 several times. If the flow of air is not diverted into the atmosphere from the valve exhaust port or if it fails to stop flowing from the hose connection, check the vacuum lines and connections. If these are tight, the valve is defective and requires replacement.

5. A leaking diaphragm will cause the

air to flow out both the hose connection and the exhaust port at the same time. If this happens, replace the valve.

Air Switching Valve (ASV) Tests

1975–77 2T-C and 20R Engines

1. Start the engine and allow it to reach normal operating temperature.

2. At curb idle, the air from the bypass valve should be discharged through the hose which runs to the ASV.

3. When the vacuum line to the ASV is disconnected, the air from the bypass valve should be diverted out through the ASV-to-air cleaner hose. Reconnect the vacuum line.

4. Disconnect the ASV-to-check valve hose and connect a pressure gauge to it.

5. Increase the engine speed. The relief valve should open when the pressure gauge registers 2.7–6.5 psi.

6. If the ASV fails any of the above tests, replace it. Reconnect all hoses.

1975–76 4M Engines

1. Start the engine and allow it to reach normal operating temperature.

2. At curb idle, air from the pump should be discharged through the hose which runs to the check valve.

3. Race the engine and allow the throttle valve to snap shut. The air from the pump should be discharged into the air cleaner.

4. Disconnect the ASV-to-check valve hose and connect a pressure gauge to it.

5. Increase the engine speed gradually. The relief valve should open when the gauge registers 3.7–7.7 psi. Reconnect the check valve hose.

6. Unfasten the wiring connector and the hoses from the solenoid valve, which is attached to the ASV. Air should pass through the solenoid valve when either the top or bottom port is blown into.

7. Connect a 12V power source to the terminals on the valve. No air should flow through the valve when either port is blown into.

8. If the solenoid valve or the ASV fail any of the above tests, replace either or both of them, as necessary.

Vacuum Delay Valve Test

1975–77 2T-C and 20R Engines

The vacuum delay valve is located in the line which runs from the intake manifold to either the vacuum surge tank (20R) or to the ASV (2T-C). To check it, proceed as follows:

1. Remove the vacuum delay valve from the vacuum line. Be sure to note which end points toward the intake manifold.

2. When air is blown in from the ASV (surge tank) side, it should pass through the valve freely.

3. When air is blown in from the intake manifold side, a resistance should be felt.

4. Replace the valve if it fails either of the above tests.

5. Install the valve in the vacuum line, being careful not to install it backward.

Check Valve Test

1. Before starting the test, check all of the hoses and connections for leaks.

2. Detach the air supply hose from the check valve.

3. Insert a suitable probe into the check valve and depress the plate. Release it; the plate should return to its original position against the valve seat. If binding is evident, replace the valve.

4. With the engine running at normal operating temperature, gradually increase its speed to 1,500 rpm. Check for exhaust gas leakage. If any is present, replace the valve assembly.

NOTE: *Vibration and flutter of the check valve at idle speed is a normal condition and does not mean that the valve should be replaced.*

Air Suction System

The Air Suction System, available only on the 3K-C engine, brings fresh, filtered air into the exhaust ports to promote better buring of hydrocarbons. It also supplies the air necessary for the oxidizing reaction in the catalytic converter.

There are no adjustments on the system and, should it malfunction, the unit must be replaced as a whole.

To check the system, look over all lines for cracks or damage. If checks indicate no problems, start the engine and put a thin sheet of paper over the inlet port of the filter. If it is drawn to the opening, the unit is operating. If not, remove the filter and test the valve opening the same way. Replace the filter, if necessary.

If there is still no indication of a draw, the valve itself is malfunctioning and must be replaced.

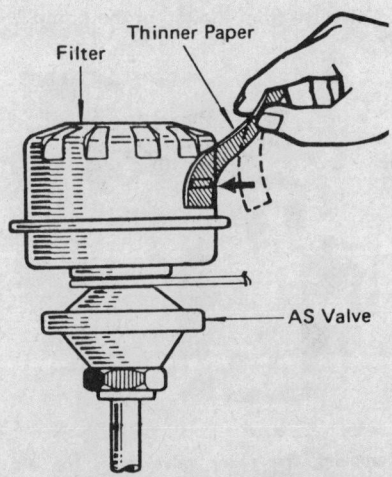

3K-C Air suction valve test

AIR INJECTION SYSTEM DIAGNOSIS CHART

Problem	Cause	Cure
1. Noisy drive belt	1a Loose belt	1a Tighten belt
	1b Seized pump	1b Replace
2. Noisy pump	2a Leaking hose	2a Trace and fix leak
	2b Loose hose	2b Tighten hose clamp
	2c Hose contacting other parts	2c Reposition hose
	2d Diverter or check valve failure	2d Replace
	2e Pump mounting loose	2e Tighten securing bolts
	2g Defective pump	2g Replace
3. No air supply	3a Loose belt	3a Tighten belt
	3b Leak in hose or at fitting	3b Trace and fix leak
	3c Defective anti-backfire valve	3c Replace
	3d Defective check valve	3d Replace
	3e Defective pump	3e Replace
4. Exhaust backfire	4a Vacuum or air leaks	4a Trace and fix leak
	4b Defective anti-backfire valve	4b Replace
	4c Sticking choke	4c Service choke
	4d Choke setting rich	4d Adjust choke

Evaporative Emission Control System

To prevent hydrocarbon emissions from entering the atmosphere, Toyota vehicles use evaporative emission control (EEC) systems. 1972 and later models use a "charcoal canister" storage system.

The charcoal canister storage system stores fuel vapors in a canister filled with activated charcoal. All models use a vacuum switching valve to purge the system. The air filter is an integral part of the charcoal canister.

Removal and Installation

Removal and installation of the various evaporative emission control system components consists of disconnecting hoses, loosening securing screws, and removing the part which is to be replaced from its mounting bracket. Installation is the reverse of removal.

NOTE: *When replacing any EEC system hoses, always use hoses that are fuel-resistant or are marked "EVAP."*

Testing

EEC System Troubleshooting

There are several things which may be checked if a malfunction of the vaporative emission control system is suspected.

1. Leaks may be traced by using a hydrocarbon tester. Run the test probe along the lines and connections. The meter will indicate the presence of a leak by a high hydrocarbon (HC) reading. This method is much more accurate than visual inspection which would only indicate the presence of leaks large enough to pass liquid.

2. Leaks may be caused by any of the following:

    a. Defective or worn hoses;

    b. Disconnected or pinched hoses;

    c. Improperly routed hoses;

    d. A defective filler cap or safety valve (sealed cap system).

NOTE: *If it becomes necessary to replace any of the hoses used in the evaporative emission control system, use only hoses which are fuel-resistant or are marked "EVAP."*

3. If the fuel tank, storage case, or thermal expansion tank collaspe, it may be the fault of clogged or pinched vent lines, a defective vapor separator, or a plugged or incorrect filler cap.

4. To test the filler cap (if it is the safety valve type), clean it and place it against your mouth. Blow into the relief valve housing. If the cap passes pressure with light blowing or if it fails to release with hard blowing, it is defective and must be replaced.

NOTE: *Use the proper cap for the type of system used; either a sealed cap or safety valve cap, as required.*

Purge Control Valve—1974–77

California models equipped with the 4M six-cylinder engine have a canister-mounted purge control valve, starting with 1974 models.

The purge control valve is connected to a carburetor port, which is located above the throttle control valve. When the engine is stopped or idling, there is no vacuum signal at the purge control valve

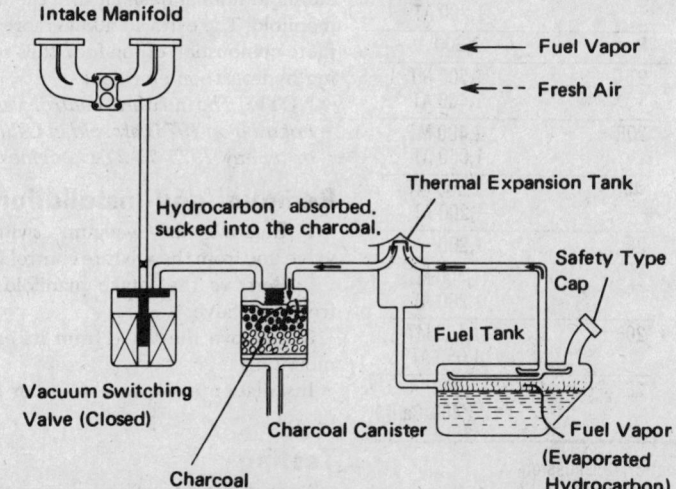

→ Fuel Vapor
- - → Fresh Air

Intake Manifold

Hydrocarbon absorbed, sucked into the charcoal.

Thermal Expansion Tank

Safety Type Cap

Fuel Tank

Vacuum Switching Valve (Closed)

Charcoal Canister

Charcoal

Fuel Vapor (Evaporated Hydrocarbon)

Schematic for charcoal storage system w/ thermal expansion tank.

so that it remains closed. When the throttle valve opens, the carburetor port is uncovered and a vacuum signal is sent to the purge control valve, which opens and allows the vapors stored in the canister to be pulled into the carburetor.

Check purge control valve operation in the following manner:

1. Note the routing of the vacuum lines and remove the charcoal canister from the car.

2. Place your finger over the purge control valve opening, which is located at the center of the canister on its top side.

3. Gently blow through the vapor intake (the other opening on the top of the canister). No resistance should be felt.

4. Uncover the purge control valve opening and blow through it. No air should be felt coming from the vapor intake or the fresh air intake (located on the bottom of the canister).

5. If the purge control valve fails either of the tests in Steps 3 or 4, replace the canister assembly. If the valve is OK, then install the canister in the car.

6. If the purge control valve still doesn't appear to be working properly when installed in the car, check for damaged vacuum lines or a clogged carburetor port.

Check Valve—1972 Corolla and All 1973–77

NOTE: *The Mark II station wagon is the only model not equipped with a check valve for 1973. All 1974–77 models have a check valve.*

Rough idling when the gas tank is full is probably caused by a defective check valve. To test it, proceed as follows:

1. Run the engine at idle.

2. Clamp the hose between the vacuum switching valve or carburetor (AM-Calif) and the charcoal canister.

3. If the engine idle becomes smooth, replace the check valve.

Exhaust Emission Control

Throttle Positioner

On Toyotas with an engine modification system, a throttle positioner is included to reduce exhaust emissions during deceleration. The positioner prevents the throttle from closing completely. Vacuum is reduced under the throttle valve which, in turn, acts on the retard chamber of the distributor vacuum unit (if so equipped). This compensates for the loss of engine braking caused by the partially open throttle.

Once the vehicle drops below a predetermined speed, the vacuum switching valve provides vacuum to the throttle positioner diaphragm; the throttle positioner retracts allowing the throttle valve

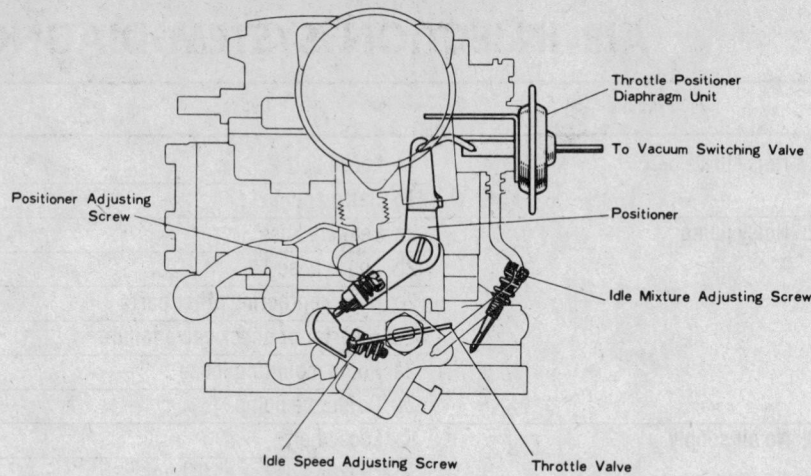

Components of the throttle positioner system.

to close completely. The distributor also is returned to normal operation.

Adjustment

1. Start the engine and allow it to reach normal operating temperature.

2. Adjust the idle speed.

NOTE: *Leave the tachometer connected after completing the idle adjustments, as it will be needed in step 5, below.*

3. Detach the vacuum line from the positioner diaphragm unit and plug the line.

4. Accelerate the engine slightly to set the throttle positioner in place.

5. Check the engine speed with a tachometer when the throttle positioner is set.

Throttle Positioner Settings (rpm)

Year	Engine	Engine rpm (positioner set)
1972–74	3K-C	1,500
	2T-C	1,400
	18R-C	1,400
	2M & 4M	1,300 MT 1,200 AT
	F	1,200
1975–76*	2T-C	1,500 MT 1,400 AT
	20R	1,400 MT 1,050 AT
	4M	1,300 MT 1,200 AT
	2F	1,200
1977	2T-C	1,400 MT 1,200 AT
	20R	1,400 MT 1,050 AT
	2F	1,200 1,400 (Calif.)

AT—Automatic Transmission
MT—Manual Transmission
* 3K-C 1,500

6. If necessary, adjust the engine speed, with the throttle positioner adjusting screw, to the specifications.

7. Connect the vacuum hose to the positioner diaphragm.

8. The throttle lever should be freed from the positioner as soon as the vacuum hose is connected. Engine idle should return to normal.

9. If the throttle positioner fails to function properly, check its linkage, and vacuum diaphragm. If there are no defects in either of these, the fault probably lies in the vacuum switching valve or the speed marker unit.

NOTE: *Due to the complexity of these two components they require special test equipment.*

Mixture Control Valve—2T-C Engines

The mixture control valve, used on all 1972–73 2T-C engines, aids in combustion of unburned fuel during periods of deceleration. The mixture control valve is operated by the vacuum switching valve during periods of deceleration to admit additional fresh air into the intake manifold. The extra air allows more complete combustion of the fuel, thus reducing hydrocarbon emissions.

NOTE: *The mixture control valve is not used on 1974 cars sold in California or on any 1975–77 2T-C engines.*

Removal and Installation

1. Remove the vacuum switching valve line from the mixture control valve.

2. Remove the intake manifold hose from the valve.

3. Remove the valve from its engine mounting.

Installation is the reverse order of removal.

Testing

1. Start the engine and allow it to idle (warmed up).

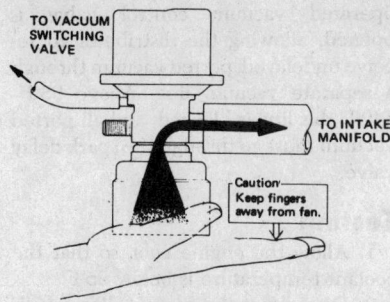

Checking the mixture control valve

2. Place your hand over the air intake at the bottom of the valve.

CAUTION: *Keep your fingers clear of the engine fan.*

3. Increase the engine speed and then release the throttle.

4. Suction should be felt at the air intake only while the engine is decelerating. Once the engine has returned to idle, no suction should be felt.

If the above test indicates a malfunction, proceed with the next step; if not, the mixture control valve is functioning properly and requires no further attention.

5. Disconnect the vacuum line from the mixture control valve. If suction can be felt underneath the valve with the engine at idle, the valve seat is defective and must be replaced.

6. Reconnect the vacuum line to the valve. Disconnect the other end of the line from the vacuum switching valve and place it in your mouth.

7. With the engine idling, suck on the end of the vacuum line to duplicate the action of the vacuum switching valve.

8. Suction at the valve air intake should only be felt for an instant. If air cannot be drawn into the valve at all, or if it is continually drawn in, replace the mixture control valve.

If the mixture control valve is functioning properly, and all of the hose and connections are in good working order, the vacuum switching valve is probably at fault.

NOTE: *Because the vacuum switching valve and related components are complex, special equipment is required to test them.*

Auxiliary Enrichment System

An auxiliary enrichment system, which Toyota calls an "Auxiliary Accelerator Pump (AAP) System", is used on 4M engines on cars sold in California starting in 1974, and on all other models, starting in 1975.

When the engine is cold, an auxiliary enrichment circuit in the carburetor is operated to squirt extra fuel into the ac-

celeration circuit in order to prevent the mixture from becoming too lean.

A thermostatic vacuum valve (warm-up sensing valve), which is threaded into the intake manifold, controls the operation of the enrichment circuit. Below a specified temperature the valve is opened and manifold vacuum is allowed to act on a diaphragm in the carburetor. The vacuum pulls the diaphragm down, allowing fuel to flow into a special chamber above it.

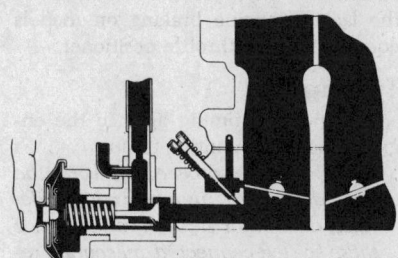

Testing the diaphragm on the auxiliary slow system.

Under sudden acceleration manifold vacuum drops momentarily, allowing the diaphragm to be pushed up by spring tension. This in turn forces the fuel from the chamber through a passage and out the accelerator pump jet.

When the coolant temperature goes above 117°F, the thermostatic vacuum valve closes, preventing the vacuum from reaching the diaphragm, which makes the enrichment system inoperative.

Tests

1. Checked for clogged, pinched, disconnected, or misrouted vacuum lines.

2. With the engine cold (below 75°F), remove the top of the air cleaner, and allow the engine to idle.

3. Disconnect the vacuum line from the carburetor AAP unit. Gasoline should squirt out the accelerator pump jet.

4. If gas doesn't squirt out of the jet, check for vacuum at the AAP vacuum line with the engine idling. If there is no

vacuum and the hoses are in good shape, the thermostatic vacuum valve is defective and must be replaced.

5. If the gas doesn't squirt out and vacuum is present at the vacuum line in step 4, the AAP unit is defective and must be replaced.

6. Repeat step 3 with the engine at normal operating temperature. If gasoline squirts out of the pump jet, the thermostatic vacuum valve is defective and must be replaced.

7. Reconnect all of the vacuum lines and install the top on the air cleaner.

Choke Return System

Because of the chance of seriously damaging the catalytic converter by operating the automobile with the choke out for long periods of time, the 3K-C engine is equipped with an automatic manual choke return system.

Utilizing a holding coil, a holding plate and a return spring, the system generates a magnetic force when the coolant temperature is below 104° F., holding the choke plate open.

However, when the coolant exceeds 104°F., the thermo switch opens, cutting off the current flow and allows the return spring to pull the choke plate open.

Most problems in this system will be electrical. Should the system malfunction, check for continuity in all circuits and replace the part not operating.

Choke Opener System

If a cold engine is driven soon after starting, the automatic choke system will close the choke plate, resulting in high levels of emissions. To combat this sitatuion on engines slated for California or high altitudes, the Toyota 2T-C engine is equipped with a system that forcibly holds the choke plate open.

When the coolant is below 140° F. the thermo wax in the TVSV closes the valve and prohibits any vacuum from acting on the choke diaphragm. This keeps the choke open. Above 140° F. the wax ex-

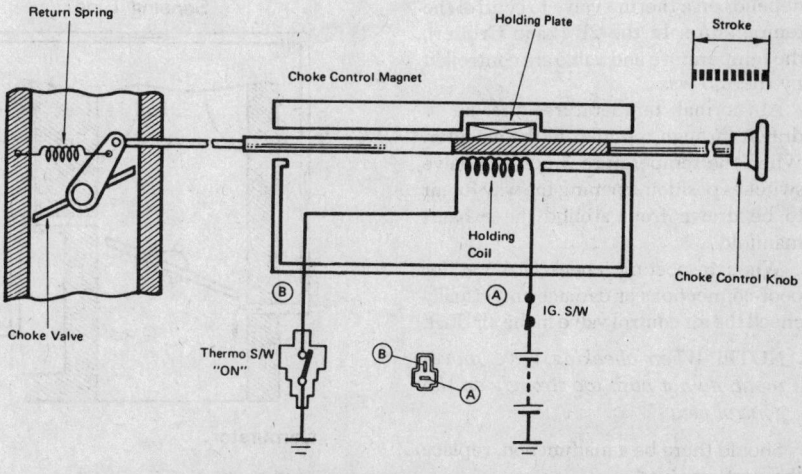

3K-C Choke return system

pands, opening the valve, and allows the choke plate to operate normally. Should the system malfunction, replace the TVSV.

Power Valve Control System-2F

In order to minimize CO while ensuring good driveability, the Land Cruiser 2F engines for California are equipped with a power valve control system on the carburetor.

Dependent on coolant temperature, the power system opens or closes turning the VSV "On." It is also influenced by the amount of pressure on the accelerator pedal. Various combinations of pedal pressure and temperature will result in more or less fuel available for use. Any breakdown in the system requires replacement of the part involved.

High Altitude Compensation System

For all engines to be sold in areas over 4,000 ft. in altitude, a system has been installed to automatically lean out the fuel mixture by supplying additional air. This also results in lower emissions.

Low atmospheric pressure allows the bellows in the system to expand and close a port, allowing more air to enter from different sources.

In the 2T-C and 20R engines, this also results in a timing advance to improve driveability.

All parts in this system must be replaced. The only adjustment available is in the timing.

Hot Air Intake—All Engines

In order to keep the temperature of the air drawn into the carburetor as constant as possible, all engines (1977) are equipped with a Hot Air Intake System (HAI).

In all engines but the 2F, the system depends on a thermo valve to control the temperature. In the 2F (Land Cruiser), the temperature and valve are controlled by thermo wax.

At normal temperatures the air is drawn through the inlet in the air filter. When the temperature drops, the valve switches position, opening the way for air to be drawn from around the exhaust manifold.

When inspecting, check all hoses for poor connections or damage and visually check the air control valve in the air duct.

NOTE: *When checking valve movement, do not push too strongly on the control face.*

Should there be a malfunction, replace the part involved.

Dual-Diaphragm Distributor

NOTE: *1973–75 Land Cruisers have a vacuum retard unit only; no vacuum advance is used.*

Some Toyota models are equipped with a dual-diaphragm distributor unit. This distributor has a retard diaphragm, as well as a diaphragm for advance. Retarding the timing helps to reduce exhaust emissions, as well as making up for the lack of engine braking on models equipped with a throttle positioner.

Testing

1. Connect a timing light to the engine. Check the ignition timing.
NOTE: *Before proceeding with the tests, disconnect any spark control devices, distributor vacuum valves, etc. If these are left connected, inaccurate results may be obtained.*
2. Remove the retard hose from the distributor and plug it. Increase the engine speed. The timing should advance. If it fails to do so, then the vacuum unit is faulty and must be replaced.
3. Check the timing with the engine at normal idle speed. Unplug the retard hose and connect it to the vacuum unit. The timing should instantly be retarded from 4 to 10 degrees. If this does not occur, the retard diaphragm has a leak and the vacuum unit must be replaced.

Spark Delay Valve

Starting in 1975, non-California Corolla models have a spark delay valve (SDV) in the distributor vacuum line. The valve has a small orifice in it, which slows down the vacuum flow to the vacuum advance unit on the distributor. By delaying the vacuum to the distributor, a reduction in HC and CO emissions is possible.

When the coolant temperature is below 95°F–140°F a coolant temperature

operated vacuum control valve is opened, allowing the distributor to receive undelayed, ported vacuum through a separate vacuum line. Above 95°F–140°F this line is blocked, and all ported vacuum must go through the spark delay valve.

Testing

1. Allow the engine cool, so that the coolant temperature is below 95°F.
2. Disconnect the vacuum line which runs from the coolant temperature operated vacuum valve to the vacuum advance unit at the advance unit end. Connect a vacuum gauge to this line.
3. Start the engine. Increase the engine speed; the gauge should indicate a vacuum.
4. Allow the engine to warm-up to normal operating temperature. Increase the engine speed; this time the vacuum gauge should read zero.
5. Replace the coolant temperature operated vacuum valve, if it fails either of these tests. Disconnect the vacuum gauge and reconnect the vacuum lines.
6. Remove the spark delay valve from the vacuum line, noting which side faces the distributor.
7. Connect a hand-operated vacuum pump which has a built-in vacuum gauge to the carburetor side of the spark delay valve.
8. Connect a vacuum gauge to the distributor side of the valve.
9. Operate the hand pump to create a vacuum. The vacuum gauge on the distributor side should show a hesitation before registering.
10. The gauge reading on the pump side should drop slightly, taking several seconds for it balance with the reading on the other gauge.
11. If steps 9 and 10 are negative, replace the spark delay valve.
12. Remove the vacuum gauge from the distributor side of the valve. Cover

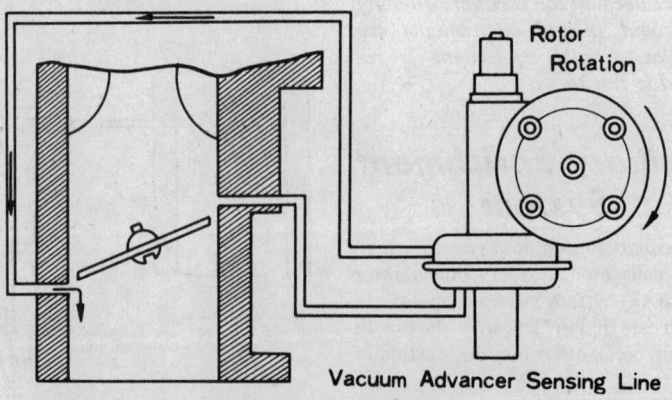

Dual-diaphragm distributor—without the vacuum switching valve.

the distributor side of the valve with your finger and operate the pump to create a vacuum of 15 in. Hg.

13. The reading on the pump gauge should remain steady, if the gauge reading drops, replace the valve.

14. Remove your finger; the reading on the gauge should drop slowly. If the reading goes to zero rapidly, replace the valve.

Engine Modifications System

Toyota also uses an assortment of engine modifications to regulate exhaust emissions. Most of these devices fall into the category of engine vacuum controls. There are three principal components used on the engine modifications system, as well as a number of smaller parts. The three major components are: a speed sensor; a computer (speed marker); and a vacuum switching valve.

The vacuum switching valve and computer circuit operates most of the emission control components. Depending upon year and engine usage, the vacuum switching valve and computer may operate the purge control for the evaporative emission control system; the transmission controlled spark (TCS) or speed controlled spark (SCS); the dual-diaphragm distributor; and the throttle positioner systems.

The functions of the evaporative emission control system, the throttle positioner, and the dual-diaphragm distributor are described in detail in the sections above. However, a word is necessary about the functions of the TCS and SCS systems before discussing the operation of the vacuum switching valve/computer circuit.

The major difference between the transmission controlled spark and speed controlled spark systems is in the manner in which systems operation is determined.

Below a predetermined speed, or any gear other than fourth, the vacuum advance unit on the distributor is rendered inoperative or, on F engines, timing is retarded. By changing the distributor advance curve in this manner, it is possible to reduce emissions of oxides of nitrogen (NO$_X$).

NOTE: *Some engines are equipped with a thermo-sensor so that the TCS or SCS system only operates when the coolant temperature is 140°–212°F.* Aside from determining the conditions outlined above, the vacuum switching valve computer circuit operates other devices in the emission control system.

The computer acts as a speed marker; at certain speeds it sends a signal to the vacuum switching valve which acts as a gate, opening and closing the emission control system vacuum circuits.

The valve used in 1972–73 contains several solenoid and valve assemblies so that different combinations of opened and closed vacuum ports are possible. This allows greater flexibility of operation for the emission control system.

System Checks

Due to the complexity of the components involved, about the only engine modification system checks which can be made without the use of special test equipment, are the following:

1. Examine the vacuum lines to see that they are not clogged, pinched, or loose.

2. Check the electrical connections for tightness and corrosion.

3. Be sure that the vacuum sources for the vacuum switching valve are not plugged.

4. On models equipped with speed controlled spark, a broken speedometer cable could also render the system inoperative.

5. Test the thermo-sensor in the following manner:

    a. Remove the lead from its center terminal.

    b. Touch one test prod of an ohmmeter to the sensor housing.

    c. Connect the other test prod in series with a 10 ohm resistor to the center terminal of the sensor.

    d. If the engine temperature is between about 140°–212°F (or 113°–217°F on 1974 California F engines), the meter should show no conductivity.

    e. If the engine is above or below these temperatures, the meter should show conductivity.

    f. Replace the thermo-sensor if it isn't working properly.

6. If everything else is in good working order, the fault probably lies in the vacuum switching valve or the computer (speed marker). About the only way to test these, without using special equipment, is by substitution of new units.

NOTE: *A faulty vacuum switching valve or computer could cause more than one of the emission control systems to fail. Therefore, if several systems are out, these two units (and the speedometer cable) would be the first things to check.*

Electric Cooling Fan

Operation

New to 3K-C engines for 1977 is an electric cooling fan. It will operate when the coolant reaches a temperature of 203° F. When the temperature drops to 190° F, the fan stops.

Removal

To remove the unit, unplug the multiconnector, remove the fan and loosen the three attaching bolts.

Installation is the reverse of removal.

Inspection

Turning on the ignition switch will cause a "click" in the fan relay. This indicates both switch and relay are operating.

For a low temperature check, unplug the thermo switch. The fan should start. To test for high temperature, allow the engine to idle to fan operating temperature.

Fluid Cooling Fan

To reduce fan noise and improve power and fuel consumption, the 1977 2F engines are equipped with a fluid coupling cooling fan.

Filled with silicon oil, the fan will vary its RPM by means of a bimetal spring opening and closing a valve with the temperature. Opening allows more oil passage and more RPM.

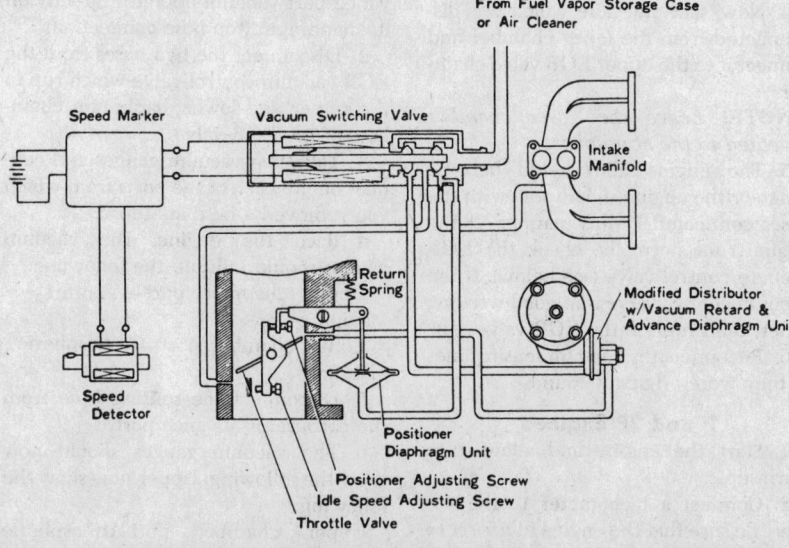

Engine modification system

Exhaust Gas Recirculation (EGR)

Starting with 1974 models, exhaust gas recirculation (EGR) is used on 18R-C, 4M, and F engines on vehicles sold in California; in 1975 EGR usage is extended to all US engines, except the 2T-C engine used in the Corolla.

In all cases, the EGR valve is controlled by the same computer and vacuum switching valve which is used to operate other emission control system components.

On 18R-C and F engines, the EGR valve is operated by vacuum supplied from a port above the throttle blades and fed through the vacuum switching valve.

On 4M engines, vacuum from the carburetor vacuum advance port flows through the vacuum switching valve to an EGR vacuum control valve. The vacuum from the advance port opens the vacuum control valve which then allows venturi vacuum to act on the chamber *above* the EGR valve diaphragm, causing the EGR valve to open. When exhaust gas recirculation is not required, the vacuum switching valve stops sending the advance port vacuum signal to the EGR vacuum control valve which closes, sending intake manifold vacuum to the chamber *below* the EGR valve disphragm. This closes the EGR valve, blocking the flow of exhaust gases to the intake manifold.

On all engines there are several conditions, determined by the computer and vacuum switching valve, which permit exhaust gas recirculation to take place:
1. Vehicle speed
2. Engine coolant temperature
3. EGR valve temperature (18R-C and F)
4. Carburetor flange temperature (18R-C)

On 18R-C and F engines equipped with EGR, the exhaust gases are carried from the exhaust manifold to the EGR valve and from the EGR valve to the carburetor, via external tubing. The F engine has an exhaust gas cooler mounted on the exhaust manifold.

On 4M engines, the EGR value is mounted on the exhaust manifold and exhaust gases from it are carried through external tubing to the intake manifold.

EGR Valve Checks

18R-C Engine and 20R
1. Allow the engine to warm up and remove the top from the air cleaner.
NOTE: *Do not remove the entire air cleaner assembly.*
2. Disconnect the hose (white tape coded), which runs from the vacuum switching valve to the EGR valve, at its EGR valve end.

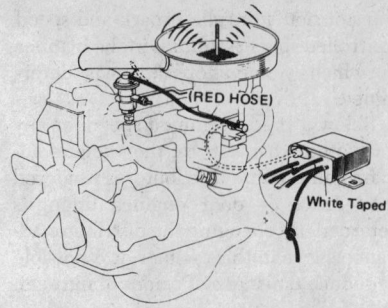

Checking the EGR valve on the 18R-C engine—20R similar

3. Remove the intake manifold hose (red coded) from the vacuum switching valve and connect it to the EGR valve. When the engine is at idle, a "hollow" sound should be heard coming from the air cleaner.
4. Disconnect the hose from the EGR valve; the hollow sound should disappear.
5. If the sound doesn't vary, the EGR valve is defective and must be replaced.
6. Reconnect the vacuum hoses as they were originally found. Install the top on the air cleaner.

4M Engine
1. Warm up the engine and allow it to idle.

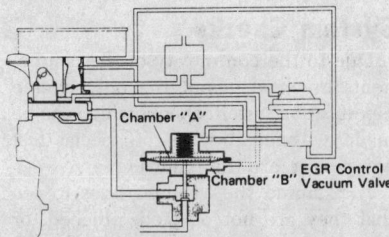

Checking the EGR valve on the 4M engine

2. Disconnect the vacuum sensing line from the *upper* vacuum chamber of the EGR valve.
3. Disconnect the sensing line from the *lower* chamber of the EGR valve.
4. Now, take the hose which was disconnected from the *lower* chamber and connect it to the upper EGR valve chamber.
NOTE: *Leave the lower chamber vented to the atmosphere.*
5. The engine idle should become rough or the engine should stall with the hoses connected in this manner. If the engine runs normally, check the EGR vacuum control valve (see below). If the vacuum control valve is in good working order, then replace the EGR valve.
6. Reconnect the vacuum sensing lines as they were originally found.

F and 2F Engines
1. Start the engine and allow it to warm up.
2. Connect a tachometer to the engine. Be sure that the engine idle is set to specifications (650 rpm).

3. Disconnect the EGR valve vacuum line (yellow coded) from the vacuum switching valve.
4. Connect a vacuum line directly to either manifold vacuum or to an alternate vacuum source (vacuum pump).
5. When the vacuum is applied to the EGR valve, the engine speed should drop about 50 rpm (to 600 rpm). If the engine speed remains the same, replace the EGR valve.
6. Disconnect the tachometer and reconnect the EGR valve vacuum line to the vacuum switching valve.

EGR Valve Thermo-Sensor
18R-C, 2F and F Engines
1. Disconnect the electrical lead which runs to the EGR valve thermo-sensor.
2. Remove the thermo-sensor from the side of the EGR valve.
3. Heat the thermo-sensor in a pan of water to one of the following temperatures:
260°F—18R-C engine
320°F—F engine
4. Connect an ohmmeter, in series with a 10 ohm resistor, between the thermo-sensor terminal and case.
5. With the ohmmeter set on the k-ohm scale, the following readings should be obtained:
2.55 k-ohms—18R-C engine
2.00 k-ohms—F engines
6. Replace the thermo-sensor if the ohmmeter readings vary considerably from those specified.
7. To install the thermo-sensor on the EGR valve, tighten it 15–21 ft lbs.
CAUTION: *Do not tighten the thermo-sensor with an impact wrench.*

EGR Vacuum Control Valve
4M Engine
1. Connect the EGR vacuum control valve hoses up, so that carburetor advance port vacuum operates directly on its diaphragm (top hose connection).
2. Disconnect the two hoses from the EGR vacuum control valve which run to the upper and lower diaphragm chambers of the EGR valve.
3. Take two vacuum gauges and connect one to each of the ports from which you removed a hose in Step 2.
4. Race the engine; the vacuum gauges should indicate the following:
Upper chamber port— Venturi vacuum
Lower chamber port—Atmospheric pressure
5. Disconnect the sensing hose from the carburetor advance port.
6. The vacuum gauges should now show the following: Upper now show the following:
Upper chamber port-Atmospheric pressure

Lower chamber port-Intake manifold vacuum

NOTE: *The atmospheric pressure reading should be nearly equal to that obtained in Step 4.*

7. Replace the EGR vacuum control valve if the readings on the vacuum gauges are incorrect.

8. Hook up the vacuum lines as they were originally found.

System Checks

If, after having completed the above tests, the EGR system still doesn't work right and everything else checks out OK, the fault probably lies in the computer or the vacuum switching valve systems. Proceed with the tests outlined under "System Checks" in the Engine Modification Section above.

NOTE: *A good indication that the fault doesn't lie in the EGR system, but rather in the vacuum supply system, would be if several emission control systems were not working properly.*

2F Thermal Reactor System and Heat Control Valve

Installed in place of the exhaust manifold on the Land Cruiser 2F engine for California, is the Thermal Reactor System. It collects the exhaust gases in a common area in order to keep their temperatures higher for a longer period of time to increase the efficiency of the exhaust gas and secondary air, restricting the release of unburned emissions.

Check the manifold for undue noises, leakage or damage and for movement of the heat control valve. Replace the manifold, if there's a problem.

Catalytic Converters

Starting in 1975 all Toyota passenger cars (except Hi-Lux and Land Cruiser) sold in California and all Mark IIs sold in the U.S., are equipped with catalytic converters. The converters are used to oxidize hydrocarbons (HC) and carbon monoxide (CO). The converters are necessary because of the stricter emission level standards for the 1975 models.

The catalysts are made of noble metals (platinum and palladium) which are bonded to individual pellets. These catalysts cause the HC and CO to break down into water and carbon dioxide (CO_2) without taking part in the reaction; hence, a catalyst life of 50,000 miles may be expected under normal conditions.

An air pump is used to supply air to the exhaust system to aid in the reaction. A thermosensor, inserted into the converter, shuts off the air supply if the catalyst temperature becomes excessive.

The same sensor circuit also causes a dash warning light labled "EXH TEMP" to come on when the catalyst temperature gets too high.

NOTE: *It is normal for the light to come on temporarily if the car is being driven downhill for long periods of time (such as descending a mountain).* The light will come on and stay on if the air injection system is malfunctioning or if the engine is misfiring.

Precautions

1. Use only unleaded fuel.

2. Avoid prolonged idling; the engine should run no longer than 20 minutes at curb idle, nor longer than 10 minutes at fast idle.

3. Reduce the fast idle speed, by quickly depressing and releasing the accelerator pedal, as soon as the coolant temperature reaches 120°F.

4. Do not disconnect any spark plug leads while the engine is running.

5. Make engine compression checks as quickly as possible.

6. Do not dispose of the catalyst in a place where anything coated with grease, gas, or oil is present; spontaneous combustion could result.

Catalyst Testing

At the present time there is no known way to reliably test catalytic converter operation in the field. The only reliable test is a 12 hour and 40 minute "soak test" (CVS) which must be done in a laboratory.

An infrared HC/CO tester is not sensitive enough to measure the higher tailpipe emissions from a partially-failed converter. Thus, a bad converter may allow enough HC and CO emissions to escape, so that the car is not in compliance with Federal (or state) standards, but still will not cause the needle on the HC/CO tester to move off zero.

A *completely* failed converter should cause the tester to show a slight reading. As a result, it should be possible to spot one of these in the shop.

As long as the driver of the car avoids severe overheating or use of leaded fuels and the car has less than 50,000 miles on it, it is safe to assume that the converter is working.

Warning Light Checks

NOTE: *The warning light comes on while the engine is being cranked, to test its operation, just like any of the other warning lights.*

1. If the warning light comes on and stays on, check the components of the air injection system, as outlined above. If these are not defective, check the ignition system for faulty leads, plugs, points, or control box.

2. If no problems can be found in step 1, check the wiring for the light for shorts or opened circuits.

3. If nothing else can be found wrong in steps 1 and 2 above, check the operation of the emission control system computer, either by substitution of a new unit, or by taking it to a service facility which has Toyota's special emission control system checker.

Converter Removal and Installation

CAUTION: *Do not perform the operation on a hot (or even warm) engine. Catalyst temperatures may go as high as 1700°F, so that any contact with the catalyst could cause severe burns.*

1. Disconnect the lead from the converter thermosensor.

2. Remove the wiring shield.

3. Unfasten the pipe clamp securing bolts at either end of the converter. Remove the clamps.

4. Push the tailpipe rearward and remove the converter, complete with thermosensor.

5. Carry the converter with the thermosensor upward to prevent the catalyst from falling out.

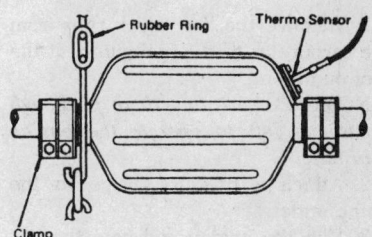

Catalytic converter removal

6. Unfasten the screws and withdraw the thermosensor and gasket.

Installation is performed in the following order:

1. Place a new gasket on the thermosensor. Push the thermosensor into the converter and secure it with its two bolts. Be careful not to drop the thermosensor.

NOTE: *Service replacement converters are provided with a plastic thermosensor guide. Slide the sensor into the guide to install it. Do not remove the guide.*

2. Install new gaskets on the converter mounting flanges.

3. Secure the converter with its mounting clamps.

4. If the converter is attached to the body with rubber O-rings, install the O-rings over the body and converter mounting hooks.

5. Install the wire protector and connect the lead to the thermosensor.

FUEL SYSTEM

Fuel Filter

Replacement

All Engines employ a disposable, inline filter, when dirty, or at recommended intervals, remove from line and replace.

Mechanical Fuel Pump

All pre-1975 Toyota vehicles use a mechanically operated fuel pump of diaphragm construction. A separate fuel filter is incorporated into the fuel line.

Removal and Installation

1. Disconnect both of the fuel lines from the pump.
2. Unfasten the bolts which attach the fuel pump to the cylinder block.
3. Withdraw the pump assembly.

Installation is performed in the reverse order of removal. Always use a new gasket when installing the fuel pump. After the pump is installed check its discharge rate. See "Testing" below.

NOTE: *Failure to use a gasket of the correct thickness could result in an improper pump discharge rate.*

Testing

1. Remove the line which runs from the carburetor to the fuel pump, at the fuel pump end.

NOTE: *Be sure that there is enough gasoline left to operate the engine briefly.*

2. Attach a pressure gauge to the pump outlet.
3. Run the engine and note the discharge pressure.
4. Check the pump discharge pressure against the specification given at the beginning of the section.
5. If the pump output is not up to specifications, replace the diaphragm spring or the entire pump assembly.
6. Reconnect the carburetor fuel line.

Electric Fuel Pump

Starting in 1975, the following Toyota models use an electric fuel pump:

Corolla (California only)
Corona
Celica
Mark II/6
Hi-Lux

The fuel pump is located inside the gas tank. It is serviced as unit; if it breaks, replace it.

Removal and Installation

1. Disconnect the negative (−) cable from the battery.
2.
   a. On sedans and hardtops, remove the trim panel from inside the trunk.
   b. On station wagons, raise the rear of the vehicle, in order to gain access to the pump.
   c. On Hi-Lux pick-ups, remove the fuel tank.
3. Remove the screws which secure the pump access plate to the tank. With-

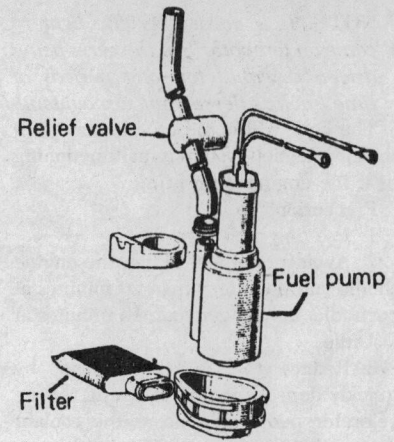

Electric fuel pump assembly

draw the plate, gasket, and pump assembly.

4. Disconnect the leads and hoses from the pump.

Installation is performed in the reverse order of removal. Use a new gasket on the pump access plate.

Testing

CAUTION: *Do not operate the fuel pump unless it is immersed in gasoline and connected to its resistor.*

1. Disconnect the lead from the oil pressure warning light sender.
2. Unfasten the line from the outlet side of the fuel filter.
3. Connect a pressure gauge to the filter outlet with a length of rubber hose.
4. Turn the ignition switch to the "ON" position, but do not start the engine.
5. Check the pressure gauge reading against the figure given in the "Tune-Up Specifications" chart above.
6. Check for a clogged filter or pinched lines if the pressure is not up to specification.
7. If there is nothing wrong with the filter or lines, replace the fuel pump.
8. Turn the ignition off and reconnect the fuel line to the filter. Connect the lead to the oil pressure sender also.

Fuel Return Cut Valve

The fuel return cut valve controls the amount of fuel returned to the gas tank according to engine load. This prevents percolation when the engine is hot and the load, light.

Inspection

Attach a long tube to the return pipe of the valve. Put a container under it to catch the fuel. With the engine at idle, fuel should go into the container.

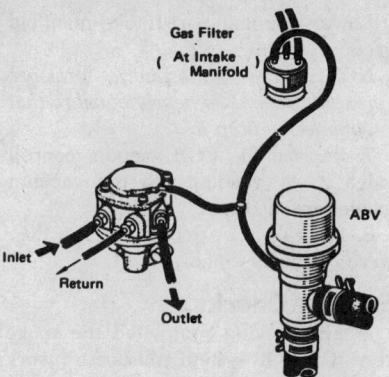

Fuel return cut valve—1977 2T-C engine

Pinch-off the vacuum line. If valve is operating correctly, the fuel flow should stop.

Fuel Cut-Off Valve

In case of an accident, a fuel cut-off valve was added to all systems in 1976. The valve, installed between the fuel filter and the carburetor, consists of two check balls that clog the fuel line if the automobile is in other than the normal wheels down position.

Combined with a check valve on the carburetor and specially designed fuel lines, the fuel cut-off system almost eliminates the chance of spilled fuel during an accident.

Carburetors

The carburetors used on Toyota models are conventional two-barrel, downdraft types similar to domestic carburetors.

The main circuits are: *primary,* for normal operational requirements; *secondary,* to supply high-speed fuel needs; *float,* to supply fuel to the primary and secondary circuits; *accelerator,* to supply fuel for quick and safe acceleration; *choke,* for reliable starting in cold weather; and *power valve,* for fuel economy. Although slight differences in appearance may be noted, these carburetors are basically alike. Of course, different jets and settings are demanded by the different engines to which they are fitted.

Removal and Installation

1. Remove the air cleaner housing, disconnect all air hoses from the air cleaner base, and disconnect the battery ground cable.

NOTE: *On 20R engines, drain the coolant to prevent it from running into the intake manifold when the carburetor is removed.*

2. Disconnect the fuel line, choke pipe, and distributor vacuum line. On 20R engines disconnect the choke coolant hose.
3. Remove the accelerator linkage. (With an automatic transmission, also

remove the throttle rod to the transmission.)

NOTE: *On Land Cruisers disconnect the magnetic valve wire from the coil terminal, if equipped.*

4. Remove the four nuts that secure the carburetor to the manifold and lift off the carburetor and gasket.

5. Cover the open manifold with a clean rag to prevent small objects from dropping into the engine.

Installation is performed in the reverse order of removal. After the engine is warmed up, check for fuel leaks and float level settings.

Overhaul

Efficient carburetion depends greatly on careful cleaning and inspection during overhaul since dirt, gum, water, or varnish in or on the carburetor parts are often responsible for poor performance.

Overhaul your carburetor in a clean, dust-free area. Carefully disassemble the carburetor, referring often to the exploded views. Keep all similar and looka-like parts segregated during disassembly and cleaning to avoid accidental interchange during assembly. Make a note of all jet sizes.

When the carburetor is disassembled, wash all parts (except diaphragms, electric choke units, pump plunger, and any other plastic, leather, fiber, or rubber parts) in clean carburetor solvent. Do not leave parts in the solvent any longer than is necessary to sufficiently loosen the deposits. Excessive cleaning may remove the special finish from the float bowl and choke valve bodies, leaving these parts unfit for service. Rinse all parts in clean solvent and blow them dry with compressed air or allow them to air dry. Wipe clean all cork, plastic, leather, and fiber parts with a clean, lint-free cloth.

Blow out all passages and jets with compressed air and be sure that there are no restrictions or blockages. Never use wire or similar tools to clean jets, fuel passages, or air bleeds. Clean all jets and valves separately to avoid accidental interchange.

Check all parts for wear or damage. If wear or damage is found, replace the defective parts. Especially check the following:

1. Check the float needle and seat for wear. If wear is found, replace the complete assembly.

2. Check the float hinge pin for wear and the float(s) for dents or distortion. Replace the float if fuel has leaked into it.

3. Check the throttle and choke shaft bores for wear or an out-of-round condition. Damage or wear to the throttle arm, shaft, or shaft bore will often require replacement of the throttle body. These parts require a close tolerance of fit; wear may allow air leakage, which could affect starting and idling.

NOTE: *Throttle shafts and bushings are not included in overhaul kits. They can be purchased separately.*

4. Inspect the idle mixture adjusting needles for burrs or grooves. Any such condition requires replacement of the needle, since you will not be able to obtain a satisfactory idle.

5. Test the accelerator pump check valves. They should pass air one way but not the other. Test for proper seating by blowing and sucking on the valve. Replace the valve if necessary. If the valve is satisfactory, wash the valve again to remove breath moisture.

6. Check the bowl cover for warped surfaces with a straightedge.

7. Closely inspect the valves and seats for wear and damage, replacing as necessary.

8. After the carburetor is assembled, check the choke valve for freedom of operation.

Carburetor overhaul kits are recommended for each overhaul. These kits contain all gaskets and new parts to replace those that deteriorate most rapidly. Failure to replace all parts supplied with the kit (especially gaskets) can result in poor performance later.

After cleaning and checking all components, reassemble the carburetor, using new parts and referring to the exploded view. When reassembling, make sure that all screws and jets are tight in their

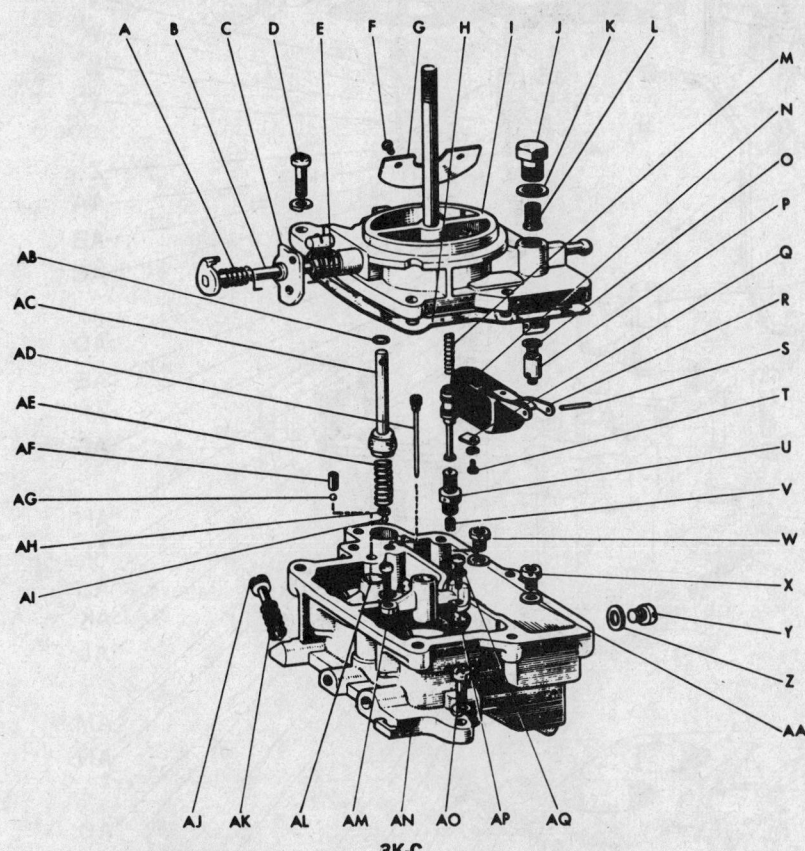

3K-C

(a)—Choke valve relief spring
(b)—Choke shaft
(c)—Choke lever
(d)—Screw
(e)—Choke return spring
(f)—Screw
(g)—Choke valve
(h)—Air horn gasket
(i)—Air horn
(j)—Main passage plug
(k)—Inlet strainer gasket
(l)—Strainer
(m)—Power piston spring
(n)—Power piston
(o)—Needle valve seat gasket
(p)—Needle valve
(q)—Power piston stopper
(r)—Float
(s)—Float lever pin
(t)—Screw
(u)—Power valve
(v)—Power jet

(w)—Primary main jet
(x)—Secondary main jet
(y)—Drain plug
(z)—Gasket
(aa)—Main jet gasket
(ab)—O-ring
(ac)—Pump plunger
(ad)—Slow jet
(ae)—Pump damping spring
(af)—Pump discharge weight
(ag)—Check ball
(ah)—Check ball retainer
(ai)—Check ball
(aj)—Throttle adjusting screw
(ak)—Spring
(al)—Primary small venturi
(am)—Secondary small venturi
(an)—Main body
(ao)—Screw
(ap)—Venturi No. 1 gasket
(aq)—Screw

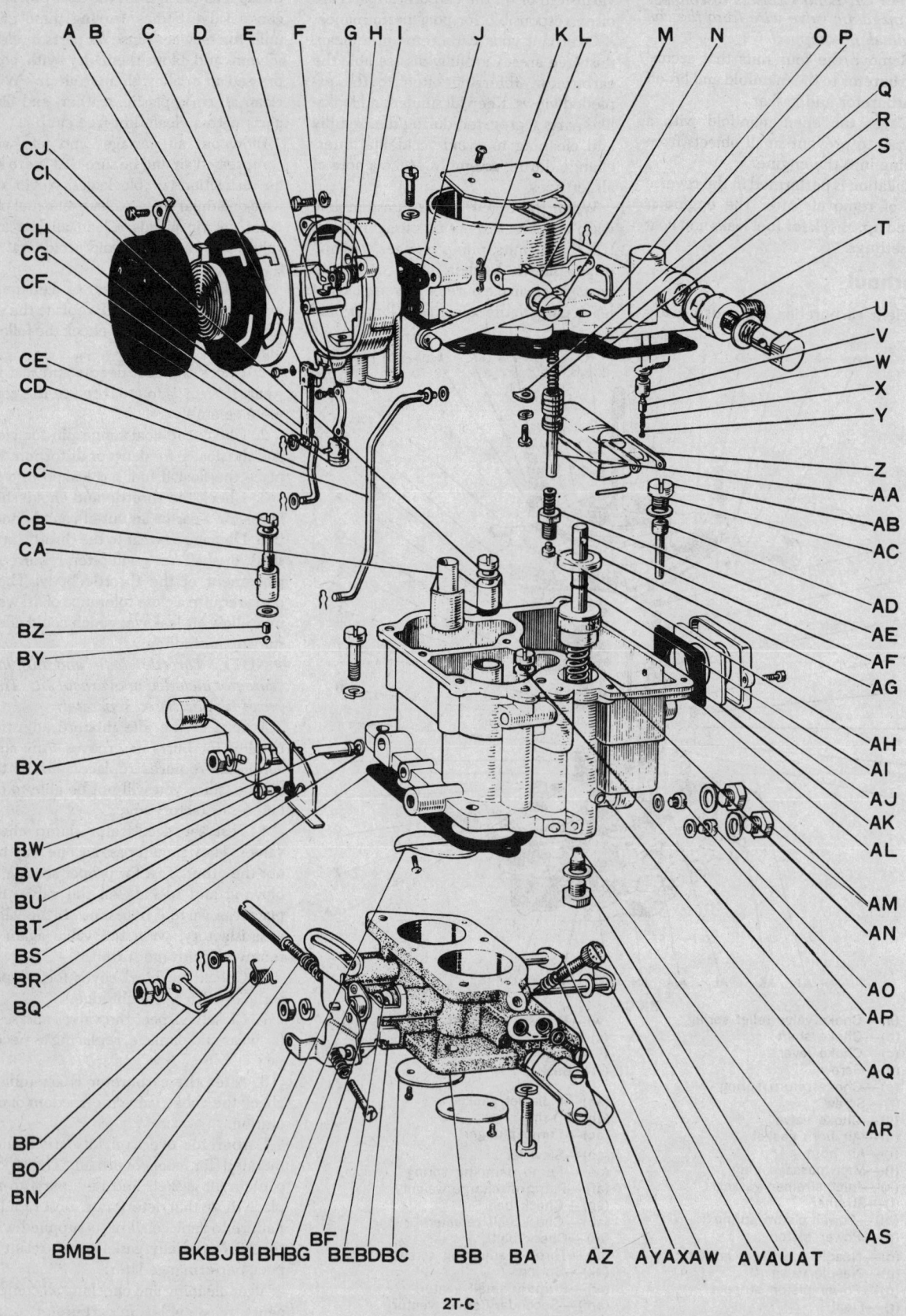

2T-C

(a)—Thermostat bimetal
(b)—Coil housing gasket
(c)—Fast idle cam follower
(d)—Coil housing plate
(e)—Piston connector
(f)—Choke shaft
(g)—Fast idle cam
(h)—Fast idle cam spring
(i)—Thermostat case
(k—Pump arm spring
(j)—Thermostat case gasket
(l)—Choke valve
(m)—Pump lever
(n)—Pump arm securing screw
(o)—Pump connecting link
(p)—Air horn
(q)—Power piston stopper
(r)—Power piston spring
(s)—Air horn gasket
(t)—Union nipple
(u)—Plug with strainer
(v)—Needle valve seat

(w)—Needle valve
(x)—Needle valve spring
(y)—Needle valve push pin
(z)—Float
(aa)—Power piston
(ab)—Slow circuit plug
(ac)—Float lever pin
(ad)—Slow jet
(ae)—Power valve
(af)—Pump plunger
(ag)—Plunger guide
(ah)—Power jet
(ai)—O-ring
(aj)—Level gauge clamp
(ak)—Level gauge glass
(al)—Gasket
(am)—Main passage plug
(an)—Pump damping spring
(ao)—Primary main jet
(ap)—Secondary main jet
(aq)—Primary air bleeder
(ar)—Body

(as)—Discharge check valve
(at)—Main passage plug
(au)—Idle adjusting screw
(av)—Primary throttle shaft
(aw)—Secondary throttle shaft
(ax)—Spring
(ay)—Main passage plug
(az)—Thermostatic valve
(ba)—Primary throttle valve
(bb)—Flange
(bc)—Secondary throttle valve
(bd)—Fast idle adjusting lever
(be)—Retaining ring
(bf)—Fast idle adjusting bolt
(bg)—Fast idle lever
(bh)—Spring
(bi)—Throttle lever collar
(bj)—High speed valve
(bk)—Primary throttle arm
(bl)—Spring
(bm)—Thoottle adjusting screw
(bn)—Secondary throttle back spring

(bo)—Throttle shaft link
(bp)—Secondary throttle lever
(bq)—Gasket
(br)—High speed valve stop lever
(bs)—Retaining ring
(bt)—High speed valve stop lever spring
(bu)—Stop lever securing screw
(bv)—High speed valve shaft
(bw)—High speed valve stopper
(bx)—High speed valve weight
(by)—Check ball
(bz)—Weight
(ca)—Pump jet
(cb)—Secondary small venturi
(cc)—Pump jet screw
(cd)—Pump connecting rod
(ce)—Connecting rod
(cf)—Vacuum piston
(cg)—Piston pin
(ch)—Sliding rod
(ci)—Primary main air bleeder
(cj)—Coil housing

2T-C

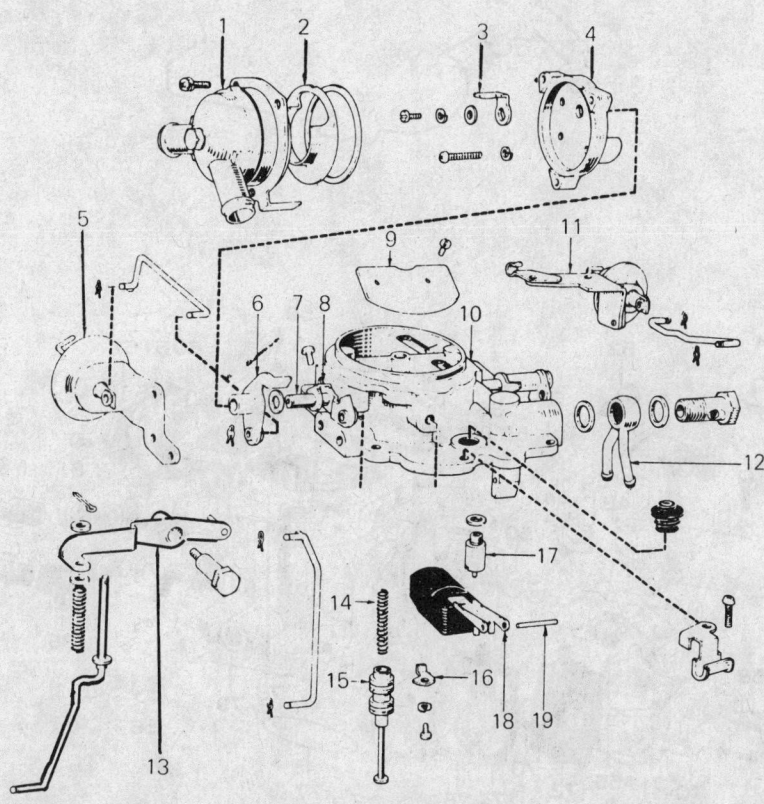

Air horn assembly—20R

1. Choke coil water housing
2. Choke housing plate
3. Choke lever
4. Choke housing body
5. Choke breaker
6. Relief lever

7. Choke shaft
8. Connecting lever
9. Choke valve
10. Air horn
11. Choke opener
12. Union

13. Pump arm
14. Spring
15. Power piston
16. Piston retainer
17. Needle valve set
18. Float
19. Float pivot pin

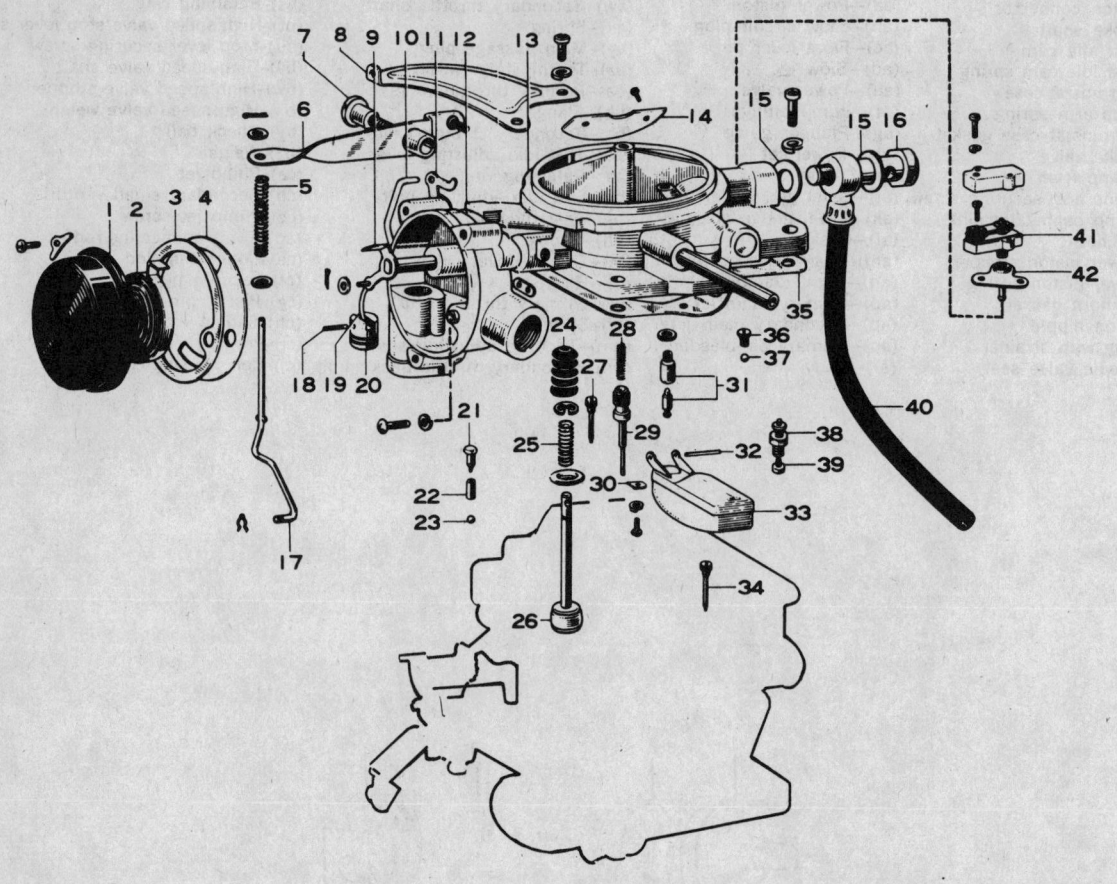

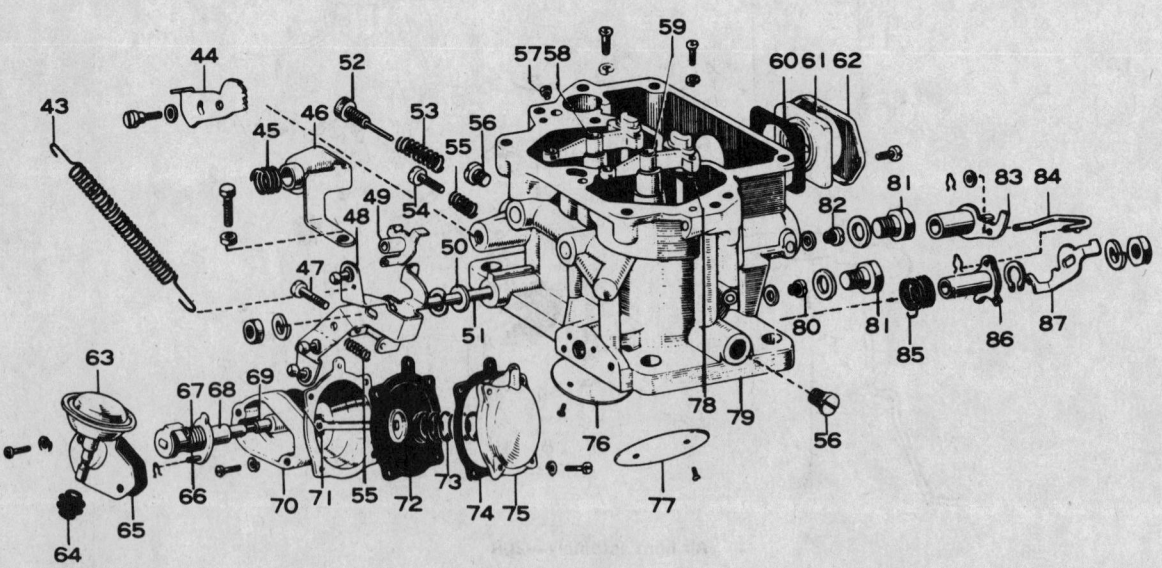

2M and 4M

1. Coil housing
2. Thermostatic bimetal coil
3. Coil housing gasket
4. Coil housing plate
5. Pump damping spring
6. Pump lever
7. Pump lever set screw
8. Back spring support
9. Choke shaft
10. Choke lever link
11. Fast idle cam lever
12. Thermostat case
13. Air horn
14. Choke valve
15. Union fitting gasket
16. Union fitting
17. Pump connecting link
18. Piston pin
19. Piston connector
20. Vacuum piston
21. Discharge weight stop
22. Pump discharge weight
23. Steel ball
24. Boot
25. Plunger return spring
26. Pump plunger
27. Primary slow jet
28. Power piston spring
29. Power piston

30. Power piston stopper
31. Needle valve
32. Float lever pin
33. Float
34. Secondary slow jet
35. Air horn gasket
36. Nut plug
37. Steel ball
38. Power valve
39. Power jet
40. Fuel hose
41. Thermostatic valve
42. Bracket
43. Primary throttle return spring
44. Fast idle cam
45. Lever return spring
46. Dash pot lever
47. Fast idle adjusting screw
48. Primary throttle lever
49. Fast idle adjusting lever
50. Throttle valve adjusting shim
51. Primary throttle shaft
52. Idle mixture adjusting screw
53. Adjusting screw spring
54. Idle speed adjusting screw
55. Adjusting screw spring
56. Nut plug
57. Pump jet plug
58. Primary small venturi

59. Secondary small venturi
60. Level gauge gasket
61. Level gauge glass
62. Level gauge clamp
63. Dash pot
64. Boot
65. Diaphragm housing cap gasket
66. Diaphragm relief lever
67. Diaphragm relief spring
68. Collar
69. Secondary throttle shaft
70. Diaphragm housing
71. Diaphragm housing gasket
72. Diaphragm rod
73. Diaphragm spring
74. Diaphragm cap gasket
75. Diaphragm housing cap
76. Primary throttle valve
77. Secondary throttle valve
78. Venturi gasket
79. Carburetor body
80. Secondary main jet
81. Main passage plug
82. Primary main jet
83. First kick lever
84. Throttle shaft link
85. Secondary throttle return spring
86. Second kick lever
87. Second kick arm

2M and 4M

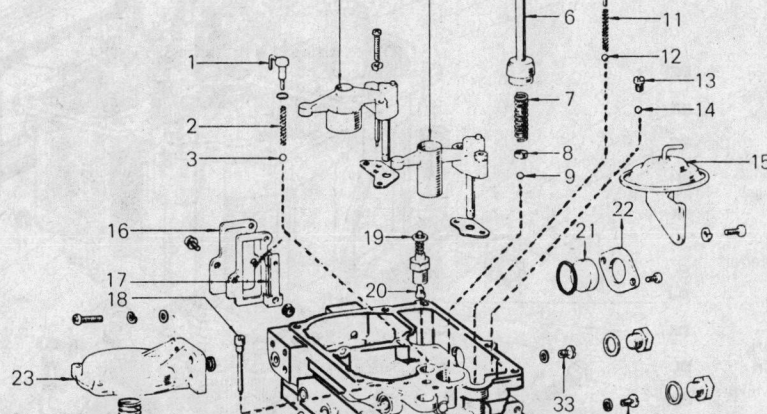

Main body assembly—20R

1. Pump jet
2. Spring
3. Outlet check ball
4. Secondary venturi
5. Primary venturi
6. Pump plunger
7. Spring
8. Ball retainer
9. Inlet check ball
10. Plug
11. Spring
12. AAP outlet check ball

13. Plug
14. AAP inlet check ball
15. Throttle positioner
16. Thermostatic valve cover
17. Thermostatic valve
18. Primary slow jet
19. Power valve
20. Power jet
21. Sight glass
22. Glass retainer
23. Diaphragm housing cap

24. Spring
25. Diaphragm
26. Housing
27. Fast idle cam
28. Solenoid valve
29. Carburetor body
30. Diaphragm
31. Spring
32. AAP housing
33. Secondary main jet
34. Primary main jet

Toyota

(a)—Choke valve relief spring
(b)—Choke lever
(c)—Choke valve spring
(d)—Choke lever adapter
(e)—Adapter gasket
(f)—Choke wire support
(g)—Choke valve
(h)—Plug
(i)—Economizer jet
(j)—Air bleeder
(k)—Air horn
(l)—Main passage plug
(m)—Plug gasket
(n)—Strainer
(o)—Power piston stopper
(p)—Power piston spring
(q)—Fitting
(r)—Needle valve seat gasket
(s)—Air horn gasket
(t)—Float pin
(u)—Needle valve seat
(v)—Power piston
(w)—Needle valve
(x)—Needle valve spring
(y)—Needle valve push pin
(z)—Float
(aa)—Lifter rod
(ab)—Slow jet
(ac)—Primary main jet
(ad)—Gasket
(ae)—Pump jet screw
(af)—Pump jet gasket
(ag)—Pump jet
(ah)—Spare jet
(ai)—Power valve
(aj)—Power jet
(ak)—Pump discharge weight
(al)—Level gauge retainer
(am)—Level gauge glass
(an)—Level gauge gasket
(ao)—Primary small venturi
(ap)—Main body
(aq)—Discharge check valve
(ar)—Plug gasket
(as)—Pump connecting link
(at)—Choke shaft
(au)—Plunger washer
(av)—Fast idle connector
(aw)—Secondary main jet
(ax)—Gasket
(ay)—Secondary main air bleeder
(az)—Gasket
(ba)—Pump damping spring
(bb)—Gasket
(bc)—Secondary small venturi
(bd)—Secondary main venturi
(be)—High speed valve stop lever
(bf)—Fast idle cam
(bg)—High speed valve stop
(bh)—High speed shaft
(bi)—High speed valve shaft lever
(bj)—Stop lever attaching screw
(bk)—High speed valve stop lever spring
(bl)—Fast idle attaching screw
(bm)—Throttle adjusting screw
(bn)—Throttle adjusting screw spring
(bo)—Secondary throttle back spring
(bp)—Secondary throttle lever
(bq)—Throttle shaft link
(br)—Fast idle adjusting screw
(bs)—Fast idle adjusting screw spring
(bt)—Primary throttle shaft arm
(bu)—Throttle lever collar
(bv)—Throttle lever
(bw)—Secondary throttle valve
(bx)—High speed valve
(by)—Primary throttle valve
(bz)—Flange
(ca)—Body to flange gasket
(cb)—Secondary throttle valve shaft
(cc)—Gasket
(cd)—Idle port plug
(ce)—Idle adjusting screw spring
(cf)—Primary throttle valve shaft
(cg)—Idle adjusting screw
(ch)—Plug

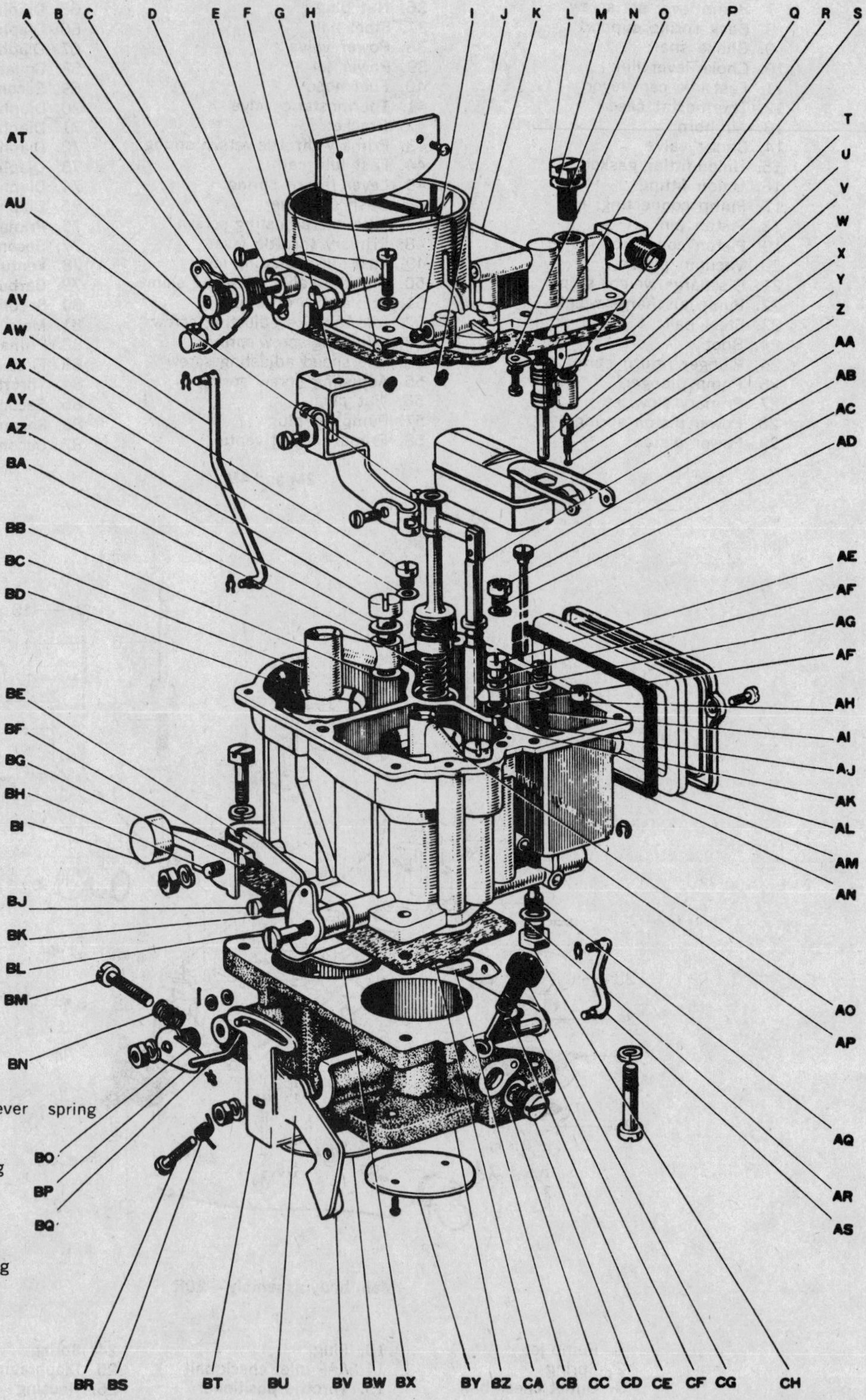

F engine—2-bbl

seats, but do not overtighten, as the tips will be distorted. Tighten all screws gradually, in rotation. Do not tighten needle valves into their seats; uneven jetting will result. Always use new gaskets. Be sure to adjust the float level when reassembling.

Float Level Adjustment

Float level adjustments are unnecessary on models equipped with a carburetor sight glass, if the fuel level falls within the lines or aligns with the dot when the engine is running.

There are two float level adjustments which may be made on Toyota carburetors. One is with the air horn inverted, so that the float is in a fully *raised* position; the other is with the air horn in an upright position, so that the float falls to the bottom of its travel.

The float level is either measured with a special carburetor float level gauge, which comes with a rebuilding kit, or with a standard wire gauge. For the proper type of gauge, as well as the points to be measured, see the chart at the end of this section.

To adjust the float level, bend the upper tab (1) or the lower tab (2).

NOTE: *Gap specifications are also given so that a float level gauge may be fabricated. Several different gauges are illustrated.*

Measuring the Float Level

3K-C lowered

3K-C raised

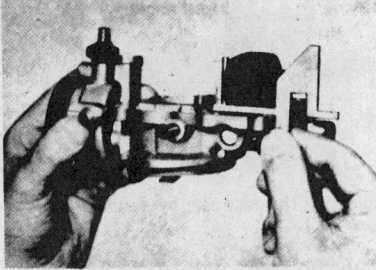

2T-C and 18R-C lowered

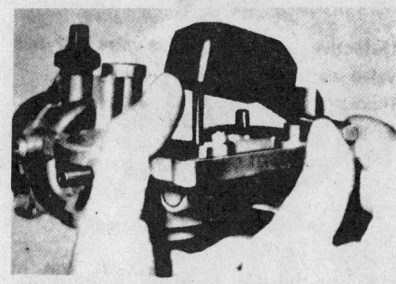

2T-C and 18R-C raised

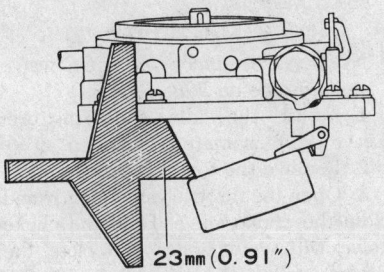

2M and 4M lowered

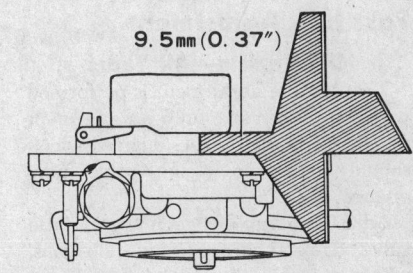

2M and 4M raised

FLOAT LEVEL ADJUSTMENTS

Engine	Gauge Type	FLOAT RAISED Measure distance between:	Gap (in.)	Gauge Type	FLOAT LOWERED Measure distance between:	Gap (in.)
3K-C	Special	Float end and air horn	0.260	Special	Lowest point of float and upper side of gauge	1.89③
2T-C	Block	Float tip and air horn	0.200	Wire	Needle valve bushing pin and float lip	0.047
18R-C	Special	Float and air horn	0.138④	Wire	Needle valve bushing pin and float tab	0.039
20R	Special	Float end and air horn	0.197	Special	Needle valve bushing pin and float tab	0.039
2M and 4M	Special	Float end and air horn	0.370①	Special	Float end and air horn	0.910②
F	Special	Float end and air horn gasket surface	0.230	Special	Float end and air horn gasket surface	0.800
2F	Special	Float end and air horn	0.161⑤	Special	Float end and air horn	0.039⑥

① 1975-76—0.394
② 1975-76—0.039
③ 1976-77—float lip gap 0.035

④ 1976-77—0.236
⑤ 1976-77—0.295
⑥ 1976-77—0.043

F engine lowered

5.8mm (0.23")

F engine raised

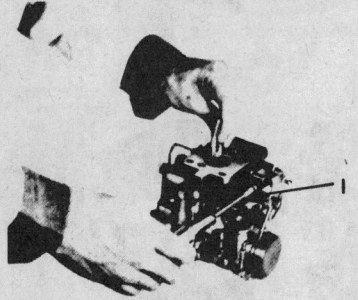

Screw-type fast idle adjustment

Adjusting the fast idle by bending the linkage.

Adjust the float level by bending the tabs on the float levers, either upper or lower, as required.

Fast Idle Adjustment

Off Vehicle—All Years

The fast idle adjustment is performed with the choke valve fully *closed,* except on the 2T-C and 18R-C engines which should have the choke valve fully *opened.*

Adjust the gap between the throttle valve edge and bore to the specifications, where given, in the chart below. Use a wire gauge to determine the gap.

The chart below also gives the proper primary throttle valve opening angle, where necessary, and the proper means of fast idle adjustment.

NOTE: *The throttle valve opening angle is measured with a gauge supplied*

in the carburetor rebuilding kit. It is also possible to make one out of cardboard by using a protractor to obtain the correct angle.

On Vehicle—1975–77

NOTE: *Disconnect the EGR valve vacuum line on 20R engines.*

1. Adjust the idle speed/mixture. Leave the tachometer connected.
2. Remove the top of the air cleaner.
3. Open the throttle valve slightly and close the choke valve. Hold the choke valve with your finger and close the throttle valve. The choke valve is now fully closed.
4. Without depressing the accelerator pedal, start the engine.
5. Check the engine fast idle speed against the chart below.
6. If the reading on the tachometer is not within specifications, adjust the fast

idle speed by turning the fast idle screw.

7. Disconnect the tachometer, install the air cleaner cover, and connect the EGR valve vacuum line if it was disconnected.

Fast Idle Speed—1975–77

2T-C (US)—3,000 rpm (1977–3,400)
2T-C (Calif.)—2,700 rpm (1977–3,000)
20R—2,400 rpm
4M (US)—2,600 rpm
4M (Calif.)—2,400 rpm
2F—1,800 rpm

Automatic Choke Adjustment

NOTE: *The automatic choke should be adjusted with the carburetor installed and the engine running. On 20R engines do not loosen the center bolt; the coolant will leak out.*

1. Check to see that the choke valve will close from fully opened when the coil housing is turned counterclockwise (2M and 4M engines—clockwise).
2. Align the mark on the coil housing with the center line on the thermostat case. In this position, the choke valve should be fully closed when the ambient temperature is 77°F.

Setting Marks

Align the setting marks on the choke housing.

3. If necessary, adjust the mixture by turning the coil housing. If the mixture is too *rich,* rotate the housing *clockwise;* if too *lean,* rotate the housing *counterclockwise.* On models equipped with the 2M and 4M engines, rotate the housing in exactly the reverse direction of the above.

NOTE: *Each graduation on the thermostat case is equivalent to 9°F.*

Choke Break Adjustment

20R Engine

1. Push the rod which comes out of the upper (choke breaker) diaphragm so that the choke valve opens.
2. Measure the choke valve opening angle. It should be 40° (38° 1976–77).
3. Adjust the angle, if necessary, by bending the relief lever link.

Initial Idle Mixture Screw Adjustment

When assembling the carburetor, turn the idle mixture screw the number of

FAST IDLE ADJUSTMENT

Engine	Throttle Valve to bore clearance (in.)	Primary throttle angle (deg)	To adjust fast idle:
3K-C	0.040①②	—	Bend the fast idle lever
2T-C	0.032③	—	Turn the fast idle adjusting screw
18R-C	0.041	13—from closed	Turn the fast idle adjusting screw
20R	0.047	—	Turn the fast idle screw
2M	—	24—from closed	Turn the fast idle adjusting screw
4M	—	16—from closed	Turn the fast idle adjusting screw
F	—	30—from closed	Bend the fast idle lever
2F	0.051	30—from closed	Bend the fast idle lever

— Not available
① 0.051 in 1976

② 0.0562 in 1977
③ 1976-77 0.043

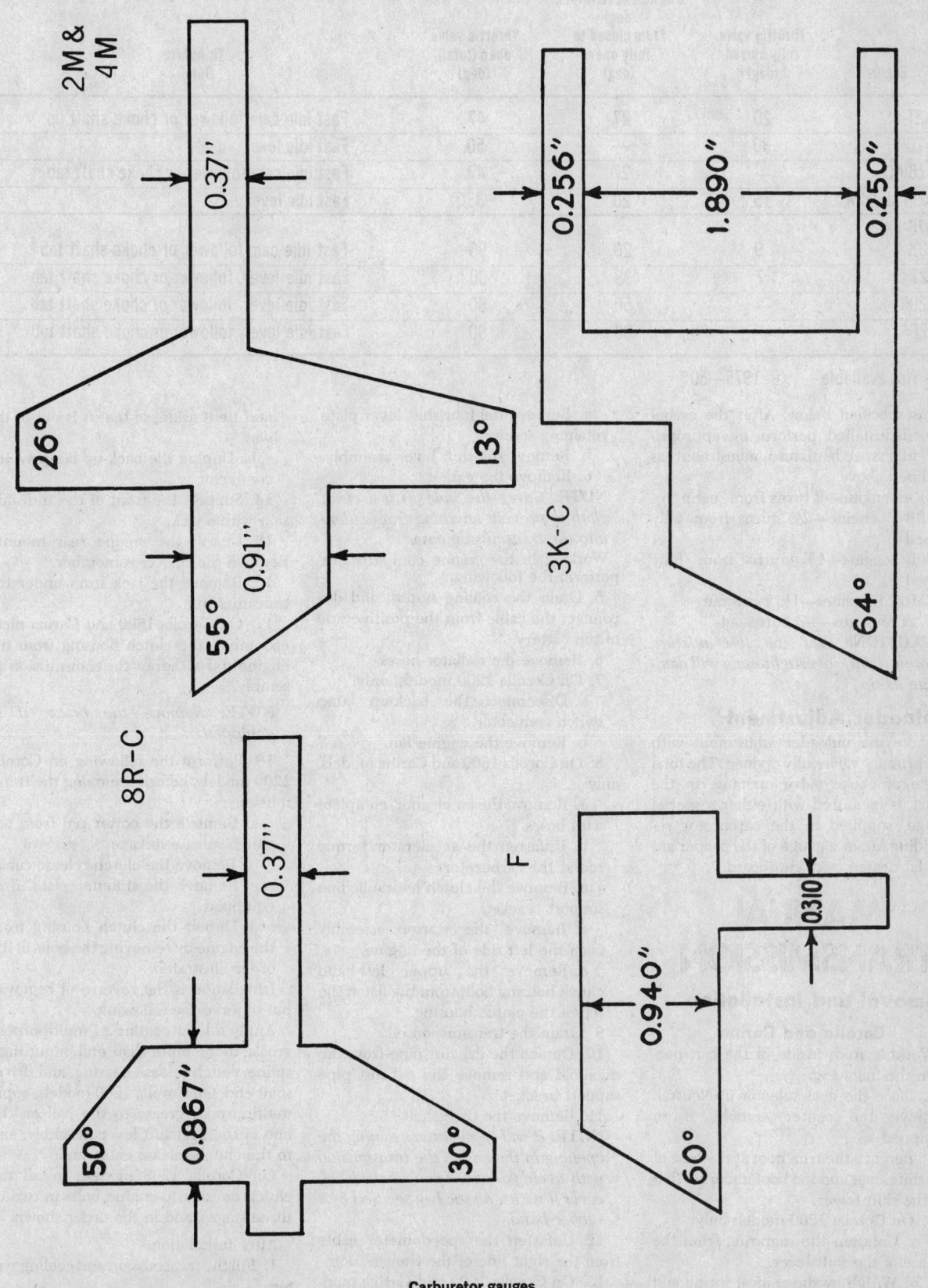

Carburetor gauges

CHOKE UNLOADER ADJUSTMENT

Engine	Throttle valve fully closed (deg)	CHOKE VALVE ANGLE (deg) From closed to fully open (deg)	Throttle valve open (total) (deg)	To Adjust Bend:
2T-C	20	27	47	Fast idle cam follower or choke shaft lip
20R	30	—	50	Fast idle lever
18R-C	—	27	47	Fast idle cam follower or choke shaft tab
2M and 4M	15	20	35①	Fast idle lever
1976-77				
3K-C	9	20	90	Fast idle cam follower or choke shaft tab
2T-C	7	38	90	Fast idle lever, follower or choke shaft tab
20R	—	50	90	Fast idle lever, follower or choke shaft tab
2F	—	38	90	Fast idle lever, follower or choke shaft tab

— Not available   ① 1975—50°

turns specified below. After the carburetor is installed, perform the appropriate idle speed/mixture adjustment as outlined above.

3K-C engine—2 turns from seating
18R-C engine—2½ turns from fully closed
20R engine—1¾ turns from fully closed
2M/4M engines—1½ turns out
F/2F engines—1¼ turns out
CAUTION: *Seat the idle mixture screw lightly; overtightening will damage its tip.*

Unloader Adjustment

Make the unloader adjustment with the primary valve fully opened. The total angle of choke valve opening, in the chart, is measured with either a special gauge, supplied in the carburetor rebuilding kit, or a gauge of the proper angle fabricated from cardboard.

MANUAL TRANSMISSION

Removal and Installation

Corolla and Carina

Working from inside of the car, perform the following:
1. Place the gear selector in Neutral. Remove the center console, if so equipped.
2. Remove the trim boot at the base of the shift lever and the boot underneath it on the shift tower.
3. On Corolla 1200 models only:
   a. Unfasten the snap-ring from the base of the shift lever.
   b. Withdraw the conical spring and the shift lever itself.
4. On Corolla 1600 and Carina models only:

a. Remove the four shift lever plate retaining screws.
   b. Remove the shift lever assembly.
   c. Remove the gasket.
NOTE: *Cover the hole with a clean cloth to prevent anything from falling into the transmission case.*
Working in the engine compartment perform the following:
5. Drain the cooling system and disconnect the cable from the positive side of the battery.
6. Remove the radiator hoses.
7. On Corolla 1200 models, only:
   a. Disconnect the back-up lamp switch connector.
   b. Remove the engine fan.
8. On Corolla 1600 and Carina models, only:
   a. Remove the air cleaner, complete with hoses.
   b. Unfasten the accelerator torque rod at the carburetor.
   c. Remove the clutch hydraulic line support bracket.
   d. Remove the starter assembly from the left side of the engine.
   e. Remove the upper left-hand clutch housing bolt, from the flat at the top of the clutch housing.
9. Drain the transmission oil.
10. Detach the exhaust pipe from the manifold and remove the exhaust pipe support bracket.
11. Remove the driveshaft.
NOTE: *It will be necessary to plug the opening in the end of the transmission with an old yoke or, if none is available, cover it with a plastic bag secured by a rubber band.*
12. Unfasten the speedometer cable from the right side of the transmission.
13. On Corolla 1600 and Carina models, only:
   a. Remove the clutch release cylinder assembly from the transmission

and tie it aside, so that it is out of the way.
   b. Unplug the back-up lamp switch connector.
14. Support the front of the transmission with a jack.
15. Unbolt the engine rear mounts. Remove the rear crossmember.
16. Remove the jack from under the transmission.
17. On Corolla 1600 and Carina models, unbolt the clutch housing from the engine and withdraw the transmission assembly.

NOTE: *Remove the brace, if so equipped.*

18. Perform the following on Corolla 1200 models, before removing the transmission:
   a. Remove the cotter pin from the clutch release linkage.
   b. Remove the clutch release cable.
   c. Remove the stiffener plate, if so equipped.
   d. Unbolt the clutch housing from the engine by removing the bolts in the order illustrated.
Installation is the reverse of removal, but observe the following.
Apply a light coating of multipurpose grease to the input shaft end, input shaft spline, clutch release bearing, and driveshaft end. On Corolla 1200 models, apply multipurpose grease to the ball on the end of the gearshift lever assembly; and to the clutch release cable end.
On Corolla 1200 models, install the clutch housing-to-engine bolts in two or three stages, and in the order shown.

After installation:
1. Fill the transmission and cooling system.
2. Adjust the clutch as detailed below.
3. Check to see that the back-up lamps function when Reverse is selected.

Corona (1972–73), Mark II/4, and Hi-Lux

1. Unfasten the cable from the positive battery terminal.

2. Remove the accelerator torque rod from its valve cover mounting.

3. Separate the downpipe from the flange and remove the flange. Remove the exhaust pipe bracket.

Raise the car with a jack and support it with jackstands.

4. Remove the parking brake equalizer support bracket.

5. Disconnect the speedometer cable and back-up lamp wiring harness from the transmission.

6. Remove the control shaft lever retainer.

7. Remove the clutch release cylinder from the transmission and set it up, out of the way.

NOTE: *Do not disconnect the hydraulic line from the release cylinder.*

8. Drain the transmission oil.

9. Remove the driveshaft.

NOTE: *To prevent oil from draining out of the transmission, install a spare U-joint or, if none is available, cover the opening with a plastic bag secured by a rubber band.*

10. Support the transmission with a jack.

11. Unfasten the rear engine mounts and remove the engine rear supporting crossmember.

12. Lower the jack.

13. Unfasten the bolts which secure the clutch housing to the cylinder block.

14. Remove the transmission toward the rear of the car.

Installation is performed in the reverse order of removal. See the notes at the end of the Corolla and Carina transmission installation section for details which require attention during installation.

NOTE: *Use a clutch guide tool, of the proper size, during installation, to locate the clutch disc.*

1974–77 Corona (4- and 5-Speed)

1. Disconnect the negative battery cable and then the positive battery-to-starter cable, complete with fusible link.

2. Drain the coolant from the radiator into a suitable clean container for re-use.

Unfasten the upper radiator hose.

3. Detach the accelerator rod and link at the firewall side.

4. Raise both ends of the car and support them with jackstands.

5. Working underneath the car, remove the exhaust pipe clamp and clutch release cylinder (Don't disconnect its hydraulic line; set the cylinder out of the way). Next, disconnect the back-up light switch lead and speedometer cable.

6. Remove the driveshaft from the transmission, after matchmarking it and the companion flange for assembly.

NOTE: *To prevent oil from draining out of the transmission, install a spare U-joint or if none is available, cover the opening with a plastic bag secured with a rubber band.*

7. Place a block of wood on the lift pad of a jack to protect the transmission, and support the transmission with it.

8. Cover the back end of the valve cover with cloths, remove the rear crossmember (See "Engine Removal"), and lower the jack.

9. Unfasten the bolts which secure the shift lever, and remove the shift lever.

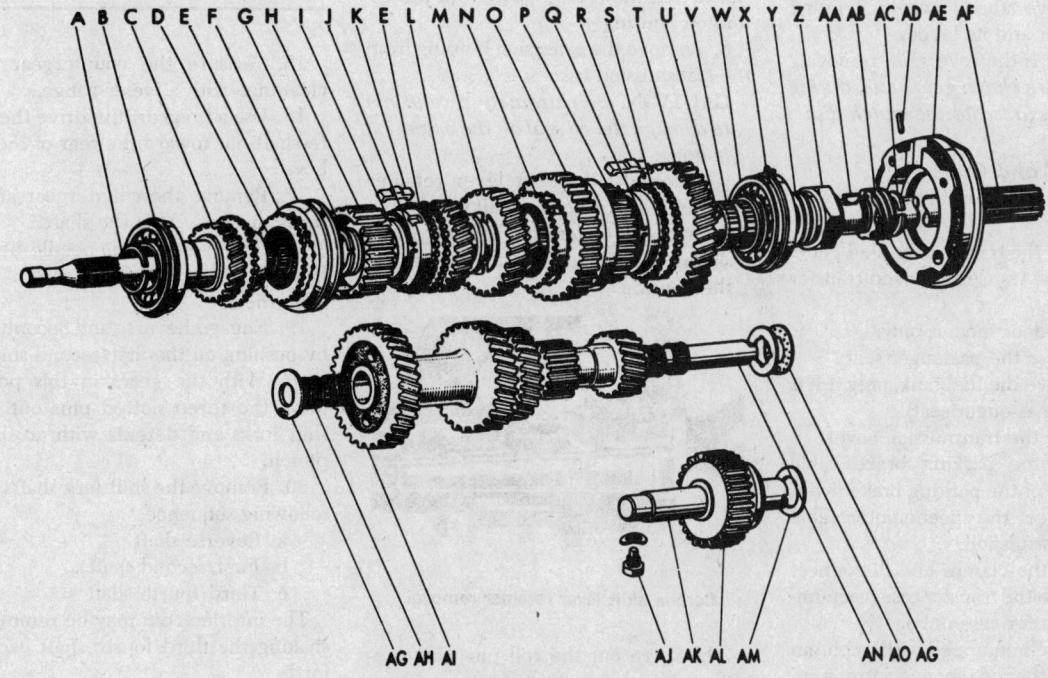

Corolla 1200 transmission components

(a)—Shaft snap-ring
(b)—Bearing (transmission front)
(c)—Input shaft
(d)—Needle roller bearing
(e)—Synchronizer ring No. 3
(f)—Transmission hub sleeve
(g)—Shaft snap-ring
(h)—Transmission clutch hub No. 2
(i)—Clutch hub spacer
(j)—Synchromesh shifting key spring No. 2
(k)—Synchromesh shifting key No. 2
(l)—Side gear
(m)—Second gear
(n)—Synchronizer ring No. 2

(o)—Reverse gear
(p)—Transmission clutch hub No. 1
(q)—Synchromesh shifting key spring No. 1
(r)—Synchromesh shifting key No. 1
(s)—Synchronizer ring No. 1
(t)—First gear
(u)—Ball
(v)—First gear bushing
(w)—Bearing (transmission rear)
(x)—Shaft snap-ring
(y)—Shim
(z)—Nut
(aa)—Woodruff key
(ab)—Speedometer drive gear

(ac)—Shaft snap-ring
(ad)—Slotted split pin
(ae)—Output shaft rear retainer
(af)—Output shaft
(ag)—Countergear thrust washer (case side)
(ah)—Needle roller bearing
(ai)—Countergear
(aj)—Shaft retaining bolt
(ak)—Reverse idler gear shaft
(al)—Reverse idler gear
(am)—Spacer
(an)—Counter shaft
(ao)—Countergear thrust washer (gear side)

10. Remove the starter motor from the clutch housing.

11. Remove the bolts which secure the clutch housing to the engine block.

12. Move the transmission and jack rearward, until the input shaft has cleared the clutch cover. Remove the transmission from underneath the car.

Installation is the reverse of removal. Be sure to apply a thin coating of grease to the input shaft splines. The clutch housing-to-cylinder block bolts should be tightened to 37–58 ft lbs. Adjust the clutch and fill the transmission with API GL-4 SAE 90 gear oil. Grease the shift lever spring seat and shift lever tip. Use the matchmarks to install the driveshaft.

Celica, Mark II/6, and Crown 2600

Perform the removal procedures as outlined for the Corolla 1600 and Carina. In addition, perform the following:

1. Remove the accelerator connecting rod from the linkage.

2. With the car jacked up and supported:

    a. Remove the left-hand, rear stone shield before removing the clutch release cylinder.

    b. Remove the flywheel housing lower cover and its braces.

Installation is the reverse of removal.

NOTE: *Use a clutch guide tool, during installation, to locate the clutch disc.*

Land Cruiser

1. Raise the vehicle and support it with jackstands.

2. Remove the transmission skid plate.

3. Drain the transmission and transfer case.

4. On two-door models only:

    a. Remove the passenger seat.

    b. Remove the fuel tank (only if it is under the passenger seat).

5. Remove the transmission cover.

6. Detach the parking brake cable from the end of the parking brake lever.

7. Disconnect the speedometer cable from the transmission.

8. Loosen the clamps and disconnect the hoses from the transfer case (vacuum-operated transfer case only).

9. On models equipped with a column shift, remove the rod pins and cotter pins, then detach the intermediate rods.

10. Disconnect the high and low shift rods.

11. Disconnect the wires from the front drive indicator light switch.

12. Raise the transmission with a jack.

13. Disconnect both front and rear U-joint yokes from the transfer case.

14. Remove the clutch housing skid plate.

15. Unfasten the bolts which attach the transmission to the transfer case.

16. Slide the transmission toward the rear of the vehicle so that the input shaft clears the clutch housing.

17. Remove the transmission transfer case assembly from under the vehicle, complete with the parking brake assembly.

Installation is the reverse of removal. Tighten the transmission mounting bolts to 52–57 ft lbs. Refill the transmission, and check the clutch linkage and shift linkage operation, after installation.

Overhaul

Corolla 1200

1. Drain the lubricant from the transmission, if you have not already done so. Clean off the magnetic plug.

2. Unfasten the lead from the back-up light switch.

3. Remove the tension spring from the clutch release fork.

4. Unfasten the throwout bearing hub clips and the release fork boot.

5. Withdraw the clutch fork and the release hub.

6. Unfasten the oil pan retaining nuts, and remove the pan complete with its gasket.

7. Remove the speedometer shaft sleeve and the driven gear from the extension housing.

8. Remove the extension housing from the transmission case.

CAUTION: *Be extremely careful not to damage the oil seal on the extension housing.*

    a. Remove the shift lever retainer by pulling the selector shaft toward the front of the extension housing while sliding the retainer toward the rear of the housing.

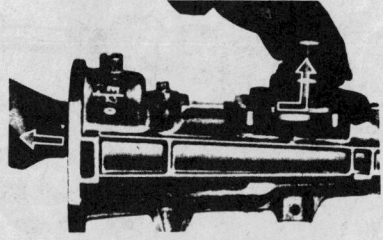

Corolla shift lever retainer removal

    b. Drive out the roll pin which secures the shift housing to the selector shaft and remove the housing.

    c. Withdraw the selector shaft, as well as its support and gasket.

10. Remove the countershaft cover and the front bearing retainer, complete with gaskets.

CAUTION: *Be careful not to damage the front bearing oil seal.*

11. Evenly loosen the five nuts which attach the transmission case cover. Withdraw the cover, gasket, and three detent springs.

CAUTION: *Be careful not to lose the*

three detent balls, as the springs keep them under compression.

12. Remove the securing bolt and withdraw the reverse idler gear shaft from the transmission case.

13. Remove the idler gear and the spacer, if installed.

14. Measure gear backlash:

    a. Set up a dial indicator, so that its plunger contacts the countergear teeth at right angles.

    b. With a screwdriver, lock each gear, in turn, to the output shaft so that it cannot move.

    c. Rock the countershaft back and forth and note the reading on the dial indicator for each gear.

    d. The specifications for each gear follow:

Gear Backlash

Gear	BACKLASH Specified	Limit
Input shaft	0.004	0.008
lst, 2nd and 3rd gears	0.004	0.008
Reverse	0.006	0.012
Reverse idler	0.007	0.012

15. Measure the countergear thrust clearance with a feeler gauge.

16. Use a brass drift to drive the countershaft out toward the rear of the gearbox.

17. Remove the countergear and the thrust washers from the shaft.

18. Remove the four needle bearings from the countershaft. Be careful not to drop them.

19. Engage Reverse and Second gears, by pushing on the first/second shift fork shaft. With the gears in this position, drive the three slotted pins out of the shift forks and detents with an 0.18 in. punch.

20. Remove the shift fork shafts in the following sequence:

    a. Reverse shaft

    b. First/second shaft

    c. Third/fourth shaft

The interlock pin may be removed by shaking the third/fourth shaft back and forth.

21. Withdraw the three detent balls from the case.

22. Remove the plug bolt from the housing (just below the slotted pin holes) and take out the two interlock pins.

23. Remove the shift forks in the following order:

    a. Reverse fork

    b. First/second fork

    c. Third/fourth fork

NOTE: *Be sure that the transmission is shifted into second gear before removing the first/second shift fork.*

24. Carefully remove the output shaft assembly from the rear of the transmission case.

25. Remove the roller bearings and fourth gear synchronizer ring from the input shaft. Use a soft brass drift to drive the input shaft toward the front of the transmission.

26. Measure the thrust clearance of the third, second and first gears with a feeler gauge.

Thrust Clearance
(in.)

Gear	Range	Limit
Third	0.004–0.010	0.020
Second	0.006–0.012	0.020
First	0.004–0.012	0.020
Countergear	0.002–0.010	0.020

27. Remove the snap-ring from the output shaft. Remove the third and fourth synchronizer assembly, clutch, hub spacer and third gear.

NOTE: *Be careful not to mix up the third and fourth gear synchronizer rings. Label them as they are removed.*

28. Remove the snap-ring which retains the speedometer drive gear. Withdraw the drive gear from the input shaft.

29. Remove the woodruff key.

30. Use a punch to straighten out the punched portion of the nut. Be careful not to damage the threaded portion of the output shaft.

31. Support the input shaft by placing reverse gear in a vise.

CAUTION: *Use aluminum plates to protect the gear teeth.*

Loosen the nut and remove it, complete with its shims.

32. Remove these items in the following order:
   a. Rear bearing retainer
   b. First gear
   c. Second gear
   d. Ball
   e. First/second gear synchronizer
   f. Synchronizer rings
   g. Second gear

33. Disassemble the components of the synchronizer assemblies. Be sure the components of the two assemblies are not mixed.

Clean all parts of the transmission and inspect them for wear or damage. Replace any parts which are defective.

Check the backlash and thrust clearance measurements made during disassembly against the specifications given in the charts above. If any of the specifications exceed the limits, replace the part(s), as necessary.

Use a dial indicator to check output shaft runout. The runout limit is 0.001 in.

Replace the front bearing, if it is rough or noisy, using a drift and press. Replace the bearing snap-ring with one of the following to obtain the minimum thrust clearance:
0.091–0.095 in.
0.097–0.101 in.
Transmission assembly is performed in the following order:

NOTE: *Always use new gaskets (apply liquid sealer) and snap-rings.*

1. Apply a thin coat of gear oil to all of the rotating surfaces prior to assembly.

2. Assemble the components of the third/fourth gear synchronizer hub:
   a. Install the key springs in the clutch hub.
   b. Place the three shifting keys into the hub slots.
   c. Install the second clutch hub into the sleeve.

NOTE: *Keep the open end of the key springs 120 degrees apart. By doing this, spring tension is kept uniform.*

3. Assemble the second/third synchronizer hub in the same manner detailed in step 2.

4. Install the second gear and its synchronizer ring, working from the back end of the output shaft. Be sure that the synchronizer is facing the proper direction. Do not mix the rings for the different gears.

5. Fit the first and second gear synchronizer hub on the output shaft, being careful to align its keys with the slots on the synchronizer ring.

6. Install first gear, complete with its synchronizer ring, bushing, and ball on the output shaft.

7. Attach the following to the output shaft:
   a. Rear bearing
   b. Shims
   c. Nut

NOTE: *If the original nut is used, change the number of shims to alter the locking position of the nut.*

8. Tighten the nut to 60–80 ft lbs, or if the torque wrench is over 20 in. long, 50–70 ft lbs. Stake the nut in place.

9. Working from the front of the output shaft, install third gear, third gear synchronizer ring, spacer, and third-/fourth synchronizer hub assembly. Be sure that the hub is facing forward.

10. Select a snap-ring to obtain a thrust clearance of less than 0.002 in. for the third/fourth synchronizer hub. Snap-rings are available in a range of sizes from 0.081–0.097 in. Install the snap-ring on the end of the output shaft.

11. Working from the rear of the output shaft, assemble the following:
   a. Snap-ring
   b. Woodruff key
   c. Speedometer drive gear
   d. Snap-ring

12. Check the thrust clearance of each gear.

13. Fit the input shaft into the transmission case with a piece of pipe which is large enough so that it drives the bearing into place, but does not damage the shaft.

14. Select the proper gasket for the bearing retainer:
   a. If the transmission case sticks out beyond the bearing installation surface, use a gasket with a thickness of 0.01 in.
   b. If the bearing installation surface protrudes beyond the transmission case, use a gasket with a thickness of 0.02 in.
   c. Apply liquid sealer to both sides of the gasket.

15. Apply grease to the lip of the bearing retainer oil seal.

16. Mount the bearing retainer and gasket in the transmission case and tighten its securing bolts to 7–12 ft lbs.

17. Install the needle bearing and the synchronizer ring onto the output shaft.

18. Slide the output shaft into the transmission case, carefully. Be sure to align the slotted pin on the bearing retainer with the grooves on the transmission case, and the notches on the ring with the proper shift keys.

19. Engage reverse gear with the second gear, then install the first/second shift fork in the groove on reverse gear. Rotate the fork half a turn around the gear.

20. Working from the rear of the transmission case, fit the first/second shift fork shaft into the case and then into the shift fork.

21. Fit the third/fourth shift fork into the groove on the clutch hub sleeve and rotate it one half turn around the sleeve.

22. Install the third/fourth shift fork shaft in the same manner outlined in step 20.

23. Engage the reverse shift fork with the center of the reverse shift arm. Fasten it with the E-ring. Fit the shaft into the transmission case and then into the fork, itself.

24. Align the slotted spring pin hole in each shift fork with the corresponding hole on each shaft.

NOTE: *Grease the pins, prior to installation.*

25. If the transmission is equipped with a pin installation hole, apply seal packing on the threads of the plug bolt and screw the bolt into the hole.

26. Install the needle roller bearings in countergear set. Be sure to grease the rollers first.

27. Install the front thrust washer in the recess on the transmission case. Install the rear gearset thrust washer and the rear case thrust washer in the recess located at the rear of the transmission case.

NOTE: *The washer which abuts the case goes into the recess first. Be sure that the embossed portion of each washer fits snugly in the case.*

28. Place the countergear into the transmission case. Measure the countergear thrust clearance with a feeler gauge; it should be 0.002–0.010 in. The thrust washer which abuts the case is available in several sizes, ranging from 0.051 to 0.-063 in., to adjust countergear thrust clearance to specifications.

29. Working from the rear of the transmission case, insert the countershaft.

NOTE: *The slot in the end of the shaft should be in a horizontal position.*

30. Install the countershaft front end cover and gasket. Tighten the securing bolts to 7–12 ft lbs.

31. Fit the groove in the reverse idler gear over the pin on the reverse shift arm. Place the gear and reverse idler shaft in the transmission case, with the shaft retaining boss facing upward.

32. Check the clearance between the reverse idler gear and the countergear end teeth when the reverse idler gear is pulled fully to the rear. If the clearance is less than 0.02 in., insert a spacer on the rear side of the reverse idler gear.

33. Align the boss on the reverse idler gear shaft with the retaining bolt boss. Tighten the retaining bolt to 7–12 ft lbs.

34. Drop the three detent balls and their compression springs into the three holes provided on the transmission case.

35. Fit the case cover and gasket over the holes. Tighten the cover securing bolts to 3–7 ft lbs.

36. Adjust the reverse shift arm pivot in the following manner:

a. Position the gears in neutral.

b. Unscrew the pivot out all of the way.

c. Adjust the clearance between the reverse idler gear teeth and the rear teeth of the countergear, so that it is 0.06 in. Adjust by turning the pivot.

d. Check the clearance between the bottom of the reverse idler gear groove and the reverse shift arm. It should be 0.02–0.06 in.

e. Adjust the pivot until both clearances are obtained.

f. Lock the pivot with the locknut and recheck both clearances.

NOTE: *Be sure that the reverse idler gear does not contact the reverse gear when the transmission is in First gear.*

37.

a. Install the support and gasket for the selector shaft through the hole in the support. Coat both sides of the gasket with sealer.

b. Fit the selector shaft through the hole in the support.

c. Attach the shift lever housing on the selector shaft, so that the pin hole is on the left side.

d. Drive the slotted pin into the shift lever housing with a brass drift.

e. Push in on the selector shaft and slide the shift lever retainer gasket and the retainer forward into place on the extension housing.

NOTE: *Apply sealer to both sides of the retainer gasket, before installation.*

f. Tighten the shift lever retainer bolts to 11–16 ft lbs.

38. Coat the extension housing oil seal lips with grease and coat the extension housing gasket with sealer on both sides.

39. Attach the extension housing to the transmission case, using care not to damage the oil seal. Tighten the housing securing bolts to 22–33 ft lbs.

40. Install the back-up light switch, if it was removed, in the following order:

a. Grease the reverse restricter pin and insert it into the extension housing.

b. Insert the compression spring, followed by the straight pin, into the housing.

c. Screw the back-up light switch into the housing and tighten it to 22–36 ft lbs.

41. Coat the speedometer gear with gear oil.

42. Install the speedometer shaft sleeve and the gear in the extension housing.

43. Position the embossed portion of the transmission oil pan gasket on the left-hand rear side of the case. Tighten the securing nuts to 4–5 ft lbs.

44. Install the drain plug and gasket on the oil pan. Tighten the plug to 27–31 ft lbs.

45. Coat the portions of the clutch release hub and fork which contact each other, with grease. Grease the inner surface of the clutch release hub.

46. Fit the boot over the release fork.

47. Install the release fork and hub. Tighten the fork securing bolt to 14–22 ft lbs.

48. Fit the release fork tension spring in place.

49. Connect the back-up light switch wiring.

50. Install the transmission in the car as outlined above.

Corolla 1600 and Carina

CAUTION: *The clutch housing, split transmission case, and extension housing are all made of aluminum. Care should be taken not to strip the threads and not to damage the machined surfaces of these components.*

1. Drain the oil from the transmission, if you have not done so during removal.

2. Remove the bolts which secure the clutch housing and withdraw the housing, with the bearing retainer, release bearing, and release fork still attached.

NOTE: *Use care not to lose the two conical springs from the bearings.*

3. Remove the bolt and withdraw the speedometer shaft sleeve and driven gear from the extension housing.

4. Remove the six bolts which retain the extension housing and separate the housing from the case.

CAUTION: *Be careful not to damage the extension housing oil seal.*

5. Remove the back-up light switch, spring and ball from the transmission case.

6. Unfasten the 14 bolts which secure the transmission case halves. Using a *wooden* mallet, tap the protrusion on the right-hand side of the case.

CAUTION: *Do not separate the halves of the case by prying them apart.*

7. Measure gear backlash, as detailed in step 14 of the Corolla 1200 transmission overhaul procedure. Make a note of the values obtained. The backlash for all gears should be 0.004–0.008 in. and the wear limit should be 0.016 in.

8. Lift the countergear set out of the right-hand half of the case.

9. Use a magnet to remove the ball from the second countergear bearing.

10. Withdraw the input and the output shafts as a unit.

11. Use a punch to drive the three slotted spring pins out of the shift forks and shift fork shafts.

NOTE: *The slotted pin cannot always be fully removed from the first/second shift fork; however, the shift fork can still be withdrawn. Do not try to force the pin out, as damage to the transmission case could result.*

12. Remove the case cover and withdraw the three detent balls and springs.

13. Remove the shift fork shafts in the following order:

a. First/second shaft

b. Pin

c. Reverse shift fork shaft

d. Third/fourth shaft

e. Pin

14. Measure the thrust of the reverse idler gear with a feeler gauge. The specified clearance is 0.002–0.020 in. and the wear limit is 0.039 in.

15. Unfasten the idler shaft retaining bolt and withdraw the shaft. Remove the gear and washer.

Thrust Clearance Specifications

Gear	Specified	Wear Limit
First	0.006-0.010	0.020
Second	0.006-0.010	0.020
Third	0.006-0.012	0.024
Reverse	0.008-0.012	0.024
Fifth①	0.006-0.010	0.020

① Optional

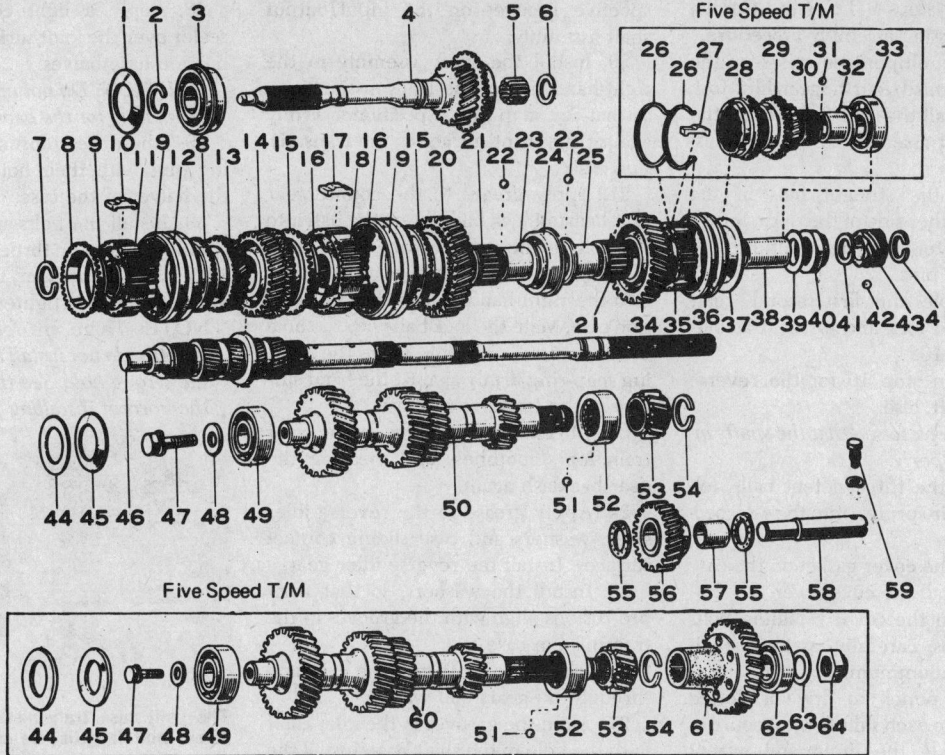

Corolla 1600 and Carina 4 and 5-speed components

1. Conical spring
2. Shaft snap-ring
3. Ball bearing
4. Input shaft
5. Roller
6. Snap-ring
7. Shaft snap-ring
8. Synchronizer ring
9. Shift-key spring
10. Shift-key
11. Clutch hub
12. Hub sleeve
13. Third gear assembly
14. Second gear assembly
15. Synchronizer ring
16. Shift-key spring
17. Shift-key

18. Clutch hub
19. Hub sleeve
20. First gear assembly
21. Needle roller bearing
22. Ball
23. First gear bushing
24. Ball bearing
25. Reverse gear bushing
26. Shift-key spring*
27. Shift-key*
28. Synchronizer ring*
29. Fifth gear assembly*
30. Needle roller bearing*
31. Ball*
32. Fifth gear bushing*
33. Ball bearing*

34. Reverse gear
35. Clutch hub
36. Hub sleeve
37. Spacer
38. Spacer (long)
39. Shim
40. Nut
41. Shaft snap-ring
42. Ball
43. Speedometer drive gear
44. Shim
45. Conical spring
46. Output shaft
47. Bolt and washer
48. Plate washer
49. Ball bearing
50. Countergear

51. Ball
52. Roller bearing
53. Reverse countergear
54. Snap-ring
55. Thrust washer—reverse idler gear
56. Reverse idler gear
57. Bushing
58. Reverse idler gear shaft
59. Shaft retaining bolt
60. Countergear*
61. Fifth-speed countergear*
62. Ball bearing*
63. Shim*
64. Nut*

* Five-speed transmission only

16. Measure the thrust clearance of the gears on the output shaft and make a note of their values.

17. Disassemble the components of the output shaft in a similar manner to that outlined in steps 27–33 of the Corolla 1200 overhaul (disassembly) procedure. Remember that five-speed transmissions have an extra gearset and related parts.

Clean all of the parts of the transmission and check them for wear or damage. Replace any defective parts.

Check the backlash and thrust clearance measurements made during disassembly against the specifications given in the charts above. If any of the specifications exceed the wear limits, replace the part(s) as necessary.

Use a dial indicator to check output shaft runout. The runout limit is 0.0012 in.; replace the shaft if it exceeds this.

Replace the front bearing, if it is rough or noisy. Use a drift and a press. Remove the snap-ring first.

For bearing installation, replacement snap-rings are available in a range of sizes (0.0925–0.1024 in.) to obtain *minimum* axial play between the input shaft and the bearing.

Assemble as follows:

NOTE: *Always use new gaskets and snap-rings. Apply gear lubricant to all sliding contact surfaces, gears, bushings and bearings.*

1. Assemble the components of the synchronizer hubs, and the output shaft, as detailed in steps 2–6 of the Corolla 1200 assembly procedures, above.

2. Install the rear bushing on the output shaft, being careful to install it in the proper direction.

3. Install the ball into the groove of the bushing and slide the bushing over the shaft.

4. Install the needle roller bearing, reverse gear, the ball and the reverse gear synchronizer hub.

5. Install the following items on the

output shaft of the four-speed transmission, in the order indicated:

   a. Large-diameter reverse gear spacer

   b. Long spacer

   c. Shims

6. Install the following items on the output shaft of the five-speed transmission in the order indicated:

   a. Ball

   b. Fifth gear synchronizer ring

   c. Fifth gear

   d. Needle roller bearing

   e. Bushing

   f. Rear support ball bearing

7. Install the shims and the nut on the end of the output shaft. Tighten it to 33–54 ft lbs and lock it with a chisel.

NOTE: *If the original nut is being used, change the number of shims to alter the locking portion of the nut.*

8. Check the thrust clearance of each gear.

9. Perform steps 9–12 of the Corolla 1200 transmission assembly procedure.

10. Apply multipurpose grease on the end of the third/fourth gearshift fork shaft and install the shift fork. Install the fork and shaft assembly in the transmission case.

11. Insert the straight pins in the grooves on either side of the third/fourth shift shaft, after applying multipurpose grease to the pins.

12. Assemble the first/second gearshift shaft and fork and install it as outlined in step 10.

13. Perform step 10 for the reverse shift fork shaft, also.

NOTE: *Check to see that the shafts interlock properly.*

14. Insert the three detent balls, followed by their springs, into their respective bores.

15. Place the cover gasket on the case and then install the cover over it.

16. Tighten the cover retaining bolts to 8–11 ft lbs, carefully, as the case is made out of aluminum.

17. Use a punch to drive a slotted spring pin into each shift fork to secure it.

18. Assemble the input and output shafts.

19. Install the shift forks into their respective grooves on the input/output shaft assembly.

20. Install the shaft assembly in the right-hand half of the transmission case, so that the snap-ring is positioned firmly against the front surface of the transmission case.

21. Apply grease to the countergear rear bearing lock ball. Insert the ball into the hole in the rear bearing outer race.

22. Place the countergear assembly into the right-hand half of the transmission case. Mate the lock ball with the hole in the transmission case. Place the bearing snap-ring firmly against the front surface of the transmission case.

23. Check the operation of the gear train for smoothness and measure the gear backlash again.

24. Apply grease to the reverse idler shaft, washers and case sliding contact surfaces. Install the reverse idler gear.

25. Install the washers, so that their protrusions align with the grooves in the transmission case.

26. Install the shaft into the case and through the gears and washers.

27. Align the grooves in the idler shaft with the hole in the shaft boss. Install the retaining bolt and washer into the boss. Torque the bolt to 9–13 ft lbs.

28. Apply a light coating of liquid sealer over the joint surfaces of the transmission case halves.

CAUTION: *Do not apply sealer to the ½ in. hole for the back-up light switch.*

29. Align the transmission case locating pins with their holes and assemble the halves of the case.

30. Install the bolts and tighten them evenly, in two or three stages, to 10.9–14.5 ft lbs. Remember, the case is aluminum, do not overtighten the bolts.

NOTE: *There are four different bolt lengths, do not install the wrong bolt in the wrong hole. See the illustration for the correct installing position.*

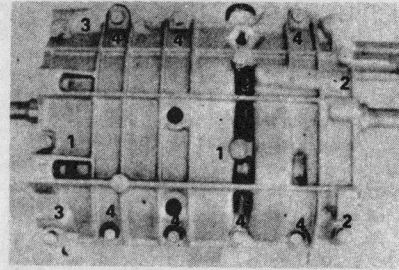

The split case transmission uses four different bolt lengths. Be careful not to mix them.

1. 3.55 in. 3. 1.77 in.
2. 2.76 in. 4. 1.26 in.

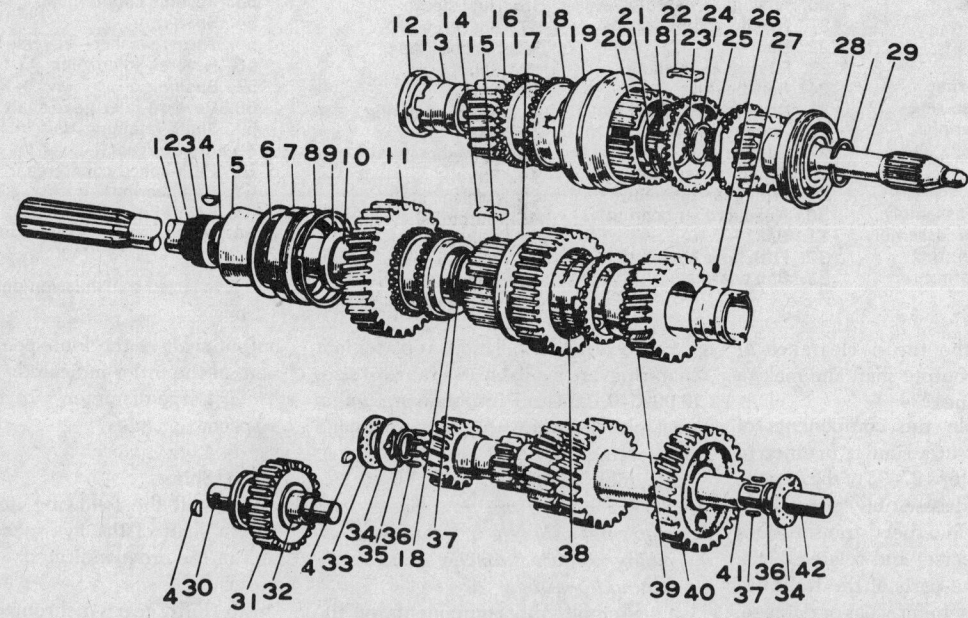

Transmission components for the Corona, Mark II, Crown and Hi-Lux—side cover type.

1. Output shaft
2. Shaft snap-ring
3. Speedometer drive gear
4. Woodruff key
5. Extension housing baffle
6. Shaft snap-ring
7. Radial ball bearing
8. Shaft snap-ring
9. Spacer
10. Bi-metal formed bushing
11. First gear
12. Second & Third gear thrust washer
13. Third gear bushing
14. Synchromesh shifting key No. 1

15. Transmission clutch hub No. 1
16. Third gear
17. Reverse gear
18. Synchronizer ring
19. Transmission sleeve
20. Transmission clutch hub No. 2
21. Synchromesh shifting key spring
22. Synchromesh shifting key No. 2
23. Shaft snap-ring
24. Hole snap-ring
25. Roller
26. Straight pin
27. Second gear bushing
28. Bushing

29. Input shaft
30. Reverse idler gear shaft
31. Reverse idler gear
32. Bi-metal formed bushing
33. Counter gear case side thrust washer
34. Counter gear side thrust washer
35. Spacer
36. Roller
37. Shaft snap-ring
38. Synchromesh shifting key spring
39. Second gear
40. Countergear
41. Tube
42. Countershaft

31. Insert the ball, spring, and washer in the back-up light switch hole. Screw in the switch assembly and tighten it to 22–36 ft lbs.

32. Fit the gasket and bolt the extension housing to the rear of the transmission. Tighten the bolts evenly, in two or three stages, to 22–33 ft lbs. Do not over-tighten.

CAUTION: *Be careful not to damage the extension housing oil seal.*

33. Install the speedometer shaft sleeve and drive gear into the extension housing. Tighten to 36–61 in. lbs.

34. Apply grease to the conical springs. Install one spring over the input shaft bearing and the other over the countershaft bearing. Install the spacer over the countershaft bearing spring, after coating the spacer with grease.

35. Install the gasket and the clutch housing. Tighten the clutch housing securing bolts, evenly and in two or three stages, to 22–33 ft lbs. Do not over-tighten.

Corona, Mark II and Hi-Lux— Side Cover

1. Remove the clutch release fork and the release bearing hub assembly. Remove the clutch housing from the gear case.

2. Remove the front bearing retainer and transmission case cover assembly.

3. Before removing the internal parts, check the countergear thrust clearance with a feeler gauge, record the reading, then pick the proper adjusting gear side thrust washer to obtain the specified clearance of 0.002–0.006 in. (1973–77 Hi-Lux—0.004–0.010 in.).

4. Remove the bolts which retain the extension housing to the transmission case. Turn and align the cut portion of the extension housing with the countershaft.

5. Use a dummy shaft and drive out the countershaft and the woodruff key to the rear. Remove the extension housing, the output shaft, and the gear assembly.

6. Remove the input shaft with the bearing.

7. Take the countergear assembly and the thrust washers out of the transmission case. Remove the dummy shaft, roller bearings, and the spacer from the countergear.

8. Using a brass rod, gently tap the reverse idler gear shaft toward the rear and remove it. Remove the reverse idler gear.

9. Check and record the following clearances; first gear thrust clearance, third gear thrust clearance, second gear thrust clearance, and clearance between snap-ring and clutch hub.

NOTE: *On 1973–77 Hi-Lux models reverse step 10 through 14; remove parts from the starting at the back and working forward.*

10. Remove the shaft snap-ring at the front end of the output shaft. Slide the synchronizer unit, synchronizer ring, third gear, third gear bushing, thrust washer, second gear bushing, second gear, synchronizer ring, clutch hub and reverse gear assembly and the synchronizer ring, out of the output shaft.

11. Remove the lock plate and speedometer driven gear assembly from the extension housing.

12. Expand the shaft snap-ring on the output shaft rear bearing with a snap-ring expander. Drive the output shaft out of the extension housing with a mallet.

13. Check and record the output shaft rear bearing thrust clearance. Remove the shaft snap-ring and speedometer drive gear, the woodruff key, and oil baffle.

14. Remove the shaft snap-rings. Place the first gear on vise anvils, and press out first gear, spacer, and the bearing from the output shaft.

15. Loosen and remove the backup light switch. Move the third and fourth shift fork into the fourth speed position (to the front).

16. Using a long drift punch, drive out the slotted spring pin which connects the shift fork to the shift fork shaft.

17. Slide the shift fork shaft out of the rear of the case cover gradually, preventing the lock ball from popping out under spring tension. Remove the lock ball, spring and the two interlock pins from the case cover.

18. Drive the slotted spring pin out of the first and second shift fork and the shift fork shaft in the same manner. Remove the shift fork shaft and the shift fork, then remove the lock ball and the spring from the case cover.

19. Remove the shift arm pivot locknut. Remove the shift arm from the case cover. Drive out the slotted spring pin, and remove the reverse shift head and the shift fork shaft. Remove the lock ball and the spring. Remove the selector outer lever and the selector lever shaft.

20. Remove the shift lever shaft lockbolt, slide out the shift lever shaft from the case cover. Be careful to prevent the lock ball from popping out under spring tension.

21. Remove the sliding shift lever, lock ball and spring. Remove the wire and shift lever lockbolt.

22. Remove the shift and selector lever shaft toward the rear side of the case.

Wash all disassembled parts thoroughly. Check the transmission case, case cover and the extension housing for cracks; check the bearing fitting portions and gasket surfaces for burrs and nicks.

Check the output shaft splines, snap-ring grooves, bearing contact surfaces, bearing fitting portions and oil seal lip contact surface for wear, scores, or damage. Check the output shaft for runout. If the runout exceeds 0.0012 in. (0.0024 in. —1973–77 Hi-Lux) replace the shaft. To measure runout, place a dial indicator on the center point of the shaft and rotate the shaft slowly to read the maximum and minimum values. The runout equals the maximum value minus the minimum value divided by two.

Check the bearings for roughness and wear. Check for noise or damage by rotating the bearing after applying a few drops of oil. To remove the input shaft bearing, remove the shaft snap-ring with a snap-ring expander, then remove the bearing from the input shaft with a puller. Check the bushings and the bearing rollers for abnormal wear. If the wear is excessive, replace the bushing/s or the bearing rollers.

Inspect the extension housing bushing for wear or scoring. To replace the bushing, press the bushing out of the extension housing to the front side. To install, align the oil grooves of the bushing and the extension housing, and press the bushing into the housing. After installing the bushing, ream the bushing to fit the outer diameter of the universal joint sleeve yoke.

Gear Backlash

Input shaft gear to countergear: 0.004 in.

Third gear to countergear: 0.004 in.

Second gear to countergear: 0.004 in.

First gear to countergear: 0.004 in.

Reverse idler gear to countergear: 0.-005 in. (1973–77 Hi-Lux—0.004–0.008 in.)

Reverse idler gear to reverse gear: 0.-005 in. (1973–77 Hi-Lux—0.004–0.008 in.)

Assembly is performed in the following order:

NOTE: *Always install new gaskets, apply liquid sealer or gasket cement when assembling. Apply a thin coating of transmission lubricant on all parts before installation. Thrust clearances of gears and bearings are important factors for smooth gear shifting. Therefore, select and assemble thrust washers, snap-rings and spacers of proper thickness.*

1. Slide the first gear onto the output shaft with the synchronizer gear toward the front of the shaft. Install the spacer, and press the bearing onto the output shaft with the snap-ring groove on the bearing toward the front of the shaft.

2. Check the first gear thrust clearance, and if necessary, select and install a thicker first gear spacer to obtain the following clearance. First gear thrust clearance: 0.004–0.008 in. A first gear spacer, 0.209–0.211 in. thick is available.

3. After installing the first gear spacer, make sure that first gear will rotate smoothly. Checking the first gear thrust clearance must be performed with the rear bearing snap-ring installed.

4. Check the clearance between the rear bearing and the snap-ring, and if necessary select and install a thicker snap-ring to obtain an output shaft rear bearing thrust clearance of 0–0.002 in. (0.004 in.—1973-77 Hi-Lux) Six thicknesses of rear bearing snap-rings are available.

5. Check the clearance between the second gear and second and third gear thrust washer while pressing the third gear bushing against the second gear, and if necessary, file off the rear end of the second gear bushing to obtain a second gear thrust clearance of 0.004–0.008 in. Five thicknesses of second and third gear thrust washers are available. A second gear bushing 1.264–1.265 in. long is available.

6. Check the clearance between the third gear and second and third gear thrust washer while pressing the clutch hub against the third gear, and if necessary, file off the front end of the third gear bushing as well as the second gear bushing to obtain 0.004–0.008 in. third gear thrust clearance. A third gear bushing 1.382–1.384 in. long is available. Make sure that gears rotate smoothly while pressing the clutch hub against third gear.

7. Check the clearance between the front end snap-ring and the clutch hub. If necessary, use a thicker front end snap-ring to obtain 0–0.002 in. (0.004 in.—1973-77 Hi-Lux) clearance between the snap-ring and clutch hub.

8. If specified clearance cannot be obtained by installing a snap-ring, select and install a thicker second and third gear thrust washer, then install a front end snap-ring of proper thickness. Front end snap-rings are available in ten thicknesses.

9. Install the oil baffle and the shaft snap-ring. Install the Woodruff key into the key groove of the output shaft.

10. Slide the speedometer drive gear onto the output shaft, then install the shaft snap-ring and secure the gear.

11. Install the shaft snap-ring into the groove of the extension housing front end. Expand the shaft snap-ring with a snap-ring expander, then assemble the output shaft into the extension housing.

NOTE: *On 1973-77 Hi-Lux models select a snap-ring that will provide a 0–0.006 in. clearance between the drive gear and the snap-ring.*

12. When assembling the output shaft, install the universal joint sleeve yoke temporarily onto the output shaft rear end to prevent damaging the extension housing bushing and the oil seal, and to properly center the output shaft.

13. Assemble the synchronizer unit by installing the two shifting springs onto the clutch hub with open ends of the springs 120° apart, so that the spring tension on each shifting key will be uniform.

14. Place the three shifting keys into the clutch hub key slots and onto the shifting springs.

CAUTION: *There are two kinds of shifting keys in this transmission. The keys with the shorter straddle length should be installed on the third and fourth synchronizer unit.*

15. Next, slide the hub sleeve onto the clutch hub. The clutch hubs and the hub sleeve of the reverse gear are matched, and should be kept together as an assembly for smooth operation.

16. Assemble the first and second synchronizer unit in the same manner as described.

17. Install the synchronizer ring, reverse gear, and synchronizer ring onto the output shaft. Align the cut portions of the synchronizer rings with the shifting keys on the clutch hub.

18. Slide the second gear bushing onto the output shaft, and align the bushing groove with the straight pin on the output shaft.

19. Install the second gear onto the bushing of the output shaft.

20. Install the second and third gear thrust washer, and align the indents of the thrust washer and the claws of the bushing.

21. Install the third gear bushing, third gear, synchronizer ring and the third and fourth synchronizer unit onto the output shaft.

22. Install the shaft snap-ring onto the output shaft.

23. Check the first gear, second gear and the third gear on the output shaft for smooth rotation, and also check the synchronizer units for smooth movement.

24. Press the bearing onto the input shaft with the snap-ring on the bearing toward the front.

25. Select and install the proper shaft snap-ring to obtain minimum thrust play on the input shaft. Shaft snap-rings are available in two sizes; No. 1 is 0.096–0.102 in. thick, No. 2 is 0.091–0.095 in. thick.

26. Coat the bearing rollers with grease, and coat the bore of the input shaft gear. Install the bearing rollers into the bore, then install the hole snap-ring.

27. Position the reverse idler gear into the transmission case with the shift fork groove toward the rear. Align the key groove of the reverse idler gear shaft and the cut portion of the transmission case, and drive the shaft through the gear and into the transmission case.

28. Secure the shaft by installing the Woodruff key. Install the collar into the countergear, then install the two needle roller bearings into both sides of the countergear.

29. Insert the dummy shaft into the countergear. Position the countergear assembly, case side thrust washers and the proper adjusting gear side thrust washer which was determined when disassembling the transmission, onto the bottom of the transmission case.

30. Countergear thrust clearance is 0.002–0.006 in. (0.004–0.010 in.—1973-77 Hi-Lux). Side thrust washers are available in different sizes. After installing the side thrust washers, make sure that the countergear rotates smoothly.

31. Install the input shaft assembly onto the transmission case.

32. Install the output shaft and gears, and the extension housing assembly with the gasket, onto the transmission case. Turn and align the cut portion of the extension housing with the countershaft bore of the transmission.

33. Next, align the bores of the transmission case and the countergear. Install the countershaft from the rear of the transmission case. Secure the countershaft by installing the woodruff key onto the end of the shaft.

34. Tighten the extension housing retaining bolts to 22–33 ft lbs.

35. Install the speedometer driven gear into the extension housing, and secure the driven gear sleeve with the lock plate.

36. Install the front bearing retainer with the gasket. Be sure to align the oil hole and the oil hole slot. Apply liquid sealer on the threads of the bolts, and torque the front bearing retainer attaching bolts to 3–5 ft lbs.

37. Install the clutch housing onto the transmission case. Lubricate the clutch release bearing hub bore with multipurpose grease, and install the clutch release fork and hub assembly onto the transmission case.

38. To assemble the transmission case cover, install the shift arm pivot onto the reverse shift arm, and insert into the case.

39. Assemble the shift and selector lever shaft together with the shift and selector lever, and secure the bolt with a wire.

40. Insert the reverse shift fork shaft compression spring and lock ball into the case, and insert the fork shaft from the rear side, then secure the shift head with a new slotted spring pin.

41. Align the fork shaft positioning groove with the shift interlock pin groove.

42. Align the reverse shift arm knob with the reverse shift fork shaft, and install the O-ring, washer and nut onto the shift arm pivot. Insert the shift interlock pin into the rear side of the case cover and the compression spring and lock ball into the front side, and assemble the shift

fork together with the first and second shift fork shaft. Secure the shift fork with a new slotted spring pin.

43. Align the shift fork shaft positioning groove with the shift interlock pin groove. Insert the two shift interlock pins into the front side of the case cover.

44. Insert the compression spring and the lock ball, and assemble the shift fork together with the third and fourth shift fork shaft, then secure the shift fork with a new slotted spring pin.

45. Install the lock ball, compression spring and reverse restricting ball holder.

46. Check all shift forks for smooth movement. Tighten to 27–32 ft lbs.

47. Install the back-up light switch on the case cover.

48. Align each shift fork and the reverse shift arm with the respective gears, and install the transmission case cover, with the gasket, onto the transmission. Torque the case cover retaining bolts to 11–16 ft lbs.

49. To adjust the shift arm pivot, loosen the locknut on the shift arm pivot, turn the shift arm pivot clockwise until friction is felt, when the reverse idler gear contacts with the first gear and/or the countergear.

50. Next from this position, turn the shift arm pivot counterclockwise approximately 90 degrees. Tighten the pivot locknut securely.

51. With the input shaft rotating, make sure that there is no noise and that the reverse idler gear does not contact other gears in the transmission.

52. If no friction is felt when the shift arm pivot is turned clockwise, set the pivot line mark at 60 degrees rearward from its horizontal position to the case cover surface.

53. If necessary, replace the oil seal in the extension housing after assembling the transmission using the oil seal puller, and pull out the oil seal together with the dust seal.

4-Speed Corona, Mark II, Celica and Crown 2600—Internal Linkage and W-40

1. Drain the oil from the transmission, if you have not already done so.

2. Unbolt and remove the clutch housing from the transmission case, with the release fork, bearing and hub still attached.

3. Unbolt the back-up light switch. Remove the reverse restrictor pin and the speedometer driven gear.

4. Remove the gearshift lever retainer.

5. Rotate the shift rod housing counterclockwise (viewed from behind) and then disconnect the rod from the shift fork shafts.

6. Unbolt and remove the extension housing.

7. Drive out the slotted pin and separate the shift rod, housing and spring.

8. Unbolt and remove the front bearing retainer. Remove the back-up light switch (W-40 only).

9. Take off both of the front countershaft covers, as well as the spacer.

10. Using an expander, remove the snap-rings from the input and countershaft bearings.

11. Remove the rear cover from the transmission case, by unfastening the bolts which secure it.

NOTE: *Use a hammer and a wooden drift to break the rear cover free of the case, if necessary.*

12. When removing the rear cover leave all of the gears and other parts attached. Mount the cover in a vise.

CAUTION: *Use a copper sheet and clamp the rear cover in the vise at the crosshatched area, to prevent damage to its joining surfaces.*

13. Withdraw the speedometer driven gear from the output shaft, using care not to lose its lockball.

14. Punch the slotted pin out of the reverse shift arm bracket bolt and remove the bracket, complete with the shift arm.

15. Remove the reverse idler shaft stop and withdraw the idler gear and shaft assembly away from the rear cover.

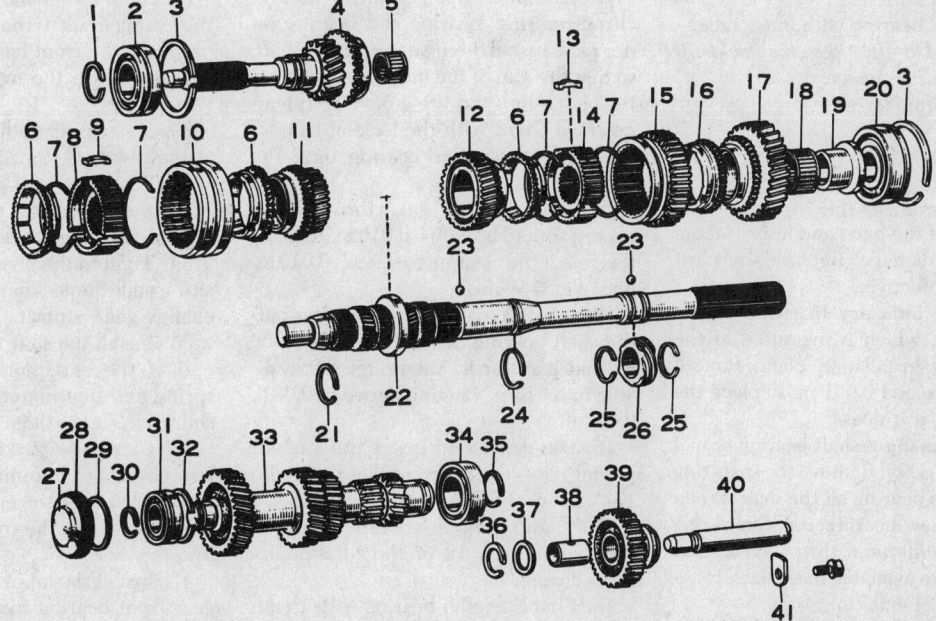

Transmission components for the Corona, Mark II, Celica, and Crown—enclosed linkage type.

1. Shaft snap-ring	11. Third gear assembly	21. Shaft snap-ring
2. Radial ball bearing	12. Second gear assembly	22. Output shaft
3. Shaft snap-ring	13. Shift-key	23. Reverse shaft restricter ball
4. Input shaft assembly	14. Clutch hub	24. Shaft snap-ring
5. Needle roller bearing	15. Reverse gear	25. Shaft snap-ring
6. Synchronizer ring	16. Synchronizer ring	26. Speedometer drive gear
7. Shift-key spring	17. First gear assembly	27. Countershaft end cover—front
8. Clutch hub	18. Needle roller bearing	28. Countershaft end cover—rear
9. Shift-key	19. First gear bearing inner race	29. Spacer
10. Hub spring	20. Radial ball bearing	30. Snap-ring

31. Radial ball bearing
32. Snap-ring
33. Countergear
34. Radial ball bearing
35. Shaft snap-ring
36. Shaft snap-ring
37. Spacer
38. Bushing
39. Reverse idler gear
40. Reverse idler shaft
41. Reverse idler shaft stop

16. Unbolt and remove the output shaft rear bearing retainer.

17. Remove the screwplug and spring from each shift fork and shaft.

18. Drive the slotted interlock pins out of each shaft. Be careful not to lose the balls.

19. Remove the shift fork shafts in the following order:
   a. Reverse
   b. First/second
   c. Third/fourth

Once the shafts have been removed, slide the shift forks off them.

20. Remove the snap-ring from the output shaft rear bearing. Push the output shaft and countershaft out, working from the rear side of the cover. Once the shafts are started, grasp them carefully and pull them forward as an assembly.

CAUTION: *Do not drop either of the shafts while removing them.*

21. Separate the input shaft and the front synchronizer ring from the output shaft.

22. Use an expander to remove the snap-ring and remove the hub and synchronizer ring, followed by third gear.

NOTE: *Remove the clutch hub by tapping it lightly with a plastic hammer.*

23. Remove the rear bearing snap-ring and press off the rear bearing.

24. Remove the following items from the output shaft, in the order listed:
   a. First gear
   b. Roller bearing with inner race
   NOTE: *Do not lose the lockballs from the inner race.*
   c. Synchronizer ring
   d. Reverse gear
   e. Clutch hub
   f. Second gear
   g. Synchronizer ring

Clean all of the parts and inspect them for wear or damage. Replace any parts which are defective.

Use a dial indicator to check output shaft runout, which is measured at the rear bearing installation point. Runout should not exceed 0.001 in. Replace the output shaft, if it does.

Replace the input shaft bearing only if it is rough or noisy. Remove the snap-ring and press the bearing off the shaft. When installing a new bearing, use a snap-ring to obtain *minimum* thrust clearance. Snap-rings are available in six sizes, ranging from 0.081–0.93 in.

Assembly is performed in the following order:

1. Apply a thin coating of gear oil to all rotating or sliding surfaces, prior to assembly.

2. Perform steps 2–3 of the Corolla 1200 transmission assembly procedure, above.

3. Assemble the synchronizer ring to third gear, and fit both of them on the output shaft.

4. Insert the third/fourth synchronizer hub on the output shaft, until it contacts the shoulder of the shaft.

NOTE: *If the hub is tight on the shaft, lightly tap it home with a wooden mallet.*

5. Select a snap-ring to provide 0.002 in. end play for the synchronizer hub and fit it onto the shaft. Snap-rings are available in a range of sizes.

6. Measure third gear thrust clearance with a feeler gauge. The clearance should be 0.004–0.010 in. Replace third gear if the clearance exceeds the limit of 0.010 in. (0.012 in.—W40).

7. Install the synchronizer ring for second gear to the gear and install the assembly on the output shaft.

8. Install the reverse gear over its clutch hub. Examine them to see that they are properly positioned and slide smoothly.

9. Install the reverse gear and hub on the output shaft so that they contact the shoulder.

10. Measure second gear thrust clearance; it should be between 0.004–0.010 in. Replace the gear if the clearance is more than 0.010 in. (0.012 in.—W40).

11. Coat the locking ball with grease. Insert it, and the roller bearing inner race, on the output shaft.

NOTE: *Be sure that the locking ball does not protrude from the shaft.*

12. Assemble first gear with its synchronizer ring, bearing and bearing inner race. Install them on the output shaft, so that the end of the inner race contacts the clutch hub and the groove on the inner race aligns with the locking ball.

13. Press the rear bearing onto the output shaft.

14. Measure first gear thrust clearance; it should be 0.004–0.010 in. Replace the gear if the clearance exceeds 0.010 in. (0.012 in.—W40).

15. Select a snap-ring for the rear output shaft bearing that will provide 0.002 in. end play for it. Snap-rings are available in six sizes, ranging between 0.081–0.093 in.

16. Use a press to insert the straight pin into the rear cover, until it protrudes ¼–5/16 in. from the cover front side.

17. Clamp the rear cover in a vise, as detailed in step 12 of the disassembly procedure.

18. Coat the roller bearing with grease and fit it over the input shaft.

19. Apply gear oil to the front synchronizer ring on the output shaft.

20. Assemble the output shaft and the input shaft.

21. Assemble the output shaft and countergear, then fit them through the holes in the rear cover. Push them in until the snap-ring sticks out beyond the rear cover. Install the snap-ring and then push the shafts back until the snap-ring is flush with the rear cover surface.

22. Install the shaft through the reverse idler gear. Insert the end of the shaft into the end of the rear cover.

23. Install the spacer on the idler shaft and secure it with a snap-ring.

24. Install the idler shaft stop.

25. Install the first/second and third/fourth shift forks into the grooves on the hub sleeves, so that the longer parts of their bosses face each other.

26. Assemble the ends of the three shift fork shafts and insert them into the rear cover. Install the interlock pins, after coating them with grease.

27. Install the shafts through the forks and drive in the slotted spring pins to secure them.

28. Insert the lockballs, followed by their springs. Tighten their plugs to 14–22 ft lbs.

29. Install the output shaft rear bearing retainer and tighten its attaching bolts to 11–16 ft lbs.

NOTE: *There should be zero clearance between the rear bearing snap-ring and the surface of the rear cover.*

30. Assemble the reverse shift arm to its bracket. Finger-tighten the pivot bolt. Install the assembly on the rear cover.

31. Drive the slotted mounting pin in, so that it protrudes 0.08–0.16 in. beyond the rear cover. Tighten the securing bolts to 11–16 ft lbs.

32. Shift the gears to reverse. Check the gear contact. If the gears are meshing properly, the front face of the idler gear will align with the front face of the reverse gear.

33. If necessary, adjust the gear mesh at the pivot.

NOTE: *When the gears are meshing properly, the slot in the pivot should be perpendicular to the rear cover.*

34. Tighten the pivot nut to 7–12 ft lbs and install the lockpin. Be careful not to change gear contact.

35. Install the shift rod from the front end of the extension housing. Fit the spring and housing onto the end of the shift rod. Secure them with a slotted pin.

36. Clean the gasket surfaces of the rear cover and transmission case. Place a new gasket over the end of the transmission case and fit the rear cover assembly into the case.

37. Install the input shaft and countergear front bearing snap-rings.

38. Install the extension housing and gasket over the rear cover, after cleaning both gasket mounting surfaces.

NOTE: *Coat the bushing bore with grease.*

39. Screw the securing bolts through the extension housing, the rear cover and into the transmission case. Tighten the bolts to 22–29 ft lbs.

40. Install the reverse restrictor pin and gasket. Tighten it to 22–29 ft lbs.

41. Push the countergear rearward, as far as it will go and measure the distance (E) in the illustration. Select a spacer to yield the *minimum* clearance which is closest to the measurement obtained. Spacers are available in various sizes.

42. Install the spacer and then the countershaft end covers.

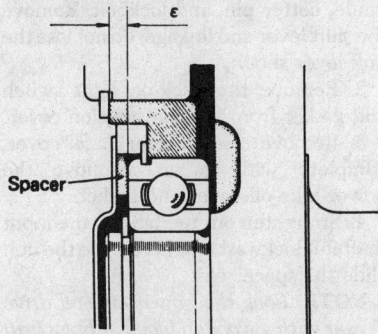

Measure the distance (E) to obtain the proper countergear spacer size.

43. Align the front bearing retainer gasket with the oil holes. Fit the bearing retainer over the gasket and tighten its securing bolts to 4.3–6.5 ft lbs evenly, in two or three stages.

44. Bolt the clutch housing onto the front of the transmission case, evenly, in two or three stages, to 36–50 ft lbs.

45. Attach the shift lever retainer to the extension housing by securing it with its bolts. Tighten the bolts to 11–16 ft lbs. (9–13 ft lbs—W40).

46. Install the speedometer driven gear and secure it with its lockplate. Tighten it to 7.2–11.6 ft lbs.

47. Install the components of the back-up light switch in the reverse order of their removal. Tighten the switch to 27–33 ft lbs.

48. Install the drain plug and its gasket. Tighten the plug to 27–33 ft lbs.

5-Speed Corona, Corolla, Hi-Lux, and Celica—W-50 and K-50

1. Perform steps 1 to 13 of the 4-speed internal shift linkage and W-40 transmission disassembly procedure, above.

NOTE: *On 5-speed transmissions there are two reverse restrictor pins instead of one. The pins are located underneath plugs on the extension housing.*

2. Remove the straight screw plugs from the shift forks and withdraw the springs.

3. Drive the slotted spring pins out of each shift fork.

4. Slide the gear shift fork shafts back and remove the forks. Be careful not to lose the two interlock pins and three balls.

4. Use an expander to remove the speedometer drive gear snap-ring and remove the drive gear. Be careful not to loose the drive gear ball.

5. Remove the snap-ring with an ex-

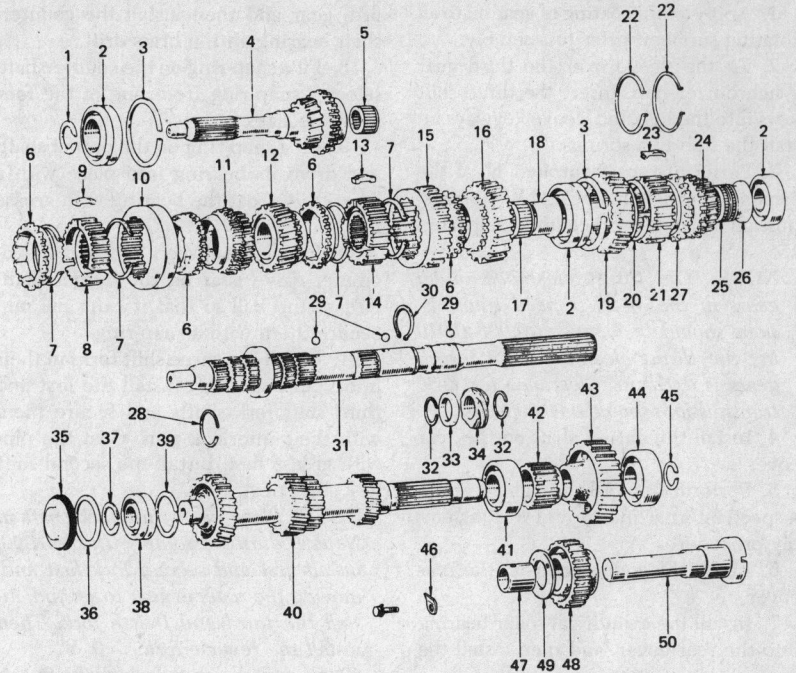

Five-speed transmission components—Celica, Corona, and Half-ton

1. Snap-ring
2. Bearing
3. Snap-ring
4. Input shaft
5. Bearing
6. Synchronizer ring
7. Synchromesh shifting key spring
8. Transmission clutch hub
9. Synchromesh shifting key
10. Transmission hub sleeve
11. Third gear
12. Second gear
13. Synchromesh shifting key
14. Transmission clutch hub
15. Reverse gear
16. First gear
17. Bearing
18. First gear bearing inner race
19. Reverse gear
20. Snap-ring
21. Transmission clutch hub
22. Synchromesh shifting key spring
23. Synchromesh shifting key
24. Fifth gear
25. Bearing
26. Fifth gear inner race
27. Synchronizer ring
28. Snap-ring
29. Ball
30. Snap-ring
31. Output shaft
32. Snap-ring
33. Spacer
34. Speedometer drive gear
35. Countershaft cover
36. Spacer
37. Snap ring
38. Bearing
39. Snap ring
40. Countergear
41. Bearing
42. Countershaft reverse gear
43. Countershaft fifth gear
44. Bearing
45. Snap-ring
46. Stop
47. Bushing
48. Reverse idler gear
49. Reverse dler gear shaft spacer
50. Reverse idler gear shaft

pander and remove the output shaft bearing with a puller.

6. Perform step 5 for the countershaft bearing.

7. Remove the fifth and reverse gears from the countershaft.

8. Remove the snap-ring, fifth gear, its synchronizer ring, needle roller bearing, and fifth gear bearing inner race from the output shaft. Be careful not to lose the fifth gear to inner race lockball.

9. Remove the reverse gear and clutch hub from the output shaft.

10. Loosen the bolt and remove the reverse idler gear stop from the rear cover. Withdraw the reverse idler shaft from the rear; remove the reverse idler gear and spacer.

11. Remove the output shaft rear bearing retainer. Remove the rear bearing snap-ring.

12. Push the countergear bearing outer race rearward, and remove the bearing. Separate the countergear from the rear cover.

13. Separate the input shaft and synchronizer ring from the output shaft.

14. Remove the output shaft from the rear cover.

15. Perform steps 22 through 24 of the 4-speed internal linkage and W-40 disassembly procedure above.

Perform the same cleaning and inspection procedures, as outlined above for the 4-speed internal linkage and the W-40 transmissions.

Asssembly is performed in the following order:

CAUTION: *The transmission case and extension housing are aluminum alloy. Take extreme care with mating surfaces.*

1. Apply a thin coating of gear oil to all rotating surfaces, prior to assembly.

2. Fit the sleeve over the third gear synchronizer hub. Insert the three shift keys into the hub and sleeve keyways install the hub two springs.

3. Perform steps 3 through 17 of the 4-speed internal linkage and W-40 transmission assembly procedure. Skip step 15.

NOTE: *The thrust clearance of all gears in the W-50 5-speed transmissions should be between 0.006–0.010 in.; the thrust clearance limit for all gears is 0.012 in. Clearance for K-50 transmissions should be 0.008–0.012 in.*

4. Install the output shaft on the rear cover.

5. Perform steps 18 through 20 of the 4-speed internal linkage and W-40 assembly procedure.

6. Install the countergear on the rear cover.

7. Install the cylindrical roller bearing into the rear cover, and then install the spacer.

8. Perform steps 21 through 23 of the 4-speed internal linkage and W-40 transmission assembly procedure.

9. Lock the reverse idler shaft on the rear cover with its stop. Check the reverse idler gear thrust clearance, it should be 0.006–0.010 in. The thrust clearance limit is 0.012 in. The K-50 transmission clearance is 0.008–0.012.

10. Install the reverse clutch hub on the reverse gear and check it for smooth engagement.

11. Fit the three shift keys into the hub keyways and secure them with the two springs and a snap-ring.

12. Slide the reverse gear hub over the output shaft until it registers against the inner race of the rear cover bearing.

NOTE: *Tap the hubs lightly into place with a wooden or plastic mallet, if necessary.*

13. Insert the inner race lockball into the output shaft bore, after greasing it so that it can't fall out.

14. Assemble fifth gear, its synchronizer ring, needle roller bearing, and race. Slide the assembly onto the output shaft until the inner bear face rests against the reverse clutch hub. Be sure that the inner race groove is aligned with the lockball. In the K-50, press each synchro ring against the gear. The clearance should be 0.039–0.029 in.

15. Secure fifth gear with a snap-ring. Select the snap-ring from one of 13 sizes available, to obtain minimum axial play.

16. Measure fifth gear thrust clearance; it should be 0.004 to 0.010 in. (K-50 0.008–0.012). The thrust clearance limit is 0.012 in.

17. Install the countershaft reverse gear so that it just rests against the bearing inner race. Install the countershaft

fifth gear and then install the countershaft bearing with a brass drift.

18. Fit a snap-ring on the countershaft; select a snap-ring from one of the four available sizes.

19. Fit a snap-ring on the output shaft, and drive its bearing into place with a brass drift. Coat the bearing with grease first.

20. Install the spacer, ball, and speedometer drive gear on the output shaft. Grease the ball so that it can't fall out. Secure them with a snap-ring.

21. Install the three shift forks in their hub sleeve grooves. Install the first and third shift fork shafts and secure them with their interlock pins. Coat the pins with grease first. Install the second shift fork shaft next.

NOTE: *Place each shift fork shaft in Neutral during assembly. In the K-50, install first and second fork first and, moving the reverse gear to second, install the third and fourth fork. Then install the reverse fork.*

22. Secure the shift fork shafts to the end cover by inserting the lockballs into their bores, followed by the lockball springs. Tighten the lockball plugs to 14–22 ft lbs, after coating the threads with sealer.

23. Use a new gasket between the transmission case and the rear cover. Slide the case into place.

24. Fit snap-rings on the input shaft and countershaft front bearings.

25. Install the shift lever housing on the end of the shifter shaft. Slide the shifter shaft into the extension housing and secure it with a slotted spring pin.

26. Install a new gasket and slide the extension housing into place, until there is about an inch of clearance between it and the rear cover.

27. Rotate the shift lever housing clockwise (as viewed from the rear) to engage the shifter shaft with the selector lever and the shift fork shaft.

28. Slide the extension housing the rest of the way home and tighten its securing bolts to 22–32 ft lbs.

29. Perform steps 42 through 44 of the 4-speed internal linkage and W-40 transmission assembly procedure.

30. Fit the restrictor pins and springs into their extension housing bores. Install the gaskets and tighten the plugs to 27–32 ft lbs.

31. Fit the shift lever retainer over the oil baffle on the extension housing and tighten it to 9–13 ft lbs.

32. Install the shift lever conical spring, large side down, and install the ball seat in the shift lever retainer.

33. Perform steps 46 through 48 of the 4-speed internal linkage and W-40 transmission assembly procedure.

34. Check to see that the input shaft has no more than 0.020 in. end-play. Put

the transmission in Neutral and see if the output shaft can be rotated freely by hand.

35. On the K-50, do not forget to hook the anti-rattle spring securely.

Land Cruiser 3-Speed

1. Remove the transfer case shift lever guide, cotter pin, and lockbolt. Remove the shift lever and linkage; do not lose the link lever shoe.

2. Remove the back-up light switch and gasket from the transmission cover.

3. Remove the transfer case cover, complete with gasket. Remove the power take-off cover and gasket.

4. Straighten out the tabs on the input shaft nut lockwasher and remove the nut. Slide the spacer off.

NOTE: *Lock the power take-off drive gear with a wooden block or brass drift to keep the shaft from turning while the nut is being removed.*

5. Loosen the five bolts which secure the transfer case to the transmission case and separate the cases with a puller. Hold the power take-off drive gear, spacer, and input gear, so that they don't drop out.

6. Unfasten the bolt and remove the gear selector outer lever.

7. Unfasten the bolts and remove the transmission case cover, complete with gasket.

8. Loosen the bolts and remove the front bearing retainer, with gasket, from the transmission case.

9. Drive the shift fork shaft out toward the front of the case with a hammer and a brass drift. Use care not to lose the fork balls, springs and pin.

10. Withdraw the first/reverse shift fork and the second/third shift fork from the transmission case. Remove the lock balls and springs.

11. Drive the countershaft rearward with a brass drift. Remove the countershaft Woodruff key.

NOTE: *The countergear should remain in the case.*

12. Remove the input shaft and bearing with a puller. Install the puller on the front of the input shaft.

13. Use a hammer and a brass drift to drive the output shaft rearward until the output shaft bearing clears the case. Do not pound on the output shaft; tap it gently.

14. Separate the bearing from the output shaft with a puller.

15. Remove the output shaft and the related components from the transmission case.

16. Use a snap-ring expander to remove the snap-ring from the front of the output shaft. Slide the synchronizer clutch hub, sleeve, synchronizer ring, second gear, and the first/reverse gearset off of the shaft.

17. Remove the countershaft drive

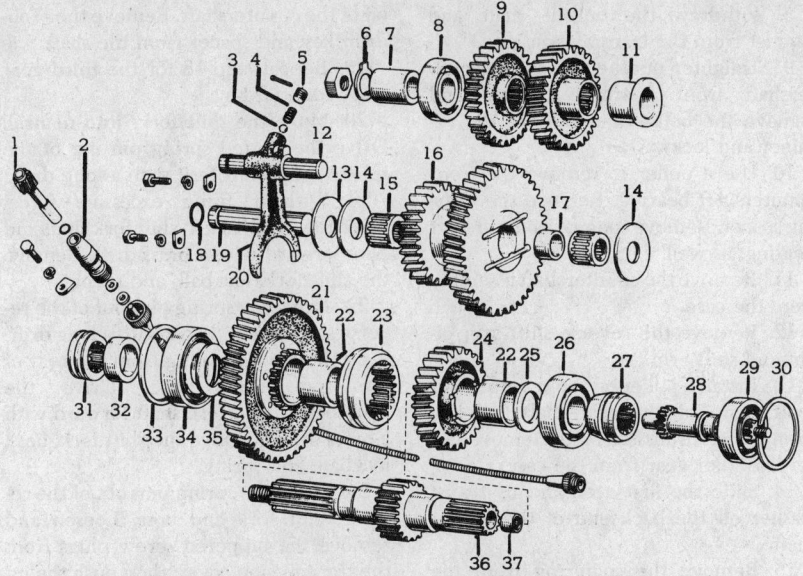

Land Cruiser three-speed transmission

1. Speedometer driven gear
2. Speedometer shaft sleeve
3. Shift fork lockball
4. Compression spring
5. Screw plug
6. Lockwasher
7. Transfer input shaft spacer
8. Bearing
9. Power take-off drive gear
10. Transfer input gear
11. Transfer input gear stop
12. Transfer high & low shift fork shaft
13. Transfer idler gear spacer
14. Washer
15. Needle roller bearing
16. Transfer idler gear
17. Spacer
18. O-ring
19. Transfer idler gear shaft
20. Transfer high and low shift fork
21. Transfer low speed output gear
22. Bushing
23. Transfer high and low clutch sleeve
24. Transfer high speed output gear
25. Washer
26. Bearing
27. Front drive clutch sleeve
28. Transfer output shaft (front)
29. Bearing
30. Snap-ring
31. Speedometer drive gear
32. Spacer
33. Adjusting shim
34. Bearing
35. Washer
36. Transfer output shaft
37. Needle roller bearing

gear, spacer, roller bearing, and washers. Note the placement of the gear thrust washers. Use care not to lose the rollers.

18. Drive the reverse idler gear shaft rearward and remove its Woodruff key.

19. Remove the reverse idler gear, rollers, and thrust washers from the case.

Wash all parts thoroughly. Check the case for cracks and burrs. Inspect the gears, replace any that are worn, cracked, or chipped. Check all internal parts for wear or damage; replace as required.

Gear Backlash

Input shaft gear-to-countershaft drive gear—0.004 in.

Second-to-countergear—0.004 in.

First/reverse gear-to-countergear—0.008 in.

Countergear-to-reverse idler gear—0.008 in.

Reverse gear-to-reverse idler gear—0.008 in.

Synchronizer ring-to-gear—0.039 in.

Transmission assembly is performed in the following order:

NOTE: *Use new gaskets, oil seals, and dust seals. Coat the gaskets with sealer.*

1. Apply a light coating of gear oil to all components, prior to assembly.

2. Grease the bore of the reverse idler gear. Insert the bearing rollers and washer in the bore.

3. Install the reverse idler gear and the two thrust washers into the case. Drive the reverse idler gear shaft through the case, by gently tapping it into place from behind. Lock the shaft into place with the Woodruff key.

4. Grease the bore of the countershaft drive gear and fit its spacer. Install the rollers in the bore and hold them in place with a heavy coating of grease. Install the washers in the bore.

5. Place the countershaft drive gear, thrust washer, and side thrust washers in the case.

6. If the bearing was removed from the input shaft, press it into place on the shaft.

7. Select a snap-ring that will give the input shaft minimum end-play, and install it on the shaft.

8. Grease bore of the input shaft, install the rollers, and then fit the snap-ring.

9. Carefully drive the input shaft assembly and bearing into the transmission case.

10. Lift the countershaft drive gear up and install the countershaft from the rear

of the case. Secure the countershaft with its Woodruff key.

11. Use a feeler gauge to measure the countershaft thrust clearance; it should be 0.002–0.008 in. Select a countergear side thrust washer of the proper size to obtain the specified thrust clearance.

12. Install the two synchronizer shifting key springs into the clutch hub, so that the open ends are 120° apart. Place the three shifting keys into the clutch hub key slots.

13. Slide the clutch hub sleeve into the clutch hub.

14. Fit second gear, its synchronizer ring, and the synchronizer assembly on the output shaft. Check second gear thrust clearance with a feeler gauge. It should be 0.003–0.009 in. Select and install the proper front output shaft snap-ring to obtain this clearance.

15. Working from the rear, slide the first/reverse gearset on the output shaft.

16. Install the output shaft assembly in the transmission case. Using a suitable brass drift, install the rear bearing over the output shaft and into the case.

17. Install both shift forks and retain them with their balls and lockpins.

18. Depress the shift fork lockballs with a screwdriver, then drive the shift fork shaft through the case, and into shift forks.

19. Install a new O-ring on the shift fork shaft and lock it in place with its pin.

20. Coat the front bearing retainer with liquid sealer and install the bearing retainer over it. Tighten the bearing retainer bolts to 11–14 ft lbs.

21. Check all parts for smooth operation and freedom of movement.

22. Install a suitable size pipe over the transmission output shaft. Place the transfer case input gear, power takeoff drive gear, and the spacers over the pipe, which should be projecting through the transfer case.

23. Coat a new gasket with liquid sealer and place the gasket between the transmission case and the transfer case.

24. Install the transfer case on the transmission case and tighten the retaining bolts to 25–30 ft lbs. Be sure to install the two short bolts from the *inside* of the transfer case.

25. Remove the pipe from the output shaft and transfer case.

26. Install the bearing over the end of the transmission output shaft and into the transfer case with a drift.

27. Fit the transfer case input shaft spacer and tighten the bearing nut to 101–108 ft lbs. Use the lockwasher to secure the nut.

28. Install the transfer case cover over its gasket.

29. Coat the gasket with liquid sealer and install the power take-off cover.

30. Install the back-up light switch and gasket.

31. Install the transfer front drive fork and its gasket on the transfer case extension housing.

32. Check all parts for smooth operation.

Land Cruiser 4-Speed

1. Perform steps 1 through 5 of the Land Cruiser three-speed transmission disassembly procedure.

2. Remove the transfer case input shaft gear stop from the transmission rear bearing retainer.

3. Remove the rear bearing retainer and gasket.

4. Remove the front bearing retainer and gasket from the transmission case.

5. Remove the input shaft and front bearing from the case with a puller.

NOTE: *Prior to removing the input shaft, align the slot in the input shaft with the countershaft drivegear. While removing the input shaft, use care not to drop the needle bearings and spacer into the transmission case.*

6. Remove the synchronizer ring.

7. Use an expander to remove the snap-ring on the output shaft rear bearing. Remove the bearing with a puller.

8. Withdraw the output shaft and gearset from the transmission case.

9. Straighten out the tabs on the countershaft front bearing retainer and remove the bolts; then remove the retainer and lockwasher.

10. Use a puller to remove the front countershaft bearing. Remove the bearing spacer. Remove the rear countershaft bearing, as well.

11. Remove the countershaft assembly from the case.

12. Remove the reverse shift arm pivot and shift arm.

13. Install a puller on the reverse idler shaft, and pull the gear shaft and key from the transmission case. Remove the reverse idler gear from the case.

14. Slide the first gear and its thrust washer off the back end of the output shaft.

15. Remove the snap-ring from the front of the output shaft; then remove the clutch hub, sleeve, synchronizer ring, and third gear from the shaft.

16. Remove the snap-ring and slide second gear and thrust washer off the shaft.

17. Slide the reverse gear synchronizer ring off the output shaft.

18. Press the countershaft drive gear

off of the countershaft. Remove the Woodruff key and spacer from the shaft.

19. Repeat step 18 for the third gear and Woodruff key.

20. Move the shift forks into neutral. Drive the slotted spring pin out of the third/fourth shift fork with a long drift.

21. Without using excessive force, drive the third/fourth shift fork shaft and plug forward with a brass drift. Remove the shift fork, lockball, and spring.

22. Drive the spring pins out of the reverse shift fork and boss with a long drift.

23. Remove the plug from the rear of the transmission case. Drive the first/second shift fork shaft forward with a brass drift. Remove the shift fork, boss, lockball, and spring.

24. Drive the spring pins out of the reverse shift fork and boss. Loosen and remove the tappered screw plugs from the transmission cover; then push the interlock rollers out with a long drift.

25. Remove the cotter pin, spring, and lockball from the shift fork boss.

26. Remove the C-washer, then withdraw the reverse return spring and plunger from the boss.

Wash all parts thoroughly. Check the case for cracks and burrs. Inspect the gears, replace any that are worn, cracked, or chipped. Check all internal parts for wear or damage; replace as required.

Gear Backlash

Input gear-to-countershaft drivegear—0.004 in.

Third gear-to-countershaft gear—0.004 in.

Second gear-to-countershaft gear—0.004 in.

First gear-to-countershaft gear—0.004 in.

Reverse gear-to-reverse idler gear—0.005 in.

To assemble the transmission:

NOTE: *Use new gaskets, oil seals, and dust seals. Coat the gaskets with sealer.*

1. Apply a light coating of gear oil to all components, prior to assembly.

2. Place the reverse idler gear in the case with its fork groove facing forward.

3. Align the Woodruff key, groove, and slot. Carefully drive the reverse idler shaft through the holes in the case, and into the gear.

NOTE: *If you install new bushings in the idler gear, be sure that their openings are at least 90° apart.*

4. Adjust the reverse idler gear position by turning the shaft arm pivot to obtain a distance of 4.49 in. between the outer rear of the transmission case and the reverse idler gear. Tighten the shift arm pivot nut. Move the gear to neutral; the distance between the front end of the gear and outer rear of the transmission case should now be 2.71 in. Adjust by rotating the shift arm pivot.

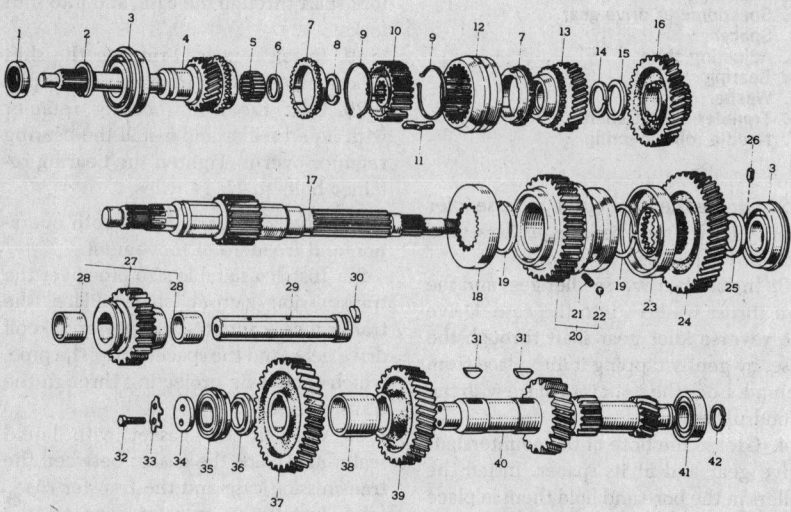

Land Cruiser four-speed transmission

1. Oil seal
2. Snap-ring
3. Bearing
4. Input shaft
5. Bearing roller
6. Bearing spacer
7. Synchronizer ring No. 2
8. Snap-ring
9. Shift-key spring
10. Clutch hub No. 2
11. Shift key No. 2
12. Hub sleeve
13. Third gear
14. Snap-ring
15. Second gear thrust washer
16. Second gear
17. Output shaft
18. Second synchronizer outer ring
19. Snap-ring
20. Synchronizer ring No. 1
21. Compression spring
22. Lockball
23. First synchronizer outer ring
24. First gear
25. First gear thrust washer
26. Straight pin
27. Reverse idler gear
28. Bushing
29. Reverse idler gear shaft
30. Woodruff key
31. Woodruff key
32. Bolt
33. Lockbolt washer
34. Lockbolt plate
35. Bearing
36. Front bearing spacer
37. Countershaft drive gear
38. Spacer
39. Counter shaft third speed gear
40. Countershaft
41. Bearing
42. Snap-ring

5. Install the Woodruff key into the groove of the countershaft and align its keyway with the countershaft third gear. Place the gear on the shaft with the long hub facing forward.

6. Slide the spacer on the countershaft and press its drivegear on, in a similar manner to third gear (step 5), with its long hub facing rearward.

7. Place the countershaft assembly into the transmission case and install the countershaft rear bearing with a press. Install the snap-ring over the end of the countershaft.

8. Install the front bearing spacer, protruded end forward, on the countershaft. Press the front bearing on, until its snap-ring registers firmly against the transmission case.

CAUTION: *Apply pressure to the outer bearing race only, to prevent damage to the bearing.*

9. Place the bearing retainer and lockwasher on the front of the countershaft. Tighten the bearing retainer bolts to 11–16 ft lbs. Bend the lockwasher tabs upward.

10. Slide second gear on the output shaft so that its synchronizer outer ring faces rearward. Select a snap-ring so that second gear has a thrust clearance of 0.004–0.012 in.

11. Slide third gear on the output shaft, so that its synchronizer cone faces forward.

12. Perform steps 12 and 13 of the Land Cruiser three-speed transmission assembly procedure.

13. Install the synchronizer ring and slide the synchronizer assembly over the output shaft. The grooves should face the rear.

14. Select a snap-ring to provide 0.008 in. thrust clearance for the clutch hub.

15. Slide the reverse gear synchronizer ring over the output shaft. Check the ring for smooth movement.

16. Slide first gear on the output shaft.

17. Place the output shaft assembly in the transmission case.

18. Fit the first gear thrust washer on the output shaft. Align the slot in the thrust washer with the output shaft pin.

19. Install the output shaft rear bearing with a press. Be sure to apply pressure on the bearing *outer* race only. Install the rear bearing and its gasket.

20. Press-fit the bearing on the input shaft. Grease the bearing rollers and install all 18 in the input shaft.

21. Place the input shaft in the transmission case, so that the synchronizer ring keyways align with the shift keys. Install the input shaft bearing spacer in the input shaft.

CAUTION: *Be sure the bearing rollers or the spacer do not fall into the transmission case during installation.*

22. Install the input shaft bearing re-

tainer and gasket. Tighten the retainer bolts to 7–11 ft lbs.

NOTE: *Make sure that all shift fork shafts are in neutral during the shift fork shaft assembly steps, below.*

23. Install the spring and return plunger in the reverse shift boss. Secure them with the C-washer. Install the ball and spring then secure them with a cotter pin.

24. Place the reverse shift fork and boss in the transmission cover. Install the fork lock-spring and ball in the cover.

25. Slide the reverse shift fork shaft through the front of the cover, its bore, shift fork and into its boss, while depressing the lockball with a screwdriver.

26. Align the holes and drive the slotted spring pin through the reverse shift fork and boss to secure them to the shaft.

27. Coat the roller with grease and install it into the interlock hole in the cover.

28. Place the first/second shift boss and fork into the cover. Install the first/second shift fork shaft and spacer from the front of the cover, after fitting its pin, and while depressing the lockball with a screwdriver.

29. Secure the first/second shift fork and boss with their slotted spring pins. Install another roller into the hole in the cover.

30. Install the third/fourth shift fork lock-spring and ball in the shift fork. Install the shift fork and shaft in the cover

and secure them with a slotted spring pin.

31. Check the shift fork assembly for smooth operation. Apply liquid sealer to the plugs and screw plug threads. Install the plugs.

32. Perform steps 22 through 31 of the Land Cruiser three-speed transmission assembly procedure.

33. Place the transmission and shift forks in neutral and install the transmission cover with gasket on the transmission case.

34. Check the transmission and transfer case for smooth operation.

Shift Linkage Adjustment

Land Cruiser—Column Shift

Shift lever adjustment:

The only adjustments which may be performed on the column shift linkages are for the length of the column-to-rods. Adjust these so that the transmission operates smoothly

Floor Shifter Adjustment

All Toyota models equipped with a floor shifter have internally-mounted shift linkages. On older models, the linkage is contained in the side cover which is bolted on the transmission case. Newer cars have the shift linkage mounted in the top of the transmission case itself.

No external adjustment is needed or possible.

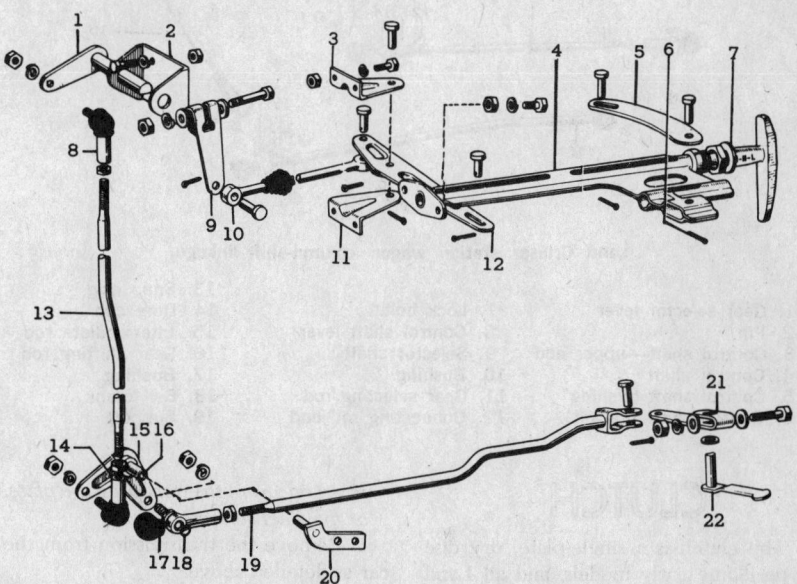

Transfer case shift linkage station wagon

1. High/low shift link	12. Front drive engagement lever
2. Shift link bracket	13. High/low connecting rod
3. Bracket	14. Connecting rod end—lower
4. Shift lever housing	15. Bell crank
5. Lever	16. Bushing
6. Cotter pin	17. Dust cap
7. Transfer range selector lever	18. Snap ring
8. Connecting rod end—upper	19. High/low shift rod
9. Shift link lever	20. Support
10. High/low shift intermediate rod	21. Transfer case high/low shift lever
11. Bracket	22. Lever

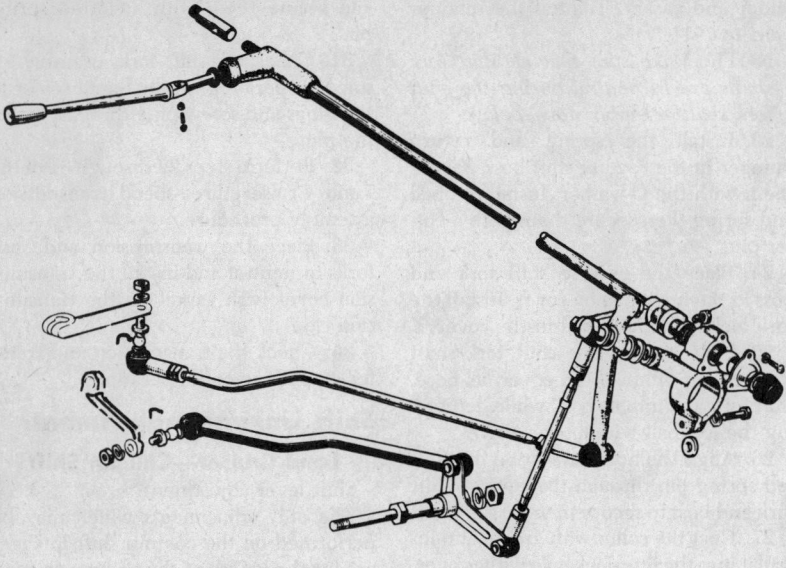

Two-door Land Cruiser column-shift linkage.

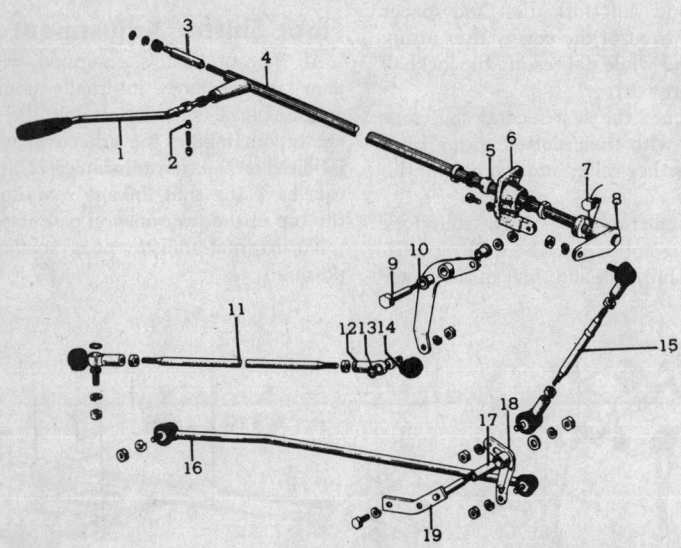

Land Cruiser station wagon column-shift linkage.

1. Gear selector lever	7. Lock bolt	13. Snap ring
2. Pin	8. Control shaft lever	14. Dust cap
3. Control shaft—upper end	9. Selector shaft	15. Intermediate rod
4. Control shaft	10. Bushing	16. Gear shifting rod
5. Control shaft bushing	11. Gear selecting rod	17. Bushing
6. Control shaft bracket	12. Connecting rod end	18. Bell crank
		19. Support

CLUTCH

The clutch is a single-plate, dry disc type. Some early models, and all Land Cruisers, use a coil-spring pressure plate. Later models use a diaphragm-spring pressure plate. Clutch release bearings are sealed ball bearing units which need no lubrication and should never be washed in any kind of solvent. All clutches, except those on the Corolla 1200 series, are hydraulically operated.

Removal and Installation

CAUTION: *Do not allow grease or oil*

to get on any of the disc, pressure plate, or flywheel surfaces.

1. Remove the transmission from the car as detailed above.

2. Remove the clutch cover and disc from the bellhousing.

3. Unfasten the release fork bearing clips. Withdraw the release bearing hub, complete with the release bearing.

4. Remove the tension spring from the clutch linkage.

5. Remove the release fork and support.

6. Punch matchmarks on the clutch cover and the pressure plate so the pres-

sure plate can be returned to its original position during installation.

7. Slowly unfasten the screws which attach the retracting springs.

NOTE: *If the screws are released too fast, the clutch assembly will fly apart, causing possible injury or loss of parts.*

8. Separate the pressure plate from the clutch cover/spring assembly.

Inspect the parts for wear or deterioration. Replace parts as required.

Installation is performed in the reverse order of removal. Several points should be noted, however:

1. Be sure to align the matchmarks on the clutch cover and pressure plate which were made during disassembly.

2. Apply a thin coating of multipurpose grease to the release bearing hub and release fork contact points. Also, pack the groove inside the clutch hub with multipurpose grease.

3. Center the clutch disc by using a clutch pilot tool or an old input shaft. Insert the pilot into the end of the input shaft front bearing and bolt the clutch to the flywheel.

NOTE: *Bolt the clutch assembly to the flywheel in two or three stages.*

4. Adjust the clutch as outlined.

Pedal Height Specifications

Model	Height (in.)	Measure between:
Corolla 1200 (All)	2.2①	Pedal pad and floor mat
Corolla 1600 ('70-'74)	2.8①	Pedal pad and floor mat
Corolla 1600 ('75-'77)	6.5	Pedal pad and floor mat
Carina (All)	6.3	Pedal pad and floor mat
Corona ('72-'73)	5.7-6.1	Pedal pad and floor mat
Corona ('74-'77)	6.3-6.7	Pedal pad and floor mat
Mark II/4 (All)	6.0-6.2	Pedal pad and top of floor panel
Mark II/6 (All)	6.2-6.6	Pedal pad and asphalt seat
Celica (All)	6.3	Pedal pad and floor mat
Crown 2600 (All)	6.8	Pedal pad and asphalt seat
Hi-Lux ('72)	6.0	Pedal pad and floor
Hi-Lux ('73-'77)	6.3	Pedal from toe-board
Land Cruiser 2-dr. (All)	6.7	Pedal pad and firewall
Station Wagon (All)	9.6	Pedal pad and firewall

① Pedal depressed

Free-Play Adjustment

Corolla 1200

1. Pull on the clutch release cable at the clutch support flange until a resistance is felt when the release bearing contacts the clutch diaphragm spring.

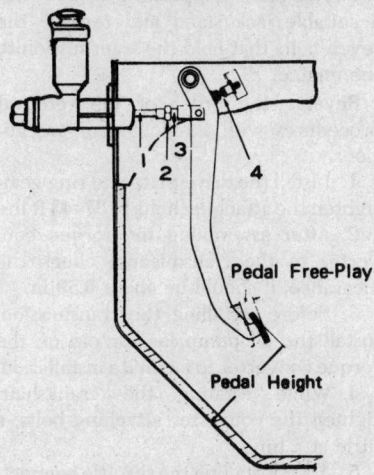

Clutch pedal adjustments

1. Master cylinder push rod
2. Push rod locknut
3. Clevis
4. Pedal stop (bolt)

2. Holding the cable in this position, measure the distance between the E-ring and the end of the wire support flange. The distance should be 5–6 threads.

3. If adjustment is required, change the position of the E-ring.

4. After completing the adjustment, check the clutch pedal free-play which should be 0.8–1.4 in. after the pedal is depressed several times.

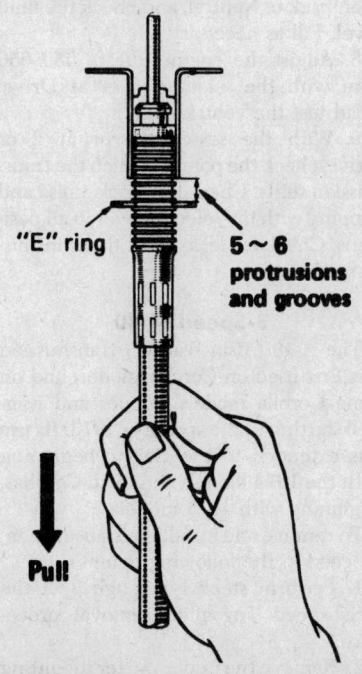

"E" ring

5~6 protrusions and grooves

Pull

Clutch release cable adjustment—Corolla 1200.

All—Except Corolla 1200

1. Adjust the clearance between the master cylinder piston and the pushrod to the specifications given in the chart below. Loosen the pushrod locknut and rotate the pushrod while depressing the clutch pedal lightly with your finger.

2. Tighten the locknut when finished the adjustment.

3. Adjust the release cylinder free-play by loosening the release cylinder pushrod locknut and rotating the pushrod until the specification in the chart is obtained.

4. Measure the clutch pedal free-play after performing the above adjustments. If it fails to fall within specifications, repeat steps 1–3 until it does.

Clutch Master Cylinder

Removal and Installation

CAUTION: *Do not spill brake fluid on the painted surfaces of the vehicle.*

1. Remove the clevis pin.
2. Detach the hydraulic line from the tube.
3. Unfasten the bolts which secure the master cylinder to the firewall. Withdraw the assembly.

Installation is performed in the reverse order of removal. Bleed the system as detailed below. Adjust the clutch pedal height and free-play.

Overhaul

1. Remove master cylinder.
2. Remove the reservoir.

3. Disengage the snap ring and take out the push rod and piston.

4. Inspect all parts for pitting and wear and replace as necessary.

5. Apply a grease compatible with rubber, to the piston seals.

6. Install the push rod and piston and secure with a snap ring and washer.

7. Install the reservoir. Torque to 22 ftlb.

8. Install master cylinder.

9. Bleed the system.

Clutch Release Cylinder

Removal and Installation

1. Plug the master cylinder cap to prevent fluid leakage.

2. Raise the front of the vehicle and support it with jackstands.

3. Remove the gravel shield, if necessary, to gain access to the release cylinder.

4. Unfasten the clutch fork return spring at the fork.

5. Detach the hydraulic line from the release cylinder.

6. Screw the release cylinder push rod in.

7. Loosen and remove the securing nuts from the release cylinder. Remove the cylinder.

Installation is performed in the reverse order of removal. Adjust the release fork-to-release cylinder free-play and bleed the hydraulic system, after installation is completed.

Overhaul

1. Remove the release cylinder.

CLUTCH PEDAL FREE-PLAY ADJUSTMENTS

Model	Master Cylinder piston to pushrod clearance (in.)	Release cylinder to release fork free-play (in.)	Pedal free-play (in.)
Corolla	0.02	1.00-1.40	1.00-1.80
Corolla 1600	0.02	0.08-0.14	0.79-1.58
Carina	0.04-0.12	0.08-0.14	1.00-1.75
Corona 2000	0.02-0.12	0.08-0.14	1.00-1.75
Corona 2000/2200⑥	—	0.08-0.12	0.04-0.28
Mark II/4	①	0.08-0.14	0.79-1.58
Mark II/6	0.02-0.12	0.08-0.12	1.20-1.80
Celica	0.04-0.12	0.08-0.14	1.00-1.75
Crown 2600	0.02-0.12	0.08-0.14③	1.40-2.20
Hi-Lux	④	0.145	1.30
Land Cruiser—2-dr	⑤	0.120	1.00
Land Cruiser—Station Wagon	⑤	0.210	1.38

① Not adjustable
② Measured at clutch pedal
③ Adjustable type only
④ Adjust by feel
⑤ Adjust so that pushrod pin will fit through clevis
⑥ 1975-77

2. Remove the pushrod, boot, piston and cup.

3. Inspect all parts for pitting and wear. Replace as necessary.

4. Coat piston seal and cup with a grease compatible with rubber.

5. Install all parts.

6. Install cylinder.

7. Bleed the system.

AUTOMATIC TRANSMISSION

All 1972 and some 1973–74 Corolla models use a two-speed Toyoglide automatic transmission as optional equipment. Starting in mid-1973 all Corona and in 1974 Celica models and some Corolla models use a three-speed transmission made by Aisin-Warner (A-40). All 1975 Corolla models use the A-40 transmission. All other models use a three-speed Toyoglide unit. Land Cruisers are not available with automatic transmissions.

This section covers routine service, basic adjustments, and transmission removal.

Removal and Installation

2-Speed Toyoglide

1. Disconnect the battery.

2. Drain all coolant from the engine and disconnect the radiator inlet hose.

3. Disconnect the throttle link from the carburetor bell-crank (remove the air filter if necessary).

4. Remove the exhaust pipe flange nuts, then jack up the car and support it on stands.

5. Drain the transmission, remove the drive shaft and remove the exhaust pipe bracket from the transmission case.

6. Disconnect the exhaust pipe and transmission shift rod from the control shaft.

7. Disconnect the throttle link rod from the throttle valve lever, then disconnect the speedometer drive cable.

8. Unbolt the torque converter from the drive plate. Remove the four bolts from the rear support and take off the crossmember. (Support the transmission with a suitable jack.)

9. Remove the clamp from the two cooler lines and disconnect both lines, then remove the seven bolts that hold the transmission case to the bellhousing.

10. Withdraw the transmission slowly so as not to damage the seal.

CAUTION: *There will be some fluid in the converter, be prepared with a drain pan.*

Installation

Reverse the order of the removal procedures, with the following precautions.

1. Do not extend the crankshaft locating dowel more than 0.315 in. from the end.

2. Tighten the drive plate to 45–47 ft lbs.

3. When installing the torque converter position the drive plate as it was during removal.

4. Tighten the drive plate to the pump impeller front disc to 7–10 ft lbs. First tighten the eight bolts finger tight, then to the specified torque.

5. When installing the transmission, align the pump drive keys of the pump impeller with the key holes of the pump drive gear.

6. After installing the transmission, adjust the throttle link connecting rod, and the selector lever.

7. Fill the transmission with automatic transmission fluid, and then start the engine. Run the engine at idle speed, with the selector lever at N (Neutral). Add fluid gradually up to the F line of the level gauge. After warming the engine, fill the transmission with automatic transmission fluid.

8. Adjust the engine idle to 600 rpm, with the selector at N (Neutral).

9. Road test the vehicle. With the selector lever at D (Drive), check the point at which the transmission shifts. Check for shock, noise and slippage, with the selector lever in all positions. Check for leakage from the transmission.

Torque Specifications

Drive plate to crankshaft: 33–39 ft lbs
Drive plate to torque converter: 8–11 ft lbs
Transmission housing to engine: 37–50 ft lbs
Transmission housing to case: 14–22 ft lbs

3-Speed Toyoglide

1. Disconnect the battery.

2. Remove the air cleaner and disconnect the accelerator torque link or the cable.

3. Disconnect the throttle link rod at the carburetor side, then disconnect the back-up light wiring at the firewall (on early models).

4. Jack up the car and support it on stands, then drain the transmission. (Use a clean receptacle so that the fluid can be checked for color, smell and foreign matter.)

5. Disconnect all shift linkage.

6. On early models, remove the cross shaft from the frame.

7. Disconnect the throttle link rod at the transmission side and remove the speedometer cable, cooler lines and parking brake equalizer bracket.

8. Loosen the exhaust flange nuts and remove the exhaust pipe clamp and bracket.

9. Remove the drive shaft and the rear mounting bracket, then lower the rear end of the transmission carefully.

10. Unbolt the torque converter from the drive plate. Support the engine with a suitable jack stand and remove the seven bolts that hold the transmission to the engine.

Reverse the order of the removal procedures with the following precautions.

1. Install the drive plate and ring gear, tighten the attaching bolts to 37–43 ft lbs.

2. After assembling the torque converter to the transmission, check the clearance, it should be about 0.59 in.

3. Before installing the transmission, install the oil pump locator pin on the torque converter to facilitate installation.

4. While rotating the crankshaft, tighten the converter attaching bolts, a little at a time.

5. After installing the throttle connecting second rod, make sure the throttle valve lever indicator aligns with the mark on the transmission with the carburetor throttle valve fully opened. If required, adjust the rod.

6. To install the transmission control rod correctly, move the transmission lever to N (Neutral), and the selector lever to Neutral. Fill the transmission with automatic transmission fluid (Type F only), then start the engine. Run the engine at idle speed and apply the brakes while moving the selector lever through all positions, then return it to Neutral.

7. After warming the engine, move the selector lever through all positions, then back to Neutral, and check the fluid level. Fill as necessary.

8. Adjust the engine idle to 550–650 rpm with the selector lever at Drive. Road test the vehicle.

9. With the selector lever at 2 or Drive, check the point at which the transmission shifts. Check for shock, noise and slipping with the selector lever in all positions. Check for leaks from the transmission.

3-Speed A-40

The A-40 (Aisin-Warner) transmission was first used on Corona models and on some Corolla models (coupes and wagons) starting in the spring of 1973. Its use was extended to the Celica, beginning with the 1974 models and to all Corollas, beginning with 1975 models.

To remove and install the transmission, proceed in the following manner:

1. Perform steps 1 through 3 of the three-speed Toyoglide removal procedure.

2. Remove the upper starter mounting nuts using a socket wrench with a long extension.

3. Raise the car and support it securely with jackstands. Drain the transmission.

4. Remove the lower starter mounting bolt and lay the starter along side of the engine. Don't let it hang by the wires.

5. Unbolt the parking brake equalizer support.

6. Matchmark the driveshaft and the companion flange, to ensure correct installation. Remove the bolts securing the driveshaft to the companion flange.

7. Slide the driveshaft straight back and out of the transmission. Use a spare U-joint yoke or tie a plastic bag over the end of the transmission to keep any fluid from dripping out.

8. Remove the bolts from the cross-shaft body bracket, the cotter pin from the manual lever, and the cross-shaft socket from the transmission.

9. Remove the exhaust pipe bracket from the torque converter bell housing.

10. Disconnect the oil cooler lines from the transmission and remove the line bracket from the bell housing.

11. Disconnect the speedometer cable from the transmission.

12. Unbolt both support braces from the bell housing.

13. Use a transmission jack to raise the transmission slightly.

14. Unbolt the rear crossmember and lower the transmission about 3 in.

15. Pry the two rubber torque converter access plugs out of their holes at the back of the engine.

16. Remove the six torque converter mounting bolts through the access hole. Rotate the engine with the crankshaft pulley.

17. Cut the head off of a bolt to make a guide pin for the torque converter. Install the pin on the converter.

18. Remove the converter bell housing-to-engine bolts.

19. Push on the end of the guide pin in order to remove the converter with the transmission. Remove the transmission rearward and then bring it out from under the car.

CAUTION: *Don't catch the throttle cable during removal.*

Installation is the reverse of removal. Be sure to note the following, however:

1. Install the two long bolts on the upper converter housing and tighten them to 36–58 ft lbs.

2. Tighten the converter-to-flex-plate bolts finger-tight, and then tighten them with a torque wrench to 11–16 ft lbs.

3. When installing the speedometer cable, make sure that the felt dust protector and washer are on the cable end.

4. Tighten the cooling line and exhaust pipe bracket mounting bolts to 37–58 ft lbs. Tighten the cooling lines to 14–22 ft lbs.

5. Align the matchmarks made on the driveshaft and the companion flange dur-

ing removal. Tighten the driveshaft mounting bolts to 11–16 ft lbs.

6. Be sure to install the oil pan drain plug. Tighten it to 11–14 ft lbs.

7. Adjust the throttle cable.

8. Fill the transmission to the proper capacity. Use only type "F" (ATF) fluid. Start the engine, run the selector through all gear ranges and place it in Park (P). Check the level on the dipstick and add type F fluid, as necessary.

9. Road test the car and check for leaks.

Pan Removal

1. Remove the oil plug and drain the fluid from the transmission.

2. Unfasten the pan securing bolts.

3. Remove the pan.

Installation is the reverse of removal. Torque the pan securing bolts to 4–6 ft lbs. Refill the transmission with fluid.

Low Servo and Band Adjustment

2 Speed

The low servo and band adjusting bolt is located on the outside of the transmission case, so it is unnecessary to remove the oil pan in order to perform the adjustment.

Adjusting the low servo and band—Corolla two-speed automatic.

1. Loosen the locknut on the adjusting bolt.

2. Tighten the bolt until it is bottomed.

3. Back off 3½ turns (3 turns—Corona) and hold the adjusting bolt securely while tightening the locknut.

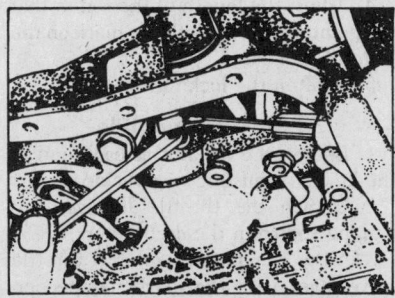

Adjusting the three-speed Toyoglide front band.

Front Band Adjustment

3 Speed

1. Remove the oil pan as outlined above.

2. Pry the band engagement lever toward the band with a screwdriver.

3. The gap between the end of the piston rod and the engagement bolt should be 0.138 in.

4. If the gap does not meet the specification, adjust it by turning the engagement bolt.

5. Install the oil pan and refill the transmission as outlined above.

Rear Band Adjustment

3 Speed

The rear band adjusting bolt is located on the outside of the case, so it is not necessary to remove the oil pan in order to adjust the band.

1. Loosen the adjusting bolt locknut and fully screw in the adjusting bolt.

2. Loosen the adjusting bolt one turn.

3. Tighten the locknut while holding the bolt so that it cannot turn.

Band Adjustments

3-Speed A-40

The A-40 transmission has no bands, and therefore no band adjustments are possible. The only external adjustments are throttle and shift linkages.

Neutral Safety Switch Adjustment

Corolla—1972–1977

The neutral safety switch used on 1972–77 Corolla models is not adjustable. If it malfunctions, it must be replaced. To do so, proceed in the following manner:

1. Remove the center console.

2. Unfasten and remove the three screws which secure the transmission selector assembly.

3. Disconnect the neutral safety switch multiconnector.

4. Slightly lift the transmission selector assembly and remove the two neutral safety switch attaching screws.

5. Withdraw the switch.

Installation is the reverse of removal. Position the selector lever in Neutral and install the switch so that installation marks align with each other.

3 Speed—Column Selector

The neutral safety switch/reverse lamp switch on the Toyoglide transmission with a column-mounted selector is located under the hood on the shift linkage. If the switch is not functioning properly, adjust as follows:

1. Loosen the switch securing bolt.

2. Move the switch so that its arm just contacts the control shaft lever when the gear selector is in Drive position.

3. Tighten the switch securing bolt.

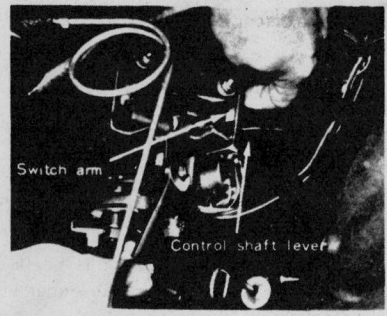

Adjusting the neutral safety switch on models wih three-speed Toyoguide and a column-mounted shift.

4. Check the operation of the switch; the car should start only in Park or Neutral and the back-up lamps should come on only when Reverse is selected.

5. If the switch cannot be adjusted so that it functions properly, replace it. Perform the adjustment as outlined.

3 Speed—Console Shift

Models with a console-mounted selector have the neutral safety switch on the linkage located beneath the console. To adjust it, proceed in the following manner:

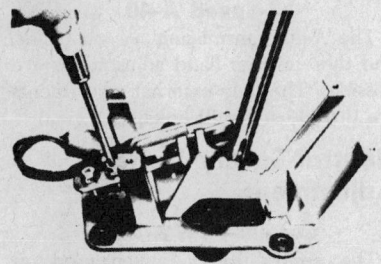

Adjusting the neutral safety switch on models with three-speed Toyoglide and a floor-mounted shift.

1. Remove the screws which secure the center console.

2. Unfasten the console multiconnector, if so equipped, and completely remove the console.

3. Adjust the switch in the manner outlined in the column selector section, above.

4. Install the console in the reverse order of removal after completion of the switch adjustment.

Shift Linkage Adjustment
2 and 3 Speed Toyoglide

1. Check all of the shift linkage bushings for wear. Replace any worn bushings.

2. Loosen the connecting rod swivel locknut.

3. Move the selector lever and check movement of the pointer in the shift quadrant.

4. When the control shaft is set in the neutral position the quadrant pointer should indicate "N" (Neutral), as well.

Steps 5–7 apply only to cars equipped with column-mounted shift levers.

5. If the pointer does not indicate Neutral, then check the drive cord adjustment.

6. Remove the steering column shroud.

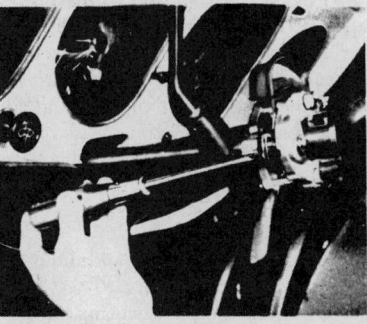

Adjusting the column-shift indicator drive cord.

7. Turn the drive cord adjuster with a phillips screwdriver until the pointer indicates Neutral.

Steps 8–10 apply to both column-mounted and floor-mounted selectors:

8. Position the manual valve lever on the transmission so that it is in the Neutral position.

9. Lock the connecting rod swivel with the locknut so that the pointer, selector, and manual valve lever are all positioned in Neutral.

10. Check the operation of the gear selector by moving it through all ranges.

3-Speed A-40

1. Check the linkage for freedom of movement.

2. Push the manual valve lever toward the front of the car, as far as it will go.

3. Bring the lever back to its third notch (Neutral).

4. Have someone hold the shift lever in Neutral, while you tighten the linkage so that it can't slip.

Throttle Linkage Adjustment
2 Speed Toyoglide

1. Loosen the locknuts on the throttle linkage connecting rod turnbuckle.

2. Have someone depress the accelerator pedal fully.

3. Hold the throttle butterfly in the fully opened position.

4. Adjust the length of the rod so that the pointer lines up with the mark on the transmission case.

5. Tighten the locknut.

3 Speed Toyoglide

1. Loosen the locknut at each end of the linkage adjusting turnbuckle.

2. Detach the throttle linkage connecting rod from the carburetor.

3. Align the pointer on the throttle valve lever with the mark stamped on the transmission case.

4. Rotate the turnbuckle so that the

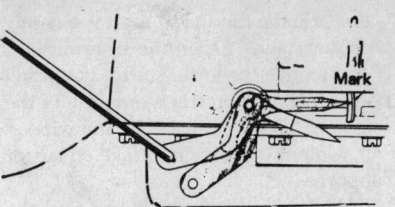

Throttle linkage aligning marks

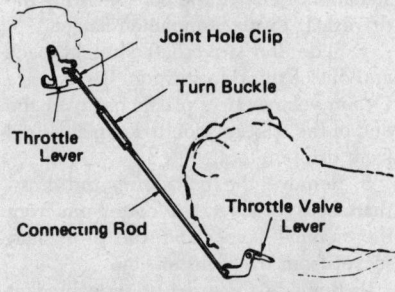

Throttle linkage components

end of the throttle linkage rod and the carburetor throttle lever are aligned.

NOTE: *The carburetor throttle valve must be fully opened during this adjustment.*

5. Tighten the turnbuckle locknuts and reconnect the throttle rod to the carburetor.

6. Open the throttle valve and check the pointer alignment with the mark on the transmission case.

7. Road-test the car. If the transmission "hunts," i.e, keeps shifting rapidly back and forth between gears at certain speeds or if it fails to downshift properly when going up hills, repeat the throttle linkage adjustment.

3-Speed A-40

1. Remove the air cleaner.

2. Confirm that the accelerator linkage opens the throttle fully. Adjust the link as necessary.

3. Peel the rubber dust boot back from the throttle cable.

4. Loosen the adjustment nuts on the throttle cable bracket (rocker cover) just enough to allow cable housing movement.

5. Have someone depress the accelerator pedal fully.

6. Adjust the cable housing so that the distance between its end the cable stop collar is 2.05 in.

7. Tighten the adjustment nuts. Make sure that the adjustment hasn't changed. Install the dust boot and the air cleaner.

DRIVE AXLES
Driveshaft and U-Joints
Removal and Installation
Passenger Cars and Hi-Lux

1. Raise the rear of the car with jacks

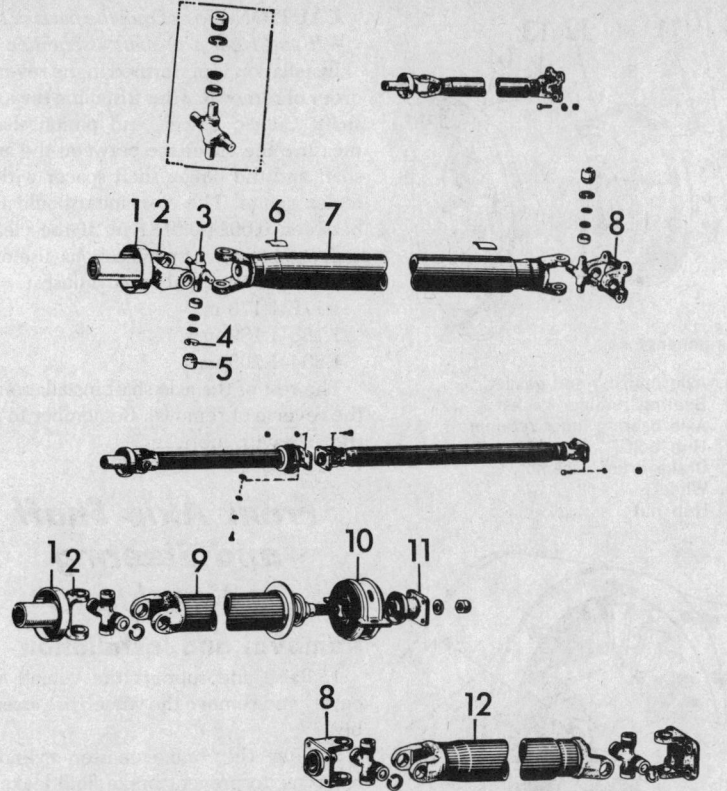

Driveshaft components—the upper illustration shows a single piece driveshaft.

1. Transmission end of driveshaft
2. U-joint yoke and sleeve
3. U-joint spider
4. Snap ring
5. U-joint spider bearing
6. Balancing weight
7. Driveshaft

8. U-joint yoke flange
9. Intermediate driveshaft assembly
10. Center bearing support
11. U-joint flange assembly
12. Driveshaft

Two-piece driveshaft only

and support the rear axle housing with jackstands.

2. Matchmark the driveshaft and companion flange. Unfasten the bolts which attach the driveshaft universal joint yoke flange to the mounting flange on the differential drive pinion.

3. On models equipped with three universal joints, perform the following:

   a. Remove the driveshaft subassembly from the U-joint sleeve yoke.

   b. Remove the center support bearing from its bracket.

4. Remove the driveshaft end from the transmission.

5. Install an old U-joint yoke in the transmission or, if none is available, use a plastic bag secured with a rubber band over the hole to keep the transmission oil from running out.

6. Remove the driveshaft from beneath the vehicle.

Installation is performed in the following order:

1. Apply multipurpose grease on the section of the U-joint sleeve which is to be inserted into the transmission.

2. Insert the driveshaft sleeve into the transmission.

CAUTION: *Be careful not to damage any of the seals.*

3. For models equipped with three U-joints and center bearings, perform the following:

   a. Adjust the center bearing clearance with no load placed on the driveline components; the top of the rubber center cushion should be 0.04 in. *behind* the center of the elongated bolt hole.

   b. Install the center bearing assembly.

NOTE: *Use the same number of washers on the center bearing bracket as were removed.*

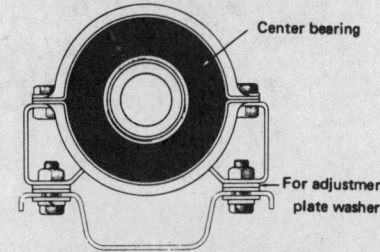

Center bearing

For adjustment plate washer

Center bearing adjustment

   c. On Hi-Lux models, match the arrow marks on the driveshaft and grease fittings.

4. Align the matchmarks. Secure the U-joint flange to the differential pinion flange with the mounting bolts.

CAUTION: *Be sure that the bolts are of the same type as those removed and that they are tightened securely.*

5. Remove the jackstands and lower the vehicle.

Land Cruiser

Land Cruiser models are equipped with two driveshafts; one runs from the transfer case to the rear differential and the other from the transfer case to the front differential. Removal and installation of both driveshafts is performed in the same manner.

1. Raise the vehicle and support it with jackstands.

2. Unfasten the bolts which secure the universal joint flange to the differential pinion flange.

3. Perform step 2 for the U-joint-to-transfer case flange bolts.

4. Withdraw the driveshaft from beneath the vehicle.

Installation is performed in the reverse order of removal.

NOTE: *Lubricate the U-joints and sliding joints with multipurpose grease before installation.*

U-Joint Overhaul

1. Mark the flange yoke and shaft for reassembly.

2. Remove the snap rings and, using a hammer and drift, drive one bearing cap most of the way out. Remove it with a pliers.

3. Drive the opposite cap out.

4. Repeat this procedure for the other two caps.

5. Remove the spider.

6. Install a new spider in the yoke.

7. Press bearing caps over spider using a vise.

8. Install snap rings.

9. Assemble drive shaft and check for smoothness of operation.

Axle Shafts

Removal and Installation

Passenger Cars and Hi-Lux

1. Raise the rear of the car and support it securely by using jackstands.

2. Drain the oil from the axle housing.

3. Remove the wheel disc, unfasten the lug nuts, and remove the wheel.

4. Punch matchmarks on the brake drum and the axle shaft to maintain rotational balance.

5. Remove the brake drum and related components, as detailed below.

6. Remove the rear bearing retaining nut.

7. Remove the backing plate attachment nuts through the access holes in the rear axle shaft flange.

8. Use a slide hammer with a suitable adapter to withdraw the axle shaft from its housing.

Toyota

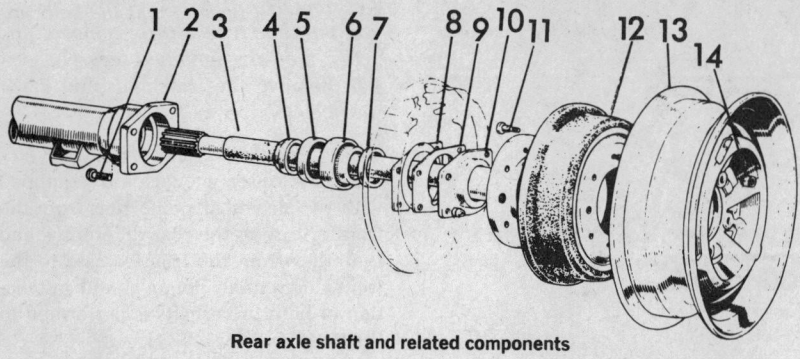

Rear axle shaft and related components

1. Backing plate set bolt
2. Rear axle housing
3. Rear axle shaft
4. Axle bearing inner retainer
5. Oil seal
6. Bearing
7. Spacer
8. Axle housing end gasket
9. Bearing retainer gasket
10. Axle bearing inner retainer
11. Hub bolt
12. Brake drum assembly
13. Wheel
14. Hub nut

CAUTION: *Use care not to damage the oil seal when removing the axle shaft.*

9. Repeat the procedure for the axle shaft on the opposite side.

CAUTION: *Be careful not to mix the components of the two sides.*

Installation is performed in the reverse order of removal. Coat the lips of the rear housing oil seal with multipurpose grease prior to installation of the rear axle shaft. Torque the bearing retaining nut to the specifications.

NOTE: *Always use new nuts, as they are the self-locking type.*

Axle Bearing Retaining Nut Specifications

Model	Torque range (ft lbs)
Corolla 1200	15-22
Corolla 1200/1600	26-38
Carina	26-38
Corona	29-36
Mark II/4	29-26
Mark II/6	43-52
Crown 2600	29-40
Hi-Lux	—

— Not available

Land Cruiser—Rear

1. Remove the hub cap and loosen the wheel nuts.

2. Raise the rear axle housing with a jack and support the rear of the vehicle with jackstands.

3. Drain the oil from the differential.

4. Remove the wheel nuts and take off the wheels.

5. Remove the brake drum and related parts, as detailed below.

6. Remove the cover from the back of the differential housing.

7. Remove the pin from the differential pinion shaft.

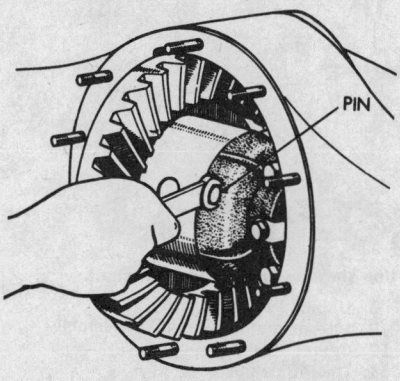

Pinion shaft pin removal on Land Cruiser models.

8. Withdraw the pinion shaft and its spacer from the case.

9. Use a mallet to *tap* the rear axle shaft toward the differential, to aid in removal of the axle shaft C-lock.

10. Remove the C-lock.

11. Withdraw the axle shaft from the housing.

12. Repeat the removal procedure for the opposite side.

CAUTION: *Do not mix the parts of the left and right axle shaft assemblies.*

Installation is performed in the reverse order of removal. After installing the axle shaft, C-lock, spacer, and pinion shaft, measure the clearance between the axle shaft and the pinion shaft spacer with a feeler gauge. The clearance should fall between 0.0024-0.0181 in. If the clearance is not within specifications, use one of the following spacers to adjust it:

1.172–1.173 in.
1.188–1.189 in.
1.204–1.205 in.

The rest of the axle shaft installation is the reverse of removal. Remember to fill the axle with lubricant.

Front Axle Shaft and Steering Knuckle

Removal and Installation

1. Raise and support the vehicle securely and remove the wheel/tire assembly.

2. Plug the brake master cylinder reservoir to prevent brake fluid leakage from the disconnected brake flexible hose.

3. Remove the outer axle shaft flange cap, and then remove the shaft snap-ring on the outer shaft.

4. Remove the bolts retaining the outer axle shaft flange onto the front axle hub, and then, screw in two service bolts into the shaft flange alternately, and remove the shaft flange with its gasket.

5. Remove the brake drum set screws and remove the brake drum. If equipped with disc brakes, remove the caliper and disc.

6. Straighten the lockwasher, and remove the front wheel bearing adjusting nuts with a front wheel adjusting nut wrench or similar tool.

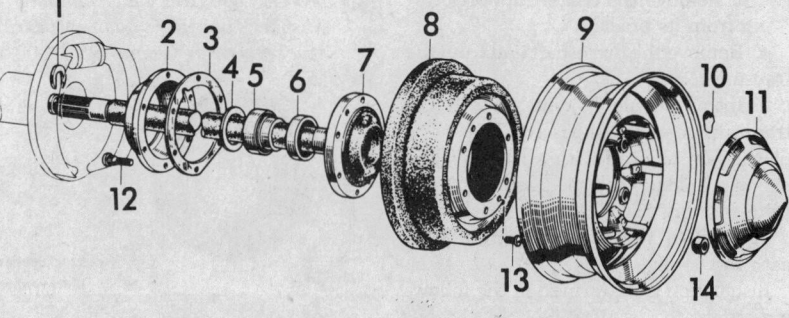

Land Cruiser rear axle shaft components

1. Rear axle shaft lock
2. Brake drum oil deflector
3. Gasket
4. Spacer
5. Wheel bearing
6. Oil seal
7. Axle shaft
8. Brake drum
9. Wheel
10. Wheel balancing weight
11. Hub cap
12. Hub bolt
13. Brake drum set bolt
14. Lug nut

7. Remove the front axle hub together with its claw washer, bearings, and oil seal.

8. Remove the clip and disconnect the brake flexible hose from the brake tube.

9. Cut and remove the lock wire and remove the bolts retaining the brake backing plate onto the steering knuckle. Remove the brake backing plate together with the brake shoes, tension springs, and the wheel cylinder still assembled to the backing plate.

10. Tap the steering knuckle spindle lightly with a soft mallet, and remove the spindle with its gasket.

NOTE: *When removing the steering knuckle spindle on a vehicle equipped with the ball joint type axle shaft joint, be prepared for the disconnection of the outer axle shaft from the joint. The joint ball will fall from the joint. Try and cushion its fall or catch it if you can.*

11. On those models equipped with the ball type axle shaft joint, slide the inner front axle shaft out of the axle housing. On those models equipped with the Birfield constant velocity joint type of axle joint, remove the entire axle shaft assembly from the axle housing.

12. Remove the screws, and take out the steering knuckle oil seal covers.

13. Remove the nuts retaining the steering knuckle arm onto the steering knuckle. Hold a short drift firmly onto the side of the dowel and strike it sharply to loosen the dowel. Remove the dowels from the steering knuckle arm.

14. Using a small drift and a hammer, tap the steering knuckle arm through the center of the steering knuckle upper bearing from the inside of the steering knuckle.

NOTE: *Do not lose the steering knuckle adjusting shim(s) that are installed between the steering knuckle arm and the steering knuckle. Record the position and thickness of the shim(s) so that they can be installed in their original positions.*

15. Remove the steering knuckle bearing cap retaining nuts, and the dowels in the same manner as in Step 13. Remove the steering knuckle bearing cap by tapping lightly with a drift and hammer from the inside of the steering knuckle. Remove the adjusting shims, following the Note given after Step 14.

16. Be careful not to drop the bearings, and remove the steering knuckle with the bearings from the axle housing.

17. Install the steering knuckle and axle shaft in the reverse order of removal. When the steering knuckle is assembled to the axle housing, the steering knuckle pivot bearing can be checked in the following manner:

a. Attach a spring scale to the end

hole of the steering knuckle arm at a right angle to the arm.

b. The force required to move the steering knuckle from side-to-side should be 4–5 lbs.

c. Adjust the bearing preload by adding or subtracting the same number of shims of the same size from both the upper and lower steering knuckle bearings.

18. On those models equipped with the ball joint type axle joint, install the inner axle with its proper spacer in position until the splines on the shaft are fully meshed with the differential side gear splines. Next, fill the steering knuckle ¾ full with grease and place the joint ball on the inner shaft end. Install the outer shaft and the front axle shaft spacer into the steering knuckle spindle and install the spindle with its gasket onto the steering knuckle.

19. On those models equipped with the Birfield constant velocity joint type axle joint, install the axle assembly into position in the axle housing until the splines on the end of the shaft mesh with the differential side gear splines. Fill the steering knuckle housing ¾ full with grease and install the steering knuckle spindle.

20. Install and assemble the remaining components in the reverse order of removal. Adjust the wheel bearing preload.

Axle Bearing and Seal

1. Remove axle shaft.

2. Remove bearing inner retainer by grinding off one edge and hammering it from the shaft.

3. Remove the bearing with a press.

4. Remove the seal with a puller.

5. Install in reverse of removal. A press and seal installer are necessary.

Differential

Removal and Installation

NOTE: *Rear axle servicing is a complex operation. Repair should not be attempted unless the special tools and knowledge required are readily available.*

Rear Carrier—All Models

1. Remove the axle shafts.

2. Disconnect the driveshaft from the pinion shaft flange.

3. Unfasten the carrier securing nuts and remove the carrier assembly.

Installation is performed in the reverse order of removal. Be sure to apply liquid sealer to both the carrier gasket and the lower carrier securing nuts.

Front Carrier—Land Cruiser

1. Remove the wheel covers and loosen the lug nuts.

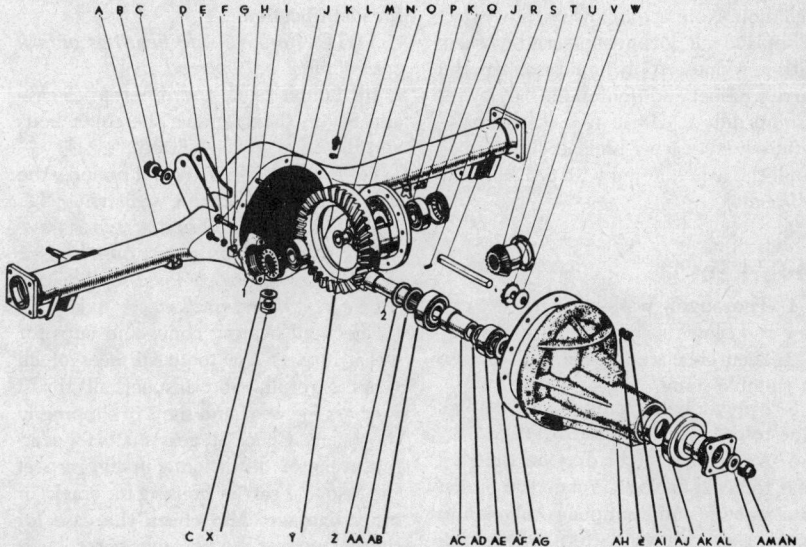

Differential components

(a)—Housing assembly	(n)—Ring gear and drive pinion 1 and 2	(aa)—Shim
(b)—Filler plug	(o)—Case	(ab)—Bearing
(c)—Gasket	(p)—Lockplate	(ac)—Spacer
(d)—Bolt	(q)—Bolt	(ad)—Shim
(e)—Lock washer	(r)—Lockpin	(ae)—Bearing
(f)—Hexagon bolt	(s)—Pinion shaft	(af)—Oil slinger
(g)—Bearing adjusting nut lock	(t)—Side gear	(ag)—Gasket
(h)—Lockwasher	(u)—Thrust washer	(ah)—Carrier
(i)—Stud	(v)—Pinion	(ai)—Nut
(j)—Bearing adjusting nut	(w)—Thrust washer	(aj)—Oil seal
(k)—Bearing	(x)—Drain plug	(ak)—Dust deflector
(l)—Breather plug	(y)—Oil reservoir	(al)—Universal joint flange
(m)—Lockwasher	(z)—Spacer	(am)—Flat washer
		(an)—Nut

2. Jack the front axle housing up and support it with jackstands.

3. Remove the lug nuts and the wheels.

4. Unfasten the bolts and disconnect the front driveshaft from the flange on the differential.

5. Drain the lubricant from the differential.

6. Remove the axle outer shaft flange cap. Unfasten the snap-ring from the shaft.

7. Unfasten the securing bolts from the axle shaft outer flange. Withdraw the flange by screwing service bolts into it alternately. Do not pry it off.

8. Straighten the lockwasher and remove the adjusting nuts with a hub nut wrench.

9. Remove the brake drum and front axle hub as an assembly.

10. Cut the lockwire and remove it. Unfasten the backing plate retaining bolts from the steering knuckle and wire the backing plate up to the front spring.

NOTE: *Do not remove the hydraulic brake line from the backing plate.*

11. Remove the spindle and gasket from the steering knuckle. Withdraw the outer shaft, front ball joint and axle inner shaft.

12. Unfasten the differential carrier retaining nuts and remove the carrier inner shaft.

Reverse the removal procedure for installation. Note the following, however:

Replace all lockwashers and gaskets with new ones. Apply liquid sealer to the carrier gasket and tighten the carrier retaining nuts to 29–40 ft lbs. Adjust the front wheel bearing preload. Remember to fill the axle housing with SAE 90 gear lubricant.

Overhaul

1. Thoroughly wash and rinse the carrier and blow dry with compressed air.

2. Securely clamp the carrier in a vise or suitable stand.

3. Apply a light coating of mechanic's blue to the teeth of the ring gear.

4. Applying a slight drag on the ring gear to avoid backlash, rotate the pinion in a smooth and continuous manner to obtain a good tooth pattern on the ring gear.

5. Next, attach a dial indicator gauge to the carrier base and check the ring gear backlash.

6. Also check ring gear runout at this time. If the tooth pattern obtained is correct, and the backlash and runout are within limits, any gear noise must come from the side gears.

7. With the dial indicator gauge set up on the carrier, check the backlash between the pinion gears and side gears. Excessive backlash usually is due to ei-

ther worn thrust washers or a worn pinion shaft.

8. Check side gear thrust clearance with a feeler gauge.

9. If everything is within specifications, test the preload on the differential drive pinion nut. Punch mark both pinion and nut in their original positions, then loosen the pinion nut about ½ turn and torque to specifications. If the punch marks line up again (within 60°) the pinion preload was correct.

10. Punch mark both the carrier and the side bearing caps for identification, remove the lock-nuts and take off the caps.

11. Remove the differential case assembly from the carrier. Do not mix the bearing cups; paint mark them for identification.

12. Remove the differential pinion nut (do not let the pinion drop out), then remove the pinion spacer, yoke and oil seal.

13. With a brass punch, drive out the pinion bearing cups.

NOTE: *This should be done only when the bearings are to be replaced.*

14. Press or pull off the drive pinion rear bearing. Avoid damaging the flat spacer behind the bearing.

15. Measure the spacer thickness and note the measurement for future use. Remove both side bearings from the differential case and mark them "L" and "R" for identification.

NOTE: *Remove side bearings only if they must be replaced.*

16. Punch mark the differential case and cover, then remove the cover bolts and the cover (where fitted).

17. Remove the shaft and pinions, the side gears and all thrust washers.

NOTE: *Some differential types have four spider pinion gears; punch mark the gears before removal so they can be correctly reinstalled.*

Check all bearing cones and cups for wear. Inspect the tooth surfaces of all gears carefully and inspect all thrust washers for wear and signs of slipping in their seats. Check all gear shafts for scoring, wear or distortion. Finally, inspect the case and carrier housing for cracks or other damage. Also check the case for signs of wear at the side gear bores, bearing cap and mounting hubs.

Assembly is performed in the following order:

1. Wash and clean all parts before installation.

2. Lightly oil all bearings and gear shafts, except the ring gear and drive pinion teeth.

3. Place the side gears and the pinion gears, with their thrust washers, into the differential case.

4. Insert the shaft and align the lock pin holes in the case and shaft.

5. Install the case cover in place and install the lock pin (bolt) and tighten the cover bolts to specification; check the play.

6. If the side bearings were removed, install them now. If the ring gear was removed, install it now. Tighten the bolts in symmetrical sequence to avoid distortion and runout.

7. Install the drive pinion bearing cups into the carrier housing, using a suitable installing tool. Make sure the cups are seated solidly.

8. Assemble the drive pinion rear bearing to the drive pinion and insert it into the carrier housing. Install the spacer and front bearing to the drive pinion; install the yoke and tighten the nut to specifications.

CAUTION: *The drive pinion oil seal is NOT installed at this point.*

9. The drive pinion preload is measured in in. lbs (not ft lbs). Adjust the preload by changing the length of the bearing spacer (between the front and rear bearings) until the required preload is obtained.

10. Place the previously assembled differential case into position in the bearing hubs and put the caps into position as marked (L and R).

11. Set the case so that there will be the least amount of backlash between the ring gear and pinion (in order to save time adjusting).

12. Install the adjusting nuts (also marked L and R) and take care not to cross-thread them.

13. Finger-tighten the bearing caps until the threads are lined up correctly, then tighten slowly.

14. Back off the right-hand adjusting nut (ring gear teeth side) and screw in the other nut until almost no backlash is felt.

15. Attach a dial indicator gauge so that it reads at right angles to the back of the ring gear, then screw in the right-hand adjusting nut until the gauge indicates that all side play has been eliminated.

16. Tighten the adjusting nut another 1 or 1½ notches (depending on the fit of the lock tabs).

17. Recheck the preload on the drive pinion as before; this time the specifications are different.

18. If too loose, readjust the side bearing preload; if too tight, adjust the ring gear backlash.

19. Install the dial indicator gauge so that it contacts the ring gear teeth at right angles. Adjust the backlash to specifications.

20. If too great, adjust by loosening the bearing cap bolts slightly and screwing the right-hand adjusting nut (ring gear teeth side) out about two notches.

21. Tighten the left-hand adjusting nut the same amount.

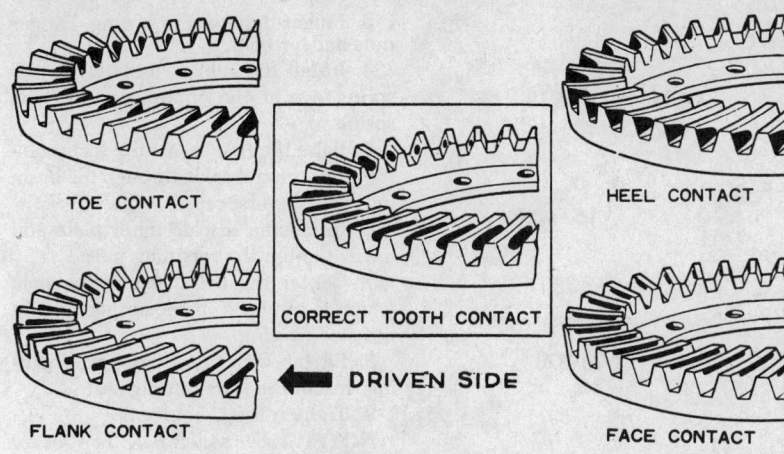

TOE CONTACT

HEEL CONTACT

CORRECT TOOTH CONTACT

← DRIVEN SIDE

FLANK CONTACT

FACE CONTACT

Ring gear tooth contact pattern

NOTE: *One notch of the adjusting nut equals about 0.002 in. of backlash.*

22. Recheck the backlash, then tighten the bearing cap nuts.

23. Using a dial indicator recheck all runout dimensions (ring gear back, ring gear outer circumference and differential case).

24. Apply a thin coat of mechanic's blue, red lead or even lipstick to the ring gear teeth. Rotate the gear several times, applying a light drag to the ring gear. Rotate the gear in both directions.

25. Inspect the tooth pattern. There are four basic tooth patterns: heel, toe,

flank and face. Most often the tooth pattern obtained will be a combination of two of these patterns and the adjustments must be made accordingly.

Heel contact Move the drive pinion in by increasing the thickness of the spacer (between the pinion head and rear bearing). Readjust backlash by moving the ring gear away from the pinion.

Face contact Adjust same as above.

Toe contact Adjust by moving the drive pinion out by reducing the thickness of the spacer. Readjust backlash.

Flank contact Adjust same as toe contact.

Continue assembling as follows:

25. Remove the drive pinion nut and install the seal into the differential carrier housing, then install the oil slinger, dust shield and yoke and retorque the pinion nut as specified.

26. Install the differential carrier assembly into the axle housing.

REAR SUSPENSION
Springs

Removal and Installation

Passenger Cars with Rear Leaf Springs, Hi-Lux, and Land Cruiser

1. Loosen the rear wheel lug nuts.

2. Raise the rear of the vehicle. Support the frame and rear axle housing with stands.

3. Remove the lug nuts and the wheel.

4. Remove the cotter pin, nut, and washer from the lower end of the shock absorber.

5. On Land Cruiser models, perform the following:

   a. Remove the cotter pins and nuts from the lower end of the stabilizer link.

   b. Detach the link from the axle housing.

DIFFERENTIAL SPECIFICATIONS

Model	BACKLASH (in.) Ring gear and pinion	Side gears	Runout (in.) Ring gear	TORQUE (ft lbs) Side bearing cap	Differential pinion nut	PINION BEARING PRELOAD (in. lbs) New	Old
Corolla							
1200	0.004-0.006	0.001-0.006	0.0016	40-47	95-110	3-5①	1-3①
1200 ('76-'77)	0.0039-0.0059	0.0008-0.0059	0.0028	40-47	65-145	7-12	4-6
Corolla							
1600 ('70-'74)	0.0004-0.056	0.0008-0.0060	0.0016	40-47	123-145	4-5①	3①
1600 ('75)	0.005-0.007	0.0020-0.0079	0.0028	37-52	79-173	2-4②④	3-4②⑤
Carina and Celica	0.005-0.007	0.003-0.008	0.0016	36-50	123-145	4-5①	2-3①
Celica ('76-'77)	0.005-0.007	0.003-0.008	0.0028	51-65	80-174	9-16	4-8
Corona							
('70-'73)	0.005-0.007	0.0008-0.0080	0.0020	36-51	123-145	4-8①	1-2①
('74-'77)	0.005-0.007	0.0020-0.0079	0.0020③	50-65	80-160	4-6④	1-3⑤
Mark'll							
2000	0.005-0.007	0.002-0.008	0.0020	36-51	123-145	4-6①	1-3①
6-cyl	0.005-0.007	0.002-0.008	0.0030	51-65	80-145	7-10①	2-4①
Crown							
2600	0.006-0.007	0.002-0.008	0.0030	51-65	80-145	16-23①	4-10①
Hi-Lux							
2000	0.005-0.007	0.002-0.008	0.0020⑥	51-65	120-152	17-23①	4-13①⑦
Land Cruiser	0.006-0.008	0.0008-0.0079	0.0040	65-80	145-175	12-15①⑧	5-8①⑦

① Without oil seal and differential gears installed
② With oil seal
③ 1976-77 and station wagon—0.0028 in.
④ 1976-77—9-15 in. lbs.
⑤ 1976-77—4-8 in. lbs.
⑥ 1976-77—0.004
⑦ 1977—8-11 in. lbs.

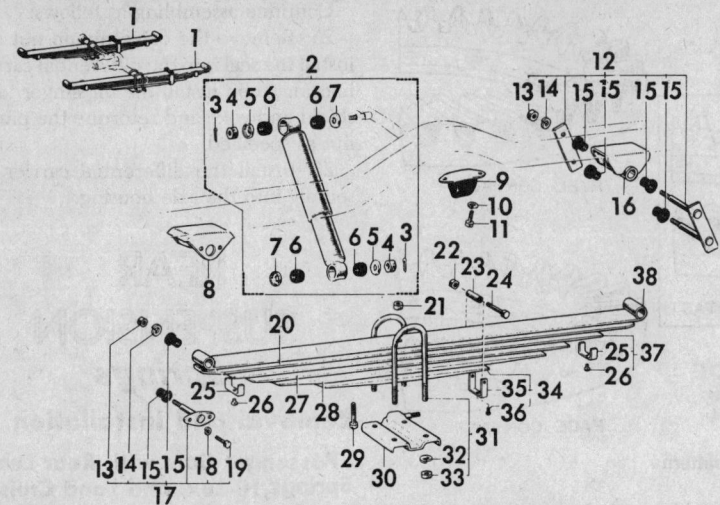

Components of the Hi-Lux rear suspension —other vehicles with leaf springs similar.

1. Rear spring
2. Rear shock absorber
3. Cotter pin
4. Castle pin
5. Shock absorber cushion washer
6. Bushing
7. Shock absorber cushion washer
8. Spring bracket
9. Rear spring bumper
10. Spring washer
11. Bolt
12. Rear spring shackle
13. Nut
14. Spring washer
15. Bushing
16. Spring bracket
17. Rear spring hanger pin
18. Spring washer
19. Bolt
20. Rear spring leaf
21. Nut
22. Nut
23. Rear spring clip bolt
24. Clip bolt
25. Rear spring clip
26. Round rivet
27. Rear spring leaf
28. Rear spring leaf No. 5
29. Rear spring center bolt
30. U-bolt seat
31. U-bolt
32. Spring washer
33. Nut
34. Rear spring leaf
35. Rear spring clip
36. Round rivet
37. Rear spring leaf
38. Rear spring leaf
39. Bumper block spacer

6. Detach the shock absorber from the spring seat pivot pin.

7. Remove the parking brake cable clamp (except Land Cruiser).

NOTE: *Remove the parking brake equalizer, if necessary.*

8. Unfasten the U-bolt nuts and remove the spring seat assemblies.

9. Adjust the height of the rear axle housing so that the weight of the rear axle is removed from the rear springs.

10. Unfasten the spring shackle retaining nuts. Withdraw the spring shackle inner plate. Carefully pry out the spring shackle with a bar.

11. Remove the spring bracket pin from the front end of the spring hanger and remove the rubber bushings.

12. Remove the spring.

CAUTION: *Use care not to damage the hydraulic brake line or the parking brake cable.*

Installation is performed in the following order:

1. Install the rubber bushings in the eye of the spring.

2. Align the eye of the spring with the spring hanger bracket and drive the pin through the bracket holes and rubber bushings.

NOTE: *Use soapy water as lubricant, if necessary, to aid in pin installation. Never use oil or grease.*

3. Finger-tighten the spring hanger nuts and/or bolts.

4. Install the rubber bushings in the spring eye at the opposite end of the spring.

5. Raise the free end of the spring. Install the spring shackle through the bushings and the bracket.

6. Install the shackle inner plate and finger-tighten the retaining nuts.

7. Center the bolt head in the hole which is provided in the spring seat on the axle housing.

8. Fit the U-bolts over the axle housing. Install the lower spring seat.

9. Tighten the U-bolt nuts.

NOTE: *Some models have two sets of nuts, while others have a nut and lockwasher.*

10. Install the parking brake cable clamp. Install the equalizer, if it was removed.

11. On passenger cars:

a. Install the shock absorber end at the spring seat. Tighten the nuts.

b. Install the wheel and lug nuts. Lower the car to the ground.

c. Bounce the car several times.

d. Tighten the spring bracket pins and shackles.

12. Hi-Lux and Land Cruiser:

a. Raise the rear axle with the jack so that the stands no longer support the frame.

b. Tighten the hanger pin and shackle nuts.

c. Install the shock absorber bushings and washers. Tighten and install the cotter pins.

d. Install the stabilizer link and hand-tighten its retaining nuts (Land Cruiser).

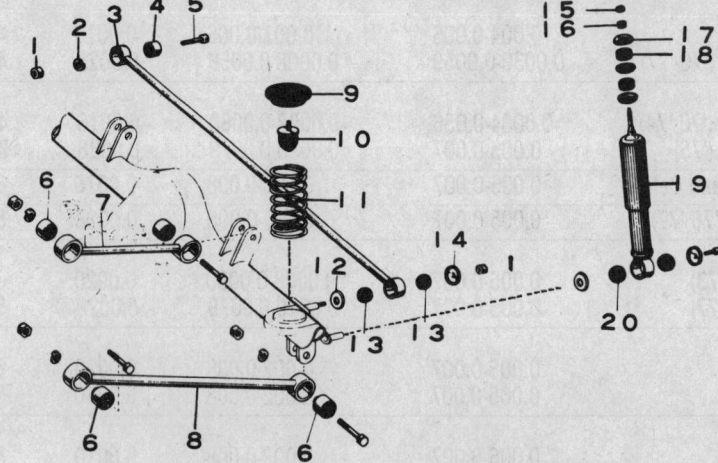

Celica and Carina rear suspension—Crown similar.

1. Nut
2. Washer
3. Lateral control rod
4. Bushing
5. Bolt
6. Bushing
7. Upper control arm
8. Lower control arm
9. Spring insulator
10. Spring bumper
11. Coil spring
12. Washer
13. Bushing
14. Washer
15. Nut
16. Nut
17. Washer
18. Bushing
19. Shock absorber
20. Bushing

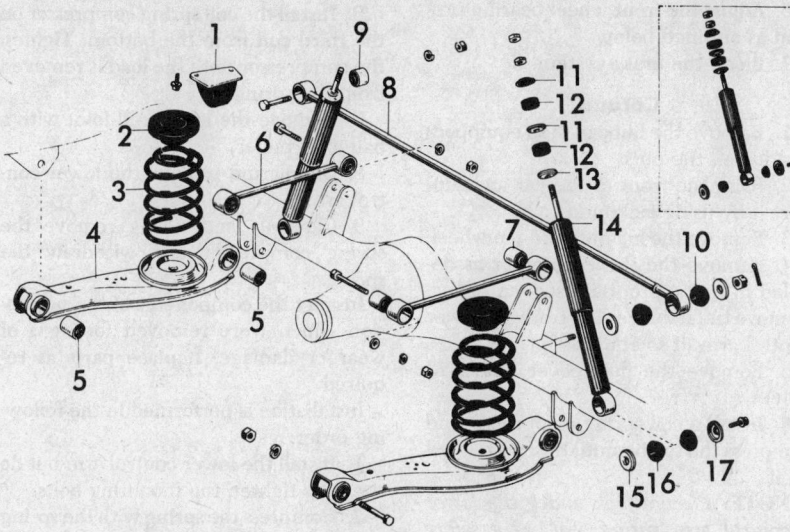

Mark II/6 rear suspension.

1. Bumper
2. Spring insulator
3. Coil spring
4. Lower control arm
5. Bushing
6. Upper control arm
7. Bushing
8. Bushing
9. Lateral control rod
10. Bushing
11. Retainer
12. Cushion
13. Retainer
14. Shock absorber
15. Washer
16. Bushing
17. Washer

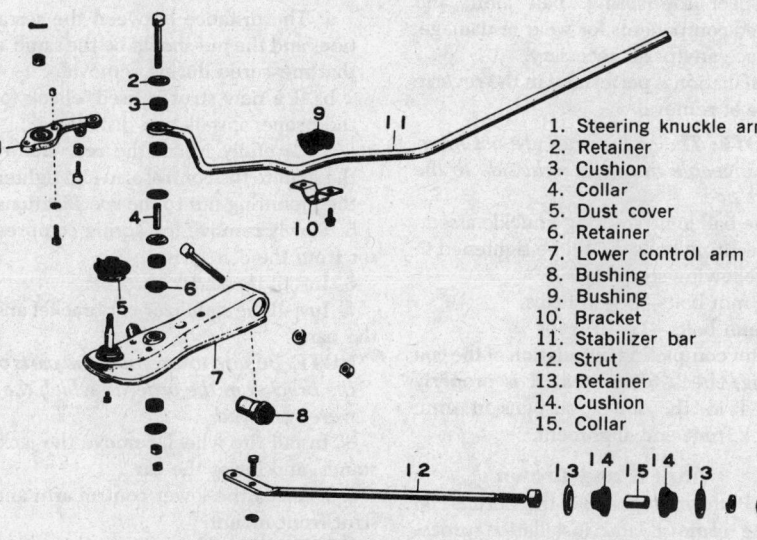

1. Steering knuckle arm
2. Retainer
3. Cushion
4. Collar
5. Dust cover
6. Retainer
7. Lower control arm
8. Bushing
9. Bushing
10. Bracket
11. Stabilizer bar
12. Strut
13. Retainer
14. Cushion
15. Collar

The components of the MacPherson strut front suspension—Corolla, Carina and Celica.

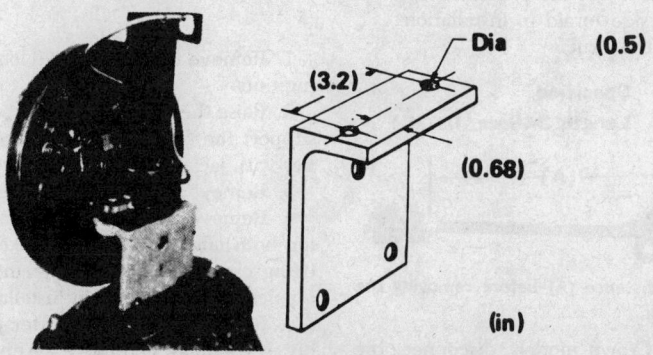

Fabricate the shock absorber bracket and mount it in a vise as shown.

e. Install the wheels, remove the stands, and lower the vehicle to the ground.

f. Tighten the stabilizer link bolts, bounce the vehicle, and tighten them again (Land Cruiser).

Passenger Cars with Coil Spring Rear Suspensions

1. Remove the hubcap and loosen the lug nuts.

2. Jack up the rear axle housing and support the frame with jackstands. Leave the jack in place under the rear axle housing.

3. Remove the lug nuts and wheel.

4. Unfasten the lower shock absorber end.

5. Slowly lower the jack under the rear axle housing until the axle is at the bottom of its travel.

6. Withdraw the coil spring, complete with its insulator.

Inspect the coil spring and insulator for wear, cracks, or weakness; replace either or both, as necessary.

Installation is performed in the reverse order of removal.

Rear Shock Absorbers

Removal and Installation

1. Jack up the rear end of the vehicle.

2. Support the rear axle housing with jackstands.

3. Unfasten the upper shock absorber retaining nuts and/or bolts from the upper frame member.

4. Depending upon the type of rear springs used, either disconnect the lower end of the shock absorber from the spring seat, or the rear axle housing, by removing its cotter pins, nuts, and/or bolts.

5. Remove the shock absorber.

Inspect the shock for wear, leaks, or other signs of damage. Test it as outlined in the front suspension shock absorber section.

Installation is performed in the reverse order from removal.

FRONT SUSPENSION
Springs

Removal and Installation

Corolla, Carina and Celica

1. Remove the hubcap and loosen the lug nuts.

2. Raise the front of the car and support it, on the chassis jacking plates provided, with jackstands.

CAUTION: *Do not support the weight of the car on the suspension arm; the arm will deform under its weight.*

3. Unfasten the lug nuts and remove the wheel.

4. Detach the front brake line from its clamp.

5. Remove the brake drum, or the caliper and wire it out of the way.

6. Unfasten the three nuts which secure the upper shock absorber mounting plate to the top of the wheel arch.

7. Remove the two bolts which attach the shock absorber lower end to the steering knuckle lower arm.

NOTE: *Press down on the suspension lower arm, in order to remove the shock absorber assembly. This must be done to clear the collars on the steering knuckle arm bolt holes when removing the shock/spring assembly.*

8. Fabricate the shock absorber/-spring assembly mounting stand. Bolt the assembly on the stand and mount the stand on a vise.

9. Use a coil spring compressor to compress the spring until it can be moved freely.

10. Remove the bearing dust cap from the top of the shock absorber assembly.

11. Use a large open-end wrench to keep the upper spring seat from turning and unfasten the 10 mm nut at the top of the shock absorber assembly.

CAUTION: *Do not use an impact wrench when loosening the nut.*

12. Remove the components from the top of the shock and withdraw the spring in its compressed state.

Check the spring for cracks and weakness. Check the dust seals and spring seats for wear or deterioration. Replace parts, as necessary.

Installation is performed in the reverse order of removal. Be sure to note the following, however:

1. Align the hole in the upper suspension support with the shock absorber piston rod end, so that they fit properly.

2. Always use a *new* nut and nylon washer on the shock absorber piston rod end when securing it to the upper suspension support. Torque the nut to 29–40 ft lbs.

CAUTION: *Do not use an impact wrench to tighten the nut.*

3. Coat the suspension support bearing with multipurpose grease prior to installation. Pack the space in the upper support with multipurpose grease, also, after installation.

4. Tighten the suspension support-to-wheel arch bolts to the following specification:

Corolla—11–16 ft lbs

Carina and Celica—14–23 ft lbs

5. Tighten the shock absorber-to-steering knuckle arm bolts to the following specifications.

Corolla—50–65 ft lbs

Carina and Celica—58–87 ft lbs

6. Adjust the front wheel bearing preload as outlined below.

7. Bleed the brake system.

Corona

1. Remove the hubcap (if so equipped) and loosen the nuts.

2. Raise the front of the car and support it by using jackstands.

3. Remove the lug nuts and the wheel.

4. Remove the shock absorber as detailed in the appropriate section below. Remove the stabilizer bar from the lower control arm (if so equipped).

5. Remove the dust cover. (1972–73 only)

6. Install a coil spring compressor and compress the spring until there is no load on it.

NOTE: *Place a jack under the lower control arm spring seat, as a safety precaution.*

7. Unfasten the lower ball joint retaining bolts and withdraw the ball joint, complete with the steering knuckle, from the lower control arm.

8. Slowly loosen the spring compressor and remove the spring. (Lower the jack).

Inspect the spring, ball joint, and related components for wear or damage. Replace any parts necessary.

Installation is performed in the reverse order of removal.

NOTE: *The coil springs are not interchangeable from the right side to the left side.*

The ball joint/steering knuckle assembly securing bolts should be tightened to the following specifications:

12 mm bolts—58–83 ft lbs

8 mm bolts—11–16 ft lbs

After completing installation of the coil spring, check to see that it is properly seated in the lower suspension arm. Check front end alignment.

Mark II and Crown

1. Perform steps 1–3 of the Corona coil spring removal and installation procedure.

2. Unfasten the stabilizer bar.

3. Measure the distance between the serrated bolt holes on the front side of the torque strut and the attachment nut on the rear side to aid in installation. Remove the strut.

Specified
Length 348mm (18.7")

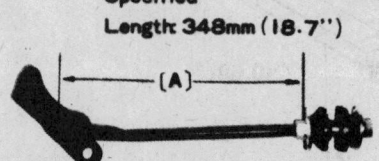

Measure distance (A) before removing the strut.

4. On Crown models, disconnect the brake line.

5. Remove the shock absorber.

6. Install the coil spring compressor on the third coil from the bottom. Tighten the compressor until the load is removed from the spring.

7. Remove the lower ball joint with a ball joint puller.

8. Unbolt and remove the lower control arm.

9. Carefully and slowly remove the spring compressor and withdraw the spring.

Inspect the components of the suspension which were removed for signs of wear or damage. Replace parts as required.

Installation is performed in the following order:

1. Install the lower control arm but do not fully tighten the mounting bolts.

2. Compress the spring with the spring compressor and install the spring.

NOTE: *Keep the spring compressed after installation.*

3. Install the lower ball joint on the steering knuckle and tighten it .

4. Install the strut on the lower control arm and temporarily install the other end on the frame.

a. The distance between the serrations and the nut should be the same as that measured during removal.

b. If a new strut is used, check for the proper installation distance.

c. Carefully install the rear side of the strut to the control arm and tighten the mounting nut to the specifications.

5. Slowly remove the spring compressor from the coil spring.

6. Install the shock absorber.

7. Install the stabilizer bar bracket and the bar.

NOTE: *Be sure to assemble the parts of the bracket in the order in which they were removed.*

8. Install the wheel, remove the jackstands, and lower the car.

9. Tighten the lower control arm and strut front mount.

NOTE: *These parts should be tightened with the equivalent of passenger weight in the car.*

10. Check the wheel alignment, after completing installation.

Hi-Lux

1. Remove the hubcap and loosen the lug nuts.

2. Raise the front end of the truck and support the front suspension crossmember with jackstands.

3. Remove the lug nuts and the wheel.

4. Remove the stabilizer bar connecting bolts and remove the bracket parts, being careful to note their removal sequence in order to aid in installation.

5. Remove the tie rod cotter pin and nut. Use a puller to remove the end of the tie rod from the knuckle arm.

6. Remove the shock absorber, as de-

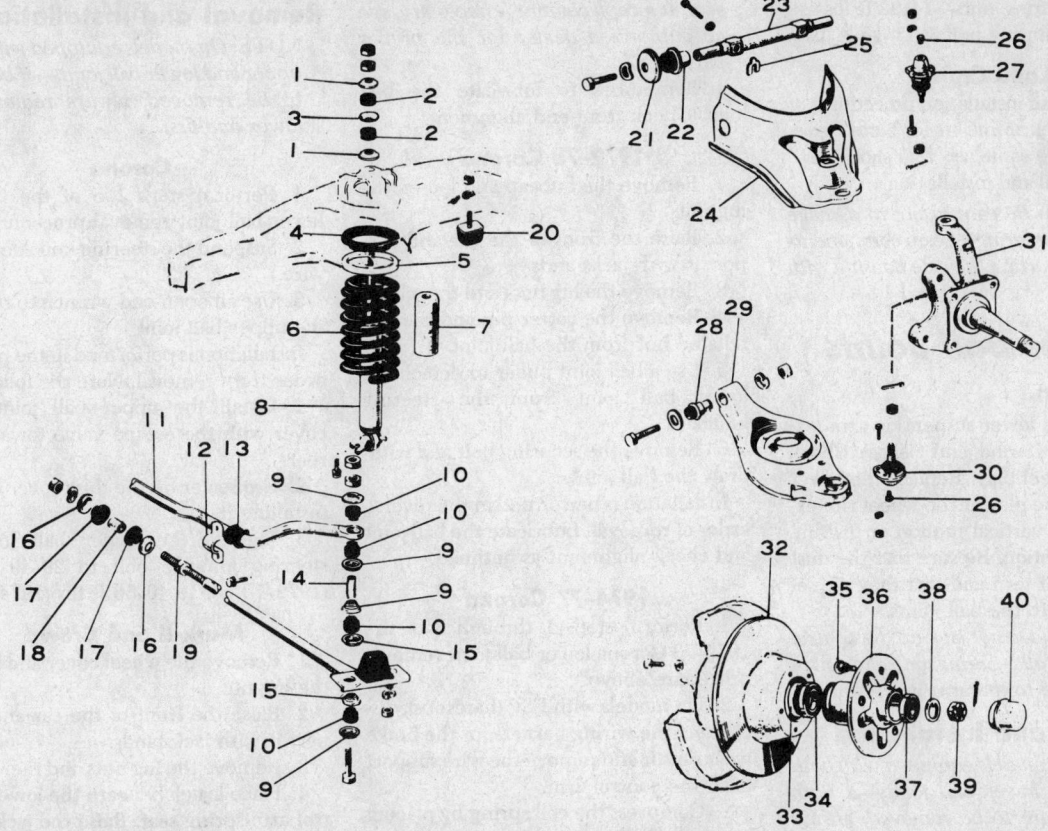

Components of the Crown front suspension —Mark II similar.

1. Washer	11. Stabilizer bar	21. Retainer	31. Steering knuckle
2. Cushion	12. Bracket	22. Bushing	32. Brake disc
3. Retainer	13. Bushing	23. Shaft	33. Oil seal
4. Insulator	14. Collar	24. Upper control arm	34. Roller bearing
5. Spacer	15. Retainer	25. Camber adjusting shim	35. Hub bolt
6. Coil spring	16. Retainer	26. Plug	36. Axle hub
7. Dust cover	17. Cushion	27. Upper ball joint	37. Roller bearing
8. Shock absorber	18. Collar	28. Bushing	38. Washer
9. Retainer	19. Strut	29. Lower control arm	39. Wheel adjusting nut
10. Cushion	20. Bumper	30. Lower ball joint	40. Hub cap

tailed in the appropriate section. Detach the brake hose.

7. Raise the lower control arm, using a jack, so that the arm is free of the steering knuckle.

8. Loosen the ball joint attachment nut and remove the ball joint puller.

9. Slowly lower the jack underneath the control arm.

CAUTION: *If the jack is lowered too fast, the spring could suddenly release, causing damage or injury.*

10. Remove the coil spring and its insulator from underneath the truck.

Inspect the coil spring, its insulator, and bumper for cracks, wear, or damage. Replace parts as necessary.

Installation is basically performed in the reverse order of removal. However, a coil spring compressor should be used to install the spring, rather than the method used for removing it.

Torque the suspension components to the following specifications:

Lower control arm—51–65 ft lbs (1976–77 33–43 ft lbs)

Ball joint—65–94 ft lbs (1972)
Ball joint—87–123 ft lbs (1973–77)

Land Cruiser

Land Cruiser models are equipped with leaf springs in the front and rear. Thus, front spring removal is performed in almost the same manner as rear spring removal. Follow the procedure outlined in the rear suspension section, above.

CAUTION: *Be careful when raising or lowering the front suspension with a jack, so as not to damage any of the steering system components.*

Front Shock Absorber

Removal and Installation

Corolla, Carina, and Celica

1. Perform the front coil spring removal procedure as outlined above for the Corolla, Carina, and Celica.

2. Remove the wheel hub and brake drum or disc.

Inspect the shock absorber and test it Inspect the other parts of the front suspension system which were removed.

Installation is performed in the reverse order of removal. See the notes at the end of coil spring installation for details.

Corona, Mark II, Crown, and Hi-Lux

1. Remove the hubcap and loosen the lug nuts.

2. Raise the front of the car and support it with jackstands.

3. Remove the lug nuts and the wheel.

4. Unfasten the double nuts at the top end of the shock absorber. Remove the cushions and cushion retainers.

5. Remove the two bolts which secure the lower end of the shock absorber to the lower control arm.

6. Remove the shock absorber.

Inspect and test the shock as detailed below.

Installation of the shock is performed in the reverse order of removal. Tighten the securing nuts and bolts to the following specifications:

Upper securing nuts—14–22 ft lbs
Lower mounting bolts—11–16 ft lbs

Land Cruiser

Removal and installation procedures of the front shock absorbers for Land Cruisers are in the same as rear shock absorber removal and installation.

CAUTION: *Be careful not to damage any of the steering system components when supporting the axle housing with a jack.*

Lower Ball Joints

Inspection

Jack up the lower suspension arm (except Corolla, Carina, and Celica). Check the front wheel play. Replace the lower ball joint if the play at the wheel rim exceeds 0.1 in. vertical motion or 0.25 in. horizontal motion. Be sure that the dust covers are not torn and that they are securely glued to the ball joints.

CAUTION: *Do not jack up the control arm on Corolla, Carina, or Celica models; damage to the arm will result.*

Removal and Installation

NOTE: *On models equipped with both upper and lower ball joints—if both ball joints are to be removed, always remove the lower and then the upper ball joint.*

Corolla 1200/1600, Carina, and Celica

The ball joint and control arm cannot be separated from each other. If one fails, then both must be replaced as an assembly, in the following manner:

1. Perform steps 1–7 of the Corolla, Carina, and Celica front coil spring removal procedure. Skip step 6.
2. Remove the stabilizer bar securing bolts.
3. Unfasten the torque strut mounting bolts.
4. Remove the control arm mounting bolt and detach the arm from the front suspension member.
5. Remove the steering knuckle arm from the control arm with a ball joint puller.

Inspect the suspension components, which were removed for wear or damage. Replace any parts, as required.

Installation is the reverse of removal. Note the following, however:

1. When installing the control arm on the suspension member, tighten the bolts partially at first.
2. Complete the assembly procedure and lower the car to the ground.
3. Bounce the front of the car several times. Allow the suspension to settle, then tighten the lower control arm bolts to 51–65 ft lbs.

CAUTION: *Use only the bolt which was designed to fit the lower control arm. If a replacement is necessary, see an authorized dealer for the proper part.*

4. Remember to lubricate the ball joint. Check front-end alignment.

1972–73 Corona

1. Remove the hubcap and loosen the lug nuts.
2. Raise the front of the car and support it with jackstands.
3. Remove the lug nuts and the wheel.
4. Remove the cotter pin and the castellated nut from the ball joint.
5. Use a ball joint puller to detach the lower ball joint from the steering knuckle.
6. Remove the securing bolt and withdraw the ball joint.

Installation is performed in the reverse order of removal. Lubricate the ball joint and check alignment as outlined.

1974–77 Corona

1. Perform steps 1 through 3 of the 1972–73 Corona lower ball joint removal procedure above.
2. On models with ESP (hardtops), disconnect the wiring harness for the brake wear sensor and remove the wire support from the control arm.
3. Compress the coil spring by placing a jack underneath the control arm and raising it.
4. Perform steps 4 and 5 of the 1972–73 Corona lower ball joint removal procedure.
5. Safety wire the steering knuckle out of the way.
6. Remove the bolt and withdraw the ball joint.

Installation is the reverse of removal. Tighten the stud nuts to 51–65 ft lbs.

Mark II and Crown

Perform steps 1–7 of the Mark II and Crown coil spring removal procedure. Skip step 3.

Installation is performed by starting with step 3 of the Mark II and Crown coil spring installation procedure. When step 3 is completed, go on to steps 5–10. Lubricate the ball joints and check alignment.

Hi-Lux

Perform steps 1–8 of the Hi-Lux coil spring removal procedure. Skip step 6.

Installation is performed in the reverse order of removal. Lubricate the ball joint. Check front end alignment.

Upper Ball Joint

Inspection

Disconnect the ball joint from the steering knuckle and check free-play by hand. Replace the ball joint, if it is noticeably loose.

Removal and Installation

NOTE: *On models equipped with both upper and lower ball joints—if both are to be removed, always remove the lower one first.*

Corona

1. Perform steps 1–5 of the Corona lower ball joint removal procedure.
2. Suspend the steering knuckle with a wire.
3. Use an open-end wrench to remove the upper ball joint.

Installation is performed in the reverse order from removal. Note the following:

1. Install the upper ball joint dust cover with the escape valve toward the rear.
2. Use sealer on the dust cover before installing it.
3. Tighten the upper ball joint-to-steering knuckle bolt to 29–40 ft lbs (1972–73); or to 40–50 ft lbs (1974–77).

Mark II and Crown

1. Remove the wheel cover and loosen the lug nut.
2. Raise the front of the car and support it with jackstands.
3. Remove the lug nuts and the wheel.
4. Place a jack beneath the lower control arm spring seat. Raise the jack until the spring bumper separates from the frame.
5. Detach the flexible hose from the dust cover.
6. Using a ball joint puller, remove the upper ball joint from the steering knuckle.
7. Use an open-end wrench to remove the ball joint from the upper control arm.

Installation is performed in the reverse order of removal. Tighten the components to the specifications. Lubricate the ball joint. Check front wheel alignment. (See below.) Remember to bleed the air from the flexible hose.

Hi-Lux

Remove and install the upper ball joint in the same manner as outlined for the lower ball joint.

Lower Control Arm

Removal and Installation

Corolla, Celica, Carina

1. Raise and support front end.
2. Remove wheel.
3. Disconnect the steering knuckle from the control arm.
4. Disconnect the tie rod, stabilizer bar and strut bar from the control arm.
5. Remove the control arm mounting bolts, and remove the arm.
6. Install in reverse of above. Tighten, but do not torque fasteners until car is on ground.
7. Lower car to ground, rock it from

side-to-side several times and torque control arm mounting bolts to 51–65 ftlb.; stabilizer bar to 16 ftlb.; strut bar to 40 ftlb.; shock absorber to 65 ftlb.

Corona

1. Raise and support the vehicle.
2. Remove the front wheel.
3. Remove the shock absorber and disconnect the stabilizer from the lower arm.
4. Install a spring compressor and fully tighten it.
5. Place a jack under the lower arm seat.
6. Disconnect the lower ball joint from the knuckle and lower the jack.
7. Remove the ball joint from the arm, remove the cam plates and bolts and take off the arm.
8. Install in reverse of above. Tighten all fasteners, but do not torque them to specification until vehicle is on ground.
9. Lower vehicle and rock it from side-to-side several times.
10. With no load in vehicle, torque the lower arm mounting bolts to 94–130 ftlb.

Corolla, Mark II, Crown

1. Remove the stabilizer bar.
2. Measure the length of the strut bar from the bolt hole (front side) to the outer edge of the securing nut at the other end.
3. Remove the shock absorber.
4. Compress the front spring with a spring compressor.
   NOTE: *It is recommended that the compressor be installed at the third coil from the bottom.*
5. Remove the lower ball joint with a puller.
6. Remove the lower arm.
7. Install the lower arm to the frame.
8. Install the ball joint and tighten the nut to 50–65 ftlb. for the Mark II and 66–96 ftlb. for the Crown.
9. Install the strut bar onto the lower arm and temporarily install the front side onto the frame.
10. Set the strut bar to the length noted before removal. If a new lower arm or strut bar is used, the measurement should be 14.16″.
11. Torque the strut bar rear end to 50–65 ftlb.
12. Remove the spring compressor and install the shock absorber.
13. Install the stabilizer bar.
14. Lower the vehicle and torque the lower arm to 65–80 ftlb. for the Mark II and 75–110 ft.lb. for the Crown. Torque the strut bar front end to 44–54 ftlb. for the Mark II and 70–110 ftlb. for the Crown.

Hi-Lux

1. Raise and support the front end.
2. Remove the coil spring.
3. Unbolt and remove the lower arm.
4. Install in reverse of removal.

Tighten fasteners but do not torque them until truck is on ground.
5. Lower truck and torque lower arm mounting bolts to 33–43 ftlb. and ball joint bolts to 22–32 ftlb.

Upper Control Arm
Removal and Installation
Corona

1. Remove the upper arm mounting nuts from inside the engine compartment, but do not remove the bolts.
2. Raise the vehicle, support the lower arm and remove the wheel.
3. On vehicles equipped with a ball joint wear sensor, remove the wiring from the clamp on the arm.
4. Remove the upper ball joint.
5. Remove the control arm mounting bolts.
6. Pry out the arm with a pry bar.
7. Install in reverse of removal. Do not tighten fasteners until vehicle is on ground.
8. Lower vehicle and torque the control arm mounting bolts to 95–130 ftlb.

Corona Mk II, Crown

1. Raise and support the vehicle at the frame.
2. Remove the flexible hose from the dust cover.
3. Jack up the lower arm and separate the ball joint from the steering knuckle with a ball joint remover.
4. Unbolt and remove the upper arm, taking note of the size and number of aligning shims.
5. Install in reverse of removal. Tighten, but do not torque, the fasteners until the car is on the ground.
6. Lower the car and torque the upper arm mounting bolts to 50–65 ftlb. for the Mk II and 37–52 ftlb for the Crown; the ball joint nut to 40–54 ftlb. for the Mk II and 70–96 ftlb. for the Crown.

Hi-Lux

1. Raise and support the truck under the frame.
2. Remove the wheel.
3. Raise the lower control arm with a jack.
4. Remove the nut from the upper ball joint stud.
5. Separate the ball joint from the steering knuckle.
6. Unbolt and remove the upper arm, taking note of the number and size of the aligning shims.
7. Installation is the reverse of removal. Replace the shims as found. Tighten fasteners, but do not torque them until the truck is on the ground.
8. Lower the truck and torque the upper arm mounting bolts to 95–153 ftlb. the ball joint stud nut to 65–94 ftlb.

Front-End Alignment

Front-end alignment measurements require the use of special equipment. Before measuring alignment or attempting to adjust it, always check the following points:

1. Be sure that the tires are properly inflated.
2. See that the wheels are properly balanced.
3. Check the ball joints to determine if they are worn or loose.
4. Check front wheel bearing adjustment.
5. Be sure that the car is on a level surface.
6. Check all suspension parts for tightness.

Caster and Camber Adjustments

Except for 1974–77 Corona
NOTE: *The MacPherson strut front suspension used on the Corolla, Carina, and Celica models cannot be adjusted for caster or camber. If measurements indicate that the suspension is out of alignment, the damaged part must be found and replaced. The same thing is true for Land Cruiser models, all of which use a solid front axle.*

Measure the caster and camber angles. If they are not within specifications, adjust them by adding or subtracting the shims on the mounting bolts between the upper control arm and the suspension member:

1. To *increase* camber, *remove* shims equally from both of the control shaft mounting bolts. Do the reverse to decrease camber.

Removing camber adjustment shims

2. To *increase* caster, add camber adjusting shims to the *rear* mounting bolt, or remove them from the front mounting bolt. Do the reverse to decrease caster.
NOTE: *Caster and camber adjustments should always be performed in a single operation.*

1974–77 Corona
Caster and camber angles are measured in the same way and with the same equipment as all the other models above. However, the method of adjustment is different:

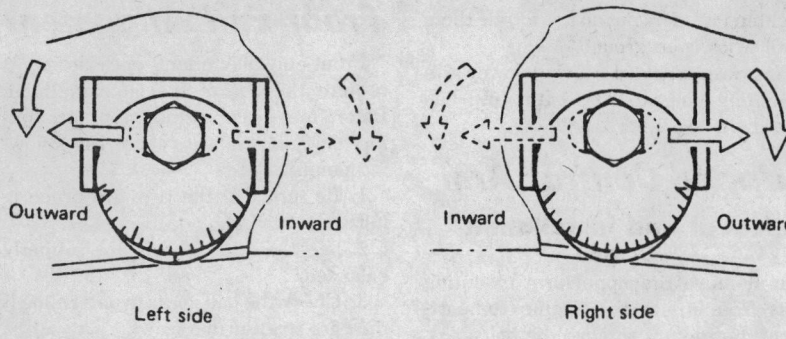

| Outward | Inward | Inward | Outward |

Left side   Right side

Front-end alignment adjusting cams—1974-77 Corona

1. Measure the camber and adjust it with the *rear* adjusting cam.

2. Measure the caster and adjust it with the *front* adjusting cam.

3. Check the caster and camber again.

4. Tighten the lower control arm mounting bolts to 94–132 ft lbs (1976–77 94–130 ft.lbs).

NOTE: *There should be no more than six graduations difference between the front and rear cams; inspect for damaged suspension parts if there is.*

Toe-in Adjustment

Measure the toe-in. Adjust it, if necessary, by loosening the tie rod end clamping bolts and rotating the tie rod adjusting tubes. Tighten the clamping bolts when finished.

NOTE: *Both tie rod ends should be the same length. If they are not, perform the adjustment until the toe-in is within specifications and the tie rod ends are equal in length.*

STEERING

Steering Wheel

Removal and Installation

Three-Spoke

CAUTION: *Do not attempt to remove or install the steering wheel by hammering on it. Damage to the energy-absorbing steering column could result.*

1. Unfasten the horn and turn signal multiconnector(s) at the base of the steering column shroud.

2. Loosen the trim pad retaining screws from the back side of the steering wheel.

3. Lift the trim pad and horn button assembly(ies) from the wheel.

4. Remove the steering wheel hub retaining nut.

5. Scratch matchmarks on the hub and shaft to aid in correct installation.

6. Use a steering wheel puller to remove the steering wheel.

Installation is the reverse of removal. Tighten the wheel retaining nut to 15–22

ft lbs, except for the Mark II/6, which should be tightened to 22–29 ft lbs.

Two-Spoke

The two-spoke steering wheel is removed in the same manner as the three-spoke, except that the trim pad should be pried off with a screwdriver. Remove the pad by lifting it toward the top of the wheel.

Four-Spoke

CAUTION: *Do not attempt to remove or install the steering wheel by hammering on it. Damage to the energy absorbing steering column could result.*

1. Unfasten the horn and turn signal connectors at the base of the steering column shroud, underneath the instrument panel.

2. Gently pry the center emblem off the front of the steering wheel.

3. Insert a wrench through the hole and remove the steering wheel retaining nut.

4. Scratch matchmarks on the hub and shaft to aid installation.

5. Use a steering wheel puller to remove the steering wheel.

Installation is the reverse of removal. Tighten the steering wheel retaining nut to 15–22 ft lbs.

Turn Signal Switch Replacement

All Models—except 1972 Mk II/4

1. Disconnect the negative (−) battery cable.

2. Remove the steering wheel, as outlined in the appropriate section above.

3. Unfasten the screws which secure the upper and lower steering column shroud halves. On 1974–75 Corona models, remove the lower instrument panel garnish first.

4. Unfasten the screws which retain the turn signal switch and remove the switch from the column. On 1974–77 Corona and on 1975–77 Corolla models, the hazard warning and windshield wiper switches are part of the assembly, and will be removed as well.

Installation is performed in the reverse order of removal.

1972 Mark II/4

1. Disconnect the negative (−) battery cable.

2. Remove the steering wheel as outlined in the appropriate section above.

3. Remove the turn signal switch housing and the turn signal switch.

Installation is performed in the reverse order of removal.

Ignition Lock/Switch

Removal and Installation

All Models—except 1972 Mark II/4

1. Disconnect the negative (−) battery cable.

2. Unfasten the ignition switch connector underneath the instrument panel.

3. Remove the screws which secure the upper and lower halves of the steering column cover. Remove the lower instrument panel garnish on 1974–77 Corona models first.

4. Turn the lock cylinder to the "ACC" position with the ignition key.

5. Push the lock cylinder stop in with a small, round object (cotter pin, punch, etc.)

NOTE: *On some models it may be necessary to remove the steering wheel and turn signal switch first.*

6. Withdraw the lock cylinder from the lock housing while depressing the stop tab.

7. To remove the ignition switch, unfasten its securing screws and withdraw the switch from the lock housing.

Installation is performed in the following order:

1. Align the locking cam with the hole in the ignition switch and insert the switch in the lock housing.

2. Secure the switch with its screw(s).

3. Make sure that both the lock cylinder and the column lock are in the "ACC" position. Slide the cylinder into the lock housing until the stop tab engages the hole in the lock.

4. The rest of installation is performed in the reverse order of removal.

1972 Mark II/4

1. Remove the steering wheel, turn signal switch housing, and turn signal switch as outlined above.

2. Remove the lock assembly retaining screw.

3. Withdraw the switch assembly from the column by pulling it out with the ignition key.

Installation is the reverse of removal.

Manual Steering Gear

Removal and Installation

Corolla, Corona

1. Remove the bolt attaching the coupling yoke to the steering worm.
2. Disconnect the relay rod from the pitman arm.
3. Remove the steering gear housing down and to the left.
4. Install in reverse of removal. Torque the housing-to-frame bolts to 25–36 ftlb.; lbs; the coupling yoke bolt to 15–20 ftlb.; the relay rod to 36–50 ftlb.

Carina, Celica, Corona Mk II, Crown, Hi-Lux

1. Remove the Pitman arm from the sector shaft with a puller.
2. Loosen the flexible coupling-to-wormshaft bolt.
3. Unbolt and remove the steering gear housing.
4. Install in reverse of removal. Torque the housing bolts to 25–36 ftlb. (37–52 for Mk II and Crown); the Pitman arm to 72–101 ftlb (80–90 for Crown, Hi-Lux); the coupling yoke bolt to 15–20 ftlb

Land Cruiser

55 Series

1. Remove the worm yokes from the worm and main shaft.
2. Remove the intermediate shaft assembly.
3. Remove the Pitman arm from the sector shaft.
4. Unbolt and remove the gear housing.
5. Install in reverse of removal. Torque the Pitman arm to 119–141 ftlb.
NOTE: *The intermediate shaft must be installed with the wheels in a straight ahead position and the steering wheel straight ahead.*

40 Series

1. Remove the horn button assembly and, using a puller, remove the steering wheel.
2. Remove the steering column jacket lower clamp.
3. Remove the turn signal switch assembly.
4. Remove the steering column access plate.
5. Remove the carburetor and oil filter. (Not necessary on 1975–76)
6. Disconnect the #1 shift rod and select rod at the ends of the shift control and select levers.
7. Remove the lower shift control bracket clamp.
8. Remove the shift control lever, select lever, control shaft lower bracket, control shaft low speed lever, and control shaft lower bracket.

9. Pull the control shaft out toward the driver's side.
10. Remove the Pitman arm with a puller.
11. Remove the steering gear box bracket cap and lift out the gear box.
12. Installation is the reverse of removal. Torque the gear box bracket cap to 75–90 ftlb. (30–40 for 1975–76); the Pitman arm to 120–140 ftlb. the steering wheel nut to 30–50 ftlb.

Adjustments

Adjustments to the manual steering gear are not necessary during normal service. Adjustments are performed only as part of overhaul.

Power Steering Pump

Removal and Installation

1. Remove the fan shroud.
2. Unfasten the nut from the center of the pump pulley.
NOTE: *Use the drive belt as a brake to keep the pulley from rotating.*
3. Withdraw the drive belt.
4. Remove the pulley and the Woodruff key from the pump shaft.
5. Detach the intake and outlet hoses from the pump reservoir.
NOTE: *Tie the hose ends up high so the fluid cannot flow out of them. Drain or plug the pump to prevent fluid leakage.*
6. Remove the bolt from the rear mounting brace.
7. Remove the front bracket bolts and withdraw the pump.
Installation is performed in the reverse order of removal. Note the following, however:
1. Tighten the pump pulley mounting bolt to 25–39 ft lbs.
2. Adjust the pump drive belt tension. The belt should deflect 0.31–0.39 in. un-

der thumb pressure applied midway between the air pump and the power steering pump.
3. Fill the reservoir with "Dexron" automatic transmission fluid. Bleed the air from the system.

Bleeding

1. Raise the front of the car and support it securely with jackstands.
2. Fill the pump reservoir with "Dexron" automatic transmission fluid.
3. Rotate the steering wheel from lock to lock several times. Add fluid as necessary.
4. With the steering wheel turned fully to one lock, crank the starter while watching the fluid level in the reservoir.
NOTE: *Do not start the engine. Operate the starter with a remote starter switch or have an assistant do it from inside of the car. Do not run the starter for prolonged periods.*
5. Repeat step 4 with the steering wheel turned to the opposite lock.
6. Start the engine. With the engine idling, turn the steering wheel from lock to lock two or three times.
7. Lower the front of the car and repeat step 6.
8. Center the wheel at the midpoint of its travel. Stop the engine.
9. The fluid level should not have risen more than 0.2 in. If it does, repeat step 7.
10. Check for fluid leakage.

Steering Linkage

Removal and Installation

Passenger Cars and Hi-Lux

1. Raise the front of the vehicle and support it with jackstands.
CAUTION: *Be sure that the vehicle is*

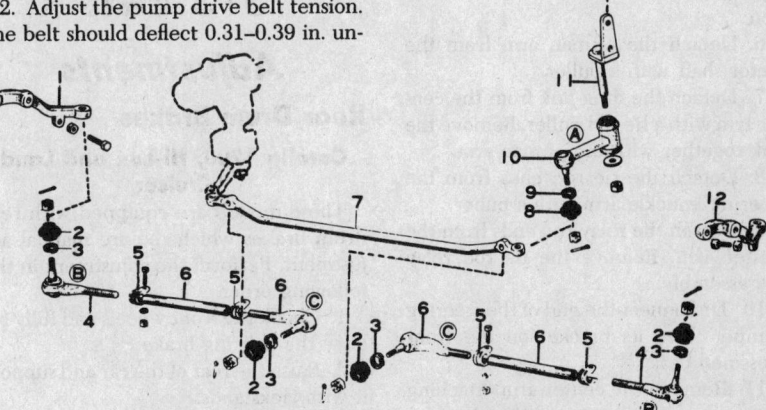

Corona steering linkage—other passenger cars similar.

1. Steering knuckle arm—right-hand
2. Dust seal
3. Clip
4. Tie rod end
5. Tie rod end clamp
6. Tie rod adjusting tube
7. Steering relay rod
8. Dust seal
9. Lock ring
10. Steering idler arm
11. Idler arm support
12. Steering knuckle arm—left-hand

(a)—Idler arm assembly
(b)—Tie rod end assembly
(c)—Tie rod adjusting tube

securely supported. *Do not support it by the lower control arms.*

2. Remove the gravel shields if they prevent access to the steering linkage.

3. Unfasten the nut and, using a puller, disconnect the pitman arm from the sector shaft.

4. Unfasten the idler arm support securing bolts and remove the support from the frame.

5. Detach the tie rod ends with a puller after removing the cotter pins and castellated nuts.

NOTE: *On Mark II/6 models, it is necessary to remove the disc brake caliper in order to gain access to the tie rod ends.*

6. Remove the steering linkage as an assembly.

Installation is performed in the reverse order of removal. Note the following, however:

1. Tighten the linkage parts to the torque figures given in the chart below.

2. Align the marks on the pitman arm and sector shaft before installing the pitman arm.

3. The self-locking nut used on some models, on the idler arm, may be reused if it cannot be turned by hand when fitted to the bolt.

4. Adjust the toe-in to specifications after completing the steering linkage installation procedure.

Land Cruiser

1. Remove the hubcaps and the lug nuts.

2. Raise the front of the vehicle and support it with jackstands.

3. Remove both front wheels.

4. Unfasten the pitman arm attaching nut.

5. Punch matchmarks on the pitman arm and the sector shaft to aid in installation.

6. Detach the pitman arm from the sector shaft with a puller.

7. Detach the drag link from the center arm with a tie rod puller. Remove the link together with the pitman arm.

8. Detach the tie rod ends from the steering knuckle arm with a puller.

9. Detach the relay rod ends from the center arm. Remove the tie rod/relay rod assembly.

10. Disconnect the end of the steering damper from its bracket on the front crossmember.

11. Remove the center arm attaching nut and use a puller to remove the arm, complete with the damper.

12. Remove the skid plate and then remove the center arm bracket from the frame.

Installation is performed in the reverse order of removal. Note the following, however:

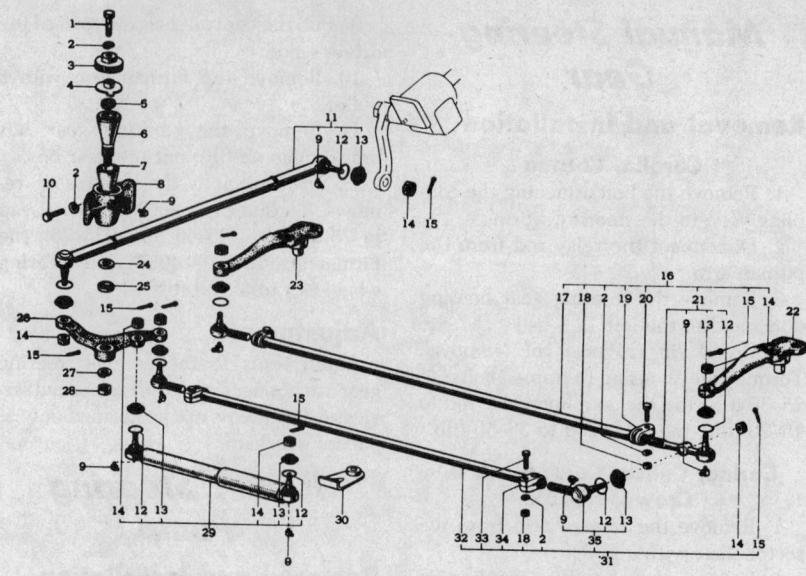

Components of the Land Cruiser steering linkage.

1. Bolt	13. Joint dust seal	25. Center arm dust lower seal
2. Lock washer	14. Lock nut	26. Steering center arm
3. Center arm shaft nut	15. Cotter pin	27. Lock washer
4. Center arm nut lock plate	16. Tie-rod assembly	28. Nut
5. Compression spring	17. Steering tie-rod	29. Steering damper
6. Center arm shaft	18. Lock nut	30. Damper bracket
7. Shaft bushing	19. Tie-rod end clamp	31. Steering relay rod assembly
8. Center arm bracket	20. Bolt	32. Steering relay rod
9. Grease fitting	21. Tie-rod end assembly	33. Bolt
10. Bolt	22. Steering knuckle arm	34. Tie-rod end clamp
11. Steering drag link assmebly	23. Steering knuckel arm	35. Relay rod end assembly
12. Set ring	24. Dust seal	

1. Align the matchmarks, which were made during removal, on the pitman arm and the sector shaft. Tighten the mounting bolt to 120–140 ft lbs.

2. Lubricate all of the rod ends and damper ends with multipurpose grease.

3. After the linkage is installed, adjust toe-in to the proper specifications.

BRAKE SYSTEMS

Adjustments

Rear Drum Brakes

Corolla 1200, Hi-Lux and Land Cruiser

These models are equipped with rear drum brakes which require manual adjustment. Perform the adjustment in the following order:

1. Chock the front wheels and fully release the parking brake.

2. Raise the rear of the car and support it with jackstands.

3. Remove the adjusting hole plug from the backing plate.

4. Expand the brake shoes by turning the adjusting wheel with a star-wheel adjuster or a thin-bladed screwdriver.

5. Pump the brake pedal several times, while expanding the shoes, so that the shoe contacts the drum evenly.

NOTE: *If the wheel still turns when your foot is removed from the brake pedal, continue expanding the shoes until the wheel locks.*

6. Back off on the adjuster, just enough so that the wheel rotates without dragging.

7. After this point is reached, continue backing off for *five* additional notches.

NOTE: *On models which have two wheel cylinders at each wheel, adjust each set of brakes separately; never adjust both at once.*

8. If the wheel still does not turn freely, back off one or two more notches. If after this, it still drags, check for worn or defective parts.

9. Pump the brake pedal again, and check wheel rotation.

10. Reverse steps 1–3.

Passenger Cars—Except Corolla 1200

These models are equipped with self-adjusting rear drum brakes. No adjustment is necessary.

Front Drum Brakes

Corolla 1200, Hi-Lux and Land Cruiser

Perform the adjustment in the same manner as detailed for the Corolla 1200, Hi-Lux and Land Cruiser.

Front Disc Brakes

Front disc brakes require no adjustment. Hydraulic pressure maintains the proper brake pad-to-disc contact at all times.

NOTE: *Because of this, the brake fluid level should be checked regularly.*

HYDRAULIC SYSTEMS
Master Cylinder

Removal and Installation

CAUTION: *Be careful not to spill brake fluid on the painted surfaces of the vehicle; it will damage the paint.*

1. Unfasten the hydraulic lines from the master cylinder.

2. Detach the hydraulic fluid pressure differential switch wiring connectors.

3. Loosen the master cylinder reservoir mounting bolt.

4. Then do one of the following:

a. On models with manual brakes, remove the master cylinder securing bolts and the clevis pin from the brake pedal. Remove the master cylinder.

b. On other models with power brakes, unfasten the nuts and remove the master cylinder assembly from the power brake unit.

Installation is performed in the reverse order of removal. Note the following, however:

1. Before tightening the master cylinder mounting nuts or bolts, screw the hydraulic line into the cylinder body, a few turns.

2. After installation is completed, bleed the master cylinder and the brake system.

Overhaul

1. Remove the reservoir caps and floats and unscrew the bolts that hold the reservoir to the main body.

2. Remove warning switches (where fitted), then remove from the rear of the cylinder, in order: boot and snap-ring, stop plate (washer), piston No. 1 with spacer, cylinder cup, spring retainer and spring.

3. Remove the end plug and gasket from the front of the cylinder, then remove the front piston stop bolt from underneath. Pull out the spring and its retainer, piston No. 2, the spacer and the cylinder cup.

4. Remove the two outlet fittings, washers, check valves and springs.

5. Remove the piston cups from their seats on the pistons only if they are to be replaced.

After washing all parts in clean brake fluid, dry with compressed air. Inspect the cylinder bore for wear, scuff marks or nicks. Cylinders may be honed slightly, but the limit is 0.006 in. It is recommended that it be replaced rather than overhauled.

Reverse the sequence of disassembly. Absolute cleanliness is important, and all parts must be coated with clean brake fluid. Bleed the master cylinder and make sure all lines are tightened correctly and do not leak. Use fluid that meets specifications (for standard brakes) and use the special disc brake fluid (DOT-3) for disc brake equipped cars.

Proportioning Valve

A proportioning valve is used on all models to reduce the hydraulic pressure to the rear brakes because of weight transfer during high speed stops. This helps to keep the rear brakes from locking up by improving front to rear brake balance.

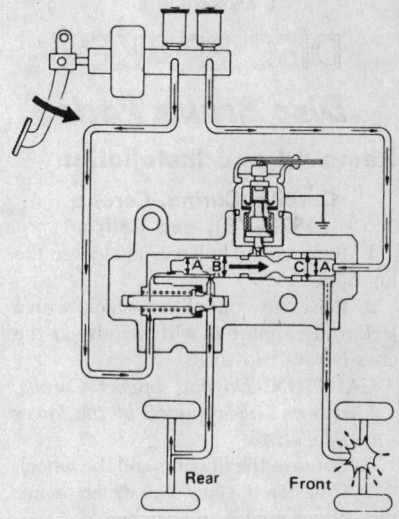

1976 proportioning bypass valve

Removal and Installation

1. Disconnect the brake lines from the valve unions.

2. Remove the valve mounting bolt, if used, and remove the valve.

NOTE: *If the proportioning valve is defective, it must be replaced as an assembly; it cannot be rebuilt.*

Installation is the reverse of removal. Bleed the brake system after it is completed.

Bleeding

CAUTION: *Do not reuse brake fluid which has been bled from the brake system.*

1. Insert a clear vinyl tube into the bleeder plug on the master cylinder or the wheel cylinders.

NOTE: *If the master cylinder has been overhauled or if air is present in it, start the bleeding procedure with the master cylinder. Otherwise, (and after bleeding the master cylinder) start with the wheel cylinder which is farthest from the master toylinder.*

2. Insert the other end of the tube into a jar which is half filled with brake fluid.

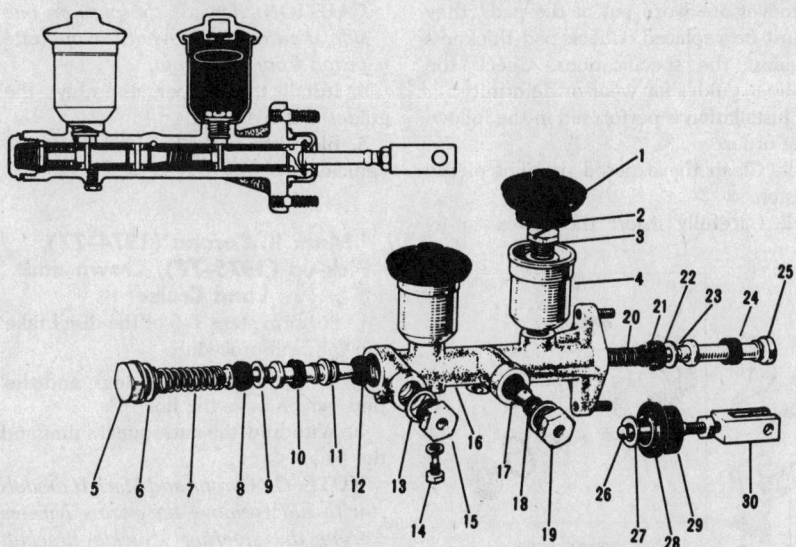

Components of the dual-tandem master cylinder.

1. Reservoir filler cap
2. Reservoir float
3. Reservoir set bolt
4. Master cylinder reservoir
5. Master cylinder plug
6. Gasket
7. Compression spring
8. Cylinder cup
9. Piston cup spacer
10. Cylinder cup
11. Master cylinder piston No. 2
12. Cylinder cup
13. Gasket
14. Piston stop bolt
15. Valve plug
16. Tandem master cylinder body
17. Compression spring
18. Master cylinder outlet check valve
19. Valve plug
20. Compression
21. Piston return spring retainer
22. Cylinder cup
23. Master cylinder piston cup spacer
24. Cylinder cup
25. Master cylinder piston No. 1
26. Master cylinder pushrod
27. Master cylinder piston stop plate
28. Hole snap-ring
29. Master cylinder boot
30. Master cylinder pusrod clevis

3. Slowly depress the brake pedal (have an assistant do it) and turn the bleeder plug 1/3–½ of a turn at the same time.

NOTE: *If the brake pedal is depressed too fast, small air bubbles will form in the brake fluid which will be very difficult to remove.*

4. Close the bleeder plug before hydraulic pressure decreases in the cylinder.

5. Repeat this procedure until the air bubbles are removed and then go on to the next wheel cylinder.

CAUTION: *Replenish the brake fluid in the master cylinder reservoir, so that it does not run out during bleeding.*

FRONT DISC BRAKES

Disc Brake Pads

Removal and Installation

Corolla, Carina, Corona (1972–73), and Celica

1. Remove the hub cap and loosen the lug nuts.

2. Raise the front of the vehicle with a jack and support it with stands on the chassis pads provided.

CAUTION: *Do not support Corolla, Carina or Celica models by the lower control arm.*

3. Remove the lug nuts and the wheel.

4. Unfasten the four clips which secure the caliper guides and remove.

5. Detach the flexible line from the caliper.

NOTE: *Be sure that the master cylinder is closed to prevent brake fluid from leaking out.*

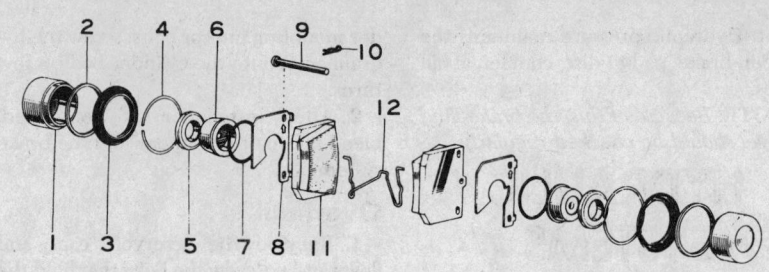

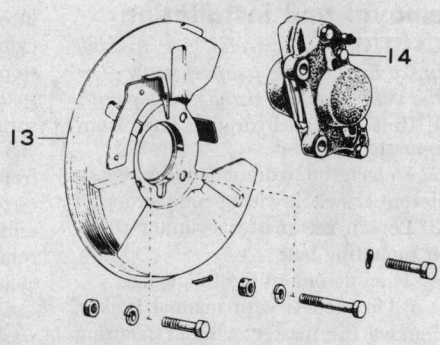

Components of the disc brake caliper—Crown 2600, Mark II, 1974–75 Corona, and 1975 Half-ton

1. Piston	6. Piston cup	11. Brake pad
2. Ring	7. O-ring	12. Anti-rattle spring
3. Cylinder boot	8. Anti-squeal shim	13. Dust cover
4. Set-ring	9. Pin	14. Caliper body
5. Spacer	10. Clip	

6. Remove the caliper assembly.

7. Remove the pads.

Inspect the pads for wear. If the grooves are worn out of the pads, they must be replaced. Check pad thickness against the specifications. Check the caliper guides for wear or deformity.

Installation is performed in the following order:

1. Clean the exposed portions of the piston.

2. Carefully insert the piston in its

caliper. If the piston is difficult to install, loosen the bleeder plug.

3. Insert the brake pads.

CAUTION: *Replace the pads on one side at a time, to prevent the opposite piston from falling out.*

4. Install the caliper assembly, the guides and the clips.

5. Bleed the brake line and lower the vehicle.

Mark II, Corona (1974–77), Pick-up (1975–77), Crown and Land Cruiser

1. Perform steps 1–3 of the disc brake pad removal procedure.

2. Remove the clips, springs, and the pins (which have the holes).

3. Withdraw the anti-squeal shims and the pads.

NOTE: *On Corona and Mark II models with ESP, remove the wiring harness from the steering knuckle bracket. Take out the pad and disconnect it from the wear sensor.*

4. Check pad thickness against the specifications.

Install the pads in the following order:

1. Clean the back of the pistons, cylinder boots and the caliper surfaces which contact the brake pads.

2. Fit the pads and anti-squeal shims into the caliper.

NOTE: *Install the shims with their arrows pointing toward the rotational direction of the disc.*

Disc brake cylinder

1. Pad support—left-hand
2. Pad support—right-hand
3. Disc brake pad
4. Disc brake caliper mounting
5. Guide
6. Cylinder support spring
7. Clip
8. Caliper assembly
9. Piston
10. Ring
11. Cylinder boot

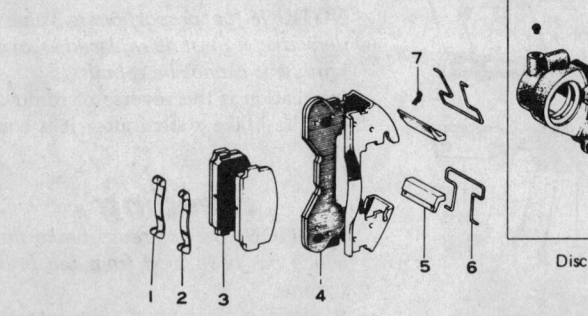

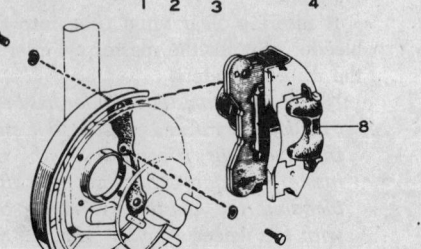

Corolla, Carina, Corona (1972-73), and Celica disc brake assembly.

3. Install the spring so that it presses correctly against the pads.

4. After completing installation, depress the brake pedal several times before lowering the car. This will provide proper operating clearance for the wheel cylinder components.

5. Install the wheel and lower the car.

Disc Brake Calipers

Removal and Installation

Corolla, Carina, Corona (1972–73), and Celica

Caliper removal and installation for these models is given as part of the brake pad removal and installation procedure. Consult the appropriate section for details.

Mark II, Corona (1974–77), Hi-Lux (1975–77), Crown and Land Cruiser

CAUTION: *Do not unfasten the bridge bolt and separate the caliper halves.*

1. Remove the wheel covers and loosen the lug nuts.

2. Raise the front of the car and support it with jackstands.

3. Remove the lug nuts and the wheel.

4. Plug the master cylinder inlet, so that the brake fluid will not run out when the hydraulic line is disconnected.

5. Remove the hydraulic line from the caliper by unfastening the union bolt.

NOTE: *On Corona and Mark II models with ESP, remove the wiring harness from the steering knuckle bracket, then remove the pad and separate the pad and wear sensor connection.*

6. Remove the lockwire and unfasten the caliper securing bolts. Withdraw the caliper assembly.

NOTE: *Shims are installed between the caliper mounting points and its body to center the caliper over the disc. Count the number of shims at each mounting point. Use care not to mix the shims from the upper and lower mounting points.*

Installation is performed in the following order:

1. If the brake disc was not removed or if the caliper was not replaced, use exactly the same number of shims as were removed.

CAUTION: *Do not mix the shims from the upper and lower mounting points.*

2. If the brake disc was removed or if the caliper was replaced, adjust the number of shims used, so that the caliper assembly is centered over the disc.

3. Tighten the caliper bolts to the following specifications:

Corona—67–87 ft lbs
Hi-Lux—67–87 ft lbs
Mark II/4—72–87 ft lbs
Mark II/6—67–87 ft lbs

Crown 2600—67–87 ft lbs

4. Install the lockwire on the caliper securing bolts.

5. Connect the hydraulic line to the caliper. Connect the wear sensor to the brake pad and install the wiring harness on the steering knuckle bracket.

6. Bleed the hydraulic system and check for leaks.

Overhaul

Corolla, Carina, Celica and 1972–73 Corona

1. Remove the caliper.

2. Carefully remove the dust boot from around the cylinder bore.

3. Apply compressed air to the brake line union to force the piston out of its bore. Be careful, the piston may come out forcefully.

4. Remove the seal from the piston. Check the piston and cylinder bore for wear and/or corrosion. Replace components as necessary.

Assembly is performed in the following order:

1. Coat all components with clean brake fluid.

2. Install the seal and piston in the cylinder bore, after coating them with the rubber lubricant supplied in the rebuilding kit. Seat the piston in the bore with your fingers.

3. Fit the boot into the groove in the cylinder bore.

4. Install the caliper cylinder assembly.

Hi-Lux, Mark II, Crown and 1974–77 Corona

1. Remove the caliper assembly from the car, and separate the pads from the caliper.

2. Remove the snap-ring and the dust boot from both caliper bores.

3. Place a block of wood between the pistons and blow them out of their bores by applying compressed air to the brake line union. Use of the wood block is to keep the pistons from striking each other.

4. Withdraw the sealing rings from the caliper bores. Do not mix the pistons; they must be returned to their original bores.

CAUTION: *Do not loosen or remove the bridge bolts which secure the halves of the caliper body.*

Check the caliper body for cracks and/or distortion. Examine the caliper bores for wear, damage, or corrosion. Replace the guide pins (with holes) if they are bent.

Assembly is performed in the following order:

1. Replace all rubber parts with new ones.

2. Coat the sealing rings and the caliper bore with the rubber grease sup-

plied in the rebuilding kit; do not use any other type of lubricant.

3. Fit the sealing rings into the grooves in the caliper bores.

4. Install the O-rings and spacers (if used) on the pistons and carefully insert each piston into its original bore. Use only finger-pressure to seat the pistons.

5. Install the boots over the bores and secure them with the snap-rings.

6. Install the calipers and the brake pads, then bleed the brake system.

Land Cruiser

NOTE: *Do not separate the caliper halves.*

1. Remove the caliper.

2. Remove the retaining pin and anti-rattle spring.

3. Remove the brake pads.

4. Remove the piston retaining ring.

5. Remove the piston boot and piston.

6. Remove the piston seal.

7. Assembly is the reverse of disassembly.

Brake Disc

Removal and Installation

1. Remove the brake pads and the caliper.

2. On Corolla, Carina, Corona (1972–73) and Celica models only:

    a. Loosen the bolts which secure the caliper mounting bracket.

    b. Withdraw the bracket, complete with the caliper support plates and springs attached.

3. Check the disc run-out, as detailed below, at this point. Make a note of the results for use during installation.

4. Remove the grease cap from the hub. Remove the cotter pin and the castellated nut.

5. Remove the wheel hub with the brake disc attached.

Inspect the disc.

Installation is performed in the following order:

1. Coat the hub oil seal lip with multipurpose grease and install the disc/hub assembly.

2. Adjust the wheel bearing preload, as detailed below.

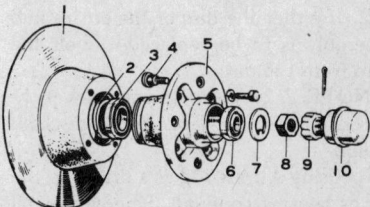

Brake disc and hub assembly

1. Disc
2. Oil seal
3. Tapered roller bearing
4. Hub bolt
5. Hub
6. Tapered roller bearing
7. Washer
8. Nut
9. Adjusting lock cap
10. Grease cap

3. Measure the disc run-out. Check it against the specifications.

NOTE: *If the wheel bearing nut is improperly tightened, disc run-out will be affected.*

4. On Corolla, Carina, Corona (1972–73) and Celica models only:

a. Install the caliper support, complete with springs. Tighten the securing nuts to the following torque specifications:

Corolla, Carina and Celica—20–40 ft lbs

Corona—65–87 ft lbs

CAUTION: *Be careful not to distort the support springs during installation.*

b. Install the support plates and the brake pads in the same positions from which they were removed.

NOTE: *Install the pad support plate with the arrow pointing in the same direction as when it was removed.*

5. Install the remainder of the components.

6. Bleed the brake system.

7. Road test the car. Check the rolling resistance of the wheel.

Inspection

Examine the disc. If it is worn, warped or scored, it must be replaced.

Check the thickness of the disc against specifications. If it is below specifications, replace it. Use a micrometer to measure the thickness. Disc run-out should be measured *before* the disc is removed and again *after* the disc is installed. Use a dial indicator mounted on a stand to determine run-out. If run-out exceeds 0.006 in. (all models), replace the disc.

NOTE: *Be sure that the wheel bearing nut is properly tightened. If it is not, an inaccurate run-out reading may be obtained. If different run-out readings are obtained with the same disc, between removal and installation, this is probably the cause.*

Wheel Bearings

Removal and Installation

1. Remove the disc/hub assembly, as detailed above.

2. If either the disc or the entire hub assembly is to be replaced, unbolt the hub from the disc.

NOTE: *If only the bearings are to be replaced, do not separate the disc and hub.*

3. Using a brass rod as a drift, tap the inner bearing cone out. Remove the oil seal and the inner bearing.

NOTE: *Throw the old oil seal away.*

4. Drive out the inner bearing cup.

5. Drive out the outer bearing cup.

Inspect the bearings and the hub for signs of wear or damage. Replace components, as necessary.

Installation is performed in the following order:

1. Install the inner bearing cup and then the outer bearing cup, by driving them into place.

CAUTION: *Use care not to cock the bearing cups in the hub.*

2. Pack the bearings, hub inner well and grease cap with multipurpose grease.

3. Install the inner bearing into the hub.

4. Carefully install a new oil seal with a soft drift.

5. Install the hub on the spindle. Be sure to install all of the washers and nuts which were removed.

6. Adjust the bearing preload.

7. Install the caliper assembly.

Preload Adjustment

1. With the front hub/disc assembly installed, tighten the castellated nut to the torque figure specified.

2. Rotate the disc back and forth, two or three times, to allow the bearing to seat properly.

3. Loosen the castellated nut until it is only finger-tight.

Measuring wheel bearing preload with a spring scale.

4. Tighten the nut firmly, using a box wrench.

5. Measure the bearing preload with a spring scale attached to a wheel mounting stud. Check it against the specifications.

Preload Specifications

Model	Initial torque setting (ft lbs)	Preload (oz)
Corolla ('72–'74)	19-23	11-25
Corolla ('75–'77)	19-23	11-25
Carina and Celica	19-24	10-22
1976-77	19-26	11-25
Corona	19-26	10-22
1976-77	19-26	12-31
Mark II	19-23	10-22
1976	19-23	11-24
Crown 2600	22	12-30
Hi-Lux	36	11-39
1976-77	36	11-31
Land Cruiser	Tighten to 43 Ft. Lbs. Loosen 1/8 to 1/5 Turn	

6. Install the cotter pin.

NOTE: *If the hole does not align with the nut (or cap) holes, tighten the nut slightly until it does.*

7. Finish installing the brake components and the wheel.

FRONT DRUM BRAKES

NOTE: *The 1976–77 Land Cruisers are equipped with front wheel disc brakes. Refer to front disc brake section.*

Brake Drums

Removal and Installation

1972–75 Hi-Lux and Land Cruiser

1. Remove the hub cap and loosen the lug nuts.

2. Raise the front of the vehicle and support it with jackstands.

3. Remove the lug nuts and the wheel.

4. On Hi-Lux models:

a. Remove the axle hub grease cap.

b. Remove the cotter pin and claw washer.

c. Unfasten the nut and withdraw the drum, complete with the hub.

5. On Land Cruiser models:

a. Unfasten the brake drum retaining screws.

b. Tap the drum lightly with a mallet to free it.

CAUTION: *Do not depress the brake pedal once the drum has been removed.*

Inspect the brake drum as detailed in the section below.

Installation is performed in the reverse order of removal. On Corolla, Corona and Hi-Lux models adjust the wheel bearing preload.

Inspection

1. Clean the drum.

2. Inspect the drum for scoring, cracks, grooves, and out of roundness. Replace or turn the drum, as required.

3. Light scoring may be removed by dressing the drum with *fine* emery cloth.

4. Heavy scoring will require the use of a brake drum lathe to turn the drum. The service limits of the drum inside diameter are as follows:

Hi-Lux—9.134 in.

Land Cruiser—11.540 in.

Brake Shoes

Removal and Installation

Hi-Lux

1. Remove the drum.

2. Remove the following parts in the order listed:

a. Shoe retaining spring pins

b. Shoe retaining springs

c. Shoe tension (return) springs

d. Shoes

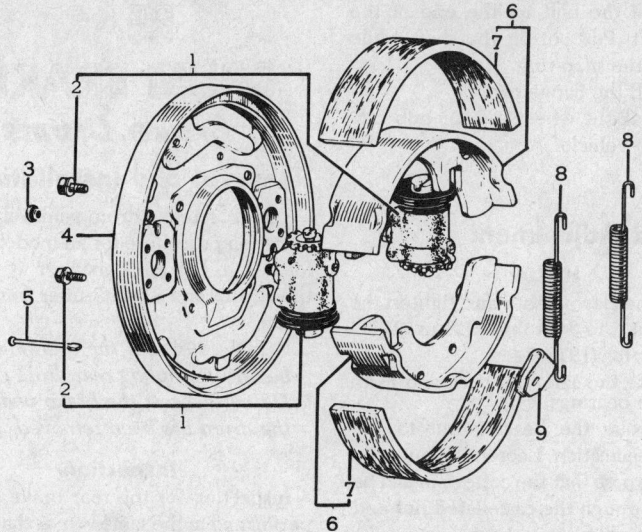

Hi-Lux front drum brake—Land Cruiser similar.

1. Front brake
2. Bolt
3. Shoe adjusting hole plug
4. Front brake backing plate
5. Shoe hold down spring pin
6. Brake shoe assembly
7. Brake shoe lining
8. Tension spring
9. Shoe hold down spring

NOTE: *Use a brake shoe removal tool to aid in removal of the tension springs.*

3. After removal, keep the brake shoes in their proper order.

CAUTION: *Be careful to keep oil or grease from contacting the lining surface.*

Inspect the brake shoes for wear, rust or damage. Inspect the brake linings for wear. The shoes should be relined if the lining thickness is less than 0.06 in.

Inspect the tension spring for deformation or weakness.

Installation is performed in the following order:

1. Coat all of the points where the brake shoes make contact with other brake assembly parts, with grease.

CAUTION: *Be careful not to get grease on the surface of the lining.*

2. Fit the upper and lower shoes into the grooves on the wheel cylinders and adjusting bolts. Install the spring pins in the shoes and then attach the retaining springs.

3. Hook the brake shoe tension springs on the upper and lower shoes with the aid of the tool used during removal.

4. Install the drum.

Land Cruiser

1. Remove the brake drum.

2. Remove the upper shoe by pulling out the end, while applying an upward force on it.

3. Depress the lower shoe and repeat the removal procedure for it.

CAUTION: *Do not interchange the upper and lower shoes. Do not allow grease to contact the lining surface.*

Inspect the shoes for wear, rust or damage. Check the linings for wear. The ser-

vice limit of lining thickness is 0.16 in.; have the shoes relined if it is less.

Inspect the springs for weakness and deformation.

Installation is performed in the following order:

1. Grease all points at which the brake shoe makes contact with other brake components.

CAUTION: *Do not allow grease to contact the lining surface.*

2. Fit the ends of the lower brake shoe into the grooves on the wheel cylinder piston and the adjusting bolt.

3. Push up on the upper brake shoe and fit it into the grooves on the piston and the adjusting bolt.

4. Hook the return springs on the brake shoes.

5. Install the brake drum.

Wheel Cylinders

Removal and Installation

Hi-Lux and Land Cruiser

1. Perform the brake drum and brake shoe removal procedures.

2. Plug the master cylinder reservoir inlet, to prevent fluid from leaking out.

3. Remove the hydraulic lines from the wheel cylinders by unfastening the union bolt.

4. Remove the wheel cylinder attachment screws and withdraw the wheel cylinders.

CAUTION: *Do not mix the right and left wheel cylinders.*

To install the wheel cylinders, proceed in the following manner:

1. Use the attaching screws to install the wheel cylinder to the backing plate.

NOTE: *The wheel cylinder adjusting nut and bolt on the right side of the brake have left-hand threads; while those on the left side have right-hand threads. Be careful not to mix them.*

2. Connect the hydraulic lines to the wheel cylinders.

CAUTION: *Use care to see that the hydraulic line is not twisted.*

3. Install the brake drum and shoes. Bleed the brake system.

General Overhaul

Remove the boots, pistons and the cups and closely inspect the bores for signs of wear, scoring and/or scuffing. When in doubt, replace or hone the wheel cylinders with a special brake hone, using clean brake fluid as lubricant. Wash residue from the bores using clean fluid; never use oil or any other solvent on any brake components. Blow dry with air and install with fresh brake fluid. The general limit for a honed cylinder is 0.005 in. oversize (Do not try to save money by reusing brake components such as cylinders and cups) The self-adjuster screws should be taken apart and all dirt and rust removed with a wire brush. Lightly coat with Lubriplate before assembly; components should turn freely.

Wheel Bearings

Removal and Installation

Hi-Lux

1. Remove the brake drum. Do not separate the drum from the hub, unless either one is to be replaced.

NOTE: *The outer bearing comes off with the brake drum.*

2. Use a puller to remove the inner bearing and the steering knuckle grease retainer.

3. Use a brass drift to remove the bearing cups from the axle hub.

Check the bearings for worn or pitted rollers. Examine the cup for signs of wear or damage. Inspect the hub itself, for defects.

Installation and packing are performed in the following order:

1. Use the brass drift to install the bearing cups in the hub.

CAUTION: *Be careful not to cock the bearing cups in the hub.*

2. Coat both the inner and outer bearings with multipurpose grease. Work the grease into the roller cages.

3. Drift the inner bearing and the steering knuckle grease retainer on the spindle.

4. Clean all of the old grease out of hub. Pack the inside of the hub with multipurpose grease.

5. Install the hub and brake drum assembly over the steering knuckle.

6. Install the outer bearing in the axle

hub and adjust the preload, as detailed below.

7. Pack the grease cap with multipurpose grease and fit it over the hub.

8. Check and adjust the brake shoe clearance. Lower the vehicle.

Land Cruiser

1. Perform steps 1–3 of the front brake drum removal procedure.

2. Remove the cap from the axle shaft outer flange. Remove the snap-ring from the shaft.

3. Remove the bolts which secure the axle shaft outer flange to the hub.

4. Install the two service bolts into the holes provided in the flange. Tighten the bolts evenly in order to loosen the flange. Withdraw the flange, complete with gasket.

CAUTION: *Never remove the flange by prying it off; oil leaks will result.*

5. Remove the set screws and withdraw the brake drum.

6. Straighten out the lockwasher and remove the adjusting nut, using a spindle nut wrench.

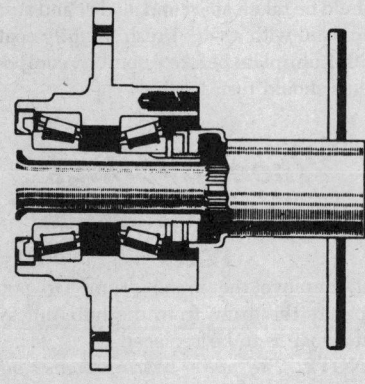

Removing the bearing adjustment nut from the Land Cruiser.

CAUTION: *Do not use a hammer and chisel to remove the nut.*

7. Remove the hub assembly, complete with the claw washer, bearings and oil seal.

NOTE: *If the bearings or cups are difficult to remove, use a puller.*

Installation and packing are performed in the following order:

1. Install the oil seal and the inner bearing cone.

2. Pack the hub with multipurpose grease, after assembling both inner and outer bearing cups to it.

3. Assemble the axle hub and brake drum.

4. Install the hub/drum assembly over the spindle then install the outer bearing.

5. Install the claw washer and adjusting nut with the spindle nut wrench.

6. Adjust the bearing preload, then install the locknut and washer.

7. Install the axle shaft flange and gasket. Tighten the retaining bolts to 11–16 ft lbs.

8. Install the bolt on the end of the outer shaft. Pull out on the shaft while installing the snap-ring.

9. Install the flange cap.

10. Install the wheel and the hub cap. Lower the vehicle.

Preload Adjustment

Hi-Lux

1. Fit the claw washer and tighten the retaining nut to 34 ft lbs—Hi-Lux (1972) or to 36 ft lbs (1973–74).

2. Rotate the axle hub back and forth to seat the bearings.

3. Retorque the bearing nut to the proper specification. Loosen the nut 1/6–1/3 of a turn, so that the cotter pin can be inserted through the castellated nut and into the spindle.

4. Install the front wheel and the lug nuts.

5. Check the wheel for free rotation. Check the axial play of the wheel by shaking it back and forth; the bearing free play should feel like it is about zero.

6. Install a *new* cotter pin and lock the retaining nut.

Land Cruiser

1. After tightening the adjusting nut with the spindle nut wrench, rotate the wheel back and forth in order to seat the bearing.

2. Loosen the adjusting nut ⅛–1/5 of a turn.

3. Check the brake drum for free rotation.

4. Install the lockwasher and the locknut. Use the spindle nut wrench to tighten the locknut.

5. Bend the tabs on the lockwasher up.

REAR DRUM BRAKES
Brake Drums
Removal and Installation

The rear brake drum removal and installation procedure for all models is performed in the same manner as that for the Hi-Lux and Land Cruiser front brake drum.

NOTE: *Release the parking brake before attempting rear drum removal. Do not depress the brake pedal, once the drum has been removed.*

Inspection

Inspection for the rear brake drum is performed in the same way as that for the front brake drum (see above).

Brake Shoes
Removal and Installation

Corolla, Carina, Celica, Corona (1974–77), and Crown

1. Remove the drum.

2. Unhook the shoe tension springs from the shoes with the aid of a brake spring removing tool.

3. Remove the brake shoe securing springs.

4. Disconnect the parking brake cable at the parking brake shoe lever.

5. Withdraw the shoes, complete with the parking brake shoe lever.

6. Unfasten the C-clip and remove the adjuster assembly from the shoes.

Inspect the shoes for wear and scoring. Replace the linings if their thickness is less than 0.04 in. (0.06 in.—Crown).

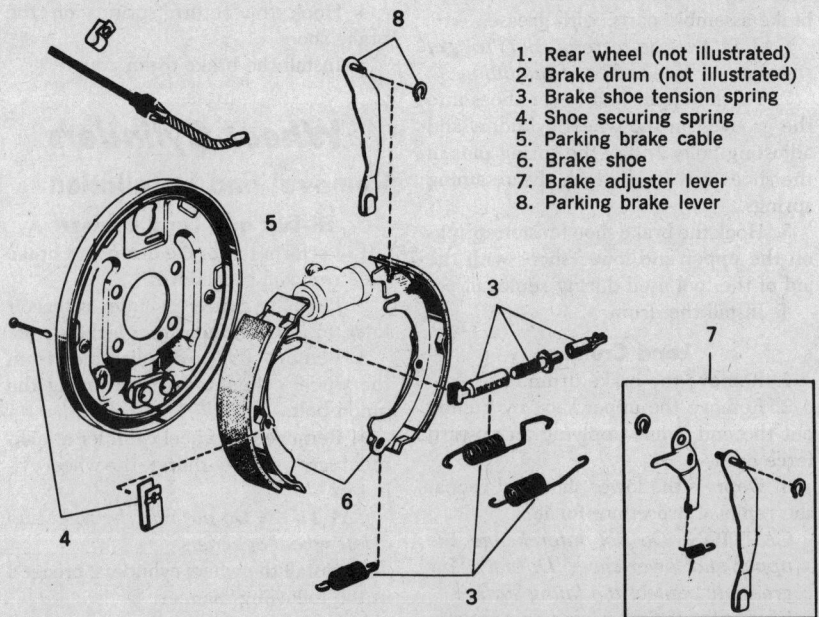

1. Rear wheel (not illustrated)
2. Brake drum (not illustrated)
3. Brake shoe tension spring
4. Shoe securing spring
5. Parking brake cable
6. Brake shoe
7. Brake adjuster lever
8. Parking brake lever

Rear brake shoe removal sequence—all models similar.

Check the tension springs to see if they are weak, distorted or rusted.

Inspect the teeth on the automatic adjuster wheel for chipping or other damage.

Installation is performed in the following order:

NOTE: *Grease the point of the shoe which slides against the backing plate. Do not get grease on the linings.*

1. Attach the parking brake shoe lever and the automatic adjuster lever to the rear of the shoe from which they were removed.

2. Fasten the parking brake cable to the lever on the brake shoe.

3. Install the automatic adjuster and fit the tension spring on the adjuster lever.

NOTE: *The tension spring should be installed on the anchor before performing step 4.*

4. Install the securing spring on the *rear* shoe and then install the securing spring on the *front* shoe.

5. Hook one end of the tension spring over the rear shoe, with the tool used during removal; then hook the other end over the front shoe.

CAUTION: *Be sure that the wheel cylinder boots are not being pinched by the ends of the shoes.*

6. Test the automatic adjuster by operating the parking brake shoe lever.

7. Install the brake drum and adjust the brakes.

Corona (1972–73) and Mark II

1. Remove the brake drum.

2. Remove the tension springs from the trailing (rear) shoe with the aid of a brake return spring removal tool.

3. Press down on the brake adjuster ratchet and move the shoe adjusting lever forward, to the center of the drum.

4. Remove the securing spring and remove the leading (front) shoe with the tension spring attached.

5. Disconnect the trailing shoe from the parking brake cable and remove the shoe retaining spring. Withdraw the shoe.

CAUTION: *Use care not to get grease on the lining surface.*

Inspect all of the parts removed for wear or damage. Check the lining thickness; it should be no less than 0.06 in. If it is less than this have the brakes relined.

Installation is performed in the following order:

1. Install the adjusting lever and ratchet on to the leading shoe. Attach the parking brake cable to the trailing shoe.

NOTE: *Use a new retaining clip.*

2. Apply non-melting lubricant to the shoe parts which contact other components of the brake.

CAUTION: *Do not allow lubricant to get on the surface of the brake lining.*

3. Install the parking brake strut on the trailing shoe with its retaining spring (rear brakes only).

4. Attach the parking brake cable to the lever (rear brakes only).

5. Fasten the trailing shoe with its securing spring.

6. Push the adjusting lever toward the center of the brake and install it with the tension spring. Fasten the shoe retaining spring.

NOTE: *The longer hook of the tension spring attaches to the leading shoe.*

7. Push the adjusting ratchet downward, while returning the lever, so that it contacts the rim of the shoe.

8. Install the retaining spring.

9. Attach the tension spring to the shoes with the tool used during removal.

10. Install the drum and adjust the brakes.

Land Cruiser and Hi-Lux

Land Cruiser rear brake shoe removal and installation procedures are identical to those for Land Cruiser front brake shoes.

The procedure for the Hi-Lux is also similar to the Land Cruiser front shoe removal procedure, except for the following points:

1. Remove and install the parking brake strut and springs along with the front shoe.

2. Disconnect the parking brake cable from the shoe lever. Remember to connect it during installation.

3. Remove and install the rear shoe complete with the parking brake shoe lever.

The service limits of the brake lining thickness, are as follows:

Hi-Lux—0.06 in.

Land Cruiser—0.16 in.

The brakes must be relined if the lining thickness falls below these specifications.

Wheel Cylinders

Removal and Installation

Passenger Cars and Hi-Lux

1. Plug the master cylinder inlet to prevent hydraulic fluid from leaking.

2. Remove the brake drums and shoes as detailed in the appropriate section above.

3. Working from behind the backing plate, disconnect the hydraulic line from the wheel cylinder.

4. Unfasten the screws retaining the wheel cylinder and withdraw the cylinder.

Installation is performed in the reverse order of removal. However, once the hydraulic line has been disconnected from the wheel cylinder, the union seat must be replaced. To replace the seat, proceed in the following manner:

NOTE: *This procedure is not required*

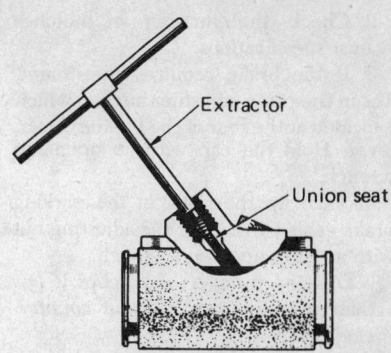

Replacing the wheel cylinder union seat

on Crown, Corona (1974–75), and Hi-Lux models.

1. Use a screw extractor with a diameter of 0.1 in. and having reverse threads, to remove the union seat from the wheel cylinder.

2. Drive in the new union seat with a 5/16 in. bar, used as a drift.

Remember to bleed the brake system after completing wheel cylinder, brake shoe and drum installation.

Land Cruiser

The front brake wheel cylinder removal procedure is performed in the same manner as the procedure for the Hi-Lux and Land Cruiser rear brakes. For details see the section dealing with these vehicles.

Overhaul

See "General Overhaul" for a description of wheel cylinder overhaul procedures.

PARKING BRAKE

Adjustments

Floor-Mounted Lever

Corolla, Carina, and Celica

1. Slowly pull the parking brake lever upward, without depressing the button on the end of it, and while counting the number of notches required until the parking brake is applied.

NOTE: *Two "clicks" are equal to one notch.*

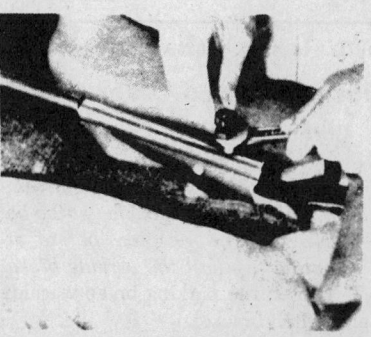

Adjusting the Corolla, Carina and Celica floor-mounted parking brake lever.

2. Check the number of notches against specifications.

3. If the brake requires adjustment, loosen the cable adjusting nut cap which is located at the rear of the parking brake lever. Hold the cap with an open-end wrench.

4. Take up the slack in the parking brake cable by rotating the adjusting nut with another open-end wrench.

   a. If the number of notches is *less* than specified, turn the nut *counterclockwise.*

   b. If the number of notches is *more* than specified, turn the nut *clockwise.*

5. Tighten the adjusting cap, using care not to disturb the setting of the adjusting nut.

6. Check the rotation of the rear wheels to be sure that the brakes are not dragging.

1974-75 Crown and 1974-76 Mark II

1. Adjust the rear brake shoes.

2. Without depressing the button, pull the parking brake handle up slowly, and count the number of notches before the brake is applied. It should take 3-6 notches; if not, proceed with step 3.

3. Loosen the locknut on the parking brake equalizer.

4. Screw the adjusting nut *in,* just enough so that the parking brake cables have no slack.

5. Hold the adjusting nut in this position while tightening the locknut.

6. Check the rotation of the rear wheels, with the parking brake off, to be sure that the brake shoes aren't dragging.

Parking Brake Adjustment

Model	Range of adjustment (notches)
Corolla 1200	7-8
Corolla 1600 ('72-'74)	5-8
Corolla 1600 ('75-'77)	2-6
Carina ('72-'74)	3-7
Celica ('72-'77)	3-7
Corona ('74-'77)	3-6
Mark II/6 ('74-'75) 1976	3-6 8-12

NOTE: Each notch equals two clicks.

Dash-Mounted Lever

Corona, Mark II, Crown and Hi-Lux

NOTE: *On Hi-Lux models, adjust the rear brake shoes, as detailed at the beginning of this chapter, before attempting to adjust the parking brake.*

1. Loosen the parking brake warning light switch bracket.

2. Push the parking brake lever in until it is stopped by the pawl.

3. Move the switch so that it will be "off" at this position but "on" when the handle is pulled out.

4. Tighten the switch bracket and push the brake lever in again.

5. Working from underneath the vehicle, loosen the locknut on the parking brake cable equalizer.

6. Screw the adjusting nut *in,* just enough so that the brake cables have no slack.

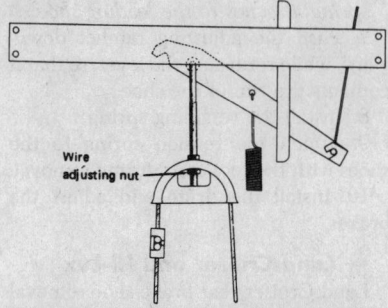

Wire adjusting nut

Adjusting the dash mounted or the 1974-75 Corona and Mark II floor-mounted parking brake from underneath the car.

7. Hold the adjusting nut in this position while tightening the locknut.

8. Check the rotation of the rear wheels to make sure that the brakes are not dragging.

9. Pull out on the parking brake lever, and count the number of notches needed to apply the parking brake. Check the number against the figures given in the chart.

Parking Brake Adjustment

Model	Adjusting Range (notches)
Corona ('72-'73)	7-12
Mark II/4	5-9
Mark II/6 ('72-'73)	8-10
Crown 2600	8-11
Hi-Lux①	6-9

① 1973-77—8-12 Notches

Land Cruiser

Land Cruiser models use a separate drum brake assembly, operating on the driveshaft, to serve as a parking brake. Adjust it as follows:

1. Push the parking brake lever all the way in, so that the brake is released.

2. Raise the rear of the vehicle and support it with jackstands.

3. Turn the parking brake adjustment shaft, which is located at the bottom of the parking brake backing plate, counterclockwise until the shoes seat against the drum.

4. Back the adjuster off one notch.

5. Apply the parking brake; the drum should be locked. Release the brake; the drum should rotate freely.

NOTE: *If the drum does not rotate freely with the brake off, loosen the adjuster one more notch.*

6. Adjust the turnbuckles on the parking brake intermediate levers and the adjusting nuts on the end of the parking brake cables, so that 6-9 notches are required to apply the parking brake (1972-75). Set for 7-12 notches for 1976-77.

Removal and Installation

Corolla, Celica, Carina—Front Cable

1. Raise and support the rear of the vehicle.

2. Remove the rear console.

3. Remove the parking brake lever adjusting cap.

4. Remove the cable lock nut.

5. Remove the parking brake lever.

6. Remove the cable from the underside and disconnect it from the equalizer.

7. Install in reverse of removal.

8. Adjust the brake.

Corolla, Celica, Carina—Rear Cables

1. Remove the front cable.

2. Disconnect the rear cables from the equalizer.

3. Disconnect the cable clamps.

4. Remove the rear brake shoe and pull the cables from the backing plates.

5. Install in reverse of removal.

6. Adjust the brake.

Corona—Floor Lever Type

1. Raise and support the vehicle.

2. Remove the drive shaft.

3. Remove the equalizer from the lever pull rod.

4. Remove the rear brake shoes.

5. Depress the cable retaining claw and remove it from the backing plate.

6. Installation is the reverse of removal.

Corona—Underdash Type

1. Raise and support the vehicle.

2. Remove the driveshaft.

3. Separate the equalizer from the front cable and remove the clip.

4. Remove the return spring.

5. Remove the pin and take off the pulley.

6. Remove the clip and lever pin and take off the front cable.

7. The rear cables are removed as in the floor lever type.

8. Installation is the reverse of removal.

Corona Mk II—Front Cable

1. Remove the parking brake signal switch wiring harness and switch bracket.

2. Slightly pull out the parking brake handle and lift the pawl to disengage the ratchet.

3. While holding the pawl, push down

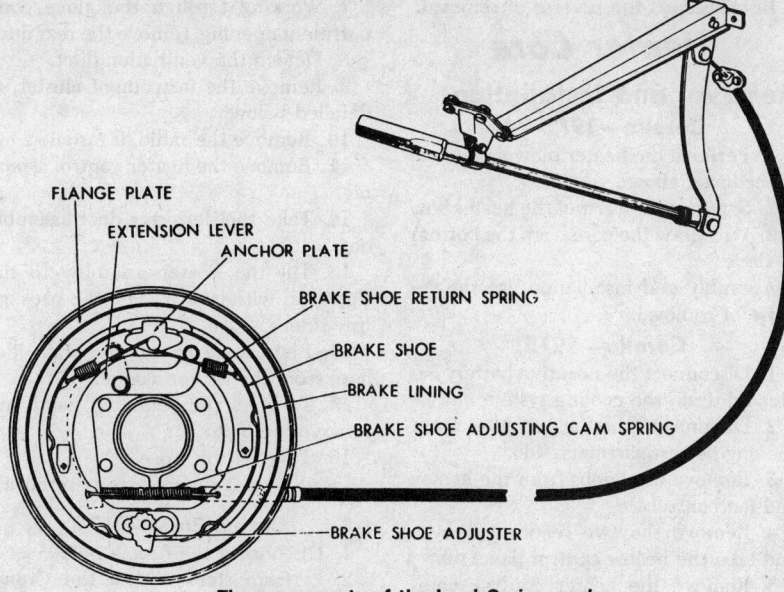

FLANGE PLATE
EXTENSION LEVER
ANCHOR PLATE
BRAKE SHOE RETURN SPRING
BRAKE SHOE
BRAKE LINING
BRAKE SHOE ADJUSTING CAM SPRING
BRAKE SHOE ADJUSTER

The components of the Land Cruiser parking brake system.

on the handle and disconnect the cable from the handle.

4. Remove the pulley, clip and bracket.

5. Remove the upper portion of the brake handle guide and remove the handle.

6. Remove the return spring and cable from the intermediate lever.

7. Remove the cable body clamp clip and remove the front cable.

8. Installation is the reverse of above.

9. Adjust the brake.

Corona Mk II—Rear Cables

1. Remove the equalizer adjusting nut and remove the pull rod.

2. Remove the cables from the equalizer.

3. Remove the retainers and clamps from the cables.

4. Remove the brake drums, disconnect the cables from the shoes and remove them from the backing plates. The retaining claw may be depressed with a pliers.

5. Installation is the reverse of removal.

Crown—Front Cable

1. Raise and support the vehicle.

2. Remove the return spring and rod from the intermediate lever and disconnect the front cable.

3. Remove the cable retaining clip at the floor pan.

4. Remove the parking brake switch bracket.

5. Remove the brake handle guide bolts.

6. Remove the pin and pulley.

7. Remove the cable-to-pulley bracket clip.

8. Push the brake handle all the way down, and, using a welding rod or bent

wire clothes hanger, depress the plunger ratchet and remove the cable end.

9. Remove the grommet and pull out the cable.

10. Install in reverse of removal.

Crown—Rear Cable

1. Raise and support the car.

2. Remove the pull rod from the intermediate lever.

3. Remove the cable retaining clamp, equalizer and support lever.

4. Disconnect the cables from the clevises at the backing plates.

5. Install in reverse of removal.

Hi-Lux

1. Raise and support the vehicle.

2. Remove the parking brake signal switch bracket.

3. Remove the pulley bracket.

4. Release the brake handle and disconnect the front cable.

5. Remove the return spring.

6. Disconnect the front cable from the inermediate lever.

7. Remove the cable clip from the crossmember.

8. Remove the pull rod nuts and disconnect the equalizer.

9. Remove the rear drums and disconnect the cables from the shoes.

10. Depress the cable retaining claws and remove the cables from the backing plates.

11. Reverse the removal procedure for installation.

12. Adjust the brake.

Land Cruiser

1. Disconnect the throttle and choke rods from the carburetor and remove them from the instrument panel.

2. Remove the driver's side heater duct.

3. Disconnect the return spring from the parking brake lever. Remove the cotter pins from both ends of the lever.

4. Remove the lever bracket bolts and the parking brake handle bolts and lower the assembly from the dash.

5. Remove the cotter pin from the lever located in the engine compartment and remove the intermediate lever pull rod.

6. Disconnect the cable from the lever.

7. Raise and support the rear end.

8. Remove the transmission shield.

9. Disconnect the driveshaft from the parking brake drum.

10. Drain the oil from the transfer case.

11. Remove the cotter pin from the transfer output shaft and remove the drum retaining nut.

12. Remove the parking brake drum.

13. Unbolt and remove the backing plate.

14. Remove the holddown and return springs, disconnect the cables and remove the parking brake shoes.

15. Installation is the reverse of removal. Torque the brake drum retaining nuts to 101–123 ft lbs. Adjust the brake.

CHASSIS ELECTRICAL
Heater Blower

NOTE: *On some models the air conditioner, if so equipped, is integral with the heater, and therefore, heater removal may differ from the procedures detailed below.*

Removal and Installation

Corolla 1972–74

1. Drain the cooling system.

2. Remove the package tray from beneath the dashboard.

3. Unfasten the two water hoses from the heater.

NOTE: *Have a container ready to catch any water which remains in the system.*

4. Unfasten the clamp and remove the defroster hose.

5. Unfasten the three heater control cables from the heater box.

6. Remove the fresh air duct.

7. Unfasten the electrical connections.

8. Unfasten the four heater box attachment bolts and withdraw the heater box.

9. Loosen the fan attachment nut by tapping it lightly and then withdraw the fan from the shaft.

CAUTION: *Do not remove the balancing weight from the fan.*

10. Unfasten the blower motor securing screws and remove the motor.

Installation is the reverse of removal. Be sure that the fan does not contact the blower housing when it is assembled. Hold the fan adapter in place, on the armature shaft while tightening the fan locknut to 43 ft lbs.

Corolla—1975

1. Disconnect the blower wiring harness.
2. Remove the right-hand defroster hose.
3. Remove the three screws which secure the blower motor and lift out the motor.
4. Separate the fan from the motor. Installation is the reverse of removal.

Carina, Corona (1972–73), Mark II/4 and Celica

1. Working from under the instrument panel, unfasten the defroster hoses from the heater box.
2. Unplug the multiconnector.
3. Loosen the mounting screws and withdraw the blower assembly.
Installation is the reverse of removal.

Mark II/6

1. Remove the center console, after removing the shift knob (manual), unfastening the wiring, connector, and undoing the console securing screws.
2. Unfasten the heater blower wiring connector.
3. Remove the three bolts which secure the blower motor to the heater box.
4. Withdraw the motor, complete with fan, from the box.
Installation is the reverse order of removal.

Corona—1974–75

1. Remove the package tray.
2. Remove the trim panel.
3. Disconnect the heater blower motor wiring harness.
4. Loosen the three screws which secure the motor to the housing and remove the motor/blower assembly.
Installation is the reverse of removal.

Crown 2600—1972

1. Unfasten the cables and remove the battery. Next remove the ignition coil and fuel filter.
2. Raise the front of the car and support it with jackstands.
3. Remove the left-hand wheel arch by unfastening its retaining bolts.
4. Unfasten the bolts which secure the heater blower motor; withdraw it, complete with the fan.
Installation is the reverse of removal.

Land Cruiser

1. Loosen the air duct clamping screws and remove the ducts.
2. Remove the air duct screen.
3. Unfasten the mounting bolts and remove the blower motor complete with fan.

Installation is the reverse of removal.

Heater Core

Removal and Installation

Corolla—1972–74

1. Perform the heater blower removal procedures, above.
2. Separate the parts of the heater box.
3. Withdraw the core from the bottom of the case.
Assembly and installation are the reverse of removal.

Corolla—1975

1. Disconnect the negative battery cable and drain the cooling system.
2. Disconnect the heater hose from the engine compartment side.
3. Remove the knobs from the heater and fan controls.
4. Remove the two securing screws, and take the heater control panel off.
5. Remove the heater control, complete with cables.
6. Disconnect the wiring harness.
7. Remove the three heater assembly securing bolts and remove the assembly.
8. Separate the core from the heater assembly.
Installation is the reverse of removal.

Carina, Corona (1972–73), Celica and Mark II (all)

1. Drain the cooling system.
2. Remove the console, if so equipped, by removing the shift knob (manual), wiring connector, and console attaching screws.
3. Remove the carpeting from the tunnel.
4. If necessary, remove the cigarette lighter and ash tray.
5. Remove the package tray, if it makes access to the heater core difficult.
6. Remove the securing screws and remove the center air outlet on the Mark II/6.
7. Remove the bottom cover/intake assembly screws and withdraw the assembly.
8. Remove the cover from the water valve.
9. Remove the water valve.
10. Remove the hose clamps and remove the hoses from the core.
11. Remove the core.
Installation is the reverse of removal.

Corona—1974–77

1. Disconnect the negative battery cable.
2. Drain the cooling system.
3. Disconnect the heater hoses from the engine.
4. Remove the center console, if so equipped.
5. Remove the package tray and disconnect the heater air duct.
6. Unfasten the screws and take the glove compartment out of the dash.

7. Working through the glove compartment opening, remove the rear duct.
8. Detach the ventilation duct.
9. Remove the instrument cluster, as detailed below.
10. Remove the radio, if installed.
11. Remove the heater control assembly.
12. Take the defroster duct assembly out.
13. Tilt the heater assembly to the right and withdraw it from the package tray side.
14. Remove the water valve and outlet hose from the heater assembly.
15. Take off the retaining band and remove the bolt.
16. Take out the core.
Installation is the reverse of removal.

Crown 2600—1972

1. Disconnect the fusible link.
2. Perform steps 1–3 of the Crown 2300 heater core removal procedure.
3. Detach the air intake door and heater control cables from the core.
4. Remove the air ducts; center, left-hand, and right-hand, as well as both defroster hoses.
5. Remove the heater core from the top of the heater box.
Installation is the reverse of removal.

Land Cruiser

Front Heater

1. Turn off the water valve.
2. Detach both hoses from the heater core.
3. Unfasten the air duct clamp.
4. Detach the defroster hoses from the heater box.
5. Unfasten its attachment bolts and withdraw the core.
Installation is the reverse of removal.

Rear Heater

1. Shut the water valve.
2. Detach both of the hoses from the rear heater core.
3. Detach the wiring from the rear heater.
4. Unfasten the bolts and lift out the core.
Installation is the reverse of removal.

Radio

CAUTION: *Never operate the radio without a speaker; severe damage to the output transistors will result. If the speaker must be replaced, use a speaker of the correct impedance (ohms) or else the output transistors will be damaged and require replacement.*

Removal and Installation

Corolla (1972–74) and Celica

1. Remove the knobs from the radio.
2. Remove the nuts from the radio control shafts.

3. Detach the antenna lead from the jack on the radio case.

4. Remove the cowl air intake duct.

5. Detach the power and speaker leads.

6. Remove the radio support nuts and bolts.

7. Remove the radio from beneath the dashboard.

8. Remove the nuts which secure the speaker through the service hole in the top of the glovebox.

9. Remove remainder of the speaker securing nuts from above the radio mounting location.

10. Remove the speaker.

Installation is the reverse of removal.

Corolla—1975–77

1. Remove the two screws from the top of the dashboard center trim panel.

2. Lift the center panel out far enough to gain access to the cigarette lighter wiring and disconnect the wiring. Remove the trim panel.

3. Unfasten the screws which secure the radio to the instrument panel braces.

4. Lift out the radio and disconnect the leads from it. Remove the radio.

Installation is the reverse of removal.

Carina and Corona (1972–73)

1. Remove the center air outlet from under the dash.

2. Unfasten the radio control mounting bracket.

3. Remove the radio control knobs and then the securing nuts from the control shafts.

4. Detach the speaker, and the power and antenna leads from the radio.

5. Withdraw the radio from underneath the dashboard.

6. Unfasten the speaker securing nuts and remove the speaker.

Installation is the reverse of removal.

Corona—1974–77

Instrument Panel-Mounted

1. Remove the two screws securing the instrument cluster surround and remove the surround.

2. Remove the knobs from the heater controls and remove the heater control face.

3. Remove the four screws which secure the center trim panel (two are behind the heater control opening).

4. Remove the radio knobs and remove the center trim panel.

5. Remove the four screws which secure the radio bracket.

6. Pull the radio far enough out to remove the antenna, power, and speaker leads.

7. Remove the radio.

Installation is the reverse of removal.

Console-Mounted

1. Remove the screws which secure the console and remove the console, by lowering the armrest rearward and lifting up on the center of the console.

2. Unplug the radio and disconnect the antenna lead.

3. Remove the radio knobs.

4. Remove the radio bracket and then remove the radio.

Installation is the reverse of removal.

Mark II/4—1972

1. Disconnect the battery.

2. Remove the left and right instrument panel moldings.

3. Remove the heater control knobs, unfasten the screws, and remove the heater control trim panel.

4. Remove the five screws and withdraw the center crash pad from the instrument panel area around the heater controls.

5. Working from beneath the dash, disconnect the radio and clock (optional) leads.

6. Unfasten the screws securing the radio and clock surrounding trim panel.

7. Remove the radio bracket. Withdraw the radio and clock assembly.

8. Remove the knobs and unfasten the nuts which secure the radio.

Installation is the reverse of removal.

Mark II/6—1972–77

1. Remove the instrument cluster housing as detailed in the appropriate section below.

2. Remove the heater control panel assembly.

3. Unfasten the two radio securing bolts.

4. Detach all of the radio leads.

5. Withdraw the radio.

Installation is the reverse of removal.

Crown 2600—1972

1. Remove the center and right-hand heater air ducts.

2. Detach the antenna, power, and speaker leads from the radio.

3. Remove the control knobs and nuts from the top of the radio panel. Remove the panel.

4. Remove the knobs and nuts from the top of the radio panel. Remove the panel.

5. Remove the four tape deck mounting screws and withdraw the tape deck, if so equipped.

6. Unfasten the radio mounting bracket and remove the radio.

Installation is the reverse of removal.

Windshield Wiper Motor

Removal and Installation

Corolla—1972–74

1. Disconnect the car battery.

2. Unfasten the wiper motor connection.

3. Detach the wiper motor from the linkage by prying it with a screwdriver.

NOTE: *It may be necessary to remove the defroster nozzle to gain access to the motor.*

4. Remove the package tray.

5. Unfasten the three wiper motor securing nuts and withdraw the motor from inside the car.

Installation is the reverse of removal.

Corolla (1975), Carina, Corona and Crown

1. Disconnect the wiper motor connector.

2. Remove the service cover and loosen the wiper motor bolts.

3. Use a screwdriver to separate the wiper link-to-motor connection.

CAUTION: *Be careful not to bend the linkage.*

4. Withdraw the wiper motor assembly.

Installation is the reverse of removal.

Celica and Mark II/4

1. Remove the access hole cover.

2. Separate the wiper and motor by prying gently with a screwdriver.

3. Remove the left and right cowl ventilators.

4. Remove the wiper arms and the linkage mounting nuts. Push the linkage pivot ports into the ventilators.

5. Loosen the wiper link connectors at their ends and with the linkage from the cowl ventilator.

6. Start the wiper motor and turn the ignition key off.

NOTE: *The wiper motor is difficult to remove when it is in the parked position. If the motor is turned off at the wiper switch, it will automatically return to this position.*

7. Unplug the connector.

8. Loosen the motor bolts and withdraw the motor.

Installation is the reverse of removal. Be sure to install the wiper motor with it in the park position by connecting the multiconnector and operating the wiper control switch. Assemble the crank.

Mark II/6 1972–76

1. Remove the cover from the service hole.

2. Set the wiper crank at 180° from park, by turning the wiper switch on and then turning the ignition switch off, once the desired position is reached.

3. Separate the link from the motor crank with a screwdriver.

4. Disconnect the wiper motor connector.

5. Unfasten the wiper motor bolts and withdraw the motor.

Installation is the reverse of removal.

Land Cruiser

1. Detach the wiper link from the motor with a screwdriver.

2. Unfasten the two bracket bolts at the rear of the motor.

3. Disconnect the wiper motor wiring.

4. Unfasten the wiper motor screws and withdraw the motor.

Installation is the reverse of removal.

Instrument Cluster

Removal and Installation

Corolla—1972–74

1. Disconnect the battery.

2. Detach the speedometer cable from the speedometer.

3. Remove the center and right-hand trim moldings from the instrument panel. (1972–73).

4. Unfasten the instrument cluster and panel molding retainer screw.

5. Remove the two nuts holding the instrument cluster from behind (1972–73).

6. Pull the cluster out slightly and disconnect the wiring.

7. Remove the cluster assembly completely.

CAUTION: *Be careful not to scratch the steering column cover.*

Installation is the reverse of removal.

Corolla—1975–77

1. Disconnect the negative battery cable.

2. Remove the instrument cluster surround.

3. Remove the center trim panel. Disconnect the cigarette lighter wiring before completely removing the panel.

4. Remove the speedometer cable and disconnect it.

5. Pull the instrument cluster out just far enough so that its wiring harness may be disconnected.

6. Remove the cluster.

Installation is the reverse of removal.

Carina

1. Remove the glove box door and withdraw the glove box slightly.

2. Disconnect the inspection lamp socket and glove box light wiring.

3. Remove the glove box.

4. Unfasten the cigarette lighter wiring and remove the ash tray.

5. Unfasten the lower crash pad screws and remove the crash pad.

NOTE: *It may be necessary to lower the steering column. Be careful, the column is the collapsible type.*

6. Loosen the radio rear screws and detach the heater cable at the heater.

7. Unfasten the instrument retaining screws and tilt the panel toward the rear.

8. Detach the speedometer cable and the wiring connectors. Remove the cluster assembly.

Installation is the reverse of removal.

Corona 1972–73

1. Disconnect the battery.

2. Remove the fuse block bolts.

3. Remove the parking brake bracket.

4. Detach the fuel gauge/warning light pod wiring and remove its screws. Pull out the pod.

5. Perform step 4 for the clock.

6. Disconnect the speedometer wiring and cable.

7. Remove the wiring clamp then push the harness toward the front.

8. Loosen the speedometer attachment screws and remove the speedometer.

NOTE: *Cover the lens with a cloth during removal.*

Installation is the reverse of removal.

Corona—1973–74

1. Disconnect the negative (−) battery cable.

2. Remove the two instrument cluster surround.

3. Remove the side air outlet control knob and the clock setting knob.

4. Lift off the panel.

5. Unfasten the five screws which secure the cluster to the instrument panel support.

6. Disconnect the speedometer cable and the instrument cluster wiring harness.

7. Lift out the cluster assembly.

Installation is the reverse of removal.

Mark II/4

1. Disconnect the battery.

2. Remove the package shelf from beneath the dashboard.

3. Remove the fuse block bracket.

4. Remove the lower left-side crash pad and the left-hand trim molding.

5. Unfasten the instrument cluster securing screws and tip the cluster slightly forward.

6. Detach the cluster wiring harness and the speedometer cable. Remove the cluster.

NOTE: *If the car is not equipped with a radio, it is much easier to remove the glove box and then remove the instrument cluster through the opening.*

Installation is the reverse of removal.

Mark II/6

1. Remove the housing from the steering column.

2. Remove the control knobs from the heater and radio.

3. Loosen the heater control floodlight and pull it out slightly.

4. Remove the nine screws which attach the cluster surround.

5. Push the upper crash pad away from the surround and slightly pull out the surround.

6. Remove the heater control floodlight from the surround.

7. Remove the panel toward the right.

8. Remove the instrument panel lower garnish moldings. Remove the ash tray.

9. Remove the heater control assembly.

10. Unfasten the dash side ventilator mounting screws.

11. Remove the radio and tape deck, if so equipped.

12. Remove the heater control bracket.

13. Remove the six cluster securing bolts and lift it out slightly.

14. Detach the speedometer cable and all of the wiring harnesses. Remove the cluster.

Installation is the reverse of removal.

NOTE: *Have the heater control floodlight installed in the cluster surround prior to its installation.*

Celica

1. Disconnect the battery.

2. Detach the heater control cables at the heater box.

3. Loosen the steering column clamping nuts and lower the column.

CAUTION: *Be careful when handling the column; it is the collapsible type. Cover the column shroud with a cloth to protect it.*

4. Loosen the instrument panel screws and tilt the panel forward.

5. Detach the speedometer cable and wiring connectors. Remove the entire panel assembly.

6. Remove the instruments from the panel as required.

Installation is the reverse of removal.

Crown 2600

1. Disconnect the battery.

2. Remove the air duct from the center air outlet.

3. Remove the radio panel from the center instrument panel.

4. Remove the radio. (See above.)

5. Unfasten the screws and remove the instrument cluster panel. Remove the cluster housing.

6. Detach the speedometer drive cable and wiring connectors by reaching through the radio opening.

7. Withdraw the instrument cluster.

Installation is the reverse of removal.

Land Cruiser and Hi-Lux

1. Working from underneath the dashboard, disconnect the speedometer cable.

2. Remove the instrument cluster retaining screws. Pull the cluster part of the way out of the panel.

3. Detach the wiring connectors and light bulbs from the cluster.

4. Remove the instrument cluster from the panel.

NOTE: *On Hi-Lux and Land Cruiser station wagon models, it will be necessary to unfasten the steering column clamping bolts and lower the column in order to remove the cluster.*

Installation is the reverse of removal.

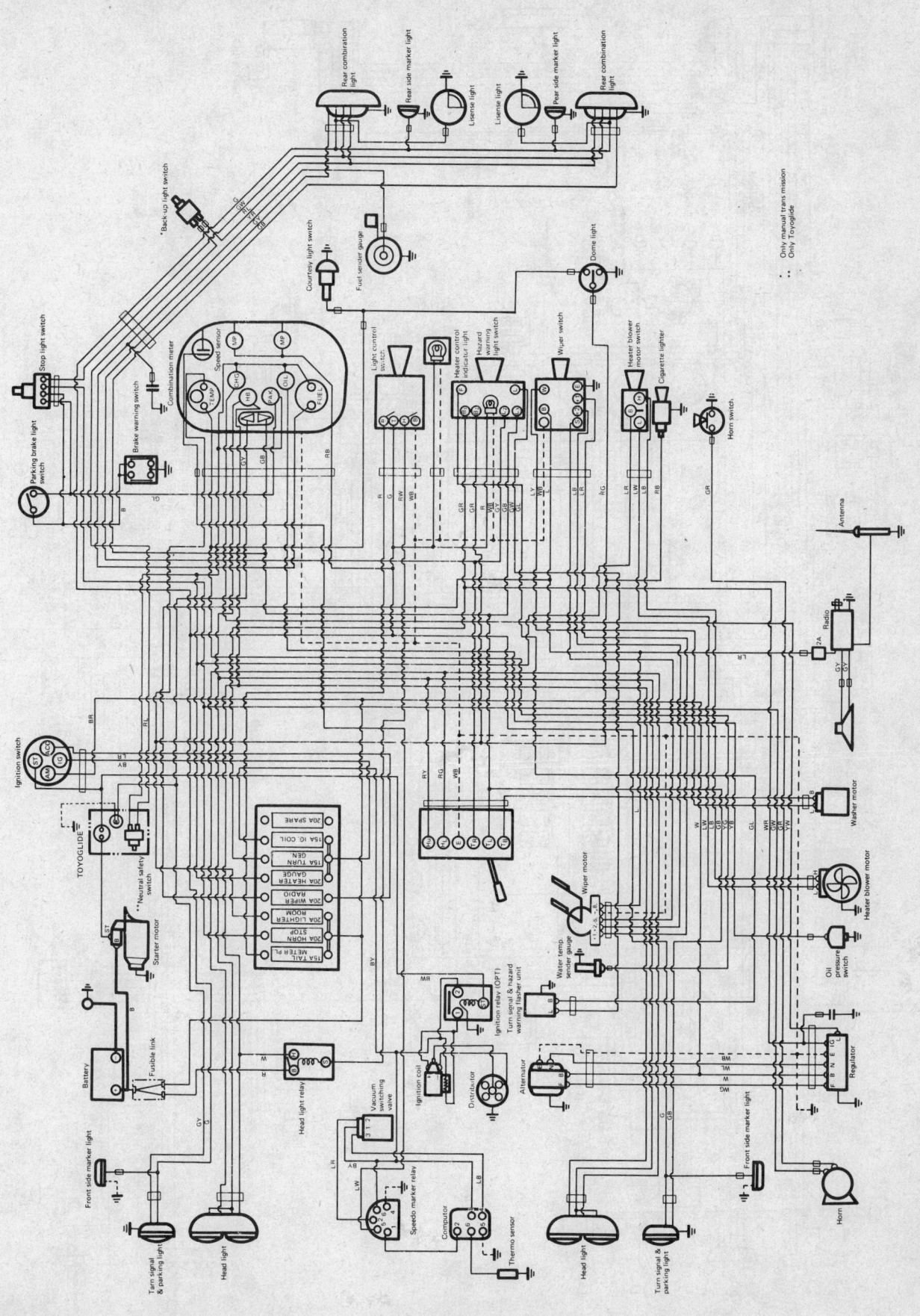

1973-75 Hi-Lux (Pick-up)

Wiring Circuits

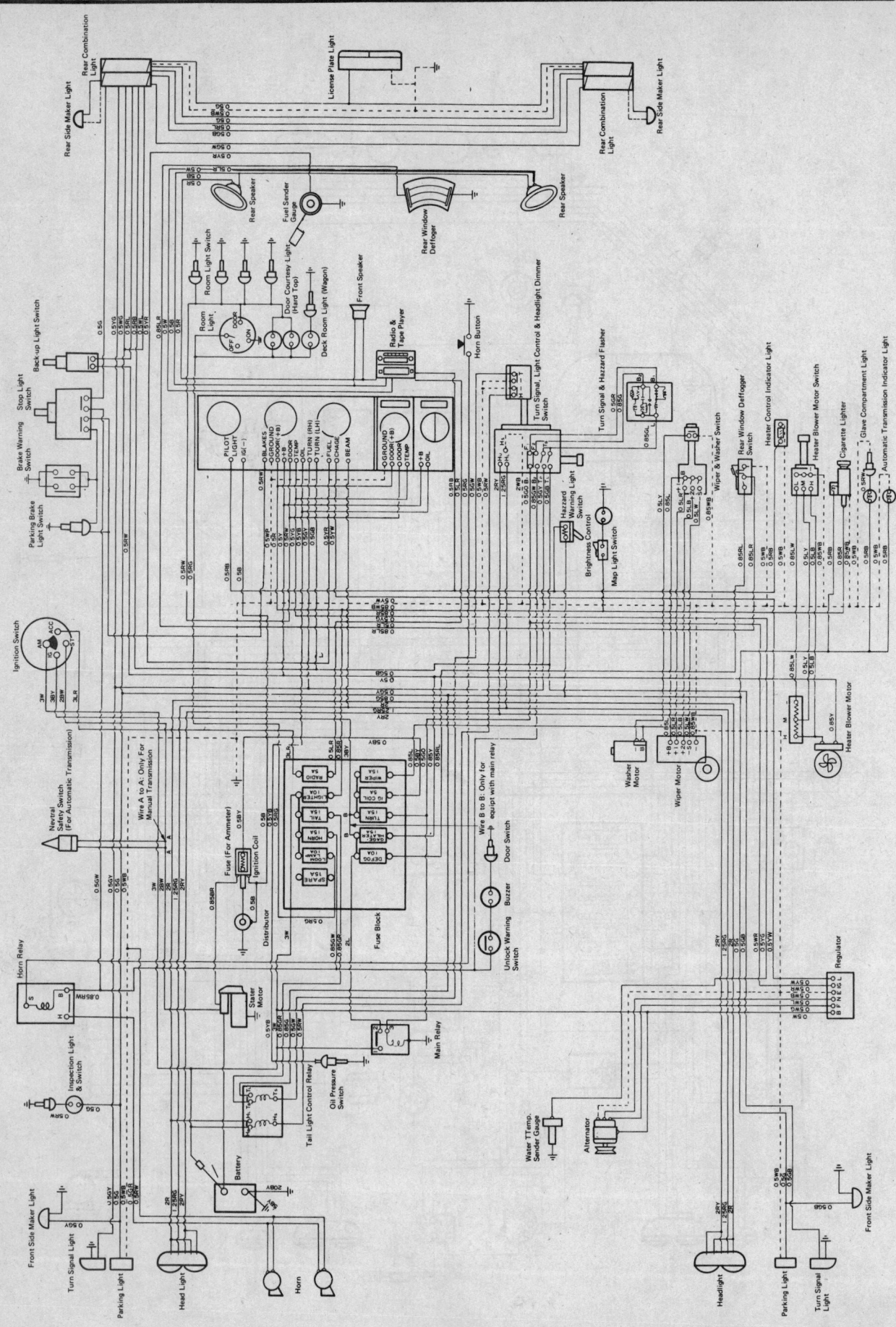

1974-77 Corona

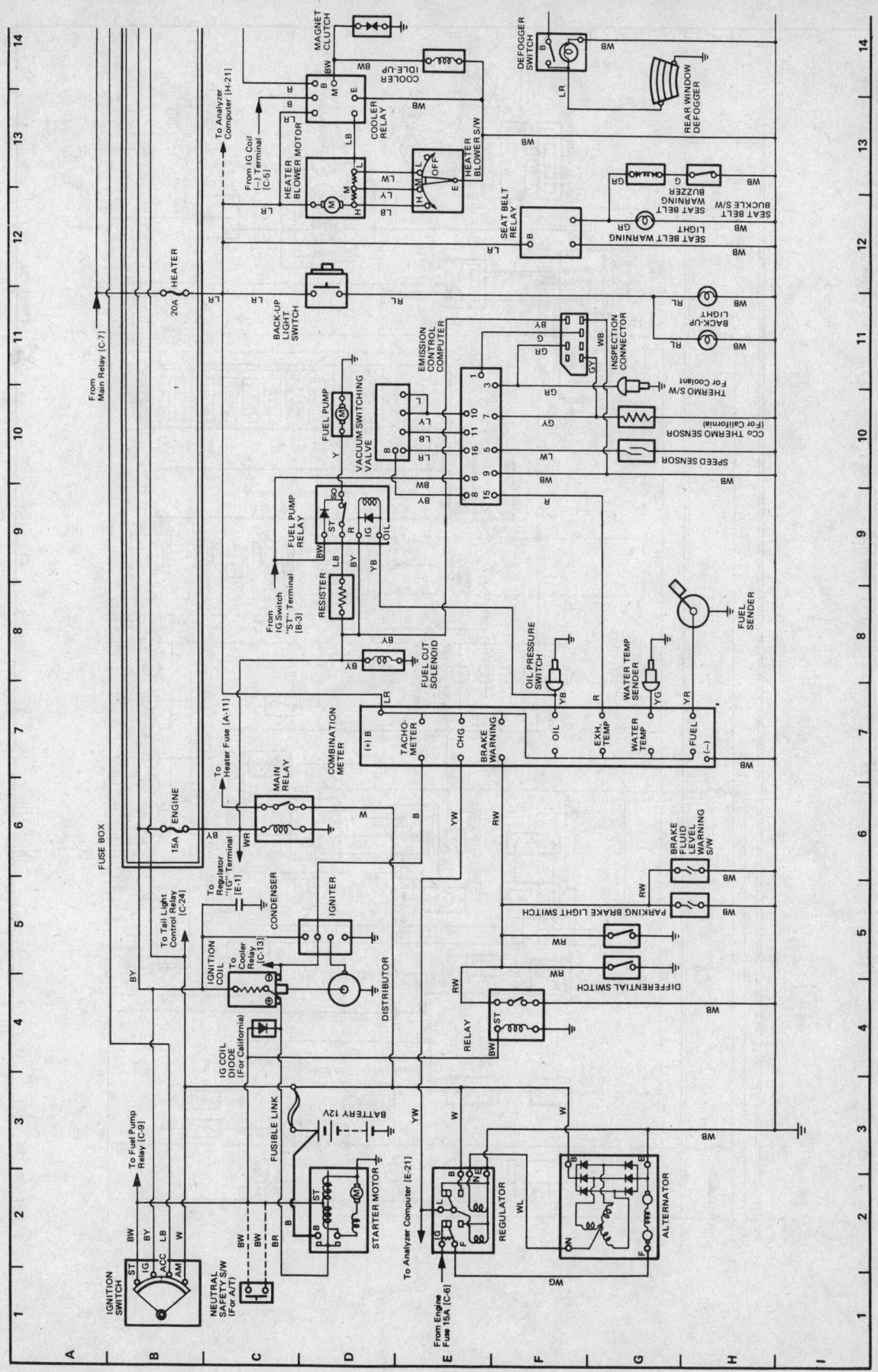

1974-76 Celica and Carina

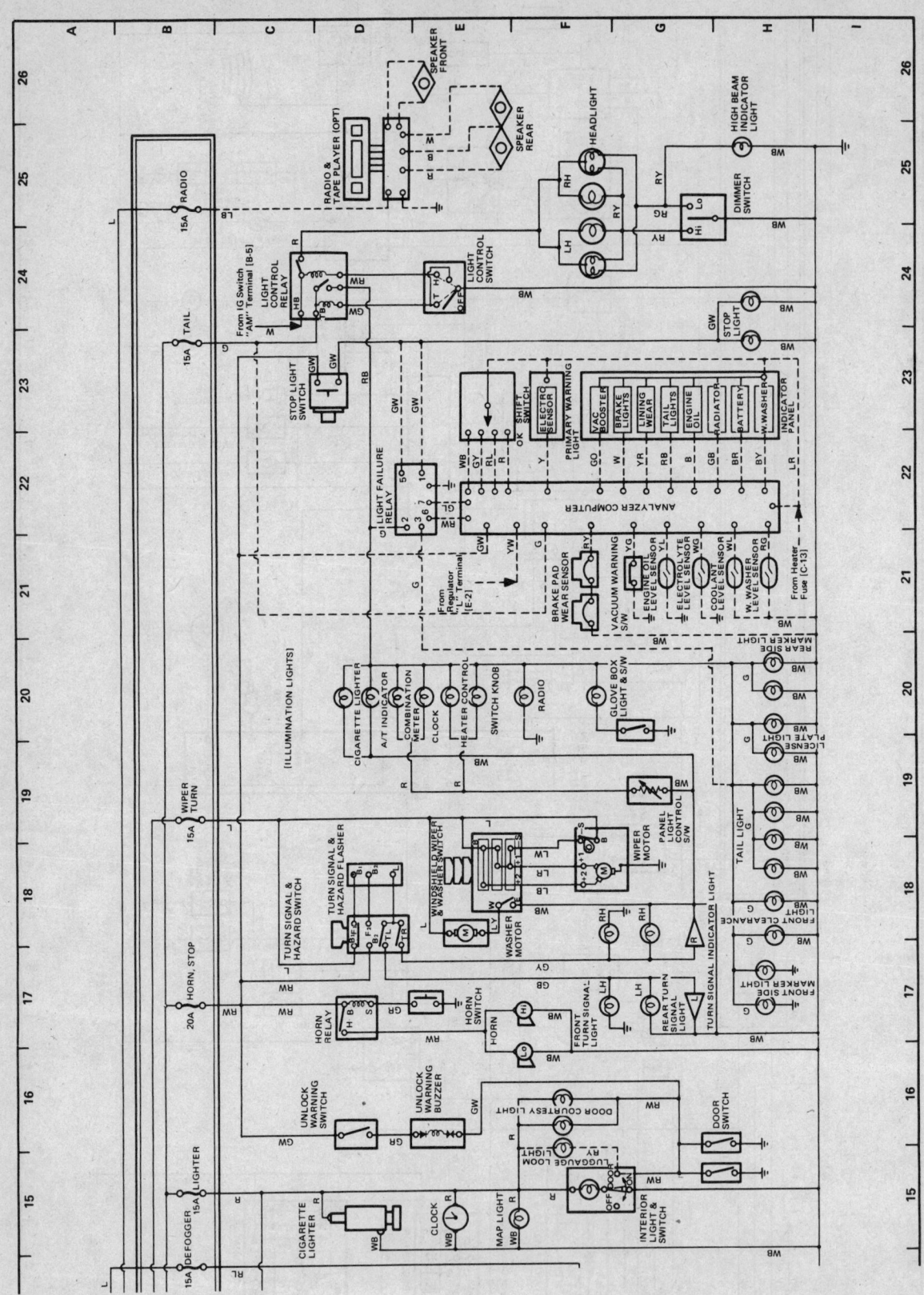

1974-76 Celica and Carina

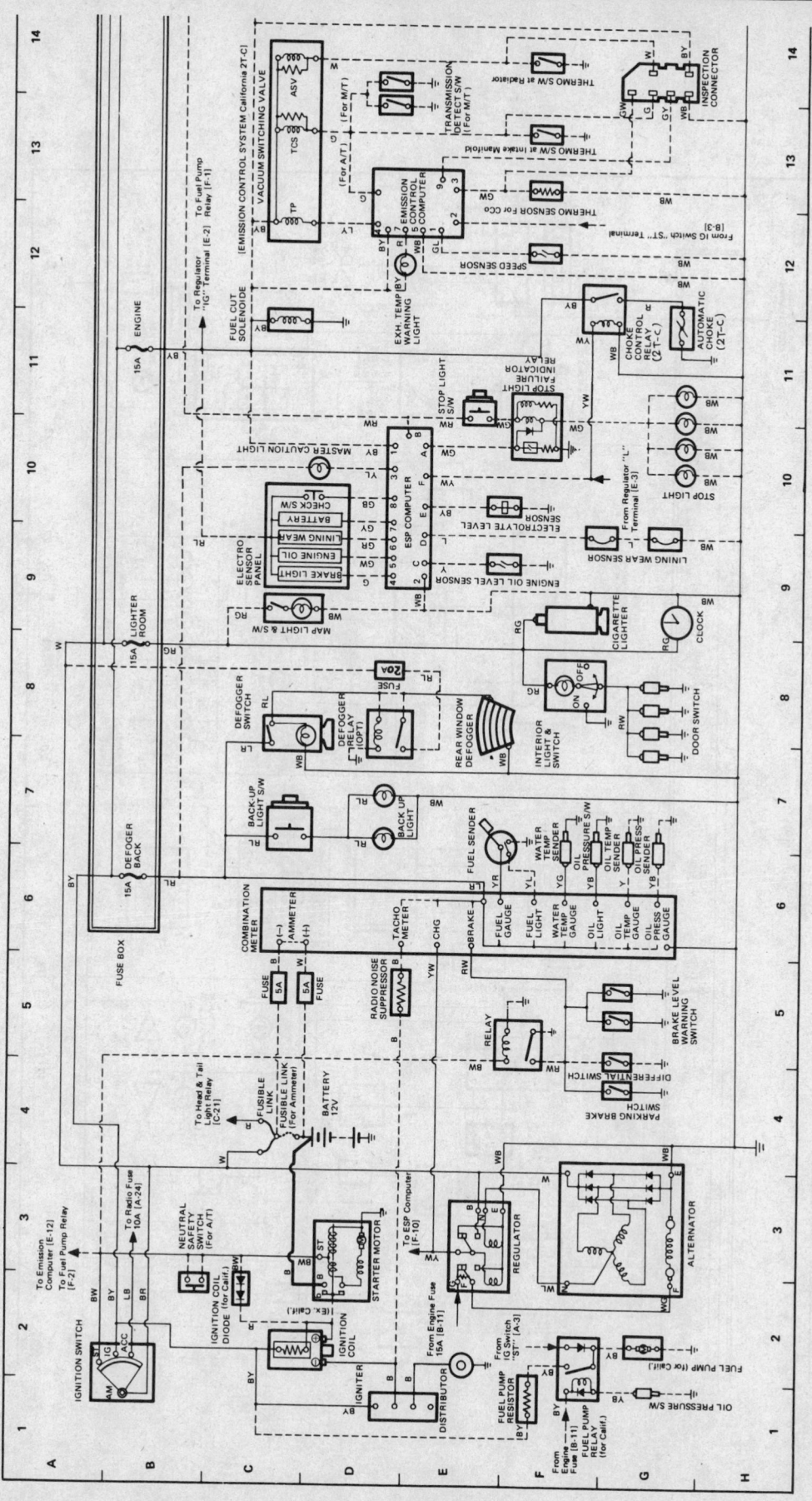

1976-77 Corolla

Wiring Circuits

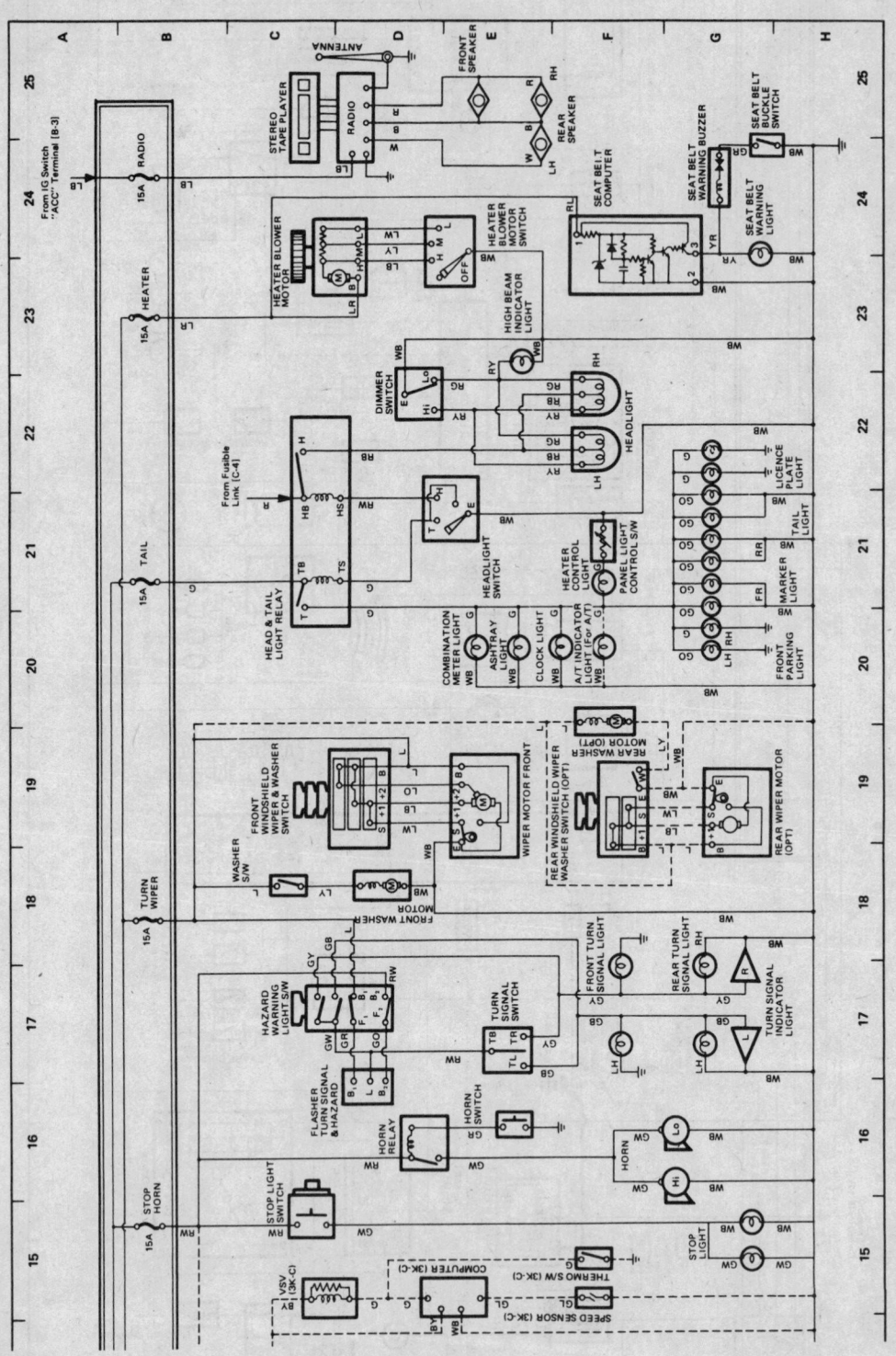

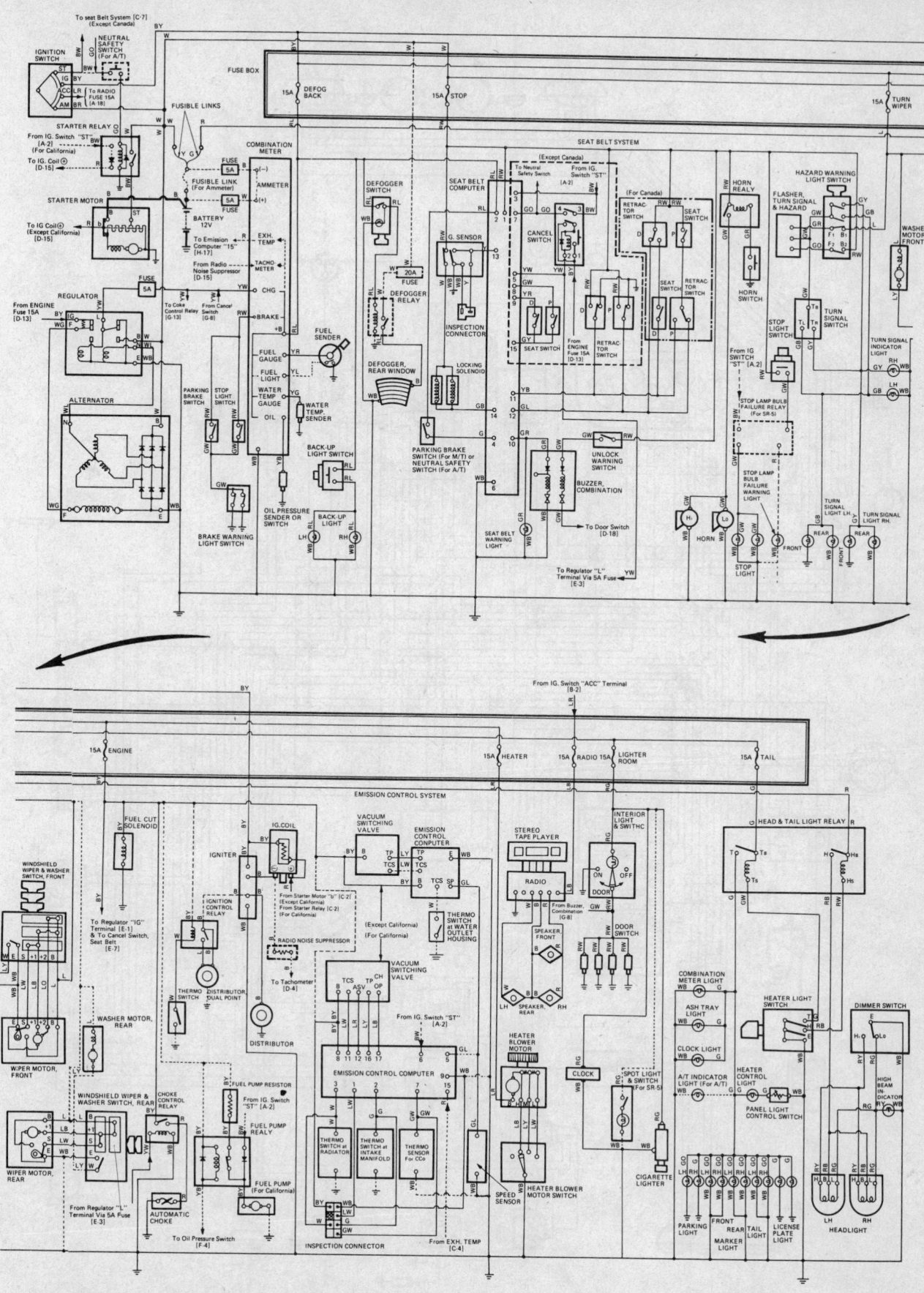

1975 Corolla

Wiring Circuits

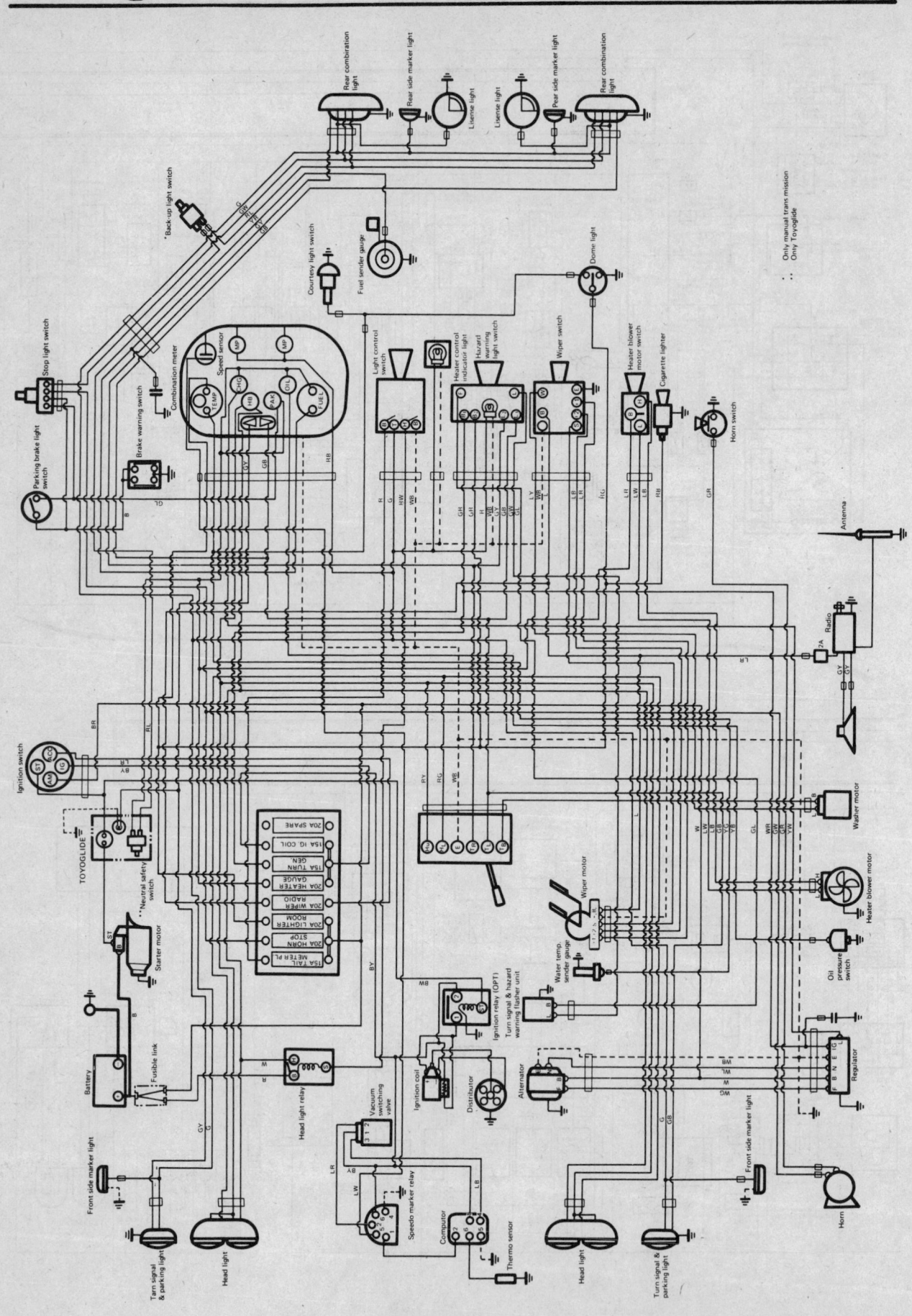

1976-77 Hi-Lux

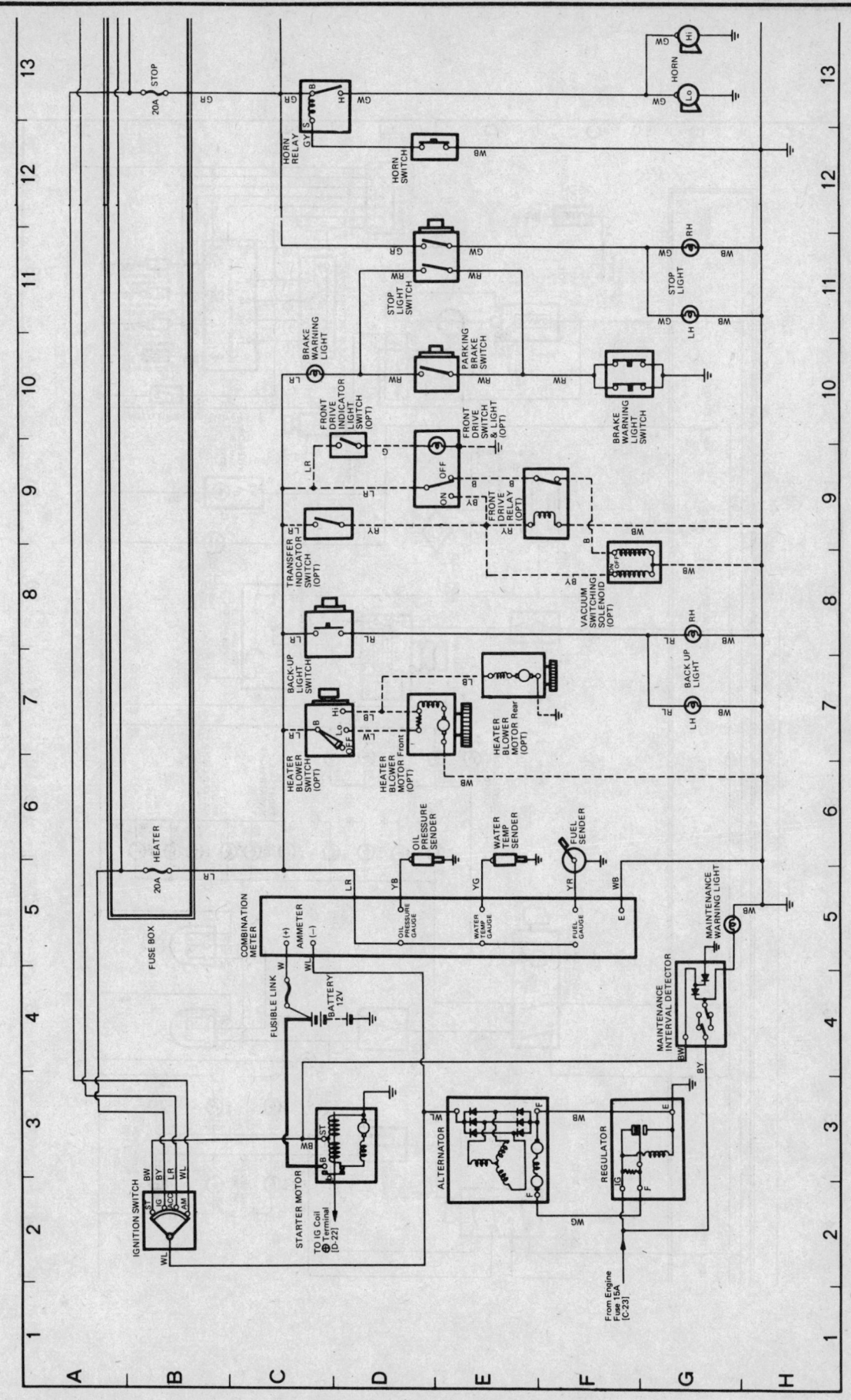

1975-77 Land Cruiser (FJ40 short wheelbase)

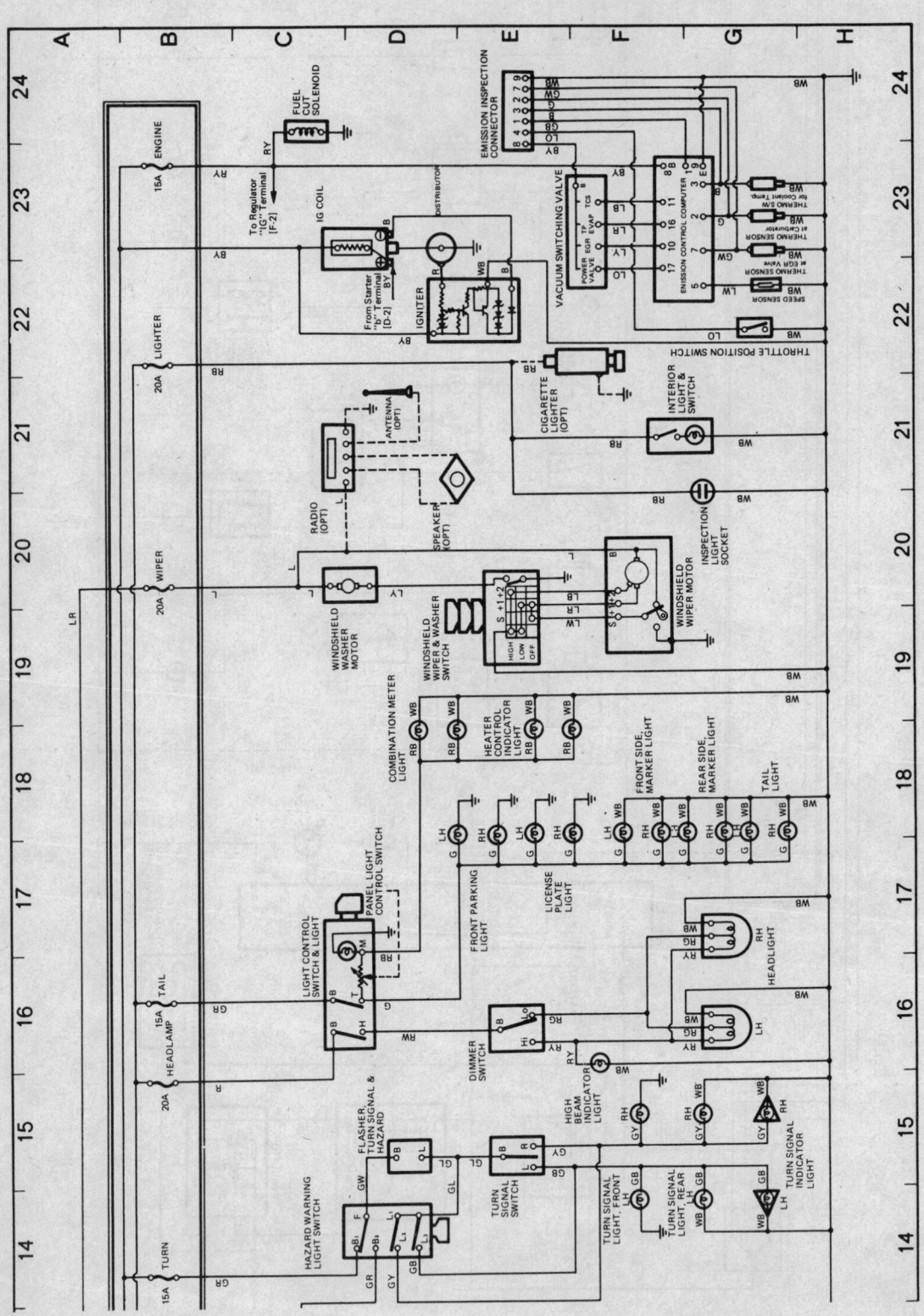

1975-77 Land Cruiser (FJ40 short wheelbase)

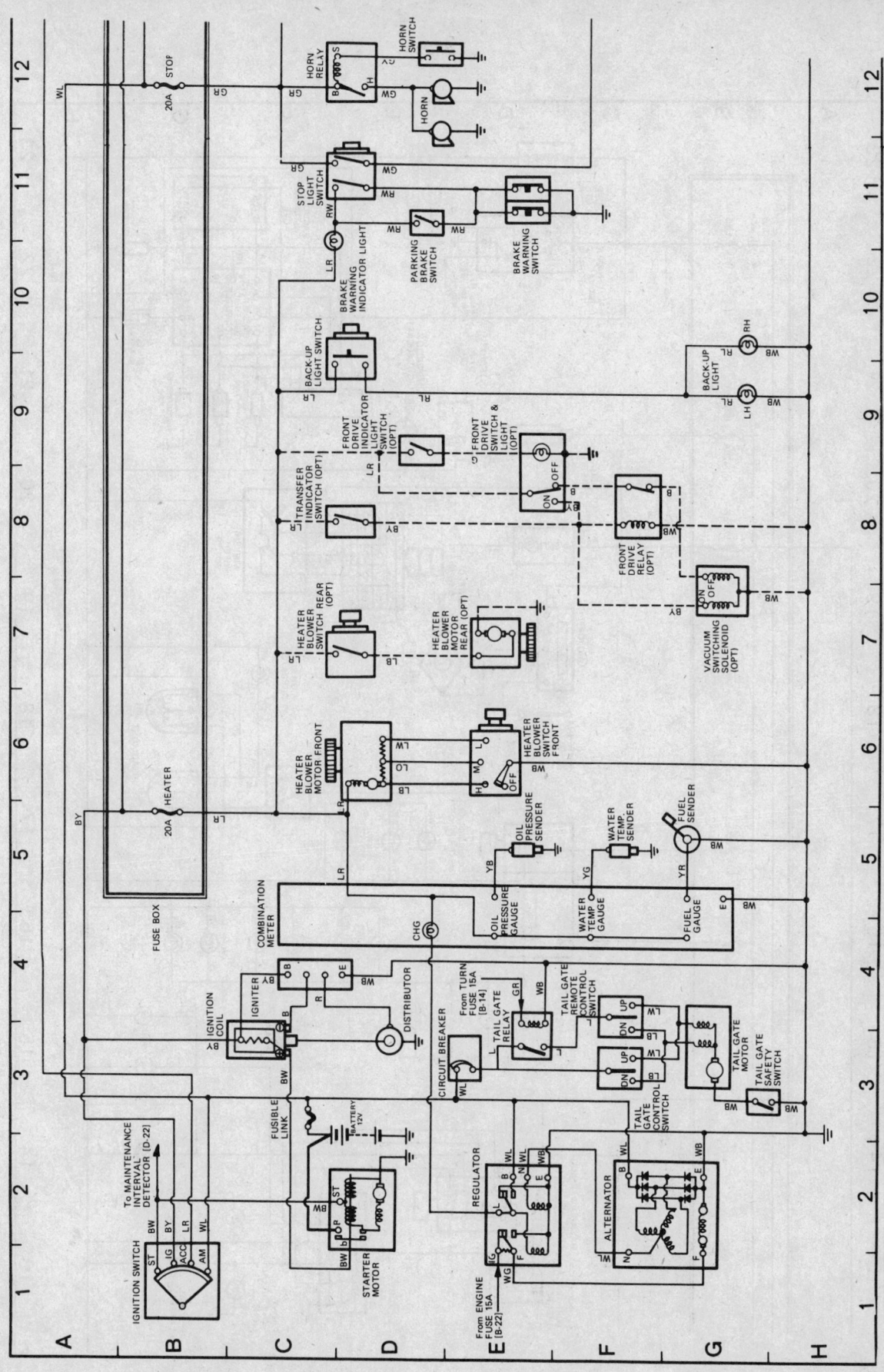

1975-77 Land Cruiser (FJ55 long wheelbase)

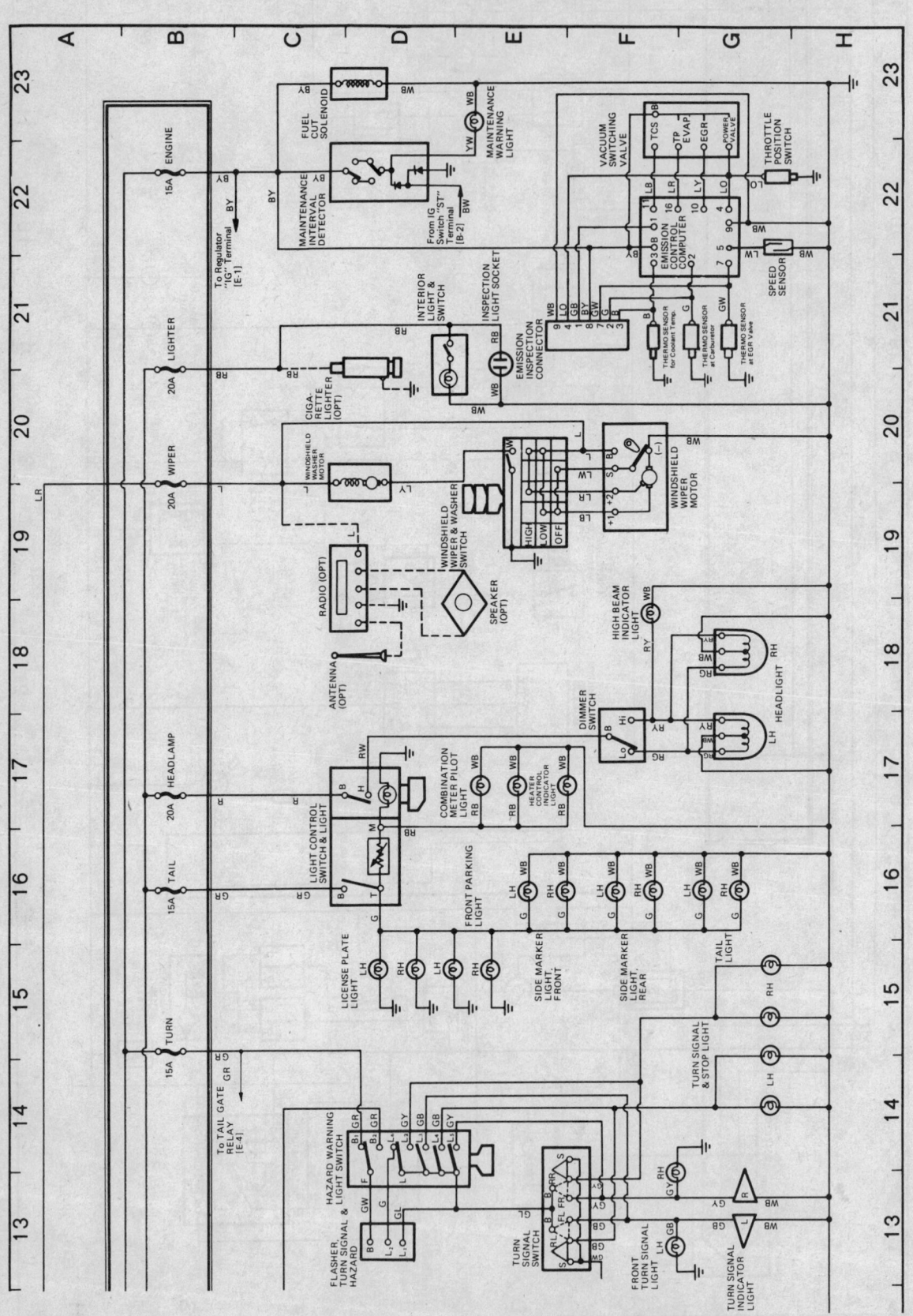

1975-77 Land Cruiser (FJ55 long wheelbase)

SPECIFICATIONS

Triumph

INTRODUCTION

In 1971, the Spitfire Mk IV was introduced. The rear suspension was modified to limit the rear roll center and the engine was strengthened by the addition of larger rod bearings and journals. A new, all-synchromesh four-speed transmission became standard equipment on the Mk IV. The Mk IV is readily identifiable by its redesigned, Stag-like rear end.

For 1973, the Spitfire engine displacement has been increased to 1493 cc; hence the Spitfire 1500. To accommodate the increased torque of the engine, the clutch diameter was increased to 7 ¼ in.

In 1971, the GT6 Mk III was introduced, retaining the same basic 1998 cc six cylinder engine and fastback/hatchback theme of the GT6+. The GT6 Mk III can be identified by its redesigned rear end treatment and large horizontal tail lights.

The TR-6 was introduced, in 1969 superseding the TR-250. The TR-6 is mechanically identical to the TR-250, except for the addition of a front anti-roll bar and wider wheels. The TR-6 is identifiable by its full width horizontal grille and its Kammback tail end treatment.

The TR-6 was discontinued after the 1976 model year. In 1975, the TR-7 was introduced. The car shares few components with former models. New features include the 2 liter overhead cam engine with an aluminum cross-flow cylinder head and an oversquare bore-to-stroke ratio; the McPherson strut front suspension; live rear axle with 4 link coil rear suspension; unitized body/frame construction; electronic ignition; self-adjusting rear drum brakes, sealed cooling system; printed instrument panel electrical circuit; and automatic choke (only on California models); and air conditioning.

MODEL IDENTIFICATION

1972-73 Spitfire Mk. IV

GT6 Mk. III

1972-76 TR-6

TR-7

SERIAL NUMBER IDENTIFICATION

All 1968 and later Triumphs have the chassis number (commission number) stamped on a plate adjacent to the driver's door striker plate and on another small plate visible through the windshield.

Engine Number

The engine number is stamped on the left side of the engine block on all models.

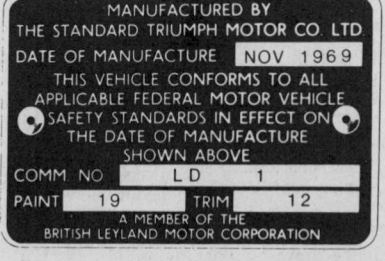

MANUFACTURED BY
THE STANDARD TRIUMPH MOTOR CO. LTD.
DATE OF MANUFACTURE   NOV 1969
THIS VEHICLE CONFORMS TO ALL
APPLICABLE FEDERAL MOTOR VEHICLE
SAFETY STANDARDS IN EFFECT ON
THE DATE OF MANUFACTURE
SHOWN ABOVE
COMM. NO.   L D   1
PAINT   19   TRIM   12
A MEMBER OF THE
BRITISH LEYLAND MOTOR CORPORATION

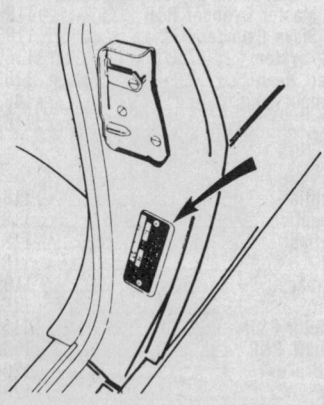

Transmission Number

The transmission number is stamped on the left side of the clutch housing (TR models), or on the top right side of the transmission case (GT6 and Spitfire models).

Rear Axle Number

The rear axle number is stamped on the housing flange on all models.

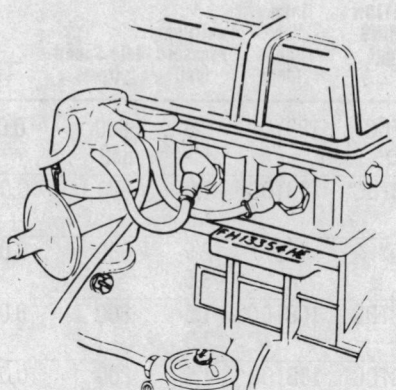

Engine number location—OHV engines

Engine number location—OHC engine

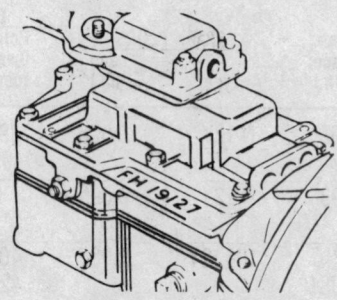

Transmission number location

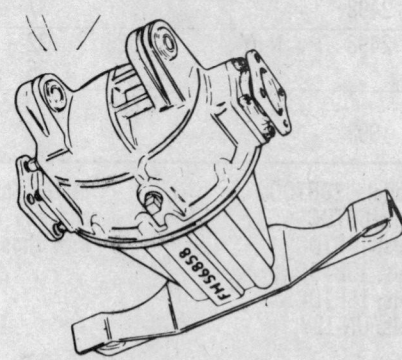

Rear axle number location—Spitfire, GT6 shown; TR series similar.

GENERAL ENGINE SPECIFICATIONS

Year & Model	Engine Displace. Cu in (cc)	Carburetor Type	Horsepower @ rpm	Torque @ rpm (ft lbs)	Bore x Stroke (in.)	Compression Ratio	Oil Pressure @ rpm (psi)
1972 Spitfire Mk IV	79.2 (1296)	Single horizontal Zenith-Stromberg 150 CDSE	48 @ 5500	61 @ 2900	2.90 x 2.992	8.0:1	40-60
1973-77 Spitfire 1500	91.0 (1493)	Single horizontal Zenith-Stromberg 150 CDSE(V)	57 @ 5000	71 @ 3000	2.90 x 3.440	7.5:1	40-60
1972-73 GT6 Mk III	122.0 (1998)	Twin horizontal Zenith-Stromberg 150 CDSE(V)	79 @ 4900	97 @ 2900	2.940 x 2.992	8.0:1	45-55
1972-76 TR-6	152.0 (2498)	Twin horizontal Zenith-Stromberg 175 CDSE(V)	106 @ 4900	133 @ 3000	2.940 x 3.740	7.75:1	70
1975-77 TR-7	122.0 (1998)	Twin horizontal* Zenith-Stromberg 175 CDSE(V)	NA	NA	3.56 x 3.07	8.0:1	60

* California: single Zenith-Stromberg 175 CD4TV

TUNE-UP SPECIFICATIONS

When analyzing compression test results, look for uniformity among cylinders, rather than specific pressures.

Year	Engine Displace. (Cu. In.)	SPARK PLUGS Type	SPARK PLUGS Gap (in.)	DISTRIBUTOR Point Dwell (deg)	DISTRIBUTOR Point Gap (in.)	IGNITION TIMING (deg) MT	IGNITION TIMING (deg) AT	Intake Valve Opens (deg)	Fuel Pump Pressure (psi)	Idle Speed (rpm)	VALVE CLEAR (in.) In	VALVE CLEAR (in.) Ex
Spitfire 1972	1296	UN-12Y	0.025	38-40	0.014-0.016	6ATDC	18BTDC	2-5-3.5	800-850	0.010	0.010

TUNE-UP SPECIFICATIONS

When analyzing compression test results, look for uniformity among cylinders, rather than specific pressures.

Year	Engine Displace. (Cu. In.)	SPARK PLUGS Type	Gap (in.)	DISTRIBUTOR Point Dwell (deg)	Point Gap (in.)	IGNITION TIMING (deg) MT	AT	Intake Valve Opens (deg)	Fuel Pump Pressure (psi)	Idle Speed (rpm)	VALVE CLEAR (in.) In	Ex
1973-75	1493	N-12Y	0.025	38-40	0.014-0.016	8BTDC ①	18BTDC		2.5-3.5	800-850	0.010	0.010
1976-77	1493	N-12Y	0.025	Electronic		10BTDC	18BTDC		1.5-2.5	800	0.010	0.010
GT6 1972-73	1998	UN-12Y	0.025	40-42	0.014-0.016	②	③		2.5-3.5	800	0.010	0.010
TR-6 1972-74	2498	N-9Y④	0.025	34-37	0.014-0.016	10BTDC	10BTDC		1.5-2.5	800	0.010	0.010
1975-76	2498	N-9Y	0.025	32-38	0.014-0.016	10BTDC	18BTDC		1.5-2.5	800	0.010	0.010
TR-7 1975-77	1998	N-11Y	0.025	Electronic		10BTDC	16BTDC		2.5-3.5	800	0.008	0.018

① 1974-75 models: 10BTDC
② 1972 models: 6BTDC
   1973 models: 12BTDC
③ 1972 models: 10BTDC
   1973 models: 18BTDC
④ 1972 models: UN-12Y

NOTE: The underhood specifications sticker often reflects tune-up specification changes made in production. Sticker figures must be used if they disagree with those in this chart.

FIRING ORDERS

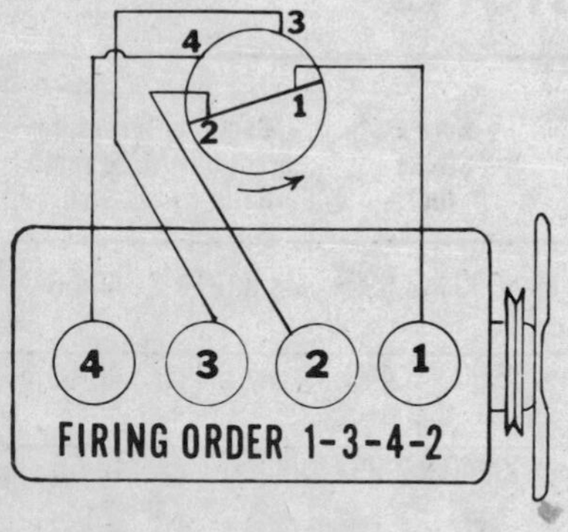

FIRING ORDER 1-3-4-2

Spitfire

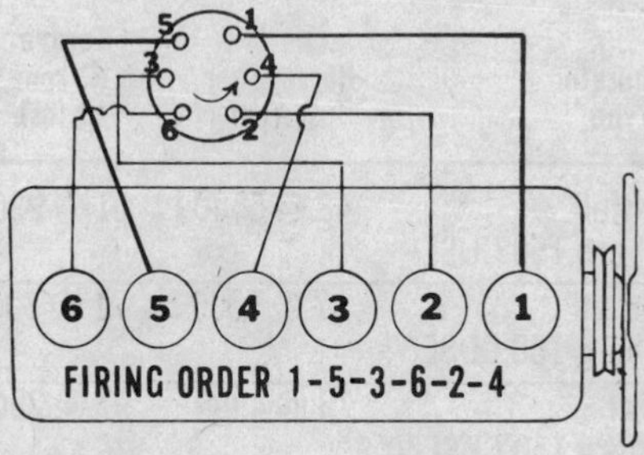

FIRING ORDER 1-5-3-6-2-4

GT6 & TR-6

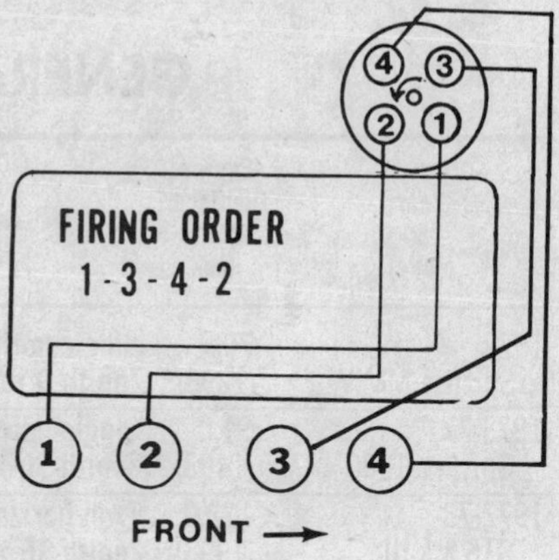

FIRING ORDER 1-3-4-2

FRONT →

TR-7

CAPACITIES

Year	Model	Engine Displacement (cc)	Engine Crankcase (qts) With Filter	Without Filter	Transmission (pts) 4-spd	With Overdrive	Drive Axis (pts)	Gasoline Tank (gals)	Cooling System (qts) W/AC	W/O AC
1972	Spitfire	1296	4.8	4.2	1.8	3.0	1.2	8.7	—	4.8
1973-77	Spitfire	1493	4.8	4.2	1.8	3.0	1.2	8.7	—	4.8
1972-73	GT-6	1998	5.4	4.8	1.8	3.0	1.2	11.7	—	6.6
1972-76	TR-6	2498	5.4	4.8	2.4	4.2	①	②	—	6.6
1975-77	TR-7	1998	4.75	4.25	2.5	—	2.75	14.4	7.75	7.75

① 1975-76 models: 2.7   1972-74 models: 3.0   ② 1974-76 models: 11.7   1972-73 models: 13.5

CRANKSHAFT AND CONNECTING ROD SPECIFICATIONS

All measurements are given in inches

Year	Engine Displace. Cu In (cc)	CRANKSHAFT				CONNECTING ROD		
		Main Brg. Journal Dia.	Main Brg. Oil Clearance	Shaft End-Play	Thrust on No.	Journal Diameter	Oil Clearance	Side Clearance
1972	79.2 (1296)	2.3115-2.3120	0.0010-0.0020	0.004-0.008	3	1.8750-1.8755	0.0005-0.0020	0.0105-0.0126
1973-77	91.0 (1493)	2.3115-2.3120	—	0.004-0.008	3	1.8750-1.8755	—	—
1972-73	122.0 (1998)	2.0005-2.0010	0.0012-0.0020	0.006-0.008	4	1.8750-1.8755	0.0010-0.0027	0.0086-0.0125
1972-76	152.0 (2498)	2.3110-2.3115	0.0015-0.0025	0.006-0.008	4	1.8750-1.8755	0.0010-0.0027	0.0070-0.0140
1975-77	122.0 (1998)	2.1260-2.1265	0.0012-0.0022	0.003-0.011	3	1.7500-1.7505	0.0008-0.0023	0.006-0.013

— Not Available

VALVE SPECIFICATIONS

Year	Engine Displace. (cc)	Seat Angle (deg)	Face Angle (deg)	Spring Test Pressure (lbs @ in.)	Spring (in.) Free Length	STEM TO GUIDE CLEARANCE (in.)		STEM DIAMETER (in.)	
						Intake	Exhaust	Intake	Exhaust
1972	1296	44.5	45	27-30 @ 1.36	1.61	0.0008-0.0023	0.0015-0.0030	0.3107-0.3112	0.3100-0.3105
1973-77	1493	44.5	45	27-30 @ 1.36	1.61③	0.0008-0.0023	0.0015-0.0030	0.3107-0.3112	0.3100-0.3105
1972-73	1998	44.5	45	①	②	0.0008-0.0023	0.0015-0.0030	0.3107-0.3112	0.3100-0.3105
1972	2498	44.5	45	—	1.52	—	—	0.3107-0.3112	0.3101-0.3106
1973-76	2498	44.5	45	—	1.14 inner 1.52 outer	0.0013-0.0017	0.0020-0.0024	0.3107-0.3112	0.3101-0.3106
1975-77	1998	44.5	45	—	1.60	0.0017-0.0023	0.0014-0.0030	0.3107-0.3113	0.3100-0.3106

① Inner—11-14 @ 1.14
Outer—27-30 @ 1.386
② Inner—1.56
Outer—1.61
— Not Available

③ 1975-77: 1.52

PISTON AND RING SPECIFICATIONS

All measurements in inches

Year	Engine Displace. (cc)	PISTON CLEARANCE		RING GAP			RING SIDE CLEARANCE		
		Crown	Skirt	Top Compression	Bottom Compression	Oil Control	Top Compression	Bottom Compression	Oil Control
1972	1296	①	②	0.012-0.022	0.012-0.022	(ends butt)	0.0020-0.0025	0.0020-0.0025	0.0028-0.0038
1973-77	1493	①	②	0.012-0.022	0.012-0.022	(ends butt)	0.0020-0.0025	0.0020-0.0025	0.0028-0.0038
1972-73	1998	0.0035-0.0042	0.0017-0.0024	0.008-0.013	0.008-0.013	0.008-0.0013	0.0019-0.0035	0.0019-0.0035	0.0007-0.0027

Triumph

PISTON AND RING SPECIFICATIONS
All measurements in inches

| Year | Engine Displace. (cc) | PISTON CLEARANCE | | RING GAP | | | RING SIDE CLEARANCE | | |
		Crown	Skirt	Top Compression	Bottom Compression	Oil Control	Top Compression	Bottom Compression	Oil Control
1972-76	2498	0.0038-0.0045	0.0021-0.0028	0.012-0.017	0.008-0.013	③	0.0010-0.0030	0.0010-0.0030	0.0010-0.0030
1975-77	1998	—	0.0005-0.0015	0.015-0.025	0.015-0.025	⑤	0.0019-0.0039	0.0015-0.0025	—

① Grade F-0.020-0.024
Grade G-0.0205-0.0260
1975-77: All 0.002-0.003 at skirt
— Not Available

② Grade F-0.0014-0.0019
Grade G-0.0013-0.0028
③ Plain oil rings-0.015-0.055
Scraper oil ring (ends butt)

TORQUE SPECIFICATIONS
All readings in ft lbs

| Year | Engine Displace. (cc) | Cylinder Head Bolts | Rod Bearing Bolts | Main Bearing Bolts | Crankshaft Pulley Bolt | Flywheel To Crankshaft Bolts | MANIFOLD | | Spark Plug |
							Intake	Exhaust	
1972	1296	42-46	38-42	50-55	90-110	①	20-25	20-25	14-20
1973-77	1493	42-46	38-42	50-55	90-110	35-40	20-25	20-25	14-20
1972-73	1998	65-70	38-42	55-60	90-100	42-46	14-16②	20-22	14-16
1972-76	2498	65-70	38-42	55-60	90-100	55-60	③	③	14-16
1975-77	1998	45-55	40-45	50-65	90-120	40-45	15-20	15-20	14-20

① Black parkerized bolt—42-50 ft lbs
Bright cadmium plated bolt—35-40 ft lbs
② Exhaust/intake attaching bolt—20-22 ft lbs

③ TR-6; outer (2)—12-14 ft lbs, inner—16-18 ft lbs

TORQUE SEQUENCES

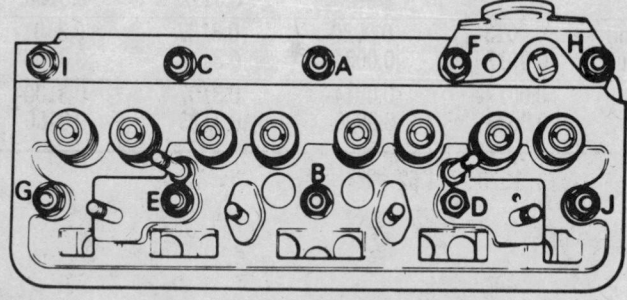

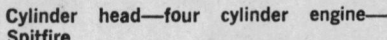

Cylinder head—four cylinder engine—Spitfire

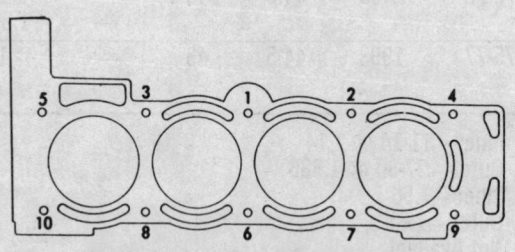

Cylinder head—four cylinder TR-7 engine

Cylinder head—six cylinder engine

BATTERY AND STARTER SPECIFICATIONS

All cars use 12 volt, negative ground electrical systems

Year	Model	BATTERY Amp Hour Capacity	STARTER						Brush Spring Tension (oz)	Min. Brush Length (in.)
			Lock Test			No Load Test				
			Amps	Volts	Torque (ft/lbs)	Amps	Volts	RPM		
1972-77	Spitfire	40	350-375	—	7.0	65	12	8000-10000	28	0.500
1972-73	GT-6	56	350-375	—	7.0	65	12	8000-10000	28	0.500
1972-76	TR-6	57	463	—	14.4	40	12	6000	36	0.710
1975-77	TR-7	50	463	—	14.4	40	12	6000	36	0.710

— Not Available

ALTERNATOR AND REGULATOR SPECIFICATIONS

Year	Model	ALTERNATOR			REGULATOR						
		Part No. or Manufacturer	Field Current @ 12v	Output (amps)	Part No. or Manufacturer	Field Relay			Regulator		
						Air Gap (in.)	Point Gap (in.)	Volts to Close	Air Gap (in.)	Point Gap (in.)	Volts @ 75°
1972	Spitfire/GT-6	Lucas 15 ACR	NA	28	NA	integral regulator					14
1973-77	Spitfire/GT-6	Lucas 16 ACR	NA	34	NA	integral regulator					14
1972-74	TR-6	Lucas 17 ACR	NA	36	NA	integral regulator					14
1975-76	TR-6	Lucas 18 ACR	NA	43	NA	integral regulator					14
1975-77	TR-7	Lucas 20 ACR	NA	66	14TR	integral regulator					14

BRAKE SPECIFICATIONS

All measurements given are (in.) unless noted

Year	Model	Lug Nut Torque (ft/lb)	Brake Disc		Brake Drum			Minimum Lining Thickness	
			Minimum Thickness	Maximum Run-Out	Diameter	Max. Machine O/S	Max. Wear Limit	Front	Rear
1972-76	Spitfire	48	NA	0.007	7.0	7.03	7.05	1/8	1/16
1972-73	GT-6	48	0.46	0.007	8.0	8.03	8.05	1/8	1/16
1972-76	TR-6	70	NA	0.007	9.0	9.03	9.05	1/8	1/16
1975-77	TR-7	72	0.375	0.007	8.0	8.03	8.05	1/8	1/16

NOTE: Minimum lining thickness is as recommended by the manufacturer. Due to variations in state inspection laws, the minimum allowable thickness may be different than recommended by the manufacturer.

WHEEL ALIGNMENT SPECIFICATIONS

Year	Model	CASTER		CAMBER		Toe-in (in.)	Steering Axis Inclination (deg)
		Range (deg)	Preferred Setting (deg)	Range (deg)	Preferred Setting (deg)		
1972-74	Spitfire	—	4.0P	—	3.0P	1/16-1/8	5.75
1975-77	Spitfire	—	4.0P	—	2.0P	1/16	6.75
1972-73	GT-6	—	3.5P	—	2.75P	1/16-1/8	6.00
1972-74	TR-6	—	2.75P	—	0.25P	1/16-1/8	8.75
1975-76	TR-6	—	2.75P	—	0.25P	1/16	9.25
1975-77	TR-7	—	3.5P	—	0.25N	1/16-1/8	11.25

P—Positive   N—Negative   — Not Available

TUNE-UP PROCEDURES

Spark Plugs

Removal and Installation

Every six months or 6,000 miles, the spark plugs should be removed for inspection. At this time they should be cleaned and regapped. At 12 month or 12,000 mile intervals, the plugs should be replaced.

Prior to removal, number each spark plug with a piece of masking tape bearing the cylinder number. Remove each spark plug wire by grasping its rubber boot and twisting slightly to free the wire from the plug. Using a 13/16 in. spark plug socket, turn the plugs counterclockwise to remove them. Do not allow any foreign matter to enter the cylinder through the spark plug holes.

If the plugs are to be reused, check the porcelain insulator for cracks and the electrodes for excessive wear. Replace the entire set if one plug is damaged. Clean the reusable plugs with a stiff wire brush, or in a sandblasting machine. Uneven wear of the center of ground electrode may be corrected by leveling off the unevenly worn section with a file. The gap must be checked with a feeler gauge. With the ground electrode positioned parallel to the center electrode, a 0.025 in. wire gauge must pass through the opening with a slight drag. If the air gap between the two electrodes is not correct, the ground electrode must be bent to bring it to specifications.

After the plugs are gapped correctly, they may be inserted into their holes and hand tightened. Be careful not to cross-thread the plugs. Torque the plugs to their proper specification. Install each numbered plug wire onto its respective plug.

Breaker Points and Condenser

Removal and Installation

Remove the distributor cap and rotor, noting their position. Inspect the contacts and replace the points if the contacts are blackened, pitted or worn excessively, if the breaker arm has lost its tension, or if the fiber rubbing block has become worn or loose. Points that appear light gray in color may be cleaned with a point file.

To replace the points and condenser, disconnect the electrical leads at the primary connection, remove the lock screw for the points and lift them straight up. Loosen the condenser retaining bracket and slide out the condenser. While the points are out, lubricate the breaker cam with a very light coating of silicone based grease. Clean the distributor base plate with alcohol to free it of any oil film that might impede completion of the ground circuit. Also clean the contact point surfaces with the solvent. Install the new points and condenser and tighten their retaining screws. Connect the electrical leads for both at the primary connection. If the point contacts are not aligned, bend the stationary arm.

To gap the contact points, turn the engine until the rubbing block on the point assembly is resting on the high point of the cam lobe. Loosen the point hold-down screw slightly and insert a feeler gauge of the specified thickness (0.014–0.016 in.) between the point contacts. Fine adjustment is made either by inserting a screwdriver into the eccentric adjusting slot on the stationary arm (late distributors) or by turning the eccentric adjusting screw on the stationary arm (early distributors). When the feeler gauge passes between the point contacts with a slight drag, tighten the hold-down screw without disturbing the setting.

If a dwell meter is available, proceed to "Dwell Angle Setting". If the meter is not available, install the rotor and cap, and proceed to "Ignition Timing Adjustment".

Dwell Angle Setting

The dwell angle is the number of degrees of distributor cam rotation through which the breaker points remain fully closed (conducting electricity). Increasing the point gap decreases dwell, while decreasing the point gap increases dwell.

Connect the positive wire of the meter to the distributor primary wire connection on the positive side of the coil, and the negative wire of the meter to a good ground on the engine (e.g. thermostat housing nut).

The dwell angle may be checked either with the engine running or with the cap and rotor removed and the engine cranking at starter speed. The meter gives a constant reading with the engine running. With the engine cranking, the reading will fluctuate between zero degrees dwell and the maximum figure for that angle. While cranking, the maximum figure is the correct one. Never attempt to change dwell angle while the ignition is on, as touching the point contacts or the primary wire connection with a metal screwdriver may result in a 12 volt shock.

To change dwell angle, loosen the point hold-down screw slightly and make the approximate correction. Tighten the hold-down screw and test the dwell with the engine cranking. If the dwell appears to be correct, install the rotor and distributor cap and test the dwell with the engine running. Take the engine through its entire rpm range and observe the dwell meter. The dwell should remain within specifications at all times. Great fluctuation of dwell at different engine speeds indicates worn distributor parts.

Following the dwell angle adjustment, the ignition timing must be checked. A 1° increase in dwell results in the ignition timing being retarded 2° and vice-versa.

Ignition Timing

Ignition Timing Preliminary Adjustment—All except electronic ignition

This procedure is used to obtain a rough initial timing setting when the distributor has been removed and the timing disturbed.

1. Adjust the gap of the breaker points as outlined under "Breaker Points Removal and Installation."

2. If the distributor was removed, install it in the engine, making sure that the drive gears are engaged. Tighten the clamp bracket.

3. Disconnect the distributor low tension lead at the coil. Hook up a 12 V test light directly to the disconnected distributor lead and to the positive terminal of the battery.

4. Rotate the engine (crankshaft) manually in the normal direction of rotation (clockwise) until the timing marks nearly coincide with the static timing figure given in the "Tune-Up Specifications" table. The test light should now be illuminated.

CAUTION: *Do not rotate the engine counterclockwise.*

5. Slowly rotate the crankshaft further in a clockwise direction until the test light just goes out. At this point, the No. 1 piston should be in its compression

TR-6 distributor alignment

GT6 distributor in firing position for No. 1 cylinder.

stroke and the rotor should be pointing at the distributor cap contact for the No. 1 spark plug wire.

6. If the timing is correct, the marks will be aligned at the static timing figure. If the timing proves to be incorrect and the marks do not properly align, loosen the distributor pinch bolt and turn the distributor until the points just open and the test light goes out. Rotate the engine one complete revolution again by hand and make sure that the light goes out at the static timing figure.

7. Disconnect the test light. Reconnect the distributor lead at the coil. Install the distributor cap, if removed.

8. Proceed to final (dynamic) timing adjustment.

Ignition Timing Adjustment

Clean the crankshaft damper and pointer on the water pump housing. Disconnect the vacuum line(s) from the intake manifold at the distributor and plug the line(s). On breakerless systems, the retard unit pipe should be connected.

Attach a tachometer to the engine and set the idle speed to specifications. Set timing to specifications. As a final check, start the engine once more to make sure that the timing marks do align.

Unplug and reconnect all disconnected hoses. Remove the timing light and tachometer from the engine.

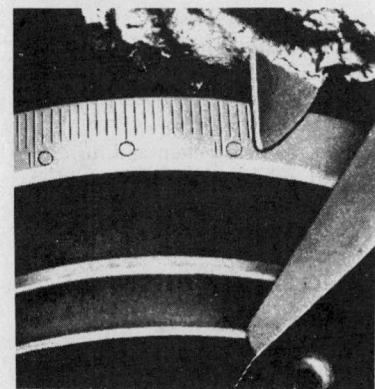

Timing marks—GT6 models, TR-6 similar

Valve Lash Adjustment

All Except TR–7

Valve clearances should be as specified with the engine cold. For the four-cylinder engines, adjust the valves as follows: turn the crankshaft until the valve to be adjusted is fully open, then rotate the crankshaft one more revolution to be sure that the valve will be fully closed. Loosen the locking nut and adjust the screw until the specified feeler gauge will just fit between the valve stem and the rocker arm. Tighten the locking nut and recheck the clearance to see that it has not changed.

Excessive clearance(exhaust valve used for example)

Valve clearance recorded	0.023 in.
Valve clearance required	0.018 in.
Valve clearance excess	0.005 in.
Plus shim thickness recorded	0.090 in.
Shim thickness required	0.095 in.

Insufficient clearance(intake valve used for example)

Valve clearance recorded	0.005 in.
Valve clearance required	0.008 in.
Insufficient clearance	0.003 in.
Shim thickness recorded	0.100 in.
Shim thickness required	0.097 in.

Valve Adjustment Sequence

Adjust These Valves	When These Are Fully Open
1 and 3	10 and 12
8 and 11	2 and 5
4 and 6	7 and 9
10 and 12	1 and 3
2 and 5	8 and 11
7 and 9	4 and 6

Adjusting valve lash—overhead valve engines

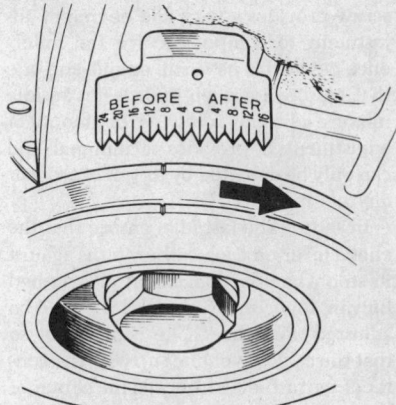

Timing marks—Spitfire Mk. IV, 1500; TR-7 similar

For the six-cylinder engines, the following sequence of valve clearance adjustments is recommended. Turn the engine clockwise and adjust as follows:

TR–7

1. Rotate the engine. Check and record each valve clearance. Clearance should be checked with the cam heel facing the tappet.

2. To adjust, remove the camshaft.

Idle speed and mixture adjusting locations—Zenith-Stromberg 150 CDSE(V) and 175 CDSE(V) carburetors

1. Fast idle screws
2. Cam pivots
3. Idling screws
4. Choke cable trunnion
5. Idle trimming screw

Remove the shim on each valve which requires adjustment. Keep them in sequence.

3. Using a micrometer, measure and record the thickness of each shim. To determine the thickness required, use the following example and install new shims where necessary.

Carburetor

Idle Speed and Mixture Adjustment

1972–74 TR–6 W/Zenith-Stromberg 175 CDSE

Idle speed is adjusted in the normal manner, which requires the use of an airflow meter to maintain the balance between carburetors. The idle trimming screw provides a very fine degree of adjustment to compensate for the difference between a new, stiff engine and one that has been broken in. It is not an idle mixture adjusting screw, as the amount of adjustment it provides is minimal and can only be detected by means of a CO or air/fuel meter.

In setting the fast idle, ensure that the choke lever on each carburetor is against its stop when the choke control is pushed fully in. If necessary, the cables should be adjusted. Pull the choke control out so that the cable pivot lines up with the center of the fast-idle screw and the center of the cam pivot point. Loosen the locknuts and unscrew both idle screws until each is just contacting the cam. Start the engine and, while it is cold, adjust the fast-idle screws an equal amount to provide an engine speed of 1,100 rpm on 1972 models and 1,500 rpm on 1973–74 models. Tighten the locknuts and recheck the fast-idle speed.

Carburetor settings for the TR–6 are as follows:
Idle CO level: 0.5–2.5% (warm engine)
Equivalent air/fuel ratio: 14.4:1–13.6:1

GT6 and Spitfire W/Zenith-Stromberg 150 CDSE

Make the following adjustments:
1. Idle speed—screw adjustment
2. Idle emission—to be used only with a fuel/air ratio meter.
3. Fast idle—simple screw adjustment.
Settings are as follows:
1972–73 GT6 1972–77 Spitfire Mk IV;
Idle CO level: 0.5–2.5% (warm engine)
Equivalent air/fuel ratio: 14.4:1–13.6:1

1975–76 TR–6 and 1975–77 TR–7 with twin carburetors

Zenith-Stromberg 175 CDSEV

1. Check that the fast idle cam is against its stop on each carburetor, and that the fast idle screw is clear of the fast idle cam.

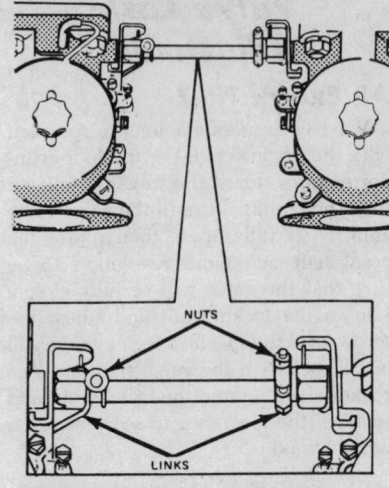

Air flow balance adjustment

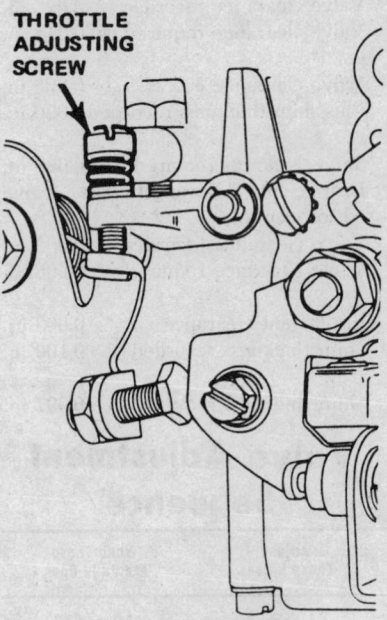

Throttle adjusting screw

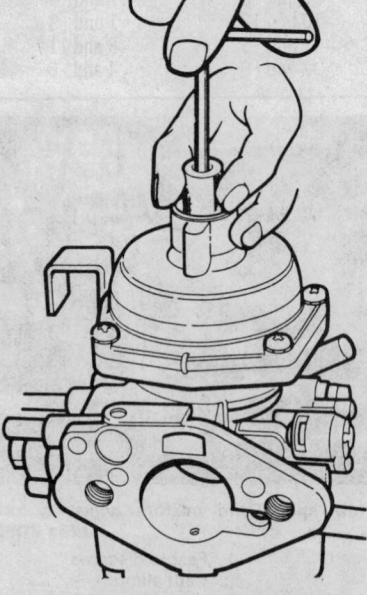

Adjusting the mixture

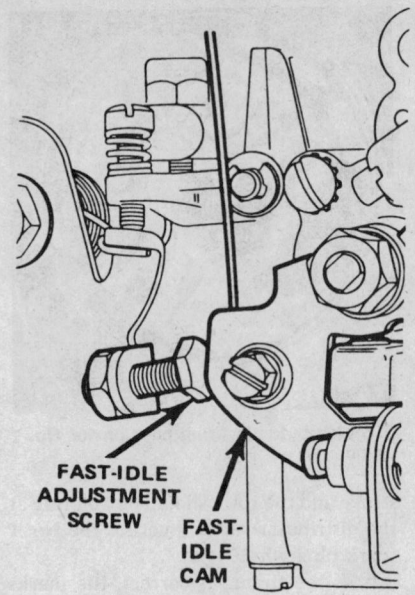

Fast idle speed adjustment

2. Run engine to normal operating temperature.

3. Using an air flow meter check flow on both carburetors.

4. If air flow is not equal, loosen one of the clamping nuts on one of the throttle interconnecting links and loosen the throttle adjusting screws enough to allow the throttles to close, then turn both screws so that they just touch their stops plus ½ turn.

5. Turn both adjusting screws just enough to achieve air flow balance.

6. Tighten the clamping nut on the interconnecting link.

7. If necessary, turn the adjusting screws equally to achieve 800 rpm.

8. Where applicable, disconnect the air pump outlet hose and plug the hose end. Insert the analyzer probe and check the CO reading against the underhood decal.

NOTE: *Do not allow the engine to idle for more than 3 minutes without a 1 minute clear-out period at 2000 rpm.*

9. If the CO level is above limits, adjust the mixture as follows:

10. Remove the piston dampers and insert a mixture adjusting tool into the dashpot. The tool must be fully engaged and held correctly to prevent tearing the diaphragm.

11. Back out to richen and turn in to lean both carburetors equally until CO is within acceptable limits. Add oil to the dampers if necessary.

1975–77 TR–7 (California) W/Zenith-Stromberg 175 CD4TV

NOTE: *When making adjustments, do not let the engine idle for more than 3 minutes without a 1 minute clear-out period at 2000 rpm.*

1. Run engine at normal operating temperature.

2. Set idle to 800 rpm.

3. Disconnect the air pump outlet hose and plug hose end.

4. Insert infrared analyzer probe and check CO readings against the underhood decal.

5. If CO readings are not within specifications, remove damper and insert mixture adjusting tool into dashpot. Tool must be inserted and held properly to avoid tearing the diaphragm.

6. Back off to enrichen and turn in to lean the mixture as required. Add oil, if necessary, to the damper.

ENGINE ELECTRICAL

Distributor

Removal and Installation

1. Detach the spring clips and remove the distributor cap, low tension wire, and vacuum connection. Remove the tachometer drive.

2. Release the clamping plate and withdraw the distributor assembly.

NOTE: *Do not loosen the pinch bolt unless the ignition timing is to be reset, and note the position of the rotor prior to removal of the assembly.*

3. If the pinch bolt has not been loosened, replace the distributor by reversing the installation procedure, and rotate the distributor rotor until it properly engages the driving shaft, then secure the clamping plate.

Alternator

Removal and Installation

1. Disconnect the electrical leads.

2. Loosen the main mounting bolt and the adjustment bracket bolts.

3. Remove the drive belt.

4. Remove the outer adjustment bracket bolt and the main mounting bolt and spacer.

5. Installation is the reverse of removal. Adjust the belt tension.

Alternator Precautions

Several precautions must be observed when performing work on alternator equipment.

1. If the battery is removed for any reason, make sure that it is reconnected with the correct polarity. Reversing the battery connections may result in damage to the one-way rectifiers.

2. Never operate the alternator with the main circuit broken. Make sure that the battery, alternator, and regulator

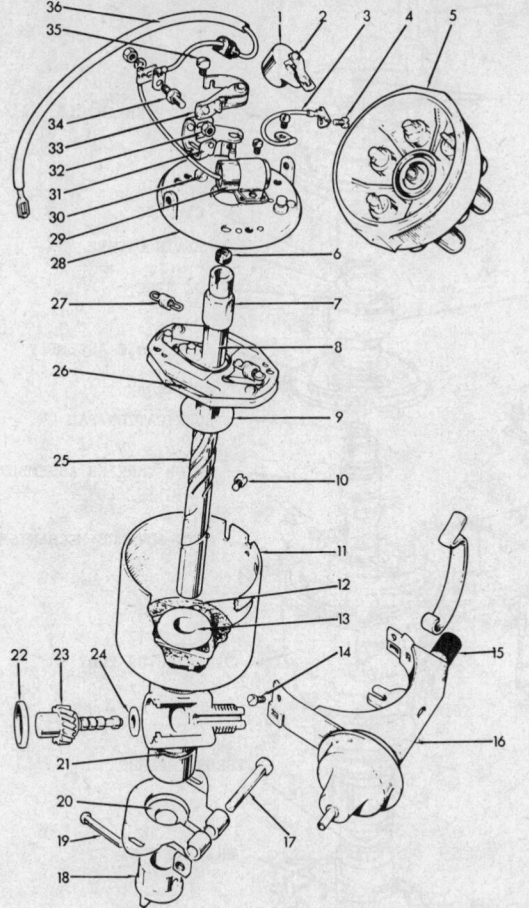

1. Rotor
2. Rotor contact
3. Mounting plate lead
4. Side screw
5. Cap
6. Oil retaining felt
7. Cam
8. Cam spindle
9. Upper thrust washer
10. Short side screw
11. Housing
12. Oil retaining felt
13. Upper sintered iron bearing
14. Side screw
15. Vernier adjustment knob
16. Vacuum advance mechanism
17. Clamp bolt
18. Coupling
19. Coupling pin
20. Lower thrust washer
21. Rubber O-ring
22. Staked plug
23. Tachometer drive gear
24. Thrust washer
25. Shaft and centrifugal advance mechanism unit
26. Weight
27. Control spring
28. Mounting plate
29. Condenser
30. Eccentric screw
31. Fixed contact
32. Terminal stud inner nut
33. Moving contact
34. Terminal stud
35. Lock screw
36. Low tension wire

Delco-Remy distributor disassembled—GT6 series, Spitfire similar

leads are not disconnected while the engine is running.

3. Never attempt to polarize an alternator.

4. When charging a battery that is installed in the vehicle, disconnect the negative battery cable.

5. When utilizing a booster battery as a starting aid, always connect it in parallel; negative to negative, and positive to positive.

6. When arc welding is to be performed on any part of the vehicle, disconnect the negative battery cable, disconnect the alternator leads, and unplug the voltage regulator.

Drive Belt Adjustment

Check the drive belt for cracks and wear. Replace it if its condition is questionable. The belt should be adjusted so that it is possible to depress the belt ap-

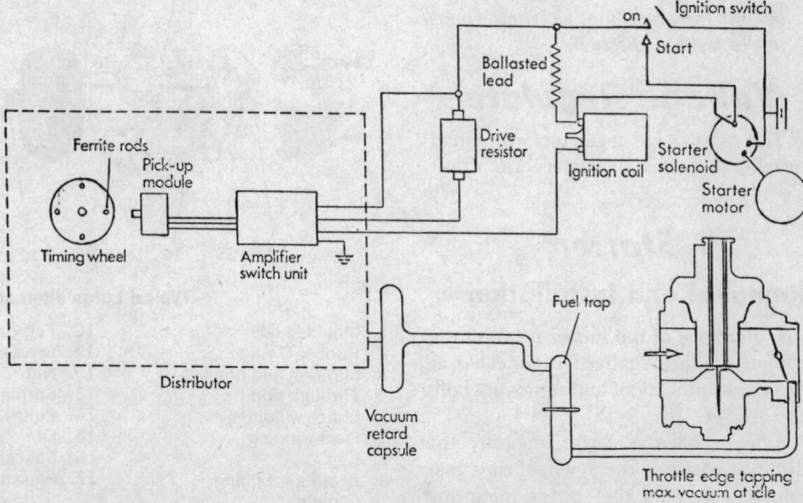

Lucas Electronic Ignition schematic

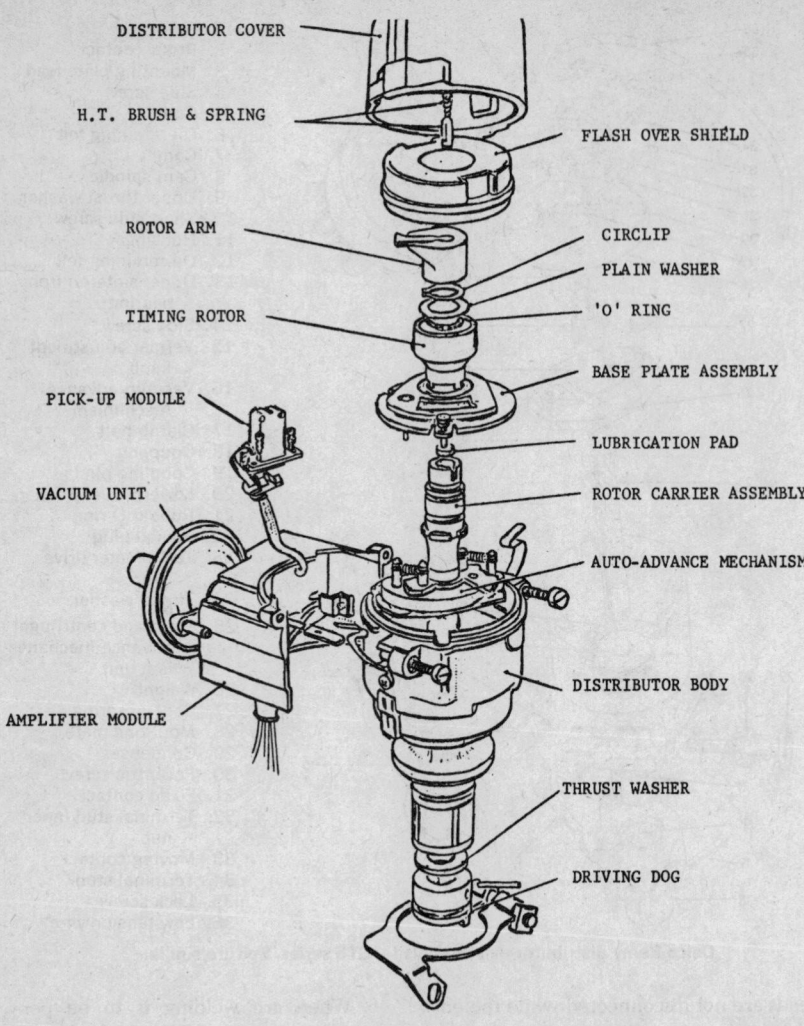

Lucas electronic (breakerless) distributor

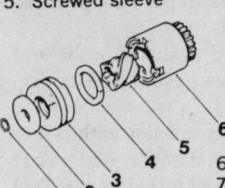

1. Jump ring
2. Shaft collar
3. Main spring
4. Buffer washer
5. Screwed sleeve

6. Pinion and barrel
7. Drive end bracket

Starter drive components—M35J

Starter Drive Replacement

M35J

1. Remove the starter.

2. Remove the two drive end bracket bolts and lockwashers.

3. Pull the drive end bracket, armature, and inertia drive assembly from the yoke.

4. Remove the four retaining bolts and lay aside the commutator end bracket.

5. Lift out the two field winding brushes and remove the commutator end bracket from the yoke.

6. Compress the main spring and ease the snap-ring from the shaft. Remove the starter drive components.

7. Installation is the reverse of removal. Lubricate the drive end bracket bushing with 10W engine oil.

M-100

The starter drive is not replaceable.

M418G

1. Remove the starter.

2. Disconnect the lead from the "STA" terminal.

3. Remove the solenoid, leaving the plunger attached to the engaging lever.

4. Remove the plunger return spring and plunger, from the engaging lever.

5. Loosen the locknut and remove the eccentric pin.

proximately ¾ in. between the pulleys of the longest run. To adjust, loosen the adjusting bolt and alternator mounting bolt, then pivot the alternator until the belt has the correct amount of free movement. Tighten the bolts in this position.

NOTE: *Do not use a metal pry bar against the aluminum alternator housing to tension the belt.*

Voltage Regulator

The AC voltage regulators are nonadjustable and must be replaced as a unit.

Starter

Removal and Installation

1. Removal of the starter requires disconnecting the negative battery cable, all terminal connections and removing bolts and starter.

2. To install the starter, measure the distance between the flywheel ring gear (pinion side) and the starter mounting face.

3. In addition, measure the distance from the starter face to the pinion end. End clearance from the starter pinion to the flywheel ring gear should be 3/32 to 5/32 in. (shims are available).

4. Connect all electrical leads.

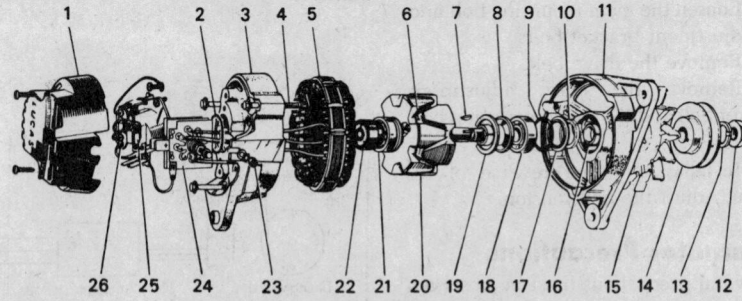

Typical Lucas alternator (15ACR shown)

1. Moulded cover
2. Rubber O-ring
3. Slip ring end bracket
4. Through bolt
5. Stator windings
6. Field winding
7. Key
8. Bearing retaining plate
9. Pressure ring
10. Felt ring
11. Drive end bracket
12. Nut
13. Spring washer
14. Pulley
15. Fan
16. Spacer
17. Pressure ring and felt ring retaining plate
18. Drive end bearing
19. Circlip
20. Rotor
21. Slip ring end bearing
22. Slip ring moulding
23. Nut
24. Rectifier pack
25. Brushbox assembly
26. Regulator unit

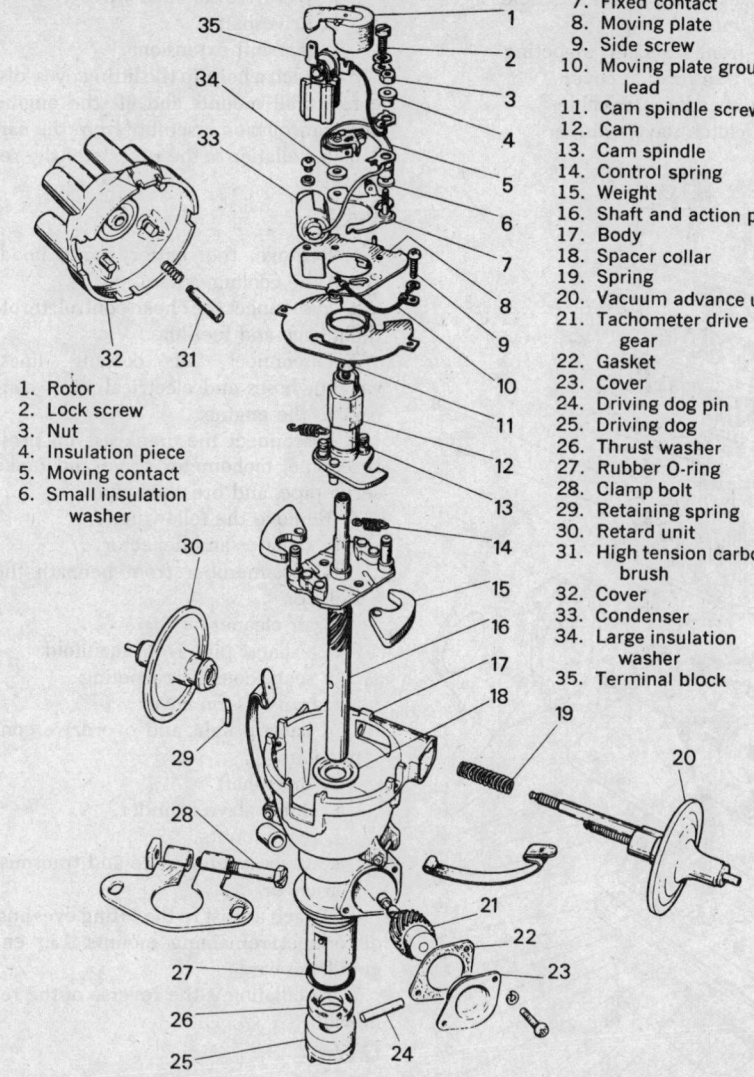

7. Fixed contact
8. Moving plate
9. Side screw
10. Moving plate ground lead
11. Cam spindle screw
12. Cam
13. Cam spindle
14. Control spring
15. Weight
16. Shaft and action plate
17. Body
18. Spacer collar
19. Spring
20. Vacuum advance unit
21. Tachometer drive gear
22. Gasket
23. Cover
24. Driving dog pin
25. Driving dog
26. Thrust washer
27. Rubber O-ring
28. Clamp bolt
29. Retaining spring
30. Retard unit
31. High tension carbon brush
32. Cover
33. Condenser
34. Large insulation washer
35. Terminal block

1. Rotor
2. Lock screw
3. Nut
4. Insulation piece
5. Moving contact
6. Small insulation washer

Lucas conventional diaphragm distributor disassembled—TR-6

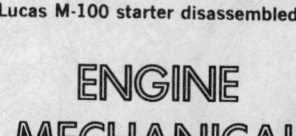

Lucas M-100 starter disassembled

ENGINE MECHANICAL
Engine Removal and Installation
Spitfire

1. Remove all electrical wires, coolant lines and vacuum hoses.
2. Remove the hood.

6. Remove the cover band and the brushes.

7. Remove the through bolts. Lightly rap the mounting bracket lugs.

8. Separate the commutator end bracket from the yoke.

9. Remove both the steel and fabric thrust washers. Note their placement.

10. Remove the rubber molding. Remove the armature and starter drive assembly.

11. Remove the engaging lever and thrust washer.

12. Using a ⅝ in. I.D. tube, over the shaft end, force the thrust collar of the snap ring toward the starter drive.

13. Remove the snap-ring.

14. Remove the thrust collar and the starter drive. Replace the entire drive assembly if the roller clutch is defective.

CAUTION: *Use a gasoline moistened cloth to clean the drive, carefully avoiding the roller clutch.*

15. Assembly is the reverse of disassembly. Lubricate the drive sleeve splines and pinion bearing.

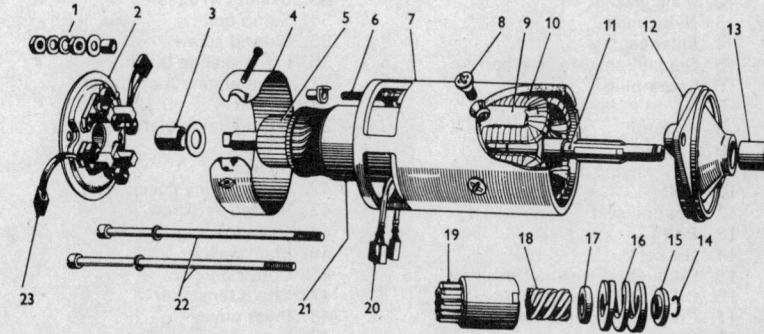

Lucas M35G starter disassembled—M35J similar.

1. Terminal post nuts and washers
2. Commutator end bracket
3. Commutator end bracket bearing bushing
4. Cover band
5. Commutator
6. Terminal post
7. Yoke
8. Pole shoe screw
9. Pole shoe
10. Field winding
11. Shaft
12. Drive end bracket
13. Drive end bracket bearing bushing
14. Ring
15. Shaft collar
16. Main spring
17. Buffer washer
18. Screwed sleeve
19. Pinion and barrel
20. Field winding brush
21. Armature
22. Through bolts
23. Ground brush

3. Disconnect and plug the fuel intake line.

4. Remove the following:
   a. air cleaners
   b. choke controls
   c. carburetor linkage
   d. exhaust pipe at manifold
   e. radiator
   f. front seats and carpeting
   g. transmission cover
   h. speedometer cable
   i. clutch slave cylinder
   j. overdrive solenoid wires
   k. driveshaft
   l. gearshift extension.

5. Attach a hoist to the lifting eyes, disconnect all mounts and lift the engine and transmission assembly from the car.

6. Installation is the reverse of the removal.

TR-6

1. Remove the battery and hood. Drain the cooling system.

2. Disconnect the choke control, throttle linkage and fuel line.

3. Disconnect all coolant lines, vacuum hoses and electrical wires connect to the engine.

4. Disconnect the crankcase oil pressure pipe, tachometer drive and brake servo pipe, and breather pipe.

5. Remove the following:
   a. radiator and deflector
   b. crossmember from beneath the radiator
   c. air cleaner
   d. exhaust pipe from manifold
   e. seats, console, carpeting
   f. transmission cover
   g. backup light and overdrive connections
   h. driveshaft
   i. clutch slave cylinder
   j. rear mounts
   k. speedometer cable and transmission cover.

6. Attach a hoist to the lifting eyes and disconnect remaining mounts. Lift engine from car.

7. Installation is the reverse of the removal.

GT6

Remove the engine/transmission as a unit.

1. Disconnect all coolant lines, vacuum hoses, electrical leads and cables.

2. Remove the hood and radiator.

3. Remove the crossmember at the sides of the engine.

4. Remove the following:
   a. seats, carpeting and transmission tunnel
   b. gearshift knob
   c. transmission cover
   d. driveshaft
   e. clutch slave cylinder
   f. speedometer cable
   g. exhaust pipe bracket
   h. rear mounting bracket
   i. fuel line
   j. exhaust pipe from manifold.

5. Attach a hoist to the engine and disconnect the mounts.

6. Raise the engine just enough to install a brake line protection plate, made according to the specifications shown.

7. Remove the engine and transmission assembly.

8. Installation is the reverse of removal.

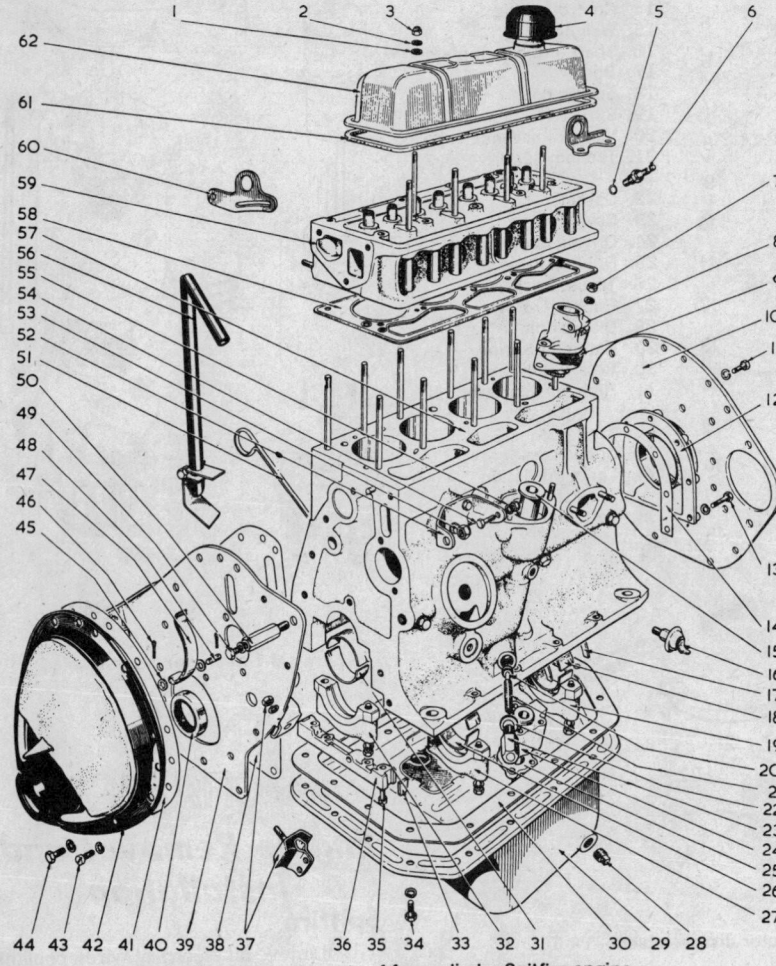

Stationary components of four cylinder Spitfire engine

1. Fiber washer	32. Front main bearing cap
2. Plain washer	33. Sealing wedges
3. Nyloc nut	34. Sump bolt
4. Filler cap	35. Slotted screw
5. Copper/asbestos washer	36. Front sealing block
6. Spark plug	37. Front engine mounting
7. Nut	38. Gasket
8. Adaptor	39. Front engine plate
9. Gasket	40. Oil seal
10. Rear engine plate	41. Gasket
11. Bolt	42. Front timing cover
12. Rear oil seal	43. Slotted setscrew
13. Bolt	44. Bolt
14. Gasket	45. Plain washer
15. Oil pump drive shaft bushing	46. Cotter pin
16. Oil pressure switch	47. Chain tensioner
17. Crankshaft thrust washer	48. Pivot pin
18. Rear bearing shell	49. Bolt
19. Rear bearing cap	50. Generator pedestal
20. Relief valve	51. Dipstick
21. Spring	52. Bracket
22. Copper washer	53. Nyloc nut
23. Cap nut	54. Bolt
24. Oil pump body	55. Nyloc nut
25. Oil pump end plate	56. Breather pipe
26. Center bearing shell	57. Cylinder block
27. Center main bearing cap	58. Cylinder head gasket
28. Drain plug	59. Cylinder head
29. Oil pan	60. Generator adjusting link
30. Oil pan gasket	61. Rocker cover gasket
31. Front bearing shell	62. Rocker cover

TR-7

Remove the engine and transmission as a unit.

1. Remove the hood.

2. Disconnect all coolant lines and electrical wires from engine.

3. Disconnect the following:

    a. brake servo hose at intake manifold

    b. vacuum hoses at intake manifold

    c. fuel line

    d. throttle linkage

    e. gear lever assembly

    f. driveshaft

    g. exhaust pipe

    h. speedometer cable

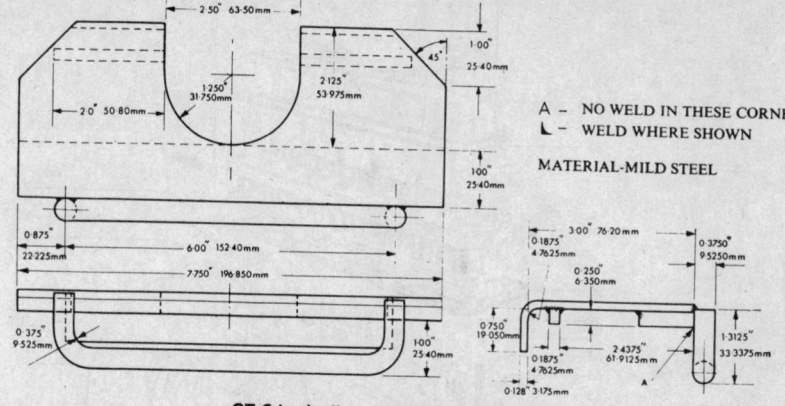

A — NO WELD IN THESE CORNERS
L — WELD WHERE SHOWN

MATERIAL-MILD STEEL

GT 6 brake line protection plate details

    i. clutch slave cylinder

    j. engine stabilizer

    k. battery ground

    l. hood lock

    m. clutch hydraulic pipe.

4. Discharge the A/C system, if equipped.

5. Raise the rear of the car.

6. Attach a hoist to the lifting eyes, support the engine weight and disconnect the front and rear supports. Lift out the engine and transmission assembly.

7. Installation is the reverse of removal.

Cylinder Head

Removal and Installation

All Models (except TR-7)

1. Disconnect the battery and drain the cooling system.

2. Remove the air cleaner(s) and the intake and exhaust manifolds.

3. Remove the drive belt. Remove the water pump.

4. Remove the rocker arm cover, the rocker assembly, and the pushrods. Be sure that all electrical and hose connections to the cylinder head have been disconnected. Remove the spark plugs.

5. Loosen and remove the cylinder head nuts in reverse order of the tightening sequence. Remove the cylinder head.

NOTE: *If the cylinder head does not lift readily, tap each side with a hammer, using a short piece of wood to help absorb the shock. Another method is to reinsert the spark plugs and crank the engine with the starter, using the engine's own compression pressure to supply the force needed to break the seal.*

6. Before replacing the cylinder head, be sure that the gasket surfaces of the head and block are perfectly clean and smooth. If any dirt is present, the gasket may leak when the head is installed. Check for the presence of dirt or carbon particles in the stud passages in the head. Also, inspect the valves and guides for wear and damage. Check valve stems for

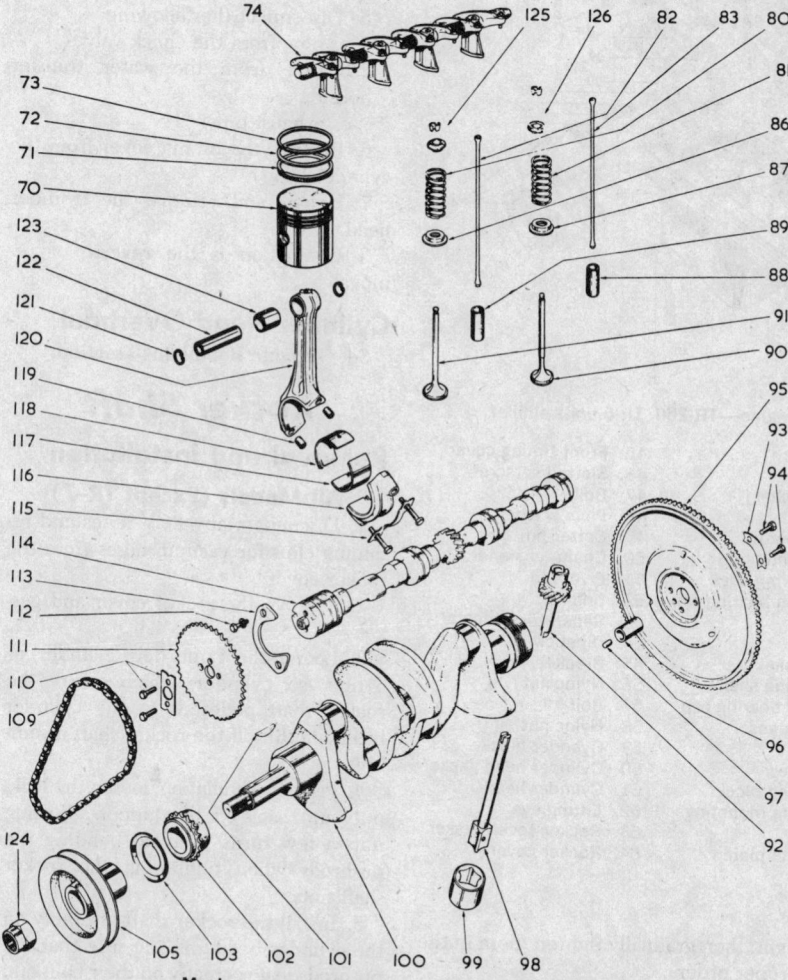

Moving components of four cylinder Spitfire engine

70. Piston	93. Lock tab	114. Camshaft
71. Oil control ring	94. Bolt	115. Bolt and locktab
72. Taper compression ring	95. Flywheel	116. Con-rod cap
73. Plain compression ring	96. Bush	117. Con-rod bearing shell— lower
74. Rocker assembly	97. Dowel	118. Con-rod bearing shell— upper
80. Spring—outer	98. Inner rotor and spindle	119. Dowels
81. Spring—inner	99. Outer rotor	120. Con-rod
82. Pushrod	100. Crankshaft	121. Circlip
83. Pushrod	101. Key	122. Piston pin
86. Spring seats	102. Sprocket	123. Piston pin bushing
87. Spring seats	103. Slinger	124. Nut
88. Tappet	105. Crankshaft pulley	125. Retainer and keeper
89. Tappet	109. Timing chain	126. Retainer and keeper
90. Exhaust valve	110. Bolts and lock tab	
91. Intake valve	111. Camshaft sprocket	
92. Distributor and oil pump drive gear	112. Bolt	
	113. Keeper plate	

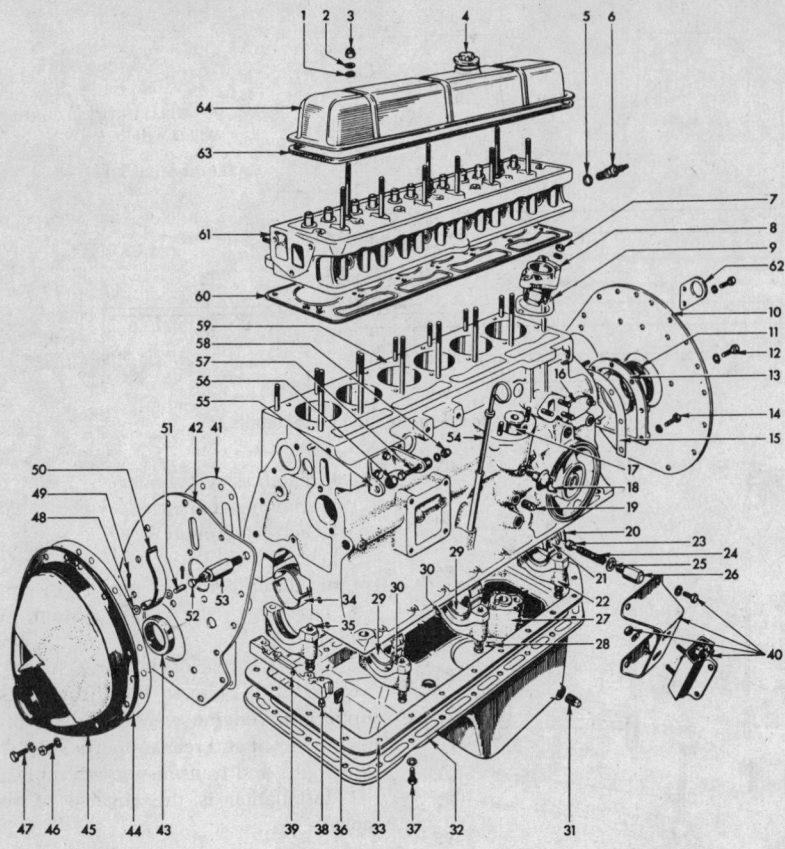

Stationary components of six cylinder GT6 engine—TR-250, TR-6 units similar

1. Fiber washer	23. Relief valve	45. Front timing cover
2. Plain washer	24. Spring	46. Slotted setscrew
3. Nyloc nut	25. Copper washer	47. Bolt
4. Filler cap	26. Cap nut	48. Plain washer
5. Copper/asbestos washer	27. Oil pump body	49. Cotter pin
6. Spark plug	28. Oil pump end plate	50. Chain tensioner
7. Nut	29. Center bearing shell	51. Pivot pin
8. Adaptor	30. Center main bearing cap	52. Bolt
9. Gasket	31. Drain plug	53. Generator pedestal
10. Rear engine plate	32. Oil pan	54. Dipstick
11. Rear oil seal	33. Oil pan gasket	55. Bracket
12. Bolt	34. Front bearing shell	56. Nyloc nut
13. Rear oil seal housing	35. Front main bearing cap	57. Bolt
14. Bolt	36. Sealing wedges	58. Nyloc nut
15. Gasket	37. Oil pan bolt	59. Cylinder block
16. Banking plate	38. Slotted screw	60. Cylinder head gasket
17. Oil pump drive shaft bushing	39. Front sealing block	61. Cylinder head
18. Oil pressure switch	40. Front engine mounting	62. Lifting eye
19. Plug	41. Gasket	63. Rocker cover gasket
20. Crankshaft thrust washer	42. Front engine plate	64. Rocker cover
21. Rear bearing shell	43. Oil seal	
22. Rear bearing cap	44. Gasket	

wear and distortion. Any valve with a head thickness less than 1/32 in. (0.8 mm.) at the seat edge should be replaced. Valve guide wear may be checked by inserting a new valve into the guide, lifting it 1/8 in. from its seat, and moving it sideways. If the movement of the valve head across the seat exceeds 0.020 in. the guide should be replaced. Valve guides must protrude above the top face of the cylinder head as follows:

GT6, Spitfire: 0.749–0.751 in.
TR–6: 0.63 in.

7. To replace the head gasket, note its markings and position it accordingly. Tighten the cylinder head nuts finger tight, then gradually tighten them in the proper order.

8. Replace the valve rocker arm assembly and reverse the cylinder head removal procedure. Check the valve clearances before running the engine, then again after a brief running period when normal temperature is reached. Make a third check after a few hundred miles and at this time check the cylinder head nuts for tightness and tighten them to the specified torque. Although tightening down the cylinder head nuts will affect valve clearances slightly, the differences will not usually be enough to warrant resetting the valves. However, the clearances should be checked.

TR–7

1. Disconnect the following:
   a. air cleaner and duct
   b. intake manifold and carburetors
   c. camshaft cover
   d. distributor cap.

2. Turn the crankshaft until the camshaft sprocket bottom bolt is accessible. Remove the bolt.

3. Anchor the sprocket to the support bracket and turn the camshaft so that the flange is in line with the groove on the front bearing cap, and the distributor arm points toward the manifold rear attachment bolt.

4. Remove the camshaft sprocket top bolt.

5. Disconnect the following:
   a. pipe from the check valve
   b. pipe from the water transfer housing
   c. exhaust pipe.

6. Remove the timing cover from the cylinder head.

7. Unbolt and remove the cylinder head.

8. Installation is the reverse of removal.

Cylinder Head Overhaul

See "Engine Rebuilding" section.

Rocker Shaft

Removal and Installation

All Models (Except TR–7)

1. Disconnect any PCV hoses and retaining clips for vacuum hoses from the rocker cover.

2. Remove the rocker cover and gasket.

3. Loosen the 4 nuts (four cylinder) or 6 nuts (six cylinder) which secure the rocker shaft pedestals to the cylinder head, and lift off the rocker shaft assembly.

4. Prior to installation, loosen the locknuts and back off the tappet adjusting nuts a few turns to avoid bending the pushrods when tightening the rocker shaft nuts.

5. Install the rocker shaft assembly on the cylinder head, making sure that the pushrods seat correctly on their balls and that the adjusting screws are located correctly. Hand tighten the rocker assembly nuts a few turns.

6. Evenly tighten the rocker shaft pedestal nuts in an order (from the front) of 3–2–4–1 to a torque of 26–32 ft lbs for 4-cylinder Spitfire engines, and in an order of 4–3–5–2–6–1 to 24–26 ft lbs for 6-cylinder GT6 series, and TR–6 engines.

Intake Manifold

Removal and Installation

1. Drain the cooling system.

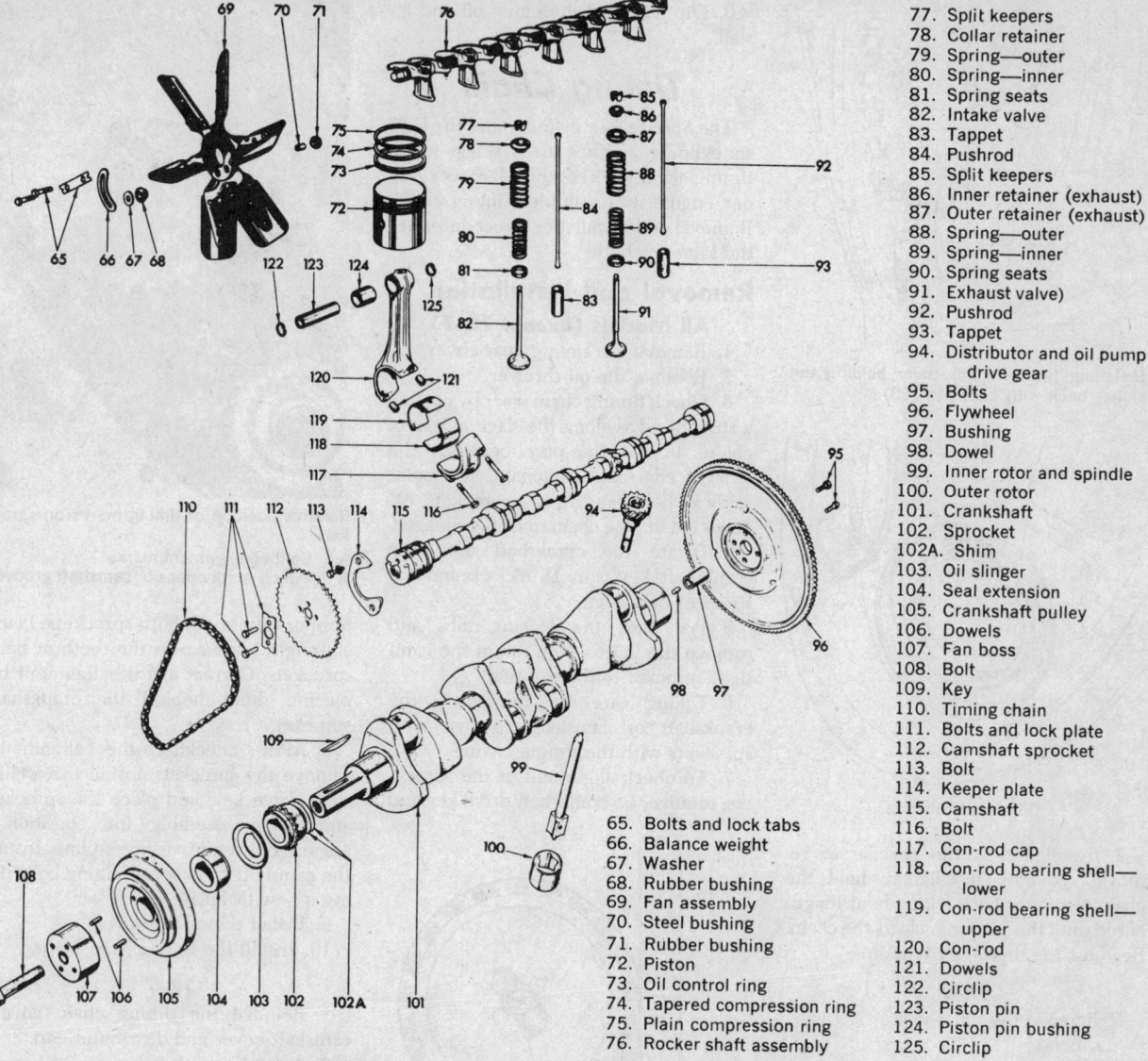

77.	Split keepers
78.	Collar retainer
79.	Spring—outer
80.	Spring—inner
81.	Spring seats
82.	Intake valve
83.	Tappet
84.	Pushrod
85.	Split keepers
86.	Inner retainer (exhaust)
87.	Outer retainer (exhaust)
88.	Spring—outer
89.	Spring—inner
90.	Spring seats
91.	Exhaust valve)
92.	Pushrod
93.	Tappet
94.	Distributor and oil pump drive gear
95.	Bolts
96.	Flywheel
97.	Bushing
98.	Dowel
99.	Inner rotor and spindle
100.	Outer rotor
101.	Crankshaft
102.	Sprocket
102A.	Shim
103.	Oil slinger
104.	Seal extension
105.	Crankshaft pulley
106.	Dowels
107.	Fan boss
108.	Bolt
109.	Key
110.	Timing chain
111.	Bolts and lock plate
112.	Camshaft sprocket
113.	Bolt
114.	Keeper plate
115.	Camshaft
116.	Bolt
117.	Con-rod cap
118.	Con-rod bearing shell—lower
119.	Con-rod bearing shell—upper
120.	Con-rod
121.	Dowels
122.	Circlip
123.	Piston pin
124.	Piston pin bushing
125.	Circlip

65.	Bolts and lock tabs
66.	Balance weight
67.	Washer
68.	Rubber bushing
69.	Fan assembly
70.	Steel bushing
71.	Rubber bushing
72.	Piston
73.	Oil control ring
74.	Tapered compression ring
75.	Plain compression ring
76.	Rocker shaft assembly

Moving components of six cylinder GT6 engine—TR-250, TR-6 units similar

2. Remove the air cleaner. Disconnect the throttle linkage spring and the choke cable(s).

3. Disconnect the vacuum lines, the fuel lines, and the water hoses from the induction assembly.

4. Remove the clamps which retain the manifold to the cylinder head and to the exhaust manifold (if so equipped). Remove the manifold.

NOTE: *If the intake manifold gasket is in need of replacement, the exhaust manifold must be removed first.*

6. Installation is the reverse of removal. Torque the nuts to specifications.

Exhaust Manifold

Removal and Installation

1. Remove the intake manifold (exc. TR-7).

2. Unbolt the exhaust manifold from the exhaust pipe.

3. Remove the manifold and discard the gasket.

4. Installation is the reverse of removal. Torque nuts to specifications.

Timing Gear Cover

Removal and Installation

Spitfire

1. Remove the drive belt.

2. Remove the fan.

3. Remove the crankshaft damper nut (accessible from below), and the damper.

NOTE: *It may be necessary to block the flywheel to stop the crankshaft from turning. Replace the nut loosely and pull off the damper with a gear puller.*

4. Remove the five screws, six bolts, and one nut which retain the timing gear cover to the engine. Lift off the cover with its gasket, taking care not to damage the seal.

5. Installation is the reverse of removal. To ease installation, hold the chain tensioner back with a bent length of rod until the tensioner clears the chain. When installing the pulley, take care to position the drive key between the pulley and the crankshaft spindle. Tighten the damper nut to specifications. Readjust the drive belt tension.

GT6, TR-6

1. Drain the cooling system. Drain the engine oil. Disconnect the overflow pipe and tank, if so equipped.

2. Remove the radiator support(s), radiator valance(s), and radiator.

3. Remove the fan, cross tube and drive belt.

4. On the TR-6, remove the U-bolts from the steering rack and ease the rack forward.

5. Remove the fan adaptor. Using a gear puller, remove the crankshaft pulley.

6. Remove the timing cover, gasket, and spacer.

Triumph

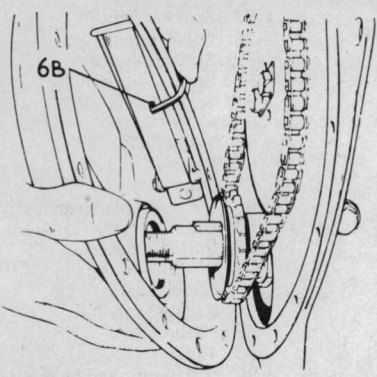

Installing timing chain cover holding tensioner back with bent rod (6B).

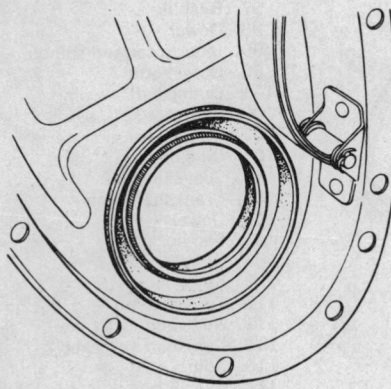

Oil seal installation

7. Installation is the reverse of removal. To ease installation, hold the chain tensioner back with a bent length of rod until the tensioner clears the chain. Readjust the drive belt tension.

TR-7

1. Remove the following:
   a. hood
   b. battery ground
   c. alternator and bracket
   d. air pump, diverter and relief valve and bracket
   e. A/C compressor brackets
   f. front sump bolts
   g. timing cover-to-head bolts
   h. timing cover center and lower left bolts
   i. fan assembly.
2. Remove the timing cover.
3. Installation is the reverse of removal.

Oil Seal Replacement

All Models (Except TR-7)

1. Remove the timing gear cover.
2. Tap out the old seal.
3. Smear the new seal with engine oil and, making sure that the cavity face of the seal faces the engine, install it into the cover using a drift or wooden block.
4. Install the timing gear cover.

TR-7

1. Remove the pulleys.
2. Pry out old seal.

3. Dip new seal in engine oil and install.

Timing Chain

The Spitfire four cylinder and the GT6 six cylinder engines use a single width timing chain whereas the TR-6 six cylinder engine uses a duplex timing chain. Removal and installation procedures are the same for both.

Removal and Installation

All Models (Except TR-7)

1. Remove the timing gear cover.
2. Remove the oil thrower.
3. Check timing chain wear by placing a straight edge along the slack length of chain. If the free-play between the straight edge and the chain, at a point midway between the two sprockets, exceeds 0.4 in., the chain must be replaced.
4. Rotate the crankshaft until the crankshaft key is at 12 o'clock and the sprocket dots align.
5. Pry back the locking tabs and remove the bolts which retain the camshaft sprocket to the camshaft.
6. Taking care not to disturb the crankshaft or camshaft, remove both sprockets with the timing chain.
7. To check alignment of the sprockets, remove the crankshaft drive key and

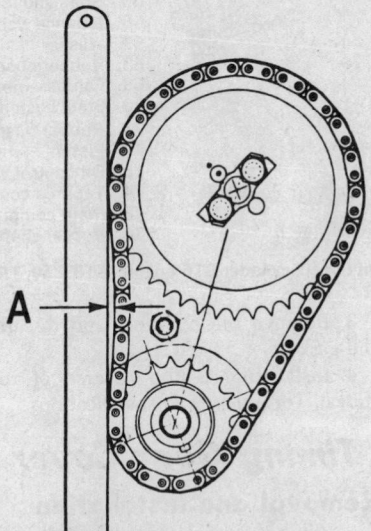

Checking timing chain slack

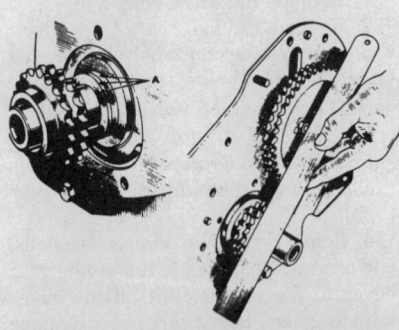

Checking sprocket alignment (right), correcting alignment with shims (A) (left).

Relative position of timing marks on sprockets.
A. Scribed alignment marks
B. Punch mark opposite camshaft groove

temporarily install both sprockets. Place a straight edge across the teeth of both sprockets. Correct any misalignment by placing shims behind the crankshaft sprocket.

8. After checking the alignment, remove the sprockets, install the crankshaft drive key, and place the sprocket and chain assembly into position—aligned dot to dot, or line to line. Install the camshaft sprocket retaining bolts using a new lockplate.
9. Install the oil thrower.
10. Install the timing gear cover.

TR-7

1. Remove the timing chain cover, camshaft cover and distributor cap.
2. Turn the crankshaft so that the camshaft timing mark is at the bottom.
3. Remove the exposed camshaft retaining bolt and turn the crankshaft until the mark is in line with the groove in the front bearing cap.

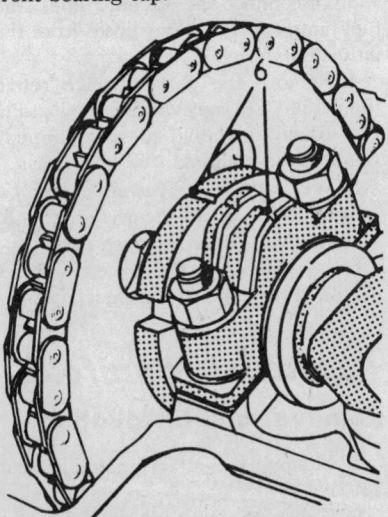

Camshaft timing marks (6)

4. Secure the camshaft sprocket to the support bracket, and remove the last sprocket bolt.

5. Remove the hydraulic tensioner and guide plate as well as the locking bolt from the adjustable chain guide.

6. Remove the common bolt between the adjustable guide and the support and remove the guide.

7. Remove the fixed guide, chain and sprocket.

8. Install the chain over the sprockets and on the engine.

9. Loosely install the fixed guide and support bracket.

10. Loosely install the adjustable guide.

11. Install a guide bolt in the timing cover center bolt hole.

12. Install the camshaft sprocket with one bolt and turn the idler shaft sprocket so that the scribed line is halfway between the guide bolt and the lower adjustable guide bolt.

13. Install and tighten the hydraulic chain tensioner.

14. Remove the nut securing the camshaft sprocket to the support bracket and install the remaining sprocket bolt.

15. Install the distributor cap, camshaft cover and timing cover.

Timing Chain Tensioner Adjustment

The tensioner is non-adjustable. The TR-7 uses a hydraulic tensioner, the others use a spring type. If the chain is not tensioned properly and is not stretched, the tensioner must be replaced. To remove the spring type tensioner, remove the timing chain cover. Spread the tensioner blades apart and slide the tensioner off the anchor pin. The hydraulic type is a simple bolt-on unit.

Installation is the reverse of removal. Make sure that the convex surface of the tensioner faces the timing chain.

Camshaft
Removal and Installation
All Models (Except TR-7)

1. Drain the cooling system. Remove the radiator valence(s) and the radiator. On TR-6 models, remove the radiator grille. On GT6 models, remove the hood.

2. Remove the timing cover.

3. Remove the timing chain and camshaft sprocket. Remove the fuel pump, the distributor driveshaft, and gear.

4. Remove the cylinder head. Remove the pushrods and lifters, keeping them in order.

5. Remove the camshaft keeper plate and slide the camshaft out.

6. Installation is the reverse of removal. Keep the camshaft end play to 0.004–0.008 in. Adjust the valve timing.

TR-7

1. Remove the cover and turn the camshaft so that the timing mark is 180° from the groove in the front bearing cap.

2. Anchor the sprocket to the support bracket and remove the exposed bolt.

3. Align the timing mark and the groove and remove the remaining bolt.

4. Number the bearing caps and remove them. Loosen the nuts evenly.

5. Remove the camshaft.

6. Install in reverse of the above.

NOTE: *when installing shaft, make sure that the mark and groove are in alignment. Torque bearing cap nuts to 3–5 ftlb.*

Piston and Connecting Rod Identification

Spitfire, GT6, TR-6

Pistons and connecting rods are installed with the open end of the bearing facing the non-thrust side of the engine and the arrow on the piston crown facing forward.

TR-7

Two types of pistons are used with this model. One is installed with the flat raised part of the piston on the right side of the engine; the other with the arrow on the piston crown facing forward.

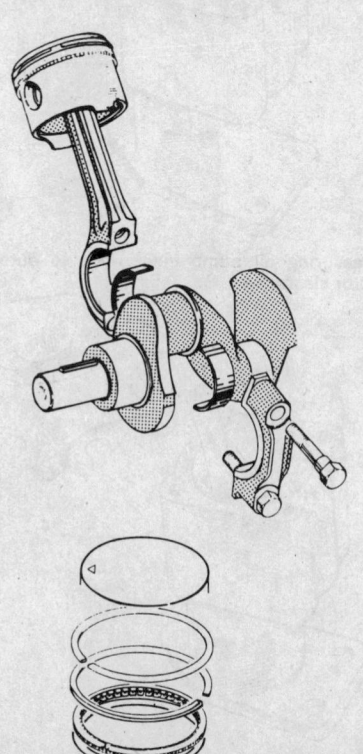

TR-6, Spitfire, GT6 piston and connecting rod

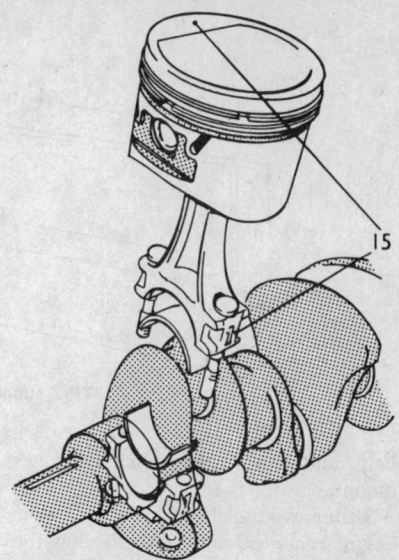

TR-7 piston assembly. The flat raised part is installed on the right; the numbered side of the rod (15) goes on the left.

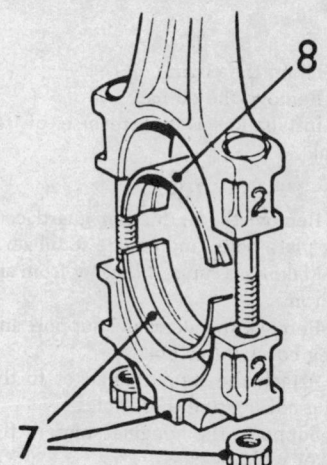

TR-7 connecting rod (7) and bearing caps (8).

ENGINE LUBRICATION

Oil Pan

Removal and Installation

Spitfire

1. Drain the engine oil.

2. Unbolt the oil pan and rest it on the crossmember.

3. Raise the engine. If necessary, rotate the crankshaft. Remove the pan.

4. Installation is the reverse of removal. The long bolts go at the rear of the pan.

GT6

1. Drain the engine oil. Drain the cooling system. Disconnect the radiator hoses.

2. Lift the engine a few inches with a hoist. Loosen the right side engine mount

Triumph

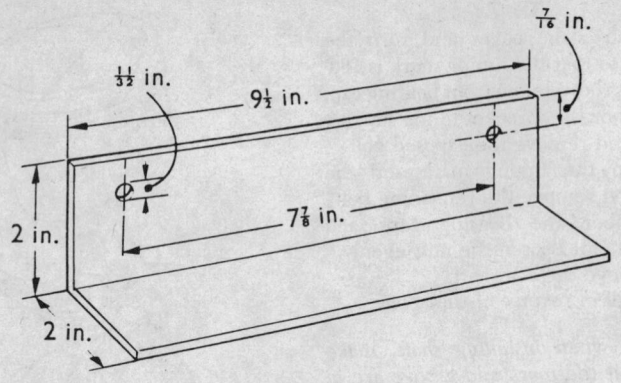

TR-7 support bracket

bolts, and remove the bolts for the left mount.

3. Remove the oil pan bolts. Lever the engine rearward sufficiently to allow the pan to clear the crossmember. Remove the pan.

4. Installation is the reverse of removal.

TR–6

1. Drain the engine oil.
2. Remove the oil pan.
3. Installation is the reverse of removal.

TR–7

1. Remove the air duct, fan guard, coupling plate bolts, and engine stabilizer.
2. Make up a support bracket from angle iron.
3. Remove the alternator support and timing cover lower bolt.
4. Attach the support bracket to the timing cover using these holes.
5. Support the engine under the bracket with a jack.
6. Remove the right engine mount and the left mount-to-frame bolts.
7. Remove the pan bolts and raise the engine far enough to remove the pan, along with the left mount.
8. Installation is the reverse of removal.

Rear Main Oil Seal Replacement

All Models (Except TR–7)

1. Remove the transmission.

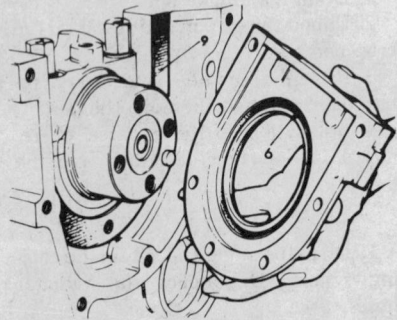

Rear main oil seal correctly positioned in housing.

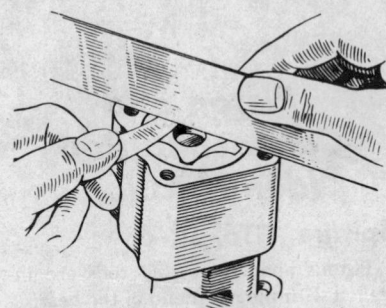

Measuring oil pump rotor end clearance

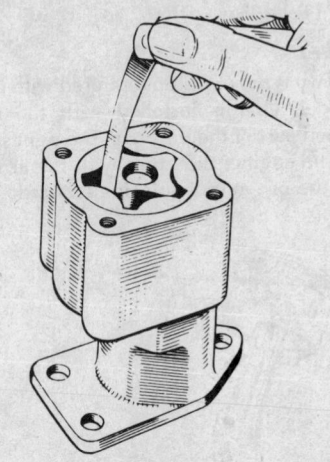

Measuring oil pump inner rotor to outer rotor clearance.

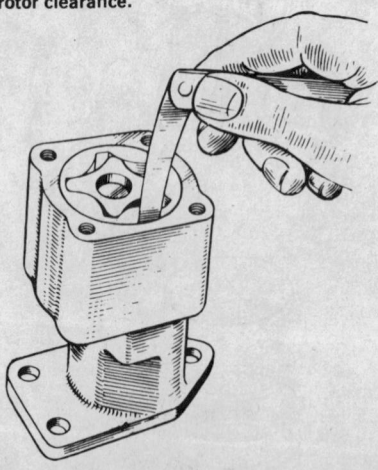

Measuring oil pump outer rotor to pump housing clearance.

2. Remove the flywheel. Remove the engine rear transmission adapter plate.

3. On the GT6, lift the engine sufficiently to provide access to the rear main seal bolts.

4. Remove the oil seal housing with gasket. Press out the old seal.

5. Smear the outside diameter of the new oil seal with grease and press it into the housing, lip toward the crankshaft.

6. Coat the crankcase face with sealing compound and smear the crankshaft with oil.

7. Using a new gasket, install the seal housing and hand-tighten the retaining bolts.

8. Position the housing to the crankcase face using a centering sleeve. After the housing is centered, tighten the bolts.

9. Further installation is the reverse of removal.

TR–7

1. Remove the transmission, clutch and flywheel.
2. Remove the two rear pan bolts and loosen the left rear pan bolt.
3. Remove the oil seal housing and pry out the seal.
4. Installation is the reverse of removal.

Oil Pump

Removal and Installation

All Models (Except TR–7)

1. Remove the dipstick, drain the oil pan, remove the oil pan and remove the oil pump from the crankcase.

2. With the oil pump assembled except for the top cover, measure the clearances between the inner and outer rotors, the outer rotor and the pump housing, and the inner rotor and the face of the pump housing. Clearances should fall within the specifications.

Oil Pump Clearances

Model	Inner Rotor to Outer Rotor (in. max.)	Outer Rotor to Pump Housing (in. max.)	Inner Rotor to Housing Face (in. max.)
Spitfire	0.010	0.0075	0.0035②
GT6	0.004①	0.0075	0.0040
TR-6	0.004①	0.0075	0.0040
TR-7	0.004①	0.008	0.004

① Min.—0.001 in.   ② Min.—0.0015 in.

3. Replace worn components and install the inner rotor in the pump housing, followed by the outer rotor, with its chamfered face leading.

4. Installation is the reverse of removal.

TR–7

1. Remove the clutch slave cylinder, bell housing nut and bolt, oil pump retaining bolts and pump.

2. Install in reverse of the above using a new O-ring.

ENGINE COOLING

Radiator

Removal and Installation

1. Drain the cooling system by opening the engine block drain cock and the radiator drain cock or by disconnecting the lower radiator hose.

2. On GT6 models, remove the air duct. On TR–6 models, remove the radiator valance and position the stay rods to one side.

3. Disconnect the remaining radiator hoses. Disconnect the overflow hose to the expansion tank.

4. Remove the radiator retaining bolts and lift out the radiator.

5. Reverse the above procedure to install, making sure that the cooling system is filled to the proper level with a 50% water, 50% ethylene glycol solution.

Water Pump

Removal and Installation

All Models (Except TR–7)

1. Drain the cooling system, and remove the fan belt.

2. Disconnect the radiator and water hoses at the thermostat housing and water pump, and disconnect the fuel supply line at the carburetors and fuel pump.

3. Remove the temperature transmitter connection.

4. Remove the water pump.

5. Installation is the reverse of removal.

TR–7

1. Remove the intake manifold with carburetors.

2. Remove the connecting tube from the water pump cover and the bottom hose from the pump.

3. Remove the pump from the block.

4. Installation is the reverse of removal.

Thermostat

All thermostats are pre-set by the manufacturer; no adjustment is necessary. Servicing is by replacement only. If a thermostat malfunction is suspected, it may be tested by placing the thermostat in water of specific temperature and watching to see if unit functions at the temperature marked on the thermostat flange.

Removal and Installation

Empty the cooling system and remove the outlet hose. Lift out the thermostat. To replace, reverse the above procedure. Be sure to replace the old gasket with a new one.

EMISSION CONTROLS

Positive Crankcase Ventilation System

Two different systems have been used on TR–6, TR–7, GT6 Mark III, Spitfire Mark IV, and Spitfire 1500 models. Both systems are closed ones, so named because they are sealed from the atmosphere.

1972–77 TR–6, 1975–77 TR–7, 1972–73 GT6 and Mark III, and all Spitfire Mark IV and 1500 models use a PCV system that draws the crankcase vapors through a combination oil strainer/flame trap in the valve cover through a metering orifice on each carburetor (Zenith-Stromberg CDSE, CD4VT or CDSE (V)) and then into the air/fuel mixture.

Component Service

The PCV system is serviced every 12 months or 12,000 miles.

Clean the crankcase breather hoses by

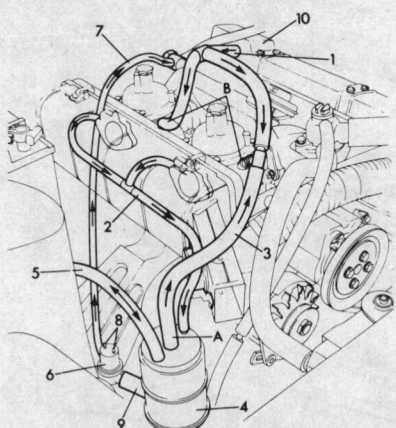

Crankcase and evaporative control purge system—1975 TR-7 (49 states)
1. Crankcase purge line
2. Carburetor float chamber vent pipe
3. Canister purge line
4. Charcoal canister
5. Fuel tank vent pipe
6. Anti dieseling valve
7. Manifold vacuum line
8. Electrical connections for anti dieseling valve
9. Purge air to canister
10. Flame arrestor
A. 3/32 in. restrictor
B. 5/16 in. restrictor

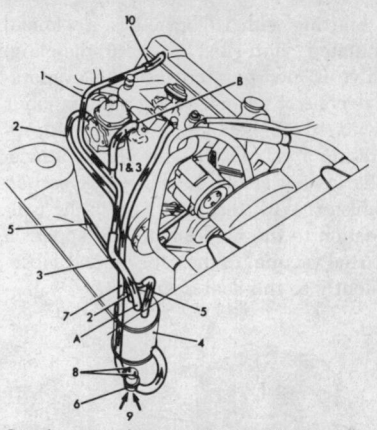

Crankcase and evaporative control purge system—1975 TR-7 (Calif.)
1. Crankcase purge line
2. Carburetor float chamber vent pipe
3. Canister purge line
4. Charcoal canister
5. Fuel tank vent pipe
6. Anti dieseling valve
7. Manifold vacuum line
8. Electrical connections for Anti dieseling valve
9. Purge air to canister
10. Flame arrestor
A. 3/32 in. restrictor
B. 5/16 in. restrictor

running a solvent soaked rag on a coat hanger through them. Remove the oil filler cap and clean it with gasoline. If the cap is gummed up, chances are that the wire screen (flame guard) at the breather hose outlet on the inside of the valve cover is also dirty. Remove the valve cover and clean the screen with solvent. Replace the valve cover gasket, if necessary.

Fuel Evaporative Control System

All 1970 and later model Triumphs have been equipped with an evaporative control system to prevent unburned fuel vapors in the fuel tank and carburetor float chambers from escaping into the atmosphere. The gas filler cap is sealed from the atmosphere on all 1970 and later models.

All 1972 and later models use a gas filler neck that extends down into the tank, thus preventing complete filling of the tank. This eliminates the need for an expansion tank that would take up much needed trunk space. A small vapor separator, located above the tank, is used instead. The vapor separator contains a restrictor valve which prevents fuel surges from reaching the carbon canister. Those vapors which do not condense and return to the fuel tank are displaced and drawn into an activated charcoal canister located in the engine compartment. The excess fuel vapors in the carburetor float chambers are also vented to the charcoal canister.

Triumph

Starting with 1973 models, a solenoid actuated anti-run on (anti-dieseling) valve is incorporated into the evaporative control system. When the ignition is switched off, the solenoid is activated, operating a valve that seals off the atmospheric vent at the bottom of the carbon canister. With the vent sealed, the connection to the intake manifold applies a partial vacuum to the canister and subsequently to the float chambers.

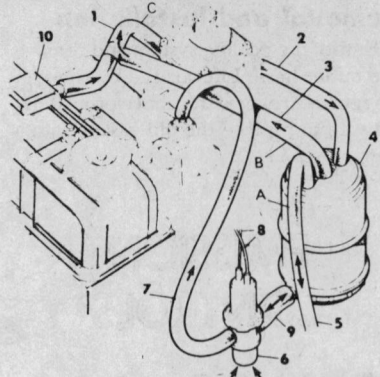
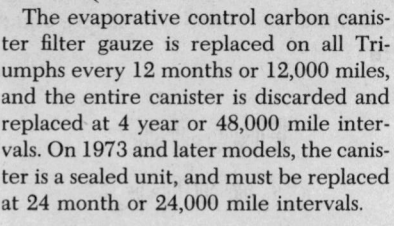
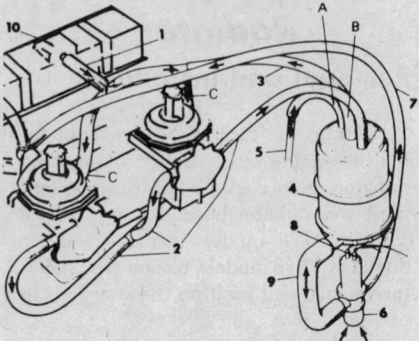

The evaporative control carbon canister filter gauze is replaced on all Triumphs every 12 months or 12,000 miles, and the entire canister is discarded and replaced at 4 year or 48,000 mile intervals. On 1973 and later models, the canister is a sealed unit, and must be replaced at 24 month or 24,000 mile intervals.

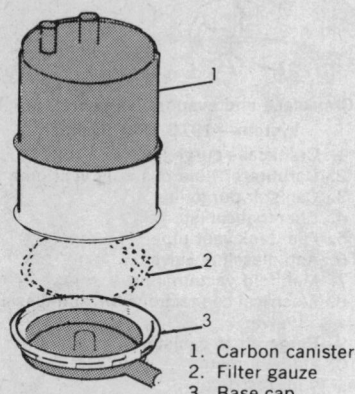

1. Carbon canister
2. Filter gauze
3. Base cap

Evaporation control system carbon canister.

1973 Spitfire crankcase and evaporative control emission system details showing anti-run on valve

1. Crankcase breather pipe
2. Vent valve connecting pipe(s)
3. Canister purge pipe
4. Evaporative control canister
5. Canister to fuel tank pipe
6. Run-on control valve
7. Vacuum control pipe
8. Solenoid connections
9. Canister to run-on control valve pipe
10. Flame arrestor
A. 1/32 in. restrictor
B. 3/32 in. restrictor
C. 3/16 in. restrictor

1973 TR-6 crankcase and evaporative control emission system details showing anti-run on valve

1. Crankcase breather pipe
2. Vent valve connecting pipes
3. Canister purge pipe
4. Evaporative control canister
5. Canister to fuel tank pipe
6. Run-on control valve
7. Vacuum control pipe
8. Solenoid connections
9. Canister to run-on control valve pipe
10. Flame arrestor
A. 1/32 in. restrictor
B. 3/32 in. restrictor
C. 5/16 in. restrictors

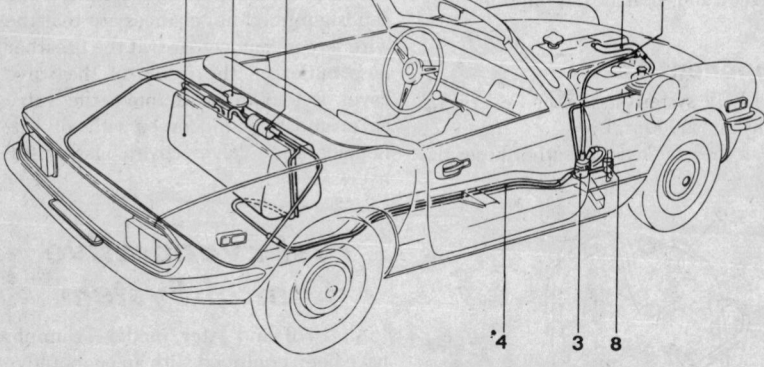
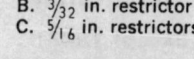

1973-74 Spitfire evaporative control system

1. Crankcase purge line
2. Canister purge line
3. Canister
4. Vapor feed line
5. Fuel tank (limited fill)
6. Sealed fuel filler cap
7. Vapor separator
8. Anti run-on valve

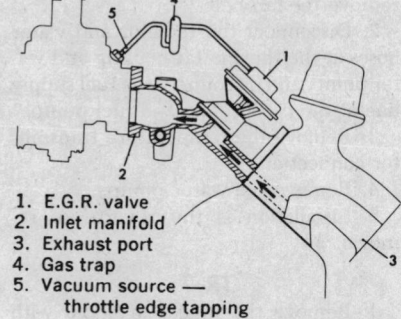

1. E.G.R. valve
2. Inlet manifold
3. Exhaust port
4. Gas trap
5. Vacuum source — throttle edge tapping

Exhaust gas recirculation system—1975 TR-7 (California)

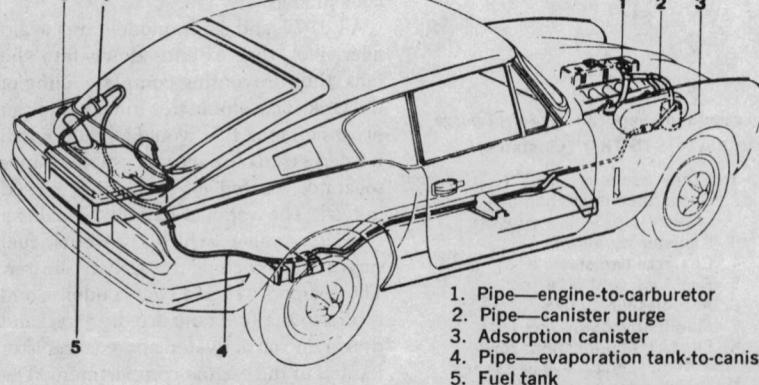

1. Pipe—engine-to-carburetor
2. Pipe—canister purge
3. Adsorption canister
4. Pipe—evaporation tank-to-canister
5. Fuel tank
6. Sealed filler cap
7. Separator tank

1972 GT6 Evaporative control system

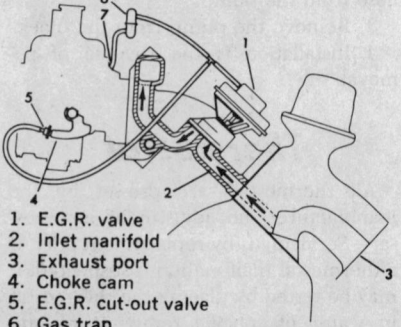

1. E.G.R. valve
2. Inlet manifold
3. Exhaust port
4. Choke cam
5. E.G.R. cut-out valve
6. Gas trap
7. Vacuum source — throttle edge tapping

Exhaust gas recirculation system—1975 TR-7 (49 states)

Exhaust Gas Recirculation System

Beginning in 1974, U.S.A. TR–6 and Spitfire 1500 models are equipped with an (EGR) system. All TR–7 models are equipped with EGR.

The EGR valve is mounted on the exhaust manifold on TR–7 models and Spitfires and located on the cylinder head on TR–6 models. The valve is controlled by a vacuum signal taken from a throttle edge tapping in the carburetor.

At 12 month or 12,000 mile intervals (1974 models), or 12,500 mile intervals (1975–77 models), the components of the EGR system must be removed for cleaning. Most common EGR valve failures stem from exhaust deposits or a cracked diaphragm. The base of the valve may be cleaned with a wire brush. Clean the valve seat and metering valve with a sand blaster or spark plug cleaning machine. On 1975–77 models, reset the EGR service reminder light (odometer actuated) using the special British Leyland Key at 12,500 mile intervals.

Exhaust Emission Control

Air Injection System

All TR–7 and Spitfire 1500 models are equipped with an air pump system. A belt driven air pump delivers filtered air under pressure to the exhaust ports. Here, the additional oxygen, supplied by the air pump, reacts with any uncombusted fuel mixture promoting an afterburning effect. To prevent a reverse flow in the air injection manifold when exhaust gas pressure exceeds air supply pressure, a non-return check valve is used. A combination diverter/relief valve is installed to divert air to the atmosphere upon deceleration to prevent backfiring in the system. The diverter/relief valve also vents pump air at high speeds to prevent pump damage.

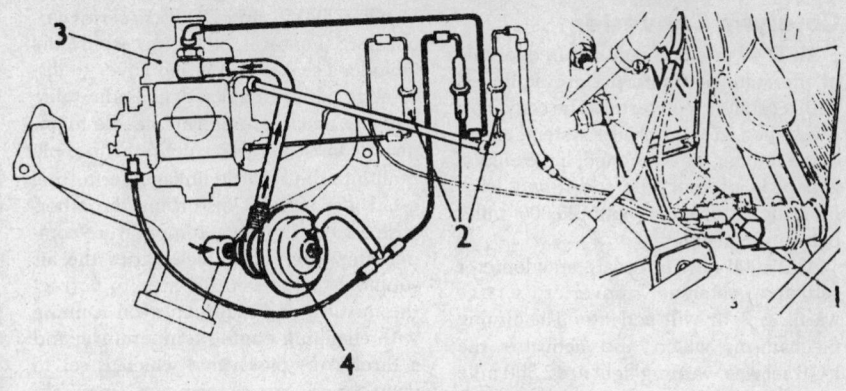

1974 Spitfire EGR system

1. Thermostatic vacuum switch
2. Vapor trap
3. Carburetor
4. E.G.R. Valve

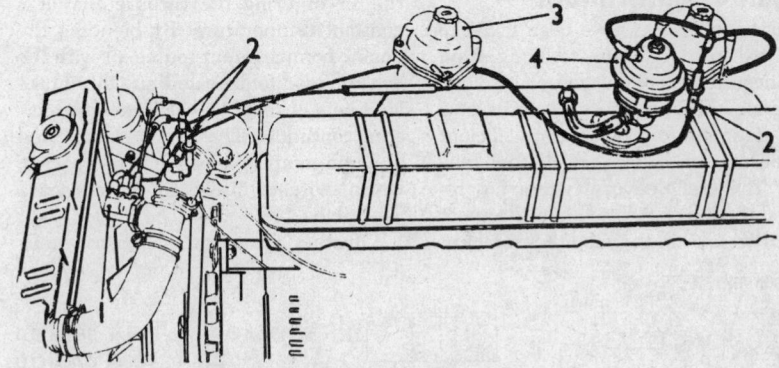

1974 TR-6 EGR system

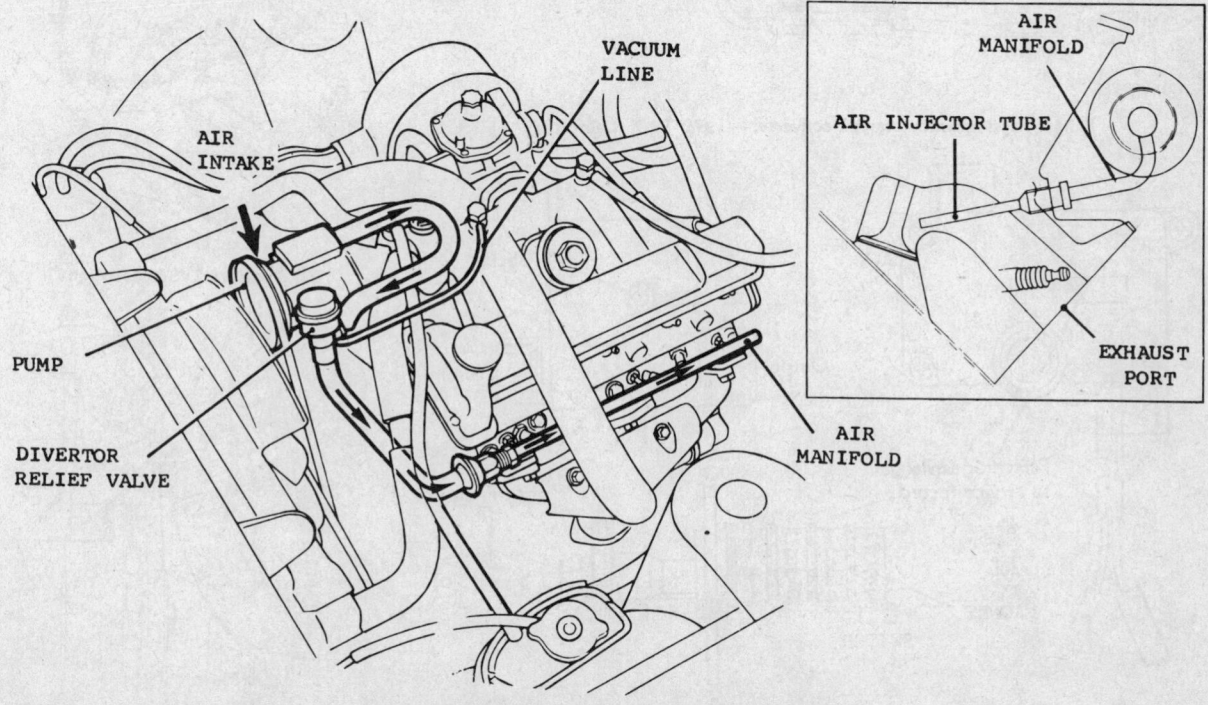

Air injection reactor system—1975 TR-7 (50 states)

Catalytic Converter

All TR–7 models manufactured for sale in the state of California are equipped with a catalytic converter. The converter is installed in the exhaust system, ahead of the muffler. It is designed, if the engine is kept in proper tune and if *only* lead-free fuel is used, to last 25,000 miles before replacement.

At 25,000 mile intervals, an odometer actuated catalytic converter service warning light will activate. The timing mechanism, which also activates the EGR service warning light at 12,500 mile intervals, may be reset (extinguished) with a special service indicator reset key available through British Leyland dealers.

Engine Modifications

Various measures have been taken to limit exhaust emissions resulting from the incomplete combustion of gasoline. Generally speaking, these measures have been designed to provide more efficient combustion of a "leaner" air/fuel mixture. The fuel delivery system has received the most attention in this respect with the use of the Zenith-Stromberg CDSE, CD4VT, and CDSE(V) series carburetors. Features of these carburetors include: a sealed and wired cover to discourage tampering; fixed, non-adjustable fuel jets; a biased metering needle to ensure a consistment air/fuel ratio; free-play built into the throttle linkage permitting a fast idle without disturbing the otherwise closed throttle; a temperature compensator assembly which varies the air supplied to the venturi area to correct the mixture and maintain even running with changing engine temperature; and a throttle by-pass valve which is set to open at a pre-determined manifold depression to admit air during deceleration.

An intake air temperature control system is used on TR–7 models to maintain the air entering the carburetor(s) at a constant temperature. By blending the engine compartment source air with the exhaust manifold heated air, the intake air is kept at roughly 99°F under all operating conditions. The system is controlled by a temperature sensitive bi-metal strip, which switches intake air sources via a flap valve.

A further reduction of exhaust emissions is gained by the use of ignition distributors that retard the spark during idling and deceleration, on all models. All models utilize distributors with centrifugal advance and vacuum retard.

1973 and 1974 Triumphs incorporate a thermostatic vacuum switch (TVS) into the vacuum retard system. The purpose of the switch is to prevent overheating during prolonged periods of idling. The TVS, located in the upper radiator hose, contains a vacuum valve which is connected in-line from the carburetor to the distributor. When the coolant temperature in the upper radiator hose reaches 220° F, a sensor in the switch vents the vacuum retard line to the atmosphere, thus negating the retard system. This, in turn, advances the ignition timing which increases the idle speed to avoid overheating. When the temperature falls below 220° F, normal vacuum retard is restored.

Other measures taken to reduce the level of exhaust emissions include a modified camshaft that reduces overlap at low engine speeds and a modified cylinder head to promote cleaner burning. Stellite faced exhaust valves are used to maintain effective valve seating over a longer period of time. All 1972 and later models are modified to achieve a lower compression ratio so that regular octane fuels may be used.

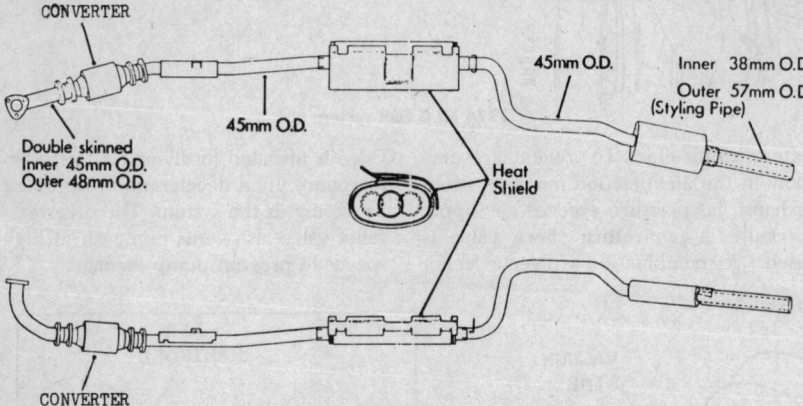

Exhaust system with catalytic converter—1975 TR-7 (California)

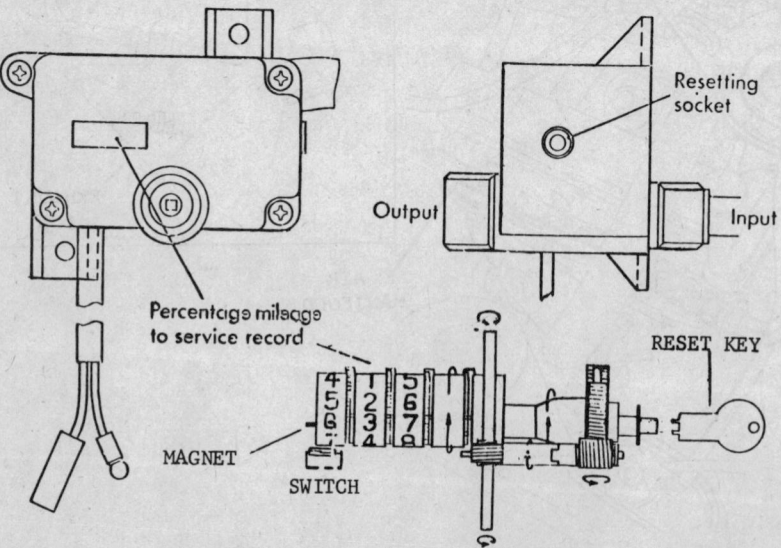

EGR/Catalytic converter service reminder mechanism

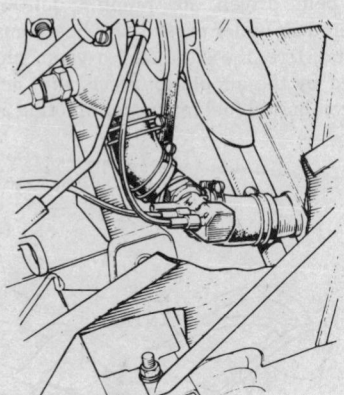

1973 Spitfire TVS installation

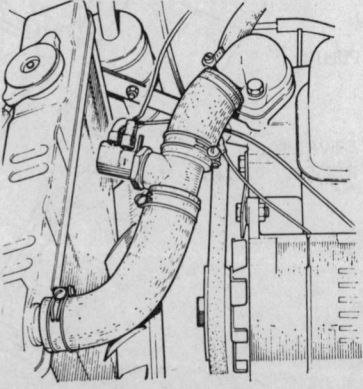

1973 TR-6 TVS installation

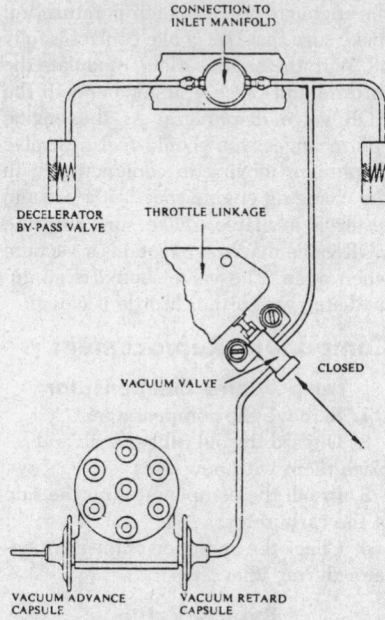

Emission control vacuum circuit—TR-6

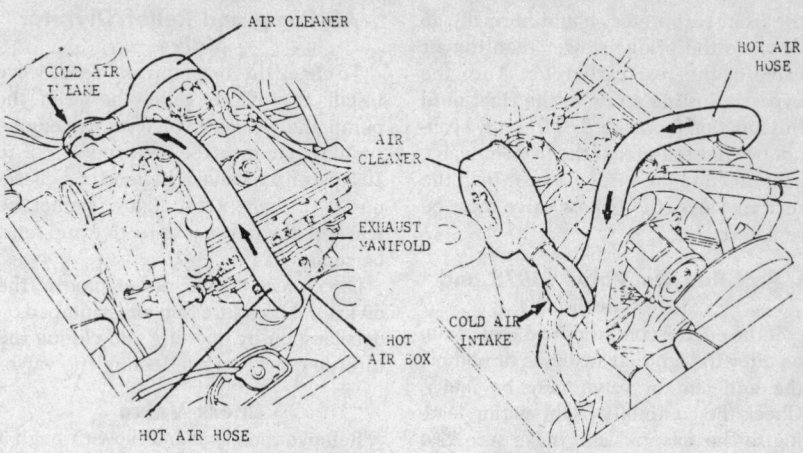

Intake air temperature control system—1975 TR-7 (California)

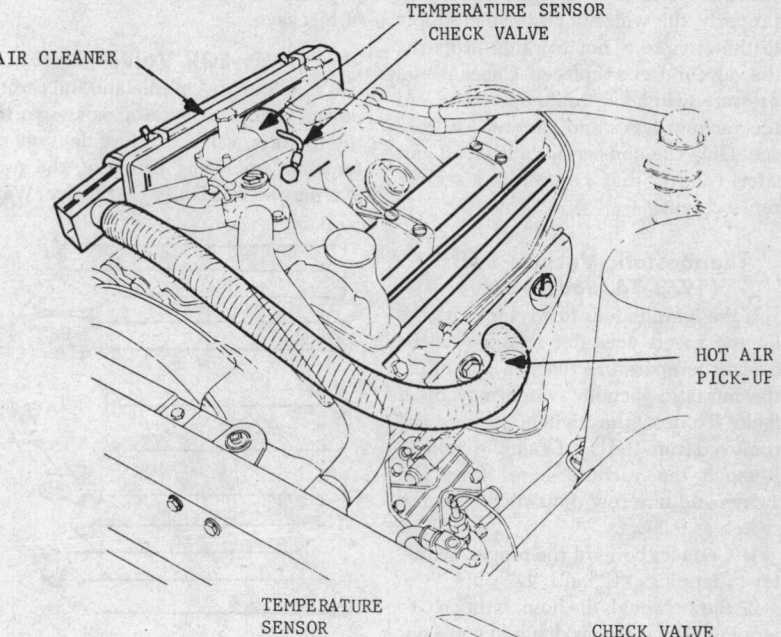

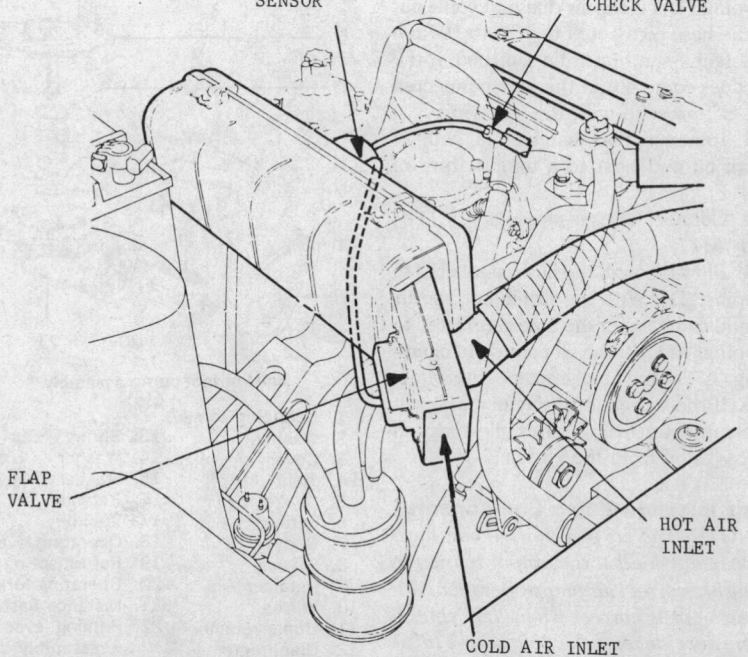

Intake air temperature control system—1975 TR-7 (49 states)

Component Testing and Adjustment

Temperature Compensator

If the idle speed drops off sharply during extended periods of idling, especially during warm weather, the temperature compensator may be in need of replacement.

1. Remove the plastic cover from the compensator

2. With the ambient temperature at or above 85° F, the valve should be able to be pressed inward with light finger pressure and then return to its position without jamming. If the valve jams and is still in operation, the temperature compensator should be replaced.

3. If properly adjusted, the valve will begin to open at 70–77° F, and be fully open at 85° F.

4. Replace the cover and check its operation during idling.

Bypass Valve

If the engine does not return to idle speed soon after the throttle is released and the throttle control linkage is properly adjusted, the bypass valve may be faulty.

1. If the engine still refuses to return to idle speed when the throttle is released, turn the bypass adjusting screw on the front carburetor to the left and manually lower the idle.

2. Run the engine briefly to approximately 2000 rpm, then release the throttle. If the engine returns to idle speed, turn the screw ½ turn further to the left. If the engine does not return to idle, replace the bypass valve as a unit.

3. Remove the air cleaner and observe the air valves. Briefly race the engine and then release the throttle. The air valve of

the front carburetor should normally go down to the bridge slower than the air valve of the rear carburetor. Turn the bypass adjusting screw to the right until this function is obtained. If the valve cannot be adjusted so that the front air valve goes down to the bridge slower than the rear air valve, the bypass valve must be replaced.

Anti-Run On Valve (1973 and later models)

If the engine continues to diesel or run on after the ignition switch is turned off, the anti-run on valve may be faulty. Check the continuity of the wiring leading to the solenoid and make sure that the electrical connections at the solenoid are tight. Then apply 12V to the solenoid with the engine running. If working properly, this will shut off the fuel supply to the engine. If not working properly, the valve must be replaced. Check the oil pressure switch for proper operation, and the vacuum hoses and canister for leakage. Only the non-serviceable (1973 and later) canister may be used as a service replacement.

Thermostatic Vacuum Switch (1973–74 models only)

If the ignition fails to advance and the engine speed does not increase as the coolant temperature reaches 220° F, the thermostatic vacuum switch may be at fault. To test the switch, it must be removed from the car. Drain the coolant. Remove the vacuum hoses from the switch and unscrew the switch. Test the switch as follows:

1. Connect hoses of the proper diameter to tappings "C" and "D".

2. Blow through the hose connected to tapping "D". If the air does not come out of the hose connected to "C", the switch is defective and must be replaced. If the air does come out of the hose connected to "C", proceed with the following.

3. Immerse the switch in a bath of clean oil and heat to a temperature of 220° F.

4. Connect hoses to tappings "C", "D", and "MT".

5. Blow through the hose connected to tapping "D". With the switch hot, the air should come out of the hose connected to tapping "MT". If the air comes out of tapping "C", or not at all, replace the switch.

6. If the switch is satisfactory, screw it back into its fitting, after cleaning all traces of oil from the switch.

Air Injection Pump Components

NOTE: *The air pump drive belt must be maintained at the proper tension to ensure correct air pump operation. Adjustment is correct when light thumb pressure deflects the belt ¾ to 1 in. at the mid-point of its longest run.*

Air Pump and Relief/Diverter Valve

To check the air pump and relief valve install a pressure gauge between the pump and relief valve. With the engine running, air must be relieved at 8.2 to 10.5 psi or the valve is in need of replacement. If the 8.2 psi figure cannot be reached, the pump is defective and must be replaced.

Disconnect the air outlet pipe at the divertor. Make sure that air is dumped on deceleration by opening and closing the throttle quickly while feeling the valve.

Check Valve

Remove the valve and blow through it orally. Air should pass from pump to manifold end, but not from the manifold to pump end. Make sure the hose is free of blockage.

EGR Valve

If a sudden loss of idle and full throttle power is noticed when it is known that the ignition, valve and fuel delivery systems are operating properly, the problem may lie in a faulty EGR valve. Warm

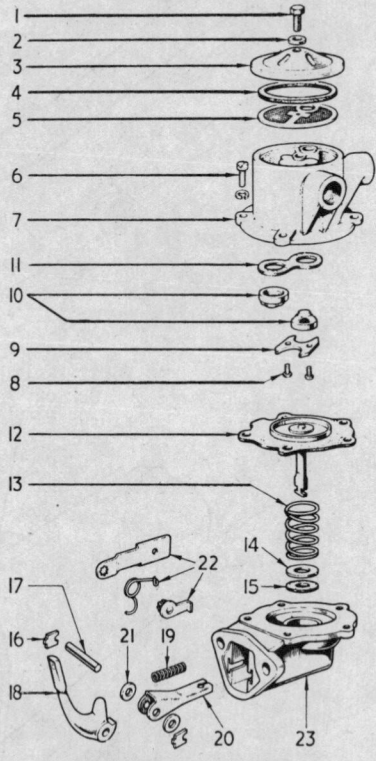

Spitfire fuel pump assembly

1. Retaining screw
2. Washer
3. Cover
4. Joint
5. Gauze
6. Screw
7. Body
8. Screws
9. Retainer
10. Valves
11. Upper retainer
12. Diaphragm assembly
13. Spring
14. Washer
15. Washer
16. Retainer
17. Spindle
18. Operating lever
19. Return spring
20. Operating fork
21. Distance washer
22. Priming lever assembly
23. Lower body

the engine to operating temperature and make sure that the choke control is fully off. With the engine idling, modulate the throttle and place a finger beneath the EGR valve diaphragm. As the engine rpm changes, you should feel the valve diaphragm moving in conjunction with the changing engine speed. If a vacuum tester is available, make sure that the EGR valve diaphragm retains a vacuum when open. The valve should close immediately when the throttle is closed.

Component Replacement

Temperature Compensator

1. Remove the compensator.
2. Discard the old rubber seals and replace them with new ones.
3. Install the compensator on the side of the carburetor.
4. Check the operation of the compensator during idle.

Bypass Valve

1. Remove the bypass valve.
2. Discard the old bypass valve-to-carburetor housing gasket.
3. Install a new gasket and bypass valve on the carburetor.
4. Check the operation of the bypass valve.

Anti-Run On Valve

1. Disconnect the electrical connections at the solenoid.
2. Disconnect and plug the evaporative piping from the valve.
3. Lift out the old valve and install the new unit. Connect the vacuum and electrical connections.

FUEL SYSTEM

Fuel Pump

All models are equipped with an AC mechanical diaphragm type fuel pump located on the left side of the engine.

Removal and Installation

To remove the fuel pump, disconnect the fuel inlet and outlet lines.

Unscrew the attaching nuts and remove the pump.

When installing, make sure that the pump lever (rocker arm) is positioned correctly above its lobe on the cam.

Fuel Pump Cleaning

Every 12,000 miles the fuel pump should be serviced. This may be accomplished by:

1. Removing the top bolt and domed cover.

2. Removing the gauze filter and thoroughly washing in a safe solvent (denatured alcohol).

3. Cleaning the sediment in the fuel bowl with a small screw driver. The pre-

ferred method for removing loosened sediment is compressed air. Wipe out the interior of the fuel bowl with a soft, clean rag.

CAUTION: *The interior of the fuel bowl must be absolutely free of grease or lint.*

4. Renewing the cork gasket if cracked or brittle. Fuel pump parts are delicate; use caution. When reassembling, be sure the filter gauze is facing down.

Carburetors

Removal and Installation

Single Zenith-Stromberg 150 CDSE, 175CD4TV

1. Remove the air cleaner.
2. Disconnect the fuel feed line, the distributor vacuum hose, the PCV hose, and the throttle return spring.
3. Remove the cotter pin, clevis pin, and washers. Disconnect the throttle cable.
4. Disconnect choke cable.
5. Remove the flange nuts and lift off the carburetor.
6. Installation is the reverse of removal.

Twin Zenith-Stromberg 150 CDSE, 175 CDSE(V)

1. Remove the air cleaner.
2. Disconnect the vacuum valve lines at each carburetor and from both sides of the vacuum valve. Disconnect the distributor vacuum hose, both fuel feed lines, the accelerator control rod (from the firewall side of the rear carburetor), and both choke cables.
3. Remove the vacuum valve bracket and the carburetor flange nuts. Remove the twin carburetor and linkage assembly.
4. Installation is the reverse of removal.

Carburetor Overhaul

Carburetors are relatively complex. Proper performance depends upon the cleanliness and proper adjustment of all internal and external components. In addition to the usual adjustments performed at the regular tune-up intervals, it eventually becomes necessary to remove, disassemble, clean, and overhaul the entire carburetor(s), in order to restore its original performance. To overhaul a carburetor, first purchase the proper rebuilding kit. Read the instructions and study the exploded view of the carburetor thoroughly prior to the actual removal and disassembly.

Carburetor Disassembly and Assembly

Zenith-Stromberg 150 CDSE(V), 175 CDSE(V)

NOTE: *Special tool (Churchill) S 353 is needed to remove the spring loaded*

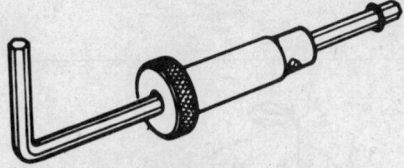

Churchill carburetor adjusting tool No.S.353 for removing and installing spring-loaded metering needle

metering needle from the air valve. If the special tool is not available, an allen wrench of the proper diameter may be used.

1. Remove the carburetor(s).
2. Remove the damper.
3. Lever out the bottom plug.
4. Drain the carburetor of oil and fuel.
5. Remove the O-ring from its plug.
6. Remove the six screws which secure the float chamber to the body.
7. Remove the float chamber.
8. Remove the float assembly by gently prying the spindle from the clip at each end.
9. Remove the needle valve.
10. Remove the four screws which secure the top cover to the body.
11. Remove the top cover.
12. Remove the spring.
13. Remove the air valve assembly.
14. Remove the four screws which secure the diaphragm and retaining ring to the air valve assembly.
15. Remove the diaphragm and retaining ring.
16. Slacken the set screw in the side of the air valve.
17. Insert tool S353 or an allen wrench of the proper diameter into the stem of the air valve, turn it counterclockwise approximately two turns, and withdraw the needle and housing by pulling firmly and straight with your fingers.
18. Remove the two screws which secure the starter box to the body.
19. Remove the starter box.
20. Remove the two screws which secure the temperature compensator to the body.
21. Remove the temperature compensator and two rubber washers of different diameters.
22. Remove the three (slotted) screws which secure the by-pass valve to the body.
23. Remove the by-pass valve and gasket.
24. Remove the two screws which secure the butterfly to the spindle.
25. Turn the spindle return spring.
26. Release the spindle return spring.
27. Withdraw the spindle and spring.
28. Remove the spindle seals from the body by hooking them out with a small screwdriver.
29. Wash all components in clean solvent. Allow them to air dry or use com-

pressed air. Place all components on a clean surface. Discard all seals and gaskets. Scrape all old gasket material from the mating surfaces.

30. Examine the condition of all components for wear, paying special attention to the needle and seat and the air valve and diaphragm which should be replaced unless in exceptionally good condition.
31. Use clean compressed air to blow through all ports, needle valve, and starter box.
32. Fit the spindle seals to the body, tapping them gently into position, with the metal casing of the seals flush with the body of the carburetor.
33. Insert the spindle, loading and locating the spindle return spring while doing so.
34. Insert the butterfly with the two protruding spots facing outboard and below the spindle. Tighten the screws.
35. Install the starter box and tighten the screws.
36. Install the by-pass valve and gasket and tighten the screws.
37. Install the temperature compensator and tighten the screws.
38. Insert the needle housing assembly into the bottom of the air valve.
39. Install tool S353 or an allen wrench of the proper diameter, turning it clockwise to engage the threads of the needle valve assembly with the adjusting screw. Then, continue turning until the slot in the needle housing is aligned with the set screw.
40. Tighten the set screw.

NOTE: *The set screw does not tighten on the needle housing but locates into the slot. This ensures that during adjustment the needle will remain in its operating position, i.e. biased by a spring in the needle housing toward the air cleaner side of the carburetor.*

41. Install the diaphragm, locating the inner tag into the recess in the air valve.
42. Install the diaphragm retaining ring and secure it with four screws.
43. Install the air valve assembly, locating the outer tag and rim of the diaphragm in the complementary recesses in the carburetor body.
44. Install the carburetor top cover with the bulge on the housing neck toward the air intake.
45. Install and evenly tighten the top cover screws.
46. Install the needle valve and sealing washers and tighten them.
47. Install the float assembly by levering the pivot pin gently into the piston.
48. Check the float height by measuring the distance between the carburetor gasket face and the highest point of the floats.

NOTE: *The float heights must be equal and set to 0.625–0.672 in. (16–17 mm).*

1. Carburetor
2. Spring—idle trimming screw
3. Idle trimming screw
4. Gasket—by-pass valve
5. By-pass valve
6. Lockwasher under (7)
7. Screw—securing (5)
8. Temperature compensator unit
9. Lockwasher under (10)
10. Screw—securing (8)
11. Cover—temperature compensator
12. Screw—securing (11)
13. Seal—on compensator body
14. Seal—inside carburetor
15. Damper rod ⎫
16. Washer ⎬ damper
17. Spacer sleeve ⎭ assembly
18. Circlip
19. Cover—air valve
20. Screws—securing (19)
21. Spring—air valve return

22. Ring—diaphragm attachment
23. Screw—securing (22) (24)
24. Diaphragm
25. Air valve
26. Screw—securing (27)
27. Needle assembly
28. Spring—idle adjusting screw
29. Idle adjusting screw
30. Throttle disc
31. Screw—securing (30)
32. Seal—throttle spindle
33. Throttle spindle
34. Spring—throttle return
35. Lever—throttle
36. Screw—fast idle
37. Locknut—securing (36)
38. Lockwasher— retaining (39)
39. Nut—throttle spindle
40. Coupling—throttle spindles
41. Connecting lever assembly
42. Clamping bolt
43. Washer—under (42)
44. Nut—securing (42)

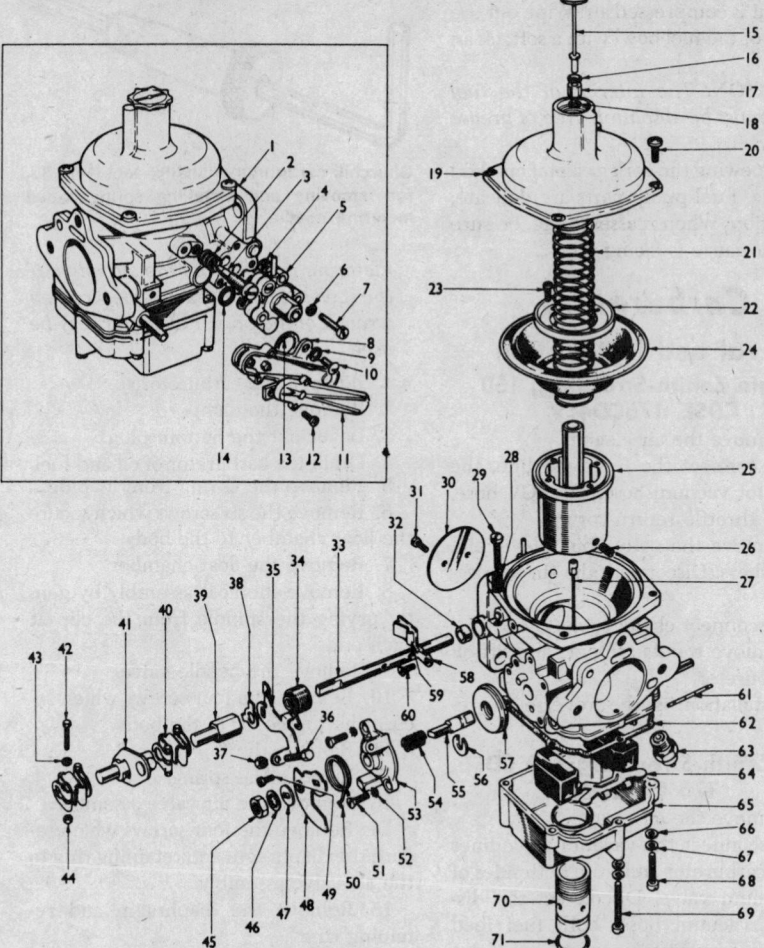

Zenith-Stromberg 150 CDSE(V), 175 CDSE(V) carburetor assembly

45. Nut
46. Shakeproof washer
47. Washer
48. Lever
49. Screw—cable attachment
50. Return spring ⎫
51. Screw ⎬ Starter
52. Shakeproof washer ⎬ box
53. Starter box cover ⎬ assembly
54. Spring
55. Spindle
56. Retainer
57. Valve plate
58. Cable abutment bracket
59. Spring clip

60. Screw—securing (58)
61. Float pivot pin
62. Gasket—float chamber
63. Needle valve
64. Float assembly
65. Float chamber cover
66. Washer—under (68/69)
67. Spring washer— under (68/69)
68. Screw—securing (65)
69. Screw—securing (65)
70. Plug
71. Rubber O-ring— for (70)

Adjust by bending the tabs while ensuring that the tab sits on the needle valve at right angles.

49. Install the float chamber gasket.

50. Install the float chamber and secure it with six screws.

51. Install the O-ring to the bottom plug.

52. Install the bottom plug.

53. Install the carburetor(s).

54. Fill the carburetor damper dashpot with a seasonal grade of engine oil until, using the damper as a dipstick, the threaded plug is 0.25 in. (6 mm) above the dashpot when resistance is felt.

55. Install the damper.

56. Adjust the idle speed, throttle linkage, and choke.

Throttle Linkage Adjustment

Single Zenith-Stromberg 150 CDSE, 175 CD4TV

1. Remove the air cleaner.

2. Loosen the throttle cable nuts. Loosen the fast idle screw to obtain maximum cam clearance. Fully close the throttle. Open the throttle by turning the screw 1½ turns clockwise.

3. Loosen the locknut and set the linkage adjusting screw until the clevis pin is moved to the engine side of the slots in the linkage straps; tighten the locknut.

NOTE: *It is necessary to have free play in the linkage to allow for a fast idle setting without interfering with the closed position of the throttle.*

4. Tighten the cable nuts so that the cable has no play and is not taut.

5. Install the air cleaner.

Twin Zenith-Stromberg 150 CDSE

1. Loosen the spring coupling bolts on both carburetor ends.

2. Fully close the throttles by unscrewing the idling screws, then open them evenly 1-½ turns. Make sure that the choke is closed and that the fast idle adjustment screw is clear of the linkage cam.

3. Place a 1/16 in. drill bit in space between the lever tongue and the lever slot edge. With the bit in position, put pressure on the stop cam and tighten the spring bolts. Remove the drill bit.

4. Loosen the vacuum valve screws. Adjust the valve to provide a 0.030 in. clearance between the valve and the lever.

5. Position the linkage so that the tongue rests in the lever slot. With the throttle at the point of opening, the valve should be fully closed.

Twin Zenith-Stromberg 175 CDSE(V)

1. Loosen the bolts on the spring couplings (both carburetor ends).

2. Adjust both idle screws to the fully closed position. Rotate the screws open exactly 1-½ turns. Make sure the fast idle adjustment screw is clear of the linkage cam. Be sure the choke linkage is fully closed.

3. Start and warm the engine to operating temperature. Adjust the idle screw to set both carburetors to the specified idle speed. Stop the engine.

4. Place a 3/32 in. drill bit in the space between the lever tongue and the lever slot edge. With the bit in position put pressure on the stop cam and tighten the spring bolts. Remove the bit.

5. Place the relay lever against the stop screw. Loosen the vacuum valve screws. Adjust the valve to 0.030 in. clearance (between the valve and the lever).

6. Move the linkage until the tongue rests in the lever slot. The valve should be fully closed (the throttle should be at the point of opening).

Float Level Adjustment

Zenith-Stromberg 150 CDSE, 175 CDSE(V) & CD4TV

1. Remove the carburetor(s) from the manifold.

2. Unscrew the cap(s) and drain the oil from the damping cylinder(s). Drain the fuel from the float chamber(s).

3. With the carburetor inverted and the float chamber cover removed, make sure that the distance between the highest point of the floats and the carburetor body is 0.625–0.672 in.

4. To adjust, bend the float tang which contacts the needle of the valve assembly. To lower the fuel level, a thin washer may be inserted beneath the needle valve assembly.

5. Install the float chamber cover with

1. Spring coupling clamp bolts
2. Throttle stop
3. Relay lever
4. Vacuum valve plunger
5. Vacuum valve securing screws

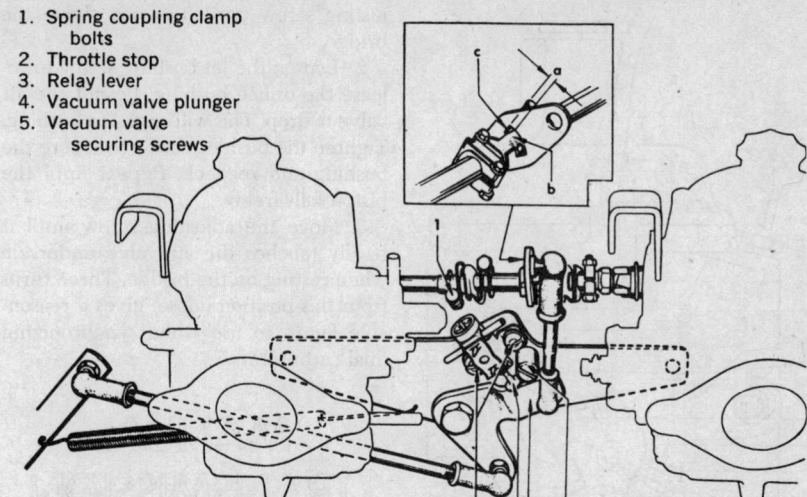

Zenith-Stromberg 150 CDSE(V) throttle linkage

1. Spring coupling clamp bolts
2. Throttle stop
3. Relay lever
4. Vacuum valve plunger
5. Vacuum valve securing screws

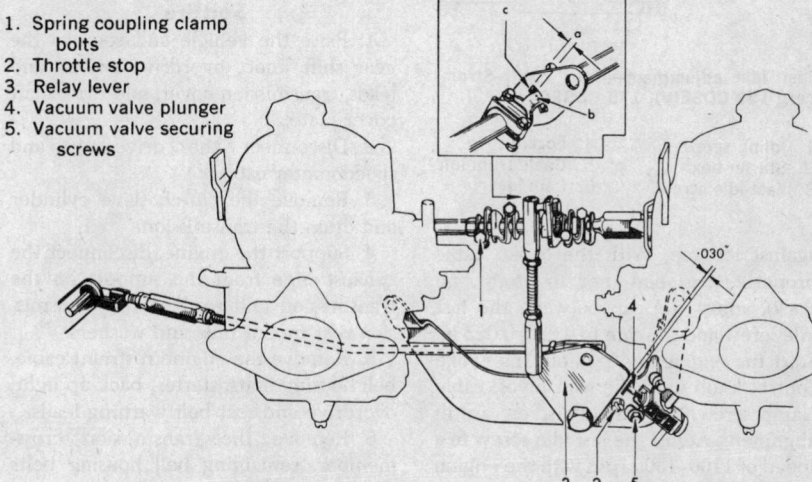

Zenith-Stromberg 175 CDSE(V) throttle linkage

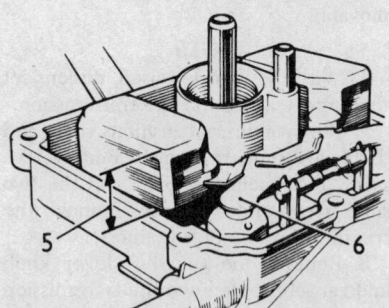

Float level adjustment—Zenith-Stromberg 150 CDSE(V), 175 CDSE(V).

a new gasket. Fill the damping cylinder(s) to ¼ in. from the top with Type A automatic transmission fluid and install the cap(s).

6. Install the carburetor(s).

Fast Idle and Choke Adjustment

Single Zenith-Stromberg 150 CDSE

Push the choke control knob fully in and make sure that the cam is positioned

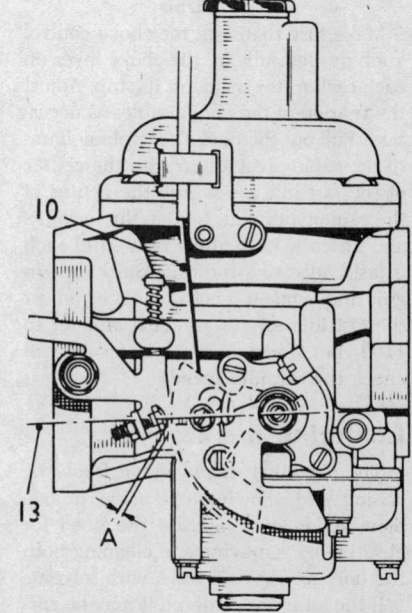

Fast idle adjustment—single Zenith-Stromberg 150 CDSE(V).

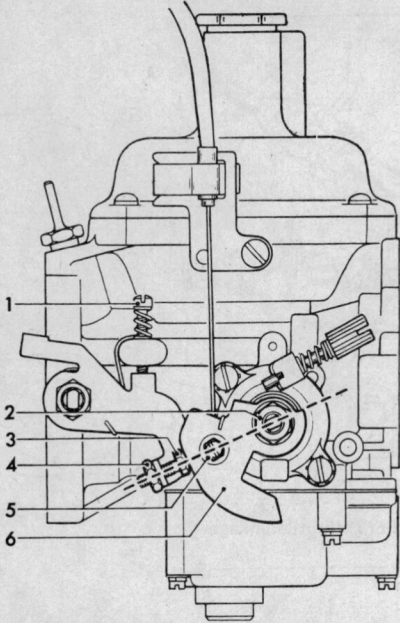

Fast idle adjustment—twin Zenith-Stromberg 150 CDSE(V), 175 CDSE(V).

1. Idling screw
2. Starter box
3. Fast-idle screw
4. Locknut
5. Cable trunnion
6. Cam lever

against its stop. With the choke cable properly tensioned (not too tight, no slack), adjust the gap between the fast idle screw and the cam to 0.020–0.025 in. Start the engine and pull out the choke control knob until the cam pivot, cable clamp screw, and fast idle screw are in alignment. Adjust the fast idle screw to a speed of 1100–1300 rpm with the engine hot and the air cleaner installed.

Twin Zenith-Stromberg 150 CDSE, 175 CDSE

Make sure that with the choke control knob pushed fully in, the choke lever on each carburetor is against its stop. Adjust the tension of the choke cables as necessary. Pull out the choke control knob until the cable pivot aligns with the center of the fast idle screw and the center of the cam pivot point. Loosen the locknuts and unscrew both idle screws until each is just contacting the cam. Start the engine and, while it is cold (68–86°F), adjust the fast idle screws an equal amount to 1100 rpm. Tighten the locknuts and recheck the fast idle speed.

Centering the Jet

The air valve should move freely by raising and allowing the valve to fall. Slow action may indicate the need for cleaning by removing and cleaning both the bore and the air valve with solvent.

If the jet is not centered it may be corrected as follows:

1. Raise the air valve and tighten the jet bushing screw. Tighten the orifice ad-

justing screw until it is just above the bridge.

2. Loosen the jet bushing screw to release the orifice bushing. Permit the air valve to drop. This will align the bushing. Tighten the bushing screw to secure the bushing and recheck. Repeat until the piston falls freely.

3. Move the adjusting screw until it barely touches the air valve underside when resting on the bridge. Three turns from this position (loose) gives a reasonable figure to use when synchronizing dual carburetors.

MANUAL TRANSMISSION

Removal and Installation

Spitfire

1. Raise the vehicle and remove the gear shift knob, overdrive switch and leads, transmission cover, and driveshaft cover plate.

2. Disconnect the driveshaft and speedometer cable.

3. Remove the clutch slave cylinder and drain the transmission.

4. Support the engine, disconnect the exhaust pipe from the support on the transmission and remove the transmission rear mount nuts and washers.

5. Remove the engine restraint cable, bell housing bolts, starter, back-up light, overdrive and seat belt warning leads.

6. Remove the transmission crossmember, remaining bell housing bolts and remove the transmission.

7. Installation is the reverse of removal.

GT6

1. With the vehicle raised, disconnect the battery and drain the transmission.

2. Remove the seat cushions, seats, and dashboard support bracket. Remove the safety belt anchoring bolts and the two small screws next to each. Remove the transmission tunnel side liners.

3. Remove the gearshift lever knob and carpeting. Remove the transmission center cover.

4. Disconnect the driveshaft from the transmission flange. Remove the slave cylinder, speedometer cable, and exhaust pipe attachment.

5. With transmission in first gear, remove the transmission cover and extension assembles. Cover the transmission.

6. From beneath the vehicle, release the mounting bracket at the rear of the transmission.

7. Place a jack under the oil pan to support the weight of the engine, detach the clutch housing flange and raise the engine until the transmission can be

removed. With the rear of the transmission raised, maneuver the clutch housing underneath the parcel shelf at the passenger side of the vehicle.

9. Installation is the reverse of removal.

TR–6

The transmission is removed, with the engine remaining in position.

1. Disconnect the battery, drain the transmission, and remove the seat cushions and carpets.

2. Disconnect the cables from the heater control switch, the control cable from the heater unit, and the lower left control cable from the center control panel. Remove the dashboard support. Remove the headlight dimmer switch, leaving the electrical connections attached.

3. Remove the center floor cover.

4. Remove the driveshaft.

5. Remove the clutch slave cylinder, allowing it to hang by its flexible hose. Remove the clutch cover plate from the lower part of the clutch housing. Disconnect the speedometer cable and the overdrive connections (if installed).

6. With a block of wood protecting the oil pan, use a jack to support the weight of the engine and transmission. The jack should be placed as far as possible toward the rear of the oil pan.

7. Remove the exhaust pipe bracket next to the hand brake, then detach the rear mounting from the transmission and crossmember.

8. Raise the engine and transmission. Remove the crossmember by sliding it forward.

9. Unbolt the clutch housing flange from the engine.

10. Remove the transmission rearward.

11. Installation is the reverse of removal.

TR–7

1. Remove the shift lever, driveshaft, exhaust pipe-to-bell housing bracket, exhaust pipe-to-rear axle supports, speedometer cable, reverse switch leads, restraint cable, transmission-to-crossmember tie-bar, and support the transmission on a jack.

2. Loosen the engine stabilizer-to-frame nut (lower), and remove the stabilizer from the engine support bracket.

3. Remove the transmission rear mount.

4. Lower the transmission and engine assembly just enough to remove the bell housing top bolts.

5. Remove the starter.

6. Disconnect the wiring harness and slave cylinder pipe from the bell housing.

7. Unbolt and remove the transmission/bell housing assembly.

8. Installation is the reverse of removal. Adjust the restraint cable as follows:

    a. Fully slack off the front nut at the rear end of the cable.

    b. Tighten the rear nut.

    c. Slack off the rear nut, hold the cable by hand and position the rear nut so that a 1/32–1/16″ clearance exists between the nut and the cable bracket.

    d. Tighten the front nut.

Overhaul

Transmission overhaul requires the use of certain special tools. If these tools are not available, the job should not be attempted.

Spitfire MK IV, Spitfire 1500
Disassembly

1. Remove the transmission.
2. Remove the bell housing and clutch lever.

3. Take out the top cover retaining bolts.

4. Lift off the top cover and extension and the joint washer.

5. Using Tool RG 421, unscrew the output flange nut and remove the washer.

6. Withdraw the output flange.

7. Unscrew the bolts retaining the rear extension to the case.

8. Withdraw the rear extension and joint washer.

9. Unscrew the retaining bolt, for the reverse idler spindle.

10. Withdraw the reverse idler spindle and distance tube.

11. Insert the needle-roller retaining tube (corresponding to the dimensions given) and remove the layshaft spindle to the rear. Allow the layshaft cluster to drop to the bottom of the transmission.

12. Using Tool No. S4235A-2, withdraw the constant pinion assembly.

13. Remove the top gear baulk ring.

14. Remove the circlip retaining the speedometer drive gear.

15. Remove the speedometer drive gear and ball.

16. Remove the snap-ring from the mainshaft ballrace.

17. Remove the circlip from the mainshaft ballrace.

18. Install the abutment plate, Tool No. S4221A-19, to the case.

19. Install Tool No. S4221A and adaptor S4221A-19/1, to the annular groove in the mainshaft center ballrace.

20. Withdraw the ballrace.

21. Tilt the mainshaft and remove it from the transmission.

22. Remove the 3rd/top synchro unit.

23. Remove the 3rd gear baulk ring.

24. From the rear of the mainshaft, remove the thrust washer.

25. Remove the 1st speed gear.

26. Remove the 1st gear baulk ring.

27. Remove the circlip. If the third gear mainshaft thrust washer has three

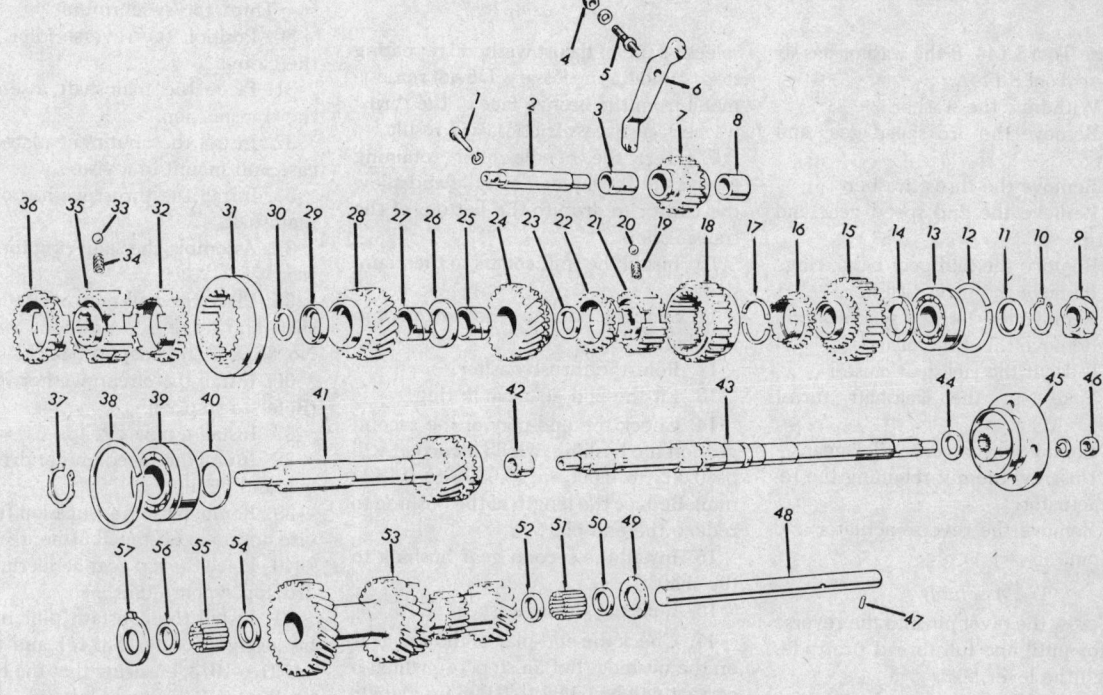

GT6 4-speed gears

1. Locating ball
2. Reverse idler spindle
4. Nyloc nut
5. Pivot pin
6. Reverse actuator
7. Reverse idler gear
8. Spacer tube
9. Speedometer driven gear
10. Circlip
11. Washer
12. Snap ring
13. Center ballrace
14. Thrust washer
15. 1st speed gear
16. Baulk ring
17. Split collars
18. 1st/2nd synchro sleeve
19. Spring
20. Ball
21. 1st/2nd synchro hub
22. Baulk ring
23. Thrust washer
24. 2nd speed gear
25. 2nd gear bushing
26. Thrust washer
27. 3rd gear bushing
28. 3rd speed gear
29. Circlip washer
30. Circlip
31. 3rd/Top synchro sleeve
32. Baulk ring
33. Ball
34. Spring
35. 3rd/Top synchro hub
36. Baulk ring
37. Circlip
38. Snap ring
39. Front ballrace
40. Oil thrower
41. Input shaft
42. Roller bearing
43. Mainshaft
44. Thrust washer
45. Coupling flange
46. Nut
47. Pin
48. Countershaft spindle
49. Rear thrust washer
50. Retaining ring
51. Needle rollers
52. Retaining ring
53. Countershaft gear cluster
54. Retaining ring
55. Needle rollers
56. Retaining ring
57. Front thrust washer

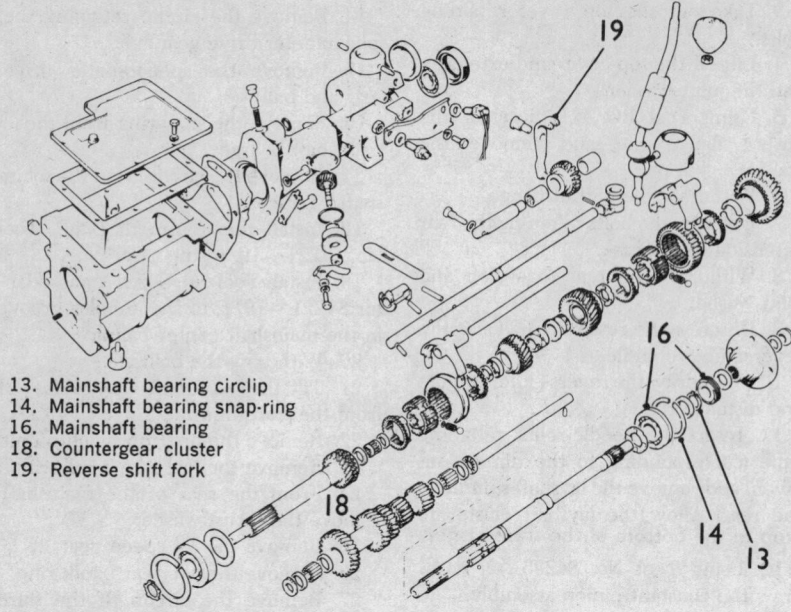

13. Mainshaft bearing circlip
14. Mainshaft bearing snap-ring
16. Mainshaft bearing
18. Countergear cluster
19. Reverse shift fork

Spitfire Mk. IV and 1500 and TR-7 transmission

lugs, use Tool S.144. If the washer has six lugs, use Tool S.144A.

28. Withdraw the washer.

29. Remove the 3rd speed gear and bushing.

30. Remove the thrust washer.

31. Remove the 2nd speed gear and bushing.

32. Remove the 2nd gear baulk ring.

33. Remove the thrust washer.

34. Remove the 1st/2nd synchro unit.

35. Remove the split collars.

36. Lift out the jackshaft cluster.

37. Take out the jackshaft thrust washer.

38. Remove the reverse idler gear.

39. Unscrew the nut retaining the reverse actuator.

40. Remove the reverse actuator and pivot pin.

Assembly

1. Screw the pivot pin into the reverse-actuator until one full thread protrudes through the lever boss.

2. Install the actuator and pivot pin into the gear casing.

3. Install the plain washer and tighten the nut.

4. Smear the front face of the jackshaft front thrust washer with grease and stick it in position in the gear casing. Insert one end of the jackshaft spindle through the casing to centralize the washer.

5. Lower the jackshaft cluster assembly into the transmission.

6. Fit the rear thrust washer in position.

7. Insert the jackshaft spindle and eject the needle-roller retaining tube.

8. Measure the jackshaft cluster end-play. Adjust the layshaft end-float to 0.-007 to 0.013 in. (0.18 to 0.33 mm), by

selective use of thrust washers, repeating steps 4 and 8 as necessary. Do not remove metal from the bronze face of the thrust washers, as excess friction will result.

9. Insert the needle-roller retaining tube, eject the layshaft spindle and allow the cluster to drop to the bottom of the transmission.

10. Install the split collars to the mainshaft.

11. Slide the 1st/2nd synchro unit onto the shaft.

12. Refit the thrust washer.

13. Fit the 2nd gear baulk ring.

14. Check the end-play of the second gear on the bushing, which if correct will be 0.002 to 0.006 in. (0.0508 to 0.1524 mm). Reduce the length of the bushing to reduce the end-play.

15. Install the second gear bushing to the shaft.

16. Refit the thrust washer.

17. Check the end-play of the 3rd gear on the bushing (Ref. in step 14), which if correct will be 0.002 to 0.006 in. (0.0508 to 0.1524 mm).

18. Install the 3rd gear bushing to the shaft.

19. Refit the washer.

20. Secure the assembly using a discarded half circlip.

21. Measure the end-play of the bushing on the mainshaft and adjust by selective use of thrust washers until an end-play of 0.000 to 0.006 in. (0.00 to 0.15 mm) is obtained. Dismantle the mainshaft.

22. Install the split collars to the mainshaft.

23. Install the 1st speed gear.

24. Install the thrust washer.

25. Install a discarded bearing inner

race to distance tube 0.784 to 0.750 in. (18.99 to 19.05 mm) long.

26. Measure the thickness of the circlip washer and assemble to the shaft.

27. Install a discarded half circlip.

28. Measure the 1st speed gear end-play and determine the thickness of the circlip washer required to provide and end-float of 0.000 to 0.002 in. (0.00 to 0.05 mm).

29. Dismantle the mainshaft. Assemble components to the mainshaft as follows:

First/second synchro unit;
Second gear baulk ring;
Thrust washer;
Second speed gear and bushing;
Thrust washer;
Third speed gear and bushing;
Washer;
Circlip, offset outermost (locate lip of clip in recess of tool No. S145);
Split collars;
First gear baulk ring;
First speed gear;
Third/top synchro unit.

30. Position the reverse idler gear in the casing.

31. Place the mainshaft assembly in the transmission.

32. Install the abutment plate on the case and mount in a vise.

33. Install the thrust washer over the mainshaft.

34. Assemble the snap-ring to the ball race.

35. Place the ball race over the mainshaft and drive into position using Tool No. S314/1 and adaptor S4221A-19/3½.

36. Install the circlip washer selected. (Refer to step 28).

37. Install a new circlip.

38. Install the speedometer drive gear, ball and circlip.

39. Remove the transmission from the vise and take off the abutment plate.

40. Place the top gear baulk ring in the 3rd/top synchro unit.

41. Install the constant pinion assembly using Tool No. S314/1 and adaptor S4221A-19/3, ensuring that the top gear baulk ring is correctly located.

42. Invert the transmission and align the jackshaft cluster and thrust washer.

43. Insert the jackshaft spindle from the gear and remove the needle-roller retaining tube.

44. Position the reverse idler gear and fit the spindle and spacer. Install the locating bolt.

45. Locate the washer on the end of the mainshaft.

46. Refit the rear extension assembly and a new joint washer.

47. Install the bolts and washers.

48. Replace the drive flange.

49. Install and tighten the nut and washer and secure the cotter pin.

50. Refit the bell housing assembly and

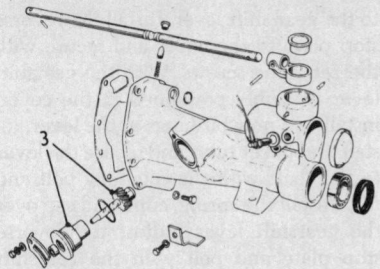

Spitfire Mk. IV, 1500 and TR-7 extension housing 3 is the speedometer pinion gear

a new joint washer. Install the clutch lever.

51. Install and tighten the bottom bolt and copper washer.

52. Select 1st gear on the top cover and the transmission.

53. Install the top cover and a new joint washer.

54. Install and tighten the bolts and washers.

GT6 Mk III

Disassembly

Disassembly procedure for the GT-6 transmission is as follows: Remove the top cover from the transmission. Twist and release the cap at the base of the gearshift lever. Remove the nylon nut and bolt to release the shaft from the gearshift lever. Lift the gearshift lever assembly from the rear extension and remove the cups along with the outer spring. Remove the snap ring from the gearshift lever, then remove the inner spring and the nylon ball. Remove the two retaining screws and take off the reverse stop plate. Remove the reverse stop bolt from the gearshift lever. Remove the threaded and tapered locking pin and extract the shaft from the extension housing and selector. Remove the rubber O-rings from the bores of the extension housing. Remove the retaining nut and withdraw the pivot bolt from the coupling fork. Extract the shaft and fiber washers from the coupling. Remove the steel pin, releasing the coupling fork from the shaft. Disassemble the selector shaft and fork assemblies by driving out the retaining plugs with a 1/8 in. (3.17 mm.) punch.

Remove the threaded, tapered locking pins from the selector shafts and forks. Release the 1st/2nd selector fork, spacer washer and sleeve by pushing the 1st/2nd selector shaft out of the cover. Remove the two interlock balls and plunger. Release the 3rd/4th selector fork by pushing the 3rd/4th selector shaft out of the cover. Release the reverse selector by pushing the reverse selector shaft out of the cover. Remove the detent plungers and springs from the cover.

Disassemble the clutch housing: Remove the release lever from its pivot pin and remove the lever and bearing. Remove the retaining bolts, releasing the

clutch housing, and remove the springs.

Disassemble the rear extension: Remove the retaining nut and extract the driving flange from the mainshaft. Remove the retaining bolts and carefully withdraw the extension from the transmission. The operation may be facilitated by lightly tapping the mounting lugs with a soft-headed hammer. Remove the paper washer and spacer washer from the mainshaft. Remove the bolt and extract the reverse spindle and spacer tube. If necessary, withdraw the ball bearing and oil seal from the extension.

Withdraw the countershaft, retaining the needle roller bearings. Using a special tool, withdraw the input shaft assembly from the transmission case. Shake out the roller bearing and remove the baulk ring. Remove the circlip and snap ring and use the special tool and adaptor to extract the ball race and oil thrower. With an abutment plate installed, remove the snap ring, circlip, and spacer washer. Withdraw the ball bearing and speedometer gear, using the special tool and adaptors used for the first ball race. Remove the abutment plate, tilt the mainshaft assembly and maneuver it from the transmission case.

Disassemble the mainshaft as follows: Remove the 3rd/4th synchronizer unit, 3rd gear baulk ring, thrust washer, 1st gear and 1st gear baulk ring. Remove the circlip, washer, 3rd gear, bushing, thrust washer, 2nd gear, bushing, thrust washer, 2nd gear baulk ring, 1st/2nd synchronizer unit, and split collars. Disassemble each synchronizer unit by pressing the hub through the sleeve. During this operation, the synchronizer unit should be placed in a suitable container to prevent the loss of the spring-loaded balls. Withdraw the countershaft assembly from the case and lift out the thrust washers. The countershaft may be further disassembled by removing the needle rollers and the retaining rings. Disassemble the reverse idler gear and actuator by taking out the idler gear, removing the securing nut, and removing the actuator and pivot pin.

Assembly

Replace the needle rollers, smearing them with grease, and insert the retaining tube. With the steel face of the front thrust washer smeared with grease, locate the washer in the transmission case. The tang should engage the recess provided. Insert the end of the countershaft spindle through the case to centralize the thrust washer. With the countershaft gear cluster assembly lowered into the case, install the rear thrust washer and insert the spindle. Measure the end clearance of the countershaft and adjust if necessary to 0.007–0.013 in. (0.178–0.330 mm) by using thrust washers of selected

thickness. If the thickness of a thrust washer must be reduced, do not remove metal from the bronze face. Insert the needle roller retaining tube and remove the countershaft spindle. Allow the gear cluster assembly to drop to the bottom of the transmission case.

Assemble the reverse idle gear mechanism by screwing the pivot pin into the actuator until a thread protrudes through the boss of the lever. Install it into the transmission case and secure it with a nut and washer. Position the reverse idler gear in the case. Install the synchronizer springs and balls to the 3rd/4th synchronizer hub and install the outer sleeve. Repeat the preceding with the 1st/2nd synchronizer unit and test the axial release loads, which should be between 19 and 21 pounds for each unit. The axial release load may be adjusted by the installation of new springs or the addition/subtraction of shims to/from the position beneath each synchronizer spring.

Measure the end clearance of each mainshaft gear on its respective bushing. Correct end clearance is 0.002–0.006 in. (0.05–0.15 mm.). End clearance may be increased by the installation of a new bushing and decreased by the reduction of the length of the bushing.

NOTE: *The reduction of bushing length will increase the end clearance of the bushings on the mainshaft.* Install the thrust washer, bushing, thrust washer, bushing and washer to the mainshaft. With the assembly secured with half a circlip, measure the total end clearance of the bushings and thrust washers on the mainshaft. The end clearance may be adjusted to the correct range of 0.004–0.010 in. (0.10–0.25 mm.) through the use of thrust washers of various thicknesses.

Determine the required thickness of the circlip washer by installing the split collars, 1st gear thrust washer, bearing inner race or spacer tube, spacer washer and half a circlip to the mainshaft, then insert a feeler gauge. Use washers of proper thickness to obtain the correct clearance of 0.000–0.002 in. (00–0.50 mm).

Install the following components on the mainshaft: 1st/2nd synchronizer unit, 2nd gear baulk ring, thrust washer, 2nd gear bushing, 2nd gear, thrust washer, 3rd gear bushing, 3rd gear, and washer. Use a special tool to install the circlip, and install the 3rd/4th synchronizer unit, split collars, 1st gear baulk ring, and 1st gear. Position the mainshaft assembly in the transmission case, install an abutment plate tool or its equivalent, and install the thrust washer.

With the transmission positioned vertically, and the abutment plate held in a vise, install the snap ring to the ball bearing and position the ball bearing over the mainshaft. Being sure that the mainshaft

Triumph

is correctly located in the abutment plate, drive the ball bearing into position, using the special tool and adaptor or their equivalents. Install the speedometer drive gear and remove the abutment plate from the transmission.

Assemble the input shaft components: Position the 4th gear baulk ring into the 3rd/4th synchronizer unit. Using the special tool and adaptor or their equivalents, press the ball bearing and oil thrower onto the input shaft and secure the ball bearing with the circlip. Install the snap ring onto the ball bearing and place the roller bearing in the bore of the input shaft. Ensuring that the baulk ring is correctly located, drive the input shaft assembly into the transmission case. Assemble the countershaft by inverting the transmission, lining up the countershaft thrust washers and gear cluster, and inserting the spindle from the rear. With the reverse idler gear correctly positioned, insert the spindle and install the spacer tube.

Assemble the rear extension: Replace the ball bearing and seal to the rear extension. Install a new gasket at the rear of the transmission and place the washer over the end of the mainshaft. Install the rear extension assembly and secure it with bolts. Replace and secure the driving flange. Torque the nut to 90–100 ft lbs. Assemble the bearing, oil seal, O-rings and driven gear and install the assembly to the extension housing, securing it with the bolt. Insert the three springs into their holes in the front face of the transmission case. Replace, if necessary, the oil seal in the clutch housing and install a new gasket to the front face of the transmission. Secure the clutch housing with bolts and washers. Replace the clutch throw-out bearing and sleeve and the release lever.

Reassemble the top cover as follows: Insert the plungers and springs into the cover and slide the 3rd/4th selector shaft into the front end of the cover. While the shaft is being slid into position, press down on the selector plunger so that the shaft will be able to pass over it and through the selector fork. The shaft should be inserted until its middle indentation engages the plunger, achieving the neutral position. Repeat the above procedure with the reverse shaft and selector. With the interlock plunger inserted into the 1st/2nd selector shaft, install the selector fork, sleeve and washer into the cover in similar fashion, ensuring that the shaft also passes through the 3rd/4th selector fork. Before the 1st/2nd selector shaft is pushed to its neutral position, insert the two interlock balls into the transverse bore which connects the shaft bores at the rear of the casting and then push the shaft further into the cover until the selector plunger engages the middle

Determining required thickness of mainshaft circlip washer.

Proper positioning of 4th gear baulk ring (36) in 3rd/4th synchronizer unit.

indentation and the balls and plunger are retained by the shafts. Use new tapered locking pins to secure the selector and forks to the shafts. Use sealing compound around the edges of the plugs before driving them into the ends of the selector shaft bores. Use a new pin to secure the fork to the shaft. If necessary, replace the "Metalistik" bushing in the shaft. Using new fiber washers, secure the shaft to the fork with the bolt and nut. Install new O-rings to the case and install the shaft through the bores of the case and through the selector. Use a new tapered locking pin when securing the selector to the shaft. Install the reverse stop bolt, locknut, nylon ball, spring and snap ring

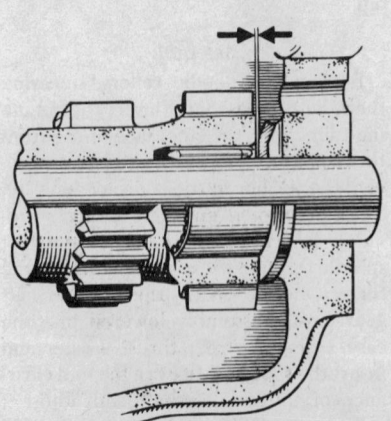
Countershaft rear thrust washer clearance

to the gear shift lever. Install the reverse stop plate to the cover and secure with the retaining screws. With the gearshift lever assembly positioned in the cover, install two new bushings to the lever, install the spacer tube, and secure the lever to the shaft with the retaining bolt and nut. Install the spring, cups, and cap over the gearshift lever. Adjust the reverse stop plate and bolt with the gearshift lever in the neutral position of the 1st/2nd gate. The clearance between the reverse stop plate and bolt should be 0.-010–0.050 in (0.26–1.27 mm) Reinstall the top cover on the transmission.

TR–6

Disassembly

Disassemble the top cover as follows: Remove the bolts, washers, top cover, and paper gasket. Remove the nut, cross pin, cover, and withdraw the gear shift lever assembly from the top cover. With the cover inverted, remove the plugs, spacer, springs, plunger, and balls. Detach the peg bolts. With the selector shafts in the neutral position, withdraw the 3rd/4th gear selector shaft, being careful to remove the interlock plunger and balls as they are released. Remove the 3rd/4th selector fork and spacer tube from the top cover. Repeat the preceding operation for the 1st/2nd and reverse gear selector shafts. Remove the retaining screws and take out the retaining plate. Remove the sealing rings from their recesses. If necessary, remove the peg bolts and remove the selectors from their shafts.

Disassemble the front cover: Remove the tapered bolt, bolt, and spring washer. Withdraw the crossshaft along with the release spring, release bearing, sleeve and fork. Remove the retaining bolts and remove the front cover, bolts, and plate.

Disassemble the rear extension: Remove the peg bolt and withdraw the speedometer drive gear assembly. Remove the cotter pin, slotted nut, and withdraw the flange. Remove the retaining bolts and detach the rear extension, using an extractor.

Remove the countershaft and reverse pinion shaft by removing the retaining screw and plate. Withdraw the input shaft assembly from the transmission. Remove the circlips, spacer washer, and withdraw the bearing. Detach the disc and, if necessary, remove the needle roller bearing.

Remove the circlip, spacer washer, and circlip, and remove the mainshaft rear bearing. After maneuvering the mainshaft assembly through the transmission top cover opening, lift out the countershaft assembly, thrust washers, and reverse gear. Remove the countershaft gears from the hub and, if necessary,

1. Thrust washer
2. Bushing—1st speed gear
3. 1st speed gear
4. Thrust washer
5. 1st speed synchro cup
6. 1st/2nd speed synchro hub
7. Synchro ball
8. Spring
9. Reverse mainshaft gear and synchro outer sleeve
10. 2nd speed synchro cup
11. Thrust washer
12. 2nd speed gear
13. Bushing—2nd speed gear
14. Bushing—3rd speed gear
15. 3rd speed gear
16. Thrust washer
17. Circlip
18. 3rd speed synchro cup
19. Synchro ball
20. Spring
21. 3rd/top synchro hub
22. Synchro sleeve
23. Top gear synchro cup
24. Circlip
25. Spacer washer
26. Circlip
27. Ball race
28. Oil deflector plate
29. Input shaft
30. Needle roller bearing
31. Mainshaft
32. Ball race
33. Circlip
34. Spacer washer
35. Circlip

36. Spacer washer
37. Rear ball race
38. Flange
39. Plain washer
40. Slotted nut
41. Cotter pin
42. Rear thrust washer
43. Needle roller bearing
44. Countershaft hub
45. 2nd speed counter-shaft gear
46. 3rd speed counter-shaft gear

47. Spacer piece
48. Countershaft gear
49. Needle roller bearing
50. Front thrust washer
51. Countershaft
52. Reverse gear shaft
53. Pivot stud
54. Nyloc nut and washer
55. Reverse gear opera-ting lever
56. Reverse gear
57. Reverse gear bushing
58. Locating plate
59. Screw

TR-6 transmission working components disassembled

remove the needle roller assemblies from the hub bore. Remove the circlip by driving a special tool beneath the circlip and then levering the 3rd gear forward to remove the circlip from its groove. Remove all mainshaft components, and remove the 1st/2nd and 3rd/4th synchronizer inner hubs from the outer sleeves (being careful to catch the springs and balls).

After disassembly is completed, clean all components and inspect for wear. The transmission case should be washed with solvent and inspected for cracks and burrs.

Assembly

Install the reverse gear in the transmission, with the selector groove to the rear. Install the reverse gear shaft, securing it with string to prevent it from sliding into the transmission. Use a stepped drift to drive a new needle roller bearing (with lettered face outward) into each end of the countershaft hub. Install the gears, spacer, and gear to the countershaft hub. Using grease to retain the countershaft thrust washers, install the washers into the transmission and lower the gear cluster into position. With the countershaft temporarily installed, measure the cluster gear end float, which should be 0.-

007–0.012 in. (0.1778–0.3048 mm). End clearance may be adjusted to within this range through the use of thrust washers of larger or smaller thickness. Remove the countershaft and drop the gear cluster to the bottom of the transmission case.

Assemble the synchronizer springs, balls and shims to the 3rd/4th synchronizer hub. Install the outer sleeve. Repeat the preceding operations with the 1st/2nd synchronizer unit. Check the axial release loads. The points of release should be as follows:

3rd/4th: 19–21 lbs
1st/2nd: 25–27 lbs

If the actual release loads observed are greater or less than those specified above, the correct loading may be achieved by adjusting the number of shims beneath each synchronizer spring.

Using a straightedge and a feeler gauge, measure the end clearance of each mainshaft gear on its bushing. The end clearance measured should be 0.004–0.006 in. (0.1–0.15 mm.), and may be increased by installing a new bushing and decreased by reducing bushing length. In the preceding adjustments, take care, as reduction of bushing length will cause the end clearance of the bush-

ings on the mainshaft to increase.

Install the thrust washer, bushings and thrust washer to the mainshaft, secure the assembly and measure the total end clearance of the bushings and thrust washers on the mainshaft. This measurement should be 0.003–0.009 in. (0.08–0.23 mm), and may be adjusted by using thrust washers available in the following thicknesses:

Color	Thickness
Plain	0.119 in. (3.02 mm)
Green	0.122 in. (3.10 mm)
Blue	0.125 in. (3.18 mm)
Orange	0.128 in. (3.25 mm)
Yellow	0.133 in. (3.38 mm)

Install the thrust washer, bushing, and thrust washer to the mainshaft. Using a special tool, assemble the race into position and install the washer and circlip. The race should be driven toward the rear to ensure that it is firmly against the circlip. Measure the 1st gear end clearance by gauging the distance between the washer and bushing. The end clearance should be 0.003–0.009 in. (0.08–0.23 mm.) and is adjustable by use of the various thrust washers described above. Prior

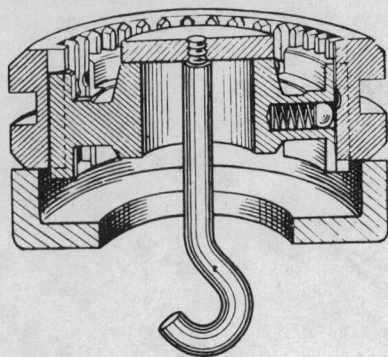

Checking synchronizer release load with spring balance.

to final assembly, all components should be removed from the mainshaft.

Assemble the mainshaft as follows: With the components placed in their proper relative positions, install them in the following order: thrust washer, gear and bushing, gear and bushing, thrust washer, a new circlip, 3rd/4th synchronizer unit with baulk ring at each side. Install a baulk ring to each side of the 1st/2nd synchronizer unit, slide the unit over the rear of the mainshaft and onto the larger splines. Install the washer, gear and bushing, and washer to the rear of the mainshaft. Pass the rear of the mainshaft through the rear bearing housing and position the shaft. With the mainshaft in position, a special tool is installed in place of the front cover. This tool consists of a plate that holds the front of the mainshaft in position. Install the circlip to the bearing and drive the bearing into position. Install the washer and circlip. Tap the rear of the mainshaft with a soft-headed mallet to take up the clearance between the circlip, washer, and bearing.

Install the disc, bearing (with circlip groove to the front), washer, and circlip to the input shaft. If necessary, a new bearing should be installed to the bore of the input shaft, with the lettered face of the bearing facing outward. Install the circlip to the bearing and install the assembly. Install the front cover as follows: With the lip of the seal toward the gears, use a special tool to drive a new seal into the front cover. With a seal protector protecting the oil seal, install the gasket and cover and secure with the retaining washers and bolts.

With a tapered pilot tool inserted to align the countershaft gears and thrust washers, insert the countershaft, pushing out the pilot tool. With the ends of the countershaft and reverse gear shafts engaged at the retaining plate, secure with the Phillips head screw. Install and secure the countershaft cover gasket and cover plate.

Assemble the rear extension as follows: Install a new gasket and the rear extension to the transmission and secure with

the retaining bolts. Install a spacer washer to the mainshaft and drive the extension ball bearing into position. With its sealing face forward, install a new oil seal. With the driving flange positioned on the mainshaft, install the washer and slotted nut. Tighten the nut to a torque of 80–120 ft lbs and install a new cotter pin. Install the speedometer drive gear assembly, and secure with a retaining bolt.

Reassemble the top cover: Install the selectors to their shafts and secure with the retaining bolts. Install new O-rings to the recesses in the rear of the top cover and install the retaining plate and secure it. With the interlock plunger positioned in the 3d/4th selector shaft, insert the shaft into the top cover. Install the selector fork, spacer tube, and retaining bolt. Install the interlock ball between the bores of the reverse and 3rd/4th selector shafts, using grease to retain the ball. Slide the reverse selector shaft into the top cover and engage it with the reverse selector fork and distance tube. Install the retaining bolt to the selector fork. With the reverse and 3rd/4th selector shafts in the neutral position, install the other interlock ball, using grease to retain it.

Install the 1st/2nd selector shaft into the top cover, inserting the shaft through the 1st/2nd selector fork and spacer tube. Install the balls and long springs to the 1st/2nd and 3rd/4th selector shaft detents. The springs may be retained by screwing the plugs so that they are flush with the machined lower face of the top cover.

NOTE: *From transmission number CT 9899, the 3rd/4th selector shaft ball and long spring have been replaced by a plunger and short spring identical to those of the reverse selector shaft.*

Install the plunger, short spring, and shim to the reverse selector shaft detent, and use the plug to retain the assembly. Use a spring balance to check the selector shaft release loads, which should be as follows:

Selector Shaft	Release Load
1st/2nd	32-34 lbs
3rd/4th	26-28 lbs
Reverse	26-28 lbs

If necessary, the spring loads may be adjusted by grinding the end of the spring (to reduce the release load) or by installing shims between the spring and plunger (to increase the load).

Replace the spring and plunger to the gearshift lever. Assemble the gearshift lever, spring and plate to the top cover, pressing the plunger with a screwdriver as the end of the gearshift lever engages the selectors. Retain the gearshift lever

Measuring end clearance of countershaft gears.

with the cap, cross pin, and nut. Install a new gasket and replace the top cover assembly to the transmission. Be sure that the reverse selector fork engages the actuating lever. Install the strap beneath the head of the rear mounting bolt.

NOTE: *With the modified gearshift lever installed in TR–6 models, the position of the gearshift lever is adjusted as follows: With the gearshift lever positioned into the 1st and 2nd gate, screw the locating pin clockwise until it just causes the gearshift lever to move, then turn the locating pin one-half turn in the counterclockwise direction and tighten the locknut. Move the gearshift lever into the reverse gate position and adjust the other locating pin in the same manner.*

TR–7

1. Remove the clutch housing.
2. Remove the top cover and interlock plate.
3. Remove the extension housing.
4. Remove the shift mechanism.
5. Remove the selector shaft and forks.
6. Remove the countershaft and let the countergear drop.
7. Remove the input shaft.
8. Install a support bracket, Triumph tool # 18G47BP, to the front of the case. Make sure that the center bolt and locknut are fully released before tightening the tool bolts.
9. Adjust the tool center bolt to fit the mainshaft and tighten the locknut.
10. Remove the reverse idler gear spindle, spacer and gear.
11. Remove the mainshaft bearing snap ring.
12. Remove the bearing-to-mainshaft circlip and remove the bearing using a puller. Remove the select-fit washer and speedometer gear.
13. Remove the support tool, without changing the center bolt setting.
14. Remove the mainshaft assembly.
15. Remove the countergear and thrust washers.
16. Remove the reverse gear lever.
17. From the mainshaft remove:
    a. thrust washer and 1st gear

b. 1st speed synchro

c. two split collars

d. 3–4 synchro hub and sleeve

e. 3rd synchro cup

f. 3rd speed gear retainer, gear, bushing, thrust washer, and retainer

g. 2nd gear and bushing

h. 2nd synchro cup

i. select-fit washer

j. select-fit washer locating ball

k. 1–2 synchro hub and sleeve

18. Mark the sleeve and synchro hub assemblies for reassembly.

19. Remove the needle bearings from each end of the countergear cluster.

20. Press out the reverse/idler bushing.

21. Clean and examine all parts for wear.

22. Coat the needle bearings with grease and install them in the countergear.

23. Install a dummy countershaft.

24. Assemble the 1–2 synchronizer and slide the sleeve into position matching up the marks made previously.

25. Check the load required to install the sleeve. It should fall between 19–27 lbs. Add or remove shims to adjust.

26. Assemble and install the 3–4 synchronizer in the same manner. Effort should be 19–21 lbs.

27. Install a new bushing on the reverse/idler gear. The bushing should be flush with the boss opposite the collar of the operating lever. Ream the bushing within 0.6585–0.6592″ diameter.

28. Check the countergear cluster end play. It should be 0.007–0.015″.

29. 1st gear end play should be 0.004–0.013″ between the split collars and thrust washer.

30. 2nd gear end play should be 0.002″ on the bushing.

31. 3rd gear end play should be 0.002–0.006″ on the bushing.

32. Adjust clearances by means of select-fit washers available on 0.003″ increments.

33. Install the input shaft.

34. Install the countershaft gear front and rear thrust washers, making sure that the tabs engage the casing slots.

35. Assemble the mainshaft components in reverse order of removal.

36. Install the mainshaft.

37. Place the reverse gear in the bottom of the case and install the reverse operating lever.

38. Install the bracket, 18G47BP to the front of the gear case, engaging the mainshaft.

39. Fit the snap ring to the mainshaft center bearing and slide the bearing onto the mainshaft with the snap ring last.

40. Drive the bearing into position.

41. Install select-fit washers to give a mainshaft end play of 0.002″. Install circlip.

42. Install the speedometer gear.

43. Remove the tool from the mainshaft and install the front bearing and snap rings, 4th speed synchronizer cup and input shaft.

44. Install the countershaft, displacing the dummy shaft.

45. Install the reverse gear, gearshaft and spacer.

46. Install the selector forks and shaft.

47. Install the selector mechanism.

48. Install the extension housing and flange.

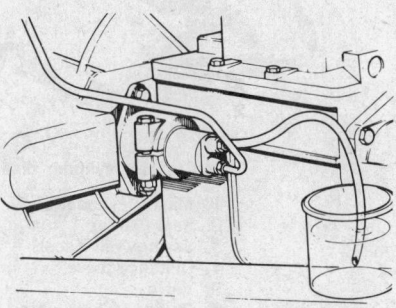

Clutch hydraulic system bleeding—Spitfire shown.

49. Install the three thrust springs to the counter gear front bearing.

50. Install the clutch housing, clutch release fork and bearing.

51. Install the drain plug, interlock plate and top cover.

CLUTCH

Removal and Installation

1. Remove the transmission.

2. In rotation, progressively loosen the bolts which retain the clutch assembly to the flywheel.

3. Lift off the clutch cover assembly (cover, diaphragm, driving plate, and pressure plate) and pull off the driven plate.

4. Installation is the reverse of removal.

Bleeding Clutch Hydraulic System

If the clutch does not disengage fully, air may have entered the hydraulic sys-

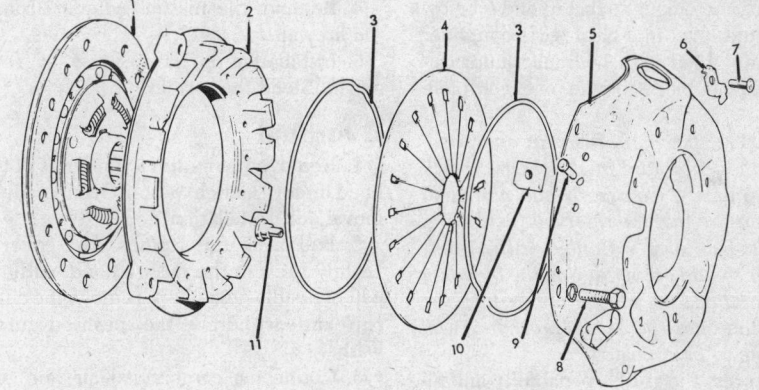

Borg and Beck clutch disassembled

1. Driven plate
2. Pressure plate
3. Fulcrum ring
4. Diaphragm spring
5. Cover pressing
6. Retractor clip
7. Rivet
8. Setscrew
9. Rivet
10. Balance weight
11. Rivet

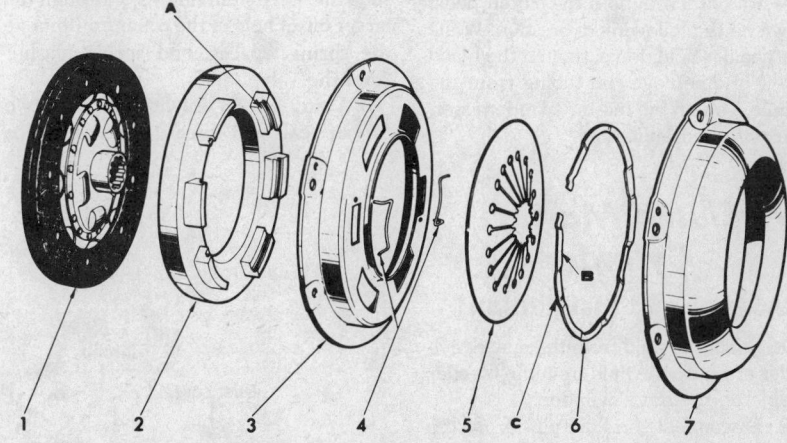

Laycock clutch disassembled

1. Driven plate
2. Pressure plate
3. Inner cover
4. Spring clips
5. Diaphragm spring
6. Circlip
7. Outer cover

Centering clutch with dummy shaft

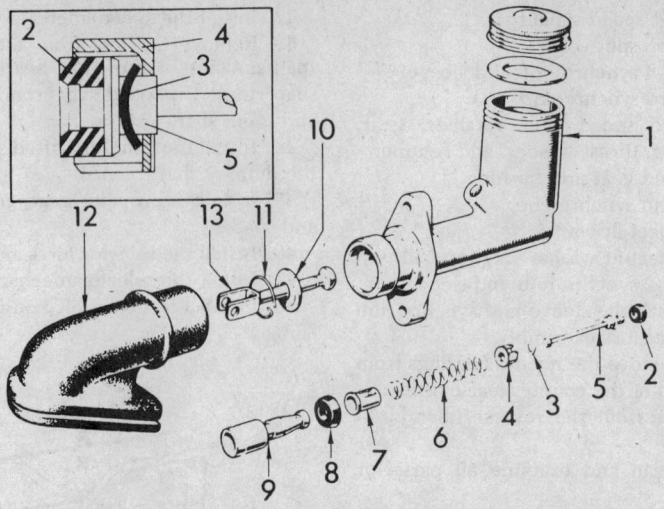

Clutch master cylinder disassembled—GT6 series shown.

1. Master cylinder body
2. Seal (valve)
3. Spring (valve seal)
4. Distance piece
5. Valve
6. Plunger return spring
7. Retainer
8. Seal (plunger)
9. Plunger
10. Abutment plate
11. Circlip
12. Dust excluder
13. Push-rod

tem through a break in the system or because the level in the reservoir has fallen too low. Bleed the system to remove the air.

Top up the clutch fluid reservoir to within ¼ in. of the FULL level. Clean the bleed nipple on the slave cylinder and attach to it a short length of tubing. Allow the tubing to hang so that its end is below the fluid level in a clean glass container partially filled with hydraulic fluid. Unscrew the bleed nipple one complete turn.

NOTE: *During the bleeding operation, the level of fluid in the reservoir will fall quickly. Constantly add new fluid to ensure that the reservoir is always at least half filled with fluid. If the reservoir should empty during the bleeding operation, air will be drawn into the system and the entire procedure will have to be repeated.*

Depress the clutch pedal fully and allow it to return normally. Repeat this operation, allowing a slight pause between each depression of the pedal. Note the appearance of the fluid being discharged into the glass container. When no bubbles are observed, hold the clutch pedal down on the following depression. While the pedal is held down, tighten the bleed screw and remove the tubing from the nipple. Top up the master cylinder reservoir with hydraulic fluid.

Clutch Master Cylinder

Removal and Installation

1. Drain the fluid from the master cylinder or pump the fluid from the bleeder nipple on the slave cylinder.

2. Disconnect the fluid pipe from the master cylinder outlet and plug the ends.

3. Pull back the protective dust cover and remove the cotter pin, washer, and clevis pin which retain the master cylinder pushrod to the top of the pedal.

4. Remove the master cylinder from the firewall.

5. Installation is the reverse of removal. Bleed the system.

Overhaul

1. Remove the master cylinder as outlined under "Clutch Master Cylinder Removal and Installation".

2. Pull back the rubber dust cover. Lightly press in the pushrod and, with a pair of needle nose pliers, remove the circlip and withdraw the pushrod and washer.

3. Connect a compressed air line to the outlet connection and, using light pressure, force out the internal parts.

4. Lift the leaf on the spring retainer and pull it free of the plunger.

5. Compress the return spring and slide the valve stem sideways through the larger offset hole of the retainer. Remove the spring, spacer, and spring washer from the valve shank.

6. Using fingers only, remove the two rubber seals and discard them. Replace with new seals. Clean all parts in methylated alcohol or in clean hydraulic fluid meeting SAE 70 R3 specifications. Lay all metal parts out to dry on a clean sheet of paper. Check the cylinder bore for pitting or scoring.

7. Reverse the above procedure to install, taking care to dip each internal part in hydraulic fluid prior to installation. Make sure that the rubber seals are installed with the lips facing the bore.

Clutch Slave Cylinder

Removal and Installation

1. On GT6 models, remove the transmission cover for access to the slave cylinder.

2. Drain the clutch hydraulic system by opening the slave cylinder bleeder nipple ½ turn and pumping on the clutch pedal.

3. Disconnect the hydraulic pipe.

4. Remove the nuts and bolts which

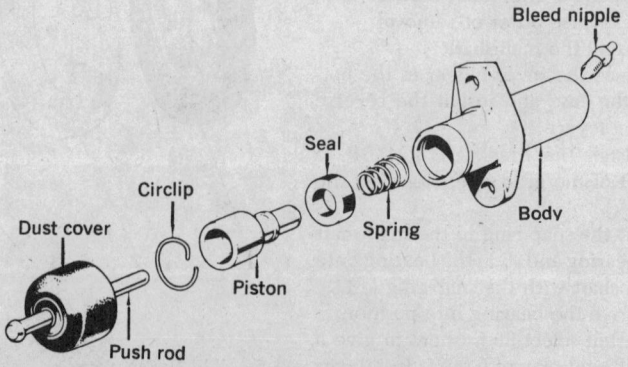

Clutch slave cylinder disassembled—GT6 series shown.

retain the cylinder to its bracket on the bellhousing. Remove the dust cover and pull the cylinder forward to clear it from the pushrod. Leave the pushrod attached to the operating shaft lever.

5. Installation is the reverse of removal. Bleed the system.

Overhaul

1. Remove the slave cylinder as outlined under "Slave Cylinder Removal and Installation".

2. Remove the rubber dust cover. Depress the piston and, using a pair of needle nose pliers, remove the circlip from the bore.

3. If the internal parts cannot be shaken out, use low pressure compressed air injected into the inlet port to force them out.

4. Remove and discard the rubber seal. Remove the return spring.

5. Clean all metal parts in methylated alcohol or in clean hydraulic fluid meeting SAE 70 R3 specifications. Lay out the parts to dry on a clean sheet of paper. Replace the cylinder body if its bore is pitted or scored. Lubricate the bore and dip each internal part in clean hydraulic fluid.

6. To assemble, insert the internal parts into the cylinder bore, using a new rubber seal. Be careful not to bend back the lips of the seal when installing in the bore. Retain the parts in the bore with the circlip.

7. Install the cylinder as outlined under "Slave Cylinder Removal and Installation".

DRIVE AXLES

Driveshaft and U-Joints

Removal and Installation

1. Remove the dashboard supports and transmission cover.

2. Remove the attaching nuts. Gently angle the transmission/engine forward to remove the driveshaft. Remove the driveshaft. Models with sliding splines do not require movement of the engine/-transmission assembly.

3. Installation is the reverse of removal.

U-Joint Overhaul

Disassembly

1. Remove the snap-ring from the forked end of the shaft. Tap the lug until the bearing cup is seen to protrude. Remove the cup with pliers.

2. Repeat the operation on the reverse side.

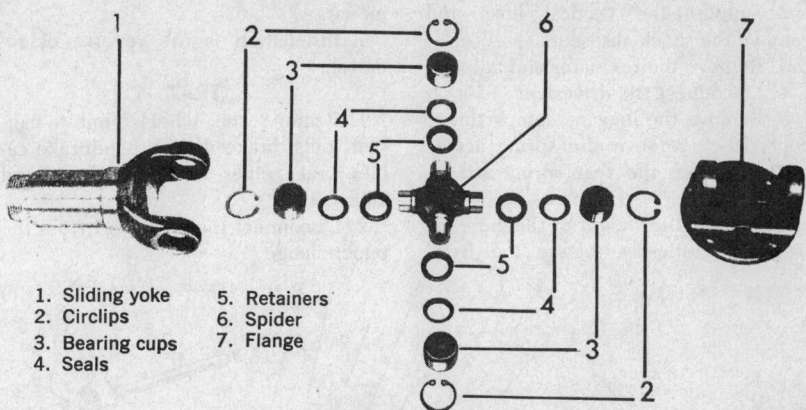

1. Sliding yoke
2. Circlips
3. Bearing cups
4. Seals
5. Retainers
6. Spider
7. Flange

Universal joint disassembled

3. Remove the flange.

4. Remove all remaining snap-rings. Rest the shaft on a block and gently tap out the remaining components.

Assembly

1. Place sealing compound on the shoulders of the new spider journals.

2. Fit oil seal retainers over the trunnions with a tubular drift. Fit the oil seals.

3. Place the trunnion into the bearing holes and fit the bearing caps and snap-rings. Make sure they are properly seated.

4. Fit the spider with the lubrication nipple toward the driveshaft. Place the other trunnion through the bearing holes in the forked end of the driveshaft and fit the cups and snap-rings.

5. Repeat the procedure on the second universal joint.

CAUTION: *Do not disassemble the sliding yoke for any reason.*

Outer Axle Shaft and Hub Assembly

Removal and Installation

All Models (Except TR–7)

1. Remove the wheel and backing plate. Remove the brake hose, attaching bracket, and brake line. Disconnect the handbrake from the attaching lever.

2. Relieve the shock absorber of load.

3. Release the radius arm.

4. Remove the universal joint coupling bolts.

5. Remove the shock absorber and jack.

6. Remove the spring eye nuts. The hub and axle shafts are now free.

7. Reinstall the vertical link to the spring attaching eye; leave the nut loose.

8. Install the shock absorber and radius arm.

9. Connect the inner and outer axle shafts. Place a load of 300 lbs in the front seats. Tighten the securing nut to the vertical link.

10. Further installation is the reverse of removal.

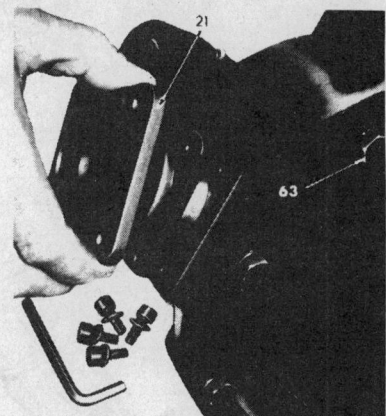

Removing inner axle shaft

Inner Axle Shaft

Removal and Installation

All Models (Except TR–7)

1. Remove the outer axle shaft.

2. Drain the rear axle.

3. Using a 3/16 in. Allen wrench, remove the Allen screws from the differential housing and remove the inner axle shaft.

4. Installation is the reverse of removal.

Halfshaft

Removal & Installation

TR–7

1. Remove the hub-to-halfshaft nut, brake drum, handbrake cable, brake pipe(s), back plate bolts, and remove the halfshaft and bearing.

2. Installation is the reverse of removal. Torque the hub nut to 100–110 ftlb.

Differential

Removal and Installation

All Models (Except TR–7)

1. Drain the rear axle. Remove the wheels and backing plate.

2. Support the vertical links and remove the shock absorbers.

3. Remove the resonator and tailpipe.

4. Disconnect the driveshaft.

5. Remove the luggage compartment floor panel; remove the spring access plate. Remove the rear spring attachments.

6. Support the weight of the differential and cautiously release the front mounts.

7. Installation is the reverse of removal.

TR-7

1. Remove the wheels, hub-to-half-shaft nuts, brake drums, handbrake cables, brake pipes, back plate bolts, and halfshafts.

2. Disconnect the driveshaft from the pinion flange.

3. Remove the differential-to-axle nuts and spring washers.

4. Ease the differential out of the axles.

5. Reverse the above to install. Torque the hub nuts to 100–110 ft lb.

Overhaul

NOTE: *Unless one has the experience and the special factory tools, especially the special spreader tool used by Tri-*

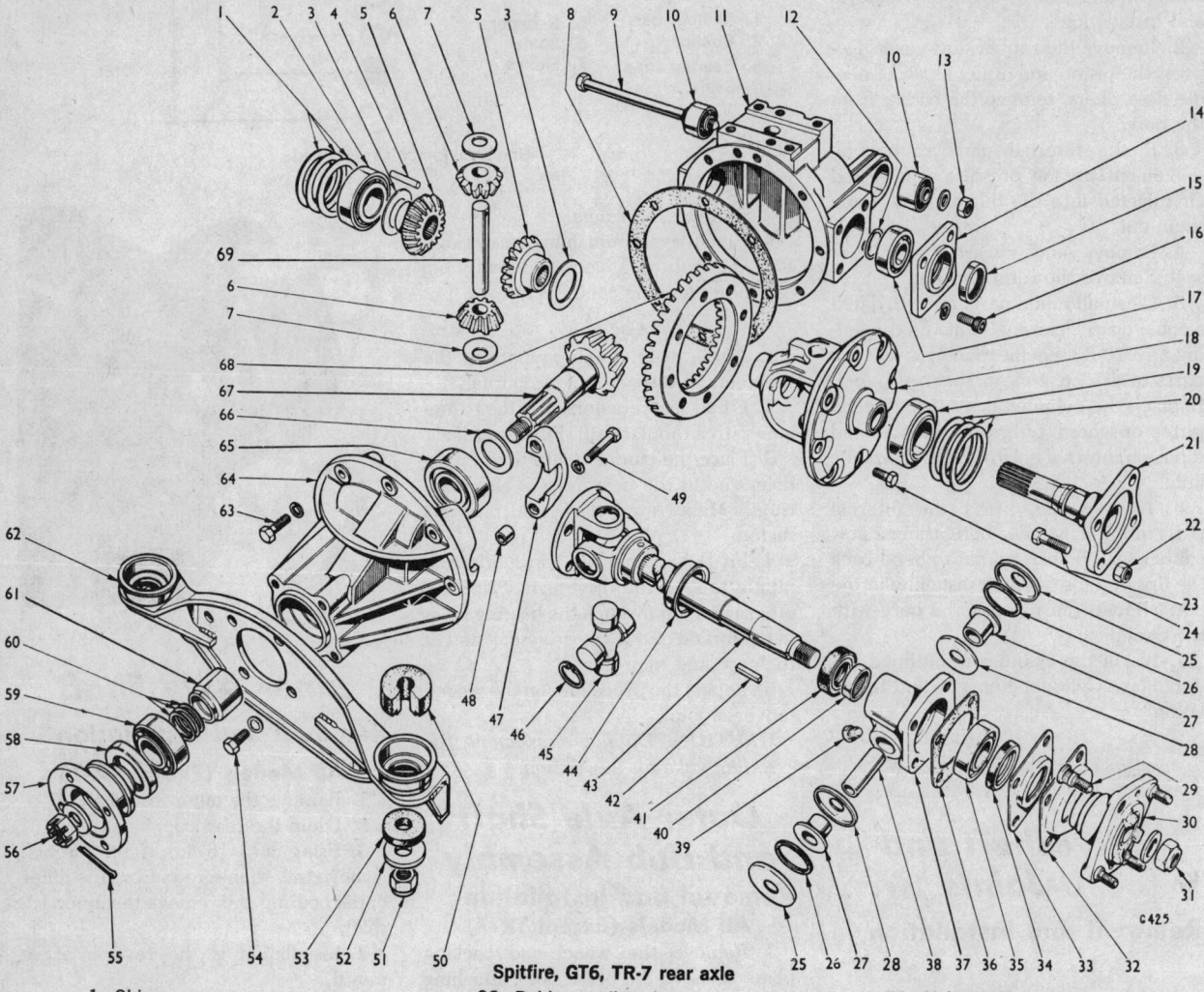

Spitfire, GT6, TR-7 rear axle

1. Shims
2. Differential side bearing
3. Thrust washer
4. Cross-shaft locking pin
5. Sun gear
6. Planet gear
7. Thrust washer
8. Gasket
9. Rear mounting bolt
10. Bushing
11. Hypoid rear casing
12. Circlip
13. Nyloc nut
14. Seal housing plate
15. Oil seal
16. Hexagon socket screw
17. Ball race
18. Differential carrier
19. Differential side bearing
20. Shims
21. Inner axle shaft
22. Nyloc nut
23. Bolt
24. Bolt
25. Shim

26. Rubber sealing ring
27. Nylon bushing
28. Shim
29. Stud
30. Hub
31. Nyloc nut
32. Grease trap
33. Outer seal housing
34. Seal
35. Ballrace
36. Gasket
37. Trunnion housing
38. Spacer tube
39. Grease plug
40. Needle roller bearing
41. Inner oil seal
42. Key
43. Outer axle shaft
44. Grease flinger
45. Universal joint assembly
46. Circlip
47. Bearing cap
48. Tubular dowel
49. Bolt
50. Mounting rubber

51. Nyloc nut
52. Plain washer
53. Rubber pad
54. Bolt
55. Cotter pin
56. Slotted nut
57. Coupling flange
58. Oil seal
59. Pinion tail bearing
60. Shims
61. Spacer
62. Mounting plate
63. Bolt
64. Hypoid nose piece casing
65. Pinion head bearing
66. Spacer
67. Pinion
68. Ring gear
69. Cross-shaft
70. Bolt
71. Lockplate
72. Brake backplate
73. Bolt
74. Nyloc nut
75. Vertical link

Luggage compartment floor panel removed showing rear leaf spring mounting bolts—Spitfire, GT6.

umph to spread the differential housing sufficiently to free the differential components, the overhaul of the differential assembly should not be attempted. The following specifications, torque figures, and tooth contact conditions are included for reference purposes.

Differential Overhaul

Spitfire, GT6, TR–7

1. Remove the differential.
2. Clamp the differential in a vise. Mark and remove the bearing caps. Remove the differential from the housing.
3. Press off the bearings and unbolt and remove the ring gear.
4. Drive out the pinion pin. Remove the side gears.
5. Remove the pinion flange cap and while holding the flange, remove the pinion shaft nut. Remove the flange.
6. Tap out the pinion assembly, and drive out the outer bearing and oil seal.
7. Drive out both bearing races.
8. Install the carrier bearings in the differential with the tapered ends toward the shafts.
9. Lubricate the bearings and install the carrier in the case.
10. Rotate the unit to seat the bearings and push the differential to one side of the case.
11. Install a dial indicator on the ring gear mounting flange and check and runout. It should not exceed 0.003″.
12. Slide the differential sideways to butt the bearing seats in either direction. Measure the lateral free-play.
13. Remove the differential and bearings. Lubricate and install the side gears.
14. Install the pinion pin. Check and record end-play.
15. Remove the pinion pin, rotate the sun gears to bring the planet gears clear of the case.
16. Lubricate the selected planet thrust washers and slide the thrust washers and planets into position. Install the pinion pin and again check end-play.

Zero backlash is required.

17. Install the ring gear assembly. Apply Loctite, or its equivalent, to the ring gear bolts.
18. Install the pinion inner bearing, spacer, washer and nut.
19. Tighten the nut gradually to obtain a 15–18 in lb. pre-load.
20. Using a dial indicator, check the measurements on the two bearing bores; add the measurements and divide by two. Twenty-two pinion head washers are available in sizes from 0.075–0.096 in.
21. Install the inner bearing. Install the pinion, spacer and bearing in the case.
22. Install a new spacer, oil seal, flange, washer and nut.
23. Gradually tighten the nut checking the bearing preload. Rotate the flange to seat the bearings and check the rotating torque. Tighten the nut to obtain a 13–20 in. lb reading.
24. Install the ring gear assembly into the case. Mesh the ring and pinion assembly. Move the ring and pinion fully in the opposite direction and check the measurement on the gauge. Check the mesh clearance.
25. To set the backlash, subtract the required backlash (0.005) from the recorded mesh clearance above. To this, add the required bearing pre-load divided by two.
26. To determine the shims required for ring gear side carrier bearing, subtract the result of step 25 from the figure recorded in step 12. To that, add the carrier bearing pre-load divided by two.
27. Install the necessary carrier bearing shims.
28. Install a spreading tool in the case and carefully stretch the case enough to permit the differential assembly to be installed.
29. Remove the spreader, install the bearing caps, bolts and spring washers.

TR–6

1. Remove ring gear and differential from case.
2. Remove the ring gear.
3. Install the differential in the case and check the flange runout. This should not exceed 0.003 in.
4. Remove the differential from the case, and press off the bearings.
5. Remove the cross-shaft locking pin and the cross-shaft.
6. Remove the planet and sun gears.
7. Remove the pinion shaft nut and the flange.
8. Remove the front mounting bracket and drive out the pinion shaft, inner bearing, spacer, and shim pack.
9. Drive out the outer bearing and seal.
10. Remove the bearing races.
11. Install the bearing races.

12. Install the outer bearing and seal.
13. Install the inner bearing, collar, flange, washer and nut.
14. Tighten the nut to obtain a pre-load of 15–18 in. lbs of preload.
15. Install a pinion gauge and dummy bearing in the case. Check the free-play to determine necessary shim thickness.
16. Install the mounting flange.
17. Install the pinion shaft and necessary shims.
18. Install the spacer flange washer and nut. Carefully tighten the nut while checking the pre-load. Torque the nut to 90–120 ft lbs. to obtain a pre-load of 15–18 in.lb.
19. Install the sun gears, planet gears and thrust washers in the housing. Insert the planet gear cross shaft and install thrust washers to obtain zero backlash.
20. Install the lock pin and secure by peening.
21. Install the inner carrier bearings, and install the case spreader.
22. Install the outer bearings to the differential and fit the differential in the case. Install a dial indicator and check the axial play of the ring gear flange.
23. Add to this measurement 0.003 in. pre-load. This figure is the necessary shim total.
24. Remove the differential and install the ring gear.
25. Install the differential.
26. Check the axial movement with a dial gauge.
27. Subtract the correct backlash (0.-004–0.006 in.) from this reading.
28. Install the necessary shim pack.
29. Release the spreader, install and tighten the bearing caps. Check the backlash at several points on the ring gear. An average reading of 0.004–0.006 in. should be indicated.
30. Install the rear cover and gasket.

Backlash between pinion and ring gears:
All: 0.004–0.006 in. (0.10–0.15 mm)
Pinion bearing preload, without oil seal:
TR–6: 15–18 in. lbs
GT6 and Spitfire: 12–16 in. lbs
Differential bearing preload, measured over both bearings:
All: 0.003 in. (0.076 mm)
Maximum run-out of ring gear, when bolted to differential carrier:
All: 0.003 in. (0.076 mm)

Differential Torque Figures

TR–6, TR–7

Ring gear to differential case: 40–45 ft lbs
Inner driving flange to inner axle: 100–110 ft lbs
Driveshaft flange to pinion:
TR–6:
90–100 ft lbs

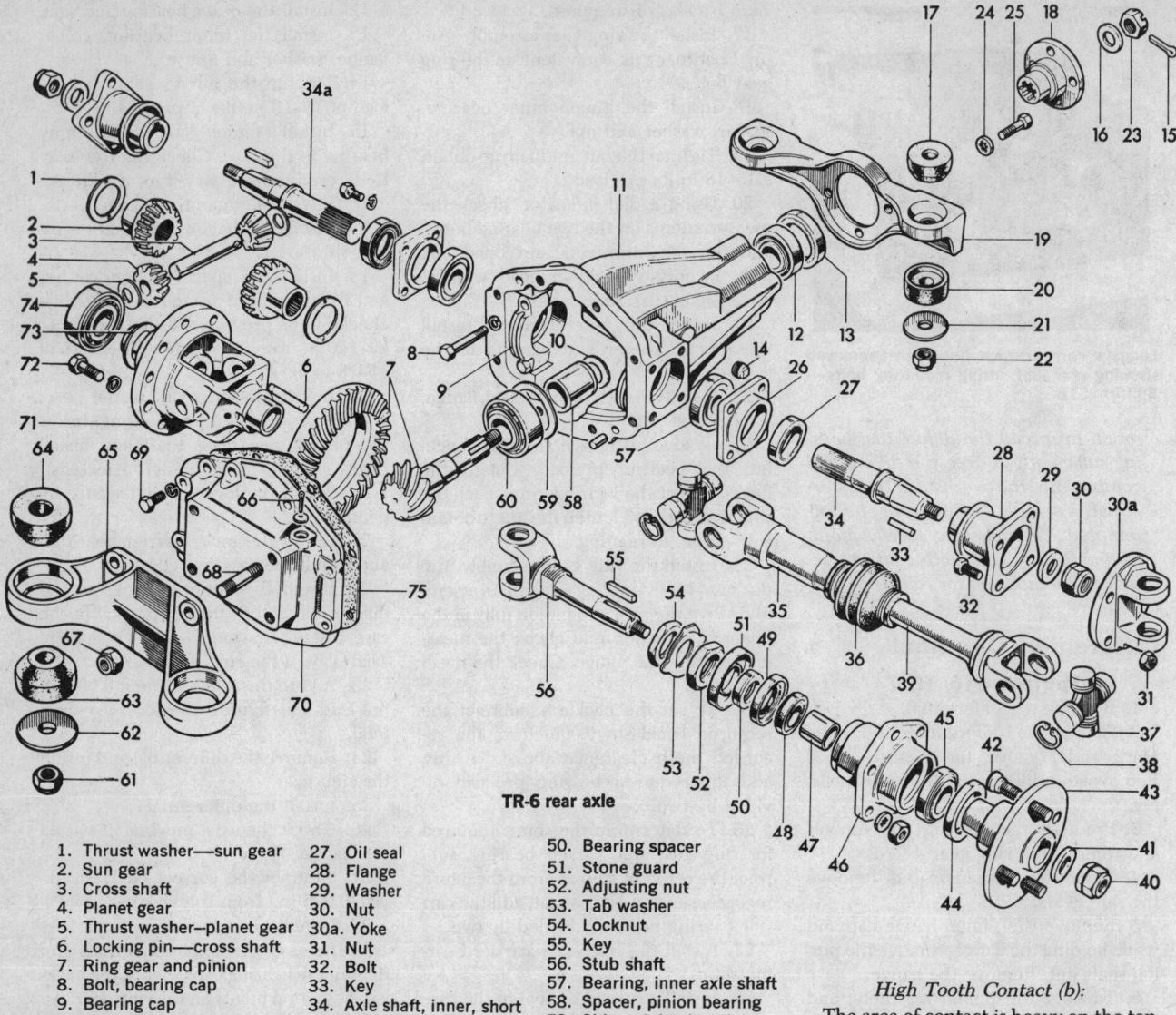

TR-6 rear axle

1. Thrust washer—sun gear	27. Oil seal	50. Bearing spacer
2. Sun gear	28. Flange	51. Stone guard
3. Cross shaft	29. Washer	52. Adjusting nut
4. Planet gear	30. Nut	53. Tab washer
5. Thrust washer–planet gear	30a. Yoke	54. Locknut
6. Locking pin—cross shaft	31. Nut	55. Key
7. Ring gear and pinion	32. Bolt	56. Stub shaft
8. Bolt, bearing cap	33. Key	57. Bearing, inner axle shaft
9. Bearing cap	34. Axle shaft, inner, short	58. Spacer, pinion bearing
10. Shim, pinion pre-loading	34a Axle shaft, inner, long	59. Shim, pinion locating
11. Axle casing	35. Axle shaft, fixed, outer	60. Head bearing, pinion
12. Tail bearing, pinion	36. Seal	61. Nut
13. Oil seal, pinion	37. Universal spider	62. Backing plate
14. Filler plug—oil level	38. Circlip	63. Buffer, lower
15. Cotter pin	39. Axle shaft, sliding, outer	64. Buffer, upper
16. Washer	40. Nut	65. Mounting, rear
17. Rubber buffer, upper	41. Washer	66. Cotter pin—breather
18. Companion flange	42. Wheel stud	67. Nut
19. Mounting, front	43. Hub	68. Stud
20. Rubber buffer, lower	44. Oil seal	69. Bolt
21. Backing plate	45. Hub bearing, outer	70. Rear cover
22. Nyloc nut	46. Bearing housing	71. Differential cage
23. Slotted nut	47. Bearing spacer, collapsible	72. Bolt
24. Lockwasher	48. Hub bearing, inner	73. Shim, pre-load
25. Bolt	49. Oil seal	74. Bearing, differential cage
26. Bearing retainer		75. Gasket, rear cover

GT6, Spitfire

Hypoid pinion flange attachment:
(GT6) 90–100 ft lbs
(Spitfire) 70–85 ft lbs
Rear hub to axle shaft: 100–110 ft lbs

Differential Tooth Contact Conditions

By painting about ten teeth of the ring gear with special paint, then moving the pinion into mesh with the painted teeth, it is possible to obtain a good impression of how the teeth are making contact. The following tooth contact conditions, along with their remedies, are keyed to the accompanying diagrams:

Ideal Contact (a):

The area of contact is distributed evenly over the tooth profile, and is closer to the toe than to the heel.

High Tooth Contact (b):

The area of contact is heavy on the top of the tooth profile of the drive gear. The pinion must be moved into deeper mesh with the drive gear.

Low Tooth Contact (c):

The contact area is heavy in the root of the drive gear tooth profile, and the pinion gear is meshed too deeply with the drive gear. The pinion must be moved away.

Toe Contact (d):

The contact area is concentrated at the small end of the driven tooth. To correct, the ring gear must be moved out of mesh by increasing the backlash.

Heel Contact (e):

The contact area is concentrated at the large end of the driven tooth. To correct, the ring gear must be moved into closer mesh with the pinion by decreasing the backlash.

CAUTION: *When decreasing the backlash, be sure to maintain the minimum backlash of 0.004 in. (0.10 mm).*

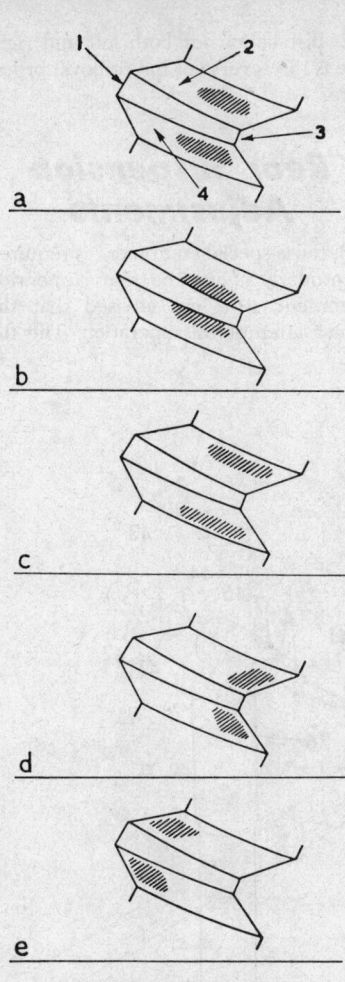

Gear tooth markings

1. Heel
2. Coasting side
3. Toe
4. Drive side

REAR SUSPENSION

Transverse Leaf Spring

Removal and Installation

1. Disconnect the brake lines. Disconnect the chassis bracket. Disconnect the handbrake.

2. Jack up the suspension vertical link. Disconnect the axle shaft and couplings.

3. On GT6 remove the radius arm mounting bolts from the chassis. Remove the shock absorber and lower vertical link.

4. Support the vertical link, and remove the eye bolt from the spring eye. Remove the luggage floor plate and slide the spring from the vehicle.

5. To replace the spring: align the spring in the recess in the differential casing. Make sure the bolt is in the correct

hole. (The spring is marked Front to indicate the proper position.)

6. Replace the studs in the casing. Make sure the shorter threaded end is down. Replace the spring clamp plate and fasten down. Install the luggage floor plate.

7. Connect the vertical link to the spring eyes. Do not tighten the spring eye nut. (Refit the radius arms at this point, if required.)

8. Raise the vertical link and install the shock absorber. Install the axle shaft. Install the handbrake brake lines.

9. Tighten the spring eye nuts with the car on the ground.

Coil Spring

Removal and Installation

1. Support the differential with a jack. Jack up the suspension arm.

2. Remove the wheel, disconnect the driveshaft, remove the shock absorber.

3. Being careful to avoid placing stress on the brake line, lower the suspension arm until the spring is free.

4. Installation is the reverse of removal.

Rear Shock Absorber

Removal and Installation

Spitfire, GT6

1. Block the front wheels. Jack the rear of the car and support the chassis.

2. Remove the wheel. Jack the vertical link to unload the shock absorber.

3. Release the lower end of the shock absorber and remove it.

4. Installation is the reverse of removal.

TR-6

1. Disconnect the shock absorber link to the suspension arm.

2. Lift the shock absorber arm and remove the link from the suspension arm, taking care not to misplace the two rubber buffers and buffer backing plates. Remove the shock absorber and link.

3. Clean away any dirt from the filler plug hole. Keeping the shock vertical, unscrew the filler plug and check the level of the fluid. Top-up to the bottom of the filler plug hole with the recommended shock absorber fluid.

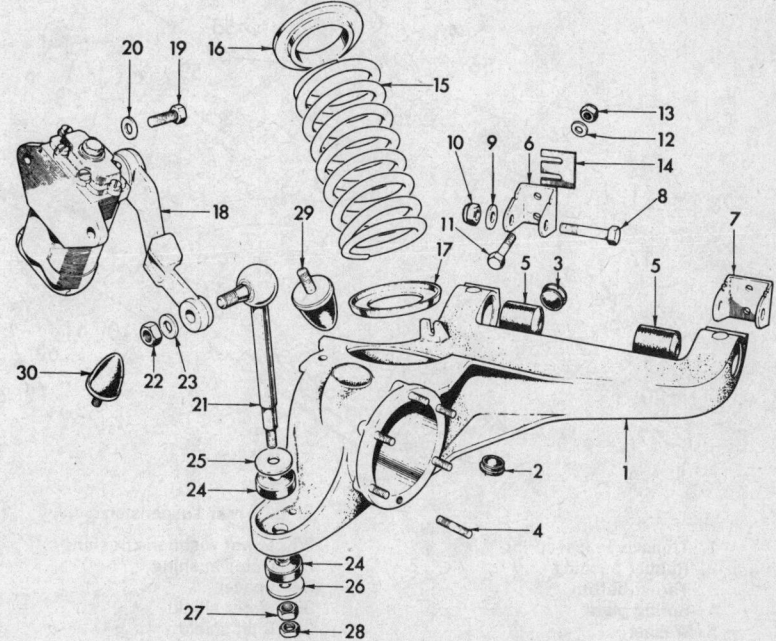

TR-6 independent coil spring rear suspension

1. Suspension arm
2. Rubber plug
3. Rubber plug
4. Stud
5. Metalastik bushing
6. Fulcrum bracket, inner
7. Fulcrum bracket, outer
8. Bolt
9. Plain washer
10. Nyloc nut
11. Bolt
12. Plain washer
13. Nyloc nut
14. Shim
15. Road spring
16. Rubber insulator
17. Rubber insulator
18. Shock absorber arm
19. Bolt
20. Washer

21. Shock absorber link
22. Nut
23. Washer
24. Rubber buffer
25. Backing plate
26. Backing plate
27. Nut
28. Locknut
29. Bump stop
30. Rebound rubber

Triumph

CAUTION: *Do not overfill the shock as the air space above the fluid is required for the proper operation of the unit. Move the shock absorber arm (lever) up and down a few times to force trapped air to the top of the unit. Recheck the fluid level. Replace the filler plug. Keeping the unit vertical, pump it several times. Discard the unit if it offers pockets of no resistance or if it becomes extremely difficult to move.*

4. Installation is the reverse of removal. Transfer the link to the new shock.

TR–7 Right side

1. Support the car, remove the wheel, gas cap and filler neck.
2. Unbolt and remove the shock absorber.

TR–7 Left side

1. Support the car, remove the wheel, access plate in the trunk, and unbolt and remove shock absorber.

2. Installation for both left and right side is the reverse of the removal procedure.

Rear Suspension Adjustments

Because special equipment is required to properly adjust the rear suspension alignment, it is not advised that the owner attempt this operation. The fol-

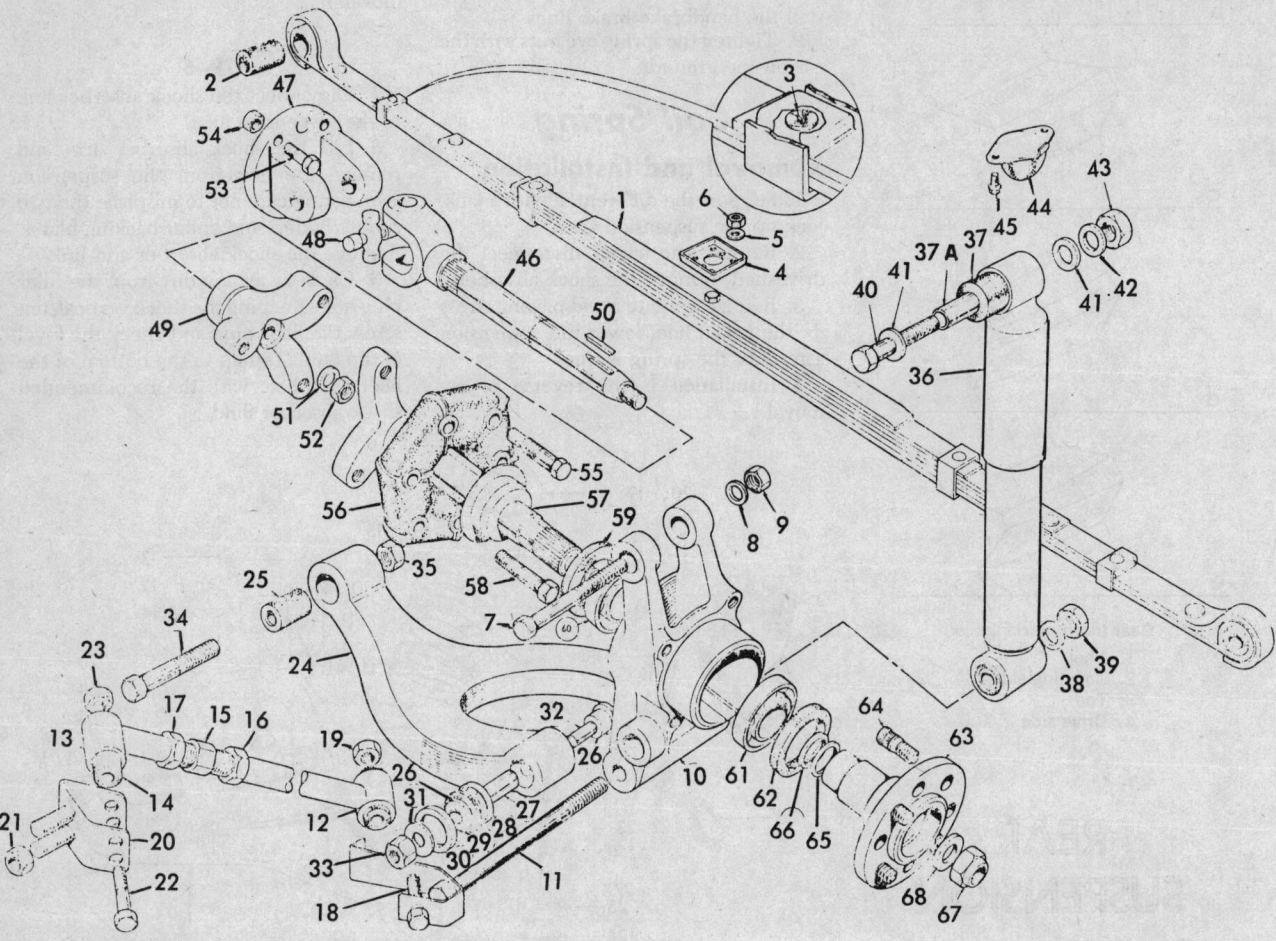

GT6 rear suspension

1. Transverse leaf spring	25. Lower wishbone bushing	47. Yoke flange
2. Rubber bushing	26. Outer bushing	48. Universal joint
3. Thrust button	27. Spacer	49. Driven flange
4. Spring plate	28. Water shield	50. Key
5. Washer	29. Dust shield	51. Washer
6. Nyloc nut	30. Water shield	52. Nyloc nut
7. Bolt	31. Washer	53. Bolt
8. Washer	32. Bolt	54. Nyloc nut
9. Nyloc nut	33. Nyloc nut	55. Bolt
10. Rear vertical link	34. Bolt	56. Rotoflex coupling
11. Bracket assembly	35. Nut	57. Outer axle shaft assembly
12. Radius arm rear eye	36. Shock absorber	58. Bolt
13. Radius arm front eye	37. Rubber bushing	59. Inner oil seal
14. Rubber bushing	37a. Sleeve	60. Inner bearing
15. Radius arm adjuster	38. Washer	61. Outer bearing
16. Locknut	39. Nyloc nut	62. Outer oil seal
17. Locknut	40. Bolt	63. Rear hub
18. Bolt	41. Washer	64. Stud
19. Nut	42. Washer	65. Adjusting spacer
20. Mounting bracket assembly	43. Nyloc nut	66. Shim
21. Nyloc nut	44. Rubber bumper	67. Nyloc nut
22. Bolt	45. Screw	68. Washer
23. Nyloc nut	46. Intermediate axle shaft	
24. Lower wishbone assembly	assembly	

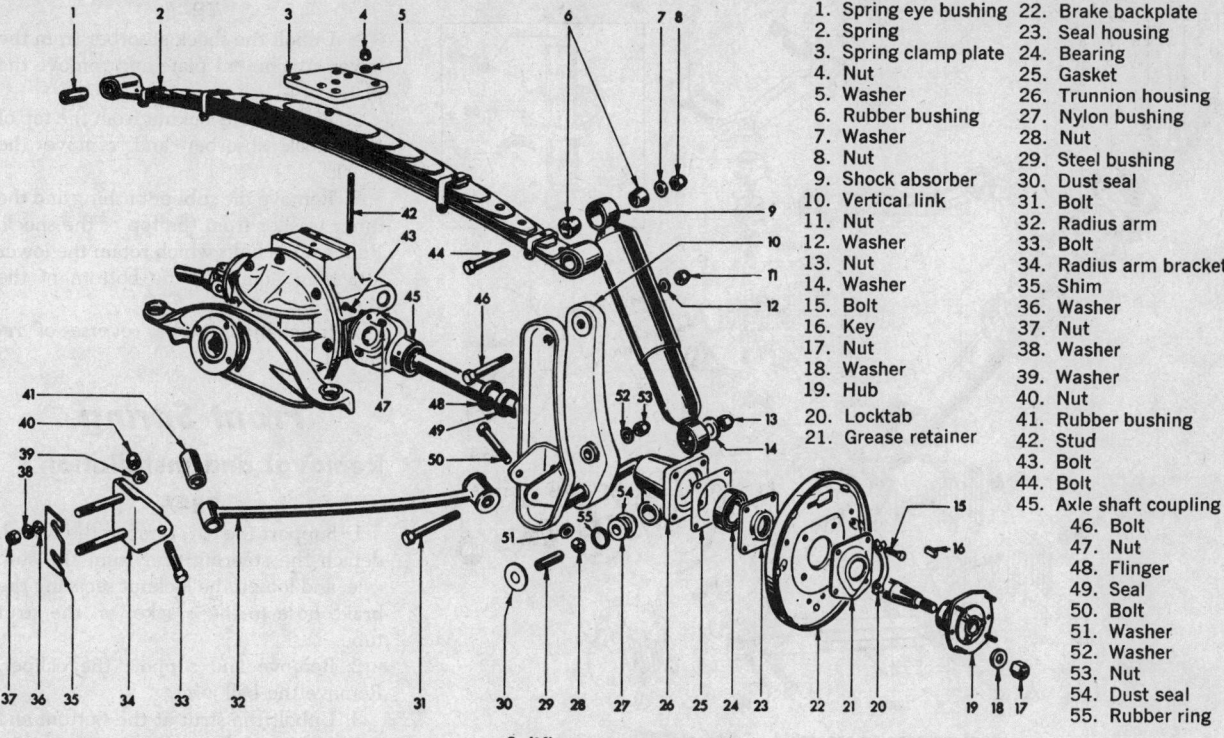

1. Spring eye bushing
2. Spring
3. Spring clamp plate
4. Nut
5. Washer
6. Rubber bushing
7. Washer
8. Nut
9. Shock absorber
10. Vertical link
11. Nut
12. Washer
13. Nut
14. Washer
15. Bolt
16. Key
17. Nut
18. Washer
19. Hub
20. Locktab
21. Grease retainer
22. Brake backplate
23. Seal housing
24. Bearing
25. Gasket
26. Trunnion housing
27. Nylon bushing
28. Nut
29. Steel bushing
30. Dust seal
31. Bolt
32. Radius arm
33. Bolt
34. Radius arm bracket
35. Shim
36. Washer
37. Nut
38. Washer
39. Washer
40. Nut
41. Rubber bushing
42. Stud
43. Bolt
44. Bolt
45. Axle shaft coupling
46. Bolt
47. Nut
48. Flinger
49. Seal
50. Bolt
51. Washer
52. Washer
53. Nut
54. Dust seal
55. Rubber ring

Spitfire rear suspension

lowing information is included for reference purposes.

Camber

Rear suspension camber angle is nonadjustable. If the camber angle is not within the specifications this indicates a weak or incorrectly set spring or excessive wear in the vertical link bushings (Spitfire, GT6) or in the suspension arm bushings (TR–6).

Toe-in/Toe-out

Rear wheel toe-in/toe-out is adjustable by means of shims. Toe-in/toe-out dimensions are influenced by vehicle load, rear spring rate, and wear factors in the vertical link linkage (Spitfire, GT6) or in the suspension arm linkage (TR–6). Unlike the front wheels, each rear wheel may be adjusted independently. Adding shims increases toe-out while removing shims decreases toe-out.

FRONT SUSPENSION

Front Spring and Shock Absorber

Removal and Installation

Spitfire, GT6

1. Loosen the bolt and nut which retain the steering trunnion to the lower control arm.
2. Unbolt the shock lower end.

3. Unbolt the front spring pad from its bracket.
4. Remove the spring and shock absorber assembly.
5. Installation is the reverse of removal. Tighten the shock with the weight of the car on the wheels.

Disassembly

Spitfire, GT6

1. Compress the spring and remove the locknut and nut which retain the shock absorber rod to its mounting flange. Remove the mounting rubbers, mounting rubber seats, and mounting flange from the shock.
2. Remove the spring compressor and remove the shock absorber from the spring.
3. Assembly is the reverse of disassembly.

Front Shock Absorber

Removal and Installation

TR–7

1. Remove the spring.
2. Using a ⅛ in. drill, remove the indentation securing the strut tube to the cap nut.
3. Remove the cap nut and lift out the cartridge.
4. Drill a ¼ in. hole to a depth of 1/16 in. at 90° to the existing notch in the cap nut.
5. Insert the cartridge and tighten the cap nut.

6. Peen the strut at a point locking the cap nut notch.

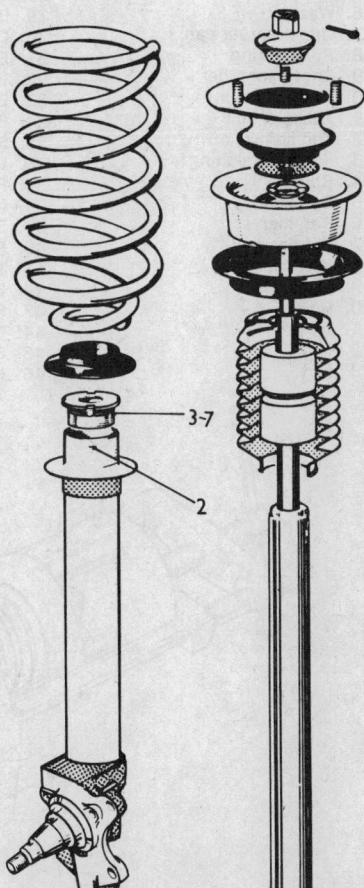

TR-7 front shock absorber showing strut tube (2) and tube cap (3).

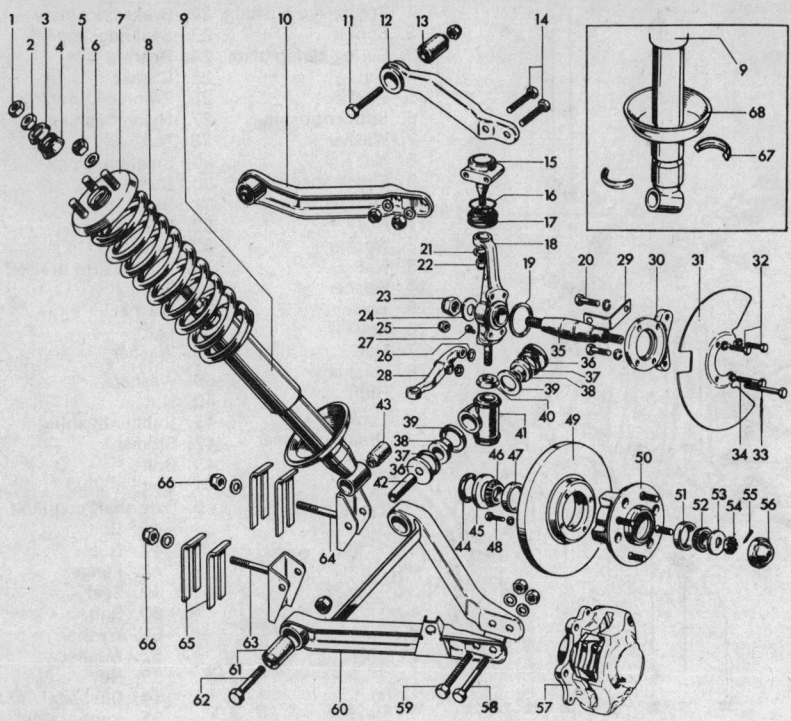

Front suspension assembly—Spitfire, GT6

1. Nut	24. Washer	47. Outer track
2. Nut	25. Nut	48. Bolt
3. Washer	26. Spacer	49. Brake disc
4. Mounting rubber	27. Plug	50. Hub
5. Nut	28. Steering arm	51. Outer track
6. Washer	29. Bracket	52. Inner race
7. Upper spring pan	30. Caliper bracket	53. Washer
8. Road spring	31. Dust shield	54. Nut
9. Shock absorber	32. Bolt	55. Cotter pin
10. Top control arm	33. Bolt	56. Grease cap
11. Fulcrum bolt	34. Bolt	57. Brake caliper
12. Top control arm	35. Spindle	58. Trunnion bolt
13. Fulcrum bushing	36. Dust seal	59. Shock absorber bolt
14. Bolt	37. Rubber ring	60. Lower control arm
15. Ball joint	38. Nylon bushing	61. Fulcrum bushing
16. Retainer	39. Dust seal	62. Bolt
17. Rubber seal	40. Rubber seal	63. Front fulcrum bracket
18. Vertical link	41. Trunnion	64. Rear fulcrum bracket
19. Rubber seal	42. Bushing	65. Shim
20. Bolt	43. Fulcrum bushing	66. Nut
21. Washer	44. Felt seal	67. Keeper
22. Nut	45. Seal holder	68. Lower spring pan
23. Nut	46. Inner race	

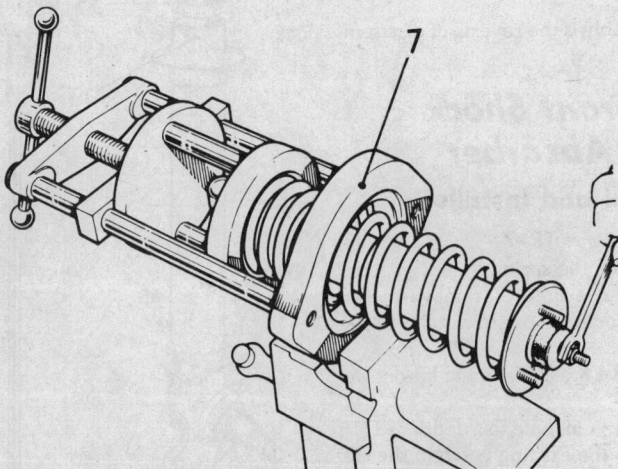

Disassembling front spring and shock absorber assembly using spring compressor (7).

TR-6

1. Unbolt the shock absorber from the lower attachment plate and remove the plate.

2. Remove the locknut from the top of the shock absorber and remove the shock.

3. Remove the rubber bushing and the inner washer from the top of the shock. Remove the bolts which retain the lower attaching points to the bottom of the shock.

4. Installation is the reverse of removal.

Front Spring

Removal and Installation

TR-7

1. Support the car, remove the wheel, detach the steering arm from the stub axle, and loosen the locknut securing the brake hose to the bracket on the strut tube.

2. Remove and support the caliper. Remove the ball joint.

3. Unbolt the strut at the bottom and swing it out of the way.

4. Compress the spring, unbolt the strut at the top and remove it from the car.

5. Installation is the reverse of removal.

TR-6

1. Remove the shock absorber.

2. Jack up the lower control arm until it is clear of the rebound stop. Disconnect the rebound stop and bracket assembly and lower the suspension. Remove the jack.

3. Compress the spring until the lower control arm assembly is horizontal. Use a wooden block between the top of the turret and the upper control arm for support.

4. Unbolt lower control arm from the spring pan. Remove the bump rubber. Replace the front lower control arm-to-spring pan bolt and bump rubber with ⅜ × 6 in. guide rods.

5. Release the spring compressor, until the spring is loose. Remove the spring pan, rubber collars, front spring, and spacer. Remove the four shock absorber lower attachment bolts.

6. Installation is the reverse of removal.

Ball Joint

Removal and Installation
All Models (Except TR-7)

1. Remove the ball joint stud washer and nut. Separate the ball joint from the vertical link.

2. Unbolt the ball joint from the lower control arm. Support the hub assembly.

3. Installation is the reverse of removal.

TR–7

1. Remove the bottom link, plastic boot, circlip and press out the ball joint housing.

2. Press a new ball joint and housing squarely into the bottom link. Do not apply pressure to the center of the housing end cap.

3. Install the circlip and plastic boot.

Upper Control Arm

Removal and Installation

Spitfire, GT 6

1. Support car, remove wheel; remove spring and shock absorber.

2. Unbolt and remove upper ball joint from upper control arm.

3. Unbolt and remove upper control arm.

4. Installation is the reverse of removal. Do not tighten control arm inner fulcrum bolts until the car is resting on the suspension.

TR–6

1. Support the car, remove the wheel, locate a jack under the lower control arm spring pad to take tension off the upper control arm, and remove the ball joint and vertical link.

2. Unbolt and remove the fulcrum bracket and upper control arm.

3. Installation is the reverse of removal.

Lower Control Arm

Removal and Installation

Spitfire, GT6

1. Support the car, remove the wheel and disconnect the sway bar from the lower control arm.

2. Unbolt the shock absorber at the bottom.

3. Unbolt and remove the control arm.

4. Installation is the reverse of removal.

TR–6

1. Support the car, remove the front wheel and spring.

2. Unbolt and remove the control arm.

3. Installation is the reverse of removal.

Front End Alignment

Toe-in

With the steering centralized, measure the toe-in. If adjustment is required, loosen the tie-rod end locknuts and the outer clip of the rubber seals. Rotate the tie-rod ends until the correct alignment is obtained. Note the reading and move the vehicle forward until the wheels rotate one-half turn, then take a second reading. This procedure allows for wheel rim run-out. Adjust the tie-rods to the mean of the

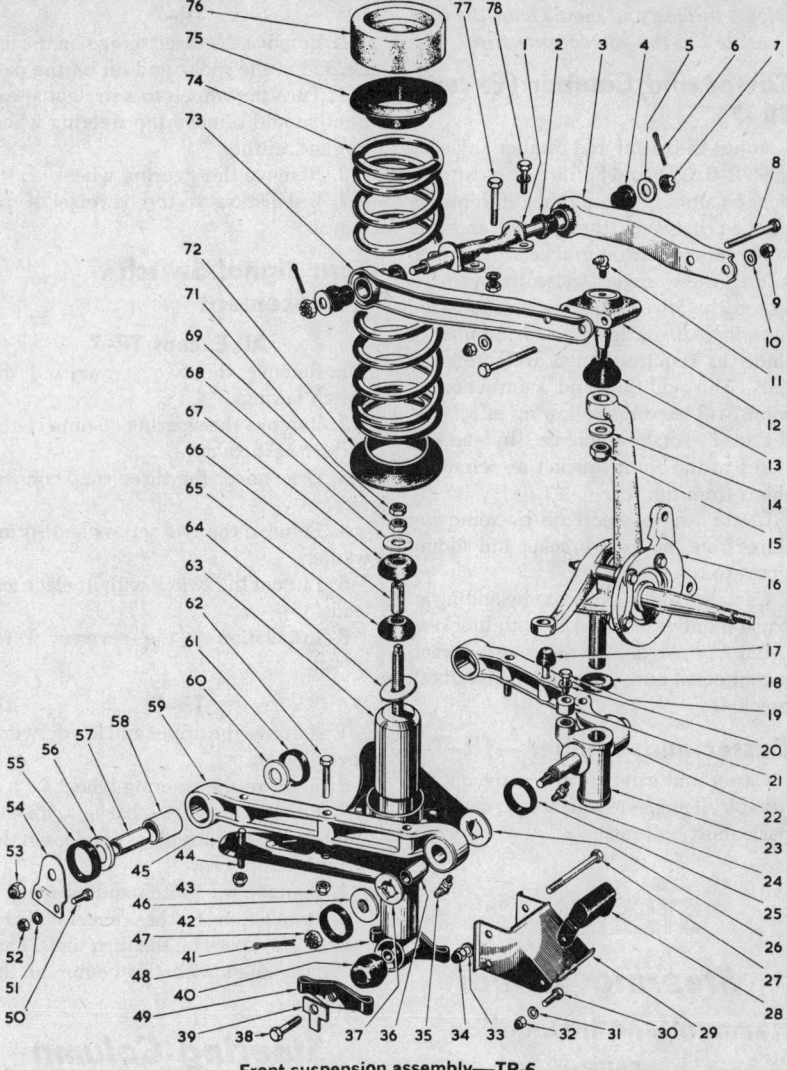

Front suspension assembly—TR-6

1. Upper inner fulcrum
2. Rubber bushing
3. Upper control arm—rear
4. Rubber bushing
5. Washer
6. Cotter pin
7. Slotted nut
8. Bolt
9. Nyloc nut
10. Plain washer
11. Grease nipple
12. Upper ball joint
13. Rubber seal
14. Plain washer
15. Nyloc nut
16. Caliper bracket and vertical link
17. Bump rubber
18. Rubber seal
19. Bolt
20. Spring washer
21. Lock stop collar
22. Lower control arm—rear
23. Lower trunnion bracket
24. Grease nipple
25. Rubber seal
26. Thrust washer
27. Bolt
28. Rebound rubber
29. Bracket
30. Bolt
31. Spring washer
32. Nyloc nut
33. Plain washer
34. Nyloc nut
35. Grease nipple
36. Bushing—nylon
37. Thrust washer
38. Bolt
39. Tab washer
40. Rubber bushing
41. Cotter pin
42. Rubber seal
43. Nyloc nut
44. Stud
45. Spring pan
46. Serrated washer
47. Slotted nut
48. Shock absorber attachment bracket—rear
49. Shock absorber attachment bracket—front
50. Bolt
51. Spring washer
52. Nut
53. Nyloc nut
54. Fulcrum bracket
55. Rubber seal
56. Thrust washer
57. Steel sleeve
58. Nylon bushing
59. Lower control arm—front
60. Thrust washer
61. Rubber seal
62. Bolt
63. Shock absorber
64. Washer
65. Rubber bushing
66. Sleeve
67. Rubber bushing
68. Washer
69. Nut
71. Locknut
72. Rubber collar
73. Upper control arm—front
74. Spring
75. Rubber collar
76. Spacer
77. Bolt
78. Bolt

two readings for greater accuracy. After adjustment, tighten the tie-rod locknut and rubber seal clips.

NOTE: *When checking toe-in or other suspension geometry, the vehicle should be static laden, on a smooth and* *level surface, and should have the tires inflated to the correct pressure.*

Caster and Camber (Except TR-7)

Adjust the caster and camber angles of the TR-6, GT6 and Spitfire front suspensions by altering the number of shims positioned between the chassis and the lower inner fulcrum brackets. When adjusting these angles, raise the vehicle, loosen the lower control arm mounting nuts, increase or decrease the number of shims as required, then retighten the nuts. The addition and subtraction of shims will have the following effects:

Caster Angle—increase by adding shims to the front bracket or removing shims from the rear.

Caster Angle—decrease by removing shims from the front bracket and adding shims to the rear.

Camber Angle—increase by adding an equal number of shims to both brackets.

Camber Angle—decrease by subtracting an equal number of shims from both brackets.

Caster and Camber—TR-7

Caster and camber angles are not adjustable. If angles are incorrect, damaged parts must be replaced.

STEERING

Steering Wheel

Removal and Installation

Spitfire

1. Pry off the steering wheel crash pad and the horn button.
2. Remove the horn brush connection.
3. Remove the steering wheel nut and washer.
4. Scribe alignment marks on the steering wheel and column.
5. Being careful not to jar the collapsible column, install a steering wheel puller and remove the wheel.
   CAUTION: *The use of a knock-off type puller may damage the column.*
6. Installation is the reverse of removal.

TR-6

1. Pry off the steering wheel crash pad and the horn button.
2. Remove the six bolts which retain the steering wheel to its support boss.
3. With the front wheels pointing straight ahead, scribe alignment marks on the support boss and steering column.
4. Remove the column nut and carefully pull the support boss from the upper inner steering column.
5. Installation is the reverse of removal.

TR-7

1. Remove the three screws on the underside of the spoke and lift off the pad.
2. Turn the wheels to a straight ahead position and remove the steering wheel nut and washer.
3. Remove the steering wheel.
4. Installation is the reverse of removal.

Turn Signal Switch Replacement

All Except TR-7

1. Remove the two screws and the switch fairings.
2. Remove the steering column clamp and harness cover.
3. Disconnect the three snap connectors.
4. Remove the two screws and spring washers.
5. Lift out the switch with its electrical leads.
6. Installation is the reverse of removal.

TR-7

1. Remove the upper and lower switch cover halves.
2. Remove the steering wheel.
3. Remove the wiring harness clip, disconnect the harness plugs and loosen the switch clamp screw.
4. Remove the switch and harness.
5. Installation is the reverse of removal. The arrow on the turn signal handle must align with the center of the column.

Steering Column Ignition Lock Switch

Spitfire, TR-6

1. Remove the steering column.
2. Remove the steering lock shroud and steering column tie-bar.
3. Either unscrew the shear-off bolts with a small chisel, or drill into the bolt heads and remove the bolts with an easy-out.
4. Remove the lock switch.
5. To install, position the lock switch to the column so that the switch dowel locates in the column drilling.
6. Install the steering lock shroud using two new shear-off bolts.
7. Evenly tighten the bolts until the heads shear.
9. Install the steering column.

TR-7

1. Disconnect the battery and remove the upper and lower switch cover halves.
2. Remove the wiring harness clip and disconnect the harness plug.
3. On vehicles with a key warning system, disconnect the single pin harness plug and the connect from below the steering column lock assembly.

4. Unbolt and remove the switch assembly.
5. Installation is the reverse of removal.

Manual Steering Gear

Adjustment

Adjust the end clearance of the pinion shaft. This should be as little as possible with the pinion still able to rotate freely. There are shims available in thicknesses of 0.004 in. and 0.010 in. to obtain minimal end clearance with free rotation. The second adjustment involves the damper cap. With the pressure pad and cap nut installed to the rack tube, tighten the cap nut to eliminate all end clearance. Measure the clearance between the nut and the housing. Put together a shim package that is equal to the clearance between the cap nut and the housing plus 0.004 in. (i.e., pack-clearance + 0.004 in.). Pack the unit with grease and install the cap nut, shim pack, spring, and pressure pad to the housing and tighten the cap nut. When the cap nut is correctly adjusted, a force of 2 lbs on a radius of 8 in. is required to rotate the pinion shaft. Check the unit and readjust if necessary by adding or subtracting shims from beneath the cap nut.

Removal and Installation

All exc TR-7

1. Place the vehicle on jack stands and remove the front wheels. Empty the cooling system and remove the bottom radiator hose.
2. Loosen and remove the bolt from the steering shaft coupling. Remove the steering rod end nuts. Pull the ball joints from the tie rod lever.
3. Remove nuts, U-bolts, and shims.

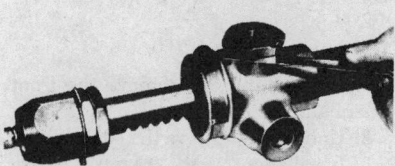

Measuring clearance between cap nut and housing.

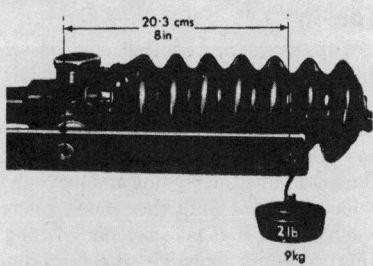

Measuring load required to turn pinion

Pull the steering unit forward. Remove the unit by pulling it through the wheel-well.

4. Count the number of pinion shaft turns required to move the gear from lock to lock. Return the shaft to the central position and move the steering wheel to straight ahead. Install the steering unit by placing the splined pinion shaft into the splined coupling.

5. Place the aluminum packing pieces behind the rack and the two front aluminum packing blocks into the dowels. These fit into holes in the rack tube.

6. Replace the U-bolts and nuts. Replace the unit in the car.

7. Place the taper pins of the tie rod ball joints into the steering levers and insert the steering washers and nuts. Replace the bolt and nut.

CAUTION: *Check the front end alignment.*

TR–7

1. Raise vehicle and set wheels to straight ahead position.

2. Scribe the pinion shaft and lower steering coupling.

3. Disconnect the rack tie rod outer ball joints from the steering arms.

4. Remove the pinch bolt securing the lower steering coupling to the rack pinion.

5. Remove the two bolts, spring washers and plain washers securing the pinion end of the rack to the sub-frame.

6. Remove the two nyloc nuts and washers and remaining bolts securing the rack to the sub-frame.

7. Disconnect the lower coupling from the pinion shaft, and remove the rack from the driver's side.

8. Installation is the reverse of removal.

BRAKE SYSTEMS

Adjustment

Disc brakes are inherently self-adjusting and therefore require no adjustments between pad changes. To adjust the rear drum brakes:

1. Block the front wheels. Release the handbrake. Raise the rear of the car so that both rear wheels clear the ground.

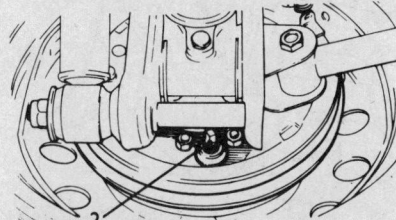

Rear drum brake adjuster (2)—Spitfire, GT6 shown; TR-6 similar

2. Turn the square-ended adjuster on the rear of the backing plate clockwise until the wheel is locked.

3. Back-off the adjuster a notch at a time until the wheel may spin freely when turned with one hand.

NOTE: *The TR-7 has self adjusting rear brakes.*

Master Cylinder

Removal and Installation

1. Remove both brake lines. Be careful not to let fluid drip out.

2. Pull out the rubber dust cover. Remove the clevis pin. (This is secured by a cotter pin.)

3. Remove the master cylinder.

4. Installation is the reverse of removal. Bleed the brakes.

Overhaul

1. Remove the master cylinder.

2. Drain the master cylinder and discard the old fluid. Remove the screws which hold the reservoir to the body.

3. Press down on the pushrod, remove the circlip, and pull out the pushrod, abutment plate, and circlip. Using an Allen wrench, remove the tipping valve nut and lift out the seal.

4. Depress the plunger and remove the tipping valve. Lightly shake the body to remove the internal parts. Pull the intermediate spring and plunger apart.

5. Raise the leaf spring of the spring retainer and lift out the valve assembly

from the plunger. Remove the spring, valve spacer, and washer spring from the valve stem.

6. Next, take the valve seal from the valve head end. Remove the seals from both plungers. Take the baffle and cap washer from the cap.

7. Replace all seals with new ones from the rebuilding kit. Thoroughly clean all other parts in clean brake fluid. Check the cylinder bore for any imperfections or coarseness. If any doubt exists as to condition, replace the cylinder.

8. Before assembling, lubricate all parts with clean brake fluid. Place seals on the plungers.

9. Place the valve seals, smaller end leading, on the valve head. Place the spring washer on the stem of the valve. It must be positioned with the flare away from the stem shoulder. Next, fit the valve spacer, legs leading.

10. Place the retainer on the stem, keyway first. Put the spring over the retainer; position the assembly on the plunger.

11. Compress the spring while the retainer is pushed behind the plunger head. To accomplish this, place the subassembly in a vise and place clean paper between each subassembly end and the vise jaws to prevent contamination.

12. Close the vise until the spring is nearly coil bound. Using a small screwdriver, press the spring retainer against the secondary plunger. Using needle nose pliers, depress the spring retainer leaf behind the plunger head. Be certain

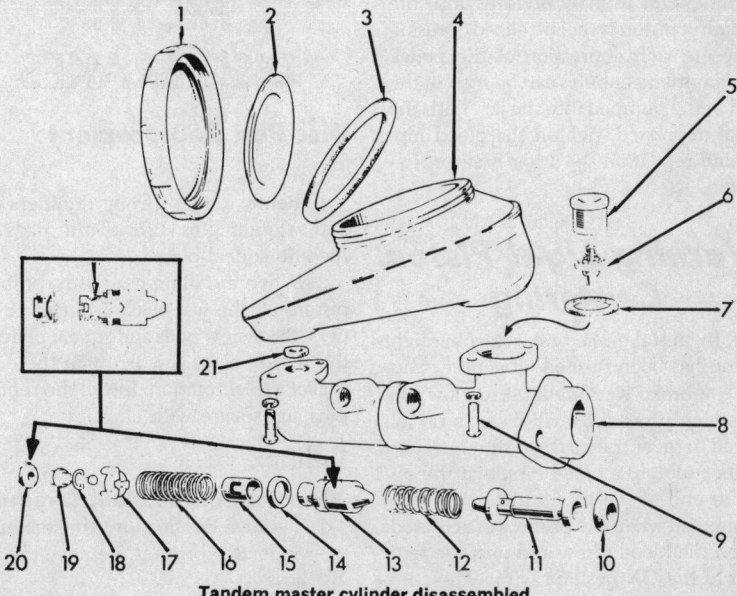

Tandem master cylinder disassembled

1. Cap	8. Body
2. Baffle plate	9. Screw—reservoir to body
3. Seal	10. Seal
4. Reservoir	11. Primary plunger
5. Tipping valve securing nut	12. Intermediate spring
6. Tipping valve	13. Secondary plunger
7. Seal—reservoir to body	14. Seal
	15. Spring retainer
16. Secondary spring	
17. Valve spacer	
18. Spring washer	
19. Valve	
20. Seal	
21. Seal—reservoir to body	

the retainer lead is properly aligned (straight) and is firmly located behind the plunger.

13. Place the spring between the plungers. Lubricate the plunger seals and the bore of the cylinder with clean brake fluid.

14. Fit the plunger assembly in the bore. Make sure the valve end is leading. Use caution to avoid seal damage. Press the plunger down into the bore and put in the tipping valve. Tighten the seal to 35–40 ft lbs.

15. Reassemble the cap washer and baffle to the cap. Place the cap on the reservoir. Assembly is now complete.

16. Install the master cylinder.

Hydraulic System Bleeding

In bleeding the rear brakes, turn the brake adjusters so that the shoes are locked against the drums. Note that the front brakes must be bled as one system, and the rear brakes as another. Attach a tube to the system bleed nipple that is farthest from the master cylinder, allowing the other end of the tube to hang submerged in a jar containing a small amount of clean brake fluid. Unscrew the bleed nipple about half a turn to allow the fluid to be pumped out. Press the brake pedal *lightly* without pushing through to the end of the stroke. If the pedal is pushed heavily or fully through its stroke, the pressure differential switch could be actuated, causing the brake warning light to glow brightly until the actuating piston is recentralized. Pausing between each depression of the pedal, pump until no bubbles can be seen in the fluid being pumped into the jar. With the pedal depressed, tighten the bleed nipple and repeat on the other brake of the system.

Warning Light Piston Centering

If, by mistake, the brake warning light piston has been pushed off center, causing the brake warning light to glow, the following procedure will have to be followed to recentralize the piston: Attach a rubber tube to a bleed nipple at the opposite end of the car to that which was being bled when the piston was actuated. Open the bleed screw and turn the ignition to the ON position without starting the engine. The brake warning light will glow, but the oil pressure warning light will be out. Push steadily on the brake pedal until the brake light dims and the oil light glows. As the piston returns to mid-position, a click will be felt on the pedal.

NOTE: *If the pedal is pushed too hard,*

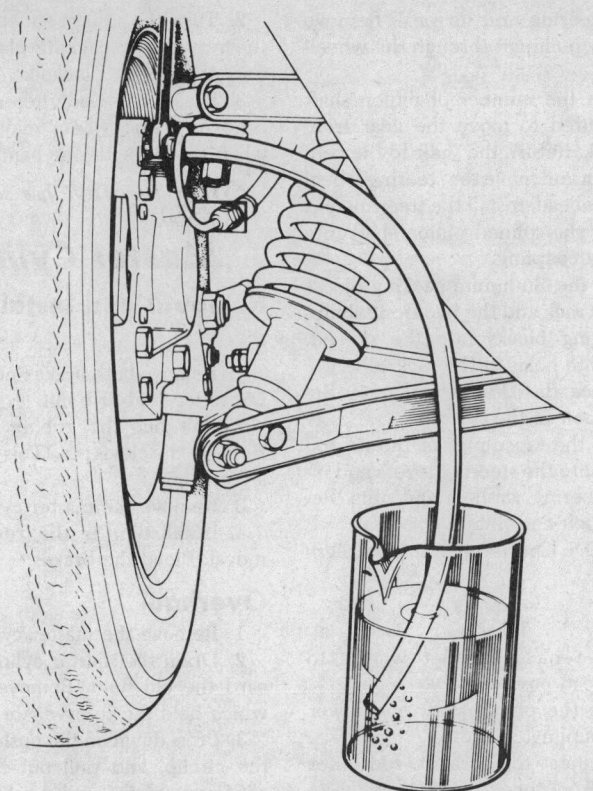

Bleeding front disc brake

the piston will move over to the other side, necessitating the repeat of the preceding operations at the other end of the car. Tighten the bleed screw.

FRONT DISC BRAKES

Disc Pad Replacement

1. Remove the spring retainers and pad retainer pins. Lift off the pads and the anti squeal plates.

2. When installing new pads, push the pistons all the way back into their cylinders. Place new pads and squeal plates on the wheel; place the arrow in the direction of wheel rotation. Install the retainer pins and secure with clips.

Caliper

Removal, Installation, Overhaul

1. Remove the line and the locknut at the supporting bracket. Remove the flexible hose.

2. Remove the bolts which hold the caliper to the support bracket; lift off the caliper and take out the pistons.

3. Remove the rubber seals from the recess. Replace all the components as needed; thoroughly clean all others. Oil all the parts and the bore with brake fluid.

Disc brake pad removal showing pads (4), spring clips (8), and pad retainer pins (9).

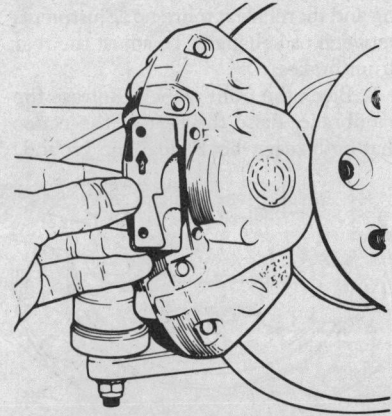

Installing brake pads with damping shim arrows pointing in direction of forward rotation

4. Place the piston seal in the cylinder recess. Locate the lips (projecting) of the dust cover in the cylinder recess. Place the closed end of the piston into the cylinder.

CAUTION: *Do not harm the polished surface.* Insert the piston to the furthest extent and engage the outer lip of the dust cover with the piston recess.

5. Install the caliper over the disc; place shims between the mounting bracket and the calipers.

6. Replace all hoses and bleed the system.

Brake Disc (Rotor)

Removal and Installation

1. Remove the caliper.

2. Remove the grease cap with a screwdriver. Remove the cotter pin, nut, and washer. Pull out the hub with the outer race and part of the inner race.

3. Remove the brake disc from the hub assembly.

NOTE: *Bearings, if needed, should only be replaced as a complete set.*

4. Install the outer bearing rings (taper outward).

5. Replace the discs. Put the inner races together and install the hub with the disc to the stub axle.

6. Install the washer and slotted nut while rotating the hub; finger tighten only. Loosen the nut to the closest cotter pin hole and mark the position by center punching the end of the stub axle and nut. Hub end-play should be 0.003–0.005 in.

If loosening the nut gives excessive play, remove the nut and file the rear face. This will correct the problem.

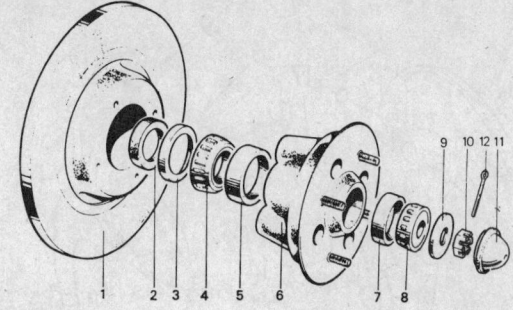

1. Brake disc
2. Oil seal
3. Oil seal cage
4. Taper bearing (inner)
5. Bearing track (inner)
6. Hub casting
7. Bearing track (outer)
8. Taper bearing (outer)
9. "D" washer
10. Slotted nut
11. Grease cap
12. Split pin

Spitfire, GT6 front hub details

Remove the nut, washer, hub, and races. Pack the hub with grease.

Place the new hub seal in the seal re-

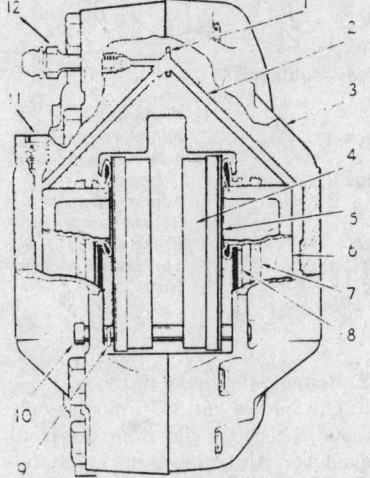

Disc caliper assembly cross-section

1. Rubber O-ring	7. Piston sealing ring
2. Fluid transfer channels	8. Dust cover
3. Caliper body	9. Retaining clip
4. Brake pad	10. Retaining pin
5. Anti-squeal plate	11. Flexible hose connection
6. Piston	12. Bleed nipple

tainer. Saturate the seal in engine oil and squeeze out the excess. Place the races and seal retainer on the hub. Be sure the seal faces inward.

Replace the hub assembly on the axle. Tighten the nut until the punch marks correspond; secure the nuts with a new cotter pin. Install the remaining parts. Be sure to replace any shims.

Wheel Bearing Adjustment

The end play of the front wheel bearings should be 0.003–0.005 in. and may be checked by a suitable dial gauge. The front wheel hub nut is provided with slots to accompany a securing cotter pin. In the event that a gauge is not available, rotate the hub, tighten the nut only sufficiently to remove looseness (5 ft lbs), then loosen the nut by one flat and secure it with a new cotter pin.

Removal and Installation

To remove bearings, remove hub and outer bearing. Reach inside hub and pull out inner bearing and oil seal.

1. Bolt
2. Spring washer
3. Nyloc nut
4. Plain washer
5. Dust shield
6. Stub axle
7. Caliper bracket
8. Tab plate
9. Bolt
10. Felt seal
11. Seal retainer
12. Bolt
13. Spring washer
14. Inner tapered race
15. Disc
16. Hub
17. Outer tapered race
18. Washer
19. Slotted nut
20. Cotter pin
21. Hub cap
22. Bolt
23. Bolt
24. Caliper unit
25. Vertical link
26. Plain washer
27. Nyloc nut
28. Distance pieces
29. Steering arm
30. Nyloc nut

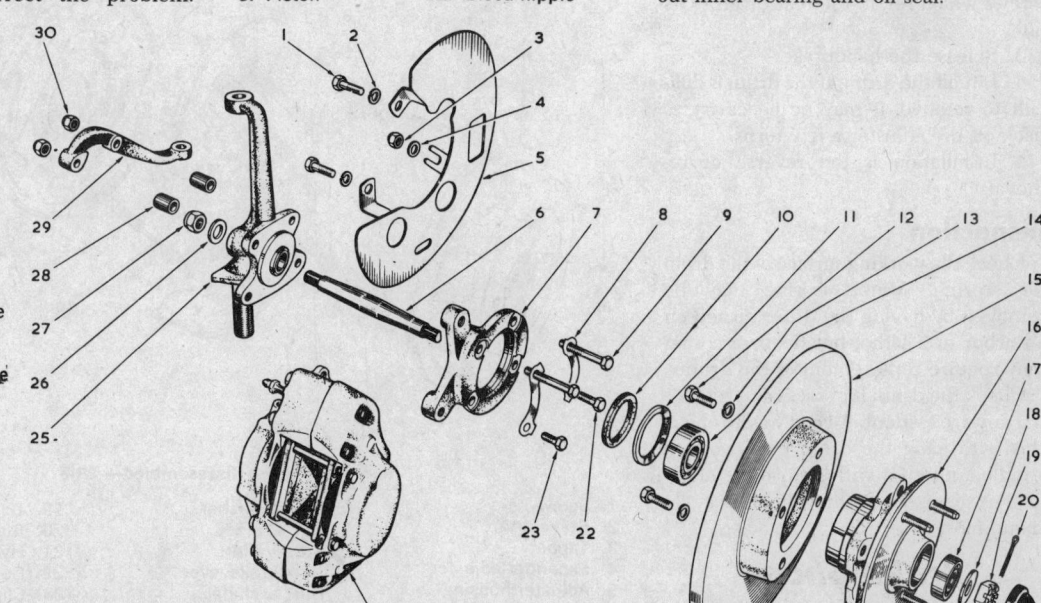

Disc and hub assembly—TR-6

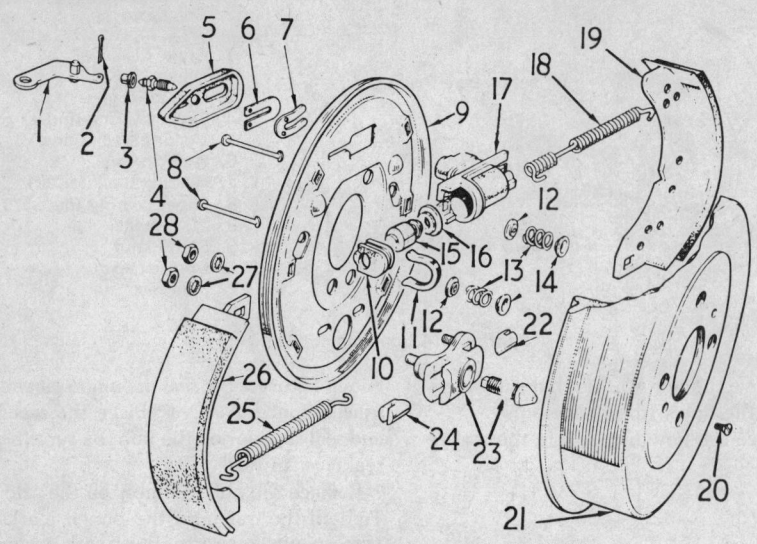

Rear drum brake disassembled—Spitfire, GT6

1. Handbrake lever	11. Clip	21. Brake drum
2. Cotter pin	12. Steady pin cups	22. Adjuster tappet
3. Dust cap	13. Springs	23. Adjuster wedge and
4. Bleed nipple	14. Steady pin cups	body
5. Dust excluder	15. Piston	24. Adjuster tappet
6. Retaining clip	16. Seal	25. Return spring
7. Retaining clip	17. Wheel cylinder	26. Brake shoe
8. Steady pins	18. Return spring	27. Shakeproof washers
9. Backplate	19. Brake shoe	28. Nuts
10. Dust excluder	20. Countersunk screw	

REAR DRUM BRAKES

Brake Drums

Removal and Installation

1. Jack up the rear of the car. Apply the handbrake.

2. Remove the two countersunk screws which retain the rear drum to its hub.

3. Release the handbrake.

4. Lift off the drum. If the drum is difficult to remove, it may be necessary to back off the adjuster a few turns.

5. Installation is the reverse of removal.

Inspection

Check the working surface of the drum for scoring. Minor scoring may be removed by having the drum turned on an arbor in a lathe, but deeper scoring may require replacement of the drum.

Check the drum for cracks and replace it if any are evident. A good way to check this is to hang the drum by a wooden handle and tap it with a small metal object. A cracked drum will emit a flat sounding note.

Brake Shoes

Removal and Installation

1. Jack up the car and support the chassis with jackstands.

2. Remove the brake drum.

3. On Spitfire and GT6 models only, remove the cotter pin from the handbrake lever. Also remove the brake shoe hold-down pins (shoe-steady pins), caps and springs.

4. On TR–6 models only, remove the spring clips, rotate the shoe-steady pins

90° and remove the pins.

5. Release the lower end of one shoe from the adjuster. Then release the upper end of the same shoe from the wheel cylinder.

6. Remove the brake shoe return springs, and lift off the shoes.

7. Installation is the reverse of removal. Shoe return springs are installed inboard.

Rear Wheel Cylinder

Removal and Installation

1. Remove the brake shoes as outlined under "Brake Shoes Removal and Installation".

2. Disconnect and plug the flexible brake hose.

3. Remove the protective rubber shield for the wheel cylinder from the rear of the backing plate and remove the horseshoe clip and spring plate which retain the cylinder.

4. Remove the wheel cylinder and handbrake lever assembly.

5. Reverse the above procedure to install, making sure to bleed the brakes.

Overhaul

1. Remove the wheel cylinder as previously described.

2. Remove the clip which retains the rubber boot to the cylinder body.

3. Remove the piston, rubber boot, and seal assembly from the cylinder body. Discard the old boot and seal.

4. Clean the piston and body in methylated alcohol or clean brake fluid

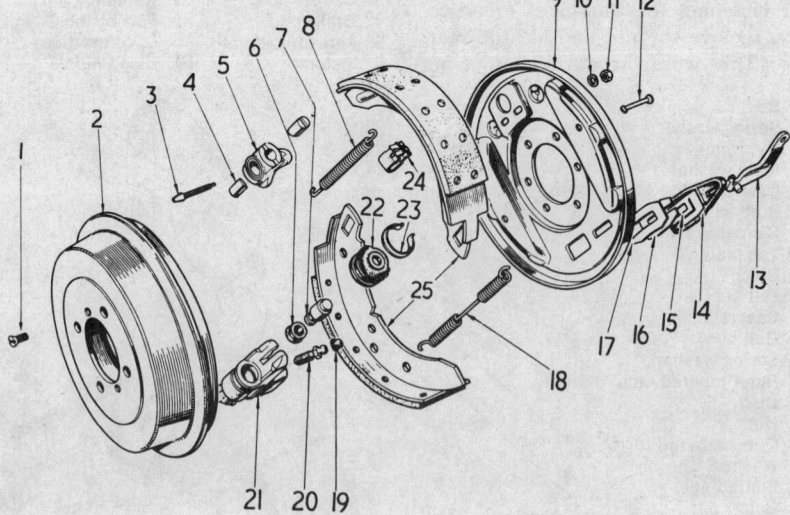

Rear drum brake disassembled—TR-6

1. Screw	10. Spring washer	19. Dust cap
2. Brake drum	11. Nut	20. Bleed nipple
3. Tappet	12. Steady pin	21. Hydraulic cylinder
4. Expander-adjuster	13. Handbrake lever	22. Dust excluders
5. Adjuster housing	14. Dust excluder	23. Clip
6. Piston seal	15. Abutment plate	24. Spring clip—steady pin
7. Piston	16. Spring plate—retaining	25. Brake shoes
8. Spring	17. Spring plate	
9. Backplate	18. Spring	

meeting SAE 70 R3 specifications. Replace the piston or body if either is corroded or scored.

5. Dip the cylinder bore, the piston, and a new seal in clean brake fluid and insert the piston and seal assembly in the bore.

6. Install the rubber boot and its retaining clip on the cylinder.

7. Install the wheel cylinder as previously described.

PARKING BRAKE

Cable Adjustment

Lift the rear wheels from the ground. Lock the brake drums by screwing each adjuster in to its fullest extent. Remove the spring and clevis pin. Adjust the clevis at each cable end by equal amounts to reduce play in the cable. The cable is overly tightened when the clevis pin cannot be inserted without straining the cables. Secure the clevis pin, hook up spring and adjust the cable brackets to give slight spring tension.

Parking Brake Cable

Removal and Installation

Spitfire (Front)

1. Remove the handbrake lever and disconnect the cable fork.

2. Disconnect the cable from the relay lever and pull the cable from the car.

3. Installation is the reverse of removal.

Spitfire (Rear)

1. Disconnect the compensator from the relay lever.

2. Unhook the cable return springs and forks from the backplate lever.

3. Remove the cable from the car.

4. Installation is the reverse of removal.

TR-6

1. Remove the clevis pins securing the cable forks to the backplate levers and remove the brake cable supports from the trailing arms.

2. Release the cables from the compensator.

3. Remove the cables.

4. Installation is the reverse of removal.

TR-7

1. Raise the body to allow access to the transmission tunnel.

2. Pull back the rubber boot and release the cable locknut.

3. Unscrew the cable from the operating rod.

4. Back off the nut to release the cable from the bracket and remove the cotter pin, washer and clevis pin retaining the cable to each operating lever.

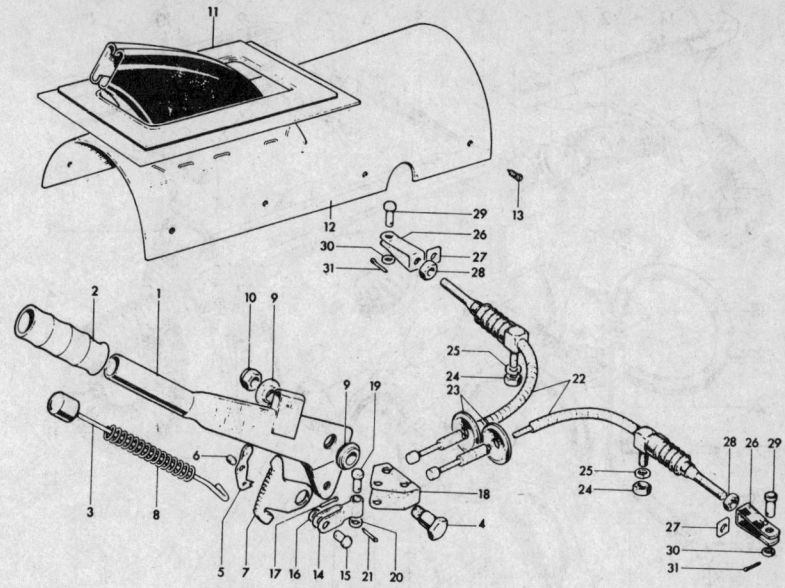

Spitfire, GT6 parking brake assembly

1. Handlever	11. Carpet trim	22. Cable assembly
2. Rubber grip	12. Cardboard cover	23. Rubber grommet
3. Operating rod, pawl	13. Screw	24. Nut
4. Fulcrum pin, hand-lever	14. Link	25. Lockwasher
5. Pawl	15. Clevis pin	26. Fork end
6. Pivot pin, pawl	16. Washer	27. Nut
7. Ratchet	17. Cotter pin	28. Locknut
8. Spring	18. Compensator	29. Clevis pin
9. Nylon washer	19. Clevis pin	30. Washer
10. Nyloc nut	20. Washer	31. Cotter pin
	21. Cotter pin	

5. Remove the trunnion nut and bolt, back off the nuts on the compensating levers and remove the cables.

6. Installation is the reverse of removal.

CHASSIS ELECTRICAL

Heater Assembly

Removal and Installation

1. Disconnect the battery and empty the cooling system.

2. Remove the heater hoses. Remove the screws which hold the water valve mounting bracket to the dash shelf. Push the bracket and valve assembly away from the dash.

3. Inside the car, remove the dashboard support bracket. Remove the passenger and driver's side parcel shelf. Remove the bracket which holds the choke and heater cable.

4. Disconnect the tachometer and speedometer cables from the back of the gauges. Pull the cables into the engine compartment. Be careful not to damage the cables or the grommet.

5. Remove the bolts which attach the heater box to the dash. Plug the heater lines. Lift out the heater.

6. Installation is the reverse of removal.

Blower Motor

Removal and Installation

1. Remove the heater.

2. Remove the screws which secure the inner and outer heater assembly.

3. Loosen the large nut in the center of the impeller. Remove the impeller from the shaft. Remove the exposed nut and lift out the motor.

4. Installation is the reverse of removal.

Windshield Wipers

Removal and Installation

1. Remove all electrical connections.

2. Make a mark on the domed cover and gearbox cover. Remove the four hold down screws. Move the gearbox and cover clear. Remove the exposed spring clip by pulling it sideways.

3. Take off the moving contact limiting switch. Remove the connecting rod.

4. Take the mounting bracket from the firewall. Move the unit to allow the

Triumph

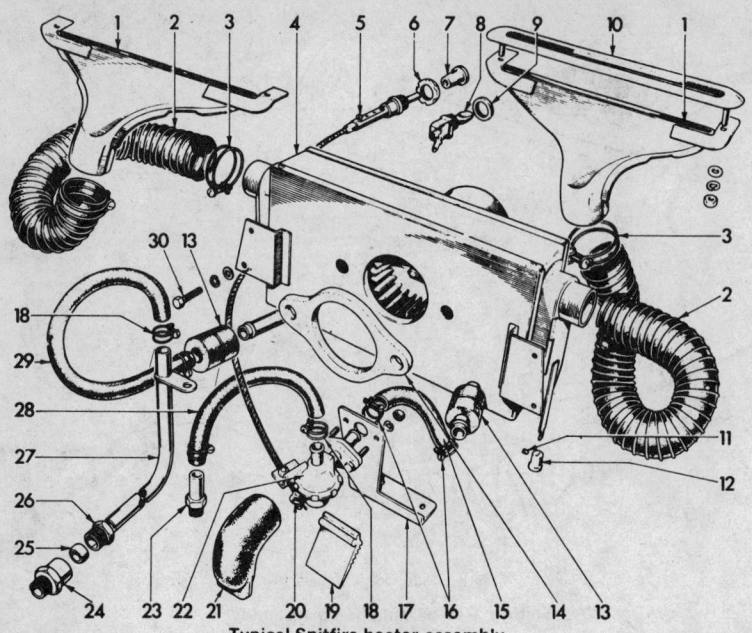

Typical Spitfire heater assembly

1. Defroster nozzle
2. Air hose
3. Hose clip
4. Heater unit
5. Heat control assembly
6. Bezel
7. Control knob
8. Blower switch
9. Bezel
10. Demister finisher
11. Screw
12. Flap knob
13. Sponge packing
14. Sealing ring
15. Water hose
16. Hose clip
17. Mounting bracket
18. Hose clip
19. Drain flap (from April 1964)
20. Water valve lever
21. Drain elbow (up to April 1964)
22. Water control valve
23. Adapter—cylinder head
24. Adapter—water pump
25. Sealing ring
26. Nut
27. Water return pipe
28. Water hose
29. Water hose
30. Bolt—heater attachment

vacuum assembly to be released. Remove the mounting bracket.

5. Installation is the reverse of removal.

Adjusting Wiper Stop (Park Position)

Loosen the four holding screws and rotate the domed cover. Rotate the cover either way until the desired stop position is achieved. Replace the cover and tighten down.

Radio
Removal and Installation

Radios used in Triumphs are dealer installed or after-market units, therefore, a common procedure is not possible.

Instruments
Removal and Installation

All instruments may be replaced individually from the back of the panel. On some models it may be necessary to loosen the panel screws to get at the instrument. Take care when working behind the panel since in most cases it is a tight fit and wires can be pulled loose without knowing it.

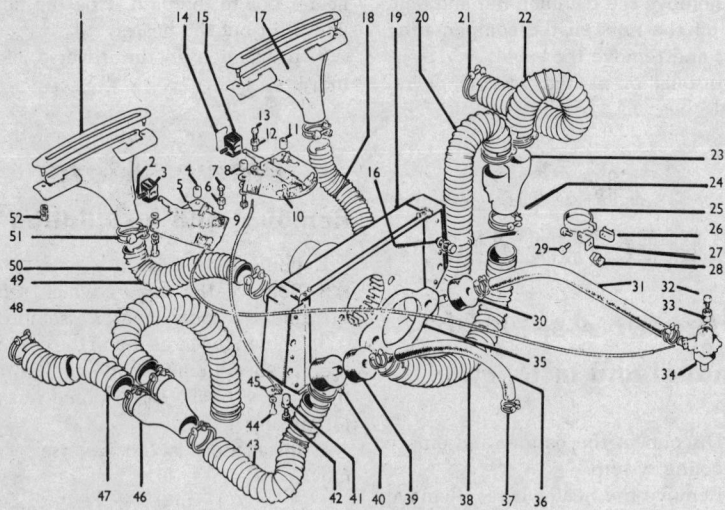

Typical GT6 + heater assembly

1. Demister outlet—capping
2. Grub screw—knob
3. Knob assembly
4. Spacer—control lever
5. Lever control—water valve
6. Trunnion—cable attachment
7. Screw—cable attachment
8. Spacer—control lever
9. Setscrew—lever control attachment
10. Lever control—ventilator and heater motor
11. Spacer—control lever
12. Trunnion ⎱ Cable
13. Screw ⎰ attachment
14. Pull boast—label
15. Knob assembly
16. Setscrew—heater attachment
17. Demister nozzle
18. Hose demister
19. Heater unit assembly
20. Hose "Y" piece to foot level vent
21. Hose clip
22. Hose "Y" piece to facia level vent
23. "Y" piece
24. Hose clip
25. Clip "Y" piece retainer
26. Fix nut
27. Bracket "Y" piece clip
28. Fix nut
29. Setscrew—bracket attachment
30. Seal—inlet and outlet pipes
31. Hose—water to valve heater
32. Screw ⎱ Cable to
33. Trunnion ⎰ water valve
34. Water control valve
35. Seal—heater blower
36. Hose—water return
37. Hose clip
38. Hose—heater to "Y" piece
39. Seal—inlet and outlet pipes
40. Hose clip
41. Trunnion ⎱ Cable
42. Screw ⎰ attachment
43. Hose—heater to "Y" piece
44. Setscrew—cable clamp attachment
45. Cable clamp
46. "Y" piece
47. Hose "Y" piece to face level vent
48. Hose "Y" piece to face level vent
49. Hose—demister
50. Setscrew—lever control attachment
51. Hose clip
52. Nut—demister nozzle attachment

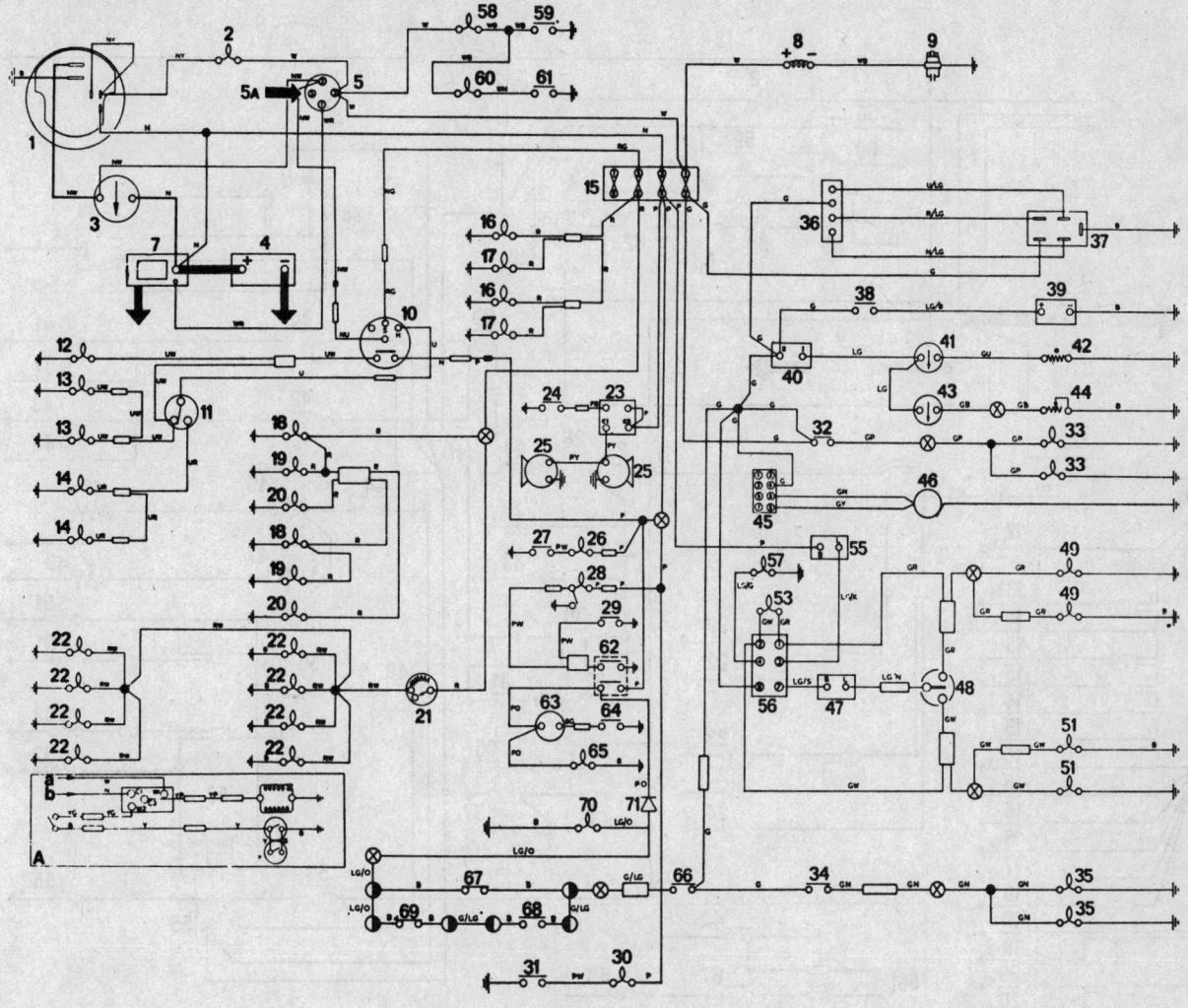

1972-74 TR-6 (1974 starter interlock not shown)

1. Alternator	26. Glovebox illumination	55. Hazard flasher unit
2. Ignition warning light	27. Glovebox illumination switch	56. Hazard switch
3. Ammeter	28. Transmission tunnel lamp	57. Hazard warning light
4. Battery	29. R.H. door switch	58. Brake line failure warning light
5. Ignition/starter switch	30. Trunk lamp	59. Brake line failure switch
5A. Ignition/starter switch	31. Trunk lamp switch	60. Oil prtssure warning light
radio supply connector	32. Stop lamp switch	61. Oil pressure switch
7. Starter motor	33. Stop lamp	62. L.H. door switch
8. Ignition coil	34. Back-up lamp switch	63. Buzzer
9. Ignition distributor	35. Back-up lamp	64. Key switch
10. Column light switch	36. Windshield wiper switch	65. Key light
11. Dimmer switch	37. Windshield wiper motor	66. Belt warning transmission switch
12. High beam warning light	38. Windshield washer switch	67. Drivers belt switch
13. High beam	39. Windshield washer pump	68. Passengers seat switch
14. Low beam	40. Voltage sabilizer	69. Passengers belt switch
15. Fuse box	41. Temperature indicator	70. Belt warning light
16. Front parking lamp	42. Temperature transmitter	71. Diode
17. Front marker lamp	43. Fuel indicator	
18. Rear marker lamp	44. Fuel tank unit	
19. Tail lamp	45. Heater switch	
20. Plate illumination lamp	46. Heater motor	**COLOR CODE**
21. Panel rheostat	47. Turn signal flasher unit	
22. Instrument illumination	48. Turn signal switch	N Brown LG Light Green
23. Horn relay	49. L.H. Flasher lamp	U Blue W White
24. Horn push	51. R.H. Flasher lamp	R Red Y Yellow
25. Horn	53. Turn signal warning light	P Purple S Slate
		G Green B Black

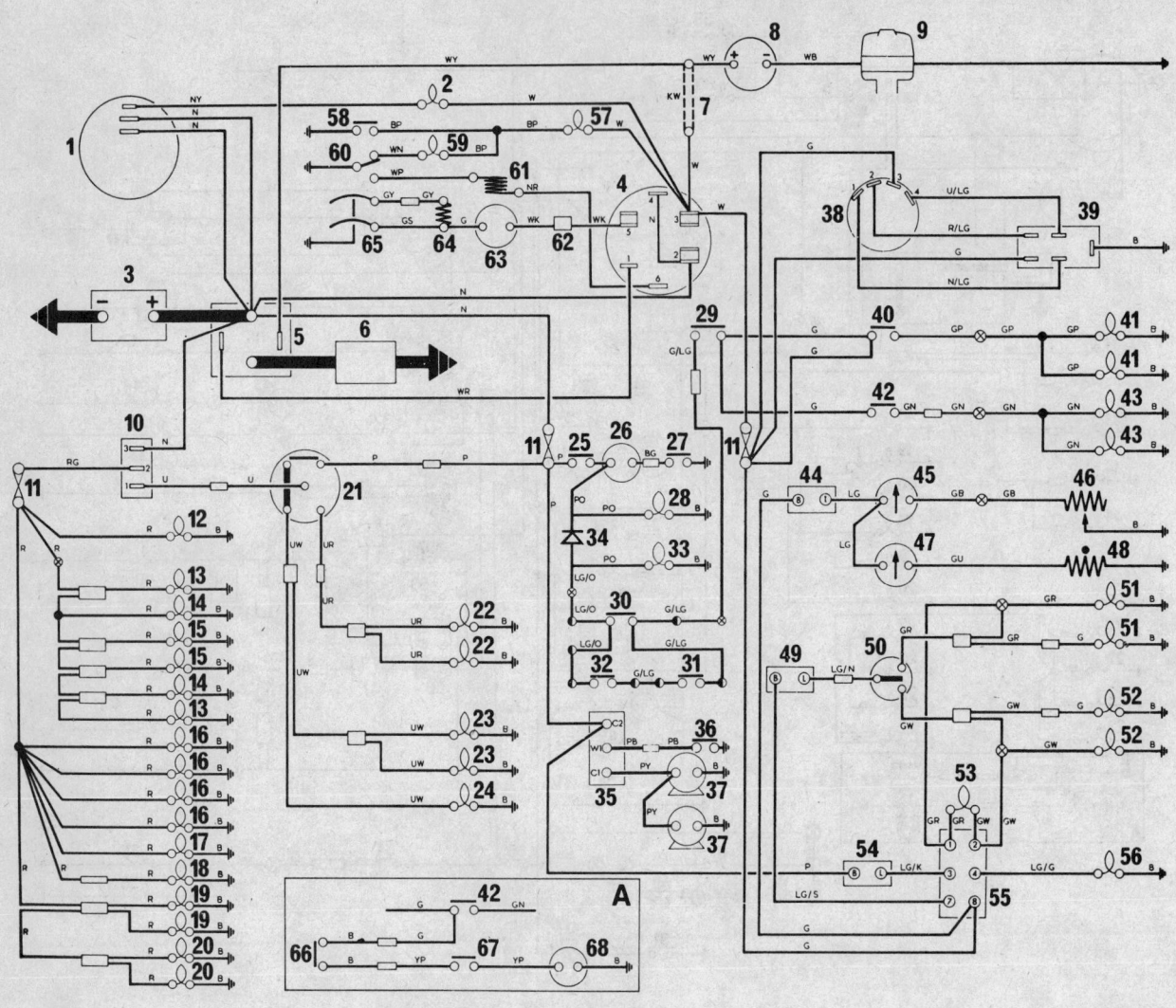

1973-74 Spitfire 1500 (1974 starter interlock not shown)

1. Alternator	24. Main beam warning light	47. Temperature indicator
2. Ignition warning light	25. L.H. door switch	48. Temperature transmitter
3. Battery	26. Buzzer	49. Turn signal flasher unit
4. Ignition/starter switch	27. Key switch	50. Turn signal switch
5. Starter solenoid	28. Key light	51. L.H. flasher lamp
6. Starter motor	29. Belt waning gearbox switch	52. R.H. flasher lamp
7. Ballast resistor wire	30. Drivers belt switch	53. Turn signal warning light
8. Ignition coil—6 volt	31. Passengers seat switch	54. Hazard flasher unit
9. Ignition distributor	32. Passengers belt switch	55. Hazard switch
10. Master light switch	33. Fasten belts warning light	56. Hazard warning light
11. Fuse	34. Diode	57. Brake warning light
12. Wipe/wash switch identification light	35. Horn relay	58. Brake line failure switch
13. Rear marker lamp	36. Horn push	59. Oil pressure warning light
14. Tail lamp	37. Horn	60. Oil pressure switch
15. Plate illumination lamp	38. Windscreen wiper switch	61. Anti run on valve
16. Instrument illumination	39. Windscreen wiper motor	62. Radio facility
17. Hazard switch identification light	40. Stop lamp switch	63. Heater motor
18. Heater control identification light	41. Stop lamp	64. Heater rheostat
19. Front parking lamp	42. Reverse lamp switch	65. Heater switch
20. Front marker lamp	43. Reverse lamp	**A. Overdrive (optional extra)**
21. Column light switch	44. Voltage stabilizer	66. Overdrive gear lever switch
22. Dip beam	45. Fuel indicator	67. Overdrive gearbox switch
23. Main beam	46. Fuel tank unit	68. Overdrive solenoid

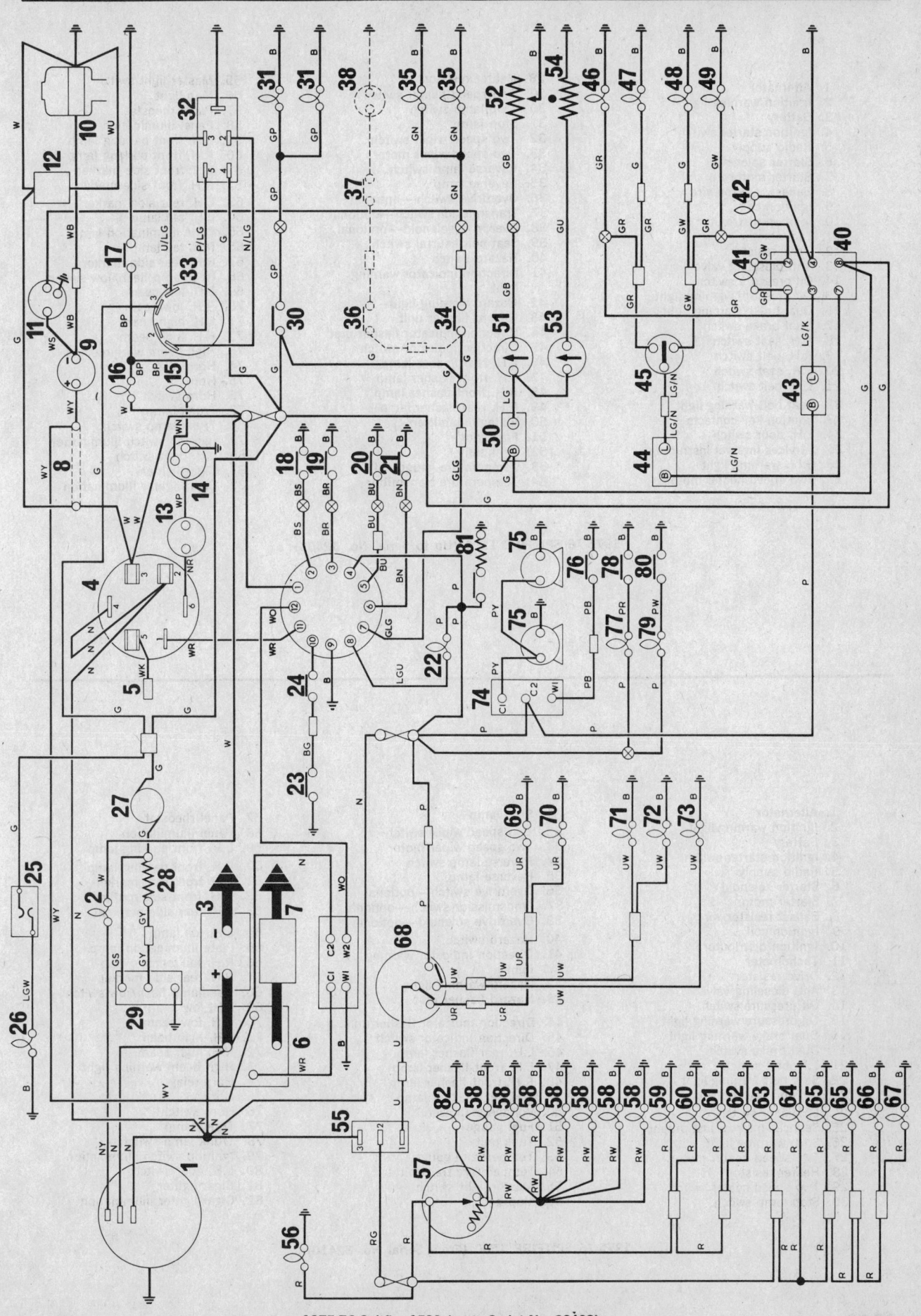

1975-76 Spitfire 1500 (up to Serial No. 32409)

Wiring Circuits

1. Alternator
2. Ignition warning light
3. Battery
4. Ignition starter switch
5. Radio supply
6. Starter solenoid
7. Starter motor
8. Ballast resistor wire
9. Ignition coil
10. Ignition distributor
11. Tachometer
12. Drive resistor
13. Anti dieseling valve
14. Oil pressure switch
15. Oil pressure warning light
16. Dual brake warning light
17. Dual brake switch
18. R.H. seat switch
19. R.H. belt switch
20. L.H. seat switch
21. L.H. belt switch
22. Seat belt warning light
23. Ignition key contacts
24. L.H. door switch
25. Services interval instrument
26. S.I.I. warning light
27. Two speed heater motor

28. Heater resistor
29. Two speed heater switch
30. Stop lamp switch
31. Stop lamp
32. Two speed wiper switch
33. Two speed wiper motor
34. Reverse lamp switch
35. Reverse lamp
36. Overdrive switch—optional
37. Transmission switch—optional
38. Overdrive solenoid—optional
39. Seat belt neutral switch
40. Hazard switch
41. Direction indicator warning light
42. Hazard warning light
43. Hazard flasher unit
44. Direction indicator flasher unit
45. Direction indicator switch
46. L.H. rear flasher lamp
47. L.H. front flasher lamp
48. R.H. front flasher lamp
49. R.H. rear flasher lamp
50. Voltage stabilizer
51. Fuel gauge
52. Tank unit
53. Temperature gauge
54. Temperature transmitter

55. Master light switch
56. Map light
57. Panel rheostat
58. Panel illumination
59. L.H. front parking lamp
60. R.H. front parking lamp
61. L.H. front side marker
62. R.H. front side marker
63. L.H. rear side marker
64. L.H. tail lamp
65. Plate illumination lamp
66. R.H. tail lamp
67. R.H. rear side marker
68. Headlamp flash/low switch
69. L.H. low beam
70. R.H. low beam
71. L.H. high beam
72. R.H. high beam
73. High beam warning light
74. Horn relay
75. Horn
76. Horn switch
77. Trunk lamp
78. Trunk lamp switch
79. Ignition switch illumination
80. L.H. door switch
81. Cigar lighter
82. Cigar lighter illumination

1975-76 SPITFIRE 1500 (Up to Serial No. 32409)

---

1. Alternator
2. Ignition warning light
3. Battery
4. Ignition starter switch
5. Radio supply
6. Starter solenoid
7. Starter motor
8. Ballast resistor wire
9. Ignition coil
10. Ignition distributor
11. Tachometer
12. Drive resistor
13. Anti dieseling valve
14. Oil pressure switch
15. Oil pressure warning light
16. Dual brake warning light
17. Dual brake switch
21. L.H. belt switch
22. Seat belt warning light
23. Ignition key contacts
24. L.H. door switch
25. Services interval instrument
26. S.I.I. warning light
27. Two speed heater motor
28. Heater resistor
29. Two speed heater switch
30. Stop lamp switch

31. Stop lamp
32. Two speed wiper switch
33. Two speed wiper motor
34. Reverse lamp switch
35. Reverse lamp
36. Overdrive switch—optional
37. Transmission switch—optional
38. Overdrive solenoid—optional
40. Hazard switch
41. Direction indicator warning light
42. Hazard warning light
43. Hazard flasher unit
44. Direction indicator flasher unit
45. Direction indicator switch
46. L.H. rear flasher lamp
47. L.H. front flasher lamp
48. R.H. front flasher lamp
49. R.H. rear flasher lamp
50. Voltage stabilizer
51. Fuel gauge
52. Tank unit
53. Temperature gauge
54. Temperature transmitter
55. Master light switch
56. Map light

57. Panel rheostat
58. Panel illumination
59. L.H. front parking lamp
60. R.H. front parking lamp
61. L.H. front side marker
62. R.H. front side marker
63. L.H. rear side marker
64. L.H. tail lamp
65. Plate illumination lamp
66. R.H. tail lamp
67. R.H. rear side marker
68. Headlamp flash/low switch
69. L.H. low beam
70. R.H. low beam
71. L.H. high beam
72. R.H. high beam
73. High beam warning light
74. Horn relay
75. Horn
76. Horn switch
77. Trunk lamp
78. Trunk lamp switch
79. Ignition switch illumination
80. L.H. door switch
81. Cigar lighter
82. Cigar lighter illumination

1975-76 SPITFIRE 1500 (From Serial No. 32410)

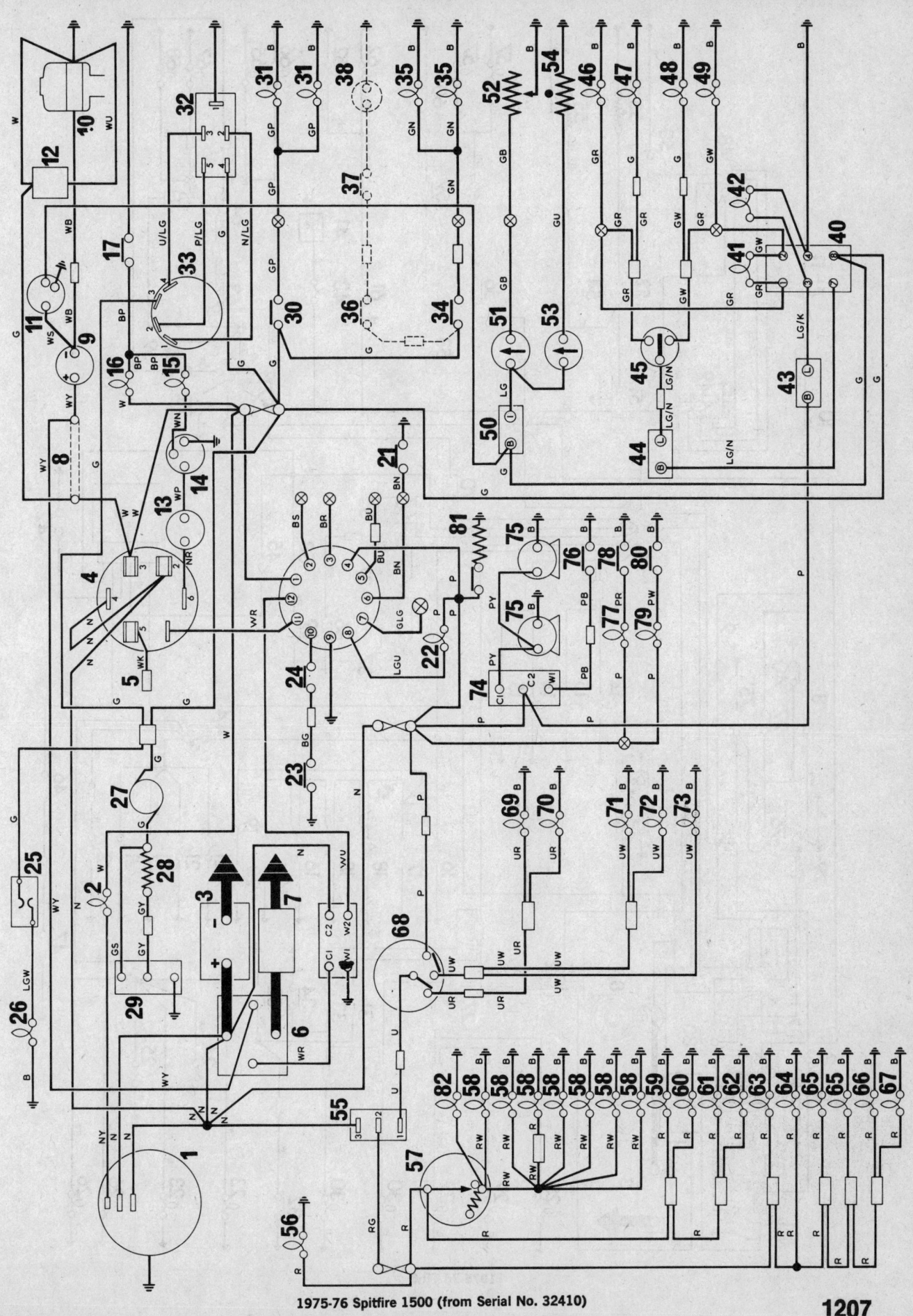

1975-76 Spitfire 1500 (from Serial No. 32410)

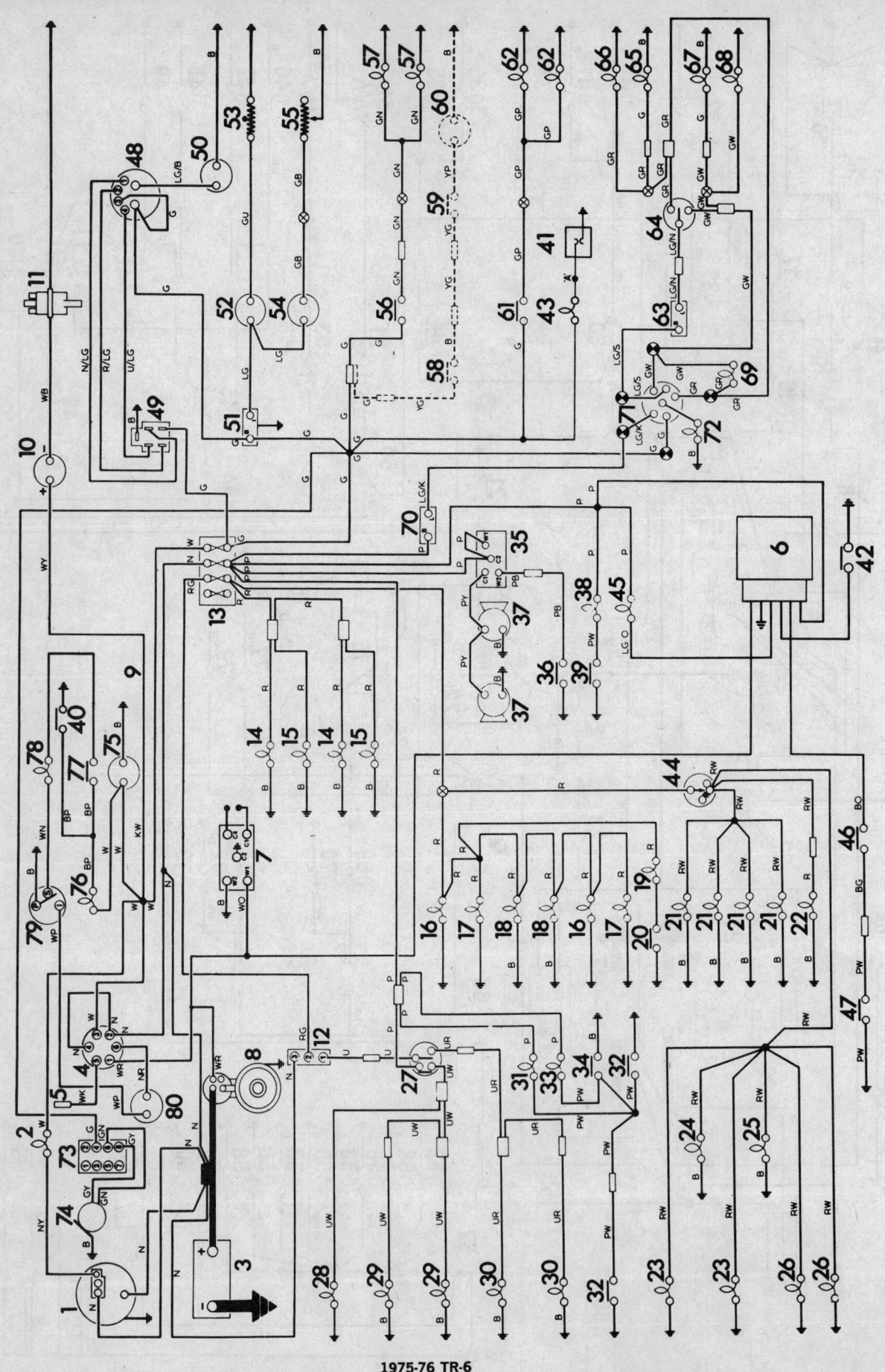

1975-76 TR-6

1. Alternator
2. Ignition warning light
3. Battery
4. Ignition/starter switch
5. Radio supply
6. Seat belt timer
7. Starter relay
8. Starter motor
9. Ballast resistor wire
10. Ignition coil
11. Ignition distributor
12. Master light switch
13. Fuse
14. Front parking lamp
15. Front marker lamp
16. Rear marker lamp
17. Tail lamp
18. Plate illumination lamp
19. Luggage boot lamp
20. Luggage boot lamp switch
21. Instrument illumination
22. Heater control identification light
23. Speedometer illumination
24. Wipe/wash switch identification light
25. Hazard switch identification light
26. Tachometer illumination
27. Headlight dipper switch
28. Main beam warning light
29. Main beam
30. Low beam

31. Key light
32. Door switch
33. Passenger light
34. Passenger light switch
35. Horn relay
36. Horn-push
37. Horn
38. Glovebox illumination
39. Glovebox illumination switch
40. Hand brake switch
41. E.G.R. service warning counter
42. Driver's seat belt switch
43. E.G.R. service warning light
44. Panel light rheostat
45. Fasten belts warning light
46. Door switch
47. Key switch
48. Windshield washer/wiper switch
49. Windshield wiper motor
50. Windshield washer pump
51. Voltage stabilizer
52. Temperature indicator
53. Temperature transmitter
54. Fuel indicator
55. Fuel tank unit
56. Reverse lamp switch
57. Reverse lamp
58. Overdrive gear lever switch
59. Overdrive transmission switch
60. Overdrive solenoid
61. Stop lamp switch
62. Stop lamp

63. Turn signal flasher unit
64. Turn signal switch
65. L.H. front flasher lamp
66. L.H. rear flasher lamp
67. R.H. front flasher lamp
68. R.H. rear flasher lamp
69. Turn signal warning light
70. Hazard flasher unit
71. Hazard switch
72. Hazard warning light
73. Heater switch
74. Heater motor
75. Battery condition indicator
76. Brake-line failure/hand brake warning indicator
77. Brake line failure switch
78. Oil pressure warning light
79. Oil pressure switch
80. Anti dieseling valve

COLOR CODE

N. Brown
U. Blue
R. Red
P. Purple
G. Green
K. Pink
LG. Light Green
W. White
Y. Yellow
S. Slate
B. Black
O. Orange

1975-76 TR-6

---

1. Alternator
2. Ignition warning light
3. Battery
4. Battery condition indicator
5. Ignition/starter switch
6. Radio supply
7. Interlock module
8. Interlock starter motor relay
9. Starter motor
10. Ballast resistor wire
11. Ignition coil
12. Ignition distributor
13. Drive resistor
14. Battery lead connector
15. Master light switch
16. Actuator—limit switch
17. Circuit breaker
18. Headlamp—run/stop relay
19. Actuator—motor
20. Main/low/flash switch
21. Main beam
22. Main beam warning light
23. Low beam
24. L.H. door switch
25. Key switch
26. Fasten belts warning light
27. Interlock—transmission switch
28. Drivers belt switch
29. Drivers seat switch
30. Passengers belt switch
31. Passengers seat switch
32. Tachometer
33. Temperature indicator
34. Temperature transmitter
35. Fuel indicator
36. Fuel warning light
37. Fuel tank unit
   U.S.A. Federal vehicles only
38. Choke warning light

39. Choke switch
   U.S.A. California vehicles only
38. Catalyst service warning light
39. Catalyst service interval indicator
40. Brake warning light
41. Brake line failure switch
42. Handbrake switch
43. Oil pressure warning light
44. Oil pressure switch
45. Anti dieseling valve
50-53. Fuse
60. Front marker lamp
61. Front parking lamp
62. Plate illumination lamp
63. Rear marker lamp
64. Tail lamp
65. Panel rheostat
66. Cigarette lighter illumination
67. Heater control illumination
68. Instrument illumination
69. Dash switch panel illumination
70. Air conditioning—control relay
71. Cold thermostat
72. Air conditioning—delay circuit flasher unit
73. Air conditioning—delay circuit relay
74. High pressure cut out
75. Compressor clutch
76. Throttle jack
77. Condenser fan motor
78. Radiator switch
79. Cigarette lighter
80. Horn relay
81. Horn
82. Horn push
83. Clock

84. Roof lamp
85. Door switch
86. Reverse lamp switch
87. Reverse lamp
88. Blower motor
89. Blower motor switch
90. Windshield washer/wiper switch
91. Windshield wiper motor
92. Windshield washer pump
93. Stop lamp switch
94. Stop lamp
95. Heated backlight switch
96. Heated backlight
97. Heated backlight warning light
98. Turn signal flasher unit
99. Turn signal switch
100. L.H. flasher lamp
101. L.H. turn signal warning light
102. R.H. turn signal warning light
103. R.H. flasher lamp
104. Hazard flasher unit
105. Hazard switch
106. Hazard warning light

COLOR CODE

B. Black
G. Green
K. Pink
LG. Light Green
N. Brown
O. Orange
P. Purple
R. Red
S. Slate
U. Blue
W. White
Y. Yellow

TRIUMPH TR-7

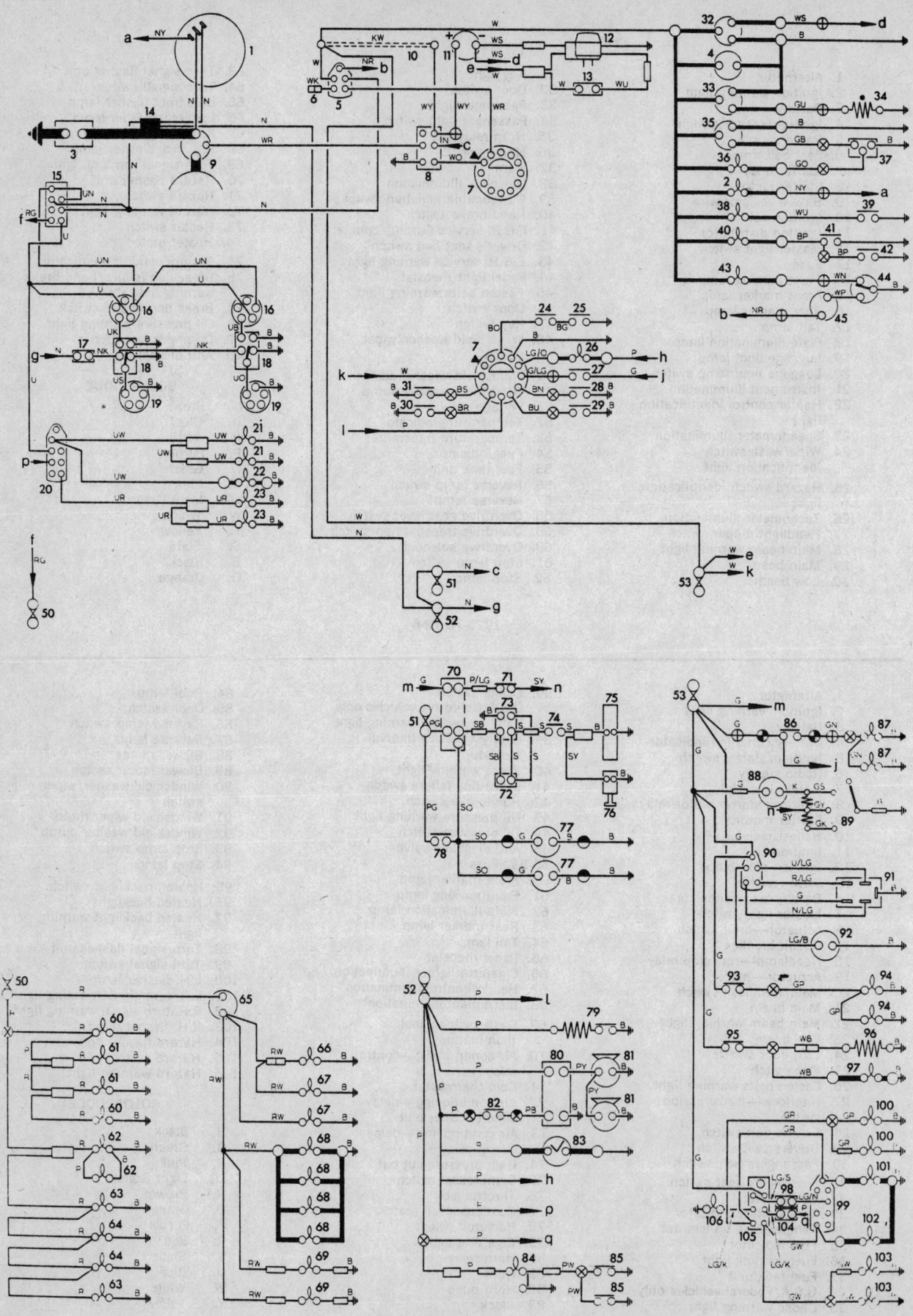

Triumph TR-7

SPECIFICATIONS

Volvo

INTRODUCTION

Since Volvo imported its first cars to this country in 1956, the company has enjoyed a reputation for building safe, reliable, durable and economical cars. Since 1970, Volvo has imported four distinctly different series of cars. The 140 series, first produced in 1967, is a four cylinder compact offered in a two-door sedan (142), four-door sedan (144), and station wagon (145) body styles. The 164, first produced in 1969, is a six cylinder luxury rendition of the 144, sharing the same sheet metal and mechanical components with the 144 from the firewall back. The 1800 series, first exported to the U.S. in 1962, is a four cylinder sports model offered through 1972 in a two-door coupe version (P1800, 1800S, 1800E), and from 1972 to 1973 in a two-door sportswagon version (1800ES).

Beginning with the 1975 model year, the 240 series replaces the 140 series in the U.S. market. This 4 cylinder compact incorporates the styling and some of the features of the Volvo Experimental Safety Vehicle. Technical improvements to ride and handling include a modified rear suspension, a completely new McPherson strut front suspension, rack and pinion steering, a wider front track and longer wheelbase. For 1976, the 260 series replaces the 164 in the U.S. market. The 260 combines the features of the 240 series with a 90° V-6 engine of light aluminum-alloy construction.

MODEL IDENTIFICATION

1972 140 series—144 shown

1973 140 series—144 shown

1974 140 series—145 shown

1975-76 240 (242 shown)

1972 164

1973 164

1212

1974-75 164

1972 1800E

1972-73 1800ES

1967-77 260 Series

SERIAL NUMBER IDENTIFICATION

Vehicle Type Designation and Chassis Number

Type designation (142, 164, 1800, etc.) and chassis number appear at several lo-cations on every Volvo. On all 140, 240, 260 series and 164 model Volvos, they are stamped into the sheet metal of the right front door pillar. On all 1800 mod-els, they are stamped into the sheet metal on the right side of the engine compart-ment. The type designation and the chas-sis number also appear on a metal plate (1) riveted to the engine side of the fire-wall. For 1972–76, they appear on the V.I.N. plate (3) located at the foot of the left door post.

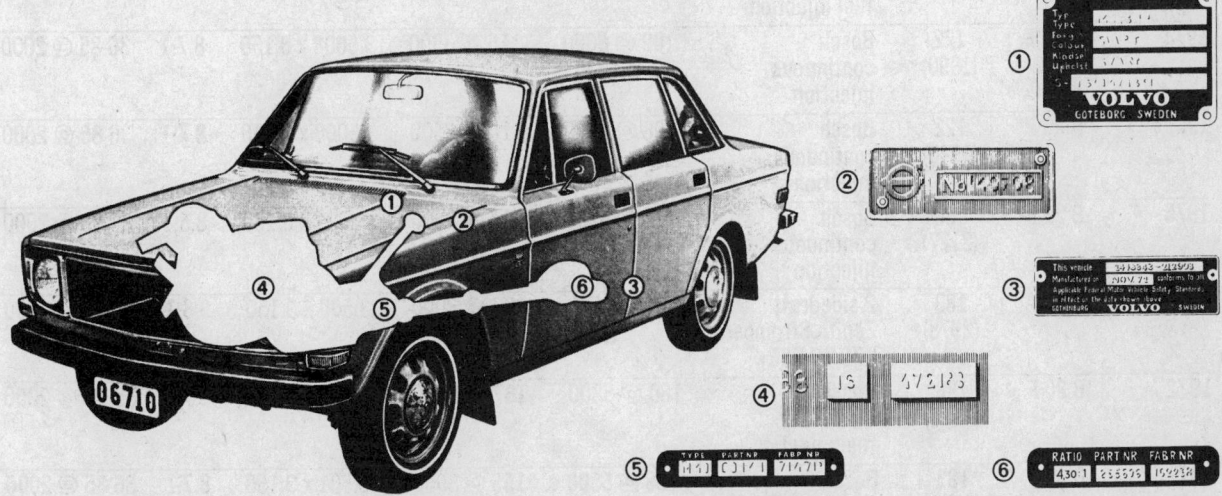

Serial number identification—1972 144 shown.

Volvo

Chassis Number Chart

Year	Model	Starting Chassis No.
1972	142	249930
	144	263070
	145	103380
	164	52790
	1800E	37550
	1800ES	1
1973	142	323400
	144	340100
	145	153730
	164	74450
	1800ES	3070
1974	142	393950
	144	428000

Year	Model	Starting Chassis No.
1974	145	210050
	164	102950
1975	242	1
	244	1
	245	1
	164	132577
1976	242	53865
	244	82980
	245	54710
	262	1
	264	9675
	265	5

Component Identification

Beginning with 1975 models, a component data plate is used to specify the manufacturer of major serviceable components. The plate is located on the right front door pillar.

Component	Manufacturer	Code
Brakes	Girling	1
	ATE	2
Carburetor	Zenith-Stromberg	1
	SU	
Fuel Pump	SEV (Marchal)	1
	Pierburg	2
	Bosch	3
Clutch	Borg and Beck	1
	Fichtel and Sachs	2
Alternator	Bosch	1
	SEV (Marchal)	2
Steering Gear	Ehrenreich	1
	Cam Gears	2
	Zahnradfabrik (ZF)	3
	TRW	4

Engine, Transmission, and Final Drive Identification

The engine type designation, part number, and serial number are given on the left side of the block (4). The last figures of the part number are stamped on a tab and are followed by the serial number stamped on the block.

The transmission type designation, serial number, and part number appear on a metal plate (5) riveted to the underside of the transmission.

The final drive reduction ratio, part number, and serial number are found on a metal plate (6) riveted to the left-hand side of the differential.

GENERAL ENGINE SPECIFICATIONS

Year		Engine Displacement Cu in. (cc)	Fuel Delivery Type	Horsepower @ rpm	Torque @ rpm (ft lbs)	Bore x Stroke (in.)	Compression Ratio	Oil Pressure @ rpm (psi)
1972	B 20 B	122 (1990)	2 sidedraft SU HIF 6	118 @ 5800	123 @ 3500	3.5004 x 3.150	9.3:1	36-85 @ 2000
1972	B 20 F	122 (1990)	Bosch electronic fuel injection	125 @ 6000	123 @ 3500	3.5008 x 3.150	8.7:1	36-85 @ 2000
1973	B 20 F	122 (1990)	Bosch electronic fuel injection	112 @ 6000	115 @ 3500	3.5008 x 3.150	8.7:1	36-85 @ 2000
1974	B 20 F	122 (1990)	Bosch continuous injection	109 @ 6000	115 @ 3500	3.5008 x 3.150	8.7:1	36-85 @ 2000
1975	B 20 F	122 (1990)	Bosch continuous injection	98 @ 6000 ①	110 @ 3500 ②	3.5008 x 3.150	8.7:1	36-85 @ 2000
1976	B 21 F	130 (2127)	Bosch continuous injection	102 @ 5200 ⑤	114 @ 2500 ⑥	3.623 x 3.150	8.5:1	35-85 @ 2000
1972	B 30 A	183 (2978)	2 sidedraft Zenith-Stromberg 175 CD 2SE	145 @ 5500	163 @ 3000	3.500 x 3.150	9.3:1	36-85 @ 2000
1972	B 30 F	183 (2978)	Bosch electronic fuel injection	160 @ 5800	167 @ 2500	3.501 x 3.150	8.7:1	36-85 @ 2000
1973-74	B 30 F	183 (2978)	Bosch electronic fuel injection	138 @ 5500	155 @ 3500	3.501 x 3.150	8.7:1	36-85 @ 2000

GENERAL ENGINE SPECIFICATIONS

Year		Engine Displacement Cu in. (cc)	Fuel Delivery Type	Horsepower @ rpm	Torque @ rpm (ft lbs)	Bore x Stroke (in.)	Compression Ratio	Oil Pressure @ rpm (psi)
1975	B 30 F	183 (2978)	Bosch electronic fuel injection	130 @ 5250 ③	150 @ 4000 ④	3.501 x 3.150	8.7:1	36-85 @ 2000
1976	B 27 F	162 (2660)	Bosch continuous injection ,	125 @ 5500 ⑦	150 @ 2750 ⑧	3.4646 x 2.8740	8.2:1	58 @ 3000

① 94 @ 6000 w/catalytic converter
② 105 @ 3500 w/catalytic converter
③ 125 @ 5250 w/catalytic converter
④ 145 @ 4000 w/catalytic converter

⑤ 99 @ 5200 in Calif.
⑥ 114 @ 2500 in Calif.
⑦ 121 @ 5500 in Calif.
⑧ 148 @ 2750 in Calif.

TUNE-UP SPECIFICATIONS

When analyzing compression test results, look for uniformity among cylinders, rather than specific pressures.

Year	Engine Displace. (Cu. in)	SPARK PLUGS Type	Gap (in.)	DISTRIBUTOR Point Dwell (deg)	Point Gap (in.)	IGNITION TIMING (deg) MT	AT	Intake Valve Opens (deg)	Fuel Pump Pressure (psi)	IDLE SPEED (rpm) MT	AT	VALVE CLEARANCE (cold) (in.) In	Ex
1972	B 20 B 122	Bosch W200T35 ②	0.030	59-65	③	10B ①	10B ①	TDC	1.56-3.55	800 800	700 700	0.020-0.022	0.020-0.022
	B 30 A 183	④	0.030	37-43	0.010 min.	10B ①	10B ①	TDC	2.10-3.50	800 800	700 700	0.020-0.022	0.020-0.022
1972-73	B 20 F 122	⑤	0.030	59-65	0.014 min.	10B ①	10B ①	5.5B	28	900	800	0.016-0.018	0.016-0.018
1972-73	B 30 F 183	Bosch W200T35	0.030	37-43	0.010 min.	10B ①	10B ①	TDC	28	900	800	0.020-0.022	0.020-0.022
1974	B 20 F 122	Bosch W200T35	0.030	59-65	0.014 min.	10B ①	10B ①	5.5B	71	900	800	0.016-0.018	0.016-0.018
	B 30 F 183	Bosch W200T35	0.030	37-43	0.010 min.	10B ①	10B ①	TDC	28	900	800	0.020-0.022	0.020-0.022
1975	B 20 F 122	Bosch W200T35	0.030	Electronic Ignition		10B ①	10B ①	5.5B	71	900	800	0.016-0.018	0.016-0.018
	B 30 F 183	Bosch W200T35	0.030	Electronic Ignition		10B ①	10B ①	TDC	28	900	800	0.020-0.022	0.020-0.022
1976	B 21 F 130	Bosch W175T30	0.030	Electronic Ignition		15B ①	15B ①	15B	64-75	900	800	0.014-0.016	0.014-0.016
	B 27 F 162	Bosch WA200T30 Champ BN9Y	0.026	Electronic Ignition		10B ①	10B ①	⑥	64-75	900	900	0.004-0.006	0.010-0.012

① @ 700 rpm
② Severe service—W225T35
③ 1969-71—0.016-0.020 in.
　 1972　—0.014 min. in.

④ 1970-72—W200T35

⑤ W225T35—Severe service
　 W200T35—Normal service
⑥ 9B—left side; 7B—right side

NOTE: The underhood specifications sticker often reflects tune-up specification changes made in production. Sticker figures must be used if they disagree with those in this chart.

FIRING ORDER

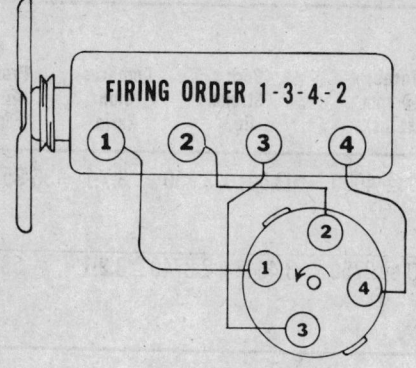

FIRING ORDER 1-3-4-2

B20B, B20F

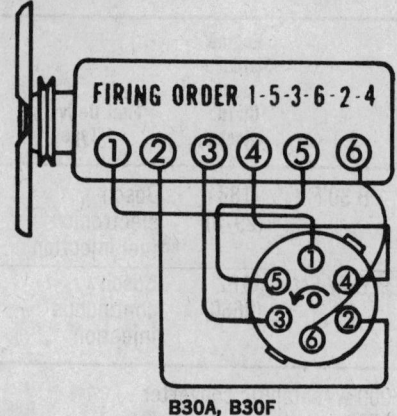

FIRING ORDER 1-5-3-6-2-4

B30A, B30F

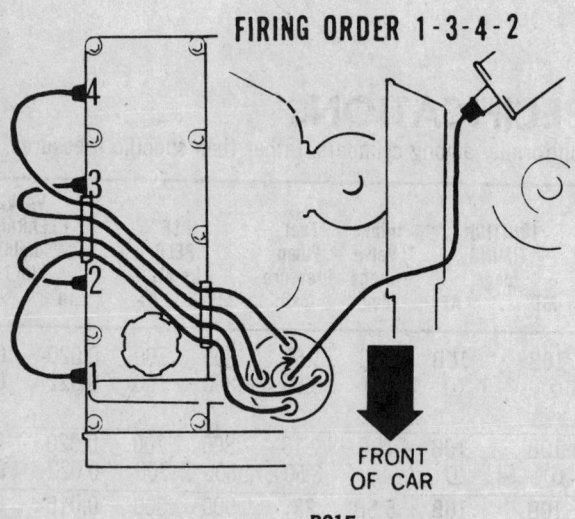

FIRING ORDER 1-3-4-2

FRONT OF CAR

B21F

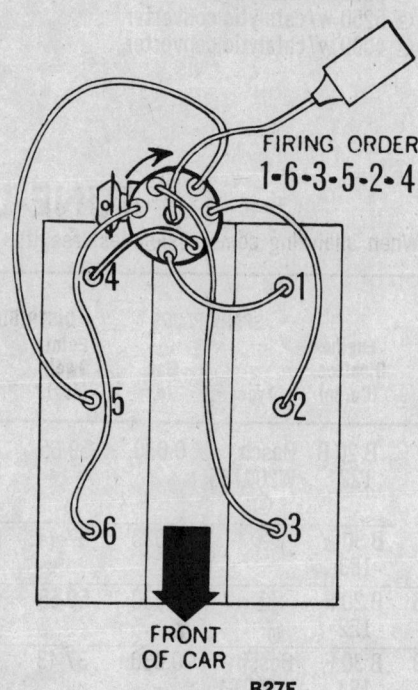

FIRING ORDER 1-6-3-5-2-4

FRONT OF CAR

B27F

CAPACITIES

Year	Model	Engine Displacement Cu in. (cc)	ENGINE CRANKCASE (qt)		TRANSMISSION (pts)		Drive Axle (pt)	Gasoline Tank (gal)	Cooling System (qt)
			With Filter	Without Filter	Manual 4 spd*	Automatic			
1972-73	142, 144, 145	122 (1990)	4.0	3.4	1.6 (3.4)	13.5	2.7	15.3	10.5
	164	183 (2978)	6.3	5.5	1.3 (3.0)	17.7	3.4	15.3	13.0
	1800	122 (1990)	4.0	3.4	(3.4)	13.5	2.7	12.0	9.0
1974	142, 144, 145	122 (1990)	4.0	3.4	1.6 (3.4)	13.5	2.7	15.8	10.0
	164	183 (2978)	6.3	5.5	(3.1)	18.0	3.4	15.8	13.0
1975	242, 244, 245	122 (1990)	4.0	3.4	1.6 (3.4)	13.5	2.7	15.8	10.0
	164	183 (2978)	6.3	5.5	(3.1)	18.0	3.4	15.8	11.0
1976	242, 244, 245	130 (2127)	4.0	3.5	1.6 (4.8)	13.8	3.4	15.8	10.0①
	262, 264, 265	162 (2660)	7.4	6.8	1.6 (4.8)	13.8	3.4	15.8	12.0

* Figures in parentheses are for overdrive transmission
① 9.8 qts w/auto trans.

CRANKSHAFT AND CONNECTING ROD SPECIFICATIONS

All measurements are given in inches

Year	Engine Displacement Cu. in. (cc)		CRANKSHAFT				CONNECTING ROD		
		Main Brg Journal Dia	Main Brg Oil Clearance	Shaft End-Play	Thrust on No.	Journal Diameter	Oil Clearance	Side Clearance
1972-73	B 20 122 (1990)	2.4981-2.4986	0.0011-0.0033	0.0018-0.0054	5	2.1299-2.1304	0.0012-0.0028	0.006-0.014
1974-75	B 20 122 (1990)	2.4981-2.4986	0.0011-0.0033	0.0018-0.0054	5	2.1255-2.1260	0.0012-0.0028	0.006-0.014
1976	B 21 130 (2127)	2.4981-2.4986	0.0011-0.0033	0.0015-0.0058	5	2.1255-2.1260	0.0009-0.0028	0.006-0.014
1972-73	B 30 183 (2978)	2.4981-2.4986	0.0011-0.0033	0.0018-0.0054	7	2.1299-2.1304	0.0012-0.0028	0.006-0.014
1974-75	B 30 183 (2978)	2.4981-2.4986	0.0011-0.0033	0.0018-0.0054	7	2.1255-2.1260	0.0012-0.0028	0.006-0.014
1976	B 27 162 (2660)	2.7576-2.7583	0.0015-0.0035	0.0028-0.0106	4	2.0578-2.0585	0.0012-0.0031	0.008-0.015

VALVE SPECIFICATIONS

Year	Engine and Displacement Cu. in. (cc)	Cylinder Head Seat Angle (deg)	Valve Face Angle (deg)	Seat Width (in.)	Spring Test Pressure (lbs @ in.)	Spring Installed Height (in.)	STEM TO GUIDE CLEARANCE (in.)		STEM DIAMETER (in.)	
							Intake	Exhaust	Intake	Exhaust
1972	B 20 B 109 (1780)	44.5	45	0.055	181.5 @ 1.18	1.81	0.0010-0.0022	0.0026-0.0037	0.3419-0.3425	0.3403-0.3409
1972-75	B 20 F 122 (1990)	44.5	45	0.08	181.5 @ 1.18	1.81	0.0012-0.0026	0.0024-0.0038	0.3132-0.3138	0.3120-0.3126
1976	B 21 F 130 (2127)	44.75	45.5	0.08	170 @ 1.06	1.77	0.0012-0.0024	0.0024-0.0035	0.3132-0.3135	0.3128-0.3126
1972	B 30 A 183 (2978)	44.5	45	0.08	145.0 @ 1.20	1.77	0.0012-0.0026	0.0024-0.0038	0.3132-0.3138	0.3120-0.3126
1972-75	B 30 F 183 (2978)	44.5	45	0.08	181.5 @ 1.18	1.81	0.0012-0.0026	0.0024-0.0038	0.3132-0.3138	0.3120-0.3126
1976	B 27 F 162 (2660)	29.5 Int 30 Exh	29.5 Int 30 Exh ①	124.3 @ 1.27	1.86	②	②	0.3136-0.3142 to 0.3140-0.3146	0.3128-0.3134 to 0.3136-0.3142

① 0.067-0.083 Intake; 0.079-0.094 Exhaust
② Tapered; valve guide 1D is 0.3150-0.3158

PISTON AND RING SPECIFICATIONS

All measurements in inches

Year	Engine Displacement Cu. In. (cc)	Piston Clearance	RING GAP			RING SIDE CLEARANCE		
			Top Compression	Bottom Compression	Oil Control	Top Compression	Bottom Compression	Oil Control
1972	B 20 B 122 (1990)	0.0014-0.0020	0.016-0.022	0.016-0.022	0.016-0.022	0.0016-0.0028	0.0016-0.0028	0.0016-0.0028

PISTON AND RING SPECIFICATIONS
All measurements in inches

Year	Engine Displacement Cu. In. (cc)	Piston Clearance	RING GAP			RING SIDE CLEARANCE		
			Top Compression	Bottom Compression	Oil Control	Top Compression	Bottom Compression	Oil Control
1972-75	B 20 F 122 (1990)	0.0016-0.0024①	0.016-0.022	0.016-0.022	0.016-0.022	0.0016-0.0028	0.0016-0.0028	0.0016-0.0028
1976	B 21 F 130 (2127)	0.0004-0.0012	0.0138-0.0217	0.0138-0.0217	0.010-0.016	0.0016-0.0028	0.0016-0.0028	0.0016-0.0028
1972	B 30 A 183 (2978)	0.0016-0.0024	0.016-0.022	0.016-0.022	0.016-0.022	0.0016-0.0028	0.0016-0.0028	0.0016-0.0028
1972-75	B 30 F 183 (2978)	0.0016-0.0024①	0.016-0.022	0.016-0.022	0.016-0.022	0.0016-0.0032	0.0016-0.0028	0.0016-0.0028
1976	B 27 F 162 (2660)	0.0008-0.0016	0.016-0.022	0.016-0.022	0.015-0.055	0.0018-0.0029	0.0010-0.0021	0.0004-0.0092

① 1974-75 piston clearance—0.0004-0.0012 in.

TORQUE SPECIFICATIONS
All readings in ft lbs

Year	Engine	Cyl. Head Bolts	Rod Bearing Bolts	Main Bearing Bolts	Crank-shaft Pulley Bolt	Flywheel-To-Crank-shaft Bolts	MANIFOLD BOLTS		Cam-shaft Nut	Spark Plug	Oil Pan
							Intake	Exhaust			
1972-73	All	65①	38-42	87-94	50-58	36-40	13-16	13-16	94-108	25-29	6-8
1974-75	All	65①	51-57	87-94	69-76②	47-51	13-16	13-16	94-108	25-29	6-8
1976	B 21 F	76-83③	43-48	85-91	107-128	47-54	15	15	32-38	25-29	8
1976	B 27 F	④	33-37	⑤	118-132	33-37	7-11	7-11	51-59	13-15	7-11

① Torque head bolts in three stages; first, torque in sequence to 29 ft lbs, then to 58 ft lbs, and finally after driving the car for 10 minutes, torque to the final figure of 65 ft lbs.
② Double pulley—80-101 ft-lbs
③ Torque head bolts in two stages; first, tighten in sequence to 43 ft-lbs, then to 76-83 ft-lbs.
④ Torque heads bolts in sequence to 7 ft-lb, then 22 ft-lb, then 44 ft-lb. Wait 10-15 minutes and slacken the bolts ½ turn. Then torque to 11-14 ft-lb and then protractor torque to 116-120° (⅓ of a turn). Finally run to operating temperature, shut off and allow to cool for 30 min. Following the sequence, slacken, torque to 11-14 ft-lb, and protractor torque to 113-117° each bolt.
⑤ Torque main bearing nuts to 22 ft-lb, in sequence. Then slacken 1st nut ½ turn, tighten to 22-26 ft-lb, and protractor torque to 73-77°. Repeat for remaining nuts following the sequence.

TORQUE SEQUENCES

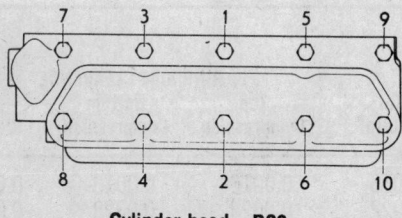

Cylinder head—B20

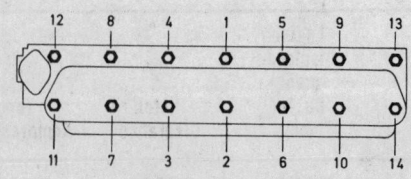

Cylinder head—B30

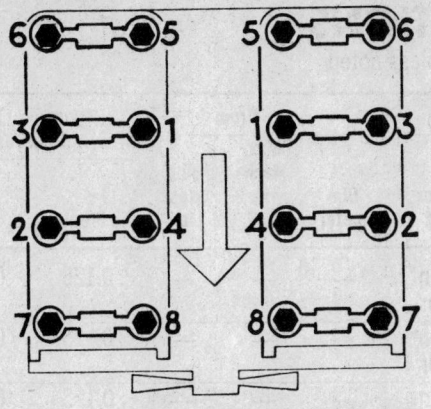

Cylinder head bolt tightening sequence—B27

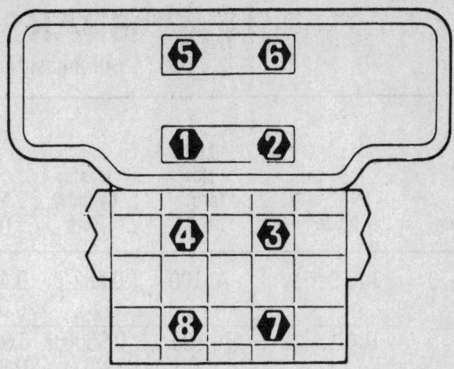

Main bearing nut tightening sequence—B27

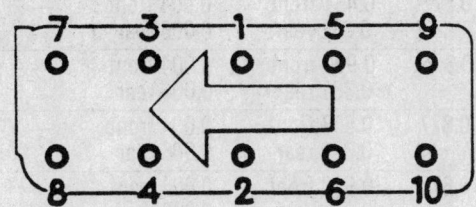

Cylinder heat bolt tightening sequence—B21

BATTERY AND STARTER SPECIFICATIONS

All cars use 12 volt, negative ground electrical systems

			Starter								
			Lock Test			No Load Test					
Year	Model	Battery Amp Hour Capacity	Amps	Volts	Torque (ft/lbs)	Amps	Volts	RPM	Brush Spring Tension (oz)	Min. Brush Length (in.)
All	140 Series, 164, 1800	60	300-350	6	—	40-50	12	6900-8100	2.53-2.86	0.60
All	240 Series, 260 Series	60①	400-490	7	—	30-50	11.5	5800-7800	3.10-3.50	0.52

① 260 series—70 amp hour battery

ALTERNATOR AND REGULATOR SPECIFICATIONS

		ALTERNATOR			REGULATOR	
Year	Vehicle Model	Part No. and Manufacturer	Output (amps.)	Min. Brush Length (in.)	Part No. and Manufacturer	Volts @ Alternator rpm (cold)
1972-75	164 140, 1800	S.E.V. Motorola 14V 34833	55	0.20	S.E.V. Motorola 14V 33544	13.1-14.4 @ 4000
1972	140	S.E.V. Motorola 14V 71270202	35	0.20	S.E.V. Motorola 14V 33525	13.1-14.4 @ 4000
1972-73	1800	Bosch K1	55	0.53	Bosch AD 14V	13.9-14.8 @ 4000
1975-76	240	14V 55A20				
1976	260	S.E.V. Marchal A14/55A 7160410	55	0.20	S.E.V. Marchal 72710502	13.5-14.1 @ 4000①

① After driving 10 minutes

BRAKE SPECIFICATIONS
All measurements given are (in.) unless noted

Year	Model	Lug Nut Torque (ft/lb)	Master Cylinder Bore	Brake Disc		Brake Drum			Minimum Lining Thickness	
				Minimum Thickness	Maximum Run-Out	Diameter	Max. Machine O/S	Max. Wear Limit	Front	Rear
1972-73	140 Series	70-100	0.882①	0.457 front 0.331 rear	0.004 front 0.006 rear	—	—	—	0.125	0.125
	164	70-100	0.950②	0.900 front 0.331 rear	0.004 front 0.006 rear	—	—	—	0.125	0.125
	1800 E/ 1800 ES	70-100	0.882	0.520 front 0.331 rear	0.004 front 0.006 rear	—	—	—	0.125	0.125
1974	140 Series	70-100	0.875	0.457 front 0.331 rear	0.004 front 0.006 rear	—	—	—	0.125	0.125
	164	70-100	0.875	0.900 front 0.331 rear	0.004 front 0.006 rear	—	—	—	0.125	0.125
1975	240 Series	70-100	0.877	0.557 front 0.331 rear	0.004 front 0.006 rear	—	—	—	0.125	0.125
	164	70-100	0.875	0.900 front 0.331 rear	0.004 front 0.006 rear	—	—	—	0.125	0.125
1976	240 Series	70-100	0.877	0.557 front 0.331 rear	0.004 front 0.006 rear	—	—	—	0.125	0.125
	260 Series	70-100	0.877	0.900 front 0.331 rear	0.004 front 0.006 rear	—	—	—	0.125	0.125

① Master cylinder bore is 0.875 starting from chassis nos; 377809 on 142, 403575 on 144, and 194933 on 145
② Master cylinder bore is 0.875 starting from chassis no. 79021

WHEEL ALIGNMENT

Year	Model	Caster Range (deg)	Camber Range (deg)	Toe-in (in.)	Steering Axis Inclination (at 0° camber)	WHEEL PIVOT RATIO (deg)	
						Inner Wheel	Outer Wheel
1972	140 series, 164	0-1P	0-1/2P	0.08-0.20	7.5	20	21.5-23.5
1972-73	1800 series	①	0-1/2P	0-0.12	8.0	20	21.5-23.5
1973	140 series, 164	1 1/2P-2P	0-1/2P	0.08-0.20	7.5	20	21.5-23.5
1974	140 series, 164	1 1/2P-2 1/2P②	0-1/2P	0-0.063	7.5	20	21.5-23.5
1975	240 series	2P-3P	1P-1 1/2P	③	12	20	20.8
1975	164	1/2P-1 1/2P	3/4N-1 1/4N	0.063-0.188	7.5	20	21.5-23.5
1976	240 series, 260 series	2P-3P	1P-1 1/2P	0.18-0.30	12	20	20.8

P Positive   N Negative
① 0-1P—165HR15 Tires
   2P-2 1/2P—185/70HR15 Tires
② w/power steering, caster is 2P-3P
③ w/manual steering—1/8 in. to 1/4 in.
   w/power steering—1/16 in. to 3/16 in.

TUNE-UP PROCEDURES

CAUTION: *When working with a running engine, make sure that there is proper ventilation. Also make sure that the transmission is in neutral, and the parking brake is firmly applied. Always keep hands, clothing, and tools well clear of the radiator fan.*

Spark Plug Removal and Installation

Every six months or 6,000 miles, the spark plugs should be removed for inspection. At this time they should be cleaned and regapped. At 12-month or 12,000-mile intervals on 1970–74 models and at 15,000 mile intervals on 1975 models, the plugs should be replaced.

Remove each spark plug wire by grasping its rubber boot on the end and twisting slightly to free the wire from the plug. Using a 13/16 in. spark plug socket, turn the plugs counterclockwise to remove them. Do not allow any foreign matter to enter the cylinders through the spark plug holes.

The gap must be checked with a feeler gauge before installing the plug in the engine. With the ground electrode positioned parallel to the center electrode, a 0.030 in. wire gauge must pass through the opening with a slight drag. If the air gap between the two electrodes is not correct, the ground electrode must be bent to bring it to specifications.

After the plugs are gapped correctly, they may be inserted into their holes and hand-tightened. Be careful not to cross-thread the plugs. Torque the plugs to the proper specification with a 13/16 in. socket and a torque wrench. Install each spark plug wire on its respective plug, making sure that each spark plug end is making good metal-to-metal contact in its wire socket.

Breaker Points and Condenser Removal and Installation

1972–74 Models

Volvo recommends that the breaker points be inspected and adjusted every six months on 6,000 miles on all 1972–74 models. They must be replaced with the condenser as a unit.

Remove the distributor cap and rotor from the top of the distributor, taking note of their placement. On fuel-injected six cylinder models, remove the breaker point protective cover. Place a screwdriver against the breaker points and ex-

Recess for adjusting contact points

amine the condition of the contacts. Replace the points if the contacts are blackened, pitted, or worn excessively, if the breaker arm has lost its tension, or if the fiber rubbing block on the breaker has become worn or loose. Contact points that have become slightly burned (light gray) may be cleaned with a point file.

To replace the points and condenser, disconnect the electrical leads for both at the primary connection. Remove the lockscrew for the contact breakers and lift them straight up. Loosen the condenser bracket retaining screw and slide out the condenser. While the points are out, lubricate the breaker cam with a very light coating of silicone-based grease. Clean the distributor base plate with alcohol to free it of any oil film that might impede completion of the ground circuit. Also clean the contact point surfaces with the solvent. Install the new points and new condenser and tighten their retaining screws. Connect the electrical leads for both at the primary connection. Make sure that the point contacts are aligned horizontally and vertically. If the points are not aligned properly, bend the stationary arm to suit.

The breaker points must be correctly gapped before proceeding any further. Turn the engine until the rubbing block on the point assembly is resting on the high point of a breaker cam lobe. Loosen the point hold-down screw slightly and insert a feeler gauge of the proper thickness between the point contacts. Fine adjustment is made by inserting a screwdriver into the adjusting recess and turning the screwdriver until the proper size feeler gauge passes between the point contacts with a slight drag. Without disturbing the setting, tighten the breaker point retaining screw.

If a dwell meter is available, proceed to "Dwell Angle Setting." A dwell meter is considered a more accurate means of measuring point gap. If the meter is not available, except on fuel-injected six cylinder models, proceed to replace the rotor in top of the distributor shaft, making sure that the tab inside the rotor aligns

with the slot on the distributor. Before replacing the rotor on fuel-injected six cylinder models, install the breaker point protection cover. Place the distributor cap on top of the distributor and snap the cap clasps into the slots on the cap. Make sure that all the spark plug wires fit snugly into the cap. Proceed to "Ignition Timing Adjustment."

Dwell Angle Setting

1972–74 Models

The dwell angle is the number of degrees of distributor cam rotation through which the breaker points remain fully closed (conducting electricity). Increasing the point gap decreases dwell, while decreasing the point gap increases dwell. On 1975–76 models with breakerless ignition, the dwell angle is electronically controlled and cannot be adjusted.

Using a dwell meter of known accuracy, connect the red lead (positive) wire of the meter to the distributor primary wire connection on the positive (+) side of the coil, and the black ground (negative) wire of the meter to a good ground on the engine (e.g. thermostat housing nut).

The dwell angle may be checked either with the distributor cap and rotor installed and the engine running, or with the cap and rotor removed and the engine cranking at starter speed. The meter gives a constant reading with the engine running. With the engine cranking ,the reading will fluctuate between zero degrees dwell and the maximum figure for that angle. While cranking, the maximum figure is the correct one for that setting.

To change the dwell angle, loosen the point retaining screw slightly and make the approximate correction. Tighten the retaining screw and test the dwell with the engine cranking. If the dwell appears to be correct, install the breaker point protective cover (if so equipped), the rotor and distributor cap and test the dwell with the engine running. Take the engine through its entire rpm range and observe the dwell meter. The dwell should remain within specifications at all times. Great fluctuation of dwell at different engine speeds indicates worn distributor parts.

Following the dwell angle adjustment, the ignition timing must be checked. A 1° increase in dwell results in the ignition timing being retarded 2° and vice versa.

Ignition Timing Adjustment

Volvo recommends that the ignition timing be checked every six months or 6,000 miles on 1972–74 models, and at 15,000 mile intervals on 1975 models.

The timing adjustment should always follow a breaker point gap and/or dwell angle adjustment (1972–74 models only), and be made with the engine at operating temperature.

Clean the crankshaft damper and pointer on the water pump housing with a solvent-soaked rag so that the marks can be seen. Connect a stroboscopic timing light to the no. 1 cylinder spark plug and to the battery, according to the manufacturer's instructions. Scribe a mark on the crankshaft damper and on the marker with chalk or luminescent (day-glo) paint to highlight the correct timing setting. On carbureted models, disconnect the vacuum advance line from the intake manifold at the distributor and plug it with a pencil, golf tee, or some other suitably small object. On fuel-injected models, disconnect and plug the distributor vacuum line and also disconnect the hose between the air cleaner and the inlet duct at the duct. On all 1973 and later models equipped with exhaust gas recirculation, disconnect and plug the vacuum hose at the EGR valve.

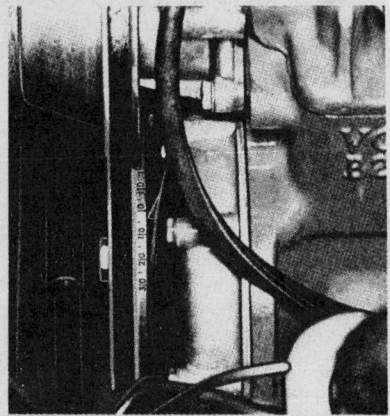

Ignition timing marks—B20, B30

Attach a tachometer to the engine and set the idle speed to specifications. With the engine running, aim the timing light at the pointer and the marks on the damper. If the marks do not coincide, stop the engine, loosen the distributor pinch bolt, and start the engine again. While observing the timing light flashes on the markers, grasp the distributor vacuum regulator and rotate the distributor until the marks do coincide. Stop the engine and tighten the distributor pinch bolt, taking care not to disturb the setting.

Reconnect all disconnected hoses and remove the timing light and tachometer from the engine.

Valve Lash Adjustment

B20 and B30 engines

The recommended maintenance inter-

Adjusting valve clearance

val for valve clearance adjustment is 12 months or 12,000 miles on 1970–74 models and 15,000 miles on 1975 models. The clearance may be checked with the engine *hot* or *cold.*

Remove the valve cover and crank the engine until number one cylinder is at Top Dead Center (TDC). TDC is the point at which both intake and exhaust valves are fully closed and the piston is on its compression stroke. To find TDC, crank the engine, preferably with a remote starter switch, until the pushrods for both valves on the subject cylinder stop falling. Stop cranking the engine. At this point, it will be easier to find TDC by turning the engine over manually. To accomplish this, remove all of the spark plugs so the compression and resistance to cranking are diminished, and remove the distributor cap so the position of the rotor may be observed. To crank the engine manually, position a socket or closed-end wrench—with a long handle for greater leverage—on the crankshaft damper bolt and turn the crankshaft in the required direction. **CAUTION:** *Do not attempt to crank the engine by grasping the viscous drive fan as damage to the fan may result.*

At TDC, the piston for the subject cylinder should be at its highest point of travel. Make a visual check or insert a screwdriver through the spark plug hole to make sure that the piston is no longer traveling upward. As an additional check, the distributor rotor should be pointed to the spark plug wire for the subject cylinder at TDC.

Number one cylinder is at TDC when the 0 degree mark on the crankshaft damper aligns with the pointer on the water pump housing. On four-cylinder models, with number one cylinder at TDC, valves (counting from the front) 1, 2, 3, and 5 may be adjusted. On six-cylinder models, with number one cylinder at TDC, valves 1, 2, 3, 6, 7, and 10 may be adjusted.

Insert a feeler gauge of the specified

thickness between the rocker arm and the valve stem. Adjustment is accomplished by loosening the locknut and turning the adjusting screw and then, without disturbing the adjustment, re-tightening the locknut.

The remainder of the valves may be adjusted in the following manner. On four-cylinder models, with no. 4 cylinder at TDC, valves (counting from the front) 4, 6, 7, and 8 may be adjusted. On six-cylinder models, with no. 6 cylinder at TDC, valves 4, 5, 8, 9, 11, and 12 may be adjusted.

B21 Engine

Valve clearance is checked every 15,000 miles. If it is necessary to adjust valve clearance, you will need three special tools: first, a valve tappet depressor tool used to push down the tappet sufficiently to remove the adjusting disc (Volvo tool #999 5022); second, a specially shaped pliers to actually remove and install the valve adjusting disc (Volvo tool #999 5026); and third, a set of varying thickness valve adjusting discs to make the necessary adjustments. We've included pictures of these special tools so that you might be able to find a suitable substitute. Otherwise, don't attempt the job.

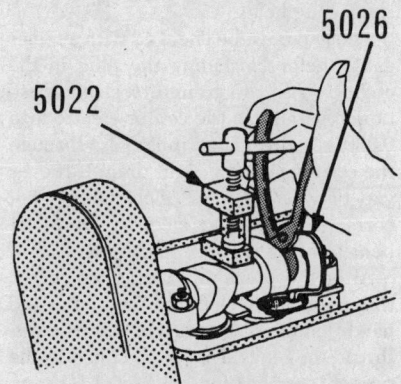

B21 Valve adjusting tools

The procedure for checking, and, if necessary, adjusting the valves is as follows;

1. Remove the valve cover. Scribe chalkmarks on the distributor body indicating each of the four spark plug wire leads in the cap. Remove the distributor cap.

2. Crank over the engine with a remote starter switch or with a wrench on the crankshaft pulley center bolt (22mm hex) until the engine is in the firing position for no. 1 cylinder. At this point, the 0 degree or TDC mark on the crankshaft pulley is aligned with the timing pointer, the rotor is pointing at the no. 1 spark plug wire cap position, and the camshaft lobes for no. 1 cylinder are pointing at the 10 o'clock and 2 o'clock positions (see illustration). At this point, the clearance between the rocker arm and valve depressor (tappet) may be

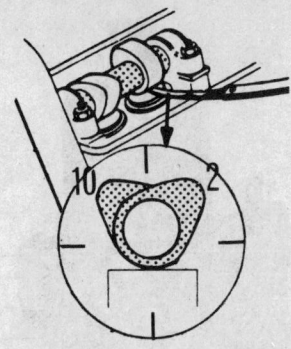

B21 Camshaft lobes at "10 and 2'clock" positions indicating that subject cylinder is in firing position and valves can be adjusted

checked for the intake and exhaust valves of cylinder no. 1, using a feeler gauge. When checking clearance, the wear limit is 0.010–0.018 in. for a cold engine, and 0.012–0.020 in. for a hot one (176°F).

3. Repeat step 2 for cylinders 3, 4, and 2 (in that order). Each time, rotate the crankshaft pulley 180° so that the rotor is pointing to the spark plug wire cap position for that cylinder, and the cam lobes are pointing at the 10 and 2 o'clock positions for the valves of that cylinder.

4. If any of the valve clearance measurements are outside the wear limit, you will have to remove the old valve adjusting disc and install a new one to bring the clearance within specifications. First, rotate the valve depressors (tappets) until their notches are at a right angle to the engine center line. Attach valve depressor tool 999 5022 to the camshaft and screw down the tool spindle until the depressor (tappet) groove is just above the edge of its bore and still accessible with the special pliers (tool no. 999 5026).

5. Remove the valve adjusting disc and measure with a micrometer. Once you've gone to all this trouble, the valve clearance should be set to much narrower tolerances; 0.014–0.016 in. for a cold engine, and 0.016–0.018 for a hot one. So, if the measured clearance had been 0.019 in. and the desired clearance 0.016 in. (for a net difference of 0.003 in., then the new valve adjusting disc should be 0.003 in. thicker than the old one to take up the clearance. Valve adjusting discs are available from Volvo in sizes from 0.130 to 0.180 in. (in 0.002 in. increments). Always oil the new disc and install it with the marks facing down.

6. Remove the valve tappet depressor tool. Rotate the engine a few times and recheck clearance. Install the valve cover with a new gasket.

B27 Engine

Valve clearance is checked every 15,000 miles. No special tools are required.

1. In order to gain access to the valve covers, disconnect or remove the following;

a. Air conditioning compressor from bracket (do not disconnect refrigerant hoses)

b. EGR valve and hoses

c. AC compressor bracket

d. Fuel injection control pressure regulator

e. Air pump

f. Vacuum pump

g. Hoses and wires from solenoid valve (Calif. only)

2. Using a 36 mm hex socket on the crankshaft pulley bolt, rotate the crankshaft to the no. 1 cylinder TDC position. At this point the "O" mark on the timing plate aligns with the crankshaft pulley notch, the distributor rotor is pointing to the no. 1 cylinder spark plug wire cap position, and both valves for no. 1 cylinder have clearance. At this position (see illustration), adjust the intake valves of cylinders no. 1, 2 and 4, and the exhaust valves of cylinders no. 1, 3 and 6. Insert a feeler gauge between the rocker arm and valve stem. Loosen the locknut and turn the adjusting screw in the required direction. Tighten the locknut and recheck clearance. Clearance is 0.004–0.006 in. intake and 0.010–0.012 in. exhaust for a cold engine and 0.006–0.008 in. in-

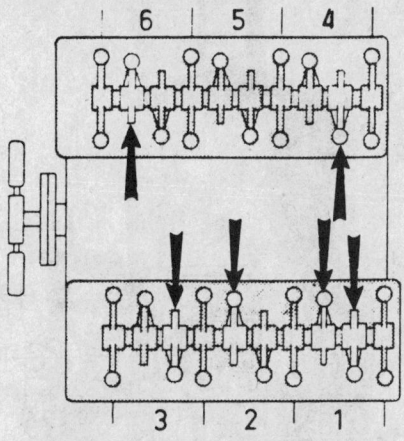

On B27, with No. 1 cylinder at TDC, adjust these valves (arrows)

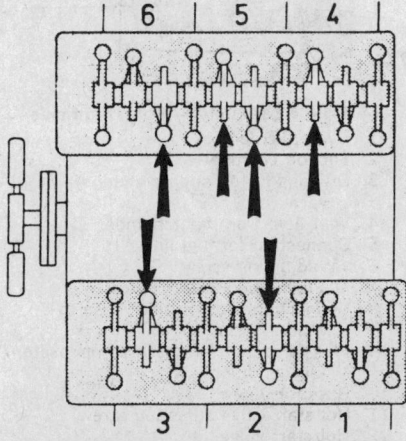

On B27, rotate crankshaft 360° and adjust remaining valves (arrows)

take and 0.012–0.014 in. exhaust for a hot engine.

3. Rotate the crankshaft pulley one full 360° turn to adjust the remaining valves. At this point, the "O" mark will again align with the pulley notch, the rotor is pointing 180° opposite its former position, and the no. 1 cylinder rockers contact the ramps of the camshaft. At this position (see illustration), adjust the intake valves of cylinders no. 3, 5 and 6, and the exhaust valves of cylinders no. 2, 4 and 5.

4. Install the valve covers with new gaskets. Connect all disconnected equipment.

Carburetor Adjustments

Idle Speed and Mixture

Stromberg 175 CD 2SE

1. Check the oil level in the damper cylinders. If the oil is not ¼ in. from the top of the spindle, top up as necessary with Type "A" automatic transmission fluid.

2. Run the engine until it has reached full operating temperature. A good way to check this is to feel the upper radiator hose. When the engine reaches operating temperature, the thermostat opens,

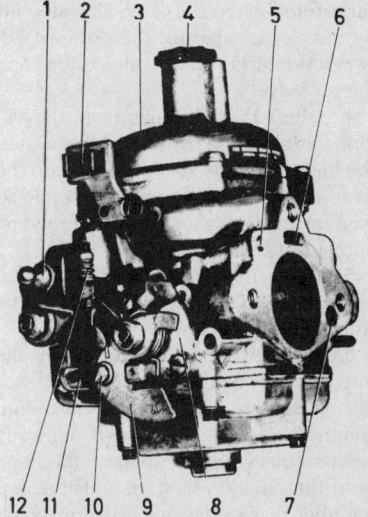

Zenith-Stromberg 175 CD2 SE carburetor—left side

1. Lever for throttle control
2. Clamp for choke wire
3. Suction chamber
4. Hydraulic damper
5. Vent drilling from floatchamber
6. Drilling for air supply under diaphragm
7. Drilling for air supply to temp. compensator and idle trimming screw
8. Cold start device
9. Cam disc for fast idle
10. Connection for choke control
11. Fast idle stop screw
12. Throttle stop screw

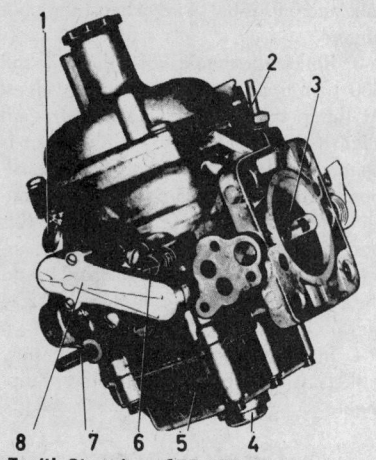

Zenith-Stromberg 175 CD2 SE carburetor—right side
1. Sealed plug
2. Connection for vacuum hose to distributor
3. Primary throttle
4. Floatchamber plug
5. Floatchamber
6. Idle trimming screw
7. Connection for fuel hose
8. Temperature compensator

filling the upper radiator hose with 180° coolant.

3. Adjust the idling speed of the engine to the specifications on the tune-up chart by turning the throttle stopscrews. Turn the screws on both carburetors equally. Check to make sure that both carburetors have the same air valve lift by visually comparing the distance between the carburetor housing bridge and the air valve.

4. Adjust the idle mixture of the engine with the idle trimming screws until the highest engine speed is attained. The basic setting is two turns counterclockwise from lock. Again, turn the screws on both carburetors equally.

5. Adjust the idling speed of the engine to specifications with the throttle stopscrews.

6. Remove the plastic caps over the mixture adjusting screws. Turn both adjusting screws equally until maximum rpm is achieved. Turn both adjusting screws equally in the opposite direction until the engine just starts to falter. Remember that, in this case, the proper setting is not when maximum rpm is reached but when the engine just starts to falter. As a further check, unscrew the adjusting screws ¼–½ of a turn. The speed should then drop a further 20–40 rpm. Turn back the screws equally to the point where the engine just starts to falter and install the plastic caps over the screws.

7. Adjust the idling speed of the engine to specifications with the throttle stopscrews.

SU HIF 6

1. Check the oil level in the damper

cylinders. If the oil is not ¼ in. from the top of the spindle, top up as necessary with Type "A" automatic transmission fluid.

2. Remove the air cleaner.

3. Adjust the fuel jets to their basic setting by lifting the air valve and turning the adjusting screw until the upper edge of the fuel jet is level with the bridge. The jet is then lowered two and one-half turns clockwise. This basic jet setting is correct for a carburetor temperature of approximately 170° F. Turning the adjusting screw a quarter turn in either direction compensates for a temperature difference of approximately 70° F. Turn the adjusting screw less than the two and one-half turns for temperatures above 170° F, and more than two and one-half turns for lower temperatures.

4. Run the engine until it has reached full operating temperature. The upper radiator hose should be very warm at this point.

5. Adjust the idling speed of the engine to the specifications on the tune-up chart by turning the throttle stop screws. Turn the screws on both carburetors equally. Check to make sure that both

SU HIF 6 carburetor—front, right side
1. Hydraulic damper
2. Suction chamber
3. Drillings for air supply under air valve
4. Vent hole from floatchamber
5. Connection for fuel line
6. Jet adjusting screw
7. Floatchamber cover
8. Connection (positive) for hose to venting filter
9. Plug for outlet for speed compensator (air condition)
10. Boss for guard
11. Hot start valve adjusting screw
12. Hot start valve
13. Outlet from floatchamber (connection for hose to venting filter)

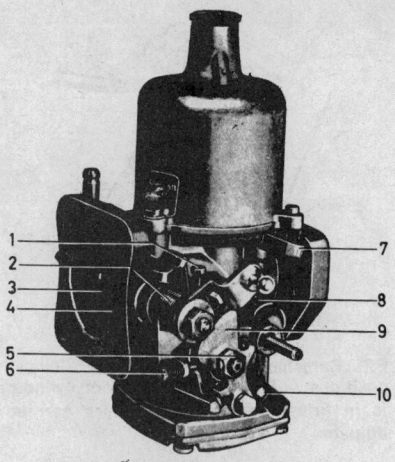

SU HIF carburetor-front, left side
1. Throttle stop screw
2. Return spring
3. Throttle
4. Overrev valve
5. Cold-start device
6. Fast-idle stop screw
7. Attachment for choke control
8. Lift pin
9. Cam disc for fast idle
10. Screw head for float shaft

carburetors have the same air valve lift by visually comparing the distance between the carburetor housing bridge and the air valve.

Bosch Electronic Fuel Injection Adjustments

Idle Speed and Mixture

The idle mixture adjustment or CO value may be set only with the use of a CO meter. This adjustment is made by attaching a CO meter to the exhaust pipe of a vehicle with a warm (176° F) engine, and turning the adjusting screw of the Bosch control unit (beneath the passenger seat) until the correct CO value is obtained. The correct value is 1–1.5 percent for cars with manual transmissions and 0.5–1.0 percent for cars with automatic transmissions. Because this operation requires highly technical skills and expensive equipment, it is best referred to a Volvo or Bosch agency. In other words, don't mess with the control unit.

The idle speed adjustment may, on the other hand, be set with a tachometer and an average amount of expertise. The check should be made with the engine idling at operating temperature (176°F). On 140 and 1800 series Volvos, remove the air cleaner-to-inlet duct hose. Check to see that the auxiliary air regulator is closed properly by removing the inlet duct-to-regulator hose and covering the opening with your hand. If the idle speed differs greatly, the engine is not fully warm or the regulator is faulty. Fit the

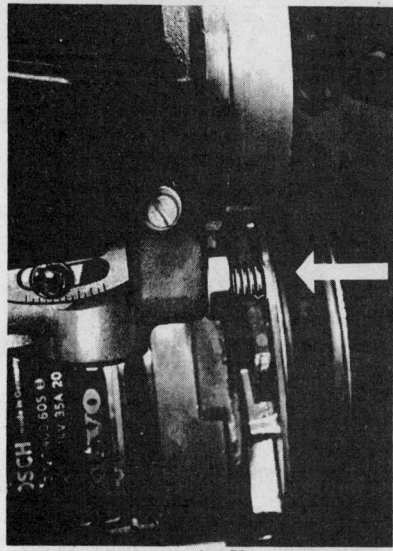

Idle speed adjusting screw—B20E, B20F with electronic fuel injection

Idle speed adjusting screw—B30F

hose again and adjust the idle speed to specifications with the idle adjusting screw. The idle adjusting screw is located on the inlet duct below the air cleaner hose opening on four-cylinder models, and inline in the auxiliary air pipe on six-cylinder models (see illustrations). On 140 and 1800 series Volvos, install the air cleaner hose.

Bosch Continuous Fuel Injection Adjustments

Idle Speed and Mixture

1974 140 series models, and all 240 and 260 series models are equipped with the continuous fuel injection system. With this system, the injectors are open all of the time, and the amount of fuel injected is directly proportional to the amount of air drawn into the intake.

1974–75 B20 F

The idle mixture adjustment or CO value may be set only with the use of a

CIS fuel injection idle CO adjustment—1974-75 B20F

CIS fuel injection idle adjustment 1974-75 B20F

CO meter. Also, a special tapered setscrew tool (see illustration) is needed to turn the mixture adjusting screw. The adjustment is made with the engine idling at curb idle speed and at operating temperature (176°F) and the CO meter attached to the exhaust pipe. 1975 models with air injection require disconnecting and plugging the air pump output hose to

prevent an erroneous CO reading. With the special setscrew tool inserted into the small hole between the fuel distributor and the bellows for the air sensor plate, engage the adjusting screw and adjust to a 1.5% CO value.

The idle speed adjustment is a simple matter of rotating the idle adjusting screw located in-line in the auxiliary air pipe. With the engine idling at operating temperature (176°F), and the transmission in neutral, adjust to 800 rpm on cars with automatic transmission, and 900 rpm on cars with manual transmission.

1976 B21F

Special Tools Required: CO meter and CO idle mixture adjusting allen wrench (Volvo tool #999 5015).

1. Disconnect and plug the air injection pump output hose and the EGR vacuum hose.

2. With the engine warmed to operating temperature (176°F), check that the idle speed is 900 rpm (manual trans) or 800 rpm (automatic) with the car idling in neutral. Adjust as necessary by rotating the air adjusting screw (knob) located beneath the intake air box.

3. With the engine at specified idle speed, check that the CO value is 2.0%. Adjust as necessary by inserting special tool #5015 into adjustment hole located between the air intake bellows and the fuel distributor. Recheck the idle speed.

CAUTION: *Do not rev the engine with the tool inserted.*

4. Stop the engine. Connect the air pump and EGR hoses.

1976 B27F

Special Tools Required: CO meter with two position switch capable of isolating left or right cylinder banks, and CO meter plumbing and fittings to screw into exhaust pipe gas pickup points; and CO idle mixture adjusting allen wrench

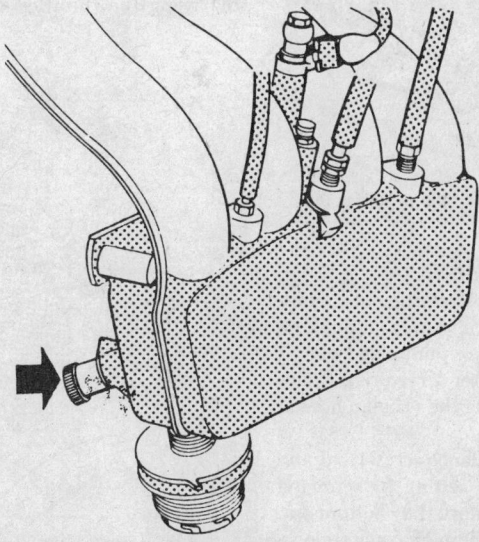

Continuous injection idle speed adjustment—B21F

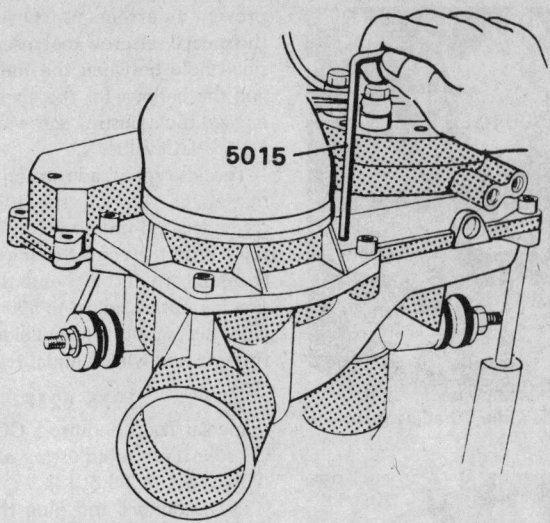

Continuous injection idle mixture (CO) adjustment—B21F

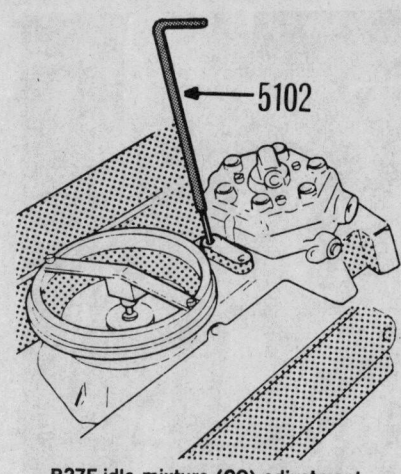

B27F idle mixture (CO) adjustment

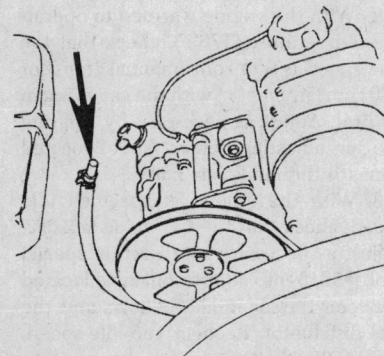

Disconnect the air pump outlet hose to adjust the mixture on B27F

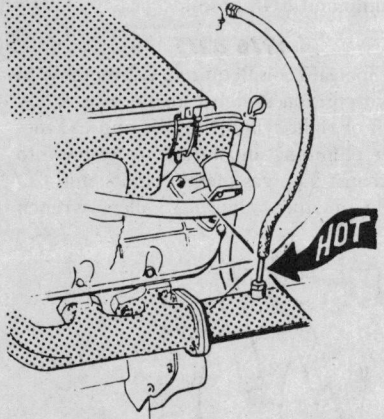

Exhaust pipe gas sample pickup points on B27F

(Volvo tool # 999 5102).

1. Remove the air cleaner and housing. Disconnect the air pump output hose (large hose on rear of pump) and plug it with a large diameter screwdriver shaft. Disconnect and plug the vacuum hose at the EGR valve.

2. Set the idle balance screws (#1 and #2) to their basic setting by screwing them in clockwise until they bottom out, and then backing them off counterclockwise 4 full turns each.

3. Start the engine and allow it to reach operating temperature (176°F). Using the idle air adjusting screw (#3), set the idle speed to 900 rpm.

4. Using the CO meter, check that the carbon monoxide level is 1.4–2.0% at 900 rpm. If necessary, adjust CO level by inserting the special allen wrench (Volvo tool # 5102) into the adjustment hole between the fuel distributor and throttle valve, and turning it clockwise to increase CO and counterclockwise to reduce CO. Before inserting the tool, remove the copper washer and plug covering the hole. Also, between adjustments, remove the tool and plug the hole to prevent a lean mixture and erroneous reading. **CAUTION:** *Do not rev the engine with the tool inserted, as the lever may become damaged.*

5. The final step is to check the CO balance between the right and left cylinder banks. Both must have an equal CO value; 1.4–2.0% at 900 rpm. Air adjusting screw #3 controls the total amount of air bypassing the throttles at idle, whereas

idle balance screws #1 and #2 divide this air to the two cylinder banks. Screw #1 is for the right (passenger) side cylinders, and screw #2 for the left (driver) side. If you decrease the airflow past screw #2, it will increase the airflow past screw #1, and vice versa. More air means a leaner mixture, and less air a richer mixture. After balancing the CO value of each cylinder bank, recheck the total CO value at 900 rpm. Stop the engine.

6. Connect the EGR hose, air pump hose, and air cleaner.

ENGINE ELECTRICAL
Distributor
Removal and Installation

1. Unsnap the distributor cap clasps and remove the cap.

2. Crank the engine until no. 1 cylinder is at Top Dead Center (TDC). At this point, the rotor should point to the spark plug wire socket for no. 1 cylinder, and the 0° timing mark on the crankshaft

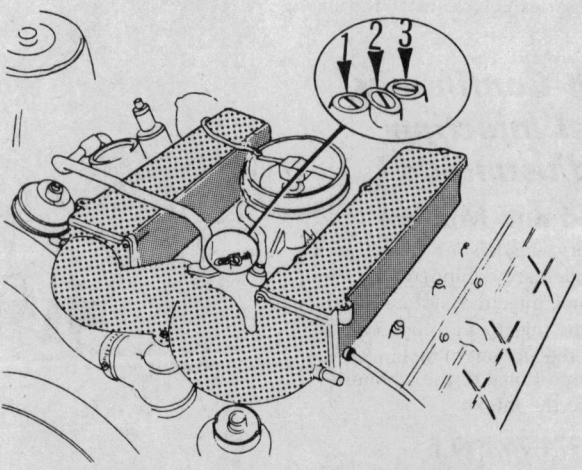

B27F idle balance (#1 and 2) and air adjusting screws (#3)

els with electronic ignition, remove the retaining screw for the primary voltage wire connector and pull it from the distributor housing.

4. Remove the vacuum hose(s) from the regulator (except on 1974 140 models). Take care not to damage the bakelite connection during removal.

5. On B20 and B30 engines, slacken the distributor attaching screw and hold-

down clamp enough to slide the distributor up and out of position. On B21 and B27 engines, remove the distributor attaching screw and lift out the distributor.

6. When ready to install the distributor, if the engine has been disturbed (cranked), find TDC for no. 1 cylinder as outlined under "Valve Lash Adjustment". If the engine has not been disturbed, install the distributor with the

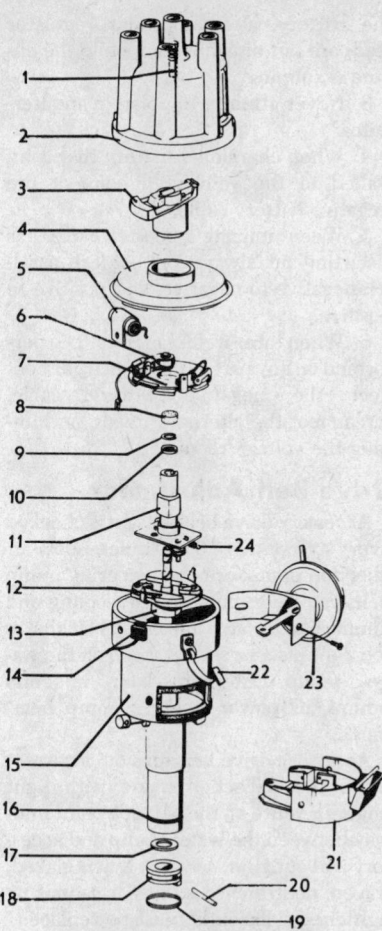

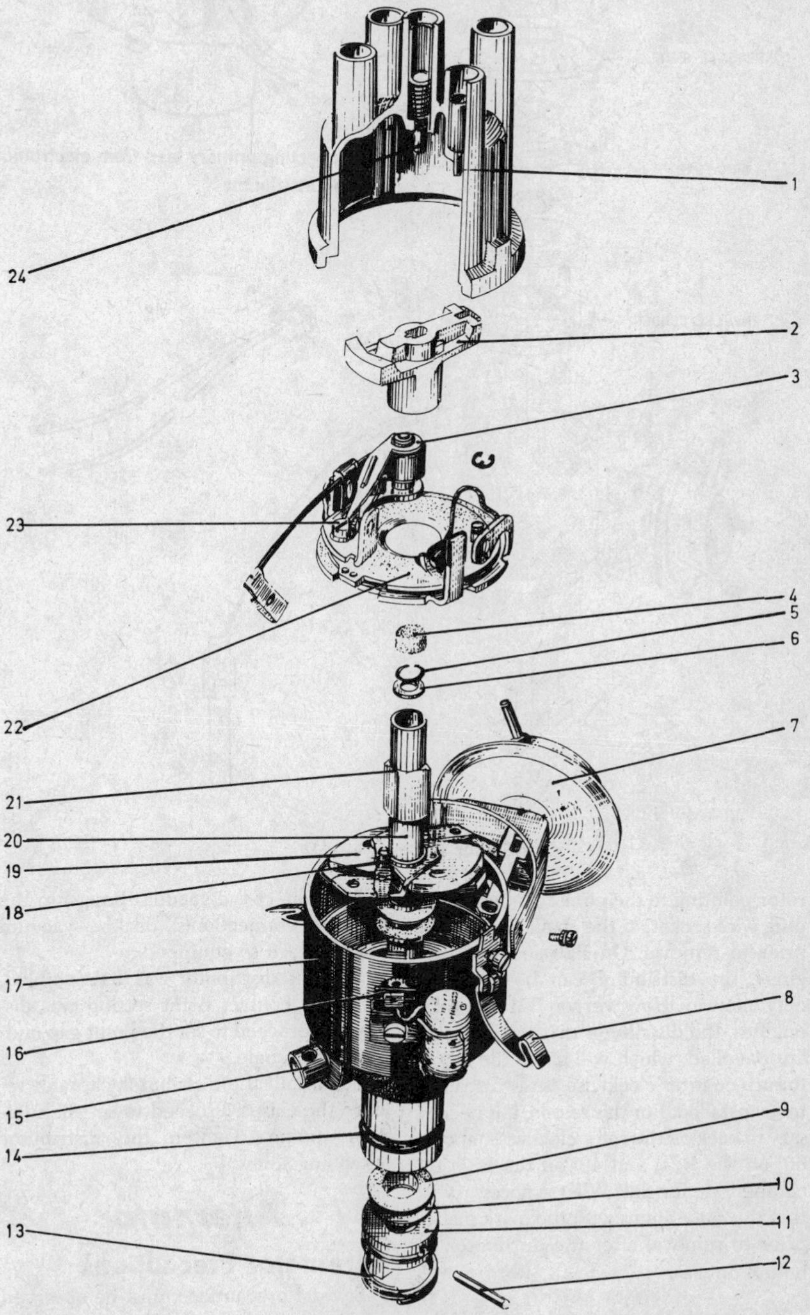

Distributor assembly—B30F

1. Rod brush (carbon)
2. Distributor cap
3. Distributor arm
4. Protective cover
5. Condenser
6. Ignition contact breaker
7. Breaker plate
8. Lubricating felt
9. Circlip
10. Washer
11. Breaker cam
12. Centrifugal weight
13. Cam for triggering contacts
14. Primary terminal
15. Distributor body
16. Rubber seal
17. Washers
18. Driving collar
19. Resilient ring
20. Lock pin
21. Contact device
22. Lock clamp for distr. cap
23. Vacuum regulator
24. Centrifugal governor spring

damper should be aligned with the pointer. For ease of assembly, scribe a chalkmark on the distributor housing to note the position of the rotor.

3. Disconnect the primary lead from the coil at its terminal on the distributor housing. On electronic fuel-injected models, disconnect the plug for the triggering contacts. On 1975 and later mod-

Distributor assembly—B20B

1. Distributor cap
2. Distributor arm
3. Contact breaker
4. Lubricating felt
5. Circlip
6. Washer
7. Vacuum regulator
8. Cap clasp
9. Fiber washer
10. Steel washer
11. Driving collar
12. Lock pin
13. Resilient ring
14. Rubber seal
15. Lubricator
16. Primary connection
17. Distributor housing
18. Centrifugal governor spring
19. Centrifugal weight
20. Breaker camshaft
21. Breaker cam
22. Breaker plate
23. Lock screw for breaker contacts
24. Rod brush (carbon)

Volvo

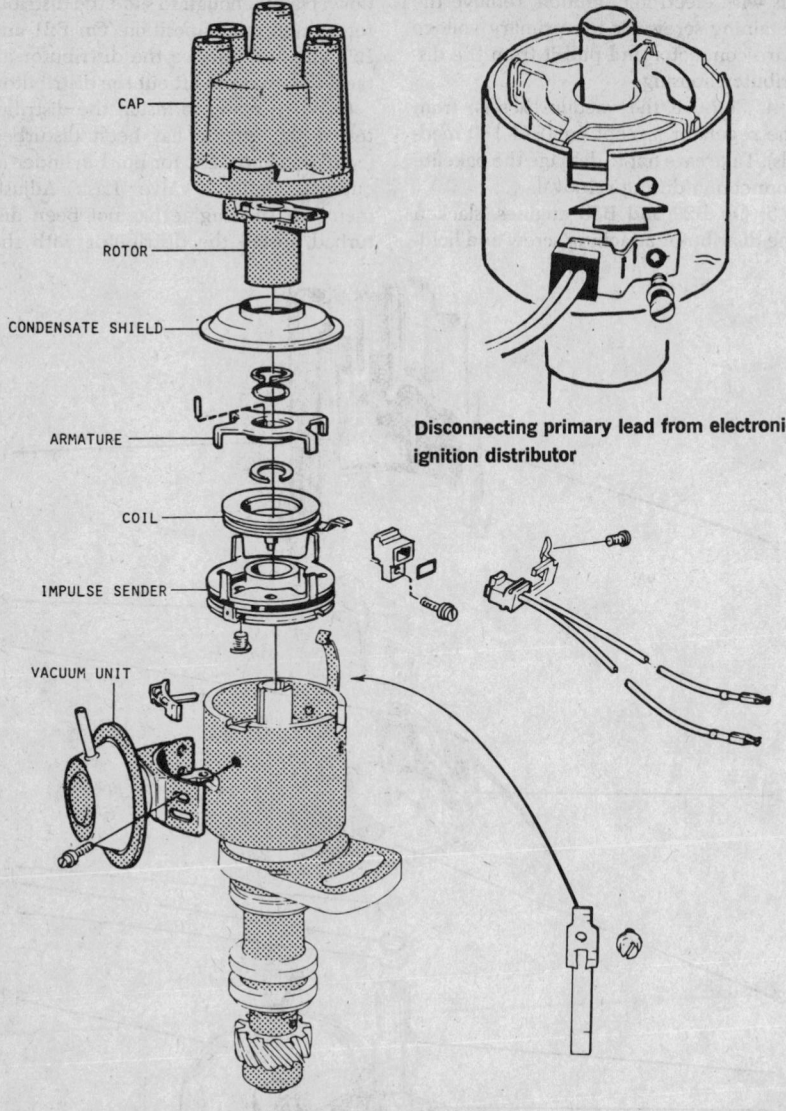

CAP

ROTOR

CONDENSATE SHIELD

ARMATURE

COIL

IMPULSE SENDER

VACUUM UNIT

Disconnecting primary lead from electronic ignition distributor

Distributor assembly—B21F

rotor pointing to the no. 1 cylinder spark plug wire socket, or the chalkmark made prior to removal. On B20 and B30 engines, the distributor can be installed only one way. However, on B21 and B27 engines, the distributor drive gear teeth are bevelled, which will cause the rotor to turn counter-clockwise as the distributor is installed. For this reason, it is necessary to back off the rotor clockwise (about 60° on the B21, and 40° on the B27) to compensate for this. What is necessary is that the rotor aligns with the mark made prior to removal after the distributor is bolted down.

7. Connect the primary lead to its terminal on the distributor housing. On electronic fuel-injected models, connect the plug for the triggering contacts. On 1975 and later models equipped with electronic ignition, push the primary voltage wire connector into its slot in the distributor housing and tighten the retaining screw.

8. Connect the vacuum hose(s) to the bakelite connection(s) on the vacuum regulator, (if so equipped).

9. If the distributor was disassembled, or if the contact point setting was disturbed, proceed to set the point gap and-/or dwell angle.

10. Install the distributor cap and secure the clasps. Proceed to set the ignition timing. Tighten the distributor attaching screw.

Alternator

Alternator Precautions

Several precautions must be observed when performing work on alternator equipment.

1. If the battery is removed for any reason, make sure that it is reconnected with the correct polarity. Reversing battery connections may result in damage to the one-way rectifiers.

2. Never operate the alternator with the main circuit broken. Make sure that the battery, alternator, and regulator leads are not disconnected while the engine is running.

3. Never attempt to polarize an alternator.

4. When charging a battery that is installed in the vehicle, disconnect the negative battery cable.

5. When utilizing a booster battery as a starting aid, always connect it in parallel; negative to negative, and positive to positive.

6. When arc welding is to be performed on any part of the vehicle, disconnect the negative battery cable, disconnect the alternator leads, and unplug the voltage regulator.

Drive Belt Adjustment

Accessory drive belt tension is checked every six months or 6,000 miles. Loose air injection pump, or power steering pump belts can cause poor engine cooling and diminish alternator output. A belt that is too tight places a severe strain on the water pump, alternator, air injection pumps, or power steering pump bearings.

Accessory drive belt tension is correct when the deflection made with light finger pressure on the belt at a point midway between the water pump and accessory is about ½ in. Any belt that is glazed, frayed, or stretched so that it cannot be tightened sufficiently must be replaced.

Incorrect belt tension is corrected by moving the driven accessory (alternator, air pump, power steering pump or air conditioning compressor) away from or toward the driving pulley. Loosen the mounting and adjusting bolts on the respective accessory and tighten them, once the belt tension is correct. Never position a metal pry bar on the rear end of the alternator, air pump or power steering pump housing; they can be deformed easily.

Alternator Removal and Installation

NOTE: *On 1975 models, it will be necessary to remove the air pump and place it to one side, to gain access to the alternator.*

1. Disconnect the negative battery cable.

2. Disconnect the electrical leads to the alternator.

3. Remove the adjusting arm-to-alternator bolt and the adjusting arm-to-engine bolt.

4. Remove the alternator mounting bolt.

5. Remove the fan belt and lift the alternator forward and out.

6. Reverse the above procedure to install, taking care to properly tension the fan (drive) belt.

1228

Voltage Regulator

Voltage Regulator Removal and Installation

1. Disconnect the negative battery cable.

2. Disconnect the leads or plug socket from the old regulator taking note of their (its) location.

3. Remove the hold-down screws from the old regulator and install the new one.

4. Connect the leads or plug socket and reconnect the negative battery cable.

Voltage Adjustment

Motorola (S.E.V. Marchal) Regulator

If the Motorola A.C. regulator is found to be defective, it must be replaced. No adjustments can be made on this unit.

The following test may be performed on the Motorola regulator to see if it is functioning properly. An ammeter, tachometer, and voltmeter are required.

1. Connect the alternator and regulator as shown in the illustration.

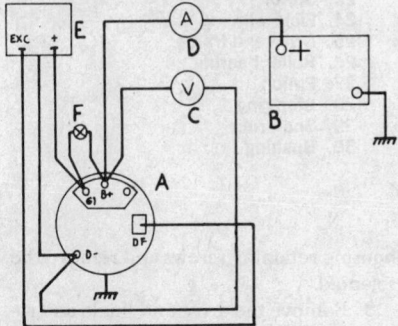

Wiring diagram for testing Motorola regulator.

A. Alternator
B. Battery 60 Ah
C. Voltmeter 0—20 amps.
D. Ammeter 0—50 amps.
E. Voltage regulator
F. Warning lamp 12 volts. 2 watts

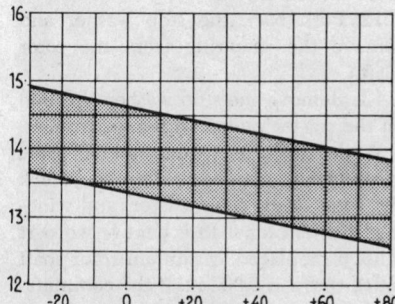

Voltage-temperature diagram for cold regulator—Motorola.

2. Run the engine at 2500 rpm (5000 alternator rpm) for 15 seconds. With no load on the alternator, and the regulator ambient temperature at 77°F, the reading on the voltmeter should be 13.1–14.4

V. For regulator ambient temperatures other than 77°F, consult the voltage-temperature diagram for cold regulator.

3. Load the alternator with 10–15 amps (high-beam headlights) while the engine is running at 2500 rpm. The voltmeter reading should again be 13.1–14.4 V. Replace the regulator if it does not fall within these limits.

4. For a more accurate indication of the regulator's performance, drive the vehicle for about 45 minutes at a minimum speed of 30 mph. The regulator will be at the correct working temperature immediately after this drive.

5. With the engine running at 2500 rpm, and the regulator ambient temperature at 77°F, the voltmeter reading should be 13.85–14.25 V. For regulator ambient temperatures other than 77°F, consult the Voltage-temperature diagram for warm regulator.

Bosch A.C. Regulator (35, 55 amp)

The Bosch A.C. regulator is fully adjustable. To determine which adjustments are necessary—if any—perform the following test. (An ammeter, 12 V control lamp, tachometer, and voltmeter are required for this test.)

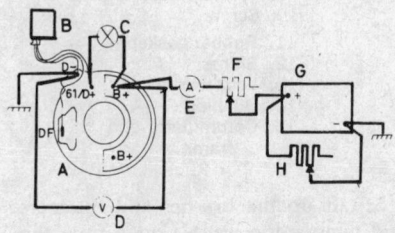

Wiring diagram for testing Bosch A.C. regulator.

A. Alternator
B. Voltage lamp 12 volts
C. Control lamp 12 volts, 2 watts
D. Voltmeter 0-20 volts
F. Regulator resistance
G. Battery 60 amperehours
H. Load resistance
E. Ammeter 0-50 amps

NOTE: *Where the numerical values differ for the 35 amp voltage regulator and the 55 amp unit, the figures for the 55 amp regulator will be given in parentheses.*

1. Connect the alternator and regulator as shown in the illustration.

NOTE: *the first reading must be taken within 30 seconds of beginning of test.*

2. While running the engine at 2000 rpm, load the alternator with 28–30 amps (44–46 for 55 amp alternator).

3. Rapidly lower the engine to idle speed or 500 rpm, and then return it to 2000 rpm. With a load of 28–30 amps (44–46 for 55 amp alternator), the voltmeter reading should be 14.0–15.0 V (13.9–14.8 V for 55 amp alternator). The

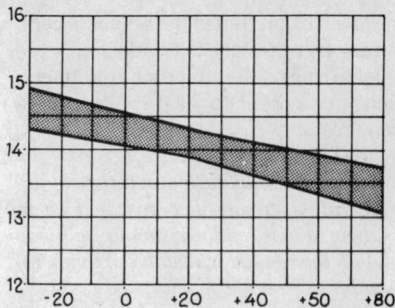

Voltage-temperature diagram for warm regulator—Motorola.

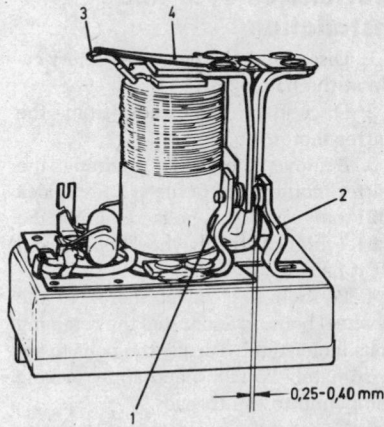

Bosch A.C. voltage adjustments

1. Regulator contact for lower control range (lower contact)
2. Regulator contact for upper control range (upper contact)
3. Spring tensioner
4. Spring upper section: Steel spring Lower section: Bimetal spring

regulator should be regulated on the left (lower) contact.

4. Reduce the alternator load to 3–8 amps. The voltmeter reading should not decrease more than 0.3 (0.4 for 55 amp. alternator) V. The regulator should be regulated on the right (upper) contact.

5. Adjustment is made by bending the stop bracket for the bimetal spring. Bending the stop bracket down lowers the regulating voltage; bending it up raises the voltage. If the voltmeter reading for the low amp alternator load decreased more than 0.3 (0.4 for 55 amp alternator) V, compared to the reading for the high amp alternator load, adjust the regulator by bending the holder for the left (lower) cont act and simultaneously adjust the gap between the right (upper) contact and the movable contact. The gap should be adjusted to 0.010–0.015 in. (0.25–0.40 mm). If the holder is bent toward the right (upper) contact, the regulating voltage under high amp alternator load will be lowered.

To avoid faulty adjustments due to

residual magnetism in the regulator core, it may be necessary to rapidly lower the engine rpm to idle after each adjustment, and then raise it to 2000 rpm to take a new reading.

NOTE: *Warm regulators may be cooled to ambient temperature by directing a stream of compressed air on them. Final readings should be made with the regulator at ambient temperature.*

Starter

Starter Removal and Installation

1. Disconnect the negative battery cable at the battery.

2. Disconnect the leads from the starter motor.

3. Remove the bolts retaining the starter motor brace to the cylinder block (B21 only) and the bolts retaining the starter motor to the flywheel housing and lift it off.

4. Position the starter motor to the flywheel housing and install the retaining bolts finger-tight. Torque the bolts to approximately 25 ft lbs, and apply locking compound to the threads.

5. Connect the starter motor leads and the negative battery cable.

Starter Drive Replacement

In order to remove the starter pinion drive, it is necessary to disassemble the starter. The procedure for disassembling the starter is as follows.

1. Remove the starter from the car as outlined in "Starter Removal and Installation."

2. Unscrew the two screws and remove the small cover from the front end of the starter shaft.

3. Unsnap the lockwasher and remove the adjusting washers from the front end of the shaft.

4. Unscrew the two screws retaining the commutator bearing shield and remove the shield.

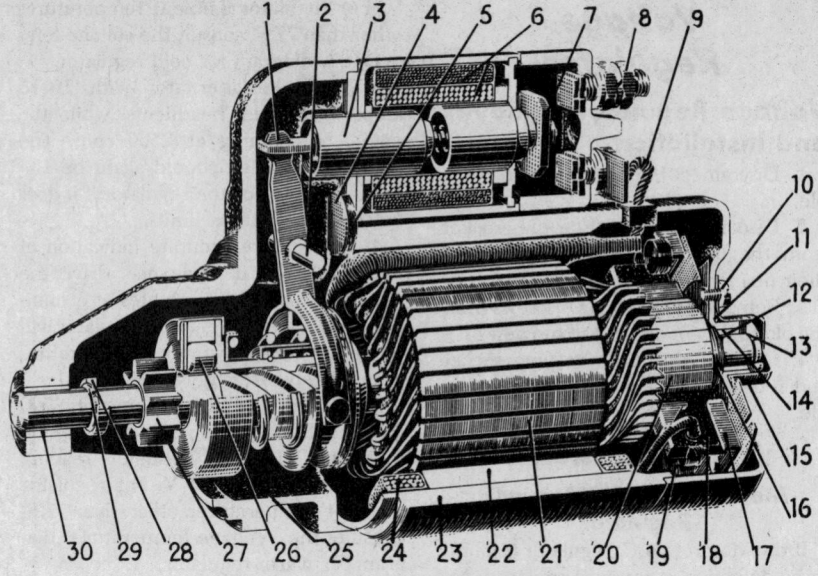

Volvo starter motor

1. Shift lever	16. Adjusting washers
2. Pivot pin	17. Brush holder
3. Plunger	18. Brush
4. Steel washer	19. Bush spring
5. Rubber washer	20. Commutator
6. Winding	21. Armature
7. Contact plate	22. Pole shoe
8. Terminal for battery	23. Stator
lead	24. Field winding
9. Terminal lead to field	25. Drive end frame
10. Screw	26. Roller bearing
11. Rubber gasket	27. Pinion
12. Shims	28. Stop ring
13. Lock washer	29. Snap ring
14. Bushing	30. Bushing
15. Commutator end	
frame	

5. Lift up the brushes and retainers and remove the brush bridge from the rotor shaft. The negative brushes are removed with the bridge while the positive brushes remain in the field winding. Do not remove the steel washer and the fiber washer at this time.

6. Unscrew the nut retaining the field terminal connection to the control solenoid.

7. Unscrew the two solenoid-to-starter housing retaining screws and remove the solenoid.

8. Remove the drive end shield and rotor from the stator.

9. Remove the rubber and metal sealing washers from the housing.

10. Unscrew the nut and remove the screw on which the engaging arm pivots.

11. Remove the rotor, with the pinion and engaging arm attached, from the drive end shield.

12. Push back the stop washer and remove the snap-ring from the rotor shaft.

13. Remove the stop washer and pull off the starter pinion with a gear puller.

While the starter is disassembled, a few quick checks may be performed. Check the rotor shaft, commutator, and windings. If the rotor shaft is bent or worn, it must be replaced. Maximum rotor shaft radial throw is 0.003 in. If the commutator is scored or worn unevenly, it should be turned. Minimum commutator diameter is 1.3 in. Check the end shield, which houses the brushes, for excessive wear. Maximum bearing clearance is 0.005 in.

14. Lubricate the starter.

15. Press the starter pinion onto the

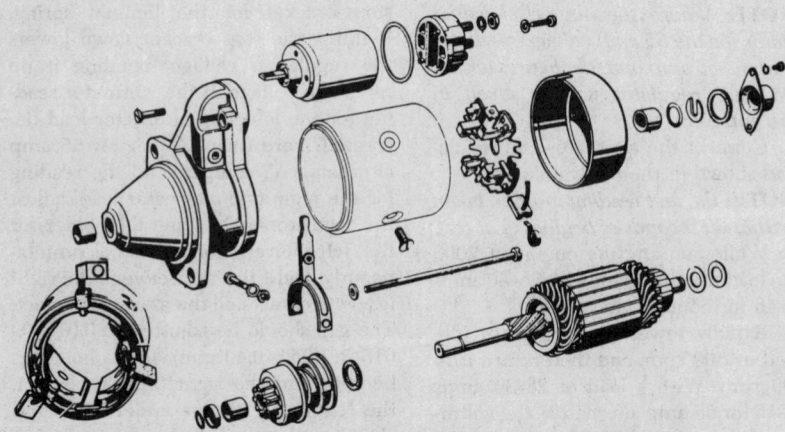

Exploded view of starter motor

rotor shaft. Install the stop washer and secure it with a new snap-ring.

16. Position the engaging arm on the pinion. Install the rotor into the drive end frame.

17. Install the screw and nut for the engaging arm pivot.

18. Install the rubber and metal sealing washers into the drive end housing.

19. Install the stator onto the rotor and drive end shield.

20. Position the solenoid so that the eyelet on the end of the solenoid plunger fits onto the engaging arm (shift lever). Tighten the solenoid retaining screws.

21. Place the metal and fiber washers on the rotor shaft.

22. Install the brush bridge on the rotor shaft and replace the brushes.

23. Fit the commutator bearing shield into position and install the retaining screws.

24. Install the adjusting washers and snap a new lockwasher into position on the end of the shaft. Make sure that the rotor axial clearance does not exceed 0.12 in. If necessary, adjust the clearance with washers, maintaining a minimum clearance of 0.002 in.

25. Replace the small cover over the front end of the shaft and install the two retaining screws.

26. Install the starter in the car as outlined in "Starter Removal and Installation."

Solenoid Replacement

Before replacing the solenoid when the starter will not crank, see if the battery has sufficient charge. If the no-crank condition persists when the battery is known to be good, connect a jumper wire between the positive terminal of the battery and the contact screw for the solenoid lead. If the solenoid engages the starter pinion, the starter switch or leads are at fault. If the starter still does not crank, replace the solenoid. To remove the solenoid, remove the starter from the car. The solenoid may be removed from the starter while installed in the car, but then aligning the solenoid plunger eyelet with the engaging arm during installation can be difficult. The procedure for replacement of the solenoid is as follows.

1. Remove the starter from the car as outlined in "Starter Removal and Installation."

2. Unscrew the two solenoid-to-starter housing retaining screws and remove the solenoid.

3. As a final test, wipe the solenoid clean and press in the armature. Test its operation by connecting it to a battery. If the solenoid still does not function, replace it with a new unit.

4. Position the new solenoid so that the eyelet on the end of the plunger fits into the engaging arm. Tighten the retaining screws.

5. Replace the starter in the car as outlined in "Starter Removal and Installation."

ENGINE MECHANICAL

All 1972–75 Volvos are equipped with either the B 20 or B 30 engine. All of these engines have evolved from those seemingly indestructible cast-iron, water-cooled, pushrod, inline fours of yesteryear. The B 20, introduced late in 1968, is a two liter (1990 cc) four-cylinder powerplant. The B 30, introduced in 1969, is a three liter (2978 cc) six-cylinder powerplant. The six-cylinder B 30 is, in effect, a stretched four-cylinder B 20. All of these engines share the same basic design.

The B 20 engine has been imported in three variations; the B 20 B, B 20 E, and the B 20 F. The B 20 B, with its 9.3:1 compression ratio and dual sidedraft carburetors (Stromberg 175 CD2 SE in 1969–70 and SU HIF in 1971–72), is standard equipment in the 140 series Volvos of 1969–72 vintage. The B 20 E, with its high-compression head (10.5:1) and Bosch electronic fuel injection, has been standard equipment in all 1970–71 1800E series, and optional in the 1971 142S (known as the 142E). Due to the decision to convert to low-lead fuels in this country, which makes high-compression engines unfeasible, the B 20 F engine was introduced in 1972. This engine incorporates Bosch electronic fuel injection with the low-compression head (8.-7:1). The B 20 F was optional on 1972 140 series models, and is standard on all 1972–73 1800 series, and all 1973 140 series models. Beginning with the 1974 model year, the B 20 F utilizes Bosch continuous (air-flow controlled) fuel injection.

The B 30 engine has been imported in two variations; the B 30 A, and the B 30 F. The B 30 A has a 9.3:1 compression ratio and is equipped with dual sidedraft Stromberg 175 CD2 SE carburetors. This engine is standard equipment on all 1969–72 164 models. The B 30 F is the same engine with a lower compression ratio (8.7:1) and Bosch electronic fuel injection; optional on 1972 164 models, and standard on 1973 and later models.

With the 1976 model year, two entirely new engines are used; a 2127 cc B21F in the 240 series and a 2660 cc B27F in the 260. Both engines use Bosch Continuous Fuel Injection, where fuel is metered according to intake air flow.

The B21F is a 130 cu. in. in-line four cylinder. Its cast iron cylinder block carries the crankshaft in five main bearings. This engine features an aluminum alloy, cross-flow cylinder head with belt-driven overhead camshaft.

The B27F is a 162 cu. in. 90° V-6, developed jointly by Volvo, Peugeot and Renault. Both the cylinder block and cross-flow cylinder heads are constructed of aluminum alloy. Wet, replaceable iron cylinder liners are used. The valves are operated by chain-driven overhead camshafts, one for each cylinder bank. In order to engineer out the roughness inherent in the 90° V-6 design, the four main crankshaft is generously counterbalanced, and the valve and ignition timing is staggered to offset the uneven firing intervals.

Engine Removal and Installation

B20, B30

All Volvo engines and transmissions are removed as a unit. In most cases, a good chain hoist will suffice. Do not attempt to lift the engine with the chain wrapped around either the oil filter or the distributor. Lifting eyes may be fabricated from heavy gauge steel or angle iron.

1. Scribe the outline of the hinges on the hood and remove the hood.

2. Drain the oil from the crankcase. Open the drain plug on the right-hand side of the engine block, disconnect the lower radiator hose at the radiator, and drain the cooling system. On Volvos with automatic transmissions, disconnect and plug the transmission oil cooler lines.

3. Remove the expansion tank, radiator cover plate, upper radiator hose, radiator, and fan shroud, if so equipped.

4. Remove the positive lead from the battery.

5. Remove the electric cables for the starter, the coil high-tension wire, the distributor lead, alternator wires, water and oil temperature sensors, and the lead for the oil pressure sensor, if so equipped.

6. Remove the vacuum hoses for the distributor advance, and the power brake booster, if so equipped. Remove the positive crankcase ventilation (PCV) hoses, and the oil pressure gauge hose at the pipe connection, if so equipped.

7a. On carbureted models, remove the air cleaner, air intake hoses, and preheating plate. Also disconnect and plug the inlet hose to the fuel pump, disconnect the choke linkage, and remove the throttle control shaft from the pedal shaft, intermediate shaft, and bracket.

7b. On electronic fuel-injected models, remove the air cleaner and intake hoses; pressure sensor hose from the inlet duct; the plug contacts for the temperature sensor, cold start valve, throttle valve switch, fuel injectors, and distributor impulse. In addition, remove the ground wire from the inlet duct, the throttle cable bracket from the inlet duct, the throttle cable from the throttle valve switch, the cold start valve fuel hose from the distribution pipe, the fuel return line from the pressure regulator, and the fuel inlet line from the distribution pipe. Remove the injectors by turning the lockrings counterclockwise and lifting them out of their bayonet fittings. The injectors should then be fitted with protective covers and plugs to prevent dirt from entering.

7c. On continuous (air-flow controlled) fuel-injected models, disconnect the rubber hose to the control pressure regulator, the plastic hose from the pressure regulator to the fuel distributor, the hose at the cold start injector, the fuel filter hose, and the fuel return hose at the fuel distributor. Remove the pipe connecting the air cleaner and the intake manifold. Disconnect the electrical leads from the cold start injector, control pressure regulator, auxilliary air valve, coolant temperature sensor and the thermal time switch (engine side). Disconnect the ground wire for the control pressure regulator. Disconnect and plug the 4 fuel hoses at the injectors. Disconnect the throttle cable from the throttle and intake manifold. Disconnect the brake booster vacuum hose. Remove the thermal time switch.

8. Disconnect the heater pipes from all models. Remove the exhaust pipe flange nuts and disconnect the exhaust pipe from the manifold. On 1973 and later models, remove the EGR valve pipe from the manifold. On models equipped with power steering, remove the steering pump bolts and place the pump and reservoir to one side.

9. On Volvos with manual transmissions, place the gearshift in neutral and remove the shifter lever. On Volvos with automatic transmissions, disconnect the control rod from the selector lever, and the ground cable from the start inhibitor switch.

10. Disconnect the wires for the back-up lights and overdrive, if so equipped. Remove the speedometer drive cable from the transmission. Remove the clamp for the exhaust manifold and the clamp for the automatic transmission filler tube, if so equipped.

11. Jack up the vehicle and place two jackstands under the front jack attachments and two more in front of the rear jack attachments.

12. Place a hydraulic jack under the transmission. On manual transmission cars, remove the return spring from the throw-out fork, and disconnect the clutch cable.

13. Separate the transmission (or overdrive) from the front universal joint by unbolting the flange. Unbolt the rear crossmember.

14. Disconnect the negative ground cable from the engine.

15. Remove the rear crossmember and rear engine mounts. Remove the lower nuts for the front engine mounts.

16. Install the lifting eyes and lifting crossbar. The lifting eyes are attached by ⅜ x 1¾ x 1 in. bolts. Lift out the engine and set it on an engine stand or rack. The engine is removed by raising its front and lowering its back while pulling forward until it clears the front crossmember, then leveling it and raising the complete unit.

17. Install the lifting apparatus on the engine. Make sure that the jackstands are located beneath the front jack attachments and in front of the rear jack attachments. Place the hydraulic jack beneath the transmission tunnel.

18. Carefully lower the engine into the engine compartment. Place the hydraulic jack under the transmission and guide the unit into place. Be careful not to damage the oil filter, or oil pressure sending unit against the exhaust pipe. Be careful not to damage the distributor against the steering column.

19. Tighten the nuts for the front engine mounts.

20. Connect the wires for the back-up lights, start inhibitor switch (automatic transmission), and overdrive, if so equipped.

21. Install the brackets for the exhaust manifold and the automatic transmission filler tube. Install the rear engine mounts and rear crossmember, then tighten the nuts.

22. Remove the hydraulic jack from the transmission and the lifting apparatus from the engine. Connect the negative ground cable to the engine.

23. Connect the front universal joint to the transmission (or overdrive) flange. Connect the speedometer drive cable.

24. On manual transmission cars, connect the clutch cable and install the return spring. Adjust clutch free-play. On automatic transmission cars, connect the control rod to the selector lever, and the ground cable to the start inhibitor switch.

25. Connect the exhaust pipe to the exhaust manifold with new gaskets and tighten the nuts. On 1973 and later models, connect the EGR valve pipe.

26. Remove the jackstands from the jack attachments and lower the vehicle.

27. Connect the heater pipes. On models with power steering, install the pump and reservoir to the engine block and adjust the drive belt tension.

28a. On continuous (air-flow controlled) fuel-injected models, install the thermal time switch and connect the hose for the brake booster. Install the throttle cable and connect the 4 fuel hoses to the injectors. Connect the control pressure regulator ground wire and the cold start injector, control pressure regulator, auxiliary air valve, temperature sensor, and thermal time switch leads. Connect the fuel hoses to the control pressure regulator and fuel distributor. Connect the hoses to the fuel filter, cold start injector, and the fuel return hose to the fuel distributor. Install the pipe between the air filter and the intake manifold.

28b. On electronic fuel-injected models, place the injectors in their bayonet fittings with new rubber seals, and turn them clockwise to install. In addition, connect the fuel inlet line and the cold start valve hose to the distribution pipe, and the return line from the pressure regulator. Install the ground wire and the throttle cable bracket to the inlet duct, and connect the throttle cable. Connect the plug contacts for the temperature sensor, cold start valve, throttle valve switch, fuel injectors, and distributor impulse. Install the pressure sensor vacuum hose, air cleaner, and intake hoses.

28c. On carbureted models, connect the fuel pump inlet hose, choke linkage, and throttle linkage. Install the preheating plate, intake hoses, and air cleaner.

29. On all models, connect the positive crankcase ventilation hoses, and the distributor vacuum advance hose. Connect the vacuum hose for the power brake booster, and the oil pressure gauge hose at the pipe connection, if so equipped.

30. Install the electric cables for the starter, the coil high-tension wire, the distributor lead, alternator wires, water and oil temperature sensors, and the lead for the oil pressure sensor, if so equipped.

31. Connect the positive lead to the battery.

32. Install the radiator and fan shroud, if so equipped, and the radiator cover plate. Install the expansion tank, the upper and lower radiator hoses, and, on automatic transmission cars, the transmission oil cooler lines. Make sure that the cooler lines clear the engine mounts and brake tubes by a generous ¾ in.

33. Fill the crankcase and cooling system.

34. Install the hood. Install the gearshift lever.

35. Start the engine and check for leaks.

B21F

1. On cars equipped with manual transmission, remove the four retaining clips and lift up the shifter boot. Then, remove the snap-ring for the shifter.

2. Remove the battery.

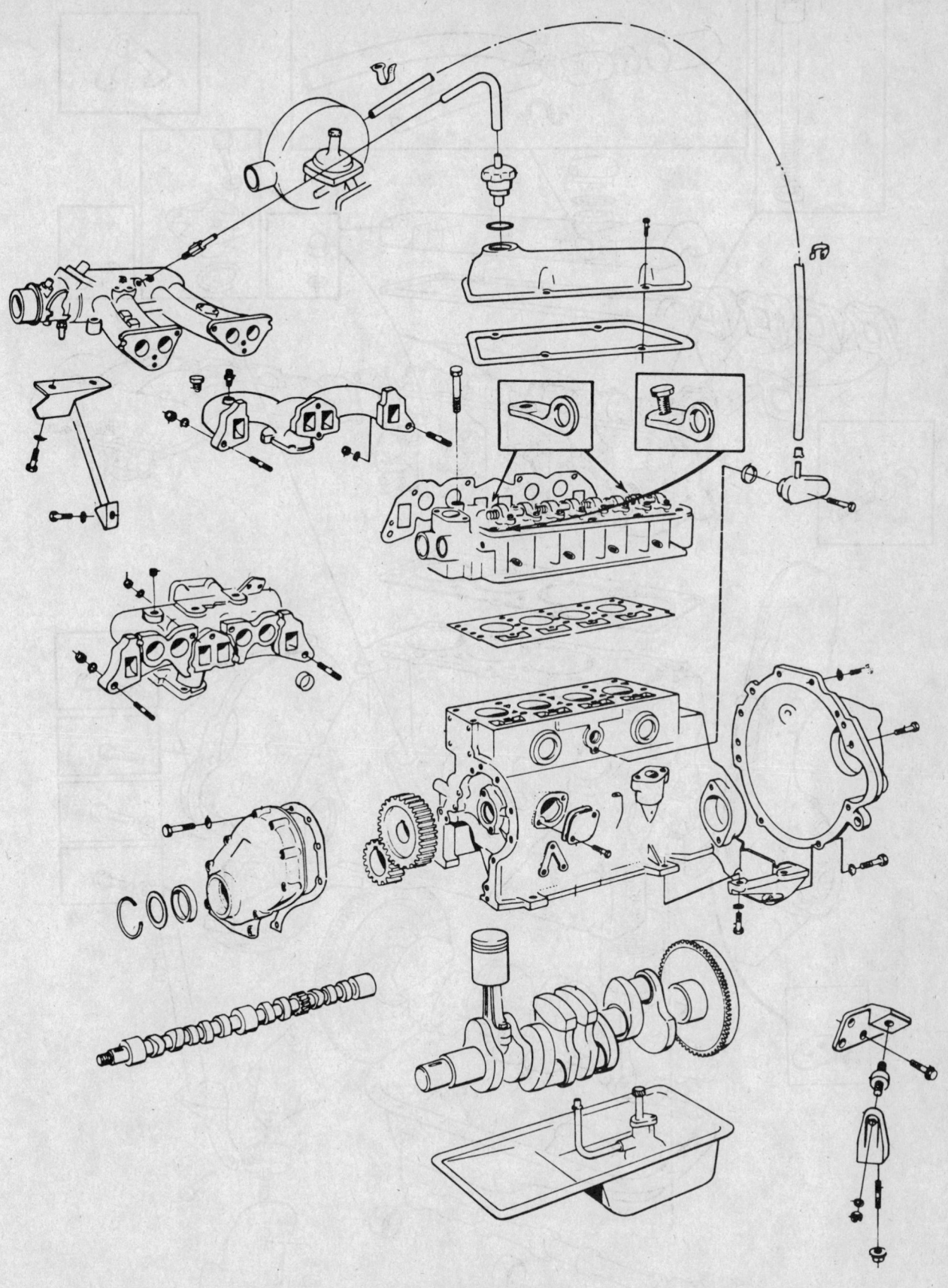

B20 engine (B30 engine similar)

Volvo

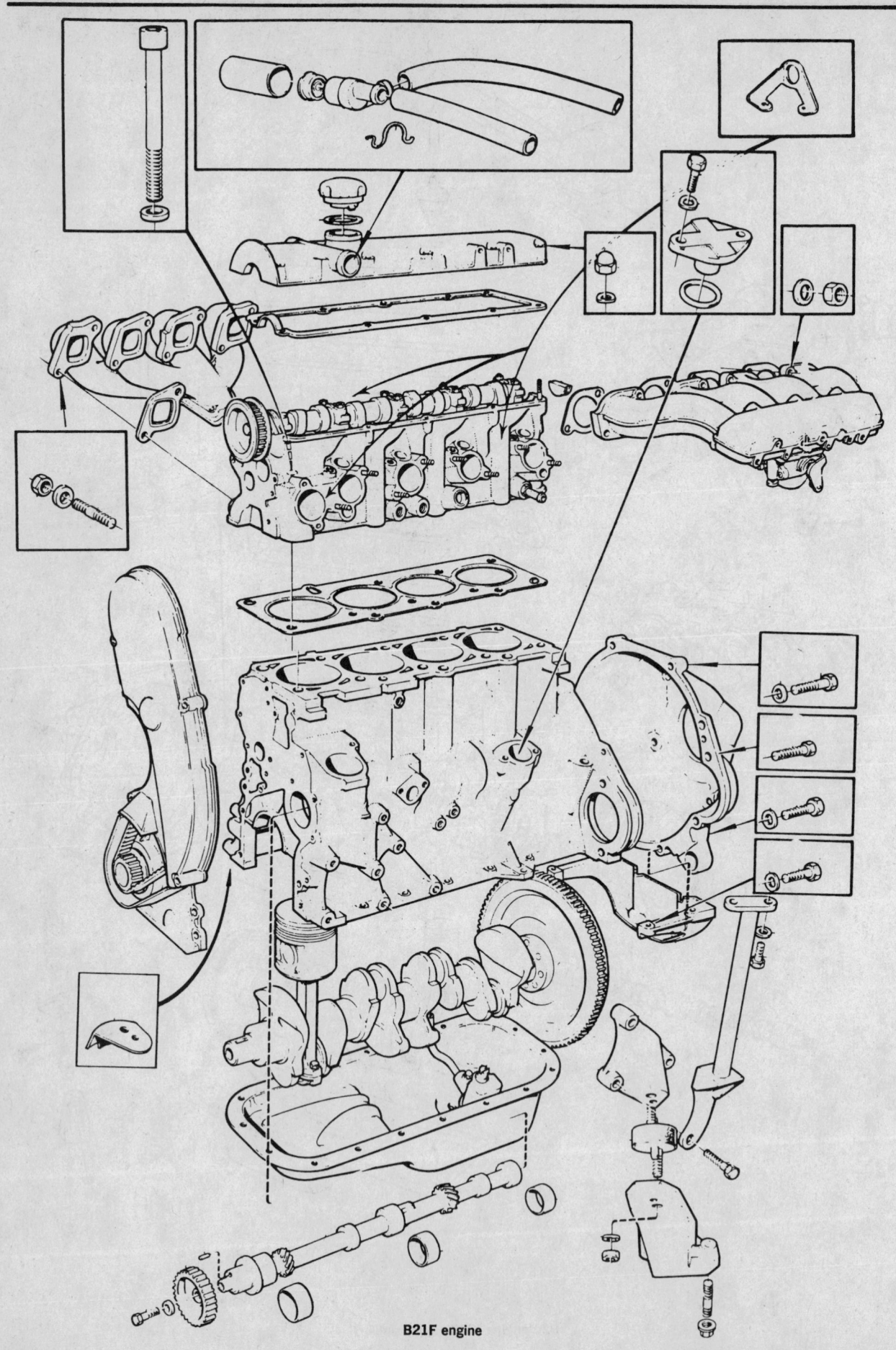

B21F engine

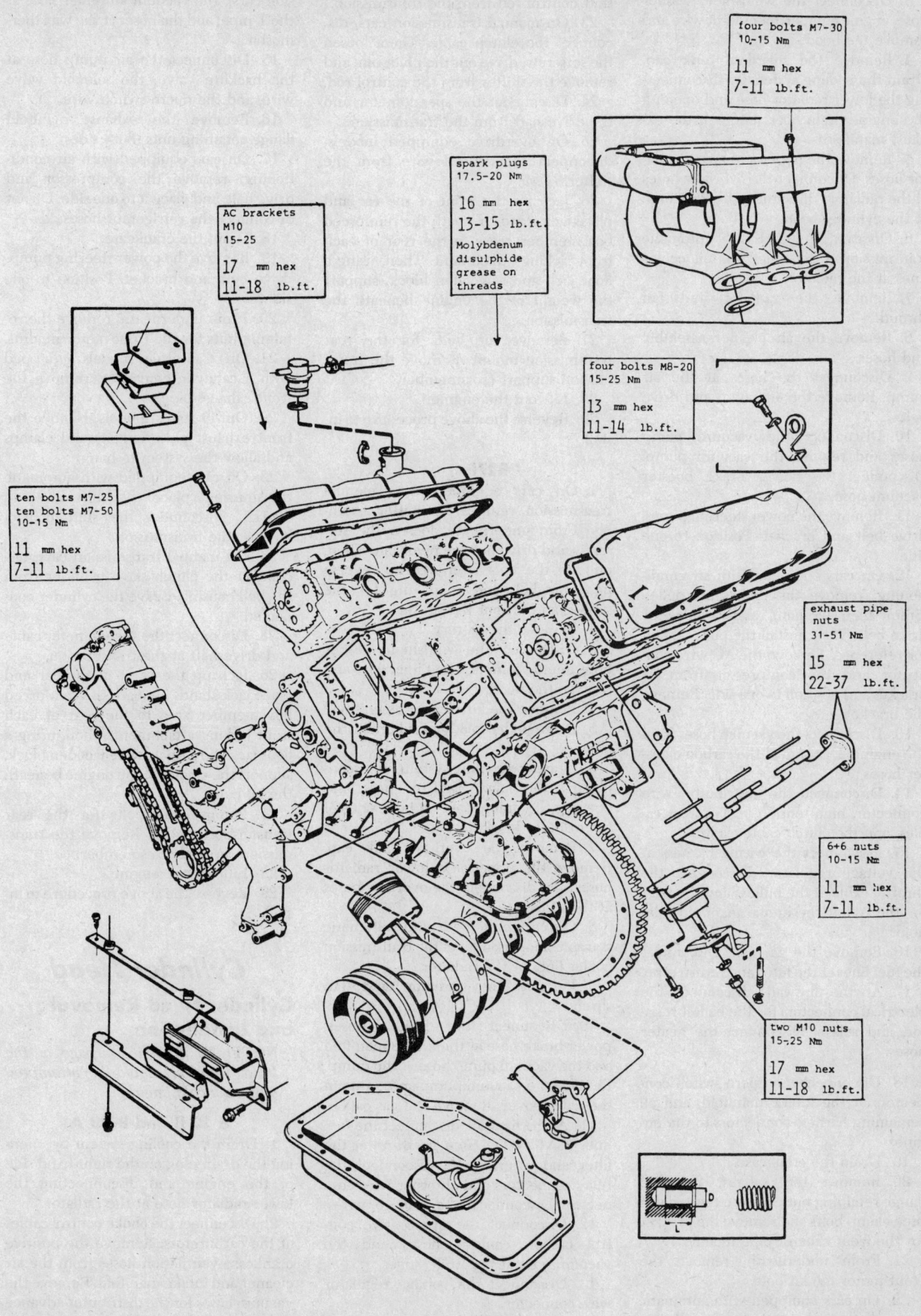

four bolts M7-30
10-15 Nm

11 mm hex

7-11 lb.ft.

spark plugs
17.5-20 Nm

16 mm hex

13-15 lb.ft.

Molybdenum
disulphide
grease on
threads

AC brackets
M10
15-25

17 mm hex

11-18 lb.ft.

four bolts M8-20
15-25 Nm

13 mm hex

11-14 lb.ft.

ten bolts M7-25
ten bolts M7-50
10-15 Nm

11 mm hex

7-11 lb.ft.

exhaust pipe
nuts
31-51 Nm

15 mm hex

22-37 lb.ft.

6+6 nuts
10-15 Nm

11 mm hex

7-11 lb.ft.

two M10 nuts
15-25 Nm

17 mm hex

11-18 lb.ft.

B27 Engine assembly

3. Disconnect the windshield washer hose, engine compartment light wire and remove the hood.

4. Remove the overflow tank cap. Drain the cooling system by disconnecting the lower radiator hose and opening the engine drain cock (beneath the exhaust manifold).

5. Remove the upper and lower radiator hoses. Disconnect the overflow hoses at the radiator. Disconnect the PCV hose at the cylinder head.

6. On cars equipped with automatic transmission, disconnect the oil cooler lines at the radiator.

7. Remove the radiator and fan shroud.

8. Remove the air cleaner assembly and hoses.

9. Disconnect the hoses at the air pump. Remove the air pump and drive belt.

10. Disconnect the vacuum pump hoses and remove the vacuum pump. Disconnect the power brake booster vacuum hose.

11. Remove the power steering pump, drive belt and bracket. Position to one side.

12. On cars equipped with air conditioning, remove the crankshaft pulley (5mm allen wrench), and compressor drive belt. Then, install the pulley again for reference. Remove the AC wire connector and the compressor from its bracket and position to one side. Remove the bracket.

13. Disconnect the vacuum hoses from the engine. Disconnect the carbon canister hoses.

14. Disconnect the distributor wire connector, high tension lead, starter cables, and the clutch cable clamp.

15. Disconnect the wiring harness at the voltage regulator. Disconnect the throttle cable at the pulley, and the wire for the AC at the intake manifold solenoid.

16. Remove the gas cap. Disconnect the fuel lines at the filter and return pipe.

17. At the firewall, disconnect the electrical connectors for the ballast resistor, and relays. Disconnect the heater hoses.

18. Disconnect the micro switch connectors at the intake manifold, and all remaining harness connectors to the engine.

19. Drain the crankcase.

20. Remove the exhaust manifold flange retaining nuts. Loosen the exhaust pipe clamp bolts and remove the bracket for the front exhaust pipe mount.

21. From underneath, remove the front motor mount bolts.

22. On cars equipped with automatic transmission, place the gear selector lever in "Park" and disconnect the gear

shift control rod from the transmission.

23. On manual transmission cars, disconnect the clutch cable. Then, loosen the setscrew, drive out the pivot pin, and remove the shifter from the control rod.

24. Disconnect the speedometer and the driveshaft from the transmission.

25. On overdrive equipped models, disconnect the control wire from the shifter.

26. Jack up the front of the car and place jack stands beneath the reinforced box member areas to the rear of each front jacking attachment. Then, using a floor jack and a wooden block, support the weight of the engine beneath the transmission.

27. Remove the bolts for the rear transmission mount. Remove the transmission support crossmember.

28. Lift out the engine.

29. Reverse the above procedure to install.

B27F

1. On cars equipped with manual transmission, remove the shifter assembly. From underneath, loosen the setscrew and drive out the pivot pin. Then, pull up the boot, remove the reverse pawl bracket, and snap ring for the shifter, and lift out the shifter.

2. Remove the battery.

3. Disconnect the windshield washer hose, engine compartment light wire and remove the hood.

4. Remove the air cleaner assembly.

5. Remove the splash guard under the engine.

6. Drain the cooling system by disconnecting the lower radiator hose and opening the drain cocks on both sides of the cylinder block.

7. Remove the overflow tank cap. Remove the upper and lower radiator hoses, and disconnect the overflow hoses at the radiator.

8. On cars equipped with automatic transmission, disconnect the transmission cooler lines at the radiator.

9. Remove the radiator and fan shroud.

10. Disconnect the heater hoses, power brake hose at the intake manifold and the vacuum pump hose at the pump. Remove the vacuum pump and o-ring in the valve cover. Remove the gas cap.

11. At the firewall, disconnect the fuel lines (CAUTION: High pressure) at the filter and return pipe, disconnect the relay connectors and all other wire connectors. Disconnect the distributor wires.

12. Disconnect the evaporative control carbon canister hoses and the vacuum hose at the EGR valve.

13. Disconnect the voltage regulator wire connector.

14. Disconnect the throttle cable (and kickdown cable on automatic transmis-

sion cars), the vacuum amplifier hose at the T-pipe, and the hoses at the wax thermostat.

15. Disconnect the air pump hose at the backfire valve, the solenoid valve wire, and the micro switch wire.

16. Remove the exhaust manifold flange retaining nuts (both sides).

17. On cars equipped with air conditioning, remove the compressor and drive belt, and place it to one side. Do not disconnect the refrigerant hoses.

18. Drain the crankcase.

19. Remove the power steering pump, drive belt, and bracket. Position to one side.

20. From underneath, remove the retaining nuts for the front motor mounts.

21. On California models equipped with a catalytic converter, remove the front exhaust pipe.

22. On 49 states models, remove the front exhaust pipe hangers and clamps and allow the system to hang.

23. On cars equipped with automatic transmission, place the shift lever in "Park". Disconnect the shift control lever at the transmission.

24. On manual transmission cars, disconnect the clutch slave cylinder from the bell housing. Leave the cylinder connected.

25. Disconnect the speedometer cable and driveshaft at the transmission.

26. Jack up the front of the car and place jack stands beneath the reinforced box member area to the rear of each front jacking attachment. Then, using a floor jack and a thick, wide wooden block, support the weight of the engine beneath the oil pan.

27. Remove the bolts for the rear transmission mount. Remove the transmission support crossmember.

28. Lift out the engine.

29. Reverse the above procedure to install.

Cylinder Head

Cylinder Head Removal and Installation

NOTE: *To prevent warpage of the head, removal should be attempted only on a cold engine.*

B 20 B and B 30 A

1. Drain the cooling system by opening the drain plug on the right-hand side of the engine and disconnecting the lower radiator hose at the radiator.

2. Disconnect the choke control cables at the carburetors. Remove the positive crankcase ventilation hoses from the air cleaner and intake manifold. Remove the vacuum hoses for the distributor advance and the power brake booster, if so equipped.

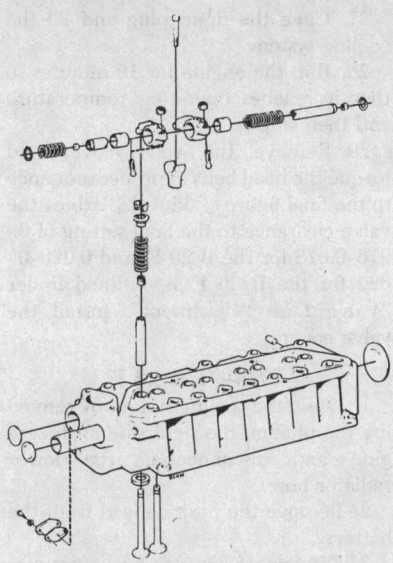

B20 Cylinder head assembly—B30 similar

3. Remove the throttle control shaft from the pedal shaft, link rods, and bracket. (Disconnect the downshift linkage on cars with automatic transmissions.)

4. Remove the air cleaner(s), inlet hose, and heat control valve hose from the engine.

5. Remove the upper radiator hose. Remove the heater hose clamp from the head.

6. Remove and plug the fuel line at the carburetors.

7. Label the spark plug wires and disconnect them from the plugs. Disconnect the coolant temperature sensor.

8. Remove the exhaust manifold preheating plate. Remove the nuts and disconnect the exhaust pipe from the exhaust manifold.

9. Unbolt the alternator adjusting arm from the head.

10. Remove the valve cover. Remove the rocker shaft and arm assembly as a unit and draw out the push rods, keeping them in order.

11. Loosen the head bolts gradually, in the same order as their tightening sequence. Remove the head bolts, noting their locations, and lift off the head. Do not attempt to pry off the head. The head may be tapped lightly with a rubber mallet to break the gasket seal. If any residual water in the cooling passages of the head falls into the combustion chambers during removal, remove it immediately and coat the cylinder walls with oil.

12. Remove the integrally cast intake and exhaust manifold.

13. Remove the old head gasket, flange gasket, and rubber sealing rings for the water pump.

14. Thoroughly clean the mating surfaces of the cylinder head and block and remove any traces of the old head gasket.

Check the mating surfaces for warpage. There is an oil feed hole for the rocker arm assembly on the tappet side, in the middle of the head. Make sure it is clean. A clogged oil feed hole may be opened with a length of thin gauge metal wire and some kerosine to dissolve some of the deposits. Clean the top of the cylinder head and the oil return holes to remove any gum or foreign deposits. Clean and oil the head bolts.

15. Install the combination intake and exhaust manifold on the head with new gaskets.

16. Install new sealing rings for the water pump.

17. Use a pair of guide studs for proper alignment of the cylinder head, head gasket, and block. Guide studs can be easily made by cutting the heads off a pair of spare head bolts. The tops of the bolts are then filed to a tapered edge and slotted so that they may be installed and removed with a screwdriver. The guide studs should be installed at opposite ends of the cylinder block.

18. Fit a new head gasket on the cylin-

Oil feed hole in cylinder head

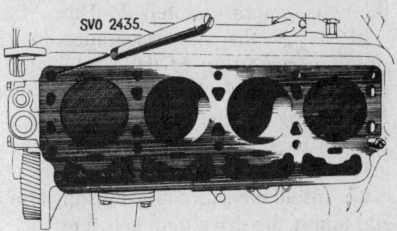

Guide stud installation

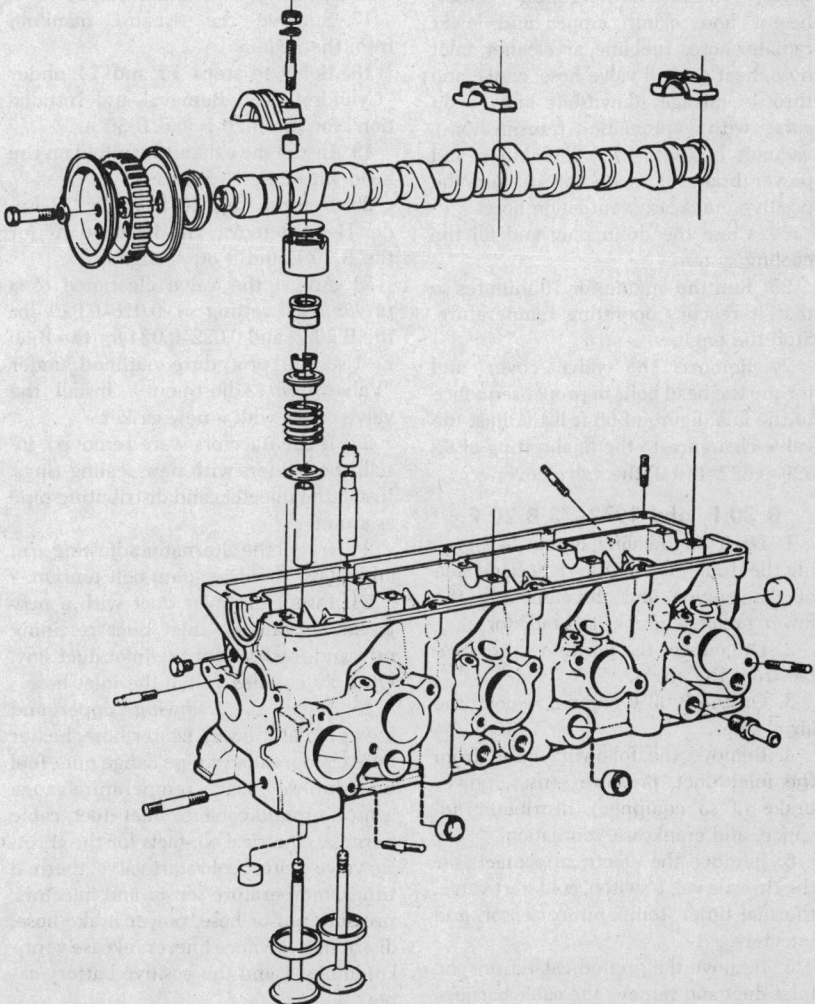

B21 Cylinder head assembly

der block with the lettering "TOP" (wide edge) facing up. Slide the gasket down over the two guide studs.

19. Carefully lower the cylinder head over the guide studs onto the block. Install, but do not tighten, two head bolts at opposite ends to secure the gasket, and remove the guide studs. Install the remaining head bolts finger-tight. Torque the head bolts in proper sequence first to 29 ft lbs, and then to 58 ft lbs.

20. Roll the pushrods on a level surface to inspect them for straightness. Replace any bent pushrods. Install the pushrods in their original positions and install the rocker shaft and arm assembly. Torque the bolts to approximately 20 ft lbs.

21. Adjust the valve clearance to a *preliminary* setting of 0.018–0.020 for the B 30 A, and 0.022–0.024 for the B 20 B. Use the procedure outlined under "Valve Lash Adjustment". Install the valve cover.

22. Install the alternator adjusting arm and adjust the drive (fan) belt tension.

23. Install the following: exhaust manifold preheating plate, exhaust pipe and flange nuts (with new gaskets), spark plug wires, coolant temperature sensor, heater hose clamp, upper and lower radiator hoses, fuel line, air cleaner, inlet hose, heat control valve hose, choke and throttle linkage (downshift linkage on cars with automatic transmissions), vacuum hoses for the distributor and power brake (if so equipped), and the positive crankcase ventilation hoses.

24. Close the drain plug and fill the cooling system.

25. Run the engine for 10 minutes so that it reaches operating temperature. Stop the engine.

26. Remove the valve cover and torque the head bolts in proper sequence to the final figure of 65 ft lbs. Adjust the valve clearance to the final setting of 0.-020–0.022. Install the valve cover.

B 30 F, and 1972–73 B 20 F

1. Drain the cooling system by opening the drain plug on the right-hand side of the engine and disconnecting the lower radiator hose at the radiator.

2. Disconnect the positive battery cable from the engine.

3. On the B 30 F engine, remove the air cleaner.

4. Remove the following hoses from the inlet duct, pressure sensor, power brake (if so equipped), distributor advance, and crankcase ventilation.

5. Remove the electrical contacts for the throttle valve switch, cold start valve, thermal timer, temperature sensor, and injectors.

6. Remove the ground cable from the inlet duct and remove the cable harness.

7. Disconnect the sensor for the coolant temperature gauge. Remove the

spark plug wires from the plugs.

8. On B 20 F engines, remove the inlet hose.

9. Disconnect the throttle control cable from the throttle valve and inlet duct.

10. Remove and pinch shut the fuel hoses from the distributing pipe.

11. Remove the upper radiator hose, the heater control valve hose, and the clamp for the heater pipe.

12. Unbolt the alternator adjusting arm from the head.

13. Remove the bolts for the inlet duct stay. Remove the inlet duct-to-cylinder head retaining nuts and disconnect the inlet duct.

14. If any cleaning or machine work is to be performed on the cylinder head, remove the fuel injectors beforehand. Turn the lockrings on the injectors counterclockwise and lift out the injectors and distributing pipe as a unit. Remove the injector holders from the head.

15. Remove the exhaust manifold-to-exhaust pipe flange nuts and disconnect the pipe.

16. Refer to steps 10 and 11 under "Cylinder Head Removal and Installation" for the B 20 B and B 30 A.

17. Remove the exhaust manifold from the head.

18. Refer to steps 13 and 14 under "Cylinder Head Removal and Installation" for the B 20 B and B 30 A.

19. Install the exhaust manifold on the head with a new gasket.

20. Refer to steps 16–20 under "Cylinder Head Removal and Installation" for the B 20 B and B 30 A engines.

21. Adjust the valve clearance to a *preliminary* setting of 0.018–0.020 for the B 20 F, and 0.022–0.024 for the B 30 F. Use the procedure outlined under "Valve Lash Adjustment". Install the valve cover with a new gasket.

22. If the injectors were removed, install the holders with new sealing rings. Install the injectors and distributing pipe as a unit.

23. Install the alternator adjusting arm and adjust the drive (fan) belt tension.

24. Install the inlet duct with a new gasket. Install the inlet duct retaining nuts and the bolts for the inlet duct stay. On B 20 engines, install the inlet hose.

25. Install the following: upper and lower radiator hoses, heater hose, heater hose clamp, exhaust pipe flange nuts, fuel line, throttle linkage, temperature gauge sensor, ground cable to inlet duct, cable harness, electrical contacts for the throttle valve switch, cold start valve, thermal timer, temperature sensor and injectors, pressure sensor hose, power brake hose, distributor advance line, crankcase ventilation hoses, and the positive battery cable.

26. On the B 30 F engine, install the air cleaner.

27. Close the drain plug and fill the cooling system.

28. Run the engine for 10 minutes so that it reaches operating temperature and then stop it.

29. Remove the valve cover and torque the head bolts in proper sequence to the final figure of 65 ft lbs. Adjust the valve clearance to the final setting of 0.-016–0.018 for the B 20 F, and 0.020–0.-022 for the B 30 F as outlined under "Valve Lash Adjustment". Install the valve cover.

1974–75 B 20 F

1. Drain the cooling system by removing the plug on the right side of the engine and disconnecting the lower radiator hose.

2. Remove the positive lead from the battery.

3. Disconnect hoses to brake vacuum booster and crankcase ventilation.

4. Remove the cold start injector hose and the fuel return hoses on both sides of the T-connection (at the control pressure regulator).

5. Remove the outlet fuel hose at the fuel filter and remove fuel filter with clamp from the firewall.

6. Disconnect the fuel hose from the fuel distributor at the control pressure regulator.

7. Disconnect electrical wires at cold start injector, auxiliary air valve, control pressure regulator and temperature sensor.

8. Remove the air cleaner connecting pipe.

9. Disconnect the throttle cable at the intake manifold.

10. Disconnect hose for heater and the upper radiator hose.

11. Remove the alternator adjustment bracket.

12. Remove the straps for the injector hoses. Remove injectors with hoses from the cylinder head, by turning the lockrings counterclockwise.

13. Remove the bracket for the intake manifold, and remove the manifold.

14. Remove exhaust manifold from exhaust pipe and cylinder head.

15. Remove ignition leads and spark plugs.

16. Remove the valve cover, rocker arm shaft and the pushrods.

17. Remove the cylinder head bolts and lift off the head. Take off the cylinder head gasket, the flange gasket and the rubber rings for the water pump.

18. Follow steps 14, 16, 17, 18, 19 and 20 under "Cylinder Head Removal and Installation" for the B 20 B, and B 30 A.

19. Install pushrods and rocker arm shaft. Adjust the valves to .45–.50 mm (.018–.020 in.) (Not final Clearance.)

20. Reverse the removal procedure to install. Then, run the engine for 10

minutes. Retighten the cylinder head bolts to 65 ft lb with a torque wrench. Re-adjust valve clearance as outlined under "Valve Lash Adjustment". Install the valve cover.

B21F

1. Disconnect the battery.

2. Remove the overflow tank cap and drain the coolant. Disconnect the upper radiator hose.

3. Remove the distributor cap and wires.

4. Remove the PCV hoses.

5. Remove the EGR valve and vacuum pump.

6. Remove the air pump, and air injection manifold.

7. Remove the exhaust manifold and header pipe bracket.

8. Remove the intake manifold. Disconnect the manifold brace and the hose clamp to the bellows for the fuel injection air/flow unit. Disconnect the throttle cable, and all vacuum hoses and electrical connectors to the fuel injection unit.

9. Remove the fuel injectors.

10. Remove the valve cover.

11. Loosen the fan shroud and remove the fan. Remove the shroud. Remove the upper belts and pulleys.

12. Remove the timing belt cover. Remove the timing belt as described later in this section.

13. Remove the camshaft (if so desired) as outlined later in this section.

14. Remove the cylinder head (10 mm allen head bolts).

15. To install, reverse the removal procedure. Oil the head bolts. Tighten the head bolts in the prescribed torque sequence first to 44 ft-lbs, then to 81 ft-lbs. After the engine has been run for 30 minutes, slacken the bolts to relieve any pre-tension, and then retorque to 81 ft-lbs. To set the valve timing, follow the steps for timing belt installation later in this section.

B27F

1. Disconnect the battery. Drain the coolant.

2. Remove the air cleaner assembly and all attaching hoses.

3. Disconnect the throttle cable. On automatic transmission equipped cars, disconnect the kick-down cable.

4. Disconnect the EGR vacuum hose and remove the pipe between the EGR valve and manifold.

5. Remove the oil filler cap, and cover the hole with a rag. Disconnect the PCV pipe from the intake manifold.

6. Remove the front section of the intake manifold.

7. Disconnect the electrical connector and fuel line at the cold start injector. Disconnect the vacuum hose, both fuel lines, and the electrical connector from the control pressure regulator.

8. Disconnect the hose, pipe, and electrical connector from the auxiliary air valve. Remove the auxiliary air valve.

9. Disconnect the electrical connector from the fuel distributor. Remove the wire looms from the intake manifolds. Disconnect the spark plug wires.

10. Disconnect the fuel injectors from their holders.

11. Disconnect the distributor vacuum hose, carbon filter hose, and diverter valve hose from the intake manifold. Also, disconnect the power brake hose and heater hose at the intake manifold.

12. Disconnect the throttle control link from its pulley.

13. On cars equipped with an EGR vacuum amplifier, disconnect the wires from the throttle micro switch and solenoid valve.

14. At the firewall, disconnect the fuel lines from the fuel filter and return line.

15. Remove the two attaching screws and lift out the fuel distributor and throttle housing assembly.

16. On cars not equipped with an EGR vacuum amplifier, disconnect the EGR valve hose from underneath the throttle housing.

17. Remove the cold start injector, rubber ring, and pipe.

18. Remove the four retaining bolts and lift off the intake manifold. Remove the rubber rings.

19. Remove the splash guard beneath the engine.

20. If removing the left cylinder head, remove the air pump from its bracket.

21. Remove the vacuum pump and o-ring in the valve cover. Remove the vacuum hoses from the wax thermostat.

22. If removing the right cylinder head, disconnect the upper radiator hose.

23. On air conditioned models, remove the AC compressor and place it to one side. Do not disconnect the refrigerant lines.

24. Disconnect the distributor leads and remove the distributor. Remove the EGR valve, bracket and pipe. At the firewall, disconnect the electrical connectors at the relays.

25. On air conditioned models, remove the rear compressor bracket.

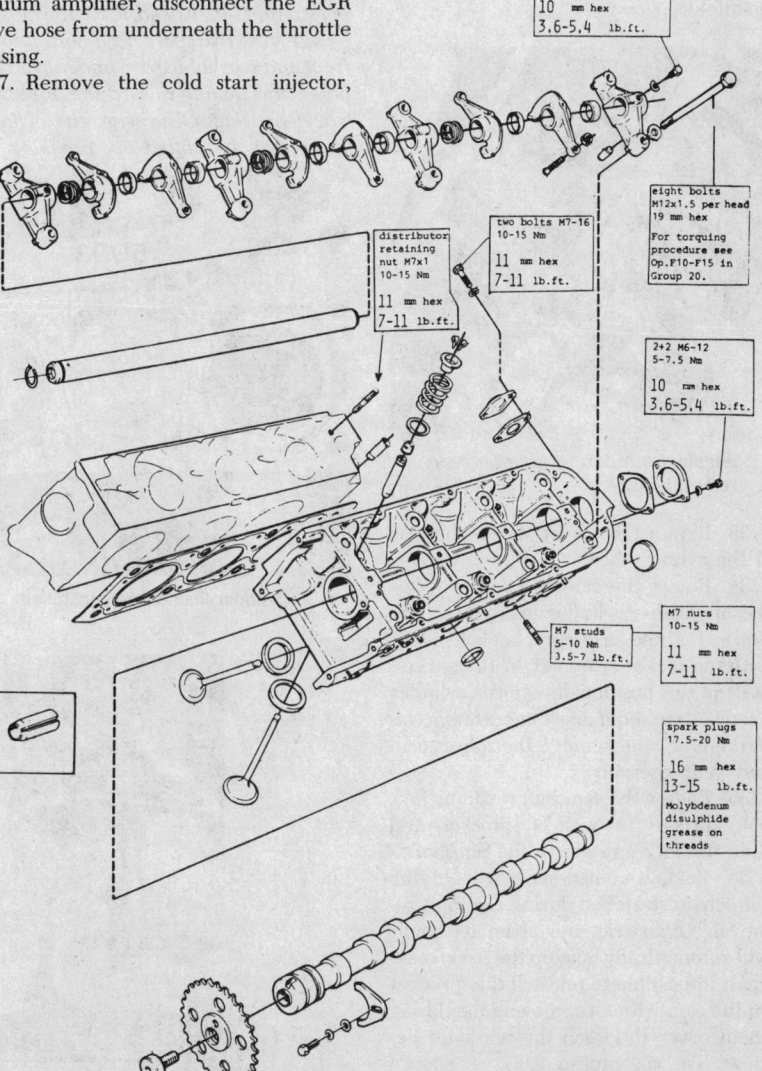

B27 Cylinder head assembly

26. Disconnect the coolant hose(s) from the water pump to the cylinder head(s). If removing the left cylinder head, disconnect the lower radiator hose at the water pump.

27. Disconnect the air injection system supply hose from the applicable cylinder head. Separate the air manifold at the rear of the engine. If removing the left cylinder head, remove the backfire valve and air hose.

28. Remove the valve cover(s).

29. On the left cylinder head, remove the allen head screw and four upper bolts to the timing gear cover. On the right cylinder head, remove the four upper bolts to the timing gear cover and the front cover plate.

30. From beneath the car, remove the exhaust pipe clamps for both header pipes.

31. If removing the right cylinder head, remove the retainer bracket bolt and pull the dipstick tube out of the crankcase.

32. Remove the applicable exhaust manifold(s).

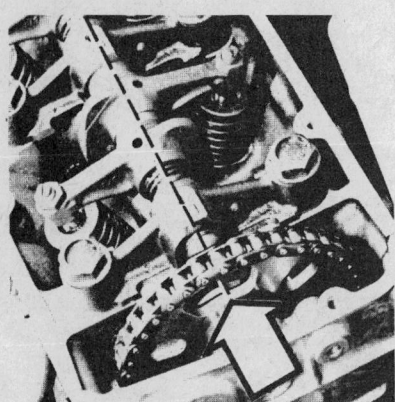

Aligning camshaft for cylinder head removal—B27

33. Remove the cover plate at the rear of the cylinder head.

34. Rotate the camshaft sprocket (for the applicable cylinder head) into position so that the large sprocket hole aligns with the rocker arm shaft. With the camshaft in this position, loosen the cylinder head bolts in sequence (same sequence as tightening), and remove the rocker arm and shaft assembly.

35. Loosen the camshaft retaining fork bolt (directly in back of sprocket) and slide the fork away from the camshaft.

36. Next, it is necessary to hold the cam chain stretched during camshaft removal. Otherwise, the chain tensioner will automatically take up the slack, making it impossible to reinstall the sprocket on the cam without removing the timing chain cover to loosen the tensioner device. To accomplish this, a special sprocket retainer tool (Volvo #999 5104) is installed over the sprocket with two

Final step of cylinder head tightening sequence is protractor torquing to 116-120 degrees (⅓ of a full turn)

bolts in the top of the timing chain cover. A bolt is then screwed into the sprocket to hold it in place.

37. Remove the camshaft sprocket center bolt and push the camshaft to the rear, so it clears the sprocket.

38. Remove the cylinder head. **NOTE:** *Do not remove the cylinder head by pulling straight up. Instead, lever the head off by inserting two spare head bolts into the front and rear inboard cylinder head bolt holes, and pulling toward the applicable wheel housing. Otherwise, the cylinder liners may be pulled up, breaking the*

Cylinder liner holders installed

Camshaft sprocket retainer tool installed—B27

lower liner seal and leaking coolant into the crankcase. If any do pull up, new liner seals must be used, and the crankcase completely drained.

39. Remove the head gasket. Clean the contact surfaces with a plastic scaper and laquer thinner.

40. If the head is going to be off for any length of time, install liner holders (Volvo special tool #999 5093) or two strips of thick stock sheet steel with holes for the head bolts, so that the liners stay pressed down against their seals. Install the hold-

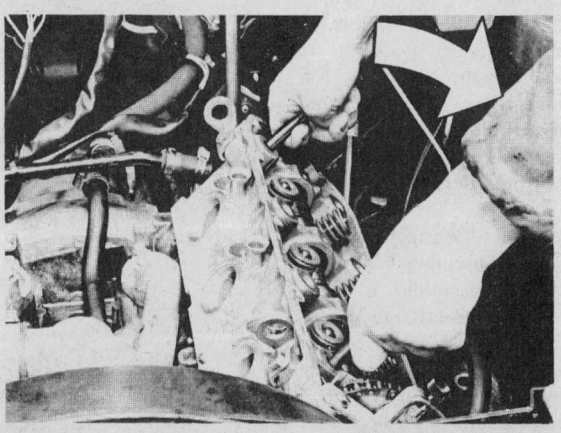

Cylinder head removal—B27F

ers widthwise between the middle four head bolt holes.

41. Reverse the above procedure to install, using the following installation notes:

a. There are a pair of guide dowels at both outboard corners of the head. If they fell down during removal, pull them back out with a puller hammer. They can be propped up with a ⅛ in. drill shank.

b. Remove the liner holders.

c. The right and left head gaskets are different.

d. Check the timing chain cover gasket. If damaged, replace only the upper section.

e. Oil the head bolt threads. Position the head on the dowels and install (hand tight) one center head bolt. Then, slide the camshaft forward into position against the sprocket and install the sprocket center bolt, and remove the retainer tool.

f. Before installing the head bolts, remove the guide dowel drill shanks, if used.

g. Using the correct tightening sequence, tighten the head bolts to 7 ft-lbs, then 22 ft-lbs, and then 44 ft-lbs. Next, slacken the head bolts (in the tightening sequence) to relieve any pre-tension. Now, tighten the bolts to 11-14 ft-lbs. *Finally, tighten the head bolts exactly one-third of a full 360° turn (116-120°) in the tightening sequence. This is critical for proper piston liner O-ring sealing. If necessary, use a protractor to ensure accuracy.*

h. Adjust the valves after completing assembly.

i. After running the engine to operating temperature, allow to cool for 30 minutes, and retorque the head bolts. Following the tightening sequence, slacken the bolts to relieve any pre-tension, then tighten to 11-14 ft-lbs, *and finally protractor torque them to 113-117° (one-third of a full turn).*

Cylinder Head Overhaul

Refer to "Cylinder Head Reconditioning" in the "Engine Rebuilding" section.

Rocker Shafts

Removal and Installation

B20, B30

1. Remove the four retaining screws and the valve cover and gasket.

2. Remove the rocker shaft-to-cylinder head bolts and lift out the shaft and rocker arms as a unit.

3. Lift out the pushrods, keeping them in order, and check them for straightness by rolling them on a flat surface. Replace any bent pushrods.

4. Inspect the rocker shaft and arms. If the shaft and rockers are coated with baked-on sludge, oil may not be reaching them. Clean out the oil feed holes in the rocker shaft with 0.020 in. wire (piano wire). If the clearance between the rocker arms and shaft exceeds 0.004 in., the rocker arm needs to be rebushed. The rocker arm bushings are press fitted, and are removed with a drift. When pressing in a new bushing, make sure that the oil hole in the bushing aligns with the hole in the arm.

5. Position the pushrods on their respective lifters. Install the the rocker shaft and arm assembly on the head, and install the retaining bolts. Step-tighten the bolts, moving front to rear, until a torque of approximately 20 ft lbs is reached.

6. Check to see that valve lash has remained within specifications. Adjust valve lash, if necessary.

7. Install the valve cover and gasket, and snugly tighten the valve cover retaining screws.

B27F

1. Disconnect the battery.

2. Remove the air cleaner assembly.

3. Disconnect the air pump bracket.

4. Remove the vacuum pump.

5. Remove the left valve cover (if so desired).

6. Tie the upper radiator hose out of the way and remove the oil filler cap and carbon canister hose.

7. On air conditioned models, remove the AC compressor from its bracket. Do not disconnect the hoses.

8. Remove the EGR valve.

9. Remove the AC compressor rear bracket.

10. Remove the control pressure regulator.

11. Disconnect any hoses or wires in the way. Remove the right valve cover (if so desired).

12. The rocker arm bolts double as cylinder head bolts. When loosening, follow the cylinder head bolt tightening sequence diagram. If removing both rocker shafts, mark them left and right.

NOTE: *Do not jar or strike head while rockers and bolts are out, as cylinder liner o-ring seals may break, necessitating teardown of engine to clean coolant out of crankcase and installation of new seals.*

13. To install, reverse removal procedure. Follow cylinder head installation procedure for proper torque sequence.

Intake and Exhaust Manifolds

Combination Manifold

Removal and Installation— Carbureted Models

1. Remove the exhaust manifold pre-heating plate 1968-72 carbureted models only. Remove the nuts and disconnect the exhaust pipe from the exhaust manifold.

2. Remove the air cleaner(s). Disconnect the throttle, choke, and downshift linkage, if so equipped. Disconnect the positive crankcase ventilation hoses, and the vacuum hoses for the distributor advance, and power brake, if so equipped.

3. Remove the nuts and slide the combination intake and exhaust manifold off the studs. Remove and discard the old manifold gasket.

4. To install, reverse the above procedure. Remember to use a new manifold gasket and exhaust pipe flange gasket in assembly. Torque the manifold retaining nuts to 13-16 ft lbs.

Inlet Duct Removal and Installation—Fuel Injected in-line engines

1. On B 30 F engines, remove the air cleaner. On B 20 F engines, remove the inlet duct-to-air cleaner hose at the inlet duct.

2. Disconnect the positive battery cable (fuel-injection models only).

3. Disconnect the throttle and downshift linkage. Remove from the inlet duct, the positive crankcase ventilation, distributor advance, pressure sensor (electronic fuel-injection models only) and power brake hoses.

4. On electronic fuel-injected models, disconnect the contact for the throttle valve switch, and remove the ground cable for the inlet duct.

5. Remove the bolts for the inlet duct stay. Remove the inlet duct-to-cylinder head retaining nuts and slide the inlet duct off the studs. Discard the old gasket.

6. To install, reverse the above procedure. Use a new inlet duct gasket. Torque the nuts to 13-16 ft lbs.

Timing Gear Cover

Removal and Installation

B 20

1. Loosen the fan (drive) belt. Remove the fan and water pump pulley. Disconnect the stabilizer attachment from the frame.

2. Remove the crankshaft pulley and bolt.

3. Remove the retaining bolts and the timing gear cover. Loosen a few oil pan bolts, being carefull not to damage the pan gasket.

4. Remove the circlip, washer, and felt ring from the cover. Replace any gasket in questionable condition. Make sure that the oil drain hole is open and clean.

5. Place the cover in position and install the retaining bolts finger-tight.

6. Center the cover with a sleeve.

Turn the sleeve while tightening and adjust the position of the cover so that that the sleeve may be easily rotated without jamming.

7. Install a new felt ring, washer, and circlip. Push them into their positions with the engaging sleeve. Check to make sure that the circlip has seated in its groove.

8. Tighten the cover bolts. Install the pulleys and fan. Tension the accessory drive belts. Tighten the stabilizer attachment firmly to the frame.

Timing Gear Cover Oil Seal Replacement

B 20

1. Remove the fan belt. Loosen the stabilizer attachment at the frame.

2. Remove the crankshaft pulley and bolt.

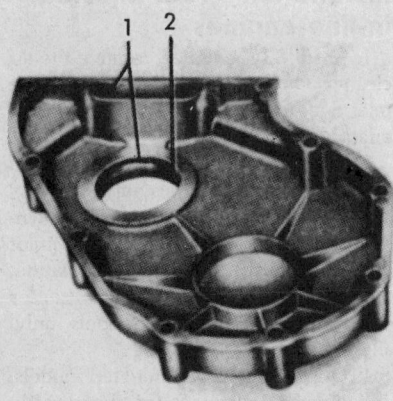

Timing gear cover—B20

1. Drain holes
2. Sealing ring

3. Remove the circlip for the washer retaining the felt ring. Check to make sure that the cover is correctly installed by inserting a 0.004 in. feeler gauge between the casing and the crankshaft hub. If the feeler gauge jams at any point, the cover must be centered.

4. Install a new felt ring. Place the washer in position and install the circlip in its groove.

5. Install the crankshaft pulley and fan. Tension the fan (drive) belt. Tighten the stabilizer attachment at the frame.

B 30

1. Drain the cooling system by opening the engine drain plug and disconnecting the lower radiator hose. On automatic transmission cars, disconnect and plug the transmission oil cooler lines at the radiator. Remove the radiator, fan shroud, and grille.

2. Remove the fan (drive) belt. Remove the bolts for the pulley and crankshaft damper.

3. Remove the center bolt and pull off the hub by hand or, if necessary, with a puller.

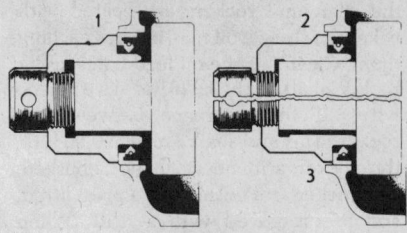

Center spindle position—B30

4. Remove the oil seal. Lubricate the sealing lip on the new seal and install the seal with a drift. The seal may be installed in one of three positions, depending on the amount of wear on the hub. With a new hub, the seal will be installed in its outer position (position 1). With a wear mark on the hub, install the seal in position 2. With two wear marks on the hub, install the seal in position 3. With three wear marks on the hub, you either have a very old engine or you have gone through more than a normal share of oil seals, and it's time to think about replacing that old hub with a new one.

5. Grease the sliding surfaces of the hub and install the hub. Note the center punch marks on the crankshaft end and hub. Install the center bolt and torque it to 50–57 ft lbs.

6. Install the crankshaft damper and pulley.

7. Install and properly tension the fan (drive) belt. Install the radiator, fan shroud, and grille. Install the lower radiator hose, close the drain plug, and fill the cooling system. On cars with automatic transmissions, connect the transmission oil cooler lines at the radiator.

Timing Belt Cover

Removal and Installation

B21F

1. Loosen the fan shroud and remove the fan. Remove the shroud.

2. Loosen the alternator, air pump, power steering pump (if so equipped), and AC compressor (if so equipped) and remove their drive belts.

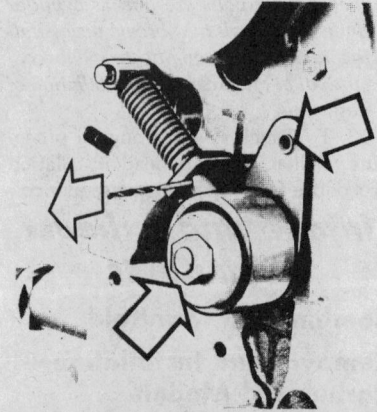

Locking tensioner spring with drill shank

3. Remove the water pump pulley.

4. Remove the four retaining bolts and lift off the timing belt cover.

5. Reverse the above procedure to install.

Timing Belt

Removal and Installation

B21F

1. Remove the timing belt cover as outlined previously.

2. To remove the tension from the belt, loosen the nut for the tensioner and press the idler roller back. The tension spring can be locked in this position by inserting the shank end of a 3mm drill bit through the pusher rod.

3. Remove the six retaining bolts and the crankshaft pulley.

4. Remove the belt, taking care not to bend it at any sharp angles. The belt should be replaced at 45,000 mile intervals, or if it becomes oil soaked or frayed.

5. If the crankshaft, idler shaft, or camshaft were disturbed while the belt was out, align each shaft with its corresponding index mark to assure proper valve timing and ignition timing, as follows:

   a. Rotate the crankshaft so that the notch in the convex crankshaft gear belt guide aligns with the embossed mark on the front cover (12 o'clock position).

   b. Rotate the idler shaft so that the dot on the idler shaft drive sprocket aligns with the notch on the timing belt rear cover (four o'clock position).

   c. Rotate the camshaft so that the notch in the camshaft sprocket inner belt guide aligns with the notch in the forward edge of the valve cover (12 o'clock position).

6. Install the timing belt (don't use any sharp tools) over the sprockets, and then over the tensioner roller. Loosen the tensioner nut and let the spring tension automatically take up the slack. Tighten the tensioner nut to 37 ft-lbs.

7. Rotate the crankshaft one full revolution clockwise, and make sure the timing marks still align.

8. Reverse steps 1–3 to install.

Timing Chain Cover

Removal and Installation

B27F

1. Remove the air cleaner and valve covers.

2. Loosen the fan shroud and remove the fan. Remove the shroud.

3. Loosen the alternator, air pump, power steering pump, and AC compressor (if so equipped) and remove their drive belts.

4. Block the flywheel from turning, remove the crankshaft pulley nut

(36mm) and the pulley.

NOTE: *Do not drop the pulley key into the crankcase.*

5. Remove the power steering pump and place to one side. Remove the pump bracket.

6. Remove the timing chain cover retaining bolts (25 11mm hex bolts), tap and remove the cover.

7. Clean the gasket contact surfaces. Place the upper gasket on the cover and the lower gasket on the block. Install the cover and tighten to 7–11 ft-lbs. Trim the gaskets flush with the valve cover.

8. Install a new crankshaft seal.

9. Block the flywheel, install the pulley (and key) and tighten the 36mm nut to 118–132 ft-lbs.

10. Reverse steps 1–5 to install.

Timing Chain
Removal and Installation
B27F

1. Remove the timing chain cover and adjacent engine accessories as outlined previously.

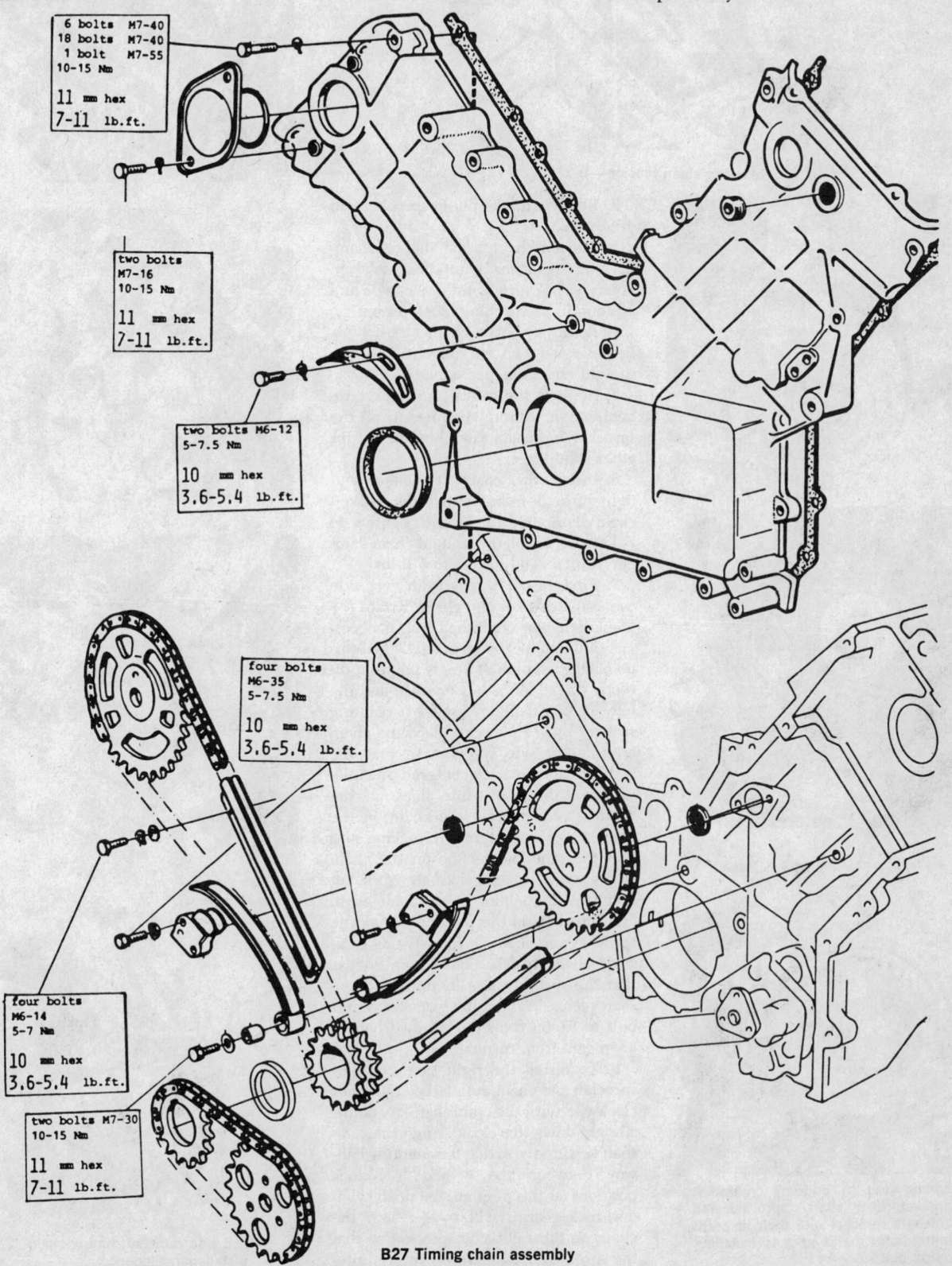

```
6 bolts   M7-40
18 bolts  M7-40
1 bolt    M7-55
10-15 Nm

11 mm hex
7-11 lb.ft.
```

```
two bolts
M7-16
10-15 Nm

11 mm hex
7-11 lb.ft.
```

```
two bolts M6-12
5-7.5 Nm

10 mm hex
3.6-5.4 lb.ft.
```

```
four bolts
M6-35
5-7.5 Nm

10 mm hex
3.6-5.4 lb.ft.
```

```
four bolts
M6-14
5-7 Nm

10 mm hex
3.6-5.4 lb.ft.
```

```
two bolts M7-30
10-15 Nm

11 mm hex
7-11 lb.ft.
```

B27 Timing chain assembly

Relieving chain tension—B-27

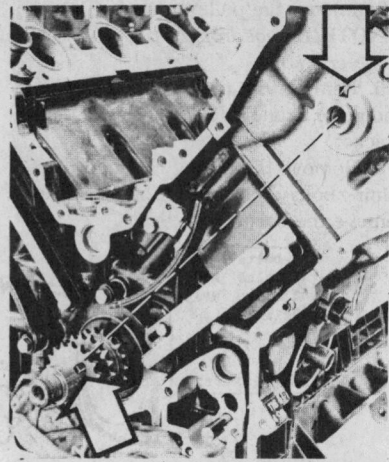

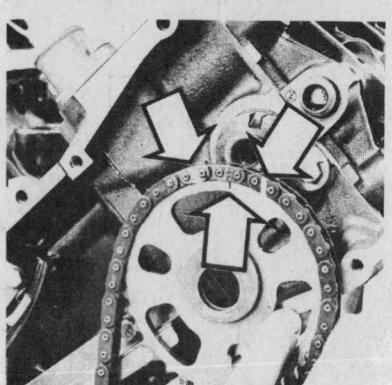

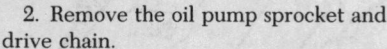

2. Remove the oil pump sprocket and drive chain.

3. Slacken the tension in both camshaft timing chains by rotating each tensioner lock ¼ turn counterclockwise and pushing in the rubbing block piston.

4. Remove both chain tensioners. Remove the two curved and the two straight chain damper/runners.

5. Remove the camshaft sprocket retaining bolt (10 mm allen head) and the sprocket and chain assembly. Repeat for other side.

6. Install the chain tensioners and tighten to 5 ft-lbs. Install the curved chain damper/runners and tighten to 7–11 ft-lbs. Install the straight chain damper/runners and torque to 5 ft-lbs.

7. First install the left (driver) side camshaft sprocket and chain. Rotate the crankshaft (use crankshaft nut, if necessary) until no. 1 cylinder is at TDC. At this point, the crankshaft key is pointing directly to the left side camshaft, and the left side camshaft key groove is pointing straight up (12 o'clock). Place the chain on the left side sprocket so that the sprocket notchmark is centered precisely between the two white lines on the chain. Then, position the chain on the crankshaft sprocket (inner), making sure that the other white line on the chain aligns with the crankshaft sprocket notch. While holding the left side chain and sprockets in this position, install the sprocket and chain on the left side camshaft (chain stretched on tension side) so that the sprocket pin fits into the camshaft recess. Tighten the sprocket center bolt to 51–59 ft-lbs (use screwdriver to keep cam from turning).

8. To install the right side camshaft sprocket and chain, rotate the crankshaft clockwise until the crankshaft key points straight down (6 o'clock). Align the camshaft key groove so that it is pointing halfway between the 8 and 9 o'clock positions (at this position, the no. 6 cylinder rocker arms will rock). Place the chain on the right side sprocket so that the sprocket notchmark is centered pre-

Aligning (top to bottom) crankshaft sprocket, idler shaft sprocket, and camshaft sprocket with their respective timing index marks prior to installing timing belt

Left side camshaft timing chain installation sequence

cisely between the two white lines on the chain. Then, position the chain on the middle crankshaft sprocket, making sure that the other white line aligns with the crankshaft sprocket notch. Then, install the sprocket and chain on the camshaft so that the sprocket notch fits into the camshaft recess. Tighten the sprocket nut to 51–59 ft-lbs.

9. Rotate the chain tensioners ¼ turn clockwise each. The chains are tensioned by rotating the crankshaft two full turns clockwise. Recheck to make sure the alignment marks coincide.

10. Install the oil pump sprocket and chain.

11. Install the timing chain cover and engine accessories as outlined previously.

Camshaft

Timing Gear and Camshaft Replacement

1. Disconnect the lower radiator hose, open the engine drain plug, and drain the cooling system. On cars with automatic transmissions, disconnect and plug the transmission oil cooler lines at the radiator. Remove the fan shroud (if so equipped) and the radiator.

2. Remove the fan and the pulley on the water pump. Remove the crankshaft bolt and remove the pulley using a puller.

3. Remove the timing gear cover. Loosen a few oil pan bolts, being careful not to damage the pan gasket.

4. Measure the tooth flank clearance. Maximum permissible gear backlash is 0.-005 in. Check to make sure that the end-play of the camshaft does not exceed 0.002 in. Camshaft end-play is determined by the shim behind the camshaft timing gear.

5. Try to align the marks on the timing gears dot to dot (or line to dot) prior to removing the gears. If this is not possible, note the correct relative position of the timing gear marks. Remove the hub from the crankshaft with a puller. Remove the

Timing gear alignment—B20 shown, B30 similar
1. Oil nozzle 2. Markings

crankshaft gear and the camshaft gear with a puller. Remove the oil jet, blow it clean, and reposition it. Oil fed through this jet lubricates the timing gears.

6. If the camshaft is being replaced, it is necessary to remove the distributor (noting its position), the distributor/oil pump driveshaft, fuel pump, valve cover, rocker shaft and arm assembly, pushrods, cylinder head, valve lifters, and the thrust flange. The camshaft may then be pulled out the front.

7. Reverse the above procedure to install. Replace the camshaft if the lobes exhibit excessive or uneven wear. Install the crankshaft and camshaft timing gears, making sure that they align in the correct relative positions. Do not push the camshaft backward, or the seal washer on the rear end may be forced out. Recheck the tooth flank clearance and the camshaft end-play.

8. Bring no. 1 piston to Top Dead Center. Install the distributor/oil pump driveshaft so that the offset position of the distributor slot (angle A) is 35° for the B 30 A and B 30 F engines, and 5° for the B 20 B, B 20 E, and B 20 F engines.

NOTE: *Make sure that the distributor-/oil pump driveshaft seats fully in the*

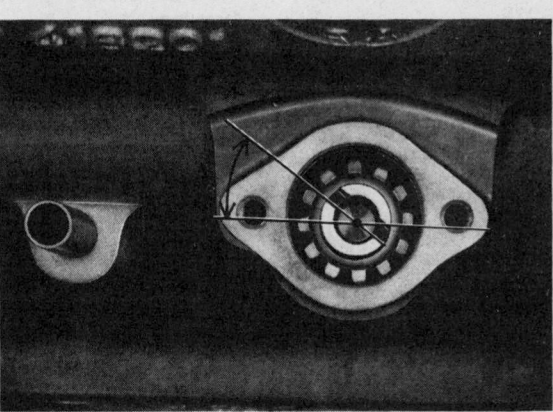

After installing camshaft, bring no. 1 piston to TDC and align distributor drive shaft "angle A" as outlined in text. Failure to do so will result in ignition timing out of syn—chronization with valve timing

Right side camshaft timing chain installation sequence

5021

B21 camshaft press tool installed

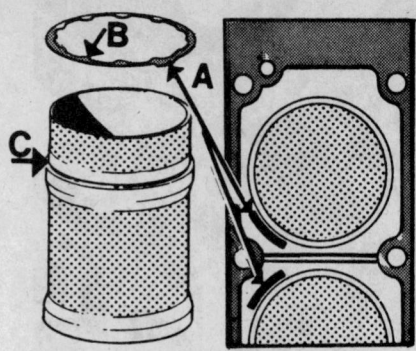

When installing B27 liner shims, color marking "A" must face up and be positioned where shown. Inside tabs "B" fit into liner groove "C"

slot at the top of the oil pump. If necessary, use a long screwdriver to turn the pump manually until the slot aligns.

9. When installing the timing case cover, make sure that the drain holes are open. Center the cover with a sleeve. Install the distributor, making sure the rotor points to the no. 1 cylinder position.

10. Install the pulleys and fan. Install the fan (drive) belt and adjust the tension. Refit the radiator hose, close the drain plug, and fill the cooling system.

11. Adjust the ignition timing.

B21F

1. Remove the timing belt cover and timing belt as outlined in their appropriate sections.

2. Remove the valve cover.

3. Remove the camshaft center bearing cap. Install special camshaft press tool (Volvo #5021) over the center bearing journal to hold the camshaft in place while removing the other bearing caps.

4. Remove the four remaining bearings caps.

5. Remove the seal from the forward edge of the camshaft.

6. Release camshaft press tool, and lift out the camshaft.

7. Reverse the above procedure to install.

B27F

1. Remove the cylinder head as outlined previously.

2. Remove the camshaft rear cover plate.

3. Remove the camshaft retaining fork at the front of the cylinder head.

4. Pull the camshaft out the rear of the head.

5. Reverse the above to install.

Pistons and Connecting Rods

Piston and Connecting Rod Positioning

On all engines, the notch or arrow stamped on top of the piston must face

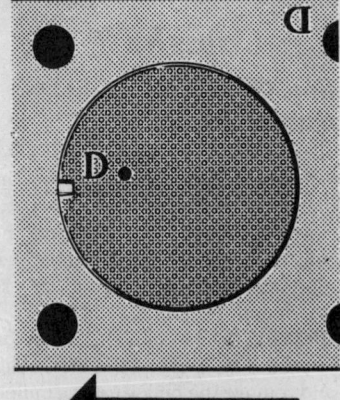

B20, B21, and B30 piston postioning; notch faces forward

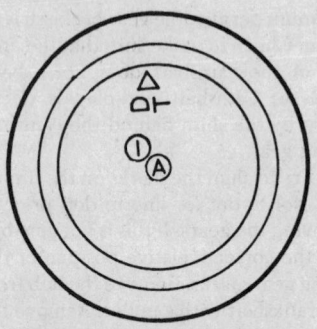

B27 piston positioning; arrowhead faces forward

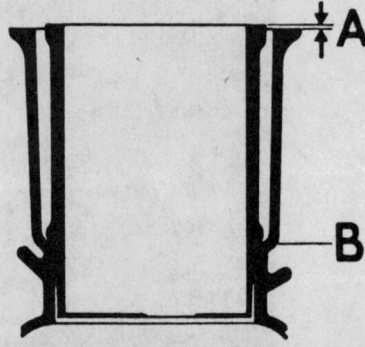

Correct B27 piston liner height "A" above block face is 0.0091 in. Shims are installed at point "B" and should be uniform for all cylinders

the front of the engine. On B20 and B30 engines, the connecting rod big end marking must face away from the camshaft side, and on the B21 the connecting rod marking must face the front of the engine.

ENGINE LUBRICATION

Oil Pan

Removal and Installation

B20 (except 240 series), B30

The oil pan may be removed from the engine while the engine is still in the chassis.

1. Place supports on the frame side members as shown. Insert a lifting hook into the lifting plate bolted to the front of the engine. Using the lifting apparatus, raise the engine until there is no weight on the front engine mounts. Remove the oil dipstick.

2. Jack up the vehicle and place jackstands under the front jacking points. Drain the crankcase oil.

3. Remove the lower nuts for the engine mounts. On 140 series models, remove the steering rods from the pitman arm and relay arm with a puller.

4. Place a hydraulic floor jack beneath the front axle member. Remove the rear bolts of the front axle member and replace them with two longer auxiliary bolts (UNC ½-13X114). Remove the front bolts for the front axle member and lower the hydraulic jack, allowing the axle member to hang on the auxiliary bolts.

5. Remove the plug for the oil temperature gauge, if so equipped, and the reinforcing bracket at the flywheel.

6. Unscrew the oil pan bolts and lower the pan. Remove the old gasket and clean the surfaces of the cylinder block and oil pan. Remove any sludge or foreign matter that has accumulated at the bottom of the pan.

1. Dowel pin
2. Core plug
3. Sealing flange
4. Circlip
5. Pilot bearing
6. Sealing ring
7. Crankshaft
8. Plug
9. Dowel pin

Rear of engine—B20, B30

7. Using a new gasket, position the pan to the cylinder block and install the oil pan bolts. Torque the bolts to 6–8 ft lbs.

8. Install the plug for the oil temperature gauge, if so equipped. Position the reinforcing bracket to the cylinder block and flywheel casing and install the bolts finger-tight. Snugly tighten the bolts for the flywheel casing and then those for the cylinder block.

9. Raise the hydraulic jack, raising the front axle member, and tighten the front bolts. Remove the auxiliary bolts and install the original rear bolts of the front axle member.

10. Install the lower nuts for the front engine mounts. On 140 series models, connect the steering rods at the pitman arm and relay arm, and fit the nuts.

11. Remove the jackstands and hydraulic jack. Lower the vehicle. Remove the lifting apparatus.

12. Insert the dipstick. Fill the crankcase with the proper amount and grade of oil.

13. Start the engine and check for leaks.

1975 240 Series (B20)

On these models, the motor mounts are located high in the chassis, permitting more than 2 inches of clearance between the bottom of the oil pan and the steering linkage and suspension. Therefore, oil pan removal is a simple matter of unbolting the attaching bolts. Always use a new gasket when installing the pan. A few daubs of oil resistant sealer on the gasket at the front and rear main seals will help prevent oil leaks. Tighten the attaching bolts to no more than 6–8 ft lbs of torque in a diagonal criss-cross pattern.

B21F

1. Attach a chain/pulley hoist to the lifting eye on the thermostat housing.

2. On air conditioned models, remove the compressor from its bracket to gain access to the motor mount.

3. Remove the retaining bolts for the left (driver side) motor mount at the cyl-

inder block.

4. Drain the crankcase.

5. Remove the splash guard.

6. Raise the engine slightly.

7. Remove the left motor mount from the chassis.

8. Remove the engine-to-clutch housing brace.

9. Remove the oil pan retaining bolts. Tap the pan loose, swivel and remove.

10. Reverse the removal procedure to install.

B27F V-6

1. Remove the splash guard.

2. Drain the crankcase.

3. Remove the oil pan retaining bolts. Swivel the pan past the stabilizer bar and remove.

4. Reverse the above to install.

Rear Main Oil Seal Replacement

1. Remove the transmission, clutch (if so equipped), and flywheel from the engine. Remove the two oil pan bolts from the bottom of the sealing flange, and loosen two more on each side so that the pressure on the sealing flange is reduced.

2. Remove the sealing flange retaining bolts and pull off the sealing flange and old gasket. Press out the sealing ring in the flange with a drift.

3. Make sure that the sealing surfaces of the flange are clean. Also make sure that the oil drain hole is not blocked by the oil pan gasket.

4. Oil the sealing ring. Install the sealing ring, sealing flange, and new gasket to the block, but do not tighten the bolts.

5. Center the flange with special SVO tool 2439 (for B 20), or 2817 (for B 30). Rotate the sleeve while tightening the flange bolts. Adjust the position of the flange if the sleeve jams. After tightening, the sleeve should rotate easily if the flange is properly positioned. Make sure that the sealing flange is seated against the underside of the block.

6. Install a new felt ring and replace

the washer and circlip. Install the sealing ring into its groove with the centering sleeve.

7. Install and tighten the oil pan bolts. Install the flywheel, clutch (if so equipped), and transmission.

Oil Pump

Replacement

B20, B30

The oil pump must be removed with the engine removed from the car.

1. Crank the engine to TDC at no. 1 cylinder. Remove the distributor.

2. Drain the crankcase and remove the oil pan. Remove the oil pump retaining bolts.

3. Disconnect the oil pump from the delivery tube by unscrewing the connecting flange. Be careful not to discard the rubber sealing rings from the sealing flange.

4. Unscrew the connecting flange and remove the delivery tube from the block.

5. To install, fit the delivery tube with sealing rings to the oil pump, and then to the block. If the tube does not seat properly in the block, it may be tapped lightly with a soft mallet. Tightly screw the connecting flanges.

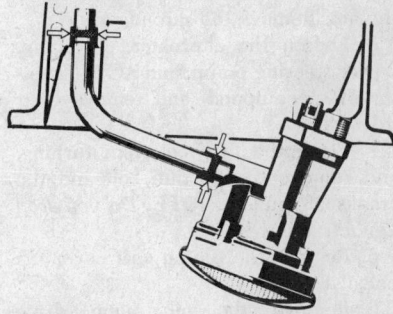

Oil pump delivery pipe seal rings—B20, B30

6. With no. 1 cylinder at TDC, install the oil pump drive and distributor. Make sure that the shaft goes down into its groove in the pump shaft. Tighten the oil pump retaining bolts.

7. Install the oil pan with a new gasket and fill the crankcase.

B21F

1. Remove the oil pan as described previously.

2. Remove the two oil pump retaining bolts, and pull the delivery tube from the block.

3. When installing, use new sealing rings at either end of the delivery tube.

B27F

The oil pump body is cast integrally with the cylinder block. It is chain driven by a separate sprocket on the crankshaft and is located behind the timing chain cover. The pick-up screen and tube are serviced by removing the oil pan. To

Oil pump—B20, 21, 27

1. Pump body
2. Spring for relief valve
3. Gear
4. Valve ball
5. Hole for oil pipe

check the pump gears or remove the oil pump cover:

1. Remove the air cleaner and valve covers.

2. Loosen the fan shroud and remove the fan. Remove the shroud.

3. Loosen the alternator, air pump, power steering pump, and AC compressor (if so equipped) and remove their drive belts.

4. Block the flywheel from turning, and remove the 36 mm bolt and the crankshaft pulley. **NOTE:** *Do not drop key into crankcase.*

5. Remove the timing gear cover (25 bolts).

6. Remove the oil pump drive sprocket and chain.

7. Remove the oil pump cover, and gears.

8. Reverse the removal procedure to install.

Oil Pump Clearance

After removing the oil pump from the engine, place the pump body in a vise. Remove the four bolts which retain the pick-up screen housing to the pump body, exposing the oil pump gears, relief valve, ball and spring. To measure the tooth flank clearance, insert a proper size feeler gauge between the engaging teeth of the oil pump gears. Proper tooth flank clearance is 0.006–0.014 in. If the clearance is not within specifications, the pump must be replaced. To measure the oil pump gear end-float, place a straightedge ruler over top of the two pump gears so that it lies flat on the pump housing at both ends, and insert a proper size feeler gauge between the top of the pump gear and the straightedge. Proper

Measuring oil pump tooth flank clearance

gear end float is 0.0008–0.0040 in. If all clearances are within specifications, reassemble the oil pump taking care to install the relief valve, ball, and spring in their original locations.

Oil Cooler

Replacement

1. Remove the plug in the oil cooler and drain the coolant.

2. Disconnect the coolant connection at the oil cooler. Remove the oil filter.

3. Unscrew the oil cooler nipple nut and remove the cooler. Remove and discard the rubber sealing ring at the cylinder block connection.

4. Install a new O-ring into the groove in the oil cooler and apply a thin layer of oil-resistant (up to 280°F) adhesive, such as Pliobond® 20, to the groove. Postion the cooler and new rubber sealing ring to the block and tighten the nipple nut to 23–25 ft lbs. Make sure that the cooler is flush against the block.

5. Install the oil filter and connect the coolant pipe. Install the cooler plug.

6. Replace the coolant, and, if necessary, the engine oil. Run the engine and check for leaks.

ENGINE COOLING
Radiator

Removal and Installation

1. Remove the radiator and expansion tank caps, disconnect the lower radiator hose, and drain the cooling system.

2. Remove the expansion tank and hose, and drain the coolant. Remove the upper radiator hose. On cars with automatic transmissions, disconnect and plug the transmission oil cooler lines at the radiator.

3. Remove the retaining bolts for the radiator and fan shroud, if so equipped,

and lift out the radiator.

4. To install, place the radiator and fan shroud in position and install the retaining bolts.

5. On automatic transmission cars, connect the oil cooler lines.

6. Install the lower and upper radiator hoses.

7. Install the expansion tank with its hose. Make sure that the overflow hose is clear of the fan and is free of any sharp bends.

8. Fill the cooling system with a 50 percent ethylene glycol, 50 percent water solution. Replace the caps.

9. Start the engine and check for leaks. After the engine has reached operating temperature make sure that the coolant level in the expansion tank is between the maximum and minimum marks.

Water Pump

Removal and Installation

B20, B30

1. Drain the cooling system and remove the radiator as previously described.

2. Loosen the fan belt by slackening the alternator adjusting bolt. Remove the fan.

3. Remove the housing bolts from the water pump. Carefully remove the aluminum housing from the engine along with all the old gasket material. Remove the sealing rings.

4. To install, position the water pump assembly to the block, using a new housing gasket and water resistant sealer, and making sure that the sealing rings on the upper side of the pump are seated fully. Press the pump upward against the cylinder head extension to seat the rings.

5. Hand-tighten the housing bolts until snug. Do not tighten the bolts more than ½ turn further to avoid cracking the housing or breaking the bolts.

6. Install the fan and adjust the (drive) belt tension.

7. Install the radiator as previously described. Fill the cooling system.

8. Start the engine and check for leaks.

B21F

1. Remove the overflow tank cap. Drain the cooling system by opening the cylinder block drain cock (beneath the exhaust manifold) and disconnecting the lower radiator hose.

2. Remove the fan and fan shroud.

3. Remove the alternator and air pump drive belts. Remove the water pump pulley.

4. Remove the timing belt cover.

5. Remove the lower radiator hose.

6. Remove the retaining bolt for the coolant pipe (beneath exhaust manifold) and pull the pipe rearward.

7. Remove the six retaining bolts and lift off the water pump.

8. Clean the gasket contact surfaces thoroughly, and use a new gasket and o-rings (especially between the cylinder head and top of water pump).

9. Reverse steps 1–7 to install.

B27F

1. Remove the front and main sections of the intake manifold.

2. Remove the overflow tank cap and drain the cooling system.

3. Disconnect both radiator hoses. On automatic transmission cars, disconnect the transmission cooler lines at the radiator. Disconnect the fan shroud. Remove the radiator and fan shroud.

4. Remove the fan.

5. Remove the hoses from the water pump to each cylinder head.

6. Remove the fan belts. Remove the water pump pulley.

7. Loosen the hose clamps at the rear of the water pump.

8. Transfer the thermal time sender and temperature sensor to the new pump.

9. Remove the water pump from the block (three bolts).

10. Transfer the thermostat cover, thermostat, and rear pump cover to the new pump.

11. Reverse the removal procedure to install.

Thermostat

Removal and Installation

1. Disconnect the lower radiator hose and drain the cooling system.

2. Remove the two bolts securing the thermostat housing to the cylinder head and carefully lift the housing free.

3. Remove all old gasket material from the mating surfaces and remove the thermostat.

4. Test the operation of the thermostat by immersing it in a container of heated water. Two types of thermostats are used on 1967–73 Volvos. Type one is a 170° unit which bears a 170 marking. It begins to open at 168–172°F and is fully open at 194°F. Type two is a 180° unit which bears an 85° marking (85° Centigrade). It begins to open at 177–181°F and is fully open at 195°F. Replace any thermostat that does not open at the correct temperature.

5. Place the thermostat, with a new gasket, in the cylinder head. Fit the thermostat housing to the head and hand-tighten the two bolts until snug. Do not tighten the bolts more than ¼ turn past snug.

6. Connect the lower radiator hose and replace the coolant.

EMISSION CONTROLS

PCV System

Volvos have been equipped with positive crankcase ventilation (PCV) systems to control crankcase vapors since the early 1960s. The present system is a closed one; it is sealed to the atmosphere. A metal filter located inline between the fresh air source and the crankcase prevents engine backfire from reaching the

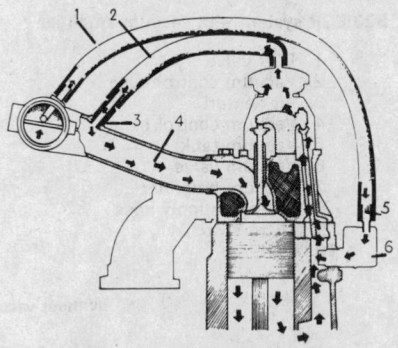

Positive crankcase ventilation system— B20E, B20F system shown

1. Hose for fresh air supply
2. Hose for crankcase gases
3. Nipple
4. Inlet duct
5. Flame guard
6. Oil trap

crankcase and oil from being drawn into the induction system.

Evaporative Control System

All post-1969 model Volvos have been equipped with an evaporative control system to prevent unburnt fuel vapors in the fuel tank and, in carbureted models, the float chambers, from escaping into the atmosphere. An expansion tank above the fuel tank provides for thermal expansion of fuel vapors in warm weather. Those vapors which do not condense and return to the fuel tank are displaced and drawn into an activated charcoal canister in the engine compartment. The charcoal canister then absorbs and stores these fuel tank vapors, along with the float chamber vapors (on carbureted models) when the engine is shut off or is idling. Throttling the engine causes the vapors to be drawn out of the canister into the carburetor venturi (on fuel-injected models, the inlet duct) and then into the combustion chambers where they are burned.

On carbureted models, the float chamber vapors are diverted from the canister to the air cleaner upon acceleration. As a result of these fumes being vented to the air cleaner, an overly rich fuel mixture may develop, leading to starting difficul-ties—especially in warm weather. A hot start valve is located inline between the float chamber and the air cleaner which returns the vapors to the charcoal canister until the engine can handle the extra-rich mixture.

Exhaust Emission Control

Various measures have been taken since 1968 to limit exhaust emissions of hydrocarbons, carbon monoxide, and more recently, oxides of nitrogen. Basic modifications include a distributor which retards the timing from its basic setting during idle, and the installation of a "hotter" 190° F thermostat in the cooling system. Fuel injection, which is inherently cleaner due to its precise regulation of the air-fuel mixture under varying rpm, engine load, and ambient temperature conditions, has been available since 1970.

Carbureted engines have incorporated many modifications including such pollutant control devices as a temperature-regulated fuel jet, an air-fuel mixture preheating chamber, and a throttle bypass or overrev valve, and measures to improve the operation and driveability of emission-controlled engines such as a constant intake air temperature device, and, as previously mentioned, a hot-start valve.

The temperature-regulated fuel mixture is accomplished differently on the Zenith-Stromberg 175 CD2 SE carburetor than on the SU HIF 6 carburetor. On the Stromberg carburetor, a temperature-sensitive bimetal spring in the temperature compensator actuates an air valve that varies the air supplied the venturi area to maintain the air-fuel ratio constant, despite changing fuel temperature. On the SU HIF carburetor, a temperature-sensitive bimetal spring raises or lowers the adjustable jet to maintain the proper air-fuel ratio at changing fuel temperatures.

On 1969 and later models, the throttle bypass or overrev valve serves to direct a regulated flow of fuel and air around the closed carburetor throttle, during engine deceleration (braking) from high speeds, and into the combustion chambers. This eliminates the over-rich surge condition that occurs when the throttle is finally opened after a period of engine braking.

On 1968 and later models, the constant intake air temperature device also aids in cold weather warm-up by providing exhaust manifold heat to the hose for the intake air. A thermostatically controlled flap regulates the mixture of intake air and exhaust heated air to an approximate temperature of 90°F.

Volvo

Exhaust Gas Recirculation System

In order to control emissions of NO_x, 1973–74 models with automatic transmission, as well as all 240 and 260 series and 1975 164 models, are equipped with an exhaust gas recirculation system. The system consists of a metering valve, a tubular pipe running from the exhaust manifold to the valve, another tubular pipe running from the valve to the inlet duct, and a vacuum hose running from the valve's diaphragm to the inlet duct in front of the air regulator shutter. The valve permits a regulated amount of exhaust gasses to enter the inlet duct and mix with the incoming intake air when the throttle is partly open. Every 12 months or 12,000 miles (1973–74) or 15,000 miles (1975–76), the system must be disassembled and cleaned. Every 24 months or 24,000 miles (1973–74) or 30,000 miles (1975–76), the valve must be replaced with a new one.

On 1974–75 B20 engines, and 1976 B21 and B27 models sold in California, the EGR system is modified to improve cold start driveability by the addition of a venturi vacuum amplifier system. The EGR system with vacuum amplifier works as follows: Venturi vacuum at the air intake is used to measure the total air flow. This weak vacuum signal controls the vacuum amplifier which regulates the EGR valve via a solenoid valve. The vacuum amplifier receives inputs both from the strong intake manifold source which is used as a power source, and from the weak air intake source which is to be amplified. The intake vacuum is stored in the vacuum reservoir and is controlled by a check valve in the amplifier. This allows a generous amount of vacuum on tap regardless of variations in engine manifold vacuum. The amplifier then continues to supply adequate vacuum at higher speeds and moderate throttle openings, when manifold vacuum normally would drop to an insufficient amount. The EGR system functions as before, except that the exhaust gasses are prevented from recirculation at idle and full throttle by a throttle angle sensing micro-switch and

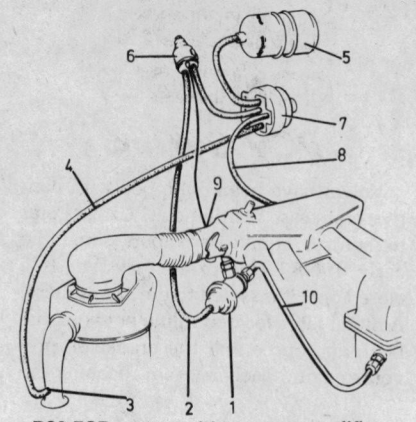

B20 EGR system with vacuum amplifier

1. EGR valve
2. Vacuum control hose
3. Air venturi
4. Vacuum control hose
5. Vacuum tank
6. Vacuum valve
7. Vacuum amplifier
8. Vacuum supply hose
9. Micro switch
10. EGR-line

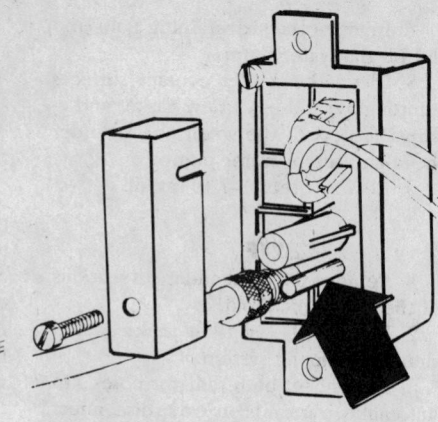

EGR, Catalytic Converter service reminder light reset button

an electrically operated solenoid valve, rather than simple vacuum as in 1973. On 1976 models, a wax thermostat blocks exhaust gas recirculation until the engine warms to 140°F.

Beginning with the 1975 model year, all Volvos are equipped with an EGR ser-

Without vacuum amplifier

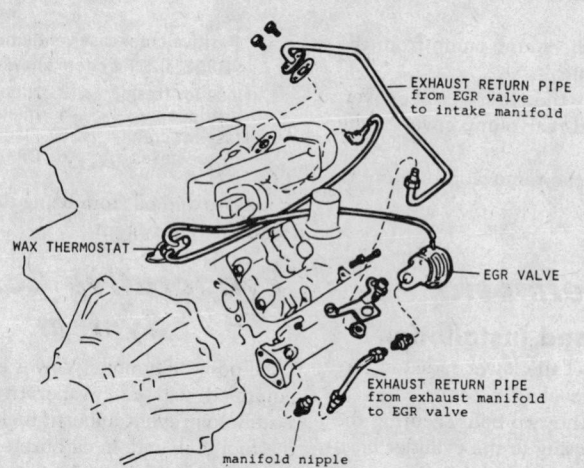

EXHAUST RETURN PIPE from EGR valve to intake manifold

WAX THERMOSTAT

EGR VALVE

EXHAUST RETURN PIPE from exhaust manifold to EGR valve

manifold nipple

With vacuum amplifier (California)

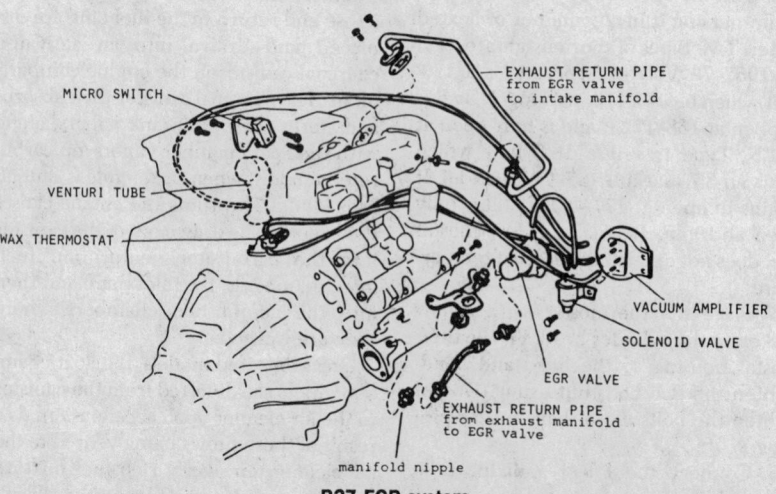

MICRO SWITCH

VENTURI TUBE

WAX THERMOSTAT

EXHAUST RETURN PIPE from EGR valve to intake manifold

VACUUM AMPLIFIER

SOLENOID VALVE

EGR VALVE

EXHAUST RETURN PIPE from exhaust manifold to EGR valve

manifold nipple

B27 EGR system

Exhaust gas recirculation valve installed—B20F shown, B30F similar.

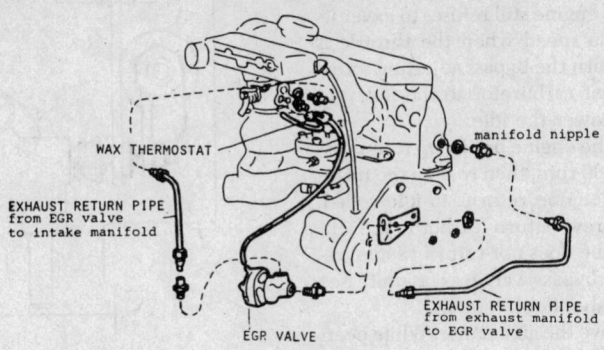

Without vacuum amplifier

WAX THERMOSTAT

manifold nipple

EXHAUST RETURN PIPE
from EGR valve
to intake manifold

EXHAUST RETURN PIPE
from exhaust manifold
to EGR valve

EGR VALVE

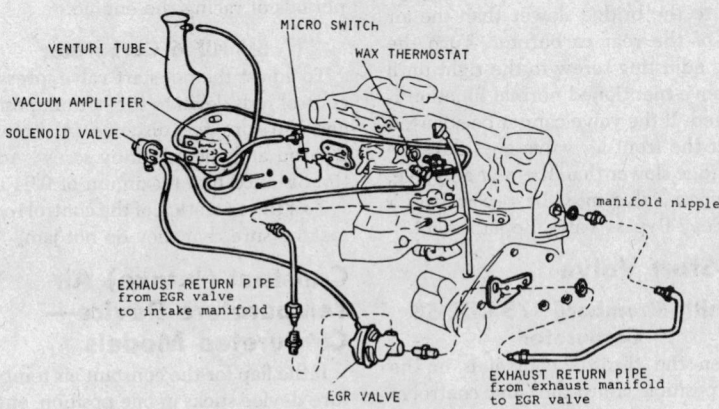

**With vacuum amplifier
(California)**

VENTURI TUBE

MICRO SWITCH

WAX THERMOSTAT

VACUUM AMPLIFIER

SOLENOID VALVE

manifold nipple

EXHAUST RETURN PIPE
from EGR valve
to intake manifold

EXHAUST RETURN PIPE
from exhaust manifold
to EGR valve

EGR VALVE

B21 EGR system

The system consists of an air pump (belt-driven), a diverter valve, a backfiring valve, and an air manifold which is attached to the exhaust manifold. Under normal conditions, air is pumped from the air pump via the diverter valve, the backfiring valve and the air manifold into the exhaust manifold ports. The air pump takes in filtered air which is then compressed and discharged to the diverter valve. The diverter valve sends the air through to the backfiring valve, except during deceleration. The diverter valve also releases some of the air into the atmosphere if the pressure is too great. The backfiring valve is a one-way valve which prevents the exhaust gasses from flowing back towards the air injection components, but allows the pump air to pass into the air manifold and exhaust manifold.

Catalytic Converter System

All 1975–76 Volvos manufactured for California, as well as all 1975 164 models equipped with manual transmission and overdrive for the 49 states, are equipped with a catalytic converter. The converters are installed in these vehicles to further control emissions of carbon monoxide and hydrocarbons which have resisted the treatment of the air injection system.

The converter is installed in the exhaust system ahead of the muffler. The converter uses platinum and palladium metals in a substrate or beaded form as

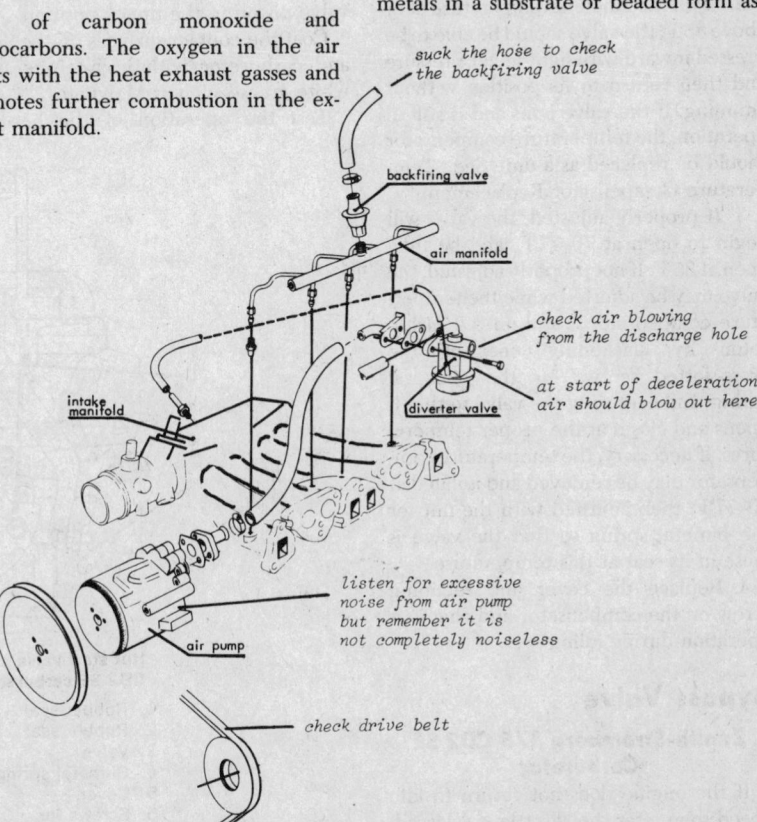

sions of carbon monoxide and hydrocarbons. The oxygen in the air reacts with the heat exhaust gasses and promotes further combustion in the exhaust manifold.

*suck the hose to check
the backfiring valve*

backfiring valve

air manifold

*check air blowing
from the discharge hole*

*at start of deceleration
air should blow out here*

intake
manifold

diverter valve

*listen for excessive
noise from air pump
but remember it is
not completely noiseless*

air pump

check drive belt

AIR system—B20

1. To air intake
2. To manifold
3. To vacuum reservoir
S. To solenoid

Vacuum amplifier connections—B20

vice reminder light which is actuated by the odometer at 15,000 mile intervals. The light may be reset by pressing a white button at the rear of the odometer.

Air Injection Reactor System

All 1975–76 Volvos are equipped with an air injection reactor system. Basically, the system injects filtered air into the exhaust manifold in order to reduce emis-

the catalyst. The catalyst and the oxygen supplied by the air pump then react with the exhaust gases producing harmless carbon dioxide and water vapor, as well as a minute amount of sulphur dioxide or sulphuric acid.

The converter is designed, if properly maintained, to last 50,000 miles as long as leaded gasoline is not used. The lead in gasoline will coat the catalytic substrate or beads, thereby preventing the reaction process, rendering the converter ineffective.

At 15,000 mile intervals, the retaining bolts for the converter must be checked for tightness. A service reminder light on the dashboard lights at 15,000 mile intervals. To extinguish the light, press the white reset button at the rear of the odometer.

Component Testing and Adjustment

Temperature Compensator

Zenith-Stromberg 175 CD2 SE Carburetor

If the idle speed drops off sharply during extended periods of idling, especially during warm weather, the temperature compensator may be in need of adjustment or replacement.

1. Remove the one screw retaining the plastic cover to the compensator and remove the cover.

2. With the ambient temperature at or above 85°F, the valve should be able to be pressed inward with light finger pressure and then return to its position without jamming. If the valve jams and is stiff in operation, the temperature compensator should be replaced as a unit. See "Temperature Compensator Replacement."

3. If properly adjusted, the valve will begin to open at 70–77°F, and be fully open at 85°F. If not properly adjusted, the valve may be adjusted while the temperature compensator is still on the carburetor by slackening one of the cross-slotted screws for the bimetal spring, and centering the valve so that it opens and closes at the proper temperatures. If necessary, the temperature compensator may be removed and isolated at 70–77°F, then adjusted with the nut for the bimetal spring so that the valve is loose in its seat at this temperature.

4. Replace the cover and retaining screw on the compensator and check its operation during idling.

Bypass Valve

Zenith-Stromberg 175 CD2 SE Carburetor

If the engine does not return to idle speed soon after the throttle is released, and the throttle control linkage is prop-

erly adjusted, the bypass valve may be in need of adjustment or replacement.

1. If the engine still refuses to lower its rpm to idle speed when the throttle is released, turn the bypass adjusting screw on the front carburetor to the left, and manually lower the idle.

2. Run the engine briefly up to approximately 2000 rpm, then release the throttle. If the engine returns to idle speed, turn the screw ½ turn further to the left. If the engine does not return to idle, replace the bypass valve as a unit. See "Bypass Valve Replacement."

3. Remove the air cleaner. While peering into the carburetor bores, observe the air valves. Briefly race the engine and then release the throttle. The air valve of the front carburetor should normally go down to the bridge slower than the air valve of the rear carburetor. Turn the bypass adjusting screw to the right until the above-mentioned normal function is obtained. If the valve cannot be adjusted so that the front air valve goes down to the bridge slower than the rear air valve, the bypass valve must be replaced as a unit. See "Bypass Valve Replacement."

Hot-Start Valve

Zenith-Stromberg 175 CD2 SE Carburetor

When the throttle control is in the idling position, adjust the valve control of the hot-start valve so that the valve is against the carburetor lever with the valve piston in the upper position.

Coat the contact surfaces on the valve and carburetor with high-temperature white grease such as Molykote®.

Test the operation of the hot-start

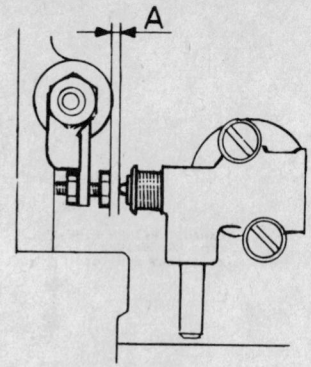

Hot start valve adjustment—SU HIF 6

valve by determining that the engine returns to idle speed after several brief periods of racing the engine.

SU HIF 6 Carburetor

To adjust the hot-start valve, press the control rods down to the bottom position and measure the distance (A) between the rod and the adjusting screw. Adjust the distance to a maximum of 0.04 in.

Test the operation of the control rods—making sure that they do not jam.

Constant (Intake) Air Temperature Device— Carbureted Models

If the flap for the constant air temperature device sticks in one position, engine operation will suffer. Normally, the flap is closed to cold air (intake hose) at an ambient temperature of 70–77° F, and closed to hot air (exhaust manifold heated) at 95–105° F.

1. The operation of the flap may be checked with the flap housing installed in

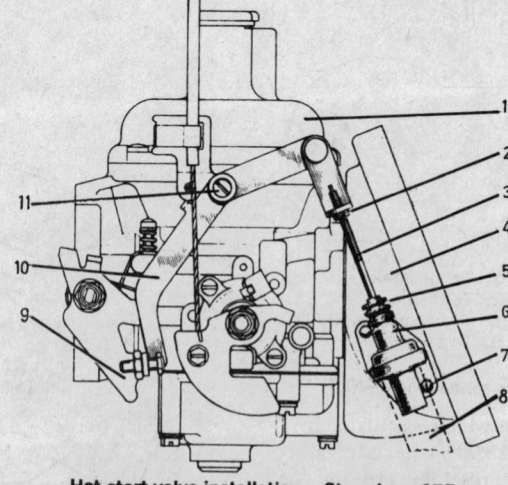

Hot start valve installation—Stromberg 175 CD2 SE carburetor.

1. Rubber seal
2. Rubber seal
3. Valve
4. Bi-metal spring
5. Cover
6. Screws for temperature compensator
7. Screw for cover
8. Cross slotted screw
9. Adjusting nut
10. Housing
11. Marking

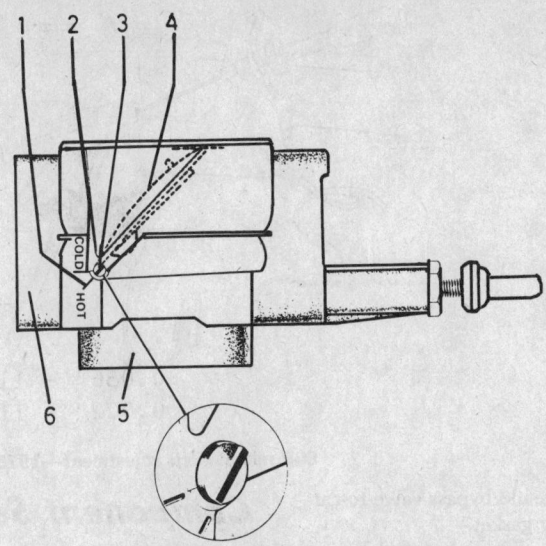

Checking constant air temperature flap function.

1. HOT—open for warm air
2. COLD—open for cold air
3. Tab
4. Flap
5. Hot air intake
6. Cold air intake

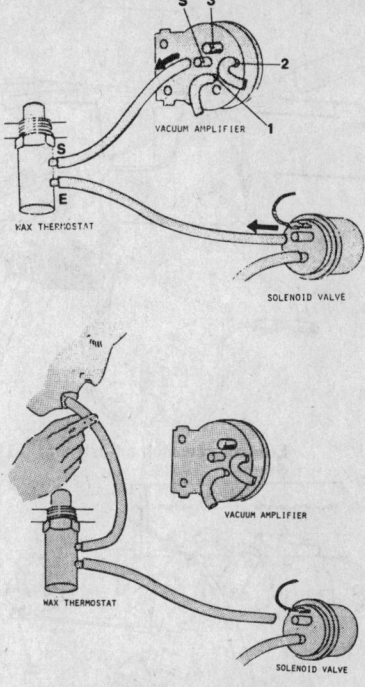

Checking wax thermostat

position. When the small tab on the flap housing points toward the mark closest the exhaust heat hose, the flap is open for cold (unheated) air. When the tab points to the mark nearest the cold air intake, the flap is open for warm (exhaust heated) air. If the tab indicates that the flap is opening and closing the air sources at the right temperatures, you may rest your soul. If not, check the operation of the flap control thermostat.

2. Disconnect the flap housing from the air intake hoses. Immerse the thermostat in lukewarm water. At a water temperature of 70–77° F, the thermostat should be in its upper (toward the flap housing) position. At 95–105° F, the thermostat should be in its lower position (away from the flap housing). If correct operation cannot be obtained, replace the thermostat and flap housing as a unit.

3. Replace the flap housing and thermostat assembly, making sure that the thermostat is centered in the middle of the air flow. Secure the hose clamp screw on top of the flap.

EGR System Checking

1976 49 States Models—B21, B27

1. With a cold engine, check the operation of the wax thermostat. Start the engine and idle. Manipulate the throttle by hand and check that the EGR valve rod does not move in and out. If it does, the thermostat is faulty. It should not operate the EGR valve until the coolant reaches 130–140°F.

2. With the engine warmed up (176°F), check that the EGR valve rod *does* move

in and out when the throttle is opened and closed. If not, the wax thermostat, hoses or EGR valve may be at fault.

3. Stop the engine. Disconnect the vacuum hose from the EGR valve. Blow through the hose. If no air passes, the wax thermostat is faulty. If air does pass, either the hose is incorrectly installed or the EGR valve is defective.

4. Finally, connect the EGR vacuum hose and start the engine. Open the throttle to 3000–4000 rpm and then quickly release. The EGR valve rod should close. If not, replace the EGR valve.

1976 California Models—B21, B27

1. With a cold engine (below 130°F coolant temperature), check the operation of the wax thermostat. Disconnect the vacuum hose at the solenoid valve and disconnect the vacuum hose at the vacuum amplifier connection "S". Suck one of the disconnected hoses. If any air passes, one of the hoses has a vacuum leak or the wax thermostat is faulty. Connect the hoses.

2. Start the engine and warm to operating temperature (176°F). Stop the engine. Disconnect the two hoses again, and suck through either of the hoses. This time the thermostat should be open, and air should pass through. If not, replace the wax thermostat.

3. Connect the hoses. Check the throttle position sensing micro-switch next. Connect a 12v test light in series between the upper wire connector and its upper terminal .   Switch the ig-

nition to the "on" position. Pull back the throttle lever and insert an 0.006 in. feeler gauge between the screw and the lever stop. When the lever is released and the throttle screw makes contact with the switch plunger, the test light should illuminate. This indicates that current is reaching the solenoid valve, the micro-switch is activating, and the fuse is good. Then, repeat by inserting an 0.008 in. feeler gauge between the screw and lever stop. This time, the test light should not light and the throttle screw should not make contact with the switch plunger. Adjust as necessary by loosening the locknut on the stopscrew and adjusting for 0.006 in. clearance.

4. Check the solenoid valve next. Start the engine and idle. Disconnect the hose from connection "1" at the amplifier. Connect a vacuum gauge and a vacuum pump to connection "1", and create a vacuum. With the engine idling, the EGR valve should remain closed (no change in rpm). If not, the solenoid valve is defective.

5. With the vacuum pump still connected, and engine idling, check that the vacuum reading does not change for 10 seconds. If the reading changes, this indicates a bad amplifier or leaking hoses.

6. Finally, with the engine idling, increase the rpm while observing the EGR valve. If the EGR valve rod does not open, check for a clogged venturi or leaking venturi vacuum hose. Then, suddenly release the throttle and check that the EGR valve rod closes. If not, the solenoid valve is faulty.

Volvo

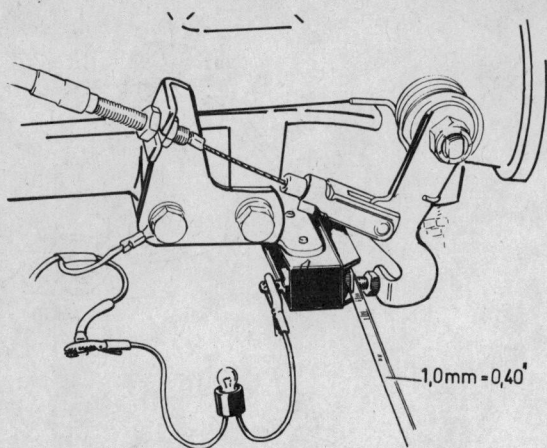

EGR microswitch adjustment—1974 B20

1,0mm = 0,40"

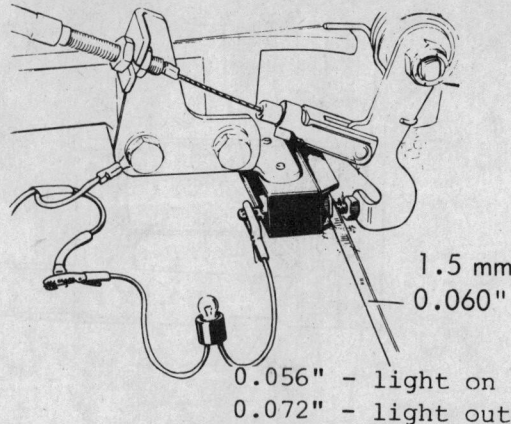

1.5 mm
0.060"

0.056" - light on
0.072" - light out

EGR microswitch adjustment—1975 B20

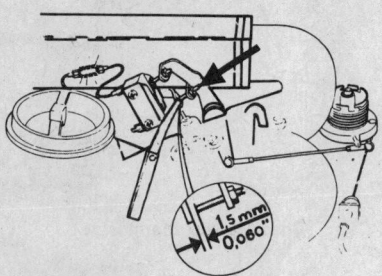

1.5 mm
0.060"

Checking micro-switch—1976

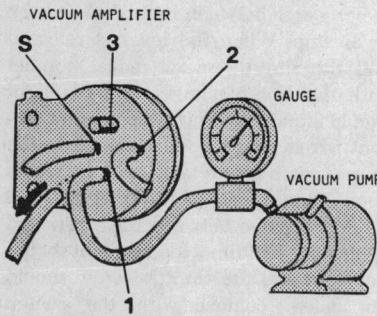

VACUUM AMPLIFIER

S 3 2

GAUGE

VACUUM PUMP

1

Checking solenoid valve

Component Replacement

Temperature Compensator

Zenith-Stromberg 175 CD2 SE Carburetor

1. Remove the retaining screws (6) and lift off the compensator.
2. Discard the old rubber seals and replace them with new ones.
3. Position the compensator to the side of the carburetor and install the retaining screws.
4. Check the operation of the compensator during idle as outlined in "Temperature Compensator Testing and Adjustment."

Bypass Valve

Zenith-Stromberg 175 CD2 SE Carburetor

1. Remove the three retaining screws and lift off the bypass valve.

2. Discard the old bypass valve-to-carburetor housing gasket.
3. Position a new gasket and bypass valve to the carburetor, making sure that the orifices and mating surfaces of the valve and gasket align, then install the three retaining screws.
4. Check the operation of the bypass valve as outlined in "Bypass Valve Testing and Adjustment."

Hot-Start Valve

Zenith-Stromberg 175 CD2 SE Carburetor

The hot-start valve on the Stromberg carburetor is riveted to the air cleaner. If cleaning is to be performed on the valve, it must be accomplished with the valve in place on the air cleaner.

SU HIF 6 Carburetor

1. Remove the two retaining screws and lift off the valve.
2. Discard the old gasket and clean the channels in the carburetor with a low-pressure air line.
3. Position the valve and new gasket to the carburetor, making sure that the gasket is aligned properly, then install the two retaining screws.
4. Adjust the position of the control rod and test the operation of the valve as outlined in "Hot-Start Valve Testing and Adjustment."

Constant Air Temperature Device Flap Housing

1. Loosen the hose clamps, and disconnect the flap housing and thermostat assembly from the hoses for the intake air, exhaust heated air, and intake manifold.
2. Install the new flap housing assembly in position and reconnect the three hoses. Make sure that the thermostat is centered in the middle of the intake air flow. Secure the hose clamp screw on top of the flap.
3. Check the operation of the new flap housing as outlined in "Constant Air Temperature Device Testing and Adjustment."

Component Service

Positive Crankcase Ventilation System

The only service required for the PCV system is the cleaning of the hoses, nipples, and metal filter every two years or 24,000 miles (1972–74) or 15,000 miles (1975–76).

Fuel Evaporative Control System

The only items requiring service in the evaporative control system are the foam plastic filter in the bottom of the charcoal canister. The canister filter is replaced every two years or 24,000 miles (1972–74) or 45,000 miles (1975–76).

FUEL SYSTEM
Fuel Pump

The mechanical pumps are used with carbureted engines, and the electrical pumps with fuel-injection.

Mechanical Type

The Pierburg PV 3025 fuel pump used on the 164, and the Pierburg APG fuel pump used on the 140 series are all camshaft-driven diaphragm types. The fuel pump is located on the left (driver's) side of the engine block.

Testing and Adjustment

No adjustments may be made to the fuel pump. Before removing the old fuel pump, the following test may be made while the pump is still installed on the engine.

CAUTION: *To avoid accidental ignition of fuel during the test, first remove the coil high-tension wire from the distributor and the coil.*

1. If a fuel pressure gauge is available, connect the gauge to the engine and operate the engine until the pressure stops rising. Stop the engine and take the read-

ing. If the reading is within the specifications given in the "Tune-Up Specifications" chart, the malfunction is not in the fuel pump. Also check the pressure drop after the engine is stopped. A large pressure drop below the minimum specification indicates leaky valves. If the pump proves to be satisfactory, check the tank and inlet line.

2. If a fuel pressure gauge is not available, disconnect the fuel line at the pump outlet, place a vessel beneath the pump outlet, and crank the engine. A good pump will force the fuel out of the outlet in steady spurts. A worn diaphragm spring may not provide proper pumping action.

3. As a further test, disconnect and plug the fuel line from the tank at the pump, and hold your thumb over the pump inlet. If the pump is functioning properly, a suction should be felt on your thumb. No suction indicates that the pump diaphragm is leaking, or that the diaphragm linkage is worn.

4. Check the crankcase for gasoline. A ruptured diaphragm may leak fuel into the engine.

Replacement

1. Disconnect and plug the inlet and outlet lines to the fuel pump.

2. Remove the two fuel pump retaining bolts and carefully pull the pump and old gasket away from the block.

3. Discard the old gasket and position a new one on the pump.

4. Mount the fuel pump and gasket to the engine block, being careful to insert the pump lever (rocker arm) in the engine block, aligning it correctly above the camshaft.

5. While holding the pump securely against the block, install the two fuel pump retaining bolts, and tighten them securely.

6. Unplug and reconnect the fuel lines to the pump.

7. Start the engine and check for fuel leaks. Also check for oil leaks where the pump attaches to the block.

Electric Type

Volvo has used electric fuel pumps on all of its fuel-injected models.

NOTE: *Volvo states that a no-start condition may occasionally occur when the car has not been started for an extended period of time. This may be due to the fuel pump sticking in one position because of foreign matter entering the pump, or corrosion forming on the rotor shaft or commutator and brushes. It is, therefore, very important to replace the inline fuel filter at its regular intervals on pre-1972 fuel-injected models, and clean the fuel tank pick-up screen every 12 months or 12,000 miles on post-1971 fuel-injected mod-*

els to prevent corrosion causing water condensation and foreign matter from entering the pump. As an additional corrosion prevention measure, add an alcohol solution or "dry gas" to the fuel, especially in winter months. If, however, the pump does become "stuck" in one position for any of the above reasons, it may be "unstuck" by lighty rapping on the pump casing with a length of hardwood such as a hammer handle, while the ignition is switched on.

Testing and Adjustment

No adjustments may be made to the fuel pump. If the pump is not functioning properly, it must be discarded and replaced. To check the function of the fuel pump, the pump should be connected to a pressure gauge. Be careful not to switch the electrical leads. If the pump fails to pump its normal capacity, or if it cannot pump that capacity at its specified rate of current consumption, it must be replaced.

Replacement

1. Remove the filler cap. Remove the electrical lead from the pump as well as the template to which the pump is mounted.

2. Clean around the hose connections. Pinch shut the fuel lines, loosen the hose clamps, and disconnect the lines.

3. Loosen the retaining nuts and remove the pump from its rubber mounts.

4. Install the new pump on its rubber mounts and tighten the retaining nuts.

5. Reconnect the fuel lines, tighten the hose clamps, and remove the pinchers.

6. Mount the template beneath the car and connect the electrical lead.

7. Start the engine and check for leaks.

Carburetors

Two different types of carburetors have been used on 1972 Volvos. A pair of sidedraft Stromberg 175 CD2 SE units were used on 1972 164 models. A pair of sidedraft SU HIF units were used on 1972 140 series models.

Removal and Installation

1. On the Stromberg carburetor, disconnect the hot-start valve control. Separate the air cleaner halves and remove the inner half from the carburetors. Remove both air cleaners.

2. Disconnect the throttle linkage by removing the link rod ball joints from the carburetors. Disconnect the choke cable, taking note of its proper location.

3. Disconnect and plug the fuel lines at the float chambers. Remove the vacuum hose for the distributor. On the SU HIF carburetor, disconnect the hot-start valve hose.

4. Remove the four (each) nuts retaining the carburetors to the intake manifold. Remove the carburetors, gaskets, and protection plate.

5. Position the protection plate, new gaskets, and carburetors on the intake manifold studs. Install the carburetor retaining nuts and tighten them evenly until they are snug against the manifold.

6. Connect the vacuum hose, fuel hoses, choke, and throttle linkage. On the SU HIF carburetor, connect the hot-start valve hose.

7. Install the inner half of the air cleaner to the carburetors. Adjust the idle speed and mixture of the carburetors as outlined in the "Tune-Up" section.

8. Fit the air cleaner halves together and, on the Stromberg carburetor, connect the hot-start valve control.

Carburetor Overhaul

Carburetors are relatively complex units. Proper performance depends upon the cleanliness and proper adjustment of all internal and external components. In addition to the usual adjustments performed at the regular tune-up intervals, it eventually becomes necessary to remove, disassemble, clean, and overhaul the entire carburetor(s), in order to restore its original performance. To overhaul a carburetor, first purchase the proper rebuilding kit. Read the instructions and study the exploded view of the carburetor thoroughly prior to the actual removal and disassembly.

After reading the detailed carburetor rebuilding instructions, the following general procedure may be used. Remove the carburetor and place it on a clean work table. Disassemble the carburetor by removing the screws securing the upper and lower sections together. Remove the damping piston, air valve, spring, metering needle, fuel jet (SU only), and float assembly, and soak all metal parts in carburetor cleaning solvent. Scrape all old gasket material from the mating surfaces. After the metal parts have been soaked to remove all gum, varnish, and dirt, rinse them off with a clean, uncontaminated, solvent solution. Blow out all passages with compressed air and allow them to air dry. Do not use drills or wire to clean the passages. Check the throttle shaft and choke disc for excessive wear. Inspect the float hinge pins for distortion. All non-metal parts that are not being replaced should be wiped clean with a lint-free cloth. After all of the parts have been sufficiently cleaned or replaced, assemble the carburetor using new gaskets and seals, and, on Zenith-Stromberg carburetors, a new air valve diaphragm. If any of the replacement seals in the SU carburetor are cork, they must first be soaked in penetrating oil for a minimum of a half hour to avoid splitting during installation.

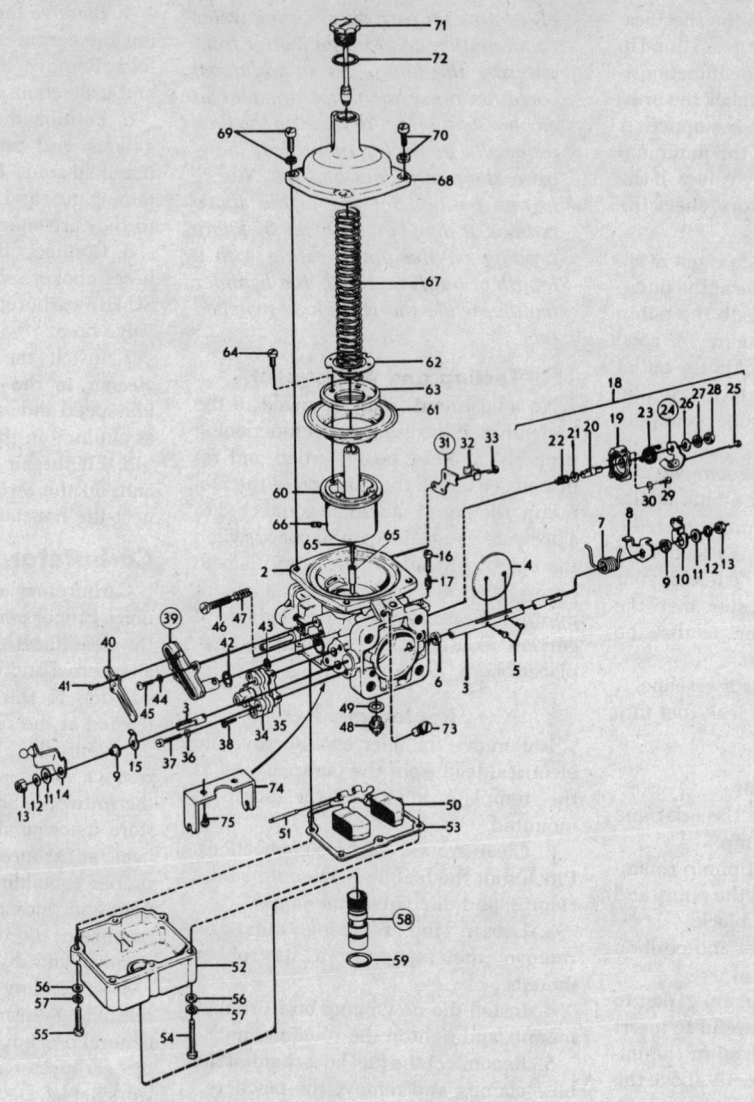

Stromberg 175 CD2 SE disassembled

2. Body
3. Throttle plate spindle
4. Throttle plate
5. Throttle plate set screws
6. Seal
7. Return spring
8. Lever
9. Bushing
10. Lever
11. Spacing masher
12. Lockwasher
13. Nut
14. Lever
15. Lever
16. Adjuster screw
17. Spring
18. Cold start device assembly
19. Cold start device housing
20. Shaft
21. Circlip
22. Spring
23. Return spring
24. Fast idle choke lever
25. Choke cable attaching screw
26. Spacing washer
27. Lockwasher

28. Nut
29. Screw
30. Lockwasher
31. Choke cable support
32. Choke cable retaining clip
33. Screw
34. By-pass valve assembly (front carb only)
35. Gasket
36. Lockwasher
37. Screw
38. Screw
39. Temperature compensator housing
40. Temperature compensator cover
41. Screw
42. Rubber seal
43. Rubber seal
44. Lockwasher
45. Screw
46. Idle trimming screw
47. Spring
48. Needle valve with seat
49. Gasket
50. Float
51. Float hinge pin

52. Floatchamber cover
53. Gasket
54. Screw
55. Screw
56. Washer
57. Lockwasher
58. Floatchamber plug
59. Gasket
60. Air valve
61. Diaphragm
62. Washer
63. Washer
64. Screw
65. Metering needle
66. Metering needle retaining set screw
67. Air valve return spring
68. Suction chamber cover
69. Screw and washer
70. Screw and washer
71. Damping piston assembly
72. Damping piston gasket
73. Plug for air conditioner speed compensator

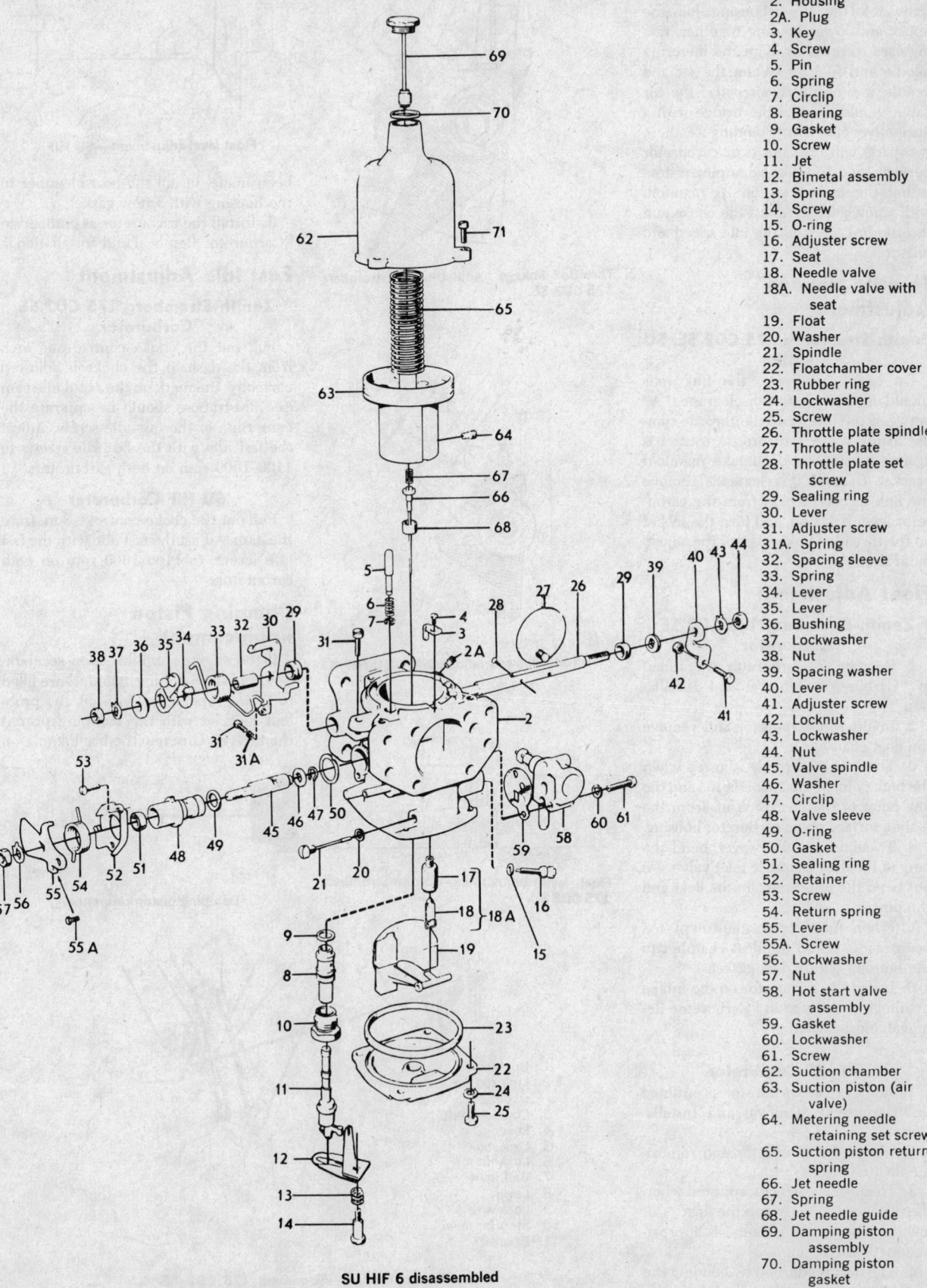

SU HIF 6 disassembled

2. Housing
2A. Plug
3. Key
4. Screw
5. Pin
6. Spring
7. Circlip
8. Bearing
9. Gasket
10. Screw
11. Jet
12. Bimetal assembly
13. Spring
14. Screw
15. O-ring
16. Adjuster screw
17. Seat
18. Needle valve
18A. Needle valve with seat
19. Float
20. Washer
21. Spindle
22. Floatchamber cover
23. Rubber ring
24. Lockwasher
25. Screw
26. Throttle plate spindle
27. Throttle plate
28. Throttle plate set screw
29. Sealing ring
30. Lever
31. Adjuster screw
31A. Spring
32. Spacing sleeve
33. Spring
34. Lever
35. Lever
36. Bushing
37. Lockwasher
38. Nut
39. Spacing washer
40. Lever
41. Adjuster screw
42. Locknut
43. Lockwasher
44. Nut
45. Valve spindle
46. Washer
47. Circlip
48. Valve sleeve
49. O-ring
50. Gasket
51. Sealing ring
52. Retainer
53. Screw
54. Return spring
55. Lever
55A. Screw
56. Lockwasher
57. Nut
58. Hot start valve assembly
59. Gasket
60. Lockwasher
61. Screw
62. Suction chamber
63. Suction piston (air valve)
64. Metering needle retaining set screw
65. Suction piston return spring
66. Jet needle
67. Spring
68. Jet needle guide
69. Damping piston assembly
70. Damping piston gasket
71. Screw

Assemble the float chamber and adjust the float height. Assemble the air valve, spring, and metering needle with set-screw into the upper housing. Join the upper and lower housing together, taking care to properly align the metering needle and fuel jet. When the jet and needle are installed correctly, the air valve should drop to the bridge with a distinctive click. Any binding of these two parts will result in poor carburetor performance. Install the damping piston. Install the carburetor on its manifold with a new gasket. Adjust the choke and throttle linkage, and the idle speed and mixture.

Throttle Linkage Adjustment

Zenith-Stromberg 175 CD2 SE, SU HIF

On each carburetor, the link rods should maintain a 0.004 in. clearance "A" between the lever and the throttle spindle flange when the throttle control is against its stop on the intake manifold bracket. To adjust this clearance, remove the link rod ball socket from the carburetor lever ball stud, and turn the socket on the threaded link rod until the adjustment is correct.

Float Adjustment

Zenith-Stromberg 175 CD2 SE Carburetor

1. Remove the carburetor as outlined in "Carburetor Removal and Installation."

2. Invert the carburetor and remove the float chamber.

3. The float is correctly adjusted when the high point of the float is 5⁄8 in., and the low point of the float is 1⁄2 in. from the sealing surface of the carburetor housing.

4. To adjust the float level, bend the tang at the float chamber inlet valve. Do not bend the arm between the float and the pin.

5. When the proper adjustment has been made, install the float chamber to the housing with a new gasket.

6. Install the carburetor on the intake manifold as outlined in "Carburetor Removal and Installation."

SU HIF Carburetor

1. Remove the carburetor as outlined in "Carburetor Removal and Installation."

2. Invert the carburetor and remove the float chamber.

3. The float is correctly adjusted when the distance "A" between the float "valley" and the housing flange is approximately 0.02–0.06 in.

4. The float is adjusted by bending the metal tab at the float chamber inlet valve.

5. When the correct adjustment has

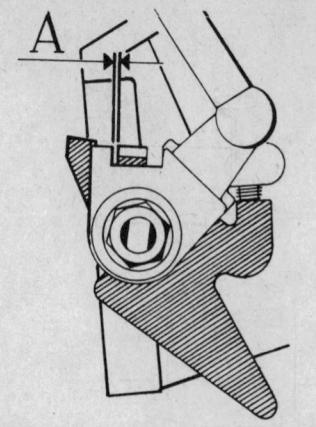

Throttle linkage adjustment—Stromberg 175 CD2 SE.

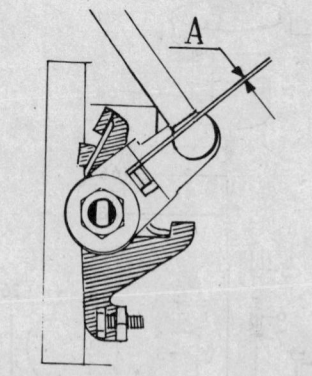

Throttle linkage adjustment—SU HIF 6

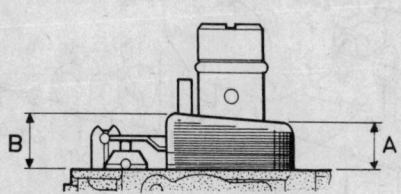

Float level adjustment—Zenith-Stromberg 175 CD2 SE.

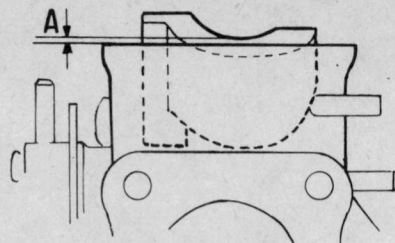

Float level adjustment—SU HIF

been made, install the float chamber to the housing with a new gasket.

6. Install the carburetor as outlined in "Carburetor Removal and Installation."

Fast Idle Adjustment

Zenith-Stromberg 175 CD2 SE Carburetor

Pull out the choke control one inch from the dash. If the choke is adjusted correctly, the mark on the rapid idle cam (see illustration) should be opposite the centerline of the fast idle screw. Adjust the fast idle with the fast idle screws to 1100–1300 rpm on both carburetors.

SU HIF Carburetor

Pull out the choke control 0.8 in. from the dash. Adjust the fast idle with the fast idle screws to 1100–1600 rpm on both carburetors.

Damping Piston Replacement

If the engine stumbles upon acceleration, and the damping cylinders are filled to their proper level with oil, the problem may be with the damping pistons themselves. Unscrew the black knobs on

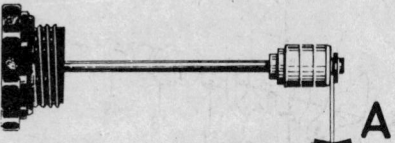

Damping piston clearance

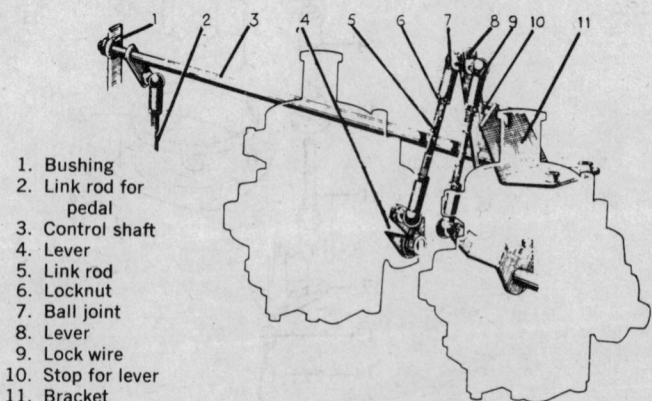

1. Bushing
2. Link rod for pedal
3. Control shaft
4. Lever
5. Link rod
6. Locknut
7. Ball joint
8. Lever
9. Lock wire
10. Stop for lever
11. Bracket

Throttle linkage—Stromberg 175 CD2 SE installation shown, SU HIF installation similar.

top of the carburetors and remove the damping pistons. If the axial clearance "A" between the bottom of the piston and the retaining clip is not 0.04–0.07 in., the damping piston must be replaced as a unit.

Electronic Fuel Injection

Volvo has made Bosch electronic fuel injection available since 1970, when it was standard equipment on the 1800 series. The system was optional on the 140 series in 1971–72, and on the 164 in 1972. For 1973, all Volvos imported into the U.S. were equipped with the system. Electronic fuel injection was retained on the 1974–75 164 series, while the 4-cylinder models went to continuous injection starting in 1974.

The complete system contains the following components electronic control unit (brain), electric fuel pump, fuel filter, fuel pressure regulator, fuel injectors, cold-start valve, inlet duct (for intake air), throttle valve switch, auxiliary air regulator, intake air temperature sensor, coolant temperature sensor, intake air pressure sensor, and the triggering contacts in the ignition distributor.

Fuel Injection System Precautions

Due to the highly sensitive nature of the Bosch electronic fuel injection system, the following special precautions must be strictly adhered to in order to avoid damage to the system.

1. Do not operate the engine with the battery disconnected.

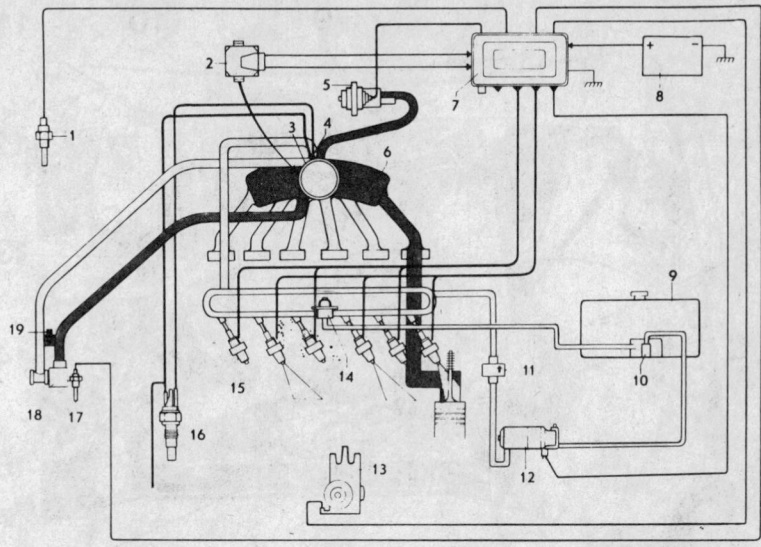

Fuel injection principle of operation—1972-73 B30F shown

1. Temperature sensor for induction air
2. Throttle valve switch
3. Throttle housing
4. Cold start valve
5. Pressure sensor
6. Inlet duct
7. Control unit (electronic)
8. Battery
9. Fuel tank
10. Fuel filter, suction side
11. Fuel filter, discharge side
12. Fuel pump
13. Triggering contacts in distributor
14. Pressure regulator
15. Injectors
16. Thermal timer contact
17. Temperature sensor for coolant
18. Auxiliary air regulator
19. Idling adjusting screw

2. Do not utilize a high-speed battery charger as a starting aid.

3. When using a high-speed battery charger to charge the battery while it is installed in the vehicle, at least one battery cable must be disconnected.

4. Do not allow the control unit to be subjected to temperatures exceeding 185° F, such as when the vehicle is being baked after painting. If there is a risk of the temperature exceeding 185° F, the

control unit must be removed.

5. The engine must not be started when the ambient temperature exceeds 158° F, or damage to the control unit will result.

6. The ignition must be in the off position when disconnecting or connecting the control unit.

7. When working on the fuel system, take care not to allow dirt to enter the system. Small dust particles may jam fuel injectors.

Component Replacement

The fuel injection system is repaired simply by replacing the defective component. There are adjustments that can be made to the pressure regulator, throttle valve, throttle valve switch, throttle stopscrew, and the fuel mixture. To make resistance checks, use an ohmmeter, and for continuity checks, a 12 V test light. If the control unit is defective, return it to a qualified repair agency and install a new unit.

Control Unit

1. On 1800 series models and 1975 164 models, disconnect the defroster hose, remove the control unit bracket retaining screws, and lower the unit to the floor. On 1971–73 140 series and 1972–74 164 models, move the passenger's front seat all the way back, unscrew the bolt securing the seat's front, move the seat forward while folding the seat bottom to the rear, remove the control unit retaining screws, and draw out the unit.

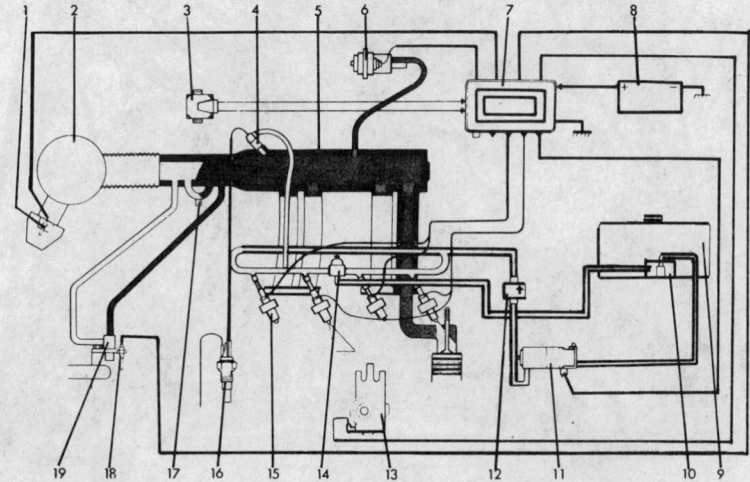

Fuel injection principle of operation—1972- 73 B20F shown.

1. Temperature sensor for induction air
2. Air cleaner
3. Throttle valve switch
4. Cold start valve
5. Inlet duct
6. Pressure sensor
7. Control unit (electronic)
8. Battery
9. Fuel tank
10. Fuel filter, suction side
11. Fuel pump
12. Fuel filter, discharge side
13. Triggering contacts in distributor
14. Pressure regulator
15. Injectors
16. Thermal timer contact
17. Idling adjusting screw
18. Temperature sensor for coolant
19. Auxiliary air regulator

Volvo

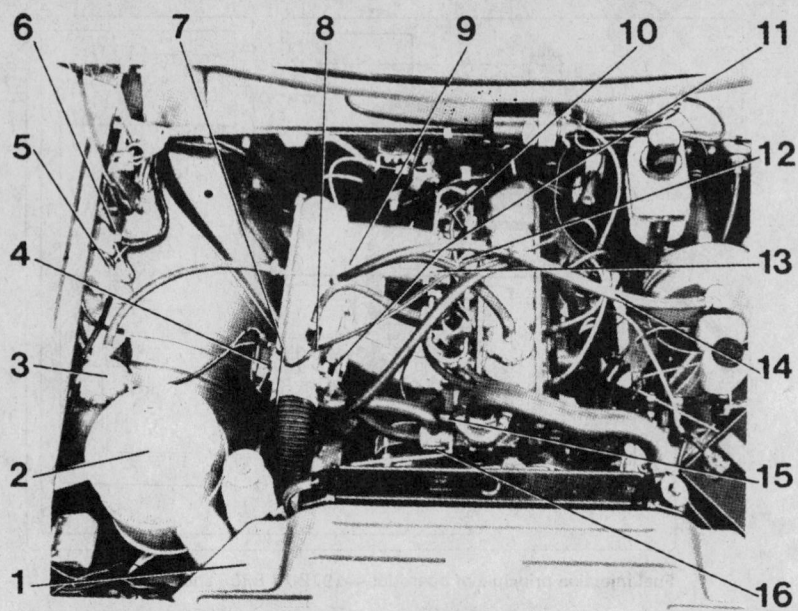

Fuel injection system installation—1972-73 B20F shown, 1970-71 B20E similar

1. Temperature sensor (induction air)
2. Air cleaner
3. Pressure sensor
4. Throttle switch
5. Pump relay
6. Main relay
7. Screw for adjusting idling (not visible)
8. Cold start valve
9. Inlet duct
10. Thermal timer
11. Stop screw for throttle valve
12. Injector
13. Pressure regulator
14. Triggering contacts
15. Temperature sensor (coolant)
16. Auxiliary air regulator

2. Remove the screw for the cap holding the cable harness to the unit. Pull out the plastic cover strip.

3. Construct a puller out of 5/64 in. welding wire to disconnect the main plug contact. Insert the puller in the rear of the control unit and pull out the plug carefully.

4. Press the plug contact firmly into the new or reconditioned control unit. Fit the plastic cover strip, retaining cap, and screw.

5. Fit the control unit into place and install its retaining screws. On 1800 series models, connect the defroster hose. On 140 series and 164 models, secure the seat front.

Pressure Regulator

If the pressure regulator cannot be adjusted to 28 psi with its adjusting nut, it must be replaced.

1. Place pinch clamps on the three fuel hoses connected to the regulator.

2. Loosen the hose clamps and remove the hoses.

3. Remove the regulator from its bracket and replace it with a new one.

4. Connect the fuel hoses to the new regulator, tighten the hose clamps, and remove the pinch clamps.

5. Start the engine and check for fuel leaks.

Fuel Injectors

1. On 164 models, remove the air cleaner.

2. Pinch shut the fuel hose to the

Removing injector—electronic fuel injection header pipe.

3. Loosen the hose clamps for the injectors and lift up the header pipe.

4. Remove the plug contacts from the injectors. Disconnect the cable harness from the distributing pipe.

5. Turn the lockrings on the injectors counterclockwise so that they loosen from their bayonet fittings. Lift out the injectors.

6. Place the new injectors, with new washers and rubber sealing rings, in position and secure them by turning the lockrings clockwise.

7. Connect the cable harness at the distributing pipe. Connect the plug contacts to the injectors.

8. Place the header pipe in position, and tighten the hose clamps. Remove the pinch clamps.

9. On 164 models, install the air cleaner.

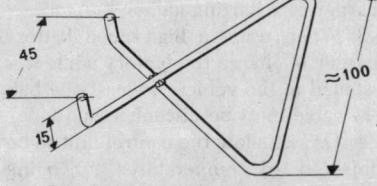

Puller for control unit plug contact

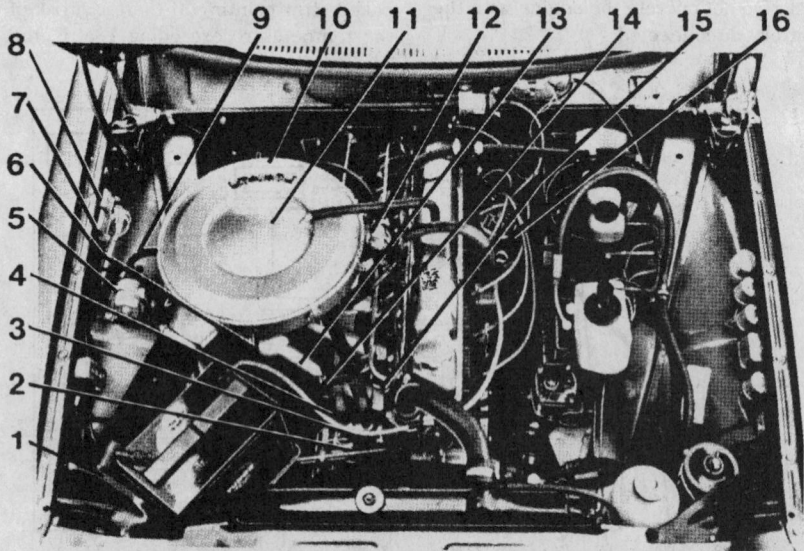

Fuel injection system installation—1972-73 B30F shown

1. Temperature sensor, induction air
2. Thermal timer
3. Auxiliary air regulator
4. Temperature sensor, coolant
5. Pressure sensor
6. Throttle switch
7. Pump relay
8. Main relay
9. Cold start valve
10. Stop screw for throttle valve
11. Air cleaner
12. Pressure regulator
13. Inlet duct
14. Screw for adjusting idling
15. Injector
16. Triggering contacts

Cold-Start Valve

1. On 164 models, remove the air cleaner.
2. Pinch shut the fuel line to the valve.
3. Remove the plug contact and the fuel hose from the valve.
4. Remove the two retaining screws and the cold-start valve from the inlet duct.
5. Place the new cold-start valve in position with packing and install the retaining screws.
6. Connect the plug contact and fuel hose to the valve. Remove the pinch clamp.
7. On 164 models, install the air cleaner.

Thermal Timer

1. Drain the cooling system.
2. Disconnect the plug contacts and unscrew the thermal timer from the cylinder head.
3. Install a new timer and connect the plug contacts.
4. Refill the cooling system.

Throttle Valve Switch

1. Disconnect the plug contact from the switch. Remove the two retaining screws and pull the switch straight out of the inlet duct.
2. Fit the new switch to the inlet duct and install the retaining screws. Connect the plug contact.
3. Adjust the switch as outlined in "Throttle Valve Switch Adjustment."

Auxiliary Air Regulator

1. Drain the cooling system.
2. Remove the plug contact from the temperature sensor and disconnect the air hoses from the regulator.
3. Remove the two retaining bolts and draw out the regulator.
4. Using a new sealing ring, position the new regulator to the cylinder head and install the retaining bolts.
5. Connect the plug contact and the two air hoses.
6. Refill the cooling system.

Intake Air Temperature Sensor

1. On 164 models, remove the right drip protection, and the air hose from the right side.
2. Disconnect the four-way plug contact from the sensor.
3. Unscrew the old sensor and install a new one, taking care not to overtighten it.
4. Plug in the four-way contact for the sensor.
5. On 164 models, install the right air hose and drip protection.

Coolant Temperature Sensor

1. Drain a portion of the cooling system so that the coolant level in the radiator and engine is below the temperature sensor.

2. Disconnect the plug contact from the sensor.
3. Unscrew the old sensor and install a new one with a new sealing ring.
4. Connect the plug contact.
5. Top up the cooling system.

Pressure Sensor

1. Disconnect the four-way plug contact and the air hose from the sensor.
2. Remove the three screws retaining the sensor to the right wheel housing.
3. Transfer the attaching bracket to the new pressure sensor.
4. Position the new sensor to the wheel well and install the retaining screws.
5. Connect the plug contact and the air hose to the sensor.

Triggering Contacts

1. Remove the distributor as outlined under "Distributor Removal and Installation."
2. Remove the two screws securing the triggering contacts holder to the distributor and then pull out the holder.
3. Lubricate the fiber pieces of the contact breaker lever on the new holder with Bosch Ft 1V4 or similar silicone cam lobe grease.

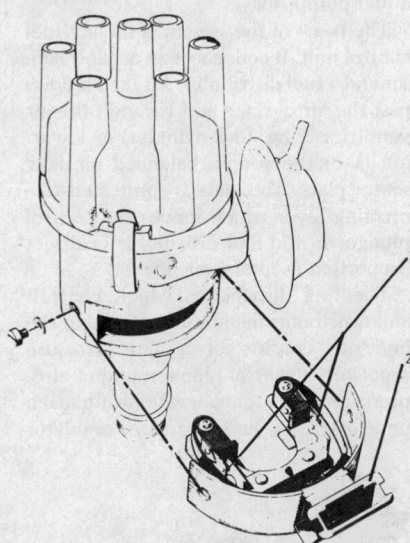

Distributor with control device—B30F shown, B20E and B20F similar
1. Triggering contacts
2. Electrical connection

4. Check to see that the rubber ring is not damaged. Replace if necessary.
5. Install the new holder in the distributor and tighten the retaining screws.
6. Install the distributor as outlined in "Distributor Removal and Installation."

Component Testing and Adjustment

Control Unit

The idle mixture may be adjusted with the slotted knob on the control unit. This operation is best performed with the use

of a CO meter. Refer to the "Fuel Injection System Idle Mixture Adjustment" for details.

The control unit may be tested only with the help of sophisticated test equipment available, again, only at the dealer level.

Pressure Regulator

The regulator may be adjusted with its adjusting nut. Pinch and disconnect the flexible fuel hose between the pressure regulator and the header pipe and insert a tee fitting and pressure gauge. Tighten the fuel connections and start the engine. Slacken the locknut and adjust the pressure to 28 psi. If the regulator cannot be adjusted properly, it must be replaced. Remove the tee fitting and gauge, and connect the fuel hoses.

Throttle Valve

The throttle valve may be adjusted with its stopscrew near the mouth of the inlet duct. Release the stopscrew locknut for the throttle valve switch, and back off the screw several turns so that it does not

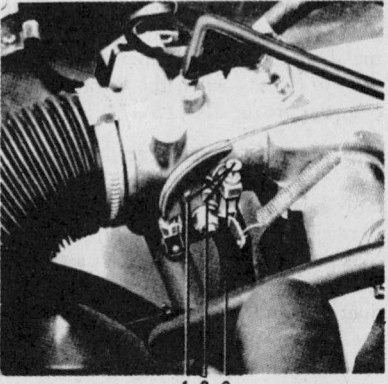

Throttle valve adjustment—B20F
1. Locknut
2. Stop screw
3. Stop on throttle valve spindle

Throttle valve adjustment—B30F
1. Stop screw
2. Locknut
3. Stop on valve spindle

lie against the throttle valve spindle stop. Make sure that the valve is completely closed. Screw in the stopscrew so that it contacts the spindle stop. At this point, turn the stopscrew 1/4–1/3 additional turn and tighten the locknut. Check to see that the switch does not jam in the closed position. Proceed to adjust the throttle valve switch as follows.

NOTE: *The stopscrew must not be used for idle adjustment.*

Throttle Valve Switch

The throttle valve switch may be adjusted with an ohmmeter. Connect the ohmmeter to the control unit (contacts 14 and 17 for four-cylinder, and contacts 9 and 14 for six-cylinder). Loosen the screws slightly so that the switch may be rotated. Scribe a mark at the upper switch screw on the inlet duct if one is not there already. Close the throttle valve by turning the switch clockwise as far as it will go. Then, observing the ohmmeter, carefully turn the switch counterclockwise until the ohmmeter registers 0 (zero). At this point, the switch is turned a further 1° counterclockwise (1/2 graduation mark at upper screw), and both switch screws are tightened. Check to make sure that the ohmmeter reading rises to infinity when the throttle valve opens approximately 1°.

Auxiliary Air Regulator

To check the operation of the auxiliary air regulator, start the engine and allow it to reach operating temperature (176° F). Make a note of the idle speed and then disconnect the hose between the inlet duct and the regulator. While covering the hose opening with your hand, check to see that the idle speed does not drop significantly over the first reading. A drop in idle speed indicates a leak in the regulator, requiring its replacement.

Continuous Fuel Injection

Continuous fuel injection is standard on all 240, 260 and 1974 140 models. It differs from electronic fuel injection in that injection takes place continuously; controlled through variation of the fuel flow rate through the injectors, rather than variation of the fuel injection duration. This system has no electronic computer. It is an electro-mechanical system that will provide suitable air/fuel mixtures to accommodate differing driving conditions.

The complete system consists of the following components: air/fuel control unit (housing both air flow sensor and fuel distributor), electric fuel pump (and fuel pressure accumulator), fuel filter, control pressure regulator, continuous fuel injectors, auxiliary air valve, cold start injec-

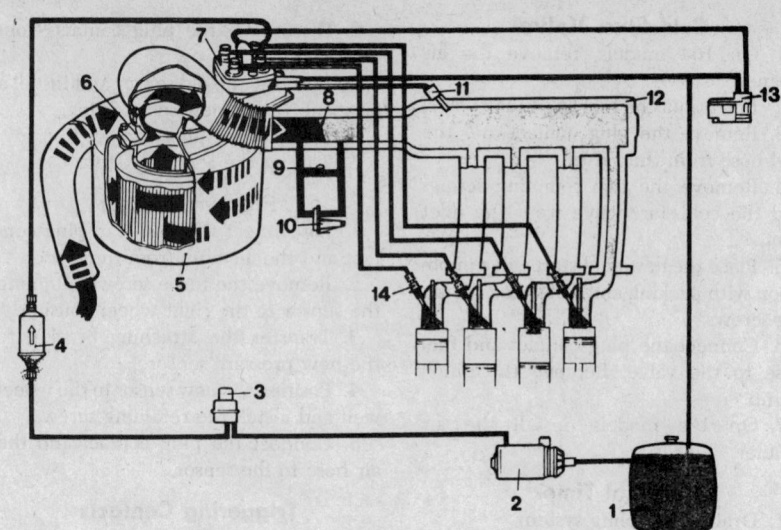

Continuous injection principle of operation—1974-75 B20F shown

1. Fuel tank
2. Fuel pump
3. Fuel accumulator
4. Fuel filter
5. Air cleaner
6. Air flow sensor
7. Fuel distributor
8. Throttle
9. Idle adjustment screw
10. Auxiliary air valve
11. Cold start injector
12. Intake manifold
13. Control pressure regulator
14. Injector

tor, thermal time switch, main relay, and a fuel pump relay.

The heart of the system is the air/fuel control unit. It consists of an air flow sensor and a fuel distributor. Intake air flows past the air cleaner and through the air venturi, raising (four cylinder) or lowering (V-6) the counterbalanced air flow sensor plate. The plate is connected to a pivoting lever which moves the control plunger in the fuel distributor in direct proportion to intake air flow.

The fuel distributor, which controls and distributes the amount of fuel to the injectors consists of a line pressure regulator, a control plunger, and (4 or 6) pressure regulator valves (one for each injector). The line pressure regulator

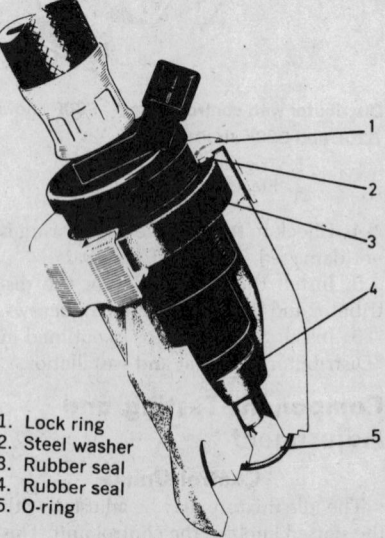

1. Lock ring
2. Steel washer
3. Rubber seal
4. Rubber seal
5. O-ring

Injector with holder—electronic fuel injection

maintains the fuel distributor inlet pressure at about 65 psi., and will recirculate fuel to the tank if pressure exceeds this value. The control plunger, which is connected to the air flow sensor plate, controls the amount of fuel available to each of the pressure regulator valves. The pressure regulator valves maintain a constant fuel pressure differential (1.4 psi) between the inlet and outlet sides of the control plunger. This is independent of the amount of fuel passing through the valves, which varies according to plunger height.

The injectors themselves are spring loaded and calibrated to open at 47–51 psi. They are not electrically operated as on the older electronic fuel injection system.

The control pressure regulator, located on the intake manifold, acts to regulate the fuel/air mixture according to engine temperature. When the engine is cold, the control pressure regulator richens the mixture (4–5 minutes max.). This is accomplished in the following manner; a certain amount of fuel is bled off into a separate control pressure system. The control pressure regulator maintains this fuel at about 52.5 psi. The regulator is connected to the upper side of the fuel distributor control plunger. When the engine temperature is below operating parameters, a bi-metal spring in the regulator senses this and reduces the fuel pressure on top of the plunger. This allows the plunger to rise further and channel more fuel to the regulator valves and injectors, thereby richening the mixture. When the engine warms, the bi-metal

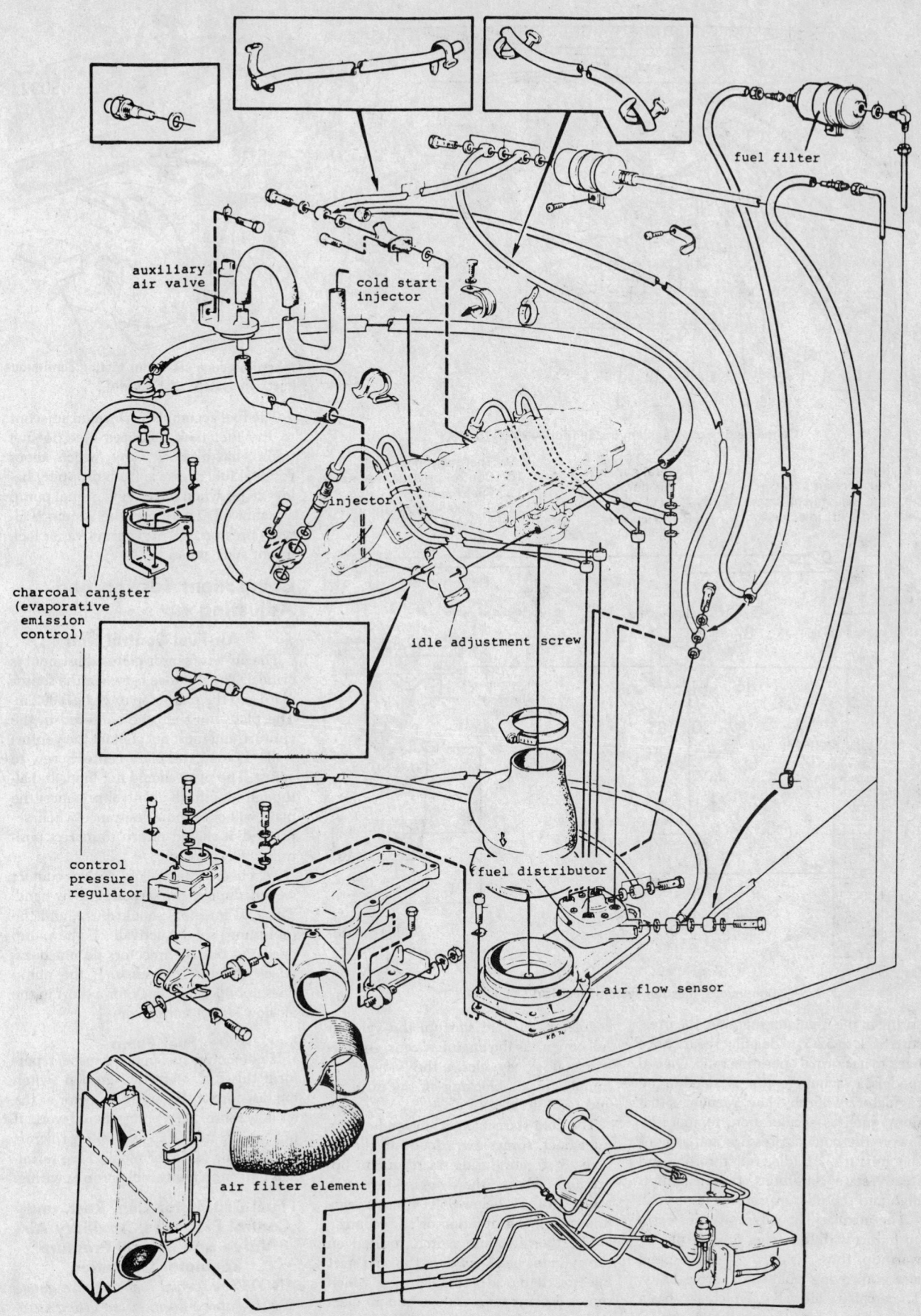

auxiliary
air valve

cold start
injector

fuel filter

injector

charcoal canister
(evaporative
emission
control)

idle adjustment screw

control
pressure
regulator

fuel distributor

air flow sensor

air filter element

Continuous injection system components—B21

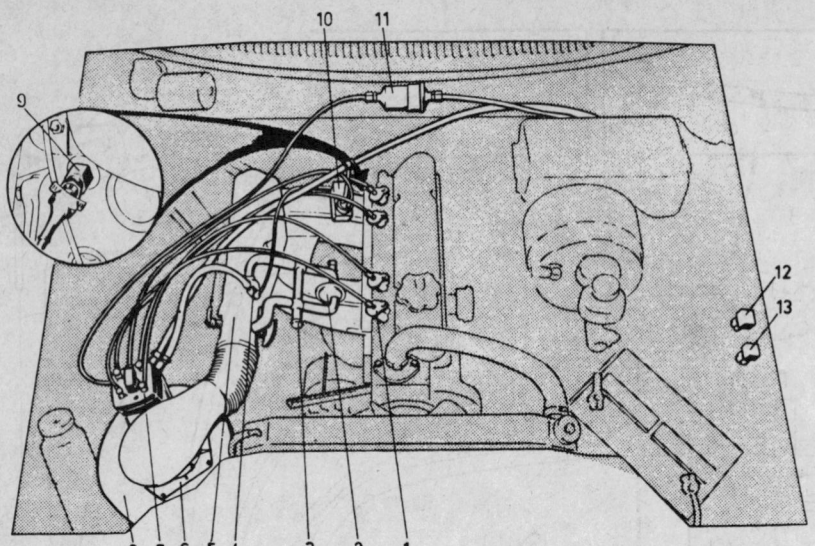

Continous injection system installation—1974-75 B20F

1. Injector
2. Auxiliary air valve
3. Idle adjustment screw
4. Cold start injector
5. Intake manifold
6. Air flow sensor
7. Fuel distributor
8. Air cleaner
9. Thermal time switch
10. Control pressure regulator
11. Fuel filter
12-13. Safety relay and pump relay

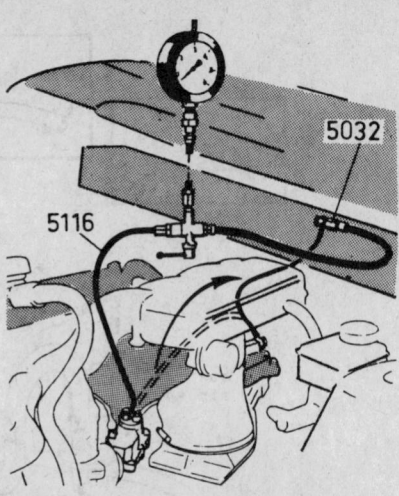

Pressure gauge set-up for testing continuous injection system B21 shown

The fuel accumulator, located adjacent to the fuel tank mounted electric fuel pump, has a check valve which keeps residual fuel pressure from dropping below 28 psi when the engine or fuel pump are shut off. Therefore, the system is always pressurized, preventing vapor lock in hot start situations.

Component Testing and Adjusting

Air-Fuel Control Unit

The air-flow sensor plate adjustment is critical. The distance between the sensor plate and the plate stop must be 0.002 in. The plate must also be centered in the venturi, and must not contact the venturi walls. Loosen the plate center screw to adjust. The plate should not bind, and although (due to the control pressure) the plate will offer some resistance when depressed, it should return to its rest position when released.

To check the air-flow sensor contact switch, depress the sensor plate by hand. The fuel injectors should buzz, and the fuel pump should activate. If the pump operates, but the injectors do not buzz, check the fuel pressures. If the pump does not operate, check for a short in the air-flow sensor connector.

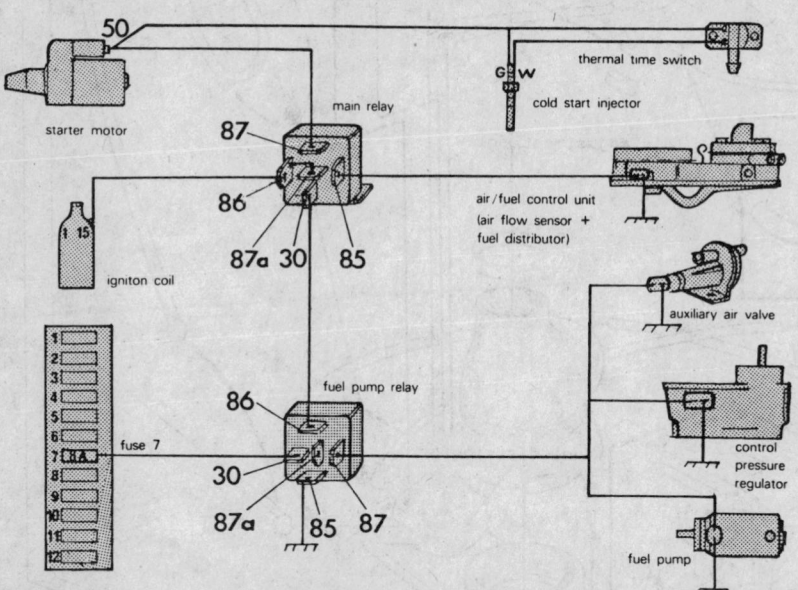

Continuous injection system electrical schematic

spring in the regulator increases the pressure back to 52.5 psi, leaning the mixture back to its normal operating ratio. On V-6 models, a vacuum feature is added to the regulator, whereby low vacuum situations, such as acceleration, temporarily lowers the control pressure and richens the mixture. At idle, full throttle, and steady state conditions, the vacuum is high and the mixture returns to normal.

The auxiliary air valve provides extra air to mix with the richer mixture during warmup, thus raising the engine speed and improving cold start driveability. The auxiliary air valve, which also has a temperature sensitive bi-metal spring, works directly with the control pressure

regulator. At cold startup, the valve is fully open. As the engine warms, an electric coil slowly closes the valve (4–5 minutes max.), blocking off the extra air and fast idle speed.

The cold start injector, located on the inlet duct, sprays extra fuel into the intake air stream during starter motor operation when the engine coolant temperature is below 95°F. It has a maximum spraying duration of 12 seconds.

The thermal time switch, located on the cylinder head, actuates the cold start injector. It has a bi-metal spring which senses coolant temperature and an electric coil which limits the cold start injector spray to 12 seconds.

Fuel Pump

If a defective fuel pump is suspect, perform this test. With the ignition switch on, disconnect the wire connector at the air flow sensor. The pump should work. If not, check fuse #7, and voltage across auxiliary air valve terminals. Live terminals indicate a faulty fuel pump or wiring.

Fuel Distributor Line, Rest, and Control Pressures, Auxiliary Air Valve and Control Pressure Regulator Operation

NOTE: *A special fuel pressure gauge with a three position tee-fitting is required to isolate the line, rest, and control pressure readings.*

Connect a pressure gauge and tee-fitting with 3-way valve in-line between the center of the fuel distributor (control pressure fuel line) and the control pressure regulator.

CAUTION: *Disconnect the coil wire (terminal 15) to prevent burning out the coil windings.* Disconnect the wire connectors at the control pressure regulator and auxiliary air valve. Switch on the ignition and and disconnect the wire connector at the air-flow sensor. The fuel pump should start.

Check the line pressure first. With the tee-fitting lever pointing to the fuel distributor, check that the line pressure is 64–75 psi. If insufficient, check fuel lines for leakage, fuel pump for delivery capacity (25.3 fluid ounces in 30 sec.), or low line pressure adjustment. If too high, check for clogged fuel return line or high line pressure adjustment. Line pressure is adjusted along with rest pressure later in this procedure.

Check the control pressure next. With the tee-fitting turned at a right angle to the hoses, check that the control pressure corresponds to those values given in the control pressure/coolant temperature graph. Depending on coolant temperature, the control pressure will be somewhere between 18–55 psi, lower for cool temperatures, higher for warm temperatures. If the control pressure is insufficient, try a new pressure regulator. If the pressure is too high, check for a clogged fuel return line, or try a new control pressure regulator. Reconnect the control pressure regulator electrical connector. After 4–5 minutes, the pressure should decrease to 44–50 psi. If not, disconnect the electrical connector at the control pressure regulator and check with a 12v test light across the terminals. No voltage indicates a defective wire. Voltage indicates a possible faulty regulator. Then, check across the terminals with an ohmmeter. Resistance indicates corroded terminals. No resistance indicates a defective control pressure regulator.

The vacuum function of the control pressure regulator on the V-6 engine is checked later in this test.

The auxiliary air valve is checked next. Disconnect the auxiliary air valve hoses. Using a dentist mirror and a flashlight, check that the valve is partly open at room temperature. Then, reconnect the wire connector at the valve and, after 4–5 min., the valve should be fully closed. If not, tap on valve and check again. If tapping closes valve, the valve is OK (engine vibrations will close valve in normal operation). If the auxiliary air valve still does not close, disconnect the connector and check the voltage across the wire connector terminals with a 12v test light. No

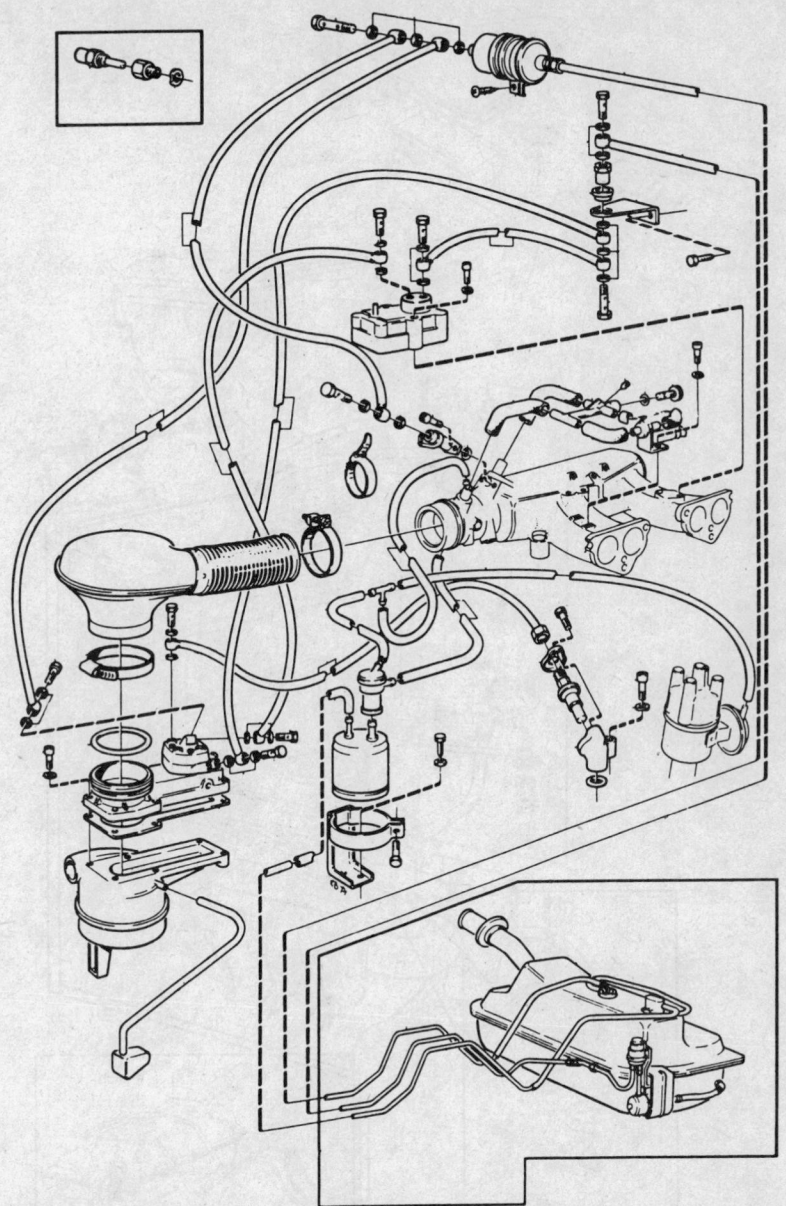

Continuous injection system components—B20

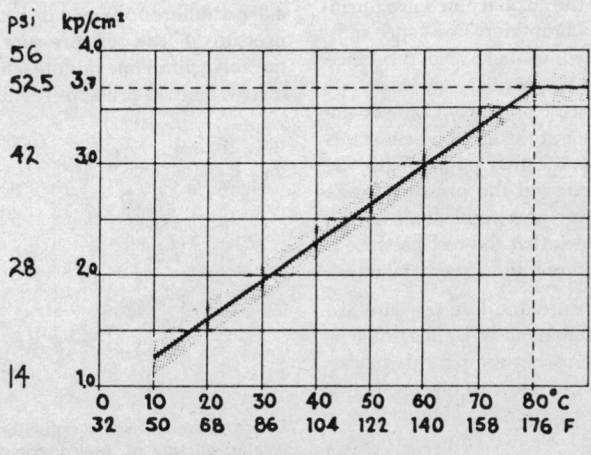

Control pressure/coolant temperature graph

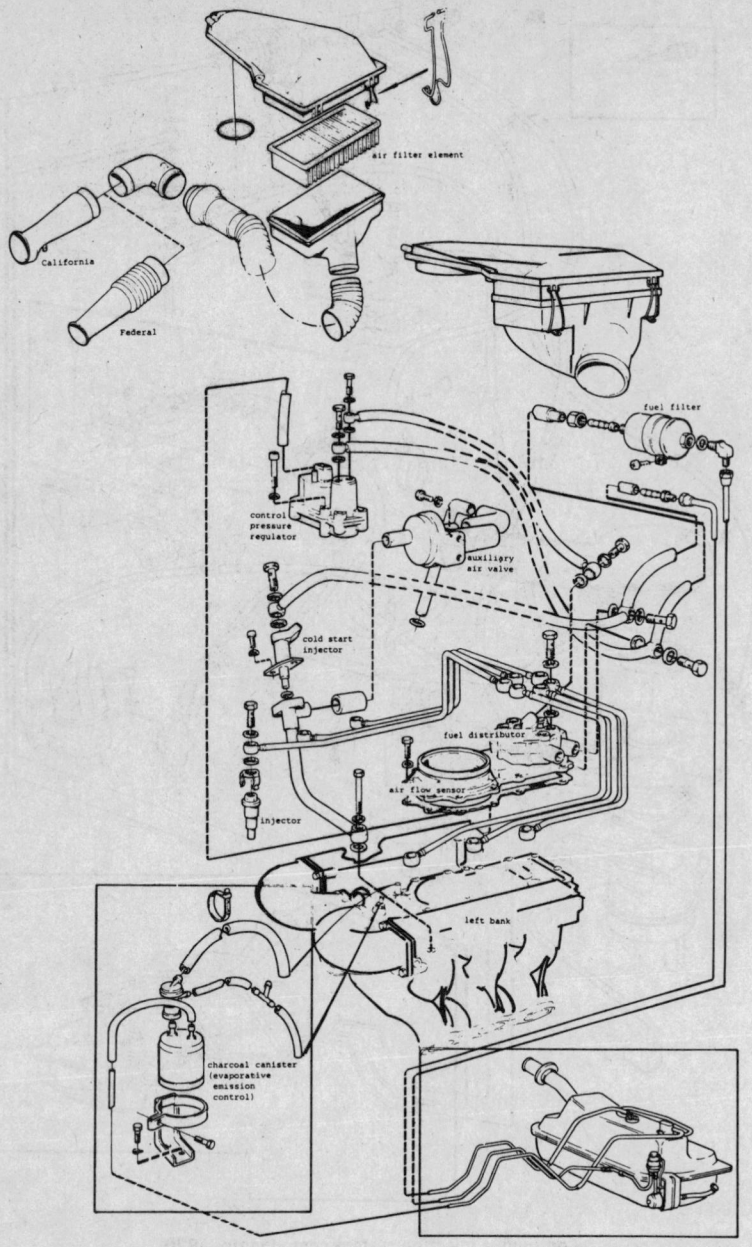

Continuous injection system components—B27

line pressure regulator or O-ring, a defective fuel pump check valve, or some external fuel leak.

The vacuum function of the V-6 control pressure regulator is checked with the pressure gauge and tee-fitting installed, and all electrical connectors installed. On a running, warm engine, with the tee-fitting positioned at a right angle to the fuel hoses, fuel pressure should be 50–55 psi. When the vacuum hose is disconnected at the regulator, the pressure should drop to 44–50 psi. If not, the regulator is defective.

Cold Start Injector

Remove the cold start injector from the intake manifold and hold over a beaker. With a cold engine (95°F or lower coolant temperature), the injector should spray during starter operation (max. 12 seconds). If not, check the voltage between the terminals of the injector when the starter is on. Voltage indicates a bad cold start injector. No voltage indicates a faulty thermal time switch or wiring.

With the starter off, disconnect the wire connector at the air-flow sensor to operate fuel pump. Check for cold start injector leakage. Maximum allowable leakage is one drop per minute.

Thermal Time Switch

Remove the cold start injector and place over a beaker. With a hot engine (coolant temperature over 95°F), the injector should not operate. If it does, the thermal time switch is defective. Also, on a cold engine, the cold start injector should not inject fuel for more than 12 seconds (during starter cranking). If it does, the thermal time switch is defective.

Continuous Fuel Injectors

The injectors are simple spring-loaded atomizers, designed to open at 47–51 psi. Critical factors are spray pattern, fuel spray quantity, and leakdown after engine is shut off.

To check spray pattern, remove the injectors, one at a time, and hold over a beaker. Switch the ignition key on and disconnect the connector at the air-flow

voltage indicates a defective wire. Next, check across the auxiliary air valve terminals with an ohmmeter. Resistance indicates corroded contacts. No resistance indicates a faulty auxiliary air valve.

Check the rest pressure. Connect the wire connector at the air-flow sensor terminal to stop the fuel pump. With the pump stopped, and the pressure gauge tee-fitting lever at a right angle to the fuel lines, check that the rest pressure is 24 psi (14 psi minimum after 10 minutes).

The rest pressure and line pressure are adjusted simultaneously by inserting or removing shims between the regulator plunger and plunger cap on the side of the fuel distributor.

Shims are available in 0.1mm and 0.5mm sizes. A 0.1mm shims makes an 0.8 psi

difference, and an 0.5mm shim makes a 4.3 psi difference in both rest and line pressure. If the rest pressure drops noticeably within one minute, check for defective control pressure regulator, leaky

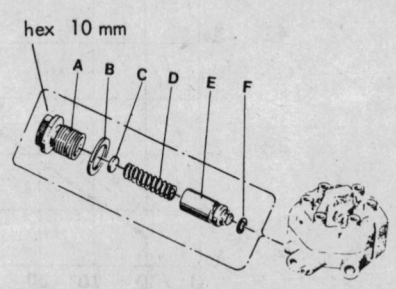

Line and rest pressure regulator plunger is located on side of fuel distributor. Add or remove shims "C" to adjust pressure

B20F injector removal. Note right-hand threads on pipe fitting

ENGINE CRANKS BUT DOES NOT START

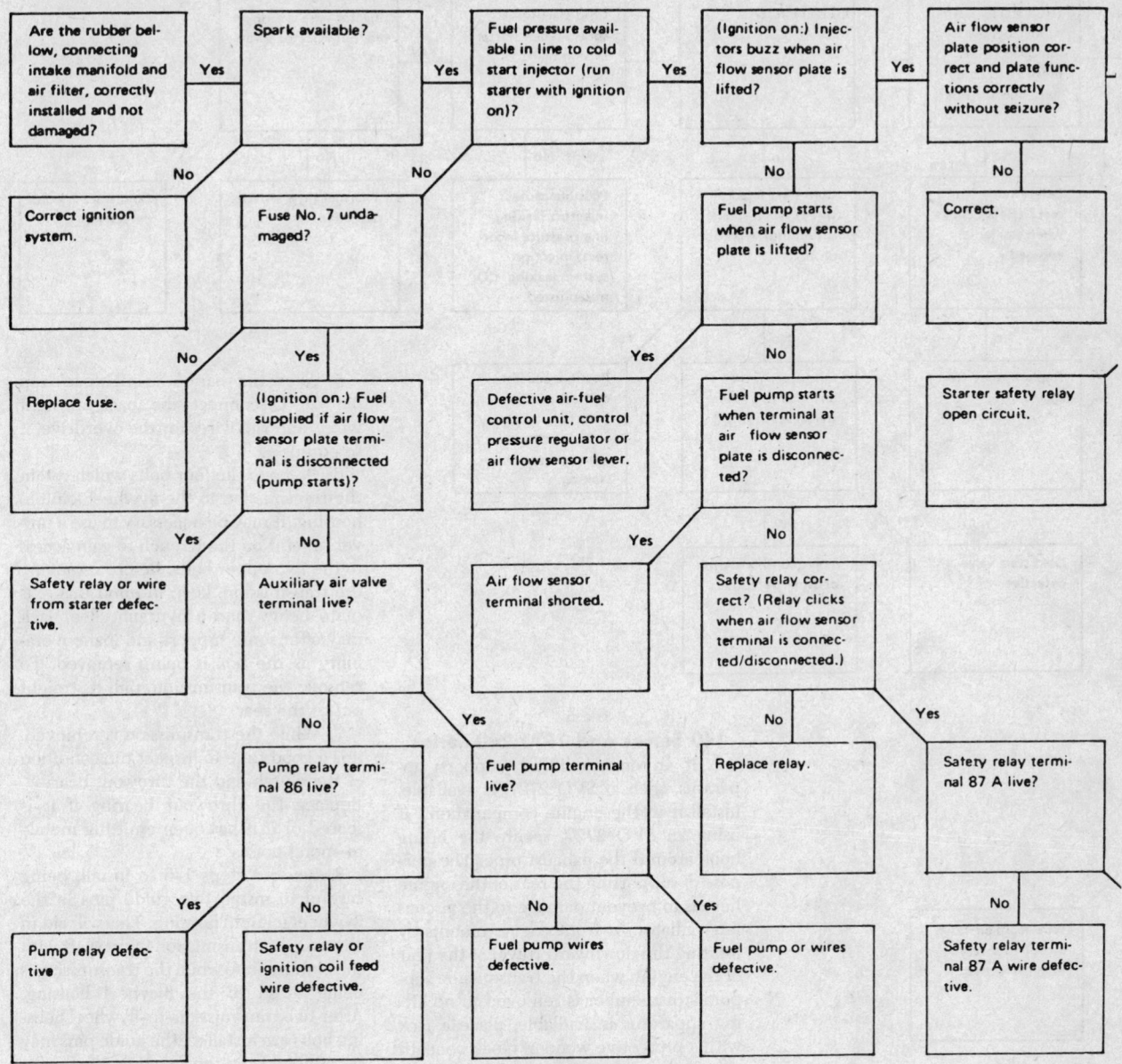

Continuous injection system troubleshooting guide

sensor to activate the fuel pump. Move the air-flow sensor plate. The injector should provide a healthy dose of uniformly atomized fuel at about a 15–25 degree wide angle.

To check injection quantity, connect the removed injectors via hoses to 4 (or 6) equal sized beakers. Switch on the ignition. Disconnect the connector at the airflow sensor to activate the fuel pump. Run (the pump) for approximately 30 seconds to pressurize the system. Then connect the connector to stop the fuel pump. Lift (four-cylinder) or depress (V-6) the air-flow sensor plate halfway until one of the beakers fills up. Check the beakers. If injection quantity deviates more than 20% between injectors, isolate problem

by swapping the lowest and highest (in fuel quantity) injectors and repeating the test. If the same injector still injects less, clean or replace that injector and fuel supply line. If the other injector is now faulty, the fuel distributor is defective.

The check for injector leak-down (when closed) can now be conducted. Injector leakage more than slight seepage may be due to air-flow sensor plate set to incorrect height, seizing of fuel distributor plunger, or internal leaks in the fuel distributor. Connect the air-flow sensor connector to deactivate the fuel pump and switch off the ignition. Check for injector leakage at rest pressure. Depress the sensor plate to open the fuel distributor slots. Maximum permissible leakage

is one drop per 15 seconds. If all injectors leak, problem may be excessive rest pressure.

MANUAL TRANSMISSION

All are fully synchronized four speed transmissions, with all forward gears in constant mesh. The M41, M46 and M410 units are equipped with Laycock-de-Normanville overdrive units, and except for the overdrive engaging switch and push plate, are identical to their M40, M45 and M400 counterparts. The heavy-duty, top cover, Volvo manufactured M40 is in-

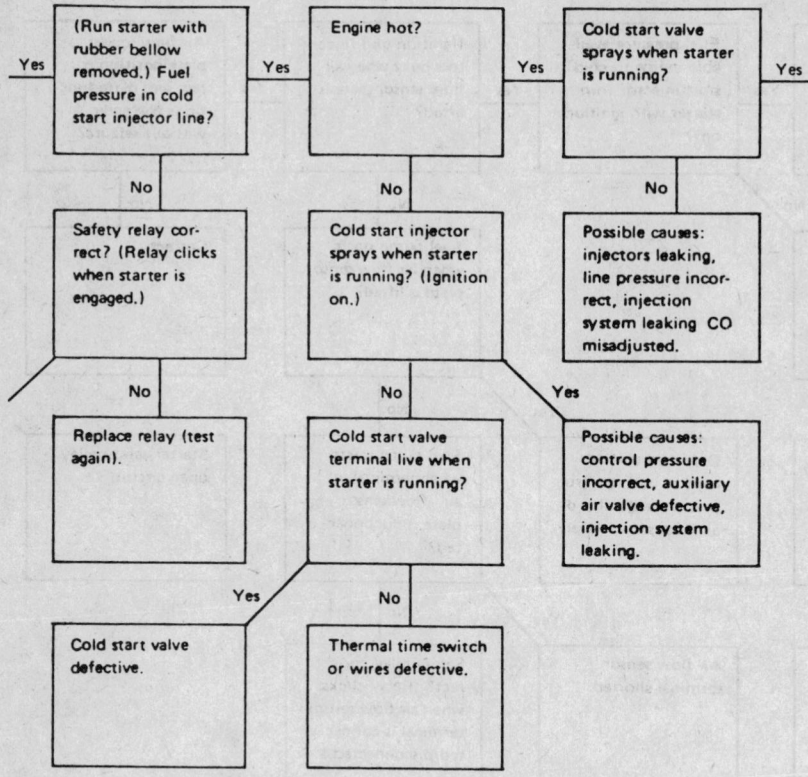

stalled as standard equipment on 140 and 1975 240 series models. The similar M41 overdrive transmission is optional on 140 and 1975 240 series models, and standard equipment on 1800E, and 1800ES models. The extra heavy-duty, top cover, ZF manufactured M400 is standard equipment on 164 models. The similar M410 overdrive transmission is optional on the 164.

The Volvo-made M45 is standard on 1976 and later 240 series models. The similar M46 overdrive transmission is optional on 240 models and standard on the 260 series.

Removal and Installation

The transmission or the transmission-overdrive assembly may be removed with the engine installed in the vehicle.

140 Series and 1975 240 series

1. If an engine lifting (support) apparatus, such as SVO 2727, is available, install it in the engine compartment. If using an SVO 2727, secure the lifting hook around the exhaust pipe. The purpose of supporting the rear of the engine here is to prevent damage to the viscous fan, radiator, or front engine mounts by limiting the downward travel of the rear of the engine when the transmission support crossmember is removed. If no lifting apparatus is available, place a jack with a protective wooden block beneath the engine oil pan. Do not place the jack under the flywheel (clutch) housing.

2. Lift up the rubber boot, unscrew the protective cover, and remove the gear shift lever from the transmission.

3. Jack up the vehicle sufficiently to allow removal of the transmission. Maintain the car at a level attitude and place jackstands beneath the jack points for support. Remove the lower drain plug from the transmission and drain the oil.

4. Slowly loosen the nuts for the transmission support crossmember. Make sure that the supporting apparatus or the jack prevent the rear of the engine from lowering. Remove the crossmember. Disconnect the front universal joint from the transmission (or overdrive) output shaft flange. Disconnect the speedometer cable. Disconnect the rear engine mount and the exhaust pipe bracket.

5. Allow the rear of the engine to drop 0.8 in. Disconnect the back-up light wires, and the wires for the overdrive, if so equipped.

6. Remove the four bolts which retain the transmission to the flywheel (clutch) housing. It may be necessary to use a universal joint on the wrench to gain access to the two upper bolts. Before removing the transmission, keep in mind that it is quite heavy, and a hydraulic floor jack may offer some support and maneuverability as the box is being removed. To remove the transmission, pull it straight out to the rear.

7. While the transmission is removed, it is a good time to inspect the condition of the clutch and the throwout bearing. Replace the throwout bearing if it is scored or if it has been emitting metal–to–metal noises.

8. Reverse steps 1–6 to install, being careful to install two guide pins in the flywheel (clutch) housing. This will aid in aligning the transmission input shaft with the clutch spline when the transmission is being fitted to the flywheel housing. After two transmission–to–flywheel housing bolts are installed, the guide pins may be removed and the remaining two bolts installed. Torque the transmission–to–flywheel housing bolts to 45 ft. lbs, and the universal joint–to–output shaft flange bolts to 25–30 ft. lbs. Fill the transmission to the proper level with oil.

164

1. Follow steps 1–3 under "Transmission Removal and Installation" for the 140 series.

2. Remove the upper radiator bolts and the exhaust manifold flange nuts. Disconnect the negative battery cable, the throttle shaft and clutch cable from the flywheel (clutch) housing.

3. Slowly loosen the nuts for the transmission support crossmember. Making sure that the rear of the engine remains supported, remove the crossmember. Disconnect the exhaust pipe bracket and the speedometer cable. Disconnect the

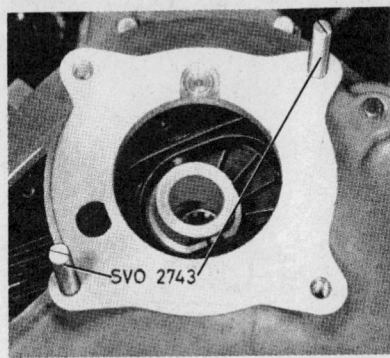

Transmission guide pins installed

front universal joint from the transmission (or overdrive) output shaft flange.

4. Lower the rear of the engine approximately 1.8 in. Disconnect the back-up light wires and the wires for the overdrive, if so equipped.

5. Place a hydraulic floor jack beneath the transmission. Remove the bolts which retain the transmission and flywheel (clutch) housing assembly to the engine. Leave the starter connected but position it to one side. Remove the transmission by pulling it straight to the rear.

6. Prior to assembly, inspect the condition of the clutch and throwout bearing. Replace the bearing if it is scored or noisy in operation.

7. Reverse steps 1–5 to install. Torque the flywheel (clutch) housing–to–engine bolts to 45 ft. lbs, and the universal joint–to–output shaft flange bolts to 25–30 ft. lbs. Fill the transmission to the proper level with oil.

1800 series (M41)

1. Remove the storage console from the transmission tunnel. Lift up the boot, unscrew the protective cover and remove the gear shift lever.

2. Disconnect the negative battery cable. Remove the radiator attaching bolts.

3. Jack up the vehicle sufficiently to allow removal of the transmission. Install jackstands. Remove the lower drain plug and drain the transmission oil.

4. Remove the bolts which retain the driveshaft to the flanges, and remove the attaching bolts for the support bearings. Pull the driveshaft approximately 0.4 in. to the rear.

5. Place a jack, with a protective wooden block, beneath the oil pan of the engine.

6. Disconnect the exhaust pipe bracket and the speedometer. Remove the rear engine mount. Slowly loosen the nuts for the transmission support crossmember making sure that the jack supports the rear of the engine.

7. Lower the engine approximately 0.8 in. Disconnect the electric cables from the transmission.

8. Remove the four bolts which secure the transmission to the flywheel (clutch)

housing. It may be necessary to use a universal joint to gain access to the two upper bolts. Support the weight of the transmission with another jack and pull the unit straight out to the rear.

9. Inspect the condition of the clutch and throwout bearing. Replace the bearing if it is scored or has been noisy in operation.

10. Reverse steps 1–8 to install, making sure to install two guide pins in the flywheel (clutch) housing to aid in aligning the transmission input shaft with the clutch spline when the transmission is being fitted to the flywheel housing. After two transmission–to–flywheel housing bolts are installed, the guide pins may be removed and the remaining two bolts installed. Torque the bolts to 45 ft. lbs. Fill the transmission to the proper level with oil.

1976–77 240, 260 Series

1. Disconnect the battery. At the firewall, disconnect the back-up light connector.

2. Jack up the front of the car and install jack stands. Loosen the setscrew and drive out the pin for the shifter rod. Disconnect the shift lever from the rod.

3. Inside the car, pull up the shift boot. Remove the fork for the reverse gear detent. Remove the snap-ring and lift up the shifter. If overdrive-equipped, disconnect the engaging switch wire.

4. On 240 Series models, disconnect the clutch cable and return spring at the throw-out fork and flywheel housing. On 260 Series models, remove the bolts retaining the slave cylinder to the flywheel housing and tie the cylinder back out of the way (do not disconnect).

5. Disconnect the exhaust pipe bracket(s) from the flywheel cover. Remove the oil pan splash guard.

6. Using a floor jack and a block of wood, support the engine beneath the oil pan. Remove the transmission support crossmember.

7. Disconnect the driveshaft. Disconnect the speedometer cable. If so equipped, disconnect the overdrive wire.

8. Remove the starter retaining bolts and pull free of the flywheel housing.

9. Support beneath the transmission using another floor jack. Remove the flywheel (bell) housing-to-engine bolts and remove the transmission.

10. Reverse steps 1–9 to install. Tighten the flywheel housing-to-engine bolts to 25–35 ft-lbs.

Overhaul

M40, M41

The following procedure applies to units without overdrive. If the transmission has overdrive, first remove the overdrive.

Disassembly

1. Place the transmission in a support fixture.

2. Unscrew the bolts for the transmission cover. Lift off the cover. Remove the springs and interlock balls for the selector rails.

3. Remove the cover over the selector rails. Unscrew the selector fork bolts.

4. Slide the selector fork backward to 1st speed position. Drive out the pin slightly (it must not foul 1st gear). Then move the selector fork forward sufficiently to allow the pin to pass in front of the gear. Drive out the pin.

5. Slide out the selector rails. When doing this, hold the selector forks so that they do not jam on the rails. Remove the selector forks.

6. Unscrew the bolts for the rear cover. Turn the cover so that it does not lock the shafts for the idler and reverse gears (early production only. On late production, there is no locking tab). Drive out the shaft for the idler gear. The shaft must be driven out backward. Let the idler gear fall into the bottom of the transmission.

7. Pull out the mainshaft.

8. Remove the cover over the input shaft. Pry out the oil seal from the cover with a screwdriver.

9. Drive out the input shaft. If necessary, remove the circlip and press the ball bearing off the shaft.

10. Take out the idler gear. Pull out the shaft for the reverse gear. Take out the reverse gear and other parts.

11a. Transmission with overdrive (M41): Remove the circlip and press off the rotor for the overdrive oil pump. Remove the circlip for the mainshaft rear bearing. Slide the engaging sleeve for 1st and 2nd forward. Place the shaft in a press and support under 1st gear. Press out the shaft.

11b. Transmissions without overdrive: Unscrew the yoke (flange) nut. Slide the engaging sleeve for 1st and 2nd forward. Place the shaft in a press and support under 1st gear. Press out the shaft with a drift.

12. Remove the synchronizing cone, thrust washer, engaging sleeves, engaging springs and snap rings from the shaft.

13. Remove the circlip on the front end of the shaft. Pull off the synchronizing hub and 3rd gear with a puller. Remove the thrust washer.

14. Remove the circlip and then the thrust washer, 2nd gear, synchronizing cone and spring.

15. Remove the oil seal from the rear cover and take out the speedometer gear. If necessary, remove the circlip and press out the ball bearing.

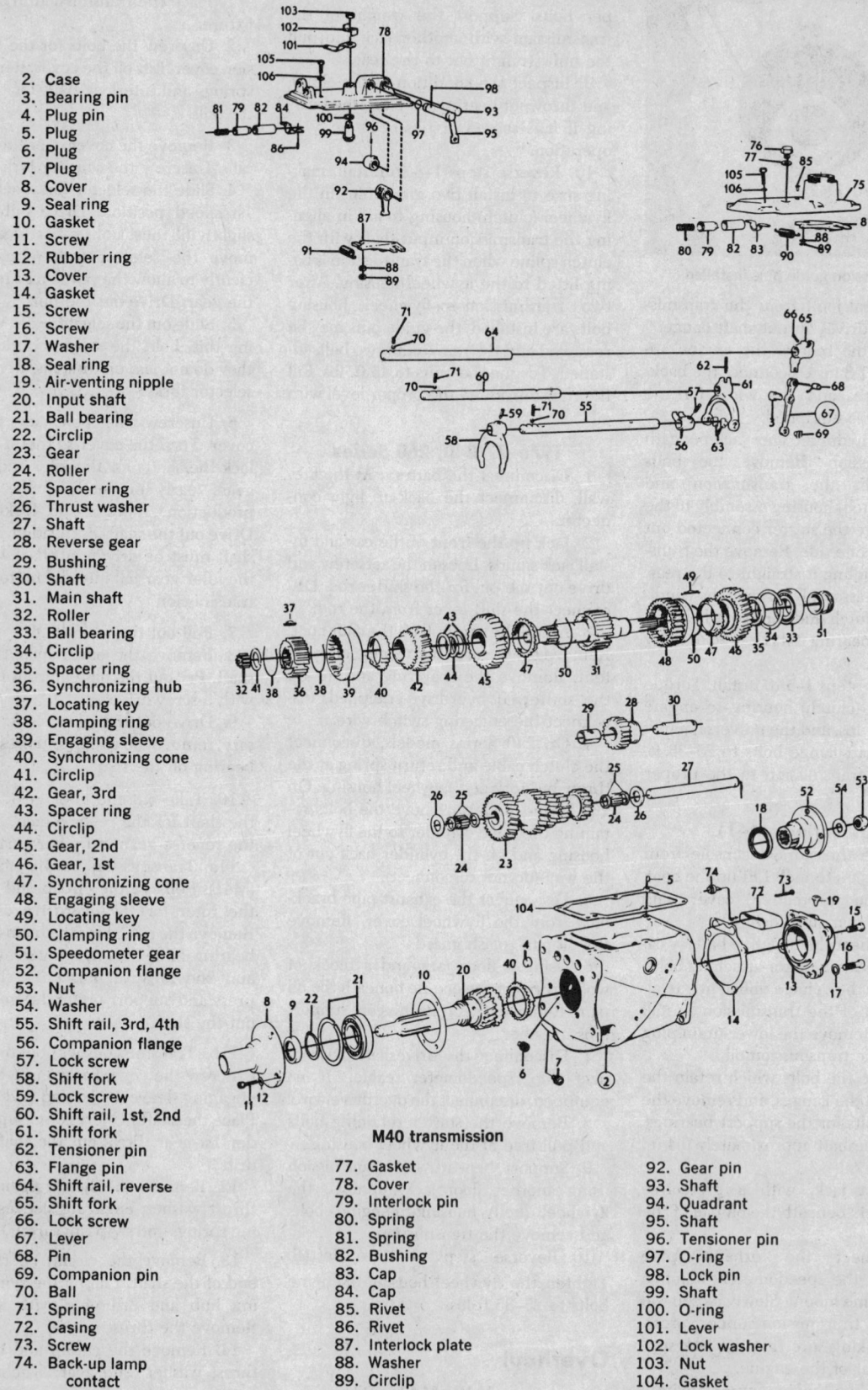

2. Case
3. Bearing pin
4. Plug pin
5. Plug
6. Plug
7. Plug
8. Cover
9. Seal ring
10. Gasket
11. Screw
12. Rubber ring
13. Cover
14. Gasket
15. Screw
16. Screw
17. Washer
18. Seal ring
19. Air-venting nipple
20. Input shaft
21. Ball bearing
22. Circlip
23. Gear
24. Roller
25. Spacer ring
26. Thrust washer
27. Shaft
28. Reverse gear
29. Bushing
30. Shaft
31. Main shaft
32. Roller
33. Ball bearing
34. Circlip
35. Spacer ring
36. Synchronizing hub
37. Locating key
38. Clamping ring
39. Engaging sleeve
40. Synchronizing cone
41. Circlip
42. Gear, 3rd
43. Spacer ring
44. Circlip
45. Gear, 2nd
46. Gear, 1st
47. Synchronizing cone
48. Engaging sleeve
49. Locating key
50. Clamping ring
51. Speedometer gear
52. Companion flange
53. Nut
54. Washer
55. Shift rail, 3rd, 4th
56. Companion flange
57. Lock screw
58. Shift fork
59. Lock screw
60. Shift rail, 1st, 2nd
61. Shift fork
62. Tensioner pin
63. Flange pin
64. Shift rail, reverse
65. Shift fork
66. Lock screw
67. Lever
68. Pin
69. Companion pin
70. Ball
71. Spring
72. Casing
73. Screw
74. Back-up lamp
    contact
75. Cover
76. Plug

M40 transmission

77. Gasket
78. Cover
79. Interlock pin
80. Spring
81. Spring
82. Bushing
83. Cap
84. Cap
85. Rivet
86. Rivet
87. Interlock plate
88. Washer
89. Circlip
90. Spring
91. Spring

92. Gear pin
93. Shaft
94. Quadrant
95. Shaft
96. Tensioner pin
97. O-ring
98. Lock pin
99. Shaft
100. O-ring
101. Lever
102. Lock washer
103. Nut
104. Gasket
105. Screw
106. Spring washer

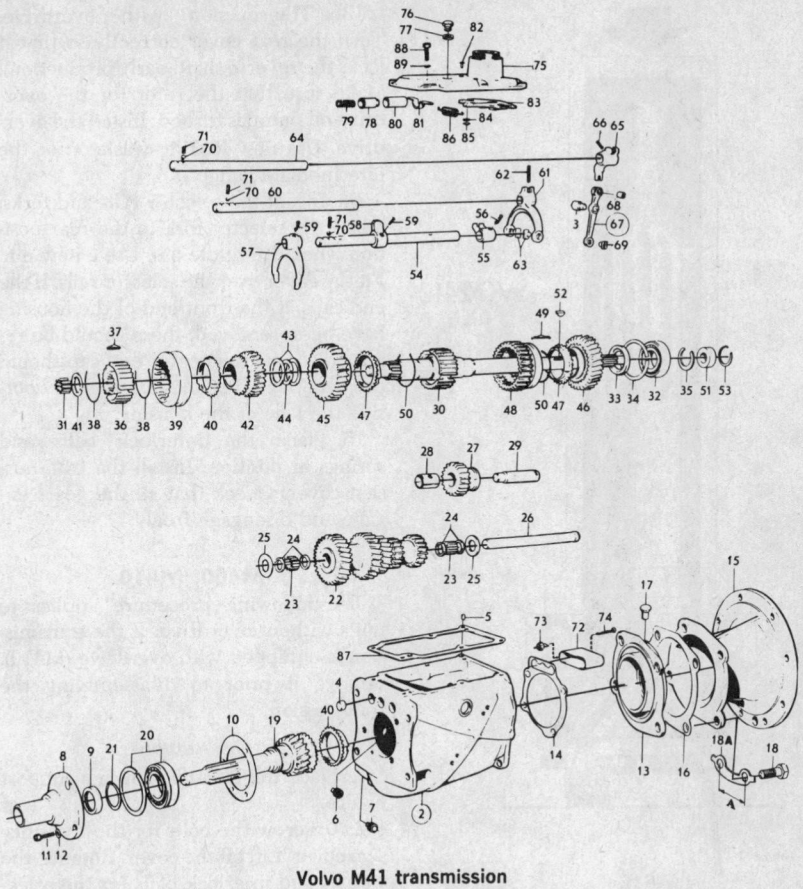

2. Case
3. Bearing pin
4. Plug
5. Pin
6. Plug
7. Plug
8. Cover
9. Seal ring
10. Gasket
11. Screw
12. Rubber ring
13. Cover
14. Gasket
15. Spacer flange
16. Gasket
17. Air-venting nipple
18. Screw
18A. Lock washer
19. Input shaft
20. Ball bearing
21. Circlip
22. Gear
23. Roller
24. Spacer ring
25. Thrust washer
26. Countershaft
27. Reverse gear
28. Bushing
29. Shaft
30. Main shaft
31. Roller
32. Ball bearing
33. Spacer ring
34. Circlip
35. Circlip
36. Synchronizing hub
37. Locating key
38. Clamping ring
39. Engaging sleeve
40. Synchronizing hub
41. Circlip

42. Gear, 3rd
43. Spacer ring
44. Circlip
45. Gear, 2nd
46. Gear
47. Synchronizing cone
48. Engaging sleeve
49. Locating key
50. Clamping ring
51. Cam
52. Key
53. Circlip
54. Shift rail, 3rd, 4th
55. Companion flange
56. Lock screw
57. Shift fork, 3rd, 4th
58. Companion flange
59. Lock screw
60. Shift rail, 1st, 2nd
61. Shift fork, 1st, 2nd
62. Tensioner pin
63. Companion pin
64. Shift rail, reverse
65. Shift fork
66. Lock screw
67. Lever
68. Pin
69. Companion pin
70. Ball
71. Spring
72. Casing
73. Back-up lamp contact
74. Screw
75. Cover
76. Plug
77. Gasket
78. Interlock pin
79. Spring
80. Bushing
81. Cap

Volvo M41 transmission

82. Rivet
83. Interlock plate
84. Washer
85. Circlip
86. Spring
87. Gasket
88. Screw
89. Spring washer

Inspection

Check the gears, particularly for cracks or chips on the tooth surfaces. Damaged or worn gears must be replaced. Check the synchronizing cones and all the other synchronizing components. Damaged or worn parts must be replaced. Check the ball bearings, particularly for scoring or cracks on the races or balls.

Assembly

1. Press the ball bearing into the rear cover. Install the circlip. There are different sizes of circlips, so select one which fits snugly into the groove.

2. Transmission without overdrive: Place the speedometer gear on the bearing in the rear cover. Press in the oil seal with a drift.

3. Install the parts for the 1st and 2nd gear synchronizer on the mainshaft. Install the snap rings.

4a. Transmission without overdrive: Install the synchronizing cone, 1st gear, and thrust washer. Place the rear cover on the shaft. Ensure that the speedometer gear is positioned correctly. Install the yoke (flange). Use a sleeve which fits into the recess in the yoke (flange), press on the cover and yoke (flange). Install the washer and nut for the yoke (flange). Tighten the nut.

4b. Transmission with overdrive (M41): Place the rear cover and ball bearing on a cushioning ring or sleeve. Install the thrust washer, 1st gear, and synchronizing cone. Press in the shaft. Select a circlip of suitable thickness and install it. Install the key, the rotor for the oil pump, and circlip.

5. Install the synchronizing cone, 2nd gear, and thrust washer on the shaft. Select a circlip which fits snugly into the groove on the shaft and install it.

6. Install the thrust washer, 3rd gear, and synchronizing cone on the shaft. Assemble the 3rd and 4th gear synchronizing parts. Install the snap rings. Then install the synchronizer on the mainshaft. Ensure that the synchronizer is correctly fitted. The turned groove should face rearward. Select a circlip of the correct thickness and install it.

7. Install the striker lever and striker. Install the reverse gear and reverse shaft. Make sure that the groove in the reverse shaft (early production) is turned correctly. The late production reverse shaft with turned groove is installed so that it projects 0.276–0.300 in. outside the housing.

8. Place a dummy shaft in the idler gear. Put in spacer washers and needles (24 in each bearing). Use grease to hold

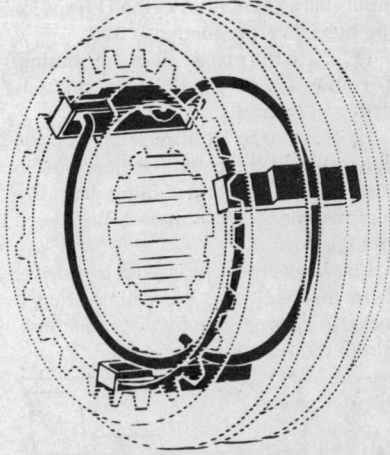

Assembling synchronizer—M40, M41

the needles and washers in position.

9. Attach the washers to the housing with grease and guide them into position, with the centering plugs. Lay the idler gear in the bottom of the housing.

10. Press the bearing onto the input shaft with the help of a drift. Select a circlip of suitable thickness and install it. Place the 14 bearing rollers for the mainshaft in position in the input shaft. Use grease to hold the rollers in place. Press the input shaft into position in the housing. Press the oil seal into the cover with

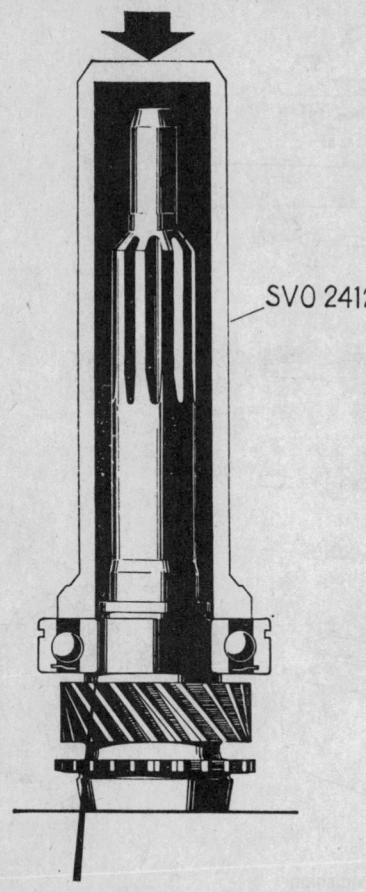

SVO 2412

Installing ball bearing on input shaft—M40, M41.

a drift. Then install the cover over the input shaft. Do not forget the O-rings for the bolts (late production).

11. Place the mainshaft in the housing. Turn the rear cover so that the countershaft can be fitted.

12. Turn the transmission upside down. Install the countershaft from the rear. Hold it against a dummy shaft. Ensure that the thrust washers do not loosen and fall down.

13a. Transmissions without overdrive: Turn the rear cover correctly so that it locks the reverse shaft (early production). Install the bolts for the cover.

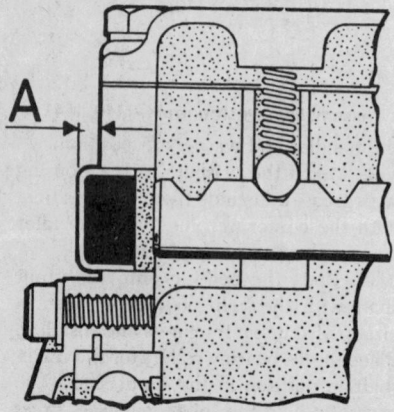

A

Installing end cap over selector rail—M40, M41.

13b. Transmission with overdrive: Turn the rear cover correctly so that it locks the reverse shaft (early production). Make sure that the rotor for the overdrive oil pump is turned. Install the overdrive. Use new locking washers for the intermediate flange.

14. Install the selector rails and forks. Move the selector fork to the rear position when fitting the pin. Use a new pin. Fit the cover over the selector rails. If the end caps at the front end of the housing have been removed, these should be replaced so that the center end cap should project about (0.16 in.) distance "A" outside the face of the housing.

15. Place the interlock balls and springs in position. Install the transmission cover. Check that all the gears engage and disengage freely.

M400, M410

The following procedure applies to units without overdrive. If the transmission is equipped with overdrive (M410), remove it prior to disassembling the transmission.

Disassembly

1. Place the transmission in a support fixture.

2. Unscrew the bolts for the transmission cover. Lift off the cover. Remove the springs and interlock balls for the selector rails.

3. Loosen the flange nut. Remove the flange using a puller.

4. Remove the throwout bearing. Remove the retaining bolts and the cover for the input shaft. Remove the bolts which retain the clutch housing to the transmission and lift off the housing.

5. Turn the transmission upside down. Using an internal, expanding bearing puller, pull out the front bearing for the intermediate shaft. Remove the rear cover, and pull out the rear bearing for the intermediate shaft.

6. Return the transmission to its normal position, taking care not to damage the teeth of the intermediate shaft as the shaft drops to the bottom of the transmission.

7. Remove the bolts for the selector forks. Push the selector rails backward and drive out the tensioning pin in the flange of the selector rails. Push out the selector rails, taking care not to jam them onto the selector forks. Remove the forks.

8. Remove the speedometer gear. Remove the rear bearing for the mainshaft on the M400 transmission with internal, expanding puller SVO 2828. If the bearing remains lodged in the case, push the mainshaft forward until the drive and synchronizers are positioned against the intermediate shaft drive. For the overdrive (M410) transmission, remove the bolt in SVO 2828 and install puller SVO

2832 in place of the bolt. Using both tools in conjunction, pull out the rear mainshaft bearing.

9. Pull out the input shaft and remove the synchronizing ring. Remove the thrust washer from the rear of the mainshaft. Push the 1st and 2nd speed engaging sleeve rearward. Lift out the mainshaft.

10. Pull out the reversing shaft and remove the reverse gear. Remove the front and rear cover oil seals with a drift.

11. If a lifting tool was used to remove the mainshaft from the case, remove it. Remove the 1st speed gear wheel, the needle bearing and the synchronizing cone.

12. Remove the engaging sleeves and the flanges for the synchronizers. Remove the synchronizing hub circlips.

13. Place the mainshaft in a press and support it under the 1st speed synchronizing hub. Press off the 2nd speed gear wheel and the 1st and 2nd speed synchronizing hub.

14. Invert the mainshaft and press off the 3rd speed gear wheel and the 4th speed synchronizing hub.

Inspection

After dismantling the mainshaft, clean all parts in an alcohol-based solvent and allow to air dry. Check the gear wheels for cracked teeth or scoring. Inspect the synchronizing cones and hubs for galling or scoring. Check all ball bearings for cracks or scoring on the bearing races or on the balls themselves. Replace all damaged or worn parts.

Assembly

1. Assemble the 1st/2nd and 3rd/4th speed synchronizers,

Position the snap-ring in the hub for the 3rd/4th speed synchronizers.

2. Position the 3rd/4th speed synchronizer, synchronizing cone, 3rd speed gear wheel and needle bearing on top of a ring type support, and after making sure that the synchronizing flange locates correctly into the synchronizing cone grooves, and that the snap-ring fits properly on the 3rd speed gear wheel, press the mainshaft into the synchronizing hub. While pressing in the mainshaft, rotate the 3rd speed gear wheel to make sure that it and the needle bearing are fitted correctly. Install the snap-ring.

3. Position the 1st/2nd speed synchronizer, synchronizing cone, 2nd speed gear wheel, and needle bearing on top of a ring type support, making sure that the engaging sleeve gear ring comes forward and the flanges fit correctly in the synchronizing cone grooves. While pressing in the mainshaft, rotate the 2nd speed gear wheel to prevent it from seizing on the shaft. Install the snap-ring.

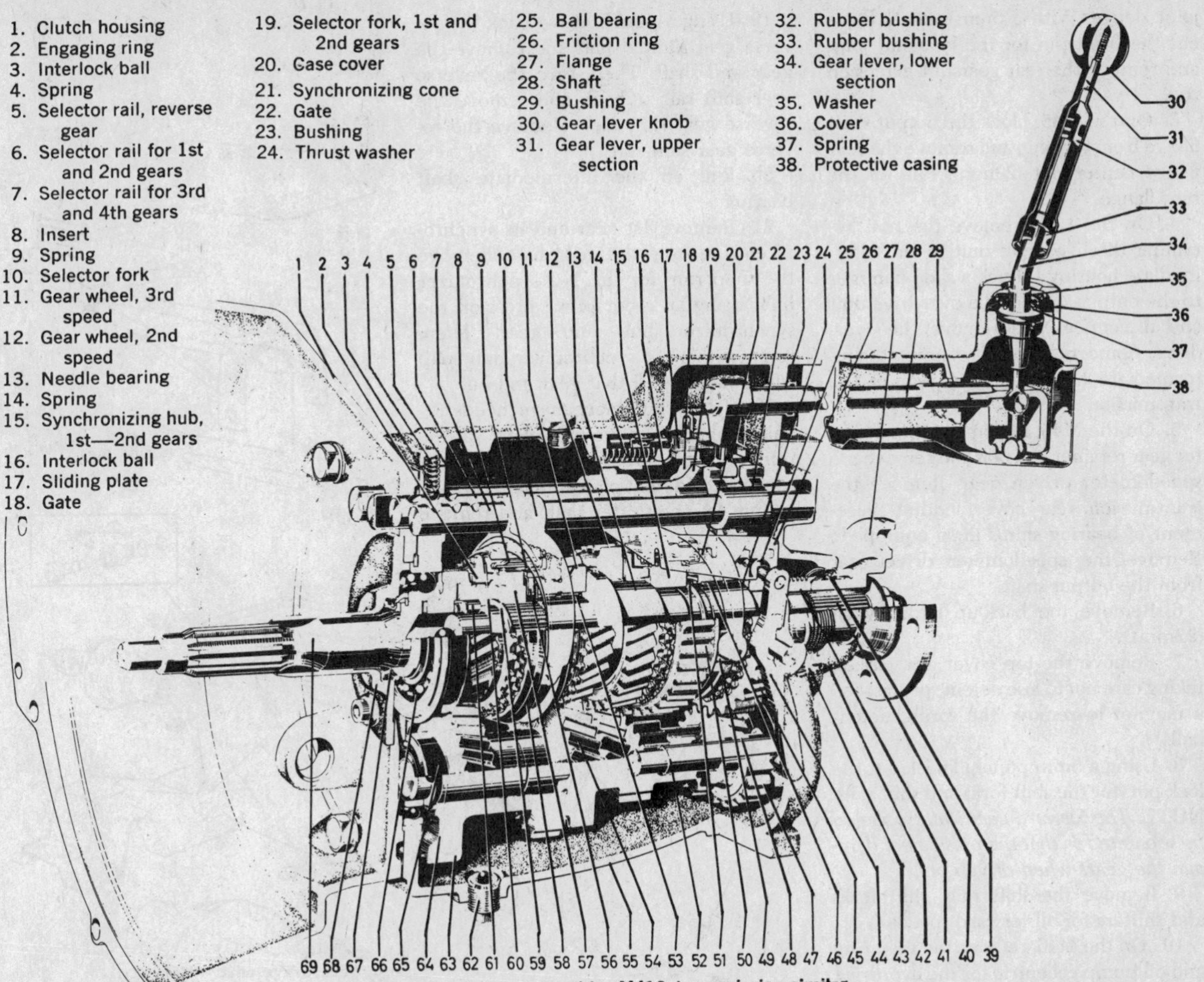

1. Clutch housing
2. Engaging ring
3. Interlock ball
4. Spring
5. Selector rail, reverse gear
6. Selector rail for 1st and 2nd gears
7. Selector rail for 3rd and 4th gears
8. Insert
9. Spring
10. Selector fork
11. Gear wheel, 3rd speed
12. Gear wheel, 2nd speed
13. Needle bearing
14. Spring
15. Synchronizing hub, 1st—2nd gears
16. Interlock ball
17. Sliding plate
18. Gate

19. Selector fork, 1st and 2nd gears
20. Case cover
21. Synchronizing cone
22. Gate
23. Bushing
24. Thrust washer

25. Ball bearing
26. Friction ring
27. Flange
28. Shaft
29. Bushing
30. Gear lever knob
31. Gear lever, upper section

32. Rubber bushing
33. Rubber bushing
34. Gear lever, lower section
35. Washer
36. Cover
37. Spring
38. Protective casing

M400 transmission assembly, M410 transmission similar.

4. Install the 1st speed gear wheel, with needle bearing and synchronizing cone, onto the mainshaft. If a lifting tool is needed to lower the mainshaft into the case, install it now.

5. Press the oil seals into the front and rear covers with a drift. Press the ball bearing onto the input shaft with a drift and cushioning ring. Install a snug fitting snap-ring into the groove.

6. Position the reverse shaft gear lever onto the bearing pin in the case. Install the reverse gear and reverse gear shaft, taking care to ensure that the reverse gear shaft lies level or is a maximum of 0.08 in. below the rear end of the case.

7. Place the intermediate shaft in the bottom of the case. Install the mainshaft. Remove the lifting tool, if used, and place the thrust washer on the mainshaft.

8. Press the rear ball bearing onto the mainshaft. If the bearing does not seat correctly in the case, the spindle on SVO tool 2831 can be screwed out and a flat iron piece placed between this and the front end of the case, then the bearing pressed in.

9. Fit the needle bearing into the input shaft. Install the loose synchronizing

cone in the synchronizer for the 3rd/4th speeds, taking care to insert the flanges in the grooves. Push the input shaft into the case and onto the mainshaft pin.

10. Turn the transmission upside down. Press on the front and rear bearings for the intermediate shaft. Install the clutch housing with a new gasket.

11. Install the selector forks, flanges,

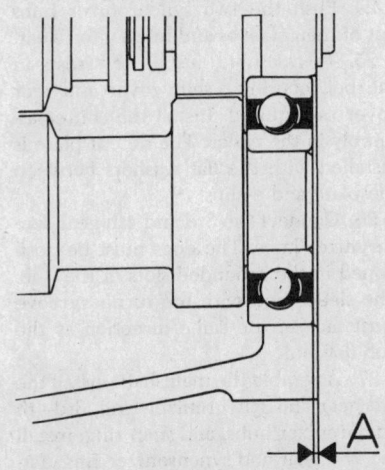

Clearance for intermediate shaft—M400, M410.

and selector rails. Make sure that the flange for the reverse gear fits correctly in the gear lever. Install the bolts and new tensioning pins.

12. Position the transmission with the rear end facing upward. Drive the intermediate shaft forward until its front bearing contacts the clutch housing. Install shims for the intermediate shaft bearing so that they lie flush or within a maximum of 0.002 in. (distance "A") of the rear end.

13. Install the speedometer gear. Install the rear cover with a new gasket, taking care to compress the gasket. Make sure that the intermediate shaft has 0.-008–0.010 in. clearance.

14. Press on the rear flange. Install the washer and nut and torque to 80–110 ft lbs.

15. Position the interlock balls and springs and install the case cover with a new gasket. Install the input shaft cover. Install the throwout bearing.

M45, M46

1. Remove the transmission and place on a work bench.

2. Remove the gearshift bracket extension assembly. Remove the gearshift

joint sleeve. With a 5mm punch, drive out the front pin for the gearshift joint and remove the rear gearshift extension rod.

3. On the M45, block the output shaft flange from turning, and remove the rear flange center nut (29mm). Pull off the rear flange.

4. On the M46, remove the nuts retaining the overdrive unit to the intermediate housing. Attach a slide hammer to the output shaft of the overdrive unit and disconnect and remove the overdrive. Remove the bolts retaining the intermediate housing to the rear of the transmission.

5. On the M45, loosen the speedometer gear retainer and bolt and remove the speedometer driven gear. Remove the transmission rear cover, noting placement of bearing shims (if so equipped). Remove the speedometer drive gear from the output shaft.

6. Remove the back-up light switch (22mm).

7. Remove the top cover and gasket, taking care not to lose detent springs. Use a magnet to remove the spring detent balls.

8. Using a 5mm punch, knock out the lock pins for the shift forks and shift rails. **NOTE:** *The forward gear shifters should be separated so that the pins do not damage the gears when driven out.*

9. Remove the shift rails, shift forks and shifters for all forward speeds.

10. On the M46, remove the snap ring and oil pump eccentric for the overdrive from the output shaft. Remove the eccentric retaining key.

11. Remove the mainshaft (output shaft) bearing inner and outer snap rings. Before removing the mainshaft bearing, place a metal spacer (guard plate Volvo #2985) between the input shaft and the front synchronizer ring to prevent damage to the ring during bearing removal. Remove the mainshaft bearing ring and pull off the bearing. Remove the bearing thrust washer.

12. Remove the flywheel (bell) housing (8mm allen head).

13. Remove the snap ring and spacer rings retaining the input shaft bearing. With the front synchronizer ring protective spacer still in place, pull out the input shaft bearing. Remove the protective plate.

14. Knock the intermediate shaft back and remove the rear outer race for the intermediate shaft. Then, knock the shaft forward and remove the front intermediate shaft outer race.

15. Remove the input shaft.

16. Lift out the 4th gear synchronizer ring.

17. Lift out the mainshaft.

18. Lift out the intermediate shaft.

19. Using a punch, drive back the reverse gear sliding shaft and remove the gear and shaft. Then, turn the reverse gear shift rail, unhook and remove the reverse gear shift fork. Remove the reverse gear shift rail.

20. Pull off the intermediate shaft bearing.

21. Remove 1st gear and its synchronizer ring from the mainshaft. Remove the snap ring for the 1–2 synchronizer hub. Using an arbor press, press off the synchronizer hub and gear. Then, remove the 3–4 synchronizer hub snap ring and press off that gear and hub.

22. If the shift mechanism needs repair, unhook the detent plate spring, remove the three retaining bolts, and remove the detent plate. Pull out the cotter pin for the shifter shaft and remove

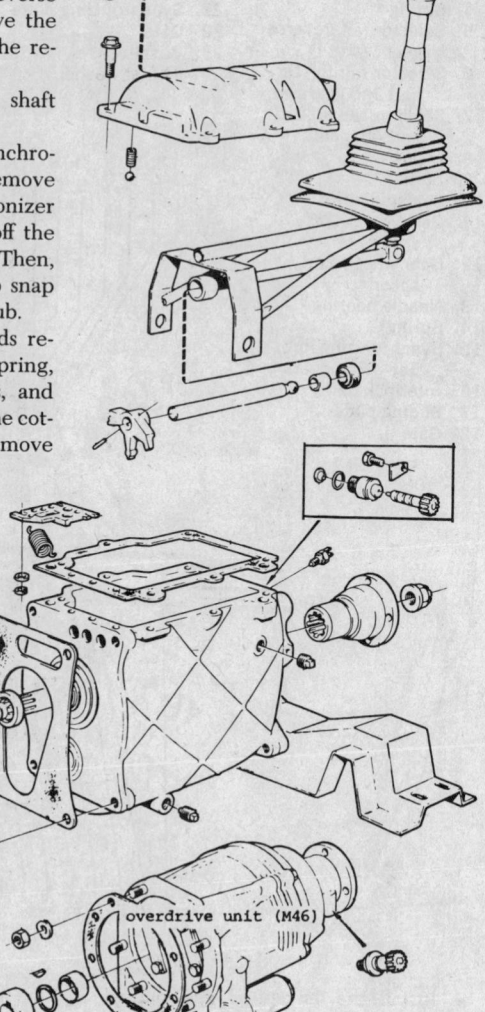

Volvo M45, M46 case and overdrive

the shaft. If necessary, remove the shaft seal at the rear of the cover.

23. If leaking, remove the bell housing seal and the rear cover seal.

24. Push the two synchronizer hubs out of their sleeves and inspect for wear.

25. To assemble, install new seals in the bell housing, shift cover and rear cover as required. Install the shifter assembly in the cover. The detent plate is installed with the flat washers between the plate and c-clips.

26. Connect the 3rd and 4th gear synchronizer hubs. The dogs must be positioned in the grounded slots in the hub. The sleeve end with the turned groove must face in the same direction as the hub flat end.

27. Assemble the mainshaft: install the 3rd gear and synchronizer ring, 3rd-4th synchronizer hubs, and snap ring; install the 2nd gear and synchronizer ring, 1st-2nd synchronizer hubs, and snap ring; install the 1st gear and synchronizer ring.

28. Press on the two intermediate shaft bearings.

29. Press on the input shaft bearing, and install its snap-ring. **NOTE:** *Do not install the spacer ring yet.*

30. Install the reverse gear shift rail (without lock pin), shift fork and shifter. Install the reverse gear and shaft. Check that the reverse gear shaft aligns flush with the outside of the case. Also, check that the clearance between the reverse gear and shift fork is 0.004–0.08 in.. Adjust as necessary by knocking the shift fork pivot in axially with a punch.

31. Lay the intermediate shaft at the bottom of the case. Position the mainshaft in the case. Slip the thrust washer, ball bearing and positioning ring over the output end of the mainshaft. Press the mainshaft bearing into place, taking care not damage the reverse gear. When the bearing seats properly, the positioning ring will butt against the case.

32. Grease and install the input shaft

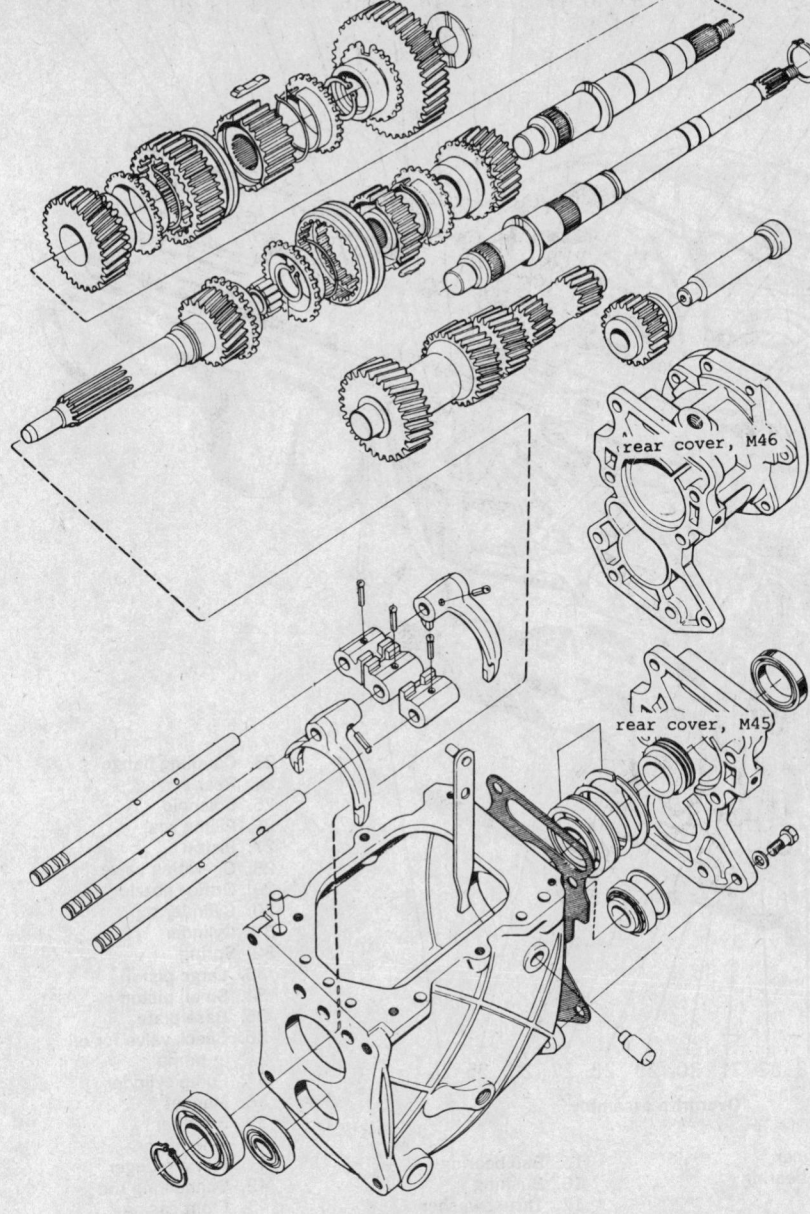

Volvo M45, M46 gear train

inner roller bearing.

33. On the M46, install the snap ring for the mainshaft bearing. Install the woodruff key, overdrive oil pump eccentric and snap ring on the mainshaft extension.

34. Position the 4th gear synchronizer ring in its hub.

35. Push the input shaft into the case all the way, so it makes contact with the mainshaft.

36. Lift up the intermediate shaft so that both bearings locate in the case.

37. Pull out the input shaft slightly to install the spacer ring. Then push the input shaft back in so that the spacer rings contacts the case.

38. Install the intermediate shaft outer bearing races.

39. Determine the shim thickness re-quired between the bell housing and the input shaft bearing. Measure how much the input shaft bearing protrudes from the case, and measure the depth of the bearing seat in the bell housing. Subtract bell housing seat depth and bell housing gasket thickness (0.25mm) from the input shaft bearing protrusion height, and then subtract from this the allowable clearance (0.01–0.15mm), and you have your required shim clearance. Shims come in 0.10, 0.15 and 0.20mm sizes.

40. Install the bell housing with shims and gasket. Tighten the bolts to 25–35 ft-lbs.

41. Install the shift forks on the synchronizer hubs (the forks are identical). Install the forward shift rails and shifters (not interchangeable) and secure with the lock pins. Drive in the pins until flush.

42. Determine the shim thickness re-quired between the rear cover and the intermediate shaft outer race, and the shim thickness between the rear cover and the mainshaft bearing. Allowable clearance is 1.98mm for the intermediate shaft outer race, and 0.24mm for the mainshaft bearing. Gasket thickness is 0.25mm. When measuring, turn the transmission case vertical with the input shaft facing down, to take any slack out of the intermediate or mainshafts.

43. On the M45, install the speedometer driving gear.

44. Install the rear cover (or inter-mediate housing on the M46) with shims and a new gasket. Tighten the bolts to 25–25 ft-lbs.

45. On the M45, install the output shaft flange. Tighten the nut to 67–88 ft-lbs. Install the speedometer driven gear and new o-ring. Install the gear retainer and bolt.

46. Position the top cover gasket with shifter detent balls and springs. Install the cover and tighten to 11–18 ft-lbs. Install the back-up light switch. Check gear operation by inserting a punch through the shift rod eye and rotating the main-shaft.

47. On the M46, install the overdrive assembly with a new gasket. Tighten the nuts to 25 ft-lbs.

48. Install a new rubber o-ring in the gearshift rod joint. Connect the gearshift rod and drive in the locking pin. Install the cover sleeve.

49. Install the gearshift bracket exten-sion assembly with the spacers, rubber washers, and flat washers shown to eliminate vibration. First install the two upper bolts flush with the spacer sleeves, and then the two lower bolts. Then, tighten all four bolts to 15–18 ft-lbs.

50. Fill the transmission with 0.8 qts (2.4 qts with overdrive M46) of 80W/90 hypoid gear oil. Install the plug(s).

NOTE: *Add oil only to the transmis-sion; the overdrive will fill automati-cally.*

51. Install the transmission.

Linkage Adjustment

Shift linkage adjustments are neither necessary nor possible on Volvo transmis-sions.

Overdrive

The overdrive unit for the M41, M46 and M410 transmissions is a planetary gear type and is mounted on the rear of the transmission. When the overdrive is

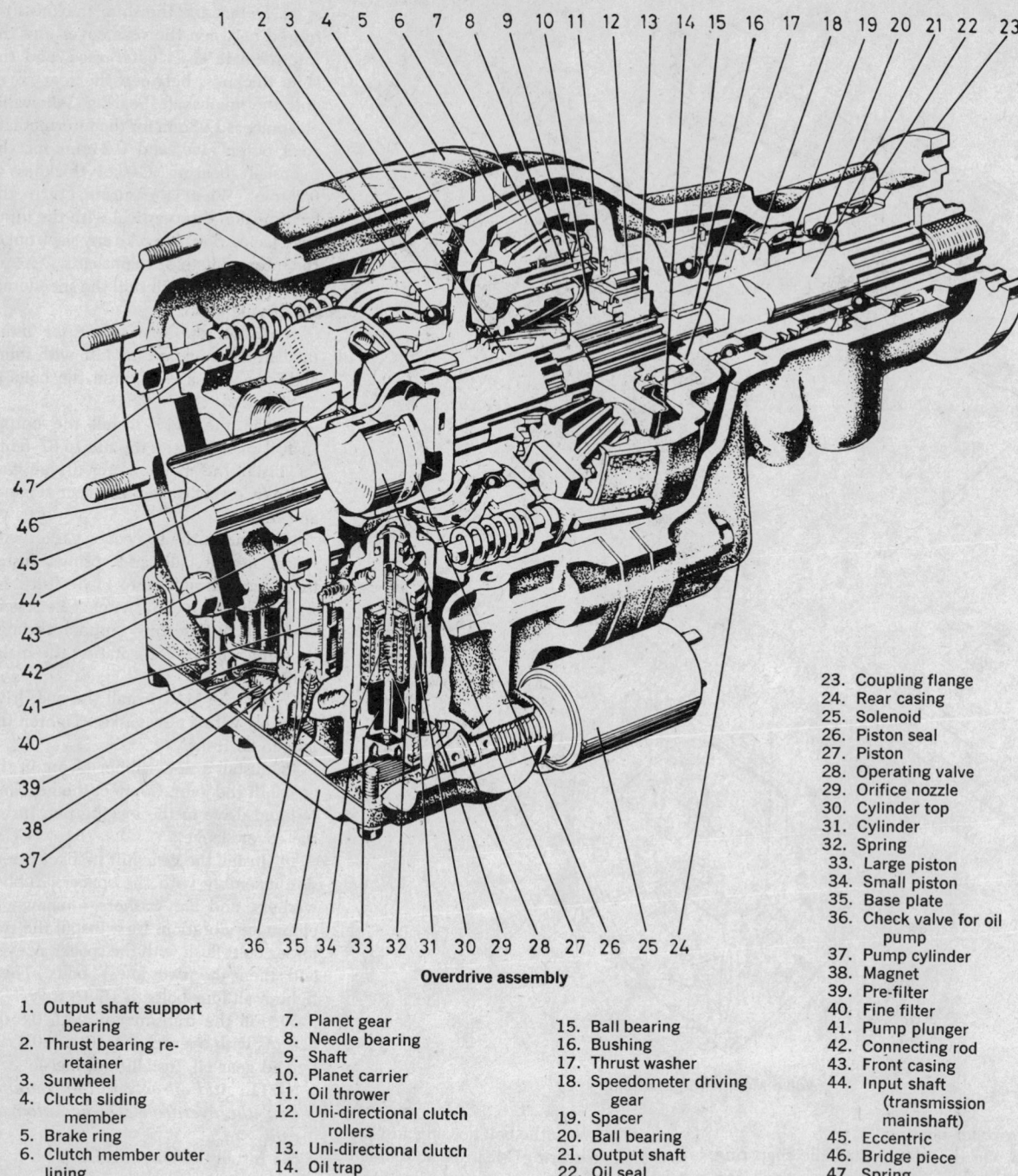

Overdrive assembly

1. Output shaft support bearing
2. Thrust bearing re-retainer
3. Sunwheel
4. Clutch sliding member
5. Brake ring
6. Clutch member outer lining
7. Planet gear
8. Needle bearing
9. Shaft
10. Planet carrier
11. Oil thrower
12. Uni-directional clutch rollers
13. Uni-directional clutch
14. Oil trap
15. Ball bearing
16. Bushing
17. Thrust washer
18. Speedometer driving gear
19. Spacer
20. Ball bearing
21. Output shaft
22. Oil seal
23. Coupling flange
24. Rear casing
25. Solenoid
26. Piston seal
27. Piston
28. Operating valve
29. Orifice nozzle
30. Cylinder top
31. Cylinder
32. Spring
33. Large piston
34. Small piston
35. Base plate
36. Check valve for oil pump
37. Pump cylinder
38. Magnet
39. Pre-filter
40. Fine filter
41. Pump plunger
42. Connecting rod
43. Front casing
44. Input shaft (transmission mainshaft)
45. Eccentric
46. Bridge piece
47. Spring

in the direct drive position (overdrive switched off) and the car is driven forward, power from the transmission mainshaft is transmitted through the freewheel rollers and uni-directional clutch to the overdrive output shaft. When the car is backing up or during periods of engine braking, torque is transmitted through the clutch sliding member which is held by spring pressure against the tapered portion of the output shaft. When the overdrive is actuated, the clutch sliding member is pressed by hydraulic pressure against the brake disc (ring), which locks the sun wheel. As a result, the output shaft of the overdrive

rotates at a higher speed than the mainshaft thereby accomplishing a 20% reduction in engine speed in relation to vehicle speed.

Removal and Installation

To facilitate removal, the vehicle should first be driven in 4th gear with the overdrive engaged, and then coasted for a few seconds with the overdrive disengaged and the clutch pedal depressed.

1. Remove the transmission from the vehicle as outlined in the applicable "Transmission Removal and Installation" section.

2. Disconnect the solenoid cables.

3. If the overdrive unit has not already been drained, remove the six bolts and the overdrive oil pan.

4. Remove the bolts which retain the overdrive unit to the transmission intermediate flange. Pull the unit straight to the rear until it clears the transmission mainshaft.

5. Reverse the above procedure to install. Install the overdrive oil pan with a new gasket. After installation of the transmission and overdrive assembly, fill the transmission (which automatically fills the overdrive) to the proper level

with the correct lubricant. Check the lubricant level in the transmission after driving 6–9 miles.

CLUTCH

All 1972 and later model Volvos are equipped with Borg and Beck or Fichtel and Sachs diaphragm spring clutches.

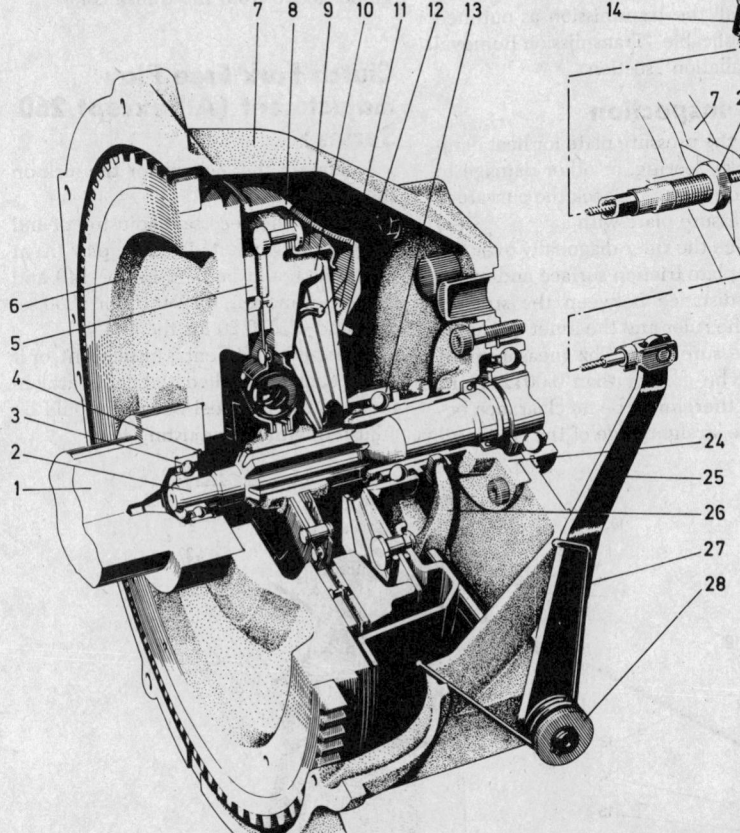

1. Crankshaft
2. Clutch plate shaft (input shaft, transmission)
3. Support bearing in crankshaft
4. Circlip
5. Clutch plate
6. Flywheel
7. Flywheel housing
8. Clutch cover
9. Retainer
10. Thrust plate
11. Support rings
12. Pressure spring
13. Throw-out bearing
14. Clutch wire
15. Washer
16. Rubber bushing
17. Washer
18. Nut
19. Rubber stop
20. Stop bracket
21. Pedal shaft
22. Clutch pedal
23. Adjusting nuts
24. Cover, transmission
25. Lever and release shaft
26. Release fork
27. Return spring
28. Washer

Clutch and clutch controls—164

The 140, 240 and 1800 series use an 8 ½ in. disc, while the carbureted 164 uses a 9 in. disc, and the fuel-injected 164 uses a 9 ½ in. disc. The 260 uses a 9 in. disc.

Removal and Installation
M40, M41

1. Remove the transmission as outlined in the applicable "Transmission Removal and Installation" procedure.

2. Remove the upper bolt for the starter motor.

3. Remove the throwout bearing. Disconnect the clutch cable at the release lever (fork), and slacken the cable sleeve at its bracket.

4. Remove the bolts which retain the flywheel (clutch) housing to the engine, and lift off the housing.

5. Remove the bolt for the release fork ball joint, and remove the ball and release fork.

6. Scribe alignment marks on the clutch and flywheel. In order to prevent warpage, slowly loosen the bolts which retain the clutch to the flywheel diagonally in rotation. Remove the bolts and lift off the clutch and pressure plate.

7. Inspect the clutch assembly as outlined under "Clutch Inspection."

8. When ready to install,
wash the pressure plate and flywheel with solvent to remove any traces of oil, and wipe them clean with a cloth.

9. Position the clutch assembly (the longest side of the hub facing backward) to the flywheel and align the bolt holes. Insert a pilot shaft (centering mandrel), or an input shaft from an old transmission of the same type, through the clutch assembly and flywheel so that the flywheel pilot bearing is centered.

10. Install the six bolts which retain the clutch assembly to the flywheel and tighten them diagonally in rotation, a few turns at a time. After all of the bolts are tightened, remove the pilot shaft (centering mandrel).

11. Install the ball and release fork in the flywheel housing.

12. Place the upper starter bolt in the housing. Position the housing to the engine and first install the four upper bolts (7/16 in.), then the lower starter bolt, and finally the two lower bolts (⅜ in.).

13. Insert the cable sleeve in its bracket and install the rear nut. Connect the cable at the release lever (fork), and install the throwout bearing.

14. Install the nut for the upper starter motor bolt.

15. Install the transmission as outlined in the applicable "Transmission Removal and Installation" section.

16. Adjust the clutch pedal free travel.

M45, M46

1. Remove the transmission as outlined under M45, M46 Removal and In-

stallation.

2. Follow steps 6,7,8, 9, and 10 under "Clutch Removal and Installation" for the M40 and M41.

3. Install the transmission as outlined under M45, M46 Removal and Installation.

4. On the 260 series, bleed the clutch hydraulic system, if necessary.

M400, M410

1. Remove the transmission as outlined in the applicable "Transmission Removal and Installation" section.

2. Scribe alignment marks on the clutch and flywheel. In order to prevent warpage, slowly loosen the bolts which retain the clutch assembly to the flywheel diagonally in rotation. Remove the bolts and lift off the clutch and pressure plate.

3. Inspect the clutch assembly as outlined under "Clutch Inspection."

4. When ready to install, wash the clutch pressure plate and flywheel with solvent to remove any traces of oil, and wipe them clean with a cloth.

5. Position the clutch assembly (the longest side of the hub facing backward)

to the flywheel and align the bolt holes. Insert a pilot shaft (centering mandrel), or an input shaft from an old transmission of the same type, through the clutch assembly and flywheel so that the flywheel pilot bearing is centered.

6. Install the six bolts which retain the clutch assembly to the flywheel, and tighten them diagonally in rotation, a few turns at a time. After all of the bolts are tightened, remove the pilot shaft (centering mandrel).

7. Install the transmission as outlined in the applicable "Transmission Removal and Installation" section.

Clutch Inspection

Check the pressure plate for heat damage, cracks, scoring, or other damage to the friction surface. Check the curvature of the pressure plate with a steel ruler. Place the ruler diagonally over the pressure plate friction surface and measure the distance between the straight edge of the ruler and the inner diameter of the pressure plate. This measurement must not be greater than 0.0012 in. In addition, there must be no clearance between the straight edge of the ruler and

the outer diameter of the pressure plate. This check should be made at several points. Replace the clutch as a unit if it proves faulty.

Check the throwout bearing by rotating it several times while applying finger pressure, so that the ball bearings roll against the inside of the races. If the bearing does not turn easily or if it binds at any point, replace it as a unit. Also make sure that the bearing slides easily on the guide sleeve from the transmission.

Clutch Fork Free Play Adjustment (All except 260 Series)

1. Loosen the locknut for the fork on the clutch cable.

2. Make the necessary adjustment and tighten the locknut. The free play (A) at the fork should be 0.12 in. for 140 and 240 series models, 0.12–0.16 for 1800 series, and 0.16–0.20 for the 164.

3. If this adjustment is insufficient, or if a new cable is installed, the sleeve attachment to the flywheel housing should be adjusted with the adjusting nuts.

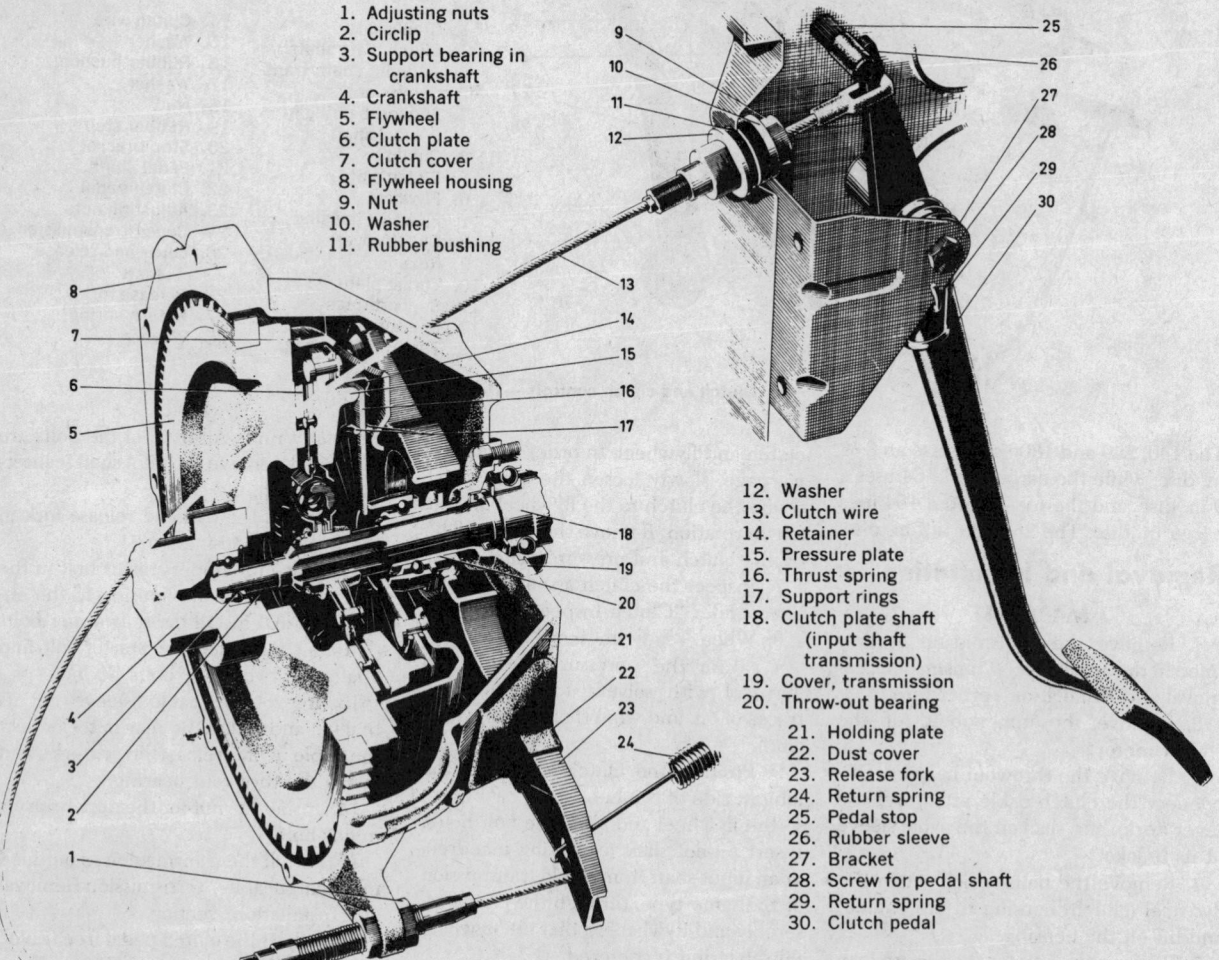

1. Adjusting nuts
2. Circlip
3. Support bearing in crankshaft
4. Crankshaft
5. Flywheel
6. Clutch plate
7. Clutch cover
8. Flywheel housing
9. Nut
10. Washer
11. Rubber bushing

12. Washer
13. Clutch wire
14. Retainer
15. Pressure plate
16. Thrust spring
17. Support rings
18. Clutch plate shaft (input shaft transmission)
19. Cover, transmission
20. Throw-out bearing

21. Holding plate
22. Dust cover
23. Release fork
24. Return spring
25. Pedal stop
26. Rubber sleeve
27. Bracket
28. Screw for pedal shaft
29. Return spring
30. Clutch pedal

Clutch and clutch controls—140 series installation shown, 1800 series similar

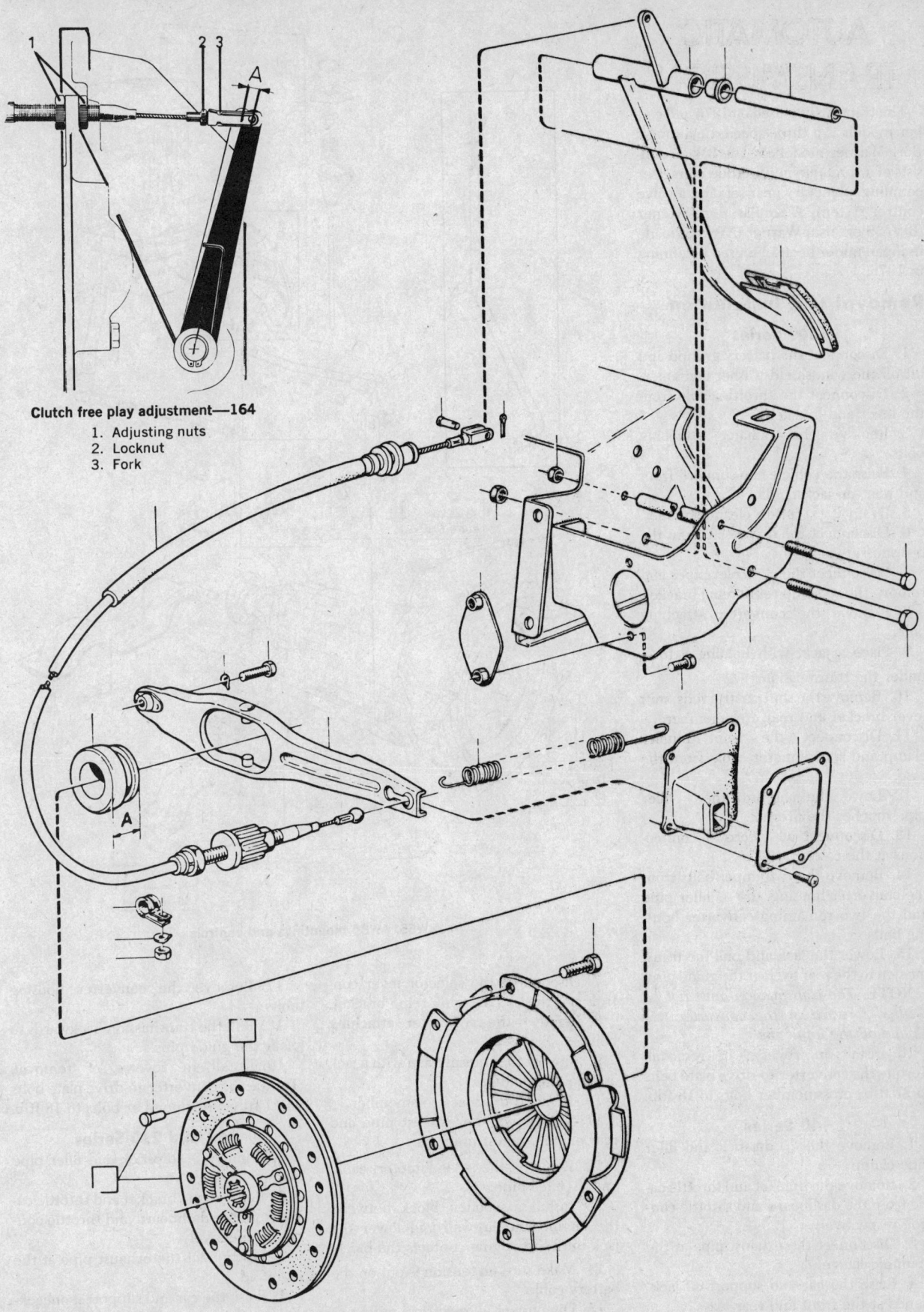

Clutch free play adjustment—164

1. Adjusting nuts
2. Locknut
3. Fork

240 series clutch linkage

Volvo

AUTOMATIC TRANSMISSION

The transmission used on 1975 and earlier models is a three-speed, dual-range, Borg-Warner model 35. The BW 35 consists of a three element torque converter coupling, planetary gear set, and a valve control system. A similar Borg-Warner (BW) 55 or Aisin-Warner (AW) 55 (made in Japan under license) is used beginning in 1976.

Removal and Installation

1800 Series

1. Disconnect the battery ground and lift off the windshield washer container.
2. Disconnect the throttle cable from the lever and bracket.
3. Remove the radiator attaching bolts.
4. Raise the vehicle and support, front and rear, on jackstands.
5. Drain   into a clean container.
6. Disconnect the driveshaft from the transmission flange.
7. Disconnect the   cooler pipes and remove the   sump reinforcing bracket.
8. Remove the converter attaching bolts.
9. Place a jack, with holding fixture, under the transmission.
10. Remove the shift control rods, shift lever bracket and rear crossmember.
11. Disconnect the front muffler clamp and speedometer cable from the case.
12. Lower the jack until the   filler pipe touches the firewall.
13. Disconnect all electrical connections at the case.
14. Remove the two upper bolts from the converter housing, the   filler pipe and the two remaining converter housing bolts.
15. Lower the jack and pull the transmission to the rear to clear the guide pins.
   NOTE: *The transmission must not be tilted forward or the converter will slide off the input shaft.*
16. Install in reverse of removal. Torque the converter-to-drive plate bolts to 27 ftlb.; crossmember bolts to 18 ftlb.

140 Series

1. Remove the   dipstick and filler pipe clamp.
2. Remove the bracket and throttle cable from the dashboard and throttle control, respectively.
3. Disconnect the exhaust pipe at the manifold flange.
4. Raise the car and support on jackstands at the front and rear axles.
5. Drain   into a clean container.
6. Disconnect the driveshaft from the transmission flange.

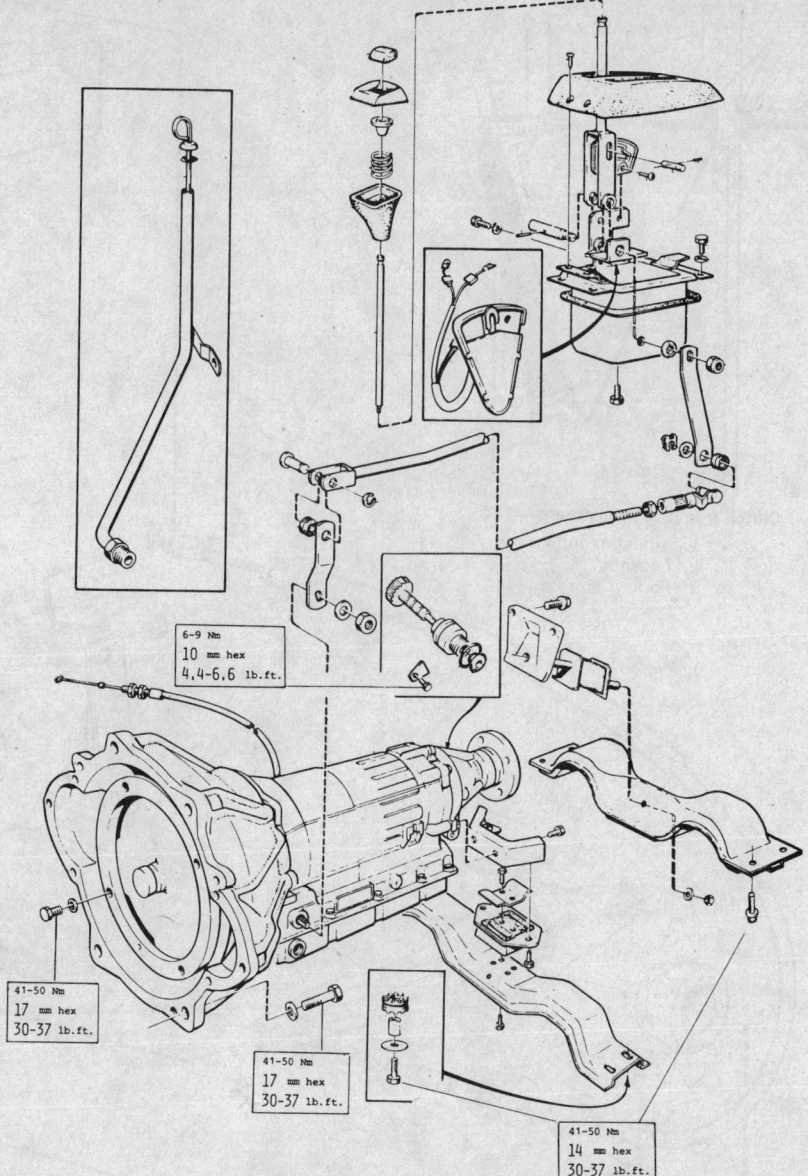

BW55, AW55 mountings and controls

6-9 Nm / 10 mm hex / 4.4-6.6 lb.ft.

41-50 Nm / 17 mm hex / 30-37 lb.ft.

41-50 Nm / 17 mm hex / 30-37 lb.ft.

41-50 Nm / 14 mm hex / 30-37 lb.ft.

7. Disconnect the selector lever controls and the   pan reinforcing bracket.
8. Remove the converter attaching bolts.
9. Support the transmission with a jack and holding fixture.
10. Remove the rear crossmember.
11. Disconnect the exhaust pipe and rear engine mount brackets.
12. Remove the speedometer cable and   filler pipe.
13. Install a wooden block between the engine and firewall and lower the jack until the engine contacts the block.
14. Make sure no tension is put on the battery cable.
15. Disconnect all electrical wiring at the transmission case.
16. Disconnect the starter cable and remove the starter.

17. Remove the converter housing bolts.
18. Pull the transmission backwards to clear the guide pins.
19. Install in reverse of removal. Torque the converter-to-drive plate bolts to 27 ftlb.; crossmember bolts to 18 ftlb.

164 and 240 Series

1. Remove   dipstick and filler pipe clamp.
2. Remove the bracket and throttle cable from the dashboard and throttle control, respectively.
3. Disconnect the exhaust pipe at the manifold.
4. Raise the car and support it on jackstands at the front and rear axles.
5. Drain   into a clean container.
6. Disconnect the driveshaft from the transmission flange.

7. Disconnect the selector lever controls and remove the reinforcing bracket from the pan.

8. Remove the torque converter attaching bolts.

9. Support the transmission with a jack equipped with a holding fixture.

10. Remove the rear crossmember.

11. Disconnect the exhaust pipe brackets and remove the speedometer cable from the case.

12. Remove the filler pipe.

13. Place a wooden block between the engine and firewall and lower the jack until the engine is against the block.

NOTE: *If the battery cable appears to stretch too much, remove it.*

14. Disconnect the starter wires, remove the converter housing bolts and pull the transmission backwards to clear the guide pins.

15. Install in reverse of removal. Torque all 14 mm bolts to 35 ftlb.

264 Series

1. Remove air cleaner.

2. Disconnect throttle cable.

3. Remove the two upper converter housing bolts.

4. Remove the filler pipe.

5. Raise the vehicle, support it front and rear with jackstands and drain the transmission into a clean container.

6. Remove the splash shield (8 bolts).

7. Disconnect the front muffler from the rubber suspensor.

8. Disconnect the driveshaft from the transmission flange.

9. Remove the exhaust pipe brackets at the rear of the transmission.

10. Remove the rear crossmember.

11. Remove the rear engine support and exhaust pipe bracket.

12. Remove the speedometer cable.

13. Disconnect the cooler lines at the transmission.

14. Remove electrical connections from transmission.

15. Remove neutral start switch.

16. Remove shift control rod.

17. Remove engine-to-transmission cover plate.

18. Remove starter motor and cover.

19. Remove converter-to-drive plate bolts.

20. Position jack, with holding fixture, under transmission.

21. Remove the two lower converter housing bolts.

22. Pull the transmission back and down to clear the guide pins.

23. Installation is the reverse of removal. Torque converter housing bolts to 35 ftlb. Torque filler pipe nut to 70 ftlb. Torque converter-to-drive plate bolts to 35 ftlb. Adjust control rod so that 1 ⅛" of thread is visible. Torque crossmember bolts to 35 ftlb.

Pan

Removal and Installation
1972–75 BW 35

1. Place the transmission selector in Park.

2. Raise the vehicle and place jackstands underneath.

3. The drain plug is located on the pan. Place a container underneath to catch the fluid. If the vehicle has been driven for any length of time, be careful, as the transmission fluid will be scalding hot.

4. After the fluid has stopped draining, remove the 15 pan retaining bolts, and lower the pan and gasket.

5. Inspect the magnetic element in the pan for metal shavings or chips. Also remove any sludge or gum from the bottom of the pan. Clean the mating surfaces of the transmission case and pan.

6. Position the pan (with a new gasket) to the case and install the 15 retaining bolts. Step torque the bolts diagonally in rotation to 8–13 ft. lbs. Coat the threads of the drain plug with Loctite®. Install the plug and a new plug gasket and torque to 8–10 ft. lbs.

7. Remove the jackstands and lower the vehicle. Refer to the capacities chart and fill the transmission to the proper level (between the MAX and MIN marks for a cold transmission) with type "F" automatic transmission fluid.

1976–77 BW55, AW55

1. Raise the car and place jackstands underneath.

2. The dipstick tube doubles as the filler tube, and when removed, the drain plug. Disconnect the tube from the side of the pan, and drain the transmission.

3. Remove the 14 pan bolts, and lower the pan and gasket (some fluid will remain in the pan).

4. Inspect the magnet (located adjacent to the filter screen) for metal particles. Check the filter screen for the pump. Remove any gum or sludge from the bottom of the pan. Clean and dry the pan and install a new gasket.

5. Position the pan and install the bolts finger tight. Then, step torque, diagonally in rotation, to 4.4–7.4 ft-lbs.

6. Connect the dipstick tube and tighten to 59–74 ft-lbs.

7. Remove the jackstands and lower the car. Refer to the capacities chart and fill the transmission to the proper level with ATF Type F.

Pump Strainer Service

1. Remove the pan as outlined in the Pan Removal and Installation section.

2. Remove the bolts which retain the front pump wire-mesh strainer to the valve body, and lower the strainer.

3. Clean the strainers in an alcohol based solvent solution.

4. Position the strainers to the valve body and install the retaining screws and bolts. Torque the bolts to 1.7–2.5 ft. lbs. (BW 35) or 3.7–4.4 ft. lbs. (BW 55 and AW 55).

5. Install the pan with a new gasket as outlined in the Pan Removal and Installation section.

Front Band Adjustment—BW 35

1. Remove the pan as outlined in the Pan Removal and Installation section.

2. Insert a 0.25 in. gauge block between the adjusting bolt and the servo cylinder. Tighten the bolt with an inch pound torque wrench to a torque of 10 in. lbs.

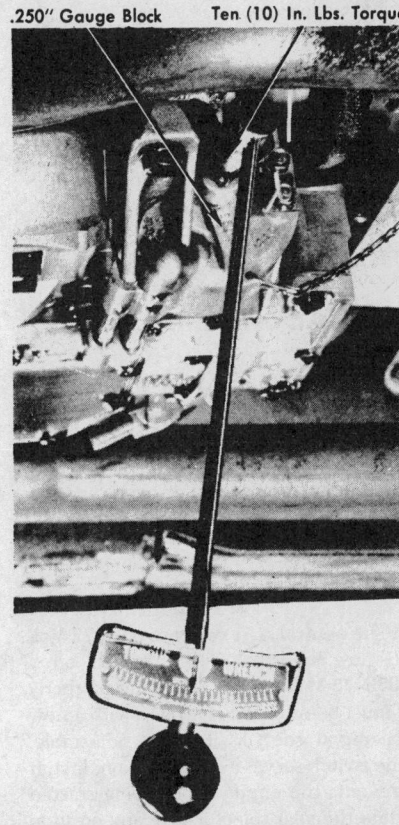

.250" Gauge Block   Ten (10) In. Lbs. Torque

Front band adjustment—Borg Warner 35

3. Adjust the position of the adjusting bolt spring. It should be 1–2 threads from the lever.

4. Remove the gauge block and torque wrench. Make sure that the long end of the adjusting bolt spring is inserted in the cam for the front brake band.

5. Install the pan as outlined in the Pan Removal and Installation section.

Rear Band Adjustment—BW 35

1. An access hole is provided in the right side of the transmission tunnel. On

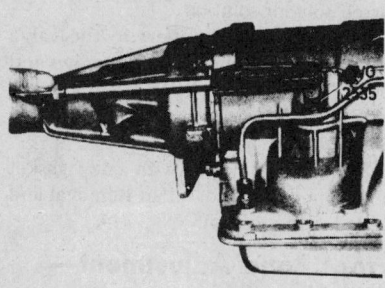

Rear band adjustment—Borg Warner Type 35

some 140 series and 164 models, it is necessary to disconnect the right heater duct. Lift up the carpet and position it to one side. Remove the rubber plug from the access hole.

2. Loosen the locknut for the adjusting screw located on the right side of the transmission case.

3. Using a 5/16 in. square socket and a foot pound torque wrench, tighten the adjusting screw to a torque of 10 ft. lbs; then back off the adjusting screw one complete turn.

4. Without disturbing the adjustment, tighten the locknut.

5. Install the rubber plug, fit the carpet, and install the heater duct, if removed.

Band Adjustments—BW55, AW55

The BW55 and AW55 transmissions are equipped with a multi-disc brake (band) system which does not require any adjustment. No provision is made for band adjustment, even at overhaul.

Neutral Start Switch Adjustment

1972–75

The neutral start switches on 1972 Volvos are adjustable. If a switch on a 1973–75 Volvo is not operating correctly it must be replaced complete with a new spacing washer, as it is not adjustable. The switch serves a dual function: first, it prevents the engine from being started while the gear selector is in any position other than Neutral or Park, and second, it closes the circuit that actuates the back-up lights when the selector is placed in Reverse. The following procedure is used to adjust the switch.

1. Check the adjustment of the gear selector as outlined under "Selector Linkage Adjustment." Place the gear selector in Drive. Firmly apply the parking brake.

2. On 1972 140 series and 164 models, remove the control lever from the transmission.

3. Loosen the locknut for the switch. Taking note of their positions, disconnect the electrical leads. Unscrew the switch

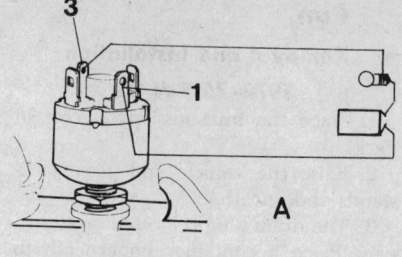

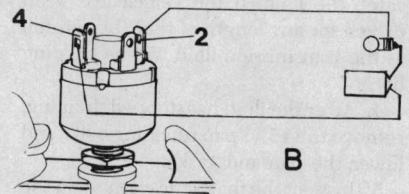

Neutral start switch adjustment—1972

(a)—Bulb connected to starter inhibitor contacts
(b)—Bulb connected to back-up light contacts

until it is held on by just a few threads.

4. On 1972 models, first connect a 12 volt test light to the start inhibitor terminals (1 and 3), and screw in the switch until the test light goes out. Disconnect the light and mark this position on the switch and transmission with a pencil. Then connect the test light to the back-up light terminals (2 and 4), and screw out the switch until the light goes on. Disconnect the light and also mark this position. The proper adjustment is midway between these two marks.

5. When the proper adjustment is achieved, tighten the locknut, taking care not to disturb the adjustment. Connect the four electrical leads.

6. On 1972 140 series and 164 models, install the control lever on the transmission.

7. Block the wheels so that the car cannot move either forward or backward. Make sure that the engine can only be started with the gear selector in Neutral or Park. Make sure that the back-up lights operate when the selector is placed in Reverse.

1976–77 Models

Some early production 1976 models have a non-adjustable neutral start switch located on the side of the case. All subse-

quent production models have an adjustable switch, located beneath the shifter quadrant on the tunnel. To adjust:

1. Remove the shifter quadrant cover.

2. Place the shifter lever in Park. Check that the round switch contact centers over the indicating line for "P" (park). If not, loosen the two switch mounting screws and align the switch.

3. Place the shifter lever in Neutral. Repeat the check and adjust as necessary.

4. Finally, check that the engine starts only in Park or Neutral, and check that the back-up lights work only in Reverse.

Gear Selector Linkage Adjustment

140 series, 164, 240, 260 series

1972–75 BW 35

1. Disconnect the shift rod from the transmission lever. Place both the transmission lever and the gear selector lever in the "2" position.

2. Adjust the length of the shift control rod so that a small clearance (distance B) of 0.04 in. is obtained between the gear selector lever inhibitor and the inhibitor plate, when the shift control rod is connected to the transmission lever.

3. Position the gear selector lever in Drive and make sure that a similar small clearance (distance A) of 0.04 in. exists between the lever inhibitor and the inhibitor plate. Disconnect the shift control rod from the transmission lever and adjust, if necessary.

4. Lock the control rod bolt with its safety clasp and tighten the locknut. Make sure that the control rod lug follows with the transmission lever.

5. After moving the transmission lever to the Park and "1" positions, make sure that the clearances A and B remain the same. In addition, make sure that the output shaft is locked with the selector lever in the Park position.

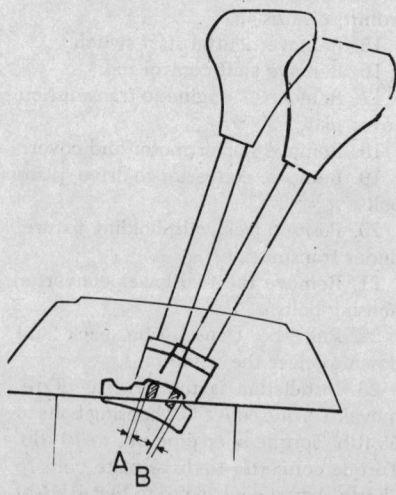

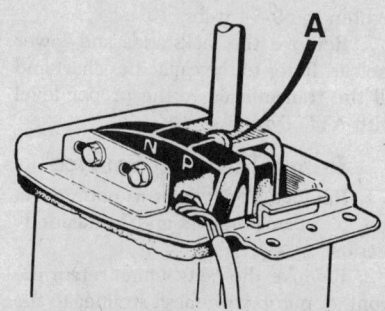

Neutral start switch adjustment—1976-77

Gear selector linkage adjustment—1972-74 140 series, 1972-75 164, 1975 240 series

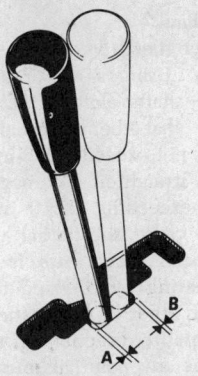

Gear selector linkage adjustment—1972-73 1800 series.

1976–77 BW55

1. With the engine off, check that the distance between the "D" position and its forward stop is equal to the distance between the "2" position and its rearward stop, when the gear selector is moved. If you are not sure, remove the gear quadrant cover, and measure.

2. If adjustment is necessary, a rough setting is made by loosening the locknut and rotating the clevis on the control rod to the transmission. A fine adjustment can be made by rotating the knurled sleeve between the control rod locknut and the pivot for the gear selector lever. Increasing the rod length will decrease clearance between the "D" position and its forward stop, and vice versa. Maximum permissable length of exposed thread between the locknut and the control rod is 1.1 in.

1800 series

1971–73 BW 35

1. Check to make sure that the transmission lever and the lever at the linkage bracket are parallel. If necessary, adjust the length of the lower control rod.

2. Disconnect the upper control rod from the intermediate lever (5). Place the gear selector in Neutral. Also set the transmission lever to its third (Neutral) position. Adjust the length of the upper control rod so that the ball socket aligns with the ball stud. Connect the control rod to the lever.

3. If the upper control rod adjustment is correct, the distances to the inhibitor plate in Neutral and Drive (A and B) should be equal.

4. Make sure that the output shaft is locked with the selector lever in the Park position.

Throttle and Downshift Cable Adjustment

1972–75 Models

Connect a tachometer to the engine and an oil pressure gauge (manometer) to the rear of the transmission (as shown) for this adjustment.

Procedure A

1. Warm up the engine and check the idle speed against specifications in the "Tune-Up Chart." Make sure that the throttle cable and cable housing (outer cable) are attached correctly.

2. On dual-carbureted engines, the threaded sleeve is then screwed to within 1/32 in. of the crimped stop on the cable.

3. Check the adjustment by making sure (with the accelerator pedal fully depressed), first, that the carburetor lever is at the full open stop position, and second, that the line pressure reading at converter stall speed is a minimum of 160 psi.

Procedure B

If the cable stop has been damaged, the adjustment disturbed, or if the transmission is not functioning properly, the throttle cable must be adjusted as follows.

1. Firmly apply the parking brake and place blocks in front and in back of the wheels.

2. Place the gear selector in Drive. Note the line pressure readings at 700 rpm and 1200 rpm. The line pressure increase between the two readings should be a minimum of 15 psi and a maximum of 20 psi for B 20 engines, and 25–30 psi for B 30 engines. The effective length of the outer cable (cable housing) must be increased if the pressure increase is lower than 15 psi (or 25 psi) and decreased if the

pressure rise is greater than 20 psi (or 30 psi). The length of the outer cable is determined by the adjuster.

Procedure C

If the cable itself has been damaged and is in need of replacement, the transmission oil pan must be removed first. Refer to "Oil Pan Removal and Installation." Adjust the new cable as follows.

NOTE: *Do not lubricate the new cable as it is pre-lubricated.*

1. With the oil pan removed, observe the position of the throttle cable cam in the transmission, in relation to the accelerator pedal position.

2. With the accelerator fully released and the carburetor lever at the idle stop, the heel of the cam must contact the full diameter of the downshift valve, taking up all of the slack in the inner throttle cable.

3. With the accelerator fully depressed and the carburetor lever at the full open stop, the constant radius area of the cam must be the point of contact with the downshift valve.

4. Make sure that the outer cable (cable housing) is correctly positioned in its adjuster.

1976–77 Models

1. First, adjust the throttle plate angle and throttle cable. Disconnect the cable at the control pulley and the linkage rod at the throttle shaft. Set the throttle plate

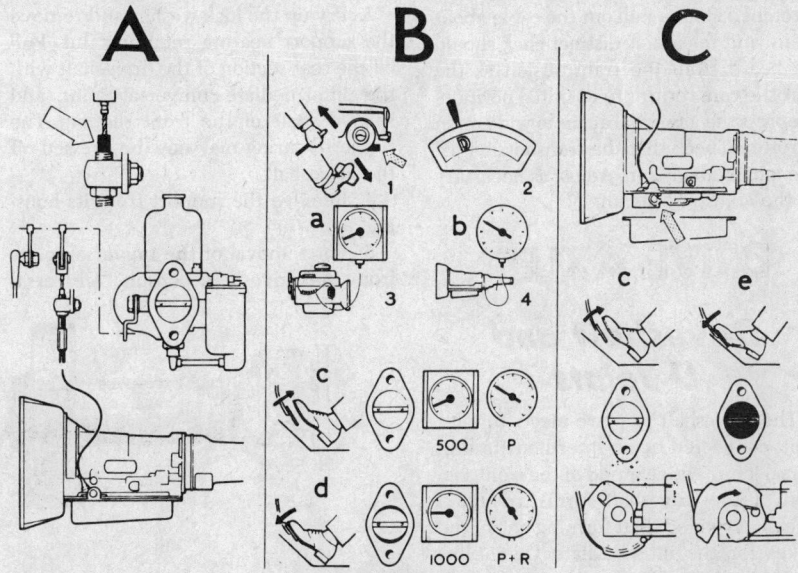

Throttle cable adjustment

(a)——Adjusting cable stop
(b)——Adjusting with tachometer and manometer
1. Chock the wheels and apply the brakes
2. Select position "D"
3. Connect a tachometer (a)
4. Connect a pressure gauge (b)
(c)——Measure pressure (P) at 500 r.p.m.
(d)——Measure pressure (P+R) at 1000 r.p.m.
(r)——Should be (15—20 lb/sq in.)
(c)——Adjust the cam in transmission
(c)——Accelerator pedal in idling position
(e)——Accelerator pedal fully depressed

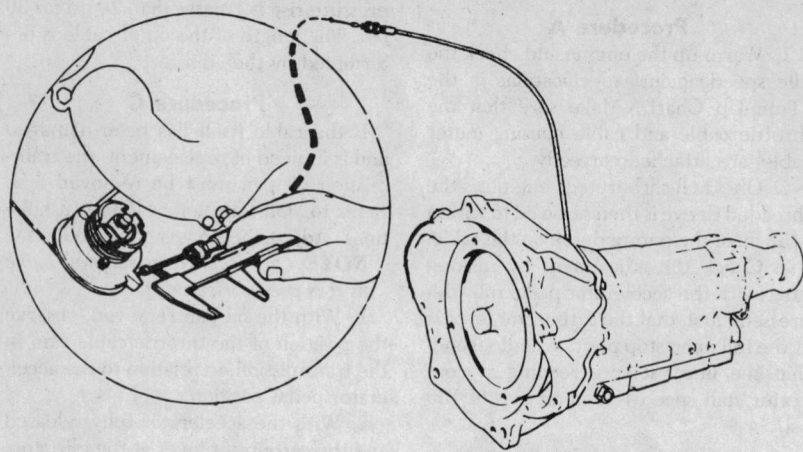

Throttle and downshift cable adjustment—1976-77 models

angle by loosening the adjusting screw locknut and backing off the screw. Then, turn in the screw until it just makes contact and then one additional turn. Tighten the locknut. Adjust the linkage rod so that it fits onto the throttle shaft pulley ball without moving the cable pulley. Attach the throttle cable to the pulley and adjust the cable sheath so that the cable is stretched but does not move the cable pulley. Finally, fully depress the gas pedal and check that the pulley contacts the full throttle abutment.

2. With the transmission cable hooked up, check that there is 0.010–0.040 in. clearance between the cable clip and the adjusting sheath. The cable should be stretched at idle. Pull out the cable about ½ in. and release. A distinct click should be heard from the transmission as the throttle cam returns to its initial position. Depress the gas pedal again to wide open throttle. Check that the transmission cable moves about 2 in. Adjust as necessary at the adjusting sheath.

DRIVE AXLES

Driveshaft and U-Joints

The driveshaft is a two-piece, tubular unit, connected by an intermediate universal joint. The rear end of the front section of the driveshaft forms a splined sleeve. A splined shaft forming one of the yokes for the intermediate U-joint fits into this sleeve. The front section is supported by a ball bearing contained in an insulated rubber housing which is attached to the bottom of the driveshaft tunnel. The front section is connected to the transmission flange, and the rear section is connected to the differential housing flange by universal joints. Each joint consists of a spider with four ground trunnions carried in the flange yokes by needle bearings.

Driveshaft and Universal Joint Removal and Installation

1. Jack up the vehicle and install safety stands.

2. Mark the relative positions of the driveshaft yokes and transmission and differential housing flanges for purposes of assembly. Remove the nuts and bolts which retain the front and rear driveshaft sections to the transmission and differential housing flanges, respectively. Remove the support bearing housing from the driveshaft tunnel, and lower the driveshaft and universal joint assembly as a unit.

3. Pry up the lock washer and remove the support bearing retaining nut. Pull off the rear section of the driveshaft with the intermediate universal joint and splined shaft of the front section. The support bearing may now be pressed off the driveshaft.

4. Remove the support from its housing.

5. For removal of the universal joints from the driveshaft, consult "Universal

Joint Overhaul."

6. Inspect the driveshaft sections for straightness. Using a dial indicator, or rolling the shafts along a flat surface, make sure that the driveshaft out-of-round does not exceed 0.010 in. Do not attempt to straighten a damaged shaft. Any shaft exceeding 0.010 in. out-of-round will cause substantial vibration, and must be replaced. Also, inspect the support bearing by pressing the races against each other by hand, and turning them in opposite directions. If the bearing binds at any point, it must be discarded and replaced.

7. Install the support bearing into its housing.

8. Press the support bearing and housing onto the front driveshaft section. Push the splined shaft of the front section, with the intermediate universal joint and rear driveshaft section, into the splined sleeve of the front section. Install the retaining nut and lock washer for the support bearing.

9. Taking note of the alignment marks made prior to removal, position the driveshaft and universal joint assembly to its flange connections and install but do not tighten its retaining nuts and bolts. Position the support bearing housing to the driveshaft tunnel and install the retaining nut. Tighten the nuts which retain the driveshaft sections to the transmission and differential housing flanges to a torque of 25–30 ft. lbs.

10. Remove the safety stands and lower the vehicle. Road test the car and check for driveline vibrations.

Universal Joint Overhaul

1. Remove the driveshaft and universal joint assembly as outlined in "Driveshaft and Universal Joint Assembly Removal and Installation."

2. Place the driveshaft section in a vise so that the joint being removed comes as

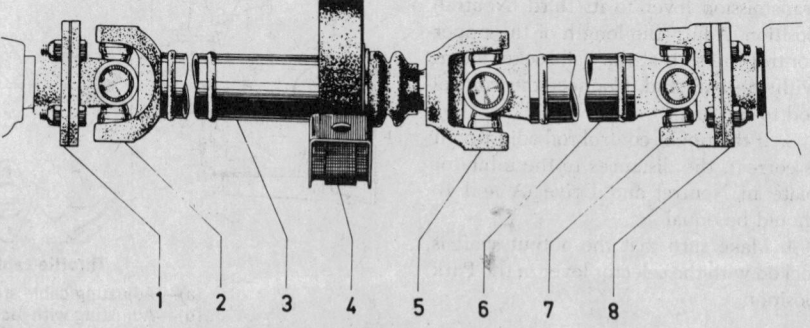

Driveshaft with support bearing
1. Flange on transmission
2. Front universal joint
3. Front section of driveshaft
4. Support bearing
5. Intermediate universal joint
6. Rear section of driveshaft
7. Rear universal joint
8. Flange on rear axle

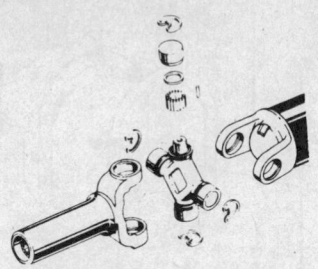

Universal joint disassembled

close as possible to the vise jaws. Do not tighten the vise any more than is necessary as the driveshaft is of tubular construction, and easily deformed.

3. Remove the snap-rings, which secure the needle bearings in the yokes, with snap-ring pliers.

4. With a hammer and a metal punch, drive the spider as far as it will go in one direction. The needle bearing should come about half-way out. Then, drive the spider as far as it will go in the other direction.

5. Drive out one of the needle bearings with a thinner punch. Remove the spider, and then drive out the other needle bearing.

6. Clean the spider and needle bearings completely. Check the frictional surfaces for wear. Replace any worn or broken parts. If the old needle bearings and spider are to be reused, fill them with molybdenum disulphide chassis grease, and make sure that the rubber seals are not damaged. If new needle bearings are used, fill them half-way with the grease.

7. To install, position the spider in the yoke and push the spider in one direction as far as it will go, so that the needle bearing can be fitted onto the spider trunnion. Then, using a drift of a slightly smaller diameter than the needle bearing sleeve, press the needle bearing in until the bearing sleeve and snap-ring can be fitted.

8. Install the other needle bearing, bearing sleeve, and snap-ring as outlined in step 7.

9. Remove the driveshaft section from the vise and repeat steps 2–8 for the other universal joints.

10. Install the driveshaft and universal joint assembly as outlined under "Driveshaft and Universal Joint Removal and Installation."

Rear Axle

All Volvos utilize a solid rear axle housing carried in two support arms. Two torque rods, connected between the axle shaft tubes and the body, limit the rear axle wind-up. A track bar controls lateral movement of the axle housing. Final drive is of the hypoid design, with the drive pinion lying below the ring gear. Each axle shaft is indexed into a splined

sleeve for the differential side gears, and supported at its outer end in a tapered roller bearing. Bearing clearance is not adjustable by use of shims as on earlier model Volvos, but instead is determined by bearing thickness. Both sides of the axle bearings are protected by oil seals.

Axle Shaft Removal and Installation, Bearing and Oil Seal Replacement

1. Raise the vehicle and install safety stands.

2. Remove the applicable wheel and tire assembly.

3. Place a wooden block beneath the brake pedal, plug the master cylinder reservoir vent hole, and remove and plug the brake line from the caliper. Be careful not to allow any brake fluid to spill onto the disc or pads. Remove the two bolts which retain brake caliper to the axle housing, and lift off the caliper. Lift off the brake disc.

4. Remove the thrust washer bolts through the holes in the axle shaft flange. Using a slide hammer, remove the axle shaft, bearing and oil seal assembly.

5. Using an arbor press, remove the axle shaft bearing and its locking ring from the axle shaft. Remove and discard the old oil seal.

6. Fill the space between the lips of the new oil seal with wheel bearing grease. Position the new seal on the axle shaft. Using an arbor press, install the bearing with a new locking ring, onto the axle shaft.

7. Thoroughly pack the bearing with wheel bearing grease. Install the axle shaft into the housing, rotating it so that it indexes with the differential. Install the bolts for the thrust washer and tighten to 36 ft. lbs.

8. Install the brake disc. Position the brake caliper to its retainer on the axle housing and install the two retaining bolts. Torque the caliper retaining bolts to 45–50 ft. lbs.

9. Unplug the brake line and connect it to the caliper. Bleed the caliper of all air trapped in the system.

10. Position the wheel and tire assembly on its lugs and hand-tighten the lug nuts. Remove the jackstands and lower the vehicle. Torque the lug nuts to 70–100 ft. lbs.

Rear Axle Housing Removal

1800 Series

1. Block the front wheels. Unscrew the rear wheel nuts and the nuts on the axle shafts. Jack up the rear. Place blocks un-

der the body in front of the rear wheels.

2. Disconnect the rear section of the driveshaft from the flange (yoke) on the pinion and disconnect the brake lines from the master cylinder to the rear axle.

3. Loosen the track bar, shock absorber and shock absorber straps from the rear axle. Disconnect the handbrake cables and the adjuster.

4. Unscrew the nuts for the support arms. Lower the rear axle and remove the springs. Loosen the bolts for the torque rod and remove the rear axle.

140 Series, 164, 240, 260 Series

1. Block the front wheels. Unscrew the rear wheel nuts. Jack up the rear of the vehicle. Place blocks in front of the rear jack attachments and lower the jack slightly. Remove the rear wheels.

2. Unscrew the upper bolts for the shock absorbers. Disconnect the handbrake cables from the lever arms and brackets on the brake backing plates.

3. Disconnect the driveshaft from the flange (yoke) on the pinion. Remove the brake line union from the differential carrier.

4. Loosen the front attaching bolt for the support arms about 1 turn. Remove the rear screws for the torque rods. Disconnect the track rod from the bracket on the differential carrier. Remove the lower attaching bolts for the springs.

5. Lower the jack until the support arms release from the springs. Remove the bolts which secure the differential carrier to the support arms. Lower the jack and pull the rear axle forward.

Differential Overhaul

Disassembly

1. Place the rear axle with the pinion pointing down. Remove the brake lines.

2. 140 Series 1970–73 1800, 164: Unscrew the bolts for the brake backing plates and retainers. The bolts are loosened through the holes in the axle shaft flanges. Pull out the axle shafts with a slide hammer.

3. Remove the inspection cover.

4. If the unit is being overhauled because of noise, the backlash and the gear tooth pattern should be checked before disassembly. Clean the teeth to avoid a misleading tooth pattern.

5. Check the alignment markings on the cap and carrier. If there are no alignment marks, or if they are difficult to see, mark one side with a punch. Remove the cap.

6. Expand the pinion carrier with a special tool. Pull out the differential carrier with ring gear. A special tool is available for this purpose.

7. Turn the assembly and allow the oil to run out. Remove the nuts for the flange. Pull the flange off with a puller. Press out the pinion.

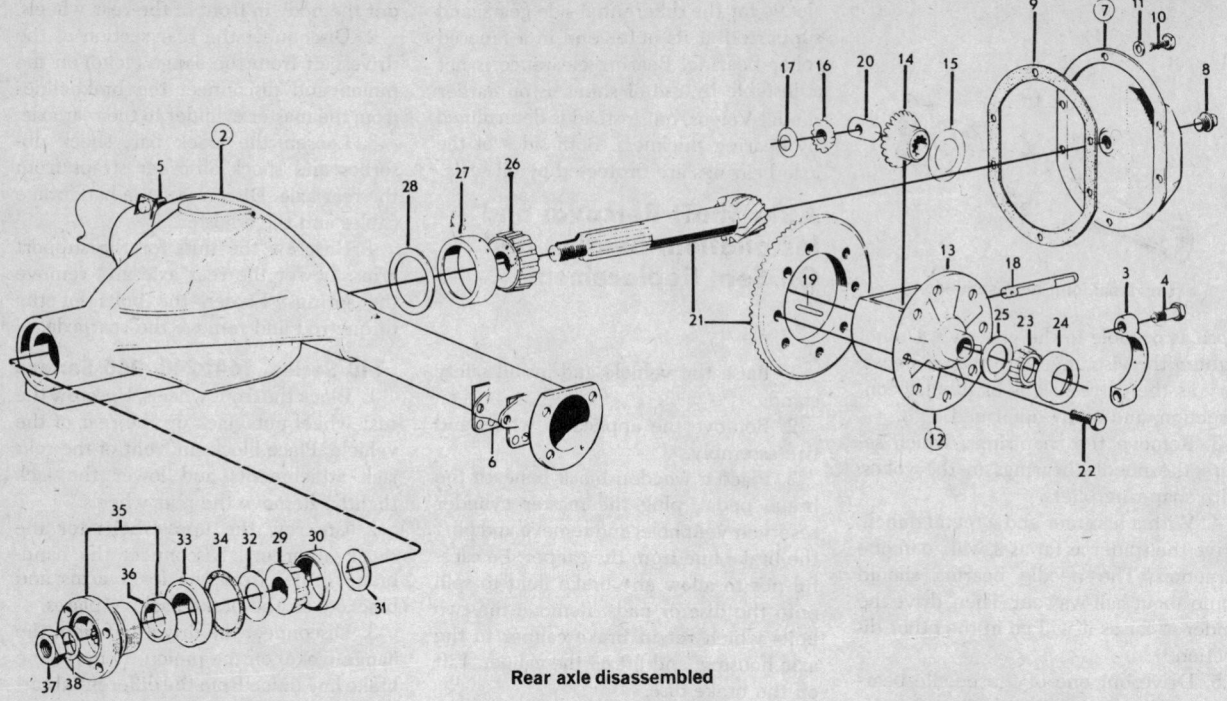

Rear axle disassembled

2. Rear axle housing
3. Bearing cap
4. Bolt
5. Anchorage point
   (track bar)
6. Anchorage point
   (support arm)
7. Inspection cover
8. Plug
9. Gasket
10. Bolt
11. Washer
12. Differential
13. Differential housing

14. Differential side
    pinion
15. Thrust washer
16. Differential side gear
17. Thrust washer
18. Pivot pin
19. Lock pin
20. Spacer sleeve
21. Ring and pinion
22. Bolt
23. Roller bearing cone
24. Roller bearing cup
25. Shim

26. Roller bearing cone
27. Roller bearing cup
28. Shim
29. Roller bearing cone
30. Roller bearing cup
31. Shim
32. Oil deflector
33. Oil seal
34. Gasket
35. Flange
36. Mud slinger
37. Nut
38. Washer

8. Drive out the front pinion bearing, the washer, and oil seal.

9. If necessary, drive out the rear bearing outer ring.

10. Clean the gasket surface. Remove all burrs with a file.

11. If necessary, pull off the rear bearing from the pinion with a puller. Slide the puller down over the rollers and press down the lock ring. Then tighten the puller until the rollers are flush against the edge of the inner race. Tap the lock ring with a hammer.

12. Loosen the ring gear bolts and remove the ring gear.

13. Drive out the lock pin, and the shaft for the differential gears. Remove the thrust block, the differential gears, and the thrust washers.

14. Remove the differential carrier bearings with a puller. Do not lose the shims.

Inspection

Clean all the parts thoroughly. Check all the bearing races and bearings. All damaged bearings and bearing races must be replaced. Check both the pinion drive and ring gear carefully for damage to the teeth. Tooth damage is caused by

incorrect break-in, wrong oil, insufficient tooth flank clearance, or faulty tooth contact.

The differential gears should also be examined for tooth damage. They should be placed in the differential carrier together with the shaft and thrust washers. Play should then be checked. If the play exceeds 0.0024 in. install thicker washers. These are available in 0.78 mm., 0.86 mm., and 0.94 mm. sizes. Also check to see whether the cylindrical part of the flange which goes into the oil seal is worn or scratched. If it is, replace the flange and the oil seal.

The pinion nut has a locking slit. In time this slit loses its effectiveness. For this reason, the nut should be replaced if it has been removed more than once. The washer under the nut should also be replaced if it is deformed.

Check the oil seals and replace them if they are damaged or worn.

Check for cracks in the rear axle casing. Make sure that the brackets for the support arms and track rod are intact.

Assembly

Great cleanliness should be observed when assembling and adjusting the diff-

erential. Dirt in a tapered roller bearing can result in inaccurate measurement. When measuring the bearing clearance or preloading, the bearing should be oiled and rotated several turns loaded.

1. Place the differential side gears and the thrust washers in the differential carrier. Then roll in the differential pinions simultaneously with the dished thrust washers.

2. Insert the thrust block and drive in the shaft.

3. Check the differential unit. If the gear play has not been measured, check it as described under "Inspection." If oversize washers are installed, check by turning the gears one turn. The turning torque should not exceed 7.23 ft.lbs. The tool for making this check can be easily made from a shortened axle shaft adapted to a suitable torque wrench. After checking the replacement of the thrust washers, install the lock pin.

4. Install the ring gear. Make sure that the contact surfaces are clean and without burrs. Tighten the bolts to 45–65 ft lbs.

NOTE: *Always use new bolts for gears in which the bolts are locked only by* *thread friction and the contact surface of the screw head.*

Pinion Installation

1. Polish the marking surface on the pinion with very fine emery cloth. Place the pinion in the casing so that the screw on the adjusting ring faces the larger part of the casing.

2. The pinion should have a certain nominal measurement to the center line of the ring gear. Due to manufacturing tolerances, there are deviations from the nominal measurement. This is indicated on the pinion.

On differentials made by Volvo, the surface is generally ground down 0.012 in. so that the deviation is always indicated by plus tolerance in hundredths of a millimeter. The plus sign is not indicated. On other units, the deviation is indicated in thousandths of an inch and with a plus or minus sign. If there is a plus sign in front of the figure, the nominal measurement is to be increased and, in the case of a minus sign, the nominal measurement is to be decreased.

To check the pinion location, use a dial indicator, an indicator retainer (SVO 2284), and a measuring tool (SVO 2393), which consists of two parts: a pinion gauge and an adjuster fixture. Place the pinion gauge on the ground end surface of the pinion and place the adjuster fixture in the differential bearing recesses. Place the indicator retainer on the drive pinion carrier and zero the indicator against the adjuster fixture. Then move the indicator retainer so that the indicator is against the pinion gauge. Read the indicator.

On a Volvo unit on which the pinion is, for example, marked 33, the pinion gauge should be 0.013 in. (0.33mm) under the adjuster fixture. On other units, if the pinion is marked 0, the adjuster fixture and pinion gauge should be at the same height; if the pinion is marked −, the pinion gauge should be higher than the adjuster fixture; and if it is marked +, the pinion gauge should be lower than the adjuster fixture. The setting is adjusted by turning the cam on the pinion until the gauge dial shows the correct figure, then locking in the adjusting ring with the lock screw. Remove the measuring tool and pinion.

3. Place the rear pinion bearing complete with the outer ring in a measuring fixture (SVO 2600). Install the plate, spring and nut. The flat side of the nut should face upward. The plate (and the bearing) should be turned forward and backward several times so that the rollers take up the correct position. Place the adjusting ring in the measuring fixture. Use an indicator retainer (SVO 2284) and a dial indicator. Place the measuring point of the gauge against the adjusting

ring and set the gauge to zero. Then place the point of the gauge against the outer ring of the bearing. The gauge now shows the required size for the shims. Measure the thickness of the shims with a micrometer. It is not always possible to obtain shims with exactly the correct thickness. However, they may not be more than 0.0012 in. thicker than the measured value but may be up to 0.0020 in. thinner.

4. Press the rear bearing on the pinion with a sleeve. The washer under the rear bearing inner ring on a new Volvo unit should not be installed after overhaul. Install the measured shims and press in both the outer rings of the bearings.

5. Install the pinion in the carrier and mount three 0.30 in. thick shims and the front pinion bearing. Tighten the pinion. If a nut remover is used when installing the pinion, the pinion must be pressed forward so that it does not strike against the bearing positions.

6. Install the pinion gauge and indicator retainer. Move the pinion down while turning it forward and backward at the same time. Set the indicator gauge to zero. Then press the pinion upward while turning it backward and forward at the same time. Read the play.

7. Remove the pinion. Remove a sufficient number of shims corresponding to the measured play plus 0.0028 in. Reinstall the pinion.

8. Then check the pinion bearings with a torque gauge. The torque gauge should show a torque of 5–10 in.lbs. for used bearings and 10–20 in.lbs. for new bearings when the pinion rotates. On new units, turning torque may be higher due to another installation method.

Check the location of the pinion with a dial indicator, an indicator retainer (SVO 2284), and a measuring tool (SVO 2393).

Differential Installation

1. Oil the adjusting rings internally and install them on the differential carrier. The ring with the oxidized adjusting ring is placed on the ring gear side. Also oil the bearing seal in the carrier. The differential carrier and adjusting rings are placed in the carrier. Use the dial indicator and adjust the ring so that the correct tooth flank clearance, 0.0060 in. is obtained. The tooth flank clearance may vary between 0.0040 in. (model 30: 0.-0052 in.) and 0.0080 in., but should be kept as near 0.0060 in. as possible. Tighten the lock bolts in the adjusting rings.

2. Coat several teeth with marking blue at three points on the ring gear. By this means a check can be kept on possible ring gear warping. Pull the pinion 10–12 turns in both directions and check the tooth pattern. When the tooth contact is correct, the contact pattern should

be vertical in the middle of the tooth but somewhat nearer to the toe than to the heel. The contact pattern on the reverse side and driving side should lie opposite each other. If the contact pattern is incorrect, the location of the pinion must be adjusted before assembly continues. If the contact pattern lies too far toward the heel on the driving side and too far toward the toe on the reverse side, the pinion should be moved inward. If the contact pattern lies too far toward the toe on the driving side and too far toward the heel on the reverse side, the pinion should be moved outward. Note that the contact pattern will lie somewhat nearer the toe when the adjusting rings are installed than when the bearings are installed.

3. When correct tooth flank clearance and contact pattern are obtained, remove the differential and adjusting ring. Place the center washer on the measuring fixture. Place a bearing in the measuring fixture and fit the plate, spring and nut. The nut should be fitted with the flat side facing downward. Turn the plate forward and backward several times. Install the dial indicator gauge and retainer. Set the gauge to zero against the adjusting ring and then place the pointer facing the bearing. Read the gauge. With a micrometer, measure the shims. The total shim thickness should correspond to the indicator reading plus 0.0028 in. Repeat with the other bearing. Keep a careful check on which side the bearing and shim are to be fitted.

4. Install the shims on the differential carrier and press on the bearings. Use a drift. When installing the second bearing, use a drift as a cushioning ring to avoid damage to the first bearing.

5. Expand the pinion carrier with a special tool. Install the differential and outer rings. Remove the tool. Install the bearing caps and tighten the bolts to 35–50 ft lbs.

6. Check the tooth flank clearance and contact pattern.

7. Install the oil slinger and the oil seal.

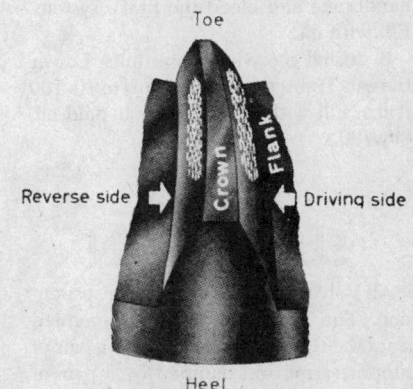

Correct tooth contact

The oil seal should be fitted with a drift. Press on the flange. Install the washer and nut. Tighten the nut to a torque of 200–220 ft lbs.

8. Install the inspection cover and gasket.

9. Install the axle shafts as outlined in the applicable "Axle Shaft Removal and Installation" procedure.

Rear Axle Housing Installation

1800 Series

1. Place the rear axle on a jack. Lift up the axle and install the torque rods. Slide the support arms into the retainers on the body and install the rubber blocks, washers, and nuts. The nuts should be tightened only a couple of turns to begin with.

2. Install the springs, retainers, and rubber blocks. Install bolts. Lift up the rear axle with the jack. Tighten the nuts for the support arms. Install the shock absorbers, shock absorber straps, and track rod.

3. Connect the universal joint at the flange, the brake hose, and the hand-brake cables. Bleed the brake system and adjust the handbrake. Fill with oil. Use only hypoid oil.

4. Install the wheels and nuts. Lower the car and tighten the wheel nuts to 70–100 ft lbs.

140 Series, 164, 240, 260 Series

1. Place the rear axle on a garage jack. Move the axle in under the car and install the bolts for the support arms and torque rods.

2. Raise the jack until the track rod attachment on the shaft is at the level with the attachment on the body. Install the track rod.

3. Install the attaching bolts for the springs. Tighten the nuts for the torque rods and support arms.

4. Install the bracket, union, and brake hoses. Connect the universal joint to the flange.

5. Install the upper bolts for the shock absorbers. Install the handbrake cable in the brackets and at the levers. Adjust the handbrake and bleed the brake system. Fill with oil.

6. Install the wheels and nuts. Lower the car. Tighten the wheel nuts to 70–100 ft lbs. Fill with oil. Use only hypoid oil, 80w/90.

REAR SUSPENSION

All Volvos use a coil spring rear suspension. The solid rear axle is suspended from the rigid frame member by a pair of support arms and damped by a pair of double-acting telescopic shock absorbers. A pair of torque rods control rear axle

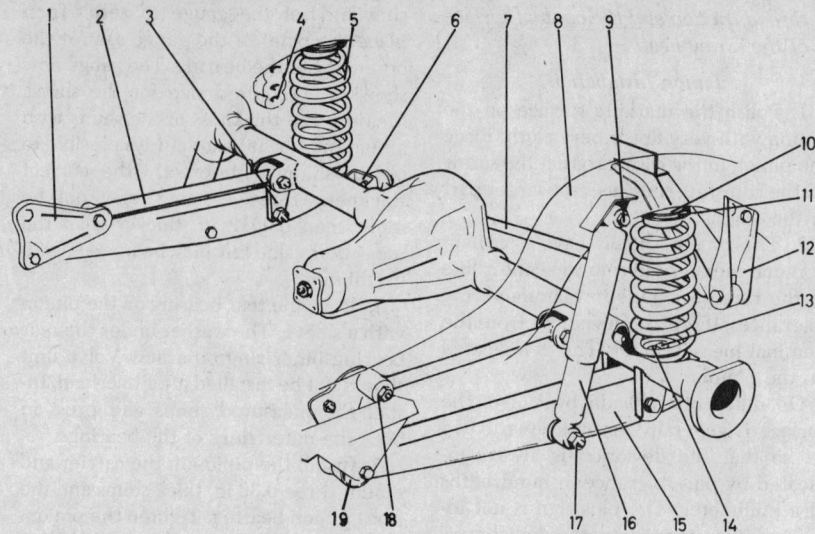

Rear suspension assembly—140 series, 164.

1. Bracket
2. Support stay
3. Bracket
4. Rubber buffer
5. Rear spring
6. Bracket
7. Track bar
8. Rear side-member
9. Shock absorber upper attachment
10. Washer
11. Rubber spacer
12. Bracket
13. Screw, lower spring attachment
14. Washer
15. Support arm
16. Shock absorber
17. Shock absorber lower attachment
18. Front support stay attachment
19. Front bushing, support arm

wind-up and a track rod limits the lateral movement of the rear axle in relation to the car. A rear stabilizer bar, attached to both rear support (trailing) arms, is installed on 240 and 260 models.

Springs

Removal and Installation

140 series, 164, 240, 260 Series

1. Remove the hub cap and loosen the lug nuts a few turns. Jack up the car and place jack stands in front of the rear jacking points. Remove the wheel and tire assembly.

2. Place a hydraulic jack beneath the rear axle housing and raise the housing sufficiently to compress the spring. Loosen the nuts for the upper and lower spring attachments.

1. Upper shock absorber bushings
2. Shock absorber
3. Rubber buffer
4. Rubber spacer
5. Spring
6. Suspension travel limiter
7. Rubber cushion
8. Lower shock absorber bushings
9. Spring attachment
10. Torque rod
11. Support stay

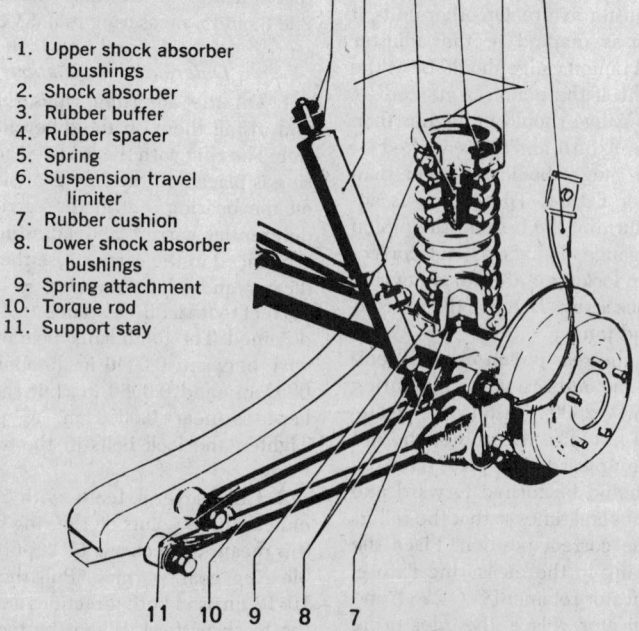

Rear suspension assembly—1800 series

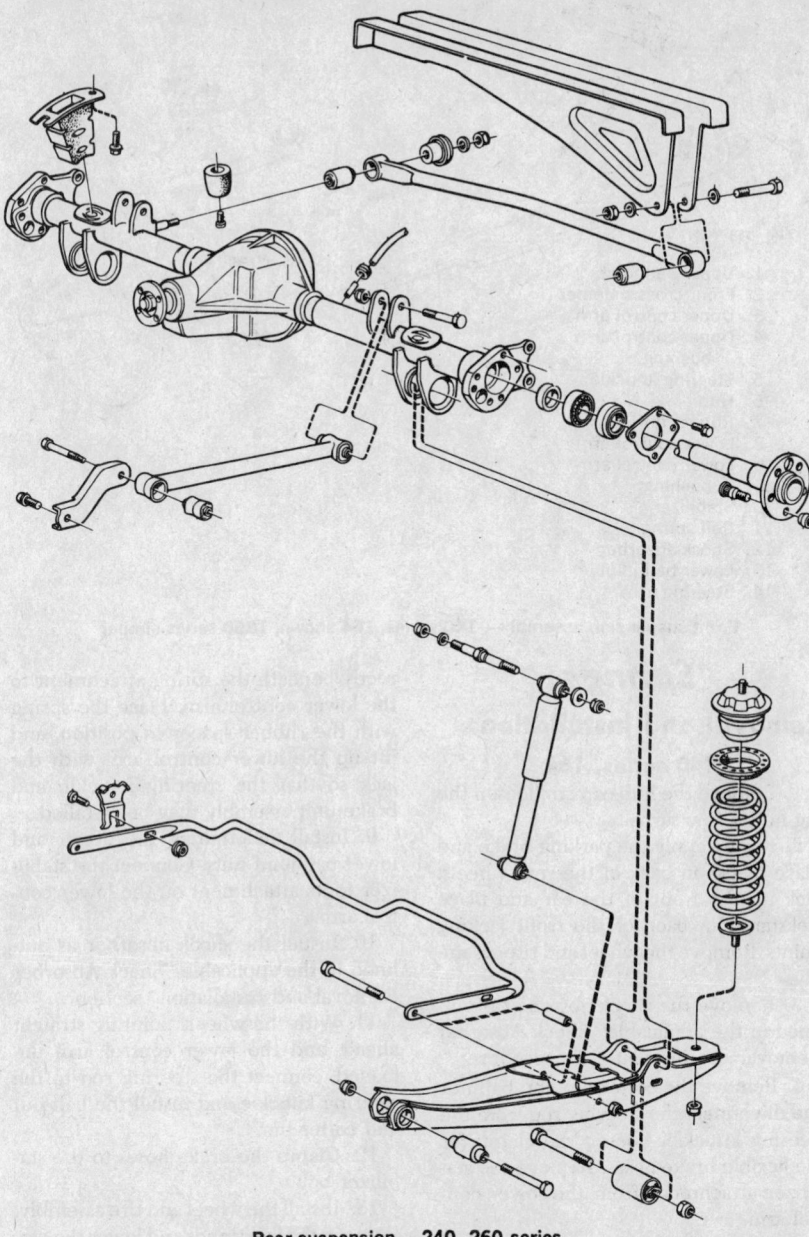

Rear suspension—240, 260 series

bly and release the parking brake.

3. Place a hydraulic jack beneath the rear axle housing and raise the jack and axle housing sufficiently to off-load the suspension downward travel limiter (shock absorber band).

4. Disconnect the shock absorber at its lower attachment. Also disconnect the suspension travel limiter (shock absorber band) at its upper attachment.

CAUTION: *Do not attempt to remove the spring until it is fully extended. As an added safety measure, a chain may be attached to the lower spring coil and secured to the axle housing.*

5. Carefully lower the jack and axle housing until the spring is fully extended. Remove the spring and rubber spacer.

6. To install, fit the rubber spacer to the top of the spring and position the spring into its upper attachment. Secure the bottom of the spring into its lower attachment, making sure that the rubber cushion on the axle housing is positioned correctly.

7. Raise the jack sufficiently so that the shock absorber may be connected to its lower attachment. Connect the suspension travel limiter to its upper attachment.

8. Install the wheel and tire assembly. Remove the jack stands and lower the car. Tighten the lug nuts to 70–100 ft lbs, and install the hub cap.

Shock Absorbers

Removal and Installation

140 series, 164, 240, 260 Series

1. Remove the hub cap and loosen the lug nuts a few turns. Place blocks in front of the front wheels. Jack up the rear of the car and place jack stands in front of the rear jacking points. Remove the wheel and tire assembly.

2. Remove the nuts and bolts which retain the shock absorber to its upper and lower attachments and remove the shock absorber. Make sure that the spacing sleeve, inside the axle support arm for the lower attachment, is not misplaced.

3. The damping effect of the shock absorber may be tested by securing the lower attachment in a vise and extending and compressing it. A properly operating shock absorber should offer approximately three times as much resistance to extending the unit as compressing it. Replace the shock absorber if it does not function as above, or if its fixed rubber bushings are damaged. Replace any leaking shock absorber.

4. To install, position the shock absorber to its upper and lower attachments. Make sure that the spacing sleeve is installed inside the axle support (trailing) arm and is aligned with the lower attachment bolt hole. Install the retain-

CAUTION: *Due to the fact that the spring is compressed under several hundred pounds of pressure, when it is freed from its lower attachment, it will attempt to suddenly return to its extended position. It is therefore imperative that the axle housing be lowered with extreme care until the spring is fully extended. As an added safety measure, a chain may be attached to the lower spring coil and secured to the axle housing.*

3. Disconnect the shock absorber at its upper attachment. Carefully lower the jack and axle housing until the spring is fully extended. Remove the spring.

4. To install, position the retaining bolt and inner washer, for the upper attachment, inside the spring and then, while holding the outer washer and rubber spacer to the upper body attachment, in-

stall the spring and inner washer to the upper attachment (sandwiching the rubber spacer), and tighten the retaining bolt.

5. Raise the jack and secure the bottom of the spring to its lower attachment with the washer and retaining bolt.

6. Connect the shock absorber to its upper attachment. Install the wheel and tire assembly.

7. Remove the jack stands and lower the car. Tighten the lug nuts to 70–100 ft lbs and install the hub cap.

1800 series

1. Remove the hub cap and loosen the lug nuts a few turns. Place blocks in front of the front wheels. Jack up the rear of the car and place jack stands in front of the rear jacking points.

2. Remove the wheel and tire assem-

ing nuts and bolts. On 240 series models, the shock fits *inside* the support arm. On all 140 series and 164 models, the shock attaches on the *outboard* side of the support arm.

5. Install the wheel and tire assembly. Remove the jack stands and lower the car. Tighten the lug nuts to 70–100 ft lbs, and install the hub cap.

1800 series

1. Fold the rear seat back forward. On 1800E models, remove the upholstery for the shelf under the rear window, and on 1800ES models, fold back the carpet for the bed, which will reveal the shock absorber upper attaching points.

2. Remove the upper nut, washers, and outer rubber bushing from the top of the shock absorber.

3. Remove the lower nut, washers, and outer rubber bushing from the bottom of the shock absorber.

4. Compress and remove the shock absorber.

5. Test the damping action of the shock absorber. Extending the unit should offer about three times as much resistance as compressing the unit. If the shock absorber is operating properly and is being reinstalled, be sure to use new rubber bushings.

6. Install inner washers and new rubber bushings, if removed, on the unit. Compress the shock absorber and position it to its upper and lower attachments.

7. Install the outer nuts, washers, and new rubber bushings first to the top and then to the bottom, of the shock absorber.

8. Replace the package shelf upholstery or the bed carpet to its original position.

FRONT SUSPENSION

140 Series, 164, 1800 Series

All 140 series, 164, and 1800 series model Volvos use a coil spring independent front suspension utilizing a pair of upper and lower control arms bolted to each side of the rigid front frame member. The coil springs and telescopic double-acting shock absorbers are bolted to the lower control arms at the bottom and seat in the crossmember at the top. A pair of steering knuckles are carried in ball joints between the upper and lower control arms. A stabilizer bar is attached to the lower control arms and to the body.

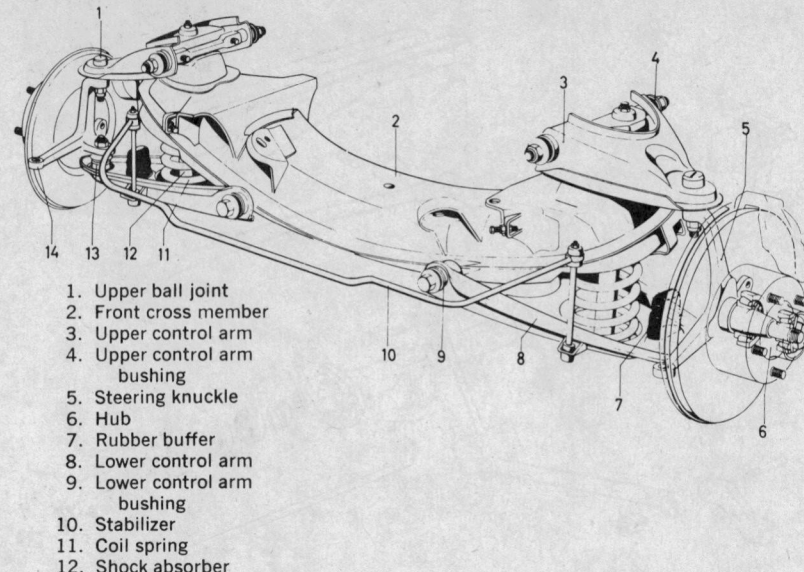

1. Upper ball joint
2. Front cross member
3. Upper control arm
4. Upper control arm bushing
5. Steering knuckle
6. Hub
7. Rubber buffer
8. Lower control arm
9. Lower control arm bushing
10. Stabilizer
11. Coil spring
12. Shock absorber
13. Lower ball joint
14. Steering arm

Front suspension assembly—140 series, 164 shown, 1800 series similar

Springs

Removal and Installation

140 series, 164

1. Remove the hub cap and loosen the lug nuts a few turns.

2. Firmly apply the parking brake and place blocks in back of the rear wheels. Jack up the front of the car and place jackstands in back of the front jacking points. Remove the wheel and tire assembly.

3. Remove the shock absorber as outlined in the applicable "Shock Absorber Removal and Installation" procedure.

4. Remove the cotter pin and ball nut and disconnect the steering rod from the steering knuckle. Loosen the clamp for the flexible brake hoses. Remove the stabilizer attachment from the lower control arm.

5. Place a jack under the lower control arm. Raise the jack to unload the lower control arm. Remove the cotter pins and loosen the nuts for the upper and lower ball joints; then rap with a hammer until they loosen from the spindle. Remove the nuts and lower the jack slightly.

6. Remove the steering knuckle with the front brake caliper and disc still connected to the brake lines. In order not to stretch the brake lines, place the brake unit on a milk crate or other suitable stand.

CAUTION: *Do not attempt to remove the spring until it is fully extended. As an added safety measure, a chain may be attached to the lower spring coil and secured to the frame.*

7. Slowly lower the jack and lower control arm to the fullest extent. Remove the spring and rubber spacer.

8. To install the spring place a jack di-

rectly beneath the spring attachment to the lower control arm. Place the spring with the rubber spacer in position, and lift up the lower control arm with the jack so that the steering knuckle and brake unit assembly may be installed.

9. Install and tighten the upper and lower ball joint nuts. Connect the stabilizer to its attachment on the lower control arm.

10. Install the shock absorber as outlined in the applicable "Shock Absorber Removal and Installation" section.

11. With the wheels pointing straight ahead, and the lower control arm unloaded, connect the steering rod to the steering knuckle and install the ball nut and cotter pin.

12. Clamp the brake hoses to the stabilizer bolt.

13. Install the wheel and tire assembly. Remove the jackstands and lower the car. Tighten the lug nuts to 70–100 ft lbs, and install the hub cap.

1800 series

1. Remove the hub cap and loosen the lug nuts a few turns.

2. Firmly apply the parking brake and place blocks in back of the rear wheels.

3. Jack up the front of the car and place jackstands beneath the front crossmember. Remove the wheel and tire assembly.

4. Remove the shock absorber as outlined in the applicable "Shock Absorber Removal and Installation" procedure.

5. Position a jack directly beneath the lower spring attachment on the lower control arm, and raise the jack until the upper control arm rubber buffer is lifted.

6. Disconnect the stabilizer from the lower control arm. Remove the cotter pin and ball nut from the lower ball joint.

CAUTION: *Do not attempt to remove the spring until it is fully extended. As an added safety measure, a chain may be attached to the lower spring coil and secured to the frame.*

7. Slowly lower the jack and lower control arm. If the lower ball joint does not release when the jack is lowered, it must be pressed out with a press tool such as SVO 2281. When the lower control arm is lowered sufficiently, carefully remove the spring, rubber spacer and washer assembly.

8. Reverse the above procedure to install, taking care to place the rubber spacer and washer correctly on top of the spring, prior to installation.

Shock Absorbers

Removal and Installation

140 series, 164

1. Remove the upper nut, washer, and outer rubber bushing.

2. Remove the two lower attaching bolts beneath the lower control arm, and pull the shock absorber assembly down and out.

3. Test the damping action of the shock absorber. Extending the unit should offer approximately three times as much resistance as compressing it. If the shock absorber is operating properly and is being reinstalled, be sure to use new rubber bushings on top.

4. Position the inner washer, spacing sleeve, and inner rubber bushing on top of the shock absorber.

5. Position the shock to its upper and lower attachments, and install the lower attaching bolts.

6. Install the outer rubber bushing, washer, and the upper nut on top of the unit. Tighten the upper nut until it makes firm contact with the spacing sleeve.

1800 series

1. Remove the upper nut, washer, and outer rubber bushing from the top of the shock absorber.

2. Remove the lower nut, washer, and outer rubber bushing from beneath the shock absorber.

3. Remove the two lower attaching bolts from beneath the lower control arm, and pull the shock absorber assembly down and out.

4. Test the damping action of the shock absorber. Extending the unit should offer approximately three times as much resistance as compressing it. If the shock absorber is operating properly and is being reinstalled, be sure to use new rubber bushings.

5. Reverse steps 1–3 to install.

Upper Ball Joint

Inspection

If the upper ball joint is worn, the wheel and tire assembly will exhibit excessive radial play when the joint is off-loaded. Place a jack beneath the lower control arm, and lift the wheel and tire assembly until clear of the ground. Make sure that the upper control arm is not making contact with the rubber stop. Firmly grasp the top and bottom of the tire and try to rock it in and out; that is, intermittently push the top of the tire towards the engine compartment, then pull it away from the car, while simultaneously doing the opposite to the bottom of the tire. Replace the upper ball joint if the radial play of the wheel and tire assembly is excessive.

NOTE: *Do not confuse possible wheel bearing play with ball joint play. It is advisable that the wheel bearing adjustment procedure in Chapter nine be followed prior to replacing the ball joint.*

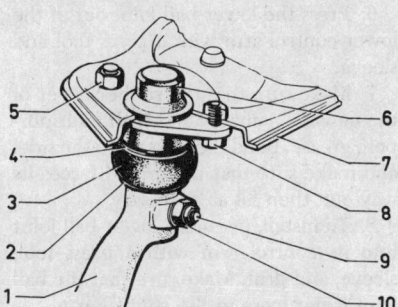

Upper ball joint attachment—1800 series

1. Spindle	7. Upper wish-
2. Circlip	bone
3. Rubber cover	8. Bolt
4. Circlip	9. Clamp bolt
5. Nut	10. Nut
6. Upper ball	
joint	

Removal and Installation

140 series, 164

1. Remove the hub cap and loosen the lug nuts a few turns.

2. Jack up the front of the vehicle and place safety stands beneath the front jacking points. Remove the wheel and tire assembly.

3. Loosen, but do not remove the nut for the upper ball joint. With a hammer, rap around the ball joint stud on the steering knuckle until it loosens. Remove the nut, and safety wire the upper end of the steering knuckle to the stabilizer bar to avoid straining the flexible brake hoses.

4. Loosen the nuts for the upper control arm shaft ½ turn. Lift up the control arm slightly and press out the old ball joint with a press tool and a sleeve.

4. Make sure that the rubber cover of the new ball joint is filled with multipurpose grease. Bend the pin end over the slot, and make sure that the grease forces its way out, then fill as necessary.

5. Press the ball joint into the upper control arm using the press tool, a sleeve, and a drift. It is imperative that the ball joint be aligned so that the slot comes in line with the longitudinal shaft of the control arm, either internally or externally, as the pin has maximum movement along this line.

6. Lower the upper control arm to its operating position, and tighten the shaft nuts to 40–45 ft lbs. Remove the safety wire; place the steering knuckle in position; install and tighten the ball nut to 60–70 ft lbs. If the pin rotates during tightening, clamp it firmly with a screw vise.

7. Install the wheel and tire assembly. Remove the safety stands and lower the vehicle. Tighten the lug nuts to 70–100 ft lbs, and install the hub cap.

1800 series

1. Remove the hub cap and loosen the lug nuts a few turns.

2. Jack up the front of the vehicle and place safety stands beneath the lower control arms. Remove the wheel and tire assembly.

3. Remove the two nuts (5) and bolts (8) which retain the ball joint to the upper control arm. Lift the upper control arm up and out of the way.

4. Remove the clamping nut (10) and bolt (9) which secure the ball joint to the steering knuckle. Remove the upper ball joint, sealing washers, and rubber cover assembly.

5. Make sure that the rubber cover of the new ball joint is filled with multipurpose (universal) grease. If the old ball joint is being reused, make sure that the rubber cover is not damaged, and fill it with grease.

6. After making sure that the sleeve and sealing washers (circlips) are positioned properly, place the ball joint assembly on the steering knuckle and install the clamping nut and bolt.

7. Lower the upper control arm into position over the ball joint and install the attaching nuts and bolts.

8. Install the wheel and tire assembly. Remove the safety stands and lower the vehicle. Tighten the lug nuts to 70–100 ft lbs, and install the hub cap.

Lower Ball Joint

Inspection

If the lower ball joint is worn, a measurement (A) taken from the ball stud to the cover of the ball joint will exceed the maximum allowable length for the ball joint when it is normally loaded. The check is made with the vehicle standing on the ground, wheels pointing straight ahead. Two types of lower ball joints have been used on late model Volvos; one utilizing a pressure spring, and the other not. The maximum allowable length for the spring type ball joint is 4.5 in. for the 140 series and 164, and 4.4 in. for the 1800 series. The maximum allowable length for the non-spring type ball joint is 3.91 in. for the 140 series and 164, and 3.76 in. for the 1800 series.

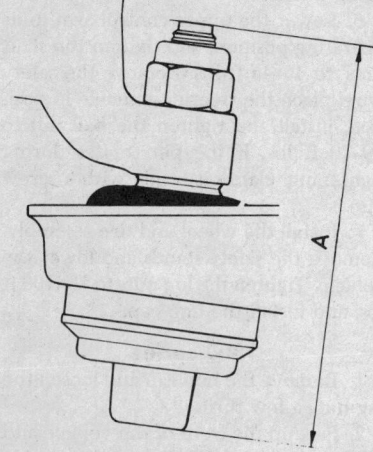

Spring type lower ball joint maximum allowable length.

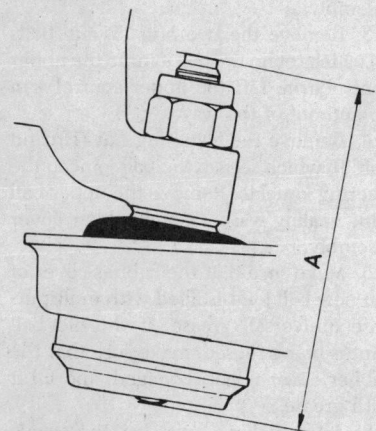

Non-spring type lower ball joint maximum allowable length.

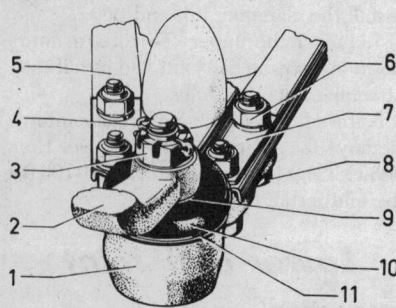

Lower ball joint attachment—1800 series

1. Lower ball joint	7. Bracket
2. Spindle	8. Bolt
3. Castle nut	9. Circlip
4. Cotter pin	10. Rubber cover
5. Lower wishbone	11. Circlip
6. Nut	

Removal and Installation

140 series, 164

1. Remove the hub cap and loosen the lug nuts a few turns.

2. Jack up the front of the vehicle and place jack stands beneath the front jacking points. Remove the wheel and tire assembly.

3. Remove the cotter pin and ball stud nut, and press the steering rod ball stud from the steering knuckle. Remove the brake lines from their bracket at the stabilizer bolt.

4. Remove the cotter pins and loosen but do not remove the nuts for both the upper and lower ball joints. Rap with a hammer until the ball joints loosen from the spindle. Place a jack beneath the lower control arm and raise it to off-load the control arm. Remove the ball joint nuts.

5. Remove the steering knuckle with the front brake unit still connected to the brake lines. In order not to stretch the brake lines, place the brake unit on a milk crate or other suitable stand.

6. Press the lower ball joint out of the lower control arm with a press tool and sleeve.

7. Make sure that the rubber cover of the new ball joint is filled with multipurpose grease. Bend the pin end to the side, and make sure that the grease forces its way out, then fill as necessary.

8. To install, press the lower ball joint into its control arm with a press tool, sleeve, and drift. Make sure that the ball joint is not loose in the control arm.

9. Position the steering knuckle and brake unit assembly in between the upper and lower control arms and tighten the ball joint stud nuts to 60–70 ft lbs (upper ball joint), and 75–90 ft lbs (lower ball joint). If the pins rotate during tightening, clamp them firmly with a screw vise.

10. Install the steering rod ball stud into the steering knuckle and tighten the stud nut. Lower the jack beneath the lower control arm slightly and with the front wheels pointing straight ahead, attach the brake lines to their bracket at the stabilizer bolt.

11. Install the wheel and tire assembly. Remove the jack stands and lower the vehicle. Tighten the lug nuts to 70–100 ft lbs, and install the hub cap.

1800 series

1. Remove the hub cap and loosen the lug nuts a few turns.

2. Jack up the front of the car and place safety stands beneath the lower control arms. Remove the wheel and tire assembly.

3. Remove the four nuts (6) and bolts (8) which retain the ball joint to the lower control arm. Remove the cotter pin and

ball stud nut which secure the steering knuckle to the ball joint.

4. Disconnect and plug the brake hoses at their retainer. Remove the ball joint from the steering knuckle by lightly rapping its attachment with a hammer.

5. Make sure that the rubber cover of the new ball joint is filled with multipurpose (universal) grease.

6. Place the ball joint, sealing washers (circlips), and sleeve into position on the steering knuckle and install the ball stud nut. Tighten the nut to 35–40 ft lbs.

7. Place the ball joint and steering knuckle assembly into position on the lower control arm and install the four retaining nuts and bolts.

8. Unplug and connect the brake hoses. Bleed the brake caliper.

9. Install the wheel and tire assembly. Remove the safety stands and lower the vehicle. Tighten the lug nuts to 70–100 ft lbs, and install the hub cap.

Upper Control Arm

Removal and Installation

1800 Series

1. Loosen the front wheel lugs, raise the car, support it on jackstands under the lower control arm and remove the wheel.

2. Remove the control arm-to-cross shaft nuts and clamps.

3. Remove the nuts at the spindle end and the bolts for the ball joint and lift off the control arm.

4. Position the new control arm and ball joint assembly. Fit the clamps and torque the nuts to 14–18 ftlb. Assemble other parts.

140 Series

1. Loosen the wheel lugs, raise the front end, support it on jackstands and remove the wheel.

2. Loosen, but do not remove, the upper ball joint nut. Remove the ball joint by hammering around the ball joint pin, on the steering knuckle.

3. Remove the nut and suspend the upper end of the axle to avoid straining the brake hose.

4. Disconnect the control arm from the cross shaft. Take note of the number and position of the shims.

5. Install in reverse of removal. Tighten the cross shaft nuts to 43 ftlb.

164 Series

1. Loosen the wheel lugs.

2. Raise and support the front end and remove the wheel.

3. Loosen, but do not remove, the ball joint nut. Tap on the knuckle, around the ball joint pin until the ball joint loosens from the axle.

4. Remove the nut and suspend the axle to avoid straining the brake hose.

5. Disconnect the control arm from the cross shaft. Note the number and location of the shims.

6. Install in reverse of the removal. Torque the cross shaft nuts to 43 ftlb.

Lower Control Arm

Removal and Installation

1800 Series

1. Loosen the wheel lugs, raise and support the front end and remove the wheels.

2. Remove the shock absorber.

3. Place a jack under the lower control arm at the spring. Raise the jack until the control arm rubber stop rises.

4. Disconnect the stabilizer bar from the lower control arm.

5. Remove the lower ball joint.

6. Slowly lower the jack and remove the spring when all tension is relieved. NOTE: The spring is under considerable pressure. The use of a spring compressor or safety chain is advised.

7. Disconnect control arm from cross shaft and remove.

8. Install in reverse of removal.

the distance between the top of the rubber stop and the bottom of the axle member should be approximately 1 ½".

140, 164 Series

1. Loosen wheel lugs, raise and support car and remove wheels.

2. Remove shock absorber.

3. Disconnect the tie rod from the steering arm with a separator tool.

4. Loosen the brake hose clamp and remove the stabilizer.

5. Place a jack under the lower control arm.

6. Loosen the ball joint nuts and tap around the ball joints with a hammer until they loosen from the knuckle.

7. Remove the nuts, lower the jack and remove the knuckle with the front brake unit. Suspend or position this assembly out of the way.

8. Lower the jack slowly and carefully, and when all tension is relieved, remove the spring.

NOTE: *The spring is under considerable pressure. It is adviseable to use a spring compressor or safety chain when removing spring.*

9. Remove the control arm shaft nut, turn the relay rod with the tie rod and remove the control arm shaft.

10. Remove the control arm.

11. Install in reverse of removal.

Front Suspension— 240, 260 Series

All 240 and 260 series Volvos use a coil spring independent front suspension utilizing a pair of McPherson-type struts

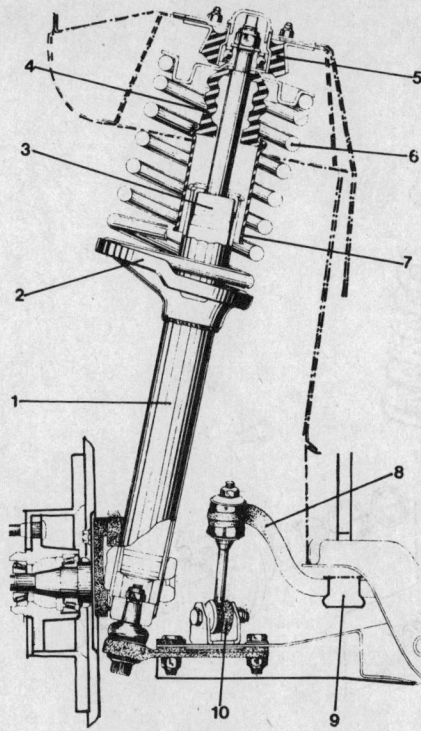

Front suspension—240, 260 series

1. Strut assembly
2. Lower spring support
3. Shock absorber
4. Rubber bumper
5. Upper attachment
6. Coil spring
7. Ruber sleeve, protecting the shock absorber
8. Stabilizer bar
9. Stabilizer bar attachment
10. Stabilizer link

located between a sheet metal tower at the top and a lower control arm at the bottom. The McPherson strut design incorporates the coil spring, shock absorber and wheel spindle into a single assembly, eliminating the need for an upper suspension control arm. The McPherson strut design provides for generous vertical suspension travel allowing the use of softer springs. The strut design is extremely sensitive to front wheel imbalance; the slightest imbalance often leading to front end wobble. Finally, the caster angle of the front suspension is preset and cannot be adjusted. If the caster angle is not up to specifications, the damaged components must be replaced as a unit.

Coil Spring

Removal and Installation

NOTE: *In order to perform the following procedure, a special coil spring compressor tool must be available. Under no circumstances should you attempt to lower and disassemble the strut assembly without the proper spring compressor tool, as serious injury could result.*

1. Remove the hub cap and loosen the lug nuts a few turns.

2. Firmly apply the parking brake and place blocks in back of the rear wheels.

3. Install the spring compressor on the spring directly beneath the sheet metal tower. Make sure that 3 coils of the spring are free between the tool attachment points. Then tighten the tool and compress the spring.

4. Jack up the front of the car with a hoist or using a floor jack at the center of the front crossmember. When the wheels are 2–3 in. off the ground, the car is high enough. Place jack stands beneath the

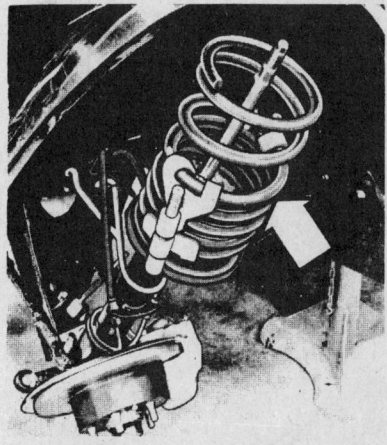

Removing coil spring from strut assembly. Note retaining wire around shock absorber to prevent strut from tilting out too far

front jacking points. Then, remove the floor jack from the crossmember (if used), and reposition it beneath the applicable lower control arm to provide support at the outer end. Remove the wheel and tire assembly.

5. Using a ball joint puller, disconnect the steering rod from the steering arm.

6. Disconnect the stabilizer bar at the link upper attachment.

7. Remove the bolt retaining the brake line bracket to the fender well.

8. Open the hood and remove the cover for the strut assembly upper attachment.

9. While keeping the strut from turning, loosen and remove the nut for the upper attachment.

10. Before lowering the strut assembly, wire or tie the strut to some stationary component, or use a holding fixture such as SVO 5045, to prevent the strut from traveling down too far and damaging the hydraulic brake lines. Then lower the jack supporting the lower arm and allow the strut to tilt out to about a 60 degree angle. At this angle, the top of the strut assembly should just protrude past the wheel well, allowing removal of the strut components from the top.

11. Lift off the spring seat, rubber bumper, and the shock absorber protec-

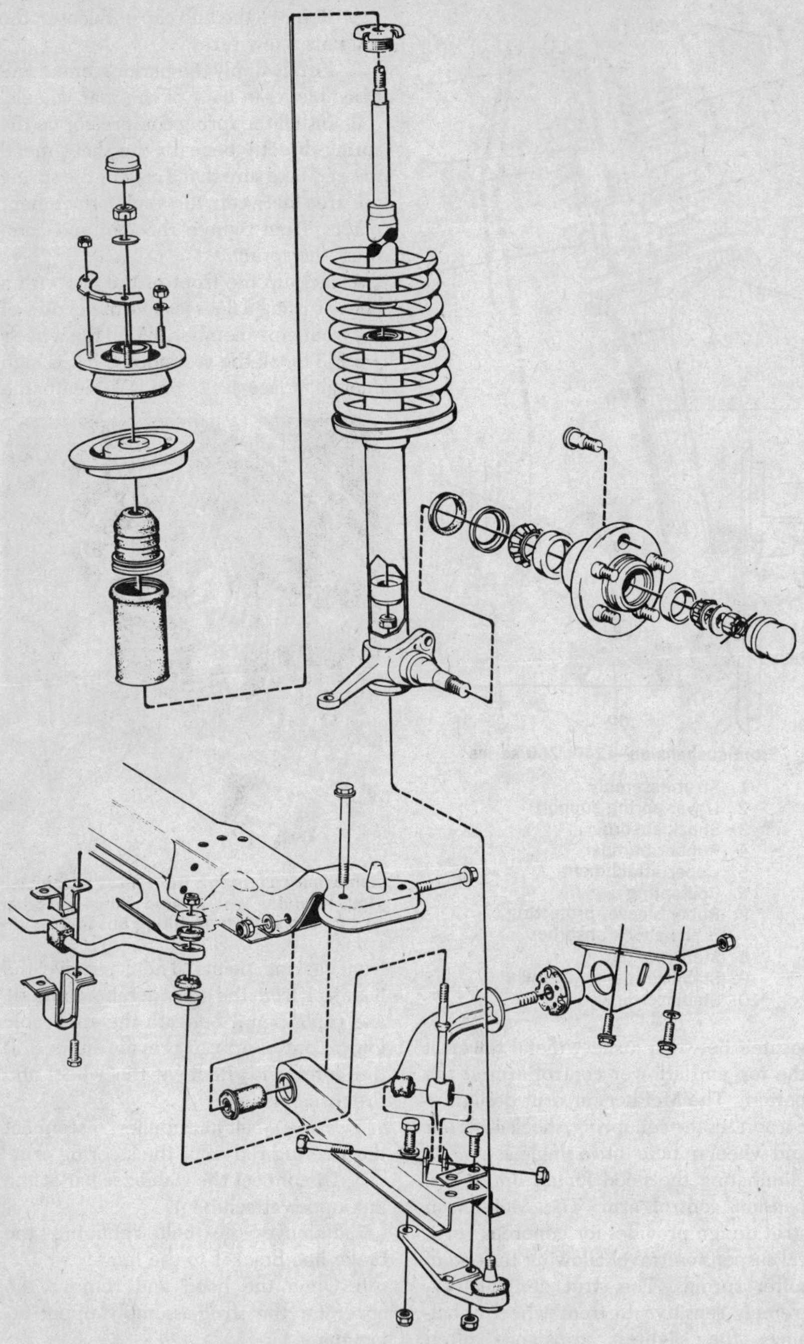

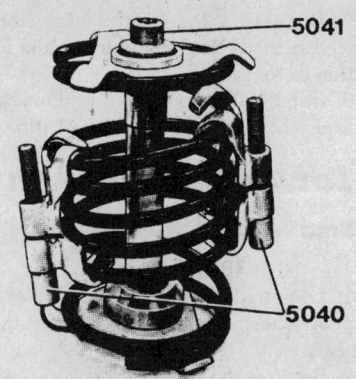

Front suspension strut—240, 260 series

If the "claw type" spring compressor does not have enough travel to release all of the spring tension, a "sandwich" type compressor will have to be used (SVO 5041) to remove the original com-pressor

16. Attach the brake line bracket to its mount. Tighten the nut retaining the stabilizer bar to the link. Connect the steering rod at the steering arm.

17. Release the coil spring compressor and install the wheel and tire assembly. Remove the jack stands and lower the car. Jounce the suspension a few times and then road test.

Shock Absorber

Removal and Installation

1. Follow steps 1–11 under "Coil Spring Removal and Installation" for the 240, 260 series.

2. While keeping the strut outer tube from turning, remove the upper shock absorber retaining nut.

3. Pull the shock absorber unit out of the outer tube (casing).

4. Install the new shock absorber unit into the outer tube and install the retaining nut. You can stop the outer tube from turning with the nut by holding the tube at the weld with a pair of channel-lock pliers.

5. Pull the shock absorber spindle to its uppermost position.

6. Follow steps 13–17 under "Coil Spring Removal and Installation" for the 240 series.

Lower Control Arm

Replacement

1. Jack up car, support on stands and remove wheels.

2. Remove stabilizer bar.

3. Remove ball joint from control arm.

4. Remove control arm front retaining bolt.

5. Remove control arm rear attachment plate.

6. Remove attachment plate from control arm.

7. Remove stabilizer link from control arm.

8. Install in reverse of removal.

tion. Remove the coil spring and compressor assembly from the strut.

12. Slowly relieve the tension on the compressor and remove it from the spring. Place the compressor on the replacement spring (making sure 3 coils separate the attachment points as before), and compress.

NOTE: *If the spring compressor does not have enough travel to fully release the spring tension, it will be necessary to use another "sandwich" type compressor to remove the original compressor once the spring is out of the car.*

13. Position the new spring and compressor on the strut assembly. Make sure the spring end is properly aligned with

the strut bracket.
NOTE: *Make sure that the compressor bolts face downwards.*

14. Install the rubber bumper and the shock absorber protection. Position the spring seat on the spring, making sure it is aligned with the spring.

15. Carefully lift and guide the strut assembly into its upper attachment in the spring tower. Connect the stabilizer bar to the stabilizer link. Guide the shock absorber spindle into the upper attachment and raise the jack beneath the lower control arm. Install the washer and nut on top of the shock absorber spindle. While holding the spindle from turning, tighten the nut to 15–25 ft lbs. Install the cover.

NOTE: *Right and left bushings are not interchangeable. The right side bushing should be turned so that the small slots point horizontally when installed. Torque the front retaining bolt to 55 ftlb., the rear busing nut to 4 ftlb., and the rear attachment bolts to 30 ftlb.*

Lower Ball Joint

Removal and Installation

Early Production Models

1. Follow steps 1–11 under "Coil Spring Removal and Installation" for the 240, 260 series.
2. While grasping the strut outer tube (casing) with a pair of locking pliers, loosen and remove the shock absorber retaining nut.
3. Pull the shock absorber unit out of the outer tube.
4. Loosen the ball joint retaining nut. Grasp the outer tube at the weld with a pair of channel-lock pliers and loosen the nut with a 19mm socket and a long extension, until the joint bracket comes loose.
5. Using a drift and hammer, loosen the conical part of the ball joint from the strut assembly.
6. Using the 19mm socket coated on the inside with vaseline or wheel bearing grease, remove the ball joint retaining nut. The grease should keep the nut from falling down into the strut tube.
7. Wire the top of the strut assembly to the sheet metal tower, and allow the strut to hang vertically. Disconnect the ball joint from the bottom of the strut assembly. Take care not to damage the brake hoses. Then, disconnect the ball joint from the lower control arm.
8. Attach the new ball joint to the lower control arm.
NOTE: *Make sure the new ball joint stud is free of grease, or the stud could be tightened too far into the cone making the rubber bellows stick to the strut.*

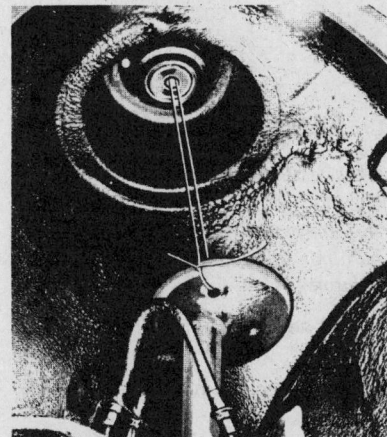

Suspending top of strut to body with wire while removing lower ball joint

9. Remove the securing wire and lift the strut assembly into position. Install the ball joint nut, and torque to 30–50 ft lbs. Stop the outer tube from turning with locking pliers at the weld.
10. Install the shock absorber and retaining nut. Tighten as in step 9. Pull the shock absorber spindle to its uppermost position.
11. Follow steps 13–17 under "Coil Spring Removal and Installation" for the 240, 260 series.

Late Production Models

1. Jack up the front of the car and install jackstands beneath the front jacking attachments.
2. Remove the tire and wheel assembly.
3. Reach in between the spring coils and loosen the shock absorber cap nut a few turns.
4. Remove the four bolts (12mm) retaining the ball joint seat to the bottom of the strut.
5. Remove the three nuts (19mm) retaining the ball joint to the lower control arm.

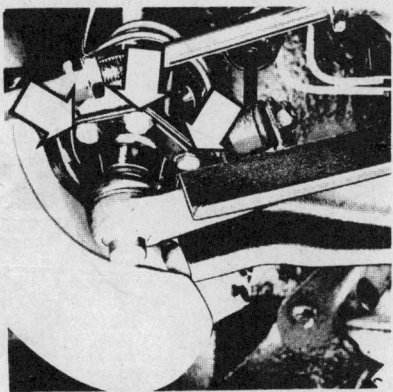

Late production type lower ball joint-to-strut retaining bolts

6. Place the ball joint and attachment assembly in a vise and remove the 19mm nut from the ball joint stud. Then, drive out the old ball joint.
7. Install the new ball joint in the attachment and tighten the stud nut to 35–50 ft-lbs.
8. Attach the ball joint assembly to the strut. Tighten to 15–20 ft-lbs.
9. Attach the ball joint assembly to the control arm. Tighten to 70–95 ft-lbs.
10. Tighten the shock absorber cap nut. Install the wheel and tire. Lower the car and road-test.

Wheel Alignment

Caster and Camber Adjustment

140 series, 164, 1800 series

The procedures for adjusting caster and camber are grouped together here as they may be performed at the same time

on these Volvos. Both adjustments are made by inserting shims between the upper control arm shaft and the sheet metal of the shock absorber tower. Loosen the bolts which retain the control arm shaft to the shock tower and insert the shims. Before each adjustment is completed, the bolts must be tightened or an erroneous measurement will be obtained. A special SVO tool (no. 2713) is available from dealers for loosening or tightening the control arm shaft bolts on the 140 series and 164 models, because gaining access to these bolts is difficult.

Caster is adjusted by either removing a shim at one of the bolts, adding a shim at the other bolt, or by transferring half of the required shim thickness from one bolt to another. Caster is adjusted to the positive side, for example, by inserting shims at the rear bolt or removing shims at the front bolt.

Camber is adjusted by either removing or adding shims of equal thickness at both bolts. Camber is increased toward the positive by removing shims, and decreased toward the negative by adding shims.

Shims are available in sizes of 0.15, 0.5, 1.0, 3.0, and 6.0 mm (0.006, 0.020, 0.039, 0.12, and 0.24 in.). Remember to torque the control arm shaft bolts to 40–50 ft lbs after making the adjustment.

240, 260 Models

Caster angle is fixed by suspension design and cannot be adjusted. If caster is not within specifications, check front end parts for damage and replace as necessary.

Camber angle, however, may be adjusted. At the strut upper attachment to the body, two of the three bolts holes are eccentric, allowing the upper end of the strut to tilt out or in as necessary. A special pivot lever tool SVO 5038, which attaches to the tops of the strut upper attachment retaining bolt threads is recommended for this job. To adjust, loosen the three retaining nuts,

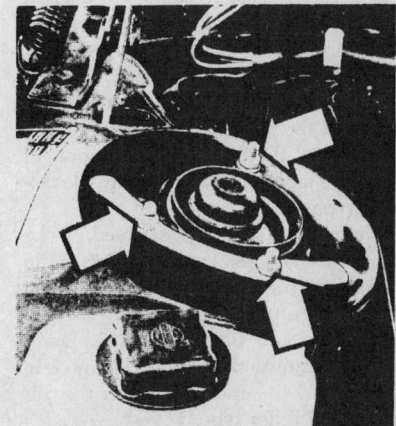

Loosen the upper strut nuts to adjust the camber on 240, 260 series

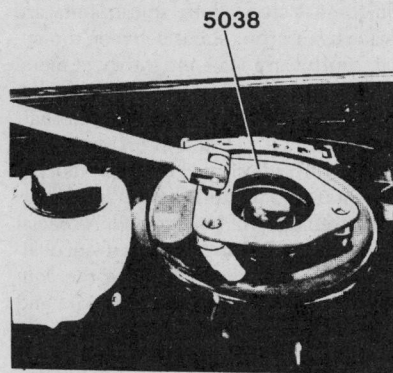

5038

Adjusting camber with special tool—240, 260 series

install the pivot lever tool, and adjust to specifications. After adjusting, torque the nuts to 15–25 ft lbs.

Toe-In Adjustment—All Models

Toe-in may be adjusted after performing the caster and camber adjustments. With a wheel spreader, measure the distance (X) between the rear of the right and left front tires, at spindle (hub) height, and then measure the distance (Y) between the front of the right and left front tires, also at spindle (hub) height. Subtract the front distance (Y) from the rear distance (X), and compare that to the specifications table. $X - Y = $ toe-in. If the adjustment is not correct, loosen the locknuts on both sides of the tie rod, and rotate the tie rod itself. Toe-in is increased by turning the tie rod in the normal forward rotation of the wheels, and reduced by turning it in the opposite direction. After the final adjustment is made, torque the locknuts to 55–65 ft lbs, being careful not to disturb the adjustment.

STEERING

All Volvos use divided steering columns that protect the driver during front end collisions. The system used on the 140 series utilizes a flange connection that breaks on impact, allowing the lower portion to travel backward but keeping the upper portion stable. The 164 uses a telescoping column and a breakaway flange at the steering box. The 1800 series utilizes the telescoping column. All 1973 and later models are collapsible column types.

The manual steering gear used on the 140 series, and 1800 series models is the Gemmer worm and roller type. The power steering gear used on the 164 series, some late production 1973 automatic transmission equipped 145 models, and 1974 140 series models, is the ZF worm and roller type.

The manual steering gear used on the 240 series is a rack and pinion type of

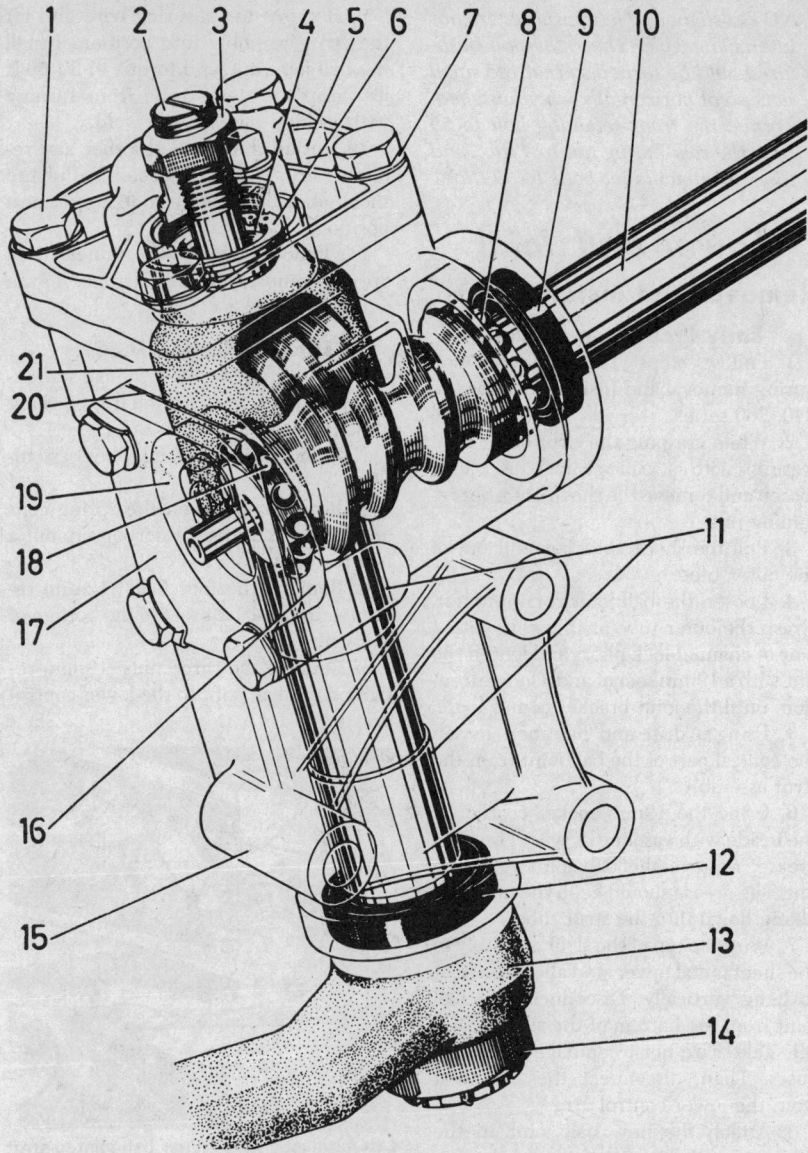

Manual steering gear—worm and roller

1. Bolt
2. Adjusting screw
3. Locknut
4. Pitman arm shaft bushing
5. Cover
6. Lock ring
7. Tab washer
8. Upper steering cam bearing
9. Oil seal, steering column
10. Steering cam
11. Pitman arm shaft bushing
12. Pitman arm shaft seal
13. Pitman arm
14. Nut
15. Housing
16. Lower bearing cap
17. Steering column cover
18. Lower cam bearing
19. Washer
20. Shims
21. Pitman arm shaft with roller

either Cam or ZF manufacture. Both units are fully enclosed, with the steering rods attached directly to the rack piston and protected by rubber bellows. However, the Cam unit is filled with steering gear oil while the ZF unit is grease-filled.

Power steering is available on all 240 series models and standard equipment on the 260. Power assist is integral with the steering rear unit, and is supplied by an engine driven pump of ZF or Saginaw manufacture. The Saginaw pump is used in the 260 series, while the ZF pump is used in the 240.

Steering Wheel

Removal and Installation

NOTE: *the use of a knock-off type steering wheel puller, or the use of a hammer may damage the collapsible column.*

140 series, 164, 240 series
1972

1. Disconnect the negative battery cable.

2. Remove the retaining screw for the upper half of the molded turn signal switch housing and lift off the housing.

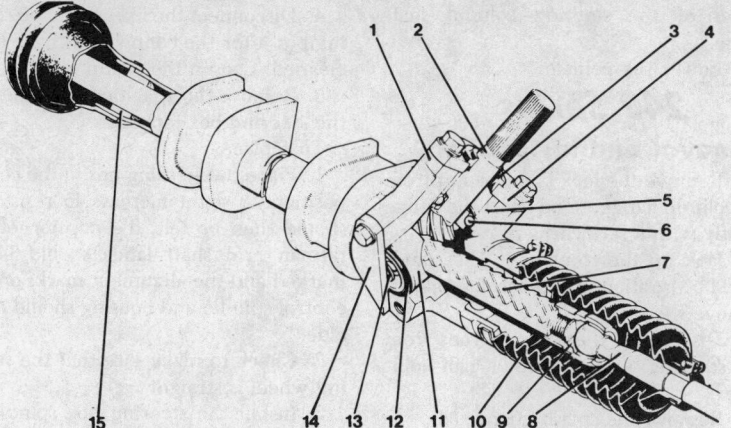

Manual steering gear assembly (cam gear)—rack & pinion type

1. Housing
2. Pinion
3. Seal
4. Pinion cover
5. Spacer sleeve
6. Upper Pinion bearing
7. Rack
8. Steering rod
9. Inner ball joint
10. Rubber bellow
11. Pre-tensioning piston
12. O-ring
13. Spring
14. Cover
15. Bushing

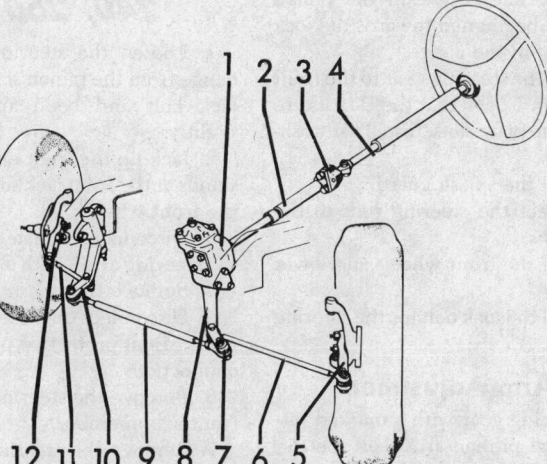

Steering linkage assembly—1800 series shown—140 series, 164 similar.

1. Steering box
2. Safety device
3. Rubber flange
4. Steering column
5. Left stering arm
6. Left steering rod
7. Ball joint
8. Pitman arm
9. Tie rod
10. Relay arm
11. Right steering rod
12. Right steering arm

3. Pry up and remove the impact protection badge from the horn ring. Disconnect the plug contact for the horn and remove the four retaining screws for the horn ring. Lift off the horn ring, noting the positions of the various springs and washers.

4. Remove the steering wheel nut.

5. With the front wheels pointing straight ahead, and the steering wheel centered, install a steering wheel puller, such as SVO 2972, and pull off the steering wheel.

6. Remove the turn signal switch flange.

7. To install, make sure that the front wheels are pointing straight ahead, then position the turn signal switch flange into the column and place the centered steer-ing wheel on the column. Install the steering wheel nut and tighten to 20–30 ft lbs.

8. Making sure that the springs and washers are positioned correctly, install the horn ring on the steering wheel and tighten the four retaining screws. Connect the horn plug contact.

9. Install the upper turn signal housing halve.

10. Connect the negative battery cable and test the operation of the horn.

1973–76

1. Disconnect the negative battery cable.

2. Remove the retaining screws for the upper half of the molded turn signal housing and lift off the housing.

3. Pry off the steering wheel impact pad.

4. Disconnect the horn plug contact.

5. Remove the steering wheel nut.

6. With the front wheels pointing straight ahead, and the steering wheel centered, install a steering wheel puller. On 164 models, use an outside circumference type, such as SVO 5003, and pull off the steering wheel. On 140, 240 and 260 models, use a universal type puller, such as SVO 2263.

7. To install, make sure that the front wheels are pointing straight ahead, then place the centered steering wheel on the column with the plug contact to the left. Install the nut and tighten to 20–30 ft lbs.

8. Connect the horn plug contact and install the impact pad.

9. Install the upper turn signal housing half.

10. Connect the negative battery cable and test the operation of the horn.

1800 series

1. Disconnect the negative battery cable.

2. Pry off the steering wheel impact pad.

3. Disconnect the horn plug contact. Remove the three retaining screws and lift off the horn ring, (if so equipped) noting the placement of the springs and washers.

4. Bend back the locking washer and remove the steering wheel nut. Mark the relative positions of the steering wheel to the column. Slacken the horn wire.

5. Install a steering wheel puller and pull off the wheel.

6. To install, place the steering wheel on the column so that the alignment marks made prior to removal line up. Install the nut and tighten to 20–30 ft lbs.

7. Connect the horn plug contact, and install the horn ring, springs, and washers with the three retaining screws (if so equipped).

8. Snap on the impact pad.

9. Connect the negative battery cable and test the operation of the horn.

Ignition Lock and Switch

Replacement

1800 series

1. Disconnect the battery ground.

2. Remove both bolts securing the switch to the lock and remove the switch.

3. Install in reverse of removal.

140, 164 Series

1. Disconnect the wiring from the switch.

2. Remove the attaching screws and lift out switch.

3. Install in reverse of removal.

240, 260 Series

1. Remove noise insulation panel and center side panel.

2. Disconnect the wires from the switch.

3. Pry out the switch with a short screwdriver.

4. Install in reverse of removal.

Manual Steering Gear

Removal and Installation

1800 Series

1. Disconnect the horn lead from the connecting block.

2. Unscrew the two nuts and remove the bolts.

3. Remove the pitman arm with a puller.

4. Unscrew and remove the three attaching bolts.

5. Lift and turn the steering box. Pull out the horn lead from the lower section of the steering column and steering box. Lift off the steering box, being careful when moving to clamp past the brake line.

To replace:

1. Place the steering box in position. Be careful when moving the clamp past the brake line. Install the attaching bolts. On P1800, insert the horn lead through the lower section of the steering column with the help of a piece of wire. Place the steering box in position and install the attaching bolts, washers, and nuts loosely.

2. Assemble the clamp to the coupling disc. Do not forget the ground lead.

3. Adjust the position of the steering box so that the upper and lower sections of the steering column form a straight line. Tighten the attaching bolts.

4. Install the pitman arm so that the alignment mark on the pitman arm shaft aligns with the mark on the pitman arm. Tighten the nut to 100–120 ft lbs.

5. Make sure that the steering wheel spokes are horizontal when the wheels are straight.

140 Series

1. Jack up the vehicle at the front.

2. Loosen the bolt at the lower steering column shaft flange. Remove the nuts and move the lower part of the flange as far down as possible on the steering cam.

3. Remove the lock nut for the pitman arm. Pull off the pitman arm.

4. Remove the nuts and bolts and lift out the steering box.

To install:

1. Place the steering box in position and tighten the bolts.

2. Install the pitman arm and tighten the nut to 135 ft lbs.

3. Move the steering wheel so that the wheels point straight and tighten both

halves of the steering column shaft flange.

4. Lower the vehicle.

240 Series

Removal and Installation

1. Remove the lock bolt and nut from the column flange. Bend apart the flange slightly with a screwdriver.

2. Jack up the front end. The stands should be positioned at the jack supports. Remove the front wheels.

3. Disconnect the steering rods from the steering arms, using a ball joint puller.

4. Remove the splash guard.

5. Disconnect the steering gear from the front axle member.

6. Disconnect the steering gear from the steering gear flange. Remove steering gear.

7. Install rubber spacers and plates for the steering gear attachment points.

8. Position the steering gear, and guide the pinion shaft into the steering shaft flange. The recess on the pinion shaft should be aligned towards the lock bolt opening in the flange.

9. Attach the steering gear to the front axle member. Check that the U-bolts are aligned in the plate slots. Install flat washers and nuts.

10. Install the splash guard.

11. Connect the steering rods to the steering arms.

12. Install the front wheels and lower the vehicle.

13. Install the lock bolt for the steering shaft flange.

Pitman Arm Adjustment

On a steering gear with a marked pitman arm and pitman arm shaft (on the steering gear), make sure that the marks align.

On a steering gear without the marks, lift up the front of the vehicle so that the front wheels are free. Turn the steering wheel to its center position (count the number of turns). Lower the vehicle. If the vehicle is correctly loaded, the wheels should now point straight forward. If the wheels do not, remove the pitman arm from the shaft with a puller. Then set the left wheel straight ahead and replace the pitman arm. The steering wheel should be in its center position. Tighten the pitman arm nut to 100–120 ft lbs.

Power Steering Gear

Removal and Installation

140 series, 164

1. Jack up the front end.

2. Drain the system.

3. Remove the lock nut for the pitman arm. Pull the pitman arm off.

4. Disconnect the lines from the steering box after the connections have been cleaned. Loosen the clamp bolt.

5. Remove the attaching bolts and pull the steering box forward.

To replace:

1. Place the steering box in the center position. A slight increase in resistance should then be felt, the position of the pitman arm shaft lands should be as marked and the alignment marks on the control spindle and housing should coincide.

2. Check to make sure that the steering wheel is straight.

3. Install the steering box spindle in the flange of the lower steering column section. Install and tighten the attaching bolts. Tighten the clamp bolt. Connect the lines. The longer delivery line should run in a curve and be clamped.

4. Point the front wheels straight and install the pitman arm. Tighten the nut to 125–141 ft lbs.

5. Fill and bleed the system.

240, 260 Series

1. Loosen the steering column shaft flange from the pinion shaft. Remove the lock bolt and bend apart the flange slightly.

2. Jack up the front end. Position jack stands at the front jack supports. Remove the front wheels.

3. Disconnect the steering rods from the steering arms, with a ball joint puller.

4. Remove the splash guard.

5. Disconnect the hoses at the steering gear. Install protective plugs in the hose connections.

6. Remove the steering gear from the front axle member.

7. Remove the steering gear by pulling down until it is free from the steering shaft flange. Then remove the unit on the left side of the vehicle.

8. Position the steering gear and attach the pinion shaft to the steering shaft flange. Take care to align the recess for the lock bolt.

9. Install right side U-bolt and bracket, but do NOT tighten the nuts.

10. Install left side retaining bolts, and tighten. Tighten the U-bolt nuts.

11. Connect the steering rods to the steering arms.

12. Install the lock bolt on the steering column flange.

13. Connect the return and pressure hoses to the steering gear.

Power Steering Pump

Removal and Installation

1. Remove all dirt and grease from around the suction line connections and from around the delivery line on the

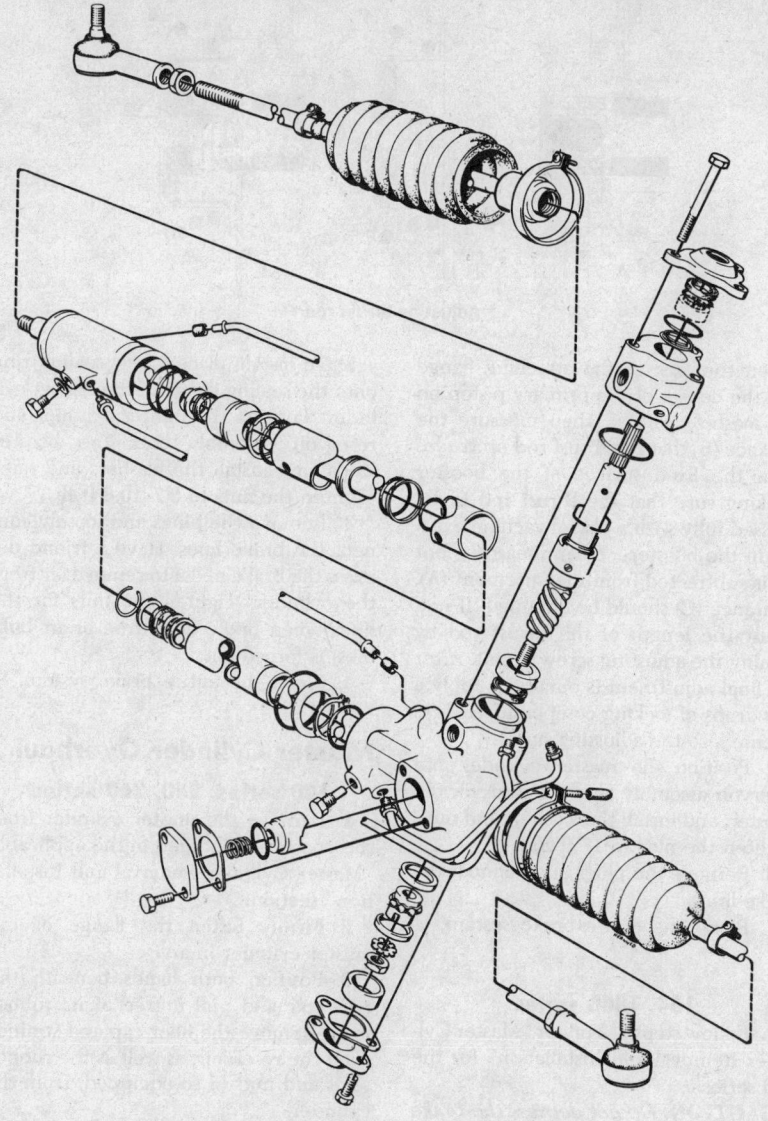

Rack & Pinion power steering gear disassembled

pump housing.

2. Using a container to catch any power steering fluid that might run out, disconnect the oil lines, and plug them to prevent dirt from entering the system.

3. Remove the tensioning bolt and the attaching bolts.

4. Clear the pump free of the fan belt and lift it out.

5. If a new pump is to be used, the old brackets, fittings, and pulley must be transferred from the old unit. The pulley may be removed with a puller, and pressed on the pump shaft with a press tool. Under no circumstances should the pulley be hammered on, as this will damage the pump bearings.

6. To install, place the pump in position and loosely fit the attaching bolts. Connect the oil lines to the pump with new seals.

7. Place the fan belt onto the pulley and adjust the fan belt tension as outlined.

8. Tighten the tensioning bolt and the attaching bolts.

9. Fill the reservoir with Type "A" automatic transmission fluid and bleed the system as outlined under "Power Steering System Bleeding"

Power Steering System Bleeding

1. Fill the reservoir up to the edge with Automatic Transmission Fluid Type "A". Raise the front wheels off the ground, and install safety stands. Place the transmission in neutral and apply the parking brake.

2. Keeping a can of ATF Type "A" within easy reach, start the engine and fill the reservoir as the level drops.

3. When the reservoir level has stopped dropping, slowly turn the steering wheel from lock to lock several times. Fill the reservoir if necessary.

4. Locate the bleeder screw on the power steering gear. Open the bleeder screw ½–1 turn, and close it when oil starts flowing out.

5. Continue to turn the steering wheel slowly until the fluid in the reservoir is free of air bubbles.

6. Stop the engine and observe the oil level in the reservoir. If the oil level rises more than ¼ in. past the level mark, air still remains in the system. Continue bleeding until the level rise is correct.

7. Remove the safety stands and lower the car.

Steering and Tie Rod Service

Bent or otherwise damaged steering rods and tie rods must be replaced, never straightened. All components of the steering linkage, including the pitman arm and idler arm (on worm and roller steering types), are connected by means of ball joints. Ball joints cannot be disassembled or adjusted, so they must also be replaced when damaged. They should also be replaced if the rubber seal is broken and the joint contaminated.

The ball joints of the steering rods are made in unit with the rods, therefore the entire rod assembly must be replaced when their ball joints become unserviceable. Maximum permissible axial (vertical) play is .120 in. After removing the cotter pins and ball stud nuts at the rod's connections, press the ball joint out of its connecting socket.

The ball joints of the tie rod may be replaced individually. After the ball joint is disconnected, the lock nut on the tie rod is loosened and the clamp bolt released. The ball joint is then screwed out of the tie rod, taking note of the number of turns. The new ball joint is screwed in the same number of turns, and the clamp bolt and lock nut tightened. The ball joint is locked to the rod with 55–65 ft lbs. of torque. The new ball joint is pressed into its connection and the ball stud nut tightened to 23–27 ft lbs.

After reconditioning of the rods and joints, the wheel alignment must be adjusted.

BRAKE SYSTEM

Volvos are equipped with a four wheel power-assisted disc brake system. The four wheel disc system utilizes a pair of four-piston, fixed calipers at the rear. The calipers are either Girling or ATE manufacture, so when ordering disc pads or caliper rebuilding kits, you must identify which you have. The discs are one-piece castings. Since 1972, 164 models have been equipped with internally vented discs.

Whenever adding to or replacing brake fluid, it is imperative that the fluid be of SAE 70 R3 (SAE J 1703) quality or better. Fluid meeting DOT 3 or DOT 4 specifications is also acceptable. Avoid mixing brake fluids from different manufacturers and never reuse old brake fluid.

Drum Brake Adjustment

1. Jack up the car and place supports under the rear axle. Release the hand brake.

2. Remove the rubber seal. Turn the wheel in its normal direction of rotation while bringing the brake shoes into contact with the drum. Use an adjusting tool to turn the adjuster screw. When the wheel can just be turned by using one hand, stop tightening the screw. Then back off the adjuster screw 1–2 notches. Install the rubber seal.

3. Repeat the adjustment procedure on the other brake. Remove the supports and lower the car.

Disc Brake Adjustment

Disc brakes require no adjustment. They should, however, be checked frequently for wear. Consult the specifications table for new pad thickness. Pads should never be allowed to wear down to less than 0.125 in., or disc damage may occur.

Hydraulic System

Master Cylinder

Removal and Installation

140 series, 240, 260 series

1. To prevent brake fluid from spilling onto and damaging the paint, place a protective cover over the fender apron, and rags beneath the master cylinder.

2. Disconnect and plug the brake lines from the master cylinder.

3. Remove the two nuts which retain the master cylinder and reservoir assembly to the vacuum booster, and lift the assembly forward, being careful not to spill any fluid on the fender. Empty out and discard the brake fluid.

CAUTION: *Do not depress the brake pedal while the master cylinder is removed.*

4. In order for the master cylinder to function properly when installed to the vacuum booster, the adjusting nut for the thrust rod of the booster must not prevent the primary piston of the master cylinder from returning to its resting position. A clearance (C) of 0.004–0.04 in. on 1971 and later models, is required between the thrust rod and primary piston with the master cylinder installed. The clearance may be adjusted by rotating the adjusting nut for the booster thrust rod in the required direction. To determine what the clearance (C) will be when the master cylinder and booster are connected, first measure the distance (A) be-

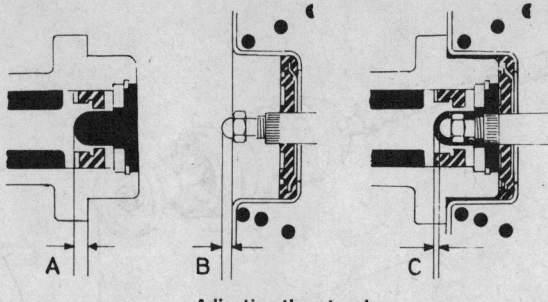

Adjusting thrust rod

tween the face of the attaching flange and the center of the primary piston on the master cylinder, then measure the distance (B) that the thrust rod protrudes from the fixed surface of the booster (making sure that the thrust rod is depressed fully with a partial vacuum existing in the booster). When measurement (B) is subtracted from measurement (A), clearance (C) should be obtained. If not, adjust the length of the thrust rod by turning the adjusting screw to suit. After the final adjustment is obtained, apply a few drops of locking compound, such as Loctite®, to the adjusting nut.

5. Position the master cylinder and reservoir assembly onto the studs for the booster, and install the washers and nuts. Tighten the nuts to 17 ft lbs.

6. Remove the plugs and connect the brake lines.

7. Bleed the entire brake system.

164, 1800 series

1. Follow steps 1–3 under "Master Cylinder Removal and Installation" for the 140 series.

CAUTION: *Do not depress the brake pedal while the master cylinder is removed.*

2. To install, place a new sealing ring onto the sealing flange of the master cylinder. Position the master cylinder and reservoir assembly onto the booster studs, and install the washers and nuts. Tighten the nuts to 8.7–10.8 ft lbs.

3. Remove the plugs and loosely connect the brake lines. Have a friend depress the brake pedal to remove air from the cylinder. Tighten the nuts for the lines when brake fluid (free of air bubbles) is forced out.

4. Bleed the entire brake system.

Master Cylinder Overhaul

140 series, 240, 260 series

1. Remove the master cylinder from the booster as outlined in the applicable "Master Cylinder Removal and Installation" section.

2. Firmly fasten the flange of the master cylinder in a vise.

3. Position both hands beneath the reservoir and pull it free of its rubber seals. Remove the filler cap and strainer from the reservoir, as well as the rubber seals and nuts (if so equipped) from the cylinder.

4. Remove the stop screw. Using a pair of snap-ring pliers, remove the snap-ring

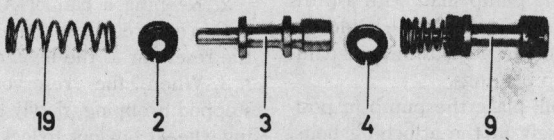

Master cylinder disassembled (with type 1 secondary piston)—140 series.

2. Piston seal	12. Circlip
3. Secondary piston	13. Cylinder housing
4. Piston seal	17. Sealing washer
9. Primary piston (assembled)	18. Stop screw
11. Thrust washer	19. Return spring

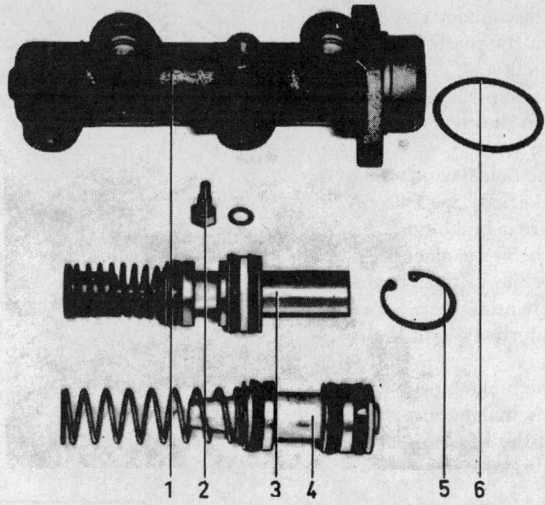

Master cylinder disassembled—164, 1800 series.

1. Cylinder housing
2. Stop screw
3. Primary piston
4. Secondary piston
5. Circlip
6. Sealing ring

from the primary piston and shake out the piston. If the secondary piston remains lodged in the bore, it may be forced out by blowing air into the stoplight switch hole.

5. Remove both the seals from the secondary piston, taking care not to damage or score the surfaces of the plunger. The old primary piston should be discarded and replaced.

6. Clean all reusable metal parts in clean brake fluid or methylated alcohol. The parts may be allowed to thoroughly air dry, or compressed air may be used. At any rate, all alcohol must be removed from the parts, as alcohol lowers the boiling temperature of brake fluid. If the inside of the cylinder is scored or scratched, the cylinder must be replaced. Minor pitting or corrosion may be removed by honing. Remember to flush the cylinder clean after honing, and make sure that the passages are clear. Check the piston for damage and proper clearance in the bore.

7. Install new seals on the secondary piston, making sure that they are positioned in the proper direction.

8. Coat the cylinder bore with brake fluid and dip the secondary piston and seals in brake fluid prior to installation. Slide the spring, spring plate, and washer onto the secondary piston and install the assembly in the bore, taking care not to damage the seals. Dip the new primary piston and seal assembly in brake fluid. Press the primary piston assembly into the bore and install a new washer and snap-ring.

9. Make sure that the hole for the stop screw is clear and install the new stop screw and sealing washer. Torque the screw to 7–9 ft lbs.

10. Check the movement of the pistons and make sure that the flow-through holes are clear. The equalizing hole is checked by inserting a 25 gauge soft copper wire through it and making sure that it is not blocked by the secondary piston seal. If it is blocked, then the master cylinder is incorrectly assembled, and you must take it through the numbers once more.

11. Install the nuts (if so equipped), new rubber seals, and washers onto the master cylinder at the reservoir connections. After making sure that the venting hole in the cap is open, install the cleaned strainer and cap. Press the reservoir into the master cylinder by hand. If the stoplight switch was removed, reinstall it.

12. Install the master cylinder as outlined in the applicable "Master Cylinder Removal and Installation" section.

164, 1800 series

1. Remove the master cylinder from the booster as outlined in the applicable "Master Cylinder Removal and Installation" section.

2. Follow steps 2–4 under "Master Cylinder Overhaul" for the 140 series.

3. Discard both the primary and secondary pistons.

4. Clean all reusable metal parts in clean brake fluid or methylated alcohol. The parts must be thoroughly dried with filtered, water-free compressed air, or air dried. All cleaning alcohol must be removed from the parts, as it lowers the boiling temperature of brake fluid. If the inside of the cylinder is scored or scratched, the cylinder must be replaced. Minor pitting and corrosion may be removed by honing. Remember to flush the cylinder clean after honing, and make sure that the passages are clear.

Check the cylinder bore for excessive wear.

5. Make sure that new rubber seals, a new brass washer and back-up ring are installed on the new secondary piston. Make sure that the rubber seals are pointing in the right direction.

6. Coat the cylinder bore with brake fluid and dip the secondary piston and seals in brake fluid prior to installation. Install the secondary piston and spring in the bore, taking care not to damage the rubber seals.

7. Make sure that the new rubber seals, metal washers, plastic washer, back-up ring, sleeve, and spring are installed on the new primary piston. Make sure that the seals are facing in the right direction.

8. On 1800 models, compress the primary piston spring and tighten the screw for the sleeve until it bottoms. Torque the screw to 1.5–2.2 ft lbs.

9. Dip the primary piston assembly in brake fluid and install it in the bore, taking care not to damage the rubber seals. While holding the piston in the bore, install the snap-ring.

10. Check that the hole for the stop screw is clear, and install the new stop screw and sealing washer. Torque the screw to 3.5–5.7 ft lbs on all 164 models and 1972 and later 1800 series models.

11. Check the movement of the pistons and make sure that the flow-through holes are clear. The equalizing hole is checked by inserting a 25 gauge (1800) or 22 gauge (164) soft copper wire through it and making sure that it is not blocked by the secondary piston seal. If it is blocked, the master cylinder will not function properly and must be reassembled.

12. Install the nuts (if so equipped), new rubber seals and washers onto the master cylinder at the reservoir connections. After making sure that the venting hole in the cap is open, install the cleaned strainer and cap. Press the reservoir into the master cylinder by hand. If the stoplight switch was removed, reinstall it.

13. Install the master cylinder as outlined in the applicable "Master Cylinder Removal and Installation" section.

Brake System Warning Valve

The brake system warning valve is located near the master cylinder in the engine compartment. The valve is centered by hydraulic pressure from the primary circuit on one side and the secondary circuit on the other. When a hydraulic imbalance exists, such as a leak in one of the calipers, the valve will move off-center toward the system with the leak and, therefore, the lowest pressure.

Volvo

When the valve moves off-center, it closes a circuit to a warning light on the dashboard, warning the driver of the imbalance. Sometimes, the valve will actuate the warning light when one of the systems is bled during normal maintenance. When this happens, the valve has to be reset.

Valve Resetting

1. Disconnect the plug contact and screw out the warning switch so that the pistons inside the valve may return to their normal position.
2. Repair and bleed the faulty hydraulic circuit.
3. Screw in the warning switch and tighten it to a torque of 10–14 ft lbs. Connect the plug contact.

Valve Replacement

1. Placing a rag beneath the valve to catch the brake fluid, loosen the pipe connections, and disconnect the six brake lines. Disconnect the electrical plug contact, and lift out the valve.
2. Connect the new warning valve in the reverse order of removal, and connect the plug contact.
3. Bleed the entire brake system.

Brake System Proportioning Valves

Each of the brake circuits has a proportioning (relief) valve located inline between the rear wheels. The purpose of these valves is to ensure that brake pressure on all four wheels compensates for the change in weight distribution under varied braking conditions. The harder the brakes are applied, the more weight there is on the front wheels. The valves regulate the hydraulic pressure to the rear wheels so that under hard braking conditions, they receive a smaller percentage of the total braking effort. This prevents premature rear wheel lock-up when the brakes are applied in emergency situations.

Valve Replacement

Sophisticated pressure testing equipment is required to troubleshoot the dual hydraulic system in order to determine if the proportioning valve(s) are in need of replacement. However, if the car is demonstrating signs of rear wheel lock-up under moderate to heavy braking pressure, and other variables such as tire pressure, tread depth, etc. have been ruled out, the valve(s) may be at fault. Rebuilding kits are available from the dealer for the valves in 1972 and earlier model Volvos. However, the valves installed in 1973 and later models are not rebuildable, and must be replaced as a unit.

1. Unscrew, disconnect and plug the brake pipe from the master cylinder, at the valve connection.
2. Slacken the connection for the flexible brake hose to the rear wheel a *maximum* of ¼ turn.
3. Remove the bolt(s) which retain the valve to the underbody, and unscrew the valve from the rear brake hose.
4. To install the valve, place a new seal on it, and screw the valve onto the rear brake hose and hand tighten. Secure the valve to the underbody with the retaining bolt(s).
5. Connect the brake pipe and tighten both connections, making sure that there is no tension on the flexible rear hose.
6. Bleed the brake system.

Bleeding Hydraulic System

Whenever a spongy brake pedal indicates that there is air in the system, or when any part of the hydraulic system has been removed for service, the system must be bled. In addition, if the level in the master cylinder reservoir is allowed to go below the minimum mark for too long a period of time, air may enter the system, necessitating bleeding.

If only one brake caliper or wheel cylinder is removed for servicing, it is usually only necessary to bleed that unit. If, however, the master cylinder, warning valve, or any of the main brake lines are removed, the entire system must be bled.

Be careful not to spill any brake fluid onto the brake disc or pads or drum and linings and, of course, the paintwork. When bleeding the entire system, the rear of the car should be raised higher than the front. Only use brake fluid bearing the designation SAE 1703 (SAE 70 R3), DOT 3, or DOT 4. Never reuse old brake fluid.

1. Check to make sure that there are

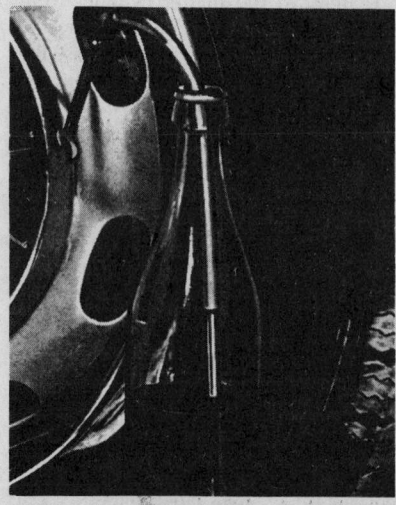

Bleeding front wheel caliper—rear caliper similar.

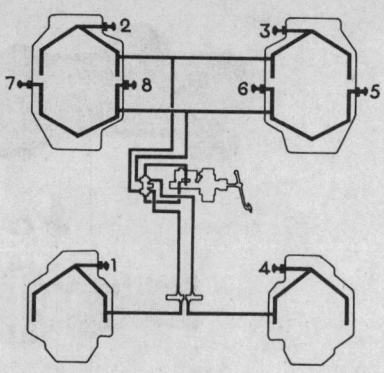

Bleeding sequence—140 series, 164, with Girling brakes.

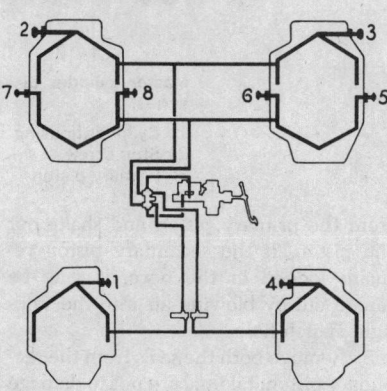

Bleeding sequence—140 series, 164, with ATE brakes.

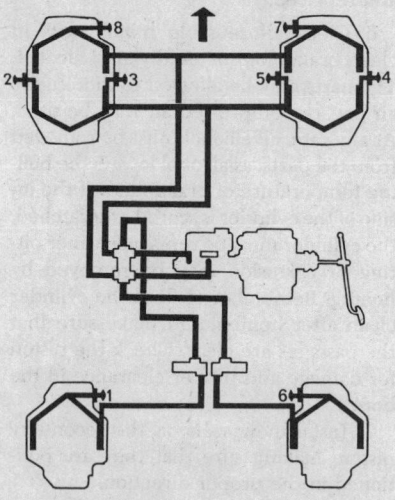

Bleeding sequence—1800 series

no mats or other materials obstructing the travel of the brake pedal. During bleeding, the full pedal travel should be 6 in. for the 140 series, and 5.5 in. for the 164 and 1800 series (providing that both circuits are bled simultaneously)
2. Disconnect the plug contact, and unscrew the electric switch from the warning valve.
3. Clean the cap and the top of the master cylinder reservoir, and make sure that the vent hole in the cap is open. Fill the reservoir to the maximum mark, if necessary. Never allow the level to dip

below the minimum mark during bleeding, as this will allow air into the system.

4. If only one brake caliper or wheel cylinder was removed, it will usually suffice to bleed only that wheel. Otherwise, prepare to bleed the entire system.

5. Remove the protective cap for the bleeder screw, and fit a 5/16 in. ring spanner wrench on the nipple. Install a tight fitting plastic hose onto the nipple, and insert the other end of the hose into a glass bottle containing clean brake fluid. The hose must hang down below the surface of the fluid, or air will be sucked into the system when the brake pedal is released. Open the bleeder screw a maximum of ½ turn. Slowly depress the brake pedal until it bottoms, pause a second or two, and then quickly release the pedal. This should be repeated until the fluid flowing into the bottle is completely free of air bubbles. Then have a friend press the pedal to the bottom and hold it there while you tighten the bleeder screw. Install the protective cap.

6. If the entire system is to be bled, follow the above procedure for the remaining nipples. Generally, it is sufficient to bleed each circuit once. However, if the pedal continues to feel spongy, repeat the bleeding sequence. Remember to keep the master cylinder reservoir level above the minimum mark.

7. Fill the reservoir with the specified brake fluid to the maximum mark.

8. Screw the electric switch into the warning valve and connect the plug contact. Tighten the switch to 10–14 ft lbs. Make sure that the warning light is actuated only when the parking brake is applied.

Stoplight Switch Adjustment

With the brake pedal in the released position, the distance (A) between the brass hub of the switch and the pedal lever should be 0.08–0.24 in. To adjust, loosen the attaching screws for the switch bracket and move the switch in the required direction.

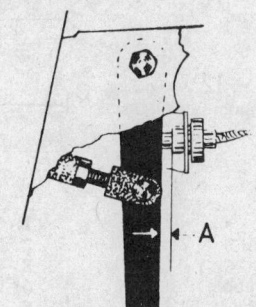

Stoplight switch adjustment

DISC BRAKES

Brake Pads

Removal and Installation

Girling Brakes

1. Remove the hub caps and loosen the lug nuts a few turns.

2. Raise the vehicle and place jackstands beneath the rear axle and the front jack attachments. Remove the wheel and tire assemblies.

3. Remove the hairpin-shaped locking clips, one lock pin then the other, together with the damping springs for the brake pads. Pull out the pads. Discard them if they are worn down to a lining thickness of ⅛ in. or less. If they are reusable, mark them for ease of assembly.

4. Carefully clean out the pad cavity. Replace any damaged dust covers. If any dirt has contaminated the cylinders, the caliper must be removed for overhaul. Inspect the brake disc as described under "Brake Discs—Inspection and Replacement".

5. Carefully depress the pistons in their cylinders so that the new pads will fit. This may be done with a screwdriver, but extra care must be exercised not to damage the rubber piston seals, the pistons, or the new pads themselves. A piston depressing tool (SVO 2809) is available from the dealer that accomplishes the job without danger to the caliper components. Remember that when the pistons are depressed in their bores, brake fluid is displaced causing the level in the master cylinder to rise, and perhaps, overflow.

6. Install the new pads and secure them with first one lock pin, then the other pin with the damping springs. Install new locking clips on the lock pins. Make sure that the pads are able to move and that the linings do not project outside

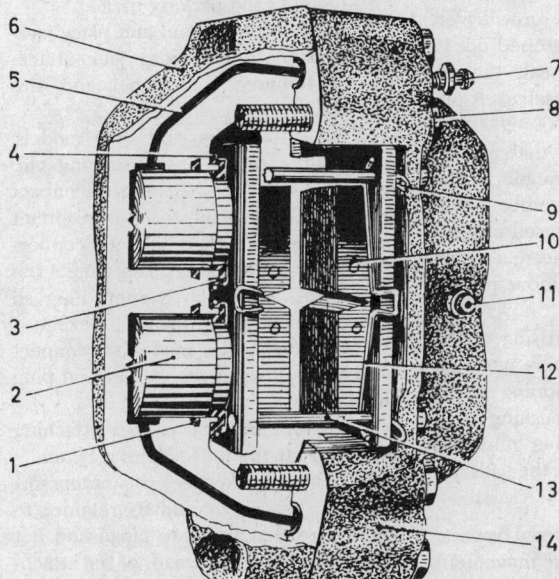

Girling front caliper assembly

1. Sealing ring
2. Piston
3. Rubber dust cover
4. Retaining ring
5. Channel
6. Outer half
7. Upper bleeder nipple
8. Bolt
9. Retaining clip
10. Brake pad
11. Lower bleeder nipple
12. Damping spring
13. Retaining pin
14. Inner half

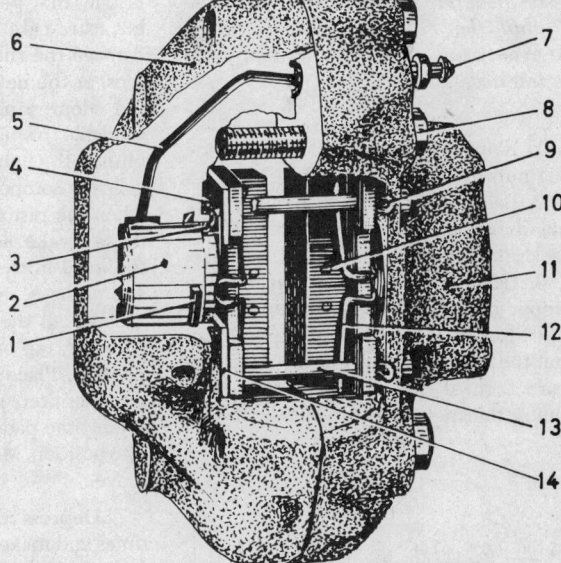

Girling rear caliper assembly

1. Sealing ring
2. Piston
3. Rubber dust cover
4. Retaining ring
5. Channel
6. Outer half
7. Bleeder nipple
8. Bolt
9. Retaining clip
10. Brake pad
11. Inner half
12. Damping spring
13. Retaining pin
14. Washer

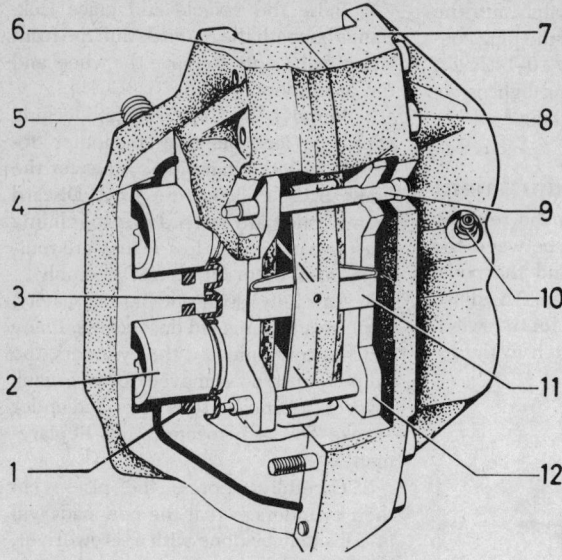

ATE front caliper assembly

1. Sealing ring
2. Piston
3. Rubber dust cover
4. Channel
5. Upper bleeder nipple
6. Outer half
7. Inner half
8. Bolt
9. Guide pin
10. Inner bleeder nipple
11. Damping spring
12. Brake pad

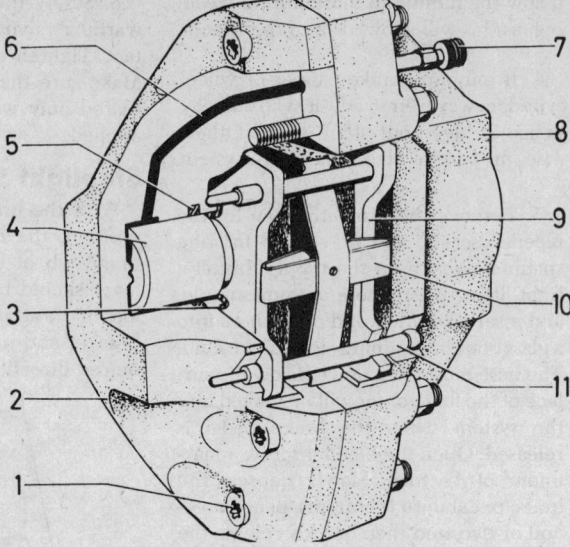

ATE rear caliper assembly

1. Bolt
2. Outer half
3. Rubber dust cover
4. Piston
5. Sealing ring
6. Channel
7. Bleeder nipple
8. Inner half
9. Brake pad
10. Damping spring
11. Guide pin

of the brake disc.

7. Depress the brake pedal several times and make sure that the movement feels normal. Bleeding is not usually necessary after pad replacement.

8. Clean the contact surfaces of the wheel and hub. Install the wheel and tire assemblies. Remove the jackstands and lower the vehicle. Tighten the lug nuts to 70–100 ft lbs, and install the hub cap.

NOTE: *If at all possible, braking should be moderate for the first 25 miles or so until the new pads seat correctly. Avoid panic stops in the beginning, unless necessary.*

Ate Brakes

1. Remove the hub caps and loosen the lug nuts a few turns.

2. Raise the vehicle and place jack stands beneath the rear axle and the front jack attachments.

3. Using a 9/64 in. drift, tap out the upper guide pin for the pads and remove and discard the tensioning spring. Tap out the lower pin. Pull out the pads. Discard them if they are worn down to a lining thickness of ⅛ in. or less. If they

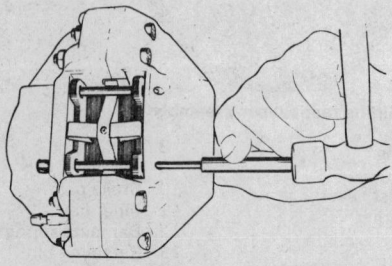

Removing guide pin—ATE brakes

are reusable, mark them for ease of assembly.

4. Carefully clean out the pad cavities. Replace any damaged dust covers. If any dirt has contaminated the cylinders, the caliper must be removed for overhaul. Inspect the brake disc as described under "Brake Discs—Inspection and Replacement".

5. Carefully depress the pistons in their cylinders so that the new pads will fit. This may be done with a screwdriver, but extra care must be exercised not to damage the rubber piston seals, the pistons, or the new pads themselves. A piston depressing tool (SVO 2809) is available from the dealer that accomplishes the job without danger to the caliper components. Remember that when the pistons are depressed in their bores, brake fluid is displaced, causing the level in the master cylinder to rise, and perhaps, overflow.

6. Install the new pads. Using only a hammer, tap one of the guide pins into position. Place a new tensioning spring into position, and while pushing it in against the pads, tap the other guide pin into position. Make sure that the pads can move.

7. Depress the brake pedal several times and make sure that the movement feels normal. Bleeding is not normally necessary after pad replacement.

8. Clean the contact surfaces of the wheel and hub. Install the wheel and tire assemblies. Remove the jackstands and lower the vehicle. Tighten the lug nuts to 70–100 ft lbs, and install the hub cap.

NOTE: *If at all possible, avoid hard or*

lengthy braking for the first 25 miles or so, until the new pads seat correctly.

Front Brake Caliper

Removal and Installation

1. Remove the hub cap and loosen the lug nuts a few turns. Block the reservoir cap vent hole to reduce leakage of brake fluid when the lines are disconnected. Firmly apply the parking brake.

2. Raise the front end and place jackstands beneath the front jack attachments. Remove the wheel and tire assembly.

3. On 140 series and 164 models, remove the brake hose retaining clip from the stabilizer bar, and disconnect the lower hose and secondary circuit brake pipe from their inboard connection underneath the car. Disconnect the upper hose from the caliper. Plug all brake connections to prevent leakage.

4. On 1800 series models, disconnect both brake lines at the caliper and plug them.

5. Remove the two caliper attaching bolts and lift the unit off the retainer.

6. To install, first check the mating surfaces of the caliper and its retainer to make sure that they are clean and not damaged. Coat the threads of the attaching bolts with a locking compound such as Loctite. Position the caliper to its retainer over the disc and install the two attaching bolts. Tighten the bolts to 65–70 ft lbs. Make sure that the caliper is parallel to the disc, and that the disc can rotate freely in the brake pads.

7. On 140 series and 164 models, con-

nect the lower brake hose and the secondary circuit brake pipe to their inboard connection and install the brake hose retaining clip to the stabilizer bar. Connect the upper brake hose to the caliper.

8. On 1800 series models, connect both brake lines to the caliper.

9. Unplug the reservoir cap vent hole. Install the wheel and tire assembly. Remove the jackstands and lower the car. Tighten the lug nuts to 70–100 ft lbs and install the hub cap.

10. Bleed the brake system as outlined under "Bleeding Hydraulic System".

Rear Brake Caliper

Removal and Installation

1. Remove the hub cap and loosen the lug nuts a few turns. Block the reservoir cap vent hole to reduce leakage of brake fluid when the line is disconnected.

2. Place blocks in front of the front wheels. Raise the rear of the car and place jackstands beneath the rear axle. Remove the wheel and tire assembly. Release the parking brake.

3. Disconnect the brake line from the caliper and plug it to prevent leakage.

4. Remove the two caliper attaching bolts and lift the unit off the retainer.

5. To install, first check the mating surfaces of the caliper and its retainer to make sure that they are clean and not damaged. Coat the threads of the attaching bolts with locking compound, such as Loctite type AV. Position the caliper to its retainer and install the two attaching bolts. Tighten the bolts to 45–50 ft lbs. Make sure that the caliper is parallel to the disc, and that the disc can rotate freely in the brake pads.

6. Connect the brake line to the caliper. Unplug the reservoir cap hole.

7. Install the wheel and tire assembly.

Remove the jackstands and lower the car. Tighten the lug nuts to 70–100 ft lbs, and install the hub cap.

8. Bleed the applicable rear brake caliper as outlined under "Bleeding Hydraulic System".

Caliper Overhaul

The following procedure applies to front calipers and rear calipers of both Girling and Ate design.

1. Remove the brake caliper from the car as outlined in the applicable "Caliper Removal and Installation" section.

2. Remove the brake pads as outlined in step 3 of the applicable "Brake Pad Removal and Installation" section.

3. Remove the retaining rings and the rubber dust covers. Place a wooden block (1) between the pistons. Using compressed air applied through the brake line connection, force the pistons toward the wooden block. Remove the pistons from their bores, taking care not to burr or scratch them.

4. Remove the sealing rings with a blunt plastic tool. Be careful not to damage the edges of the grooves. Screw out the bleeder nipple(s), and on front calipers, remove the external connecting pipe.

NOTE: *It is not necessary to separate the caliper halves. Assembling the halves would require special pressure testing equipment.*

5. Clean all reusable metal parts in clean brake fluid or methylated alcohol. Dry all parts with compressed air or allow to air dry. Make sure that all of the passages are clear. All alcohol must be removed from the parts as alcohol lowers the boiling temperature of brake fluid. If any of the cylinders are scored or scratched, the entire housing must be replaced. Minor scratching may be removed from the pistons by fine polish-

ing. Replace any piston that is damaged or worn.

6. Coat the mating surfaces of the pistons and cylinders with brake fluid.

7. Install new sealing rings in the cylinders.

8. On Girling brakes and Ate front brakes, press the pistons into their bores with the large diameter end facing inward. Make sure that the pistons are installed straight and are not scratched in the process.

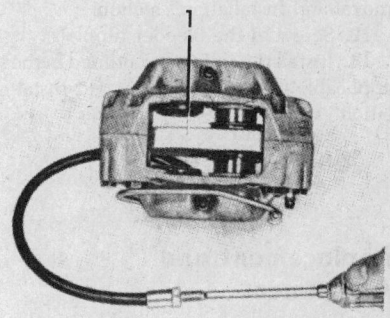

Removing pistons with compressed air

9. On Ate rear brakes, check to make sure that the pistons are in the proper positions to prevent brake squeal. The piston recess should incline 20° in relation to the lower guide area on the caliper. Check the location of the piston with template SVO 2919. When the template is placed against the one recess, the distance (A) to the other recess may be no greater than 0.039 in. If the location of

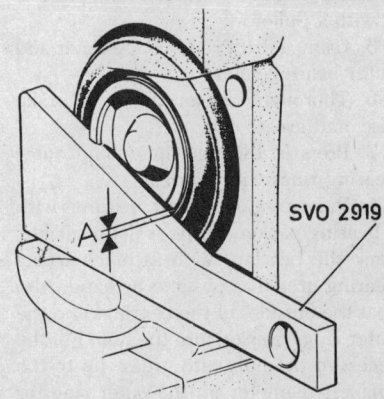

Checking location of rear caliper pistons—ATE brakes.

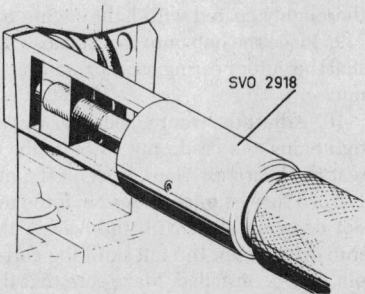

Adjusting location of rear caliper pistons—ATE brakes.

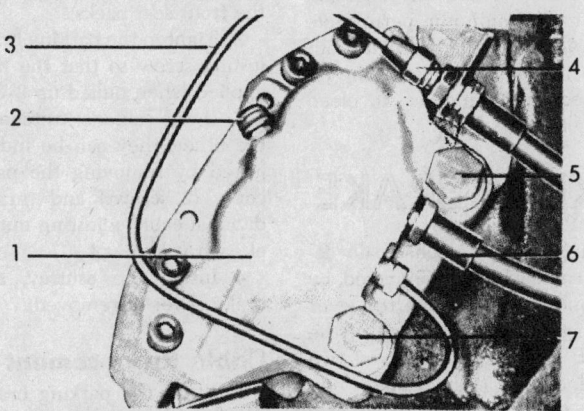

Front caliper installed—ATE shown, Girling similar

1. Front wheel brake caliper
2. Lower bleeder nipple
3. Upper bleeder nipple
4. Connection for lower wheel unit cylinder
5. Attaching bolt
6. Connection for upper wheel unit cylinder
7. Attaching bolt

the piston needs adjusting, press SVO 2918 against the piston and force out the shoes by screwing in the handle. Turn the piston in the required direction, release the tool, and re-measure with the template. Repeat this operation for the other piston.

10. Place the new rubber dust covers on the pistons and housing. Install the new retaining rings.

11. Install the brake pads as outlined in step 6 of the applicable "Brake Pad Removal and Installation" section.

12. Screw in the bleeder nipple(s).

13. Install the caliper as outlined in the applicable "Caliper Removal and Installation" section.

Front Wheel Bearings

Replacement and Adjustment

1. Remove the hub cap, and loosen the lug nuts a few turns.

2. Firmly apply the parking brake. Jack up the front of the car and place jackstands beneath the lower control arms. Remove the wheel and tire assembly.

3. Remove the front caliper as outlined in "Front Caliper Removal and Installation".

4. Pry off the grease cap. Remove the cotter pin and castle nut. Use a hub puller to pull off the hub. If the inner bearing remains lodged on the stub axle, remove it with a puller.

5. Using a drift, remove the inner and outer bearing rings.

6. Thoroughly clean the hub, brake disc, and grease cap.

7. Press in the new inner and outer bearing rings with a drift.

8. Press grease into both bearings with a bearing packer. If one is not available, pack the bearings with as much wheel bearing grease as possible by hand. Also coat the outsides of the bearings and the outer rings pressed into the hub. Fill the recess in the hub with grease up to the smallest diameter on the outer ring for the outer bearing. Place the inner bearing in position in the hub and press its seal in with a drift. The felt ring should be thoroughly coated with light engine oil.

9. Place the hub onto the stub axle. Install the outer bearing, washer, and castle nut.

10. Adjust the front wheel bearings by tightening the castle nut to 50 ft lbs to seat the bearings. Then, back off the nut 1/3 of a turn counterclockwise. If the nut slot does not align with the hole in the stub axle, loosen the nut until the cotter pin may be installed. Make sure that the wheel spins freely without any side play.

11. Fill the grease cap halfway with wheel bearing grease, and install it on the hub.

12. Install the front caliper as outlined in "Front Caliper Removal and Installation".

13. Install the wheel and tire assembly. Remove the jackstands and lower the car. Tighten the lug nuts to 70–100 ft lbs, and install the hub cap.

Brake Discs

Inspection and Replacement

Remove the hub cap, loosen the lug nuts, raise the car, and remove the wheel and tire assembly. The friction surface on both sides of the disc should be examined for surface deviations such as scoring or corrosion. Minor radial scratches and small rust spots may be removed by turning or fine polishing the disc. The lateral run-out of the disc must not exceed 0.004 in. for the front, and 0.006 in. for the rear, measured at the outer edge of the disc. Do not mistake a faulty wheel bearing adjustment, or an improperly mounted disc for lateral runout. Actual disc thickness, which varies from model to model (see specifications), should not vary more than 0.0012 in. when taken at several points on the same disc. If the disc is worn at any point to less than the minimum permissible thickness (see specifications), it must be replaced.

When removing the disc, either to have it machined or replaced, the brake line must be disconnected from the caliper and plugged, the two bolts attaching the caliper to its retainer removed, and the caliper lifted off. The disc is then removed by unscrewing its two philips head retaining screws and rapping on the inside of the disc with a plastic hammer or rubber mallet. Machining should be performed in unit with the hub, and should be equal on both sides. After machining, recheck the disc thickness and compare it to the minimum permissible thickness value on the specifications chart. To install the disc, reverse the removal procedure, taking care to bleed the brake caliper.

PARKING BRAKE

The parking brake is mechanically actuated by a cable which is connected, by means of a pull rod and linkage, to a lever mounted on the floor to the left of the driver's seat. The brake consists of two miniature duo-servo drum brakes, one mounted at each end of the rear axle housing inside the hub of the rear brake discs.

Adjustment

1972–74 Models

The parking brake should be fully engaged when the lever is pulled up to the third or fourth notch. If it does not, adjust as follows.

1. Apply the parking brake. Remove the rear hub caps and loosen the lug nuts a few turns.

2. Place blocks in front of the front wheels. Jack up the rear end and place jackstands beneath the rear axle. Remove the wheel and tire assemblies. Release the parking brake.

3. Make sure that the brake pads are not stuck to their discs. Disconnect the cable from the lever.

4. Rotate the disc until the adjusting screw hole aligns with the serrations on the adjusting screw. Insert a screwdriver, and adjust the shoes by moving the handle of the screwdriver upward. When the disc cannot be rotated easily, stop adjusting the shoes. Turn the adjusting screw back 4 or 5 serrations. Make sure that the shoes do not drag by hand turning the disc in its normal direction of rotation. A slight drag is permissible. However, if there is a heavy drag, back off the adjusting screw 2 or 3 serrations more. Connect the cable to the lever.

5. Repeat the adjusting procedure for the other wheel.

6. Apply the parking brake lever and make sure that the parking brake is fully engaged with the lever at the third or fourth notch. If not, tighten the cable. This is accomplished by loosening the locknuts and screwing in the block on the pull rod. After adjusting, tighten the locknuts. Make sure that there is approximately the same braking effect on both rear wheels.

7. Install the wheel and tire assemblies. Remove the jackstands and lower the car. Tighten the lug nuts to 70–100 ft lbs and install the hub caps.

1975–77 Models

1. Remove the rear ashtray (between the front seat backs).

2. Tighten the parking brake cable adjusting screw so that the brake is fully applied when pulled up 2–3 notches.

3. If one cable is stretched more than the other, they can be individually adjusted by removing the parking brake cover (2 screws) and turning the individual cable adjusting nut at the front of each yoke pivot.

4. Install the ashtray, and parking brake cover (if removed).

Cable Replacement

1. Apply the parking brake. Remove the hub caps for the rear wheels and loosen the lug nuts a few turns.

2. Place blocks in front of the front wheels. Jack up the rear end and place jackstands beneath the rear axle. Remove the wheel and tire assembly. Release the parking brake.

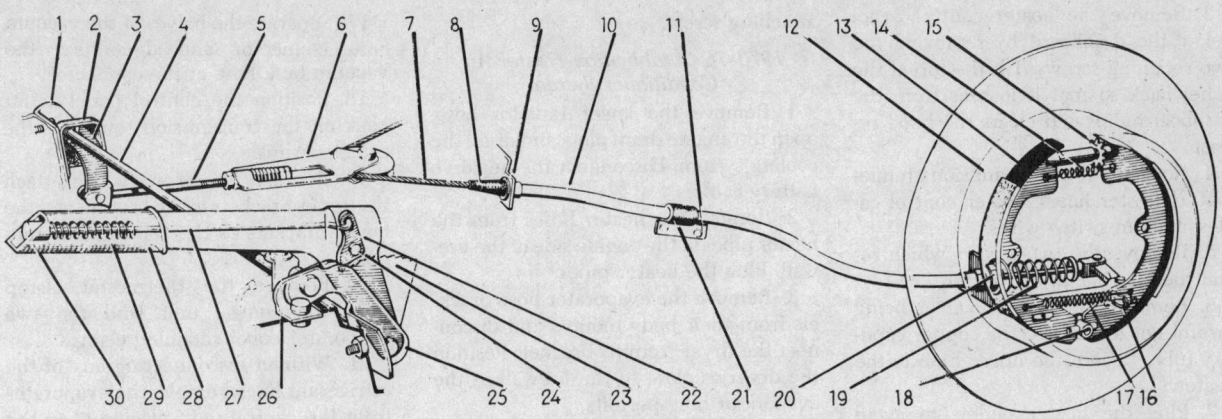

Parking brake—1972-74 140, 1972-75 164 and 1972-73 1800

1. Inside support attachment
2. Rubber cover
3. Lever
4. Shaft
5. Pull rod
6. Block
7. Rubber cover
9. Front attachment
10. Cable sleeve
11. Attachment

12. Brake drum
13. Brake shoe (secondary shoe)
14. Return spring
15. Adjusting device
16. Lever
17. Movable rod
18. Anchor bolt
19. Return spring
20. Rear attachment
21. Rubber cable guide

22. Pawl
23. Ratchet segment
24. Rivet
25. Outside support
    attachment
26. Warning valve switch
27. Push rod
28. Parking brake lever
29. Spring
30. Push button

Adjusting parking brake (vehicles equipped with rear disc brakes).

3. Remove the bolt and the wheel from the pulley.

4. Remove the rubber cover for the front attachment of the cable sleeve and nut, as well as the attachment for the rubber suspension ring on the frame. Remove the cable from the other side of the attachment in the same manner.

5. Hold the return spring in position. Pry up the lock and remove the lock pin so that the cable releases from the lever.

6. Remove the return spring with washers. Loosen the nut for the rear attachment of the cable sleeve. Lift the cable forward, after loosening both sides of the attachments, and remove it.

6. To install, first adjust the rear brake shoes of the parking brake as outlined in steps 3, 4, and 5 under "Parking Brake Adjustment".

7. Install new rubber cable guides for the cable suspension. Place the cable in position in the rear attachment and tighten the nut. Install the washers and return spring. Oil the lock pin and install it, together with the cable, on the lever. Install the attachment and rubber cable guide on the frame.

8. Install the cable in the same manner on the side of the vehicle.

9. Place the cable sleeve in position in the front attachments and install the rubber covers.

10. Lubricate and install the pulley on the pull rod. Adjust the pulley so that the parking brake is fully engaged with the lever at the third or fourth notch.

11. Install the wheel and tire assemblies. Remove the jackstands and lower the vehicle. Tighten the lug nut to 70–100 ft lbs and install the hub caps.

Parking Brake Shoe Replacement

1. Remove the rear ashtray and back off the adjusting screw so that the cable goes slack.
2. Jack up and support the rear end.
3. Remove the wheels.
4. Remove the brake line-to-axle clamp.
5. Remove the caliper retaining bolts and suspend the caliper out of the way.
6. Unbolt and remove the brake drum.
7. Unhook the return springs and remove the shoes.
8. Install in reverse of the above. Adjust the parking brake.

CHASSIS ELECTRICAL

Heater

Heater Unit Removal and Installation

140 series, 164, 240 series

1972

1. Remove the lower radiator hose, open the engine drain plug, and drain the cooling system. Disconnect the negative battery cable.

2. Remove the control valve hoses.

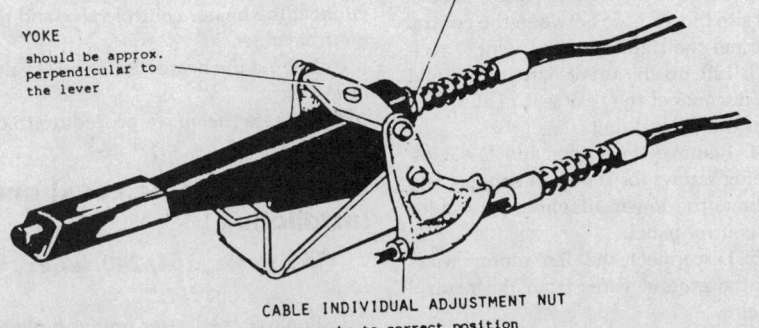

MAIN ADJUSTING SCREW

YOKE
should be approx. perpendicular to the lever

CABLE INDIVIDUAL ADJUSTMENT NUT
adjust yoke to correct position

Parking brake cable adjustment—1975-77

Volvo

3. Remove the heater control panel below the dashboard by removing the two retaining screws. Tilt the top of the panel back so that it loosens from the dashboard clips and clears the hood release.

4. Remove the transmission tunnel mat, defroster hoses, heater control cables, and fan switch wires.

5. Remove the two screws which retain the fuse box to the heater.

6. Remove the control valve, being careful not to damage the copper capillary tube. Loosen the upper hose to the heater.

7. Plug the heater outlets to avoid spilling coolant upon removal. Loosen the heater unit ground cables, remove the four retaining screws, loosen the drain hose, and lift out the heater unit and control valve from their brackets.

8. Reverse the above procedure to install.

1973–76 Standard Heating System

1. Remove the lower radiator hose, open the engine drain plug, and drain the cooling system. Disconnect the negative battery cable.

2. Remove the center panel and the left-hand defroster hose.

3. Lift up the driveshaft tunnel mat, disconnect the front and rear attaching screws of the rear seat heater ducts, and then remove the ducts from the heater.

4. Disconnect the heater control valve and air-mix cables from their shutters.

5. Disconnect and plug the pressure hose at the heater. Also plug the heater pipes to prevent residual coolant from spilling onto the carpet.

6. Remove the attaching screws which secure the left-hand upper bracket to the dashboard and the left-hand lower bracket to the transmission tunnel.

7. Remove the glovebox by unscrewing the four attaching screws, removing the glovebox door stop, and disconnecting the wires from the glovebox courtesy light.

8. Disconnect the defroster and floor heating cables from their levers.

9. Disconnect the fan motor wires at the switch contact plate.

10. Remove the attaching screws which secure the right-hand upper bracket to the dashboard and the right-hand lower bracket to the transmission tunnel.

11. Remove the right-hand defroster hose. Disconnect the hose between the heater and the dashboard circular vents. Lift the heater unit to the right, and then out of the vehicle.

12. Reverse the above procedure to install, taking care to ensure that the air vent rubber seal is properly located, and that the fan motor ground cable is attached to the upper right-hand bracket

attaching screw.

1973–76 Combination Heater-Air Conditioner System

1. Remove the lower radiator hose, open the engine drain plug, and drain the cooling system. Disconnect the negative battery cable.

2. Remove the heater hoses from the heater pipes at the engine side of the firewall. Plug the heater pipes.

3. Remove the evaporator hose brackets from their body mounts and disconnect the dryer from its bracket. Position the dryer as close to the firewall as the evaporator hose permits.

4. Remove the instrument cluster by removing the steering column molded casings, removing the bracket retaining screw and lowering it toward the steering column, removing the four instrument cluster retaining screws, disconnecting the speedometer cable, tilting the speedometer out of its snap fitting, moving the cluster forward and disconnecting the electrical plug contacts, then lifting the cluster out of the vehicle.

5. Remove the air hose between the central unit and the left inner air vent. Remove the hose from the vacuum motor for the left defroster nozzle.

6. Remove the left-side panel from the central unit.

7. Lift up the driveshaft tunnel mat and disconnect the rear seat heater duct from the central unit.

8. Remove the heater pipes from the passenger side of the firewall.

9. Remove the upper and lower attaching screws for the left support leg. Remove the attaching screws which secure the upper bracket to the dashboard and the lower bracket to the transmission tunnel.

NOTE: If the upper bracket screw holes are slotted, the screws need only be slackened a few turns.

10. Remove the right-side panel from the central unit.

11. Remove the glovebox by unscrewing the four attaching screws, removing the glovebox door stop, and disconnecting the glovebox courtesy light wires.

12. Remove the right defroster nozzle, and also the air hose between the central unit and the right inner air vent.

13. Lift up the driveshaft tunnel mat and disconnect the rear seat heater duct from the central unit.

14. Remove the upper and lower attaching screws for the right support leg. Remove the lower attaching screws for the control panel.

15. Disconnect the fan motor wires and the ground wires from the control panel.

16. Disconnect the yellow lead cable from its plug contact.

17. Separate the halves of the vacuum hose connector and disconnect the vacuum tank hose at the connector.

18. Position the control panel as far back on the transmission tunnel as the cables permit.

19. Remove the screws which attach the upper brackets to the firewall and the lower brackets to the transmission tunnel.

20. Remove the thermostat clamp from the central unit, and the two evaporator cover retaining clamps.

21. Without disconnecting any of the refrigerant lines, remove the evaporator from the central unit, placing it on the right-hand side of the firewall.

22. Remove the molded dashboard padding from beneath the glovebox.

23. Remove the retaining clamps for the right outer vent duct, and remove the duct. Pry off the locking retainer for the turbine (blower), and remove the turbine. Remove the clamps which retain the blower housing (inner end) to the central unit and remove the housing.

24. Remove the passenger's front seat cushion and lift the central unit forward and onto the floor of the vehicle. Be careful not to place undue stress on the connected refrigerant lines.

25. Reverse the above procedure to install, taking care to ensure that the evaporator pipes and thermostat capillary are enclosed in sealing compound, that the drainage tubes are inserted in their respective transmission tunnel holes, and that the ground cables are connected.

1800 series

1. Disconnect the lower radiator hose, open the engine drain plug, and drain the cooling system. Disconnect the negative battery cable.

2. Disconnect the heater hoses from the heater core pipe and the control valve pipe. Disconnect the fan motor wires.

3. Disconnect the fresh air intake from the heater.

4. Remove the four heater-to-firewall attaching nuts.

5. Remove the defroster hoses. Disconnect the heater control valve and the control cables.

6. Lift out the heater and control valve as a unit.

7. Reverse the above procedure to install.

Blower Motor Removal and Installation

140 series, 164, 240 series

1972

1. Remove the heater unit as outlined in "Heater Unit Removal and Installation."

2. Remove the four rubber bushings on the sides of the heater unit.

3. Scribe marks on both sides of the fan housing to facilitate assembly. Remove the spring clips and separate the housing halves.

4. Mark the mounting plate's relative position to the fan housing. Straighten the tabs and separate the mounting plate from the housing.

5. Remove the retaining screws and separate the fan motor from the mounting plate.

6. Reverse the above procedure to install, being careful to apply soft sealer to the housing halves.

1973–76 Standard Heating System

1. Remove the heater unit as outlined in "Heater Unit Removal and Installation."

2. Place the unit on its side with the control valve facing upward. Remove the spring clips and separate the housing halves.

3. Lift out the old fan motor and replace it with a new unit, making sure that the support leg without the "foot" points to the output for the defroster channel.

4. Assemble the heater housing halves with new spring clips, and seal the joint without clips with soft sealing compound.

5. Install the heater unit as outlined in "Heater Unit Removal and Installation."

1973–76 Combination Heater-Air Conditioner System

In order to remove the blower motor, both the right and left turbines (blower wheels) must first be removed. The heater unit does not have to be removed.

1. Disconnect the negative battery cable.

2. Lift the carpet and remove the central unit side panels.

3. Remove the retaining screws for the control panel and move the panel as far back on the transmission tunnel as the electrical cables will permit.

4. Remove the attaching screws for the rear seat heater ducts and disconnect the ducts from the central unit.

5. Remove the instrument cluster as outlined in "Instrument Cluster Removal and Installation."

6. Remove the glovebox by unscrewing the four attaching screws, removing the glovebox door stop, and disconnecting the wires from the glovebox courtesy light. Remove the molded dashboard padding from beneath the glovebox.

7. Disconnect the vacuum hoses to the left and right defroster nozzle vacuum motors, then remove the nozzles and the left and right air ducts.

8. Remove the air hoses between the left and right inside air vents.

9. Remove the clamps on the central unit outer ends, and remove the ends.

10. Pry off the locking retainer for the

turbines (blower wheels), and remove both left and right turbines.

11. Position the heater control valve capillary tube to one side.

12. Remove the left inner end (blower housing) from the central unit.

13. Unscrew the three retaining screws and remove the fan motor retainer.

14. Disconnect the plug contact from the fan motor control panel. Release the tabs of the electric cables from the plug contact, and, removing the rubber grommet, pull the electrical cables down through the central unit right opening.

15. Remove the fan motor from the left opening.

16. Reverse the above procedure to install.

1800 series

NOTE: *The fan motor and fan are replaced as a unit.*

1. Remove the valve cover and place a rag over the rocker arm assembly.

2. Disconnect the fan motor wires at the fan terminals.

3. Remove the six retaining screws and remove the fan motor from the heater assembly.

4. Reverse the above procedure to install.

Heater Core Removal and Installation

140 series, 164, 240 series

1972

1. Remove the heater unit as outlined in "Heater Unit Removal and Installation."

2. Remove the four rubber bushings on the sides of the heater unit.

3. Scribe marks on both sides of the fan housing to facilitate assembly. Remove the spring clips and separate the housing halves.

4. Separate the heater core from the housing half, taking care not to damage the sensitive body for the control valve.

5. Reverse the above procedure to install, being careful to apply soft sealer to the housing halves.

1973–76 Standard Heating System

1. Remove the heater unit as outlined in "Heater Unit Removal and Installation."

2. Place the unit on its side with the control valve facing upward. Remove the spring clips and separate the housing halves.

3. Disconnect the capillary tube from the heater core and then lift out the core.

4. Reverse the above procedure to install, being careful to transfer the foam plastic packing to the new heater core, and to install the fragile capillary tube carefully on the core.

1973–76 Combination Heater-Air Conditioner System

1. Remove the combination heater-air conditioner unit as outlined under "Heater Unit Removal and Installation."

2. Remove the left outer end of the central unit. Remove the locking retainer and the turbine (blower wheel).

3. Remove the two retaining screws for the left transmission tunnel bracket.

4. Remove the lockring for the left intake shutter shaft.

5. Remove the three retaining screws and lift off the inner end.

6. Remove the three retaining screws for the fan motor retainer.

7. Disconnect the heater hoses at the heater core.

8. Remove the clamps which retain the central unit halves together, lift off the left half, and remove the heater core.

9. Reverse the above procedure to install, taking care to transfer the foam plastic packing to the new heater core.

1800 series

1. Remove the heater unit as outlined in "Heater Unit Removal and Installation."

2. Remove the fan motor as outlined in "Blower Motor Removal and Installation."

3. Remove the screws securing the heater housing halves together and then separate the halves.

4. Remove the heater core from the housing.

5. Install the new or reconditioned core in the housing. Check the operation of the shutters for binding or looseness.

6. Install the thermostat capillary tube on the core.

7. Apply new soft sealing compound to the housing halves prior to assembly.

8. Reverse the above procedure to install.

Radio

Radio Removal and Installation

1. Disconnect the negative battery cable.

2. Remove the radio control knobs by pulling them straight out. Remove the control shaft retaining nuts.

3. Disconnect the speaker wires, the power lead (either at the fuse box or the in-line fuse connection), and the antenna cable from its jack on the radio.

4. Remove the hardware which attaches the radio to its mounting (support) bracket(s), and slide it back and down from the dash.

5. Reverse the above procedure to install.

Windshield Wipers

Motor Removal and Installation

140 series, 164, 240 series

1972

1. Disconnect the negative battery cable.
2. Remove the wiper arm and blade assemblies.
3. Remove the molded panel from under the dash.
4. Remove the heater switch.
5. Remove the instrument cluster as outlined in "Instrument Cluster Removal and Installation."
6. Remove the intermediate defroster nozzle and disconnect the hoses.
7. Remove the retaining bolts and lower the wiper motor.
8. Reverse the above procedure to install.

1973–76

1. Disconnect the negative battery cable.
2. Disconnect the drive link from the wiper motor lever by unsnapping the locking tab underneath the dashboard.
3. Open the hood and disconnect the plug contact from the motor, located on the firewall.
4. Remove the three attaching screws and lift out the motor.
5. Reverse the above procedure to install, taking care to transfer the rubber seal, rubber damper, and spacer sleeves to the new motor.

Windshield Wiper Unit (complete) Removal and Installation

1800 series

1. Disconnect the negative battery cable.
2. Remove the wiper arm and blade assemblies. Unscrew the wiper arm shaft retaining nuts, and then lift off the washers and rubber seals.
3. Disconnect the electrical wires at the wiper motor.

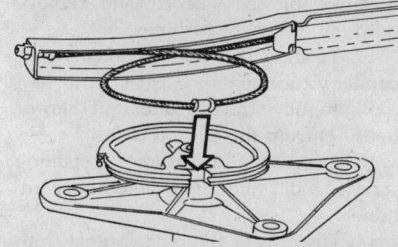

Installing cable for drive link and parallel drive link, left hand side—1973-75 140 series, 164, 240 series

4. Remove the two wiper motor retaining bolts and lower the motor and linkage assembly out from under the dash.
5. Reverse the above procedure to install.

Tailgate Window Wiper

Motor Removal and Installation

145

1. Disconnect the negative battery cable.
2. Remove the upholstered finish panel on the inside of the tailgate.
3. Remove the screws which retain the reinforcing bracket beneath the wiper motor.
4. Disconnect the wiper link arm. Bend the reinforcing bracket to one side and lower the wiper motor until it is clear of the bracket.
5. Disconnect the electrical wires from the motor and remove the motor.
6. Reverse the above procedure to install.

Instruments

Instrument Cluster Removal and Installation

A voltage stabilizer feeds a 10 V current to both the temperature gauges and the fuel gauge. Electrical malfunctions in these gauges must be checked with an ohmmeter, not a 12 V test light. If malfunctions occur simultaneously in all three of the gauges that are fed by the stabilizer, the stabilizer itself is probably malfunctioning. When replacing the voltage stabilizer, the new unit must fit in the same position as the old one. If the stabilizer is not located correctly in the dash, the voltage output may be altered.

140 series, 164, 240 series

1972

1. Disconnect the negative battery cable.
2. Remove the two screws which retain the control panel.
3. Remove the two retaining screws and lower the molded panel beneath the dashboard.
4. Pull the upper section of the cluster outward so it loosens from its retaining clips. Loosen the panel from the hood release mechanism.
5. Move the control panel—with the short side first—through the dashboard opening.
6. Disconnect the heater controls and the speedometer cable. Remove the flange nuts for the instrumentation.
7. Rotate the instrument cluster slightly, so that the electrical connections may be removed from the reverse side.
8. Lift out the cluster from the dashboard.
9. Reverse the above procedure to install.

1973–76

1. Disconnect the negative battery cable.
2. Remove the molded plastic casings from the steering column.
3. Remove the bracket retaining screw and lower the bracket toward the steering column.
4. Remove the cluster attaching screws.
5. Disconnect the speedometer cable.
6. Tilt the cluster out of its snap fitting and disconnect the plug contact. On vehicles equipped with a tachometer, disconnect the tachometer sending wire.
7. Lift the cluster out of the dashboard.
8. Reverse the above procedure to install.

1800 series

The 1800 series Volvos are equipped with a tachometer, coolant temperature gauge, oil temperature gauge, speedometer (with odometer, tripmeter, and warning lamps), fuel gauge, oil pressure gauge, and clock. Each of these instruments must be removed separately. When replacing an instrument, first disconnect the negative battery cable, then disconnect the electrical connections on the instrument's reverse side. Remove the retaining nuts and attaching bracket, and pull the instrument straight out.

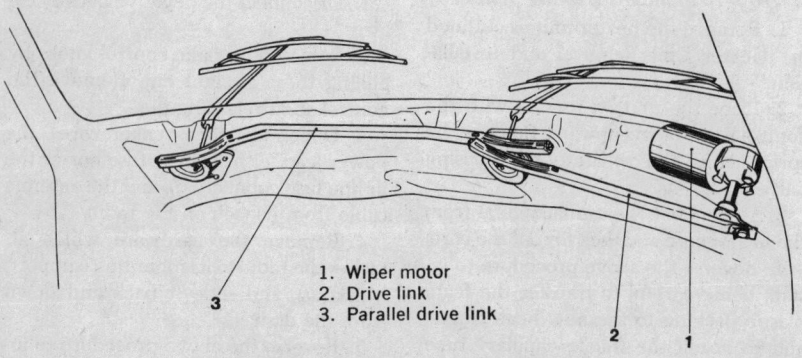

1. Wiper motor
2. Drive link
3. Parallel drive link

Windshield wiper unit—1973-75 140

1. Battery
2. Connection plate
3. Ignition switch
4. Ignition coil
5. Distributor
6. Spark plugs
7. Starter motor
8. Alternator
9. Voltage regulator
10. Fuse box
11. Light switch
12. Bulb integrity sensor
13. Step relay for upper and lower beams and headlight flasher
14. Upper beam
15. Lower beam
16. Position lamp
17. Tail lamp
18. Side marker lamp
19. License plate lamp
20. Stop light switch
21. Stop lamp
22. Conn at instrument
23. Contact on transmission
24. Back-up lamp
25. Flasher unit
26. Turn indicator lever
27. Hazard warning signal switch
28. Front turn signal lamp
29. Rear turn signal lamp
30. Conn at instrument
31. Conn at instrument

32. Brake failure pilot lamp
33. Conn at instrument
34. Tachometer
35. Thermometer
36. Fuel meter
37. Voltage stabilizer
38. Turn signal light pilot lamp
39. Diode
40. Upper beam pilot lamp
41. Bulb integrity sensor
42. Charging pilot lamp
43. Parking brake pilot lamp
44. Choke pilot lamp
45. Oil pressure pilot lamp
46. Contact, passenger's seat
47. Contact, driver's seat
48. Parking brake contact
49. Luggage comp. light
50. Temperature gauge
51. Oil pressure guard
52. Brake failure contact
53. Starter cut-out relay
54. Fuel level gauge
55. Horn
56. Horn ring
57. Windshield wiper/wash switch
58. Windshield wiper
59. Windshield washer
60. Fan switch
61. Fan
62. El heated rear window switch
63. El heated rear window

64. Clock
65. Cigar lighter
66. Instrument lighting rheostat
67. Instrument lighting
68. Control panel lighting
69. Gear Selector lighting
70. Glove box contact
71. Glove box lamp
72. Interior lamp
73. Door contact, driver's side
74. Door contact, passenger's side
75. EGR/CAT Warning lamp
76. Belt interlock unit
77. EGR/CAT Warning contact
78. Safety belt pilot lamp
79. Safety belt contact, pass. seat
80. Safety belt contact, driver's seat
81. Junction
82. Overdrive lever M 410
83. Overdrive contact on transmission M 410
84. Overdrive solenoid on transmission M 410
85. Overdrive pilot lamp
86. Buckle lighting
87. Relay for window lifts
88. Supplementary air valve
89. Heating element with thermostat, driver's seat

90. Heating element, driver's seat
91. Switch for window lift r.h.
92. Switch for window lift l.h.
93. Switch for compressor
94. Thermostat
95. Solenoid on compressor
96. Solenoid valve
97. Relay for fuel pump
98. Main relay, fuel injection
99. Starting valve
100. Temperature-time contact
101. Injection control unit
102. Fuel pump
103. Flop valve contact
104. Pressure sensor
105. Temperature sensor I
106. Temperature sensor II
107. Injection valves
108. Release contact
109. Resistor
110. Rear ash tray lighting
111. Engine comp. lighting
112. Motor for window lift r.h.
113. Motor for window lift l.h.
114. Ignition control unit
115. Relay for headlamp wiper
116. Headlamp wiper
117. Contact on transmission M 410
118. Relay for back-up lamp
119. Relay for AC

1975 240

1. Battery
2. Connection plate
3. Ignition switch
4. Ignition coil
5. Distributor
6. Spark plugs
7. Starter motor
8. Alternator
9. Charging relay
10. Fuse box
11. Light switch
12. Lamp failure warning unit
13. Step relay for upper and lower beams and headlight flasher
14. Upper beam
15. Lower beam
16. Position lamp
17. Observation light
18. Tail lamp
19. Side marker lamp
20. License plate lamp
21. Stop light switch
22. Stop lamp
23. Contact on gearbox M 40, M 41
24. Contact on gearbox BW 35
25. Back up lamp
26. Turn signal switch
27. Hazard warning signal switch
28. Flasher unit

29. Front turn signal lamp
30. Rear turn signal lamp
31. Conn at instrument
32. Conn at instrument
33. Conn at instrument
34. Conn at instrument
35. Oil pressure pilot lamp
36. Choke pilot lamp
37. Parking brake pilot lamp
38. Brake failure pilot lamp
39. EGR—pilot lamp
40. Charging pilot lamp
41. Lamp failure pilot lamp
42. Upper beam pilot lamp
43. Turn signal light pilot lamp
44. Overdrive pilot lamp
45. Safety belt pilot lamp, front
46. Engine comp. lighting
47. Buckle lighting
48. Rear ash tray lighting
49. Gear selector lighting
50. Instrument lighting rheostat
51. Instrument lighting
52. Control panel lighting
53. Glove comp. lamp
54. Interior lamp
55. Door contact, driver's side
56. Door contact, passenger's side
57. Fuel level gauge
58. Temperature gauge

59. Oil pressure guard
60. Choke control contact
61. Parking brake contact
62. Brake failure contact
63. EGR-warning contact
64. Safety belt contact, pass. seat
65. Safety belt contact, driver's seat
66. Contact, passenger's seat
68. Light buzzer
72. Tachometer
73. Fuel meter
74. Thermometer
75. Voltage stabilizer
76. Horn
77. Horn ring
78. Cigar lighter
79. Fan
80. Fan switch
81. Windshield wiper/wash switch
82. Windshield wiper
83. Windshield washer
84. Relay for headlamp wiper
85. Headlamp wiper
86. Rear window wiper/wash switch
87. Rear window wiper
88. Rear window washer
89. Rear door contact

90. Rear interior lighting
91. El heated rear window switch
92. El heated rear window
93. Overdrive switch M 41
94. Overdrive contact on gearbox M 41
95. Overdrive solenoid on gearbox M 41
96. Heating element with thermostat, driver's seat
97. Heating element, driver's seat
98. Clock
99. Diode
100. Junction
102. Belt reminder
103. Temperature-time contact
105. Air metering device
106. Main relay, fuel injection
107. Relay for fuel pump
108. Fuel pump
109. Pressure regulating valve
110. Supplementary air valve
111. Resistor
112. Ignition control unit
113. Solenoid on compressor
114. Solenoid valve
115. Switch, AC compressor
116. Thermostat
118. Relay for back-up lamp

1975 164

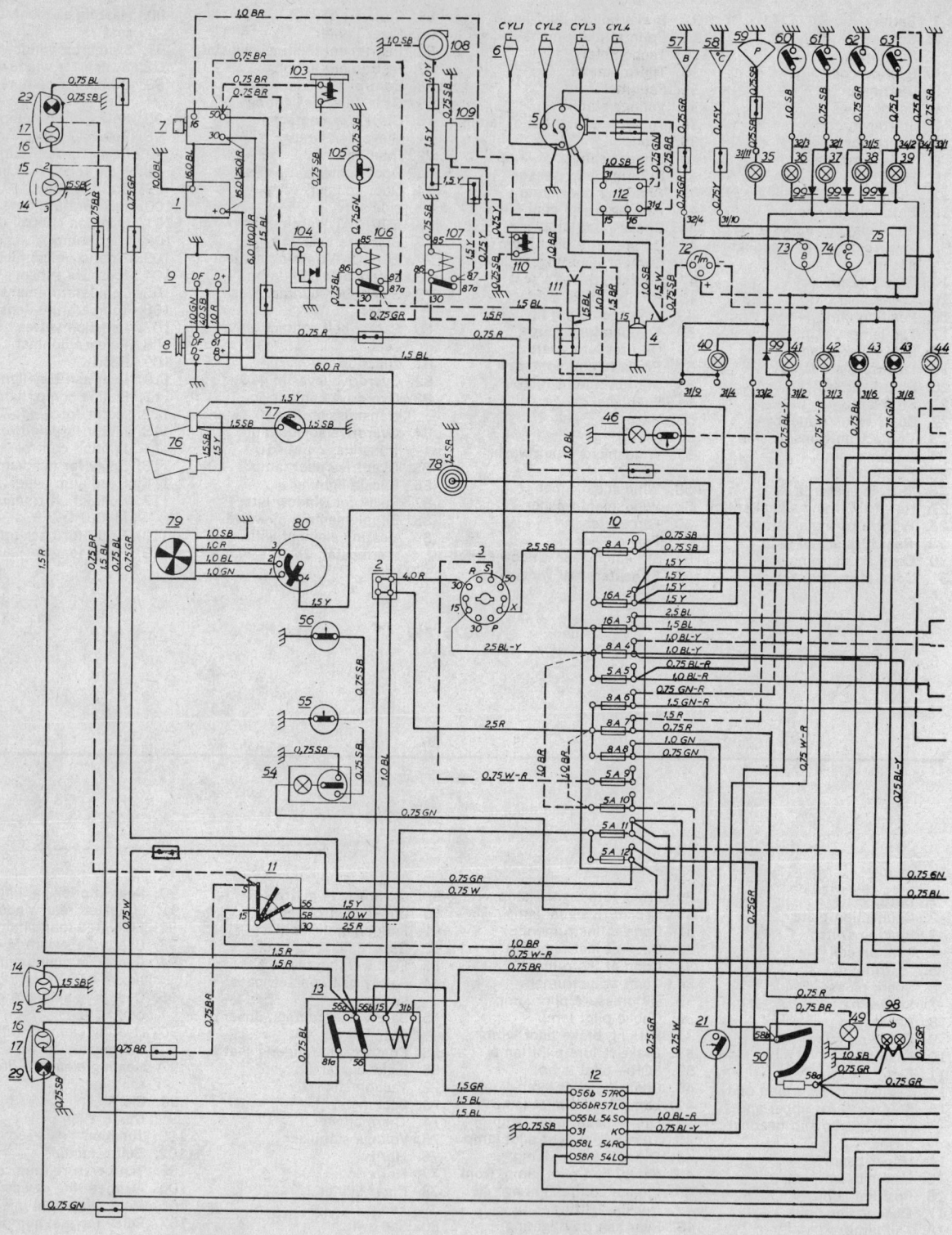

Color Code

SB = Black	W = White	BR = Brown	BL = Blue
GR = Grey	R = Red	Y = Yellow	GN = Green

1975 240

FÄRGBETECKNING / COLOUR INDICATION		
SB	SVART	BLACK
GR	GRÅ	GREY
W	VIT	WHITE
R	RÖD	RED
BR	BRUN	BROWN
Y	GUL	YELLOW
BL	BLÅ	BLUE
GN	GRÖN	GREEN

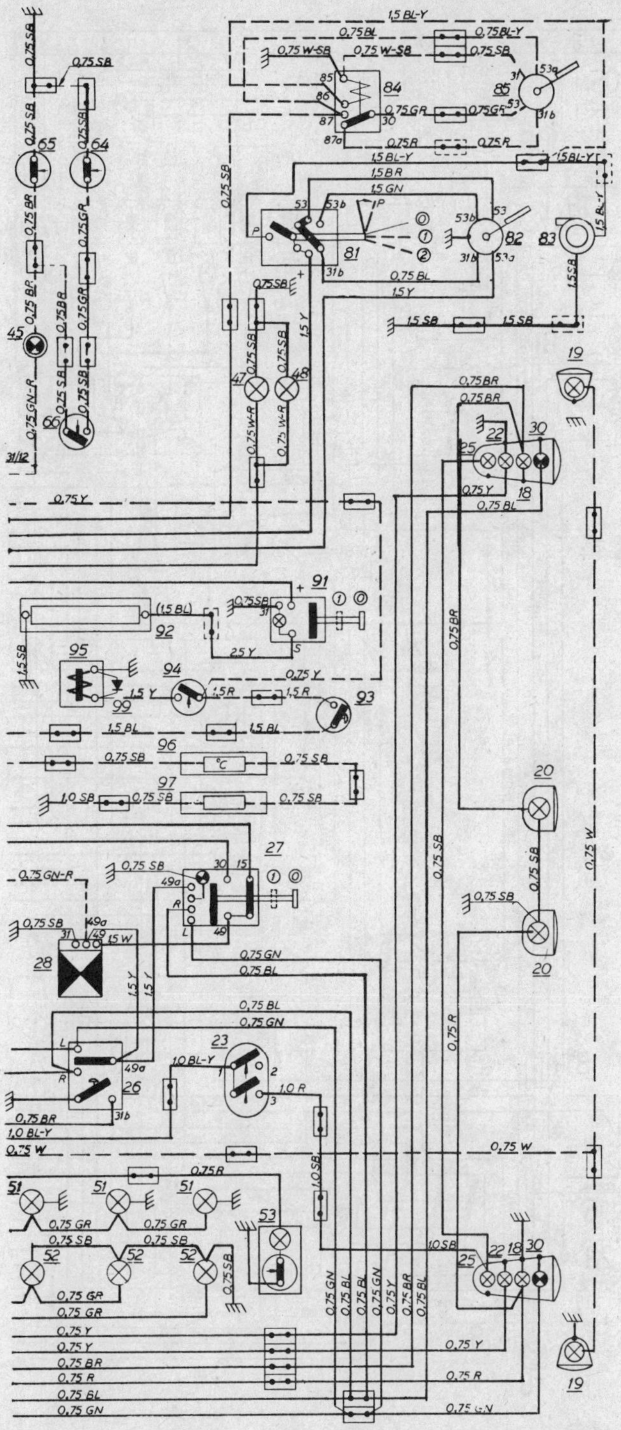

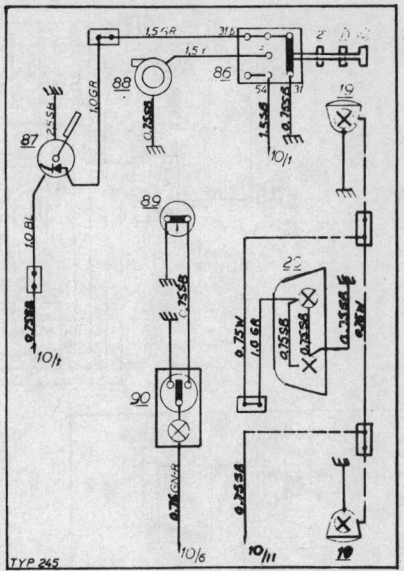

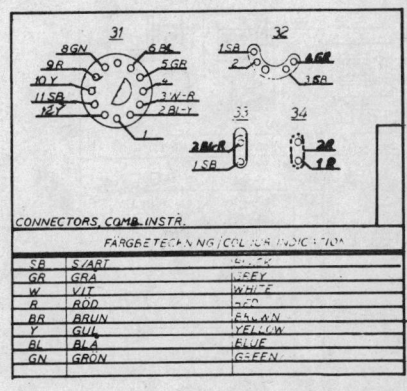

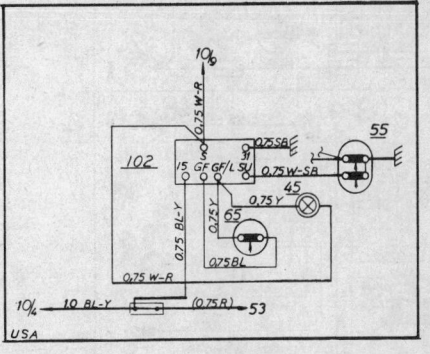

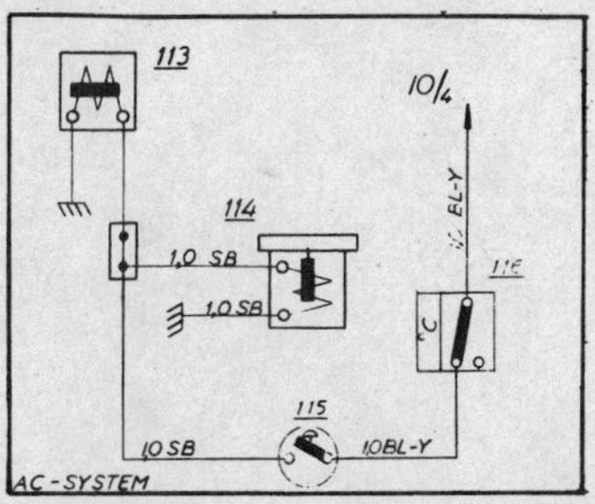

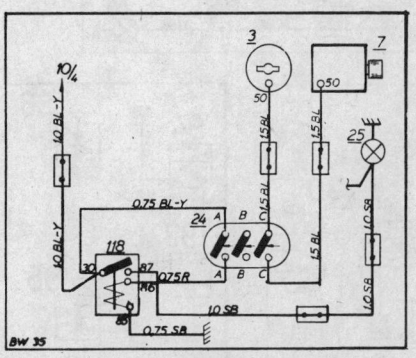

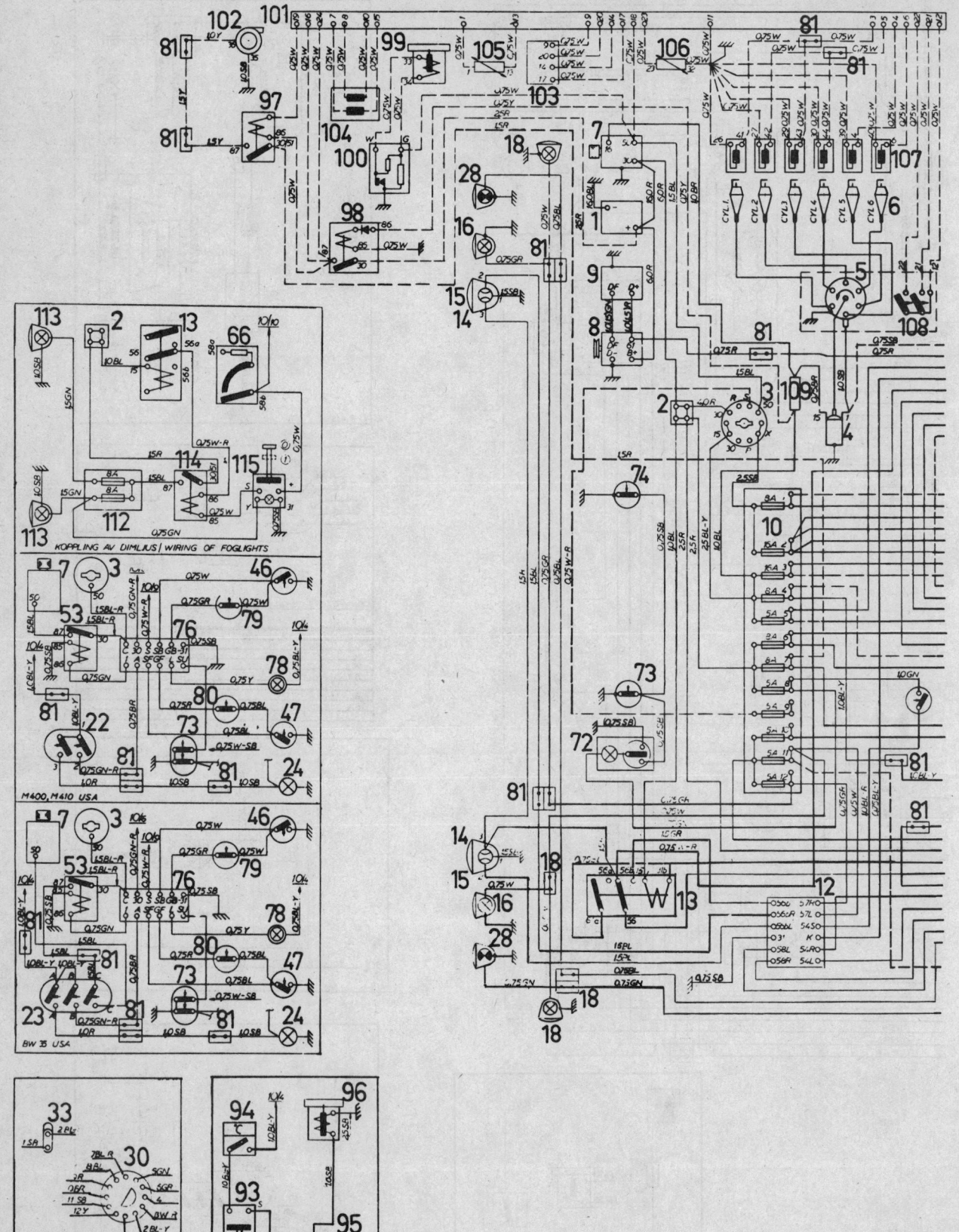

1975 164

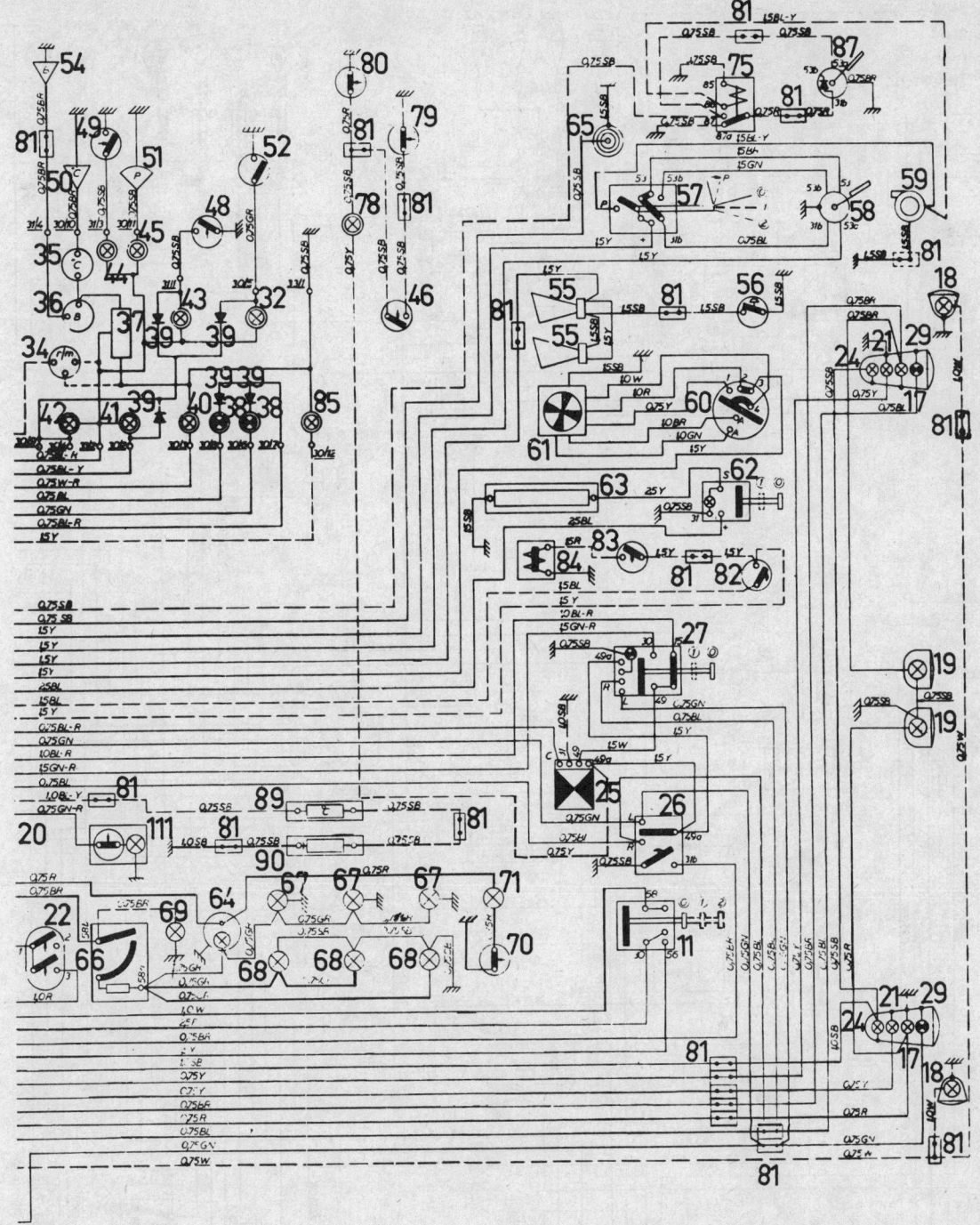

Color Code

SB = Black	W = White	BR = Brown	BL = Blue
GR = Grey	R = Red	Y = Yellow	GN = Green

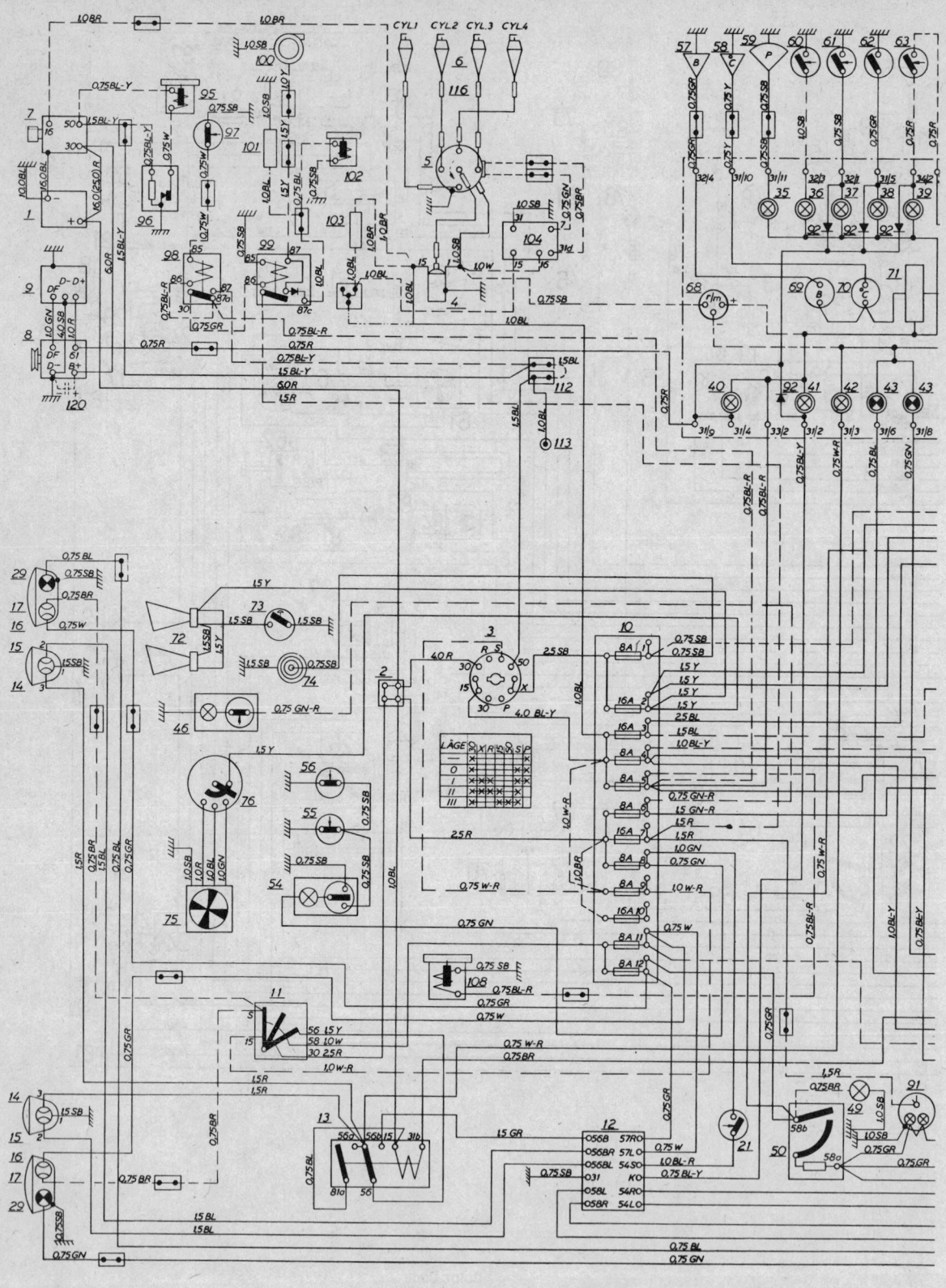

Color Code

SB = Black	W = White	BR = Brown	BL = Blue
GR = Grey	R = Red	Y = Yellow	GN = Green

1976 240

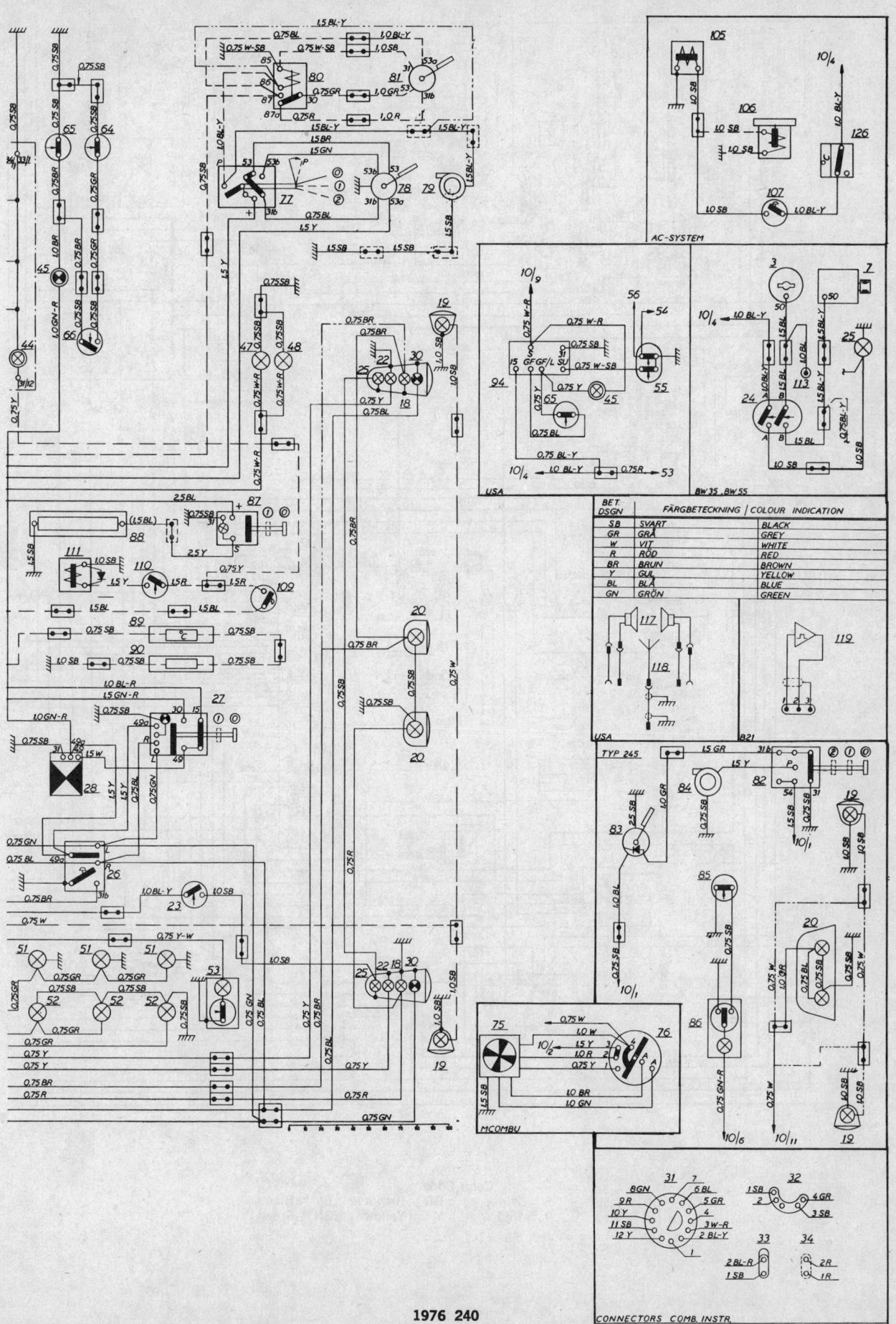

BET. DSGN	FÄRGBETECKNING	COLOUR INDICATION
SB	SVART	BLACK
GR	GRÅ	GREY
W	VIT	WHITE
R	RÖD	RED
BR	BRUN	BROWN
Y	GUL	YELLOW
BL	BLÅ	BLUE
GN	GRÖN	GREEN

AC-SYSTEM

USA

BW35, BW55

TYP 245

MCOMBU

CONNECTORS COMB. INSTR.

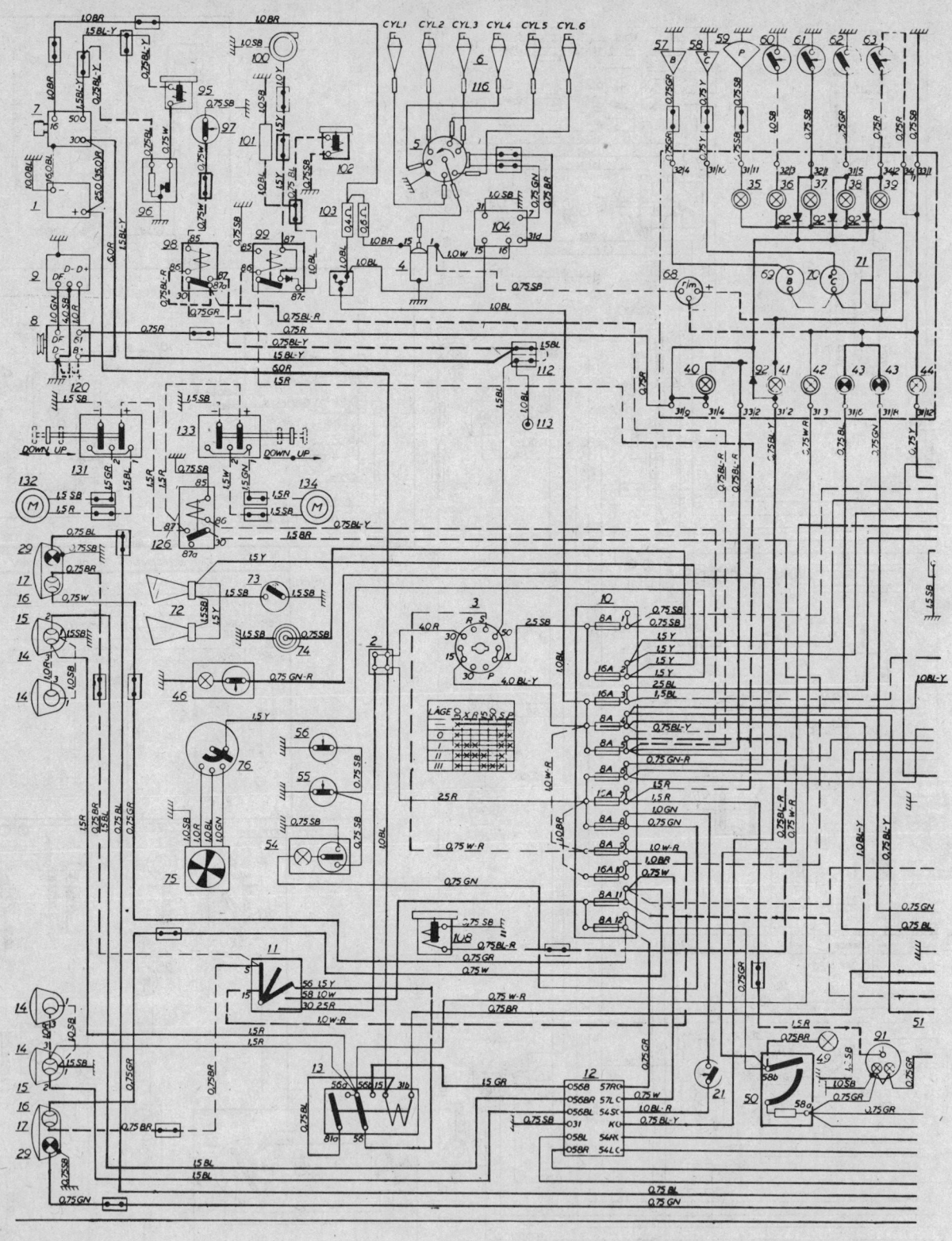

CYL1 CYL2 CYL3 CYL4 CYL5 CYL6

Color Code

SB = Black	W = White	BR = Brown	BL = Blue
GR = Grey	R = Red	Y = Yellow	GN = Green

1976 260

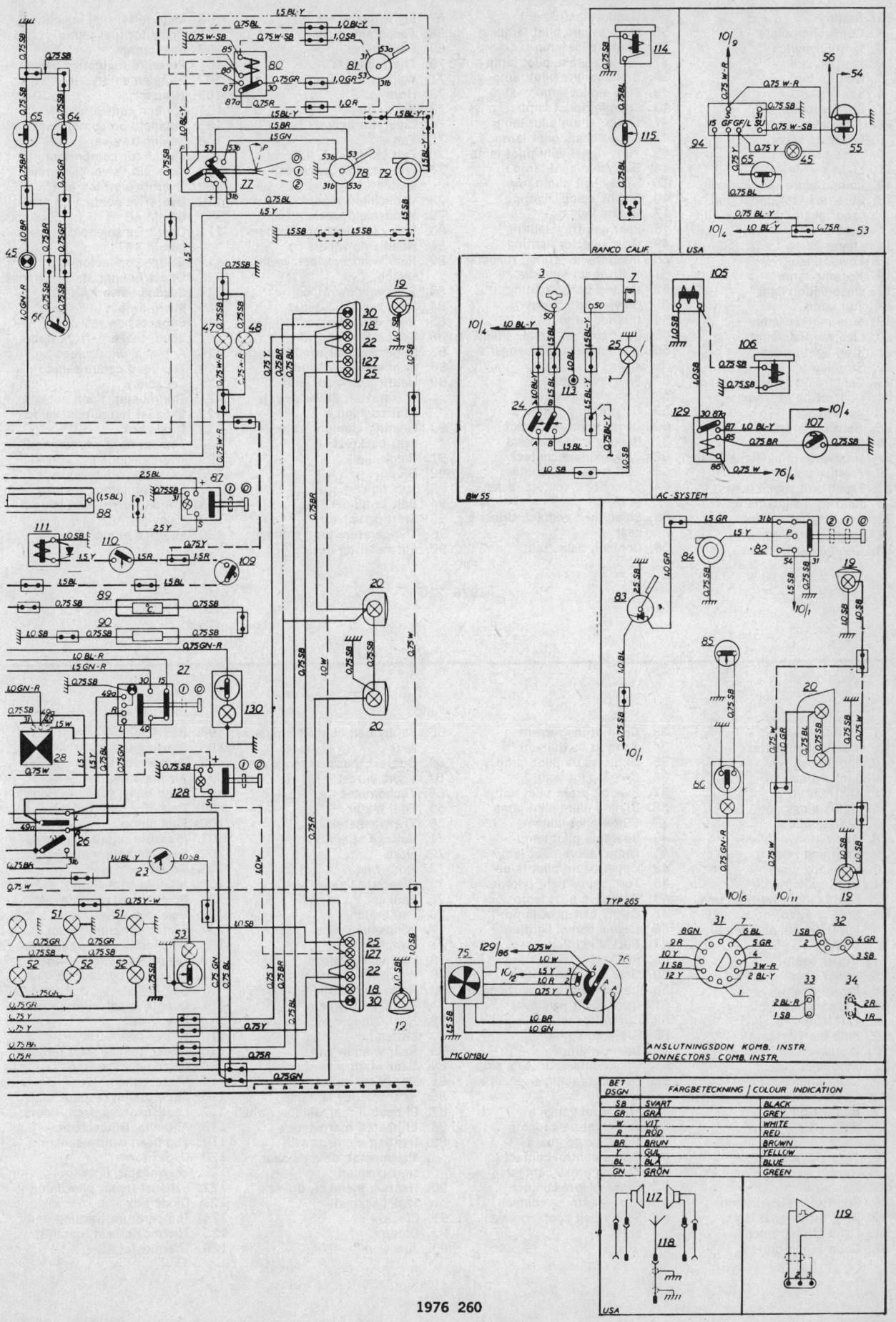

Wiring Circuits

1. Battery
2. Connection plate
3. Ignition switch
4. Ignition coil
5. Distributor
6. Spark plugs
7. Starter motor
8. Alternator
9. Charging relay
10. Fuse box
11. Light switch
12. Lamp failure warning unit
13. Step relay for upper and lower beams and headlight flasher
14. Upper beam
15. Lower beam
16. Position lamp
17. Observation light
18. Tail lamp
19. Side marker lamp
20. License plate lamp
21. Stop light switch
22. Stop lamp
23. Contact on gearbox, manual
24. Contact on gearbox, automatic
25. Back up lamp
26. Turn signal switch
27. Hazard warning signal switch
28. Flasher unit
29. Front turn signal lamp
30. Rear turn signal lamp
31. Conn at instrument
32. Conn at instrument
33. Conn at instrument

34. Conn at instrument
35. Oil pressure pilot lamp
36. Choke pilot lamp
37. Parking brake pilot lamp
38. Brake failure pilot lamp
39. EGR—pilot lamp
40. Charging pilot lamp
41. Lamp failure pilot lamp
42. Upper beam pilot lamp
43. Turn signal light pilot lamp
44. Overdrive pilot lamp
45. Safety belt pilot lamp
46. Engine comp. lighting
47. Buckle lighting
48. Rear ash tray lighting
49. Gear selector lighting
50. Instrument lighting rheostat
51. Instrument lighting
52. Control panel lighting
53. Glove comp. lamp
54. Interior lamp
55. Door contact, driver's side
56. Door contact, passenger's side
57. Fuel level gauge
58. Temperature gauge
59. Oil pressure gauge
60. Choke control contact
61. Parking brake contact
62. Brake failure contact
63. EGR—warning contact
64. Safety belt contact, pass. seat
65. Safety belt contact, driver's seat
66. Contact, pass. seat

67. Light buzzer
68. Tachometer
69. Fuel meter
70. Thermometer
71. Voltage stabilizer
72. Horn
73. Horn ring
74. Cigarette lighter
75. Fan
76. Fan switch
77. Windshield wiper/wash switch
78. Windshield wiper
79. Windshield washer
80. Relay for headlamp wipers
81. Headlamp wipers
82. Rear window wiper/wash switch
83. Rear window wiper
84. Rear window washer
85. Rear door contact
86. Rear interior lighting
87. El heated rear window switch
88. El heated rear window
89. Heating element with thermostat, driver's seat, seat cushion
90. Heating element, driver's seat backrest
91. Clock
92. Diode
93. Junction
94. Belt reminder
95. Starting valve
96. Temperature-time contact
97. Air metering device

98. Main relay, fuel injection
99. Relay for fuel pump
100. Fuel pump
101. Pressure regulating valve
102. Supplementary air valve
103. Resistor
104. Ignition control unit
105. Solenoid on compressor
106. Solenoid valve
107. Switch for compressor
108. Solenoid valve, carburetor
109. Overdrive switch M 46
110. Overdrive contact on gearbox M 46
111. Overdrive solenoid on gearbox M 46
112. Bridge connector
113. Under bonnet start terminal
114. Second valve RANCO
115. Micro switch
116. Suppression resistor
117. Loudspeakers, front doors
118. Antenna, windscreen
119. Top dead centre sensor
120. Capacitor
121. Thermostat, floor
122. Exhaust temp. pilot lamp
123. Diode box
124. Temperature warning unit
125. Thermoelement, catalyst
126. Relay for window lifts
127. Rear fog lamp
128. Switch for rear fog lamp
129. Relay for AC
130. Luggage comp. light

1976 240

---

1. Battery
2. Connection plate
3. Ignition switch
4. Ignition coil
5. Distributor
6. Spark plugs
7. Starter motor
8. Alternator
9. Charging relay
10. Fuse box
11. Light switch
12. Lamp failure warning unit
13. Step relay for upper and lower beams and headlight flasher
14. Upper beam
15. Lower beam
16. Position lamp
17. Observation light
18. Tail lamp
19. Side marker lamp
20. License plate lamp
21. Stop light switch
22. Stop lamp
23. Contact on gearbox, manual
24. Contact on gearbox, automatic
25. Back up lamp
26. Turn signal switch
27. Hazard warning signal switch
28. Flasher unit
29. Front turn signal lamp
30. Rear turn signal lamp
31. Conn at instrument
32. Conn at instrument

33. Conn at instrument
34. Conn at instrument
35. Oil pressure pilot lamp
36. Choke pilot lamp
37. Parking brake pilot lamp
38. Brake failure pilot lamp
39. EGR—pilot lamp
40. Charging pilot lamp
41. Lamp failure pilot lamp
42. Upper beam pilot lamp
43. Turn signal light pilot lamp
44. Overdrive pilot lamp
45. Safety belt pilot lamp
46. Engine comp. lighting
47. Buckle lighting
48. Rear ash tray lighting
49. Gear selector lighting
50. Instrument lighting rheostat
51. Instrument lighting
52. Control panel lighting
53. Glove comp. lamp
54. Interior lamp
55. Door contact, driver's side
56. Door contact, passenger's side
57. Fuel level gauge
58. Temperature gauge
59. Oil pressure guard
60. Choke control contact
61. Parking brake contact
62. Brake failure contact
63. EGR—warning contact
64. Safety belt contact, pass. seat

65. Safety belt contact, driver's seat
66. Contact, pass. seat
67. Light buzzer
68. Tachometer
69. Fuel meter
70. Thermometer
71. Voltage stabilizer
72. Horn
73. Horn ring
74. Cigarette lighter
75. Fan
76. Fan switch
77. Windshield wiper/wash switch
78. Windshield wiper
79. Windshield washer
80. Relay for headlamp wipers
81. Headlamp wipers
82. Rear window wiper/wash switch
83. Rear window wiper
84. Rear window washer
85. Rear door contact
86. Rear interior lighting
87. El heated rear window switch
88. El heated rear window
89. Heating element with thermostat, driver's seat, seat cushion
90. Heating element, driver's seat backrest
91. Clock
92. Diode
93. Junction

94. Belt reminder
95. Starting valve
96. Temperature-time contact
97. Air metering device
98. Main relay, fuel injection
99. Relay for fuel pump
100. Fuel pump
101. Pressure regulating valve
102. Supplementary air valve
103. Resistor
104. Ignition control unit
105. Solenoid on compressor
106. Solenoid valve
107. Switch for compressor
108. Solenoid valve, carburetor
109. Overdrive switch M 46
110. Overdrive contact on gearbox M 46
111. Overdrive solenoid on gearbox M 46
112. Bridge connector
113. Under bonnet start terminal
114. Solenoid valve RANCO
115. Micro switch
116. Suppression resistor
117. Loudspeakers, front doors
118. Antenna, windscreen
119. Top dead centre sensor
120. Capacitor
121. Thermostat, floor
122. Exhaust temp. pilot lamp
123. Diode box
124. Temperature warning unit
125. Thermoelement, catalyst
126. Thermostat AC

1976 260

SPECIFICATIONS

INTRODUCTION

In 1932, Ferdinand Porsche produced prototypes for the NSU company of Germany which eventually led to the design of the Volkswagen. The prototypes had a rear mounted, air-cooled engine, torsion bar suspension, and the spare tire mounted at an angle in the front luggage compartment. In 1936, Porsche produced three Volkswagen prototypes, one of which was a 995 cc, horizontally opposed four cylinder automobile. Passenger car development was sidetracked during World War II, when all attention was on military vehicles. In 1945, Volkswagen production began and 1,785 Beetles were built. The Volkswagen convertible was introduced in 1949, the same year that only two Volkswagens were sold in the United States. 1950 marked the beginning of the sunroof models and the transporter series. The Karmann Ghia was introduced in 1956, and remained in the same basic styling format until its demise in 1974. The 1500 Squareback and Fastback were introduced in the United States in 1966 to start the Type 3 series. The Type 4 was imported into the U.S.A. beginning with the 1971 model.

Type numbers are the way Volkswagen designates its various groups of models. The Type 1 group contains the Beetle, Super Beetle, the Karmann Ghia, and the "Thing". Type 2 vehicles are the Delivery Van, the Micro Bus, the Kombi and the Campmobile. The Type 3 designation is for the Fastback and the Squareback sedans. The Type 4 is for the 411 and 412 sedans and wagon. These type numbers will be used throughout the book when it is necessary to refer to models.

The upright fan engine refers to the engine used in the Type 1 and 2 (1970–71) vehicles. This engine has the engine cooling fan mounted on the top of the engine and is driven by the generator. The fan is mounted vertically in contrast to a horizontally mounted fan. The suitcase engine is a comparatively new engine and was designed as a more compact unit to fit in the Type 3, 4 and 1972 and later Type 2 engine compartments. On this engine, the cooling fan is mounted on the crankshaft giving the engine a rectangular shape similar to that of a suitcase.

MODEL IDENTIFICATION
Basic Body Types

Type 1 Beetle (left) and Super Beetle (right)

Type 1 Super Beetle Convertible (Model 15)

Type 1 Karmann Ghia (Model 14)

Type 1 Karmann Ghia Convertible (Model 14)

Type 1 Thing (Model 181)

Type 2 Bus (Model 22)

Type 2 Van (Model 21)

Type 2 Campmobile (Model 23)

Type 3 Fastback (Model 31)

Type 3 Squareback (Model 36)

Type 4 411 4-Door Sedan (1971-72 Model 41)

Type 4 412 4-Door Sedan
(1973-74 Model 41)

Type 4 411 Station Wagon
(1971-72 Model 46)

Type 4 412 Station Wagon
(1973-74 Model 46)

SERIAL NUMBER IDENTIFICATION

Vehicle (Chassis) Number

The first two numbers are the first two digits of the car's model number and the third digit stands for the car's model year. For example a 0 as the third digit means that the car was produced during the 1970 model year, a 1 would signify 1971, and so forth.

The chassis number is on the frame tunnel under the back seat in the Type 1, 3, and 4. In the Type 2, the chassis number is on the right engine cover plate in the engine compartment and behind the front passenger's seat. All models also

have an identification plate bearing the chassis number on the top of the instrument panel at the driver's side. This plate is easily visible through the windshield and aids in rapid identification.

Another identification plate bearing the vehicle's serial number and paint, body, and assembly codes, is found in the luggage compartment of Type 1, 3 and 4 vehicles.

Engine Number

On Type 1 and 2 vehicles, which have the upright engine cooling fan housing, the engine number is on the crankcase flange for the generator support. The

On Type 3 and 4 suitcase engines, the number is along the crankcase joint be-

tween the oil cooler and the air cleaner. On 1972 and later Type 2 models with the suitcase engine, the number is stamped on the crankcase near the ignition coil and below the crankcase breather. The engine can be identified by the letter or pair of letters preceding the serial number. Engine specifications are listed according to the letters and model year.

Transmission Identification

Transmission identification marks are stamped into the bellhousing or on the final drive housing.

Identification plate in luggage compartment
(Karmann Ghia shown)

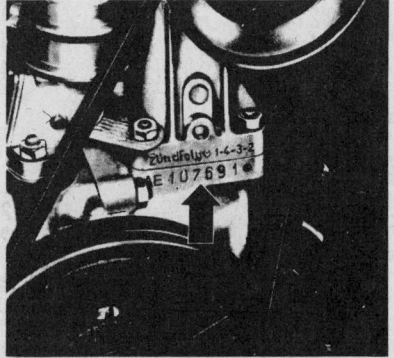

Engine number location on upright fan engine

Chassis number location on dashboard
(Karmann Ghia shown)

Chassis number location under rear seat
(Karmann Ghia shown)

Engine number location on the "upright fan" engine

CHASSIS NUMBER CHART

Model Year	Vehicle	Model No.	From			To		
				Chassis Number				
1972	Beetle/Super Beetle	111/113	112	2000	001	112	3200	000
	Karmann Ghia	14	142	2000	001	142	3200	000
	Beetle Convertible	15	152	2000	001	152	3200	000
	Van	21	212	2000	001	212	2300	000
	Bus	22	222	2000	001	222	2300	000
	Camper, Kombi	23	232	2000	001	232	2300	000
	Type 3 Fastback	31	312	2000	001	312	2500	000
	Type 3 Squareback	36	362	2000	001	362	2500	000
	411 2 Door	41	412	2000	001	412	2100	000
	411 4 Door	42	422	2000	001	422	2100	000
	411 Wagon	46	462	2000	001	462	2100	000
1973	Beetle	11	113	2000	001	113	3200	000
	Super Beetle	13	133	2000	001	133	3200	000
	Karmann Ghia	14	143	2000	001	143	3200	000
	Beetle Convertible	15	153	2000	001	153	3200	000
	Thing	181	183	2000	001	183	3200	000
	Van	21	213	2000	001	213	2300	000
	Bus	22	223	2000	001	223	2300	000
	Camper, Kombi	23	233	2000	001	233	2300	000
	Type 3 Fastback	31	313	2000	001	313	2500	000
	Type 3 Squareback	36	363	2000	001	363	2500	000
	412 2 Door	41	413	2000	001	413	2100	000
	412 4 Door	42	423	2000	001	423	2100	000
	412 Wagon	46	463	2000	001	463	2100	000
1974	Beetle	11	114	2000	001	114	3200	000
	Super Beetle	13	134	2000	001	134	3200	000
	Karmann Ghia	14	144	2000	001	144	3200	000
	Beetle Convertible	15	154	2000	001	154	3200	000
	Thing	181	184	2000	001	184	3200	000
	Van	21	214	2000	001	214	2300	000
	Bus	22	224	2000	001	224	2300	000
	Camper, Kombi	23	234	2000	001	234	2300	000
	412 2 Door	41	414	2000	001	414	2100	000
	412 4 Door	42	424	2000	001	424	2100	000
	412 Wagon	46	464	2000	001	464	2100	000
1975	Beetle	11	115	2000	001	115	3200	000
	Beetle Convertible	15	155	2000	001	155	3200	000
	Thing	181	185	2000	001	185	3200	000
	Van	21	215	2000	001	215	2300	000
	Bus	22	225	2000	001	225	2300	000
	Camper, Kombi	23	235	2000	001	235	2300	000
1976	Beetle	11	116	2000	001	—		
	Beetle Convertible	15	156	2000	001	—		
	Bus	22	226	2000	001	—		
	Camper, Kombi	23	236	2000	001	—		
1977	Beetle	11	117	2000	001	—		
	Beetle Convertible	15	157	2000	001	—		
	Bus	22	227	2000	001	—		
	Camper, Kombi	23	237	2000	001	—		

ENGINE IDENTIFICATION CHART

Engine Code Letter	Type Vehicle	First Production Year	Last Production Year ①	Engine Type	Common Designation
AE	1, 2	1971	1972	Upright Fan	1600
AH (Calif.)	1	1972	1974	Upright Fan	1600
AK	1	1973	1974	Upright Fan	1600
AM (181)	1	1973	1974	Upright Fan	1600
AJ	1	1975	In Production	Upright Fan	1600
CB	2	1972	1973	Suitcase	1700
CD	2	1973	1973	Suitcase	1700
AW	2	1974	1974	Suitcase	1800
ED	2	1975	1975	Suitcase	1800
GD	2	1976	In Production	Suitcase	2000
U	3	1968	1973	Suitcase	1600
X	3	1972	1973	Suitcase	1600
EA	4	1972	1974	Suitcase	1700
EB (Calif.)	4	1973	1973	Suitcase	1700
EC	4	1974	1974	Suitcase	1800

① In production as of the publication of this book.

GENERAL ENGINE SPECIFICATIONS

Year	Engine Code	Displacement (cc)	Horsepower @ rpm	Torque @ rpm (ft lbs)	Bore x Stroke (in.)	Ratio Compression	Oil Pressure @ rpm (psi)
1972	AE	1584	46/4000	72/2000	3.37 x 2.72	7.3:1	42
1972-74	AK	1584	46/4000	72/2000	3.37 x 2.72	7.3:1	42
1972-74	AH①, AM	1584	46/4000	72/2000	3.37 x 2.72	7.5:1	42
1972-73	CB	1679	63/4800	81/3200	3.54 x 2.60	7.3:1	42
1973	CD	1679	59/4200	82/3200	3.54 x 2.60	7.3:1	42
1972-73	U	1584	65/4600	87/2800	3.37 x 2.72	7.7:1	42
1972-73	X	1584	52/4000	77/2200	3.37 x 2.72	7.3:1	42
1972-74	EA	1679	76/4900	95/2700	3.54 x 2.60	8.2:1	42
1973	EB①	1679	69/5000	87/2700	3.54 x 2.60	7.3:1	42
1974	EC	1795	72/4800	91/3400	3.66 x 2.60	7.3:1	42
1974	AW	1795	65/4200	92/3000	3.66 x 2.60	7.3:1	42
1975-77	AJ	1584	48/4200	73.1/2800	3.37 x 2.72	7.3:1	42
1975	ED	1795	67/4400	90/2400	3.66 x 2.60	7.3:1	42
1976-77	GD	1970	67/4200	101/3000	3.70 x 2.80	7.3:1	42

① California only
② Type 2—7.7:1

FIRING ORDERS

A general firing order diagram is shown because distributor positioning varies from model to model. All VW distributors have a scribed notch on the housing which locates the No. 1 rotor position. The firing order of all VW engines is 1-4-3-2. Correct re-wiring of the distributor cap would then begin at the No. 1 notch and proceed clockwise in the firing order.

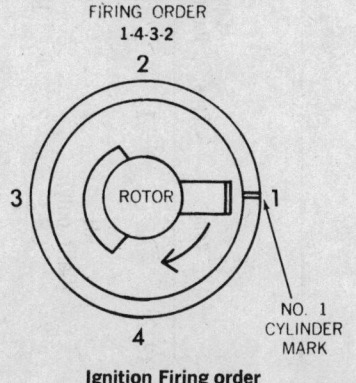

DISTRIBUTOR FIRING ORDER 1-4-3-2

ROTOR

NO. 1 CYLINDER MARK

Ignition Firing order

FRONT OF CAR

ENGINE FROM TOP

CYLINDER NUMBERING

VALVE SPECIFICATIONS

Year	Vehicle Type Displacement	Seat Angle (deg) Intake	Seat Angle (deg) Exhaust	Face Angle (deg) Intake	Face Angle (deg) Exhaust	Valve Seat Width (in.) Intake	Valve Seat Width (in.) Exhaust	Spring Test Pressure (lbs @ in.)	Valve Guide Inside Dia (in.) Intake	Valve Guide Inside Dia (in.) Exhaust	Stem to Guide Clearance (in.) Intake	Stem to Guide Clearance (in.) Exhaust	Stem Diameter (in.) Intake	Stem Diameter (in.) Exhaust
1972-77	1, 2, 3 1600	45	45	45	45	0.05-0.10	0.05-0.10	117.7-134.8 @ 1.22	0.3150-0.3157	0.3150[1]-0.3157	0.009-0.010	0.009-0.010	0.3125-0.3129	0.3113-[2]0.3117
1972-77	2, 4 1700, 1800, 2000	30	45	30	45	0.07-0.08	0.078-0.098	168-186 @ 1.14	0.3150-0.3157	0.3534-0.3538	0.018	0.014	0.3125-0.3129	0.3507-0.3511

[1] On 1975-77 Type 1 models, exhaust valve guide inside diameter is 0.353-0.354 in.
[2] On 1975-77 Type 1 models, exhaust valve stem diameter is 0.350-0.351 in.

TUNE-UP SPECIFICATIONS

Year	Code	Type	Common Designation	Spark Plugs Type	Spark Plugs Gap (in.)	Distributor Point Dwell (deg)	Distributor Point Gap (in.)	Ignition Timing (deg) MT	Ignition Timing (deg) AT	Fuel Pump Pressure (psi) @ 4000 rpm	Compression Pressure (psi)	Idle Speed (rpm) MT	Idle Speed (rpm) AT	Valve Clearance (in.) Cold In	Valve Clearance (in.) Cold Ex
1972	AE	1	1600	W145T1 L88A	.024	44-50	.016	5ATDC[1]	5ATDC[1]	3.5	107-135	800-900	900-1000	.006	.006
	AH (Calif. only)	1	1600	W145T1 L88A	.024	44-50	.016	5ATDC[1]	5ATDC[1]	3.5	107-135	800-900	900-1000	.006	.006
	CB	2	1700	W145T2 N88	.024	44-50	.016	5ATDC[1]	—	5.0	100-135	800-900	—	.006	.006
	U, X	3	1600	W145T1 L88A	.024	44-50	.016	5BTDC[2]	5BTDC[2]	28	107-135	800-900	900-1000	.006	.006
	EA	4	1700	W175T2	.024	44-50	.016	27BTDC[3]	27BTDC[3]	28	128-156	800-900	900-1000	.006	.006
1973	AK	1	1600	W145T1 L88A	.024	44-50	.016	5ATDC [1][4]	5ATDC [1][4]	3.5	107-135	800-900	900-1000	.006	.006
	AH, AM (Calif. only and Thing)	1	1600	W145T1 L88A	.024	44-50	.016	5ATDC [1][4]	5ATDC [1][4]	3.5	107-135	800-900	900-1000	.006	.006
	CB	2	1700	W145T2 N88	.024	44-50	.016	10ATDC[1]	—	5.0	100-135	800-900	—	.006	.008
	CD	2	1700	W145T2 N88	.024	44-50	.016	—	5ATDC[1]	5.0	100-135	—	900-1000	.006	.008
	U, X	3	1600	W145T1 L88A	.024	44-50	.016	5BTDC[2]	5BTDC[2]	28	107-135	800-900	900-1000	.006	.006
	EA	4	1700	W175T2 N88	.024	44-50	.016	27BTDC[3]	27BTDC[3]	28	128-156	800-900	900-1000	.006	.006
	EB (Calif. only)	4	1700	W175T2 N88	.024	44-50	.016	27BTDC[3]	27BTDC[3]	28	107-135	800-900	900-1000	.006	.006

TUNE-UP SPECIFICATIONS (Con't)

	Code	Type	Common Designation	Spark Plugs Type	Spark Plugs Gap (in.)	Distributor Point Dwell (deg)	Distributor Point Gap (in.)	Ignition Timing (deg) MT	Ignition Timing (deg) AT	Fuel Pump Pressure (psi) @ 4000 rpm	Compression Pressure (psi)	Idle Speed (rpm) MT	Idle Speed (rpm) AT	Valve Clearance (in.) Cold In	Valve Clearance (in.) Cold Ex
1974	AK	1	1600	W145T1 L88A	.024	44-50	0.16	7½BTDC ②	7½BTDC ②	3.5	107-135	800-900	900-1000	.006	.006
	AH, AM (Calif. only and Thing)	1	1600	W145T1 L88A	.024	44-50	0.16	5ATDC ①	5ATDC ①	3.5	107-135	800-900	900-1000	.006	.006
	AW	2	1800	W175T2 N88	.024	44-50	.016	10ATDC ①	5ATDC ①	5.0	85-135	800-900	900-1000	.006	.008
	EA	4	1700	W175T2 N88	.024	44-50	.016	27BTDC ③	—	28	128-156	800-900	—	.006	.006
	EC	4	1800	W175T2 N88	.024	44-50	.016	—	7½BTDC ②	28	85-135	—	900-1000	.006	.006
1975	AJ	1	1600	W145M1 L288	.024	44-50	.016	5ATDC ⑤	TDC ⑤	28	85-135	875	875	.006	.006
	ED	2	1800	W145M2 N288	.024	44-50	.016	5ATDC ⑤	5ATDC ⑤	28	85-135	900	900	.006	.006
1976	AJ	1	1600	Bosch W145M1 Champ L288	.024	44-50	.016	5ATDC ⑤	TDC ⑤	28	85-135	875	925	.006	.006
	GD	2	2000	Bosch W145M2 Champ N288	.028	44-50	.016	7½BTDC ⑤	7½BTDC ⑤	28	85-135	900	950	.006	.006
1977	AJ	1	1600	Bosch M145M1 Champ N288	.028	44-50	.016	5ATDC ⑤	5ATDC ⑤	28	85-135	800-950	800-950	.006	.006
	GD	2	2000	Bosch M145M2 Champ N288	.028	44-50	.016	7½BTDC ⑤	7½BTDC ⑤	28	85-135	800-950	850-1000	.006	.006

① At idle, throttle valve closed (Types 1 & 2), vacuum hose(s) on

② At idle, throttle valve closed (Types 1 & 2), vacuum hose(s) off

③ At 3,500 rpm, vacuum hose(s) off

④ From March 1973, vehicles with single diaphragm distributor (one vacuum hose); adjust timing to 7½° BTDC with hose disconnected and plugged. The starting serial numbers for those type 1 vehicles using the single diaphragm distributors are # 113 2674 897 (manual trans.) and 113 2690 032 (auto. stick shift)

⑤ Carbon canister hose at air cleaner disconnected; at idle; vacuum hose(s) on

MT   Manual Transmission
AT   Automatic Transmission
BTDC   Before Top Dead Center
ATDC   After Top Dead Center

TORQUE SPECIFICATIONS

(All readings in ft lbs)

Year	Type Vehicle	Cylinder Head Nuts	Rod Bearing Bolts	Generator Pulley	Crankshaft Pulley Bolt	Flywheel to Crankshaft Bolts	Fan to Hub	Hub to Crank-shaft	Crankcase Half Nuts Sealing Nuts	Crankcase Half Nuts Non-Sealing Nuts	Drive Plate to Crank-shaft	Spark plugs	Oil Strainer Cover
1972-77	1	23	22-25	40-47	29-36	253	—	—	18	14	—	25	5
1972-77	2/1700, 1800, 2000	23	24	—	—	80	14	23	23	14	61	22	7-9
1972-73	3	23	22-25	40-47	94-108	253	—	—	18	14	—	25	5
1972-74	4	23	24	—	—	80	14	23	23	14	61	22	7-9

CAPACITIES CHART

Year	Type and Model	Engine Displacement (cc)	Engine Crankcase (qts) With Filter	Engine Crankcase (qts) Without	Transaxle (pts) Manual	Transaxle (pts) Automatic Conv.	Transaxle (pts) Automatic Final Drive	Gasoline Tank (gals)
1972-77	1, 111, 114	1600	—	2.5	6.3	7.6	6.3①	10.6
1972-77	1, 113, 115	1600	—	2.5	6.3	7.6	6.3①	11.1
1972-71	2, All	1600	—	2.5	7.4	12.6②	3.0	15.8
1972-77	2, All	1700, 1800, 2000	3.7	3.2	7.4	12.6②	3.0	15.8
1972-73	3, All	1600	—	2.5	6.3	12.6②	2.1	10.6
1972-74	4, All	1700, 1800	3.7	3.2	5.3	12.6②	2.1	13.2

Conv—Torque Converter   ① 5.3 when changed   ② 6.3 when changed

TYPE 4 ENGINE AND TRANSMISSION ASSEMBLY CENTERING SPECIFICATIONS

Offset between vehicle center and engine/transmission unit center	1.0 in
Center of left measuring hole to center of right measuring hole	44.3±0.04 in.
Center of left measuring hole to center of rib on transmission	23.1±0.02 in.
Center of right measuring hole to center of rib on transmission	21.2±0.02 in.

UNLOADED REAR TORSION BAR SETTINGS

Type	Model	Transmission	Setting	Range
1	all	all	20° 30'	+50'
2	221, 223, 226	Manual	21° 10'	+50'
2	222	Manual	23°	+50'
2③	221, 223	all	20°	+50'
2④	222	all	23°	+50'
3	311	Manual	23°	+50'
3	311	Automatic	24°	+50'
3	361	all	21° 30'	+50'

③ From chassis 212 2 000 001 (1972-up)
④ From chassis 212 2 000 001 (1972-up)

TORQUE SEQUENCES

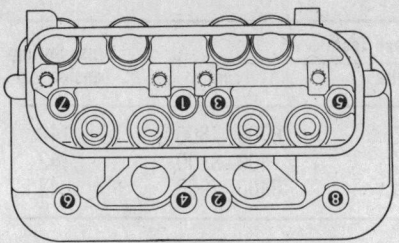

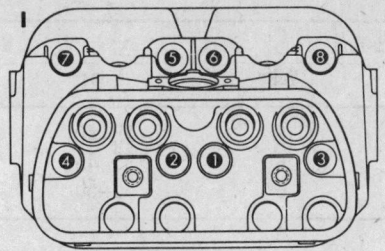

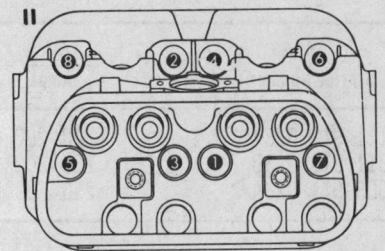

Cylinder head torque sequence—
1700, 1800 cc

For 1600cc engines, the cylinder head nuts should initially be tightened to 7 ft-lbs in order I, then tightened to the recommended torque in order II

CRANKSHAFT AND CONNECTING ROD SPECIFICATIONS

(All measurements are given in inches)

Year	Type Engine	Crankshaft						Thrust on No	Connecting Rods		
		Main Bearing Journal Dia		Main Bearing Oil Clearance			Crankshaft End-Play		Journal Dia	Oil Clearance	Endplay
		No. 1, 2, 3	No. 4	No. 1, 3	No. 2	No. 4					
1972-77	1, 2, 3 1600	2.1640- 2.1648	1.5739- 1.5748	0.0016- 0.004	0.001- 0.003	0.002- 0.004	0.0027- 0.005	1 at flywheel	2.1644- 2.1653	0.0008- 0.0027	0.004- 0.016
1972-77	2, 4 1700, 1800, 2000	2.3609- 2.3617	1.5739- 1.5748	0.002- 0.004	0.0012- 0.0035	0.002- 0.004	0.0027- 0.005	1 at flywheel	2.1644-① 2.1653	0.0008- 0.0027	0.004- 0.016

① On 1977 Type 2/2000 models, connecting rod journal diameter is 1.968 in. (50 mm)

PISTON AND RING SPECIFICATIONS

(All measurements in inches)

Year	Type, Engine Displacement	Piston Clearance	Ring Gap			Ring Side Clearance		
			Top Compression	Bottom Compression	Oil Control	Top Compression	Bottom Compression	Oil Control
1972-77	1, 2, 3 1600	0.0016- 0.0023	0.012- 0.018	0.012- 0.018	0.010- 0.016	0.0027- 0.0039	0.002- 0.0027	0.0011- 0.0019
1972-77	2, 4 1700, 1800, 2000	0.0016- 0.0023	0.014- 0.021	0.012- 0.022	0.010- 0.016	0.0023- 0.0035	0.0016- 0.0027	0.0008- 0.0019

ALTERNATOR, GENERATOR, AND REGULATOR SPECIFICATIONS

Year	Type	Generator	Alternator			Regulator	
		Maximum Output (Amps)	Maximum Output (Amps)	Stator Winding Resistance (Ohms)	Exciter Winding Resistance (Ohms)	Load Current (Amps)	Regulating Voltage Under Load (Volts)
1972-73	1	30	—	—	—	25①	12.5-14.5
1973-77	1	—	50	0.13 ± 0.013	4.0 ± 0.4	25-30	13.8-14.9②
1972-73	2/1700	—	55	0.13 ± 0.013	4.0 ± 0.4	25-30	13.8-14.9②
1974-77	2/1800, 2000	—	55	0.13 ± 0.013	4.0 ± 0.4	25-30	13.8-14.9②
1972-73	3	30	—	—	—	25①	12.5-14.5
1971-74	4	—	55	0.13 ± 0.013	4.0 ± 0.4	25-30	13.8-14.9②

① @ 2000-2500 generator rpm
② @ 2000 engine rpm
— Not Applicable

STARTER SPECIFICATIONS

Starter Number	Lock Test		No-Load Test			Brush Spring Tension (oz)
	Amps	Volts	Amps	Volts	rpm	
111 911 023A	270–290	6	25–40	12	6700–7800	42
311 911 023B	250–300	6	35–45	12	7400–8100	42
003 911 023A	250–300	6	35–50	12	6400–7900	42

BRAKE SPECIFICATIONS

All measurements given are (in.) unless noted

Year	Model	Lug Nut Torque (ft/lb)	Master Cylinder Bore	Brake Disc		Brake Drum			Minimum Lining Thickness	
				Minimum Thickness	Maximum Run-Out	Diameter	Max. Machine O/S	Max. Wear Limit	Front	Rear
1972-77	Type 1 (Beetle)	87-94	0.750	—	—	9.059	9.10	9.114	0.100	0.100
1972-77	Type 1 (Super Beetle)	87-94	0.750	—	—	9.768 (fr) 9.059 (rr)	9.80 (fr) 9.10 (rr)	9.823 (fr) 9.114 (rr)	0.100	0.100
1972-74	Karmann Ghia	87-94	0.938	0.335	0.0008	9.059	9.10	9.114	0.079	0.100
1971-77	Type 2 (Bus)	87-94	0.938	0.472	0.0008	9.920	9.97	9.98	0.079	0.100
1972-73	Type 3	87-94	0.750	0.393	0.0008	9.768	9.80	9.82	0.079	0.100
1972-74	Type 4	87-94	0.750	0.393	0.0008	9.768	9.80	9.82	0.079	0.100

NOTE: Minimum lining thickness is as recommended by the manufacturer. Due to variations in state inspection regulations, the minimum allowable thickness may be different than recommended by the manufacturer.
(fr)—Front
(rr)—rear
——Not Applicable

WHEEL ALIGNMENT SPECIFICATIONS

Year	Model	FRONT AXLE					REAR AXLE		
		CASTER		CAMBER			CAMBER		
		Range (deg)	Pref Setting (deg)	Range (deg)	Pref Setting (deg)	Toe-in (in.)	Range (deg)	Pref Setting (deg)	Toe-in (deg)
1972-77	Type 1	±1°	+3° 20'	±20'	+30'	+0.071-+0.213	±40'	−1°	0'±15'
1972-74	Type 1①	±35'	+2°	+20'-40'	+1°	+0.071-+0.231	±40'	−1° ③	0'±15'
1972-77	Type 2	±40'	+3°	±20'	+40'	0.0-+0.136	±30'	−50'	+10'±20'
1972-73	Type 3	±40'	+4°	±20'	+1° 20'	+0.118-+0.260	±40'	−1° 20'	0'±15'②
1972-74	Type 4	±35'	+1° 45'	+25'-30'	+1° 10'	+0.024-+0.165	±30'	−1°	+10'±15'

① Super Beetle
② Squareback given; Sedan 5'±15'
③ Model 181 (Thing); +20'

TUNE-UP PROCEDURES

This section gives specific procedures on how to tune-up your Volkswagen and is intended to be as complete and basic as possible.

CAUTION: *When working with a running engine, make sure that the transmission is in Neutral (unless otherwise specified) and the parking brake is fully applied. When the ignition is turned on and the engine running, do not grasp the ignition wires, distributor cap, or coil wire, as a shock in excess of 20,000 volts may result. Whenever working around the distributor, even if the engine is not running, make sure that the ignition is switched off. Always keep hands, clothing, jewelry, and long hair clear of the cooling fan and pulleys. Also, stay clear of the hot exhaust manifolds and catalytic converter (if so equipped).*

Spark Plugs

Before attempting any work on the cylinder head, it is very important to note that the cylinder head is cast aluminum alloy. It is extremely easy to damage threads in the cylinder head. Care must be taken not to cross-thread the spark plugs or any bolts or studs. Never overtighten the spark plugs, bolts, or studs.

CAUTION: *To prevent seizure, always lubricate the spark plug threads with liquid silicon or Never-Seez.*

To avoid cross-threading the spark plugs, always start the plugs in their threads with your fingers. Never force the plugs into the cylinder head. Do not use a wrench until you are certain that the plug is correctly threaded.

VW spark plugs should be cleaned and regapped every 6,000 miles and replaced every 12,000.

Removal and Installation

To install the spark plugs, remove the spark plug wire from the plug. Grasp the plug connector and, while removing, do not pull on the wire. Using a 13/16 in. spark plug socket, remove the old spark plugs. Examine the threads of the old plugs; if one or more of the plugs have aluminum clogged threads, it will be necessary to rethread the spark plug hole. See the following section for the necessary information.

Obtain the proper heat range and type of new plug. Set the gap by bending the side electrode only. Do not bend the center electrode to adjust the gap. The proper gap is listed in the "Tune-Up Specifications" chart. Lubricate the plug threads.

Start each new plug in its hole using your fingers. Tighten the plug several turns by hand to assure that the plug is not cross-threaded. Using a wrench, tighten the plug just enough to compress the gasket. Do not overtighten the plug.

RETHREADING SPARK PLUG HOLE

It is possible to repair light damage to spark plug hole threads by using a spark plug hole tap of the proper diameter and thread. Plenty of grease should be used on the tap to catch any metal chips. Exercise caution when using the tap as it is possible to cut a second set of threads instead of straightening the old ones.

If the old threads are beyond repair, then the hole must be drilled and tapped to accept a steel bushing or Heli-Coil. It is not always necessary to remove the cylinder head to rethread the spark plug holes. Bushing kits, Heli-Coil kits, and spark plug hole taps are available at most auto parts stores. Heli-Coil information is contained in the "Engine Rebuilding" section of this book.

Breaker Points and Condenser

Removal and Installation

1. Release the spring clips which secure the distributor cap and lift the cap from the distributor. Pull the rotor from the distributor shaft.
2. Disconnect the points wire from the condenser snap connection inside the distributor.
3. Remove the locking screw from the stationary breaker point.
4. To remove the condenser which is located on the outside of the distributor, remove the screw which secures the condenser bracket and condenser connection to the distributor.

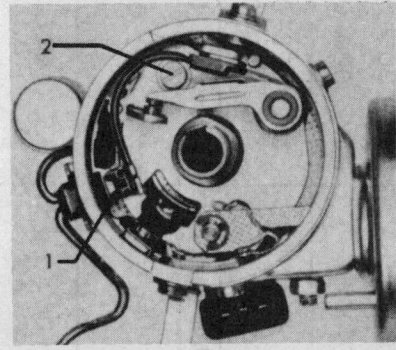

Breaker point removal is accomplished by disconnecting snap connection (1) and removing attaching screw (2)

5. Disconnect the condenser wire from the coil.
6. With a clean rag, wipe the excess oil from the breaker plate.

NOTE: *Make sure that the new point contacts are clean and oil free.*

7. Installation of the points and condenser is the reverse of the above; however, it will be necessary to adjust the point gap, (or dwell), and check the timing. Lubricate the point cam with a small amount of lithium or white grease. Set the dwell, or gap, before the ignition timing.

Point Gap Adjustment

1. Remove the distributor cap and rotor.

Checking point gap with feeler gauge

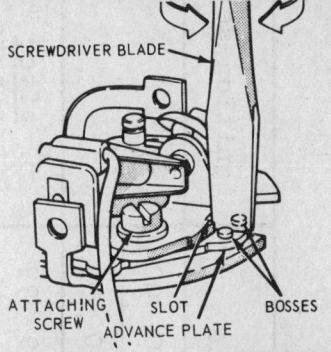

Adjusting point gap by moving stationary arm with screwdriver

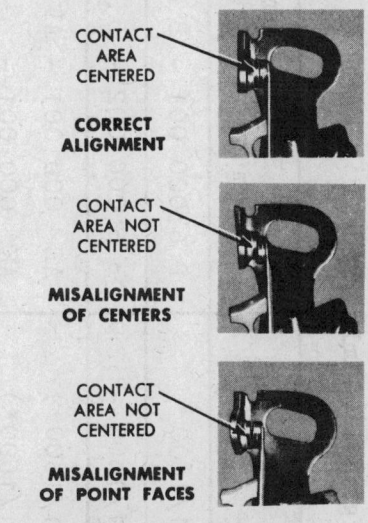

Breaker point alignment guide

Ignition timing Type 1

Type	Engine number from	to	Ignition setting	Marking	Speed rpm	Remarks
1/1600	B 6 000 001 -	B 6 440 900	0°			Vacuum hose off
1/1600 - M 9	B 6 000 002 -	B 6 440 899				Vacuum hoses on
1/1600*	AE 000 001 -	AE 999 999	5° after TDC (see note 1 on page 1)		850 ± 50	Vacuum hoses on
1/1600*	AK 000 001 -					
1/1600*	AH 000 001 -					
18/1600*	AM 000 001 -					
1/1600**	AK 120 009 -		7.5° before TDC			Vacuum hose off
1/1600**	AII 090 024 -					

Ignition timing Type 2

Type	Engine number from	to	Ignition setting	Marking	Speed rpm	Remarks
2/1600	B 5 000 001 - B 5 230 000		0°			
2/1600	AE 0 000 002 -		5° after TDC (see note 1 on page 1)		850 ± 50	Vacuum hose off
2/1700	CB 000 001 -	062 000	5° after TDC		900 ± 50	Vacuum hoses on

*) Double acting vacuum
**) Single acting vacuum

Explanation of M-equipment listed in the table:
M 9 = Automatic Stick Shift
M 27 = Exhaust gas recirculation (Automatic Stick Shift / California)

Timing mark identification—Types 1, 2, 3 and 4

Ignition timing Type 2 (Cont'd)

Type	Engine number from — to	Ignition setting	Marking	Speed rpm	Remarks
2/1700	CB 062 001 –	10° after TDC		900 ± 50	Vacuum hoses on
2/1700-M 249	CD 000 001	5° after TDC		950 ± 50	Vacuum hoses on

Ignition timing Type 3

Type	Engine number from — to	Ignition setting	Marking	Speed rpm	Remarks
3/1600	U 0 000 001 – U 0 502 000	0°			Vacuum hose off
3/1600	U 5 000 000 – U 5 057 000	5° before TDC (see note 1 on page 1)		850 ± 50	Vacuum hoses off
3/1600-M 27	X 0 000 001 – X 0 004 000				
3/1600	U 5 057 001 –	5° before TDC			Vacuum hose off
3/1600-M 27	X 0 004 001 –				

Ignition timing Type 4

Type	Engine number from — to	Ignition setting	Marking	Speed rpm	Remarks
4/1700	W 0 000 001 –	27° before TDC		3500	Vacuum hose or hoses off
4/1700	EA 000 001 –				
4/1700-M 27	EB 000 001 –				

Explanation of M-equipment listed:

M 249 = Automatic transmission

M 27 = Exhaust gas recirculation (automatic transmission / California)

Timing mark identification—Types 1, 2, 3 and 4

2. Turn the engine by hand until the fiber rubbing block on the movable breaker point rests on a high point of the cam lobe. The point gap is the maximum distance between the points and must be set at the top of a cam lobe.

3. Using a screwdriver, loosen the locking screw of the stationary breaker point.

4. Move the stationary point plate so that the gap is set as specified and then tighten the screw. Make sure that the feeler gauge is clean. After tightening the screw, recheck the gap.

Dwell Angle

1. Setting the dwell angle with a dwell meter achieves the same effect as setting the point gap but offers better accuracy.

NOTE: *The dwell must be set before setting the timing. Setting the dwell will alter the timing, but when the timing is set, the dwell will not change.*

2. Attach the positive lead of the dwell meter to that coil terminal which has a wire leading to the distributor. The negative lead should be attached to a good ground.

3. Remove the distributor cap and rotor. Turn the ignition ON and turn the engine over using a starter or a starter button. Read the dwell from the meter and open or close the points to adjust the dwell.

NOTE: *Increasing the gap decreases the dwell and decreasing the gap increases the dwell.*

Dwell specifications are listed in the "Tune-Up Specifications" chart.

4. Reinstall the cap and rotor and start the engine. Check the dwell and reset it if necessary.

Ignition Timing

Dwell or point gap must be set before the timing is set. Also, the idle speed must be set to specifications.

NOTE: *The engine must be warmed up before the timing is set (oil temperature of 122°F-158°F).*

1. Remove the No. 1 spark plug wire from the distributor cap and attach the timing light lead. Disconnect the vacuum hose if so advised by the "Tune-Up Specifications" chart (and re-adjust the idle speed if necessary).

2. Start the engine and run it at the specified rpm. Aim the timing light at the crankshaft pulley on upright fan engines and at the engine cooling fan on the suitcase engines. The rubber plug in the fan housing will have to be removed before the timing marks on the suitcase engine can be seen.

3. Read the timing and rotate the distributor accordingly.

NOTE: *Rotate the distributor in the*

opposite direction of normal rotor rotation to advance the timing. Retard the timing by turning the distributor in the normal direction of rotor rotation.

4. It is necessary to loosen the clamp at the base of the distributor before the distributor can be rotated. It may also be necessary to put a small amount of white paint or chalk on the timing marks to make them more visible.

Valve Lash

NOTE: *The engine must be as cool as possible before adjusting the valves.*

Adjust the valves as follows:

1. Remove the distributor cap and turn the engine until the rotor points to the No. one spark plug wire post in the distributor cap. To bring the piston to exactly top dead center (TDC) on the compression stroke, align the crankshaft timing marks on TDC.

2. Remove the rocker arm covers. At TDC, the pushrods should be down and there should be clearance between the rocker arms and valve stems of both valves of the subject cylinder.

3. With the proper feeler gauge, check the clearance between the adjusting screw and the valve stem of both valves for the No. 1 cylinder. If the feeler gauge slides in snugly without being forced, the clearance is correct. It is better that the clearance is a little loose than a little tight.

4. If the clearance is incorrect, the lock-nut must be loosened and the adjust-

No. 1 piston at Top Dead Center—Type 1, 2/1600

No. 1 piston at Top Dead Center—Type 3

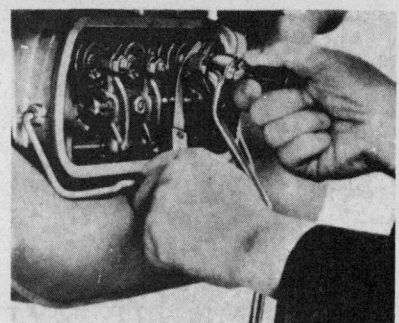

Checking valve clearance with feeler gauge

ing screw turned until the proper clearance is obtained. After tightening down the lock nut, it is then advisable to recheck the clearance. It is possible to alter the adjustment when tightening the lock-nut.

5. The valves are adjusted in a 1–2–3–4 (exact opposite of firing [1–4–3–2] order) sequence. To adjust cylinders 2 through 4, the distributor rotor must be pointed at the appropriate distributor cap post 90° apart from each other. Align the crankshaft timing marks for each cylinder, remembering that the piston must be at TDC on the compression stroke when the valves are adjusted.

NOTE: *Always use new valve cover gaskets.*

Fuel System Adjustments

Carburetor Idle Speed and Mixture

A carburetor adjustment should be performed only after all other variables in a tune-up have been checked and adjusted. This includes checking valve clearance, spark plug gap, breaker point gap and/or dwell angle, and ignition timing. Prior to making any carburetor adjustments, the engine should be brought to operating temperature (122–158° F oil temperature) and you should make sure that the automatic choke is fully open and off the fast idle cam. Once you have performed all of the preliminary steps, shut off the engine and hook up a tachometer. Connect the hot lead to the distributor side of the ignition coil and the ground wire to an engine bolt or other good metal to metal connection. Keep the wire clear of the fan.

NOTE: *An improper carburetor adjustment may have an adverse effect on exhaust emission levels. If any doubt exists, check your state laws regarding the adjusting of emission control equipment.*

Solex 34 PICT-3
(1972–74 Type 1 Models, and Solex 34 PICT-4 (1973–74 Type 1 California Models)

1. Start the engine and bring it to operating temperature. Make sure the car is in neutral.

2. Shut off the engine.

3. Slowly turn in the idle mixture (volume control) screw until it bottoms. Then, carefully counting the complete revolutions of the screwdriver, turn it out 2½ to 3 turns.

4. With a tachometer connected to the engine as previously described, start the engine.

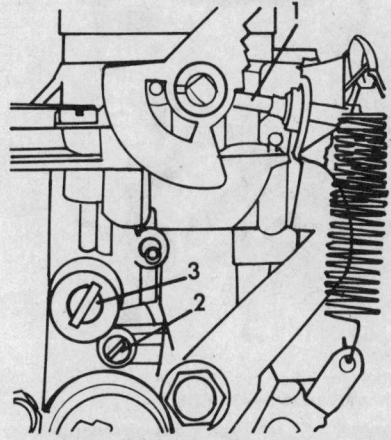

Solex 34 PICT-3 Idle Adjustments

5. Using the idle speed (bypass) screw, adjust the idle speed to specifications. Then, using the idle mixture (volume control) screw, adjust until the fastest idle is obtained. Observing the tachometer, turn the volume control screw until the engine speed drops by 20–30 rpm.

6. Finally, using the bypass screw, adjust the idle to specifications.

Solex 34 PDSIT-2/3 Twin Carb (1972–74 Type 2 Models)

Periodic Adjustment

1. Start the engine and bring it to operating temperature (122–158° F oil temperature). Make sure the car is in neutral and the parking brake firmly applied.

2. Using the central idle speed adjusting screw (4) on the left carburetor, adjust the idle speed to that listed in the "Tune-Up Specifications" chart.

3a. If a CO meter/exhaust analyzer is available, adjust the carbon monoxide (CO) level to 1–3% CO using the central mixture control screw (5) also on the left carburetor.

3b. If a CO meter is not available, the following procedure is used: First, slowly

Type 2 Twin Carb Adjustments—34 PDSIT-2

(left carburetor shown)

1. Synchronizing screw
2. Central idling system left end piece
3. Central idling system left end connecting hose
4. Central idling (idle speed) adjusting screw
5. Central mixture control screw
6. Throttle linkage ball socket

turn the central mixture control screw (5) in (clockwise) until the engine speed drops noticeably, then turn the screw out (counterclockwise) until maximum idle speed is attained. Next, turn the screw in once again until rpm drops by 20–50 rpm. Finally, turn the screw out ¼ turn.

4. Recheck the idle speed, and adjust as necessary using the central idle speed adjusting screw (4) on the left carburetor.

5. If a satisfactory idle cannot be obtained using this procedure, proceed to "Basic Adjustment."

Basic Adjustment

Whenever a carburetor has been removed for service, or if a new or rebuilt carburetor has been installed, a basic carburetor adjustment should be performed.

NOTE: *The throttle valve setting (distance "a") must be 0.004 in.*

NOTE: *An exhaust analyzer/CO meter and tachometer is required for this adjustment.*

1. Check the synchronization of the carburetors as outlined under "Balancing Multiple Carburetor Installations."

2. Disconnect the throttle linkage rod from the right carburetor.

3. Disconnect the vacuum retard hose from the distributor.

4. Disconnect the cut-off valve wire at the central idling system. Disconnect and plug the left side air pump hose (1973–74 models).

5. Turn the idle volume control screws (6) in on both carburetors until they contact their seats.

CAUTION: *Do not force the screws or the tips may become distorted.*

Then, turn both screws out exactly 2½ turns.

6. Start the engine and bring it to operating temperature (122–158° F oil tem-

perature). Set the idle speed to 500–700 rpm by equally adjusting both volume control screws (6).

7. Disconnect the wire from the electromagnetic idling cut-off valve (smaller of the two valves) at the left carburetor and note the decrease in idle speed. Then, repeat this operation for the right carburetor. The idle speed drop should be equal for both sides. If not, readjust the volume control screws accordingly.

8. Connect the wire for the cut-off valve at the central idling system. Unplug, and connect the left air pump hose. Connect the vacuum retard hose.

9. Take the engine through the upper rpm range for a few quick bursts. Then, adjust the idle speed to specifications as outlined under steps 2–5 of "Periodic Adjustment."

Balancing Multiple Carburetor Installations

Synchronizing 1972–74 Type 2 Twin Carb

If a carburetor has been removed or disassembled, or if any part of the linkage has been repaired, the carburetors must be synchronized prior to performing any idle adjustments. To synchronize the carburetors, a special instrument is used to measure air flow, such as the UniSyn® or Auto-Syn®. This commonly available device measures the vacuum created inside the carburetors and provides an index for adjusting the carburetors equally. In order to use the air flow gauge on the 34 PDSIT carburetors, a special diameter adaptor (or a small frozen juice can with both ends removed) must be used.

1. Disconnect the linkage connecting rod from the lower socket of the right carburetor. Without moving the throttle valve from its closed position, check the ball and socket alignment of the linkage for the right carburetor. If the ball and socket at the *right* carburetor do not align *perfectly,* adjust, as necessary, using the

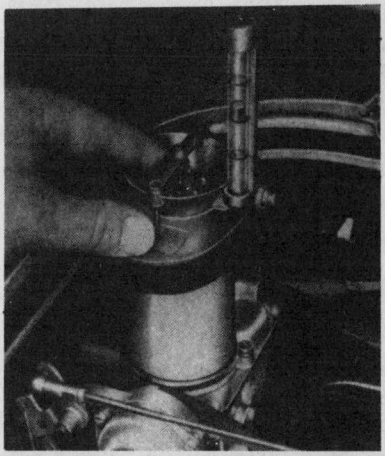

Air flow meter positioned over the left carburetor

Terminal connection for central idling system electromagnetic cut-off valve—30 PDSIT—2

On 34 PDSIT—⅔ carburetors, the throttle valve closing gap (distance "a") must be 0.004 in

Volume control screw—34 PDSIT—⅔ carburetors

Terminal connection for idling cut-off valve of both left and right carburetors—34 PDSIT—⅔

synchronizing screw (1) at the *left* carburetor. Connect the linkage. Hook up a tachometer.

2. Remove the air cleaner ducts from the tops of both carburetors, taking care to leave the central idle system connecting hose (3) and left end piece (2) connected.

3. Start the engine and bring it to operating temperature (122–158° F oil temperature). Make sure the choke flaps are fully open. Using the air flow meter, balance the carburetors using the synchronizing screw (1) on the left carburetor, at 2,000 to 3,000 rpm. After balancing, install the air cleaners.

4. Adjust the idle speed to specifications.

Fuel Injection Idle Speed

All Type 3 and Type 4, 1975–76 Type 1 and Type 2

The idle speed is adjusted by a screw located on the left side of the intake air distributor. To adjust the idle speed, loosen the lock nut (Type 3 only) and turn the screw with a screwdriver until the idle speed is adjusted to specification.

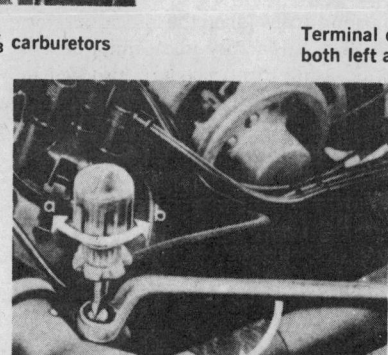

Fuel Injection Idle speed adjustments—Type 3

    a. slower
    b. faster
    c. tighten locknut

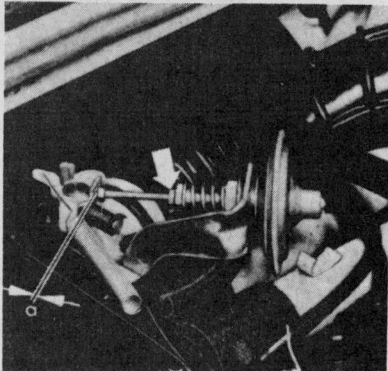

Idling speed regulator dashpot adjustment–Type 4

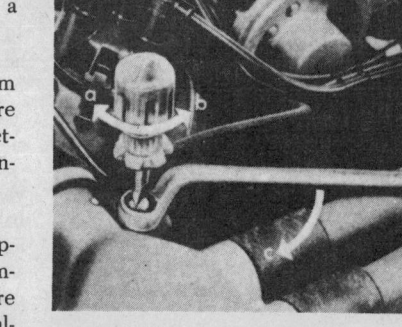

Fuel Injection idle speed adjustment—Type 4

On Type 4 and 1975–76 Type 2 models equipped with automatic transmission, the idling speed regulator dashpot must also be adjusted. With the car idling in neutral at 900 rpm, firmly apply the parking brake, bock the front wheels, and place the transmission in drive. Under this load, the car should idle at 600–700 rpm. Check that clearance "a" between the end of the dashpot plunger and the bracket is 0.002–0.004 in. Adjust as necessary with the M5 bolt indicated by the arrow (see illustration).

Fuel injection idle speed (by-pass screw) adjustment—
1975-77 Type 1

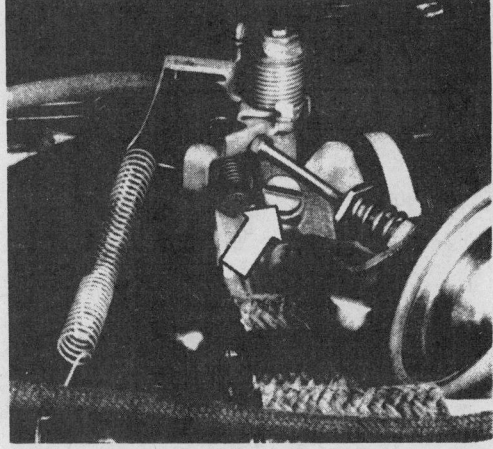

Fuel injection idle speed (by-pass screw) adjustment—
1975-77 Type 2

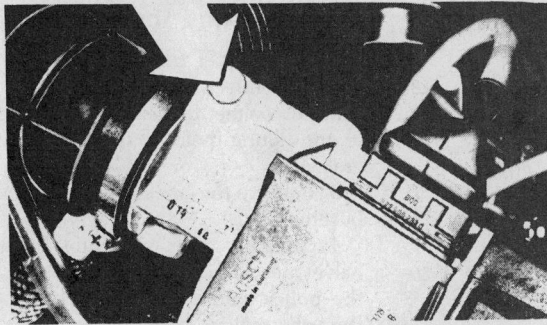

Fuel injection idle mixture adjustment—1975-77
Type 2. Remove plug (arrow) and adjust CO to 1.1%

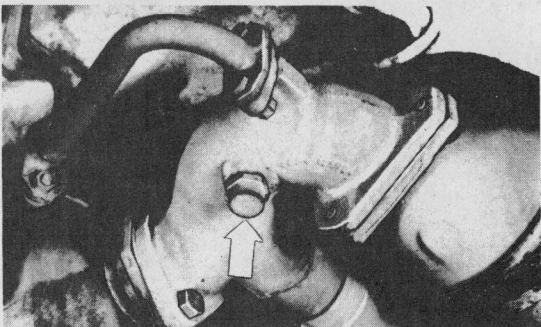

On 1975-77 Type 1 and Type 2 California models, check
CO ahead of catalytic converter at probe receptacle
(arrow)

ENGINE ELECTRICAL

Distributor

Removal and Installation

1. Take off the vacuum hose(s) at the distributor.

2. Disconnect the coil wire and remove the distributor cap.

3. Disconnect the condenser wire.

4. Bring No. 1 cylinder to top dead center (TDC) on the compression stroke by rotating the engine so that the rotor points to the No. 1 spark plug wire tower on the distributor cap and the timing marks are aligned at 0°. Mark the rotor-to-distributor relationship. Also, match mark the distributor housing-to-crankcase relationship.

5. Unscrew the distributor retaining screw on the crankcase and lift the distributor out.

6. If the engine has been rotated since the distributor was removed, bring the No. 1 cylinder to TDC on the compression stroke and align the timing marks on 0°. Align the match marks and insert the distributor into the crankcase. If the match marks are gone, have the rotor pointing to the No. 1 spark plug wire tower upon insertion.

7. Replace the distributor retaining screw and reconnect the condenser and coil wires. Reinstall the distributor cap.

8. Retime the engine.

Distributor Driveshaft

Removal and Installation

1. On carbureted engines, remove the fuel pump.

Type 4 timing mark and rotor alignment

2. Bring the engine to TDC on the compression stroke of No. 1 cylinder. Align the timing marks at 0°.

3. Remove the distributor.

4. Remove the spacer spring from the driveshaft.

5. Grasp the shaft and turn it slowly to the left while withdrawing it from its bore.

6. Remove the washer found under the shaft.

CAUTION: *Make sure that this washer does not fall down into the engine.*

7. To install, make sure that the engine is at TDC on the compression stroke for No. 1 cylinder with the timing marks aligned at 0°.

8. Replace the washer and insert the shaft into its bore.

NOTE: *Due to the slant of the teeth on the drive gears, the shaft must be rotated slightly to the left when it is inserted into the crankcase.*

9. When the shaft is properly inserted, the offset slot in the drive shaft of Type 1 and 2/1600 engines will be perpendicular to the crankcase joint and the slot offset will be facing the crankshaft pulley. On Type 3, the slot will form a 60° angle with the crankcase joint and the slot offset will be facing the oil cooler. On Type 4 engines, and Type 2/1700, 2/1800 and 2/2000 engines, the slot should be about 12° out of parallel with the center line of

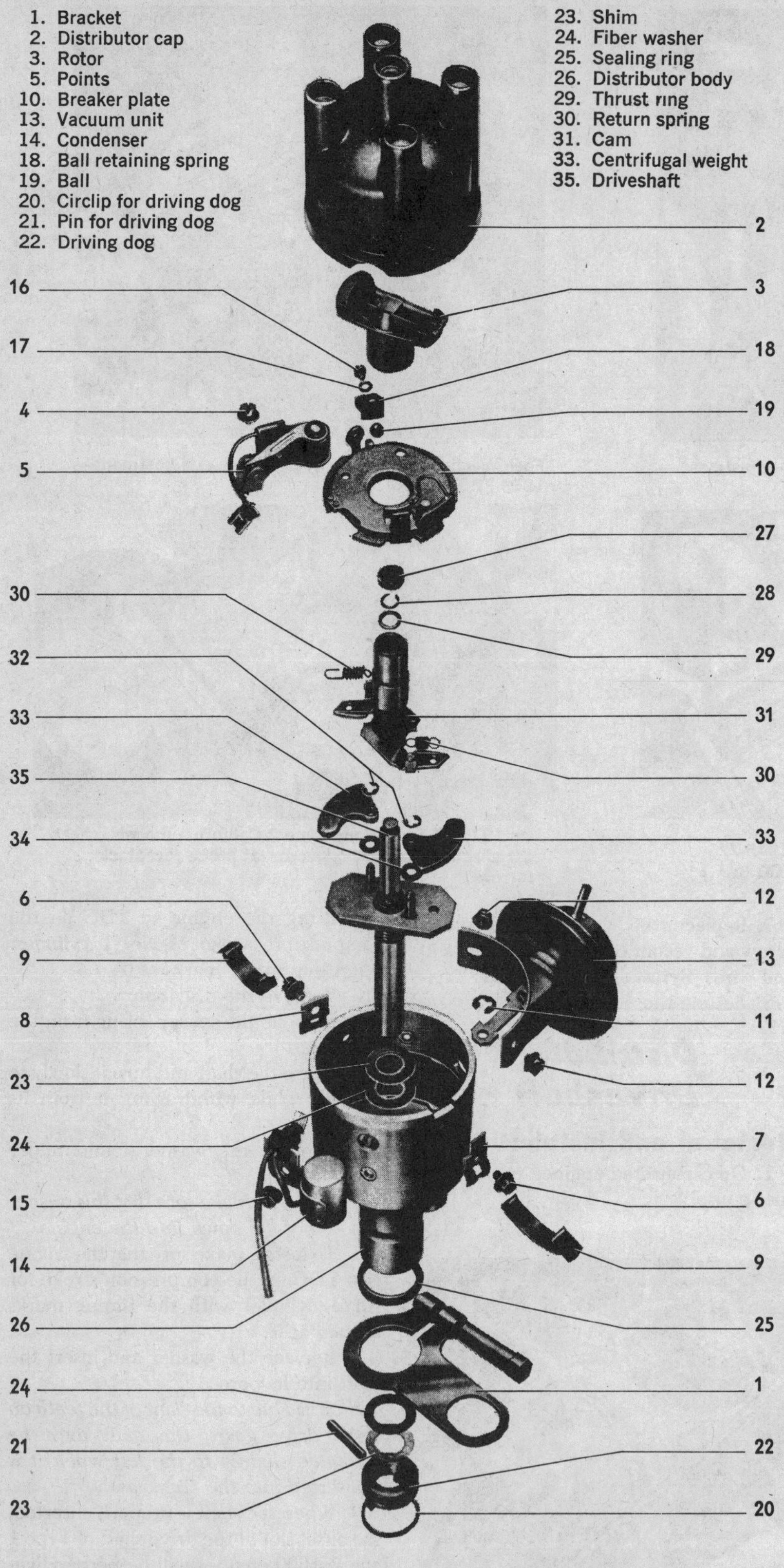

1. Bracket
2. Distributor cap
3. Rotor
5. Points
10. Breaker plate
13. Vacuum unit
14. Condenser
18. Ball retaining spring
19. Ball
20. Circlip for driving dog
21. Pin for driving dog
22. Driving dog

23. Shim
24. Fiber washer
25. Sealing ring
26. Distributor body
29. Thrust ring
30. Return spring
31. Cam
33. Centrifugal weight
35. Driveshaft

Distributor with vacuum and centrifugal advance

the engine and the slot offset should be facing outside the engine.

10. Reinstall the spacer spring.

11. Reinstall the distributor and fuel pump, if removed.

12. Retime the engine

Generator
Alternator

Alternator Precautions

1. Battery polarity should be checked before any connections, such as jumper cables or battery charger leads, are made. Reversing the battery connections will damage the diodes in the alternator. It is recommended that the battery cables be disconnected before connecting a battery charger.

2. The battery must never be disconnected while the alternator is running.

3. Always disconnect the battery ground lead before working on the charging system, especially when replacing an alternator.

4. Do not short across or ground any alternator or regulator terminals.

5. If electric arc welding has to be done to the car, first disconnect the battery and alternator cables. Never start the car with the welding unit attached.

Removal and Installation

Types 1 and 2/1600

1. Disconnect the battery.

2. Disconnect the leads from the generator, noting their position on the generator.

3. Remove the air cleaner and the carburetor.

4. Separate the generator pulley halves, noting the number and position of the pulley shims, and remove the belt from the pulley.

5. Remove the retaining strap from the generator.

6. Remove the cooling air thermostat.

7. Remove the hot air hoses from the fan housing, take out the fan housing screws, and lift off the housing.

8. The generator, fan, and fan cover may be removed as an assembly.

9. Remove the fan from the generator by unscrewing the special nut and pulling the fan off the keyed generator shaft. Note the position of any shims found on Type 2 generators, from chassis number 219000001, as these shims are used to maintain a gap of 0.047 in. between the fan and the fan cover. The Type 1 gap is 0.08 in.

10. Reverse the above steps to install. When reinstalling the generator, the cooling air intake slot in the fan cover

Alignment of Type 3 generator

2. Distributor cap
3. Rotor
6. Points
8. Vacuum unit
9. Condenser
10. Holding spring
16. Ball retaining spring
17. Ball
18. Breaker plate
22. Return spring

23. Distributor cam
25. Flyweight
27. Circlip for drive dog
28. Pin for drive dog
29. Drive dog
30. 0.1 mm compensating washer
32. Distributor shaft
33. Distributor housing
34. Rubber sealing ring
35. Fuel injection trigger contacts

must face downward and the generator pulley must align with the crankshaft pulley.

Type 2/1800, 2/2000 (Fuel Injected)

1. Disconnect the negative battery cable.

2. Disconnect the alternator wiring harness at the voltage regulator and starter.

3. Pull out the dipstick and remove the oil filler neck.

4. Loosen the alternator adjusting bolt and remove the drive belt.

5. Remove the right rear engine cover plate and the alternator cover plate.

6. Disconnect the warm air duct at the right side, and remove the heat exchanger bracket and connecting pipe from the blower.

Fuel injection distributor

Type 3 distributor driveshaft alignment

Type 1 and 2/1600 distributor driveshaft alignment

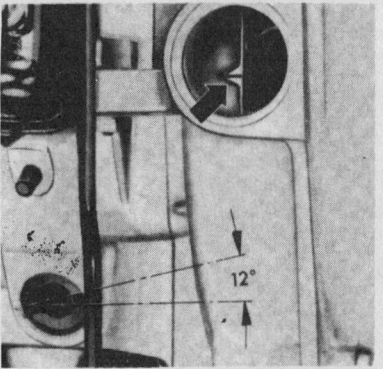

Type 4 distributor driveshaft alignment

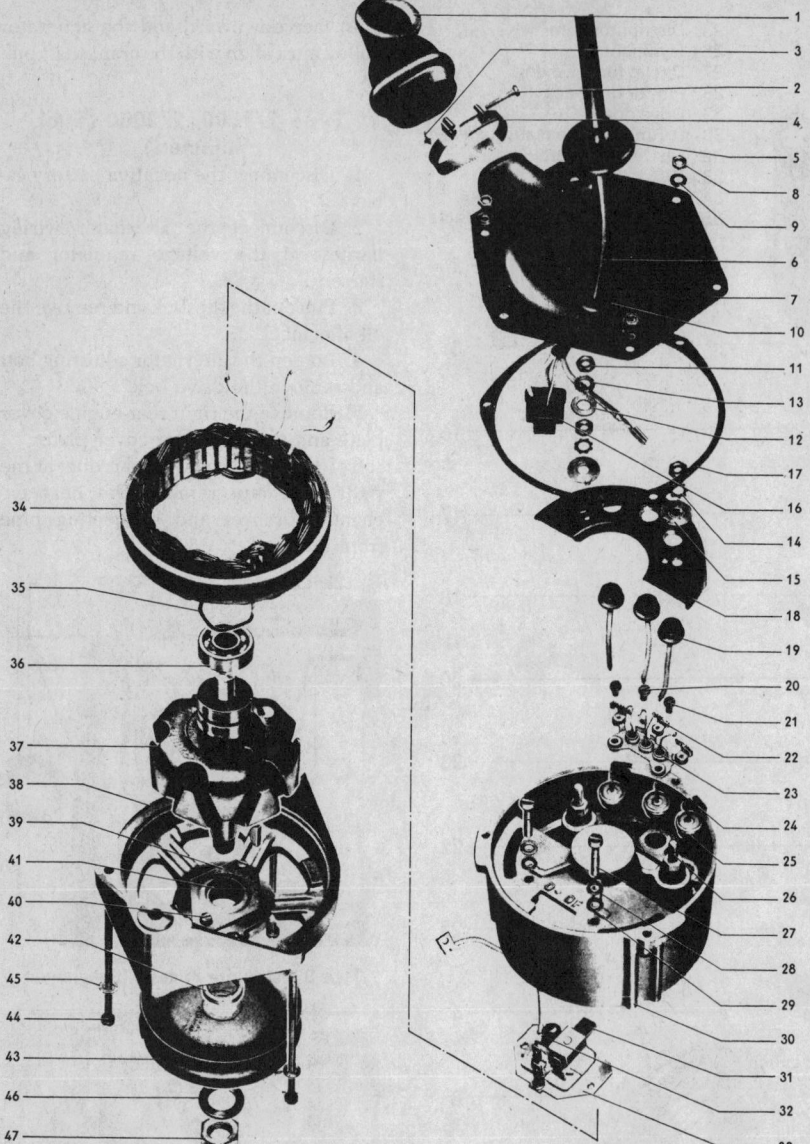

1. Elbow
2. Screw for hose clip
3. Threaded portion for hose clip
4. Cable hose clamp
5. Rubber grommet
6. Alternator wiring harness
7. Intake cover for alternator
8. Hex nut
9. Lockwasher
10. Rubber grommet for intake cover
11. B+ connection hex nut
12. Washer
13. Washer
14. Star washer
15. Contact disc
16. Three pin plug
17. Intake cover gasket
18. Positive diode carrier
19. Positive diodes
20. Screw
21. Stator winding connection screw
22. Exciter diode carrier
23. Exciter diodes
24. Seal
25. Negative diodes
26. Positive diode carrier pin
27. Brush holder screw
28. Washer
29. Spring washer
30. Alternator housing
31. Carbon brush
32. Brush retaining spring
33. Brush holder
34. Stator
35. Spring washer
36. Slip ring ball bearings
37. Claw pole rotor
38. End plate
39. Bearing end plate
40. Screw
41. Drive end ball bearing
42. Intermediate ring
43. Pulley
44. Housing bolt
45. Washer
46. Washer
47. Nut

Exploded view of 55 amp alternator used in Type 2/1700, 2/1800, and Type 4 models

1. Nut for pulley
2. Special washer
3. Shim
4. Pulley
5. End plate
6. End ring
7. Through-bolt
8. Washer
9. Screw
10. Washer
11. End plate with carbon brushes
12. Spring
13. Carbon brushes
14. Screw
15. Ball bearing
16. Splash shield
18. Splash shield
19. Retaining plate
20. Woodruff key
21. Splash shield
22. Armature
23. Armature flange
24. Gasket
25. Field coil
26. Housing
27. Field screw

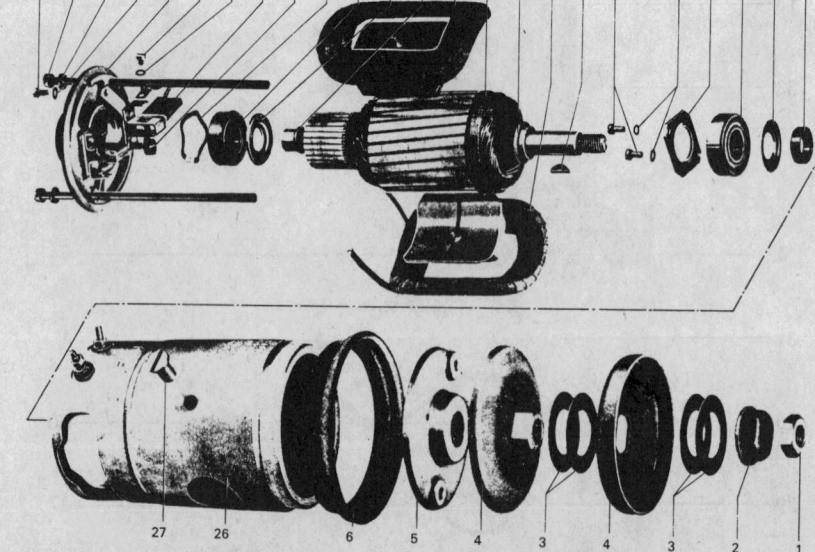
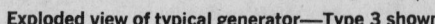

Exploded view of typical generator—Type 3 shown

7. Disconnect the cool air intake elbow at the alternator. Remove the attaching bolt and lift out the alternator from above.

8. Reverse the above procedure to install, taking care to ensure that the rubber grommet on the intake cover for the wiring harness is installed correctly. After installation, adjust the drive belt so that moderate thumb pressure midway on the belt depresses the belt about ½ in.

Type 3

1. Remove the cooling air intake cover and disconnect the battery.

2. Loosen the fan belt adjustment and remove the fan belt. Removal of the belt is accomplished by removing the nut in the center of the generator pulley and removing the outer pulley half.

3. Remove the two nuts which hold the generator securing strap in place and then remove the strap.

4. Disconnect the generator wiring.

5. Remove the generator.

6. Installation is the reverse of the above. Install the generator so that the mark on the generator housing is in line with the notch on the clamping strap. The generator pulley must be aligned with the crankshaft pulley. Make sure that the boot which seals the generator to the air intake housing is properly placed.

Type 4

The factory procedure recommends removing the engine to remove the alternator. However, it is possible to reach the alternator by first removing the right heater box.

1. Disconnect the battery.

2. The following is the alternator removal and installation procedure after removing the engine; however, all bolts and connections listed below must be removed, except the engine cooling fan, if the right heater box is removed to gain access to the alternator.

3. Remove the engine.

4. Remove the dipstick, if necessary, and the rear engine cover plate.

5. Remove the fan belt.

6. Remove the lower alternator belt and the alternator cover plate.

7. Disconnect the wiring harness from the alternator.

8. Remove the allen-head screws which attach the engine cooling fan, then remove the fan.

9. Remove the rubber elbow from the fan housing.

NOTE: *This elbow must be in position upon installation because it provides cooling air for the alternator.*

10. Remove the alternator adjusting bracket.

11. Remove the alternator.

12. Installation is the reverse of the

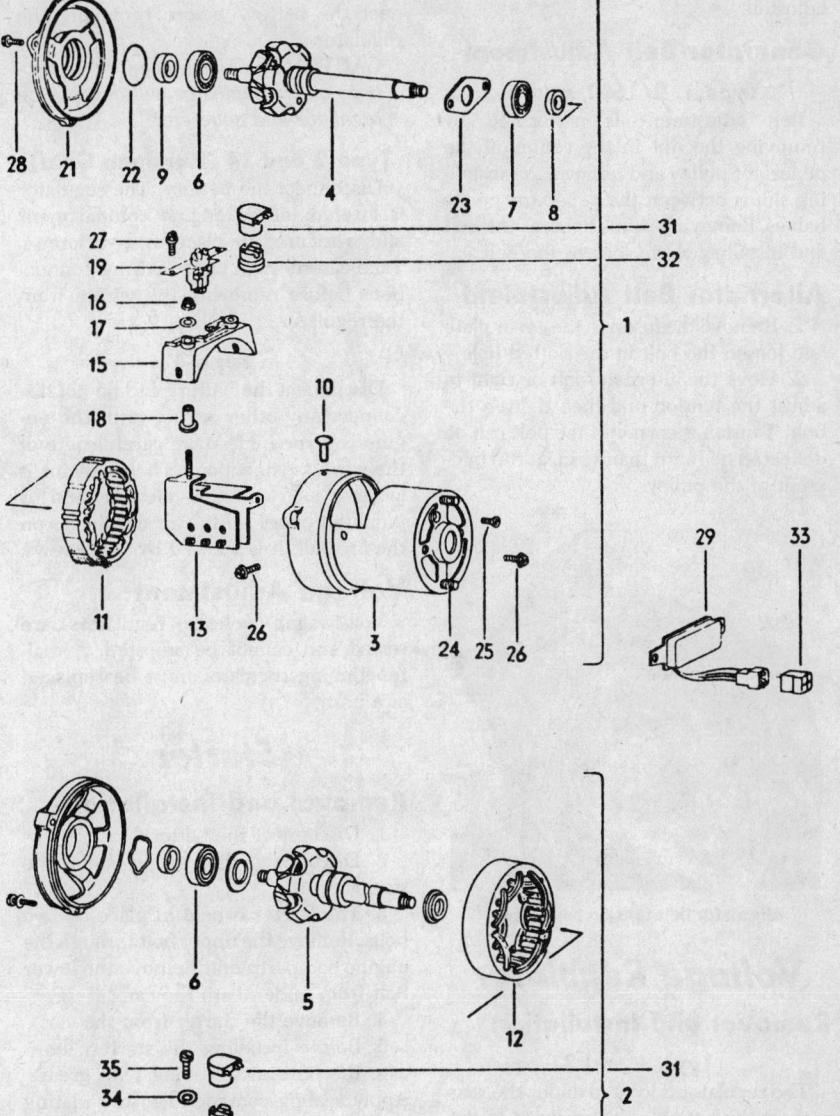

Exploded view of 50 amp alternator used in Type 1/1600 models

1. Motorola alternator	13. Diode carrier	25. Diode carrier screw
2. Bosch alternator	14. Diode carrier	26. Retaining plate screw
3. Housing	15. Diode carrier retainer	27. Brush holder cover screw
4. Claw-pole rotor	16. B+ terminal nut	28. End plate screw
5. Claw-pole rotor	17. B+ terminal insulating washer	29. Voltage regulator
6. End plate ball bearing	18. B+ terminal insulating bushing	30. Voltage regulator
7. Ball bearing	19. Brush holder	31. Boot
8. Fan end spacer ring	20. Carbon brush holder plate	32. Terminal sleeve housing
9. Drive end spacer ring	21. End plate	33. Terminal pin housing
10. Rotor locating plate	22. O-ring	34. Spring washer
11. Stator winding	23. Retaining plate	35. Screw
12. Stator winding	24. Fan cover bolt	

VW Types 1,2,3,4

above. Make sure that the belt is properly adjusted.

Generator Belt Adjustment

Type 1, 2/1600, and 3

Belt adjustment is performed by removing the nut in the center of the generator pulley and removing or installing shims between the generator pulley halves. Removing shims tightens the belt and installing shims loosens the belt.

Alternator Belt Adjustment

1. Remove the insert in the cover plate and loosen the bolt in the slotted hole.

2. Move the alternator left or right to adjust the tension and then tighten the bolt. Tension is correct if the bolt can be deflected no more than ½ in. at the midpoint of the pulleys.

Alternator belt tension adjustment

Voltage Regulator

Removal and Installation

Type 1 and 3

The regulator is located under the rear seat on the left side. It is secured to the frame by two screws. Take careful note of the wiring connections before removing

the wiring from the regulator. Disconnect the battery before removing the regulator.

CAUTION: *Interchanging the connections on the regulator will destroy the regulator and generator.*

Type 2 and 14 (Karmann Ghia)

Disconnect the battery. The regulator is located in the engine compartment and is secured in place by two screws. Take careful note of the wiring connections before removing the wiring from the regulator.

Type 4

Disconnect the battery and do not disconnect any other wiring until the engine is turned off. Make careful note of the wiring connections. The regulator is located near the air cleaner and is mounted either on the air cleaner or on the firewall. It is secured by two screws.

Voltage Adjustment

Volkswagen voltage regulators are sealed and cannot be adjusted. A malfunctioning regulator must be replaced as a unit.

Starter

Removal and Installation

1. Disconnect the battery.

2. Disconnect the wiring from the starter.

3. The starter is held in place by two bolts. Remove the upper bolt through the engine compartment. Remove the lower bolt from underneath the car.

4. Remove the starter from the car.

5. Before installing the starter, lubricate the outboard bushing with grease. Apply sealing compound to the mating surfaces between the starter and the transmission.

6. Place the long starter bolt in its hole in the starter and locate the starter on the transmission housing. Install the other bolt.

7. Connect the starter wiring and battery cables.

Solenoid Replacement

1. Remove the starter.

2. Remove the nut which secures the connector strip at the end of the solenoid.

3. Take out the two retaining screws on the mounting bracket and withdraw the solenoid after it has been unhooked from its actuating lever.

4. When replacing a defective solenoid with a new one, care should be taken to see that the distance (a) in the accompanying diagram is 19 mm when the magnet is drawn inside the solenoid.

5. Installation is the reverse of removal. In order to facilitate engagement of the actuating rod, the pinion should be pulled out as far as possible when inserting the solenoid.

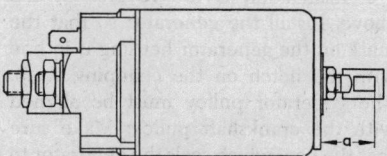

Solenoid adjustment

Battery

The electrical system of the Volkswagen is a negative grounded type. In most VW models, the battery is located under the right-hand side of the rear seat. In Karmann Ghia, Type 2 and 4 models, it is located in the engine compartment.

Removal and Installation

1. Disconnect the battery cables. Note the position of the battery cables for in-

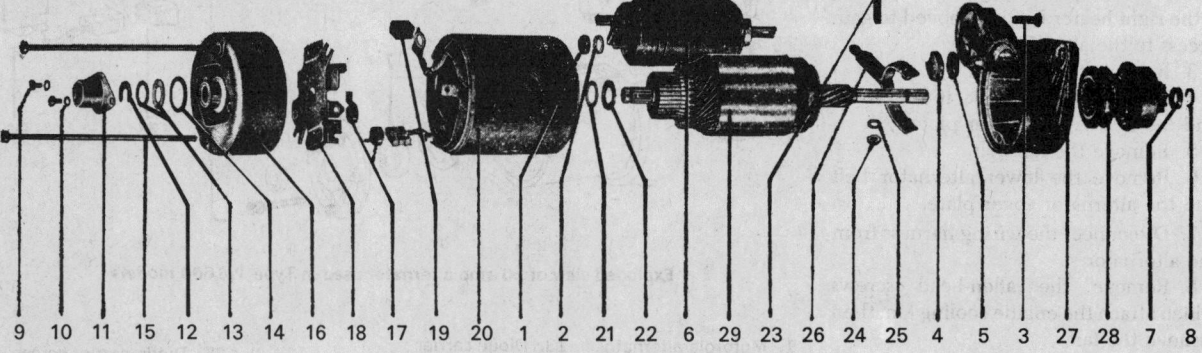

Exploded view of Bosch no. 311 911 023B starter

1. Nut	11. End cap	21. Insulating washer
2. Lockwasher	12. C-washer	22. Thrust washer
3. Screw	13. Shim	23. Pin
4. Rubber seal	14. Sealing ring	24. Nut
5. Disc	15. Housing screw	25. Lockwasher
6. Solenoid switch	16. End plate	26. Operating lever
7. Stop-ring	17. Spring	27. Drive end plate
8. Circlip	18. Brush holder	28. Drive pinion
9. Screw	19. Rubber grommet	29. Armature
10. Washer	20. Housing	

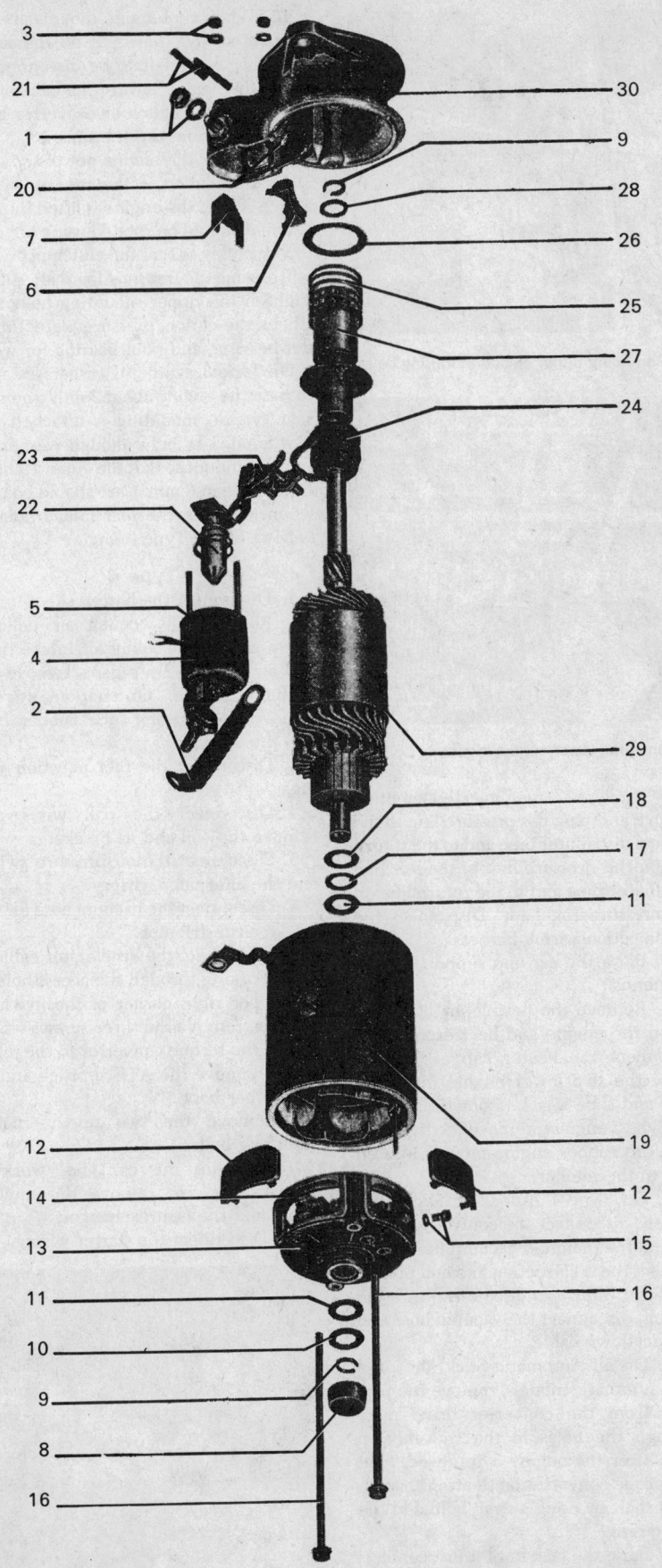

1. Nut and lockwasher
2. Connecting strip
3. Nut and lockwasher
4. Solenoid
5. Insulating disc
6. Seal
7. Insulating plate
8. Cap
9. Circlip
10. Steel washer
11. Bronze washer
12. Brush inspection cover
13. Commutator end plate
14. Brush holder
15. Screw and lockwasher
16. Housing screws
17. Dished washer
18. Steel washer
19. Housing and field windings
20. Spring clip
21. Pin
22. Solenoid core
23. Linkage
24. Bushing
25. Spring
26. Washer
27. Drive pinion
28. Dished washer
29. Armature
30. Mounting bracket

stallation. The small diameter battery post is the negative terminal. The negative battery cable is usually black.

2. Undo the battery holddown strap and lift the battery out of its holder.

3. Install the battery in its holder and replace the clamp. Reconnect the battery cables.

ENGINE MECHANICAL

The Volkswagen engine is a flat four cylinder design. This four cycle, overhead valve engine has two pairs of horizontally opposed cylinders. All rear-engined VW models are air.cooled.

The Type 1 and 2/1600 engine is known as an upright fan engine, that is, the engine cooling fan is mounted vertically on top of the engine and is driven by the generator shaft. The Type 2/1700, Type 2/1800, Type 3 and 4 engine, although of the same basic design, i.e. flat four, has the cooling fan driven by the crankshaft and is therefore mounted on the front of the engine. This type of engine is known as the suitcase engine.

Because it is air cooled, the VW engine is slightly noisier than a water cooled engine. This is due to the lack of water jacketing around the cylinders which provides sound deadening on water cooled engines. In addition, air cooled engines tend to run at somewhat higher temperatures, necessitating larger operating clearances to allow more room for the expansion of the parts. These larger operating clearances cause an increase in noise level over a water cooled engine.

The crankshaft of all Volkswagen engines is mounted in a two piece crankcase. The halves are machined to very

Exploded view of VW no. 111 911 023A starter

close tolerances and line bored as a pair and, therefore, should always be replaced in pairs. When fitting them, it is necessary to coat only the mating surfaces with sealing compound and tighten them down to the correct torque. No gasket is used.

The pistons and cylinders are identical on any particular engine. However, it is not possible to interchange pistons and cylinders between engines. The four pistons each have three rings, two compression rings and one oil scraper. Each piston is attached to its connecting rod with a fully floating piston pin.

Each pair of cylinders shares a detachable cylinder head made of light aluminum alloy casting. The cylinder head contains the valves for both cylinders. Shrunk-in valve guides and valve seats are used.

Engine Removal and Installation

Type 1, 2, and 3

The Volkswagen engine is mounted on the transmission, which in turn is attached to the frame. In the Type 1 and 2 models, there are two bolts and two studs attaching the engine to the transmission. Type 3 engines have an extra mounting at the rear of the engine. Type 3 engines with automatic transmissions have front and rear engine and transmission mounts. At the front, the gearbox is supported by the rear tubular crossmember; at the rear, a crossmember is bolted to the crankcase and mounted to the body at either end.

When removing the engine from the car, it is recommended that the rear of the car be about 3 ft off the ground. Remove the engine by bringing it out from underneath the car. Proceed with the following steps to remove the engine.

1. Disconnect the battery ground cable.

2. Disconnect the generator wiring.

3. Remove the air cleaner. On Type 1 engines, remove the rear engine cover plate. On Type 2/1600 cc engines, remove the rear crossmember.

4. Disconnect the throttle cable and remove the electrical connections to the automatic choke, coil, electromagnetic cutoff jet, and the oil pressure sending unit.

5. Disconnect the fuel hose at the front engine cover plate and seal it to prevent leakage.

6. On Type 3 models, remove the oil dipstick and the rubber boot between the oil filter and the body.

7. Remove the cooling air intake bellows on Type 3 engines after loosening the clip that secures the unit.

8. On Type 3 models, remove the warm air hose.

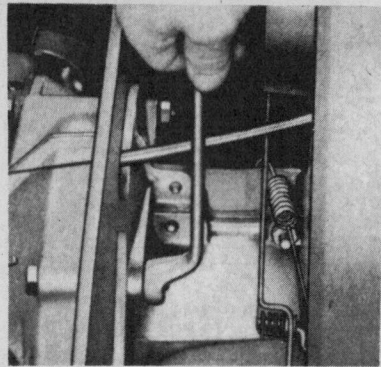

Removing upper engine mounting bolts

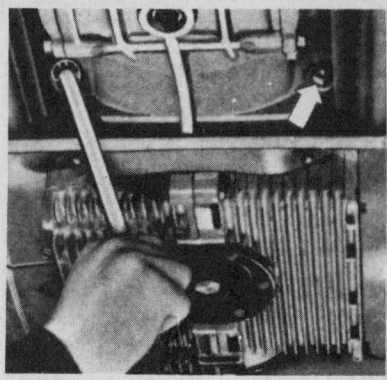

Removing lower engine mounting bolts

9. On Type 3 fuel injected engines, remove and plug the pressure line to the left fuel distributor pipe and to the return line on the pressure line to the left fuel distributor pipe and to the return line on the pressure regulator. Disconnect the fuel injection wiring harness.

10. Raise the car and support it with jackstands.

11. Remove the flexible air hoses between the engine and heat exchangers, disconnect the heater flap cables, unscrew the two lower engine mounting nuts, and slide a jack under the engine. On Type 2 engines, remove the two bolts from the rubber engine mounts located next to the muffler.

12. On Type 1 Automatic Stick Shift models, disconnect the control valve cable and the manifold vacuum hoses. Disconnect the ATF suction line and plug it. On Type 3 fully automatic transmission models, disconnect the vacuum hose and the kickdown cable.

13. On all Automatic Stick Shift and fully automatic models, remove the four bolts from the converter drive plate through the holes in the transmission case. After the engine is removed, hold the torque converter on the transmission input shaft by using a strap bolted to the bellhousing.

14. Raise the jack until it just contacts the engine and have an assistant hold the two upper mounting bolts so that the nuts can be removed from the bottom.

15. When the engine mounts are disconnected and there are no remaining cables or wires left to be disconnected, move the engine toward the back of the car so that the clutch or converter plate disengages from the transmission.

16. Lower the engine out of the car.

17. Installation is the reverse of the above. When the engine is lifted into position, it should be rotated using the generator pulley so that the clutch plate hub will engage the transmission shaft splines. Tighten the upper mounting bolts first. Check the clutch, pressure plate, throwout bearing, and pilot bearing for wear.

On Type 3, synthetic washers are used to raise the engine about 3 mm when the rear engine mounting is attached and tightened. Use only enough washers in the rear mount so that the engine is lifted no more than 3 mm. Care should be used when installing the rear intake housing bellows of the Type 3 engine.

Type 4

1. Disconnect the battery.

2. Remove the cooling air bellows, warm air hoses, cooling air intake duct, and air cleaner. On sedans, remove the cooling air fan. On station wagons, remove the dipstick tube rubber boot and the dipstick.

3. Disconnect the fuel injection wiring.

4. Disconnect the coil wires and remove the coil and its bracket.

5. Disconnect the oil pressure switch and the alternator wiring.

6. Disconnect the vacuum hose for the intake air distributor.

7. Disconnect the accelerator cable.

8. Working through the access hole at the upper right corner of the flywheel housing, remove the three screws which secure the torque converter to the drive plate. Remove the ATF dipstick and the rubber boot.

9. Remove the two upper engine mounting bolts.

10. Jack up the car and, working beneath the car, remove the muffler shield and the heat exchanger.

11. Disconnect the starter wiring.

Access hole for torque converter bolts— Type 4

Engine carrier screw location upon installation of engine—Type 4

12. Remove the heater booster exhaust pipe.

13. Remove the two lower engine mounting nuts.

14. Jack up the engine slightly and remove the four engine carrier screws.

NOTE: *Do not loosen the mountings on the body or the engine-transmission assembly will have to be recentralized in the chassis.*

15. Remove the engine from the car.

16. Reverse the removal procedures to install the engine. Install the engine on the lower engine mounting studs and then locate the engine in the engine carrier. When installing the engine in the carrier, lift the engine up so that the four screws are at the top of the elongated holes and tighten them in this position. If it is necessary to raise or lower the engine for adjustment purposes, use the threaded shaft. After the engine is installed, make sure that the rubber buffer is centered in the rear axle carrier. Make sure that the engine carrier is vertical and parallel to the engine fan housing. Readjust it if necessary by moving the brackets on the side members.

Checking that engine carrier is vertical and parallel to the fan housing—Type 4

Cylinder Head

Removal and Installation

In order to remove the cylinder head from either pair of cylinders, it is necessary to lower the engine.

1. Remove the valve cover and gasket. Remove the rocker arm assembly. Unbolt the intake manifold from the cylinder head. The cylinder head is held in place by eight studs. Since the cylinder head also holds the cylinders in place in the VW engine, and the cylinders are not going to be removed, it will be necessary to hold the cylinders in place after the head is removed.

2. After the rocker arm cover, rocker arm retaining nuts, and rocker arm assembly have been removed, the cylinder head nuts can be removed and the cylinder head lifted off.

3. When reinstalling the cylinder head, the head should be checked for cracks both in the combustion chamber and in the intake and exhaust ports. Cracked heads must be replaced.

4. Spark plug threads should be checked. New seals should be used on the pushrod tube ends and they should be checked for proper seating.

5. The pushrod tubes should be turned so that the seam faces upward. In order to ensure perfect sealing, used tubes should be stretched slightly before they are reinstalled.

6. Install the cylinder head. Using new rocker shaft stud seals, install the pushrods and rocker shaft assembly.

NOTE: *Pay careful attention to the orientation of the shaft as described in the "Rocker Shaft" section.*

7. Torque the cylinder head in three stages. Adjust the valve clearance. Using a new gasket, install the rocker cover. It may be necessary to readjust the valves after the engine has been run a few minutes and allowed to cool.

Valve Seats

On all air-cooled VW engines, the valve seats are shrunk-fit into the cylinder head. This usually involves freezing the seat with liquid nitrogen or some other refrigerant to about 200°F below zero, and heating up the cylinder head to approximately 400°F. Due to the extreme temperatures required to shrink-fit these items, and because of the extra care needed when working with metals at these extreme temperatures, it is advised that this operation be referred to an experienced repair shop.

Cylinder Head Overhaul and Valve Guide Replacement

See the "Engine Rebuilding" section at the end of this book.

Rocker Shafts

Rocker Shaft Removal and Installation

1. Before the valve rocker assembly can be reached, it is necessary to lever off the clip that retains the valve cover and

On types 1, 2/1600, and 3, install the rocker shaft with the chamfer out and the slot up

On Types 2/1700, 2/1800, and 4, install the rocker shaft with the chamfer out and the slots down

then remove the valve cover.

2. Remove the rocker arm retaining nuts, the rocker arm shaft, and the rocker arms. Remove the stud seals.

3. Before installing the rocker arm mechanism, be sure that the parts are as clean as possible.

4. Install new stud seals. On Type 1, 2/1600, and 3, install the rocker shaft assembly with the chamfered edges of the rocker shaft supports pointing outward and the slots pointing upward. On Type 4 and Type 2/1700, 2/1800, 2/2000 models, the chamfered edges must point outward and the slots must face downward, and the pushrod tube retaining wire must engage the slots in the rocker arm shaft supports as well as the grooves in the pushrod tubes.

5. Tighten the retaining nuts to the proper torque. Use only the copper colored nuts that were supplied with the engine.

6. Make sure that the ball ends of the push rods are centered in the sockets of the rocker arms.

7. Adjust the valve clearance. Install the valve cover using a new gasket.

Intake Manifold

Removal and Installation

Single Carburetor Engines

1. Disconnect the battery.
2. Disconnect the generator wiring.

1. Cylinder head cover
2. Gasket
3. Nut
4. Spring washer
5. Rocker shaft
6. Clip
7. Thrust washer
8. Spring washer
9. Rocker arm
10. Adjusting screw
11. Nut
12. Support
13. Stud seal
14. Nut
15. Washer

16a. Type 1, Type 2/1600 cylinder head
16b. Type 3 cylinder head
17. Thermostat link
18. Valve cotter
19. Spring cap
20. Valve spring
21. Oil deflector ring
22. Intake valve
23. Exhaust valve
24. Intake valve guide
25. Exhaust valve guide
26. Pushrod tube
27. Sealing ring
28. Pushrod

Cylinder head exploded view—Types 1/1600, 2/1600, 3/1600

3. Remove the generator. It will be necessary to loosen the fan housing and tilt it back to gain clearance to remove the generator.

4. Disconnect the choke and the accelerator cable.

5. On some models it will be necessary to remove the carburetor from the manifold.

6. Unbolt the manifold from the cylinder head and remove the manifold from the engine.

7. Reverse the above to install. Always use new gaskets.

Twin Carburetor Engines

1. Remove the carburetors.

2. Disconnect the tubes from the central idling system mixture distributor.

3. Disconnect all vacuum lines. Label them for purposes of installation.

4. Remove the nuts and bolts retaining the manifolds to the cylinder heads.

Carefully lift off each manifold.

5. Reverse the above procedure to install, taking care to carefully clean all mating surfaces to the carburetors and cylinder heads. Always use new gaskets.

Fuel Injection Engines

1. Remove the air cleaner.

2. Remove the pressure switch which is mounted under the right pair of intake manifold pipes. Disconnect the injector wiring.

3. Remove the fuel injectors by removing the two nuts which secure them in place. On Type 3, do not separate the pair of injectors; they can be removed as a pair and must be left in the injector plate. See Step 7 for proper injector installation.

4. After removing the intake manifold outer cover plate, remove the two screws which secure the manifold inner cover plate.

5. The manifold may be removed by

removing the two nuts and washers which hold the manifold flange to the cylinder head.

6. Installation is the reverse of the above. The inner manifold cover should be installed first, but leave the cover loose until the outer cover and manifold are in place. Always use new gaskets.

7. Connect the fuel hoses to the injectors, if removed, after assembling the injectors with the injector retainer plate in place. Make sure that the sleeves are in place on the injector securing studs. Carefully slip the injectors into the manifold and install the securing nuts. Never force the injectors in or out of the manifold. Reconnect the injector wiring.

Intake Air Distributor
Removal and Installation

Fuel Injected Engines

The intake air distributor is located at

the center of the engine at the junction of the intake manifold pipes.

NOTE: *It is not necessary to remove the distributor if only the manifold pipes are to be removed.*

1. Remove the air cleaner and pressure switch which are located under the right pair of manifold pipes.

2. Push the four rubber hoses onto the intake manifold pipes.

3. Remove the accelerator cable and the throttle valve switch.

4. Disconnect the accelerator cable.

5. Disconnect the vacuum hoses leading to the ignition distributor and the pressure sensor and disconnect the hose running to the auxiliary air regulator.

6. Remove those bolts under the air distributor which secure the air distributor to the crankcase and remove the air distributor.

7. Installation is the reverse of removal.

Mufflers, Tailpipes, Heat Exhangers

Removal and Installation

Muffler, Type 1 and 2/1600

1. Working under the hood, disconnect the pre-heater hoses.

2. Remove the pre-heater pipe protection plate on each side of the engine. The plates are secured by three screws.

3. Remove the crankshaft pulley cover plate.

4. Remove the rear engine cover plate from the engine compartment. It is held in place by screws at the center, right, and left sides.

5. Remove the four intake manifold preheat pipe bolts. There are two bolts on each side of the engine.

6. Disconnect the warm air channel clamps at the left and right side of the engine.

7. Disconnect the heat exchanger clamps at the left and right side of the engine.

8. Remove the muffler from the engine.

9. Installation is the reverse of the above. Always use new gaskets to install the muffler.

Muffler, Type 3

The muffler is secured to the heat exchangers with clamps and, on some models, to the body with bolts at the top and at the ends.

Muffler, Type 4, 2/1700, 2/1800, 2/2000

The muffler is secured to the left and right heat exchangers by three bolts. There is a bracket at the left end of the muffler. Always use new gaskets when installing a new muffler.

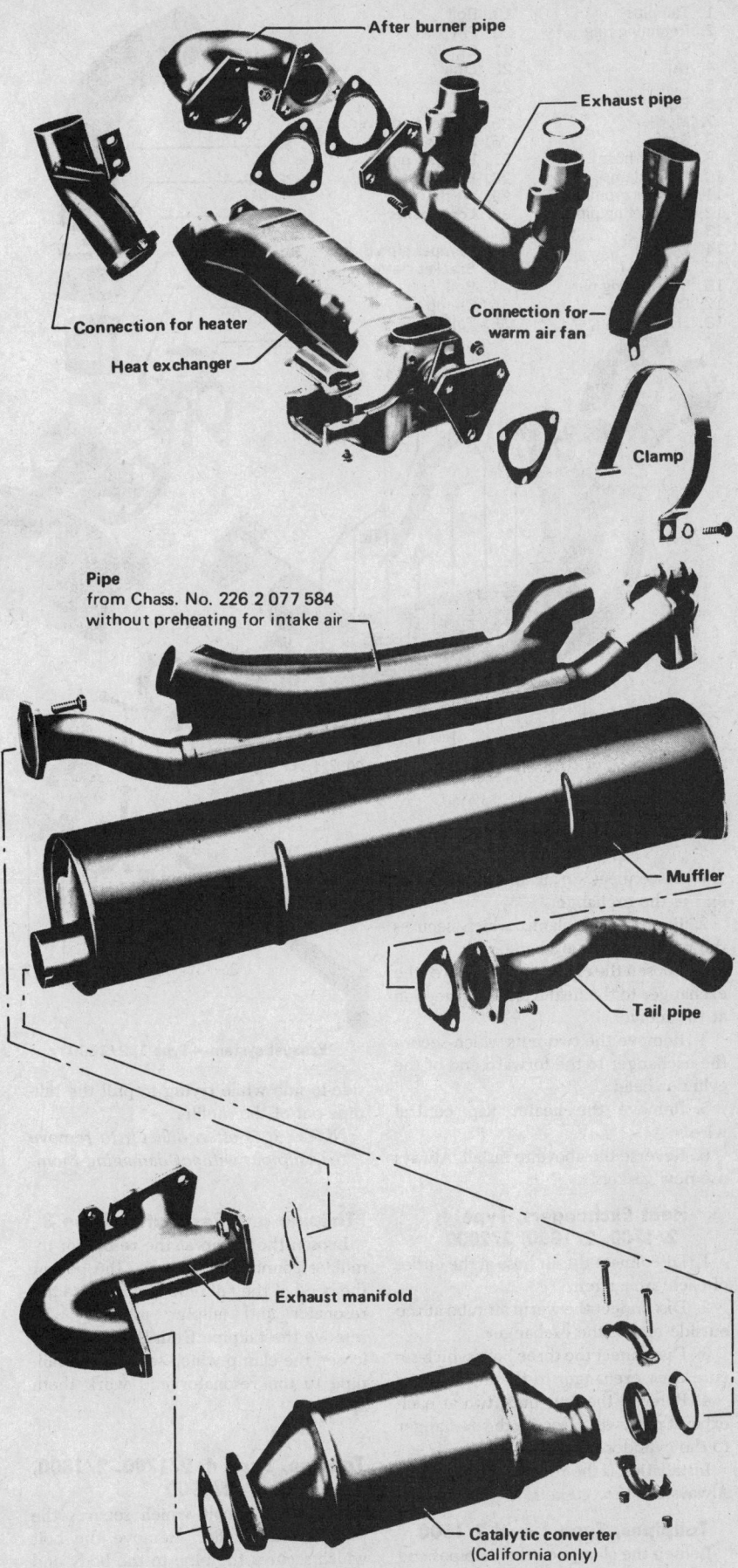

Pipe from Chass. No. 226 2 077 584 without preheating for intake air

Exhaust system—1975-77 Type 2/1800, 2/2000

1. Tail pipe
2. Retaining ring
3. Seal
4. Nut
5. Clamp
6. Bolt
7. Muffler
8. Seal
9. Heater hose
10. Hose clamp
11. Rubber grommet
12. Connecting pipe
13. Gasket
14. Gasket
15. Gasket
16. Self-locking nut
17. Clamp
18. Heat exchanger
19. Bolt
20. Pin
21. Circlip
22. Link
23. Pin
24. Pin
25. Heater flap lever
26. Return spring
27. Damper pipe
28. Bolt
29. Washer
30. Lockwasher
31. Bolt
32. Damper pipe bracket
33. Bracket clamp
34. Bolt
35. Clamp
36. Tailpipe

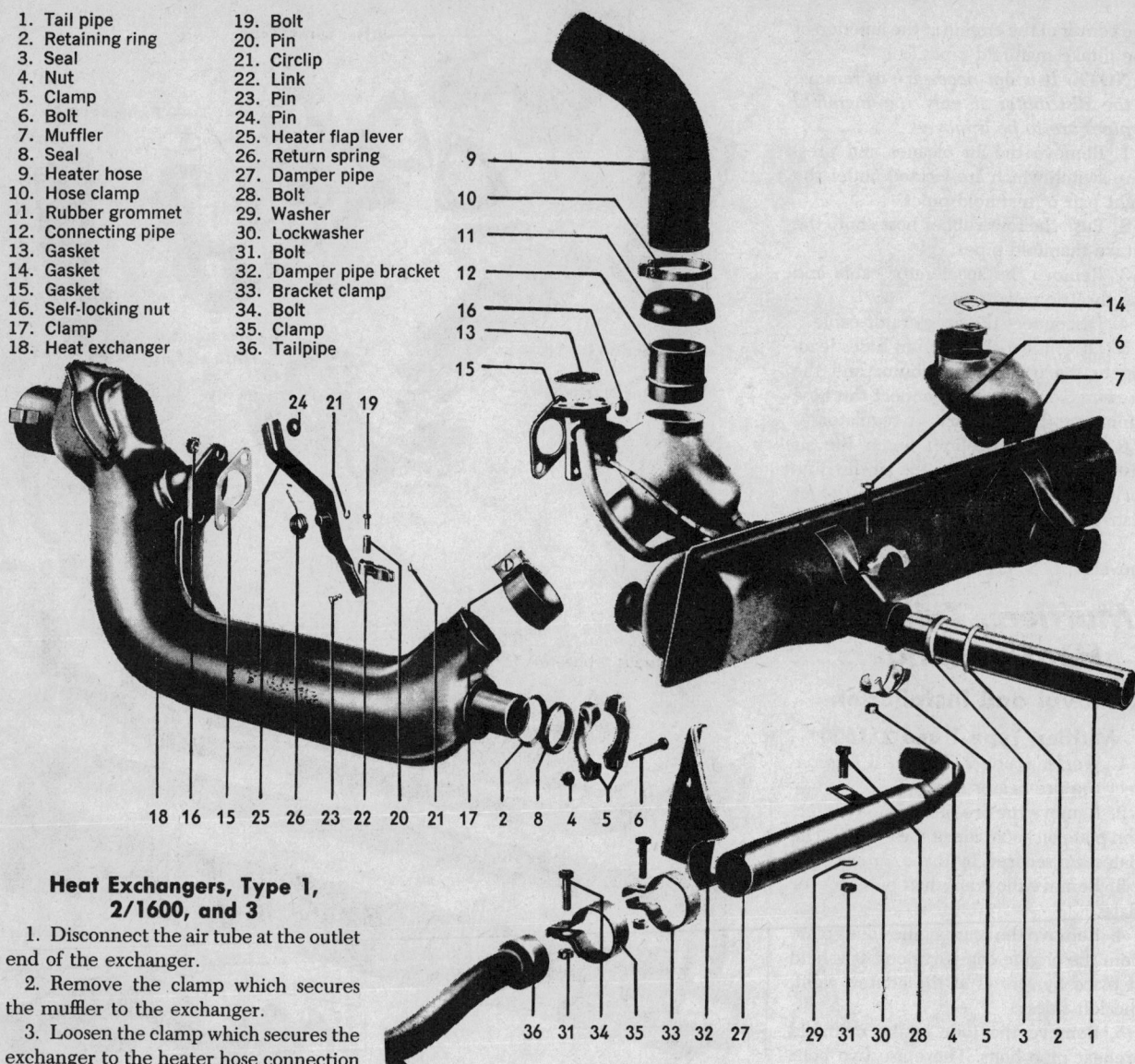

Exhaust system—Type 1, 2/1600

Heat Exchangers, Type 1, 2/1600, and 3

1. Disconnect the air tube at the outlet end of the exchanger.

2. Remove the clamp which secures the muffler to the exchanger.

3. Loosen the clamp which secures the exchanger to the heater hose connection at the muffler.

4. Remove the two nuts which secure the exchanger to the forward end of the cylinder head.

5. Remove the heater flap control wire.

6. Reverse the above to install. Always use new gaskets.

Heat Exchangers, Type 4, 2/1700, 2/1800, 2/2000

1. Disconnect the air hose at the outlet of each exchanger.

2. Disconnect the warm air tube at the outside end of the exchanger.

3. Disconnect the three bolts which secure each exchanger to the muffler.

4. Remove the four nuts, two at each exhaust port, which secure the exchanger to the cylinder head.

Installation is the reverse of the above. Always use new gaskets.

Tailpipes, Type 1 and 2/1600

Loosen the clamps on the tailpipes and apply penetrating oil. Work the pipe side-to-side while trying to pull the tailpipe out of the muffler.

NOTE: *It is often difficult to remove the tailpipes without damaging them.*

Tailpipe and Resonator, Type 3

Loosen the clamp at the resonator-to-muffler connection. Remove the bolt at the bend of the tail pipe and remove the resonator and tailpipe assembly. To remove the tailpipe from the resonator, loosen the clamp which secures the tailpipe to the resonator and work them apart.

Tailpipe, Type 4, 2/1700, 2/1800, 2/1900

Remove the bolt which secures the pipe to the muffler. Remove the bolt which secures the pipe to the body and remove the pipe.

Pistons and Cylinders

Pistons and cylinders are matched according to their size. When replacing pistons and cylinders, make sure that they are properly sized.

NOTE: *See the "Engine Rebuilding" section for cylinder refinishing.*

Cylinder Removal and Installation

1. Remove the engine. Remove the cylinder head, pushrod tubes, and the deflector plate.

2. Slide the cylinder out of its groove in the crankcase and off the piston. Matchmark the cylinders for reassembly. The cylinders must be returned to their original bore in the crankcase. If a cylinder is to be replaced, it must be replaced with a matching piston.

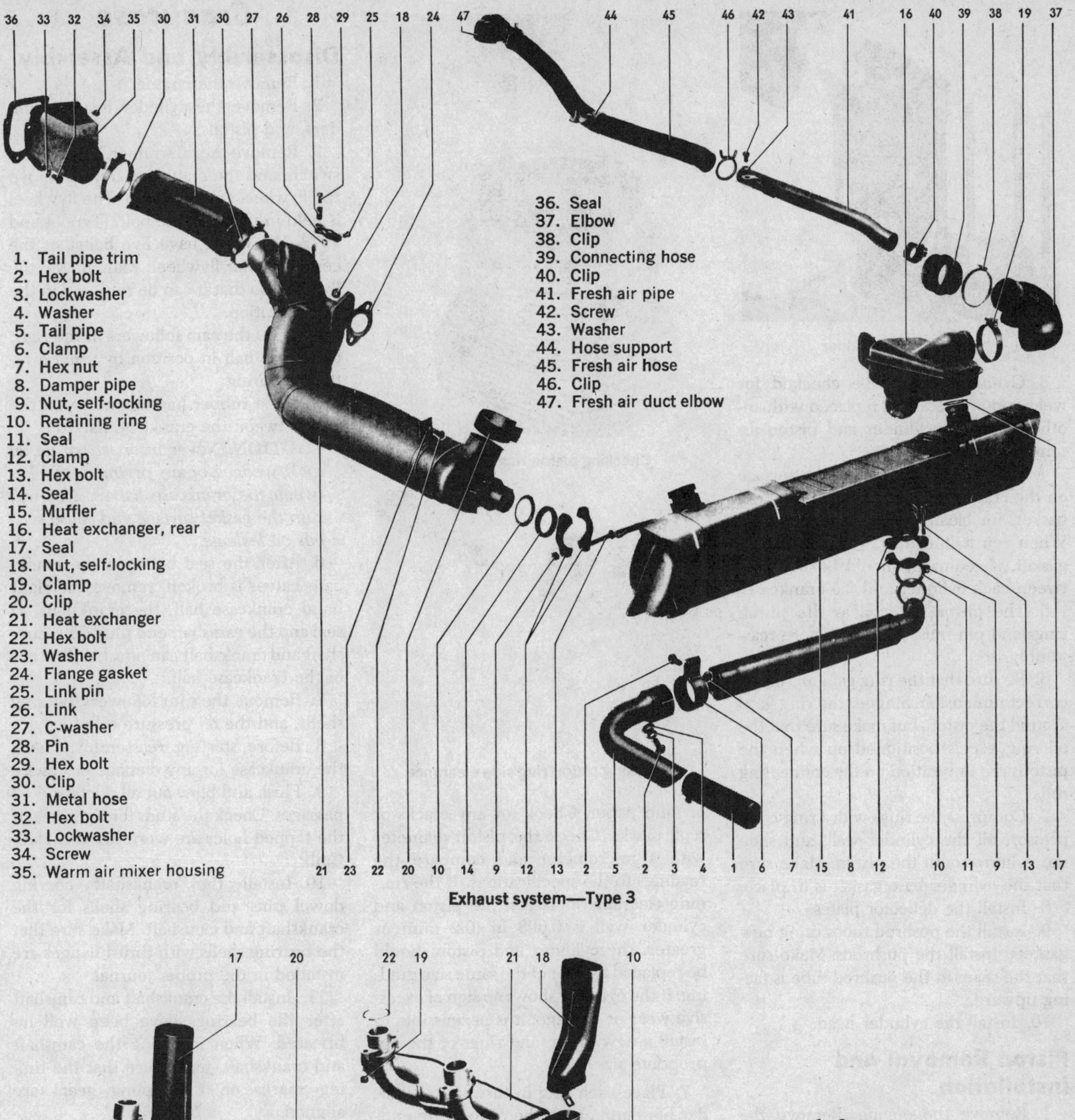

1. Tail pipe trim
2. Hex bolt
3. Lockwasher
4. Washer
5. Tail pipe
6. Clamp
7. Hex nut
8. Damper pipe
9. Nut, self-locking
10. Retaining ring
11. Seal
12. Clamp
13. Hex bolt
14. Seal
15. Muffler
16. Heat exchanger, rear
17. Seal
18. Nut, self-locking
19. Clamp
20. Clip
21. Heat exchanger
22. Hex bolt
23. Washer
24. Flange gasket
25. Link pin
26. Link
27. C-washer
28. Pin
29. Hex bolt
30. Clip
31. Metal hose
32. Hex bolt
33. Lockwasher
34. Screw
35. Warm air mixer housing

36. Seal
37. Elbow
38. Clip
39. Connecting hose
40. Clip
41. Fresh air pipe
42. Screw
43. Washer
44. Hose support
45. Fresh air hose
46. Clip
47. Fresh air duct elbow

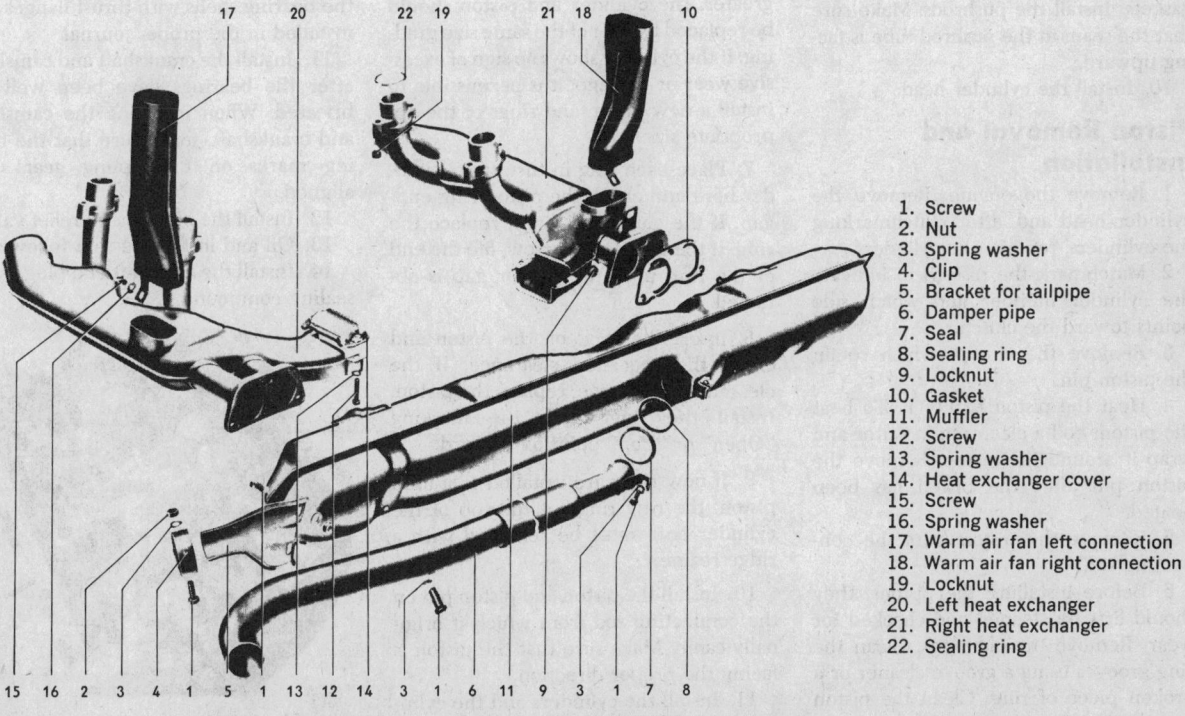

Exhaust system—Type 3

1. Screw
2. Nut
3. Spring washer
4. Clip
5. Bracket for tailpipe
6. Damper pipe
7. Seal
8. Sealing ring
9. Locknut
10. Gasket
11. Muffler
12. Screw
13. Spring washer
14. Heat exchanger cover
15. Screw
16. Spring washer
17. Warm air fan left connection
18. Warm air fan right connection
19. Locknut
20. Left heat exchanger
21. Right heat exchanger
22. Sealing ring

Exhaust system—Type 2/1700, 2/1800, and Type 4

Installing a cylinder

3. Cylinders should be checked for wear and, if necessary, replaced with another matched cylinder and piston assembly of the same size.

4. Check the cylinder seating surface on the crankcase, cylinder shoulder, and gasket, for cleanliness and deep scores. When reinstalling the cylinders, a new gasket, if required, should be used between each cylinder and the crankcase.

5. The piston, as well as the piston rings and pin must be oiled before reassembly.

6. Be sure that the ring gaps are of the correct dimension. Stagger the ring gaps around the piston, but make sure that the oil ring gap is positioned up when the pistons are in position on the connecting rods.

7. Compress the rings with a ring compressor, oil the cylinder wall, and slide the cylinder onto the piston. Make sure that the cylinder base gasket is in place.

8. Install the deflector plates.

9. Install the pushrod tubes using new gaskets. Install the pushrods. Make sure that the seam in the pushrod tube is facing upward.

10. Install the cylinder head.

Piston Removal and Installation

1. Remove the engine. Remove the cylinder head and, after matchmarking the cylinders, remove the cylinders.

2. Matchmark the pistons to indicate the cylinder number and which side points toward the clutch.

3. Remove the circlips which retain the piston pin.

4. Heat the piston to 176 F. To heat the piston, boil a clean rag in water and wrap it around the piston. Remove the piston pin after the piston has been heated.

5. Remove the piston from the connecting rod.

6. Before installing the pistons, they should first be cleaned and checked for wear. Remove the old rings. Clean the ring grooves using a groove cleaner or a broken piece of ring. Clean the piston with solvent but do not use a wire brush

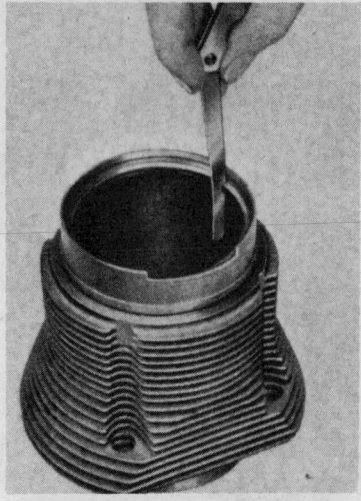

Checking piston ring end-gap

Checking piston ring side clearance

or sand paper. Check for any cracks or scuff marks. Check the piston diameter with a micrometer and compare the readings to the specifications. If the running clearance between the piston and cylinder wall is 0.008 in (0.2 mm) or greater, the cylinder and piston should be replaced by a set of the same size grading. If the cylinder shows no sign of excessive wear or damage, it is permissible to install a new piston and rings of the appropriate size.

7. Place each ring in turn in its cylinder bore and check the piston ring end-gap. If the gap is too large, replace the ring. If the gap is too narrow, file the end of the ring until the proper gap is obtained.

8. Insert the rings on the piston and check the ring side clearance. If the clearance is too large, replace the piston. Install the rings with the marking "Oben" or "Top" pointing upward.

9. If new rings are installed in a used piston, the ring ridge at the top of the cylinder bore must be removed with a ridge reamer.

10. Install the piston and piston pin on the connecting rod from which it originally came. Make sure that the piston is facing the proper direction.

11. Install the cylinders and the cylinder heads.

Crankcase

Disassembly and Assembly

1. Remove the engine.

2. Remove the cylinder heads, cylinders, and pistons.

3. Remove the oil strainer, oil pressure switch, and the crankcase nuts. Remove the flywheel and oil pump. The flywheel is held in place by the bolt. (Type 4 and 1972–76 Type 2 have five bolts), at the center of the flywheel. Matchmark the flywheel so that it can be replaced in the same position.

4. Keep the cam followers in the right crankcase half in position by using a retaining spring.

5. Use a rubber hammer to break the seal between the crankcase halves.

CAUTION: *Never insert sharp metal tools, wedges, or any prying device between the crankcase halves. This will ruin the gasket surface and cause serious oil leakage.*

6. After the seal between the crankcase halves is broken, remove the right hand crankcase half, the crankshaft oil seal and the camshaft end plug. The camshaft and crankshaft can now be lifted out of the crankcase half.

7. Remove the cam followers, bearing shells, and the oil pressure relief valve.

8. Before starting reassembly, check the crankcase for any damage or cracks.

9. Flush and blow out all ducts and oil passages. Check the studs for tightness. If the tapped holes are worn install a Heli-Coil.

10. Install the crankshaft bearing dowel pins and bearing shells for the crankshaft and camshaft. Make sure that the bearing shells with thrust flanges are installed in the proper journal.

11. Install the crankshaft and camshaft after the bearings have been well lubricated. When installing the camshaft and crankshaft, make sure that the timing marks on the timing gears are aligned.

12. Install the oil pressure relief valve.

13. Oil and install the cam followers.

14. Install the camshaft end plug using sealing compound.

Check dowel pins for tightness

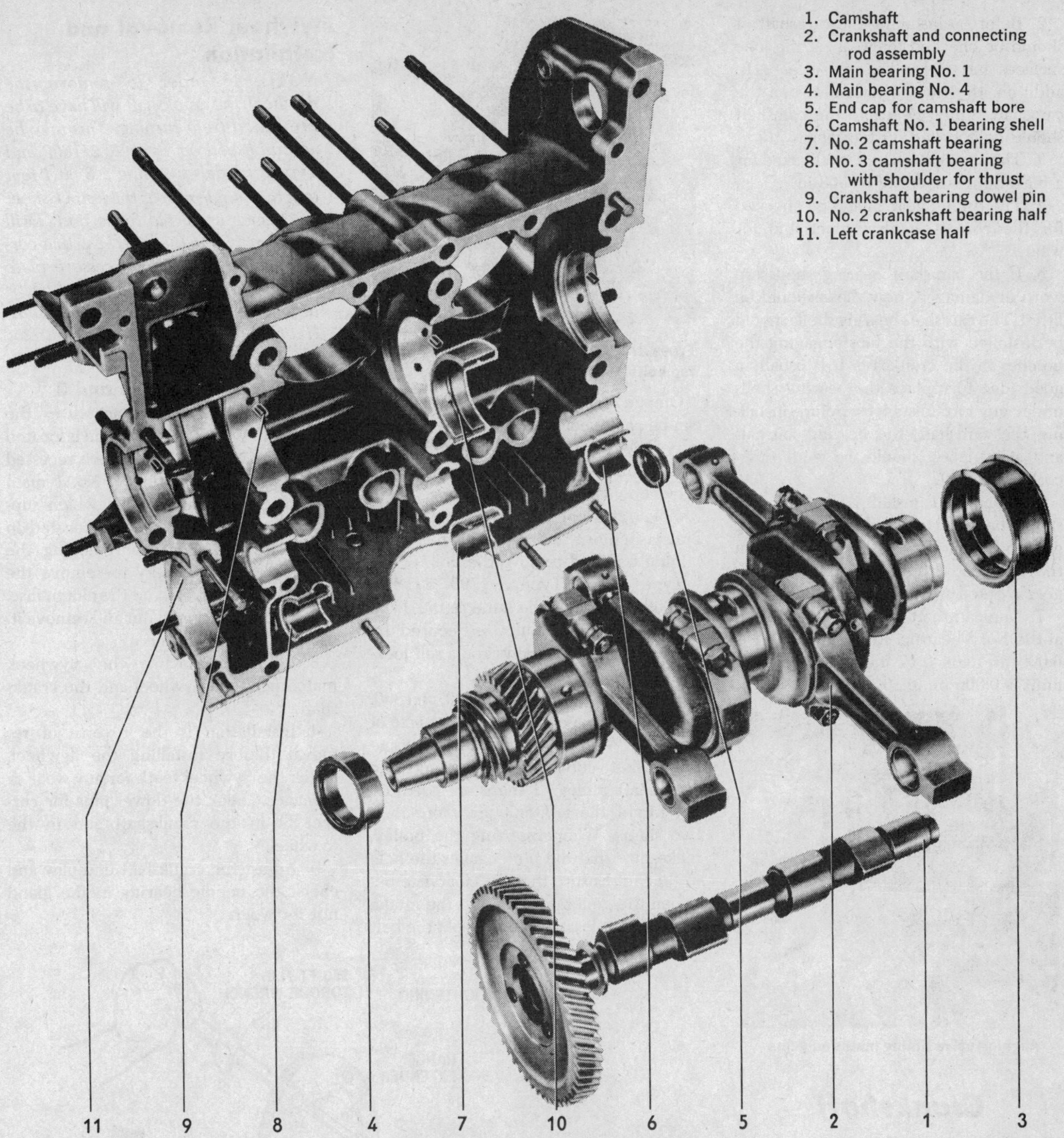

1. Camshaft
2. Crankshaft and connecting rod assembly
3. Main bearing No. 1
4. Main bearing No. 4
5. End cap for camshaft bore
6. Camshaft No. 1 bearing shell
7. No. 2 camshaft bearing
8. No. 3 camshaft bearing with shoulder for thrust
9. Crankshaft bearing dowel pin
10. No. 2 crankshaft bearing half
11. Left crankcase half

Crankcase half assembly—Type 2/1700, 2/1800, and Type 4

15. Install the thrust washers and crankshaft oil seal. The oil seal must rest squarely on the bottom of its recess in the crankcase. The thrust washers at the flywheel end of the crankshaft are shims used to set the crankshaft end-play.

16. Spread a thin film of sealing compound on the crankcase joining faces and place the two halves together. Torque the nuts in several stages. Tighten the 8 mm nut located next to the 12 mm stud of the No. 1 crankshaft bearing first. As the crankcase halves are being torqued, continually check the crankshaft for ease of rotation.

17. Crankshaft end-play is checked when the flywheel is installed. It is ad-

Tighten the 8 mm nut located next to the 12 mm stud of the No. 1 crankcase bearing first on Type 1, 2/1600 and 3 models

justed by varying the number and thickness of the shims located behind the flywheel. Measure the end-play with a dial indicator mounted against the flywheel, and attached firmly to the crankcase.

Camshaft and Timing Gears

Removal and Installation

1. Removal of the camshaft requires splitting the crankcases. See "Crankcase Disassembly". The camshaft and its bearing shells are then removed from the crankcase halves.

2. Before reinstalling the camshaft, it should be checked for wear on the lobe surfaces and on the bearing surfaces. In addition, the riveted joint between the camshaft timing gear and the camshaft should be checked for tightness.

3. The camshaft should be checked for a maximum run-out of 0.0008 in.

4. The timing gear should be checked for the correct tooth contact and for wear.

5. If the camshaft bearing shells are worn or damaged, new shells should be fitted. The camshaft bearing shells should be installed with the tabs engaging the notches in the crankcase. It is usually a good idea to replace the bearing shells under any circumstances. Before installing the camshaft, the bearing journals and cam lobes should be generously coated with oil.

6. When the camshaft is installed, care should be taken to ensure that the timing gear tooth marked (0) is located between the two teeth of the crankshaft timing gear marked with a center punch.

7. The camshaft end-play is measured at the No. 3 bearing. End-play is 0.0015–0.005 in. (0.04–0.12 mm) and the wear limit is 0.006 in. (0.16 mm).

Aligning valve timing marks on gears

Crankshaft

Crankshaft Pulley Removal and Installation

On the Type 1 and 2/1600, the crankshaft pulley can be removed while the engine is still in the car. However, in this instance it is necessary for the rear cover plate of the engine to be removed. Remove the cover plate after taking out the screws in the cover plate below the crankshaft pulley. Remove the fan belt and the crankshaft pulley securing screw. Using a puller, remove the crankshaft pulley. The crankshaft pulley should be checked for proper seating and belt contact. The oil return thread should be cleaned and lubricated with oil. The crankshaft pulley should be installed in the reverse sequence. Check for oil leaks after installing the pulley.

Types 2/1700, 2/1800, and Type 4 engine fan bolts

On the Type 3, the crankshaft pulley can be removed only when the engine is out of the car and the muffler, generator, and cooling air intake housing are removed. After these parts have been removed, take out the plastic cap in the pulley. Remove the crankshaft pulley retaining bolt and remove the pulley.

Type 4 and Type 2/1700, 2/1800, 2/2000 removal is the same as the Type 3. However, the pulley is secured by three socket head screws and a self locking nut.

Installation for Type 2/1700, 2/1800, 2/2000, 3 and 4 engines is the reverse of removal. When installing, use a new paper gasket between the fan and the crankshaft pulley. If shims are used, do not forget them. Don't use more than two shims. When inserting the pulley, make sure that the pin engages the hole in the fan. Ensure that the clearance between the generator belt and the intake housing is at least 4 mm and that the belt is parallel to the housing.

Flywheel Removal and Installation

NOTE: *In order to remove the flywheel, the crankshaft will have to be prevented from turning. This may be accomplished on Type 1, 2/1600 and Type 3 models by using a 3 or 4 foot length of angle iron or thick stock sheet steel, such as an old fence post. Drill out two holes in the metal bar that correspond to two of the pressure plate retaining bolt holes. The metal bar is installed as per the accompanying illustration.*

Types 1, 2/1600, and 3

1. The flywheel is attached to the crankshaft with a gland nut and is located by four dowel pins. An oil seal is recessed in the crankcase casting at No. 1 main bearing. A needle bearing, which supports the main driveshaft, is located in the gland nut. Prior to removing the flywheel, it is necessary to remove the clutch pressure plate and the clutch disc.

2. Loosen the gland nut and remove it, using a 36 mm wrench.

3. Before removing the flywheel, matchmark the flywheel and the crankshaft.

4. Installation is the reverse of removal. Before installing the flywheel, check the flywheel teeth for any wear or damage. Check the dowel pins for correct fit in the crankshaft and in the flywheel.

5. Adjust the crankshaft end-play and check the needle bearing in the gland nut for wear.

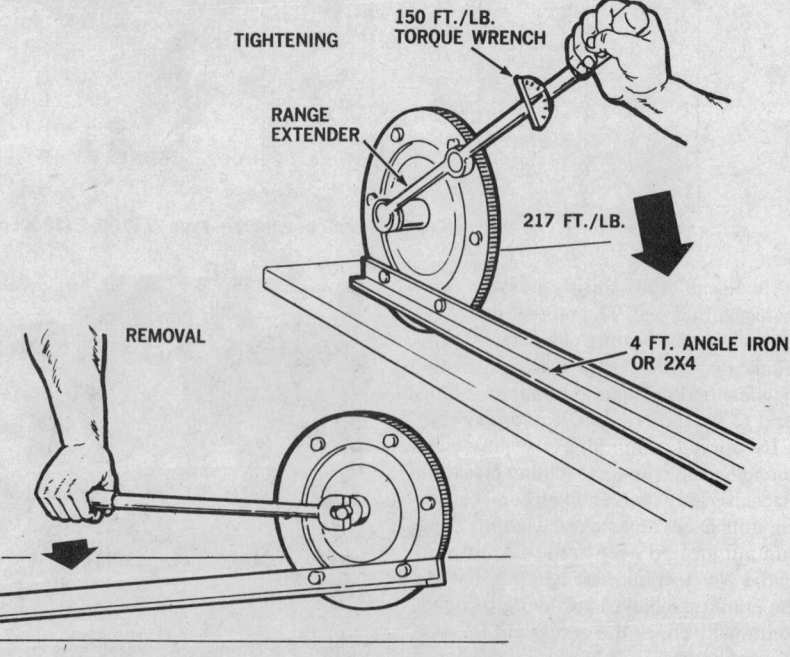

Removing/installing flywheel on 1600 cc engines using special bar

Type 2/1700, 2/1800, 2/2000 and 4

Removal and installation is similar to the Type 1, 2/1600, and 3 except that the flywheel is secured to the crankshaft by five socket head screws.

Crankshaft Oil Seal (Flywheel End)

Replacement

This seal is removed after removing the flywheel. After the flywheel is removed, inspect the surface on the flywheel joining flange where the seal makes contact. If there is a deep groove or any other damage, the flywheel must be replaced. Remove the oil seal by prying it out of its bore. Before installing a new seal, clean the crankcase oil seal recess and coat it thinly with a sealing compound. Be sure that the seal rests squarely on the bottom of its recess. Make sure that the correct side of the seal is facing outward, that is, the lip of the seal should be facing the inside of the crankcase. Reinstall the flywheel after coating the oil seal contact surface with oil.

NOTE: *Be careful not to damage the seal when sliding the flywheel into place.*

Crankshaft Removal and Installation

NOTE: *See the "Engine Rebuilding" section for crankshaft refinishing procedures.*

1. Removal of the crankshaft requires splitting the crankcase. See "Crankcase Disassembly".

2. After the crankcase is opened, the crankshaft can then be lifted out.

3. The crankshaft bearings are held in place by dowel pins. These pins must be checked for tightness.

4. When installing the bearings, make sure that the oil holes in the shells are properly aligned. Be sure that the bearing shells are seated properly on their dowel pins. Bearing shells are available in three undersizes. Measure the crankshaft bearing journals to determine the proper bearing size. Place one half of the No. 2 crankshaft bearing in the crankcase. Slide the No. 1 bearing on the crankshaft so that the dowel pin hole is toward the flywheel and the oil groove faces toward the fan. The No. 3 bearing is installed with the dowel pin hole facing toward the crankshaft web.

5. To remove the No. 3 main bearing, remove the distributor gear circlip and the distributor drive gear. Mild heat (176° F) must be applied to remove the gear. Next slide the spacer off of the crankshaft.

6. The crankshaft timing gear should now be pressed off the crankshaft after mild heating.

7. When the timing gear is reinstalled, the chamfer must face towards the No. 3 bearing. The No. 3 bearing can then be replaced. When removing and installing the gears on the crankshaft, be careful not to damage the No. 4 bearing journal.

8. When all of the crankshaft bearings are in place, lift the crankshaft and the connecting rod assembly into the crankcase and align the valve timing marks.

9. Install the crankcase half and reassemble the engine.

Connecting Rods

Removal and Installation

NOTE: *See the "Engine Rebuilding" section for additional information.*

1. After splitting the crankcase (See "Crankcase Disassembly"), remove the crankshaft and the connecting rod assembly.

2. Remove the connecting rods, clamping bolts, and the connecting rod caps.

3. Inspect the piston pin bushing. With a new bushing, the correct clearance is indicated by a light finger push fit of the pin at room temperature.

4. Reinsert the new connecting rod

Measuring the connecting rod side clearance

Staking the connecting rod bolt

bearings after all parts have been thoroughly cleaned.

5. Assemble the connecting rods on the crankshaft, making sure that the rods are oriented properly on the crankshaft. The identification numbers stamped on the connecting rods and connecting rod caps must be on the same side. Note that the marks on the connecting rods are pointing upward, while the rods are pointing toward their respective cylinders. Lubricate the bearing shells before installing them.

6. Tighten the connecting rod bolts to the specified torque. A slight pre-tension between the bearing halves, which is likely to occur when tightening the connecting rod bolts, can be eliminated by gently striking the side of the bearing cap with a hammer.

7. Do not install the connecting rod in the engine unless it swings freely on its journal.

8. Using a peening chisel, secure the connecting rod bolts in place.

9. Failure to swing freely on the journal may be caused by improper side clearance, improper bearing clearance, or failure to lubricate the rod before assembly.

Tapping the connecting rod cap to relieve pre-tension

cylinder 1   cylinder 2

cylinder 3   cylinder 4

Forge marks on connecting rods must face up

ENGINE LUBRICATION

Oil Strainer

Removal and Installation

The oil strainer can be easily removed by removing the retaining nuts, washers, oil strainer plate, strainer, and gaskets. The Type 2/1700, 2/1800, 2/2000 and Type 4 strainer is secured by a single bolt at the center of the strainer. Once taken out, the strainer must be thoroughly cleaned and all traces of oil gaskets removed prior to installing new ones.

The suction pipe should be checked for tightness and proper position. When the strainer is installed, be sure that the suction pipe is correctly seated in the strainer. If necessary, the strainer may be bent slightly. The measurement from the strainer flange to the tip of the suction pipe should be 10 mm. The measurement from the flange to the bottom of the strainer should be 6 mm. The cap nuts on Types 1, 2/1600, and 3 must not be overtightened. The Type 4 and Type 2/1700, 2/1800, 2/2000 have a spin-off replaceable oil filter as well as the strainer in the crankcase. The oil filter is located at the left rear corner of the engine.

Oil Cooler

Removal and Installation

The Type 1 and 2/1600 oil cooler is located under the engine cooling fan housing at the left side of the engine. The Type 3 cooler is located at the same position but is mounted horizontally. The Type 4 and Type 2/1700, 2/1800, 2/2000 coolers are mounted near the oil filter, at the left corner of the engine.

The oil cooler may be removed without taking the engine out of the car. On Types 1 and 2/1600, the engine fan housing must be removed. On the Type 3, the cooler is accessible through the left-hand cylinder cover plate. The Type 4 and

Oil cooler spacers on suitcase engines

Type 2/1700, 2/1800, 2/2000 cooler is accessible through the left side engine cowling, working either in the engine compartment or from underneath the car.

The oil cooler can be removed after the three retaining nuts have been taken off. The gaskets should be removed along with the cooler and replaced with new gaskets. If the cooler is leaking, check the oil pressure relief valve. The studs and bracket on the cooler should be checked for tightness. Make certain that the hollow ribs of the cooler do not touch one another. The cooler must not be clogged with dirt. Clean the contact surfaces on the crankcase, install new gaskets, and attach the oil cooler. Types 3, 4 and 2/1700, 2/1800, 2/2000 have a spacer ring between the crankcase and the cooler at each securing screw. If these rings are omitted, the seals may be squeezed too tightly, resulting in oil stoppage and resultant engine damage. Use double retaining nuts and locking compound on the cooler studs.

Oil Pump

Removal and Installation

1. On Types 1 and 2/1600, the pump can be removed while the engine is in the car, but it is first necessary to remove the cover plate, the crankshaft pulley, and the cover plate under the pulley.

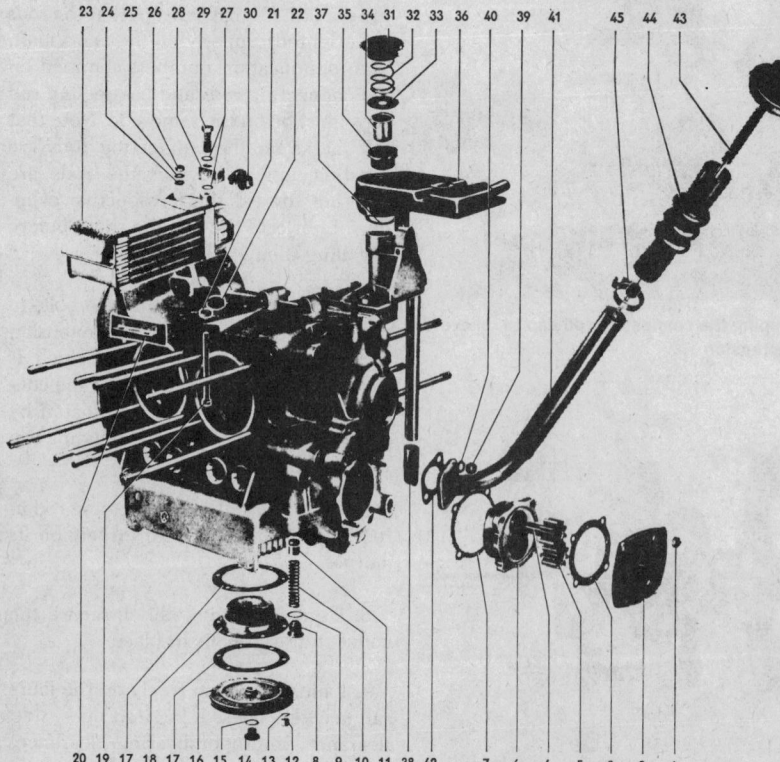

1. Sealing nut
2. Oil pump cover
3. Cover gasket
4. Drive shaft
5. Oil pump gear
6. Oil pump housing
7. Housing gasket
8. Plug
9. Seal
10. Spring
11. Relief valve piston
12. Cap nut
13. Seal
14. Oil drain plug
15. Seal
16. Oil strainer cover
17. Gasket
18. Oil strainer
19. Bolt
20. Plate under oil cooler
21. Spacer
22. Oil cooler seal
23. Oil cooler
24. Washer
25. Lockwasher
26. Nut
27. Seal
28. Oil pressure switch connection
29. Gland nut for connection
30. Oil pressure switch
31. Plastic plug
32. Spring
33. Washer
34. Sleeve
35. Gland nut
36. Oil breather
37. Seal
38. Valve for cleaner
39. Nut
40. Lockwasher
41. Oil filler neck
42. Gasket
43. Dipstick
44. Boot
45. Clamp

Lubricating System—Type 3

1. Oil filter cover
2. Oil filter
3. Nut
4. Spring washer
5. Oil filter seal
6. Oil vent
7. Seal
8. Oil dipstick
9. Dipstick
10. Bellows
11. Nut
12. Spring washer
13. Oil filler
14. Gasket
15. Nut
16. Spring washer
17. Oil pump housing
18. Pump housing seal
19. Locknut
20. Spring washer
21. Oil pump cover
22. Pump cover sealing ring
23. Oil pump gear
24. Driveshaft
25. Oil pressure switch
26. Screw
27. Sealing ring
28. Spring
29. Piston for oil relief valve
30. Screw
31. Sealing ring
32. Spring
33. Piston for oil pressure control valve
34. Nut
35. Sealing ring
36. Oil strainer closing cover
37. Seal
38. Oil strainer
39. Closing screw
40. Sealing ring

41. Nut
42. Spring washer
43. Washer
44. Oil cooler
45. Oil cooler sealing ring
46. Oil filter
47. Nut
48. Spring washer
49. Oil filter intermediate flange
50. Seal

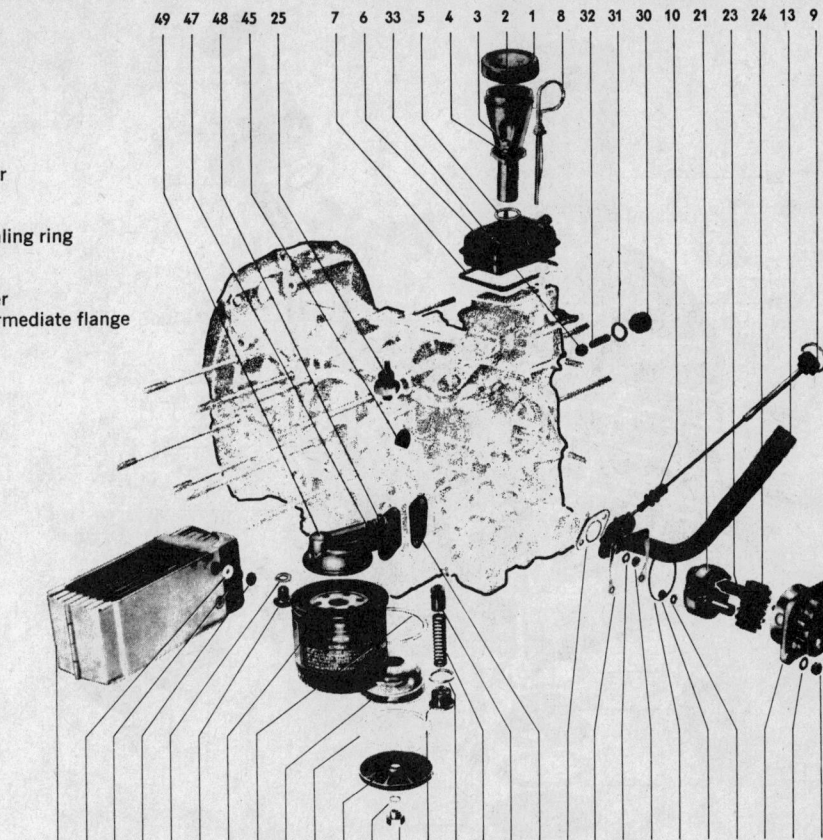

Lubricating System—Types 2/1700, 2/1800, 4

2. On Types 3, 4 and 2/1700, 2/1800, 2/2000 the oil pump can be taken out only after the engine is removed from the car and the air intake housing, the belt pulley fan housing, and fan are dismantled.

3. On the Automatic Stick Shift models, the torque converter oil pump is driven by the engine oil pump.

4. On Type 1, 2/1600 and 3 remove the nuts from the oil pump cover and then remove the cover and its gasket. Remove the gears and take out the pump with a special extractor that pulls the body out of the crankcase. Care should be taken so as not to damage the inside of the pump housing.

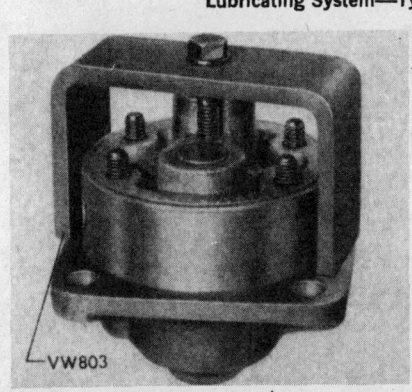
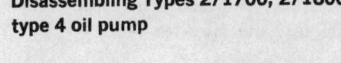

Disassembling Types 2/1700, 2/1800, and type 4 oil pump

5. On Type 4 and Type 2/1700, 2/1800, 2/2000 engines, remove the four pump securing nuts and, prying on either side of the pump, pry the pump assembly out of the crankcase.

6. To disassemble the pump, the pump cover must be pressed apart.

7. Prior to assembly, check the oil pump body for wear, especially the gear seating surface. If the pump body is worn, the result will be loss of oil pressure. Check the driven gear shaft for tightness and, if necessary, peen it tightly into place or replace the pump housing. The gears should be checked for excessive wear, backlash, and end-play. Maximum end-play without a gasket is 1 mm (0.004 in.). The end-play can be checked using a T-square and a feeler gauge. Check the mating surfaces of the pump body and the crankcase for damage and cleanliness. Install the pump into the crankcase with a new gasket. Do not use any sealing compound.

8. Turn the camshaft several revolutions in order to center the pump body opposite the slot in the camshaft.

9. On Type 1, 2/1600, and 3 the cover may now be installed.

10. On Type 4 and Type 2/1700, 2/1800, 2/2000 models, the pump was installed complete.

11. Tighten the securing nuts.

Removing oil pump housing—Types 1, 2/1600, 3

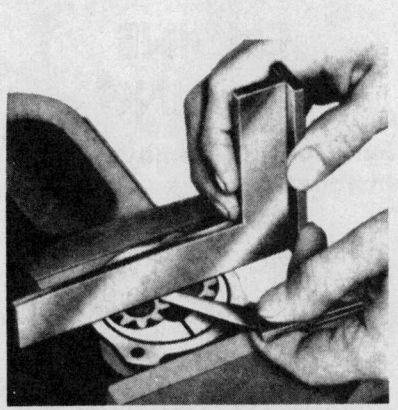

Checking oil pump end-play

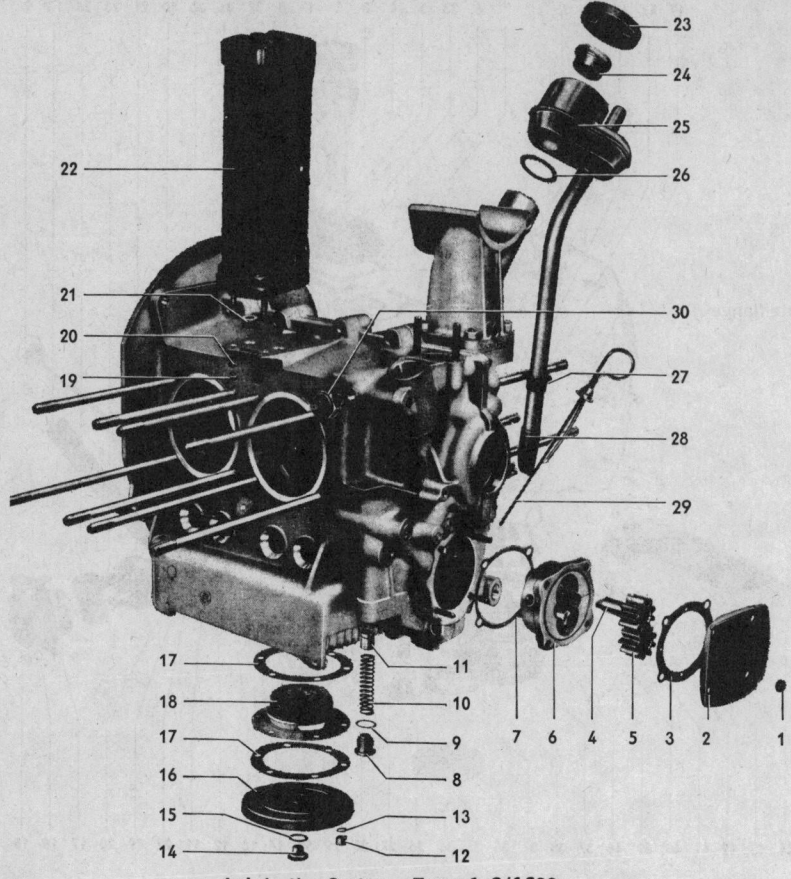

Lubricating System—Types 1, 2/1600

1. Sealing nut	16. Oil strainer cover
2. Oil pump cover	17. Gasket
3. Pump cover gasket	18. Oil strainer
4. Driveshaft	19. Nut
5. Oil pump gear	20. Lockwasher
6. Oil pump housing	21. Oil cooler seal
7. Housing gasket	22. Oil cooler
8. Plug	23. Oil filler neck cap
9. Seal	24. Breather gland nut
10. Spring	25. Oil filler and breather assembly
11. Relief valve piston	26. Seal
12. Cap nut	27. Grommet
13. Seal	28. Breather rubber valve
14. Oil drain plug	29. Dipstick
15. Seal	30. Oil pressure switch

Oil Pressure Relief Valve

Removal and Installation

The oil pressure relief valve is removed by unscrewing the end plug and removing the gasket ring, spring, and plunger. If the plunger sticks in its bore, it can be removed by screwing a 10 mm tap into it.

On 1600 cc engines, the valve is located to the left of the oil pump. On Automatic Stick Shift models, it is located in the oil pump housing. On 1700, 1800 and 2000 engines, the valve is located beside the oil filter.

Before installing the valve, check the plunger for any signs of seizure. If necessary, the plunger should be replaced. If there is any doubt about the condition of the spring, it should also be replaced. When installing the relief valve, be careful that you do not scratch the bore. Reinstall the plug with a new gasket.

Type 4 and Type 2/1700, 2/1800, 2/2000 engines have a second oil pressure relief valve located just to the right of, and below the oil filter.

ENGINE COOLING

Fan Housing Removal and Installation

Type 1 and 2/1600

1. Remove the two heater hoses and the generator strap.

2. Pull out the lead wire from the coil. Remove the distributor cap and take off the spark plug connectors.

3. Remove the retaining screws that are located on both sides of the fan housing. Remove the rear hood.

4. Remove the outer half of the generator pulley and remove the fan belt.

5. Remove the thermostat securing screw and take out the thermostat.

6. Remove the lower part of the carburetor pre-heater duct.

7. The fan housing can now be removed with the generator. After removal, check the fan housing for damage and for loose air deflector plates.

8. Installation is the reverse of the above.

9. Make sure that the thermostat connecting rod is inserted into its hole in the cylinder head. The fan housing should be fitted properly on the cylinder cover plates so that there is no loss of cooling air.

Fan Removal and Installation

Type 1 and 2/1600

1. Remove the generator and fan assembly as described in the "Generator Removal and Installation" section.

2. While holding the fan, unscrew the fan retaining nut and take off the fan, spacer washers, and the hub.

3. To install, place the hub on the generator shaft, making sure that the woodruff key is securely positioned.

4. Insert the spacer washers. The clearance between the fan and the fan cover is 0.06–0.07 in. Place the fan into position and tighten its retaining nut. Correct the spacing by inserting the proper number of spacer washers. Place any extra washers between the lockwasher and the fan.

5. Reinstall the generator and the fan assembly.

Fan Housing and Fan Removal and Installation

Type 2/1700, 2/1800, 2/2000

1. On 1973–74 models, the air injection pump and related parts must first be removed. Loosen the air pump adjusting and retaining bolts, lower the pump and remove the drive belt. Remove the pump and bracket retaining bolts and remove the air pump and retaining brackets. Unbolt and remove the extension shaft and pulley assembly from the fan and fan housing. Using a 12 point allen wrench, loosen the alternator drive belt adjusting bolt. Then, remove the timing scale, fan and crankshaft pulley assembly, and the alternator drive belt.

2. On 1972 and 1975–76 models without the air injection pump, pry out the alternator cover insert, and, using a 12 point allen wrench, loosen the alternator adjusting bolt. Remove the alternator drive belt, the ignition timing scale and the grille over the fan. Remove the three socket head screws attaching the fan and crankshaft assembly to the crankshaft

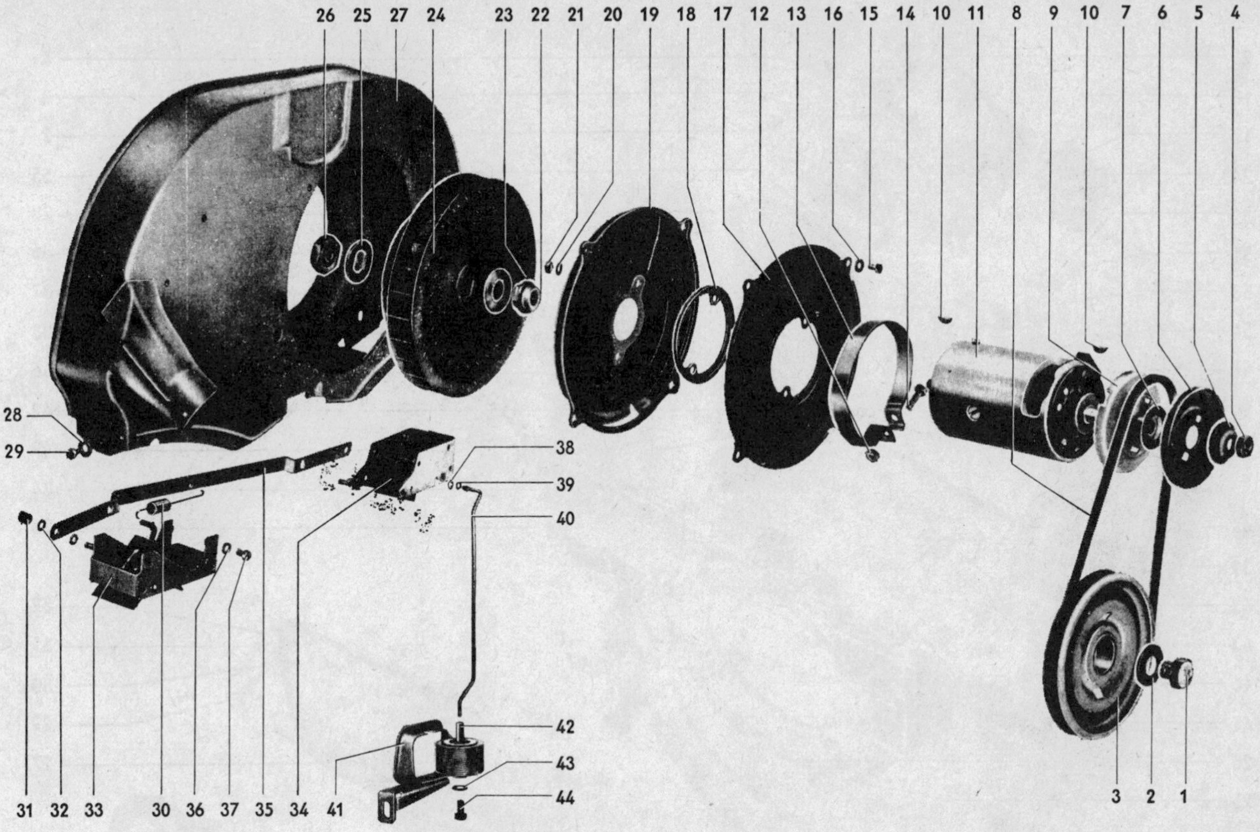

Numbers across top: 26 25 27 24   23 22 21 20 19 18 17 12 13 16 15 14 10 11 8 9 10 7 6 5 4

28
29

38
39
40

42
43
44

31 32 33   30 36 37 35 34 41

3 2 1

Cooling System—Types 1, 2/1600

1. Pulley bolt	16. Lockwasher	31. Spring
2. Dished washer	17. Outer fan cover	32. Washer
3. Crankshaft pulley	18. Reinforcement flange	33. Left cooling air regulator
4. Pulley nut	19. Inner fan cover	34. Right cooling air regulator
5. Special washer	20. Lockwasher	35. Cooling air regulator connecting rod
6. Rear pulley half	21. Nut	36. Washer
7. Spacer washer	22. Fan hub	37. Cheese head screw
8. V-belt	23. Shim	38. Lockwasher
9. Front pulley half	24. Fan	39. Washer
10. Woodruff key	25. Lockwasher	40. Connecting rod
11. Generator	26. Special nut	41. Thermostat bracket
12. Nut	27. Cheese head screw	42. Thermostat
13. Strap	28. Washer	43. Lockwasher
14. Bolt	29. Cheese head screw	44. Bolt
15. Bolt	30. Return spring	

and remove the fan and pulley.

3. Disconnect the cooling air control cable at the flap control shaft.

4. On models so equipped, pull out the rubber elbow for the alternator from the front half of the fan housing.

5. Remove the four nuts retaining the fan housing to the engine crankcase. The assembled fan housing may then be removed by pulling it to the rear and off the engine. It is not necessary to separate the fan housing halves or remove the alternator to remove the fan housing.

6. Reverse the above procedure to install, taking care to adjust the alternator and air pump drive belts (1973–74 models) so that moderate thumb pressure deflects the belt about ½ in. when applied at a point midway between the longest run. Also, adjust the cooling air control cable as outlined in this section.

Type 3

1. Remove the crankshaft pulley, the rear fan housing half, and the fan.

2. Unhook the linkage and spring at the right-hand air control flap.

3. Remove the screws for the front half of the housing and remove the housing.

4. Install the front half and ensure the correct sealing of the cylinder cover plates.

Type 3 fan housing nuts

5. Replace and tighten the two lower mounting screws slightly.

6. Turn the two halves of the fan housing to the left until the left crankcase half is contacted by the front lug.

7. Fully tighten the two lower mounting screws.

8. Loosen the nuts at the breather support until it can be moved.

9. Insert and tighten the mounting screws of the upper fan housing half. Tighten the breather support nuts fully.

10. Connect the linkage and spring to the right-hand air control flap.

11. Install the fan and the rear half of the fan housing.

Type 4

1. Remove the engine. Remove the fan belt.

2. Remove the allen head screws and remove the belt pulley and fan as an assembly.

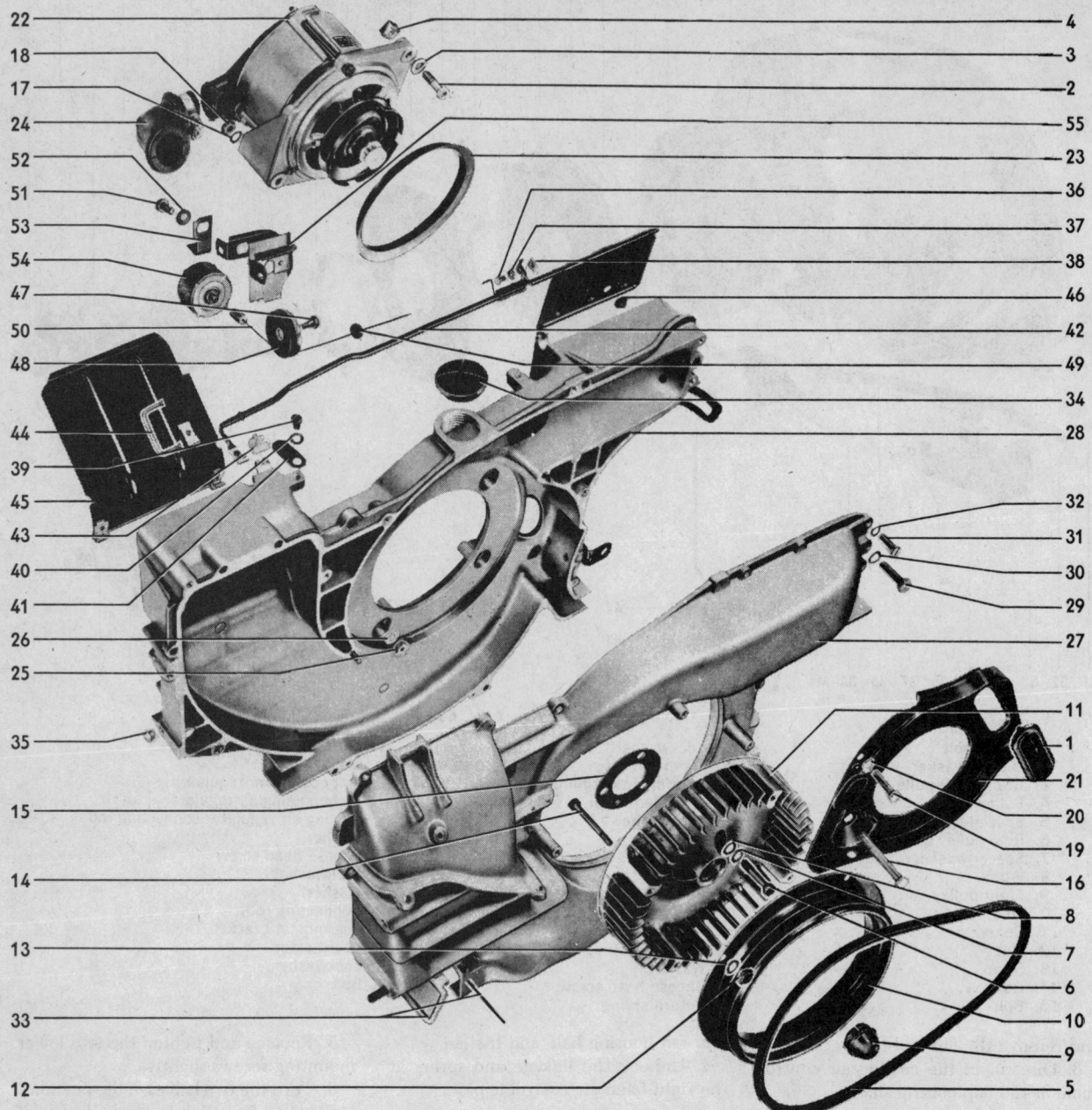

22 — 4
18 — 3
17 — 2
24 — 55
52 — 23
51 — 36
53 — 37
54 — 38
47 — 46
50 — 42
48 — 49
— 34
44 — 28
39
45 — 32
43 — 31
40 — 30
41 — 29
26 — 27
25
35 — 11
— 1
15 — 21
— 20
14 — 19
— 16
13 — 8
— 7
33 — 6
— 10
12 — 9
— 5

Cooling System—Types 2/1700, 2/1800, 4

1. Cover plate insert
2. Socket head capscrew
3. Spring washer
4. Nut
5. Belt
6. Socket head capscrew
7. Spring washer
8. Flat washer
9. Cap
10. Crankshaft pulley
11. Fan
12. Nut
13. Spring nut
14. Socket head capscrew
15. Spacer
16. Bolt
17. Spring washer
18. Nut

19. Screw
20. Spring washer
21. Alternator cover plate
22. Alternator
23. Alternator sealing ring
24. Alternator elbow
25. Nut
26. Spring washer
27. Fan housing—rear half
28. Fan housing—front half
29. Bolt
30. Spring washer
31. Screw
32. Spring washer
33. Air non-return flap
34. Inspection hole cover
35. Plug
36. Bolt

37. Washer
38. Nut
39. Screw
40. Spring washer
41. Shaft retaining spring
42. Right flap and shaft
43. Bearing
44. Flap link
45. Left flap
46. Plug
47. Bolt
48. Cooling air control cable roller
49. Sealing washer
50. Cooling air control cable
51. Bolt
52. Washer
53. Thermostat washer
54. Thermostat
55. Thermostat bracket

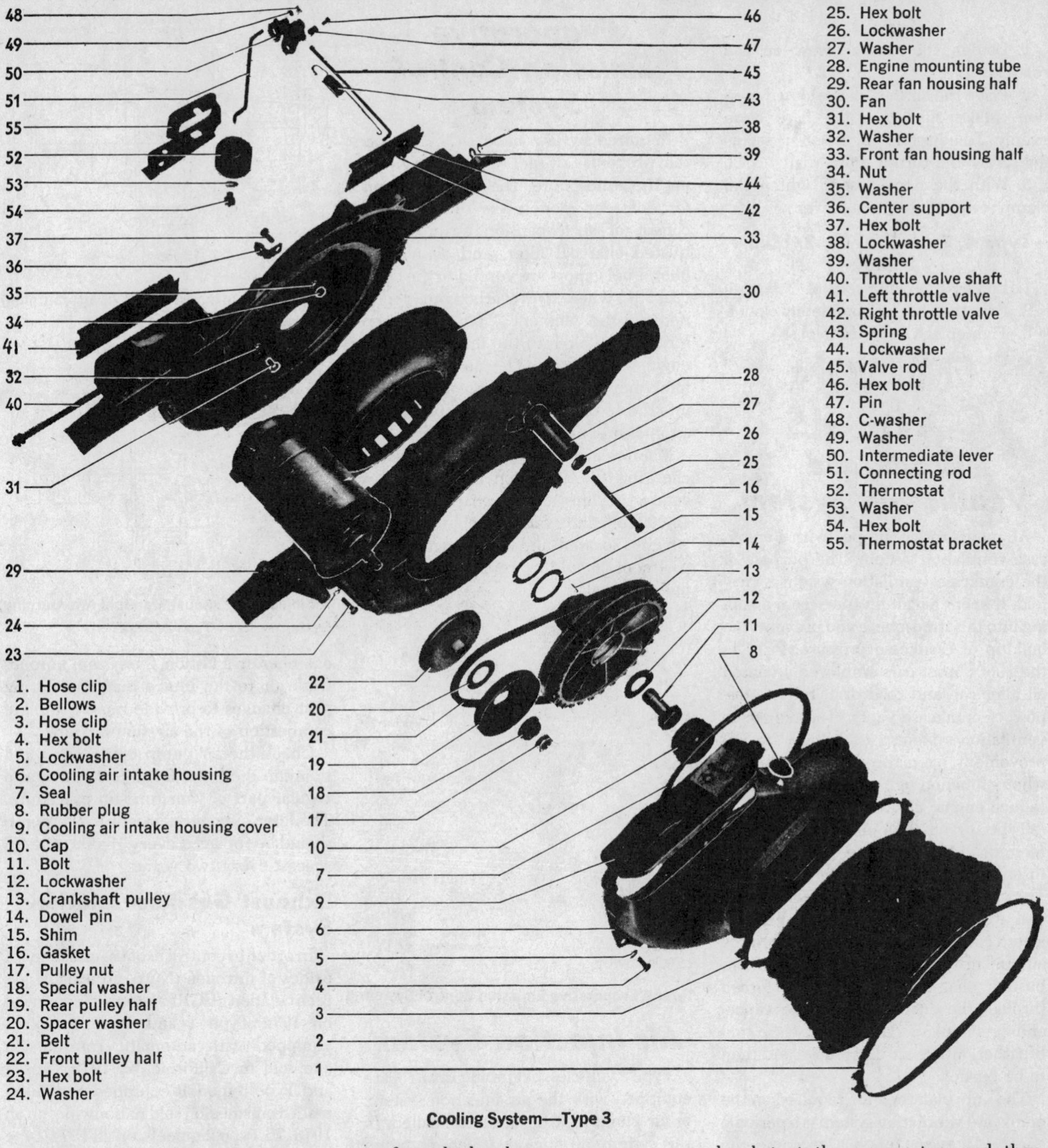

48	46
49	47
50	45
51	43
55	38
52	39
53	44
54	42
37	33
36	
35	30
34	
41	
32	
40	28
	27
	26
31	25
	16
	15
	14
29	13
	12
24	11
23	8

25. Hex bolt
26. Lockwasher
27. Washer
28. Engine mounting tube
29. Rear fan housing half
30. Fan
31. Hex bolt
32. Washer
33. Front fan housing half
34. Nut
35. Washer
36. Center support
37. Hex bolt
38. Lockwasher
39. Washer
40. Throttle valve shaft
41. Left throttle valve
42. Right throttle valve
43. Spring
44. Lockwasher
45. Valve rod
46. Hex bolt
47. Pin
48. C-washer
49. Washer
50. Intermediate lever
51. Connecting rod
52. Thermostat
53. Washer
54. Hex bolt
55. Thermostat bracket

1. Hose clip
2. Bellows
3. Hose clip
4. Hex bolt
5. Lockwasher
6. Cooling air intake housing
7. Seal
8. Rubber plug
9. Cooling air intake housing cover
10. Cap
11. Bolt
12. Lockwasher
13. Crankshaft pulley
14. Dowel pin
15. Shim
16. Gasket
17. Pulley nut
18. Special washer
19. Rear pulley half
20. Spacer washer
21. Belt
22. Front pulley half
23. Hex bolt
24. Washer

Cooling System—Type 3

NOTE: *It is not necessary to remove the alternator to remove the fan housing.*

3. Remove the spacer and the alternator cover plate.

4. Disconnect the cooling air regulating cable at the shaft.

5. Remove the nuts and remove both halves of the fan housing at the same time.

6. Installation is the reverse of the above.

Air Flap and Thermostat Adjustment

Type 1 and 2/1600

1. Loosen the thermostat bracket securing nut and disconnect the thermo-stat from the bracket.

2. Push the thermostat upwards to fully open the air flaps.

3. Reposition the thermostat bracket so that the thermostat contacts the bracket at the upper stop, and then tighten the bracket nut.

4. Reconnect the thermostat to the bracket.

Engine cooling air thermostat

Type 4 air flap cable control

Type 3

1. Loosen the clamp screw on the relay lever.

2. Place the air flaps in the closed position. Make sure that the flaps close evenly. To adjust a flap, loosen its securing screw and turn it on its shaft.

3. With the flaps closed, tighten the clamp screw on the relay lever.

Type 4, Type 2/1700, 2/1800, 2/2000

1. Loosen the cable control.

2. Push the air flaps completely closed.

3. Tighten the cable control.

EMISSION CONTROLS

Crankcase Ventilation System

All models are equipped with a crankcase ventilation system. The purpose of the crankcase ventilation system is twofold. It keeps harmful vapors from escaping into the atmosphere and prevents the buildup of crankcase pressure. Prior to the 1960s, most cars employed a vented oil filler cap and road draft tube to dispose of crankcase vapor. The crankcase ventilation systems now in use are improvement over the old method and, when functioning properly, will not reduce engine efficiency.

Type 1 and 2 crankcase vapors are recirculated from the oil breather through a rubber hose to the air cleaner. The vapors then join the air/fuel mixture and are burned in the engine. Fuel injected cars mix crankcase vapors into the air/fuel mixture to be burned in the combustion chambers. Fresh air is forced through the engine to evacuate vapors and recirculate them into the oil breather, intake air distributor, and then to be burned.

The only maintenance required on the crankcase ventilation system is a periodic check. At every tune-up, examine the hoses for clogging or deterioration. Clean or replace the hoses as required.

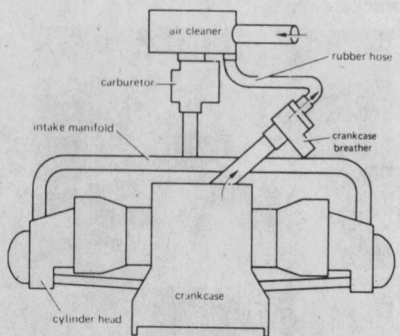

Crankcase ventilation system—Types 1, 2/1600

Evaporative Emission Control System

Required by law since 1971, this system prevents raw fuel vapors from entering the atmosphere. The various systems for different models are similar. They consist of an expansion chamber, activated charcoal filter, and connecting lines. Fuel vapors are vented to the charcoal filter where hydrocarbons are deposited on the element. The engine fan forces fresh air into the filter when the engine is running. The air purges the filter and the hydrocarbons are forced into the air cleaner to become part of the air/fuel mixture and burned.

Maintenance of this system consists of checking the condition of the various connecting lines and the charcoal filter at 10,000 mile intervals. The charcoal filter, which is located under the engine compartment, should be replaced at 48,000 mile intervals.

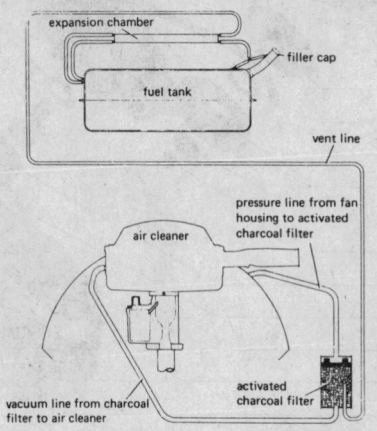

Typical Evaporative Emission Control System

Air Injection System

Type 2 vehicles, beginning in 1973, are equipped with the air injection system, or air pump as it is sometimes called. In this system, an engine driven air pump delivers fresh air to the engine exhaust ports. The additional air is used to promote afterburning of any unburned mixture as they leave the combustion

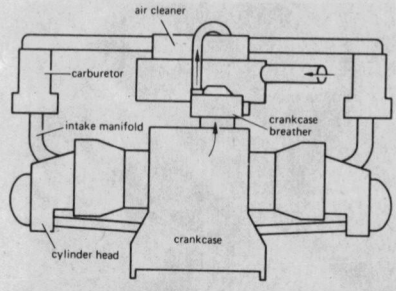

Crankcase ventilation system—Types 2/1700, 2/1800

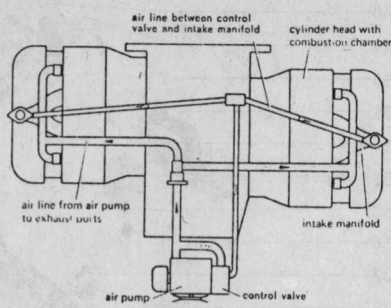

Air injection (exhaust manifold afterburning) System—1973 Type 2/1700

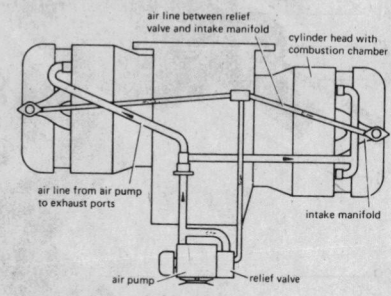

Air injection (Exhaust Manifold Afterburning) System—1974 Type 2/1800

chamber. In addition, the system supplies fresh air to the intake manifold during gear changes to provide more complete combustion of the air/fuel mixture.

Check the air pump belt tension and examine the hoses for deterioration as a regular part of your tune-up procedure. The filter element adjacent to the pump should be replaced every 18,000 miles or at least every two years.

Exhaust Gas Recirculation System

In order to control exhaust emissions of oxides of nitrogen (NOx), an exhaust gas recirculation (EGR) system is employed on 1972 Type 1 and Type 3 models equipped with automatic transmission and sold in California, on 1973 Type 1 and Type 3 models equipped with automatic transmission sold nationwide, on all 1973–76 Type 2 models, on all 1974 Type 4 models equipped with automatic transmission, and on all 1974–76 Type 1 models. The system lowers peak flame temperature during combustion by introducing a small (about 10%) percentage of

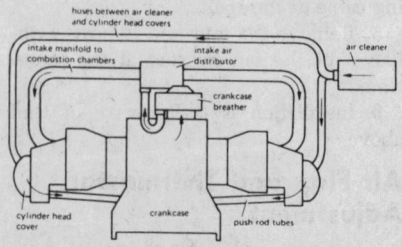

Crankcase ventilation system—Types 3, 4

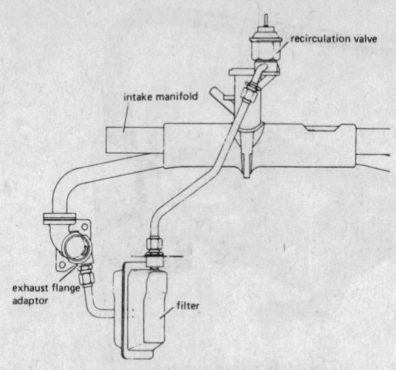

Exhaust Gas Recirculation System—1973-74 Type 1

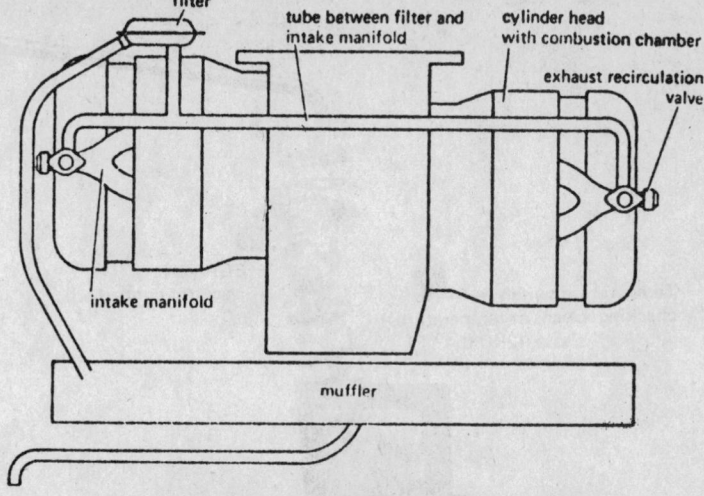

Exhaust Gas Recirculation System—1973 Type 2/1700

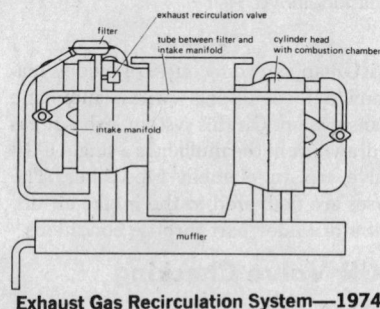

Exhaust Gas Recirculation System—1974

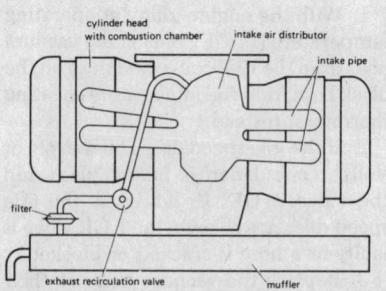

Exhaust Gas Recirculation System—1974 Type 4

relatively inert exhaust gas into the intake charge. Since the exhaust gas contains little or no oxygen, it cannot react with nor influence the air/fuel mixture. However, the exhaust gas does (by volume) take up space in the combustion chambers (space that would otherwise be occupied by a heat-producing, explosive air/fuel mixture), and does serve to lower peak combustion chamber temperature. The amount of exhaust gas directed to the combustion chambers is infinitely variable by means of a vacuum operated EGR valve. For system specifics, see the vehicle type breakdown under "General Description."

General Description

Type 1

For 1972, EGR is used only on automatic stick shift models sold in California. Exhaust gas is drawn from the left hand rear exhaust flange and then cooled in a cooling coil. From here, the gas is filtered in a cyclone filter and finally channelled to the intake manifold, via the EGR valve. The valve permits exhaust gas recirculation during part throttle applications, but not during idling or wide open throttle.

All 1973 models (nationwide) equipped with the automatic stick shift transmission use an EGR system. As in '72, the gas is drawn from the left rear exhaust flange. However, instead of the cooling coil and cyclone filter, a replaceable element type filter is used. The remainder of the system remains unchanged from 1972.

All 1974 Type 1 cars, regardless of equipment, are equipped with EGR. The system uses the element type filter and EGR valve which recirculates exhaust gases during part throttle applications as before. However, to improve driveability, all California models use a two stage EGR valve (one stage in the 49 states), and California models equipped with an automatic use an electric throttle valve switch to further limit exhaust gas recirculation to part throttle applications (EGR permitted only between 12° to 72° on a scale of 90° throttle valve rotation).

EGR is installed on all 1975–76 models. All applications use the element type filter and single stage EGR valve. Recirculations occurs during part throttle applications as before. The system is controlled by a throttle valve switch which measures throttle position, and an intake air sensor which reacts to engine vacuum. Beginning in 1975, an odometer actuated EGR reminder light (on the dashboard) is used to inform the driver that it is time to service the EGR system. The reminder light measures elapsed mileage and lights at 15,000 mile intervals. A reset button is located behind the switch.

Type 2

Type 2 models use an EGR system be-

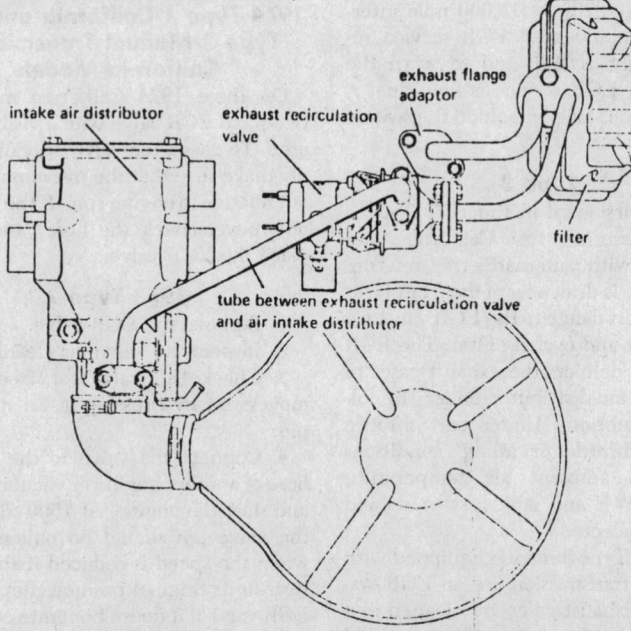

Exhaust Gas Recirculation System—1973 Type 3

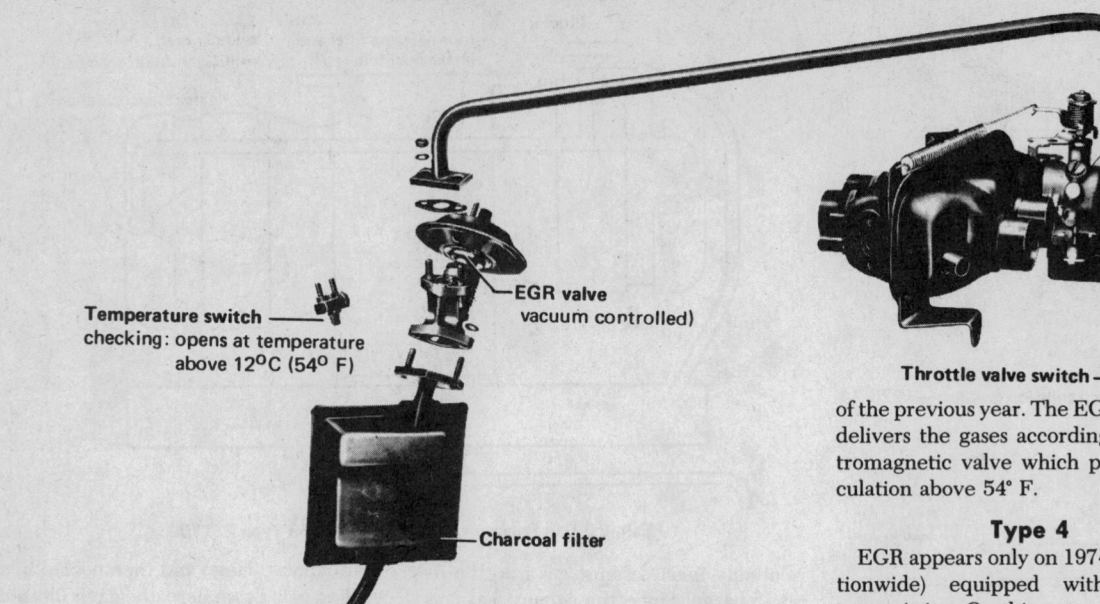

Temperature switch —
checking: opens at temperature
above 12°C (54° F)

EGR valve
vacuum controlled)

Charcoal filter

EGR system—1975-77 Type 2

Throttle valve switch —

ginning in 1973. All models use two valves; one at each manifold. Exhaust gas is taken from the muffler, cleaned in a replaceable element type filter, then directed to both intake manifolds, via the EGR valves. On models equipped with manual transmission, recirculation is vacuum controlled and occurs *both* during part *and* full throttle applications. On models equipped with the automatic, recirculation is controlled both by throttle position and engine compartment (ambient) temperature. When the ambient temperature exceeds 54° F, a sensor switch (located above the battery) opens, permitting EGR during part throttle applications.

All 1974 Type 2 models use EGR, but there are three different systems used. All models use one central EGR valve. Exhaust gas is taken from #4 exhaust port, cleaned in an element type filter, and then directed to both intake manifolds via the single EGR valve. Models equipped with manual transmission and sold in the 49 states use a single stage EGR valve which allows recirculation according to the vacuum signal in the left carburetor during part throttle applications. Models equipped with manual transmission and sold in California use a two stage EGR valve which recirculates exhaust gases during part throttle openings in two steps. During the first stage, EGR is controlled by the vacuum in the

left carburetor. The second stage controls EGR according to the throttle position of the right carburetor. Finally, all models equipped with automatic transmission (nationwide) use a single stage EGR valve which controls recirculation according to throttle valve position and engine cooling air temperature. When the cooling system air reaches 185° F, a sensor switch (located between the coil and distributor) opens, permitting EGR during part throttle applications.

All 1975–76 Type 2 models utilize an EGR system. A single stage EGR valve and element type filter are used on all applications. Recirculation occurs during part throttle openings, and is controlled by throttle position, engine vacuum, and engine compartment temperature (54° F cutoff as in 1973). At 15,000 mile intervals, a dash mounted EGR service reminder light is activated to warn the driver that EGR service is now due. A reset button is located behind the switch.

Type 3

EGR is first used in the 1972 Type 3 models destined for California and equipped with automatic transmission. Exhaust gas is drawn from the front right hand exhaust flange to the EGR valve via a container and cyclone filter. The EGR valve then delivers the exhaust gases to the intake air distributor under the following conditions; Under part throttle (not full throttle or idling) conditions when the ambient air temperature reaches 65° F *and* only first or second gears are selected.

All 1973 Type 3 models equipped with automatic transmission use an EGR system. The exhaust gases are cleaned in a replaceable element type filter in 1973 instead of the cyclone filter and container

of the previous year. The EGR valve then delivers the gases according to an electromagnetic valve which permits recirculation above 54° F.

Type 4

EGR appears only on 1974 models (nationwide) equipped with automatic transmission. On this system, exhaust gas is drawn from the muffler to a single EGR valve via an element type filter. The gases are delivered to the intake air distributor under part throttle conditions.

EGR Valve Checking

1972–74 Type 1 (Except 1974 California Models)

1. With the engine idling at operating temperature (176° F), pull off the vacuum hose from the EGR valve and push on the black hose from the intake air preheating thermostat instead.

2. If the idle speed drops off sharply or stalls, recirculation is taking place and the valve is OK. If, however, the idle speed does not change, the EGR valve is faulty or a hose is cracked or blocked.

3. Replace the vacuum hoses to their original locations.

1974 Type 1 California and 1974 Type 2 Manual Transmission California Models

On these 1974 California models, a two-stage EGR valve with a visible pin is used. To check the valve operation, simply make sure that the pin moves in and out relative to engine rpm. If the pin does not move, check the hoses and/or replace the EGR valve.

1973 Type 2

1. Remove the EGR valve.

2. Inspect the valve for cleanliness.

3. Check the valve for freedom of movement by pressing in on the valve pin.

4. Connect the valve to the vacuum hose of another engine or vacuum source and start the engine. At 1500–2000 rpm the valve pin should be pulled in and when the speed is reduced it should return to its original position. Replace the EGR valve if it doesn't operate correctly.

5. Replace the washer and install the valve.

6. Repeat this operation on the second valve.

1974 Type 2 w/Manual Transmission (Except California Models)

1. With the engine idling at operating temperature, pull off the vacuum hose at the tee-fitting for the EGR valve and push on the hose from the flow valve of the air pump to the fitting instead.

2. If idle speed drops sharply or stalls, the valve is OK. If the rpm does not change, a hose is blocked or the valve is faulty.

3. Replace the hoses to their original locations.

1972–73 Type 3

1. Remove the EGR valve.

2. Reconnect the vacuum hose and place the valve on the base.

3. Start the engine. If it doesn't stall, the vacuum line between the valve base and the intake manifold is clogged and must be cleaned.

4. Run the engine at 2000–3000 rpm. The closing pin of the EGR valve should pull in 0.15 in. (4 mm) and immediately return to its original position at idle. Replace the EGR valve if it doesn't operate correctly.

5. Install the EGR valve using new seals.

Catalytic Converter System

All 1975–76 Type 1 and 2 models sold in California are equipped with a catalytic converter. The converter is installed in the exhaust system, upstream and adjacent to the muffler.

Catalytic converters change noxious emissions of hydrocarbons (HC) and carbon monoxide (CO) into harmless carbon dioxide and water vapor. The reaction takes place inside the converter at great heat using platinum and palladium metals as the catalyst. If the engine is operated on lead-free fuel, they are designed to last 50,000 miles before replacement. now must not exceed 6 seconds. If it does, go back to step 4. If it doesn't, shut off the engine, disconnect the tachometer, and have a cigar.

Deceleration Control

All 1975–76 Type 2 models, as well as those 1975–76 Type 1 models equipped with manual transmission, are equipped with deceleration control to prevent an overly rich fuel mixture from reaching the exhaust. During deceleration, a vacuum valve (manual transmission) or electrical transmission switch (automatic transmission) opens, bypassing the closed throttle plate and allowing air to enter the combustion chambers.

Throttle Valve Positioner

1972 Type 1 models with manual transmission sold in California use a throttle valve positioner to hold the throttle butterfly slightly open during deceleration to prevent an excessively rich mixture from reaching the combustion chambers. The throttle valve positioner consists of two parts connected by a hose. The operating part is mounted on the carburetor, connected to the throttle valve arm. It regulates fast idle speed. The control section (altitude corrector) is located at the left side of the engine compartment. It controls throttle valve closing time.

Adjustment

NOTE: *The car should first be warmed to operating temperature (122–158° F) for this adjustment. Make sure the choke plate is open.*

1. Hook up a tachometer (0–3000 rpm sweep minimum) to the engine with the positive lead to the distributor side of the coil and the negative lead to a good ground. You will also need a stop watch or a good wristwatch with a second hand.

CAUTION: *Keep yourself, any clothing, jewelry, long locks (of hair), or tools etc. well clear of the engine belts and pulleys. Make sure you are in a well ventilated area.*

2. Start the engine and let it idle in neutral. Make a check of the fast idle speed by pulling the fast idle lever back so that it contacts the lever stop on the carburetor. The tachometer should read 1450–1650 rpm. If the fast idle is not within specifications, turn the adjusting screw (on the lever stop, not on the lever as required. Disconnect the tachometer.

3. Take the car for a warmup drive. Recheck the fast idle as in steps 1 and 2. The tachometer reading should not exceed 1700 rpm.

4. Now, make a check of the throttle valve closing time and get your watch handy. Pull the throttle lever away from the fast idle lever until the tachometer reads 3000 rpm. While keeping an eye on the second hand of your watch, release the throttle lever and check the time elapsed until the engine reaches idle speed (800–900 rpm). The closing time should be 2.5–4.5 seconds. If the closing time is not within specifications, adjust the control section at the left side of the engine compartment. After loosening the lock screw, turn the adjusting screw (1) clockwise to increase closing time and counterclockwise to decrease closing time. Recheck the adjustment. If it is within specifications, tighten the lock screw and disconnect the tachometer.

5. Take the car for another test drive Once again, recheck the closing time as in step 4.

FUEL SYSTEM

Mechanical Fuel Pump

All 1972–74 Type 1 and 2 models utilize a mechanical fuel pump. The pump is located to the left of the generator/alternator on Type 1 and 2/1600 models, and located next to the flywheel on dual carburetor Type 2 models. On Type 1 and 2/1600 models the pump is pushrod operated by an eccentric on the distributor driveshaft. On Type 2/1700 and 2/1800 twin carb models the pump is operated by a pushrod which rides on a camshaft eccentric.

Removal and Installation

Types 1, 2/1600

1. Disconnect the fuel lines at the pump and plug them to prevent leakage.

2. Remove the two securing nuts.

3. Remove the fuel pump. If necessary, the pushrod, gaskets, and intermediate flange may also be removed.

4. When installing the fuel pump, it is necessary to check the fuel pump pushrod stroke. This is done by measuring the distance that the pushrod projects above the intermediate flange when both gaskets are in place. The rod must project ½ inch.

5. Fill the cavity in the lower part of the fuel pump housing with grease. Total pushrod length is 4.252 in. for all Type 2/1600 and for Type 1 models equipped with generators. Pushrod length is 3.937 in. for all 1973–74 Type 1 models equipped with alternators. Replace any worn pushrod.

6. Using new gaskets, install the fuel pump and tighten the two securing nuts.

7. Install the fuel hoses.

Types 2/1700 and 2/1800 Twin Carb

1. Remove the engine.

2. Once the engine is removed, remove the upper and lower deflector plates and the carburetor preheater connection to gain access to the pump mounting bolts (adjacent to the flywheel).

3. Disconnect and plug the fuel lines to the carburetor.

4. Remove the two retaining bolts and lift off the fuel pump, gaskets and intermediate flange.

5. Reverse the above procedure to install, using new gaskets.

1. Screw
2. Washer
3. Screw
4. Upper pump cover
5. Gasket
6. Cut-off valve spring
7. Cut-off valve diaphragm
8. Fuel filter plug
10. Fuel filter
14. Inspection cover
16. Operating lever spring
17. Operating lever
18. Pump diaghragm with spring and guide halves attached
19. Pump housing
21. Pushrod
22. Intermediate flange

Exploded view of fuel pump—1972 Type 3

pump is 3.5 psi at 3,400 rpm for the Type 1 and 4,000 rpm for the Type 2. The maximum fuel pump pressure developed by the Type 2 Twin carb fuel pump is 5 psi at 3800 rpm.

All fuel pumps deliver 400 cc of fuel per minute.

The only adjustment possible is performed by varying the thickness of the fuel pump flange gaskets. Varying the thickness of the gaskets will change the stroke of the fuel pump pushrod. This adjustment is not meant to compensate for a pump in bad condition; therefore, do not attempt to vary the height of the pushrod to any great extent.

The fuel pumps used on 1972–74 Type 2 models may be disassembled for cleaning or repairs. All other mechanical pumps are permanently sealed and must be replaced if found defective.

Electric Fuel Pump

All Type 3 and Type 4 models, as well as 1975–76 Type 1 and Type 2 models have an electric pump. The fuel pump is located near the front axle.

Removal and Installation

1. Disconnect the fuel pump wiring. Pull the plug from the pump but do not pull on the wiring.

2. Disconnect the fuel hoses and plug them to prevent any leakage.

3. Remove the two nuts which secure the pump and then remove the pump.

4. Reconnect the fuel pump hoses and wiring and install the pump on the vehicle.

Adjustments

Electric fuel pump pressure is 28 psi. Fuel pump pressure is determined by a pressure regulator which diverts part of the fuel pump output to the gas tank when 28 psi is reached. The regulator, located on the engine firewall, has a screw and lock nut on its end. Loosen the lock nut and adjust the screw to adjust the pressure. Do not force the screw in or out if it does not turn.

Remember to coat the pushrod and lever with grease.

NOTE: *Prior to installation of the fuel pump, check the action of the camshaft eccentric driven pushrod. Install just the intermediate flange on the engine with 2 gaskets underneath and one on top. Turn the engine over by hand until the pushrod is on the highest point of the camshaft eccentric. Then, measure the distance between the tip of the pushrod and the top gasket surface. Adjust, as necessary, to 0.2 in. by removing or installing gaskets under the intermediate flange. Total pushrod length should be 5.492 in. minimum. Replace, if worn.*

Testing and Adjusting

The maximum fuel pump pressure developed by the Type 1 and 2/1600 fuel

Type 3 electric fuel pump location

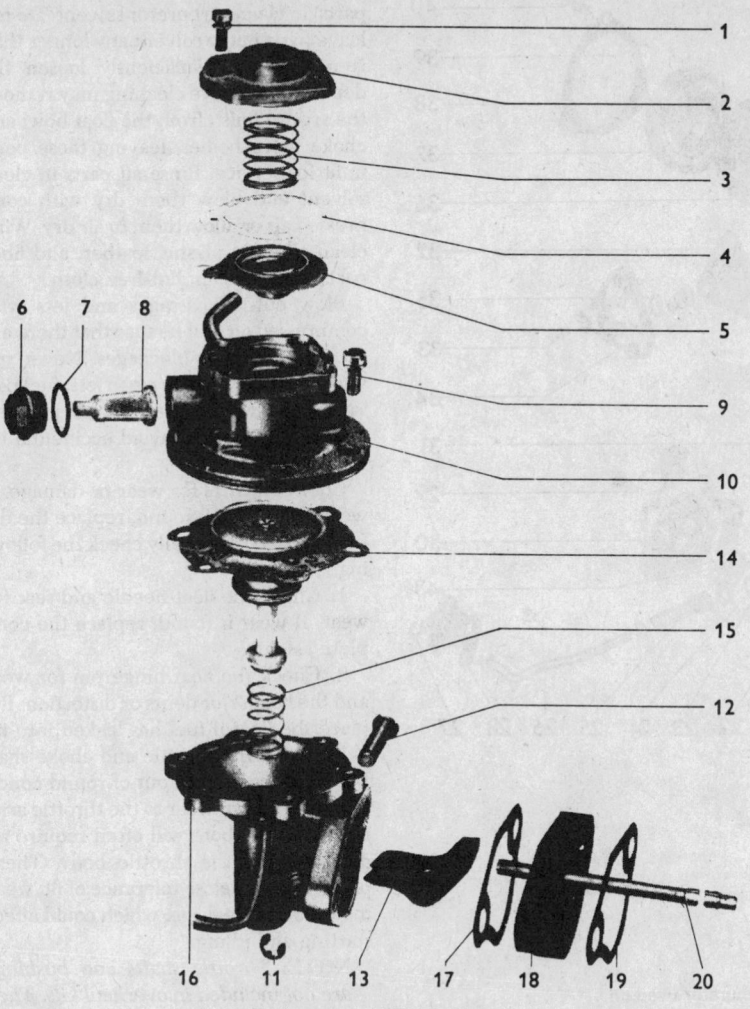

Fuel pump—1972-74 Type 2

1. Screw
2. Cover
3. Cut-off diaphragm spring
4. Cut-off diaphragm gasket
5. Cut-off diaphragm
6. Plug
7. Washer
8. Filter
9. Screw
10. Pump upper part
11. Circlip
12. Lever shaft
13. Pump lever
14. Diaphragm and spring
15. Diaphragm spring
16. Pump lower part
17. Gasket
18. Intermediate
19. Gasket
20. Push rod

1975-77 Type 2 electric fuel pump location (1) and filter (2)

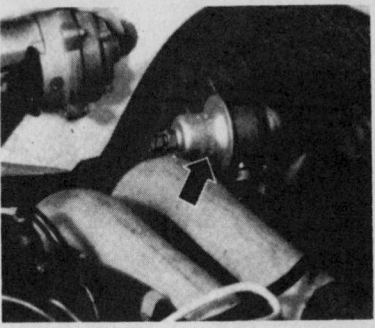

Fuel pressure regulator with locknut and adjusting screw at the left end of the regulator

Carburetors

Carburetors are used on all Type 1 and 2 models through 1974. A single downdraft unit is used on all Type 1 models. Beginning with the 1972 model year, the Type 2 utilizes twin carburetion.

Removal and Installation

Type 1 and 2/1600

1. Remove the air cleaner.
2. Disconnect the fuel hose.
3. Disconnect the vacuum hoses.
4. Remove the automatic choke cable and remove the wire for the electromagnetic pilot jet.
5. Disconnect the accelerator cable at the throttle valve lever.
6. Remove the two nuts securing the carburetor on the intake manifold and then remove the carburetor from the engine.
7. Using a new gasket, install the carburetor on the manifold.
8. Reconnect the fuel and vacuum hoses, the automatic choke cable, and the wiring for the pilot jet.
9. Reconnect the throttle cable and adjust it so that at full throttle there is a gap of 0.04 in. between the throttle valve lever and its stop on the lower portion of the carburetor body.

NOTE: *Open the throttle valve by hand and tighten the adjustment screw, then have an assistant open the throttle and recheck the adjustment.*

Type 2/1700 and 2/1800 Twin Carb

1. Remove the air cleaner.
2. Disconnect and plug the fuel line(s).
3. Disconnect the electrical leads for the automatic choke, pilot jet cut-off valve, and idle mixture cut-off valve.
4. If removing the left carburetor, disconnect the vacuum line, the idle mixture line for the central idling system, and the idle air intake line from the top of the carburetor.
5. Remove the linkage cross shaft bracket retaining bolt. Disconnect the return spring and the pull rod and release the linkage from both carburetors.

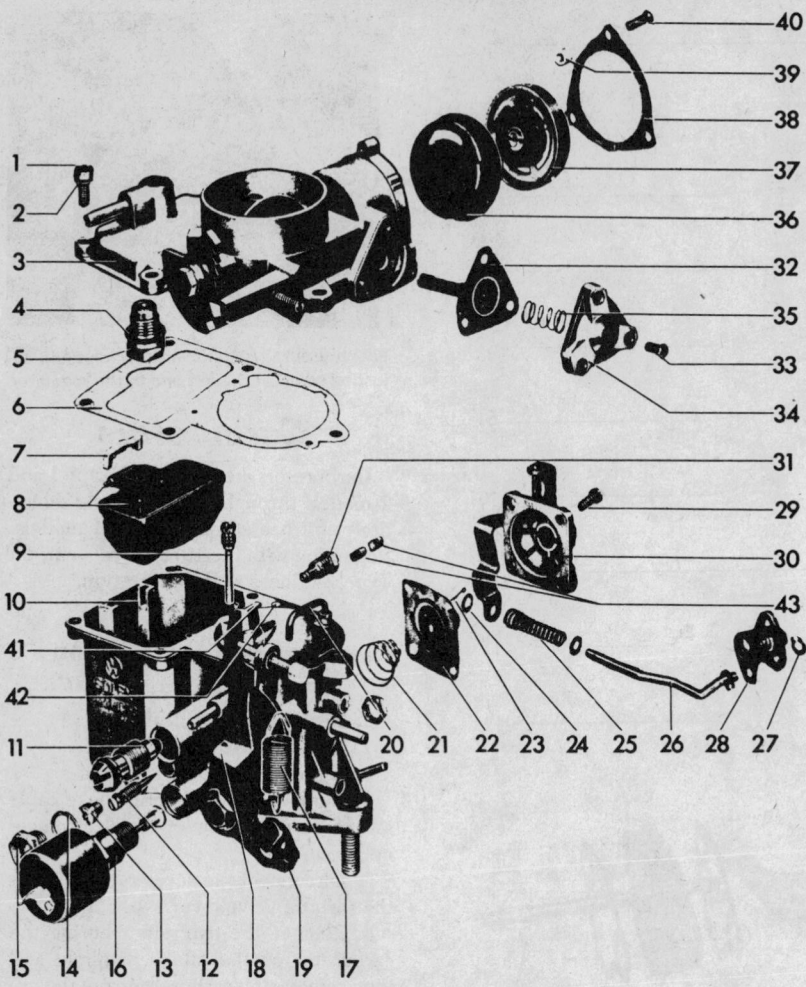

Exploded view of Solex 34 PICT-3 carburetor used on 1972-74 Type 1

1. Carburetor screw, upper part
2. Spring washer
3. Carburetor upper part
4. Float needle valve washer
5. Float needle valve
6. Washer
7. Float pin retainer
8. Float and pin
9. Air correction jet and emulsion tube
10. Carburetor lower part
11. By-pass screw
12. Volume control screw
13. Main jet
14. Plug washer
15. Plug
16. By-pass air cut-off valve
17. Return spring
18. Fast idling lever
19. Throttle valve lever and stop screw
20. Accelerator pump injection pipe
21. Diaphragm spring
22. Accelerator pump diaphragm
23. Cotter pin
24. Washer
25. Connecting rod spring
26. Connecting rod
27. Clip
28. Bell crank lever
29. Countersunk head screw
30. Pump cover
31. Pilot jet
32. Vacuum diaphragm
33. Countersunk head screw
34. Vacuum diaphragm cover
35. Vacuum diaphragm spring
36. Plastic cap
37. Insert with spring and heater element
38. Cover retaining ring
39. Retaining ring spacer
40. Retaining ring screw
41. Pilot air drilling
42. Auxiliary air drilling
43. Auxiliary fuel jet and plug

6. Remove the carburetor retaining nuts and remove the carburetor(s).

7. Reverse the above procedure to install, taking care to use new gaskets. After installation, synchronize the carburetors as outlined under "Fuel Adjustments" in Tune-Up Procedures.

Overhaul

Efficient carburetion depends greatly on careful cleaning and inspection during overhaul, since dirt, gum, water, or varnish in or on the carburetor parts are often responsible for poor performance.

Overhaul your carburetor in a clean, dust-free area. Carefully disassemble the carburetor, referring often to the exploded views. Keep all similar and looka-like parts segregated during disassembly and cleaning to avoid accidental interchange during assembly. Make a note of all jet sizes.

When the carburetor is disassembled, wash all parts (except diaphragms, electric choke units, pump plunger, and any other plastic, leather, fiber, or rubber parts) in clean carburetor solvent. Do not leave parts in the solvent any longer than is necessary to sufficiently loosen the deposits. Excessive cleaning may remove the special finish from the float bowl and choke valve bodies, leaving these parts unfit for service. Rinse all parts in clean solvent and blow them dry with compressed air or allow them to air dry. Wipe clean all cork, plastic, leather, and fiber parts with a clean, lint-free cloth.

Blow out all passages and jets with compressed air and be sure that there are no restrictions or blockages. Never use wire or similar tools to clean jets, fuel passages, or air bleeds. Clean all jets and valves separately to avoid accidental interchange.

Check all parts for wear or damage. If wear or damage is found, replace the defective parts. Especially check the following:

1. Check the float needle and seat for wear. If wear is found, replace the complete assembly.

2. Check the float hinge pin for wear and the float(s) for dents or distortion. Replace the float if fuel has leaked into it.

3. Check the throttle and choke shaft bores for wear or an out-of-round condition. Damage or wear to the throttle arm, shaft, or shaft bore will often require replacement of the throttle body. These parts require a close tolerance of fit; wear may allow air leakage, which could affect starting and idling.

NOTE: *Throttle shafts and bushings are not included in overhaul kits. They can be purchased separately.*

4. Inspect the idle mixture adjusting needles for burrs or grooves. Any such condition requires replacement of the needle, since you will not be able to obtain a satisfactory idle.

5. Test the accelerator pump check valves. They should pass air one way but not the other. Test for proper seating by blowing and sucking on the valve. Replace the valve if necessary. If the valve is satisfactory, wash the valve again to remove breath moisture.

6. Check the bowl cover for warped surfaces with a straight edge.

7. Closely inspect the valves and seats for wear and damage, replacing as necessary.

8. After the carburetor is assembled, check the choke valve for freedom of operation.

Carburetor overhaul kits are recommended for each overhaul. These kits contain all gaskets and new parts to replace those that deteriorate most rapidly. Failure to replace all parts supplied with the kit (especially gaskets) can result in poor performance later.

Some carburetor manufacturers supply overhaul kits of three basic types: minor repair; major repair; and gasket kits.

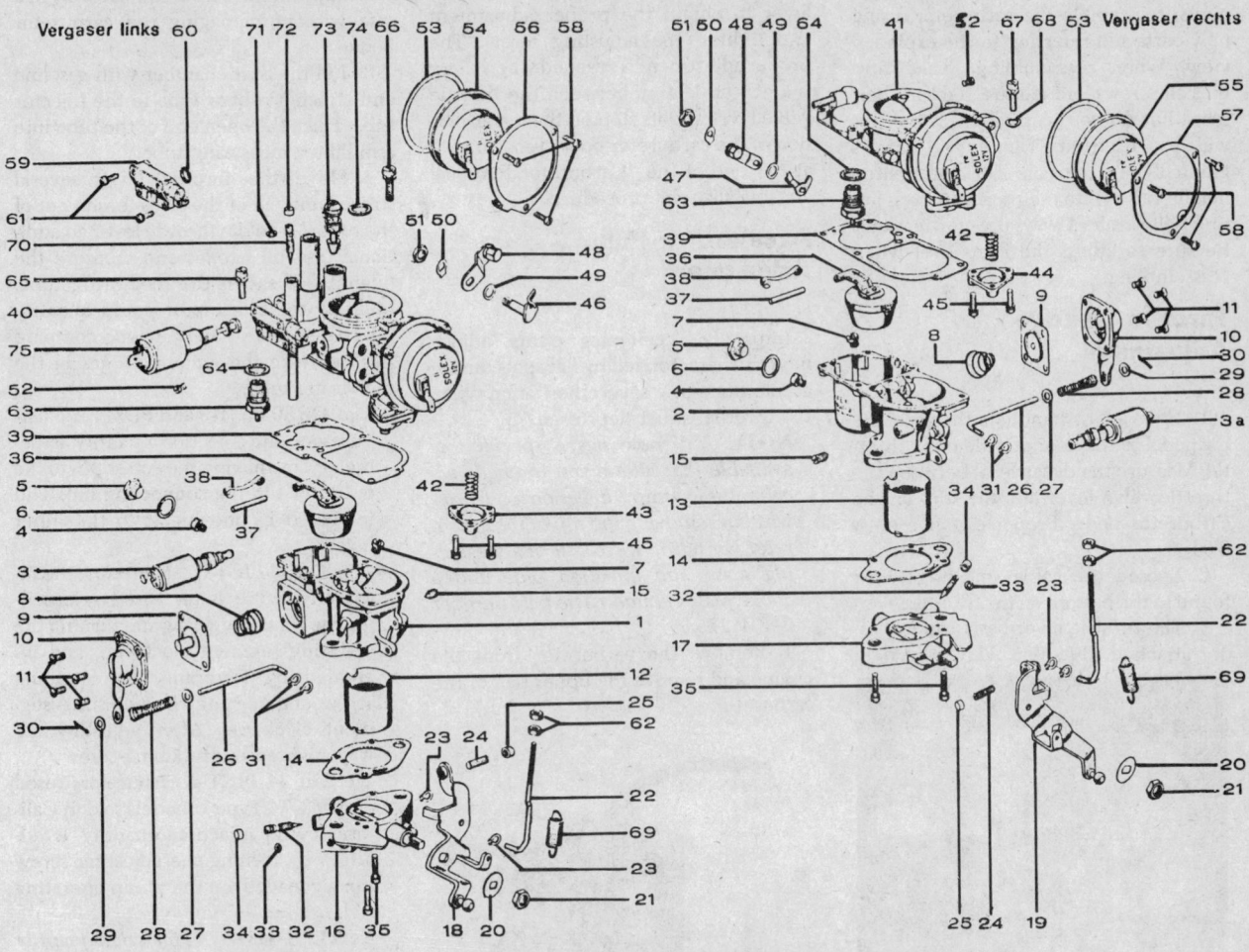

Vergaser links 60 71 72 73 74 66 53 54 56 58

51 50 48 49 64 41 52 67 68 53 Vergaser rechts

Exploded view of twin Solex 34 PDSIT 2/3 carburetors used on 1972-74 Type 2/1700, 2/1800

1. Carburetor body—34 PDSIT-2
2. Carburetor body—34 PDSIT-3
3. Electromagnetic idling cutoff valve—34 PDSIT-2
3a. Electromagnetic idling cutoff valve—34 PDSIT-3
4. Main jet
5. Main jet cover plug
6. Main jet cover plug seal
7. Air correction jet
8. Pump diaphragm spring
9. Pump diaphragm
10. Accelerator pump cover
11. Screws
12. Venturi—34 PDSIT-2
13. Venturi—34 PDSIT-3
14. Throttle body gasket
15. Venturi setscrew
16. Throttle body—34 PDSIT-2
17. Throttle body—34 PDSIT-3
18. Throttle arm—34 PDSIT-2
19. Throttle arm—34 PDSIT-3
20. Special washer
21. Nut
22. Connecting rod
23. Circlip
24. Throttle valve opening adjusting screw
25. Plug
26. Connecting link
27. Washer
28. Connecting link spring
29. Washer
30. Cotter pin
31. Circlip
32. Idle mixture screw
33. O-ring
34. Plug
35. Throttle body screws

36. Float
37. Float pin
38. Float pin retainer
39. Gasket
40. Carburetor upper part (air horn) with idle mixture enrichment—34 PDSIT-2
41. Carburetor upper part (air horn)—34 PDSIT-3
42. Vacuum diaphragm spring
43. Vacuum diaphragm cover—34 PDSIT-2
44. Vacuum diaphragm cover—34 PDSIT-3
45. Screws
53. Choke heating element gasket
54. Choke heating element—34 PDSIT-2
55. Choke heating element—34 PDSIT-3
56. Choke cover retaining ring—34 PDSIT-2
57. Choke cover retaining ring—34 PDSIT-3
58. Screws
59. Idle mixture enrichment unit
60. O-ring
61. Screws
62. Connecting rod locknuts
63. Float valve
64. Float valve washer
65. Screws
66. Screws
67. Screws
68. Washer
69. Throttle return spring
70. Idle mixture screw
71. O-ring
72. Plug
73. Idle speed adjusting screw
74. O-ring
75. Central idling system electromagnetic cutoff valve
Vergaser links—left carburetor (34 PDSIT-2)
Vergaser rechts—right carburetor (34 PDSIT-3)

After cleaning and checking all components, reassemble the carburetor, using new parts and referring to the exploded view. When reassembling, make sure that all screws and jets are tight in their seats, but do not overtighten as the tips will be distorted. Tighten all screws gradually, in rotation. Do not tighten needle valves into their seats: uneven jetting will result. Always use new gaskets. Be sure to adjust the float level when reassembling.

Throttle Linkage Adjustment

1. Have an assistant hold the accelerator pedal to the floor at wide open throttle. Measure the distance (a) between the throttle valve lever and the stop on the carburetor body. Proper distance (a) is 0.04 in.

2. Loosen the cable adjusting screw found in the bottom on the throttle lever.

3. The throttle lever has a rigid cylinder attached to its end. Move the rigid

portion in or out of the end of the throttle lever to obtain the proper adjustment and tighten the adjusting screw. The proper adjustment is reached when there is a gap of 0.04 in. between the throttle valve lever and its stop on the lower portion of the carburetor body. See the note at the end of the "Carburetor Removal and Installation" procedure.

Accelerator Pump Adjustment

Improper accelerator pump adjustment is characterized by flat spots during acceleration or a severe hesitation when the throttle is first depressed.

NOTE: *VW now has a special tool available that allows you to check accelerator pump injection quantity without removing the top of the carburetor (air horn). It consists of a measuring glass, and injection pipe and a choke plate retainer. The part number is VW 119.*

1. Remove the carburetor from the engine and remove the upper half of the carburetor.

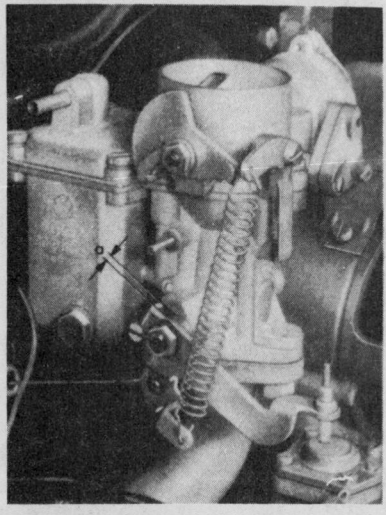

Full-throttle clearance (distance a) should be 0.04 in. on single carburetor engines

Measuring accelerator pump output

2. Support the carburetor securely in a vise without damaging the carburetor body.

3. Fill the float chamber with gasoline and attach a rubber tube to the injector tube. Place the open end of the tube into a milliliter measuring tube.

4. Move the throttle lever several strokes until all of the air is forced out of the tube. Move the throttle lever an additional ten full strokes and measure the quantity of gas in the measuring tube. Multiply the accelerator pump quantity injected specification by 10 and compare this figure to the amount of gas in the measuring tube.

5. a. On 30 PICT-3 and PDSIT 2/3 carburetors, the injection quantity is decreased by moving the cotter pin to the outer hole in the connecting link, and increased by moving it to the inner hole.

b. On 34 PICT-3 carburetors, the injection quantity is decreased by loosening the retaining screw and turning the adjusting segment clockwise, and increased by loosening the retaining screw and turning the adjusting segment clockwise. After adjusting, always tighten the retaining screw.

c. On 34 PICT-4 carburetors (used on 1973–74 Type 1 models sold in California), the injection quantity is adjusted by turning the adjusting screw (spring loaded) on the pump operating rod.

NOTE: *Below 70° F, injection quantity is 1.7 cm³ per stroke. Above 78° F, injector quantity is 1.1 cm³ per stroke.*

Float and Fuel Level Adjustment

A properly assembled carburetor has a preset float level. For the float level to be correct the fiber washer under the needle valve seat must be installed and be of the proper thickness. See the "Carburetor Specifications Chart".

Accelerator pump injection quantity adjusting segment for 1973-74 Type 1 models with alternator. Dotted line shows position of adjusting segment for 1972-73 Type 1 models with generator (Solex 34-PICT-3)

Accelerator pump injection quantity adjusting nut for 1973-74 Type 1 California models (Solex 34-PICT-4)

The only way to adjust the float level, if it is absolutely necessary, and still retain proper seating of the needle in the needle valve seat, is to vary the thickness of the fiber washer beneath the seat. Washers are available in thicknesses of 0.50 mm, 0.80 mm, 1.00 mm, and 1.50 mm.

Throttle Valve Gap

34 PDSIT 2/3 Carburetors

Carburetor Removed

1. Remove the carburetor from the car.

2. Loosen the two nuts on the automatic choke connecting rod and insert a 0.028 in. wire gauge or drill between the throttle valve and the side of the venturi.

3. Move the two nuts up or down on the connecting rod until the throttle valve gap is adjusted and tighten the two nuts.

NOTE: *The choke valve must be closed for proper adjustment.*

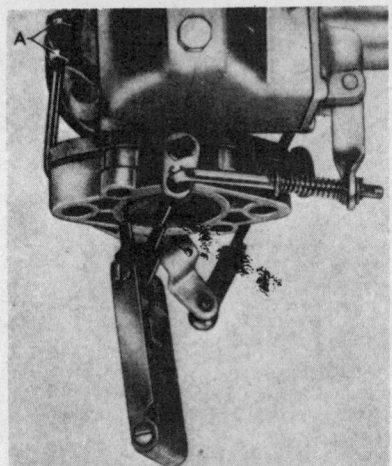

Adjusting throttle valve gap with adjusting nuts (A)

Carburetor Installed

1. Back out the idle speed screw until the throttle valve is completely closed.

2. Turn the idle speed screw until it just touches the throttle lever.

3. Close the choke valve.

4. Place a 0.09 in. drill or wire gauge between the idle screw and the throttle valve lever. Adjust the two nuts on the automatic choke connecting rod either up or down until the drill can be easily pulled out.

5. It will be necessary to rebalance the carburetors on dual carburetor models.

Fast Idle Adjustment

1. The fast idle speed is adjusted by means of a screw located at the upper end of the throttle valve arm. This screw rests against a cam with steps cut into its edge.

2. To adjust the fast idle, start the engine and rotate the cam so that the fast idle screw is resting against the highest step on the fast idle cam. The fast idle speed should be approximately 1500 rpm.

3. Turn the fast idle screw either in or out until the proper idle speed is obtained.

4. On dual carburetor engines it is necessary to adjust the fast idle on only one of the carburetors. There is a direct mechanical connection between the two carburetors and if one carburetor is adjusted the other will automatically be adjusted.

Dashpot Adjustment

1972–74 Type 1 with Manual Transmission

NOTE: *The car must be fully warmed up and the choke plate open.*

1. Check that the distance (a) between the tip of the dashpot and the throttle lever is 0.040 in. with the dashpot plunger fully retracted and the throttle fully closed on the warm running position of the fast idle cam.

2. To adjust, loosen the two locknuts on the dashpot mounting bracket, and raise or lower the dashpot as needed.

1972–74 Type 2 Twin Carb

NOTE: *This adjustment is required only if the dashpot has been removed or the linkage disassembled.*

1. Check that the distance between the tip of the plunger and the tab on the linkage is 0.0015 in. while holding the dashpot plunger in the retracted position.

2. To adjust, loosen the two locknuts on the dashpot mounting bracket, and raise or lower the dashpot as required.

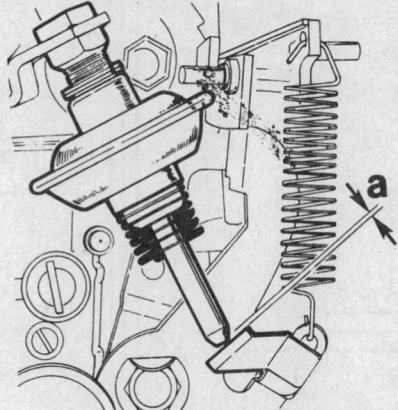

Dashpot adjustment on 1972-74 Type 1 models. Distance "a" is 0.040 in.

Accelerator Cable Replacement

1. Disconnect the cable from the accelerator pedal.

2. Disconnect the cable from the throttle lever.

3. Pull the cable from the accelerator pedal end and then remove it from the car.

4. Grease the cable before sliding it into its housing.

5. Slide the cable into its housing and push it through its guide tubes. It may be necessary to raise the car and start the cable into the segments of guide tube found under the car.

6. Install one cable end into the accelerator cable. Slip the other end into the throttle valve lever and adjust the cable.

NOTE: *Make sure that the rubber boot at the rear end of the cable is properly seated so that water will not enter the guide tubes.*

Electronic Fuel Injection—Non-Air Flow Controlled

The Bosch Electronic fuel injection system used on all Type 3 models, and on Type 4 through 1974 models (except 1974 models equipped with an automatic), consists of two parts. One part consists of the actual injection components: the injectors, the fuel pump, pressure regulator, and related wiring and hoses. The second part consists of the injection controls and engine operating characteristics sensors: a manifold vacuum sensor that monitors engine load, trigger contacts used to determine when and which pair of injectors will operate, three temperature sensors used to control air fuel mixture enrichment, a cold starting valve for additional cold starting fuel enrichment, a throttle valve switch used to cut off fuel during decleration, and the brain box used to analyze information about engine operating characteristics and, after processing this information, to control the electrically operated injectors.

It is absolutely imperative that no adjustments other than those found in the following pages be performed. The controls for this fuel injection system are extremely sensitive and easily damaged when subject to abuse. Never attempt to test the brain box without proper training and the proper equipment. The dealer is the best place to have any needed work performed.

CAUTION: *Whenever a fuel injection component is to be removed or installed, the battery should be disconnected and the ignition turned OFF.*

It is not recommended that the inexperienced mechanic work on any portion of the fuel injection system.

Air Flow Controlled Electronic Fuel Injection

1974 Type 4 models equipped with au-

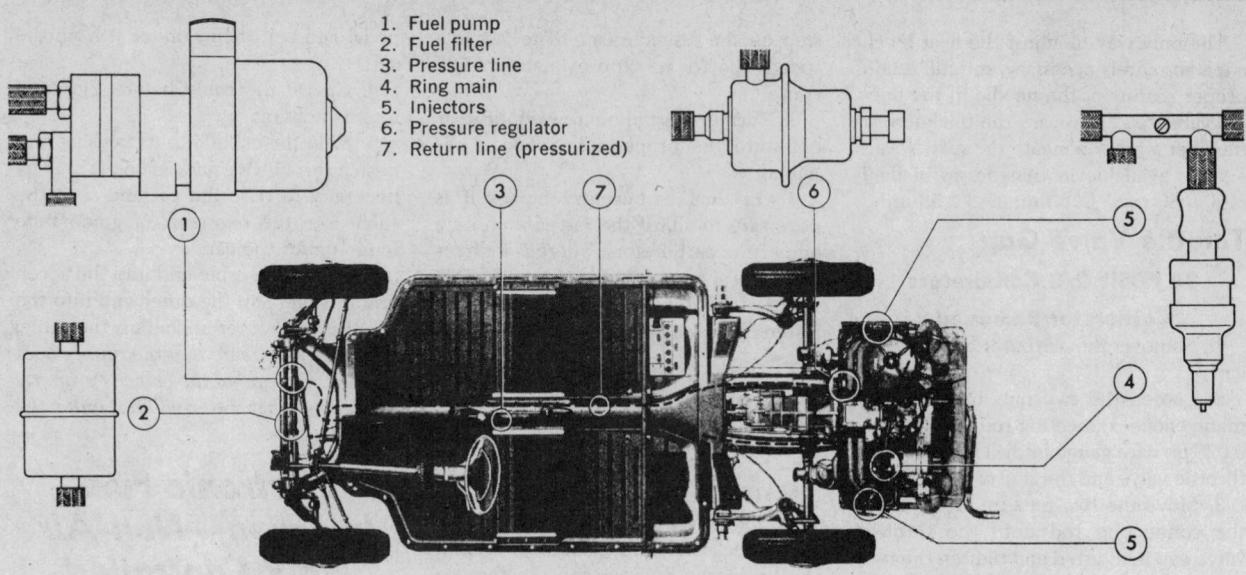

1. Fuel pump
2. Fuel filter
3. Pressure line
4. Ring main
5. Injectors
6. Pressure regulator
7. Return line (pressurized)

Location of fuel injection components—Type 3

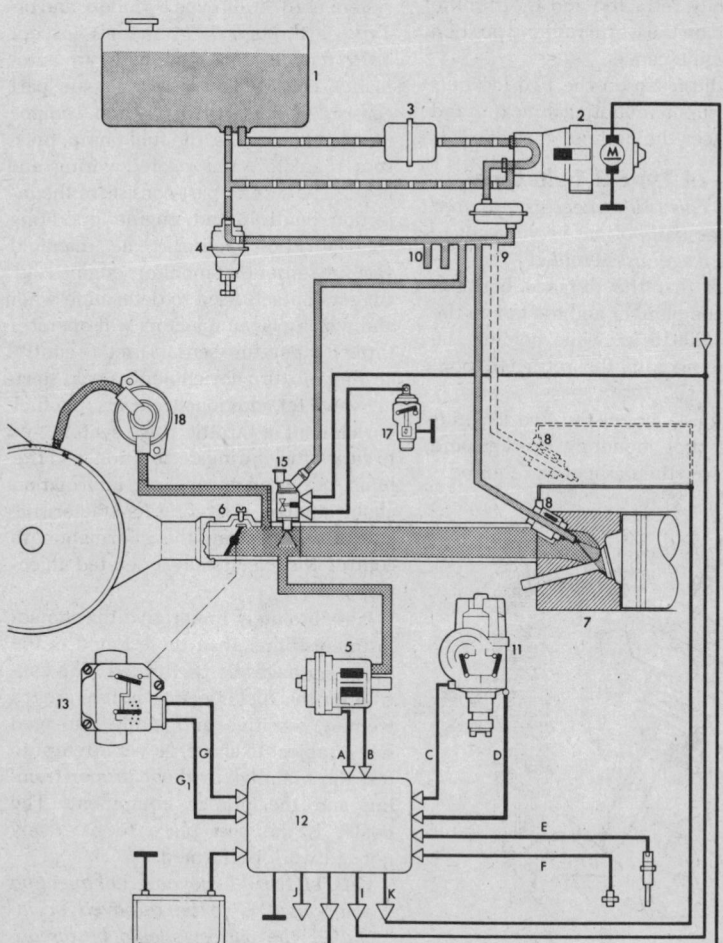

Schematic of fuel injection—1972 and later Federal

1. Fuel tank
2. Fuel pump
3. Fuel filter
4. Pressure regulator
5. Pressure sensor
6. Intake air distributor
7. Cylinder head
8. Injectors
9. Fuel distributor pipe
10. Fuel distributor pipe with connection for cold starting device
11. Distributor with trigger contacts (distributor contact I, distributor contact II)
12. Control unit
13. Throttle valve switch with acceleration enrichment
15. Cold starting valve
17. Thermostat for cold starting device
18. Auxiliary air regulator
A + B. from pressure sensor (load condition signal)
C + D. from distributor contacts (engine speed and releasing signal)
E + F. from temperature sensors (warmup signal)
G. from throttle valve switch (fuel supply cut-off when coasting)
G1. Acceleration enrichment
I. from starter, terminal 50 solenoid switch (signal for enrichening mixture when starting)
J. to the injectors, cylinders 1 and 4
K. to the injectors, cylinders 2 and 3

It also controls the electric fuel pump by shutting it off when intake air stops. It is located between the air cleaner and the intake air distributor.

Ignition contact breaker points—these are the regular points inside the distributor. When the points open, all four injectors are triggered. The points also send engine speed signals to the control unit. No separate triggering contacts are used.

Throttle valve switch—provides only for full load enrichment. This switch is not adjustable.

Temperature sensor I—senses intake temperature as before. It is now located in the intake air sensor.

Temperature sensor II—senses cylinder head temperature as before.

Control unit (brain box)—contains only 80 components compared to the old systems 300.

tomatic transmission, as well as all 1975–76 Type 1 and Type 2 models, are equipped with an improved system known as the Air Flow Controlled Electronic Fuel Injection System. With this system, some of the electronic sensors and wiring are eliminated, and the con-

trol box is smaller. Instead fuel is metered according to intake air flow.

The system consists of the following components;

Intake air sensor—measures intake air volume and temperature and sends voltage signals to the control unit (brain box).

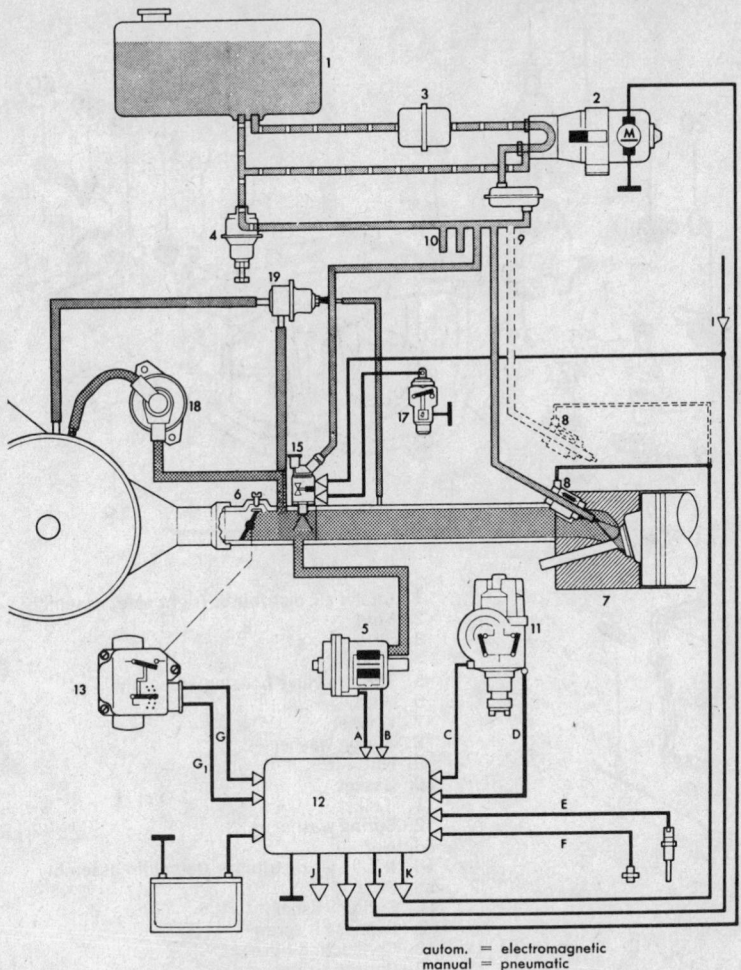

1. Fuel tank
2. Fuel pump
3. Fuel filter
4. Pressure regulator
5. Pressure sensor
6. Intake air distributor
7. Cylinders head
8. Injectors
9. Fuel distributor pipe
10. Fuel distributor pipe with connection for cold starting device
11. Distributor with trigger contacts (contacts I and II)
12. Electronic control unit
13. Throttle valve switch with acceleration enrichment
14. Pressure switch
15. Cold starting valve
17. Thermostat for cold starting device
18. Auxiliary air regulator
19. Deceleration mixture control valve
A + B. from pressure sensor (load condition signal)
C + D. from distributor contacts (engine speed and releasing signal)
E + F. from temperature sensors (warmup signal)
G. from throttle valve switch (full throttle signal, Type 3 only)
G1. Acceleration enrichment
I. from starter, terminal 50 solenoid switch (signal for enrichening mixture when starting)
J. to the injectors, cylinders 1 and 4
K. to the injectors, cylinders 2 and 3

autom. = electromagnetic
manual = pneumatic

Schematic of fuel injection—1972 and later California

Pressure regulator—is connected by a vacuum hose to the intake air distributor and is no longer adjustable. It adjusts fuel pressure according to manifold vacuum.

Auxiliary air regulator—provides more air during cold warmup.

Electronic Control Box

All work concerning the control box is to be performed by the dealer. Do not remove the control box and take it to a dealer because the dealer will not be able to test it without the vehicle. Do not disconnect the control box unless the battery is disconnected and the ignition is OFF.

Fuel Injectors

There are two types of injectors. One type is secured in place by a ring that holds a single injector. The second type of injector is secured to the intake manifold in pairs by a common bracket.

Removal and Installation

Single Injectors

1. Remove the nut which secures the injector bracket to the manifold.

2. If the injector is not going to be replaced, do not disconnect the fuel line.

Disconnect the injector wiring.

3. Gently slide the injector bracket up the injector and pull the injector from the intake manifold. Be careful not to damage the inner and outer rubber seal-

ing rings. These sealing rings are used to seal the injector to the manifold and must be replaced if they show any sign of deterioration.

4. Installation is the reverse of removal. Be careful not to damage the injector tip or contaminate the injector with dirt.

Paired Injectors

1. Disconnect the injector wiring.

2. Remove the two nuts which secure the injector bracket to the manifold. Slide the bracket up the injector. Do not disconnect the fuel lines if the injector is not going to be replaced.

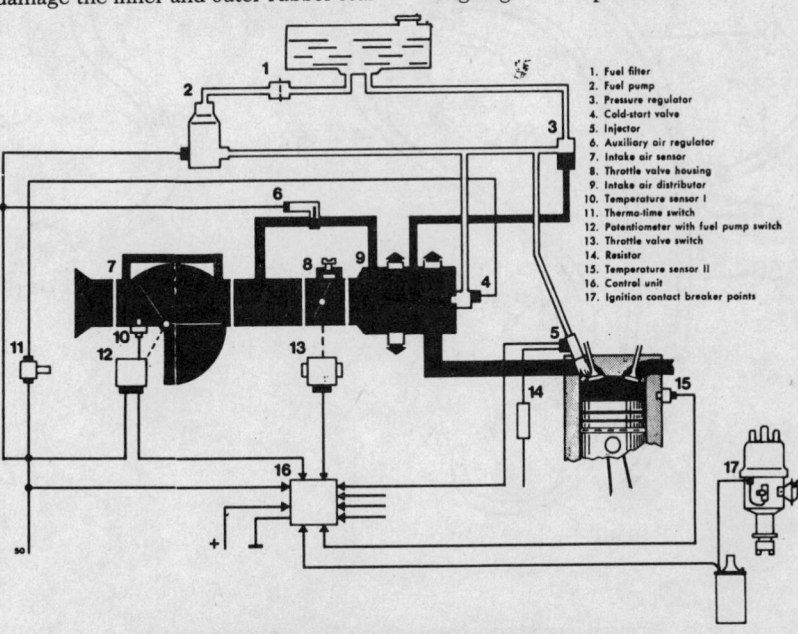

1. Fuel filter
2. Fuel pump
3. Pressure regulator
4. Cold-start valve
5. Injector
6. Auxiliary air regulator
7. Intake air sensor
8. Throttle valve housing
9. Intake air distributor
10. Temperature sensor I
11. Thermo-time switch
12. Potentiometer with fuel pump switch
13. Throttle valve switch
14. Resistor
15. Temperature sensor II
16. Control unit
17. Ignition contact breaker points

Schematic of airflow controlled fuel injection system—1975-77 models

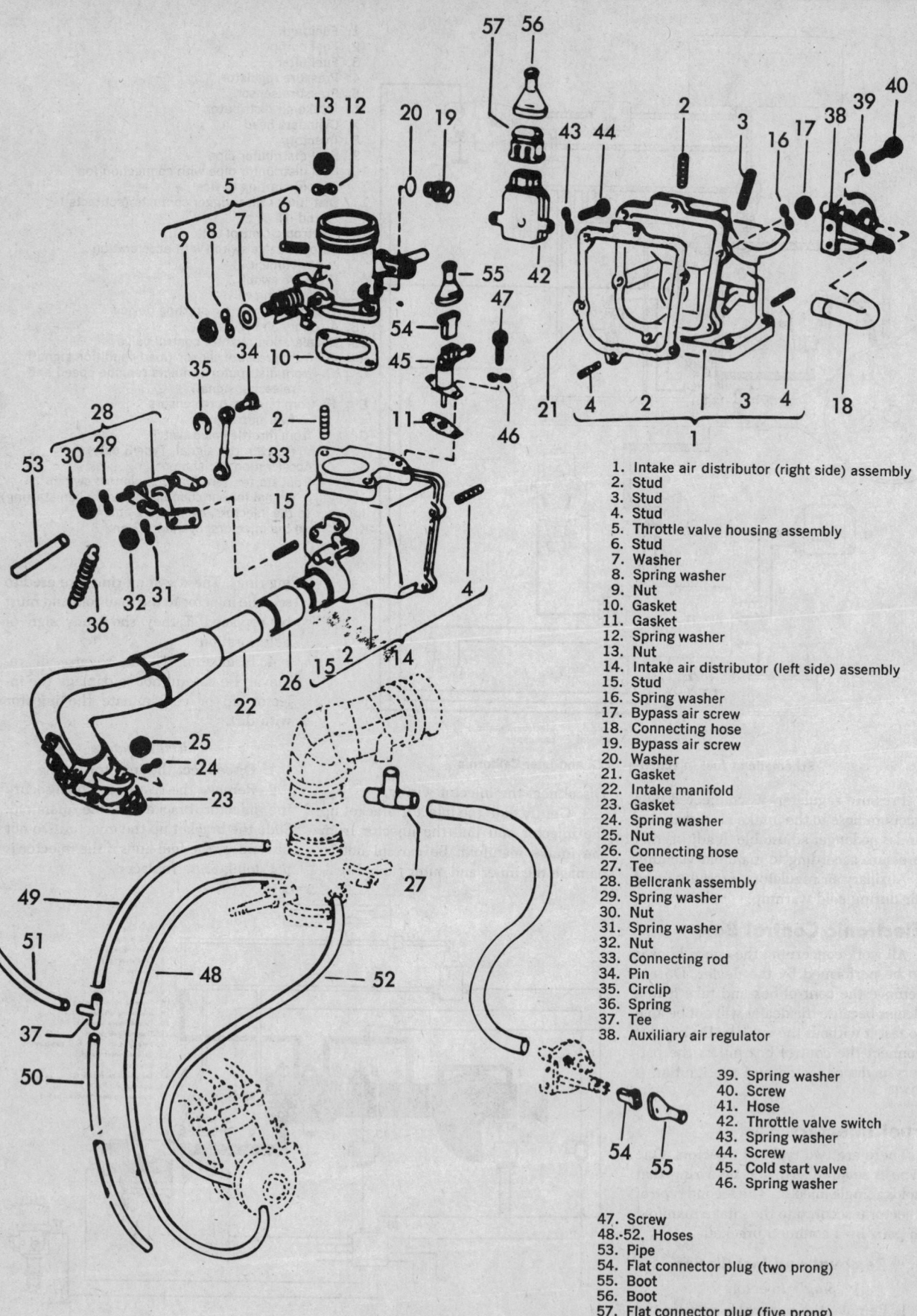

57 56

13 12   20 19   2   3   16 17 38 39 40

43 44

5
9 8 7 6

55

42

54

47

45

35 34

2

46

11

53 30 29 33

15

28

32 31

36

15 2 14

26

22

25
24

23

27

49

51

48   52

37

50

54 55

1. Intake air distributor (right side) assembly
2. Stud
3. Stud
4. Stud
5. Throttle valve housing assembly
6. Stud
7. Washer
8. Spring washer
9. Nut
10. Gasket
11. Gasket
12. Spring washer
13. Nut
14. Intake air distributor (left side) assembly
15. Stud
16. Spring washer
17. Bypass air screw
18. Connecting hose
19. Bypass air screw
20. Washer
21. Gasket
22. Intake manifold
23. Gasket
24. Spring washer
25. Nut
26. Connecting hose
27. Tee
28. Bellcrank assembly
29. Spring washer
30. Nut
31. Spring washer
32. Nut
33. Connecting rod
34. Pin
35. Circlip
36. Spring
37. Tee
38. Auxiliary air regulator

39. Spring washer
40. Screw
41. Hose
42. Throttle valve switch
43. Spring washer
44. Screw
45. Cold start valve
46. Spring washer

47. Screw
48.-52. Hoses
53. Pipe
54. Flat connector plug (two prong)
55. Boot
56. Boot
57. Flat connector plug (five prong)

Exploded view of components for air flow controlled electronic fuel injection system used in 1975 Type 1 and Type 2 vehicles—Type 1 system shown; Type 2 similar

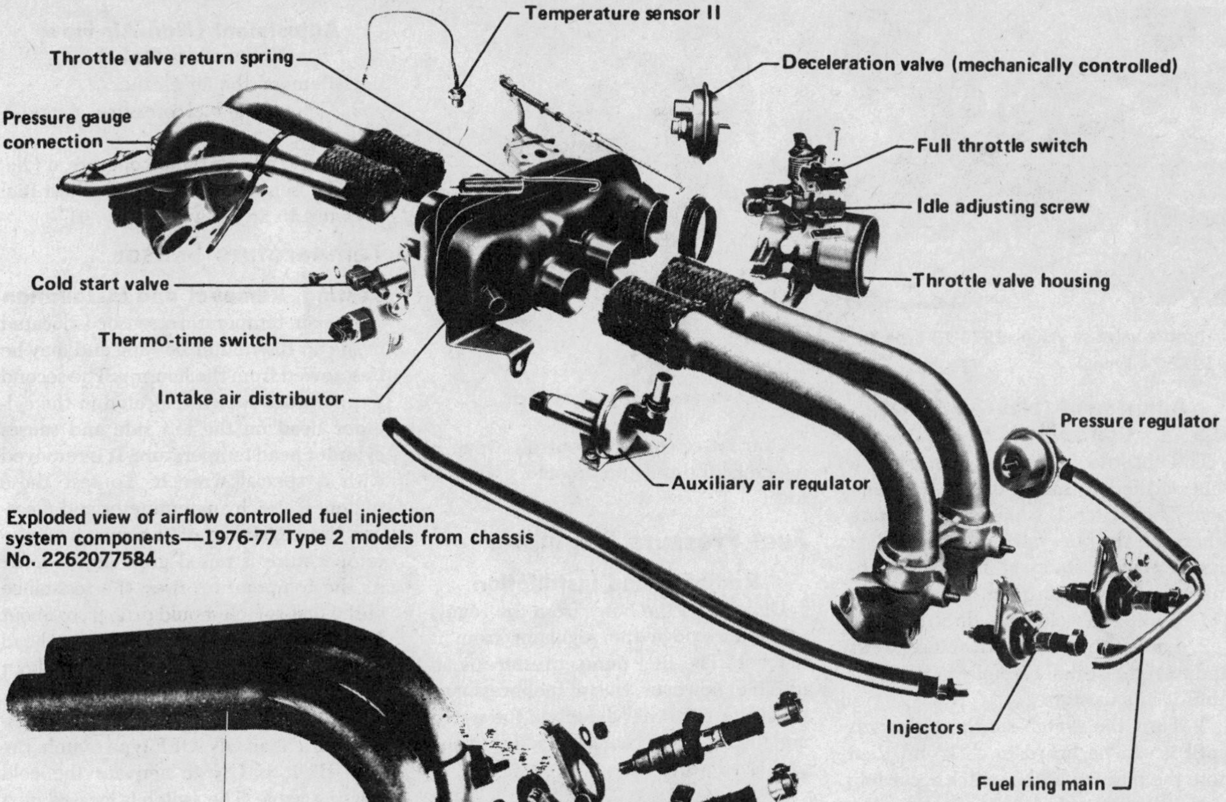

Temperature sensor II

Throttle valve return spring

Deceleration valve (mechanically controlled)

Pressure gauge connection

Full throttle switch

Idle adjusting screw

Cold start valve

Throttle valve housing

Thermo-time switch

Intake air distributor

Pressure regulator

Auxiliary air regulator

Injectors

Fuel ring main

Exploded view of airflow controlled fuel injection system components—1976-77 Type 2 models from chassis No. 2262077584

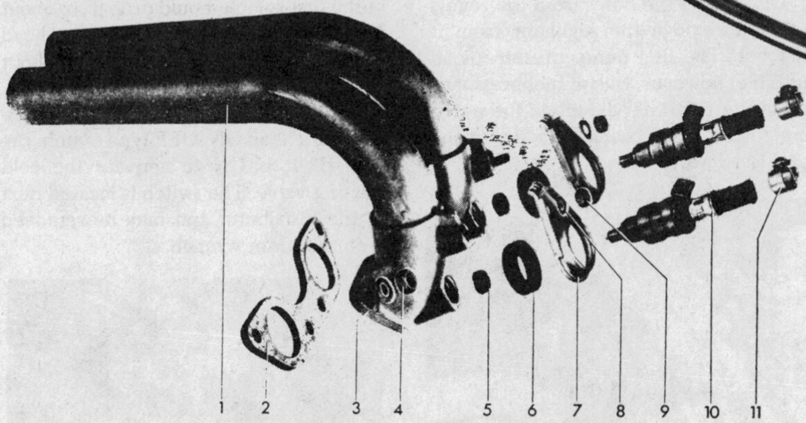

1 2   3 4   5 6 7 8 9 10 11

Individually mounted fuel injectors

1. Intake manifold
2. Intake manifold gasket
3. Lock washer
4. Inner sealing bushing
5. Outer sealing bushing
6. Outer sealing bushing
7. Retainer
8. Lock washer
9. Nut
10. Fuel injector
11. Hose connection with clamp

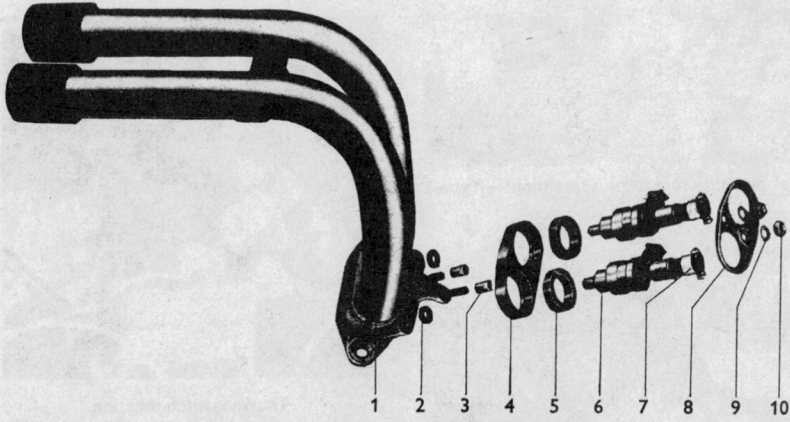

1 2 3   4   5   6   7   8   9   10

Paired fuel injectors

1. Intake manifolds with injector seats
2. Injector inner locating sealing bushings
3. Sleeves
4. Injector plate
5. Injector outer locating bushings
6. Electromagnetic fuel injector
7. Hose connection with clamp
8. Injector retainer
9. Lock washer
10. Nut

3. Gently slide the pair of injectors out of their bores along with the rubber sealing rings, injector plate, and the inner and outer injector locating bushings. It may be necessary to remove the inner bushings from the intake manifold after the injectors are removed since they sometimes lodge within the manifold.

NOTE: *There are two sleeves that fit over the injector bracket studs. Be careful not to lose them.*

4. Upon installation, place the injector bracket, the outer locating bushings, the injector plate, and the inner locating bushings on the pair of injectors in that order.

5. Gently slip the injector assembly into the manifold and install the bracket nuts. Be careful not to damage the injector tips or contaminate the injectors with dirt.

6. Reconnect the injector wiring.

Throttle Valve Switch

Removal and Installation

1. Remove the air filter.

2. The switch is located on the throttle valve housing. Disconnect the throttle valve return spring.

3. Remove the throttle valve assembly but do not disconnect the bowden wire for the throttle valve or the connecting hoses to the ignition distributor.

4. Remove the throttle valve, switch securing screws and remove the switch.

5. Reverse the above steps to install. It will be necessary to adjust the switch after installation.

Throttle valve switch on 1970-73 Type 3, 1972-74 Type 4

Adjustment (Non-Air Flow Controlled Only)

The throttle valve switch is used to shut off the fuel supply during deceleration. The switch is supposed to operate when the throttle valve is opened 2°. A degree scale is stamped into the attachment plate for adjustment purposes.

1. Completely close the throttle valve.
2. Loosen the switch attaching screws and turn the switch carefully to the right until it hits its stop.
3. Turn the switch slowly to the left until it can be heard to click and then note the position of the switch according to the degree scale.
4. Continue to turn the switch another 2°. The distance between any two marks on the degree scale is 2°.
5. Tighten the screws and recheck the adjustment.

Cold Start Valve

Removal and Installation

The cold start valve is located near the thermo-switch and is secured to the air intake distributor by two screws. This valve sometimes jams open and causes excesssive consumption, rough idle, and low power output.

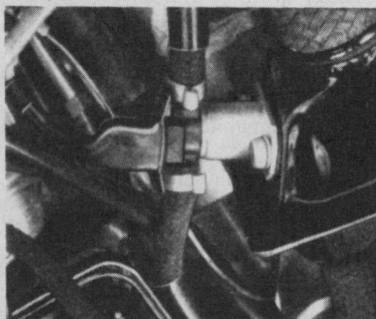

Cold start valve location

Trigger Contacts (Non-Air Flow Controlled Only)

Removal and Installation

The trigger contacts are located in the base of the distributor and are secured by two screws. These contacts are supplied in pairs and are not adjustable. Do not attempt to replace just one set of contacts.

1374

Removing trigger contacts

One set of contacts controls a pair of injectors and tells the injectors when to fire.

Fuel Pressure Regulator

Removal and Installation

Disconnect the hoses from the regulator and remove the regulator from its bracket. The fuel pump pressure is adjustable; however, lack of fuel pressure is usually due to other defects in the system and the regulator should be adjusted only as a last resort.

Fuel pressure regulator test gauge installation

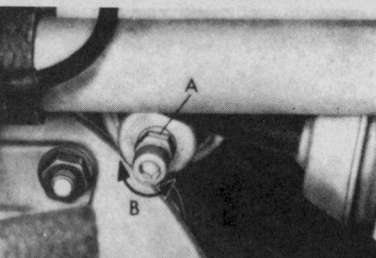

Fuel pressure regulator adjustment—Type 3

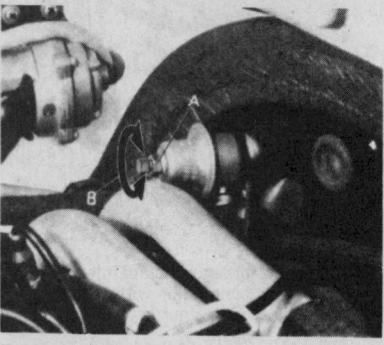

Fuel pressure regulator adjustment—Type 4

Adjustment (Non-Air Flow Controlled Only)

1. Remove the air cleaner.
2. Connect a fuel pressure gauge.

3. Start the engine and operate at idle.
4. Loosen locknut "A" and adjust fuel pressure to 28 psi with screw "B".

Temperature Sensor

Testing, Removal and Installation

The air temperature sensor is located in the air distributor housing and may be unscrewed from the housing. The second temperature switch is located in the cylinder head on the left side and senses cylinder head temperature. It is removed with a special wrench. To test these switches, attach an ohmmeter and measure the resistance of the switch as the temperature is raised gradually to 212°. As the temperature rises, the resistance of the first switch should drop from about 200 ohms to 80 ohms. The cylinder head switch resistance should drop from about 1700 ohms to 190 ohms at 212°.

The third switch is actually a thermoswitch and is an ON/OFF type switch. Below 41° it is ON to activate the cold starting valve. The switch is located next to the distributor and may be removed with a 24 mm wrench.

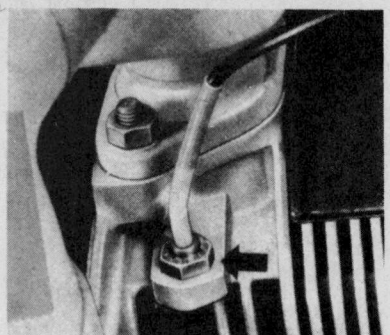

Cylinder head temperature sensing switch

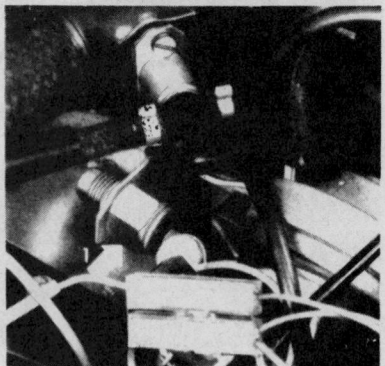

Thermoswitch location

Pressure Sensor (Non-Air Flow Controlled Only)

Removal and Installation

1. The sensor is secured to the firewall by two screws. Remove the screws and

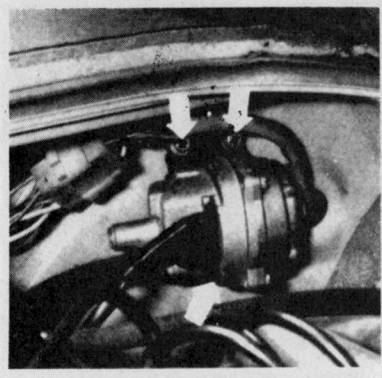

Pressure sensor retaining screws

disconnect the wiring.

2. Remove the pressure connection and immediately plug the connection into the sensor.

3. Always keep the connection plugged as the bellows inside the sensor is sensitive to the smallest pieces of dirt. Reverse the above steps to install.

4. Do not disassemble the sensor. There are no adjustments possible for the sensor.

NOTE: *Do not reverse the square electrical plug when reconnecting the sensor wiring.*

Troubleshooting

There are very few items to check without the special tester used by the dealer.

It is possible to check the fuel pressure by inserting a fuel pressure gauge in the line after the pressure regulator. Insert the gauge using a T-fitting. Turn on the key and check the pressure. If the pressure is low, check for leaking injectors, restricted lines, clogged fuel filters, damaged pressure regulator, bad fuel pump, water in the gas and resultant corrosion of the injectors, or a leaking or jammed cold start valve.

CLUTCH

The clutch used in all models is a single dry disc mounted on the flywheel with a diaphragm spring type pressure plate. The release bearing is the ball bearing type and does not require lubrication. On Types 1, 2, and 3, the clutch is engaged mechanically via a cable which attaches to the clutch pedal. On the Type 4, the clutch is engaged hydraulically, using a clutch pedal operated master cylinder and a bell housing mounted slave cylinder.

Removal and Installation
Manual Transmission

1. Remove the engine.

2. Remove the pressure plate securing bolts one turn at a time until all spring pressure is released.

3. Remove the bolts and remove the clutch assembly.

NOTE: *Notice which side of the clutch disc faces the flywheel and install the new disc in the same direction.*

4. Before installing the new clutch, check the condition of the flywheel. It should not have excessive heat cracks and the friction surface should not be scored or warped. Check the condition of the throw out bearing. If the bearing is worn, replace it.

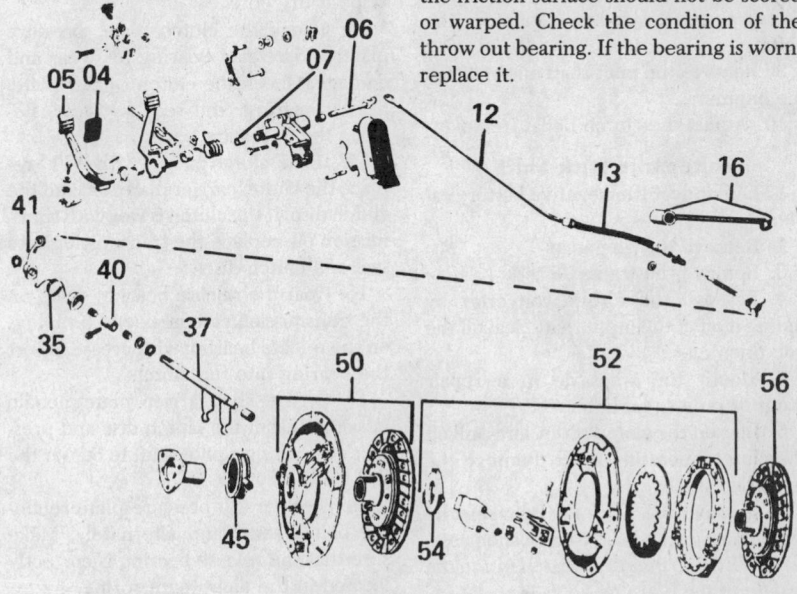

Clutch Control—Type 1

4. Clutch pedal pad	37. Clutch cross shaft
5. Clutch pedal	40. Bushing—operating shaft
6. Clutch pedal shaft	41. Clutch operating lever
7. Bushings for pedal cluster	45. Clutch release bearing
12. Clutch cable	50. Clutch
13. Clutch cable sleeve	52. Pressure plate
16. Angle plate for clutch cable	54. Clutch release plate
35. Clutch return spring	56. Clutch disc

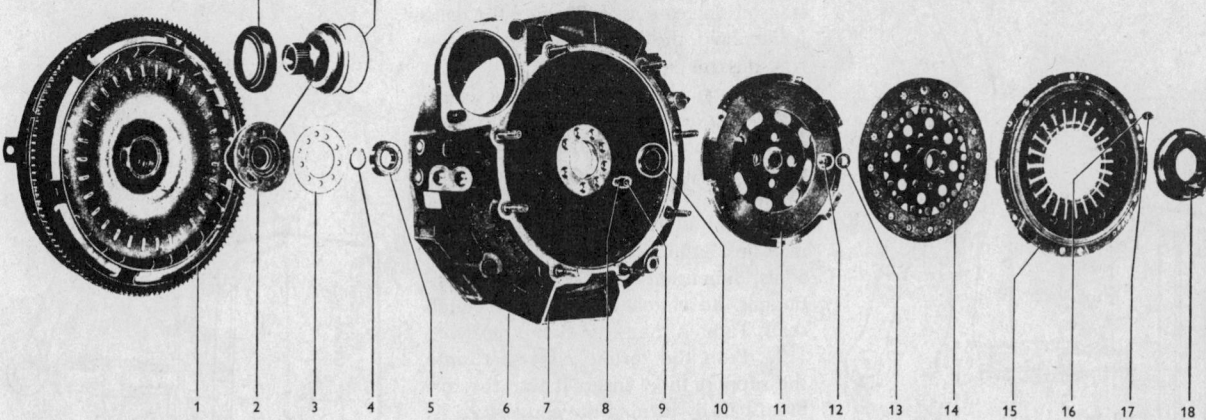

Automatic Stick Shift clutch assembly

1. Torque converter	8. Spring washer	15. Diaphragm clutch pressure plate
2. One-way clutch support	9. Socket head screw	16. Spring washer
3. Gasket	10. Seal	17. Socket head screw
4. Circlip for carrier plate	11. Clutch carrier plate	18. Release bearing
5. Ball bearing	12. Needle bearing	19. Seal/converter
6. O-ring for stud	13. Seal/carrier plate	20. O-ring/one-way clutch support
7. Converter housing	14. Clutch plate	

5. Lubricate the pilot bearing in the end of the crankshaft with grease.

6. Insert a pilot shaft, used for centering the clutch disc, through the clutch disc and place the disc against the flywheel. The pilot shaft will hold the disc in place.

7. Place the pressure plate over the disc and loosely install the bolts.

NOTE: *Make sure the correct side of the clutch disc is facing outward. The disc will rub the flywheel if it is incorrectly positioned.*

8. After making sure that the pressure plate aligning dowels will fit into the pressure plate, gradually tighten the bolts.

9. Remove the pilot shaft and reinstall the engine.

10. Adjust the clutch pedal free-play.

Automatic Stick Shift

1. Disconnect the negative battery cable.

2. Remove the engine.

3. Remove the transaxle.

4. Remove the torque converter by sliding it off of the input shaft. Seal off the hub opening.

5. Mount the transaxle in a repair stand or on a suitable bench.

6. Loosen the clamp screw and pull off the clutch operating lever. Remove the transmission cover.

7. Remove the hex nuts between the clutch housing and the transmission case.

NOTE: *Two nuts are located inside the differential housing.*

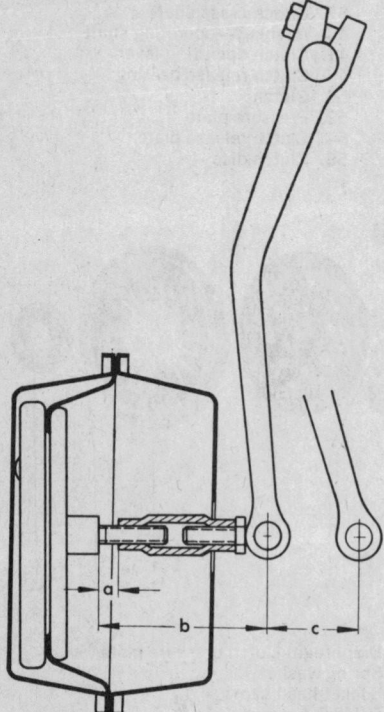

Automatic Stick Shift basic clutch adjusting dimensions

8. The oil need not be drained if the clutch is removed with the cover opening up and the gearshift housing breather blocked.

9. Pull the transmission from the clutch housing studs.

10. Turn the clutch lever shaft to disengage the release bearing.

11. Remove both lower engine mounting bolts.

12. Loosen the clutch retaining bolts gradually and alternately to prevent distortion. Remove the bolts, pressure plate, clutch plate, and release bearing.

13. Do not wash the release bearing. Wipe it dry only.

14. Check the clutch plate, pressure plate, and release bearing for wear and damage. Check the clutch carrier plate, needle bearing, and seat for wear. Replace the necessary parts.

15. If the clutch is wet with ATF, replace the clutch carrier plate seal and the clutch disc. If the clutch is wet with transmission oil, replace the transmission case seal and clutch disc.

16. Coat the release bearing guide on the transmission case neck and both lugs on the release bearing with grease. Insert the bearing into the clutch.

17. Grease the carrier plate needle bearing. Install the clutch disc and pressure plate using a pilot shaft to center the disc on the flywheel.

18. Tighten the pressure plate retaining bolts evenly and alternately. Make sure that the release bearing is correctly located in the diaphragm spring.

19. Insert the lower engine mounting bolts from the front. Replace the sealing rings if necessary. Some units have aluminum sealing rings and cap nuts.

20. Push the transmission onto the converter housing studs. Insert the clutch lever shaft behind the release bearing lugs. Push the release bearing onto the transmission case neck. Tighten the bolts which hold the clutch housing to the transmission case.

21. Install the clutch operating lever.

22. It is necessary to adjust the basic clutch setting. The clutch operating lever should contact the clutch housing. Tighten the lever clamp screw slightly.

23. First adjust dimension (a) to 0.335 in. Adjust dimension (b) to 3.03 in. Finally adjust dimension (c) to 1.6 in. by repositioning the clutch lever on the clutch shaft. Tighten the lever clamp screw.

24. Push the torque converter onto the support tube. Insert it into the turbine shaft by turning the converter.

25. Check the clutch play after installing the transaxle and engine.

Clutch Cable Adjustment

Manual Transmission—
Types 1, 2, 3

1. Check the clutch pedal travel by

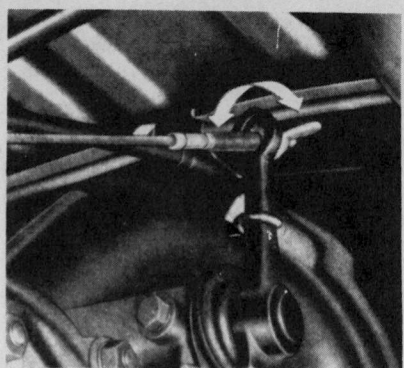

Wing nut for clutch cable adjustment

measuring the distance the pedal travels toward the floor until pressure is exerted against the clutch. The distance is ⅜ to ¾ in.

2. To adjust the clutch, jack up the rear of the car and support it on jackstands.

3. Remove the left rear wheel.

4. Adjust the cable tension by turning the wing nut on the end of the clutch cable. Turning the wing nut counterclockwise decreases pedal free-play, turning it clockwise increases free-play.

5. When the adjustment is completed, the wings of the wing nut must be horizontal so that the lugs on the nut engage the recesses in the clutch lever.

6. Push on the clutch pedal several times and check the pedal free-play.

7. Install the wheel and lower the car.

Automatic Stick Shift Type 1

The adjustment is made on the linkage between the clutch arm and the vacuum servo unit. To check the clutch play:

1. Disconnect the servo vacuum hose.

2. Measure the clearance between the upper edge of the servo unit mounting bracket and the lower edge of the adjusting turnbuckle. If the clearance (e) is 0.16

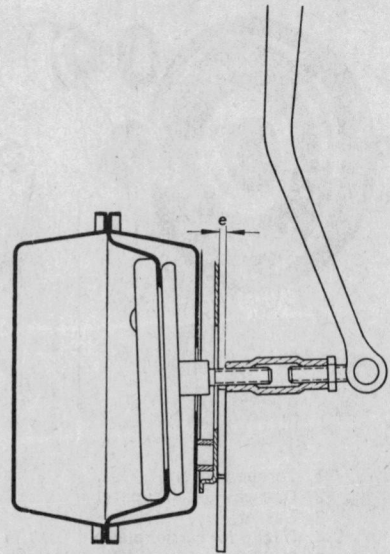

Checking clutch adjustment—Automatic Stick Shift

Adjusting Automatic Stick Shift Clutch—(d) is 0.25 in., measured between locknut and turnbuckle

in. or more, the clutch needs adjustment.

3. Reconnect the vacuum hose.

To adjust the clutch:

1. Disconnect the servo vacuum hose.

2. Loosen the turnbuckle locknut and back it off completely to the lever arm. Then turn the servo turnbuckle against the locknut. Now back off the turnbuckle 5–5½ turns. The distance between the locknut and the turnbuckle should be 0.25 in.

3. Tighten the locknut against the adjusting sleeve.

4. Reconnect the vacuum hose and road test the vehicle. The clutch is properly adjusted when Reverse gear can be engaged silently and the clutch does not slip on acceleration. If the clutch arm contacts the clutch housing, there is no more adjustment possible and the clutch plate must be replaced.

The speed of engagement of the Automatic Stick Shift clutch is regulated by the vacuum operated valve rather than by the driver's foot. The adjusting screw is on top of the valve under a small protective cap. Adjust the valve as follows:

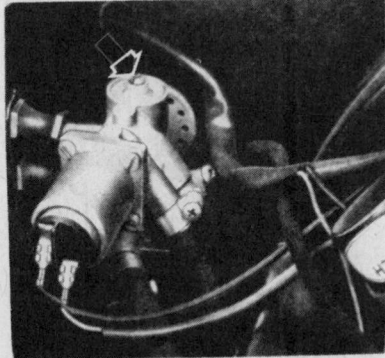

Speed of engagement adjusting screw

1. Remove the cap.

2. To slow the engagement, turn the adjusting screw ¼–½ turn clockwise. To speed engagement, turn the screw counterclockwise.

3. Replace the cap.

4. Test operation by shifting from Second to First at 44 mph without depressing the accelerator. The shift should take

exactly one second to occur.

Clutch Cable Replacement

Types 1, 2, 3

1. Jack up the car and remove the left rear wheel.

2. Disconnect the cable from the clutch operating lever.

3. Remove the rubber boot from the end of the guide tube and off the end of the cable.

4. On Type 1, unbolt the pedal cluster and remove it from the car. It will also be necessary to disconnect the brake master cylinder push rod and throttle cable from the pedal cluster. On Type 2, remove the cover under the pedal cluster, then remove the pin from the clevis on the end of the clutch cable. On Type 3, remove the frame head cover and remove the pin from the clevis on the end of the clutch cable.

5. Pull the cable out of its guide tube from the pedal cluster end.

6. Installation is the reverse of the above.

NOTE: *Grease the cable before installing it and readjust the clutch pedal free-play.*

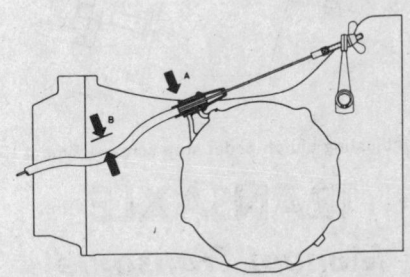

For smooth clutch action, dimension B should be 1.0–1.7 in. Adjust cable to provide slight sag at point B by installing spacer washers at point A

Clutch Master Cylinder

Removal and Installation

Type 4

1. Siphon the hydraulic fluid from the master cylinder (clutch) reservoir.

2. Pull back the carpeting from the pedal area and lay down some absorbent rags.

3. Pull the elbow connection from the top of the master cylinder.

4. Disconnect and plug the pressure line from the rear of the master cylinder.

5. Remove the master cylinder mounting bolts and remove the cylinder to the rear.

6. Reverse the above procedure to install, taking care to bleed the system and adjust pedal free-play.

Clutch Slave Cylinder

Removal and Installation

Type 4

1. Locate the slave cylinder on the bell housing.

2. Disconnect and plug the pressure line from the slave cylinder.

3. Disconnect the return spring from the pushrod.

4. Remove the retaining circlip from the boot and remove the boot.

5. Remove the circlip and slide the slave cylinder rearwards from its mount.

6. Remove the spring clip from the mount.

7. Reverse the above procedure to install, taking care to bleed the system and adjust pedal free-play.

Clutch System Bleeding and Adjustment

Type 4

Whenever air enters the clutch hydraulic system due to leakage, or if any part of the system is removed for service, the system must be bled. The hydraulic system uses high quality brake fluid meeting SAE J1703 or DOT 3 or DOT 4 specifications. Brake fluid is highly corrosive to paint finishes and care should be exercised that no spillage occurs. The procedure is as follows;

1. Top up the clutch fluid reservoir and make sure the cap vent is open.

2. Locate the slave cylinder bleed nipple and remove all dirt and grease from the valve. Attach a hose to the nipple and submerge the other end of the hose in a jar containing a few inches of clean brake fluid.

3. Find a friend to operate the clutch pedal. When your friend depresses the

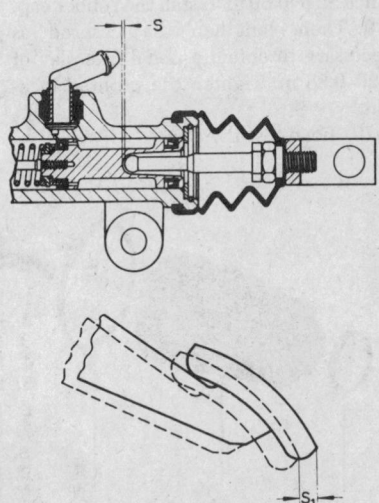

Adjusting clutch pedal free play—Type 4

1. Boot
2. Lockring
3. Stop ring
4. Secondary cup
5. Piston

6. Cup washer
7. Primary cup
8. Spring and spring plate
9. Cylinder

10. Elbow
11. Sealing plug
12. Seal
13. Residual pressure valve

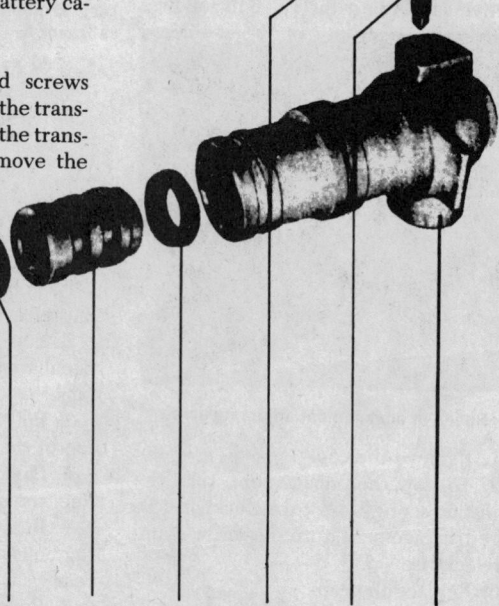

Type 4 clutch master cylinder

clutch pedal slowly to the floor, open the bleeder valve about one turn. Have your friend keep the pedal on the floor until you close the bleeder valve. Repeat this operation several times until no air bubbles are emitted from the tube.

NOTE: *Keep a close check on the fluid level in the fluid reservoir. Never let the level fall below the ½ full mark.*

4. After bleeding, discard the old fluid and top up the reservoir.

5. The clutch pedal should have a free-play of 0.20–0.28 in., and a 7 in. total travel. If either of the above are not to specifications, adjust the master cylinder as follows. (Steps 6–9).

6. Loosen the master cylinder pushrod locknut and shorten the pushrod length slightly.

7. Loosen the master cylinder bolts and push the cylinder as far forward as it will go. Retighten the bolts.

8. Remove the rubber cap from the clutch pedal stop screw and adjust distance S2 to 0.89 in. Install the rubber cap.

9. Then, lengthen the pushrod as necessary to obtain a pedal free-play of 0.20–0.28 in. Tighten the pushrod locknut.

10. Road-test the car.

Adjusting clutch pedal stop screw—Type 4

TRANSAXLE

Manual Transaxle

Removal and Installation

1. Disconnect the negative battery cable.

2. Remove the engine.

3. Remove the socket head screws which secure the drive shafts to the transmission. Remove the bolts from the transmission end first and then remove the shafts.

NOTE: *It is not necessary to remove the drive shafts entirely from the car if the car does not have to be moved while the transaxle is out.*

4. Disconnect the clutch cable from the clutch lever and remove the clutch cable and its guide tube from the transaxle. Loosen the square head bolt at the shift linkage coupling located near the rear of the transaxle. Slide the coupling off the inner shaft lever. There is an access plate under the rear seat to reach the coupling on Type 1 and 3. It is necessary to work under the car to reach the coupling on Type 2 models.

5. Disconnect the starter wiring.

1. Pushrod
2. Retaining ring
3. Boot
4. Retaining ring
5. Lockspring
6. Piston
7. Cup
8. Cylinder
9. Bleeder valve
10. Cap

Type 4 clutch slave cylinder

Shift linkage coupling

6. Disconnect the back-up light switch wiring.

7. Remove the front transaxle mounting bolts.

8. Support the transaxle with a jack and remove the transmission carrier bolts.

9. Carefully lower the jack and remove the transaxle from the car.

10. To install, jack the transaxle into position and loosely install the bolts.

11. Tighten the transmission carrier bolts first, then tighten the front mounting nuts.

12. Install the drive shaft bolts with new lockwashers. The lockwashers should be positioned on the bolt with the convex side toward the screw head.

13. Reconnect the wiring, the clutch cable, and the shift linkage.

NOTE: *It may be necessary to align the transmission so that the driveshaft joints do not rub the frame.*

14. Install the engine.

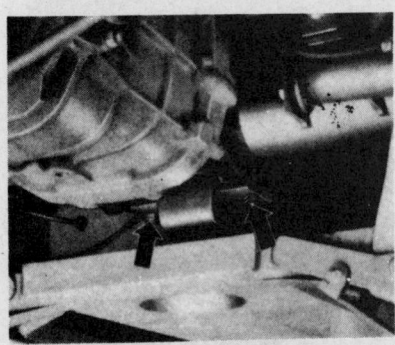

Front transaxle mounting bolts

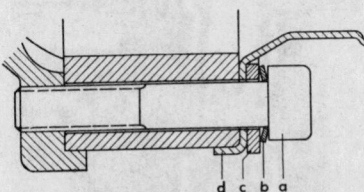

Drive axle bolts and washer positioning
a. Socket head screws
b. Lock washer
c. Spacer
d. Protective cap

Automatic Stick Shift Transaxle

Removal and Installation

1. Disconnect the negative battery cable.

2. Remove the engine.

3. Make a bracket to hold the torque converter in place. If a bracket is not used, the converter will slide off the transmission input shaft.

4. Detach the gearshift rod coupling.

5. Disconnect the drive shafts at the transmission end. If the driveshafts are not going to be repaired, it is not necessary to detach the wheel end.

6. Disconnect the ATF hoses from the transmission. Seal the open ends. Disconnect the temperature switch, neutral safety switch, and the back-up light switch.

7. Pull off the vacuum servo hose.

8. Disconnect the starter wiring.

9. Remove the front transaxle mounting nuts.

10. Loosen the rear transaxle mounting bolts. Support the transaxle and remove the bolts.

11. Lower the axle and remove it from the car.

12. With the torque converter bracket still in place, raise the axle into the car.

13. Tighten the nuts for the front transmission mounting. Insert the rear mounting bolts but do not tighten them at this time.

14. Replace the vacuum servo hose.

15. Connect the ATF hoses, using new washers. The washers are seals.

16. Connect the temperature switch and starter cables.

17. Install the drive shafts, using new washers. Turn the convex sides of the washers toward the screw head.

18. Align the transaxle so that the inner drive shaft joints do not rub on the frame fork and then tighten the rear mounting bolts.

19. Insert the shift rod coupling, tighten the screw, and secure it with wire.

20. Remove the torque converter bracket, and install the engine.

21. After installing the engine, bleed the ATF lines if return flow has not started after 2–3 minutes.

Shift Linkage Adjustment

1. The Volkswagen shift linkage is not adjustable. When shifting becomes difficult or there is an excessive amount of play in the linkage, check the shifting mechanism for worn parts. Make sure the shift linkage coupling is tightly connected to the inner shaft lever located at the rear of the transaxle under the rear seat. Worn parts may be found in the shift lever mechanism and the supports for the linkage rod sometimes wear out.

2. The gear shift lever can be removed after the front floor mat has been lifted.

3. After the two retaining screws have been removed from the gear shift lever ball housing, the gear shift lever, ball housing, rubber boot, and spring are removed as a unit.

CAUTION: *Carefully mark the position of the stop plate and note the position of the turned up ramp at the side of the stop plate. Normally the ramp is turned up and on the right hand side of the hole.*

4. Installation is the reverse of removal.

5. Lubricate all moving parts with grease.

6. Test the gear shift pattern. If there is difficulty in shifting, adjust the stop plate back and forth in its slotted holes.

Drive Shaft and Constant Velocity U-Joint

Removal and Installation

1. Remove the bolts which secure the joints at each end of the shaft, tilt the shaft down, and remove the shaft.

2. Loosen the clamps which secure the rubber boot to the axle and slide the boot back on the axle.

3. Drive the stamped steel cover off the joint with a drift.

NOTE: *After the cover is removed, do not tilt the ball hub as the balls will fall out of the hub.*

4. Remove the circlip from the end of the axle and press the axle out of the joint.

5. Reverse the above steps to install. The position of the dished washer is dependent on the type of transmission. On automatic transmissions, it is placed between the ball hub and the circlip. On manual transmissions, it is placed between the ball hub and the shoulder on the shaft. Be sure to pack the joint with grease.

NOTE: *The chamfer on the splined inside diameter of the ball hub faces the shoulder on the driveshaft.*

AUTOMATIC TRANSMISSION

Removal and Installation

NOTE: *The engine and transmission must be removed as an assembly on the Type 4 and Type 2/1700, 2/1800, 2/2000.*

1. Remove the battery ground cable.

2. On the sedan, remove the cooling air intake duct with the heating fan and hoses. Remove the cooling air intake con-

nection and bellows, then detach the hoses to the air cleaner.

3. On the station wagons, remove the warm air hoses and air cleaner. Remove the boot between the dipstick tube and the body and the boot between the oil filler neck and the body. Disconnect the cooling air bellows at the body.

4. Disconnect the wires at the regulator and the alternator wires at the snap-connector located by the regulator. Disconnect the auxiliary air regulator and the oil pressure switch at the snap connectors located by the distributor.

5. Disconnect the fuel injection wiring on Type 3 and 4 models. There are 12 connections and they are listed as follows:

    a. Fuel injector cylinder 2, 2-pole, protective gray cap

    b. Fuel injector cylinder 1, 2-pole, protective black cap

    c. Starter, 1-pole, white

    d. Throttle valve switch, 4-pole

    e. Distributor, 3-pole

    f. Thermo switch, 1-pole, white

    g. Cold start valve, 3-pole

    h. Temperature sensor crankcase, 2-pole

    i. Ground connection, 3-pole, white wires

    j. Temperature sensor for the cylinder head, 1-pole

    k. Fuel injector cylinder 3, 2-pole, protective black cap

    l. Fuel injector cylinder 4, 2-pole, protective gray cap

6. Disconnect the accelerator cable.

7. Disconnect the right fuel return line.

8. Raise the car.

9. Disconnect the hoses from the heat exchangers.

10. Disconnect the starter wires and push the engine wiring harness through the engine cover plate.

11. Disconnect the fuel supply line and plug it.

12. Remove the heater booster exhaust pipe.

13. Remove the rear axles and cover the ends to protect them from dirt.

14. Remove the selector cable by unscrewing the cable sleeve.

15. Remove the wire from the kickdown switch.

16. Remove the bolts from the rubber transmission mountings, taking careful note of the position, number, and thickness of the spacers that are present.

CAUTION: *These spacers must be reinstalled exactly as they were removed. Do not detach the transmission carrier from the body.*

17. Support the engine and transmission assembly in such a way that it may be lowered and moved rearward at the same time.

18. Remove the engine carrier bolts and the engine and transmission assem-

Engine carrier bolts positioned at the top of their elongated holes

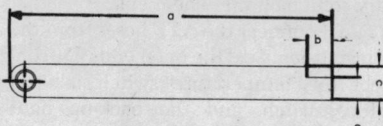

Buffer alignment gauges
    a. 5.095 in.
    b. 0.472 in.
    c. 0.590 in.
    d. 0.393, 0.433, and 0.472 in.

bly from the car.

19. Matchmark the flywheel and the torque converter and remove the three attaching bolts.

20. Remove the engine-to-transmission bolts and separate the engine and transmission.

CAUTION: *Exercise care when separating the engine and transmission as the torque converter will easily slip off the input shaft if the transmission is tilted downward.*

21. Installation is as follows. Install and tighten the engine-to-transmission bolts after aligning the match marks on the flywheel and converter.

22. Making sure the match marks are aligned, install the converter-to-flywheel bolts.

23. Make sure the rubber buffer is in place and the two securing studs do not project more than 0.7 in. from the transmission case.

24. Tie a cord to the slot in the engine compartment seal. This will make positioning the seal easier.

25. Lift the assembly far enough to allow the accelerator cable to be pushed through the front engine cover.

26. Continue lifting the assembly into place. Slide the rubber buffer into the locating tube in the rear axle carrier.

27. Insert the engine carrier bolts and raise the engine until the bolts are at the top of their elongated slots. Tighten the bolts.

NOTE: *A set of three gauges must be obtained to check the alignment of the rubber buffer in its locating tube. The dimensions are given in the illustration as is the measuring technique. The rubber buffer is centered horizontally*

where the 11 mm gauge can be inserted on both sides. The buffer is located vertically when the 10 mm gauge can be inserted on the bottom side and the 12 mm gauge can be inserted on the top side. See steps 28 and 29 for adjustment procedure.

28. Install the rubber transmission mount bolts with spacers of the correct thickness. The purpose of the spacers is to center the rubber buffer vertically in its support tube. The buffer is not supposed to carry any weight; it absorbs torsional forces only.

29. To locate the buffer horizontally in its locating tube, the engine carrier must be vertical and parallel to the fan housing. It is adjusted by moving the engine carrier bolts in elongated slots. Further travel may be obtained by moving the brackets attached to the body. It may be necessary to adjust the two rear suspension wishbones with the center of the transmission after the rubber buffer is horizontally centered. Take the car to a dealer or alignment specialist to align the rear suspension.

30. Adjust the selector lever cable.

31. Connect the wire to the kickdown switch.

32. Install the rear axles. Make sure the lockwashers are placed with the convex side out.

33. Reconnect the fuel hoses and heat exchanger hoses. Install the pipe for the heater booster.

34. Lower the car and pull the engine compartment seal into place with the cord.

35. Reconnect the fuel injection and

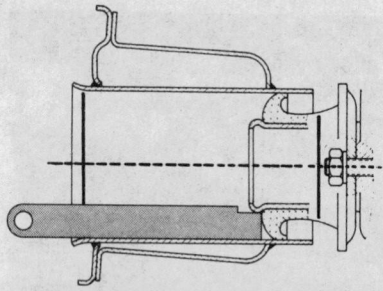

Measuring procedure or centering the buffer

Checking the position of the engine carrier

engine wiring. Push the starter wires through the engine cover plate and connect the wires to the starter.

36. Install the intake duct with the fan and hoses, also the cooling air intake.

Pan Removal and Installation

1. Some models have a drain plug in the pan. Remove the plug and drain the transmission. On models without the plug, loosen the pan bolts 2–3 turns and lower one corner of the pan to drain.

2. Remove the pan bolts and remove the pan from the transmission.
NOTE: *It may be necessary to tap the pan with a rubber hammer to loosen it.*

3. Use a new gasket and install the pan. Tighten the bolts loosely until the pan is properly in place, then tighten the bolts fully, moving in a diagonal pattern.
NOTE: *Do not overtighten the bolts.*

4. Refill the transmission with ATF.

5. At 5 minute intervals, retighten the pan bolts two or three times.

Filter Service

The Volkswagen automatic transmission has a filter screen secured by a screw to the bottom of the valve body. Remove the pan and remove the filter screen from the valve body.

CAUTION: *Never use a cloth that will leave the slightest bit of lint in the transmission when cleaning transmission parts. The lint will expand when exposed to transmission fluid and clog the valve body and filter.*

Clean the filter screen with compressed air.

Front (Second) Band Adjustment

Tighten the front band adjusting screw to 7 ft lbs. Then loosen the screw and tighten it to 3.5 ft lbs. From this position, loosen the screw exactly 1¾ to 2 turns and tighten the locknut.

Rear (First) Band Adjustment

Tighten the rear band adjusting screw to 7 ft lbs. Then loosen the screw and retighten it to 3.5 ft lbs. From this position, loosen the screw exactly 3¼ to 3½ turns and tighten the locknut.

Kickdown Switch Adjustment

Type 3

1. Disconnect the accelerator cable return spring.

2. Move the throttle to the fully open position. Adjust the accelerator cable to give 0.02–0.04 in. clearance between the stop and the end of the throttle valve lever.

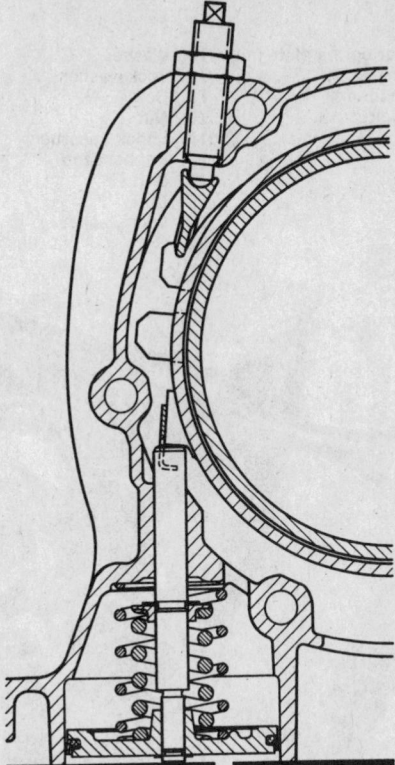

Front band assembly adjustment screw at top

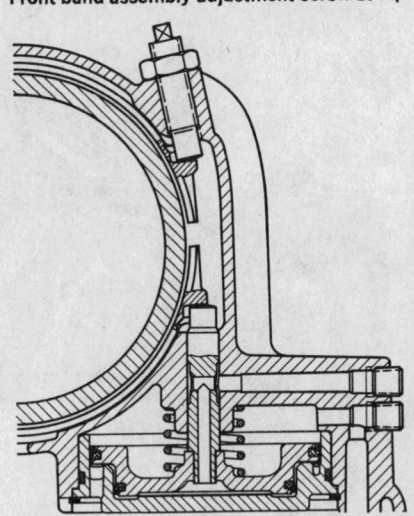

Rear band assembly adjustment screw at top

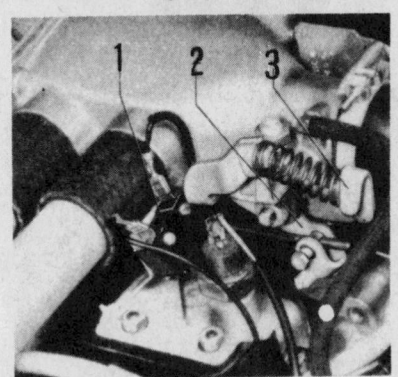

Kickdown Switch—Type 3
1. Kickdown switch
2. Accelerator cable lever
3. Throttle valve lever

3. When the accelerator cable is adjusted and the throttle is moved to the fully open position, the kickdown switch should click. The ignition switch must be ON for this test.

4. To adjust the switch, loosen the switch securing screws and slide the switch back and forth until the test in Step 3 is satisfied.

5. Reconnect the accelerator cable return spring.

Type 4

The Type 4 switch is not adjustable.

Shift Linkage Adjustment

Make sure the shifting cable is not kinked or bent and that the linkage and cable are properly lubricated.

1. Move the gear shift lever to the Park position.

2. Loosen the clamp which holds the front and rear halves of the shifting rod together. Loosen the clamping bolts on the transmission lever.

3. Press the lever on the transmission rearward as far as possible. Spring pressure will be felt. The manual valve must be on the stop in the valve body.

4. Holding the transmission lever against its stop, tighten the clamping bolt.

5. Holding the rear shifting rod half, push the front half forward to take up any clearance and tighten the clamp bolt.

6. Test the shift pattern.

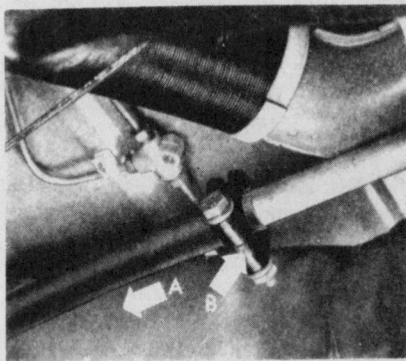

Clamp securing shift linkage rod halves

REAR SUSPENSION

Diagonal Arm Suspension—Types 1, 2, 3

Diagonal Arm Removal and Installation

1. Remove the wheel shaft nuts.
CAUTION: *Do not raise the car to remove the nuts. They can be safely removed only if the weight on the car is on its wheels.*

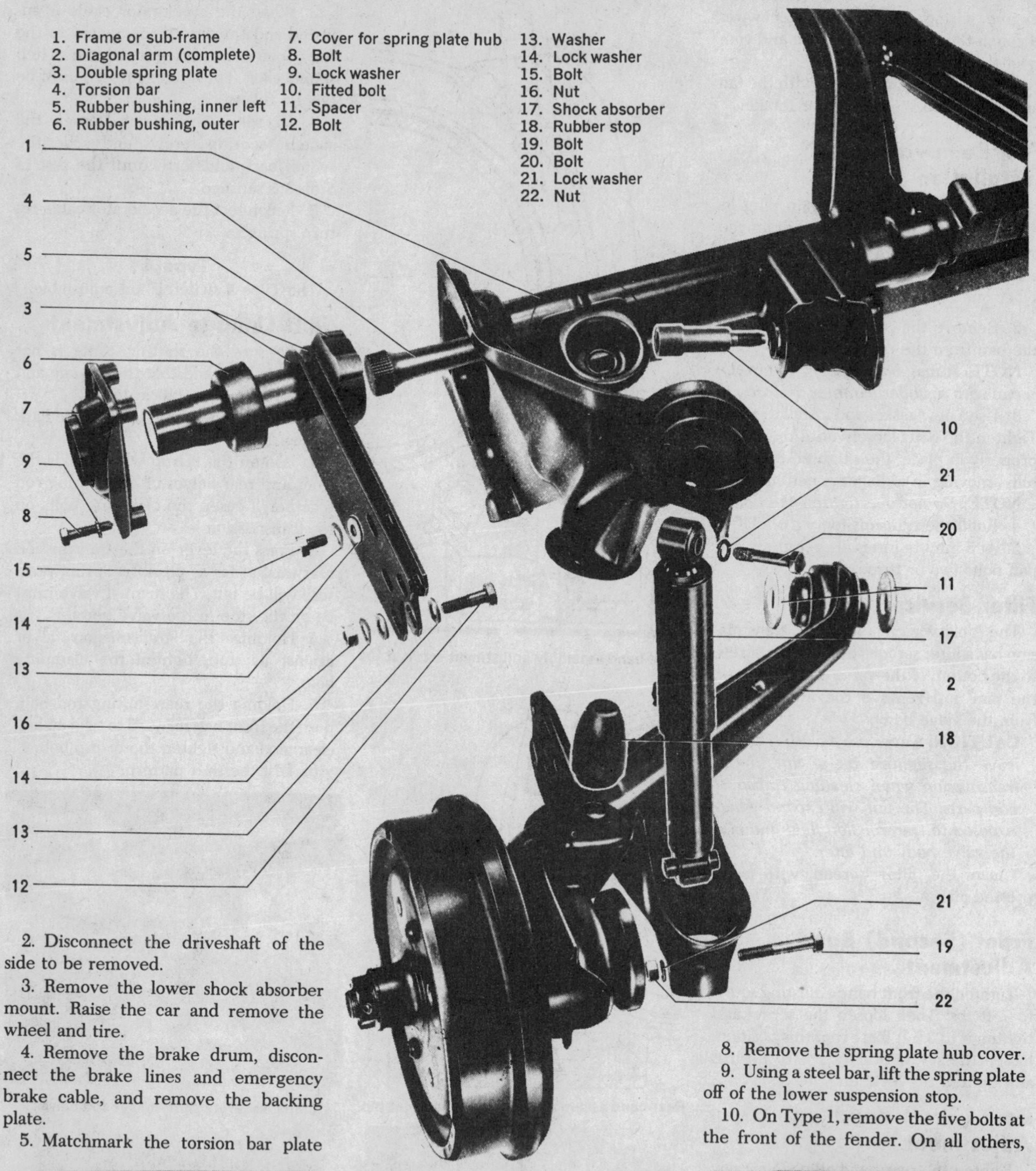

1. Frame or sub-frame
2. Diagonal arm (complete)
3. Double spring plate
4. Torsion bar
5. Rubber bushing, inner left
6. Rubber bushing, outer
7. Cover for spring plate hub
8. Bolt
9. Lock washer
10. Fitted bolt
11. Spacer
12. Bolt
13. Washer
14. Lock washer
15. Bolt
16. Nut
17. Shock absorber
18. Rubber stop
19. Bolt
20. Bolt
21. Lock washer
22. Nut
1
4
5
3
6
7
9
8
15
14
13
16
14
13
12
10
21
20
11
17
2
18
21
19
22

Diagonal arm rear suspension—Types 1, 2, and 3

2. Disconnect the driveshaft of the side to be removed.

3. Remove the lower shock absorber mount. Raise the car and remove the wheel and tire.

4. Remove the brake drum, disconnect the brake lines and emergency brake cable, and remove the backing plate.

5. Matchmark the torsion bar plate and the diagonal arm with a cold chisel.

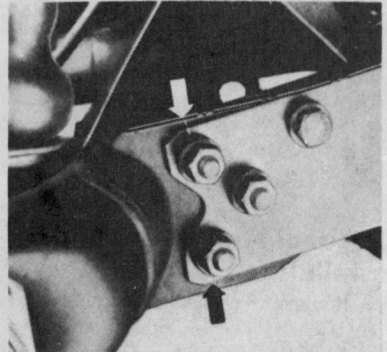

Matchmarking torsion bar and diagonal arm with cold chisel

6. Remove the four bolts and nuts which secure the plate to the diagonal arm.

7. Remove the pivot bolts for the diagonal arm and remove the arm from the car.

NOTE: *Take careful note of the washers at the pivot bolts. These washers are used to determine alignment and they must be put back in the same place.*

8. Remove the spring plate hub cover.

9. Using a steel bar, lift the spring plate off of the lower suspension stop.

10. On Type 1, remove the five bolts at the front of the fender. On all others,

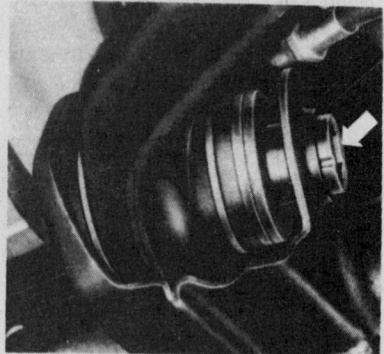

Proper positioning of diagonal arm pivot bolt with both spacer washers on the outside

1. Rear axle carrier
2. A-arm (left/right)
3. Coil spring with plastic tube
4. Shock absorber
5. Bracket—inner (eccentric)
6. Bracket—outer left/right
7. Eccentric bolt
8. Eccentric washer
9. Bolt
10. Bolt
11. Damping ring, shock absorber
12. Damping washer, shock absorber
13. Spacer sleeve
14. Self-locking nut
15. Damping ring, rear axle carrier
16. Damping bushing, rear axle carrier
17. Plate
18. Plate
19. Nut
20. Lock washer
21. Cover plate
22. Bolt
23. Lock washer
24. Bolt
25. Lock washer

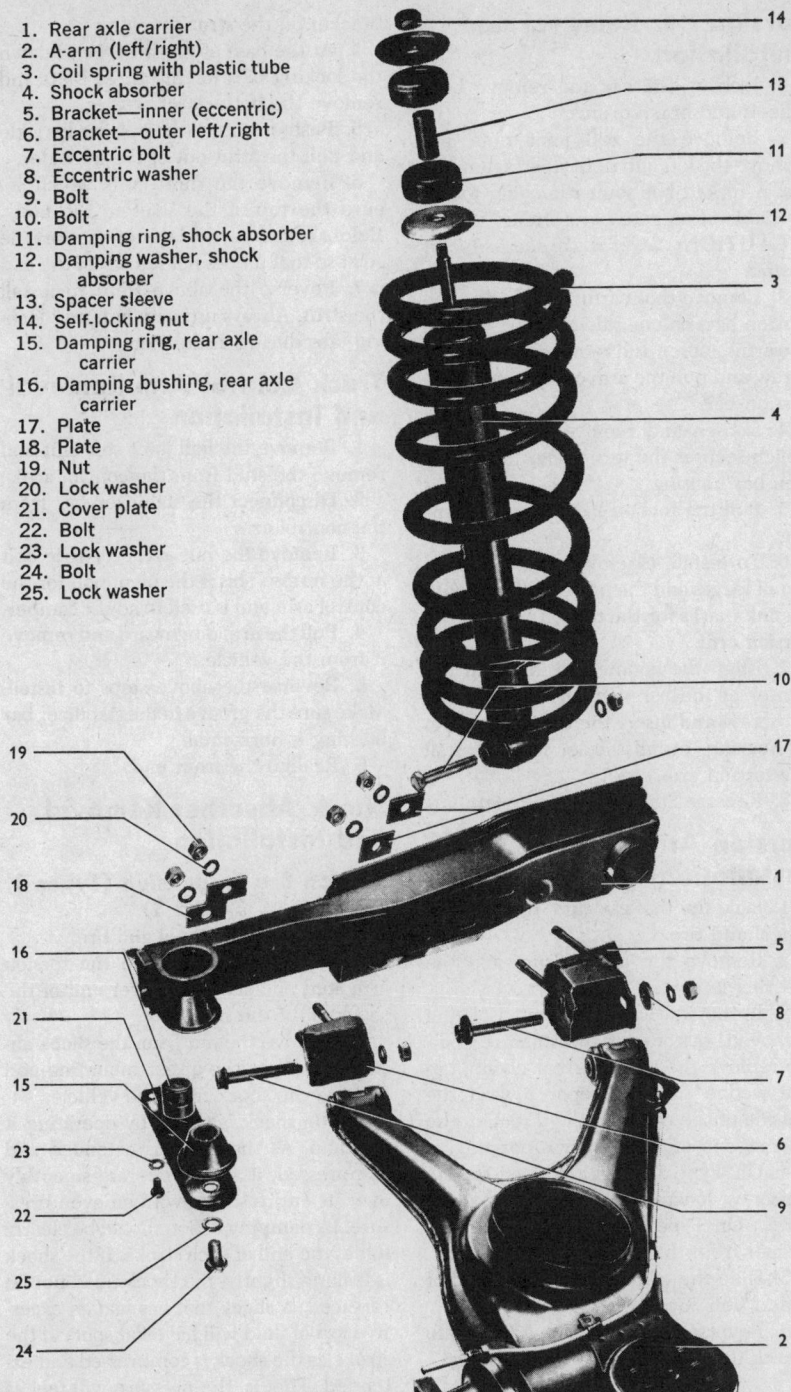

A-Arm rear suspension—Type 4

17. Install the backing plate, parking brake cable, and brake lines.

18. Reconnect the shock absorber. Install the brake drum and wheel shaft nuts.

19. Reconnect the drive shaft. Bleed the brakes.

20. Install the wheel and tire.

21. Check the suspension alignment.

A-Arm Suspension— Type 4

A-Arm Removal and Installation

1. Raise the car and place it on jackstands. Securely block up the A-arm.

CAUTION: *The A-arm must be securely supported when the shock absorber is disconnected to prevent the spring tension from being released suddenly. The shock absorber is the lower stop for the suspension.*

2. Disconnect the driveshaft.

3. Disconnect the handbrake cable at the brake lever and remove it.

4. Disconnect the brake lines and the stabilizer bar if equipped.

5. With the vehicle on the ground or the A-arm securely supported, remove the lower shock absorber mounting bolt.

6. Slowly release the A-arm and remove the coil springs.

7. Mark the position of the brackets or the eccentric bolts, whichever are removed, with a chisel. Remove the nuts which secure the brackets in the rear axle carrier, or the pivot bolts in the bonded rubber bushings, and remove the A-arm.

8. Loosely install the A-arm. If the pivot bolts were removed, install them loosely. If the eccentric bolts and brackets were removed, install them, aligning the chisel marks, and then tighten them.

9. Insert the coil spring and slowly compress it into place. Install the lower shock absorber mount.

10. Reverse Steps 1–4 to complete.

Shock Absorber Removal and Installation

Diagonal Arm Suspension

The shock absorber is secured at the top and bottom by a through bolt. Raise the car and remove the bolts. Remove the shock absorber from the car.

A-Arm Suspension

The shock absorber is the lower stop for the suspension.

CAUTION: *The A-arm must be securely supported when the shock absorber is disconnected to prevent the spring tension from being released suddenly.*

Leaving the car on the ground or raising the car and securely supporting the A-arm, remove the lower shock absorber

remove the cover in the side of the fender.

11. Remove the spring plate and pull the torsion bar out of its housing.

NOTE: *There are left and right torsion bars designated by an (L) or (R) on the end face. (Coat any rubber bushings with talcum powder upon installation. Do not use graphite, silicon, or grease.*

12. To install, insert the torsion bar, outer bushing, and spring plate. The torsion bar is properly adjusted when the spring plate, with no load, is the specified number of degrees below a horizontal position.

13. Using two bolts, loosely secure the spring plate hub cover. Place a thick nut between the leaves of the spring plate.

14. Lift the spring plate up to the lower suspension stop and install the remaining bolts into the hub cover. Tighten the hub cover bolts.

15. Install the diagonal arm pivot bolt and washers and peen it with a chisel. There must always be at least one washer on the outside end of the bolt.

16. Align the chisel marks and attach the diagonal arm to the spring plate.

through bolt. To gain access to the upper shock mounting, remove the access panel for each shock located at the sides of the rear luggage shelf. Remove the self locking nut from the shock absorber shaft and remove the shock. Installation is the reverse of removal.

Rear Suspension Adjustments

Type 1, Diagonal Arm Suspension

The only adjustment is the toe-in adjustment. The adjustment is performed by varying the number of washers at the diagonal arm pivot. There must always be one washer located on the outboard side of the pivot.

Type 2, 3, Diagonal Arm Suspension

The transmission and engine assembly position in the vehicle is adjustable. It is necessary that the assembly be correctly centered before the suspension is aligned. It may be adjusted by moving the engine and transmission brackets in their elongated slots.

The distance between the diagonal arms may be adjusted by moving the washers at the A-arm pivots. The washers may be positioned only two ways. Either both washers on the outboard side of the pivot or a single washer on each side of the pivot. To adjust the distance, position the diagonal arms and move the washers in the same manner at both pivots.

The wheel track angle may be adjusted by moving the diagonal arm flange in the elongated slot in the spring plate.

The toe-in adjusted by positioning the washers and the diagonal arm pivot.

Type 4, A-Arm Suspension

The toe-in is adjusted by the eccentric A-arm pivot bolts.

The rubber buffer centralization procedure is given in the "Type 4 Transaxle Removal and Installation" procedure.

The track width can be adjusted by loosening the A-arm mounting bracket bolts and moving the brackets in or out to the proper position.

FRONT SUSPENSION

Torsion Bar Suspension—Types 1, 2, 3 (Except Super Beetle and Beetle Convertible Through 1975)

Torsion Bar Removal and Installation

1. Jack up the car and remove both wheels and brake drums.
2. Remove the ball joint nuts and remove the left and right steering knuckles. A forked ball joint removing tool is available at an auto parts store.
   CAUTION: *Never strike the ball joint stud.*
3. Remove those arms attached to the torsion bars on one side only. To remove the arms, loosen and remove the arm set-screw and pull the arm off the end of the torsion bar.
4. Loosen and remove the set-screw which secures the torsion bar to the torsion bar housing.
5. Pull the torsion bar out of its housing.
6. To install, carefully note the number of leaves and the position of the countersink marks for the torsion bar and the torsion arm.
7. Align the countersink mark in the center of the bar with the hole for the set-screw and insert the torsion bar into its housing. Install the set screw. Install the torsion arm.
8. Reverse Steps 1–3 to complete.

Torsion Arm Removal and Installation

1. Jack up the car and remove the wheel and tire.
2. Remove the brake drum and the steering knuckle.
3. If the lower torsion arm is being removed, disconnect the stabilizer bar. To remove the stabilizer bar clamp, tap the wedge shaped keeper toward the outside of the car or in the direction the narrow end of the keeper is pointing.
4. On Type 1 and 2, back off on the set-screw locknut and remove the set-screw. On Type 3, remove the bolt and keeper from the end of the torsion bar.
5. Slide the torsion arm off the end of the torsion bar.
6. Reverse the above steps to install. Check the camber and toe-in settings.

Strut Suspension— Type 1 Super Beetle, Beetle Convertible Through 1975, and all Type 4

Suspension Strut Removal and Installation

1. Jack up the car and remove the wheel and tire.
2. If the left strut is to be removed, remove the speedometer cable from the steering knuckle.
3. Disconnect the brake line from the bracket on the strut.
4. At the base of the strut, bend down the locking tabs for the three bolts and remove the bolts.
5. Push down on the steering knuckle and pull the strut out of the knuckle.
6. Remove the three nuts which secure the top of the strut to the body. Before removing the last nut, support the strut so that it does not fall out of the car.
7. Reverse the above steps to install the strut. Always use new nuts and locking tabs during installation.

Track Control Arm Removal and Installation

1. Remove the ball joint stud nut and remove the stud from the control arm.
2. Disconnect the stabilizer bar from the control arm.
3. Remove the nut and eccentric bolt at the frame. This is the pivot bolt for the control arm and is used to adjust camber.
4. Pull the arm downward and remove it from the vehicle.
5. Reverse the above steps to install. Make sure the groove in the stabilizer bar bushing is horizontal.
6. Realign the front end.

Shock Absorber Removal and Installation

Torsion Bar Suspension (Types 1, 2, and 3)

1. Remove the wheel and tire.
2. Remove the nut from the torsion arm stud and slide the lower end of the shock off of the stud.
3. Remove the nut from the shock absorber shaft at the upper mounting and remove the shock from the vehicle.
4. The shock is tested by operating it by hand. As the shock is extended and compressed, it should operate smoothly over its entire stroke with an even pressure. Its damping action should be clearly felt at the end of each stroke. If the shock is leaking slightly, the shock need not be replaced. A shock that has had an excessive loss of fluid will have flat spots in the stroke as the shock is compressed and extended. That is, the pressure will feel as though it has been suddenly released for a short distance during the stroke.
5. Installation is the reverse of Steps 1–3.

Strut Suspension (Super Beetle and Type 4)

In this type suspension system, the shock absorber is actually the supporting vertical member.

1. Remove the strut.
2. It is necessary to disassemble the strut to replace the shock absorber. To remove the spring, it must be compressed. The proper type compressor is available at an auto parts store.
3. Remove the nut from the end of the

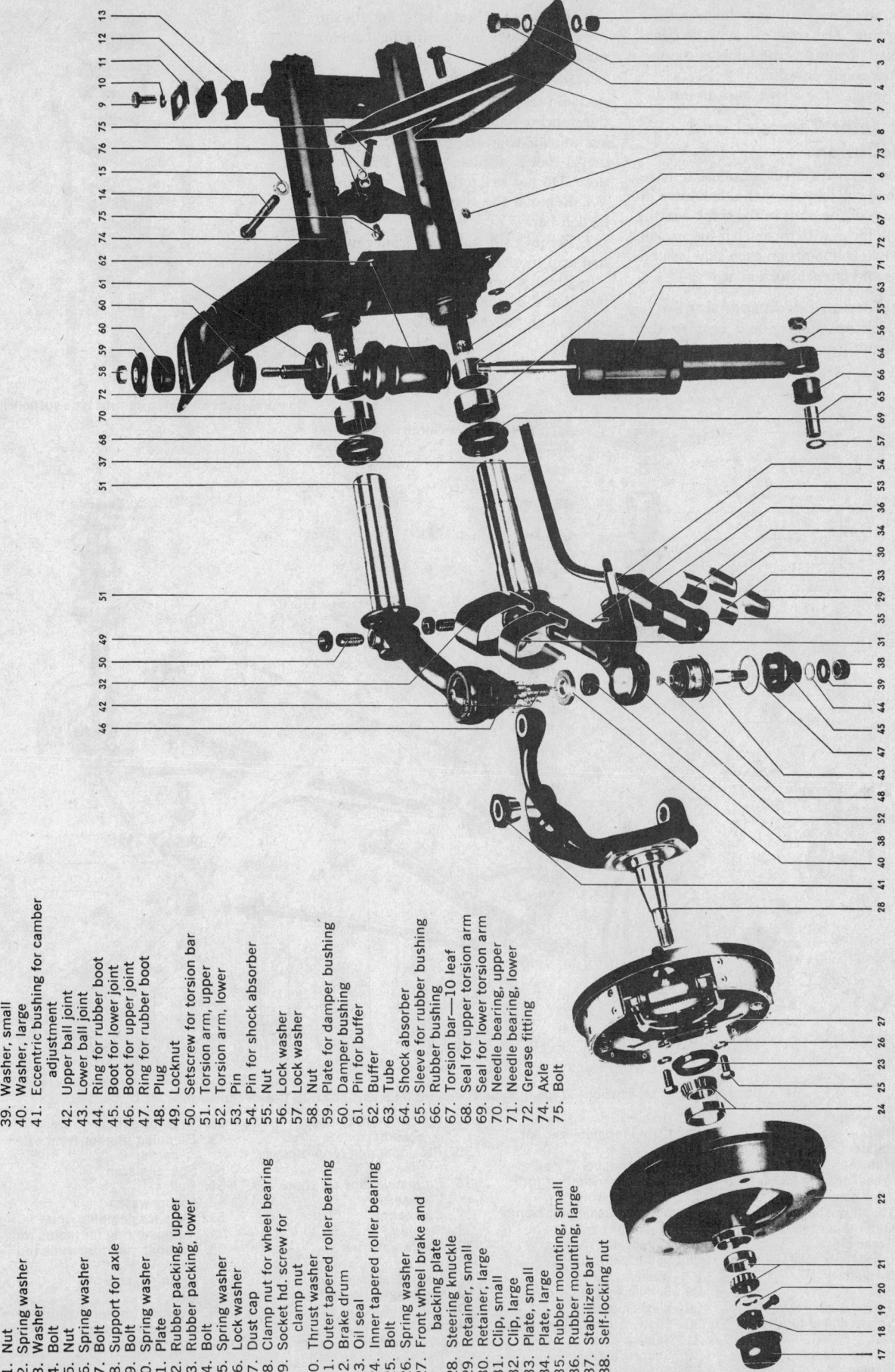

Torsion bar front suspension—Types 1 (Beetle, Karmann Ghia, Thing), 2 and 3

1. Nut
2. Spring washer
3. Washer
4. Bolt
5. Nut
6. Spring washer
7. Bolt
8. Support for axle
9. Bolt
10. Spring washer
11. Plate
12. Rubber packing, upper
13. Rubber packing, lower
14. Bolt
15. Spring washer
16. Lock washer
17. Dust cap
18. Clamp nut for wheel bearing
19. Socket hd. screw for clamp nut
20. Thrust washer
21. Outer tapered roller bearing
22. Brake drum
23. Oil seal
24. Inner tapered roller bearing
25. Bolt
26. Spring washer
27. Front wheel brake and backing plate
28. Steering knuckle
29. Retainer, small
30. Retainer, large
31. Clip, small
32. Clip, large
33. Plate, small
34. Plate, large
35. Rubber mounting, small
36. Rubber mounting, large
37. Stabilizer bar
38. Self-locking nut

39. Washer, small
40. Washer, large
41. Eccentric bushing for camber adjustment
42. Upper ball joint
43. Lower ball joint
44. Ring for rubber boot
45. Boot for lower joint
46. Boot for upper joint
47. Ring for rubber boot
48. Plug
49. Locknut
50. Setscrew for torsion bar
51. Torsion arm, upper
52. Torsion arm, lower
53. Pin
54. Pin for shock absorber
55. Nut
56. Lock washer
57. Lock washer
58. Nut
59. Plate for damper bushing
60. Damper bushing
61. Pin for buffer
62. Buffer
63. Tube
64. Shock absorber
65. Sleeve for rubber bushing
66. Rubber bushing
67. Torsion bar—10 leaf
68. Seal for upper torsion arm
69. Seal for lower torsion arm
70. Needle bearing, upper
71. Needle bearing, lower
72. Grease fitting
74. Axle
75. Bolt

shock absorber shaft and slowly release the spring. The strut can now be disassembled. Testing is the same as the torsion bar shock absorber.

4. Reverse the above steps to install.

Ball Joint Removal and Installation

Vehicles with strut suspension have only one ball joint on each side located at the base of the strut in the track control arm. Vehicles with torsion bar suspension have two ball joints on each side located at the end of each torsion arm.

Torsion Bar Suspension

1. Jack up the car and remove the wheel and tire.

2. Remove the brake drum and disconnect the brake line from the backing plate.

3. Remove the nut from each ball joint stud and remove the ball joint stud from the steering knuckle. Remove the steering knuckle from the car. A ball joint removal tool is available at an auto parts store. Do not strike the ball joint stud.

4. Remove the torsion arm from the torsion bar.

5. Remove the ball joint from the torsion arm by pressing it out.

6. Press a new ball joint in, making sure that the square notch in the joint is in line with the notch in the torsion arm eye.

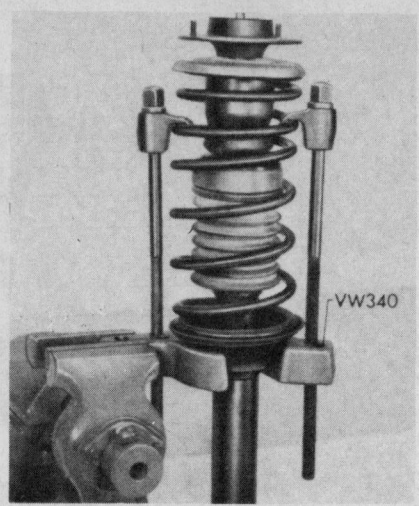

Compressing coil spring of strut type suspension

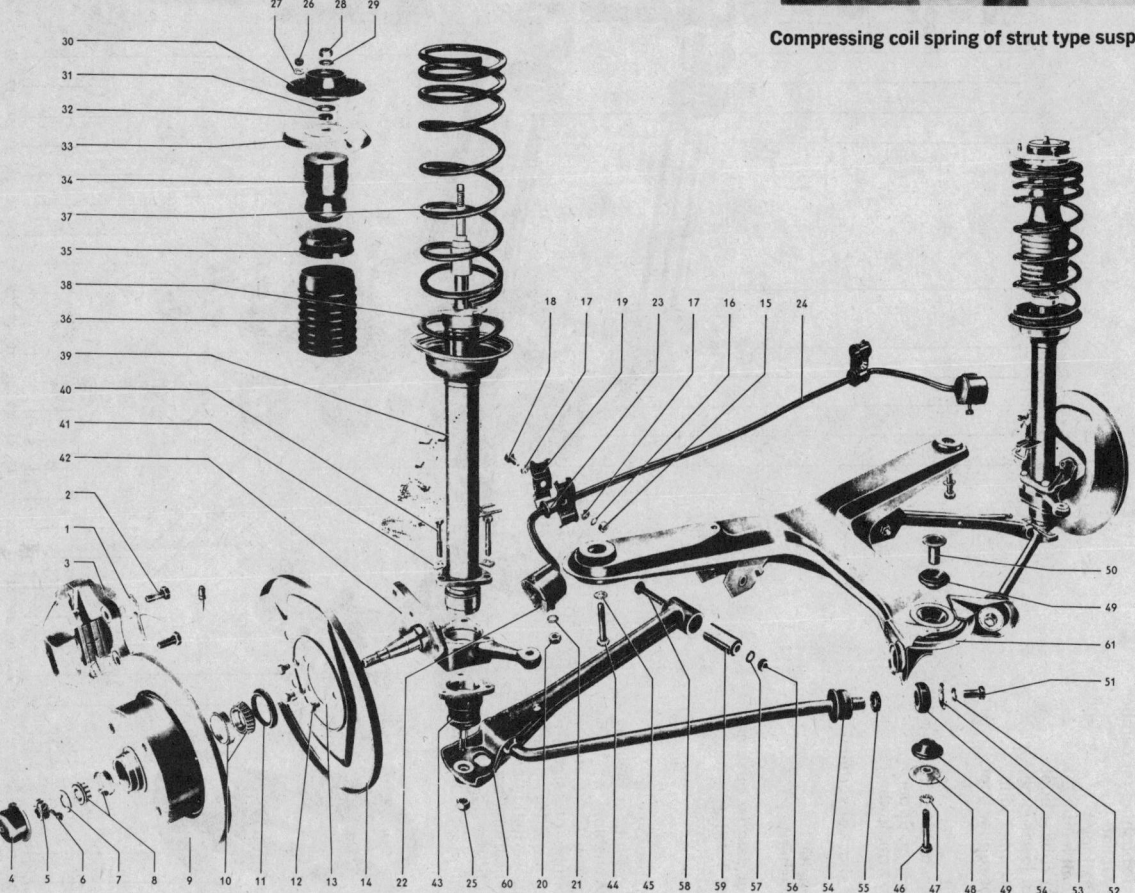

Strut type front suspension—Type 4, Type 1 Super Beetle and 1971-75 Beetle convertible

1. Lockplate
2. Bolt
3. Caliper
4. Hub cap
5. Wheel bearing locknut
6. Allen screw for locknut
7. Thrust washer
8. Outer taper roller bearing
9. Brake disc
10. Inner taper roller bearing
11. Oil seal
12. Bolt
13. Spring washer
14. Splash shield for disc
15. Nut
16. Spring washer
17. Washer
18. Bolt
19. Clamp for stabilizer bar
20. Nut
21. Spring washer
22. Stabilizer mounting for control arm
23. Rubber bushing for clamp
24. Stabilizer bar
25. Self-locking nut
26. Self-locking nut
27. Washer
28. Self-locking nut
29. Washer, small
30. Suspension strut bearing
31. Sealing plate
32. Spacer ring
33. Spring plate
34. Rubber stop for shock absorber
35. Retaining ring for protective tube
36. Protective tube for shock absorber
37. Coil spring
38. Damping ring, coil spring
39. Shock absorber
40. Bolt
41. Lock washer
42. Steering knuckle
43. Ball joint
44. Bolt
45. Lock washer
46. Bolt
47. Lock washer
48. Seat for damping ring
49. Damping ring for front axle carrier
50. Spacer sleeve
51. Bolt
52. Spring washer
53. Plate for damping ring
54. Damping ring for radius rod
55. Locating ring for radius rod
56. Nut
57. Spring washer
58. Bolt
59. Bushing for track control arm
60. Track control arm
61. Front axle carrier

A notched ball joint on a car with a torsion bar suspension indicates that it is oversized

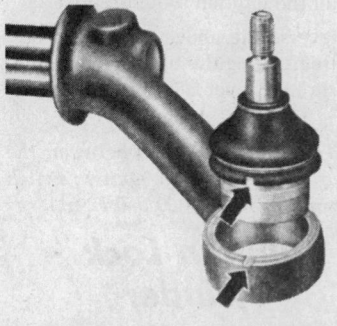

Align the square notch in the ball joint with the notch in the torsion arm upon installation

NOTE: *Ball joints are supplied in different sizes designated by V-notches in the ring around the side of the joint. When replacing a ball joint, make sure that the new part has the same number of V-notches. If it has no notches, the replacement joint should have no notches.*

7. Reverse Steps 1–4 to complete the installation.

Strut Suspension

1. Jack up the car and remove the wheel and tire.

2. Remove the nut from the ball joint stud and remove the stud from the track control arm.

3. Bend back the locking tab and remove the three ball joint securing screws.

4. Pull the track control arm downward and remove the ball joint from the strut.

5. Reverse the above steps to install.

Ball Joint Inspection

Torsion Bar Suspension

1. A quick initial inspection can be made with the vehicle on the ground.

2. Grasp the top of the tire and vigorously pull the top of the tire in and out. Test both sides in this manner.

3. If the ball joints are excessively worn, there will be an audible tap as the ball moves around in its socket. Excess play can sometimes be felt through the tire.

4. A more rigorous test may be performed by jacking the car under the lower torsion arm and inserting a lever under the tire.

5. Lift up gently on the lever so as to pry the tire upward.

6. If the ball joints are worn, the tire will move upward ⅛–¼ in. or more.

7. If the tire displays excessive movement, have an assistant inspect each joint, as the tire is pried upward, to determine which ball joint is defective.

Strut Suspension

1. Raise the car and support it under the frame. The wheel must be clear of the ground.

2. With a lever, apply upward pressure to the track control arm.

3. Apply the pressure gently and slowly; it is important that only enough pressure is exerted to check the play in the ball joint and not compress the suspension.

4. Using a vernier caliper, measure the distance between the control arm and the lower edge of the ball joint flange. Record the reading.

5. Release the pressure on the track control arm and again measure the distance between the control arm and the lower edge of the ball joint flange.

6. Record the reading.

7. Subtract the higher reading from the lower reading. If the difference is more than 0.10 in., the ball joint should be replaced.

NOTE: *Remember that even in a new joint there will be measurable play because the ball in the ball joint is spring loaded.*

Front End Alignment

Caster Adjustment

Caster is the forward or backward tilt of the spindle. Forward tilt is negative caster and backward tilt is positive caster. Caster is not adjustable on either the torsion bar or the strut suspensions.

Camber Adjustment

Camber is the tilt of the top of the wheel, inward or outward, from true vertical. Outward tilt is positive, inward tilt is negative.

Torsion Bar Suspension

The upper ball joint on each side is mounted in an eccentric bushing. The bushing has a hex head and it may be rotated in either direction using a wrench.

Strut Suspension

The track control arm pivots on an eccentric bolt. Camber is adjusted by loosening the nut and rotating the bolt.

Toe-in Adjustment

Toe-in is the adjustment made to make the front wheels point slightly into the front. Toe-in is adjusted on both types of front suspensions by adjusting the length of the tie-rod sleeves.

STEERING

Steering Wheel Removal and Installation

1. Disconnect the negative battery cable.

2. Remove the center emblem. This emblem will gently pry off the wheel, or is attached by screws from the back of the steering wheel.

3. Remove the nut from the steering shaft. This is a right-hand thread.

NOTE: *Mark the steering shaft and steering wheel so that the wheel may be installed in the same position on the shaft.*

4. Using a steering wheel puller, remove the wheel from the splined steering shaft. Do not strike the end of the steering shaft.

5. Reverse the above steps to install. Make sure to align the match marks made on the steering wheel and steering shaft. The gap between the turn signal switch housing and the back of the wheel is 0.08–0.12 in.

Correct gap (a) between steering wheel and column

Turn Signal Switch Removal and Installation

1. Disconnect the negative battery cable.

2. Remove the steering wheel.

3. Remove the four turn signal switch securing screws.

Turn signal switch retaining screws

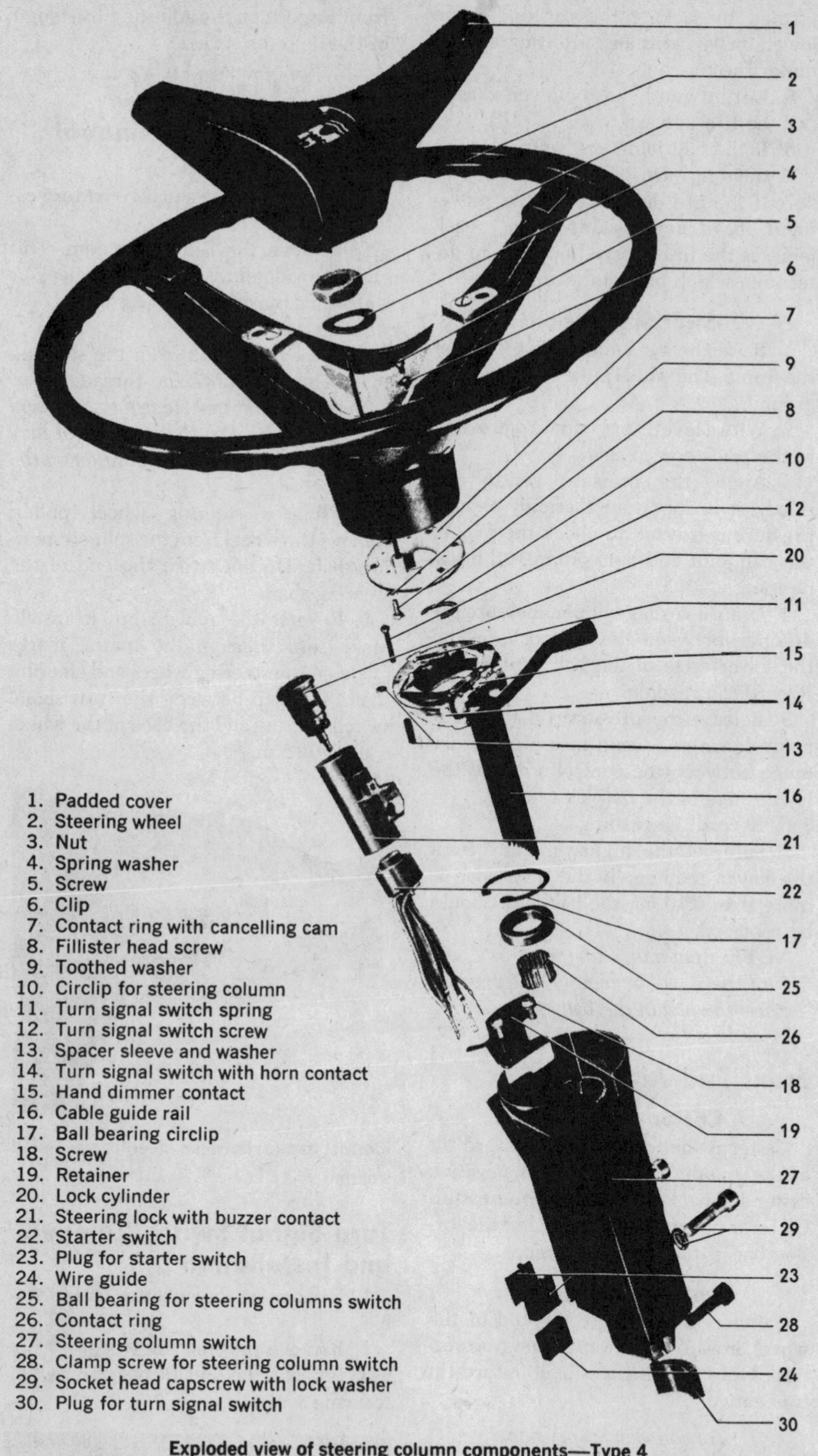

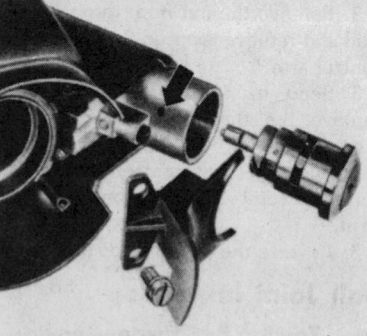

1. Padded cover
2. Steering wheel
3. Nut
4. Spring washer
5. Screw
6. Clip
7. Contact ring with cancelling cam
8. Fillister head screw
9. Toothed washer
10. Circlip for steering column
11. Turn signal switch spring
12. Turn signal switch screw
13. Spacer sleeve and washer
14. Turn signal switch with horn contact
15. Hand dimmer contact
16. Cable guide rail
17. Ball bearing circlip
18. Screw
19. Retainer
20. Lock cylinder
21. Steering lock with buzzer contact
22. Starter switch
23. Plug for starter switch
24. Wire guide
25. Ball bearing for steering columns switch
26. Contact ring
27. Steering column switch
28. Clamp screw for steering column switch
29. Socket head capscrew with lock washer
30. Plug for turn signal switch

Exploded view of steering column components—Type 4

4. Disconnect the turn signal switch wiring plug under the steering column.

5. Pull the switch and wiring guide rail up and out of the steering column.

6. Reverse the above steps to install. Make sure the spacers located behind the switch, if installed originally, are in position. The distance between the steering wheel and the steering column housing is 0.08–0.12 in. Install the switch with the lever in the central position.

Ignition Switch

Removal and Installation

On Type 3 cars, the fuse box must be removed. It is not necessary to remove the turn signal switch. Disconnect the steering column wiring at the block located behind the instrument panel and pull the column wiring harness into the passenger compartment.

1. Remove the steering wheel.

2. Remove the circlip on the steering shaft.

3. Insert the key and turn the switch to the ON position.

4. Remove the three securing screws and slide the switch assembly from the steering column tube.

5. After removing the wiring retainer, press the ignition switch wiring block upward and out of the housing and disconnect the wiring.

6. Remove the lock cylinder and the steering lock mechanism.

7. Remove the ignition switch screw and pull the ignition switch rearward.

8. Reverse the above steps to install. When reinstalling the turn signal switch, make sure the lever is in the center position.

NOTE: *The distance (a) between the steering wheel and the ignition switch housing is 2–3 mm (0.08–0.12 in.).*

Ignition Lock Cylinder

Removal and Installation

1. Remove the ignition switch.

2. With the key in the cylinder and turned to the ON position, pull the lock cylinder out far enough so the securing pin can be depressed through a hole in the side of the lock cylinder housing.

3. As the pin is depressed, pull the lock cylinder out of its housing.

4. To install the lock cylinder, gently push the cylinder into its housing. Make sure the pin engages correctly and that the retainer fits easily in place. Do not force any parts together; when they are correctly aligned, they will fit easily together.

Access hole for depressing lock cylinder retaining pin

Steering Linkage Removal and Installation

1. All tie-rod ends are secured by a nut which holds the tapered tie-rod end stud into a matching tapered hole. There are several ways to remove the tapered stud from its hole after the nut has been

removed.

2. First, there are several types of removal tools available from auto parts stores. These tools include directions for their use. One of the most commonly available tools is the fork shaped tool which is a wedge that is forced under the tie-rod end. This tool should be used with caution because instead of removing the tie-rod end from its hole it may pull the ball out of its socket, ruining the tie-rod end.

3. It is also possible to remove the tie-rod end by holding a heavy hammer on one side of the tapered hole and striking the opposite side of the hole sharply with another hammer. The stud will pop out of

its hole, usually.

CAUTION: *Never strike the end of the tie-rod end stud. It is impossible to remove the tie-rod end in this manner.*

4. Once the tie-rod end stud has been removed, turn the tie-rod end out of the adjusting sleeve.

5. On the pieces of the steering linkage that are not used to adjust the toe-in, the tie-rod end is welded in place and it will be necessary to replace the whole assembly.

6. When reassembling the steering linkage, never put lubricant in the tapered hole.

Manual Steering Gear Adjustment

There are three types of steering gear boxes. The first type is the roller type, identified by the square housing cover secured by four screws, one at each corner. The second type is the worm and peg type, identified by an asymetric housing cover with the adjusting screw located at one side of the housing cover.

The third type is the rack and pinion type used on 1975 Super Beetles and 1975–76 Beetle Convertibles.

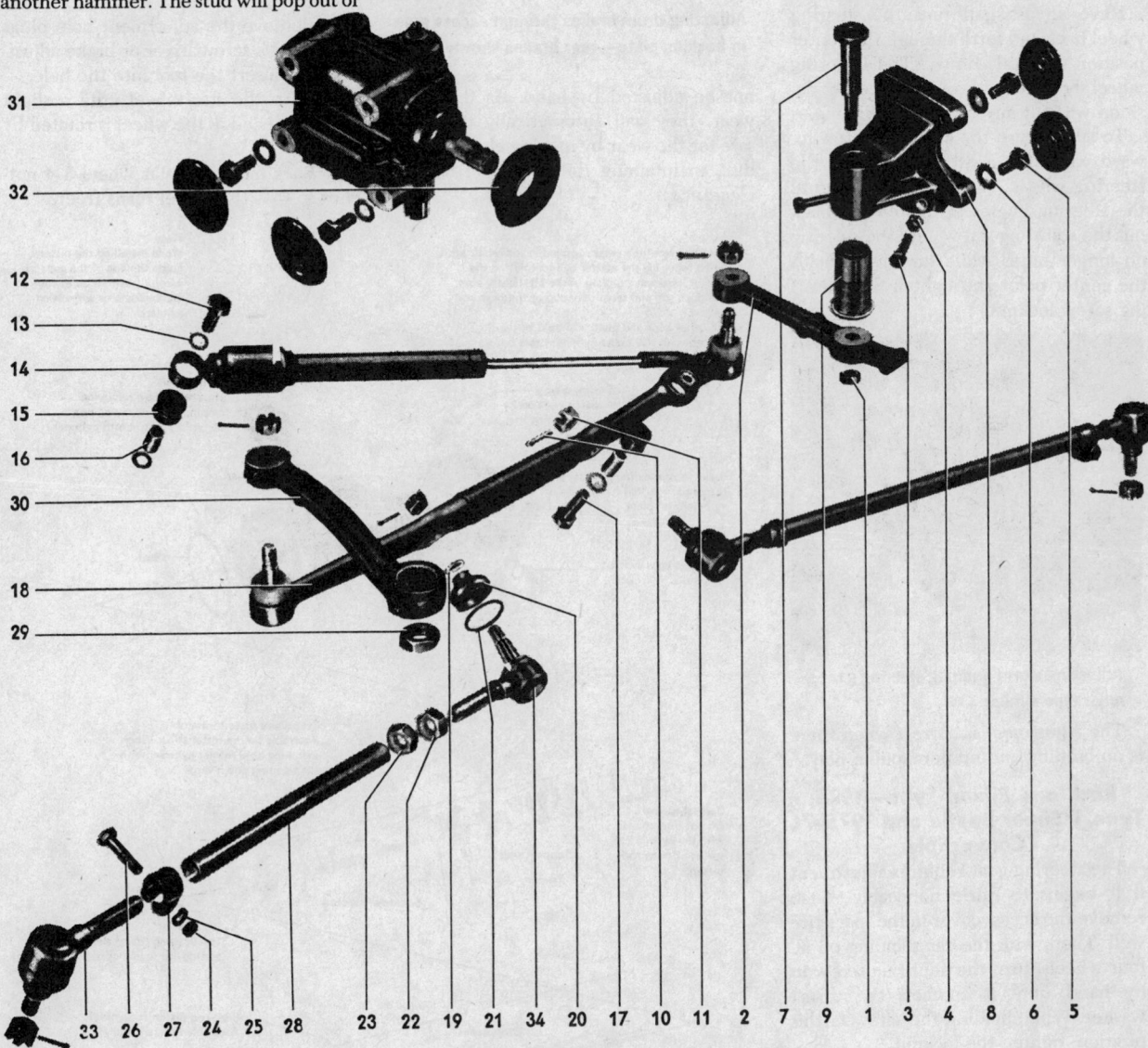

Type 4 steering linkage

1. Nut	9. Idler arm bushing	17. Bolt
2. Idler arm	10. Cotter pin	18. Center tie-rod
3. Bolt	11. Nut	19. Boot seal
4. Nut	12. Bolt	20. Boot
5. Bolt	13. Lockwasher	21. Boot ring
6. Lockwasher	14. Steering damper	22. Nut
7. Bolt	15. Bushing	23. Tapered ring
8. Idler arm bracket	16. Sleeve	24. Nut

Worm and Roller Types—Types 1, 3, 4 and 1973–76 Type 2 Models

Disconnect the steering linkage from the pitman arm and make sure the gearbox mounting bolts are tight. Have an assistant rotate the steering wheel so that the pitman arm moves alternately 10° to the left and then 10° to the right of the straight ahead position. Turn the adjusting screw in until no further play can be felt while moving the pitman arm. Tighten the adjusting screw locknut and recheck the adjustment.

Worm and Peg Type—1972 Type 2 Models

Have an assistant turn the steering wheel back and forth through the center position several times. The steering wheel should turn through the center position without any noticeable binding.

To adjust, turn the adjusting screw inward while the assistant is turning the steering wheel. Turn the screw in until the steering begins to tighten up. Back out the adjusting screw until the steering no longer binds while turning through the center point and tighten the adjusting screw locknut.

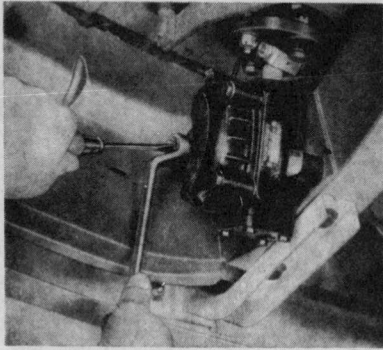

Adjusting worm and peg steering gear—roller type similar

The adjustment is correct when there is no binding and no perceptible play.

Rack and Pinion Type—1975 Type 1 Super Beetle and 1975–76 Convertible

The steering gear requires adjustment if it begins to rattle noticeably. First, remove the access cover in the spare tire well. Then, with the car standing on all four wheels, turn the adjusting screw in by hand until it contacts the thrust washer. While holding the screw in this position, tighten the locknut.

The adjustment is correct when there is no binding and the steering self-centers properly.

BRAKES

Brake Adjustment

Disc brakes are self adjusting and can-

Adjusting drum brakes through access hole in backing plate—rear brakes shown

not be adjusted by hand. As the pads wear, they will automatically compensate for the wear by moving closer to the disc, maintaining the proper operating clearance.

Drum brakes, however, must be manually adjusted to take up excess clearance as the shoes wear.

1. To adjust drum brakes, both front and rear, it is necessary to jack up the car and support it on a jackstand. The wheel must spin freely.

2. On the backing plate there are four inspection holes with a rubber plug in each hole. Two of the holes are for checking the thickness of the brake lining and the other two are used for adjustment.

NOTE: *There is an adjustment for each brake shoe. That means that on each wheel it is necessary to make two adjustments, one for each shoe on that wheel.*

3. Remove the adjustment hole plugs and, using a screwdriver or brake adjusting tool, insert the tool into the hole.

4. Turn the star wheel until a slight drag is noticed as the wheel is rotated by hand.

5. Back off on the star wheel 3–4 notches so that the wheel turns freely.

Note
Always use all the parts supplied in the repair kit when repairing the master cylinder. Using the silicon lubricant supplied in the kit, lightly coat the push rod and secondary cup of the push rod piston.
All other cups and pistons should be lightly coated with VW brake cylinder paste before installation.

Note
When installing the pistons, guide the lips of the cups in carefully with a blunt tool (screwdriver or something similar).

Sealing plug
Moisten with brake fluid and press in reservoir

Stop screw
Unscrew before removing circlip, when installing push secondary piston into cylinder.

Brake master cylinder housing
If scored or rusted renew master cylinder complete.

Washer

Brake light switch
3-pole.

Seal

Secondary piston (assembly)
Assemble before installation. When installing hold master cylinder with the opening downwards

Conical spring
Do not interchange with the cylindrical spring of push rod piston.

Support ring

Primary cup

Cup washer

Secondary piston

Piston seal
Install using fitting sleeve. Fit with sealing lips facing opposite directions

Push rod piston (assembly)
Assemble before installation

Stop sleeve

Support ring

Plastic washer

Stroke limiting screw
Tighten.

Cylindrical spring
Do not interchange with conical spring

Support ring

Primary cup

Push rod piston

Washer

Secondary cup
Sealing lips towards cylinder

Circlip

1972-77 Type 2 master cylinder

6. Perform the same adjustment on the other shoe.

NOTE: *One of the star wheels in each wheel has left-hand threads and the other star wheel has right-hand threads.*

7. Repeat the above procedure on each wheel with drum brakes.

Master Cylinder

Removal and Installation

1. Drain the brake fluid from the master cylinder reservoir.

CAUTION: *Do not get any brake fluid on the paint, as it will dissolve the paint.*

2. On Type 3, remove the master cylinder cover plate.

3. Pull the plastic elbows out of the rubber sealing rings on the top of the master cylinder.

4. Remove the two bolts which secure the master cylinder to the frame and remove the cylinder. Note the spacers on the Type 1 between the frame and the master cylinder.

5. To install, bolt the master cylinder to the frame. Do not forget the spacers on the Type 1.

6. Lubricate the elbows with brake fluid and insert them into the rubber seals.

7. If necessary, adjust the brake pedal free travel. On Type 1, 3, and 4, adjust the length of the master cylinder pushrod so that there is 5–7 mm of brake pedal free-play before the pushrod contacts the master cylinder piston. On Type 2, the free-play is properly adjusted when the length of the pushrod, measured between the ball end and the center of the clevis pin hole, is 4.17 in.

8. Refill the master cylinder reservoir and bleed the brakes.

Master Cylinder Overhaul

1. Remove the master cylinder from the car.

2. Remove the rubber sealing boot.

3. Remove the stop screw and sealing ring on the top of the unit.

4. Insert a screwdriver in the master cylinder piston, exert inward pressure, and remove the snap-ring from its groove in the end of the unit. The internal parts are spring loaded and must be kept from flying out when the snap-ring is removed.

5. Carefully remove the internal parts of the unit and make note of their order and the orientation of the internal parts. If parts remain in the cylinder bore, they may be removed with a wire hook or very gentle application of low pressure air to the stop screw hole. Cover the end of the cylinder bore with a rag and stand away from the open end of the bore when using compressed air.

6. Use alcohol or brake fluid to clean the master cylinder and its parts.

7. It may be necessary to hone the cylinder bore, or clean it by lightly sanding it with emery cloth. Clean thoroughly after honing or sanding. Lubricate the bore with brake fluid before reassembly.

8. Holding the master cylinder with the open end downward, place the cup washer, primary cup, support washer, spring retainer, and spring onto the front brake circuit piston and insert the piston vertically into the master cylinder bore.

9. Assemble the rear brake circuit piston, cup washer, primary cup, support washer, spring retainer, stop sleeve, spring, and stroke limiting screw and insert the assembly into the master cylinder.

10. Install the stop washer and snapring.

11. Install the stop screw and seal, making sure the hole for the screw is not blocked by the piston. If the hole is blocked, it will be necessary to push the piston further in until the screw can be turned in.

NOTE: *Some Type 2 vehicles have a brake servo*

12. Install the master cylinder and bleed the brakes.

Hydraulic System Bleeding

The hydraulic brake system must be bled any time one of the lines is disconnected or air enters the system.

Manual Bleeding

This method requires two people, one to depress the brake pedal and the other to open the bleeder nipples.

1. Remove the reservoir caps and fill the reservoir.

2. Attach a bleeder hose and a clear container as outlined in the pressure bleeding procedure.

3. Have the assistant depress the brake pedal to the floor several times and then have him hold the pedal to the floor. With the pedal to the floor, open the bleeder nipple until the fluid flow ceases and then close the nipple. Repeat this sequence until there are no more air bubbles in the fluid.

NOTE: *As the air is gradually forced out of the system, it will no longer be possible to force the brake pedal to the floor.*

Periodically check the master cylinder for an adequate supply of fluid. Keep the master cylinder reservoir full of fluid to prevent air from entering the system. If the reservoir does run dry during bleeding, it will be necessary to rebleed the entire system.

Front Disc Brakes

Brake Pad

Removal and Installation

1. Loosen but do not remove the reservoir cover.

2. Jack up the car and remove the wheel and tire.

3. Using a punch, remove the two pins which retain the disc brake pads in the caliper.

NOTE: *If the pads are to be reused, mark the pads to insure that they are reinstalled in the same caliper and on the same side of the disc. Do not invert the pads. Changing pads from one location to another can cause uneven braking.*

4. If the pads are not going to be reused, force a wedge between the disc and the pad and pry the piston back into the caliper as far as possible.

5. Using compressed air, blow away the brake dust. Pull the old pad out of the caliper and insert a new one.

6. Now insert the wedge between the disc and pad on the opposite side and force that piston into the caliper. Remove the old pad and insert a new one.

7. If the old pads are to be reused, it is not necessary to push the piston into the caliper. Pull the pads from the caliper and reinstall the pads when necessary.

8. Install a new brake pad spreader spring and insert the retaining pins. Be careful not to shear the split clamping bushing from the pin. Insert the pin from the inside of the caliper and drive it to the outside.

9. Pump the brake pedal several times to take up the clearance between the pads and the disc before driving the car.

10. Install the wheel and tire and carefully road test the car. Apply the brakes gently for 500 to 1000 miles to properly break in the pads and prevent glazing them.

Brake Caliper

Removal and Installation

1. Jack up the car and remove the wheel and tire.

2. Remove the brake pads.

3. Disconnect the brake line from the caliper.

4. Remove the two bolts which secure the caliper to the steering knuckle and remove the caliper from the vehicle.

5. Reverse the above steps to install the caliper and bleed the brakes after the caliper is installed.

Overhaul

Clean all parts in alcohol or brake fluid.

1. Remove the caliper from the vehicle.

2. Remove the piston retaining plates.

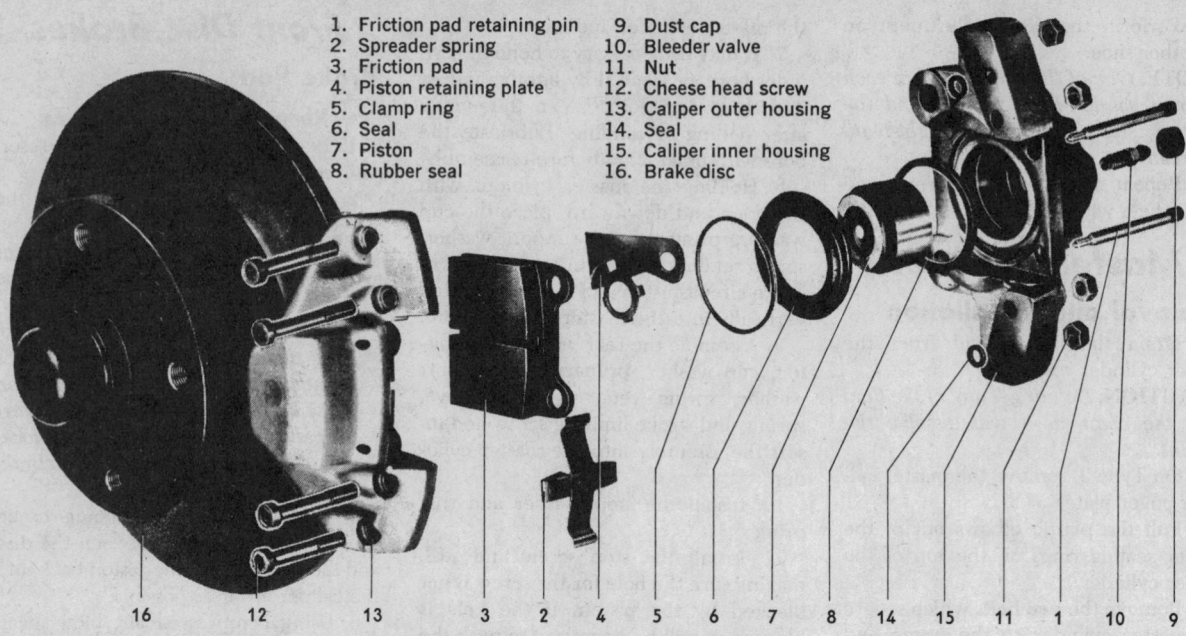

1. Friction pad retaining pin
2. Spreader spring
3. Friction pad
4. Piston retaining plate
5. Clamp ring
6. Seal
7. Piston
8. Rubber seal
9. Dust cap
10. Bleeder valve
11. Nut
12. Cheese head screw
13. Caliper outer housing
14. Seal
15. Caliper inner housing
16. Brake disc

Front disc brake assembly—Types 1 (Karmann Ghia) and 3

3. Pry out the seal spring ring using a small screwdriver. Do not damage the seal beneath the ring.

4. Remove the seal with a plastic or hard rubber rod. Do not use sharp edged or metal tools.

5. Rebuild one piston at a time. Securely clamp one piston in place so that it cannot come out of its bore. Place a block of wood between the two pistons and apply air pressure to the brake fluid port.

CAUTION: *Use extreme care with this technique because the piston can fly out of the caliper with tremendous force.*

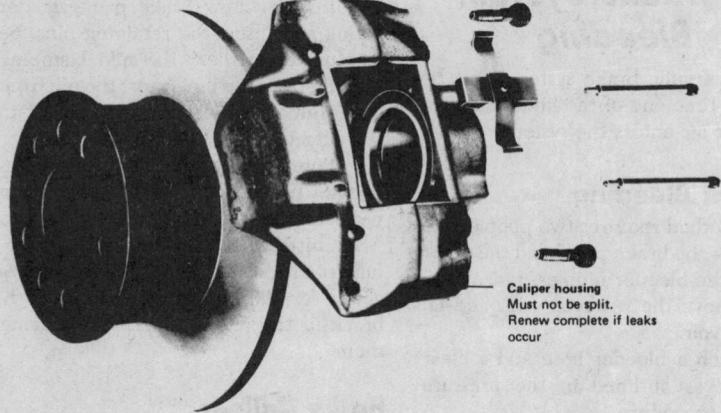

Caliper housing
Must not be split.
Renew complete if leaks
occur

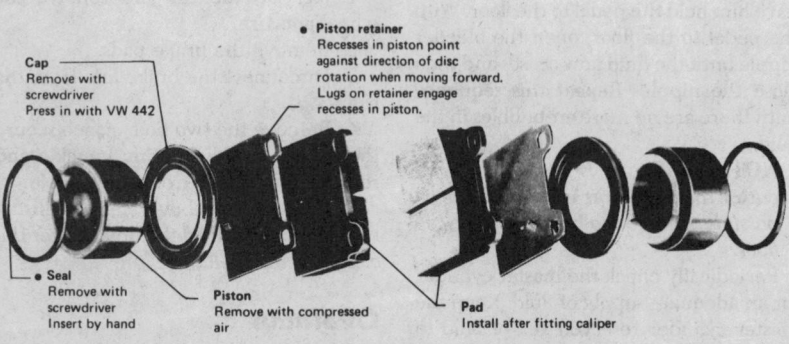

Cap
Remove with
screwdriver
Press in with VW 442

Piston retainer
Recesses in piston point
against direction of disc
rotation when moving forward.
Lugs on retainer engage
recesses in piston.

• Seal
Remove with
screwdriver
Insert by hand

Piston
Remove with compressed
air

Pad
Install after fitting caliper

• = Parts in repair kit

ATE front disc brake assembly—1971-75 Type 2

6. Remove the rubber seal at the bottom of the piston bore using a rubber or plastic tool.

7. Check the bore and piston for wear, rust, and pitting.

8. Install a new seal in the bottom of the bore and lubricate the bore and seal with brake fluid.

9. Gently insert the piston, making sure it does not cock and jam in the bore.

10. Install the new outer seal and new spring ring.

11. Install the piston retaining plate.

12. Repeat the above procedure on the other piston. Never rebuild only one side of a caliper.

Brake Disc

Removal and Installation

1. Jack up the car and remove the wheel and tire.

2. Remove the caliper.

3. On Type 2, remove the three socket head bolts which secure the disc to the hub and remove the disc from the hub. Sometimes the disc is rusted to the hub. Spray penetrating oil on the seam and tap the disc with a lead or brass hammer. If it still does not come off, screw three 8 mm by 40 screws into the socket head holes. Tighten the screws evenly and pull the disc from the hub.

4. On Type 1, 3, and 4, remove the wheel bearing cover. On the left side it will be necessary to remove the small clip which secures the end of the speedometer cable to the cover.

5. Unscrew the wheel bearing nut and remove the nut and outer wheel bearing.

6. Pull the disc off of the spindle.

7. To remove the wheel bearing races, see the "Wheel Bearing Removal and In-

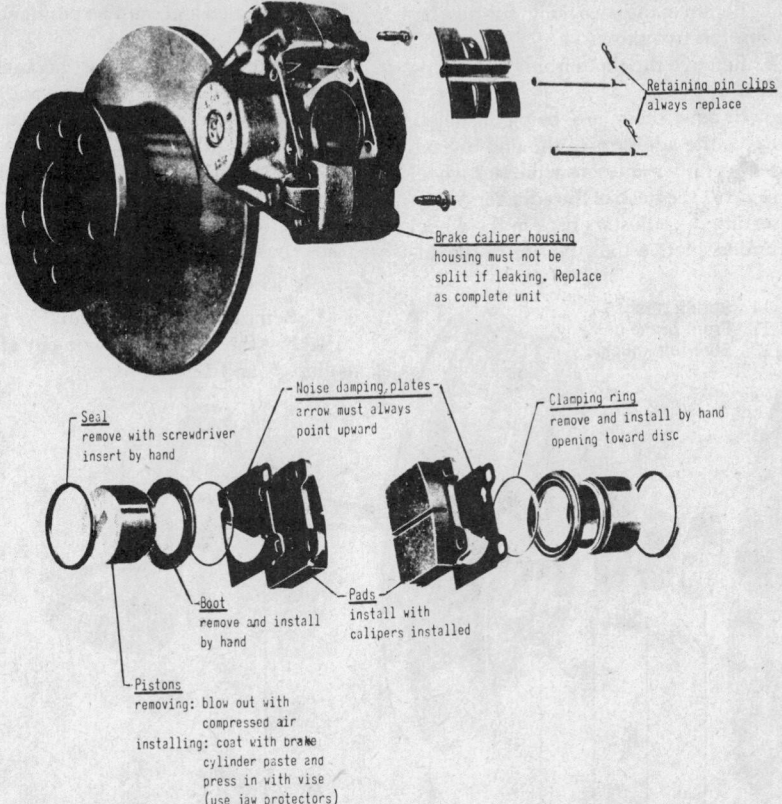

Seal
remove with screwdriver
insert by hand

Noise damping plates
arrow must always
point upward

Clamping ring
remove and install by hand
opening toward disc

Boot
remove and install
by hand

Pads
install with
calipers installed

Pistons
removing: blow out with
compressed air
installing: coat with brake
cylinder paste and
press in with vise
(use jaw protectors)

Brake caliper housing
housing must not be
split if leaking. Replace
as complete unit

Retaining pin clips
always replace

Girling front disc brake assembly—1975-77 Type 2

its race in the hub and tap a new seal into the hub. Lubricate the sealing surface of the seal with grease.

10. Install the hub on the spindle and install the outer wheel bearing.

11. Adjust the wheel bearing and install the dust cover.

12. Install the caliper (if equipped with disc brakes).

Adjustment

The bearing may be adjusted by feel or by a dial indicator.

To adjust the bearing by feel, tighten the adjusting nut so that all the play is taken up in the bearing. There will be a slight amount of drag on the wheel if it is hand spun. Back off fully on the adjusting nut and retighten very lightly. There should be no drag when the wheel is hand spun and there should be no perceptible play in the bearing when the wheel is grasped and wiggled from side to side.

To use a dial indicator, remove the dust cover and mount a dial indicator against the hub. Grasp the wheel at the side and pull the wheel in and out along the axis of the spindle. Read the axial play on the dial indicator. Screw the adjusting nut in or out to obtain 0.001–0.005 in. of axial play. Secure the adjusting nut and recheck the axial play.

Front Wheel Bearings

Removal and Installation

1. Jack up the car and remove the wheel and tire.

2. Remove the caliper and disc (if equipped with disc brakes) or brake drum.

3. To remove the inside wheel bearing, pry the dust seal out of the hub with a screwdriver. Lift out the bearing and its inner race.

4. To remove the outer race for either the inner or outer wheel bearing, insert a long punch into the hub opposite the end from which the race is to be removed. The race rests against a shoulder in the hub. The shoulder has two notches cut into it so that it is possible to place the end of the punch directly against the back side of the race and drive it out of the hub.

5. Carefully clean the hub.

6. Install new races in the hub. Drive them in with a soft faced hammer or a large piece of pipe of the proper diameter. Lubricate the races with a light coating of wheel bearing grease.

7. Force wheel bearing grease into the sides of the tapered roller bearings so that all the spaces are filled.

8. Place a small amount of grease inside the hub.

9. Place the inner wheel bearing into

Front Drum Brakes

Brake Drum

Removal and Installation

1. Jack up the car and remove the wheel and tire.

2. On the left side, remove the clip which secures the speedometer cable to the wheel bearing dust cover. Remove the dust cover.

3. Remove the wheel bearing adjusting nut and slide the brake drum off of the spindle. It may be necessary to back off on the brake shoe star wheels so that there is enough clearance to remove the drum.

4. Installation is the reverse of removal. Adjust the wheel bearings after installing the drum.

CAUTION: *Do not forget to readjust the brake shoes if they were disturbed during removal.*

Inspection

If the brake drums are scored or cracked, they must be replaced or machined. If the vehicle pulls to one side or exhibits a pulsating braking action, the drum is probably out of round and should be checked at a machine shop. The drum may have a smooth even surface and still be out of round. The drum should be free of surface cracks and dark spots.

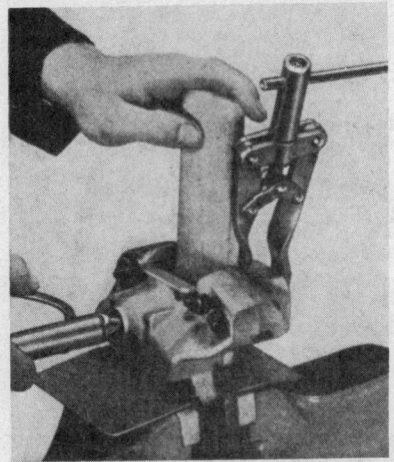

Clamping a caliper piston in place and applying compressed air to the brake hose port

stallation" procedure.

8. Installation is the reverse of the above. Make sure the wheel bearing is properly adjusted.

Inspection

Visually check the rotor for excessive scoring. Minor scores will not affect the performance; however, if the scores are over 1/32 in., it is necessary to replace the disc or have it resurfaced. The disc must be 0.02 in. over the wear limit to be resurfaced. The disc must be free of surface cracks and discoloration (heat bluing). Hand spin the disc and make sure that it does not wobble from side to side.

Brake Linings

Removal and Installation

Type 1

1. Jack up the car and remove the wheel and tire.

2. Remove the brake drum.

3. Remove the small disc and spring which secure each shoe to the backing plate.

1. Speedometer cable circlip
2. Hub cap dust cover
3. Clamp nut allen screw
4. Wheel bearing clamp nut
5. Thrust washer
6. Outer taper roller bearing
7. Brake drum
8. Drum seal (grease)
9. Inner taper roller bearing
10. Bolt

4. Remove the two long springs between the two shoes.

5. Remove the shoes from the backing plate.

6. If new shoes are being installed, remove the adjusters in the end of each wheel cylinder and screw the star wheel up against the head of the adjuster. When inserting the adjusters back in the wheel cylinders, notice that the slot in the ad-

11. Spring washer
12. Front brake unit
13. Steering knuckle

juster is angled and must be positioned as illustrated.

7. Position new shoes on the backing plate. The slot in the shoes and the stronger return spring must be at the wheel cylinder end.

8. Install the disc and spring which secure the shoe to the backing plate.

9. Install the brake drum and adjust the wheel bearing.

Type 2

1. Remove the brake drum.

2. Pry the rear brake shoe out of the adjuster, and detach the re-

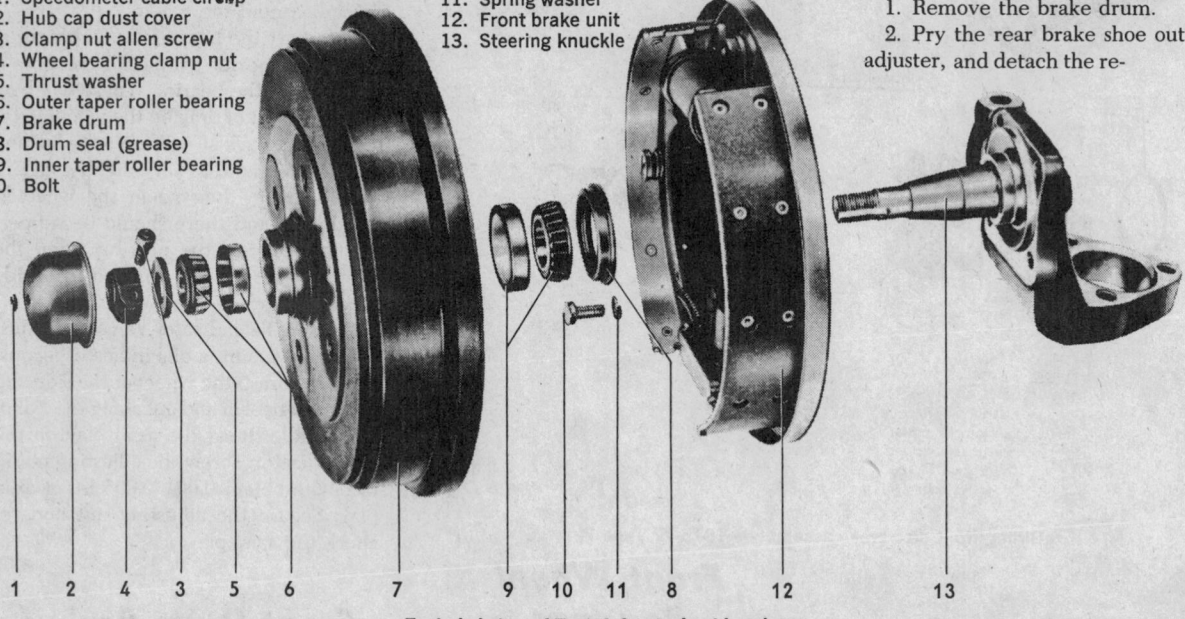

Exploded view of Type 1 front wheel bearings

Front wheel brake

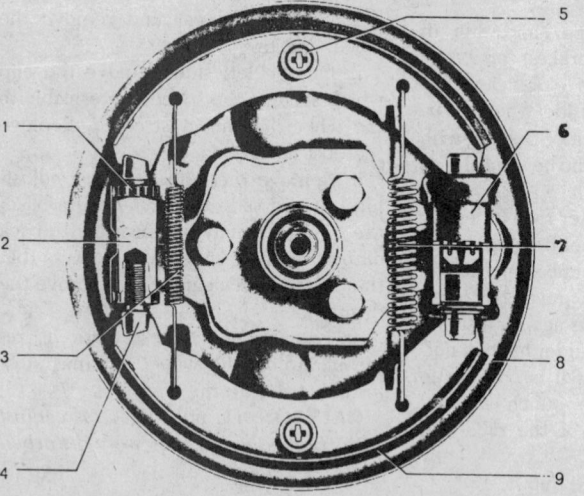

Rear wheel brake

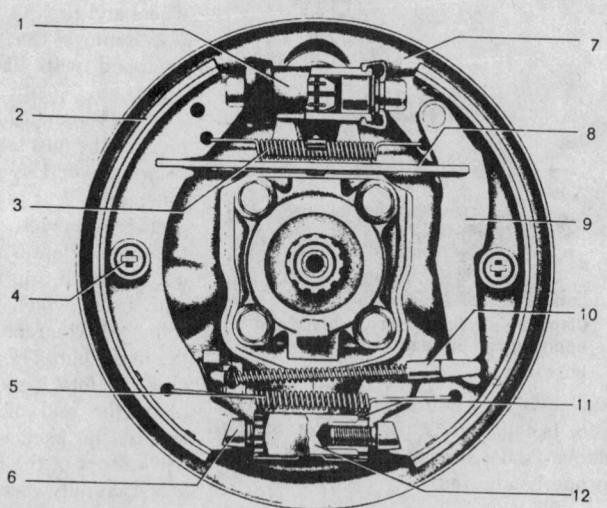

Front and rear drum brakes—Type 1

FRONT
1. Adjusting screw
2. Anchor block
3. Front return spring
4. Adjusting nut
5. Guide spring with cup and pin
6. Cylinder
7. Rear return spring
8. Back plate
9. Brake shoe with lining

REAR
1. Cylinder
2. Brake shoe with lining
3. Upper return spring
4. Spring with cup and pin
5. Lower return spring
6. Adjusting screw
7. Back plate
8. Connecting link
9. Lever

10. Brake cable
11. Adjusting nut
12. Anchor block

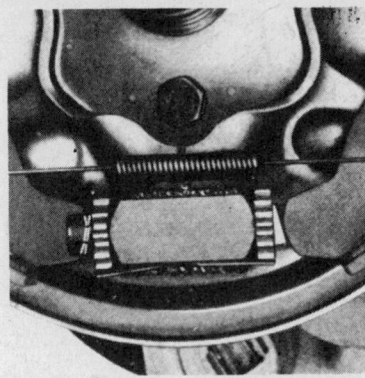

The notched adjusters must be positioned as shown

For proper installation, Type 1 brake shoes must have notches in shoes on wheel cylinder side

turn springs. Remove the forward shoe.

3. If new shoes are to be installed, screw the star wheel up against the head of the adjuster.

4. Install the rear brake shoe.

5. Attach the return spring to the front brake shoe and then to the rear shoe.

6. Position the front brake shoe in the slot of the adjusting screw and lever it into position in the same manner as it was removed. Make sure that the return springs do not touch the brake line be-

tween the upper and lower wheel cylinders.

7. Install the brake drum and adjust the wheel bearings.

Wheel Cylinder

Removal and Installation

1. Remove the brake shoes.

2. On Type 1, disconnect the brake line from the rear of the cylinder. On Type 2, disconnect the brake line from the rear of the cylinder and the transfer line from the front of the cylinder.

3. Remove the bolts which secure the cylinder to the backing plate and remove the cylinder from the vehicle.

4. Reverse the above steps to install and bleed the brakes.

Overhaul

1. Remove the wheel cylinder.

2. Remove the brake adjusters and remove the rubber boot from each end.

NOTE: *The Type 2 cylinder has only one rubber boot, piston, and cup. The rebuilding procedures are the same.*

3. On Type 1, push in on one of the pistons to force out the opposite piston and rubber cup. On Type 2, remove the piston and cup by blowing compressed air into the brake hose hole.

4. Wash the pistons and cylinder in clean brake fluid or alcohol.

5. Inspect the cylinder bore for signs of pitting, scoring, and excessive wear. If it is badly scored or pitted, the whole cylinder should be replaced. It is possible to remove the glaze and light scores with crocus cloth or a brake cylinder hone. Before rebuilding the cylinder, make sure the bleeder screw is free. If the bleeder is rusted shut or broken off, replace the entire cylinder.

6. Dip the new pistons and rubber cups in brake fluid. Place the spring in the bore and insert the rubber cups into the bore against the spring. The concave

side of the rubber cup should face inward.

7. Place the pistons in the bore and install the rubber boot.

8. Install the cylinder and bleed the brakes after the shoes and drum are in place. Make sure that the brakes are adjusted.

Rear Drum Brakes

Brake Drum

Removal and Installation

Type 1, 2, 3

1. With the wheels still on the ground, remove the cotter pin from the slotted nut on the rear axle and remove the nut from the axle.

CAUTION: *Make sure the emergency brake is now released.*

2. Jack up the car and remove the wheel and tire.

3. The brake drum is splined to the rear axle and the drum should slip off the axle. However, the drum sometimes rusts on the splines and it is necessary to

Removing rear brake drum using puller—Types 1, 2, and 3

1. Boot
2. Piston
3. Cup
4. Cup expander
5. Spring
6. Housing
7. Bleeder valve
8. Dust cap
9. Adjusting nut
10. Adjusting screw

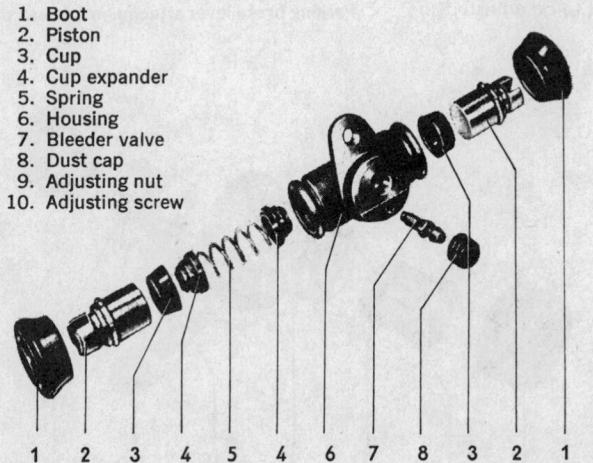

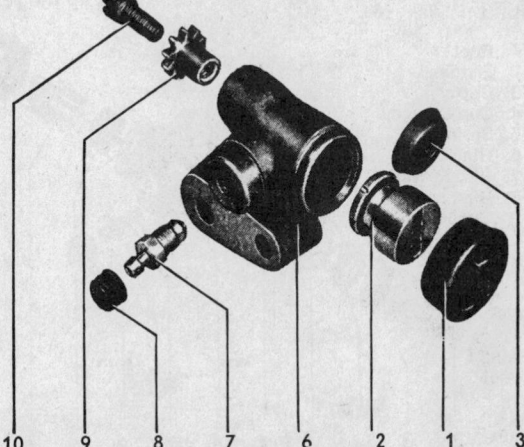

1 2 3 4 5 4 6 7 8 3 2 1   10 9 8 7 6 2 1 3

Front wheel cylinders disassembled—Type 1 (left), Type 2 (right)

remove the drum using a puller.

4. Before installing the drum, lubricate the splines. Install the drum on the axle and tighten the nut on the axle. Line up a slot in the nut with a hole in the axle and insert a cotter pin. Never loosen the nut to align the slot and hole.

Type 4

The drum is held in place by the wheel lugs. Jack up the car and remove the wheel and tire. After the wheel is removed, there are two small screws that secure the drum to the hub and they must be removed before the drum will slip off the hub.

Inspection

Inspection is the same as given in the "Front Drum Brake" section.

Brake Lining

Removal and Installation

1. Remove the brake drum.
2. Remove both shoe retaining springs.

Rear wheel brake assembly—Parking brake cable disconnected

3. Disconnect the lower return spring.
4. Disconnect the hand brake cable from the lever attached to the rear shoe.
5. Remove the upper return spring and clip.

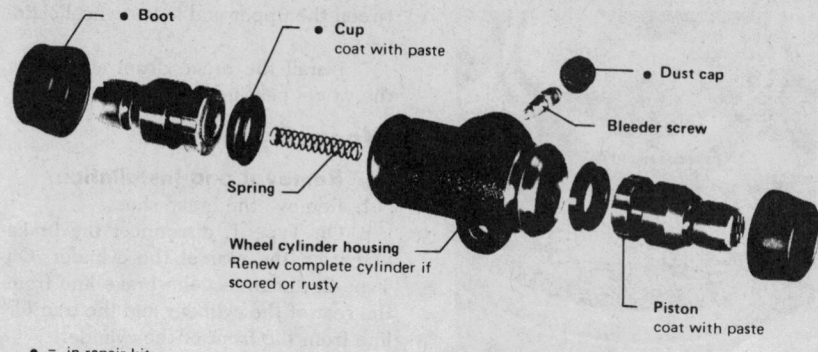

1971-77 Type 2 rear wheel cylinder

- Boot
- Cup — coat with paste
- Dust cap
- Bleeder screw
- Spring
- Wheel cylinder housing — Renew complete cylinder if scored or rusty
- Piston — coat with paste

● = in repair kit

6. Remove the brake shoes and connecting link.
7. Remove the emergency brake lever from the rear shoe.
8. Lubricate the adjusting screws and the star wheel against the head of the adjusting screw.
9. Reverse Steps 1–7 to install the shoes.
10. Adjust the brakes.

Wheel Cylinder

Removal and Installation

Remove the brake drum and brake shoes. Disconnect the brake line from the cylinder and remove the bolts which secure the cylinder to the backing plate. Remove the cylinder from the vehicle.

Overhaul

Overhaul is the same as given in the "Front Drum Brake" section.

Parking Brake

Cable Adjustment

Brake cable adjustment is performed at the handbrake lever in the passenger compartment. There is a cable for each rear wheel and there are two adjusting nuts at the lever.

To adjust the cable, loosen the locknut. Jack up the rear wheel to be adjusted so

that it can be hand spun. Turn the adjusting nut until a very slight drag is felt as the wheel is spun. Then back off on the adjusting nut until the lever can be pulled up three notches.

CAUTION: *Never pull up on the handbrake lever with the cables disconnected.*

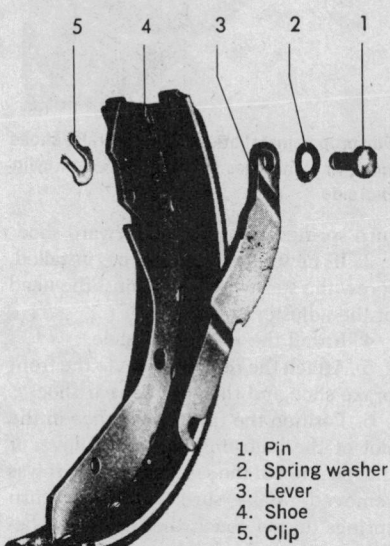

1. Pin
2. Spring washer
3. Lever
4. Shoe
5. Clip

Parking brake lever attachment to rear shoe

1. Boot
2. Piston
3. Cup
4. Cup expander
5. Spring
6. Housing
7. Bleeder valve
8. Dust cap
9. Circlip

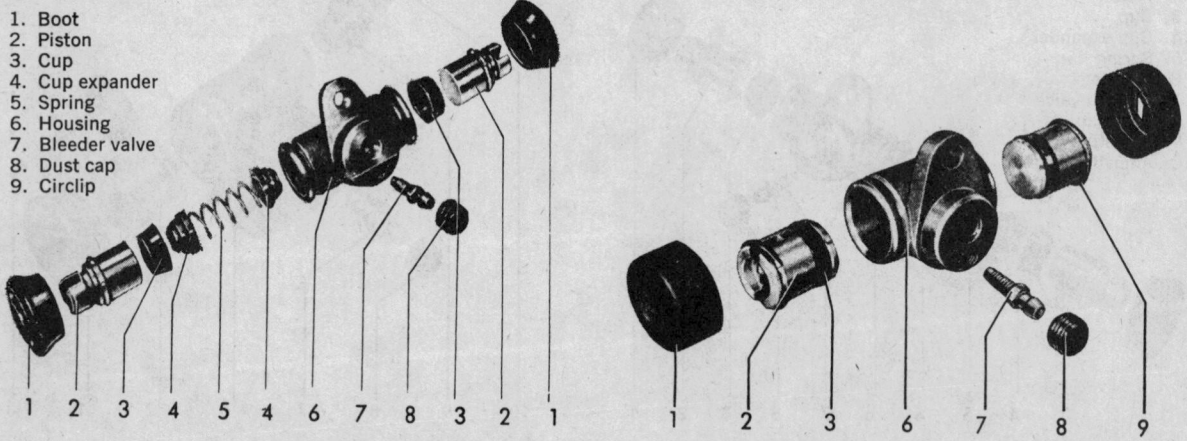

Rear wheel cylinder disassembled—Types 1, 3, and 4 (left), Type 2 (right)

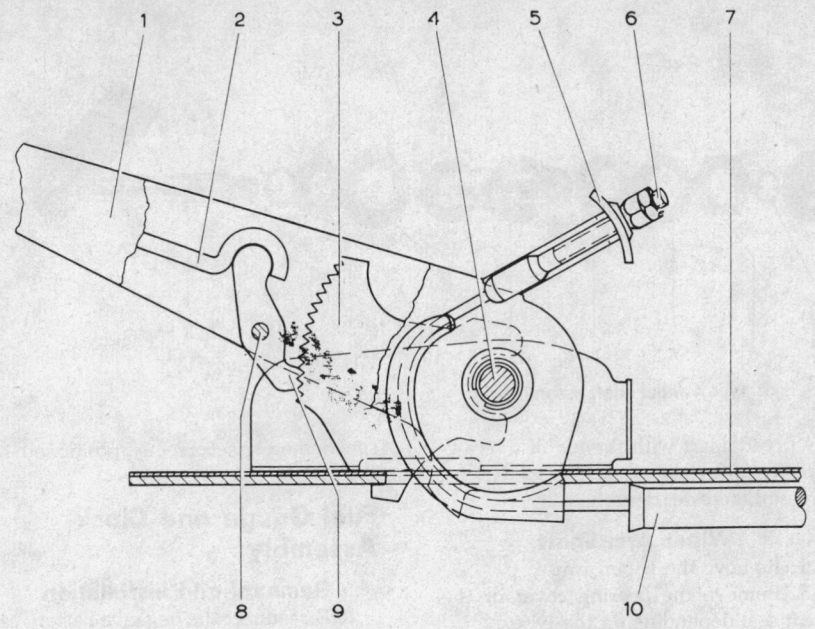

Parking brake hand lever and cable end assembly

1. Hand brake lever
2. Pawl rod
3. Ratchet segment
4. Lever pin
5. Cable compensator
6. Brake cable
7. Frame
8. Pawl pin
9. Pawl
10. Cable guide tube

Parking brake cable adjusting nuts

Cable

Removal and Installation

1. Disconnect the cables at the hand-brake lever by removing the two nuts which secure the cables to the lever. Pull the cables rearward to remove that end from the lever bracket.

2. Remove the brake drum and detach the cable end from the lever attached to the rear brake shoe.

3. Remove the brake cable bracket from the backing plate and remove the cable from the vehicle.

4. Reverse the above steps to install and adjust the cable.

CHASSIS ELECTRICAL

Heater

The Volkswagen heating system has no electrical blower. The engine cooling fan blows air over the engine and out through the cooling ducts. If the heater flaps are opened, then a portion of the heated air from the engine is diverted to the passenger compartment. An auxiliary gas heater is optional on Types 1, 2, and 3, and standard on Type 4.

Cable for Heater Outlet

Removal and Installation

Types 1, 2, 3

1. Remove the rear air outlet, hose, and heater pipe as an assembly.
2. Remove the hose from the outlet and from the pipe.
3. Remove the pin which attaches the cable to the flap in the heater pipe.
NOTE: *The pin is push-fit.*
4. Remove the heater pipe from the outlet.
5. Bend up the tabs which secure the cable shielding to the outlet.
6. Disconnect the opposite end from the heater controls and remove the cable.
7. Reverse the above steps to install.

Windshield Wipers

Motor Removal and Installation

Type 1

1. Disconnect the battery ground cable.
2. Loosen the clamp screws and remove the wiper arms.
3. Remove the wiper bearing nuts as well as the washers. Take off the outer bearing seals.
4. Remove the back of the instrument panel from the luggage compartment.
5. Disconnect the cable from the wiper motor.
6. Remove the glove compartment box.
7. Remove the screw which secures the wiper frame to the body.
8. Remove the frame and motor with the linkage.

NOTE: *The ball joints at the ends of the linkage may be slipped apart by gently popping the ball and socket apart with a screwdriver. Always lubricate the joints upon reassembly.*

9. Remove the lock and spring washers from the motor driveshaft and remove the connecting rod. Matchmark the motor and frame to ensure proper realignment when the motor is reinstalled.
10. Remove the nut located at the base of the motor driveshaft, and the nut at the side of the driveshaft, and remove the motor from the frame.
11. To install, reverse the above steps and heed the following reminders.
12. The pressed lug on the wiper frame must engage the groove in the wiper bearing. Make sure that the wiper spindles are perpendicular to the plane of the windshield.
13. Check the linkage bushings for wear.
14. The hollow side of the links must face toward the frame with the angled end of the driving link toward the right bearing.
15. The inner bearing seal should be placed so that the shoulder of the rubber molding faces the wiper arm.

Type 2

1. Disconnect the ground wire from the battery.
2. Remove both wiper arms.
3. Remove the bearing cover and nut.
4. Remove the heater branch connections under the instrument panel.
5. Disconnect the wiper motor wiring.
6. Remove the wiper motor securing screw and remove the motor.
7. Reverse the above steps to install.

1. Cap nut
2. Lock washer
3. Wiper arm
4. Bearing cover
5. Circlip
6. Nut
7. Washer
8. Seal
9. Shaft bearing
10. Spring washer
11. Brass nut
12. Spring washer
13. Wiper shaft

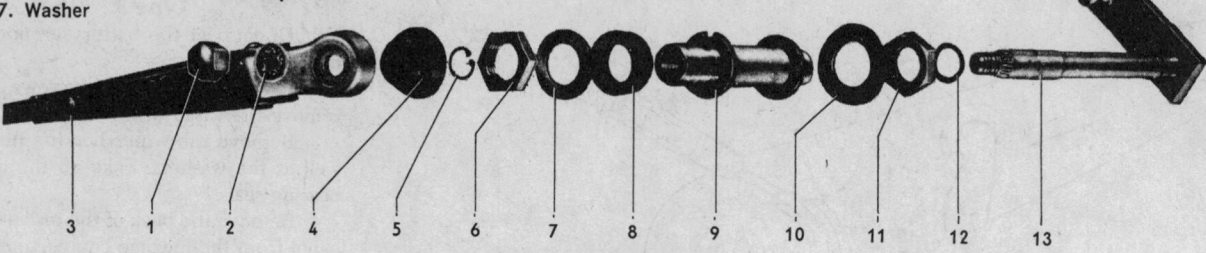

Type 4 wiper shaft assembly

Type 3

1. Disconnect the negative battery cable.

2. Remove the ashtray and glove compartment.

3. Remove the fresh air controls.

4. Remove the cover for the heater and water drainage hoses.

5. Disconnect the motor wiring.

6. Remove the wiper arms.

7. Remove the bearing covers and nuts, washers, and outer bearing seals.

8. Remove the wiper motor securing screws and remove the motor.

9. Reverse the above steps to install.

Type 4

1. Disconnect the negative battery cable.

2. Remove the wiper arms.

3. Remove the bearing cover and remove the nut under it.

4. Remove the steering column cover and the hoses running between the fresh air control box and the vents.

5. Remove the clock but do not disconnect the wiring.

6. Remove the left fresh air and defroster vent. Disconnect the air hose from the vent.

7. Disconnect the wiring for the motor at the windshield wiper switch. Remove the ground wire from the motor gear cover.

8. Remove the motor securing screw and remove the motor frame and motor assembly downward and to the right.

9. Reverse the above steps to install.

Linkage Removal and Installation

The windshield wiper linkage is secured at the ends by a ball and socket type joint. The ball and joint may be gen-tly pryed apart with the aid of a screwdriver. Always lubricate the joints with grease before reassembly.

Wiper Arm Shaft

1. Remove the wiper arm.

2. Remove the bearing cover or the shaft seal depending on the type.

3. On Type 4, remove the shaft circlip.

4. Remove the large wiper shaft bearing securing nut and remove the accompanying washer and rubber seal.

5. Disconnect the wiper linkage from the wiper arm shaft.

6. Working from inside the car, slide the shaft out of its bearing.

NOTE: *It may be necessary to lightly tap the shaft out of its bearing. Use a soft face hammer.*

7. Reverse the above steps to install.

Instrument Cluster

Speedometer

Removal and Installation

1. Disconnect the negative battery cable.

2. Disconnect the speedometer light bulb wires.

3. Unscrew the knurled nut which secures the speedometer cable to the back of the speedometer. Pull the cable from the back of the speedometer.

4. Using a 4 mm allen wrench, remove the two knurled nuts which secure the speedometer brackets. Remove the brackets.

5. Remove the speedometer from the dashboard by sliding it out toward the steering wheel.

6. Reverse the above steps to install. Before fully tightening the nuts for the speedometer brackets, make sure the speedometer is correctly positioned in the dash.

Fuel Gauge and Clock Assembly

Removal and Installation

1. Disconnect the negative battery cable.

2. Disconnect the wiring from the back of the assembly.

3. Remove the knurled nuts and brackets which secure the assembly in the dash. Use a 4 mm allen wrench.

4. Remove the assembly by gently sliding it toward the steering wheel and out of the dash.

5. The fuel gauge is secured into the base of the clock by two screws. Remove the screws and slip the fuel gauge out of the clock.

6. Reverse the above steps to install. Make sure the clock and fuel gauge assembly is properly centered in the dash before fully tightening the nuts.

Fuse Box Location

All major circuits are protected from overloading or short circuiting by fuses. A 12 position fusebox is located beneath the dashboard near the steering column, or located in the luggage compartment on some air conditioned models.

When a fuse blows, the cause should be investigated. Never install a fuse of a larger capacity than specified and never use foil or a bolt or nail in place of a fuse. However, always carry a few spares in case of emergency. There are 10 8 amp (white) fuses and two 16 amp (red) fuses in the VW fusebox. Circuits number 9 and 10 use the 16 amp fuses. To replace a fuse, pry off the clear plastic cover at either end of the subject fuse.

NOTE: No wiring diagrams are published by the manufacturer after 1972.

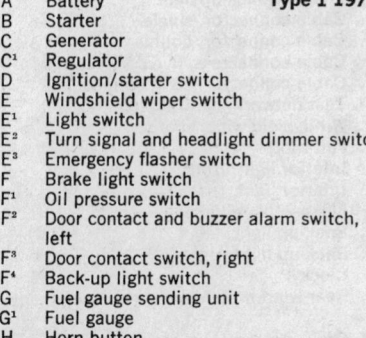

Type 1 1972

A	Battery
B	Starter
C	Generator
C^1	Regulator
D	Ignition/starter switch
E	Windshield wiper switch
E^1	Light switch
E^2	Turn signal and headlight dimmer switch
E^3	Emergency flasher switch
F	Brake light switch
F^1	Oil pressure switch
F^2	Door contact and buzzer alarm switch, left
F^3	Door contact switch, right
F^4	Back-up light switch
G	Fuel gauge sending unit
G^1	Fuel gauge
H	Horn button
H^1	Horn
H^5	Ignition key warning buzzer
J	Dimmer relay
J^2	Emergency flasher relay
J^6	Fuel gauge vibrator
K^1	High beam warning light
K^2	Generator charging warning light
K^3	Oil pressure warning light
K^5	Turn signal warning light
K^6	Emergency flasher warning light
K^7	Dual circuit brake warning light
L^1	Sealed-Beam unit, left headlight
L^2	Sealed-Beam unit, right headlight
L^{10}	Instrument panel light
M^1	Parking light, left
M^2	Tail/brake light, right
M^4	Tail/brake light, left
M^5	Turn signal and parking light front left
M^6	Turn signal, rear, left
M^7	Turn signal and parking light front right
M^8	Turn signal, rear, right
M^{11}	Side marker, light, front
N	Ignition coil
N^1	Automatic choke
N^3	Electromagnetic pilot jet
O	Distributor
P^1	Spark plug connector, No. 1 cylinder
P^2	Spark plug connector, No. 2 cylinder
P^3	Spark plug connector, No. 3 cylinder
P^4	Spark plug connector, No. 4 cylinder
Q^1	Spark plug, No. 1 cylinder
Q^2	Spark plug, No. 2 cylinder
Q^3	Spark plug, No. 3 cylinder
Q^4	Spark plug, No. 4 cylinder
S	Fuse box
S^1	Back-up light in-line fuse
T	Cable adapter
T^1	Cable connector, single
T^2	Cable connector, double
T^3	Cable connector, triple
T^4	Cable connector (four connections)
T^5	Cable connector (five connections)
T^{20}	Test network, central plug
V	Windshield wiper motor
W	Interior light
X	License plate light
X^1	Back-up light, left
X^2	Back-up light, right
①	Ground strap from battery to frame
②	Ground strap from transmission to frame
④	Ground cable from front axle to frame

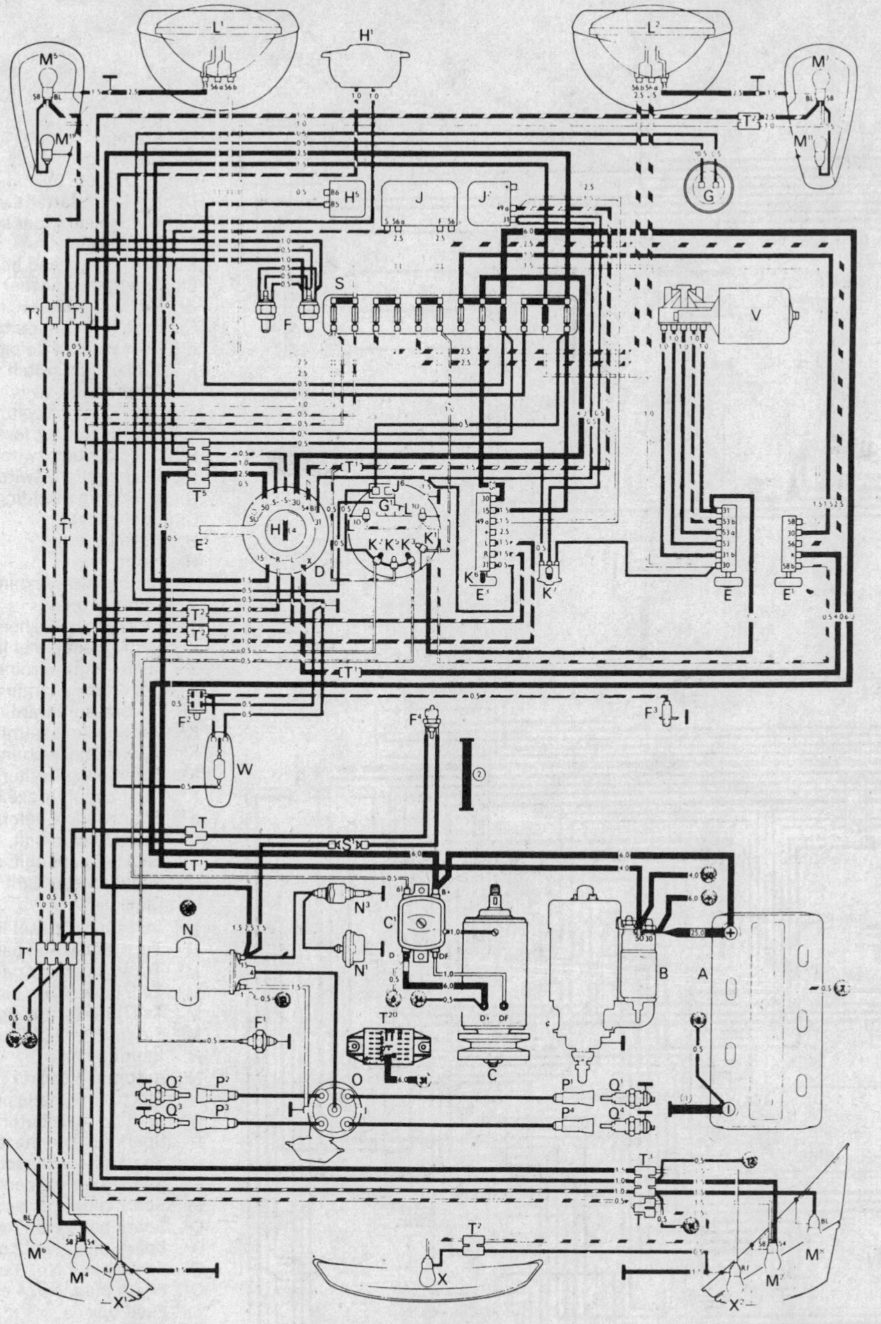

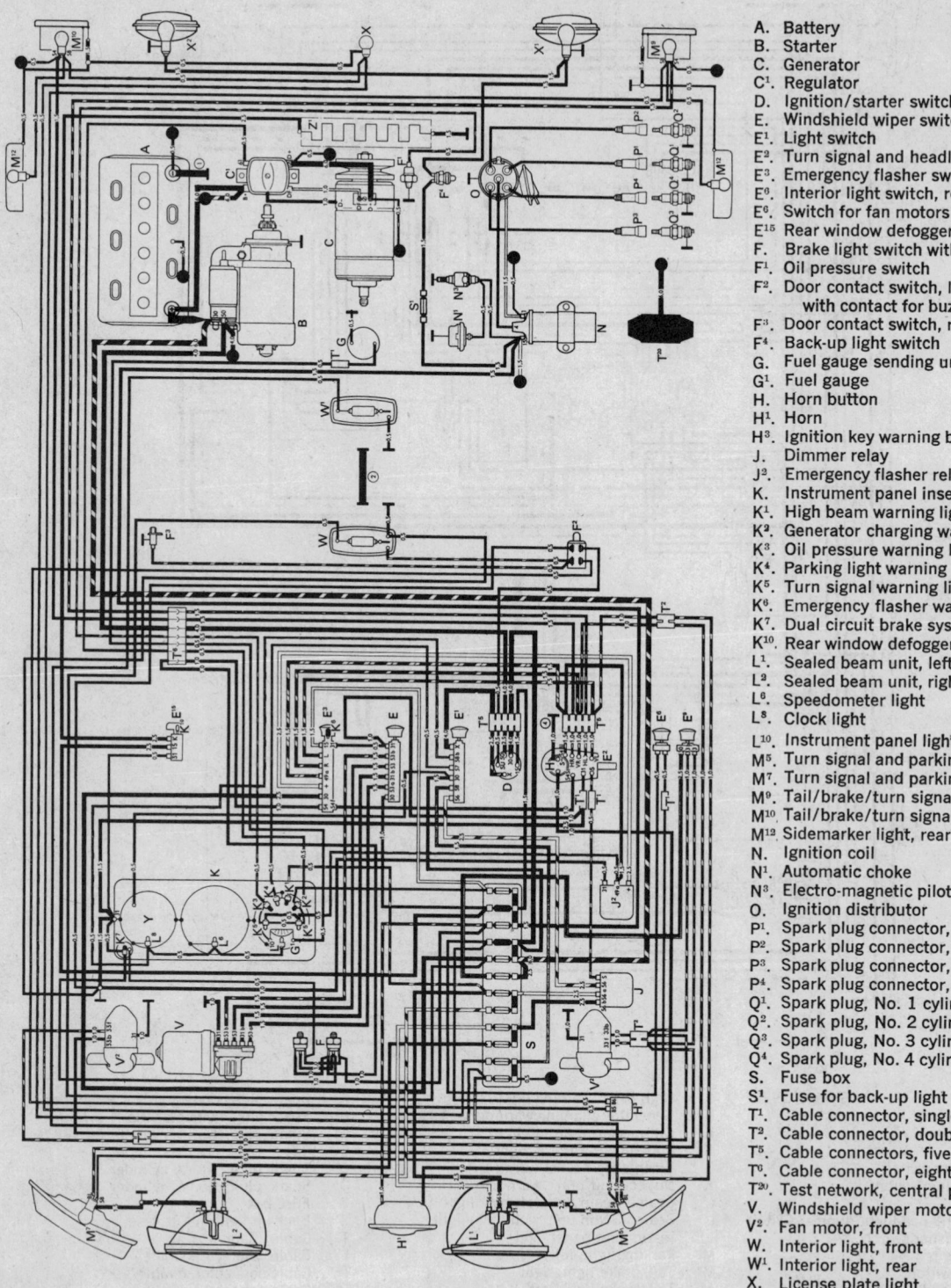

Type 2 1972

A. Battery
B. Starter
C. Generator
C¹. Regulator
D. Ignition/starter switch
E. Windshield wiper switch
E¹. Light switch
E². Turn signal and headlight dimmer switch
E³. Emergency flasher switch
E⁶. Interior light switch, rear
E⁹. Switch for fan motors
E¹⁵ Rear window defogger switch
F. Brake light switch with warning switch
F¹. Oil pressure switch
F². Door contact switch, left, with contact for buzzer
F³. Door contact switch, right
F⁴. Back-up light switch
G. Fuel gauge sending unit
G¹. Fuel gauge
H. Horn button
H¹. Horn
H³. Ignition key warning buzzer
J. Dimmer relay
J². Emergency flasher relay
K. Instrument panel insert
K¹. High beam warning light
K². Generator charging warning light
K³. Oil pressure warning light
K⁴. Parking light warning light
K⁵. Turn signal warning light
K⁶. Emergency flasher warning light
K⁷. Dual circuit brake system warning light
K¹⁰. Rear window defogger warning light
L¹. Sealed beam unit, left headlight
L². Sealed beam unit, right headlight
L⁶. Speedometer light
L⁸. Clock light
L¹⁰. Instrument panel light
M⁵. Turn signal and parking light, front, left
M⁷. Turn signal and parking light, front, right
M⁹. Tail/brake/turn signal light, left
M¹⁰. Tail/brake/turn signal light, right
M¹². Sidemarker light, rear
N. Ignition coil
N¹. Automatic choke
N³. Electro-magnetic pilot jet
O. Ignition distributor
P¹. Spark plug connector, No. 1 cylinder
P². Spark plug connector, No. 2 cylinder
P³. Spark plug connector, No. 3 cylinder
P⁴. Spark plug connector, No. 4 cylinder
Q¹. Spark plug, No. 1 cylinder
Q². Spark plug, No. 2 cylinder
Q³. Spark plug, No. 3 cylinder
Q⁴. Spark plug, No. 4 cylinder
S. Fuse box
S¹. Fuse for back-up light
T¹. Cable connector, single
T². Cable connector, double
T⁵. Cable connectors, five connections
T⁹. Cable connector, eight connections
T²⁰. Test network, central plug
V. Windshield wiper motor
V². Fan motor, front
W. Interior light, front
W¹. Interior light, rear
X. License plate light
X¹. Back-up light, left
X². Back-up light, right
Y. Clock
Z¹. Rear window defogger heating element

① Ground strap from battery to frame
② Ground strap from transmission to the frame
④ Ground cable from horn button to steering coupling

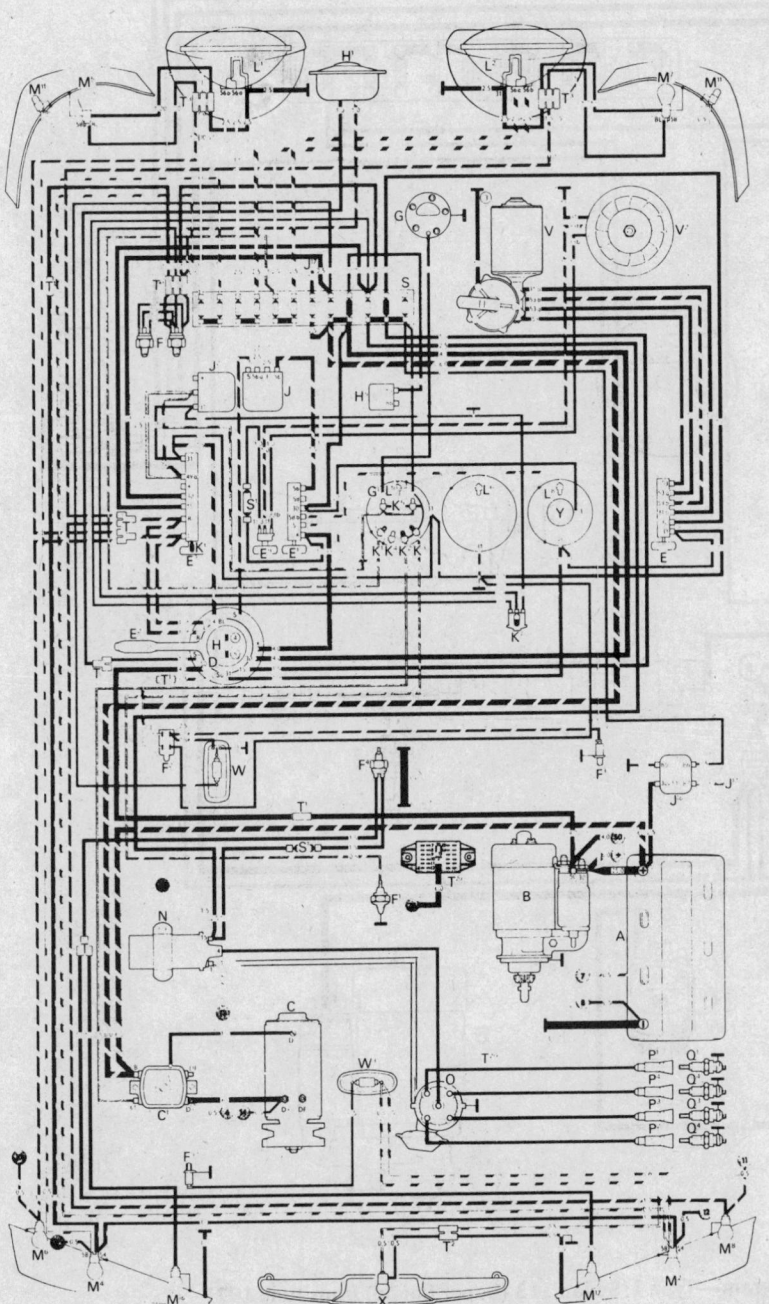

Type 3 1972

A	Battery
B	Starter
C	Generator
C¹	Regulator
D	Ignition/starter switch
E	Windshield wiper switch
E¹	Light switch
E²	Turn signal and headlight dimmer switch
E³	Emergency flasher switch
E⁹	Fresh air fan motor switch
F	Brake light switch
F¹	Oil pressure switch
F²	Door contact and buzzzer alarm switch, left
F³	Door contact switch, right
F⁴	Back-up light switch
F⁵	Luggage compartment light switch
G	Fuel gauge sending unit
G¹	Fuel gauge
H	Horn button
H¹	Horn
H⁵	Ignition key warning buzzer
J	Dimmer relay
J²	Emergency flasher relay
J¹⁶	Power supply relay for fuel injection
J¹⁷	Connection to fuel pump relay
K¹	High beam warning light
K²	Generator charging warning light
K³	Oil pressure warning light
K⁴	Parking light warning light
K⁵	Turn signal warning light
K⁶	Emergency flasher warning light
K⁷	Dual brake circuit warning light
L¹	Sealed-Beam unit left headlight
L²	Sealed-Beam unit right headlight
L⁶	Speedometer light
L⁸	Clock light
L¹⁰	Instrument panel light
M²	Tail/brake light, right
M⁴	Tail/brake light, left
M⁵	Turn signal and parking light, front, left
M⁶	Turn signal, rear, left
M⁷	Turn signal and parking light, front, right
M⁸	Turn signal, rear, right
M¹¹	Side marker light, front
M¹⁶	Back-up light, left
M¹⁷	Back-up light, right
N	Ignition coil
O	Distributor
P¹	Spark plug connector, No. 1 cylinder
P²	Spark plug connector, No. 2 cylinder
P³	Spark plug connector, No. 3 cylinder
P⁴	Spark plug connector, No. 4 cylinder
Q¹	Spark plug, No. 1 cylinder
Q²	Spark plug, No. 2 cylinder
Q³	Spark plug, No. 3 cylinder
Q⁴	Spark plug, No. 4 cylinder
S	Fuse box
S¹	In-line fuse for back-up lights and fresh air fan motor
T	Cable adapter
T¹	Cable connector, single
T²	Cable connector, double
T³	Cable connector, triple
T²⁰	Test network, central plug
V	Windshield wiper motor
V²	Fresh air motor front
W	Interior light
W³	Luggage compartment light
X	License plate light
Y	Clock
①	Ground strap from battery to frame
②	Ground strap from transmission to frame
④	Ground cable from horn to steering coupling
⑤	Ground cable from front axle to frame

Test network

The orange colored spots are the connections in the test network which are wired to the central plug. The numbers in the spots correspond to the terminals in the central plug.

Wiring Circuits

Test network

The circles with the numbers 5 and 31 are connections in the test network which are wired to the central plug.
The numbers in the circles correspond to the terminals in the central plug.

Color of cables:

sw = black
ro = red
ws = white
br = brown
bl = blue
gn = green
ge = yellow

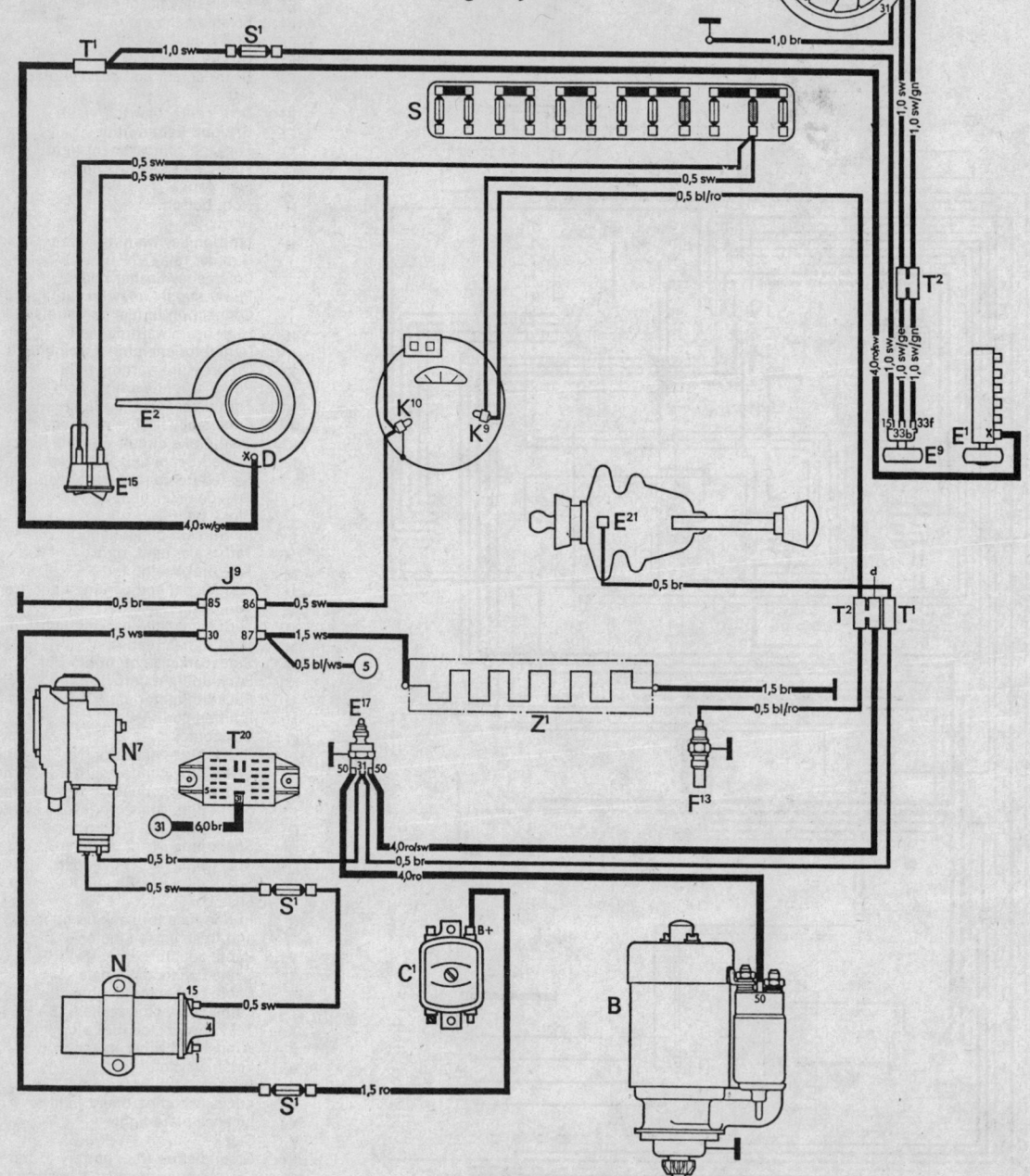

Supplemental wiring diagram—Type 1/Sedan 113 (Super Beetle) from June 1971

B	Starter
C^1	Regulator
D	Ignition / starter switch
d	To ignition / starter switch, terminal 50
E^1	Light switch
E^2	Turn signal and headlight dimmer switch
E^9	Fan motor switch
E^{15}	Rear window defogger switch
E^{17}	Starter cut-out switch
E^{21}	Contact at selector lever
F^{13}	ATF temperature control switch
J^9	Rear window defogger relay
K^9	ATF temperature warning light
K^{10}	Rear window defogger warning light
N	Ignition coil
N^7	Automatic Stick Shift control valve
S	Fuse box
S^1	Fuse for: rear window defogger, Automatic Stick Shift control valve, fan motor
T^1	Cable connector, single
T^2	Cable connector, double
T^{20}	Test network, central plug
V^2	Fan motor
Z^1	Rear window defogger heating element

1402

SPECIFICATIONS

VW Dasher / Rabbit / Scirocco

INTRODUCTION

The Dasher is a unique VW. Most of its features are the opposite of those traditionally associated with VW cars, such as air cooling, rear engine, and torsion bar suspension. It is front wheel drive with a water-cooled, in-line, overhead camshaft engine. Suspension is by coil springs, with McPherson strut spring/shock units at the front. Steering is by rack and pinion, and radial ply tires are standard equipment. The front suspension is designed with negative roll radius. This safety feature keeps the car straight when drag on the front tires is not equal, as would happen with one wheel on wet pavement and one wheel on dry pavement.

The Rabbit and the Scirocco share most of the Dasher's unique features. The most striking difference is that the engine is mounted transversely. The rear wheels are suspended by trailing arms connected by a torsion beam and shock absorber/strut units.

MODEL IDENTIFICATION

Rabbit

Scirocco

Dasher

SERIAL NUMBER IDENTIFICATION

Vehicle Identification Plate

The Dasher vehicle identification plate is riveted to the inner right fender. On the Rabbit and Scirocco, the plate is on top of the body crossmember above the grille.

Chassis Number

The chassis number is located on the driver's side windshield pillar and is visible through the windshield. The Dasher

Dasher chassis number

Rabbit, Scirocco chassis number

chassis number is also stamped on the firewall over the windshield washer reservoir. The Rabbit and Scirocco chassis number is also on top of the right suspension strut mounting and appears on the vehicle identification plate.

Engine Number

The engine number is stamped on the left side (front on the Rabbit and Scirocco) of the engine block between the fuel pump and the distributor.

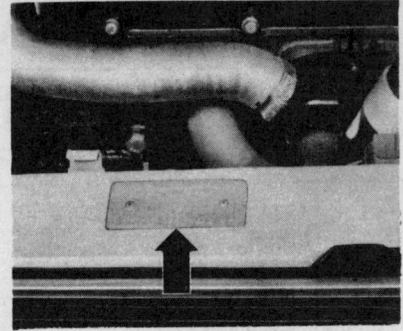

identification plate

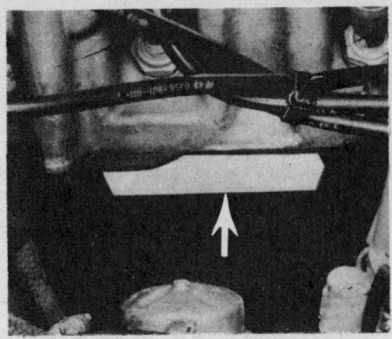

engine number location

GENERAL ENGINE SPECIFICATIONS

Year, Model	Engine Cu in Displacement (cc)	Carburetor Type	Horsepower @ rpm (SAE)	Torque @ rpm (ft lbs) (SAE)	Bore x Stroke (in)	Compression Ratio	Oil Pressure @ rpm (psi)
1974-75 Dasher	89.7 (1,471)	2 bbl Solex	75 @ 5,800	81 @ 4,000	3.01 x 3.15	8.5:1	40 @ 2,500
1975 Scirocco, Rabbit	89.7 (1,471)	2 bbl Zenith	70 @ 6,000	81 @ 3,500	3.01 x 3.15	8.2:1	40 @ 2,500
1976-77 Dasher	96.8 (1588)	CSI Fuel inj.	81 @ 5,800	90 @ 3,300	3.13 x 3.15	8.0:1	40 @ 2,500
1976 Rabbit, Scirocco Scirocco	96.8 (1588)	2 bbl Zenith	71 @ 5,600	82 @ 3,300	3.13 x 3.15	8.2:1	40 @ 2,500
1977 Rabbit, Scirocco	96.8 (1588)	CSI Fuel inj.	81 @ 5,800	90 @ 3,300	3.13 x 3.15	8.0:1	40 @ 2,500
1977 Rabbit (Diesel)	89.7 (1471)	Fuel Inj.	48 @ 5,000	58 @ 5,000	3.01 x 3.15	23.5:1	27 @ 2,000

TUNE-UP SPECIFICATIONS

Year, Model	Engine Displacement (cc)	Spark Plugs		Distributor		Ignition Timing (deg)	Intake Valve Opens (deg)	Compression Pressure (psi)	Idle Speed (rpm)	Valve Clearance (in)	
		Type	Gap (in.)	Point Dwell (deg)	Point Gap (in)					In ▲	Ex ▲
1974 Dasher	1,471	W175 T30 N8Y	0.024-0.028	44-50 ①	0.016	3 ATDC @ idle	4 BTDC	142-184	850-1000	0.008-0.012	0.016-0.020
1975 Dasher	1,471	W200 T30 N8Y	0.024-0.028	44-50	0.016	3 ATDC @ idle	4 BTDC	142-184	850-1000	0.008-0.012	0.016-0.020
1975 Scirocco, Rabbit	1,471	W200 T30 N8Y	0.024-0.028	44-50	0.016	3 ATDC @ idle	4 BTDC	142-184	900-1000	0.008-0.012	0.016-0.020
1976-77 Dasher	1588	W215 T30 N7Y	0.024-0.028	44-50	0.016	3 ATDC @ idle	4 BTDC	142-184	850-1000	0.008-0.012	0.016-0.020
1976-77 Rabbit, Scirocco	1588	W215 T30 N7Y	0.024-0.028	44-50	0.016	3 ATDC @ idle	4 BTDC	142-184	900-1000	0.008-0.012	0.016-0.020

NOTE: The underhood specifications sticker often reflects tune-up specification changes made in production. Sticker figures must be used if they disagree with those in this chart.

① 47°-53°—California

▲ NOTE: Valve clearance need not be adjusted unless it varies more than 0.002 in. from specification.

DIESEL TUNE-UP SPECIFICATIONS

| Model | VALVE CLEARANCE (cold) ① | | Intake valve opens (deg) | Injection pump setting (deg) | INJECTION NOZZLE PRESSURE (psi) | | Idle speed (rpm) ③ | Cranking compression pressure (psi) |
	Intake (in.)	Exhaust (in.)			New	Used		
1977 Diesel Rabbit	0.008-0.012	0.016-0.020	N.A.	Align marks	1849	1706	850-950	398 minimum

① Warm clearance given—Cold clearance: Intake 0.006-0.010
Exhaust 0.014-0.018
Valve clearance need not be adjusted unless it varies more
than 0.002 in. from specification.
N.A. Not Available

FIRING ORDER

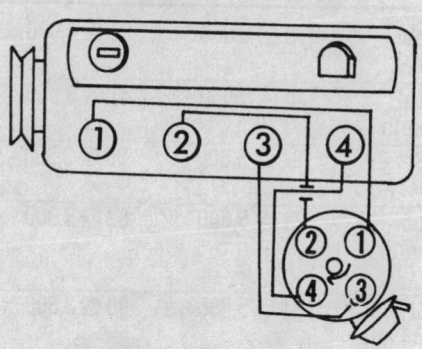

Firing order: 1-3-4-2

CAPACITIES

| Year | Model | Engine Displacement Cu in (cc) | Engine Crankcase (qts) | | Transmission (pts) | | Drive Axle (pts) | Gasoline Tank (gals) | Cooling, System (pts) |
			With Filter	Without Filter	Manual	Automatic			
1974-75	Dasher	89.7 (1,471)	3.7	3.1	3.4①	12.8②	3.0	12.1③	12.7
1975	Scirocco, Rabbit	89.7 (1,471)	3.7	3.1	2.6	12.8②	1.6	12.1	13.6
1976	Dasher	96.8 (1588)	3.7	3.2	5.4	12.8②	3.0	12.1	12.8
1976	Rabbit, Scirocco	96.8 (1588)	3.7	3.2	5.4	12.8②	3.0	12.1	13.8
1977	Dasher	96.8 (1588)	3.7	3.2	3.4	12.4②	1.6	12.1	12.6
1977	Rabbit, Scirocco	96.8 (1588)	3.7	3.5	2.6	12.8②	1.6	12.1	9.8
1977	Rabbit (Diesel)	89.7 (1471)	3.7	3.2	2.6	—	1.6	10.9	12.6

① At change, initial amount 4.2 pts.
② Dry refill; normal refill is 6.4 pts.
③ Doesn't include 1.3 gal reserve.
— Not Applicable

CRANKSHAFT AND CONNECTING ROD SPECIFICATIONS

All measurements are given in inches.

| Model | Crankshaft | | | | Connecting Rod | | |
	Main Brg. Journal Dia.	Main Brg. Oil Clearance	Shaft End-Play	Thrust on No.	Journal Diameter	Oil Clearance	Side Clearance (max.)
1974-77 Dasher, Rabbit, Scirocco	2.126	0.001-0.003	0.003-0.007	3	1.811	0.001-0.003	0.015

NOTE: Main and connecting rod bearings are available in three undersizes.

VALVE SPECIFICATIONS

| Model | Seat Angle (deg) | Spring Test Pressure (lbs. @ in.) | Stem to Guide Clearance (in.) | | Stem Diameter (in.) | |
			Intake	Exhaust	Intake	Exhaust
1974-77 Dasher, Rabbit, Scirocco	45	96-106① @ 0.92 in.	0.001-0.002	0.001-0.002	0.314	0.313

① Outer spring, inner spring test pressure is 46-51 lbs. @ 0.72 in.

NOTE: Exhaust valves must be ground by hand.

PISTON AND RING SPECIFICATIONS

(All measurements in inches)

| Model | Piston Clearance | Ring Gap | | | Ring Side Clearance | | |
		Top Compression	Bottom Compression	Oil Control	Top Compression	Bottom Compression	Oil Control
1974-77 Dasher, Rabbit, Scirocco	0.001-0.003	0.001-0.002	0.001-0.002	0.001-0.002	0.001-0.002	0.001-0.002	0.001-0.002
1977 Diesel Rabbit	0.001-0.003	0.012-0.020	0.012-0.020	0.010-0.016	0.001-0.002	0.002-0.003	0.002-0.003

NOTE: Three piston sizes are available to accommodate over-bores up to 0.040 in.

TORQUE SPECIFICATIONS

(All readings in ft lbs)

| Model | Cylinder Head Bolts | Rod Bearing Bolts* | Main Bearing Bolts | Crankshaft Pulley Bolt | Flywheel To Crankshaft Bolts | Manifold | |
						Intake	Exhaust
1974-77 Dasher	56①	30	47	58	36	18	18

TORQUE SPECIFICATIONS

(All readings in ft lbs)

Model	Cylinder Head Bolts	Rod* Bearing Bolts	Main Bearing Bolts	Crankshaft Pulley Bolt	Flywheel To Crankshaft Bolts	Manifold	
						Intake	Exhaust
1974-77 Rabbit, Scirocco	54①	33	47	58	54②	18	18
1977 Diesel Rabbit	69①	33	47	56	54②	18	18

① Cold, 62 ft. lbs. warm.
② Pressure plate to crankshaft bolts.
* Always use new bolts.

TORQUE SEQUENCES

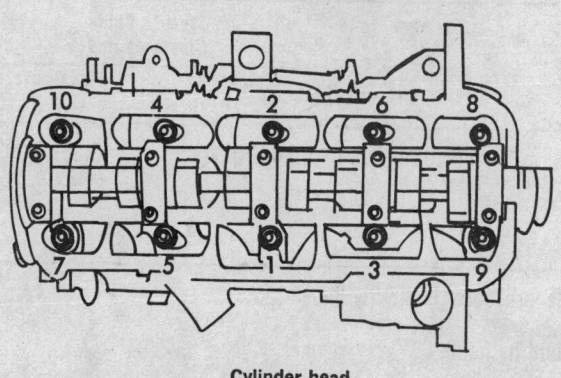

Cylinder head

BRAKE SPECIFICATIONS

Year	Model	Lug Nut Torque (ft/lbs)	Master Cylinder Bore	Brake Disc		Brake Drum			Minimum Brake Lining Thickness*	
				Minimum Thickness	Maximum Run-out	Diameter	Maximum Machine o/s	Max. Wear Limit	Front	Rear
1974-77	Dasher	65	0.82	0.41	0.004	7.87	7.90	7.97	0.078	0.098
1975-77	Rabbit, Scirroco	65	0.82	0.41	0.004	7.08	7.10	7.12	0.078	0.098

* NOTE: Minimum lining thickness is as recommended by manufacturer. Due to variations in state inspection regulations, the minimum thickness may be different than that recommended by the manufacturer.

BATTERY AND STARTER SPECIFICATIONS

(All models use 12 volt, negative ground system)

Year	Model	Battery Amp Hour Capacity	Lock Test			No Load Test			Brush Spring Tension (oz)	Minimum Brush Length (in)
			Amps	Volts	Torque (ft/lbs)	Amps	Volts	RPM		
1974-77	All	45/54*	280-370	7.5	2.42	33-55	11.5	6000-8000	35.5	0.5

* w/AC

WHEEL ALIGNMENT

| Year | Model | CASTER* | | CAMBER | | Toe-in (in.) | Steering Axis Inclination* (deg) |
		Range (deg)	Pref Setting (deg)	Range (deg)	Pref Setting (deg)		
1974-77	Dasher	0°-1°	0°30′	0°5′-0°55′	0°30′	0.08	10°30′
1975-76	Rabbit, Scirocco	+1°30′-2°30′	+2°	+0°-1°	+30′	0.08	10°30′
1977	Rabbit, Scirocco	+1°20′-2°20′	+1°50′	−10′-+50′	+20′	0.08	10°30′

* Not adjustable

Rear Wheel Alignment

Camber (Not Adjustable)   Rabbit (to Ch. No. 176 3 241 690)—1°N ± 30′
Rabbit (from Ch. No. 176 3 261 691)—1¼°N ± 30′

Scirocco (all)—1°N ± 30′
Dasher (all)—½°N ± 30′

Toe-In (Not Adustable)   Rabbit—0° ± 15′
Scirocco (to Ch. No. 536 2 031 722)—10′P ± 30′
Scirocco (from Ch. No. 536 2 031 723)—20′P ± 30′
Dasher—±25′

TUNE-UP PROCEDURES

VW recommends a tune-up, including new points and plugs, at 10,000 mile intervals.

Spark Plugs

The firing order is 1–3–4–2, with No. 1 cylinder at the front (right on the Rabbit and Scirocco) of the engine.

1. Grasp the spark plug boot and pull it straight out. Don't pull on the wire.
2. Place the spark plug socket firmly on the plug and screw the spark plug out. **NOTE:** *The cylinder head is aluminum alloy, which is easily stripped of threads. Remove the plugs only when the engine is cold.*

If removal is difficult, loosen the plug only slightly and drip penetrating oil onto the threads.

3. Inspect the plugs and clean or discard them. The recommended spark plug gap is listed in the "Tune-Up Specifications" chart.
4. Torque the new spark plugs to 22 ft lbs. Install the ignition wire boots firmly.

Breaker Points and Condenser

Snap off the two retaining clips on the distributor cap. Remove the cap and examine it for cracks, deterioration, or carbon tracking. Replace the cap, if necessary, by transferring one wire at a time from the old cap to the new one.

Examine the rotor for corrosion or wear and replace it if questionable. Remove the dust shield. Check the points for pitting and burning. Slight imperfections on the contact surface may be filed off with a point file. It is best to replace the breaker point set. Always replace the condenser when you replace the point set.

To replace the breaker points:

1. Remove the rotor.
2. Unsnap the point connector from the terminal at the side of the distributor. Remove the retaining screw, and lift out the point set.
3. Install the new point set, making sure that the pin on the bottom engages the hole in the breaker plate.
4. Install the wire connector and the retaining screws (hand-tight).
5. Turn the engine until the breaker arm rubbing block is on the high point of one of the cam lobes.
6. A 0.016 in. feeler gauge should just slip through the points. If the gap is incor-

rect, pivot a screwdriver in the point set notch and the two projections on the breaker plate to bring it within specifications.

7. When the gap is correct, tighten the retaining screw.
8. Lubricate the distributor cam with silicone grease.
9. Install the dust cover, rotor and distributor cap.
10. Check the dwell angle and the ignition timing.
11. The condenser is mounted on the outside of the distributor. Undo the mounting screw and the terminal block to replace.

Dwell Angle

The dwell angle or cam angle is the number of degrees that the distributor cam rotates while the points are closed. There is an inverse relationship between dwell angle and point gap. Increasing the point gap will decrease the dwell angle

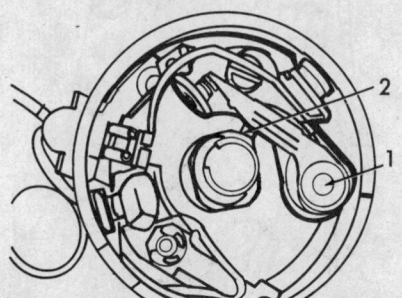

Breaker points and condenser—Lubricate at (1) with a drop of engine oil and at (2) with silicone (high melting point) grease

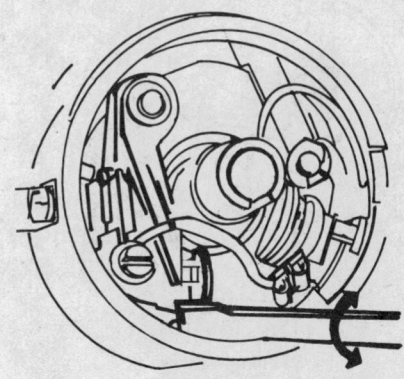

Adjusting point gap

and vice versa. Checking the dwell angle with a meter is a far more accurate method of measuring point opening than the feeler gauge method.

After setting the point gap to specification with a feeler gauge, check the dwell angle. Attach the dwell meter. The negative lead is grounded and the positive lead is connected to the primary wire, Terminal No. 1 that runs from the coil to the distributor. Start the engine, let it idle and reach operating temperature, and observe the dwell on the meter. The reading should fall within the allowable range. If it does not, the gap will have to be reset. Dwell can also be checked with the engine cranking.

Ignition Timing

Ignition timing is always adjusted after the points are gapped (dwell angle changed) since altering the dwell affects the timing.

1. Attach a timing light. Hook-up a dwell/tachometer.

2. Locate the timing mark opening in the clutch or torque convertor housing at the rear of the engine directly behind the distributor. The 0°T mark stands for TDC or 0°. The 3 mark to the right means 3° ATDC. Mark them with chalk so that they will be more visible. Don't disconnect the vacuum line.

3. Start the engine and allow it to reach normal operating temperature. The engine should be at normal idle speed.

4. Shine the timing light at the marks.

5. The 3° line and the V-shaped pointer should be aligned.

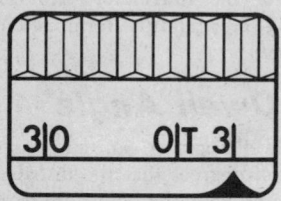

Timing mark aligned at 3° ATDC

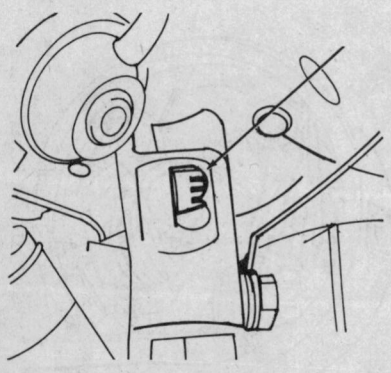

Timing window

6. If not, loosen the distributor hold down bolt and rotate the distributor very slowly to align the marks.

7. Tighten the mounting nut when the ignition timing is correct.

8. Recheck the timing when the distributor is secured.

Valve Lash

Check the valve clearance every 20,-000 miles in firing order, with the engine at normal operating temperature.

1. Remove the camshaft cover and the distributor cap.

2. Set the engine at TDC on No. 1 cylinder by aligning the 0°T mark on the flywheel with the pointer and aligning the distributor rotor with the No. 1 cylinder mark on the rim of the distributor body.

NOTE: *Always turn the crankshaft in the normal direction of rotation. There is a hole in the body behind the front license plate through which a wrench can be used on the crankshaft on the Dasher.*

3. The valve clearances of cylinder No. 1 should be checked when the valves of No. 4 cylinder overlap, i.e. when both No. 4 cylinder valves move in opposite directions simultaneously. It may be necessary to move the crankshaft slightly to find this position. When this happens, the exhaust valve is closing and the intake opening. Check and note the clearance of both the intake and exhaust valves for No. 1 cylinder.

4. Turn the crankshaft 180° (90° at the distributor rotor) in the normal direction of rotation. Check and note the valve clearances of cylinder No. 3 at the overlap position of cylinder No. 2.

5. Turn the crankshaft 180°. Check and note the valve clearances of cylinder No. 4 at the overlap position of cylinder No. 1.

6. Turn the crankshaft 180°. Check and note the valve clearances of cylinder No. 2 at the overlap position of cylinder No. 3.

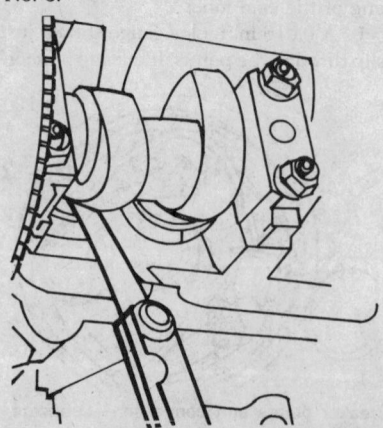

Checking valve clearance with a feeler gauge

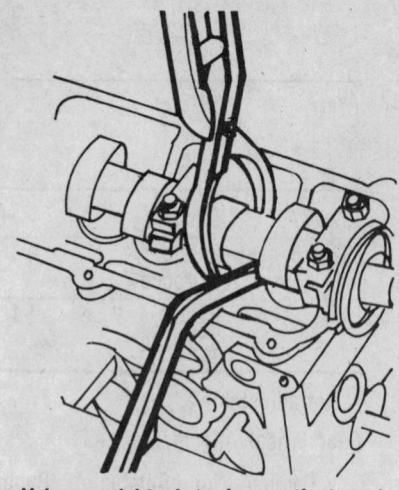

Using special tools to depress the tappet and remove the tappet clearance disc

7. Compare the noted clearances with those listed in the Tune-Up Specifications Chart. Adjustment is made by replacing the tappet clearance disc in the top of each tappet. These are available in 26 sizes ranging from 3.0 mm (0.119 in) to 4.25 mm (0.166 in) in increments of 0.05 mm (0.002 in). The thickness of each disc is marked on the bottom.

NOTE: *If a valve clearance deviates 0.-002 in or less from the specified clearance, it need not be adjusted.*

8. To remove a tappet clearance disc, turn the cylinder to TDC and press down the tappet so that the disc can be lifted out. A special tool is available from VW for this operation. Once the disc is removed, check its size and determine what size will be needed to produce the required adjustment.

NOTE: *Before depressing the tappets, turn them so their openings are at right angles to the camshaft.*

9. Install the required disc and turn the tappet back to its normal direction. When all the clearances have been corrected, recheck valve clearances.

Carburetor

The Dasher carburetor is a Solex 32/35 DIDTA two barrel unit with a vacuum operated secondary barrel. The Rabbit and Scirocco use a Zenith 32/32–2B2 two barrel carburetor with a vacuum operated secondary barrel and dual floats.

Idle Speed Adjustment

1. Start the engine and run it until normal operating temperature is reached.

2. Hook-up a tachometer to the engine and observe the idle speed.

3. If the idle speed is not as specified, turn the curb idle screw to correct it. Make sure that you are turning the correct screw. Do not mistake the idle mixture screw for the curb idle screw.

Idle speed adjustment screw (all carbureted models)

Idle Mixture Adjustment

This adjustment should only be performed with a CO meter. Notice that the Dasher California idle mixture screw is in a different location.

All 1974 Dasher Models Except California

1. Run the engine until it reaches normal operating temperature.
2. Ignition timing should be correctly set at 3° ATDC.
3. Idle speed should be as specified in tune-up chart.
4. Adjust the CO level with idle mixture screw to 0.4–1.6%.

1974 California Dasher Models and all 1975 Dasher Models

1. Run the engine until it reaches normal operating temperature.
2. Disconnect the hose that connects the air injection pump and the air manifold at the pump and plug it.
3. Ignition timing should be adjusted to 3° ATDC and idle speed set at specified rpm.
4. Adjust the CO level with the idle mixture screw to 1.5%.

Carburetor mixture screw—1974 California Dasher and all 1975 Dashers

5. Unplug and connect the air injection pump hose. The CO level should now fall below 1%.

1975 Rabbit, Scirocco

1. Run the engine until it reaches normal operating temperature.
2. Check the ignition timing and idle speed are as specified.
3. Adjust the CO level with the idle mixture screw to 2%.

CIS Fuel Injection

Idle and CO Adjustment

The following adjustments can be made *only* with a CO meter and the CO adjusting tool (VW–P377).
1. Run the engine until it reaches normal operating temperature.
2. Adjust the ignition timing to specification with the vacuum hoses connected and the engine at idle.
3. Adjust the idle speed to specification.
4. Remove the charcoal filter hose from the air cleaner.
5. Turn the headlight high beams and A/C on.
6. Remove the plug from the CO adjusting hole and insert adjustment tool

Rabbit and Scirocco idle mixture adjustment screw

Idle speed adjustment screw—CIS fuel injection models

Vacuum unit second stage

Water heated* choke

Dashpot

Vacuum pickup for ignition

Vacuum pickup for EGR valve

Idle mixture adjusting screw

Idle speed adjusting screw

Carburetor mixture screw—1974 Dasher (except California)

CO adjusting tool installed—CIS fuel injection

VW–P377. Turn the adjustment screw clockwise to raise the percentage of CO and counterclockwise to lower the percentage of CO.

CAUTION: Do Not *push the adjustment tool down or accelerate the engine with the tool in place.*

7. Remove the tool after each adjustment and accelerate the engine briefly before reading the percentage of CO. The correct CO values are as follows:

CO percentages are:

Dasher	California maximum	0.5%
	USA maximum-auto trans	
1.0%		
	manual trans	1.5%
Rabbit & Scirocco	California maximum	0.3%
	USA maximum-auto trans	
1.0%		
	manual trans	1.5%

ENGINE ELECTRICAL
Distributor

The distributor is a single breaker point unit. It has both centrifugal and vacuum advance mechanisms. A vacuum retard system works only at idle.

The distributor is gear driven by an intermediate shaft which also drives the fuel pump. The distributor shaft also turns the oil pump.

Removal and Installation

1. Disconnect the coil high tension wire.
2. Detach the primary wire.
3. Remove the distributor cap.
4. Turn the engine until the rotor aligns with the index mark on the outer edge of the distributor. This is the No. 1 position. Mark the bottom of the distributor housing and its mounting flange on the engine.
5. Remove the bolt and lift off the retaining flange. Lift the distributor straight out of the engine.

If the engine has not been disturbed while the distributor was out i.e., the crankshaft was not turned, then reinstall the distributor in the reverse order of removal. Carefully align the marks.

If the engine has been rotated while the distributor was out, then proceed as follows:

1. Turn the crankshaft so that No. 1 piston is on its compression stroke and the 0˚T timing mark is aligned with the V-shaped pointer.
2. Turn the distributor so that the rotor points approximately 15° before the No. 1 cylinder position on the distributor.
3. Insert the distributor into the en-

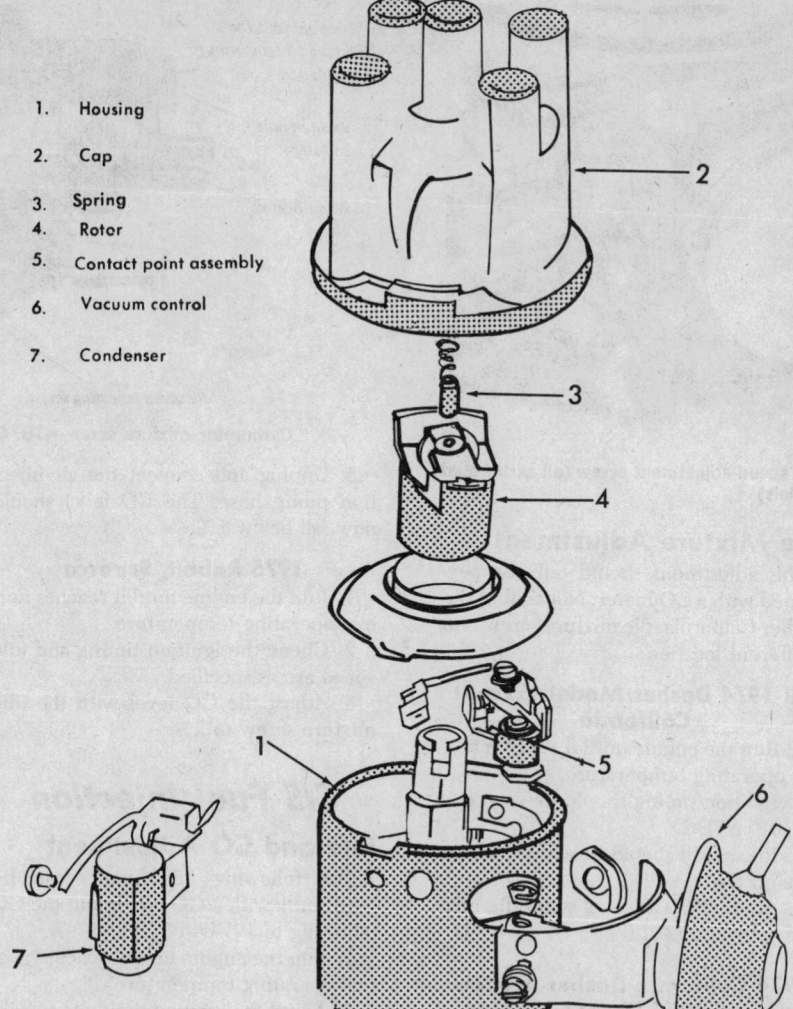

1. Housing
2. Cap
3. Spring
4. Rotor
5. Contact point assembly
6. Vacuum control
7. Condenser

Exploded view of distributor

gine block. If the oil pump drive doesn't engage, remove the distributor and, using a long screwdriver turn the pump shaft so that it is parallel to the centerline of the crankshaft.

4. Install the distributor, aligning the marks. Tighten the retaining nut.

5. Install the cap. Adjust the ignition timing.

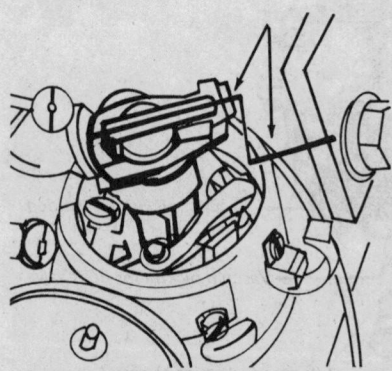

Rotor alignment with the notch for No. 1 cylinder

Alternator

Alternator Precautions

An alternating current (AC) generator (alternator) is used. Unlike the direct current (DC) generators used in many older cars, there are several precautions which must be strictly observed in order to avoid damaging the unit. They are:

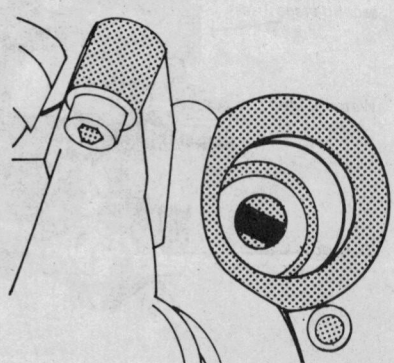

The oil pump drive should be parallel to the crankshaft

1. Reversing the battery connections will result in damage to the diodes.

2. Booster batteries should be connected from negative to negative, and positive to positive.

3. Never use a fast charger as a booster to start cars with AC circuits.

4. When servicing the battery with a fast charger, always disconnect the car battery cables.

5. Never attempt to polarize an AC generator.

6. Avoid long soldering times when replacing diodes or transistors. Prolonged heat is damaging to AC generators.

7. Do not use test lamps of more than 12 volts (V) for checking diode continuity.

8. Do not short across or ground any of the terminals on the AC generator.

9. The polarity of the battery, generator, and regulator must be matched and considered before making any electrical connections within the system.

10. Never operate the AC generator on an open circuit. Make sure that all connections within the circuit are clean and tight.

11. Disconnect the battery terminals when performing any service on the electrical system. This will eliminate the possibility of accidental reversal of polarity.

12. Disconnect the battery ground cable if arc welding is to be done on any part of the car.

Removal and Installation

The alternator and voltage regulator are combined in one housing. No voltage adjustment can be made with this unit. The regulator can be replaced without removing the alternator. Unbolt the regulator and remove from the rear.

1. Disconnect the battery cables.

2. Remove the multi-connector retaining bracket and unplug the connector from the rear of the alternator.

3. Loosen and remove the top mounting nut and bolt.

4. Using a socket inserted through the timing belt cover (it is not necessary to remove the cover), loosen the lower mounting bolt.

Removing the lower alternator bolt through the timing cover

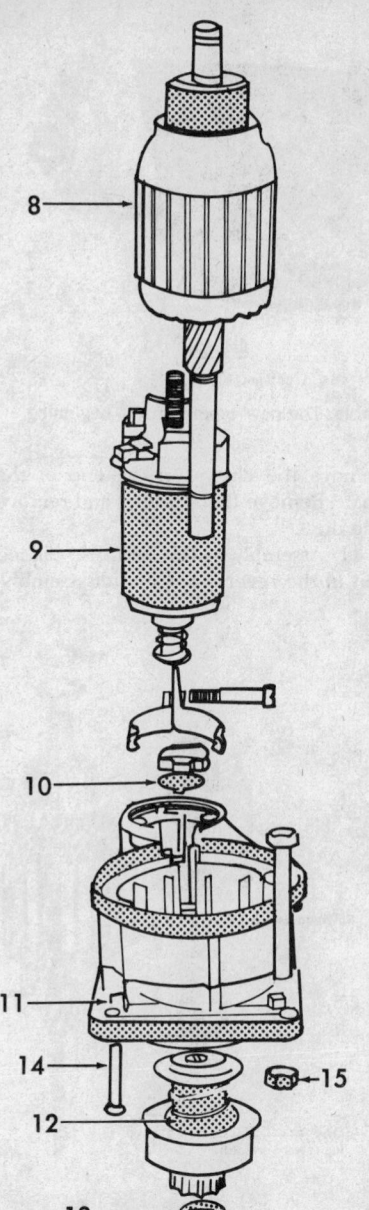
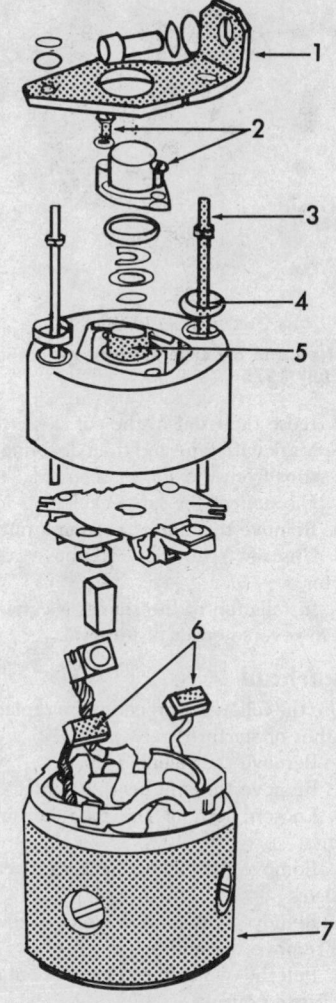

1. Mounting bracket		9. Solenoid	
2. End cap screws		10. Disc	
3. Housing screws		11. Mounting housing	
4. Cupped washer		12. Drive pinion	
5. End plate bushing		13. Stop ring	
6. Brushes		14. Solenoid bolt	
7. Field coil housing		15. Starter bolt and nut	
8. Armature		16. Circlip	

Exploded view of Dasher starter

5. Swing the alternator over and remove the alternator belt.

6. Remove the lower nut and bolt.

7. Remove the alternator.

8. Install the alternator with the lower bolt. *Do not* tighten it at this point.

9. Install the alternator belt over the pulleys.

10. Loosely install the top mounting bolt and pivot the alternator until the belt is correctly tensioned.

11. Tighten the top and bottom bolts to 14 ft lbs.

12. Connect the alternator and battery wires.

Belt Replacement and Tensioning

1. Loosen the top alternator mounting

bolt.

2. Using a socket inserted through the timing belt cover loosen the lower mounting bolt.

3. Using a pry bar swing the alternator over and remove the belt.

4. Slip the new belt over the pulleys.

5. Pry the alternator over until the belt deflection midway between the crankshaft pulley and the alternator pulley is ⅜–9/16 in. (10–15 mm).

6. Securely tighten the mounting bolts.

Starter

Removal and Installation

1. Disconnect the battery ground cable.

New type
(Part No. 055-911-023B)

Old type
(Part No. 055-911-023)

New and old type starters are not interchangeable. The new type is used beginning July 1975

2. Raise the front of the car.

3. Mark with tape and then disconnect the wires from the starter solenoid.

4. Disconnect the large cable.

5. Remove the starter retaining nuts.

6. Unscrew the bolt. Remove the starter.

7. Installation of the starter is carried out in reverse order of removal.

Overhaul

Use the following procedure to replace brushes or starter drive.

1. Remove the solenoid.

2. Remove the end bearing cap.

3. Loosen both of the long housing screws.

4. Remove the lockwasher and spacer washers.

5. Remove the long housing screws and remove the end cover.

6. Pull the two field coil brushes out of the brush housing.

7. Remove the brush housing assembly.

8. Loosen the nut on the solenoid housing, remove the sealing disc, and remove the solenoid operating lever.

9. Loosen the large screws on the side of the starter body and remove the field coil along with the brushes.

NOTE: *If the brushes require replacement, the field coil and brushes and/or the brush housing and its brushes must be replaced as a unit.*

10. If the starter drive is being replaced, push the stop ring down and

remove the circlip on the end of the shaft. Remove the stop-ring and remove the drive.

11. Assembly of the starter is carried out in the reverse order of disassembly.

Use a gear puller to install the stop-ring in its groove. Use a new circlip on the shaft.

Solenoid Replacement

1. Remove the starter.

2. Remove the nut which secures the connector strip on the end of the solenoid.

3. Take out the two retaining screws on the mounting bracket and pull out the solenoid after it has been unhooked from the operating lever.

4. Installation is the reverse of removal. In order to facilitate engagement of the lever, the pinion should be pulled out as far as possible when inserting the solenoid.

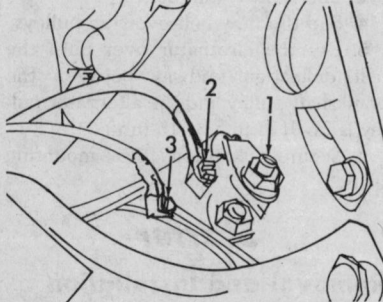

Starter electrical connections—(A) solenoid, (B) coil, (C) positive battery cable

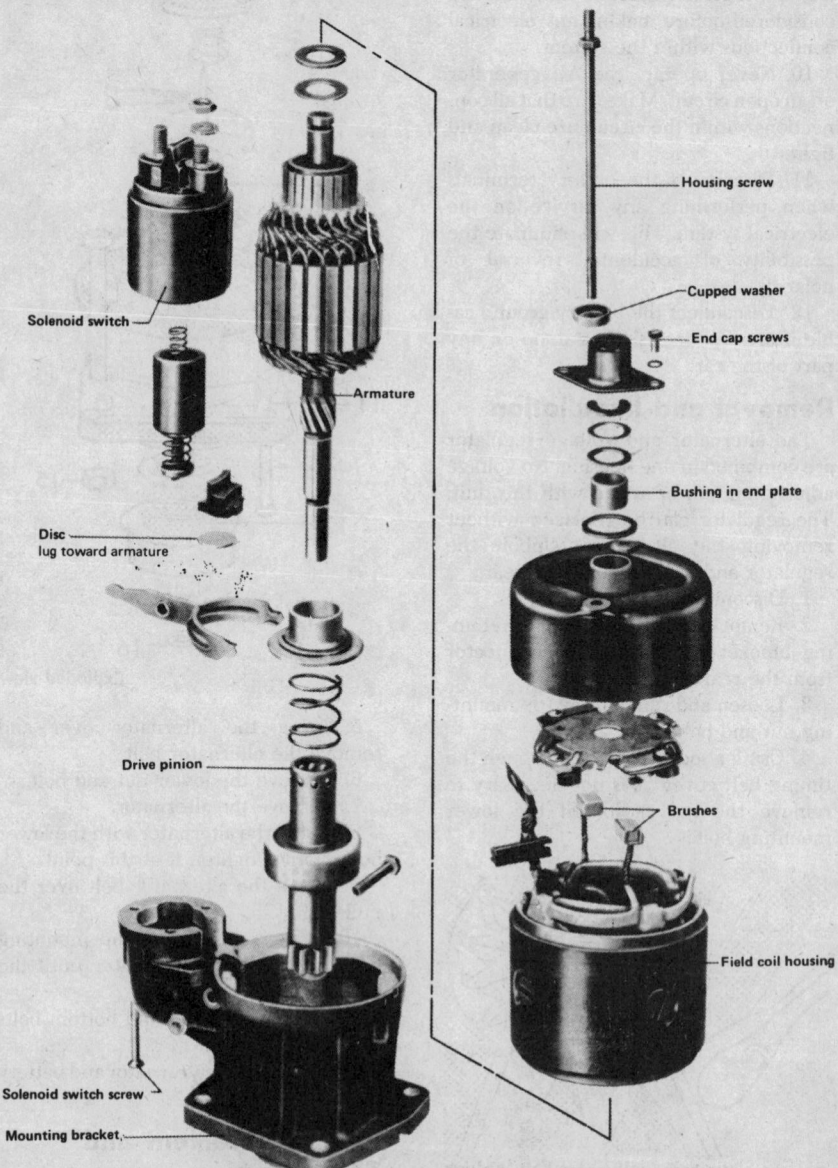

Solenoid switch

Armature

Disc
lug toward armature

Drive pinion

Solenoid switch screw

Mounting bracket

Housing screw

Cupped washer

End cap screws

Bushing in end plate

Brushes

Field coil housing

Exploded view of Rabbit, Scirocco starter

ENGINE MECHANICAL

The engine is an inline four cylinder unit with single overhead camshaft. It is inclined 30° to the right (to the rear in the Rabbit and Scirocco). The crankshaft runs in five bearings with thrust taken on the center bearing. The cylinder block is cast iron. A steel reinforced rubber belt drives the intermediate shaft and camshaft. The intermediate shaft drives the oil pump, distributor and fuel pump.

The cylinder head is lightweight aluminum alloy. The intake and exhaust manifolds are mounted on the same side of the cylinder head. The valves are opened and closed by camshaft lobes operating on cupped cam followers which fit over the valves and springs. This design results in lighter valve train weight and fewer moving parts.

Engine Removal and Installation

Dasher

1. Disconnect the battery cables.
2. Remove the exhaust manifold heater hose and breather hose from the air cleaner.
3. Remove the air cleaner assembly.
4. Pull the clip off the accelerator cable and detach the cable.
5. Loosen the upper adjustment nut on the clutch cable and detach it.
6. Disconnect the fuel line from the fuel pump, plug it, and place it out of the way.
7. Detach emission control hoses.
8. On 1974 models, disconnect relay plate fuse box. Bend the harness clip open.
9. Disconnect the wiring from the alternator.
10. Detach the clip and remove the heater cable.

CAUTION: Do Not *disconnect refrigerant lines on cars equipped with air conditioning.*

11. On cars with air conditioning;
    a. Remove the horn, compressor and condenser assemblies.
    b. Move the compressor and condensers out of the way, without disconnecting the refrigerant lines.
    c. Disconnect the vacuum hoses.
12. Disconnect the front engine mount and remove the mount bracket.
13. Drain the coolant from the radiator. The plug is located near the lower hose. Drain the cylinder block at the plug near the starter.
14. Disconnect the electrical wire from the coil and distributor, oil pressure and temperature sending units, fan and

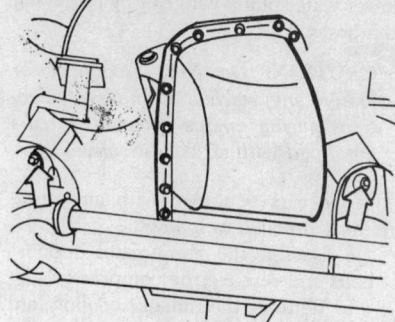

Dasher engine side mounts

A fixture of this type can be arranged to support the Dasher transmission, or a floor jack can be used

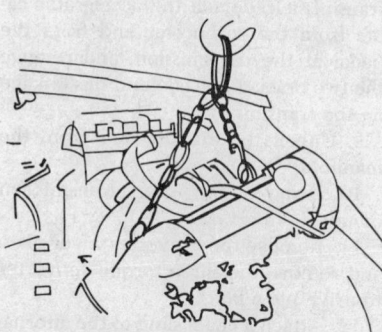

Lifting the Dasher engine out of the car. Note how it must be turned for removal

the thermal switch on the radiator.
15. Disconnect the radiator and heater hoses from the engine. Detach the heater valve cable.
16. Loosen the radiator shroud retainers. Remove the mounting bolts and nuts and lift out the radiator and fan.
17. Raise the front of the car and safely support it.
18. Remove the starter.
19. Disconnect the exhaust pipe from the manifold.
20. Detach the engine side mounts.
21. Loosen the upper engine-to-transmission bolts. Remove the lower bolts. If the car is equipped with an automatic transmission, remove the three torque converter-to-flywheel bolts by working through the starter hole. Use a bar to hold the flywheel.
22. Support the transmission with a floor jack.

23. Lower the car until the wheels are on the ground.
24. Attach the hoist to the engine lift points.
25. Raise the engine/transmission until the transmission touches the steering.
26. Adjust your jack or support so that the transmission is held firmly.
27. Remove the upper engine-to-transmission bolts.
28. Pry the engine and transmission apart and remove the intermediate plate. Install a bar or cable to the torque converter housing on automatic cars to prevent the converter from falling out.
29. Remove the engine by slowly lifting and turning simultaneously.

CAUTION: *Do this very carefully to avoid damaging the driveshafts or transmission.*

30. Installation is the reverse of removal. Be careful not to damage the input shaft of the transmission during installation. Install new torque converter mounting bolts. Tighten the torque converter bolts to 25 ft lbs, engine to transaxle bolts to 40 ft lbs, and the engine mount bolts to 32 ft lbs.

Rabbit and Scirocco With Manual Transmission

The engine and transmission are removed as an assembly.

1. Disconnect the battery ground cable.
2. Drain the coolant by unbolting the lower water pump flange or by removing the hoses.

CAUTION: Do Not *disconnect or loosen any refrigerant hose connections during engine removal on cars equipped with air conditioning.*

3. On cars equipped with air conditioning:
    a. Loosen the compressor support bolts and remove the compressor.
    b. Remove the radiator cooling fan, air ducts and radiator.
    c. Remove the condenser.

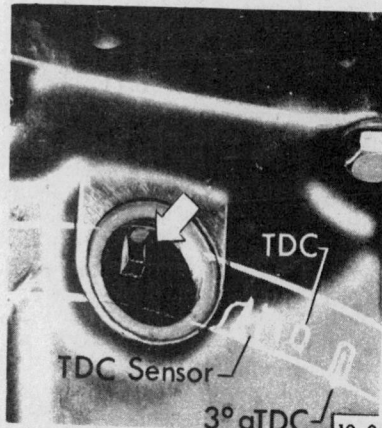

Aligning flywheel for manual transmission and engine separation—Rabbit, Scirocco

d. Place the air conditioning compressor and condenser out of the way without disconnecting any refrigerant lines.

4. Remove the radiator with the air ducts and fan.

5. Detach all the electrical wires connecting the engine to the body.

6. Disconnect and plug the fuel line at the fuel pump. Detach the coolant hoses at the left end of the engine. Disconnect the accelerator cable and remove the air cleaner.

7. Disconnect the speedometer cable from the transmission. Detach the clutch cable.

8. Remove the engine support to the right of the starter.

9. Remove the headlight caps inside the engine compartment.

10. Unbolt the driveshafts from the transmission and wire them up.

11. Unbolt the exhaust pipe from the manifold and unbolt the exhaust pipe brace.

12. Unbolt the transmission rear mount from the body (alongside the tunnel).

13. Detach the ground strap from the transmission and body.

14. Remove the shift linkage.

15. Attach a chain sling to the alternator bracket and the lifting eye at the left end of the engine. Lift the engine and transmission slightly.

16. Detach the engine carrier from the body and remove the left transmission carrier.

17. Lift the engine/transmission assembly carefully out of the car.

18. To separate the engine and transmission, turn the flywheel to align the lug on the flywheel (to the left of TDC) with the pointer in the opening. Remove the cover plate over the driveshaft flange and remove the engine to transmission bolts and the transmission housing cover plate.

To install the engine:

19. To attach the transmission to the engine, the recess in the flywheel edge must be at 3:00 O'Clock (facing the left end of the engine). Torque the engine to transmission bolts to 40 ft lbs. Lift the engine/transmission assembly into place and loosely attach the left transmission carrier to the transmission. Align the assembly, then bolt the engine and transmission carrier to the body. Torque the 10 mm bolts to 29 ft lbs. Torque the driveshaft flange bolts to 32 ft lbs. Refill the cooling system.

Rabbit and Scirocco With Automatic Transmission

The engine and transmission are removed as an assembly.

1. Disconnect both battery cables.

2. Drain the coolant by unbolting the lower water pump flange or by removing the hoses.

CAUTION: *Do Not disconnect or loosen any refrigerant hose connections during engine removal on cars equipped with air conditioning.*

3. On cars equipped with air conditioning, proceed as follows:

a. Loosen the compressor support bolts and remove the compressor.

b. Remove the radiator cooling fan, air ducts, and radiator.

c. Remove the condenser.

d. Place the air conditioning components out of the way without disconnecting any refrigerant lines.

4. Remove the radiator with the air ducts and fan.

5. Remove the air cleaner.

6. Detach the speedometer cable from the transmission.

7. Detach all electrical wires connecting the engine to the body. Detach the coolant hoses.

8. Remove the screws holding the accelerator cable bracket to the carburetor float bowl, shift into P, detach the end of the gearshift selector cable from the transmission, detach the accelerator cable from the carburetor and from the pedal at the transmission, and remove the two bracket bolts behind this linkage on the transmission.

9. Unbolt the exhaust pipe from the manifold.

10. Remove the rear transmission mount.

11. Remove the converter cover plate and remove the three torque converter to drive plate bolts.

12. Attach a chain sling to the alternator bracket and the lifting eye at the left end of the engine. It may be necessary to remove the alternator. Lift the engine and transmission slightly.

13. Detach the engine front mounting support; remove the left transmission carrier and the right engine carrier.

14. Lift the engine/transmission assembly carefully out of the car.

15. The transmission can now be detached from the engine.

To install the engine:

16. The engine to transmission bolts should be torqued to 40 ft lbs. Lift the engine/transmission assembly into place and install the left transmission carrier, tightening first the body, then the transmission bolts. Lower the assembly to attach the engine carrier to the body, tightening the bolts to 40 ft lbs. Install the engine mounting support. Torque converter bolts should be torqued to 21 ft lbs and drive shaft bolts to 32 ft lbs. Refill the cooling system. Check the adjustment of transmission and carburetor linkages.

Cylinder Head

Removal and Installation Carbureted Engines

The engine should be cold before the cylinder head can be removed. The head is retained by 10 allen head bolts. It can be removed without removing the intake and exhaust manifolds.

1. Disconnect the battery ground cable.

2. Drain the cooling system.

3. Remove the air cleaner. Disconnect the fuel line.

4. Disconnect the radiator, heater, and choke hoses.

5. Disconnect all electrical wires. Remove the spark plug wires.

6. Separate the exhaust manifold from the exhaust pipe.

7. Disconnect the EGR line from the exhaust manifold. Remove the EGR valve and filter from the intake manifold.

8. Remove the carburetor.

9. Disconnect the air pump fittings.

10. Remove the timing belt cover and belt.

11. Loosen the cylinder head bolts in the reverse of the tightening sequence.

12. Remove the bolts and lift the head straight off.

13. Install the new cylinder head gasket with the word TOP or OBEN up.

14. Install bolts No. 7 and 8 first, these holes are smaller and will properly locate the gasket and cylinder head.

15. Install the remaining bolts. Tighten them in three stages in the sequence shown. Cylinder head bolt torque (cold) is 55 ft lbs.

NOTE: *After approximately 300 miles, retighten the cylinder head bolts. Torque them hot to 61 ft lbs.*

16. Install the remaining components in the reverse order of removal.

Removal and Installation— Fuel Injected Engines

1. Disconnect the battery ground cable.

2. Drain the cooling system.

3. Disconnect the air duct from the throttle valve assembly.

4. Disconnect the throttle cable from the throttle valve assembly.

5. Remove the injectors and disconnect the line from the cold start valve.

6. Disconnect the radiator and heater hoses.

7. Disconnect the vacuum and PCV lines (label lines for installation).

8. Remove the auxiliary air regulator from the intake manifold.

9. Disconnect all electrical lines and remove the spark plugs (label all lines and wires for installation).

10. Separate the exhaust manifold

1. Valve keeper
2. Valve springs
3. Valve stem seal
4. Lower valve spring seat
5. Valve guide
6. Cylinder head bolt
7. Valves
8. Cylinder head gasket
9. Cylinder head

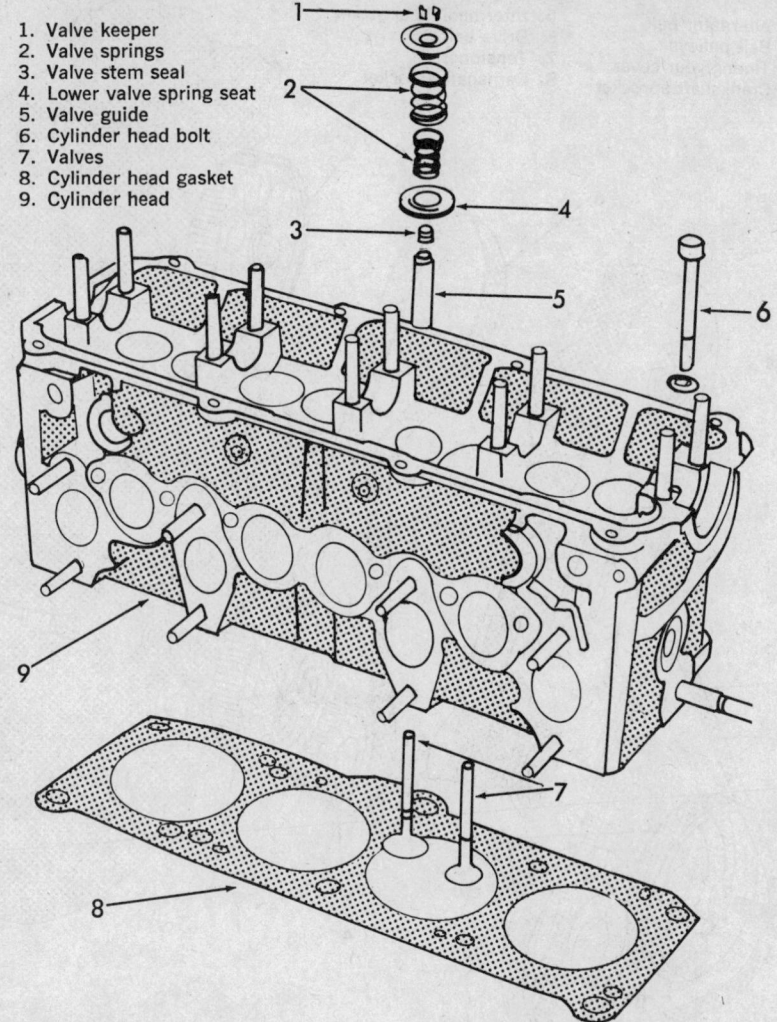

Exploded view of cylinder head showing valve train components

from the exhaust pipe.

11. Remove the EGR line from the exhaust manifold.

12. Remove the intake manifold.

13. Remove the timing belt cover and belt.

14. Loosen the cylinder head bolts in the reverse of the tightening sequence.

15. Remove the bolts and lift the head straight off.

16. Check the flatness of the cylinder block.

17. Install the new cylinder head gasket with the word TOP or OBEN facing upward.

18. Install bolts No. 7 and 8 first, these holes are smaller and will properly locate the gasket and cylinder head.

19. Install the remaining bolts. Tighten them in the three stage sequence shown in the illustration. Cylinder head bolts must be torqued cold to 54 ft. lbs.

NOTE: *After 300 miles, retighten the cylinder head bolts.*

20. Install the remaining components in the reverse order of removal.

Overhaul

Valve guides are a shrink fit. Always install new valve seals when doing a valve job. Valve seats are not replaceable, the cylinder head should be replaced if the valve pocket depth exceeds 0.354 in. (9 mm) for intake valves and/or 0.378 in. (9.6 mm) for exhaust valves.

Refer to general information section under Engine Overhaul.

Intake Manifold

Removal and Installation— Carbureted Models

1. Remove the air cleaner. Drain the cooling system.

2. Disconnect the accelerator cable.

3. Disconnect the EGR valve connections.

4. Detach all electrical leads.

5. Disconnect the coolant hoses.

6. Disconnect the fuel line from the carburetor.

7. Remove the vacuum hoses from the carburetor.

8. Loosen and remove the retaining bolts and lift off the manifold.

9. Install a new gasket. Install the manifold and tighten the bolts from the inside out. Tightening torque is 18 ft lbs.

10. Install the remaining components in the reverse order of removal. Refill the cooling system.

Removal and Installation— Fuel Injected Models

1. Disconnect the air duct from the throttle valve body. Drain the cooling system.

2. Disconnect the accelerator cable.

3. Remove the injectors and disconnect the line from the cold start valve.

4. Disconnect all coolant hoses.

5. Disconnect all vacuum and emission control hoses (label all hoses for installation).

6. Remove the auxiliary air regulator.

7. Disconnect all electrical lines (label all wires for installation).

8. Disconnect the EGR line from the exhaust manifold.

9. Loosen and remove the retaining bolts and lift off the manifold.

10. Install a new gasket. Install the manifold and tighten the bolts to 18 ft. lbs.

11. Install the remaining components in the reverse order of removal.

Exhaust Manifold

1. Disconnect the EGR tube from the exhaust manifold.

2. Remove the interfering air pump components if so equipped.

3. Remove the air cleaner hose from the exhaust manifold.

4. Disconnect the intake manifold support.

5. Separate the exhaust pipe from the manifold.

6. Remove the retaining nuts and remove the manifold.

7. Clean the cylinder head and manifold mating surfaces.

8. Install the exhaust manifold using a new gasket.

9. Tighten the nuts to 18 ft lbs. Work from the inside out.

10. Install the remaining components in the reverse order of removal. Use a new manifold flange gasket.

Timing Belt Cover

Removal and Installation

1. Loosen the alternator mounting bolts.

2. Pivot the alternator and slip the drive belt off the sprockets.

3. Unscrew the cover retaining nuts and remove the cover.

4. Reposition the spacers on the studs

and then install the washers and nuts.

5. Install the alternator belt and adjust its tension.

Timing Belt

NOTE: *The timing belt is designed to last for more than 60,000 miles and does not normally require tension adjustments. If the belt is removed or replaced, the basic valve timing must be checked and the belt retensioned.*

Removal, Installation, and Tensioning

1. Remove the timing belt cover.

2. While holding the large hex on the tension sprocket, loosen the pulley locknut.

3. Release the tensioner from the timing belt.

4. Slide the belt off the three toothed sprockets and remove it.

5. Turn the crankshaft until no. 1 cyl-

1. Alternator belt
2. Belt pulleys
3. Timing gear cover
4. Crankshaft sprocket
5. Intermediate sprocket
6. Drive belt
7. Tensioner
8. Camshaft sprocket

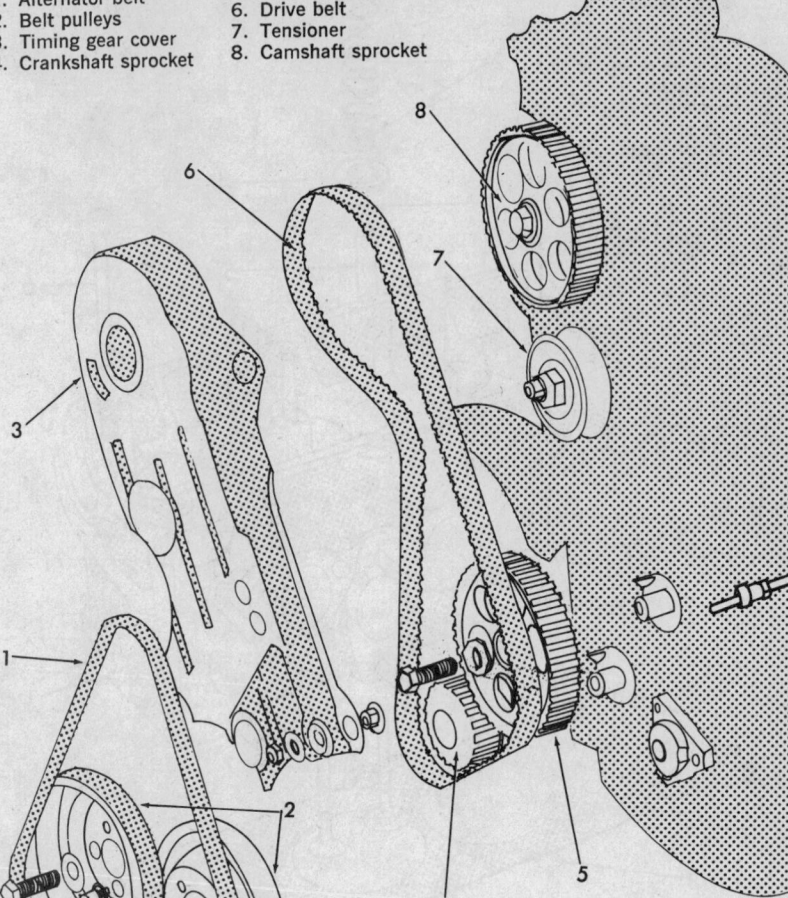

Exploded view of camshaft drive arrangement

Turn the tensioner (R) toward (a) to tighten the belt and toward (b) to loosen. Check the tension at (c)

0°T or TDC mark on the flywheel

inder is at TDC. At this point, the 0°T mark will be aligned with the pointer on the bell housing.

6. Align the timing mark on the rear face of the camshaft pulley with the camshaft cover gasket on the left.

7. Align the V-notch in the crankshaft pulley with the dot mark on the intermediate shaft. The distributor rotor

should be pointing to the No. 1 cylinder mark on the rim of the distributor.

CAUTION: *If the timing marks are not correctly aligned, valve timing will be incorrect. Poor performance and serious engine damage can result from improper valve timing.*

8. Install the belt on the sprockets.

9. Adjust the tensioner by turning the large tensioner hex to the right. Tension is correct when you can just twist the belt

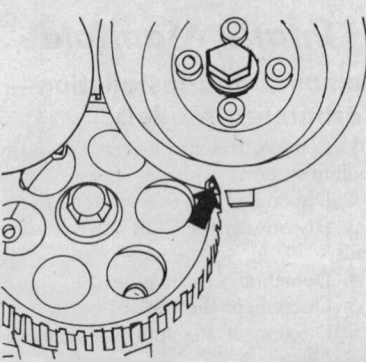

Crankshaft pulley and intermediate shaft sprocket alignment

Camshaft sprocket alignment

90° with two fingers at the midpoint. Tighten the locknut to 32 ft. lbs.

10. Install the timing belt cover and check the ignition timing.

Timing Sprockets

Removal and Installation

The camshaft, intermediate shaft, and crankshaft sprockets are located by keys on their respective shafts and each is retained by a bolt. To remove any or all of the pulleys, first remove the timing belt cover and belt.

NOTE: *When removing the crankshaft pulley, don't remove the four allen head bolts which hold the outer belt pulley to the timing belt sprocket.*

1. Remove the center bolt.

2. Gently pry the sprocket off the shaft. If the gear does not come off easily, use a gear puller. Don't hammer on the sprocket.

3. Remove the sprocket and key.

4. Install in the reverse order of removal.

5. Tighten the center bolt to 58 ft. lbs.

6. Install the timing belt, check the valve timing, tension the belt, and install the cover.

Camshaft

Removal and Installation

1. Remove the timing belt.

2. Remove the camshaft sprocket.

3. Remove the air cleaner.

4. Remove the camshaft cover.

5. Unscrew and remove the No. 1, 3, and 5 bearing caps (No. 1 is at the front).

6. Unscrew the No. 2 and 4 bearing caps, diagonally and in increments.

7. Lift the camshaft out of the cylinder head.

8. Lubricate the camshaft journals and lobes with assembly lube or gear oil before installing it in the cylinder head.

9. Replace the camshaft oil seal with a new one whenever the cam is removed.

10. Install the No. 1, 3, and 5 bearing caps and tighten the nuts to 14 ft. lbs. The caps should be installed so they read right side up from the driver's seat.

11. Install the No. 2 and 4 bearing caps and diagonally tighten the nuts to 14 ft. lbs.

NOTE: *If checking end play, install a dial indicator so that the feeler touches the camshaft snout. Endplay should be no more than 0.006 in. (0.15 mm.).*

12. Replace the seal in the No. 1 bearing cap. If necessary, replace the end plug in the cylinder head.

13. Install the camshaft cover.

14. Install the camshaft pulley and the timing belt.

15. Check the valve clearance.

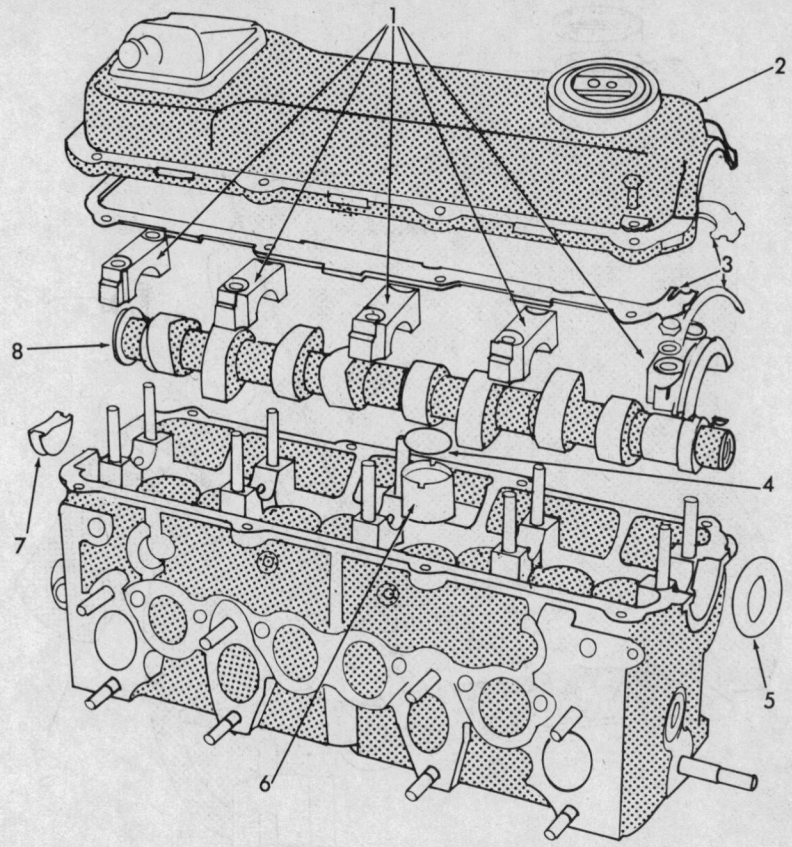

Exploded view of camshaft assembly

1. Camshaft bearing caps
2. Camshaft cover
3. Gasket
4. Valve adjusting disc
5. Oil seal
6. Cam follower
7. End plug
8. Camshaft

Pistons and Connecting Rods

The pistons must be installed in the block with the arrow at the edge of the crown facing to the front of the car. The connecting rod and cap alignment casting grooves must face the intermediate shaft. New connecting rod bolts must always be used. The pistons must be heated to 140°F in an oven before the piston pins can be pressed in. Three piston oversizes are available to accommodate overbores up to 0.040 in.

There is a piston size code stamped on the cylinder block above the water pump.

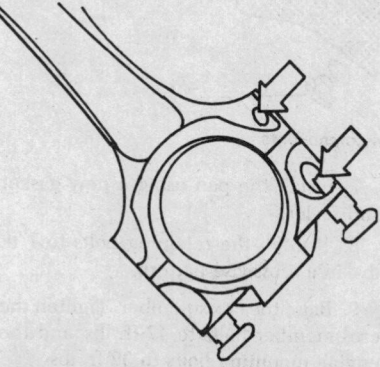

The connecting rod and cap alignment casting grooves must face the intermediate shaft

ENGINE LUBRICATION

The lubrication system is a conventional wet-sump design. The gear type oil pump is driven by the intermediate shaft. A pressure relief valve limits pressure and prevents extreme pressure from developing in the system. All oil is filtered by a full flow replaceable filter. A bypass valve assures lubrication in the event the filter becomes plugged. The oil pressure switch is located at the end of the cylinder head gallery (the end of the system) to assure accurate pressure readings.

Oil Pan

Removal and Installation

Dasher

1. Drain the oil pan.

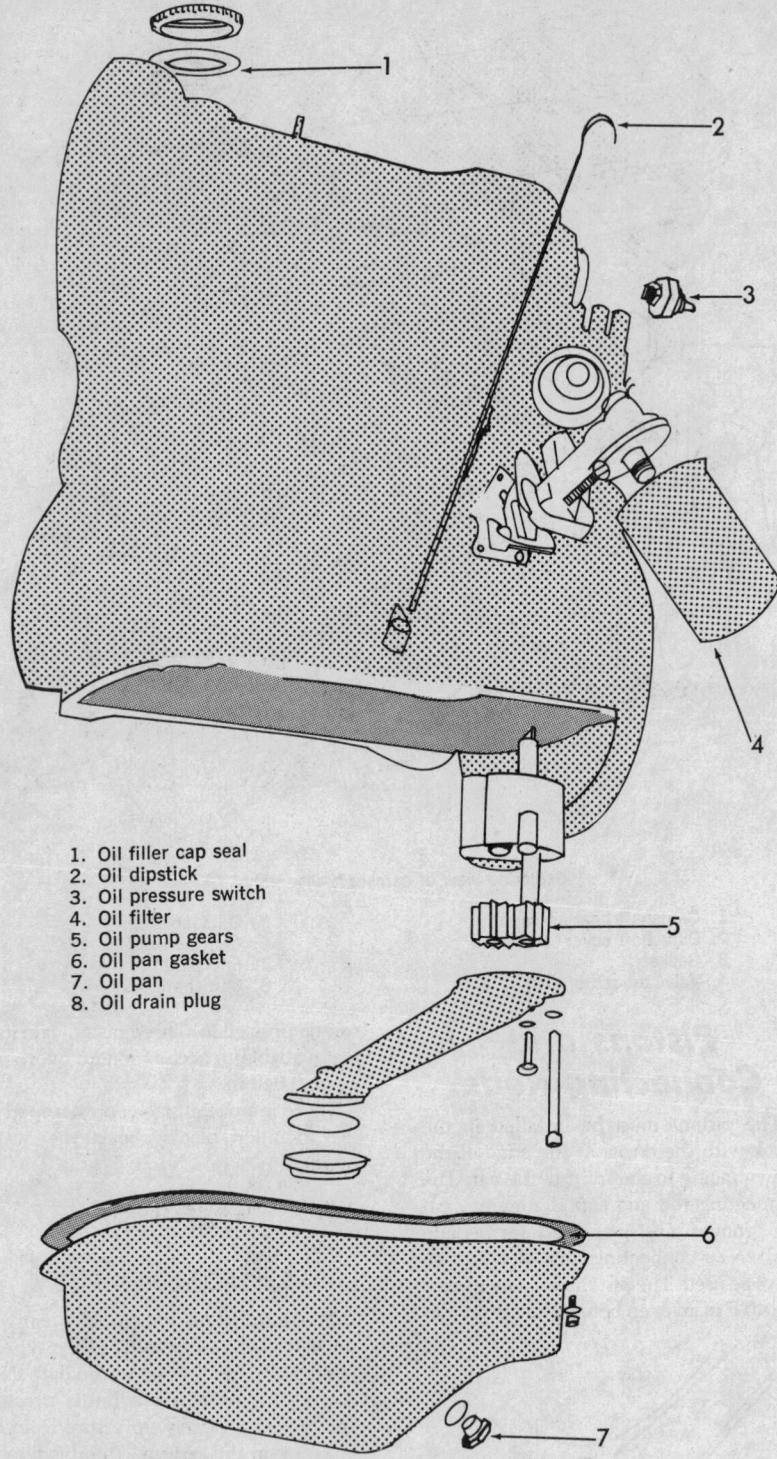

1. Oil filler cap seal
2. Oil dipstick
3. Oil pressure switch
4. Oil filter
5. Oil pump gears
6. Oil pan gasket
7. Oil pan
8. Oil drain plug

Lubrication system components

2. Support and slightly raise the engine with an overhead hoist.

3. Gradually loosen the engine crossmember mounting bolts. Remove the left and right side engine mounts.

4. Lower the crossmember very carefully.

5. Loosen and remove the allen head, oil pan retaining bolts.

6. Lower the pan from the car.

7. Install the pan using a new gasket and sealer.

8. Tighten the retaining bolts to 7 ft. lbs. in a crosswise pattern.

9. Raise the crossmember. Tighten the crossmember bolts to 42 ft. lbs. and the engine mounting bolts to 32 ft. lbs.

10. Refill the engine with oil. Start the engine and check for leaks.

Rabbit & Scirocco

1. Drain the engine oil.

2. Loosen and remove the bolts retaining the oil pan.

3. Lower the pan from the car.

4. Install the pan using a new oil pan gasket.

5. Tighten the retaining bolts to 7 ft. lbs. in a criss-cross pattern.

6. Refill the engine with oil. Start the engine and examine the pan for leaks.

Rear Main Oil Seal
Replacement

The rear main oil seal is located in a housing on the rear of the cylinder block. To replace the seal on the Dasher, it is necessary to remove the transmission and perform the work from underneath the car or remove the engine and perform the work on an engine stand or work bench.

See "Transmission Removal and Installation." On the Rabbit and Scirocco, the engine should be removed from the car.

1. Remove the transmission and flywheel.

2. Using a screwdriver, very carefully pry the old seal out of the support ring.

3. Remove the seal.

4. Lightly oil the replacement seal and then press it into place using a circular piece of flat metal. Be careful not to damage the seal or score the crankshaft.

5. Install the flywheel and transmission. Flywheel-to-engine bolts are tightened to 36 ft. lbs.

Oil Pump
Removal and Installation

1. Remove the oil pan.

2. Remove the two mounting bolts.

3. Pull the oil pump down and out of the engine.

4. Unscrew the two bolts and separate the pump halves.

5. Remove the driveshaft and gear from the upper body.

6. Clean the bottom half in solvent. Pry up the metal edges to remove the filter screen for cleaning.

7. Examine the gears and driveshaft for wear or damage. Replace them if necessary.

8. Reassemble the pump halves.

9. Prime the pump with oil and install in the reverse order of removal.

ENGINE COOLING

The cooling system consists of a belt driven, external water pump, thermostat, radiator, and thermostatically con-

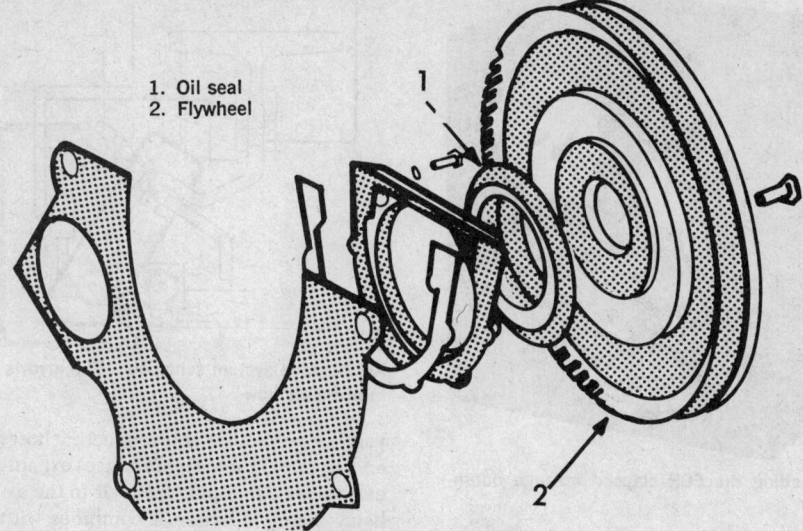

1. Oil seal
2. Flywheel

Rear main oil seal assembly

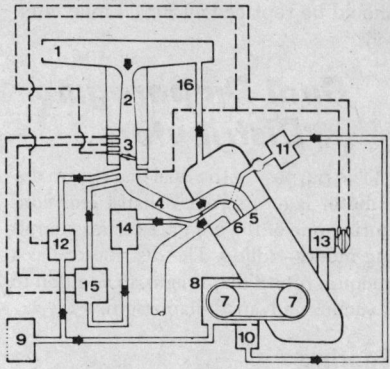

**Emission control system schematic.
The arrows indicate flow**

1. Air cleaner
2. Carburetor venturi
3. Throttle valve
4. Intake manifold
5. Cylinder head intake port
6. Cylinder head exhaust port
7. Belt drive for air pump
8. Air pump
9. Air pump filter
10. Pressure relief valve
11. Check valve
12. Diverter valve
13. Distributor
14. EGR filter
15. EGR valve
16. Crankcase ventilation

trolled electric cooling fan. When the engine is cold the thermostat is closed and blocks the water from the radiator so the coolant is circulated only through the engine. When the engine warms up, the thermostat opens and the radiator is included in the coolant circuit. The thermostatic switch is in the bottom of the radiator and turns the electrical fan on at 199°F, off at 186°F. This reduces power loss and engine noise.

Radiator and Fan

Removal and Installation

1. Drain the cooling system.
2. Remove the inner shroud mounting bolts.
3. Disconnect the lower radiator hose.
4. Disconnect the thermostatic switch lead.
5. Remove the lower radiator shroud.
6. Remove the lower radiator mounting units.
7. Disconnect the upper radiator hose.
8. Detach the upper radiator shroud.
9. Disconnect the heater and intake manifold hoses.
10. Remove the side mounting bolts and lift the radiator and fan out as an assembly.
11. Installation is the reverse of removal.

Thermostat

Removal and Installation

The thermostat is located in the bottom radiator hose neck on the water pump.

1. Drain the cooling system.
2. Remove the two retaining bolts from the lower water pump neck.

NOTE: *It isn't necessary to disconnect the hose.*

3. Move the neck, with the hoses attached, out of the way.
4. Remove the thermostat.
5. Install a new seal on the water pump neck.
6. Install the thermostat with the spring end up.
7. Replace the water pump neck and tighten the two retaining bolts.

Water Pump

Removal and Installation

1. Drain the cooling system.
2. Remove the alternator and drive belt.
3. Remove the timing belt cover.
4. Disconnect the lower radiator hose, engine hose, and heater hose from the water pump.
5. Remove the four pump retaining bolts. Notice where the different length bolts are located.
6. Turn the pump slightly and lift it out of the engine block.
7. Installation is the reverse of removal. Use a new seal on the mating surface with the engine.

EMISSION CONTROLS

Crankcase Ventilation

The crankcase ventilation system keeps harmful vapor byproducts of combustion from escaping into the atmosphere and prevents the building of crankcase pressure which can lead to oil leaking. Crankcase vapors are recirculated from the camshaft cover through a hose to the air cleaner. Here they are mixed with the air/fuel mixture and burned in the combustion chamber.

Service

The only maintenance required on the crankcase ventilation system is a periodic check. At every tune up, examine the hoses for clogging or deterioration. Clean or replace the hoses as necessary.

Evaporative Emission Control System

This system prevents the escape of raw fuel vapors (unburned hydrocarbons or HC) into the atmosphere. The system consists of a sealed carburetor, unvented fuel tank filter cap, fuel tank expansion chamber, an activated charcoal filter canister and connector hoses. Fuel vapors which reach the filter deposit hydrocarbons on the surface of the charcoal filter element. Fresh air enters the filter when the engine is running and forces the hydrocarbons to the air cleaner where they join the air/fuel mixture and are burned.

Service

Maintenance of the system requires checking the condition of the various connector hoses and the charcoal filter at 10,000 mile intervals. The charcoal filter should be replaced at 50,000 mile intervals.

Dual Diaphragm Distributors

The purpose of the dual diaphragm distributor is to improve exhaust emissions during one of the engine's dirtier operating modes—idling. The distributor has a vacuum retard diaphragm, in addition to a vacuum advance diaphragm.

Testing

1. Connect a timing light to the engine. Check the ignition timing.
2. Remove the retard hose from the distributor and plug it. Increase the engine speed. The ignition timing should advance. If it doesn't, then the vacuum unit is faulty and must be replaced.

Exhaust Gas Recirculation (EGR)

To reduce NOx (oxides of nitrogen) emissions, metered amounts of exhaust gases are added to the air/fuel mixture. The recirculated exhaust gas lowers the peak flame temperature during combustion. Exhaust gas from the manifold passes through a filter where it is cleaned. The vacuum operated EGR valve controls the volume of this exhaust gas which is allowed into the intake manifold. There is no EGR at idle, partial at slight throttle and full EGR at mid-throttle. California models are equipped with a dual chamber EGR valve.

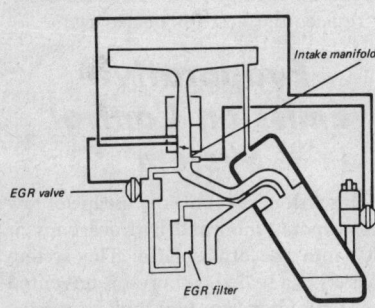

EGR system schematic

Testing

All Models Except California

1. Disconnect the vacuum line from the EGR valve.
2. Disconnect the vacuum hose from the distributor vacuum unit.
3. Start the engine and allow it to idle.
4. Connect the distributor vacuum hose to the EGR valve. The engine should stumble or stall.
5. If the idle stays even, the EGR line is clogged or the EGR valve is defective.

Resetting the EGR elapsed mileage odometer

California Models

1. Disconnect both vacuum lines from the EGR valve.
2. Disconnect the hose from the distributor vacuum unit.
3. Start the engine and let it idle.
4. Connect the distributor vacuum line to each EGR connector. The engine should stumble or stall.
NOTE: *The right connector should affect the engine less than the left.*
5. If the idle stays even during Step 4, the EGR line is clogged or the valve is defective. If the idle remains steady during only one vacuum line connection, the EGR valve is defective.

Maintenance

The only required maintenance is that the EGR filter be replaced at 15,000 mile or two year intervals.

1. Disconnect the filter EGR line fittings.
2. Remove the filter and discard.
3. Install the new filter into the EGR lines and securely tighten the fittings.
4. Reset the EGR elapsed mileage odometer by pressing the white button marked "EGR".

Removal and Installation

EGR Valve

1. Disconnect the vacuum hose from the EGR valve.
2. Unbolt the EGR line fitting on the opposite side of the valve.
3. Remove the two retaining bolts and lift the EGR valve from the intake manifold.
4. Install the EGR valve in the reverse order of removal. Use a new gasket at the intake manifold.

Air Injection

This system includes a belt-driven air pump, filter, check valve, anti-backfire

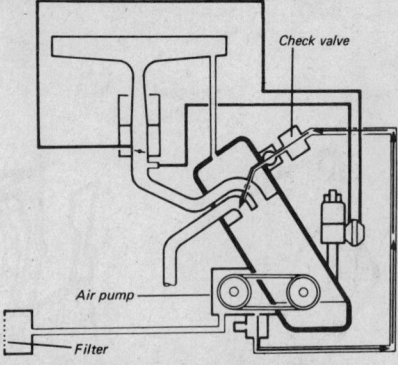

Air injection system schematic. The arrows indicate air flow

valve or gulp valve, and connecting hoses and air lines. The system reduces exhaust emissions by pumping fresh air to the exhaust manifold where it combines with the hot exhaust gas to burn away excess hydrocarbons and reduce carbon monoxide.

Maintenance

Required maintenance on the air pump involves visually checking the pump, control valves, hoses and lines every 10,000 miles. Clean the air pump filter element at this interval. The filter element should be replaced every 20,000 miles or two years.

Testing and Service

Air Pump System

1. Remove and clean the air manifold.
2. Blow compressed air into the anti-backfire valve in the direction of the air flow.
3. Clean or replace the air pump filter.
4. Start the engine.
5. Exhaust gas should flow equally from each air inlet.
6. With the engine idling, block the relief valve air outlet—only a slight pressure should be felt if the system is operating properly.

Anti-Backfire Valve

1. Disconnect the air pump filter line from the anti-backfire valve.
2. Briefly disconnect the anti-backfire valve vacuum line with the engine running. There should be a noticeable vacuum.
3. Replace the anti-backfire valve if the engine backfires.

Catalytic Converter

Maintenance

Required maintenance on the catalytic converter involves checking the condition of the ceramic insert every 30,000 miles. As this interval is reached, a indicator light on the dash will glow. Once service to the converter is performed, the

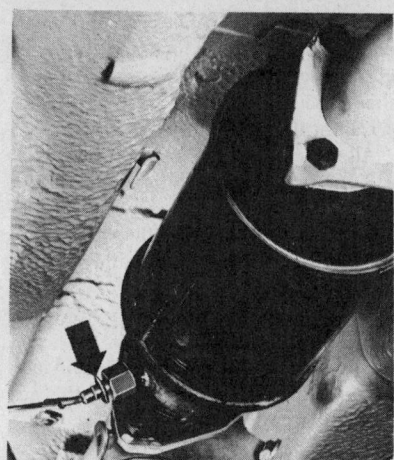

Checking catalytic converter—arrow indicates the temperature sensor

Resetting the catalytic converter elapsed mileage odometer

odometer must be reset. Disconnect wire.

Testing and Service

CAUTION: *Do Not drop or strike the converter assembly or damage to the ceramic insert will result.*

Damage and overheating of the catalytic converter, indicated by the flickering of the "CAT" warning light, can be caused by the following:

1. Engine misfire caused by faulty spark plug, ignition wires and so on.
2. Improper ignition timing.
3. CO valve set too high.
4. Faulty air pump diverter valve.
5. Faulty temperature sensor.
6. Engine under strain caused by trailer hauling, high speed driving in hot weather, etc.

A faulty converter is indicated by one of the following symptoms:

1. Poor engine performance.
2. The engine stalls.
3. Rattling in the exhaust system.
4. A CO reading greater than 0.4% at the tail pipe.

Check or replace the converter as follows:

1. Disconnect the temperature sensor.
2. Loosen and remove the bolts holding the converter to the exhaust system and the chassis.
3. Remove the converter.
4. Hold the converter up to a strong light and look through both ends, checking for blockages. If the converter is blocked, replace it.
5. Install the converter in the reverse order of removal.
6. Reset the elapsed mileage odometer by pushing the white button marked "CAT".

FUEL SYSTEM

Fuel Pump— Carbureted Engines

Cleaning

The filter screen can be removed from the pump and cleaned.

1. Remove the center cover screw.
2. Remove the screen and gasket. Clean the screen in solvent.
3. Replace the screen.
4. Install a new gasket and replace the cover.

NOTE: *Make sure the depression in the pump cover engages the projection on the body of the pump.*

Removal and Installation

The pump cannot be repaired and must be replaced when defective.

Exploded view of fuel pump

1. Screen
2. Gasket
3. Cover
4. Plastic flange
5. Flange seal

1. Disconnect and plug both fuel lines.
2. Remove the two allen head retaining bolts.
3. Remove the fuel pump and its plastic flange.
4. Replace the pump in the reverse order of removal. Use a new flange seal.

Fuel Pump—CIS Engines (Fuel Injection)

Testing—Electrical

1. Have an assistant operate the starter. Listen at the rear wheel to determine if the pump is running.
2. If the pump is not running, check the fuse on the front of the fuel pump relay.
3. If the fuse is good, replace the fuel pump relay.
4. If the fuel pump still does not operate, the fuel pump is faulty and must be replaced.

Testing—Fuel Pump Delivery

1. Check the condition of the fuel filter, make sure it is clean.
2. Connect a jumper wire between the #1 terminal on the ignition coil and ground.
3. Disconnect the return fuel line and hold in a measuring container with a capacity of 1 quart or 1000cc.
4. Have an assistant run the starter for 30 seconds while watching the quantity of fuel delivered.
5. If less than ¾ quart or 750 cc of fuel is delivered in 30 seconds, replace the fuel pump.

Removal and Installation

1. Support the car on a lift and remove the right rear wheel.
2. Remove the gas tank filler cap to release the pressure.
3. Clean all fuel line connections *thoroughly*.
4. Disconnect the fuel line from the gas tank and the line to the fuel accumulator.
5. Disconnect the electrical connector.
6. Loosen and remove the retaining nuts and remove the fuel pump.
7. Install the new fuel pump in the reverse order of removal. Make sure that new seal washers are installed on the fuel discharge line.

Carburetor

1974–75

Removal and Installation

1. Remove the air cleaner.

1423

2. Disconnect the fuel line, being careful not to spill any fuel on the hot engine components.

3. Drain some of the coolant and then disconnect the choke hoses.

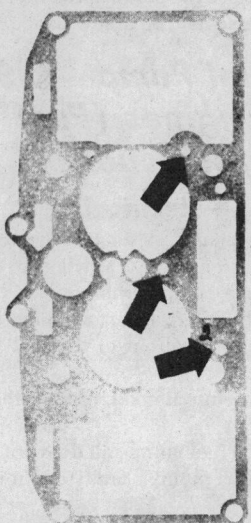

Old type (1975)
Pt. No. 055 129 281A

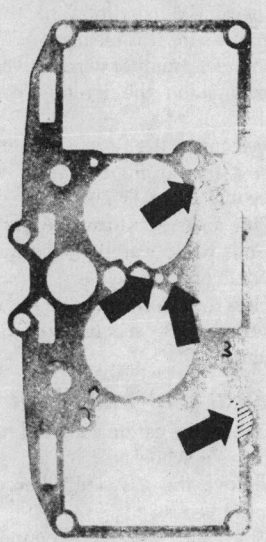

New type (1976)
Pt. No. 049 129 281

New and old type carburetor gaskets are not interchangeable

4. Disconnect the distributor and EGR valve vacuum lines.

5. Disconnect the electrical lead for the idle cut-off valve.

6. Remove the clip which secures the throttle linkage to the carburetor. Detach the linkage, being careful not to lose any washers or bushings.

7. Unbolt the carburetor from the manifold and remove it.

8. Use a new gasket when replacing the carburetor. Don't overtighten the nuts.

Automatic Choke Adjustment

Dasher

The standard adjustment on all versions of the automatic choke is with the two notches aligned with the notch on the housing. To adjust, loosen the three clamping screws and move the outer part of the choke unit.

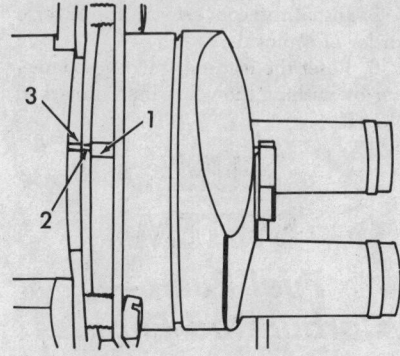

The Dasher automatic choke is correctly adjusted when (1) the choke cover, (2) the adjusting ring, and (3) the mark on the carburetor housing are aligned

Internal Choke Adjustment

Dasher

If after performing the automatic choke adjustment, the choke doesn't operate correctly, use the following procedure.

1. Remove the choke cover with the coolant hoses attached and place it out of the way.

2. The control notch should be 180° opposite the adjusting notch. If not turn it with a screwdriver.

3. Reassemble the choke cover and adjust the choke.

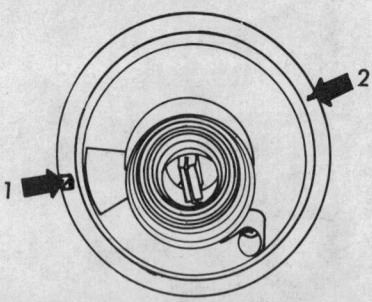

Dasher internal choke adjustment—(1) the adjusting notch, and (2) the control notch

Throttle Gap Adjustment

Dasher

This adjustment is made with the carburetor removed.

1. Close the choke tightly. The stop lever should rest on the highest step of the stepped washer, holding the throttle open slightly.

2. Check the gap between the lower edge of the throttle valve and the housing wall with a drill. The measurement should be:

California 0.0255 in. (0.65 mm)
All Others 0.0314 in. (0.80 mm)

3. Adjust the primary gap by means of the two bolts on the connecting rod.

4. The secondary throttle should only be adjusted when it is definitely incorrectly adjusted.

   a. Loosen the adjusting screw until the throttle valve closes.

   b. Turn the screw in ½ turn and lock

   c. Adjust idle mixture after this adjustment.

Rabbit, Scirocco

This adjustment is made with the carburetor removed.

1. Close the choke valve fully.

2. Use a drill to check the primary throttle valve opening. Insert the drill between the lower edge of the throttle valve and the inner side of the carburetor bore. The gap should be 0.018–0.020 in.

3. Adjust the gap by turning the linkage screw.

Throttle gap adjusting screw, Rabbit and Scirocco

Fast Idle Cam Adjustment

Rabbit, Scirocco

This is set at the factory and need not be adjusted unless disturbed. To adjust, remove the plastic cap and tighten the screw ¼ turn beyond the point at which it just contacts the fast idle cam.

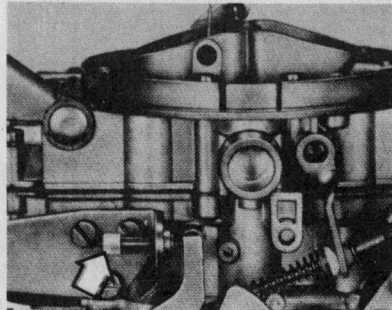

Fast idle cam adjusting screw, Rabbit and Scirocco

Choke Gap Adjustment

Rabbit, Scirocco

1. Remove the automatic choke cover.
2. Open the choke valve all the way. Push the vacuum unit rod in to the stop.
3. Check the gap between the upper edge of the choke valve and the inner side of the carburetor bore. It should be 0.130–0.147 in.
4. Adjust the gap by turning the screw on the choke vacuum unit.

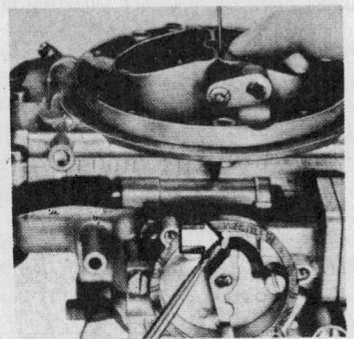

Measuring choke gap on the Rabbit and Scirocco carburetor

Fuel Level Adjustment

Dasher

This adjustment is made with the carburetor installed on the engine. Incorrect fuel level can cause stalling or high-speed miss.

1. Idle the engine for one minute.
2. Stop the engine. Remove the air cleaner.
3. Detach the fuel line.
4. Remove the five carburetor cover mounting screws.
5. Plug the fuel inlet with a finger and lift off the carburetor cover and gasket. Set them to the side, leaving the linkages attached.
6. Using a sliding T-scale, measure the distance from the top of the carburetor cover (air horn) to the upper edge of the float. It should be 0.61–.69 in.
7. The measurement may be corrected by varying the thickness of the

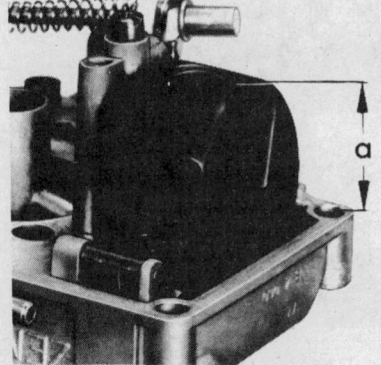

Float adjustment

fiber sealing ring under the float needle valve.

Rabbit, Scirocco

1. Remove and invert the top of the carburetor.
2. The distance between the bottom of the float and the gasket surface of the top of the carburetor should be 1.102 in. for the primary float and 1.118 in. for the secondary.
3. Adjust by bending the float arm.

Throttle Linkage Adjustment

Throttle linkage adjustments are not normally required. However, it is a good idea to make sure that the throttle valve(s) in the carburetor open all the way when the accelerator pedal is held in the wide-open position. Only the primary throttle valve will open; the secondary throttle is vacuum operated.

Overhaul

Efficient carburetion depends greatly on careful cleaning and inspection during overhaul since dirt, gum, water, or varnish in or on the carburetor parts are often responsible for poor performance.

Overhaul the carburetor in a clean, dust-free area. Carefully disassemble the carburetor, referring often to a diagram. Keep all similar and look-alike parts segregated during disassembly and cleaning to avoid accidental interchange during assembly. Make a note of all jet sizes.

When the carburetor is disassembled, wash all parts (except diaphragms, electric choke units, pump plunger, and any other plastic, leather, fiber, or rubber parts) in clean carburetor solvent. Do not leave parts in the solvent any longer than is necessary to sufficiently loosen the deposits. Excessive cleaning may remove the special finish from the float bowl and choke valve bodies, leaving these parts unfit for service. Rinse all parts in clean solvent and blow them dry with compressed air or allow them to air dry. Wipe clean all cork, plastic, leather, and fiber parts with a clean, lint-free cloth.

Blow out all passages and jets with compressed air and be sure that there are no restrictions or blockages. Never use wire or similar tools to clean jets, fuel passages, or air bleeds. Clean all jets and valves separately to avoid accidental interchange.

Check all parts for wear or damage. If wear or damage is found, replace the defective parts. Especially check the following;

1. Check the float needle and seat for wear. If wear is found, replace the complete assembly.
2. Check the float hinge pin for wear

Jet identification for the main body of the Zenith 32/32-2B2 carburetor

1. Secondary full load enrichment
2. Primary air correction jet
3. Secondary air correction jet
4. Primary idle air and fuel jets*
5. Secondary idle air and fuel jets*
6. Primary auxiliary air and fuel jets*

* The fuel jets are below the air jets

and the float(s) for dents or distortion. Replace the float if fuel has leaked into it.

3. Check the throttle and choke shaft bores for wear or an out-of-round condition. Damage or wear to the throttle arm, shaft, or shaft bore will often require replacement of the throttle body. These parts require a close tolerance of fit; wear may allow air leakage, which could adversely affect starting and idling.

NOTE: *Throttle shafts and bushings are not included in overhaul kits. They can be purchased separately.*

4. Inspect the idle mixture adjusting needles for burrs or grooves. Any such condition requires replacement of the needle, since you will not be able to obtain a satisfactory idle.
5. Test the accelerator pump check valves. They should pass air one way but not the other. Test for proper seating by blowing and sucking on the valve. Replace the valve if necessary. If the valve is satisfactory, wash the valve again to remove breath moisture.
6. Check the bowl cover for warped surfaces with a straightedge.
7. Closely inspect the valves and seats for wear and damage, replacing as necessary.

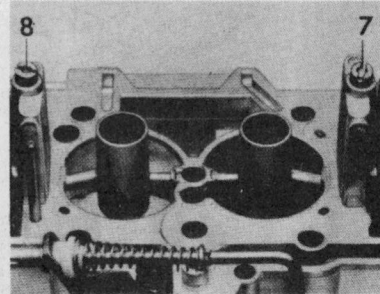

The primary main jet (7) and the secondary main jet (8) are mounted in the top of the carburetor Zenith 32/32-2B2

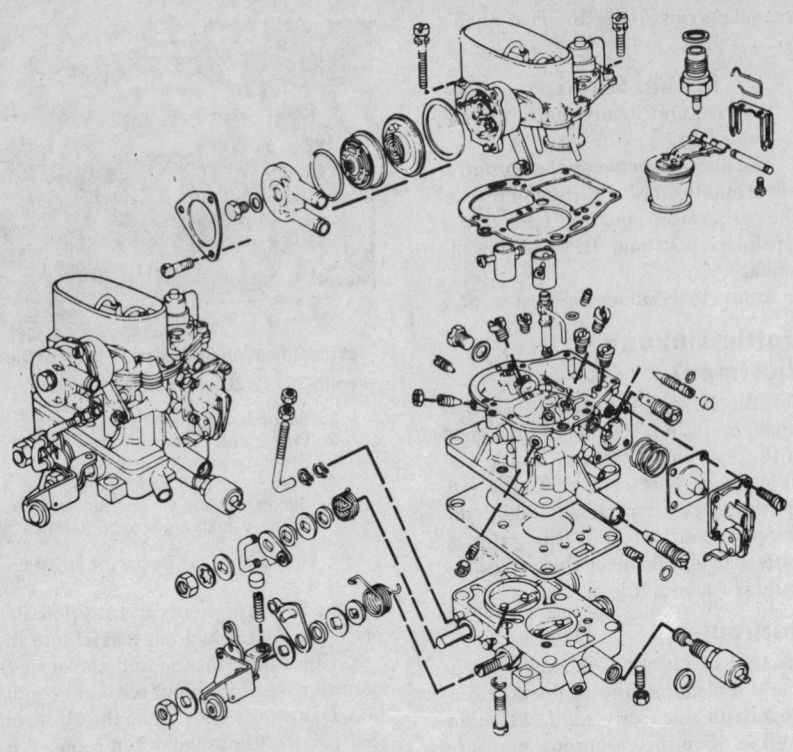

Exploded view of Solex 32/35 DIDTA carburetor

8. After the carburetor is assembled, check the choke valve for freedom of operation.

Carburetor overhaul kits are recommended for each overhaul. These kits contain all gaskets and new parts to replace those that deteriorate most rapidly. Failure to replace all parts supplied with the kit (especially gaskets) can result in poor performance later.

After cleaning and checking all components, reassemble the carburetor, using new parts and referring to the exploded view. When reassembling, make sure that all screws and jets are tight in their seats, but do not overtighten, as the tips will be distorted. Tighten all screws gradually, in rotation. Do not tighten needle valves into their seats; uneven jetting will result. Always use new gaskets.

Be sure to adjust the float level when reassembling.

Fuel Injection

Air Flow Sensor-Testing and Adjustment

Sensor Plate Lever and Control Plunger

1. Run the engine for a short time at idle.

2. Remove the air duct from the air flow sensor assembly.

3. Using a magnet, lift the sensor plate. A light even resistance must be felt over the sensor plates entire travel.

NOTE: *Make certain that the air sensor plate is centered in the air cone. If adjustment is necessary, proceed as follows:*

  a. Loosen the centering bolt slightly.

  b. Run a 0.004 in. (0.10 mm) feeler gauge around the perimeter of the air gap.

  c. Tighten the centering bolt.

4. No resistance must be felt when the sensor plate is moved rapidly up and down. If resistance is felt, the air sensor must be replaced.

5. If the sensor plate is hard to move upward but moves freely down, the control plunger is sticking. Remove the fuel distributor and clean the control plunger in solvent. If after installation the plunger still sticking, the fuel distributor must be replaced.

Sensor Plate Rest Position

1. Remove the air duct from the air flow sensor assembly.

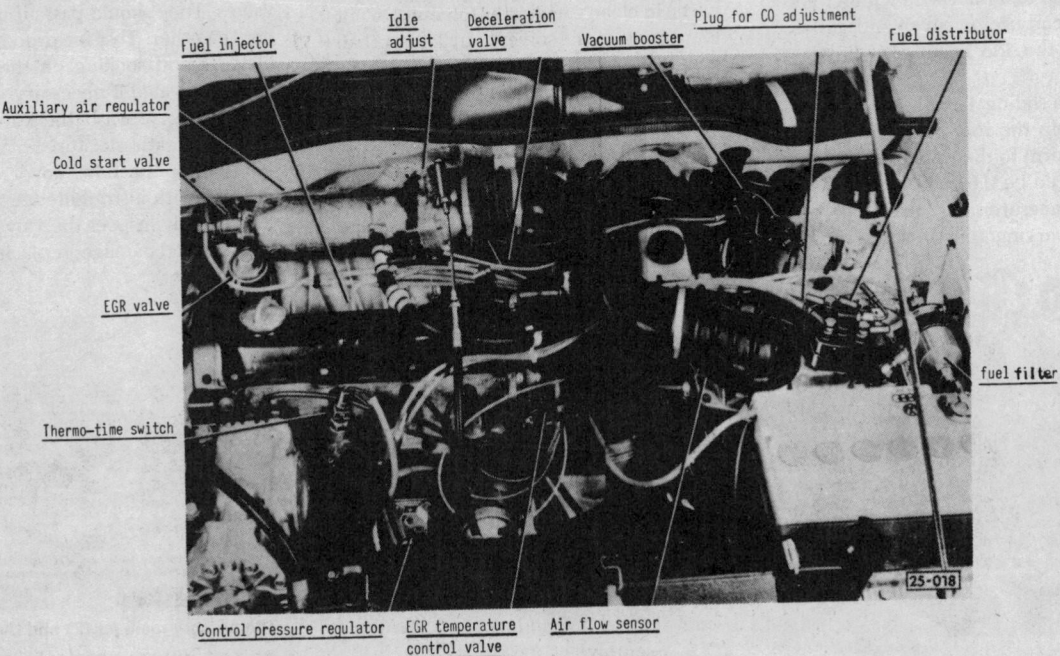

CIS fuel injection components

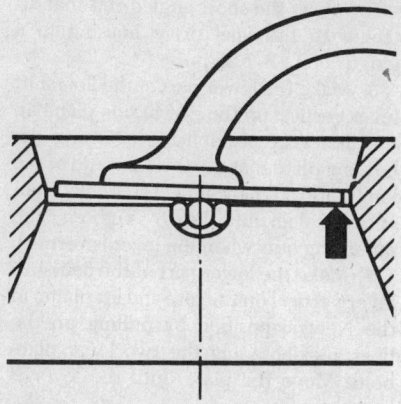

Aligning the air flow sensor plate with the edge of the air cone

2. Loosen the fuel line to the control pressure regulator at the fuel distributor. Wrap a cloth around the fitting to prevent fuel from spilling.

3. The upper edge of the sensor plate must be flush with the edge of the air cone. If it is too high, the plate can be adjusted. The plate can be lowered no more than 0.019 in (0.5 mm).

4. Adjust the spring stop by bending the wire bracket.

5. Check the CO level and adjust if necessary.

Thermo-Time Switch-Testing

NOTE: *To properly perform the following tests, the engine must be cold with the water temperature below 95 F (35 C).*

1. Disconnect the electrical connector from the cold start valve on the end of the intake manifold.

2. Connect a test light across the cold start valve terminals.

3. Connect a jumper wire from the #1 terminal on the ignition coil to a good ground.

4. Have an assistant operate the starter. If the test light fails to light after 8 seconds, the thermo-time switch is defective and should be replaced.

Adjusting the air flow sensor spring stop

Cold Start Valve—Testing

1. Remove the electrical connector from the cold start valve.

NOTE: *Do not remove the fuel line from the cold start valve.*

2. Remove the cold start valve from the manifold and point the nozzle into a measuring container.

3. Connect a jumper wire from one terminial of the cold start valve to terminial #15 on the ignition coil.

4. Connect a second jumper wire from the other cold start valve terminial to ground.

5. Remove the fuel pump relay and bridge the relay plate terminials #L13 and #L14 with a fused (8 amp) jumper wire.

6. Have assistant turn the ignition switch on while observing the fuel spray pattern from the cold start valve. The spray pattern from the nozzle must be cone-shaped and steady, if not replace the valve.

7. Turn the ignition switch off.

8. Wipe the nozzle dry with clean rag and check for leakage. If drops form within one minute, the valve is defective and must be replaced.

Auxiliary Air Regulator—Testing

NOTE: *The engine must be cold to perform this test.*

1. Remove the hose from the auxiliary air regulator and plug.

2. Observe gate valve with the aid of a mirror. The valve must be open. If the valve is not open, replace the regulator.

3. Run the engine at idle for 5 minutes. Again check the gate valve, it should be closed. If the valve did not close, replace the auxiliary air regulator.

Control Pressure Regulator—Testing

1. Remove the electrical connector from the control pressure regulator.

2. Connect a ohmmeter across the terminials in the regulator socket and measure the resistance. The reading should be approximately 20 ohms. If reading is not within specifications, replace the control pressure regulator.

Fuel Injectors—Testing

1. Remove the injector but leave it connected to the fuel line.

2. Point the injector into a measuring container.

3. Remove the fuel pump relay and bridge the relay plate terminals #L13 and L14 with a fused (8 amp) jumper wire.

4. Remove the air duct from the air flow sensor.

5. Have an assistant turn the ignition switch on.

6. Lift the air flow sensor plate with a magnet and observe the injector nozzle spray pattern. The spray pattern must be cone shaped and even, if not replace the injector.

7. Turn the ignition off and hold the injector horizontally it should not drip.

NOTE: *One or more injectors may be checked at the same time.*

8. Moisten the rubber seals on the injectors with fuel before installing.

9. Press the injectors firmly into place.

Fuel Distributor—Removal and Installation

1. Clean the fuel line connections at the fuel distributor. Disconnect the lines, making sure that they are labeled for installation.

2. Remove the fuel distributor retaining bolts.

NOTE: *When removing the fuel distributor watch underneath to make sure that the control plunger does not fall out.*

3. Carefully remove the fuel distributor.

4. If the control plunger has been removed, moisten it with gasoline before installing. The small shoulder on the plunger is inserted first.

5. Reinstall the fuel distributor using new O-rings.

MANUAL TRANSMISSION

Transaxle Removal and Installation

Dasher

1. Disconnect the battery ground cable.

2. Disconnect the exhaust pipe from the manifold and its bracket on the transaxle.

3. Remove the square-headed bolt on the shift linkage.

4. Press the shift linkage coupling off.

5. Disconnect the clutch cable.

6. Disconnect the speedometer cable.

7. Detach the axle shafts from the transaxle.

8. Remove the starter.

9. Remove the inspection plate.

10. Remove the engine-to-transaxle bolts.

11. Remove the transaxle crossmember.

12. Support the transaxle with a jack.

13. Pry the transaxle out from the engine.

14. Lift the transaxle out of the car with an assistant.

15. Install the transaxle in the reverse order of removal. Tighten the engine-to-

transaxle bolts to 40 ft. lbs. and axle drive-shaft bolts to 25 ft. lbs.

Rabbit, Scirocco

The engine and transaxle may be removed together as explained under Engine Removal and Installation or the transaxle may be removed alone, as explained here.

1. Disconnect the battery ground cable.
2. Support the left end of the engine at the lifting eye.
3. Remove the left transmission mount (between the transmission and the firewall).
4. Turn the engine until the lug on the flywheel (to the left of the TDC mark) aligns with the flywheel timing pointer.
5. Detach the speedometer drive cable, backup light wire, and clutch cable.
6. Remove the engine to transmission bolts.
7. Disconnect the shift linkage.
8. Detach the transmission ground strap.
9. Remove the starter.
10. Remove the engine mounting support near the starter.
11. Remove the rear transmission mount.
12. Unbolt and wire up the driveshafts.
13. From underneath, remove the bolts for the large cover plate, but don't remove it. Unbolt the small cover plate on the firewall side of the engine. Remove the engine to transmission nut immediately below the small plate.
14. Press the transmission off the dowels and remove it from below the car.

To install the transaxle:

15. The recess in the flywheel edge must be at 3:00 o'clock (facing the left end of the engine). Tighten the engine to transmission bolts to 47 ft lbs. Tighten the engine mounting support bolts to 47 ft lbs. Tighten the driveshaft bolts to 32 ft lbs.
16. Check the adjustment of the shift linkage.

Shift Linkage Adjustment

Dasher

1. Shift into neutral.
2. Remove the round floor cover.
3. Loosen the nuts and move the bearing housing so that the shift lever inclines approximately 5° to the rear.
4. Tighten the nuts.
5. Shift into second gear.
6. Loosen the stop plate bolts.
7. Adjust the plate so that the shift lever has ⅜–⅝ in. lateral movement at the shift knob.

NOTE: *Moving the plate to the right increases play; moving the plate to the left decreases play.*

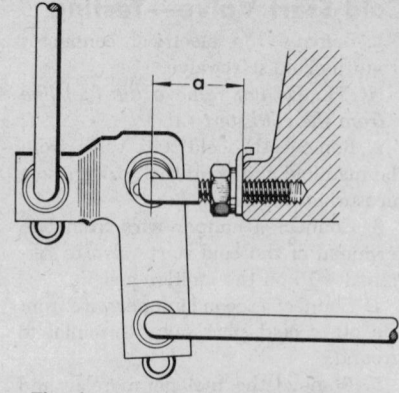

The short angled rod on the Rabbit and Scirocco shift linkage is to be adjusted to a length (a) of 1.18- 1.25 in.

8. Tighten the bolts. Check the shift pattern and make sure that reverse engages easily.

Rabbit, Scirocco

1. Adjust the long rod over the left driveshaft coupling to a length of 6.42–6.50 in.

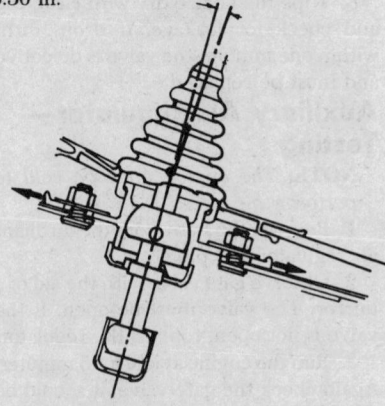

Dasher manual transmission neutral shift lever adjustment

2. Adjust the short angled rod that attaches to the final drive housing to a length of 1.18–1.25 in.
3. Make the lower part of the floorshift lever vertical (in the side to side plane) in the first gear position by loosening the bearing plate that supports the end of the long shift rod that connects to the bottom of the floorshift lever. Tighten the mounting nuts when the lever is vertical.
4. Make the lower part of the floorshift lever vertical (in the fore and aft plane) in the Neutral position by pulling up the boot and loosening the two lever plate bolts. Move the plate until the lever is vertical.

CLUTCH

Pedal Free Play Adjustment

Clutch pedal free play should be ⅝ in. Pedal free play is the distance the pedal can be depressed before the linkage starts to act on the throwout bearing.

1. Adjust the clutch pedal free play by

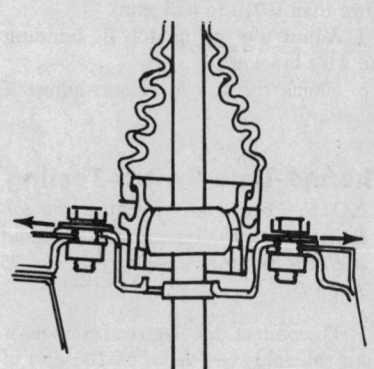

Dasher manual transmission second gear shift lever adjustment

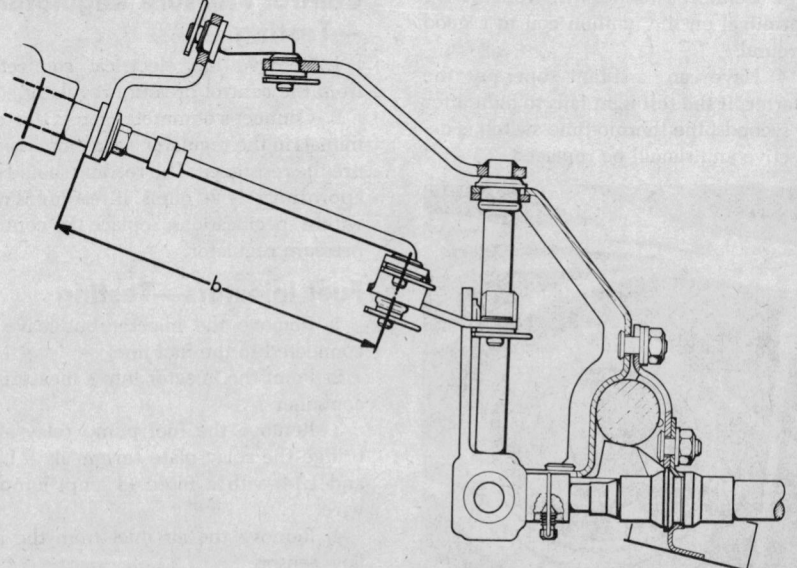

The long rod on the Rabbit and Scirocco shift linkage is to be adjusted to a length (b) of 6.42-6.50 in.

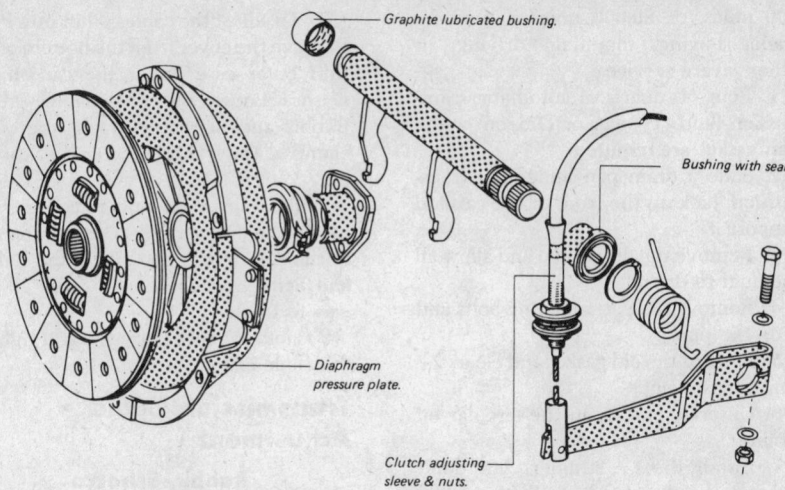

Dasher clutch components, the adjusting sleeve and nuts are adjacent to the oil filter in the engine compartment

loosening the two nuts on the cable near the oil filter on the Dasher. On the Rabbit and Scirocco, the cable adjustment point is on the front of the transmission.

2. After obtaining the correct free play, tighten the adjusting nuts.

Removal and Installation

Dasher

1. Remove the transaxle.
2. Match mark the flywheel and pressure plate if the pressure plate is being reused.
3. Gradually loosen the pressure plate bolts one or two turns at a time in a criss-cross pattern to prevent distortion.
4. Remove the pressure plate and disc.
5. Check the clutch disc for uneven or excessive lining wear. Examine the pressure plate for cracking, scorching, or scoring. Replace any questionable components.

6. Install the clutch disc and pressure plate. Use a dummy shaft to keep the disc centered.
7. Gradually tighten the pressure-plate-to-flywheel bolts in a criss-cross pattern. Tighten the bolts to 24 ft. lbs.
8. Install the throwout bearing.
9. Install the transaxle on the engine.
10. Replace the transaxle.

Rabbit, Scirocco

1. Remove the transmission.
2. Attach a toothed flywheel holder and gradually loosen the flywheel to pressure plate bolts one or two turns at a time in a crisscross pattern to prevent distortion.
3. Remove the flywheel and the clutch disc.
4. Use a screwdriver to remove the re-

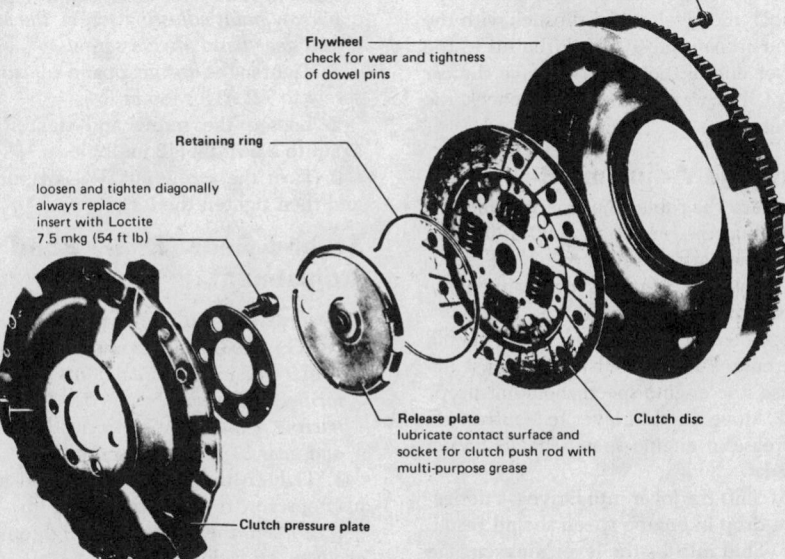

Flywheel
check for wear and tightness of dowel pins

loosen and tighten diagonally
2 mkg (14 ft lb)

Retaining ring

loosen and tighten diagonally
always replace
insert with Loctite
7.5 mkg (54 ft lb)

Release plate
lubricate contact surface and socket for clutch push rod with multi-purpose grease

Clutch disc

Clutch pressure plate

The Rabbit and Scirocco clutch, the pressure plate is bolted to the crankshaft and the clutch is actuated by a pushrod working on the release plate

lease plate retaining ring. Remove the release plate.

5. Lock the pressure plate in place and unbolt it from the crankshaft. Loosen the bolts one or two turns at a time in a criss-cross pattern to prevent distortion.
6. On installation, use new bolts to attach the pressure plate to the crankshaft. Use a thread locking compound and torque the bolts in a diagonal pattern to 54 ft lbs.
7. Lubricate the clutch disc splines with multi-purpose grease. Lubricate the release plate contact surface and pushrod socket with multi-purpose grease. Install the release plate, retaining ring, and clutch disc.
8. Install a dummy shaft to align the clutch disc.
9. Install the flywheel, tightening the bolts one or two turns at a time in a criss-cross pattern to prevent distortion. Torque the bolts to 14 ft lbs.
10. Replace the transmission.

Automatic Transmission

Transaxle Removal and Installation

Dasher

1. Disconnect the battery ground cable.
2. Raise the car on a chassis hoist.
3. Remove the lockplates and remove the axle shaft bolts. Wire the shafts up.
4. Disconnect the vacuum hose. Remove the torque converter guard plate. Disconnect the kickdown switch wire.
5. Use pliers to unscrew the speedometer cable nut.
6. Support the transaxle.
7. Remove the upper engine to transaxle bolts.
8. Remove the starter and remove the three torque converter bolts through the starter opening.
9. Unbolt the small crossmember at the rear of the transmission.
10. Lower the transaxle slightly.
11. Detach the shift linkage cable at the transmission.
12. Remove the lower engine to transaxle bolts.
13. Separate the transaxle from the engine and lower it. Secure the torque converter in the transmission with a strap. Reverse the procedure on installation. Torque the engine to transaxle bolts to 40 ft lbs and the torque converter bolts to 20–23 ft lbs. New torque converter bolts and washers must be used. Torque the axle shaft bolts to 28 ft lbs.
14. Check the shift linkage adjustment.

Rabbit, Scirocco

The engine and transaxle may be removed together as explained under Engine Removal and Installation or the transaxle may be removed alone, as explained here.

1. Disconnect both battery cables.
2. Disconnect the speedometer cable at the transmission.
3. Support the left end of the engine at the lifting eye. Attach a hoist to the transaxle.
4. Unbolt the rear transmission carrier from the body then from the transaxle. Unbolt the left side carrier from the body.
5. Unbolt the right driveshaft and wire it up.
6. Remove the starter.
7. Remove the three converter to drive plate bolts.
8. Shift into P and disconnect the floorshift linkage at the transmission.
9. Remove the accelerator and carburetor cable bracket at the transmission.
10. Unbolt the left side transmission carrier from the transmission.
11. Unbolt the front transmission mount from the transmission.
12. Unbolt the bottom of the engine from the transmission. Lift the transaxle slightly, swing the left driveshaft up, remove the rest of the bolts, pull the transmission off the mounting dowels, and lower the transaxle out of the car. Secure the converter so it doesn't fall out.

CAUTION: *Don't tilt the torque converter.*

13. Push the transmission onto the mounting dowels and install two bolts. Lift the unit until the left driveshaft can be installed and install the rest of the bolts. Torque them to 39 ft lbs.
14. Tighten the front transmission mount bolts to 39 ft lbs. Install the left side transmission carrier to the transmission.
15. Connect the accelerator and carburetor cable bracket. Connect the floorshift linkage.
16. Tighten the torque converter to drive plate bolts to 22 ft lbs. Torque the driveshaft bolts to 32 ft lbs.
17. Install the rear transmission carrier and make sure that the left side carrier is aligned in the center of the body mount. Bolt the left side carrier to the body.
18. Connect the speedometer cable and the battery cables.

Pan Removal and Installation, Strainer Service

Dasher

VW recommends that the automatic transmission fluid be replaced every 30,-000 miles, or 20,000 miles if used for trailer towing, mountain driving, or other severe service.

1. Four (4) quarts of automatic transmission fluid (Type A or Dexron) **and a pan gasket are required.**
2. Slide a drain pan under the transmission. Jack up the front of the car and support it.
3. Remove the drain plug and allow all the fluid to drain.
4. Remove the pan retaining bolts and drop the pan.
5. Discard the old gasket and clean the pan with solvent.
6. Unscrew and clean the circular oil strainer.
7. Install the   strainer, but don't tighten the bolt too much—specified torque is only 4 ft lbs.
8. Refill the transmission with about 2¾ qts. of fluid. Check the level with the dipstick. Run the car for a few minutes and check again.

Rabbit, Scirocco

1. Remove the drain plug and let the fluid drain into a pan.
2. Remove the pan bolts and take off the pan.
3. Discard the old gasket and clean the pan out. Be very careful not to get any threads or lint from rags into the pan.
4. The filter needn't be replaced unless the fluid is dirty and burnt smelling. The specified torque for the strainer screws is 2 ft lbs.
5. Replace the pan with a new gasket and tighten the bolts, in a cross-cross pattern, to 14 ft lbs.
6. Using a long-necked funnel, pour in 2½ qts of Dextron automatic transmission fluid through the dipstick tube. Start the engine and shift through all the transmission ranges with the car stationary. Check the level on the dipstick with the lever in Neutral. It should be up to the lower end of the dipstick. Drive the car until it is warmed up and recheck the level.

Linkage Adjustment

Check the cable adjustment as follows:
1. Run the engine at 1000–1200 rpm with the parking brake on.
2. Select Reverse—a drop in engine speed should be noticed.
3. Select Park—engine speed should increase. Pull the shift lever against Reverse, the engine speed shouldn't drop.
4. Move the shift lever to Neutral—an increase in engine speed should be noticed.
5. Shift the lever into Drive—a noticeable drop in engine speed should result.
6. Shift into 1—the lever must engage without having to overcome any resistance.

7. To adjust the cable—Shift into Park. Remove the cover from the bottom of the shift lever case under the car on the Dasher. Loosen the cable clamp. On the Rabbit and Scirocco, loosen the cable clamp at the transmission end of the cable.
8. Press the lever on the Dasher transmission against spring tension all the way to the stop at the rear. Press the Rabbit and Scirocco transmission lever all the way to the left.
9. Hold the lever in place and tighten the cable clamp.

Transmission Cable Adjustment

Rabbit, Scirocco

1. At the carburetor, make sure that the throttle is closed, the choke is off, and the fast idle cam is out of action. Detach the cable end at the transmission.
2. Press the lever at the transmission end of the cable toward the cable.
3. You should be able to insert the cable end into the transmission lever without moving the lever.
4. Adjust the cable length to correct.

Kickdown Switch Check

Dasher

1. Turn the ignition switch ON.
2. Floor the accelerator—you should hear an audible click from the solenoid on the transmission.
3. Replace the solenoid if no sound is heard.

First Gear (Front) Band Adjustment

Dasher

NOTE: *The transmission must be horizontal when band adjustments are performed. The first gear band has a narrow point adjusting screw, the second gear band a wide screw.*

1. Tighten the first gear band adjusting screw to 7.2 ft. lbs (86 in lbs).
2. Loosen the screw and tighten it again to 3.5 ft. lb. (42 in. lb).
3. Turn the screw out 3¼–3½ turns and then tighten the locknut.

Second Gear (Rear) Band Adjustment

Dasher, Rabbit, Scirocco

NOTE: *The transmission must be horizontal when band adjustments are performed. The first gear band has a narrow point adjusting screw, the second gear band a wide screw.*

1. Tighten the second gear band adjusting screw to 7.2 ft. lb. (86 in. lb).
2. Loosen the screw and tighten it again to 3.6 ft. lb. (43 in. lb).
3. Turn the screw out 2½ turns and then tighten the locknut.

Neutral Start Switch

The combination neutral start and backup light switch is mounted inside the shifter housing.

DRIVE AXLES

Halfshaft Removal and Installation

1. Remove the front axle nut.

NOTE: *Use a long breaker bar with an extension (length of pipe).*

2. Raise and support the car.

3. Remove the allen head bolts retaining the axle shaft to the transaxle.

NOTE: *If you are removing the right axle shaft, detach the exhaust pipe from the manifold and the transaxle bracket.*

4. Pull the axle shaft out and up and place it on top of the transaxle.

5. Turn the steering wheel all the way to the side of the shaft being removed. Pull the axle shaft from the steering knuckle.

6. Installation is the reverse of removal. Tighten the transaxle bolts to 25 ft. lbs. The axle nut is tightened to 180–216 ft. lbs.

Pulling the Dasher axle shaft from the steering knuckle

REAR SUSPENSION

The Dasher rear suspension has a rear axle beam containing a full length torsion bar. A trailing arm is welded to the axle beam tube on each side. The trailing arms mount to the unit body in rubber bushings. A coil spring provides the suspension at each wheel. A Panhard rod locates the axle against side forces.

The Rabbit and Scirocco rear suspension uses an exposed cross-chassis torsion beam connecting two trailing arms. Coil spring/shock absorber units are mounted to the body and to the trailing arms.

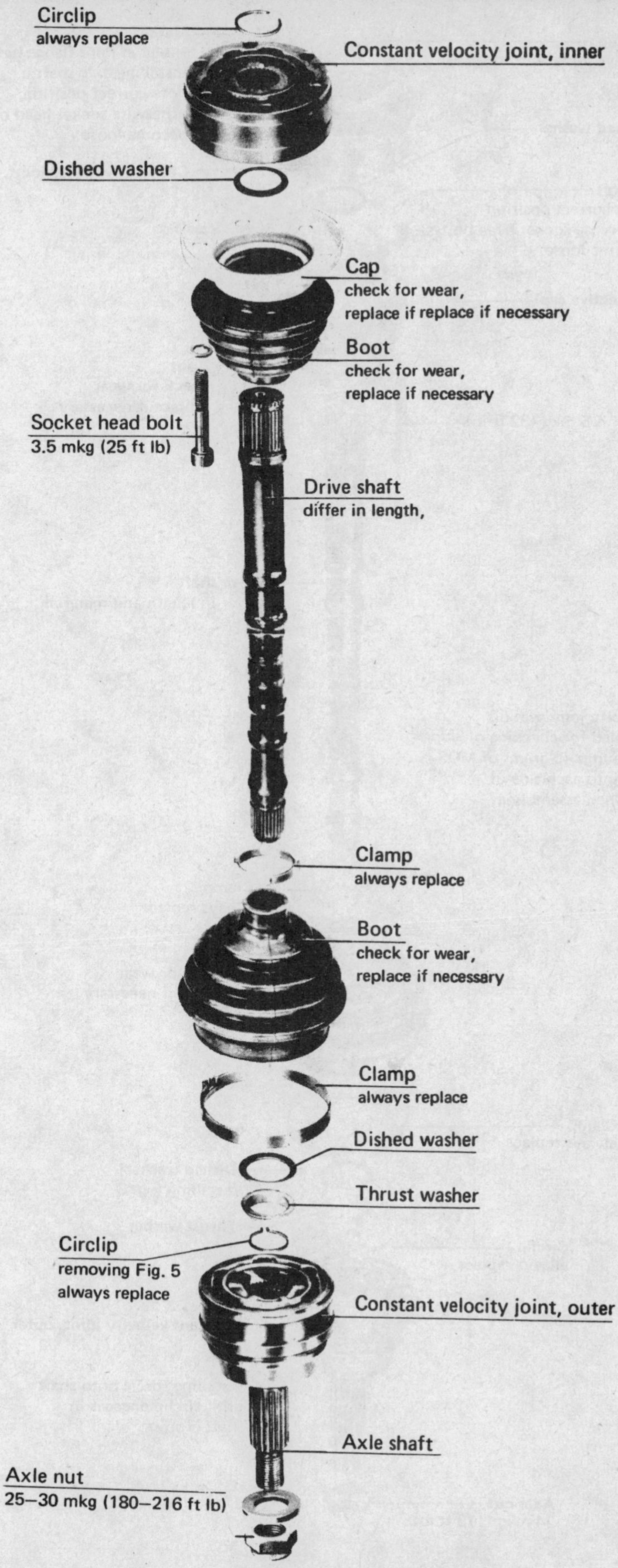

Circlip
always replace

Constant velocity joint, inner

Dished washer

Cap
check for wear,
replace if replace if necessary

Boot
check for wear,
replace if necessary

Socket head bolt
3.5 mkg (25 ft lb)

Drive shaft
differ in length,

Clamp
always replace

Boot
check for wear,
replace if necessary

Clamp
always replace

Dished washer

Thrust washer

Circlip
removing Fig. 5
always replace

Constant velocity joint, outer

Axle shaft

Axle nut
25–30 mkg (180–216 ft lb)

Dasher axle shaft

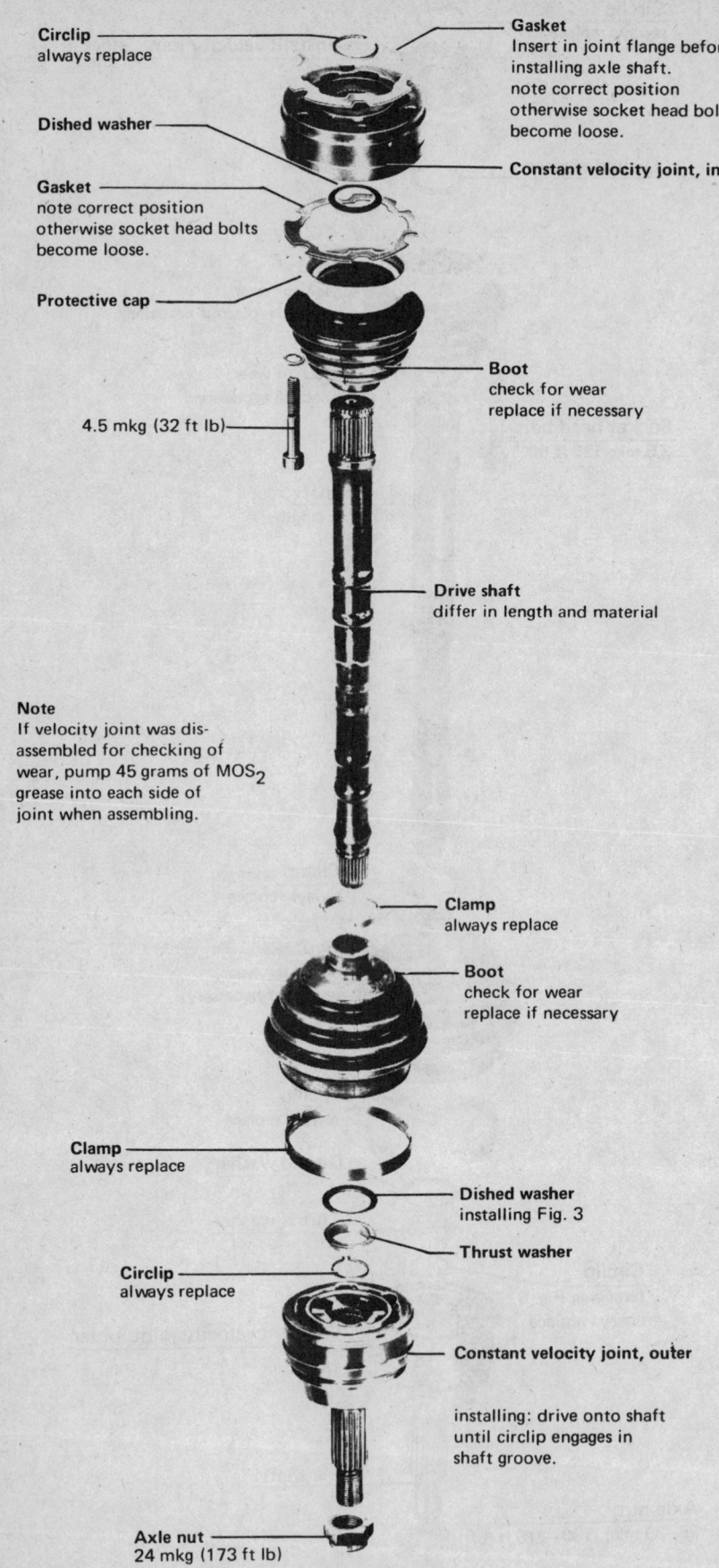

Circlip
always replace

Dished washer

Gasket
note correct position
otherwise socket head bolts
become loose.

Protective cap

4.5 mkg (32 ft lb)

Note
If velocity joint was disassembled for checking of
wear, pump 45 grams of MOS$_2$
grease into each side of
joint when assembling.

Clamp
always replace

Clamp
always replace

Circlip
always replace

Axle nut
24 mkg (173 ft lb)

Gasket
Insert in joint flange before
installing axle shaft.
note correct position
otherwise socket head bolts
become loose.

Constant velocity joint, inner

Boot
check for wear
replace if necessary

Drive shaft
differ in length and material

Boot
check for wear
replace if necessary

Dished washer
installing Fig. 3

Thrust washer

Constant velocity joint, outer

installing: drive onto shaft
until circlip engages in
shaft groove.

Rabbit Scirocco axle shaft

Coil Springs

Removal & Installation

Dasher Only

1. Raise the car on a lift.
2. Support the axle.
3. Install spring compressor on the coil spring, and remove.
4. Installation is the reverse of removal.

NOTE: *It is not necessary to replace both springs if only one is damaged.*

Shock Absorbers

Removal and Installation

Dasher

1. With the car on the ground, remove the lower shock mounting bolt and nut.
2. Raise and support the car.
3. Unscrew and remove the upper retaining bolt.
4. Remove the shock absorber.
5. Install the upper retaining bolt and tighten the bolt to 43 ft. lb.
6. Insert the lower retaining bolt and nut. Tighten to 43 ft. lb.

Strut Assembly

Removal & Installation

Rabbit & Scirocco Only

1. Raise the car on a lift.
2. Support the axle, but do not put any load on the springs.
3. Remove the rubber guard from inside the car.
4. Remove the nut, washer and mounting disc.
5. Unbolt the strut assembly from the rear axle and remove it.
6. Installation is the reverse of removal.

The struts can be disassembled with the use of a spring compressor. The sloted nut at the top of the strut is removed with the assembly mounted in a suitable vise.

FRONT SUSPENSION

The front suspension is a simple strut design. It consists of a lower control arm, ball joint, and suspension strut. In a McPherson strut design, such as this, the shock absorber strut serves as a locating member of the suspension as well as a damper. A shock absorber insert is located inside the strut. A coil spring is used. A stabilizer bar is used to reduce front body roll on the Dasher.

Ball Joint

Removal and Installation

1. Jack up the front of the car and support it on stands.

2. Matchmark the ball joint-to-control arm position on the Dasher.

3. Remove the retaining bolt and nut.

4. Pry the lower control arm and ball joint down and out of the strut.

5. Remove the two ball joint-to-lower control arm retaining nuts and bolts on the Dasher. Drill out the rivets on the Rabbit and Scirocco; enlarge the holes to 21/64 in.

6. Remove the ball joint assembly.

7. Install the Dasher ball joint in the reverse order of removal. If no parts were installed other than the ball joint, align the match marks made in Step 2. No camber adjustment is necessary if this is done. Pull the ball joint into alignment with pliers. Tighten the two control arm bolts to 47 ft lb and the strut-to-ball-joint bolt to 18 ft lb.

8. On the Rabbit and Scirocco, bolt the new ball joint in place. Torque the bolts to 18 ft lbs. Tighten the retaining bolt for the ball joint stud to 21 ft lbs.

Shock Absorber

Removal and Installation

Since the shock absorber cartridge is contained within the strut assembly, it is necessary to remove the strut and then compress the coil spring in order to remove the shock.

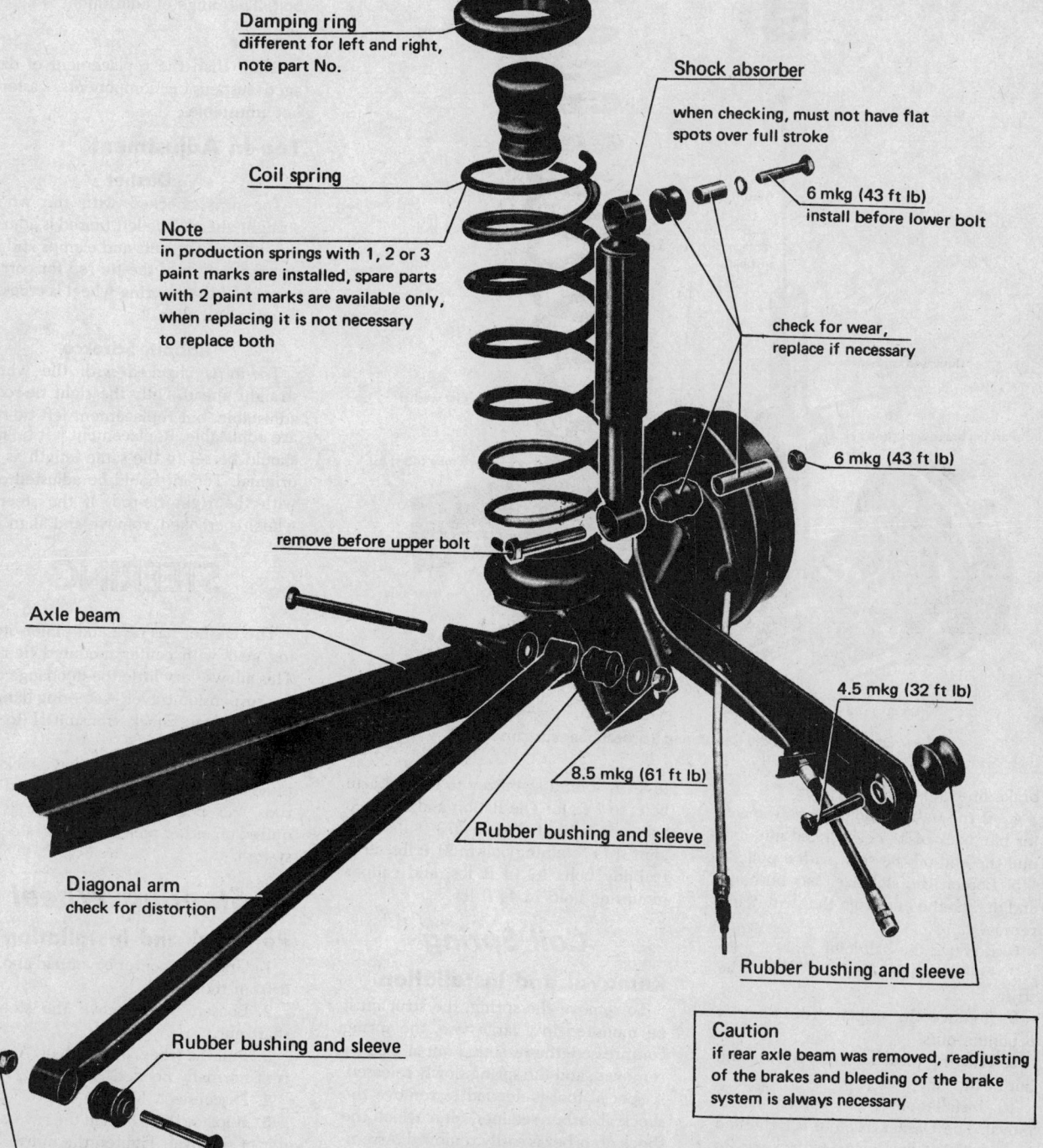

Damping ring
different for left and right, note part No.

Coil spring

Note
in production springs with 1, 2 or 3 paint marks are installed, spare parts with 2 paint marks are available only, when replacing it is not necessary to replace both

Shock absorber

when checking, must not have flat spots over full stroke

6 mkg (43 ft lb)
install before lower bolt

check for wear, replace if necessary

6 mkg (43 ft lb)

remove before upper bolt

Axle beam

4.5 mkg (32 ft lb)

8.5 mkg (61 ft lb)

Rubber bushing and sleeve

Diagonal arm
check for distortion

Rubber bushing and sleeve

Rubber bushing and sleeve

Caution
if rear axle beam was removed, readjusting of the brakes and bleeding of the brake system is always necessary

8.5 mkg (61 ft lb)

Dasher rear suspension

Strut

Removal and Installation

1. With the car on the ground, remove the front axle nut. Loosen the wheel bolts.

2. Raise and support the front of the car. Remove the wheels.

3. Remove the brake caliper from the strut and hang it with wire. Detach the

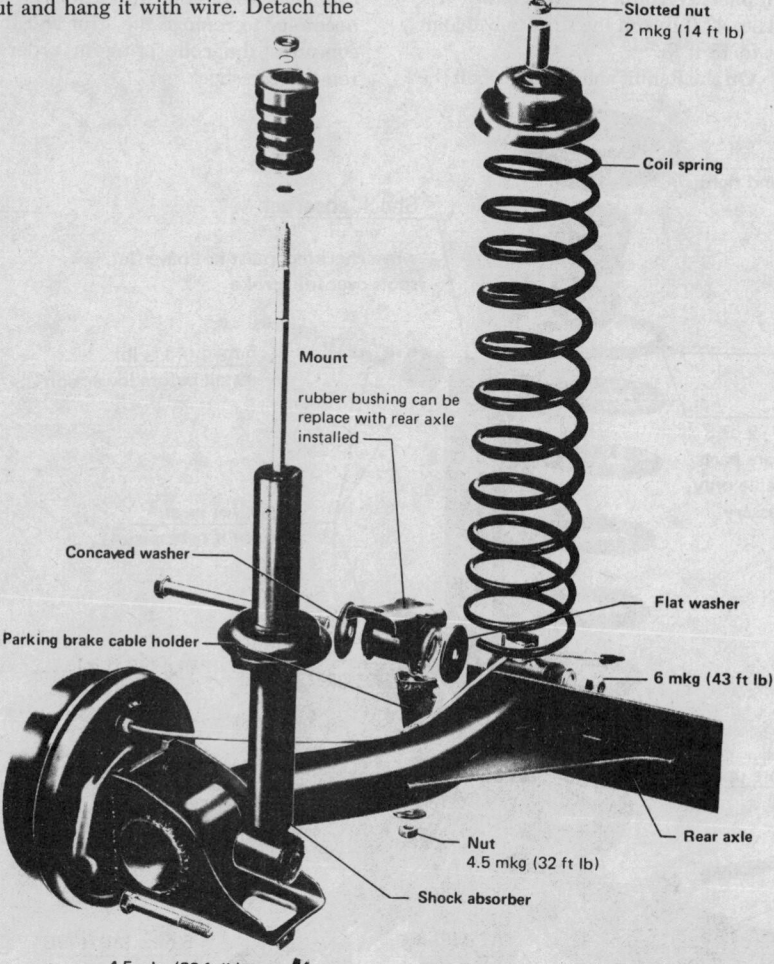

3.5 mkg (25 ft lb)

Slotted nut
2 mkg (14 ft lb)

Coil spring

Mount

rubber bushing can be
replace with rear axle
installed

Concaved washer

Parking brake cable holder

Flat washer

6 mkg (43 ft lb)

Nut
4.5 mkg (32 ft lb)

Rear axle

Shock absorber

4.5 mkg (32 ft lb)

Exploded view of the Rabbit and Scirocco rear suspension

brake line clips from the strut.

4. At the tie-rod end, remove the cotter pin, back off the castellated nut, and pull the end off the strut with a puller.

5. Loosen the stabilizer bar bushings and detach the end from the strut being removed.

6. Remove the ball joint.

7. Pull the axle driveshaft from the strut.

8. Remove the upper strut-to-fender retaining nuts.

9. Pull the strut assembly down and out of the car.

10. Installation is the reverse of removal. The Dasher axle nut is tightened to 180–216 ft lbs, lower control arm to strut bolt to 16 ft lb, caliper to strut bolts

to 44 ft lb and stabilizer to control arm bolts to 7 ft. lb. The Rabbit and Scirocco axle nut is tightened to 173 ft lbs, ball joint stud retaining bolt to 21 ft lbs, strut to body bolts to 14 ft lbs, and caliper mounting bolts to 44 ft lbs.

Coil Spring

Removal and Installation

To remove the spring, the strut must be mounted in a large vise, the spring compressed, the retaining nut and cover removed, and the spring slowly released. A special tool is needed to remove the shock absorber retainer, after which the shock absorber is easily removed. Assembly is the reverse of removal.

Front End Alignment

Camber Adjustment

Dasher

Camber is adjusted by loosening the two ball joint-to-lower control arm bolts, and moving the ball joint in or out as necessary.

Rabbit, Scirocco

Camber is adjusted by loosening the nuts of the two bolts holding the top of the wheel bearing housing to the bottom of the strut, and turning the top eccentric bolt. The range of adjustment is 2°.

Caster

Other than the replacement of damaged suspension components, caster is not adjustable.

Toe-In Adjustment

Dasher

Toe-in is checked with the wheels straight ahead. The left tie rod is adjustable. Loosen the nuts and clamps and adjust the length of the tie rod for correct toe-out. If the steering wheel is crooked, remove and align it.

Rabbit, Scirocco

Toe-in is checked with the wheels straight ahead. Only the right tie-rod is adjustable, but replacement left tie-rods are adjustable. Replacement left tie-rods should be set to the same length as the original. Toe-in should be adjusted only with the right tie-rod. If the steering wheel is crooked, remove and align it.

STEERING

The Dasher has rack and pinion steering gear with center mounted tie-rods. This allows very little toe-in change during suspension travel. A steering damper reduces road shock transmittal to the steering wheel.

The Rabbit and Scirocco have rack and pinion steering with end mounted tie-rods. No periodic maintenance is required on either rack and pinion steering system.

Steering Wheel

Removal and Installation

1. Grasp the center cover pad and pull it from the wheel.

2. Loosen and remove the steering shaft nut.

3. Pull the wheel off the shaft. A puller isn't normally needed.

4. Disconnect the horn wire.

5. Replace the wheel in the reverse order of removal. Tighten the nut to 36 ft lb.

Turn Signal and Headlight Dimmer Switch Replacement

1. Disconnect the battery ground cable.
2. Remove the steering wheel.
3. Remove the switch retaining screws.
4. Pry the switch housing off the column.
5. Disconnect the electrical plugs at the back of the switch.
6. Remove the switch housing.
7. Replace in the reverse order of removal.

Ignition Switch and Steering Lock

Removal and Installation

NOTE: *The access hole for removing the lock cylinder may be missing. Before the lock cylinder can be removed, drill a hole according to following dimensions:*
a=7/16 in.
b=7/16 in.
Drill the hole ⅛ in. deep.

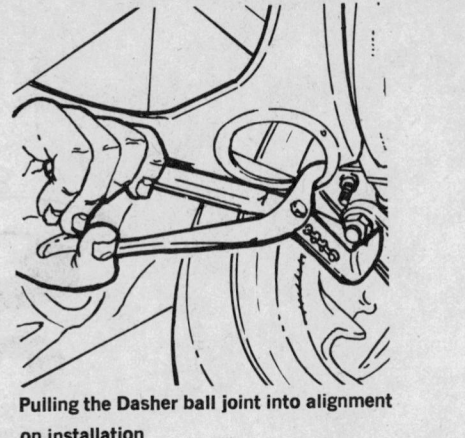

Pulling the Dasher ball joint into alignment on installation

1. Remove the steering wheel and turn signal switch. Remove the steering column shaft covers.
2. The lock is clamped to the steering column with special bolts whose heads shear off on installation. These must be drilled out in order to remove the switch.
3. On replacement, make sure that the lock tang is aligned with the slot in the steering column.

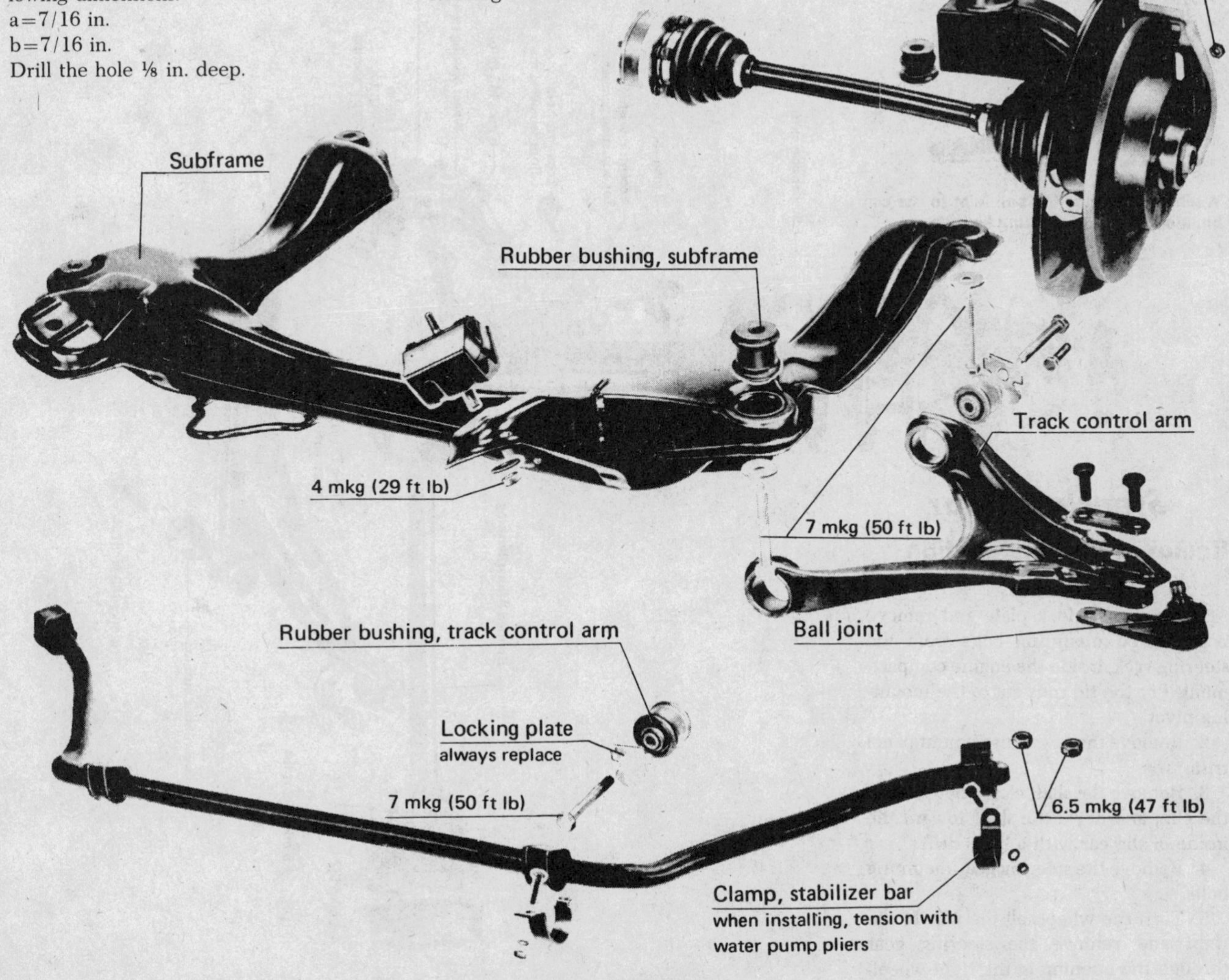

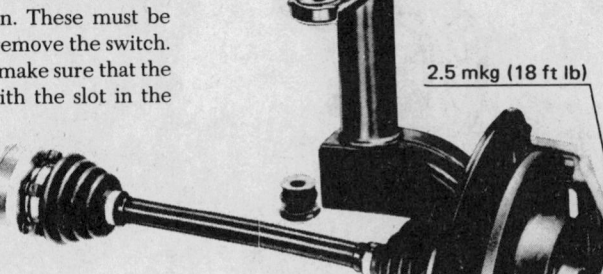

2.5 mkg (18 ft lb)

Subframe

Rubber bushing, subframe

Track control arm

4 mkg (29 ft lb)

7 mkg (50 ft lb)

Rubber bushing, track control arm

Ball joint

Locking plate
always replace

7 mkg (50 ft lb)

6.5 mkg (47 ft lb)

Clamp, stabilizer bar
when installing, tension with water pump pliers

Dasher front suspension

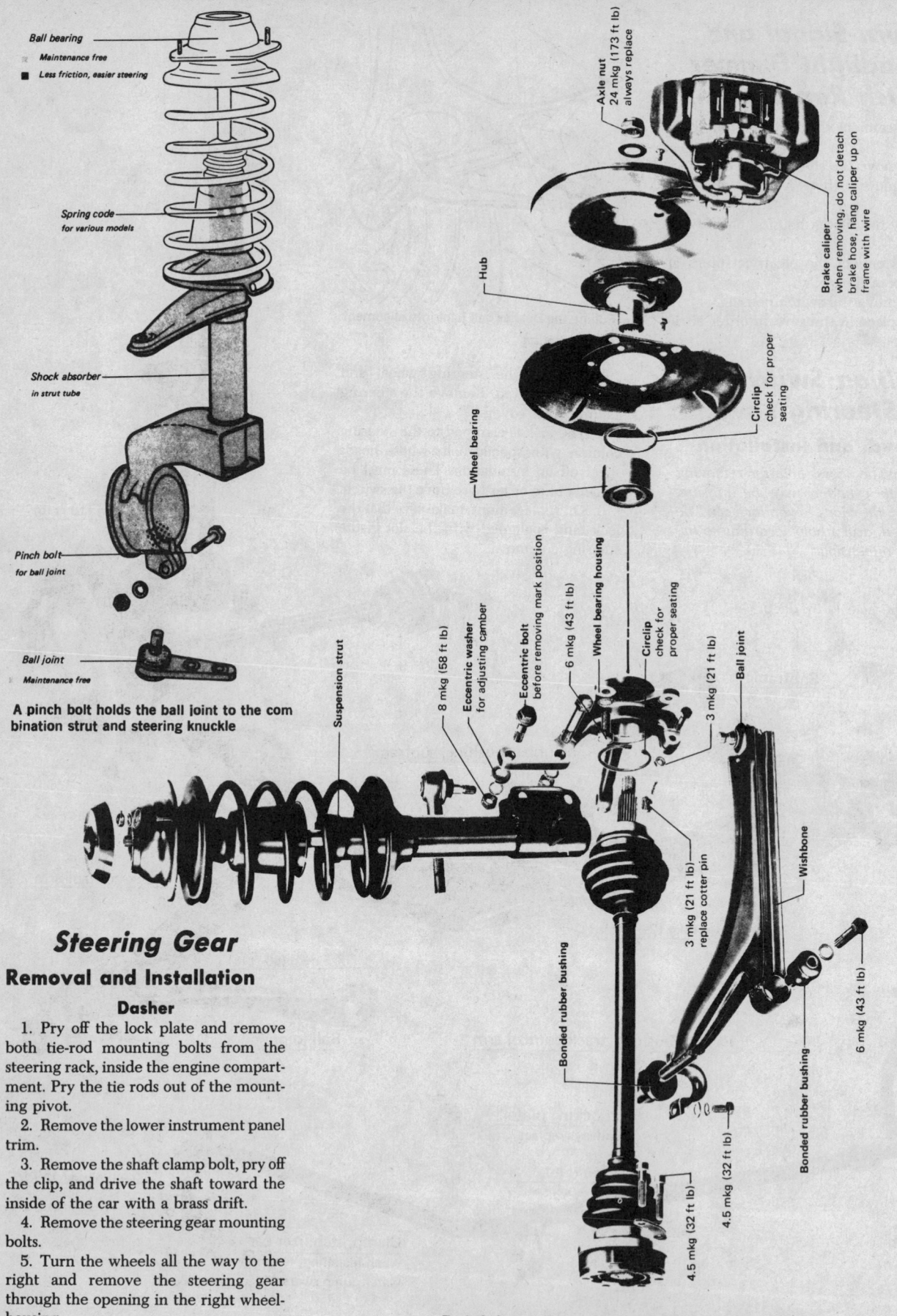

Ball bearing
- Maintenance free
- Less friction, easier steering

Spring code
for various models

Shock absorber
in strut tube

Pinch bolt
for ball joint

Ball joint
Maintenance free

A pinch bolt holds the ball joint to the combination strut and steering knuckle

Axle nut
24 mkg (173 ft lb)
always replace

Hub

Wheel bearing

Brake caliper
when removing, do not detach
brake hose, hang caliper up on
frame with wire

Circlip
check for proper
seating

Suspension strut

8 mkg (58 ft lb)

Eccentric washer
for adjusting camber

Eccentric bolt
before removing mark position

6 mkg (43 ft lb)

Wheel bearing housing

Circlip
check for
proper seating

3 mkg (21 ft lb)

Ball joint

3 mkg (21 ft lb)
replace cotter pin

Wishbone

Bonded rubber bushing

Bonded rubber bushing

6 mkg (43 ft lb)

4.5 mkg (32 ft lb)

4.5 mkg (32 ft lb)

Steering Gear

Removal and Installation

Dasher

1. Pry off the lock plate and remove both tie-rod mounting bolts from the steering rack, inside the engine compartment. Pry the tie rods out of the mounting pivot.

2. Remove the lower instrument panel trim.

3. Remove the shaft clamp bolt, pry off the clip, and drive the shaft toward the inside of the car with a brass drift.

4. Remove the steering gear mounting bolts.

5. Turn the wheels all the way to the right and remove the steering gear through the opening in the right wheelhousing.

Exploded view of the Rabbit and Scirocco front suspension

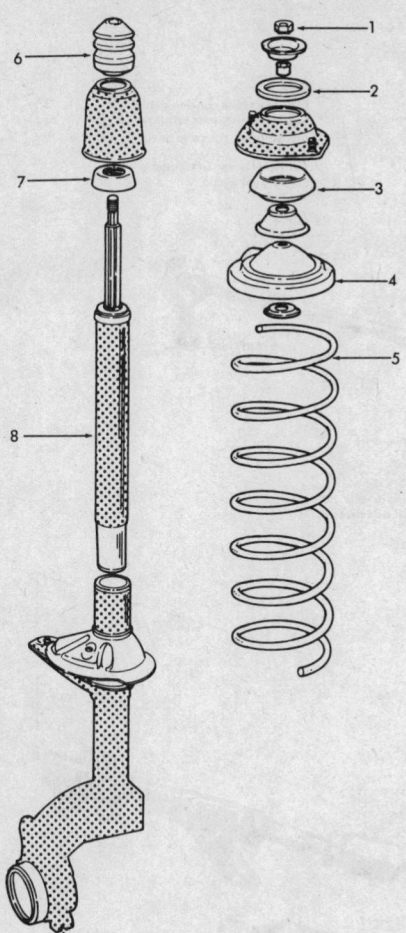

1. Cotter pin
2. Tie-rod
3. Axle driveshaft
4. Circlip
5. Retainer nut
6. Brake caliper
7. Wheel bearing
8. Hub
9. Brake disc
10. Axle nut

Dasher strut exploded view

1. Suspension strut nut
2. End collar
3. Rubber damper
4. Coil spring cap
5. Coil spring
6. Bumper
7. Threaded cap
8. Shock absorber

Dimensions for drilling ignition lock cylinder hole (if not equipped)

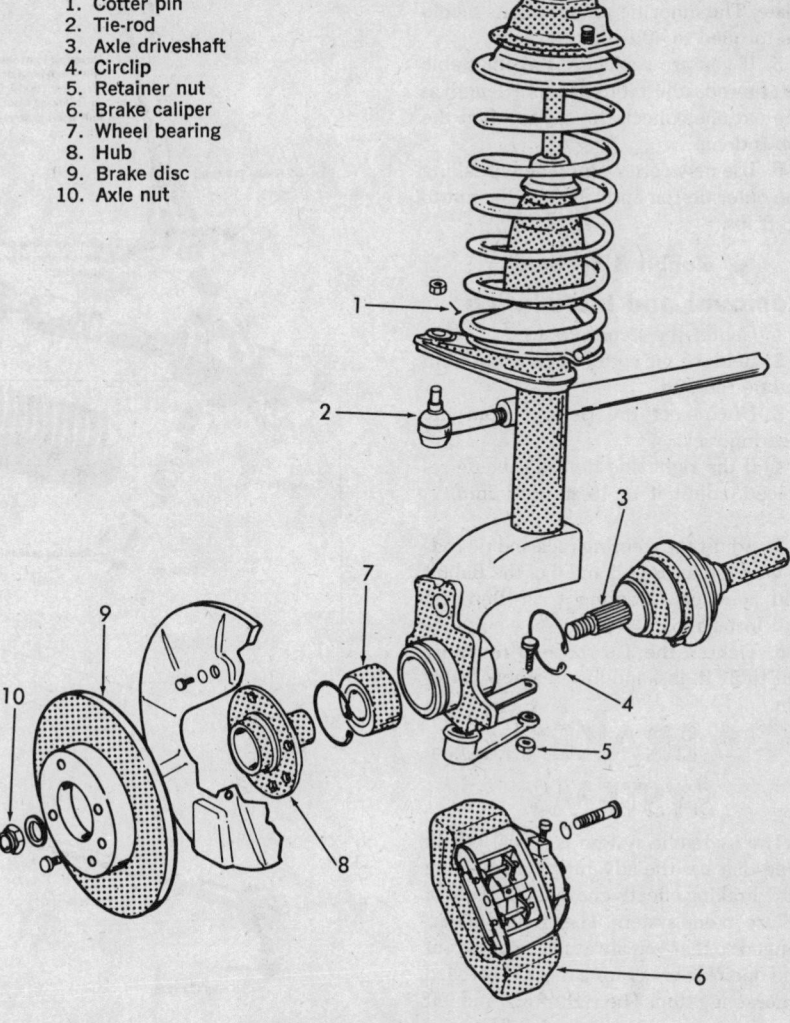

Dasher strut installation details

6. For installation, temporarily install the tie-rod mounting pivot to the rack with both mounting bolts. Remove one bolt, install the tie-rod, and replace the bolt. Do the same on the other tie-rod. Make sure to install the lock plate.

Torque the tie-rod bolts to 39 ft lbs, the mounting pivot bolt to 15 ft lbs, and the steering gear to body mounting bolts to 15 ft lbs.

Rabbit & Scirocco

1. Disconnect the steering shaft universal joint and wire up out of the way.

2. Disconnect the tie rods at the steering rack and wire up and out of the way.

3. Remove the steering rack and drive.

4. Install the steering rack and drive and torque the attaching hardware to 14 ft. lbs.

5. Set the steering rack with equal distances between the housing on the right side and left side.

6. Install the tie rods and screw both sides in until a equal distance is reached on both rods.

7. Tighten the steering gear adjusting screw until it touches the thrust washer.

Tighten the lock nut.

8. Install the steering shaft.

9. Check the front end alignment.

Steering Linkage

Tie-Rod Removal and Installation

Dasher

1. Raise the car and remove the front wheels.

2. Disconnect the outer end of the steering tie-rod from the steering knuckle by removing the cotter pin and nut and pressing out the tie-rod end. A small puller or press is required to free the tie-rod end.

3. Under the hood, pry off the lock plate and remove the mounting bolts from both tie-rod inner ends. Pry the tie-rod out of the mounting pivot.

4. First install the mounting pivot to the rack with both mounting bolts. Remove one bolt, install the tie-rod, and

replace the bolt. Do the same on the other tie-rod. Be sure to install the lock plate. The inner tie-rod end bolts should be torqued to 40 ft lbs.

5. If you are replacing the adjustable left tie-rod, adjust it to the same length as the old one. Check the toe-in when the job is done.

6. Use new cotter pins when installing the outer tie-rod ends. Torque the nut to 28 ft lbs.

Rabbit & Scirocco
Removal and Installation

1. Center the steering rack.

2. Remove the cotter pin and nut from the tie rod end.

3. Disconnect the tie rod from the steering rack.

4. If the right side tie rod is being replaced, adjust it to 15 in. (381 mm)

5. Adjust the steering rack and tie rods as outlined in steps 5 and 6 of the Rabbit and Scirocco "Steering Gear Removal and Installation".

6. Tighten the Tie rod end retaining nut to 21 ft. lbs. and install a new cotter pin.

BRAKE
SYSTEMS

The hydraulic system is a dual circuit type that has the advantage of retaining 50% braking effectiveness in the event of failure in one system. The circuits are arranged so that you always have one front and one rear brake for a more controlled emergency stop. The right front and left rear are in one circuit; the left front and right rear are in the second circuit.

There is also a brake failure switch and a proportioning valve.

The brake failure unit is a hydraulic valve/electrical switch which warns of

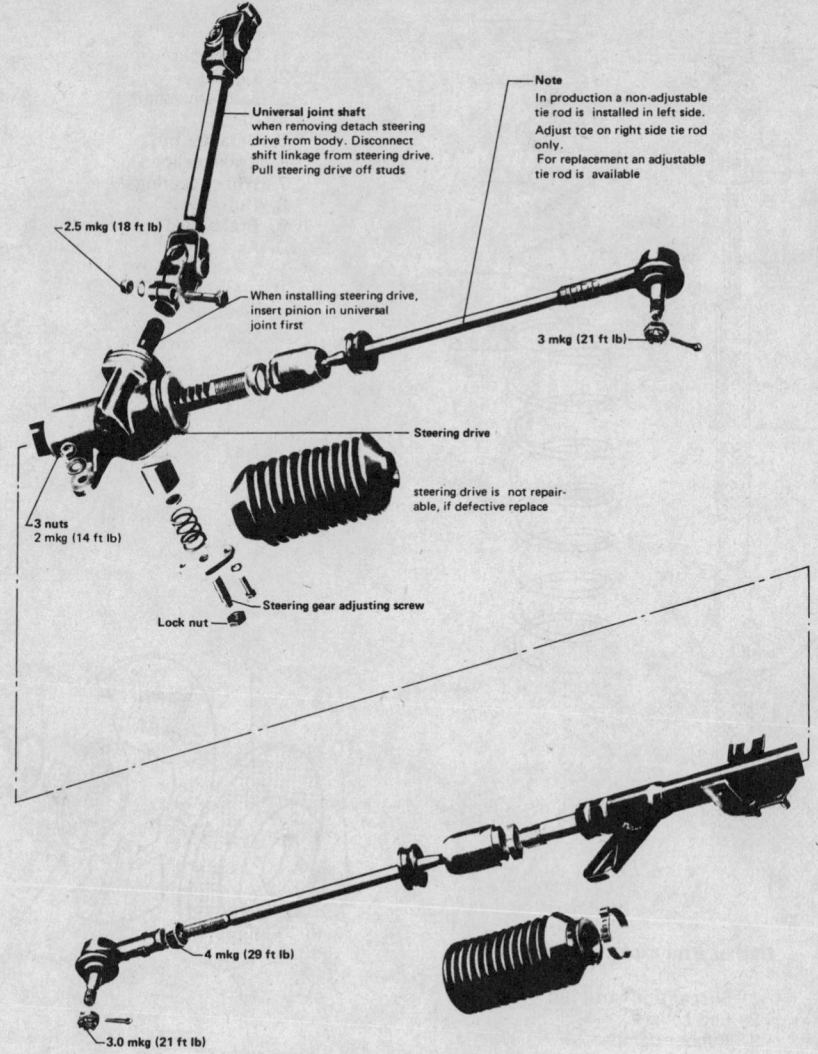

Note
In production a non-adjustable tie rod is installed in left side. Adjust toe on right side tie rod only. For replacement an adjustable tie rod is available

Universal joint shaft when removing detach steering drive from body. Disconnect shift linkage from steering drive. Pull steering drive off studs

2.5 mkg (18 ft lb)

When installing steering drive, insert pinion in universal joint first

3 mkg (21 ft lb)

Steering drive

steering drive is not repairable, if defective replace

3 nuts 2 mkg (14 ft lb)

Steering gear adjusting screw

Lock nut

4 mkg (29 ft lb)

3.0 mkg (21 ft lb)

Rabbit and Scirocco steering gear

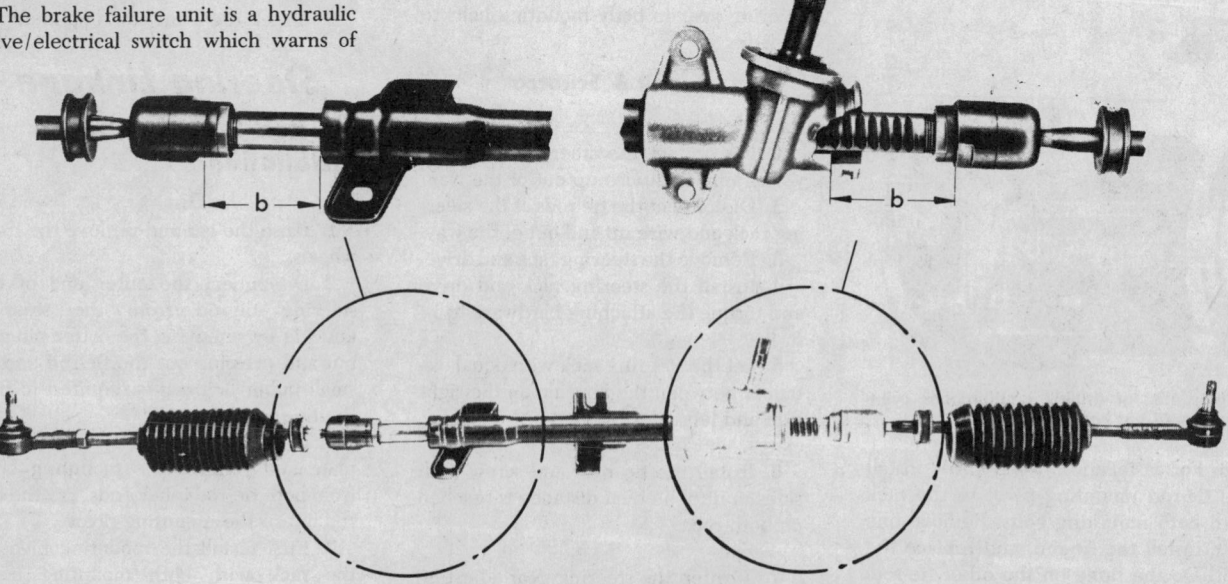

Adjusting Rabbit and Scirocco tie-rod position. b = 2.64 in.

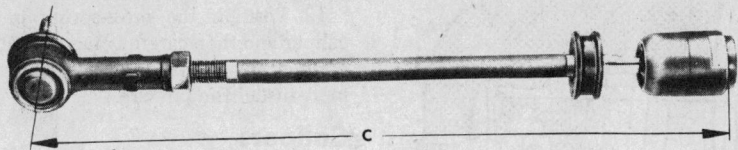

Right side tie-rod adjustment—Rabbit and Scirocco

brake problems by the warning light on the instrument panel. A piston inside the switch is kept centered by one brake system pressure on one side and the other system pressure on the opposite side. Should a failure occur in one system, the piston would go to the "failed" side and complete an electrical circuit to the warning lamp. This switch also functions as a parking brake reminder light and will go out when the parking brake is released. The proportioning valve, actually two separate valves on manual transmission Dasher sedans, provides balanced front-to-rear braking during hard stops.

Extreme brake line pressure will overcome the spring pressure on the piston within the valve causing it to proportionately restrict pressure to the rear brakes. In this manner, the rear brakes are kept from locking. The proportioner doesn't operate under normal braking conditions.

Adjustment

The front disc brakes require no adjustment, as disc brakes automatically adjust themselves to compensate for pad wear. The rear drum brakes must be adjusted whenever free travel is one third or more of the total pedal travel.

NOTE: *On all models except manual transmission Dasher sedans, it is necessary to push the brake proportioning lever toward the rear axle to relieve the pressure in the right rear brake line.*

1. Raise the rear of the car. Place the jack under the center of the Dasher torsion bar/axle. The jack pad should be at least 4 in. square, otherwise you may damage the axle. Raise the Rabbit and Scirocco on a chassis lift.

2. Block the front wheels and release the parking brake. Step on the brake pedal hard to center the linings.

3. Remove the rubber plug from the rear of the backing plate on each wheel.

4. Insert a brake adjusting tool or wide-bladed screwdriver and turn the adjuster wheel clockwise until the brakes drag as you turn the wheel in the forward direction.

5. Turn the adjuster in the opposite direction until you just pass the point of drag.

6. Repeat on the other wheel.

7. Lower the car and road test. Readjust, if necessary.

Master Cylinder

Removal and Installation

1. Disconnect and plug the brake lines.

2. Disconnect the electrical plug from the sending unit for the brake failure switch.

3. Remove the two master cylinder mounting nuts.

4. Lift the master cylinder and reservoir out of the engine compartment being careful not to spill any fluid on the fender. Empty out and discard the brake fluid.

CAUTION: *Do not depress the brake pedal while the master cylinder is removed.*

5. Position the master cylinder and reservoir assembly onto the studs for the booster and install the washers and nuts. Tighten the nuts to no more than 10 ft. lbs.

6. Remove the plugs and connect the brake lines.

7. Bleed the entire brake system.

Overhaul

1. Remove the master cylinder from the booster.

2. Firmly mount the master cylinder in a vise. Use clean rags to protect the cylinder from the vise jaws.

3. Grasp the plastic reservoir and pull it out of the rubber plugs. Remove the plugs.

4. In the center of the cylinder there is a stop screw; remove it. Discard the stop screw seal, there should be a new one in the rebuilding kit.

5. At the end of the master cylinder is a snap-ring (circlip); remove it, using snap-ring pliers.

6. Shake out the secondary piston assembly. If the primary piston remains

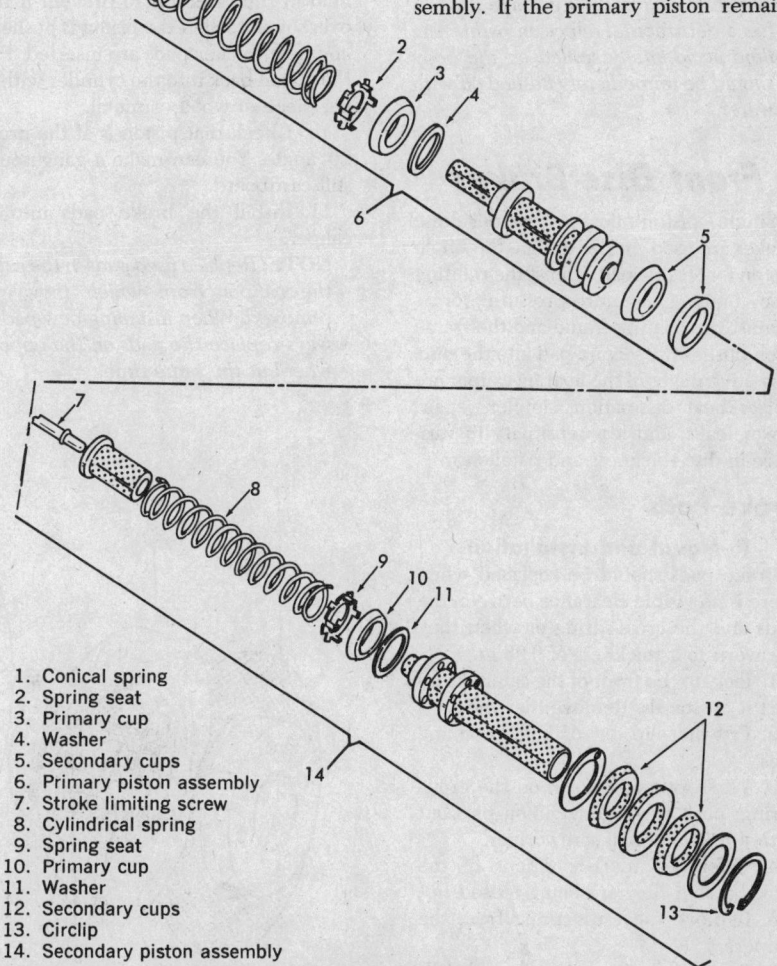

1. Conical spring
2. Spring seat
3. Primary cup
4. Washer
5. Secondary cups
6. Primary piston assembly
7. Stroke limiting screw
8. Cylindrical spring
9. Spring seat
10. Primary cup
11. Washer
12. Secondary cups
13. Circlip
14. Secondary piston assembly

Master cylinder internal components

lodged in the bore, it can be forced by applying compressed air to the open line fitting.

7. Disassemble the secondary piston. The two secondary springs will be replaced with those in the rebuilding kit. Save the washers and spacers.

8. Carefully clamp the secondary piston. Slightly compress the spring and screw out the stroke limiting bolt.

9. Remove the secondary piston stop sleeve bolt, spring, spring seat, and support washer.

10. Replace all the parts with those supplied in the overhaul kit.

11. Clean all metal parts in alcohol and dry them with compressed air.

12. Check every part you are reusing. NOTE: *Keep a close check on the brake fluid in the reservoir and top it up as necessary throughout the bleeding process.*

13. Keep repeating this procedure until no more air bubbles can be seen coming from the hose in the brake fluid.

14. Remove the bleeder hose and install the dust cover.

15. Continue the bleeding at each wheel in sequence. NOTE: *Don't spill any brake fluid; it has a detrimental effect on paint. Any fluid accidentally spilled on the body should be immediately flushed off with water.*

Front Disc Brakes

Single piston floating caliper disc brakes are used. In this design, the single piston forces one pad against the rotating disc brake. Counter pressure forces against the floating frame and the frame then pushes the second pad into the disc. The advantages of the floating caliper are better heat dissipation, simpler repair, fewer leaks, and less sensitivity to variance-in-disc thickness and parallelism.

Brake Pads

Removal and Installation

Brake pads should be replaced when there is no visible clearance between the pads and the cross-spring or when they are worn to a thickness of 0.08 in.

1. Jack up the front of the car and support it on stands. Remove the wheels.

2. Pry the clip out of both retaining pins.

3. While pressing down on the cross-spring, push the pad retaining pins out with a drift or small screwdriver.

4. Reference mark positions of the brake pads if they are being reused.

5. Remove the cross-spring from the caliper.

6. Remove the inner brake pad. VW has a special tool for this purpose, but by

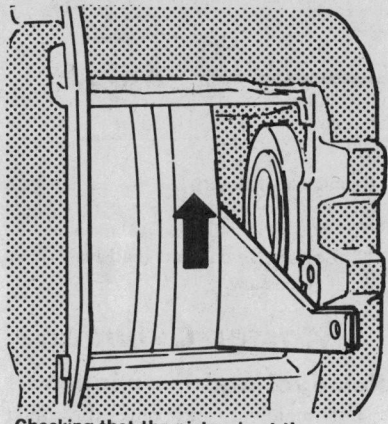

Checking that the piston is at the correct 20° angle

using a small drift or punch you can pry the pad out of the caliper until it can be gripped by a pair of pliers and removed.

7. The outer brake pad is positioned in a notch. Use a flat, smooth piece of hardwood or metal to press the floating caliper frame and piston cylinder outward.

8. Grip the outer pad and remove it.

9. Siphon out about half of the brake fluid in the reservoir to prevent it from overflowing when the piston is pushed in and new thicker pads are inserted. Press the piston back into the cylinder with the flat piece of wood or metal.

10. Check that piston is at the proper 20° angle. You can make a gauge out of stiff cardboard.

11. Install the brake pads into the caliper. NOTE: *Replace used pads in the side of the caliper from which they were removed. When installing new pads always replace the pads on the opposite wheel at the same time.*

12. Position the cross-spring in the caliper and then carefully tap the pad retaining pins into place with a small hammer. Install the pin clip.

Calipers

Removal and Installation

1. Jack up and support the front of the car.

2. Remove the brake pads.

3. If you are removing the caliper for overhaul, disconnect and plug the brake line at the caliper. If not, do not remove the hose—hang it by a wire.

4. Remove the two caliper-to-strut retaining bolts and remove the caliper.

5. Install the caliper using the reverse of the removal procedure. Tighten the two retaining bolts to 43 ft. lbs.

6. Bleed the brakes.

Overhaul

1. Remove the caliper.

2. Mount the caliper in a soft-jawed vise or place cloths over the jaws to protect the caliper.

3. Pry the fixed mounting frame off the floating frame.

4. Separate the caliper cylinder from the floating frame by prying it and the guide spring off the frame. Use a brass drift to lightly tap on the cylinder and place a piece of wood under the piston to protect it.

5. Using pliers remove the piston clamp ring. Remove and discard the rubber dust cover, a new one should be supplied with the rebuilding kit.

6. Remove the piston from the cylinder. If it is stubborn, remove the bleeder screw and blow it out with compressed air.

CAUTION: *Hold the piston over a*

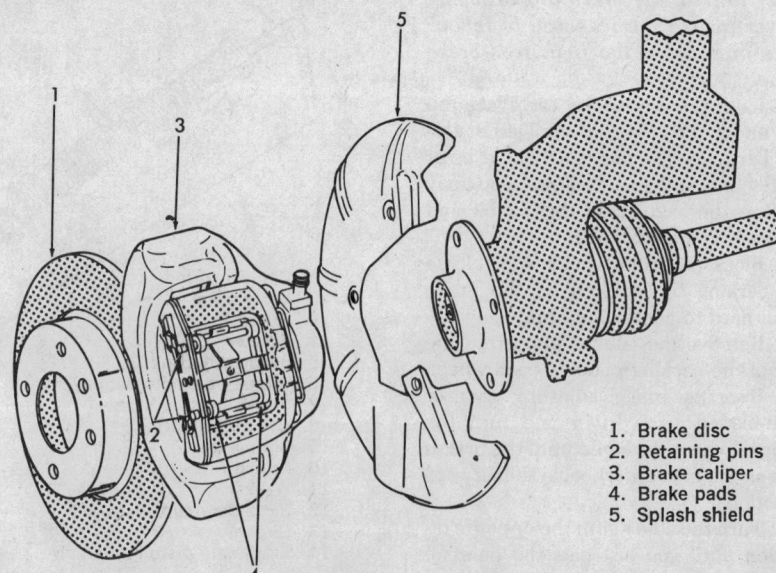

1. Brake disc
2. Retaining pins
3. Brake caliper
4. Brake pads
5. Splash shield

Caliper and disc mounting

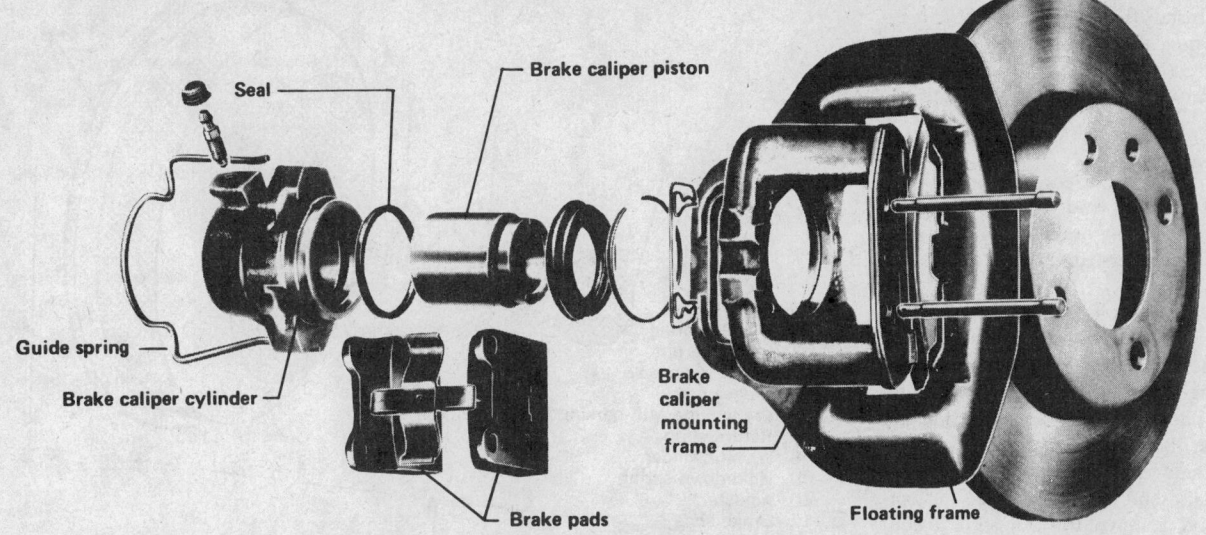

Seal — Brake caliper piston

Guide spring

Brake caliper cylinder

Brake caliper mounting frame

Floating frame

Brake pads

Exploded view of Teves or Girling caliper. Either are used

block of wood when doing this as the piston will fly out with considerable force.

7. When the piston pops out of the caliper, remove the rubber seal with a wood or plastic pin to avoid damaging the seal groove.

8. Clean all metal parts in alcohol. Inspect the pistons and their bores, they must be free of scoring and pitting. Replace the cylinder if there is any damage.

9. Discard all rubber parts. The caliper rebuilding kit includes new boots and seals which should be used as the caliper is reassembled.

10. Lightly coat the cylinder bore, piston, and seal with brake assembly paste or fresh brake fluid.

11. Using a vise, install the piston into the cylinder.

12. Position the guide spring in the groove of the brake cylinder and using a brass drift install the cylinder on the floating frame.

13. Place the mounting frame in the guide spring and slip it onto the floating frame. The fixed frame has two grooves which position it over the raised ribs of the floating frame.

14. Install the caliper and bleed the brakes.

Brake Disc

Inspection

Brake discs may be checked for lateral run-out while on the car. This check will require a dial indicator gauge and stand to mount it on the caliper. VW has a special tool for this purpose which mounts the dial indicator to the caliper, but it can also be mounted on the shaft of a C-clamp attached to the outside of the caliper.

1. Remove the wheel and reinstall the wheel bolts (tightened to 65 ft. lbs) to retain the disc to the hub.

2. Mount the dial indicator securely to the caliper. The feeler should touch the disc about ½-in. below the outer edge.

3. Rotate the disc and observe the gauge. Radial run-out (wobble) must not exceed 0.004 in. A disc which exceeds this specification must be replaced or refinished.

4. Brake discs which have excessive radial runout, sharp ridges, or scoring can be refinished. finish grinding must be done on both sides of disc to prevent squeaking and vibrating. Discs which have only light grooves and are otherwise acceptable can be used without refinishing.

The standard disc is 0.47 in thick. It should not be ground to less than 0.39 in. (0.41 for Rabbit and Scirocco).

Removal and Installation

1. Loosen the wheel bolts. Remove the hub cap.

2. Jack up the front of the car and place it on stands. Remove the wheel(s).

3. Remove the caliper.

4. Remove the disc-to-hub retaining screw.

5. Remove the disk with a sharp pull by hand, or use a suitable puller.

6. The disc is installed in the reverse order of removal. Install the caliper and bleed the brakes.

7. Install the wheel and lower the car. Tighten the wheel bolts diagonally to 65 ft lbs.

Front Wheel Bearings

There is no front wheel bearing adjustment. The bearing is pressed into the steering knuckle. Axle nut torque is 180–216 ft lbs for the Dasher and 174 ft lbs for the Rabbit and Scirocco. The axle nut should be tightened only with the wheels resting on the ground.

Drum Brakes

Brake Drums

Removal and Installation

1. Loosen the wheel bolts.

2. Jack up the rear of the car and support it on stands. Remove the wheel(s).

3. Pry off the hub cap.

4. Remove and discard the cotter pin.

5. Remove the castellated nut, hex nut, and washers. On front brakes, remove the screw holding the drum.

6. Pull off the brake drum. Be careful not to lose the inner race of the outer bearing.

NOTE: *If the drum does not come off easily, remove the rubber cover at the backing plate and back off the brake adjuster with an adjusting tool or wide-bladed screwdriver. If unsuccessful, use a puller. Never heat the drum or beat on it with a hammer.*

7. Check the brake drum for any cracks, scores, grooves, or an out-of-round condition. Replace a drum that shows cracking. Smooth out light scoring with fine emery cloth. If scoring is extensive have the drum turned. Never have a drum turned more than 0.030 in (0.020 for the Rabbit and Scirocco).

8. The stub axle bearings in the brake drum must be pressed out for replacement. Always use new seals on reassembly. The outer bearing race is retained by a snap-ring (circlip) on the Dasher.

9. After greasing the bearings and installing them in the drum with new seals, place the drum onto the stub axle.

10. Install the washer and the hex nut. Tighten the nut and then loosen it. Retighten the nut slightly so that the washer between the nut and the bearing can just be moved with a screwdriver. Correct bearing play is 0.001–.003 in.

11. Install the castellated nut and insert a new cotter pin. Fill the hub cap with grease and install it.

12. Install the wheel and lower the car.

Brake Shoes

Removal and Installation

1. Remove the brake drum.

2. Using pliers, disconnect the lower spring.

3. Disconnect the anchor spring and pins from each shoe.

4. Detach the parking brake cable by pressing back the spring with needle-nosed pliers and then disconnecting the cable at the lever.

5. Remove the second lower spring.

6. Raise one brake shoe from the bottom and remove the adjusting mechanism.

7. Lift the brake shoes and remove the upper springs. Remove both brake shoes.

8. Clean and inspect all brake parts. Spray solvents which do not affect linings are available for brake cleaning. Do not spray rubber parts with solvent.

9. Check the wheel cylinders for boot condition and leaking.

10. Inspect the replacement shoes for nicks or burrs; lubricate the backing plate contact points with Lubriplate, lubricate the brake cable, lever and adjuster, and then assemble.

11. Reverse the removal procedure for assembly. When completed, install the drum and make an initial adjustment by turning the adjuster wheel until a slight drag is felt between the shoes and drum, and back off about ¼ turn. Adjust the brakes.

Wheel Cylinders

Removal and Installation

1. Remove the brake shoes.

2. Loosen the brake line on the rear of the cylinder, but do not pull the line away from the cylinder or it may bend.

3. Remove the bolts and lockwashers that attach the wheel cylinder to the backing plate and remove the cylinder.

4. Position the new wheel cylinder on the backing plate and install the cylinder attaching bolts and lockwashers.

5. Attach the brake line.

6. Install the brakes and bleed the system.

Overhaul

1. Remove the brakes.

2. Place a bucket or some newspapers under the brake backing plate to catch the brake fluid that will run out of the wheel cylinder.

3. Remove the boots from the ends of the wheel cylinders.

4. Push one piston toward the center

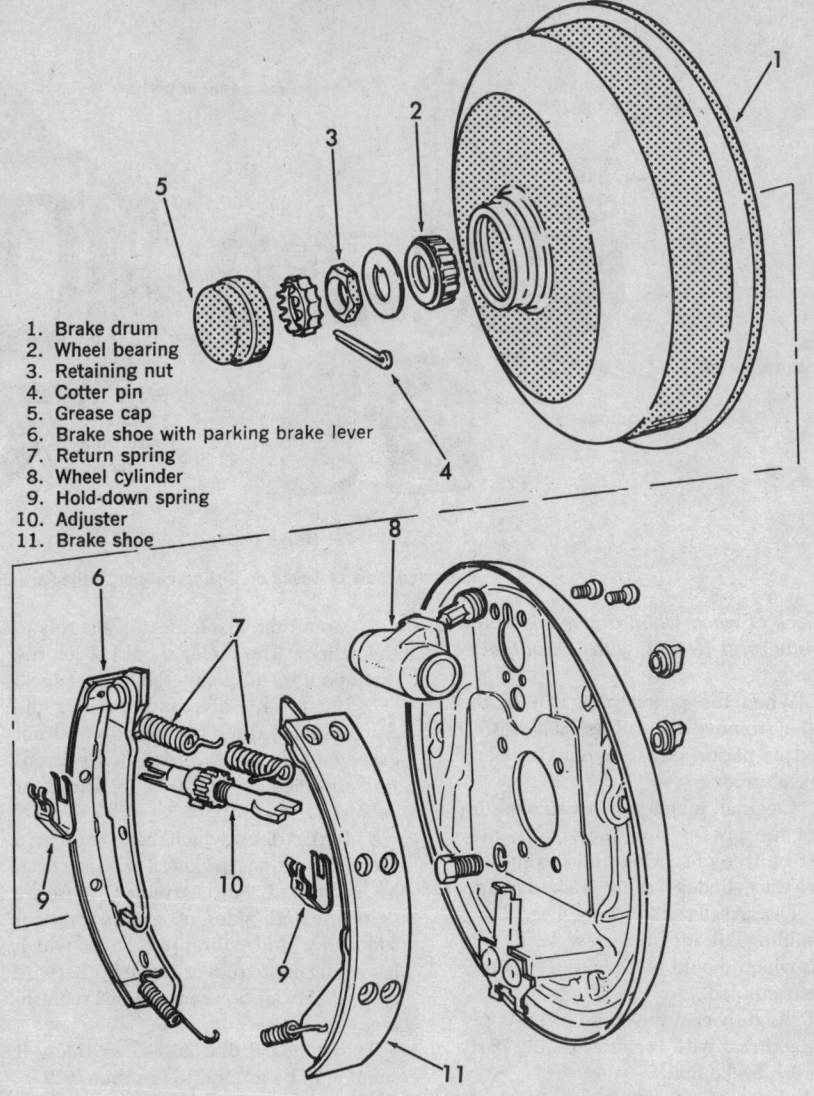

1. Brake drum
2. Wheel bearing
3. Retaining nut
4. Cotter pin
5. Grease cap
6. Brake shoe with parking brake lever
7. Return spring
8. Wheel cylinder
9. Hold-down spring
10. Adjuster
11. Brake shoe

Dasher rear brake, drum, and wheel bearing assembly, the Rabbit and Scirocco are similar but there is no inner wheel bearing snap-ring

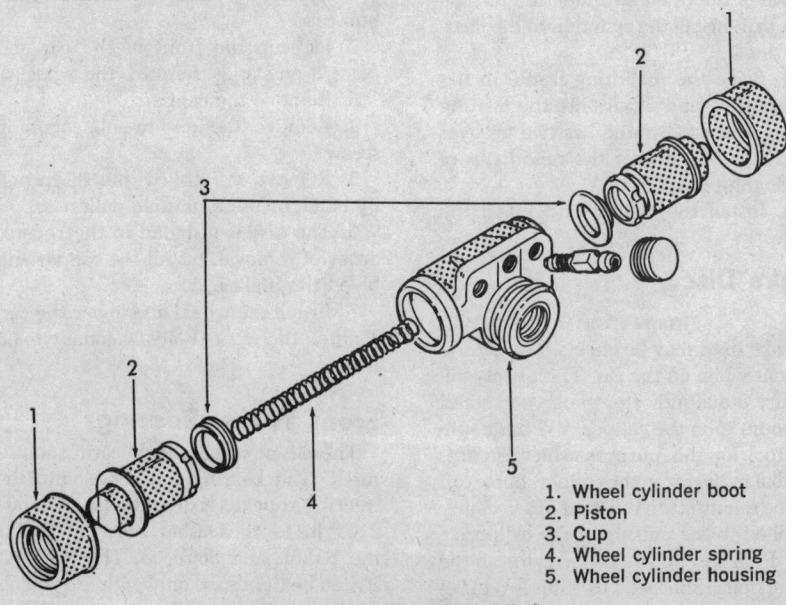

1. Wheel cylinder boot
2. Piston
3. Cup
4. Wheel cylinder spring
5. Wheel cylinder housing

Exploded view of the wheel cylinder

of the cylinder to force the opposite piston and cup out the other end of the cylinder. Reach in the open end of the cylinder and push the spring, cup, and piston out of the cylinder.

5. Remove the bleeder screw from the rear of the cylinder, on the back of the backing plate.

6. Inspect the inside of the wheel cylinder. If it is scored in any way, the cylinder must be honed with a wheel cylinder hone or fine emery paper, and finished with crocus cloth if emery paper is used. If the inside of the cylinder is excessively worn, the cylinder will have to be replaced, as only 0.003 in. of material can be removed from the cylinder walls. Whenever honing or cleaning wheel cylinders, keep a small amount of brake fluid in the cylinder to serve as a lubricant.

7. Clean any foreign matter from the pistons. The sides of the pistons must be smooth for the wheel cylinders to operate properly.

8. Clean the cylinder bore with alcohol and a lint-free rag. Pull the rag through the bore several times to remove all foreign matter and dry the cylinder.

9. Install the bleeder screw and the return spring in the cylinder.

10. Coat new cylinder cups with new brake fluid and install them in the cylinder. Make sure they are square in the bore or they will leak.

11. Install the pistons in the cylinder after coating them with new brake fluid.

12. Coat the insides of the boots with new brake fluid and install them on the cylinder. Install and bleed the brakes.

Rear Wheel Bearings

Rear wheel bearing adjustment is covered under Brake Drum Removal and Installation.

Parking Brake

Cable

Adjustment

Dasher parking brake adjustment is made at the cable compensator, which is attached to the lever push rod. On the Rabbit and Scirocco, adjustment is made at the cable end nuts on top of the handbrake lever.

1. Block the front wheels. Raise the rear of the car.

2. Apply the parking brake so that the lever is on the second notch.

3. The Dasher adjustment is made directly under the passenger compartment.

4. Tighten the compensator nut or adjusting nuts until both rear wheels can just be turned by hand. On the Rabbit and Scirocco, you shouldn't be able to turn them at all.

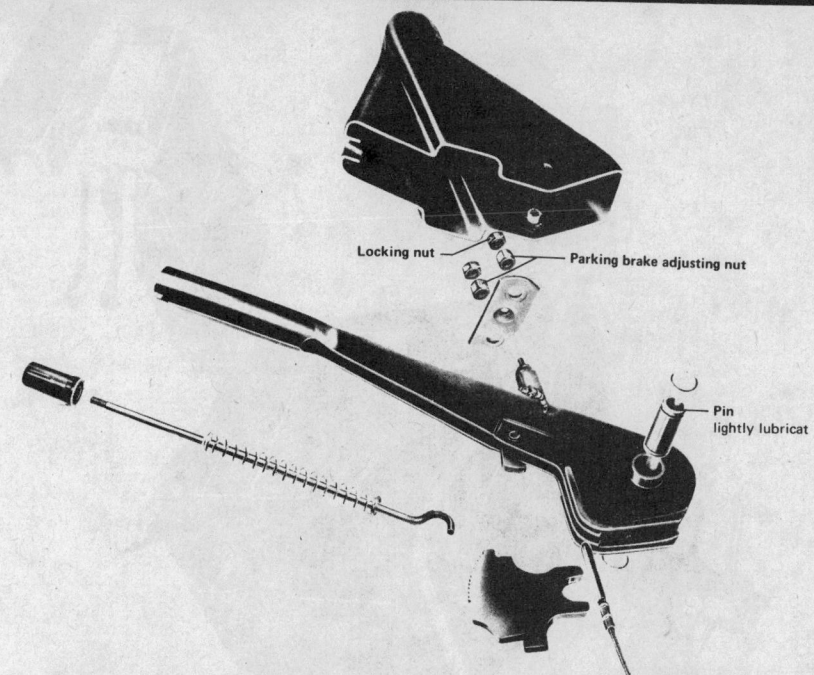

Rabbit and Scirocco parking brake, only one of the two brake cables is shown here

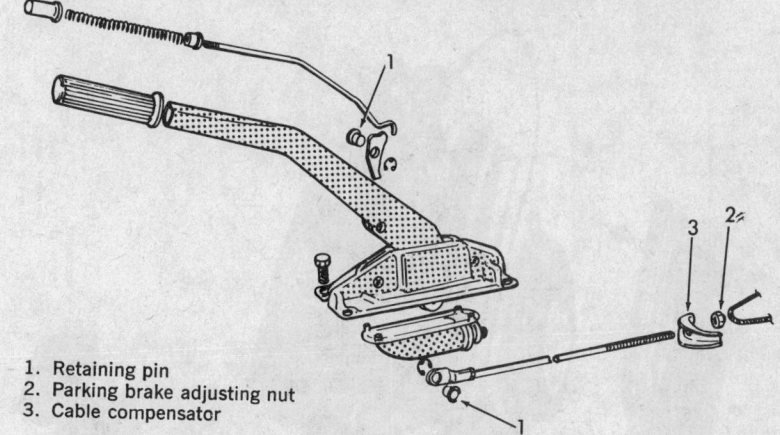

1. Retaining pin
2. Parking brake adjusting nut
3. Cable compensator

Dasher parking brake linkage and adjusting point

5. Release the parking brake lever and check that both wheels can be easily turned.

6. Lubricate the Dasher compensator with chassis grease.

CHASSIS ELECTRICAL

Heater

The heater core and blower are contained in the heater assembly which is removed and disassembled to service either component. The heater assembly is located in the passenger compartment under the center of the dash.

Removal and Installation

1. Disconnect the battery ground cable.

2. Drain the cooling system.

3. Remove the windshield washer container from its mounts. Remove the ignition coil.

4. Disconnect the two hoses from the heater core connections at the firewall.

5. Unplug the electrical connector.

6. Remove the heater control knobs on the dash.

7. Remove the two retaining screws and remove the controls from the dash complete with brackets.

8. Pull the cable connection off the electric motor.

9. Disconnect the cable from the lever on the round knob.

10. Using a screwdriver, pry the retaining clip off the fresh air housing (the front portion of the heater).

11. Remove the fresh air housing complete with the controls.

12. Detach the left and right air hoses.

13. Remove the heater-to-dash panel mounting screws and lower the heater

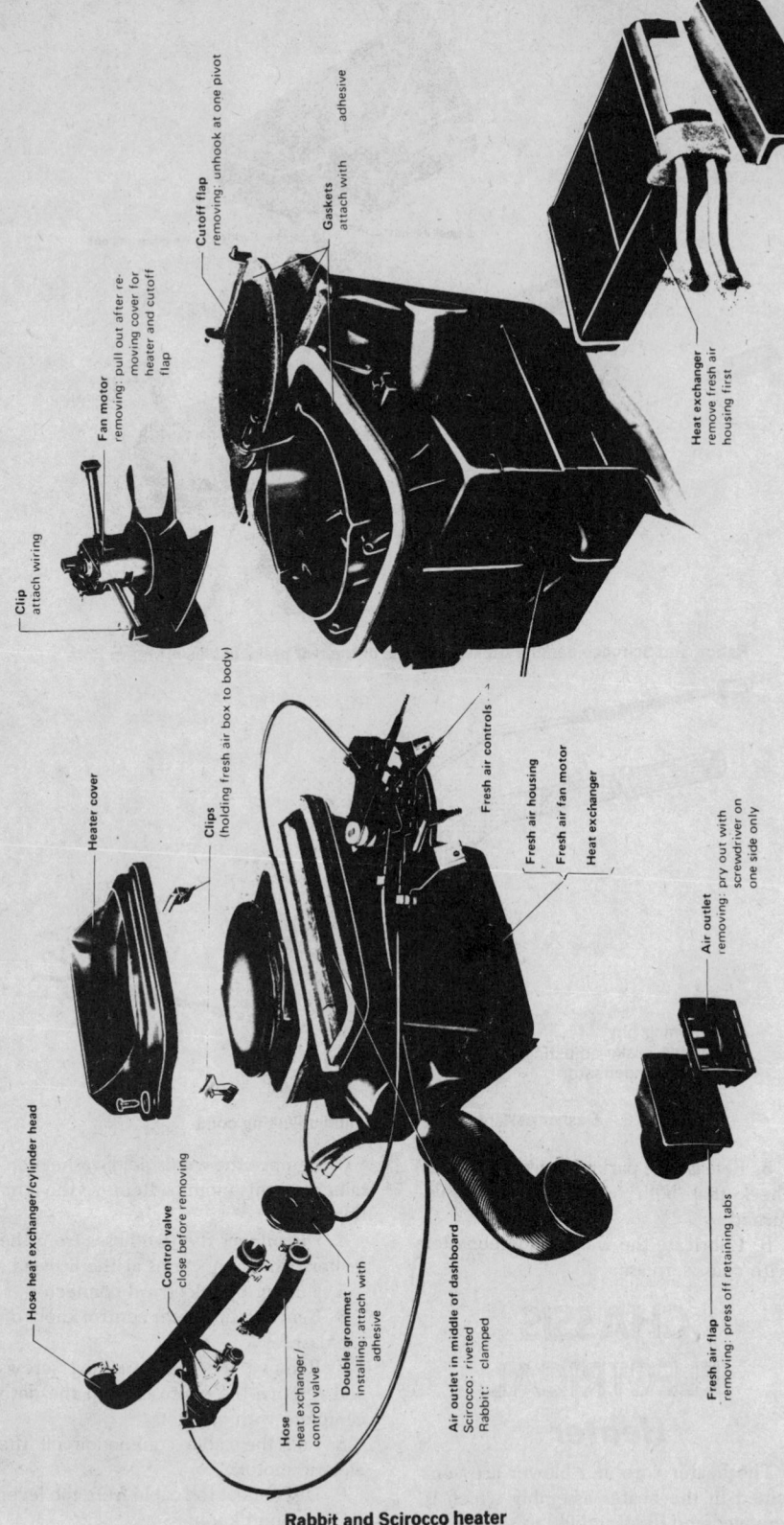

Rabbit and Scirocco heater

Labels on diagram (top illustration):
- Cutoff flap — removing: unhook at one pivot
- Gaskets — attach with adhesive
- Fan motor — removing: pull out after removing cover for heater and cutoff flap
- Clip — attach wiring
- Heat exchanger — remove fresh air housing first

Labels on diagram (bottom illustration):
- Heater cover
- Clips (holding fresh air box to body)
- Fresh air controls
- Fresh air housing
- Fresh air fan motor
- Heat exchanger
- Air outlet — removing: pry out with screwdriver on one side only
- Hose heat exchanger/cylinder head
- Control valve — close before removing
- Hose heat exchanger/control valve
- Double grommet — installing: attach with adhesive
- Air outlet in middle of dashboard Scirocco: riveted Rabbit: clamped
- Fresh air flap — removing: press off retaining tabs

Windshield Wiper Motor

Removal and Installation

Dasher

1. Unplug the multi-connector from the wiper motor.

2. Remove the three motor-to-linkage bracket retaining screws.

3. Carefully pry the motor crank out of the two linkage arms.

4. Remove the motor from the car.

5. Install the motor in the reverse order of removal. The crank arm should be at a right angle to the motor.

Rabbit, Scirocco

When removing the wiper motor, leave the mounting frame in place. Do not remove the wiper drive crank from the motor shaft—if it must be removed for any reason, matchmark the shaft, motor, and crank for reinstallation.

1. Access is with the hood open. Disconnect the battery ground cable.

2. Detach the connecting rods from the motor crank arm.

3. Pull off the wiring plug.

4. Remove the 4 mounting bolts. You may have to energize the motor for access to the top bolt.

5. Remove the motor. Reverse the procedure for installation.

Instrument Cluster

Removal and Installation

Dasher

1. Disconnect the battery ground cable.

2. Unscrew the speedometer cable from the rear of the cluster.

3. Using needle-nosed pliers, detach the retaining springs on either side of the cluster.

4. Pivot the instrument cluster out of the dash.

5. Disconnect the multi-connector plug at the rear of the cluster.

6. Remove the cluster from the dash.

7. Installation is the reverse of removal.

Rabbit, Scirocco

1. Disconnect the battery ground cable.

2. Remove the fresh air controls trim plate.

3. Remove the radio or glove box.

4. Unscrew the speedometer drive cable from the back of the speedometer. Detach the electrical plug.

5. Remove the attaching screw inside the radio/glove box opening.

6. Remove the instrument cluster. Reverse the procedure for installation.

assembly.

14. Pull out the two pins and remove the heater cover. Unscrew and remove the fan motor.

15. Separate the heater halves to remove the heater core.

16. Installation is the reverse of removal. Refill the cooling system.

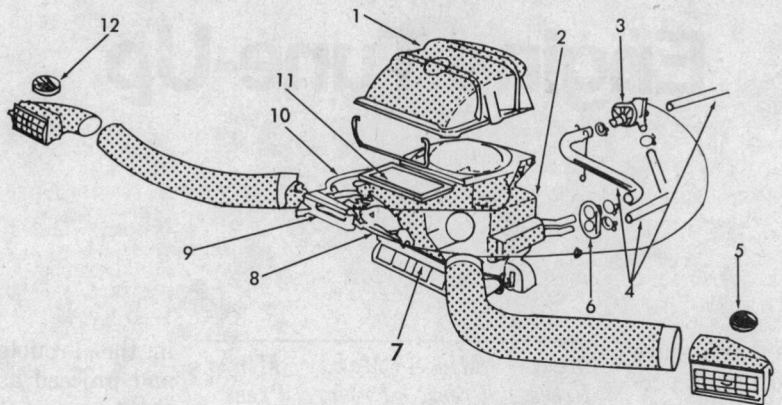

Dasher heater assembly

1. Heater cover
2. Main heater assembly
3. Heater valve
4. Heater hoses
5. Vent for side windows
6. Double grommet
7. Control flap cable
8. Heater valve cable
9. Heater controls
10. Cutoff flap cable
11. Fresh air housing
12. Vent for side windows

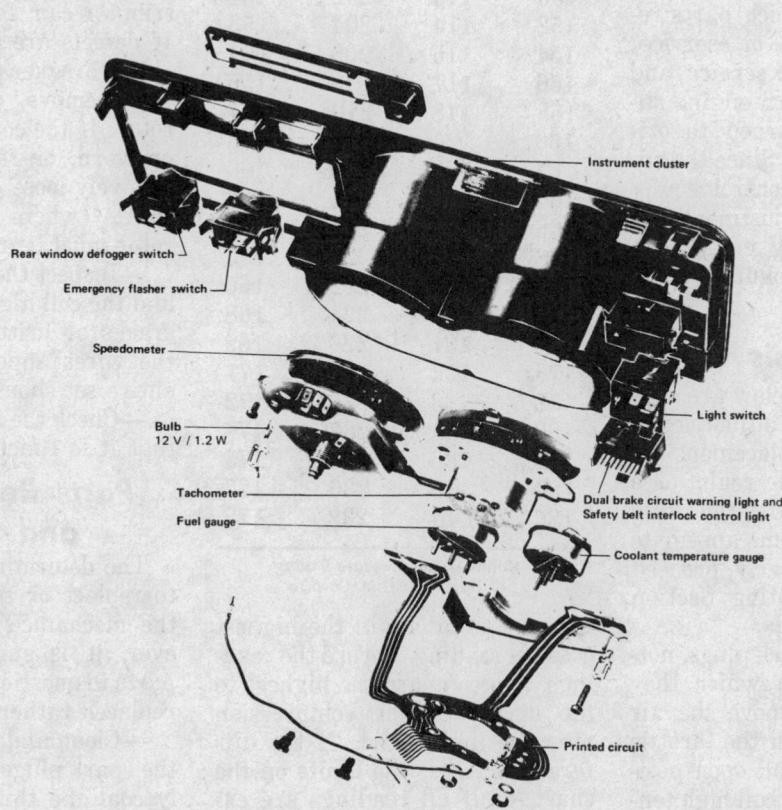

- Instrument cluster
- Rear window defogger switch
- Emergency flasher switch
- Speedometer
- Bulb 12 V / 1.2 W
- Tachometer
- Fuel gauge
- Light switch
- Dual brake circuit warning light and Safety belt interlock control light
- Coolant temperature gauge
- Printed circuit

Exploded view of Rabbit and Scirocco instrument cluster

Engine Tune-Up

Engine tune-up is a procedure performed to restore engine performance, deteriorated due to normal wear and loss of adjustment. The three major areas considered in a routine tune-up are compression, ignition, and carburetion, although valve adjustment may be included.

A tune-up is performed in three steps: *analysis*, in which it is determined whether normal wear is responsible for performance loss, and which parts require replacement or service; *parts replacement or service*; and *adjustment*, in which engine adjustments are returned to original specifications. Since the advent of emission control equipment, precision adjustment has become increasingly critical, in order to maintain pollutant emission levels.

Analysis

The procedures below are used to indicate where adjustments, parts service or replacement are necessary within the realm of a normal tune-up. If, following these tests, all systems appear to be functioning properly, proceed to the Troubleshooting Section for further diagnosis.

—Remove all spark plugs, noting the cylinder in which they were installed. Remove the air cleaner, and position the throttle and choke in the full open position. Disconnect the coil high tension lead from the coil and the distributor cap. Insert a compression gauge into the spark plug port of each cylinder, in succession, and crank the engine with

Maxi. Press. Lbs. Sq. In.	Min. Press. Lbs. Sq. In.	Max. Press. Lbs. Sq. In.	Min. Press. Lbs. Sq. In.
134	101	188	141
136	102	190	142
138	104	192	144
140	105	194	145
142	107	196	147
146	110	198	148
148	111	200	150
150	113	202	151
152	114	204	153
154	115	206	154
156	117	208	156
158	118	210	157
160	120	212	158
162	121	214	160
164	123	216	162
166	124	218	163
168	126	220	165
170	127	222	166
172	129	224	168
174	131	226	169
176	132	228	171
178	133	230	172
180	135	232	174
182	136	234	175
184	138	236	177
186	140	238	178

Compression pressure limits
Ⓒ Buick Div. G.M. Corp.)

the starter to obtain the highest possible reading. Record the readings, and compare the highest to the lowest on the compression pressure limit chart. If the difference exceeds the limits on the chart, or if all readings are excessively low, proceed to a wet compression check (see Troubleshooting Section).

—Evaluate the spark plugs according to the spark plug chart

in the Troubleshooting Section, and proceed as indicated in the chart.

—Remove the distributor cap, and inspect it inside and out for cracks and/or carbon tracks, and inside for excessive wear or burning of the rotor contacts. If any of these faults are evident, the cap must be replaced.

—Check the breaker points for burning, pitting or wear, and the contact heel resting on the distributor cam for excessive wear. If defects are noted, replace the entire breaker point set.

—Remove and inspect the rotor. If the contacts are burned or worn, or if the rotor is excessively loose on the distributor shaft (where applicable), the rotor must be replaced.

—Inspect the spark plug leads and the coil high tension lead for cracks or brittleness. If any of the wires appear defective, the entire set should be replaced.

—Check the air filter to ensure that it is functioning properly.

Parts Replacement and Service

The determination of whether to replace or service parts is at the mechanic's discretion; however, it is suggested that any parts in questionable condition be replaced rather than reused.

—Clean and regap, or replace, the spark plugs as needed. Lightly coat the threads with engine oil and install the plugs. CAUTION: *Do not over-torque taper-seat spark plugs, or plugs being installed in aluminum cylinder heads.*

Engine Tune-Up

SPARK PLUG TORQUE

Thread size	Cast-Iron Heads	Aluminum Heads
10 mm.	14	11
14 mm.	30	27
18 mm.	34*	32
7/8 in.—18	37	35

* 17 ft. lbs. for tapered plugs using no gaskets.

—If the distributor cap is to be reused, clean the inside with a dry rag, and remove corrosion from the rotor contact points with fine emery cloth. Remove the spark plug wires one by one, and clean the wire ends and the inside of the towers. If the boots are loose, they should be replaced.

If the cap is to be replaced, transfer the wires one by one, cleaning the wire ends and replacing the boots if necessary.

—If the original points are to remain in service, clean them lightly with emery cloth, lubricate the contact heel with grease specifically designed for this purpose. Rotate the crankshaft until the heel rests on a high point of the distributor cam, and adjust the point gap to specifications.

When replacing the points, remove the original points and condenser, and wipe out the inside of the distributor housing with a clean, dry rag. Lightly lubricate the contact heel and pivot point, and install the points and condenser. Rotate the crankshaft until the heel rests on a high point of the distributor cam, and adjust the point gap to specifications. NOTE: *Always replace the condenser when changing the points.*

—If the rotor is to be reused, clean the contacts with solvent. Do not alter the spring tension of the rotor center contact. Install the rotor and the distributor cap.

—Replace the coil high tension

lead and/or the spark plug leads as necessary.

—Clean the carburetor using a spray solvent (e.g., Gumout Spray). Remove the varnish from the throttle bores, and clean the linkage. Disconnect and plug the fuel line, and run the engine until it runs out of fuel. Partially fill the float chamber with solvent, and reconnect the fuel line. In extreme cases, the jets can be pressure flushed by inserting a rubber plug into the float vent, running the spray nozzle through it, and spraying the solvent until it squirts out of the venturi fuel dump.

—Clean and tighten all wiring connections in the primary electrical circuit.

Additional Services

The following services *should* be performed in conjunction with a routine tune-up to ensure efficient performance.

—Inspect the battery and fill to the proper level with distilled water. Remove the cable clamps, clean clamps and posts thoroughly, coat the posts lightly with petroleum jelly, reinstall and tighten.

—Inspect all belts, replace and/or adjust as necessary.

—Test the PCV valve (if so equipped), and clean or replace as indicated. Clean all crankcase ventilation hoses, or replace if cracked or hardened.

—Adjust the valves (if necessary) to manufacturer's specifications.

Adjustments

—Connect a dwell-tachometer between the distributor primary lead and ground. Remove the distributor cap and rotor (unless equipped with Delco externally adjustable distributor). With the ignition off, crank the engine with a remote starter switch and

measure the point dwell angle. Adjust the dwell angle to specifications. NOTE: *Increasing the gap decreases the dwell angle and vice-versa.* Install the rotor and distributor cap.

—Connect a timing light according to the manufacturer's specifications. Identify the proper timing marks with chalk or paint. NOTE: *Luminescent (day-glo) paint is excellent for this purpose.* Start the engine, and run it until it reaches operating temperature. Disconnect and plug any distributor vacuum lines, and adjust idle to the speed required to adjust timing, according to specifications. Loosen the distributor clamp and adjust timing to specifications by rotating the distributor in the engine. NOTE: *To advance timing, rotate distributor opposite normal direction of rotor rotation, and vice-versa.*

—Synchronize the throttles and mixture of multiple carburetors (if so equipped) according to procedures given in the individual car sections.

—Adjust the idle speed, mixture, and idle quality, as specified in the car sections. Final idle adjustments should be made with the air cleaner installed. CAUTION: *Due to strict emission control requirements on 1969 and later models, special test equipment (CO meter, SUN Tester) may be necessary to properly adjust idle mixture to specifications.*

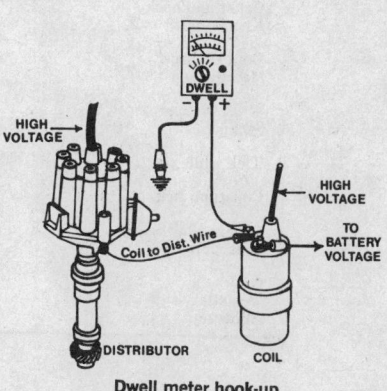

Dwell meter hook-up

Engine Troubleshooting

The following section is designed to aid in the rapid diagnosis of engine problems. The systematic format is used to diagnose problems ranging from engine starting difficulties to the need for engine overhaul. It is assumed that the user is equipped with basic hand tools and test equipment (tach-dwell meter, timing light, voltmeter, and ohmmeter).

Troubleshooting is divided into two sections. The first, *General Diagnosis*, is used to locate the problem area. In the second, *Specific Diagnosis*, the problem is systematically evaluated.

SPECIFIC DIAGNOSIS

This section is arranged so that following each test, instructions are given to proceed to another, until a problem is diagnosed.

INDEX

Group		Topic
1	*	Battery
2	*	Cranking system
3	*	Primary electrical system
4	*	Secondary electrical system
5	*	Fuel system
6	*	Engine compression
7	**	Engine vacuum
8	**	Secondary electrical system
9	**	Valve train
10	**	Exhaust system
11	**	Cooling system
12	**	Engine lubrication

*—The engine need not be running.   **—The engine must be running.

General Diagnosis

PROBLEM: Symptom	Begin diagnosis at Section Two, Number ——
Engine won't start:	
Starter doesn't turn	1.1, 2.1
Starter turns, engine doesn't	2.1
Starter turns engine very slowly	1.1, 2.4
Starter turns engine normally	3.1, 4.1
Starter turns engine very quickly	6.1
Engine fires intermittently	4.1
Engine fires consistently	5.1, 6.1
Engine runs poorly:	
Hard starting	3.1, 4.1, 5.1, 8.1
Rough idle	4.1, 5.1, 8.1
Stalling	3.1, 4.1, 5.1, 8.1
Engine dies at high speeds	4.1, 5.1
Hesitation (on acceleration from standing stop)	5.1, 8.1
Poor pickup	4.1, 5.1, 8.1
Lack of power	3.1, 4.1, 5.1, 8.1
Backfire through the carburetor	4.1, 8.1, 9.1
Backfire through the exhaust	4.1, 8.1, 9.1
Blue exhaust gases	6.1, 7.1
Black exhaust gases	5.1
Running on (after the ignition is shut off)	3.1, 8.1
Susceptible to moisture	4.1
Engine misfires under load	4.1, 7.1, 8.4, 9.1
Engine misfires at speed	4.1, 8.4
Engine misfires at idle	3.1, 4.1, 5.1, 7.1, 8.4

PROBLEM: Symptom	Probable Cause
Engine noises: ①	
Metallic grind while starting	Starter drive not engaging completely
Constant grind or rumble	*Starter drive not releasing, worn main bearings
Constant knock	Worn connecting rod bearings
Knock under load	Fuel octane too low, worn connecting rod bearings
Double knock	Loose piston pin
Metallic tap	*Collapsed or sticky valve lifter, excessive valve clearance, excessive end play in a rotating shaft
Scrape	*Fan belt contacting a stationary surface
Tick while starting	S.U. electric fuel pump (normal), starter brushes
Constant tick	*Generator brushes, shreaded fan belt
Squeal	*Improperly tensioned fan belt
Hiss or roar	*Steam escaping through a leak in the cooling system or the radiator overflow vent
Whistle	*Vacuum leak
Wheeze	Loose or cracked spark plug

①—It is extremely difficult to evaluate vehicle noises. While the above are general definitions of engine noises, those starred (*) should be considered as possibly originating elsewhere in the car. To aid diagnosis, the following list considers other potential sources of these sounds.

Metallic grind:
Throwout bearing; transmission gears, bearings, or synchronizers; differential bearings, gears; something metallic in contact with brake drum or disc.

Metallic tap:
U-joints; fan-to-radiator (or shroud) contact.

Scrape:
Brake shoe or pad dragging; tire to body contact; suspension contacting undercarriage or exhaust; something non-metallic contacting brake shoe or drum.

Tick:
Transmission gears; differential gears; lack of radio suppression; resonant vibration of body panels; windshield wiper motor or transmission; heater motor and blower.

Squeal:
Brake shoe or pad not fully releasing; tires (excessive wear, uneven wear, improper inflation); front or rear wheel alignment (most commonly due to improper toe-in).

Hiss or whistle:
Wind leaks (body or window); heater motor and blower fan.

Roar:
Wheel bearings; wind leaks (body and window).

SAMPLE SECTION

Test and Procedure	Results and Indications	Proceed to
4.1—Check for spark: Hold each spark plug wire approximately ¼″ from ground with gloves or a heavy, dry rag. Crank the engine and observe the spark.	If no spark is evident:	4.2
	If spark is good in some cases:	4.3
	If spark is good in all cases:	4.6

DIAGNOSIS

Test and Procedure	Results and Indications	Proceed to
1.1—Inspect the battery visually for case condition (corrosion, cracks) and water level.	If case is cracked, replace battery:	1.4
	If the case is intact, remove corrosion with a solution of baking soda and water (CAUTION: *do not get the solution into the battery*), and fill with water:	1.2

1.2—Check the battery cable connections: Insert a screwdriver between the battery post and the cable clamp. Turn the headlights on high beam, and observe them as the screwdriver is gently twisted to ensure good metal to metal contact.

If the lights brighten, remove and clean the clamp and post; coat the post with petroleum jelly, install and tighten the clamp: **1.4**

If no improvement is noted: **1.3**

Testing battery cable connections using a screwdriver

1.3—Test the state of charge of the battery using an individual cell tester or hydrometer.

Spec. Grav. Reading	Charged Condition
1.260-1.280	Fully Charged
1.230-1.250	Three Quarter Charged
1.200-1.220	One Half Charged
1.170-1.190	One Quarter Charged
1.140-1.160	Just About Flat
1.110-1.130	All The Way Down

If indicated, charge the battery. NOTE: *If no obvious reason exists for the low state of charge (i.e., battery age, prolonged storage), the charging system should be tested:* **1.4**

Electrolyte temperature (°F) / Specific gravity correction

+120	+.016
+100	+.012 / +.008	ADD to reading
+80	+.004 / no correction
+60	−.004 / −.008
+40	−.012 / −.016
+20	−.020 / −.024	SUBTRACT from reading
0	−.028 / −.032
−20	−.036 / −.040

The effect of temperature on the specific gravity of battery electrolyte

Test and Procedure	Results and Indications	Proceed to
1.4—Visually inspect battery cables for cracking, bad connection to ground, or bad connection to starter.	If necessary, tighten connections or replace the cables:	2.1

Tests in Group 2 are performed with coil high tension lead disconnected to prevent accidental starting.

Test and Procedure	Results and Indications	Proceed to
2.1—Test the starter motor and solenoid: Connect a jumper from the battery post of the solenoid (or relay) to the ignition switch post of the solenoid (or relay).	If starter turns the engine normally:	2.2
	If the starter buzzes, or turns the engine very slowly:	2.4
	If no response, replace the solenoid (or relay).	3.1
	If the starter turns, but the engine doesn't, ensure that the flywheel ring gear is intact. If the gear is undamaged, replace the starter drive.	3.1
2.2—Determine whether ignition override switches are functioning properly (clutch start switch, neutral safety switch), by connecting a jumper across the switch(es), and turning the ignition switch to "start".	If starter operates, adjust or replace switch:	3.1
	If the starter doesn't operate:	2.3

Test and Procedure	Results and Indications	Proceed to
2.3—Check the ignition switch "start" position: Connect a 12V test lamp between the starter post of the solenoid (or relay) and ground. Turn the ignition switch to the "start" position, and jiggle the key.	If the lamp doesn't light when the switch is turned, check the ignition switch for loose connections, cracked insulation, or broken wires. Repair or replace as necessary:	3.1
	If the lamp flickers when the key is jiggled, replace the ignition switch.	3.3

Checking the ignition switch "start" position

2.4—Remove and bench test the starter.	If the starter does not meet specifications, repair or replace as needed:	3.1
	If the starter is operating properly:	2.5
2.5—Determine whether the engine can turn freely: Remove the spark plugs, and check for water in the cylinders. Check for water on the dipstick, or oil in the radiator. Attempt to turn the engine using an 18″ flex drive and socket on the crankshaft pulley nut or bolt.	If the engine will turn freely only with the spark plugs out, and hydrostatic lock (water in the cylinders) is ruled out, check valve timing:	9.2
	If engine will not turn freely, and it is known that the clutch and transmission are free, the engine must be disassembled for further evaluation.	
3.1—Check the ignition switch "on" position: Connect a jumper wire between the distributor side of the coil and ground, and a 12V test lamp between the switch side of the coil and ground. Remove the high tension lead from the coil. Turn the ignition switch on and jiggle the key.	If the lamp lights:	3.2
	If the lamp flickers when the key is jiggled, replace the ignition switch:	3.3
	If the lamp doesn't light, check for loose or open connections. If none are found, remove the ignition switch and check for continuity. If the switch is faulty, replace it:	

Checking the ignition switch "on" position

3.2—Check the ballast resistor or resistance wire for an open circuit, using an ohmmeter.	Replace the resistor or the resistance wire if the resistance is zero.	3.3
3.3—Visually inspect the breaker points for burning, pitting, or excessive wear. Gray coloring of the point contact surfaces is normal. Rotate the crankshaft until the contact heel rests on a high point of the distributor cam, and adjust the point gap to specifications.	If the breaker points are intact, clean the contact surfaces with fine emery cloth, and adjust the point gap to specifications. If pitted or worn, replace the points and condenser, and adjust the gap to specifications: NOTE: *Always lubricate the distributor cam according to manufacturer's recommendations when servicing the breaker points.*	3.3 3.4

Test and Procedure	Results and Indications	Proceed to
3.4—Connect a dwell meter between the distributor primary lead and ground. Crank the engine and observe the point dwell angle.	If necessary, adjust the point dwell angle: NOTE: *Increasing the point gap decreases the dwell angle, and vice-versa.*	3.6
	If dwell meter shows little or no reading:	3.5

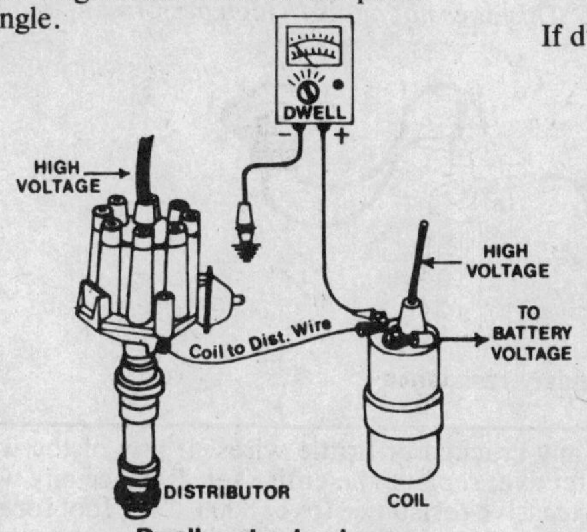

Dwell meter hook-up

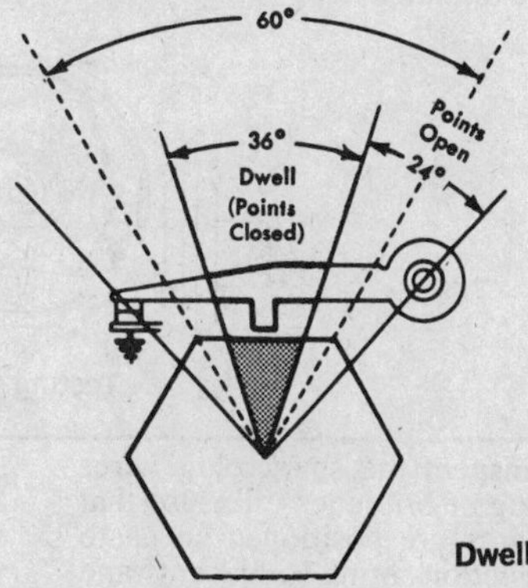

Dwell angle

| 3.5—Check the condenser for short: Connect an ohmmeter across the condenser body and the pigtail lead. | If any reading other than infinite resistance is noted, replace the condenser: | 3.6 |

Checking the condenser for short

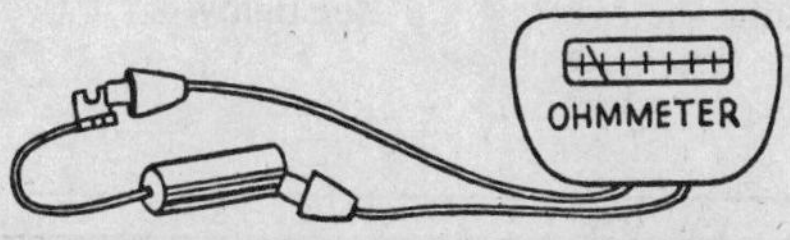

| 3.6—Test the coil primary resistance: Connect an ohmmeter across the coil primary terminals, and read the resistance on the low scale. Note whether an external ballast resistor or resistance wire is utilized. | Coils utilizing ballast resistors or resistance wires should have approximately 1.0 resistance; coils with internal resistors should have approximately 4.0 resistance. If values far from the above are noted, replace the coil: | 4.1 |

Testing the coil primary resistance

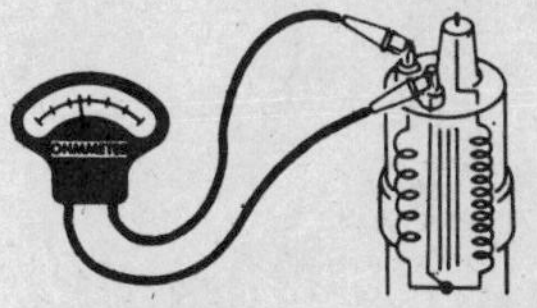

4.1—Check for spark: Hold each spark plug wire approximately 1/4" from ground with gloves or a heavy, dry rag. Crank the engine, and observe the spark.	If no spark is evident:	4.2
	If spark is good in some cylinders:	4.3
	If spark is good in all cylinders:	4.6
4.2—Check for spark at the coil high tension lead: Remove the coil high tension lead from the distributor and position it approximately 1/4" from ground. Crank the engine and observe spark. CAUTION: *This test should not be performed on cars equipped with transistorized ignition.*	If the spark is good and consistent:	4.3
	If the spark is good but intermittent, test the primary electrical system starting at 3.3:	3.3
	If the spark is weak or non-existent, replace the coil high tension lead, clean and tighten all connections and retest. If no improvement is noted:	4.4
4.3—Visually inspect the distributor cap and rotor for burned or corroded contacts, cracks, carbon tracks, or moisture. Also check the fit of the rotor on the distributor shaft (where applicable).	If moisture is present, dry thoroughly, and retest per 4.1:	4.1
	If burned or excessively corroded contacts, cracks, or carbon tracks are noted, replace the defective part(s) and retest per 4.1:	4.1
	If the rotor and cap appear intact, or are only slightly corroded, clean the contacts thoroughly (including the cap towers and spark plug wire ends) and retest per 4.1: If the spark is good in all cases: If the spark is poor in all cases:	4.6 4.5

Test and Procedure	Results and Indications	Proceed to
4.4—Check the coil secondary resistance: Connect an ohmmeter across the distributor side of the coil and the coil tower. Read the resistance on the high scale of the ohmmeter.	The resistance of a satisfactory coil should be between 4K and 10K . If the resistance is considerably higher (i.e., 40K) replace the coil, and retest per 4.1: NOTE: *This does not apply to high performance coils.*	4.1

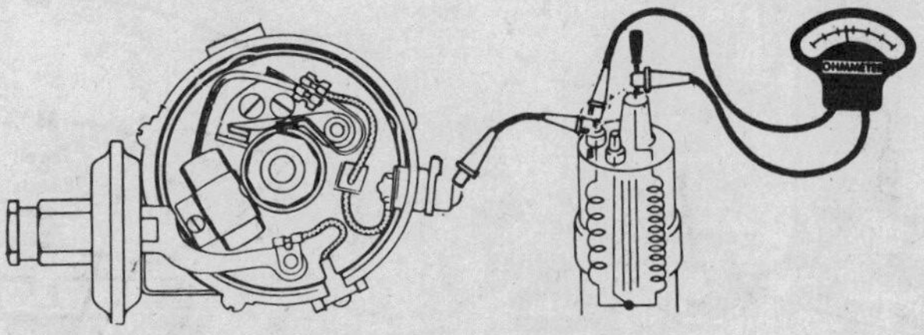

Testing the coil secondary resistance

Test and Procedure	Results and Indications	Proceed to
4.5—Visually inspect the spark plug wires for cracking or brittleness. Ensure that no two wires are positioned so as to cause induction firing (adjacent and parallel). Remove each wire, one by one, and check resistance with an ohmmeter.	Replace any cracked or brittle wires. If any of the wires are defective, replace the entire set. Replace any wires with excessive resistance (over 8000 per foot for suppression wire), and separate any wires that might cause induction firing.	4.6
4.6—Remove the spark plugs, noting the cylinders from which they were removed, and evaluate according to the chart below.	See below.	See below.

Condition	Cause	Remedy	Proceed/to
Electrodes eroded, light brown deposits.	Normal wear. Normal wear is indicated by approximately .001″ wear per 1000 miles.	Clean and regap the spark plug if wear is not excessive: Replace the spark plug if excessively worn:	4.7
Carbon fouling (black, dry, fluffy deposits).	If present on one or two plugs:		
	Faulty high tension lead(s).	Test the high tension leads:	4.5
	Burnt or sticking valve(s).	Check the valve train: (Clean and regap the plugs in either case.)	9.1
	If present on most or all plugs: Overly rich fuel mixture, due to restricted air filter, improper carburetor adjustment, improper choke or heat riser adjustment or operation.	Check the fuel system:	5.1

Test and Procedure	Results and Indications		Proceed to
Oil fouling (wet black deposits)	Worn engine components. NOTE: *Oil fouling may occur in new or recently rebuilt engines until broken in.*	Check engine vacuum and compression:	6.1
		Replace with new spark plug.	

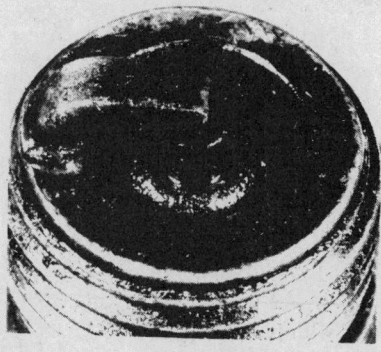

Lead fouling (gray, black, red, green, tan, or yellow deposits, which appear glazed or cinderlike).	Combustion by-products.	Clean and regap the plugs: (Use plugs of a different heat range if the problem recurs.)	4.7

Gap bridging (deposits lodged between the electrodes).	Incomplete combustion, or transfer of deposits from the combustion chamber.	Replace the spark plugs.

Engine Troubleshooting

Test and Procedure	Results and Indications	Proceed to
Overheating (burnt electrodes, and extremely white insulator with small black spots).	Ignition timing advanced too far.	Adjust timing to specifications:	8.2
	Overly lean fuel mixture.	Check the fuel system:	5.1
	Spark plugs not seated properly.	Clean spark plug seat and install a new gasket washer: (Replace the spark plugs in all cases.)	4.7

Pre-ignition (melted or severely burned electrodes, blistered or cracked insulators, or metallic deposits on the insulator).	Incorrect spark plug heat range.	Replace with plugs of the proper heat range:	4.7
	Ignition timing advanced too far.	Adjust timing to specifications:	8.2
	Spark plugs not being cooled efficiently.	Clean the spark plug seat, and check the cooling system:	11.1
	Fuel mixture too lean	Check the fuel system:	5.1
	Poor compression.	Check compression:	6.1
	Fuel grade too low.	Use higher octane fuel:	4.7

4.7—Determine the static ignition timing: Using the flywheel or crankshaft pulley timing marks as a guide, locate top dead center on the *compression* stroke of the No. 1 cylinder. Remove the distributor cap.	Adjust the distributor so that the rotor points toward the No. 1 tower in the distributor cap, and the points are just opening:	4.8
4.8—Check coil polarity: Connect a voltmeter negative lead to the coil high tension lead, and the positive lead to ground (NOTE: *reverse the hook-up for positive ground cars*). Crank the engine momentarily.	If the voltmeter reads up-scale, the polarity is correct:	5.1
	If the voltmeter reads down-scale, reverse the coil polarity (switch the primary leads):	5.1

Checking coil polarity

5.1—Determine that the air filter is functioning efficiently: Hold paper elements up to a strong light, and attempt to see light through the filter.	Clean permanent air filters in solvent (or manufacturer's recommendation), and allow to dry. Replace paper elements through which light cannot be seen:	5.2

Test and Procedure	Results and Indications	Proceed to
5.2—Determine whether a flooding condition exists: Flooding is identified by a strong gasoline odor, and excessive gasoline present in the throttle bore(s) of the carburetor.	If flooding is not evident:	5.3
	If flooding is evident, permit the gasoline to dry for a few moments and restart. If flooding doesn't recur:	5.6
	If flooding is persistant:	5.5
5.3—Check that fuel is reaching the carburetor: Detach the fuel line at the carburetor inlet. Hold the end of the line in a cup (not styrofoam), and crank the engine.	If fuel flows smoothly:	5.6
	If fuel doesn't flow (NOTE: *Make sure that there is fuel in the tank*), or flows erratically:	5.4
5.4—Test the fuel pump: Disconnect all fuel lines from the fuel pump. Hold a finger over the input fitting, crank the engine (with electric pump, turn the ignition or pump on), and feel for suction.	If suction is evident, blow out the fuel line to the tank with low pressure compressed air until bubbling is heard from the fuel filler neck. Also blow out the carburetor fuel line (both ends disconnected):	5.6
	If no suction is evident, replace or repair the fuel pump: NOTE: *Repeated oil fouling of the spark plugs, or a no-start condition, could be the result of a ruptured vacuum booster pump diaphragm, through which oil or gasoline is being drawn into the intake manifold (where applicable).*	5.6
5.5—Check the needle and seat: Tap the carburetor in the area of the needle and seat.	If flooding stops, a gasoline additive (e.g., Gumout) will often cure the problem:	5.6
	If flooding continues, check the fuel pump for excessive pressure at the caruburetor (according to specifications). If the pressure is normal, the needle and seat must be removed and checked, and/or the float level adjusted:	5.6
5.6—Test the accelerator pump by looking into the throttle bores while operating the throttle.	If the accelerator pump appears to be operating normally:	5.7
	If the accelerator pump is not operating, the pump must be reconditioned. Where possible, service the pump with the carburetor(s) installed on the engine. If necessary, remove the carburetor. Prior to removal:	5.7
5.7—Determine whether the carburetor main fuel system is functioning: Spray a commercial starting fluid into the carburetor while attempting to start the engine.	If the engine starts, runs for a few seconds, and dies:	5.8
	If the engine doesn't start:	6.1
5.8—Uncommon fuel system malfunctions: See below:	If the problem is solved:	6.1
	If the problem remains, remove and recondition the carburetor.	

Engine Troubleshooting

Condition	Indication	Test	Usual Weather Conditions	Remedy
Vapor lock	Car will not restart shortly after running.	Cool the components of the fuel system until the engine starts.	Hot to very hot	Ensure that the exhaust manifold heat control valve is operating. Check with the vehicle manufacturer for the recommended solution to vapor lock on the model in question.
Carburetor icing	Car will not idle, stalls at low speeds.	Visually inspect the throttle plate area of the throttle bores for frost.	High humidity, 32-40 F.	Ensure that the exhaust manifold heat control valve is operating, and that the intake manifold heat riser is not blocked.
Water in the fuel	Engine sputters and stalls; may not start.	Pump a small amount of fuel into a glass jar. Allow to stand, and inspect for droplets or a layer of water.	High humidity, extreme temperature changes.	For droplets, use one or two cans of commercial gas dryer (Dry Gas) For a layer of water, the tank must be drained, and the fuel lines blown out with compressed air.

Test and Procedure	Results and Indications	Proceed to
6.1—Test engine compression: Remove all spark plugs. Insert a compression gauge into a spark plug port, crank the engine to obtain the maximum reading, and record.	If compression is within limits on all cylinders:	7.1
	If guage reading is extremely low on all cylinders:	6.2
	If gauge reading is low on one or two cylinders: (If gauge readings are identical and low on two or more adjacent cylinders, the head gasket must be replaced.)	6.2

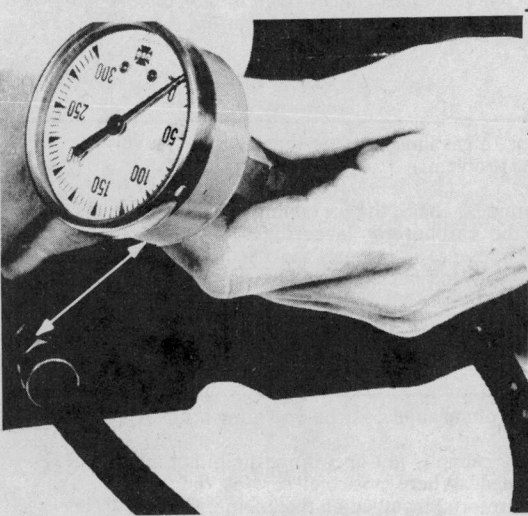

Testing compression

Maxi. Press. Lbs. Sq. In.	Min. Press. Lbs. Sq. In.	Maxi. Press. Lbs. Sq. In.	Min. Press. Lbs. Sq. In.	Max. Press. Lbs. Sq. In.	Min. Press. Lbs. Sq. In.	Max. Press. Lbs. Sq. In.	Min. Press. Lbs. Sq. In.
134	101	162	121	188	141	214	160
136	102	164	123	190	142	216	162
138	104	166	124	192	144	218	163
140	105	168	126	194	145	220	165
142	107	170	127	196	147	222	166
146	110	172	129	198	148	224	168
148	111	174	131	200	150	226	169
150	113	176	132	202	151	228	171
152	114	178	133	204	153	230	172
154	115	180	135	206	154	232	174
156	117	182	136	208	156	234	175
158	118	184	138	210	157	236	177
160	120	186	140	212	158	238	178

Compression pressure limits

Test and Procedure	Results and Indications	Proceed to
6.2—Test engine compression (wet): Squirt approximately 30 cc. of engine oil into each cylinder, and retest per 6.1.	If the readings improve, worn or cracked rings or broken pistons are indicated:	
	If the readings do not improve, burned or excessively carboned valves or a jumped timing chain are indicated: NOTE: *A jumped timing chain is often indicated by difficult cranking.*	7.1
7.1—Perform a vacuum check of the engine: Attach a vacuum gauge to the intake manifold beyond the throttle plate. Start the engine, and observe the action of the needle over the range of engine speeds.	See below.	See below

Reading	Indications	Proceed to
Steady, from 17-22 in. Hg.	Normal.	8.1
Low and steady.	Late ignition or valve timing, or low compression:	6.1
Very low.	Vacuum leak:	
Needle fluctuates as engine speed increases.	Ignition miss, blown cylinder head gasket, leaking valve or weak valve spring:	6.1, 8.3
Gradual drop in reading at idle.	Excessive back pressure in the exhaust system:	10.1
Intermittent fluctuation at idle.	Ignition miss, sticking valve:	8.3, 9.1
Drifting needle.	Improper idle mixture adjustment, carburetors not synchronized (where applicable), or minor intake leak. Synchronize the carburetors, adjust the idle, and retest. If the condition persists:	7.2
High and steady.	Early ignition timing:	8.2

7.2—Attach a vacuum gauge per 7.1, and test for an intake manifold leak. Squirt a small amount of oil around the intake manifold gaskets, carburetor gaskets, plugs and fittings. Obsserve the action of the vacuum gauge.

If the reading improves, replace the indicated gasket, or seal the indicated fitting or plug: 8.1

If the reading remains low: 7.3

Reading	Indications	Proceed to
7.3—Test all vacuum hoses and accessories for leaks as described in 7.2. Also check the carburetor body (dashpots, automatic choke mechanism, throttle shafts) for leaks in the same manner.	If the reading improves, service or replace the offending part(s): If the reading remains low:	**8.1** **6.1**
8.1—Check the point dwell angle: Connect a dwell meter between the distributor primary wire and ground. Start the engine, and observe the dwell angle from idle to 3000 rpm.	If necessary, adjust the dwell angle. NOTE: *Increasing the point gap reduces the dwell angle and vice-versa.* If the dwell angle moves outside specifications as engine speed increases, the distributor should be removed and checked for cam accuracy, shaft endplay and concentricity, bushing wear, and adequate point arm tension (NOTE: *Most of these items may be checked with the distributor installed in the engine, using an oscilloscope):*	**8.2**
8.2—Connect a timing light (per manufacturer's recommendation) and check the dynamic ignition timing. Disconnect and plug the vacuum hose(s) to the distributor if specified, start the engine, and observe the timing marks at the specified engine speed.	If the timing is not correct, adjust to specifications by rotating the distributor in the engine: (Advance timing by rotating distributor opposite normal direction of rotor rotation, retard timing by rotating distributor in same direction as rotor rotation.)	**8.3**
8.3—Check the operation of the distributor advance mechanism(s): To test the mechanical advance, disconnect the vacuum advance, and observe the timing marks with a timing light as the engine speed is increased from idle. If the mark moves smoothly, without hesitation, it may be assumed that the mechanical advance is functioning properly. To test vacuum advance and/or retard systems, alternately crimp and release the vacuum line, and observe the timing mark for movement. If movement is noted, the system is operating.	If the systems are functioning: If the systems are not functioning, remove the distributor, and test on a distributor tester:	**8.4** **8.4**
8.4—Locate an ignition miss: With the engine running, remove each spark plug wire, one by one, until one is found that doesn't cause the engine to roughen and slow down.	When the missing cylinder is identified:	**4.1**
9.1—Evaluate the valve train: Remove the valve cover, and ensure that the valves are adjusted to specifications. A mechanic's stethoscope may be used to aid in the diagnosis of the valve train. By pushing the probe on or near push rods or rockers, valve noise often can be isolated. A timing light also may be used to diagnose valve problems. Connect the light according to manufacturer's recommendations, and start the engine. Vary the firing moment of the light by increasing the engine speed (and therefore the ignition advance), and moving the trigger from cylinder to cylinder. Observe the movement of each valve.	See below	**See below**

Observation	Probable Cause	Remedy	Proceed to
Metallic tap heard through the stethoscope.	Sticking hydraulic lifter or excessive valve clearance.	Adjust valve. If tap persists, remove and replace the lifter:	**10.0**
Metallic tap through the stethoscope, able to push the rocker arm (lifter side) down by hand.	Collapsed valve lifter.	Remove and replace the lifter:	**10.1**
Erratic, irregular motion of the valve stem.*	Sticking valve, burned valve.	Recondition the valve and/or valve guide:	**Next Chapter-ter**
Eccentric motion of the pushrod at the rocker arm.*	Bent pushrod.	Replace the pushrod:	**10.1**
Valve retainer bounces as the valve closes.*	Weak valve spring or damper.	Remove and test the spring and damper. Replace if necessary:	**10.1**

*—When observed with a timing light.

Test and Procedure	Results and Indications	Proceed to
9.2—Check the valve timing: Locate top dead center of the No. 1 piston, and install a degree wheel or tape on the crankshaft pulley or damper with zero corresponding to an index mark on the engine. Rotate the crankshaft in its direction of rotation, and observe the opening of the No. 1 cylinder intake valve. The opening should correspond with the correct mark on the degree wheel according to specifications.	If the timing is not correct, the timing cover must be removed for further investigation:	
10.1—Determine whether the exhaust manifold heat control valve is operating: Operate the valve by hand to determine whether it is free to move. If the valve is free, run the engine to operating temperature and observe the action of the valve, to ensure that it is opening.	If the valve sticks, spray it with a suitable solvent, open and close the valve to free it, and retest. If the valve functions properly:	**10.2**
	If the valve does not free, or does not operate, replace the valve:	**10.2**
10.2—Ensure that there are no exhaust restrictions: Visually inspect the exhaust system for kinks, dents, or crushing. Also note that gases are flowing freely from the tailpipe at all engine speeds, indicating no restriction in the muffler or resonator.	Replace any damaged portion of the system:	**11.1**
11.1—Visually inspect the fan belt for glazing, cracks, and fraying, and replace if necessary. Tighten the belt so that the longest span has approximately 1/2" play at its midpoint under thumb pressure.	Replace or tighten the fan belt as necessary:	**11.2**

Checking the fan belt tension
(© Outboard Marine Corp.)

Test and Procedure	Results and Indications	Proceed to
11.2—Check the fluid level of the cooling system.	If full or slightly low, fill as necessary:	**11.5**
	If extremely low:	**11.3**
11.3—Visually inspect the external portions of the cooling system (radiator, radiator hoses, thermostat elbow, water pump seals, heater hoses, etc.) for leaks. If none are found, pressurize the cooling system to 14-15 psi.	If cooling system holds the pressure:	**11.5**
	If cooling system loses pressure rapidly, reinspect external parts of the system for leaks under pressure. If none are found, check dipstick for coolant in crankcase. If no coolant is present, but pressure loss continues:	**11.4**
	If coolant is evident in crankcase, remove cylinder head(s), and check gasket(s). If gaskets are intact, block and cylinder heads(s) should be checked for cracks or holes.	
	If the gasket(s) is blown, replace, and purge the crankcase of coolant:	**12.6**
	NOTE: *Occasionally, due to atmospheric and driving conditions, condensation of water can occur in the crankcase. This causes the oil to appear milky white. To remedy, run the engine until hot, and change the oil and oil filter.*	
11.4—Check for combustion leaks into the cooling system: Pressurize the cooling system as above. Start the engine, and observe the pressure gauge. If the needle fluctuates, remove each spark plug wire, one by one, noting which cylinder(s) reduce or eliminate the fluctuation.	Cylinders which reduce or eliminate the fluctuation, when the spark plug wire is removed, are leaking into the cooling system. Replace the head gasket on the affected cylinder bank(s).	

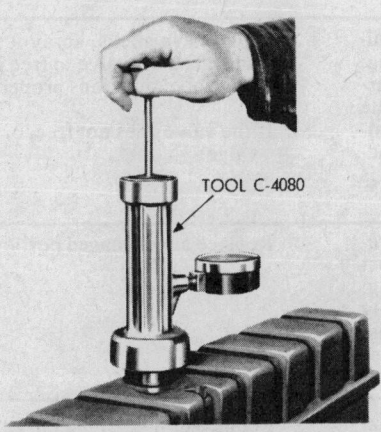

Radiator pressure tester

TOOL C-4080

11.6—Test the thermostat: Start the engine cold, remove the radiator cap, and insert a thermometer into the radiator. Allow the engine to idle. After a short while, there will be a sudden, rapid increase in coolant temperature. The temperature at which this sharp rise stops is the thermostat opening temperature.	If the thermostat opens at or about the specified temperature:	**11.7**
	If the temperature doesn't increase: (If the temperature increases slowly and gradually, replace the thermostat.)	**11.7**
11.5—Check the radiator pressure cap: Attach a radiator pressure tester to the radiator cap (wet the seal prior to installation). Quickly pump up the pressure, noting the point at which the cap releases.	If the cap releases within ± 1 psi of the specified rating, it is operating properly:	**11.6**
	If the cap releases at more than ± 1 psi of the specified rating. It should be replaced:	**11.6**

Test and Procedure	Results and Indications	Proceed to

Testing the radiator pressure cap

Test and Procedure	Results and Indications	Proceed to
11.7—Check the water pump: Remove the thermostat elbow and the thermostat, disconnect the coil high tension lead (to prevent starting), and crank the engine momentarily.	If coolant flows, replace the thermostat and retest per 11.6:	**11.6**
	If coolant doesn't flow, reverse flush the cooling system to alleviate any blockage that might exist. If system is not blocked, and coolant will not flow, recondition the water pump.	
12.1—Check the oil pressure gauge or warning light: If the gauge shows low pressure, or the light is on, for no obvious reason, remove the oil pressure sender. Install an accurate oil pressure gauge and run the engine momentarily.	If oil pressure builds normally, run engine for a few moments to determine that it is functioning normally, and replace the sender.	
	If the pressure remains low:	**12.2**
	If the pressure surges:	**12.3**
	If the oil pressure is zero:	**12.3**
12.2—Visually inspect the oil: If the oil is watery or very thin, milky, or foamy, replace the oil and oil filter.	If the oil is normal:	**12.3**
	If after replacing oil the pressure remains low:	**12.3**
	If after replacing oil the pressure becomes normal:	
12.3—Inspect the oil pressure relief valve and spring, to ensure that it is not sticking or stuck. Remove and thoroughly clean the valve, spring, and the valve body.	If the oil pressure improves:	
	If no improvement is noted:	**12.4**

Oil pressure relief valve
(© British Leyland Motors)

Test and Procedure	Results and Indications	Proceed to
12.4—Check to ensure that the oil pump is not cavitating (sucking air instead of oil): See that the crankcase is neither over nor underfull, and that the pickup in the sump is in the proper position and free from sludge.	Fill or drain the crankcase to the proper capacity, and clean the pickup screen in solvent if necessary. If no improvement is noted:	**12.5**
12.5—Inspect the oil pump drive and the oil pump:	If the pump drive or the oil pump appear to be defective, service as necessary and retest per 12.1:	**12.1**
	If the pump drive and pump appear to be operating normally, the engine should be disassembled to determine where blockage exists.	
12.6—Purge the engine of ethylene glycol coolant: Completely drain the crankcase and the oil filter. Obtain a commercial solvent, designated for this purpose, and follow the instructions precisely. Following this, install a new oil filter and refill the crankcase with the proper viscosity oil. The next oil and filter change should follow shortly thereafter (1000 miles).		

Engine Rebuilding

This section describes, in detail, the procedures involved in rebuilding a typical engine. The procedures specifically refer to an inline engine, however, they are basically identical to those used in rebuilding engines of nearly all design and configurations. Procedures for servicing atypical engines (i.e., horizontally opposed) are described in the appropriate section, although in most cases, cylinder head reconditioning procedures described in this chapter will apply.

The section is divided into two sections. The first, Cylinder Head Reconditioning, assumes that the cylinder head is removed from the engine, all manifolds are removed, and the cylinder head is on a workbench. The camshaft should be removed from overhead cam cylinder heads. The second section, Cylinder Block Reconditioning, covers the block, pistons, connecting rods and crankshaft. It is assumed that the engine is mounted on a work stand, and the cylinder head and all accessories are removed.

Procedures are identified as follows:
Unmarked—Basic procedures that must be performed in order to successfully complete the rebuilding process.
Starred (*)—Procedures that should be performed to ensure maximum performance and engine life.
Double starred (**)—Procedures that may be performed to increase engine performance and reliability. These procedures are usually reserved for extremely heavy-duty or competition usage.

In many cases, a choice of methods is also provided. Methods are identified in the same manner as procedures. The choice of method for a procedure is at the discretion of the user.

The tools required for the basic rebuilding procedure should, with minor exceptions, be those included in a mechanic's tool kit. An accurate torque wrench, and a dial indicator (reading in thousandths) mounted on a universal base should be available. Bolts and nuts with no torque specification should be tightened according to size (see chart). Special tools, where required, all are readily available from the major tool suppliers (i.e., Craftsman, Snap-On, K-D). The services of a competent automotive machine shop must also be readily available.

When assembling the engine, any parts that will be in frictional contact must be pre-lubricated, to provide protection on initial start-up. Vortex Pre-Lube or any product specifically formulated for this purpose may be used. NOTE: *Do not use engine oil.* Where semi-permanent (locked but removable) installation of bolts or nuts is desired, threads should be cleaned and coated with Loctite. Studs may be permanently installed using Loctite Stud and Bearing Mount.

Aluminum has become increasingly popular for use in engines, due to its low weight and excellent heat transfer characteristics. The following precautions must be observed when handling aluminum engine parts:
—Never hot-tank aluminum parts.
—Remove all aluminum parts (identification tags, etc.) from engine parts before hot-tanking (otherwise they will be removed during the process).
—Always coat threads lightly with engine oil or anti-seize compounds before installation, to prevent seizure.
—Never over-torque bolts or spark plugs in aluminum threads. Should stripping occur, threads can be restored according to the following procedure, using Heli-Coil thread inserts:

Tap drill the hole with the stripped threads to the specified size (see chart). Using the specified tap (NOTE: *Heli-Coil tap sizes refer to the size thread being replaced, rather than the actual tap size*), tap the hole for the Heli-Coil. Place the insert on the proper installation tool (see chart). Apply pressure on the insert while winding it clockwise into the hole, until the top of the insert is one turn below the surface. Remove the installation tool, and break the installation tang from the bottom of the insert by moving it up and down. If the Heli-Coil must be removed, tap the removal tool firmly into the hole, so that it engages the top thread, and turn the tool counter-clockwise to extract the insert.

There are also several other types of thread repair devices available. Snapped bolts or studs may be removed, using a stud extractor (unthreaded) or Vise-Grip pliers (threaded). Penetrating oil (e.g., Liquid Wrench) will often aid in breaking frozen threads. In cases where the stud or bolt is flush with, or below the surface, proceed as follows:

Drill a hole in the broken stud or bolt, approximately 1/2 its diameter. Select a screw extractor (e.g., Easy-Out) of the proper size, and tap it into the stud or bolt. Turn the extractor counterclockwise to remove the stud or bolt.

TORQUE (ft lbs)*

U.S.

| Bolt Diameter (inches) | Bolt Grade (SAE) | | | | Wrench Size (inches) | |
	1 and 2	5	6	8	Bolt	Nut
1/4	5	7	10	10.5	3/8	7/16
5/16	9	14	19	22	1/2	9/16
3/8	15	25	34	37	9/16	5/8
7/16	24	40	55	60	5/8	3/4
1/2	37	60	85	92	3/4	13/16
9/16	53	88	120	132	7/8	7/8
5/8	74	120	167	180	15/16	1
3/4	120	200	280	296	1-1/8	1-1/8
7/8	190	302	440	473	1-5/16	1-5/16
1	282	466	660	714	1-1/2	1-1/2

Metric

| Bolt Diameter (mm) | Bolt Grade | | | | Wrench Size (mm) Bolt and Nut |
	5D	8G	10K	12K	
6	5	6	8	10	10
8	10	16	22	27	14
10	19	31	40	49	17
12	34	54	70	86	19
14	55	89	117	137	22
16	83	132	175	208	24
18	111	182	236	283	27
22	182	284	394	464	32
24	261	419	570	689	36

*—Torque values are for lightly oiled bolts. CAUTION: Bolts threaded into aluminum require much less torque.

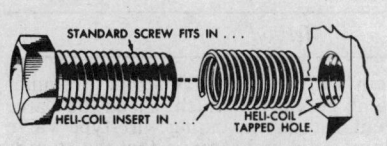

Heli-Coil installation
(© Chrysler Corp.)

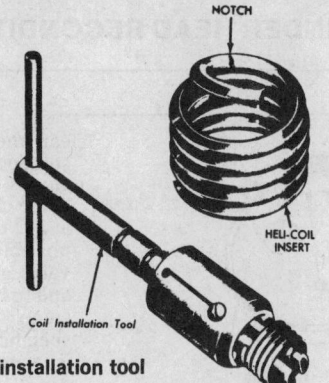

Heli-Coil and installation tool

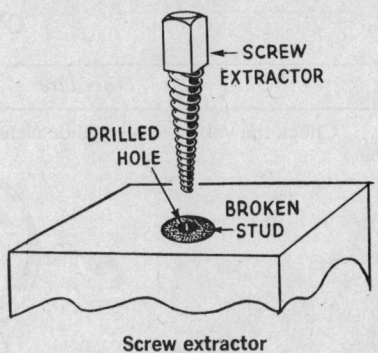

Screw extractor

Heli-Coil Insert			Drill	Tap	Insert. Tool	Extract-ing Tool
Thread Size	Part No.	Insert Length (In.)	Size	Part No.	Part No.	Part No.
1/2 -20	1185-4	3/8	17/64 (.266)	4 CPB	528-4N	1227-6
5/16-18	1185-5	15/32	Q (.332)	5 CPB	528-5N	1227-6
3/8 -16	1185-6	9/16	X (.397)	6 CPB	528-6N	1227-6
7/16-14	1185-7	21/32	29/64 (.453)	7 CPB	528-7N	1227-16
1/2 -13	1185-8	3/4	33/64 (.516)	8 CPB	528-8N	1227-16

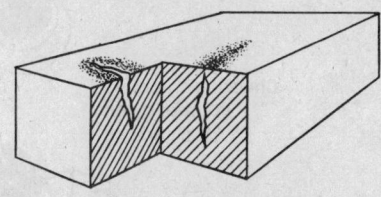

Magnaflux indication of cracks

Magnaflux and Zyglo are inspection techniques used to locate material flaws, such as stress cracks. Magnafluxing coats the part with fine magnetic particles, and subjects the part to a magnetic field. Cracks cause breaks in the magnetic field, which are outlined by the particles. Since Magnaflux is a magnetic process, it is applicable only to ferrous materials. The Zyglo process coats the material with a fluorescent dye penetrant, and then subjects it to blacklight inspection, under which cracks glow brightly. Parts made of any material may be tested using Zyglo. While Magnaflux and Zyglo are excellent for general inspection, and locating hidden defects, specific checks of suspected cracks may be made at lower cost and more readily using spot check dye. The dye is sprayed onto the suspected area, wiped off, and the area is then sprayed with a developer. Cracks then will show up brightly. Spot check dyes will only indicate surface cracks; therefore, structural cracks below the surface may escape detection. When questionable, the part should be tested using Magnaflux or Zyglo.

CYLINDER HEAD RECONDITIONING

Procedure	Method
Identify the valves:	Invert the cylinder head, and number the valve faces front to rear, using a permanent felt-tip marker.

Valve identification

Procedure	Method
Remove the rocker arms:	Remove the rocker arms with shaft(s) or balls and nuts. Wire the sets of rockers, balls and nuts together, and identify according to the corresponding valve.
Remove the valves and springs:	Using an appropriate valve spring compressor (depending on the configuration of the cylinder head), compress the valve springs. Lift out the keepers with needlenose pliers, release the compressor, and remove the valve, spring, and spring retainer.

Engine Rebuilding

CYLINDER HEAD RECONDITIONING

Procedure	Method

Check the valve stem-to-guide clearance:

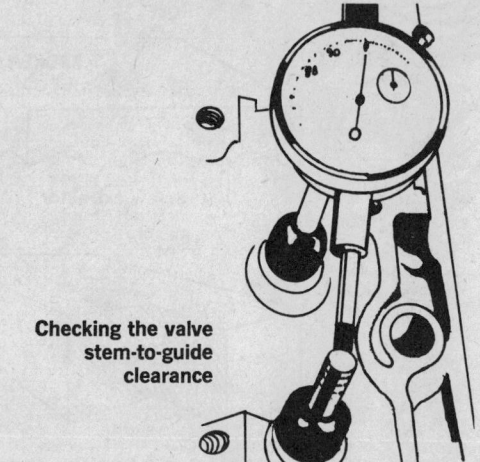

Checking the valve stem-to-guide clearance

Clean the valve stem with lacquer thinner or a similar solvent to remove all gum and varnish. Clean the valve guides using solvent and an expanding wire-type valve guide cleaner. Mount a dial indicator so that the stem is at 90° to the valve stem, as close to the valve guide as possible. Move the valve off its seat, and measure the valve guide-to-stem clearance by moving the stem back and forth to actuate the dial indicator. Measure the valve stems using a micrometer, and compare to specifications, to determine whether stem or guide wear is responsible for excessive clearance.

De-carbon the cylinder head and valves:

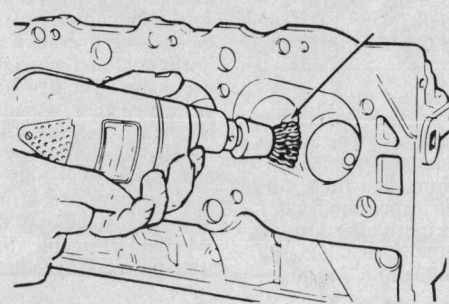

Removing carbon from the cylinder head

Chip carbon away from the valve heads, combustion chambers, and ports, using a chisel made of hardwood. Remove the remaining deposits with a stiff wire brush. NOTE: *Ensure that the deposits are actually removed, rather than burnished.*

Hot-tank the cylinder head:

Have the cylinder head hot-tanked to remove grease, corrosion, and scale from the water passages. NOTE: *In the case of overhead cam cylinder heads, consult the operator to determine whether the camshaft bearings will be damaged by the caustic solution.*

Degrease the remaining cylinder head parts:

Using solvent (i.e., Gunk), clean the rockers, rocker shaft(s) (where applicable), rocker balls and nuts, springs, spring retainers, and keepers. Do not remove the protective coating from the springs.

Check the cylinder head for warpage:

1
2
3

1 & 3 CHECK DIAGONALLY
2 CHECK ACROSS CENTER

Checking the cylinder head for warpage

Place a straight-edge across the gasket surface of the cylinder head. Using feeler gauges, determine the clearance at the center of the straight-edge. Measure across both diagonals, along the longitudinal centerline, and across the cylinder head at several points. If warpage exceeds .003″ in a 6″ span, or .006″ over the total length, the cylinder head must be resurfaced. NOTE: *If warpage exceeds the manufacturers maximum tolerance for material removal, the cylinder head must be replaced. When milling the cylinder heads of V-type engines, the intake manifold mounting position is altered, and must be corrected by milling the manifold flange a proportionate amount.*

CYLINDER HEAD RECONDITIONING

Procedure	Method
** Porting and gasket matching:	** Coat the manifold flanges of the cylinder head with Prussian blue dye. Glue intake and exhaust gaskets to the cylinder head in their installed position using rubber cement and scribe the outline of the ports on the manifold flanges. Remove the gaskets. Using a small cutter in a hand-held power tool (i.e., Dremel Moto-Tool), gradually taper the walls of the port out to the scribed outline of the gasket. Further enlargement of the ports should include the removal of sharp edges and radiusing of sharp corners. Do not alter the valve guides. NOTE: *The most efficient port configuration is determined only by extensive testing. Therefore, it is best to consult someone experienced with the head in question to determine the optimum alterations.*

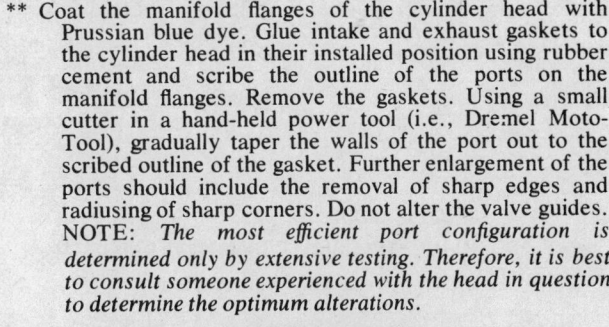

Port configuration before and after
gasket matching

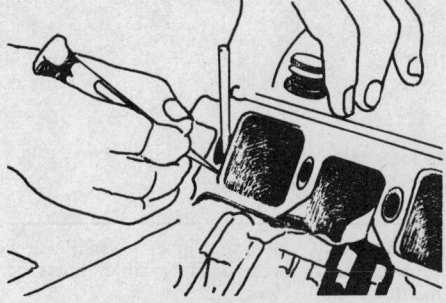

Marking the cylinder head for
gasket matching

Procedure	Method
** Polish the ports:	** Using a grinding stone with the above mentioned tool, polish the walls of the intake and exhaust ports, and combustion chamber. Use progressively finer stones until all surface imperfections are removed. NOTE: *Through testing, it has been determined that a smooth surface is more effective than a mirror polished surface in intake ports, and vice-versa in exhaust ports.*

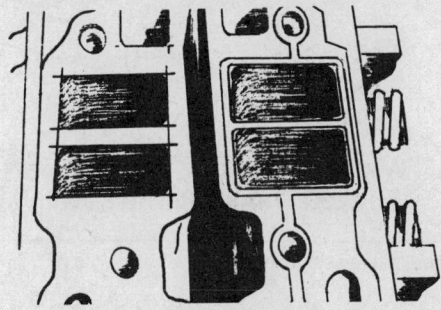

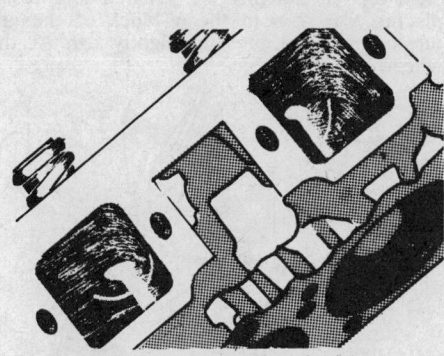

Relieved and polished ports

Procedure	Method
* Knurling the valve guides:	* Valve guides which are not excessively worn or distorted may, in some cases, be knurled rather than replaced. Knurling is a process in which metal is displaced and raised, thereby reducing clearance. Knurling also provides excellent oil control. The possibility of knurling rather than replacing valve guides should be discussed with a machinist.

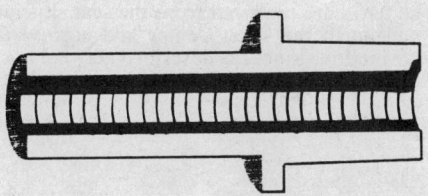

Cut-away view of a knurled valve guide

CYLINDER HEAD RECONDITIONING

Procedure	Method

Replacing the valve guides: NOTE: *Valve guides should only be replaced if damaged or if an oversize valve stem is not available.*

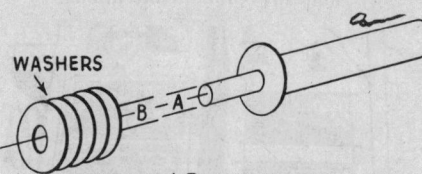

A - VALVE GUIDE I.D.
B - SLIGHTLY SMALLER THAN VALVE GUIDE O.D.

Valve guide removal tool

WASHERS

A - VALVE GUIDE I.D.
B - LARGER THAN THE VALVE GUIDE O.D.

Valve guide installation tool (with washers used during installation)

Depending on the type of cylinder head, valve guides may be pressed, hammered, or shrunk in. In cases where the guides are shrunk into the head, replacement should be left to an equipped machine shop. In other cases, the guides are replaced as follows: Press or tap the valve guides out of the head using a stepped drift (see illustration). Determine the height above the boss that the guide must extend, and obtain a stack of washers, their I.D. similar to the guide's O.D., of that height. Place the stack of washers on the guide, and insert the guide into the boss. NOTE: *Valve guides are often tapered or beveled for installation.* Using the stepped installation tool (see illustration), press or tap the guides into position. Ream the guides according to the size of the valve stem.

Replacing valve seat inserts:

Replacement of valve seat inserts which are worn beyond resurfacing or broken, if feasible, must be done by a machine shop.

Resurfacing (grinding) the valve face:

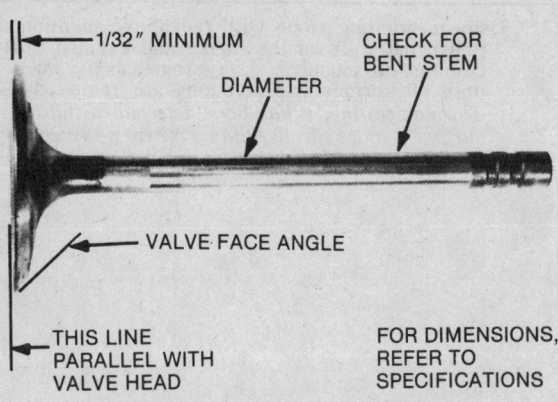

1/32" MINIMUM

DIAMETER

CHECK FOR BENT STEM

VALVE FACE ANGLE

THIS LINE PARALLEL WITH VALVE HEAD

FOR DIMENSIONS, REFER TO SPECIFICATIONS

Critical valve dimensions

Using a valve grinder, resurface the valves according to specifications. CAUTION: *Valve face angle is not always identical to valve seat angle.* A minimum margin of $^1/_{32}''$ should remain after grinding the valve. The valve stem top should also be squared and resurfaced, by placing the stem in the V-block of the grinder, and turning it while pressing lightly against the grinding wheel.

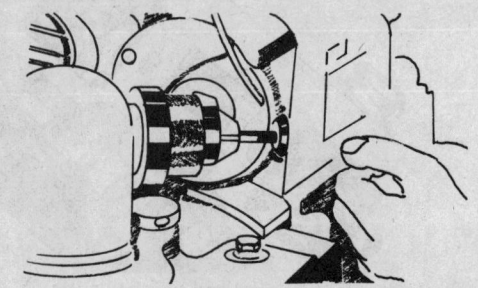

Grinding a valve

---

* **Resurfacing the valve seats using a grinder:**

Valve grinder

Grinding a valve seat
(© Subaru)

Select a pilot of the correct size, and a coarse stone of the correct seat angle. Lubricate the pilot if necessary, and install the tool in the valve guide. Move the stone on and off the seat at approximately two cycles per second, until all flaws are removed from the seat. Install a fine stone, and finish the seat. Center and narrow the seat using correction stones, as described above.

CYLINDER HEAD RECONDITIONING

Procedure	Method
Resurfacing the valve seats using reamers:	Select a reamer of the correct seat angle, slightly larger than the diameter of the valve seat, and assemble it with a pilot of the correct size. Install the pilot into the valve guide, and using steady pressure, turn the reamer clockwise. CAUTION: *Do not turn the reamer counter-clockwise.* Remove only as much material as necessary to clean the seat. Check the concentricity of the seat (see below). If the dye method is not used, coat the valve face with Prussian blue dye, install and rotate it on the valve seat. Using the dye marked area as a centering guide, center and narrow the valve seat to specifications with correction cutters. NOTE: *When no specifications are available, minimum seat width for exhaust valves should be $5/64''$, intake valves $1/16''$.* After making correction cuts, check the position of the valve seat on the valve face using Prussian blue dye.

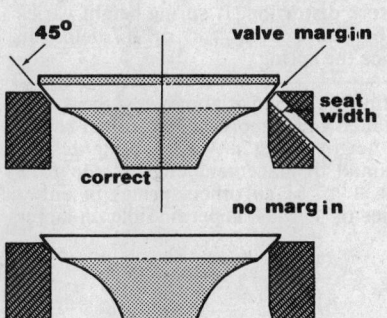

45° valve margin

seat width

correct

no margin

incorrect

Valve seat width and centering

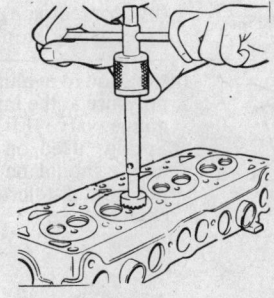

Reaming the valve seat (© Outboard Marine Corp)

Checking the valve seat concentricity:	Coat the valve face with Prussian blue dye, install the valve, and rotate it on the valve seat. If the entire seat becomes coated, and the valve is known to be concentric, the seat is concentric.
	* Install the dial gauge pilot into the guide, and rest of the arm on the valve seat. Zero the gauge, and rotate the arm around the seat. Run-out should not exceed .002″.

Checking the valve seat concentricity using a dial gauge

* Lapping the valves: NOTE: *Valve lapping is done to ensure efficient sealing of resurfaced valves and seats. Valve lapping alone is not recommended for use as a resurfacing procedure.*	* Invert the cylinder head, lightly lubricate the valve stems, and install the valves in the head as numbered. Coat valve seats with fine grinding compound, and attach the lapping tool suction cup to a valve head (NOTE: *Moisten the suction cup*). Rotate the tool between the palms, changing position and lifting the tool often to prevent grooving. Lap the valve until a smooth, polished seat is evident. Remove the valve and tool, and rinse away all traces of grinding compound.
	** Fasten a suction cup to a piece of drill rod, and mount the rod in a hand drill. Proceed as above, using the hand drill as a lapping tool. CAUTION: *Due to the higher speeds involved when using the hand drill, care must be exercised to avoid grooving the seat. Lift the tool and change direction of rotation often.*

HAND DRILL

ROD

SUCTION CUP

Hand lapping the valves

Home made mechanical valve lapping tool

CYLINDER HEAD RECONDITIONING

Procedure	Method

Check the valve springs:

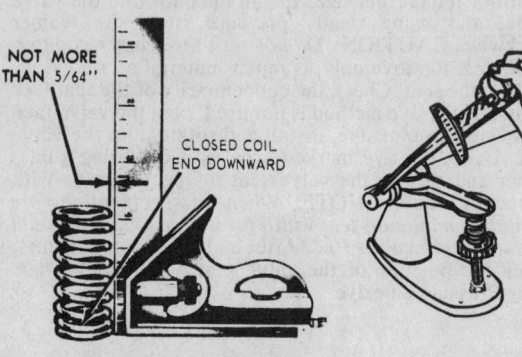

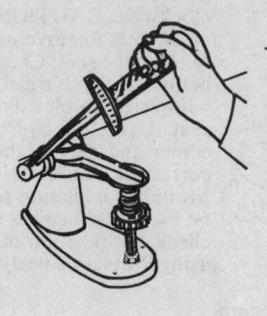

NOT MORE THAN 5/64"

CLOSED COIL END DOWNWARD

Checking the valve spring free length and squareness

(© Outboard Marine Corp.)

Place the spring on a flat surface next to a square. Measure the height of the spring, and rotate it against the edge of the square to measure distortion. If spring height varies (by comparison) by more than $1/16''$ or if distortion exceeds $1/16''$, replace the spring.

** In addition to evaluating the spring as above, test the spring pressure at the installed and compressed (installed height minus valve lift) height using a valve spring tester. Springs used on small displacement engines (up to 3 liters) should be ∓ 1 lb. of all other springs in either position. A tolerance of ∓ 5 lbs. is permissible on larger engines.

* Install valve stem seals:

RETAINER
SPRING
INTAKE VALVE
SEAL

Valve stem seal installation

* Due to the pressure differential that exists at the ends of the intake valve guides (atmospheric pressure above, manifold vacuum below), oil is drawn through the valve guides into the intake port. This has been alleviated somewhat since the addition of positive crankcase ventilation, which lowers the pressure above the guides. Several types of valve stem seals are available to reduce blow-by. Certain seals simply slip over the stem and guide boss, while others require that the boss be machined. Recently, Teflon guide seals have become popular. Consult a parts supplier or machinist concerning availability and suggested usages. NOTE: *When installing seals, ensure that a small amount of oil is able to pass the seal to lubricate the valve guides; otherwise, excessive wear may result.*

Install the valves:

Lubricate the valve stems, and install the valves in the cylinder head as numbered. Lubricate and position the seals (if used, see above) and the valve springs. Install the spring retainers, compress the springs, and insert the keys using needlenose pliers or a tool designed for this purpose. NOTE: *Retain the keys with wheel bearing grease during installation.*

Checking valve spring installed height:

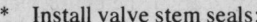

GRIND OUT THIS PORTION

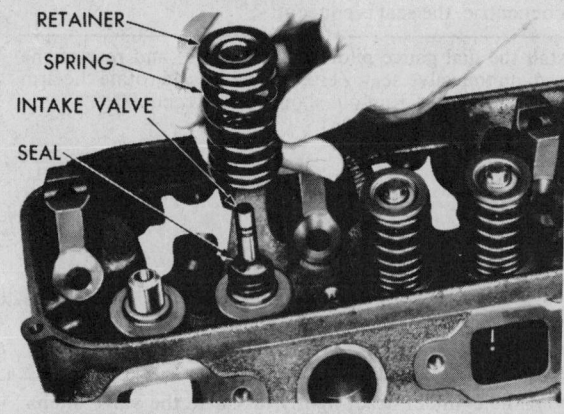

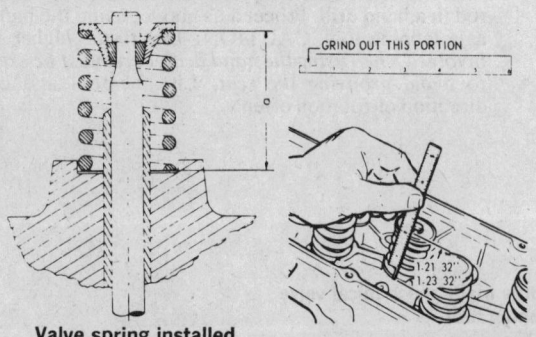

Valve spring installed height dimension
(© Porsche)

Measuring valve spring installed height (© Outboard Marine Corp.)

Measure the distance between the spring pad and the lower edge of the spring retainer, and compare to specifications. If the installed height is incorrect, add shim washers between the spring pad and the spring. CAUTION: *Use only washers designed for this purpose.*

CYLINDER HEAD RECONDITIONING

Procedure	Method

** CC'ing the combustion chambers:

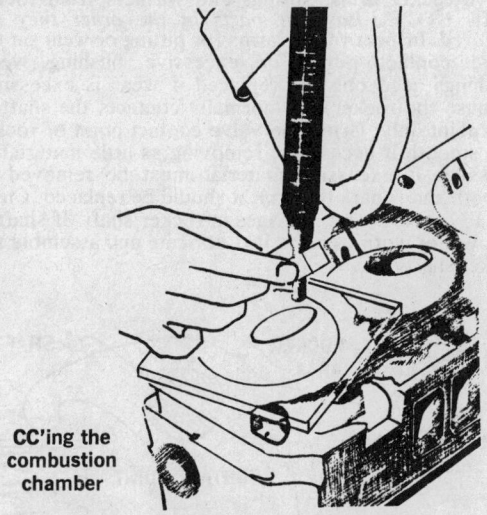

CC'ing the combustion chamber

** Invert the cylinder head and place a bead of sealer around a combustion chamber. Install an apparatus designed for this purpose (burette mounted on a clear plate; see illustration) over the combustion chamber, and fill with the specified fluid to an even mark on the burette. Record the burette reading, and fill the combustion chamber with fluid. (NOTE: *A hole drilled in the plate will permit air to escape*). Subtract the burette reading, with the combustion chamber filled, from the previous reading, to determine combustion chamber volume in cc's. Duplicate this procedure in all combustion chambers on the cylinder head, and compare the readings. The volume of all combustion chambers should be made equal to that of the largest. Combustion chamber volume may be increased in two ways. When only a small change is required (usually), a small cutter or coarse stone may be used to remove material from the combustion chamber. NOTE: *Check volume frequently.* Remove material over a wide area, so as not to change the configuration of the combustion chamber. When a larger change is required, the valve seat may be sunk (lowered into the head). NOTE: *When altering valve seat, remember to compensate for the change in spring installed height.*

Inspect the rocker arms, balls, studs, and nuts (where applicable):

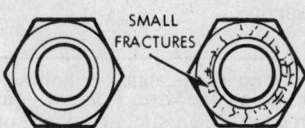

Stress cracks in rocker nuts
(© Ford Motor Co.)

Visually inspect the rocker arms, balls, studs, and nuts for cracks, galling, burning, scoring, or wear. If all parts are intact, liberally lubricate the rocker arms and balls, and install them on the cylinder head. If wear is noted on a rocker arm at the point of valve contact, grind it smooth and square, removing as little material as possible. Replace the rocker arm if excessively worn. If a rocker stud shows signs of wear, it must be replaced (see below). If a rocker nut shows stress cracks, replace it. If an exhaust ball is galled or burned, substitute the intake ball from the same cylinder (if it is intact), and install a new intake ball. NOTE: *Avoid using new rocker balls on exhaust valves.*

Replacing rocker studs:

Reaming the stud bore for oversize rocker studs
(© Buick Div. G.M. Corp.)

In order to remove a threaded stud, lock two nuts on the stud, and unscrew the stud using the lower nut. Coat the lower threads of the new stud with Loctite, and install.

Two alternative methods are available for replacing pressed in studs. Remove the damaged stud using a stack of washers and a nut (see illustration). In the first, the boss is reamed .005-.006″ oversize, and an oversize stud pressed in. Control the stud extension over the boss using washers, in the same manner as valve guides. Before installing the stud, coat it with white lead and grease. To retain the stud more positively drill a hole through the stud and boss, and install a roll pin. In the second method, the boss is tapped, and a threaded stud installed. Retain the stud using Loctite Stud and Bearing Mount.

Extracting a pressed in rocker stud
(© Buick Div. G.M. Corp.)

FLAT WASHERS

AS STUD BEGINS TO PULL UP, IT WILL BE NECESSARY TO REMOVE THE NUT AND ADD MORE WASHERS.

CYLINDER HEAD RECONDITIONING

Procedure	Method

Inspect the rocker shaft(s) and rocker arms (where applicable):

Remove rocker arms, springs and washers from rocker shaft. NOTE: *Lay out parts in the order they are removed.* Inspect rocker arms for pitting or wear on the valve contact point, or excessive bushing wear. Bushings need only be replaced if wear is excessive, because the rocker arm normally contacts the shaft at one point only. Grind the valve contact point of rocker arm smooth if necessary, removing as little material as possible. If excessive material must be removed to smooth and square the arm, it should be replaced. Clean out all oil holes and passages in rocker shaft. If shaft is grooved or worn, replace it. Lubricate and assemble the rocker shaft.

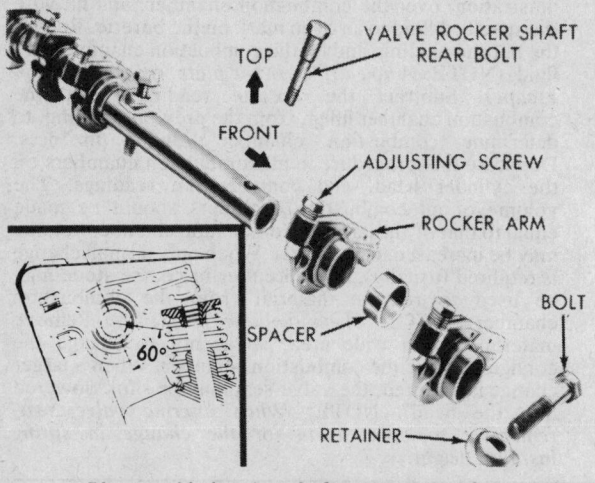

VALVE ROCKER SHAFT REAR BOLT

TOP

FRONT

ADJUSTING SCREW

ROCKER ARM

SPACER

BOLT

RETAINER

60°

Disassembled rocker shaft parts arranged for inspection

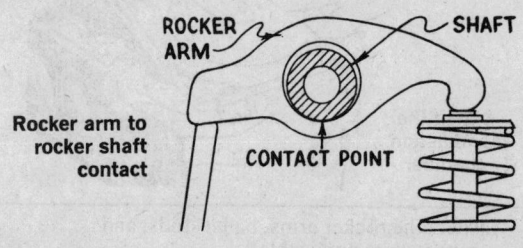

ROCKER ARM

SHAFT

Rocker arm to rocker shaft contact

CONTACT POINT

Inspect the camshaft bushings and the camshaft (overhead cam engines):

See next section.

Inspect the pushrods:

Remove the pushrods, and, if hollow, clean out the oil passages using fine wire. Roll each pushrod over a piece of clean glass. If a distinct clicking sound is heard as the pushrod rolls, the rod is bent, and must be replaced.

* The length of all pushrods must be equal. Measure the length of the pushrods, compare to specifications, and replace as necessary.

Inspect the valve lifters:

Remove lifters from their bores, and remove gum and varnish, using solvent. Clean walls of lifter bores. Check lifters for concave wear as illustrated. If face is worn concave, replace lifter, and carefully inspect the camshaft. Lightly lubricate lifter and insert it into its bore. If play is excessive, an oversize lifter must be installed (where possible). Consult a machinist concerning feasibility. If play is satisfactory, remove, lubricate, and reinstall the lifter.

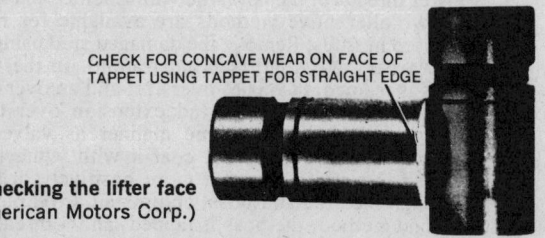

CHECK FOR CONCAVE WEAR ON FACE OF TAPPET USING TAPPET FOR STRAIGHT EDGE

Checking the lifter face
(© American Motors Corp.)

* Testing hydraulic lifter leak down:

Submerge lifter in a container of kerosene. Chuck a used pushrod or its equivalent into a drill press. Position container of kerosene so pushrod acts on the lifter plunger. Pump lifter with the drill press, until resistance increases. Pump several more times to bleed any air out of lifter. Apply very firm, constant pressure to the lifter, and observe rate at which fluid bleeds out of lifter. If the fluid bleeds very quickly (less than 15 seconds), lifter is defective. If the time exceeds 60 seconds, lifter is sticking. In either case, recondition or replace lifter. If lifter is operating properly (leak down time 15-60 seconds), lubricate and install it.

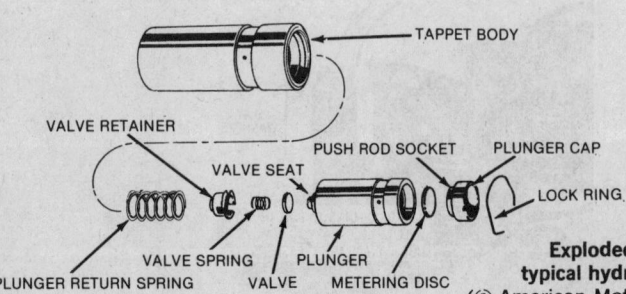

TAPPET BODY

VALVE RETAINER

PUSH ROD SOCKET

VALVE SEAT

PLUNGER CAP

LOCK RING

VALVE SPRING

PLUNGER

PLUNGER RETURN SPRING

VALVE

METERING DISC

Exploded view of a typical hydraulic lifter
(© American Motors Corp.)

CYLINDER BLOCK RECONDITIONING

Procedure	Method

Checking the main bearing clearance:

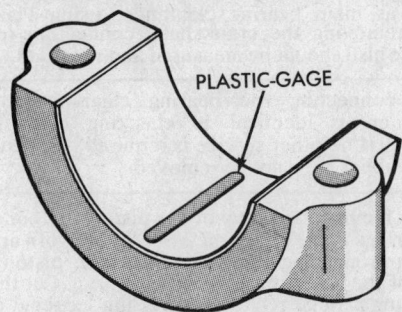

PLASTIC-GAGE

Installing Plastigage on lower bearing shell (© Chrysler Corp.)

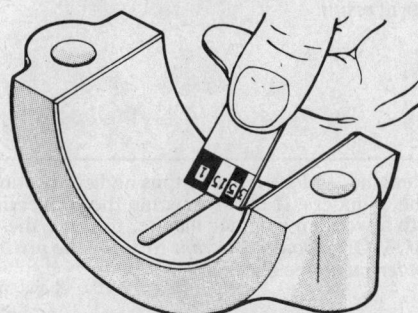

Measuring Plastigage to determine bearing clearance (© Chrysler Corp.)

Invert engine, and remove cap from the bearing to be checked. Using a clean, dry rag, thoroughly clean all oil from crankshaft journal and bearing insert. NOTE: *Plastigage is soluble in oil; therefore, oil on the journal or bearing could result in erroneous readings.* Place a piece of Plastigage along the full length of journal, reinstall cap, and torque to specifications. Remove bearing cap, and determine bearing clearance by comparing width of Plastigage to the scale on Plastigage envelope. Journal taper is determined by comparing width of the Plastigage strip near its ends. Rotate crankshaft 90° and retest, to determine journal eccentricity. NOTE: *Do not rotate crankshaft with Plastigage installed.* If bearing insert and journal appear intact, and are within tolerances, no further main bearing service is required. If bearing or journal appear defective, cause of failure should be determined before replacement.

* Remove crankshaft from block (see below). Measure the main bearing journals at each end twice (90° apart) using a micrometer, to determine diameter, journal taper and eccentricity. If journals are within tolerances, reinstall bearing caps at their specified torque. Using a telescope gauge and micrometer, measure bearing I.D. parallel to piston axis and at 30° on each side of piston axis. Subtract journal O.D. from bearing I.D. to determine oil clearance. If crankshaft journals appear defective, or do not meet tolerances, there is no need to measure bearings; for the crankshaft will require grinding and/or undersize bearings will be required. If bearing appears defective, cause for failure should be determined prior to replacement.

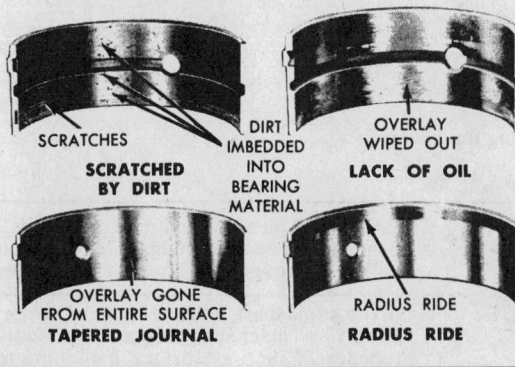

SCRATCHES — SCRATCHED BY DIRT

DIRT IMBEDDED INTO BEARING MATERIAL

OVERLAY WIPED OUT — LACK OF OIL

BRIGHT (POLISHED) SECTIONS — IMPROPER SEATING

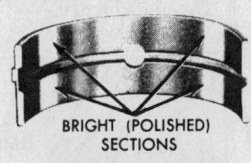

OVERLAY GONE FROM ENTIRE SURFACE — TAPERED JOURNAL

RADIUS RIDE — RADIUS RIDE

CRATERS OR POCKETS — FATIGUE FAILURE

Causes of bearing failure (© Ford Motor Co.)

Removing the crankshaft:

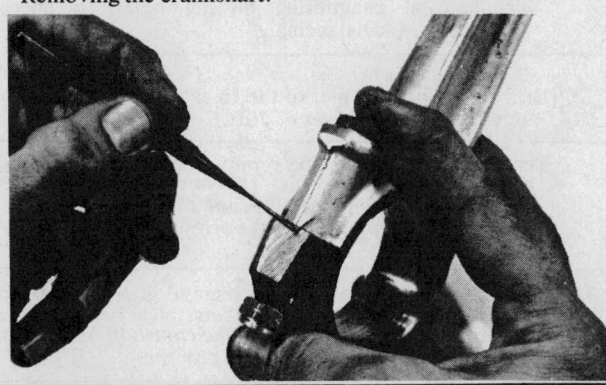

Connecting rod matching marks

Using a punch, mark the corresponding main bearing caps and saddles according to position (i.e., one punch on the front main cap and saddle, two on the second, three on the third, etc.). Using number stamps, identify the corresponding connecting rods and caps, according to cylinder (if no numbers are present). Remove the main and connecting rod caps, and place sleeves of plastic tubing over the connecting rod bolts, to protect the journals as the crankshaft is removed. Lift the crankshaft out of the block.

CYLINDER BLOCK RECONDITIONING

Procedure	Method
Checking the connecting rod bearing clearance:	Connecting rod bearing clearance is checked in the same manner as main bearing clearance, using Plastigage. Before removing the crankshaft, connecting rod side clearance also should be measured and recorded.
	* Checking connecting rod bearing clearance, using a micrometer, is identical to checking main bearing clearance. If no other service is required, the piston and rod assemblies need not be removed.
Remove the ridge from the top of the cylinder:	In order to facilitate removal of the piston and connecting rod, the ridge at the top of the cylinder (unworn area; see illustration) must be removed. Place the piston at the bottom of the bore, and cover it with a rag. Cut the ridge away using a ridge reamer, exercising extreme care to avoid cutting too deeply. Remove the rag, and remove cuttings that remain on the piston. CAUTION: *If the ridge is not removed, and new rings are installed, damage to rings will result.*

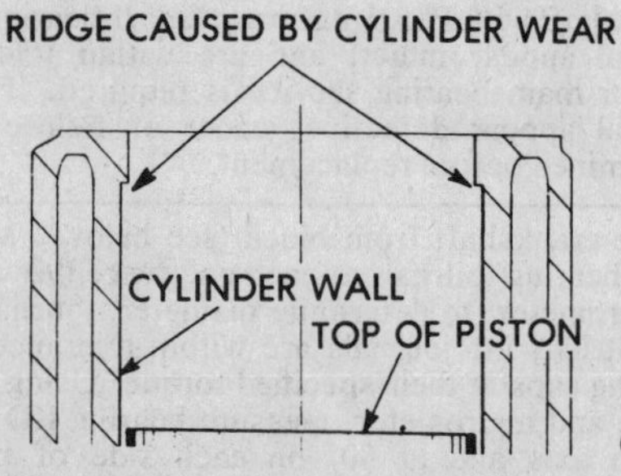

RIDGE CAUSED BY CYLINDER WEAR

CYLINDER WALL

TOP OF PISTON

Cylinder bore ridge
(© Pontiac Div. G.M. Corp.)

Procedure	Method
Removing the piston and connecting rod:	Invert the engine, and push the pistons and connecting rods out of the cylinders. If necessary, tap the connecting rod boss with a wooden hammer handle, to force the piston out. CAUTION: *Do not attempt to force the piston past the cylinder ridge* (see above).

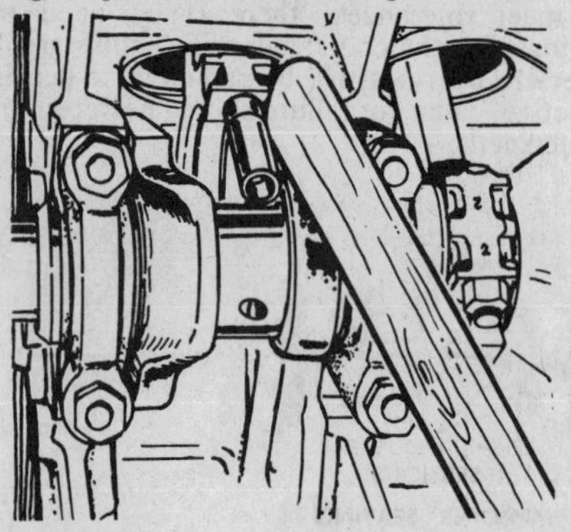

Removing the piston

Procedure	Method
Service the crankshaft:	Ensure that all oil holes and passages in the crankshaft are open and free of sludge. If necessary, have the crankshaft ground to the largest possible undersize.
	** Have the crankshaft Magnafluxed, to locate stress cracks. Consult a machinist concerning additional service procedures, such as surface hardening (e.g., nitriding, Tuftriding) to improve wear characteristics, cross drilling and chamfering the oil holes to improve lubrication, and balancing.
Removing freeze plugs:	Drill a hole in the center of the freeze plugs, and pry them out using a screwdriver or drift.
Remove the oil gallery plugs:	Threaded plugs should be removed using an appropriate (usually square) wrench. To remove soft, pressed in plugs, drill a hole in the plug, and thread in a sheet metal screw. Pull the plug out by the screw using pliers.
Hot-tank the block:	Have the block hot-tanked to remove grease, corrosion, and scale from the water jackets. NOTE: *Consult the operator to determine whether the camshaft bearings will be damaged during the hot-tank process.*

CYLINDER BLOCK RECONDITIONING

Procedure	Method
Check the block for cracks:	Visually inspect the block for cracks or chips. The most common locations are as follows: Adjacent to freeze plugs. Between the cylinders and water jackets. Adjacent to the main bearing saddles. At the extreme bottom of the cylinders. Check only suspected cracks using spot check dye (see introduction). If a crack is located, consult a machinist concerning possible repairs.
	** Magnaflux the block to locate hidden cracks. If cracks are located, consult a machinist about feasibility of repair.
Install the oil gallery plugs and freeze plugs:	Coat freeze plugs with sealer and tap into position using a piece of pipe, slightly smaller than the plug, as a driver. To ensure retention, stake the edges of the plugs. Coat threaded oil gallery plugs with sealer and install. Drive replacement soft plugs into block using a large drift as a driver.
	* Rather than reinstalling lead plugs, drill and tap the holes, and install threaded plugs.
Check the bore diameter and surface:	Visually inspect the cylinder bores for roughness, scoring, or scuffing. If evident, the cylinder bore must be bored or honed oversize to eliminate imperfections, and the smallest possible oversize piston used. The new pistons should be given to the machinist with the block, so that the cylinders can be bored or honed exactly to the piston size (plus clearance). If no flaws are evident, measure the bore diameter using a telescope gauge and micrometer, or dial guage, parallel and perpendicular to the engine centerline, at the top (below the ridge) and bottom of the bore. Subtract the bottom measurements from the top to determine taper, and the parallel to the centerline measurements from the perpendicular measurements to determine eccentricity. If the measurements are not within specifications, the cylinder must be bored or honed, and an oversize piston installed. If the measurements are within specifications the cylinder may be used as is, with only finish honing (see below). NOTE: *Prior to submitting the block for boring, perform the following operation(s).*

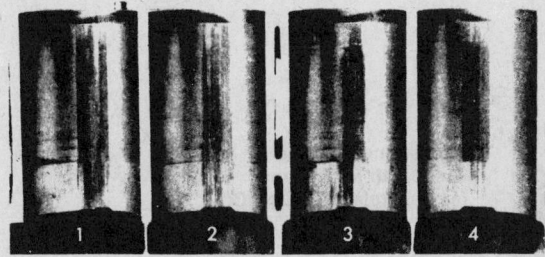

1, 2, 3 Piston skirt seizure resulted in this pattern. Engine must be rebored

4. Piston skirt and oil ring seizure caused this damage. Engine must be rebored

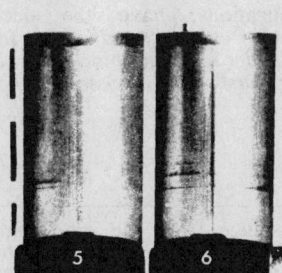

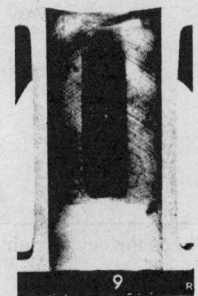

5, 6 Score marks caused by a split piston skirt. Damage is not serious enough to warrant reboring

7. Ring seized longitudinally, causing a score mark 1 3/16″ wide, on the land side of the piston groove. The honing pattern is destroyed and the cylinder must be rebored

8. Result of oil ring seizure. Engine must be rebored

9. Oil ring seizure here was not serious enough to warrant reboring. The honing marks are still visible

Cylinder wall damage
(© Daimler-Benz A.G.)

CYLINDER BLOCK RECONDITIONING

Procedure	Method

Check the bore diameter and surface:

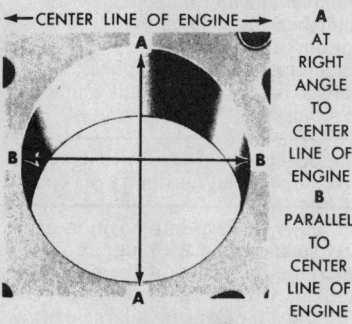

Cylinder bore measuring
positions
(© Ford Motor Co.)

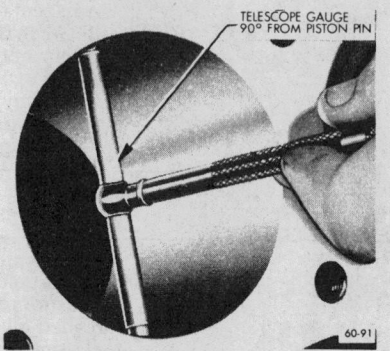

Measuring the cylinder bore
with a telescope gauge
(© Buick Div. G.M. Corp.)

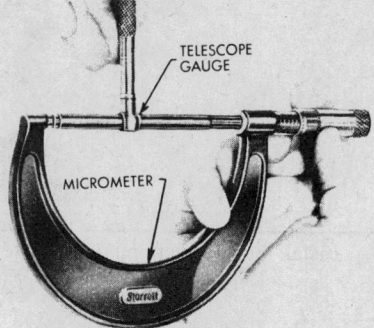

Determining the cylinder bore
by measuring the telescope
gauge with a micrometer
(© Buick Div. G.M. Corp.)

Measuring the cylinder bore
with a dial gauge
(© Chevrolet Div. G.M. Corp.)

Check the block deck for warpage:

Using a straightedge and feeler gauges, check the block deck for warpage in the same manner that the cylinder head is checked (see Cylinder Head Reconditioning). If warpage exceeds specifications, have the deck resurfaced. NOTE: *In certain cases a specification for total material removal (Cylinder head and block deck) is provided. This specification must not be exceeded.*

---

* Check the deck height:

The deck height is the distance from the crankshaft centerline to the block deck. To measure, invert the engine, and install the crankshaft, retaining it with the center main cap. Measure the distance from the crankshaft journal to the block deck, parallel to the cylinder centerline. Measure the diameter of the end (front and rear) main journals, parallel to the centerline of the cylinders, divide the diameter in half, and subtract it from the previous measurement. The results of the front and rear measurements should be identical. If the difference exceeds .005″, the deck height should be corrected. NOTE: *Block deck height and warpage should be corrected at the same time.*

CYLINDER BLOCK RECONDITIONING

Procedure	*Method*

Check the cylinder block bearing alignment:

Checking main bearing saddle alignment

Remove the upper bearing inserts. Place a straightedge in the bearing saddles along the centerline of the crankshaft. If clearance exists between the straightedge and the center saddle, the block must be alignbored.

Clean and inspect the pistons and connecting rods:

RING EXPANDER

Removing the piston rings

Using a ring expander, remove the rings from the piston. Remove the retaining rings (if so equipped) and remove piston pin. NOTE: *If the piston pin must be pressed out, determine the proper method and use the proper tools; otherwise the piston will distort.* Clean the ring grooves using an appropriate tool, exercising care to avoid cutting too deeply. Thoroughly clean all carbon and varnish from the piston with solvent. CAUTION: *Do not use a wire brush or caustic solvent on pistons.* Inspect the pistons for scuffing, scoring, cracks, pitting, or excessive ring groove wear. If wear is evident, the piston must be replaced. Check the connecting rod length by measuring the rod from the inside of the large end to the inside of the small end using calipers (see illustration). All connecting rods should be equal length. Replace any rod that differs from the others in the engine.

* Have the connecting rod alignment checked in an alignment fixture by a machinist. Replace any twisted or bent rods.

---

* Magnaflux the connecting rods to locate stress cracks. If cracks are found, replace the connecting rod.

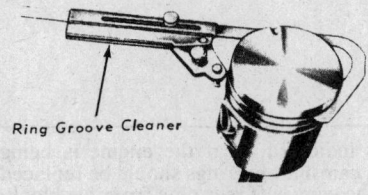

Ring Groove Cleaner

Cleaning the piston ring grooves
(© Ford Motor Co.)

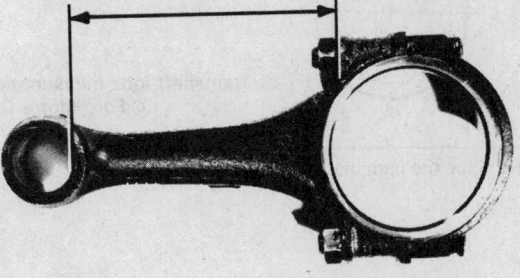

Connecting rod length checking dimension

Fit the pistons to the cylinders:

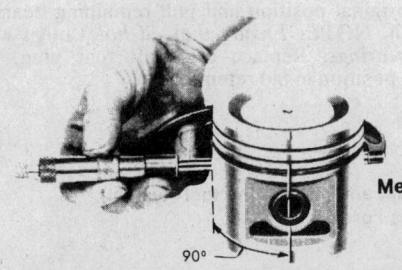

Measuring the piston for fitting
(© Buick Div. G.M. Corp.)

90°

Using a telescope gauge and micrometer, or a dial gauge, measure the cylinder bore diameter perpendicular to the piston pin, $2^{1}/_{2}''$ below the deck. Measure the piston perpendicular to its pin on the skirt. The difference between the two measurements is the piston clearance. If the clearance is within specifications or slightly below (after boring or honing), finish honing is all that is required. If the clearance is excessive, try to obtain a slightly larger piston to bring clearance within specifications. Where this is not possible, obtain the first oversize piston, and hone (or if necessary, bore) the cylinder to size.

CYLINDER BLOCK RECONDITIONING

Procedure	Method
Assemble the pistons and connecting rods:  **Installing piston pin lock rings**	Inspect piston pin, connecting rod small end bushing, and piston bore for galling, scoring, or excessive wear. If evident, replace defective part(s). Measure the I.D. of the piston boss and connecting rod small end, and the O.D. of the piston pin. If within specifications, assemble piston pin and rod. CAUTION: *If piston pin must be pressed in, determine the proper method and use the proper tools; otherwise the piston will distort.* Install the lock rings; ensure that they seat properly. If the parts are not within specifications, determine the service method for the type of engine. In some cases, piston and pin are serviced as an assembly when either is defective. Others specify reaming the piston and connecting rods for an oversize pin. If the connecting rod bushing is worn, it may in many cases be replaced. Reaming the piston and replacing the rod bushing are machine shop operations.
Clean and inspect the camshaft: 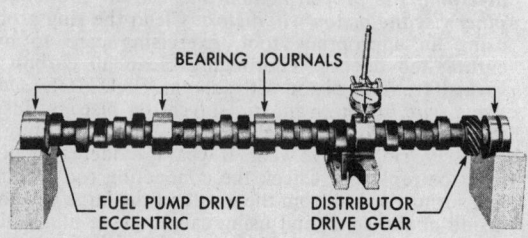 BEARING JOURNALS FUEL PUMP DRIVE ECCENTRIC DISTRIBUTOR DRIVE GEAR **Checking the camshaft for straightness** (© Chevrolet Motor Div. G.M. Corp.)	Degrease the camshaft, using solvent, and clean out all oil holes. Visually inspect cam lobes and bearing journals for excessive wear. If a lobe is questionable, check all lobes as indicated below. If a journal or lobe is worn, the camshaft must be reground or replaced. NOTE: *If a journal is worn, there is a good chance that the bushings are worn.* If lobes and journals appear intact, place the front and rear journals in V-blocks, and rest a dial indicator on the center journal. Rotate the camshaft to check straightness. If deviation exceeds .001", replace the camshaft.
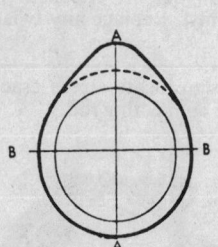 **Camshaft lobe measurement** (© Ford Motor Co.)	* Check the camshaft lobes with a micrometer, by measuring the lobes from the nose to base and again at 90° (see illustration). The lift is determined by subtracting the second measurement from the first. If all exhaust lobes and all intake lobes are not identical, the camshaft must be reground or replaced.
Replace the camshaft bearings: 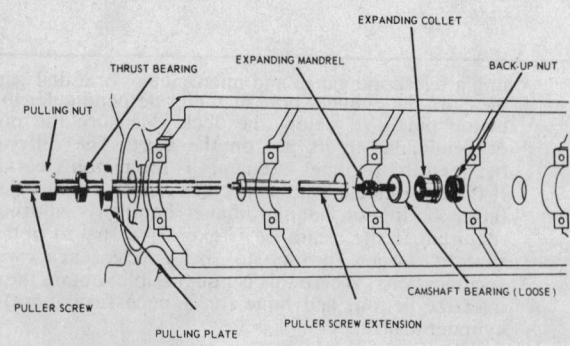 EXPANDING COLLET THRUST BEARING EXPANDING MANDREL BACK-UP NUT PULLING NUT PULLER SCREW PULLING PLATE PULLER SCREW EXTENSION CAMSHAFT BEARING (LOOSE) **Camshaft removal and installation tool (typical)** (© Ford Motor Co.)	If excessive wear is indicated, or if the engine is being completely rebuilt, camshaft bearings should be replaced as follows: Drive the camshaft rear plug from the block. Assemble the removal puller with its shoulder on the bearing to be removed. Gradually tighten the puller nut until bearing is removed. Remove remaining bearings, leaving the front and rear for last. To remove front and rear bearings, reverse position of the tool, so as to pull the bearings in toward the center of the block. Leave the tool in this position, pilot the new front and rear bearings on the installer, and pull them into position: Return the tool to its original position and pull remaining bearings into position. NOTE: *Ensure that oil holes align when installing bearings.* Replace camshaft rear plug, and stake it into position to aid retention.

CYLINDER BLOCK RECONDITIONING

Procedure	Method
Finish hone the cylinders: 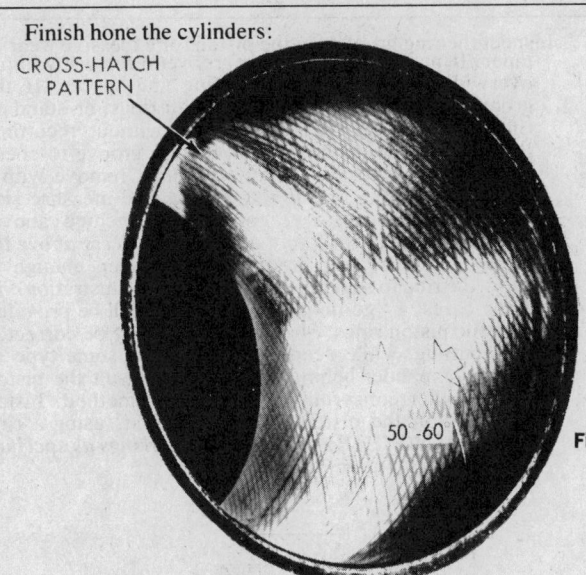 **Finish honed cylinder** (© Chrysler Corp.)	Chuck a flexible drive hone into a power drill, and insert it into the cylinder. Start the hone, and move it up and down in the cylinder at a rate which will produce approximately a 60° cross-hatch pattern (see illustration). NOTE: *Do not extend the hone below the cylinder bore.* After developing the pattern, remove the hone and recheck piston fit. Wash the cylinders with a detergent and water solution to remove abrasive dust, dry, and wipe several times with a rag soaked in engine oil.
Check piston ring end-gap: 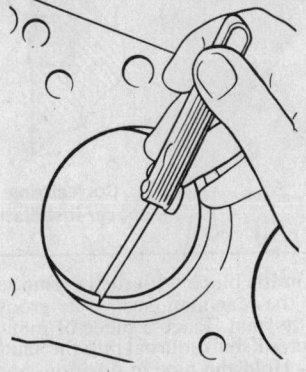 **Checking ring end-gap** (© Outboard Marine Corp.)	Compress the piston rings to be used in a cylinder, one at a time, into that cylinder, and press them approximately 1″ below the deck with an inverted piston. Using feeler guages, measure the ring end-gap, and compare to specifications. Pull the ring out of the cylinder and file the ends with a fine file to obtain proper clearance. CAUTION: *If inadequate ring end-gap is utilized, ring breakage will result.*
Install the camshaft:	Liberally lubricate the camshaft lobes and journals, and slide the camshaft into the block. CAUTION: *Exercise extreme care to avoid damaging the bearings when inserting the camshaft.* Install and tighten the camshaft thrust plate retaining bolts.
Check camshaft end-play:	Using feeler gauges, determine whether the clearance between the camshaft boss (or gear) and backing plate is within specifications. Install shims behind the thrust plate, or reposition the camshaft gear and retest end-play. In some cases, adjustment is by replacing the thrust plate.
	* Mount a dial indicator stand so that the stem of the dial indicator rests on the nose of the camshaft, parallel to the camshaft axis. Push the camshaft as far in as possible and zero the gauge. Move the camshaft outward to determine the amount of camshaft endplay. If the endplay is not within tolerance, install shims behind the thrust plate, or reposition the camshaft gear and retest.

DIAL INDICATOR

CAMSHAFT

0.0025″-0.0075″

Checking camshaft end-play with a feeler gauge

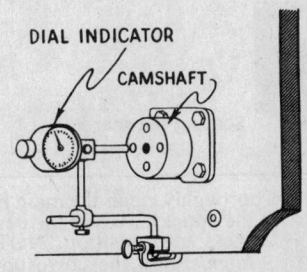

Checking camshaft end-play with a dial indicator

(© Outboard Marine Corp.)

CYLINDER BLOCK RECONDITIONING

Procedure	Method
Install the piston rings: 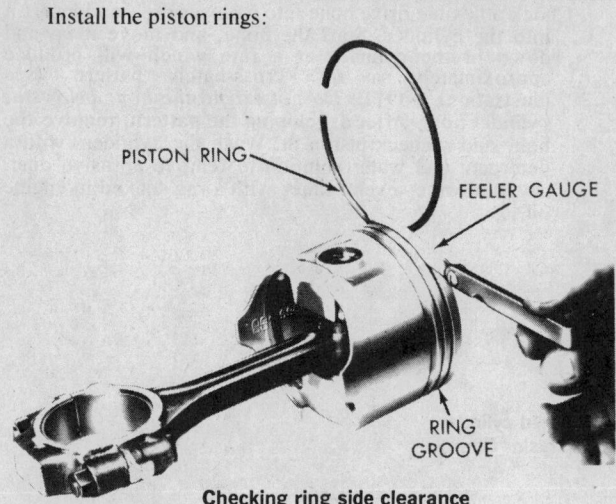Checking ring side clearance ((C) Chrysler Corp.)	Inspect the ring grooves in the piston for excessive wear or taper. If necessary, recut the groove(s) for use with an overwidth ring or a standard ring and spacer. If the groove is worn uniformly, overwidth rings, or standard rings and spacers may be installed without recutting. Roll the outside of the ring around the groove to check for burrs or deposits. If any are found, remove with a fine file. Hold the ring in the groove, and measure side clearance. If necessary, correct as indicated above. NOTE: *Always install any additional spacers above the piston ring.* The ring groove must be deep enough to allow the ring to seat below the lands (see illustration). In many cases, a ''go-no-go'' depth gauge will be provided with the piston rings. Shallow grooves may be corrected by recutting, while deep grooves require some type of filler or expander behind the piston. Consult the piston ring supplier concerning the suggested method. Install the rings on the piston, lowest ring first, using a ring expander. NOTE: *Position the ring markings as specified by the manufacturer (see car section).*

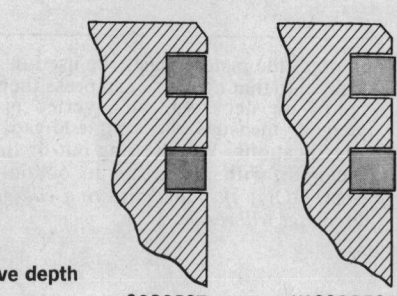

Piston groove depth   CORRECT   INCORRECT

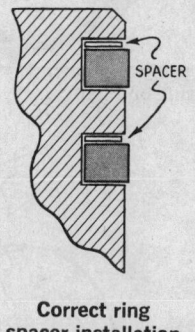

Correct ring spacer installation

Procedure	Method
Install the rear main seal (where applicable): 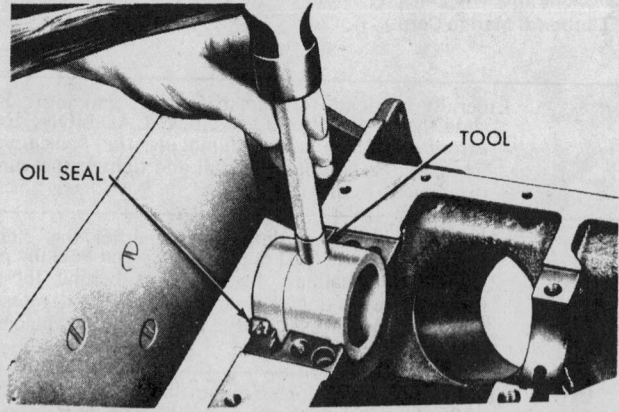**Seating the rear main seal**	Position the block with the bearing saddles facing upward. Lay the rear main seal in its groove and press it lightly into its seat. Place a piece of pipe the same diameter as the crankshaft journal into the saddle, and firmly seat the seal. Hold the pipe in position, and trim the ends of the seal flush if required.
Install the crankshaft:	Thoroughly clean the main bearing saddles and caps. Place the upper halves of the bearing inserts on the saddles and press into position. NOTE: *Ensure that the oil holes align.* Press the corresponding bearing inserts into the main bearing caps. Lubricate the upper main bearings, and lay the crankshaft in position. Place a strip of

CYLINDER BLOCK RECONDITIONING

Procedure	Method

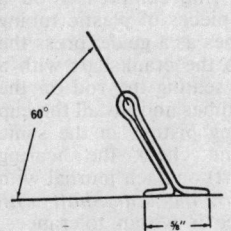

Home made bearing roll-out pin
(© Pontiac Div. G.M. Corp.)

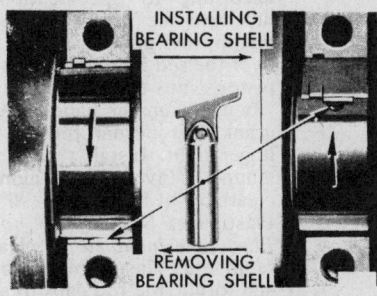

Removal and installation of upper bearing insert using a roll-out pin
(© Buick Div. G.M. Corp.)

Plastigage on each of the crankshaft journals, install the main caps, and torque to specifications. Remove the main caps, and compare the Plastigage to the scale on the Plastigage envelope. If clearances are within tolerances, remove the Plastigage, turn the crankshaft 90°, wipe off all oil and retest. If all clearances are correct, remove all Plastigage, thoroughly lubricate the main caps and bearing journals, and install the main caps. If clearances are not within tolerance, the upper bearing inserts may be removed, without removing the crankshaft, using a bearing roll out pin (see illustration). Roll in a bearing that will provide proper clearance, and retest. Torque all main caps, excluding the thrust bearing cap, to specifications. Tighten the thrust bearing cap finger tight. To properly align the thrust bearing, pry the crankshaft the extent of its axial travel several times, the last movement held toward the front of the engine, and torque the thrust bearing cap to specifications. Determine the crankshaft end-play (see below), and bring within tolerance with thrust washers.

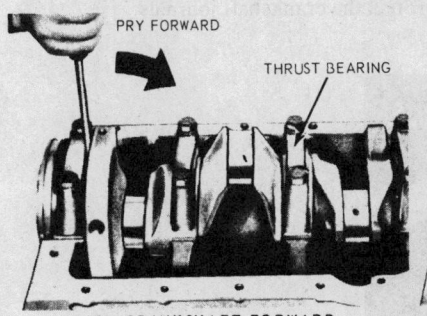
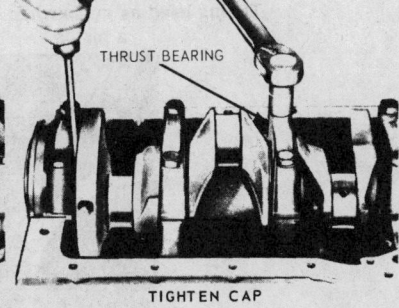

Aligning the thrust bearing
(© Ford Motor Co.)

Measure crankshaft end-play:

Mount a dial indicator stand on the front of the block, with the dial indicator stem resting on the nose of the crankshaft, parallel to the crankshaft axis. Pry the crankshaft the extent of its travel rearward, and zero the indicator. Pry the crankshaft forward and record crankshaft end-play. NOTE: *Crankshaft end-play also may be measured at the thrust bearing, using feeler gauges* (see illustration).

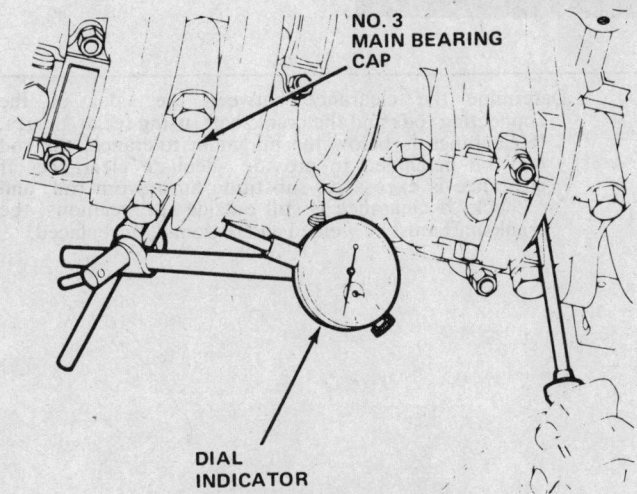

Checking crankshaft end-play with a dial indicator

Checking crankshaft end-play with a feeler gauge

CYLINDER BLOCK RECONDITIONING

Procedure	Method

Install the pistons:

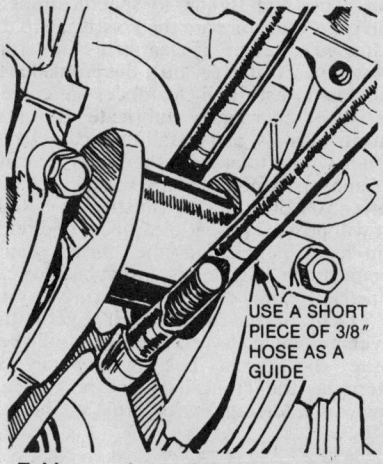

USE A SHORT PIECE OF 3/8" HOSE AS A GUIDE

Tubing used as guide when installing a piston

Press the upper connecting rod bearing halves into the connecting rods, and the lower halves into the connecting rod caps. Position the piston ring gaps according to specifications (see car section), and lubricate the pistons. Install a ring compresser on a piston, and press two long (8") pieces of plastic tubing over the rod bolts. Using the tubes as a guide, press the pistons into the bores and onto the crankshaft with a wooden hammer handle. After seating the rod on the crankshaft journal, remove the tubes and install the cap finger tight. Install the remaining pistons in the same manner. Invert the engine and check the bearing clearance at two points (90° apart) on each journal with Plastigage. NOTE: *Do not turn the crankshaft with Plastigage installed.* If clearance is within tolerances, remove *all* Plastigage, thoroughly lubricate the journals, and torque the rod caps to specifications. If clearance is not within specifications, install different thickness bearing inserts and recheck. CAUTION: *Never shim or file the connecting rods or caps.* Always install plastic tube sleeves over the rod bolts when the caps are not installed, to protect the crankshaft journals.

Installing a piston

Check connecting rod side clearance:

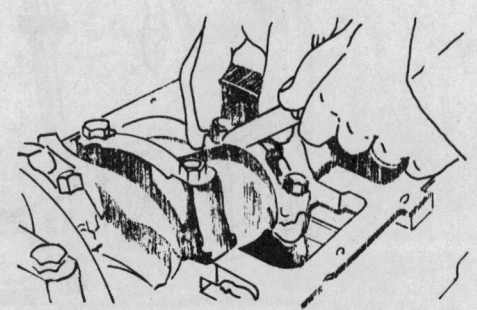

Checking connecting rod side clearance

Determine the clearance between the sides of the connecting rods and the crankshaft, using feeler gauges. If clearance is below the minimum tolerance, the rod may be machined to provide adequate clearance. If clearance is excessive, substitute an unworn rod, and recheck. If clearance is still outside specficiations, the crankshaft must be welded and reground, or replaced.

CYLINDER BLOCK RECONDITIONING

Procedure	Method
Inspect the timing chain:	Visually inspect the timing chain for broken or loose links, and replace the chain if any are found. If the chain will flex sideways, it must be replaced. Install the timing chain as specified. NOTE: *If the original timing chain is to be reused, install it in its original position.*
Check timing gear backlash and runout:	Mount a dial indicator with its stem resting on a tooth of the camshaft gear (as illustrated). Rotate the gear until all slack is removed, and zero the indicator. Rotate the gear in the opposite direction until slack is removed, and record gear backlash. Mount the indicator with its stem resting on the edge of the camshaft gear, parallel to the axis of the camshaft. Zero the indicator, and turn the camshaft gear one full turn, recording the runout. If either backlash or runout exceed specifications, replace the worn gear(s).

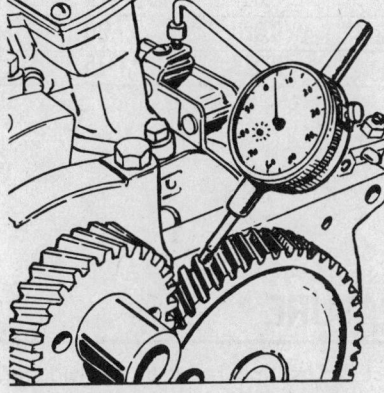

Checking camshaft gear backlash

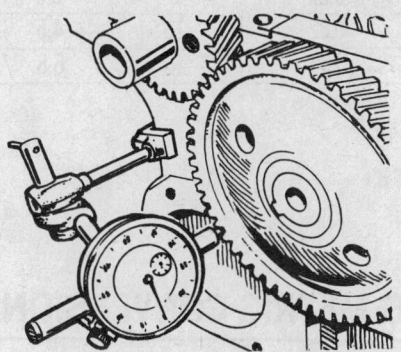

Checking camshaft gear runout

Completing the Rebuilding Process

Following the above procedures, complete the rebuilding process as follows:

Fill the oil pump with oil, to prevent cavitating (sucking air) on initial engine start up. Install the oil pump and the pickup tube on the engine. Coat the oil pan gasket as necessary, and install the gasket and the oil pan. Mount the flywheel and the crankshaft vibration damper or pulley on the crankshaft. NOTE: *Always use new bolts when installing the flywheel.* Inspect the clutch shaft pilot bushing in the crankshaft. If the bushing is excessively worn, remove it with an expanding puller and a slide hammer, and tap a new bushing into place.

Position the engine, cylinder head side up. Lubricate the lifters, and install them into their bores. Install the cylinder head, and torque it as specified in the car section. Insert the pushrods (where applicable), and install the rocker shaft(s) (if so equipped) or position the rocker arms on the pushrods. If solid lifters are utilized, adjust the valves to the "cold" specifications.

Mount the intake and exhaust manifolds, the carburetor(s), the distributor and spark plugs. Adjust the point gap and the static ignition timing. Mount all accessories and install the engine in the car. Fill the radiator with coolant, and the crankcase with high quality engine

Break-in Procedure

Start the engine, and allow it to run at low speed for a few minutes, while checking for leaks. Stop the engine, check the oil level, and fill as necessary. Restart the engine, and fill the cooling system to capactiy. Check the point dwell angle and adjust the ignition timing and the valves. Run the engine at low to medium speed (800-2500 rpm) for approximately 1/2 hour, and retorque the cylinder head bolts. Road test the car, and check again for leaks.

Follow the manufacturer's recommended engine break-in procedure and maintenance schedule for new engines.

Metric Conversion

ENGLISH TO METRIC CONVERSION: MASS (WEIGHT)

Current mass measurement is expressed in pounds and ounces (lbs. & ozs.). The metric unit of mass (or weight) is the kilogram (kg). Even although this table does not show conversion of masses (weights) larger than 15 lbs, it is easy to calculate larger units by following the data immediately below.

To convert ounces (oz.) to grams (g): multiply th number of ozs. by 28
To convert grams (g) to ounces (oz.): multiply the number of grams by .035

To convert pounds (lbs.) to kilograms (kg): multiply the number of lbs. by .45
To convert kilograms (kg) to pounds (lbs.): multiply the number of kilograms by 2.2

lbs	kg	lbs	kg	oz	kg	oz	kg
0.1	0.04	0.9	0.41	0.1	0.003	0.9	0.024
0.2	0.09	1	0.4	0.2	0.005	1	0.03
0.3	0.14	2	0.9	0.3	0.008	2	0.06
0.4	0.18	3	1.4	0.4	0.011	3	0.08
0.5	0.23	4	1.8	0.5	0.014	4	0.11
0.6	0.27	5	2.3	0.6	0.017	5	0.14
0.7	0.32	10	4.5	0.7	0.020	10	0.28
0.8	0.36	15	6.8	0.8	0.023	15	0.42

ENGLISH TO METRIC CONVERSION: TEMPERATURE

To convert Fahrenheit (°F) to Celsius (°C): take number of °F and subtract 32; multiply result by 5; divide result by 9

To convert Celsius (°C) to Fahrenheit (°F): take number of °C and multiply by 9; divide result by 5; add 32 to total

Fahrenheit (F)		Celsius (C)		Fahrenheit (F)		Celsius (C)		Fahrenheit (F)		Celsius (C)	
°F	°C	°C	°F	°F	°C	°C	°F	°F	°C	°C	°F
−40	−40	−38	−36.4	80	26.7	18	64.4	215	101.7	80	176
−35	−37.2	−36	−32.8	85	29.4	20	68	220	104.4	85	185
−30	−34.4	−34	−29.2	90	32.2	22	71.6	225	107.2	90	194
−25	−31.7	−32	−25.6	95	35.0	24	75.2	230	110.0	95	202
−20	−28.9	−30	−22	100	37.8	26	78.8	235	112.8	100	212
−15	−26.1	−28	−18.4	105	40.6	28	82.4	240	115.6	105	221
−10	−23.3	−26	−14.8	110	43.3	30	86	245	118.3	110	230
−5	−20.6	−24	−11.2	115	46.1	32	89.6	250	121.1	115	239
0	−17.8	−22	−7.6	120	48.9	34	93.2	255	123.9	120	248
1	−17.2	−20	−4	125	51.7	36	96.8	260	126.6	125	257
2	−16.7	−18	−0.4	130	54.4	38	100.4	265	129.4	130	266
3	−16.1	−16	3.2	135	57.2	40	104	270	132.2	135	275
4	−15.6	−14	6.8	140	60.0	42	107.6	275	135.0	140	284
5	−15.0	−12	10.4	145	62.8	44	112.2	280	137.8	145	293
10	−12.2	−10	14	150	65.6	46	114.8	285	140.6	150	302
15	−9.4	−8	17.6	155	68.3	48	118.4	290	143.3	155	311
20	−6.7	−6	21.2	160	71.1	50	122	295	146.1	160	320
25	−3.9	−4	24.8	165	73.9	52	125.6	300	148.9	165	329
30	−1.1	−2	28.4	170	76.7	54	129.2	305	151.7	170	338
35	1.7	0	32	175	79.4	56	132.8	310	154.4	175	347
40	4.4	2	35.6	180	82.2	58	136.4	315	157.2	180	356
45	7.2	4	39.2	185	85.0	60	140	320	160.0	185	365
50	10.0	6	42.8	190	87.8	62	143.6	325	162.8	190	374
55	12.8	8	46.4	195	90.6	64	147.2	330	165.6	195	383
60	15.6	10	50	200	93.3	66	150.8	335	168.3	200	392
65	18.3	12	53.6	205	96.1	68	154.4	340	171.1	205	401
70	21.1	14	57.2	210	98.9	70	158	345	173.9	210	410
75	23.9	16	60.8	212	100.0	75	167	350	176.7	215	414

ENGLISH TO METRIC CONVERSION: LENGTH

To convert inches (ins.) to millimeters (mm): multiply number of inches by 25.4

To convert millimeters (mm) to inches (ins.): multiply number of millimeters by .04

Inches		Decimals	Milli-meters	Inches to millimeters inches	mm	Inches		Decimals	Milli-meters	Inches to millimeters inches	mm
	1/64	0.051625	0.3969	0.0001	0.00254		33/64	0.515625	13.0969	0.6	15.24
1/32		0.03125	0.7937	0.0002	0.00508	17/32		0.53125	13.4937	0.7	17.78
	3/64	0.046875	1.1906	0.0003	0.00762		35/64	0.546875	13.8906	0.8	20.32
1/16		0.0625	1.5875	0.0004	0.01016	9/16		0.5625	14.2875	0.9	22.86
	5/64	0.078125	1.9844	0.0005	0.01270		37/64	0.578125	14.6844	1	25.4
3/32		0.09375	2.3812	0.0006	0.01524	19/32		0.59375	15.0812	2	50.8
	7/64	0.109375	2.7781	0.0007	0.01778		39/64	0.609375	15.4781	3	76.2
1/8		0.125	3.1750	0.0008	0.02032	5/8		0.625	15.8750	4	101.6
	9/64	0.140625	3.5719	0.0009	0.02286		41/64	0.640625	16.2719	5	127.0
5/32		0.15625	3.9687	.001	0.0254	21/32		0.65625	16.6687	6	152.4
	11/64	0.171875	4.3656	0.002	0.0508		43/64	0.671875	17.0656	7	177.8
3/16		0.1875	4.7625	0.003	0.0762	11/16		0.6875	17.4625	8	203.2
	13/64	0.203125	5.1594	0.004	0.1016		45/64	0.703125	17.8594	9	228.6
7/32		0.21875	5.5562	0.005	0.1270	23/32		0.71875	18.2562	10	254.0
	15/64	0.234375	5.9531	0.006	0.1524		47/64	0.734375	18.6531	11	279.4
1/4		0.25	6.3500	0.007	0.1778	3/4		0.75	19.0500	12	304.8
	17/64	0.265625	6.7469	0.008	0.2032		49/64	0.765625	19.4469	13	330.2
9/32		0.28125	7.1437	0.009	0.2286	25/32		0.78125	19.8437	14	355.6
	19/64	0.296875	7.5406	0.01	0.254		51/64	0.796875	20.2406	15	381.0
5/16		0.3125	7.9375	0.02	0.508	13/16		0.8125	20.6375	16	406.4
	21/64	0.328125	8.3344	0.03	0.762		53/64	0.828125	21.0344	17	431.8
11/32		0.34375	8.7312	0.04	1.016	27/32		0.84375	21.4312	18	457.2
	23/64	0.359375	9.1281	0.05	1.270		55/64	0.859375	21.8281	19	482.6
3/8		0.375	9.5250	0.06	1.524	7/8		0.875	22.2250	20	508.0
	25/64	0.390625	9.9219	0.07	1.778		57/64	0.890625	22.6219	21	533.4
13/32		0.40625	10.3187	0.08	2.032	29/32		0.90625	23.0187	22	558.8
	27/64	0.421875	10.7156	0.09	2.286		59/64	0.921875	23.4156	23	584.2
7/16		0.4375	11.1125	0.1	2.54	15/16		0.9375	23.8125	24	609.6
	29/64	0.453125	11.5094	0.2	5.08		61/64	0.953125	24.2094	25	635.0
15/32		0.46875	11.9062	0.3	7.62	31/32		0.96875	24.6062	26	660.4
	31/64	0.484375	12.3031	0.4	10.16		63/64	0.984375	25.0031	27	690.6
1/2		0.5	12.7000	0.5	12.70						

ENGLISH TO METRIC CONVERSION: TORQUE

To convert foot-pounds (ft./lbs.) to Newton-meters: multiply the number of ft./lbs. by 1.3

To convert inch-pounds (in./lbs.) to Newton-meters: multiply the number of in./lbs. by .11

in lbs	N-m	in lbs	N-m	in lbs	N-m	in lbs	N-m	in lbs	N-m
0.1	0.01	1	0.11	10	1.13	19	2.15	28	3.16
0.2	0.02	2	0.23	11	1.24	20	2.26	29	3.28
0.3	0.03	3	0.34	12	1.36	21	2.37	30	3.39
0.4	0.04	4	0.45	13	1.47	22	2.49	31	3.50
0.5	0.06	5	0.56	14	1.58	23	2.60	32	3.62
0.6	0.07	6	0.68	15	1.70	24	2.71	33	3.73
0.7	0.08	7	0.78	16	1.81	25	2.82	34	3.84
0.8	0.09	8	0.90	17	1.92	26	2.94	35	3.95
0.9	0.10	9	1.02	18	2.03	27	3.05	36	4.07

Metric Conversion

ENGLISH TO METRIC CONVERSION: TORQUE

Torque is now expressed as either foot-pounds (ft./lbs.) or inch-pounds (in./lbs.). The metric measurement unit for torque is the Newton-meter (Nm). This unit—the Nm—will be used for all SI metric torque references, both the present ft./lbs. and in./lbs.

ft lbs	N-m	ft lbs	N-m	ft lbs	N-m	ft lbs	N-m
0.1	0.1	33	44.7	74	100.3	115	155.9
0.2	0.3	34	46.1	75	101.7	116	157.3
0.3	0.4	35	47.4	76	103.0	117	158.6
0.4	0.5	36	48.8	77	104.4	118	160.0
0.5	0.7	37	50.7	78	105.8	119	161.3
0.6	0.8	38	51.5	79	107.1	120	162.7
0.7	1.0	39	52.9	80	108.5	121	164.0
0.8	1.1	40	54.2	81	109.8	122	165.4
0.9	1.2	41	55.6	82	111.2	123	166.8
1	1.3	42	56.9	83	112.5	124	168.1
2	2.7	43	58.3	84	113.9	125	169.5
3	4.1	44	59.7	85	115.2	126	170.8
4	5.4	45	61.0	86	116.6	127	172.2
5	6.8	46	62.4	87	118.0	128	173.5
6	8.1	47	63.7	88	119.3	129	174.9
7	9.5	48	65.1	89	120.7	130	176.2
8	10.8	49	66.4	90	122.0	131	177.6
9	12.2	50	67.8	91	123.4	132	179.0
10	13.6	51	69.2	92	124.7	133	180.3
11	14.9	52	70.5	93	126.1	134	181.7
12	16.3	53	71.9	94	127.4	135	183.0
13	17.6	54	73.2	95	128.8	136	184.4
14	18.9	55	74.6	96	130.2	137	185.7
15	20.3	56	75.9	97	131.5	138	187.1
16	21.7	57	77.3	98	132.9	139	188.5
17	23.0	58	78.6	99	134.2	140	189.8
18	24.4	59	80.0	100	135.6	141	191.2
19	25.8	60	81.4	101	136.9	142	192.5
20	27.1	61	82.7	102	138.3	143	193.9
21	28.5	62	84.1	103	139.6	144	195.2
22	29.8	63	85.4	104	141.0	145	196.6
23	31.2	64	86.8	105	142.4	146	198.0
24	32.5	65	88.1	106	143.7	147	199.3
25	33.9	66	89.5	107	145.1	148	200.7
26	35.2	67	90.8	108	146.4	149	202.0
27	36.6	68	92.2	109	147.8	150	203.4
28	38.0	69	93.6	110	149.1	151	204.7
29	39.3	70	94.9	111	150.5	152	206.1
30	40.7	71	96.3	112	151.8	153	207.4
31	42.0	72	97.6	113	153.2	154	208.8
32	43.4	73	99.0	114	154.6	155	210.2

ENGLISH TO METRIC CONVERSION: FORCE

Force is presently measured in pounds (lbs.). This type of measurement is used to measure spring pressure, specifically how many pounds it takes to compress a spring. Our present force unit (the pound) will be replaced in SI metric measurements by the Newton (N). This term will eventually see use in specifications for electric motor brush spring pressures, valve spring pressures, etc.

To convert pounds (lbs.) to Newton (N): multiply the number of lbs. by 4.45

lbs	N	lbs	N	lbs	N	oz	N
0.01	0.04	21	93.4	59	262.4	1	0.3
0.02	0.09	22	97.9	60	266.9	2	0.6
0.03	0.13	23	102.3	61	271.3	3	0.8
0.04	0.18	24	106.8	62	275.8	4	1.1
0.05	0.22	25	111.2	63	280.2	5	1.4
0.06	0.27	26	115.6	64	284.6	6	1.7
0.07	0.31	27	120.1	65	289.1	7	2.0
0.08	0.36	28	124.6	66	293.6	8	2.2
0.09	0.40	29	129.0	67	298.0	9	2.5
0.1	0.4	30	133.4	68	302.5	10	2.8
0.2	0.9	31	137.9	69	306.9	11	3.1
0.3	1.3	32	142.3	70	311.4	12	3.3
0.4	1.8	33	146.8	71	315.8	13	3.6
0.5	2.2	34	151.2	72	320.3	14	3.9
0.6	2.7	35	155.7	73	324.7	15	4.2
0.7	3.1	36	160.1	74	329.2	16	4.4
0.8	3.6	37	164.6	75	333.6	17	4.7
0.9	4.0	38	169.0	76	338.1	18	5.0
1	4.4	39	173.5	77	342.5	19	5.3
2	8.9	40	177.9	78	347.0	20	5.6
3	13.4	41	182.4	79	351.4	21	5.8
4	17.8	42	186.8	80	355.9	22	6.1
5	22.2	43	191.3	81	360.3	23	6.4
6	26.7	44	195.7	82	364.8	24	6.7
7	31.1	45	200.2	83	369.2	25	7.0
8	35.6	46	204.6	84	373.6	26	7.2
9	40.0	47	209.1	85	378.1	27	7.5
10	44.5	48	213.5	86	382.6	28	7.8
11	48.9	49	218.0	87	387.0	29	8.1
12	53.4	50	224.4	88	391.4	30	8.3
13	57.8	51	226.9	89	395.9	31	8.6
14	62.3	52	231.3	90	400.3	32	8.9
15	66.7	53	235.8	91	404.8	33	9.2
16	71.2	54	240.2	92	409.2	34	9.4
17	75.6	55	244.6	93	413.7	35	9.7
18	80.1	56	249.1	94	418.1	36	10.0
19	84.5	57	253.6	95	422.6	37	10.3
20	89.0	58	258.0	96	427.0	38	10.6

Metric Conversion

ENGLISH TO METRIC CONVERSION: LIQUID CAPACITY

Liquid or fluid capacity is presently expressed as pints, quarts or gallons, or a combination of all of these. In the metric system the liter (l) will become the basic unit. Fractions of a liter would be expressed as deciliters, centiliters, or most frequently (and commonly) as milliliters.

To convert pints (pts.) to liters (l): multiply the number of pints by .47
To convert liters (l) to pints (pts.): multiply the number of liters by 2.1
To convert quarts (qts.) to liters (l): multiply the number of quarts by .95

To convert liters (l) to quarts (qts.): multiply the number of liters by 1.06
To convert gallons (gals.) to liters (l): multiply the number of gallons by 3.8
To convert liters (l) to gallons (gals.): multiply the number of liters by .26

gals	liters	qts	liters	pts	liters
0.1	0.38	0.1	0.10	0.1	0.05
0.2	0.76	0.2	0.19	0.2	0.10
0.3	1.1	0.3	0.28	0.3	0.14
0.4	1.5	0.4	0.38	0.4	0.19
0.5	1.9	0.5	0.47	0.5	0.24
0.6	2.3	0.6	0.57	0.6	0.28
0.7	2.6	0.7	0.66	0.7	0.33
0.8	3.0	0.8	0.76	0.8	0.38
0.9	3.4	0.9	0.85	0.9	0.43
1	3.8	1	1.0	1	0.5
2	7.6	2	1.9	2	1.0
3	11.4	3	2.8	3	1.4
4	15.1	4	3.8	4	1.9
5	18.9	5	4.7	5	2.4
6	22.7	6	5.7	6	2.8
7	26.5	7	6.6	7	3.3
8	30.3	8	7.6	8	3.8
9	34.1	9	8.5	9	4.3
10	37.8	10	9.5	10	4.7
11	41.6	11	10.4	11	5.2
12	45.4	12	11.4	12	5.7
13	49.2	13	12.3	13	6.2
14	53.0	14	13.2	14	6.6
15	56.8	15	14.2	15	7.1
16	60.6	16	15.1	16	7.6
17	64.3	17	16.1	17	8.0
18	68.1	18	17.0	18	8.5
19	71.9	19	18.0	19	9.0
20	75.7	20	18.9	20	9.5
21	79.5	21	19.9	21	9.9
22	83.2	22	20.8	22	10.4
23	87.0	23	21.8	23	10.9
24	90.8	24	22.7	24	11.4
25	94.6	25	23.6	25	11.8
26	98.4	26	24.6	26	12.3
27	102.2	27	25.5	27	12.8
28	106.0	28	26.5	28	13.2
29	110.0	29	27.4	29	13.7
30	113.5	30	28.4	30	14.2

ENGLISH TO METRIC CONVERSION: PRESSURE

The basic unit of pressure measurement used today is expressed as pounds per square inch (psi). The metric unit for psi will be the kilopascal (kPa). This will apply to either fluid pressure or air pressure, and will be frequently seen in tire pressure readings, oil pressure specifications, fuel pump pressure, etc.

To convert pounds per square inch (psi) to kilopascals (kPa): multiply the number of psi by 6.89

Psi	kPa	Psi	kPa	Psi	kPa	Psi	kPa
0.1	0.7	37	255.1	82	565.4	127	875.6
0.2	1.4	38	262.0	83	572.3	128	882.5
0.3	2.1	39	268.9	84	579.2	129	889.4
0.4	2.8	40	275.8	85	586.0	130	896.3
0.5	3.4	41	282.7	86	592.9	131	903.2
0.6	4.1	42	289.6	87	599.8	132	910.1
0.7	4.8	43	296.5	88	606.7	133	917.0
0.8	5.5	44	303.4	89	613.6	134	923.9
0.9	6.2	45	310.3	90	620.5	135	930.8
1	6.9	46	317.2	91	627.4	136	937.7
2	13.8	47	324.0	92	634.3	137	944.6
3	20.7	48	331.0	93	641.2	138	951.5
4	27.6	49	337.8	94	648.1	139	958.4
5	34.5	50	344.7	95	655.0	140	965.2
6	41.4	51	351.6	96	661.9	141	972.2
7	48.3	52	358.5	97	668.8	142	979.0
8	55.2	53	365.4	98	675.7	143	985.9
9	62.1	54	372.3	99	682.6	144	992.8
10	69.0	55	379.2	100	689.5	145	999.7
11	75.8	56	386.1	101	696.4	146	1006.6
12	82.7	57	393.0	102	703.3	147	1013.5
13	89.6	58	399.9	103	710.2	148	1020.4
14	96.5	59	406.8	104	717.0	149	1027.3
15	103.4	60	413.7	105	723.9	150	1034.2
16	110.3	61	420.6	106	730.8	151	1041.1
17	117.2	62	427.5	107	737.7	152	1048.0
18	124.1	63	434.4	108	744.6	153	1054.9
19	131.0	64	441.3	109	751.5	154	1061.8
20	137.9	65	448.2	110	758.4	155	1068.7
21	144.8	66	455.0	111	765.3	156	1075.6
22	151.7	67	461.9	112	772.2	157	1082.5
23	158.6	68	468.8	113	779.1	158	1089.4
24	165.5	69	475.7	114	786.0	159	1096.3
25	172.4	70	482.6	115	792.9	160	1103.2
26	179.3	71	489.5	116	799.8	161	1110.0
27	186.2	72	496.4	117	806.7	162	1116.9
28	193.0	73	503.3	118	813.6	163	1123.8
29	200.0	74	510.2	119	820.5	164	1130.7
30	206.8	75	517.1	120	827.4	165	1137.6
31	213.7	76	524.0	121	834.3	166	1144.5
32	220.6	77	530.9	122	841.2	167	1151.4
33	227.5	78	537.8	123	848.0	168	1158.3
34	234.4	79	544.7	124	854.9	169	1165.2
35	241.3	80	551.6	125	861.8	170	1172.1
36	248.2	81	558.5	126	868.7	171	1179.0

ENGLISH TO METRIC CONVERSION: PRESSURE

The basic unit of pressure measurement used today is expressed as pounds per square inch (psi). The metric unit for psi will be the kilopascal (kPa). This will apply to either fluid pressure or air pressure, and will be frequently seen in tire pressure readings, oil pressure specifications, fuel pump pressure, etc.

To convert pounds per square inch (psi) to kilopascals (kPa): multiply the number of psi by 6.89

Psi	kPa	Psi	kPa	Psi	kPa	Psi	kPa
172	1185.9	216	1489.3	260	1792.6	304	2096.0
173	1192.8	217	1496.2	261	1799.5	305	2102.9
174	1199.7	218	1503.1	262	1806.4	306	2109.8
175	1206.6	219	1510.0	263	1813.3	307	2116.7
176	1213.5	220	1516.8	264	1820.2	308	2123.6
177	1220.4	221	1523.7	265	1827.1	309	2130.5
178	1227.3	222	1530.6	266	1834.0	310	2137.4
179	1234.2	223	1537.5	267	1840.9	311	2144.3
180	1241.0	224	1544.4	268	1847.8	312	2151.2
181	1247.9	225	1551.3	269	1854.7	313	2158.1
182	1254.8	226	1558.2	270	1861.6	314	2164.9
183	1261.7	227	1565.1	271	1868.5	315	2171.8
184	1268.6	228	1572.0	272	1875.4	316	2178.7
185	1275.5	229	1578.9	273	1882.3	317	2185.6
186	1282.4	230	1585.8	274	1889.2	318	2192.5
187	1289.3	231	1592.7	275	1896.1	319	2199.4
188	1296.2	232	1599.6	276	1903.0	320	2206.3
189	1303.1	233	1606.5	277	1909.8	321	2213.2
190	1310.0	234	1613.4	278	1916.7	322	2220.1
191	1316.9	235	1620.3	279	1923.6	323	2227.0
192	1323.8	236	1627.2	280	1930.5	324	2233.9
193	1330.7	237	1634.1	281	1937.4	325	2240.8
194	1337.6	238	1641.0	282	1944.3	326	2247.7
195	1344.5	239	1647.8	283	1951.2	327	2254.6
196	1351.4	240	1654.7	284	1958.1	328	2261.5
197	1358.3	241	1661.6	285	1965.0	329	2268.4
198	1365.2	242	1668.5	286	1971.9	330	2275.3
199	1372.0	243	1675.4	287	1978.8	331	2282.2
200	1378.9	244	1682.3	288	1985.7	332	2289.1
201	1385.8	245	1689.2	289	1992.6	333	2295.9
202	1392.7	246	1696.1	290	1999.5	334	2302.8
203	1399.6	247	1703.0	291	2006.4	335	2309.7
204	1406.5	248	1709.9	292	2013.3	336	2316.6
205	1413.4	249	1716.8	293	2020.2	337	2323.5
206	1420.3	250	1723.7	294	2027.1	338	2330.4
207	1427.2	251	1730.6	295	2034.0	339	2337.3
208	1434.1	252	1737.5	296	2040.8	240	2344.2
209	1441.0	253	1744.4	297	2047.7	341	2351.1
210	1447.9	254	1751.3	298	2054.6	342	2358.0
211	1454.8	255	1758.2	299	2061.5	343	2364.9
212	1461.7	256	1765.1	300	2068.4	344	2371.8
213	1468.7	257	1772.0	301	2075.3	345	2378.7
214	1475.5	258	1778.8	302	2082.2	346	2385.6
215	1482.4	259	1785.7	303	2089.1	347	2392.5

THE METRIC SYSTEM

How It Works

The metric system is based on multiples of 10, like our money (100 cents = $1; or 10 pennies = 1 dime, 10 dimes = $1). The foundation of the metric system is the meter (which is a little more than 39 inches in length).

This meter is divided into 1000 parts, each part is called a millimeter. Do not confuse the millimeter with a millionth of a meter just because it sounds like a million. One millimeter is 1/1000th of a meter.

Now if we take 10 millimeters in a row, they equal 1 centimeter, and 100 centimeters equal 1 meter. To repeat:

1. 10 millimeters = 1 centimeter
2. 100 centimeters = 1 meter
3. 1000 millimeters = 1 meter

Since one meter is actually 39.37 inches, a millimeter (mm) is .03937 inches. For all but the most precise work this is rounded off to .0394 in. And there are 25.4 millimeters in one inch.

Four Main Areas

The things that are measured in the customary English system (the one we use) and the metric system—or SI—(the one all other countries are or will be using) can be lumped into four main groupings:

1. Length
2. Area
3. Volume
4. Mass (Weight)

When we describe a vehicle as being 4.557 meters in length, powered by a 2000 cubic centimeter engine, with a mass weight of 1210 kilograms and with a front seat area of .83 square meter, we are using all four groups of SI measurements.

To describe the same vehicle in the English system, we would say it is 179.4 inches in length, powered by a 122 cubic inch displacement engine, weighing 2679 pounds, and has a front seat area of 1 square yard.

As you can see, there is more to the metric system than picturing a meter being divided into 100 or 1000 equal parts. This is simply a measurement of length. One must know area, volume and weight (in SI terms this is now called mass), as well.

For most practical purposes, you won't be using any more terms or units of measurement that you now use. The most commonly used units of measure are:

to measure length   meter
                          millimeter
to measure weight   kilogram
(mass)   gram

to measure volume   liter
                          cubic
                          centimeter
to measure area   square meter
                          square
                          milimeter

There are other units, of course, but you're not likely to see them in a professional automotive service manual.

In normal professional automotive service, we will be dealing often with such prefixes as milli (m) numerical value 0.001; centi (c) numerical value 0.01; and kilo (k) numerical value 1000. For exam-

BASIC UNITS IN METRIC MEASUREMENT

Quantity	Name of Unit	Symbol
length	meter	m
mass (weight)	kilogram	kg
time	second	s
electric current	ampere	A
electric potential	volt	V
electric energy	kilowatt-hour	kW·h
road speed	kilometers per hr.	km/h
temperature	celsius	°C
torque	newton meters	Nm
luminous intensity	candela	cd

The quantity expressions shown above are some of the most common now used. Not all of these, however, are approved metric standards that are used in the SI measurement method. These are ones that will most likely be encountered in the future in many areas of the automotive service world. Remember, wherever you see a period (·) placed midway between the height of figures, it means the same as today's multiplication (×) sign. The decimal point (.) will continue to be positioned between figures at the bottom of a line.

ple, if the distance between town A and town B is 10,000 meters, it is expressed more simply as 10 kilometers.

Practical Applications

The most common measure of volume affecting automotive service dealers is the liter. Every time an imported car has its oil drained, cooling system serviced or gearbox oil changed, the refill quantity will likely be specified in liters. If the book says 4.5 liters of oil are needed when the filter is changed, how much is that? A quart is a bit less than a liter. How close would four quarts come to filling the crankcase? Five quarts? A quart equals .9461 (liter). Four quarts adds to 3.7841—not enough to do the job. One more quart brings the total to 4.731. That's less than half a pint over full, and close enough for most jobs.

Suppose the front wheel toe-in spec calls for 3 millimeters. Where should the gauge be set if it's calibrated in fractions of an inch? Since 1 mm equals approximately .039 in. the spec equals .117 in. An eighth of an inch has the decimal equivalent of .125 in. Few could argue that ⅛ in. wouldn't be a reasonable setting.

The number that throws many professional mechanics for a complete loss is torque spec. Torque is stated as a new unit with a new name—newton meters, abbreviated Nm.

One foot pound (ft/lb) equals 1.356 Nm. If the specs call for a cylinder head to be torqued to 50 Nm, the correct torque wrench setting in ft/lb is 37. An alternate metric term, kilogram/meters (Kg/m) are not to be used with SI units. They are part of the old gravimetric system.

Look at it this way:

A foot pound is bigger than a newton meter. Converting Nm to ft/lb will always produce a smaller number. As seen above, 50 Nm = 37 ft/lb.

METRIC FRACTIONS EXPRESSED AS PREFIXES

Prefix	SI Symbol	Multiplication Factors	Example of use
mega	M	$1\ 000\ 000 = 10^6$	**mega**watt—1 million watts
kilo	k	$1\ 000 = 10^3$	**kilo**meter—1000 meters
hecto	h	$100 = 10^2$	**hecto**liter—100 liters
deka	da	$10 = 10^1$	**deka**gram—10 grams
deci	d	$0.1 = 10^{-1}$	**deci**liter—1/10th of a liter
centi	c	$0.01 = 10^{-2}$	**centi**meter—1/100th of a meter
milli	m	$0.001 = 10^{-3}$	**milli**liter—1/1000th of a liter
micro	μ	$0.000\ 001 = 10^{-6}$	**micro**second—1 millionth of a second

Prefixes are used to express fractions of any given quantity or measurement in the SI method. Some of these terms many mechanics will be familiar with today—because they've been using them for a long time. For instance, imported cars measure their engine displacement in cubic centimeters—therefore the centimeter is a commonly used term right now, one you are probably quite familiar with. Power station electrical output is stated as so many megawatts, which when converted tells us how many millions of watts of electrical energy can be generated by a power plant.